AMERICAN

SALARIES

AND

WAGES

SURVEY

AMERICAN

SALARIES

AND

WAGES

SURVEY

Tenth Edition

Statistical Data Derived
from More Than 590
Government, Business &
News Sources

Joyce P. Simkin

GALE
CENGAGE Learning

Detroit • New York • San Francisco • New Haven, Conn • Waterville, Maine • London

American Salaries and Wages Survey, 10th Edition

Joyce P. Simkin, Editor

Project Editor: Jeffrey Wilson

Editorial: Monique D. Magee, Robert Lazich, Susan M. Turner, Editorial Code and Data, Inc.

Manufacturing: Rita Wimberley

For product information and technology assistance, contact us at
Gale Customer Support, 1-800-877-4253.
For permission to use material from this text or product,
submit all requests online at **www.cengage.com/permissions.**
Further permissions questions can be emailed to
permissionrequest@cengage.com

While every effort has been made to ensure the reliability of the information presented in this publication, Gale, a part of Cengage Learning, does not guarantee the accuracy of the data contained herein. Gale accepts no payment for listing; and inclusion in the publication of any organization, agency, institution, publication, service, or individual does not imply endorsement of the editors or publisher. Errors brought to the attention of the publisher and verified to the satisfaction of the publisher will be corrected in future editions.

EDITORIAL DATA PRIVACY POLICY. Does this publication contain information about you as an individual? If so, for more information about our editorial data privacy policies, please see our Privacy Statement at www.gale.com.

Gale, Cengage Learning
27500 Drake Rd.
Farmington Hills, MI, 48331-3535

ISBN-13: 978-1-4144-1907-7
ISBN-10: 1-4144-1907-4

ISSN 1055-7628

Printed in the United States of America
1 2 3 4 5 6 7 13 12 11 10 09

CONTENTS

INTRODUCTION

American Salaries & Wages Survey (*ASWS*), now in its tenth edition, is a compilation of 2,355 occupational combinations (2,796 occupations) and their corresponding salaries obtained from 597 sources—federal, state and city government, as well as various trade associations and journals.

Incorporating wage data for the period 2003 through 2009, *ASWS* provides extensive compensation information for industry, economic planners and developers, human resources professionals, employment counselors, job seekers, and job changers. Most of the data shown were collected in May 2007 and released, for the first time, in May 2008.

Features of this edition include:

• Data from 597 sources.

• More than 86,960 individual entries.

• 2,355 occupational combinations representing 2,796 occupations.

• 629 geographical areas, including national data and 29 regions, 3 territories, 51 states, and 550 cities, of which 541 are reported as 245 metropolitan statistical areas and 296 as independent cities or urbanized counties.

• Occupational outline of contents with numerous cross references.

• Geographical outline of contents.

• Updated employment statistics for 2006 and 2016.

• Complete source listings for further research.

Sources

During the first decade of the twenty-first century publishers of trade journals, magazines, and newspapers have struggled. Since 2007, many have lost their battles and either cut back significantly on their publishing activities or stopped publishing all together. The economic recession that began in December 2007 has complicated this situation from the perspective of a researcher into salary and wage data. By putting pressure on all sectors of the economy, the recession has also impacted industry, trade, and professional associations. These associations conduct annual wage surveys of their members. Typically, these groups survey members of their professional societies to obtain data and report wages across the nation or within U.S. regions. Fewer large salary surveys are being conducted and fewer yet are being published by the shrinking number of trade journals on the market today.

This decline in unique source materials has meant that the research portion of producing *ASWS* has become a greater challenge with each edition since the turn of the century. All efforts are made to scour the data landscape gathering salary and wage data: (1) from all reliable sources; (2) covering as broad a spectrum of occupations as possible, and (3) from as large and varied a number of sources as possible.

In order to provide a comprehensive data base, wage information was sought at the city level, the county or state region level, the state level, the U.S. region level, and the national level. Most Federal data are from the Occupational Employment Statistics (OES) semi-annual survey, published annually. It samples and contacts approximately 200,000 establishments semi-annually and about 1.2 million establishments over a three year period. Data from this program are available for 800 detailed occupations, 30 more occupations than in past years. Other occupations were identified using a variety of sources.

Occupational Titles

Federal data—and state data reported through the Federal government—follow the Standard Occupational Classification System (SOC). This system has now been adopted by the Occupational Employment Statistics program of the Bureau of Labor Statistics.

Occupational titles from other sources follow no particular standard. They are reproduced essentially as reported. Therefore it is possible to find both *Registered Nurse* under R and *Nurse Practitioner* under N. The Outline of Contents provides a cross-referenced alphabetical listing of all titles to help the user identify all variants of an occupation. Thus *Nurse* provides references to *Registered Nurse* and vice versa.

Wage Denominations

Wage figures presented in *ASWS* are given in the form provided by the original source—hourly, daily, weekly, monthly, or annual. A wage conversion chart is provided for your convenience in Appendix II. The denomination type is referred to by its first letter in the wage denomination column (H for hourly, W for weekly, etc.). The number of wage calculations varies from source to source; one source may provide only an average wage figure, another may report only a median. Many reports, however, give three or more calculated wage amounts—a mid-level value such as average or median, as well as a low and a high value. In some cases, ranges are provided. Occasionally the low and high figures will be replaced by or supplemented with percentile or quartile figures. *ASWS* presents, wherever possible, three points on the wage spectrum: Low, Mid, and High. The ideal entry will show Lowest Wage Paid, Average Wage Paid, and Highest Wage Paid. But these figures are not always available; therefore, a coding system is used to specify what type of wage amount is being presented. For example,

FQ stands for First Quartile and means that 25% of the workers surveyed earned less than the dollar amount shown.

TQ stands for Third Quartile and means that 75% of the workers surveyed earned less than the dollar amount shown and 25% earned more than the dollar amount shown. All abbreviations of wage types are listed in alphabetical order at the bottom of every page in the data section.

Organization

Outlines of Contents

ASWS includes two outlines of contents providing access to the salaries listed. The Outline of Contents provides the reader with the means to find all listings of an occupation, despite variations in naming conventions. It lists the primary occupational classifications found in the main body of *ASWS,* in alphabetical order. In addition, the outline supplies derivations of those titles and cross-references them to their base forms. For example, the primary occupational title, Engineer, can be found in the data section. The Outline of Contents provides several additional titles, including:

> *Aerospace Engineer*
> *Agricultural Engineer*
> *Biomedical Engineer*
> *Environmental Engineer*
> *Fuel Cell Engineer*
> *Locomotive Engineer*
> *Nuclear Engineer*

The reader is advised to check the Outline of Contents when seeking wage information about a particular occupation in order to locate all available entries. The Geographic Outline is a listing of geographic locations down to the state level and the primary occupations provided for those locations. Metro areas and cities are not listed individually because the same occupations tend to be present at the state and local levels.

Main Body

The main body of *ASWS* is organized alphabetically by primary occupation first, then by secondary occupation and/or industry designation, then by geographic area. Data are presented in an eight-column table. The following is an explanation of these data columns from left to right.

Occupation/Type/Industry Column–

Lists the primary occupational title (e.g., Accountant), the secondary occupational title/type (e.g., Systems Software) and/or the industry designation (e.g., Aerospace & Defense or

Manufacturing). In cases where both a secondary title and an industry designation are provided, the secondary title precedes the industry.

Location Column–

Specifies the geographical area to which the data refer. The column is organized by size of region in descending order: national data, U.S. regional (e.g., Southwest) data, statewide data, metropolitan statistical area (MSA) and New England city and town area (NECTA) data, county data, and city data. If the area is smaller than a U.S. state, the location is followed by its two-letter postal code (e.g., MI for Michigan). *Please note:* Cities appear alphabetically by state, so that California cities will appear ahead of those located in New Jersey, for instance.

Wage Denomination (Per) Column–

Specifies intervals at which the wage amount is paid to the employee. The single-letter codes are translated at the bottom of each page. Wages may be given in hourly, daily, weekly, monthly, or annual denominations. A wage conversion table is provided in Appendix II.

Low, Mid, and High Columns–

The columns list the wage figures for each entry in U.S. dollars. Each amount is followed by an explanatory code. A typical code is AW, standing for Average Wage, or MW, standing for Median Wage. Sometimes references to "quartiles" may be found. The third quartile (TQ) wage, for instance, means that 75% of individuals earned less than the amount shown and 25% earned more.

Source Column–

Alphanumeric codes in this column refer to titles of sources from which data were obtained. A code like CABLS means that the source for this entry is the Bureau of Labor Statistics, based on data supplied by the State of California. These codes are explained in Appendix I.

Date Column–

Specifies the dates to which respective entries refer. If a particular source did not report a precise date, an approximate date ("2009") is provided.

Code Listings Block–

An explanation for all wage codes is shown at the bottom of each page. These abbreviations may also be found in the Abbreviations Table, Appendix III.

ASWS has four appendices, some of which have been mentioned above.

Appendix I - Sources

Appendix I lists 597 organizations which contributed data from one or multiple wage surveys or job banks. The appendix is organized alphabetically by source codes.

Appendix II - Wage Conversion Table

Appendix II is a table that translates an hourly wage into ·its weekly, monthly, and annual equivalents. The reader, however, should note that these equivalencies are only approximate since wages reported in hourly formats may pertain to work weeks of different lengths.

Appendix III - Abbreviations

Appendix III lists and explains the abbreviations used throughout *ASWS*. Source abbreviations, of course, are explained in Appendix I.

Appendix IV - Employment by Occupation, 2006 and 2016

Appendix IV reproduces a portion of the BLS Occupational Matrix, a data base that lists 754 detailed occupations and shows total employment in 2006 together with projections to the year 2016. The appendix provides three presentations—alphabetical, by largest employment, and by growth—to help the user gain further insight into wage trends in the United States.

Data Limitations

A number of points should be kept in mind when using *ASWS* for wage information. *ASWS* is a compilation of a large number of sources. Some are scientific surveys, some are job offers, and some are themselves compilations of other sources. No attempt was made to standardize the data from these sources. Therefore, the user should take great care drawing general conclusions. Variations and/or skewed data occur in title derivations, wage calculations, job descriptions, and methodology. Note, however, that data from the government surveys (sources that end in BLS) are largely comparable place to place. But, government survey data for some smaller metropolitan statistical areas may be skewed due to a low survey response rate.

In this edition, occupational titles are generally more uniform and follow Federal naming conventions much more consistently than in the first four editions. Ambiguous titles, however, continue to exist.

The editors have made a limited effort to edit the occupational titles presented. Grammatical forms and punctuation have been made consistent whenever possible. Titles are presented in singular forms (Nurse *vs* Nurses).

It is important to bear in mind that wage variations between different entries with the same occupational title may be due to differences in job responsibilities.

ASWS provides base salary figures only. Unless otherwise specified, supplemental compensation —i.e., fringe benefits, overtime, bonuses, etc.—have not been included. Wage figures shown do not include any cost of living adjustment.

Acknowledgments

ASWS was initially suggested to Gale by Ms. Flower L. Hund, Central Missouri State University, Warrensburg, MO. From the start, the editors have attempted to realize, in practice, Ms. Hund's original concepts; to the extent that they have succeeded, the credit is Ms. Hund's; she is, however, in no way responsible for shortcomings in *ASWS*. The editors would like to thank the many individuals in state government and in associations who helped in the creation of *ASWS* by providing reports, data, clarifications, and permissions.

Comments and Suggestions

Comments on *ASWS* or suggestions for improvement of its usefulness, format, and coverage are always welcome. Although we have made every effort to be as accurate and consistent as possible, errors may be noted by others; we will appreciate having these called to our attention. Please contact:

American Salaries & Wages Survey
Gale, Cengage Learning
27500 Drake Road
Farmington Hills, MI 48331-3535
Phone: (248)-699-GALE
Toll-free: (800) 347-GALE
Fax: (248) 699-8068
E-mail: BusinessProducts@cengage.com
URL: gale.cengage.com

OUTLINE OF CONTENTS

GEOGRAPHICAL OUTLINE OF CONTENTS

Geographical Outline of Contents

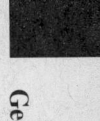

Indiana - continued:

Meeting and Convention Planner
Mental Health and Substance Abuse Social Worker
Mental Health Counselor
Merchandise Displayer and Window Trimmer
Metal-Refining Furnace Operator and Tender
Meter Reader
Microbiologist
Middle School Teacher
Milling and Planing Machine Setter, Operator, and Tender
Millwright
Mine Cutting and Channeling Machine Operator
Mining and Geological Engineer
Mixing and Blending Machine Setter, Operator, and Tender
Mobile Heavy Equipment Mechanic
Model Maker
Molder, Shaper, and Caster
Molding, Coremaking, and Casting Machine Setter, Operator, and Tender
Motion Picture Projectionist
Motorboat Mechanic
Motorcycle Mechanic
Multi-Media Artist and Animator
Multiple Machine Tool Setter, Operator, and Tender
Museum Technician and Conservator
Music Director and Composer
Musical Instrument Repairer and Tuner
Musician and Singer
Natural Sciences Manager
Network and Computer Systems Administrator
Network Systems and Data Communications Analyst
New Accounts Clerk
Nonfarm Animal Caretaker
Nuclear Medicine Technologist
Numerical Tool and Process Control Programmer
Nursing Aide, Orderly, and Attendant
Nursing Instructor and Teacher
Obstetrician and Gynecologist
Occupational Health and Safety Specialist
Occupational Health and Safety Technician
Occupational Therapist
Occupational Therapist Aide
Occupational Therapist Assistant
Office Clerk
Office Machine Operator
Operating Engineer and Other Construction Equipment Operator
Operations Research Analyst
Ophthalmic Laboratory Technician
Optician, Dispensing
Optometrist
Order Clerk

Orthotist and Prosthetist
Outdoor Power Equipment and Other Small Engine Mechanic
Packaging and Filling Machine Operator and Tender
Packer and Packager
Painter
Painting, Coating, and Decorating Worker
Paper Goods Machine Setter, Operator, and Tender
Paperhanger
Paralegal and Legal Assistant
Parking Enforcement Worker
Parking Lot Attendant
Parts Salesperson
Patternmaker
Paving, Surfacing, and Tamping Equipment Operator
Payroll and Timekeeping Clerk
Pediatrician
Personal and Home Care Aide
Personal Financial Advisor
Pest Control Worker
Pesticide Handler, Sprayer, and Applicator
Petroleum Pump System Operator, Refinery Operator, and Gauger
Pharmacist
Pharmacy Aide
Pharmacy Technician
Philosophy and Religion Teacher
Photographer
Photographic Process Worker
Photographic Processing Machine Operator
Physical Therapist
Physical Therapist Aide
Physical Therapist Assistant
Physician Assistant
Physicist
Physics Teacher
Pile-Driver Operator
Pipelayer
Plasterer and Stucco Mason
Plating and Coating Machine Setter, Operator, and Tender
Plumber, Pipefitter, and Steamfitter
Podiatrist
Police, Fire, and Ambulance Dispatcher
Police and Sheriff's Patrol Officer
Political Science Teacher
Postal Service Clerk
Postal Service Mail Carrier
Postal Service Mail Sorter, Processor, and Processing Machine Operator
Postmaster and Mail Superintendent
Pourer and Caster
Power Distributor and Dispatcher
Power Plant Operator
Prepress Technician and Worker
Preschool Teacher
Presser
Printing Machine Operator
Private Detective and Investigator

Probation Officer and Correctional Treatment Specialist
Procurement Clerk
Producer and Director
Production, Planning, and Expediting Clerk
Proofreader and Copy Marker
Property, Real Estate, and Community Association Manager
Psychiatric Aide
Psychiatric Technician
Psychiatrist
Psychology Teacher
Public Address System and Other Announcer
Public Relations Manager
Public Relations Specialist
Pump Operator
Purchasing Agent
Purchasing Agent and Buyer
Purchasing Manager
Radiation Therapist
Radio and Television Announcer
Radio Mechanic
Radiologic Technologist and Technician
Rail Car Repairer
Rail-Track Laying and Maintenance Equipment Operator
Railroad Brake, Signal, and Switch Operator
Railroad Conductor and Yardmaster
Real Estate Broker
Real Estate Sales Agent
Receptionist and Information Clerk
Recreation and Fitness Studies Teacher
Recreation Worker
Recreational Therapist
Recreational Vehicle Service Technician
Refractory Materials Repairer
Refuse and Recyclable Material Collector
Registered Nurse
Rehabilitation Counselor
Reinforcing Iron and Rebar Worker
Reporter and Correspondent
Reservation and Transportation Ticket Agent and Travel Clerk
Residential Advisor
Respiratory Therapist
Respiratory Therapy Technician
Retail Salesperson
Rigger
Rock Splitter
Rolling Machine Setter, Operator, and Tender
Roof Bolter
Roofer
Roustabout
Sailor and Marine Oiler
Sales Engineer
Sales Manager
Sales Representative
Sawing Machine Setter, Operator, and Tender, Wood

Secondary School Teacher
Secretary
Securities, Commodities, and Financial Services Sales Agent
Security and Fire Alarm Systems Installer
Security Guard
Self-Enrichment Education Teacher
Separating, Filtering, Clarifying, Precipitating, and Still Machine Setter, Operator, and Tender
Septic Tank Servicer and Sewer Pipe Cleaner
Service Station Attendant
Set and Exhibit Designer
Sewer
Sewing Machine Operator
Shampooer
Sheet Metal Worker
Ship Engineer
Shipping, Receiving, and Traffic Clerk
Shoe and Leather Worker and Repairer
Signal and Track Switch Repairer
Skin Care Specialist
Slaughterer and Meat Packer
Slot Key Person
Social and Community Service Manager
Social and Human Service Assistant
Social Science Research Assistant
Social Work Teacher
Sociology Teacher
Soil and Plant Scientist
Sound Engineering Technician
Special Education Teacher
Speech-Language Pathologist
Stationary Engineer and Boiler Operator
Statistical Assistant
Statistician
Stock Clerk and Order Filler
Stonemason
Structural Iron and Steel Worker
Structural Metal Fabricator and Fitter
Substance Abuse and Behavioral Disorder Counselor
Surgical Technologist
Survey Researcher
Surveying and Mapping Technician
Surveyor
Switchboard Operator
Tailor, Dressmaker, and Custom Sewer
Tank Car, Truck, and Ship Loader
Taper
Tax Examiner, Collector, and Revenue Agent
Tax Preparer
Taxi Driver and Chauffeur
Teacher Assistant
Team Assembler
Technical Writer
Telecommunications Equipment Installer and Repairer

Geographical Outline of Contents

Kentucky - continued:

Emergency Medical Technician and Paramedic

Employment, Recruitment, and Placement Specialist

Engine and Other Machine Assembler

Engineering Manager

Engineering Teacher

English Language and Literature Teacher

Environmental Engineer

Environmental Engineering Technician

Environmental Science and Protection Technician

Environmental Scientist and Specialist

Epidemiologist

Etcher and Engraver

Excavating and Loading Machine and Dragline Operator

Executive Secretary and Administrative Assistant

Explosives Worker, Ordnance Handling Expert, and Blaster

Extruding, Forming, Pressing, and Compacting Machine Setter, Operator, and Tender

Extruding and Drawing Machine Setter, Operator, and Tender

Extruding and Forming Machine Setter, Operator, and Tender

Faller

Family and General Practitioner

Farm, Ranch, and Other Agricultural Manager

Farm Equipment Mechanic

Farmworker

Farmworker and Laborer

Fence Erector

Fiberglass Laminator and Fabricator

File Clerk

Film and Video Editor

Financial Analyst

Financial Examiner

Financial Manager

Fine Artist, Including Painter, Sculptor, and Illustrator

Fire Fighter

Fire Inspector and Investigator

First-Line Supervisor/Manager

Fitness Trainer and Aerobics Instructor

Floor Layer

Floor Sander and Finisher

Floral Designer

Food and Tobacco Roasting, Baking, and Drying Machine Operator and Tender

Food Batchmaker

Food Cooking Machine Operator and Tender

Food Preparation Worker

Food Scientist and Technologist

Food Server

Food Service Manager

Foreign Language and Literature Teacher

Forensic Science Technician

Forest and Conservation Technician

Forging Machine Setter, Operator, and Tender

Foundry Mold and Coremaker

Funeral Attendant

Funeral Director

Furnace, Kiln, Oven, Drier, and Kettle Operator and Tender

Furniture Finisher

Gaming and Sports Book Writer and Runner

Gaming Supervisor

Gas Plant Operator

General and Operations Manager

Geography Teacher

Geological and Petroleum Technician

Geoscientist

Glazier

Grader and Sorter

Graphic Designer

Grinding, Lapping, Polishing, and Buffing Machine Tool Setter, Operator, and Tender

Grinding and Polishing Worker

Hairdresser, Hairstylist, and Cosmetologist

Hazardous Materials Removal Worker

Health and Safety Engineer

Health Educator

Health Specialties Teacher

Heat Treating Equipment Setter, Operator, and Tender

Heating, Air Conditioning, and Refrigeration Mechanic and Installer

Helper

Highway Maintenance Worker

Historian

History Teacher

Hoist and Winch Operator

Home Appliance Repairer

Home Economics Teacher

Home Health Aide

Host and Hostess

Hotel, Motel, and Resort Desk Clerk

Human Resources Assistant

Hydrologist

Industrial Engineer

Industrial Engineering Technician

Industrial Machinery Mechanic

Industrial Production Manager

Industrial Truck and Tractor Operator

Inspector, Tester, Sorter, Sampler, and Weigher

Instructional Coordinator

Insulation Worker

Insurance Appraiser

Insurance Claims and Policy Processing Clerk

Insurance Sales Agent

Insurance Underwriter

Interior Designer

Internist

Interpreter and Translator

Interviewer

Janitor and Cleaner

Jeweler and Precious Stone and Metal Worker

Job Printer

Kindergarten Teacher

Laborer and Freight, Stock, and Material Mover

Landscape Architect

Landscaping and Groundskeeping Worker

Lathe and Turning Machine Tool Setter, Operator, and Tender

Laundry and Dry-Cleaning Worker

Law Clerk

Law Teacher

Lawyer

Lay-Out Worker

Legal Secretary

Librarian

Library Assistant

Library Science Teacher

Library Technician

Licensed Practical and Licensed Vocational Nurse

Lifeguard, Ski Patrol, and Other Recreational Protective Service Worker

Loading Machine Operator

Loan Counselor

Loan Interviewer and Clerk

Loan Officer

Locker Room, Coatroom, and Dressing Room Attendant

Locksmith and Safe Repairer

Locomotive Engineer

Lodging Manager

Log Grader and Scaler

Logging Equipment Operator

Logistician

Machine Feeder and Offbearer

Machinist

Maid and Housekeeping Cleaner

Mail Clerk and Mail Machine Operator

Maintenance and Repair Worker

Maintenance Worker

Management Analyst

Manicurist and Pedicurist

Manufactured Building and Mobile Home Installer

Market Research Analyst

Marketing Manager

Marriage and Family Therapist

Massage Therapist

Materials Engineer

Materials Scientist

Mathematical Science Teacher

Meat, Poultry, and Fish Cutter and Trimmer

Mechanical Door Repairer

Mechanical Drafter

Mechanical Engineer

Mechanical Engineering Technician

Medic

Medical and Clinical Laboratory Technician

Medical and Clinical Laboratory Technologist

Medical and Health Services Manager

Medical and Public Health Social Worker

Medical Appliance Technician

Medical Assistant

Medical Equipment Preparer

Medical Equipment Repairer

Medical Records and Health Information Technician

Medical Scientist

Medical Secretary

Medical Transcriptionist

Meeting and Convention Planner

Mental Health and Substance Abuse Social Worker

Mental Health Counselor

Merchandise Displayer and Window Trimmer

Metal-Refining Furnace Operator and Tender

Meter Reader

Microbiologist

Middle School Teacher

Milling and Planing Machine Setter, Operator, and Tender

Millwright

Mine Cutting and Channeling Machine Operator

Mining and Geological Engineer

Mixing and Blending Machine Setter, Operator, and Tender

Mobile Heavy Equipment Mechanic

Model

Model Maker

Molder, Shaper, and Caster

Molding, Coremaking, and Casting Machine Setter, Operator, and Tender

Motion Picture Projectionist

Motorboat Mechanic

Motorcycle Mechanic

Multi-Media Artist and Animator

Multiple Machine Tool Setter, Operator, and Tender

Museum Technician and Conservator

Music Director and Composer

Musical Instrument Repairer and Tuner

Natural Sciences Manager

Network and Computer Systems Administrator

Network Systems and Data Communications Analyst

New Accounts Clerk

Nonfarm Animal Caretaker

Nuclear Medicine Technologist

Numerical Tool and Process Control Programmer

Nursing Aide, Orderly, and Attendant

Nursing Instructor and Teacher

Mississippi

Accountant and Auditor
Administrative Law Judge, Adjudicator, and Hearing Officer
Administrative Services Manager
Adult Literacy, Remedial Education, and GED Teacher and Instructor
Advertising and Promotions Manager
Advertising Sales Agent
Aerospace Engineer
Agricultural and Food Science Technician
Agricultural Engineer
Agricultural Equipment Operator
Agricultural Inspector
Agricultural Sciences Teacher
Air Traffic Controller
Aircraft Mechanic and Service Technician
Airline Pilot, Copilot, and Flight Engineer
Alderman
Ambulance Driver and Attendant
Amusement and Recreation Attendant
Anesthesiologist
Animal Control Worker
Animal Scientist
Anthropologist and Archeologist
Appraiser and Assessor of Real Estate
Arbitrator, Mediator, and Conciliator
Architect
Architectural and Civil Drafter
Architecture Teacher
Art, Drama, and Music Teacher
Art Director
Athletic Trainer
Atmospheric, Earth, Marine, and Space Sciences Teacher
Atmospheric and Space Scientist
Audio and Video Equipment Technician
Audiologist
Automotive Body and Related Repairer
Automotive Glass Installer and Repairer
Automotive Service Technician and Mechanic
Avionics Technician
Baggage Porter and Bellhop
Bailiff
Baker
Bartender
Bill and Account Collector
Billing and Posting Clerk and Machine Operator
Bindery Worker
Biological Science Teacher
Biological Technician
Biomedical Engineer
Boilermaker
Bookkeeping, Accounting, and Auditing Clerk

Brickmason and Blockmason
Bridge and Lock Tender
Broadcast News Analyst
Broadcast Technician
Brokerage Clerk
Budget Analyst
Building Inspector
Bus and Truck Mechanic and Diesel Engine Specialist
Bus Driver
Business Teacher
Butcher and Meat Cutter
Cabinetmaker and Bench Carpenter
Camera Operator
Captain, Mate, and Pilot of Water Vessels
Cardiovascular Technologist and Technician
Cargo and Freight Agent
Carpenter
Carpet Installer
Cartographer and Photogrammetrist
Cashier
Cement Mason and Concrete Finisher
Cementing and Gluing Machine Operator and Tender
Chef and Head Cook
Chemical Engineer
Chemical Equipment Operator and Tender
Chemical Plant and System Operator
Chemical Technician
Chemist
Chemistry Teacher
Chief Executive
Child, Family, and School Social Worker
Child Care Worker
Chiropractor
Choreographer
City Clerk
City Engineer
City Manager
City Planner
Civil Engineer
Civil Engineering Technician
Claims Adjuster, Examiner, and Investigator
Cleaner of Vehicles and Equipment
Cleaning, Washing, and Metal Pickling Equipment Operator and Tender
Clergy
Clinical, Counseling, and School Psychologist
Coach and Scout
Coating, Painting, and Spraying Machine Setter, Operator, and Tender
Coil Winder, Taper, and Finisher
Coin, Vending, and Amusement Machine Servicer and Repairer
Combined Food Preparation and Serving Worker
Commercial and Industrial Designer
Commercial Diver

Commercial Pilot
Communications Teacher
Compensation, Benefits, and Job Analysis Specialist
Compensation and Benefits Manager
Compliance Officer
Computer, Automated Teller, and Office Machine Repairer
Computer and Information Scientist
Computer and Information Systems Manager
Computer-Controlled Machine Tool Operator
Computer Hardware Engineer
Computer Operator
Computer Programmer
Computer Science Teacher
Computer Software Engineer
Computer Support Specialist
Computer Systems Analyst
Concierge
Conservation Scientist
Construction and Building Inspector
Construction Laborer
Construction Manager
Control and Valve Installer and Repairer
Conveyor Operator and Tender
Cook
Cooling and Freezing Equipment Operator and Tender
Correctional Officer and Jailer
Cost Estimator
Counter and Rental Clerk
Counter Attendant
Courier and Messenger
Court, Municipal, and License Clerk
Court Clerk
Court Reporter
Crane and Tower Operator
Credit Analyst
Credit Authorizer, Checker, and Clerk
Criminal Justice and Law Enforcement Teacher
Crossing Guard
Crushing, Grinding, and Polishing Machine Setter, Operator, and Tender
Customer Service Representative
Cutter and Trimmer
Cutting, Punching, and Press Machine Setter, Operator, and Tender
Cutting and Slicing Machine Setter, Operator, and Tender
Data Entry Keyer
Database Administrator
Demonstrator and Product Promoter
Dental Assistant
Dental Hygienist
Dental Laboratory Technician
Dentist
Derrick Operator
Desktop Publisher
Detective and Criminal Investigator
Diagnostic Medical Sonographer

Dietetic Technician
Dietitian and Nutritionist
Dining Room and Cafeteria Attendant and Bartender Helper
Director
Dishwasher
Dispatcher
Door-to-Door Sales Worker, News and Street Vendor, and Related Worker
Drilling and Boring Machine Tool Setter, Operator, and Tender
Driver/Sales Worker
Drywall and Ceiling Tile Installer
Earth Driller
Economics Teacher
Economist
Editor
Education Administrator
Education Teacher
Educational, Vocational, and School Counselor
Electric Motor, Power Tool, and Related Repairer
Electrical and Electronic Engineering Technician
Electrical and Electronic Equipment Assembler
Electrical and Electronics Drafter
Electrical and Electronics Installer and Repairer
Electrical and Electronics Repairer
Electrical Engineer
Electrical Power-Line Installer and Repairer
Electrician
Electro-Mechanical Technician
Electromechanical Equipment Assembler
Electronic Equipment Installer and Repairer
Electronic Home Entertainment Equipment Installer and Repairer
Electronics Engineer
Elementary School Teacher
Eligibility Interviewer
Embalmer
Emergency Management Specialist
Emergency Medical Technician and Paramedic
Employment, Recruitment, and Placement Specialist
Engine and Other Machine Assembler
Engineering Manager
Engineering Teacher
English Language and Literature Teacher
Environmental Engineer
Environmental Engineering Technician
Environmental Science and Protection Technician
Environmental Science Teacher
Environmental Scientist and Specialist

Geographical Outline of Contents

Missouri

Accountant and Auditor
Actuary
Administrative Law Judge, Adjudicator, and Hearing Officer
Administrative Services Manager
Adult Literacy, Remedial Education, and GED Teacher and Instructor
Advertising and Promotions Manager
Advertising Sales Agent
Aerospace Engineer
Aerospace Engineering and Operations Technician
Agent and Business Manager
Agricultural and Food Science Technician
Agricultural Engineer
Agricultural Equipment Operator
Agricultural Inspector
Agricultural Sciences Teacher
Air Traffic Controller
Aircraft Cargo Handling Supervisor
Aircraft Maintenance Specialist
Aircraft Mechanic and Service Technician
Airline Pilot, Copilot, and Flight Engineer
Ambulance Driver and Attendant
Amusement and Recreation Attendant
Animal Breeder
Animal Control Worker
Animal Scientist
Animal Trainer
Anthropologist and Archeologist
Anthropology and Archeology Teacher
Appraiser and Assessor of Real Estate
Arbitrator, Mediator, and Conciliator
Architect
Architectural and Civil Drafter
Architecture Teacher
Archivist
Area, Ethnic, and Cultural Studies Teacher
Art, Drama, and Music Teacher
Art Director
Athlete and Sports Competitor
Athletic Trainer
Atmospheric, Earth, Marine, and Space Sciences Teacher
Atmospheric and Space Scientist
Audio and Video Equipment Technician
Audio-Visual Collections Specialist
Audiologist
Automotive Body and Related Repairer
Automotive Glass Installer and Repairer
Automotive Service Technician and Mechanic
Avionics Technician
Baggage Porter and Bellhop

Bailiff
Baker
Barber
Bartender
Bicycle Repairer
Bill and Account Collector
Billing and Posting Clerk and Machine Operator
Bindery Worker
Biochemist and Biophysicist
Biological Science Teacher
Biological Technician
Biomedical Engineer
Boilermaker
Bookbinder
Bookkeeping, Accounting, and Auditing Clerk
Brickmason and Blockmason
Bridge and Lock Tender
Broadcast News Analyst
Broadcast Technician
Brokerage Clerk
Budget Analyst
Bus and Truck Mechanic and Diesel Engine Specialist
Bus Driver
Business Teacher
Butcher and Meat Cutter
Cabinetmaker and Bench Carpenter
Camera Operator
Captain, Mate, and Pilot of Water Vessels
Cardiovascular Technologist and Technician
Cargo and Freight Agent
Carpenter
Carpet Installer
Cartographer and Photogrammetrist
Cashier
CDL Examiner
Cement Mason and Concrete Finisher
Cementing and Gluing Machine Operator and Tender
Chef and Head Cook
Chemical Engineer
Chemical Equipment Operator and Tender
Chemical Plant and System Operator
Chemical Technician
Chemist
Chemistry Teacher
Chief Executive
Child, Family, and School Social Worker
Child Care Worker
Chiropractor
Choreographer
Civil Engineer
Civil Engineering Technician
Claims Adjuster, Examiner, and Investigator
Cleaner of Vehicles and Equipment
Cleaning, Washing, and Metal Pickling Equipment Operator and Tender
Clergy

Clerical Services Supervisor
Clinical, Counseling, and School Psychologist
Coach and Scout
Coating, Painting, and Spraying Machine Setter, Operator, and Tender
Coil Winder, Taper, and Finisher
Coin, Vending, and Amusement Machine Servicer and Repairer
Combined Food Preparation and Serving Worker
Commercial and Industrial Designer
Commercial Diver
Commercial Pilot
Communications Teacher
Compensation, Benefits, and Job Analysis Specialist
Compensation and Benefits Manager
Compliance Officer
Computer, Automated Teller, and Office Machine Repairer
Computer and Information Scientist
Computer and Information Systems Manager
Computer-Controlled Machine Tool Operator
Computer Hardware Engineer
Computer Operator
Computer Programmer
Computer Science Teacher
Computer Software Engineer
Computer Support Specialist
Computer Systems Analyst
Concierge
Conservation Scientist
Construction and Building Inspector
Construction Laborer
Construction Manager
Continuous Mining Machine Operator
Control and Valve Installer and Repairer
Conveyor Operator and Tender
Cook
Cooling and Freezing Equipment Operator and Tender
Correctional Officer and Jailer
Correspondence Clerk
Cost Estimator
Costume Attendant
Counter and Rental Clerk
Counter Attendant
Courier and Messenger
Court, Municipal, and License Clerk
Court Reporter
Craft Artist
Crane and Tower Operator
Credit Analyst
Credit Authorizer, Checker, and Clerk
Crime Laboratory Quality Assurance Coordinator
Criminal Justice and Law Enforcement Teacher
Criminalist Supervisor
Crossing Guard

Crushing, Grinding, and Polishing Machine Setter, Operator, and Tender
Curator
Customer Service Representative
Cutter and Trimmer
Cutting, Punching, and Press Machine Setter, Operator, and Tender
Cutting and Slicing Machine Setter, Operator, and Tender
Dancer
Data Entry Keyer
Database Administrator
Demonstrator and Product Promoter
Dental Assistant
Dental Hygienist
Dental Laboratory Technician
Dentist
Desktop Publisher
Detective and Criminal Investigator
Diagnostic Medical Sonographer
Dietetic Technician
Dietitian and Nutritionist
Dining Room and Cafeteria Attendant and Bartender Helper
Dishwasher
Dispatcher
Door-to-Door Sales Worker, News and Street Vendor, and Related Worker
Dredge Operator
Drilling and Boring Machine Tool Setter, Operator, and Tender
Driver/Sales Worker
Drywall and Ceiling Tile Installer
Earth Driller
Economics Teacher
Economist
Editor
Education Administrator
Education Teacher
Educational, Vocational, and School Counselor
Electric Motor, Power Tool, and Related Repairer
Electrical and Electronic Engineering Technician
Electrical and Electronic Equipment Assembler
Electrical and Electronics Drafter
Electrical and Electronics Installer and Repairer
Electrical and Electronics Repairer
Electrical Engineer
Electrical Power-Line Installer and Repairer
Electrician
Electro-Mechanical Technician
Electromechanical Equipment Assembler
Electronic Equipment Installer and Repairer
Electronic Home Entertainment Equipment Installer and Repairer
Electronics Engineer
Elementary School Teacher

Geographical Outline of Contents

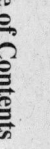

Geographical Outline of Contents

Geographical Outline of Contents

Geographical Outline of Contents

OCCUPATIONS

Occupation/Type/Industry	Location	Per	Low	Mid	High	Source	Date
1st Class Petty Officer							
U.S. Navy, Active Duty, Pay Grade E-6	United States	M	2176 LO		3370 HI	DOD1	2009
1st Sergeant							
U.S. Army, Active Duty, Pay Grade E-8	United States	M	3619 LO		5161 HI	DOD1	2009
U.S. Marines, Active Duty, Pay Grade E-8	United States	M	3619 LO		5161 HI	DOD1	2009
2D Animator	United States	W		2080 MW		TAG	1/08
2nd Class Petty Officer							
U.S. Navy, Active Duty, Pay Grade E-5	United States	M	1994 LO		2828 HI	DOD1	2009
3D Animator	United States	W		1745 MW		TAG	1/08
3rd Class Petty Officer							
U.S. Navy, Active Duty, Pay Grade E-4	United States	M	1827 LO		2219 HI	DOD1	2009
747 Load Planner	United States	H		14.50 AW		AVJOB01	2009
911 Director	Riverdale, GA	Y	56824 LO		86464 HI	GACTY01	2008
	Livingston County, MI	Y			93060 HI	LCPP	2009
911 Operator	Washington, GA	Y	19060 LO		28262 HI	GACTY01	2008
	Baltimore, MD	Y	26702 LO			BMAG	2009
	Cincinnati, OH	Y	40748 LO		42428 HI	COHSS	10/08
A&P Mechanic	United States	Y		52562 AW		AMT	2008
Account Executive							
State Government	Ohio	H	19.88 LO		26.28 HI	ODAS	2008
Accountant							
Partner in Accounting Firm	Middle Atlantic	Y	112000 LO		164000 HI	ACTT	2009
Accountant and Auditor	Alabama	Y	39640 FQ	50090 MW	65650 TQ	USBLS	5/07
	Birmingham-Hoover MSA, AL	Y	42730 FQ	52290 MW	67350 TQ	USBLS	5/07
	Montgomery MSA, AL	Y	40300 FQ	51080 MW	66260 TQ	USBLS	5/07
	Alaska	Y	42440 FQ	52660 MW	65720 TQ	USBLS	5/07
	Anchorage MSA, AK	Y	42370 FQ	52600 MW	69100 TQ	USBLS	5/07
	Arizona	Y	40250 FQ	50090 MW	64210 TQ	USBLS	5/07
	Phoenix-Mesa-Scottsdale MSA, AZ	Y	40590 FQ	50250 MW	63810 TQ	USBLS	5/07
	Tucson MSA, AZ	Y	40850 FQ	50550 MW	68340 TQ	USBLS	5/07
	Arkansas	Y	35660 FQ	45000 MW	59390 TQ	USBLS	5/07
	Fort Smith MSA, AR-OK	Y	32880 FQ	40390 MW	52680 TQ	USBLS	5/07
	Little Rock-North Little Rock MSA, AR	Y	37170 FQ	47370 MW	66030 TQ	USBLS	5/07
	California	H	23.21 FQ	29.88 MW	38.91 TQ	CABLS	1/08-3/08
	Fresno MSA, CA	H	21.22 FQ	25.69 MW	32.35 TQ	CABLS	1/08-3/08
	Los Angeles-Long Beach-Glendale PMSA, CA	H	22.03 FQ	29.19 MW	39.61 TQ	CABLS	1/08-3/08
	Oakland-Fremont-Hayward MSA, CA	H	26.77 FQ	32.15 MW	40.11 TQ	CABLS	1/08-3/08
	Oxnard-Thousand Oaks-Ventura MSA, CA	H	22.74 FQ	29.39 MW	36.84 TQ	CABLS	1/08-3/08
	Riverside-San Bernardino-Ontario MSA, CA	H	22.62 FQ	27.77 MW	34.46 TQ	CABLS	1/08-3/08
	Sacramento-Arden Arcade-Roseville MSA, CA	H	22.38 FQ	27.62 MW	35.29 TQ	CABLS	1/08-3/08
	San Diego-Carlsbad-San Marcos MSA, CA	H	23.47 FQ	29.08 MW	37.08 TQ	CABLS	1/08-3/08

AE	Average entry wage	**AW**	Average wage paid	**FQ**	First quartile wage	**LO** Lowest wage paid · **MTC** Median total compensation · **TCC** Total cash compensation
AER	Average entry range	**AWR**	Average wage range	**H**	Hourly	**LR** Low end range · **MW** Median wage paid · **TQ** Third quartile wage
AEX	Average experienced wage	**AXR**	Average experienced range	**HI**	Highest wage paid	**M** Monthly · **MWR** Median wage range · **W** Weekly
ATC	Average total compensation	**D**	Daily	**HR**	High end range	**MCC** Median cash compensation · **S** See annotated source · **Y** Yearly

1

Occupation/Type/Industry	Location	Per	Low	Mid	High	Source	Date
Accountant and Auditor	San Francisco-San Mateo-Redwood PMSA, CA	H	26.76 FQ	34.87 MW	43.83 TQ	CABLS	1/08-3/08
	San Jose-Sunnyvale-Santa Clara MSA, CA	H	26.89 FQ	34.25 MW	43.40 TQ	CABLS	1/08-3/08
	Santa Ana-Anaheim-Irvine PMSA, CA	Y	46290 FQ	59660 MW	75750 TQ	USBLS	5/07
	Colorado	Y	44660 FQ	57840 MW	78440 TQ	USBLS	5/07
	Denver-Aurora MSA, CO	Y	46080 FQ	59620 MW	80310 TQ	USBLS	5/07
	Connecticut	H	21.57 AE	30.89 MW		CTBLS	1/08-3/08
	Bridgeport-Stamford-Norwalk MSA, CT	Y	54750 FQ	69040 MW	88820 TQ	USBLS	5/07
	Hartford-West Hartford-East Hartford MSA, CT	Y	48040 FQ	59930 MW	76130 TQ	USBLS	5/07
	Waterbury MSA, CT	Y	45710 FQ	55380 MW	68820 TQ	USBLS	5/07
	Delaware	Y	44100 FQ	57680 MW	75500 TQ	USBLS	5/07
	Wilmington PMSA, DE-MD-NJ	Y	46220 FQ	59940 MW	78150 TQ	USBLS	5/07
	District of Columbia	Y	49110 FQ	65840 MW	89960 TQ	USBLS	5/07
	Washington-Arlington-Alexandria MSA, DC-VA-MD-WV	Y	50760 FQ	66440 MW	88970 TQ	USBLS	5/07
	Florida	Y	41380 FQ	53200 MW	70050 TQ	USBLS	5/07
	Fort Lauderdale-Pompano Beach-Deerfield Beach PMSA, FL	Y	43560 FQ	56230 MW	73690 TQ	USBLS	5/07
	Jacksonville MSA, FL	Y	41730 FQ	51670 MW	66390 TQ	USBLS	5/07
	Miami-Fort Lauderdale-Miami Beach MSA, FL	Y	43650 FQ	56810 MW	74530 TQ	USBLS	5/07
	Orlando-Kissimmee MSA, FL	Y	40180 FQ	50730 MW	69940 TQ	USBLS	5/07
	Tampa-St. Petersburg-Clearwater MSA, FL	Y	41720 FQ	53240 MW	68550 TQ	USBLS	5/07
	West Palm Beach-Boca Raton-Boynton Beach PMSA, FL	Y	46730 FQ	59110 MW	75660 TQ	USBLS	5/07
	Georgia	Y	43870 FQ	55940 MW	74010 TQ	USBLS	5/07
	Atlanta-Sandy Springs-Marietta MSA, GA	Y	45440 FQ	57770 MW	76590 TQ	USBLS	5/07
	Hawaii	Y	38810 FQ	48180 MW	60620 TQ	USBLS	5/07
	Honolulu MSA, HI	Y	38530 FQ	47800 MW	60760 TQ	USBLS	5/07
	Idaho	Y	37710 FQ	46630 MW	60270 TQ	USBLS	5/07
	Boise City-Nampa MSA, ID	Y	38560 FQ	46990 MW	58710 TQ	USBLS	5/07
	Illinois	Y	46320 FQ	59910 MW	79550 TQ	USBLS	5/07
	Chicago-Naperville-Joliet MSA, IL-IN-WI	Y	47810 FQ	61530 MW	81350 TQ	USBLS	5/07
	Indiana	Y	41060 FQ	53300 MW	69790 TQ	USBLS	5/07
	Gary PMSA, IN	Y	38640 FQ	48730 MW	61160 TQ	USBLS	5/07
	Indianapolis-Carmel MSA, IN	Y	42930 FQ	57300 MW	75640 TQ	USBLS	5/07
	Iowa	Y	39510 FQ	49790 MW	63890 TQ	USBLS	5/07
	Des Moines-West Des Moines MSA, IA	Y	39960 FQ	51020 MW	64200 TQ	USBLS	5/07
	Kansas	Y	41290 FQ	50250 MW	63610 TQ	USBLS	5/07
	Wichita MSA, KS	Y	43410 FQ	51500 MW	65810 TQ	USBLS	5/07
	Kentucky	Y	39004 FQ	50103 MW	63999 TQ	KYBLS	2008
	Louisville-Jefferson County MSA, KY-IN	Y	40190 FQ	50580 MW	64550 TQ	USBLS	5/07
	Louisiana	H	18.43 FQ	23.06 MW	29.59 TQ	LABLS	1/08-3/08
	Baton Rouge MSA, LA	Y	39180 FQ	47240 MW	57650 TQ	USBLS	5/07
	Lake Charles MSA, LA	Y	34760 FQ	44550 MW	55320 TQ	USBLS	5/07
	New Orleans-Metairie-Kenner MSA, LA	Y	42020 FQ	53070 MW	72620 TQ	USBLS	5/07
	Shreveport-Bossier City MSA, LA	Y	36700 FQ	45910 MW	58440 TQ	USBLS	5/07
	Maine	Y	39190 FQ	48110 MW	62620 TQ	USBLS	5/07
	Portland-South Portland-Biddeford MSA, ME	Y	41330 FQ	49030 MW	63320 TQ	USBLS	5/07
	Maryland	Y		63750 MW		MDBLS	3/08
	Baltimore-Towson MSA, MD	Y	47200 FQ	60780 MW	77430 TQ	USBLS	5/07
	Bethesda-Gaithersburg-Frederick PMSA, MD	Y	51660 FQ	67850 MW	89350 TQ	USBLS	5/07
	Hagerstown-Martinsburg MSA, MD-WV	Y	39780 FQ	50630 MW	65970 TQ	USBLS	5/07
	Massachusetts	Y	48970 FQ	61490 MW	78090 TQ	USBLS	5/07

AE   Average entry wage   AW   Average wage paid   FQ   First quartile wage   LO   Lowest wage paid   MTC   Median total compensation   TCC   Total cash compensation
AER   Average entry range   AWR   Average wage range   H   Hourly   LR   Low end range   MW   Median wage paid   TQ   Third quartile wage
AEX   Average experienced wage   AXR   Average experienced range   HI   Highest wage paid   M   Monthly   MWR   Median wage range   W   Weekly
ATC   Average total compensation   D   Daily   HR   High end range   MCC   Median cash compensation   S   See annotated source   Y   Yearly

Occupation/Type/Industry	Location	Per	Low	Mid	High	Source	Date
Accountant and Auditor	Boston-Cambridge-Quincy NECTA, MA	Y	50280 FQ	63610 MW	79990 TQ	USBLS	5/07
	Worcester MSA, MA-CT	Y	48090 FQ	58420 MW	73960 TQ	USBLS	5/07
	Michigan	Y	44460 FQ	55650 MW	71580 TQ	USBLS	5/07
	Ann Arbor MSA, MI	Y	41630 FQ	51410 MW	62760 TQ	USBLS	5/07
	Detroit-Warren-Livonia MSA, MI	Y	46020 FQ	57280 MW	74970 TQ	USBLS	5/07
	Grand Rapids-Wyoming MSA, MI	Y	44300 FQ	56320 MW	69140 TQ	USBLS	5/07
	Muskegon-Norton Shores MSA, MI	Y	44970 FQ	53960 MW	88510 TQ	USBLS	5/07
	Warren-Troy-Farmington Hills PMSA, MI	Y	45260 FQ	55950 MW	72990 TQ	USBLS	5/07
	Minnesota	Y	47816 FQ	58054 MW	72068 TQ	MNBLS	10/08-12/08
	Duluth-Superior MSA, MN-WI	Y	43416 FQ	51694 MW	63810 TQ	MNBLS	10/08-12/08
	Minneapolis-Saint Paul MSA, MN-WI	Y	49286 FQ	59723 MW	75050 TQ	MNBLS	10/08-12/08
	Rochester MSA, MN	Y	45150 FQ	53134 MW	64717 TQ	MNBLS	10/08-12/08
	Mississippi	Y	36630 FQ	45950 MW	62360 TQ	USBLS	5/07
	Jackson MSA, MS	Y	36030 FQ	44910 MW	60470 TQ	USBLS	5/07
	Missouri	Y	38780 FQ	50840 MW	65860 TQ	USBLS	5/07
	Kansas City MSA, MO-KS	Y	41420 FQ	52490 MW	66760 TQ	USBLS	5/07
	St. Louis MSA, MO-IL	Y	42710 FQ	54630 MW	70530 TQ	USBLS	5/07
	Montana	Y	37300 FQ	47490 MW	62810 TQ	USBLS	5/07
	Billings MSA, MT	Y	35100 FQ	45650 MW	58130 TQ	USBLS	5/07
	Nebraska	Y	42250 FQ	52350 MW	66540 TQ	USBLS	5/07
	Lincoln MSA, NE	Y	40400 FQ	50240 MW	61110 TQ	USBLS	5/07
	Omaha-Council Bluffs MSA, NE-IA	Y	43850 FQ	55020 MW	70940 TQ	USBLS	5/07
	Nevada	H	20.33 FQ	25.27 MW	31.82 TQ	NVBLS	5/08
	Carson City MSA, NV	H	21.13 FQ	25.87 MW	33.25 TQ	NVBLS	5/08
	Las Vegas-Paradise MSA, NV	H	20.26 FQ	25.40 MW	32.11 TQ	NVBLS	5/08
	New Hampshire	H	19.32 AE	25.43 MW	30.96 AEX	NHBLS	6/08
	Manchester MSA, NH	Y	43870 FQ	52310 MW	65740 TQ	USBLS	5/07
	Nashua NECTA, NH-MA	Y	45670 FQ	55680 MW	71170 TQ	USBLS	5/07
	New Jersey	Y	54880 FQ	68890 MW	87170 TQ	USBLS	5/07
	Camden PMSA, NJ	Y	49590 FQ	61710 MW	77290 TQ	USBLS	5/07
	Edison PMSA, NJ	Y	55290 FQ	69630 MW	89560 TQ	USBLS	5/07
	Newark-Union PMSA, NJ-PA	Y	56190 FQ	71300 MW	89910 TQ	USBLS	5/07
	New Mexico	Y	39630 FQ	49000 MW	64060 TQ	USBLS	5/07
	Albuquerque MSA, NM	Y	42620 FQ	51810 MW	68970 TQ	USBLS	5/07
	New York	Y	54090 FQ	67650 MW	88600 TQ	USBLS	5/07
	Albany-Schenectady-Troy MSA, NY	Y	47880 FQ	58080 MW	72390 TQ	USBLS	5/07
	Buffalo-Niagara Falls MSA, NY	Y	47350 FQ	59540 MW	74510 TQ	USBLS	5/07
	Kingston MSA, NY	Y	46430 FQ	54330 MW	83230 TQ	USBLS	5/07
	Nassau-Suffolk PMSA, NY	Y	55330 FQ	70560 MW	94000 TQ	USBLS	5/07
	New York-Northern New Jersey-Long Island MSA, NY-NJ-PA	Y	56760 FQ	71190 MW	92000 TQ	USBLS	5/07
	North Carolina	Y	43450 FQ	54070 MW	68600 TQ	USBLS	5/07
	Charlotte-Gastonia-Concord MSA, NC-SC	Y	44840 FQ	55730 MW	70890 TQ	USBLS	5/07
	Raleigh-Cary MSA, NC	Y	44280 FQ	54920 MW	68680 TQ	USBLS	5/07
	North Dakota	Y	34540 FQ	43410 MW	53800 TQ	USBLS	5/07
	Fargo MSA, ND-MN	Y	38100 FQ	45240 MW	54180 TQ	USBLS	5/07
	Ohio	Y	43140 FQ	53970 MW	68840 TQ	USBLS	5/07
	Cincinnati-Middletown MSA, OH-KY-IN	Y	44180 FQ	56090 MW	70960 TQ	USBLS	5/07
	Cleveland-Elyria-Mentor MSA, OH	Y	43670 FQ	54460 MW	71580 TQ	USBLS	5/07
	Columbus MSA, OH	Y	42540 FQ	52850 MW	68490 TQ	USBLS	5/07
	Dayton MSA, OH	Y	44880 FQ	56960 MW	76360 TQ	USBLS	5/07
	Springfield MSA, OH	Y	43230 FQ	49580 MW	59810 TQ	USBLS	5/07
	Oklahoma	Y	35550 FQ	45770 MW	60130 TQ	USBLS	5/07
	Oklahoma City MSA, OK	Y	34870 FQ	44350 MW	58150 TQ	USBLS	5/07
	Tulsa MSA, OK	Y	37530 FQ	48350 MW	61990 TQ	USBLS	5/07
	Oregon	H	21.31 FQ	26.40 MW	33.91 TQ	ORBLS	5/08
	Eugene-Springfield MSA, OR	Y	42760 FQ	52760 MW	69980 TQ	USBLS	5/07
	Portland-Vancouver-Beaverton MSA, OR-WA	Y	45240 FQ	56360 MW	71950 TQ	USBLS	5/07

AE	Average entry wage	AW	Average wage paid	FQ	First quartile wage
AER	Average entry range	AWR	Average wage range	H	Hourly
AEX	Average experienced wage	AXR	Average experienced range	HI	Highest wage paid
ATC	Average total compensation	D	Daily	HR	High end range

LO	Lowest wage paid	MTC	Median total compensation	TCC	Total cash compensation
LR	Low end range	MW	Median wage paid	TQ	Third quartile wage
M	Monthly	MWR	Median wage range	W	Weekly
MCC	Median cash compensation	S	See annotated source	Y	Yearly

Occupation/Type/Industry	Location	Per	Low	Mid	High	Source	Date
Accountant and Auditor	Pennsylvania	Y	43100 FQ	56700 MW	77120 TQ	USBLS	5/07
	Allentown-Bethlehem-Easton MSA, PA-NJ	Y	42520 FQ	55680 MW	74090 TQ	USBLS	5/07
	Philadelphia-Camden-Wilmington MSA, PA-NJ-DE-MD	Y	48520 FQ	62420 MW	83810 TQ	USBLS	5/07
	Pittsburgh MSA, PA	Y	40710 FQ	52530 MW	74210 TQ	USBLS	5/07
	Rhode Island	Y	49620 FQ	59880 MW	73290 TQ	USBLS	5/07
	Providence-Fall River-Warwick MSA, RI-MA	Y	49280 FQ	59650 MW	73270 TQ	USBLS	5/07
	South Carolina	Y	38660 FQ	49820 MW	65120 TQ	USBLS	5/07
	Charleston-North Charleston MSA, SC	Y	42690 FQ	54340 MW	68700 TQ	USBLS	5/07
	Columbia MSA, SC	Y	38670 FQ	49050 MW	64350 TQ	USBLS	5/07
	Spartanburg MSA, SC	Y	40570 FQ	51790 MW	68000 TQ	USBLS	5/07
	South Dakota	Y	40081 FQ	47765 MW	58915 TQ	SDBLS	7/08-9/08
	Sioux Falls MSA, SD	Y	43538 FQ	51399 MW	62052 TQ	SDBLS	7/08-9/08
	Tennessee	Y	39550 FQ	49670 MW	64080 TQ	USBLS	5/07
	Memphis MSA, TN-MS-AR	Y	42870 FQ	53160 MW	68370 TQ	USBLS	5/07
	Nashville-Davidson-Murfreesboro MSA, TN	Y	41600 FQ	51160 MW	64690 TQ	USBLS	5/07
	Texas	Y	41910 FQ	55150 MW	73220 TQ	USBLS	5/07
	Austin-Round Rock MSA, TX	Y	39930 FQ	57060 MW	75710 TQ	USBLS	5/07
	Brownsville-Harlingen MSA, TX	Y	34270 FQ	43010 MW	54780 TQ	USBLS	5/07
	Dallas-Fort Worth-Arlington MSA, TX	Y	44220 FQ	57980 MW	77560 TQ	USBLS	5/07
	El Paso MSA, TX	Y	37210 FQ	48580 MW	61310 TQ	USBLS	5/07
	Houston-Sugar Land-Baytown MSA, TX	Y	44830 FQ	57960 MW	75600 TQ	USBLS	5/07
	San Antonio MSA, TX	Y	39190 FQ	50980 MW	66650 TQ	USBLS	5/07
	Utah	Y	41570 FQ	54150 MW	72700 TQ	USBLS	5/07
	Salt Lake City MSA, UT	Y	42710 FQ	55240 MW	73080 TQ	USBLS	5/07
	Vermont	Y	45120 FQ	54940 MW	67170 TQ	USBLS	5/07
	Burlington-South Burlington MSA, VT	Y	47450 FQ	56850 MW	70500 TQ	USBLS	5/07
	Virginia	Y	45560 FQ	60090 MW	80250 TQ	USBLS	5/07
	Lynchburg MSA, VA	Y	35620 FQ	47150 MW	68800 TQ	USBLS	5/07
	Richmond MSA, VA	Y	46420 FQ	58900 MW	76130 TQ	USBLS	5/07
	Virginia Beach-Norfolk-Newport News MSA, VA-NC	Y	40870 FQ	53360 MW	71630 TQ	USBLS	5/07
	Washington	H	23.69 FQ	28.96 MW	36.07 TQ	WABLS	3/08
	Seattle-Tacoma-Bellevue MSA, WA	Y	50140 FQ	61190 MW	75730 TQ	USBLS	5/07
	West Virginia	Y	35920 FQ	44994 MW	61518 TQ	WVBLS	7/08-9/08
	Charleston MSA, WV	Y	35060 FQ	42300 MW	53540 TQ	USBLS	5/07
	Wisconsin	Y	44560 FQ	54730 MW	68780 TQ	USBLS	5/07
	Milwaukee-Waukesha-West Allis MSA, WI	Y	46480 FQ	57240 MW	73880 TQ	USBLS	5/07
	Wyoming	Y	38447 FQ	46846 MW	61521 TQ	WYBLS	9/08
	Cheyenne MSA, WY	Y	37362 FQ	43384 MW	51932 TQ	WYBLS	9/08
	Puerto Rico	Y	24230 FQ	30330 MW	40080 TQ	USBLS	5/07
	San Juan-Caguas-Guaynabo MSA, PR	Y	24940 FQ	31060 MW	40720 TQ	USBLS	5/07
	Virgin Islands	Y	34750 FQ	40600 MW	49560 TQ	USBLS	5/07
	Guam	Y	28160 FQ	35640 MW	45110 TQ	USBLS	5/07
Accountant Manager	Middle Atlantic	Y	68000 LO		92000 HI	ACTT	2009
Accounting Assistant							
Municipal Government	Seaside, CA	S	1719 LO		2026 HI	SSSS	8/08
Accounting Technician							
Municipal Government	Seaside, CA	S	1863 LO		2202 HI	SSSS	8/08
Activities Aide							
State Government	Ohio	H	14.36 LO		15.41 HI	ODAS	2008
Activity Director							
Nursing Home	United States	Y		38304 AW		MLTCN02	2008
Activity Therapy Specialist							
State Government	Ohio	H	15.62 LO		21.77 HI	ODAS	2008

AE	Average entry wage	**AW**	Average wage paid	**FQ**	First quartile wage	**LO**	Lowest wage paid	**MTC**	Median total compensation
AER	Average entry range	**AWR**	Average wage range	**H**	Hourly	**LR**	Low end range	**MW**	Median wage paid
AEX	Average experienced wage	**AXR**	Average experienced range	**HI**	Highest wage paid	**M**	Monthly	**MWR**	Median wage range
ATC	Average total compensation	**D**	Daily	**HR**	High end range	**MCC**	Median cash compensation	**S**	See annotated source

TCC	Total cash compensation		
TQ	Third quartile wage		
W	Weekly		
Y	Yearly		

Occupation/Type/Industry	Location	Per	Low	Mid	High	Source	Date
Actor	Arkansas	H	6.77 FQ	7.16 MW	7.56 TQ	USBLS	5/07
	California	H	8.97 FQ	11.94 MW	20.49 MW	CABLS	1/08-3/08
	Colorado	H	8.20 FQ	12.48 MW	22.75 TQ	USBLS	5/07
	Connecticut	H	13.55 AE	18.53 MW		CTBLS	1/08-3/08
	District of Columbia	H	10.12 FQ	14.70 MW	21.74 TQ	USBLS	5/07
	Florida	H	8.36 FQ	9.60 MW	15.71 TQ	USBLS	5/07
	Georgia	H	16.26 FQ	20.62 MW	64.04 TQ	USBLS	5/07
	Idaho	H	6.75 FQ	8.39 MW	14.05 TQ	USBLS	5/07
	Illinois	H	10.27 FQ	19.30 MW	27.43 TQ	USBLS	5/07
	Indiana	H	9.38 FQ	11.32 MW	13.81 TQ	USBLS	5/07
	Kansas	H	6.34 FQ	7.26 MW	11.91 TQ	USBLS	5/07
	Louisiana	H	8.65 FQ	16.95 MW	33.15 TQ	LABLS	1/08-3/08
	Maine	H	12.56 FQ	14.29 MW	16.93 TQ	USBLS	5/07
	Michigan	H	7.80 FQ	8.53 MW	9.26 TQ	USBLS	5/07
	Minnesota	H	11.15 FQ	13.07 MW	17.76 TQ	MNBLS	10/08-12/08
	Nevada	H	20.37 FQ	23.25 MW	26.73 TQ	NVBLS	5/08
	New York	H	14.21 FQ	37.93 MW	47.32 TQ	USBLS	5/07
	North Carolina	H	6.83 FQ	7.48 MW	11.40 TQ	USBLS	5/07
	Ohio	H	7.63 FQ	8.70 MW	11.63 TQ	USBLS	5/07
	Pennsylvania	H	9.11 FQ	13.21 MW	18.26 TQ	USBLS	5/07
	South Carolina	H	8.84 FQ	11.08 MW	15.69 TQ	USBLS	5/07
	South Dakota	H	10.89 FQ	11.70 MW	12.50 TQ	SDBLS	7/08-9/08
	Tennessee	H	6.55 FQ	8.11 MW	17.19 TQ	USBLS	5/07
	Utah	H	9.00 FQ	13.59 MW	15.74 TQ	USBLS	5/07
	Virginia	H	11.92 FQ	17.06 MW	26.59 TQ	USBLS	5/07
	Washington	H	11.47 FQ	20.93 MW	51.79 TQ	WABLS	3/08
	Wisconsin	H	11.08 FQ	14.57 MW	25.58 TQ	USBLS	5/07
Network Program Commercial	United States	S	422 LO		1354 HI	AFTRA1	10/30/06-10/29/08
Actuary	Alabama	Y	44920 FQ	51060 MW	83180 TQ	USBLS	5/07
	Birmingham-Hoover MSA, AL	Y	45710 FQ	52880 MW	87180 TQ	USBLS	5/07
	Arizona	Y	58230 FQ	73020 MW	96180 TQ	USBLS	5/07
	Phoenix-Mesa-Scottsdale MSA, AZ	Y	58270 FQ	73490 MW	97150 TQ	USBLS	5/07
	California	H	31.65 FQ	41.87 MW	54.91 TQ	CABLS	1/08-3/08
	Los Angeles-Long Beach-Glendale PMSA, CA	H	31.07 FQ	44.76 MW	59.92 TQ	CABLS	1/08-3/08
	Oakland-Fremont-Hayward MSA, CA	H	36.93 FQ	43.98 MW	50.24 TQ	CABLS	1/08-3/08
	Sacramento-Arden Arcade-Roseville MSA, CA	H	31.70 FQ	41.79 MW	54.33 TQ	CABLS	1/08-3/08
	San Francisco-San Mateo-Redwood PMSA, CA	H	33.18 FQ	42.99 MW	57.60 TQ	CABLS	1/08-3/08
	Santa Ana-Anaheim-Irvine PMSA, CA	Y	59510 FQ	80130 MW	101170 TQ	USBLS	5/07
	Colorado	Y	69790 FQ	91530 MW	122610 TQ	USBLS	5/07
	Denver-Aurora MSA, CO	Y	71180 FQ	91980 MW	122940 TQ	USBLS	5/07
	Connecticut	H	28.67 AE	48.59 MW		CTBLS	1/08-3/08
	Bridgeport-Stamford-Norwalk MSA, CT	Y	71090 FQ	96260 MW	142130 TQ	USBLS	5/07
	Hartford-West Hartford-East Hartford MSA, CT	Y	66010 FQ	89830 MW	119430 TQ	USBLS	5/07
	Delaware	Y	77290 FQ	111830 MW	142120 TQ	USBLS	5/07
	Wilmington PMSA, DE-MD-NJ	Y	78580 FQ	113090 MW	143300 TQ	USBLS	5/07
	District of Columbia	Y	66200 FQ	86940 MW	112740 TQ	USBLS	5/07
	Washington-Arlington-Alexandria MSA, DC-VA-MD-WV	Y	66580 FQ	91230 MW	127290 TQ	USBLS	5/07
	Florida	Y	60490 FQ	85280 MW	109730 TQ	USBLS	5/07
	Fort Lauderdale-Pompano Beach-Deerfield Beach PMSA, FL	Y	78830 FQ	100820 MW	128410 TQ	USBLS	5/07
	Jacksonville MSA, FL	Y	72880 FQ	114650 MW	133100 TQ	USBLS	5/07
	Miami-Fort Lauderdale-Miami Beach MSA, FL	Y	65300 FQ	85900 MW	109300 TQ	USBLS	5/07
	Tampa-St. Petersburg-Clearwater MSA, FL	Y	59120 FQ	76330 MW	97280 TQ	USBLS	5/07
	Georgia	Y	61670 FQ	79310 MW	107490 TQ	USBLS	5/07
	Atlanta-Sandy Springs-Marietta MSA, GA	Y	61900 FQ	79190 MW	109040 TQ	USBLS	5/07
	Boise City-Nampa MSA, ID	Y	105310 FQ	119780 MW	137190 TQ	USBLS	5/07

AE Average entry wage	**AW** Average wage paid	**FQ** First quartile wage	**LO** Lowest wage paid	**MTC** Median total compensation	**TCC** Total cash compensation
AER Average entry range	**AWR** Average wage range	**H** Hourly	**LR** Low end range	**MW** Median wage paid	**TQ** Third quartile wage
AEX Average experienced wage	**AXR** Average experienced range	**HI** Highest wage paid	**M** Monthly	**MWR** Median wage range	**W** Weekly
ATC Average total compensation	**D** Daily	**HR** High end range	**MCC** Median cash compensation	**S** See annotated source	**Y** Yearly

Occupation/Type/Industry	Location	Per	Low	Mid	High	Source	Date
Actuary	Illinois	Y	64080 FQ	85270 MW	112080 TQ	USBLS	5/07
	Chicago-Naperville-Joliet MSA, IL-IN-WI	Y	66430 FQ	88200 MW	119220 TQ	USBLS	5/07
	Indiana	Y	57650 FQ	85880 MW	114150 TQ	USBLS	5/07
	Indianapolis-Carmel MSA, IN	Y	49920 FQ	77980 MW	98990 TQ	USBLS	5/07
	Iowa	Y	57590 FQ	82580 MW	116660 TQ	USBLS	5/07
	Des Moines-West Des Moines MSA, IA	Y	56010 FQ	76800 MW	113090 TQ	USBLS	5/07
	Kansas	Y	55080 FQ	81080 MW	117210 TQ	USBLS	5/07
	Wichita MSA, KS	Y	46050 FQ	56240 MW	79770 TQ	USBLS	5/07
	Kentucky	Y	68005 FQ	89380 MW	127056 TQ	KYBLS	2008
	Louisville-Jefferson County MSA, KY-IN	Y	65320 FQ	87730 MW	124640 TQ	USBLS	5/07
	Louisiana	H	30.04 FQ	43.12 MW	57.29 TQ	LABLS	1/08-3/08
	Maine	Y	44970 FQ	53980 MW	63440 TQ	USBLS	5/07
	Portland-South Portland-Biddeford MSA, ME	Y	44690 FQ	53460 MW	63160 TQ	USBLS	5/07
	Maryland	Y		98500 MW		MDBLS	3/08
	Baltimore-Towson MSA, MD	Y	61350 FQ	93080 MW	117220 TQ	USBLS	5/07
	Bethesda-Gaithersburg-Frederick PMSA, MD	Y	69320 FQ	101350 MW	129500 TQ	USBLS	5/07
	Massachusetts	Y	65940 FQ	89420 MW	125450 TQ	USBLS	5/07
	Boston-Cambridge-Quincy NECTA, MA	Y	64820 FQ	88430 MW	124730 TQ	USBLS	5/07
	Worcester MSA, MA-CT	Y	66420 FQ	77580 MW	134470 TQ	USBLS	5/07
	Michigan	Y	48740 FQ	62840 MW	98110 TQ	USBLS	5/07
	Detroit-Warren-Livonia MSA, MI	Y	47270 FQ	53090 MW	84360 TQ	USBLS	5/07
	Warren-Troy-Farmington Hills PMSA, MI	Y	46580 FQ	51880 MW	79390 TQ	USBLS	5/07
	Minnesota	Y	68632 FQ	91523 MW	124260 TQ	MNBLS	10/08-12/08
	Minneapolis-Saint Paul MSA, MN-WI	Y	68266 FQ	91450 MW	124919 TQ	MNBLS	10/08-12/08
	Missouri	Y	59840 FQ	101540 MW		USBLS	5/07
	Kansas City MSA, MO-KS	Y	60170 FQ	90110 MW	125550 TQ	USBLS	5/07
	St. Louis MSA, MO-IL	Y	65380 FQ	102770 MW		USBLS	5/07
	Nebraska	Y	57500 FQ	78340 MW	108970 TQ	USBLS	5/07
	Omaha-Council Bluffs MSA, NE-IA	Y	59330 FQ	78740 MW	111930 TQ	USBLS	5/07
	Nevada	H	23.34 FQ	25.75 MW	38.50 TQ	NVBLS	5/08
	Las Vegas-Paradise MSA, NV	H	22.54 FQ	24.15 MW	25.76 TQ	NVBLS	5/08
	New Hampshire	H	27.07 AE	37.65 MW	51.33 AEX	NHBLS	6/08
	Manchester MSA, NH	Y	62880 FQ	72660 MW	93360 TQ	USBLS	5/07
	New Jersey	Y	68660 FQ	90750 MW	123670 TQ	USBLS	5/07
	Camden PMSA, NJ	Y	88900 FQ	116280 MW	145350 TQ	USBLS	5/07
	Newark-Union PMSA, NJ-PA	Y	70700 FQ	94830 MW	121920 TQ	USBLS	5/07
	Trenton-Ewing MSA, NJ	Y	67910 FQ	91400 MW	140460 TQ	USBLS	5/07
	New Mexico	Y	105630 FQ	130400 MW	145170 TQ	USBLS	5/07
	Albuquerque MSA, NM	Y	108470 FQ	131170 MW	145580 TQ	USBLS	5/07
	New York	Y	58090 FQ	88020 MW	123530 TQ	USBLS	5/07
	Albany-Schenectady-Troy MSA, NY	Y	58350 FQ	73060 MW	90680 TQ	USBLS	5/07
	Buffalo-Niagara Falls MSA, NY	Y	53950 FQ	104730 MW	121500 TQ	USBLS	5/07
	Nassau-Suffolk PMSA, NY	Y	70850 FQ	110850 MW	126040 TQ	USBLS	5/07
	New York-Northern New Jersey-Long Island MSA, NY-NJ-PA	Y	64810 FQ	90810 MW	124930 TQ	USBLS	5/07
	North Carolina	Y	57880 FQ	78500 MW	114400 TQ	USBLS	5/07
	Charlotte-Gastonia-Concord MSA, NC-SC	Y	66250 FQ	99990 MW	142190 TQ	USBLS	5/07
	Raleigh-Cary MSA, NC	Y	56470 FQ	74710 MW	112080 TQ	USBLS	5/07
	Ohio	Y	60690 FQ	77430 MW	100970 TQ	USBLS	5/07
	Cincinnati-Middletown MSA, OH-KY-IN	Y	61780 FQ	79020 MW	102840 TQ	USBLS	5/07
	Cleveland-Elyria-Mentor MSA, OH	Y	66380 FQ	77450 MW	106780 TQ	USBLS	5/07
	Columbus MSA, OH	Y	60300 FQ	76820 MW	100350 TQ	USBLS	5/07
	Oklahoma	Y	36220 FQ	53500 MW	85820 TQ	USBLS	5/07
	Oklahoma City MSA, OK	Y	40050 FQ	56870 MW	95490 TQ	USBLS	5/07
	Oregon	H	36.85 FQ	48.23 MW	69.23 TQ	ORBLS	5/08

Occupation/Type/Industry	Location	Per	Low	Mid	High	Source	Date
Actuary	Portland-Vancouver-Beaverton MSA, OR-WA	Y	70710 FQ	96350 MW	135590 TQ	USBLS	5/07
	Pennsylvania	Y	69770 FQ	98280 MW	137800 TQ	USBLS	5/07
	Allentown-Bethlehem-Easton MSA, PA-NJ	Y	69850 FQ	99760 MW	136850 TQ	USBLS	5/07
	Philadelphia-Camden-Wilmington MSA, PA-NJ-DE-MD	Y	72760 FQ	104590 MW	141670 TQ	USBLS	5/07
	Pittsburgh MSA, PA	Y	60290 FQ	78970 MW	104190 TQ	USBLS	5/07
	Rhode Island	Y	59990 FQ	81010 MW	122880 TQ	USBLS	5/07
	Providence-Fall River-Warwick MSA, RI-MA	Y	58940 FQ	80390 MW	118930 TQ	USBLS	5/07
	South Carolina	Y	55110 FQ	70820 MW	93300 TQ	USBLS	5/07
	Tennessee	Y	56070 FQ	66780 MW	103470 TQ	USBLS	5/07
	Nashville-Davidson-Murfreesboro MSA, TN	Y	49700 FQ	57140 MW	63140 TQ	USBLS	5/07
	Texas	Y	63780 FQ	91690 MW	132170 TQ	USBLS	5/07
	Austin-Round Rock MSA, TX	Y	60470 FQ	79760 MW	117770 TQ	USBLS	5/07
	Dallas-Fort Worth-Arlington MSA, TX	Y	70410 FQ	101070 MW	143480 TQ	USBLS	5/07
	Houston-Sugar Land-Baytown MSA, TX	Y	57970 FQ	76230 MW	119250 TQ	USBLS	5/07
	San Antonio MSA, TX	Y	63300 FQ	84830 MW	125710 TQ	USBLS	5/07
	Utah	Y	57600 FQ	72100 MW	103300 TQ	USBLS	5/07
	Salt Lake City MSA, UT	Y	57970 FQ	71470 MW	98260 TQ	USBLS	5/07
	Virginia	Y	62810 FQ	87260 MW	135860 TQ	USBLS	5/07
	Richmond MSA, VA	Y	64890 FQ	89210 MW	124090 TQ	USBLS	5/07
	Washington	H	29.48 FQ	37.16 MW	53.56 TQ	WABLS	3/08
	Seattle-Tacoma-Bellevue MSA, WA	Y	59620 FQ	75090 MW	106150 TQ	USBLS	5/07
	West Virginia	Y	59721 FQ	93262 MW	118774 TQ	WVBLS	7/08-9/08
	Wisconsin	Y	64760 FQ	85050 MW	125100 TQ	USBLS	5/07
	Milwaukee-Waukesha-West Allis MSA, WI	Y	64270 FQ	85270 MW	131620 TQ	USBLS	5/07
	Puerto Rico	Y	36150 FQ	50390 MW	59500 TQ	USBLS	5/07
	San Juan-Caguas-Guaynabo MSA, PR	Y	36150 FQ	50390 MW	59500 TQ	USBLS	5/07
Acupuncturist	Rhode Island	Y		50000-60000 AWR		RIM01	2009
ADA Coordinator Judicial Branch, State Government	New Hampshire	Y			83086 HI	NHUL03	2008
Adaptive Equipment Technician State Government	Ohio	H	16.78 LO		19.88 HI	ODAS	2008
Adjutant General National Guard	Massachusetts	Y			200000 HI	BGLOBE1	2008
Administrative Law Attorney Examiner State Government	Ohio	H	19.70 LO		45.31 HI	ODAS	2008
Administrative Law Judge, Adjudicator, and Hearing Officer	Alabama	Y	83800 FQ	126220 MW		USBLS	5/07
	Montgomery MSA, AL	Y	85550 FQ	98920 MW	136940 TQ	USBLS	5/07
	Alaska	Y	65510 FQ	76260 MW	89710 TQ	USBLS	5/07
	Arizona	Y	56230 FQ	64680 MW	94960 TQ	USBLS	5/07
	Phoenix-Mesa-Scottsdale MSA, AZ	Y	57460 FQ	65300 MW	95740 TQ	USBLS	5/07
	Arkansas	Y	33240 FQ	39130 MW	52950 TQ	USBLS	5/07
	Little Rock-North Little Rock MSA, AR	Y	33040 FQ	38500 MW	50210 TQ	USBLS	5/07
	California	H	46.27 FQ	55.48 MW	62.45 TQ	CABLS	1/08-3/08
	Riverside-San Bernardino-Ontario MSA, CA	H	49.17 FQ	56.93 MW	63.96 TQ	CABLS	1/08-3/08
	San Diego-Carlsbad-San Marcos MSA, CA	H	49.27 FQ	56.78 MW	63.17 TQ	CABLS	1/08-3/08
	Connecticut	H	33.45 AE	39.85 MW		CTBLS	1/08-3/08

AE	Average entry wage	AW	Average wage paid	FQ	First quartile wage	LO	Lowest wage paid	MTC	Median total compensation	TCC	Total cash compensation
AER	Average entry range	AWR	Average wage range	H	Hourly	LR	Low end range	MW	Median wage paid	TQ	Third quartile wage
AEX	Average experienced wage	AXR	Average experienced range	HI	Highest wage paid	M	Monthly	MWR	Median wage range	W	Weekly
ATC	Average total compensation	D	Daily	HR	High end range	MCC	Median cash compensation	S	See annotated source	Y	Yearly

7

Occupation/Type/Industry	Location	Per	Low	Mid	High	Source	Date
Administrative Law Judge, Adjudicator, and Hearing Officer							
	Hartford-West Hartford-East Hartford MSA, CT	Y	71550 FQ	82180 MW	104960 TQ	USBLS	5/07
	Delaware	Y	38830 FQ	48430 MW	79630 TQ	USBLS	5/07
	Miami-Fort Lauderdale-Miami Beach MSA, FL	Y	69780 FQ	87290 MW	128410 TQ	USBLS	5/07
	Tampa-St. Petersburg-Clearwater MSA, FL	Y	36900 FQ	84400 MW	122470 TQ	USBLS	5/07
	Hawaii	Y	68630 FQ	80290 MW	93210 TQ	USBLS	5/07
	Idaho	Y	47250 FQ	55140 MW	64990 TQ	USBLS	5/07
	Illinois	Y	48160 FQ	58550 MW	73030 TQ	USBLS	5/07
	Indiana	Y	38650 FQ	89600 MW	132480 TQ	USBLS	5/07
	Kansas	Y	79430 FQ	92900 MW	127930 TQ	USBLS	5/07
	Louisiana	H	11.43 FQ	28.87 MW	52.03 TQ	LABLS	1/08-3/08
	New Orleans-Metairie-Kenner MSA, LA	Y	69610 FQ	101020 MW	140730 TQ	USBLS	5/07
	Maine	Y	39130 FQ	48060 MW	63360 TQ	USBLS	5/07
	Maryland	Y		121075		MDBLS	3/08
	Baltimore-Towson MSA, MD	Y	108540 FQ	118180 MW	127850 TQ	USBLS	5/07
	Massachusetts	Y	59740 FQ	73580 MW	95090 TQ	USBLS	5/07
	Boston-Cambridge-Quincy NECTA, MA	Y	56860 FQ	72870 MW	97140 TQ	USBLS	5/07
	Michigan	Y	76690 FQ	92340 MW	104660 TQ	USBLS	5/07
	Detroit-Warren-Livonia MSA, MI	Y	84230 FQ	96400 MW	126180 TQ	USBLS	5/07
	Warren-Troy-Farmington Hills PMSA, MI	Y	84910 FQ	97340 MW	137200 TQ	USBLS	5/07
	Minnesota	Y	85518 FQ	117198 MW	134011 TQ	MNBLS	10/08-12/08
	Minneapolis-Saint Paul MSA, MN-WI	Y	85508 FQ	117679 MW	134251 TQ	MNBLS	10/08-12/08
	Mississippi	Y	36390 FQ	92110 MW	130760 TQ	USBLS	5/07
	Missouri	Y	54520 FQ	84240 MW	134790 TQ	USBLS	5/07
	Kansas City MSA, MO-KS	Y	86490 FQ	103370 MW	145540 TQ	USBLS	5/07
	St. Louis MSA, MO-IL	Y	58400 FQ	92990 MW	133180 TQ	USBLS	5/07
	Montana	Y	47520 FQ	57820 MW	78850 TQ	USBLS	5/07
	Nebraska	Y	37710 FQ	83870 MW	120090 TQ	USBLS	5/07
	Omaha-Council Bluffs MSA, NE-IA	Y	36950 FQ	76200 MW	103930 TQ	USBLS	5/07
	New Hampshire	H	17.46 AE	24.15 MW	31.94 AEX	NHBLS	6/08
	New Jersey	Y	74510 FQ	93540 MW	116430 TQ	USBLS	5/07
	Camden PMSA, NJ	Y	71030 FQ	88440 MW	138520 TQ	USBLS	5/07
	Newark-Union PMSA, NJ-PA	Y	78020 FQ	100230 MW	120700 TQ	USBLS	5/07
	New Mexico	Y	34200 FQ	71500 MW	90110 TQ	USBLS	5/07
	Albuquerque MSA, NM	Y	29300 FQ	35550 MW	94970 TQ	USBLS	5/07
	Nassau-Suffolk PMSA, NY	Y	66340 FQ	76300 MW	103720 TQ	USBLS	5/07
	North Dakota	Y	64750 FQ	94150 MW	138990 TQ	USBLS	5/07
	Cincinnati-Middletown MSA, OH-KY-IN	Y	43750 FQ	60720 MW	87500 TQ	USBLS	5/07
	Cleveland-Elyria-Mentor MSA, OH	Y	46260 FQ	77250 MW	103220 TQ	USBLS	5/07
	Dayton MSA, OH	Y	47530 FQ	73910 MW	98170 TQ	USBLS	5/07
	Oklahoma	Y	36530 FQ	55970 MW	112270 TQ	USBLS	5/07
	Oregon	H	21.75 FQ	28.02 MW	39.41 TQ	ORBLS	5/08
	Portland-Vancouver-Beaverton MSA, OR-WA	Y	44380 FQ	62820 MW	91180 TQ	USBLS	5/07
	Rhode Island	Y	67000 FQ	87110 MW	112680 TQ	USBLS	5/07
	Providence-Fall River-Warwick MSA, RI-MA	Y	67490 FQ	85400 MW	111090 TQ	USBLS	5/07
	South Carolina	Y	39990 FQ	50340 MW	103200 TQ	USBLS	5/07
	Columbia MSA, SC	Y	42050 FQ	51730 MW	95650 TQ	USBLS	5/07
	South Dakota	Y	41768 FQ	64860 MW	99245 TQ	SDBLS	7/08-9/08
	Tennessee	Y	37070 FQ	55630 MW	115960 TQ	USBLS	5/07
	Memphis MSA, TN-MS-AR	Y	40230 FQ	69720 MW	107640 TQ	USBLS	5/07
	Nashville-Davidson-Murfreesboro MSA, TN	Y	36080 FQ	67190 MW	104040 TQ	USBLS	5/07
	Texas	Y	33590 FQ	69040 MW	107450 TQ	USBLS	5/07
	Dallas-Fort Worth-Arlington MSA, TX	Y	72120 FQ	105700 MW	138140 TQ	USBLS	5/07
	Houston-Sugar Land-Baytown MSA, TX	Y	67490 FQ	87460 MW	119170 TQ	USBLS	5/07

AE	Average entry wage	AW	Average wage paid	FQ	First quartile wage	LO Lowest wage paid	MTC Median total compensation	TCC Total cash compensation
AER	Average entry range	AWR	Average wage range	H	Hourly	LR Low end range	MW Median wage paid	TQ Third quartile wage
AEX	Average experienced wage	AXR	Average experienced range	HI	Highest wage paid	M Monthly	MWR Median wage range	W Weekly
ATC	Average total compensation	D	Daily	HR	High end range	MCC Median cash compensation	S See annotated source	Y Yearly

Occupation/Type/Industry	Location	Per	Low	Mid	High	Source	Date
Administrative Law Judge, Adjudicator, and Hearing Officer	Utah	Y	47900 FQ	61260 MW	85660 TQ	USBLS	5/07
	Salt Lake City MSA, UT	Y	52040 FQ	66590 MW	93770 TQ	USBLS	5/07
	Virginia	Y	48750 FQ	66700 MW	92740 TQ	USBLS	5/07
	Virginia Beach-Norfolk-Newport News MSA, VA-NC	Y	47770 FQ	62770 MW	132530 TQ	USBLS	5/07
	Washington	H	33.09 FQ	37.20 MW	43.44 TQ	WABLS	3/08
	Seattle-Tacoma-Bellevue MSA, WA	Y	65950 FQ	77200 MW	98540 TQ	USBLS	5/07
	Spokane MSA, WA	Y	67640 FQ	75400 MW	82820 TQ	USBLS	5/07
	West Virginia	Y	70272 FQ	104925 MW		WVBLS	7/08-9/08
	Wisconsin	Y	67950 FQ	94880 MW	136130 TQ	USBLS	5/07
	Milwaukee-Waukesha-West Allis MSA, WI	Y	89240 FQ	101980 MW	135140 TQ	USBLS	5/07
	Puerto Rico	Y	59790 FQ	74540 MW	97950 TQ	USBLS	5/07
	San Juan-Caguas-Guaynabo MSA, PR	Y	52230 FQ	66810 MW	75150 TQ	USBLS	5/07
Administrative Services Director Municipal Government	Walnut Creek, CA	Y	132321 LO		183837 HI	WCSWP	7/11/08
Administrative Services Manager	Alabama	Y	45380 FQ	63930 MW	83530 TQ	USBLS	5/07
	Birmingham-Hoover MSA, AL	Y	55970 FQ	74000 MW	89450 TQ	USBLS	5/07
	Alaska	Y	42740 FQ	56360 MW	73780 TQ	USBLS	5/07
	Anchorage MSA, AK	Y	46080 FQ	59580 MW	76190 TQ	USBLS	5/07
	Arizona	Y	36060 FQ	49790 MW	67550 TQ	USBLS	5/07
	Phoenix-Mesa-Scottsdale MSA, AZ	Y	36080 FQ	49210 MW	66670 TQ	USBLS	5/07
	Tucson MSA, AZ	Y	37190 FQ	54630 MW	71990 TQ	USBLS	5/07
	Yuma MSA, AZ	Y	41770 FQ	58210 MW	70960 TQ	USBLS	5/07
	Arkansas	Y	40320 FQ	54500 MW	76750 TQ	USBLS	5/07
	Little Rock-North Little Rock MSA, AR	Y	45800 FQ	62490 MW	86080 TQ	USBLS	5/07
	California	H	29.03 FQ	39.40 MW	52.43 TQ	CABLS	1/08-3/08
	Bakersfield MSA, CA	H	24.08 FQ	34.64 MW	48.04 TQ	CABLS	1/08-3/08
	Los Angeles-Long Beach-Glendale PMSA, CA	H	30.82 FQ	40.70 MW	55.79 TQ	CABLS	1/08-3/08
	Oakland-Fremont-Hayward MSA, CA	H	31.29 FQ	42.79 MW	54.66 TQ	CABLS	1/08-3/08
	Riverside-San Bernardino-Ontario MSA, CA	H	24.70 FQ	34.32 MW	43.31 TQ	CABLS	1/08-3/08
	Sacramento-Arden Arcade-Roseville MSA, CA	H	26.96 FQ	35.00 MW	46.42 TQ	CABLS	1/08-3/08
	San Diego-Carlsbad-San Marcos MSA, CA	H	27.75 FQ	41.06 MW	54.41 TQ	CABLS	1/08-3/08
	San Francisco-San Mateo-Redwood PMSA, CA	H	30.19 FQ	42.19 MW	57.18 TQ	CABLS	1/08-3/08
	San Jose-Sunnyvale-Santa Clara MSA, CA	H	35.57 FQ	44.88 MW	59.01 TQ	CABLS	1/08-3/08
	Santa Ana-Anaheim-Irvine PMSA, CA	Y	63880 FQ	80540 MW	103520 TQ	USBLS	5/07
	Santa Rosa-Petaluma MSA, CA	H	29.53 FQ	38.14 MW	52.62 TQ	CABLS	1/08-3/08
	Colorado	Y	54140 FQ	72430 MW	95340 TQ	USBLS	5/07
	Denver-Aurora MSA, CO	Y	55150 FQ	73900 MW	96440 TQ	USBLS	5/07
	Connecticut	H	27.21 AE	37.79 MW		CTBLS	1/08-3/08
	Bridgeport-Stamford-Norwalk MSA, CT	Y	56750 FQ	75460 MW	95940 TQ	USBLS	5/07
	Hartford-West Hartford-East Hartford MSA, CT	Y	66660 FQ	86750 MW	102390 TQ	USBLS	5/07
	Delaware	Y	61630 FQ	80230 MW	105200 TQ	USBLS	5/07
	Wilmington PMSA, DE-MD-NJ	Y	65370 FQ	81780 MW	110860 TQ	USBLS	5/07
	District of Columbia	Y	53300 FQ	70650 MW	95610 TQ	USBLS	5/07
	Washington-Arlington-Alexandria MSA, DC-VA-MD-WV	Y	56190 FQ	76490 MW	100800 TQ	USBLS	5/07
	Florida	Y	59030 FQ	83600 MW	107390 TQ	USBLS	5/07
	Fort Lauderdale-Pompano Beach-Deerfield Beach PMSA, FL	Y	59470 FQ	84360 MW	108230 TQ	USBLS	5/07
	Jacksonville MSA, FL	Y	70510 FQ	89620 MW	111850 TQ	USBLS	5/07

AE Average entry wage	**AW** Average wage paid	**FQ** First quartile wage	**LO** Lowest wage paid	**MTC** Median total compensation **TCC** Total cash compensation
AER Average entry range	**AWR** Average wage range	**H** Hourly	**LR** Low end range	**MW** Median wage paid **TQ** Third quartile wage
AEX Average experienced wage	**AXR** Average experienced range	**HI** Highest wage paid	**M** Monthly	**MWR** Median wage range **W** Weekly
ATC Average total compensation **D** Daily		**HR** High end range	**MCC** Median cash compensation **S** See annotated source	**Y** Yearly

Occupation/Type/Industry	Location	Per	Low	Mid	High	Source	Date
Administrative Services Manager	Miami-Fort Lauderdale-Miami Beach MSA, FL	Y	60400 FQ	87890 MW	114840 TQ	USBLS	5/07
	Orlando-Kissimmee MSA, FL	Y	57120 FQ	80630 MW	110830 TQ	USBLS	5/07
	Tampa-St. Petersburg-Clearwater MSA, FL	Y	55100 FQ	81040 MW	103180 TQ	USBLS	5/07
	West Palm Beach-Boca Raton-Boynton Beach PMSA, FL	Y	61210 FQ	87240 MW	113320 TQ	USBLS	5/07
	Georgia	Y	44370 FQ	61130 MW	86480 TQ	USBLS	5/07
	Atlanta-Sandy Springs-Marietta MSA, GA	Y	47390 FQ	64270 MW	92590 TQ	USBLS	5/07
	Macon MSA, GA	Y	42550 FQ	61350 MW	79960 TQ	USBLS	5/07
	Hawaii	Y	45590 FQ	60800 MW	78630 TQ	USBLS	5/07
	Honolulu MSA, HI	Y	46080 FQ	63250 MW	81540 TQ	USBLS	5/07
	Idaho	Y	29320 FQ	44400 MW	70490 TQ	USBLS	5/07
	Boise City-Nampa MSA, ID	Y	32570 FQ	55900 MW	78800 TQ	USBLS	5/07
	Coeur d'Alene MSA, ID	Y	28530 FQ	39890 MW	52650 TQ	USBLS	5/07
	Illinois	Y	39770 FQ	54400 MW	77010 TQ	USBLS	5/07
	Champaign-Urbana MSA, IL	Y	35280 FQ	44280 MW	57740 TQ	USBLS	5/07
	Chicago-Naperville-Joliet MSA, IL-IN-WI	Y	42670 FQ	59080 MW	84320 TQ	USBLS	5/07
	Indiana	Y	44520 FQ	60900 MW	82150 TQ	USBLS	5/07
	Gary PMSA, IN	Y	48390 FQ	63130 MW	79280 TQ	USBLS	5/07
	Indianapolis-Carmel MSA, IN	Y	48980 FQ	66030 MW	86550 TQ	USBLS	5/07
	Iowa	Y	53500 FQ	72460 MW	93610 TQ	USBLS	5/07
	Des Moines-West Des Moines MSA, IA	Y	61860 FQ	77630 MW	95770 TQ	USBLS	5/07
	Sioux City MSA, IA-NE-SD	Y	45050 FQ	61260 MW	77480 TQ	USBLS	5/07
	Kansas	Y	46840 FQ	63290 MW	84720 TQ	USBLS	5/07
	Lawrence MSA, KS	Y	43090 FQ	54520 MW	74150 TQ	USBLS	5/07
	Topeka MSA, KS	Y	48210 FQ	60160 MW	81460 TQ	USBLS	5/07
	Wichita MSA, KS	Y	52060 FQ	71360 MW	94000 TQ	USBLS	5/07
	Kentucky	Y	52229 FQ	67931 MW	79955 TQ	KYBLS	2008
	Louisville-Jefferson County MSA, KY-IN	Y	47800 FQ	60730 MW	80730 TQ	USBLS	5/07
	Louisiana	H	18.44 FQ	25.10 MW	32.21 TQ	LABLS	1/08-3/08
	Baton Rouge MSA, LA	Y	40900 FQ	52110 MW	67110 TQ	USBLS	5/07
	New Orleans-Metairie-Kenner MSA, LA	Y	36170 FQ	52920 MW	67740 TQ	USBLS	5/07
	Maine	Y	43450 FQ	56630 MW	73310 TQ	USBLS	5/07
	Portland-South Portland-Biddeford MSA, ME	Y	49650 FQ	62520 MW	78440 TQ	USBLS	5/07
	Maryland	Y		69200 MW		MDBLS	3/08
	Baltimore-Towson MSA, MD	Y	47930 FQ	64710 MW	82780 TQ	USBLS	5/07
	Bethesda-Gaithersburg-Frederick PMSA, MD	Y	56970 FQ	75580 MW	100350 TQ	USBLS	5/07
	Massachusetts	Y	58350 FQ	74790 MW	96020 TQ	USBLS	5/07
	Boston-Cambridge-Quincy NECTA, MA	Y	61040 FQ	77230 MW	100050 TQ	USBLS	5/07
	Worcester MSA, MA-CT	Y	56330 FQ	71940 MW	91260 TQ	USBLS	5/07
	Michigan	Y	47780 FQ	67460 MW	87030 TQ	USBLS	5/07
	Detroit-Warren-Livonia MSA, MI	Y	53540 FQ	73600 MW	94640 TQ	USBLS	5/07
	Grand Rapids-Wyoming MSA, MI	Y	45040 FQ	63640 MW	78670 TQ	USBLS	5/07
	Lansing-East Lansing MSA, MI	Y	53970 FQ	67160 MW	80550 TQ	USBLS	5/07
	Warren-Troy-Farmington Hills PMSA, MI	Y	45680 FQ	70760 MW	94040 TQ	USBLS	5/07
	Minnesota	Y	64717 FQ	79523 MW	98363 TQ	MNBLS	10/08-12/08
	Duluth-Superior MSA, MN-WI	Y	59118 FQ	74935 MW	86415 TQ	MNBLS	10/08-12/08
	Minneapolis-Saint Paul MSA, MN-WI	Y	66271 FQ	80972 MW	99948 TQ	MNBLS	10/08-12/08
	Rochester MSA, MN	Y	56024 FQ	77322 MW	105147 TQ	MNBLS	10/08-12/08
	Mississippi	Y	31690 FQ	46170 MW	66830 TQ	USBLS	5/07
	Gulfport-Biloxi MSA, MS	Y	31090 FQ	44260 MW	75730 TQ	USBLS	5/07
	Hattiesburg MSA, MS	Y	31360 FQ	40880 MW	61580 TQ	USBLS	5/07
	Jackson MSA, MS	Y	35360 FQ	54270 MW	73100 TQ	USBLS	5/07
	Missouri	Y	52920 FQ	70090 MW	94430 TQ	USBLS	5/07
	Kansas City MSA, MO-KS	Y	54810 FQ	71710 MW	91470 TQ	USBLS	5/07
	St. Louis MSA, MO-IL	Y	47750 FQ	67640 MW	92630 TQ	USBLS	5/07
	Montana	Y	36000 FQ	45950 MW	65180 TQ	USBLS	5/07
	Billings MSA, MT	Y	40440 FQ	50240 MW	74330 TQ	USBLS	5/07
	Nebraska	Y	43670 FQ	61510 MW	84530 TQ	USBLS	5/07

AE Average entry wage	**AW** Average wage paid	**FQ** First quartile wage	**LO** Lowest wage paid	**MTC** Median total compensation	**TCC** Total cash compensation
AER Average entry range	**AWR** Average wage range	**H** Hourly	**LR** Low end range	**MW** Median wage paid	**TQ** Third quartile wage
AEX Average experienced wage	**AXR** Average experienced range	**HI** Highest wage paid	**M** Monthly	**MWR** Median wage range	**W** Weekly
ATC Average total compensation	**D** Daily	**HR** High end range	**MCC** Median cash compensation	**S** See annotated source	**Y** Yearly

Occupation/Type/Industry	Location	Per	Low	Mid	High	Source	Date
Administrative Services Manager	Omaha-Council Bluffs MSA, NE-IA	Y	46990 FQ	67840 MW	88470 TQ	USBLS	5/07
	Nevada	H	21.68 FQ	29.15 MW	38.47 TQ	NVBLS	5/08
	Las Vegas-Paradise MSA, NV	H	21.50 FQ	27.52 MW	38.06 TQ	NVBLS	5/08
	Manchester MSA, NH	Y	51880 FQ	65490 MW	86530 TQ	USBLS	5/07
	Nashua NECTA, NH-MA	Y	57240 FQ	90210 MW	114190 TQ	USBLS	5/07
	New Jersey	Y	72760 FQ	89660 MW	110820 TQ	USBLS	5/07
	Camden PMSA, NJ	Y	75170 FQ	89250 MW	111840 TQ	USBLS	5/07
	Edison PMSA, NJ	Y	69500 FQ	88240 MW	110650 TQ	USBLS	5/07
	Newark-Union PMSA, NJ-PA	Y	73290 FQ	89770 MW	111190 TQ	USBLS	5/07
	New Mexico	Y	42500 FQ	57210 MW	75740 TQ	USBLS	5/07
	Albuquerque MSA, NM	Y	44950 FQ	58920 MW	75160 TQ	USBLS	5/07
	New York	Y	72530 FQ	90420 MW	113620 TQ	USBLS	5/07
	Albany-Schenectady-Troy MSA, NY	Y	68790 FQ	83810 MW	105730 TQ	USBLS	5/07
	Binghamton MSA, NY	Y	57610 FQ	70430 MW	88020 TQ	USBLS	5/07
	Buffalo-Niagara Falls MSA, NY	Y	60810 FQ	76000 MW	92780 TQ	USBLS	5/07
	Kingston MSA, NY	Y	70180 FQ	85170 MW	100240 TQ	USBLS	5/07
	Nassau-Suffolk PMSA, NY	Y	72330 FQ	90330 MW	117560 TQ	USBLS	5/07
	New York-Northern New Jersey-Long Island MSA, NY-NJ-PA	Y	75720 FQ	92960 MW	117470 TQ	USBLS	5/07
	Utica-Rome MSA, NY	Y	61830 FQ	76850 MW	94650 TQ	USBLS	5/07
	North Carolina	Y	51580 FQ	65630 MW	84210 TQ	USBLS	5/07
	Charlotte-Gastonia-Concord MSA, NC-SC	Y	53830 FQ	66060 MW	83480 TQ	USBLS	5/07
	Durham MSA, NC	Y	51540 FQ	68760 MW	93220 TQ	USBLS	5/07
	Raleigh-Cary MSA, NC	Y	51090 FQ	63460 MW	83080 TQ	USBLS	5/07
	North Dakota	Y	46190 FQ	59270 MW	73400 TQ	USBLS	5/07
	Fargo MSA, ND-MN	Y	49240 FQ	65240 MW	76850 TQ	USBLS	5/07
	Ohio	Y	57300 FQ	73070 MW	93250 TQ	USBLS	5/07
	Cincinnati-Middletown MSA, OH-KY-IN	Y	58100 FQ	74410 MW	97030 TQ	USBLS	5/07
	Cleveland-Elyria-Mentor MSA, OH	Y	60740 FQ	74150 MW	91650 TQ	USBLS	5/07
	Columbus MSA, OH	Y	61080 FQ	76420 MW	99630 TQ	USBLS	5/07
	Dayton MSA, OH	Y	60720 FQ	73910 MW	94250 TQ	USBLS	5/07
	Oklahoma	Y	31850 FQ	46930 MW	65340 TQ	USBLS	5/07
	Oklahoma City MSA, OK	Y	34160 FQ	47960 MW	69720 TQ	USBLS	5/07
	Tulsa MSA, OK	Y	33710 FQ	49560 MW	65670 TQ	USBLS	5/07
	Oregon	H	26.99 FQ	34.55 MW	45.19 TQ	ORBLS	5/08
	Portland-Vancouver-Beaverton MSA, OR-WA	Y	58860 FQ	74360 MW	96520 TQ	USBLS	5/07
	Pennsylvania	Y	44030 FQ	62250 MW	86760 TQ	USBLS	5/07
	Allentown-Bethlehem-Easton MSA, PA-NJ	Y	49350 FQ	68390 MW	87960 TQ	USBLS	5/07
	Lancaster MSA, PA	Y	41420 FQ	58460 MW	82850 TQ	USBLS	5/07
	Philadelphia-Camden-Wilmington MSA, PA-NJ-DE-MD	Y	56370 FQ	77010 MW	100520 TQ	USBLS	5/07
	Pittsburgh MSA, PA	Y	37460 FQ	49300 MW	78370 TQ	USBLS	5/07
	Rhode Island	Y	68850 FQ	87160 MW	109290 TQ	USBLS	5/07
	Providence-Fall River-Warwick MSA, RI-MA	Y	67140 FQ	84990 MW	104280 TQ	USBLS	5/07
	South Carolina	Y	41320 FQ	55560 MW	73430 TQ	USBLS	5/07
	Charleston-North Charleston MSA, SC	Y	38400 FQ	51560 MW	71510 TQ	USBLS	5/07
	Columbia MSA, SC	Y	44260 FQ	56320 MW	69870 TQ	USBLS	5/07
	South Dakota	Y	58839 FQ	69619 MW	82821 TQ	SDBLS	7/08-9/08
	Sioux Falls MSA, SD	Y	61265 FQ	71681 MW	84161 TQ	SDBLS	7/08-9/08
	Tennessee	Y	33950 FQ	48670 MW	71260 TQ	USBLS	5/07
	Clarksville MSA, TN-KY	Y	32430 FQ	50490 MW	59730 TQ	USBLS	5/07
	Johnson City MSA, TN	Y	32160 FQ	81970 MW	98070 TQ	USBLS	5/07
	Kingsport-Bristol-Bristol MSA, TN-VA	Y	28430 FQ	50840 MW	75100 TQ	USBLS	5/07
	Knoxville MSA, TN	Y	35480 FQ	51560 MW	69520 TQ	USBLS	5/07
	Memphis MSA, TN-MS-AR	Y	38660 FQ	51670 MW	78250 TQ	USBLS	5/07
	Nashville-Davidson-Murfreesboro MSA, TN	Y	33940 FQ	50010 MW	73440 TQ	USBLS	5/07
	Texas	Y	56120 FQ	78040 MW	105800 TQ	USBLS	5/07
	Austin-Round Rock MSA, TX	Y	63930 FQ	80340 MW	118380 TQ	USBLS	5/07

AE	Average entry wage	AW	Average wage paid	FQ	First quartile wage
AER	Average entry range	AWR	Average wage range	H	Hourly
AEX	Average experienced wage	AXR	Average experienced range	HI	Highest wage paid
ATC	Average total compensation	D	Daily	HR	High end range

LO	Lowest wage paid	MTC	Median total compensation
LR	Low end range	MW	Median wage paid
M	Monthly	MWR	Median wage range
MCC	Median cash compensation	S	See annotated source

TCC	Total cash compensation
TQ	Third quartile wage
W	Weekly
Y	Yearly

Occupation/Type/Industry	Location	Per	Low	Mid	High	Source	Date
Administrative Services Manager	Dallas-Fort Worth-Arlington						
	MSA, TX	Y	57170 FQ	81710 MW	109470 TQ	USBLS	5/07
	El Paso MSA, TX	Y	55990 FQ	80640 MW	96900 TQ	USBLS	5/07
	Houston-Sugar Land-Baytown						
	MSA, TX	Y	63090 FQ	84790 MW	115510 TQ	USBLS	5/07
	San Antonio MSA, TX	Y	48440 FQ	69020 MW	91470 TQ	USBLS	5/07
	Utah	Y	50170 FQ	63410 MW	80990 TQ	USBLS	5/07
	Ogden-Clearfield MSA, UT	Y	48790 FQ	59500 MW	76360 TQ	USBLS	5/07
	Salt Lake City MSA, UT	Y	51920 FQ	65070 MW	83910 TQ	USBLS	5/07
	Vermont	Y	31840 FQ	48040 MW	74370 TQ	USBLS	5/07
	Burlington-South Burlington						
	MSA, VT	Y	43620 FQ	67750 MW	88290 TQ	USBLS	5/07
	Virginia	Y	54540 FQ	78250 MW	101190 TQ	USBLS	5/07
	Charlottesville MSA, VA	Y	49230 FQ	66910 MW	81890 TQ	USBLS	5/07
	Richmond MSA, VA	Y	44010 FQ	66510 MW	90960 TQ	USBLS	5/07
	Virginia Beach-Norfolk-						
	Newport News MSA, VA-NC	Y	58420 FQ	76710 MW	94470 TQ	USBLS	5/07
	Washington	H	34.87 FQ	43.48 MW	51.94 TQ	WABLS	3/08
	Seattle-Tacoma-Bellevue						
	MSA, WA	Y	72880 FQ	90160 MW	109180 TQ	USBLS	5/07
	West Virginia	Y	43848 FQ	57707 MW	70384 TQ	WVBLS	7/08-9/08
	Charleston MSA, WV	Y	48530 FQ	59020 MW	71300 TQ	USBLS	5/07
	Wisconsin	Y	51020 FQ	67790 MW	86830 TQ	USBLS	5/07
	Milwaukee-Waukesha-West						
	Allis MSA, WI	Y	57000 FQ	73610 MW	92170 TQ	USBLS	5/07
	Wyoming	Y	39522 FQ	56039 MW	66117 TQ	WYBLS	9/08
	Cheyenne MSA, WY	Y	54646 FQ	60859 MW	66892 TQ	WYBLS	9/08
	Puerto Rico	Y	36610 FQ	45360 MW	59210 TQ	USBLS	5/07
	San Juan-Caguas-Guaynabo						
	MSA, PR	Y	36710 FQ	45270 MW	58140 TQ	USBLS	5/07
	Virgin Islands	Y	44850 FQ	55520 MW	71530 TQ	USBLS	5/07
	Guam	Y	29730 FQ	37430 MW	48170 TQ	USBLS	5/07
Administrative Specialist							
Municipal Government	Cincinnati, OH	Y	45117 LO		60634 HI	COHSS	10/08
Administrative Systems Manager							
Municipal Government	Lincoln Park, MI	Y			46311 HI	NHERLD2	2009
Administrator of Physician							
Practices	United States	Y			89640-		
					138959 HR	CRDB03	2009
Admissions Coordinator							
Nursing Home	United States	Y		40034 MW		MLTCN04	2008-2009
Admitting and Discharging Clerk	United States	Y		26400 AW		HCC02	2009
Adult Literacy, Remedial							
Education, and GED Teacher							
and Instructor	Alabama	Y	24240 FQ	35970 MW	49660 TQ	USBLS	5/07
	Birmingham-Hoover MSA, AL	Y	32750 FQ	37440 MW	49010 TQ	USBLS	5/07
	Mobile MSA, AL	Y	35110 FQ	37650 MW	40280 TQ	USBLS	5/07
	Alaska	Y	33680 FQ	37130 MW	40640 TQ	USBLS	5/07
	Anchorage MSA, AK	Y	32660 FQ	36920 MW	41180 TQ	USBLS	5/07
	Arizona	Y	33150 FQ	38040 MW	47720 TQ	USBLS	5/07
	Phoenix-Mesa-Scottsdale						
	MSA, AZ	Y	33020 FQ	37820 MW	47050 TQ	USBLS	5/07
	Tucson MSA, AZ	Y	34530 FQ	40310 MW	51760 TQ	USBLS	5/07
	Yuma MSA, AZ	Y	31530 FQ	37770 MW	48900 TQ	USBLS	5/07
	Arkansas	Y	34720 FQ	42270 MW	48550 TQ	USBLS	5/07
	Little Rock-North Little Rock						
	MSA, AR	Y	40730 FQ	48680 MW	57010 TQ	USBLS	5/07
	California	H	23.09 FQ	31.43 MW	40.71 TQ	CABLS	1/08-3/08
	Los Angeles-Long Beach-						
	Glendale PMSA, CA	H	28.00 FQ	37.68 MW	44.20 TQ	CABLS	1/08-3/08
	Oakland-Fremont-Hayward						
	MSA, CA	H	25.99 FQ	28.59 MW	31.47 TQ	CABLS	1/08-3/08
	Riverside-San Bernardino-						
	Ontario MSA, CA	H	23.04 FQ	30.05 MW	40.63 TQ	CABLS	1/08-3/08
	Sacramento-Arden Arcade-						
	Roseville MSA, CA	H	19.20 FQ	22.77 MW	29.66 TQ	CABLS	1/08-3/08

AE	Average entry wage	AW	Average wage paid	FQ	First quartile wage	LO	Lowest wage paid	MTC	Median total compensation	TCC	Total cash compensation
AER	Average entry range	AWR	Average wage range	H	Hourly	LR	Low end range	MW	Median wage paid	TQ	Third quartile wage
AEX	Average experienced wage	AXR	Average experienced range	HI	Highest wage paid	M	Monthly	MWR	Median wage range	W	Weekly
ATC	Average total compensation	D	Daily	HR	High end range	MCC	Median cash compensation	S	See annotated source	Y	Yearly

Occupation/Type/Industry	Location	Per	Low	Mid	High	Source	Date
Adult Literacy, Remedial Education, and GED Teacher and Instructor							
	San Diego-Carlsbad-San Marcos MSA, CA	H	12.00 FQ	21.71 MW	30.01 TQ	CABLS	1/08-3/08
	San Francisco-San Mateo-Redwood PMSA, CA	H	16.48 FQ	22.60 MW	26.92 TQ	CABLS	1/08-3/08
	San Jose-Sunnyvale-Santa Clara MSA, CA	H	13.30 FQ	14.56 MW	22.69 TQ	CABLS	1/08-3/08
	Santa Ana-Anaheim-Irvine PMSA, CA	Y	42930 FQ	57210 MW	81120 TQ	USBLS	5/07
	Colorado	Y	31870 FQ	37000 MW	44860 TQ	USBLS	5/07
	Denver-Aurora MSA, CO	Y	32250 FQ	37070 MW	43240 TQ	USBLS	5/07
	Connecticut	H	12.64 AE	24.99 MW		CTBLS	1/08-3/08
	Bridgeport-Stamford-Norwalk MSA, CT	Y	31270 FQ	46610 MW	53910 TQ	USBLS	5/07
	Hartford-West Hartford-East Hartford MSA, CT	Y	43600 FQ	55610 MW	61340 TQ	USBLS	5/07
	Norwich-New London MSA, CT-RI	Y	52350 FQ	55800 MW	59250 TQ	USBLS	5/07
	Wilmington PMSA, DE-MD-NJ	Y	42440 FQ	51130 MW	61170 TQ	USBLS	5/07
	District of Columbia	Y	23760 FQ	34140 MW	46020 TQ	USBLS	5/07
	Washington-Arlington-Alexandria MSA, DC-VA-MD-WV	Y	34020 FQ	44890 MW	50960 TQ	USBLS	5/07
	Florida	Y	38500 FQ	45750 MW	57000 TQ	USBLS	5/07
	Jacksonville MSA, FL	Y	33480 FQ	37260 MW	40790 TQ	USBLS	5/07
	Miami-Fort Lauderdale-Miami Beach MSA, FL	Y	44710 FQ	51350 MW	66420 TQ	USBLS	5/07
	Orlando-Kissimmee MSA, FL	Y	41690 FQ	45180 MW	48670 TQ	USBLS	5/07
	Tampa-St. Petersburg-Clearwater MSA, FL	Y	41100 FQ	49150 MW	62530 TQ	USBLS	5/07
	West Palm Beach-Boca Raton-Boynton Beach PMSA, FL	Y	23730 FQ	43440 MW	58460 TQ	USBLS	5/07
	Georgia	Y	33050 FQ	38830 MW	47200 TQ	USBLS	5/07
	Atlanta-Sandy Springs-Marietta MSA, GA	Y	34110 FQ	40830 MW	48080 TQ	USBLS	5/07
	Hawaii	Y	41550 FQ	45560 MW	49230 TQ	USBLS	5/07
	Idaho	Y	27010 FQ	31610 MW	37700 TQ	USBLS	5/07
	Illinois	Y	30650 FQ	46250 MW	56330 TQ	USBLS	5/07
	Chicago-Naperville-Joliet MSA, IL-IN-WI	Y	29030 FQ	46040 MW	55260 TQ	USBLS	5/07
	Indiana	Y	26090 FQ	37550 MW	56920 TQ	USBLS	5/07
	Gary PMSA, IN	Y	22820 FQ	25920 MW	37410 TQ	USBLS	5/07
	Indianapolis-Carmel MSA, IN	Y	27720 FQ	32150 MW	53770 TQ	USBLS	5/07
	Iowa	Y	25920 FQ	31220 MW	41090 TQ	USBLS	5/07
	Des Moines-West Des Moines MSA, IA	Y	43480 FQ	49630 MW	57300 TQ	USBLS	5/07
	Kansas	Y	27220 FQ	34180 MW	42790 TQ	USBLS	5/07
	Wichita MSA, KS	Y	29790 FQ	42760 MW	51600 TQ	USBLS	5/07
	Kentucky	Y	27178 FQ	33817 MW	43598 TQ	KYBLS	2008
	Louisville-Jefferson County MSA, KY-IN	Y	28010 FQ	33530 MW	46890 TQ	USBLS	5/07
	Louisiana	Y		35536 AW		LABLS	1/08-3/08
	Baton Rouge MSA, LA	Y	19740 FQ	22890 MW	25770 TQ	USBLS	5/07
	New Orleans-Metairie-Kenner MSA, LA	Y	31110 FQ	42950 MW	47740 TQ	USBLS	5/07
	Maine	Y	38940 FQ	42610 MW	46410 TQ	USBLS	5/07
	Maryland	Y		45800 MW		MDBLS	3/08
	Baltimore-Towson MSA, MD	Y	23910 FQ	28710 MW	43170 TQ	USBLS	5/07
	Bethesda-Gaithersburg-Frederick PMSA, MD	Y	44130 FQ	47500 MW	50880 TQ	USBLS	5/07
	Massachusetts	Y	34960 FQ	42620 MW	52360 TQ	USBLS	5/07
	Barnstable Town MSA, MA	Y	25550 FQ	43410 MW	49710 TQ	USBLS	5/07
	Boston-Cambridge-Quincy NECTA, MA	Y	37850 FQ	46360 MW	54980 TQ	USBLS	5/07
	Worcester MSA, MA-CT	Y	19040 FQ	31080 MW	41780 TQ	USBLS	5/07
	Michigan	Y	23420 FQ	34410 MW	46760 TQ	USBLS	5/07
	Detroit-Warren-Livonia MSA, MI	Y	22430 FQ	25190 MW	38020 TQ	USBLS	5/07

AE Average entry wage	**AW** Average wage paid	**FQ** First quartile wage	**LO** Lowest wage paid	**MTC** Median total compensation	**TCC** Total cash compensation
AER Average entry range	**AWR** Average wage range	**H** Hourly	**LR** Low end range	**MW** Median wage paid	**TQ** Third quartile wage
AEX Average experienced wage	**AXR** Average experienced range	**HI** Highest wage paid	**M** Monthly	**MWR** Median wage range	**W** Weekly
ATC Average total compensation	**D** Daily	**HR** High end range	**MCC** Median cash compensation	**S** See annotated source	**Y** Yearly

Occupation/Type/Industry	Location	Per	Low	Mid	High	Source	Date
Adult Literacy, Remedial Education, and GED Teacher and Instructor							
	Grand Rapids-Wyoming MSA, MI	Y	37150 FQ	50570 MW	57830 TQ	USBLS	5/07
	Warren-Troy-Farmington Hills PMSA, MI	Y	21670 FQ	33280 MW	54720 TQ	USBLS	5/07
	Minnesota	Y	27965 FQ	36827 MW	46818 TQ	MNBLS	10/08-12/08
	Duluth-Superior MSA, MN-WI	Y	36691 FQ	44966 MW	59760 TQ	MNBLS	10/08-12/08
	Minneapolis-Saint Paul MSA, MN-WI	Y	28007 FQ	36408 MW	45040 TQ	MNBLS	10/08-12/08
	Mississippi	Y	22210 FQ	30680 MW	42290 TQ	USBLS	5/07
	Jackson MSA, MS	Y	15570 FQ	29830 MW	39990 TQ	USBLS	5/07
	Missouri	Y	33420 FQ	37400 MW	45890 TQ	USBLS	5/07
	Kansas City MSA, MO-KS	Y	31660 FQ	34190 MW	36770 TQ	USBLS	5/07
	St. Louis MSA, MO-IL	Y	35350 FQ	41070 MW	49990 TQ	USBLS	5/07
	Montana	Y	27560 FQ	31460 MW	40050 TQ	USBLS	5/07
	Nebraska	Y	26370 FQ	29940 MW	38270 TQ	USBLS	5/07
	Omaha-Council Bluffs MSA, NE-IA	Y	27220 FQ	29700 MW	37710 TQ	USBLS	5/07
	Nevada	H	17.28 FQ	21.50 MW	26.63 TQ	NVBLS	5/08
	Las Vegas-Paradise MSA, NV	H	17.03 FQ	21.24 MW	26.53 TQ	NVBLS	5/08
	New Hampshire	H	14.36 AE	22.59 MW	27.24 AEX	NHBLS	6/08
	New Jersey	Y	45890 FQ	57960 MW	70770 TQ	USBLS	5/07
	Camden PMSA, NJ	Y	49590 FQ	66080 MW	74660 TQ	USBLS	5/07
	Edison PMSA, NJ	Y	45730 FQ	57900 MW	71710 TQ	USBLS	5/07
	Newark-Union PMSA, NJ-PA	Y	42990 FQ	55870 MW	67950 TQ	USBLS	5/07
	New Mexico	Y	25500 FQ	29700 MW	36900 TQ	USBLS	5/07
	Albuquerque MSA, NM	Y	26330 FQ	28950 MW	33680 TQ	USBLS	5/07
	New York	Y	42510 FQ	56960 MW	74190 TQ	USBLS	5/07
	Albany-Schenectady-Troy MSA, NY	Y	48320 FQ	58540 MW	71040 TQ	USBLS	5/07
	Buffalo-Niagara Falls MSA, NY	Y	31650 FQ	49080 MW	59220 TQ	USBLS	5/07
	Nassau-Suffolk PMSA, NY	Y	45740 FQ	58690 MW	73520 TQ	USBLS	5/07
	New York-Northern New Jersey-Long Island MSA, NY-NJ-PA	Y	45630 FQ	60290 MW	75740 TQ	USBLS	5/07
	Utica-Rome MSA, NY	Y	50110 FQ	57030 MW	81280 TQ	USBLS	5/07
	North Carolina	Y	31690 FQ	37450 MW	45030 TQ	USBLS	5/07
	Charlotte-Gastonia-Concord MSA, NC-SC	Y	33000 FQ	37010 MW	41270 TQ	USBLS	5/07
	Raleigh-Cary MSA, NC	Y	30980 FQ	36750 MW	44920 TQ	USBLS	5/07
	Winston-Salem MSA, NC	Y	42470 FQ	46330 MW	50390 TQ	USBLS	5/07
	Ohio	Y	33790 FQ	45410 MW	60460 TQ	USBLS	5/07
	Cincinnati-Middletown MSA, OH-KY-IN	Y	30230 FQ	35800 MW	50550 TQ	USBLS	5/07
	Cleveland-Elyria-Mentor MSA, OH	Y	38530 FQ	51950 MW	72550 TQ	USBLS	5/07
	Columbus MSA, OH	Y	48560 FQ	59790 MW	73470 TQ	USBLS	5/07
	Dayton MSA, OH	Y	30140 FQ	36750 MW	47630 TQ	USBLS	5/07
	Oklahoma	Y	32120 FQ	36870 MW	43330 TQ	USBLS	5/07
	Oklahoma City MSA, OK	Y	35060 FQ	39790 MW	46220 TQ	USBLS	5/07
	Tulsa MSA, OK	Y	27490 FQ	37210 MW	44510 TQ	USBLS	5/07
	Oregon	H	15.07 FQ	20.08 MW	28.74 TQ	ORBLS	5/08
	Portland-Vancouver-Beaverton MSA, OR-WA	Y	29610 FQ	35670 MW	44330 TQ	USBLS	5/07
	Pennsylvania	Y	33230 FQ	41280 MW	49700 TQ	USBLS	5/07
	Allentown-Bethlehem-Easton MSA, PA-NJ	Y	37690 FQ	44460 MW	51470 TQ	USBLS	5/07
	Philadelphia-Camden-Wilmington MSA, PA-NJ-DE-MD	Y	36210 FQ	45240 MW	58090 TQ	USBLS	5/07
	Pittsburgh MSA, PA	Y	27700 FQ	34300 MW	39950 TQ	USBLS	5/07
	Rhode Island	Y	35420 FQ	39100 MW	46580 TQ	USBLS	5/07
	Providence-Fall River-Warwick MSA, RI-MA	Y	35440 FQ	39170 MW	45890 TQ	USBLS	5/07
	South Carolina	Y	40790 FQ	47830 MW	56780 TQ	USBLS	5/07
	Charleston-North Charleston MSA, SC	Y	41630 FQ	49520 MW	59080 TQ	USBLS	5/07
	Columbia MSA, SC	Y	43860 FQ	48500 MW	53420 TQ	USBLS	5/07
	South Dakota	Y	25199 FQ	30377 MW	35962 TQ	SDBLS	7/08-9/08

AE	Average entry wage	**AW**	Average wage paid	**FQ**	First quartile wage
AER	Average entry range	**AWR**	Average wage range	**H**	Hourly
AEX	Average experienced wage	**AXR**	Average experienced range	**HI**	Highest wage paid
ATC	Average total compensation	**D**	Daily	**HR**	High end range

LO	Lowest wage paid	**MTC**	Median total compensation	**TCC** Total cash compensation
LR	Low end range	**MW**	Median wage paid	**TQ** Third quartile wage
M	Monthly	**MWR**	Median wage range	**W** Weekly
MCC	Median cash compensation	**S**	See annotated source	**Y** Yearly

Occupation/Type/Industry	Location	Per	Low	Mid	High	Source	Date
Adult Literacy, Remedial Education, and GED Teacher and Instructor	Sioux Falls MSA, SD	Y	25384 FQ	29839 MW	34253 TQ	SDBLS	7/08-9/08
	Tennessee	Y	30360 FQ	40250 MW	50830 TQ	USBLS	5/07
	Memphis MSA, TN-MS-AR	Y	47500 FQ	53240 MW	58470 TQ	USBLS	5/07
	Nashville-Davidson-Murfreesboro MSA, TN	Y	27350 FQ	38330 MW	47690 TQ	USBLS	5/07
	Texas	Y	29450 FQ	41900 MW	50870 TQ	USBLS	5/07
	Austin-Round Rock MSA, TX	Y	19880 FQ	34170 MW	38460 TQ	USBLS	5/07
	Dallas-Fort Worth-Arlington MSA, TX	Y	34360 FQ	45290 MW	51590 TQ	USBLS	5/07
	El Paso MSA, TX	Y	31950 FQ	47960 MW	62610 TQ	USBLS	5/07
	Houston-Sugar Land-Baytown MSA, TX	Y	36320 FQ	43120 MW	53740 TQ	USBLS	5/07
	San Antonio MSA, TX	Y	33470 FQ	40420 MW	46230 TQ	USBLS	5/07
	Utah	Y	27250 FQ	38050 MW	49190 TQ	USBLS	5/07
	Salt Lake City MSA, UT	Y	41680 FQ	48040 MW	54630 TQ	USBLS	5/07
	Vermont	Y	33240 FQ	39390 MW	47720 TQ	USBLS	5/07
	Burlington-South Burlington MSA, VT	Y	35560 FQ	40760 MW	49310 TQ	USBLS	5/07
	Virginia	Y	35900 FQ	47410 MW	55020 TQ	USBLS	5/07
	Lynchburg MSA, VA	Y	28860 FQ	35600 MW	44550 TQ	USBLS	5/07
	Richmond MSA, VA	Y	38140 FQ	49360 MW	57450 TQ	USBLS	5/07
	Virginia Beach-Norfolk-Newport News MSA, VA-NC	Y	47490 FQ	51470 MW	56250 TQ	USBLS	5/07
	Washington	H	15.81 FQ	19.46 MW	24.66 TQ	WABLS	3/08
	Seattle-Tacoma-Bellevue MSA, WA	Y	32320 FQ	42240 MW	52480 TQ	USBLS	5/07
	West Virginia	Y	25450 FQ	31959 MW	44282 TQ	WVBLS	7/08-9/08
	Wisconsin	Y	39880 FQ	50120 MW	66840 TQ	USBLS	5/07
	Milwaukee-Waukesha-West Allis MSA, WI	Y	33620 FQ	43690 MW	61130 TQ	USBLS	5/07
	Wyoming	Y	32972 FQ	47279 MW	55809 TQ	WYBLS	9/08
	Puerto Rico	Y	20510 FQ	27570 MW	34240 TQ	USBLS	5/07
	San Juan-Caguas-Guaynabo MSA, PR	Y	20500 FQ	28420 MW	34480 TQ	USBLS	5/07
Advertising and Promotions Manager	Alabama	Y	42040 FQ	58490 MW	84870 TQ	USBLS	5/07
	Birmingham-Hoover MSA, AL	Y	46220 FQ	63480 MW	93540 TQ	USBLS	5/07
	Alaska	Y	42370 FQ	54810 MW	65550 TQ	USBLS	5/07
	Anchorage MSA, AK	Y	48790 FQ	58470 MW	66240 TQ	USBLS	5/07
	Arizona	Y	43200 FQ	61150 MW	91840 TQ	USBLS	5/07
	Phoenix-Mesa-Scottsdale MSA, AZ	Y	44800 FQ	66400 MW	93600 TQ	USBLS	5/07
	Tucson MSA, AZ	Y	37350 FQ	46180 MW	66720 TQ	USBLS	5/07
	Arkansas	Y	48800 FQ	67300 MW	102680 TQ	USBLS	5/07
	Little Rock-North Little Rock MSA, AR	Y	53830 FQ	73920 MW	105000 TQ	USBLS	5/07
	California	H	30.37 FQ	39.85 MW	55.18 TQ	CABLS	1/08-3/08
	Fresno MSA, CA	H	25.99 FQ	31.48 MW	47.28 TQ	CABLS	1/08-3/08
	Los Angeles-Long Beach-Glendale PMSA, CA	H	34.64 FQ	41.22 MW	55.91 TQ	CABLS	1/08-3/08
	Oakland-Fremont-Hayward MSA, CA	H	26.87 FQ	35.79 MW	49.11 TQ	CABLS	1/08-3/08
	Riverside-San Bernardino-Ontario MSA, CA	H	21.37 FQ	31.67 MW	40.40 TQ	CABLS	1/08-3/08
	Sacramento-Arden Arcade-Roseville MSA, CA	H	22.86 FQ	34.45 MW	44.91 TQ	CABLS	1/08-3/08
	San Diego-Carlsbad-San Marcos MSA, CA	H	25.84 FQ	36.36 MW	51.74 TQ	CABLS	1/08-3/08
	San Francisco-San Mateo-Redwood PMSA, CA	H	30.89 FQ	47.69 MW	67.63 TQ	CABLS	1/08-3/08
	San Jose-Sunnyvale-Santa Clara MSA, CA	H	34.74 FQ	44.01 MW	57.16 TQ	CABLS	1/08-3/08
	Santa Ana-Anaheim-Irvine PMSA, CA	Y	66800 FQ	81480 MW	111870 TQ	USBLS	5/07
	Colorado	Y	47370 FQ	72850 MW	110570 TQ	USBLS	5/07
	Boulder MSA, CO	Y	48110 FQ	56160 MW	99370 TQ	USBLS	5/07
	Colorado Springs MSA, CO	Y	38880 FQ	50800 MW	80970 TQ	USBLS	5/07
	Denver-Aurora MSA, CO	Y	58700 FQ	84570 MW	125690 TQ	USBLS	5/07

AE	Average entry wage	**AW**	Average wage paid	**FQ**	First quartile wage	
AER	Average entry range	**AWR**	Average wage range	**H**	Hourly	
AEX	Average experienced wage	**AXR**	Average experienced range	**HI**	Highest wage paid	
ATC	Average total compensation	**D**	Daily	**HR**	High end range	

LO	Lowest wage paid	**MTC**	Median total compensation	**TCC**	Total cash compensation
LR	Low end range	**MW**	Median wage paid	**TQ**	Third quartile wage
M	Monthly	**MWR**	Median wage range	**W**	Weekly
MCC	Median cash compensation	**S**	See annotated source	**Y**	Yearly

Occupation/Type/Industry	Location	Per	Low	Mid	High	Source	Date
Advertising and Promotions Manager	Connecticut	H	25.36 AE	37.78 MW		CTBLS	1/08-3/08
	Bridgeport-Stamford-Norwalk MSA, CT	Y	72480 FQ	93830 MW	143320 TQ	USBLS	5/07
	Hartford-West Hartford-East Hartford MSA, CT	Y	58790 FQ	69240 MW	94020 TQ	USBLS	5/07
	New Haven MSA, CT	Y	54950 FQ	66720 MW	77060 TQ	USBLS	5/07
	Delaware	Y	45690 FQ	63310 MW	97610 TQ	USBLS	5/07
	Wilmington PMSA, DE-MD-NJ	Y	47980 FQ	66470 MW	101050 TQ	USBLS	5/07
	District of Columbia	Y	54000 FQ	79560 MW	104920 TQ	USBLS	5/07
	Washington-Arlington-Alexandria MSA, DC-VA-MD-WV	Y	51730 FQ	73230 MW	101950 TQ	USBLS	5/07
	Florida	Y	56630 FQ	82180 MW	121440 TQ	USBLS	5/07
	Fort Lauderdale-Pompano Beach-Deerfield Beach PMSA, FL	Y	47050 FQ	65500 MW	99690 TQ	USBLS	5/07
	Jacksonville MSA, FL	Y	68930 FQ	89320 MW	122250 TQ	USBLS	5/07
	Miami-Fort Lauderdale-Miami Beach MSA, FL	Y	57790 FQ	80040 MW	127050 TQ	USBLS	5/07
	Orlando-Kissimmee MSA, FL	Y	51100 FQ	72590 MW	115510 TQ	USBLS	5/07
	Sarasota-Bradenton-Venice MSA, FL	Y	75270 FQ	98600 MW		USBLS	5/07
	Tampa-St. Petersburg-Clearwater MSA, FL	Y	73000 FQ	93750 MW	120270 TQ	USBLS	5/07
	West Palm Beach-Boca Raton-Boynton Beach PMSA, FL	Y	67080 FQ	90380 MW		USBLS	5/07
	Georgia	Y	51920 FQ	78660 MW	105170 TQ	USBLS	5/07
	Atlanta-Sandy Springs-Marietta MSA, GA	Y	54820 FQ	83620 MW	109720 TQ	USBLS	5/07
	Hawaii	Y	49870 FQ	70940 MW	93040 TQ	USBLS	5/07
	Honolulu MSA, HI	Y	50050 FQ	70720 MW	85340 TQ	USBLS	5/07
	Idaho	Y	34320 FQ	43840 MW	60650 TQ	USBLS	5/07
	Boise City-Nampa MSA, ID	Y	36140 FQ	42070 MW	59120 TQ	USBLS	5/07
	Illinois	Y	50340 FQ	74240 MW	121410 TQ	USBLS	5/07
	Chicago-Naperville-Joliet MSA, IL-IN-WI	Y	52950 FQ	77840 MW	125160 TQ	USBLS	5/07
	Indiana	Y	51240 FQ	69860 MW	89590 TQ	USBLS	5/07
	Indianapolis-Carmel MSA, IN	Y	62590 FQ	76470 MW	95300 TQ	USBLS	5/07
	Iowa	Y	41190 FQ	54880 MW	68460 TQ	USBLS	5/07
	Des Moines-West Des Moines MSA, IA	Y	44600 FQ	58530 MW	69570 TQ	USBLS	5/07
	Kansas	Y	37320 FQ	49740 MW	80240 TQ	USBLS	5/07
	Wichita MSA, KS	Y	41860 FQ	53560 MW	77880 TQ	USBLS	5/07
	Kentucky	Y	43159 FQ	53429 MW	75253 TQ	KYBLS	2008
	Louisville-Jefferson County MSA, KY-IN	Y	50020 FQ	66010 MW	83400 TQ	USBLS	5/07
	Louisiana	H	18.83 FQ	23.66 MW	30.88 TQ	LABLS	1/08-3/08
	Baton Rouge MSA, LA	Y	42910 FQ	52550 MW	65670 TQ	USBLS	5/07
	New Orleans-Metairie-Kenner MSA, LA	Y	38130 FQ	47960 MW	65530 TQ	USBLS	5/07
	Maine	Y	43860 FQ	56210 MW	65790 TQ	USBLS	5/07
	Portland-South Portland-Biddeford MSA, ME	Y	50690 FQ	59140 MW	65600 TQ	USBLS	5/07
	Maryland	Y		87850 MW		MDBLS	3/08
	Baltimore-Towson MSA, MD	Y	60030 FQ	103430 MW	135740 TQ	USBLS	5/07
	Bethesda-Gaithersburg-Frederick PMSA, MD	Y	48030 FQ	67280 MW	95260 TQ	USBLS	5/07
	Hagerstown-Martinsburg MSA, MD-WV	Y	47990 FQ	66680 MW	106930 TQ	USBLS	5/07
	Massachusetts	Y	70720 FQ	97980 MW		USBLS	5/07
	Boston-Cambridge-Quincy NECTA, MA	Y	77790 FQ	103710 MW		USBLS	5/07
	Worcester MSA, MA-CT	Y	45710 FQ	67210 MW	105930 TQ	USBLS	5/07
	Michigan	Y	52860 FQ	79840 MW	108970 TQ	USBLS	5/07
	Detroit-Warren-Livonia MSA, MI	Y	64260 FQ	88680 MW	115510 TQ	USBLS	5/07
	Grand Rapids-Wyoming MSA, MI	Y	47300 FQ	59100 MW	72030 TQ	USBLS	5/07
	Warren-Troy-Farmington Hills PMSA, MI	Y	65700 FQ	89760 MW	116940 TQ	USBLS	5/07

AE	Average entry wage	AW	Average wage paid	FQ	First quartile wage
AER	Average entry range	AWR	Average wage range	H	Hourly
AEX	Average experienced wage	AXR	Average experienced range	HI	Highest wage paid
ATC	Average total compensation	D	Daily	HR	High end range

LO	Lowest wage paid	MTC	Median total compensation
LR	Low end range	MW	Median wage paid
M	Monthly	MWR	Median wage range
MCC	Median cash compensation	S	See annotated source

TCC	Total cash compensation
TQ	Third quartile wage
W	Weekly
Y	Yearly

Occupation/Type/Industry	Location	Per	Low	Mid	High	Source	Date
Advertising and Promotions Manager	Minnesota	Y	85059 FQ	109155 MW	137442 TQ	MNBLS	10/08-12/08
	Duluth-Superior MSA, MN-WI	Y	60953 FQ	73267 MW	94985 TQ	MNBLS	10/08-12/08
	Minneapolis-Saint Paul MSA, MN-WI	Y	87374 FQ	111855 MW	139580 TQ	MNBLS	10/08-12/08
	Mississippi	Y	39600 FQ	50010 MW	74990 TQ	USBLS	5/07
	Jackson MSA, MS	Y	38030 FQ	58740 MW	84090 TQ	USBLS	5/07
	Missouri	Y	45810 FQ	66670 MW	102470 TQ	USBLS	5/07
	Kansas City MSA, MO-KS	Y	43640 FQ	70480 MW	105810 TQ	USBLS	5/07
	St. Louis MSA, MO-IL	Y	50500 FQ	69160 MW	103980 TQ	USBLS	5/07
	Montana	Y	27580 FQ	40450 MW	58500 TQ	USBLS	5/07
	Nebraska	Y	52660 FQ	62190 MW	81190 TQ	USBLS	5/07
	Omaha-Council Bluffs MSA, NE-IA	Y	47770 FQ	68370 MW	92420 TQ	USBLS	5/07
	Nevada	H	23.14 FQ	34.10 MW	45.12 TQ	NVBLS	5/08
	Las Vegas-Paradise MSA, NV	H	25.17 FQ	34.95 MW	47.06 TQ	NVBLS	5/08
	New Hampshire	H	17.43 AE	28.65 MW	37.11 AEX	NHBLS	6/08
	New Jersey	Y	79350 FQ	113270 MW		USBLS	5/07
	Camden PMSA, NJ	Y	54810 FQ	100720 MW	141110 TQ	USBLS	5/07
	Edison PMSA, NJ	Y	65870 FQ	108060 MW	138620 TQ	USBLS	5/07
	Newark-Union PMSA, NJ-PA	Y	84200 FQ	109950 MW		USBLS	5/07
	New Mexico	Y	38190 FQ	53260 MW	76010 TQ	USBLS	5/07
	Albuquerque MSA, NM	Y	39030 FQ	61310 MW	83270 TQ	USBLS	5/07
	New York	Y	79630 FQ	117010 MW		USBLS	5/07
	Albany-Schenectady-Troy MSA, NY	Y	60600 FQ	77230 MW	107730 TQ	USBLS	5/07
	Buffalo-Niagara Falls MSA, NY	Y	48770 FQ	72940 MW	141980 TQ	USBLS	5/07
	Nassau-Suffolk PMSA, NY	Y	71780 FQ	125240 MW		USBLS	5/07
	New York-Northern New Jersey-Long Island MSA, NY-NJ-PA	Y	83580 FQ	120740 MW		USBLS	5/07
	North Carolina	Y	47120 FQ	64910 MW	91790 TQ	USBLS	5/07
	Charlotte-Gastonia-Concord MSA, NC-SC	Y	53310 FQ	64160 MW	96560 TQ	USBLS	5/07
	Greensboro-High Point MSA, NC	Y	54100 FQ	67250 MW	80300 TQ	USBLS	5/07
	Raleigh-Cary MSA, NC	Y	43700 FQ	61900 MW	94270 TQ	USBLS	5/07
	North Dakota	Y	46270 FQ	76180 MW	109170 TQ	USBLS	5/07
	Ohio	Y	51340 FQ	73330 MW	96410 TQ	USBLS	5/07
	Cincinnati-Middletown MSA, OH-KY-IN	Y	47360 FQ	69030 MW	90330 TQ	USBLS	5/07
	Cleveland-Elyria-Mentor MSA, OH	Y	55620 FQ	86990 MW	124500 TQ	USBLS	5/07
	Columbus MSA, OH	Y	53530 FQ	76420 MW	104540 TQ	USBLS	5/07
	Dayton MSA, OH	Y	36390 FQ	62750 MW	83210 TQ	USBLS	5/07
	Oklahoma	Y	40130 FQ	50580 MW	66820 TQ	USBLS	5/07
	Oklahoma City MSA, OK	Y	38620 FQ	46480 MW	60270 TQ	USBLS	5/07
	Tulsa MSA, OK	Y	45760 FQ	59020 MW	73220 TQ	USBLS	5/07
	Oregon	H	23.62 FQ	35.38 MW	52.95 TQ	ORBLS	5/08
	Portland-Vancouver-Beaverton MSA, OR-WA	Y	54330 FQ	84410 MW	115740 TQ	USBLS	5/07
	Pennsylvania	Y	54450 FQ	78780 MW	112140 TQ	USBLS	5/07
	Allentown-Bethlehem-Easton MSA, PA-NJ	Y	51210 FQ	76400 MW	99850 TQ	USBLS	5/07
	Philadelphia-Camden-Wilmington MSA, PA-NJ-DE-MD	Y	65120 FQ	91990 MW	138990 TQ	USBLS	5/07
	Pittsburgh MSA, PA	Y	49360 FQ	66680 MW	95310 TQ	USBLS	5/07
	Rhode Island	Y	50210 FQ	67440 MW	84680 TQ	USBLS	5/07
	Providence-Fall River-Warwick MSA, RI-MA	Y	52610 FQ	69180 MW	90480 TQ	USBLS	5/07
	South Carolina	Y	45910 FQ	58870 MW	85270 TQ	USBLS	5/07
	Charleston-North Charleston MSA, SC	Y	53150 FQ	59360 MW	72090 TQ	USBLS	5/07
	Columbia MSA, SC	Y	45640 FQ	58060 MW	82750 TQ	USBLS	5/07
	South Dakota	Y	60730 FQ	74784 MW	94740 TQ	SDBLS	7/08-9/08
	Tennessee	Y	36660 FQ	52490 MW	80620 TQ	USBLS	5/07
	Memphis MSA, TN-MS-AR	Y	34060 FQ	49480 MW	79780 TQ	USBLS	5/07
	Nashville-Davidson-Murfreesboro MSA, TN	Y	38650 FQ	54340 MW	74170 TQ	USBLS	5/07
	Texas	Y	55780 FQ	78290 MW	105960 TQ	USBLS	5/07

AE	Average entry wage	AW	Average wage paid	LO	Lowest wage paid	MTC	Median total compensation	TCC	Total cash compensation
AER	Average entry range	AWR	Average wage range	LR	Low end range	MW	Median wage paid	TQ	Third quartile wage
AEX	Average experienced wage	AXR	Average experienced range	HI	Highest wage paid	MWR	Median wage range	W	Weekly
ATC	Average total compensation	D	Daily	HR	High end range	MCC	Median cash compensation	S	See annotated source	Y	Yearly

Occupation/Type/Industry	Location	Per	Low	Mid	High	Source	Date
Advertising and Promotions Manager	Austin-Round Rock MSA, TX	Y	64220 FQ	83310 MW	104240 TQ	USBLS	5/07
	Dallas-Fort Worth-Arlington MSA, TX	Y	58310 FQ	82940 MW		USBLS	5/07
	Houston-Sugar Land-Baytown MSA, TX	Y	52490 FQ	75960 MW	91950 TQ	USBLS	5/07
	San Antonio MSA, TX	Y	56630 FQ	73820 MW	85340 TQ	USBLS	5/07
	Utah	Y	49890 FQ	72960 MW	112410 TQ	USBLS	5/07
	Salt Lake City MSA, UT	Y	54370 FQ	98450 MW	119120 TQ	USBLS	5/07
	Vermont	Y	49040 FQ	72440 MW	88330 TQ	USBLS	5/07
	Virginia	Y	42720 FQ	69480 MW	101460 TQ	USBLS	5/07
	Richmond MSA, VA	Y	41890 FQ	63890 MW		USBLS	5/07
	Virginia Beach-Norfolk-Newport News MSA, VA-NC	Y	38620 FQ	71880 MW	88200 TQ	USBLS	5/07
	Washington	H	36.28 FQ	46.68 MW	58.27 TQ	WABLS	3/08
	Seattle-Tacoma-Bellevue MSA, WA	Y	80890 FQ	97520 MW	120460 TQ	USBLS	5/07
	West Virginia	Y	39824 FQ	50148 MW	61259 TQ	WVBLS	7/08-9/08
	Charleston MSA, WV	Y	43480 FQ	50990 MW	61920 TQ	USBLS	5/07
	Wisconsin	Y	48990 FQ	68910 MW	90530 TQ	USBLS	5/07
	Milwaukee-Waukesha-West Allis MSA, WI	Y	52430 FQ	72460 MW	94710 TQ	USBLS	5/07
	Wyoming	Y	35820 FQ	40238 MW	64818 TQ	WYBLS	9/08
	Puerto Rico	Y	43730 FQ	60110 MW	83480 TQ	USBLS	5/07
	San Juan-Caguas-Guaynabo MSA, PR	Y	43690 FQ	59820 MW	83100 TQ	USBLS	5/07
	Guam	Y	28930 FQ	37490 MW	46990 TQ	USBLS	5/07
Advertising Sales Agent	Alabama	Y	27970 FQ	43610 MW	65390 TQ	USBLS	5/07
	Birmingham-Hoover MSA, AL	Y	28600 FQ	48260 MW	76220 TQ	USBLS	5/07
	Alaska	Y	29510 FQ	35960 MW	45670 TQ	USBLS	5/07
	Arizona	Y	32060 FQ	41750 MW	52370 TQ	USBLS	5/07
	Phoenix-Mesa-Scottsdale MSA, AZ	Y	34440 FQ	42890 MW	51000 TQ	USBLS	5/07
	Tucson MSA, AZ	Y	28560 FQ	43540 MW	58980 TQ	USBLS	5/07
	Arkansas	Y	25900 FQ	33970 MW	46000 TQ	USBLS	5/07
	Little Rock-North Little Rock MSA, AR	Y	29740 FQ	40140 MW	51910 TQ	USBLS	5/07
	California	H	16.18 FQ	22.86 MW	33.21 TQ	CABLS	1/08-3/08
	Los Angeles-Long Beach-Glendale PMSA, CA	H	16.03 FQ	21.70 MW	33.01 TQ	CABLS	1/08-3/08
	Oakland-Fremont-Hayward MSA, CA	H	18.87 FQ	25.18 MW	31.79 TQ	CABLS	1/08-3/08
	Riverside-San Bernardino-Ontario MSA, CA	H	18.50 FQ	23.37 MW	38.72 TQ	CABLS	1/08-3/08
	Sacramento-Arden Arcade-Roseville MSA, CA	H	16.08 FQ	22.99 MW	32.55 TQ	CABLS	1/08-3/08
	San Diego-Carlsbad-San Marcos MSA, CA	H	18.98 FQ	24.86 MW	37.25 TQ	CABLS	1/08-3/08
	San Francisco-San Mateo-Redwood PMSA, CA	H	18.31 FQ	26.14 MW	35.99 TQ	CABLS	1/08-3/08
	San Jose-Sunnyvale-Santa Clara MSA, CA	H	20.34 FQ	24.49 MW	33.98 TQ	CABLS	1/08-3/08
	Santa Ana-Anaheim-Irvine PMSA, CA	Y	29710 FQ	40830 MW	62730 TQ	USBLS	5/07
	Colorado	Y	30710 FQ	43640 MW	65730 TQ	USBLS	5/07
	Denver-Aurora MSA, CO	Y	33910 FQ	48960 MW	69690 TQ	USBLS	5/07
	Connecticut	H	14.72 AE	23.65 MW		CTBLS	1/08-3/08
	Bridgeport-Stamford-Norwalk MSA, CT	Y	41590 FQ	59340 MW	100890 TQ	USBLS	5/07
	Hartford-West Hartford-East Hartford MSA, CT	Y	31410 FQ	41450 MW	64130 TQ	USBLS	5/07
	New Haven MSA, CT	Y	34650 FQ	46660 MW	61810 TQ	USBLS	5/07
	Delaware	Y	33160 FQ	51010 MW	95970 TQ	USBLS	5/07
	Wilmington PMSA, DE-MD-NJ	Y	34550 FQ	54990 MW	123670 TQ	USBLS	5/07
	District of Columbia	Y	38130 FQ	58920 MW	102030 TQ	USBLS	5/07
	Washington-Arlington-Alexandria MSA, DC-VA-MD-WV	Y	32700 FQ	49730 MW	73170 TQ	USBLS	5/07
	Florida	Y	29520 FQ	39010 MW	57170 TQ	USBLS	5/07

AE	Average entry wage	**AW**	Average wage paid	**FQ**	First quartile wage	**LO**	Lowest wage paid	**MTC** Median total compensation	**TCC** Total cash compensation
AER	Average entry range	**AWR**	Average wage range	**H**	Hourly	**LR**	Low end range	**MW** Median wage paid	**TQ** Third quartile wage
AEX	Average experienced wage	**AXR**	Average experienced range	**HI**	Highest wage paid	**M**	Monthly	**MWR** Median wage range	**W** Weekly
ATC	Average total compensation	**D**	Daily	**HR**	High end range	**MCC**	Median cash compensation	**S** See annotated source	**Y** Yearly

Occupation/Type/Industry	Location	Per	Low	Mid	High	Source	Date
Advertising Sales Agent	Fort Lauderdale-Pompano Beach-Deerfield Beach PMSA, FL	Y	31850 FQ	40720 MW	59280 TQ	USBLS	5/07
	Jacksonville MSA, FL	Y	27920 FQ	33570 MW	49920 TQ	USBLS	5/07
	Miami-Fort Lauderdale-Miami Beach MSA, FL	Y	29820 FQ	39600 MW	63200 TQ	USBLS	5/07
	Orlando-Kissimmee MSA, FL	Y	29200 FQ	40940 MW	52280 TQ	USBLS	5/07
	Tampa-St. Petersburg-Clearwater MSA, FL	Y	29740 FQ	39610 MW	63580 TQ	USBLS	5/07
	West Palm Beach-Boca Raton-Boynton Beach PMSA, FL	Y	28260 FQ	36040 MW	63220 TQ	USBLS	5/07
	Georgia	Y	30440 FQ	44390 MW	66130 TQ	USBLS	5/07
	Atlanta-Sandy Springs-Marietta MSA, GA	Y	35520 FQ	50770 MW	77020 TQ	USBLS	5/07
	Macon MSA, GA	Y	22620 FQ	26910 MW	35800 TQ	USBLS	5/07
	Hawaii	Y	37290 FQ	51810 MW	66170 TQ	USBLS	5/07
	Honolulu MSA, HI	Y	43150 FQ	57890 MW	72780 TQ	USBLS	5/07
	Idaho	Y	29640 FQ	42870 MW	58230 TQ	USBLS	5/07
	Boise City-Nampa MSA, ID	Y	30390 FQ	48670 MW	59550 TQ	USBLS	5/07
	Illinois	Y	27810 FQ	40620 MW	60000 TQ	USBLS	5/07
	Chicago-Naperville-Joliet MSA, IL-IN-WI	Y	30310 FQ	43270 MW	65270 TQ	USBLS	5/07
	Indiana	Y	26040 FQ	38660 MW	53500 TQ	USBLS	5/07
	Indianapolis-Carmel MSA, IN	Y	33300 FQ	48230 MW	58930 TQ	USBLS	5/07
	Iowa	Y	24140 FQ	33040 MW	54110 TQ	USBLS	5/07
	Davenport-Moline-Rock Island MSA, IA-IL	Y	21170 FQ	31010 MW	54720 TQ	USBLS	5/07
	Des Moines-West Des Moines MSA, IA	Y	26920 FQ	34830 MW	60820 TQ	USBLS	5/07
	Iowa City MSA, IA	Y	27690 FQ	41020 MW	48440 TQ	USBLS	5/07
	Waterloo-Cedar Falls MSA, IA	Y	28260 FQ	50050 MW	78670 TQ	USBLS	5/07
	Kansas	Y	24820 FQ	34800 MW	49710 TQ	USBLS	5/07
	Wichita MSA, KS	Y	22390 FQ	31990 MW	45870 TQ	USBLS	5/07
	Kentucky	Y	25699 FQ	34848 MW	49996 TQ	KYBLS	2008
	Elizabethtown MSA, KY	Y	26180 FQ	34560 MW	42210 TQ	USBLS	5/07
	Louisville-Jefferson County MSA, KY-IN	Y	27960 FQ	35790 MW	51820 TQ	USBLS	5/07
	Louisiana	H	12.88 FQ	17.30 MW	24.39 TQ	LABLS	1/08-3/08
	Baton Rouge MSA, LA	Y	28800 FQ	36660 MW	63500 TQ	USBLS	5/07
	Lafayette MSA, LA	Y	33820 FQ	39890 MW	54030 TQ	USBLS	5/07
	New Orleans-Metairie-Kenner MSA, LA	Y	29870 FQ	39750 MW	55160 TQ	USBLS	5/07
	Maine	Y	25400 FQ	34530 MW	43620 TQ	USBLS	5/07
	Portland-South Portland-Biddeford MSA, ME	Y	28180 FQ	38240 MW	54150 TQ	USBLS	5/07
	Maryland	Y		48250 MW		MDBLS	3/08
	Baltimore-Towson MSA, MD	Y	34590 FQ	49950 MW	75390 TQ	USBLS	5/07
	Bethesda-Gaithersburg-Frederick PMSA, MD	Y	30480 FQ	48890 MW	68010 TQ	USBLS	5/07
	Massachusetts	Y	32500 FQ	44590 MW	74920 TQ	USBLS	5/07
	Boston-Cambridge-Quincy NECTA, MA	Y	32620 FQ	45410 MW	83180 TQ	USBLS	5/07
	Lynn-Peabody-Salem NECTA, MA	Y	38290 FQ	47410 MW	67250 TQ	USBLS	5/07
	Worcester MSA, MA-CT	Y	34690 FQ	46040 MW	64750 TQ	USBLS	5/07
	Michigan	Y	31430 FQ	46050 MW	73810 TQ	USBLS	5/07
	Detroit-Warren-Livonia MSA, MI	Y	35630 FQ	50370 MW	95760 TQ	USBLS	5/07
	Grand Rapids-Wyoming MSA, MI	Y	26850 FQ	37640 MW	66170 TQ	USBLS	5/07
	Warren-Troy-Farmington Hills PMSA, MI	Y	32850 FQ	46330 MW	80910 TQ	USBLS	5/07
	Minnesota	Y	29982 FQ	38072 MW	52311 TQ	MNBLS	10/08-12/08
	Duluth-Superior MSA, MN-WI	Y	27441 FQ	36405 MW	48916 TQ	MNBLS	10/08-12/08
	Minneapolis-Saint Paul MSA, MN-WI	Y	33061 FQ	39698 MW	56701 TQ	MNBLS	10/08-12/08
	Rochester MSA, MN	Y	19817 FQ	29432 MW	49241 TQ	MNBLS	10/08-12/08
	Mississippi	Y	23040 FQ	29980 MW	43010 TQ	USBLS	5/07
	Jackson MSA, MS	Y	23100 FQ	36910 MW	55370 TQ	USBLS	5/07
	Missouri	Y	23900 FQ	36250 MW	52910 TQ	USBLS	5/07
	Kansas City MSA, MO-KS	Y	31090 FQ	39910 MW	63870 TQ	USBLS	5/07
	St. Joseph MSA, MO-KS	Y	20310 FQ	41630 MW	53780 TQ	USBLS	5/07

AE	Average entry wage	AW	Average wage paid	FQ First quartile wage
AER	Average entry range	AWR	Average wage range	H Hourly
AEX	Average experienced wage	AXR	Average experienced range	HI Highest wage paid
ATC	Average total compensation	D	Daily	HR High end range

LO Lowest wage paid
LR Low end range
M Monthly
MCC Median cash compensation

MTC Median total compensation
MW Median wage paid
MWR Median wage range
S See annotated source

TCC Total cash compensation
TQ Third quartile wage
W Weekly
Y Yearly

Advertising Sales Agent

Occupation/Type/Industry	Location	Per	Low	Mid	High	Source	Date
Advertising Sales Agent	St. Louis MSA, MO-IL	Y	26500 FQ	42170 MW	57890 TQ	USBLS	5/07
	Springfield MSA, MO	Y	21610 FQ	31020 MW	59860 TQ	USBLS	5/07
	Montana	Y	19830 FQ	27230 MW	38840 TQ	USBLS	5/07
	Billings MSA, MT	Y	19490 FQ	27490 MW	44740 TQ	USBLS	5/07
	Nebraska	Y	23700 FQ	32570 MW	47790 TQ	USBLS	5/07
	Omaha-Council Bluffs MSA, NE-IA	Y	29380 FQ	37800 MW	55220 TQ	USBLS	5/07
	Nevada	H	14.60 FQ	21.10 MW	43.11 TQ	NVBLS	5/08
	Las Vegas-Paradise MSA, NV	H	14.91 FQ	21.97 MW	45.84 TQ	NVBLS	5/08
	New Hampshire	H	13.50 AE	19.79 MW	26.48 AEX	NHBLS	6/08
	Manchester MSA, NH	Y	40110 FQ	43160 MW	46180 TQ	USBLS	5/07
	Nashua NECTA, NH-MA	Y	28540 FQ	37930 MW	81260 TQ	USBLS	5/07
	New Jersey	Y	30820 FQ	46640 MW	77260 TQ	USBLS	5/07
	Atlantic City MSA, NJ	Y	27550 FQ	33150 MW	45460 TQ	USBLS	5/07
	Camden PMSA, NJ	Y	29190 FQ	47320 MW	63780 TQ	USBLS	5/07
	Edison PMSA, NJ	Y	29670 FQ	43140 MW	61100 TQ	USBLS	5/07
	Newark-Union PMSA, NJ-PA	Y	33160 FQ	51440 MW	89540 TQ	USBLS	5/07
	New Mexico	Y	25750 FQ	40000 MW	57250 TQ	USBLS	5/07
	Albuquerque MSA, NM	Y	30210 FQ	47860 MW	60210 TQ	USBLS	5/07
	New York	Y	37850 FQ	53330 MW	74310 TQ	USBLS	5/07
	Albany-Schenectady-Troy MSA, NY	Y	30270 FQ	39540 MW	56330 TQ	USBLS	5/07
	Buffalo-Niagara Falls MSA, NY	Y	24070 FQ	32330 MW	49840 TQ	USBLS	5/07
	Ithaca MSA, NY	Y	18150 FQ	49340 MW	59710 TQ	USBLS	5/07
	Kingston MSA, NY	Y	34790 FQ	45010 MW	62360 TQ	USBLS	5/07
	Nassau-Suffolk PMSA, NY	Y	43250 FQ	63190 MW	76500 TQ	USBLS	5/07
	New York-Northern New Jersey-Long Island MSA, NY-NJ-PA	Y	39180 FQ	55200 MW	76040 TQ	USBLS	5/07
	North Carolina	Y	28540 FQ	38280 MW	57010 TQ	USBLS	5/07
	Charlotte-Gastonia-Concord MSA, NC-SC	Y	28940 FQ	45070 MW	76190 TQ	USBLS	5/07
	Raleigh-Cary MSA, NC	Y	31090 FQ	40280 MW	51470 TQ	USBLS	5/07
	North Dakota	Y	25700 FQ	37870 MW	56090 TQ	USBLS	5/07
	Fargo MSA, ND-MN	Y	29940 FQ	44020 MW	59470 TQ	USBLS	5/07
	Ohio	Y	27830 FQ	38300 MW	51720 TQ	USBLS	5/07
	Canton-Massillon MSA, OH	Y	31560 FQ	40770 MW	51160 TQ	USBLS	5/07
	Cincinnati-Middletown MSA, OH-KY-IN	Y	28340 FQ	39020 MW	53680 TQ	USBLS	5/07
	Cleveland-Elyria-Mentor MSA, OH	Y	32200 FQ	40630 MW	48980 TQ	USBLS	5/07
	Columbus MSA, OH	Y	29400 FQ	38380 MW	53890 TQ	USBLS	5/07
	Dayton MSA, OH	Y	28070 FQ	43200 MW	60050 TQ	USBLS	5/07
	Oklahoma	Y	26050 FQ	31640 MW	53120 TQ	USBLS	5/07
	Oklahoma City MSA, OK	Y	26660 FQ	31080 MW	61910 TQ	USBLS	5/07
	Tulsa MSA, OK	Y	28730 FQ	37640 MW	50900 TQ	USBLS	5/07
	Oregon	H	13.43 FQ	18.50 MW	29.95 TQ	ORBLS	5/08
	Portland-Vancouver-Beaverton MSA, OR-WA	Y	28400 FQ	40600 MW	69910 TQ	USBLS	5/07
	Pennsylvania	Y	30290 FQ	42920 MW	61490 TQ	USBLS	5/07
	Allentown-Bethlehem-Easton MSA, PA-NJ	Y	27220 FQ	36620 MW	59430 TQ	USBLS	5/07
	Philadelphia-Camden-Wilmington MSA, PA-NJ-DE-MD	Y	35870 FQ	49010 MW	70850 TQ	USBLS	5/07
	Pittsburgh MSA, PA	Y	28440 FQ	42620 MW	59720 TQ	USBLS	5/07
	York-Hanover MSA, PA	Y	27460 FQ	32060 MW	50060 TQ	USBLS	5/07
	Rhode Island	Y	37810 FQ	50890 MW	67120 TQ	USBLS	5/07
	Providence-Fall River-Warwick MSA, RI-MA	Y	35580 FQ	48430 MW	64830 TQ	USBLS	5/07
	South Carolina	Y	27370 FQ	39150 MW	52700 TQ	USBLS	5/07
	Charleston-North Charleston MSA, SC	Y	32030 FQ	44360 MW	76620 TQ	USBLS	5/07
	Columbia MSA, SC	Y	26390 FQ	36300 MW	54720 TQ	USBLS	5/07
	Spartanburg MSA, SC	Y	27620 FQ	31710 MW	86820 TQ	USBLS	5/07
	South Dakota	Y	27384 FQ	33592 MW	44963 TQ	SDBLS	7/08-9/08
	Sioux Falls MSA, SD	Y	30369 FQ	40121 MW	54570 TQ	SDBLS	7/08-9/08
	Tennessee	Y	26960 FQ	35170 MW	47860 TQ	USBLS	5/07
	Knoxville MSA, TN	Y	24030 FQ	29900 MW	42380 TQ	USBLS	5/07
	Memphis MSA, TN-MS-AR	Y	27090 FQ	35780 MW	48400 TQ	USBLS	5/07

Occupation/Type/Industry	Location	Per	Low	Mid	High	Source	Date
Advertising Sales Agent	Nashville-Davidson-Murfreesboro MSA, TN	Y	28120 FQ	37470 MW	50240 TQ	USBLS	5/07
	Texas	Y	26190 FQ	38820 MW	58240 TQ	USBLS	5/07
	Austin-Round Rock MSA, TX	Y	27250 FQ	39760 MW	57470 TQ	USBLS	5/07
	Dallas-Fort Worth-Arlington MSA, TX	Y	28350 FQ	42930 MW	62880 TQ	USBLS	5/07
	El Paso MSA, TX	Y	24730 FQ	34190 MW	52280 TQ	USBLS	5/07
	Houston-Sugar Land-Baytown MSA, TX	Y	28100 FQ	37410 MW	56590 TQ	USBLS	5/07
	Midland MSA, TX	Y	23230 FQ	34700 MW	43870 TQ	USBLS	5/07
	San Antonio MSA, TX	Y	34890 FQ	51850 MW	73520 TQ	USBLS	5/07
	Utah	Y	30230 FQ	40050 MW	70380 TQ	USBLS	5/07
	Salt Lake City MSA, UT	Y	32950 FQ	43730 MW	71430 TQ	USBLS	5/07
	Vermont	Y	27590 FQ	37150 MW	48990 TQ	USBLS	5/07
	Burlington-South Burlington MSA, VT	Y	29010 FQ	41500 MW	50100 TQ	USBLS	5/07
	Virginia	Y	26740 FQ	38460 MW	62890 TQ	USBLS	5/07
	Charlottesville MSA, VA	Y	25470 FQ	48940 MW	109410 TQ	USBLS	5/07
	Richmond MSA, VA	Y	26370 FQ	44970 MW	75590 TQ	USBLS	5/07
	Virginia Beach-Norfolk-Newport News MSA, VA-NC	Y	30150 FQ	41180 MW	63450 TQ	USBLS	5/07
	Washington	H	16.49 FQ	22.23 MW	32.74 TQ	WABLS	3/08
	Seattle-Tacoma-Bellevue MSA, WA	Y	38310 FQ	51730 MW	74970 TQ	USBLS	5/07
	West Virginia	Y	22715 FQ	30387 MW	42251 TQ	WVBLS	7/08-9/08
	Charleston MSA, WV	Y	22020 FQ	31870 MW	55130 TQ	USBLS	5/07
	Wisconsin	Y	28530 FQ	38870 MW	56420 TQ	USBLS	5/07
	Milwaukee-Waukesha-West Allis MSA, WI	Y	32800 FQ	47910 MW	61920 TQ	USBLS	5/07
	Wyoming	Y	24595 FQ	31833 MW	52623 TQ	WYBLS	9/08
	Cheyenne MSA, WY	Y	31924 FQ	55869 MW	62238 TQ	WYBLS	9/08
	Puerto Rico	Y	16950 FQ	26030 MW	37660 TQ	USBLS	5/07
	San Juan-Caguas-Guaynabo MSA, PR	Y	18680 FQ	29120 MW	40310 TQ	USBLS	5/07
	Guam	Y	19850 FQ	28660 MW	35720 TQ	USBLS	5/07
Advertising Sales Director	Midwest	Y		118000 ATC		FOLIO01	2/25/08-4/9/08
	Northeast	Y		132000 ATC		FOLIO01	2/25/08-4/9/08
	South	Y		97000 ATC		FOLIO01	2/25/08-4/9/08
	West	Y		129000 ATC		FOLIO01	2/25/08-4/9/08
Aerobics and Fitness Instructor Cruise Ship	United States	M	1800 LO		2200 HI	CRU04	2008
Aeronautics Inspector Department of Safety	New Hampshire	Y		54524 AW		NHUL03	2008
Aerospace Engineer	United States	Y	54008 LO		121679 HI	WSJ01	2008
	Alabama	Y	80110 FQ	93870 MW	110480 TQ	USBLS	5/07
	Arizona	Y	61110 FQ	77180 MW	105410 TQ	USBLS	5/07
	Phoenix-Mesa-Scottsdale MSA, AZ	Y	58980 FQ	67470 MW	106740 TQ	USBLS	5/07
	Arkansas	Y	85140 FQ	94360 MW	102250 TQ	USBLS	5/07
	Little Rock-North Little Rock MSA, AR	Y	56440 FQ	66130 MW	78030 TQ	USBLS	5/07
	California	H	39.88 FQ	48.70 MW	59.22 TQ	CABLS	1/08-3/08
	Los Angeles-Long Beach-Glendale PMSA, CA	H	41.14 FQ	49.51 MW	59.69 TQ	CABLS	1/08-3/08
	Oakland-Fremont-Hayward MSA, CA	H	49.19 FQ			CABLS	1/08-3/08
	Riverside-San Bernardino-Ontario MSA, CA	H	34.45 FQ	40.41 MW	62.75 TQ	CABLS	1/08-3/08
	San Diego-Carlsbad-San Marcos MSA, CA	H	38.03 FQ	46.22 MW	54.19 TQ	CABLS	1/08-3/08
	San Francisco-San Mateo-Redwood PMSA, CA	H	37.84 FQ	46.41 MW	58.40 TQ	CABLS	1/08-3/08
	San Jose-Sunnyvale-Santa Clara MSA, CA	H	40.19 FQ	49.68 MW	59.98 TQ	CABLS	1/08-3/08
	Colorado	Y	68400 FQ	88270 MW	110660 TQ	USBLS	5/07
	Denver-Aurora MSA, CO	Y	63350 FQ	84520 MW	103370 TQ	USBLS	5/07
	Connecticut	H	28.22 AE	37.33 MW		CTBLS	1/08-3/08

AE Average entry wage	**AW** Average wage paid	**FQ** First quartile wage	**LO** Lowest wage paid	**MTC** Median total compensation	**TCC** Total cash compensation
AER Average entry range	**AWR** Average wage range	**H** Hourly	**LR** Low end range	**MW** Median wage paid	**TQ** Third quartile wage
AEX Average experienced wage	**AXR** Average experienced range	**HI** Highest wage paid	**M** Monthly	**MWR** Median wage range	**W** Weekly
ATC Average total compensation	**D** Daily	**HR** High end range	**MCC** Median cash compensation	**S** See annotated source	**Y** Yearly

Occupation/Type/Industry	Location	Per	Low	Mid	High	Source	Date
Aerospace Engineer	Bridgeport-Stamford-Norwalk MSA, CT	Y	70130 FQ	81070 MW	91900 TQ	USBLS	5/07
	Hartford-West Hartford-East Hartford MSA, CT	Y	65970 FQ	80360 MW	97170 TQ	USBLS	5/07
	Delaware	Y	57370 FQ	71980 MW	87700 TQ	USBLS	5/07
	District of Columbia	Y	88770 FQ	111360 MW	129110 TQ	USBLS	5/07
	Washington-Arlington-Alexandria MSA, DC-VA-MD-WV	Y	88760 FQ	108850 MW	129550 TQ	USBLS	5/07
	Florida	Y	61650 FQ	78000 MW	95020 TQ	USBLS	5/07
	Fort Lauderdale-Pompano Beach-Deerfield Beach PMSA, FL	Y	53990 FQ	64590 MW	76620 TQ	USBLS	5/07
	Jacksonville MSA, FL	Y	68070 FQ	78280 MW	90870 TQ	USBLS	5/07
	Miami-Fort Lauderdale-Miami Beach MSA, FL	Y	63530 FQ	77860 MW	95020 TQ	USBLS	5/07
	Orlando-Kissimmee MSA, FL	Y	57830 FQ	70940 MW	88480 TQ	USBLS	5/07
	West Palm Beach-Boca Raton-Boynton Beach PMSA, FL	Y	72830 FQ	86420 MW	102710 TQ	USBLS	5/07
	Georgia	Y	64380 FQ	80260 MW	96750 TQ	USBLS	5/07
	Illinois	Y	63890 FQ	77620 MW	104780 TQ	USBLS	5/07
	Chicago-Naperville-Joliet MSA, IL-IN-WI	Y	75640 FQ	95920 MW	112510 TQ	USBLS	5/07
	Indiana	Y	70880 FQ	84640 MW	95660 TQ	USBLS	5/07
	Indianapolis-Carmel MSA, IN	Y	68410 FQ	81930 MW	94340 TQ	USBLS	5/07
	Kansas	Y	61690 FQ	74900 MW	92260 TQ	USBLS	5/07
	Wichita MSA, KS	Y	61680 FQ	74910 MW	92240 TQ	USBLS	5/07
	Kentucky	Y	74499 FQ	93864 MW	111054 TQ	KYBLS	2008
	Louisiana	H	29.71 FQ	36.68 MW	48.66 TQ	LABLS	1/08-3/08
	New Orleans-Metairie-Kenner MSA, LA	Y	62320 FQ	77300 MW	101070 TQ	USBLS	5/07
	Maryland	Y		93950 MW		MDBLS	3/08
	Baltimore-Towson MSA, MD	Y	78510 FQ	88780 MW	98950 TQ	USBLS	5/07
	Massachusetts	Y	77930 FQ	98460 MW	118770 TQ	USBLS	5/07
	Boston-Cambridge-Quincy NECTA, MA	Y	85790 FQ	104170 MW	121110 TQ	USBLS	5/07
	Michigan	Y	61080 FQ	78900 MW	97510 TQ	USBLS	5/07
	Detroit-Warren-Livonia MSA, MI	Y	72220 FQ	88180 MW	102420 TQ	USBLS	5/07
	Warren-Troy-Farmington Hills PMSA, MI	Y	71420 FQ	87370 MW	102050 TQ	USBLS	5/07
	Minnesota	Y	61549 FQ	73340 MW	84890 TQ	MNBLS	10/08-12/08
	Minneapolis-Saint Paul MSA, MN-WI	Y	61549 FQ	73340 MW	84890 TQ	MNBLS	10/08-12/08
	Mississippi	Y	63890 FQ	82670 MW	96060 TQ	USBLS	5/07
	Gulfport-Biloxi MSA, MS	Y	65240 FQ	83730 MW	96250 TQ	USBLS	5/07
	Kansas City MSA, MO-KS	Y	96990 FQ	111050 MW	123320 TQ	USBLS	5/07
	Nebraska	Y	60070 FQ	70120 MW	83820 TQ	USBLS	5/07
	Nevada	H	38.94 FQ	50.98 MW	61.42 TQ	NVBLS	5/08
	Las Vegas-Paradise MSA, NV	H	43.54 FQ	54.56 MW		NVBLS	5/08
	New Hampshire	H	35.46 AE	51.18 MW	57.80 AEX	NHBLS	6/08
	Manchester MSA, NH	Y	87800 FQ	105650 MW	128800 TQ	USBLS	5/07
	New Jersey	Y	81300 FQ	98260 MW	115620 TQ	USBLS	5/07
	Newark-Union PMSA, NJ-PA	Y	81800 FQ	101040 MW	116010 TQ	USBLS	5/07
	New Mexico	Y	79530 FQ	97370 MW	125830 TQ	USBLS	5/07
	Albuquerque MSA, NM	Y	79490 FQ	97200 MW	132280 TQ	USBLS	5/07
	Buffalo-Niagara Falls MSA, NY	Y	61830 FQ	86670 MW	127760 TQ	USBLS	5/07
	Nassau-Suffolk PMSA, NY	Y	73160 FQ	92330 MW	113480 TQ	USBLS	5/07
	New York-Northern New Jersey-Long Island MSA, NY-NJ-PA	Y	77040 FQ	96100 MW	114760 TQ	USBLS	5/07
	North Carolina	Y	64470 FQ	74240 MW	88080 TQ	USBLS	5/07
	Ohio	Y	71950 FQ	86570 MW	106400 TQ	USBLS	5/07
	Cleveland-Elyria-Mentor MSA, OH	Y	87470 FQ	102640 MW	121580 TQ	USBLS	5/07
	Columbus MSA, OH	Y	70230 FQ	76250 MW	82470 TQ	USBLS	5/07
	Dayton MSA, OH	Y	80010 FQ	94360 MW	111670 TQ	USBLS	5/07
	Oklahoma	Y	66510 FQ	81940 MW	95250 TQ	USBLS	5/07
	Oklahoma City MSA, OK	Y	70500 FQ	84290 MW	95810 TQ	USBLS	5/07
	Tulsa MSA, OK	Y	61830 FQ	77790 MW	94960 TQ	USBLS	5/07

AE	Average entry wage	AW	Average wage paid	FQ	First quartile wage	LO	Lowest wage paid	MTC	Median total compensation	TCC	Total cash compensation
AER	Average entry range	AWR	Average wage range	H	Hourly	LR	Low end range	MW	Median wage paid	TQ	Third quartile wage
AEX	Average experienced wage	AXR	Average experienced range	HI	Highest wage paid	M	Monthly	MWR	Median wage range	W	Weekly
ATC	Average total compensation	D	Daily	HR	High end range	MCC	Median cash compensation	S	See annotated source	Y	Yearly

Occupation/Type/Industry	Location	Per	Low	Mid	High	Source	Date
Aerospace Engineer	Portland-Vancouver-Beaverton MSA, OR-WA	Y	61690 FQ	74420 MW	83950 TQ	USBLS	5/07
	Pennsylvania	Y	76170 FQ	89740 MW	105300 TQ	USBLS	5/07
	Philadelphia-Camden-Wilmington MSA, PA-NJ-DE-MD	Y	75490 FQ	89280 MW	104820 TQ	USBLS	5/07
	South Carolina	Y	75830 FQ	88450 MW	101750 TQ	USBLS	5/07
	Tennessee	Y	75920 FQ	91000 MW	103530 TQ	USBLS	5/07
	Texas	Y	75010 FQ	94290 MW	114830 TQ	USBLS	5/07
	Austin-Round Rock MSA, TX	Y	54290 FQ	88120 MW	115160 TQ	USBLS	5/07
	Dallas-Fort Worth-Arlington MSA, TX	Y	79000 FQ	96160 MW	115110 TQ	USBLS	5/07
	Houston-Sugar Land-Baytown MSA, TX	Y	75660 FQ	95840 MW	117250 TQ	USBLS	5/07
	San Antonio MSA, TX	Y	67170 FQ	79610 MW	100490 TQ	USBLS	5/07
	Utah	Y	67900 FQ	80380 MW	93760 TQ	USBLS	5/07
	Ogden-Clearfield MSA, UT	Y	69750 FQ	82730 MW	93950 TQ	USBLS	5/07
	Salt Lake City MSA, UT	Y	66480 FQ	78090 MW	95100 TQ	USBLS	5/07
	Virginia	Y	86990 FQ	104910 MW	125250 TQ	USBLS	5/07
	Virginia Beach-Norfolk-Newport News MSA, VA-NC	Y	85320 FQ	102040 MW	120250 TQ	USBLS	5/07
	Washington	H	36.01 FQ	43.34 MW	51.60 TQ	WABLS	3/08
	Seattle-Tacoma-Bellevue MSA, WA	Y	73680 FQ	88590 MW	105370 TQ	USBLS	5/07
	West Virginia	Y	64461 FQ	79316 MW	98487 TQ	WVBLS	7/08-9/08
	Wisconsin	Y	58040 FQ	71650 MW	91300 TQ	USBLS	5/07
	Milwaukee-Waukesha-West Allis MSA, WI	Y	57030 FQ	63380 MW	84680 TQ	USBLS	5/07
Aerospace Engineering and Operations Technician	Alabama	Y	31650 FQ	51920 MW	60660 TQ	USBLS	5/07
	California	H	25.11 FQ	28.70 MW	34.13 TQ	CABLS	1/08-3/08
	Colorado	Y	53200 FQ	58200 MW	63750 TQ	USBLS	5/07
	Connecticut	H	19.30 AE	23.31 MW		CTBLS	1/08-3/08
	Florida	Y	49820 FQ	55970 MW	63140 TQ	USBLS	5/07
	Hawaii	Y	62340 FQ	70900 MW	77790 TQ	USBLS	5/07
	Illinois	Y	30560 FQ	39510 MW	46890 TQ	USBLS	5/07
	Indiana	Y	37820 FQ	48270 MW	58600 TQ	USBLS	5/07
	Kansas	Y	44710 FQ	49700 MW	54710 TQ	USBLS	5/07
	Maryland	Y		52375 MW		MDBLS	3/08
	Massachusetts	Y	42100 FQ	54780 MW	63750 TQ	USBLS	5/07
	Michigan	Y	41080 FQ	50170 MW	63490 TQ	USBLS	5/07
	Missouri	Y	53370 FQ	60420 MW	65800 TQ	USBLS	5/07
	New Jersey	Y	41890 FQ	53070 MW	70230 TQ	USBLS	5/07
	New Mexico	Y	30620 FQ	46370 MW	62490 TQ	USBLS	5/07
	New York	Y	42010 FQ	48170 MW	57200 TQ	USBLS	5/07
	North Carolina	Y	46230 FQ	51280 MW	57620 TQ	USBLS	5/07
	Ohio	Y	37590 FQ	48650 MW	61960 TQ	USBLS	5/07
	Oklahoma	Y	39410 FQ	58600 MW	90760 TQ	USBLS	5/07
	Texas	Y	51570 FQ	65660 MW	76940 TQ	USBLS	5/07
	Utah	Y	41660 FQ	49550 MW	58360 TQ	USBLS	5/07
	Virginia	Y	48250 FQ	65970 MW	79440 TQ	USBLS	5/07
	Washington	H	23.11 FQ	27.97 MW	32.63 TQ	WABLS	3/08
	Wisconsin	Y	30590 FQ	47610 MW	60350 TQ	USBLS	5/07
Agency Director							
Barber Examiners Board	Nebraska	Y			52220 HI	NEST	2008
Corn Board	Nebraska	Y			108767 HI	NEST	2008
Ethanol Board	Nebraska	Y			103257 HI	NEST	2008
Wheat Board	Nebraska	Y			63036 HI	NEST	2008
Agent and Business Manager							
Artists, Performers, and Athletes	Alabama	Y	31230 FQ	35290 MW	43360 TQ	USBLS	5/07
Artists, Performers, and Athletes	Birmingham-Hoover MSA, AL	Y	30420 FQ	32750 MW	35560 TQ	USBLS	5/07
Artists, Performers, and Athletes	Arizona	Y	31750 FQ	37570 MW	52540 TQ	USBLS	5/07
Artists, Performers, and Athletes	Phoenix-Mesa-Scottsdale MSA, AZ	Y	33610 FQ	38180 MW	55440 TQ	USBLS	5/07
Artists, Performers, and Athletes	California	H	23.01 FQ	38.17 MW		CABLS	1/08-3/08
Artists, Performers, and Athletes	Los Angeles-Long Beach-Glendale PMSA, CA	H	22.45 FQ	37.63 MW		CABLS	1/08-3/08
Artists, Performers, and Athletes	San Diego-Carlsbad-San Marcos MSA, CA	H	30.93 FQ	46.02 MW	51.53 TQ	CABLS	1/08-3/08

AE	Average entry wage	AW	Average wage paid	FQ	First quartile wage	LO Lowest wage paid	MTC Median total compensation	TCC Total cash compensation
AER	Average entry range	AWR	Average wage range	H	Hourly	LR Low end range	MW Median wage paid	TQ Third quartile wage
AEX	Average experienced wage	AXR	Average experienced range	HI	Highest wage paid	M Monthly	MWR Median wage range	W Weekly
ATC	Average total compensation	D	Daily	HR	High end range	MCC Median cash compensation	S See annotated source	Y Yearly

23

Occupation/Type/Industry	Location	Per	Low	Mid	High	Source	Date
Agent and Business Manager							
Artists, Performers, and Athletes	San Francisco-San Mateo-Redwood PMSA, CA	H	16.69 FQ	34.88 MW	68.00 TQ	CABLS	1/08-3/08
Artists, Performers, and Athletes	Santa Ana-Anaheim-Irvine PMSA, CA	Y	46290 FQ	56580 MW	73500 TQ	USBLS	5/07
Artists, Performers, and Athletes	Colorado	Y	41310 FQ	53640 MW	69790 TQ	USBLS	5/07
Artists, Performers, and Athletes	Connecticut	H	14.58 AE	16.38 MW		CTBLS	1/08-3/08
Artists, Performers, and Athletes	Bridgeport-Stamford-Norwalk MSA, CT	Y	31210 FQ	42210 MW	50890 TQ	USBLS	5/07
Artists, Performers, and Athletes	Washington-Arlington-Alexandria MSA, DC-VA-MD-WV	Y	46000 FQ	75140 MW	96020 TQ	USBLS	5/07
Artists, Performers, and Athletes	Florida	Y	34360 FQ	51450 MW	75360 TQ	USBLS	5/07
Artists, Performers, and Athletes	Fort Lauderdale-Pompano Beach-Deerfield Beach PMSA, FL	Y	37590 FQ	46570 MW	85070 TQ	USBLS	5/07
Artists, Performers, and Athletes	Miami-Fort Lauderdale-Miami Beach MSA, FL	Y	42500 FQ	67940 MW	82170 TQ	USBLS	5/07
Artists, Performers, and Athletes	West Palm Beach-Boca Raton-Boynton Beach PMSA, FL	Y	69860 FQ	74460 MW	79050 TQ	USBLS	5/07
Artists, Performers, and Athletes	Georgia	Y	37770 FQ	45770 MW	84710 TQ	USBLS	5/07
Artists, Performers, and Athletes	Atlanta-Sandy Springs-Marietta MSA, GA	Y	37760 FQ	44810 MW	80660 TQ	USBLS	5/07
Artists, Performers, and Athletes	Hawaii	Y	45000 FQ	71890 MW	81410 TQ	USBLS	5/07
Artists, Performers, and Athletes	Honolulu MSA, HI	Y	46600 FQ	73990 MW	82550 TQ	USBLS	5/07
Artists, Performers, and Athletes	Illinois	Y	53990 FQ	70270 MW	80230 TQ	USBLS	5/07
Artists, Performers, and Athletes	Chicago-Naperville-Joliet MSA, IL-IN-WI	Y	55280 FQ	70890 MW	80220 TQ	USBLS	5/07
Artists, Performers, and Athletes	Indiana	Y	17330 FQ	24540 MW	79900 TQ	USBLS	5/07
Artists, Performers, and Athletes	Kentucky	Y	40204 FQ	50355 MW	125775 TQ	KYBLS	2008
Artists, Performers, and Athletes	Louisville-Jefferson County MSA, KY-IN	Y	31890 FQ	38320 MW	106780 TQ	USBLS	5/07
Artists, Performers, and Athletes	Louisiana	H	13.69 FQ	15.41 MW	17.32 TQ	LABLS	1/08-3/08
Artists, Performers, and Athletes	Maryland	Y		41800 MW		MDBLS	3/08
Artists, Performers, and Athletes	Massachusetts	Y	36930 FQ	54490 MW	72540 TQ	USBLS	5/07
Artists, Performers, and Athletes	Boston-Cambridge-Quincy NECTA, MA	Y	36040 FQ	53290 MW	68700 TQ	USBLS	5/07
Artists, Performers, and Athletes	Michigan	Y	21400 FQ	34700 MW	42930 TQ	USBLS	5/07
Artists, Performers, and Athletes	Warren-Troy-Farmington Hills PMSA, MI	Y	31970 FQ	36090 MW	39960 TQ	USBLS	5/07
Artists, Performers, and Athletes	Minnesota	Y	38828 FQ	57606 MW	107309 TQ	MNBLS	10/08-12/08
Artists, Performers, and Athletes	Minneapolis-Saint Paul MSA, MN-WI	Y	38818 FQ	53613 MW	110542 TQ	MNBLS	10/08-12/08
Artists, Performers, and Athletes	Missouri	Y	41400 FQ	47190 MW	52850 TQ	USBLS	5/07
Artists, Performers, and Athletes	Kansas City MSA, MO-KS	Y	25610 FQ	29600 MW	61710 TQ	USBLS	5/07
Artists, Performers, and Athletes	St. Louis MSA, MO-IL	Y	44270 FQ	48390 MW	53460 TQ	USBLS	5/07
Artists, Performers, and Athletes	Nevada	H	29.89 FQ	37.13 MW	47.80 TQ	NVBLS	5/08
Artists, Performers, and Athletes	Las Vegas-Paradise MSA, NV	H	33.78 FQ	37.99 MW	53.11 TQ	NVBLS	5/08
Artists, Performers, and Athletes	New Jersey	Y	30300 FQ	43440 MW	74910 TQ	USBLS	5/07
Artists, Performers, and Athletes	Newark-Union PMSA, NJ-PA	Y	37590 FQ	48700 MW	73910 TQ	USBLS	5/07
Artists, Performers, and Athletes	New York	Y	62360 FQ	79460 MW	119020 TQ	USBLS	5/07
Artists, Performers, and Athletes	New York-Northern New Jersey-Long Island MSA, NY-NJ-PA	Y	54800 FQ	78270 MW	117000 TQ	USBLS	5/07
Artists, Performers, and Athletes	North Carolina	Y	33320 FQ	42930 MW	62230 TQ	USBLS	5/07
Artists, Performers, and Athletes	Charlotte-Gastonia-Concord MSA, NC-SC	Y	32420 FQ	39010 MW	61660 TQ	USBLS	5/07
Artists, Performers, and Athletes	Ohio	Y	38030 FQ	76230 MW	116790 TQ	USBLS	5/07
Artists, Performers, and Athletes	Cincinnati-Middletown MSA, OH-KY-IN	Y	47250 FQ	92460 MW	137280 TQ	USBLS	5/07
Artists, Performers, and Athletes	Cleveland-Elyria-Mentor MSA, OH	Y	33850 FQ	59560 MW	108280 TQ	USBLS	5/07
Artists, Performers, and Athletes	Portland-Vancouver-Beaverton MSA, OR-WA	Y	26730 FQ	30300 MW	55540 TQ	USBLS	5/07
Artists, Performers, and Athletes	Pennsylvania	Y	28130 FQ	34060 MW	75110 TQ	USBLS	5/07
Artists, Performers, and Athletes	Philadelphia-Camden-Wilmington MSA, PA-NJ-DE-MD	Y	28760 FQ	32790 MW	67630 TQ	USBLS	5/07
Artists, Performers, and Athletes	Pittsburgh MSA, PA	Y	34050 FQ	75280 MW	94820 TQ	USBLS	5/07
Artists, Performers, and Athletes	South Carolina	Y	32450 FQ	57780 MW	80490 TQ	USBLS	5/07
Artists, Performers, and Athletes	Tennessee	Y	34080 FQ	67030 MW	128430 TQ	USBLS	5/07

AE	Average entry wage	AW	Average wage paid	FQ	First quartile wage	LO	Lowest wage paid	MTC	Median total compensation	TCC	Total cash compensation
AER	Average entry range	AWR	Average wage range	H	Hourly	LR	Low end range	MW	Median wage paid	TQ	Third quartile wage
AEX	Average experienced wage	AXR	Average experienced range	HI	Highest wage paid	M	Monthly	MWR	Median wage range	W	Weekly
ATC	Average total compensation	D	Daily	HR	High end range	MCC	Median cash compensation	S	See annotated source	Y	Yearly

24

Occupation/Type/Industry	Location	Per	Low	Mid	High	Source	Date
Agent and Business Manager							
Artists, Performers, and Athletes	Nashville-Davidson-Murfreesboro MSA, TN	Y	34800 FQ	77990 MW	137780 TQ	USBLS	5/07
Artists, Performers, and Athletes	Texas	Y	34270 FQ	44940 MW	60650 TQ	USBLS	5/07
Artists, Performers, and Athletes	Houston-Sugar Land-Baytown MSA, TX	Y	31130 FQ	48450 MW	99800 TQ	USBLS	5/07
Artists, Performers, and Athletes	Virginia	Y	48930 FQ	76340 MW	99260 TQ	USBLS	5/07
Artists, Performers, and Athletes	Wisconsin	Y	27320 FQ	38930 MW	55190 TQ	USBLS	5/07
Agricultural and Food Science Technician							
	Alabama	Y	29160 FQ	34450 MW	43060 TQ	USBLS	5/07
	Arkansas	Y	21870 FQ	28530 MW	37540 TQ	USBLS	5/07
	California	H	14.24 FQ	17.89 MW	21.93 TQ	CABLS	1/08-3/08
	Los Angeles-Long Beach-Glendale PMSA, CA	H	15.55 FQ	18.45 MW	21.32 TQ	CABLS	1/08-3/08
	Oakland-Fremont-Hayward MSA, CA	H	17.29 FQ	21.75 MW	26.34 TQ	CABLS	1/08-3/08
	Riverside-San Bernardino-Ontario MSA, CA	H	17.25 FQ	20.04 MW	24.97 TQ	CABLS	1/08-3/08
	Sacramento-Arden Arcade-Roseville MSA, CA	H	13.04 FQ	14.44 MW	15.97 TQ	CABLS	1/08-3/08
	San Diego-Carlsbad-San Marcos MSA, CA	L	11.60 FQ	13.95 MW	16.83 TQ	CABLS	1/08-3/08
	San Jose-Sunnyvale-Santa Clara MSA, CA	H	12.16 FQ	15.73 MW	18.78 TQ	CABLS	1/08-3/08
	Santa Ana-Anaheim-Irvine PMSA, CA	Y	27950 FQ	35310 MW	40310 TQ	USBLS	5/07
	Stockton MSA, CA	H	11.31 FQ	12.97 MW	17.41 TQ	CABLS	1/08-3/08
	Colorado	Y	28460 FQ	32290 MW	41080 TQ	USBLS	5/07
	Connecticut	H	16.62 AE	22.07 MW		CTBLS	1/08-3/08
	Hartford-West Hartford-East Hartford MSA, CT	Y	33510 FQ	41110 MW	48040 TQ	USBLS	5/07
	District of Columbia	Y	41480 FQ	49130 MW	59890 TQ	USBLS	5/07
	Washington-Arlington-Alexandria MSA, DC-VA-MD-WV	Y	32370 FQ	45010 MW	53750 TQ	USBLS	5/07
	Florida	Y	27260 FQ	32360 MW	37480 TQ	USBLS	5/07
	Miami-Fort Lauderdale-Miami Beach MSA, FL	Y	31390 FQ	36280 MW	46800 TQ	USBLS	5/07
	Georgia	Y	29330 FQ	35090 MW	41760 TQ	USBLS	5/07
	Atlanta-Sandy Springs-Marietta MSA, GA	Y	29300 FQ	38070 MW	45870 TQ	USBLS	5/07
	Hawaii	Y	33260 FQ	38320 MW	44990 TQ	USBLS	5/07
	Honolulu MSA, HI	Y	31870 FQ	36520 MW	41270 TQ	USBLS	5/07
	Idaho	Y	27760 FQ	38110 MW	46160 TQ	USBLS	5/07
	Boise City-Nampa MSA, ID	Y	40330 FQ	44760 MW	53030 TQ	USBLS	5/07
	Illinois	Y	26880 FQ	31810 MW	41780 TQ	USBLS	5/07
	Champaign-Urbana MSA, IL	Y	28510 FQ	31840 MW	38820 TQ	USBLS	5/07
	Chicago-Naperville-Joliet MSA, IL-IN-WI	Y	26820 FQ	31540 MW	43110 TQ	USBLS	5/07
	Indianapolis-Carmel MSA, IN	Y	41590 FQ	49960 MW	62780 TQ	USBLS	5/07
	Iowa	Y	26170 FQ	32590 MW	40280 TQ	USBLS	5/07
	Des Moines-West Des Moines MSA, IA	Y	21670 FQ	26240 MW	34730 TQ	USBLS	5/07
	Sioux City MSA, IA-NE-SD	Y	27880 FQ	31880 MW	39840 TQ	USBLS	5/07
	Kansas	Y	22130 FQ	32640 MW	49730 TQ	USBLS	5/07
	Wichita MSA, KS	Y	25050 FQ	29050 MW	33410 TQ	USBLS	5/07
	Kentucky	Y	26925 FQ	31392 MW	36890 TQ	KYBLS	2008
	Louisiana	H	12.79 FQ	17.11 MW	21.31 TQ	LABLS	1/08-3/08
	Maryland	Y		40325 MW		MDBLS	3/08
	Baltimore-Towson MSA, MD	Y	35850 FQ	42160 MW	50260 TQ	USBLS	5/07
	Massachusetts	Y	29750 FQ	37440 MW	51050 TQ	USBLS	5/07
	Boston-Cambridge-Quincy NECTA, MA	Y	29870 FQ	42090 MW	63290 TQ	USBLS	5/07
	Michigan	Y	24230 FQ	34080 MW	43380 TQ	USBLS	5/07
	Minnesota	Y	31303 FQ	37549 MW	45238 TQ	MNBLS	10/08-12/08
	Minneapolis-Saint Paul MSA, MN-WI	Y	34619 FQ	40206 MW	48398 TQ	MNBLS	10/08-12/08
	Mississippi	Y	18210 FQ	33640 MW	51570 TQ	USBLS	5/07
	Missouri	Y	28010 FQ	33330 MW	40660 TQ	USBLS	5/07
	Kansas City MSA, MO-KS	Y	31860 FQ	41330 MW	53350 TQ	USBLS	5/07
	St. Louis MSA, MO-IL	Y	33130 FQ	38530 MW	44990 TQ	USBLS	5/07

AE	Average entry wage	AW	Average wage paid	FQ	First quartile wage	LO	Lowest wage paid	MTC	Median total compensation	TCC	Total cash compensation
AER	Average entry range	AWR	Average wage range	H	Hourly	LR	Low end range	MW	Median wage paid	TQ	Third quartile wage
AEX	Average experienced wage	AXR	Average experienced range	HI	Highest wage paid	M	Monthly	MWR	Median wage range	W	Weekly
ATC	Average total compensation	D	Daily	HR	High end range	MCC	Median cash compensation	S	See annotated source	Y	Yearly

Occupation/Type/Industry	Location	Per	Low	Mid	High	Source	Date
Agricultural and Food Science Technician							
	Montana	Y	23590 FQ	29690 MW	36640 TQ	USBLS	5/07
	Nebraska	Y	27730 FQ	33960 MW	39770 TQ	USBLS	5/07
	Omaha-Council Bluffs MSA, NE-IA	Y	25140 FQ	29060 MW	33800 TQ	USBLS	5/07
	New Hampshire	H	14.29 AE	18.40 MW	21.77 AEX	NHBLS	6/08
	New Jersey	Y	35490 FQ	44670 MW	54310 TQ	USBLS	5/07
	Newark-Union PMSA, NJ-PA	Y	40610 FQ	47810 MW	55100 TQ	USBLS	5/07
	New Mexico	Y	21470 FQ	24390 MW	27960 TQ	USBLS	5/07
	New York	Y	28410 FQ	34480 MW	41530 TQ	USBLS	5/07
	New York-Northern New Jersey-Long Island MSA, NY-NJ-PA	Y	26230 FQ	33680 MW	43740 TQ	USBLS	5/07
	North Carolina	Y	27980 FQ	33680 MW	39770 TQ	USBLS	5/07
	Durham MSA, NC	Y	26240 FQ	32070 MW	37360 TQ	USBLS	5/07
	North Dakota	Y	26610 FQ	32330 MW	39610 TQ	USBLS	5/07
	Fargo MSA, ND-MN	Y	28260 FQ	33500 MW	40210 TQ	USBLS	5/07
	Ohio	Y	27740 FQ	34690 MW	46350 TQ	USBLS	5/07
	Cincinnati-Middletown MSA, OH-KY-IN	Y	29050 FQ	32990 MW	38600 TQ	USBLS	5/07
	Columbus MSA, OH	Y	27820 FQ	35210 MW	49320 TQ	USBLS	5/07
	Dayton MSA, OH	Y	31600 FQ	50310 MW	75840 TQ	USBLS	5/07
	Oklahoma	Y	28430 FQ	40170 MW	49650 TQ	USBLS	5/07
	Oregon	H	12.54 FQ	14.70 MW	18.43 TQ	ORBLS	5/08
	Portland-Vancouver-Beaverton MSA, OR-WA	Y	28130 FQ	35180 MW	40550 TQ	USBLS	5/07
	Pennsylvania	Y	22900 FQ	29900 MW	40740 TQ	USBLS	5/07
	Philadelphia-Camden-Wilmington MSA, PA-NJ-DE-MD	Y	28710 FQ	36780 MW	46480 TQ	USBLS	5/07
	South Carolina	Y	25540 FQ	30940 MW	44320 TQ	USBLS	5/07
	South Dakota	Y	24173 FQ	28059 MW	32400 TQ	SDBLS	7/08-9/08
	Tennessee	Y	31120 FQ	39160 MW	47990 TQ	USBLS	5/07
	Nashville-Davidson-Murfreesboro MSA, TN	Y	35930 FQ	43640 MW	49320 TQ	USBLS	5/07
	Texas	Y	23860 FQ	29140 MW	34850 TQ	USBLS	5/07
	Austin-Round Rock MSA, TX	Y	21180 FQ	27370 MW	31320 TQ	USBLS	5/07
	Corpus Christi MSA, TX	Y	26540 FQ	32530 MW	41370 TQ	USBLS	5/07
	Dallas-Fort Worth-Arlington MSA, TX	Y	27050 FQ	31650 MW	35670 TQ	USBLS	5/07
	El Paso MSA, TX	Y	25160 FQ	29660 MW	35130 TQ	USBLS	5/07
	Houston-Sugar Land-Baytown MSA, TX	Y	25020 FQ	31660 MW	36180 TQ	USBLS	5/07
	San Antonio MSA, TX	Y	21080 FQ	22840 MW	28910 TQ	USBLS	5/07
	Utah	Y	28520 FQ	34720 MW	39160 TQ	USBLS	5/07
	Salt Lake City MSA, UT	Y	23650 FQ	30050 MW	36240 TQ	USBLS	5/07
	Virginia	Y	23390 FQ	27700 MW	33080 TQ	USBLS	5/07
	Richmond MSA, VA	Y	25870 FQ	29200 MW	36240 TQ	USBLS	5/07
	Washington	H	13.03 FQ	15.60 MW	19.70 TQ	WABLS	3/08
	Seattle-Tacoma-Bellevue MSA, WA	Y	28510 FQ	36180 MW	43910 TQ	USBLS	5/07
	Wisconsin	Y	26840 FQ	32920 MW	38150 TQ	USBLS	5/07
	Green Bay MSA, WI	Y	27290 FQ	31080 MW	37240 TQ	USBLS	5/07
	Milwaukee-Waukesha-West Allis MSA, WI	Y	32470 FQ	36450 MW	41800 TQ	USBLS	5/07
	Wyoming	Y	32296 FQ	38694 MW	45869 TQ	WYBLS	9/08
	Puerto Rico	Y	20360 FQ	22540 MW	24690 TQ	USBLS	5/07
	San Juan-Caguas-Guaynabo MSA, PR	Y	17830 FQ	22180 MW	25220 TQ	USBLS	5/07
Agricultural Engineer	Arizona	Y	60190 FQ	76240 MW	92220 TQ	USBLS	5/07
	California	H	29.44 FQ	34.96 MW	41.46 TQ	CABLS	1/08-3/08
	Colorado	Y	59620 FQ	76570 MW	93640 TQ	USBLS	5/07
	Florida	Y	59430 FQ	71130 MW	85370 TQ	USBLS	5/07
	Georgia	Y	61630 FQ	72870 MW	82320 TQ	USBLS	5/07
	Idaho	Y	43730 FQ	52120 MW	72400 TQ	USBLS	5/07
	Illinois	Y	62590 FQ	73480 MW	87350 TQ	USBLS	5/07
	Indiana	Y	51870 FQ	59300 MW	73680 TQ	USBLS	5/07
	Iowa	Y	55150 FQ	64100 MW	83550 TQ	USBLS	5/07
	Kansas	Y	51810 FQ	68500 MW	87360 TQ	USBLS	5/07
	Kentucky	Y	54490 FQ	65457 MW	96595 TQ	KYBLS	2008
	Louisiana	H	30.67 FQ	35.15 MW	40.43 TQ	LABLS	1/08-3/08

AE Average entry wage	**AW** Average wage paid	**FQ** First quartile wage	**LO** Lowest wage paid	**MTC** Median total compensation	**TCC** Total cash compensation
AER Average entry range	**AWR** Average wage range	**H** Hourly	**LR** Low end range	**MW** Median wage paid	**TQ** Third quartile wage
AEX Average experienced wage	**AXR** Average experienced range	**HI** Highest wage paid	**M** Monthly	**MWR** Median wage range	**W** Weekly
ATC Average total compensation	**D** Daily	**HR** High end range	**MCC** Median cash compensation	**S** See annotated source	**Y** Yearly

Occupation/Type/Industry	Location	Per	Low	Mid	High	Source	Date
Agricultural Engineer	Maryland	Y		87150 MW		MDBLS	3/08
	Minnesota	Y	49308 FQ	60147 MW	87412 TQ	MNBLS	10/08-12/08
	Mississippi	Y	49850 FQ	66880 MW	85380 TQ	USBLS	5/07
	Missouri	Y	58130 FQ	67510 MW	79320 TQ	USBLS	5/07
	Nebraska	Y	48360 FQ	60530 MW	73280 TQ	USBLS	5/07
	New Jersey	Y	57460 FQ	65030 MW	73510 TQ	USBLS	5/07
	North Carolina	Y	57370 FQ	75760 MW	98430 TQ	USBLS	5/07
	North Dakota	Y	62890 FQ	69660 MW	75570 TQ	USBLS	5/07
	Ohio	Y	53630 FQ	71660 MW	83500 TQ	USBLS	5/07
	Oregon	H	23.77 FQ	38.72 MW	47.73 TQ	ORBLS	5/08
	Pennsylvania	Y	52420 FQ	56510 MW	60680 TQ	USBLS	5/07
	South Dakota	Y	39672 FQ	49290 MW	63102 TQ	SDBLS	7/08-9/08
	Tennessee	Y	55740 FQ	64820 MW	79750 TQ	USBLS	5/07
	Texas	Y	59500 FQ	75470 MW	105240 TQ	USBLS	5/07
	Vermont	Y	49580 FQ	57520 MW	71630 TQ	USBLS	5/07
	Washington	H	23.40 FQ	31.93 MW	37.18 TQ	WABLS	3/08
	Wisconsin	Y	57060 FQ	66230 MW	79030 TQ	USBLS	5/07
	Puerto Rico	Y	45840 FQ	55900 MW	72690 TQ	USBLS	5/07
Agricultural Equipment Operator	Alabama	Y	14460 FQ	16710 MW	18940 TQ	USBLS	5/07
	Arizona	Y	15470 FQ	17430 MW	19290 TQ	USBLS	5/07
	Arkansas	Y	15370 FQ	18030 MW	22490 TQ	USBLS	5/07
	California	H	8.88 FQ	10.20 MW	12.47 TQ	CABLS	1/08-3/08
	Colorado	Y	28210 FQ	32240 MW	37760 TQ	USBLS	5/07
	Florida	Y	16680 FQ	20900 MW	26040 TQ	USBLS	5/07
	Georgia	Y	13490 FQ	16630 MW	27810 TQ	USBLS	5/07
	Idaho	Y	17870 FQ	21230 MW	27830 TQ	USBLS	5/07
	Illinois	Y	22440 FQ	27580 MW	34740 TQ	USBLS	5/07
	Indiana	Y	20700 FQ	24110 MW	29430 TQ	USBLS	5/07
	Iowa	Y	21610 FQ	25860 MW	29690 TQ	USBLS	5/07
	Kansas	Y	20380 FQ	24490 MW	31610 TQ	USBLS	5/07
	Kentucky	Y	22599 FQ	26777 MW	30089 TQ	KYBLS	2008
	Louisiana	H	8.10 FQ	8.77 MW	9.81 TQ	LABLS	1/08-3/08
	Maryland	Y		29025 MW		MDBLS	3/08
	Michigan	Y	17270 FQ	18650 MW	20020 TQ	USBLS	5/07
	Minnesota	Y	25767 FQ	29308 MW	32817 TQ	MNBLS	10/08-12/08
	Mississippi	Y	16790 FQ	19060 MW	22820 TQ	USBLS	5/07
	Missouri	Y	16320 FQ	19050 MW	23670 TQ	USBLS	5/07
	Montana	Y	22590 FQ	24900 MW	32720 TQ	USBLS	5/07
	Nebraska	Y	20480 FQ	23400 MW	27370 TQ	USBLS	5/07
	New Mexico	Y	18090 FQ	20090 MW	24600 TQ	USBLS	5/07
	New York	Y	23110 FQ	25720 MW	29020 TQ	USBLS	5/07
	North Carolina	Y	15020 FQ	18770 MW	25230 TQ	USBLS	5/07
	North Dakota	Y	21360 FQ	27460 MW	32530 TQ	USBLS	5/07
	Ohio	Y	24020 FQ	28440 MW	33690 TQ	USBLS	5/07
	Oklahoma	Y	18500 FQ	21250 MW	24620 TQ	USBLS	5/07
	Oregon	H	9.78 FQ	11.78 MW	13.98 TQ	ORBLS	5/08
	Pennsylvania	Y	32570 FQ	36560 MW	44770 TQ	USBLS	5/07
	South Carolina	Y	14480 FQ	20110 MW	28890 TQ	USBLS	5/07
	South Dakota	Y	22428 FQ	23815 MW	25215 TQ	SDBLS	7/08-9/08
	Tennessee	Y	19210 FQ	22640 MW	26810 TQ	USBLS	5/07
	Texas	Y	14090 FQ	17020 MW	20840 TQ	USBLS	5/07
	Utah	Y	21270 FQ	23540 MW	29860 TQ	USBLS	5/07
	Vermont	Y	19380 FQ	24530 MW	29520 TQ	USBLS	5/07
	Virginia	Y	15810 FQ	22580 MW	29290 TQ	USBLS	5/07
	Washington	H	9.15 FQ	11.06 MW	15.63 TQ	WABLS	3/08
	Wisconsin	Y	25250 FQ	29490 MW	34490 TQ	USBLS	5/07
	Wyoming	Y	14385 FQ	18080 MW	22466 TQ	WYBLS	9/08
	Puerto Rico	Y	12180 FQ	13540 MW	14910 TQ	USBLS	5/07
Agricultural Inspector	Alabama	Y	30210 FQ	39960 MW	46350 TQ	USBLS	5/07
	Birmingham-Hoover MSA, AL	Y	30290 FQ	36060 MW	43530 TQ	USBLS	5/07
	Alaska	Y	15840 FQ	20510 MW	24790 TQ	USBLS	5/07
	Arizona	Y	28700 FQ	34140 MW	39540 TQ	USBLS	5/07
	Phoenix-Mesa-Scottsdale MSA, AZ	Y	29760 FQ	36130 MW	45210 TQ	USBLS	5/07
	Arkansas	Y	30820 FQ	38710 MW	45480 TQ	USBLS	5/07
	Little Rock-North Little Rock MSA, AR	Y	27080 FQ	30680 MW	37460 TQ	USBLS	5/07
	California	H	14.94 FQ	20.73 MW	26.03 TQ	CABLS	1/08-3/08
	Los Angeles-Long Beach-Glendale PMSA, CA	H	15.70 FQ	23.78 MW	28.85 TQ	CABLS	1/08-3/08

AE Average entry wage	**AW** Average wage paid	**FQ** First quartile wage	**LO** Lowest wage paid	**MTC** Median total compensation	**TCC** Total cash compensation
AER Average entry range	**AWR** Average wage range	**H** Hourly	**LR** Low end range	**MW** Median wage paid	**TQ** Third quartile wage
AEX Average experienced wage	**AXR** Average experienced range	**HI** Highest wage paid	**M** Monthly	**MWR** Median wage range	**W** Weekly
ATC Average total compensation	**D** Daily	**HR** High end range	**MCC** Median cash compensation	**S** See annotated source	**Y** Yearly

27

Agricultural Inspector

Occupation/Type/Industry	Location	Per	Low	Mid	High	Source	Date
Agricultural Inspector	Sacramento-Arden Arcade-Roseville MSA, CA	H	10.00 FQ	21.95 MW	27.44 TQ	CABLS	1/08-3/08
	San Diego-Carlsbad-San Marcos MSA, CA	H	25.15 FQ	29.04 MW	32.37 TQ	CABLS	1/08-3/08
	San Jose-Sunnyvale-Santa Clara MSA, CA	H	11.95 FQ	14.60 MW	17.76 TQ	CABLS	1/08-3/08
	Stockton MSA, CA	H	10.13 FQ	11.99 MW	18.57 TQ	CABLS	1/08-3/08
	Colorado	Y	31840 FQ	41140 MW	48140 TQ	USBLS	5/07
	Denver-Aurora MSA, CO	Y	24320 FQ	34970 MW	48770 TQ	USBLS	5/07
	Connecticut	H	23.53 AE	30.56 MW		CTBLS	1/08-3/08
	Hartford-West Hartford-East Hartford MSA, CT	Y	58380 FQ	65170 MW	74150 TQ	USBLS	5/07
	Delaware	Y	36150 FQ	42680 MW	47130 TQ	USBLS	5/07
	Florida	Y	29960 FQ	36700 MW	48210 TQ	USBLS	5/07
	Miami-Fort Lauderdale-Miami Beach MSA, FL	Y	29120 FQ	33360 MW	43970 TQ	USBLS	5/07
	Orlando-Kissimmee MSA, FL	Y	37450 FQ	53730 MW	59100 TQ	USBLS	5/07
	Tampa-St. Petersburg-Clearwater MSA, FL	Y	29060 FQ	33080 MW	42940 TQ	USBLS	5/07
	Georgia	Y	27810 FQ	35490 MW	44360 TQ	USBLS	5/07
	Idaho	Y	31030 FQ	36610 MW	42390 TQ	USBLS	5/07
	Boise City-Nampa MSA, ID	Y	31500 FQ	37600 MW	44520 TQ	USBLS	5/07
	Illinois	Y	32890 FQ	43880 MW	51430 TQ	USBLS	5/07
	Chicago-Naperville-Joliet MSA, IL-IN-WI	Y	30560 FQ	43930 MW	53850 TQ	USBLS	5/07
	Indiana	Y	30020 FQ	39000 MW	45530 TQ	USBLS	5/07
	Indianapolis-Carmel MSA, IN	Y	40910 FQ	43680 MW	46440 TQ	USBLS	5/07
	Iowa	Y	30770 FQ	39990 MW	48230 TQ	USBLS	5/07
	Davenport-Moline-Rock Island MSA, IA-IL	Y	33650 FQ	41560 MW	47420 TQ	USBLS	5/07
	Des Moines-West Des Moines MSA, IA	Y	34280 FQ	42620 MW	48970 TQ	USBLS	5/07
	Kansas	Y	34010 FQ	38660 MW	45690 TQ	USBLS	5/07
	Kentucky	Y	32530 FQ	38448 MW	46262 TQ	KYBLS	2008
	Louisville-Jefferson County MSA, KY-IN	Y	27050 FQ	31940 MW	40230 TQ	USBLS	5/07
	New Orleans-Metairie-Kenner MSA, LA	Y	48710 FQ	56060 MW	62150 TQ	USBLS	5/07
	Maine	Y	32930 FQ	36460 MW	40070 TQ	USBLS	5/07
	Maryland	Y		44025 MW		MDBLS	3/08
	Baltimore-Towson MSA, MD	Y	35520 FQ	42500 MW	48130 TQ	USBLS	5/07
	Michigan	Y	26090 FQ	51470 MW	60230 TQ	USBLS	5/07
	Minnesota	Y	35673 FQ	44020 MW	52841 TQ	MNBLS	10/08-12/08
	Duluth-Superior MSA, MN-WI	Y	39025 FQ	47466 MW	57436 TQ	MNBLS	10/08-12/08
	Minneapolis-Saint Paul MSA, MN-WI	Y	37265 FQ	45917 MW	56350 TQ	MNBLS	10/08-12/08
	Mississippi	Y	30890 FQ	39980 MW	45870 TQ	USBLS	5/07
	Missouri	Y	31380 FQ	37770 MW	46260 TQ	USBLS	5/07
	Kansas City MSA, MO-KS	Y	30490 FQ	45000 MW	59470 TQ	USBLS	5/07
	St. Louis MSA, MO-IL	Y	25990 FQ	34620 MW	46270 TQ	USBLS	5/07
	Montana	Y	21480 FQ	24860 MW	30640 TQ	USBLS	5/07
	Nebraska	Y	34290 FQ	41360 MW	47710 TQ	USBLS	5/07
	Nevada	H	11.07 FQ	12.15 MW	14.00 TQ	NVBLS	5/08
	New Jersey	Y	39650 FQ	45320 MW	53050 TQ	USBLS	5/07
	Camden PMSA, NJ	Y	39720 FQ	45400 MW	51690 TQ	USBLS	5/07
	Newark-Union PMSA, NJ-PA	Y	40130 FQ	49180 MW	58870 TQ	USBLS	5/07
	New York	Y	39880 FQ	47000 MW	55500 TQ	USBLS	5/07
	Nassau-Suffolk PMSA, NY	Y	37580 FQ	44560 MW	53710 TQ	USBLS	5/07
	New York-Northern New Jersey-Long Island MSA, NY-NJ-PA	Y	41060 FQ	47600 MW	56110 TQ	USBLS	5/07
	North Carolina	Y	31570 FQ	38270 MW	44790 TQ	USBLS	5/07
	Charlotte-Gastonia-Concord MSA, NC-SC	Y	33200 FQ	40210 MW	45800 TQ	USBLS	5/07
	North Dakota	Y	34690 FQ	40030 MW	57040 TQ	USBLS	5/07
	Ohio	Y	31340 FQ	42330 MW	48840 TQ	USBLS	5/07
	Oregon	H	12.56 FQ	15.61 MW	23.91 TQ	ORBLS	5/08
	Portland-Vancouver-Beaverton MSA, OR-WA	Y	26450 FQ	39460 MW	51550 TQ	USBLS	5/07
	Philadelphia-Camden-Wilmington MSA, PA-NJ-DE-MD	Y	39610 FQ	46890 MW	55410 TQ	USBLS	5/07

AE	Average entry wage	AW	Average wage paid	FQ	First quartile wage	LO	Lowest wage paid	MTC	Median total compensation	TCC	Total cash compensation
AER	Average entry range	AWR	Average wage range	H	Hourly	LR	Low end range	MW	Median wage paid	TQ	Third quartile wage
AEX	Average experienced wage	AXR	Average experienced range	HI	Highest wage paid	M	Monthly	MWR	Median wage range	W	Weekly
ATC	Average total compensation	D	Daily	HR	High end range	MCC	Median cash compensation	S	See annotated source	Y	Yearly

28

Occupation/Type/Industry	Location	Per	Low	Mid	High	Source	Date
Agricultural Inspector	South Carolina	Y	28640 FQ	35750 MW	43390 TQ	USBLS	5/07
	South Dakota	Y	30646 FQ	38217 MW	45218 TQ	SDBLS	7/08-9/08
	Sioux Falls MSA, SD	Y	35476 FQ	39599 MW	45935 TQ	SDBLS	7/08-9/08
	Tennessee	Y	25960 FQ	34580 MW	42270 TQ	USBLS	5/07
	Memphis MSA, TN-MS-AR	Y	18860 FQ	26990 MW	36640 TQ	USBLS	5/07
	Nashville-Davidson-Murfreesboro MSA, TN	Y	35370 FQ	42350 MW	48690 TQ	USBLS	5/07
	Texas	Y	35440 FQ	44040 MW	49380 TQ	USBLS	5/07
	Dallas-Fort Worth-Arlington MSA, TX	Y	33840 FQ	42910 MW	49790 TQ	USBLS	5/07
	Houston-Sugar Land-Baytown MSA, TX	Y	44820 FQ	48140 MW	51410 TQ	USBLS	5/07
	San Antonio MSA, TX	Y	36730 FQ	43130 MW	48140 TQ	USBLS	5/07
	Utah	Y	29420 FQ	35560 MW	43280 TQ	USBLS	5/07
	Virginia	Y	35050 FQ	43880 MW	50010 TQ	USBLS	5/07
	Richmond MSA, VA	Y	35540 FQ	44580 MW	54070 TQ	USBLS	5/07
	Virginia Beach-Norfolk-Newport News MSA, VA-NC	Y	24840 FQ	42730 MW	48340 TQ	USBLS	5/07
	Washington	H	14.46 FQ	18.00 MW	22.15 TQ	WABLS	3/08
	Seattle-Tacoma-Bellevue MSA, WA	Y	27070 FQ	33580 MW	44290 TQ	USBLS	5/07
	Wisconsin	Y	35270 FQ	41320 MW	47860 TQ	USBLS	5/07
	Wyoming	Y	32582 FQ	43422 MW	49769 TQ	WYBLS	9/08
	Puerto Rico	Y	17940 FQ	21390 MW	24510 TQ	USBLS	5/07
	San Juan-Caguas-Guaynabo MSA, PR	Y	17590 FQ	20800 MW	23630 TQ	USBLS	5/07
Agricultural Manager	United States	Y		53720 MW		MSN01	2009
Agricultural Products Inspector State Government	Rhode Island	Y	45773 LO		49775 HI	AFT02	3/1/08
Agricultural Sciences Teacher Postsecondary	Arizona	Y	57060 FQ	70030 MW	93350 TQ	USBLS	5/07
Postsecondary	California	Y		85391 AW		CABLS	1/08-3/08
Postsecondary	Colorado	Y	43030 FQ	62370 MW	83780 TQ	USBLS	5/07
Postsecondary	Florida	Y	64280 FQ	79150 MW	96610 TQ	USBLS	5/07
Postsecondary	Illinois	Y	47040 FQ	67220 MW	91120 TQ	USBLS	5/07
Postsecondary	Iowa	Y	64090 FQ	88400 MW	105960 TQ	USBLS	5/07
Postsecondary	Kansas	Y	61350 FQ	82290 MW	98840 TQ	USBLS	5/07
Postsecondary	Kentucky	Y	64519 FQ	80067 MW	98296 TQ	KYBLS	2008
Postsecondary	Louisiana	Y		53683 AW		LABLS	1/08-3/08
Postsecondary	Maryland	Y		79875 MW		MDBLS	3/08
Postsecondary	Minnesota	Y	65901 FQ	78362 MW	91262 TQ	MNBLS	10/08-12/08
Postsecondary	Mississippi	Y	60040 FQ	75160 MW	90880 TQ	USBLS	5/07
Postsecondary	Missouri	Y	42310 FQ	59730 MW	81480 TQ	USBLS	5/07
Postsecondary	Montana	Y	36550 FQ	51720 MW	63100 TQ	USBLS	5/07
Postsecondary	New Jersey	Y	58170 FQ	75180 MW	107590 TQ	USBLS	5/07
Postsecondary	New Mexico	Y	54600 FQ	61640 MW	116710 TQ	USBLS	5/07
Postsecondary	New York	Y	50320 FQ	60760 MW	79760 TQ	USBLS	5/07
Postsecondary	North Dakota	Y	67500 FQ	78660 MW	90970 TQ	USBLS	5/07
Postsecondary	Oklahoma	Y	33920 FQ	43970 MW	55500 TQ	USBLS	5/07
Postsecondary	Pennsylvania	Y	74360 FQ	89160 MW	104620 TQ	USBLS	5/07
Postsecondary	Tennessee	Y	30390 FQ	59450 MW	77770 TQ	USBLS	5/07
Postsecondary	Texas	Y	66510 FQ	89400 MW	114670 TQ	USBLS	5/07
Postsecondary	Utah	Y	53150 FQ	62320 MW	82700 TQ	USBLS	5/07
Postsecondary	Vermont	Y	42960 FQ	50460 MW	63400 TQ	USBLS	5/07
Postsecondary	Wisconsin	Y	60210 FQ	75890 MW	100260 TQ	USBLS	5/07
Postsecondary	Wyoming	Y	57413 FQ	66858 MW	81869 TQ	WYBLS	9/08
Agriculture Enforcement Agent State Government	Ohio	H	19.88 LO		26.28 HI	ODAS	2008
Agronomist	United States	Y		48514 AW		AGPRO	2007
Air Base Fire Training Officer	Ohio	H	17.78 LO		21.65 HI	ODAS	2008
Air Pollution Specialist	California	Y	46836 LO		86568 HI	SBEE01	2008
Air Quality Engineer State Government	Ohio	H	21.77 LO		36.59 HI	ODAS	2008
Air Traffic Controller	Alabama	Y	66000 FQ	89300 MW	103340 TQ	USBLS	5/07

AE Average entry wage	**AW** Average wage paid	**FQ** First quartile wage	**LO** Lowest wage paid	**MTC** Median total compensation	**TCC** Total cash compensation
AER Average entry range	**AWR** Average wage range	**H** Hourly	**LR** Low end range	**MW** Median wage paid	**TQ** Third quartile wage
AEX Average experienced wage	**AXR** Average experienced range	**HI** Highest wage paid	**M** Monthly	**MWR** Median wage range	**W** Weekly
ATC Average total compensation	**D** Daily	**HR** High end range	**MCC** Median cash compensation	**S** See annotated source	**Y** Yearly

Occupation/Type/Industry	Location	Per	Low	Mid	High	Source	Date
Air Traffic Controller	Alaska	Y	70370 FQ	88450 MW	114090 TQ	USBLS	5/07
	Arizona	Y	65500 FQ	95640 MW	124900 TQ	USBLS	5/07
	Arkansas	Y	49170 FQ	84610 MW	102170 TQ	USBLS	5/07
	California	H	37.32 FQ	57.28 MW		CABLS	1/08-3/08
	Colorado	Y	103820 FQ	129230 MW		USBLS	5/07
	Connecticut	H	26.99 AE	32.52 MW		CTBLS	1/08-3/08
	Florida	Y	83930 FQ	118310 MW	143340 TQ	USBLS	5/07
	Georgia	Y	80930 FQ	125160 MW		USBLS	5/07
	Hawaii	Y	59610 FQ	92530 MW	117410 TQ	USBLS	5/07
	Idaho	Y	48250 FQ	64840 MW	97650 TQ	USBLS	5/07
	Illinois	Y	99440 FQ	133180 MW		USBLS	5/07
	Indiana	Y	94090 FQ	124670 MW		USBLS	5/07
	Iowa	Y	68570 FQ	87420 MW	100390 TQ	USBLS	5/07
	Kansas	Y	96770 FQ	123410 MW	145090 TQ	USBLS	5/07
	Louisiana	H	27.07 FQ	36.53 MW	44.77 TQ	LABLS	1/08-3/08
	Maryland	Y		119750 MW		MDBLS	3/08
	Massachusetts	Y	55230 FQ	72790 MW	120920 TQ	USBLS	5/07
	Minnesota	Y	108341 FQ	139832 MW		MNBLS	10/08-12/08
	Mississippi	Y	64250 FQ	81670 MW	95620 TQ	USBLS	5/07
	Missouri	Y	89780 FQ	114630 MW	135390 TQ	USBLS	5/07
	Montana	Y	72200 FQ	89040 MW	98370 TQ	USBLS	5/07
	Nebraska	Y	83120 FQ	92270 MW	101410 TQ	USBLS	5/07
	New Jersey	Y	89150 FQ	108630 MW	128520 TQ	USBLS	5/07
	New Mexico	Y	72630 FQ	113110 MW	129460 TQ	USBLS	5/07
	North Dakota	Y	62790 FQ	74720 MW	88340 TQ	USBLS	5/07
	Ohio	Y	94770 FQ	124720 MW		USBLS	5/07
	Oregon	H	36.14 FQ	47.73 MW	58.97 TQ	ORBLS	5/08
	Pennsylvania	Y	56530 FQ	100340 MW	132620 TQ	USBLS	5/07
	South Carolina	Y	59030 FQ	81870 MW	95900 TQ	USBLS	5/07
	South Dakota	Y	60371 FQ	70108 MW	87671 TQ	SDBLS	7/08-9/08
	Tennessee	Y	86070 FQ	119650 MW	144610 TQ	USBLS	5/07
	Texas	Y	72300 FQ	111740 MW	145510 TQ	USBLS	5/07
	Washington	H	25.86 FQ	52.80 MW	69.26 TQ	WABLS	3/08
	West Virginia	Y	68773 FQ	85166 MW	98215 TQ	WVBLS	7/08-9/08
	Wisconsin	Y	84310 FQ	98600 MW	117350 TQ	USBLS	5/07
	Wyoming	Y	54893 FQ	66329 MW	78645 TQ	WYBLS	9/08
Aircraft Attendant							
State Government	Ohio	H	15.41 LO		17.03 HI	ODAS	2008
Aircraft Cabin Cleaner	United States	H		8.50 AW		AVJOB03	2009
Aircraft Cargo Handling Supervisor	Alaska	Y	29720 FQ	37520 MW	49880 TQ	USBLS	5/07
	Anchorage MSA, AK	Y	28970 FQ	34240 MW	46310 TQ	USBLS	5/07
	Arizona	Y	24550 FQ	29170 MW	47070 TQ	USBLS	5/07
	Phoenix-Mesa-Scottsdale MSA, AZ	Y	23900 FQ	28290 MW	34860 TQ	USBLS	5/07
	California	H	14.32 FQ	16.96 MW	25.84 TQ	CABLS	1/08-3/08
	Los Angeles-Long Beach-Glendale PMSA, CA	H	15.19 FQ	18.00 MW	25.64 TQ	CABLS	1/08-3/08
	Oakland-Fremont-Hayward MSA, CA	H	14.01 FQ	15.68 MW	18.41 TQ	CABLS	1/08-3/08
	Riverside-San Bernardino-Ontario MSA, CA	H	13.71 FQ	15.04 MW	19.06 TQ	CABLS	1/08-3/08
	San Diego-Carlsbad-San Marcos MSA, CA	H	13.93 FQ	15.41 MW	33.26 TQ	CABLS	1/08-3/08
	San Francisco-San Mateo-Redwood PMSA, CA	H	14.22 FQ	16.92 MW	26.11 TQ	CABLS	1/08-3/08
	San Jose-Sunnyvale-Santa Clara MSA, CA	H	15.08 FQ	17.82 MW	31.36 TQ	CABLS	1/08-3/08
	Colorado	Y	27830 FQ	37020 MW	49210 TQ	USBLS	5/07
	Denver-Aurora MSA, CO	Y	24670 FQ	33580 MW	45040 TQ	USBLS	5/07
	Connecticut	H	13.90 AE	15.42 MW		CTBLS	1/08-3/08
	Washington-Arlington-Alexandria MSA, DC-VA-MD-WV	Y	34140 FQ	44070 MW	56000 TQ	USBLS	5/07
	Florida	Y	27900 FQ	32690 MW	42410 TQ	USBLS	5/07
	Fort Lauderdale-Pompano Beach-Deerfield Beach PMSA, FL	Y	23300 FQ	26770 MW	32860 TQ	USBLS	5/07

AE	Average entry wage	**AW**	Average wage paid	**FQ**	First quartile wage	**LO**	Lowest wage paid	**MTC** Median total compensation	**TCC** Total cash compensation
AER	Average entry range	**AWR**	Average wage range	**H**	Hourly	**LR**	Low end range	**MW** Median wage paid	**TQ** Third quartile wage
AEX	Average experienced wage	**AXR**	Average experienced range	**HI**	Highest wage paid	**M**	Monthly	**MWR** Median wage range	**W** Weekly
ATC	Average total compensation	**D**	Daily	**HR**	High end range	**MCC**	Median cash compensation	**S** See annotated source	**Y** Yearly

Occupation/Type/Industry	Location	Per	Low	Mid	High	Source	Date
Aircraft Cargo Handling Supervisor	Miami-Fort Lauderdale-Miami Beach MSA, FL	Y	26740 FQ	32540 MW	39760 TQ	USBLS	5/07
	Orlando-Kissimmee MSA, FL	Y	27870 FQ	30680 MW	45630 TQ	USBLS	5/07
	Georgia	Y	35580 FQ	53640 MW	77450 TQ	USBLS	5/07
	Atlanta-Sandy Springs-Marietta MSA, GA	Y	36050 FQ	55540 MW	79480 TQ	USBLS	5/07
	Idaho	Y	25710 FQ	29250 MW	37110 TQ	USBLS	5/07
	Illinois	Y	41880 FQ	55650 MW	78670 TQ	USBLS	5/07
	Chicago-Naperville-Joliet MSA, IL-IN-WI	Y	41670 FQ	53410 MW	78560 TQ	USBLS	5/07
	Indiana	Y	24510 FQ	33420 MW	39500 TQ	USBLS	5/07
	Kentucky	Y	20846 FQ	24192 MW	31801 TQ	KYBLS	2008
	Louisville-Jefferson County MSA, KY-IN	Y	20120 FQ	23280 MW	30330 TQ	USBLS	5/07
	Louisiana	H	16.81 FQ	20.27 MW	24.37 TQ	LABLS	1/08-3/08
	Maryland	Y		48625 MW		MDBLS	3/08
	Baltimore-Towson MSA, MD	Y	40860 FQ	48060 MW	60790 TQ	USBLS	5/07
	Massachusetts	Y	36670 FQ	51330 MW	79730 TQ	USBLS	5/07
	Boston-Cambridge-Quincy NECTA, MA	Y	34620 FQ	50330 MW	80450 TQ	USBLS	5/07
	Michigan	Y	47700 FQ	57380 MW	71810 TQ	USBLS	5/07
	Detroit-Warren-Livonia MSA, MI	Y	46350 FQ	58230 MW	73170 TQ	USBLS	5/07
	Minneapolis-Saint Paul MSA, MN-WI	Y	31231 FQ	40948 MW	52724 TQ	MNBLS	10/08-12/08
	Missouri	Y	33520 FQ	38240 MW	50860 TQ	USBLS	5/07
	Kansas City MSA, MO-KS	Y	26260 FQ	28850 MW	41040 TQ	USBLS	5/07
	Nebraska	Y	26430 FQ	28620 MW	32710 TQ	USBLS	5/07
	Nevada	H	12.41 FQ	15.56 MW	22.00 TQ	NVBLS	5/08
	Las Vegas-Paradise MSA, NV	H	12.35 FQ	15.03 MW	22.70 TQ	NVBLS	5/08
	New Jersey	Y	33760 FQ	39440 MW	47080 TQ	USBLS	5/07
	Newark-Union PMSA, NJ-PA	Y	33180 FQ	37880 MW	45760 TQ	USBLS	5/07
	New Mexico	Y	27950 FQ	33580 MW	47290 TQ	USBLS	5/07
	Albuquerque MSA, NM	Y	26570 FQ	31380 MW	35240 TQ	USBLS	5/07
	New York	Y	39500 FQ	52820 MW	68930 TQ	USBLS	5/07
	New York-Northern New Jersey-Long Island MSA, NY-NJ-PA	Y	37160 FQ	49200 MW	60590 TQ	USBLS	5/07
	North Carolina	Y	29000 FQ	33270 MW	39140 TQ	USBLS	5/07
	Ohio	Y	51100 FQ	60730 MW	76330 TQ	USBLS	5/07
	Oklahoma	Y	54530 FQ	67720 MW	75650 TQ	USBLS	5/07
	Tulsa MSA, OK	Y	61740 FQ	70490 MW	76700 TQ	USBLS	5/07
	Oregon	H	18.98 FQ	26.71 MW	33.87 TQ	ORBLS	5/08
	Portland-Vancouver-Beaverton MSA, OR-WA	Y	37800 FQ	54810 MW	68350 TQ	USBLS	5/07
	Pennsylvania	Y	29200 FQ	39940 MW	62410 TQ	USBLS	5/07
	Philadelphia-Camden-Wilmington MSA, PA-NJ-DE-MD	Y	29010 FQ	36230 MW	48730 TQ	USBLS	5/07
	Columbia MSA, SC	Y	43890 FQ	47160 MW	50430 TQ	USBLS	5/07
	Tennessee	Y	26940 FQ	30570 MW	35720 TQ	USBLS	5/07
	Memphis MSA, TN-MS-AR	Y	30190 FQ	32760 MW	36690 TQ	USBLS	5/07
	Texas	Y	27820 FQ	34750 MW	52760 TQ	USBLS	5/07
	Dallas-Fort Worth-Arlington MSA, TX	Y	33090 FQ	48310 MW	59590 TQ	USBLS	5/07
	Houston-Sugar Land-Baytown MSA, TX	Y	18960 FQ	24110 MW	38680 TQ	USBLS	5/07
	Utah	Y	23500 FQ	27330 MW	34950 TQ	USBLS	5/07
	Salt Lake City MSA, UT	Y	23020 FQ	26500 MW	31110 TQ	USBLS	5/07
	Virginia	Y	34430 FQ	46780 MW	58680 TQ	USBLS	5/07
	Washington	H	15.22 FQ	25.76 MW	33.94 TQ	WABLS	3/08
	Seattle-Tacoma-Bellevue MSA, WA	Y	29620 FQ	50670 MW	67580 TQ	USBLS	5/07
	Wisconsin	Y	28660 FQ	32840 MW	36980 TQ	USBLS	5/07
	Milwaukee-Waukesha-West Allis MSA, WI	Y	27850 FQ	33150 MW	39810 TQ	USBLS	5/07
	Wyoming	Y	37632 FQ	55085 MW	63210 TQ	WYBLS	9/08
Aircraft Interior Fitter	United States	H		14.50 AW		AVJOB07	2009
Aircraft Interior Mechanic	United States	H		19.00 AW		AVJOB07	2009

AE	Average entry wage	AW	Average wage paid	FQ	First quartile wage	LO	Lowest wage paid	MTC	Median total compensation
AER	Average entry range	AWR	Average wage range	H	Hourly	LR	Low end range	MW	Median wage paid
AEX	Average experienced wage	AXR	Average experienced range	HI	Highest wage paid	M	Monthly	MWR	Median wage range
ATC	Average total compensation	D	Daily	HR	High end range	MCC	Median cash compensation	S	See annotated source

TCC Total cash compensation
TQ Third quartile wage
W Weekly
Y Yearly

Occupation/Type/Industry	Location	Per	Low	Mid	High	Source	Date
Aircraft Maintenance Specialist							
State Highway Patrol	Missouri	S	1613 LO		2362 HI	MSHPSS	7/1/08
Aircraft Mechanic and Service Technician							
	Alabama	Y	32760 FQ	39040 MW	45840 TQ	USBLS	5/07
	Birmingham-Hoover MSA, AL	Y	41620 FQ	45730 MW	49830 TQ	USBLS	5/07
	Alaska	Y	43600 FQ	54140 MW	67030 TQ	USBLS	5/07
	Anchorage MSA, AK	Y	45220 FQ	55150 MW	68240 TQ	USBLS	5/07
	Arizona	Y	41630 FQ	48280 MW	57890 TQ	USBLS	5/07
	Phoenix-Mesa-Scottsdale MSA, AZ	Y	41610 FQ	49680 MW	59490 TQ	USBLS	5/07
	Tucson MSA, AZ	Y	42510 FQ	47980 MW	55830 TQ	USBLS	5/07
	Yuma MSA, AZ	Y	42560 FQ	45790 MW	49110 TQ	USBLS	5/07
	Arkansas	Y	33080 FQ	39170 MW	45620 TQ	USBLS	5/07
	Little Rock-North Little Rock MSA, AR	Y	38720 FQ	43840 MW	48930 TQ	USBLS	5/07
	California	H	22.79 FQ	27.34 MW	31.02 TQ	CABLS	1/08-3/08
	Los Angeles-Long Beach-Glendale PMSA, CA	H	24.31 FQ	28.31 MW	35.32 TQ	CABLS	1/08-3/08
	Oakland-Fremont-Hayward MSA, CA	H	24.39 FQ	31.65 MW	39.42 TQ	CABLS	1/08-3/08
	Riverside-San Bernardino-Ontario MSA, CA	H	16.65 FQ	23.34 MW	29.97 TQ	CABLS	1/08-3/08
	Sacramento-Arden Arcade-Roseville MSA, CA	H	22.53 FQ	26.44 MW	29.80 TQ	CABLS	1/08-3/08
	San Diego-Carlsbad-San Marcos MSA, CA	H	22.33 FQ	25.96 MW	29.32 TQ	CABLS	1/08-3/08
	San Jose-Sunnyvale-Santa Clara MSA, CA	H	20.19 FQ	26.12 MW	30.36 TQ	CABLS	1/08-3/08
	Santa Ana-Anaheim-Irvine PMSA, CA	Y	38130 FQ	52710 MW	59940 TQ	USBLS	5/07
	Colorado	Y	43990 FQ	53710 MW	60600 TQ	USBLS	5/07
	Denver-Aurora MSA, CO	Y	51400 FQ	56720 MW	62320 TQ	USBLS	5/07
	Connecticut	H	19.67 AE	25.21 MW		CTBLS	1/08-3/08
	Bridgeport-Stamford-Norwalk MSA, CT	Y	50660 FQ	56110 MW	61370 TQ	USBLS	5/07
	Hartford-West Hartford-East Hartford MSA, CT	Y	42020 FQ	46150 MW	50360 TQ	USBLS	5/07
	Delaware	Y	43790 FQ	50420 MW	58460 TQ	USBLS	5/07
	Wilmington PMSA, DE-MD-NJ	Y	43230 FQ	52060 MW	60330 TQ	USBLS	5/07
	Washington-Arlington-Alexandria MSA, DC-VA-MD-WV	Y	40390 FQ	48400 MW	58370 TQ	USBLS	5/07
	Florida	Y	37690 FQ	45390 MW	54700 TQ	USBLS	5/07
	Fort Lauderdale-Pompano Beach-Deerfield Beach PMSA, FL	Y	31570 FQ	42350 MW	55530 TQ	USBLS	5/07
	Jacksonville MSA, FL	Y	42010 FQ	45990 MW	50000 TQ	USBLS	5/07
	Miami-Fort Lauderdale-Miami Beach MSA, FL	Y	37070 FQ	45670 MW	56690 TQ	USBLS	5/07
	Orlando-Kissimmee MSA, FL	Y	41340 FQ	49610 MW	59040 TQ	USBLS	5/07
	Tampa-St. Petersburg-Clearwater MSA, FL	Y	40930 FQ	46950 MW	57120 TQ	USBLS	5/07
	West Palm Beach-Boca Raton-Boynton Beach PMSA, FL	Y	39420 FQ	46350 MW	60470 TQ	USBLS	5/07
	Georgia	Y	42890 FQ	48950 MW	57300 TQ	USBLS	5/07
	Atlanta-Sandy Springs-Marietta MSA, GA	Y	47750 FQ	55890 MW	61760 TQ	USBLS	5/07
	Hawaii	Y	45530 FQ	56070 MW	64070 TQ	USBLS	5/07
	Honolulu MSA, HI	Y	47920 FQ	57230 MW	64870 TQ	USBLS	5/07
	Idaho	Y	30990 FQ	42290 MW	50720 TQ	USBLS	5/07
	Boise City-Nampa MSA, ID	Y	31350 FQ	44620 MW	53370 TQ	USBLS	5/07
	Illinois	Y	43660 FQ	54450 MW	61190 TQ	USBLS	5/07
	Chicago-Naperville-Joliet MSA, IL-IN-WI	Y	48460 FQ	56750 MW	62750 TQ	USBLS	5/07
	Indiana	Y	40590 FQ	56690 MW	76570 TQ	USBLS	5/07
	Fort Wayne MSA, IN	Y	50100 FQ	56000 MW	61300 TQ	USBLS	5/07
	Gary PMSA, IN	Y	38920 FQ	46020 MW	60990 TQ	USBLS	5/07
	Indianapolis-Carmel MSA, IN	Y	41810 FQ	63670 MW	83280 TQ	USBLS	5/07
	Iowa	Y	37630 FQ	45550 MW	53340 TQ	USBLS	5/07

AE	Average entry wage	AW	Average wage paid	FQ	First quartile wage	
AER	Average entry range	AWR	Average wage range	H	Hourly	
AEX	Average experienced wage	AXR	Average experienced range	HI	Highest wage paid	
ATC	Average total compensation	D	Daily	HR	High end range	

LO	Lowest wage paid	MTC	Median total compensation	TCC	Total cash compensation
LR	Low end range	MW	Median wage paid	TQ	Third quartile wage
M	Monthly	MWR	Median wage range	W	Weekly
MCC	Median cash compensation	S	See annotated source	Y	Yearly

Occupation/Type/Industry	Location	Per	Low	Mid	High	Source	Date
Aircraft Mechanic and Service Technician	Des Moines-West Des Moines MSA, IA	Y	41440 FQ	47800 MW	55750 TQ	USBLS	5/07
	Kansas	Y	41690 FQ	50670 MW	56890 TQ	USBLS	5/07
	Wichita MSA, KS	Y	43650 FQ	51640 MW	57330 TQ	USBLS	5/07
	Kentucky	Y	45895 FQ	51731 MW	64656 TQ	KYBLS	2008
	Louisiana	H	20.03 FQ	23.35 MW	27.60 TQ	LABLS	1/08-3/08
	New Orleans-Metairie-Kenner MSA, LA	Y	40630 FQ	46080 MW	52470 TQ	USBLS	5/07
	Maine	Y	38610 FQ	44280 MW	49720 TQ	USBLS	5/07
	Portland-South Portland-Biddeford MSA, ME	Y	34850 FQ	41070 MW	45740 TQ	USBLS	5/07
	Maryland	Y		48425 MW		MDBLS	3/08
	Baltimore-Towson MSA, MD	Y	40830 FQ	45940 MW	55070 TQ	USBLS	5/07
	Bethesda-Gaithersburg-Frederick PMSA, MD	Y	32360 FQ	40000 MW	46830 TQ	USBLS	5/07
	Massachusetts	Y	44390 FQ	53950 MW	62680 TQ	USBLS	5/07
	Boston-Cambridge-Quincy NECTA, MA	Y	46480 FQ	58030 MW	79290 TQ	USBLS	5/07
	Springfield MSA, MA-CT	Y	42870 FQ	48060 MW	57100 TQ	USBLS	5/07
	Michigan	Y	41370 FQ	51220 MW	59550 TQ	USBLS	5/07
	Detroit-Warren-Livonia MSA, MI	Y	47280 FQ	55920 MW	62260 TQ	USBLS	5/07
	Warren-Troy-Farmington Hills PMSA, MI	Y	45730 FQ	54290 MW	61650 TQ	USBLS	5/07
	Minnesota	Y	42765 FQ	54230 MW	63230 TQ	MNBLS	10/08-12/08
	Duluth-Superior MSA, MN-WI	Y	36419 FQ	45303 MW	51177 TQ	MNBLS	10/08-12/08
	Minneapolis-Saint Paul MSA, MN-WI	Y	51933 FQ	59716 MW	66377 TQ	MNBLS	10/08-12/08
	Mississippi	Y	42770 FQ	46530 MW	50360 TQ	USBLS	5/07
	Jackson MSA, MS	Y	43900 FQ	48750 MW	56200 TQ	USBLS	5/07
	Missouri	Y	43360 FQ	54850 MW	61270 TQ	USBLS	5/07
	Kansas City MSA, MO-KS	Y	38900 FQ	55600 MW	62010 TQ	USBLS	5/07
	St. Louis MSA, MO-IL	Y	42090 FQ	53450 MW	60450 TQ	USBLS	5/07
	Montana	Y	35290 FQ	42150 MW	49880 TQ	USBLS	5/07
	Billings MSA, MT	Y	32670 FQ	38930 MW	44420 TQ	USBLS	5/07
	Nebraska	Y	34400 FQ	41050 MW	46870 TQ	USBLS	5/07
	Omaha-Council Bluffs MSA, NE-IA	Y	36940 FQ	43330 MW	48880 TQ	USBLS	5/07
	Nevada	H	20.01 FQ	25.32 MW	30.40 TQ	NVBLS	5/08
	Las Vegas-Paradise MSA, NV	H	20.41 FQ	25.71 MW	31.14 TQ	NVBLS	5/08
	New Hampshire	H	17.36 AE	22.43 MW	26.46 AEX	NHBLS	6/08
	Manchester MSA, NH	Y	36870 FQ	44070 MW	54280 TQ	USBLS	5/07
	Nashua NECTA, NH-MA	Y	37870 FQ	43930 MW	51820 TQ	USBLS	5/07
	New Jersey	Y	49640 FQ	57560 MW	64160 TQ	USBLS	5/07
	Camden PMSA, NJ	Y	54530 FQ	58480 MW	62450 TQ	USBLS	5/07
	Edison PMSA, NJ	Y	43690 FQ	53900 MW	64190 TQ	USBLS	5/07
	Newark-Union PMSA, NJ-PA	Y	47740 FQ	57380 MW	64490 TQ	USBLS	5/07
	New Mexico	Y	40390 FQ	45450 MW	51440 TQ	USBLS	5/07
	Albuquerque MSA, NM	Y	40050 FQ	46910 MW	55690 TQ	USBLS	5/07
	New York	Y	43970 FQ	51940 MW	57750 TQ	USBLS	5/07
	Albany-Schenectady-Troy MSA, NY	Y	39890 FQ	54690 MW	61230 TQ	USBLS	5/07
	Buffalo-Niagara Falls MSA, NY	Y	46650 FQ	53440 MW	59840 TQ	USBLS	5/07
	Nassau-Suffolk PMSA, NY	Y	35890 FQ	43670 MW	50710 TQ	USBLS	5/07
	New York-Northern New Jersey-Long Island MSA, NY-NJ-PA	Y	45730 FQ	53870 MW	59850 TQ	USBLS	5/07
	Utica-Rome MSA, NY	Y	34490 FQ	39530 MW	44710 TQ	USBLS	5/07
	North Carolina	Y	35640 FQ	42360 MW	47190 TQ	USBLS	5/07
	Raleigh-Cary MSA, NC	Y	41150 FQ	47710 MW	56060 TQ	USBLS	5/07
	North Dakota	Y	33820 FQ	41030 MW	49770 TQ	USBLS	5/07
	Fargo MSA, ND-MN	Y	31460 FQ	42820 MW	55270 TQ	USBLS	5/07
	Ohio	Y	36130 FQ	50010 MW	60210 TQ	USBLS	5/07
	Cincinnati-Middletown MSA, OH-KY-IN	Y	40350 FQ	51950 MW	58390 TQ	USBLS	5/07
	Cleveland-Elyria-Mentor MSA, OH	Y	26500 FQ	35560 MW	49940 TQ	USBLS	5/07
	Columbus MSA, OH	Y	36880 FQ	45970 MW	56080 TQ	USBLS	5/07
	Dayton MSA, OH	Y	39790 FQ	51970 MW	59380 TQ	USBLS	5/07
	Oklahoma	Y	42990 FQ	50340 MW	58180 TQ	USBLS	5/07

AE Average entry wage	**AW** Average wage paid	**FQ** First quartile wage	**LO** Lowest wage paid	**MTC** Median total compensation	**TCC** Total cash compensation
AER Average entry range	**AWR** Average wage range	**H** Hourly	**LR** Low end range	**MW** Median wage paid	**TQ** Third quartile wage
AEX Average experienced wage	**AXR** Average experienced range	**HI** Highest wage paid	**M** Monthly	**MWR** Median wage range	**W** Weekly
ATC Average total compensation	**D** Daily	**HR** High end range	**MCC** Median cash compensation	**S** See annotated source	**Y** Yearly

Occupation/Type/Industry	Location	Per	Low	Mid	High	Source	Date
Aircraft Mechanic and Service Technician	Oklahoma City MSA, OK	Y	40290 FQ	44360 MW	48500 TQ	USBLS	5/07
	Tulsa MSA, OK	Y	52850 FQ	57150 MW	61450 TQ	USBLS	5/07
	Oregon	H	19.37 FQ	24.26 MW	28.89 TQ	ORBLS	5/08
	Portland-Vancouver-Beaverton MSA, OR-WA	Y	39420 FQ	50960 MW	60040 TQ	USBLS	5/07
	Pennsylvania	Y	39710 FQ	45150 MW	50700 TQ	USBLS	5/07
	Allentown-Bethlehem-Easton MSA, PA-NJ	Y	28070 FQ	31540 MW	42540 TQ	USBLS	5/07
	Philadelphia-Camden-Wilmington MSA, PA-NJ-DE-MD	Y	41910 FQ	47750 MW	55390 TQ	USBLS	5/07
	Rhode Island	Y	40060 FQ	44740 MW	49330 TQ	USBLS	5/07
	Providence-Fall River-Warwick MSA, RI-MA	Y	40240 FQ	44800 MW	49290 TQ	USBLS	5/07
	South Carolina	Y	37490 FQ	43220 MW	48320 TQ	USBLS	5/07
	Charleston-North Charleston MSA, SC	Y	41590 FQ	45760 MW	49920 TQ	USBLS	5/07
	Columbia MSA, SC	Y	41410 FQ	45880 MW	50540 TQ	USBLS	5/07
	South Dakota	Y	32592 FQ	40576 MW	48049 TQ	SDBLS	7/08-9/08
	Sioux Falls MSA, SD	Y	34296 FQ	41078 MW	47690 TQ	SDBLS	7/08-9/08
	Tennessee	Y	44470 FQ	62660 MW	76640 TQ	USBLS	5/07
	Nashville-Davidson-Murfreesboro MSA, TN	Y	41520 FQ	47620 MW	55790 TQ	USBLS	5/07
	Texas	Y	38610 FQ	46970 MW	56240 TQ	USBLS	5/07
	Austin-Round Rock MSA, TX	Y	40080 FQ	46650 MW	54330 TQ	USBLS	5/07
	Dallas-Fort Worth-Arlington MSA, TX	Y	42480 FQ	51820 MW	59480 TQ	USBLS	5/07
	El Paso MSA, TX	Y	42920 FQ	47330 MW	52200 TQ	USBLS	5/07
	Houston-Sugar Land-Baytown MSA, TX	Y	39500 FQ	52770 MW	64520 TQ	USBLS	5/07
	San Antonio MSA, TX	Y	34200 FQ	41550 MW	45970 TQ	USBLS	5/07
	Utah	Y	42340 FQ	48460 MW	57640 TQ	USBLS	5/07
	Salt Lake City MSA, UT	Y	40210 FQ	48910 MW	62130 TQ	USBLS	5/07
	Vermont	Y	40300 FQ	44990 MW	49980 TQ	USBLS	5/07
	Burlington-South Burlington MSA, VT	Y	41980 FQ	46060 MW	50570 TQ	USBLS	5/07
	Virginia	Y	39100 FQ	45630 MW	55890 TQ	USBLS	5/07
	Richmond MSA, VA	Y	43220 FQ	50800 MW	59070 TQ	USBLS	5/07
	Virginia Beach-Norfolk-Newport News MSA, VA-NC	Y	37770 FQ	44080 MW	48900 TQ	USBLS	5/07
	Washington	H	20.07 FQ	26.01 MW	31.77 TQ	WABLS	3/08
	Seattle-Tacoma-Bellevue MSA, WA	Y	42080 FQ	55110 MW	66160 TQ	USBLS	5/07
	West Virginia	Y	40752 FQ	47332 MW	53450 TQ	WVBLS	7/08-9/08
	Wisconsin	Y	39040 FQ	46880 MW	55650 TQ	USBLS	5/07
	Appleton MSA, WI	Y	42860 FQ	50810 MW	57380 TQ	USBLS	5/07
	Milwaukee-Waukesha-West Allis MSA, WI	Y	39100 FQ	47000 MW	56150 TQ	USBLS	5/07
	Wyoming	Y	37224 FQ	45792 MW	53393 TQ	WYBLS	9/08
	Cheyenne MSA, WY	Y	39020 FQ	46803 MW	54390 TQ	WYBLS	9/08
	Puerto Rico	Y	43260 FQ	53390 MW	60690 TQ	USBLS	5/07
	San Juan-Caguas-Guaynabo MSA, PR	Y	44490 FQ	56080 MW	62140 TQ	USBLS	5/07
	Guam	Y	36610 FQ	54170 MW	59700 TQ	USBLS	5/07
Aircraft Structure, Surfaces, Rigging, and Systems Assembler	Alabama	Y	26600 FQ	31580 MW	53510 TQ	USBLS	5/07
	Arizona	Y	28870 FQ	42150 MW	48690 TQ	USBLS	5/07
	Arkansas	Y	26680 FQ	31470 MW	47830 TQ	USBLS	5/07
	California	H	19.51 FQ	27.28 MW	29.96 TQ	CABLS	1/08-3/08
	Colorado	Y	22810 FQ	29620 MW	42950 TQ	USBLS	5/07
	Connecticut	H	15.04 AE	24.00 MW		CTBLS	1/08-3/08
	Delaware	Y	28430 FQ	35090 MW	40580 TQ	USBLS	5/07
	Florida	Y	34280 FQ	41520 MW	48500 TQ	USBLS	5/07
	Georgia	Y	26660 FQ	31450 MW	43140 TQ	USBLS	5/07
	Kansas	Y	34560 FQ	41910 MW	47500 TQ	USBLS	5/07
	Maryland	Y		25200 MW		MDBLS	3/08
	New Jersey	Y	34120 FQ	37210 MW	42830 TQ	USBLS	5/07
	New York	Y	26860 FQ	35730 MW	47870 TQ	USBLS	5/07
	Ohio	Y	27610 FQ	31710 MW	38860 TQ	USBLS	5/07

AE Average entry wage	**AW** Average wage paid	**FQ** First quartile wage	**LO** Lowest wage paid	**MTC** Median total compensation	**TCC** Total cash compensation
AER Average entry range	**AWR** Average wage range	**H** Hourly	**LR** Low end range	**MW** Median wage paid	**TQ** Third quartile wage
AEX Average experienced wage	**AXR** Average experienced range	**HI** Highest wage paid	**M** Monthly	**MWR** Median wage range	**W** Weekly
ATC Average total compensation	**D** Daily	**HR** High end range	**MCC** Median cash compensation	**S** See annotated source	**Y** Yearly

Occupation/Type/Industry	Location	Per	Low	Mid	High	Source	Date
Aircraft Structure, Surfaces,							
Rigging, and Systems Assembler	Oklahoma	Y	29980 FQ	42630 MW	48510 TQ	USBLS	5/07
	Oregon	H	14.40 FQ	19.05 MW	22.14 TQ	ORBLS	5/08
	South Dakota	Y	24683 FQ	28172 MW	32543 TQ	SDBLS	7/08-9/08
	Tennessee	Y	27320 FQ	40740 MW	49270 TQ	USBLS	5/07
	Texas	Y	30430 FQ	42140 MW	53310 TQ	USBLS	5/07
	Utah	Y	29780 FQ	38720 MW	44520 TQ	USBLS	5/07
	Virginia	Y	29850 FQ	34540 MW	39120 TQ	USBLS	5/07
	West Virginia	Y	31140 FQ	41484 MW	50862 TQ	WVBLS	7/08-9/08
Airfield Operations Specialist	Alaska	Y	43490 FQ	53050 MW	64460 TQ	USBLS	5/07
	Anchorage MSA, AK	Y	43070 FQ	53120 MW	64440 TQ	USBLS	5/07
	Arizona	Y	28070 FQ	30840 MW	36210 TQ	USBLS	5/07
	Phoenix-Mesa-Scottsdale MSA, AZ	Y	27950 FQ	30570 MW	35290 TQ	USBLS	5/07
	California	H	20.62 FQ	27.46 MW	35.17 TQ	CABLS	1/08-3/08
	Los Angeles-Long Beach-Glendale PMSA, CA	H	18.10 FQ	21.39 MW	27.15 TQ	CABLS	1/08-3/08
	Oakland-Fremont-Hayward MSA, CA	H	26.79 FQ	30.80 MW	40.83 TQ	CABLS	1/08-3/08
	Riverside-San Bernardino-Ontario MSA, CA	H	22.24 FQ	25.03 MW	29.86 TQ	CABLS	1/08-3/08
	San Diego-Carlsbad-San Marcos MSA, CA	H	15.64 FQ	20.65 MW	30.53 TQ	CABLS	1/08-3/08
	Colorado	Y	32510 FQ	43090 MW	52940 TQ	USBLS	5/07
	Denver-Aurora MSA, CO	Y	35230 FQ	46820 MW	56880 TQ	USBLS	5/07
	Washington-Arlington-Alexandria MSA, DC-VA-MD-WV	Y	30500 FQ	35230 MW	39900 TQ	USBLS	5/07
	Florida	Y	34660 FQ	41300 MW	50880 TQ	USBLS	5/07
	Jacksonville MSA, FL	Y	39140 FQ	45970 MW	53190 TQ	USBLS	5/07
	Orlando-Kissimmee MSA, FL	Y	28910 FQ	35320 MW	48950 TQ	USBLS	5/07
	West Palm Beach-Boca Raton-Boynton Beach PMSA, FL	Y	41940 FQ	47280 MW	54420 TQ	USBLS	5/07
	Idaho	Y	42870 FQ	46370 MW	49940 TQ	USBLS	5/07
	Illinois	Y	42160 FQ	45550 MW	48990 TQ	USBLS	5/07
	Chicago-Naperville-Joliet MSA, IL-IN-WI	Y	42130 FQ	45560 MW	48970 TQ	USBLS	5/07
	Indiana	Y	45200 FQ	84690 MW	94660 TQ	USBLS	5/07
	Indianapolis-Carmel MSA, IN	Y	83300 FQ	90320 MW	97490 TQ	USBLS	5/07
	Iowa	Y	21870 FQ	24290 MW	28010 TQ	USBLS	5/07
	Kansas	Y	43630 FQ	51730 MW	84740 TQ	USBLS	5/07
	Wichita MSA, KS	Y	49560 FQ	78740 MW	90170 TQ	USBLS	5/07
	Louisiana	H	20.94 FQ	23.50 MW	26.12 TQ	LABLS	1/08-3/08
	Maryland	Y		43025		MDBLS	3/08
	Massachusetts	Y	37700 FQ	41170 MW	44610 TQ	USBLS	5/07
	Michigan	Y	37290 FQ	46670 MW	57020 TQ	USBLS	5/07
	Detroit-Warren-Livonia MSA, MI	Y	38530 FQ	45690 MW	50980 TQ	USBLS	5/07
	Minnesota	Y	23615 FQ	26019 MW	32063 TQ	MNBLS	10/08-12/08
	Minneapolis-Saint Paul MSA, MN-WI	Y	23407 FQ	25613 MW	30731 TQ	MNBLS	10/08-12/08
	Nevada	H	19.55 FQ	29.01 MW	36.57 TQ	NVBLS	5/08
	New Jersey	Y	18690 FQ	22120 MW	43930 TQ	USBLS	5/07
	New York	Y	34420 FQ	42550 MW	57660 TQ	USBLS	5/07
	New York-Northern New Jersey-Long Island MSA, NY-NJ-PA	Y	34820 FQ	44400 MW	59390 TQ	USBLS	5/07
	North Carolina	Y	24930 FQ	35800 MW	44750 TQ	USBLS	5/07
	Charlotte-Gastonia-Concord MSA, NC-SC	Y	33100 FQ	35820 MW	38530 TQ	USBLS	5/07
	Ohio	Y	25700 FQ	42130 MW	47270 TQ	USBLS	5/07
	Cleveland-Elyria-Mentor MSA, OH	Y	41690 FQ	45020 MW	48350 TQ	USBLS	5/07
	Oklahoma	Y	40390 FQ	45550 MW	50160 TQ	USBLS	5/07
	Oregon	H	13.45 FQ	18.17 MW	25.03 TQ	ORBLS	5/08
	Portland-Vancouver-Beaverton MSA, OR-WA	Y	27350 FQ	37560 MW	51440 TQ	USBLS	5/07
	Pennsylvania	Y	38270 FQ	53370 MW	75660 TQ	USBLS	5/07
	Philadelphia-Camden-Wilmington MSA, PA-NJ-DE-MD	Y	28430 FQ	45270 MW	61230 TQ	USBLS	5/07

AE Average entry wage	**AW** Average wage paid	**FQ** First quartile wage	**LO** Lowest wage paid	**MTC** Median total compensation	**TCC** Total cash compensation
AER Average entry range	**AWR** Average wage range	**H** Hourly	**LR** Low end range	**MW** Median wage paid	**TQ** Third quartile wage
AEX Average experienced wage	**AXR** Average experienced range	**HI** Highest wage paid	**M** Monthly	**MWR** Median wage range	**W** Weekly
ATC Average total compensation	**D** Daily	**HR** High end range	**MCC** Median cash compensation	**S** See annotated source	**Y** Yearly

Occupation/Type/Industry	Location	Per	Low	Mid	High	Source	Date
Airfield Operations Specialist	Pittsburgh MSA, PA	Y	27640 FQ	41620 MW	66440 TQ	USBLS	5/07
	South Carolina	Y	26750 FQ	32660 MW	47660 TQ	USBLS	5/07,
	Tennessee	Y	19860 FQ	21500 MW	23140 TQ	USBLS	5/07
	Texas	Y	31720 FQ	36100 MW	49280 TQ	USBLS	5/07
	Dallas-Fort Worth-Arlington MSA, TX	Y	40050 FQ	47790 MW	60030 TQ	USBLS	5/07
	Houston-Sugar Land-Baytown MSA, TX	Y	30250 FQ	33420 MW	36580 TQ	USBLS	5/07
	Utah	Y	28620 FQ	35280 MW	40790 TQ	USBLS	5/07
	Salt Lake City MSA, UT	Y	29540 FQ	37180 MW	43150 TQ	USBLS	5/07
	Virginia	Y	29650 FQ	34930 MW	39780 TQ	USBLS	5/07
	Washington	H	20.97 FQ	26.04 MW	36.42 TQ	WABLS	3/08
	Seattle-Tacoma-Bellevue MSA, WA	Y	46100 FQ	59010 MW	78500 TQ	USBLS	5/07
	Wisconsin	Y	18120 FQ	23080 MW	53940 TQ	USBLS	5/07
Airline Captain							
Narrowbody Plane	United States	H	82.00-196.00 LR		100.00-200.00 HR	APC	7/08
Small Narrowbody Plane	United States	H	61.00-84.00 LR		90.00-121.00 HR	APC	7/08
Widebody Plane	United States	H	92.00-228.00 LR		117.00-239.00 HR	APC	7/08
Airline Pilot, Copilot, and Flight Engineer	Alabama	Y	77100 FQ	87810 MW	96670 TQ	USBLS	5/07
	Alaska	Y	70350 FQ	109480 MW		USBLS	5/07
	Arizona	Y	108320 FQ			USBLS	5/07
	Santa Ana-Anaheim-Irvine PMSA, CA	Y	85900 FQ			USBLS	5/07
	Colorado	Y	97730 FQ			USBLS	5/07
	Denver-Aurora MSA, CO	Y	104360 FQ			USBLS	5/07
	Delaware	Y	58380 FQ	83420 MW	107630 TQ	USBLS	5/07
	Washington-Arlington-Alexandria MSA, DC-VA-MD-WV	Y	89810 FQ			USBLS	5/07
	Florida	Y	85160 FQ			USBLS	5/07
	Fort Lauderdale-Pompano Beach-Deerfield Beach PMSA, FL	Y	37900 FQ	65330 MW	77730 TQ	USBLS	5/07
	Miami-Fort Lauderdale-Miami Beach MSA, FL	Y	81590 FQ			USBLS	5/07
	Orlando-Kissimmee MSA, FL	Y	99660 FQ			USBLS	5/07
	Tampa-St. Petersburg-Clearwater MSA, FL	Y	56340 FQ	73040 MW	89020 TQ	USBLS	5/07
	Georgia	Y	78170 FQ	125520 MW		USBLS	5/07
	Atlanta-Sandy Springs-Marietta MSA, GA	Y	78260 FQ	126470 MW		USBLS	5/07
	Hawaii	Y	57960 FQ	83250 MW	106650 TQ	USBLS	5/07
	Honolulu MSA, HI	Y	58220 FQ	82090 MW	106030 TQ	USBLS	5/07
	Boise City-Nampa MSA, ID	Y	28380 FQ	56790 MW	81940 TQ	USBLS	5/07
	Illinois	Y	141590 FQ			USBLS	5/07
	Indianapolis-Carmel MSA, IN	Y	104390 FQ	136450 MW		USBLS	5/07
	Iowa	Y	78420 FQ	91380 MW	102340 TQ	USBLS	5/07
	Kansas	Y	69240 FQ	83540 MW	96400 TQ	USBLS	5/07
	Wichita MSA, KS	Y	73080 FQ	88340 MW	101590 TQ	USBLS	5/07
	Louisiana	Y		81758 AW		LABLS	1/08-3/08
	Maine	Y	94620 FQ			USBLS	5/07
	Massachusetts	Y	84320 FQ			USBLS	5/07
	Boston-Cambridge-Quincy NECTA, MA	Y	131920 FQ			USBLS	5/07
	Michigan	Y	98480 FQ			USBLS	5/07
	Warren-Troy-Farmington Hills PMSA, MI	Y	125530 FQ			USBLS	5/07
	Minneapolis-Saint Paul MSA, MN-WI	Y	74488 FQ	89802 MW	102307 TQ	MNBLS	10/08-12/08
	Mississippi	Y	68410 FQ	87260 MW	101070 TQ	USBLS	5/07
	Jackson MSA, MS	Y	57350 FQ	91610 MW		USBLS	5/07
	Kansas City MSA, MO-KS	Y	64630 FQ	87400 MW	110700 TQ	USBLS	5/07
	Montana	Y	32500 FQ	38750 MW	45090 TQ	USBLS	5/07
	Billings MSA, MT	Y	32290 FQ	37500 MW	42500 TQ	USBLS	5/07
	Nebraska	Y	75060 FQ	86110 MW	96090 TQ	USBLS	5/07

AE	Average entry wage	**AW**	Average wage paid	**FQ**	First quartile wage	**LO** Lowest wage paid	**MTC** Median total compensation	**TCC** Total cash compensation
AER	Average entry range	**AWR**	Average wage range	**H**	Hourly	**LR** Low end range	**MW** Median wage paid	**TQ** Third quartile wage
AEX	Average experienced wage	**AXR**	Average experienced range	**HI**	Highest wage paid	**M** Monthly	**MWR** Median wage range	**W** Weekly
ATC	Average total compensation	**D**	Daily	**HR**	High end range	**MCC** Median cash compensation	**S** See annotated source	**Y** Yearly

Occupation/Type/Industry	Location	Per	Low	Mid	High	Source	Date
Airline Pilot, Copilot, and Flight Engineer	New Jersey	Y	100110 FQ	123570 MW		USBLS	5/07
	Edison PMSA, NJ	Y	77540 FQ	109400 MW	131080 TQ	USBLS	5/07
	Newark-Union PMSA, NJ-PA	Y	100910 FQ	124470 MW		USBLS	5/07
	New Mexico	Y	52440 FQ	66840 MW	92150 TQ	USBLS	5/07
	New York	Y	132010 FQ			USBLS	5/07
	Albany-Schenectady-Troy MSA, NY	Y	66610 FQ	83790 MW	98580 TQ	USBLS	5/07
	Buffalo-Niagara Falls MSA, NY	Y	73140 FQ	83810 MW	99150 TQ	USBLS	5/07
	Nassau-Suffolk PMSA, NY	Y	83730 FQ	95560 MW	108980 TQ	USBLS	5/07
	New York-Northern New Jersey-Long Island MSA, NY-NJ-PA	Y	117080 FQ			USBLS	5/07
	Ohio	Y	53730 FQ	71440 MW		USBLS	5/07
	Cleveland-Elyria-Mentor MSA, OH	Y	52120 FQ	60790 MW	88070 TQ	USBLS	5/07
	Dayton MSA, OH	Y	90480 FQ	102050 MW	121790 TQ	USBLS	5/07
	Oklahoma	Y	72730 FQ	93580 MW	110090 TQ	USBLS	5/07
	Oklahoma City MSA, OK	Y	88790 FQ	100950 MW	115920 TQ	USBLS	5/07
	Tulsa MSA, OK	Y	31430 FQ	44310 MW	89670 TQ	USBLS	5/07
	Allentown-Bethlehem-Easton MSA, PA-NJ	Y	28690 FQ	44860 MW	63240 TQ	USBLS	5/07
	Pittsburgh MSA, PA	Y	90270 FQ	123740 MW	145430 TQ	USBLS	5/07
	Rhode Island	Y	81690 FQ	88480 MW	95290 TQ	USBLS	5/07
	Providence-Fall River-Warwick MSA, RI-MA	Y	81360 FQ	88270 MW	95190 TQ	USBLS	5/07
	Columbia MSA, SC	Y	49340 FQ	56150 MW	75200 TQ	USBLS	5/07
	South Dakota	Y	42200 FQ	52619 MW	63340 TQ	SDBLS	7/08-9/08
	Sioux Falls MSA, SD	Y	39862 FQ	46336 MW	56051 TQ	SDBLS	7/08-9/08
	Tennessee	Y	74300 FQ	95970 MW		USBLS	5/07
	Memphis MSA, TN-MS-AR	Y	76190 FQ	98640 MW		USBLS	5/07
	Nashville-Davidson-Murfreesboro MSA, TN	Y	58630 FQ	76870 MW	94630 TQ	USBLS	5/07
	Texas	Y	88890 FQ			USBLS	5/07
	Austin-Round Rock MSA, TX	Y	33540 FQ	44460 MW	85520 TQ	USBLS	5/07
	San Antonio MSA, TX	Y	64670 FQ	90510 MW	102890 TQ	USBLS	5/07
	Virginia	Y	86050 FQ	145190 MW		USBLS	5/07
	Richmond MSA, VA	Y	55140 FQ	74660 MW	87860 TQ	USBLS	5/07
	Virginia Beach-Norfolk-Newport News MSA, VA-NC	Y	48420 FQ	73300 MW	114100 TQ	USBLS	5/07
	Cheyenne MSA, WY	Y	54963 FQ	70231 MW	82976 TQ	WYBLS	9/08
	Puerto Rico	Y	45230 FQ	59940 MW	80610 TQ	USBLS	5/07
	San Juan-Caguas-Guaynabo MSA, PR	Y	36250 FQ	56450 MW	75310 TQ	USBLS	5/07
Airline Reservation Sales Agent	United States	H		9.99 AW		AVJOB05	2009
Airman U.S. Air Force, Active Duty, Pay Grade E-2	United States	M		1569 AW		DOD1	2009
Airman 1st Class U.S. Air Force, Active Duty, Pay Grade E-3	United States	M	1650 LO		1860 HI	DOD1	2009
Airplane Pilot Basic and Theatrical Agreement, Weekly Basis	United States	W	2828 LO			SAG01	7/1/07-6/30/08
Airport Design and Construction Manager	Colorado Springs, CO	M	6194 LO			COSPRS	1/1/09
Airport Maintenance Manager	Colorado Springs, CO	M	5606 LO			COSPRS	1/1/09
Airport Maintenance Worker	Cincinnati, OH	Y	39113 LO		40748 HI	COHSS	10/08
Airport Manager	Livingston County, MI	Y			69781 HI	LCPP	2009
	Bismarck, ND	M			6906 HI	NDLC01	2008
	Cincinnati, OH	Y	67078 LO		90555 HI	COHSS	10/08
Airport Master Electrician	Colorado Springs, CO	M	4025 LO			COSPRS	1/1/09
Airport Operations Agent	Colorado Springs, CO	M	4442 LO			COSPRS	1/1/09

AE	Average entry wage	AW	Average wage paid	FQ	First quartile wage	LO	Lowest wage paid	MTC Median total compensation TCC Total cash compensation
AER	Average entry range	AWR	Average wage range	H	Hourly	LR	Low end range	MW Median wage paid TQ Third quartile wage
AEX	Average experienced wage	AXR	Average experienced range	HI	Highest wage paid	M	Monthly	MWR Median wage range W Weekly
ATC	Average total compensation	D	Daily	HR	High end range	MCC	Median cash compensation	S See annotated source Y Yearly

Occupation/Type/Industry	Location	Per	Low	Mid	High	Source	Date
Airport Security Screener	United States	Y		34934 AW		USATOD04	2008
Alderman	Alton, IL	Y			7606 HI	TEL01	2008
	Yazoo City, MS	Y			18153 HI	MML	2008
Allocator							
Apparel Industry	United States	Y		59000 MW		247FASH	2009
Alternative Education Principal							
Consolidated School District	Hartland, MI	Y			89045 HI	LCPP	2009
Ambulance Driver and Attendant							
Except Emergency Medical Technicians	Alabama	Y	15380 FQ	17730 MW	20650 TQ	USBLS	5/07
Except Emergency Medical Technicians	Birmingham-Hoover MSA, AL	Y	19480 FQ	21420 MW	23210 TQ	USBLS	5/07
Except Emergency Medical Technicians	Arizona	Y	19000 FQ	22200 MW	26850 TQ	USBLS	5/07
Except Emergency Medical Technicians	Phoenix-Mesa-Scottsdale MSA, AZ	Y	21440 FQ	24130 MW	29470 TQ	USBLS	5/07
Except Emergency Medical Technicians	Arkansas	Y	14720 FQ	16090 MW	23500 TQ	USBLS	5/07
Except Emergency Medical Technicians	California	H	9.67 FQ	11.54 MW	14.55 TQ	CABLS	1/08-3/08
Except Emergency Medical Technicians	Bakersfield MSA, CA	H	9.00 FQ	10.21 MW	11.99 TQ	CABLS	1/08-3/08
Except Emergency Medical Technicians	Los Angeles-Long Beach-Glendale PMSA, CA	H	10.67 FQ	13.12 MW	15.95 TQ	CABLS	1/08-3/08
Except Emergency Medical Technicians	Oakland-Fremont-Hayward MSA, CA	H	10.19 FQ	11.37 MW	14.19 TQ	CABLS	1/08-3/08
Except Emergency Medical Technicians	Riverside-San Bernardino-Ontario MSA, CA	H	9.75 FQ	10.61 MW	11.58 TQ	CABLS	1/08-3/08
Except Emergency Medical Technicians	San Diego-Carlsbad-San Marcos MSA, CA	H	8.34 FQ	8.98 MW	11.04 TQ	CABLS	1/08-3/08
Except Emergency Medical Technicians	San Francisco-San Mateo-Redwood PMSA, CA	H	9.65 FQ	12.26 MW	17.06 TQ	CABLS	1/08-3/08
Except Emergency Medical Technicians	Santa Ana-Anaheim-Irvine PMSA, CA	Y	20110 FQ	23610 MW	28820 TQ	USBLS	5/07
Except Emergency Medical Technicians	Colorado	Y	18570 FQ	21540 MW	23800 TQ	USBLS	5/07
Except Emergency Medical Technicians	Denver-Aurora MSA, CO	Y	17300 FQ	19820 MW	23260 TQ	USBLS	5/07
Except Emergency Medical Technicians	Connecticut	H	9.17 AE	11.77 MW		CTBLS	1/08-3/08
Except Emergency Medical Technicians	Hartford-West Hartford-East Hartford MSA, CT	Y	21770 FQ	31390 MW	41360 TQ	USBLS	5/07
Except Emergency Medical Technicians	Delaware	Y	20970 FQ	22860 MW	24800 TQ	USBLS	5/07
Except Emergency Medical Technicians	Washington-Arlington-Alexandria MSA, DC-VA-MD-WV	Y	23930 FQ	28800 MW	36350 TQ	USBLS	5/07
Except Emergency Medical Technicians	Florida	Y	16180 FQ	18380 MW	22240 TQ	USBLS	5/07
Except Emergency Medical Technicians	Fort Lauderdale-Pompano Beach-Deerfield Beach PMSA, FL	Y	16240 FQ	17710 MW	19470 TQ	USBLS	5/07
Except Emergency Medical Technicians	Miami-Fort Lauderdale-Miami Beach MSA, FL	Y	15890 FQ	17800 MW	21100 TQ	USBLS	5/07
Except Emergency Medical Technicians	Tampa-St. Petersburg-Clearwater MSA, FL	Y	15600 FQ	17410 MW	19700 TQ	USBLS	5/07
Except Emergency Medical Technicians	Georgia	Y	13980 FQ	17860 MW	26280 TQ	USBLS	5/07
Except Emergency Medical Technicians	Atlanta-Sandy Springs-Marietta MSA, GA	Y	14000 FQ	17900 MW	23810 TQ	USBLS	5/07
Except Emergency Medical Technicians	Idaho	Y	21930 FQ	36790 MW	67580 TQ	USBLS	5/07
Except Emergency Medical Technicians	Illinois	Y	15140 FQ	17040 MW	21740 TQ	USBLS	5/07
Except Emergency Medical Technicians	Chicago-Naperville-Joliet MSA, IL-IN-WI	Y	15850 FQ	18190 MW	24330 TQ	USBLS	5/07
Except Emergency Medical Technicians	Indiana	Y	16710 FQ	19740 MW	24950 TQ	USBLS	5/07
Except Emergency Medical Technicians	Gary PMSA, IN	Y	17910 FQ	22560 MW	26120 TQ	USBLS	5/07
Except Emergency Medical Technicians	Indianapolis-Carmel MSA, IN	Y	16210 FQ	18230 MW	25300 TQ	USBLS	5/07
Except Emergency Medical Technicians	Iowa	Y	16070 FQ	19970 MW	22680 TQ	USBLS	5/07
Except Emergency Medical Technicians	Kansas	Y	16700 FQ	18060 MW	19460 TQ	USBLS	5/07
Except Emergency Medical Technicians	Kentucky	Y	16845 FQ	19474 MW	26997 TQ	KYBLS	2008
Except Emergency Medical Technicians	Louisiana	H	7.30 FQ	9.27 MW	11.23 TQ	LABLS	1/08-3/08
Except Emergency Medical Technicians	New Orleans-Metairie-Kenner MSA, LA	Y	16830 FQ	18750 MW	22390 TQ	USBLS	5/07
Except Emergency Medical Technicians	Maine	Y	14920 FQ	15950 MW	18500 TQ	USBLS	5/07
Except Emergency Medical Technicians	Maryland	Y		29575 MW		MDBLS	3/08
Except Emergency Medical Technicians	Baltimore-Towson MSA, MD	Y	24970 FQ	29340 MW	43300 TQ	USBLS	5/07
Except Emergency Medical Technicians	Massachusetts	Y	20810 FQ	23260 MW	27250 TQ	USBLS	5/07
Except Emergency Medical Technicians	Boston-Cambridge-Quincy NECTA, MA	Y	21220 FQ	24080 MW	28660 TQ	USBLS	5/07
Except Emergency Medical Technicians	Worcester MSA, MA-CT	Y	21270 FQ	23210 MW	26780 TQ	USBLS	5/07

AE Average entry wage	**AW** Average wage paid	**FQ** First quartile wage	**LO** Lowest wage paid	**MTC** Median total compensation	**TCC** Total cash compensation
AER Average entry range	**AWR** Average wage range	**H** Hourly	**LR** Low end range	**MW** Median wage paid	**TQ** Third quartile wage
AEX Average experienced wage	**AXR** Average experienced range	**HI** Highest wage paid	**M** Monthly	**MWR** Median wage range	**W** Weekly
ATC Average total compensation	**D** Daily	**HR** High end range	**MCC** Median cash compensation	**S** See annotated source	**Y** Yearly

Occupation/Type/Industry	Location	Per	Low	Mid	High	Source	Date
Ambulance Driver and Attendant							
Except Emergency Medical Technicians	Michigan	Y	15160 FQ	21290 MW	26170 TQ	USBLS	5/07
Except Emergency Medical Technicians	Detroit-Warren-Livonia MSA, MI	Y	14730 FQ	15240 MW	22880 TQ	USBLS	5/07
Except Emergency Medical Technicians	Warren-Troy-Farmington Hills PMSA, MI	Y	14730 FQ	15210 MW	22910 TQ	USBLS	5/07
Except Emergency Medical Technicians	Minnesota	Y	15209 FQ	21930 MW	25082 TQ	MNBLS	10/08-12/08
Except Emergency Medical Technicians	Mississippi	Y	13400 FQ	16290 MW	21800 TQ	USBLS	5/07
Except Emergency Medical Technicians	Missouri	Y	21340 FQ	24580 MW	31860 TQ	USBLS	5/07
Except Emergency Medical Technicians	St. Louis MSA, MO-IL	Y	16340 FQ	21040 MW	23960 TQ	USBLS	5/07
Except Emergency Medical Technicians	Montana	Y	19450 FQ	22180 MW	24580 TQ	USBLS	5/07
Except Emergency Medical Technicians	Nebraska	Y	18770 FQ	21690 MW	24580 TQ	USBLS	5/07
Except Emergency Medical Technicians	Nevada	H	11.10 FQ	12.97 MW	14.91 TQ	NVBLS	5/08
Except Emergency Medical Technicians	New Hampshire	H	7.51 AE	11.77 MW	12.88 AEX	NHBLS	6/08
Except Emergency Medical Technicians	New Jersey	Y	20970 FQ	23890 MW	28350 TQ	USBLS	5/07
Except Emergency Medical Technicians	Camden PMSA, NJ	Y	19980 FQ	23630 MW	28380 TQ	USBLS	5/07
Except Emergency Medical Technicians	Edison PMSA, NJ	Y	22110 FQ	24270 MW	27380 TQ	USBLS	5/07
Except Emergency Medical Technicians	Newark-Union PMSA, NJ-PA	Y	22120 FQ	25970 MW	38590 TQ	USBLS	5/07
Except Emergency Medical Technicians	New Mexico	Y	16020 FQ	17340 MW	18630 TQ	USBLS	5/07
Except Emergency Medical Technicians	New York	Y	18930 FQ	22770 MW	27020 TQ	USBLS	5/07
Except Emergency Medical Technicians	Nassau-Suffolk PMSA, NY	Y	20960 FQ	22860 MW	25290 TQ	USBLS	5/07
Except Emergency Medical Technicians	New York-Northern New Jersey-Long Island MSA, NY-NJ-PA	Y	20240 FQ	23530 MW	27690 TQ	USBLS	5/07
Except Emergency Medical Technicians	North Carolina	Y	19090 FQ	22550 MW	26650 TQ	USBLS	5/07
Except Emergency Medical Technicians	Charlotte-Gastonia-Concord MSA, NC-SC	Y	21480 FQ	23890 MW	27170 TQ	USBLS	5/07
Except Emergency Medical Technicians	Raleigh-Cary MSA, NC	Y	22690 FQ	25360 MW	27590 TQ	USBLS	5/07
Except Emergency Medical Technicians	North Dakota	Y	17260 FQ	21170 MW	24900 TQ	USBLS	5/07
Except Emergency Medical Technicians	Ohio	Y	16720 FQ	18430 MW	20910 TQ	USBLS	5/07
Except Emergency Medical Technicians	Cincinnati-Middletown MSA, OH-KY-IN	Y	17310 FQ	18730 MW	20200 TQ	USBLS	5/07
Except Emergency Medical Technicians	Cleveland-Elyria-Mentor MSA, OH	Y	17380 FQ	19410 MW	21870 TQ	USBLS	5/07
Except Emergency Medical Technicians	Columbus MSA, OH	Y	18100 FQ	20030 MW	22200 TQ	USBLS	5/07
Except Emergency Medical Technicians	Dayton MSA, OH	Y	16100 FQ	17360 MW	18610 TQ	USBLS	5/07
Except Emergency Medical Technicians	Oklahoma	Y	16460 FQ	18860 MW	22480 TQ	USBLS	5/07
Except Emergency Medical Technicians	Tulsa MSA, OK	Y	17300 FQ	18890 MW	22710 TQ	USBLS	5/07
Except Emergency Medical Technicians	Oregon	H	9.59 FQ	11.10 MW	13.18 TQ	ORBLS	5/08
Except Emergency Medical Technicians	Pennsylvania	Y	15750 FQ	18500 MW	23140 TQ	USBLS	5/07
Except Emergency Medical Technicians	Allentown-Bethlehem-Easton MSA, PA-NJ	Y	16900 FQ	21270 MW	26230 TQ	USBLS	5/07
Except Emergency Medical Technicians	Erie MSA, PA	Y	16750 FQ	18200 MW	19620 TQ	USBLS	5/07
Except Emergency Medical Technicians	Philadelphia-Camden-Wilmington MSA, PA-NJ-DE-MD	Y	18620 FQ	22190 MW	25340 TQ	USBLS	5/07
Except Emergency Medical Technicians	Pittsburgh MSA, PA	Y	17070 FQ	19920 MW	31040 TQ	USBLS	5/07
Except Emergency Medical Technicians	Rhode Island	Y	20880 FQ	22710 MW	24640 TQ	USBLS	5/07
Except Emergency Medical Technicians	Providence-Fall River-Warwick MSA, RI-MA	Y	20950 FQ	22860 MW	24820 TQ	USBLS	5/07
Except Emergency Medical Technicians	South Carolina	Y	16780 FQ	18620 MW	21580 TQ	USBLS	5/07
Except Emergency Medical Technicians	Charleston-North Charleston MSA, SC	Y	17320 FQ	18800 MW	22620 TQ	USBLS	5/07
Except Emergency Medical Technicians	Columbia MSA, SC	Y	16870 FQ	18630 MW	21550 TQ	USBLS	5/07
Except Emergency Medical Technicians	Tennessee	Y	21550 FQ	24080 MW	27900 TQ	USBLS	5/07
Except Emergency Medical Technicians	Memphis MSA, TN-MS-AR	Y	16050 FQ	21990 MW	25750 TQ	USBLS	5/07
Except Emergency Medical Technicians	Nashville-Davidson-Murfreesboro MSA, TN	Y	21260 FQ	23720 MW	26520 TQ	USBLS	5/07
Except Emergency Medical Technicians	Texas	Y	17540 FQ	21050 MW	24550 TQ	USBLS	5/07
Except Emergency Medical Technicians	Dallas-Fort Worth-Arlington MSA, TX	Y	21580 FQ	27300 MW	31270 TQ	USBLS	5/07
Except Emergency Medical Technicians	Houston-Sugar Land-Baytown MSA, TX	Y	18830 FQ	21090 MW	23300 TQ	USBLS	5/07
Except Emergency Medical Technicians	San Antonio MSA, TX	Y	16310 FQ	18890 MW	22590 TQ	USBLS	5/07
Except Emergency Medical Technicians	Vermont	Y	18350 FQ	19760 MW	21630 TQ	USBLS	5/07
Except Emergency Medical Technicians	Virginia	Y	14910 FQ	20040 MW	23940 TQ	USBLS	5/07
Except Emergency Medical Technicians	Washington	H	9.96 FQ	11.45 MW	13.45 TQ	WABLS	3/08
Except Emergency Medical Technicians	Seattle-Tacoma-Bellevue MSA, WA	Y	22720 FQ	25810 MW	29610 TQ	USBLS	5/07
Except Emergency Medical Technicians	West Virginia	Y	14105 FQ	15475 MW	17838 TQ	WVBLS	7/08-9/08
Except Emergency Medical Technicians	Wisconsin	Y	15770 FQ	20280 MW	25130 TQ	USBLS	5/07

AE	Average entry wage	AW	Average wage paid	FQ	First quartile wage
AER	Average entry range	AWR	Average wage range	H	Hourly
AEX	Average experienced wage	AXR	Average experienced range	HI	Highest wage paid
ATC	Average total compensation	D	Daily	HR	High end range

LO	Lowest wage paid	MTC	Median total compensation	TCC	Total cash compensation
LR	Low end range	MW	Median wage paid	TQ	Third quartile wage
M	Monthly	MWR	Median wage range	W	Weekly
MCC	Median cash compensation	S	See annotated source	Y	Yearly

Occupation/Type/Industry	Location	Per	Low	Mid	High	Source	Date
Ambulance Driver and Attendant							
Except Emergency Medical Technicians	Milwaukee-Waukesha-West Allis MSA, WI	Y	18990 FQ	21030 MW	23160 TQ	USBLS	5/07
Except Emergency Medical Technicians	Wyoming	Y	12898 FQ	14104 MW	15311 TQ	WYBLS	9/08
Except Emergency Medical Technicians	Puerto Rico	Y	12270 FQ	13440 MW	14610 TQ	USBLS	5/07
Except Emergency Medical Technicians	San Juan-Caguas-Guaynabo MSA, PR	Y	12320 FQ	13480 MW	14640 TQ	USBLS	5/07
Amusement and Recreation Attendant							
	Alabama	Y	12850 FQ	14500 MW	17560 TQ	USBLS	5/07
	Birmingham-Hoover MSA, AL	Y	13110 FQ	15120 MW	18370 TQ	USBLS	5/07
	Alaska	Y	16930 FQ	18390 MW	20130 TQ	USBLS	5/07
	Anchorage MSA, AK	Y	16810 FQ	18000 MW	19430 TQ	USBLS	5/07
	Arizona	Y	15130 FQ	17010 MW	20330 TQ	USBLS	5/07
	Phoenix-Mesa-Scottsdale MSA, AZ	Y	15200 FQ	17290 MW	20710 TQ	USBLS	5/07
	Tucson MSA, AZ	Y	14810 FQ	15640 MW	17540 TQ	USBLS	5/07
	Arkansas	Y	14450 FQ	15770 MW	18580 TQ	USBLS	5/07
	Little Rock-North Little Rock MSA, AR	Y	14190 FQ	15230 MW	17980 TQ	USBLS	5/07
	California	H	8.10 FQ	8.91 MW	9.90 TQ	CABLS	1/08-3/08
	Fresno MSA, CA	H	8.00 FQ	8.47 MW	9.21 TQ	CABLS	1/08-3/08
	Los Angeles-Long Beach-Glendale PMSA, CA	H	8.11 FQ	8.81 MW	9.58 TQ	CABLS	1/08-3/08
	Oakland-Fremont-Hayward MSA, CA	H	8.16 FQ	8.98 MW	10.30 TQ	CABLS	1/08-3/08
	Oxnard-Thousand Oaks-Ventura MSA, CA	H	8.00 FQ	8.53 MW	9.55 TQ	CABLS	1/08-3/08
	Riverside-San Bernardino-Ontario MSA, CA	H	8.00 FQ	8.52 MW	9.42 TQ	CABLS	1/08-3/08
	Sacramento-Arden Arcade-Roseville MSA, CA	H	8.07 FQ	8.76 MW	9.53 TQ	CABLS	1/08-3/08
	San Diego-Carlsbad-San Marcos MSA, CA	H	8.00 FQ	8.74 MW	9.72 TQ	CABLS	1/08-3/08
	San Francisco-San Mateo-Redwood PMSA, CA	H	8.74 FQ	9.82 MW	11.39 TQ	CABLS	1/08-3/08
	San Jose-Sunnyvale-Santa Clara MSA, CA	H	8.05 FQ	9.13 MW	10.77 TQ	CABLS	1/08-3/08
	Santa Ana-Anaheim-Irvine PMSA, CA	Y	17380 FQ	19390 MW	21650 TQ	USBLS	5/07
	Colorado	Y	15500 FQ	17840 MW	21150 TQ	USBLS	5/07
	Denver-Aurora MSA, CO	Y	15470 FQ	17330 MW	19800 TQ	USBLS	5/07
	Connecticut	H	8.55 AE	9.73 MW		CTBLS	1/08-3/08
	Bridgeport-Stamford-Norwalk MSA, CT	Y	18610 FQ	22230 MW	27970 TQ	USBLS	5/07
	Hartford-West Hartford-East Hartford MSA, CT	Y	16930 FQ	18660 MW	24290 TQ	USBLS	5/07
	Delaware	Y	15760 FQ	18940 MW	23730 TQ	USBLS	5/07
	Wilmington PMSA, DE-MD-NJ	Y	15400 FQ	18500 MW	23260 TQ	USBLS	5/07
	District of Columbia	Y	15680 FQ	19270 MW	35140 TQ	USBLS	5/07
	Washington-Arlington-Alexandria MSA, DC-VA-MD-WV	Y	14120 FQ	15930 MW	19440 TQ	USBLS	5/07
	Florida	Y	14790 FQ	15960 MW	19440 TQ	USBLS	5/07
	Cape Coral-Fort Myers MSA, FL	Y	14920 FQ	16010 MW	19470 TQ	USBLS	5/07
	Fort Lauderdale-Pompano Beach-Deerfield Beach PMSA, FL	Y	14930 FQ	17390 MW	23640 TQ	USBLS	5/07
	Jacksonville MSA, FL	Y	14730 FQ	16110 MW	18860 TQ	USBLS	5/07
	Lakeland MSA, FL	Y	14550 FQ	15260 MW	16130 TQ	USBLS	5/07
	Miami-Fort Lauderdale-Miami Beach MSA, FL	Y	15050 FQ	17560 MW	22980 TQ	USBLS	5/07
	Orlando-Kissimmee MSA, FL	Y	14830 FQ	15880 MW	19130 TQ	USBLS	5/07
	Tampa-St. Petersburg-Clearwater MSA, FL	Y	14510 FQ	15220 MW	17130 TQ	USBLS	5/07
	West Palm Beach-Boca Raton-Boynton Beach PMSA, FL	Y	15010 FQ	16850 MW	21960 TQ	USBLS	5/07
	Georgia	Y	12970 FQ	14860 MW	18250 TQ	USBLS	5/07
	Atlanta-Sandy Springs-Marietta MSA, GA	Y	12900 FQ	14790 MW	18430 TQ	USBLS	5/07

AE Average entry wage	**AW** Average wage paid	**FQ** First quartile wage	**LO** Lowest wage paid	**MTC** Median total compensation	**TCC** Total cash compensation
AER Average entry range	**AWR** Average wage range	**H** Hourly	**LR** Low end range	**MW** Median wage paid	**TQ** Third quartile wage
AEX Average experienced wage	**AXR** Average experienced range	**HI** Highest wage paid	**M** Monthly	**MWR** Median wage range	**W** Weekly
ATC Average total compensation	**D** Daily	**HR** High end range	**MCC** Median cash compensation	**S** See annotated source	**Y** Yearly

Occupation/Type/Industry	Location	Per	Low	Mid	High	Source	Date
Amusement and Recreation Attendant							
	Hawaii	Y	17490 FQ	22400 MW	27530 TQ	USBLS	5/07
	Honolulu MSA, HI	Y	15530 FQ	17410 MW	22120 TQ	USBLS	5/07
	Idaho	Y	13910 FQ	17800 MW	24310 TQ	USBLS	5/07
	Boise City-Nampa MSA, ID	Y	15940 FQ	21060 MW	29570 TQ	USBLS	5/07
	Illinois	Y	15390 FQ	17530 MW	21240 TQ	USBLS	5/07
	Chicago-Naperville-Joliet MSA, IL-IN-WI	Y	15460 FQ	17670 MW	21260 TQ	USBLS	5/07
	Indiana	Y	13320 FQ	15480 MW	18370 TQ	USBLS	5/07
	Elkhart-Goshen MSA, IN	Y	12330 FQ	13290 MW	14240 TQ	USBLS	5/07
	Gary PMSA, IN	Y	12990 FQ	14980 MW	18510 TQ	USBLS	5/07
	Indianapolis-Carmel MSA, IN	Y	13470 FQ	15690 MW	18400 TQ	USBLS	5/07
	Iowa	Y	14150 FQ	15430 MW	17730 TQ	USBLS	5/07
	Cedar Rapids MSA, IA	Y	13920 FQ	14950 MW	16890 TQ	USBLS	5/07
	Des Moines-West Des Moines MSA, IA	Y	14140 FQ	15430 MW	18040 TQ	USBLS	5/07
	Dubuque MSA, IA	Y	14200 FQ	15450 MW	17110 TQ	USBLS	5/07
	Kansas	Y	13260 FQ	15410 MW	18730 TQ	USBLS	5/07
	Wichita MSA, KS	Y	15160 FQ	19200 MW	22240 TQ	USBLS	5/07
	Kentucky	Y	13650 FQ	15772 MW	18736 TQ	KYBLS	2008
	Lexington-Fayette MSA, KY	Y	13330 FQ	15740 MW	18960 TQ	USBLS	5/07
	Louisville-Jefferson County MSA, KY-IN	Y	13050 FQ	14860 MW	17090 TQ	USBLS	5/07
	Louisiana	H	6.04 FQ	6.70 MW	7.48 TQ	LABLS	1/08-3/08
	Baton Rouge MSA, LA	Y	12470 FQ	13630 MW	14800 TQ	USBLS	5/07
	Houma-Bayou Cane-Thibodaux MSA, LA	Y	12260 FQ	13750 MW	15250 TQ	USBLS	5/07
	Lake Charles MSA, LA	Y	12560 FQ	13920 MW	15530 TQ	USBLS	5/07
	New Orleans-Metairie-Kenner MSA, LA	Y	12830 FQ	14380 MW	17040 TQ	USBLS	5/07
	Maine	Y	15740 FQ	17790 MW	20840 TQ	USBLS	5/07
	Portland-South Portland-Biddeford MSA, ME	Y	15180 FQ	16890 MW	19200 TQ	USBLS	5/07
	Maryland	Y		16300 MW		MDBLS	3/08
	Baltimore-Towson MSA, MD	Y	14300 FQ	15530 MW	18910 TQ	USBLS	5/07
	Bethesda-Gaithersburg-Frederick PMSA, MD	Y	14620 FQ	17060 MW	19450 TQ	USBLS	5/07
	Massachusetts	Y	16660 FQ	19270 MW	24300 TQ	USBLS	5/07
	Boston-Cambridge-Quincy NECTA, MA	Y	17970 FQ	21580 MW	26820 TQ	USBLS	5/07
	Worcester MSA, MA-CT	Y	16330 FQ	18340 MW	22690 TQ	USBLS	5/07
	Michigan	Y	15380 FQ	17010 MW	20170 TQ	USBLS	5/07
	Detroit-Warren-Livonia MSA, MI	Y	15620 FQ	17490 MW	20270 TQ	USBLS	5/07
	Flint MSA, MI	Y	15150 FQ	15660 MW	17610 TQ	USBLS	5/07
	Grand Rapids-Wyoming MSA, MI	Y	15920 FQ	17690 MW	20910 TQ	USBLS	5/07
	Warren-Troy-Farmington Hills PMSA, MI	Y	15720 FQ	17720 MW	20690 TQ	USBLS	5/07
	Minnesota	Y	15788 FQ	18036 MW	20514 TQ	MNBLS	10/08-12/08
	Duluth-Superior MSA, MN-WI	Y	14993 FQ	16342 MW	21058 TQ	MNBLS	10/08-12/08
	Minneapolis-Saint Paul MSA, MN-WI	Y	16342 FQ	18485 MW	20786 TQ	MNBLS	10/08-12/08
	Rochester MSA, MN	Y	16001 FQ	17609 MW	19935 TQ	MNBLS	10/08-12/08
	Mississippi	Y	13640 FQ	16510 MW	23680 TQ	USBLS	5/07
	Jackson MSA, MS	Y	13380 FQ	15650 MW	21690 TQ	USBLS	5/07
	Missouri	Y	14770 FQ	16570 MW	20330 TQ	USBLS	5/07
	Kansas City MSA, MO-KS	Y	14560 FQ	16800 MW	21400 TQ	USBLS	5/07
	St. Louis MSA, MO-IL	Y	14890 FQ	16410 MW	19220 TQ	USBLS	5/07
	Montana	Y	14160 FQ	15640 MW	21010 TQ	USBLS	5/07
	Billings MSA, MT	Y	14100 FQ	15420 MW	21240 TQ	USBLS	5/07
	Great Falls MSA, MT	Y	13890 FQ	14990 MW	16230 TQ	USBLS	5/07
	Nebraska	Y	12980 FQ	14780 MW	17400 TQ	USBLS	5/07
	Omaha-Council Bluffs MSA, NE-IA	Y	13270 FQ	15160 MW	17750 TQ	USBLS	5/07
	Las Vegas-Paradise MSA, NV	H	6.79 FQ	8.17 MW	10.12 TQ	NVBLS	5/08
	New Hampshire	H	6.92 AE	8.81 MW	10.49 AEX	NHBLS	6/08
	Manchester MSA, NH	Y	12670 FQ	14010 MW	16550 TQ	USBLS	5/07
	Nashua NECTA, NH-MA	Y	15480 FQ	17350 MW	19440 TQ	USBLS	5/07
	Rochester-Dover MSA, NH-ME	Y	13080 FQ	14800 MW	20580 TQ	USBLS	5/07
	New Jersey	Y	15770 FQ	17730 MW	21410 TQ	USBLS	5/07

AE	Average entry wage	AW	Average wage paid	FQ	First quartile wage	LO	Lowest wage paid	MTC	Median total compensation	TCC	Total cash compensation
AER	Average entry range	AWR	Average wage range	H	Hourly	LR	Low end range	MW	Median wage paid	TQ	Third quartile wage
AEX	Average experienced wage	AXR	Average experienced range	HI	Highest wage paid	M	Monthly	MWR	Median wage range	W	Weekly
ATC	Average total compensation	D	Daily	HR	High end range	MCC	Median cash compensation	S	See annotated source	Y	Yearly

Occupation/Type/Industry	Location	Per	Low	Mid	High	Source	Date
Amusement and Recreation Attendant	Camden PMSA, NJ	Y	15900 FQ	17960 MW	21270 TQ	USBLS	5/07
	Edison PMSA, NJ	Y	15580 FQ	17260 MW	20740 TQ	USBLS	5/07
	Newark-Union PMSA, NJ-PA	Y	16140 FQ	18250 MW	22810 TQ	USBLS	5/07
	New Mexico	Y	14720 FQ	18340 MW	22190 TQ	USBLS	5/07
	Albuquerque MSA, NM	Y	13730 FQ	16970 MW	22020 TQ	USBLS	5/07
	Las Cruces MSA, NM	Y	16910 FQ	18390 MW	19930 TQ	USBLS	5/07
	New York	Y	15510 FQ	17490 MW	21290 TQ	USBLS	5/07
	Albany-Schenectady-Troy MSA, NY	Y	15400 FQ	17080 MW	19140 TQ	USBLS	5/07
	Binghamton MSA, NY	Y	14920 FQ	15460 MW	17340 TQ	USBLS	5/07
	Buffalo-Niagara Falls MSA, NY	Y	15620 FQ	17680 MW	21250 TQ	USBLS	5/07
	Nassau-Suffolk PMSA, NY	Y	16500 FQ	18650 MW	22170 TQ	USBLS	5/07
	New York-Northern New Jersey-Long Island MSA, NY-NJ-PA	Y	15850 FQ	18060 MW	22150 TQ	USBLS	5/07
	North Carolina	Y	14240 FQ	15820 MW	18500 TQ	USBLS	5/07
	Charlotte-Gastonia-Concord MSA, NC-SC	Y	14340 FQ	16630 MW	19540 TQ	USBLS	5/07
	Raleigh-Cary MSA, NC	Y	15470 FQ	16820 MW	18250 TQ	USBLS	5/07
	North Dakota	Y	13050 FQ	15170 MW	17860 TQ	USBLS	5/07
	Fargo MSA, ND-MN	Y	14860 FQ	16830 MW	18600 TQ	USBLS	5/07
	Ohio	Y	14850 FQ	15610 MW	18410 TQ	USBLS	5/07
	Canton-Massillon MSA, OH	Y	14920 FQ	15680 MW	17240 TQ	USBLS	5/07
	Cincinnati-Middletown MSA, OH-KY-IN	Y	14720 FQ	15290 MW	16480 TQ	USBLS	5/07
	Cleveland-Elyria-Mentor MSA, OH	Y	14810 FQ	15910 MW	19630 TQ	USBLS	5/07
	Columbus MSA, OH	Y	15390 FQ	17120 MW	19590 TQ	USBLS	5/07
	Dayton MSA, OH	Y	15300 FQ	16570 MW	20260 TQ	USBLS	5/07
	Mansfield MSA, OH	Y	14530 FQ	14800 MW	15080 TQ	USBLS	5/07
	Oklahoma	Y	13020 FQ	14830 MW	19200 TQ	USBLS	5/07
	Oklahoma City MSA, OK	Y	12670 FQ	14010 MW	15800 TQ	USBLS	5/07
	Tulsa MSA, OK	Y	13190 FQ	15390 MW	20350 TQ	USBLS	5/07
	Oregon	H	8.57 FQ	9.15 MW	10.22 TQ	ORBLS	5/08
	Medford MSA, OR	Y	16710 FQ	17780 MW	18860 TQ	USBLS	5/07
	Portland-Vancouver-Beaverton MSA, OR-WA	Y	17430 FQ	18600 MW	20580 TQ	USBLS	5/07
	Pennsylvania	Y	14520 FQ	15730 MW	18790 TQ	USBLS	5/07
	Allentown-Bethlehem-Easton MSA, PA-NJ	Y	14810 FQ	16250 MW	19950 TQ	USBLS	5/07
	Philadelphia-Camden-Wilmington MSA, PA-NJ-DE-MD	Y	15220 FQ	17480 MW	20910 TQ	USBLS	5/07
	Pittsburgh MSA, PA	Y	14340 FQ	15210 MW	17540 TQ	USBLS	5/07
	Rhode Island	Y	17360 FQ	19930 MW	23030 TQ	USBLS	5/07
	Providence-Fall River-Warwick MSA, RI-MA	Y	17350 FQ	19730 MW	23080 TQ	USBLS	5/07
	South Carolina	Y	13270 FQ	15390 MW	18560 TQ	USBLS	5/07
	Charleston-North Charleston MSA, SC	Y	13900 FQ	16410 MW	19740 TQ	USBLS	5/07
	Columbia MSA, SC	Y	13590 FQ	16110 MW	18300 TQ	USBLS	5/07
	South Dakota	Y	14231 FQ	16663 MW	19597 TQ	SDBLS	7/08-9/08
	Sioux Falls MSA, SD	Y	14313 FQ	17121 MW	22352 TQ	SDBLS	7/08-9/08
	Tennessee	Y	13600 FQ	16440 MW	19720 TQ	USBLS	5/07
	Memphis MSA, TN-MS-AR	Y	13190 FQ	15280 MW	18310 TQ	USBLS	5/07
	Nashville-Davidson-Murfreesboro MSA, TN	Y	17050 FQ	19220 MW	24910 TQ	USBLS	5/07
	Texas	Y	13120 FQ	15080 MW	19610 TQ	USBLS	5/07
	Austin-Round Rock MSA, TX	Y	13660 FQ	16320 MW	20630 TQ	USBLS	5/07
	Beaumont-Port Arthur MSA, TX	Y	13310 FQ	15590 MW	18530 TQ	USBLS	5/07
	Dallas-Fort Worth-Arlington MSA, TX	Y	13330 FQ	15600 MW	21070 TQ	USBLS	5/07
	El Paso MSA, TX	Y	12370 FQ	13760 MW	15160 TQ	USBLS	5/07
	Houston-Sugar Land-Baytown MSA, TX	Y	13120 FQ	15070 MW	18910 TQ	USBLS	5/07
	San Antonio MSA, TX	Y	12830 FQ	14470 MW	16440 TQ	USBLS	5/07
	Utah	Y	13380 FQ	15540 MW	18840 TQ	USBLS	5/07
	Logan MSA, UT-ID	Y	13370 FQ	15380 MW	17810 TQ	USBLS	5/07
	Salt Lake City MSA, UT	Y	14300 FQ	16970 MW	20130 TQ	USBLS	5/07

AE	Average entry wage	AW	Average wage paid	FQ	First quartile wage
AER	Average entry range	AWR	Average wage range	H	Hourly
AEX	Average experienced wage	AXR	Average experienced range	HI	Highest wage paid
ATC	Average total compensation	D	Daily	HR	High end range

LO	Lowest wage paid	MTC	Median total compensation
LR	Low end range	MW	Median wage paid
M	Monthly	MWR	Median wage range
MCC	Median cash compensation	S	See annotated source

TCC	Total cash compensation
TQ	Third quartile wage
W	Weekly
Y	Yearly

Occupation/Type/Industry	Location	Per	Low	Mid	High	Source	Date
Amusement and Recreation Attendant	Vermont	Y	17240 FQ	19000 MW	21960 TQ	USBLS	5/07
	Burlington-South Burlington MSA, VT	Y	17840 FQ	20350 MW	23910 TQ	USBLS	5/07
	Virginia	Y	13270 FQ	15390 MW	18640 TQ	USBLS	5/07
	Richmond MSA, VA	Y	14430 FQ	16620 MW	18790 TQ	USBLS	5/07
	Virginia Beach-Norfolk-Newport News MSA, VA-NC	Y	12870 FQ	14380 MW	16700 TQ	USBLS	5/07
	Washington	H	8.58 FQ	9.16 MW	10.19 TQ	WABLS	3/08
	Seattle-Tacoma-Bellevue MSA, WA	Y	17680 FQ	18970 MW	21670 TQ	USBLS	5/07
	West Virginia	Y	14103 FQ	15283 MW	18847 TQ	WVBLS	7/08-9/08
	Charleston MSA, WV	Y	13410 FQ	14380 MW	16020 TQ	USBLS	5/07
	Wisconsin	Y	14930 FQ	16690 MW	19680 TQ	USBLS	5/07
	Milwaukee-Waukesha-West Allis MSA, WI	Y	15010 FQ	17200 MW	19470 TQ	USBLS	5/07
	Wyoming	Y	16303 FQ	19840 MW	26990 TQ	WYBLS	9/08
	Cheyenne MSA, WY	Y	13486 FQ	15515 MW	17878 TQ	WYBLS	9/08
	Puerto Rico	Y	12550 FQ	13960 MW	15490 TQ	USBLS	5/07
	San Juan-Caguas-Guaynabo MSA, PR	Y	12560 FQ	13980 MW	15560 TQ	USBLS	5/07
	Virgin Islands	Y	16420 FQ	18820 MW	22500 TQ	USBLS	5/07
	Guam	Y	12690 FQ	14100 MW	15780 TQ	USBLS	5/07
Amusement Ride and Game Inspector State Government	Ohio	H	16.35 LO		21.77 HI	ODAS	2008
Analytical Laboratory Specialist State Government	Minnesota	Y	39087 LO		57336 HI	AFT02	3/1/08
Anesthesiologist	Sacramento-Arden Arcade-Roseville MSA, CA	H	56.88 FQ	63.06 MW		CABLS	1/08-3/08
	Connecticut	H	69.40 AE	93.16 AW		CTBLS	1/08-3/08
	Idaho	Y	133920 FQ			USBLS	5/07
	Illinois	Y	122210 FQ			USBLS	5/07
	Champaign-Urbana MSA, IL	Y	135950 FQ			USBLS	5/07
	Chicago-Naperville-Joliet MSA, IL-IN-WI	Y	63710 FQ			USBLS	5/07
	Louisiana	Y		184865 AW		LABLS	1/08-3/08
	Baton Rouge MSA, LA	Y	127310 FQ			USBLS	5/07
	Warren-Troy-Farmington Hills PMSA, MI	Y	139660 FQ			USBLS	5/07
	Minnesota	Y		200927 AW		MNBLS	10/08-12/08
	Minneapolis-Saint Paul MSA, MN-WI	Y		201597 AW		MNBLS	10/08-12/08
	Mississippi	Y	118700 FQ			USBLS	5/07
	Jackson MSA, MS	Y	109720 FQ	138730 MW		USBLS	5/07
	Nebraska	Y	115390 FQ			USBLS	5/07
	Omaha-Council Bluffs MSA, NE-IA	Y	39160 FQ	50940 MW	114340 TQ	USBLS	5/07
	New Mexico	Y	113320 FQ			USBLS	5/07
	Albuquerque MSA, NM	Y	122460 FQ			USBLS	5/07
	North Carolina	Y	139390 FQ			USBLS	5/07
	Oklahoma	Y	137660 FQ			USBLS	5/07
	Oklahoma City MSA, OK	Y	142460 FQ			USBLS	5/07
	Tulsa MSA, OK	Y	139310 FQ			USBLS	5/07
	Pennsylvania	Y	122360 FQ			USBLS	5/07
	Allentown-Bethlehem-Easton MSA, PA-NJ	Y	134090 FQ	145580 MW		USBLS	5/07
	Philadelphia-Camden-Wilmington MSA, PA-NJ-DE-MD	Y	132830 FQ			USBLS	5/07
	Pittsburgh MSA, PA	Y	124130 FQ			USBLS	5/07
	South Dakota	Y	140935 FQ			SDBLS	7/08-9/08
	Sioux Falls MSA, SD	Y	136307 FQ			SDBLS	7/08-9/08
	Dallas-Fort Worth-Arlington MSA, TX	Y	144470 FQ			USBLS	5/07
	Houston-Sugar Land-Baytown MSA, TX	Y	50140 FQ			USBLS	5/07
	Burlington-South Burlington MSA, VT	Y	143630 FQ			USBLS	5/07

AE Average entry wage	**AW** Average wage paid	**FQ** First quartile wage	**LO** Lowest wage paid	**MTC** Median total compensation	**TCC** Total cash compensation
AER Average entry range	**AWR** Average wage range	**H** Hourly	**LR** Low end range	**MW** Median wage paid	**TQ** Third quartile wage
AEX Average experienced wage	**AXR** Average experienced range	**HI** Highest wage paid	**M** Monthly	**MWR** Median wage range	**W** Weekly
ATC Average total compensation	**D** Daily	**HR** High end range	**MCC** Median cash compensation	**S** See annotated source	**Y** Yearly

Occupation/Type/Industry	Location	Per	Low	Mid	High	Source	Date
Anesthesiologist	West Virginia	Y		200505 AW		WVBLS	7/08-9/08
	Wyoming	Y		182066 AW		WYBLS	9/08
	Puerto Rico	Y	20690 FQ	51820 MW		USBLS	5/07
	San Juan-Caguas-Guaynabo MSA, PR	Y	139270 FQ			USBLS	5/07
Animal Behaviorist	United States	Y		35000-90000 AWR		NCBSC	2006
Animal Breeder	California	H	17.39 FQ	18.81 MW	20.21 TQ	CABLS	1/08-3/08
	Florida	Y	18070 FQ	22870 MW	51550 TQ	USBLS	5/07
	Georgia	Y	19820 FQ	22160 MW	33040 TQ	USBLS	5/07
	Illinois	Y	16520 FQ	18490 MW	20510 TQ	USBLS	5/07
	Indiana	Y	21020 FQ	23000 MW	25320 TQ	USBLS	5/07
	Iowa	Y	19770 FQ	22960 MW	32180 TQ	USBLS	5/07
	Kentucky	Y	21009 FQ	23001 MW	24996 TQ	KYBLS	2008
	Maryland	Y		33900 MW		MDBLS	3/08
	Missouri	Y	19140 FQ	22800 MW	40840 TQ	USBLS	5/07
	Ohio	Y	23880 FQ	30910 MW	40380 TQ	USBLS	5/07
	Oklahoma	Y	20610 FQ	27380 MW	36130 TQ	USBLS	5/07
	Pennsylvania	Y	19270 FQ	26420 MW	39650 TQ	USBLS	5/07
	Texas	Y	31190 FQ	34690 MW	37870 TQ	USBLS	5/07
	Virginia	Y	22870 FQ	27450 MW	33120 TQ	USBLS	5/07
	Wisconsin	Y	24330 FQ	33650 MW	47030 TQ	USBLS	5/07
Animal Control Director	Vidalia, GA	Y	17160 LO		24586 HI	GACTY01	2008
	Livingston County, MI	Y			65926 HI	LCPP	2009
Animal Control Worker	Alabama	Y	21150 FQ	25750 MW	31570 TQ	USBLS	5/07
	Birmingham-Hoover MSA, AL	Y	22380 FQ	25680 MW	31230 TQ	USBLS	5/07
	Alaska	Y	36400 FQ	42600 MW	48920 TQ	USBLS	5/07
	Arizona	Y	26930 FQ	30170 MW	34730 TQ	USBLS	5/07
	Phoenix-Mesa-Scottsdale MSA, AZ	Y	28030 FQ	30790 MW	35120 TQ	USBLS	5/07
	Arkansas	Y	20610 FQ	24630 MW	29390 TQ	USBLS	5/07
	Little Rock-North Little Rock MSA, AR	Y	22290 FQ	25470 MW	29890 TQ	USBLS	5/07
	California	H	16.57 FQ	21.38 MW	24.50 TQ	CABLS	1/08-3/08
	Oakland-Fremont-Hayward MSA, CA	H	21.44 FQ	23.28 MW	25.13 TQ	CABLS	1/08-3/08
	Riverside-San Bernardino-Ontario MSA, CA	H	14.90 FQ	17.86 MW	21.89 TQ	CABLS	1/08-3/08
	Sacramento-Arden Arcade-Roseville MSA, CA	H	16.80 FQ	18.90 MW	21.70 TQ	CABLS	1/08-3/08
	San Diego-Carlsbad-San Marcos MSA, CA	H	18.44 FQ	21.51 MW	23.80 TQ	CABLS	1/08-3/08
	San Francisco-San Mateo-Redwood PMSA, CA	H	18.54 FQ	21.88 MW	24.36 TQ	CABLS	1/08-3/08
	San Jose-Sunnyvale-Santa Clara MSA, CA	H	20.83 FQ	24.93 MW	29.15 TQ	CABLS	1/08-3/08
	Santa Ana-Anaheim-Irvine PMSA, CA	Y	37130 FQ	44950 MW	50130 TQ	USBLS	5/07
	Colorado	Y	31140 FQ	36940 MW	43570 TQ	USBLS	5/07
	Denver-Aurora MSA, CO	Y	33990 FQ	39460 MW	45440 TQ	USBLS	5/07
	Connecticut	H	9.85 AE	15.01 MW		CTBLS	1/08-3/08
	Bridgeport-Stamford-Norwalk MSA, CT	Y	20470 FQ	23860 MW	36010 TQ	USBLS	5/07
	Hartford-West Hartford-East Hartford MSA, CT	Y	28940 FQ	39390 MW	46340 TQ	USBLS	5/07
	New Haven MSA, CT	Y	20520 FQ	28440 MW	37510 TQ	USBLS	5/07
	Washington-Arlington-Alexandria MSA, DC-VA-MD-WV	Y	30070 FQ	37630 MW	47970 TQ	USBLS	5/07
	Florida	Y	25080 FQ	30020 MW	36700 TQ	USBLS	5/07
	Fort Lauderdale-Pompano Beach-Deerfield Beach PMSA, FL	Y	31970 FQ	36840 MW	41600 TQ	USBLS	5/07
	Jacksonville MSA, FL	Y	22720 FQ	25890 MW	29400 TQ	USBLS	5/07
	Miami-Fort Lauderdale-Miami Beach MSA, FL	Y	28980 FQ	36650 MW	43930 TQ	USBLS	5/07
	Orlando-Kissimmee MSA, FL	Y	25920 FQ	29250 MW	33710 TQ	USBLS	5/07
	Tampa-St. Petersburg-Clearwater MSA, FL	Y	29390 FQ	34360 MW	39580 TQ	USBLS	5/07

Occupation/Type/Industry	Location	Per	Low	Mid	High	Source	Date
Animal Control Worker	Georgia	Y	22340 FQ	26940 MW	31360 TQ	USBLS	5/07
	Atlanta-Sandy Springs- Marietta MSA, GA	Y	24790 FQ	28450 MW	33240 TQ	USBLS	5/07
	Hawaii	Y	33130 FQ	35890 MW	38660 TQ	USBLS	5/07
	Idaho	Y	21790 FQ	27310 MW	35210 TQ	USBLS	5/07
	Illinois	Y	20030 FQ	28050 MW	37940 TQ	USBLS	5/07
	Chicago-Naperville-Joliet MSA, IL-IN-WI	Y	25340 FQ	32840 MW	42060 TQ	USBLS	5/07
	Indiana	Y	21440 FQ	27130 MW	31040 TQ	USBLS	5/07
	Gary PMSA, IN	Y	20720 FQ	23490 MW	29190 TQ	USBLS	5/07
	Indianapolis-Carmel MSA, IN	Y	25890 FQ	28430 MW	30920 TQ	USBLS	5/07
	Iowa	Y	17770 FQ	27840 MW	35590 TQ	USBLS	5/07
	Kansas	Y	20880 FQ	24270 MW	29500 TQ	USBLS	5/07
	Kentucky	Y	19870 FQ	24684 MW	31415 TQ	KYBLS	2008
	Louisville-Jefferson County MSA, KY-IN	Y	23880 FQ	29250 MW	33970 TQ	USBLS	5/07
	Louisiana	H	8.81 FQ	10.77 MW	13.00 TQ	LABLS	1/08-3/08
	Maine	Y	15820 FQ	21400 MW	25920 TQ	USBLS	5/07
	Portland-South Portland- Biddeford MSA, ME	Y	19690 FQ	22720 MW	28600 TQ	USBLS	5/07
	Maryland	Y		35325 MW		MDBLS	3/08
	Baltimore-Towson MSA, MD	Y	27210 FQ	31210 MW	37350 TQ	USBLS	5/07
	Massachusetts	Y	21930 FQ	32140 MW	40840 TQ	USBLS	5/07
	Boston-Cambridge-Quincy NECTA, MA	Y	28530 FQ	36540 MW	45720 TQ	USBLS	5/07
	Springfield MSA, MA-CT	Y	24260 FQ	32860 MW	36760 TQ	USBLS	5/07
	Worcester MSA, MA-CT	Y	16180 FQ	18170 MW	31800 TQ	USBLS	5/07
	Michigan	Y	26890 FQ	33710 MW	40310 TQ	USBLS	5/07
	Detroit-Warren-Livonia MSA, MI	Y	27730 FQ	35930 MW	43300 TQ	USBLS	5/07
	Warren-Troy-Farmington Hills PMSA, MI	Y	24430 FQ	33280 MW	43090 TQ	USBLS	5/07
	Minnesota	Y	22751 FQ	30227 MW	44667 TQ	MNBLS	10/08-12/08
	Duluth-Superior MSA, MN-WI	Y	22490 FQ	26871 MW	39721 TQ	MNBLS	10/08-12/08
	Minneapolis-Saint Paul MSA, MN-WI	Y	22584 FQ	27216 MW	43987 TQ	MNBLS	10/08-12/08
	Mississippi	Y	18460 FQ	21990 MW	25200 TQ	USBLS	5/07
	Missouri	Y	20060 FQ	26100 MW	30900 TQ	USBLS	5/07
	Kansas City MSA, MO-KS	Y	26900 FQ	30420 MW	35900 TQ	USBLS	5/07
	St. Louis MSA, MO-IL	Y	23410 FQ	29440 MW	37140 TQ	USBLS	5/07
	Montana	Y	23210 FQ	28780 MW	34160 TQ	USBLS	5/07
	Nebraska	Y	23330 FQ	27690 MW	36470 TQ	USBLS	5/07
	Nevada	H	16.21 FQ	21.87 MW	25.82 TQ	NVBLS	5/08
	Las Vegas-Paradise MSA, NV	H	21.73 FQ	25.40 MW	31.37 TQ	NVBLS	5/08
	New Hampshire	H	9.03 AE	11.47 MW	14.61 AEX	NHBLS	6/08
	New Jersey	Y	26660 FQ	32880 MW	43690 TQ	USBLS	5/07
	Edison PMSA, NJ	Y	27840 FQ	33510 MW	41400 TQ	USBLS	5/07
	Newark-Union PMSA, NJ-PA	Y	25290 FQ	31620 MW	41920 TQ	USBLS	5/07
	New Mexico	Y	18930 FQ	23960 MW	30030 TQ	USBLS	5/07
	Albuquerque MSA, NM	Y	18130 FQ	26520 MW	32580 TQ	USBLS	5/07
	New York	Y	23480 FQ	28320 MW	33120 TQ	USBLS	5/07
	Albany-Schenectady-Troy MSA, NY	Y	21110 FQ	23300 MW	30360 TQ	USBLS	5/07
	Binghamton MSA, NY	Y	27160 FQ	29800 MW	32400 TQ	USBLS	5/07
	Buffalo-Niagara Falls MSA, NY	Y	24900 FQ	29030 MW	34440 TQ	USBLS	5/07
	Nassau-Suffolk PMSA, NY	Y	33300 FQ	44430 MW	56120 TQ	USBLS	5/07
	New York-Northern New Jersey-Long Island MSA, NY- NJ-PA	Y	28470 FQ	34560 MW	45310 TQ	USBLS	5/07
	North Carolina	Y	22660 FQ	27310 MW	32000 TQ	USBLS	5/07
	Charlotte-Gastonia-Concord MSA, NC-SC	Y	27040 FQ	29410 MW	33350 TQ	USBLS	5/07
	Raleigh-Cary MSA, NC	Y	29190 FQ	32850 MW	37290 TQ	USBLS	5/07
	Ohio	Y	23110 FQ	28980 MW	36620 TQ	USBLS	5/07
	Cincinnati-Middletown MSA, OH-KY-IN	Y	22100 FQ	26460 MW	31930 TQ	USBLS	5/07
	Cleveland-Elyria-Mentor MSA, OH	Y	26500 FQ	30660 MW	42530 TQ	USBLS	5/07
	Columbus MSA, OH	Y	25200 FQ	29070 MW	32970 TQ	USBLS	5/07
	Oklahoma	Y	18340 FQ	24900 MW	30230 TQ	USBLS	5/07
	Oklahoma City MSA, OK	Y	26430 FQ	30020 MW	36650 TQ	USBLS	5/07

AE	Average entry wage	AW	Average wage paid	FQ	First quartile wage
AER	Average entry range	AWR	Average wage range	H	Hourly
AEX	Average experienced wage	AXR	Average experienced range	HI	Highest wage paid
ATC	Average total compensation	D	Daily	HR	High end range

LO	Lowest wage paid	MTC	Median total compensation	TCC	Total cash compensation
LR	Low end range	MW	Median wage paid	TQ	Third quartile wage
M	Monthly	MWR	Median wage range	W	Weekly
MCC	Median cash compensation	S	See annotated source	Y	Yearly

Occupation/Type/Industry	Location	Per	Low	Mid	High	Source	Date
Animal Control Worker	Tulsa MSA, OK	Y	18360 FQ	26930 MW	31060 TQ	USBLS	5/07
	Oregon	H	16.08 FQ	18.58 MW	21.84 TQ	ORBLS	5/08
	Portland-Vancouver-Beaverton MSA, OR-WA	Y	34710 FQ	40160 MW	45820 TQ	USBLS	5/07
	Pennsylvania	Y	25870 FQ	34230 MW	39160 TQ	USBLS	5/07
	Philadelphia-Camden-Wilmington MSA, PA-NJ-DE-MD	Y	26650 FQ	34070 MW	41470 TQ	USBLS	5/07
	Pittsburgh MSA, PA	Y	30460 FQ	35970 MW	39680 TQ	USBLS	5/07
	Rhode Island	Y	27440 FQ	32980 MW	37780 TQ	USBLS	5/07
	Providence-Fall River-Warwick MSA, RI-MA	Y	25020 FQ	31300 MW	37080 TQ	USBLS	5/07
	South Carolina	Y	22610 FQ	26400 MW	30280 TQ	USBLS	5/07
	South Dakota	Y	22464 FQ	25189 MW	30213 TQ	SDBLS	7/08-9/08
	Tennessee	Y	21040 FQ	26160 MW	30110 TQ	USBLS	5/07
	Memphis MSA, TN-MS-AR	Y	24770 FQ	27970 MW	30710 TQ	USBLS	5/07
	Nashville-Davidson-Murfreesboro MSA, TN	Y	21160 FQ	25110 MW	30420 TQ	USBLS	5/07
	Texas	Y	22200 FQ	27090 MW	32380 TQ	USBLS	5/07
	Austin-Round Rock MSA, TX	Y	21530 FQ	25100 MW	30380 TQ	USBLS	5/07
	Dallas-Fort Worth-Arlington MSA, TX	Y	27740 FQ	32000 MW	37850 TQ	USBLS	5/07
	Houston-Sugar Land-Baytown MSA, TX	Y	24080 FQ	28630 MW	33360 TQ	USBLS	5/07
	San Antonio MSA, TX	Y	21860 FQ	27630 MW	31610 TQ	USBLS	5/07
	Utah	Y	26720 FQ	30280 MW	34730 TQ	USBLS	5/07
	Salt Lake City MSA, UT	Y	28150 FQ	32000 MW	37320 TQ	USBLS	5/07
	Vermont	Y	18600 FQ	20940 MW	23790 TQ	USBLS	5/07
	Virginia	Y	26130 FQ	30720 MW	38290 TQ	USBLS	5/07
	Richmond MSA, VA	Y	25270 FQ	29700 MW	37100 TQ	USBLS	5/07
	Virginia Beach-Norfolk-Newport News MSA, VA-NC	Y	27800 FQ	30790 MW	35640 TQ	USBLS	5/07
	Washington	H	13.80 FQ	18.20 MW	23.09 TQ	WABLS	3/08
	Seattle-Tacoma-Bellevue MSA, WA	Y	40550 FQ	46050 MW	50930 TQ	USBLS	5/07
	West Virginia	Y	16785 FQ	20685 MW	25890 TQ	WVBLS	7/08-9/08
	Charleston MSA, WV	Y	17510 FQ	19870 MW	28280 TQ	USBLS	5/07
	Wisconsin	Y	16040 FQ	19620 MW	27420 TQ	USBLS	5/07
	Wyoming	Y	29182 FQ	32371 MW	37141 TQ	WYBLS	9/08
Animal Inspector	Orange, MA	Y			650 HI	FRCOG	2009
Animal Scientist	California	H	16.36 FQ	28.60 MW	35.57 TQ	CABLS	1/08-3/08
	Florida	Y	38310 FQ	57460 MW	92640 TQ	USBLS	5/07
	Georgia	Y	39960 FQ	58110 MW	69800 TQ	USBLS	5/07
	Iowa	Y	51340 FQ	60130 MW	75330 TQ	USBLS	5/07
	Kansas	Y	52220 FQ	55670 MW	59120 TQ	USBLS	5/07
	Kentucky	Y	40398 FQ	48234 MW	59872 TQ	KYBLS	2008
	Maryland	Y		73575 MW		MDBLS	3/08
	Minnesota	Y	41597 FQ	49946 MW	93553 TQ	MNBLS	10/08-12/08
	Mississippi	Y	28430 FQ	34770 MW	56510 TQ	USBLS	5/07
	Missouri	Y	44850 FQ	66200 MW	84210 TQ	USBLS	5/07
	Nebraska	Y	42900 FQ	74620 MW	93150 TQ	USBLS	5/07
	New Jersey	Y	70110 FQ	78390 MW	89670 TQ	USBLS	5/07
	Oregon	H	17.99 FQ	19.70 MW	24.16 TQ	ORBLS	5/08
	South Dakota	Y	33311 FQ	37124 MW	40444 TQ	SDBLS	7/08-9/08
	Texas	Y	36800 FQ	44380 MW	54680 TQ	USBLS	5/07
	Wisconsin	Y	32550 FQ	46450 MW	72000 TQ	USBLS	5/07
Animal Trainer	Alabama	Y	15370 FQ	32600 MW	37550 TQ	USBLS	5/07
	Arizona	Y	17180 FQ	20030 MW	26720 TQ	USBLS	5/07
	Phoenix-Mesa-Scottsdale MSA, AZ	Y	17090 FQ	19800 MW	25590 TQ	USBLS	5/07
	California	H	9.94 FQ	13.25 MW	18.57 TQ	CABLS	1/08-3/08
	Los Angeles-Long Beach-Glendale PMSA, CA	H	10.82 FQ	14.35 MW	21.11 TQ	CABLS	1/08-3/08
	Oakland-Fremont-Hayward MSA, CA	H	9.55 FQ	10.88 MW	13.94 TQ	CABLS	1/08-3/08
	Riverside-San Bernardino-Ontario MSA, CA	H	8.59 FQ	9.94 MW	13.62 TQ	CABLS	1/08-3/08
	Sacramento-Arden Arcade-Roseville MSA, CA	H	8.00 FQ	9.19 MW	10.96 TQ	CABLS	1/08-3/08

AE	Average entry wage	AW	Average wage paid	FQ	First quartile wage	LO	Lowest wage paid	MTC Median total compensation TCC Total cash compensation
AER	Average entry range	AWR	Average wage range	H	Hourly	LR	Low end range	MW Median wage paid TQ Third quartile wage
AEX	Average experienced wage	AXR	Average experienced range	HI	Highest wage paid	M	Monthly	MWR Median wage range W Weekly
ATC	Average total compensation	D	Daily	HR	High end range	MCC	Median cash compensation	S See annotated source Y Yearly

Occupation/Type/Industry	Location	Per	Low	Mid	High	Source	Date
Animal Trainer	San Diego-Carlsbad-San Marcos MSA, CA	H	10.55 FQ	13.60 MW	17.38 TQ	CABLS	1/08-3/08
	San Francisco-San Mateo-Redwood PMSA, CA	H	13.14 FQ	18.12 MW	22.93 TQ	CABLS	1/08-3/08
	Santa Ana-Anaheim-Irvine PMSA, CA	Y	18900 FQ	25700 MW	30840 TQ	USBLS	5/07
	Colorado	Y	21020 FQ	23490 MW	27250 TQ	USBLS	5/07
	Denver-Aurora MSA, CO	Y	21380 FQ	24200 MW	29340 TQ	USBLS	5/07
	Connecticut	H	8.12 AE	11.53 MW		CTBLS	1/08-3/08
	Delaware	Y	30660 FQ	36540 MW	41800 TQ	USBLS	5/07
	Wilmington PMSA, DE-MD-NJ	Y	24960 FQ	34310 MW	40440 TQ	USBLS	5/07
	Washington-Arlington-Alexandria MSA, DC-VA-MD-WV	Y	21820 FQ	27290 MW	40920 TQ	USBLS	5/07
	Florida	Y	20360 FQ	25670 MW	33300 TQ	USBLS	5/07
	Fort Lauderdale-Pompano Beach-Deerfield Beach PMSA, FL	Y	21780 FQ	24330 MW	27140 TQ	USBLS	5/07
	Miami-Fort Lauderdale-Miami Beach MSA, FL	Y	22940 FQ	27060 MW	32860 TQ	USBLS	5/07
	Orlando-Kissimmee MSA, FL	Y	27000 FQ	34070 MW	45900 TQ	USBLS	5/07
	Tampa-St. Petersburg-Clearwater MSA, FL	Y	15450 FQ	24760 MW	30640 TQ	USBLS	5/07
	Georgia	Y	21260 FQ	32190 MW	42150 TQ	USBLS	5/07
	Atlanta-Sandy Springs-Marietta MSA, GA	Y	18540 FQ	25080 MW	42760 TQ	USBLS	5/07
	Hawaii	Y	15530 FQ	20080 MW	29040 TQ	USBLS	5/07
	Honolulu MSA, HI	Y	18920 FQ	22670 MW	30240 TQ	USBLS	5/07
	Idaho	Y	18200 FQ	20530 MW	25870 TQ	USBLS	5/07
	Illinois	Y	22820 FQ	29070 MW	39340 TQ	USBLS	5/07
	Chicago-Naperville-Joliet MSA, IL-IN-WI	Y	22650 FQ	29380 MW	38920 TQ	USBLS	5/07
	Indiana	Y	17460 FQ	20630 MW	26070 TQ	USBLS	5/07
	Iowa	Y	21270 FQ	24850 MW	32180 TQ	USBLS	5/07
	Kansas	Y	16170 FQ	17890 MW	21150 TQ	USBLS	5/07
	Kentucky	Y	26903 FQ	31232 MW	36513 TQ	KYBLS	2008
	Louisville-Jefferson County MSA, KY-IN	Y	17660 FQ	31350 MW	37370 TQ	USBLS	5/07
	Louisiana	H	7.43 FQ	8.55 MW	9.71 TQ	LABLS	1/08-3/08
	New Orleans-Metairie-Kenner MSA, LA	Y	14990 FQ	17680 MW	19960 TQ	USBLS	5/07
	Maryland	Y		24725 MW		MDBLS	3/08
	Baltimore-Towson MSA, MD	Y	22970 FQ	25670 MW	35010 TQ	USBLS	5/07
	Massachusetts	Y	20160 FQ	23860 MW	37350 TQ	USBLS	5/07
	Boston-Cambridge-Quincy NECTA, MA	Y	18300 FQ	25240 MW	31570 TQ	USBLS	5/07
	Michigan	Y	18530 FQ	21780 MW	24780 TQ	USBLS	5/07
	Detroit-Warren-Livonia MSA, MI	Y	18040 FQ	21190 MW	23760 TQ	USBLS	5/07
	Warren-Troy-Farmington Hills PMSA, MI	Y	17890 FQ	20980 MW	23510 TQ	USBLS	5/07
	Minnesota	Y	27561 FQ	53669 MW	70305 TQ	MNBLS	10/08-12/08
	Minneapolis-Saint Paul MSA, MN-WI	Y	47783 FQ	59451 MW	72615 TQ	MNBLS	10/08-12/08
	Missouri	Y	18890 FQ	23240 MW	30960 TQ	USBLS	5/07
	Kansas City MSA, MO-KS	Y	16440 FQ	17870 MW	21070 TQ	USBLS	5/07
	St. Louis MSA, MO-IL	Y	21470 FQ	23590 MW	25860 TQ	USBLS	5/07
	Nebraska	Y	18910 FQ	21380 MW	23480 TQ	USBLS	5/07
	Omaha-Council Bluffs MSA, NE-IA	Y	19740 FQ	22960 MW	29210 TQ	USBLS	5/07
	Las Vegas-Paradise MSA, NV	H	9.02 FQ	10.05 MW	11.30 TQ	NVBLS	5/08
	New Hampshire	H	12.17 AE	17.01 MW	17.93 AEX	NHBLS	6/08
	New Jersey	Y	29610 FQ	36580 MW	41440 TQ	USBLS	5/07
	Camden PMSA, NJ	Y	33630 FQ	36360 MW	39210 TQ	USBLS	5/07
	Edison PMSA, NJ	Y	28270 FQ	35890 MW	42910 TQ	USBLS	5/07
	Newark-Union PMSA, NJ-PA	Y	32370 FQ	35810 MW	38840 TQ	USBLS	5/07
	New Mexico	Y	17510 FQ	19630 MW	23340 TQ	USBLS	5/07
	Albuquerque MSA, NM	Y	17350 FQ	19200 MW	22450 TQ	USBLS	5/07
	New York	Y	25050 FQ	36170 MW	48420 TQ	USBLS	5/07
	Nassau-Suffolk PMSA, NY	Y	24940 FQ	39160 MW	68140 TQ	USBLS	5/07

Occupation/Type/Industry	Location	Per	Low	Mid	High	Source	Date
Animal Trainer	New York-Northern New Jersey-Long Island MSA, NY-NJ-PA	Y	27390 FQ	36780 MW	46000 TQ	USBLS	5/07
	North Carolina	Y	17340 FQ	20370 MW	30610 TQ	USBLS	5/07
	Ohio	Y	17920 FQ	21260 MW	30840 TQ	USBLS	5/07
	Cincinnati-Middletown MSA, OH-KY-IN	Y	33040 FQ	36930 MW	43380 TQ	USBLS	5/07
	Columbus MSA, OH	Y	18710 FQ	28350 MW	38280 TQ	USBLS	5/07
	Oklahoma	Y	16640 FQ	18640 MW	22930 TQ	USBLS	5/07
	Oklahoma City MSA, OK	Y	15880 FQ	18330 MW	26890 TQ	USBLS	5/07
	Tulsa MSA, OK	Y	17490 FQ	19020 MW	21520 TQ	USBLS	5/07
	Oregon	H	10.45 FQ	12.23 MW	20.90 TQ	ORBLS	5/08
	Pennsylvania	Y	16880 FQ	20060 MW	30480 TQ	USBLS	5/07
	Philadelphia-Camden-Wilmington MSA, PA-NJ-DE-MD	Y	21870 FQ	30900 MW	37750 TQ	USBLS	5/07
	South Carolina	Y	18050 FQ	24990 MW	30560 TQ	USBLS	5/07
	Charleston-North Charleston MSA, SC	Y	22030 FQ	27060 MW	32920 TQ	USBLS	5/07
	Tennessee	Y	18320 FQ	26210 MW	43010 TQ	USBLS	5/07
	Texas	Y	18430 FQ	26540 MW	31410 TQ	USBLS	5/07
	Austin-Round Rock MSA, TX	Y	26430 FQ	28560 MW	30690 TQ	USBLS	5/07
	Dallas-Fort Worth-Arlington MSA, TX	Y	18690 FQ	28340 MW	37000 TQ	USBLS	5/07
	Houston-Sugar Land-Baytown MSA, TX	Y	18000 FQ	23840 MW	30540 TQ	USBLS	5/07
	San Antonio MSA, TX	Y	19290 FQ	25120 MW	42720 TQ	USBLS	5/07
	Utah	Y	22870 FQ	31130 MW	44960 TQ	USBLS	5/07
	Virginia	Y	22350 FQ	28440 MW	42880 TQ	USBLS	5/07
	Richmond MSA, VA	Y	20820 FQ	24880 MW	27890 TQ	USBLS	5/07
	Virginia Beach-Norfolk-Newport News MSA, VA-NC	Y	29980 FQ	44240 MW	48190 TQ	USBLS	5/07
	Washington	H	11.11 FQ	13.81 MW	19.65 TQ	WABLS	3/08
	Seattle-Tacoma-Bellevue MSA, WA	Y	22450 FQ	28500 MW	43080 TQ	USBLS	5/07
	West Virginia	Y	18596 FQ	22257 MW	32846 TQ	WVBLS	7/08-9/08
	Charleston MSA, WV	Y	20010 FQ	29180 MW	34960 TQ	USBLS	5/07
	Wisconsin	Y	19540 FQ	23180 MW	30690 TQ	USBLS	5/07
Anthropologist and Archeologist	Alaska	Y	52830 FQ	68110 MW	80550 TQ	USBLS	5/07
	Arizona	Y	39160 FQ	53980 MW	61050 TQ	USBLS	5/07
	California	H	23.74 FQ	29.88 MW	37.18 TQ	CABLS	1/08-3/08
	Colorado	Y	35060 FQ	43130 MW	56340 TQ	USBLS	5/07
	Connecticut	H	11.89 AE	15.48 MW		CTBLS	1/08-3/08
	District of Columbia	Y	33000 FQ	40740 MW	60420 TQ	USBLS	5/07
	Florida	Y	37770 FQ	47400 MW	68170 TQ	USBLS	5/07
	Hawaii	Y	42980 FQ	66330 MW	86550 TQ	USBLS	5/07
	Idaho	Y	48400 FQ	60840 MW	73640 TQ	USBLS	5/07
	Illinois	Y	29310 FQ	53650 MW	70370 TQ	USBLS	5/07
	Kentucky	Y	49490 FQ	62939 MW	73799 TQ	KYBLS	2008
	Louisiana	H	23.42 FQ	28.92 MW	34.89 TQ	LABLS	1/08-3/08
	Maryland	Y		35350 MW		MDBLS	3/08
	Massachusetts	Y	35870 FQ	47560 MW	76470 TQ	USBLS	5/07
	Michigan	Y	45270 FQ	56200 MW	69360 TQ	USBLS	5/07
	Minnesota	Y	52311 FQ	67669 MW	76636 TQ	MNBLS	10/08-12/08
	Mississippi	Y	31760 FQ	37580 MW	62660 TQ	USBLS	5/07
	Missouri	Y	27850 FQ	42200 MW	61920 TQ	USBLS	5/07
	Montana	Y	56350 FQ	63890 MW	74350 TQ	USBLS	5/07
	Nevada	H	24.01 FQ	28.74 MW	33.87 TQ	NVBLS	5/08
	New Jersey	Y	37240 FQ	52520 MW	60360 TQ	USBLS	5/07
	New Mexico	Y	37880 FQ	49050 MW	62880 TQ	USBLS	5/07
	New York	Y	50680 FQ	65970 MW	86010 TQ	USBLS	5/07
	North Carolina	Y	35400 FQ	41790 MW	58970 TQ	USBLS	5/07
	Oregon	H	19.15 FQ	23.31 MW	32.53 TQ	ORBLS	5/08
	Pennsylvania	Y	40240 FQ	65480 MW	81860 TQ	USBLS	5/07
	South Carolina	Y	32200 FQ	37880 MW	67880 TQ	USBLS	5/07
	Tennessee	Y	28590 FQ	37600 MW	61390 TQ	USBLS	5/07
	Texas	Y	36680 FQ	46840 MW	63450 TQ	USBLS	5/07
	Vermont	Y	38650 FQ	50470 MW	59580 TQ	USBLS	5/07
	Virginia	Y	39980 FQ	59110 MW	84290 TQ	USBLS	5/07
	West Virginia	Y	35059 FQ	43411 MW	49773 TQ	WVBLS	7/08-9/08
	Wisconsin	Y	49360 FQ	62120 MW	73180 TQ	USBLS	5/07

AE Average entry wage	**AW** Average wage paid	**FQ** First quartile wage	**LO** Lowest wage paid	**MTC** Median total compensation	**TCC** Total cash compensation	
AER Average entry range	**AWR** Average wage range	**H** Hourly	**LR** Low end range	**MW** Median wage paid	**TQ** Third quartile wage	
AEX Average experienced wage	**AXR** Average experienced range	**HI** Highest wage paid	**M** Monthly	**MWR** Median wage range	**W** Weekly	
ATC Average total compensation	**D** Daily	**HR** High end range	**MCC** Median cash compensation	**S** See annotated source	**Y** Yearly	

Occupation/Type/Industry	Location	Per	Low	Mid	High	Source	Date
Anthropologist and Archeologist	Wyoming	Y	38896 FQ	50490 MW	64583 TQ	WYBLS	9/08
Anthropology and Archeology Teacher							
Postsecondary	Arizona	Y	48510 FQ	58270 MW	79190 TQ	USBLS	5/07
Postsecondary	Phoenix-Mesa-Scottsdale MSA, AZ	Y	30770 FQ	50320 MW	76920 TQ	USBLS	5/07
Postsecondary	California	Y		81997 AW		CABLS	1/08-3/08
Postsecondary	Los Angeles-Long Beach-Glendale PMSA, CA	Y		76398 AW		CABLS	1/08-3/08
Postsecondary	Riverside-San Bernardino-Ontario MSA, CA	Y		87637 AW		CABLS	1/08-3/08
Postsecondary	Sacramento-Arden Arcade-Roseville MSA, CA	Y		82797 AW		CABLS	1/08-3/08
Postsecondary	San Diego-Carlsbad-San Marcos MSA, CA	Y		77823 AW		CABLS	1/08-3/08
Postsecondary	Santa Ana-Anaheim-Irvine PMSA, CA	Y	71290 FQ	83190 MW	97800 TQ	USBLS	5/07
Postsecondary	Colorado	Y	45530 FQ	57870 MW	72770 TQ	USBLS	5/07
Postsecondary	Denver-Aurora MSA, CO	Y	41870 FQ	57260 MW	69850 TQ	USBLS	5/07
Postsecondary	District of Columbia	Y	43790 FQ	56770 MW	74850 TQ	USBLS	5/07
Postsecondary	Washington-Arlington-Alexandria MSA, DC-VA-MD-WV	Y	45980 FQ	62360 MW	85020 TQ	USBLS	5/07
Postsecondary	Florida	Y	54980 FQ	67740 MW	80020 TQ	USBLS	5/07
Postsecondary	Tampa-St. Petersburg-Clearwater MSA, FL	Y	53470 FQ	64710 MW	83170 TQ	USBLS	5/07
Postsecondary	Georgia	Y	50650 FQ	61320 MW	79080 TQ	USBLS	5/07
Postsecondary	Atlanta-Sandy Springs-Marietta MSA, GA	Y	51860 FQ	60460 MW	76400 TQ	USBLS	5/07
Postsecondary	Hawaii	Y	51630 FQ	66280 MW	79170 TQ	USBLS	5/07
Postsecondary	Illinois	Y	50380 FQ	63750 MW	84740 TQ	USBLS	5/07
Postsecondary	Chicago-Naperville-Joliet MSA, IL-IN-WI	Y	50240 FQ	69250 MW	90180 TQ	USBLS	5/07
Postsecondary	Indiana	Y	48350 FQ	58810 MW	73460 TQ	USBLS	5/07
Postsecondary	Iowa	Y	55560 FQ	68670 MW	83260 TQ	USBLS	5/07
Postsecondary	Kentucky	Y	45510 FQ	58124 MW	73958 TQ	KYBLS	2008
Postsecondary	Maine	Y	57270 FQ	74360 MW	95750 TQ	USBLS	5/07
Postsecondary	Maryland	Y		72000 MW		MDBLS	3/08
Postsecondary	Massachusetts	Y	57030 FQ	74400 MW	95590 TQ	USBLS	5/07
Postsecondary	Boston-Cambridge-Quincy NECTA, MA	Y	57330 FQ	74350 MW	99400 TQ	USBLS	5/07
Postsecondary	Michigan	Y	54670 FQ	67110 MW	85180 TQ	USBLS	5/07
Postsecondary	Minnesota	Y	47048 FQ	59634 MW	75265 TQ	MNBLS	10/08-12/08
Postsecondary	Minneapolis-Saint Paul MSA, MN-WI	Y	47927 FQ	62177 MW	76824 TQ	MNBLS	10/08-12/08
Postsecondary	Missouri	Y	42320 FQ	50370 MW	70020 TQ	USBLS	5/07
Postsecondary	St. Louis MSA, MO-IL	Y	42790 FQ	51830 MW	73050 TQ	USBLS	5/07
Postsecondary	New Hampshire	Y	41153 AE	49964 MW	72658 AEX	NHBLS	6/08
Postsecondary	New Jersey	Y	52430 FQ	67840 MW	89980 TQ	USBLS	5/07
Postsecondary	Edison PMSA, NJ	Y	63420 FQ	84670 MW	118610 TQ	USBLS	5/07
Postsecondary	Newark-Union PMSA, NJ-PA	Y	48240 FQ	63470 MW	81030 TQ	USBLS	5/07
Postsecondary	New Mexico	Y	54560 FQ	62470 MW	76100 TQ	USBLS	5/07
Postsecondary	Albuquerque MSA, NM	Y	55710 FQ	63800 MW	77110 TQ	USBLS	5/07
Postsecondary	New York	Y	57410 FQ	74740 MW	100750 TQ	USBLS	5/07
Postsecondary	New York-Northern New Jersey-Long Island MSA, NY-NJ-PA	Y	55410 FQ	72790 MW	94930 TQ	USBLS	5/07
Postsecondary	North Carolina	Y	47280 FQ	65540 MW	90960 TQ	USBLS	5/07
Postsecondary	Ohio	Y	52860 FQ	66280 MW	82370 TQ	USBLS	5/07
Postsecondary	Cincinnati-Middletown MSA, OH-KY-IN	Y	42020 FQ	55400 MW	72400 TQ	USBLS	5/07
Postsecondary	Cleveland-Elyria-Mentor MSA, OH	Y	55700 FQ	67700 MW	82070 TQ	USBLS	5/07
Postsecondary	Columbus MSA, OH	Y	65970 FQ	76890 MW	90870 TQ	USBLS	5/07
Postsecondary	Portland-Vancouver-Beaverton MSA, OR-WA	Y	57340 FQ	77680 MW	111620 TQ	USBLS	5/07
Postsecondary	Pennsylvania	Y	54650 FQ	72610 MW	96570 TQ	USBLS	5/07
Postsecondary	Philadelphia-Camden-Wilmington MSA, PA-NJ-DE-MD	Y	53850 FQ	70180 MW	94710 TQ	USBLS	5/07
Postsecondary	Rhode Island	Y	53860 FQ	80640 MW	115850 TQ	USBLS	5/07

AE	Average entry wage	AW	Average wage paid	FQ	First quartile wage
AER	Average entry range	AWR	Average wage range	H	Hourly
AEX	Average experienced wage	AXR	Average experienced range	HI	Highest wage paid
ATC	Average total compensation	D	Daily	HR	High end range

LO	Lowest wage paid	MTC	Median total compensation
LR	Low end range	MW	Median wage paid
M	Monthly	MWR	Median wage range
MCC	Median cash compensation	S	See annotated source

TCC	Total cash compensation
TQ	Third quartile wage
W	Weekly
Y	Yearly

Occupation/Type/Industry	Location	Per	Low	Mid	High	Source	Date
Anthropology and Archeology Teacher							
Postsecondary	Providence-Fall River-Warwick MSA, RI-MA	Y	53860 FQ	80640 MW	115850 TQ	USBLS	5/07
Postsecondary	South Carolina	Y	32630 FQ	45900 MW	59100 TQ	USBLS	5/07
Postsecondary	South Dakota	Y	54304 FQ	60498 MW	79494 TQ	SDBLS	7/08-9/08
Postsecondary	Tennessee	Y	38640 FQ	58120 MW	69800 TQ	USBLS	5/07
Postsecondary	Texas	Y	48080 FQ	64560 MW	93320 TQ	USBLS	5/07
Postsecondary	Austin-Round Rock MSA, TX	Y	52360 FQ	66590 MW	108880 TQ	USBLS	5/07
Postsecondary	San Antonio MSA, TX	Y	41130 FQ	46500 MW	51680 TQ	USBLS	5/07
Postsecondary	Virginia	Y	44810 FQ	57710 MW	75050 TQ	USBLS	5/07
Postsecondary	Washington	Y		62971 AW		WABLS	3/08
Postsecondary	Seattle-Tacoma-Bellevue MSA, WA	Y	44760 FQ	56560 MW	72410 TQ	USBLS	5/07
Postsecondary	Wisconsin	Y	44580 FQ	51670 MW	70260 TQ	USBLS	5/07
Apiary Specialist							
State Government	Ohio	H	17.22 LO		21.77 HI	ODAS	2008
Apple Certified System Administrator	United States	Y		65520 AW		CERT01	8/1/07-9/5/07
Application Support Specialist							
State Government	Delaware	Y	39998 LO		59996 HI	AFT02	3/1/08
Applicator	United States	Y		39351 AW		AGPRO	2007
Appraiser and Assessor of Real Estate							
	Alabama	Y	33430 FQ	45000 MW	64970 TQ	USBLS	5/07
	Birmingham-Hoover MSA, AL	Y	42500 FQ	50930 MW	70110 TQ	USBLS	5/07
	Anchorage MSA, AK	Y	47400 FQ	57750 MW	75110 TQ	USBLS	5/07
	Arizona	Y	27980 FQ	38490 MW	56220 TQ	USBLS	5/07
	Phoenix-Mesa-Scottsdale MSA, AZ	Y	34270 FQ	42580 MW	64240 TQ	USBLS	5/07
	Tucson MSA, AZ	Y	21140 FQ	23340 MW	38600 TQ	USBLS	5/07
	Arkansas	Y	23030 FQ	29640 MW	41690 TQ	USBLS	5/07
	Little Rock-North Little Rock MSA, AR	Y	27190 FQ	37660 MW	47890 TQ	USBLS	5/07
	California	H	25.94 FQ	33.73 MW	40.98 TQ	CABLS	1/08-3/08
	Los Angeles-Long Beach-Glendale PMSA, CA	H	30.44 FQ	37.91 MW	45.02 TQ	CABLS	1/08-3/08
	Oakland-Fremont-Hayward MSA, CA	H	25.39 FQ	31.70 MW	39.32 TQ	CABLS	1/08-3/08
	Riverside-San Bernardino-Ontario MSA, CA	H	22.04 FQ	29.57 MW	40.17 TQ	CABLS	1/08-3/08
	Sacramento-Arden Arcade-Roseville MSA, CA	H	27.68 FQ	32.71 MW	38.35 TQ	CABLS	1/08-3/08
	San Diego-Carlsbad-San Marcos MSA, CA	H	26.83 FQ	29.96 MW	34.28 TQ	CABLS	1/08-3/08
	San Francisco-San Mateo-Redwood PMSA, CA	H	34.88 FQ	41.36 MW	56.11 TQ	CABLS	1/08-3/08
	San Jose-Sunnyvale-Santa Clara MSA, CA	H	27.94 FQ	34.83 MW	40.62 TQ	CABLS	1/08-3/08
	Santa Ana-Anaheim-Irvine PMSA, CA	Y	55430 FQ	71190 MW	80510 TQ	USBLS	5/07
	Colorado	Y	29400 FQ	44350 MW	67110 TQ	USBLS	5/07
	Denver-Aurora MSA, CO	Y	26500 FQ	46070 MW	69110 TQ	USBLS	5/07
	Connecticut	H	17.99 AE	29.64 MW		CTBLS	1/08-3/08
	Bridgeport-Stamford-Norwalk MSA, CT	Y	34510 FQ	56440 MW	71190 TQ	USBLS	5/07
	Hartford-West Hartford-East Hartford MSA, CT	Y	49310 FQ	64830 MW	75940 TQ	USBLS	5/07
	Norwich-New London MSA, CT-RI	Y	38650 FQ	53160 MW	67070 TQ	USBLS	5/07
	Delaware	Y	33820 FQ	41150 MW	50580 TQ	USBLS	5/07
	Wilmington PMSA, DE-MD-NJ	Y	37580 FQ	44670 MW	66570 TQ	USBLS	5/07
	District of Columbia	Y	48210 FQ	61200 MW	78780 TQ	USBLS	5/07
	Washington-Arlington-Alexandria MSA, DC-VA-MD-WV	Y	49470 FQ	62120 MW	84910 TQ	USBLS	5/07
	Florida	Y	35190 FQ	48770 MW	71490 TQ	USBLS	5/07

AE	Average entry wage	AW	Average wage paid	FQ	First quartile wage
AER	Average entry range	AWR	Average wage range	H	Hourly
AEX	Average experienced wage	AXR	Average experienced range	HI	Highest wage paid
ATC	Average total compensation	D	Daily	HR	High end range

LO	Lowest wage paid	MTC	Median total compensation	TCC	Total cash compensation
LR	Low end range	MW	Median wage paid	TQ	Third quartile wage
M	Monthly	MWR	Median wage range	W	Weekly
MCC	Median cash compensation	S	See annotated source	Y	Yearly

Occupation/Type/Industry	Location	Per	Low	Mid	High	Source	Date
Appraiser and Assessor of Real Estate							
	Fort Lauderdale-Pompano Beach-Deerfield Beach PMSA, FL	Y	33530 FQ	38390 MW	61900 TQ	USBLS	5/07
	Jacksonville MSA, FL	Y	33920 FQ	44810 MW	64260 TQ	USBLS	5/07
	Miami-Fort Lauderdale-Miami Beach MSA, FL	Y	36130 FQ	57150 MW	84080 TQ	USBLS	5/07
	Orlando-Kissimmee MSA, FL	Y	31670 FQ	40380 MW	80070 TQ	USBLS	5/07
	Tampa-St. Petersburg-Clearwater MSA, FL	Y	46500 FQ	61820 MW	79960 TQ	USBLS	5/07
	West Palm Beach-Boca Raton-Boynton Beach PMSA, FL	Y	54060 FQ	62160 MW	86280 TQ	USBLS	5/07
	Georgia	Y	29450 FQ	38790 MW	54520 TQ	USBLS	5/07
	Atlanta-Sandy Springs-Marietta MSA, GA	Y	32260 FQ	42830 MW	59190 TQ	USBLS	5/07
	Macon MSA, GA	Y	28810 FQ	38620 MW	53100 TQ	USBLS	5/07
	Hawaii	Y	42980 FQ	54770 MW	64220 TQ	USBLS	5/07
	Honolulu MSA, HI	Y	42200 FQ	54140 MW	64040 TQ	USBLS	5/07
	Idaho	Y	26290 FQ	35440 MW	47700 TQ	USBLS	5/07
	Boise City-Nampa MSA, ID	Y	35240 FQ	48720 MW	62580 TQ	USBLS	5/07
	Coeur d'Alene MSA, ID	Y	32940 FQ	38060 MW	44200 TQ	USBLS	5/07
	Illinois	Y	28410 FQ	38680 MW	57690 TQ	USBLS	5/07
	Chicago-Naperville-Joliet MSA, IL-IN-WI	Y	33130 FQ	45590 MW	70660 TQ	USBLS	5/07
	Indiana	Y	24770 FQ	31770 MW	39860 TQ	USBLS	5/07
	Fort Wayne MSA, IN	Y	34130 FQ	38140 MW	52770 TQ	USBLS	5/07
	Gary PMSA, IN	Y	27100 FQ	33990 MW	39540 TQ	USBLS	5/07
	Indianapolis-Carmel MSA, IN	Y	32560 FQ	37690 MW	50310 TQ	USBLS	5/07
	Iowa	Y	30710 FQ	42810 MW	51440 TQ	USBLS	5/07
	Des Moines-West Des Moines MSA, IA	Y	28460 FQ	37790 MW	50460 TQ	USBLS	5/07
	Iowa City MSA, IA	Y	42290 FQ	46470 MW	51460 TQ	USBLS	5/07
	Waterloo-Cedar Falls MSA, IA	Y	38690 FQ	46310 MW	57470 TQ	USBLS	5/07
	Kansas	Y	29040 FQ	36990 MW	48600 TQ	USBLS	5/07
	Wichita MSA, KS	Y	28690 FQ	32720 MW	41260 TQ	USBLS	5/07
	Kentucky	Y	33845 FQ	42107 MW	73678 TQ	KYBLS	2008
	Louisville-Jefferson County MSA, KY-IN	Y	22710 FQ	28800 MW	62590 TQ	USBLS	5/07
	Louisiana	H	13.82 FQ	19.02 MW	24.45 TQ	LABLS	1/08-3/08
	Baton Rouge MSA, LA	Y	29650 FQ	38610 MW	53210 TQ	USBLS	5/07
	New Orleans-Metairie-Kenner MSA, LA	Y	25220 FQ	37130 MW	52360 TQ	USBLS	5/07
	Maine	Y	33640 FQ	41840 MW	50420 TQ	USBLS	5/07
	Portland-South Portland-Biddeford MSA, ME	Y	37800 FQ	45430 MW	55660 TQ	USBLS	5/07
	Maryland	Y		55550 MW		MDBLS	3/08
	Baltimore-Towson MSA, MD	Y	31580 FQ	48500 MW	63630 TQ	USBLS	5/07
	Bethesda-Gaithersburg-Frederick PMSA, MD	Y	55430 FQ	59790 MW	64450 TQ	USBLS	5/07
	Massachusetts	Y	39150 FQ	65690 MW	88530 TQ	USBLS	5/07
	Boston-Cambridge-Quincy NECTA, MA	Y	57090 FQ	81400 MW	102560 TQ	USBLS	5/07
	Worcester MSA, MA-CT	Y	34300 FQ	43920 MW	68460 TQ	USBLS	5/07
	Michigan	Y	34280 FQ	47580 MW	66740 TQ	USBLS	5/07
	Detroit-Warren-Livonia MSA, MI	Y	38570 FQ	53840 MW	72150 TQ	USBLS	5/07
	Grand Rapids-Wyoming MSA, MI	Y	34370 FQ	54090 MW	62110 TQ	USBLS	5/07
	Warren-Troy-Farmington Hills PMSA, MI	Y	38160 FQ	56730 MW	73420 TQ	USBLS	5/07
	Minnesota	Y	41820 FQ	49046 MW	62746 TQ	MNBLS	10/08-12/08
	Duluth-Superior MSA, MN-WI	Y	45928 FQ	52935 MW	60870 TQ	MNBLS	10/08-12/08
	Minneapolis-Saint Paul MSA, MN-WI	Y	42227 FQ	49286 MW	67397 TQ	MNBLS	10/08-12/08
	Rochester MSA, MN	Y	42236 FQ	48054 MW	63789 TQ	MNBLS	10/08-12/08
	Mississippi	Y	29730 FQ	40130 MW	51130 TQ	USBLS	5/07
	Jackson MSA, MS	Y	39360 FQ	47870 MW	53670 TQ	USBLS	5/07
	Missouri	Y	26390 FQ	37110 MW	49490 TQ	USBLS	5/07
	Kansas City MSA, MO-KS	Y	29120 FQ	36780 MW	54120 TQ	USBLS	5/07
	St. Louis MSA, MO-IL	Y	26430 FQ	33250 MW	42400 TQ	USBLS	5/07
	Montana	Y	15510 FQ	33700 MW	44460 TQ	USBLS	5/07
	Billings MSA, MT	Y	34340 FQ	39180 MW	44340 TQ	USBLS	5/07

AE	Average entry wage	**AW**	Average wage paid	**FQ**	First quartile wage
AER	Average entry range	**AWR**	Average wage range	**H**	Hourly
AEX	Average experienced wage	**AXR**	Average experienced range	**HI**	Highest wage paid
ATC	Average total compensation	**D**	Daily	**HR**	High end range

LO	Lowest wage paid	**MTC**	Median total compensation	**TCC**	Total cash compensation
LR	Low end range	**MW**	Median wage paid	**TQ**	Third quartile wage
M	Monthly	**MWR**	Median wage range	**W**	Weekly
MCC	Median cash compensation	**S**	See annotated source	**Y**	Yearly

Appraiser and Assessor of Real Estate

Occupation/Type/Industry	Location	Per	Low	Mid	High	Source	Date
Appraiser and Assessor of Real Estate	Nebraska	Y	32260 FQ	43040 MW	55660 TQ	USBLS	5/07
	Omaha-Council Bluffs MSA, NE-IA	Y	42530 FQ	48910 MW	64130 TQ	USBLS	5/07
	Nevada	H	25.91 FQ	34.78 MW	39.38 TQ	NVBLS	5/08
	Las Vegas-Paradise MSA, NV	H	29.97 FQ	35.84 MW	39.69 TQ	NVBLS	5/08
	New Hampshire	H	17.72 AE	28.40 MW	40.36 AEX	NHBLS	6/08
	Manchester MSA, NH	Y	42640 FQ	56440 MW	66890 TQ	USBLS	5/07
	Nashua NECTA, NH-MA	Y	44240 FQ	51370 MW	103600 TQ	USBLS	5/07
	New Jersey	Y	51070 FQ	66910 MW	78590 TQ	USBLS	5/07
	Camden PMSA, NJ	Y	36810 FQ	56960 MW	71970 TQ	USBLS	5/07
	Edison PMSA, NJ	Y	48810 FQ	64350 MW	80090 TQ	USBLS	5/07
	Newark-Union PMSA, NJ-PA	Y	48370 FQ	68950 MW	81120 TQ	USBLS	5/07
	New Mexico	Y	28220 FQ	38040 MW	45830 TQ	USBLS	5/07
	Albuquerque MSA, NM	Y	31000 FQ	40330 MW	45680 TQ	USBLS	5/07
	Santa Fe MSA, NM	Y	40610 FQ	46930 MW	56860 TQ	USBLS	5/07
	New York	Y	36580 FQ	47300 MW	63590 TQ	USBLS	5/07
	Albany-Schenectady-Troy MSA, NY	Y	39480 FQ	54510 MW	71710 TQ	USBLS	5/07
	Buffalo-Niagara Falls MSA, NY	Y	35910 FQ	47080 MW	57120 TQ	USBLS	5/07
	Kingston MSA, NY	Y	32880 FQ	38340 MW	46420 TQ	USBLS	5/07
	Nassau-Suffolk PMSA, NY	Y	34930 FQ	51290 MW	74860 TQ	USBLS	5/07
	New York-Northern New Jersey-Long Island MSA, NY-NJ-PA	Y	47660 FQ	65790 MW	83270 TQ	USBLS	5/07
	North Carolina	Y	33300 FQ	43130 MW	62080 TQ	USBLS	5/07
	Charlotte-Gastonia-Concord MSA, NC-SC	Y	36140 FQ	52800 MW	66630 TQ	USBLS	5/07
	Raleigh-Cary MSA, NC	Y	42420 FQ	52770 MW	64530 TQ	USBLS	5/07
	North Dakota	Y	31000 FQ	37880 MW	54580 TQ	USBLS	5/07
	Ohio	Y	31880 FQ	40450 MW	59710 TQ	USBLS	5/07
	Cincinnati-Middletown MSA, OH-KY-IN	Y	35110 FQ	49790 MW	72200 TQ	USBLS	5/07
	Cleveland-Elyria-Mentor MSA, OH	Y	27910 FQ	40020 MW	60730 TQ	USBLS	5/07
	Columbus MSA, OH	Y	37700 FQ	44920 MW	71790 TQ	USBLS	5/07
	Oklahoma	Y	22930 FQ	28060 MW	40280 TQ	USBLS	5/07
	Oklahoma City MSA, OK	Y	26000 FQ	31500 MW	45060 TQ	USBLS	5/07
	Tulsa MSA, OK	Y	21560 FQ	24270 MW	35810 TQ	USBLS	5/07
	Oregon	H	19.83 FQ	24.23 MW	30.29 TQ	ORBLS	5/08
	Portland-Vancouver-Beaverton MSA, OR-WA	Y	41700 FQ	51870 MW	76000 TQ	USBLS	5/07
	Pennsylvania	Y	31170 FQ	42850 MW	66010 TQ	USBLS	5/07
	Allentown-Bethlehem-Easton MSA, PA-NJ	Y	18540 FQ	28460 MW	40330 TQ	USBLS	5/07
	Philadelphia-Camden-Wilmington MSA, PA-NJ-DE-MD	Y	47370 FQ	64800 MW	74180 TQ	USBLS	5/07
	Pittsburgh MSA, PA	Y	31430 FQ	41820 MW	59670 TQ	USBLS	5/07
	Rhode Island	Y	46420 FQ	57380 MW	68680 TQ	USBLS	5/07
	Providence-Fall River-Warwick MSA, RI-MA	Y	44150 FQ	56080 MW	70110 TQ	USBLS	5/07
	South Carolina	Y	29690 FQ	37300 MW	53310 TQ	USBLS	5/07
	Charleston-North Charleston MSA, SC	Y	30140 FQ	36980 MW	60100 TQ	USBLS	5/07
	Columbia MSA, SC	Y	32200 FQ	38040 MW	61800 TQ	USBLS	5/07
	South Dakota	Y	31813 FQ	38875 MW	60128 TQ	SDBLS	7/08-9/08
	Sioux Falls MSA, SD	Y	37823 FQ	70696 MW	85358 TQ	SDBLS	7/08-9/08
	Tennessee	Y	32550 FQ	44370 MW	59980 TQ	USBLS	5/07
	Memphis MSA, TN-MS-AR	Y	34680 FQ	50760 MW	71020 TQ	USBLS	5/07
	Nashville-Davidson-Murfreesboro MSA, TN	Y	31860 FQ	40460 MW	52960 TQ	USBLS	5/07
	Texas	Y	33060 FQ	47440 MW	68010 TQ	USBLS	5/07
	Austin-Round Rock MSA, TX	Y	54610 FQ	59880 MW	65340 TQ	USBLS	5/07
	Dallas-Fort Worth-Arlington MSA, TX	Y	40210 FQ	60460 MW	90080 TQ	USBLS	5/07
	El Paso MSA, TX	Y	30450 FQ	42490 MW	51650 TQ	USBLS	5/07
	Houston-Sugar Land-Baytown MSA, TX	Y	35870 FQ	42590 MW	56030 TQ	USBLS	5/07
	Utah	Y	31040 FQ	39090 MW	51860 TQ	USBLS	5/07
	Salt Lake City MSA, UT	Y	35060 FQ	46220 MW	63570 TQ	USBLS	5/07

AE	Average entry wage	AW	Average wage paid	FQ	First quartile wage	LO	Lowest wage paid	MTC	Median total compensation	TCC	Total cash compensation
AER	Average entry range	AWR	Average wage range	H	Hourly	LR	Low end range	MW	Median wage paid	TQ	Third quartile wage
AEX	Average experienced wage	AXR	Average experienced range	HI	Highest wage paid	M	Monthly	MWR	Median wage range	W	Weekly
ATC	Average total compensation	D	Daily	HR	High end range	MCC	Median cash compensation	S	See annotated source	Y	Yearly

52

Occupation/Type/Industry	Location	Per	Low	Mid	High	Source	Date
Appraiser and Assessor of Real Estate	Vermont	Y	26950 FQ	40310 MW	65040 TQ	USBLS	5/07
	Burlington-South Burlington MSA, VT	Y	30480 FQ	56430 MW	76170 TQ	USBLS	5/07
	Virginia	Y	35710 FQ	52000 MW	72640 TQ	USBLS	5/07
	Richmond MSA, VA	Y	46590 FQ	59570 MW	76110 TQ	USBLS	5/07
	Virginia Beach-Norfolk-Newport News MSA, VA-NC	Y	33310 FQ	51110 MW	66850 TQ	USBLS	5/07
	Washington	H	20.42 FQ	25.65 MW	31.93 TQ	WABLS	3/08
	Bremerton-Silverdale MSA, WA	Y	39600 FQ	45600 MW	62850 TQ	USBLS	5/07
	Seattle-Tacoma-Bellevue MSA, WA	Y	43080 FQ	54890 MW	68950 TQ	USBLS	5/07
	West Virginia	Y	22792 FQ	29846 MW	41439 TQ	WVBLS	7/08-9/08
	Charleston MSA, WV	Y	21260 FQ	26660 MW	35930 TQ	USBLS	5/07
	Huntington-Ashland MSA, WV-KY-OH	Y	19280 FQ	25110 MW	49170 TQ	USBLS	5/07
	Wisconsin	Y	39850 FQ	50320 MW	66050 TQ	USBLS	5/07
	Green Bay MSA, WI	Y	43740 FQ	50310 MW	59080 TQ	USBLS	5/07
	Milwaukee-Waukesha-West Allis MSA, WI	Y	46050 FQ	54640 MW	71590 TQ	USBLS	5/07
	Wyoming	Y	31719 FQ	47978 MW	90714 TQ	WYBLS	9/08
	Puerto Rico	Y	20830 FQ	25880 MW	31510 TQ	USBLS	5/07
	San Juan-Caguas-Guaynabo MSA, PR	Y	21890 FQ	26830 MW	31900 TQ	USBLS	5/07
Appraiser Specialist State Government	Ohio	H	19.88 LO		26.28 HI	ODAS	2008
Aquarium Exhibit Designer	Seattle, WA	H	22.01 LO		25.62 HI	CSSS	2007
Aquarium Guide	Seattle, WA	H	13.45 LO		15.68 HI	CSSS	2008
Aquatic Biologist	Ingham County, MI	Y			35600-63246 HR	LSJ01	6/07
Aquatic Center Director Public Schools	Howell, MI	Y			64816 HI	LCPP	2009
Aquatics Attendant Municipal Government	Seaside, CA	S	679 LO		899 HI	SSSS	8/08
Aquatics Specialist Municipal Government	Carlsbad, CA	S	1800 LO		2188 HI	CCSS01	8/5/08
Arbitrator, Mediator, and Conciliator	Alabama	Y	33540 FQ	37100 MW	40760 TQ	USBLS	5/07
	Birmingham-Hoover MSA, AL	Y	33550 FQ	36940 MW	40320 TQ	USBLS	5/07
	Arizona	Y	44580 FQ	52860 MW	63470 TQ	USBLS	5/07
	Phoenix-Mesa-Scottsdale MSA, AZ	Y	45760 FQ	53370 MW	64050 TQ	USBLS	5/07
	Arkansas	Y	61510 FQ	66410 MW	71700 TQ	USBLS	5/07
	Little Rock-North Little Rock MSA, AR	Y	61970 FQ	66820 MW	71900 TQ	USBLS	5/07
	California	H	19.39 FQ	31.30 MW	40.71 TQ	CABLS	1/08-3/08
	Los Angeles-Long Beach-Glendale PMSA, CA	H	20.01 FQ	33.01 MW	45.90 TQ	CABLS	1/08-3/08
	Oakland-Fremont-Hayward MSA, CA	H	36.36 FQ	40.56 MW	56.98 TQ	CABLS	1/08-3/08
	Riverside-San Bernardino-Ontario MSA, CA	H	14.99 FQ	33.66 MW	38.02 TQ	CABLS	1/08-3/08
	Sacramento-Arden Arcade-Roseville MSA, CA	H	25.65 FQ	38.88 MW	51.45 TQ	CABLS	1/08-3/08
	San Diego-Carlsbad-San Marcos MSA, CA	H	29.97 FQ	34.78 MW	40.44 TQ	CABLS	1/08-3/08
	San Francisco-San Mateo-Redwood PMSA, CA	H	22.14 FQ	26.35 MW	36.88 TQ	CABLS	1/08-3/08
	San Jose-Sunnyvale-Santa Clara MSA, CA	H	29.00 FQ	36.52 MW		CABLS	1/08-3/08
	Santa Ana-Anaheim-Irvine PMSA, CA	Y	38750 FQ	66220 MW	79190 TQ	USBLS	5/07
	Colorado	Y	51370 FQ	62020 MW	77120 TQ	USBLS	5/07

AE	Average entry wage	AW	Average wage paid	FQ	First quartile wage	LO Lowest wage paid	MTC Median total compensation	TCC Total cash compensation
AER	Average entry range	AWR	Average wage range	H	Hourly	LR Low end range	MW Median wage paid	TQ Third quartile wage
AEX	Average experienced wage	AXR	Average experienced range	HI	Highest wage paid	M Monthly	MWR Median wage range	W Weekly
ATC	Average total compensation	D	Daily	HR	High end range	MCC Median cash compensation	S See annotated source	Y Yearly

Occupation/Type/Industry	Location	Per	Low	Mid	High	Source	Date
Arbitrator, Mediator, and Conciliator	Connecticut	H	21.65 AE	36.23 MW		CTBLS	1/08-3/08
	Hartford-West Hartford-East Hartford MSA, CT	Y	61300 FQ	78130 MW	95910 TQ	USBLS	5/07
	Delaware	Y	38170 FQ	45700 MW	54200 TQ	USBLS	5/07
	District of Columbia	Y	39430 FQ	50500 MW	65700 TQ	USBLS	5/07
	Washington-Arlington-Alexandria MSA, DC-VA-MD-WV	Y	34780 FQ	42210 MW	67290 TQ	USBLS	5/07
	Florida	Y	34270 FQ	38880 MW	46610 TQ	USBLS	5/07
	Miami-Fort Lauderdale-Miami Beach MSA, FL	Y	44720 FQ	50370 MW	63710 TQ	USBLS	5/07
	Georgia	Y	36610 FQ	45710 MW	58540 TQ	USBLS	5/07
	Atlanta-Sandy Springs-Marietta MSA, GA	Y	38320 FQ	49860 MW	63840 TQ	USBLS	5/07
	Idaho	Y	38960 FQ	49050 MW	58510 TQ	USBLS	5/07
	Boise City-Nampa MSA, ID	Y	39030 FQ	48330 MW	57730 TQ	USBLS	5/07
	Illinois	Y	56920 FQ	83910 MW	98680 TQ	USBLS	5/07
	Chicago-Naperville-Joliet MSA, IL-IN-WI	Y	49670 FQ	73430 MW	96680 TQ	USBLS	5/07
	Indiana	Y	35330 FQ	47230 MW	63170 TQ	USBLS	5/07
	Indianapolis-Carmel MSA, IN	Y	41280 FQ	51710 MW	66980 TQ	USBLS	5/07
	Iowa	Y	45910 FQ	79420 MW	94120 TQ	USBLS	5/07
	Des Moines-West Des Moines MSA, IA	Y	50850 FQ	81060 MW	92310 TQ	USBLS	5/07
	Kansas	Y	14930 FQ	45220 MW	73280 TQ	USBLS	5/07
	Louisiana	H	18.78 FQ	27.46 MW	45.21 TQ	LABLS	1/08-3/08
	Maine	Y	37840 FQ	46160 MW	57890 TQ	USBLS	5/07
	Maryland	Y		38925 MW		MDBLS	3/08
	Baltimore-Towson MSA, MD	Y	35320 FQ	37750 MW	40190 TQ	USBLS	5/07
	Massachusetts	Y	43520 FQ	55750 MW	93480 TQ	USBLS	5/07
	Boston-Cambridge-Quincy NECTA, MA	Y	50040 FQ	65070 MW	96270 TQ	USBLS	5/07
	Worcester MSA, MA-CT	Y	42320 FQ	47200 MW	103140 TQ	USBLS	5/07
	Michigan	Y	51280 FQ	88040 MW	109200 TQ	USBLS	5/07
	Detroit-Warren-Livonia MSA, MI	Y	87450 FQ	104840 MW	120700 TQ	USBLS	5/07
	Minnesota	Y	59886 FQ	74114 MW	89264 TQ	MNBLS	10/08-12/08
	Minneapolis-Saint Paul MSA, MN-WI	Y	62763 FQ	75997 MW	103178 TQ	MNBLS	10/08-12/08
	Mississippi	Y	21910 FQ	26050 MW	35230 TQ	USBLS	5/07
	Missouri	Y	40520 FQ	51130 MW	68940 TQ	USBLS	5/07
	Kansas City MSA, MO-KS	Y	38680 FQ	51510 MW	81610 TQ	USBLS	5/07
	St. Louis MSA, MO-IL	Y	48910 FQ	56350 MW	82020 TQ	USBLS	5/07
	Montana	Y	44950 FQ	49630 MW	53960 TQ	USBLS	5/07
	Nevada	H	31.42 FQ	36.17 MW	41.02 TQ	NVBLS	5/08
	Las Vegas-Paradise MSA, NV	H	30.74 FQ	35.34 MW	40.05 TQ	NVBLS	5/08
	New Jersey	Y	50110 FQ	76180 MW	101430 TQ	USBLS	5/07
	New York	Y	46780 FQ	54740 MW	90650 TQ	USBLS	5/07
	Albany-Schenectady-Troy MSA, NY	Y	70440 FQ	90550 MW	110020 TQ	USBLS	5/07
	Buffalo-Niagara Falls MSA, NY	Y	45080 FQ	48550 MW	52110 TQ	USBLS	5/07
	Nassau-Suffolk PMSA, NY	Y	48240 FQ	80990 MW	94520 TQ	USBLS	5/07
	New York-Northern New Jersey-Long Island MSA, NY-NJ-PA	Y	46060 FQ	51120 MW	79190 TQ	USBLS	5/07
	North Carolina	Y	31860 FQ	43960 MW	51660 TQ	USBLS	5/07
	Ohio	Y	42310 FQ	54700 MW	65590 TQ	USBLS	5/07
	Cincinnati-Middletown MSA, OH-KY-IN	Y	14730 FQ	35750 MW	61360 TQ	USBLS	5/07
	Cleveland-Elyria-Mentor MSA, OH	Y	52050 FQ	60940 MW	74830 TQ	USBLS	5/07
	Columbus MSA, OH	Y	40450 FQ	48950 MW	61820 TQ	USBLS	5/07
	Oklahoma	Y	34320 FQ	48800 MW	73910 TQ	USBLS	5/07
	Oregon	H	22.44 FQ	29.06 MW	42.18 TQ	ORBLS	5/08
	Portland-Vancouver-Beaverton MSA, OR-WA	Y	53410 FQ	79300 MW	93870 TQ	USBLS	5/07
	Pennsylvania	Y	15020 FQ	37520 MW	64070 TQ	USBLS	5/07

AE	Average entry wage	AW	Average wage paid	FQ	First quartile wage	LO	Lowest wage paid	MTC	Median total compensation	TCC	Total cash compensation

AE   Average entry wage   AW   Average wage paid   FQ   First quartile wage   LO   Lowest wage paid   MTC Median total compensation TCC Total cash compensation
AER Average entry range   AWR Average wage range   H   Hourly   LR   Low end range   MW   Median wage paid   TQ   Third quartile wage
AEX Average experienced wage AXR Average experienced range HI   Highest wage paid   M   Monthly   MWR Median wage range   W   Weekly
ATC Average total compensation D   Daily   HR   High end range   MCC Median cash compensation S   See annotated source   Y   Yearly

Occupation/Type/Industry	Location	Per	Low	Mid	High	Source	Date
Arbitrator, Mediator, and Conciliator	Philadelphia-Camden-Wilmington MSA, PA-NJ-DE-MD	Y	14850 FQ	35760 MW	68020 TQ	USBLS	5/07
	Pittsburgh MSA, PA	Y	55790 FQ	60460 MW	65130 TQ	USBLS	5/07
	South Carolina	Y	27400 FQ	30780 MW	46460 TQ	USBLS	5/07
	Columbia MSA, SC	Y	26630 FQ	28850 MW	31780 TQ	USBLS	5/07
	Tennessee	Y	56200 FQ	70240 MW	90150 TQ	USBLS	5/07
	Memphis MSA, TN-MS-AR	Y	62010 FQ	78920 MW	93230 TQ	USBLS	5/07
	Texas	Y	38300 FQ	54030 MW	64980 TQ	USBLS	5/07
	Dallas-Fort Worth-Arlington MSA, TX	Y	34200 FQ	40900 MW	59750 TQ	USBLS	5/07
	Utah	Y	27800 FQ	34450 MW	45420 TQ	USBLS	5/07
	Washington	H	27.49 FQ	34.48 MW	39.59 TQ	WABLS	3/08
	Seattle-Tacoma-Bellevue MSA, WA	Y	63500 FQ	75870 MW	93930 TQ	USBLS	5/07
	Charleston MSA, WV	Y	27630 FQ	30750 MW	36730 TQ	USBLS	5/07
	Puerto Rico	Y	27160 FQ	33130 MW	39250 TQ	USBLS	5/07
	San Juan-Caguas-Guaynabo MSA, PR	Y	27160 FQ	33130 MW	39250 TQ	USBLS	5/07
Arboriculturist							
Municipal Government	Seattle, WA	H	24.21 LO		28.27 HI	CSSS	2007
Arborist							
Municipal Government	Seattle, WA	H	34.12 LO		39.67 HI	CSSS	2008
Architect							
Except Landscape and Naval	Alabama	Y	51750 FQ	69150 MW	87200 TQ	USBLS	5/07
Except Landscape and Naval	Birmingham-Hoover MSA, AL	Y	47540 FQ	60700 MW	82070 TQ	USBLS	5/07
Except Landscape and Naval	Montgomery MSA, AL	Y	58730 FQ	73560 MW	84020 TQ	USBLS	5/07
Except Landscape and Naval	Alaska	Y	54360 FQ	65130 MW	82420 TQ	USBLS	5/07
Except Landscape and Naval	Anchorage MSA, AK	Y	53780 FQ	63680 MW	79720 TQ	USBLS	5/07
Except Landscape and Naval	Arizona	Y	43410 FQ	62990 MW	78980 TQ	USBLS	5/07
Except Landscape and Naval	Phoenix-Mesa-Scottsdale MSA, AZ	Y	50410 FQ	68280 MW	82410 TQ	USBLS	5/07
Except Landscape and Naval	Tucson MSA, AZ	Y	28860 FQ	40520 MW	62540 TQ	USBLS	5/07
Except Landscape and Naval	Arkansas	Y	52040 FQ	69480 MW	105060 TQ	USBLS	5/07
Except Landscape and Naval	Fayetteville-Springdale-Rogers MSA, AR-MO	Y	51470 FQ	71180 MW	88420 TQ	USBLS	5/07
Except Landscape and Naval	Little Rock-North Little Rock MSA, AR	Y	58580 FQ	81440 MW	138880 TQ	USBLS	5/07
Except Landscape and Naval	California	H	29.42 FQ	37.25 MW	47.16 TQ	CABLS	1/08-3/08
Except Landscape and Naval	Los Angeles-Long Beach-Glendale PMSA, CA	H	28.57 FQ	36.95 MW	47.03 TQ	CABLS	1/08-3/08
Except Landscape and Naval	Modesto MSA, CA	H	32.44 FQ	35.15 MW	38.09 TQ	CABLS	1/08-3/08
Except Landscape and Naval	Oakland-Fremont-Hayward MSA, CA	H	31.66 FQ	37.43 MW	49.27 TQ	CABLS	1/08-3/08
Except Landscape and Naval	Oxnard-Thousand Oaks-Ventura MSA, CA	H	38.42 FQ	67.33 MW		CABLS	1/08-3/08
Except Landscape and Naval	Riverside-San Bernardino-Ontario MSA, CA	H	28.88 FQ	34.69 MW	46.66 TQ	CABLS	1/08-3/08
Except Landscape and Naval	Sacramento-Arden Arcade-Roseville MSA, CA	H	31.03 FQ	37.25 MW	44.65 TQ	CABLS	1/08-3/08
Except Landscape and Naval	San Diego-Carlsbad-San Marcos MSA, CA	H	28.97 FQ	38.44 MW	50.60 TQ	CABLS	1/08-3/08
Except Landscape and Naval	San Francisco-San Mateo-Redwood PMSA, CA	H	28.74 FQ	35.86 MW	45.32 TQ	CABLS	1/08-3/08
Except Landscape and Naval	San Jose-Sunnyvale-Santa Clara MSA, CA	H	28.69 FQ	38.61 MW	49.39 TQ	CABLS	1/08-3/08
Except Landscape and Naval	Santa Ana-Anaheim-Irvine PMSA, CA	Y	63720 FQ	76800 MW	98680 TQ	USBLS	5/07
Except Landscape and Naval	Colorado	Y	44260 FQ	60510 MW	87560 TQ	USBLS	5/07
Except Landscape and Naval	Denver-Aurora MSA, CO	Y	41970 FQ	57320 MW	84810 TQ	USBLS	5/07
Except Landscape and Naval	Connecticut	H	26.81 AE	38.98 MW		CTBLS	1/08-3/08
Except Landscape and Naval	Bridgeport-Stamford-Norwalk MSA, CT	Y	60320 FQ	84180 MW	103340 TQ	USBLS	5/07
Except Landscape and Naval	Hartford-West Hartford-East Hartford MSA, CT	Y	63100 FQ	76760 MW	95990 TQ	USBLS	5/07
Except Landscape and Naval	Delaware	Y	57620 FQ	74180 MW	90680 TQ	USBLS	5/07
Except Landscape and Naval	Wilmington PMSA, DE-MD-NJ	Y	60320 FQ	78320 MW	94670 TQ	USBLS	5/07

AE	Average entry wage	**AW**	Average wage paid	**FQ**	First quartile wage	**LO**	Lowest wage paid	**MTC** Median total compensation	**TCC** Total cash compensation
AER	Average entry range	**AWR**	Average wage range	**H**	Hourly	**LR**	Low end range	**MW** Median wage paid	**TQ** Third quartile wage
AEX	Average experienced wage	**AXR**	Average experienced range	**HI**	Highest wage paid	**M**	Monthly	**MWR** Median wage range	**W** Weekly
ATC	Average total compensation	**D**	Daily	**HR**	High end range	**MCC**	Median cash compensation	**S** See annotated source	**Y** Yearly

Occupation/Type/Industry	Location	Per	Low	Mid	High	Source	Date
Architect							
Except Landscape and Naval	District of Columbia	Y	53320 FQ	73310 MW	95500 TQ	USBLS	5/07
Except Landscape and Naval	Washington-Arlington-Alexandria MSA, DC-VA-MD-WV	Y	55380 FQ	73850 MW	94890 TQ	USBLS	5/07
Except Landscape and Naval	Florida	Y	43310 FQ	56640 MW	75570 TQ	USBLS	5/07
Except Landscape and Naval	Cape Coral-Fort Myers MSA, FL	Y	48560 FQ	111950 MW	125510 TQ	USBLS	5/07
Except Landscape and Naval	Fort Lauderdale-Pompano Beach-Deerfield Beach PMSA, FL	Y	36230 FQ	46070 MW	66420 TQ	USBLS	5/07
Except Landscape and Naval	Jacksonville MSA, FL	Y	46020 FQ	61500 MW	78050 TQ	USBLS	5/07
Except Landscape and Naval	Miami-Fort Lauderdale-Miami Beach MSA, FL	Y	41420 FQ	56350 MW	74130 TQ	USBLS	5/07
Except Landscape and Naval	Orlando-Kissimmee MSA, FL	Y	43590 FQ	55300 MW	78790 TQ	USBLS	5/07
Except Landscape and Naval	Tampa-St. Petersburg-Clearwater MSA, FL	Y	42990 FQ	54580 MW	68340 TQ	USBLS	5/07
Except Landscape and Naval	West Palm Beach-Boca Raton-Boynton Beach PMSA, FL	Y	40660 FQ	50510 MW	70900 TQ	USBLS	5/07
Except Landscape and Naval	Georgia	Y	51590 FQ	72150 MW	97160 TQ	USBLS	5/07
Except Landscape and Naval	Atlanta-Sandy Springs-Marietta MSA, GA	Y	52490 FQ	73910 MW	98870 TQ	USBLS	5/07
Except Landscape and Naval	Savannah MSA, GA	Y	34350 FQ	45080 MW	61290 TQ	USBLS	5/07
Except Landscape and Naval	Hawaii	Y	52960 FQ	65150 MW	78380 TQ	USBLS	5/07
Except Landscape and Naval	Honolulu MSA, HI	Y	54840 FQ	65720 MW	78750 TQ	USBLS	5/07
Except Landscape and Naval	Idaho	Y	45960 FQ	63030 MW	76230 TQ	USBLS	5/07
Except Landscape and Naval	Boise City-Nampa MSA, ID	Y	53700 FQ	67840 MW	77780 TQ	USBLS	5/07
Except Landscape and Naval	Illinois	Y	49440 FQ	67900 MW	90430 TQ	USBLS	5/07
Except Landscape and Naval	Chicago-Naperville-Joliet MSA, IL-IN-WI	Y	49170 FQ	67750 MW	90860 TQ	USBLS	5/07
Except Landscape and Naval	Indiana	Y	45060 FQ	58970 MW	81940 TQ	USBLS	5/07
Except Landscape and Naval	Evansville MSA, IN-KY	Y	54530 FQ	83540 MW	124930 TQ	USBLS	5/07
Except Landscape and Naval	Gary PMSA, IN	Y	29620 FQ	47670 MW	78360 TQ	USBLS	5/07
Except Landscape and Naval	Indianapolis-Carmel MSA, IN	Y	48270 FQ	62660 MW	89620 TQ	USBLS	5/07
Except Landscape and Naval	Iowa	Y	47690 FQ	62560 MW	78100 TQ	USBLS	5/07
Except Landscape and Naval	Davenport-Moline-Rock Island MSA, IA-IL	Y	62770 FQ	81780 MW	95730 TQ	USBLS	5/07
Except Landscape and Naval	Des Moines-West Des Moines MSA, IA	Y	48630 FQ	62480 MW	74830 TQ	USBLS	5/07
Except Landscape and Naval	Waterloo-Cedar Falls MSA, IA	Y	45580 FQ	85490 MW	108090 TQ	USBLS	5/07
Except Landscape and Naval	Kansas	Y	49090 FQ	61240 MW	76430 TQ	USBLS	5/07
Except Landscape and Naval	Wichita MSA, KS	Y	42350 FQ	48220 MW	60840 TQ	USBLS	5/07
Except Landscape and Naval	Kentucky	Y	42145 FQ	59072 MW	72769 TQ	KYBLS	2008
Except Landscape and Naval	Louisville-Jefferson County MSA, KY-IN	Y	46290 FQ	61380 MW	73210 TQ	USBLS	5/07
Except Landscape and Naval	Louisiana	H	20.05 FQ	28.35 MW	35.04 TQ	LABLS	1/08-3/08
Except Landscape and Naval	Baton Rouge MSA, LA	Y	41310 FQ	68470 MW	78500 TQ	USBLS	5/07
Except Landscape and Naval	New Orleans-Metairie-Kenner MSA, LA	Y	47460 FQ	58800 MW	70040 TQ	USBLS	5/07
Except Landscape and Naval	Maine	Y	49660 FQ	58520 MW	67710 TQ	USBLS	5/07
Except Landscape and Naval	Portland-South Portland-Biddeford MSA, ME	Y	50700 FQ	58980 MW	68540 TQ	USBLS	5/07
Except Landscape and Naval	Maryland	Y		75025 MW		MDBLS	3/08
Except Landscape and Naval	Baltimore-Towson MSA, MD	Y	52550 FQ	67580 MW	89460 TQ	USBLS	5/07
Except Landscape and Naval	Bethesda-Gaithersburg-Frederick PMSA, MD	Y	68440 FQ	80860 MW	96850 TQ	USBLS	5/07
Except Landscape and Naval	Massachusetts	Y	62120 FQ	76930 MW	97580 TQ	USBLS	5/07
Except Landscape and Naval	Boston-Cambridge-Quincy NECTA, MA	Y	62410 FQ	77360 MW	99050 TQ	USBLS	5/07
Except Landscape and Naval	Worcester MSA, MA-CT	Y	46150 FQ	63110 MW	88700 TQ	USBLS	5/07
Except Landscape and Naval	Michigan	Y	53980 FQ	65490 MW	79240 TQ	USBLS	5/07
Except Landscape and Naval	Detroit-Warren-Livonia MSA, MI	Y	55410 FQ	65890 MW	77560 TQ	USBLS	5/07
Except Landscape and Naval	Grand Rapids-Wyoming MSA, MI	Y	63110 FQ	76890 MW	94840 TQ	USBLS	5/07
Except Landscape and Naval	Warren-Troy-Farmington Hills PMSA, MI	Y	53240 FQ	64010 MW	74270 TQ	USBLS	5/07
Except Landscape and Naval	Minnesota	Y	58044 FQ	74041 MW	95206 TQ	MNBLS	10/08-12/08
Except Landscape and Naval	Duluth-Superior MSA, MN-WI	Y	54058 FQ	66016 MW	142286 TQ	MNBLS	10/08-12/08
Except Landscape and Naval	Minneapolis-Saint Paul MSA, MN-WI	Y	58756 FQ	74941 MW	95436 TQ	MNBLS	10/08-12/08
Except Landscape and Naval	Rochester MSA, MN	Y	63595 FQ	83370 MW	94521 TQ	MNBLS	10/08-12/08

Occupation/Type/Industry	Location	Per	Low	Mid	High	Source	Date
Architect							
Except Landscape and Naval	Mississippi	Y	40310 FQ	53170 MW	68150 TQ	USBLS	5/07
Except Landscape and Naval	Jackson MSA, MS	Y	43170 FQ	54930 MW	81540 TQ	USBLS	5/07
Except Landscape and Naval	Missouri	Y	44680 FQ	62370 MW	82830 TQ	USBLS	5/07
Except Landscape and Naval	Kansas City MSA, MO-KS	Y	48490 FQ	65830 MW	85530 TQ	USBLS	5/07
Except Landscape and Naval	St. Louis MSA, MO-IL	Y	51880 FQ	65370 MW	83330 TQ	USBLS	5/07
Except Landscape and Naval	Montana	Y	35650 FQ	46400 MW	59600 TQ	USBLS	5/07
Except Landscape and Naval	Billings MSA, MT	Y	36800 FQ	47920 MW	63770 TQ	USBLS	5/07
Except Landscape and Naval	Nebraska	Y	48800 FQ	66120 MW	87620 TQ	USBLS	5/07
Except Landscape and Naval	Omaha-Council Bluffs MSA, NE-IA	Y	51270 FQ	69210 MW	92470 TQ	USBLS	5/07
Except Landscape and Naval	Nevada	H	25.11 FQ	31.76 MW	42.33 TQ	NVBLS	5/08
Except Landscape and Naval	Las Vegas-Paradise MSA, NV	H	23.85 FQ	31.12 MW	41.15 TQ	NVBLS	5/08
Except Landscape and Naval	New Hampshire	H	21.51 AE	28.36 MW	39.91 AEX	NHBLS	6/08
Except Landscape and Naval	Manchester MSA, NH	Y	45590 FQ	52210 MW	60660 TQ	USBLS	5/07
Except Landscape and Naval	New Jersey	Y	59960 FQ	74970 MW	91430 TQ	USBLS	5/07
Except Landscape and Naval	Camden PMSA, NJ	Y	56170 FQ	70700 MW	83760 TQ	USBLS	5/07
Except Landscape and Naval	Edison PMSA, NJ	Y	65060 FQ	88340 MW	104620 TQ	USBLS	5/07
Except Landscape and Naval	Newark-Union PMSA, NJ-PA	Y	57030 FQ	67680 MW	83780 TQ	USBLS	5/07
Except Landscape and Naval	Trenton-Ewing MSA, NJ	Y	58630 FQ	72300 MW	93900 TQ	USBLS	5/07
Except Landscape and Naval	New Mexico	Y	51300 FQ	63400 MW	80050 TQ	USBLS	5/07
Except Landscape and Naval	Albuquerque MSA, NM	Y	54990 FQ	68930 MW	81930 TQ	USBLS	5/07
Except Landscape and Naval	New York	Y	55260 FQ	74430 MW	96640 TQ	USBLS	5/07
Except Landscape and Naval	Albany-Schenectady-Troy MSA, NY	Y	57780 FQ	72810 MW	97140 TQ	USBLS	5/07
Except Landscape and Naval	Buffalo-Niagara Falls MSA, NY	Y	43570 FQ	57000 MW	70550 TQ	USBLS	5/07
Except Landscape and Naval	Nassau-Suffolk PMSA, NY	Y	67050 FQ	86360 MW	103760 TQ	USBLS	5/07
Except Landscape and Naval	New York-Northern New Jersey-Long Island MSA, NY-NJ-PA	Y	57780 FQ	76640 MW	97840 TQ	USBLS	5/07
Except Landscape and Naval	North Carolina	Y	52380 FQ	64040 MW	83810 TQ	USBLS	5/07
Except Landscape and Naval	Charlotte-Gastonia-Concord MSA, NC-SC	Y	58360 FQ	69960 MW	89990 TQ	USBLS	5/07
Except Landscape and Naval	Raleigh-Cary MSA, NC	Y	44540 FQ	58950 MW	78560 TQ	USBLS	5/07
Except Landscape and Naval	North Dakota	Y	41420 FQ	51580 MW	65080 TQ	USBLS	5/07
Except Landscape and Naval	Fargo MSA, ND-MN	Y	39250 FQ	49790 MW	62140 TQ	USBLS	5/07
Except Landscape and Naval	Ohio	Y	56550 FQ	69700 MW	86210 TQ	USBLS	5/07
Except Landscape and Naval	Cincinnati-Middletown MSA, OH-KY-IN	Y	57390 FQ	71300 MW	86020 TQ	USBLS	5/07
Except Landscape and Naval	Cleveland-Elyria-Mentor MSA, OH	Y	54040 FQ	63890 MW	78590 TQ	USBLS	5/07
Except Landscape and Naval	Columbus MSA, OH	Y	60940 FQ	74540 MW	98350 TQ	USBLS	5/07
Except Landscape and Naval	Dayton MSA, OH	Y	51570 FQ	62450 MW	78670 TQ	USBLS	5/07
Except Landscape and Naval	Oklahoma	Y	46850 FQ	61280 MW	79410 TQ	USBLS	5/07
Except Landscape and Naval	Oklahoma City MSA, OK	Y	53340 FQ	65790 MW	82220 TQ	USBLS	5/07
Except Landscape and Naval	Tulsa MSA, OK	Y	40030 FQ	56820 MW	74130 TQ	USBLS	5/07
Except Landscape and Naval	Oregon	H	21.19 FQ	27.47 MW	34.45 TQ	ORBLS	5/08
Except Landscape and Naval	Portland-Vancouver-Beaverton MSA, OR-WA	Y	44560 FQ	57970 MW	72010 TQ	USBLS	5/07
Except Landscape and Naval	Pennsylvania	Y	55730 FQ	73230 MW	95180 TQ	USBLS	5/07
Except Landscape and Naval	Allentown-Bethlehem-Easton MSA, PA-NJ	Y	62010 FQ	72740 MW	81230 TQ	USBLS	5/07
Except Landscape and Naval	Philadelphia-Camden-Wilmington MSA, PA-NJ-DE-MD	Y	56680 FQ	75940 MW	95110 TQ	USBLS	5/07
Except Landscape and Naval	Pittsburgh MSA, PA	Y	55020 FQ	70830 MW	95110 TQ	USBLS	5/07
Except Landscape and Naval	Rhode Island	Y	60050 FQ	72150 MW	82290 TQ	USBLS	5/07
Except Landscape and Naval	Providence-Fall River-Warwick MSA, RI-MA	Y	60450 FQ	72310 MW	82510 TQ	USBLS	5/07
Except Landscape and Naval	South Carolina	Y	56930 FQ	72580 MW	90430 TQ	USBLS	5/07
Except Landscape and Naval	Charleston-North Charleston MSA, SC	Y	55060 FQ	70750 MW	88250 TQ	USBLS	5/07
Except Landscape and Naval	Columbia MSA, SC	Y	63630 FQ	70960 MW	77710 TQ	USBLS	5/07
Except Landscape and Naval	South Dakota	Y	59551 FQ	67603 MW	96015 TQ	SDBLS	7/08-9/08
Except Landscape and Naval	Sioux Falls MSA, SD	Y	61595 FQ	70787 MW	105568 TQ	SDBLS	7/08-9/08
Except Landscape and Naval	Tennessee	Y	52760 FQ	65290 MW	80290 TQ	USBLS	5/07
Except Landscape and Naval	Memphis MSA, TN-MS-AR	Y	49400 FQ	57970 MW	80400 TQ	USBLS	5/07
Except Landscape and Naval	Nashville-Davidson-Murfreesboro MSA, TN	Y	57000 FQ	70260 MW	84290 TQ	USBLS	5/07
Except Landscape and Naval	Texas	Y	48580 FQ	64280 MW	86260 TQ	USBLS	5/07
Except Landscape and Naval	Austin-Round Rock MSA, TX	Y	47880 FQ	56650 MW	70550 TQ	USBLS	5/07

AE	Average entry wage	AW	Average wage paid	FQ	First quartile wage	LO	Lowest wage paid	MTC	Median total compensation	TCC	Total cash compensation
AER	Average entry range	AWR	Average wage range	H	Hourly	LR	Low end range	MW	Median wage paid	TQ	Third quartile wage
AEX	Average experienced wage	AXR	Average experienced range	HI	Highest wage paid	M	Monthly	MWR	Median wage range	W	Weekly
ATC	Average total compensation	D	Daily	HR	High end range	MCC	Median cash compensation	S	See annotated source	Y	Yearly

Occupation/Type/Industry	Location	Per	Low	Mid	High	Source	Date
Architect							
Except Landscape and Naval	Dallas-Fort Worth-Arlington MSA, TX	Y	48970 FQ	66330 MW	85290 TQ	USBLS	5/07
Except Landscape and Naval	El Paso MSA, TX	Y	39330 FQ	60970 MW	77400 TQ	USBLS	5/07
Except Landscape and Naval	Houston-Sugar Land-Baytown MSA, TX	Y	52260 FQ	71240 MW	96820 TQ	USBLS	5/07
Except Landscape and Naval	San Antonio MSA, TX	Y	47830 FQ	63280 MW	81070 TQ	USBLS	5/07
Except Landscape and Naval	Utah	Y	61180 FQ	71110 MW	87850 TQ	USBLS	5/07
Except Landscape and Naval	Salt Lake City MSA, UT	Y	61330 FQ	71450 MW	89390 TQ	USBLS	5/07
Except Landscape and Naval	Vermont	Y	49130 FQ	63860 MW	86020 TQ	USBLS	5/07
Except Landscape and Naval	Burlington-South Burlington MSA, VT	Y	46500 FQ	71580 MW	92580 TQ	USBLS	5/07
Except Landscape and Naval	Virginia	Y	53350 FQ	67500 MW	85910 TQ	USBLS	5/07
Except Landscape and Naval	Richmond MSA, VA	Y	56470 FQ	65740 MW	76100 TQ	USBLS	5/07
Except Landscape and Naval	Virginia Beach-Norfolk-Newport News MSA, VA-NC	Y	53330 FQ	65930 MW	87990 TQ	USBLS	5/07
Except Landscape and Naval	Washington	H	27.18 FQ	32.99 MW	40.29 TQ	WABLS	3/08
Except Landscape and Naval	Seattle-Tacoma-Bellevue MSA, WA	Y	57150 FQ	68770 MW	83070 TQ	USBLS	5/07
Except Landscape and Naval	West Virginia	Y	64469 FQ	76886 MW	96643 TQ	WVBLS	7/08-9/08
Except Landscape and Naval	Wisconsin	Y	47500 FQ	63540 MW	81770 TQ	USBLS	5/07
Except Landscape and Naval	Milwaukee-Waukesha-West Allis MSA, WI	Y	49940 FQ	66910 MW	83610 TQ	USBLS	5/07
Except Landscape and Naval	Wyoming	Y	46612 FQ	52370 MW	67012 TQ	WYBLS	9/08
Except Landscape and Naval	Casper MSA, WY	Y	38702 FQ	45892 MW	64192 TQ	WYBLS	9/08
Except Landscape and Naval	Cheyenne MSA, WY	Y	47650 FQ	52796 MW	75223 TQ	WYBLS	9/08
Except Landscape and Naval	Puerto Rico	Y	34140 FQ	41060 MW	65030 TQ	USBLS	5/07
Except Landscape and Naval	San Juan-Caguas-Guaynabo MSA, PR	Y	33980 FQ	40760 MW	64840 TQ	USBLS	5/07
Except Landscape and Naval	Guam	Y	35790 FQ	48420 MW	69960 TQ	USBLS	5/07
State Government	Connecticut	Y	67888 HI		93926 HI	AFT02	3/1/08
State Government	Indiana	Y	38454 LO		68770 HI	AFT02	3/1/08
State Government	Utah	Y	39533 LO		62679 HI	AFT02	3/1/08
Architect Intern							
Municipal Government	Cincinnati, OH	Y	44033 LO		60634 HI	COHSS	10/08
Architect of the Capitol							
Federal Government	United States	Y			167800 HI	CRS02	1/08
Architectural and Civil Drafter	Alabama	Y	30240 FQ	40520 MW	51910 TQ	USBLS	5/07
	Birmingham-Hoover MSA, AL	Y	30490 FQ	42440 MW	52150 TQ	USBLS	5/07
	Montgomery MSA, AL	Y	35060 FQ	47860 MW	56200 TQ	USBLS	5/07
	Alaska	Y	39810 FQ	46780 MW	55790 TQ	USBLS	5/07
	Anchorage MSA, AK	Y	38620 FQ	45980 MW	55640 TQ	USBLS	5/07
	Arizona	Y	32980 FQ	39940 MW	52820 TQ	USBLS	5/07
	Phoenix-Mesa-Scottsdale MSA, AZ	Y	32620 FQ	39560 MW	52450 TQ	USBLS	5/07
	Tucson MSA, AZ	Y	35330 FQ	43280 MW	55450 TQ	USBLS	5/07
	Arkansas	Y	29070 FQ	36040 MW	47150 TQ	USBLS	5/07
	Little Rock-North Little Rock MSA, AR	Y	33450 FQ	40100 MW	57600 TQ	USBLS	5/07
	California	H	19.50 FQ	24.70 MW	30.07 TQ	CABLS	1/08-3/08
	Los Angeles-Long Beach-Glendale PMSA, CA	H	18.53 FQ	24.79 MW	30.14 TQ	CABLS	1/08-3/08
	Oakland-Fremont-Hayward MSA, CA	H	23.53 FQ	27.79 MW	32.25 TQ	CABLS	1/08-3/08
	Riverside-San Bernardino-Ontario MSA, CA	H	19.06 FQ	24.37 MW	32.25 TQ	CABLS	1/08-3/08
	Sacramento-Arden Arcade-Roseville MSA, CA	H	18.86 FQ	22.27 MW	27.64 TQ	CABLS	1/08-3/08
	San Diego-Carlsbad-San Marcos MSA, CA	H	18.00 FQ	22.11 MW	27.89 TQ	CABLS	1/08-3/08
	San Francisco-San Mateo-Redwood PMSA, CA	H	22.14 FQ	26.17 MW	31.06 TQ	CABLS	1/08-3/08
	San Jose-Sunnyvale-Santa Clara MSA, CA	H	23.23 FQ	29.67 MW	49.34 TQ	CABLS	1/08-3/08
	Santa Ana-Anaheim-Irvine PMSA, CA	Y	39830 FQ	51400 MW	60000 TQ	USBLS	5/07
	Colorado	Y	36650 FQ	45730 MW	53840 TQ	USBLS	5/07
	Denver-Aurora MSA, CO	Y	39430 FQ	46910 MW	53790 TQ	USBLS	5/07
	Connecticut	H	17.64 AE	23.61 MW		CTBLS	1/08-3/08

AE Average entry wage	**AW** Average wage paid	**FQ** First quartile wage	**LO** Lowest wage paid	**MTC** Median total compensation	**TCC** Total cash compensation
AER Average entry range	**AWR** Average wage range	**H** Hourly	**LR** Low end range	**MW** Median wage paid	**TQ** Third quartile wage
AEX Average experienced wage	**AXR** Average experienced range	**HI** Highest wage paid	**M** Monthly	**MWR** Median wage range	**W** Weekly
ATC Average total compensation	**D** Daily	**HR** High end range	**MCC** Median cash compensation	**S** See annotated source	**Y** Yearly

Occupation/Type/Industry	Location	Per	Low	Mid	High	Source	Date
Architectural and Civil Drafter	Bridgeport-Stamford-Norwalk MSA, CT	Y	42250 FQ	49060 MW	58970 TQ	USBLS	5/07
	Hartford-West Hartford-East Hartford MSA, CT	Y	39920 FQ	46920 MW	54380 TQ	USBLS	5/07
	Delaware	Y	34420 FQ	41540 MW	50360 TQ	USBLS	5/07
	Wilmington PMSA, DE-MD-NJ	Y	34280 FQ	41060 MW	50010 TQ	USBLS	5/07
	District of Columbia	Y	41610 FQ	47920 MW	59590 TQ	USBLS	5/07
	Washington-Arlington-Alexandria MSA, DC-VA-MD-WV	Y	35820 FQ	44160 MW	52570 TQ	USBLS	5/07
	Florida	Y	31120 FQ	40600 MW	51700 TQ	USBLS	5/07
	Fort Lauderdale-Pompano Beach-Deerfield Beach PMSA, FL	Y	31240 FQ	42070 MW	52710 TQ	USBLS	5/07
	Jacksonville MSA, FL	Y	31220 FQ	40040 MW	49480 TQ	USBLS	5/07
	Miami-Fort Lauderdale-Miami Beach MSA, FL	Y	30480 FQ	41110 MW	53050 TQ	USBLS	5/07
	Orlando-Kissimmee MSA, FL	Y	31660 FQ	41610 MW	53740 TQ	USBLS	5/07
	Pensacola-Ferry Pass-Brent MSA, FL	Y	23480 FQ	28790 MW	37680 TQ	USBLS	5/07
	Tampa-St. Petersburg-Clearwater MSA, FL	Y	35190 FQ	43170 MW	54430 TQ	USBLS	5/07
	West Palm Beach-Boca Raton-Boynton Beach PMSA, FL	Y	35940 FQ	47850 MW	57600 TQ	USBLS	5/07
	Georgia	Y	33460 FQ	42490 MW	53270 TQ	USBLS	5/07
	Atlanta-Sandy Springs-Marietta MSA, GA	Y	33350 FQ	43550 MW	54630 TQ	USBLS	5/07
	Hawaii	Y	32660 FQ	42970 MW	53190 TQ	USBLS	5/07
	Honolulu MSA, HI	Y	31750 FQ	42290 MW	53030 TQ	USBLS	5/07
	Idaho	Y	28170 FQ	36790 MW	44400 TQ	USBLS	5/07
	Boise City-Nampa MSA, ID	Y	26890 FQ	36730 MW	44720 TQ	USBLS	5/07
	Illinois	Y	35120 FQ	42680 MW	52290 TQ	USBLS	5/07
	Chicago-Naperville-Joliet MSA, IL-IN-WI	Y	34140 FQ	41720 MW	52420 TQ	USBLS	5/07
	Indiana	Y	33390 FQ	39560 MW	51210 TQ	USBLS	5/07
	Evansville MSA, IN-KY	Y	32400 FQ	36990 MW	41530 TQ	USBLS	5/07
	Gary PMSA, IN	Y	28120 FQ	32340 MW	41320 TQ	USBLS	5/07
	Indianapolis-Carmel MSA, IN	Y	36490 FQ	45450 MW	59120 TQ	USBLS	5/07
	Iowa	Y	34670 FQ	43020 MW	52770 TQ	USBLS	5/07
	Des Moines-West Des Moines MSA, IA	Y	36230 FQ	43960 MW	56150 TQ	USBLS	5/07
	Kansas	Y	32060 FQ	38480 MW	47350 TQ	USBLS	5/07
	Wichita MSA, KS	Y	33550 FQ	39110 MW	45390 TQ	USBLS	5/07
	Kentucky	Y	33623 FQ	39803 MW	47439 TQ	KYBLS	2008
	Lexington-Fayette MSA, KY	Y	32550 FQ	41480 MW	50540 TQ	USBLS	5/07
	Louisville-Jefferson County MSA, KY-IN	Y	32930 FQ	38480 MW	45810 TQ	USBLS	5/07
	Louisiana	H	14.62 FQ	19.63 MW	26.49 TQ	LABLS	1/08-3/08
	Baton Rouge MSA, LA	Y	27130 FQ	43280 MW	60790 TQ	USBLS	5/07
	New Orleans-Metairie-Kenner MSA, LA	Y	35080 FQ	43240 MW	52370 TQ	USBLS	5/07
	Maine	Y	34280 FQ	39040 MW	48580 TQ	USBLS	5/07
	Portland-South Portland-Biddeford MSA, ME	Y	34330 FQ	39320 MW	51000 TQ	USBLS	5/07
	Maryland	Y		43775 MW		MDBLS	3/08
	Baltimore-Towson MSA, MD	Y	36070 FQ	43320 MW	50080 TQ	USBLS	5/07
	Bethesda-Gaithersburg-Frederick PMSA, MD	Y	32280 FQ	41160 MW	52180 TQ	USBLS	5/07
	Massachusetts	Y	39540 FQ	47290 MW	58420 TQ	USBLS	5/07
	Boston-Cambridge-Quincy NECTA, MA	Y	39620 FQ	47170 MW	58680 TQ	USBLS	5/07
	Worcester MSA, MA-CT	Y	45630 FQ	54450 MW	71820 TQ	USBLS	5/07
	Michigan	Y	35880 FQ	43830 MW	52480 TQ	USBLS	5/07
	Detroit-Warren-Livonia MSA, MI	Y	35480 FQ	44240 MW	55380 TQ	USBLS	5/07
	Grand Rapids-Wyoming MSA, MI	Y	41350 FQ	45560 MW	49820 TQ	USBLS	5/07
	Warren-Troy-Farmington Hills PMSA, MI	Y	34940 FQ	43320 MW	54220 TQ	USBLS	5/07
	Minnesota	Y	39505 FQ	47770 MW	60147 TQ	MNBLS	10/08-12/08
	Duluth-Superior MSA, MN-WI	Y	34703 FQ	40321 MW	50930 TQ	MNBLS	10/08-12/08

AE	Average entry wage	AW	Average wage paid	FQ	First quartile wage	LO	Lowest wage paid
AER	Average entry range	AWR	Average wage range	H	Hourly	LR	Low end range
AEX	Average experienced wage	AXR	Average experienced range	HI	Highest wage paid	M	Monthly
ATC	Average total compensation	D	Daily	HR	High end range	MCC	Median cash compensation

MTC	Median total compensation	TCC	Total cash compensation
MW	Median wage paid	TQ	Third quartile wage
MWR	Median wage range	W	Weekly
S	See annotated source	Y	Yearly

Occupation/Type/Industry	Location	Per	Low	Mid	High	Source	Date
Architectural and Civil Drafter	Minneapolis-Saint Paul MSA, MN-WI	Y	41849 FQ	50825 MW	63840 TQ	MNBLS	10/08-12/08
	Rochester MSA, MN	Y	36760 FQ	44092 MW	54617 TQ	MNBLS	10/08-12/08
	Mississippi	Y	27410 FQ	35440 MW	44340 TQ	USBLS	5/07
	Jackson MSA, MS	Y	25810 FQ	34450 MW	41450 TQ	USBLS	5/07
	Missouri	Y	30830 FQ	37930 MW	46610 TQ	USBLS	5/07
	Kansas City MSA, MO-KS	Y	33920 FQ	41430 MW	49090 TQ	USBLS	5/07
	St. Louis MSA, MO-IL	Y	32820 FQ	38650 MW	47290 TQ	USBLS	5/07
	Montana	Y	26340 FQ	33460 MW	41490 TQ	USBLS	5/07
	Billings MSA, MT	Y	27280 FQ	34370 MW	41250 TQ	USBLS	5/07
	Nebraska	Y	32520 FQ	39220 MW	48570 TQ	USBLS	5/07
	Omaha-Council Bluffs MSA, NE-IA	Y	33250 FQ	41590 MW	53140 TQ	USBLS	5/07
	Nevada	H	17.94 FQ	21.63 MW	25.54 TQ	NVBLS	5/08
	Las Vegas-Paradise MSA, NV	H	18.28 FQ	21.53 MW	25.12 TQ	NVBLS	5/08
	New Hampshire	H	17.38 AE	21.71 MW	24.80 AEX	NHBLS	6/08
	Manchester MSA, NH	Y	40140 FQ	44050 MW	48380 TQ	USBLS	5/07
	Nashua NECTA, NH-MA	Y	36240 FQ	42240 MW	51680 TQ	USBLS	5/07
	New Jersey	Y	34840 FQ	44430 MW	56660 TQ	USBLS	5/07
	Camden PMSA, NJ	Y	35670 FQ	43470 MW	51840 TQ	USBLS	5/07
	Edison PMSA, NJ	Y	37360 FQ	44830 MW	53610 TQ	USBLS	5/07
	Newark-Union PMSA, NJ-PA	Y	31270 FQ	45240 MW	61840 TQ	USBLS	5/07
	New Mexico	Y	31690 FQ	37660 MW	46340 TQ	USBLS	5/07
	Albuquerque MSA, NM	Y	33290 FQ	38530 MW	46260 TQ	USBLS	5/07
	New York	Y	40250 FQ	48400 MW	59550 TQ	USBLS	5/07
	Albany-Schenectady-Troy MSA, NY	Y	37700 FQ	45000 MW	53530 TQ	USBLS	5/07
	Buffalo-Niagara Falls MSA, NY	Y	30460 FQ	39300 MW	46320 TQ	USBLS	5/07
	Nassau-Suffolk PMSA, NY	Y	38060 FQ	47170 MW	60030 TQ	USBLS	5/07
	New York-Northern New Jersey-Long Island MSA, NY-NJ-PA	Y	39590 FQ	48550 MW	60110 TQ	USBLS	5/07
	North Carolina	Y	35210 FQ	43460 MW	50700 TQ	USBLS	5/07
	Charlotte-Gastonia-Concord MSA, NC-SC	Y	39680 FQ	46450 MW	53120 TQ	USBLS	5/07
	Greensboro-High Point MSA, NC	Y	35420 FQ	40290 MW	48540 TQ	USBLS	5/07
	Raleigh-Cary MSA, NC	Y	37100 FQ	44380 MW	50460 TQ	USBLS	5/07
	North Dakota	Y	28710 FQ	35230 MW	45150 TQ	USBLS	5/07
	Fargo MSA, ND-MN	Y	26220 FQ	31680 MW	41140 TQ	USBLS	5/07
	Ohio	Y	35240 FQ	42440 MW	50630 TQ	USBLS	5/07
	Cincinnati-Middletown MSA, OH-KY-IN	Y	36440 FQ	41550 MW	48530 TQ	USBLS	5/07
	Cleveland-Elyria-Mentor MSA, OH	Y	40600 FQ	46090 MW	53970 TQ	USBLS	5/07
	Columbus MSA, OH	Y	34570 FQ	41940 MW	50260 TQ	USBLS	5/07
	Dayton MSA, OH	Y	33740 FQ	37580 MW	45410 TQ	USBLS	5/07
	Oklahoma	Y	33230 FQ	42430 MW	49530 TQ	USBLS	5/07
	Oklahoma City MSA, OK	Y	34060 FQ	40850 MW	48150 TQ	USBLS	5/07
	Tulsa MSA, OK	Y	32970 FQ	44480 MW	51060 TQ	USBLS	5/07
	Oregon	H	16.13 FQ	19.17 MW	24.21 TQ	ORBLS	5/08
	Portland-Vancouver-Beaverton MSA, OR-WA	Y	33320 FQ	39700 MW	50000 TQ	MNBLS	5/07
	Pennsylvania	Y	31970 FQ	39150 MW	48390 TQ	USBLS	5/07
	Allentown-Bethlehem-Easton MSA, PA-NJ	Y	33570 FQ	40020 MW	49730 TQ	USBLS	5/07
	Philadelphia-Camden-Wilmington MSA, PA-NJ-DE-MD	Y	33460 FQ	40840 MW	49560 TQ	USBLS	5/07
	Pittsburgh MSA, PA	Y	32880 FQ	41360 MW	51960 TQ	USBLS	5/07
	York-Hanover MSA, PA	Y	34660 FQ	41340 MW	47680 TQ	USBLS	5/07
	Rhode Island	Y	38730 FQ	45520 MW	54830 TQ	USBLS	5/07
	Providence-Fall River-Warwick MSA, RI-MA	Y	39180 FQ	45870 MW	54530 TQ	USBLS	5/07
	South Carolina	Y	35590 FQ	43880 MW	53660 TQ	USBLS	5/07
	Charleston-North Charleston MSA, SC	Y	42300 FQ	47920 MW	56250 TQ	USBLS	5/07
	Columbia MSA, SC	Y	33840 FQ	42300 MW	49000 TQ	USBLS	5/07
	South Dakota	Y	27810 FQ	31024 MW	36599 TQ	SDBLS	7/08-9/08
	Sioux Falls MSA, SD	Y	27956 FQ	32636 MW	43405 TQ	SDBLS	7/08-9/08
	Tennessee	Y	35090 FQ	43080 MW	54490 TQ	USBLS	5/07

AE	Average entry wage	AW	Average wage paid	FQ	First quartile wage	LO	Lowest wage paid	MTC	Median total compensation	TCC	Total cash compensation
AER	Average entry range	AWR	Average wage range	H	Hourly	LR	Low end range	MW	Median wage paid	TQ	Third quartile wage
AEX	Average experienced wage	AXR	Average experienced range	HI	Highest wage paid	M	Monthly	MWR	Median wage range	W	Weekly
ATC	Average total compensation	D	Daily	HR	High end range	MCC	Median cash compensation	S	See annotated source	Y	Yearly

Occupation/Type/Industry	Location	Per	Low	Mid	High	Source	Date
Architectural and Civil Drafter	Memphis MSA, TN-MS-AR	Y	36940 FQ	44680 MW	54360 TQ	USBLS	5/07
	Nashville-Davidson-Murfreesboro MSA, TN	Y	34820 FQ	43520 MW	55540 TQ	USBLS	5/07
	Texas	Y	33570 FQ	41450 MW	51540 TQ	USBLS	5/07
	Austin-Round Rock MSA, TX	Y	32410 FQ	37300 MW	44250 TQ	USBLS	5/07
	Corpus Christi MSA, TX	Y	30450 FQ	37380 MW	45280 TQ	USBLS	5/07
	Dallas-Fort Worth-Arlington MSA, TX	Y	36410 FQ	43930 MW	53420 TQ	USBLS	5/07
	El Paso MSA, TX	Y	20900 FQ	30680 MW	36620 TQ	USBLS	5/07
	Houston-Sugar Land-Baytown MSA, TX	Y	38930 FQ	47640 MW	58280 TQ	USBLS	5/07
	San Antonio MSA, TX	Y	31730 FQ	35860 MW	40080 TQ	USBLS	5/07
	Utah	Y	31650 FQ	37830 MW	47580 TQ	USBLS	5/07
	Provo-Orem MSA, UT	Y	33040 FQ	40260 MW	51240 TQ	USBLS	5/07
	Salt Lake City MSA, UT	Y	32180 FQ	38530 MW	48920 TQ	USBLS	5/07
	Vermont	Y	36850 FQ	44070 MW	49390 TQ	USBLS	5/07
	Burlington-South Burlington MSA, VT	Y	42600 FQ	46150 MW	49900 TQ	USBLS	5/07
	Virginia	Y	33760 FQ	41940 MW	49260 TQ	USBLS	5/07
	Richmond MSA, VA	Y	35540 FQ	43280 MW	50860 TQ	USBLS	5/07
	Virginia Beach-Norfolk-Newport News MSA, VA-NC	Y	31870 FQ	38710 MW	46550 TQ	USBLS	5/07
	Washington	H	18.02 FQ	21.32 MW	26.52 TQ	WABLS	3/08
	Seattle-Tacoma-Bellevue MSA, WA	Y	38070 FQ	44860 MW	56760 TQ	USBLS	5/07
	West Virginia	Y	34756 FQ	47282 MW	59833 TQ	WVBLS	7/08-9/08
	Charleston MSA, WV	Y	35740 FQ	44310 MW	56160 TQ	USBLS	5/07
	Wisconsin	Y	34580 FQ	40690 MW	50660 TQ	USBLS	5/07
	Milwaukee-Waukesha-West Allis MSA, WI	Y	34620 FQ	40470 MW	53600 TQ	USBLS	5/07
	Wyoming	Y	32453 FQ	38785 MW	45445 TQ	WYBLS	9/08
	Cheyenne MSA, WY	Y	36259 FQ	47423 MW	53681 TQ	WYBLS	9/08
	Puerto Rico	Y	20940 FQ	24280 MW	29430 TQ	USBLS	5/07
	San Juan-Caguas-Guaynabo MSA, PR	Y	21280 FQ	24500 MW	29710 TQ	USBLS	5/07
	Guam	Y	26160 FQ	33050 MW	39720 TQ	USBLS	5/07
Architecture Teacher							
Postsecondary	Alabama	Y	45620 FQ	60810 MW	92790 TQ	USBLS	5/07
Postsecondary	California	Y		76234 AW		CABLS	1/08-3/08
Postsecondary	Colorado	Y	51520 FQ	57920 MW	70440 TQ	USBLS	5/07
Postsecondary	Florida	Y	60230 FQ	71580 MW	79820 TQ	USBLS	5/07
Postsecondary	Georgia	Y	50080 FQ	61740 MW	77350 TQ	USBLS	5/07
Postsecondary	Illinois	Y	51520 FQ	60870 MW	78800 TQ	USBLS	5/07
Postsecondary	Indiana	Y	52750 FQ	60330 MW	75770 TQ	USBLS	5/07
Postsecondary	Iowa	Y	74430 FQ	84930 MW	101980 TQ	USBLS	5/07
Postsecondary	Kansas	Y	56380 FQ	70870 MW	92120 TQ	USBLS	5/07
Postsecondary	Louisiana	Y		81171 AW		LABLS	1/08-3/08
Postsecondary	Maryland	Y		70850 MW		MDBLS	3/08
Postsecondary	Massachusetts	Y	61570 FQ	80930 MW	94880 TQ	USBLS	5/07
Postsecondary	Michigan	Y	49730 FQ	68470 MW	82790 TQ	USBLS	5/07
Postsecondary	Mississippi	Y	62210 FQ	72810 MW	80890 TQ	USBLS	5/07
Postsecondary	Missouri	Y	59950 FQ	73290 MW	81590 TQ	USBLS	5/07
Postsecondary	Nebraska	Y	37060 FQ	41100 MW	58700 TQ	USBLS	5/07
Postsecondary	New Jersey	Y	60900 FQ	79530 MW	102580 TQ	USBLS	5/07
Postsecondary	New Mexico	Y	46240 FQ	57910 MW	71790 TQ	USBLS	5/07
Postsecondary	New York	Y	63160 FQ	78830 MW	93480 TQ	USBLS	5/07
Postsecondary	North Carolina	Y	45960 FQ	59580 MW	75830 TQ	USBLS	5/07
Postsecondary	Ohio	Y	70830 FQ	83230 MW	96940 TQ	USBLS	5/07
Postsecondary	Pennsylvania	Y	54940 FQ	70350 MW	91210 TQ	USBLS	5/07
Postsecondary	Rhode Island	Y	59540 FQ	78360 MW	90110 TQ	USBLS	5/07
Postsecondary	South Dakota	Y	45789 FQ	49953 MW	54151 TQ	SDBLS	7/08-9/08
Postsecondary	Texas	Y	43150 FQ	59370 MW	74960 TQ	USBLS	5/07
Postsecondary	Utah	Y	53920 FQ	64920 MW	89810 TQ	USBLS	5/07
Postsecondary	Virginia	Y	53200 FQ	67700 MW	81390 TQ	USBLS	5/07
Postsecondary	Wisconsin	Y	52360 FQ	66570 MW	81640 TQ	USBLS	5/07
Postsecondary	Puerto Rico	Y	32970 FQ	35760 MW	42860 TQ	USBLS	5/07
Archivist	United States	Y		40286 AW		LIBJ	2007
	Alabama	Y	41230 FQ	51490 MW	59780 TQ	USBLS	5/07
	Alaska	Y	42530 FQ	49940 MW	60610 TQ	USBLS	5/07
	Arizona	Y	33790 FQ	42990 MW	53700 TQ	USBLS	5/07

AE	Average entry wage	AW	Average wage paid	FQ	First quartile wage	LO	Lowest wage paid	MTC	Median total compensation	TCC	Total cash compensation
AER	Average entry range	AWR	Average wage range	H	Hourly	LR	Low end range	MW	Median wage paid	TQ	Third quartile wage
AEX	Average experienced wage	AXR	Average experienced range	HI	Highest wage paid	M	Monthly	MWR	Median wage range	W	Weekly
ATC	Average total compensation	D	Daily	HR	High end range	MCC	Median cash compensation	S	See annotated source	Y	Yearly

Occupation/Type/Industry	Location	Per	Low	Mid	High	Source	Date
Archivist	Arkansas	Y	29270 FQ	43220 MW	65260 TQ	USBLS	5/07
	California	H	16.77 FQ	19.65 MW	27.47 TQ	CABLS	1/08-3/08
	Los Angeles-Long Beach-Glendale PMSA, CA	H	15.61 FQ	18.27 MW	26.49 TQ	CABLS	1/08-3/08
	Oakland-Fremont-Hayward MSA, CA	H	13.34 FQ	15.35 MW	28.12 TQ	CABLS	1/08-3/08
	Riverside-San Bernardino-Ontario MSA, CA	H	14.38 FQ	21.37 MW	27.77 TQ	CABLS	1/08-3/08
	Sacramento-Arden Arcade-Roseville MSA, CA	H	24.88 FQ	28.08 MW	30.64 TQ	CABLS	1/08-3/08
	San Diego-Carlsbad-San Marcos MSA, CA	H	13.88 FQ	17.88 MW	27.95 TQ	CABLS	1/08-3/08
	San Francisco-San Mateo-Redwood PMSA, CA	H	20.30 FQ	22.77 MW	34.40 TQ	CABLS	1/08-3/08
	Santa Ana-Anaheim-Irvine PMSA, CA	Y	35370 FQ	37750 MW	40130 TQ	USBLS	5/07
	Colorado	Y	36580 FQ	46650 MW	60340 TQ	USBLS	5/07
	Denver-Aurora MSA, CO	Y	39000 FQ	49400 MW	64240 TQ	USBLS	5/07
	Connecticut	H	11.00 AE	13.26 MW		CTBLS	1/08-3/08
	Delaware	Y	34930 FQ	37600 MW	40330 TQ	USBLS	5/07
	District of Columbia	Y	50610 FQ	59770 MW	71570 TQ	USBLS	5/07
	Washington-Arlington-Alexandria MSA, DC-VA-MD-WV	Y	48540 FQ	61850 MW	79380 TQ	USBLS	5/07
	Florida	Y	29930 FQ	35210 MW	40670 TQ	USBLS	5/07
	Tampa-St. Petersburg-Clearwater MSA, FL	Y	27810 FQ	32860 MW	39200 TQ	USBLS	5/07
	Georgia	Y	39340 FQ	52600 MW	65530 TQ	USBLS	5/07
	Atlanta-Sandy Springs-Marietta MSA, GA	Y	48570 FQ	59210 MW	72170 TQ	USBLS	5/07
	Illinois	Y	37050 FQ	47120 MW	60730 TQ	USBLS	5/07
	Chicago-Naperville-Joliet MSA, IL-IN-WI	Y	36260 FQ	46990 MW	61360 TQ	USBLS	5/07
	Indiana	Y	26650 FQ	30960 MW	38970 TQ	USBLS	5/07
	Kansas	Y	22510 FQ	27300 MW	46010 TQ	USBLS	5/07
	Kentucky	Y	31591 FQ	41820 MW	53497 TQ	KYBLS	2008
	Louisiana	H	12.98 FQ	18.46 MW	24.23 TQ	LABLS	1/08-3/08
	Maine	Y	37520 FQ	42460 MW	47330 TQ	USBLS	5/07
	Maryland	Y		53075 MW		MDBLS	3/08
	Baltimore-Towson MSA, MD	Y	34780 FQ	43560 MW	52560 TQ	USBLS	5/07
	Bethesda-Gaithersburg-Frederick PMSA, MD	Y	34100 FQ	42180 MW	49170 TQ	USBLS	5/07
	Massachusetts	Y	38920 FQ	49250 MW	61770 TQ	USBLS	5/07
	Boston-Cambridge-Quincy NECTA, MA	Y	41600 FQ	52290 MW	66550 TQ	USBLS	5/07
	Michigan	Y	32490 FQ	42520 MW	55100 TQ	USBLS	5/07
	Detroit-Warren-Livonia MSA, MI	Y	37710 FQ	45280 MW	54720 TQ	USBLS	5/07
	Minnesota	Y	34651 FQ	42393 MW	51976 TQ	MNBLS	10/08-12/08
	Minneapolis-Saint Paul MSA, MN-WI	Y	36670 FQ	44485 MW	52698 TQ	MNBLS	10/08-12/08
	Missouri	Y	33160 FQ	39020 MW	58470 TQ	USBLS	5/07
	Jefferson City MSA, MO	Y	34900 FQ	37760 MW	40410 TQ	USBLS	5/07
	Kansas City MSA, MO-KS	Y	28850 FQ	40350 MW	67000 TQ	USBLS	5/07
	St. Louis MSA, MO-IL	Y	32960 FQ	52380 MW	69430 TQ	USBLS	5/08
	Nevada	H	16.56 FQ	18.77 MW	23.44 TQ	NVBLS	5/08
	New Hampshire	H	15.03 AE	18.43 MW	21.33 AEX	NHBLS	6/08
	New Jersey	Y	30660 FQ	40680 MW	59780 TQ	USBLS	5/07
	New York	Y	37080 FQ	48340 MW	60620 TQ	USBLS	5/07
	Buffalo-Niagara Falls MSA, NY	Y	23310 FQ	25750 MW	33670 TQ	USBLS	5/07
	New York-Northern New Jersey-Long Island MSA, NY-NJ-PA	Y	41030 FQ	52680 MW	62700 TQ	USBLS	5/07
	North Carolina	Y	29890 FQ	35630 MW	45190 TQ	USBLS	5/07
	Charlotte-Gastonia-Concord MSA, NC-SC	Y	27940 FQ	30240 MW	32460 TQ	USBLS	5/07
	Ohio	Y	27250 FQ	31730 MW	46610 TQ	USBLS	5/07
	Oklahoma	Y	26760 FQ	32170 MW	41380 TQ	USBLS	5/07
	Oklahoma City MSA, OK	Y	26000 FQ	30880 MW	48520 TQ	USBLS	5/07
	Oregon	H	14.65 FQ	23.46 MW	30.09 TQ	ORBLS	5/08
	Pennsylvania	Y	29210 FQ	39850 MW	55240 TQ	USBLS	5/07

AE	Average entry wage	AW	Average wage paid	FQ	First quartile wage	LO	Lowest wage paid	MTC	Median total compensation	TCC	Total cash compensation
AER	Average entry range	AWR	Average wage range	H	Hourly	LR	Low end range	MW	Median wage paid	TQ	Third quartile wage
AEX	Average experienced wage	AXR	Average experienced range	HI	Highest wage paid	M	Monthly	MWR	Median wage range	W	Weekly
ATC	Average total compensation	D	Daily	HR	High end range	MCC	Median cash compensation	S	See annotated source	Y	Yearly

Occupation/Type/Industry	Location	Per	Low	Mid	High	Source	Date
Archivist	Philadelphia-Camden-Wilmington MSA, PA-NJ-DE-MD	Y	28130 FQ	36850 MW	54900 TQ	USBLS	5/07
	Pittsburgh MSA, PA	Y	30280 FQ	47930 MW	59080 TQ	USBLS	5/07
	Rhode Island	Y	42340 FQ	53670 MW	66940 TQ	USBLS	5/07
	Providence-Fall River-Warwick MSA, RI-MA	Y	42340 FQ	53670 MW	66940 TQ	USBLS	5/07
	South Carolina	Y	29370 FQ	34480 MW	39160 TQ	USBLS	5/07
	South Dakota	Y	30434 FQ	35373 MW	45330 TQ	SDBLS	7/08-9/08
	Tennessee	Y	27490 FQ	32740 MW	38220 TQ	USBLS	5/07
	Texas	Y	35770 FQ	45380 MW	62600 TQ	USBLS	5/07
	Dallas-Fort Worth-Arlington MSA, TX	Y	39420 FQ	49470 MW	69050 TQ	USBLS	5/07
	Houston-Sugar Land-Baytown MSA, TX	Y	35330 FQ	44000 MW	50390 TQ	USBLS	5/07
	Utah	Y	31130 FQ	36130 MW	41550 TQ	USBLS	5/07
	Salt Lake City MSA, UT	Y	30990 FQ	36110 MW	42000 TQ	USBLS	5/07
	Vermont	Y	33920 FQ	40230 MW	49600 TQ	USBLS	5/07
	Virginia	Y	31770 FQ	48300 MW	64460 TQ	USBLS	5/07
	Washington	H	18.62 FQ	22.52 MW	27.34 TQ	WABLS	3/08
	Seattle-Tacoma-Bellevue MSA, WA	Y	37080 FQ	45180 MW	55450 TQ	USBLS	5/07
	Wisconsin	Y	36190 FQ	42650 MW	51210 TQ	USBLS	5/07
	Wyoming	Y	31112 FQ	38042 MW	48121 TQ	WYBLS	9/08
Area, Ethnic, and Cultural Studies Teacher							
Postsecondary	Arizona	Y	47390 FQ	55860 MW	65560 TQ	USBLS	5/07
Postsecondary	California	Y		98979 AW		CABLS	1/08-3/08
Postsecondary	Colorado	Y	40990 FQ	54140 MW	78370 TQ	USBLS	5/07
Postsecondary	District of Columbia	Y	45680 FQ	56940 MW	75530 TQ	USBLS	5/07
Postsecondary	Florida	Y	50410 FQ	62280 MW	78440 TQ	USBLS	5/07
Postsecondary	Georgia	Y	43660 FQ	52830 MW	67410 TQ	USBLS	5/07
Postsecondary	Hawaii	Y	46190 FQ	57890 MW	76380 TQ	USBLS	5/07
Postsecondary	Illinois	Y	43380 FQ	55610 MW	73860 TQ	USBLS	5/07
Postsecondary	Indiana	Y	43470 FQ	57100 MW	72500 TQ	USBLS	5/07
Postsecondary	Kentucky	Y	39621 FQ	57658 MW	77324 TQ	KYBLS	2008
Postsecondary	Louisiana	Y		57572 AW		LABLS	1/08-3/08
Postsecondary	Maryland	Y		67450 MW		MDBLS	3/08
Postsecondary	Massachusetts	Y	49920 FQ	64510 MW	97120 TQ	USBLS	5/07
Postsecondary	Michigan	Y	45810 FQ	53120 MW	81730 TQ	USBLS	5/07
Postsecondary	Minnesota	Y	42581 FQ	58180 MW	76761 TQ	MNBLS	10/08-12/08
Postsecondary	Missouri	Y	51950 FQ	81590 MW	98450 TQ	USBLS	5/07
Postsecondary	Montana	Y	27050 FQ	34120 MW	45140 TQ	USBLS	5/07
Postsecondary	New Jersey	Y	52120 FQ	68180 MW	95170 TQ	USBLS	5/07
Postsecondary	New Mexico	Y	43780 FQ	50890 MW	65190 TQ	USBLS	5/07
Postsecondary	New York	Y	52090 FQ	67590 MW	98450 TQ	USBLS	5/07
Postsecondary	North Carolina	Y	40560 FQ	54850 MW	72580 TQ	USBLS	5/07
Postsecondary	Ohio	Y	47090 FQ	62460 MW	84090 TQ	USBLS	5/07
Postsecondary	Pennsylvania	Y	46750 FQ	60500 MW	98130 TQ	USBLS	5/07
Postsecondary	South Carolina	Y	41510 FQ	51140 MW	67160 TQ	USBLS	5/07
Postsecondary	South Dakota	Y	34192 FQ	38743 MW	48947 TQ	SDBLS	7/08-9/08
Postsecondary	Tennessee	Y	38150 FQ	46040 MW	55490 TQ	USBLS	5/07
Postsecondary	Texas	Y	27820 FQ	46770 MW	69710 TQ	USBLS	5/07
Postsecondary	Vermont	Y	44860 FQ	53150 MW	61670 TQ	USBLS	5/07
Postsecondary	Virginia	Y	34970 FQ	53850 MW	71810 TQ	USBLS	5/07
Postsecondary	Washington	Y		63420 AW		WABLS	3/08
Postsecondary	Wisconsin	Y	39600 FQ	56760 MW	81230 TQ	USBLS	5/07
Postsecondary	Wyoming	Y	52033 FQ	80393 MW	99973 TQ	WYBLS	9/08
Armorer							
State Government	Ohio	H	21.12 LO		26.63 HI	ODAS	2008
Arson Investigator							
State Government	Ohio	H	21.77 LO		31.86 HI	ODAS	2008
Art, Drama, and Music Teacher							
Postsecondary	Alabama	Y	38290 FQ	47990 MW	63250 TQ	USBLS	5/07
Postsecondary	Birmingham-Hoover MSA, AL	Y	34730 FQ	44250 MW	58950 TQ	USBLS	5/07
Postsecondary	Alaska	Y	46470 FQ	66870 MW	83120 TQ	USBLS	5/07
Postsecondary	Arizona	Y	35130 FQ	49620 MW	61460 TQ	USBLS	5/07

AE Average entry wage	**AW** Average wage paid	**FQ** First quartile wage	**LO** Lowest wage paid	**MTC** Median total compensation	**TCC** Total cash compensation
AER Average entry range	**AWR** Average wage range	**H** Hourly	**LR** Low end range	**MW** Median wage paid	**TQ** Third quartile wage
AEX Average experienced wage	**AXR** Average experienced range	**HI** Highest wage paid	**M** Monthly	**MWR** Median wage range	**W** Weekly
ATC Average total compensation	**D** Daily	**HR** High end range	**MCC** Median cash compensation	**S** See annotated source	**Y** Yearly

Occupation/Type/Industry	Location	Per	Low	Mid	High	Source	Date
Art, Drama, and Music Teacher							
Postsecondary	Phoenix-Mesa-Scottsdale MSA, AZ	Y	33450 FQ	45810 MW	57030 TQ	USBLS	5/07
Postsecondary	Tucson MSA, AZ	Y	53660 FQ	63430 MW	71840 TQ	USBLS	5/07
Postsecondary	Arkansas	Y	34780 FQ	46120 MW	56850 TQ	USBLS	5/07
Postsecondary	Little Rock-North Little Rock MSA, AR	Y	26070 FQ	38700 MW	51380 TQ	USBLS	5/07
Postsecondary	California	Y		85504 AW		CABLS	1/08-3/08
Postsecondary	Los Angeles-Long Beach-Glendale PMSA, CA	Y		79648 AW		CABLS	1/08-3/08
Postsecondary	Oakland-Fremont-Hayward MSA, CA	Y		101747 AW		CABLS	1/08-3/08
Postsecondary	Riverside-San Bernardino-Ontario MSA, CA	Y		89072 AW		CABLS	1/08-3/08
Postsecondary	Sacramento-Arden Arcade-Roseville MSA, CA	Y		83935 AW		CABLS	1/08-3/08
Postsecondary	San Diego-Carlsbad-San Marcos MSA, CA	Y		88980 AW		CABLS	1/08-3/08
Postsecondary	San Francisco-San Mateo-Redwood PMSA, CA	Y		93010 AW		CABLS	1/08-3/08
Postsecondary	Santa Ana-Anaheim-Irvine PMSA, CA	Y	66580 FQ	84020 MW	104330 TQ	USBLS	5/07
Postsecondary	Colorado	Y	37300 FQ	48380 MW	62100 TQ	USBLS	5/07
Postsecondary	Denver-Aurora MSA, CO	Y	39380 FQ	49840 MW	61190 TQ	USBLS	5/07
Postsecondary	Hartford-West Hartford-East Hartford MSA, CT	Y	40440 FQ	60820 MW	75800 TQ	USBLS	5/07
Postsecondary	Delaware	Y	32740 FQ	53070 MW	71500 TQ	USBLS	5/07
Postsecondary	Wilmington PMSA, DE-MD-NJ	Y	30380 FQ	49260 MW	71540 TQ	USBLS	5/07
Postsecondary	District of Columbia	Y	40080 FQ	56230 MW	75590 TQ	USBLS	5/07
Postsecondary	Washington-Arlington-Alexandria MSA, DC-VA-MD-WV	Y	37270 FQ	55180 MW	74550 TQ	USBLS	5/07
Postsecondary	Florida	Y	39730 FQ	53310 MW	70550 TQ	USBLS	5/07
Postsecondary	Fort Lauderdale-Pompano Beach-Deerfield Beach PMSA, FL	Y	50800 FQ	64170 MW	75470 TQ	USBLS	5/07
Postsecondary	Jacksonville MSA, FL	Y	34540 FQ	43760 MW	56170 TQ	USBLS	5/07
Postsecondary	Miami-Fort Lauderdale-Miami Beach MSA, FL	Y	50400 FQ	68650 MW	77070 TQ	USBLS	5/07
Postsecondary	Orlando-Kissimmee MSA, FL	Y	33090 FQ	44560 MW	58630 TQ	USBLS	5/07
Postsecondary	Tampa-St. Petersburg-Clearwater MSA, FL	Y	40300 FQ	54230 MW	72280 TQ	USBLS	5/07
Postsecondary	Georgia	Y	41310 FQ	51420 MW	63730 TQ	USBLS	5/07
Postsecondary	Atlanta-Sandy Springs-Marietta MSA, GA	Y	44620 FQ	54580 MW	65470 TQ	USBLS	5/07
Postsecondary	Hawaii	Y	50380 FQ	60310 MW	73540 TQ	USBLS	5/07
Postsecondary	Honolulu MSA, HI	Y	51750 FQ	61550 MW	74750 TQ	USBLS	5/07
Postsecondary	Illinois	Y	32040 FQ	48690 MW	64700 TQ	USBLS	5/07
Postsecondary	Chicago-Naperville-Joliet MSA, IL-IN-WI	Y	33410 FQ	49880 MW	67870 TQ	USBLS	5/07
Postsecondary	Indiana	Y	41270 FQ	52160 MW	71800 TQ	USBLS	5/07
Postsecondary	Gary PMSA, IN	Y	39980 FQ	48420 MW	64280 TQ	USBLS	5/07
Postsecondary	Indianapolis-Carmel MSA, IN	Y	37840 FQ	49810 MW	69390 TQ	USBLS	5/07
Postsecondary	Iowa	Y	44920 FQ	57310 MW	71600 TQ	USBLS	5/07
Postsecondary	Des Moines-West Des Moines MSA, IA	Y	45550 FQ	56840 MW	72980 TQ	USBLS	5/07
Postsecondary	Kansas	Y	38520 FQ	52650 MW	69270 TQ	USBLS	5/07
Postsecondary	Wichita MSA, KS	Y	51470 FQ	60950 MW	76430 TQ	USBLS	5/07
Postsecondary	Kentucky	Y	39549 FQ	53981 MW	70969 TQ	KYBLS	2008
Postsecondary	Louisville-Jefferson County MSA, KY-IN	Y	40610 FQ	59160 MW	87460 TQ	USBLS	5/07
Postsecondary	Louisiana	Y		49426 AW		LABLS	1/08-3/08
Postsecondary	New Orleans-Metairie-Kenner MSA, LA	Y	35250 FQ	46420 MW	64390 TQ	USBLS	5/07
Postsecondary	Maine	Y	47050 FQ	59470 MW	73130 TQ	USBLS	5/07
Postsecondary	Portland-South Portland-Biddeford MSA, ME	Y	44590 FQ	56620 MW	70200 TQ	USBLS	5/07
Postsecondary	Maryland	Y		55700 MW		MDBLS	3/08
Postsecondary	Baltimore-Towson MSA, MD	Y	40760 FQ	57010 MW	75550 TQ	USBLS	5/07
Postsecondary	Bethesda-Gaithersburg-Frederick PMSA, MD	Y	29790 FQ	42560 MW	74880 TQ	USBLS	5/07

AE Average entry wage	**AW** Average wage paid	**FQ** First quartile wage	**LO** Lowest wage paid	**MTC** Median total compensation	**TCC** Total cash compensation
AER Average entry range	**AWR** Average wage range	**H** Hourly	**LR** Low end range	**MW** Median wage paid	**TQ** Third quartile wage
AEX Average experienced wage	**AXR** Average experienced range	**HI** Highest wage paid	**M** Monthly	**MWR** Median wage range	**W** Weekly
ATC Average total compensation	**D** Daily	**HR** High end range	**MCC** Median cash compensation	**S** See annotated source	**Y** Yearly

Occupation/Type/Industry	Location	Per	Low	Mid	High	Source	Date
Art, Drama, and Music Teacher							
Postsecondary	Massachusetts	Y	50990 FQ	69010 MW	88220 TQ	USBLS	5/07
Postsecondary	Boston-Cambridge-Quincy NECTA, MA	Y	52100 FQ	69840 MW	88700 TQ	USBLS	5/07
Postsecondary	Worcester MSA, MA-CT	Y	42450 FQ	59660 MW	75530 TQ	USBLS	5/07
Postsecondary	Michigan	Y	30310 FQ	45170 MW	62510 TQ	USBLS	5/07
Postsecondary	Detroit-Warren-Livonia MSA, MI	Y	28410 FQ	31460 MW	50120 TQ	USBLS	5/07
Postsecondary	Grand Rapids-Wyoming MSA, MI	Y	29490 FQ	44610 MW	85090 TQ	USBLS	5/07
Postsecondary	Warren-Troy-Farmington Hills PMSA, MI	Y	30640 FQ	44620 MW	60800 TQ	USBLS	5/07
Postsecondary	Minnesota	Y	42340 FQ	54121 MW	71718 TQ	MNBLS	10/08-12/08
Postsecondary	Duluth-Superior MSA, MN-WI	Y	41545 FQ	50783 MW	68015 TQ	MNBLS	10/08-12/08
Postsecondary	Minneapolis-Saint Paul MSA, MN-WI	Y	42665 FQ	56642 MW	74376 TQ	MNBLS	10/08-12/08
Postsecondary	Mississippi	Y	41550 FQ	50030 MW	61180 TQ	USBLS	5/07
Postsecondary	Jackson MSA, MS	Y	39400 FQ	46830 MW	56540 TQ	USBLS	5/07
Postsecondary	Missouri	Y	42480 FQ	56640 MW	73330 TQ	USBLS	5/07
Postsecondary	Kansas City MSA, MO-KS	Y	41490 FQ	53300 MW	67890 TQ	USBLS	5/07
Postsecondary	St. Louis MSA, MO-IL	Y	38460 FQ	56150 MW	72720 TQ	USBLS	5/07
Postsecondary	Montana	Y	35270 FQ	48200 MW	56640 TQ	USBLS	5/07
Postsecondary	Nebraska	Y	35340 FQ	48340 MW	63030 TQ	USBLS	5/07
Postsecondary	Omaha-Council Bluffs MSA, NE-IA	Y	34220 FQ	47340 MW	64780 TQ	USBLS	5/07
Postsecondary	New Jersey	Y	46260 FQ	61230 MW	83480 TQ	USBLS	5/07
Postsecondary	Camden PMSA, NJ	Y	50010 FQ	59280 MW	68270 TQ	USBLS	5/07
Postsecondary	Edison PMSA, NJ	Y	50960 FQ	72120 MW	96710 TQ	USBLS	5/07
Postsecondary	Newark-Union PMSA, NJ-PA	Y	42880 FQ	55630 MW	73750 TQ	USBLS	5/07
Postsecondary	New Mexico	Y	41160 FQ	46880 MW	58500 TQ	USBLS	5/07
Postsecondary	New York	Y	48870 FQ	67340 MW	91320 TQ	USBLS	5/07
Postsecondary	Albany-Schenectady-Troy MSA, NY	Y	52770 FQ	79430 MW	115570 TQ	USBLS	5/07
Postsecondary	Buffalo-Niagara Falls MSA, NY	Y	25080 FQ	35750 MW	46030 TQ	USBLS	5/07
Postsecondary	Nassau-Suffolk PMSA, NY	Y	42480 FQ	47590 MW	57290 TQ	USBLS	5/07
Postsecondary	New York-Northern New Jersey-Long Island MSA, NY-NJ-PA	Y	47940 FQ	66100 MW	89990 TQ	USBLS	5/07
Postsecondary	North Carolina	Y	39570 FQ	50040 MW	61310 TQ	USBLS	5/07
Postsecondary	Charlotte-Gastonia-Concord MSA, NC-SC	Y	34950 FQ	43630 MW	56240 TQ	USBLS	5/07
Postsecondary	Raleigh-Cary MSA, NC	Y	34960 FQ	45250 MW	55950 TQ	USBLS	5/07
Postsecondary	North Dakota	Y	38850 FQ	46650 MW	58120 TQ	USBLS	5/07
Postsecondary	Fargo MSA, ND-MN	Y	38060 FQ	45530 MW	56610 TQ	USBLS	5/07
Postsecondary	Grand Forks MSA, ND-MN	Y	46720 FQ	60580 MW	75720 TQ	USBLS	5/07
Postsecondary	Ohio	Y	36380 FQ	50630 MW	66440 TQ	USBLS	5/07
Postsecondary	Cincinnati-Middletown MSA, OH-KY-IN	Y	37020 FQ	50470 MW	68540 TQ	USBLS	5/07
Postsecondary	Cleveland-Elyria-Mentor MSA, OH	Y	30680 FQ	43030 MW	58720 TQ	USBLS	5/07
Postsecondary	Columbus MSA, OH	Y	41110 FQ	54760 MW	71910 TQ	USBLS	5/07
Postsecondary	Dayton MSA, OH	Y	30830 FQ	46940 MW	63990 TQ	USBLS	5/07
Postsecondary	Oklahoma	Y	28960 FQ	40670 MW	54570 TQ	USBLS	5/07
Postsecondary	Oklahoma City MSA, OK	Y	32330 FQ	44960 MW	61710 TQ	USBLS	5/07
Postsecondary	Tulsa MSA, OK	Y	21050 FQ	35170 MW	45790 TQ	USBLS	5/07
Postsecondary	Portland-Vancouver-Beaverton MSA, OR-WA	Y	39630 FQ	59240 MW	80100 TQ	USBLS	5/07
Postsecondary	Pennsylvania	Y	41400 FQ	53000 MW	71770 TQ	USBLS	5/07
Postsecondary	Allentown-Bethlehem-Easton MSA, PA-NJ	Y	46190 FQ	59880 MW	80870 TQ	USBLS	5/07
Postsecondary	Philadelphia-Camden-Wilmington MSA, PA-NJ-DE-MD	Y	42610 FQ	55440 MW	73830 TQ	USBLS	5/07
Postsecondary	Pittsburgh MSA, PA	Y	35900 FQ	51370 MW	66780 TQ	USBLS	5/07
Postsecondary	Rhode Island	Y	49040 FQ	61420 MW	87710 TQ	USBLS	5/07
Postsecondary	Providence-Fall River-Warwick MSA, RI-MA	Y	49080 FQ	61550 MW	87560 TQ	USBLS	5/07
Postsecondary	South Carolina	Y	42840 FQ	52770 MW	65240 TQ	USBLS	5/07
Postsecondary	Charleston-North Charleston MSA, SC	Y	52160 FQ	59580 MW	69050 TQ	USBLS	5/07
Postsecondary	Columbia MSA, SC	Y	42900 FQ	52830 MW	67740 TQ	USBLS	5/07

AE	Average entry wage	AW	Average wage paid	FQ	First quartile wage	LO	Lowest wage paid	MTC	Median total compensation	TCC	Total cash compensation
AER	Average entry range	AWR	Average wage range	H	Hourly	LR	Low end range	MW	Median wage paid	TQ	Third quartile wage
AEX	Average experienced wage	AXR	Average experienced range	HI	Highest wage paid	M	Monthly	MWR	Median wage range	W	Weekly
ATC	Average total compensation	D	Daily	HR	High end range	MCC	Median cash compensation	S	See annotated source	Y	Yearly

Occupation/Type/Industry	Location	Per	Low	Mid	High	Source	Date
Art, Drama, and Music Teacher							
Postsecondary	South Dakota	Y	40628 FQ	49587 MW	63813 TQ	SDBLS	7/08-9/08
Postsecondary	Tennessee	Y	39320 FQ	50420 MW	67750 TQ	USBLS	5/07
Postsecondary	Memphis MSA, TN-MS-AR	Y	40250 FQ	49430 MW	62000 TQ	USBLS	5/07
Postsecondary	Nashville-Davidson-Murfreesboro MSA, TN	Y	41190 FQ	56040 MW	89770 TQ	USBLS	5/07
Postsecondary	Texas	Y	36430 FQ	51100 MW	68060 TQ	USBLS	5/07
Postsecondary	Austin-Round Rock MSA, TX	Y	18580 FQ	50260 MW	71020 TQ	USBLS	5/07
Postsecondary	Dallas-Fort Worth-Arlington MSA, TX	Y	34340 FQ	49410 MW	66100 TQ	USBLS	5/07
Postsecondary	El Paso MSA, TX	Y	33460 FQ	43330 MW	59570 TQ	USBLS	5/07
Postsecondary	Houston-Sugar Land-Baytown MSA, TX	Y	43450 FQ	59290 MW	81440 TQ	USBLS	5/07
Postsecondary	San Antonio MSA, TX	Y	35300 FQ	49070 MW	61770 TQ	USBLS	5/07
Postsecondary	Utah	Y	41260 FQ	48440 MW	57610 TQ	USBLS	5/07
Postsecondary	Salt Lake City MSA, UT	Y	37520 FQ	46170 MW	56870 TQ	USBLS	5/07
Postsecondary	Vermont	Y	41960 FQ	49380 MW	59350 TQ	USBLS	5/07
Postsecondary	Burlington-South Burlington MSA, VT	Y	43830 FQ	51030 MW	58640 TQ	USBLS	5/07
Postsecondary	Virginia	Y	41890 FQ	55550 MW	75620 TQ	USBLS	5/07
Postsecondary	Richmond MSA, VA	Y	42830 FQ	54080 MW	68040 TQ	USBLS	5/07
Postsecondary	Virginia Beach-Norfolk-Newport News MSA, VA-NC	Y	42940 FQ	54530 MW	64720 TQ	USBLS	5/07
Postsecondary	Washington	Y		51911 AW		WABLS	3/08
Postsecondary	Seattle-Tacoma-Bellevue MSA, WA	Y	40770 FQ	48550 MW	59380 TQ	USBLS	5/07
Postsecondary	Spokane MSA, WA	Y	41220 FQ	51390 MW	62340 TQ	USBLS	5/07
Postsecondary	West Virginia	Y	41674 FQ	52847 MW	66462 TQ	WVBLS	7/08-9/08
Postsecondary	Wisconsin	Y	38780 FQ	48710 MW	62710 TQ	USBLS	5/07
Postsecondary	Milwaukee-Waukesha-West Allis MSA, WI	Y	37870 FQ	50500 MW	67960 TQ	USBLS	5/07
Postsecondary	Wyoming	Y	44514 FQ	54182 MW	66599 TQ	WYBLS	9/08
Art Director	Alabama	Y	37730 FQ	46290 MW	66420 TQ	USBLS	5/07
	Birmingham-Hoover MSA, AL	Y	40800 FQ	51900 MW	72910 TQ	USBLS	5/07
	Alaska	Y	40420 FQ	47630 MW	79590 TQ	USBLS	5/07
	Arizona	Y	38340 FQ	46570 MW	60270 TQ	USBLS	5/07
	Phoenix-Mesa-Scottsdale MSA, AZ	Y	38020 FQ	46210 MW	59940 TQ	USBLS	5/07
	Tucson MSA, AZ	Y	41270 FQ	47860 MW	65130 TQ	USBLS	5/07
	Arkansas	Y	29610 FQ	37590 MW	53530 TQ	USBLS	5/07
	Little Rock-North Little Rock MSA, AR	Y	31740 FQ	36020 MW	40310 TQ	USBLS	5/07
	California	H	30.24 FQ	42.72 MW	61.57 TQ	CABLS	1/08-3/08
	Los Angeles-Long Beach-Glendale PMSA, CA	H	30.43 FQ	44.60 MW	65.36 TQ	CABLS	1/08-3/08
	Oakland-Fremont-Hayward MSA, CA	H	27.78 FQ	38.88 MW	51.77 TQ	CABLS	1/08-3/08
	Oxnard-Thousand Oaks-Ventura MSA, CA	H	31.98 FQ	47.36 MW	54.80 TQ	CABLS	1/08-3/08
	Riverside-San Bernardino-Ontario MSA, CA	H	23.44 FQ	33.43 MW	59.88 TQ	CABLS	1/08-3/08
	Sacramento-Arden Arcade-Roseville MSA, CA	H	23.61 FQ	28.94 MW	35.76 TQ	CABLS	1/08-3/08
	San Diego-Carlsbad-San Marcos MSA, CA	H	31.69 FQ	38.32 MW	50.95 TQ	CABLS	1/08-3/08
	San Francisco-San Mateo-Redwood PMSA, CA	H	33.15 FQ	46.89 MW	67.54 TQ	CABLS	1/08-3/08
	San Jose-Sunnyvale-Santa Clara MSA, CA	H	40.01 FQ	54.57 MW	69.97 TQ	CABLS	1/08-3/08
	Santa Ana-Anaheim-Irvine PMSA, CA	Y	62220 FQ	81450 MW	116090 TQ	USBLS	5/07
	Colorado	Y	47000 FQ	63210 MW	78500 TQ	USBLS	5/07
	Boulder MSA, CO	Y	42000 FQ	48910 MW	57580 TQ	USBLS	5/07
	Denver-Aurora MSA, CO	Y	56680 FQ	70620 MW	84800 TQ	USBLS	5/07
	Connecticut	H	21.47 AE	31.80 MW		CTBLS	1/08-3/08
	Bridgeport-Stamford-Norwalk MSA, CT	Y	49040 FQ	65920 MW	90210 TQ	USBLS	5/07
	Hartford-West Hartford-East Hartford MSA, CT	Y	54080 FQ	70910 MW	86130 TQ	USBLS	5/07
	Delaware	Y	52410 FQ	61230 MW	82850 TQ	USBLS	5/07

AE   Average entry wage   AW   Average wage paid   FQ   First quartile wage   LO   Lowest wage paid   MTC   Median total compensation   TCC   Total cash compensation
AER Average entry range   AWR Average wage range   H   Hourly   LR   Low end range   MW   Median wage paid   TQ   Third quartile wage
AEX Average experienced wage   AXR Average experienced range   HI   Highest wage paid   M   Monthly   MWR   Median wage range   W   Weekly
ATC Average total compensation   D   Daily   HR   High end range   MCC   Median cash compensation   S   See annotated source   Y   Yearly

66

Occupation/Type/Industry	Location	Per	Low	Mid	High	Source	Date
Art Director	Wilmington PMSA, DE-MD-NJ	Y	53700 FQ	62190 MW	84330 TQ	USBLS	5/07
	District of Columbia	Y	51320 FQ	71930 MW	89250 TQ	USBLS	5/07
	Washington-Arlington-Alexandria MSA, DC-VA-MD-WV	Y	56220 FQ	72440 MW	89330 TQ	USBLS	5/07
	Florida	Y	44980 FQ	54590 MW	70660 TQ	USBLS	5/07
	Fort Lauderdale-Pompano Beach-Deerfield Beach PMSA, FL	Y	44290 FQ	53680 MW	73600 TQ	USBLS	5/07
	Jacksonville MSA, FL	Y	40620 FQ	47190 MW	56410 TQ	USBLS	5/07
	Miami-Fort Lauderdale-Miami Beach MSA, FL	Y	44380 FQ	53710 MW	70530 TQ	USBLS	5/07
	Orlando-Kissimmee MSA, FL	Y	51700 FQ	67160 MW	86260 TQ	USBLS	5/07
	Tampa-St. Petersburg-Clearwater MSA, FL	Y	45410 FQ	50740 MW	65870 TQ	USBLS	5/07
	West Palm Beach-Boca Raton-Boynton Beach PMSA, FL	Y	42890 FQ	65030 MW	90930 TQ	USBLS	5/07
	Georgia	Y	41620 FQ	63950 MW	96180 TQ	USBLS	5/07
	Atlanta-Sandy Springs-Marietta MSA, GA	Y	43330 FQ	65180 MW	98090 TQ	USBLS	5/07
	Hawaii	Y	39710 FQ	46630 MW	59510 TQ	USBLS	5/07
	Honolulu MSA, HI	Y	39040 FQ	45420 MW	59310 TQ	USBLS	5/07
	Idaho	Y	38110 FQ	49370 MW	77060 TQ	USBLS	5/07
	Boise City-Nampa MSA, ID	Y	43260 FQ	51880 MW	85270 TQ	USBLS	5/07
	Illinois	Y	48430 FQ	60090 MW	81010 TQ	USBLS	5/07
	Chicago-Naperville-Joliet MSA, IL-IN-WI	Y	49350 FQ	61250 MW	82960 TQ	USBLS	5/07
	Peoria MSA, IL	Y	42640 FQ	51900 MW	72360 TQ	USBLS	5/07
	Indiana	Y	40570 FQ	54990 MW	69400 TQ	USBLS	5/07
	Indianapolis-Carmel MSA, IN	Y	40560 FQ	53340 MW	63570 TQ	USBLS	5/07
	Iowa	Y	48330 FQ	57330 MW	70460 TQ	USBLS	5/07
	Des Moines-West Des Moines MSA, IA	Y	52520 FQ	57310 MW	62410 TQ	USBLS	5/07
	Kansas	Y	38760 FQ	47780 MW	60410 TQ	USBLS	5/07
	Kentucky	Y	50018 FQ	60072 MW	91524 TQ	KYBLS	2008
	Louisville-Jefferson County MSA, KY-IN	Y	45730 FQ	65080 MW	95460 TQ	USBLS	5/07
	Louisiana	H	20.18 FQ	22.43 MW	27.28 TQ	LABLS	1/08-3/08
	Maine	Y	49890 FQ	66570 MW	90210 TQ	USBLS	5/07
	Portland-South Portland-Biddeford MSA, ME	Y	50640 FQ	67460 MW	87730 TQ	USBLS	5/07
	Maryland	Y		66575 MW		MDBLS	3/08
	Baltimore-Towson MSA, MD	Y	50710 FQ	64750 MW	80840 TQ	USBLS	5/07
	Bethesda-Gaithersburg-Frederick PMSA, MD	Y	55160 FQ	68190 MW	75540 TQ	USBLS	5/07
	Massachusetts	Y	59630 FQ	80250 MW	115300 TQ	USBLS	5/07
	Boston-Cambridge-Quincy NECTA, MA	Y	62520 FQ	82550 MW	122400 TQ	USBLS	5/07
	Springfield MSA, MA-CT	Y	43030 FQ	75780 MW	97500 TQ	USBLS	5/07
	Worcester MSA, MA-CT	Y	49040 FQ	68730 MW	88960 TQ	USBLS	5/07
	Michigan	Y	48370 FQ	66890 MW	93630 TQ	USBLS	5/07
	Detroit-Warren-Livonia MSA, MI	Y	51900 FQ	73380 MW	100130 TQ	USBLS	5/07
	Grand Rapids-Wyoming MSA, MI	Y	46900 FQ	58410 MW	79210 TQ	USBLS	5/07
	Warren-Troy-Farmington Hills PMSA, MI	Y	50010 FQ	72290 MW	96870 TQ	USBLS	5/07
	Minnesota	Y	53964 FQ	77420 MW	101107 TQ	MNBLS	10/08-12/08
	Duluth-Superior MSA, MN-WI	Y	36900 FQ	44611 MW	50773 TQ	MNBLS	10/08-12/08
	Minneapolis-Saint Paul MSA, MN-WI	Y	63798 FQ	83279 MW	109811 TQ	MNBLS	10/08-12/08
	Rochester MSA, MN	Y	70510 FQ	78727 MW	86516 TQ	MNBLS	10/08-12/08
	Mississippi	Y	32840 FQ	43910 MW	64330 TQ	USBLS	5/07
	Jackson MSA, MS	Y	42080 FQ	55360 MW	77670 TQ	USBLS	5/07
	Missouri	Y	40750 FQ	61350 MW	88940 TQ	USBLS	5/07
	Kansas City MSA, MO-KS	Y	40280 FQ	55530 MW	74280 TQ	USBLS	5/07
	St. Louis MSA, MO-IL	Y	56240 FQ	78060 MW	96210 TQ	USBLS	5/07
	Montana	Y	37780 FQ	45630 MW	62100 TQ	USBLS	5/07
	Nebraska	Y	38840 FQ	53690 MW	69040 TQ	USBLS	5/07
	Omaha-Council Bluffs MSA, NE-IA	Y	47550 FQ	59140 MW	82450 TQ	USBLS	5/07

AE Average entry wage	**AW** Average wage paid	**FQ** First quartile wage	**LO** Lowest wage paid	**MTC** Median total compensation	**TCC** Total cash compensation
AER Average entry range	**AWR** Average wage range	**H** Hourly	**LR** Low end range	**MW** Median wage paid	**TQ** Third quartile wage
AEX Average experienced wage	**AXR** Average experienced range	**HI** Highest wage paid	**M** Monthly	**MWR** Median wage range	**W** Weekly
ATC Average total compensation	**D** Daily	**HR** High end range	**MCC** Median cash compensation	**S** See annotated source	**Y** Yearly

Art Director

Occupation/Type/Industry	Location	Per	Low	Mid	High	Source	Date
Art Director	Nevada	H	21.80 FQ	26.93 MW	39.39 TQ	NVBLS	5/08
	Las Vegas-Paradise MSA, NV	H	22.36 FQ	27.41 MW	40.53 TQ	NVBLS	5/08
	New Hampshire	H	20.59 AE	25.62 MW	39.30 AEX	NHBLS	6/08
	New Jersey	Y	67970 FQ	79460 MW	99310 TQ	USBLS	5/07
	Camden PMSA, NJ	Y	62880 FQ	74060 MW	94230 TQ	USBLS	5/07
	Edison PMSA, NJ	Y	68780 FQ	76840 MW	85120 TQ	USBLS	5/07
	Newark-Union PMSA, NJ-PA	Y	64140 FQ	85020 MW	111950 TQ	USBLS	5/07
	New Mexico	Y	42560 FQ	47130 MW	55810 TQ	USBLS	5/07
	Albuquerque MSA, NM	Y	43170 FQ	47000 MW	50890 TQ	USBLS	5/07
	New York	Y	73460 FQ	101010 MW	139420 TQ	USBLS	5/07
	Albany-Schenectady-Troy MSA, NY	Y	56440 FQ	64450 MW	88870 TQ	USBLS	5/07
	Buffalo-Niagara Falls MSA, NY	Y	37600 FQ	59800 MW	80190 TQ	USBLS	5/07
	Nassau-Suffolk PMSA, NY	Y	57040 FQ	70870 MW	88890 TQ	USBLS	5/07
	New York-Northern New Jersey-Long Island MSA, NY-NJ-PA	Y	73920 FQ	97690 MW	133920 TQ	USBLS	5/07
	North Carolina	Y	41120 FQ	52700 MW	70690 TQ	USBLS	5/07
	Charlotte-Gastonia-Concord MSA, NC-SC	Y	45110 FQ	56390 MW	69030 TQ	USBLS	5/07
	Raleigh-Cary MSA, NC	Y	43970 FQ	73750 MW	133770 TQ	USBLS	5/07
	Ohio	Y	50600 FQ	74980 MW	103620 TQ	USBLS	5/07
	Cincinnati-Middletown MSA, OH-KY-IN	Y	64630 FQ	84710 MW	107640 TQ	USBLS	5/07
	Cleveland-Elyria-Mentor MSA, OH	Y	48980 FQ	65850 MW	92420 TQ	USBLS	5/07
	Columbus MSA, OH	Y	50810 FQ	86560 MW	124010 TQ	USBLS	5/07
	Dayton MSA, OH	Y	43150 FQ	50330 MW	88940 TQ	USBLS	5/07
	Oklahoma	Y	32260 FQ	40960 MW	63470 TQ	USBLS	5/07
	Oklahoma City MSA, OK	Y	30840 FQ	35950 MW	48630 TQ	USBLS	5/07
	Oregon	H	27.06 FQ	31.55 MW	43.75 TQ	ORBLS	5/08
	Portland-Vancouver-Beaverton MSA, OR-WA	Y	56920 FQ	68700 MW	97460 TQ	USBLS	5/07
	Pennsylvania	Y	41120 FQ	56060 MW	79650 TQ	USBLS	5/07
	Allentown-Bethlehem-Easton MSA, PA-NJ	Y	45950 FQ	56330 MW	62560 TQ	USBLS	5/07
	Philadelphia-Camden-Wilmington MSA, PA-NJ-DE-MD	Y	40900 FQ	58270 MW	82060 TQ	USBLS	5/07
	Pittsburgh MSA, PA	Y	45600 FQ	69180 MW	106920 TQ	USBLS	5/07
	Rhode Island	Y	42790 FQ	52020 MW	74930 TQ	USBLS	5/07
	Providence-Fall River-Warwick MSA, RI-MA	Y	38540 FQ	50310 MW	72870 TQ	USBLS	5/07
	South Carolina	Y	37890 FQ	47370 MW	60500 TQ	USBLS	5/07
	South Dakota	Y	46264 FQ	57067 MW	71637 TQ	SDBLS	7/08-9/08
	Sioux Falls MSA, SD	Y	48670 FQ	59087 MW	73398 TQ	SDBLS	7/08-9/08
	Tennessee	Y	39300 FQ	47300 MW	58550 TQ	USBLS	5/07
	Memphis MSA, TN-MS-AR	Y	35280 FQ	41630 MW	54240 TQ	USBLS	5/07
	Nashville-Davidson-Murfreesboro MSA, TN	Y	47080 FQ	53590 MW	63270 TQ	USBLS	5/07
	Texas	Y	49400 FQ	67280 MW	93050 TQ	USBLS	5/07
	Austin-Round Rock MSA, TX	Y	53640 FQ	71760 MW	101380 TQ	USBLS	5/07
	Dallas-Fort Worth-Arlington MSA, TX	Y	54730 FQ	73110 MW	95720 TQ	USBLS	5/07
	Houston-Sugar Land-Baytown MSA, TX	Y	44940 FQ	60970 MW	89790 TQ	USBLS	5/07
	San Antonio MSA, TX	Y	45030 FQ	50400 MW	66020 TQ	USBLS	5/07
	Utah	Y	50770 FQ	69200 MW	82530 TQ	USBLS	5/07
	Salt Lake City MSA, UT	Y	50270 FQ	70290 MW	82760 TQ	USBLS	5/07
	Vermont	Y	44530 FQ	59650 MW	94490 TQ	USBLS	5/07
	Virginia	Y	52430 FQ	66560 MW	85520 TQ	USBLS	5/07
	Richmond MSA, VA	Y	44290 FQ	52990 MW	75700 TQ	USBLS	5/07
	Virginia Beach-Norfolk-Newport News MSA, VA-NC	Y	52580 FQ	58510 MW	71730 TQ	USBLS	5/07
	Washington	H	29.02 FQ	35.66 MW	43.14 TQ	WABLS	3/08
	Seattle-Tacoma-Bellevue MSA, WA	Y	62690 FQ	74960 MW	89840 TQ	USBLS	5/07
	West Virginia	Y	42636 FQ	54712 MW	84981 TQ	WVBLS	7/08-9/08
	Wisconsin	Y	47330 FQ	63600 MW	82140 TQ	USBLS	5/07
	Milwaukee-Waukesha-West Allis MSA, WI	Y	47960 FQ	64070 MW	81310 TQ	USBLS	5/07

Occupation/Type/Industry	Location	Per	Low	Mid	High	Source	Date
Art Director	Wyoming	Y	23919 FQ	33891 MW	41225 TQ	WYBLS	9/08
	Puerto Rico	Y	30870 FQ	43300 MW	62130 TQ	USBLS	5/07
	San Juan-Caguas-Guaynabo MSA, PR	Y	31360 FQ	43520 MW	62680 TQ	USBLS	5/07
Arts Instructor							
Municipal Library	Carlsbad, CA	H	12.00 LO		30.00 HI	CCSS	1/1/08
Asphalt Plant Equipment Operator							
Municipal Government	Cincinnati, OH	Y	40851 LO		43372 HI	COHSS	10/08
Asphalt Raker							
Municipal Government	Cincinnati, OH	Y	36517 LO		37647 HI	COHSS	10/08
Municipal Government	Seattle, WA	H	21.56 LO		23.23 HI	CSSS	2007
Assembly Staffer							
State Government	California	Y		51996 MW		SBEE	2008
Assessor	Handy Township, MI	Y			65000 HI	LCPP	2009
Assessor Clerk	Charlemont, MA	Y			20000 HI	FRCOG	2009
Assistant Attorney General							
Department of Justice	New Hampshire	Y		58542 AW		NHUL03	2008
Assistant Brewer	United States	H		9.86-14.60 AWR		NBREW	2008
Assistant Chaplain							
State Government	Ohio	H	16.51 LO		19.78 HI	ODAS	2008
Assistant City Archivist	Seattle, WA	H	29.34 LO		34.12 HI	CSSS	2008
Assistant City Attorney	Walnut Creek, CA	Y	116535 LO		162341 HI	WCSWP	7/11/08
Assistant Clerk of the Legislature	Nebraska	Y			120363 HI	NEST	2008
Assistant District Forest Manager							
State Government	Ohio	H	25.40 LO		33.16 HI	ODAS	2008
Assistant Fire Alarm Operator and Dispatcher							
Municipal Government	Cincinnati, OH	Y	38340 LO		43264 HI	COHSS	10/08
Assistant Fire Chief	Roswell, GA	Y	60599 LO		96958 HI	GACTY01	2008
Assistant Librarian	Bernardston, MA	H			11.00 HI	FRCOG	2009
Assistant Lottery Ticket Sales Regional Manager	Ohio	H	25.40 LO		33.16 HI	ODAS	2008
Assistant Museum Curator	United States	Y		42642 MW		WSJ08	2008
Assistant Personnel Manager							
State Government	Arkansas	Y	31093 LO		53876 HI	AFT02	3/1/08
Assistant Plumber							
State Government	Ohio	H	14.85 LO		16.35 HI	ODAS	2008
Assistant Police Chief	Dublin, GA	Y			49057 HI	GACTY01	2008
	Marietta, GA	Y	71997 LO		108459 HI	GACTY01	2008
	Rome, GA	Y	50000 LO		80000 HI	GACTY01	2008
Assistant Press Secretary and Director of Television							
White House Staff	United States	Y			100300 HI	WPOST02	2008
Assistant Press Secretary to the First Lady							
White House Staff	United States	Y			43000 HI	WPOST02	2008
Assistant Principal	North Carolina	M	3781 LO		5839 HI	NCSS	2008-2009

AE Average entry wage	**AW** Average wage paid	**FQ** First quartile wage	**LO** Lowest wage paid	**MTC** Median total compensation	**TCC** Total cash compensation
AER Average entry range	**AWR** Average wage range	**H** Hourly	**LR** Low end range	**MW** Median wage paid	**TQ** Third quartile wage
AEX Average experienced wage	**AXR** Average experienced range	**HI** Highest wage paid	**M** Monthly	**MWR** Median wage range	**W** Weekly
ATC Average total compensation	**D** Daily	**HR** High end range	**MCC** Median cash compensation	**S** See annotated source	**Y** Yearly

Occupation/Type/Industry	Location	Per	Low	Mid	High	Source	Date
Assistant Professor of Astronomy	United States	Y	45000-50000 AE			NOAO	2008
Assistant Public Defender	Ohio	H	16.23 LO		49.50 HI	ODAS	2008
Assistant Statue/Decorative Artwork Restorer State Government	Ohio	H	17.72 LO		21.77 HI	ODAS	2008
Assistant Supervisor of Building Permits	Cincinnati, OH	Y	37150 LO		49926 HI	COHSS	10/08
Assistant Supervisor of Parking Services	Cincinnati, OH	Y	37150 LO		49926 HI	COHSS	10/08
Assistant to the President and Chief of Staff White House Staff	United States	Y			172200 HI	WPOST02	2008
Assistant to the President and Chief of Staff to the First Lady White House Staff	United States	Y			172200 HI	WPOST02	2008
Assistant to the President for Speechwriting White House Staff	United States	Y			172200 HI	WPOST02	2008
Assistant Turf Manager Municipal Government	Cincinnati, OH	Y	37647 LO		40748 HI	COHSS	10/08
Assistive Technology Specialist Master's Degree, Public Schools	Wake County, NC	Y	44272 LO		73062 HI	WCPS	2008-2009
Associate Accountant State Government	New York	Y	58406 LO		71732 HI	AFT02	3/1/08
Associate Biochemist State Government	New York	Y	58406 LO		71732 HI	AFT02	3/1/08
Associate Bridge Engineer State Government	California	Y	75504 LO		91740 HI	AFT02	3/1/08
Associate Economist State Government	New York	Y	58406 LO		71732 HI	AFT02	3/1/08
Associate Geologist State Government	California	Y	59520 LO		71760 HI	AFT02	3/1/08
Associate Justice of the Supreme Court Federal Government	United States	Y			208100 HI	CRS02	1/08
Associate Park Planner Municipal Government	Gresham, OR	Y	49920 LO		63792 HI	GOSS	1/1/09
Associate Professor Accounting/Taxation Economics/Managerial Economics	United States United States	Y Y		108500 AW 85900 AW		AACSB AACSB	2007-2008 2007-2008
Associate Superintendent of Business Public Schools	Howell, MI	Y			125898 HI	LCPP	2009
Astrobiologist	United States	Y	50000 LO		100000 HI	JYI	2008
Astronaut	United States	Y	65140 LO		100701 HI	NASA	2008
Astronomer	Colorado Orlando, FL Hawaii Maryland	Y Y Y Y	64940 FQ 59180 FQ	91850 MW 110960 AW 82250 MW 132575 MW	116880 TQ 126930 TQ	USBLS SALEX USBLS MDBLS	5/07 7/08 5/07 3/08

AE	Average entry wage	AW	Average wage paid	FQ	First quartile wage	LO	Lowest wage paid	MTC	Median total compensation	TCC	Total cash compensation
AER	Average entry range	AWR	Average wage range	H	Hourly	LR	Low end range	MW	Median wage paid	TQ	Third quartile wage
AEX	Average experienced wage	AXR	Average experienced range	HI	Highest wage paid	M	Monthly	MWR	Median wage range	W	Weekly
ATC	Average total compensation	D	Daily	HR	High end range	MCC	Median cash compensation	S	See annotated source	Y	Yearly

Occupation/Type/Industry	Location	Per	Low	Mid	High	Source	Date
Astronomer	Massachusetts	Y	106190 FQ	124180 MW	145390 TQ	USBLS	5/07
	New York-Manhattan, NY	Y		135352 AW		SALEX	7/08
	Ohio	Y	82010 FQ	90240 MW	98880 TQ	USBLS	5/07
	Texas	Y	49820 FQ	75780 MW	123320 TQ	USBLS	5/07
•	Virginia	Y	82320 FQ	118180 MW	141430 TQ	USBLS	5/07
Astrophysicist	United States	Y		60200 AW		SUSA04	2009
Athlete and Sports Competitor	Arkansas	Y	14990 FQ	22290 MW	32410 TQ	USBLS	5/07
	California	Y		79864 AW		CABLS	1/08-3/08
	Colorado	Y	21960 FQ	29470 MW	45680 TQ	USBLS	5/07
	District of Columbia	Y	52260 FQ	78630 MW	122460 TQ	USBLS	5/07
	Florida	Y	15350 FQ	29030 MW	55610 TQ	USBLS	5/07
	Georgia	Y	14990 FQ	50690 MW	85950 TQ	USBLS	5/07
	Illinois	Y	15400 FQ	26460 MW	49560 TQ	USBLS	5/07
	Indiana	Y	25270 FQ	32580 MW	55620 TQ	USBLS	5/07
	Iowa	Y	31740 FQ	74640 MW	96780 TQ	USBLS	5/07
	Kentucky	Y	28610 FQ	41939 MW	58523 TQ	KYBLS	2008
	Louisiana	Y		46129 AW		LABLS	1/08-3/08
	Maryland	Y		32675 MW		MDBLS	3/08
	Massachusetts	Y	28340 FQ	42730 MW	69190 TQ	USBLS	5/07
	Michigan	Y	29300 FQ	36620 MW	63240 TQ	USBLS	5/07
	Missouri	Y	39710 FQ			USBLS	5/07
	Montana	Y	28090 FQ	31650 MW	54560 TQ	USBLS	5/07
	Nebraska	Y	44620 FQ	51280 MW	63140 TQ	USBLS	5/07
	New Hampshire	Y	17850 AE	35531 MW	38051 AEX	NHBLS	6/08
	New Jersey	Y	29170 FQ	48320 MW	117390 TQ	USBLS	5/07
	New York	Y	48890 FQ	106290 MW		USBLS	5/07
	North Carolina	Y	15970 FQ	50920 MW		USBLS	5/07
	Ohio	Y	28900 FQ	46840 MW	61850 TQ	USBLS	5/07
	Pennsylvania	Y	15900 FQ	34350 MW	62460 TQ	USBLS	5/07
	South Carolina	Y	22240 FQ	26140 MW	44970 TQ	USBLS	5/07
	South Dakota	Y	25836 FQ	34286 MW	55191 MW	SDBLS	7/08-9/08
	Texas	Y	21460 FQ	40140 MW	92460 TQ	USBLS	5/07
	Virginia	Y	24830 FQ	39100 MW	71950 TQ	USBLS	5/07
	Washington	Y		80184 AW		WABLS	3/08
	West Virginia	Y	24600 FQ	33709 MW	55088 TQ	WVBLS	7/08-9/08
	Wisconsin	Y	18710 FQ	29410 MW	49570 TQ	USBLS	5/07
Athletic Coordinator							
Public High School	Baldwin County, AL	S			9550 HI	BCPSSS	2008-2009
Athletic Director							
Community Schools	Fowlerville, MI	Y			64960 HI	LCPP	2009
Consolidated School District	Hartland Township, MI	Y			85000 HI	LCPP	2009
Athletic Trainer	United States	Y		36560 AW		OOSE01	5/06
	Alabama	Y	28690 FQ	36050 MW	42040 TQ	USBLS	5/07
	Birmingham-Hoover MSA, AL	Y	26880 FQ	35510 MW	41150 TQ	USBLS	5/07
	Arizona	Y	28520 FQ	36280 MW	44160 TQ	USBLS	5/07
	Phoenix-Mesa-Scottsdale MSA, AZ	Y	28090 FQ	35870 MW	43760 TQ	USBLS	5/07
	Arkansas	Y	34850 FQ	44450 MW	60590 TQ	USBLS	5/07
	Little Rock-North Little Rock MSA, AR	Y	30420 FQ	41570 MW	59300 TQ	USBLS	5/07
	California	Y		38230 AW		CABLS	1/08-3/08
	Los Angeles-Long Beach-Glendale PMSA, CA	Y		33318 AW		CABLS	1/08-3/08
	Oakland-Fremont-Hayward MSA, CA	Y		44382 MW		CABLS	1/08-3/08
	Riverside-San Bernardino-Ontario MSA, CA	Y		34292 AW		CABLS	1/08-3/08
	Sacramento-Arden Arcade-Roseville MSA, CA	Y		45408 AW		CABLS	1/08-3/08
	San Diego-Carlsbad-San Marcos MSA, CA	Y		46198 AW		CABLS	1/08-3/08
	San Francisco-San Mateo-Redwood PMSA, CA	Y		38353 AW		CABLS	1/08-3/08
	San Jose-Sunnyvale-Santa Clara MSA, CA	Y		48495 AW		CABLS	1/08-3/08
	Santa Ana-Anaheim-Irvine PMSA, CA	Y	21570 FQ	23960 MW	28810 TQ	USBLS	5/07
	Colorado	Y	24080 FQ	30250 MW	38920 TQ	USBLS	5/07

AE	Average entry wage	AW	Average wage paid	FQ	First quartile wage	LO	Lowest wage paid	MTC	Median total compensation	TCC	Total cash compensation
AER	Average entry range	AWR	Average wage range	H	Hourly	LR	Low end range	MW	Median wage paid	TQ	Third quartile wage
AEX	Average experienced wage	AXR	Average experienced range	HI	Highest wage paid	M	Monthly	MWR	Median wage range	W	Weekly
ATC	Average total compensation	D	Daily	HR	High end range	MCC	Median cash compensation	S	See annotated source	Y	Yearly

Occupation/Type/Industry	Location	Per	Low	Mid	High	Source	Date
Athletic Trainer	Denver-Aurora MSA, CO	Y	23290 FQ	26220 MW	36590 TQ	USBLS	5/07
	Wilmington PMSA, DE-MD-NJ	Y	38040 FQ	44540 MW	48670 TQ	USBLS	5/07
	District of Columbia	Y	39370 FQ	46450 MW	56050 TQ	USBLS	5/07
	Washington-Arlington-Alexandria MSA, DC-VA-MD-WV	Y	36320 FQ	43830 MW	53760 TQ	USBLS	5/07
	Florida	Y	30980 FQ	37630 MW	45570 TQ	USBLS	5/07
	Fort Lauderdale-Pompano Beach-Deerfield Beach PMSA, FL	Y	37800 FQ	43550 MW	47650 TQ	USBLS	5/07
	Jacksonville MSA, FL	Y	24460 FQ	28360 MW	32180 TQ	USBLS	5/07
	Miami-Fort Lauderdale-Miami Beach MSA, FL	Y	35460 FQ	40540 MW	47270 TQ	USBLS	5/07
	Orlando-Kissimmee MSA, FL	Y	37350 FQ	42370 MW	52700 TQ	USBLS	5/07
	Tampa-St. Petersburg-Clearwater MSA, FL	Y	31960 FQ	37660 MW	45450 TQ	USBLS	5/07
	West Palm Beach-Boca Raton-Boynton Beach PMSA, FL	Y	34310 FQ	36890 MW	39560 TQ	USBLS	5/07
	Georgia	Y	33110 FQ	37470 MW	44820 TQ	USBLS	5/07
	Atlanta-Sandy Springs-Marietta MSA, GA	Y	33180 FQ	37350 MW	44540 TQ	USBLS	5/07
	Hawaii	Y	40400 FQ	44670 MW	49440 TQ	USBLS	5/07
	Honolulu MSA, HI	Y	38720 FQ	43020 MW	49360 TQ	USBLS	5/07
	Illinois	Y	32540 FQ	42110 MW	52420 TQ	USBLS	5/07
	Chicago-Naperville-Joliet MSA, IL-IN-WI	Y	34540 FQ	45160 MW	56390 TQ	USBLS	5/07
	Indiana	Y	34030 FQ	38120 MW	45010 TQ	USBLS	5/07
	Indianapolis-Carmel MSA, IN	Y	34770 FQ	38620 MW	45890 TQ	USBLS	5/07
	Iowa	Y	30050 FQ	35260 MW	40260 TQ	USBLS	5/07
	Des Moines-West Des Moines MSA, IA	Y	18840 FQ	32830 MW	37440 TQ	USBLS	5/07
	Kansas	Y	30350 FQ	36120 MW	41100 TQ	USBLS	5/07
	Kentucky	Y	35133 FQ	40206 MW	47867 TQ	KYBLS	2008
	Louisville-Jefferson County MSA, KY-IN	Y	32260 FQ	37710 MW	52960 TQ	USBLS	5/07
	Louisiana	Y		37135 AW		LABLS	1/08-3/08
	Maine	Y	35000 FQ	39090 MW	47470 TQ	USBLS	5/07
	Maryland	Y		41350 MW		MDBLS	3/08
	Baltimore-Towson MSA, MD	Y	28900 FQ	37270 MW	50650 TQ	USBLS	5/07
	Massachusetts	Y	21900 FQ	38700 MW	54450 TQ	USBLS	5/07
	Boston-Cambridge-Quincy NECTA, MA	Y	21660 FQ	38120 MW	54990 TQ	USBLS	5/07
	Worcester MSA, MA-CT	Y	18180 FQ	20360 MW	35150 TQ	USBLS	5/07
	Michigan	Y	35960 FQ	41390 MW	48550 TQ	USBLS	5/07
	Detroit-Warren-Livonia MSA, MI	Y	34720 FQ	39550 MW	46560 TQ	USBLS	5/07
	Grand Rapids-Wyoming MSA, MI	Y	37970 FQ	41310 MW	45700 TQ	USBLS	5/07
	Warren-Troy-Farmington Hills PMSA, MI	Y	34170 FQ	43340 MW	51700 TQ	USBLS	5/07
	Minnesota	Y	36209 FQ	40143 MW	46264 TQ	MNBLS	10/08-12/08
	Duluth-Superior MSA, MN-WI	Y	34525 FQ	38783 MW	44422 TQ	MNBLS	10/08-12/08
	Minneapolis-Saint Paul MSA, MN-WI	Y	37444 FQ	41179 MW	49141 TQ	MNBLS	10/08-12/08
	Mississippi	Y	31750 FQ	38650 MW	45290 TQ	USBLS	5/07
	Jackson MSA, MS	Y	34500 FQ	40020 MW	45910 TQ	USBLS	5/07
	Missouri	Y	29820 FQ	36940 MW	47090 TQ	USBLS	5/07
	Kansas City MSA, MO-KS	Y	19530 FQ	34570 MW	43690 TQ	USBLS	5/07
	St. Louis MSA, MO-IL	Y	36930 FQ	47320 MW	70690 TQ	USBLS	5/07
	Montana	Y	15840 FQ	27670 MW	32120 TQ	USBLS	5/07
	Nebraska	Y	33270 FQ	39640 MW	47110 TQ	USBLS	5/07
	Omaha-Council Bluffs MSA, NE-IA	Y	30730 FQ	35620 MW	40630 TQ	USBLS	5/07
	Nevada	Y	28659 FQ	38246 MW	57022 TQ	NVBLS	5/08
	Las Vegas-Paradise MSA, NV	Y	37270 FQ	46552 MW	61449 TQ	NVBLS	5/08
	Reno-Sparks MSA, NV	Y	24897 FQ	30286 MW	57869 TQ	NVBLS	5/08
	New Hampshire	Y	30664 AE	40887 MW	49887 AEX	NHBLS	6/08
	Manchester MSA, NH	Y	34160 FQ	40430 MW	52130 TQ	USBLS	5/07
	New Jersey	Y	40980 FQ	49980 MW	60500 TQ	USBLS	5/07
	Camden PMSA, NJ	Y	48420 FQ	55630 MW	63660 TQ	USBLS	5/07
	Edison PMSA, NJ	Y	43100 FQ	50510 MW	59610 TQ	USBLS	5/07

AE	Average entry wage	AW	Average wage paid	FQ	First quartile wage
AER	Average entry range	AWR	Average wage range	H	Hourly
AEX	Average experienced wage	AXR	Average experienced range	HI	Highest wage paid
ATC	Average total compensation	D	Daily	HR	High end range

LO	Lowest wage paid	MTC	Median total compensation	TCC	Total cash compensation
LR	Low end range	MW	Median wage paid	TQ	Third quartile wage
M	Monthly	MWR	Median wage range	W	Weekly
MCC	Median cash compensation	S	See annotated source	Y	Yearly

Occupation/Type/Industry	Location	Per	Low	Mid	High	Source	Date
Athletic Trainer	Newark-Union PMSA, NJ-PA	Y	35610 FQ	43610 MW	54030 TQ	USBLS	5/07
	New Mexico	Y	17790 FQ	22780 MW	32810 TQ	USBLS	5/07
	Albuquerque MSA, NM	Y	17340 FQ	19080 MW	30280 TQ	USBLS	5/07
	New York	Y	28280 FQ	35560 MW	46910 TQ	USBLS	5/07
	Albany-Schenectady-Troy MSA, NY	Y	27080 FQ	34250 MW	40710 TQ	USBLS	5/07
	Buffalo-Niagara Falls MSA, NY	Y	33230 FQ	37110 MW	45970 TQ	USBLS	5/07
	Nassau-Suffolk PMSA, NY	Y	27240 FQ	30090 MW	51010 TQ	USBLS	5/07
	New York-Northern New Jersey-Long Island MSA, NY-NJ-PA	Y	30380 FQ	41810 MW	58380 TQ	USBLS	5/07
	North Carolina	Y	31780 FQ	36970 MW	43100 TQ	USBLS	5/07
	Charlotte-Gastonia-Concord MSA, NC-SC	Y	32530 FQ	37410 MW	41940 TQ	USBLS	5/07
	Raleigh-Cary MSA, NC	Y	32910 FQ	37180 MW	45560 TQ	USBLS	5/07
	North Dakota	Y	30590 FQ	36790 MW	44900 TQ	USBLS	5/07
	Ohio	Y	34590 FQ	39740 MW	46520 TQ	USBLS	5/07
	Cincinnati-Middletown MSA, OH-KY-IN	Y	34690 FQ	39870 MW	46850 TQ	USBLS	5/07
	Cleveland-Elyria-Mentor MSA, OH	Y	35440 FQ	39900 MW	45630 TQ	USBLS	5/07
	Columbus MSA, OH	Y	31200 FQ	38140 MW	47120 TQ	USBLS	5/07
	Dayton MSA, OH	Y	35630 FQ	41530 MW	47090 TQ	USBLS	5/07
	Oklahoma	Y	29620 FQ	38960 MW	46370 TQ	USBLS	5/07
	Oklahoma City MSA, OK	Y	33520 FQ	41720 MW	51810 TQ	USBLS	5/07
	Tulsa MSA, OK	Y	22630 FQ	32850 MW	41490 TQ	USBLS	5/07
	Oregon	Y	36022 FQ	43335 MW	50891 TQ	ORBLS	5/08
	Portland-Vancouver-Beaverton MSA, OR-WA	Y	34060 FQ	41880 MW	49010 TQ	USBLS	5/07
	Pennsylvania	Y	31430 FQ	36320 MW	41940 TQ	USBLS	5/07
	Allentown-Bethlehem-Easton MSA, PA-NJ	Y	30160 FQ	35690 MW	42220 TQ	USBLS	5/07
	Philadelphia-Camden-Wilmington MSA, PA-NJ-DE-MD	Y	35100 FQ	40930 MW	47990 TQ	USBLS	5/07
	Pittsburgh MSA, PA	Y	31050 FQ	35270 MW	39730 TQ	USBLS	5/07
	Rhode Island	Y	36680 FQ	44180 MW	51240 TQ	USBLS	5/07
	Providence-Fall River-Warwick MSA, RI-MA	Y	36300 FQ	43610 MW	50440 TQ	USBLS	5/07
	South Carolina	Y	33810 FQ	38730 MW	47150 TQ	USBLS	5/07
	Tennessee	Y	33010 FQ	37820 MW	46080 TQ	USBLS	5/07
	Memphis MSA, TN-MS-AR	Y	30190 FQ	37910 MW	49460 TQ	USBLS	5/07
	Nashville-Davidson-Murfreesboro MSA, TN	Y	34430 FQ	38830 MW	46110 TQ	USBLS	5/07
	Texas	Y	31840 FQ	42620 MW	54470 TQ	USBLS	5/07
	Austin-Round Rock MSA, TX	Y	44260 FQ	49310 MW	56870 TQ	USBLS	5/07
	Corpus Christi MSA, TX	Y	34420 FQ	39730 MW	48440 TQ	USBLS	5/07
	Dallas-Fort Worth-Arlington MSA, TX	Y	33340 FQ	40850 MW	59180 TQ	USBLS	5/07
	El Paso MSA, TX	Y	14720 FQ	18140 MW	30930 TQ	USBLS	5/07
	Houston-Sugar Land-Baytown MSA, TX	Y	24340 FQ	41800 MW	50470 TQ	USBLS	5/07
	San Antonio MSA, TX	Y	42600 FQ	50310 MW	59730 TQ	USBLS	5/07
	Utah	Y	32970 FQ	37320 MW	44610 TQ	USBLS	5/07
	Salt Lake City MSA, UT	Y	31710 FQ	35720 MW	39430 TQ	USBLS	5/07
	Vermont	Y	37060 FQ	42880 MW	48120 TQ	USBLS	5/07
	Burlington-South Burlington MSA, VT	Y	36100 FQ	40580 MW	46070 TQ	USBLS	5/07
	Virginia	Y	26910 FQ	33450 MW	40060 TQ	USBLS	5/07
	Richmond MSA, VA	Y	29880 FQ	35210 MW	40050 TQ	USBLS	5/07
	Virginia Beach-Norfolk-Newport News MSA, VA-NC	Y	28530 FQ	31910 MW	37620 TQ	USBLS	5/07
	Washington	Y		42682 AW		WABLS	3/08
	Seattle-Tacoma-Bellevue MSA, WA	Y	32980 FQ	37960 MW	48620 TQ	USBLS	5/07
	West Virginia	Y	27654 FQ	33928 MW	41024 TQ	WVBLS	7/08-9/08
	Wisconsin	Y	35760 FQ	42490 MW	48400 TQ	USBLS	5/07
	Milwaukee-Waukesha-West Allis MSA, WI	Y	32980 FQ	41900 MW	48160 TQ	USBLS	5/07

AE Average entry wage	**AW** Average wage paid	**FQ** First quartile wage	**LO** Lowest wage paid	**MTC** Median total compensation	**TCC** Total cash compensation
AER Average entry range	**AWR** Average wage range	**H** Hourly	**LR** Low end range	**MW** Median wage paid	**TQ** Third quartile wage
AEX Average experienced wage	**AXR** Average experienced range	**HI** Highest wage paid	**M** Monthly	**MWR** Median wage range	**W** Weekly
ATC Average total compensation	**D** Daily	**HR** High end range	**MCC** Median cash compensation	**S** See annotated source	**Y** Yearly

Occupation/Type/Industry	Location	Per	Low	Mid	High	Source	Date
Atmospheric, Earth, Marine, and Space Sciences Teacher							
Postsecondary	Alabama	Y	42740 FQ	59180 MW	76740 TQ	USBLS	5/07
Postsecondary	Arizona	Y	48130 FQ	68170 MW	97560 TQ	USBLS	5/07
Postsecondary	California	Y		97912 AW		CABLS	1/08-3/08
Postsecondary	Colorado	Y	37690 FQ	59990 MW	85350 TQ	USBLS	5/07
Postsecondary	District of Columbia	Y	42740 FQ	51560 MW	76480 TQ	USBLS	5/07
Postsecondary	Florida	Y	46110 FQ	63670 MW	81840 TQ	USBLS	5/07
Postsecondary	Georgia	Y	51990 FQ	63150 MW	75030 TQ	USBLS	5/07
Postsecondary	Hawaii	Y	61250 FQ	77030 MW	115190 TQ	USBLS	5/07
Postsecondary	Illinois	Y	46270 FQ	61760 MW	81870 TQ	USBLS	5/07
Postsecondary	Indiana	Y	44760 FQ	58210 MW	83540 TQ	USBLS	5/07
Postsecondary	Iowa	Y	57350 FQ	73550 MW	92300 TQ	USBLS	5/07
Postsecondary	Kansas	Y	63790 FQ	78350 MW	110590 TQ	USBLS	5/07
Postsecondary	Kentucky	Y	52077 FQ	61236 MW	82696 TQ	KYBLS	2008
Postsecondary	Maine	Y	58340 FQ	77390 MW	97640 TQ	USBLS	5/07
Postsecondary	Maryland	Y		93200 MW		MDBLS	3/08
Postsecondary	Massachusetts	Y	68420 FQ	92290 MW	120760 TQ	USBLS	5/07
Postsecondary	Michigan	Y	54900 FQ	70720 MW	82830 TQ	USBLS	5/07
Postsecondary	Minnesota	Y	47540 FQ	64353 MW	99255 TQ	MNBLS	10/08-12/08
Postsecondary	Mississippi	Y	56670 FQ	65300 MW	80100 TQ	USBLS	5/07
Postsecondary	Missouri	Y	48770 FQ	63400 MW	91700 TQ	USBLS	5/07
Postsecondary	New Mexico	Y	57500 FQ	69940 MW	87100 TQ	USBLS	5/07
Postsecondary	New York	Y	53970 FQ	79420 MW	109430 TQ	USBLS	5/07
Postsecondary	North Carolina	Y	53270 FQ	73690 MW	95720 TQ	USBLS	5/07
Postsecondary	North Dakota	Y	53600 FQ	72290 MW	85350 TQ	USBLS	5/07
Postsecondary	Ohio	Y	56150 FQ	73430 MW	96150 TQ	USBLS	5/07
Postsecondary	Oklahoma	Y	28830 FQ	36010 MW	52470 TQ	USBLS	5/07
Postsecondary	Pennsylvania	Y	50650 FQ	73470 MW	102630 TQ	USBLS	5/07
Postsecondary	South Carolina	Y	44570 FQ	54980 MW	65960 TQ	USBLS	5/07
Postsecondary	Tennessee	Y	35080 FQ	43860 MW	49540 TQ	USBLS	5/07
Postsecondary	Texas	Y	44600 FQ	69610 MW	100680 TQ	USBLS	5/07
Postsecondary	Utah	Y	54730 FQ	71170 MW	99920 TQ	USBLS	5/07
Postsecondary	Virginia	Y	51970 FQ	68300 MW	93980 TQ	USBLS	5/07
Postsecondary	Washington	Y		72851 AW		WABLS	3/08
Postsecondary	Wisconsin	Y	49300 FQ	63230 MW	82930 TQ	USBLS	5/07
Postsecondary	Wyoming	Y	60699 FQ	76739 MW	102430 TQ	WYBLS	9/08
Atmospheric and Space Scientist	Arizona	Y	60360 FQ	79150 MW	94580 TQ	USBLS	5/07
	California	H	30.11 FQ	45.31 MW	57.45 TQ	CABLS	1/08-3/08
	Colorado	Y	56740 FQ	82320 MW	103470 TQ	USBLS	5/07
	Connecticut	H	17.59 AE	33.23 MW		CTBLS	1/08-3/08
	District of Columbia	Y	83870 FQ	100200 MW	120830 TQ	USBLS	5/07
	Florida	Y	43200 FQ	69710 MW	93370 TQ	USBLS	5/07
	Georgia	Y	49010 FQ	66240 MW	89280 TQ	USBLS	5/07
	Hawaii	Y	72740 FQ	90540 MW	106820 TQ	USBLS	5/07
	Idaho	Y	70060 FQ	84940 MW	97490 TQ	USBLS	5/07
	Illinois	Y	36420 FQ	40280 MW	72780 TQ	USBLS	5/07
	Indiana	Y	64920 FQ	81230 MW	97980 TQ	USBLS	5/07
	Iowa	Y	59450 FQ	72590 MW	89790 TQ	USBLS	5/07
	Kansas	Y	33040 FQ	68880 MW	89710 TQ	USBLS	5/07
	Kentucky	Y	71558 FQ	85189 MW	101208 TQ	KYBLS	2008
	Louisiana	H	31.96 FQ	38.50 MW	46.62 TQ	LABLS	1/08-3/08
	Maryland	Y		93800 MW		MDBLS	3/08
	Massachusetts	Y	47860 FQ	69620 MW	96010 TQ	USBLS	5/07
	Michigan	Y	64710 FQ	86680 MW	116260 TQ	USBLS	5/07
	Minnesota	Y	41503 FQ	54089 MW	78697 TQ	MNBLS	10/08-12/08
	Mississippi	Y	55220 FQ	70700 MW	86020 TQ	USBLS	5/07
	Missouri	Y	73840 FQ	88540 MW	99810 TQ	USBLS	5/07
	Montana	Y	64470 FQ	82100 MW	92400 TQ	USBLS	5/07
	Nebraska	Y	66930 FQ	82480 MW	95140 TQ	USBLS	5/07
	Nevada	H	24.24 FQ	36.24 MW	47.09 TQ	NVBLS	5/08
	New Hampshire	H	19.64 AE	25.31 MW	30.79 AEX	NHBLS	6/08
	New Jersey	Y	80340 FQ	99590 MW	119200 TQ	USBLS	5/07
	New Mexico	Y	28700 FQ	35290 MW	82750 TQ	USBLS	5/07
	New York	Y	59370 FQ	79650 MW	96130 TQ	USBLS	5/07
	North Carolina	Y	68320 FQ	85630 MW	100420 TQ	USBLS	5/07
	North Dakota	Y	62230 FQ	81640 MW	93340 TQ	USBLS	5/07
	Ohio	Y	71970 FQ	84630 MW	100550 TQ	USBLS	5/07
	Oregon	H	28.57 FQ	33.88 MW	44.42 TQ	ORBLS	5/08
	Pennsylvania	Y	54170 FQ	81270 MW	96310 TQ	USBLS	5/07
	South Carolina	Y	59040 FQ	79020 MW	97050 TQ	USBLS	5/07

AE	Average entry wage	AW	Average wage paid	FQ	First quartile wage
AER	Average entry range	AWR	Average wage range	H	Hourly
AEX	Average experienced wage	AXR	Average experienced range	HI	Highest wage paid
ATC	Average total compensation	D	Daily	HR	High end range

LO	Lowest wage paid	MTC	Median total compensation	TCC	Total cash compensation
LR	Low end range	MW	Median wage paid	TQ	Third quartile wage
M	Monthly	MWR	Median wage range	W	Weekly
MCC	Median cash compensation	S	See annotated source	Y	Yearly

Occupation/Type/Industry	Location	Per	Low	Mid	High	Source	Date
Atmospheric and Space Scientist	South Dakota	Y	37801 FQ	72813 MW	94524 TQ	SDBLS	7/08-9/08
	Tennessee	Y	66580 FQ	78940 MW	93770 TQ	USBLS	5/07
	Texas	Y	36430 FQ	68430 MW	90500 TQ	USBLS	5/07
	Utah	Y	64390 FQ	84060 MW	100290 TQ	USBLS	5/07
	Virginia	Y	67930 FQ	84120 MW	98690 TQ	USBLS	5/07
	Washington	H	27.53 FQ	35.20 MW	43.24 TQ	WABLS	3/08
	Wisconsin	Y	46570 FQ	65510 MW	87910 TQ	USBLS	5/07
	Wyoming	Y	50991 FQ	73799 MW	90204 TQ	WYBLS	9/08
Attendance Specialist							
Public Schools	Baldwin County, AL	Y	42278 LO		45851 HI	BCPSSS	2008-2009
Attorney							
First-Year Associate, Top Law Firm	Seattle, WA	Y	100000 LO		130000 HI	BIZJ01	2008
State Government	Georgia	Y	43063 LO		75523 HI	AFT02	3/1/08
Attorney General	Michigan	Y			124900 HI	LSJ01	6/07
	Nebraska	Y			95000 HI	NEST	2008
Attorney Supervisor							
State Government	Arkansas	Y	50267 LO		83708 HI	AFT02	3/1/08
Au Pair	United States	W			176.85 HI	AIFS	7/24/08-7/23/09
Au Pair Extraordinaire	United States	W			250.00 HI	AIFS	7/24/08-7/23/09
Audio and Video Equipment Technician	Alabama	Y	17310 FQ	21650 MW	31500 TQ	USBLS	5/07
	Birmingham-Hoover MSA, AL	Y	17380 FQ	19560 MW	25690 TQ	USBLS	5/07
	Alaska	Y	32590 FQ	39400 MW	59480 TQ	USBLS	5/07
	Anchorage MSA, AK	Y	33710 FQ	39960 MW	59980 TQ	USBLS	5/07
	Arizona	Y	20970 FQ	29250 MW	42290 TQ	USBLS	5/07
	Phoenix-Mesa-Scottsdale MSA, AZ	Y	20000 FQ	28870 MW	43760 TQ	USBLS	5/07
	Tucson MSA, AZ	Y	24570 FQ	29620 MW	37020 TQ	USBLS	5/07
	Arkansas	Y	24400 FQ	31510 MW	44150 TQ	USBLS	5/07
	Little Rock-North Little Rock MSA, AR	Y	26410 FQ	33280 MW	42970 TQ	USBLS	5/07
	California	H	12.70 FQ	17.88 MW	24.90 TQ	CABLS	1/08-3/08
	Los Angeles-Long Beach-Glendale PMSA, CA	H	11.90 FQ	16.64 MW	24.27 TQ	CABLS	1/08-3/08
	Oakland-Fremont-Hayward MSA, CA	H	15.16 FQ	19.34 MW	23.09 TQ	CABLS	1/08-3/08
	Riverside-San Bernardino-Ontario MSA, CA	H	16.75 FQ	18.78 MW	22.91 TQ	CABLS	1/08-3/08
	San Diego-Carlsbad-San Marcos MSA, CA	H	13.43 FQ	16.64 MW	20.76 TQ	CABLS	1/08-3/08
	San Francisco-San Mateo-Redwood PMSA, CA	H	14.43 FQ	19.16 MW	27.01 TQ	CABLS	1/08-3/08
	San Jose-Sunnyvale-Santa Clara MSA, CA	H	16.02 FQ	21.43 MW	29.58 TQ	CABLS	1/08-3/08
	Santa Ana-Anaheim-Irvine PMSA, CA	Y	37330 FQ	49440 MW	57380 TQ	USBLS	5/07
	Colorado	Y	23190 FQ	30250 MW	41870 TQ	USBLS	5/07
	Colorado Springs MSA, CO	Y	26670 FQ	30730 MW	40230 TQ	USBLS	5/07
	Denver-Aurora MSA, CO	Y	22320 FQ	29040 MW	42160 TQ	USBLS	5/07
	Connecticut	H	12.06 AE	19.41 MW		CTBLS	1/08-3/08
	Bridgeport-Stamford-Norwalk MSA, CT	Y	38100 FQ	43230 MW	47430 TQ	USBLS	5/07
	Hartford-West Hartford-East Hartford MSA, CT	Y	27530 FQ	36960 MW	48350 TQ	USBLS	5/07
	Norwich-New London MSA, CT-RI	Y	15910 FQ	28120 MW	42680 TQ	USBLS	5/07
	Delaware	Y	32590 FQ	37430 MW	43380 TQ	USBLS	5/07
	Wilmington PMSA, DE-MD-NJ	Y	32720 FQ	37480 MW	43350 TQ	USBLS	5/07
	District of Columbia	Y	34290 FQ	44540 MW	55410 TQ	USBLS	5/07
	Washington-Arlington-Alexandria MSA, DC-VA-MD-WV	Y	34290 FQ	42690 MW	51490 TQ	USBLS	5/07
	Florida	Y	26700 FQ	33290 MW	40110 TQ	USBLS	5/07

AE Average entry wage	AW Average wage paid	FQ First quartile wage	LO Lowest wage paid
AER Average entry range	AWR Average wage range	H Hourly	LR Low end range
AEX Average experienced wage	AXR Average experienced range	HI Highest wage paid	M Monthly
ATC Average total compensation	D Daily	HR High end range	MCC Median cash compensation

MTC Median total compensation	TCC Total cash compensation
MW Median wage paid	TQ Third quartile wage
MWR Median wage range	W Weekly
S See annotated source	Y Yearly

Audio and Video Equipment Technician

Occupation/Type/Industry	Location	Per	Low	Mid	High	Source	Date
Audio and Video Equipment Technician							
	Fort Lauderdale-Pompano Beach-Deerfield Beach PMSA, FL	Y	27690 FQ	31360 MW	37830 TQ	USBLS	5/07
	Jacksonville MSA, FL	Y	22750 FQ	29580 MW	37270 TQ	USBLS	5/07
	Miami-Fort Lauderdale-Miami Beach MSA, FL	Y	28390 FQ	34470 MW	39840 TQ	USBLS	5/07
	Orlando-Kissimmee MSA, FL	Y	27080 FQ	34230 MW	43150 TQ	USBLS	5/07
	Tampa-St. Petersburg-Clearwater MSA, FL	Y	27990 FQ	33820 MW	40600 TQ	USBLS	5/07
	West Palm Beach-Boca Raton-Boynton Beach PMSA, FL	Y	27810 FQ	35900 MW	43800 TQ	USBLS	5/07
	Georgia	Y	23800 FQ	31990 MW	45800 TQ	USBLS	5/07
	Atlanta-Sandy Springs-Marietta MSA, GA	Y	23150 FQ	29600 MW	43400 TQ	USBLS	5/07
	Hawaii	Y	32050 FQ	38950 MW	45900 TQ	USBLS	5/07
	Honolulu MSA, HI	Y	31180 FQ	39510 MW	45950 TQ	USBLS	5/07
	Idaho	Y	27890 FQ	41300 MW	49570 TQ	USBLS	5/07
	Boise City-Nampa MSA, ID	Y	29440 FQ	43830 MW	51280 TQ	USBLS	5/07
	Illinois	Y	26990 FQ	36070 MW	50320 TQ	USBLS	5/07
	Chicago-Naperville-Joliet MSA, IL-IN-WI	Y	27080 FQ	36420 MW	49430 TQ	USBLS	5/07
	Indiana	Y	21890 FQ	32290 MW	49590 TQ	USBLS	5/07
	Fort Wayne MSA, IN	Y	16650 FQ	27220 MW	36380 TQ	USBLS	5/07
	Gary PMSA, IN	Y	20090 FQ	22940 MW	41750 TQ	USBLS	5/07
	Indianapolis-Carmel MSA, IN	Y	25100 FQ	40090 MW	53910 TQ	USBLS	5/07
	Iowa	Y	21950 FQ	36770 MW	45710 TQ	USBLS	5/07
	Des Moines-West Des Moines MSA, IA	Y	33900 FQ	42670 MW	49360 TQ	USBLS	5/07
	Kansas	Y	25270 FQ	31540 MW	43630 TQ	USBLS	5/07
	Kentucky	Y	28399 FQ	36773 MW	48152 TQ	KYBLS	2008
	Louisville-Jefferson County MSA, KY-IN	Y	29330 FQ	40160 MW	60620 TQ	USBLS	5/07
	Louisiana	H	12.45 FQ	16.32 MW	21.49 TQ	LABLS	1/08-3/08
	Baton Rouge MSA, LA	Y	18880 FQ	23860 MW	36610 TQ	USBLS	5/07
	New Orleans-Metairie-Kenner MSA, LA	Y	32460 FQ	38120 MW	56220 TQ	USBLS	5/07
	Maine	Y	29230 FQ	36210 MW	43440 TQ	USBLS	5/07
	Portland-South Portland-Biddeford MSA, ME	Y	29440 FQ	35700 MW	44130 TQ	USBLS	5/07
	Maryland	Y		43550 MW		MDBLS	3/08
	Baltimore-Towson MSA, MD	Y	33530 FQ	42440 MW	49160 TQ	USBLS	5/07
	Bethesda-Gaithersburg-Frederick PMSA, MD	Y	37700 FQ	43430 MW	48350 TQ	USBLS	5/07
	Massachusetts	Y	31230 FQ	38580 MW	47820 TQ	USBLS	5/07
	Boston-Cambridge-Quincy NECTA, MA	Y	32090 FQ	39840 MW	49050 TQ	USBLS	5/07
	Worcester MSA, MA-CT	Y	25750 FQ	33990 MW	43850 TQ	USBLS	5/07
	Michigan	Y	22610 FQ	29550 MW	40600 TQ	USBLS	5/07
	Detroit-Warren-Livonia MSA, MI	Y	24480 FQ	31190 MW	48330 TQ	USBLS	5/07
	Grand Rapids-Wyoming MSA, MI	Y	25050 FQ	29090 MW	35810 TQ	USBLS	5/07
	Warren-Troy-Farmington Hills PMSA, MI	Y	22860 FQ	29460 MW	68370 TQ	USBLS	5/07
	Minnesota	Y	32171 FQ	39076 MW	50020 TQ	MNBLS	10/08-12/08
	Duluth-Superior MSA, MN-WI	Y	18329 FQ	32558 MW	48011 TQ	MNBLS	10/08-12/08
	Minneapolis-Saint Paul MSA, MN-WI	Y	34399 FQ	40248 MW	52248 TQ	MNBLS	10/08-12/08
	Rochester MSA, MN	Y	28135 FQ	40035 MW	48948 TQ	MNBLS	10/08-12/08
	Mississippi	Y	25540 FQ	30020 MW	36160 TQ	USBLS	5/07
	Jackson MSA, MS	Y	26950 FQ	31110 MW	36750 TQ	USBLS	5/07
	Missouri	Y	26090 FQ	34060 MW	44940 TQ	USBLS	5/07
	Kansas City MSA, MO-KS	Y	27620 FQ	34960 MW	46800 TQ	USBLS	5/07
	St. Louis MSA, MO-IL	Y	25530 FQ	35360 MW	52030 TQ	USBLS	5/07
	Montana	Y	20280 FQ	23750 MW	30100 TQ	USBLS	5/07
	Billings MSA, MT	Y	21500 FQ	24330 MW	30140 TQ	USBLS	5/07
	Nebraska	Y	25240 FQ	29070 MW	37250 TQ	USBLS	5/07
	Omaha-Council Bluffs MSA, NE-IA	Y	25290 FQ	29870 MW	40060 TQ	USBLS	5/07
	Nevada	H	22.90 FQ	27.55 MW	30.68 TQ	NVBLS	5/08
	Las Vegas-Paradise MSA, NV	H	23.53 FQ	27.74 MW	30.73 TQ	NVBLS	5/08

AE Average entry wage	**AW** Average wage paid	**FQ** First quartile wage	**LO** Lowest wage paid	**MTC** Median total compensation	**TCC** Total cash compensation
AER Average entry range	**AWR** Average wage range	**H** Hourly	**LR** Low end range	**MW** Median wage paid	**TQ** Third quartile wage
AEX Average experienced wage	**AXR** Average experienced range	**HI** Highest wage paid	**M** Monthly	**MWR** Median wage range	**W** Weekly
ATC Average total compensation	**D** Daily	**HR** High end range	**MCC** Median cash compensation	**S** See annotated source	**Y** Yearly

Occupation/Type/Industry	Location	Per	Low	Mid	High	Source	Date
Audio and Video Equipment Technician	New Hampshire	H	10.08 AE	16.06 MW	20.37 AEX	NHBLS	6/08
	New Jersey	Y	32310 FQ	45090 MW	59700 TQ	USBLS	5/07
	Camden PMSA, NJ	Y	26370 FQ	37500 MW	50280 TQ	USBLS	5/07
	Newark-Union PMSA, NJ-PA	Y	31840 FQ	43670 MW	53280 TQ	USBLS	5/07
	New Mexico	Y	24420 FQ	29580 MW	40590 TQ	USBLS	5/07
	Albuquerque MSA, NM	Y	24810 FQ	29500 MW	40700 TQ	USBLS	5/07
	New York	Y	33440 FQ	44010 MW	56830 TQ	USBLS	5/07
	Buffalo-Niagara Falls MSA, NY	Y	29400 FQ	35400 MW	44570 TQ	USBLS	5/07
	Nassau-Suffolk PMSA, NY	Y	33400 FQ	42320 MW	50200 TQ	USBLS	5/07
	New York-Northern New Jersey-Long Island MSA, NY-NJ-PA	Y	35020 FQ	46130 MW	59740 TQ	USBLS	5/07
	North Carolina	Y	27090 FQ	33940 MW	43670 TQ	USBLS	5/07
	Charlotte-Gastonia-Concord MSA, NC-SC	Y	26140 FQ	33970 MW	41050 TQ	USBLS	5/07
	Raleigh-Cary MSA, NC	Y	30300 FQ	37530 MW	50520 TQ	USBLS	5/07
	Winston-Salem MSA, NC	Y	26580 FQ	30310 MW	38980 TQ	USBLS	5/07
	North Dakota	Y	19360 FQ	25690 MW	35780 TQ	USBLS	5/07
	Ohio	Y	26160 FQ	32290 MW	42760 TQ	USBLS	5/07
	Cincinnati-Middletown MSA, OH-KY-IN	Y	27730 FQ	32970 MW	42370 TQ	USBLS	5/07
	Cleveland-Elyria-Mentor MSA, OH	Y	26730 FQ	34610 MW	40900 TQ	USBLS	5/07
	Columbus MSA, OH	Y	19280 FQ	29010 MW	38990 TQ	USBLS	5/07
	Dayton MSA, OH	Y	28510 FQ	39820 MW	51040 TQ	USBLS	5/07
	Oklahoma	Y	20920 FQ	27220 MW	33340 TQ	USBLS	5/07
	Oklahoma City MSA, OK	Y	23580 FQ	29070 MW	36780 TQ	USBLS	5/07
	Oregon	H	11.40 FQ	15.68 MW	21.49 TQ	ORBLS	5/08
	Eugene-Springfield MSA, OR	Y	21910 FQ	30830 MW	43280 TQ	USBLS	5/07
	Portland-Vancouver-Beaverton MSA, OR-WA	Y	24180 FQ	34110 MW	47620 TQ	USBLS	5/07
	Pennsylvania	Y	26760 FQ	38950 MW	47090 TQ	USBLS	5/07
	Philadelphia-Camden-Wilmington MSA, PA-NJ-DE-MD	Y	32310 FQ	41040 MW	46970 TQ	USBLS	5/07
	Pittsburgh MSA, PA	Y	19990 FQ	29350 MW	41470 TQ	USBLS	5/07
	Rhode Island	Y	32540 FQ	39600 MW	56350 TQ	USBLS	5/07
	Providence-Fall River-Warwick MSA, RI-MA	Y	26150 FQ	34040 MW	45830 TQ	USBLS	5/07
	South Carolina	Y	22290 FQ	27590 MW	35490 TQ	USBLS	5/07
	Charleston-North Charleston MSA, SC	Y	21900 FQ	25360 MW	29860 TQ	USBLS	5/07
	South Dakota	Y	18497 FQ	20360 MW	31263 TQ	SDBLS	7/08-9/08
	Sioux Falls MSA, SD	Y	19767 FQ	29474 MW	37006 TQ	SDBLS	7/08-9/08
	Tennessee	Y	24790 FQ	32670 MW	43100 TQ	USBLS	5/07
	Memphis MSA, TN-MS-AR	Y	25040 FQ	41930 MW	49140 TQ	USBLS	5/07
	Nashville-Davidson-Murfreesboro MSA, TN	Y	25480 FQ	32680 MW	41340 TQ	USBLS	5/07
	Texas	Y	25700 FQ	30410 MW	40770 TQ	USBLS	5/07
	Austin-Round Rock MSA, TX	Y	27430 FQ	31900 MW	37520 TQ	USBLS	5/07
	Dallas-Fort Worth-Arlington MSA, TX	Y	30000 FQ	37370 MW	48930 TQ	USBLS	5/07
	El Paso MSA, TX	Y	22700 FQ	26470 MW	30190 TQ	USBLS	5/07
	Houston-Sugar Land-Baytown MSA, TX	Y	26210 FQ	29270 MW	41300 TQ	USBLS	5/07
	San Antonio MSA, TX	Y	24470 FQ	31960 MW	40760 TQ	USBLS	5/07
	Utah	Y	22530 FQ	31290 MW	40650 TQ	USBLS	5/07
	Salt Lake City MSA, UT	Y	23470 FQ	33630 MW	42760 TQ	USBLS	5/07
	Virginia	Y	25690 FQ	33930 MW	42420 TQ	USBLS	5/07
	Richmond MSA, VA	Y	24740 FQ	35280 MW	45230 TQ	USBLS	5/07
	Virginia Beach-Norfolk-Newport News MSA, VA-NC	Y	24410 FQ	31770 MW	39600 TQ	USBLS	5/07
	Washington	H	11.63 FQ	15.40 MW	20.89 TQ	WABLS	3/08
	Seattle-Tacoma-Bellevue MSA, WA	Y	25450 FQ	34900 MW	46130 TQ	USBLS	5/07
	West Virginia	Y	20132 FQ	25700 MW	36366 TQ	WVBLS	7/08-9/08
	Wisconsin	Y	23380 FQ	30960 MW	40790 TQ	USBLS	5/07
	Milwaukee-Waukesha-West Allis MSA, WI	Y	21310 FQ	26470 MW	37670 TQ	USBLS	5/07
	Wyoming	Y	29468 FQ	34323 MW	45311 TQ	WYBLS	9/08

AE Average entry wage	**AW** Average wage paid	**FQ** First quartile wage	**LO** Lowest wage paid	**MTC** Median total compensation	**TCC** Total cash compensation
AER Average entry range	**AWR** Average wage range	**H** Hourly	**LR** Low end range	**MW** Median wage paid	**TQ** Third quartile wage
AEX Average experienced wage	**AXR** Average experienced range	**HI** Highest wage paid	**M** Monthly	**MWR** Median wage range	**W** Weekly
ATC Average total compensation	**D** Daily	**HR** High end range	**MCC** Median cash compensation	**S** See annotated source	**Y** Yearly

Occupation/Type/Industry	Location	Per	Low	Mid	High	Source	Date
Audio and Video Equipment Technician	Puerto Rico	Y	20710 FQ	23090 MW	25480 TQ	USBLS	5/07
	San Juan-Caguas-Guaynabo MSA, PR	Y	20880 FQ	23180 MW	25500 TQ	USBLS	5/07
	Guam	Y	16320 FQ	18390 MW	23810 TQ	USBLS	5/07
Audio-Visual Collections Specialist	Alabama	Y	20340 FQ	23430 MW	31110 TQ	USBLS	5/07
	Arizona	Y	23480 FQ	38050 MW	50860 TQ	USBLS	5/07
	Phoenix-Mesa-Scottsdale MSA, AZ	Y	24210 FQ	41310 MW	52040 TQ	USBLS	5/07
	California	H	16.38 FQ	19.80 MW	23.41 TQ	CABLS	1/08-3/08
	Los Angeles-Long Beach-Glendale PMSA, CA	H	15.08 FQ	19.51 MW	22.24 TQ	CABLS	1/08-3/08
	Oakland-Fremont-Hayward MSA, CA	H	20.05 FQ	23.13 MW	27.35 TQ	CABLS	1/08-3/08
	Riverside-San Bernardino-Ontario MSA, CA	H	14.87 FQ	17.81 MW	22.33 TQ	CABLS	1/08-3/08
	Sacramento-Arden Arcade-Roseville MSA, CA	H	22.50 FQ	27.46 MW	31.26 TQ	CABLS	1/08-3/08
	San Diego-Carlsbad-San Marcos MSA, CA	H	16.54 FQ	19.19 MW	22.04 TQ	CABLS	1/08-3/08
	San Francisco-San Mateo-Redwood PMSA, CA	H	16.81 FQ	18.92 MW	22.40 TQ	CABLS	1/08-3/08
	San Jose-Sunnyvale-Santa Clara MSA, CA	H	17.67 FQ	20.87 MW	23.18 TQ	CABLS	1/08-3/08
	Connecticut	H	17.97 AE	29.28 MW		CTBLS	1/08-3/08
	District of Columbia	Y	25190 FQ	36560 MW	48300 TQ	USBLS	5/07
	Washington-Arlington-Alexandria MSA, DC-VA-MD-WV	Y	28280 FQ	37540 MW	48110 TQ	USBLS	5/07
	Florida	Y	33130 FQ	46070 MW	52490 TQ	USBLS	5/07
	Georgia	Y	30500 FQ	45630 MW	58160 TQ	USBLS	5/07
	Atlanta-Sandy Springs-Marietta MSA, GA	Y	30800 FQ	47640 MW	60400 TQ	USBLS	5/07
	Hawaii	Y	29490 FQ	45380 MW	62390 TQ	USBLS	5/07
	Honolulu MSA, HI	Y	30660 FQ	47310 MW	63260 TQ	USBLS	5/07
	Idaho	Y	46300 FQ	54060 MW	59640 TQ	USBLS	5/07
	Boise City-Nampa MSA, ID	Y	46060 FQ	52650 MW	57920 TQ	USBLS	5/07
	Illinois	Y	26880 FQ	36080 MW	46720 TQ	USBLS	5/07
	Chicago-Naperville-Joliet MSA, IL-IN-WI	Y	27070 FQ	37780 MW	49990 TQ	USBLS	5/07
	Indiana	Y	26050 FQ	34240 MW	47930 TQ	USBLS	5/07
	Indianapolis-Carmel MSA, IN	Y	31240 FQ	35140 MW	43380 TQ	USBLS	5/07
	Iowa	Y	25640 FQ	31080 MW	49140 TQ	USBLS	5/07
	Kentucky	Y	23062 FQ	30386 MW	41383 TQ	KYBLS	2008
	Louisiana	H	16.63 FQ	19.74 MW	23.02 TQ	LABLS	1/08-3/08
	Maine	Y	27940 FQ	30190 MW	32350 TQ	USBLS	5/07
	Maryland	Y		42900 MW		MDBLS	3/08
	Baltimore-Towson MSA, MD	Y	40850 FQ	45560 MW	50480 TQ	USBLS	5/07
	Massachusetts	Y	33580 FQ	43200 MW	56790 TQ	USBLS	5/07
	Boston-Cambridge-Quincy NECTA, MA	Y	38590 FQ	50060 MW	60190 TQ	USBLS	5/07
	Michigan	Y	36200 FQ	50090 MW	60690 TQ	USBLS	5/07
	Detroit-Warren-Livonia MSA, MI	Y	27150 FQ	46050 MW	57180 TQ	USBLS	5/07
	Minnesota	Y	48586 FQ	60053 MW	68820 TQ	MNBLS	10/08-12/08
	Duluth-Superior MSA, MN-WI	Y	53556 FQ	59655 MW	65200 TQ	MNBLS	10/08-12/08
	Minneapolis-Saint Paul MSA, MN-WI	Y	48283 FQ	60325 MW	70662 TQ	MNBLS	10/08-12/08
	Rochester MSA, MN	Y	50430 FQ	59408 MW	67099 TQ	MNBLS	10/08-12/08
	Missouri	Y	23800 FQ	33830 MW	47260 TQ	USBLS	5/07
	New Jersey	Y	36100 FQ	43710 MW	51780 TQ	USBLS	5/07
	Camden PMSA, NJ	Y	39910 FQ	43910 MW	47960 TQ	USBLS	5/07
	New York	Y	24020 FQ	31990 MW	45940 TQ	USBLS	5/07
	Nassau-Suffolk PMSA, NY	Y	31250 FQ	43750 MW	70950 TQ	USBLS	5/07
	New York-Northern New Jersey-Long Island MSA, NY-NJ-PA	Y	24400 FQ	37840 MW	52410 TQ	USBLS	5/07
	North Carolina	Y	28300 FQ	35690 MW	49910 TQ	USBLS	5/07
	Ohio	Y	39090 FQ	53460 MW	67480 TQ	USBLS	5/07

AE	Average entry wage	AW	Average wage paid	FQ	First quartile wage	LO	Lowest wage paid	MTC	Median total compensation	TCC	Total cash compensation
AER	Average entry range	AWR	Average wage range	H	Hourly	LR	Low end range	MW	Median wage paid	TQ	Third quartile wage
AEX	Average experienced wage	AXR	Average experienced range	HI	Highest wage paid	M	Monthly	MWR	Median wage range	W	Weekly
ATC	Average total compensation	D	Daily	HR	High end range	MCC	Median cash compensation	S	See annotated source	Y	Yearly

Occupation/Type/Industry	Location	Per	Low	Mid	High	Source	Date
Audio-Visual Collections Specialist	Cincinnati-Middletown MSA, OH-KY-IN	Y	49770 FQ	59790 MW	69710 TQ	USBLS	5/07
	Cleveland-Elyria-Mentor MSA, OH	Y	37040 FQ	49350 MW	65110 TQ	USBLS	5/07
	Columbus MSA, OH	Y	45240 FQ	56050 MW	72950 TQ	USBLS	5/07
	Dayton MSA, OH	Y	36600 FQ	47730 MW	67510 TQ	USBLS	5/07
	Oklahoma	Y	22370 FQ	32280 MW	41950 TQ	USBLS	5/07
	Oklahoma City MSA, OK	Y	24080 FQ	32980 MW	39080 TQ	USBLS	5/07
	Tulsa MSA, OK	Y	14560 FQ	37520 MW	46620 TQ	USBLS	5/07
	Oregon	H	10.72 FQ	13.66 MW	16.81 TQ	ORBLS	5/08
	Portland-Vancouver-Beaverton MSA, OR-WA	Y	32500 FQ	38340 MW	47100 TQ	USBLS	5/07
	Pennsylvania	Y	29750 FQ	35080 MW	43480 TQ	USBLS	5/07
	Philadelphia-Camden-Wilmington MSA, PA-NJ-DE-MD	Y	31690 FQ	38240 MW	46530 TQ	USBLS	5/07
	Pittsburgh MSA, PA	Y	32610 FQ	36600 MW	44490 TQ	USBLS	5/07
	South Carolina	Y	22160 FQ	29830 MW	40430 TQ	USBLS	5/07
	Tennessee	Y	30130 FQ	42380 MW	64690 TQ	USBLS	5/07
	Texas	Y	31280 FQ	46100 MW	57560 TQ	USBLS	5/07
	Austin-Round Rock MSA, TX	Y	36350 FQ	53850 MW	64520 TQ	USBLS	5/07
	Dallas-Fort Worth-Arlington MSA, TX	Y	43370 FQ	54630 MW	67750 TQ	USBLS	5/07
	Houston-Sugar Land-Baytown MSA, TX	Y	43090 FQ	51180 MW	58190 TQ	USBLS	5/07
	Utah	Y	22660 FQ	27790 MW	35430 TQ	USBLS	5/07
	Vermont	Y	25260 FQ	32210 MW	49350 TQ	USBLS	5/07
	Virginia	Y	26420 FQ	36310 MW	46920 TQ	USBLS	5/07
	Washington	H	15.68 FQ	18.41 MW	22.98 TQ	WABLS	3/08
	Wisconsin	Y	19990 FQ	32700 MW	47340 TQ	USBLS	5/07
	Wyoming	Y	42219 FQ	65091 MW	76613 TQ	WYBLS	9/08
	Puerto Rico	Y	18190 FQ	27740 MW	35230 TQ	USBLS	5/07
	San Juan-Caguas-Guaynabo MSA, PR	Y	16940 FQ	26380 MW	35090 TQ	USBLS	5/07
Audio-Visual Production Specialist State Government	Ohio	H	19.88 LO		26.28 HI	ODAS	2008
Audiologist	Alabama	Y	44660 FQ	50290 MW	60480 TQ	USBLS	5/07
	Birmingham-Hoover MSA, AL	Y	43290 FQ	47840 MW	52050 TQ	USBLS	5/07
	Phoenix-Mesa-Scottsdale MSA, AZ	Y	41300 FQ	55310 MW	63810 TQ	USBLS	5/07
	Arkansas	Y	45120 FQ	55760 MW	64340 TQ	USBLS	5/07
	California	H	27.19 FQ	34.00 MW	42.50 TQ	CABLS	1/08-3/08
	Los Angeles-Long Beach-Glendale PMSA, CA	H	28.30 FQ	34.84 MW	39.61 TQ	CABLS	1/08-3/08
	Oakland-Fremont-Hayward MSA, CA	H	26.90 FQ	33.00 MW	42.78 TQ	CABLS	1/08-3/08
	Riverside-San Bernardino-Ontario MSA, CA	H	29.18 FQ	36.05 MW	42.81 TQ	CABLS	1/08-3/08
	Sacramento-Arden Arcade-Roseville MSA, CA	H	31.74 FQ	38.73 MW	48.07 TQ	CABLS	1/08-3/08
	San Diego-Carlsbad-San Marcos MSA, CA	H	24.43 FQ	29.54 MW	41.54 TQ	CABLS	1/08-3/08
	San Francisco-San Mateo-Redwood PMSA, CA	H	47.72 FQ	66.60 MW		CABLS	1/08-3/08
	San Jose-Sunnyvale-Santa Clara MSA, CA	H	18.83 FQ	28.29 MW	34.64 TQ	CABLS	1/08-3/08
	Santa Ana-Anaheim-Irvine PMSA, CA	Y	53260 FQ	58800 MW	70920 TQ	USBLS	5/07
	Colorado	Y	49700 FQ	58810 MW	68210 TQ	USBLS	5/07
	Denver-Aurora MSA, CO	Y	56890 FQ	63660 MW	74940 TQ	USBLS	5/07
	Connecticut	H	23.58 AE	29.69 MW		CTBLS	1/08-3/08
	Bridgeport-Stamford-Norwalk MSA, CT	Y	56650 FQ	65380 MW	77150 TQ	USBLS	5/07
	District of Columbia	Y	53690 FQ	67490 MW	82500 TQ	USBLS	5/07
	Washington-Arlington-Alexandria MSA, DC-VA-MD-WV	Y	42940 FQ	69360 MW	82010 TQ	USBLS	5/07
	Florida	Y	48760 FQ	63010 MW	79760 TQ	USBLS	5/07

AE	Average entry wage	AW	Average wage paid	FQ	First quartile wage	LO	Lowest wage paid	MTC	Median total compensation
AER	Average entry range	AWR	Average wage range	H	Hourly	LR	Low end range	MW	Median wage paid
AEX	Average experienced wage	AXR	Average experienced range	HI	Highest wage paid	M	Monthly	MWR	Median wage range
ATC	Average total compensation	D	Daily	HR	High end range	MCC	Median cash compensation	S	See annotated source

TCC	Total cash compensation
TQ	Third quartile wage
W	Weekly
Y	Yearly

Occupation/Type/Industry	Location	Per	Low	Mid	High	Source	Date
Audiologist	Fort Lauderdale-Pompano Beach-Deerfield Beach PMSA, FL	Y	52040 FQ	59500 MW	76760 TQ	USBLS	5/07
	Miami-Fort Lauderdale-Miami Beach MSA, FL	Y	51030 FQ	60050 MW	81870 TQ	USBLS	5/07
	Orlando-Kissimmee MSA, FL	Y	43280 FQ	47210 MW	53180 TQ	USBLS	5/07
	Pensacola-Ferry Pass-Brent MSA, FL	Y	44110 FQ	51650 MW	74070 TQ	USBLS	5/07
	Tampa-St. Petersburg-Clearwater MSA, FL	Y	78340 FQ	85960 MW	93890 TQ	USBLS	5/07
	Georgia	Y	55410 FQ	67350 MW	74570 TQ	USBLS	5/07
	Atlanta-Sandy Springs-Marietta MSA, GA	Y	62480 FQ	69230 MW	75480 TQ	USBLS	5/07
	Hawaii	Y	58470 FQ	65350 MW	79450 TQ	USBLS	5/07
	Honolulu MSA, HI	Y	58520 FQ	65590 MW	79960 TQ	USBLS	5/07
	Idaho	Y	50570 FQ	57570 MW	63960 TQ	USBLS	5/07
	Boise City-Nampa MSA, ID	Y	53040 FQ	58410 MW	66500 TQ	USBLS	5/07
	Illinois	Y	46500 FQ	60320 MW	73880 TQ	USBLS	5/07
	Chicago-Naperville-Joliet MSA, IL-IN-WI	Y	47080 FQ	61400 MW	75430 TQ	USBLS	5/07
	Indiana	Y	48080 FQ	56400 MW	65760 TQ	USBLS	5/07
	Indianapolis-Carmel MSA, IN	Y	53980 FQ	59980 MW	67750 TQ	USBLS	5/07
	Iowa	Y	44890 FQ	53870 MW	61790 TQ	USBLS	5/07
	Des Moines-West Des Moines MSA, IA	Y	47600 FQ	55940 MW	60780 TQ	USBLS	5/07
	Kansas	Y	44170 FQ	53570 MW	64540 TQ	USBLS	5/07
	Wichita MSA, KS	Y	44410 FQ	51910 MW	63190 TQ	USBLS	5/07
	Kentucky	Y	52060 FQ	61686 MW	77281 TQ	KYBLS	2008
	Louisville-Jefferson County MSA, KY-IN	Y	49900 FQ	58720 MW	84490 TQ	USBLS	5/07
	Louisiana	H	23.79 FQ	30.35 MW	35.13 TQ	LABLS	1/08-3/08
	Baton Rouge MSA, LA	Y	47250 FQ	56430 MW	68160 TQ	USBLS	5/07
	Maryland	Y		65850 MW		MDBLS	3/08
	Baltimore-Towson MSA, MD	Y	40710 FQ	58330 MW	69740 TQ	USBLS	5/07
	Bethesda-Gaithersburg-Frederick PMSA, MD	Y	69650 FQ	81950 MW	89790 TQ	USBLS	5/07
	Massachusetts	Y	51770 FQ	62240 MW	73100 TQ	USBLS	5/07
	Boston-Cambridge-Quincy NECTA, MA	Y	49570 FQ	60720 MW	72220 TQ	USBLS	5/07
	Michigan	Y	52540 FQ	59010 MW	67900 TQ	USBLS	5/07
	Ann Arbor MSA, MI	Y	44010 FQ	56640 MW	64400 TQ	USBLS	5/07
	Detroit-Warren-Livonia MSA, MI	Y	54950 FQ	63890 MW	74880 TQ	USBLS	5/07
	Grand Rapids-Wyoming MSA, MI	Y	52710 FQ	56470 MW	60210 TQ	USBLS	5/07
	Warren-Troy-Farmington Hills PMSA, MI	Y	57300 FQ	65930 MW	76980 TQ	USBLS	5/07
	Minnesota	Y	52572 FQ	64332 MW	78456 TQ	MNBLS	10/08-12/08
	Duluth-Superior MSA, MN-WI	Y	61434 FQ	71645 MW	82013 TQ	MNBLS	10/08-12/08
	Minneapolis-Saint Paul MSA, MN-WI	Y	45615 FQ	61852 MW	76196 TQ	MNBLS	10/08-12/08
	Mississippi	Y	36180 FQ	39890 MW	46660 TQ	USBLS	5/07
	Missouri	Y	46650 FQ	57140 MW	68090 TQ	USBLS	5/07
	Kansas City MSA, MO-KS	Y	42490 FQ	48430 MW	59900 TQ	USBLS	5/07
	St. Louis MSA, MO-IL	Y	50000 FQ	60940 MW	69790 TQ	USBLS	5/07
	Nebraska	Y	40850 FQ	52600 MW	60490 TQ	USBLS	5/07
	Omaha-Council Bluffs MSA, NE-IA	Y	47850 FQ	57170 MW	64430 TQ	USBLS	5/07
	New Jersey	Y	58200 FQ	69150 MW	81090 TQ	USBLS	5/07
	Camden PMSA, NJ	Y	57480 FQ	63660 MW	73920 TQ	USBLS	5/07
	Edison PMSA, NJ	Y	49280 FQ	64720 MW	73030 TQ	USBLS	5/07
	Newark-Union PMSA, NJ-PA	Y	64910 FQ	79670 MW	91940 TQ	USBLS	5/07
	New Mexico	Y	20020 FQ	49830 MW	58250 TQ	USBLS	5/07
	Albuquerque MSA, NM	Y	51190 FQ	55570 MW	59750 TQ	USBLS	5/07
	New York	Y	55040 FQ	64590 MW	79480 TQ	USBLS	5/07
	Albany-Schenectady-Troy MSA, NY	Y	44950 FQ	49670 MW	65680 TQ	USBLS	5/07
	Buffalo-Niagara Falls MSA, NY	Y	42260 FQ	54640 MW	60100 TQ	USBLS	5/07
	Nassau-Suffolk PMSA, NY	Y	61060 FQ	74240 MW	90620 TQ	USBLS	5/07

AE	Average entry wage	AW	Average wage paid	FQ	First quartile wage	LO	Lowest wage paid	MTC	Median total compensation	TCC	Total cash compensation
AER	Average entry range	AWR	Average wage range	H	Hourly	LR	Low end range	MW	Median wage paid	TQ	Third quartile wage
AEX	Average experienced wage	AXR	Average experienced range	HI	Highest wage paid	M	Monthly	MWR	Median wage range	W	Weekly
ATC	Average total compensation	D	Daily	HR	High end range	MCC	Median cash compensation	S	See annotated source	Y	Yearly

Occupation/Type/Industry	Location	Per	Low	Mid	High	Source	Date
Audiologist	New York-Northern New Jersey-Long Island MSA, NY-NJ-PA	Y	59420 FQ	70880 MW	83890 TQ	USBLS	5/07
	North Carolina	Y	49980 FQ	57730 MW	65570 TQ	USBLS	5/07
	Charlotte-Gastonia-Concord MSA, NC-SC	Y	49850 FQ	56030 MW	62100 TQ	USBLS	5/07
	Raleigh-Cary MSA, NC	Y	48960 FQ	56850 MW	71990 TQ	USBLS	5/07
	North Dakota	Y	38110 FQ	48730 MW	61480 TQ	USBLS	5/07
	Ohio	Y	45820 FQ	52980 MW	62490 TQ	USBLS	5/07
	Cleveland-Elyria-Mentor MSA, OH	Y	51990 FQ	58840 MW	66820 TQ	USBLS	5/07
	Columbus MSA, OH	Y	45440 FQ	53670 MW	61360 TQ	USBLS	5/07
	Dayton MSA, OH	Y	49100 FQ	57340 MW	66810 TQ	USBLS	5/07
	Oklahoma	Y	42150 FQ	49420 MW	61600 TQ	USBLS	5/07
	Oklahoma City MSA, OK	Y	42650 FQ	53960 MW	64950 TQ	USBLS	5/07
	Oregon	H	25.90 FQ	32.32 MW	37.81 TQ	ORBLS	5/08
	Portland-Vancouver-Beaverton MSA, OR-WA	Y	55440 FQ	69980 MW	77740 TQ	USBLS	5/07
	Pennsylvania	Y	29070 FQ	44120 MW	55630 TQ	USBLS	5/07
	Allentown-Bethlehem-Easton MSA, PA-NJ	Y	43980 FQ	47190 MW	50450 TQ	USBLS	5/07
	Pittsburgh MSA, PA	Y	44200 FQ	49960 MW	58500 TQ	USBLS	5/07
	Rhode Island	Y	57800 FQ	62840 MW	67120 TQ	USBLS	5/07
	Providence-Fall River-Warwick MSA, RI-MA	Y	58670 FQ	63440 MW	68390 TQ	USBLS	5/07
	South Carolina	Y	51550 FQ	62580 MW	77560 TQ	USBLS	5/07
	South Dakota	Y	50770 FQ	55295 MW	60934 TQ	SDBLS	7/08-9/08
	Sioux Falls MSA, SD	Y	50548 FQ	54441 MW	59262 TQ	SDBLS	7/08-9/08
	Tennessee	Y	48570 FQ	84650 MW	112200 TQ	USBLS	5/07
	Memphis MSA, TN-MS-AR	Y	44110 FQ	48000 MW	56770 TQ	USBLS	5/07
	Nashville-Davidson-Murfreesboro MSA, TN	Y	58330 FQ	98260 MW	117220 TQ	USBLS	5/07
	Texas	Y	46730 FQ	57340 MW	66990 TQ	USBLS	5/07
	Dallas-Fort Worth-Arlington MSA, TX	Y	52760 FQ	59260 MW	67890 TQ	USBLS	5/07
	Houston-Sugar Land-Baytown MSA, TX	Y	45590 FQ	56220 MW	69950 TQ	USBLS	5/07
	San Antonio MSA, TX	Y	43410 FQ	55640 MW	63090 TQ	USBLS	5/07
	Utah	Y	49630 FQ	55230 MW	60720 TQ	USBLS	5/07
	Salt Lake City MSA, UT	Y	51510 FQ	55970 MW	60560 TQ	USBLS	5/07
	Virginia	Y	44100 FQ	55530 MW	73730 TQ	USBLS	5/07
	Richmond MSA, VA	Y	71290 FQ	76290 MW	81350 TQ	USBLS	5/07
	Virginia Beach-Norfolk-Newport News MSA, VA-NC	Y	47990 FQ	54410 MW	60960 TQ	USBLS	5/07
	Washington	H	24.44 FQ	28.92 MW	34.60 TQ	WABLS	3/08
	Seattle-Tacoma-Bellevue MSA, WA	Y	51890 FQ	62150 MW	74610 TQ	USBLS	5/07
	West Virginia	Y	38574 FQ	50135 MW	62885 TQ	WVBLS	7/08-9/08
	Wisconsin	Y	49850 FQ	61880 MW	74420 TQ	USBLS	5/07
	Milwaukee-Waukesha-West Allis MSA, WI	Y	57360 FQ	67670 MW	74740 TQ	USBLS	5/07
	Wyoming	Y	31751 FQ	54412 MW	62621 TQ	WYBLS	9/08
Auditor	Golden Valley, ND	M			800 HI	NDLC02	2008
	Washington	Y			116950 HI	WCC	9/1/08
Automation/Control Engineer	United States	Y		85395 AW		AUTOM	2008
Automation Professional	Midwest	Y		82378 AW		AUTOM	2008
	New England	Y		90779 AW		AUTOM	2008
	Pacific Northwest	Y		96211 AW		AUTOM	2008
Automotive or Other Transportation Equipment Manufacturing	United States	Y		73929 AW		AUTOM	2008
Engineering/Construction	United States	Y		102983 AW		AUTOM	2008
Training/Education	United States	Y		55313 AW		AUTOM	2008
Automotive Body and Related Repairer	Alabama	Y	26000 FQ	33780 MW	48710 TQ	USBLS	5/07
	Birmingham-Hoover MSA, AL	Y	27540 FQ	36210 MW	53100 TQ	USBLS	5/07
	Alaska	Y	49360 FQ	57200 MW	64550 TQ	USBLS	5/07
	Anchorage MSA, AK	Y	49900 FQ	57430 MW	64900 TQ	USBLS	5/07
	Arizona	Y	28590 FQ	35250 MW	45130 TQ	USBLS	5/07

AE Average entry wage	**AW** Average wage paid	**FQ** First quartile wage	**LO** Lowest wage paid	**MTC** Median total compensation	**TCC** Total cash compensation
AER Average entry range	**AWR** Average wage range	**H** Hourly	**LR** Low end range	**MW** Median wage paid	**TQ** Third quartile wage
AEX Average experienced wage	**AXR** Average experienced range	**HI** Highest wage paid	**M** Monthly	**MWR** Median wage range	**W** Weekly
ATC Average total compensation	**D** Daily	**HR** High end range	**MCC** Median cash compensation	**S** See annotated source	**Y** Yearly

Occupation/Type/Industry	Location	Per	Low	Mid	High	Source	Date
Automotive Body and Related Repairer							
	Phoenix-Mesa-Scottsdale MSA, AZ	Y	28980 FQ	35490 MW	47100 TQ	USBLS	5/07
	Tucson MSA, AZ	Y	30680 FQ	35380 MW	40880 TQ	USBLS	5/07
	Yuma MSA, AZ	Y	22870 FQ	30160 MW	39970 TQ	USBLS	5/07
	Arkansas	Y	26260 FQ	32330 MW	39180 TQ	USBLS	5/07
	Fayetteville-Springdale-Rogers MSA, AR-MO	Y	27140 FQ	35080 MW	44520 TQ	USBLS	5/07
	Little Rock-North Little Rock MSA, AR	Y	26380 FQ	35330 MW	41980 TQ	USBLS	5/07
	California	H	13.81 FQ	19.47 MW	25.64 TQ	CABLS	1/08-3/08
	Los Angeles-Long Beach-Glendale PMSA, CA	H	12.98 FQ	16.50 MW	23.29 TQ	CABLS	1/08-3/08
	Oakland-Fremont-Hayward MSA, CA	H	20.17 FQ	26.29 MW	31.19 TQ	CABLS	1/08-3/08
	Riverside-San Bernardino-Ontario MSA, CA	H	9.74 FQ	13.52 MW	17.66 TQ	CABLS	1/08-3/08
	Sacramento-Arden Arcade-Roseville MSA, CA	H	19.74 FQ	22.47 MW	25.32 TQ	CABLS	1/08-3/08
	San Diego-Carlsbad-San Marcos MSA, CA	H	13.00 FQ	19.53 MW	28.11 TQ	CABLS	1/08-3/08
	San Francisco-San Mateo-Redwood PMSA, CA	H	17.74 FQ	23.82 MW	29.55 TQ	CABLS	1/08-3/08
	San Jose-Sunnyvale-Santa Clara MSA, CA	H	13.97 FQ	21.40 MW	25.33 TQ	CABLS	1/08-3/08
	Santa Ana-Anaheim-Irvine PMSA, CA	Y	31510 FQ	45560 MW	60140 TQ	USBLS	5/07
	Stockton MSA, CA	H	16.05 FQ	19.03 MW	22.22 TQ	CABLS	1/08-3/08
	Colorado	Y	33160 FQ	44700 MW	59020 TQ	USBLS	5/07
	Boulder MSA, CO	Y	38080 FQ	52130 MW	89340 TQ	USBLS	5/07
	Denver-Aurora MSA, CO	Y	34470 FQ	46910 MW	61050 TQ	USBLS	5/07
	Connecticut	H	13.48 AE	19.21 MW		CTBLS	1/08-3/08
	Bridgeport-Stamford-Norwalk MSA, CT	Y	33710 FQ	39370 MW	51250 TQ	USBLS	5/07
	Hartford-West Hartford-East Hartford MSA, CT	Y	29700 FQ	39340 MW	48480 TQ	USBLS	5/07
	New Haven MSA, CT	Y	29150 FQ	37180 MW	46350 TQ	USBLS	5/07
	Norwich-New London MSA, CT-RI	Y	28380 FQ	35480 MW	41460 TQ	USBLS	5/07
	Delaware	Y	27030 FQ	37480 MW	47810 TQ	USBLS	5/07
	Wilmington PMSA, DE-MD-NJ	Y	29670 FQ	39670 MW	50050 TQ	USBLS	5/07
	District of Columbia	Y	30880 FQ	35620 MW	43110 TQ	USBLS	5/07
	Washington-Arlington-Alexandria MSA, DC-VA-MD-WV	Y	25470 FQ	45630 MW	62890 TQ	USBLS	5/07
	Florida	Y	26790 FQ	33900 MW	44180 TQ	USBLS	5/07
	Fort Lauderdale-Pompano Beach-Deerfield Beach PMSA, FL	Y	28090 FQ	36340 MW	47850 TQ	USBLS	5/07
	Jacksonville MSA, FL	Y	26740 FQ	36390 MW	46080 TQ	USBLS	5/07
	Miami-Fort Lauderdale-Miami Beach MSA, FL	Y	25940 FQ	31300 MW	43020 TQ	USBLS	5/07
	Orlando-Kissimmee MSA, FL	Y	23150 FQ	32940 MW	40380 TQ	USBLS	5/07
	Sarasota-Bradenton-Venice MSA, FL	Y	32980 FQ	36100 MW	40250 TQ	USBLS	5/07
	Tampa-St. Petersburg-Clearwater MSA, FL	Y	29610 FQ	38380 MW	52540 TQ	USBLS	5/07
	West Palm Beach-Boca Raton-Boynton Beach PMSA, FL	Y	28580 FQ	32660 MW	38140 TQ	USBLS	5/07
	Georgia	Y	30930 FQ	37460 MW	50270 TQ	USBLS	5/07
	Atlanta-Sandy Springs-Marietta MSA, GA	Y	32600 FQ	38620 MW	51320 TQ	USBLS	5/07
	Hawaii	Y	25580 FQ	33670 MW	40860 TQ	USBLS	5/07
	Honolulu MSA, HI	Y	25770 FQ	33660 MW	40060 TQ	USBLS	5/07
	Idaho	Y	20200 FQ	25520 MW	40440 TQ	USBLS	5/07
	Boise City-Nampa MSA, ID	Y	18690 FQ	22340 MW	28970 TQ	USBLS	5/07
	Illinois	Y	31640 FQ	39500 MW	48500 TQ	USBLS	5/07
	Chicago-Naperville-Joliet MSA, IL-IN-WI	Y	32140 FQ	40100 MW	50470 TQ	USBLS	5/07
	Indiana	Y	29420 FQ	37340 MW	48780 TQ	USBLS	5/07
	Gary PMSA, IN	Y	33140 FQ	46030 MW	66810 TQ	USBLS	5/07

AE	Average entry wage	AW	Average wage paid	FQ First quartile wage
AER	Average entry range	AWR	Average wage range	H Hourly
AEX	Average experienced wage	AXR	Average experienced range	HI Highest wage paid
ATC	Average total compensation	D	Daily	HR High end range

LO	Lowest wage paid	MTC Median total compensation	TCC Total cash compensation
LR	Low end range	MW Median wage paid	TQ Third quartile wage
M	Monthly	MWR Median wage range	W Weekly
MCC	Median cash compensation	S See annotated source	Y Yearly

Occupation/Type/Industry	Location	Per	Low	Mid	High	Source	Date
Automotive Body and Related Repairer							
	Indianapolis-Carmel MSA, IN	Y	32950 FQ	41670 MW	50740 TQ	USBLS	5/07
	Iowa	Y	25000 FQ	31810 MW	39190 TQ	USBLS	5/07
	Cedar Rapids MSA, IA	Y	29170 FQ	36160 MW	41030 TQ	USBLS	5/07
	Davenport-Moline-Rock Island MSA, IA-IL	Y	24780 FQ	33630 MW	43100 TQ	USBLS	5/07
	Des Moines-West Des Moines MSA, IA	Y	22260 FQ	35010 MW	41450 TQ	USBLS	5/07
	Sioux City MSA, IA-NE-SD	Y	26540 FQ	34090 MW	38920 TQ	USBLS	5/07
	Kansas	Y	25040 FQ	32460 MW	38400 TQ	USBLS	5/07
	Wichita MSA, KS	Y	25490 FQ	32820 MW	39740 TQ	USBLS	5/07
	Kentucky	Y	25826 FQ	34828 MW	42395 TQ	KYBLS	2008
	Louisville-Jefferson County MSA, KY-IN	Y	31970 FQ	37710 MW	46440 TQ	USBLS	5/07
	Louisiana	H	13.64 FQ	16.98 MW	21.76 TQ	LABLS	1/08-3/08
	Baton Rouge MSA, LA	Y	28080 FQ	35250 MW	45300 TQ	USBLS	5/07
	New Orleans-Metairie-Kenner MSA, LA	Y	30540 FQ	35970 MW	46100 TQ	USBLS	5/07
	Maine	Y	22890 FQ	28590 MW	35640 TQ	USBLS	5/07
	Portland-South Portland-Biddeford MSA, ME	Y	29470 FQ	37560 MW	45290 TQ	USBLS	5/07
	Maryland	Y		40650 MW		MDBLS	3/08
	Baltimore-Towson MSA, MD	Y	33360 FQ	38690 MW	46790 TQ	USBLS	5/07
	Bethesda-Gaithersburg-Frederick PMSA, MD	Y	31130 FQ	42690 MW	59850 TQ	USBLS	5/07
	Massachusetts	Y	31470 FQ	42500 MW	52000 TQ	USBLS	5/07
	Boston-Cambridge-Quincy NECTA, MA	Y	33450 FQ	44580 MW	53590 TQ	USBLS	5/07
	Worcester MSA, MA-CT	Y	29710 FQ	44000 MW	52160 TQ	USBLS	5/07
	Michigan	Y	29000 FQ	39670 MW	54800 TQ	USBLS	5/07
	Detroit-Warren-Livonia MSA, MI	Y	30020 FQ	46070 MW	58170 TQ	USBLS	5/07
	Grand Rapids-Wyoming MSA, MI	Y	28570 FQ	34340 MW	43230 TQ	USBLS	5/07
	Warren-Troy-Farmington Hills PMSA, MI	Y	36890 FQ	50780 MW	60440 TQ	USBLS	5/07
	Minnesota	Y	33251 FQ	42010 MW	53380 TQ	MNBLS	10/08-12/08
	Duluth-Superior MSA, MN-WI	Y	20863 FQ	34090 MW	41108 TQ	MNBLS	10/08-12/08
	Minneapolis-Saint Paul MSA, MN-WI	Y	38884 FQ	47674 MW	60282 TQ	MNBLS	10/08-12/08
	Rochester MSA, MN	Y	35388 FQ	40222 MW	47502 TQ	MNBLS	10/08-12/08
	Mississippi	Y	24770 FQ	30740 MW	39290 TQ	USBLS	5/07
	Hattiesburg MSA, MS	Y	28190 FQ	33990 MW	39380 TQ	USBLS	5/07
	Jackson MSA, MS	Y	25720 FQ	30360 MW	37560 TQ	USBLS	5/07
	Pascagoula MSA, MS	Y	21710 FQ	27270 MW	39070 TQ	USBLS	5/07
	Missouri	Y	31550 FQ	42700 MW	55670 TQ	USBLS	5/07
	Kansas City MSA, MO-KS	Y	33410 FQ	38960 MW	56490 TQ	USBLS	5/07
	St. Louis MSA, MO-IL	Y	39600 FQ	48610 MW	57110 TQ	USBLS	5/07
	Montana	Y	22920 FQ	31500 MW	39300 TQ	USBLS	5/07
	Billings MSA, MT	Y	19950 FQ	24570 MW	37350 TQ	USBLS	5/07
	Nebraska	Y	25520 FQ	33610 MW	40600 TQ	USBLS	5/07
	Omaha-Council Bluffs MSA, NE-IA	Y	26460 FQ	37000 MW	44770 TQ	USBLS	5/07
	Nevada	H	14.24 FQ	19.54 MW	24.64 TQ	NVBLS	5/08
	Las Vegas-Paradise MSA, NV	H	15.59 FQ	21.14 MW	25.51 TQ	NVBLS	5/08
	New Hampshire	H	12.97 AE	17.49 MW	20.91 AEX	NHBLS	6/08
	Manchester MSA, NH	Y	30730 FQ	38180 MW	46950 TQ	USBLS	5/07
	Nashua NECTA, NH-MA	Y	31300 FQ	35480 MW	43570 TQ	USBLS	5/07
	Portsmouth MSA, NH-ME	Y	33280 FQ	43250 MW	50390 TQ	USBLS	5/07
	New Jersey	Y	30860 FQ	39580 MW	49380 TQ	USBLS	5/07
	Camden PMSA, NJ	Y	30450 FQ	40440 MW	51630 TQ	USBLS	5/07
	Edison PMSA, NJ	Y	27730 FQ	37910 MW	49130 TQ	USBLS	5/07
	Newark-Union PMSA, NJ-PA	Y	27410 FQ	38510 MW	49970 TQ	USBLS	5/07
	New Mexico	Y	26300 FQ	31790 MW	42290 TQ	USBLS	5/07
	Albuquerque MSA, NM	Y	26190 FQ	31660 MW	41920 TQ	USBLS	5/07
	New York	Y	25890 FQ	32020 MW	41660 TQ	USBLS	5/07
	Albany-Schenectady-Troy MSA, NY	Y	25860 FQ	30280 MW	41300 TQ	USBLS	5/07
	Buffalo-Niagara Falls MSA, NY	Y	26970 FQ	34120 MW	45690 TQ	USBLS	5/07
	Ithaca MSA, NY	Y	33480 FQ	41580 MW	55440 TQ	USBLS	5/07
	Nassau-Suffolk PMSA, NY	Y	24180 FQ	30590 MW	40390 TQ	USBLS	5/07

AE	Average entry wage	AW	Average wage paid	FQ	First quartile wage	LO	Lowest wage paid
AER	Average entry range	AWR	Average wage range	H	Hourly	LR	Low end range
AEX	Average experienced wage	AXR	Average experienced range	HI	Highest wage paid	M	Monthly
ATC	Average total compensation	D	Daily	HR	High end range	MCC	Median cash compensation

MTC	Median total compensation	TCC	Total cash compensation
MW	Median wage paid	TQ	Third quartile wage
MWR	Median wage range	W	Weekly
S	See annotated source	Y	Yearly

Occupation/Type/Industry	Location	Per	Low	Mid	High	Source	Date
Automotive Body and Related Repairer							
	New York-Northern New Jersey-Long Island MSA, NY-NJ-PA	Y	26230 FQ	35040 MW	46960 TQ	USBLS	5/07
	North Carolina	Y	28700 FQ	37700 MW	51060 TQ	USBLS	5/07
	Charlotte-Gastonia-Concord MSA, NC-SC	Y	35620 FQ	47170 MW	58110 TQ	USBLS	5/07
	Raleigh-Cary MSA, NC	Y	27830 FQ	35220 MW	46790 TQ	USBLS	5/07
	North Dakota	Y	24420 FQ	33210 MW	40880 TQ	USBLS	5/07
	Fargo MSA, ND-MN	Y	26570 FQ	36110 MW	52000 TQ	USBLS	5/07
	Ohio	Y	26850 FQ	34790 MW	47300 TQ	USBLS	5/07
	Cincinnati-Middletown MSA, OH-KY-IN	Y	31620 FQ	40820 MW	50600 TQ	USBLS	5/07
	Cleveland-Elyria-Mentor MSA, OH	Y	27250 FQ	42310 MW	56680 TQ	USBLS	5/07
	Columbus MSA, OH	Y	27570 FQ	36170 MW	49660 TQ	USBLS	5/07
	Dayton MSA, OH	Y	29080 FQ	35600 MW	45560 TQ	USBLS	5/07
	Oklahoma	Y	21980 FQ	29000 MW	39330 TQ	USBLS	5/07
	Oklahoma City MSA, OK	Y	22310 FQ	29430 MW	44170 TQ	USBLS	5/07
	Tulsa MSA, OK	Y	24340 FQ	31520 MW	37450 TQ	USBLS	5/07
	Oregon	H	14.14 FQ	17.72 MW	25.34 TQ	ORBLS	5/08
	Portland-Vancouver-Beaverton MSA, OR-WA	Y	29930 FQ	37290 MW	53700 TQ	USBLS	5/07
	Pennsylvania	Y	28440 FQ	35120 MW	43570 TQ	USBLS	5/07
	Allentown-Bethlehem-Easton MSA, PA-NJ	Y	29600 FQ	36560 MW	44310 TQ	USBLS	5/07
	Philadelphia-Camden-Wilmington MSA, PA-NJ-DE-MD	Y	31660 FQ	39810 MW	47910 TQ	USBLS	5/07
	Pittsburgh MSA, PA	Y	29310 FQ	34310 MW	40490 TQ	USBLS	5/07
	Rhode Island	Y	31680 FQ	38630 MW	45670 TQ	USBLS	5/07
	Providence-Fall River-Warwick MSA, RI-MA	Y	32100 FQ	39060 MW	45680 TQ	USBLS	5/07
	South Carolina	Y	27800 FQ	34790 MW	43890 TQ	USBLS	5/07
	Charleston-North Charleston MSA, SC	Y	28370 FQ	35910 MW	42610 TQ	USBLS	5/07
	Columbia MSA, SC	Y	32820 FQ	38060 MW	48940 TQ	USBLS	5/07
	South Dakota	Y	26570 FQ	31144 MW	37491 TQ	SDBLS	7/08-9/08
	Rapid City MSA, SD	Y	29351 FQ	34054 MW	41073 TQ	SDBLS	7/08-9/08
	Sioux Falls MSA, SD	Y	26883 FQ	30614 MW	35216 TQ	SDBLS	7/08-9/08
	Tennessee	Y	24500 FQ	32430 MW	43390 TQ	USBLS	5/07
	Memphis MSA, TN-MS-AR	Y	28360 FQ	33170 MW	43010 TQ	USBLS	5/07
	Nashville-Davidson-Murfreesboro MSA, TN	Y	26640 FQ	34650 MW	52630 TQ	USBLS	5/07
	Texas	Y	25290 FQ	30580 MW	38810 TQ	USBLS	5/07
	Austin-Round Rock MSA, TX	Y	29710 FQ	35050 MW	40280 TQ	USBLS	5/07
	Beaumont-Port Arthur MSA, TX	Y	18970 FQ	32110 MW	37590 TQ	USBLS	5/07
	Dallas-Fort Worth-Arlington MSA, TX	Y	24170 FQ	28570 MW	36740 TQ	USBLS	5/07
	El Paso MSA, TX	Y	22890 FQ	26470 MW	30520 TQ	USBLS	5/07
	Houston-Sugar Land-Baytown MSA, TX	Y	27140 FQ	32740 MW	42710 TQ	USBLS	5/07
	San Antonio MSA, TX	Y	25860 FQ	30940 MW	40000 TQ	USBLS	5/07
	Utah	Y	26360 FQ	35950 MW	48010 TQ	USBLS	5/07
	Ogden-Clearfield MSA, UT	Y	30350 FQ	38890 MW	57120 TQ	USBLS	5/07
	Salt Lake City MSA, UT	Y	24640 FQ	36890 MW	54940 TQ	USBLS	5/07
	Vermont	Y	28090 FQ	32790 MW	36930 TQ	USBLS	5/07
	Burlington-South Burlington MSA, VT	Y	27830 FQ	32890 MW	38480 TQ	USBLS	5/07
	Virginia	Y	23910 FQ	35360 MW	51050 TQ	USBLS	5/07
	Richmond MSA, VA	Y	33560 FQ	40460 MW	46650 TQ	USBLS	5/07
	Roanoke MSA, VA	Y	27670 FQ	30220 MW	36310 TQ	USBLS	5/07
	Virginia Beach-Norfolk-Newport News MSA, VA-NC	Y	28840 FQ	38110 MW	54380 TQ	USBLS	5/07
	Washington	H	15.24 FQ	19.00 MW	25.10 TQ	WABLS	3/08
	Seattle-Tacoma-Bellevue MSA, WA	Y	31580 FQ	41090 MW	55100 TQ	USBLS	5/07
	West Virginia	Y	21900 FQ	30202 MW	37745 TQ	WVBLS	7/08-9/08
	Charleston MSA, WV	Y	26040 FQ	32340 MW	46430 TQ	USBLS	5/07
	Huntington-Ashland MSA, WV-KY-OH	Y	23570 FQ	31070 MW	35640 TQ	USBLS	5/07

AE	Average entry wage	AW	Average wage paid	FQ	First quartile wage
AER	Average entry range	AWR	Average wage range	H	Hourly
AEX	Average experienced wage	AXR	Average experienced range	HI	Highest wage paid
ATC	Average total compensation	D	Daily	HR	High end range

LO	Lowest wage paid	MTC	Median total compensation
LR	Low end range	MW	Median wage paid
M	Monthly	MWR	Median wage range
		MCC	Median cash compensation

TCC	Total cash compensation
TQ	Third quartile wage
W	Weekly
S	See annotated source
Y	Yearly

Occupation/Type/Industry	Location	Per	Low	Mid	High	Source	Date
Automotive Body and Related Repairer							
	Wisconsin	Y	28380 FQ	34750 MW	40690 TQ	USBLS	5/07
	Appleton MSA, WI	Y	31380 FQ	36840 MW	42780 TQ	USBLS	5/07
	Milwaukee-Waukesha-West Allis MSA, WI	Y	27820 FQ	36040 MW	43760 TQ	USBLS	5/07
	Racine MSA, WI	Y	32170 FQ	35850 MW	40290 TQ	USBLS	5/07
	Wyoming	Y	31680 FQ	38948 MW	46692 TQ	WYBLS	9/08
	Cheyenne MSA, WY	Y	32722 FQ	38135 MW	47029 TQ	WYBLS	9/08
	Puerto Rico	Y	12900 FQ	14690 MW	17200 TQ	USBLS	5/07
	San Juan-Caguas-Guaynabo MSA, PR	Y	12930 FQ	14740 MW	17360 TQ	USBLS	5/07
	Guam	Y	16850 FQ	21750 MW	27600 TQ	USBLS	5/07
Automotive Glass Installer and Repairer							
	Alabama	Y	18660 FQ	23190 MW	31730 TQ	USBLS	5/07
	Alaska	Y	31100 FQ	38050 MW	45850 TQ	USBLS	5/07
	Arizona	Y	26110 FQ	30760 MW	39980 TQ	USBLS	5/07
	Phoenix-Mesa-Scottsdale MSA, AZ	Y	25720 FQ	30890 MW	46020 TQ	USBLS	5/07
	Tucson MSA, AZ	Y	26910 FQ	34420 MW	39910 TQ	USBLS	5/07
	Arkansas	Y	22400 FQ	26770 MW	30750 TQ	USBLS	5/07
	Little Rock-North Little Rock MSA, AR	Y	21710 FQ	26080 MW	30400 TQ	USBLS	5/07
	California	H	10.83 FQ	14.10 MW	22.27 TQ	CABLS	1/08-3/08
	Los Angeles-Long Beach-Glendale PMSA, CA	H	10.13 FQ	10.92 MW	11.70 TQ	CABLS	1/08-3/08
	Riverside-San Bernardino-Ontario MSA, CA	H	13.26 FQ	16.53 MW	24.39 TQ	CABLS	1/08-3/08
	San Francisco-San Mateo-Redwood PMSA, CA	H	18.08 FQ	23.41 MW	28.89 TQ	CABLS	1/08-3/08
	Santa Ana-Anaheim-Irvine PMSA, CA	Y	21920 FQ	25450 MW	43270 TQ	USBLS	5/07
	Colorado	Y	25480 FQ	28010 MW	31040 TQ	USBLS	5/07
	Colorado Springs MSA, CO	Y	25530 FQ	27180 MW	28840 TQ	USBLS	5/07
	Denver-Aurora MSA, CO	Y	27710 FQ	30130 MW	32520 TQ	USBLS	5/07
	Connecticut	H	16.00 AE	18.84 MW		CTBLS	1/08-3/08
	Washington-Arlington-Alexandria MSA, DC-VA-MD-WV	Y	30210 FQ	34650 MW	40490 TQ	USBLS	5/07
	Florida	Y	21830 FQ	34490 MW	41540 TQ	USBLS	5/07
	Fort Lauderdale-Pompano Beach-Deerfield Beach PMSA, FL	Y	35440 FQ	41620 MW	46780 TQ	USBLS	5/07
	Miami-Fort Lauderdale-Miami Beach MSA, FL	Y	19210 FQ	34320 MW	43500 TQ	USBLS	5/07
	Tampa-St. Petersburg-Clearwater MSA, FL	Y	33140 FQ	35630 MW	38090 TQ	USBLS	5/07
	Georgia	Y	36330 FQ	42050 MW	47560 TQ	USBLS	5/07
	Atlanta-Sandy Springs-Marietta MSA, GA	Y	39560 FQ	43430 MW	46850 TQ	USBLS	5/07
	Idaho	Y	20090 FQ	26170 MW	31020 TQ	USBLS	5/07
	Illinois	Y	28250 FQ	32160 MW	39970 TQ	USBLS	5/07
	Chicago-Naperville-Joliet MSA, IL-IN-WI	Y	28780 FQ	31610 MW	37800 TQ	USBLS	5/07
	Indiana	Y	21380 FQ	29300 MW	35120 TQ	USBLS	5/07
	Indianapolis-Carmel MSA, IN	Y	28790 FQ	31600 MW	35010 TQ	USBLS	5/07
	Iowa	Y	21320 FQ	25980 MW	32810 TQ	USBLS	5/07
	Kansas	Y	26160 FQ	29720 MW	35680 TQ	USBLS	5/07
	Kentucky	Y	27416 FQ	32460 MW	39718 TQ	KYBLS	2008
	Louisville-Jefferson County MSA, KY-IN	Y	27700 FQ	36910 MW	42110 TQ	USBLS	5/07
	Louisiana	H	9.04 FQ	11.20 MW	13.31 TQ	LABLS	1/08-3/08
	Maine	Y	24110 FQ	27100 MW	30660 TQ	USBLS	5/07
	Maryland	Y		33325 MW		MDBLS	3/08
	Bethesda-Gaithersburg-Frederick PMSA, MD	Y	29750 FQ	34270 MW	39080 TQ	USBLS	5/07
	Massachusetts	Y	28440 FQ	35490 MW	43560 TQ	USBLS	5/07
	Boston-Cambridge-Quincy NECTA, MA	Y	29090 FQ	39430 MW	50270 TQ	USBLS	5/07
	Worcester MSA, MA-CT	Y	32120 FQ	35840 MW	39400 TQ	USBLS	5/07
	Michigan	Y	32640 FQ	37960 MW	45890 TQ	USBLS	5/07

AE	Average entry wage	AW	Average wage paid	FQ	First quartile wage	LO	Lowest wage paid	MTC	Median total compensation	TCC	Total cash compensation
AER	Average entry range	AWR	Average wage range	H	Hourly	LR	Low end range	MW	Median wage paid	TQ	Third quartile wage
AEX	Average experienced wage	AXR	Average experienced range	HI	Highest wage paid	M	Monthly	MWR	Median wage range	W	Weekly
ATC	Average total compensation	D	Daily	HR	High end range	MCC	Median cash compensation	S	See annotated source	Y	Yearly

Occupation/Type/Industry	Location	Per	Low	Mid	High	Source	Date
Automotive Glass Installer and Repairer	Detroit-Warren-Livonia MSA, MI	Y	35280 FQ	41460 MW	56040 TQ	USBLS	5/07
	Grand Rapids-Wyoming MSA, MI	Y	32020 FQ	35030 MW	39270 TQ	USBLS	5/07
	Warren-Troy-Farmington Hills PMSA, MI	Y	35940 FQ	47160 MW	58840 TQ	USBLS	5/07
	Minnesota	Y	37248 FQ	43751 MW	49195 TQ	MNBLS	10/08-12/08
	Duluth-Superior MSA, MN-WI	Y	31153 FQ	35433 MW	39870 TQ	MNBLS	10/08-12/08
	Minneapolis-Saint Paul MSA, MN-WI	Y	38894 FQ	44779 MW	49489 TQ	MNBLS	10/08-12/08
	Mississippi	Y	18880 FQ	29540 MW	36160 TQ	USBLS	5/07
	Missouri	Y	29590 FQ	34710 MW	40840 TQ	USBLS	5/07
	Kansas City MSA, MO-KS	Y	27090 FQ	30360 MW	40090 TQ	USBLS	5/07
	St. Louis MSA, MO-IL	Y	30560 FQ	34990 MW	41570 TQ	USBLS	5/07
	Montana	Y	25980 FQ	32530 MW	37090 TQ	USBLS	5/07
	Nebraska	Y	20420 FQ	25120 MW	31040 TQ	USBLS	5/07
	Nevada	H	16.56 FQ	19.66 MW	33.84 TQ	NVBLS	5/08
	New Hampshire	H	14.24 AE	17.51 MW	19.24 AEX	NHBLS	6/08
	New Jersey	Y	15050 FQ	25700 MW	35440 TQ	USBLS	5/07
	Camden PMSA, NJ	Y	15050 FQ	15050 MW	15050 TQ	USBLS	5/07
	Newark-Union PMSA, NJ-PA	Y	22890 FQ	25190 MW	43300 TQ	USBLS	5/07
	New Mexico	Y	18640 FQ	21020 MW	23140 TQ	USBLS	5/07
	Albuquerque MSA, NM	Y	21010 FQ	22450 MW	23880 TQ	USBLS	5/07
	New York	Y	22770 FQ	28610 MW	33280 TQ	USBLS	5/07
	Buffalo-Niagara Falls MSA, NY	Y	22250 FQ	24580 MW	34330 TQ	USBLS	5/07
	New York-Northern New Jersey-Long Island MSA, NY-NJ-PA	Y	23030 FQ	29730 MW	34290 TQ	USBLS	5/07
	North Carolina	Y	24520 FQ	30550 MW	35650 TQ	USBLS	5/07
	North Dakota	Y	22030 FQ	26370 MW	33630 TQ	USBLS	5/07
	Ohio	Y	27270 FQ	33320 MW	42000 TQ	USBLS	5/07
	Cincinnati-Middletown MSA, OH-KY-IN	Y	31370 FQ	38440 MW	48330 TQ	USBLS	5/07
	Cleveland-Elyria-Mentor MSA, OH	Y	27140 FQ	32730 MW	39790 TQ	USBLS	5/07
	Columbus MSA, OH	Y	24590 FQ	37440 MW	51850 TQ	USBLS	5/07
	Oklahoma	Y	25810 FQ	30930 MW	38250 TQ	USBLS	5/07
	Oklahoma City MSA, OK	Y	29790 FQ	34430 MW	39050 TQ	USBLS	5/07
	Oregon	H	12.32 FQ	17.21 MW	22.18 TQ	ORBLS	5/08
	Portland-Vancouver-Beaverton MSA, OR-WA	Y	31590 FQ	38210 MW	45060 TQ	USBLS	5/07
	Pennsylvania	Y	25240 FQ	30450 MW	36560 TQ	USBLS	5/07
	Allentown-Bethlehem-Easton MSA, PA-NJ	Y	22960 FQ	29280 MW	36620 TQ	USBLS	5/07
	Philadelphia-Camden-Wilmington MSA, PA-NJ-DE-MD	Y	15050 FQ	33440 MW	38010 TQ	USBLS	5/07
	Rhode Island	Y	25420 FQ	28430 MW	32860 TQ	USBLS	5/07
	Providence-Fall River-Warwick MSA, RI-MA	Y	25920 FQ	29200 MW	39370 TQ	USBLS	5/07
	South Carolina	Y	19770 FQ	29980 MW	38550 TQ	USBLS	5/07
	Charleston-North Charleston MSA, SC	Y	18470 FQ	24600 MW	35370 TQ	USBLS	5/07
	South Dakota	Y	24281 FQ	29915 MW	40022 TQ	SDBLS	7/08-9/08
	Tennessee	Y	26530 FQ	35690 MW	42620 TQ	USBLS	5/07
	Memphis MSA, TN-MS-AR	Y	31440 FQ	39200 MW	44410 TQ	USBLS	5/07
	Texas	Y	20950 FQ	26740 MW	32090 TQ	USBLS	5/07
	Dallas-Fort Worth-Arlington MSA, TX	Y	25910 FQ	28910 MW	34020 TQ	USBLS	5/07
	El Paso MSA, TX	Y	24640 FQ	27810 MW	31830 TQ	USBLS	5/07
	Houston-Sugar Land-Baytown MSA, TX	Y	19060 FQ	24650 MW	31170 TQ	USBLS	5/07
	Utah	Y	25460 FQ	33120 MW	37630 TQ	USBLS	5/07
	Salt Lake City MSA, UT	Y	25410 FQ	30750 MW	36810 TQ	USBLS	5/07
	Vermont	Y	42100 FQ	49420 MW	54710 TQ	USBLS	5/07
	Burlington-South Burlington MSA, VT	Y	48080 FQ	52080 MW	56200 TQ	USBLS	5/07
	Virginia	Y	26510 FQ	31280 MW	38560 TQ	USBLS	5/07
	Richmond MSA, VA	Y	24390 FQ	33730 MW	40760 TQ	USBLS	5/07

AE	Average entry wage	AW	Average wage paid	FQ	First quartile wage
AER	Average entry range	AWR	Average wage range	H	Hourly
AEX	Average experienced wage	AXR	Average experienced range	HI	Highest wage paid
ATC	Average total compensation	D	Daily	HR	High end range

LO	Lowest wage paid	MTC	Median total compensation
LR	Low end range	MW	Median wage paid
M	Monthly	MWR	Median wage range
		MCC	Median cash compensation

		TCC	Total cash compensation
		TQ	Third quartile wage
		W	Weekly
S	See annotated source	Y	Yearly

Occupation/Type/Industry	Location	Per	Low	Mid	High	Source	Date
Automotive Glass Installer and Repairer							
	Virginia Beach-Norfolk-Newport News MSA, VA-NC	Y	25290 FQ	28220 MW	31120 TQ	USBLS	5/07
	Washington	H	14.78 FQ	17.68 MW	20.01 TQ	WABLS	3/08
	Seattle-Tacoma-Bellevue MSA, WA	Y	30720 FQ	36560 MW	41600 TQ	USBLS	5/07
	West Virginia	Y	22769 FQ	33463 MW	38520 TQ	WVBLS	7/08-9/08
	Wisconsin	Y	30890 FQ	39610 MW	46830 TQ	USBLS	5/07
	Wyoming	Y	26594 FQ	30026 MW	33501 TQ	WYBLS	9/08
	Puerto Rico	Y	12690 FQ	14260 MW	17330 TQ	USBLS	5/07
	San Juan-Caguas-Guaynabo MSA, PR	Y	12690 FQ	14260 MW	17330 TQ	USBLS	5/07
Automotive Service Technician and Mechanic							
	Alabama	Y	21560 FQ	29530 MW	40200 TQ	USBLS	5/07
	Birmingham-Hoover MSA, AL	Y	21890 FQ	31560 MW	42920 TQ	USBLS	5/07
	Alaska	Y	34770 FQ	47840 MW	59300 TQ	USBLS	5/07
	Anchorage MSA, AK	Y	37900 FQ	47780 MW	58860 TQ	USBLS	5/07
	Fairbanks MSA, AK	Y	34540 FQ	54360 MW	63650 TQ	USBLS	5/07
	Arizona	Y	26500 FQ	37790 MW	49650 TQ	USBLS	5/07
	Phoenix-Mesa-Scottsdale MSA, AZ	Y	25860 FQ	37520 MW	50190 TQ	USBLS	5/07
	Tucson MSA, AZ	Y	28890 FQ	38960 MW	48210 TQ	USBLS	5/07
	Arkansas	Y	20900 FQ	28300 MW	38210 TQ	USBLS	5/07
	Little Rock-North Little Rock MSA, AR	Y	24990 FQ	34390 MW	44130 TQ	USBLS	5/07
	California	H	13.65 FQ	18.75 MW	25.46 TQ	CABLS	1/08-3/08
	Bakersfield MSA, CA	H	11.41 FQ	17.67 MW	24.87 TQ	CABLS	1/08-3/08
	Los Angeles-Long Beach-Glendale PMSA, CA	H	12.43 FQ	16.29 MW	23.79 TQ	CABLS	1/08-3/08
	Oakland-Fremont-Hayward MSA, CA	H	16.68 FQ	22.73 MW	29.82 TQ	CABLS	1/08-3/08
	Riverside-San Bernardino-Ontario MSA, CA	H	12.70 FQ	17.43 MW	23.25 TQ	CABLS	1/08-3/08
	Sacramento-Arden Arcade-Roseville MSA, CA	H	16.59 FQ	21.09 MW	26.16 TQ	CABLS	1/08-3/08
	San Diego-Carlsbad-San Marcos MSA, CA	H	14.67 FQ	20.34 MW	25.39 TQ	CABLS	1/08-3/08
	San Francisco-San Mateo-Redwood PMSA, CA	H	17.18 FQ	24.54 MW	29.60 TQ	CABLS	1/08-3/08
	San Jose-Sunnyvale-Santa Clara MSA, CA	H	15.38 FQ	23.28 MW	29.54 TQ	CABLS	1/08-3/08
	Santa Ana-Anaheim-Irvine PMSA, CA	Y	26300 FQ	36150 MW	52860 TQ	USBLS	5/07
	Colorado	Y	24480 FQ	34910 MW	48450 TQ	USBLS	5/07
	Denver-Aurora MSA, CO	Y	24570 FQ	35350 MW	48710 TQ	USBLS	5/07
	Connecticut	H	13.19 AE	19.54 MW		CTBLS	1/08-3/08
	Bridgeport-Stamford-Norwalk MSA, CT	Y	31880 FQ	42820 MW	53990 TQ	USBLS	5/07
	Hartford-West Hartford-East Hartford MSA, CT	Y	29670 FQ	38470 MW	49070 TQ	USBLS	5/07
	Delaware	Y	25500 FQ	33600 MW	42790 TQ	USBLS	5/07
	Wilmington PMSA, DE-MD-NJ	Y	25520 FQ	34290 MW	45020 TQ	USBLS	5/07
	District of Columbia	Y	27850 FQ	41860 MW	50960 TQ	USBLS	5/07
	Washington-Arlington-Alexandria MSA, DC-VA-MD-WV	Y	30920 FQ	41400 MW	55820 TQ	USBLS	5/07
	Florida	Y	23910 FQ	32140 MW	42990 TQ	USBLS	5/07
	Fort Lauderdale-Pompano Beach-Deerfield Beach PMSA, FL	Y	24520 FQ	30850 MW	42300 TQ	USBLS	5/07
	Jacksonville MSA, FL	Y	23260 FQ	31000 MW	40560 TQ	USBLS	5/07
	Miami-Fort Lauderdale-Miami Beach MSA, FL	Y	24100 FQ	31730 MW	44100 TQ	USBLS	5/07
	Orlando-Kissimmee MSA, FL	Y	24210 FQ	34810 MW	45340 TQ	USBLS	5/07
	Tampa-St. Petersburg-Clearwater MSA, FL	Y	23970 FQ	32720 MW	41550 TQ	USBLS	5/07
	West Palm Beach-Boca Raton-Boynton Beach PMSA, FL	Y	26590 FQ	36210 MW	47290 TQ	USBLS	5/07
	Georgia	Y	23640 FQ	32900 MW	43940 TQ	USBLS	5/07

AE Average entry wage	**AW** Average wage paid	**FQ** First quartile wage	**LO** Lowest wage paid	**MTC** Median total compensation	**TCC** Total cash compensation
AER Average entry range	**AWR** Average wage range	**H** Hourly	**LR** Low end range	**MW** Median wage paid	**TQ** Third quartile wage
AEX Average experienced wage	**AXR** Average experienced range	**HI** Highest wage paid	**M** Monthly	**MWR** Median wage range	**W** Weekly
ATC Average total compensation	**D** Daily	**HR** High end range	**MCC** Median cash compensation	**S** See annotated source	**Y** Yearly

Occupation/Type/Industry	Location	Per	Low	Mid	High	Source	Date
Automotive Service Technician and Mechanic							
	Atlanta-Sandy Springs-Marietta MSA, GA	Y	25890 FQ	35780 MW	46270 TQ	USBLS	5/07
	Hawaii	Y	27010 FQ	33410 MW	43690 TQ	USBLS	5/07
	Honolulu MSA, HI	Y	27470 FQ	33020 MW	43910 TQ	USBLS	5/07
	Idaho	Y	22960 FQ	31540 MW	41470 TQ	USBLS	5/07
	Boise City-Nampa MSA, ID	Y	23930 FQ	32020 MW	41080 TQ	USBLS	5/07
	Illinois	Y	26810 FQ	36340 MW	49600 TQ	USBLS	5/07
	Chicago-Naperville-Joliet MSA, IL-IN-WI	Y	27380 FQ	37470 MW	53380 TQ	USBLS	5/07
	Indiana	Y	24270 FQ	32830 MW	43400 TQ	USBLS	5/07
	Gary PMSA, IN	Y	21430 FQ	30380 MW	39620 TQ	USBLS	5/07
	Indianapolis-Carmel MSA, IN	Y	26880 FQ	37470 MW	48950 TQ	USBLS	5/07
	Iowa	Y	22850 FQ	30540 MW	40420 TQ	USBLS	5/07
	Des Moines-West Des Moines MSA, IA	Y	27830 FQ	36850 MW	46520 TQ	USBLS	5/07
	Waterloo-Cedar Falls MSA, IA	Y	23750 FQ	29930 MW	36110 TQ	USBLS	5/07
	Kansas	Y	24540 FQ	32280 MW	42500 TQ	USBLS	5/07
	Wichita MSA, KS	Y	23370 FQ	31350 MW	39290 TQ	USBLS	5/07
	Kentucky	Y	22328 FQ	29047 MW	38120 TQ	KYBLS	2008
	Louisville-Jefferson County MSA, KY-IN	Y	24330 FQ	30920 MW	40010 TQ	USBLS	5/07
	Louisiana	H	10.39 FQ	14.35 MW	19.05 TQ	LABLS	1/08-3/08
	Baton Rouge MSA, LA	Y	22040 FQ	29920 MW	39280 TQ	USBLS	5/07
	New Orleans-Metairie-Kenner MSA, LA	Y	22530 FQ	31610 MW	42050 TQ	USBLS	5/07
	Maine	Y	25200 FQ	30030 MW	36990 TQ	USBLS	5/07
	Lewiston-Auburn MSA, ME	Y	21790 FQ	26790 MW	33670 TQ	USBLS	5/07
	Portland-South Portland-Biddeford MSA, ME	Y	27770 FQ	33690 MW	41960 TQ	USBLS	5/07
	Maryland	Y		38475 MW		MDBLS	3/08
	Baltimore-Towson MSA, MD	Y	25460 FQ	35620 MW	48010 TQ	USBLS	5/07
	Bethesda-Gaithersburg-Frederick PMSA, MD	Y	35230 FQ	47780 MW	59270 TQ	USBLS	5/07
	Massachusetts	Y	29550 FQ	37770 MW	48210 TQ	USBLS	5/07
	Boston-Cambridge-Quincy NECTA, MA	Y	33180 FQ	40690 MW	51800 TQ	USBLS	5/07
	Worcester MSA, MA-CT	Y	27330 FQ	31890 MW	42900 TQ	USBLS	5/07
	Michigan	Y	27020 FQ	38150 MW	51260 TQ	USBLS	5/07
	Ann Arbor MSA, MI	Y	32660 FQ	51970 MW	65930 TQ	USBLS	5/07
	Detroit-Warren-Livonia MSA, MI	Y	29340 FQ	43810 MW	59070 TQ	USBLS	5/07
	Grand Rapids-Wyoming MSA, MI	Y	32230 FQ	40010 MW	50480 TQ	USBLS	5/07
	Warren-Troy-Farmington Hills PMSA, MI	Y	30620 FQ	45170 MW	61640 TQ	USBLS	5/07
	Minnesota	Y	29150 FQ	37017 MW	46541 TQ	MNBLS	10/08-12/08
	Duluth-Superior MSA, MN-WI	Y	26852 FQ	32380 MW	42146 TQ	MNBLS	10/08-12/08
	Minneapolis-Saint Paul MSA, MN-WI	Y	31678 FQ	40069 MW	50506 TQ	MNBLS	10/08-12/08
	Rochester MSA, MN	Y	28950 FQ	34085 MW	43559 TQ	MNBLS	10/08-12/08
	Mississippi	Y	21020 FQ	27000 MW	37560 TQ	USBLS	5/07
	Jackson MSA, MS	Y	24060 FQ	28830 MW	36140 TQ	USBLS	5/07
	Missouri	Y	22840 FQ	32790 MW	43600 TQ	USBLS	5/07
	Kansas City MSA, MO-KS	Y	25050 FQ	35270 MW	46200 TQ	USBLS	5/07
	St. Louis MSA, MO-IL	Y	29330 FQ	37930 MW	47010 TQ	USBLS	5/07
	Montana	Y	25780 FQ	32860 MW	43740 TQ	USBLS	5/07
	Billings MSA, MT	Y	28930 FQ	37010 MW	47520 TQ	USBLS	5/07
	Nebraska	Y	24790 FQ	31310 MW	40470 TQ	USBLS	5/07
	Omaha-Council Bluffs MSA, NE-IA	Y	26400 FQ	36330 MW	46440 TQ	USBLS	5/07
	Nevada	H	13.70 FQ	18.55 MW	24.01 TQ	NVBLS	5/08
	Carson City MSA, NV	H	11.65 FQ	18.05 MW	24.87 TQ	NVBLS	5/08
	Las Vegas-Paradise MSA, NV	H	13.49 FQ	18.04 MW	23.75 TQ	NVBLS	5/08
	New Hampshire	H	12.56 AE	18.29	22.03 AEX	NHBLS	6/08
	Manchester MSA, NH	Y	28780 FQ	38910 MW	46620 TQ	USBLS	5/07
	Nashua NECTA, NH-MA	Y	28210 FQ	36950 MW	50190 TQ	USBLS	5/07
	Portsmouth MSA, NH-ME	Y	26560 FQ	36740 MW	44760 TQ	USBLS	5/07
	New Jersey	Y	28760 FQ	37300 MW	48550 TQ	USBLS	5/07
	Camden PMSA, NJ	Y	30070 FQ	38760 MW	49500 TQ	USBLS	5/07
	Edison PMSA, NJ	Y	26250 FQ	36630 MW	49590 TQ	USBLS	5/07
	Newark-Union PMSA, NJ-PA	Y	29790 FQ	37760 MW	47130 TQ	USBLS	5/07

AE	Average entry wage	AW	Average wage paid	FQ	First quartile wage
AER	Average entry range	AWR	Average wage range	H	Hourly
AEX	Average experienced wage	AXR	Average experienced range	HI	Highest wage paid
ATC	Average total compensation	D	Daily	HR	High end range

LO	Lowest wage paid	MTC	Median total compensation
LR	Low end range	MW	Median wage paid
M	Monthly	MWR	Median wage range
MCC	Median cash compensation	S	See annotated source

TCC	Total cash compensation
TQ	Third quartile wage
W	Weekly
Y	Yearly

Occupation/Type/Industry	Location	Per	Low	Mid	High	Source	Date
Automotive Service Technician and Mechanic	Trenton-Ewing MSA, NJ	Y	29430 FQ	38050 MW	52180 TQ	USBLS	5/07
	Vineland-Millville-Bridgeton MSA, NJ	Y	27400 FQ	38260 MW	45200 TQ	USBLS	5/07
	New Mexico	Y	22600 FQ	31230 MW	41800 TQ	USBLS	5/07
	Albuquerque MSA, NM	Y	24080 FQ	33860 MW	43270 TQ	USBLS	5/07
	Las Cruces MSA, NM	Y	23260 FQ	32910 MW	42750 TQ	USBLS	5/07
	New York	Y	24140 FQ	33220 MW	46470 TQ	USBLS	5/07
	Albany-Schenectady-Troy MSA, NY	Y	27900 FQ	39680 MW	48310 TQ	USBLS	5/07
	Binghamton MSA, NY	Y	23440 FQ	27830 MW	32500 TQ	USBLS	5/07
	Buffalo-Niagara Falls MSA, NY	Y	19980 FQ	30570 MW	40060 TQ	USBLS	5/07
	Glens Falls MSA, NY	Y	26500 FQ	33200 MW	38000 TQ	USBLS	5/07
	Nassau-Suffolk PMSA, NY	Y	28530 FQ	39910 MW	55280 TQ	USBLS	5/07
	New York-Northern New Jersey-Long Island MSA, NY-NJ-PA	Y	27140 FQ	36970 MW	51480 TQ	USBLS	5/07
	North Carolina	Y	26220 FQ	33760 MW	45490 TQ	USBLS	5/07
	Charlotte-Gastonia-Concord MSA, NC-SC	Y	28660 FQ	38550 MW	50440 TQ	USBLS	5/07
	Raleigh-Cary MSA, NC	Y	26530 FQ	34350 MW	45790 TQ	USBLS	5/07
	Winston-Salem MSA, NC	Y	21840 FQ	31410 MW	43100 TQ	USBLS	5/07
	North Dakota	Y	23970 FQ	30840 MW	39580 TQ	USBLS	5/07
	Fargo MSA, ND-MN	Y	27010 FQ	35380 MW	46860 TQ	USBLS	5/07
	Ohio	Y	24920 FQ	33710 MW	44100 TQ	USBLS	5/07
	Cincinnati-Middletown MSA, OH-KY-IN	Y	24730 FQ	32070 MW	45910 TQ	USBLS	5/07
	Cleveland-Elyria-Mentor MSA, OH	Y	26900 FQ	37400 MW	47510 TQ	USBLS	5/07
	Columbus MSA, OH	Y	26690 FQ	35330 MW	46110 TQ	USBLS	5/07
	Dayton MSA, OH	Y	23280 FQ	33110 MW	41440 TQ	USBLS	5/07
	Oklahoma	Y	20740 FQ	29370 MW	41010 TQ	USBLS	5/07
	Oklahoma City MSA, OK	Y	22230 FQ	31300 MW	42140 TQ	USBLS	5/07
	Tulsa MSA, OK	Y	21810 FQ	29900 MW	41940 TQ	USBLS	5/07
	Oregon	H	13.21 FQ	18.00 MW	23.01 TQ	ORBLS	5/08
	Portland-Vancouver-Beaverton MSA, OR-WA	Y	25860 FQ	35860 MW	46780 TQ	USBLS	5/07
	Pennsylvania	Y	24980 FQ	32680 MW	41710 TQ	USBLS	5/07
	Allentown-Bethlehem-Easton MSA, PA-NJ	Y	26080 FQ	34990 MW	43160 TQ	USBLS	5/07
	Erie MSA, PA	Y	24740 FQ	31570 MW	43890 TQ	USBLS	5/07
	Philadelphia-Camden-Wilmington MSA, PA-NJ-DE-MD	Y	28890 FQ	37650 MW	47020 TQ	USBLS	5/07
	Pittsburgh MSA, PA	Y	24590 FQ	31510 MW	40530 TQ	USBLS	5/07
	Rhode Island	Y	30120 FQ	37260 MW	45650 TQ	USBLS	5/07
	Providence-Fall River-Warwick MSA, RI-MA	Y	28810 FQ	35470 MW	44490 TQ	USBLS	5/07
	South Carolina	Y	22340 FQ	29980 MW	40060 TQ	USBLS	5/07
	Charleston-North Charleston MSA, SC	Y	22620 FQ	32780 MW	42170 TQ	USBLS	5/07
	Columbia MSA, SC	Y	26100 FQ	33460 MW	40780 TQ	USBLS	5/07
	South Dakota	Y	27126 FQ	32004 MW	38773 TQ	SDBLS	7/08-9/08
	Sioux Falls MSA, SD	Y	27111 FQ	32968 MW	40961 TQ	SDBLS	7/08-9/08
	Tennessee	Y	20410 FQ	29910 MW	40810 TQ	USBLS	5/07
	Clarksville MSA, TN-KY	Y	17950 FQ	23900 MW	33410 TQ	USBLS	5/07
	Memphis MSA, TN-MS-AR	Y	23970 FQ	33900 MW	47310 TQ	USBLS	5/07
	Nashville-Davidson-Murfreesboro MSA, TN	Y	22320 FQ	33570 MW	43260 TQ	USBLS	5/07
	Texas	Y	24310 FQ	33040 MW	43890 TQ	USBLS	5/07
	Austin-Round Rock MSA, TX	Y	30620 FQ	39350 MW	48880 TQ	USBLS	5/07
	Dallas-Fort Worth-Arlington MSA, TX	Y	25110 FQ	34040 MW	45180 TQ	USBLS	5/07
	El Paso MSA, TX	Y	21720 FQ	27060 MW	35300 TQ	USBLS	5/07
	Houston-Sugar Land-Baytown MSA, TX	Y	26170 FQ	36460 MW	46720 TQ	USBLS	5/07
	San Antonio MSA, TX	Y	26860 FQ	34410 MW	42330 TQ	USBLS	5/07
	Utah	Y	25900 FQ	34860 MW	46170 TQ	USBLS	5/07
	Logan MSA, UT-ID	Y	22450 FQ	30950 MW	38830 TQ	USBLS	5/07
	Ogden-Clearfield MSA, UT	Y	23670 FQ	37260 MW	48330 TQ	USBLS	5/07
	Salt Lake City MSA, UT	Y	27160 FQ	36640 MW	50370 TQ	USBLS	5/07

AE	Average entry wage	AW	Average wage paid	FQ	First quartile wage	LO	Lowest wage paid	MTC	Median total compensation	TCC	Total cash compensation
AER	Average entry range	AWR	Average wage range	H	Hourly	LR	Low end range	MW	Median wage paid	TQ	Third quartile wage
AEX	Average experienced wage	AXR	Average experienced range	HI	Highest wage paid	M	Monthly	MWR	Median wage range	W	Weekly
ATC	Average total compensation	D	Daily	HR	High end range	MCC	Median cash compensation	S	See annotated source	Y	Yearly

Occupation/Type/Industry	Location	Per	Low	Mid	High	Source	Date
Automotive Service Technician and Mechanic	Vermont	Y	24400 FQ	31530 MW	39100 TQ	USBLS	5/07
	Burlington-South Burlington MSA, VT	Y	26410 FQ	34170 MW	41940 TQ	USBLS	5/07
	Virginia	Y	26980 FQ	35430 MW	47090 TQ	USBLS	5/07
	Richmond MSA, VA	Y	29480 FQ	36710 MW	46550 TQ	USBLS	5/07
	Virginia Beach-Norfolk-Newport News MSA, VA-NC	Y	26680 FQ	33490 MW	44610 TQ	USBLS	5/07
	Washington	H	14.75 FQ	19.31 MW	24.18 TQ	WABLS	3/08
	Bremerton-Silverdale MSA, WA	Y	32640 FQ	43570 MW	51190 TQ	USBLS	5/07
	Olympia MSA, WA	Y	35370 FQ	43000 MW	49900 TQ	USBLS	5/07
	Seattle-Tacoma-Bellevue MSA, WA	Y	33940 FQ	43830 MW	53470 TQ	USBLS	5/07
	West Virginia	Y	19514 FQ	25443 MW	33831 TQ	WVBLS	7/08-9/08
	Charleston MSA, WV	Y	20320 FQ	25400 MW	35890 TQ	WVBLS	5/07
	Wisconsin	Y	25930 FQ	34330 MW	43540 TQ	USBLS	5/07
	Milwaukee-Waukesha-West Allis MSA, WI	Y	26250 FQ	38590 MW	47360 TQ	USBLS	5/07
	Wyoming	Y	26621 FQ	32926 MW	42526 TQ	WYBLS	9/08
	Cheyenne MSA, WY	Y	24903 FQ	29247 MW	34607 TQ	WYBLS	9/08
	Puerto Rico	Y	13760 FQ	17100 MW	22210 TQ	USBLS	5/07
	Aguadilla-Isabela-San Sebastian MSA, PR	Y	12600 FQ	14040 MW	15990 TQ	USBLS	5/07
	San German-Cabo Rojo MSA, PR	Y	12230 FQ	13360 MW	14480 TQ	USBLS	5/07
	San Juan-Caguas-Guaynabo MSA, PR	Y	14010 FQ	17920 MW	22910 TQ	USBLS	5/07
	Virgin Islands	Y	25310 FQ	27910 MW	30860 TQ	USBLS	5/07
	Guam	Y	21010 FQ	27160 MW	31530 TQ	USBLS	5/07
Automotive Street Cleaning Equipment Operator Municipal Government	Cincinnati, OH	Y	39917 LO		43264 HI	COHSS	10/08
Automotive Tire Repair Worker State Government	Ohio	H	14.36 LO		15.41 HI	ODAS	2008
Automotive Upholsterer Municipal Government	Cincinnati, OH	Y	41597 LO		44936 HI	COHSS	10/08
Autoworker Chrysler LLC	United States	H		30.00 AW		CHITRI	2008
General Motors Corp., New Hire	United States	H		14.00-16.23 HR		CNNM	2008
General Motors Corp., United Auto Workers	United States	H		29.78 AW		SFCHN	2008
Honda Motor Corp.	United States	H		27.62 AW		CHITRI	2008
Toyota Motor Corp.	United States	H		30.00 AW		CHITRI	2008
Aviation Director	Colorado Springs, CO	M	10313 LO			COSPRS	1/1/09
Aviation Installer	United States	H		19.50 AW		AVJOB06	2009
Aviation Specialist Department of Transportation	Michigan	H	20.20 LO		30.90 HI	MDOT	10/1/07
Avionics Technician	Alabama	Y	32660 FQ	36640 MW	41830 TQ	USBLS	5/07
	Birmingham-Hoover MSA, AL	Y	30520 FQ	43730 MW	48460 TQ	USBLS	5/07
	Alaska	Y	41780 FQ	58790 MW	69480 TQ	USBLS	5/07
	Anchorage MSA, AK	Y	45570 FQ	59410 MW	69770 TQ	USBLS	5/07
	Arizona	Y	35130 FQ	43360 MW	50780 TQ	USBLS	5/07
	Phoenix-Mesa-Scottsdale MSA, AZ	Y	35410 FQ	43910 MW	51310 TQ	USBLS	5/07
	Tucson MSA, AZ	Y	40270 FQ	45210 MW	51650 TQ	USBLS	5/07
	Arkansas	Y	35120 FQ	42880 MW	49770 TQ	USBLS	5/07
	Little Rock-North Little Rock MSA, AR	Y	36820 FQ	44060 MW	50550 TQ	USBLS	5/07
	California	H	21.75 FQ	25.59 MW	28.52 TQ	CABLS	1/08-3/08
	Los Angeles-Long Beach-Glendale PMSA, CA	H	21.71 FQ	25.33 MW	28.12 TQ	CABLS	1/08-3/08

AE Average entry wage	**AW** Average wage paid	**FQ** First quartile wage	**LO** Lowest wage paid	**MTC** Median total compensation	**TCC** Total cash compensation
AER Average entry range	**AWR** Average wage range	**H** Hourly	**LR** Low end range	**MW** Median wage paid	**TQ** Third quartile wage
AEX Average experienced wage	**AXR** Average experienced range	**HI** Highest wage paid	**M** Monthly	**MWR** Median wage range	**W** Weekly
ATC Average total compensation	**D** Daily	**HR** High end range	**MCC** Median cash compensation	**S** See annotated source	**Y** Yearly

Occupation/Type/Industry	Location	Per	Low	Mid	High	Source	Date
Avionics Technician	Oakland-Fremont-Hayward MSA, CA	H	17.01 FQ	18.41 MW	24.62 TQ	CABLS	1/08-3/08
	Riverside-San Bernardino-Ontario MSA, CA	H	20.32 FQ	22.64 MW	28.36 TQ	CABLS	1/08-3/08
	Sacramento-Arden Arcade-Roseville MSA, CA	H	21.82 FQ	25.60 MW	29.02 TQ	CABLS	1/08-3/08
	San Diego-Carlsbad-San Marcos MSA, CA	H	21.95 FQ	25.62 MW	28.93 TQ	CABLS	1/08-3/08
	Santa Ana-Anaheim-Irvine PMSA, CA	Y	47880 FQ	53600 MW	58730 TQ	USBLS	5/07
	Colorado	Y	44250 FQ	52980 MW	58880 TQ	USBLS	5/07
	Denver-Aurora MSA, CO	Y	47870 FQ	54470 MW	59380 TQ	USBLS	5/07
	Connecticut	H	21.05 AE	25.61 MW		CTBLS	1/08-3/08
	Hartford-West Hartford-East Hartford MSA, CT	Y	45380 FQ	50190 MW	69160 TQ	USBLS	5/07
	Delaware	Y	35820 FQ	44200 MW	53040 TQ	USBLS	5/07
	Washington-Arlington-Alexandria MSA, DC-VA-MD-WV	Y	43920 FQ	49250 MW	57680 TQ	USBLS	5/07
	Florida	Y	38560 FQ	44930 MW	51370 TQ	USBLS	5/07
	Fort Lauderdale-Pompano Beach-Deerfield Beach PMSA, FL	Y	42590 FQ	49230 MW	64730 TQ	USBLS	5/07
	Miami-Fort Lauderdale-Miami Beach MSA, FL	Y	38050 FQ	45750 MW	57420 TQ	USBLS	5/07
	Orlando-Kissimmee MSA, FL	Y	41970 FQ	48720 MW	58410 TQ	USBLS	5/07
	Georgia	Y	42560 FQ	47150 MW	53220 TQ	USBLS	5/07
	Hawaii	Y	52730 FQ	58830 MW	66680 TQ	USBLS	5/07
	Honolulu MSA, HI	Y	53360 FQ	59310 MW	67660 TQ	USBLS	5/07
	Idaho	Y	19800 FQ	31480 MW	40770 TQ	USBLS	5/07
	Illinois	Y	35060 FQ	48120 MW	56460 TQ	USBLS	5/07
	Chicago-Naperville-Joliet MSA, IL-IN-WI	Y	41880 FQ	52890 MW	57750 TQ	USBLS	5/07
	Indiana	Y	51220 FQ	56360 MW	61080 TQ	USBLS	5/07
	Indianapolis-Carmel MSA, IN	Y	51980 FQ	56700 MW	61300 TQ	USBLS	5/07
	Iowa	Y	22800 FQ	40630 MW	48330 TQ	USBLS	5/07
	Kansas	Y	43170 FQ	49940 MW	55860 TQ	USBLS	5/07
	Wichita MSA, KS	Y	43410 FQ	50170 MW	55990 TQ	USBLS	5/07
	Kentucky	Y	44284 FQ	49025 MW	55066 TQ	KYBLS	2008
	Louisiana	H	16.26 FQ	21.11 MW	25.04 TQ	LABLS	1/08-3/08
	New Orleans-Metairie-Kenner MSA, LA	Y	39660 FQ	45280 MW	51870 TQ	USBLS	5/07
	Maryland	Y		50825 MW		MDBLS	3/08
	Baltimore-Towson MSA, MD	Y	44880 FQ	50670 MW	56280 TQ	USBLS	5/07
	Massachusetts	Y	41700 FQ	56450 MW	65090 TQ	USBLS	5/07
	Michigan	Y	38700 FQ	47560 MW	57200 TQ	USBLS	5/07
	Detroit-Warren-Livonia MSA, MI	Y	39210 FQ	48880 MW	58290 TQ	USBLS	5/07
	Warren-Troy-Farmington Hills PMSA, MI	Y	36710 FQ	45840 MW	54850 TQ	USBLS	5/07
	Minnesota	Y	46132 FQ	55352 MW	63912 TQ	MNBLS	10/08-12/08
	Minneapolis-Saint Paul MSA, MN-WI	Y	45576 FQ	53517 MW	63870 TQ	MNBLS	10/08-12/08
	Mississippi	Y	44050 FQ	49280 MW	57630 TQ	USBLS	5/07
	St. Louis MSA, MO-IL	Y	34310 FQ	47660 MW	59330 TQ	USBLS	5/07
	Montana	Y	35340 FQ	42050 MW	47750 TQ	USBLS	5/07
	Nebraska	Y	42530 FQ	56120 MW	62130 TQ	USBLS	5/07
	Omaha-Council Bluffs MSA, NE-IA	Y	53920 FQ	58600 MW	63270 TQ	USBLS	5/07
	Nevada	H	18.09 FQ	20.03 MW	27.87 TQ	NVBLS	5/08
	Las Vegas-Paradise MSA, NV	H	17.31 FQ	18.59 MW	19.87 TQ	NVBLS	5/08
	New Hampshire	H	17.81 AE	22.20 MW	25.31 AEX	NHBLS	6/08
	Nashua NECTA, NH-MA	Y	37060 FQ	43650 MW	49400 TQ	USBLS	5/07
	New Jersey	Y	46620 FQ	55100 MW	62290 TQ	USBLS	5/07
	Newark-Union PMSA, NJ-PA	Y	41140 FQ	47100 MW	53710 TQ	USBLS	5/07
	New Mexico	Y	38150 FQ	42950 MW	51010 TQ	USBLS	5/07
	Albuquerque MSA, NM	Y	37500 FQ	41480 MW	52160 TQ	USBLS	5/07
	New York	Y	41100 FQ	47940 MW	55540 TQ	USBLS	5/07
	Nassau-Suffolk PMSA, NY	Y	38390 FQ	44730 MW	50190 TQ	USBLS	5/07
	New York-Northern New Jersey-Long Island MSA, NY-NJ-PA	Y	41490 FQ	48540 MW	57310 TQ	USBLS	5/07

AE	Average entry wage	**AW**	Average wage paid	**FQ**	First quartile wage
AER	Average entry range	**AWR**	Average wage range	**H**	Hourly
AEX	Average experienced wage	**AXR**	Average experienced range	**HI**	Highest wage paid
ATC	Average total compensation	**D**	Daily	**HR**	High end range

LO	Lowest wage paid	**MTC**	Median total compensation	**TCC**	Total cash compensation
LR	Low end range	**MW**	Median wage paid	**TQ**	Third quartile wage
M	Monthly	**MWR**	Median wage range	**W**	Weekly
MCC	Median cash compensation	**S**	See annotated source	**Y**	Yearly

Occupation/Type/Industry	Location	Per	Low	Mid	High	Source	Date
Avionics Technician	North Carolina	Y	42790 FQ	47720 MW	53950 TQ	USBLS	5/07
	Ohio	Y	46210 FQ	56550 MW	63730 TQ	USBLS	5/07
	Cincinnati-Middletown MSA, OH-KY-IN	Y	45640 FQ	51620 MW	57840 TQ	USBLS	5/07
	Cleveland-Elyria-Mentor MSA, OH	Y	39680 FQ	51800 MW	60720 TQ	USBLS	5/07
	Columbus MSA, OH	Y	52820 FQ	57010 MW	61290 TQ	USBLS	5/07
	Dayton MSA, OH	Y	33730 FQ	37250 MW	42260 TQ	USBLS	5/07
	Oklahoma	Y	47590 FQ	54860 MW	60140 TQ	USBLS	5/07
	Oklahoma City MSA, OK	Y	42700 FQ	46080 MW	49560 TQ	USBLS	5/07
	Oregon	H	18.35 FQ	22.25 MW	26.94 TQ	ORBLS	5/08
	Portland-Vancouver-Beaverton MSA, OR-WA	Y	39460 FQ	46500 MW	55730 TQ	USBLS	5/07
	Pennsylvania	Y	42030 FQ	49890 MW	62230 TQ	USBLS	5/07
	Philadelphia-Camden-Wilmington MSA, PA-NJ-DE-MD	Y	46040 FQ	58010 MW	66340 TQ	USBLS	5/07
	Pittsburgh MSA, PA	Y	42250 FQ	46510 MW	54220 TQ	USBLS	5/07
	South Carolina	Y	41360 FQ	44820 MW	49000 TQ	USBLS	5/07
	South Dakota	Y	29549 FQ	36343 MW	40941 TQ	SDBLS	7/08-9/08
	Sioux Falls MSA, SD	Y	29549 FQ	36343 MW	40941 TQ	SDBLS	7/08-9/08
	Texas	Y	38850 FQ	47130 MW	56770 TQ	USBLS	5/07
	Corpus Christi MSA, TX	Y	46880 FQ	52950 MW	58400 TQ	USBLS	5/07
	Dallas-Fort Worth-Arlington MSA, TX	Y	38180 FQ	48070 MW	57870 TQ	USBLS	5/07
	Houston-Sugar Land-Baytown MSA, TX	Y	36460 FQ	52190 MW	61400 TQ	USBLS	5/07
	Utah	Y	43310 FQ	48360 MW	55380 TQ	USBLS	5/07
	Salt Lake City MSA, UT	Y	30990 FQ	44460 MW	55370 TQ	USBLS	5/07
	Virginia	Y	35090 FQ	41210 MW	49380 TQ	USBLS	5/07
	Virginia Beach-Norfolk-Newport News MSA, VA-NC	Y	33420 FQ	35860 MW	39840 TQ	USBLS	5/07
	Washington	H	17.84 FQ	20.84 MW	24.88 TQ	WABLS	3/08
	Seattle-Tacoma-Bellevue MSA, WA	Y	38080 FQ	44070 MW	53420 TQ	USBLS	5/07
	West Virginia	Y	42047 FQ	46667 MW	51287 TQ	WVBLS	7/08-9/08
	Wisconsin	Y	35410 FQ	41130 MW	47210 TQ	USBLS	5/07
	Milwaukee-Waukesha-West Allis MSA, WI	Y	36900 FQ	44940 MW	54400 TQ	USBLS	5/07
	Wyoming	Y	30329 FQ	42592 MW	50396 TQ	WYBLS	9/08
Background Painter	United States	W		1800 MW		TAG	1/08
Baggage Porter and Bellhop	Alabama	Y	12670 FQ	14150 MW	15890 TQ	USBLS	5/07
	Alaska	Y	16360 FQ	19480 MW	25540 TQ	USBLS	5/07
	Anchorage MSA, AK	Y	16360 FQ	20590 MW	29300 TQ	USBLS	5/07
	Arizona	Y	15060 FQ	16380 MW	19160 TQ	USBLS	5/07
	Phoenix-Mesa-Scottsdale MSA, AZ	Y	15100 FQ	16460 MW	18870 TQ	USBLS	5/07
	Tucson MSA, AZ	Y	14820 FQ	15700 MW	19380 TQ	USBLS	5/07
	Arkansas	Y	15380 FQ	17070 MW	19020 TQ	USBLS	5/07
	Little Rock-North Little Rock MSA, AR	Y	14850 FQ	16370 MW	18730 TQ	USBLS	5/07
	California	H	8.47 FQ	9.72 MW	12.80 TQ	CABLS	1/08-3/08
	Los Angeles-Long Beach-Glendale PMSA, CA	H	8.40 FQ	9.71 MW	11.70 TQ	CABLS	1/08-3/08
	Oakland-Fremont-Hayward MSA, CA	H	8.94 FQ	17.32 MW	28.02 TQ	CABLS	1/08-3/08
	Riverside-San Bernardino-Ontario MSA, CA	H	8.44 FQ	9.49 MW	17.49 TQ	CABLS	1/08-3/08
	Sacramento-Arden Arcade-Roseville MSA, CA	H	8.10 FQ	9.17 MW	11.06 TQ	CABLS	1/08-3/08
	San Diego-Carlsbad-San Marcos MSA, CA	H	8.30 FQ	9.17 MW	11.52 TQ	CABLS	1/08-3/08
	San Francisco-San Mateo-Redwood PMSA, CA	H	10.24 FQ	12.22 MW	16.54 TQ	CABLS	1/08-3/08
	San Jose-Sunnyvale-Santa Clara MSA, CA	H	8.47 FQ	9.36 MW	11.29 TQ	CABLS	1/08-3/08
	Santa Ana-Anaheim-Irvine PMSA, CA	Y	16150 FQ	17530 MW	19100 TQ	USBLS	5/07
	Colorado	Y	15540 FQ	19600 MW	23300 TQ	USBLS	5/07
	Denver-Aurora MSA, CO	Y	15770 FQ	20820 MW	23660 TQ	USBLS	5/07

Occupation/Type/Industry	Location	Per	Low	Mid	High	Source	Date
Baggage Porter and Bellhop	Connecticut	H	8.14 AE	10.04 MW		CTBLS	1/08-3/08
	Hartford-West Hartford-East Hartford MSA, CT	Y	20260 FQ	22410 MW	24840 TQ	USBLS	5/07
	Norwich-New London MSA, CT-RI	Y	15940 FQ	16060 MW	22420 TQ	USBLS	5/07
	Delaware	Y	15380 FQ	17180 MW	21090 TQ	USBLS	5/07
	District of Columbia	Y	16780 FQ	19520 MW	26770 TQ	USBLS	5/07
	Washington-Arlington-Alexandria MSA, DC-VA-MD-WV	Y	18710 FQ	21990 MW	28150 TQ	USBLS	5/07
	Florida	Y	14740 FQ	15770 MW	21040 TQ	USBLS	5/07
	Cape Coral-Fort Myers MSA, FL	Y	14540 FQ	15300 MW	17000 TQ	USBLS	5/07
	Fort Lauderdale-Pompano Beach-Deerfield Beach PMSA, FL	Y	15250 FQ	17600 MW	21750 TQ	USBLS	5/07
	Jacksonville MSA, FL	Y	14870 FQ	16850 MW	20770 TQ	USBLS	5/07
	Miami-Fort Lauderdale-Miami Beach MSA, FL	Y	14890 FQ	16320 MW	22390 TQ	USBLS	5/07
	Orlando-Kissimmee MSA, FL	Y	14650 FQ	15460 MW	18380 TQ	USBLS	5/07
	Tampa-St. Petersburg-Clearwater MSA, FL	Y	14750 FQ	16350 MW	31270 TQ	USBLS	5/07
	West Palm Beach-Boca Raton-Boynton Beach PMSA, FL	Y	14800 FQ	16020 MW	23760 TQ	USBLS	5/07
	Georgia	Y	12990 FQ	14800 MW	20000 TQ	USBLS	5/07
	Atlanta-Sandy Springs-Marietta MSA, GA	Y	13110 FQ	15050 MW	22680 TQ	USBLS	5/07
	Savannah MSA, GA	Y	14700 FQ	17330 MW	19150 TQ	USBLS	5/07
	Hawaii	Y	15740 FQ	18070 MW	23670 TQ	USBLS	5/07
	Honolulu MSA, HI	Y	15640 FQ	17650 MW	26600 TQ	USBLS	5/07
	Idaho	Y	15100 FQ	16930 MW	18770 TQ	USBLS	5/07
	Illinois	Y	16130 FQ	18210 MW	24110 TQ	USBLS	5/07
	Chicago-Naperville-Joliet MSA, IL-IN-WI	Y	16190 FQ	18250 MW	24130 TQ	USBLS	5/07
	Indiana	Y	14960 FQ	17920 MW	21920 TQ	USBLS	5/07
	Gary PMSA, IN	Y	15430 FQ	20890 MW	23390 TQ	USBLS	5/07
	Indianapolis-Carmel MSA, IN	Y	14790 FQ	18100 MW	23140 TQ	USBLS	5/07
	Iowa	Y	14390 FQ	16280 MW	18550 TQ	USBLS	5/07
	Des Moines-West Des Moines MSA, IA	Y	14110 FQ	15380 MW	18280 TQ	USBLS	5/07
	Kentucky	Y	14132 FQ	17547 MW	24011 TQ	KYBLS	2008
	Louisville-Jefferson County MSA, KY-IN	Y	15350 FQ	18860 MW	24550 TQ	USBLS	5/07
	Louisiana	H	6.57 FQ	7.88 MW	9.49 TQ	LABLS	1/08-3/08
	Baton Rouge MSA, LA	Y	13300 FQ	15630 MW	19730 TQ	USBLS	5/07
	New Orleans-Metairie-Kenner MSA, LA	Y	14410 FQ	17510 MW	22500 TQ	USBLS	5/07
	Maine	Y	17230 FQ	19820 MW	23320 TQ	USBLS	5/07
	Portland-South Portland-Biddeford MSA, ME	Y	17340 FQ	20260 MW	23820 TQ	USBLS	5/07
	Maryland	Y		31925 MW		MDBLS	3/08
	Baltimore-Towson MSA, MD	Y	16380 FQ	31760 MW	35560 TQ	USBLS	5/07
	Bethesda-Gaithersburg-Frederick PMSA, MD	Y	18660 FQ	27990 MW	35240 TQ	USBLS	5/07
	Massachusetts	Y	17470 FQ	21720 MW	33150 TQ	USBLS	5/07
	Boston-Cambridge-Quincy NECTA, MA	Y	17080 FQ	20670 MW	32850 TQ	USBLS	5/07
	Michigan	Y	17580 FQ	34250 MW	38000 TQ	USBLS	5/07
	Warren-Troy-Farmington Hills PMSA, MI	Y	15620 FQ	18690 MW	24290 TQ	USBLS	5/07
	Mississippi	Y	13370 FQ	15480 MW	18440 TQ	USBLS	5/07
	Jackson MSA, MS	Y	12460 FQ	13820 MW	15190 TQ	USBLS	5/07
	Missouri	Y	14950 FQ	19160 MW	31300 TQ	USBLS	5/07
	Kansas City MSA, MO-KS	Y	14810 FQ	20430 MW	39750 TQ	USBLS	5/07
	St. Louis MSA, MO-IL	Y	15260 FQ	19430 MW	30420 TQ	USBLS	5/07
	Springfield MSA, MO	Y	14800 FQ	16860 MW	27290 TQ	USBLS	5/07
	Montana	Y	14170 FQ	15540 MW	20120 TQ	USBLS	5/07
	Nebraska	Y	14040 FQ	16180 MW	18710 TQ	USBLS	5/07
	Omaha-Council Bluffs MSA, NE-IA	Y	13400 FQ	15230 MW	18250 TQ	USBLS	5/07
	Las Vegas-Paradise MSA, NV	H	9.02 FQ	10.75 MW	12.32 TQ	NVBLS	5/08
	Reno-Sparks MSA, NV	H	6.45 FQ	7.35 MW	9.52 TQ	NVBLS	5/08

AE	Average entry wage	AW	Average wage paid	FQ	First quartile wage
AER	Average entry range	AWR	Average wage range	H	Hourly
AEX	Average experienced wage	AXR	Average experienced range	HI	Highest wage paid
ATC	Average total compensation	D	Daily	HR	High end range

LO	Lowest wage paid	MTC	Median total compensation	TCC	Total cash compensation
LR	Low end range	MW	Median wage paid	TQ	Third quartile wage
M	Monthly	MWR	Median wage range	W	Weekly
MCC	Median cash compensation	S	See annotated source	Y	Yearly

Baggage Porter and Bellhop

Occupation/Type/Industry	Location	Per	Low	Mid	High	Source	Date
Baggage Porter and Bellhop	New Hampshire	H	7.94 AE	10.63 MW	12.57 AEX	NHBLS	6/08
	New Jersey	Y	15390 FQ	17400 MW	21530 TQ	USBLS	5/07
	Edison PMSA, NJ	Y	16040 FQ	18570 MW	22730 TQ	USBLS	5/07
	Newark-Union PMSA, NJ-PA	Y	15170 FQ	15430 MW	17620 TQ	USBLS	5/07
	New Mexico	Y	13020 FQ	15040 MW	18880 TQ	USBLS	5/07
	Albuquerque MSA, NM	Y	12730 FQ	14530 MW	16740 TQ	USBLS	5/07
	New York	Y	19400 FQ	26180 MW	34710 TQ	USBLS	5/07
	Albany-Schenectady-Troy MSA, NY	Y	21960 FQ	30730 MW	34440 TQ	USBLS	5/07
	Buffalo-Niagara Falls MSA, NY	Y	16450 FQ	20410 MW	34010 TQ	USBLS	5/07
	Nassau-Suffolk PMSA, NY	Y	17160 FQ	21120 MW	25280 TQ	USBLS	5/07
	New York-Northern New Jersey-Long Island MSA, NY-NJ-PA	Y	18050 FQ	25020 MW	33390 TQ	USBLS	5/07
	North Carolina	Y	18520 FQ	30840 MW	34770 TQ	USBLS	5/07
	Raleigh-Cary MSA, NC	Y	19650 FQ	30410 MW	37320 TQ	USBLS	5/07
	North Dakota	Y	13010 FQ	14790 MW	17860 TQ	USBLS	5/07
	Ohio	Y	15090 FQ	18910 MW	25780 TQ	USBLS	5/07
	Cincinnati-Middletown MSA, OH-KY-IN	Y	14740 FQ	15950 MW	18490 TQ	USBLS	5/07
	Cleveland-Elyria-Mentor MSA, OH	Y	14780 FQ	15360 MW	19510 TQ	USBLS	5/07
	Columbus MSA, OH	Y	20090 FQ	25340 MW	33570 TQ	USBLS	5/07
	Dayton MSA, OH	Y	14880 FQ	16870 MW	22940 TQ	USBLS	5/07
	Oklahoma	Y	12830 FQ	14430 MW	16360 TQ	USBLS	5/07
	Oklahoma City MSA, OK	Y	14620 FQ	17640 MW	26270 TQ	USBLS	5/07
	Tulsa MSA, OK	Y	12940 FQ	14570 MW	19180 TQ	USBLS	5/07
	Oregon	H	8.62 FQ	9.37 MW	11.29 TQ	ORBLS	5/08
	Portland-Vancouver-Beaverton MSA, OR-WA	Y	17270 FQ	18590 MW	20710 TQ	USBLS	5/07
	Pennsylvania	Y	14940 FQ	18660 MW	29810 TQ	USBLS	5/07
	Allentown-Bethlehem-Easton MSA, PA-NJ	Y	16150 FQ	17920 MW	19550 TQ	USBLS	5/07
	Philadelphia-Camden-Wilmington MSA, PA-NJ-DE-MD	Y	14540 FQ	16730 MW	23090 TQ	USBLS	5/07
	Pittsburgh MSA, PA	Y	15720 FQ	28370 MW	33900 TQ	USBLS	5/07
	Rhode Island	Y	17010 FQ	18280 MW	19550 TQ	USBLS	5/07
	Providence-Fall River-Warwick MSA, RI-MA	Y	17010 FQ	18280 MW	19550 TQ	USBLS	5/07
	South Carolina	Y	13670 FQ	16150 MW	19990 TQ	USBLS	5/07
	Charleston-North Charleston MSA, SC	Y	13750 FQ	16780 MW	23410 TQ	USBLS	5/07
	South Dakota	Y	17123 FQ	19717 MW	23193 TQ	SDBLS	7/08-9/08
	Sioux Falls MSA, SD	Y	18618 FQ	21158 MW	24268 TQ	SDBLS	7/08-9/08
	Tennessee	Y	14720 FQ	20230 MW	34780 TQ	USBLS	5/07
	Memphis MSA, TN-MS-AR	Y	16860 FQ	27450 MW	35830 TQ	USBLS	5/07
	Nashville-Davidson-Murfreesboro MSA, TN	Y	12830 FQ	14790 MW	18790 TQ	USBLS	5/07
	Texas	Y	13070 FQ	14930 MW	18620 TQ	USBLS	5/07
	Austin-Round Rock MSA, TX	Y	12690 FQ	14130 MW	16040 TQ	USBLS	5/07
	Dallas-Fort Worth-Arlington MSA, TX	Y	13130 FQ	15080 MW	18800 TQ	USBLS	5/07
	Houston-Sugar Land-Baytown MSA, TX	Y	13340 FQ	15580 MW	19680 TQ	USBLS	5/07
	San Antonio MSA, TX	Y	13320 FQ	15840 MW	19910 TQ	USBLS	5/07
	Utah	Y	12930 FQ	14530 MW	17060 TQ	USBLS	5/07
	Salt Lake City MSA, UT	Y	12950 FQ	14490 MW	16860 TQ	USBLS	5/07
	Vermont	Y	17140 FQ	18950 MW	21140 TQ	USBLS	5/07
	Virginia	Y	17400 FQ	20680 MW	25080 TQ	USBLS	5/07
	Charlottesville MSA, VA	Y	15800 FQ	17190 MW	18570 TQ	USBLS	5/07
	Richmond MSA, VA	Y	16590 FQ	17930 MW	19320 TQ	USBLS	5/07
	Virginia Beach-Norfolk-Newport News MSA, VA-NC	Y	13630 FQ	16170 MW	18960 TQ	USBLS	5/07
	Washington	H	12.35 FQ	15.10 MW	18.00 TQ	WABLS	3/08
	Seattle-Tacoma-Bellevue MSA, WA	Y	25200 FQ	31770 MW	37420 TQ	USBLS	5/07
	West Virginia	Y	14203 FQ	15468 MW	20578 TQ	WVBLS	7/08-9/08
	Wisconsin	Y	14690 FQ	16510 MW	23390 TQ	USBLS	5/07
	Milwaukee-Waukesha-West Allis MSA, WI	Y	14630 FQ	17850 MW	31800 TQ	USBLS	5/07

AE	Average entry wage	AW	Average wage paid	FQ	First quartile wage	LO	Lowest wage paid	MTC	Median total compensation	TCC	Total cash compensation
AER	Average entry range	AWR	Average wage range	H	Hourly	LR	Low end range	MW	Median wage paid	TQ	Third quartile wage
AEX	Average experienced wage	AXR	Average experienced range	HI	Highest wage paid	M	Monthly	MWR	Median wage range	W	Weekly
ATC	Average total compensation	D	Daily	HR	High end range	MCC	Median cash compensation	S	See annotated source	Y	Yearly

Occupation/Type/Industry	Location	Per	Low	Mid	High	Source	Date
Baggage Porter and Bellhop	Wyoming	Y	15252 FQ	18200 MW	22064 TQ	WYBLS	9/08
	Puerto Rico	Y	12520 FQ	13790 MW	15150 TQ	USBLS	5/07
	San Juan-Caguas-Guaynabo MSA, PR	Y	12540 FQ	13780 MW	15120 TQ	USBLS	5/07
	Virgin Islands	Y	14110 FQ	15630 MW	18130 TQ	USBLS	5/07
	Guam	Y	12490 FQ	13840 MW	15220 TQ	USBLS	5/07
Bailiff	Alabama	Y	23920 FQ	31320 MW	37510 TQ	USBLS	5/07
	Arizona	Y	24630 FQ	31480 MW	40160 TQ	USBLS	5/07
	Arkansas	Y	19390 FQ	27230 MW	35400 TQ	USBLS	5/07
	California	H	21.35 FQ	23.27 MW	25.26 TQ	CABLS	1/08-3/08
	Colorado	Y	27030 FQ	31470 MW	48790 TQ	USBLS	5/07
	Florida	Y	35700 FQ	42150 MW	52620 TQ	USBLS	5/07
	Georgia	Y	14090 FQ	18080 MW	22600 TQ	USBLS	5/07
	Idaho	Y	27610 FQ	31770 MW	41020 TQ	USBLS	5/07
	Indiana	Y	26050 FQ	28980 MW	32260 TQ	USBLS	5/07
	Kansas	Y	24110 FQ	35840 MW	46300 TQ	USBLS	5/07
	Kentucky	Y	17743 FQ	21471 MW	25912 TQ	KYBLS	2008
	Louisiana	H	10.15 FQ	12.65 MW	15.54 TQ	LABLS	1/08-3/08
	Maine	Y	25900 FQ	28350 MW	30770 TQ	USBLS	5/07
	Maryland	Y		36125 MW		MDBLS	3/08
	Massachusetts	Y	41560 FQ	51230 MW	71600 TQ	USBLS	5/07
	Michigan	Y	29370 FQ	32600 MW	40300 TQ	USBLS	5/07
	Minnesota	Y	25909 FQ	31262 MW	38561 TQ	MNBLS	10/08-12/08
	Mississippi	Y	16290 FQ	19870 MW	23890 TQ	USBLS	5/07
	Missouri	Y	23250 FQ	27640 MW	31810 TQ	USBLS	5/07
	Montana	Y	14940 FQ	21690 MW	25260 TQ	USBLS	5/07
	Nebraska	Y	30610 FQ	44070 MW	49070 TQ	USBLS	5/07
	Nevada	H	17.71 FQ	23.28 MW	28.50 TQ	NVBLS	5/08
	New Hampshire	H	9.18 AE	13.48 MW	17.36 AEX	NHBLS	6/08
	New Jersey	Y	25940 FQ	30590 MW	36940 TQ	USBLS	5/07
	New Mexico	Y	22970 FQ	25390 MW	29280 TQ	USBLS	5/07
	New York	Y	39710 FQ	54010 MW	60070 TQ	USBLS	5/07
	North Carolina	Y	26690 FQ	30730 MW	35910 TQ	USBLS	5/07
	Ohio	Y	28370 FQ	35420 MW	45570 TQ	USBLS	5/07
	Oklahoma	Y	26510 FQ	28640 MW	30770 TQ	USBLS	5/07
	Oregon	H	15.81 FQ	18.63 MW	21.02 TQ	ORBLS	5/08
	Pennsylvania	Y	30850 FQ	40640 MW	48370 TQ	USBLS	5/07
	South Carolina	Y	15620 FQ	22230 MW	25890 TQ	USBLS	5/07
	South Dakota	Y	17815 FQ	18999 MW	20183 TQ	SDBLS	7/08-9/08
	Tennessee	Y	19030 FQ	25310 MW	32400 TQ	USBLS	5/07
	Texas	Y	26350 FQ	33050 MW	42480 TQ	USBLS	5/07
	Utah	Y	31560 FQ	35550 MW	39800 TQ	USBLS	5/07
	Virginia	Y	28630 FQ	33300 MW	39820 TQ	USBLS	5/07
	Washington	H	15.92 FQ	20.77 MW	23.62 TQ	WABLS	3/08
	West Virginia	Y	23161 FQ	25726 MW	32909 TQ	WVBLS	7/08-9/08
	Wisconsin	Y	18760 FQ	22570 MW	29170 TQ	USBLS	5/07
	Wyoming	Y	20743 FQ	32243 MW	43726 TQ	WYBLS	9/08
	Puerto Rico	Y	23220 FQ	27500 MW	30410 TQ	USBLS	5/07
Baker	Alabama	Y	15000 FQ	20330 MW	27440 TQ	USBLS	5/07
	Birmingham-Hoover MSA, AL	Y	17190 FQ	23040 MW	28250 TQ	USBLS	5/07
	Alaska	Y	25880 FQ	31830 MW	40350 TQ	USBLS	5/07
	Anchorage MSA, AK	Y	27490 FQ	35710 MW	42060 TQ	USBLS	5/07
	Arizona	Y	17740 FQ	22460 MW	28120 TQ	USBLS	5/07
	Phoenix-Mesa-Scottsdale MSA, AZ	Y	17810 FQ	22280 MW	27960 TQ	USBLS	5/07
	Tucson MSA, AZ	Y	18250 FQ	24420 MW	29430 TQ	USBLS	5/07
	Arkansas	Y	15340 FQ	17530 MW	19890 TQ	USBLS	5/07
	Little Rock-North Little Rock MSA, AR	Y	14390 FQ	15920 MW	18650 TQ	USBLS	5/07
	California	H	9.28 FQ	11.65 MW	15.60 TQ	CABLS	1/08-3/08
	Los Angeles-Long Beach-Glendale PMSA, CA	H	8.90 FQ	11.18 MW	16.13 TQ	CABLS	1/08-3/08
	Oakland-Fremont-Hayward MSA, CA	H	11.27 FQ	13.86 MW	16.83 TQ	CABLS	1/08-3/08
	Riverside-San Bernardino-Ontario MSA, CA	H	8.66 FQ	10.09 MW	13.54 TQ	CABLS	1/08-3/08
	Sacramento-Arden Arcade-Roseville MSA, CA	H	12.09 FQ	14.49 MW	19.95 TQ	CABLS	1/08-3/08
	San Diego-Carlsbad-San Marcos MSA, CA	H	8.99 FQ	11.14 MW	14.72 TQ	CABLS	1/08-3/08

AE	Average entry wage	AW	Average wage paid	FQ	First quartile wage
AER	Average entry range	AWR	Average wage range	H	Hourly
AEX	Average experienced wage	AXR	Average experienced range	HI	Highest wage paid
ATC	Average total compensation	D	Daily	HR	High end range

LO	Lowest wage paid	MTC	Median total compensation
LR	Low end range	MW	Median wage paid
M	Monthly	MWR	Median wage range
MCC	Median cash compensation	S	See annotated source

TCC	Total cash compensation
TQ	Third quartile wage
W	Weekly
Y	Yearly

Occupation/Type/Industry	Location	Per	Low	Mid	High	Source	Date
Baker	San Francisco-San Mateo-Redwood PMSA, CA	H	9.84 FQ	11.81 MW	16.29 TQ	CABLS	1/08-3/08
	San Jose-Sunnyvale-Santa Clara MSA, CA	H	9.66 FQ	12.78 MW	16.69 TQ	CABLS	1/08-3/08
	Santa Ana-Anaheim-Irvine PMSA, CA	Y	18060 FQ	21090 MW	26450 TQ	USBLS	5/07
	Colorado	Y	20610 FQ	26580 MW	34320 TQ	USBLS	5/07
	Denver-Aurora MSA, CO	Y	22150 FQ	28920 MW	36890 TQ	USBLS	5/07
	Connecticut	H	9.06 AE	11.49		CTBLS	1/08-3/08
	Bridgeport-Stamford-Norwalk MSA, CT	Y	19880 FQ	25630 MW	30610 TQ	USBLS	5/07
	Danbury MSA, CT	Y	21170 FQ	25690 MW	30570 TQ	USBLS	5/07
	Hartford-West Hartford-East Hartford MSA, CT	Y	18880 FQ	22600 MW	28590 TQ	USBLS	5/07
	New Haven MSA, CT	Y	21440 FQ	24950 MW	33720 TQ	USBLS	5/07
	Delaware	Y	18200 FQ	21980 MW	27170 TQ	USBLS	5/07
	Wilmington PMSA, DE-MD-NJ	Y	19790 FQ	23540 MW	29080 TQ	USBLS	5/07
	District of Columbia	Y	21960 FQ	26680 MW	32140 TQ	USBLS	5/07
	Washington-Arlington-Alexandria MSA, DC-VA-MD-WV	Y	21690 FQ	26640 MW	33650 TQ	USBLS	5/07
	Florida	Y	17230 FQ	21490 MW	26510 TQ	USBLS	5/07
	Fort Lauderdale-Pompano Beach-Deerfield Beach PMSA, FL	Y	21940 FQ	24780 MW	28420 TQ	USBLS	5/07
	Jacksonville MSA, FL	Y	18500 FQ	22920 MW	30070 TQ	USBLS	5/07
	Miami-Fort Lauderdale-Miami Beach MSA, FL	Y	16380 FQ	22200 MW	26820 TQ	USBLS	5/07
	Orlando-Kissimmee MSA, FL	Y	16120 FQ	18520 MW	23740 TQ	USBLS	5/07
	Tampa-St. Petersburg-Clearwater MSA, FL	Y	18730 FQ	21770 MW	24830 TQ	USBLS	5/07
	West Palm Beach-Boca Raton-Boynton Beach PMSA, FL	Y	15170 FQ	20650 MW	25520 TQ	USBLS	5/07
	Georgia	Y	17380 FQ	21500 MW	27140 TQ	USBLS	5/07
	Atlanta-Sandy Springs-Marietta MSA, GA	Y	17460 FQ	21090 MW	25780 TQ	USBLS	5/07
	Hawaii	Y	18990 FQ	23850 MW	34680 TQ	USBLS	5/07
	Honolulu MSA, HI	Y	17930 FQ	21720 MW	29830 TQ	USBLS	5/07
	Idaho	Y	18440 FQ	22520 MW	27920 TQ	USBLS	5/07
	Boise City-Nampa MSA, ID	Y	19170 FQ	22270 MW	26450 TQ	USBLS	5/07
	Illinois	Y	17870 FQ	21620 MW	26920 TQ	USBLS	5/07
	Chicago-Naperville-Joliet MSA, IL-IN-WI	Y	17950 FQ	21790 MW	27300 TQ	USBLS	5/07
	Peoria MSA, IL	Y	17920 FQ	23800 MW	28360 TQ	USBLS	5/07
	Indiana	Y	18060 FQ	22330 MW	29750 TQ	USBLS	5/07
	Gary PMSA, IN	Y	16950 FQ	21060 MW	28030 TQ	USBLS	5/07
	Indianapolis-Carmel MSA, IN	Y	21310 FQ	25590 MW	32650 TQ	USBLS	5/07
	Terre Haute MSA, IN	Y	17930 FQ	20850 MW	23520 TQ	USBLS	5/07
	Iowa	Y	17320 FQ	21380 MW	26770 TQ	USBLS	5/07
	Des Moines-West Des Moines MSA, IA	Y	19590 FQ	23320 MW	28170 TQ	USBLS	5/07
	Kansas	Y	15100 FQ	18670 MW	22870 TQ	USBLS	5/07
	Wichita MSA, KS	Y	14990 FQ	18620 MW	23200 TQ	USBLS	5/07
	Kentucky	Y	16978 FQ	21080 MW	29043 TQ	KYBLS	2008
	Louisville-Jefferson County MSA, KY-IN	Y	17450 FQ	20030 MW	23700 TQ	USBLS	5/07
	Louisiana	H	7.29 FQ	8.97 MW	11.02 TQ	LABLS	1/08-3/08
	Baton Rouge MSA, LA	Y	14230 FQ	18090 MW	23020 TQ	USBLS	5/07
	New Orleans-Metairie-Kenner MSA, LA	Y	17100 FQ	20820 MW	24120 TQ	USBLS	5/07
	Maine	Y	19630 FQ	24170 MW	28950 TQ	USBLS	5/07
	Lewiston-Auburn MSA, ME	Y	20380 FQ	22920 MW	25760 TQ	USBLS	5/07
	Portland-South Portland-Biddeford MSA, ME	Y	20700 FQ	24100 MW	27930 TQ	USBLS	5/07
	Maryland	Y		26475 MW		MDBLS	3/08
	Baltimore-Towson MSA, MD	Y	19280 FQ	25930 MW	32340 TQ	USBLS	5/07
	Bethesda-Gaithersburg-Frederick PMSA, MD	Y	21810 FQ	28940 MW	35620 TQ	USBLS	5/07
	Massachusetts	Y	19620 FQ	24070 MW	31000 TQ	USBLS	5/07
	Boston-Cambridge-Quincy NECTA, MA	Y	19590 FQ	24170 MW	30790 TQ	USBLS	5/07

AE	Average entry wage	AW	Average wage paid	FQ	First quartile wage	LO	Lowest wage paid	MTC	Median total compensation	TCC Total cash compensation
AER	Average entry range	AWR	Average wage range	H	Hourly	LR	Low end range	MW	Median wage paid	TQ Third quartile wage
AEX	Average experienced wage	AXR	Average experienced range	HI	Highest wage paid	M	Monthly	MWR	Median wage range	W Weekly
ATC	Average total compensation	D	Daily	HR	High end range	MCC	Median cash compensation	S	See annotated source	Y Yearly

Occupation/Type/Industry	Location	Per	Low	Mid	High	Source	Date
Baker	Springfield MSA, MA-CT	Y	19690 FQ	24190 MW	31710 TQ	USBLS	5/07
	Worcester MSA, MA-CT	Y	18950 FQ	24230 MW	30910 TQ	USBLS	5/07
	Michigan	Y	17500 FQ	21140 MW	26380 TQ	USBLS	5/07
	Detroit-Warren-Livonia MSA, MI	Y	19310 FQ	24200 MW	30750 TQ	USBLS	5/07
	Grand Rapids-Wyoming MSA, MI	Y	17100 FQ	18890 MW	22910 TQ	USBLS	5/07
	Warren-Troy-Farmington Hills PMSA, MI	Y	18670 FQ	23470 MW	30790 TQ	USBLS	5/07
	Minnesota	Y	19924 FQ	25035 MW	31670 TQ	MNBLS	10/08-12/08
	Duluth-Superior MSA, MN-WI	Y	19085 FQ	24320 MW	29908 TQ	MNBLS	10/08-12/08
	Minneapolis-Saint Paul MSA, MN-WI	Y	20370 FQ	25937 MW	33578 TQ	MNBLS	10/08-12/08
	Rochester MSA, MN	Y	21476 FQ	26762 MW	35356 TQ	MNBLS	10/08-12/08
	Mississippi	Y	17020 FQ	19540 MW	22680 TQ	USBLS	5/07
	Jackson MSA, MS	Y	17360 FQ	19820 MW	22760 TQ	USBLS	5/07
	Missouri	Y	15890 FQ	20060 MW	26510 TQ	USBLS	5/07
	Joplin MSA, MO	Y	13940 FQ	14350 MW	14770 TQ	USBLS	5/07
	Kansas City MSA, MO-KS	Y	17430 FQ	20910 MW	27880 TQ	USBLS	5/07
	St. Louis MSA, MO-IL	Y	18480 FQ	23540 MW	27930 TQ	USBLS	5/07
	Montana	Y	17920 FQ	21540 MW	26130 TQ	USBLS	5/07
	Billings MSA, MT	Y	17290 FQ	20440 MW	25690 TQ	USBLS	5/07
	Nebraska	Y	16990 FQ	20140 MW	25940 TQ	USBLS	5/07
	Omaha-Council Bluffs MSA, NE-IA	Y	17750 FQ	22250 MW	27970 TQ	USBLS	5/07
	Nevada	H	10.18 FQ	13.34 MW	16.73 TQ	NVBLS	5/08
	Las Vegas-Paradise MSA, NV	H	10.34 FQ	14.12 MW	16.98 TQ	NVBLS	5/08
	New Hampshire	H	8.86 AE	11.81 MW	14.04 AEX	NHBLS	6/08
	Manchester MSA, NH	Y	18720 FQ	22620 MW	27910 TQ	USBLS	5/07
	Nashua NECTA, NH-MA	Y	22080 FQ	24690 MW	38730 TQ	USBLS	5/07
	New Jersey	Y	18670 FQ	24480 MW	31970 TQ	USBLS	5/07
	Camden PMSA, NJ	Y	20040 FQ	26230 MW	32920 TQ	USBLS	5/07
	Edison PMSA, NJ	Y	20060 FQ	24590 MW	33530 TQ	USBLS	5/07
	Newark-Union PMSA, NJ-PA	Y	19140 FQ	25510 MW	31300 TQ	USBLS	5/07
	New Mexico	Y	18170 FQ	22070 MW	25650 TQ	USBLS	5/07
	Albuquerque MSA, NM	Y	18190 FQ	22330 MW	26700 TQ	USBLS	5/07
	Las Cruces MSA, NM	Y	20730 FQ	23080 MW	25880 TQ	USBLS	5/07
	New York	Y	18760 FQ	23400 MW	30280 TQ	USBLS	5/07
	Albany-Schenectady-Troy MSA, NY	Y	18720 FQ	22190 MW	27740 TQ	USBLS	5/07
	Buffalo-Niagara Falls MSA, NY	Y	18130 FQ	21230 MW	24780 TQ	USBLS	5/07
	Nassau-Suffolk PMSA, NY	Y	21890 FQ	27190 MW	40900 TQ	USBLS	5/07
	New York-Northern New Jersey-Long Island MSA, NY-NJ-PA	Y	19000 FQ	24650 MW	33770 TQ	USBLS	5/07
	Utica-Rome MSA, NY	Y	18170 FQ	23580 MW	27430 TQ	USBLS	5/07
	North Carolina	Y	17610 FQ	20990 MW	24750 TQ	USBLS	5/07
	Charlotte-Gastonia-Concord MSA, NC-SC	Y	19840 FQ	23580 MW	26810 TQ	USBLS	5/07
	Raleigh-Cary MSA, NC	Y	18640 FQ	22660 MW	27970 TQ	USBLS	5/07
	North Dakota	Y	15940 FQ	19650 MW	23110 TQ	USBLS	5/07
	Fargo MSA, ND-MN	Y	18880 FQ	22300 MW	26660 TQ	USBLS	5/07
	Grand Forks MSA, ND-MN	Y	18170 FQ	23380 MW	28260 TQ	USBLS	5/07
	Ohio	Y	18010 FQ	21970 MW	26890 TQ	USBLS	5/07
	Cincinnati-Middletown MSA, OH-KY-IN	Y	20340 FQ	24510 MW	29160 TQ	USBLS	5/07
	Cleveland-Elyria-Mentor MSA, OH	Y	19110 FQ	22820 MW	27610 TQ	USBLS	5/07
	Columbus MSA, OH	Y	17870 FQ	21630 MW	27010 TQ	USBLS	5/07
	Dayton MSA, OH	Y	17440 FQ	21480 MW	25270 TQ	USBLS	5/07
	Oklahoma	Y	15420 FQ	18490 MW	23540 TQ	USBLS	5/07
	Oklahoma City MSA, OK	Y	15330 FQ	18120 MW	23370 TQ	USBLS	5/07
	Tulsa MSA, OK	Y	16310 FQ	19950 MW	24720 TQ	USBLS	5/07
	Oregon	H	10.33 FQ	12.53 MW	15.69 TQ	ORBLS	5/08
	Portland-Vancouver-Beaverton MSA, OR-WA	Y	22560 FQ	28400 MW	35010 TQ	USBLS	5/07
	Pennsylvania	Y	18630 FQ	23050 MW	28460 TQ	USBLS	5/07
	Allentown-Bethlehem-Easton MSA, PA-NJ	Y	19090 FQ	24230 MW	30010 TQ	USBLS	5/07

AE	Average entry wage	AW	Average wage paid	FQ	First quartile wage
AER	Average entry range	AWR	Average wage range	H	Hourly
AEX	Average experienced wage	AXR	Average experienced range	HI	Highest wage paid
ATC	Average total compensation	D	Daily	HR	High end range

LO	Lowest wage paid	MTC	Median total compensation
LR	Low end range	MW	Median wage paid
M	Monthly	MWR	Median wage range
MCC	Median cash compensation	S	See annotated source

TCC	Total cash compensation
TQ	Third quartile wage
W	Weekly
Y	Yearly

Occupation/Type/Industry	Location	Per	Low	Mid	High	Source	Date
Baker	Philadelphia-Camden- Wilmington MSA, PA-NJ-DE- MD	Y	21050 FQ	25770 MW	31220 TQ	USBLS	5/07
	Pittsburgh MSA, PA	Y	17750 FQ	22130 MW	26330 TQ	USBLS	5/07
	Reading MSA, PA	Y	19410 FQ	21770 MW	24910 TQ	USBLS	5/07
	York-Hanover MSA, PA	Y	20750 FQ	25350 MW	29350 TQ	USBLS	5/07
	Rhode Island	Y	21620 FQ	26720 MW	33290 TQ	USBLS	5/07
	Providence-Fall River- Warwick MSA, RI-MA	Y	20620 FQ	25530 MW	32420 TQ	USBLS	5/07
	South Carolina	Y	16700 FQ	19440 MW	25700 TQ	USBLS	5/07
	Charleston-North Charleston MSA, SC	Y	16740 FQ	18280 MW	20330 TQ	USBLS	5/07
	Columbia MSA, SC	Y	17680 FQ	20170 MW	23880 TQ	USBLS	5/07
	South Dakota	Y	18604 FQ	21936 MW	27635 TQ	SDBLS	7/08-9/08
	Rapid City MSA, SD	Y	18512 FQ	21255 MW	23790 TQ	SDBLS	7/08-9/08
	Sioux Falls MSA, SD	Y	19467 FQ	22917 MW	27026 TQ	SDBLS	7/08-9/08
	Tennessee	Y	16470 FQ	20000 MW	23850 TQ	USBLS	5/07
	Memphis MSA, TN-MS-AR	Y	20160 FQ	22990 MW	29750 TQ	USBLS	5/07
	Nashville-Davidson- Murfreesboro MSA, TN	Y	20370 FQ	22730 MW	26070 TQ	USBLS	5/07
	Texas	Y	15960 FQ	19670 MW	24470 TQ	USBLS	5/07
	Austin-Round Rock MSA, TX	Y	18700 FQ	22260 MW	25440 TQ	USBLS	5/07
	Dallas-Fort Worth-Arlington MSA, TX	Y	17600 FQ	21520 MW	26140 TQ	USBLS	5/07
	El Paso MSA, TX	Y	12920 FQ	14990 MW	18710 TQ	USBLS	5/07
	Houston-Sugar Land-Baytown MSA, TX	Y	16540 FQ	20470 MW	24250 TQ	USBLS	5/07
	San Antonio MSA, TX	Y	20540 FQ	24690 MW	30020 TQ	USBLS	5/07
	Utah	Y	17350 FQ	21850 MW	29130 TQ	USBLS	5/07
	Salt Lake City MSA, UT	Y	17930 FQ	22680 MW	31110 TQ	USBLS	5/07
	Vermont	Y	20770 FQ	24030 MW	28600 TQ	USBLS	5/07
	Burlington-South Burlington MSA, VT	Y	21180 FQ	24890 MW	28820 TQ	USBLS	5/07
	Virginia	Y	19250 FQ	23400 MW	29720 TQ	USBLS	5/07
	Lynchburg MSA, VA	Y	17320 FQ	21520 MW	28640 TQ	USBLS	5/07
	Richmond MSA, VA	Y	17520 FQ	19700 MW	24760 TQ	USBLS	5/07
	Virginia Beach-Norfolk- Newport News MSA, VA-NC	Y	18950 FQ	22590 MW	26710 TQ	USBLS	5/07
	Washington	H	11.51 FQ	14.37 MW	17.64 TQ	WABLS	3/08
	Seattle-Tacoma-Bellevue MSA, WA	Y	25150 FQ	30650 MW	37380 TQ	USBLS	5/07
	West Virginia	Y	16450 FQ	19042 MW	24097 TQ	WVBLS	7/08-9/08
	Charleston MSA, WV	Y	14630 FQ	17430 MW	20470 TQ	USBLS	5/07
	Huntington-Ashland MSA, WV-KY-OH	Y	13610 FQ	16110 MW	18630 TQ	USBLS	5/07
	Wisconsin	Y	17950 FQ	21760 MW	26830 TQ	USBLS	5/07
	Milwaukee-Waukesha-West Allis MSA, WI	Y	18690 FQ	22670 MW	27580 TQ	USBLS	5/07
	Wyoming	Y	17690 FQ	20887 MW	27364 TQ	WYBLS	9/08
	Cheyenne MSA, WY	Y	19851 FQ	23391 MW	27924 TQ	WYBLS	9/08
	Puerto Rico	Y	12510 FQ	13930 MW	15630 TQ	USBLS	5/07
	Aguadilla-Isabela-San Sebastian MSA, PR	Y	12220 FQ	13320 MW	14430 TQ	USBLS	5/07
	San Juan-Caguas-Guaynabo MSA, PR	Y	12630 FQ	14200 MW	16320 TQ	USBLS	5/07
	Virgin Islands	Y	20230 FQ	23240 MW	27080 TQ	USBLS	5/07
	Guam	Y	12830 FQ	14680 MW	18090 TQ	USBLS	5/07
Bakery Manager							
Small Organization	United States	Y	38996 FQ	43578 MW	48160 TQ	ALA02	2008
Ballet Dancer							
New York City Ballet	New York, NY	Y			80000- 120000 HR	NYT02	2007
Band Director							
Public High School	Baldwin County, AL	S			8426 HI	BCPSSS	2008-2009
Bank Examiner							
State Government	Iowa	Y	36254 LO		99320 HI	AFT02	3/1/08
State Government	Maine	Y	29411 LO		39770 HI	AFT02	3/1/08
State Government	New York	Y	49992 LO		61757 HI	AFT02	3/1/08

AE	Average entry wage	AW	Average wage paid	FQ	First quartile wage	LO	Lowest wage paid	MTC	Median total compensation
AER	Average entry range	AWR	Average wage range	H	Hourly	LR	Low end range	MW	Median wage paid
AEX	Average experienced wage	AXR	Average experienced range	HI	Highest wage paid	M	Monthly	MWR	Median wage range
ATC	Average total compensation	D	Daily	HR	High end range	MCC	Median cash compensation	S	See annotated source

TCC	Total cash compensation
TQ	Third quartile wage
W	Weekly
Y	Yearly

Occupation/Type/Industry	Location	Per	Low	Mid	High	Source	Date
Banking Commissioner	New Hampshire	Y			99928 HI	NHUL03	2008
Bankruptcy Judge							
Federal Government	United States	Y			155756 HI	CRS02	1/08
Barber	Alabama	Y	17200 FQ	18350 MW	19500 TQ	USBLS	5/07
	Arizona	Y	16320 FQ	18450 TQ	21180 TQ	USBLS	5/07
	California	H	9.29 FQ	10.84 MW	14.17 TQ	CABLS	1/08-3/08
	Connecticut	H	8.38 AE	11.08 MW		CTBLS	1/08-3/08
	Delaware	Y	23890 FQ	27800 MW	33640 TQ	USBLS	5/07
	District of Columbia	Y	15010 FQ	15450 MW	20500 TQ	USBLS	5/07
	Florida	Y	15560 FQ	18700 MW	27060 TQ	USBLS	5/07
	Georgia	Y	26650 FQ	31490 MW	57320 TQ	USBLS	5/07
	Idaho	Y	12550 FQ	13860 MW	15180 TQ	USBLS	5/07
	Illinois	Y	21510 FQ	23190 MW	24910 TQ	USBLS	5/07
	Indiana	Y	15330 FQ	23460 MW	33960 TQ	USBLS	5/07
	Louisiana	H	10.40 FQ	11.49 MW	12.98 TQ	LABLS	1/08-3/08
	Maryland	Y		21800 MW		MDBLS	3/08
	Massachusetts	Y	17180 FQ	20600 MW	29300 TQ	USBLS	5/07
	Michigan	Y	22250 FQ	26780 MW	31780 TQ	USBLS	5/07
	Missouri	Y	20510 FQ	22350 MW	24550 TQ	USBLS	5/07
	New Jersey	Y	18670 FQ	28160 MW	38550 TQ	USBLS	5/07
	New Mexico	Y	13570 FQ	16410 MW	19220 TQ	USBLS	5/07
	New York	Y	16430 FQ	18940 MW	23180 TQ	USBLS	5/07
	Ohio	Y	21480 FQ	24830 MW	27940 TQ	USBLS	5/07
	Oklahoma	Y	25560 FQ	27590 MW	29610 TQ	USBLS	5/07
	Pennsylvania	Y	24280 FQ	26840 MW	29490 TQ	USBLS	5/07
	Rhode Island	Y	15450 FQ	15500 MW	15560 TQ	USBLS	5/07
	Tennessee	Y	17270 FQ	21730 MW	28020 TQ	USBLS	5/07
	Texas	Y	13670 FQ	16230 MW	33340 TQ	USBLS	5/07
	Virginia	Y	14630 FQ	18070 MW	22620 TQ	USBLS	5/07
	Washington	H	12.56 FQ	15.22 MW	17.06 TQ	WABLS	3/08
	Wisconsin	Y	19550 FQ	22690 MW	28430 TQ	USBLS	5/07
	Puerto Rico	Y	16300 FQ	17650 MW	19310 TQ	USBLS	5/07
Barber Inspector							
State Government	Ohio	H	17.22 LO		21.77 HI	ODAS	2008
Barista	United States	Y		18202 AW		NDAY01	2009
Bartender	Alabama	Y	12880 FQ	14650 MW	17210 TQ	USBLS	5/07
	Birmingham-Hoover MSA, AL	Y	12960 FQ	14810 MW	18060 TQ	USBLS	5/07
	Alaska	Y	19910 FQ	22910 MW	26490 TQ	USBLS	5/07
	Anchorage MSA, AK	Y	20340 FQ	24730 MW	28230 TQ	USBLS	5/07
	Arizona	Y	14670 FQ	15450 MW	19060 TQ	USBLS	5/07
	Phoenix-Mesa-Scottsdale MSA, AZ	Y	14720 FQ	15580 MW	20670 TQ	USBLS	5/07
	Tucson MSA, AZ	Y	14620 FQ	15350 MW	18250 TQ	USBLS	5/07
	Arkansas	Y	14390 FQ	15630 MW	18880 TQ	USBLS	5/07
	Fort Smith MSA, AR-OK	Y	14470 FQ	15810 MW	18370 TQ	USBLS	5/07
	Little Rock-North Little Rock MSA, AR	Y	14560 FQ	15890 MW	18990 TQ	USBLS	5/07
	California	H	8.00 FQ	8.77 MW	9.89 TQ	CABLS	1/08-3/08
	Fresno MSA, CA	H	8.03 FQ	8.66 MW	9.30 TQ	CABLS	1/08-3/08
	Los Angeles-Long Beach-Glendale PMSA, CA	H	8.00 FQ	8.60 MW	9.38 TQ	CABLS	1/08-3/08
	Oakland-Fremont-Hayward MSA, CA	H	8.03 FQ	8.94 MW	10.35 TQ	CABLS	1/08-3/08
	Riverside-San Bernardino-Ontario MSA, CA	H	8.00 FQ	8.64 MW	9.60 TQ	CABLS	1/08-3/08
	Sacramento-Arden Arcade-Roseville MSA, CA	H	8.04 FQ	8.91 MW	10.80 TQ	CABLS	1/08-3/08
	San Diego-Carlsbad-San Marcos MSA, CA	H	8.00 FQ	8.70 MW	9.70 TQ	CABLS	1/08-3/08
	San Francisco-San Mateo-Redwood PMSA, CA	H	8.77 FQ	9.85 MW	11.81 TQ	CABLS	1/08-3/08
	San Jose-Sunnyvale-Santa Clara MSA, CA	H	8.00 FQ	8.68 MW	9.83 TQ	CABLS	1/08-3/08
	Santa Ana-Anaheim-Irvine PMSA, CA	Y	16050 FQ	17230 MW	19180 TQ	USBLS	5/07
	Colorado	Y	14810 FQ	15710 MW	20780 TQ	USBLS	5/07
	Denver-Aurora MSA, CO	Y	14780 FQ	15580 MW	20920 TQ	USBLS	5/07
	Connecticut	H	8.26 AE	9.19 MW		CTBLS	1/08-3/08

AE	Average entry wage	AW	Average wage paid	FQ	First quartile wage	LO	Lowest wage paid	MTC	Median total compensation	TCC	Total cash compensation
AER	Average entry range	AWR	Average wage range	H	Hourly	LR	Low end range	MW	Median wage paid	TQ	Third quartile wage
AEX	Average experienced wage	AXR	Average experienced range	HI	Highest wage paid	M	Monthly	MWR	Median wage range	W	Weekly
ATC	Average total compensation	D	Daily	HR	High end range	MCC	Median cash compensation	S	See annotated source	Y	Yearly

Occupation/Type/Industry	Location	Per	Low	Mid	High	Source	Date
Bartender	Bridgeport-Stamford-Norwalk MSA, CT	Y	16650 FQ	18300 MW	21660 TQ	USBLS	5/07
	Hartford-West Hartford-East Hartford MSA, CT	Y	17000 FQ	20230 MW	26810 TQ	USBLS	5/07
	Delaware	Y	15340 FQ	17740 MW	21440 TQ	USBLS	5/07
	Wilmington PMSA, DE-MD-NJ	Y	15720 FQ	18310 MW	22030 TQ	USBLS	5/07
	District of Columbia	Y	16390 FQ	22080 MW	28920 TQ	USBLS	5/07
	Washington-Arlington-Alexandria MSA, DC-VA-MD-WV	Y	15510 FQ	20580 MW	27110 TQ	USBLS	5/07
	Florida	Y	14930 FQ	17860 MW	23440 TQ	USBLS	5/07
	Fort Lauderdale-Pompano Beach-Deerfield Beach PMSA, FL	Y	14950 FQ	18140 MW	23830 TQ	USBLS	5/07
	Jacksonville MSA, FL	Y	14660 FQ	16000 MW	20300 TQ	USBLS	5/07
	Miami-Fort Lauderdale-Miami Beach MSA, FL	Y	15450 FQ	19290 MW	26220 TQ	USBLS	5/07
	Orlando-Kissimmee MSA, FL	Y	14870 FQ	17620 MW	22880 TQ	USBLS	5/07
	Tampa-St. Petersburg-Clearwater MSA, FL	Y	14860 FQ	17210 MW	22110 TQ	USBLS	5/07
	West Palm Beach-Boca Raton-Boynton Beach PMSA, FL	Y	16580 FQ	23370 MW	30130 TQ	USBLS	5/07
	Georgia	Y	13100 FQ	15200 MW	20640 TQ	USBLS	5/07
	Atlanta-Sandy Springs-Marietta MSA, GA	Y	13040 FQ	15060 MW	21110 TQ	USBLS	5/07
	Hawaii	Y	18700 FQ	26220 MW	38940 TQ	USBLS	5/07
	Honolulu MSA, HI	Y	16600 FQ	21980 MW	33860 TQ	USBLS	5/07
	Idaho	Y	12890 FQ	14600 MW	17960 TQ	USBLS	5/07
	Boise City-Nampa MSA, ID	Y	12920 FQ	14610 MW	17900 TQ	USBLS	5/07
	Illinois	Y	14910 FQ	16510 MW	19990 TQ	USBLS	5/07
	Chicago-Naperville-Joliet MSA, IL-IN-WI	Y	15050 FQ	17200 MW	21710 TQ	USBLS	5/07
	Indiana	Y	13660 FQ	16390 MW	20180 TQ	USBLS	5/07
	Gary PMSA, IN	Y	13420 FQ	15610 MW	19470 TQ	USBLS	5/07
	Indianapolis-Carmel MSA, IN	Y	14180 FQ	18400 MW	24300 TQ	USBLS	5/07
	Iowa	Y	14180 FQ	15480 MW	18300 TQ	USBLS	5/07
	Des Moines-West Des Moines MSA, IA	Y	14150 FQ	15630 MW	19190 TQ	USBLS	5/07
	Kansas	Y	13080 FQ	15060 MW	18860 TQ	USBLS	5/07
	Lawrence MSA, KS	Y	14650 FQ	17870 MW	21970 TQ	USBLS	5/07
	Wichita MSA, KS	Y	12870 FQ	14740 MW	17250 TQ	USBLS	5/07
	Kentucky	Y	13297 FQ	15045 MW	18176 TQ	KYBLS	2008
	Elizabethtown MSA, KY	Y	12790 FQ	14610 MW	16420 TQ	USBLS	5/07
	Louisville-Jefferson County MSA, KY-IN	Y	12800 FQ	14410 MW	17300 TQ	USBLS	5/07
	Louisiana	H	6.19 FQ	7.03 MW	8.34 TQ	LABLS	1/08-3/08
	Baton Rouge MSA, LA	Y	13060 FQ	15040 MW	17850 TQ	USBLS	5/07
	New Orleans-Metairie-Kenner MSA, LA	Y	12870 FQ	14580 MW	17820 TQ	USBLS	5/07
	Maine	Y	15030 FQ	16730 MW	22450 TQ	USBLS	5/07
	Portland-South Portland-Biddeford MSA, ME	Y	15050 FQ	17220 MW	25460 TQ	USBLS	5/07
	Maryland	Y		16050 MW		MDBLS	3/08
	Baltimore-Towson MSA, MD	Y	14170 FQ	15270 MW	18870 TQ	USBLS	5/07
	Bethesda-Gaithersburg-Frederick PMSA, MD	Y	14590 FQ	17190 MW	24940 TQ	USBLS	5/07
	Hagerstown-Martinsburg MSA, MD-WV	Y	14440 FQ	16120 MW	20540 TQ	USBLS	5/07
	Massachusetts	Y	17120 FQ	21830 MW	28550 TQ	USBLS	5/07
	Boston-Cambridge-Quincy NECTA, MA	Y	17740 FQ	24840 MW	29720 TQ	USBLS	5/07
	Worcester MSA, MA-CT	Y	16080 FQ	18620 MW	24560 TQ	USBLS	5/07
	Michigan	Y	15190 FQ	16030 MW	19580 TQ	USBLS	5/07
	Detroit-Warren-Livonia MSA, MI	Y	15390 FQ	16660 MW	20490 TQ	USBLS	5/07
	Grand Rapids-Wyoming MSA, MI	Y	15140 FQ	15770 MW	18520 TQ	USBLS	5/07
	Warren-Troy-Farmington Hills PMSA, MI	Y	15300 FQ	16230 MW	20220 TQ	USBLS	5/07
	Minnesota	Y	16415 FQ	19928 MW	24508 TQ	MNBLS	10/08-12/08
	Duluth-Superior MSA, MN-WI	Y	15286 FQ	16677 MW	20179 TQ	MNBLS	10/08-12/08

AE Average entry wage	**AW** Average wage paid	**FQ** First quartile wage	**LO** Lowest wage paid	**MTC** Median total compensation	**TCC** Total cash compensation
AER Average entry range	**AWR** Average wage range	**H** Hourly	**LR** Low end range	**MW** Median wage paid	**TQ** Third quartile wage
AEX Average experienced wage	**AXR** Average experienced range	**HI** Highest wage paid	**M** Monthly	**MWR** Median wage range	**W** Weekly
ATC Average total compensation	**D** Daily	**HR** High end range	**MCC** Median cash compensation	**S** See annotated source	**Y** Yearly

Occupation/Type/Industry	Location	Per	Low	Mid	High	Source	Date
Bartender	Minneapolis-Saint Paul MSA, MN-WI	Y	16969 FQ	21277 MW	25637 TQ	MNBLS	10/08-12/08
	Rochester MSA, MN	Y	15612 FQ	19220 MW	24592 TQ	MNBLS	10/08-12/08
	Mississippi	Y	13540 FQ	15880 MW	18990 TQ	USBLS	5/07
	Gulfport-Biloxi MSA, MS	Y	14730 FQ	17550 MW	20840 TQ	USBLS	5/07
	Jackson MSA, MS	Y	13510 FQ	15880 MW	19390 TQ	USBLS	5/07
	Missouri	Y	14620 FQ	16030 MW	20330 TQ	USBLS	5/07
	Kansas City MSA, MO-KS	Y	14080 FQ	15110 MW	18570 TQ	USBLS	5/07
	St. Louis MSA, MO-IL	Y	14930 FQ	16770 MW	21440 TQ	USBLS	5/07
	Montana	Y	14330 FQ	16030 MW	18960 TQ	USBLS	5/07
	Billings MSA, MT	Y	13900 FQ	15010 MW	16750 TQ	USBLS	5/07
	Nebraska	Y	13090 FQ	15090 MW	18430 TQ	USBLS	5/07
	Omaha-Council Bluffs MSA, NE-IA	Y	14110 FQ	16780 MW	19910 TQ	USBLS	5/07
	Nevada	H	7.17 FQ	9.90 MW	14.89 TQ	NVBLS	5/08
	Las Vegas-Paradise MSA, NV	H	7.56 FQ	11.57 MW	15.65 TQ	NVBLS	5/08
	New Hampshire	H	6.52 AE	8.53 MW	11.25 AEX	NHBLS	6/08
	Manchester MSA, NH	Y	15940 FQ	19010 MW	22740 TQ	USBLS	5/07
	Nashua NECTA, NH-MA	Y	15670 FQ	19000 MW	22710 TQ	USBLS	5/07
	New Jersey	Y	16450 FQ	23540 MW	29870 TQ	USBLS	5/07
	Camden PMSA, NJ	Y	18160 FQ	24000 MW	30260 TQ	USBLS	5/07
	Edison PMSA, NJ	Y	18220 FQ	23860 MW	30890 TQ	USBLS	5/07
	Newark-Union PMSA, NJ-PA	Y	17070 FQ	23540 MW	29510 TQ	USBLS	5/07
	Trenton-Ewing MSA, NJ	Y	15620 FQ	23020 MW	29590 TQ	USBLS	5/07
	New Mexico	Y	12680 FQ	14210 MW	16070 TQ	USBLS	5/07
	Albuquerque MSA, NM	Y	12550 FQ	14000 MW	15560 TQ	USBLS	5/07
	Las Cruces MSA, NM	Y	12640 FQ	14080 MW	15640 TQ	USBLS	5/07
	New York	Y	15860 FQ	20920 MW	31770 TQ	USBLS	5/07
	Albany-Schenectady-Troy MSA, NY	Y	15670 FQ	17210 MW	24680 TQ	USBLS	5/07
	Buffalo-Niagara Falls MSA, NY	Y	15390 FQ	17290 MW	21900 TQ	USBLS	5/07
	Ithaca MSA, NY	Y	15230 FQ	16140 MW	19430 TQ	USBLS	5/07
	Nassau-Suffolk PMSA, NY	Y	17230 FQ	26490 MW	34220 TQ	USBLS	5/07
	New York-Northern New Jersey-Long Island MSA, NY-NJ-PA	Y	18480 FQ	25320 MW	34370 TQ	USBLS	5/07
	Syracuse MSA, NY	Y	15200 FQ	15690 MW	19420 TQ	USBLS	5/07
	North Carolina	Y	14180 FQ	15770 MW	21310 TQ	USBLS	5/07
	Charlotte-Gastonia-Concord MSA, NC-SC	Y	14010 FQ	15450 MW	21750 TQ	USBLS	5/07
	Raleigh-Cary MSA, NC	Y	14290 FQ	16520 MW	24530 TQ	USBLS	5/07
	North Dakota	Y	13250 FQ	15420 MW	18540 TQ	USBLS	5/07
	Fargo MSA, ND-MN	Y	12970 FQ	14490 MW	16580 TQ	USBLS	5/07
	Ohio	Y	14700 FQ	15280 MW	17030 TQ	USBLS	5/07
	Cincinnati-Middletown MSA, OH-KY-IN	Y	14540 FQ	15170 MW	17030 TQ	USBLS	5/07
	Cleveland-Elyria-Mentor MSA, OH	Y	14840 FQ	15600 MW	17600 TQ	USBLS	5/07
	Columbus MSA, OH	Y	14850 FQ	15710 MW	18500 TQ	USBLS	5/07
	Dayton MSA, OH	Y	14520 FQ	14800 MW	15080 TQ	USBLS	5/07
	Springfield MSA, OH	Y	14560 FQ	14860 MW	15690 TQ	USBLS	5/07
	Oklahoma	Y	13360 FQ	15630 MW	18760 TQ	USBLS	5/07
	Oklahoma City MSA, OK	Y	13420 FQ	15740 MW	19310 TQ	USBLS	5/07
	Tulsa MSA, OK	Y	14050 FQ	16620 MW	19270 TQ	USBLS	5/07
	Oregon	H	8.74 FQ	9.52 MW	10.92 TQ	ORBLS	5/08
	Portland-Vancouver-Beaverton MSA, OR-WA	Y	17980 FQ	19870 MW	24530 TQ	USBLS	5/07
	Pennsylvania	Y	14520 FQ	15810 MW	19350 TQ	USBLS	5/07
	Allentown-Bethlehem-Easton MSA, PA-NJ	Y	14650 FQ	16430 MW	19650 TQ	USBLS	5/07
	Philadelphia-Camden-Wilmington MSA, PA-NJ-DE-MD	Y	15100 FQ	18060 MW	23400 TQ	USBLS	5/07
	Pittsburgh MSA, PA	Y	14380 FQ	15410 MW	18460 TQ	USBLS	5/07
	Rhode Island	Y	15770 FQ	17110 MW	19740 TQ	USBLS	5/07
	Providence-Fall River-Warwick MSA, RI-MA	Y	15900 FQ	17620 MW	21130 TQ	USBLS	5/07
	South Carolina	Y	13030 FQ	14930 MW	18660 TQ	USBLS	5/07
	Charleston-North Charleston MSA, SC	Y	12890 FQ	14700 MW	19210 TQ	USBLS	5/07
	Columbia MSA, SC	Y	13010 FQ	14840 MW	17250 TQ	USBLS	5/07

AE Average entry wage	**AW** Average wage paid	**FQ** First quartile wage	**LO** Lowest wage paid	**MTC** Median total compensation	**TCC** Total cash compensation
AER Average entry range	**AWR** Average wage range	**H** Hourly	**LR** Low end range	**MW** Median wage paid	**TQ** Third quartile wage
AEX Average experienced wage	**AXR** Average experienced range	**HI** Highest wage paid	**M** Monthly	**MWR** Median wage range	**W** Weekly
ATC Average total compensation **D** Daily		**HR** High end range	**MCC** Median cash compensation **S** See annotated source		**Y** Yearly

Occupation/Type/Industry	Location	Per	Low	Mid	High	Source	Date
Bartender	South Dakota	Y	14368 FQ	17144 MW	19555 TQ	SDBLS	7/08-9/08
	Sioux Falls MSA, SD	Y	14112 FQ	17101 MW	20422 TQ	SDBLS	7/08-9/08
	Tennessee	Y	12740 FQ	14320 MW	16880 TQ	USBLS	5/07
	Kingsport-Bristol-Bristol MSA, TN-VA	Y	13530 FQ	15860 MW	19600 TQ	USBLS	5/07
	Memphis MSA, TN-MS-AR	Y	13050 FQ	14900 MW	18640 TQ	USBLS	5/07
	Nashville-Davidson-Murfreesboro MSA, TN	Y	12600 FQ	14070 MW	15780 TQ	USBLS	5/07
	Texas	Y	13050 FQ	14890 MW	19910 TQ	USBLS	5/07
	Austin-Round Rock MSA, TX	Y	13970 FQ	17230 MW	21260 TQ	USBLS	5/07
	Beaumont-Port Arthur MSA, TX	Y	13150 FQ	14990 MW	18440 TQ	USBLS	5/07
	Dallas-Fort Worth-Arlington MSA, TX	Y	13280 FQ	15450 MW	22550 TQ	USBLS	5/07
	El Paso MSA, TX	Y	12560 FQ	13780 MW	15000 TQ	USBLS	5/07
	Houston-Sugar Land-Baytown MSA, TX	Y	13220 FQ	15350 MW	21140 TQ	USBLS	5/07
	San Antonio MSA, TX	Y	12750 FQ	14340 MW	18600 TQ	USBLS	5/07
	Utah	Y	14010 FQ	17820 MW	23170 TQ	USBLS	5/07
	St. George MSA, UT	Y	14190 FQ	18910 MW	27050 TQ	USBLS	5/07
	Salt Lake City MSA, UT	Y	14510 FQ	19570 MW	24080 TQ	USBLS	5/07
	Vermont	Y	16670 FQ	19110 MW	23700 TQ	USBLS	5/07
	Burlington-South Burlington MSA, VT	Y	16590 FQ	19540 MW	24780 TQ	USBLS	5/07
	Virginia	Y	14640 FQ	19180 MW	24790 TQ	USBLS	5/07
	Charlottesville MSA, VA	Y	14260 FQ	19600 MW	23990 TQ	USBLS	5/07
	Richmond MSA, VA	Y	14670 FQ	19020 MW	24090 TQ	USBLS	5/07
	Virginia Beach-Norfolk-Newport News MSA, VA-NC	Y	13810 FQ	16980 MW	22150 TQ	USBLS	5/07
	Washington	H	12.72 FQ	14.18 MW	15.73 TQ	WABLS	3/08
	Seattle-Tacoma-Bellevue MSA, WA	Y	27070 FQ	29850 MW	33070 TQ	USBLS	5/07
	West Virginia	Y	14189 FQ	15440 MW	18508 TQ	WVBLS	7/08-9/08
	Charleston MSA, WV	Y	14220 FQ	15960 MW	19350 TQ	USBLS	5/07
	Wisconsin	Y	15540 FQ	17630 MW	20140 TQ	USBLS	5/07
	Milwaukee-Waukesha-West Allis MSA, WI	Y	16690 FQ	18960 MW	22880 TQ	USBLS	5/07
	Wyoming	Y	13548 FQ	15443 MW	18382 TQ	WYBLS	9/08
	Casper MSA, WY	Y	13044 FQ	14450 MW	15961 TQ	WYBLS	9/08
	Cheyenne MSA, WY	Y	13469 FQ	15210 MW	17795 TQ	WYBLS	9/08
	Puerto Rico	Y	12640 FQ	14040 MW	15930 TQ	USBLS	5/07
	San Juan-Caguas-Guaynabo MSA, PR	Y	12720 FQ	14160 MW	16770 TQ	USBLS	5/07
	Virgin Islands	Y	14730 FQ	17120 MW	19690 TQ	USBLS	5/07
	Guam	Y	13050 FQ	14950 MW	17250 TQ	USBLS	5/07
Baseball Player							
Major League Baseball	United States	Y		395000-3175000 MW		USATOD07	2008
Major League Baseball, Catcher	United States	Y		3676514 AW		MLBPA	2008
Major League Baseball, Designated Hitter	United States	Y		7506036 AW		MLBPA	2008
Major League Baseball, First Base	United States	Y		7118519 AW		MLBPA	2008
Major League Baseball, Outfielder	United States	Y		4756939 AW		MLBPA	2008
Major League Baseball, Relief Pitcher	United States	Y		1859796 AW		MLBPA	2008
Major League Baseball, Second Base	United States	Y		3547171 AW		MLBPA	2008
Major League Baseball, Shortstop	United States	Y		4978402 AW		MLBPA	2008
Major League Baseball, Starting Pitcher	United States	Y		4429366 AW		MLBPA	2008
Major League Baseball, Third Base	United States	Y		6588419 AW		MLBPA	2008
Baseball Stadium Staff							
Major League Baseball	United States	H	7.50 LO		18.00 HI	ABCN02	2009
Basketball Coach							
University of Pittsburgh	Pittsburgh, PA	Y			1300000 HI	PPGAZ	2009
Basketball Player							
National Basketball Association	United States	Y		2679197-5841590 AWR		HOOPS	2007-2008
Women's National Basketball Association	United States	Y	34500 LO		95000 HI	IHOOPS	2008
Battalion Chief	Seaside, CA	S	2490 LO		3018 HI	SSSS	8/08
	Colorado Springs, CO	M			8195 HI	COSPRS	1/1/09

Occupation/Type/Industry	Location	Per	Low	Mid	High	Source	Date
Battalion Chief	Gresham, OR	Y	74916 LO		97428 HI	GOSS01	7/1/08
Beach and Pool Manager							
Municipal Government	Seattle, WA	H	15.84 LO		18.94 HI	CSSS	2008
Behavioral Clinician							
State Government	Indiana	Y	32604 LO		56264 HI	AFT02	3/1/08
Bicycle Repairer	Arizona	Y	17510 FQ	19150 MW	22040 TQ	USBLS	5/07
	California	H	10.08 FQ	12.24 MW	15.23 TQ	CABLS	1/08-3/08
	Colorado	Y	17200 FQ	19030 MW	22720 TQ	USBLS	5/07
	Connecticut	H	8.61 AE	12.52 MW		CTBLS	1/08-3/08
	Florida	Y	19690 FQ	24620 MW	30060 TQ	USBLS	5/07
	Georgia	Y	21530 FQ	24180 MW	33270 TQ	USBLS	5/07
	Idaho	Y	17240 FQ	19420 MW	24950 TQ	USBLS	5/07
	Illinois	Y	16970 FQ	18620 MW	22580 TQ	USBLS	5/07
	Indiana	Y	17750 FQ	21200 MW	26690 TQ	USBLS	5/07
	Iowa	Y	17010 FQ	20990 MW	23840 TQ	USBLS	5/07
	Kansas	Y	13320 FQ	19600 MW	27160 TQ	USBLS	5/07
	Kentucky	Y	24307 FQ	32184 MW	37895 TQ	KYBLS	2008
	Maine	Y	16080 FQ	17220 MW	18370 TQ	USBLS	5/07
	Maryland	Y		25600 MW		MDBLS	3/08
	Massachusetts	Y	21540 FQ	24280 MW	28380 TQ	USBLS	5/07
	Michigan	Y	16410 FQ	19020 MW	23290 TQ	USBLS	5/07
	Minnesota	Y	20769 FQ	28552 MW	35296 TQ	MNBLS	10/08-12/08
	Missouri	Y	18630 FQ	22770 MW	25450 TQ	USBLS	5/07
	Montana	Y	15020 FQ	17850 MW	22070 TQ	USBLS	5/07
	Nebraska	Y	14780 FQ	18460 MW	22560 TQ	USBLS	5/07
	Nevada	H	6.47 FQ	7.87 MW	9.20 TQ	NVBLS	5/08
	New Hampshire	H	9.75 AE	11.17 MW	13.25 AEX	NHBLS	6/08
	New Jersey	Y	15610 FQ	21810 MW	27890 TQ	USBLS	5/07
	New Mexico	Y	17310 FQ	20430 MW	23380 TQ	USBLS	5/07
	New York	Y	19520 FQ	22660 MW	28730 TQ	USBLS	5/07
	North Carolina	Y	20860 FQ	24880 MW	29340 TQ	USBLS	5/07
	North Dakota	Y	15820 FQ	18670 MW	24200 TQ	USBLS	5/07
	Ohio	Y	19730 FQ	21890 MW	24890 TQ	USBLS	5/07
	Oregon	H	9.07 FQ	10.91 MW	13.26 TQ	ORBLS	5/08
	Pennsylvania	Y	16080 FQ	25960 MW	28830 TQ	USBLS	5/07
	South Dakota	Y	19046 FQ	21396 MW	24274 TQ	SDBLS	7/08-9/08
	Tennessee	Y	21460 FQ	25120 MW	27870 TQ	USBLS	5/07
	Texas	Y	16790 FQ	21370 MW	23890 TQ	USBLS	5/07
	Utah	Y	19050 FQ	21010 MW	23300 TQ	USBLS	5/07
	Vermont	Y	18090 FQ	21800 MW	25380 TQ	USBLS	5/07
	Virginia	Y	19940 FQ	22210 MW	29850 TQ	USBLS	5/07
	Washington	H	9.36 FQ	10.84 MW	12.33 TQ	WABLS	3/08
	Wisconsin	Y	18470 FQ	21920 MW	24930 TQ	USBLS	5/07
Bike Messenger	Minnesota	Y			19000-40000 HR	MMTHLY	2008
Bill and Account Collector	Alabama	Y	19900 FQ	24350 MW	30190 TQ	USBLS	5/07
	Birmingham-Hoover MSA, AL	Y	22730 FQ	28090 MW	34980 TQ	USBLS	5/07
	Montgomery MSA, AL	Y	18590 FQ	20670 MW	26090 TQ	USBLS	5/07
	Alaska	Y	30830 FQ	37250 MW	44240 TQ	USBLS	5/07
	Anchorage MSA, AK	Y	31100 FQ	38830 MW	46120 TQ	USBLS	5/07
	Arizona	Y	23900 FQ	29100 MW	35240 TQ	USBLS	5/07
	Phoenix-Mesa-Scottsdale MSA, AZ	Y	24040 FQ	29460 MW	35620 TQ	USBLS	5/07
	Tucson MSA, AZ	Y	23070 FQ	27120 MW	33410 TQ	USBLS	5/07
	Arkansas	Y	21260 FQ	25100 MW	30900 TQ	USBLS	5/07
	Little Rock-North Little Rock MSA, AR	Y	21820 FQ	26060 MW	31690 TQ	USBLS	5/07
	California	H	14.24 FQ	17.18 MW	20.78 TQ	CABLS	1/08-3/08
	Bakersfield MSA, CA	H	11.68 FQ	14.22 MW	18.25 TQ	CABLS	1/08-3/08
	Los Angeles-Long Beach-Glendale PMSA, CA	H	14.01 FQ	17.19 MW	21.12 TQ	CABLS	1/08-3/08
	Oakland-Fremont-Hayward MSA, CA	H	16.41 FQ	18.95 MW	22.49 TQ	CABLS	1/08-3/08
	Riverside-San Bernardino-Ontario MSA, CA	H	13.31 FQ	15.11 MW	17.51 TQ	CABLS	1/08-3/08
	Sacramento-Arden Arcade-Roseville MSA, CA	H	13.86 FQ	16.25 MW	20.98 TQ	CABLS	1/08-3/08

AE	Average entry wage	AW	Average wage paid	FQ	First quartile wage	LO	Lowest wage paid	MTC	Median total compensation	TCC	Total cash compensation
AER	Average entry range	AWR	Average wage range	H	Hourly	LR	Low end range	MW	Median wage paid	TQ	Third quartile wage
AEX	Average experienced wage	AXR	Average experienced range	HI	Highest wage paid	M	Monthly	MWR	Median wage range	W	Weekly
ATC	Average total compensation	D	Daily	HR	High end range	MCC	Median cash compensation	S	See annotated source	Y	Yearly

103

Bill and Account Collector

Occupation/Type/Industry	Location	Per	Low	Mid	High	Source	Date
Bill and Account Collector	San Diego-Carlsbad-San Marcos MSA, CA	H	14.25 FQ	16.49 MW	19.69 TQ	CABLS	1/08-3/08
	San Francisco-San Mateo-Redwood PMSA, CA	H	17.84 FQ	21.55 MW	25.77 TQ	CABLS	1/08-3/08
	San Jose-Sunnyvale-Santa Clara MSA, CA	H	15.79 FQ	20.76 MW	25.28 TQ	CABLS	1/08-3/08
	Santa Ana-Anaheim-Irvine PMSA, CA	Y	31510 FQ	36370 MW	41570 TQ	USBLS	5/07
	Colorado	Y	25510 FQ	30550 MW	37070 TQ	USBLS	5/07
	Denver-Aurora MSA, CO	Y	26260 FQ	31280 MW	38270 TQ	USBLS	5/07
	Connecticut	H	14.66 AE	18.24 MW		CTBLS	1/08-3/08
	Bridgeport-Stamford-Norwalk MSA, CT	Y	32780 FQ	38650 MW	46410 TQ	USBLS	5/07
	Hartford-West Hartford-East Hartford MSA, CT	Y	31800 FQ	36320 MW	41330 TQ	USBLS	5/07
	Delaware	Y	26740 FQ	31710 MW	37760 TQ	USBLS	5/07
	Wilmington PMSA, DE-MD-NJ	Y	27310 FQ	32320 MW	38310 TQ	USBLS	5/07
	District of Columbia	Y	34950 FQ	42290 MW	53500 TQ	USBLS	5/07
	Washington-Arlington-Alexandria MSA, DC-VA-MD-WV	Y	30180 FQ	36070 MW	44310 TQ	USBLS	5/07
	Florida	Y	24420 FQ	28830 MW	34190 TQ	USBLS	5/07
	Fort Lauderdale-Pompano Beach-Deerfield Beach PMSA, FL	Y	23390 FQ	29280 MW	35600 TQ	USBLS	5/07
	Jacksonville MSA, FL	Y	25060 FQ	29140 MW	33700 TQ	USBLS	5/07
	Miami-Fort Lauderdale-Miami Beach MSA, FL	Y	23810 FQ	28840 MW	35140 TQ	USBLS	5/07
	Orlando-Kissimmee MSA, FL	Y	24700 FQ	28940 MW	34460 TQ	USBLS	5/07
	Tampa-St. Petersburg-Clearwater MSA, FL	Y	25670 FQ	29330 MW	34690 TQ	USBLS	5/07
	West Palm Beach-Boca Raton-Boynton Beach PMSA, FL	Y	22660 FQ	27320 MW	32350 TQ	USBLS	5/07
	Georgia	Y	23760 FQ	28400 MW	34470 TQ	USBLS	5/07
	Athens-Clarke County MSA, GA	Y	20320 FQ	24140 MW	29070 TQ	USBLS	5/07
	Atlanta-Sandy Springs-Marietta MSA, GA	Y	24740 FQ	29330 MW	35910 TQ	USBLS	5/07
	Macon MSA, GA	Y	26700 FQ	30480 MW	34540 TQ	USBLS	5/07
	Hawaii	Y	26690 FQ	31690 MW	37900 TQ	USBLS	5/07
	Honolulu MSA, HI	Y	26710 FQ	32210 MW	39790 TQ	USBLS	5/07
	Idaho	Y	23080 FQ	27630 MW	32410 TQ	USBLS	5/07
	Boise City-Nampa MSA, ID	Y	23760 FQ	27880 MW	32700 TQ	USBLS	5/07
	Pocatello MSA, ID	Y	24890 FQ	29230 MW	39380 TQ	USBLS	5/07
	Illinois	Y	24090 FQ	30510 MW	37520 TQ	USBLS	5/07
	Chicago-Naperville-Joliet MSA, IL-IN-WI	Y	24860 FQ	31600 MW	38530 TQ	USBLS	5/07
	Indiana	Y	23920 FQ	28180 MW	33290 TQ	USBLS	5/07
	Gary PMSA, IN	Y	22060 FQ	26710 MW	32310 TQ	USBLS	5/07
	Indianapolis-Carmel MSA, IN	Y	25370 FQ	29290 MW	34710 TQ	USBLS	5/07
	South Bend-Mishawaka MSA, IN-MI	Y	26060 FQ	30550 MW	35480 TQ	USBLS	5/07
	Iowa	Y	25280 FQ	29270 MW	34330 TQ	USBLS	5/07
	Cedar Rapids MSA, IA	Y	27450 FQ	30980 MW	35580 TQ	USBLS	5/07
	Des Moines-West Des Moines MSA, IA	Y	26990 FQ	31170 MW	36710 TQ	USBLS	5/07
	Kansas	Y	21230 FQ	25870 MW	31710 TQ	USBLS	5/07
	Topeka MSA, KS	Y	21440 FQ	23780 MW	27910 TQ	USBLS	5/07
	Wichita MSA, KS	Y	23360 FQ	27850 MW	32800 TQ	USBLS	5/07
	Kentucky	Y	22833 FQ	28495 MW	34395 TQ	KYBLS	2008
	Louisville-Jefferson County MSA, KY-IN	Y	25480 FQ	29400 MW	36060 TQ	USBLS	5/07
	Louisiana	H	10.51 FQ	12.63 MW	14.97 TQ	LABLS	1/08-3/08
	Baton Rouge MSA, LA	Y	22390 FQ	26290 MW	31640 TQ	USBLS	5/07
	Houma-Bayou Cane-Thibodaux MSA, LA	Y	22740 FQ	26850 MW	29930 TQ	USBLS	5/07
	New Orleans-Metairie-Kenner MSA, LA	Y	24040 FQ	28260 MW	33530 TQ	USBLS	5/07
	Shreveport-Bossier City MSA, LA	Y	22880 FQ	25850 MW	29940 TQ	USBLS	5/07
	Maine	Y	25710 FQ	29770 MW	35480 TQ	USBLS	5/07

AE	Average entry wage	AW	Average wage paid	FQ	First quartile wage	LO	Lowest wage paid	MTC	Median total compensation	TCC	Total cash compensation
AER	Average entry range	AWR	Average wage range	H	Hourly	LR	Low end range	MW	Median wage paid	TQ	Third quartile wage
AEX	Average experienced wage	AXR	Average experienced range	HI	Highest wage paid	M	Monthly	MWR	Median wage range	W	Weekly
ATC	Average total compensation	D	Daily	HR	High end range	MCC	Median cash compensation	S	See annotated source	Y	Yearly

104

Bill and Account Collector

Occupation/Type/Industry	Location	Per	Low	Mid	High	Source	Date
Bill and Account Collector	Bangor MSA, ME	Y	26640 FQ	29200 MW	32300 TQ	USBLS	5/07
	Lewiston-Auburn MSA, ME	Y	22900 FQ	26760 MW	30530 TQ	USBLS	5/07
	Portland-South Portland-Biddeford MSA, ME	Y	27270 FQ	31960 MW	38650 TQ	USBLS	5/07
	Maryland	Y		34250 MW		MDBLS	3/08
	Baltimore-Towson MSA, MD	Y	28050 FQ	33380 MW	39020 TQ	USBLS	5/07
	Bethesda-Gaithersburg-Frederick PMSA, MD	Y	28800 FQ	34340 MW	41200 TQ	USBLS	5/07
	Cumberland MSA, MD-WV	Y	20100 FQ	23200 MW	27570 TQ	USBLS	5/07
	Massachusetts	Y	30170 FQ	35900 MW	42550 TQ	USBLS	5/07
	Boston-Cambridge-Quincy NECTA, MA	Y	31240 FQ	36760 MW	43720 TQ	USBLS	5/07
	New Bedford MSA, MA	Y	32400 FQ	36980 MW	43240 TQ	USBLS	5/07
	Worcester MSA, MA-CT	Y	30080 FQ	35710 MW	43700 TQ	USBLS	5/07
	Michigan	Y	28040 FQ	33880 MW	39510 TQ	USBLS	5/07
	Detroit-Warren-Livonia MSA, MI	Y	30820 FQ	35800 MW	40890 TQ	USBLS	5/07
	Grand Rapids-Wyoming MSA, MI	Y	28480 FQ	33950 MW	41190 TQ	USBLS	5/07
	Warren-Troy-Farmington Hills PMSA, MI	Y	30070 FQ	34910 MW	39830 TQ	USBLS	5/07
	Minnesota	Y	26280 FQ	31369 MW	38790 TQ	MNBLS	10/08-12/08
	Duluth-Superior MSA, MN-WI	Y	28413 FQ	32254 MW	40414 TQ	MNBLS	10/08-12/08
	Minneapolis-Saint Paul MSA, MN-WI	Y	26998 FQ	32014 MW	39571 TQ	MNBLS	10/08-12/08
	Rochester MSA, MN	Y	31208 FQ	36107 MW	42253 TQ	MNBLS	10/08-12/08
	Mississippi	Y	20360 FQ	23750 MW	28740 TQ	USBLS	5/07
	Jackson MSA, MS	Y	20940 FQ	24450 MW	29800 TQ	USBLS	5/07
	Pascagoula MSA, MS	Y	21870 FQ	24720 MW	30240 TQ	USBLS	5/07
	Missouri	Y	22830 FQ	27760 MW	33350 TQ	USBLS	5/07
	Jefferson City MSA, MO	Y	19930 FQ	22060 MW	24770 TQ	USBLS	5/07
	Kansas City MSA, MO-KS	Y	21570 FQ	26970 MW	33040 TQ	USBLS	5/07
	St. Louis MSA, MO-IL	Y	24370 FQ	28900 MW	35030 TQ	USBLS	5/07
	Montana	Y	23690 FQ	27940 MW	34450 TQ	USBLS	5/07
	Billings MSA, MT	Y	25050 FQ	28690 MW	34000 TQ	USBLS	5/07
	Nebraska	Y	23100 FQ	27330 MW	31810 TQ	USBLS	5/07
	Omaha-Council Bluffs MSA, NE-IA	Y	24420 FQ	28110 MW	32460 TQ	USBLS	5/07
	Nevada	H	12.73 FQ	14.81 MW	17.54 TQ	NVBLS	5/08
	Las Vegas-Paradise MSA, NV	H	12.61 FQ	14.61 MW	17.24 TQ	NVBLS	5/08
	New Hampshire	H	11.93 AE	14.39 MW	16.73 AEX	NHBLS	6/08
	Manchester MSA, NH	Y	23830 FQ	33730 MW	40080 TQ	USBLS	5/07
	Nashua NECTA, NH-MA	Y	24520 FQ	27160 MW	29890 TQ	USBLS	5/07
	Rochester-Dover MSA, NH-ME	Y	26690 FQ	29000 MW	32460 TQ	USBLS	5/07
	New Jersey	Y	28240 FQ	33670 MW	41100 TQ	USBLS	5/07
	Camden PMSA, NJ	Y	26200 FQ	31380 MW	39850 TQ	USBLS	5/07
	Edison PMSA, NJ	Y	29410 FQ	34860 MW	40720 TQ	USBLS	5/07
	Newark-Union PMSA, NJ-PA	Y	29160 FQ	34130 MW	41560 TQ	USBLS	5/07
	New Mexico	Y	22800 FQ	26840 MW	31530 TQ	USBLS	5/07
	Albuquerque MSA, NM	Y	23250 FQ	27370 MW	32150 TQ	USBLS	5/07
	Las Cruces MSA, NM	Y	19280 FQ	23570 MW	28500 TQ	USBLS	5/07
	New York	Y	25010 FQ	31590 MW	39930 TQ	USBLS	5/07
	Albany-Schenectady-Troy MSA, NY	Y	27430 FQ	32650 MW	38490 TQ	USBLS	5/07
	Buffalo-Niagara Falls MSA, NY	Y	20950 FQ	25370 MW	31850 TQ	USBLS	5/07
	Kingston MSA, NY	Y	22630 FQ	26880 MW	31870 TQ	USBLS	5/07
	Nassau-Suffolk PMSA, NY	Y	28510 FQ	35440 MW	42640 TQ	USBLS	5/07
	New York-Northern New Jersey-Long Island MSA, NY-NJ-PA	Y	29590 FQ	35690 MW	43830 TQ	USBLS	5/07
	North Carolina	Y	23910 FQ	29140 MW	34960 TQ	USBLS	5/07
	Charlotte-Gastonia-Concord MSA, NC-SC	Y	26930 FQ	30610 MW	35440 TQ	USBLS	5/07
	Durham MSA, NC	Y	25660 FQ	34310 MW	46990 TQ	USBLS	5/07
	Raleigh-Cary MSA, NC	Y	27820 FQ	32900 MW	37730 TQ	USBLS	5/07
	North Dakota	Y	18790 FQ	23610 MW	30020 TQ	USBLS	5/07
	Fargo MSA, ND-MN	Y	17300 FQ	19000 MW	27440 TQ	USBLS	5/07
	Ohio	Y	24330 FQ	28370 MW	33410 TQ	USBLS	5/07
	Cincinnati-Middletown MSA, OH-KY-IN	Y	26230 FQ	29930 MW	35350 TQ	USBLS	5/07

Occupation/Type/Industry	Location	Per	Low	Mid	High	Source	Date
Bill and Account Collector	Cleveland-Elyria-Mentor MSA, OH	Y	23890 FQ	27880 MW	32740 TQ	USBLS	5/07
	Columbus MSA, OH	Y	24430 FQ	28110 MW	32780 TQ	USBLS	5/07
	Dayton MSA, OH	Y	24360 FQ	28140 MW	34340 TQ	USBLS	5/07
	Oklahoma	Y	22250 FQ	26970 MW	32340 TQ	USBLS	5/07
	Oklahoma City MSA, OK	Y	22430 FQ	26890 MW	31880 TQ	USBLS	5/07
	Tulsa MSA, OK	Y	24220 FQ	28240 MW	33260 TQ	USBLS	5/07
	Oregon	H	13.19 FQ	15.56 MW	18.43 TQ	ORBLS	5/08
	Eugene-Springfield MSA, OR	Y	27020 FQ	33620 MW	39630 TQ	USBLS	5/07
	Portland-Vancouver-Beaverton MSA, OR-WA	Y	28160 FQ	32810 MW	38000 TQ	USBLS	5/07
	Pennsylvania	Y	23420 FQ	28860 MW	35880 TQ	USBLS	5/07
	Allentown-Bethlehem-Easton MSA, PA-NJ	Y	21450 FQ	25020 MW	31780 TQ	USBLS	5/07
	Philadelphia-Camden-Wilmington MSA, PA-NJ-DE-MD		26150 FQ	31670 MW	38780 TQ	USBLS	5/07
	Pittsburgh MSA, PA	Y	24220 FQ	28920 MW	34340 TQ	USBLS	5/07
	York-Hanover MSA, PA	Y	22930 FQ	25910 MW	31680 TQ	USBLS	5/07
	Rhode Island	Y	27280 FQ	32470 MW	38700 TQ	USBLS	5/07
	Providence-Fall River-Warwick MSA, RI-MA	Y	27230 FQ	32220 MW	38600 TQ	USBLS	5/07
	South Carolina	Y	22610 FQ	27120 MW	32090 TQ	USBLS	5/07
	Charleston-North Charleston MSA, SC	Y	23310 FQ	26900 MW	32140 TQ	USBLS	5/07
	Columbia MSA, SC	Y	22650 FQ	26990 MW	31630 TQ	USBLS	5/07
	South Dakota	Y	23297 FQ	26843 MW	31628 TQ	SDBLS	7/08-9/08
	Rapid City MSA, SD	Y	23584 FQ	27431 MW	32138 TQ	SDBLS	7/08-9/08
	Sioux Falls MSA, SD	Y	24668 FQ	28405 MW	32635 TQ	SDBLS	7/08-9/08
	Tennessee	Y	24000 FQ	28490 MW	33580 TQ	USBLS	5/07
	Johnson City MSA, TN	Y	24770 FQ	29380 MW	34600 TQ	USBLS	5/07
	Memphis MSA, TN-MS-AR	Y	23330 FQ	28980 MW	34190 TQ	USBLS	5/07
	Nashville-Davidson-Murfreesboro MSA, TN	Y	26200 FQ	30530 MW	35990 TQ	USBLS	5/07
	Texas	Y	22960 FQ	29100 MW	35570 TQ	USBLS	5/07
	Austin-Round Rock MSA, TX	Y	25370 FQ	29470 MW	34690 TQ	USBLS	5/07
	Dallas-Fort Worth-Arlington MSA, TX	Y	25930 FQ	31150 MW	37190 TQ	USBLS	5/07
	El Paso MSA, TX	Y	20290 FQ	25740 MW	30340 TQ	USBLS	5/07
	Houston-Sugar Land-Baytown MSA, TX	Y	24280 FQ	30980 MW	36970 TQ	USBLS	5/07
	San Antonio MSA, TX	Y	20930 FQ	24550 MW	30480 TQ	USBLS	5/07
	Utah	Y	23690 FQ	28390 MW	32820 TQ	USBLS	5/07
	Logan MSA, UT-ID	Y	19010 FQ	23390 MW	27790 TQ	USBLS	5/07
	Salt Lake City MSA, UT	Y	24350 FQ	28820 MW	33130 TQ	USBLS	5/07
	Vermont	Y	27410 FQ	31550 MW	37130 TQ	USBLS	5/07
	Burlington-South Burlington MSA, VT	Y	29200 FQ	33250 MW	39200 TQ	USBLS	5/07
	Virginia	Y	25340 FQ	30310 MW	36850 TQ	USBLS	5/07
	Lynchburg MSA, VA	Y	24230 FQ	30620 MW	39620 TQ	USBLS	5/07
	Richmond MSA, VA	Y	27300 FQ	31460 MW	37140 TQ	USBLS	5/07
	Virginia Beach-Norfolk-Newport News MSA, VA-NC	Y	23040 FQ	27610 MW	31730 TQ	USBLS	5/07
	Washington	H	13.67 FQ	16.84 MW	20.06 TQ	WABLS	3/08
	Seattle-Tacoma-Bellevue MSA, WA	Y	28640 FQ	35450 MW	41520 TQ	USBLS	5/07
	West Virginia	Y	22457 FQ	26154 MW	30457 TQ	WVBLS	7/08-9/08
	Charleston MSA, WV	Y	21500 FQ	24560 MW	28930 TQ	USBLS	5/07
	Parkersburg-Marietta-Vienna MSA, WV-OH	Y	21650 FQ	25580 MW	29310 TQ	USBLS	5/07
	Wisconsin	Y	25480 FQ	29110 MW	34090 TQ	USBLS	5/07
	Green Bay MSA, WI	Y	25670 FQ	29130 MW	34180 TQ	USBLS	5/07
	Milwaukee-Waukesha-West Allis MSA, WI	Y	24810 FQ	28900 MW	34120 TQ	USBLS	5/07
	Wyoming	Y	22406 FQ	27431 MW	35564 TQ	WYBLS	9/08
	Cheyenne MSA, WY	Y	23621 FQ	29752 MW	35526 TQ	WYBLS	9/08
	Puerto Rico	Y	13850 FQ	17080 MW	21960 TQ	USBLS	5/07
	San Juan-Caguas-Guaynabo MSA, PR	Y	13940 FQ	17300 MW	22330 TQ	USBLS	5/07
	Virgin Islands	Y	25410 FQ	28610 MW	32580 TQ	USBLS	5/07
	Guam	Y	16650 FQ	21010 MW	28300 TQ	USBLS	5/07

AE Average entry wage	**AW** Average wage paid	**FQ** First quartile wage	**LO** Lowest wage paid	**MTC** Median total compensation	**TCC** Total cash compensation
AER Average entry range	**AWR** Average wage range	**H** Hourly	**LR** Low end range	**MW** Median wage paid	**TQ** Third quartile wage
AEX Average experienced wage	**AXR** Average experienced range	**HI** Highest wage paid	**M** Monthly	**MWR** Median wage range	**W** Weekly
ATC Average total compensation	**D** Daily	**HR** High end range	**MCC** Median cash compensation	**S** See annotated source	**Y** Yearly

Occupation/Type/Industry	Location	Per	Low	Mid	High	Source	Date
Billing Advocate	United States	H		50.00- 100.00 AW		USNEWS04	2008
Billing and Posting Clerk and Machine Operator							
	Alabama	Y	21690 FQ	25790 MW	30560 TQ	USBLS	5/07
	Birmingham-Hoover MSA, AL	Y	24410 FQ	28460 MW	32790 TQ	USBLS	5/07
	Mobile MSA, AL	Y	21340 FQ	25660 MW	29580 TQ	USBLS	5/07
	Alaska	Y	31420 FQ	35860 MW	41370 TQ	USBLS	5/07
	Anchorage MSA, AK	Y	31880 FQ	35760 MW	40280 TQ	USBLS	5/07
	Arizona	Y	24470 FQ	29620 MW	35510 TQ	USBLS	5/07
	Flagstaff MSA, AZ	Y	21620 FQ	26730 MW	31180 TQ	USBLS	5/07
	Phoenix-Mesa-Scottsdale MSA, AZ	Y	25290 FQ	30430 MW	36190 TQ	USBLS	5/07
	Tucson MSA, AZ	Y	22960 FQ	27100 MW	32210 TQ	USBLS	5/07
	Arkansas	Y	20950 FQ	24710 MW	29510 TQ	USBLS	5/07
	Little Rock-North Little Rock MSA, AR	Y	22660 FQ	26610 MW	31620 TQ	USBLS	5/07
	Pine Bluff MSA, AR	Y	21500 FQ	23690 MW	27830 TQ	USBLS	5/07
	California	H	13.16 FQ	15.83 MW	19.42 TQ	CABLS	1/08-3/08
	Los Angeles-Long Beach-Glendale PMSA, CA	H	12.83 FQ	15.44 MW	19.46 TQ	CABLS	1/08-3/08
	Oakland-Fremont-Hayward MSA, CA	H	13.79 FQ	17.40 MW	21.74 TQ	CABLS	1/08-3/08
	Riverside-San Bernardino-Ontario MSA, CA	H	12.56 FQ	15.04 MW	17.61 TQ	CABLS	1/08-3/08
	Sacramento-Arden Arcade-Roseville MSA, CA	H	13.85 FQ	16.20 MW	19.20 TQ	CABLS	1/08-3/08
	San Diego-Carlsbad-San Marcos MSA, CA	H	13.48 FQ	15.75 MW	18.61 TQ	CABLS	1/08-3/08
	San Francisco-San Mateo-Redwood PMSA, CA	H	15.71 FQ	19.81 MW	25.97 TQ	CABLS	1/08-3/08
	San Jose-Sunnyvale-Santa Clara MSA, CA	H	15.29 FQ	17.95 MW	21.83 TQ	CABLS	1/08-3/08
	Santa Ana-Anaheim-Irvine PMSA, CA	Y	28360 FQ	33930 MW	40870 TQ	USBLS	5/07
	Stockton MSA, CA	H	13.34 FQ	15.68 MW	19.26 TQ	CABLS	1/08-3/08
	Colorado	Y	26480 FQ	31300 MW	37780 TQ	USBLS	5/07
	Denver-Aurora MSA, CO	Y	27480 FQ	33210 MW	39480 TQ	USBLS	5/07
	Connecticut	H	13.45 AE	17.20 MW		CTBLS	1/08-3/08
	Bridgeport-Stamford-Norwalk MSA, CT	Y	30340 FQ	36280 MW	43720 TQ	USBLS	5/07
	Hartford-West Hartford-East Hartford MSA, CT	Y	29280 FQ	33650 MW	39210 TQ	USBLS	5/07
	Delaware	Y	26730 FQ	31980 MW	38420 TQ	USBLS	5/07
	Wilmington PMSA, DE-MD-NJ	Y	28420 FQ	33450 MW	39550 TQ	USBLS	5/07
	District of Columbia	Y	30970 FQ	38030 MW	46940 TQ	USBLS	5/07
	Washington-Arlington-Alexandria MSA, DC-VA-MD-WV	Y	29410 FQ	35640 MW	43380 TQ	USBLS	5/07
	Florida	Y	24180 FQ	28520 MW	33260 TQ	USBLS	5/07
	Fort Lauderdale-Pompano Beach-Deerfield Beach PMSA, FL	Y	26250 FQ	30170 MW	34790 TQ	USBLS	5/07
	Jacksonville MSA, FL	Y	24710 FQ	28350 MW	31910 TQ	USBLS	5/07
	Miami-Fort Lauderdale-Miami Beach MSA, FL	Y	24640 FQ	29170 MW	34460 TQ	USBLS	5/07
	Orlando-Kissimmee MSA, FL	Y	23440 FQ	27430 MW	32540 TQ	USBLS	5/07
	Tampa-St. Petersburg-Clearwater MSA, FL	Y	24740 FQ	29330 MW	35000 TQ	USBLS	5/07
	West Palm Beach-Boca Raton-Boynton Beach PMSA, FL	Y	25750 FQ	29950 MW	36360 TQ	USBLS	5/07
	Georgia	Y	25310 FQ	29810 MW	35530 TQ	USBLS	5/07
	Atlanta-Sandy Springs-Marietta MSA, GA	Y	27740 FQ	32320 MW	37780 TQ	USBLS	5/07
	Hawaii	Y	26450 FQ	31670 MW	36880 TQ	USBLS	5/07
	Honolulu MSA, HI	Y	27010 FQ	32220 MW	37230 TQ	USBLS	5/07
	Idaho	Y	20820 FQ	26210 MW	31120 TQ	USBLS	5/07
	Boise City-Nampa MSA, ID	Y	21810 FQ	26420 MW	31570 TQ	USBLS	5/07
	Illinois	Y	26260 FQ	31430 MW	37880 TQ	USBLS	5/07
	Chicago-Naperville-Joliet MSA, IL-IN-WI	Y	27610 FQ	32740 MW	38940 TQ	USBLS	5/07

AE	Average entry wage	AW	Average wage paid	FQ	First quartile wage	LO	Lowest wage paid	MTC	Median total compensation	TCC	Total cash compensation
AER	Average entry range	AWR	Average wage range	H	Hourly	LR	Low end range	MW	Median wage paid	TQ	Third quartile wage
AEX	Average experienced wage	AXR	Average experienced range	HI	Highest wage paid	M	Monthly	MWR	Median wage range	W	Weekly
ATC	Average total compensation	D	Daily	HR	High end range	MCC	Median cash compensation	S	See annotated source	Y	Yearly

Occupation/Type/Industry	Location	Per	Low	Mid	High	Source	Date
Billing and Posting Clerk and Machine Operator	Indiana	Y	24060 FQ	28270 MW	33070 TQ	USBLS	5/07
	Gary PMSA, IN	Y	24490 FQ	28550 MW	33670 TQ	USBLS	5/07
	Indianapolis-Carmel MSA, IN	Y	25940 FQ	30380 MW	35970 TQ	USBLS	5/07
	Iowa	Y	23890 FQ	28120 MW	32630 TQ	USBLS	5/07
	Davenport-Moline-Rock Island MSA, IA-IL	Y	21160 FQ	24720 MW	30700 TQ	USBLS	5/07
	Des Moines-West Des Moines MSA, IA	Y	26620 FQ	30350 MW	35410 TQ	USBLS	5/07
	Kansas	Y	23230 FQ	27800 MW	32590 TQ	USBLS	5/07
	Wichita MSA, KS	Y	23510 FQ	27290 MW	31190 TQ	USBLS	5/07
	Kentucky	Y	24275 FQ	28445 MW	33370 TQ	KYBLS	2008
	Bowling Green MSA, KY	Y	23620 FQ	26970 MW	30070 TQ	USBLS	5/07
	Louisville-Jefferson County MSA, KY-IN	Y	26180 FQ	29710 MW	35030 TQ	USBLS	5/07
	Owensboro MSA, KY	Y	23540 FQ	27170 MW	31020 TQ	USBLS	5/07
	Louisiana	H	10.38 FQ	12.37 MW	14.65 TQ	LABLS	1/08-3/08
	Baton Rouge MSA, LA	Y	21750 FQ	25890 MW	29940 TQ	USBLS	5/07
	Houma-Bayou Cane-Thibodaux MSA, LA	Y	22180 FQ	26130 MW	31050 TQ	USBLS	5/07
	New Orleans-Metairie-Kenner MSA, LA	Y	23290 FQ	26990 MW	31520 TQ	USBLS	5/07
	Maine	Y	23460 FQ	27580 MW	31490 TQ	USBLS	5/07
	Portland-South Portland-Biddeford MSA, ME	Y	27240 FQ	30440 MW	34710 TQ	USBLS	5/07
	Maryland	Y		33300 MW		MDBLS	3/08
	Baltimore-Towson MSA, MD	Y	27340 FQ	32670 MW	38390 TQ	USBLS	5/07
	Bethesda-Gaithersburg-Frederick PMSA, MD	Y	29360 FQ	34770 MW	41220 TQ	USBLS	5/07
	Massachusetts	Y	28020 FQ	33300 MW	38930 TQ	USBLS	5/07
	Boston-Cambridge-Quincy NECTA, MA	Y	29900 FQ	34860 MW	40990 TQ	USBLS	5/07
	Worcester MSA, MA-CT	Y	28720 FQ	34060 MW	38210 TQ	USBLS	5/07
	Michigan	Y	26930 FQ	31500 MW	37730 TQ	USBLS	5/07
	Detroit-Warren-Livonia MSA, MI	Y	28300 FQ	33150 MW	39470 TQ	USBLS	5/07
	Grand Rapids-Wyoming MSA, MI	Y	25870 FQ	30250 MW	35870 TQ	USBLS	5/07
	Warren-Troy-Farmington Hills PMSA, MI	Y	27960 FQ	32460 MW	39200 TQ	USBLS	5/07
	Minnesota	Y	28486 FQ	33763 MW	39727 TQ	MNBLS	10/08-12/08
	Duluth-Superior MSA, MN-WI	Y	25135 FQ	29090 MW	33659 TQ	MNBLS	10/08-12/08
	Minneapolis-Saint Paul MSA, MN-WI	Y	29881 FQ	35012 MW	40455 TQ	MNBLS	10/08-12/08
	Rochester MSA, MN	Y	36689 FQ	42795 MW	49000 TQ	MNBLS	10/08-12/08
	Mississippi	Y	21550 FQ	25350 MW	30120 TQ	USBLS	5/07
	Jackson MSA, MS	Y	22450 FQ	26730 MW	30650 TQ	USBLS	5/07
	Missouri	Y	23270 FQ	28240 MW	33950 TQ	USBLS	5/07
	Kansas City MSA, MO-KS	Y	27420 FQ	31830 MW	37240 TQ	USBLS	5/07
	St. Louis MSA, MO-IL	Y	24120 FQ	29080 MW	34710 TQ	USBLS	5/07
	Montana	Y	20190 FQ	24690 MW	30620 TQ	USBLS	5/07
	Billings MSA, MT	Y	16790 FQ	21380 MW	27800 TQ	USBLS	5/07
	Nebraska	Y	23990 FQ	28050 MW	32460 TQ	USBLS	5/07
	Omaha-Council Bluffs MSA, NE-IA	Y	25940 FQ	29270 MW	34230 TQ	USBLS	5/07
	Nevada	H	12.49 FQ	14.80 MW	17.92 TQ	NVBLS	5/08
	Las Vegas-Paradise MSA, NV	H	12.80 FQ	15.05 MW	18.15 TQ	NVBLS	5/08
	New Hampshire	H	12.41 AE	15.49 MW	17.54 AEX	NHBLS	6/08
	Manchester MSA, NH	Y	27670 FQ	32090 MW	37160 TQ	USBLS	5/07
	Nashua NECTA, NH-MA	Y	29710 FQ	34100 MW	39320 TQ	USBLS	5/07
	Portsmouth MSA, NH-ME	Y	26840 FQ	30020 MW	34490 TQ	USBLS	5/07
	New Jersey	Y	28750 FQ	34500 MW	40330 TQ	USBLS	5/07
	Atlantic City MSA, NJ	Y	27470 FQ	32940 MW	37450 TQ	USBLS	5/07
	Camden PMSA, NJ	Y	27660 FQ	32830 MW	37970 TQ	USBLS	5/07
	Edison PMSA, NJ	Y	28740 FQ	34320 MW	39980 TQ	USBLS	5/07
	Newark-Union PMSA, NJ-PA	Y	30130 FQ	36010 MW	42930 TQ	USBLS	5/07
	New Mexico	Y	21640 FQ	25940 MW	31110 TQ	USBLS	5/07
	Albuquerque MSA, NM	Y	23590 FQ	27570 MW	32300 TQ	USBLS	5/07
	New York	Y	26990 FQ	32410 MW	38910 TQ	USBLS	5/07
	Albany-Schenectady-Troy MSA, NY	Y	26180 FQ	30450 MW	35460 TQ	USBLS	5/07

AE	Average entry wage	AW	Average wage paid	FQ	First quartile wage	LO	Lowest wage paid	MTC	Median total compensation	TCC	Total cash compensation
AER	Average entry range	AWR	Average wage range	H	Hourly	LR	Low end range	MW	Median wage paid	TQ	Third quartile wage
AEX	Average experienced wage	AXR	Average experienced range	HI	Highest wage paid	M	Monthly	MWR	Median wage range	W	Weekly
ATC	Average total compensation	D	Daily	HR	High end range	MCC	Median cash compensation	S	See annotated source	Y	Yearly

Occupation/Type/Industry	Location	Per	Low	Mid	High	Source	Date
Billing and Posting Clerk and Machine Operator	Buffalo-Niagara Falls MSA, NY	Y	24400 FQ	28250 MW	32240 TQ	USBLS	5/07
	Nassau-Suffolk PMSA, NY	Y	28980 FQ	34510 MW	40630 TQ	USBLS	5/07
	New York-Northern New Jersey-Long Island MSA, NY-NJ-PA	Y	29170 FQ	35060 MW	41160 TQ	USBLS	5/07
	North Carolina	Y	25140 FQ	29290 MW	34300 TQ	USBLS	5/07
	Charlotte-Gastonia-Concord MSA, NC-SC	Y	27420 FQ	31730 MW	36550 TQ	USBLS	5/07
	Raleigh-Cary MSA, NC	Y	26900 FQ	30470 MW	35790 TQ	USBLS	5/07
	North Dakota	Y	21750 FQ	25310 MW	30240 TQ	USBLS	5/07
	Fargo MSA, ND-MN	Y	22350 FQ	26620 MW	31110 TQ	USBLS	5/07
	Grand Forks MSA, ND-MN	Y	23400 FQ	27130 MW	31790 TQ	USBLS	5/07
	Ohio	Y	24540 FQ	28830 MW	33800 TQ	USBLS	5/07
	Canton-Massillon MSA, OH	Y	24760 FQ	27830 MW	31150 TQ	USBLS	5/07
	Cincinnati-Middletown MSA, OH-KY-IN	Y	26570 FQ	30600 MW	36180 TQ	USBLS	5/07
	Cleveland-Elyria-Mentor MSA, OH	Y	25840 FQ	29910 MW	35430 TQ	USBLS	5/07
	Columbus MSA, OH	Y	25670 FQ	30160 MW	35270 TQ	USBLS	5/07
	Dayton MSA, OH	Y	25600 FQ	28940 MW	32730 TQ	USBLS	5/07
	Oklahoma	Y	20800 FQ	25440 MW	30290 TQ	USBLS	5/07
	Oklahoma City MSA, OK	Y	21430 FQ	26280 MW	30630 TQ	USBLS	5/07
	Tulsa MSA, OK	Y	22730 FQ	27350 MW	32150 TQ	USBLS	5/07
	Oregon	H	13.23 FQ	15.48 MW	18.15 TQ	ORBLS	5/08
	Eugene-Springfield MSA, OR	Y	27200 FQ	31360 MW	36330 TQ	USBLS	5/07
	Portland-Vancouver-Beaverton MSA, OR-WA	Y	27310 FQ	32210 MW	37810 TQ	USBLS	5/07
	Pennsylvania	Y	24200 FQ	28760 MW	34760 TQ	USBLS	5/07
	Allentown-Bethlehem-Easton MSA, PA-NJ	Y	26570 FQ	30600 MW	36770 TQ	USBLS	5/07
	Philadelphia-Camden-Wilmington MSA, PA-NJ-DE-MD	Y	26900 FQ	32210 MW	38260 TQ	USBLS	5/07
	Pittsburgh MSA, PA	Y	23680 FQ	27760 MW	32180 TQ	USBLS	5/07
	Rhode Island	Y	24060 FQ	29040 MW	34800 TQ	USBLS	5/07
	Providence-Fall River-Warwick MSA, RI-MA	Y	24320 FQ	29070 MW	34860 TQ	USBLS	5/07
	South Carolina	Y	23710 FQ	27750 MW	31880 TQ	USBLS	5/07
	Charleston-North Charleston MSA, SC	Y	23160 FQ	27580 MW	32830 TQ	USBLS	5/07
	Columbia MSA, SC	Y	24710 FQ	27950 MW	31230 TQ	USBLS	5/07
	South Dakota	Y	20321 FQ	23684 MW	28318 TQ	SDBLS	7/08-9/08
	Sioux Falls MSA, SD	Y	21363 FQ	24208 MW	28677 TQ	SDBLS	7/08-9/08
	Tennessee	Y	23470 FQ	27900 MW	32460 TQ	USBLS	5/07
	Johnson City MSA, TN	Y	21130 FQ	24180 MW	30010 TQ	USBLS	5/07
	Memphis MSA, TN-MS-AR	Y	25490 FQ	29670 MW	34530 TQ	USBLS	5/07
	Nashville-Davidson-Murfreesboro MSA, TN	Y	25580 FQ	29490 MW	34830 TQ	USBLS	5/07
	Texas	Y	23580 FQ	28640 MW	34240 TQ	USBLS	5/07
	Austin-Round Rock MSA, TX	Y	26260 FQ	30200 MW	35530 TQ	USBLS	5/07
	Dallas-Fort Worth-Arlington MSA, TX	Y	26300 FQ	30680 MW	36380 TQ	USBLS	5/07
	El Paso MSA, TX	Y	18050 FQ	22620 MW	28600 TQ	USBLS	5/07
	Houston-Sugar Land-Baytown MSA, TX	Y	26190 FQ	30720 MW	36050 TQ	USBLS	5/07
	San Antonio MSA, TX	Y	23890 FQ	28560 MW	33520 TQ	USBLS	5/07
	Utah	Y	22480 FQ	26570 MW	31400 TQ	USBLS	5/07
	Ogden-Clearfield MSA, UT	Y	21700 FQ	25680 MW	30490 TQ	USBLS	5/07
	St. George MSA, UT	Y	18100 FQ	20760 MW	27110 TQ	USBLS	5/07
	Salt Lake City MSA, UT	Y	22860 FQ	26930 MW	31710 TQ	USBLS	5/07
	Vermont	Y	25670 FQ	29810 MW	35180 TQ	USBLS	5/07
	Burlington-South Burlington MSA, VT	Y	26100 FQ	30310 MW	35590 TQ	USBLS	5/07
	Virginia	Y	25450 FQ	30510 MW	37160 TQ	USBLS	5/07
	Richmond MSA, VA	Y	27010 FQ	31880 MW	37890 TQ	USBLS	5/07
	Virginia Beach-Norfolk-Newport News MSA, VA-NC	Y	24410 FQ	28560 MW	33380 TQ	USBLS	5/07
	Washington	H	13.56 FQ	16.09 MW	18.60 TQ	WABLS	3/08
	Olympia MSA, WA	Y	28340 FQ	31710 MW	37100 TQ	USBLS	5/07

AE	Average entry wage	AW	Average wage paid	FQ	First quartile wage
AER	Average entry range	AWR	Average wage range	H	Hourly
AEX	Average experienced wage	AXR	Average experienced range	HI	Highest wage paid
ATC	Average total compensation	D	Daily	HR	High end range

LO	Lowest wage paid	MTC	Median total compensation	TCC	Total cash compensation
LR	Low end range	MW	Median wage paid	TQ	Third quartile wage
M	Monthly	MWR	Median wage range	W	Weekly
MCC	Median cash compensation	S	See annotated source	Y	Yearly

Occupation/Type/Industry	Location	Per	Low	Mid	High	Source	Date
Billing and Posting Clerk and Machine Operator	Seattle-Tacoma-Bellevue MSA, WA	Y	30750 FQ	35560 MW	40190 TQ	USBLS	5/07
	West Virginia	Y	20789 FQ	24407 MW	29525 TQ	WVBLS	7/08-9/08
	Charleston MSA, WV	Y	21760 FQ	26620 MW	31030 TQ	USBLS	5/07
	Wisconsin	Y	26200 FQ	30280 MW	35520 TQ	USBLS	5/07
	Milwaukee-Waukesha-West Allis MSA, WI	Y	26460 FQ	31150 MW	36230 TQ	USBLS	5/07
	Wyoming	Y	23012 FQ	27422 MW	32297 TQ	WYBLS	9/08
	Cheyenne MSA, WY	Y	23053 FQ	25305 MW	29011 TQ	WYBLS	9/08
	Puerto Rico	Y	13430 FQ	15850 MW	19810 TQ	USBLS	5/07
	San Juan-Caguas-Guaynabo MSA, PR	Y	13520 FQ	16040 MW	20180 TQ	USBLS	5/07
	Virgin Islands	Y	19550 FQ	22070 MW	25310 TQ	USBLS	5/07
	Guam	Y	17090 FQ	20480 MW	25950 TQ	USBLS	5/07
Bindery Operator State Government	Ohio	H	16.09 LO		18.36 HI	ODAS	2008
Bindery Worker	Alabama	Y	19650 FQ	24510 MW	30710 TQ	USBLS	5/07
	Birmingham-Hoover MSA, AL	Y	21680 FQ	27020 MW	34830 TQ	USBLS	5/07
	Alaska	Y	20900 FQ	27450 MW	36860 TQ	USBLS	5/07
	Anchorage MSA, AK	Y	17790 FQ	22470 MW	30650 TQ	USBLS	5/07
	Arizona	Y	19070 FQ	22880 MW	31100 TQ	USBLS	5/07
	Phoenix-Mesa-Scottsdale MSA, AZ	Y	20430 FQ	23920 MW	33520 TQ	USBLS	5/07
	Tucson MSA, AZ	Y	16490 FQ	18240 MW	23680 TQ	USBLS	5/07
	Arkansas	Y	19080 FQ	23690 MW	32820 TQ	USBLS	5/07
	Little Rock-North Little Rock MSA, AR	Y	18290 FQ	22810 MW	33210 TQ	USBLS	5/07
	California	H	9.53 FQ	11.41 MW	15.10 TQ	CABLS	1/08-3/08
	Los Angeles-Long Beach-Glendale PMSA, CA	H	10.08 FQ	11.61 MW	15.62 TQ	CABLS	1/08-3/08
	Oakland-Fremont-Hayward MSA, CA	H	9.74 FQ	12.09 MW	16.64 TQ	CABLS	1/08-3/08
	Riverside-San Bernardino-Ontario MSA, CA	H	8.73 FQ	9.73 MW	11.41 TQ	CABLS	1/08-3/08
	Sacramento-Arden Arcade-Roseville MSA, CA	H	9.81 FQ	11.63 MW	14.44 TQ	CABLS	1/08-3/08
	San Diego-Carlsbad-San Marcos MSA, CA	H	9.04 FQ	12.38 MW	17.25 TQ	CABLS	1/08-3/08
	San Francisco-San Mateo-Redwood PMSA, CA	H	10.20 FQ	11.32 MW	14.77 TQ	CABLS	1/08-3/08
	San Jose-Sunnyvale-Santa Clara MSA, CA	H	10.63 FQ	12.34 MW	14.20 TQ	CABLS	1/08-3/08
	Santa Ana-Anaheim-Irvine PMSA, CA	Y	17570 FQ	20720 MW	28970 TQ	USBLS	5/07
	Colorado	Y	22140 FQ	27790 MW	33270 TQ	USBLS	5/07
	Boulder MSA, CO	Y	27990 FQ	32320 MW	35220 TQ	USBLS	5/07
	Denver-Aurora MSA, CO	Y	21740 FQ	27200 MW	32500 TQ	USBLS	5/07
	Connecticut	H	9.63 AE	13.56 MW		CTBLS	1/08-3/08
	Bridgeport-Stamford-Norwalk MSA, CT	Y	24150 FQ	29340 MW	36910 TQ	USBLS	5/07
	Hartford-West Hartford-East Hartford MSA, CT	Y	22900 FQ	28390 MW	35030 TQ	USBLS	5/07
	Delaware	Y	21710 FQ	28300 MW	35240 TQ	USBLS	5/07
	Wilmington PMSA, DE-MD-NJ	Y	21230 FQ	25930 MW	33100 TQ	USBLS	5/07
	District of Columbia	Y	35460 FQ	44270 MW	54900 TQ	USBLS	5/07
	Washington-Arlington-Alexandria MSA, DC-VA-MD-WV	Y	25940 FQ	32250 MW	40210 TQ	USBLS	5/07
	Florida	Y	18460 FQ	24020 MW	31900 TQ	USBLS	5/07
	Fort Lauderdale-Pompano Beach-Deerfield Beach PMSA, FL	Y	19660 FQ	26980 MW	34960 TQ	USBLS	5/07
	Jacksonville MSA, FL	Y	17180 FQ	19240 MW	23000 TQ	USBLS	5/07
	Miami-Fort Lauderdale-Miami Beach MSA, FL	Y	18120 FQ	24440 MW	32570 TQ	USBLS	5/07
	Orlando-Kissimmee MSA, FL	Y	21330 FQ	26260 MW	32500 TQ	USBLS	5/07
	Tampa-St. Petersburg-Clearwater MSA, FL	Y	20430 FQ	25180 MW	34640 TQ	USBLS	5/07

AE Average entry wage	**AW** Average wage paid	**FQ** First quartile wage	**LO** Lowest wage paid	**MTC** Median total compensation	**TCC** Total cash compensation
AER Average entry range	**AWR** Average wage range	**H** Hourly	**LR** Low end range	**MW** Median wage paid	**TQ** Third quartile wage
AEX Average experienced wage	**AXR** Average experienced range	**HI** Highest wage paid	**M** Monthly	**MWR** Median wage range	**W** Weekly
ATC Average total compensation	**D** Daily	**HR** High end range	**MCC** Median cash compensation	**S** See annotated source	**Y** Yearly

Occupation/Type/Industry	Location	Per	Low	Mid	High	Source	Date
Bindery Worker	West Palm Beach-Boca Raton-Boynton Beach PMSA, FL	Y	21780 FQ	26920 MW	36500 TQ	USBLS	5/07
	Georgia	Y	19160 FQ	25070 MW	36700 TQ	USBLS	5/07
	Atlanta-Sandy Springs-Marietta MSA, GA	Y	19650 FQ	25390 MW	36050 TQ	USBLS	5/07
	Hawaii	Y	15920 FQ	24720 MW	31840 TQ	USBLS	5/07
	Honolulu MSA, HI	Y	15760 FQ	19650 MW	34220 TQ	USBLS	5/07
	Idaho	Y	21900 FQ	23810 MW	26270 TQ	USBLS	5/07
	Illinois	Y	19270 FQ	26990 MW	36760 TQ	USBLS	5/07
	Chicago-Naperville-Joliet MSA, IL-IN-WI	Y	19350 FQ	27780 MW	39940 TQ	USBLS	5/07
	Rockford MSA, IL	Y	23420 FQ	27870 MW	31690 TQ	USBLS	5/07
	Indiana	Y	20770 FQ	28430 MW	37180 TQ	USBLS	5/07
	Indianapolis-Carmel MSA, IN	Y	20060 FQ	25860 MW	34610 TQ	USBLS	5/07
	Terre Haute MSA, IN	Y	22320 FQ	25040 MW	28090 TQ	USBLS	5/07
	Iowa	Y	21160 FQ	25740 MW	30750 TQ	USBLS	5/07
	Des Moines-West Des Moines MSA, IA	Y	22510 FQ	26590 MW	31250 TQ	USBLS	5/07
	Kansas	Y	18130 FQ	22220 MW	26860 TQ	USBLS	5/07
	Topeka MSA, KS	Y	17080 FQ	20070 MW	30020 TQ	USBLS	5/07
	Wichita MSA, KS	Y	18460 FQ	22830 MW	27940 TQ	USBLS	5/07
	Kentucky	Y	23221 FQ	29942 MW	36559 TQ	KYBLS	2008
	Louisville-Jefferson County MSA, KY-IN	Y	21440 FQ	26080 MW	33870 TQ	USBLS	5/07
	Louisiana	H	7.30 FQ	9.66 MW	12.35 TQ	LABLS	1/08-3/08
	Baton Rouge MSA, LA	Y	16250 FQ	18270 MW	23160 TQ	USBLS	5/07
	New Orleans-Metairie-Kenner MSA, LA	Y	13920 FQ	18940 MW	25700 TQ	USBLS	5/07
	Maine	Y	20510 FQ	26130 MW	31490 TQ	USBLS	5/07
	Portland-South Portland-Biddeford MSA, ME	Y	25580 FQ	29510 MW	32950 TQ	USBLS	5/07
	Maryland	Y		29800 MW		MDBLS	3/08
	Baltimore-Towson MSA, MD	Y	22050 FQ	27980 MW	34620 TQ	USBLS	5/07
	Bethesda-Gaithersburg-Frederick PMSA, MD	Y	23600 FQ	29690 MW	36160 TQ	USBLS	5/07
	Massachusetts	Y	22810 FQ	31500 MW	41120 TQ	USBLS	5/07
	Boston-Cambridge-Quincy NECTA, MA	Y	24810 FQ	36060 MW	45010 TQ	USBLS	5/07
	Lynn-Peabody-Salem NECTA, MA	Y	25420 FQ	35980 MW	44480 TQ	USBLS	5/07
	Worcester MSA, MA-CT	Y	20980 FQ	27830 MW	35800 TQ	USBLS	5/07
	Michigan	Y	24340 FQ	29570 MW	35660 TQ	USBLS	5/07
	Ann Arbor MSA, MI	Y	23660 FQ	28240 MW	34890 TQ	USBLS	5/07
	Detroit-Warren-Livonia MSA, MI	Y	24260 FQ	29460 MW	36790 TQ	USBLS	5/07
	Grand Rapids-Wyoming MSA, MI	Y	24040 FQ	30570 MW	35760 TQ	USBLS	5/07
	Warren-Troy-Farmington Hills PMSA, MI	Y	23570 FQ	29050 MW	37270 TQ	USBLS	5/07
	Minnesota	Y	25274 FQ	31680 MW	41166 TQ	MNBLS	10/08-12/08
	Duluth-Superior MSA, MN-WI	Y	18701 FQ	26922 MW	32593 TQ	MNBLS	10/08-12/08
	Minneapolis-Saint Paul MSA, MN-WI	Y	25875 FQ	31774 MW	41270 TQ	MNBLS	10/08-12/08
	Rochester MSA, MN	Y	26554 FQ	28881 MW	40106 TQ	MNBLS	10/08-12/08
	Mississippi	Y	24000 FQ	26230 MW	28650 TQ	USBLS	5/07
	Jackson MSA, MS	Y	21650 FQ	24460 MW	35980 TQ	USBLS	5/07
	Missouri	Y	21160 FQ	26600 MW	34840 TQ	USBLS	5/07
	Kansas City MSA, MO-KS	Y	20640 FQ	24900 MW	31300 TQ	USBLS	5/07
	St. Louis MSA, MO-IL	Y	20990 FQ	27140 MW	36660 TQ	USBLS	5/07
	Springfield MSA, MO	Y	18910 FQ	23140 MW	28420 TQ	USBLS	5/07
	Montana	Y	17680 FQ	21910 MW	27000 TQ	USBLS	5/07
	Nebraska	Y	21110 FQ	25520 MW	34320 TQ	USBLS	5/07
	Omaha-Council Bluffs MSA, NE-IA	Y	23050 FQ	28310 MW	34890 TQ	USBLS	5/07
	Nevada	H	10.00 FQ	12.58 MW	15.41 TQ	NVBLS	5/08
	Las Vegas-Paradise MSA, NV	H	9.91 FQ	11.27 MW	15.13 TQ	NVBLS	5/08
	New Hampshire	H	10.90 AE	15.31 MW	16.89 AEX	NHBLS	6/08
	New Jersey	Y	19220 FQ	25390 MW	35900 TQ	USBLS	5/07
	Camden PMSA, NJ	Y	19850 FQ	23550 MW	36130 TQ	USBLS	5/07
	Edison PMSA, NJ	Y	16010 FQ	22180 MW	31170 TQ	USBLS	5/07
	Newark-Union PMSA, NJ-PA	Y	20290 FQ	27920 MW	38970 TQ	USBLS	5/07
	New Mexico	Y	18490 FQ	21970 MW	24800 TQ	USBLS	5/07

AE	Average entry wage	AW	Average wage paid	FQ	First quartile wage
AER	Average entry range	AWR	Average wage range	H	Hourly
AEX	Average experienced wage	AXR	Average experienced range	HI	Highest wage paid
ATC	Average total compensation	D	Daily	HR	High end range

LO	Lowest wage paid	MTC	Median total compensation	TCC	Total cash compensation
LR	Low end range	MW	Median wage paid	TQ	Third quartile wage
M	Monthly	MWR	Median wage range	W	Weekly
MCC	Median cash compensation	S	See annotated source	Y	Yearly

Bindery Worker

Occupation/Type/Industry	Location	Per	Low	Mid	High	Source	Date
Bindery Worker	Albuquerque MSA, NM	Y	19180 FQ	22320 MW	25030 TQ	USBLS	5/07
	New York	Y	20610 FQ	26860 MW	34260 TQ	USBLS	5/07
	Albany-Schenectady-Troy MSA, NY	Y	23460 FQ	28330 MW	34920 TQ	USBLS	5/07
	Buffalo-Niagara Falls MSA, NY	Y	25590 FQ	29870 MW	36230 TQ	USBLS	5/07
	Nassau-Suffolk PMSA, NY	Y	18830 FQ	26900 MW	35170 TQ	USBLS	5/07
	New York-Northern New Jersey-Long Island MSA, NY-NJ-PA	Y	19730 FQ	26210 MW	35250 TQ	USBLS	5/07
	North Carolina	Y	19280 FQ	23970 MW	30170 TQ	USBLS	5/07
	Charlotte-Gastonia-Concord MSA, NC-SC	Y	21040 FQ	25220 MW	29890 TQ	USBLS	5/07
	Raleigh-Cary MSA, NC	Y	24220 FQ	32610 MW	41190 TQ	USBLS	5/07
	North Dakota	Y	16020 FQ	19970 MW	28700 TQ	USBLS	5/07
	Bismarck MSA, ND	Y	15090 FQ	19120 MW	31360 TQ	USBLS	5/07
	Fargo MSA, ND-MN	Y	18900 FQ	24110 MW	31710 TQ	USBLS	5/07
	Ohio	Y	22280 FQ	29320 MW	36150 TQ	USBLS	5/07
	Cincinnati-Middletown MSA, OH-KY-IN	Y	23040 FQ	28460 MW	34120 TQ	USBLS	5/07
	Cleveland-Elyria-Mentor MSA, OH	Y	25490 FQ	33250 MW	40930 TQ	USBLS	5/07
	Columbus MSA, OH	Y	23410 FQ	28960 MW	35420 TQ	USBLS	5/07
	Dayton MSA, OH	Y	18790 FQ	24570 MW	28340 TQ	USBLS	5/07
	Oklahoma	Y	19530 FQ	23860 MW	28940 TQ	USBLS	5/07
	Oklahoma City MSA, OK	Y	20750 FQ	23300 MW	28490 TQ	USBLS	5/07
	Tulsa MSA, OK	Y	18580 FQ	25400 MW	29560 TQ	USBLS	5/07
	Oregon	H	11.84 FQ	14.60 MW	18.86 TQ	ORBLS	5/08
	Portland-Vancouver-Beaverton MSA, OR-WA	Y	23980 FQ	29620 MW	39600 TQ	USBLS	5/07
	Pennsylvania	Y	21080 FQ	27710 MW	36610 TQ	USBLS	5/07
	Allentown-Bethlehem-Easton MSA, PA-NJ	Y	23800 FQ	26550 MW	29750 TQ	USBLS	5/07
	Lancaster MSA, PA	Y	23100 FQ	33090 MW	40890 TQ	USBLS	5/07
	Philadelphia-Camden-Wilmington MSA, PA-NJ-DE-MD	Y	22140 FQ	27330 MW	36160 TQ	USBLS	5/07
	Pittsburgh MSA, PA	Y	16540 FQ	22220 MW	31450 TQ	USBLS	5/07
	Rhode Island	Y	18130 FQ	24520 MW	32740 TQ	USBLS	5/07
	Providence-Fall River-Warwick MSA, RI-MA	Y	18200 FQ	22190 MW	27710 TQ	USBLS	5/07
	South Carolina	Y	14720 FQ	21190 MW	29450 TQ	USBLS	5/07
	Columbia MSA, SC	Y	19600 FQ	23350 MW	30580 TQ	USBLS	5/07
	South Dakota	Y	22227 FQ	25692 MW	30833 TQ	SDBLS	7/08-9/08
	Sioux Falls MSA, SD	Y	23819 FQ	27075 MW	31715 TQ	SDBLS	7/08-9/08
	Tennessee	Y	20180 FQ	24830 MW	31160 TQ	USBLS	5/07
	Memphis MSA, TN-MS-AR	Y	18890 FQ	24980 MW	33670 TQ	USBLS	5/07
	Nashville-Davidson-Murfreesboro MSA, TN	Y	20320 FQ	25070 MW	30960 TQ	USBLS	5/07
	Texas	Y	18420 FQ	23140 MW	30820 TQ	USBLS	5/07
	Austin-Round Rock MSA, TX	Y	18020 FQ	22330 MW	28820 TQ	USBLS	5/07
	Dallas-Fort Worth-Arlington MSA, TX	Y	18610 FQ	24110 MW	32930 TQ	USBLS	5/07
	El Paso MSA, TX	Y	18550 FQ	22560 MW	30600 TQ	USBLS	5/07
	Houston-Sugar Land-Baytown MSA, TX	Y	18740 FQ	24020 MW	30520 TQ	USBLS	5/07
	San Antonio MSA, TX	Y	18530 FQ	22280 MW	28540 TQ	USBLS	5/07
	Utah	Y	21320 FQ	27090 MW	32270 TQ	USBLS	5/07
	Salt Lake City MSA, UT	Y	19700 FQ	27330 MW	33460 TQ	USBLS	5/07
	Vermont	Y	25360 FQ	27940 MW	31820 TQ	USBLS	5/07
	Burlington-South Burlington MSA, VT	Y	25020 FQ	27280 MW	29640 TQ	USBLS	5/07
	Virginia	Y	23870 FQ	30380 MW	37790 TQ	USBLS	5/07
	Richmond MSA, VA	Y	21020 FQ	29100 MW	37190 TQ	USBLS	5/07
	Virginia Beach-Norfolk-Newport News MSA, VA-NC	Y	17930 FQ	24790 MW	31120 TQ	USBLS	5/07
	Washington	H	10.07 FQ	12.92 MW	16.38 TQ	WABLS	3/08
	Seattle-Tacoma-Bellevue MSA, WA	Y	20190 FQ	26320 MW	33330 TQ	USBLS	5/07
	West Virginia	Y	19338 FQ	23370 MW	30914 TQ	WVBLS	7/08-9/08
	Wisconsin	Y	21390 FQ	25700 MW	32880 TQ	USBLS	5/07

AE	Average entry wage	AW	Average wage paid	FQ	First quartile wage	LO	Lowest wage paid	MTC	Median total compensation	TCC	Total cash compensation
AER	Average entry range	AWR	Average wage range	H	Hourly	LR	Low end range	MW	Median wage paid	TQ	Third quartile wage
AEX	Average experienced wage	AXR	Average experienced range	HI	Highest wage paid	M	Monthly	MWR	Median wage range	W	Weekly
ATC	Average total compensation	D	Daily	HR	High end range	MCC	Median cash compensation	S	See annotated source	Y	Yearly

112

Occupation/Type/Industry	Location	Per	Low	Mid	High	Source	Date
Bindery Worker	Milwaukee-Waukesha-West Allis MSA, WI	Y	22150 FQ	27600 MW	35540 TQ	USBLS	5/07
	Wyoming	Y	16575 FQ	19200 MW	23135 TQ	WYBLS	9/08
	Puerto Rico	Y	13010 FQ	14850 MW	17770 TQ	USBLS	5/07
	San Juan-Caguas-Guaynabo MSA, PR	Y	12940 FQ	14660 MW	17580 TQ	USBLS	5/07
Biochemist and Biophysicist	Arkansas	Y	48500 FQ	64770 MW	89390 TQ	USBLS	5/07
	California	H	34.04 FQ	42.93 MW	53.00 TQ	CABLS	1/08-3/08
	Los Angeles-Long Beach-Glendale PMSA, CA	H	32.65 FQ	43.53 MW	50.90 TQ	CABLS	1/08-3/08
	Oakland-Fremont-Hayward MSA, CA	H	34.34 FQ	40.41 MW	48.50 TQ	CABLS	1/08-3/08
	Riverside-San Bernardino-Ontario MSA, CA	H	34.48 FQ	41.61 MW	50.61 TQ	CABLS	1/08-3/08
	Sacramento-Arden Arcade-Roseville MSA, CA	H	36.40 FQ	41.48 MW	48.48 TQ	CABLS	1/08-3/08
	San Diego-Carlsbad-San Marcos MSA, CA	H	31.18 FQ	39.24 MW	55.28 TQ	CABLS	1/08-3/08
	San Francisco-San Mateo-Redwood PMSA, CA	H	35.21 FQ	43.91 MW	50.29 TQ	CABLS	1/08-3/08
	San Jose-Sunnyvale-Santa Clara MSA, CA	H	35.13 FQ	43.80 MW	55.12 TQ	CABLS	1/08-3/08
	Santa Ana-Anaheim-Irvine PMSA, CA	Y	83520 FQ	95440 MW	105760 TQ	USBLS	5/07
	Colorado	Y	57310 FQ	79670 MW	95150 TQ	USBLS	5/07
	Denver-Aurora MSA, CO	Y	38720 FQ	70290 MW	85830 TQ	USBLS	5/07
	Connecticut	H	31.44 AE	41.46 MW		CTBLS	1/08-3/08
	Delaware	Y	74840 FQ	115840 MW	128310 TQ	USBLS	5/07
	Wilmington PMSA, DE-MD-NJ	Y	75470 FQ	116000 MW	128390 TQ	USBLS	5/07
	District of Columbia	Y	53900 FQ	75270 MW	112280 TQ	USBLS	5/07
	Washington-Arlington-Alexandria MSA, DC-VA-MD-WV	Y	43770 FQ	65360 MW	95730 TQ	USBLS	5/07
	Florida	Y	48720 FQ	63940 MW	83020 TQ	USBLS	5/07
	Illinois	Y	66350 FQ	75550 MW	96510 TQ	USBLS	5/07
	Chicago-Naperville-Joliet MSA, IL-IN-WI	Y	66470 FQ	75660 MW	96660 TQ	USBLS	5/07
	Indiana	Y	65920 FQ	81800 MW	109110 TQ	USBLS	5/07
	Indianapolis-Carmel MSA, IN	Y	68630 FQ	83250 MW	111280 TQ	USBLS	5/07
	Louisiana	H	16.68 FQ	19.32 MW	24.44 TQ	LABLS	1/08-3/08
	Maryland	Y		51125 MW		MDBLS	3/08
	Baltimore-Towson MSA, MD	Y	44660 FQ	50490 MW	60800 TQ	USBLS	5/07
	Bethesda-Gaithersburg-Frederick PMSA, MD	Y	32620 FQ	45620 MW	65970 TQ	USBLS	5/07
	Massachusetts	Y	67520 FQ	86180 MW	105850 TQ	USBLS	5/07
	Boston-Cambridge-Quincy NECTA, MA	Y	70620 FQ	89850 MW	109250 TQ	USBLS	5/07
	Worcester MSA, MA-CT	Y	62380 FQ	79850 MW	107720 TQ	USBLS	5/07
	Michigan	Y	39810 FQ	51650 MW	80960 TQ	USBLS	5/07
	Minnesota	Y	57783 FQ	73183 MW	89096 TQ	MNBLS	10/08-12/08
	Minneapolis-Saint Paul MSA, MN-WI	Y	57416 FQ	72252 MW	88500 TQ	MNBLS	10/08-12/08
	Missouri	Y	44250 FQ	74830 MW	103510 TQ	USBLS	5/07
	Kansas City MSA, MO-KS	Y	37280 FQ	104420 MW	117880 TQ	USBLS	5/07
	St. Louis MSA, MO-IL	Y	54850 FQ	77670 MW	107110 TQ	USBLS	5/07
	Nebraska	Y	39600 FQ	54050 MW	75860 TQ	USBLS	5/07
	Nevada	H	17.67 FQ	20.23 MW	22.71 TQ	NVBLS	5/08
	New Jersey	Y	79280 FQ	111500 MW		USBLS	5/07
	Camden PMSA, NJ	Y	51900 FQ	99780 MW	122710 TQ	USBLS	5/07
	Edison PMSA, NJ	Y	87850 FQ	111720 MW	140560 TQ	USBLS	5/07
	Newark-Union PMSA, NJ-PA	Y	74610 FQ			USBLS	5/07
	New York	Y	59260 FQ	80400 MW	108260 TQ	USBLS	5/07
	Albany-Schenectady-Troy MSA, NY	Y	57160 FQ	77530 MW	108460 TQ	USBLS	5/07
	Buffalo-Niagara Falls MSA, NY	Y	52230 FQ	68590 MW	95790 TQ	USBLS	5/07
	Nassau-Suffolk PMSA, NY	Y	46360 FQ	79090 MW	116290 TQ	USBLS	5/07
	New York-Northern New Jersey-Long Island MSA, NY-NJ-PA	Y	72930 FQ	101800 MW	142830 TQ	USBLS	5/07

AE	Average entry wage	AW	Average wage paid	FQ	First quartile wage
AER	Average entry range	AWR	Average wage range	H	Hourly
AEX	Average experienced wage	AXR	Average experienced range	HI	Highest wage paid
ATC	Average total compensation	D	Daily	HR	High end range

LO	Lowest wage paid	MTC	Median total compensation	TCC	Total cash compensation
LR	Low end range	MW	Median wage paid	TQ	Third quartile wage
M	Monthly	MWR	Median wage range	W	Weekly
MCC	Median cash compensation	S	See annotated source	Y	Yearly

Occupation/Type/Industry	Location	Per	Low	Mid	High	Source	Date
Biochemist and Biophysicist	North Carolina	Y	49410 FQ	65010 MW	87970 TQ	USBLS	5/07
	Raleigh-Cary MSA, NC	Y	55630 FQ	69900 MW	92100 TQ	USBLS	5/07
	Ohio	Y	39300 FQ	50200 MW	72500 TQ	USBLS	5/07
	Cincinnati-Middletown MSA, OH-KY-IN	Y	42020 FQ	51280 MW	70020 TQ	USBLS	5/07
	Cleveland-Elyria-Mentor MSA, OH	Y	42570 FQ	51030 MW	72000 TQ	USBLS	5/07
	Columbus MSA, OH	Y	32760 FQ	47650 MW	74040 TQ	USBLS	5/07
	Pennsylvania	Y	61390 FQ	86530 MW	115640 TQ	USBLS	5/07
	Philadelphia-Camden-Wilmington MSA, PA-NJ-DE-MD	Y	66830 FQ	95830 MW	124350 TQ	USBLS	5/07
	Pittsburgh MSA, PA	Y	62960 FQ	86470 MW	110450 TQ	USBLS	5/07
	South Carolina	Y	46520 FQ	63580 MW	73020 TQ	USBLS	5/07
	Tennessee	Y	39100 FQ	46630 MW	58170 TQ	USBLS	5/07
	Nashville-Davidson-Murfreesboro MSA, TN	Y	35830 FQ	38630 MW	41370 TQ	USBLS	5/07
	Texas	Y	47710 FQ	66420 MW	92730 TQ	USBLS	5/07
	Austin-Round Rock MSA, TX	Y	46980 FQ	60310 MW	89590 TQ	USBLS	5/07
	Dallas-Fort Worth-Arlington MSA, TX	Y	59390 FQ	90710 MW		USBLS	5/07
	Houston-Sugar Land-Baytown MSA, TX	Y	42990 FQ	59520 MW	97500 TQ	USBLS	5/07
	Utah	Y	39470 FQ	57120 MW	79350 TQ	USBLS	5/07
	Salt Lake City MSA, UT	Y	38470 FQ	55420 MW	73080 TQ	USBLS	5/07
	Virginia	Y	50400 FQ	72610 MW	95810 TQ	USBLS	5/07
	Washington	H	20.70 FQ	27.96 MW	35.80 TQ	WABLS	3/08
	Seattle-Tacoma-Bellevue MSA, WA	Y	48550 FQ	60000 MW	73900 TQ	USBLS	5/07
	West Virginia	Y	60327 FQ	74293 MW	93694 TQ	WVBLS	7/08-9/08
	Wisconsin	Y	41550 FQ	46700 MW	72320 TQ	USBLS	5/07
Bioenergy Process Engineer							
Master's Degree, Experience	Tech Valley, NY	Y	50000-70000 LR			TVC05	2008
Biological Aide							
Fish and Game Commission	New Hampshire	Y		14980 AW		NHUL03	2008
Biological Science Teacher							
Postsecondary	Alabama	Y	48850 FQ	66940 MW	96330 TQ	USBLS	5/07
Postsecondary	Birmingham-Hoover MSA, AL	Y	50780 FQ	72330 MW	101860 TQ	USBLS	5/07
Postsecondary	Huntsville MSA, AL	Y	43330 FQ	51350 MW	67360 TQ	USBLS	5/07
Postsecondary	Alaska	Y	69880 FQ	80430 MW	98410 TQ	USBLS	5/07
Postsecondary	Anchorage MSA, AK	Y	65710 FQ	77420 MW	93480 TQ	USBLS	5/07
Postsecondary	Arizona	Y	49300 FQ	60550 MW	79460 TQ	USBLS	5/07
Postsecondary	Phoenix-Mesa-Scottsdale MSA, AZ	Y	41400 FQ	56930 MW	75540 TQ	USBLS	5/07
Postsecondary	Arkansas	Y	42830 FQ	55670 MW	70000 TQ	USBLS	5/07
Postsecondary	Little Rock-North Little Rock MSA, AR	Y	40640 FQ	49570 MW	59780 TQ	USBLS	5/07
Postsecondary	California	Y		103819 AW		CABLS	1/08-3/08
Postsecondary	Los Angeles-Long Beach-Glendale PMSA, CA	Y		84642 AW		CABLS	1/08-3/08
Postsecondary	Oakland-Fremont-Hayward MSA, CA	Y		102537 AW		CABLS	1/08-3/08
Postsecondary	Riverside-San Bernardino-Ontario MSA, CA	Y		101993 AW		CABLS	1/08-3/08
Postsecondary	Sacramento-Arden Arcade-Roseville MSA, CA	Y		113550 AW		CABLS	1/08-3/08
Postsecondary	San Francisco-San Mateo-Redwood PMSA, CA	Y		109202 AW		CABLS	1/08-3/08
Postsecondary	Santa Ana-Anaheim-Irvine PMSA, CA	Y	74300 FQ	91680 MW	114720 TQ	USBLS	5/07
Postsecondary	Colorado	Y	44380 FQ	58330 MW	81130 TQ	USBLS	5/07
Postsecondary	Denver-Aurora MSA, CO	Y	40270 FQ	49620 MW	65430 TQ	USBLS	5/07
Postsecondary	Wilmington PMSA, DE-MD-NJ	Y	44720 FQ	61820 MW	81910 TQ	USBLS	5/07
Postsecondary	District of Columbia	Y	47300 FQ	66080 MW	89960 TQ	USBLS	5/07
Postsecondary	Washington-Arlington-Alexandria MSA, DC-VA-MD-WV	Y	51670 FQ	69260 MW	93470 TQ	USBLS	5/07

AE	Average entry wage	AW	Average wage paid	FQ	First quartile wage	LO	Lowest wage paid	MTC	Median total compensation	TCC	Total cash compensation
AER	Average entry range	AWR	Average wage range	H	Hourly	LR	Low end range	MW	Median wage paid	TQ	Third quartile wage
AEX	Average experienced wage	AXR	Average experienced range	HI	Highest wage paid	M	Monthly	MWR	Median wage range	W	Weekly
ATC	Average total compensation	D	Daily	HR	High end range	MCC	Median cash compensation	S	See annotated source	Y	Yearly

114

Occupation/Type/Industry	Location	Per	Low	Mid	High	Source	Date
Biological Science Teacher							
Postsecondary	Florida	Y	47690 FQ	66720 MW	81580 TQ	USBLS	5/07
Postsecondary	Fort Lauderdale-Pompano Beach-Deerfield Beach PMSA, FL	Y	58950 FQ	72800 MW	83000 TQ	USBLS	5/07
Postsecondary	Jacksonville MSA, FL	Y	42870 FQ	53650 MW	79570 TQ	USBLS	5/07
Postsecondary	Miami-Fort Lauderdale-Miami Beach MSA, FL	Y	60430 FQ	72900 MW	80590 TQ	USBLS	5/07
Postsecondary	Orlando-Kissimmee MSA, FL	Y	37250 FQ	54610 MW	74370 TQ	USBLS	5/07
Postsecondary	Tampa-St. Petersburg-Clearwater MSA, FL	Y	44670 FQ	61090 MW	86900 TQ	USBLS	5/07
Postsecondary	West Palm Beach-Boca Raton-Boynton Beach PMSA, FL	Y	48750 FQ	59060 MW	76270 TQ	USBLS	5/07
Postsecondary	Georgia	Y	47250 FQ	62950 MW	90670 TQ	USBLS	5/07
Postsecondary	Atlanta-Sandy Springs-Marietta MSA, GA	Y	49230 FQ	65860 MW	95280 TQ	USBLS	5/07
Postsecondary	Hawaii	Y	64770 FQ	92710 MW	118660 TQ	USBLS	5/07
Postsecondary	Honolulu MSA, HI	Y	71380 FQ	97090 MW	120890 TQ	USBLS	5/07
Postsecondary	Illinois	Y	50060 FQ	66820 MW	94560 TQ	USBLS	5/07
Postsecondary	Chicago-Naperville-Joliet MSA, IL-IN-WI	Y	48620 FQ	63780 MW	87470 TQ	USBLS	5/07
Postsecondary	Indiana	Y	51320 FQ	63010 MW	84290 TQ	USBLS	5/07
Postsecondary	Gary PMSA, IN	Y	46460 FQ	55750 MW	66660 TQ	USBLS	5/07
Postsecondary	Indianapolis-Carmel MSA, IN	Y	50380 FQ	62760 MW	80850 TQ	USBLS	5/07
Postsecondary	Iowa	Y	46380 FQ	61560 MW	84640 TQ	USBLS	5/07
Postsecondary	Davenport-Moline-Rock Island MSA, IA-IL	Y	40060 FQ	53710 MW	61140 TQ	USBLS	5/07
Postsecondary	Des Moines-West Des Moines MSA, IA	Y	47580 FQ	64340 MW	72530 TQ	USBLS	5/07
Postsecondary	Waterloo-Cedar Falls MSA, IA	Y	48130 FQ	56140 MW	64390 TQ	USBLS	5/07
Postsecondary	Kansas	Y	43270 FQ	61150 MW	79900 TQ	USBLS	5/07
Postsecondary	Wichita MSA, KS	Y	45510 FQ	68540 MW	81330 TQ	USBLS	5/07
Postsecondary	Kentucky	Y	44976 FQ	57241 MW	80203 TQ	KYBLS	2008
Postsecondary	Louisiana	Y		59468 AW		LABLS	1/08-3/08
Postsecondary	Baton Rouge MSA, LA	Y	52260 FQ	63830 MW	79410 TQ	USBLS	5/07
Postsecondary	New Orleans-Metairie-Kenner MSA, LA	Y	44420 FQ	52340 MW	72300 TQ	USBLS	5/07
Postsecondary	Maine	Y	50330 FQ	61580 MW	82810 TQ	USBLS	5/07
Postsecondary	Portland-South Portland-Biddeford MSA, ME	Y	50680 FQ	60690 MW	80670 TQ	USBLS	5/07
Postsecondary	Maryland	Y		77725 MW		MDBLS	3/08
Postsecondary	Baltimore-Towson MSA, MD	Y	56670 FQ	83190 MW	118560 TQ	USBLS	5/07
Postsecondary	Bethesda-Gaithersburg-Frederick PMSA, MD	Y	54810 FQ	65900 MW	86050 TQ	USBLS	5/07
Postsecondary	Massachusetts	Y	63290 FQ	89580 MW	128770 TQ	USBLS	5/07
Postsecondary	Boston-Cambridge-Quincy NECTA, MA	Y	66190 FQ	96840 MW	142630 TQ	USBLS	5/07
Postsecondary	Worcester MSA, MA-CT	Y	58970 FQ	75590 MW	103390 TQ	USBLS	5/07
Postsecondary	Michigan	Y	49340 FQ	67220 MW	86600 TQ	USBLS	5/07
Postsecondary	Ann Arbor MSA, MI	Y	68190 FQ	78130 MW	107460 TQ	USBLS	5/07
Postsecondary	Detroit-Warren-Livonia MSA, MI	Y	38230 FQ	69310 MW	92450 TQ	USBLS	5/07
Postsecondary	Warren-Troy-Farmington Hills PMSA, MI	Y	30970 FQ	61780 MW	87520 TQ	USBLS	5/07
Postsecondary	Minnesota	Y	43366 FQ	55261 MW	71499 TQ	MNBLS	10/08-12/08
Postsecondary	Duluth-Superior MSA, MN-WI	Y	43774 FQ	56464 MW	70222 TQ	MNBLS	10/08-12/08
Postsecondary	Minneapolis-Saint Paul MSA, MN-WI	Y	43460 FQ	56705 MW	76604 TQ	MNBLS	10/08-12/08
Postsecondary	Mississippi	Y	46990 FQ	58670 MW	77150 TQ	USBLS	5/07
Postsecondary	Jackson MSA, MS	Y	44010 FQ	55610 MW	71820 TQ	USBLS	5/07
Postsecondary	Missouri	Y	44600 FQ	62220 MW	85550 TQ	USBLS	5/07
Postsecondary	Kansas City MSA, MO-KS	Y	43180 FQ	57160 MW	77440 TQ	USBLS	5/07
Postsecondary	St. Louis MSA, MO-IL	Y	43030 FQ	58210 MW	77460 TQ	USBLS	5/07
Postsecondary	Montana	Y	37970 FQ	48360 MW	60850 TQ	USBLS	5/07
Postsecondary	Nebraska	Y	44150 FQ	60290 MW	78660 TQ	USBLS	5/07
Postsecondary	Omaha-Council Bluffs MSA, NE-IA	Y	50040 FQ	68760 MW	83960 TQ	USBLS	5/07
Postsecondary	New Hampshire	Y	42918 AE	72836 MW	96713 AEX	NHBLS	6/08
Postsecondary	Manchester MSA, NH	Y	53710 FQ	72570 MW	80590 TQ	USBLS	5/07
Postsecondary	New Jersey	Y	50870 FQ	73940 MW	102440 TQ	USBLS	5/07
Postsecondary	Camden PMSA, NJ	Y	51850 FQ	75400 MW	105550 TQ	USBLS	5/07
Postsecondary	Edison PMSA, NJ	Y	57260 FQ	83810 MW	110770 TQ	USBLS	5/07

AE	Average entry wage	AW	Average wage paid	FQ	First quartile wage
AER	Average entry range	AWR	Average wage range	H	Hourly
AEX	Average experienced wage	AXR	Average experienced range	HI	Highest wage paid
ATC	Average total compensation	D	Daily	HR	High end range

LO	Lowest wage paid	MTC	Median total compensation	TCC	Total cash compensation
LR	Low end range	MW	Median wage paid	TQ	Third quartile wage
M	Monthly	MWR	Median wage range	W	Weekly
MCC	Median cash compensation	S	See annotated source	Y	Yearly

Occupation/Type/Industry	Location	Per	Low	Mid	High	Source	Date

Biological Science Teacher

Occupation/Type/Industry	Location	Per	Low	Mid	High	Source	Date
Postsecondary	Newark-Union PMSA, NJ-PA	Y	43970 FQ	66520 MW	95240 TQ	USBLS	5/07
Postsecondary	New Mexico	Y	45330 FQ	54770 MW	68730 TQ	USBLS	5/07
Postsecondary	Albuquerque MSA, NM	Y	43630 FQ	49970 MW	64900 TQ	USBLS	5/07
Postsecondary	New York	Y	51450 FQ	70460 MW	96430 TQ	USBLS	5/07
Postsecondary	Albany-Schenectady-Troy MSA, NY	Y	50100 FQ	72020 MW	95410 TQ	USBLS	5/07
Postsecondary	Nassau-Suffolk PMSA, NY	Y	51760 FQ	64500 MW	89710 TQ	USBLS	5/07
Postsecondary	New York-Northern New Jersey-Long Island MSA, NY-NJ-PA	Y	52010 FQ	72210 MW	97750 TQ	USBLS	5/07
Postsecondary	North Carolina	Y	48880 FQ	60960 MW	86840 TQ	USBLS	5/07
Postsecondary	Charlotte-Gastonia-Concord MSA, NC-SC	Y	47530 FQ	56310 MW	74800 TQ	USBLS	5/07
Postsecondary	Winston-Salem MSA, NC	Y	49710 FQ	70930 MW	119480 TQ	USBLS	5/07
Postsecondary	North Dakota	Y	35450 FQ	46380 MW	61590 TQ	USBLS	5/07
Postsecondary	Fargo MSA, ND-MN	Y	41420 FQ	49730 MW	65680 TQ	USBLS	5/07
Postsecondary	Ohio	Y	48790 FQ	68750 MW	91540 TQ	USBLS	5/07
Postsecondary	Cincinnati-Middletown MSA, OH-KY-IN	Y	48570 FQ	70170 MW	97120 TQ	USBLS	5/07
Postsecondary	Cleveland-Elyria-Mentor MSA, OH	Y	44410 FQ	62520 MW	80110 TQ	USBLS	5/07
Postsecondary	Columbus MSA, OH	Y	69390 FQ	84460 MW	101780 TQ	USBLS	5/07
Postsecondary	Dayton MSA, OH	Y	43250 FQ	64240 MW	86410 TQ	USBLS	5/07
Postsecondary	Oklahoma	Y	38090 FQ	57630 MW	84240 TQ	USBLS	5/07
Postsecondary	Oklahoma City MSA, OK	Y	46960 FQ	68680 MW	95860 TQ	USBLS	5/07
Postsecondary	Tulsa MSA, OK	Y	36460 FQ	48030 MW	58930 TQ	USBLS	5/07
Postsecondary	Portland-Vancouver-Beaverton MSA, OR-WA	Y	52900 FQ	74600 MW	96830 TQ	USBLS	5/07
Postsecondary	Pennsylvania	Y	47850 FQ	67210 MW	93190 TQ	USBLS	5/07
Postsecondary	Allentown-Bethlehem-Easton MSA, PA-NJ	Y	51230 FQ	76040 MW	105390 TQ	USBLS	5/07
Postsecondary	Philadelphia-Camden-Wilmington MSA, PA-NJ-DE-MD	Y	51190 FQ	73250 MW	100270 TQ	USBLS	5/07
Postsecondary	Pittsburgh MSA, PA	Y	43300 FQ	61050 MW	84130 TQ	USBLS	5/07
Postsecondary	Rhode Island	Y	51780 FQ	68110 MW	92390 TQ	USBLS	5/07
Postsecondary	Providence-Fall River-Warwick MSA, RI-MA	Y	51630 FQ	67920 MW	91280 TQ	USBLS	5/07
Postsecondary	South Carolina	Y	48130 FQ	57820 MW	71250 TQ	USBLS	5/07
Postsecondary	Charleston-North Charleston MSA, SC	Y	46680 FQ	51830 MW	60570 TQ	USBLS	5/07
Postsecondary	Columbia MSA, SC	Y	49400 FQ	66340 MW	81960 TQ	USBLS	5/07
Postsecondary	South Dakota	Y	51743 FQ	67365 MW	95968 TQ	SDBLS	7/08-9/08
Postsecondary	Sioux Falls MSA, SD	Y	40750 FQ	55582 MW	74200 TQ	SDBLS	7/08-9/08
Postsecondary	Tennessee	Y	44510 FQ	58580 MW	93820 TQ	USBLS	5/07
Postsecondary	Memphis MSA, TN-MS-AR	Y	52020 FQ	71860 MW	113750 TQ	USBLS	5/07
Postsecondary	Nashville-Davidson-Murfreesboro MSA, TN	Y	47350 FQ	62500 MW	93110 TQ	USBLS	5/07
Postsecondary	Texas	Y	63440 FQ	93760 MW		USBLS	5/07
Postsecondary	Austin-Round Rock MSA, TX	Y	49910 FQ	79320 MW	104280 TQ	USBLS	5/07
Postsecondary	Dallas-Fort Worth-Arlington MSA, TX	Y	52920 FQ	81310 MW		USBLS	5/07
Postsecondary	El Paso MSA, TX	Y	54700 FQ	65190 MW	98750 TQ	USBLS	5/07
Postsecondary	Houston-Sugar Land-Baytown MSA, TX	Y	68580 FQ	110360 MW		USBLS	5/07
Postsecondary	Utah	Y	48600 FQ	62140 MW	83120 TQ	USBLS	5/07
Postsecondary	Salt Lake City MSA, UT	Y	45630 FQ	67400 MW	90200 TQ	USBLS	5/07
Postsecondary	Vermont	Y	46390 FQ	54920 MW	68440 TQ	USBLS	5/07
Postsecondary	Virginia	Y	45320 FQ	62530 MW	85580 TQ	USBLS	5/07
Postsecondary	Lynchburg MSA, VA	Y	29560 FQ	51210 MW	58750 TQ	USBLS	5/07
Postsecondary	Richmond MSA, VA	Y	45790 FQ	67810 MW	92580 TQ	USBLS	5/07
Postsecondary	Virginia Beach-Norfolk-Newport News MSA, VA-NC	Y	50590 FQ	64350 MW	79040 TQ	USBLS	5/07
Postsecondary	Washington	Y		78354 AW		WABLS	3/08
Postsecondary	West Virginia	Y	51156 FQ	67165 MW	97287 TQ	WVBLS	7/08-9/08
Postsecondary	Wisconsin	Y	46490 FQ	59790 MW	85130 TQ	USBLS	5/07
Postsecondary	Milwaukee-Waukesha-West Allis MSA, WI	Y	46030 FQ	60150 MW	82160 TQ	USBLS	5/07
Postsecondary	Wyoming	Y	49727 FQ	60945 MW	73286 TQ	WYBLS	9/08
Postsecondary	Puerto Rico	Y	44350 FQ	51870 MW	71400 TQ	USBLS	5/07

Occupation/Type/Industry	Location	Per	Low	Mid	High	Source	Date
Biological Science Teacher							
Postsecondary	San Juan-Caguas-Guaynabo MSA, PR	Y	47800 FQ	57010 MW	75180 TQ	USBLS	5/07
Biological Technician	Alabama	Y	28020 FQ	34140 MW	40230 TQ	USBLS	5/07
	Alaska	Y	29970 FQ	35290 MW	39880 TQ	USBLS	5/07
	Anchorage MSA, AK	Y	24500 FQ	31480 MW	38010 TQ	USBLS	5/07
	Arizona	Y	23040 FQ	28920 MW	38160 TQ	USBLS	5/07
	Phoenix-Mesa-Scottsdale MSA, AZ	Y	20740 FQ	27210 MW	37790 TQ	USBLS	5/07
	Tucson MSA, AZ	Y	25800 FQ	34230 MW	47780 TQ	USBLS	5/07
	Arkansas	Y	26980 FQ	33690 MW	40960 TQ	USBLS	5/07
	California	H	16.34 FQ	20.50 MW	26.32 TQ	CABLS	1/08-3/08
	Los Angeles-Long Beach-Glendale PMSA, CA	H	14.58 FQ	17.50 MW	22.28 TQ	CABLS	1/08-3/08
	Oakland-Fremont-Hayward MSA, CA	H	17.83 FQ	22.63 MW	29.44 TQ	CABLS	1/08-3/08
	Riverside-San Bernardino-Ontario MSA, CA	H	14.16 FQ	17.28 MW	20.27 TQ	CABLS	1/08-3/08
	Sacramento-Arden Arcade-Roseville MSA, CA	H	15.66 FQ	19.71 MW	27.52 TQ	CABLS	1/08-3/08
	San Diego-Carlsbad-San Marcos MSA, CA	H	15.73 FQ	20.66 MW	25.23 TQ	CABLS	1/08-3/08
	San Francisco-San Mateo-Redwood PMSA, CA	H	18.76 FQ	21.69 MW	25.42 TQ	CABLS	1/08-3/08
	San Jose-Sunnyvale-Santa Clara MSA, CA	H	21.37 FQ	25.96 MW	33.19 TQ	CABLS	1/08-3/08
	Santa Ana-Anaheim-Irvine PMSA, CA	Y	29820 FQ	35520 MW	45620 TQ	USBLS	5/07
	Stockton MSA, CA	H	17.75 FQ	19.68 MW	23.92 TQ	CABLS	1/08-3/08
	Colorado	Y	32450 FQ	39700 MW	51210 TQ	USBLS	5/07
	Connecticut	H	17.09 AE	20.06 MW		CTBLS	1/08-3/08
	Bridgeport-Stamford-Norwalk MSA, CT	Y	43320 FQ	51390 MW	60010 TQ	USBLS	5/07
	Hartford-West Hartford-East Hartford MSA, CT	Y	36920 FQ	43250 MW	59460 TQ	USBLS	5/07
	Delaware	Y	54790 FQ	59270 MW	63760 TQ	USBLS	5/07
	Dover MSA, DE	Y	21840 FQ	25500 MW	41060 TQ	USBLS	5/07
	Wilmington PMSA, DE-MD-NJ	Y	56030 FQ	60100 MW	64200 TQ	USBLS	5/07
	District of Columbia	Y	33380 FQ	43590 MW	51470 TQ	USBLS	5/07
	Washington-Arlington-Alexandria MSA, DC-VA-MD-WV	Y	35940 FQ	46160 MW	57920 TQ	USBLS	5/07
	Florida	Y	24460 FQ	32110 MW	39900 TQ	USBLS	5/07
	Fort Lauderdale-Pompano Beach-Deerfield Beach PMSA, FL	Y	18670 FQ	21760 MW	25800 TQ	USBLS	5/07
	Jacksonville MSA, FL	Y	25220 FQ	28140 MW	30980 TQ	USBLS	5/07
	Miami-Fort Lauderdale-Miami Beach MSA, FL	Y	21430 FQ	28540 MW	40900 TQ	USBLS	5/07
	Orlando-Kissimmee MSA, FL	Y	23700 FQ	31880 MW	37530 TQ	USBLS	5/07
	Tampa-St. Petersburg-Clearwater MSA, FL	Y	30520 FQ	35860 MW	42320 TQ	USBLS	5/07
	Georgia	Y	24480 FQ	34240 MW	46190 TQ	USBLS	5/07
	Atlanta-Sandy Springs-Marietta MSA, GA	Y	22070 FQ	25760 MW	43520 TQ	USBLS	5/07
	Hawaii	Y	26800 FQ	30160 MW	36370 TQ	USBLS	5/07
	Idaho	Y	20550 FQ	26180 MW	35010 TQ	USBLS	5/07
	Boise City-Nampa MSA, ID	Y	26280 FQ	30260 MW	36330 TQ	USBLS	5/07
	Illinois	Y	27210 FQ	33690 MW	46870 TQ	USBLS	5/07
	Chicago-Naperville-Joliet MSA, IL-IN-WI	Y	26990 FQ	32520 MW	45900 TQ	USBLS	5/07
	Indiana	Y	23340 FQ	29910 MW	42230 TQ	USBLS	5/07
	Gary PMSA, IN	Y	25710 FQ	29160 MW	35570 TQ	USBLS	5/07
	Indianapolis-Carmel MSA, IN	Y	22690 FQ	25270 MW	45640 TQ	USBLS	5/07
	Kansas	Y	27910 FQ	32990 MW	38390 TQ	USBLS	5/07
	Louisiana	H	10.42 FQ	13.27 MW	18.41 TQ	LABLS	1/08-3/08
	New Orleans-Metairie-Kenner MSA, LA	Y	24400 FQ	30630 MW	40410 TQ	USBLS	5/07
	Maine	Y	30290 FQ	36250 MW	43650 TQ	USBLS	5/07
	Maryland	Y		41775 MW		MDBLS	3/08

AE	Average entry wage	AW	Average wage paid	FQ	First quartile wage
AER	Average entry range	AWR	Average wage range	H	Hourly
AEX	Average experienced wage	AXR	Average experienced range	HI	Highest wage paid
ATC	Average total compensation	D	Daily	HR	High end range

LO Lowest wage paid MTC Median total compensation TCC Total cash compensation
LR Low end range MW Median wage paid TQ Third quartile wage
M Monthly MWR Median wage range W Weekly
MCC Median cash compensation S See annotated source Y Yearly

Biological Technician

Occupation/Type/Industry	Location	Per	Low	Mid	High	Source	Date
Biological Technician	Baltimore-Towson MSA, MD	Y	31220 FQ	36850 MW	47240 TQ	USBLS	5/07
	Bethesda-Gaithersburg-Frederick PMSA, MD	Y	39160 FQ	49440 MW	61900 TQ	USBLS	5/07
	Massachusetts	Y	39060 FQ	47570 MW	61330 TQ	USBLS	5/07
	Boston-Cambridge-Quincy NECTA, MA	Y	41530 FQ	49480 MW	64650 TQ	USBLS	5/07
	Worcester MSA, MA-CT	Y	34600 FQ	40600 MW	50460 TQ	USBLS	5/07
	Michigan	Y	27620 FQ	32940 MW	42700 TQ	USBLS	5/07
	Detroit-Warren-Livonia MSA, MI	Y	28940 FQ	33800 MW	41690 TQ	USBLS	5/07
	Grand Rapids-Wyoming MSA, MI	Y	21560 FQ	24560 MW	28490 TQ	USBLS	5/07
	Warren-Troy-Farmington Hills PMSA, MI	Y	27460 FQ	33180 MW	49700 TQ	USBLS	5/07
	Minnesota	Y	36942 FQ	47697 MW	61141 TQ	MNBLS	10/08-12/08
	Duluth-Superior MSA, MN-WI	Y	37297 FQ	44475 MW	49863 TQ	MNBLS	10/08-12/08
	Minneapolis-Saint Paul MSA, MN-WI	Y	34818 FQ	42142 MW	54330 TQ	MNBLS	10/08-12/08
	Mississippi	Y	29850 FQ	37250 MW	45740 TQ	USBLS	5/07
	Missouri	Y	25150 FQ	32910 MW	40070 TQ	USBLS	5/07
	Kansas City MSA, MO-KS	Y	29690 FQ	35070 MW	41750 TQ	USBLS	5/07
	St. Louis MSA, MO-IL	Y	24580 FQ	32470 MW	39480 TQ	USBLS	5/07
	Montana	Y	25720 FQ	30590 MW	37950 TQ	USBLS	5/07
	Nebraska	Y	27360 FQ	33530 MW	40290 TQ	USBLS	5/07
	Nevada	H	13.51 FQ	15.45 MW	19.14 TQ	NVBLS	5/08
	New Hampshire	H	12.88 AE	17.16 MW	21.77 AEX	NHBLS	6/08
	Manchester MSA, NH	Y	34310 FQ	41830 MW	52970 TQ	USBLS	5/07
	New Jersey	Y	37780 FQ	45550 MW	53570 TQ	USBLS	5/07
	Camden PMSA, NJ	Y	33790 FQ	41700 MW	47940 TQ	USBLS	5/07
	Edison PMSA, NJ	Y	38640 FQ	47170 MW	54910 TQ	USBLS	5/07
	Newark-Union PMSA, NJ-PA	Y	37360 FQ	44140 MW	51730 TQ	USBLS	5/07
	New Mexico	Y	29010 FQ	37850 MW	55870 TQ	USBLS	5/07
	New York	Y	32090 FQ	38250 MW	47540 TQ	USBLS	5/07
	Albany-Schenectady-Troy MSA, NY	Y	27910 FQ	32730 MW	41310 TQ	USBLS	5/07
	Buffalo-Niagara Falls MSA, NY	Y	27280 FQ	35530 MW	43490 TQ	USBLS	5/07
	Nassau-Suffolk PMSA, NY	Y	33440 FQ	41370 MW	48340 TQ	USBLS	5/07
	New York-Northern New Jersey-Long Island MSA, NY-NJ-PA	Y	35220 FQ	42980 MW	52780 TQ	USBLS	5/07
	Syracuse MSA, NY	Y	21030 FQ	26580 MW	33360 TQ	USBLS	5/07
	North Carolina	Y	31360 FQ	37970 MW	47510 TQ	USBLS	5/07
	Charlotte-Gastonia-Concord MSA, NC-SC	Y	23750 FQ	32600 MW	36480 TQ	USBLS	5/07
	Raleigh-Cary MSA, NC	Y	35840 FQ	43380 MW	54540 TQ	USBLS	5/07
	North Dakota	Y	22670 FQ	27820 MW	36450 TQ	USBLS	5/07
	Ohio	Y	28440 FQ	33200 MW	38910 TQ	USBLS	5/07
	Cincinnati-Middletown MSA, OH-KY-IN	Y	28180 FQ	33050 MW	40200 TQ	USBLS	5/07
	Cleveland-Elyria-Mentor MSA, OH	Y	29040 FQ	34290 MW	41850 TQ	USBLS	5/07
	Columbus MSA, OH	Y	30630 FQ	33840 MW	37220 TQ	USBLS	5/07
	Dayton MSA, OH	Y	24640 FQ	31090 MW	36890 TQ	USBLS	5/07
	Oklahoma	Y	17000 FQ	25400 MW	33140 TQ	USBLS	5/07
	Oklahoma City MSA, OK	Y	16340 FQ	22950 MW	31610 TQ	USBLS	5/07
	Tulsa MSA, OK	Y	28460 FQ	32740 MW	37310 TQ	USBLS	5/07
	Oregon	H	13.17 FQ	16.09 MW	19.43 TQ	ORBLS	5/08
	Portland-Vancouver-Beaverton MSA, OR-WA	Y	29740 FQ	34840 MW	40190 TQ	USBLS	5/07
	Pennsylvania	Y	29140 FQ	36060 MW	46460 TQ	USBLS	5/07
	Allentown-Bethlehem-Easton MSA, PA-NJ	Y	28940 FQ	36770 MW	50690 TQ	USBLS	5/07
	Philadelphia-Camden-Wilmington MSA, PA-NJ-DE-MD	Y	32270 FQ	43010 MW	56750 TQ	USBLS	5/07
	Pittsburgh MSA, PA	Y	26910 FQ	32120 MW	39620 TQ	USBLS	5/07
	South Carolina	Y	26520 FQ	35040 MW	43020 TQ	USBLS	5/07
	Charleston-North Charleston MSA, SC	Y	30050 FQ	38600 MW	46020 TQ	USBLS	5/07
	Columbia MSA, SC	Y	29960 FQ	35780 MW	39730 TQ	USBLS	5/07
	South Dakota	Y	24657 FQ	29347 MW	36133 TQ	SDBLS	7/08-9/08

AE Average entry wage	AW Average wage paid	FQ First quartile wage	LO Lowest wage paid	MTC Median total compensation	TCC Total cash compensation
AER Average entry range	AWR Average wage range	H Hourly	LR Low end range	MW Median wage paid	TQ Third quartile wage
AEX Average experienced wage	AXR Average experienced range	HI Highest wage paid	M Monthly	MWR Median wage range	W Weekly
ATC Average total compensation	D Daily	HR High end range	MCC Median cash compensation	S See annotated source	Y Yearly

Occupation/Type/Industry	Location	Per	Low	Mid	High	Source	Date
Biological Technician	Sioux Falls MSA, SD	Y	27065 FQ	29333 MW	31605 TQ	SDBLS	7/08-9/08
	Tennessee	Y	27620 FQ	32540 MW	40600 TQ	USBLS	5/07
	Memphis MSA, TN-MS-AR	Y	28720 FQ	33240 MW	43250 TQ	USBLS	5/07
	Nashville-Davidson-Murfreesboro MSA, TN	Y	27550 FQ	32610 MW	40250 TQ	USBLS	5/07
	Texas	Y	28750 FQ	36070 MW	45740 TQ	USBLS	5/07
	Austin-Round Rock MSA, TX	Y	26930 FQ	29440 MW	32220 TQ	USBLS	5/07
	Beaumont-Port Arthur MSA, TX	Y	26340 FQ	30000 MW	39570 TQ	USBLS	5/07
	Dallas-Fort Worth-Arlington MSA, TX	Y	33140 FQ	37170 MW	46820 TQ	USBLS	5/07
	Houston-Sugar Land-Baytown MSA, TX	Y	32660 FQ	39150 MW	48590 TQ	USBLS	5/07
	San Antonio MSA, TX	Y	31100 FQ	38950 MW	49000 TQ	USBLS	5/07
	Utah	Y	25250 FQ	29310 MW	35780 TQ	USBLS	5/07
	Logan MSA, UT-ID	Y	23890 FQ	28520 MW	34340 TQ	USBLS	5/07
	Salt Lake City MSA, UT	Y	26390 FQ	30030 MW	36840 TQ	USBLS	5/07
	Vermont	Y	28800 FQ	34830 MW	45860 TQ	USBLS	5/07
	Burlington-South Burlington MSA, VT	Y	29410 FQ	36990 MW	51650 TQ	USBLS	5/07
	Virginia	Y	28570 FQ	36460 MW	46530 TQ	USBLS	5/07
	Richmond MSA, VA	Y	37940 FQ	50150 MW	58040 TQ	USBLS	5/07
	Virginia Beach-Norfolk-Newport News MSA, VA-NC	Y	22260 FQ	29430 MW	36590 TQ	USBLS	5/07
	Washington	H	15.58 FQ	18.36 MW	22.23 TQ	WABLS	3/08
	Seattle-Tacoma-Bellevue MSA, WA	Y	33340 FQ	39150 MW	47440 TQ	USBLS	5/07
	West Virginia	Y	22848 FQ	32203 MW	43911 TQ	WVBLS	7/08-9/08
	Charleston MSA, WV	Y	17290 FQ	19250 MW	43300 TQ	USBLS	5/07
	Wisconsin	Y	27590 FQ	34430 MW	42850 TQ	USBLS	5/07
	Milwaukee-Waukesha-West Allis MSA, WI	Y	38620 FQ	44640 MW	50000 TQ	USBLS	5/07
	Wyoming	Y	29500 FQ	34712 MW	40281 TQ	WYBLS	9/08
	Puerto Rico	Y	26330 FQ	31520 MW	36580 TQ	USBLS	5/07
	San Juan-Caguas-Guaynabo MSA, PR	Y	32300 FQ	35360 MW	38470 TQ	USBLS	5/07
Biomedical Engineer	Alabama	Y	47720 FQ	71370 MW	90550 TQ	USBLS	5/07
	Arizona	Y	39070 FQ	48770 MW	66080 TQ	USBLS	5/07
	Phoenix-Mesa-Scottsdale MSA, AZ	Y	37950 FQ	46530 MW	67660 TQ	USBLS	5/07
	California	H	35.75 FQ	44.24 MW	52.62 TQ	CABLS	1/08-3/08
	Los Angeles-Long Beach-Glendale PMSA, CA	H	34.25 FQ	43.09 MW	51.91 TQ	CABLS	1/08-3/08
	Oakland-Fremont-Hayward MSA, CA	H	34.26 FQ	42.72 MW	51.54 TQ	CABLS	1/08-3/08
	San Diego-Carlsbad-San Marcos MSA, CA	H	30.91 FQ	37.69 MW	45.83 TQ	CABLS	1/08-3/08
	San Francisco-San Mateo-Redwood PMSA, CA	H	40.55 FQ	48.19 MW	57.53 TQ	CABLS	1/08-3/08
	San Jose-Sunnyvale-Santa Clara MSA, CA	H	37.29 FQ	48.65 MW	60.82 TQ	CABLS	1/08-3/08
	Santa Ana-Anaheim-Irvine PMSA, CA	Y	77990 FQ	92900 MW	104710 TQ	USBLS	5/07
	Colorado	Y	69460 FQ	81770 MW	100080 TQ	USBLS	5/07
	Denver-Aurora MSA, CO	Y	64900 FQ	80540 MW	96720 TQ	USBLS	5/07
	Connecticut	H	30.82 AE	40.81 MW		CTBLS	1/08-3/08
	District of Columbia	Y	45990 FQ	56030 MW	71890 TQ	USBLS	5/07
	Washington-Arlington-Alexandria MSA, DC-VA-MD-WV	Y	53390 FQ	70030 MW	95080 TQ	USBLS	5/07
	Florida	Y	56200 FQ	68210 MW	83250 TQ	USBLS	5/07
	Fort Lauderdale-Pompano Beach-Deerfield Beach PMSA, FL	Y	65540 FQ	84740 MW	100950 TQ	USBLS	5/07
	Miami-Fort Lauderdale-Miami Beach MSA, FL	Y	53500 FQ	65610 MW	78800 TQ	USBLS	5/07
	Tampa-St. Petersburg-Clearwater MSA, FL	Y	71600 FQ	82990 MW	95600 TQ	USBLS	5/07
	Georgia	Y	44330 FQ	54290 MW	66900 TQ	USBLS	5/07
	Atlanta-Sandy Springs-Marietta MSA, GA	Y	48670 FQ	57780 MW	70260 TQ	USBLS	5/07

AE	Average entry wage	AW	Average wage paid	FQ	First quartile wage	LO	Lowest wage paid	MTC	Median total compensation	TCC	Total cash compensation
AER	Average entry range	AWR	Average wage range	H	Hourly	LR	Low end range	MW	Median wage paid	TQ	Third quartile wage
AEX	Average experienced wage	AXR	Average experienced range	HI	Highest wage paid	M	Monthly	MWR	Median wage range	W	Weekly
ATC	Average total compensation	D	Daily	HR	High end range	MCC	Median cash compensation	S	See annotated source	Y	Yearly

Occupation/Type/Industry	Location	Per	Low	Mid	High	Source	Date
Biomedical Engineer	Illinois	Y	55650 FQ	64880 MW	113240 TQ	USBLS	5/07
	Chicago-Naperville-Joliet MSA, IL-IN-WI	Y	55350 FQ	63250 MW	105850 TQ	USBLS	5/07
	Indiana	Y	51590 FQ	60130 MW	71390 TQ	USBLS	5/07
	Indianapolis-Carmel MSA, IN	Y	47760 FQ	54600 MW	61180 TQ	USBLS	5/07
	Iowa	Y	54790 FQ	66360 MW	78800 TQ	USBLS	5/07
	Kansas	Y	56070 FQ	65230 MW	94510 TQ	USBLS	5/07
	Kentucky	Y	41453 FQ	48635 MW	62849 TQ	KYBLS	2008
	Louisiana	H	19.33 FQ	22.99 MW	33.15 TQ	LABLS	1/08-3/08
	New Orleans-Metairie-Kenner MSA, LA	Y	46970 FQ	59220 MW	88350 TQ	USBLS	5/07
	Maryland	Y		83300 MW		MDBLS	3/08
	Baltimore-Towson MSA, MD	Y	57560 FQ	76350 MW	121840 TQ	USBLS	5/07
	Bethesda-Gaithersburg-Frederick PMSA, MD	Y	60330 FQ	81400 MW	97920 TQ	USBLS	5/07
	Massachusetts	Y	66600 FQ	84170 MW	108930 TQ	USBLS	5/07
	Boston-Cambridge-Quincy NECTA, MA	Y	65300 FQ	81470 MW	102440 TQ	USBLS	5/07
	Worcester MSA, MA-CT	Y	70540 FQ	80740 MW	99150 TQ	USBLS	5/07
	Michigan	Y	48070 FQ	65760 MW	89240 TQ	USBLS	5/07
	Detroit-Warren-Livonia MSA, MI	Y	40550 FQ	67390 MW	80600 TQ	USBLS	5/07
	Minnesota	Y	72921 FQ	89692 MW	108995 TQ	MNBLS	10/08-12/08
	Minneapolis-Saint Paul MSA, MN-WI	Y	73926 FQ	90906 MW	110042 TQ	MNBLS	10/08-12/08
	Mississippi	Y	34740 FQ	46350 MW	62980 TQ	USBLS	5/07
	Missouri	Y	57170 FQ	71500 MW	86800 TQ	USBLS	5/07
	Kansas City MSA, MO-KS	Y	58290 FQ	67720 MW	94870 TQ	USBLS	5/07
	St. Louis MSA, MO-IL	Y	58630 FQ	69120 MW	82030 TQ	USBLS	5/07
	Montana	Y	52860 FQ	60430 MW	70660 TQ	USBLS	5/07
	Nebraska	Y	46140 FQ	54370 MW	61880 TQ	USBLS	5/07
	Omaha-Council Bluffs MSA, NE-IA	Y	45620 FQ	53090 MW	60400 TQ	USBLS	5/07
	Nevada	H	28.14 FQ	32.77 MW	37.38 TQ	NVBLS	5/08
	New Hampshire	H	21.15 AE	22.63 MW	32.37 AEX	NHBLS	6/08
	New Jersey	Y	62610 FQ	74550 MW	90180 TQ	USBLS	5/07
	Edison PMSA, NJ	Y	64280 FQ	74640 MW	88700 TQ	USBLS	5/07
	Newark-Union PMSA, NJ-PA	Y	59650 FQ	81720 MW	97880 TQ	USBLS	5/07
	New Mexico	Y	50600 FQ	65070 MW	75970 TQ	USBLS	5/07
	New York	Y	61260 FQ	80100 MW	101900 TQ	USBLS	5/07
	Albany-Schenectady-Troy MSA, NY	Y	57660 FQ	77360 MW	108520 TQ	USBLS	5/07
	Nassau-Suffolk PMSA, NY	Y	79750 FQ	92830 MW	110190 TQ	USBLS	5/07
	New York-Northern New Jersey-Long Island MSA, NY-NJ-PA	Y	62910 FQ	77590 MW	96540 TQ	USBLS	5/07
	North Carolina	Y	57720 FQ	73570 MW	92090 TQ	USBLS	5/07
	Raleigh-Cary MSA, NC	Y	59720 FQ	82330 MW	106470 TQ	USBLS	5/07
	Ohio	Y	54080 FQ	67860 MW	83150 TQ	USBLS	5/07
	Cleveland-Elyria-Mentor MSA, OH	Y	54580 FQ	67580 MW	84470 TQ	USBLS	5/07
	Dayton MSA, OH	Y	41650 FQ	80690 MW	112500 TQ	USBLS	5/07
	Oklahoma	Y	41920 FQ	55950 MW	76300 TQ	USBLS	5/07
	Oregon	H	24.41 FQ	28.41 MW	37.26 TQ	ORBLS	5/08
	Portland-Vancouver-Beaverton MSA, OR-WA	Y	53560 FQ	64450 MW	91230 TQ	USBLS	5/07
	Pennsylvania	Y	51790 FQ	61210 MW	81610 TQ	USBLS	5/07
	Philadelphia-Camden-Wilmington MSA, PA-NJ-DE-MD	Y	56440 FQ	69710 MW	96910 TQ	USBLS	5/07
	Pittsburgh MSA, PA	Y	49540 FQ	68020 MW	92830 TQ	USBLS	5/07
	South Carolina	Y	49840 FQ	83540 MW	94320 TQ	USBLS	5/07
	Charleston-North Charleston MSA, SC	Y	47420 FQ	86590 MW	95660 TQ	USBLS	5/07
	Tennessee	Y	54670 FQ	71630 MW	93100 TQ	USBLS	5/07
	Memphis MSA, TN-MS-AR	Y	54040 FQ	67780 MW	91420 TQ	USBLS	5/07
	Nashville-Davidson-Murfreesboro MSA, TN	Y	55710 FQ	75330 MW	87870 TQ	USBLS	5/07
	Texas	Y	39830 FQ	56090 MW	74000 TQ	USBLS	5/07
	Dallas-Fort Worth-Arlington MSA, TX	Y	54730 FQ	65440 MW	79210 TQ	USBLS	5/07

Occupation/Type/Industry	Location	Per	Low	Mid	High	Source	Date
Biomedical Engineer	Houston-Sugar Land-Baytown						
	MSA, TX	Y	46150 FQ	58750 MW	73140 TQ	USBLS	5/07
	Utah	Y	58560 FQ	77510 MW	98320 TQ	USBLS	5/07
	Salt Lake City MSA, UT	Y	57920 FQ	71100 MW	84520 TQ	USBLS	5/07
	Virginia	Y	50640 FQ	62880 MW	114590 TQ	USBLS	5/07
	Washington	H	27.77 FQ	36.97 MW	45.21 TQ	WABLS	3/08
	Seattle-Tacoma-Bellevue						
	MSA, WA	Y	56080 FQ	75890 MW	92600 TQ	USBLS	5/07
	Wisconsin	Y	63230 FQ	81410 MW	99030 TQ	USBLS	5/07
	Milwaukee-Waukesha-West						
	Allis MSA, WI	Y	65940 FQ	80810 MW	100050 TQ	USBLS	5/07
	Puerto Rico	Y	29900 FQ	43700 MW	50110 TQ	USBLS	5/07
	San Juan-Caguas-Guaynabo						
	MSA, PR	Y	29600 FQ	43710 MW	49950 TQ	USBLS	5/07
Biopharmaceutical Professional							
Female, Regulatory Affairs	United States	Y		87810 AW		BPHARM	9/07-12/07
Male, Regulatory Affairs	United States	Y		116974 AW		BPHARM	9/07-12/07
Bituminous Plant Inspector							
State Government	Ohio	H	15.09 LO		17.03 HI	ODAS	2008
Blood Bank Technology-Specialist							
Bench Tech	United States	Y		50000 AW		HCCD01	2008
Board Director							
Top 200 Companies in the United States	United States	Y		200000 MW		BWEEK02	2008
Board Member							
Tax Appeals	Ohio	H	35.44 LO		75.94 HI	ODAS	2008
Board of Governors Member							
Federal Reserve	United States	Y			172000 HI	CSM03	2008
Body Shop Repairman							
Public Schools	Baldwin County, AL	Y	30964 LO		38886 HI	BCPSSS	2008-2009
Boiler Inspector							
Department of Labor	New Hampshire	Y			61379 HI	NHUL03	2008
State Government	Ohio	H	19.88 LO		26.28 HI	ODAS	2008
Boiler Repair Worker							
State Government	Ohio	H	15.41 LO		17.03 HI	ODAS	2008
Boilermaker	Alabama	Y	28220 FQ	37630 MW	44080 TQ	USBLS	5/07
	Arizona	Y	29150 FQ	38650 MW	51470 TQ	USBLS	5/07
	Phoenix-Mesa-Scottsdale						
	MSA, AZ	Y	29440 FQ	39020 MW	54180 TQ	USBLS	5/07
	Arkansas	Y	33530 FQ	41140 MW	48150 TQ	USBLS	5/07
	California	H	24.62 FQ	31.28 MW	36.66 TQ	CABLS	1/08-3/08
	Los Angeles-Long Beach-						
	Glendale PMSA, CA	H	26.70 FQ	33.42 MW	37.40 TQ	CABLS	1/08-3/08
	Oakland-Fremont-Hayward						
	MSA, CA	H	24.61 FQ	29.78 MW	35.60 TQ	CABLS	1/08-3/08
	Colorado	Y	40500 FQ	46880 MW	55980 TQ	USBLS	5/07
	Connecticut	H	24.67 AE	28.04 MW		CTBLS	1/08-3/08
	Delaware	Y	61700 FQ	67910 MW	73460 TQ	USBLS	5/07
	Wilmington PMSA, DE-MD-						
	NJ	Y	61700 FQ	67910 MW	73460 TQ	USBLS	5/07
	Washington-Arlington-						
	Alexandria MSA, DC-VA-						
	MD-WV	Y	48160 FQ	55580 MW	63970 TQ	USBLS	5/07
	Florida	Y	36950 FQ	42780 MW	49620 TQ	USBLS	5/07
	Tampa-St. Petersburg-						
	Clearwater MSA, FL	Y	34910 FQ	38560 MW	43410 TQ	USBLS	5/07
	Georgia	Y	42570 FQ	48450 MW	60030 TQ	USBLS	5/07
	Atlanta-Sandy Springs-						
	Marietta MSA, GA	Y	42170 FQ	47520 MW	58820 TQ	USBLS	5/07
	Hawaii	Y	45160 FQ	52550 MW	59200 TQ	USBLS	5/07
	Illinois	Y	53940 FQ	67940 MW	77560 TQ	USBLS	5/07
	Chicago-Naperville-Joliet						
	MSA, IL-IN-WI	Y	54030 FQ	64570 MW	75730 TQ	USBLS	5/07
	Indiana	Y	38950 FQ	52210 MW	61130 TQ	USBLS	5/07

AE	Average entry wage	AW	Average wage paid	FQ	First quartile wage	LO	Lowest wage paid	MTC	Median total compensation	TCC	Total cash compensation
AER	Average entry range	AWR	Average wage range	H	Hourly	LR	Low end range	MW	Median wage paid	TQ	Third quartile wage
AEX	Average experienced wage	AXR	Average experienced range	HI	Highest wage paid	M	Monthly	MWR	Median wage range	W	Weekly
ATC	Average total compensation	D	Daily	HR	High end range	MCC	Median cash compensation	S	See annotated source	Y	Yearly

Occupation/Type/Industry	Location	Per	Low	Mid	High	Source	Date
Boilermaker	Evansville MSA, IN-KY	Y	41890 FQ	54450 MW	62780 TQ	USBLS	5/07
	Gary PMSA, IN	Y	54130 FQ	58680 MW	63380 TQ	USBLS	5/07
	Indianapolis-Carmel MSA, IN	Y	35430 FQ	39740 MW	49300 TQ	USBLS	5/07
	Iowa	Y	39530 FQ	45590 MW	51430 TQ	USBLS	5/07
	Kentucky	Y	43048 FQ	54444 MW	62296 TQ	KYBLS	2008
	Louisville-Jefferson County MSA, KY-IN	Y	50370 FQ	55160 MW	60030 TQ	USBLS	5/07
	Louisiana	H	18.79 FQ	21.14 MW	24.11 TQ	LABLS	1/08-3/08
	Baton Rouge MSA, LA	Y	40430 FQ	44910 MW	50940 TQ	USBLS	5/07
	New Orleans-Metairie-Kenner MSA, LA	Y	38630 FQ	44540 MW	51070 TQ	USBLS	5/07
	Maine	Y	31760 FQ	39260 MW	50050 TQ	USBLS	5/07
	Portland-South Portland-Biddeford MSA, ME	Y	31210 FQ	37360 MW	53530 TQ	USBLS	5/07
	Maryland	Y		64125 MW		MDBLS	3/08
	Baltimore-Towson MSA, MD	Y	54170 FQ	65550 MW	72090 TQ	USBLS	5/07
	Massachusetts	Y	48400 FQ	54210 MW	59760 TQ	USBLS	5/07
	Boston-Cambridge-Quincy NECTA, MA	Y	52740 FQ	56720 MW	60810 TQ	USBLS	5/07
	Worcester MSA, MA-CT	Y	41460 FQ	48990 MW	57200 TQ	USBLS	5/07
	Michigan	Y	45100 FQ	52180 MW	64630 TQ	USBLS	5/07
	Detroit-Warren-Livonia MSA, MI	Y	45970 FQ	52530 MW	60550 TQ	USBLS	5/07
	Grand Rapids-Wyoming MSA, MI	Y	34100 FQ	65030 MW	72740 TQ	USBLS	5/07
	Minnesota	Y	39678 FQ	46560 MW	58026 TQ	MNBLS	10/08-12/08
	Minneapolis-Saint Paul MSA, MN-WI	Y	37486 FQ	42871 MW	55581 TQ	MNBLS	10/08-12/08
	Mississippi	Y	37650 FQ	46260 MW	58980 TQ	USBLS	5/07
	Missouri	Y	32730 FQ	43040 MW	55200 TQ	USBLS	5/07
	Kansas City MSA, MO-KS	Y	46040 FQ	56150 MW	67640 TQ	USBLS	5/07
	Nevada	H	25.83 FQ	33.29 MW	36.66 TQ	NVBLS	5/08
	New Jersey	Y	44850 FQ	60910 MW	71710 TQ	USBLS	5/07
	Camden PMSA, NJ	Y	32450 FQ	38580 MW	47000 TQ	USBLS	5/07
	Edison PMSA, NJ	Y	59290 FQ	67630 MW	76180 TQ	USBLS	5/07
	Newark-Union PMSA, NJ-PA	Y	36620 FQ	51140 MW	64430 TQ	USBLS	5/07
	New Mexico	Y	39920 FQ	43760 MW	47560 TQ	USBLS	5/07
	New York	Y	35740 FQ	46570 MW	68880 TQ	USBLS	5/07
	Albany-Schenectady-Troy MSA, NY	Y	37340 FQ	52690 MW	64580 TQ	USBLS	5/07
	New York-Northern New Jersey-Long Island MSA, NY-NJ-PA	Y	46930 FQ	64460 MW	82990 TQ	USBLS	5/07
	North Carolina	Y	30270 FQ	40510 MW	50670 TQ	USBLS	5/07
	Fargo MSA, ND-MN	Y	39930 FQ	49150 MW	68230 TQ	USBLS	5/07
	Ohio	Y	46650 FQ	61670 MW	72360 TQ	USBLS	5/07
	Cincinnati-Middletown MSA, OH-KY-IN	Y	42030 FQ	59140 MW	68670 TQ	USBLS	5/07
	Cleveland-Elyria-Mentor MSA, OH	Y	52290 FQ	67010 MW	75520 TQ	USBLS	5/07
	Oklahoma	Y	32010 FQ	37220 MW	43130 TQ	USBLS	5/07
	Oklahoma City MSA, OK	Y	29210 FQ	32320 MW	38890 TQ	USBLS	5/07
	Tulsa MSA, OK	Y	33160 FQ	36880 MW	40950 TQ	USBLS	5/07
	Oregon	H	21.55 FQ	25.33 MW	33.13 TQ	ORBLS	5/08
	Portland-Vancouver-Beaverton MSA, OR-WA	Y	44640 FQ	53800 MW	68530 TQ	USBLS	5/07
	Pennsylvania	Y	41250 FQ	54960 MW	67810 TQ	USBLS	5/07
	Philadelphia-Camden-Wilmington MSA, PA-NJ-DE-MD	Y	46010 FQ	64810 MW	72300 TQ	USBLS	5/07
	Pittsburgh MSA, PA	Y	36870 FQ	52840 MW	59020 TQ	USBLS	5/07
	South Carolina	Y	42120 FQ	47220 MW	57090 TQ	USBLS	5/07
	South Dakota	Y	31026 FQ	43806 MW	56451 TQ	SDBLS	7/08-9/08
	Tennessee	Y	39870 FQ	54330 MW	60500 TQ	USBLS	5/07
	Texas	Y	37480 FQ	48780 MW	59260 TQ	USBLS	5/07
	Beaumont-Port Arthur MSA, TX	Y	36920 FQ	46960 MW	58140 TQ	USBLS	5/07
	Dallas-Fort Worth-Arlington MSA, TX	Y	35950 FQ	44790 MW	51080 TQ	USBLS	5/07
	Houston-Sugar Land-Baytown MSA, TX	Y	38040 FQ	51020 MW	60280 TQ	USBLS	5/07
	Utah	Y	43340 FQ	52360 MW	59650 TQ	USBLS	5/07

AE	Average entry wage	AW	Average wage paid	FQ First quartile wage
AER	Average entry range	AWR	Average wage range	H Hourly
AEX	Average experienced wage	AXR	Average experienced range	HI Highest wage paid
ATC	Average total compensation	D	Daily	HR High end range

LO	Lowest wage paid	MTC	Median total compensation
LR	Low end range	MW	Median wage paid
M	Monthly	MWR	Median wage range
MCC	Median cash compensation	S	See annotated source

TCC	Total cash compensation
TQ	Third quartile wage
W	Weekly
Y	Yearly

Occupation/Type/Industry	Location	Per.	Low	Mid	High	Source	Date
Boilermaker	Virginia	Y	40610 FQ	46040 MW	51760 TQ	USBLS	5/07
	Virginia Beach-Norfolk-Newport News MSA, VA-NC	Y	40200 FQ	46200 MW	53580 TQ	USBLS	5/07
	Washington	H	20.26 FQ	23.06 MW	25.87 TQ	WABLS	3/08
	Seattle-Tacoma-Bellevue MSA, WA	Y	42330 FQ	46430 MW	50530 TQ	USBLS	5/07
	West Virginia	Y	56739 FQ	66577 MW	75125 TQ	WVBLS	7/08-9/08
	Wisconsin	Y	51010 FQ	57740 MW	64050 TQ	USBLS	5/07
	Puerto Rico	Y	14160 FQ	18760 MW	42510 TQ	USBLS	5/07
	San Juan-Caguas-Guaynabo MSA, PR	Y	13050 FQ	14780 MW	16400 TQ	USBLS	5/07
	Virgin Islands	Y	27640 FQ	30170 MW	35280 TQ	USBLS	5/07
Bookbinder	Alabama	Y	25710 FQ	38810 MW	43540 TQ	USBLS	5/07
	Arkansas	Y	21100 FQ	25020 MW	40030 TQ	USBLS	5/07
	California	H	10.32 FQ	13.79 MW	19.53 TQ	CABLS	1/08-3/08
	Connecticut	H	9.36 AE	13.64 MW		CTBLS	1/08-3/08
	Florida	Y	31210 FQ	39380 MW	44400 TQ	USBLS	5/07
	Georgia	Y	13230 FQ	15280 MW	24470 TQ	USBLS	5/07
	Illinois	Y	19020 FQ	30740 MW	39790 TQ	USBLS	5/07
	Indiana	Y	15080 FQ	21620 MW	28800 TQ	USBLS	5/07
	Iowa	Y	27700 FQ	31470 MW	42080 TQ	USBLS	5/07
	Kansas	Y	24350 FQ	37800 MW	43690 TQ	USBLS	5/07
	Kentucky	Y	17709 FQ	19834 MW	25077 TQ	KYBLS	2008
	Maryland	Y		40100 MW		MDBLS	3/08
	Massachusetts	Y	18660 FQ	22890 MW	28260 TQ	USBLS	5/07
	Michigan	Y	24190 FQ	29190 MW	34440 TQ	USBLS	5/07
	Minnesota	Y	26559 FQ	43032 MW	53036 TQ	MNBLS	10/08-12/08
	Missouri	Y	19380 FQ	28120 MW	38200 TQ	USBLS	5/07
	New York	Y	19050 FQ	29360 MW	42200 TQ	USBLS	5/07
	North Carolina	Y	19780 FQ	23350 MW	29500 TQ	USBLS	5/07
	Ohio	Y	20670 FQ	24790 MW	33660 TQ	USBLS	5/07
	Pennsylvania	Y	23790 FQ	32820 MW	37560 TQ	USBLS	5/07
	South Carolina	Y	25930 FQ	31180 MW	36610 TQ	USBLS	5/07
	South Dakota	Y	21783 FQ	25075 MW	28544 TQ	SDBLS	7/08-9/08
	Tennessee	Y	22190 FQ	26530 MW	31510 TQ	USBLS	5/07
	Texas	Y	26470 FQ	38050 MW	71300 TQ	USBLS	5/07
	Utah	Y	17880 FQ	20070 MW	21950 TQ	USBLS	5/07
	Virginia	Y	19020 FQ	30200 MW	37410 TQ	USBLS	5/07
	Wisconsin	Y	21940 FQ	29490 MW	42350 TQ	USBLS	5/07
	Puerto Rico	Y	14310 FQ	17310 MW	20320 TQ	USBLS	5/07
Bookkeeping, Accounting, and Auditing Clerk	Alabama	Y	21900 FQ	27610 MW	34130 TQ	USBLS	5/07
	Birmingham-Hoover MSA, AL	Y	23950 FQ	29820 MW	37190 TQ	USBLS	5/07
	Mobile MSA, AL	Y	22260 FQ	27040 MW	32860 TQ	USBLS	5/07
	Alaska	Y	30150 FQ	37030 MW	45400 TQ	USBLS	5/07
	Anchorage MSA, AK	Y	30700 FQ	37720 MW	45930 TQ	USBLS	5/07
	Arizona	Y	26120 FQ	31350 MW	38310 TQ	USBLS	5/07
	Phoenix-Mesa-Scottsdale MSA, AZ	Y	26700 FQ	32110 MW	39200 TQ	USBLS	5/07
	Tucson MSA, AZ	Y	25040 FQ	29990 MW	36790 TQ	USBLS	5/07
	Arkansas	Y	21830 FQ	26930 MW	32920 TQ	USBLS	5/07
	Little Rock-North Little Rock MSA, AR	Y	23820 FQ	29480 MW	35990 TQ	USBLS	5/07
	California	H	14.29 FQ	17.62 MW	21.62 TQ	CABLS	1/08-3/08
	Los Angeles-Long Beach-Glendale PMSA, CA	H	14.07 FQ	17.46 MW	21.42 TQ	CABLS	1/08-3/08
	Modesto MSA, CA	H	13.63 FQ	16.17 MW	19.14 TQ	CABLS	1/08-3/08
	Oakland-Fremont-Hayward MSA, CA	H	15.61 FQ	19.21 MW	23.29 TQ	CABLS	1/08-3/08
	Riverside-San Bernardino-Ontario MSA, CA	H	13.52 FQ	16.40 MW	19.67 TQ	CABLS	1/08-3/08
	Sacramento-Arden Arcade-Roseville MSA, CA	H	14.45 FQ	17.38 MW	20.39 TQ	CABLS	1/08-3/08
	San Diego-Carlsbad-San Marcos MSA, CA	H	14.20 FQ	17.32 MW	20.70 TQ	CABLS	1/08-3/08
	San Francisco-San Mateo-Redwood PMSA, CA	H	16.31 FQ	20.09 MW	24.78 TQ	CABLS	1/08-3/08
	San Jose-Sunnyvale-Santa Clara MSA, CA	H	16.38 FQ	20.59 MW	24.49 TQ	CABLS	1/08-3/08

AE	Average entry wage	AW	Average wage paid	FQ	First quartile wage
AER	Average entry range	AWR	Average wage range	H	Hourly
AEX	Average experienced wage	AXR	Average experienced range	HI	Highest wage paid
ATC	Average total compensation	D	Daily	HR	High end range

LO	Lowest wage paid	MTC	Median total compensation	TCC	Total cash compensation
LR	Low end range	MW	Median wage paid	TQ	Third quartile wage
M	Monthly	MWR	Median wage range	W	Weekly
MCC	Median cash compensation	S	See annotated source	Y	Yearly

Occupation/Type/Industry	Location	Per	Low	Mid	High	Source	Date
Bookkeeping, Accounting, and Auditing Clerk	Santa Ana-Anaheim-Irvine PMSA, CA	Y	30370 FQ	36700 MW	44600 TQ	USBLS	5/07
	Colorado	Y	26100 FQ	32970 MW	40010 TQ	USBLS	5/07
	Denver-Aurora MSA, CO	Y	28210 FQ	34820 MW	41580 TQ	USBLS	5/07
	Connecticut	H	13.52 AE	18.68 MW		CTBLS	1/08-3/08
	Bridgeport-Stamford-Norwalk MSA, CT	Y	32390 FQ	40310 MW	49410 TQ	USBLS	5/07
	Hartford-West Hartford-East Hartford MSA, CT	Y	30850 FQ	37740 MW	46050 TQ	USBLS	5/07
	Delaware	Y	27570 FQ	34420 MW	41790 TQ	USBLS	5/07
	Wilmington PMSA, DE-MD-NJ	Y	29290 FQ	35950 MW	44180 TQ	USBLS	5/07
	District of Columbia	Y	34020 FQ	40650 MW	48060 TQ	USBLS	5/07
	Washington-Arlington-Alexandria MSA, DC-VA-MD-WV	Y	31550 FQ	38650 MW	47030 TQ	USBLS	5/07
	Florida	Y	24930 FQ	30180 MW	37120 TQ	USBLS	5/07
	Fort Lauderdale-Pompano Beach-Deerfield Beach PMSA, FL	Y	25600 FQ	31780 MW	39000 TQ	USBLS	5/07
	Jacksonville MSA, FL	Y	24920 FQ	30000 MW	36280 TQ	USBLS	5/07
	Miami-Fort Lauderdale-Miami Beach MSA, FL	Y	25790 FQ	31630 MW	39110 TQ	USBLS	5/07
	Orlando-Kissimmee MSA, FL	Y	24360 FQ	29510 MW	35920 TQ	USBLS	5/07
	Sarasota-Bradenton-Venice MSA, FL	Y	25410 FQ	30790 MW	38280 TQ	USBLS	5/07
	Tampa-St. Petersburg-Clearwater MSA, FL	Y	25670 FQ	30540 MW	36850 TQ	USBLS	5/07
	West Palm Beach-Boca Raton-Boynton Beach PMSA, FL	Y	26500 FQ	32520 MW	40710 TQ	USBLS	5/07
	Georgia	Y	23880 FQ	29990 MW	37070 TQ	USBLS	5/07
	Atlanta-Sandy Springs-Marietta MSA, GA	Y	26190 FQ	32510 MW	39120 TQ	USBLS	5/07
	Hawaii	Y	26360 FQ	32340 MW	39010 TQ	USBLS	5/07
	Honolulu MSA, HI	Y	26100 FQ	32360 MW	39490 TQ	USBLS	5/07
	Idaho	Y	21690 FQ	27530 MW	33430 TQ	USBLS	5/07
	Boise City-Nampa MSA, ID	Y	23630 FQ	28900 MW	34810 TQ	USBLS	5/07
	Pocatello MSA, ID	Y	18930 FQ	25380 MW	30010 TQ	USBLS	5/07
	Illinois	Y	26150 FQ	32620 MW	40170 TQ	USBLS	5/07
	Chicago-Naperville-Joliet MSA, IL-IN-WI	Y	27550 FQ	34230 MW	41760 TQ	USBLS	5/07
	Rockford MSA, IL	Y	26230 FQ	30690 MW	37210 TQ	USBLS	5/07
	Indiana	Y	24230 FQ	29610 MW	36650 TQ	USBLS	5/07
	Gary PMSA, IN	Y	24450 FQ	30260 MW	37310 TQ	USBLS	5/07
	Indianapolis-Carmel MSA, IN	Y	26670 FQ	32520 MW	40690 TQ	USBLS	5/07
	Iowa	Y	22350 FQ	28000 MW	34290 TQ	USBLS	5/07
	Des Moines-West Des Moines MSA, IA	Y	26860 FQ	31800 MW	37870 TQ	USBLS	5/07
	Iowa City MSA, IA	Y	22270 FQ	28200 MW	35490 TQ	USBLS	5/07
	Kansas	Y	21720 FQ	27220 MW	32750 TQ	USBLS	5/07
	Wichita MSA, KS	Y	23160 FQ	27900 MW	32400 TQ	USBLS	5/07
	Kentucky	Y	23135 FQ	28838 MW	35459 TQ	KYBLS	2008
	Louisville-Jefferson County MSA, KY-IN	Y	24630 FQ	29450 MW	35830 TQ	USBLS	5/07
	Louisiana	H	11.05 FQ	13.76 MW	16.96 TQ	LABLS	1/08-3/08
	Baton Rouge MSA, LA	Y	25770 FQ	30640 MW	36830 TQ	USBLS	5/07
	New Orleans-Metairie-Kenner MSA, LA	Y	25770 FQ	31300 MW	38160 TQ	USBLS	5/07
	Maine	Y	25250 FQ	29840 MW	35600 TQ	USBLS	5/07
	Portland-South Portland-Biddeford MSA, ME	Y	27020 FQ	31480 MW	37130 TQ	USBLS	5/07
	Maryland	Y		37025 MW		MDBLS	3/08
	Baltimore-Towson MSA, MD	Y	29490 FQ	36100 MW	44270 TQ	USBLS	5/07
	Bethesda-Gaithersburg-Frederick PMSA, MD	Y	32080 FQ	39450 MW	48220 TQ	USBLS	5/07
	Massachusetts	Y	30420 FQ	36830 MW	44230 TQ	USBLS	5/07
	Barnstable Town MSA, MA	Y	28430 FQ	35240 MW	42000 TQ	USBLS	5/07
	Boston-Cambridge-Quincy NECTA, MA	Y	32290 FQ	38200 MW	45580 TQ	USBLS	5/07
	Worcester MSA, MA-CT	Y	29190 FQ	35590 MW	42440 TQ	USBLS	5/07
	Michigan	Y	26520 FQ	31910 MW	38950 TQ	USBLS	5/07

AE Average entry wage	**AW** Average wage paid	**FQ** First quartile wage	**LO** Lowest wage paid	**MTC** Median total compensation	**TCC** Total cash compensation
AER Average entry range	**AWR** Average wage range	**H** Hourly	**LR** Low end range	**MW** Median wage paid	**TQ** Third quartile wage
AEX Average experienced wage	**AXR** Average experienced range	**HI** Highest wage paid	**M** Monthly	**MWR** Median wage range	**W** Weekly
ATC Average total compensation	**D** Daily	**HR** High end range	**MCC** Median cash compensation	**S** See annotated source	**Y** Yearly

Occupation/Type/Industry	Location	Per	Low	Mid	High	Source	Date
Bookkeeping, Accounting, and Auditing Clerk	Detroit-Warren-Livonia MSA, MI	Y	28440 FQ	34210 MW	40900 TQ	USBLS	5/07
	Flint MSA, MI	Y	26840 FQ	31750 MW	38490 TQ	USBLS	5/07
	Grand Rapids-Wyoming MSA, MI	Y	26030 FQ	31040 MW	36840 TQ	USBLS	5/07
	Lansing-East Lansing MSA, MI	Y	27650 FQ	33550 MW	41830 TQ	USBLS	5/07
	Warren-Troy-Farmington Hills PMSA, MI	Y	28520 FQ	34530 MW	41310 TQ	USBLS	5/07
	Minnesota	Y	28195 FQ	34325 MW	40528 TQ	MNBLS	10/08-12/08
	Duluth-Superior MSA, MN-WI	Y	25582 FQ	30703 MW	37801 TQ	MNBLS	10/08-12/08
	Minneapolis-Saint Paul MSA, MN-WI	Y	31317 FQ	36688 MW	42329 TQ	MNBLS	10/08-12/08
	Rochester MSA, MN	Y	28345 FQ	32835 MW	38466 TQ	MNBLS	10/08-12/08
	Mississippi	Y	24410 FQ	29070 MW	35550 TQ	USBLS	5/07
	Jackson MSA, MS	Y	26510 FQ	31820 MW	39020 TQ	USBLS	5/07
	Missouri	Y	22990 FQ	29160 MW	36520 TQ	USBLS	5/07
	Kansas City MSA, MO-KS	Y	24910 FQ	31240 MW	38340 TQ	USBLS	5/07
	St. Louis MSA, MO-IL	Y	26200 FQ	31630 MW	38630 TQ	USBLS	5/07
	Montana	Y	21430 FQ	27470 MW	33860 TQ	USBLS	5/07
	Billings MSA, MT	Y	22730 FQ	28510 MW	34740 TQ	USBLS	5/07
	Nebraska	Y	22190 FQ	27720 MW	33580 TQ	USBLS	5/07
	Omaha-Council Bluffs MSA, NE-IA	Y	25280 FQ	30250 MW	36960 TQ	USBLS	5/07
	Nevada	H	12.61 FQ	15.10 MW	18.70 TQ	NVBLS	5/08
	Las Vegas-Paradise MSA, NV	H	12.68 FQ	15.01 MW	18.41 TQ	NVBLS	5/08
	New Hampshire	H	11.48 AE	16.04 MW	18.82 AEX	NHBLS	6/08
	Manchester MSA, NH	Y	30320 FQ	35080 MW	40980 TQ	USBLS	5/07
	Nashua NECTA, NH-MA	Y	26760 FQ	33480 MW	40160 TQ	USBLS	5/07
	Rochester-Dover MSA, NH-ME	Y	24680 FQ	32070 MW	37870 TQ	USBLS	5/07
	New Jersey	Y	29660 FQ	36680 MW	44960 TQ	USBLS	5/07
	Camden PMSA, NJ	Y	29420 FQ	35160 MW	41470 TQ	USBLS	5/07
	Edison PMSA, NJ	Y	28810 FQ	35930 MW	43990 TQ	USBLS	5/07
	Newark-Union PMSA, NJ-PA	Y	30680 FQ	38090 MW	46290 TQ	USBLS	5/07
	New Mexico	Y	21950 FQ	27650 MW	34230 TQ	USBLS	5/07
	Albuquerque MSA, NM	Y	24240 FQ	28960 MW	35720 TQ	USBLS	5/07
	New York	Y	27640 FQ	34530 MW	42330 TQ	USBLS	5/07
	Albany-Schenectady-Troy MSA, NY	Y	27060 FQ	32430 MW	38510 TQ	USBLS	5/07
	Buffalo-Niagara Falls MSA, NY	Y	25190 FQ	29910 MW	36690 TQ	USBLS	5/07
	Ithaca MSA, NY	Y	27150 FQ	32230 MW	37760 TQ	USBLS	5/07
	Nassau-Suffolk PMSA, NY	Y	29760 FQ	36340 MW	44210 TQ	USBLS	5/07
	New York-Northern New Jersey-Long Island MSA, NY-NJ-PA	Y	29880 FQ	37130 MW	45610 TQ	USBLS	5/07
	North Carolina	Y	24700 FQ	29970 MW	36310 TQ	USBLS	5/07
	Charlotte-Gastonia-Concord MSA, NC-SC	Y	26030 FQ	31650 MW	37390 TQ	USBLS	5/07
	Raleigh-Cary MSA, NC	Y	26390 FQ	31690 MW	38680 TQ	USBLS	5/07
	North Dakota	Y	22590 FQ	27050 MW	32090 TQ	USBLS	5/07
	Fargo MSA, ND-MN	Y	24170 FQ	28650 MW	34470 TQ	USBLS	5/07
	Ohio	Y	24980 FQ	30680 MW	37480 TQ	USBLS	5/07
	Cincinnati-Middletown MSA, OH-KY-IN	Y	26500 FQ	32070 MW	38900 TQ	USBLS	5/07
	Cleveland-Elyria-Mentor MSA, OH	Y	25830 FQ	31220 MW	37820 TQ	USBLS	5/07
	Columbus MSA, OH	Y	27170 FQ	32900 MW	39270 TQ	USBLS	5/07
	Dayton MSA, OH	Y	24280 FQ	30390 MW	38630 TQ	USBLS	5/07
	Oklahoma	Y	21290 FQ	26780 MW	32760 TQ	USBLS	5/07
	Oklahoma City MSA, OK	Y	23280 FQ	28590 MW	34990 TQ	USBLS	5/07
	Tulsa MSA, OK	Y	22450 FQ	28020 MW	34710 TQ	USBLS	5/07
	Oregon	H	12.99 FQ	15.57 MW	18.84 TQ	ORBLS	5/08
	Portland-Vancouver-Beaverton MSA, OR-WA	Y	28220 FQ	33990 MW	40390 TQ	USBLS	5/07
	Salem MSA, OR	Y	26720 FQ	31390 MW	37790 TQ	USBLS	5/07
	Pennsylvania	Y	24000 FQ	30240 MW	37620 TQ	USBLS	5/07
	Allentown-Bethlehem-Easton MSA, PA-NJ	Y	24090 FQ	29950 MW	36970 TQ	USBLS	5/07
	Erie MSA, PA	Y	24040 FQ	28270 MW	33640 TQ	USBLS	5/07

AE	Average entry wage	AW	Average wage paid	FQ	First quartile wage	LO	Lowest wage paid	MTC	Median total compensation	TCC	Total cash compensation
AER	Average entry range	AWR	Average wage range	H	Hourly	LR	Low end range	MW	Median wage paid	TQ	Third quartile wage
AEX	Average experienced wage	AXR	Average experienced range	HI	Highest wage paid	M	Monthly	MWR	Median wage range	W	Weekly
ATC	Average total compensation	D	Daily	HR	High end range	MCC	Median cash compensation	S	See annotated source	Y	Yearly

Occupation/Type/Industry	Location	Per	Low	Mid	High	Source	Date
Bookkeeping, Accounting, and Auditing Clerk	Philadelphia-Camden-Wilmington MSA, PA-NJ-DE-MD	Y	28210 FQ	34830 MW	42080 TQ	USBLS	5/07
	Pittsburgh MSA, PA	Y	23010 FQ	28860 MW	35600 TQ	USBLS	5/07
	Rhode Island	Y	29500 FQ	34730 MW	40420 TQ	USBLS	5/07
	Providence-Fall River-Warwick MSA, RI-MA	Y	29330 FQ	34610 MW	40280 TQ	USBLS	5/07
	South Carolina	Y	23080 FQ	28540 MW	34770 TQ	USBLS	5/07
	Charleston-North Charleston MSA, SC	Y	24220 FQ	29680 MW	35790 TQ	USBLS	5/07
	Columbia MSA, SC	Y	24360 FQ	28940 MW	35050 TQ	USBLS	5/07
	South Dakota	Y	21927 FQ	25296 MW	29887 TQ	SDBLS	7/08-9/08
	Sioux Falls MSA, SD	Y	23315 FQ	27021 MW	31519 TQ	SDBLS	7/08-9/08
	Tennessee	Y	23260 FQ	29050 MW	36030 TQ	USBLS	5/07
	Knoxville MSA, TN	Y	22550 FQ	27680 MW	34450 TQ	USBLS	5/07
	Memphis MSA, TN-MS-AR	Y	26000 FQ	31390 MW	38150 TQ	USBLS	5/07
	Nashville-Davidson-Murfreesboro MSA, TN	Y	25340 FQ	30760 MW	37800 TQ	USBLS	5/07
	Texas	Y	23660 FQ	29850 MW	36830 TQ	USBLS	5/07
	Austin-Round Rock MSA, TX	Y	24290 FQ	30870 MW	37450 TQ	USBLS	5/07
	Dallas-Fort Worth-Arlington MSA, TX	Y	26460 FQ	32210 MW	38590 TQ	USBLS	5/07
	El Paso MSA, TX	Y	21600 FQ	27010 MW	32170 TQ	USBLS	5/07
	Houston-Sugar Land-Baytown MSA, TX	Y	26110 FQ	32030 MW	38880 TQ	USBLS	5/07
	San Antonio MSA, TX	Y	22230 FQ	27920 MW	34750 TQ	USBLS	5/07
	Utah	Y	23250 FQ	28280 MW	33560 TQ	USBLS	5/07
	Salt Lake City MSA, UT	Y	24800 FQ	29420 MW	34890 TQ	USBLS	5/07
	Vermont	Y	25990 FQ	31200 MW	37350 TQ	USBLS	5/07
	Burlington-South Burlington MSA, VT	Y	27160 FQ	32860 MW	38310 TQ	USBLS	5/07
	Virginia	Y	26580 FQ	33420 MW	41320 TQ	USBLS	5/07
	Richmond MSA, VA	Y	28190 FQ	34390 MW	41250 TQ	USBLS	5/07
	Virginia Beach-Norfolk-Newport News MSA, VA-NC	Y	25890 FQ	31610 MW	38290 TQ	USBLS	5/07
	Washington	H	13.74 FQ	16.84 MW	20.09 TQ	WABLS	3/08
	Seattle-Tacoma-Bellevue MSA, WA	Y	29960 FQ	36380 MW	43570 TQ	USBLS	5/07
	West Virginia	Y	21257 FQ	26376 MW	33369 TQ	WVBLS	7/08-9/08
	Charleston MSA, WV	Y	22300 FQ	26710 MW	32190 TQ	USBLS	5/07
	Wheeling MSA, WV-OH	Y	20490 FQ	26540 MW	32770 TQ	USBLS	5/07
	Wisconsin	Y	24800 FQ	29970 MW	36480 TQ	USBLS	5/07
	Milwaukee-Waukesha-West Allis MSA, WI	Y	26380 FQ	31640 MW	38330 TQ	USBLS	5/07
	Wyoming	Y	23229 FQ	28671 MW	34918 TQ	WYBLS	9/08
	Cheyenne MSA, WY	Y	22851 FQ	27150 MW	33822 TQ	WYBLS	9/08
	Puerto Rico	Y	15980 FQ	19380 MW	23830 TQ	USBLS	5/07
	San Juan-Caguas-Guaynabo MSA, PR	Y	16430 FQ	19860 MW	24140 TQ	USBLS	5/07
	Virgin Islands	Y	21090 FQ	24560 MW	28840 TQ	USBLS	5/07
	Guam	Y	17970 FQ	23530 MW	30610 TQ	USBLS	5/07
Bookmobile Operator	Ohio	H	15.41 LO		17.03 HI	ODAS	2008
Border Patrol Agent	United States	Y	35000-45000 LR			CRDB02	2009
Bosun							
Cruise Ship	United States	M	1600 LO		1800 HI	CRU02	2008
Botanist	United States	Y		67218 AW		OOH03	2007
Braillist							
Public Schools	North Carolina	M	2055 LO		3403 HI	NCSS	2008-2009
Brand/Product Manager	United States	Y		90100 MW		CNNM02	2007
Apparel Industry	United States	Y		84750 MW		247FASH	2009
Breath Alcohol Testing Inspector							
State Government	Ohio	H	16.35 LO		19.88 HI	ODAS	2008

AE Average entry wage	**AW** Average wage paid	**FQ** First quartile wage	**LO** Lowest wage paid	**MTC** Median total compensation	**TCC** Total cash compensation
AER Average entry range	**AWR** Average wage range	**H** Hourly	**LR** Low end range	**MW** Median wage paid	**TQ** Third quartile wage
AEX Average experienced wage	**AXR** Average experienced range	**HI** Highest wage paid	**M** Monthly	**MWR** Median wage range	**W** Weekly
ATC Average total compensation	**D** Daily	**HR** High end range	**MCC** Median cash compensation	**S** See annotated source	**Y** Yearly

Occupation/Type/Industry	Location	Per	Low	Mid	High	Source	Date
Brewery Manager	United States	Y		42700-111500 AWR		NBREW1	8/08-9/08
Brickmason and Blockmason	Alabama	Y	29480 FQ	38270 MW	44340 TQ	USBLS	5/07
	Birmingham-Hoover MSA, AL	Y	38580 FQ	43340 MW	47460 TQ	USBLS	5/07
	Alaska	Y	53490 FQ	65640 MW	73420 TQ	USBLS	5/07
	Anchorage MSA, AK	Y	54560 FQ	68270 MW	74480 TQ	USBLS	5/07
	Arizona	Y	26380 FQ	35760 MW	46220 TQ	USBLS	5/07
	Flagstaff MSA, AZ	Y	21720 FQ	25010 MW	31000 TQ	USBLS	5/07
	Phoenix-Mesa-Scottsdale MSA, AZ	Y	27170 FQ	37330 MW	46550 TQ	USBLS	5/07
	Tucson MSA, AZ	Y	28640 FQ	39030 MW	61510 TQ	USBLS	5/07
	Arkansas	Y	27480 FQ	37210 MW	44150 TQ	USBLS	5/07
	Little Rock-North Little Rock MSA, AR	Y	29860 FQ	40530 MW	45360 TQ	USBLS	5/07
	California	H	15.16 FQ	21.40 MW	29.05 TQ	CABLS	1/08-3/08
	Los Angeles-Long Beach-Glendale PMSA, CA	H	14.50 FQ	20.14 MW	30.17 TQ	CABLS	1/08-3/08
	Oakland-Fremont-Hayward MSA, CA	H	23.49 FQ	29.12 MW	35.15 TQ	CABLS	1/08-3/08
	Riverside-San Bernardino-Ontario MSA, CA	H	14.28 FQ	18.31 MW	25.75 TQ	CABLS	1/08-3/08
	Sacramento-Arden Arcade-Roseville MSA, CA	H	18.78 FQ	27.67 MW	35.99 TQ	CABLS	1/08-3/08
	San Diego-Carlsbad-San Marcos MSA, CA	H	21.85 FQ	27.65 MW	33.90 TQ	CABLS	1/08-3/08
	San Francisco-San Mateo-Redwood PMSA, CA	H	23.83 FQ	32.34 MW	39.07 TQ	CABLS	1/08-3/08
	San Jose-Sunnyvale-Santa Clara MSA, CA	H	21.86 FQ	25.13 MW	29.09 TQ	CABLS	1/08-3/08
	Santa Ana-Anaheim-Irvine PMSA, CA	Y	21040 FQ	29790 MW	40740 TQ	USBLS	5/07
	Colorado	Y	30310 FQ	42610 MW	48660 TQ	USBLS	5/07
	Denver-Aurora MSA, CO	Y	29060 FQ	39930 MW	47810 TQ	USBLS	5/07
	Connecticut	H	17.76 AE	24.67 MW		CTBLS	1/08-3/08
	Bridgeport-Stamford-Norwalk MSA, CT	Y	48230 FQ	54630 MW	62410 TQ	USBLS	5/07
	Danbury MSA, CT	Y	31250 FQ	42360 MW	61780 TQ	USBLS	5/07
	Hartford-West Hartford-East Hartford MSA, CT	Y	44830 FQ	50790 MW	60500 TQ	USBLS	5/07
	Delaware	Y	34460 FQ	48690 MW	58070 TQ	USBLS	5/07
	Wilmington PMSA, DE-MD-NJ	Y	42030 FQ	50880 MW	58500 TQ	USBLS	5/07
	District of Columbia	Y	51170 FQ	55180 MW	59270 TQ	USBLS	5/07
	Washington-Arlington-Alexandria MSA, DC-VA-MD-WV	Y	40010 FQ	48780 MW	55570 TQ	USBLS	5/07
	Florida	Y	28240 FQ	37210 MW	45060 TQ	USBLS	5/07
	Fort Lauderdale-Pompano Beach-Deerfield Beach PMSA, FL	Y	39610 FQ	44520 MW	48570 TQ	USBLS	5/07
	Jacksonville MSA, FL	Y	29240 FQ	40610 MW	47950 TQ	USBLS	5/07
	Lakeland MSA, FL	Y	33260 FQ	38760 MW	44550 TQ	USBLS	5/07
	Miami-Fort Lauderdale-Miami Beach MSA, FL	Y	30520 FQ	41230 MW	46970 TQ	USBLS	5/07
	Orlando-Kissimmee MSA, FL	Y	32400 FQ	42150 MW	48070 TQ	USBLS	5/07
	Tampa-St. Petersburg-Clearwater MSA, FL	Y	28240 FQ	32660 MW	39980 TQ	USBLS	5/07
	West Palm Beach-Boca Raton-Boynton Beach PMSA, FL	Y	32570 FQ	39980 MW	45590 TQ	USBLS	5/07
	Georgia	Y	31310 FQ	37080 MW	41590 TQ	USBLS	5/07
	Atlanta-Sandy Springs-Marietta MSA, GA	Y	35470 FQ	39750 MW	44380 TQ	USBLS	5/07
	Hawaii	Y	52850 FQ	58970 MW	64850 TQ	USBLS	5/07
	Honolulu MSA, HI	Y	54170 FQ	61740 MW	66860 TQ	USBLS	5/07
	Idaho	Y	31430 FQ	40180 MW	50380 TQ	USBLS	5/07
	Boise City-Nampa MSA, ID	Y	30980 FQ	40100 MW	51060 TQ	USBLS	5/07
	Illinois	Y	47680 FQ	65650 MW	73860 TQ	USBLS	5/07
	Champaign-Urbana MSA, IL	Y	42760 FQ	47870 MW	51860 TQ	USBLS	5/07
	Chicago-Naperville-Joliet MSA, IL-IN-WI	Y	48030 FQ	68070 MW	74970 TQ	USBLS	5/07
	Indiana	Y	34300 FQ	46740 MW	57690 TQ	USBLS	5/07

AE	Average entry wage	AW	Average wage paid	FQ	First quartile wage	LO	Lowest wage paid	MTC	Median total compensation
AER	Average entry range	AWR	Average wage range	H	Hourly	LR	Low end range	MW	Median wage paid
AEX	Average experienced wage	AXR	Average experienced range	HI	Highest wage paid	M	Monthly	MWR	Median wage range
ATC	Average total compensation	D	Daily	HR	High end range	MCC	Median cash compensation	S	See annotated source

TCC	Total cash compensation
TQ	Third quartile wage
W	Weekly
Y	Yearly

Occupation/Type/Industry	Location	Per	Low	Mid	High	Source	Date
Brickmason and Blockmason	Gary PMSA, IN	Y	35610 FQ	41170 MW	65610 TQ	USBLS	5/07
	Indianapolis-Carmel MSA, IN	Y	42250 FQ	51820 MW	58900 TQ	USBLS	5/07
	Iowa	Y	33210 FQ	41170 MW	52140 TQ	USBLS	5/07
	Des Moines-West Des Moines MSA, IA	Y	44980 FQ	54640 MW	60210 TQ	USBLS	5/07
	Dubuque MSA, IA	Y	37800 FQ	51000 MW	65420 TQ	USBLS	5/07
	Kansas	Y	31430 FQ	40630 MW	48880 TQ	USBLS	5/07
	Wichita MSA, KS	Y	38190 FQ	42840 MW	47730 TQ	USBLS	5/07
	Kentucky	Y	32290 FQ	39838 MW	47121 TQ	KYBLS	2008
	Louisville-Jefferson County MSA, KY-IN	Y	30030 FQ	36160 MW	43320 TQ	USBLS	5/07
	Owensboro MSA, KY	Y	33980 FQ	40150 MW	48550 TQ	USBLS	5/07
	Louisiana	H	16.43 FQ	18.95 MW	21.56 TQ	LABLS	1/08-3/08
	Baton Rouge MSA, LA	Y	33300 FQ	38740 MW	45110 TQ	USBLS	5/07
	New Orleans-Metairie-Kenner MSA, LA	Y	33660 FQ	37750 MW	44490 TQ	USBLS	5/07
	Maine	Y	31090 FQ	38960 MW	47750 TQ	USBLS	5/07
	Portland-South Portland-Biddeford MSA, ME	Y	25730 FQ	31840 MW	50370 TQ	USBLS	5/07
	Maryland	Y		48625 MW		MDBLS	3/08
	Baltimore-Towson MSA, MD	Y	34780 FQ	41950 MW	57890 TQ	USBLS	5/07
	Bethesda-Gaithersburg-Frederick PMSA, MD	Y	39710 FQ	47590 MW	55030 TQ	USBLS	5/07
	Massachusetts	Y	61310 FQ	76850 MW	86180 TQ	USBLS	5/07
	Boston-Cambridge-Quincy NECTA, MA	Y	68810 FQ	78940 MW	86580 TQ	USBLS	5/07
	Worcester MSA, MA-CT	Y	56810 FQ	71900 MW	82390 TQ	USBLS	5/07
	Michigan	Y	40730 FQ	50230 MW	61740 TQ	USBLS	5/07
	Detroit-Warren-Livonia MSA, MI	Y	42480 FQ	55000 MW	66490 TQ	USBLS	5/07
	Grand Rapids-Wyoming MSA, MI	Y	31690 FQ	43870 MW	48040 TQ	USBLS	5/07
	Lansing-East Lansing MSA, MI	Y	39880 FQ	50580 MW	59610 TQ	USBLS	5/07
	Warren-Troy-Farmington Hills PMSA, MI	Y	42710 FQ	58380 MW	67940 TQ	USBLS	5/07
	Minnesota	Y	45527 FQ	59986 MW	74645 TQ	MNBLS	10/08-12/08
	Duluth-Superior MSA, MN-WI	Y	56361 FQ	61008 MW	66467 TQ	MNBLS	10/08-12/08
	Minneapolis-Saint Paul MSA, MN-WI	Y	49205 FQ	63569 MW	76743 TQ	MNBLS	10/08-12/08
	Rochester MSA, MN	Y	42068 FQ	66936 MW	74083 TQ	MNBLS	10/08-12/08
	Mississippi	Y	25960 FQ	32660 MW	46000 TQ	USBLS	5/07
	Jackson MSA, MS	Y	26760 FQ	30590 MW	40970 TQ	USBLS	5/07
	Missouri	Y	45260 FQ	57200 MW	65190 TQ	USBLS	5/07
	Kansas City MSA, MO-KS	Y	50260 FQ	60540 MW	69360 TQ	USBLS	5/07
	St. Louis MSA, MO-IL	Y	50660 FQ	57700 MW	63980 TQ	USBLS	5/07
	Montana	Y	32290 FQ	42150 MW	50790 TQ	USBLS	5/07
	Billings MSA, MT	Y	29790 FQ	38350 MW	57310 TQ	USBLS	5/07
	Nebraska	Y	31690 FQ	43020 MW	52300 TQ	USBLS	5/07
	Omaha-Council Bluffs MSA, NE-IA	Y	36220 FQ	44500 MW	51790 TQ	USBLS	5/07
	Nevada	H	16.27 FQ	20.82 MW	25.31 TQ	NVBLS	5/08
	Las Vegas-Paradise MSA, NV	H	15.79 FQ	20.51 MW	24.73 TQ	NVBLS	5/08
	New Hampshire	H	15.37 AE	21.27 MW	24.53 AEX	NHBLS	6/08
	Manchester MSA, NH	Y	32040 FQ	36080 MW	41230 TQ	USBLS	5/07
	Nashua NECTA, NH-MA	Y	38890 FQ	51040 MW	55700 TQ	USBLS	5/07
	New Jersey	Y	39930 FQ	63520 MW	73930 TQ	USBLS	5/07
	Camden PMSA, NJ	Y	45050 FQ	66090 MW	74630 TQ	USBLS	5/07
	Edison PMSA, NJ	Y	41550 FQ	59020 MW	71450 TQ	USBLS	5/07
	Newark-Union PMSA, NJ-PA	Y	36490 FQ	66490 MW	75590 TQ	USBLS	5/07
	New Mexico	Y	28360 FQ	35870 MW	45650 TQ	USBLS	5/07
	Albuquerque MSA, NM	Y	27580 FQ	34980 MW	45020 TQ	USBLS	5/07
	New York	Y	38550 FQ	52560 MW	72870 TQ	USBLS	5/07
	Albany-Schenectady-Troy MSA, NY	Y	53190 FQ	58610 MW	63530 TQ	USBLS	5/07
	Buffalo-Niagara Falls MSA, NY	Y	42050 FQ	51630 MW	61290 TQ	USBLS	5/07
	Nassau-Suffolk PMSA, NY	Y	35540 FQ	48800 MW	84360 TQ	USBLS	5/07
	New York-Northern New Jersey-Long Island MSA, NY-NJ-PA	Y	37370 FQ	58450 MW	77560 TQ	USBLS	5/07
	North Carolina	Y	27830 FQ	35100 MW	41940 TQ	USBLS	5/07
	Asheville MSA, NC	Y	28870 FQ	41230 MW	46600 TQ	USBLS	5/07

AE	Average entry wage	AW	Average wage paid	FQ	First quartile wage	LO	Lowest wage paid	MTC	Median total compensation	TCC	Total cash compensation
AER	Average entry range	AWR	Average wage range	H	Hourly	LR	Low end range	MW	Median wage paid	TQ	Third quartile wage
AEX	Average experienced wage	AXR	Average experienced range	HI	Highest wage paid	M	Monthly	MWR	Median wage range	W	Weekly
ATC	Average total compensation	D	Daily	HR	High end range	MCC	Median cash compensation	S	See annotated source	Y	Yearly

Occupation/Type/Industry	Location	Per	Low	Mid	High	Source	Date
Brickmason and Blockmason	Charlotte-Gastonia-Concord MSA, NC-SC	Y	29360 FQ	39410 MW	47070 TQ	USBLS	5/07
	Greensboro-High Point MSA, NC	Y	31240 FQ	35610 MW	40160 TQ	USBLS	5/07
	Raleigh-Cary MSA, NC	Y	30940 FQ	36810 MW	40850 TQ	USBLS	5/07
	North Dakota	Y	38220 FQ	46060 MW	54790 TQ	USBLS	5/07
	Fargo MSA, ND-MN	Y	38180 FQ	50080 MW	58680 TQ	USBLS	5/07
	Ohio	Y	36360 FQ	49930 MW	57380 TQ	USBLS	5/07
	Cincinnati-Middletown MSA, OH-KY-IN	Y	43040 FQ	51460 MW	57980 TQ	USBLS	5/07
	Cleveland-Elyria-Mentor MSA, OH	Y	30120 FQ	52110 MW	59000 TQ	USBLS	5/07
	Columbus MSA, OH	Y	27820 FQ	39270 MW	51140 TQ	USBLS	5/07
	Dayton MSA, OH	Y	44940 FQ	51930 MW	58490 TQ	USBLS	5/07
	Oklahoma	Y	31490 FQ	40750 MW	46890 TQ	USBLS	5/07
	Oklahoma City MSA, OK	Y	36510 FQ	43090 MW	53370 TQ	USBLS	5/07
	Tulsa MSA, OK	Y	35170 FQ	42430 MW	47400 TQ	USBLS	5/07
	Oregon	H	19.41 FQ	25.44 MW	30.25 TQ	ORBLS	5/08
	Portland-Vancouver-Beaverton MSA, OR-WA	Y	42040 FQ	54550 MW	62230 TQ	USBLS	5/07
	Pennsylvania	Y	36820 FQ	45740 MW	56930 TQ	USBLS	5/07
	Allentown-Bethlehem-Easton MSA, PA-NJ	Y	26850 FQ	30180 MW	43690 TQ	USBLS	5/07
	Erie MSA, PA	Y	39640 FQ	50630 MW	56300 TQ	USBLS	5/07
	Philadelphia-Camden-Wilmington MSA, PA-NJ-DE-MD	Y	42490 FQ	51700 MW	65230 TQ	USBLS	5/07
	Pittsburgh MSA, PA	Y	36120 FQ	42510 MW	56440 TQ	USBLS	5/07
	York-Hanover MSA, PA	Y	43940 FQ	53150 MW	60020 TQ	USBLS	5/07
	Rhode Island	Y	37290 FQ	46670 MW	65560 TQ	USBLS	5/07
	Providence-Fall River-Warwick MSA, RI-MA	Y	38480 FQ	49470 MW	69940 TQ	USBLS	5/07
	South Carolina	Y	26010 FQ	33940 MW	39670 TQ	USBLS	5/07
	Charleston-North Charleston MSA, SC	Y	22420 FQ	33040 MW	41380 TQ	USBLS	5/07
	Columbia MSA, SC	Y	23070 FQ	29670 MW	36160 TQ	USBLS	5/07
	Florence MSA, SC	Y	26880 FQ	29600 MW	33410 TQ	USBLS	5/07
	South Dakota	Y	32469 FQ	41220 MW	52192 TQ	SDBLS	7/08-9/08
	Sioux Falls MSA, SD	Y	30650 FQ	33852 MW	40162 TQ	SDBLS	7/08-9/08
	Tennessee	Y	32810 FQ	42650 MW	48300 TQ	USBLS	5/07
	Knoxville MSA, TN	Y	28170 FQ	36040 MW	44230 TQ	USBLS	5/07
	Memphis MSA, TN-MS-AR	Y	34570 FQ	42400 MW	46730 TQ	USBLS	5/07
	Nashville-Davidson-Murfreesboro MSA, TN	Y	35950 FQ	45620 MW	52540 TQ	USBLS	5/07
	Texas	Y	30840 FQ	38020 MW	43670 TQ	USBLS	5/07
	Austin-Round Rock MSA, TX	Y	31010 FQ	39440 MW	44960 TQ	USBLS	5/07
	Dallas-Fort Worth-Arlington MSA, TX	Y	31940 FQ	39430 MW	45940 TQ	USBLS	5/07
	El Paso MSA, TX	Y	25710 FQ	34520 MW	39130 TQ	USBLS	5/07
	Houston-Sugar Land-Baytown MSA, TX	Y	32260 FQ	37140 MW	41330 TQ	USBLS	5/07
	San Antonio MSA, TX	Y	30440 FQ	36690 MW	40800 TQ	USBLS	5/07
	Utah	Y	33050 FQ	41820 MW	48660 TQ	USBLS	5/07
	Ogden-Clearfield MSA, UT	Y	41500 FQ	47760 MW	53450 TQ	USBLS	5/07
	Salt Lake City MSA, UT	Y	34800 FQ	40660 MW	46610 TQ	USBLS	5/07
	Vermont	Y	28680 FQ	45340 MW	53130 TQ	USBLS	5/07
	Virginia	Y	36410 FQ	43310 MW	49790 TQ	USBLS	5/07
	Richmond MSA, VA	Y	38000 FQ	42830 MW	47430 TQ	USBLS	5/07
	Roanoke MSA, VA	Y	40330 FQ	44040 MW	47680 TQ	USBLS	5/07
	Virginia Beach-Norfolk-Newport News MSA, VA-NC	Y	36240 FQ	43190 MW	49820 TQ	USBLS	5/07
	Washington	H	25.75 FQ	28.70 MW	31.83 TQ	WABLS	3/08
	Seattle-Tacoma-Bellevue MSA, WA	Y	55890 FQ	61390 MW	68020 TQ	USBLS	5/07
	West Virginia	Y	30669 FQ	47427 MW	57573 TQ	WVBLS	7/08-9/08
	Charleston MSA, WV	Y	39520 FQ	47540 MW	52670 TQ	USBLS	5/07
	Wheeling MSA, WV-OH	Y	32630 FQ	43240 MW	50960 TQ	USBLS	5/07
	Wisconsin	Y	44250 FQ	54130 MW	63820 TQ	USBLS	5/07
	Green Bay MSA, WI	Y	36820 FQ	51870 MW	57550 TQ	USBLS	5/07
	Milwaukee-Waukesha-West Allis MSA, WI	Y	51240 FQ	60150 MW	69120 TQ	USBLS	5/07
	Wyoming	Y	30973 FQ	42127 MW	50561 TQ	WYBLS	9/08

AE Average entry wage	**AW** Average wage paid	**FQ** First quartile wage	**LO** Lowest wage paid	**MTC** Median total compensation	**TCC** Total cash compensation
AER Average entry range	**AWR** Average wage range	**H** Hourly	**LR** Low end range	**MW** Median wage paid	**TQ** Third quartile wage
AEX Average experienced wage	**AXR** Average experienced range	**HI** Highest wage paid	**M** Monthly	**MWR** Median wage range	**W** Weekly
ATC Average total compensation	**D** Daily	**HR** High end range	**MCC** Median cash compensation	**S** See annotated source	**Y** Yearly

Occupation/Type/Industry	Location	Per	Low	Mid	High	Source	Date
Brickmason and Blockmason	Puerto Rico	Y	16800 FQ	18840 MW	28170 TQ	USBLS	5/07
	San Juan-Caguas-Guaynabo MSA, PR	Y	17130 FQ	19050 MW	28770 TQ	USBLS	5/07
	Virgin Islands	Y	30040 FQ	33900 MW	38210 TQ	USBLS	5/07
Bridge and Lock Tender	Alabama	Y	43600 FQ	48350 MW	54940 TQ	USBLS	5/07
	California	H	17.58 FQ	19.97 MW	24.23 TQ	CABLS	1/08-3/08
	Florida	Y	21790 FQ	27970 MW	41610 TQ	USBLS	5/07
	Indiana	Y	41120 FQ	46900 MW	53790 TQ	USBLS	5/07
	Kentucky	Y	43654 FQ	47688 MW	51646 TQ	KYBLS	2008
	Louisiana	H	10.97 FQ	14.46 MW	18.81 TQ	LABLS	1/08-3/08
	Massachusetts	Y	31250 FQ	35350 MW	39110 TQ	USBLS	5/07
	Michigan	Y	30860 FQ	40230 MW	48960 TQ	USBLS	5/07
	Minnesota	Y	44662 FQ	53504 MW	60329 TQ	MNBLS	10/08-12/08
	Mississippi	Y	20810 FQ	37680 MW	50110 TQ	USBLS	5/07
	Missouri	Y	43960 FQ	50620 MW	57540 TQ	USBLS	5/07
	New Jersey	Y	31100 FQ	40340 MW	46740 TQ	USBLS	5/07
	Ohio	Y	38310 FQ	43100 MW	47220 TQ	USBLS	5/07
	Oregon	H	9.05 FQ	16.52 MW	19.69 TQ	ORBLS	5/08
	Pennsylvania	Y	34740 FQ	43610 MW	49030 TQ	USBLS	5/07
	Tennessee	Y	42770 FQ	45500 MW	48230 TQ	USBLS	5/07
	Texas	Y	30220 FQ	43980 MW	54130 TQ	USBLS	5/07
	West Virginia	Y	43576 FQ	46673 MW	49771 TQ	WVBLS	7/08-9/08
	Wisconsin	Y	37670 FQ	43770 MW	50680 TQ	USBLS	5/07
Bridge Construction Superintendent							
Department of Transportation	New Hampshire	Y		56680 AW		NHUL03	2008
Bridge Inspector	United States	Y		48471 AW		AFT01	2008
Department of Transportation	New Hampshire	Y		45801 AW		NHUL03	2008
Bridge Operator							
Department of Transportation	Michigan	H	14.41 LO		22.64 HI	MDOT	10/1/07
Bridge Safety Officer							
Department of Transportation	Michigan	H	14.17 LO		20.47 HI	MDOT	10/1/07
Broadcast News Analyst	Alabama	Y	35250 FQ	51750 MW	76010 TQ	USBLS	5/07
	Arizona	Y	27100 FQ	50240 MW	80460 TQ	USBLS	5/07
	Arkansas	Y	23530 FQ	38500 MW	57200 TQ	USBLS	5/07
	California	H	18.24 FQ	30.57 MW	46.69 TQ	CABLS	1/08-3/08
	Colorado	Y	40560 FQ	67460 MW		USBLS	5/07
	District of Columbia	Y	34050 FQ	58910 MW	89430 TQ	USBLS	5/07
	Florida	Y	45070 FQ	80330 MW	142380 TQ	USBLS	5/07
	Georgia	Y	32620 FQ	54210 MW	89650 TQ	USBLS	5/07
	Idaho	Y	25720 FQ	32010 MW	39760 TQ	USBLS	5/07
	Illinois	Y	31730 FQ	52400 MW	96000 TQ	USBLS	5/07
	Indiana	Y	34070 FQ	61900 MW	101430 TQ	USBLS	5/07
	Iowa	Y	27720 FQ	37710 MW	51840 TQ	USBLS	5/07
	Kansas	Y	22310 FQ	29120 MW	43780 TQ	USBLS	5/07
	Kentucky	Y	18844 FQ	25181 MW	50967 TQ	KYBLS	2008
	Louisiana	H	15.11 FQ	24.01 MW	46.30 TQ	LABLS	1/08-3/08
	Maryland	Y		63125 MW		MDBLS	3/08
	Massachusetts	Y	36580 FQ	69860 MW		USBLS	5/07
	Michigan	Y	28670 FQ	47340 MW	119050 TQ	USBLS	5/07
	Minnesota	Y	35529 FQ	52907 MW	133268 TQ	MNBLS	10/08-12/08
	Mississippi	Y	24390 FQ	38490 MW	62270 TQ	USBLS	5/07
	Missouri	Y	42060 FQ	69300 MW	108710 TQ	USBLS	5/07
	Montana	Y	15360 FQ	21100 MW	31770 TQ	USBLS	5/07
	Nebraska	Y	23990 FQ	30320 MW	42680 TQ	USBLS	5/07
	Nevada	H	18.81 FQ	31.16 MW	54.09 TQ	NVBLS	5/08
	New Jersey	Y	29380 FQ	47320 MW	93930 TQ	USBLS	5/07
	New Mexico	Y	38360 FQ	61120 MW	108900 TQ	USBLS	5/07
	New York	Y	29660 FQ	46430 MW	96010 TQ	USBLS	5/07
	North Carolina	Y	34280 FQ	55100 MW	95360 TQ	USBLS	5/07
	Ohio	Y	34610 FQ	62180 MW	98680 TQ	USBLS	5/07
	Oklahoma	Y	27060 FQ	41170 MW	92120 TQ	USBLS	5/07
	Oregon	H	15.96 FQ	23.09 MW	36.24 TQ	ORBLS	5/08
	South Carolina	Y	32030 FQ	35910 MW	48820 TQ	USBLS	5/07
	South Dakota	Y	30198 FQ	36236 MW	50181 TQ	SDBLS	7/08-9/08
	Tennessee	Y	40730 FQ	62230 MW	102020 TQ	USBLS	5/07

AE	Average entry wage	AW	Average wage paid	FQ	First quartile wage	LO	Lowest wage paid	MTC	Median total compensation	TCC	Total cash compensation
AER	Average entry range	AWR	Average wage range	H	Hourly	LR	Low end range	MW	Median wage paid	TQ	Third quartile wage
AEX	Average experienced wage	AXR	Average experienced range	HI	Highest wage paid	M	Monthly	MWR	Median wage range	W	Weekly
ATC	Average total compensation	D	Daily	HR	High end range	MCC	Median cash compensation	S	See annotated source	Y	Yearly

Occupation/Type/Industry	Location	Per	Low	Mid	High	Source	Date
Broadcast News Analyst	Texas	Y	29730 FQ	44070 MW	81850 TQ	USBLS	5/07
	Utah	Y	30270 FQ	47430 MW	79270 TQ	USBLS	5/07
	Virginia	Y	34800 FQ	55480 MW	91960 TQ	USBLS	5/07
	Washington	H	16.46 FQ	28.66 MW	62.90 TQ	WABLS	3/08
	West Virginia	Y	16129 FQ	21938 MW	29413 TQ	WVBLS	7/08-9/08
	Wisconsin	Y	30570 FQ	40770 MW	61830 TQ	USBLS	5/07
	Wyoming	Y	16569 FQ	24114 MW	29738 TQ	WYBLS	9/08
	Puerto Rico	Y	26490 FQ	37050 MW	64790 TQ	USBLS	
Broadcast Technician	Alabama	Y	19400 FQ	25090 MW	41810 TQ	USBLS	5/07
	Birmingham-Hoover MSA, AL	Y	18800 FQ	25360 MW	43050 TQ	USBLS	5/07
	Arizona	Y	26040 FQ	33270 MW	44450 TQ	USBLS	5/07
	Phoenix-Mesa-Scottsdale MSA, AZ	Y	27130 FQ	35140 MW	49560 TQ	USBLS	5/07
	Tucson MSA, AZ	Y	28960 FQ	34720 MW	40200 TQ	USBLS	5/07
	Arkansas	Y	20290 FQ	22640 MW	25280 TQ	USBLS	5/07
	Little Rock-North Little Rock MSA, AR	Y	20750 FQ	22870 MW	25400 TQ	USBLS	5/07
	California	H	10.98 FQ	15.46 MW	24.31 TQ	CABLS	1/08-3/08
	Los Angeles-Long Beach-Glendale PMSA, CA	H	11.46 FQ	15.97 MW	23.69 TQ	CABLS	1/08-3/08
	Oakland-Fremont-Hayward MSA, CA	H	17.05 FQ	33.50 MW	37.82 TQ	CABLS	1/08-3/08
	Riverside-San Bernardino-Ontario MSA, CA	H	10.48 FQ	12.20 MW	21.38 TQ	CABLS	1/08-3/08
	Sacramento-Arden Arcade-Roseville MSA, CA	H	11.36 FQ	16.10 MW	24.58 TQ	CABLS	1/08-3/08
	San Diego-Carlsbad-San Marcos MSA, CA	H	10.74 FQ	14.55 MW	26.14 TQ	CABLS	1/08-3/08
	San Francisco-San Mateo-Redwood PMSA, CA	H	10.76 FQ	18.65 MW	37.15 TQ	CABLS	1/08-3/08
	San Jose-Sunnyvale-Santa Clara MSA, CA	H	9.07 FQ	16.12 MW	30.62 TQ	CABLS	1/08-3/08
	Santa Ana-Anaheim-Irvine PMSA, CA	Y	23150 FQ	37550 MW	62880 TQ	USBLS	5/07
	Colorado	Y	25980 FQ	41670 MW	60660 TQ	USBLS	5/07
	Denver-Aurora MSA, CO	Y	33270 FQ	50640 MW	64540 TQ	USBLS	5/07
	Connecticut	H	10.81 AE	19.91 MW		CTBLS	1/08-3/08
	Hartford-West Hartford-East Hartford MSA, CT	Y	26690 FQ	40960 MW	54860 TQ	USBLS	5/07
	Delaware	Y	26890 FQ	35630 MW	71800 TQ	USBLS	5/07
	District of Columbia	Y	32750 FQ	55920 MW	74190 TQ	USBLS	5/07
	Washington-Arlington-Alexandria MSA, DC-VA-MD-WV	Y	28970 FQ	44300 MW	71210 TQ	USBLS	5/07
	Florida	Y	28270 FQ	37900 MW	50490 TQ	USBLS	5/07
	Fort Lauderdale-Pompano Beach-Deerfield Beach PMSA, FL	Y	36270 FQ	49460 MW	59600 TQ	USBLS	5/07
	Jacksonville MSA, FL	Y	29020 FQ	37430 MW	49330 TQ	USBLS	5/07
	Miami-Fort Lauderdale-Miami Beach MSA, FL	Y	30250 FQ	40990 MW	55050 TQ	USBLS	5/07
	Orlando-Kissimmee MSA, FL	Y	30450 FQ	40440 MW	52700 TQ	USBLS	5/07
	Tampa-St. Petersburg-Clearwater MSA, FL	Y	28210 FQ	38350 MW	54620 TQ	USBLS	5/07
	West Palm Beach-Boca Raton-Boynton Beach PMSA, FL	Y	24940 FQ	34370 MW	44710 TQ	USBLS	5/07
	Georgia	Y	25950 FQ	33640 MW	42420 TQ	USBLS	5/07
	Atlanta-Sandy Springs-Marietta MSA, GA	Y	28470 FQ	35070 MW	43040 TQ	USBLS	5/07
	Hawaii	Y	17520 FQ	22720 MW	35700 TQ	USBLS	5/07
	Honolulu MSA, HI	Y	17390 FQ	22380 MW	38140 TQ	USBLS	5/07
	Idaho	Y	16480 FQ	20890 MW	31180 TQ	USBLS	5/07
	Boise City-Nampa MSA, ID	Y	19730 FQ	24220 MW	40490 TQ	USBLS	5/07
	Illinois	Y	25260 FQ	39500 MW	53680 TQ	USBLS	5/07
	Chicago-Naperville-Joliet MSA, IL-IN-WI	Y	25840 FQ	42030 MW	55310 TQ	USBLS	5/07
	Indiana	Y	20900 FQ	28750 MW	38860 TQ	USBLS	5/07
	Indianapolis-Carmel MSA, IN	Y	27670 FQ	35420 MW	46920 TQ	USBLS	5/07
	Iowa	Y	21720 FQ	28480 MW	38580 TQ	USBLS	5/07
	Des Moines-West Des Moines MSA, IA	Y	19980 FQ	28240 MW	40140 TQ	USBLS	5/07

AE	Average entry wage	AW	Average wage paid	FQ	First quartile wage
AER	Average entry range	AWR	Average wage range	H	Hourly
AEX	Average experienced wage	AXR	Average experienced range	HI	Highest wage paid
ATC	Average total compensation	D	Daily	HR	High end range

LO	Lowest wage paid	MTC	Median total compensation	TCC	Total cash compensation
LR	Low end range	MW	Median wage paid	TQ	Third quartile wage
M	Monthly	MWR	Median wage range	W	Weekly
MCC	Median cash compensation	S	See annotated source	Y	Yearly

Occupation/Type/Industry	Location	Per	Low	Mid	High	Source	Date
Broadcast Technician	Waterloo-Cedar Falls MSA, IA	Y	26080 FQ	34590 MW	39360 TQ	USBLS	5/07
	Kansas	Y	23270 FQ	30800 MW	38000 TQ	USBLS	5/07
	Topeka MSA, KS	Y	22370 FQ	26330 MW	31640 TQ	USBLS	5/07
	Wichita MSA, KS	Y	22730 FQ	30090 MW	39210 TQ	USBLS	5/07
	Kentucky	Y	21425 FQ	29772 MW	45759 TQ	KYBLS	2008
	Louisville-Jefferson County MSA, KY-IN	Y	21240 FQ	26420 MW	46700 TQ	USBLS	5/07
	Louisiana	H	9.52 FQ	12.73 MW	17.63 TQ	LABLS	1/08-3/08
	Baton Rouge MSA, LA	Y	21770 FQ	29540 MW	38670 TQ	USBLS	5/07
	Maine	Y	18790 FQ	25030 MW	32440 TQ	USBLS	5/07
	Bangor MSA, ME	Y	24020 FQ	27620 MW	34120 TQ	USBLS	5/07
	Portland-South Portland-Biddeford MSA, ME	Y	17140 FQ	21290 MW	29340 TQ	USBLS	5/07
	Maryland	Y		33800 MW		MDBLS	3/08
	Baltimore-Towson MSA, MD	Y	28170 FQ	41590 MW	56010 TQ	USBLS	5/07
	Massachusetts	Y	22500 FQ	27490 MW	48840 TQ	USBLS	5/07
	Boston-Cambridge-Quincy NECTA, MA	Y	22280 FQ	25530 MW	39480 TQ	USBLS	5/07
	Springfield MSA, MA-CT	Y	17310 FQ	26770 MW	60690 TQ	USBLS	5/07
	Worcester MSA, MA-CT	Y	37500 FQ	47950 MW	66990 TQ	USBLS	5/07
	Michigan	Y	26650 FQ	34460 MW	50520 TQ	USBLS	5/07
	Detroit-Warren-Livonia MSA, MI	Y	30450 FQ	41120 MW	68550 TQ	USBLS	5/07
	Grand Rapids-Wyoming MSA, MI	Y	25590 FQ	31280 MW	46060 TQ	USBLS	5/07
	Warren-Troy-Farmington Hills PMSA, MI	Y	28570 FQ	36840 MW	57870 TQ	USBLS	5/07
	Minnesota	Y	29315 FQ	37758 MW	48900 TQ	MNBLS	10/08-12/08
	Duluth-Superior MSA, MN-WI	Y	27923 FQ	36021 MW	40970 TQ	MNBLS	10/08-12/08
	Minneapolis-Saint Paul MSA, MN-WI	Y	29723 FQ	38501 MW	51578 TQ	MNBLS	10/08-12/08
	Rochester MSA, MN	Y	34261 FQ	42600 MW	49103 TQ	MNBLS	10/08-12/08
	Mississippi	Y	19530 FQ	25780 MW	32910 TQ	USBLS	5/07
	Jackson MSA, MS	Y	22760 FQ	26440 MW	30650 TQ	USBLS	5/07
	Missouri	Y	23560 FQ	28690 MW	39150 TQ	USBLS	5/07
	Kansas City MSA, MO-KS	Y	27770 FQ	36190 MW	51060 TQ	USBLS	5/07
	St. Louis MSA, MO-IL	Y	25020 FQ	28400 MW	33550 TQ	USBLS	5/07
	Montana	Y	14610 FQ	16960 MW	22800 TQ	USBLS	5/07
	Nebraska	Y	17640 FQ	24940 MW	41730 TQ	USBLS	5/07
	Omaha-Council Bluffs MSA, NE-IA	Y	22150 FQ	35210 MW	45570 TQ	USBLS	5/07
	Nevada	H	11.55 FQ	14.30 MW	22.68 TQ	NVBLS	5/08
	Las Vegas-Paradise MSA, NV	H	13.09 FQ	16.45 MW	28.99 TQ	NVBLS	5/08
	Reno-Sparks MSA, NV	H	8.17 FQ	10.49 MW	14.34 TQ	NVBLS	5/08
	New Hampshire	H	10.10 AE	13.71 MW	18.95 AEX	NHBLS	6/08
	New Jersey	Y	41120 FQ	58740 MW	81730 TQ	USBLS	5/07
	New Mexico	Y	18090 FQ	24880 MW	30940 TQ	USBLS	5/07
	Albuquerque MSA, NM	Y	18610 FQ	24640 MW	32430 TQ	USBLS	5/07
	New York	Y	38430 FQ	48750 MW	65540 TQ	USBLS	5/07
	Albany-Schenectady-Troy MSA, NY	Y	25140 FQ	40850 MW	66750 TQ	USBLS	5/07
	Buffalo-Niagara Falls MSA, NY	Y	28730 FQ	43300 MW	52690 TQ	USBLS	5/07
	Nassau-Suffolk PMSA, NY	Y	39680 FQ	47500 MW	56960 TQ	USBLS	5/07
	New York-Northern New Jersey-Long Island MSA, NY-NJ-PA	Y	42370 FQ	52200 MW	76150 TQ	USBLS	5/07
	Syracuse MSA, NY	Y	22110 FQ	38530 MW	69970 TQ	USBLS	5/07
	North Carolina	Y	22960 FQ	32710 MW	44150 TQ	USBLS	5/07
	Charlotte-Gastonia-Concord MSA, NC-SC	Y	25680 FQ	34780 MW	43980 TQ	USBLS	5/07
	Durham MSA, NC	Y	31130 FQ	43520 MW	49260 TQ	USBLS	5/07
	Raleigh-Cary MSA, NC	Y	26900 FQ	34230 MW	46370 TQ	USBLS	5/07
	North Dakota	Y	25950 FQ	29200 MW	35660 TQ	USBLS	5/07
	Bismarck MSA, ND	Y	27040 FQ	29120 MW	31200 TQ	USBLS	5/07
	Fargo MSA, ND-MN	Y	23310 FQ	29060 MW	55270 TQ	USBLS	5/07
	Ohio	Y	19450 FQ	34180 MW	52670 TQ	USBLS	5/07
	Cincinnati-Middletown MSA, OH-KY-IN	Y	21330 FQ	37510 MW	58690 TQ	USBLS	5/07
	Cleveland-Elyria-Mentor MSA, OH	Y	19200 FQ	39550 MW	56500 TQ	USBLS	5/07
	Columbus MSA, OH	Y	23240 FQ	37490 MW	55670 TQ	USBLS	5/07

AE	Average entry wage	AW	Average wage paid	FQ	First quartile wage
AER	Average entry range	AWR	Average wage range	H	Hourly
AEX	Average experienced wage	AXR	Average experienced range	HI	Highest wage paid
ATC	Average total compensation	D	Daily	HR	High end range

LO	Lowest wage paid	MTC	Median total compensation	TCC	Total cash compensation
LR	Low end range	MW	Median wage paid	TQ	Third quartile wage
M	Monthly	MWR	Median wage range	W	Weekly
MCC	Median cash compensation	S	See annotated source	Y	Yearly

Occupation/Type/Industry	Location	Per	Low	Mid	High	Source	Date
Broadcast Technician	Dayton MSA, OH	Y	19570 FQ	35170 MW	54180 TQ	USBLS	5/07
	Oklahoma	Y	18040 FQ	24830 MW	32790 TQ	USBLS	5/07
	Oklahoma City MSA, OK	Y	23280 FQ	29310 MW	38650 TQ	USBLS	5/07
	Tulsa MSA, OK	Y	17520 FQ	24300 MW	32010 TQ	USBLS	5/07
	Oregon	H	10.08 FQ	12.90 MW	18.77 TQ	ORBLS	5/08
	Portland-Vancouver-Beaverton MSA, OR-WA	Y	20360 FQ	26910 MW	44700 TQ	USBLS	5/07
	Pennsylvania	Y	20780 FQ	32430 MW	49460 TQ	USBLS	5/07
	Allentown-Bethlehem-Easton MSA, PA-NJ	Y	19780 FQ	23770 MW	33520 TQ	USBLS	5/07
	Philadelphia-Camden-Wilmington MSA, PA-NJ-DE-MD	Y	23310 FQ	32790 MW	55010 TQ	USBLS	5/07
	Pittsburgh MSA, PA	Y	15040 FQ	20020 MW	39580 TQ	USBLS	5/07
	Providence-Fall River-Warwick MSA, RI-MA	Y	23130 FQ	34080 MW	52700 TQ	USBLS	5/07
	South Carolina	Y	17700 FQ	22540 MW	28730 TQ	USBLS	5/07
	Charleston-North Charleston MSA, SC	Y	16800 FQ	20720 MW	24110 TQ	USBLS	5/07
	Columbia MSA, SC	Y	22550 FQ	26570 MW	32320 TQ	USBLS	5/07
	South Dakota	Y	19250 FQ	22661 MW	34420 TQ	SDBLS	7/08-9/08
	Sioux Falls MSA, SD	Y	18664 FQ	20615 MW	24468 TQ	SDBLS	7/08-9/08
	Tennessee	Y	23360 FQ	34370 MW	46950 TQ	USBLS	5/07
	Nashville-Davidson-Murfreesboro MSA, TN	Y	23870 FQ	42980 MW	50870 TQ	USBLS	5/07
	Texas	Y	16300 FQ	21760 MW	31330 TQ	USBLS	5/07
	Austin-Round Rock MSA, TX	Y	22850 FQ	30380 MW	51400 TQ	USBLS	5/07
	Dallas-Fort Worth-Arlington MSA, TX	Y	21020 FQ	28460 MW	41810 TQ	USBLS	5/07
	El Paso MSA, TX	Y	13340 FQ	15330 MW	17400 TQ	USBLS	5/07
	Houston-Sugar Land-Baytown MSA, TX	Y	19850 FQ	23860 MW	33610 TQ	USBLS	5/07
	San Antonio MSA, TX	Y	18380 FQ	22770 MW	30330 TQ	USBLS	5/07
	Utah	Y	23160 FQ	31240 MW	39620 TQ	USBLS	5/07
	Salt Lake City MSA, UT	Y	21710 FQ	29050 MW	37880 TQ	USBLS	5/07
	Vermont	Y	17590 FQ	19840 MW	29650 TQ	USBLS	5/07
	Burlington-South Burlington MSA, VT	Y	18010 FQ	22050 MW	35970 TQ	USBLS	5/07
	Virginia	Y	22770 FQ	29190 MW	47940 TQ	USBLS	5/07
	Richmond MSA, VA	Y	21450 FQ	24500 MW	31020 TQ	USBLS	5/07
	Virginia Beach-Norfolk-Newport News MSA, VA-NC	Y	21950 FQ	26480 MW	38930 TQ	USBLS	5/07
	Washington	H	13.94 FQ	17.69 MW	23.33 TQ	WABLS	3/08
	Seattle-Tacoma-Bellevue MSA, WA	Y	29160 FQ	36210 MW	50570 TQ	USBLS	5/07
	West Virginia	Y	15279 FQ	19164 MW	27876 TQ	WVBLS	7/08-9/08
	Charleston MSA, WV	Y	18710 FQ	21500 MW	24180 TQ	USBLS	5/07
	Wisconsin	Y	20390 FQ	28060 MW	46920 TQ	USBLS	5/07
	Green Bay MSA, WI	Y	19640 FQ	24740 MW	34620 TQ	USBLS	5/07
	Milwaukee-Waukesha-West Allis MSA, WI	Y	23680 FQ	43340 MW	56010 TQ	USBLS	5/07
	Wyoming	Y	19628 FQ	28138 MW	40085 TQ	WYBLS	9/08
	Cheyenne MSA, WY	Y	20945 FQ	27185 MW	38329 TQ	WYBLS	9/08
	Puerto Rico	Y	16190 FQ	20360 MW	23820 TQ	USBLS	5/07
	San Juan-Caguas-Guaynabo MSA, PR	Y	16420 FQ	20620 MW	23960 TQ	USBLS	5/07
Broadcasting Engineer							
State Government	Ohio	H	16.35 LO		19.88 HI	ODAS	2008
Brokerage Clerk	Alabama	Y	27550 FQ	32340 MW	37630 TQ	USBLS	5/07
	Birmingham-Hoover MSA, AL	Y	28180 FQ	33090 MW	38290 TQ	USBLS	5/07
	Alaska	Y	30660 FQ	37610 MW	44020 TQ	USBLS	5/07
	Arizona	Y	28370 FQ	33950 MW	39710 TQ	USBLS	5/07
	Phoenix-Mesa-Scottsdale MSA, AZ	Y	28220 FQ	33440 MW	39800 TQ	USBLS	5/07
	Tucson MSA, AZ	Y	34230 FQ	36930 MW	39880 TQ	USBLS	5/07
	Arkansas	Y	27850 FQ	32800 MW	37730 TQ	USBLS	5/07
	Little Rock-North Little Rock MSA, AR	Y	29640 FQ	34350 MW	38660 TQ	USBLS	5/07
	California	H	16.54 FQ	20.65 MW	24.96 TQ	CABLS	1/08-3/08

AE	Average entry wage	AW	Average wage paid	FQ	First quartile wage	LO	Lowest wage paid	MTC	Median total compensation	TCC	Total cash compensation
AER	Average entry range	AWR	Average wage range	H	Hourly	LR	Low end range	MW	Median wage paid	TQ	Third quartile wage
AEX	Average experienced wage	AXR	Average experienced range	HI	Highest wage paid	M	Monthly	MWR	Median wage range	W	Weekly
ATC	Average total compensation	D	Daily	HR	High end range	MCC	Median cash compensation	S	See annotated source	Y	Yearly

Occupation/Type/Industry	Location	Per	Low	Mid	High	Source	Date
Brokerage Clerk	Los Angeles-Long Beach-Glendale PMSA, CA	H	17.24 FQ	21.55 MW	25.95 TQ	CABLS	1/08-3/08
	Oakland-Fremont-Hayward MSA, CA	H	18.67 FQ	23.23 MW	26.94 TQ	CABLS	1/08-3/08
	Riverside-San Bernardino-Ontario MSA, CA	H	16.31 FQ	20.28 MW	23.25 TQ	CABLS	1/08-3/08
	Sacramento-Arden Arcade-Roseville MSA, CA	H	15.27 FQ	16.94 MW	18.76 TQ	CABLS	1/08-3/08
	San Diego-Carlsbad-San Marcos MSA, CA	H	15.48 FQ	18.23 MW	22.14 TQ	CABLS	1/08-3/08
	San Francisco-San Mateo-Redwood PMSA, CA	H	17.15 FQ	21.80 MW	25.35 TQ	CABLS	1/08-3/08
	San Jose-Sunnyvale-Santa Clara MSA, CA	H	19.09 FQ	22.68 MW	27.34 TQ	CABLS	1/08-3/08
	Santa Ana-Anaheim-Irvine PMSA, CA	Y	35800 FQ	43310 MW	52340 TQ	USBLS	5/07.
	Colorado	Y	28940 FQ	33810 MW	41870 TQ	USBLS	5/07
	Denver-Aurora MSA, CO	Y	29810 FQ	35370 MW	42990 TQ	USBLS	5/07
	Connecticut	H	14.98 AE	19.25 MW		CTBLS	1/08-3/08
	Bridgeport-Stamford-Norwalk MSA, CT	Y	32570 FQ	39220 MW	53070 TQ	USBLS	5/07
	Hartford-West Hartford-East Hartford MSA, CT	Y	33420 FQ	38890 MW	46360 TQ	USBLS	5/07
	New Haven MSA, CT	Y	34110 FQ	39980 MW	47270 TQ	USBLS	5/07
	Delaware	Y	31010 FQ	37520 MW	45880 TQ	USBLS	5/07
	Wilmington PMSA, DE-MD-NJ	Y	31760 FQ	38520 MW	46390 TQ	USBLS	5/07
	District of Columbia	Y	33010 FQ	40010 MW	47490 TQ	USBLS	5/07
	Washington-Arlington-Alexandria MSA, DC-VA-MD-WV	Y	33040 FQ	38030 MW	46240 TQ	USBLS	5/07
	Florida	Y	27060 FQ	31490 MW	38170 TQ	USBLS	5/07
	Fort Lauderdale-Pompano Beach-Deerfield Beach PMSA, FL	Y	28730 FQ	35010 MW	42560 TQ	USBLS	5/07
	Jacksonville MSA, FL	Y	26070 FQ	29600 MW	33900 TQ	USBLS	5/07
	Lakeland MSA, FL	Y	27750 FQ	35750 MW	41900 TQ	USBLS	5/07
	Miami-Fort Lauderdale-Miami Beach MSA, FL	Y	29680 FQ	36120 MW	44610 TQ	USBLS	5/07
	Orlando-Kissimmee MSA, FL	Y	27530 FQ	31190 MW	37320 TQ	USBLS	5/07
	Tampa-St. Petersburg-Clearwater MSA, FL	Y	26440 FQ	30560 MW	35850 TQ	USBLS	5/07
	West Palm Beach-Boca Raton-Boynton Beach PMSA, FL	Y	29720 FQ	35870 MW	48920 TQ	USBLS	5/07
	Georgia	Y	27540 FQ	33280 MW	41800 TQ	USBLS	5/07
	Atlanta-Sandy Springs-Marietta MSA, GA	Y	27580 FQ	33680 MW	42680 TQ	USBLS	5/07
	Hawaii	Y	29640 FQ	36610 MW	47530 TQ	USBLS	5/07
	Honolulu MSA, HI	Y	28670 FQ	34800 MW	44090 TQ	USBLS	5/07
	Idaho	Y	31830 FQ	36690 MW	43250 TQ	USBLS	5/07
	Boise City-Nampa MSA, ID	Y	32630 FQ	37180 MW	43270 TQ	USBLS	5/07
	Illinois	Y	31550 FQ	39740 MW	49600 TQ	USBLS	5/07
	Chicago-Naperville-Joliet MSA, IL-IN-WI	Y	31790 FQ	40060 MW	49710 TQ	USBLS	5/07
	Indiana	Y	30500 FQ	36350 MW	45380 TQ	USBLS	5/07
	Fort Wayne MSA, IN	Y	29140 FQ	35030 MW	41530 TQ	USBLS	5/07
	Indianapolis-Carmel MSA, IN	Y	32120 FQ	38350 MW	48400 TQ	USBLS	5/07
	Iowa	Y	27690 FQ	31980 MW	37770 TQ	USBLS	5/07
	Des Moines-West Des Moines MSA, IA	Y	28600 FQ	32490 MW	38200 TQ	USBLS	5/07
	Kansas	Y	24610 FQ	29890 MW	35650 TQ	USBLS	5/07
	Wichita MSA, KS	Y	22580 FQ	26750 MW	32540 TQ	USBLS	5/07
	Kentucky	Y	28099 FQ	35777 MW	46333 TQ	KYBLS	2008
	Louisville-Jefferson County MSA, KY-IN	Y	30070 FQ	37590 MW	46270 TQ	USBLS	5/07
	Louisiana	H	12.95 FQ	14.57 MW	17.69 TQ	LABLS	1/08-3/08
	New Orleans-Metairie-Kenner MSA, LA	Y	27390 FQ	31570 MW	37280 TQ	USBLS	5/07
	Maine	Y	31500 FQ	39120 MW	46710 TQ	USBLS	5/07
	Portland-South Portland-Biddeford MSA, ME	Y	31790 FQ	39760 MW	47500 TQ	USBLS	5/07
	Maryland	Y		40800 MW		MDBLS	3/08

AE Average entry wage	**AW** Average wage paid	**FQ** First quartile wage	**LO** Lowest wage paid	**MTC** Median total compensation	**TCC** Total cash compensation
AER Average entry range	**AWR** Average wage range	**H** Hourly	**LR** Low end range	**MW** Median wage paid	**TQ** Third quartile wage
AEX Average experienced wage	**AXR** Average experienced range	**HI** Highest wage paid	**M** Monthly	**MWR** Median wage range	**W** Weekly
ATC Average total compensation	**D** Daily	**HR** High end range	**MCC** Median cash compensation	**S** See annotated source	**Y** Yearly

Brokerage Clerk

Occupation/Type/Industry	Location	Per	Low	Mid	High	Source	Date
Brokerage Clerk	Baltimore-Towson MSA, MD	Y	34030 FQ	40790 MW	48410 TQ	USBLS	5/07
	Bethesda-Gaithersburg-Frederick PMSA, MD	Y	31380 FQ	35840 MW	42990 TQ	USBLS	5/07
	Massachusetts	Y	34220 FQ	38140 MW	43330 TQ	USBLS	5/07
	Boston-Cambridge-Quincy NECTA, MA	Y	34420 FQ	38240 MW	43340 TQ	USBLS	5/07
	Worcester MSA, MA-CT	Y	34840 FQ	38690 MW	44730 TQ	USBLS	5/07
	Michigan	Y	28840 FQ	35980 MW	45510 TQ	USBLS	5/07
	Detroit-Warren-Livonia MSA, MI	Y	29300 FQ	37200 MW	46040 TQ	USBLS	5/07
	Warren-Troy-Farmington Hills PMSA, MI	Y	29290 FQ	37290 MW	46730 TQ	USBLS	5/07
	Minnesota	Y	35876 FQ	42568 MW	50468 TQ	MNBLS	10/08-12/08
	Minneapolis-Saint Paul MSA, MN-WI	Y	36604 FQ	43151 MW	50947 TQ	MNBLS	10/08-12/08
	Rochester MSA, MN	Y	29711 FQ	33210 MW	39423 TQ	MNBLS	10/08-12/08
	Mississippi	Y	25330 FQ	29670 MW	34950 TQ	USBLS	5/07
	Jackson MSA, MS	Y	24010 FQ	29320 MW	34600 TQ	USBLS	5/07
	Missouri	Y	28070 FQ	31690 MW	37230 TQ	USBLS	5/07
	Kansas City MSA, MO-KS	Y	27140 FQ	31950 MW	39220 TQ	USBLS	5/07
	St. Louis MSA, MO-IL	Y	28440 FQ	32130 MW	37360 TQ	USBLS	5/07
	Montana	Y	20740 FQ	27950 MW	37230 TQ	USBLS	5/07
	Nebraska	Y	27500 FQ	30670 MW	35010 TQ	USBLS	5/07
	Omaha-Council Bluffs MSA, NE-IA	Y	27200 FQ	30020 MW	33240 TQ	USBLS	5/07
	Nevada	H	13.14 FQ	14.70 MW	19.26 TQ	NVBLS	5/08
	Las Vegas-Paradise MSA, NV	H	12.85 FQ	14.17 MW	17.23 TQ	NVBLS	5/08
	Reno-Sparks MSA, NV	H	16.10 FQ	20.53 MW	22.99 TQ	NVBLS	5/08
	New Hampshire	H	12.48 AE	16.57 MW	19.79 AEX	NHBLS	6/08
	New Jersey	Y	32380 FQ	39780 MW	48280 TQ	USBLS	5/07
	Edison PMSA, NJ	Y	34260 FQ	40100 MW	49530 TQ	USBLS	5/07
	Newark-Union PMSA, NJ-PA	Y	31980 FQ	39000 MW	45630 TQ	USBLS	5/07
	New Mexico	Y	29920 FQ	40400 MW	47930 TQ	USBLS	5/07
	New York	Y	33430 FQ	43390 MW	56090 TQ	USBLS	5/07
	Albany-Schenectady-Troy MSA, NY	Y	30650 FQ	35490 MW	41810 TQ	USBLS	5/07
	Buffalo-Niagara Falls MSA, NY	Y	31530 FQ	43220 MW	55260 TQ	USBLS	5/07
	Nassau-Suffolk PMSA, NY	Y	31230 FQ	39380 MW	52160 TQ	USBLS	5/07
	New York-Northern New Jersey-Long Island MSA, NY-NJ-PA	Y	33980 FQ	42950 MW	55110 TQ	USBLS	5/07
	North Carolina	Y	30820 FQ	36170 MW	42090 TQ	USBLS	5/07
	Charlotte-Gastonia-Concord MSA, NC-SC	Y	32690 FQ	37600 MW	44670 TQ	USBLS	5/07
	Raleigh-Cary MSA, NC	Y	31940 FQ	36570 MW	41260 TQ	USBLS	5/07
	North Dakota	Y	23130 FQ	27150 MW	31700 TQ	USBLS	5/07
	Ohio	Y	29610 FQ	34700 MW	40760 TQ	USBLS	5/07
	Cincinnati-Middletown MSA, OH-KY-IN	Y	29750 FQ	35410 MW	41320 TQ	USBLS	5/07
	Cleveland-Elyria-Mentor MSA, OH	Y	29570 FQ	34650 MW	41690 TQ	USBLS	5/07
	Columbus MSA, OH	Y	30560 FQ	35560 MW	42020 TQ	USBLS	5/07
	Oklahoma	Y	24290 FQ	30130 MW	40380 TQ	USBLS	5/07
	Oklahoma City MSA, OK	Y	23930 FQ	27680 MW	33320 TQ	USBLS	5/07
	Tulsa MSA, OK	Y	30190 FQ	38950 MW	47610 TQ	USBLS	5/07
	Oregon	H	14.52 FQ	16.89 MW	20.34 TQ	ORBLS	5/08
	Portland-Vancouver-Beaverton MSA, OR-WA	Y	29910 FQ	34170 MW	40350 TQ	USBLS	5/07
	Pennsylvania	Y	26910 FQ	32330 MW	40130 TQ	USBLS	5/07
	Allentown-Bethlehem-Easton MSA, PA-NJ	Y	28760 FQ	33760 MW	41550 TQ	USBLS	5/07
	Philadelphia-Camden-Wilmington MSA, PA-NJ-DE-MD	Y	28020 FQ	34710 MW	43080 TQ	USBLS	5/07
	Pittsburgh MSA, PA	Y	26700 FQ	32060 MW	37700 TQ	USBLS	5/07
	Rhode Island	Y	30200 FQ	35940 MW	44570 TQ	USBLS	5/07
	Providence-Fall River-Warwick MSA, RI-MA	Y	30110 FQ	36080 MW	44720 TQ	USBLS	5/07
	South Carolina	Y	24730 FQ	28380 MW	31770 TQ	USBLS	5/07
	Charleston-North Charleston MSA, SC	Y	24310 FQ	29380 MW	35420 TQ	USBLS	5/07

AE Average entry wage	**AW** Average wage paid	**FQ** First quartile wage	**LO** Lowest wage paid	**MTC** Median total compensation	**TCC** Total cash compensation
AER Average entry range	**AWR** Average wage range	**H** Hourly	**LR** Low end range	**MW** Median wage paid	**TQ** Third quartile wage
AEX Average experienced wage	**AXR** Average experienced range	**HI** Highest wage paid	**M** Monthly	**MWR** Median wage range	**W** Weekly
ATC Average total compensation **D** Daily		**HR** High end range	**MCC** Median cash compensation	**S** See annotated source	**Y** Yearly

Occupation/Type/Industry	Location	Per	Low	Mid	High	Source	Date
Brokerage Clerk	Columbia MSA, SC	Y	26200 FQ	32010 MW	36750 TQ	USBLS	5/07
	South Dakota	Y	30026 FQ	35987 MW	40351 TQ	SDBLS	7/08-9/08
	Sioux Falls MSA, SD	Y	32371 FQ	37585 MW	41872 TQ	SDBLS	7/08-9/08
	Tennessee	Y	29400 FQ	35070 MW	40560 TQ	USBLS	5/07
	Memphis MSA, TN-MS-AR	Y	34850 FQ	39650 MW	45660 TQ	USBLS	5/07
	Nashville-Davidson-Murfreesboro MSA, TN	Y	30430 FQ	35500 MW	40320 TQ	USBLS	5/07
	Texas	Y	28800 FQ	36820 MW	45840 TQ	USBLS	5/07
	Austin-Round Rock MSA, TX	Y	28570 FQ	34200 MW	40220 TQ	USBLS	5/07
	Dallas-Fort Worth-Arlington MSA, TX	Y	29390 FQ	38720 MW	47710 TQ	USBLS	5/07
	Houston-Sugar Land-Baytown MSA, TX	Y	27880 FQ	35340 MW	44540 TQ	USBLS	5/07
	San Antonio MSA, TX	Y	35160 FQ	40440 MW	48600 TQ	USBLS	5/07
	Utah	Y	26300 FQ	30620 MW	35560 TQ	USBLS	5/07
	Salt Lake City MSA, UT	Y	27480 FQ	31430 MW	35730 TQ	USBLS	5/07
	Vermont	Y	26650 FQ	30950 MW	37300 TQ	USBLS	5/07
	Burlington-South Burlington MSA, VT	Y	26000 FQ	31300 MW	37700 TQ	USBLS	5/07
	Virginia	Y	30330 FQ	35140 MW	40270 TQ	USBLS	5/07
	Richmond MSA, VA	Y	29990 FQ	34550 MW	39190 TQ	USBLS	5/07
	Virginia Beach-Norfolk-Newport News MSA, VA-NC	Y	27380 FQ	32520 MW	40130 TQ	USBLS	5/07
	Washington	H	16.17 FQ	18.86 MW	23.03 TQ	WABLS	3/08
	Bremerton-Silverdale MSA, WA	Y	28640 FQ	31740 MW	43870 TQ	USBLS	5/07
	Seattle-Tacoma-Bellevue MSA, WA	Y	34390 FQ	40380 MW	48550 TQ	USBLS	5/07
	West Virginia	Y	27597 FQ	32816 MW	41211 TQ	WVBLS	7/08-9/08
	Wisconsin	Y	28830 FQ	33380 MW	40020 TQ	USBLS	5/07
	Milwaukee-Waukesha-West Allis MSA, WI	Y	28800 FQ	33680 MW	40740 TQ	USBLS	5/07
	Puerto Rico	Y	32090 FQ	38560 MW	47910 TQ	USBLS	5/07
Budget Analyst	Alabama	Y	49520 FQ	60770 MW	75120 TQ	USBLS	5/07
	Birmingham-Hoover MSA, AL	Y	41610 FQ	52610 MW	68910 TQ	USBLS	5/07
	Alaska	Y	51060 FQ	60830 MW	73750 TQ	USBLS	5/07
	Anchorage MSA, AK	Y	55080 FQ	65460 MW	76450 TQ	USBLS	5/07
	Arizona	Y	47150 FQ	57250 MW	68580 TQ	USBLS	5/07
	Phoenix-Mesa-Scottsdale MSA, AZ	Y	46870 FQ	57310 MW	69450 TQ	USBLS	5/07
	Tucson MSA, AZ	Y	50010 FQ	57850 MW	67650 TQ	USBLS	5/07
	Arkansas	Y	40130 FQ	52720 MW	62920 TQ	USBLS	5/07
	Little Rock-North Little Rock MSA, AR	Y	41090 FQ	53140 MW	62870 TQ	USBLS	5/07
	California	H	27.31 FQ	34.81 MW	44.03 TQ	CABLS	1/08-3/08
	Los Angeles-Long Beach-Glendale PMSA, CA	H	27.62 FQ	35.27 MW	43.83 TQ	CABLS	1/08-3/08
	Modesto MSA, CA	H	23.10 FQ	28.94 MW	37.77 TQ	CABLS	1/08-3/08
	Oakland-Fremont-Hayward MSA, CA	H	31.18 FQ	39.85 MW	49.26 TQ	CABLS	1/08-3/08
	Riverside-San Bernardino-Ontario MSA, CA	H	23.78 FQ	29.58 MW	36.92 TQ	CABLS	1/08-3/08
	Sacramento-Arden Arcade-Roseville MSA, CA	H	26.03 FQ	29.74 MW	35.88 TQ	CABLS	1/08-3/08
	San Diego-Carlsbad-San Marcos MSA, CA	H	25.97 FQ	31.90 MW	38.55 TQ	CABLS	1/08-3/08
	San Francisco-San Mateo-Redwood PMSA, CA	H	30.58 FQ	39.28 MW	48.38 TQ	CABLS	1/08-3/08
	San Jose-Sunnyvale-Santa Clara MSA, CA	H	33.14 FQ	42.78 MW	50.83 TQ	CABLS	1/08-3/08
	Santa Ana-Anaheim-Irvine PMSA, CA	Y	59260 FQ	72840 MW	88050 TQ	USBLS	5/07
	Colorado	Y	53990 FQ	63150 MW	77960 TQ	USBLS	5/07
	Denver-Aurora MSA, CO	Y	54530 FQ	63910 MW	79800 TQ	USBLS	5/07
	Connecticut	H	26.18 AE	33.96 MW		CTBLS	1/08-3/08
	Bridgeport-Stamford-Norwalk MSA, CT	Y	47240 FQ	61430 MW	74700 TQ	USBLS	5/07
	Danbury MSA, CT	Y	57870 FQ	65690 MW	73260 TQ	USBLS	5/07
	Hartford-West Hartford-East Hartford MSA, CT	Y	60020 FQ	70740 MW	81350 TQ	USBLS	5/07
	Delaware	Y	47020 FQ	57040 MW	69180 TQ	USBLS	5/07

AE	Average entry wage	AW	Average wage paid	FQ	First quartile wage	LO	Lowest wage paid	MTC	Median total compensation	TCC	Total cash compensation
AER	Average entry range	AWR	Average wage range	H	Hourly	LR	Low end range	MW	Median wage paid	TQ	Third quartile wage
AEX	Average experienced wage	AXR	Average experienced range	HI	Highest wage paid	M	Monthly	MWR	Median wage range	W	Weekly
ATC	Average total compensation	D	Daily	HR	High end range	MCC	Median cash compensation	S	See annotated source	Y	Yearly

Budget Analyst

Occupation/Type/Industry	Location	Per	Low	Mid	High	Source	Date
Budget Analyst	Wilmington PMSA, DE-MD-NJ	Y	52240 FQ	60240 MW	71760 TQ	USBLS	5/07
	District of Columbia	Y	57440 FQ	74480 MW	90460 TQ	USBLS	5/07
	Washington-Arlington-Alexandria MSA, DC-VA-MD-WV	Y	60220 FQ	77610 MW	94280 TQ	USBLS	5/07
	Florida	Y	45850 FQ	56780 MW	70570 TQ	USBLS	5/07
	Fort Lauderdale-Pompano Beach-Deerfield Beach PMSA, FL	Y	46760 FQ	55730 MW	67740 TQ	USBLS	5/07
	Jacksonville MSA, FL	Y	45810 FQ	57350 MW	72010 TQ	USBLS	5/07
	Miami-Fort Lauderdale-Miami Beach MSA, FL	Y	49240 FQ	61750 MW	76660 TQ	USBLS	5/07
	Orlando-Kissimmee MSA, FL	Y	42240 FQ	53790 MW	67150 TQ	USBLS	5/07
	Tampa-St. Petersburg-Clearwater MSA, FL	Y	47700 FQ	57860 MW	71760 TQ	USBLS	5/07
	West Palm Beach-Boca Raton-Boynton Beach PMSA, FL	Y	44340 FQ	51450 MW	64160 TQ	USBLS	5/07
	Georgia	Y	48480 FQ	61000 MW	77010 TQ	USBLS	5/07
	Atlanta-Sandy Springs-Marietta MSA, GA	Y	51070 FQ	64520 MW	80730 TQ	USBLS	5/07
	Hawaii	Y	53370 FQ	61640 MW	73700 TQ	USBLS	5/07
	Honolulu MSA, HI	Y	53650 FQ	61890 MW	74270 TQ	USBLS	5/07
	Idaho	Y	45200 FQ	53180 MW	62330 TQ	USBLS	5/07
	Boise City-Nampa MSA, ID	Y	45430 FQ	53920 MW	63540 TQ	USBLS	5/07
	Illinois	Y	56720 FQ	71590 MW	88480 TQ	USBLS	5/07
	Chicago-Naperville-Joliet MSA, IL-IN-WI	Y	58530 FQ	73970 MW	92180 TQ	USBLS	5/07
	Indiana	Y	46020 FQ	59970 MW	73930 TQ	USBLS	5/07
	Gary PMSA, IN	Y	42500 FQ	54740 MW	63890 TQ	USBLS	5/07
	Indianapolis-Carmel MSA, IN	Y	46370 FQ	62080 MW	73710 TQ	USBLS	5/07
	Iowa	Y	44510 FQ	57370 MW	70690 TQ	USBLS	5/07
	Des Moines-West Des Moines MSA, IA	Y	55300 FQ	66440 MW	77950 TQ	USBLS	5/07
	Kansas	Y	43860 FQ	54610 MW	69600 TQ	USBLS	5/07
	Wichita MSA, KS	Y	48360 FQ	58440 MW	70930 TQ	USBLS	5/07
	Kentucky	Y	45969 FQ	54649 MW	65452 TQ	KYBLS	2008
	Louisville-Jefferson County MSA, KY-IN	Y	45120 FQ	54820 MW	67090 TQ	USBLS	5/07
	Louisiana	H	16.72 FQ	22.67 MW	29.08 TQ	LABLS	1/08-3/08
	Baton Rouge MSA, LA	Y	33920 FQ	43060 MW	54920 TQ	USBLS	5/07
	New Orleans-Metairie-Kenner MSA, LA	Y	42620 FQ	52890 MW	66820 TQ	USBLS	5/07
	Maine	Y	48250 FQ	57290 MW	67800 TQ	USBLS	5/07
	Portland-South Portland-Biddeford MSA, ME	Y	56560 FQ	65560 MW	74560 TQ	USBLS	5/07
	Maryland	Y		68600 MW		MDBLS	3/08
	Baltimore-Towson MSA, MD	Y	48200 FQ	59770 MW	79150 TQ	USBLS	5/07
	Bethesda-Gaithersburg-Frederick PMSA, MD	Y	62230 FQ	82150 MW	95590 TQ	USBLS	5/07
	Massachusetts	Y	55620 FQ	68050 MW	84740 TQ	USBLS	5/07
	Boston-Cambridge-Quincy NECTA, MA	Y	57300 FQ	70520 MW	86710 TQ	USBLS	5/07
	Worcester MSA, MA-CT	Y	46180 FQ	63150 MW	76610 TQ	USBLS	5/07
	Michigan	Y	52900 FQ	63400 MW	80310 TQ	USBLS	5/07
	Detroit-Warren-Livonia MSA, MI	Y	56540 FQ	73470 MW	90180 TQ	USBLS	5/07
	Grand Rapids-Wyoming MSA, MI	Y	41800 FQ	53030 MW	69390 TQ	USBLS	5/07
	Warren-Troy-Farmington Hills PMSA, MI	Y	54380 FQ	65200 MW	77520 TQ	USBLS	5/07
	Minnesota	Y	51027 FQ	61871 MW	75665 TQ	MNBLS	10/08-12/08
	Duluth-Superior MSA, MN-WI	Y	42237 FQ	60390 MW	76937 TQ	MNBLS	10/08-12/08
	Minneapolis-Saint Paul MSA, MN-WI	Y	50631 FQ	61860 MW	76885 TQ	MNBLS	10/08-12/08
	Mississippi	Y	42250 FQ	54170 MW	64660 TQ	USBLS	5/07
	Jackson MSA, MS	Y	36470 FQ	42240 MW	57060 TQ	USBLS	5/07
	Missouri	Y	47400 FQ	58650 MW	72830 TQ	USBLS	5/07
	Kansas City MSA, MO-KS	Y	42350 FQ	55280 MW	73150 TQ	USBLS	5/07
	St. Louis MSA, MO-IL	Y	50000 FQ	60800 MW	74690 TQ	USBLS	5/07
	Montana	Y	42680 FQ	51340 MW	61350 TQ	USBLS	5/07
	Nebraska	Y	43740 FQ	54910 MW	70270 TQ	USBLS	5/07

Occupation/Type/Industry	Location	Per	Low	Mid	High	Source	Date
Budget Analyst	Omaha-Council Bluffs MSA, NE-IA	Y	48500 FQ	58900 MW	72550 TQ	USBLS	5/07
	Nevada	H	26.18 FQ	31.01 MW	40.03 TQ	NVBLS	5/08
	Las Vegas-Paradise MSA, NV	H	25.87 FQ	31.02 MW	40.72 TQ	NVBLS	5/08
	New Hampshire	H	25.20 AE	32.64 MW	36.23 AEX	NHBLS	6/08
	New Jersey	Y	59060 FQ	73340 MW	87960 TQ	USBLS	5/07
	Camden PMSA, NJ	Y	55150 FQ	66520 MW	79740 TQ	USBLS	5/07
	Edison PMSA, NJ	Y	62910 FQ	80290 MW	93550 TQ	USBLS	5/07
	Newark-Union PMSA, NJ-PA	Y	56580 FQ	66710 MW	81480 TQ	USBLS	5/07
	New Mexico	Y	46180 FQ	56280 MW	67190 TQ	USBLS	5/07
	Albuquerque MSA, NM	Y	49330 FQ	58240 MW	68930 TQ	USBLS	5/07
	New York	Y	49400 FQ	60830 MW	75530 TQ	USBLS	5/07
	Albany-Schenectady-Troy MSA, NY	Y	47300 FQ	57750 MW	69890 TQ	USBLS	5/07
	Buffalo-Niagara Falls MSA, NY	Y	50130 FQ	59930 MW	72570 TQ	USBLS	5/07
	Nassau-Suffolk PMSA, NY	Y	50340 FQ	59550 MW	72360 TQ	USBLS	5/07
	New York-Northern New Jersey-Long Island MSA, NY-NJ-PA	Y	55440 FQ	68850 MW	85650 TQ	USBLS	5/07
	North Carolina	Y	45310 FQ	56500 MW	70050 TQ	USBLS	5/07
	Charlotte-Gastonia-Concord MSA, NC-SC	Y	46030 FQ	54230 MW	66250 TQ	USBLS	5/07
	Raleigh-Cary MSA, NC	Y	46270 FQ	62890 MW	74640 TQ	USBLS	5/07
	North Dakota	Y	49580 FQ	59460 MW	69650 TQ	USBLS	5/07
	Ohio	Y	49440 FQ	63560 MW	78380 TQ	USBLS	5/07
	Cincinnati-Middletown MSA, OH-KY-IN	Y	50680 FQ	65890 MW	81260 TQ	USBLS	5/07
	Cleveland-Elyria-Mentor MSA, OH	Y	53050 FQ	63180 MW	77400 TQ	USBLS	5/07
	Columbus MSA, OH	Y	50080 FQ	65210 MW	78450 TQ	USBLS	5/07
	Dayton MSA, OH	Y	59360 FQ	71680 MW	85110 TQ	USBLS	5/07
	Oklahoma	Y	42430 FQ	56130 MW	67760 TQ	USBLS	5/07
	Oklahoma City MSA, OK	Y	43070 FQ	58320 MW	70090 TQ	USBLS	5/07
	Tulsa MSA, OK	Y	45350 FQ	61530 MW	73470 TQ	USBLS	5/07
	Oregon	H	23.54 FQ	27.74 MW	32.62 TQ	ORBLS	5/08
	Portland-Vancouver-Beaverton MSA, OR-WA	Y	51080 FQ	59960 MW	72000 TQ	USBLS	5/07
	Salem MSA, OR	Y	44860 FQ	51220 MW	60060 TQ	USBLS	5/07
	Pennsylvania	Y	49120 FQ	62670 MW	76930 TQ	USBLS	5/07
	Allentown-Bethlehem-Easton MSA, PA-NJ	Y	45700 FQ	59960 MW	75410 TQ	USBLS	5/07
	Philadelphia-Camden-Wilmington MSA, PA-NJ-DE-MD	Y	55640 FQ	68360 MW	81080 TQ	USBLS	5/07
	Pittsburgh MSA, PA	Y	42960 FQ	53370 MW	67230 TQ	USBLS	5/07
	Reading MSA, PA	Y	47390 FQ	69210 MW	77490 TQ	USBLS	5/07
	Rhode Island	Y	54830 FQ	68980 MW	83830 TQ	USBLS	5/07
	Providence-Fall River-Warwick MSA, RI-MA	Y	55020 FQ	69240 MW	83990 TQ	USBLS	5/07
	South Carolina	Y	41990 FQ	52220 MW	64170 TQ	USBLS	5/07
	Charleston-North Charleston MSA, SC	Y	35460 FQ	51250 MW	64760 TQ	USBLS	5/07
	Columbia MSA, SC	Y	45780 FQ	55560 MW	65840 TQ	USBLS	5/07
	South Dakota	Y	40109 FQ	49830 MW	63808 TQ	SDBLS	7/08-9/08
	Sioux Falls MSA, SD	Y	46492 FQ	58010 MW	67566 TQ	SDBLS	7/08-9/08
	Tennessee	Y	46280 FQ	57910 MW	72910 TQ	USBLS	5/07
	Memphis MSA, TN-MS-AR	Y	49870 FQ	64590 MW	82820 TQ	USBLS	5/07
	Nashville-Davidson-Murfreesboro MSA, TN	Y	46870 FQ	57120 MW	71030 TQ	USBLS	5/07
	Texas	Y	50270 FQ	61870 MW	77630 TQ	USBLS	5/07
	Austin-Round Rock MSA, TX	Y	43190 FQ	56450 MW	63210 TQ	USBLS	5/07
	Dallas-Fort Worth-Arlington MSA, TX	Y	51360 FQ	62040 MW	73990 TQ	USBLS	5/07
	El Paso MSA, TX	Y	50760 FQ	57640 MW	66160 TQ	USBLS	5/07
	Houston-Sugar Land-Baytown MSA, TX	Y	53890 FQ	69680 MW	85380 TQ	USBLS	5/07
	San Antonio MSA, TX	Y	51080 FQ	60660 MW	73050 TQ	USBLS	5/07
	Utah	Y	47930 FQ	59000 MW	71660 TQ	USBLS	5/07
	Salt Lake City MSA, UT	Y	47080 FQ	57400 MW	65590 TQ	USBLS	5/07
	Vermont	Y	47100 FQ	55520 MW	63930 TQ	USBLS	5/07

AE Average entry wage	**AW** Average wage paid	**FQ** First quartile wage	**LO** Lowest wage paid	**MTC** Median total compensation	**TCC** Total cash compensation
AER Average entry range	**AWR** Average wage range	**H** Hourly	**LR** Low end range	**MW** Median wage paid	**TQ** Third quartile wage
AEX Average experienced wage	**AXR** Average experienced range	**HI** Highest wage paid	**M** Monthly	**MWR** Median wage range	**W** Weekly
ATC Average total compensation	**D** Daily	**HR** High end range	**MCC** Median cash compensation	**S** See annotated source	**Y** Yearly

Occupation/Type/Industry	Location	Per	Low	Mid	High	Source	Date
Budget Analyst	Burlington-South Burlington						
	MSA, VT	Y	44640 FQ	52590 MW	60370 TQ	USBLS	5/07
	Virginia	Y	57110 FQ	72330 MW	91690 TQ	USBLS	5/07
	Richmond MSA, VA	Y	54090 FQ	64600 MW	78440 TQ	USBLS	5/07
	Virginia Beach-Norfolk-						
	Newport News MSA, VA-NC	Y	52030 FQ	61250 MW	73260 TQ	USBLS	5/07
	Washington	H	24.11 FQ	30.01 MW	36.30 TQ	WABLS	3/08
	Seattle-Tacoma-Bellevue						
	MSA, WA	Y	55900 FQ	67060 MW	78120 TQ	USBLS	5/07
	West Virginia	Y	38815 FQ	52988 MW	66999 TQ	WVBLS	7/08-9/08
	Wisconsin	Y	51090 FQ	60260 MW	72790 TQ	USBLS	5/07
	Milwaukee-Waukesha-West						
	Allis MSA, WI	Y	55400 FQ	69000 MW	81510 TQ	USBLS	5/07
	Wyoming	Y	51798 FQ	62664 MW	87577 TQ	WYBLS	9/08
	Cheyenne MSA, WY	Y	55372 FQ	85211 MW	96258 TQ	WYBLS	9/08
	Puerto Rico	Y	26940 FQ	35350 MW	44840 TQ	USBLS	5/07
	San Juan-Caguas-Guaynabo						
	MSA, PR	Y	27000 FQ	34980 MW	43080 TQ	USBLS	5/07
	Virgin Islands	Y	37930 FQ	46860 MW	59260 TQ	USBLS	5/07
	Guam	Y	35170 FQ	50760 MW	60000 TQ	USBLS	5/07
Budget Director							
Municipal Government	Pueblo, CO	Y			136500 HI	PCHIEF	2009
Budget Officer							
State Supreme Court	Michigan	Y			89554 HI	LSJ02	7/11/07
Building Improvement Secretary							
Public Schools	Baldwin County, AL	Y	26991 LO		35427 HI	BCPSSS	2008-2009
Building Inspector	Seaside, CA	S	2402 LO		2852 HI	SSSS	8/08
	Walnut Creek, CA	Y	71429 LO		86207 HI	WCSWP	6/27/08
	D'Iberville, MS	Y			53076 HI	MML	2008
	Tunica, MS	Y			16188 HI	MML	2008
	Bismarck, ND	M			4352 HI	NDLC01	2008
	Ohio	H	18.36 LO		23.87 HI	ODAS	2008
Building Official	Brighton Township, MI	Y			64899 HI	LCPP	2009
Building Trades Worker							
Municipal Government	Walnut Creek, CA	Y	55897 LO		67117 HI	WCSWP	6/27/08
Bus and Truck Mechanic and							
Diesel Engine Specialist	Alabama	Y	27560 FQ	34050 MW	40410 TQ	USBLS	5/07
	Birmingham-Hoover MSA, AL	Y	31720 FQ	37750 MW	45740 TQ	USBLS	5/07
	Alaska	Y	39730 FQ	47560 MW	59950 TQ	USBLS	5/07
	Anchorage MSA, AK	Y	38150 FQ	46050 MW	57900 TQ	USBLS	5/07
	Arizona	Y	29660 FQ	36590 MW	44850 TQ	USBLS	5/07
	Phoenix-Mesa-Scottsdale						
	MSA, AZ	Y	29450 FQ	36670 MW	45320 TQ	USBLS	5/07
	Tucson MSA, AZ	Y	33090 FQ	37940 MW	44610 TQ	USBLS	5/07
	Arkansas	Y	26970 FQ	33800 MW	41050 TQ	USBLS	5/07
	Fayetteville-Springdale-Rogers						
	MSA, AR-MO	Y	27870 FQ	35110 MW	42100 TQ	USBLS	5/07
	Little Rock-North Little Rock						
	MSA, AR	Y	30850 FQ	37660 MW	45570 TQ	USBLS	5/07
	California	H	17.37 FQ	21.69 MW	26.37 TQ	CABLS	1/08-3/08
	Los Angeles-Long Beach-						
	Glendale PMSA, CA	H	18.59 FQ	22.26 MW	26.63 TQ	CABLS	1/08-3/08
	Oakland-Fremont-Hayward						
	MSA, CA	H	21.93 FQ	27.02 MW	31.47 TQ	CABLS	1/08-3/08
	Riverside-San Bernardino-						
	Ontario MSA, CA	H	15.85 FQ	19.86 MW	23.32 TQ	CABLS	1/08-3/08
	Sacramento-Arden Arcade-						
	Roseville MSA, CA	H	18.78 FQ	23.99 MW	27.41 TQ	CABLS	1/08-3/08
	San Diego-Carlsbad-San						
	Marcos MSA, CA	H	18.39 FQ	21.41 MW	24.98 TQ	CABLS	1/08-3/08
	San Francisco-San Mateo-						
	Redwood PMSA, CA	H	18.90 FQ	23.36 MW	29.07 TQ	CABLS	1/08-3/08
	San Jose-Sunnyvale-Santa						
	Clara MSA, CA	H	19.20 FQ	23.76 MW	32.61 TQ	CABLS	1/08-3/08

AE	Average entry wage	**AW**	Average wage paid	**FQ**	First quartile wage
AER	Average entry range	**AWR**	Average wage range	**H**	Hourly
AEX	Average experienced wage	**AXR**	Average experienced range	**HI**	Highest wage paid
ATC	Average total compensation	**D**	Daily	**HR**	High end range

LO	Lowest wage paid	**MTC**	Median total compensation	**TCC**	Total cash compensation
LR	Low end range	**MW**	Median wage paid	**TQ**	Third quartile wage
M	Monthly	**MWR**	Median wage range	**W**	Weekly
MCC	Median cash compensation	**S**	See annotated source	**Y**	Yearly

Occupation/Type/Industry	Location	Per	Low	Mid	High	Source	Date
Bus and Truck Mechanic and Diesel Engine Specialist							
	Santa Ana-Anaheim-Irvine PMSA, CA	Y	40720 FQ	51940 MW	58950 TQ	USBLS	5/07
	Colorado	Y	34650 FQ	41640 MW	49570 TQ	USBLS	5/07
	Denver-Aurora MSA, CO	Y	35760 FQ	42930 MW	50630 TQ	USBLS	5/07
	Connecticut	H	16.42 AE	22.33 MW		CTBLS	1/08-3/08
	Bridgeport-Stamford-Norwalk MSA, CT	Y	36090 FQ	45240 MW	53940 TQ	USBLS	5/07
	Hartford-West Hartford-East Hartford MSA, CT	Y	38510 FQ	46880 MW	56390 TQ	USBLS	5/07
	Delaware	Y	33500 FQ	42080 MW	50310 TQ	USBLS	5/07
	Dover MSA, DE	Y	31490 FQ	36110 MW	41440 TQ	USBLS	5/07
	Wilmington PMSA, DE-MD-NJ	Y	34820 FQ	43770 MW	51860 TQ	USBLS	5/07
	District of Columbia	Y	42970 FQ	47910 MW	54490 TQ	USBLS	5/07
	Washington-Arlington-Alexandria MSA, DC-VA-MD-WV	Y	36170 FQ	44510 MW	54500 TQ	USBLS	5/07
	Florida	Y	32450 FQ	38750 MW	47150 TQ	USBLS	5/07
	Fort Lauderdale-Pompano Beach-Deerfield Beach PMSA, FL	Y	35970 FQ	43310 MW	52150 TQ	USBLS	5/07
	Jacksonville MSA, FL	Y	33200 FQ	40000 MW	48940 TQ	USBLS	5/07
	Miami-Fort Lauderdale-Miami Beach MSA, FL	Y	35010 FQ	42230 MW	51090 TQ	USBLS	5/07
	Orlando-Kissimmee MSA, FL	Y	32770 FQ	39770 MW	47120 TQ	USBLS	5/07
	Tampa-St. Petersburg-Clearwater MSA, FL	Y	30280 FQ	35980 MW	42580 TQ	USBLS	5/07
	West Palm Beach-Boca Raton-Boynton Beach PMSA, FL	Y	34520 FQ	40440 MW	48600 TQ	USBLS	5/07
	Georgia	Y	31040 FQ	38860 MW	48170 TQ	USBLS	5/07
	Atlanta-Sandy Springs-Marietta MSA, GA	Y	34890 FQ	42330 MW	50850 TQ	USBLS	5/07
	Hawaii	Y	37750 FQ	47530 MW	57870 TQ	USBLS	5/07
	Honolulu MSA, HI	Y	40630 FQ	49210 MW	58140 TQ	USBLS	5/07
	Idaho	Y	30790 FQ	37800 MW	46670 TQ	USBLS	5/07
	Boise City-Nampa MSA, ID	Y	34630 FQ	43020 MW	54230 TQ	USBLS	5/07
	Idaho Falls MSA, ID	Y	27420 FQ	31530 MW	37600 TQ	USBLS	5/07
	Illinois	Y	33260 FQ	42740 MW	52180 TQ	USBLS	5/07
	Chicago-Naperville-Joliet MSA, IL-IN-WI	Y	38030 FQ	46690 MW	55220 TQ	USBLS	5/07
	Indiana	Y	30250 FQ	36850 MW	44320 TQ	USBLS	5/07
	Elkhart-Goshen MSA, IN	Y	32620 FQ	37630 MW	46230 TQ	USBLS	5/07
	Gary PMSA, IN	Y	35300 FQ	42200 MW	47690 TQ	USBLS	5/07
	Indianapolis-Carmel MSA, IN	Y	31440 FQ	37900 MW	45510 TQ	USBLS	5/07
	South Bend-Mishawaka MSA, IN-MI	Y	33580 FQ	39420 MW	46710 TQ	USBLS	5/07
	Terre Haute MSA, IN	Y	25010 FQ	32420 MW	39720 TQ	USBLS	5/07
	Iowa	Y	28100 FQ	33990 MW	40350 TQ	USBLS	5/07
	Des Moines-West Des Moines MSA, IA	Y	32540 FQ	37820 MW	45340 TQ	USBLS	5/07
	Iowa City MSA, IA	Y	24530 FQ	33750 MW	42930 TQ	USBLS	5/07
	Kansas	Y	28520 FQ	35580 MW	44440 TQ	USBLS	5/07
	Wichita MSA, KS	Y	30290 FQ	34920 MW	42000 TQ	USBLS	5/07
	Kentucky	Y	28485 FQ	35169 MW	42781 TQ	KYBLS	2008
	Elizabethtown MSA, KY	Y	22940 FQ	27190 MW	31330 TQ	USBLS	5/07
	Louisville-Jefferson County MSA, KY-IN	Y	30640 FQ	36790 MW	44020 TQ	USBLS	5/07
	Owensboro MSA, KY	Y	26360 FQ	29300 MW	32390 TQ	USBLS	5/07
	Louisiana	H	13.57 FQ	16.62 MW	19.96 TQ	LABLS	1/08-3/08
	Baton Rouge MSA, LA	Y	31720 FQ	37870 MW	45820 TQ	USBLS	5/07
	New Orleans-Metairie-Kenner MSA, LA	Y	30620 FQ	35410 MW	43420 TQ	USBLS	5/07
	Shreveport-Bossier City MSA, LA	Y	26350 FQ	32490 MW	42080 TQ	USBLS	5/07
	Maine	Y	28810 FQ	34210 MW	40360 TQ	USBLS	5/07
	Portland-South Portland-Biddeford MSA, ME	Y	33600 FQ	38180 MW	44180 TQ	USBLS	5/07
	Maryland	Y		44525 MW		MDBLS	3/08
	Baltimore-Towson MSA, MD	Y	32890 FQ	43140 MW	52250 TQ	USBLS	5/07
	Bethesda-Gaithersburg-Frederick PMSA, MD	Y	31850 FQ	41520 MW	50500 TQ	USBLS	5/07

AE	Average entry wage	AW	Average wage paid	FQ	First quartile wage	LO	Lowest wage paid	MTC	Median total compensation	TCC	Total cash compensation
AER	Average entry range	AWR	Average wage range	H	Hourly	LR	Low end range	MW	Median wage paid	TQ	Third quartile wage
AEX	Average experienced wage	AXR	Average experienced range	HI	Highest wage paid	M	Monthly	MWR	Median wage range	W	Weekly
ATC	Average total compensation	D	Daily	HR	High end range	MCC	Median cash compensation	S	See annotated source	Y	Yearly

140

Occupation/Type/Industry	Location	Per	Low	Mid	High	Source	Date
Bus and Truck Mechanic and Diesel Engine Specialist	Massachusetts	Y	35650 FQ	43130 MW	49760 TQ	USBLS	5/07
	Boston-Cambridge-Quincy NECTA, MA	Y	34460 FQ	43450 MW	50140 TQ	USBLS	5/07
	Worcester MSA, MA-CT	Y	39060 FQ	44920 MW	51500 TQ	USBLS	5/07
	Michigan	Y	32330 FQ	40990 MW	49650 TQ	USBLS	5/07
	Detroit-Warren-Livonia MSA, MI	Y	39210 FQ	45660 MW	54270 TQ	USBLS	5/07
	Grand Rapids-Wyoming MSA, MI	Y	29880 FQ	40490 MW	50280 TQ	USBLS	5/07
	Warren-Troy-Farmington Hills PMSA, MI	Y	34820 FQ	45280 MW	56850 TQ	USBLS	5/07
	Minnesota	Y	36136 FQ	42408 MW	50055 TQ	MNBLS	10/08-12/08
	Duluth-Superior MSA, MN-WI	Y	35706 FQ	43793 MW	58059 TQ	MNBLS	10/08-12/08
	Minneapolis-Saint Paul MSA, MN-WI	Y	38003 FQ	44475 MW	51461 TQ	MNBLS	10/08-12/08
	Rochester MSA, MN	Y	33601 FQ	39158 MW	45557 TQ	MNBLS	10/08-12/08
	Mississippi	Y	25200 FQ	30140 MW	36860 TQ	USBLS	5/07
	Hattiesburg MSA, MS	Y	26480 FQ	31880 MW	39040 TQ	USBLS	5/07
	Jackson MSA, MS	Y	26960 FQ	34140 MW	40960 TQ	USBLS	5/07
	Missouri	Y	29370 FQ	37340 MW	45170 TQ	USBLS	5/07
	Kansas City MSA, MO-KS	Y	29460 FQ	36010 MW	43540 TQ	USBLS	5/07
	St. Joseph MSA, MO-KS	Y	25960 FQ	29240 MW	34180 TQ	USBLS	5/07
	St. Louis MSA, MO-IL	Y	34740 FQ	41430 MW	46510 TQ	USBLS	5/07
	Montana	Y	29630 FQ	36850 MW	48730 TQ	USBLS	5/07
	Billings MSA, MT	Y	30850 FQ	36670 MW	51970 TQ	USBLS	5/07
	Nebraska	Y	28960 FQ	38490 MW	50840 TQ	USBLS	5/07
	Omaha-Council Bluffs MSA, NE-IA	Y	27780 FQ	34740 MW	41820 TQ	USBLS	5/07
	Nevada	H	18.75 FQ	22.65 MW	27.04 TQ	NVBLS	5/08
	Las Vegas-Paradise MSA, NV	H	18.88 FQ	22.22 MW	26.15 TQ	NVBLS	5/08
	New Hampshire	H	15.93 AE	20.53 MW	23.15 AEX	NHBLS	6/08
	Manchester MSA, NH	Y	38420 FQ	43500 MW	49820 TQ	USBLS	5/07
	Nashua NECTA, NH-MA	Y	37590 FQ	44700 MW	50600 TQ	USBLS	5/07
	New Jersey	Y	36840 FQ	45100 MW	54330 TQ	USBLS	5/07
	Camden PMSA, NJ	Y	34000 FQ	41470 MW	50420 TQ	USBLS	5/07
	Edison PMSA, NJ	Y	34940 FQ	42470 MW	53330 TQ	USBLS	5/07
	Newark-Union PMSA, NJ-PA	Y	41990 FQ	49240 MW	58210 TQ	USBLS	5/07
	Vineland-Millville-Bridgeton MSA, NJ	Y	36120 FQ	41820 MW	46800 TQ	USBLS	5/07
	New Mexico	Y	27150 FQ	33530 MW	40810 TQ	USBLS	5/07
	Albuquerque MSA, NM	Y	32450 FQ	37960 MW	45050 TQ	USBLS	5/07
	New York	Y	34990 FQ	45180 MW	54180 TQ	USBLS	5/07
	Albany-Schenectady-Troy MSA, NY	Y	31940 FQ	38940 MW	47400 TQ	USBLS	5/07
	Buffalo-Niagara Falls MSA, NY	Y	32950 FQ	39140 MW	45390 TQ	USBLS	5/07
	Nassau-Suffolk PMSA, NY	Y	36640 FQ	47820 MW	60010 TQ	USBLS	5/07
	New York-Northern New Jersey-Long Island MSA, NY-NJ-PA	Y	40120 FQ	49770 MW	57030 TQ	USBLS	5/07
	North Carolina	Y	30670 FQ	36910 MW	44380 TQ	USBLS	5/07
	Charlotte-Gastonia-Concord MSA, NC-SC	Y	34140 FQ	40690 MW	47240 TQ	USBLS	5/07
	Durham MSA, NC	Y	34270 FQ	39030 MW	46030 TQ	USBLS	5/07
	Raleigh-Cary MSA, NC	Y	31090 FQ	38980 MW	48250 TQ	USBLS	5/07
	North Dakota	Y	29360 FQ	35180 MW	41150 TQ	USBLS	5/07
	Fargo MSA, ND-MN	Y	31320 FQ	36080 MW	41200 TQ	USBLS	5/07
	Ohio	Y	30290 FQ	37160 MW	45480 TQ	USBLS	5/07
	Canton-Massillon MSA, OH	Y	26300 FQ	33220 MW	37500 TQ	USBLS	5/07
	Cincinnati-Middletown MSA, OH-KY-IN	Y	32500 FQ	40210 MW	47240 TQ	USBLS	5/07
	Cleveland-Elyria-Mentor MSA, OH	Y	32080 FQ	40340 MW	48590 TQ	USBLS	5/07
	Columbus MSA, OH	Y	32610 FQ	38080 MW	46100 TQ	USBLS	5/07
	Dayton MSA, OH	Y	32800 FQ	40060 MW	47290 TQ	USBLS	5/07
	Oklahoma	Y	26110 FQ	32600 MW	39210 TQ	USBLS	5/07
	Oklahoma City MSA, OK	Y	28540 FQ	34080 MW	40600 TQ	USBLS	5/07
	Tulsa MSA, OK	Y	29970 FQ	35200 MW	39750 TQ	USBLS	5/07
	Oregon	H	16.61 FQ	19.87 MW	23.55 TQ	ORBLS	5/08
	Portland-Vancouver-Beaverton MSA, OR-WA	Y	36730 FQ	43650 MW	50260 TQ	USBLS	5/07

AE	Average entry wage	AW	Average wage paid	FQ	First quartile wage	LO	Lowest wage paid	MTC	Median total compensation	TCC	Total cash compensation
AER	Average entry range	AWR	Average wage range	H	Hourly	LR	Low end range	MW	Median wage paid	TQ	Third quartile wage
AEX	Average experienced wage	AXR	Average experienced range	HI	Highest wage paid	M	Monthly	MWR	Median wage range	W	Weekly
ATC	Average total compensation	D	Daily	HR	High end range	MCC	Median cash compensation	S	See annotated source	Y	Yearly

Occupation/Type/Industry	Location	Per	Low	Mid	High	Source	Date
Bus and Truck Mechanic and Diesel Engine Specialist	Pennsylvania	Y	30040 FQ	37420 MW	45130 TQ	USBLS	5/07
	Allentown-Bethlehem-Easton MSA, PA-NJ	Y	33050 FQ	38920 MW	47100 TQ	USBLS	5/07
	Philadelphia-Camden-Wilmington MSA, PA-NJ-DE-MD	Y	35500 FQ	43000 MW	49980 TQ	USBLS	5/07
	Pittsburgh MSA, PA	Y	28970 FQ	36160 MW	44580 TQ	USBLS	5/07
	Rhode Island	Y	34170 FQ	39520 MW	46620 TQ	USBLS	5/07
	Providence-Fall River-Warwick MSA, RI-MA	Y	34230 FQ	39630 MW	46670 TQ	USBLS	5/07
	South Carolina	Y	28330 FQ	33390 MW	40360 TQ	USBLS	5/07
	Charleston-North Charleston MSA, SC	Y	29550 FQ	34670 MW	39620 TQ	USBLS	5/07
	Columbia MSA, SC	Y	30320 FQ	36750 MW	44890 TQ	USBLS	5/07
	South Dakota	Y	28867 FQ	33329 MW	38686 TQ	SDBLS	7/08-9/08
	Sioux Falls MSA, SD	Y	29219 FQ	33838 MW	39446 TQ	SDBLS	7/08-9/08
	Tennessee	Y	29210 FQ	36430 MW	43480 TQ	USBLS	5/07
	Memphis MSA, TN-MS-AR	Y	32430 FQ	38090 MW	45110 TQ	USBLS	5/07
	Nashville-Davidson-Murfreesboro MSA, TN	Y	31700 FQ	38730 MW	45140 TQ	USBLS	5/07
	Texas	Y	26840 FQ	34000 MW	42260 TQ	USBLS	5/07
	Austin-Round Rock MSA, TX	Y	30280 FQ	39220 MW	46800 TQ	USBLS	5/07
	Dallas-Fort Worth-Arlington MSA, TX	Y	30510 FQ	37990 MW	45240 TQ	USBLS	5/07
	El Paso MSA, TX	Y	21760 FQ	27050 MW	33150 TQ	USBLS	5/07
	Houston-Sugar Land-Baytown MSA, TX	Y	28640 FQ	35290 MW	43000 TQ	USBLS	5/07
	San Antonio MSA, TX	Y	24390 FQ	31500 MW	39660 TQ	USBLS	5/07
	Utah	Y	31950 FQ	38240 MW	44940 TQ	USBLS	5/07
	Salt Lake City MSA, UT	Y	34480 FQ	40340 MW	46820 TQ	USBLS	5/07
	Vermont	Y	29620 FQ	35330 MW	41830 TQ	USBLS	5/07
	Burlington-South Burlington MSA, VT	Y	30720 FQ	36620 MW	44260 TQ	USBLS	5/07
	Virginia	Y	31500 FQ	37640 MW	45500 TQ	USBLS	5/07
	Lynchburg MSA, VA	Y	28610 FQ	35620 MW	41930 TQ	USBLS	5/07
	Richmond MSA, VA	Y	32910 FQ	38820 MW	46180 TQ	USBLS	5/07
	Virginia Beach-Norfolk-Newport News MSA, VA-NC	Y	32810 FQ	37340 MW	43340 TQ	USBLS	5/07
	Washington	H	17.87 FQ	21.52 MW	25.11 TQ	WABLS	3/08
	Seattle-Tacoma-Bellevue MSA, WA	Y	40260 FQ	47500 MW	55440 TQ	USBLS	5/07
	Spokane MSA, WA	Y	32970 FQ	38900 MW	44800 TQ	USBLS	5/07
	West Virginia	Y	25141 FQ	29765 MW	35757 TQ	WVBLS	7/08-9/08
	Charleston MSA, WV	Y	25610 FQ	29490 MW	35150 TQ	USBLS	5/07
	Huntington-Ashland MSA, WV-KY-OH	Y	27410 FQ	31530 MW	39360 TQ	USBLS	5/07
	Wisconsin	Y	30680 FQ	37230 MW	44790 TQ	USBLS	5/07
	Milwaukee-Waukesha-West Allis MSA, WI	Y	35340 FQ	43050 MW	49860 TQ	USBLS	5/07
	Wyoming	Y	33665 FQ	43775 MW	54293 TQ	WYBLS	9/08
	Cheyenne MSA, WY	Y	35458 FQ	38843 MW	43296 TQ	WYBLS	9/08
	Puerto Rico	Y	16150 FQ	19940 MW	25280 TQ	USBLS	5/07
	San Juan-Caguas-Guaynabo MSA, PR	Y	16850 FQ	20680 MW	26080 TQ	USBLS	5/07
	Virgin Islands	Y	28300 FQ	32930 MW	41710 TQ	USBLS	5/07
	Guam	Y	19470 FQ	25590 MW	32290 TQ	USBLS	5/07
Bus Driver							
Recreation Department	Seaside, CA	S	796 LO		976 HI	SSSS	8/08
School	Alabama	Y	12390 FQ	13720 MW	15120 TQ	USBLS	5/07
School	Birmingham-Hoover MSA, AL	Y	12420 FQ	13890 MW	15430 TQ	USBLS	5/07
School	Tuscaloosa MSA, AL	Y	12200 FQ	13490 MW	14780 TQ	USBLS	5/07
School	Alaska	Y	27200 FQ	31030 MW	37050 TQ	USBLS	5/07
School	Anchorage MSA, AK	Y	26320 FQ	31250 MW	36900 TQ	USBLS	5/07
School	Arizona	Y	19930 FQ	23120 MW	26930 TQ	USBLS	5/07
School	Phoenix-Mesa-Scottsdale MSA, AZ	Y	20720 FQ	23920 MW	27670 TQ	USBLS	5/07
School	Tucson MSA, AZ	Y	19220 FQ	21830 MW	24510 TQ	USBLS	5/07
School	Arkansas	Y	15220 FQ	20230 MW	23390 TQ	USBLS	5/07
School	Fayetteville-Springdale-Rogers MSA, AR-MO	Y	15920 FQ	20850 MW	23600 TQ	USBLS	5/07

AE	Average entry wage	AW	Average wage paid	FQ	First quartile wage
AER	Average entry range	AWR	Average wage range	H	Hourly
AEX	Average experienced wage	AXR	Average experienced range	HI	Highest wage paid
ATC	Average total compensation	D	Daily	HR	High end range

LO	Lowest wage paid	MTC	Median total compensation	TCC	Total cash compensation
LR	Low end range	MW	Median wage paid	TQ	Third quartile wage
M	Monthly	MWR	Median wage range	W	Weekly
MCC	Median cash compensation	S	See annotated source	Y	Yearly

Bus Driver

Occupation/Type/Industry	Location	Per	Low	Mid	High	Source	Date
Bus Driver							
School	Little Rock-North Little Rock MSA, AR	Y	18500 FQ	21420 MW	24350 TQ	USBLS	5/07
School	California	H	12.63 FQ	15.14 MW	18.32 TQ	CABLS	1/08-3/08
School	Bakersfield MSA, CA	H	10.45 FQ	14.25 MW	18.01 TQ	CABLS	1/08-3/08
School	Los Angeles-Long Beach-Glendale PMSA, CA	H	11.83 FQ	14.16 MW	17.72 TQ	CABLS	1/08-3/08
School	Oakland-Fremont-Hayward MSA, CA	H	14.19 FQ	16.26 MW	18.67 TQ	CABLS	1/08-3/08
School	Riverside-San Bernardino-Ontario MSA, CA	H	11.90 FQ	14.10 MW	16.38 TQ	CABLS	1/08-3/08
School	Sacramento-Arden Arcade-Roseville MSA, CA	H	11.08 FQ	14.68 MW	17.41 TQ	CABLS	1/08-3/08
School	San Diego-Carlsbad-San Marcos MSA, CA	H	12.38 FQ	16.22 MW	19.26 TQ	CABLS	1/08-3/08
School	San Francisco-San Mateo-Redwood PMSA, CA	H	12.75 FQ	16.07 MW	18.04 TQ	CABLS	1/08-3/08
School	San Jose-Sunnyvale-Santa Clara MSA, CA	H	15.92 FQ	17.92 MW	20.54 TQ	CABLS	1/08-3/08
School	Santa Ana-Anaheim-Irvine PMSA, CA	Y	28020 FQ	33830 MW	41590 TQ	USBLS	5/07
School	Colorado	Y	24740 FQ	28870 MW	33500 TQ	USBLS	5/07
School	Denver-Aurora MSA, CO	Y	27250 FQ	30710 MW	35740 TQ	USBLS	5/07
School	Pueblo MSA, CO	Y	20830 FQ	24490 MW	30000 TQ	USBLS	5/07
School	Connecticut	H	11.44 AE	14.11 MW		CTBLS	1/08-3/08
School	Bridgeport-Stamford-Norwalk MSA, CT	Y	29180 FQ	33130 MW	36360 TQ	USBLS	5/07
School	Hartford-West Hartford-East Hartford MSA, CT	Y	24310 FQ	27170 MW	29940 TQ	USBLS	5/07
School	Waterbury MSA, CT	Y	24440 FQ	28550 MW	35020 TQ	USBLS	5/07
School	Delaware	Y	17420 FQ	25630 MW	30350 TQ	USBLS	5/07
School	Dover MSA, DE	Y	14290 FQ	14750 MW	25070 TQ	USBLS	5/07
School	Wilmington PMSA, DE-MD-NJ	Y	25120 FQ	28130 MW	31160 TQ	USBLS	5/07
School	District of Columbia	Y	27770 FQ	31040 MW	35840 TQ	USBLS	5/07
School	Washington-Arlington-Alexandria MSA, DC-VA-MD-WV	Y	26110 FQ	31030 MW	36790 TQ	USBLS	5/07
School	Florida	Y	21070 FQ	24570 MW	29740 TQ	USBLS	5/07
School	Jacksonville MSA, FL	Y	14470 FQ	18180 MW	23710 TQ	USBLS	5/07
School	Miami-Fort Lauderdale-Miami Beach MSA, FL	Y	21510 FQ	24960 MW	29070 TQ	USBLS	5/07
School	Orlando-Kissimmee MSA, FL	Y	22400 FQ	25350 MW	29170 TQ	USBLS	5/07
School	Tallahassee MSA, FL	Y	20740 FQ	24450 MW	32080 TQ	USBLS	5/07
School	Tampa-St. Petersburg-Clearwater MSA, FL	Y	22520 FQ	25470 MW	29690 TQ	USBLS	5/07
School	West Palm Beach-Boca Raton-Boynton Beach PMSA, FL	Y	17100 FQ	19430 MW	23180 TQ	USBLS	5/07
School	Georgia	Y	13160 FQ	15470 MW	27400 TQ	USBLS	5/07
School	Atlanta-Sandy Springs-Marietta MSA, GA	Y	14090 FQ	18970 MW	31680 TQ	USBLS	5/07
School	Hawaii	Y	26580 FQ	32220 MW	36950 TQ	USBLS	5/07
School	Honolulu MSA, HI	Y	25380 FQ	29420 MW	36480 TQ	USBLS	5/07
School	Idaho	Y	24950 FQ	27900 MW	30550 TQ	USBLS	5/07
School	Boise City-Nampa MSA, ID	Y	26430 FQ	28470 MW	30590 TQ	USBLS	5/07
School	Pocatello MSA, ID	Y	26260 FQ	28160 MW	30130 TQ	USBLS	5/07
School	Illinois	Y	20990 FQ	26770 MW	32030 TQ	USBLS	5/07
School	Chicago-Naperville-Joliet MSA, IL-IN-WI	Y	23380 FQ	27290 MW	31560 TQ	USBLS	5/07
School	Indiana	Y	18400 FQ	28470 MW	37720 TQ	USBLS	5/07
School	Elkhart-Goshen MSA, IN	Y	33050 FQ	35750 MW	38530 TQ	USBLS	5/07
School	Evansville MSA, IN-KY	Y	17620 FQ	24400 MW	30760 TQ	USBLS	5/07
School	Gary PMSA, IN	Y	19310 FQ	26640 MW	31170 TQ	USBLS	5/07
School	Indianapolis-Carmel MSA, IN	Y	27600 FQ	37010 MW	44200 TQ	USBLS	5/07
School	Iowa	Y	21010 FQ	28060 MW	35080 TQ	USBLS	5/07
School	Des Moines-West Des Moines MSA, IA	Y	27390 FQ	30470 MW	34460 TQ	USBLS	5/07
School	Kansas	Y	20520 FQ	23630 MW	27900 TQ	USBLS	5/07
School	Wichita MSA, KS	Y	20450 FQ	22550 MW	25570 TQ	USBLS	5/07
School	Kentucky	Y	25820 FQ	29194 MW	33044 TQ	KYBLS	2008
School	Louisville-Jefferson County MSA, KY-IN	Y	25810 FQ	30160 MW	36390 TQ	USBLS	5/07

AE	Average entry wage	AW	Average wage paid	FQ	First quartile wage	LO	Lowest wage paid	MTC	Median total compensation
AER	Average entry range	AWR	Average wage range	H	Hourly	LR	Low end range	MW	Median wage paid
AEX	Average experienced wage	AXR	Average experienced range	HI	Highest wage paid	M	Monthly	MWR	Median wage range
ATC	Average total compensation	D	Daily	HR	High end range	MCC	Median cash compensation	S	See annotated source

TCC Total cash compensation
TQ Third quartile wage
W Weekly
Y Yearly

Bus Driver

Occupation/Type/Industry	Location	Per	Low	Mid	High	Source	Date
School	Louisiana	H	6.29 FQ	7.29 MW	8.72 TQ	LABLS	1/08-3/08
School	Baton Rouge MSA, LA	Y	13230 FQ	15320 MW	18300 TQ	USBLS	5/07
School	New Orleans-Metairie-Kenner MSA, LA	Y	13970 FQ	17250 MW	21900 TQ	USBLS	5/07
School	Maine	Y	23910 FQ	27370 MW	31300 TQ	USBLS	5/07
School	Bangor MSA, ME	Y	15180 FQ	21250 MW	25570 TQ	USBLS	5/07
School	Portland-South Portland-Biddeford MSA, ME	Y	24810 FQ	28540 MW	33860 TQ	USBLS	5/07
School	Maryland	Y	.	28675 MW		MDBLS	3/08
School	Baltimore-Towson MSA, MD	Y	21890 FQ	26250 MW	29060 TQ	USBLS	5/07
School	Salisbury MSA, MD	Y	16880 FQ	19080 MW	23690 TQ	USBLS	5/07
School	Massachusetts	Y	22850 FQ	30430 MW	35460 TQ	USBLS	5/07
School	Boston-Cambridge-Quincy NECTA, MA	Y	19410 FQ	28350 MW	33900 TQ	USBLS	5/07
School	Springfield MSA, MA-CT	Y	25170 FQ	29350 MW	38810 TQ	USBLS	5/07
School	Worcester MSA, MA-CT	Y	25120 FQ	29620 MW	32980 TQ	USBLS	5/07
School	Michigan	Y	25960 FQ	31130 MW	36100 TQ	USBLS	5/07
School	Detroit-Warren-Livonia MSA, MI	Y	24790 FQ	31680 MW	37240 TQ	USBLS	5/07
School	Flint MSA, MI	Y	25590 FQ	28540 MW	31680 TQ	USBLS	5/07
School	Grand Rapids-Wyoming MSA, MI	Y	29580 FQ	33000 MW	36120 TQ	USBLS	5/07
School	Muskegon-Norton Shores MSA, MI	Y	26290 FQ	30050 MW	34240 TQ	USBLS	5/07
School	Warren-Troy-Farmington Hills PMSA, MI	Y	27380 FQ	34210 MW	39070 TQ	USBLS	5/07
School	Southfield, MI	H	16.10 LO		20.31 HI	DNEWS01	2008
School	Minnesota	Y	25061 FQ	30627 MW	35527 TQ	MNBLS	10/08-12/08
School	Duluth-Superior MSA, MN-WI	Y	15782 FQ	21233 MW	26320 TQ	MNBLS	10/08-12/08
School	Minneapolis-Saint Paul MSA, MN-WI	Y	27787 FQ	31980 MW	36276 TQ	MNBLS	10/08-12/08
School	Rochester MSA, MN	Y	24574 FQ	28333 MW	33864 TQ	MNBLS	10/08-12/08
School	Mississippi	Y	12680 FQ	14260 MW	16380 TQ	USBLS	5/07
School	Hattiesburg MSA, MS	Y	12710 FQ	14360 MW	19950 TQ	USBLS	5/07
School	Jackson MSA, MS	Y	12500 FQ	14010 MW	15520 TQ	USBLS	5/07
School	Missouri	Y	18120 FQ	24270 MW	29910 TQ	USBLS	5/07
School	Kansas City MSA, MO-KS	Y	21430 FQ	24640 MW	28460 TQ	USBLS	5/07
School	St. Louis MSA, MO-IL	Y	19010 FQ	27310 MW	33330 TQ	USBLS	5/07
School	Montana	Y	20320 FQ	24370 MW	29450 TQ	USBLS	5/07
School	Billings MSA, MT	Y	16020 FQ	24420 MW	28650 TQ	USBLS	5/07
School	Nebraska	Y	19190 FQ	24330 MW	29720 TQ	USBLS	5/07
School	Omaha-Council Bluffs MSA, NE-IA	Y	23810 FQ	28490 MW	40460 TQ	USBLS	5/07
School	Nevada	H	12.94 FQ	15.27 MW	17.52 TQ	NVBLS	5/08
School	Las Vegas-Paradise MSA, NV	H	12.64 FQ	15.56 MW	17.71 TQ	NVBLS	5/08
School	New Hampshire	H	9.71 AE	12.77 MW	14.44 AEX	NHBLS	6/08
School	Manchester MSA, NH	Y	18750 FQ	21820 MW	24010 TQ	USBLS	5/07
School	Nashua NECTA, NH-MA	Y	25280 FQ	28490 MW	33020 TQ	USBLS	5/07
School	New Jersey	Y	24540 FQ	28900 MW	33970 TQ	USBLS	5/07
School	Atlantic City MSA, NJ	Y	26370 FQ	28430 MW	30800 TQ	USBLS	5/07
School	Camden PMSA, NJ	Y	24530 FQ	28000 MW	31490 TQ	USBLS	5/07
School	Edison PMSA, NJ	Y	24940 FQ	29560 MW	34920 TQ	USBLS	5/07
School	Newark-Union PMSA, NJ-PA	Y	25700 FQ	30670 MW	36040 TQ	USBLS	5/07
School	New Mexico	Y	14880 FQ	19950 MW	24740 TQ	USBLS	5/07
School	Albuquerque MSA, NM	Y	16680 FQ	20440 MW	25580 TQ	USBLS	5/07
School	New York	Y	26280 FQ	31900 MW	37750 TQ	USBLS	5/07
School	Albany-Schenectady-Troy MSA, NY	Y	26590 FQ	31160 MW	36890 TQ	USBLS	5/07
School	Buffalo-Niagara Falls MSA, NY	Y	23180 FQ	28260 MW	36640 TQ	USBLS	5/07
School	Glens Falls MSA, NY	Y	22540 FQ	26910 MW	34500 TQ	USBLS	5/07
School	Nassau-Suffolk PMSA, NY	Y	28490 FQ	32930 MW	38170 TQ	USBLS	5/07
School	New York-Northern New Jersey-Long Island MSA, NY-NJ-PA	Y	26540 FQ	32120 MW	38170 TQ	USBLS	5/07
School	Syracuse MSA, NY	Y	23800 FQ	36620 MW	44320 TQ	USBLS	5/07
School	North Carolina	Y	20370 FQ	23320 MW	26590 TQ	USBLS	5/07
School	Charlotte-Gastonia-Concord MSA, NC-SC	Y	21510 FQ	24290 MW	27140 TQ	USBLS	5/07
School	Raleigh-Cary MSA, NC	Y	18610 FQ	22120 MW	26490 TQ	USBLS	5/07
School	North Dakota	Y	23510 FQ	29510 MW	38380 TQ	USBLS	5/07

AE	Average entry wage	AW	Average wage paid	FQ	First quartile wage	LO	Lowest wage paid	MTC	Median total compensation	TCC	Total cash compensation
AER	Average entry range	AWR	Average wage range	H	Hourly	LR	Low end range	MW	Median wage paid	TQ	Third quartile wage
AEX	Average experienced wage	AXR	Average experienced range	HI	Highest wage paid	M	Monthly	MWR	Median wage range	W	Weekly
ATC	Average total compensation	D	Daily	HR	High end range	MCC	Median cash compensation	S	See annotated source	Y	Yearly

Occupation/Type/Industry	Location	Per	Low	Mid	High	Source	Date
Bus Driver							
School	Fargo MSA, ND-MN	Y	15450 FQ	24350 MW	30890 TQ	USBLS	5/07
School	Ohio	Y	23370 FQ	28280 MW	33760 TQ	USBLS	5/07
School	Cincinnati-Middletown MSA, OH-KY-IN	Y	24130 FQ	27440 MW	31290 TQ	USBLS	5/07
School	Cleveland-Elyria-Mentor MSA, OH	Y	24820 FQ	32660 MW	38650 TQ	USBLS	5/07
School	Columbus MSA, OH	Y	22980 FQ	27880 MW	32000 TQ	USBLS	5/07
School	Dayton MSA, OH	Y	20380 FQ	26940 MW	31220 TQ	USBLS	5/07
School	Oklahoma	Y	13390 FQ	16360 MW	22120 TQ	USBLS	5/07
School	Oklahoma City MSA, OK	Y	13170 FQ	15500 MW	20650 TQ	USBLS	5/07
School	Tulsa MSA, OK	Y	14930 FQ	20470 MW	23830 TQ	USBLS	5/07
School	Oregon	H	11.56 FQ	13.26 MW	14.96 TQ	ORBLS	5/08
School	Portland-Vancouver-Beaverton MSA, OR-WA	Y	25530 FQ	28530 MW	33180 TQ	USBLS	5/07
School	Pennsylvania	Y	17710 FQ	23770 MW	30330 TQ	USBLS	5/07
School	Allentown-Bethlehem-Easton MSA, PA-NJ	Y	15740 FQ	27210 MW	33320 TQ	USBLS	5/07
School	Philadelphia-Camden-Wilmington MSA, PA-NJ-DE-MD	Y	23980 FQ	28630 MW	32940 TQ	USBLS	5/07
School	Pittsburgh MSA, PA	Y	16870 FQ	21750 MW	28750 TQ	USBLS	5/07
School	Rhode Island	Y	25050 FQ	28160 MW	31800 TQ	USBLS	5/07
School	Providence-Fall River-Warwick MSA, RI-MA	Y	24850 FQ	28460 MW	32710 TQ	USBLS	5/07
School	South Carolina	Y	14530 FQ	17860 MW	21910 TQ	USBLS	5/07
School	Charleston-North Charleston MSA, SC	Y	17750 FQ	20990 MW	23650 TQ	USBLS	5/07
School	Columbia MSA, SC	Y	13720 FQ	16460 MW	19440 TQ	USBLS	5/07
School	Spartanburg MSA, SC	Y	19090 FQ	22740 MW	27190 TQ	USBLS	5/07
School	South Dakota	Y	22743 FQ	25265 MW	28937 TQ	SDBLS	7/08-9/08
School	Sioux Falls MSA, SD	Y	25658 FQ	29865 MW	33670 TQ	SDBLS	7/08-9/08
School	Tennessee	Y	13380 FQ	16220 MW	24120 TQ	USBLS	5/07
School	Knoxville MSA, TN	Y	14600 FQ	18970 MW	25340 TQ	USBLS	5/07
School	Memphis MSA, TN-MS-AR	Y	13230 FQ	15400 MW	21110 TQ	USBLS	5/07
School	Nashville-Davidson-Murfreesboro MSA, TN	Y	19440 FQ	23640 MW	28400 TQ	USBLS	5/07
School	Texas	Y	14690 FQ	20030 MW	25900 TQ	USBLS	5/07
School	Austin-Round Rock MSA, TX	Y	21640 FQ	25680 MW	29400 TQ	USBLS	5/07
School	Dallas-Fort Worth-Arlington MSA, TX	Y	15700 FQ	22240 MW	27940 TQ	USBLS	5/07
School	El Paso MSA, TX	Y	15990 FQ	21440 MW	26160 TQ	USBLS	5/07
School	Houston-Sugar Land-Baytown MSA, TX	Y	14800 FQ	19770 MW	26630 TQ	USBLS	5/07
School	San Antonio MSA, TX	Y	15910 FQ	19790 MW	24750 TQ	USBLS	5/07
School	Utah	Y	23290 FQ	30850 MW	35870 TQ	USBLS	5/07
School	Salt Lake City MSA, UT	Y	26200 FQ	30950 MW	35610 TQ	USBLS	5/07
School	Vermont	Y	23820 FQ	27500 MW	30710 TQ	USBLS	5/07
School	Burlington-South Burlington MSA, VT	Y	21290 FQ	26610 MW	30270 TQ	USBLS	5/07
School	Virginia	Y	18790 FQ	24590 MW	31310 TQ	USBLS	5/07
School	Richmond MSA, VA	Y	17160 FQ	23520 MW	27570 TQ	USBLS	5/07
School	Virginia Beach-Norfolk-Newport News MSA, VA-NC	Y	22190 FQ	25040 MW	29230 TQ	USBLS	5/07
School	Washington	H	14.29 FQ	16.17 MW	17.75 TQ	WABLS	3/08
School	Seattle-Tacoma-Bellevue MSA, WA	Y	31840 FQ	34800 MW	37640 TQ	USBLS	5/07
School	West Virginia	Y	19378 FQ	22450 MW	25411 TQ	WVBLS	7/08-9/08
School	Charleston MSA, WV	Y	19850 FQ	22370 MW	24880 TQ	USBLS	5/07
School	Wisconsin	Y	21220 FQ	24160 MW	28510 TQ	USBLS	5/07
School	Milwaukee-Waukesha-West Allis MSA, WI	Y	21260 FQ	23270 MW	25590 TQ	USBLS	5/07
School	Wyoming	Y	15643 FQ	23656 MW	29658 TQ	WYBLS	9/08
School	Cheyenne MSA, WY	Y	22559 FQ	25359 MW	29925 TQ	WYBLS	9/08
School	Puerto Rico	Y	12310 FQ	13580 MW	14860 TQ	USBLS	5/07
School	San Juan-Caguas-Guaynabo MSA, PR	Y	12260 FQ	13460 MW	14670 TQ	USBLS	5/07
School	Virgin Islands	Y	19770 FQ	23720 MW	34930 TQ	USBLS	5/07
Transit and Intercity	Alabama	Y	14410 FQ	18160 MW	27340 TQ	USBLS	5/07
Transit and Intercity	Birmingham-Hoover MSA, AL	Y	28480 FQ	32680 MW	35850 TQ	USBLS	5/07
Transit and Intercity	Montgomery MSA, AL	Y	16050 FQ	17420 MW	18790 TQ	USBLS	5/07
Transit and Intercity	Alaska	Y	27750 FQ	34270 MW	44770 TQ	USBLS	5/07

AE	Average entry wage	AW	Average wage paid	FQ	First quartile wage	LO	Lowest wage paid	MTC	Median total compensation	TCC	Total cash compensation
AER	Average entry range	AWR	Average wage range	H	Hourly	LR	Low end range	MW	Median wage paid	TQ	Third quartile wage
AEX	Average experienced wage	AXR	Average experienced range	HI	Highest wage paid	M	Monthly	MWR	Median wage range	W	Weekly
ATC	Average total compensation	D	Daily	HR	High end range	MCC	Median cash compensation	S	See annotated source	Y	Yearly

Occupation/Type/Industry	Location	Per	Low	Mid	High	Source	Date
Bus Driver							
Transit and Intercity	Anchorage MSA, AK	Y	26010 FQ	31480 MW	44690 TQ	USBLS	5/07
Transit and Intercity	Arizona	Y	21160 FQ	23850 MW	29460 TQ	USBLS	5/07
Transit and Intercity	Phoenix-Mesa-Scottsdale MSA, AZ	Y	20880 FQ	23060 MW	25280 TQ	USBLS	5/07
Transit and Intercity	Tucson MSA, AZ	Y	24000 FQ	30650 MW	36080 TQ	USBLS	5/07
Transit and Intercity	Arkansas	Y	18890 FQ	23690 MW	35890 TQ	USBLS	5/07
Transit and Intercity	California	H	14.78 FQ	17.94 MW	22.38 TQ	CABLS	1/08-3/08
Transit and Intercity	Los Angeles-Long Beach-Glendale PMSA, CA	H	15.02 FQ	17.12 MW	20.13 TQ	CABLS	1/08-3/08
Transit and Intercity	Oakland-Fremont-Hayward MSA, CA	H	12.78 FQ	18.36 MW	21.59 TQ	CABLS	1/08-3/08
Transit and Intercity	Oxnard-Thousand Oaks-Ventura MSA, CA	H	12.98 FQ	14.79 MW	18.01 TQ	CABLS	1/08-3/08
Transit and Intercity	Riverside-San Bernardino-Ontario MSA, CA	H	13.02 FQ	16.25 MW	18.58 TQ	CABLS	1/08-3/08
Transit and Intercity	Sacramento-Arden Arcade-Roseville MSA, CA	H	12.88 FQ	16.72 MW	23.75 TQ	CABLS	1/08-3/08
Transit and Intercity	San Diego-Carlsbad-San Marcos MSA, CA	H	12.03 FQ	15.40 MW	20.71 TQ	CABLS	1/08-3/08
Transit and Intercity	San Jose-Sunnyvale-Santa Clara MSA, CA	H	16.78 FQ	21.90 MW	27.88 TQ	CABLS	1/08-3/08
Transit and Intercity	Santa Ana-Anaheim-Irvine PMSA, CA	Y	28550 FQ	36920 MW	46080 TQ	USBLS	5/07
Transit and Intercity	Stockton MSA, CA	H	13.44 FQ	16.38 MW	20.58 TQ	CABLS	1/08-3/08
Transit and Intercity	Colorado	Y	24000 FQ	28970 MW	35120 TQ	USBLS	5/07
Transit and Intercity	Denver-Aurora MSA, CO	Y	23870 FQ	28530 MW	34370 TQ	USBLS	5/07
Transit and Intercity	Connecticut	H	10.72 AE	13.23 MW		CTBLS	1/08-3/08
Transit and Intercity	Bridgeport-Stamford-Norwalk MSA, CT	Y	25900 FQ	32330 MW	45050 TQ	USBLS	5/07
Transit and Intercity	Hartford-West Hartford-East Hartford MSA, CT	Y	24580 FQ	27540 MW	30630 TQ	USBLS	5/07
Transit and Intercity	Norwich-New London MSA, CT-RI	Y	20710 FQ	24260 MW	26930 TQ	USBLS	5/07
Transit and Intercity	Delaware	Y	26840 FQ	30270 MW	40580 TQ	USBLS	5/07
Transit and Intercity	Wilmington PMSA, DE-MD-NJ	Y	26930 FQ	30340 MW	40780 TQ	USBLS	5/07
Transit and Intercity	Washington-Arlington-Alexandria MSA, DC-VA-MD-WV	Y	27650 FQ	34200 MW	44960 TQ	USBLS	5/07
Transit and Intercity	Florida	Y	22240 FQ	29230 MW	37690 TQ	USBLS	5/07
Transit and Intercity	Fort Lauderdale-Pompano Beach-Deerfield Beach PMSA, FL	Y	20140 FQ	22370 MW	26070 TQ	USBLS	5/07
Transit and Intercity	Jacksonville MSA, FL	Y	32580 FQ	35920 MW	39210 TQ	USBLS	5/07
Transit and Intercity	Miami-Fort Lauderdale-Miami Beach MSA, FL	Y	23080 FQ	30280 MW	40200 TQ	USBLS	5/07
Transit and Intercity	Orlando-Kissimmee MSA, FL	Y	19990 FQ	24980 MW	35290 TQ	USBLS	5/07
Transit and Intercity	Sarasota-Bradenton-Venice MSA, FL	Y	25110 FQ	28010 MW	31450 TQ	USBLS	5/07
Transit and Intercity	Tampa-St. Petersburg-Clearwater MSA, FL	Y	26150 FQ	33870 MW	38190 TQ	USBLS	5/07
Transit and Intercity	West Palm Beach-Boca Raton-Boynton Beach PMSA, FL	Y	26540 FQ	35640 MW	45600 TQ	USBLS	5/07
Transit and Intercity	Georgia	Y	20310 FQ	29770 MW	36260 TQ	USBLS	5/07
Transit and Intercity	Athens-Clarke County MSA, GA	Y	23410 FQ	27550 MW	31090 TQ	USBLS	5/07
Transit and Intercity	Atlanta-Sandy Springs-Marietta MSA, GA	Y	24120 FQ	34140 MW	37810 TQ	USBLS	5/07
Transit and Intercity	Hawaii	Y	25380 FQ	38110 MW	55370 TQ	USBLS	5/07
Transit and Intercity	Honolulu MSA, HI	Y	26590 FQ	44330 MW	57380 TQ	USBLS	5/07
Transit and Intercity	Idaho	Y	19580 FQ	23510 MW	31800 TQ	USBLS	5/07
Transit and Intercity	Boise City-Nampa MSA, ID	Y	23950 FQ	27870 MW	32530 TQ	USBLS	5/07
Transit and Intercity	Illinois	Y	32580 FQ	45820 MW	57880 TQ	USBLS	5/07
Transit and Intercity	Champaign-Urbana MSA, IL	Y	24110 FQ	40160 MW	52160 TQ	USBLS	5/07
Transit and Intercity	Rockford MSA, IL	Y	21730 FQ	23650 MW	26160 TQ	USBLS	5/07
Transit and Intercity	Indiana	Y	20520 FQ	28600 MW	35420 TQ	USBLS	5/07
Transit and Intercity	Gary PMSA, IN	Y	13780 FQ	23790 MW	30850 TQ	USBLS	5/07
Transit and Intercity	Indianapolis-Carmel MSA, IN	Y	23880 FQ	33960 MW	38050 TQ	USBLS	5/07
Transit and Intercity	South Bend-Mishawaka MSA, IN-MI	Y	22220 FQ	27470 MW	36950 TQ	USBLS	5/07
Transit and Intercity	Iowa	Y	18070 FQ	22990 MW	30190 TQ	USBLS	5/07

AE	Average entry wage	AW	Average wage paid	FQ	First quartile wage	LO	Lowest wage paid
AER	Average entry range	AWR	Average wage range	H	Hourly	LR	Low end range
AEX	Average experienced wage	AXR	Average experienced range	HI	Highest wage paid	M	Monthly
ATC	Average total compensation	D	Daily	HR	High end range	MCC	Median cash compensation

MTC	Median total compensation	TCC	Total cash compensation
MW	Median wage paid	TQ	Third quartile wage
MWR	Median wage range	W	Weekly
S	See annotated source	Y	Yearly

Occupation/Type/Industry	Location	Per	Low	Mid	High	Source	Date
Bus Driver							
Transit and Intercity	Des Moines-West Des Moines MSA, IA	Y	22210 FQ	29180 MW	34040 TQ	USBLS	5/07
Transit and Intercity	Kansas	Y	17030 FQ	20380 MW	25400 TQ	USBLS	5/07
Transit and Intercity	Kentucky	Y	21374 FQ	25510 MW	36086 TQ	KYBLS	2008
Transit and Intercity	Louisiana	H	8.84 FQ	13.34 MW	17.28 TQ	LABLS	1/08-3/08
Transit and Intercity	New Orleans-Metairie-Kenner MSA, LA	Y	17760 FQ	28790 MW	36160 TQ	USBLS	5/07
Transit and Intercity	Maine	Y	22870 FQ	26990 MW	31830 TQ	USBLS	5/07
Transit and Intercity	Bangor MSA, ME	Y	26220 FQ	28100 MW	30210 TQ	USBLS	5/07
Transit and Intercity	Portland-South Portland-Biddeford MSA, ME	Y	25160 FQ	29660 MW	45260 TQ	USBLS	5/07
Transit and Intercity	Maryland	Y		33575 MW		MDBLS	3/08
Transit and Intercity	Bethesda-Gaithersburg-Frederick PMSA, MD	Y	33790 FQ	37150 MW	45450 TQ	USBLS	5/07
Transit and Intercity	Massachusetts	Y	26860 FQ	31600 MW	38110 TQ	USBLS	5/07
Transit and Intercity	Boston-Cambridge-Quincy NECTA, MA	Y	26620 FQ	30600 MW	36220 TQ	USBLS	5/07
Transit and Intercity	Michigan	Y	24150 FQ	28990 MW	34360 TQ	USBLS	5/07
Transit and Intercity	Detroit-Warren-Livonia MSA, MI	Y	24580 FQ	30880 MW	35430 TQ	USBLS	5/07
Transit and Intercity	Grand Rapids-Wyoming MSA, MI	Y	19210 FQ	23240 MW	26980 TQ	USBLS	5/07
Transit and Intercity	Warren-Troy-Farmington Hills PMSA, MI	Y	23330 FQ	28730 MW	35100 TQ	USBLS	5/07
Transit and Intercity	Minnesota	Y	24354 FQ	32843 MW	44797 TQ	MNBLS	10/08-12/08
Transit and Intercity	Rochester MSA, MN	Y	21545 FQ	23624 MW	28394 TQ	MNBLS	10/08-12/08
Transit and Intercity	Mississippi	Y	15190 FQ	19600 MW	24750 TQ	USBLS	5/07
Transit and Intercity	Jackson MSA, MS	Y	17970 FQ	25080 MW	30700 TQ	USBLS	5/07
Transit and Intercity	Missouri	Y	22850 FQ	30250 MW	40760 TQ	USBLS	5/07
Transit and Intercity	Kansas City MSA, MO-KS	Y	20730 FQ	27080 MW	33740 TQ	USBLS	5/07
Transit and Intercity	St. Louis MSA, MO-IL	Y	21980 FQ	29690 MW	42360 TQ	USBLS	5/07
Transit and Intercity	Montana	Y	23120 FQ	26290 MW	30750 TQ	USBLS	5/07
Transit and Intercity	Nebraska	Y	20560 FQ	24580 MW	36990 TQ	USBLS	5/07
Transit and Intercity	Omaha-Council Bluffs MSA, NE-IA	Y	20720 FQ	28080 MW	41430 TQ	USBLS	5/07
Transit and Intercity	Nevada	H	12.53 FQ	15.10 MW	17.52 TQ	NVBLS	5/08
Transit and Intercity	Las Vegas-Paradise MSA, NV	H	12.58 FQ	15.04 MW	17.73 TQ	NVBLS	5/08
Transit and Intercity	New Hampshire	H	12.81 AE	14.78 MW	16.07 AEX	NHBLS	6/08
Transit and Intercity	New Jersey	Y	26150 FQ	30320 MW	37260 TQ	USBLS	5/07
Transit and Intercity	Camden PMSA, NJ	Y	28560 FQ	34600 MW	38810 TQ	USBLS	5/07
Transit and Intercity	Edison PMSA, NJ	Y	26120 FQ	29560 MW	35200 TQ	USBLS	5/07
Transit and Intercity	Newark-Union PMSA, NJ-PA	Y	28290 FQ	34860 MW	40210 TQ	USBLS	5/07
Transit and Intercity	New Mexico	Y	22070 FQ	25350 MW	30190 TQ	USBLS	5/07
Transit and Intercity	New York	Y	36990 FQ	45350 MW	52780 TQ	USBLS	5/07
Transit and Intercity	Albany-Schenectady-Troy MSA, NY	Y	23250 FQ	27040 MW	31400 TQ	USBLS	5/07
Transit and Intercity	Buffalo-Niagara Falls MSA, NY	Y	20190 FQ	22640 MW	27650 TQ	USBLS	5/07
Transit and Intercity	Nassau-Suffolk PMSA, NY	Y	25550 FQ	31000 MW	37270 TQ	USBLS	5/07
Transit and Intercity	New York-Northern New Jersey-Long Island MSA, NY-NJ-PA	Y	34900 FQ	44060 MW	52140 TQ	USBLS	5/07
Transit and Intercity	North Carolina	Y	19660 FQ	25900 MW	33790 TQ	USBLS	5/07
Transit and Intercity	Charlotte-Gastonia-Concord MSA, NC-SC	Y	27590 FQ	34210 MW	44930 TQ	USBLS	5/07
Transit and Intercity	Raleigh-Cary MSA, NC	Y	19030 FQ	22440 MW	25570 TQ	USBLS	5/07
Transit and Intercity	North Dakota	Y	20360 FQ	23680 MW	29230 TQ	USBLS	5/07
Transit and Intercity	Ohio	Y	29340 FQ	39020 MW	46270 TQ	USBLS	5/07
Transit and Intercity	Cincinnati-Middletown MSA, OH-KY-IN	Y	29270 FQ	37890 MW	45550 TQ	USBLS	5/07
Transit and Intercity	Cleveland-Elyria-Mentor MSA, OH	Y	28440 FQ	38800 MW	46790 TQ	USBLS	5/07
Transit and Intercity	Columbus MSA, OH	Y	29850 FQ	40190 MW	46660 TQ	USBLS	5/07
Transit and Intercity	Dayton MSA, OH	Y	29300 FQ	42250 MW	46890 TQ	USBLS	5/07
Transit and Intercity	Oklahoma	Y	16330 FQ	19260 MW	25840 TQ	USBLS	5/07
Transit and Intercity	Oklahoma City MSA, OK	Y	17640 FQ	22240 MW	34440 TQ	USBLS	5/07
Transit and Intercity	Tulsa MSA, OK	Y	19550 FQ	21920 MW	25310 TQ	USBLS	5/07
Transit and Intercity	Pennsylvania	Y	23270 FQ	28700 MW	37890 TQ	USBLS	5/07
Transit and Intercity	Allentown-Bethlehem-Easton MSA, PA-NJ	Y	25720 FQ	29550 MW	36310 TQ	USBLS	5/07

AE	Average entry wage	AW	Average wage paid	FQ	First quartile wage
AER	Average entry range	AWR	Average wage range	H	Hourly
AEX	Average experienced wage	AXR	Average experienced range	HI	Highest wage paid
ATC	Average total compensation	D	Daily	HR	High end range

LO	Lowest wage paid	MTC	Median total compensation
LR	Low end range	MW	Median wage paid
M	Monthly	MWR	Median wage range
MCC	Median cash compensation	S	See annotated source

TCC	Total cash compensation		
TQ	Third quartile wage		
W	Weekly		
Y	Yearly		

Occupation/Type/Industry	Location	Per	Low	Mid	High	Source	Date
Bus Driver							
Transit and Intercity	Philadelphia-Camden-Wilmington MSA, PA-NJ-DE-MD	Y	21150 FQ	26280 MW	33440 TQ	USBLS	5/07
Transit and Intercity	Pittsburgh MSA, PA	Y	26760 FQ	36380 MW	46030 TQ	USBLS	5/07
Transit and Intercity	Rhode Island	Y	27140 FQ	33820 MW	46340 TQ	USBLS	5/07
Transit and Intercity	Providence-Fall River-Warwick MSA, RI-MA	Y	28470 FQ	38210 MW	45270 TQ	USBLS	5/07
Transit and Intercity	South Carolina	Y	16140 FQ	18800 MW	24630 TQ	USBLS	5/07
Transit and Intercity	Charleston-North Charleston MSA, SC	Y	16470 FQ	19170 MW	29180 TQ	USBLS	5/07
Transit and Intercity	Columbia MSA, SC	Y	17720 FQ	19930 MW	26780 TQ	USBLS	5/07
Transit and Intercity	South Dakota	Y	20416 FQ	23562 MW	28334 TQ	SDBLS	7/08-9/08
Transit and Intercity	Sioux Falls MSA, SD	Y	24793 FQ	29015 MW	33732 TQ	SDBLS	7/08-9/08
Transit and Intercity	Tennessee	Y	14720 FQ	19130 MW	27110 TQ	USBLS	5/07
Transit and Intercity	Nashville-Davidson-Murfreesboro MSA, TN	Y	18520 FQ	26070 MW	34840 TQ	USBLS	5/07
Transit and Intercity	Texas	Y	24660 FQ	33300 MW	38220 TQ	USBLS	5/07
Transit and Intercity	Austin-Round Rock MSA, TX	Y	27340 FQ	35480 MW	39940 TQ	USBLS	5/07
Transit and Intercity	Dallas-Fort Worth-Arlington MSA, TX	Y	22680 FQ	33160 MW	37600 TQ	USBLS	5/07
Transit and Intercity	El Paso MSA, TX	Y	22990 FQ	29020 MW	33690 TQ	USBLS	5/07
Transit and Intercity	Houston-Sugar Land-Baytown MSA, TX	Y	27700 FQ	34540 MW	38620 TQ	USBLS	5/07
Transit and Intercity	Utah	Y	25650 FQ	32290 MW	35710 TQ	USBLS	5/07
Transit and Intercity	Provo-Orem MSA, UT	Y	24510 FQ	33710 MW	37700 TQ	USBLS	5/07
Transit and Intercity	Salt Lake City MSA, UT	Y	25640 FQ	31970 MW	35210 TQ	USBLS	5/07
Transit and Intercity	Vermont	Y	25330 FQ	27390 MW	29400 TQ	USBLS	5/07
Transit and Intercity	Burlington-South Burlington MSA, VT	Y	26240 FQ	28250 MW	30260 TQ	USBLS	5/07
Transit and Intercity	Virginia	Y	23960 FQ	29110 MW	35320 TQ	USBLS	5/07
Transit and Intercity	Richmond MSA, VA	Y	24930 FQ	34800 MW	38770 TQ	USBLS	5/07
Transit and Intercity	Virginia Beach-Norfolk-Newport News MSA, VA-NC	Y	22220 FQ	26890 MW	33900 TQ	USBLS	5/07
Transit and Intercity	Washington	H	15.21 FQ	19.44 MW	22.89 TQ	WABLS	3/08
Transit and Intercity	Olympia MSA, WA	Y	32560 FQ	37410 MW	42370 TQ	USBLS	5/07
Transit and Intercity	Seattle-Tacoma-Bellevue MSA, WA	Y	29290 FQ	41950 MW	52060 TQ	USBLS	5/07
Transit and Intercity	West Virginia	Y	21023 FQ	24534 MW	30363 TQ	WVBLS	7/08-9/08
Transit and Intercity	Wisconsin	Y	26560 FQ	38530 MW	44240 TQ	USBLS	5/07
Transit and Intercity	Milwaukee-Waukesha-West Allis MSA, WI	Y	36270 FQ	41940 MW	45660 TQ	USBLS	5/07
Transit and Intercity	Wyoming	Y	18052 FQ	22728 MW	31545 TQ	WYBLS	9/08
Transit and Intercity	Cheyenne MSA, WY	Y	18479 FQ	20537 MW	23333 TQ	WYBLS	9/08
Transit and Intercity	Puerto Rico	Y	18200 FQ	22460 MW	25790 TQ	USBLS	5/07
Transit and Intercity	San Juan-Caguas-Guaynabo MSA, PR	Y	20270 FQ	23010 MW	26390 TQ	USBLS	5/07
Transit and Intercity	Virgin Islands	Y	21900 FQ	32810 MW	36720 TQ	USBLS	5/07
Transit and Intercity	Guam	Y	13440 FQ	15720 MW	19060 TQ	USBLS	5/07
Bus Mechanic	Southfield, MI	H	21.84 LO		29.74 HI	DNEWS01	2008
Busboy	United States	Y		16320 AW		RIMAG	2007
Business Analyst							
State Government	Ohio	H	24.90 LO		34.83 HI	ODAS	2008
Business Intelligence Analyst	United States	Y	78250 LO		108250 HI	FREEP08	2009
Business License Specialist							
Municipal Government	Gresham, OR	Y	34896 LO		44568 HI	GOSS	1/1/09
Business Teacher							
Postsecondary	Alabama	Y	48450 FQ	72240 MW	96440 TQ	USBLS	5/07
Postsecondary	Birmingham-Hoover MSA, AL	Y	58680 FQ	80050 MW	102120 TQ	USBLS	5/07
Postsecondary	Alaska	Y	45810 FQ	49940 MW	55430 TQ	USBLS	5/07
Postsecondary	Anchorage MSA, AK	Y	45680 FQ	49600 MW	53540 TQ	USBLS	5/07
Postsecondary	Arizona	Y	46470 FQ	67860 MW	108340 TQ	USBLS	5/07
Postsecondary	Phoenix-Mesa-Scottsdale MSA, AZ	Y	53040 FQ	71840 MW	113180 TQ	USBLS	5/07
Postsecondary	Tucson MSA, AZ	Y	46590 FQ	101910 MW	141610 TQ	USBLS	5/07
Postsecondary	Arkansas	Y	38670 FQ	55400 MW	76600 TQ	USBLS	5/07

AE Average entry wage	**AW** Average wage paid	**FQ** First quartile wage	**LO** Lowest wage paid	**MTC** Median total compensation	**TCC** Total cash compensation
AER Average entry range	**AWR** Average wage range	**H** Hourly	**LR** Low end range	**MW** Median wage paid	**TQ** Third quartile wage
AEX Average experienced wage	**AXR** Average experienced range	**HI** Highest wage paid	**M** Monthly	**MWR** Median wage range	**W** Weekly
ATC Average total compensation	**D** Daily	**HR** High end range	**MCC** Median cash compensation	**S** See annotated source	**Y** Yearly

Occupation/Type/Industry	Location	Per	Low	Mid	High	Source	Date
Business Teacher							
Postsecondary	Little Rock-North Little Rock MSA, AR	Y	31180 FQ	50650 MW	90400 TQ	USBLS	5/07
Postsecondary	California	Y		87586 AW		CABLS	1/08-3/08
Postsecondary	Los Angeles-Long Beach-Glendale PMSA, CA	Y		85514 AW		CABLS	1/08-3/08
Postsecondary	Oakland-Fremont-Hayward MSA, CA	Y		79874 AW		CABLS	1/08-3/08
Postsecondary	Riverside-San Bernardino-Ontario MSA, CA	Y		86201 AW		CABLS	1/08-3/08
Postsecondary	Sacramento-Arden Arcade-Roseville MSA, CA	Y		97851 AW		CABLS	1/08-3/08
Postsecondary	San Diego-Carlsbad-San Marcos MSA, CA	Y		87421 AW		CABLS	1/08-3/08
Postsecondary	San Francisco-San Mateo-Redwood PMSA, CA	Y		100435 AW		CABLS	1/08-3/08
Postsecondary	San Jose-Sunnyvale-Santa Clara MSA, CA	Y		85565 AW		CABLS	1/08-3/08
Postsecondary	Santa Ana-Anaheim-Irvine PMSA, CA	Y	52230 FQ	73170 MW	99630 TQ	USBLS	5/07
Postsecondary	Colorado	Y	46040 FQ	60080 MW	89510 TQ	USBLS	5/07
Postsecondary	Denver-Aurora MSA, CO	Y	46010 FQ	57080 MW	91670 TQ	USBLS	5/07
Postsecondary	Delaware	Y	58800 FQ	77220 MW	108760 TQ	USBLS	5/07
Postsecondary	Wilmington PMSA, DE-MD-NJ	Y	61730 FQ	86230 MW	117990 TQ	USBLS	5/07
Postsecondary	District of Columbia	Y	42260 FQ	67880 MW	92520 TQ	USBLS	5/07
Postsecondary	Washington-Arlington-Alexandria MSA, DC-VA-MD-WV	Y	50020 FQ	76020 MW	94790 TQ	USBLS	5/07
Postsecondary	Florida	Y	51130 FQ	72220 MW	95270 TQ	USBLS	5/07
Postsecondary	Fort Lauderdale-Pompano Beach-Deerfield Beach PMSA, FL	Y	54280 FQ	73580 MW	91960 TQ	USBLS	5/07
Postsecondary	Jacksonville MSA, FL	Y	46650 FQ	75750 MW	97590 TQ	USBLS	5/07
Postsecondary	Miami-Fort Lauderdale-Miami Beach MSA, FL	Y	57610 FQ	71910 MW	84150 TQ	USBLS	5/07
Postsecondary	Orlando-Kissimmee MSA, FL	Y	45590 FQ	70360 MW	103670 TQ	USBLS	5/07
Postsecondary	West Palm Beach-Boca Raton-Boynton Beach PMSA, FL	Y	51160 FQ	80980 MW	112160 TQ	USBLS	5/07
Postsecondary	Georgia	Y	44510 FQ	66390 MW	106110 TQ	USBLS	5/07
Postsecondary	Atlanta-Sandy Springs-Marietta MSA, GA	Y	48880 FQ	75460 MW	121740 TQ	USBLS	5/07
Postsecondary	Hawaii	Y	54730 FQ	81260 MW	113780 TQ	USBLS	5/07
Postsecondary	Honolulu MSA, HI	Y	59860 FQ	80470 MW	118070 TQ	USBLS	5/07
Postsecondary	Boise City-Nampa MSA, ID	Y	41480 FQ	54330 MW	65920 TQ	USBLS	5/07
Postsecondary	Illinois	Y	42800 FQ	60210 MW	88100 TQ	USBLS	5/07
Postsecondary	Chicago-Naperville-Joliet MSA, IL-IN-WI	Y	43740 FQ	61510 MW	90560 TQ	USBLS	5/07
Postsecondary	Indiana	Y	42650 FQ	58620 MW	92500 TQ	USBLS	5/07
Postsecondary	Gary PMSA, IN	Y	50060 FQ	68740 MW	89490 TQ	USBLS	5/07
Postsecondary	Indianapolis-Carmel MSA, IN	Y	38040 FQ	46950 MW	79630 TQ	USBLS	5/07
Postsecondary	Terre Haute MSA, IN	Y	49170 FQ	56780 MW	82440 TQ	USBLS	5/07
Postsecondary	Iowa	Y	40700 FQ	58180 MW	90140 TQ	USBLS	5/07
Postsecondary	Cedar Rapids MSA, IA	Y	43740 FQ	51000 MW	61220 TQ	USBLS	5/07
Postsecondary	Des Moines-West Des Moines MSA, IA	Y	36690 FQ	51120 MW	78920 TQ	USBLS	5/07
Postsecondary	Kansas	Y	36470 FQ	58530 MW	84910 TQ	USBLS	5/07
Postsecondary	Wichita MSA, KS	Y	44270 FQ	64530 MW	89950 TQ	USBLS	5/07
Postsecondary	Kentucky	Y	44759 FQ	63953 MW	95618 TQ	KYBLS	2008
Postsecondary	Louisville-Jefferson County MSA, KY-IN	Y	49320 FQ	75550 MW	106090 TQ	USBLS	5/07
Postsecondary	Louisiana	Y		49802 AW		LABLS	1/08-3/08
Postsecondary	Baton Rouge MSA, LA	Y	38910 FQ	45100 MW	51650 TQ	USBLS	5/07
Postsecondary	New Orleans-Metairie-Kenner MSA, LA	Y	32430 FQ	39160 MW	51340 TQ	USBLS	5/07
Postsecondary	Maine	Y	45400 FQ	56500 MW	82300 TQ	USBLS	5/07
Postsecondary	Portland-South Portland-Biddeford MSA, ME	Y	46510 FQ	58430 MW	88460 TQ	USBLS	5/07
Postsecondary	Maryland	Y		83225 MW		MDBLS	3/08
Postsecondary	Baltimore-Towson MSA, MD	Y	54740 FQ	74170 MW	95310 TQ	USBLS	5/07
Postsecondary	Bethesda-Gaithersburg-Frederick PMSA, MD	Y	59340 FQ	92550 MW		USBLS	5/07

AE	Average entry wage	AW	Average wage paid	FQ	First quartile wage	LO	Lowest wage paid	MTC	Median total compensation	TCC	Total cash compensation
AER	Average entry range	AWR	Average wage range	H	Hourly	LR	Low end range	MW	Median wage paid	TQ	Third quartile wage
AEX	Average experienced wage	AXR	Average experienced range	HI	Highest wage paid	M	Monthly	MWR	Median wage range	W	Weekly
ATC	Average total compensation	D	Daily	HR	High end range	MCC	Median cash compensation	S	See annotated source	Y	Yearly

Business Teacher

Occupation/Type/Industry	Location	Per	Low	Mid	High	Source	Date
Postsecondary	Massachusetts	Y	65340 FQ	89250 MW	130390 TQ	USBLS	5/07
Postsecondary	Boston-Cambridge-Quincy NECTA, MA	Y	71280 FQ	94950 MW	130720 TQ	USBLS	5/07
Postsecondary	Worcester MSA, MA-CT	Y	79000 FQ	135680 MW		USBLS	5/07
Postsecondary	Michigan	Y	34840 FQ	69920 MW	93100 TQ	USBLS	5/07
Postsecondary	Detroit-Warren-Livonia MSA, MI	Y	27690 FQ	34490 MW	70830 TQ	USBLS	5/07
Postsecondary	Warren-Troy-Farmington Hills PMSA, MI	Y	29510 FQ	36360 MW	66820 TQ	USBLS	5/07
Postsecondary	Minnesota	Y	46441 FQ	57479 MW	70599 TQ	MNBLS	10/08-12/08
Postsecondary	Duluth-Superior MSA, MN-WI	Y	43114 FQ	58170 MW	80590 TQ	MNBLS	10/08-12/08
Postsecondary	Minneapolis-Saint Paul MSA, MN-WI	Y	47718 FQ	58504 MW	71384 TQ	MNBLS	10/08-12/08
Postsecondary	Mississippi	Y	44660 FQ	57850 MW	78510 TQ	USBLS	5/07
Postsecondary	Gulfport-Biloxi MSA, MS	Y	41270 FQ	47660 MW	58630 TQ	USBLS	5/07
Postsecondary	Jackson MSA, MS	Y	40840 FQ	54250 MW	66090 TQ	USBLS	5/07
Postsecondary	Missouri	Y	40650 FQ	64790 MW	97040 TQ	USBLS	5/07
Postsecondary	Kansas City MSA, MO-KS	Y	39300 FQ	56760 MW	86690 TQ	USBLS	5/07
Postsecondary	St. Louis MSA, MO-IL	Y	40940 FQ	63730 MW	97460 TQ	USBLS	5/07
Postsecondary	Montana	Y	39370 FQ	47650 MW	58800 TQ	USBLS	5/07
Postsecondary	Nebraska	Y	39840 FQ	51410 MW	74710 TQ	USBLS	5/07
Postsecondary	Omaha-Council Bluffs MSA, NE-IA	Y	37140 FQ	51030 MW	78250 TQ	USBLS	5/07
Postsecondary	Nevada	Y	36864 FQ	49703 MW	101829 TQ	NVBLS	5/08
Postsecondary	Reno-Sparks MSA, NV	Y	40552 FQ	49284 MW	114901 TQ	NVBLS	5/08
Postsecondary	New Hampshire	Y	39760 AE	65644 MW	102134 AEX	NHBLS	6/08
Postsecondary	New Jersey	Y	51100 FQ	72070 MW	93590 TQ	USBLS	5/07
Postsecondary	Edison PMSA, NJ	Y	59820 FQ	77400 MW	97240 TQ	USBLS	5/07
Postsecondary	Newark-Union PMSA, NJ-PA	Y	51190 FQ	74570 MW	94380 TQ	USBLS	5/07
Postsecondary	New Mexico	Y	46770 FQ	62850 MW	79180 TQ	USBLS	5/07
Postsecondary	Albuquerque MSA, NM	Y	39850 FQ	54810 MW	86490 TQ	USBLS	5/07
Postsecondary	New York	Y	48780 FQ	69270 MW	95010 TQ	USBLS	5/07
Postsecondary	Albany-Schenectady-Troy MSA, NY	Y	59060 FQ	89000 MW	114400 TQ	USBLS	5/07
Postsecondary	Buffalo-Niagara Falls MSA, NY	Y	38230 FQ	60130 MW	87800 TQ	USBLS	5/07
Postsecondary	Nassau-Suffolk PMSA, NY	Y	45490 FQ	62580 MW	95010 TQ	USBLS	5/07
Postsecondary	New York-Northern New Jersey-Long Island MSA, NY-NJ-PA	Y	50080 FQ	70330 MW	94720 TQ	USBLS	5/07
Postsecondary	Utica-Rome MSA, NY	Y	40810 FQ	55500 MW	76810 TQ	USBLS	5/07
Postsecondary	North Carolina	Y	45470 FQ	57530 MW	82160 TQ	USBLS	5/07
Postsecondary	Charlotte-Gastonia-Concord MSA, NC-SC	Y	41590 FQ	59740 MW	89150 TQ	USBLS	5/07
Postsecondary	Raleigh-Cary MSA, NC	Y	41810 FQ	51340 MW	87890 TQ	USBLS	5/07
Postsecondary	North Dakota	Y	41870 FQ	61840 MW	89760 TQ	USBLS	5/07
Postsecondary	Fargo MSA, ND-MN	Y	50000 FQ	62300 MW	77760 TQ	USBLS	5/07
Postsecondary	Ohio	Y	36020 FQ	57170 MW	87250 TQ	USBLS	5/07
Postsecondary	Cincinnati-Middletown MSA, OH-KY-IN	Y	37660 FQ	59850 MW	91710 TQ	USBLS	5/07
Postsecondary	Cleveland-Elyria-Mentor MSA, OH	Y	36860 FQ	58880 MW	86570 TQ	USBLS	5/07
Postsecondary	Columbus MSA, OH	Y	29630 FQ	67030 MW	100420 TQ	USBLS	5/07
Postsecondary	Dayton MSA, OH	Y	33800 FQ	51280 MW	76830 TQ	USBLS	5/07
Postsecondary	Oklahoma	Y	33490 FQ	44670 MW	62730 TQ	USBLS	5/07
Postsecondary	Oklahoma City MSA, OK	Y	33160 FQ	45060 MW	64770 TQ	USBLS	5/07
Postsecondary	Tulsa MSA, OK	Y	32470 FQ	43650 MW	58080 TQ	USBLS	5/07
Postsecondary	Portland-Vancouver-Beaverton MSA, OR-WA	Y	51360 FQ	85060 MW	108870 TQ	USBLS	5/07
Postsecondary	Pennsylvania	Y	44000 FQ	66890 MW	92950 TQ	USBLS	5/07
Postsecondary	Allentown-Bethlehem-Easton MSA, PA-NJ	Y	58160 FQ	82280 MW	119430 TQ	USBLS	5/07
Postsecondary	Erie MSA, PA	Y	47220 FQ	69100 MW	82350 TQ	USBLS	5/07
Postsecondary	Philadelphia-Camden-Wilmington MSA, PA-NJ-DE-MD	Y	44150 FQ	69290 MW	94330 TQ	USBLS	5/07
Postsecondary	Pittsburgh MSA, PA	Y	46050 FQ	67520 MW	102720 TQ	USBLS	5/07
Postsecondary	Rhode Island	Y	60890 FQ	87940 MW	107660 TQ	USBLS	5/07
Postsecondary	Providence-Fall River-Warwick MSA, RI-MA	Y	59320 FQ	86830 MW	106880 TQ	USBLS	5/07
Postsecondary	South Carolina	Y	50760 FQ	61000 MW	82600 TQ	USBLS	5/07

AE	Average entry wage	AW	Average wage paid	FQ	First quartile wage	LO	Lowest wage paid	MTC	Median total compensation	TCC	Total cash compensation
AER	Average entry range	AWR	Average wage range	H	Hourly	LR	Low end range	MW	Median wage paid	TQ	Third quartile wage
AEX	Average experienced wage	AXR	Average experienced range	HI	Highest wage paid	M	Monthly	MWR	Median wage range	W	Weekly
ATC	Average total compensation	D	Daily	HR	High end range	MCC	Median cash compensation	S	See annotated source	Y	Yearly

Occupation/Type/Industry	Location	Per	Low	Mid	High	Source	Date
Business Teacher							
Postsecondary	Charleston-North Charleston MSA, SC	Y	55670 FQ	72140 MW	85760 TQ	USBLS	5/07
Postsecondary	Columbia MSA, SC	Y	55640 FQ	63050 MW	100720 TQ	USBLS	5/07
Postsecondary	South Dakota	Y	45940 FQ	57392 MW	76101 TQ	SDBLS	7/08-9/08
Postsecondary	Sioux Falls MSA, SD	Y	43588 FQ	51110 MW	61242 TQ	SDBLS	7/08-9/08
Postsecondary	Tennessee	Y	42410 FQ	55660 MW	83220 TQ	USBLS	5/07
Postsecondary	Memphis MSA, TN-MS-AR	Y	43130 FQ	55210 MW	95360 TQ	USBLS	5/07
Postsecondary	Nashville-Davidson-Murfreesboro MSA, TN	Y	41660 FQ	55190 MW	78500 TQ	USBLS	5/07
Postsecondary	Texas	Y	36990 FQ	63580 MW	93400 TQ	USBLS	5/07
Postsecondary	Austin-Round Rock MSA, TX	Y	38310 FQ	79610 MW	128710 TQ	USBLS	5/07
Postsecondary	Dallas-Fort Worth-Arlington MSA, TX	Y	33170 FQ	60650 MW	95000 TQ	USBLS	5/07
Postsecondary	El Paso MSA, TX	Y	46380 FQ	64020 MW	93750 TQ	USBLS	5/07
Postsecondary	Houston-Sugar Land-Baytown MSA, TX	Y	52110 FQ	76900 MW	133900 TQ	USBLS	5/07
Postsecondary	San Antonio MSA, TX	Y	36770 FQ	65860 MW	101190 TQ	USBLS	5/07
Postsecondary	Utah	Y	49580 FQ	64450 MW	93820 TQ	USBLS	5/07
Postsecondary	Salt Lake City MSA, UT	Y	47850 FQ	59590 MW	100550 TQ	USBLS	5/07
Postsecondary	Vermont	Y	44380 FQ	56810 MW	72440 TQ	USBLS	5/07
Postsecondary	Burlington-South Burlington MSA, VT	Y	49920 FQ	63070 MW	80610 TQ	USBLS	5/07
Postsecondary	Virginia	Y	44850 FQ	71850 MW	94810 TQ	USBLS	5/07
Postsecondary	Richmond MSA, VA	Y	47510 FQ	77180 MW	111690 TQ	USBLS	5/07
Postsecondary	Virginia Beach-Norfolk-Newport News MSA, VA-NC	Y	49320 FQ	81290 MW	120240 TQ	USBLS	5/07
Postsecondary	Washington	Y		74873 AW		WABLS	3/08
Postsecondary	Seattle-Tacoma-Bellevue MSA, WA	Y	43520 FQ	58590 MW	93440 TQ	USBLS	5/07
Postsecondary	West Virginia	Y	44337 FQ	61982 MW	91163 TQ	WVBLS	7/08-9/08
Postsecondary	Wisconsin	Y	46190 FQ	67300 MW	87850 TQ	USBLS	5/07
Postsecondary	Milwaukee-Waukesha-West Allis MSA, WI	Y	43130 FQ	63800 MW	89280 TQ	USBLS	5/07
Postsecondary	Wyoming	Y	46653 FQ	65350 MW	90888 TQ	WYBLS	9/08
Postsecondary	Puerto Rico	Y	28180 FQ	43140 MW	62950 TQ	USBLS	5/07
Postsecondary	San Juan-Caguas-Guaynabo MSA, PR	Y	28280 FQ	44640 MW	64110 TQ	USBLS	5/07
Postsecondary	Virgin Islands	Y	40800 FQ	53580 MW	71300 TQ	USBLS	5/07
Business Transformation Analyst							
State Government	Ohio	H	23.04 LO		30.13 HI	ODAS	2008
Butcher and Meat Cutter	Alabama	Y	20770 FQ	24500 MW	29420 TQ	USBLS	5/07
	Birmingham-Hoover MSA, AL	Y	21490 FQ	25510 MW	29850 TQ	USBLS	5/07
	Alaska	Y	32360 FQ	39890 MW	46280 TQ	USBLS	5/07
	Anchorage MSA, AK	Y	34060 FQ	40710 MW	46000 TQ	USBLS	5/07
	Fairbanks MSA, AK	Y	28940 FQ	42240 MW	49860 TQ	USBLS	5/07
	Arizona	Y	25530 FQ	33810 MW	42480 TQ	USBLS	5/07
	Phoenix-Mesa-Scottsdale MSA, AZ	Y	25970 FQ	34330 MW	42710 TQ	USBLS	5/07
	Tucson MSA, AZ	Y	27140 FQ	33770 MW	42420 TQ	USBLS	5/07
	Arkansas	Y	19850 FQ	22980 MW	26840 TQ	USBLS	5/07
	Jonesboro MSA, AR	Y	17260 FQ	20580 MW	26140 TQ	USBLS	5/07
	Little Rock-North Little Rock MSA, AR	Y	21520 FQ	27110 MW	32540 TQ	USBLS	5/07
	California	H	9.98 FQ	13.62 MW	19.04 TQ	CABLS	1/08-3/08
	Bakersfield MSA, CA	H	9.23 FQ	13.31 MW	18.34 TQ	CABLS	1/08-3/08
	Los Angeles-Long Beach-Glendale PMSA, CA	H	9.57 FQ	11.77 MW	14.89 TQ	CABLS	1/08-3/08
	Oakland-Fremont-Hayward MSA, CA	H	13.16 FQ	17.49 MW	21.01 TQ	CABLS	1/08-3/08
	Riverside-San Bernardino-Ontario MSA, CA	H	9.44 FQ	12.86 MW	17.05 TQ	CABLS	1/08-3/08
	Sacramento-Arden Arcade-Roseville MSA, CA	H	15.74 FQ	19.88 MW	22.31 TQ	CABLS	1/08-3/08
	San Diego-Carlsbad-San Marcos MSA, CA	H	10.23 FQ	13.85 MW	19.19 TQ	CABLS	1/08-3/08
	San Francisco-San Mateo-Redwood PMSA, CA	H	11.32 FQ	16.67 MW	21.93 TQ	CABLS	1/08-3/08
	San Jose-Sunnyvale-Santa Clara MSA, CA	H	9.56 FQ	14.97 MW	21.10 TQ	CABLS	1/08-3/08

AE Average entry wage	**AW** Average wage paid	**FQ** First quartile wage	**LO** Lowest wage paid	**MTC** Median total compensation	**TCC** Total cash compensation
AER Average entry range	**AWR** Average wage range	**H** Hourly	**LR** Low end range	**MW** Median wage paid	**TQ** Third quartile wage
AEX Average experienced wage	**AXR** Average experienced range	**HI** Highest wage paid	**M** Monthly	**MWR** Median wage range	**W** Weekly
ATC Average total compensation	**D** Daily	**HR** High end range	**MCC** Median cash compensation	**S** See annotated source	**Y** Yearly

Occupation/Type/Industry	Location	Per	Low	Mid	High	Source	Date
Butcher and Meat Cutter	Santa Ana-Anaheim-Irvine						
	PMSA, CA	Y	17930 FQ	20360 MW	30680 TQ	USBLS	5/07
	Colorado	Y	22130 FQ	29130 MW	36540 TQ	USBLS	5/07
	Denver-Aurora MSA, CO	Y	22600 FQ	29180 MW	36590 TQ	USBLS	5/07
	Connecticut	H	12.32 AE	19.26 MW		CTBLS	1/08-3/08
	Bridgeport-Stamford-Norwalk						
	MSA, CT	Y	31740 FQ	41520 MW	49660 TQ	USBLS	5/07
	Hartford-West Hartford-East						
	Hartford MSA, CT	Y	32930 FQ	40770 MW	49080 TQ	USBLS	5/07
	Waterbury MSA, CT	Y	30620 FQ	38870 MW	49010 TQ	USBLS	5/07
	Delaware	Y	27820 FQ	33920 MW	39700 TQ	USBLS	5/07
	Wilmington PMSA, DE-MD-						
	NJ	Y	24340 FQ	34700 MW	40700 TQ	USBLS	5/07
	District of Columbia	Y	23200 FQ	27630 MW	37030 TQ	USBLS	5/07
	Washington-Arlington-						
	Alexandria MSA, DC-VA-						
	MD-WV	Y	28330 FQ	36500 MW	43160 TQ	USBLS	5/07
	Florida	Y	19850 FQ	26220 MW	31710 TQ	USBLS	5/07
	Fort Lauderdale-Pompano						
	Beach-Deerfield Beach						
	PMSA, FL	Y	18580 FQ	26160 MW	32250 TQ	USBLS	5/07
	Jacksonville MSA, FL	Y	21930 FQ	25990 MW	31440 TQ	USBLS	5/07
	Miami-Fort Lauderdale-Miami						
	Beach MSA, FL	Y	16880 FQ	23350 MW	30830 TQ	USBLS	5/07
	Orlando-Kissimmee MSA, FL	Y	19750 FQ	26540 MW	31440 TQ	USBLS	5/07
	Tampa-St. Petersburg-						
	Clearwater MSA, FL	Y	21370 FQ	26670 MW	32190 TQ	USBLS	5/07
	West Palm Beach-Boca Raton-						
	Boynton Beach PMSA, FL	Y	22850 FQ	27690 MW	32490 TQ	USBLS	5/07
	Georgia	Y	20090 FQ	24000 MW	29460 TQ	USBLS	5/07
	Atlanta-Sandy Springs-						
	Marietta MSA, GA	Y	20930 FQ	25860 MW	31150 TQ	USBLS	5/07
	Macon MSA, GA	Y	17600 FQ	22180 MW	30000 TQ	USBLS	5/07
	Hawaii	Y	32310 FQ	37380 MW	43080 TQ	USBLS	5/07
	Honolulu MSA, HI	Y	33210 FQ	37980 MW	44420 TQ	USBLS	5/07
	Idaho	Y	22850 FQ	28680 MW	34570 TQ	USBLS	5/07
	Boise City-Nampa MSA, ID	Y	21690 FQ	29050 MW	35110 TQ	USBLS	5/07
	Illinois	Y	19010 FQ	24590 MW	33870 TQ	USBLS	5/07
	Chicago-Naperville-Joliet						
	MSA, IL-IN-WI	Y	19000 FQ	24530 MW	34240 TQ	USBLS	5/07
	Indiana	Y	22380 FQ	26500 MW	30650 TQ	USBLS	5/07
	Gary PMSA, IN	Y	22940 FQ	30080 MW	36350 TQ	USBLS	5/07
	Indianapolis-Carmel MSA, IN	Y	24800 FQ	28680 MW	32540 TQ	USBLS	5/07
	Iowa	Y	18630 FQ	23030 MW	28450 TQ	USBLS	5/07
	Des Moines-West Des Moines						
	MSA, IA	Y	18790 FQ	23480 MW	29030 TQ	USBLS	5/07
	Sioux City MSA, IA-NE-SD	Y	20240 FQ	26790 MW	29620 TQ	USBLS	5/07
	Waterloo-Cedar Falls MSA, IA	Y	18780 FQ	26020 MW	30400 TQ	USBLS	5/07
	Kansas	Y	18440 FQ	24930 MW	35120 TQ	USBLS	5/07
	Wichita MSA, KS	Y	17110 FQ	19540 MW	32350 TQ	USBLS	5/07
	Kentucky	Y	20120 FQ	26575 MW	31792 TQ	KYBLS	2008
	Louisville-Jefferson County						
	MSA, KY-IN	Y	22430 FQ	28190 MW	33120 TQ	USBLS	5/07
	Louisiana	H	8.28 FQ	10.74 MW	13.33 TQ	LABLS	1/08-3/08
	Baton Rouge MSA, LA	Y	18020 FQ	22880 MW	28790 TQ	USBLS	5/07
	Lafayette MSA, LA	Y	20250 FQ	22880 MW	26140 TQ	USBLS	5/07
	New Orleans-Metairie-Kenner						
	MSA, LA	Y	16900 FQ	23800 MW	29140 TQ	USBLS	5/07
	Maine	Y	24410 FQ	31310 MW	37660 TQ	USBLS	5/07
	Portland-South Portland-						
	Biddeford MSA, ME	Y	30050 FQ	35530 MW	40570 TQ	USBLS	5/07
	Maryland	Y		35025 MW		MDBLS	3/08
	Baltimore-Towson MSA, MD	Y	26680 FQ	34130 MW	40570 TQ	USBLS	5/07
	Bethesda-Gaithersburg-						
	Frederick PMSA, MD	Y	32330 FQ	36810 MW	41440 TQ	USBLS	5/07
	Hagerstown-Martinsburg						
	MSA, MD-WV	Y	24650 FQ	31360 MW	37870 TQ	USBLS	5/07
	Massachusetts	Y	26510 FQ	36410 MW	48640 TQ	USBLS	5/07
	Barnstable Town MSA, MA	Y	42410 FQ	54070 MW	59260 TQ	USBLS	5/07
	Boston-Cambridge-Quincy						
	NECTA, MA	Y	26140 FQ	34490 MW	47690 TQ	USBLS	5/07
	Worcester MSA, MA-CT	Y	26780 FQ	37430 MW	46620 TQ	USBLS	5/07

AE	Average entry wage	AW	Average wage paid	FQ	First quartile wage
AER	Average entry range	AWR	Average wage range	H	Hourly
AEX	Average experienced wage	AXR	Average experienced range	HI	Highest wage paid
ATC	Average total compensation	D	Daily	HR	High end range

LO	Lowest wage paid	MTC	Median total compensation	TCC	Total cash compensation
LR	Low end range	MW	Median wage paid	TQ	Third quartile wage
M	Monthly	MWR	Median wage range	W	Weekly
MCC	Median cash compensation	S	See annotated source	Y	Yearly

Occupation/Type/Industry	Location	Per	Low	Mid	High	Source	Date
Butcher and Meat Cutter	Michigan	Y	21450 FQ	28460 MW	35790 TQ	USBLS	5/07
	Ann Arbor MSA, MI	Y	25740 FQ	33930 MW	39490 TQ	USBLS	5/07
	Detroit-Warren-Livonia MSA, MI	Y	21060 FQ	30890 MW	38010 TQ	USBLS	5/07
	Grand Rapids-Wyoming MSA, MI	Y	23960 FQ	28010 MW	32010 TQ	USBLS	5/07
	Warren-Troy-Farmington Hills PMSA, MI	Y	23410 FQ	31270 MW	37340 TQ	USBLS	5/07
	Minnesota	Y	26850 FQ	34790 MW	45904 TQ	MNBLS	10/08-12/08
	Duluth-Superior MSA, MN-WI	Y	31774 FQ	39196 MW	44442 TQ	MNBLS	10/08-12/08
	Minneapolis-Saint Paul MSA, MN-WI	Y	29006 FQ	40057 MW	50589 TQ	MNBLS	10/08-12/08
	Rochester MSA, MN	Y	25524 FQ	31897 MW	42025 TQ	MNBLS	10/08-12/08
	Mississippi	Y	19190 FQ	23610 MW	29040 TQ	USBLS	5/07
	Jackson MSA, MS	Y	19200 FQ	23230 MW	28260 TQ	USBLS	5/07
	Missouri	Y	19550 FQ	25250 MW	33100 TQ	USBLS	5/07
	Kansas City MSA, MO-KS	Y	21620 FQ	31510 MW	38170 TQ	USBLS	5/07
	St. Louis MSA, MO-IL	Y	21830 FQ	27910 MW	36500 TQ	USBLS	5/07
	Montana	Y	20050 FQ	25990 MW	29780 TQ	USBLS	5/07
	Billings MSA, MT	Y	19130 FQ	25580 MW	29870 TQ	USBLS	5/07
	Nebraska	Y	21220 FQ	24810 MW	30220 TQ	USBLS	5/07
	Omaha-Council Bluffs MSA, NE-IA	Y	21730 FQ	24260 MW	28260 TQ	USBLS	5/07
	Nevada	H	10.97 FQ	15.09 MW	20.13 TQ	NVBLS	5/08
	Las Vegas-Paradise MSA, NV	H	9.67 FQ	14.24 MW	19.28 TQ	NVBLS	5/08
	New Hampshire	H	12.38 AE	17.26 MW	19.26 AEX	NHBLS	6/08
	Manchester MSA, NH	Y	26520 FQ	32130 MW	38390 TQ	USBLS	5/07
	Nashua NECTA, NH-MA	Y	31120 FQ	36830 MW	41000 TQ	USBLS	5/07
	New Jersey	Y	29500 FQ	42750 MW	48410 TQ	USBLS	5/07
	Camden PMSA, NJ	Y	28380 FQ	39890 MW	45050 TQ	USBLS	5/07
	Edison PMSA, NJ	Y	37130 FQ	45120 MW	50940 TQ	USBLS	5/07
	Newark-Union PMSA, NJ-PA	Y	34910 FQ	44070 MW	49350 TQ	USBLS	5/07
	Trenton-Ewing MSA, NJ	Y	28880 FQ	38160 MW	44730 TQ	USBLS	5/07
	New Mexico	Y	20570 FQ	29290 MW	38530 TQ	USBLS	5/07
	Albuquerque MSA, NM	Y	21330 FQ	29500 MW	39300 TQ	USBLS	5/07
	New York	Y	25380 FQ	35150 MW	47760 TQ	USBLS	5/07
	Albany-Schenectady-Troy MSA, NY	Y	26700 FQ	31520 MW	36930 TQ	USBLS	5/07
	Buffalo-Niagara Falls MSA, NY	Y	25880 FQ	32830 MW	37990 TQ	USBLS	5/07
	Nassau-Suffolk PMSA, NY	Y	35260 FQ	50040 MW	57120 TQ	USBLS	5/07
	New York-Northern New Jersey-Long Island MSA, NY-NJ-PA	Y	26210 FQ	40970 MW	51100 TQ	USBLS	5/07
	North Carolina	Y	19140 FQ	25290 MW	30850 TQ	USBLS	5/07
	Charlotte-Gastonia-Concord MSA, NC-SC	Y	22790 FQ	27900 MW	32150 TQ	USBLS	5/07
	Raleigh-Cary MSA, NC	Y	25190 FQ	29970 MW	33980 TQ	USBLS	5/07
	North Dakota	Y	17570 FQ	21920 MW	27630 TQ	USBLS	5/07
	Fargo MSA, ND-MN	Y	21140 FQ	24130 MW	32620 TQ	USBLS	5/07
	Ohio	Y	21310 FQ	28870 MW	35290 TQ	USBLS	5/07
	Cincinnati-Middletown MSA, OH-KY-IN	Y	24740 FQ	29890 MW	36460 TQ	USBLS	5/07
	Cleveland-Elyria-Mentor MSA, OH	Y	21530 FQ	29180 MW	35470 TQ	USBLS	5/07
	Columbus MSA, OH	Y	27340 FQ	33680 MW	37410 TQ	USBLS	5/07
	Dayton MSA, OH	Y	25890 FQ	30860 MW	35310 TQ	USBLS	5/07
	Oklahoma	Y	18070 FQ	22130 MW	28130 TQ	USBLS	5/07
	Oklahoma City MSA, OK	Y	18860 FQ	24000 MW	30780 TQ	USBLS	5/07
	Tulsa MSA, OK	Y	18030 FQ	21540 MW	25840 TQ	USBLS	5/07
	Oregon	H	12.84 FQ	16.78 MW	18.96 MW	ORBLS	5/08
	Portland-Vancouver-Beaverton MSA, OR-WA	Y	25670 FQ	34860 MW	39600 TQ	USBLS	5/07
	Pennsylvania	Y	23270 FQ	28730 MW	35230 TQ	USBLS	5/07
	Allentown-Bethlehem-Easton MSA, PA-NJ	Y	24830 FQ	32830 MW	42280 TQ	USBLS	5/07
	Philadelphia-Camden-Wilmington MSA, PA-NJ-DE-MD	Y	25080 FQ	31470 MW	39230 TQ	USBLS	5/07
	Pittsburgh MSA, PA	Y	21940 FQ	26810 MW	30900 TQ	USBLS	5/07
	Rhode Island	Y	23470 FQ	34830 MW	43270 TQ	USBLS	5/07

AE	Average entry wage	AW	Average wage paid	FQ	First quartile wage	LO	Lowest wage paid	MTC Median total compensation	TCC Total cash compensation
AER	Average entry range	AWR	Average wage range	H	Hourly	LR	Low end range	MW Median wage paid	TQ Third quartile wage
AEX	Average experienced wage	AXR	Average experienced range	HI	Highest wage paid	M	Monthly	MWR Median wage range	W Weekly
ATC	Average total compensation	D	Daily	HR	High end range	MCC	Median cash compensation	S See annotated source	Y Yearly

Occupation/Type/Industry	Location	Per	Low	Mid	High	Source	Date
Butcher and Meat Cutter	Providence-Fall River-						
	Warwick MSA, RI-MA	Y	24570 FQ	35180 MW	43730 TQ	USBLS	5/07
	South Carolina	Y	20740 FQ	26050 MW	29700 TQ	USBLS	5/07
	Charleston-North Charleston						
	MSA, SC	Y	20020 FQ	26330 MW	31230 TQ	USBLS	5/07
	Columbia MSA, SC	Y	18590 FQ	24510 MW	29510 TQ	USBLS	5/07
	South Dakota	Y	22089 FQ	25315 MW	30622 TQ	SDBLS	7/08-9/08
	Sioux Falls MSA, SD	Y	22689 FQ	26544 MW	31995 TQ	SDBLS	7/08-9/08
	Tennessee	Y	21640 FQ	26720 MW	31280 TQ	USBLS	5/07
	Clarksville MSA, TN-KY	Y	20810 FQ	24440 MW	34910 TQ	USBLS	5/07
	Memphis MSA, TN-MS-AR	Y	20190 FQ	26840 MW	32410 TQ	USBLS	5/07
	Nashville-Davidson-						
	Murfreesboro MSA, TN	Y	21950 FQ	27430 MW	32400 TQ	USBLS	5/07
	Texas	Y	18430 FQ	24260 MW	30160 TQ	USBLS	5/07
	Austin-Round Rock MSA, TX	Y	22940 FQ	28400 MW	33560 TQ	USBLS	5/07
	Dallas-Fort Worth-Arlington						
	MSA, TX	Y	19430 FQ	24920 MW	30960 TQ	USBLS	5/07
	El Paso MSA, TX	Y	16700 FQ	18740 MW	25560 TQ	USBLS	5/07
	Houston-Sugar Land-Baytown						
	MSA, TX	Y	19460 FQ	26490 MW	32410 TQ	USBLS	5/07
	San Antonio MSA, TX	Y	17980 FQ	22170 MW	28020 TQ	USBLS	5/07
	Utah	Y	22940 FQ	29280 MW	34710 TQ	USBLS	5/07
	St. George MSA, UT	Y	21850 FQ	28430 MW	34430 TQ	USBLS	5/07
	Salt Lake City MSA, UT	Y	23720 FQ	29910 MW	34720 TQ	USBLS	5/07
	Vermont	Y	27570 FQ	33630 MW	38320 TQ	USBLS	5/07
	Burlington-South Burlington						
	MSA, VT	Y	28510 FQ	34070 MW	38470 TQ	USBLS	5/07
	Virginia	Y	23350 FQ	28690 MW	37760 TQ	USBLS	5/07
	Richmond MSA, VA	Y	23700 FQ	29580 MW	37020 TQ	USBLS	5/07
	Virginia Beach-Norfolk-						
	Newport News MSA, VA-NC	Y	26530 FQ	31060 MW	37850 TQ	USBLS	5/07
	Washington	H	12.96 FQ	19.48 MW	22.05 TQ	WABLS	3/08
	Seattle-Tacoma-Bellevue						
	MSA, WA	Y	39540 FQ	43670 MW	47250 TQ	USBLS	5/07
	West Virginia	Y	17685 FQ	26125 MW	32298 TQ	WVBLS	7/08-9/08
	Charleston MSA, WV	Y	14750 FQ	20460 MW	30420 TQ	USBLS	5/07
	Wisconsin	Y	23480 FQ	31960 MW	37700 TQ	USBLS	5/07
	Milwaukee-Waukesha-West						
	Allis MSA, WI	Y	26000 FQ	34600 MW	39280 TQ	USBLS	5/07
	Wyoming	Y	23162 FQ	28419 MW	32649 TQ	WYBLS	9/08
	Cheyenne MSA, WY	Y	19755 FQ	24993 MW	31587 TQ	WYBLS	9/08
	Puerto Rico	Y	12910 FQ	14780 MW	17820 TQ	USBLS	5/07
	San Juan-Caguas-Guaynabo						
	MSA, PR	Y	13260 FQ	15420 MW	18470 TQ	USBLS	5/07
	Virgin Islands	Y	22630 FQ	26370 MW	30500 TQ	USBLS	5/07
	Guam	Y	16710 FQ	20830 MW	28790 TQ	USBLS	5/07
Buyer							
Men's Clothing	United States	Y		110500 MW		247FASH	2009
Municipal Government	Cincinnati, OH	Y	45117 LO		60634 HI	COHSS	10/08
Women's Knits and Wovens	United States	Y		92000 MW		247FASH	2009
Cabinet Level Official							
Federal Government	United States	Y			191300 HI	CRS02	1/08
Cabinetmaker and Bench Carpenter	Alabama	Y	19880 FQ	22890 MW	28460 TQ	USBLS	5/07
	Birmingham-Hoover MSA, AL	Y	23050 FQ	29570 MW	35030 TQ	USBLS	5/07
	Alaska	Y	26330 FQ	31580 MW	38410 TQ	USBLS	5/07
	Anchorage MSA, AK	Y	26160 FQ	31820 MW	38660 TQ	USBLS	5/07
	Arizona	Y	21320 FQ	27340 MW	34340 TQ	USBLS	5/07
	Phoenix-Mesa-Scottsdale						
	MSA, AZ	Y	21030 FQ	27170 MW	34380 TQ	USBLS	5/07
	Tucson MSA, AZ	Y	25370 FQ	29910 MW	33880 TQ	USBLS	5/07
	Yuma MSA, AZ	Y	21710 FQ	25950 MW	33460 TQ	USBLS	5/07
	Arkansas	Y	18820 FQ	22940 MW	29210 TQ	USBLS	5/07
	Fayetteville-Springdale-Rogers						
	MSA, AR-MO	Y	19410 FQ	21940 MW	25190 TQ	USBLS	5/07
	Little Rock-North Little Rock						
	MSA, AR	Y	19900 FQ	26000 MW	33490 TQ	USBLS	5/07
	California	H	10.61 FQ	13.98 MW	18.21 TQ	CABLS	1/08-3/08
	Bakersfield MSA, CA	H	10.50 FQ	11.57 MW	12.93 TQ	CABLS	1/08-3/08

AE	Average entry wage	AW	Average wage paid	FQ	First quartile wage	LO	Lowest wage paid	MTC	Median total compensation	TCC	Total cash compensation
AER	Average entry range	AWR	Average wage range	H	Hourly	LR	Low end range	MW	Median wage paid	TQ	Third quartile wage
AEX	Average experienced wage	AXR	Average experienced range	HI	Highest wage paid	M	Monthly	MWR	Median wage range	W	Weekly
ATC	Average total compensation	D	Daily	HR	High end range	MCC	Median cash compensation	S	See annotated source	Y	Yearly

154

Occupation/Type/Industry	Location	Per	Low	Mid	High	Source	Date
Cabinetmaker and Bench Carpenter	Los Angeles-Long Beach-Glendale PMSA, CA	H	9.06 FQ	11.61 MW	15.14 TQ	CABLS	1/08-3/08
	Oakland-Fremont-Hayward MSA, CA	H	14.70 FQ	18.80 MW	26.50 TQ	CABLS	1/08-3/08
	Riverside-San Bernardino-Ontario MSA, CA	H	10.83 FQ	14.15 MW	18.21 TQ	CABLS	1/08-3/08
	Sacramento-Arden Arcade-Roseville MSA, CA	H	10.87 FQ	12.96 MW	15.92 TQ	CABLS	1/08-3/08
	San Diego-Carlsbad-San Marcos MSA, CA	H	12.82 FQ	15.86 MW	19.47 TQ	CABLS	1/08-3/08
	San Francisco-San Mateo-Redwood PMSA, CA	H	13.62 FQ	17.95 MW	23.42 TQ	CABLS	1/08-3/08
	San Jose-Sunnyvale-Santa Clara MSA, CA	H	13.18 FQ	15.19 MW	19.03 TQ	CABLS	1/08-3/08
	Santa Ana-Anaheim-Irvine PMSA, CA	Y	20140 FQ	27690 MW	39050 TQ	USBLS	5/07
	Stockton MSA, CA	H	9.15 FQ	13.80 MW	15.98 TQ	CABLS	1/08-3/08
	Colorado	Y	22550 FQ	28140 MW	36730 TQ	USBLS	5/07
	Denver-Aurora MSA, CO	Y	21790 FQ	25220 MW	34130 TQ	USBLS	5/07
	Connecticut	H	11.24 AE	16.83 MW		CTBLS	1/08-3/08
	Bridgeport-Stamford-Norwalk MSA, CT	Y	22900 FQ	30360 MW	41760 TQ	USBLS	5/07
	Hartford-West Hartford-East Hartford MSA, CT	Y	26110 FQ	32250 MW	41500 TQ	USBLS	5/07
	Delaware	Y	25560 FQ	34240 MW	42760 TQ	USBLS	5/07
	Wilmington PMSA, DE-MD-NJ	Y	24940 FQ	33770 MW	45090 TQ	USBLS	5/07
	Washington-Arlington-Alexandria MSA, DC-VA-MD-WV	Y	27860 FQ	35640 MW	45330 TQ	USBLS	5/07
	Florida	Y	22260 FQ	28930 MW	36280 TQ	USBLS	5/07
	Fort Lauderdale-Pompano Beach-Deerfield Beach PMSA, FL	Y	15870 FQ	24420 MW	32320 TQ	USBLS	5/07
	Jacksonville MSA, FL	Y	26200 FQ	30980 MW	36360 TQ	USBLS	5/07
	Miami-Fort Lauderdale-Miami Beach MSA, FL	Y	20350 FQ	28420 MW	35520 TQ	USBLS	5/07
	Orlando-Kissimmee MSA, FL	Y	24880 FQ	31030 MW	36280 TQ	USBLS	5/07
	Tampa-St. Petersburg-Clearwater MSA, FL	Y	21690 FQ	28600 MW	35310 TQ	USBLS	5/07
	West Palm Beach-Boca Raton-Boynton Beach PMSA, FL	Y	27180 FQ	34370 MW	44440 TQ	USBLS	5/07
	Georgia	Y	21080 FQ	26460 MW	31600 TQ	USBLS	5/07
	Atlanta-Sandy Springs-Marietta MSA, GA	Y	22230 FQ	27280 MW	31300 TQ	USBLS	5/07
	Hawaii	Y	23320 FQ	28620 MW	37570 TQ	USBLS	5/07
	Honolulu MSA, HI	Y	24050 FQ	30130 MW	38360 TQ	USBLS	5/07
	Idaho	Y	19600 FQ	24120 MW	30410 TQ	USBLS	5/07
	Boise City-Nampa MSA, ID	Y	18760 FQ	22360 MW	27880 TQ	USBLS	5/07
	Illinois	Y	27920 FQ	37620 MW	46900 TQ	USBLS	5/07
	Chicago-Naperville-Joliet MSA, IL-IN-WI	Y	28930 FQ	39340 MW	48140 TQ	USBLS	5/07
	Indiana	Y	22230 FQ	26810 MW	32070 TQ	USBLS	5/07
	Gary PMSA, IN	Y	18710 FQ	28120 MW	36220 TQ	USBLS	5/07
	Indianapolis-Carmel MSA, IN	Y	21830 FQ	26770 MW	32540 TQ	USBLS	5/07
	Iowa	Y	20330 FQ	24250 MW	31040 TQ	USBLS	5/07
	Des Moines-West Des Moines MSA, IA	Y	22310 FQ	31610 MW	38890 TQ	USBLS	5/07
	Kansas	Y	20270 FQ	25010 MW	30410 TQ	USBLS	5/07
	Wichita MSA, KS	Y	20300 FQ	26060 MW	31160 TQ	USBLS	5/07
	Kentucky	Y	21249 FQ	27208 MW	32941 TQ	KYBLS	2008
	Lexington-Fayette MSA, KY	Y	25440 FQ	29050 MW	35580 TQ	USBLS	5/07
	Louisville-Jefferson County MSA, KY-IN	Y	25880 FQ	32090 MW	36070 TQ	USBLS	5/07
	Louisiana	H	8.69 FQ	11.18 MW	13.60 TQ	LABLS	1/08-3/08
	Baton Rouge MSA, LA	Y	23380 FQ	27410 MW	30910 TQ	USBLS	5/07
	New Orleans-Metairie-Kenner MSA, LA	Y	21130 FQ	25810 MW	31360 TQ	USBLS	5/07
	Maine	Y	24980 FQ	29800 MW	36010 TQ	USBLS	5/07
	Portland-South Portland-Biddeford MSA, ME	Y	26630 FQ	32190 MW	37150 TQ	USBLS	5/07

Cabinetmaker and Bench Carpenter

Occupation/Type/Industry	Location	Per	Low	Mid	High	Source	Date
Cabinetmaker and Bench Carpenter	Maryland	Y		34300 MW		MDBLS	3/08
	Baltimore-Towson MSA, MD	Y	27110 FQ	32740 MW	38950 TQ	USBLS	5/07
	Bethesda-Gaithersburg-Frederick PMSA, MD	Y	31930 FQ	36620 MW	41410 TQ	USBLS	5/07
	Massachusetts	Y	27380 FQ	33700 MW	42330 TQ	USBLS	5/07
	Boston-Cambridge-Quincy NECTA, MA	Y	27490 FQ	35360 MW	43220 TQ	USBLS	5/07
	Worcester MSA, MA-CT	Y	27860 FQ	31040 MW	44760 TQ	USBLS	5/07
	Michigan	Y	26080 FQ	32350 MW	39220 TQ	USBLS	5/07
	Detroit-Warren-Livonia MSA, MI	Y	29390 FQ	35850 MW	42420 TQ	USBLS	5/07
	Grand Rapids-Wyoming MSA, MI	Y	27800 FQ	31190 MW	40450 TQ	USBLS	5/07
	Muskegon-Norton Shores MSA, MI	Y	24760 FQ	29810 MW	34920 TQ	USBLS	5/07
	Warren-Troy-Farmington Hills PMSA, MI	Y	28600 FQ	34700 MW	40950 TQ	USBLS	5/07
	Minnesota	Y	29773 FQ	34977 MW	41249 TQ	MNBLS	10/08-12/08
	Duluth-Superior MSA, MN-WI	Y	23905 FQ	33826 MW	39010 TQ	MNBLS	10/08-12/08
	Minneapolis-Saint Paul MSA, MN-WI	Y	31763 FQ	37071 MW	42566 TQ	MNBLS	10/08-12/08
	Rochester MSA, MN	Y	31043 FQ	36280 MW	44100 TQ	MNBLS	10/08-12/08
	Mississippi	Y	19340 FQ	23560 MW	28750 TQ	USBLS	5/07
	Jackson MSA, MS	Y	18050 FQ	21740 MW	28190 TQ	USBLS	5/07
	Missouri	Y	21200 FQ	25910 MW	33530 TQ	USBLS	5/07
	Jefferson City MSA, MO	Y	21880 FQ	23870 MW	30430 TQ	USBLS	5/07
	Joplin MSA, MO	Y	18760 FQ	21740 MW	26050 TQ	USBLS	5/07
	Kansas City MSA, MO-KS	Y	22680 FQ	27600 MW	33030 TQ	USBLS	5/07
	St. Louis MSA, MO-IL	Y	27910 FQ	35900 MW	41960 TQ	USBLS	5/07
	Montana	Y	20410 FQ	27440 MW	34230 TQ	USBLS	5/07
	Billings MSA, MT	Y	17960 FQ	20560 MW	28770 TQ	USBLS	5/07
	Nebraska	Y	22200 FQ	25550 MW	30720 TQ	USBLS	5/07
	Omaha-Council Bluffs MSA, NE-IA	Y	21620 FQ	25480 MW	29200 TQ	USBLS	5/07
	Nevada	H	11.73 FQ	14.84 MW	18.64 TQ	NVBLS	5/08
	Las Vegas-Paradise MSA, NV	H	11.54 FQ	15.09 MW	19.07 TQ	NVBLS	5/08
	New Hampshire	H	12.91 AE	16.16 MW	18.70 AEX	NHBLS	6/08
	Manchester MSA, NH	Y	35640 FQ	40820 MW	44530 TQ	USBLS	5/07
	Nashua NECTA, NH-MA	Y	33060 FQ	39320 MW	45050 TQ	USBLS	5/07
	New Jersey	Y	28520 FQ	35540 MW	47480 TQ	USBLS	5/07
	Camden PMSA, NJ	Y	28630 FQ	36460 MW	46000 TQ	USBLS	5/07
	Edison PMSA, NJ	Y	29880 FQ	37290 MW	51490 TQ	USBLS	5/07
	Newark-Union PMSA, NJ-PA	Y	27320 FQ	36690 MW	49490 TQ	USBLS	5/07
	New Mexico	Y	20820 FQ	24300 MW	30860 TQ	USBLS	5/07
	Albuquerque MSA, NM	Y	21160 FQ	23970 MW	30360 TQ	USBLS	5/07
	New York	Y	24230 FQ	30410 MW	39460 TQ	USBLS	5/07
	Albany-Schenectady-Troy MSA, NY	Y	26650 FQ	29710 MW	33750 TQ	USBLS	5/07
	Buffalo-Niagara Falls MSA, NY	Y	27780 FQ	31670 MW	37380 TQ	USBLS	5/07
	Nassau-Suffolk PMSA, NY	Y	22260 FQ	34940 MW	50380 TQ	USBLS	5/07
	New York-Northern New Jersey-Long Island MSA, NY-NJ-PA	Y	25770 FQ	32940 MW	45590 TQ	USBLS	5/07
	North Carolina	Y	21150 FQ	26410 MW	31870 TQ	USBLS	5/07
	Charlotte-Gastonia-Concord MSA, NC-SC	Y	19760 FQ	26040 MW	32310 TQ	USBLS	5/07
	Winston-Salem MSA, NC	Y	18410 FQ	22000 MW	28550 TQ	USBLS	5/07
	North Dakota	Y	23530 FQ	28860 MW	33640 TQ	USBLS	5/07
	Fargo MSA, ND-MN	Y	25200 FQ	29620 MW	34840 TQ	USBLS	5/07
	Grand Forks MSA, ND-MN	Y	23220 FQ	27440 MW	31750 TQ	USBLS	5/07
	Ohio	Y	22720 FQ	28410 MW	34630 TQ	USBLS	5/07
	Cincinnati-Middletown MSA, OH-KY-IN	Y	24460 FQ	29700 MW	35980 TQ	USBLS	5/07
	Cleveland-Elyria-Mentor MSA, OH	Y	24390 FQ	30060 MW	41770 TQ	USBLS	5/07
	Columbus MSA, OH	Y	25970 FQ	29500 MW	33460 TQ	USBLS	5/07
	Dayton MSA, OH	Y	25620 FQ	32370 MW	39820 TQ	USBLS	5/07
	Oklahoma	Y	18680 FQ	23000 MW	29380 TQ	USBLS	5/07
	Oklahoma City MSA, OK	Y	18020 FQ	21200 MW	27960 TQ	USBLS	5/07
	Tulsa MSA, OK	Y	20690 FQ	25080 MW	30480 TQ	USBLS	5/07

AE Average entry wage	**AW** Average wage paid	**FQ** First quartile wage	**LO** Lowest wage paid	**MTC** Median total compensation	**TCC** Total cash compensation
AER Average entry range	**AWR** Average wage range	**H** Hourly	**LR** Low end range	**MW** Median wage paid	**TQ** Third quartile wage
AEX Average experienced wage	**AXR** Average experienced range	**HI** Highest wage paid	**M** Monthly	**MWR** Median wage range	**W** Weekly
ATC Average total compensation	**D** Daily	**HR** High end range	**MCC** Median cash compensation	**S** See annotated source	**Y** Yearly

Occupation/Type/Industry	Location	Per	Low	Mid	High	Source	Date
Cabinetmaker and Bench Carpenter	Oregon	H	11.38 FQ	13.80 MW	17.04 TQ	ORBLS	5/08
	Portland-Vancouver-Beaverton MSA, OR-WA	Y	24800 FQ	30800 MW	39430 TQ	USBLS	5/07
	Salem MSA, OR	Y	24670 FQ	29310 MW	35210 TQ	USBLS	5/07
	Pennsylvania	Y	25240 FQ	30340 MW	38230 TQ	USBLS	5/07
	Allentown-Bethlehem-Easton MSA, PA-NJ	Y	26320 FQ	31270 MW	38100 TQ	USBLS	5/07
	Philadelphia-Camden-Wilmington MSA, PA-NJ-DE-MD	Y	33050 FQ	39500 MW	45720 TQ	USBLS	5/07
	Pittsburgh MSA, PA	Y	24140 FQ	30010 MW	37580 TQ	USBLS	5/07
	Reading MSA, PA	Y	26670 FQ	30930 MW	37150 TQ	USBLS	5/07
	Rhode Island	Y	26590 FQ	33960 MW	40760 TQ	USBLS	5/07
	Providence-Fall River-Warwick MSA, RI-MA	Y	26790 FQ	33830 MW	40310 TQ	USBLS	5/07
	South Carolina	Y	18980 FQ	23360 MW	28970 TQ	USBLS	5/07
	Charleston-North Charleston MSA, SC	Y	26490 FQ	34920 MW	40840 TQ	USBLS	5/07
	Columbia MSA, SC	Y	19770 FQ	25470 MW	30800 TQ	USBLS	5/07
	South Dakota	Y	21720 FQ	24505 MW	28702 TQ	SDBLS	7/08-9/08
	Sioux Falls MSA, SD	Y	22431 FQ	25242 MW	29309 TQ	SDBLS	7/08-9/08
	Tennessee	Y	19740 FQ	25940 MW	30930 TQ	USBLS	5/07
	Memphis MSA, TN-MS-AR	Y	21860 FQ	28690 MW	34410 TQ	USBLS	5/07
	Nashville-Davidson-Murfreesboro MSA, TN	Y	24640 FQ	28460 MW	31690 TQ	USBLS	5/07
	Texas	Y	19090 FQ	24190 MW	29190 TQ	USBLS	5/07
	Austin-Round Rock MSA, TX	Y	23390 FQ	27500 MW	31460 TQ	USBLS	5/07
	Beaumont-Port Arthur MSA, TX	Y	19950 FQ	24110 MW	29430 TQ	USBLS	5/07
	Corpus Christi MSA, TX	Y	19010 FQ	21820 MW	25150 TQ	USBLS	5/07
	Dallas-Fort Worth-Arlington MSA, TX	Y	18890 FQ	24140 MW	29380 TQ	USBLS	5/07
	El Paso MSA, TX	Y	17810 FQ	22300 MW	25840 TQ	USBLS	5/07
	Houston-Sugar Land-Baytown MSA, TX	Y	20860 FQ	25780 MW	31810 TQ	USBLS	5/07
	San Antonio MSA, TX	Y	17740 FQ	21580 MW	27430 TQ	USBLS	5/07
	Utah	Y	20890 FQ	24250 MW	31110 TQ	USBLS	5/07
	Salt Lake City MSA, UT	Y	20610 FQ	23850 MW	30070 TQ	USBLS	5/07
	Vermont	Y	24880 FQ	28710 MW	34700 TQ	USBLS	5/07
	Burlington-South Burlington MSA, VT	Y	25690 FQ	30150 MW	49410 TQ	USBLS	5/07
	Virginia	Y	22520 FQ	27970 MW	34810 TQ	USBLS	5/07
	Richmond MSA, VA	Y	21040 FQ	26340 MW	31490 TQ	USBLS	5/07
	Virginia Beach-Norfolk-Newport News MSA, VA-NC	Y	25210 FQ	31570 MW	38170 TQ	USBLS	5/07
	Washington	H	12.28 FQ	15.00 MW	18.87 TQ	WABLS	3/08
	Seattle-Tacoma-Bellevue MSA, WA	Y	25780 FQ	31070 MW	38420 TQ	USBLS	5/07
	West Virginia	Y	20374 FQ	28940 MW	36413 TQ	WVBLS	7/08-9/08
	Wisconsin	Y	25250 FQ	30050 MW	35870 TQ	USBLS	5/07
	Milwaukee-Waukesha-West Allis MSA, WI	Y	26030 FQ	31290 MW	39180 TQ	USBLS	5/07
	Wyoming	Y	21804 FQ	26004 MW	41476 TQ	WYBLS	9/08
	Puerto Rico	Y	12530 FQ	14100 MW	16220 TQ	USBLS	5/07
	San German-Cabo Rojo MSA, PR	Y	12720 FQ	14430 MW	16500 TQ	USBLS	5/07
	San Juan-Caguas-Guaynabo MSA, PR	Y	12880 FQ	14730 MW	18160 TQ	USBLS	5/07
	Virgin Islands	Y	27540 FQ	30440 MW	34040 TQ	USBLS	5/07
Calculations Assistant Department of Transportation	Michigan	H	13.71 LO		20.33 HI	MDOT	10/1/07
Call Center Manager	United States	Y		53800 AW		BUS201	2005-2006
Call Center Regional Director	United States	Y		105200 AW		IOMA06	2008
Call Center Representative	United States	Y		24361 MW		IOMA06	2008
Call Center Supervisor In-House	United States	Y	38600 LO		49200 HI	IOMA06	2008

AE Average entry wage	**AW** Average wage paid	**FQ** First quartile wage	**LO** Lowest wage paid	**MTC** Median total compensation	**TCC** Total cash compensation
AER Average entry range	**AWR** Average wage range	**H** Hourly	**LR** Low end range	**MW** Median wage paid	**TQ** Third quartile wage
AEX Average experienced wage	**AXR** Average experienced range	**HI** Highest wage paid	**M** Monthly	**MWR** Median wage range	**W** Weekly
ATC Average total compensation	**D** Daily	**HR** High end range	**MCC** Median cash compensation	**S** See annotated source	**Y** Yearly

Occupation/Type/Industry	Location	Per	Low	Mid	High	Source	Date
Call Center Supervisor							
Outsourced	United States	Y	26400 LO		39600 HI	IOMA06	2008
Camera and Photographic Equipment Repairer	Alabama	Y	27020 FQ	37990 MW	44040 TQ	USBLS	5/07
	Arizona	Y	24440 FQ	29440 MW	33880 TQ	USBLS	5/07
	California	H	17.54 FQ	21.81 MW	31.32 TQ	CABLS	1/08-3/08
	Colorado	Y	38520 FQ	41500 MW	44850 TQ	USBLS	5/07
	Connecticut	H	19.06 AE	21.92 MW		CTBLS	1/08-3/08
	Florida	Y	24430 FQ	30950 MW	37300 TQ	USBLS	5/07
	Georgia	Y	24100 FQ	28200 MW	31100 TQ	USBLS	5/07
	Illinois	Y	34900 FQ	40030 MW	44120 TQ	USBLS	5/07
	Iowa	Y	23790 FQ	43420 MW	58320 TQ	USBLS	5/07
	Kentucky	Y	35171 FQ	46430 MW	50632 TQ	KYBLS	2008
	Louisiana	H	9.67 FQ	13.27 MW	16.48 TQ	LABLS	1/08-3/08
	Maine	Y	31410 FQ	44660 MW	48880 TQ	USBLS	5/07
	Maryland	Y		41550 MW		MDBLS	3/08
	Massachusetts	Y	30560 FQ	38960 MW	45350 TQ	USBLS	5/07
	Michigan	Y	32180 FQ	46100 MW	79410 TQ	USBLS	5/07
	Minnesota	Y	29338 FQ	36681 MW	45639 TQ	MNBLS	10/08-12/08
	New Jersey	Y	16990 FQ	22870 MW	40160 TQ	USBLS	5/07
	New Mexico	Y	17340 FQ	18910 MW	25330 TQ	USBLS	5/07
	New York	Y	32650 FQ	37830 MW	48720 TQ	USBLS	5/07
	North Carolina	Y	30890 FQ	35800 MW	47830 TQ	USBLS	5/07
	Ohio	Y	31770 FQ	39190 MW	44150 TQ	USBLS	5/07
	Oregon	H	14.92 FQ	18.15 MW	25.83 TQ	ORBLS	5/08
	Pennsylvania	Y	35000 FQ	43930 MW	49240 TQ	USBLS	5/07
	Tennessee	Y	30850 FQ	35770 MW	43020 TQ	USBLS	5/07
	Texas	Y	22860 FQ	35720 MW	48670 TQ	USBLS	5/07
	Virginia	Y	23020 FQ	28080 MW	32910 TQ	USBLS	5/07
	Washington	H	16.59 FQ	19.77 MW	26.99 TQ	WABLS	3/08
	Wisconsin	Y	31750 FQ	48250 MW	57920 TQ	USBLS	5/07
	Puerto Rico	Y	21750 FQ	28880 MW	58670 TQ	USBLS	5/07
Camera Operator							
Television, Video, and Motion Picture	Alabama	Y	23140 FQ	29370 MW	38380 TQ	USBLS	5/07
Television, Video, and Motion Picture	Birmingham-Hoover MSA, AL	Y	25470 FQ	29580 MW	35900 TQ	USBLS	5/07
Television, Video, and Motion Picture	Arizona	Y	36930 FQ	41930 MW	61350 TQ	USBLS	5/07
Television, Video, and Motion Picture	Phoenix-Mesa-Scottsdale MSA, AZ	Y	37330 FQ	42110 MW	62770 TQ	USBLS	5/07
Television, Video, and Motion Picture	Arkansas	Y	17340 FQ	24410 MW	35620 TQ	USBLS	5/07
Television, Video, and Motion Picture	Little Rock-North Little Rock MSA, AR	Y	22240 FQ	31260 MW	36830 TQ	USBLS	5/07
Television, Video, and Motion Picture	California	H	16.05 FQ	24.02 MW	37.30 TQ	CABLS	1/08-3/08
Television, Video, and Motion Picture	Los Angeles-Long Beach-Glendale PMSA, CA	H	16.22 FQ	24.30 MW	38.43 TQ	CABLS	1/08-3/08
Television, Video, and Motion Picture	Oakland-Fremont-Hayward MSA, CA	H	28.81 FQ	45.25 MW	49.19 TQ	CABLS	1/08-3/08
Television, Video, and Motion Picture	Riverside-San Bernardino-Ontario MSA, CA	H	22.70 FQ	25.02 MW	28.25 TQ	CABLS	1/08-3/08
Television, Video, and Motion Picture	Sacramento-Arden Arcade-Roseville MSA, CA	H	10.86 FQ	15.55 MW	20.83 TQ	CABLS	1/08-3/08
Television, Video, and Motion Picture	San Diego-Carlsbad-San Marcos MSA, CA	H	19.26 FQ	23.62 MW	29.38 TQ	CABLS	1/08-3/08
Television, Video, and Motion Picture	San Francisco-San Mateo-Redwood PMSA, CA	H	20.46 FQ	33.37 MW	38.44 TQ	CABLS	1/08-3/08
Television, Video, and Motion Picture	San Jose-Sunnyvale-Santa Clara MSA, CA	H	15.28 FQ	17.48 MW	23.41 TQ	CABLS	1/08-3/08
Television, Video, and Motion Picture	Santa Ana-Anaheim-Irvine PMSA, CA	Y	62470 FQ	77580 MW	91020 TQ	USBLS	5/07
Television, Video, and Motion Picture	Colorado	Y	26440 FQ	38390 MW	52410 TQ	USBLS	5/07
Television, Video, and Motion Picture	Colorado Springs MSA, CO	Y	20700 FQ	22610 MW	33430 TQ	USBLS	5/07
Television, Video, and Motion Picture	Denver-Aurora MSA, CO	Y	34790 FQ	44460 MW	57050 TQ	USBLS	5/07
Television, Video, and Motion Picture	Connecticut	H	15.01 AE	26.45 MW		CTBLS	1/08-3/08
Television, Video, and Motion Picture	Bridgeport-Stamford-Norwalk MSA, CT	Y	20440 FQ	28320 MW	31630 TQ	USBLS	5/07
Television, Video, and Motion Picture	Delaware	Y	40870 FQ	45720 MW	53270 TQ	USBLS	5/07
Television, Video, and Motion Picture	District of Columbia	Y	47550 FQ	55320 MW	63660 TQ	USBLS	5/07
Television, Video, and Motion Picture	Washington-Arlington-Alexandria MSA, DC-VA-MD-WV	Y	40430 FQ	54890 MW	72220 TQ	USBLS	5/07
Television, Video, and Motion Picture	Florida	Y	24820 FQ	34790 MW	47030 TQ	USBLS	5/07

AE Average entry wage	**AW** Average wage paid	**FQ** First quartile wage	**LO** Lowest wage paid	**MTC** Median total compensation	**TCC** Total cash compensation
AER Average entry range	**AWR** Average wage range	**H** Hourly	**LR** Low end range	**MW** Median wage paid	**TQ** Third quartile wage
AEX Average experienced wage	**AXR** Average experienced range	**HI** Highest wage paid	**M** Monthly	**MWR** Median wage range	**W** Weekly
ATC Average total compensation	**D** Daily	**HR** High end range	**MCC** Median cash compensation	**S** See annotated source	**Y** Yearly

Occupation/Type/Industry	Location	Per	Low	Mid	High	Source	Date
Camera Operator							
Television, Video, and Motion Picture	Cape Coral-Fort Myers MSA, FL	Y	31200 FQ	39690 MW	48990 TQ	USBLS	5/07
Television, Video, and Motion Picture	Fort Lauderdale-Pompano Beach-Deerfield Beach PMSA, FL	Y	27570 FQ	35550 MW	50040 TQ	USBLS	5/07
Television, Video, and Motion Picture	Jacksonville MSA, FL	Y	25090 FQ	32650 MW	44430 TQ	USBLS	5/07
Television, Video, and Motion Picture	Orlando-Kissimmee MSA, FL	Y	24420 FQ	35300 MW	49580 TQ	USBLS	5/07
Television, Video, and Motion Picture	Tampa-St. Petersburg-Clearwater MSA, FL	Y	38740 FQ	46590 MW	53400 TQ	USBLS	5/07
Television, Video, and Motion Picture	West Palm Beach-Boca Raton-Boynton Beach PMSA, FL	Y	20530 FQ	36510 MW	51980 TQ	USBLS	5/07
Television, Video, and Motion Picture	Atlanta-Sandy Springs-Marietta MSA, GA	Y	43760 FQ	49800 MW	61940 TQ	USBLS	5/07
Television, Video, and Motion Picture	Hawaii	Y	25130 FQ	31490 MW	43820 TQ	USBLS	5/07
Television, Video, and Motion Picture	Honolulu MSA, HI	Y	24110 FQ	29190 MW	40490 TQ	USBLS	5/07
Television, Video, and Motion Picture	Boise City-Nampa MSA, ID	Y	16320 FQ	27920 MW	51600 TQ	USBLS	5/07
Television, Video, and Motion Picture	Illinois	Y	25200 FQ	38530 MW	52650 TQ	USBLS	5/07
Television, Video, and Motion Picture	Chicago-Naperville-Joliet MSA, IL-IN-WI	Y	29720 FQ	42310 MW	54970 TQ	USBLS	5/07
Television, Video, and Motion Picture	Indianapolis-Carmel MSA, IN	Y	37620 FQ	56850 MW	75230 TQ	USBLS	5/07
Television, Video, and Motion Picture	Iowa	Y	24020 FQ	35510 MW	46900 TQ	USBLS	5/07
Television, Video, and Motion Picture	Des Moines-West Des Moines MSA, IA	Y	27630 FQ	41330 MW	49380 TQ	USBLS	5/07
Television, Video, and Motion Picture	Kansas	Y	14310 FQ	26900 MW	49930 TQ	USBLS	5/07
Television, Video, and Motion Picture	Wichita MSA, KS	Y	14120 FQ	22050 MW	31310 TQ	USBLS	5/07
Television, Video, and Motion Picture	Kentucky	Y	30057 FQ	41076 MW	53768 TQ	KYBLS	2008
Television, Video, and Motion Picture	Louisville-Jefferson County MSA, KY-IN	Y	28370 FQ	36180 MW	47790 TQ	USBLS	5/07
Television, Video, and Motion Picture	Louisiana	H	9.07 FQ	13.72 MW	21.76 TQ	LABLS	1/08-3/08
Television, Video, and Motion Picture	Maine	Y	22500 FQ	27860 MW	34130 TQ	USBLS	5/07
Television, Video, and Motion Picture	Portland-South Portland-Biddeford MSA, ME	Y	24160 FQ	29740 MW	35000 TQ	USBLS	5/07
Television, Video, and Motion Picture	Maryland	Y		57050 MW		MDBLS	3/08
Television, Video, and Motion Picture	Baltimore-Towson MSA, MD	Y	47940 FQ	57850 MW	64430 TQ	USBLS	5/07
Television, Video, and Motion Picture	Bethesda-Gaithersburg-Frederick PMSA, MD	Y	36920 FQ	52650 MW	65450 TQ	USBLS	5/07
Television, Video, and Motion Picture	Massachusetts	Y	42400 FQ	49130 MW	57030 TQ	USBLS	5/07
Television, Video, and Motion Picture	Boston-Cambridge-Quincy NECTA, MA	Y	45680 FQ	50860 MW	58680 TQ	USBLS	5/07
Television, Video, and Motion Picture	Michigan	Y	27670 FQ	48640 MW	71230 TQ	USBLS	5/07
Television, Video, and Motion Picture	Grand Rapids-Wyoming MSA, MI	Y	21430 FQ	23220 MW	26520 TQ	USBLS	5/07
Television, Video, and Motion Picture	Minnesota	Y	17806 FQ	27086 MW	43805 TQ	MNBLS	10/08-12/08
Television, Video, and Motion Picture	Duluth-Superior MSA, MN-WI	Y	14762 FQ	15662 MW	22295 TQ	MNBLS	10/08-12/08
Television, Video, and Motion Picture	Minneapolis-Saint Paul MSA, MN-WI	Y	24847 FQ	39746 MW	48461 TQ	MNBLS	10/08-12/08
Television, Video, and Motion Picture	Mississippi	Y	20860 FQ	33800 MW	42430 TQ	USBLS	5/07
Television, Video, and Motion Picture	Jackson MSA, MS	Y	13670 FQ	17770 MW	32460 TQ	USBLS	5/07
Television, Video, and Motion Picture	Missouri	Y	23440 FQ	30920 MW	43770 TQ	USBLS	5/07
Television, Video, and Motion Picture	Kansas City MSA, MO-KS	Y	27650 FQ	30760 MW	35690 TQ	USBLS	5/07
Television, Video, and Motion Picture	St. Louis MSA, MO-IL	Y	37770 FQ	51240 MW	66270 TQ	USBLS	5/07
Television, Video, and Motion Picture	Springfield MSA, MO	Y	14610 FQ	22330 MW	32900 TQ	USBLS	5/07
Television, Video, and Motion Picture	Montana	Y	21060 FQ	25980 MW	44380 TQ	USBLS	5/07
Television, Video, and Motion Picture	Nebraska	Y	30900 FQ	38300 MW	46670 TQ	USBLS	5/07
Television, Video, and Motion Picture	Omaha-Council Bluffs MSA, NE-IA	Y	31550 FQ	39420 MW	48410 TQ	USBLS	5/07
Television, Video, and Motion Picture	Nevada	H	11.84 FQ	15.85 MW	22.58 TQ	NVBLS	5/08
Television, Video, and Motion Picture	Las Vegas-Paradise MSA, NV	H	13.13 FQ	17.60 MW	22.15 TQ	NVBLS	5/08
Television, Video, and Motion Picture	New Hampshire	H	14.94 AE	16.70 MW	17.39 AEX	NHBLS	6/08
Television, Video, and Motion Picture	New Jersey	Y	49510 FQ	60700 MW	70430 TQ	USBLS	5/07
Television, Video, and Motion Picture	New Mexico	Y	29970 FQ	53870 MW	113770 TQ	USBLS	5/07
Television, Video, and Motion Picture	Albuquerque MSA, NM	Y	28900 FQ	37090 MW	114840 TQ	USBLS	5/07
Television, Video, and Motion Picture	New York	Y	30080 FQ	42370 MW	53970 TQ	USBLS	5/07
Television, Video, and Motion Picture	Albany-Schenectady-Troy MSA, NY	Y	47100 FQ	71250 MW	81030 TQ	USBLS	5/07
Television, Video, and Motion Picture	Buffalo-Niagara Falls MSA, NY	Y	22120 FQ	32000 MW	45720 TQ	USBLS	5/07
Television, Video, and Motion Picture	Nassau-Suffolk PMSA, NY	Y	31380 FQ	43140 MW	49490 TQ	USBLS	5/07
Television, Video, and Motion Picture	New York-Northern New Jersey-Long Island MSA, NY-NJ-PA	Y	32270 FQ	43930 MW	55290 TQ	USBLS	5/07

AE	Average entry wage	AW	Average wage paid	FQ	First quartile wage	LO	Lowest wage paid	MTC	Median total compensation	TCC Total cash compensation
AER	Average entry range	AWR	Average wage range	H	Hourly	LR	Low end range	MW	Median wage paid	TQ Third quartile wage
AEX	Average experienced wage	AXR	Average experienced range	HI	Highest wage paid	M	Monthly	MWR	Median wage range	W Weekly
ATC	Average total compensation	D	Daily	HR	High end range	MCC	Median cash compensation	S	See annotated source	Y Yearly

Camera Operator

Occupation/Type/Industry	Location	Per	Low	Mid	High	Source	Date
Camera Operator							
Television, Video, and Motion Picture	North Carolina	Y	23640 FQ	36380 MW	45670 TQ	USBLS	5/07
Television, Video, and Motion Picture	Charlotte-Gastonia-Concord MSA, NC-SC	Y	32820 FQ	39780 MW	47510 TQ	USBLS	5/07
Television, Video, and Motion Picture	North Dakota	Y	17040 FQ	23320 MW	31660 TQ	USBLS	5/07
Television, Video, and Motion Picture	Fargo MSA, ND-MN	Y	17840 FQ	24250 MW	35040 TQ	USBLS	5/07
Television, Video, and Motion Picture	Ohio	Y	34960 FQ	47790 MW	62680 TQ	USBLS	5/07
Television, Video, and Motion Picture	Cincinnati-Middletown MSA, OH-KY-IN	Y	33000 FQ	58200 MW	64880 TQ	USBLS	5/07
Television, Video, and Motion Picture	Cleveland-Elyria-Mentor MSA, OH	Y	34690 FQ	54360 MW	68920 TQ	USBLS	5/07
Television, Video, and Motion Picture	Columbus MSA, OH	Y	38050 FQ	51340 MW	67140 TQ	USBLS	5/07
Television, Video, and Motion Picture	Dayton MSA, OH	Y	42150 FQ	54350 MW	60380 TQ	USBLS	5/07
Television, Video, and Motion Picture	Oklahoma	Y	26910 FQ	32630 MW	44820 TQ	USBLS	5/07
Television, Video, and Motion Picture	Oklahoma City MSA, OK	Y	27630 FQ	32120 MW	43830 TQ	USBLS	5/07
Television, Video, and Motion Picture	Tulsa MSA, OK	Y	26270 FQ	35460 MW	49030 TQ	USBLS	5/07
Television, Video, and Motion Picture	Pennsylvania	Y	26780 FQ	37110 MW	52970 TQ	USBLS	5/07
Television, Video, and Motion Picture	Philadelphia-Camden-Wilmington MSA, PA-NJ-DE-MD	Y	40690 FQ	48020 MW	60330 TQ	USBLS	5/07
Television, Video, and Motion Picture	Pittsburgh MSA, PA	Y	20700 FQ	28930 MW	44090 TQ	USBLS	5/07
Television, Video, and Motion Picture	Rhode Island	Y	23460 FQ	37670 MW	48320 TQ	USBLS	5/07
Television, Video, and Motion Picture	Providence-Fall River-Warwick MSA, RI-MA	Y	23460 FQ	37670 MW	48320 TQ	USBLS	5/07
Television, Video, and Motion Picture	South Carolina	Y	20800 FQ	27800 MW	42910 TQ	USBLS	5/07
Television, Video, and Motion Picture	Charleston-North Charleston MSA, SC	Y	20620 FQ	29050 MW	62990 TQ	USBLS	5/07
Television, Video, and Motion Picture	Columbia MSA, SC	Y	22110 FQ	30550 MW	46340 TQ	USBLS	5/07
Television, Video, and Motion Picture	South Dakota	Y	17829 FQ	20112 MW	24269 TQ	SDBLS	7/08-9/08
Television, Video, and Motion Picture	Sioux Falls MSA, SD	Y	17943 FQ	21785 MW	26097 TQ	SDBLS	7/08-9/08
Television, Video, and Motion Picture	Tennessee	Y	22300 FQ	37170 MW	55180 TQ	USBLS	5/07
Television, Video, and Motion Picture	Memphis MSA, TN-MS-AR	Y	31590 FQ	50120 MW	61940 TQ	USBLS	5/07
Television, Video, and Motion Picture	Nashville-Davidson-Murfreesboro MSA, TN	Y	32740 FQ	44770 MW	59860 TQ	USBLS	5/07
Television, Video, and Motion Picture	Texas	Y	19340 FQ	29140 MW	42100 TQ	USBLS	5/07
Television, Video, and Motion Picture	Austin-Round Rock MSA, TX	Y	21440 FQ	25580 MW	28380 TQ	USBLS	5/07
Television, Video, and Motion Picture	Dallas-Fort Worth-Arlington MSA, TX	Y	27340 FQ	30850 MW	41320 TQ	USBLS	5/07
Television, Video, and Motion Picture	Houston-Sugar Land-Baytown MSA, TX	Y	28850 FQ	41060 MW	45540 TQ	USBLS	5/07
Television, Video, and Motion Picture	San Antonio MSA, TX	Y	27290 FQ	36950 MW	49810 TQ	USBLS	5/07
Television, Video, and Motion Picture	Utah	Y	41730 FQ	52770 MW	61330 TQ	USBLS	5/07
Television, Video, and Motion Picture	Salt Lake City MSA, UT	Y	42030 FQ	52790 MW	62400 TQ	USBLS	5/07
Television, Video, and Motion Picture	Virginia	Y	36960 FQ	51770 MW	73610 TQ	USBLS	5/07
Television, Video, and Motion Picture	Richmond MSA, VA	Y	26570 FQ	31400 MW	36990 TQ	USBLS	5/07
Television, Video, and Motion Picture	Virginia Beach-Norfolk-Newport News MSA, VA-NC	Y	45310 FQ	57070 MW	68020 TQ	USBLS	5/07
Television, Video, and Motion Picture	Washington	H	19.28 FQ	27.27 MW	33.26 TQ	WABLS	3/08
Television, Video, and Motion Picture	Seattle-Tacoma-Bellevue MSA, WA	Y	41960 FQ	57740 MW	70620 TQ	USBLS	5/07
Television, Video, and Motion Picture	West Virginia	Y	21575 FQ	44687 MW	58156 TQ	WVBLS	7/08-9/08
Television, Video, and Motion Picture	Wisconsin	Y	17290 FQ	30190 MW	49000 TQ	USBLS	5/07
Television, Video, and Motion Picture	Milwaukee-Waukesha-West Allis MSA, WI	Y	15540 FQ	32720 MW	50840 TQ	USBLS	5/07
Television, Video, and Motion Picture	Puerto Rico	Y	25340 FQ	32330 MW	39040 TQ	USBLS	5/07
Television, Video, and Motion Picture	San Juan-Caguas-Guaynabo MSA, PR	Y	25650 FQ	32370 MW	38940 TQ	USBLS	5/07
Television, Video, and Motion Picture	Guam	Y	16210 FQ	20360 MW	26240 TQ	USBLS	5/07
Camp Service Aide							
Municipal Government	Seattle, WA	H	14.83 LO		15.96 HI	CSSS	2008
Campaign Finance Auditor							
Municipal Government	Seattle, WA	H	29.34 LO		34.12 HI	CSSS	2008
Campground Attendant							
State Government	Ohio	H	14.03 LO		15.41 HI	ODAS	2008
Campus Sustainability Officer	United States	Y		44200-79200 AWR		AASH	2007

AE	Average entry wage	AW	Average wage paid	FQ	First quartile wage
AER	Average entry range	AWR	Average wage range	H	Hourly
AEX	Average experienced wage	AXR	Average experienced range	HI	Highest wage paid
ATC	Average total compensation	D	Daily	HR	High end range

LO	Lowest wage paid	MTC	Median total compensation
LR	Low end range	MW	Median wage paid
M	Monthly	MWR	Median wage range
MCC	Median cash compensation	S	See annotated source

TCC	Total cash compensation
TQ	Third quartile wage
W	Weekly
Y	Yearly

Occupation/Type/Industry	Location	Per	Low	Mid	High	Source	Date
Canal Maintenance Supervisor							
State Government	Ohio	H	17.78 LO		21.65 HI	ODAS	2008
Cancer/Tumor Registrar	United States	Y		39800 AW		AHIP	2008
Canteen Worker							
Public Schools	Baldwin County, AL	Y	12511 LO		14012 HI	BCPSSS	2008-2009
Captain							
Cruise Ship	United States	M	5800 LO		9800 HI	CRU02	2008
Department of Corrections	New Hampshire	Y		66958 AW		NHUL03	2008
Fire Department	Atlanta, GA	Y	52553 LO		54459 HI	GACTY01	2008
Police Department	Holly Springs, GA	Y	45000 LO		53000 HI	GACTY01	2008
Captain, Mate, and Pilot of Water Vessels	Alabama	Y	40010 FQ	55870 MW	66860 TQ	USBLS	5/07
	Alaska	Y	39580 FQ	49820 MW	63410 TQ	USBLS	5/07
	Arkansas	Y	42870 FQ	52370 MW	70820 TQ	USBLS	5/07
	California	H	18.68 FQ	25.91 MW	35.29 TQ	CABLS	1/08-3/08
	Connecticut	H	13.07 AE	28.03 MW		CTBLS	1/08-3/08
	Delaware	Y	31000 FQ	39640 MW	45850 TQ	USBLS	5/07
	Georgia	Y	40650 FQ	51370 MW	59200 TQ	USBLS	5/07
	Hawaii	Y	34790 FQ	41270 MW	49720 TQ	USBLS	5/07
	Idaho	Y	13330 FQ	16900 MW	34640 TQ	USBLS	5/07
	Illinois	Y	33610 FQ	51700 MW	62180 TQ	USBLS	5/07
	Indiana	Y	52240 FQ	67250 MW	79660 TQ	USBLS	5/07
	Iowa	Y	43390 FQ	57840 MW	71480 TQ	USBLS	5/07
	Kentucky	Y	43999 FQ	71478 MW	82571 TQ	KYBLS	2008
	Louisiana	H	22.86 FQ	31.38 MW	39.95 TQ	LABLS	1/08-3/08
	Maryland	Y		38425 MW		MDBLS	3/08
	Massachusetts	Y	32770 FQ	42740 MW	57410 TQ	USBLS	5/07
	Michigan	Y	32750 FQ	43770 MW	67500 TQ	USBLS	5/07
	Minnesota	Y	44433 FQ	56709 MW	64615 TQ	MNBLS	10/08-12/08
	Mississippi	Y	51650 FQ	60000 MW	69440 TQ	USBLS	5/07
	Missouri	Y	35980 FQ	57020 MW	73740 TQ	USBLS	5/07
	Nevada	H	15.61 FQ	20.80 MW	23.62 TQ	NVBLS	5/08
	New Jersey	Y	32390 FQ	48180 MW	76760 TQ	USBLS	5/07
	New York	Y	37420 FQ	49340 MW	67120 TQ	USBLS	5/07
	North Carolina	Y	22520 FQ	37780 MW	45920 TQ	USBLS	5/07
	Ohio	Y	32910 FQ	53390 MW	65920 TQ	USBLS	5/07
	Oklahoma	Y	39110 FQ	55910 MW	73700 TQ	USBLS	5/07
	Oregon	H	23.19 FQ	28.56 MW	33.84 TQ	ORBLS	5/08
	Pennsylvania	Y	46750 FQ	58040 MW	70890 TQ	USBLS	5/07
	Rhode Island	Y	37750 FQ	47140 MW	59790 TQ	USBLS	5/07
	South Carolina	Y	30880 FQ	38410 MW	51110 TQ	USBLS	5/07
	Texas	Y	48240 FQ	57760 MW	68370 TQ	USBLS	5/07
	Virginia	Y	46490 FQ	59480 MW	81780 TQ	USBLS	5/07
	Washington	H	25.27 FQ	32.43 MW	39.78 TQ	WABLS	3/08
	Wisconsin	Y	34420 FQ	46560 MW	66580 TQ	USBLS	5/07
	Puerto Rico	Y	32630 FQ	39910 MW	61060 TQ	USBLS	5/07
	Virgin Islands	Y	31210 FQ	36290 MW	44320 TQ	USBLS	5/07
	Guam	Y	31970 FQ	42030 MW	48790 TQ	USBLS	5/07
Card Punch Operator							
Municipal Government	Cincinnati, OH	Y	32519 LO		34475 HI	COHSS	10/08
Cardiologist							
Interventional	United States	Y			811000 HI	APHYS	6/03-6/06
Invasive	United States	Y			647000 HI	APHYS	6/03-6/06
Noninvasive	United States	Y			599000 HI	APHYS	6/03-6/06
Pediatric	United States	Y		234613 AW		CEJ01	2008
Cardiovascular Technologist and Technician	Alabama	Y	23990 FQ	34250 MW	48020 TQ	USBLS	5/07
	Birmingham-Hoover MSA, AL	Y	30300 FQ	41660 MW	53330 TQ	USBLS	5/07
	Arizona	Y	31510 FQ	39550 MW	52850 TQ	USBLS	5/07
	Phoenix-Mesa-Scottsdale MSA, AZ	Y	32490 FQ	41160 MW	54300 TQ	USBLS	5/07
	Tucson MSA, AZ	Y	33580 FQ	42920 MW	55430 TQ	USBLS	5/07
	Arkansas	Y	25430 FQ	43760 MW	56220 TQ	USBLS	5/07
	Little Rock-North Little Rock MSA, AR	Y	36010 FQ	52290 MW	60570 TQ	USBLS	5/07

AE	Average entry wage	AW	Average wage paid	FQ	First quartile wage
AER	Average entry range	AWR	Average wage range	H	Hourly
AEX	Average experienced wage	AXR	Average experienced range	HI	Highest wage paid
ATC	Average total compensation	D	Daily	HR	High end range

LO Lowest wage paid · LR Low end range · M Monthly · MCC Median cash compensation · MTC Median total compensation · MW Median wage paid · MWR Median wage range · S See annotated source · TCC Total cash compensation · TQ Third quartile wage · W Weekly · Y Yearly

Occupation/Type/Industry	Location	Per	Low	Mid	High	Source	Date
Cardiovascular Technologist and Technician	California	H	18.96 FQ	26.78 MW	33.72 TQ	CABLS	1/08-3/08
	Los Angeles-Long Beach-Glendale PMSA, CA	H	18.36 FQ	28.47 MW	35.52 TQ	CABLS	1/08-3/08
	Oakland-Fremont-Hayward MSA, CA	H	20.04 FQ	24.39 MW	31.65 TQ	CABLS	1/08-3/08
	Riverside-San Bernardino-Ontario MSA, CA	H	18.07 FQ	24.89 MW	31.02 TQ	CABLS	1/08-3/08
	Sacramento-Arden Arcade-Roseville MSA, CA	H	16.99 FQ	22.73 MW	30.86 TQ	CABLS	1/08-3/08
	San Diego-Carlsbad-San Marcos MSA, CA	H	20.56 FQ	27.90 MW	32.53 TQ	CABLS	1/08-3/08
	San Francisco-San Mateo-Redwood PMSA, CA	H	20.68 FQ	27.85 MW	32.90 TQ	CABLS	1/08-3/08
	San Jose-Sunnyvale-Santa Clara MSA, CA	H	24.31 FQ	32.56 MW	48.53 TQ	CABLS	1/08-3/08
	Santa Ana-Anaheim-Irvine PMSA, CA	Y	38380 FQ	54810 MW	69040 TQ	USBLS	5/07
	Colorado	Y	31410 FQ	42000 MW	65180 TQ	USBLS	5/07
	Denver-Aurora MSA, CO	Y	31660 FQ	39450 MW	61210 TQ	USBLS	5/07
	Connecticut	H	15.14 AE	23.94 MW		CTBLS	1/08-3/08
	Bridgeport-Stamford-Norwalk MSA, CT	Y	37210 FQ	52490 MW	63700 TQ	USBLS	5/07
	Hartford-West Hartford-East Hartford MSA, CT	Y	32390 FQ	43800 MW	59480 TQ	USBLS	5/07
	Delaware	Y	37850 FQ	53360 MW	61410 TQ	USBLS	5/07
	Wilmington PMSA, DE-MD-NJ	Y	38370 FQ	53500 MW	61640 TQ	USBLS	5/07
	District of Columbia	Y	36140 FQ	47130 MW	58230 TQ	USBLS	5/07
	Washington-Arlington-Alexandria MSA, DC-VA-MD-WV	Y	39150 FQ	55570 MW	66720 TQ	USBLS	5/07
	Florida	Y	24600 FQ	32340 MW	50690 TQ	USBLS	5/07
	Fort Lauderdale-Pompano Beach-Deerfield Beach PMSA, FL	Y	25660 FQ	30980 MW	48100 TQ	USBLS	5/07
	Jacksonville MSA, FL	Y	27450 FQ	40370 MW	52530 TQ	USBLS	5/07
	Miami-Fort Lauderdale-Miami Beach MSA, FL	Y	25030 FQ	31150 MW	47950 TQ	USBLS	5/07
	Orlando-Kissimmee MSA, FL	Y	25580 FQ	40540 MW	54580 TQ	USBLS	5/07
	Sarasota-Bradenton-Venice MSA, FL	Y	25870 FQ	30310 MW	53360 TQ	USBLS	5/07
	Tampa-St. Petersburg-Clearwater MSA, FL	Y	25400 FQ	36990 MW	55860 TQ	USBLS	5/07
	West Palm Beach-Boca Raton-Boynton Beach PMSA, FL	Y	25320 FQ	38430 MW	51210 TQ	USBLS	5/07
	Georgia	Y	27200 FQ	38570 MW	55690 TQ	USBLS	5/07
	Atlanta-Sandy Springs-Marietta MSA, GA	Y	27030 FQ	35750 MW	56900 TQ	USBLS	5/07
	Savannah MSA, GA	Y	29060 FQ	43140 MW	57120 TQ	USBLS	5/07
	Hawaii	Y	36240 FQ	56090 MW	69890 TQ	USBLS	5/07
	Honolulu MSA, HI	Y	37230 FQ	61240 MW	70560 TQ	USBLS	5/07
	Idaho	Y	33210 FQ	51600 MW	62790 TQ	USBLS	5/07
	Boise City-Nampa MSA, ID	Y	37650 FQ	51280 MW	62040 TQ	USBLS	5/07
	Illinois	Y	33040 FQ	43380 MW	58830 TQ	USBLS	5/07
	Chicago-Naperville-Joliet MSA, IL-IN-WI	Y	33420 FQ	43580 MW	58790 TQ	USBLS	5/07
	Rockford MSA, IL	Y	25920 FQ	46240 MW	83010 TQ	USBLS	5/07
	Indiana	Y	28440 FQ	41080 MW	55960 TQ	USBLS	5/07
	Gary PMSA, IN	Y	30610 FQ	41990 MW	54570 TQ	USBLS	5/07
	Indianapolis-Carmel MSA, IN	Y	33210 FQ	50750 MW	63710 TQ	USBLS	5/07
	Iowa	Y	32710 FQ	40370 MW	48260 TQ	USBLS	5/07
	Des Moines-West Des Moines MSA, IA	Y	33870 FQ	40380 MW	46840 TQ	USBLS	5/07
	Kansas	Y	30800 FQ	49200 MW	63780 TQ	USBLS	5/07
	Kentucky	Y	26349 FQ	34458 MW	52185 TQ	KYBLS	2008
	Louisville-Jefferson County MSA, KY-IN	Y	27890 FQ	39450 MW	52290 TQ	USBLS	5/07
	Louisiana	H	10.79 FQ	15.52 MW	23.22 TQ	LABLS	1/08-3/08
	Baton Rouge MSA, LA	Y	16970 FQ	19080 MW	44980 TQ	USBLS	5/07
	New Orleans-Metairie-Kenner MSA, LA	Y	23190 FQ	44810 MW	59290 TQ	USBLS	5/07

AE	Average entry wage	AW	Average wage paid	FQ First quartile wage
AER	Average entry range	AWR	Average wage range	H Hourly
AEX	Average experienced wage	AXR	Average experienced range	HI Highest wage paid
ATC	Average total compensation	D	Daily	HR High end range

LO Lowest wage paid · LR Low end range · M Monthly · MCC Median cash compensation · MTC Median total compensation · MW Median wage paid · MWR Median wage range · S See annotated source · TCC Total cash compensation · TQ Third quartile wage · W Weekly · Y Yearly

Occupation/Type/Industry	Location	Per	Low	Mid	High	Source	Date
Cardiovascular Technologist and Technician	Maine	Y	38910 FQ	51960 MW	62230 TQ	USBLS	5/07
	Portland-South Portland-Biddeford MSA, ME	Y	39320 FQ	49500 MW	61370 TQ	USBLS	5/07
	Maryland	Y		50550 MW		MDBLS	3/08
	Baltimore-Towson MSA, MD	Y	36200 FQ	50320 MW	59730 TQ	USBLS	5/07
	Bethesda-Gaithersburg-Frederick PMSA, MD	Y	41770 FQ	52300 MW	60750 TQ	USBLS	5/07
	Salisbury MSA, MD	Y	24930 FQ	30580 MW	43900 TQ	USBLS	5/07
	Massachusetts	Y	34550 FQ	49600 MW	70230 TQ	USBLS	5/07
	Boston-Cambridge-Quincy NECTA, MA	Y	36210 FQ	49820 MW	70410 TQ	USBLS	5/07
	Springfield MSA, MA-CT	Y	33200 FQ	50040 MW	65790 TQ	USBLS	5/07
	Worcester MSA, MA-CT	Y	36960 FQ	58440 MW	74690 TQ	USBLS	5/07
	Michigan	Y	34610 FQ	45880 MW	56020 TQ	USBLS	5/07
	Detroit-Warren-Livonia MSA, MI	Y	34030 FQ	45470 MW	56390 TQ	USBLS	5/07
	Grand Rapids-Wyoming MSA, MI	Y	39640 FQ	46870 MW	55670 TQ	USBLS	5/07
	Lansing-East Lansing MSA, MI	Y	42430 FQ	48430 MW	57100 TQ	USBLS	5/07
	Warren-Troy-Farmington Hills PMSA, MI	Y	34850 FQ	46330 MW	56440 TQ	USBLS	5/07
	Minnesota	Y	41671 FQ	51411 MW	65441 TQ	MNBLS	10/08-12/08
	Minneapolis-Saint Paul MSA, MN-WI	Y	44276 FQ	56192 MW	71132 TQ	MNBLS	10/08-12/08
	Rochester MSA, MN	Y	38082 FQ	45088 MW	52360 TQ	MNBLS	10/08-12/08
	Mississippi	Y	30850 FQ	41940 MW	51930 TQ	USBLS	5/07
	Jackson MSA, MS	Y	34100 FQ	43220 MW	53110 TQ	USBLS	5/07
	Missouri	Y	27590 FQ	38310 MW	53780 TQ	USBLS	5/07
	Kansas City MSA, MO-KS	Y	33480 FQ	52680 MW	71400 TQ	USBLS	5/07
	St. Louis MSA, MO-IL	Y	27440 FQ	36640 MW	52000 TQ	USBLS	5/07
	Springfield MSA, MO	Y	24170 FQ	36050 MW	55270 TQ	USBLS	5/07
	Montana	Y	30710 FQ	45440 MW	57770 TQ	USBLS	5/07
	Billings MSA, MT	Y	38110 FQ	43940 MW	52100 TQ	USBLS	5/07
	Nebraska	Y	27440 FQ	41840 MW	58680 TQ	USBLS	5/07
	Omaha-Council Bluffs MSA, NE-IA	Y	26360 FQ	34740 MW	48950 TQ	USBLS	5/07
	Nevada	H	16.57 FQ	21.38 MW	29.04 TQ	NVBLS	5/08
	Las Vegas-Paradise MSA, NV	H	17.27 FQ	21.92 MW	28.83 TQ	NVBLS	5/08
	New Hampshire	H	16.15 AE	24.60 MW	28.68 AEX	NHBLS	6/08
	Manchester MSA, NH	Y	33910 FQ	39920 MW	55840 TQ	USBLS	5/07
	Nashua NECTA, NH-MA	Y	38630 FQ	48120 MW	58090 TQ	USBLS	5/07
	New Jersey	Y	46260 FQ	57800 MW	71600 TQ	USBLS	5/07
	Camden PMSA, NJ	Y	40360 FQ	56540 MW	68240 TQ	USBLS	5/07
	Edison PMSA, NJ	Y	44880 FQ	55770 MW	64460 TQ	USBLS	5/07
	Newark-Union PMSA, NJ-PA	Y	50680 FQ	58680 MW	69000 TQ	USBLS	5/07
	New Mexico	Y	29080 FQ	44390 MW	58280 TQ	USBLS	5/07
	Albuquerque MSA, NM	Y	27400 FQ	32030 MW	46760 TQ	USBLS	5/07
	New York	Y	39280 FQ	50430 MW	62490 TQ	USBLS	5/07
	Albany-Schenectady-Troy MSA, NY	Y	31320 FQ	40810 MW	53080 TQ	USBLS	5/07
	Buffalo-Niagara Falls MSA, NY	Y	37790 FQ	52600 MW	61350 TQ	USBLS	5/07
	Nassau-Suffolk PMSA, NY	Y	45050 FQ	59090 MW	70750 TQ	USBLS	5/07
	New York-Northern New Jersey-Long Island MSA, NY-NJ-PA	Y	42470 FQ	54550 MW	66860 TQ	USBLS	5/07
	North Carolina	Y	41290 FQ	50800 MW	59530 TQ	USBLS	5/07
	Charlotte-Gastonia-Concord MSA, NC-SC	Y	43120 FQ	51200 MW	58600 TQ	USBLS	5/07
	Raleigh-Cary MSA, NC	Y	45800 FQ	53190 MW	59530 TQ	USBLS	5/07
	North Dakota	Y	29510 FQ	37470 MW	48430 TQ	USBLS	5/07
	Ohio	Y	34780 FQ	46450 MW	57610 TQ	USBLS	5/07
	Cincinnati-Middletown MSA, OH-KY-IN	Y	34180 FQ	45700 MW	57440 TQ	USBLS	5/07
	Cleveland-Elyria-Mentor MSA, OH	Y	36450 FQ	47730 MW	57860 TQ	USBLS	5/07
	Columbus MSA, OH	Y	34450 FQ	47810 MW	59330 TQ	USBLS	5/07
	Dayton MSA, OH	Y	31020 FQ	42740 MW	56060 TQ	USBLS	5/07
	Mansfield MSA, OH	Y	43780 FQ	56210 MW	61570 TQ	USBLS	5/07
	Oklahoma	Y	22670 FQ	29420 MW	45960 TQ	USBLS	5/07
	Oklahoma City MSA, OK	Y	22720 FQ	27710 MW	45180 TQ	USBLS	5/07

AE	Average entry wage	AW	Average wage paid	FQ	First quartile wage	LO	Lowest wage paid
AER	Average entry range	AWR	Average wage range	H	Hourly	LR	Low end range
AEX	Average experienced wage	AXR	Average experienced range	HI	Highest wage paid	M	Monthly
ATC	Average total compensation	D	Daily	HR	High end range	MCC	Median cash compensation

MTC	Median total compensation	TCC	Total cash compensation
MW	Median wage paid	TQ	Third quartile wage
MWR	Median wage range	W	Weekly
S	See annotated source	Y	Yearly

Occupation/Type/Industry	Location	Per	Low	Mid	High	Source	Date
Cardiovascular Technologist and Technician	Tulsa MSA, OK	Y	22620 FQ	30820 MW	47640 TQ	USBLS	5/07
	Oregon	H	17.05 FQ	28.33 MW	35.18 TQ	ORBLS	5/08
	Eugene-Springfield MSA, OR	Y	39780 FQ	56710 MW	66180 TQ	USBLS	5/07
	Portland-Vancouver-Beaverton MSA, OR-WA	Y	37140 FQ	61930 MW	74360 TQ	USBLS	5/07
	Pennsylvania	Y	30440 FQ	41970 MW	55730 TQ	USBLS	5/07
	Allentown-Bethlehem-Easton MSA, PA-NJ	Y	43430 FQ	56790 MW	75990 TQ	USBLS	5/07
	Philadelphia-Camden-Wilmington MSA, PA-NJ-DE-MD	Y	35520 FQ	47490 MW	59730 TQ	USBLS	5/07
	Pittsburgh MSA, PA	Y	27070 FQ	34350 MW	48940 TQ	USBLS	5/07
	York-Hanover MSA, PA	Y	30720 FQ	36350 MW	50960 TQ	USBLS	5/07
	Rhode Island	Y	40750 FQ	59310 MW	73050 TQ	USBLS	5/07
	Providence-Fall River-Warwick MSA, RI-MA	Y	29960 FQ	39570 MW	65850 TQ	USBLS	5/07
	South Carolina	Y	31470 FQ	43960 MW	55470 TQ	USBLS	5/07
	Charleston-North Charleston MSA, SC	Y	35130 FQ	43370 MW	53020 TQ	USBLS	5/07
	Columbia MSA, SC	Y	32900 FQ	41780 MW	50580 TQ	USBLS	5/07
	South Dakota	Y	35232 FQ	44757 MW	54268 TQ	SDBLS	7/08-9/08
	Sioux Falls MSA, SD	Y	37471 FQ	44939 MW	53988 TQ	SDBLS	7/08-9/08
	Tennessee	Y	26310 FQ	35780 MW	53140 TQ	USBLS	5/07
	Memphis MSA, TN-MS-AR	Y	25610 FQ	30490 MW	51550 TQ	USBLS	5/07
	Nashville-Davidson-Murfreesboro MSA, TN	Y	34380 FQ	46070 MW	58610 TQ	USBLS	5/07
	Texas	Y	31010 FQ	44400 MW	56680 TQ	USBLS	5/07
	Austin-Round Rock MSA, TX	Y	43590 FQ	52070 MW	59470 TQ	USBLS	5/07
	Corpus Christi MSA, TX	Y	41630 FQ	50620 MW	59100 TQ	USBLS	5/07
	Dallas-Fort Worth-Arlington MSA, TX	Y	31800 FQ	46130 MW	57720 TQ	USBLS	5/07
	Houston-Sugar Land-Baytown MSA, TX	Y	30160 FQ	39640 MW	52990 TQ	USBLS	5/07
	San Antonio MSA, TX	Y	32290 FQ	42270 MW	53380 TQ	USBLS	5/07
	Utah	Y	24910 FQ	44640 MW	60070 TQ	USBLS	5/07
	Provo-Orem MSA, UT	Y	36340 FQ	51860 MW	60320 TQ	USBLS	5/07
	Vermont	Y	35280 FQ	46990 MW	57360 TQ	USBLS	5/07
	Virginia	Y	34010 FQ	53050 MW	62890 TQ	USBLS	5/07
	Richmond MSA, VA	Y	30660 FQ	43220 MW	57830 TQ	USBLS	5/07
	Virginia Beach-Norfolk-Newport News MSA, VA-NC	Y	35740 FQ	53890 MW	61210 TQ	USBLS	5/07
	Washington	H	19.65 FQ	28.97 MW	35.13 TQ	WABLS	3/08
	Seattle-Tacoma-Bellevue MSA, WA	Y	40250 FQ	63720 MW	74980 TQ	USBLS	5/07
	West Virginia	Y	23003 FQ	37232 MW	51773 TQ	WVBLS	7/08-9/08
	Wisconsin	Y	33470 FQ	46690 MW	60530 TQ	USBLS	5/07
	Milwaukee-Waukesha-West Allis MSA, WI	Y	32850 FQ	44570 MW	59760 TQ	USBLS	5/07
	Wyoming	Y	41985 FQ	51115 MW	62430 TQ	WYBLS	9/08
	Puerto Rico	Y	16370 FQ	19320 MW	24590 TQ	USBLS	5/07
	San Juan-Caguas-Guaynabo MSA, PR	Y	16330 FQ	19010 MW	24010 TQ	USBLS	5/07
Career Coach	United States	H	100.00 LO		250.00 HI	WSJ04	2007
Cargo and Freight Agent	Alabama	Y	28850 FQ	34960 MW	41660 TQ	USBLS	5/07
	Birmingham-Hoover MSA, AL	Y	28920 FQ	34210 MW	41810 TQ	USBLS	5/07
	Mobile MSA, AL	Y	31010 FQ	34870 MW	37710 TQ	USBLS	5/07
	Alaska	Y	26320 FQ	32840 MW	43040 TQ	USBLS	5/07
	Anchorage MSA, AK	Y	29970 FQ	37080 MW	47000 TQ	USBLS	5/07
	Arizona	Y	26070 FQ	34350 MW	45280 TQ	USBLS	5/07
	Phoenix-Mesa-Scottsdale MSA, AZ	Y	25480 FQ	32400 MW	43850 TQ	USBLS	5/07
	Tucson MSA, AZ	Y	41530 FQ	45280 MW	48920 TQ	USBLS	5/07
	Arkansas	Y	29970 FQ	36330 MW	45720 TQ	USBLS	5/07
	Little Rock-North Little Rock MSA, AR	Y	31360 FQ	37860 MW	53420 TQ	USBLS	5/07
	California	H	15.35 FQ	20.14 MW	25.13 TQ	CABLS	1/08-3/08
	Los Angeles-Long Beach-Glendale PMSA, CA	H	15.32 FQ	20.35 MW	26.17 TQ	CABLS	1/08-3/08

AE Average entry wage	**AW** Average wage paid	**FQ** First quartile wage	**LO** Lowest wage paid	**MTC** Median total compensation **TCC** Total cash compensation
AER Average entry range	**AWR** Average wage range	**H** Hourly	**LR** Low end range	**MW** Median wage paid **TQ** Third quartile wage
AEX Average experienced wage	**AXR** Average experienced range	**HI** Highest wage paid	**M** Monthly	**MWR** Median wage range **W** Weekly
ATC Average total compensation **D** Daily		**HR** High end range	**MCC** Median cash compensation	**S** See annotated source **Y** Yearly

Occupation/Type/Industry	Location	Per	Low	Mid	High	Source	Date
Cargo and Freight Agent	Oakland-Fremont-Hayward MSA, CA	H	15.40 FQ	20.65 MW	28.51 TQ	CABLS	1/08-3/08
	Riverside-San Bernardino-Ontario MSA, CA	H	14.54 FQ	18.47 MW	22.79 TQ	CABLS	1/08-3/08
	Sacramento-Arden Arcade-Roseville MSA, CA	H	15.31 FQ	21.30 MW	24.61 TQ	CABLS	1/08-3/08
	San Diego-Carlsbad-San Marcos MSA, CA	H	13.12 FQ	16.83 MW	22.65 TQ	CABLS	1/08-3/08
	San Francisco-San Mateo-Redwood PMSA, CA	H	16.70 FQ	19.77 MW	24.43 TQ	CABLS	1/08-3/08
	San Jose-Sunnyvale-Santa Clara MSA, CA	H	13.70 FQ	18.09 MW	22.85 TQ	CABLS	1/08-3/08
	Santa Ana-Anaheim-Irvine PMSA, CA	Y	33550 FQ	43260 MW	49650 TQ	USBLS	5/07
	Colorado	Y	33590 FQ	40740 MW	48860 TQ	USBLS	5/07
	Denver-Aurora MSA, CO	Y	33270 FQ	40330 MW	48240 TQ	USBLS	5/07
	Connecticut	H	11.14 AE	20.61 MW		CTBLS	1/08-3/08
	Bridgeport-Stamford-Norwalk MSA, CT	Y	26910 FQ	47920 MW	74450 TQ	USBLS	5/07
	Hartford-West Hartford-East Hartford MSA, CT	Y	36260 FQ	42260 MW	50540 TQ	USBLS	5/07
	Delaware	Y	25360 FQ	32250 MW	43800 TQ	USBLS	5/07
	Wilmington PMSA, DE-MD-NJ	Y	26250 FQ	38260 MW	50170 TQ	USBLS	5/07
	District of Columbia	Y	39620 FQ	43210 MW	46800 TQ	USBLS	5/07
	Washington-Arlington-Alexandria MSA, DC-VA-MD-WV	Y	24860 FQ	32750 MW	47680 TQ	USBLS	5/07
	Florida	Y	26610 FQ	32540 MW	43790 TQ	USBLS	5/07
	Fort Lauderdale-Pompano Beach-Deerfield Beach PMSA, FL	Y	29400 FQ	35910 MW	47200 TQ	USBLS	5/07
	Jacksonville MSA, FL	Y	28250 FQ	36370 MW	46090 TQ	USBLS	5/07
	Miami-Fort Lauderdale-Miami Beach MSA, FL	Y	27330 FQ	32930 MW	43580 TQ	USBLS	5/07
	Orlando-Kissimmee MSA, FL	Y	18710 FQ	26810 MW	37450 TQ	USBLS	5/07
	Tallahassee MSA, FL	Y	35770 FQ	42730 MW	47510 TQ	USBLS	5/07
	Tampa-St. Petersburg-Clearwater MSA, FL	Y	25480 FQ	31520 MW	46790 TQ	USBLS	5/07
	West Palm Beach-Boca Raton-Boynton Beach PMSA, FL	Y	27460 FQ	31830 MW	42470 TQ	USBLS	5/07
	Georgia	Y	25560 FQ	32760 MW	43690 TQ	USBLS	5/07
	Atlanta-Sandy Springs-Marietta MSA, GA	Y	24990 FQ	32110 MW	44620 TQ	USBLS	5/07
	Hawaii	Y	19150 FQ	30110 MW	42270 TQ	USBLS	5/07
	Honolulu MSA, HI	Y	19330 FQ	30880 MW	43850 TQ	USBLS	5/07
	Idaho	Y	31840 FQ	39170 MW	45660 TQ	USBLS	5/07
	Boise City-Nampa MSA, ID	Y	33830 FQ	43610 MW	48040 TQ	USBLS	5/07
	Illinois	Y	27340 FQ	36550 MW	47190 TQ	USBLS	5/07
	Chicago-Naperville-Joliet MSA, IL-IN-WI	Y	27270 FQ	36610 MW	47250 TQ	USBLS	5/07
	Rockford MSA, IL	Y	28360 FQ	35060 MW	38630 TQ	USBLS	5/07
	Indiana	Y	31270 FQ	38790 MW	46880 TQ	USBLS	5/07
	Fort Wayne MSA, IN	Y	22880 FQ	29490 MW	44370 TQ	USBLS	5/07
	Gary PMSA, IN	Y	34630 FQ	42670 MW	52440 TQ	USBLS	5/07
	Indianapolis-Carmel MSA, IN	Y	32310 FQ	39760 MW	46940 TQ	USBLS	5/07
	Iowa	Y	31460 FQ	38830 MW	47680 TQ	USBLS	5/07
	Des Moines-West Des Moines MSA, IA	Y	34190 FQ	39190 MW	45860 TQ	USBLS	5/07
	Kansas	Y	35890 FQ	44130 MW	49780 TQ	USBLS	5/07
	Wichita MSA, KS	Y	37730 FQ	44120 MW	48710 TQ	USBLS	5/07
	Kentucky	Y	28800 FQ	36226 MW	47274 TQ	KYBLS	2008
	Louisville-Jefferson County MSA, KY-IN	Y	28810 FQ	35370 MW	45670 TQ	USBLS	5/07
	Louisiana	H	14.11 FQ	18.06 MW	24.77 TQ	LABLS	1/08-3/08
	New Orleans-Metairie-Kenner MSA, LA	Y	31010 FQ	39610 MW	52850 TQ	USBLS	5/07
	Maine	Y	34440 FQ	40360 MW	47570 TQ	USBLS	5/07
	Maryland	Y		35300 MW		MDBLS	3/08
	Baltimore-Towson MSA, MD	Y	25490 FQ	34290 MW	45300 TQ	USBLS	5/07
	Massachusetts	Y	33160 FQ	41750 MW	51710 TQ	USBLS	5/07

AE	Average entry wage	**AW**	Average wage paid	**FQ** First quartile wage	**LO** Lowest wage paid	**MTC** Median total compensation	**TCC** Total cash compensation
AER	Average entry range	**AWR**	Average wage range	**H** Hourly	**LR** Low end range	**MW** Median wage paid	**TQ** Third quartile wage
AEX	Average experienced wage	**AXR**	Average experienced range	**HI** Highest wage paid	**M** Monthly	**MWR** Median wage range	**W** Weekly
ATC	Average total compensation	**D**	Daily	**HR** High end range	**MCC** Median cash compensation	**S** See annotated source	**Y** Yearly

165

Cargo and Freight Agent

Occupation/Type/Industry	Location	Per	Low	Mid	High	Source	Date
Cargo and Freight Agent	Boston-Cambridge-Quincy NECTA, MA	Y	32930 FQ	40970 MW	50520 TQ	USBLS	5/07
	Michigan	Y	27180 FQ	37410 MW	52840 TQ	USBLS	5/07
	Detroit-Warren-Livonia MSA, MI	Y	27860 FQ	36910 MW	54900 TQ	USBLS	5/07
	Grand Rapids-Wyoming MSA, MI	Y	40440 FQ	50320 MW	56610 TQ	USBLS	5/07
	Warren-Troy-Farmington Hills PMSA, MI	Y	23060 FQ	27410 MW	37560 TQ	USBLS	5/07
	Minnesota	Y	38395 FQ	45222 MW	52914 TQ	MNBLS	10/08-12/08
	Minneapolis-Saint Paul MSA, MN-WI	Y	36063 FQ	42391 MW	51030 TQ	MNBLS	10/08-12/08
	Rochester MSA, MN	Y	35248 FQ	42470 MW	55551 TQ	MNBLS	10/08-12/08
	Mississippi	Y	26670 FQ	34270 MW	41750 TQ	USBLS	5/07
	Jackson MSA, MS	Y	29800 FQ	37810 MW	45200 TQ	USBLS	5/07
	Missouri	Y	34000 FQ	42430 MW	48960 TQ	USBLS	5/07
	Kansas City MSA, MO-KS	Y	30880 FQ	38630 MW	45980 TQ	USBLS	5/07
	St. Louis MSA, MO-IL	Y	35670 FQ	43850 MW	50100 TQ	USBLS	5/07
	Montana	Y	22340 FQ	28030 MW	39410 TQ	USBLS	5/07
	Nebraska	Y	39220 FQ	46070 MW	54240 TQ	USBLS	5/07
	Omaha-Council Bluffs MSA, NE-IA	Y	20140 FQ	28850 MW	40170 TQ	USBLS	5/07
	Nevada	H	14.52 FQ	19.28 MW	22.85 TQ	NVBLS	5/08
	Las Vegas-Paradise MSA, NV	H	14.59 FQ	19.40 MW	22.86 TQ	NVBLS	5/08
	New Hampshire	H	14.69 AE	21.10 MW	24.82 AEX	NHBLS	6/08
	Manchester MSA, NH	Y	26090 FQ	34910 MW	48480 TQ	USBLS	5/07
	Nashua NECTA, NH-MA	Y	39300 FQ	42230 MW	45170 TQ	USBLS	5/07
	New Jersey	Y	31670 FQ	39450 MW	48130 TQ	USBLS	5/07
	Camden PMSA, NJ	Y	36720 FQ	43860 MW	55480 TQ	USBLS	5/07
	Edison PMSA, NJ	Y	31360 FQ	39820 MW	51360 TQ	USBLS	5/07
	Newark-Union PMSA, NJ-PA	Y	30310 FQ	39520 MW	47430 TQ	USBLS	5/07
	New Mexico	Y	29870 FQ	35780 MW	42430 TQ	USBLS	5/07
	Albuquerque MSA, NM	Y	29620 FQ	35490 MW	42040 TQ	USBLS	5/07
	New York	Y	27230 FQ	35860 MW	45180 TQ	USBLS	5/07
	Albany-Schenectady-Troy MSA, NY	Y	28360 FQ	31480 MW	35940 TQ	USBLS	5/07
	Buffalo-Niagara Falls MSA, NY	Y	24280 FQ	29880 MW	37680 TQ	USBLS	5/07
	Nassau-Suffolk PMSA, NY	Y	30510 FQ	39310 MW	47450 TQ	USBLS	5/07
	New York-Northern New Jersey-Long Island MSA, NY-NJ-PA	Y	28390 FQ	37720 MW	46550 TQ	USBLS	5/07
	Syracuse MSA, NY	Y	35960 FQ	40110 MW	44320 TQ	USBLS	5/07
	North Carolina	Y	29330 FQ	35990 MW	43270 TQ	USBLS	5/07
	Charlotte-Gastonia-Concord MSA, NC-SC	Y	24270 FQ	34860 MW	42330 TQ	USBLS	5/07
	Raleigh-Cary MSA, NC	Y	32050 FQ	38540 MW	45550 TQ	USBLS	5/07
	North Dakota	Y	26840 FQ	31990 MW	41170 TQ	USBLS	5/07
	Fargo MSA, ND-MN	Y	33010 FQ	39210 MW	54370 TQ	USBLS	5/07
	Ohio	Y	27270 FQ	32160 MW	39200 TQ	USBLS	5/07
	Cincinnati-Middletown MSA, OH-KY-IN	Y	27640 FQ	33450 MW	40760 TQ	USBLS	5/07
	Cleveland-Elyria-Mentor MSA, OH	Y	27540 FQ	35410 MW	45320 TQ	USBLS	5/07
	Columbus MSA, OH	Y	28600 FQ	33290 MW	38070 TQ	USBLS	5/07
	Dayton MSA, OH	Y	23160 FQ	27070 MW	36180 TQ	USBLS	5/07
	Oklahoma	Y	30030 FQ	39360 MW	47920 TQ	USBLS	5/07
	Oklahoma City MSA, OK	Y	32640 FQ	41890 MW	48550 TQ	USBLS	5/07
	Tulsa MSA, OK	Y	23070 FQ	34860 MW	44440 TQ	USBLS	5/07
	Oregon	H	14.66 FQ	17.31 MW	22.21 TQ	ORBLS	5/08
	Eugene-Springfield MSA, OR	Y	34140 FQ	38690 MW	43830 TQ	USBLS	5/07
	Portland-Vancouver-Beaverton MSA, OR-WA	Y	30650 FQ	38750 MW	55920 TQ	USBLS	5/07
	Pennsylvania	Y	27310 FQ	32670 MW	43670 TQ	USBLS	5/07
	Allentown-Bethlehem-Easton MSA, PA-NJ	Y	30240 FQ	45430 MW	54180 TQ	USBLS	5/07
	Philadelphia-Camden-Wilmington MSA, PA-NJ-DE-MD	Y	30940 FQ	36650 MW	51440 TQ	USBLS	5/07
	Pittsburgh MSA, PA	Y	24450 FQ	30510 MW	37480 TQ	USBLS	5/07
	Rhode Island	Y	25640 FQ	29930 MW	43480 TQ	USBLS	5/07

AE	Average entry wage	AW	Average wage paid	FQ First quartile wage
AER	Average entry range	AWR	Average wage range	H Hourly
AEX	Average experienced wage	AXR	Average experienced range	HI Highest wage paid
ATC	Average total compensation	D	Daily	HR High end range

LO Lowest wage paid · LR Low end range · M Monthly · MCC Median cash compensation · MTC Median total compensation · MW Median wage paid · MWR Median wage range · S See annotated source · TCC Total cash compensation · TQ Third quartile wage · W Weekly · Y Yearly

Occupation/Type/Industry	Location	Per	Low	Mid	High	Source	Date
Cargo and Freight Agent	Providence-Fall River-Warwick MSA, RI-MA	Y	25640 FQ	29810 MW	43210 TQ	USBLS	5/07
	South Carolina	Y	27070 FQ	34430 MW	42670 TQ	USBLS	5/07
	Charleston-North Charleston MSA, SC	Y	29230 FQ	37550 MW	43890 TQ	USBLS	5/07
	Columbia MSA, SC	Y	27210 FQ	30150 MW	41130 TQ	USBLS	5/07
	South Dakota	Y	38136 FQ	45607 MW	55483 TQ	SDBLS	7/08-9/08
	Rapid City MSA, SD	Y	33084 FQ	38659 MW	44348 TQ	SDBLS	7/08-9/08
	Sioux Falls MSA, SD	Y	39028 FQ	46296 MW	55940 TQ	SDBLS	7/08-9/08
	Tennessee	Y	32810 FQ	38050 MW	43890 TQ	USBLS	5/07
	Nashville-Davidson-Murfreesboro MSA, TN	Y	31310 FQ	41250 MW	47920 TQ	USBLS	5/07
	Texas	Y	26450 FQ	33890 MW	44180 TQ	USBLS	5/07
	Austin-Round Rock MSA, TX	Y	24820 FQ	30990 MW	44000 TQ	USBLS	5/07
	Dallas-Fort Worth-Arlington MSA, TX	Y	25510 FQ	31800 MW	43530 TQ	USBLS	5/07
	El Paso MSA, TX	Y	30350 FQ	38210 MW	44230 TQ	USBLS	5/07
	Houston-Sugar Land-Baytown MSA, TX	Y	28020 FQ	34390 MW	43170 TQ	USBLS	5/07
	San Antonio MSA, TX	Y	35770 FQ	43150 MW	47920 TQ	USBLS	5/07
	Utah	Y	20570 FQ	26290 MW	38270 TQ	USBLS	5/07
	Salt Lake City MSA, UT	Y	20600 FQ	24600 MW	36850 TQ	USBLS	5/07
	Vermont	Y	22700 FQ	28560 MW	34090 TQ	USBLS	5/07
	Virginia	Y	30560 FQ	38160 MW	49420 TQ	USBLS	5/07
	Richmond MSA, VA	Y	38990 FQ	48850 MW	55990 TQ	USBLS	5/07
	Virginia Beach-Norfolk-Newport News MSA, VA-NC	Y	31170 FQ	37180 MW	46950 TQ	USBLS	5/07
	Washington	H	19.51 FQ	24.71 MW	31.23 TQ	WABLS	3/08
	Seattle-Tacoma-Bellevue MSA, WA	Y	39250 FQ	49080 MW	63620 TQ	USBLS	5/07
	West Virginia	Y	23668 FQ	25758 MW	31096 TQ	WVBLS	7/08-9/08
	Charleston MSA, WV	Y	22380 FQ	23930 MW	25480 TQ	USBLS	5/07
	Wisconsin	Y	24280 FQ	33490 MW	42790 TQ	USBLS	5/07
	Milwaukee-Waukesha-West Allis MSA, WI	Y	29510 FQ	37730 MW	45560 TQ	USBLS	5/07
	Puerto Rico	Y	21920 FQ	30310 MW	45420 TQ	USBLS	5/07
	San Juan-Caguas-Guaynabo MSA, PR	Y	22110 FQ	30560 MW	45540 TQ	USBLS	5/07
	Virgin Islands	Y	18150 FQ	26150 MW	36290 TQ	USBLS	5/07
	Guam	Y	22910 FQ	42150 MW	47140 TQ	USBLS	5/07
Carpenter	Alabama	Y	24140 FQ	28860 MW	34620 TQ	USBLS	5/07
	Birmingham-Hoover MSA, AL	Y	26870 FQ	32100 MW	38530 TQ	USBLS	5/07
	Alaska	Y	43910 FQ	53920 MW	64360 TQ	USBLS	5/07
	Anchorage MSA, AK	Y	43260 FQ	57460 MW	68030 TQ	USBLS	5/07
	Arizona	Y	24700 FQ	33290 MW	42290 TQ	USBLS	5/07
	Phoenix-Mesa-Scottsdale MSA, AZ	Y	24460 FQ	33430 MW	42700 TQ	USBLS	5/07
	Tucson MSA, AZ	Y	26760 FQ	35160 MW	44200 TQ	USBLS	5/07
	Yuma MSA, AZ	Y	23700 FQ	30680 MW	39310 TQ	USBLS	5/07
	Arkansas	Y	26380 FQ	30650 MW	36490 TQ	USBLS	5/07
	Little Rock-North Little Rock MSA, AR	Y	27120 FQ	31410 MW	36450 TQ	USBLS	5/07
	California	H	18.44 FQ	24.53 MW	30.49 TQ	CABLS	1/08-3/08
	Fresno MSA, CA	H	11.67 FQ	16.52 MW	23.15 TQ	CABLS	1/08-3/08
	Los Angeles-Long Beach-Glendale PMSA, CA	H	16.41 FQ	22.76 MW	30.02 TQ	CABLS	1/08-3/08
	Oakland-Fremont-Hayward MSA, CA	H	23.12 FQ	28.72 MW	34.64 TQ	CABLS	1/08-3/08
	Riverside-San Bernardino-Ontario MSA, CA	H	17.13 FQ	22.71 MW	27.67 TQ	CABLS	1/08-3/08
	Sacramento-Arden Arcade-Roseville MSA, CA	H	20.11 FQ	25.16 MW	29.92 TQ	CABLS	1/08-3/08
	San Diego-Carlsbad-San Marcos MSA, CA	H	17.41 FQ	22.58 MW	28.22 TQ	CABLS	1/08-3/08
	San Francisco-San Mateo-Redwood PMSA, CA	H	23.42 FQ	30.22 MW	35.40 TQ	CABLS	1/08-3/08
	San Jose-Sunnyvale-Santa Clara MSA, CA	H	21.72 FQ	26.67 MW	32.07 TQ	CABLS	1/08-3/08
	Santa Ana-Anaheim-Irvine PMSA, CA	Y	38260 FQ	50450 MW	64200 TQ	USBLS	5/07
	Colorado	Y	29340 FQ	37500 MW	48570 TQ	USBLS	5/07

AE	Average entry wage	AW	Average wage paid	FQ	First quartile wage
AER	Average entry range	AWR	Average wage range	H	Hourly
AEX	Average experienced wage	AXR	Average experienced range	HI	Highest wage paid
ATC	Average total compensation	D	Daily	HR	High end range

LO	Lowest wage paid	MTC	Median total compensation	TCC	Total cash compensation
LR	Low end range	MW	Median wage paid	TQ	Third quartile wage
M	Monthly	MWR	Median wage range	W	Weekly
MCC	Median cash compensation	S	See annotated source	Y	Yearly

Carpenter

Occupation/Type/Industry	Location	Per	Low	Mid	High	Source	Date
Carpenter	Denver-Aurora MSA, CO	Y	30000 FQ	37800 MW	47560 TQ	USBLS	5/07
	Connecticut	H	16.12 AE	23.30 MW		CTBLS	1/08-3/08
	Bridgeport-Stamford-Norwalk MSA, CT	Y	38430 FQ	49820 MW	58850 TQ	USBLS	5/07
	Hartford-West Hartford-East Hartford MSA, CT	Y	36650 FQ	47110 MW	56400 TQ	USBLS	5/07
	New Haven MSA, CT	Y	35670 FQ	43770 MW	54150 TQ	USBLS	5/07
	Delaware	Y	32710 FQ	40580 MW	51890 TQ	USBLS	5/07
	Wilmington PMSA, DE-MD-NJ	Y	36910 FQ	45440 MW	55050 TQ	USBLS	5/07
	District of Columbia	Y	42910 FQ	49570 MW	55740 TQ	USBLS	5/07
	Washington-Arlington-Alexandria MSA, DC-VA-MD-WV	Y	33290 FQ	41200 MW	50750 TQ	USBLS	5/07
	Florida	Y	26750 FQ	32470 MW	39530 TQ	USBLS	5/07
	Fort Lauderdale-Pompano Beach-Deerfield Beach PMSA, FL	Y	25860 FQ	31840 MW	40140 TQ	USBLS	5/07
	Jacksonville MSA, FL	Y	27540 FQ	33740 MW	41840 TQ	USBLS	5/07
	Miami-Fort Lauderdale-Miami Beach MSA, FL	Y	27240 FQ	32700 MW	40160 TQ	USBLS	5/07
	Orlando-Kissimmee MSA, FL	Y	27530 FQ	33670 MW	39110 TQ	USBLS	5/07
	Tampa-St. Petersburg-Clearwater MSA, FL	Y	25390 FQ	30960 MW	37110 TQ	USBLS	5/07
	West Palm Beach-Boca Raton-Boynton Beach PMSA, FL	Y	29300 FQ	35010 MW	43580 TQ	USBLS	5/07
	Georgia	Y	25000 FQ	31560 MW	38810 TQ	USBLS	5/07
	Atlanta-Sandy Springs-Marietta MSA, GA	Y	26650 FQ	33630 MW	40730 TQ	USBLS	5/07
	Hawaii	Y	44020 FQ	58330 MW	71720 TQ	USBLS	5/07
	Honolulu MSA, HI	Y	43120 FQ	59640 MW	72980 TQ	USBLS	5/07
	Idaho	Y	24220 FQ	30510 MW	40710 TQ	USBLS	5/07
	Boise City-Nampa MSA, ID	Y	21950 FQ	28740 MW	38930 TQ	USBLS	5/07
	Pocatello MSA, ID	Y	24460 FQ	27810 MW	32500 TQ	USBLS	5/07
	Illinois	Y	37810 FQ	57780 MW	73290 TQ	USBLS	5/07
	Chicago-Naperville-Joliet MSA, IL-IN-WI	Y	41720 FQ	64670 MW	75670 TQ	USBLS	5/07
	Peoria MSA, IL	Y	36700 FQ	44560 MW	54900 TQ	USBLS	5/07
	Rockford MSA, IL	Y	32430 FQ	38480 MW	50130 TQ	USBLS	5/07
	Indiana	Y	28350 FQ	36820 MW	49860 TQ	USBLS	5/07
	Gary PMSA, IN	Y	29990 FQ	42300 MW	61600 TQ	USBLS	5/07
	Indianapolis-Carmel MSA, IN	Y	31380 FQ	39540 MW	50850 TQ	USBLS	5/07
	Iowa	Y	26060 FQ	32110 MW	41500 TQ	USBLS	5/07
	Des Moines-West Des Moines MSA, IA	Y	31430 FQ	39400 MW	47570 TQ	USBLS	5/07
	Kansas	Y	28400 FQ	35390 MW	45350 TQ	USBLS	5/07
	Topeka MSA, KS	Y	28810 FQ	34540 MW	40570 TQ	USBLS	5/07
	Wichita MSA, KS	Y	27200 FQ	32410 MW	39280 TQ	USBLS	5/07
	Kentucky	Y	26380 FQ	32964 MW	41470 TQ	KYBLS	2008
	Elizabethtown MSA, KY	Y	25880 FQ	29940 MW	37540 TQ	USBLS	5/07
	Louisville-Jefferson County MSA, KY-IN	Y	28940 FQ	35140 MW	42490 TQ	USBLS	5/07
	Louisiana	H	12.84 FQ	15.61 MW	18.72 TQ	LABLS	1/08-3/08
	Baton Rouge MSA, LA	Y	31610 FQ	36280 MW	41120 TQ	USBLS	5/07
	New Orleans-Metairie-Kenner MSA, LA	Y	27670 FQ	34650 MW	41510 TQ	USBLS	5/07
	Shreveport-Bossier City MSA, LA	Y	25720 FQ	30310 MW	36590 TQ	USBLS	5/07
	Maine	Y	28440 FQ	32710 MW	38540 TQ	USBLS	5/07
	Portland-South Portland-Biddeford MSA, ME	Y	30150 FQ	35660 MW	42500 TQ	USBLS	5/07
	Maryland	Y		40425 MW		MDBLS	3/08
	Baltimore-Towson MSA, MD	Y	32970 FQ	40980 MW	49590 TQ	USBLS	5/07
	Bethesda-Gaithersburg-Frederick PMSA, MD	Y	34520 FQ	41830 MW	49530 TQ	USBLS	5/07
	Hagerstown-Martinsburg MSA, MD-WV	Y	26670 FQ	32400 MW	37570 TQ	USBLS	5/07
	Massachusetts	Y	39060 FQ	49160 MW	62340 TQ	USBLS	5/07
	Boston-Cambridge-Quincy NECTA, MA	Y	42510 FQ	52400 MW	66350 TQ	USBLS	5/07
	Worcester MSA, MA-CT	Y	34140 FQ	40840 MW	47760 TQ	USBLS	5/07
	Michigan	Y	31520 FQ	40970 MW	53230 TQ	USBLS	5/07

AE	Average entry wage	AW	Average wage paid	FQ	First quartile wage	LO	Lowest wage paid	MTC	Median total compensation	TCC	Total cash compensation
AER	Average entry range	AWR	Average wage range	H	Hourly	LR	Low end range	MW	Median wage paid	TQ	Third quartile wage
AEX	Average experienced wage	AXR	Average experienced range	HI	Highest wage paid	M	Monthly	MWR	Median wage range	W	Weekly
ATC	Average total compensation	D	Daily	HR	High end range	MCC	Median cash compensation	S	See annotated source	Y	Yearly

Carpenter

Occupation/Type/Industry	Location	Per	Low	Mid	High	Source	Date
Carpenter	Detroit-Warren-Livonia MSA, MI	Y	37130 FQ	47330 MW	60040 TQ	USBLS	5/07
	Grand Rapids-Wyoming MSA, MI	Y	28490 FQ	37500 MW	46130 TQ	USBLS	5/07
	Warren-Troy-Farmington Hills PMSA, MI	Y	37790 FQ	46780 MW	59040 TQ	USBLS	5/07
	Minnesota	Y	34482 FQ	43345 MW	56909 TQ	MNBLS	10/08-12/08
	Duluth-Superior MSA, MN-WI	Y	34366 FQ	42407 MW	51355 TQ	MNBLS	10/08-12/08
	Minneapolis-Saint Paul MSA, MN-WI	Y	37950 FQ	48351 MW	63622 TQ	MNBLS	10/08-12/08
	Rochester MSA, MN	Y	36060 FQ	43343 MW	50846 TQ	MNBLS	10/08-12/08
	Mississippi	Y	23700 FQ	29040 MW	34880 TQ	USBLS	5/07
	Jackson MSA, MS	Y	25630 FQ	30900 MW	36060 TQ	USBLS	5/07
	Missouri	Y	29590 FQ	42120 MW	58160 TQ	USBLS	5/07
	Kansas City MSA, MO-KS	Y	31710 FQ	43040 MW	64800 TQ	USBLS	5/07
	St. Louis MSA, MO-IL	Y	40170 FQ	53740 MW	64160 TQ	USBLS	5/07
	Montana	Y	26630 FQ	32430 MW	38820 TQ	USBLS	5/07
	Billings MSA, MT	Y	22770 FQ	29320 MW	37540 TQ	USBLS	5/07
	Nebraska	Y	25540 FQ	30250 MW	37080 TQ	USBLS	5/07
	Omaha-Council Bluffs MSA, NE-IA	Y	27250 FQ	32080 MW	39810 TQ	USBLS	5/07
	Nevada	H	16.76 FQ	21.43 MW	27.58 TQ	NVBLS	5/08
	Las Vegas-Paradise MSA, NV	H	16.88 FQ	21.43 MW	27.74 TQ	NVBLS	5/08
	New Hampshire	H	14.45 AE	18.88 MW	22.20 AEX	NHBLS	6/08
	Manchester MSA, NH	Y	38380 FQ	44140 MW	50060 TQ	USBLS	5/07
	Nashua NECTA, NH-MA	Y	29370 FQ	36650 MW	46030 TQ	USBLS	5/07
	New Jersey	Y	36180 FQ	48360 MW	69500 TQ	USBLS	5/07
	Camden PMSA, NJ	Y	35590 FQ	47740 MW	59710 TQ	USBLS	5/07
	Edison PMSA, NJ	Y	35270 FQ	47400 MW	69850 TQ	USBLS	5/07
	Newark-Union PMSA, NJ-PA	Y	38630 FQ	48140 MW	70640 TQ	USBLS	5/07
	Ocean City MSA, NJ	Y	32250 FQ	42980 MW	52020 TQ	USBLS	5/07
	New Mexico	Y	25600 FQ	31120 MW	39210 TQ	USBLS	5/07
	Albuquerque MSA, NM	Y	25110 FQ	31230 MW	40150 TQ	USBLS	5/07
	New York	Y	33540 FQ	45500 MW	62630 TQ	USBLS	5/07
	Albany-Schenectady-Troy MSA, NY	Y	32820 FQ	39650 MW	47530 TQ	USBLS	5/07
	Buffalo-Niagara Falls MSA, NY	Y	30240 FQ	38320 MW	47630 TQ	USBLS	5/07
	Nassau-Suffolk PMSA, NY	Y	38270 FQ	50770 MW	67370 TQ	USBLS	5/07
	New York-Northern New Jersey-Long Island MSA, NY-NJ-PA	Y	37930 FQ	50900 MW	73220 TQ	USBLS	5/07
	North Carolina	Y	26170 FQ	30510 MW	36200 TQ	USBLS	5/07
	Charlotte-Gastonia-Concord MSA, NC-SC	Y	27370 FQ	32200 MW	38670 TQ	USBLS	5/07
	Durham MSA, NC	Y	25800 FQ	29900 MW	35420 TQ	USBLS	5/07
	Raleigh-Cary MSA, NC	Y	25950 FQ	30730 MW	36510 TQ	USBLS	5/07
	North Dakota	Y	27020 FQ	31310 MW	37140 TQ	USBLS	5/07
	Fargo MSA, ND-MN	Y	28120 FQ	32660 MW	37600 TQ	USBLS	5/07
	Ohio	Y	28170 FQ	36050 MW	47250 TQ	USBLS	5/07
	Cincinnati-Middletown MSA, OH-KY-IN	Y	29510 FQ	37590 MW	46110 TQ	USBLS	5/07
	Cleveland-Elyria-Mentor MSA, OH	Y	31190 FQ	38130 MW	55690 TQ	USBLS	5/07
	Columbus MSA, OH	Y	30270 FQ	38060 MW	46360 TQ	USBLS	5/07
	Dayton MSA, OH	Y	27260 FQ	37390 MW	48410 TQ	USBLS	5/07
	Oklahoma	Y	23290 FQ	28570 MW	34470 TQ	USBLS	5/07
	Lawton MSA, OK	Y	20690 FQ	30760 MW	41940 TQ	USBLS	5/07
	Oklahoma City MSA, OK	Y	23620 FQ	29920 MW	36830 TQ	USBLS	5/07
	Tulsa MSA, OK	Y	25230 FQ	28570 MW	32270 TQ	USBLS	5/07
	Oregon	H	14.10 FQ	18.03 MW	24.14 TQ	ORBLS	5/08
	Portland-Vancouver-Beaverton MSA, OR-WA	Y	28740 FQ	38600 MW	52510 TQ	USBLS	5/07
	Pennsylvania	Y	29180 FQ	38090 MW	48810 TQ	USBLS	5/07
	Allentown-Bethlehem-Easton MSA, PA-NJ	Y	32030 FQ	41400 MW	51060 TQ	USBLS	5/07
	Philadelphia-Camden-Wilmington MSA, PA-NJ-DE-MD	Y	35790 FQ	45460 MW	58360 TQ	USBLS	5/07
	Pittsburgh MSA, PA	Y	29230 FQ	39920 MW	50500 TQ	USBLS	5/07
	Rhode Island	Y	35020 FQ	40140 MW	47570 TQ	USBLS	5/07

AE	Average entry wage	AW	Average wage paid	FQ	First quartile wage	LO	Lowest wage paid	MTC	Median total compensation	TCC	Total cash compensation
AER	Average entry range	AWR	Average wage range	H	Hourly	LR	Low end range	MW	Median wage paid	TQ	Third quartile wage
AEX	Average experienced wage	AXR	Average experienced range	HI	Highest wage paid	M	Monthly	MWR	Median wage range	W	Weekly
ATC	Average total compensation	D	Daily	HR	High end range	MCC	Median cash compensation	S	See annotated source	Y	Yearly

Occupation/Type/Industry	Location	Per	Low	Mid	High	Source	Date
Carpenter	Providence-Fall River- Warwick MSA, RI-MA	Y	35330 FQ	41760 MW	52660 TQ	USBLS	5/07
	South Carolina	Y	26420 FQ	31110 MW	37370 TQ	USBLS	5/07
	Charleston-North Charleston MSA, SC	Y	28250 FQ	33030 MW	38060 TQ	USBLS	5/07
	Columbia MSA, SC	Y	26590 FQ	31000 MW	38460 TQ	USBLS	5/07
	South Dakota	Y	26317 FQ	30268 MW	34674 TQ	SDBLS	7/08-9/08
	Rapid City MSA, SD	Y	26738 FQ	30808 MW	35052 TQ	SDBLS	7/08-9/08
	Sioux Falls MSA, SD	Y	27541 FQ	31354 MW	36345 TQ	SDBLS	7/08-9/08
	Tennessee	Y	24980 FQ	30240 MW	36960 TQ	USBLS	5/07
	Clarksville MSA, TN-KY	Y	24880 FQ	29390 MW	34630 TQ	USBLS	5/07
	Memphis MSA, TN-MS-AR	Y	25280 FQ	30710 MW	38320 TQ	USBLS	5/07
	Nashville-Davidson- Murfreesboro MSA, TN	Y	25550 FQ	31230 MW	37880 TQ	USBLS	5/07
	Texas	Y	24760 FQ	29850 MW	36450 TQ	USBLS	5/07
	Austin-Round Rock MSA, TX	Y	25560 FQ	31090 MW	41460 TQ	USBLS	5/07
	Corpus Christi MSA, TX	Y	22010 FQ	25240 MW	30100 TQ	USBLS	5/07
	Dallas-Fort Worth-Arlington MSA, TX	Y	25480 FQ	30510 MW	37760 TQ	USBLS	5/07
	El Paso MSA, TX	Y	18730 FQ	25840 MW	30290 TQ	USBLS	5/07
	Houston-Sugar Land-Baytown MSA, TX	Y	25800 FQ	31040 MW	37180 TQ	USBLS	5/07
	San Antonio MSA, TX	Y	26340 FQ	29800 MW	35440 TQ	USBLS	5/07
	Utah	Y	27330 FQ	33150 MW	40190 TQ	USBLS	5/07
	Salt Lake City MSA, UT	Y	27070 FQ	34320 MW	42350 TQ	USBLS	5/07
	Vermont	Y	31080 FQ	36760 MW	42890 TQ	USBLS	5/07
	Burlington-South Burlington MSA, VT	Y	33560 FQ	39370 MW	45930 TQ	USBLS	5/07
	Virginia	Y	27970 FQ	34890 MW	43760 TQ	USBLS	5/07
	Lynchburg MSA, VA	Y	24720 FQ	29870 MW	37180 TQ	USBLS	5/07
	Richmond MSA, VA	Y	29320 FQ	36710 MW	45000 TQ	USBLS	5/07
	Virginia Beach-Norfolk- Newport News MSA, VA-NC	Y	27070 FQ	33560 MW	40620 TQ	USBLS	5/07
	Washington	H	16.47 FQ	21.50 MW	27.84 TQ	WABLS	3/08
	Seattle-Tacoma-Bellevue MSA, WA	Y	35410 FQ	46890 MW	60580 TQ	USBLS	5/07
	West Virginia	Y	26933 FQ	32224 MW	41110 TQ	WVBLS	7/08-9/08
	Charleston MSA, WV	Y	27950 FQ	33100 MW	41990 TQ	USBLS	5/07
	Wisconsin	Y	30090 FQ	38110 MW	51060 TQ	USBLS	5/07
	Milwaukee-Waukesha-West Allis MSA, WI	Y	36790 FQ	46770 MW	59000 TQ	USBLS	5/07
	Wyoming	Y	30202 FQ	37793 MW	47751 TQ	WYBLS	9/08
	Cheyenne MSA, WY	Y	28351 FQ	34107 MW	42932 TQ	WYBLS	9/08
	Puerto Rico	Y	15460 FQ	17400 MW	19130 TQ	USBLS	5/07
	San Juan-Caguas-Guaynabo MSA, PR	Y	16210 FQ	17790 MW	19390 TQ	USBLS	5/07
	Virgin Islands	Y	31390 FQ	36050 MW	40970 TQ	USBLS	5/07
	Guam	Y	24440 FQ	26840 MW	29480 TQ	USBLS	5/07
Carpet Installer	Alabama	Y	18580 FQ	29810 MW	37080 TQ	USBLS	5/07
	Alaska	Y	30710 FQ	53620 MW	60090 TQ	USBLS	5/07
	Anchorage MSA, AK	Y	34040 FQ	56240 MW	61400 TQ	USBLS	5/07
	Arizona	Y	20280 FQ	23630 MW	31070 TQ	USBLS	5/07
	Phoenix-Mesa-Scottsdale MSA, AZ	Y	20850 FQ	23720 MW	33290 TQ	USBLS	5/07
	Tucson MSA, AZ	Y	16350 FQ	25210 MW	28570 TQ	USBLS	5/07
	Arkansas	Y	28900 FQ	33540 MW	37680 TQ	USBLS	5/07
	California	H	15.39 FQ	19.25 MW	25.15 TQ	CABLS	1/08-3/08
	Los Angeles-Long Beach- Glendale PMSA, CA	H	15.71 FQ	17.69 MW	19.66 TQ	CABLS	1/08-3/08
	Oakland-Fremont-Hayward MSA, CA	H	18.53 FQ	22.94 MW	29.04 TQ	CABLS	1/08-3/08
	Riverside-San Bernardino- Ontario MSA, CA	H	15.80 FQ	17.97 MW	24.59 TQ	CABLS	1/08-3/08
	Sacramento-Arden Arcade- Roseville MSA, CA	H	16.87 FQ	23.09 MW	28.12 TQ	CABLS	1/08-3/08
	San Diego-Carlsbad-San Marcos MSA, CA	H	12.47 FQ	16.96 MW	22.87 TQ	CABLS	1/08-3/08
	San Jose-Sunnyvale-Santa Clara MSA, CA	H	14.27 FQ	19.13 MW	25.91 TQ	CABLS	1/08-3/08
	Santa Ana-Anaheim-Irvine PMSA, CA	Y	35310 FQ	43700 MW	50780 TQ	USBLS	5/07

AE	Average entry wage	AW	Average wage paid	FQ	First quartile wage
AER	Average entry range	AWR	Average wage range	H	Hourly
AEX	Average experienced wage	AXR	Average experienced range	HI	Highest wage paid
ATC	Average total compensation	D	Daily	HR	High end range

LO	Lowest wage paid	MTC	Median total compensation	TCC	Total cash compensation
LR	Low end range	MW	Median wage paid	TQ	Third quartile wage
M	Monthly	MWR	Median wage range	W	Weekly
MCC	Median cash compensation	S	See annotated source	Y	Yearly

Occupation/Type/Industry	Location	Per	Low	Mid	High	Source	Date
Carpet Installer	Stockton MSA, CA	H	12.99 FQ	14.36 MW	15.71 TQ	CABLS	1/08-3/08
	Colorado	Y	21610 FQ	30790 MW	36690 TQ	USBLS	5/07
	Denver-Aurora MSA, CO	Y	19530 FQ	30620 MW	36440 TQ	USBLS	5/07
	Connecticut	H	12.10 AE	16.72 MW		CTBLS	1/08-3/08
	Wilmington PMSA, DE-MD-NJ	Y	41660 FQ	45830 MW	49990 TQ	USBLS	5/07
	Washington-Arlington-Alexandria MSA, DC-VA-MD-WV	Y	22390 FQ	26830 MW	41280 TQ	USBLS	5/07
	Florida	Y	21800 FQ	26310 MW	42560 TQ	USBLS	5/07
	Fort Lauderdale-Pompano Beach-Deerfield Beach PMSA, FL	Y	37590 FQ	43470 MW	49030 TQ	USBLS	5/07
	Miami-Fort Lauderdale-Miami Beach MSA, FL	Y	30330 FQ	40430 MW	47060 TQ	USBLS	5/07
	Orlando-Kissimmee MSA, FL	Y	23660 FQ	26090 MW	31330 TQ	USBLS	5/07
	Tampa-St. Petersburg-Clearwater MSA, FL	Y	15760 FQ	25590 MW	43630 TQ	USBLS	5/07
	Georgia	Y	19590 FQ	22790 MW	31210 TQ	USBLS	5/07
	Atlanta-Sandy Springs-Marietta MSA, GA	Y	21970 FQ	26600 MW	40680 TQ	USBLS	5/07
	Hawaii	Y	25160 FQ	34590 MW	55260 TQ	USBLS	5/07
	Honolulu MSA, HI	Y	25320 FQ	34450 MW	55230 TQ	USBLS	5/07
	Idaho	Y	23110 FQ	33600 MW	53840 TQ	USBLS	5/07
	Illinois	Y	37580 FQ	60870 MW	72730 TQ	USBLS	5/07
	Chicago-Naperville-Joliet MSA, IL-IN-WI	Y	41200 FQ	65320 MW	74210 TQ	USBLS	5/07
	Indiana	Y	26920 FQ	34160 MW	41620 TQ	USBLS	5/07
	Indianapolis-Carmel MSA, IN	Y	27740 FQ	34480 MW	40400 TQ	USBLS	5/07
	Iowa	Y	21700 FQ	28650 MW	36580 TQ	USBLS	5/07
	Davenport-Moline-Rock Island MSA, IA-IL	Y	23550 FQ	32130 MW	39620 TQ	USBLS	5/07
	Kansas	Y	33240 FQ	38430 MW	53650 TQ	USBLS	5/07
	Kentucky	Y	24215 FQ	30228 MW	38565 TQ	KYBLS	2008
	Louisville-Jefferson County MSA, KY-IN	Y	25500 FQ	29690 MW	35910 TQ	USBLS	5/07
	Louisiana	H	13.38 FQ	17.26 MW	21.71 TQ	LABLS	1/08-3/08
	New Orleans-Metairie-Kenner MSA, LA	Y	22810 FQ	27110 MW	34920 TQ	USBLS	5/07
	Maine	Y	23080 FQ	30530 MW	37030 TQ	USBLS	5/07
	Portland-South Portland-Biddeford MSA, ME	Y	28240 FQ	33130 MW	38480 TQ	USBLS	5/07
	Maryland	Y		30900 MW		MDBLS	3/08
	Baltimore-Towson MSA, MD	Y	31120 FQ	43720 MW	55560 TQ	USBLS	5/07
	Massachusetts	Y	34170 FQ	57270 MW	73650 TQ	USBLS	5/07
	Boston-Cambridge-Quincy NECTA, MA	Y	20030 FQ	62150 MW	77410 TQ	USBLS	5/07
	Michigan	Y	28210 FQ	41330 MW	55690 TQ	USBLS	5/07
	Detroit-Warren-Livonia MSA, MI	Y	34450 FQ	46740 MW	62950 TQ	USBLS	5/07
	Grand Rapids-Wyoming MSA, MI	Y	29300 FQ	35470 MW	48270 TQ	USBLS	5/07
	Warren-Troy-Farmington Hills PMSA, MI	Y	39970 FQ	57740 MW	68020 TQ	USBLS	5/07
	Minnesota	Y	38719 FQ	58479 MW	71336 TQ	MNBLS	10/08-12/08
	Minneapolis-Saint Paul MSA, MN-WI	Y	40521 FQ	63569 MW	73223 TQ	MNBLS	10/08-12/08
	Mississippi	Y	22960 FQ	26610 MW	31590 TQ	USBLS	5/07
	Missouri	Y	32950 FQ	49860 MW	57130 TQ	USBLS	5/07
	Kansas City MSA, MO-KS	Y	37440 FQ	52220 MW	58570 TQ	USBLS	5/07
	St. Louis MSA, MO-IL	Y	32360 FQ	49300 MW	57310 TQ	USBLS	5/07
	Nebraska	Y	27010 FQ	31270 MW	39340 TQ	USBLS	5/07
	Omaha-Council Bluffs MSA, NE-IA	Y	20720 FQ	29830 MW	36230 TQ	USBLS	5/07
	Nevada	H	16.45 FQ	20.58 MW	26.77 TQ	NVBLS	5/08
	Las Vegas-Paradise MSA, NV	H	16.35 FQ	21.98 MW	27.89 TQ	NVBLS	5/08
	New Hampshire	H	13.78 AE	18.39 MW	20.49 AEX	NHBLS	6/08
	Nashua NECTA, NH-MA	Y	31510 FQ	36760 MW	43570 TQ	USBLS	5/07
	New Jersey	Y	32960 FQ	49640 MW	70680 TQ	USBLS	5/07
	Camden PMSA, NJ	Y	52080 FQ	67120 MW	73830 TQ	USBLS	5/07
	Edison PMSA, NJ	Y	30910 FQ	52680 MW	75990 TQ	USBLS	5/07
	Newark-Union PMSA, NJ-PA	Y	35300 FQ	53020 MW	70260 TQ	USBLS	5/07

AE	Average entry wage	**AW**	Average wage paid	**FQ**	First quartile wage	**LO** Lowest wage paid	**MTC** Median total compensation	**TCC** Total cash compensation
AER	Average entry range	**AWR**	Average wage range	**H**	Hourly	**LR** Low end range	**MW** Median wage paid	**TQ** Third quartile wage
AEX	Average experienced wage	**AXR**	Average experienced range	**HI**	Highest wage paid	**M** Monthly	**MWR** Median wage range	**W** Weekly
ATC	Average total compensation	**D**	Daily	**HR**	High end range	**MCC** Median cash compensation	**S** See annotated source	**Y** Yearly

Occupation/Type/Industry	Location	Per	Low	Mid	High	Source	Date
Carpet Installer	New Mexico	Y	24040 FQ	31620 MW	44500 TQ	USBLS	5/07
	New York	Y	34790 FQ	49440 MW	76640 TQ	USBLS	5/07
	Nassau-Suffolk PMSA, NY	Y	37600 FQ	59020 MW	85640 TQ	USBLS	5/07
	New York-Northern New Jersey-Long Island MSA, NY-NJ-PA	Y	36030 FQ	52370 MW	76890 TQ	USBLS	5/07
	North Carolina	Y	23310 FQ	28160 MW	34430 TQ	USBLS	5/07
	Charlotte-Gastonia-Concord MSA, NC-SC	Y	22910 FQ	30520 MW	36870 TQ	USBLS	5/07
	North Dakota	Y	18410 FQ	24440 MW	29130 TQ	USBLS	5/07
	Ohio	Y	23720 FQ	34680 MW	49600 TQ	USBLS	5/07
	Cincinnati-Middletown MSA, OH-KY-IN	Y	27750 FQ	34290 MW	42140 TQ	USBLS	5/07
	Cleveland-Elyria-Mentor MSA, OH	Y	26640 FQ	49220 MW	55220 TQ	USBLS	5/07
	Oklahoma	Y	20970 FQ	23410 MW	27890 TQ	USBLS	5/07
	Oklahoma City MSA, OK	Y	21930 FQ	24090 MW	28820 TQ	USBLS	5/07
	Oregon	H	12.48 FQ	18.16 MW	22.84 TQ	ORBLS	5/08
	Portland-Vancouver-Beaverton MSA, OR-WA	Y	28060 FQ	42430 MW	48560 TQ	USBLS	5/07
	Pennsylvania	Y	26800 FQ	34940 MW	43400 TQ	USBLS	5/07
	Allentown-Bethlehem-Easton MSA, PA-NJ	Y	33430 FQ	36660 MW	40180 TQ	USBLS	5/07
	Philadelphia-Camden-Wilmington MSA, PA-NJ-DE-MD	Y	33890 FQ	43790 MW	67850 TQ	USBLS	5/07
	Pittsburgh MSA, PA	Y	25700 FQ	31370 MW	38270 TQ	USBLS	5/07
	Rhode Island	Y	28430 FQ	31580 MW	38830 TQ	USBLS	5/07
	Providence-Fall River-Warwick MSA, RI-MA	Y	28800 FQ	32200 MW	38000 TQ	USBLS	5/07
	South Carolina	Y	23340 FQ	27430 MW	31010 TQ	USBLS	5/07
	South Dakota	Y	23309 FQ	26400 MW	34765 TQ	SDBLS	7/08-9/08
	Tennessee	Y	22920 FQ	28510 MW	33630 TQ	USBLS	5/07
	Memphis MSA, TN-MS-AR	Y	20910 FQ	28320 MW	35520 TQ	USBLS	5/07
	Texas	Y	22500 FQ	26690 MW	34390 TQ	USBLS	5/07
	Dallas-Fort Worth-Arlington MSA, TX	Y	22270 FQ	24720 MW	31290 TQ	USBLS	5/07
	El Paso MSA, TX	Y	18520 FQ	25160 MW	29540 TQ	USBLS	5/07
	Houston-Sugar Land-Baytown MSA, TX	Y	31340 FQ	39390 MW	44450 TQ	USBLS	5/07
	Utah	Y	29930 FQ	35010 MW	38160 TQ	USBLS	5/07
	Salt Lake City MSA, UT	Y	29440 FQ	34730 MW	37780 TQ	USBLS	5/07
	Vermont	Y	28280 FQ	33250 MW	38330 TQ	USBLS	5/07
	Burlington-South Burlington MSA, VT	Y	30800 FQ	35990 MW	40070 TQ	USBLS	5/07
	Virginia	Y	24030 FQ	33300 MW	39390 TQ	USBLS	5/07
	Richmond MSA, VA	Y	20050 FQ	33010 MW	36520 TQ	USBLS	5/07
	Virginia Beach-Norfolk-Newport News MSA, VA-NC	Y	32310 FQ	37620 MW	47720 TQ	USBLS	5/07
	Washington	H	9.14 FQ	10.76 MW	19.31 TQ	WABLS	3/08
	West Virginia	Y	24192 FQ	31353 MW	47006 TQ	WVBLS	7/08-9/08
	Wisconsin	Y	29720 FQ	37970 MW	56600 TQ	USBLS	5/07
	Green Bay MSA, WI	Y	48370 FQ	56910 MW	61830 TQ	USBLS	5/07
	Milwaukee-Waukesha-West Allis MSA, WI	Y	30850 FQ	48780 MW	59850 TQ	USBLS	5/07
	Wyoming	Y	23601 FQ	30424 MW	44314 TQ	WYBLS	9/08
Carpet Layer	Minnesota	H		23.08 MW		MMTHLY	2008
Carpool Coordinator Department of Transportation	New Hampshire	Y			31234 HI	NHUL03	2008
Carriage Operator Department of Transportation	New Hampshire	Y		37564 AW		NHUL03	2008
Cartographer	United States	Y		42870 AW		SUSA02	2008
Department of Environmental Quality	Oregon	M	1980 LO		3548 HI	ODEQSS	11/1/08
Cartographer and Photogrammetrist	Alabama	Y	38070 FQ	43660 MW	51520 TQ	USBLS	5/07
	Birmingham-Hoover MSA, AL	Y	43630 FQ	49950 MW	62860 TQ	USBLS	5/07
	Alaska	Y	46580 FQ	52360 MW	64040 TQ	USBLS	5/07

AE	Average entry wage	AW	Average wage paid	FQ	First quartile wage	LO	Lowest wage paid	MTC Median total compensation	TCC Total cash compensation
AER	Average entry range	AWR	Average wage range	H	Hourly	LR	Low end range	MW Median wage paid	TQ Third quartile wage
AEX	Average experienced wage	AXR	Average experienced range	HI	Highest wage paid	M	Monthly	MWR Median wage range	W Weekly
ATC	Average total compensation	D	Daily	HR	High end range	MCC	Median cash compensation	S See annotated source	Y Yearly

Occupation/Type/Industry	Location	Per	Low	Mid	High	Source	Date
Cartographer and Photogrammetrist							
	Anchorage MSA, AK	Y	45790 FQ	51000 MW	63440 TQ	USBLS	5/07
	Arizona	Y	42660 FQ	50080 MW	66940 TQ	USBLS	5/07
	Phoenix-Mesa-Scottsdale MSA, AZ	Y	42770 FQ	49160 MW	68030 TQ	USBLS	5/07
	Arkansas	Y	34290 FQ	44970 MW	58190 TQ	USBLS	5/07
	Little Rock-North Little Rock MSA, AR	Y	32940 FQ	41980 MW	57600 TQ	USBLS	5/07
	California	H	24.49 FQ	29.36 MW	36.11 TQ	CABLS	1/08-3/08
	Los Angeles-Long Beach-Glendale PMSA, CA	H	22.60 FQ	27.89 MW	32.78 TQ	CABLS	1/08-3/08
	Oakland-Fremont-Hayward MSA, CA	H	19.23 FQ	28.57 MW	36.01 TQ	CABLS	1/08-3/08
	Riverside-San Bernardino-Ontario MSA, CA	H	21.88 FQ	26.70 MW	30.54 TQ	CABLS	1/08-3/08
	Sacramento-Arden Arcade-Roseville MSA, CA	H	25.93 FQ	30.52 MW	36.29 TQ	CABLS	1/08-3/08
	San Diego-Carlsbad-San Marcos MSA, CA	H	25.51 FQ	28.47 MW	33.16 TQ	CABLS	1/08-3/08
	San Francisco-San Mateo-Redwood PMSA, CA	H	33.19 FQ	40.16 MW	48.15 TQ	CABLS	1/08-3/08
	San Jose-Sunnyvale-Santa Clara MSA, CA	H	26.21 FQ	29.65 MW	34.32 TQ	CABLS	1/08-3/08
	Santa Ana-Anaheim-Irvine PMSA, CA	Y	44440 FQ	54200 MW	66880 TQ	USBLS	5/07
	Colorado	Y	44920 FQ	59170 MW	76720 TQ	USBLS	5/07
	Denver-Aurora MSA, CO	Y	51480 FQ	68880 MW	82620 TQ	USBLS	5/07
	Connecticut	H	20.59 AE	25.11 MW		CTBLS	1/08-3/08
	Washington-Arlington-Alexandria MSA, DC-VA-MD-WV	Y	58990 FQ	77550 MW	94310 TQ	USBLS	5/07
	Tampa-St. Petersburg-Clearwater MSA, FL	Y	33370 FQ	40320 MW	46830 TQ	USBLS	5/07
	Georgia	Y	36650 FQ	47120 MW	64300 TQ	USBLS	5/07
	Atlanta-Sandy Springs-Marietta MSA, GA	Y	40850 FQ	51020 MW	69120 TQ	USBLS	5/07
	Hawaii	Y	42360 FQ	45990 MW	50020 TQ	USBLS	5/07
	Idaho	Y	36470 FQ	44910 MW	55650 TQ	USBLS	5/07
	Boise City-Nampa MSA, ID	Y	40600 FQ	49760 MW	61220 TQ	USBLS	5/07
	Illinois	Y	29880 FQ	37780 MW	57010 TQ	USBLS	5/07
	Chicago-Naperville-Joliet MSA, IL-IN-WI	Y	29870 FQ	37080 MW	48320 TQ	USBLS	5/07
	Indiana	Y	32700 FQ	40760 MW	49550 TQ	USBLS	5/07
	Indianapolis-Carmel MSA, IN	Y	33770 FQ	45180 MW	53660 TQ	USBLS	5/07
	Kansas	Y	34130 FQ	42420 MW	52510 TQ	USBLS	5/07
	Kentucky	Y	31859 FQ	39856 MW	48293 TQ	KYBLS	2008
	Louisville-Jefferson County MSA, KY-IN	Y	28890 FQ	34950 MW	44490 TQ	USBLS	5/07
	Louisiana	H	18.17 FQ	22.40 MW	31.81 TQ	LABLS	1/08-3/08
	New Orleans-Metairie-Kenner MSA, LA	Y	37780 FQ	43740 MW	49560 TQ	USBLS	5/07
	Maine	Y	35840 FQ	44650 MW	57800 TQ	USBLS	5/07
	Maryland	Y		71975 MW		MDBLS	3/08
	Baltimore-Towson MSA, MD	Y	37490 FQ	43550 MW	54350 TQ	USBLS	5/07
	Massachusetts	Y	39370 FQ	47570 MW	68120 TQ	USBLS	5/07
	Boston-Cambridge-Quincy NECTA, MA	Y	46170 FQ	64180 MW	81500 TQ	USBLS	5/07
	Worcester MSA, MA-CT	Y	36560 FQ	46870 MW	60480 TQ	USBLS	5/07
	Michigan	Y	42830 FQ	54010 MW	64250 TQ	USBLS	5/07
	Minnesota	Y	42989 FQ	54926 MW	67418 TQ	MNBLS	10/08-12/08
	Duluth-Superior MSA, MN-WI	Y	45249 FQ	52007 MW	57950 TQ	MNBLS	10/08-12/08
	Minneapolis-Saint Paul MSA, MN-WI	Y	54811 FQ	62836 MW	73968 TQ	MNBLS	10/08-12/08
	Mississippi	Y	35760 FQ	40600 MW	47530 TQ	USBLS	5/07
	Jackson MSA, MS	Y	44190 FQ	47700 MW	51140 TQ	USBLS	5/07
	Missouri	Y	36420 FQ	45760 MW	60730 TQ	USBLS	5/07
	Kansas City MSA, MO-KS	Y	39720 FQ	51060 MW	65400 TQ	USBLS	5/07
	St. Louis MSA, MO-IL	Y	35980 FQ	42570 MW	54610 TQ	USBLS	5/07
	Montana	Y	34230 FQ	41210 MW	50030 TQ	USBLS	5/07
	Nebraska	Y	38010 FQ	48620 MW	61740 TQ	USBLS	5/07
	Nevada	H	25.73 FQ	32.03 MW	37.58 TQ	NVBLS	5/08
	Las Vegas-Paradise MSA, NV	H	27.29 FQ	34.24 MW	38.65 TQ	NVBLS	5/08

Occupation/Type/Industry	Location	Per	Low	Mid	High	Source	Date
Cartographer and Photogrammetrist	New Hampshire	H	15.64 AE	18.58 MW	22.15 AEX	NHBLS	6/08
	New Jersey	Y	49600 FQ	67260 MW	77080 TQ	USBLS	5/07
	Edison PMSA, NJ	Y	48140 FQ	60910 MW	77650 TQ	USBLS	5/07
	Newark-Union PMSA, NJ-PA	Y	42980 FQ	63960 MW	71280 TQ	USBLS	5/07
	New Mexico	Y	36450 FQ	43170 MW	50250 TQ	USBLS	5/07
	Albuquerque MSA, NM	Y	40110 FQ	46540 MW	53840 TQ	USBLS	5/07
	New York	Y	46240 FQ	55390 MW	66340 TQ	USBLS	5/07
	Nassau-Suffolk PMSA, NY	Y	54800 FQ	62860 MW	73690 TQ	USBLS	5/07
	New York-Northern New Jersey-Long Island MSA, NY-NJ-PA	Y	47920 FQ	60950 MW	73190 TQ	USBLS	5/07
	North Carolina	Y	35490 FQ	43290 MW	53650 TQ	USBLS	5/07
	Charlotte-Gastonia-Concord MSA, NC-SC	Y	33280 FQ	40590 MW	47980 TQ	USBLS	5/07
	Raleigh-Cary MSA, NC	Y	40330 FQ	52770 MW	63410 TQ	USBLS	5/07
	North Dakota	Y	22490 FQ	36440 MW	51600 TQ	USBLS	5/07
	Ohio	Y	36350 FQ	43420 MW	50390 TQ	USBLS	5/07
	Cleveland-Elyria-Mentor MSA, OH	Y	33300 FQ	37160 MW	43910 TQ	USBLS	5/07
	Columbus MSA, OH	Y	44560 FQ	48830 MW	53410 TQ	USBLS	5/07
	Oklahoma	Y	31990 FQ	36760 MW	40970 TQ	USBLS	5/07
	Oklahoma City MSA, OK	Y	32700 FQ	36470 MW	39940 TQ	USBLS	5/07
	Oregon	H	19.54 FQ	23.26 MW	28.95 TQ	ORBLS	5/08
	Portland-Vancouver-Beaverton MSA, OR-WA	Y	42710 FQ	51230 MW	68050 TQ	USBLS	5/07
	Pennsylvania	Y	30380 FQ	37080 MW	45740 TQ	USBLS	5/07
	Philadelphia-Camden-Wilmington MSA, PA-NJ-DE-MD	Y	39370 FQ	46410 MW	56090 TQ	USBLS	5/07
	Pittsburgh MSA, PA	Y	33610 FQ	38980 MW	45820 TQ	USBLS	5/07
	South Carolina	Y	36780 FQ	44820 MW	56620 TQ	USBLS	5/07
	Columbia MSA, SC	Y	39580 FQ	47450 MW	58040 TQ	USBLS	5/07
	South Dakota	Y	35979 FQ	40677 MW	50566 TQ	SDBLS	7/08-9/08
	Tennessee	Y	35460 FQ	39610 MW	48500 TQ	USBLS	5/07
	Nashville-Davidson-Murfreesboro MSA, TN	Y	36880 FQ	41060 MW	48330 TQ	USBLS	5/07
	Texas	Y	44350 FQ	59860 MW	77930 TQ	USBLS	5/07
	Austin-Round Rock MSA, TX	Y	43200 FQ	51640 MW	71760 TQ	USBLS	5/07
	Dallas-Fort Worth-Arlington MSA, TX	Y	48320 FQ	58540 MW	71120 TQ	USBLS	5/07
	Houston-Sugar Land-Baytown MSA, TX	Y	57160 FQ	78340 MW	87510 TQ	USBLS	5/07
	Utah	Y	43350 FQ	52310 MW	66710 TQ	USBLS	5/07
	Salt Lake City MSA, UT	Y	44020 FQ	52280 MW	63960 TQ	USBLS	5/07
	Vermont	Y	28290 FQ	34580 MW	43590 TQ	USBLS	5/07
	Virginia	Y	42830 FQ	61340 MW	85800 TQ	USBLS	5/07
	Richmond MSA, VA	Y	38630 FQ	46420 MW	58910 TQ	USBLS	5/07
	Virginia Beach-Norfolk-Newport News MSA, VA-NC	Y	35900 FQ	47560 MW	67130 TQ	USBLS	5/07
	Washington	H	25.03 FQ	29.21 MW	34.79 TQ	WABLS	3/08
	Seattle-Tacoma-Bellevue MSA, WA	Y	46910 FQ	60400 MW	73150 TQ	USBLS	5/07
	West Virginia	Y	49685 FQ	77079 MW	91275 TQ	WVBLS	7/08-9/08
	Wisconsin	Y	39840 FQ	49680 MW	60670 TQ	USBLS	5/07
	Wyoming	Y	35034 FQ	43138 MW	51190 TQ	WYBLS	9/08
	Puerto Rico	Y	18840 FQ	24750 MW	29810 TQ	USBLS	5/07
	San Juan-Caguas-Guaynabo MSA, PR	Y	18840 FQ	24750 MW	29810 TQ	USBLS	5/07
Cartographer Supervisor State Government	Ohio	H	19.19 LO		23.76 HI	ODAS	2008
Cashier	Alabama	Y	13000 FQ	14950 MW	17910 TQ	USBLS	5/07
	Birmingham-Hoover MSA, AL	Y	13700 FQ	16370 MW	19180 TQ	USBLS	5/07
	Huntsville MSA, AL	Y	13270 FQ	15540 MW	18710 TQ	USBLS	5/07
	Mobile MSA, AL	Y	12840 FQ	14640 MW	17350 TQ	USBLS	5/07
	Alaska	Y	19070 FQ	22110 MW	25830 TQ	USBLS	5/07
	Anchorage MSA, AK	Y	18710 FQ	21630 MW	24980 TQ	USBLS	5/07
	Arizona	Y	15840 FQ	18310 MW	22480 TQ	USBLS	5/07
	Phoenix-Mesa-Scottsdale MSA, AZ	Y	16130 FQ	18510 MW	22760 TQ	USBLS	5/07

AE Average entry wage	**AW** Average wage paid	**FQ** First quartile wage	**LO** Lowest wage paid	**MTC** Median total compensation	**TCC** Total cash compensation
AER Average entry range	**AWR** Average wage range	**H** Hourly	**LR** Low end range	**MW** Median wage paid	**TQ** Third quartile wage
AEX Average experienced wage	**AXR** Average experienced range	**HI** Highest wage paid	**M** Monthly	**MWR** Median wage range	**W** Weekly
ATC Average total compensation	**D** Daily	**HR** High end range	**MCC** Median cash compensation	**S** See annotated source	**Y** Yearly

Occupation/Type/Industry	Location	Per	Low	Mid	High	Source	Date
Cashier	Tucson MSA, AZ	Y	15710 FQ	18180 MW	22380 TQ	USBLS	5/07
	Arkansas	Y	14220 FQ	15360 MW	17760 TQ	USBLS	5/07
	Little Rock-North Little Rock MSA, AR	Y	14490 FQ	15920 MW	18430 TQ	USBLS	5/07
	California	H	8.25 FQ	9.18 MW	11.42 TQ	CABLS	1/08-3/08
	Los Angeles-Long Beach-Glendale PMSA, CA	H	8.15 FQ	9.01 MW	10.82 TQ	CABLS	1/08-3/08
	Oakland-Fremont-Hayward MSA, CA	H	8.63 FQ	9.98 MW	14.57 TQ	CABLS	1/08-3/08
	Riverside-San Bernardino-Ontario MSA, CA	H	8.14 FQ	8.97 MW	10.58 TQ	CABLS	1/08-3/08
	Sacramento-Arden Arcade-Roseville MSA, CA	H	8.25 FQ	9.25 MW	11.60 TQ	CABLS	1/08-3/08
	San Diego-Carlsbad-San Marcos MSA, CA	H	8.28 FQ	9.18 MW	11.33 TQ	CABLS	1/08-3/08
	San Francisco-San Mateo-Redwood PMSA, CA	H	9.07 FQ	10.99 MW	14.59 TQ	CABLS	1/08-3/08
	San Jose-Sunnyvale-Santa Clara MSA, CA	H	8.66 FQ	10.03 MW	13.08 TQ	CABLS	1/08-3/08
	Santa Ana-Anaheim-Irvine PMSA, CA	Y	16880 FQ	18610 MW	22190 TQ	USBLS	5/07
	Santa Rosa-Petaluma MSA, CA	H	8.56 FQ	9.91 MW	13.12 TQ	CABLS	1/08-3/08
	Colorado	Y	16460 FQ	19270 MW	23490 TQ	USBLS	5/07
	Denver-Aurora MSA, CO	Y	17240 FQ	19930 MW	23980 TQ	USBLS	5/07
	Connecticut	H	8.43 AE	9.20 MW		CTBLS	1/08-3/08
	Bridgeport-Stamford-Norwalk MSA, CT	Y	17190 FQ	18960 MW	22390 TQ	USBLS	5/07
	Hartford-West Hartford-East Hartford MSA, CT	Y	17200 FQ	18940 MW	22120 TQ	USBLS	5/07
	New Haven MSA, CT	Y	17230 FQ	18970 MW	22300 TQ	USBLS	5/07
	Delaware	Y	15830 FQ	18020 MW	21160 TQ	USBLS	5/07
	Wilmington PMSA, DE-MD-NJ	Y	16120 FQ	18290 MW	21610 TQ	USBLS	5/07
	District of Columbia	Y	17470 FQ	20780 MW	25030 TQ	USBLS	5/07
	Washington-Arlington-Alexandria MSA, DC-VA-MD-WV	Y	16160 FQ	18640 MW	23280 TQ	USBLS	5/07
	Florida	Y	14990 FQ	16730 MW	19220 TQ	USBLS	5/07
	Fort Lauderdale-Pompano Beach-Deerfield Beach PMSA, FL	Y	15070 FQ	16950 MW	19570 TQ	USBLS	5/07
	Jacksonville MSA, FL	Y	14880 FQ	16330 MW	18920 TQ	USBLS	5/07
	Miami-Fort Lauderdale-Miami Beach MSA, FL	Y	14910 FQ	16560 MW	19200 TQ	USBLS	5/07
	Orlando-Kissimmee MSA, FL	Y	14990 FQ	16660 MW	19440 TQ	USBLS	5/07
	Sarasota-Bradenton-Venice MSA, FL	Y	15810 FQ	17770 MW	19970 TQ	USBLS	5/07
	Tampa-St. Petersburg-Clearwater MSA, FL	Y	15060 FQ	16800 MW	19050 TQ	USBLS	5/07
	West Palm Beach-Boca Raton-Boynton Beach PMSA, FL	Y	15310 FQ	17310 MW	19730 TQ	USBLS	5/07
	Georgia	Y	13480 FQ	15930 MW	18910 TQ	USBLS	5/07
	Atlanta-Sandy Springs-Marietta MSA, GA	Y	13860 FQ	16710 MW	19670 TQ	USBLS	5/07
	Savannah MSA, GA	Y	13590 FQ	15930 MW	18330 TQ	USBLS	5/07
	Hawaii	Y	16620 FQ	18810 MW	22930 TQ	USBLS	5/07
	Honolulu MSA, HI	Y	16480 FQ	18450 MW	22130 TQ	USBLS	5/07
	Idaho	Y	14090 FQ	16920 MW	19800 TQ	USBLS	5/07
	Boise City-Nampa MSA, ID	Y	15400 FQ	17900 MW	21080 TQ	USBLS	5/07
	Illinois	Y	15280 FQ	17280 MW	19790 TQ	USBLS	5/07
	Champaign-Urbana MSA, IL	Y	15060 FQ	16740 MW	18850 TQ	USBLS	5/07
	Chicago-Naperville-Joliet MSA, IL-IN-WI	Y	15560 FQ	17700 MW	20380 TQ	USBLS	5/07
	Indiana	Y	13740 FQ	16240 MW	18890 TQ	USBLS	5/07
	Gary PMSA, IN	Y	14410 FQ	16980 MW	19390 TQ	USBLS	5/07
	Indianapolis-Carmel MSA, IN	Y	14900 FQ	17160 MW	19390 TQ	USBLS	5/07
	South Bend-Mishawaka MSA, IN-MI	Y	13960 FQ	16140 MW	18920 TQ	USBLS	5/07
	Iowa	Y	14350 FQ	15940 MW	18630 TQ	USBLS	5/07
	Des Moines-West Des Moines MSA, IA	Y	15470 FQ	17640 MW	19940 TQ	USBLS	5/07
	Kansas	Y	13610 FQ	16030 MW	18690 TQ	USBLS	5/07

Cashier

Occupation/Type/Industry	Location	Per	Low	Mid	High	Source	Date
Cashier	Wichita MSA, KS	Y	13620 FQ	16240 MW	19080 TQ	USBLS	5/07
	Kentucky	Y	13534 FQ	15722 MW	18770 TQ	KYBLS	2008
	Louisville-Jefferson County MSA, KY-IN	Y	14010 FQ	16670 MW	19260 TQ	USBLS	5/07
	Louisiana	H	6.21 FQ	7.06 MW	8.39 TQ	LABLS	1/08-3/08
	Baton Rouge MSA, LA	Y	13230 FQ	15360 MW	18200 TQ	USBLS	5/07
	Lake Charles MSA, LA	Y	12770 FQ	14370 MW	16700 TQ	USBLS	5/07
	New Orleans-Metairie-Kenner MSA, LA	Y	13260 FQ	15380 MW	18500 TQ	USBLS	5/07
	Maine	Y	15660 FQ	17460 MW	19500 TQ	USBLS	5/07
	Portland-South Portland-Biddeford MSA, ME	Y	16400 FQ	18050 MW	19860 TQ	USBLS	5/07
	Maryland	Y		18175 MW		MDBLS	3/08
	Baltimore-Towson MSA, MD	Y	15450 FQ	17920 MW	21720 TQ	USBLS	5/07
	Bethesda-Gaithersburg-Frederick PMSA, MD	Y	15980 FQ	18510 MW	23850 TQ	USBLS	5/07
	Massachusetts	Y	16840 FQ	18620 MW	21680 TQ	USBLS	5/07
	Boston-Cambridge-Quincy NECTA, MA	Y	16930 FQ	18780 MW	22050 TQ	USBLS	5/07
	Worcester MSA, MA-CT	Y	16760 FQ	18450 MW	21280 TQ	USBLS	5/07
	Michigan	Y	15410 FQ	17290 MW	20540 TQ	USBLS	5/07
	Detroit-Warren-Livonia MSA, MI	Y	15590 FQ	17960 MW	22170 TQ	USBLS	5/07
	Grand Rapids-Wyoming MSA, MI	Y	15460 FQ	17460 MW	20900 TQ	USBLS	5/07
	Warren-Troy-Farmington Hills PMSA, MI	Y	15670 FQ	18080 MW	22260 TQ	USBLS	5/07
	Minnesota	Y	15641 FQ	17887 MW	20387 TQ	MNBLS	10/08-12/08
	Duluth-Superior MSA, MN-WI	Y	14594 FQ	15976 MW	19269 TQ	MNBLS	10/08-12/08
	Minneapolis-Saint Paul MSA, MN-WI	Y	16617 FQ	18690 MW	21759 TQ	MNBLS	10/08-12/08
	Rochester MSA, MN	Y	16056 FQ	18006 MW	20084 TQ	MNBLS	10/08-12/08
	Mississippi	Y	13150 FQ	15170 MW	18200 TQ	USBLS	5/07
	Hattiesburg MSA, MS	Y	13230 FQ	15340 MW	18130 TQ	USBLS	5/07
	Jackson MSA, MS	Y	13310 FQ	15540 MW	18460 TQ	USBLS	5/07
	Missouri	Y	14710 FQ	16220 MW	19140 TQ	USBLS	5/07
	Joplin MSA, MO	Y	14730 FQ	16140 MW	18920 TQ	USBLS	5/07
	Kansas City MSA, MO-KS	Y	15170 FQ	17310 MW	19830 TQ	USBLS	5/07
	St. Louis MSA, MO-IL	Y	15050 FQ	17180 MW	20070 TQ	USBLS	5/07
	Springfield MSA, MO	Y	14500 FQ	15580 MW	18270 TQ	USBLS	5/07
	Montana	Y	14420 FQ	16320 MW	19230 TQ	USBLS	5/07
	Billings MSA, MT	Y	14350 FQ	16160 MW	19820 TQ	USBLS	5/07
	Great Falls MSA, MT	Y	14300 FQ	15930 MW	18920 TQ	USBLS	5/07
	Missoula MSA, MT	Y	14390 FQ	16400 MW	19510 TQ	USBLS	5/07
	Nebraska	Y	13450 FQ	15770 MW	18430 TQ	USBLS	5/07
	Lincoln MSA, NE	Y	13260 FQ	15430 MW	18090 TQ	USBLS	5/07
	Omaha-Council Bluffs MSA, NE-IA	Y	14620 FQ	16990 MW	19320 TQ	USBLS	5/07
	Nevada	H	7.94 FQ	9.15 MW	11.27 TQ	NVBLS	5/08
	Las Vegas-Paradise MSA, NV	H	7.99 FQ	9.22 MW	11.43 TQ	NVBLS	5/08
	New Hampshire	H	7.64 AE	9.11 MW	10.21 AEX	NHBLS	6/08
	Manchester MSA, NH	Y	16250 FQ	18260 MW	21570 TQ	USBLS	5/07
	Nashua NECTA, NH-MA	Y	16120 FQ	17960 MW	20570 TQ	USBLS	5/07
	Rochester-Dover MSA, NH-ME	Y	16720 FQ	19120 MW	22030 TQ	USBLS	5/07
	New Jersey	Y	15820 FQ	17880 MW	21070 TQ	USBLS	5/07
	Camden PMSA, NJ	Y	15980 FQ	17960 MW	20850 TQ	USBLS	5/07
	Edison PMSA, NJ	Y	15890 FQ	17840 MW	20620 TQ	USBLS	5/07
	Newark-Union PMSA, NJ-PA	Y	15740 FQ	17870 MW	21420 TQ	USBLS	5/07
	New Mexico	Y	13350 FQ	15660 MW	19390 TQ	USBLS	5/07
	Albuquerque MSA, NM	Y	13370 FQ	15730 MW	19320 TQ	USBLS	5/07
	New York	Y	15420 FQ	17070 MW	19740 TQ	USBLS	5/07
	Albany-Schenectady-Troy MSA, NY	Y	15670 FQ	17480 MW	19930 TQ	USBLS	5/07
	Buffalo-Niagara Falls MSA, NY	Y	15200 FQ	16040 MW	19080 TQ	USBLS	5/07
	Nassau-Suffolk PMSA, NY	Y	16020 FQ	18170 MW	21440 TQ	USBLS	5/07
	New York-Northern New Jersey-Long Island MSA, NY-NJ-PA	Y	15680 FQ	17730 MW	20970 TQ	USBLS	5/07
	North Carolina	Y	14430 FQ	16250 MW	18760 TQ	USBLS	5/07

AE	Average entry wage	AW	Average wage paid	FQ First quartile wage
AER	Average entry range	AWR	Average wage range	H Hourly
AEX	Average experienced wage	AXR	Average experienced range	HI Highest wage paid
ATC	Average total compensation	D	Daily	HR High end range

LO	Lowest wage paid	MTC Median total compensation	TCC Total cash compensation
LR	Low end range	MW Median wage paid	TQ Third quartile wage
M	Monthly	MWR Median wage range	W Weekly
MCC Median cash compensation	S See annotated source	Y Yearly	

Cashier

Occupation/Type/Industry	Location	Per	Low	Mid	High	Source	Date
Cashier	Charlotte-Gastonia-Concord MSA, NC-SC	Y	15130 FQ	17270 MW	19460 TQ	USBLS	5/07
	Raleigh-Cary MSA, NC	Y	14990 FQ	17110 MW	19260 TQ	USBLS	5/07
	Winston-Salem MSA, NC	Y	14240 FQ	15730 MW	18230 TQ	USBLS	5/07
	North Dakota	Y	13210 FQ	15360 MW	18200 TQ	USBLS	5/07
	Fargo MSA, ND-MN	Y	14050 FQ	16340 MW	18720 TQ	USBLS	5/07
	Ohio	Y	14940 FQ	16000 MW	18910 TQ	USBLS	5/07
	Canton-Massillon MSA, OH	Y	14800 FQ	15600 MW	18240 TQ	USBLS	5/07
	Cincinnati-Middletown MSA, OH-KY-IN	Y	15000 FQ	16680 MW	19610 TQ	USBLS	5/07
	Cleveland-Elyria-Mentor MSA, OH	Y	15100 FQ	16370 MW	19250 TQ	USBLS	5/07
	Columbus MSA, OH	Y	15300 FQ	17150 MW	19900 TQ	USBLS	5/07
	Dayton MSA, OH	Y	15030 FQ	16410 MW	19600 TQ	USBLS	5/07
	Oklahoma	Y	13070 FQ	15050 MW	17960 TQ	USBLS	5/07
	Oklahoma City MSA, OK	Y	13400 FQ	15730 MW	18510 TQ	USBLS	5/07
	Tulsa MSA, OK	Y	13250 FQ	15430 MW	18320 TQ	USBLS	5/07
	Oregon	H	8.56 FQ	9.22 MW	11.14 TQ	ORBLS	5/08
	Medford MSA, OR	Y	17520 FQ	18860 MW	22900 TQ	USBLS	5/07
	Portland-Vancouver-Beaverton MSA, OR-WA	Y	17660 FQ	19240 MW	23620 TQ	USBLS	5/07
	Salem MSA, OR	Y	17490 FQ	18770 MW	21460 TQ	USBLS	5/07
	Pennsylvania	Y	14720 FQ	16380 MW	18980 TQ	USBLS	5/07
	Allentown-Bethlehem-Easton MSA, PA-NJ	Y	15200 FQ	16980 MW	19200 TQ	USBLS	5/07
	Erie MSA, PA	Y	14500 FQ	15650 MW	18580 TQ	USBLS	5/07
	Philadelphia-Camden-Wilmington MSA, PA-NJ-DE-MD	Y	15450 FQ	17530 MW	20180 TQ	USBLS	5/07
	Pittsburgh MSA, PA	Y	14580 FQ	15970 MW	18800 TQ	USBLS	5/07
	Rhode Island	Y	16540 FQ	18240 MW	20810 TQ	USBLS	5/07
	Providence-Fall River-Warwick MSA, RI-MA	Y	16480 FQ	18110 MW	20360 TQ	USBLS	5/07
	South Carolina	Y	13200 FQ	15310 MW	18080 TQ	USBLS	5/07
	Charleston-North Charleston MSA, SC	Y	13160 FQ	15200 MW	17960 TQ	USBLS	5/07
	Columbia MSA, SC	Y	13160 FQ	15230 MW	17930 TQ	USBLS	5/07
	Florence MSA, SC	Y	12780 FQ	14380 MW	16740 TQ	USBLS	5/07
	Spartanburg MSA, SC	Y	13360 FQ	15640 MW	18430 TQ	USBLS	5/07
	South Dakota	Y	14249 FQ	16885 MW	19323 TQ	SDBLS	7/08-9/08
	Sioux Falls MSA, SD	Y	15806 FQ	18232 MW	21009 TQ	SDBLS	7/08-9/08
	Tennessee	Y	13400 FQ	15700 MW	18510 TQ	USBLS	5/07
	Memphis MSA, TN-MS-AR	Y	13940 FQ	16450 MW	19230 TQ	USBLS	5/07
	Nashville-Davidson-Murfreesboro MSA, TN	Y	13970 FQ	16640 MW	19390 TQ	USBLS	5/07
	Texas	Y	13670 FQ	16160 MW	18750 TQ	USBLS	5/07
	Austin-Round Rock MSA, TX	Y	15830 FQ	17820 MW	20080 TQ	USBLS	5/07
	Dallas-Fort Worth-Arlington MSA, TX	Y	14610 FQ	17200 MW	19660 TQ	USBLS	5/07
	El Paso MSA, TX	Y	12830 FQ	14580 MW	17170 TQ	USBLS	5/07
	Houston-Sugar Land-Baytown MSA, TX	Y	14060 FQ	16610 MW	18950 TQ	USBLS	5/07
	San Antonio MSA, TX	Y	13790 FQ	16350 MW	18710 TQ	USBLS	5/07
	Utah	Y	14210 FQ	17020 MW	19720 TQ	USBLS	5/07
	Salt Lake City MSA, UT	Y	14980 FQ	17710 MW	20410 TQ	USBLS	5/07
	Vermont	Y	16860 FQ	18330 MW	20260 TQ	USBLS	5/07
	Burlington-South Burlington MSA, VT	Y	16950 FQ	18400 MW	20590 TQ	USBLS	5/07
	Virginia	Y	14110 FQ	16820 MW	19550 TQ	USBLS	5/07
	Richmond MSA, VA	Y	14410 FQ	16970 MW	19310 TQ	USBLS	5/07
	Virginia Beach-Norfolk-Newport News MSA, VA-NC	Y	13470 FQ	15800 MW	18550 TQ	USBLS	5/07
	Washington	H	8.87 FQ	9.92 MW	12.77 TQ	WABLS	3/08
	Seattle-Tacoma-Bellevue MSA, WA	Y	18490 FQ	21510 MW	28670 TQ	USBLS	5/07
	West Virginia	Y	13757 FQ	14927 MW	16445 TQ	WVBLS	7/08-9/08
	Charleston MSA, WV	Y	13430 FQ	14560 MW	16070 TQ	USBLS	5/07
	Wisconsin	Y	15000 FQ	16890 MW	19540 TQ	USBLS	5/07
	Milwaukee-Waukesha-West Allis MSA, WI	Y	15110 FQ	17100 MW	19750 TQ	USBLS	5/07
	Racine MSA, WI	Y	14890 FQ	16980 MW	20860 TQ	USBLS	5/07
	Wyoming	Y	14866 FQ	17567 MW	20030 TQ	WYBLS	9/08

AE	Average entry wage	AW	Average wage paid	FQ	First quartile wage
AER	Average entry range	AWR	Average wage range	H	Hourly
AEX	Average experienced wage	AXR	Average experienced range	HI	Highest wage paid
ATC	Average total compensation	D	Daily	HR	High end range

LO	Lowest wage paid	MTC	Median total compensation	TCC	Total cash compensation
LR	Low end range	MW	Median wage paid	TQ	Third quartile wage
M	Monthly	MWR	Median wage range	W	Weekly
MCC	Median cash compensation	S	See annotated source	Y	Yearly

Occupation/Type/Industry	Location	Per	Low	Mid	High	Source	Date
Cashier	Cheyenne MSA, WY	Y	15276 FQ	17791 MW	20319 TQ	WYBLS	9/08
	Puerto Rico	Y	12360 FQ	13590 MW	14820 TQ	USBLS	5/07
	San Juan-Caguas-Guaynabo MSA, PR	Y	12370 FQ	13610 MW	14850 TQ	USBLS	5/07
	Virgin Islands	Y	14380 FQ	16000 MW	18650 TQ	USBLS	5/07
	Guam	Y	12610 FQ	14080 MW	15830 TQ	USBLS	5/07
Casino Dealer/Croupier							
Cruise Ship	United States	M	1900 LO		2600 HI	CRU01	2008
CDL Examiner							
State Highway Patrol	Missouri	S	1299 LO		1843 HI	MSHPSS	7/1/08
Celebrant/Religious Leader	United States	Y		48300 MW		CNNM04	2007
Cement Gun Nozzle Operator							
Municipal Government	Cincinnati, OH	Y	40748 LO		43264 HI	COHSS	10/08
Cement Mason and Concrete Finisher	Alabama	Y	23750 FQ	28570 MW	34050 TQ	USBLS	5/07
	Birmingham-Hoover MSA, AL	Y	26370 FQ	31340 MW	38980 TQ	USBLS	5/07
	Montgomery MSA, AL	Y	21420 FQ	27320 MW	31060 TQ	USBLS	5/07
	Alaska	Y	48200 FQ	62910 MW	73730 TQ	USBLS	5/07
	Anchorage MSA, AK	Y	47140 FQ	65990 MW	75080 TQ	USBLS	5/07
	Arizona	Y	29000 FQ	35080 MW	41180 TQ	USBLS	5/07
	Flagstaff MSA, AZ	Y	25490 FQ	34810 MW	40490 TQ	USBLS	5/07
	Phoenix-Mesa-Scottsdale MSA, AZ	Y	30140 FQ	36180 MW	42630 TQ	USBLS	5/07
	Tucson MSA, AZ	Y	26730 FQ	31850 MW	36600 TQ	USBLS	5/07
	Arkansas	Y	25060 FQ	28670 MW	33530 TQ	USBLS	5/07
	Little Rock-North Little Rock MSA, AR	Y	25880 FQ	29020 MW	33100 TQ	USBLS	5/07
	California	H	16.49 FQ	21.85 MW	28.14 TQ	CABLS	1/08-3/08
	Los Angeles-Long Beach-Glendale PMSA, CA	H	17.00 FQ	22.59 MW	28.21 TQ	CABLS	1/08-3/08
	Modesto MSA, CA	H	13.56 FQ	17.04 MW	22.30 TQ	CABLS	1/08-3/08
	Oakland-Fremont-Hayward MSA, CA	H	21.33 FQ	25.47 MW	29.59 TQ	CABLS	1/08-3/08
	Riverside-San Bernardino-Ontario MSA, CA	H	16.89 FQ	20.65 MW	26.15 TQ	CABLS	1/08-3/08
	Sacramento-Arden Arcade-Roseville MSA, CA	H	16.95 FQ	22.06 MW	27.49 TQ	CABLS	1/08-3/08
	San Diego-Carlsbad-San Marcos MSA, CA	H	20.46 FQ	26.74 MW	32.06 TQ	CABLS	1/08-3/08
	San Francisco-San Mateo-Redwood PMSA, CA	H	18.00 FQ	24.79 MW	29.34 TQ	CABLS	1/08-3/08
	San Jose-Sunnyvale-Santa Clara MSA, CA	H	14.60 FQ	22.22 MW	28.45 TQ	CABLS	1/08-3/08
	Santa Ana-Anaheim-Irvine PMSA, CA	Y	34260 FQ	46790 MW	61330 TQ	USBLS	5/07
	Colorado	Y	28040 FQ	33990 MW	39600 TQ	USBLS	5/07
	Denver-Aurora MSA, CO	Y	29050 FQ	34990 MW	39850 TQ	USBLS	5/07
	Connecticut	H	15.96 AE	22.02 MW		CTBLS	1/08-3/08
	Bridgeport-Stamford-Norwalk MSA, CT	Y	36730 FQ	53230 MW	66430 TQ	USBLS	5/07
	Hartford-West Hartford-East Hartford MSA, CT	Y	41240 FQ	49480 MW	62390 TQ	USBLS	5/07
	New Haven MSA, CT	Y	31350 FQ	36130 MW	42690 TQ	USBLS	5/07
	Delaware	Y	33820 FQ	40660 MW	47100 TQ	USBLS	5/07
	Dover MSA, DE	Y	33200 FQ	38650 MW	44300 TQ	USBLS	5/07
	Wilmington PMSA, DE-MD-NJ	Y	37650 FQ	43260 MW	49200 TQ	USBLS	5/07
	District of Columbia	Y	35120 FQ	39980 MW	48500 TQ	USBLS	5/07
	Washington-Arlington-Alexandria MSA, DC-VA-MD-WV	Y	28290 FQ	35140 MW	41830 TQ	USBLS	5/07
	Florida	Y	24990 FQ	29950 MW	36530 TQ	USBLS	5/07
	Cape Coral-Fort Myers MSA, FL	Y	27560 FQ	34570 MW	41650 TQ	USBLS	5/07
	Fort Lauderdale-Pompano Beach-Deerfield Beach PMSA, FL	Y	23920 FQ	29670 MW	36050 TQ	USBLS	5/07

AE Average entry wage	**AW** Average wage paid	**FQ** First quartile wage	**LO** Lowest wage paid	**MTC** Median total compensation	**TCC** Total cash compensation
AER Average entry range	**AWR** Average wage range	**H** Hourly	**LR** Low end range	**MW** Median wage paid	**TQ** Third quartile wage
AEX Average experienced wage	**AXR** Average experienced range	**HI** Highest wage paid	**M** Monthly	**MWR** Median wage range	**W** Weekly
ATC Average total compensation	**D** Daily	**HR** High end range	**MCC** Median cash compensation	**S** See annotated source	**Y** Yearly

Occupation/Type/Industry	Location	Per	Low	Mid	High	Source	Date
Cement Mason and Concrete Finisher	Jacksonville MSA, FL	Y	28060 FQ	35310 MW	43090 TQ	USBLS	5/07
	Miami-Fort Lauderdale-Miami Beach MSA, FL	Y	23280 FQ	28840 MW	35960 TQ	USBLS	5/07
	Orlando-Kissimmee MSA, FL	Y	27610 FQ	31460 MW	37040 TQ	USBLS	5/07
	Tampa-St. Petersburg-Clearwater MSA, FL	Y	24490 FQ	28310 MW	33080 TQ	USBLS	5/07
	West Palm Beach-Boca Raton-Boynton Beach PMSA, FL	Y	23900 FQ	28440 MW	35300 TQ	USBLS	5/07
	Georgia	Y	23130 FQ	28860 MW	35110 TQ	USBLS	5/07
	Atlanta-Sandy Springs-Marietta MSA, GA	Y	25360 FQ	30600 MW	36330 TQ	USBLS	5/07
	Hawaii	Y	45830 FQ	57540 MW	66020 TQ	USBLS	5/07
	Honolulu MSA, HI	Y	47420 FQ	57910 MW	66520 TQ	USBLS	5/07
	Idaho	Y	21840 FQ	27330 MW	37690 TQ	USBLS	5/07
	Boise City-Nampa MSA, ID	Y	21280 FQ	26650 MW	36940 TQ	USBLS	5/07
	Illinois	Y	39280 FQ	58950 MW	73190 TQ	USBLS	5/07
	Chicago-Naperville-Joliet MSA, IL-IN-WI	Y	40910 FQ	63890 MW	74630 TQ	USBLS	5/07
	Indiana	Y	27260 FQ	35060 MW	44600 TQ	USBLS	5/07
	Gary PMSA, IN	Y	29760 FQ	39380 MW	55530 TQ	USBLS	5/07
	Indianapolis-Carmel MSA, IN	Y	27900 FQ	38110 MW	46290 TQ	USBLS	5/07
	South Bend-Mishawaka MSA, IN-MI	Y	31960 FQ	38060 MW	45650 TQ	USBLS	5/07
	Iowa	Y	24710 FQ	29860 MW	35850 TQ	USBLS	5/07
	Cedar Rapids MSA, IA	Y	28210 FQ	36520 MW	41120 TQ	USBLS	5/07
	Des Moines-West Des Moines MSA, IA	Y	29660 FQ	34080 MW	39180 TQ	USBLS	5/07
	Iowa City MSA, IA	Y	26690 FQ	31900 MW	38150 TQ	USBLS	5/07
	Kansas	Y	26160 FQ	31700 MW	39560 TQ	USBLS	5/07
	Wichita MSA, KS	Y	24330 FQ	29800 MW	35470 TQ	USBLS	5/07
	Kentucky	Y	25141 FQ	30716 MW	38507 TQ	KYBLS	2008
	Louisville-Jefferson County MSA, KY-IN	Y	23860 FQ	29380 MW	36370 TQ	USBLS	5/07
	Louisiana	H	11.92 FQ	13.99 MW	16.51 TQ	LABLS	1/08-3/08
	Baton Rouge MSA, LA	Y	27060 FQ	30630 MW	35690 TQ	USBLS	5/07
	New Orleans-Metairie-Kenner MSA, LA	Y	26560 FQ	30180 MW	36000 TQ	USBLS	5/07
	Maine	Y	25550 FQ	29060 MW	32910 TQ	USBLS	5/07
	Lewiston-Auburn MSA, ME	Y	24680 FQ	31400 MW	39560 TQ	USBLS	5/07
	Portland-South Portland-Biddeford MSA, ME	Y	25830 FQ	30910 MW	37620 TQ	USBLS	5/07
	Maryland	Y		37500 MW		MDBLS	3/08
	Baltimore-Towson MSA, MD	Y	32640 FQ	38600 MW	45340 TQ	USBLS	5/07
	Bethesda-Gaithersburg-Frederick PMSA, MD	Y	20150 FQ	25270 MW	38570 TQ	USBLS	5/07
	Massachusetts	Y	36310 FQ	42920 MW	50350 TQ	USBLS	5/07
	Barnstable Town MSA, MA	Y	31990 FQ	35290 MW	39170 TQ	USBLS	5/07
	Boston-Cambridge-Quincy NECTA, MA	Y	40630 FQ	45860 MW	52210 TQ	USBLS	5/07
	Worcester MSA, MA-CT	Y	38890 FQ	47130 MW	71290 TQ	USBLS	5/07
	Michigan	Y	31420 FQ	38730 MW	47920 TQ	USBLS	5/07
	Detroit-Warren-Livonia MSA, MI	Y	36390 FQ	43230 MW	51550 TQ	USBLS	5/07
	Grand Rapids-Wyoming MSA, MI	Y	31270 FQ	36650 MW	42260 TQ	USBLS	5/07
	Warren-Troy-Farmington Hills PMSA, MI	Y	36120 FQ	43420 MW	50950 TQ	USBLS	5/07
	Minnesota	Y	37233 FQ	47361 MW	59659 TQ	MNBLS	10/08-12/08
	Duluth-Superior MSA, MN-WI	Y	37971 FQ	46033 MW	57752 TQ	MNBLS	10/08-12/08
	Minneapolis-Saint Paul MSA, MN-WI	Y	41849 FQ	50016 MW	61261 TQ	MNBLS	10/08-12/08
	Rochester MSA, MN	Y	30180 FQ	38881 MW	51538 TQ	MNBLS	10/08-12/08
	Mississippi	Y	21480 FQ	25610 MW	30540 TQ	USBLS	5/07
	Jackson MSA, MS	Y	18830 FQ	24200 MW	32410 TQ	USBLS	5/07
	Missouri	Y	25790 FQ	32890 MW	48100 TQ	USBLS	5/07
	Kansas City MSA, MO-KS	Y	28750 FQ	36660 MW	47230 TQ	USBLS	5/07
	St. Louis MSA, MO-IL	Y	34670 FQ	52020 MW	59320 TQ	USBLS	5/07
	Montana	Y	27040 FQ	32000 MW	40570 TQ	USBLS	5/07
	Billings MSA, MT	Y	26960 FQ	33440 MW	44550 TQ	USBLS	5/07
	Nebraska	Y	24270 FQ	29260 MW	35560 TQ	USBLS	5/07

AE	Average entry wage	AW	Average wage paid	FQ	First quartile wage
AER	Average entry range	AWR	Average wage range	H	Hourly
AEX	Average experienced wage	AXR	Average experienced range	HI	Highest wage paid
ATC	Average total compensation	D	Daily	HR	High end range

LO	Lowest wage paid	MTC	Median total compensation	TCC	Total cash compensation
LR	Low end range	MW	Median wage paid	TQ	Third quartile wage
M	Monthly	MWR	Median wage range	W	Weekly
MCC	Median cash compensation	S	See annotated source	Y	Yearly

Occupation/Type/Industry	Location	Per	Low	Mid	High	Source	Date
Cement Mason and Concrete Finisher							
	Omaha-Council Bluffs MSA, NE-IA	Y	26740 FQ	32000 MW	40040 TQ	USBLS	5/07
	Nevada	H	16.68 FQ	21.12 TQ	27.52 TQ	NVBLS	5/08
	Las Vegas-Paradise MSA, NV	H	15.71 FQ	20.51 MW	27.75 TQ	NVBLS	5/08
	New Hampshire	H	12.91 AE	16.96 MW	19.51 AEX	NHBLS	6/08
	Nashua NECTA, NH-MA	Y	27090 FQ	32180 MW	36460 TQ	USBLS	5/07
	New Jersey	Y	31870 FQ	50060 MW	62280 TQ	USBLS	5/07
	Camden PMSA, NJ	Y	32800 FQ	58920 MW	79310 TQ	USBLS	5/07
	Edison PMSA, NJ	Y	27800 FQ	42840 MW	57930 TQ	USBLS	5/07
	Newark-Union PMSA, NJ-PA	Y	36340 FQ	51260 MW	60640 TQ	USBLS	5/07
	New Mexico	Y	25860 FQ	30000 MW	36370 TQ	USBLS	5/07
	Albuquerque MSA, NM	Y	26610 FQ	30030 MW	35800 TQ	USBLS	5/07
	New York	Y	35930 FQ	48570 MW	66990 TQ	USBLS	5/07
	Albany-Schenectady-Troy MSA, NY	Y	37220 FQ	44030 MW	49560 TQ	USBLS	5/07
	Buffalo-Niagara Falls MSA, NY	Y	26870 FQ	34990 MW	53050 TQ	USBLS	5/07
	Glens Falls MSA, NY	Y	26940 FQ	31990 MW	35250 TQ	USBLS	5/07
	Nassau-Suffolk PMSA, NY	Y	39440 FQ	48210 MW	62110 TQ	USBLS	5/07
	New York-Northern New Jersey-Long Island MSA, NY-NJ-PA	Y	39240 FQ	55040 MW	68730 TQ	USBLS	5/07
	North Carolina	Y	23350 FQ	27610 MW	31770 TQ	USBLS	5/07
	Charlotte-Gastonia-Concord MSA, NC-SC	Y	26300 FQ	29710 MW	34620 TQ	USBLS	5/07
	Durham MSA, NC	Y	24910 FQ	32250 MW	37350 TQ	USBLS	5/07
	Raleigh-Cary MSA, NC	Y	23540 FQ	28230 MW	32630 TQ	USBLS	5/07
	North Dakota	Y	25140 FQ	30030 MW	36390 TQ	USBLS	5/07
	Fargo MSA, ND-MN	Y	24750 FQ	32260 MW	40000 TQ	USBLS	5/07
	Ohio	Y	30790 FQ	38730 MW	49970 TQ	USBLS	5/07
	Cincinnati-Middletown MSA, OH-KY-IN	Y	27780 FQ	35670 MW	46720 TQ	USBLS	5/07
	Cleveland-Elyria-Mentor MSA, OH	Y	33630 FQ	48930 MW	60300 TQ	USBLS	5/07
	Columbus MSA, OH	Y	33820 FQ	37730 MW	44060 TQ	USBLS	5/07
	Dayton MSA, OH	Y	27870 FQ	36170 MW	46710 TQ	USBLS	5/07
	Oklahoma	Y	23940 FQ	28540 MW	33210 TQ	USBLS	5/07
	Oklahoma City MSA, OK	Y	23910 FQ	29400 MW	35120 TQ	USBLS	5/07
	Tulsa MSA, OK	Y	24990 FQ	28670 MW	32520 TQ	USBLS	5/07
	Oregon	H	13.96 FQ	17.54 MW	21.87 TQ	ORBLS	5/08
	Portland-Vancouver-Beaverton MSA, OR-WA	Y	27040 FQ	35470 MW	50400 TQ	USBLS	5/07
	Pennsylvania	Y	29550 FQ	37550 MW	48050 TQ	USBLS	5/07
	Allentown-Bethlehem-Easton MSA, PA-NJ	Y	29260 FQ	33770 MW	41270 TQ	USBLS	5/07
	Philadelphia-Camden-Wilmington MSA, PA-NJ-DE-MD	Y	35110 FQ	45480 MW	60430 TQ	USBLS	5/07
	Pittsburgh MSA, PA	Y	35400 FQ	43900 MW	50330 TQ	USBLS	5/07
	Reading MSA, PA	Y	30750 FQ	38810 MW	47790 TQ	USBLS	5/07
	Rhode Island	Y	38240 FQ	44290 MW	59390 TQ	USBLS	5/07
	Providence-Fall River-Warwick MSA, RI-MA	Y	37910 FQ	45290 MW	63250 TQ	USBLS	5/07
	South Carolina	Y	24330 FQ	28870 MW	33530 TQ	USBLS	5/07
	Charleston-North Charleston MSA, SC	Y	24530 FQ	27680 MW	31010 TQ	USBLS	5/07
	Columbia MSA, SC	Y	27370 FQ	31190 MW	34720 TQ	USBLS	5/07
	South Dakota	Y	24626 FQ	28435 MW	32648 TQ	SDBLS	7/08-9/08
	Sioux Falls MSA, SD	Y	24548 FQ	28582 MW	32966 TQ	SDBLS	7/08-9/08
	Tennessee	Y	24120 FQ	28320 MW	32450 TQ	USBLS	5/07
	Memphis MSA, TN-MS-AR	Y	23200 FQ	28040 MW	33580 TQ	USBLS	5/07
	Nashville-Davidson-Murfreesboro MSA, TN	Y	23270 FQ	27600 MW	32280 TQ	USBLS	5/07
	Texas	Y	22970 FQ	26980 MW	30740 TQ	USBLS	5/07
	Austin-Round Rock MSA, TX	Y	21460 FQ	25240 MW	28810 TQ	USBLS	5/07
	Brownsville-Harlingen MSA, TX	Y	17320 FQ	20220 MW	23910 TQ	USBLS	5/07
	Dallas-Fort Worth-Arlington MSA, TX	Y	24960 FQ	28470 MW	32320 TQ	USBLS	5/07
	El Paso MSA, TX	Y	21460 FQ	24960 MW	29010 TQ	USBLS	5/07

AE	Average entry wage	AW	Average wage paid	FQ	First quartile wage
AER	Average entry range	AWR	Average wage range	H	Hourly
AEX	Average experienced wage	AXR	Average experienced range	HI	Highest wage paid
ATC	Average total compensation	D	Daily	HR	High end range

LO	Lowest wage paid	MTC	Median total compensation
LR	Low end range	MW	Median wage paid
M	Monthly	MWR	Median wage range
MCC	Median cash compensation	S	See annotated source

TCC	Total cash compensation
TQ	Third quartile wage
W	Weekly
Y	Yearly

Occupation/Type/Industry	Location	Per	Low	Mid	High	Source	Date
Cement Mason and Concrete Finisher							
	Houston-Sugar Land-Baytown MSA, TX	Y	23420 FQ	27260 MW	31330 TQ	USBLS	5/07
	San Antonio MSA, TX	Y	21910 FQ	25670 MW	29420 TQ	USBLS	5/07
	Utah	Y	26800 FQ	32270 MW	38940 TQ	USBLS	5/07
	Salt Lake City MSA, UT	Y	26420 FQ	31250 MW	38520 TQ	USBLS	5/07
	Vermont	Y	26190 FQ	31080 MW	39240 TQ	USBLS	5/07
	Burlington-South Burlington MSA, VT	Y	30760 FQ	36040 MW	41840 TQ	USBLS	5/07
	Virginia	Y	26460 FQ	32140 MW	38250 TQ	USBLS	5/07
	Richmond MSA, VA	Y	25690 FQ	31470 MW	36530 TQ	USBLS	5/07
	Virginia Beach-Norfolk-Newport News MSA, VA-NC	Y	24460 FQ	32160 MW	37090 TQ	USBLS	5/07
	Washington	H	16.03 FQ	22.98 MW	28.69 TQ	WABLS	3/08
	Seattle-Tacoma-Bellevue MSA, WA	Y	36220 FQ	51220 MW	60310 TQ	USBLS	5/07
	West Virginia	Y	26629 FQ	35739 MW	51453 TQ	WVBLS	7/08-9/08
	Charleston MSA, WV	Y	48540 FQ	55170 MW	60260 TQ	USBLS	5/07
	Wisconsin	Y	30850 FQ	39970 MW	51560 TQ	USBLS	5/07
	Milwaukee-Waukesha-West Allis MSA, WI	Y	39270 FQ	47810 MW	57530 TQ	USBLS	5/07
	Wyoming	Y	27803 FQ	33346 MW	38024 TQ	WYBLS	9/08
	Cheyenne MSA, WY	Y	27801 FQ	33021 MW	38157 TQ	WYBLS	9/08
	Puerto Rico	Y	13900 FQ	16400 MW	18600 TQ	USBLS	5/07
	San Juan-Caguas-Guaynabo MSA, PR	Y	14240 FQ	16800 MW	18870 TQ	USBLS	5/07
	Virgin Islands	Y	31280 FQ	35930 MW	39920 TQ	USBLS	5/07
	Guam	Y	23490 FQ	25820 MW	28710 TQ	USBLS	5/07
Cementing and Gluing Machine Operator and Tender							
	Alabama	Y	17850 FQ	21170 MW	26280 TQ	USBLS	5/07
	Arizona	Y	25300 FQ	28260 MW	31870 TQ	USBLS	5/07
	Phoenix-Mesa-Scottsdale MSA, AZ	Y	25200 FQ	28210 MW	31790 TQ	USBLS	5/07
	Arkansas	Y	21630 FQ	26730 MW	35230 TQ	USBLS	5/07
	Little Rock-North Little Rock MSA, AR	Y	20010 FQ	24910 MW	28780 TQ	USBLS	5/07
	California	H	8.99 FQ	12.08 MW	16.39 TQ	CABLS	1/08-3/08
	Los Angeles-Long Beach-Glendale PMSA, CA	H	8.62 FQ	10.46 MW	14.13 TQ	CABLS	1/08-3/08
	Oakland-Fremont-Hayward MSA, CA	H	11.95 FQ	14.07 MW	20.75 TQ	CABLS	1/08-3/08
	Riverside-San Bernardino-Ontario MSA, CA	H	9.80 FQ	18.07 MW	36.22 TQ	CABLS	1/08-3/08
	Sacramento-Arden Arcade-Roseville MSA, CA	H	8.73 FQ	10.13 MW	13.74 TQ	CABLS	1/08-3/08
	San Diego-Carlsbad-San Marcos MSA, CA	H	13.76 FQ	18.88 MW	36.22 TQ	CABLS	1/08-3/08
	San Francisco-San Mateo-Redwood PMSA, CA	H	9.91 FQ	12.48 MW	14.36 TQ	CABLS	1/08-3/08
	Santa Ana-Anaheim-Irvine PMSA, CA	Y	18650 FQ	23520 MW	31120 TQ	USBLS	5/07
	Colorado	Y	22220 FQ	29610 MW	36990 TQ	USBLS	5/07
	Denver-Aurora MSA, CO	Y	22110 FQ	29720 MW	38130 TQ	USBLS	5/07
	Connecticut	H	12.14 AE	15.24 MW		CTBLS	1/08-3/08
	Bridgeport-Stamford-Norwalk MSA, CT	Y	29470 FQ	38350 MW	47660 TQ	USBLS	5/07
	Hartford-West Hartford-East Hartford MSA, CT	Y	26140 FQ	32050 MW	38740 TQ	USBLS	5/07
	Delaware	Y	17840 FQ	19660 MW	22250 TQ	USBLS	5/07
	Florida	Y	20800 FQ	26950 MW	35200 TQ	USBLS	5/07
	Jacksonville MSA, FL	Y	29980 FQ	36380 MW	44790 TQ	USBLS	5/07
	Miami-Fort Lauderdale-Miami Beach MSA, FL	Y	15080 FQ	17050 MW	19450 TQ	USBLS	5/07
	Tampa-St. Petersburg-Clearwater MSA, FL	Y	21310 FQ	29320 MW	37190 TQ	USBLS	5/07
	Georgia	Y	15900 FQ	23640 MW	32560 TQ	USBLS	5/07
	Atlanta-Sandy Springs-Marietta MSA, GA	Y	24610 FQ	32630 MW	38280 TQ	USBLS	5/07
	Illinois	Y	22390 FQ	31430 MW	39050 TQ	USBLS	5/07

AE	Average entry wage	**AW**	Average wage paid	**FQ**	First quartile wage
AER	Average entry range	**AWR**	Average wage range	**H**	Hourly
AEX	Average experienced wage	**AXR**	Average experienced range	**HI**	Highest wage paid
ATC	Average total compensation	**D**	Daily	**HR**	High end range

LO	Lowest wage paid	**MTC**	Median total compensation	**TCC**	Total cash compensation
LR	Low end range	**MW**	Median wage paid	**TQ**	Third quartile wage
M	Monthly	**MWR**	Median wage range	**W**	Weekly
MCC	Median cash compensation	**S**	See annotated source	**Y**	Yearly

Occupation/Type/Industry	Location	Per	Low	Mid	High	Source	Date
Cementing and Gluing Machine Operator and Tender	Chicago-Naperville-Joliet MSA, IL-IN-WI	Y	22640 FQ	32720 MW	39910 TQ	USBLS	5/07
	Indiana	Y	20000 FQ	24480 MW	31410 TQ	USBLS	5/07
	Indianapolis-Carmel MSA, IN	Y	21020 FQ	26440 MW	35400 TQ	USBLS	5/07
	Iowa	Y	20070 FQ	27140 MW	35130 TQ	USBLS	5/07
	Kansas	Y	27640 FQ	33320 MW	38110 TQ	USBLS	5/07
	Kentucky	Y	17062 FQ	23404 MW	30354 TQ	KYBLS	2008
	Louisville-Jefferson County MSA, KY-IN	Y	21630 FQ	24810 MW	30590 TQ	USBLS	5/07
	Louisiana	H	10.78 FQ	14.30 MW	17.67 TQ	LABLS	1/08-3/08
	Maine	Y	24260 FQ	27620 MW	30470 TQ	USBLS	5/07
	Portland-South Portland-Biddeford MSA, ME	Y	26090 FQ	28510 MW	30850 TQ	USBLS	5/07
	Maryland	Y		30675 MW		MDBLS	3/08
	Baltimore-Towson MSA, MD	Y	25730 FQ	34920 MW	41450 TQ	USBLS	5/07
	Massachusetts	Y	24790 FQ	31080 MW	35650 TQ	USBLS	5/07
	Boston-Cambridge-Quincy NECTA, MA	Y	26870 FQ	31870 MW	36310 TQ	USBLS	5/07
	Worcester MSA, MA-CT	Y	25410 FQ	28880 MW	33050 TQ	USBLS	5/07
	Michigan	Y	24910 FQ	27790 MW	30680 TQ	USBLS	5/07
	Detroit-Warren-Livonia MSA, MI	Y	26070 FQ	27910 MW	29780 TQ	USBLS	5/07
	Grand Rapids-Wyoming MSA, MI	Y	22050 FQ	24530 MW	34220 TQ	USBLS	5/07
	Minnesota	Y	26373 FQ	30779 MW	38429 TQ	MNBLS	10/08-12/08
	Minneapolis-Saint Paul MSA, MN-WI	Y	26756 FQ	32717 MW	39943 TQ	MNBLS	10/08-12/08
	Mississippi	Y	18950 FQ	23170 MW	27310 TQ	USBLS	5/07
	Missouri	Y	17740 FQ	23070 MW	32600 TQ	USBLS	5/07
	Kansas City MSA, MO-KS	Y	19670 FQ	23680 MW	33770 TQ	USBLS	5/07
	St. Louis MSA, MO-IL	Y	20280 FQ	26960 MW	35240 TQ	USBLS	5/07
	Montana	Y	28640 FQ	33880 MW	37010 TQ	USBLS	5/07
	Nebraska	Y	27010 FQ	41780 MW	46890 TQ	USBLS	5/07
	Omaha-Council Bluffs MSA, NE-IA	Y	22050 FQ	26610 MW	30430 TQ	USBLS	5/07
	Nevada	H	9.98 FQ	11.43 MW	13.55 TQ	NVBLS	5/08
	New Hampshire	H	8.35 AE	11.02 MW	12.67 AEX	NHBLS	6/08
	New Jersey	Y	18430 FQ	24110 MW	30240 TQ	USBLS	5/07
	Camden PMSA, NJ	Y	21160 FQ	28060 MW	41000 TQ	USBLS	5/07
	Edison PMSA, NJ	Y	15690 FQ	24820 MW	34010 TQ	USBLS	5/07
	Newark-Union PMSA, NJ-PA	Y	17580 FQ	21900 MW	28130 TQ	USBLS	5/07
	New York	Y	21510 FQ	28480 MW	36960 TQ	USBLS	5/07
	Albany-Schenectady-Troy MSA, NY	Y	27100 FQ	29740 MW	34190 TQ	USBLS	5/07
	Nassau-Suffolk PMSA, NY	Y	16700 FQ	19680 MW	23550 TQ	USBLS	5/07
	New York-Northern New Jersey-Long Island MSA, NY-NJ-PA	Y	18300 FQ	24510 MW	31820 TQ	USBLS	5/07
	North Carolina	Y	20960 FQ	25470 MW	31030 TQ	USBLS	5/07
	Charlotte-Gastonia-Concord MSA, NC-SC	Y	24760 FQ	29990 MW	36480 TQ	USBLS	5/07
	Raleigh-Cary MSA, NC	Y	22020 FQ	24850 MW	36660 TQ	USBLS	5/07
	Ohio	Y	23090 FQ	29050 MW	35930 TQ	USBLS	5/07
	Cincinnati-Middletown MSA, OH-KY-IN	Y	23960 FQ	30440 MW	35810 TQ	USBLS	5/07
	Cleveland-Elyria-Mentor MSA, OH	Y	24070 FQ	32710 MW	38490 TQ	USBLS	5/07
	Columbus MSA, OH	Y	19120 FQ	24060 MW	27710 TQ	USBLS	5/07
	Oregon	H	11.64 FQ	14.77 MW	17.28 TQ	ORBLS	5/08
	Portland-Vancouver-Beaverton MSA, OR-WA	Y	23670 FQ	37440 MW	46310 TQ	USBLS	5/07
	Pennsylvania	Y	22380 FQ	27220 MW	33350 TQ	USBLS	5/07
	Allentown-Bethlehem-Easton MSA, PA-NJ	Y	22340 FQ	31220 MW	34380 TQ	USBLS	5/07
	Philadelphia-Camden-Wilmington MSA, PA-NJ-DE-MD	Y	26000 FQ	29690 MW	37030 TQ	USBLS	5/07
	Pittsburgh MSA, PA	Y	18970 FQ	22520 MW	27540 TQ	USBLS	5/07
	Rhode Island	Y	18730 FQ	22240 MW	26450 TQ	USBLS	5/07
	Providence-Fall River-Warwick MSA, RI-MA	Y	22180 FQ	27590 MW	32380 TQ	USBLS	5/07

AE	Average entry wage	AW	Average wage paid	FQ	First quartile wage	LO	Lowest wage paid	MTC	Median total compensation	TCC	Total cash compensation
AER	Average entry range	AWR	Average wage range	H	Hourly	LR	Low end range	MW	Median wage paid	TQ	Third quartile wage
AEX	Average experienced wage	AXR	Average experienced range	HI	Highest wage paid	M	Monthly	MWR	Median wage range	W	Weekly
ATC	Average total compensation	D	Daily	HR	High end range	MCC	Median cash compensation	S	See annotated source	Y	Yearly

Occupation/Type/Industry	Location	Per	Low	Mid	High	Source	Date
Cementing and Gluing Machine Operator and Tender	South Carolina	Y	18690 FQ	24950 MW	40670 TQ	USBLS	5/07
	South Dakota	Y	21894 FQ	24486 MW	29040 TQ	SDBLS	7/08-9/08
	Tennessee	Y	23450 FQ	28760 MW	34010 TQ	USBLS	5/07
	Clarksville MSA, TN-KY	Y	26820 FQ	30730 MW	35580 TQ	USBLS	5/07
	Memphis MSA, TN-MS-AR	Y	25050 FQ	32620 MW	36160 TQ	USBLS	5/07
	Nashville-Davidson-Murfreesboro MSA, TN	Y	25460 FQ	30130 MW	34920 TQ	USBLS	5/07
	Texas	Y	18540 FQ	22570 MW	28830 TQ	USBLS	5/07
	Austin-Round Rock MSA, TX	Y	16850 FQ	19270 MW	22560 TQ	USBLS	5/07
	Dallas-Fort Worth-Arlington MSA, TX	Y	18770 FQ	22960 MW	30460 TQ	USBLS	5/07
	Houston-Sugar Land-Baytown MSA, TX	Y	15650 FQ	20710 MW	26310 TQ	USBLS	5/07
	San Antonio MSA, TX	Y	20390 FQ	23070 MW	26950 TQ	USBLS	5/07
	Utah	Y	18050 FQ	23980 MW	29160 TQ	USBLS	5/07
	Salt Lake City MSA, UT	Y	17110 FQ	21770 MW	27990 TQ	USBLS	5/07
	Virginia	Y	16580 FQ	22820 MW	28500 TQ	USBLS	5/07
	Richmond MSA, VA	Y	13940 FQ	22890 MW	30420 TQ	USBLS	5/07
	Roanoke MSA, VA	Y	20030 FQ	22540 MW	25460 TQ	USBLS	5/07
	Washington	H	11.60 FQ	14.41 MW	19.21 TQ	WABLS	3/08
	West Virginia	Y	20870 FQ	25022 MW	28103 TQ	WVBLS	7/08-9/08
	Wisconsin	Y	23650 FQ	29990 MW	36640 TQ	USBLS	5/07
	Milwaukee-Waukesha-West Allis MSA, WI	Y	26460 FQ	31330 MW	35360 TQ	USBLS	5/07
	Puerto Rico	Y	13360 FQ	17490 MW	29490 TQ	USBLS	5/07
	San Juan-Caguas-Guaynabo MSA, PR	Y	13360 FQ	17490 MW	29490 TQ	USBLS	5/07
Cemetery Maintenance Supervisor	Colorado Springs, CO	M	4276 LO			COSPRS	1/1/09
Cemetery Manager	Colorado Springs, CO	M	6194 LO			COSPRS	1/1/09
Cemetery Superintendent Adjutant General	New Hampshire	Y		48149 AW		NHUL03	2008
Census Worker	United States	H	9.75 LO		14.50 HI	BRADEH	2009
Centrifuge Operator State Government	Ohio	H	14.53 LO		16.35 HI	ODAS	2008
Certified Alcoholism and/or Drug Abuse Counselor	Massachusetts	Y		29622 AW		MASS	2008
Certified Landscape Technician	United States	Y	20000-29999 LR		80000-99999 HR	AMNUR	2007
Certified Nurse Anesthetist	United States	Y	125000 AE	134000-154000 AWR		CCRUN01	2008
Certified Nurse Specialist	United States	Y	68000 AE			CCRUN01	2008
Certified Public Accountant Partner in a Firm with Annual Net Fees of More Than $2 Million	United States	Y		369000 AW		ACTECH	2008
Certified Safety Professional	United States	Y		99244 AW		SCOMP	1/08
Chancellor Ivy Tech Community College-Bloomington	Bloomington, IN	Y			131300 HI	HERT	2008-2009
University of Massachusetts Medical School	Worcester, MA	Y			609470 HI	BGLOBE3	2009
University of Pittsburgh	Pittsburgh, PA	Y			460000 HI	PPGAZ	2009
Chancellor of Schools	District of Columbia	Y			275000 HI	USNEWS03	2008
Change of Ownership Coordinator State Lottery	Tennessee	Y			32397 HI	THETN	2008
Chaplain State Government	Ohio	H	22.60 LO		31.62 HI	ODAS	2008

AE	Average entry wage	AW	Average wage paid	FQ	First quartile wage	LO	Lowest wage paid	MTC	Median total compensation	TCC	Total cash compensation
AER	Average entry range	AWR	Average wage range	H	Hourly	LR	Low end range	MW	Median wage paid	TQ	Third quartile wage
AEX	Average experienced wage	AXR	Average experienced range	HI	Highest wage paid	M	Monthly	MWR	Median wage range	W	Weekly
ATC	Average total compensation	D	Daily	HR	High end range	MCC	Median cash compensation	S	See annotated source	Y	Yearly

Occupation/Type/Industry	Location	Per	Low	Mid	High	Source	Date
Chaplain							
United States House of Representatives	United States	Y			167800 HI	CRS01	1/08
United States Senate	United States	Y			149000 HI	CRS01	1/08
Chauffeur	United States	H		13.92 AW		LCT01	2008
New Hampshire Veterans Home	New Hampshire	Y		27403 AW		NHUL03	2008
Chef and Head Cook	Alabama	Y	22650 FQ	30850 MW	43000 TQ	USBLS	5/07
	Birmingham-Hoover MSA, AL	Y	30370 FQ	41300 MW	49020 TQ	USBLS	5/07
	Arizona	Y	27600 FQ	36940 MW	48560 TQ	USBLS	5/07
	Flagstaff MSA, AZ	Y	22750 FQ	25900 MW	31150 TQ	USBLS	5/07
	Phoenix-Mesa-Scottsdale MSA, AZ	Y	29000 FQ	38690 MW	49910 TQ	USBLS	5/07
	Tucson MSA, AZ	Y	27140 FQ	36510 MW	46080 TQ	USBLS	5/07
	Yuma MSA, AZ	Y	20760 FQ	26550 MW	39360 TQ	USBLS	5/07
	Arkansas	Y	24440 FQ	30840 MW	39180 TQ	USBLS	5/07
	Little Rock-North Little Rock MSA, AR	Y	25670 FQ	30780 MW	40260 TQ	USBLS	5/07
	California	H	14.60 FQ	19.55 MW	26.07 TQ	CABLS	1/08-3/08
	Los Angeles-Long Beach-Glendale PMSA, CA	H	14.63 FQ	19.17 MW	23.66 TQ	CABLS	1/08-3/08
	Oakland-Fremont-Hayward MSA, CA	H	15.08 FQ	18.92 MW	27.44 TQ	CABLS	1/08-3/08
	Riverside-San Bernardino-Ontario MSA, CA	H	13.64 FQ	19.19 MW	27.90 TQ	CABLS	1/08-3/08
	Sacramento-Arden Arcade-Roseville MSA, CA	H	13.98 FQ	18.08 MW	24.46 TQ	CABLS	1/08-3/08
	San Diego-Carlsbad-San Marcos MSA, CA	H	16.32 FQ	23.31 MW	31.70 TQ	CABLS	1/08-3/08
	San Francisco-San Mateo-Redwood PMSA, CA	H	14.60 FQ	21.96 MW	28.93 TQ	CABLS	1/08-3/08
	San Jose-Sunnyvale-Santa Clara MSA, CA	H	13.88 FQ	18.60 MW	25.14 TQ	CABLS	1/08-3/08
	Santa Ana-Anaheim-Irvine PMSA, CA	Y	25890 FQ	37800 MW	49610 TQ	USBLS	5/07
	Colorado	Y	29160 FQ	37760 MW	47890 TQ	USBLS	5/07
	Boulder MSA, CO	Y	26690 FQ	32830 MW	38410 TQ	USBLS	5/07
	Denver-Aurora MSA, CO	Y	31020 FQ	38810 MW	47450 TQ	USBLS	5/07
	Connecticut	H	14.43 AE	21.44 MW		CTBLS	1/08-3/08
	Bridgeport-Stamford-Norwalk MSA, CT	Y	32940 FQ	44430 MW	58900 TQ	USBLS	5/07
	Hartford-West Hartford-East Hartford MSA, CT	Y	33100 FQ	41740 MW	52280 TQ	USBLS	5/07
	Delaware	Y	32060 FQ	40940 MW	52900 TQ	USBLS	5/07
	Dover MSA, DE	Y	30020 FQ	36130 MW	50830 TQ	USBLS	5/07
	Wilmington PMSA, DE-MD-NJ	Y	34490 FQ	43640 MW	53860 TQ	USBLS	5/07
	District of Columbia	Y	39990 FQ	47960 MW	61670 TQ	USBLS	5/07
	Washington-Arlington-Alexandria MSA, DC-VA-MD-WV	Y	33780 FQ	43940 MW	56630 TQ	USBLS	5/07
	Florida	Y	30490 FQ	41780 MW	55470 TQ	USBLS	5/07
	Fort Lauderdale-Pompano Beach-Deerfield Beach PMSA, FL	Y	29910 FQ	40320 MW	52560 TQ	USBLS	5/07
	Jacksonville MSA, FL	Y	28570 FQ	33720 MW	47890 TQ	USBLS	5/07
	Miami-Fort Lauderdale-Miami Beach MSA, FL	Y	32890 FQ	43300 MW	55620 TQ	USBLS	5/07
	Orlando-Kissimmee MSA, FL	Y	29000 FQ	45220 MW	67340 TQ	USBLS	5/07
	Tampa-St. Petersburg-Clearwater MSA, FL	Y	29700 FQ	47290 MW	57940 TQ	USBLS	5/07
	West Palm Beach-Boca Raton-Boynton Beach PMSA, FL	Y	33630 FQ	43940 MW	57990 TQ	USBLS	5/07
	Georgia	Y	24560 FQ	31950 MW	44670 TQ	USBLS	5/07
	Atlanta-Sandy Springs-Marietta MSA, GA	Y	26300 FQ	34750 MW	46360 TQ	USBLS	5/07
	Hawaii	Y	33600 FQ	45360 MW	62060 TQ	USBLS	5/07
	Honolulu MSA, HI	Y	34070 FQ	45780 MW	62610 TQ	USBLS	5/07
	Idaho	Y	15420 FQ	19140 MW	29860 TQ	USBLS	5/07
	Illinois	Y	23830 FQ	32990 MW	46220 TQ	USBLS	5/07
	Chicago-Naperville-Joliet MSA, IL-IN-WI	Y	26850 FQ	35490 MW	47660 TQ	USBLS	5/07

AE Average entry wage	**AW** Average wage paid	**FQ** First quartile wage	**LO** Lowest wage paid	**MTC** Median total compensation	**TCC** Total cash compensation
AER Average entry range	**AWR** Average wage range	**H** Hourly	**LR** Low end range	**MW** Median wage paid	**TQ** Third quartile wage
AEX Average experienced wage	**AXR** Average experienced range	**HI** Highest wage paid	**M** Monthly	**MWR** Median wage range	**W** Weekly
ATC Average total compensation	**D** Daily	**HR** High end range	**MCC** Median cash compensation	**S** See annotated source	**Y** Yearly

Occupation/Type/Industry	Location	Per	Low	Mid	High	Source	Date
Chef and Head Cook	Indiana	Y	25220 FQ	31970 MW	42330 TQ	USBLS	5/07
	Gary PMSA, IN	Y	29110 FQ	41820 MW	54470 TQ	USBLS	5/07
	Indianapolis-Carmel MSA, IN	Y	28070 FQ	36120 MW	46130 TQ	USBLS	5/07
	Iowa	Y	27410 FQ	35590 MW	45450 TQ	USBLS	5/07
	Des Moines-West Des Moines MSA, IA	Y	18670 FQ	36190 MW	45180 TQ	USBLS	5/07
	Kansas	Y	20460 FQ	25730 MW	32530 TQ	USBLS	5/07
	Wichita MSA, KS	Y	21180 FQ	24770 MW	37290 TQ	USBLS	5/07
	Kentucky	Y	29650 FQ	39116 MW	51576 TQ	KYBLS	2008
	Louisville-Jefferson County MSA, KY-IN	Y	29740 FQ	39690 MW	49670 TQ	USBLS	5/07
	Louisiana	H	12.73 FQ	15.97 MW	20.39 TQ	LABLS	1/08-3/08
	Baton Rouge MSA, LA	Y	23320 FQ	29720 MW	37640 TQ	USBLS	5/07
	Houma-Bayou Cane-Thibodaux MSA, LA	Y	19120 FQ	41690 MW	47170 TQ	USBLS	5/07
	New Orleans-Metairie-Kenner MSA, LA	Y	27400 FQ	33230 MW	44000 TQ	USBLS	5/07
	Maine	Y	30230 FQ	36690 MW	45200 TQ	USBLS	5/07
	Portland-South Portland-Biddeford MSA, ME	Y	33050 FQ	37550 MW	45910 TQ	USBLS	5/07
	Maryland	Y		40825 MW		MDBLS	3/08
	Baltimore-Towson MSA, MD	Y	33350 FQ	40910 MW	51230 TQ	USBLS	5/07
	Bethesda-Gaithersburg-Frederick PMSA, MD	Y	27820 FQ	39230 MW	49580 TQ	USBLS	5/07
	Massachusetts	Y	31940 FQ	40300 MW	53160 TQ	USBLS	5/07
	Boston-Cambridge-Quincy NECTA, MA	Y	32880 FQ	40770 MW	55090 TQ	USBLS	5/07
	Worcester MSA, MA-CT	Y	33130 FQ	40340 MW	48110 TQ	USBLS	5/07
	Michigan	Y	26340 FQ	33460 MW	46550 TQ	USBLS	5/07
	Detroit-Warren-Livonia MSA, MI	Y	29940 FQ	39320 MW	52820 TQ	USBLS	5/07
	Grand Rapids-Wyoming MSA, MI	Y	27590 FQ	30690 MW	41740 TQ	USBLS	5/07
	Warren-Troy-Farmington Hills PMSA, MI	Y	28960 FQ	36590 MW	50730 TQ	USBLS	5/07
	Minnesota	Y	33584 FQ	40223 MW	50010 TQ	MNBLS	10/08-12/08
	Duluth-Superior MSA, MN-WI	Y	27352 FQ	33730 MW	41342 TQ	MNBLS	10/08-12/08
	Minneapolis-Saint Paul MSA, MN-WI	Y	34263 FQ	40516 MW	49362 TQ	MNBLS	10/08-12/08
	Rochester MSA, MN	Y	32139 FQ	57638 MW	75015 TQ	MNBLS	10/08-12/08
	Mississippi	Y	20450 FQ	25840 MW	35740 TQ	USBLS	5/07
	Jackson MSA, MS	Y	20620 FQ	31980 MW	36610 TQ	USBLS	5/07
	Missouri	Y	23570 FQ	33850 MW	45300 TQ	USBLS	5/07
	Kansas City MSA, MO-KS	Y	20540 FQ	31540 MW	40830 TQ	USBLS	5/07
	St. Louis MSA, MO-IL	Y	27350 FQ	36870 MW	48750 TQ	USBLS	5/07
	Springfield MSA, MO	Y	23100 FQ	35770 MW	51200 TQ	USBLS	5/07
	Montana	Y	24210 FQ	29580 MW	36280 TQ	USBLS	5/07
	Billings MSA, MT	Y	18620 FQ	23690 MW	35400 TQ	USBLS	5/07
	Nebraska	Y	22860 FQ	29850 MW	39710 TQ	USBLS	5/07
	Omaha-Council Bluffs MSA, NE-IA	Y	25910 FQ	32160 MW	44350 TQ	USBLS	5/07
	Nevada	H	16.53 FQ	19.51 MW	25.17 TQ	NVBLS	5/08
	Carson City MSA, NV	H	15.45 FQ	17.39 MW	19.78 TQ	NVBLS	5/08
	Las Vegas-Paradise MSA, NV	H	16.82 FQ	19.69 MW	25.59 TQ	NVBLS	5/08
	New Hampshire	H	13.13 AE	17.38 MW	21.15 AEX	NHBLS	6/08
	Manchester MSA, NH	Y	28530 FQ	35620 MW	46990 TQ	USBLS	5/07
	Nashua NECTA, NH-MA	Y	33510 FQ	38470 MW	44360 TQ	USBLS	5/07
	New Jersey	Y	37420 FQ	46040 MW	58360 TQ	USBLS	5/07
	Camden PMSA, NJ	Y	34790 FQ	46470 MW	63000 TQ	USBLS	5/07
	Edison PMSA, NJ	Y	40340 FQ	49240 MW	63730 TQ	USBLS	5/07
	Newark-Union PMSA, NJ-PA	Y	34540 FQ	43760 MW	54560 TQ	USBLS	5/07
	New Mexico	Y	22700 FQ	30450 MW	48570 TQ	USBLS	5/07
	Albuquerque MSA, NM	Y	25560 FQ	35130 MW	52100 TQ	USBLS	5/07
	Santa Fe MSA, NM	Y	23280 FQ	30110 MW	57420 TQ	USBLS	5/07
	New York	Y	36240 FQ	46310 MW	60790 TQ	USBLS	5/07
	Albany-Schenectady-Troy MSA, NY	Y	15720 FQ	30930 MW	41880 TQ	USBLS	5/07
	Buffalo-Niagara Falls MSA, NY	Y	34110 FQ	40450 MW	49170 TQ	USBLS	5/07
	Glens Falls MSA, NY	Y	34170 FQ	43600 MW	50660 TQ	USBLS	5/07
	Ithaca MSA, NY	Y	45090 FQ	69750 MW	86630 TQ	USBLS	5/07
	Nassau-Suffolk PMSA, NY	Y	38220 FQ	50740 MW	66920 TQ	USBLS	5/07

AE Average entry wage	**AW** Average wage paid	**FQ** First quartile wage	**LO** Lowest wage paid	**MTC** Median total compensation	**TCC** Total cash compensation
AER Average entry range	**AWR** Average wage range	**H** Hourly	**LR** Low end range	**MW** Median wage paid	**TQ** Third quartile wage
AEX Average experienced wage	**AXR** Average experienced range	**HI** Highest wage paid	**M** Monthly	**MWR** Median wage range	**W** Weekly
ATC Average total compensation	**D** Daily	**HR** High end range	**MCC** Median cash compensation	**S** See annotated source	**Y** Yearly

Occupation/Type/Industry	Location	Per	Low	Mid	High	Source	Date
Chef and Head Cook	New York-Northern New Jersey-Long Island MSA, NY-NJ-PA	Y	38460 FQ	48450 MW	63710 TQ	USBLS	5/07
	Utica-Rome MSA, NY	Y	41970 FQ	46340 MW	50720 TQ	USBLS	5/07
	North Carolina	Y	24960 FQ	33570 MW	45080 TQ	USBLS	5/07
	Charlotte-Gastonia-Concord MSA, NC-SC	Y	25720 FQ	32290 MW	49320 TQ	USBLS	5/07
	Raleigh-Cary MSA, NC	Y	25270 FQ	34300 MW	44530 TQ	USBLS	5/07
	North Dakota	Y	22000 FQ	28190 MW	36190 TQ	USBLS	5/07
	Fargo MSA, ND-MN	Y	21210 FQ	24540 MW	32330 TQ	USBLS	5/07
	Ohio	Y	30560 FQ	38380 MW	49180 TQ	USBLS	5/07
	Cincinnati-Middletown MSA, OH-KY-IN	Y	30920 FQ	36500 MW	48280 TQ	USBLS	5/07
	Cleveland-Elyria-Mentor MSA, OH	Y	34180 FQ	41640 MW	50920 TQ	USBLS	5/07
	Columbus MSA, OH	Y	32950 FQ	39960 MW	52190 TQ	USBLS	5/07
	Dayton MSA, OH	Y	29180 FQ	34190 MW	46140 TQ	USBLS	5/07
	Oklahoma	Y	14320 FQ	21890 MW	30640 TQ	USBLS	5/07
	Oklahoma City MSA, OK	Y	13440 FQ	18190 MW	31360 TQ	USBLS	5/07
	Tulsa MSA, OK	Y	19010 FQ	24050 MW	29770 TQ	USBLS	5/07
	Oregon	H	13.81 FQ	16.57 MW	20.74 TQ	ORBLS	5/08
	Portland-Vancouver-Beaverton MSA, OR-WA	Y	28450 FQ	34440 MW	44190 TQ	USBLS	5/07
	Pennsylvania	Y	27470 FQ	34120 MW	45430 TQ	USBLS	5/07
	Allentown-Bethlehem-Easton MSA, PA-NJ	Y	28000 FQ	33680 MW	40090 TQ	USBLS	5/07
	Philadelphia-Camden-Wilmington MSA, PA-NJ-DE-MD	Y	32500 FQ	41460 MW	53320 TQ	USBLS	5/07
	Pittsburgh MSA, PA	Y	26390 FQ	32030 MW	39130 TQ	USBLS	5/07
	York-Hanover MSA, PA	Y	26780 FQ	32800 MW	38470 TQ	USBLS	5/07
	Providence-Fall River-Warwick MSA, RI-MA	Y	34570 FQ	47640 MW	57850 TQ	USBLS	5/07
	South Carolina	Y	24620 FQ	32330 MW	42900 TQ	USBLS	5/07
	Charleston-North Charleston MSA, SC	Y	32160 FQ	37640 MW	44310 TQ	USBLS	5/07
	Columbia MSA, SC	Y	26730 FQ	29890 MW	34730 TQ	USBLS	5/07
	Florence MSA, SC	Y	19630 FQ	24720 MW	34510 TQ	USBLS	5/07
	Myrtle Beach-Conway-North Myrtle Beach MSA, SC	Y	18140 FQ	28720 MW	37320 TQ	USBLS	5/07
	Spartanburg MSA, SC	Y	23830 FQ	30310 MW	39800 TQ	USBLS	5/07
	South Dakota	Y	29849 FQ	33583 MW	39985 TQ	SDBLS	7/08-9/08
	Sioux Falls MSA, SD	Y	28689 FQ	31540 MW	39029 TQ	SDBLS	7/08-9/08
	Tennessee	Y	23740 FQ	30650 MW	39910 TQ	USBLS	5/07
	Memphis MSA, TN-MS-AR	Y	22130 FQ	28880 MW	41070 TQ	USBLS	5/07
	Nashville-Davidson-Murfreesboro MSA, TN	Y	28430 FQ	35220 MW	44660 TQ	USBLS	5/07
	Texas	Y	26980 FQ	35940 MW	49290 TQ	USBLS	5/07
	Austin-Round Rock MSA, TX	Y	29380 FQ	35830 MW	48660 TQ	USBLS	5/07
	Dallas-Fort Worth-Arlington MSA, TX	Y	31630 FQ	40580 MW	52660 TQ	USBLS	5/07
	El Paso MSA, TX	Y	22500 FQ	35620 MW	53560 TQ	USBLS	5/07
	Houston-Sugar Land-Baytown MSA, TX	Y	28150 FQ	38220 MW	52600 TQ	USBLS	5/07
	San Antonio MSA, TX	Y	24990 FQ	32400 MW	44160 TQ	USBLS	5/07
	Utah	Y	29240 FQ	35430 MW	44440 TQ	USBLS	5/07
	Salt Lake City MSA, UT	Y	30680 FQ	36140 MW	45370 TQ	USBLS	5/07
	Vermont	Y	29740 FQ	35590 MW	45320 TQ	USBLS	5/07
	Burlington-South Burlington MSA, VT	Y	27830 FQ	31490 MW	44810 TQ	USBLS	5/07
	Virginia	Y	31710 FQ	39850 MW	51180 TQ	USBLS	5/07
	Richmond MSA, VA	Y	31870 FQ	36660 MW	47790 TQ	USBLS	5/07
	Virginia Beach-Norfolk-Newport News MSA, VA-NC	Y	30660 FQ	36080 MW	43060 TQ	USBLS	5/07
	Washington	H	17.71 FQ	21.82 MW	26.19 TQ	WABLS	3/08
	Seattle-Tacoma-Bellevue MSA, WA	Y	38150 FQ	45770 MW	55530 TQ	USBLS	5/07
	West Virginia	Y	26866 FQ	39750 MW	60120 TQ	WVBLS	7/08-9/08
	Charleston MSA, WV	Y	29200 FQ	48250 MW	59650 TQ	USBLS	5/07
	Wisconsin	Y	24470 FQ	30520 MW	39190 TQ	USBLS	5/07
	Appleton MSA, WI	Y	24220 FQ	27190 MW	30640 TQ	USBLS	5/07

AE Average entry wage	**AW** Average wage paid	**FQ** First quartile wage	**LO** Lowest wage paid	**MTC** Median total compensation	**TCC** Total cash compensation
AER Average entry range	**AWR** Average wage range	**H** Hourly	**LR** Low end range	**MW** Median wage paid	**TQ** Third quartile wage
AEX Average experienced wage	**AXR** Average experienced range	**HI** Highest wage paid	**M** Monthly	**MWR** Median wage range	**W** Weekly
ATC Average total compensation	**D** Daily	**HR** High end range	**MCC** Median cash compensation	**S** See annotated source	**Y** Yearly

Occupation/Type/Industry	Location	Per	Low	Mid	High	Source	Date
Chef and Head Cook	Milwaukee-Waukesha-West Allis MSA, WI	Y	25690 FQ	32020 MW	42310 TQ	USBLS	5/07
	Wyoming	Y	23778 FQ	30609 MW	40262 TQ	WYBLS	9/08
	Cheyenne MSA, WY	Y	22091 FQ	26834 MW	40042 TQ	WYBLS	9/08
	Puerto Rico	Y	22640 FQ	28670 MW	36740 TQ	USBLS	5/07
	San Juan-Caguas-Guaynabo MSA, PR	Y	22470 FQ	28240 MW	35720 TQ	USBLS	5/07
	Virgin Islands	Y	38180 FQ	43100 MW	52880 TQ	USBLS	5/07
	Guam	Y	21150 FQ	29460 MW	39960 TQ	USBLS	5/07
Chemical Engineer	United States	Y		95231 AW		CHEMPR	2008
	Alabama	Y	67040 FQ	81850 MW	98240 TQ	USBLS	5/07
	Arizona	Y	58680 FQ	73310 MW	90630 TQ	USBLS	5/07
	Phoenix-Mesa-Scottsdale MSA, AZ	Y	59020 FQ	73390 MW	89900 TQ	USBLS	5/07
	Tucson MSA, AZ	Y	58490 FQ	77370 MW	94850 TQ	USBLS	5/07
	Arkansas	Y	56560 FQ	78720 MW	93560 TQ	USBLS	5/07
	California	H	33.14 FQ	42.83 MW	52.62 TQ	CABLS	1/08-3/08
	Los Angeles-Long Beach-Glendale PMSA, CA	H	34.17 FQ	43.53 MW	53.33 TQ	CABLS	1/08-3/08
	Oakland-Fremont-Hayward MSA, CA	H	30.84 FQ	39.17 MW	53.29 TQ	CABLS	1/08-3/08
	Riverside-San Bernardino-Ontario MSA, CA	H	30.63 FQ	34.92 MW	44.94 TQ	CABLS	1/08-3/08
	Sacramento-Arden Arcade-Roseville MSA, CA	H	37.98 FQ	42.08 MW	46.15 TQ	CABLS	1/08-3/08
	San Diego-Carlsbad-San Marcos MSA, CA	H	30.81 FQ	43.29 MW	49.81 TQ	CABLS	1/08-3/08
	San Francisco-San Mateo-Redwood PMSA, CA	H	44.96 FQ	50.27 MW	58.59 TQ	CABLS	1/08-3/08
	San Jose-Sunnyvale-Santa Clara MSA, CA	H	36.69 FQ	44.84 MW	56.59 TQ	CABLS	1/08-3/08
	Santa Ana-Anaheim-Irvine PMSA, CA	Y	64600 FQ	83560 MW	100240 TQ	USBLS	5/07
	Colorado	Y	62060 FQ	81900 MW	102460 TQ	USBLS	5/07
	Denver-Aurora MSA, CO	Y	64120 FQ	79120 MW	95900 TQ	USBLS	5/07
	Connecticut	H	26.94 AE	40.14 MW		CTBLS	1/08-3/08
	Bridgeport-Stamford-Norwalk MSA, CT	Y	60370 FQ	85900 MW	106580 TQ	USBLS	5/07
	Delaware	Y	77740 FQ	94580 MW	118870 TQ	USBLS	5/07
	Wilmington PMSA, DE-MD-NJ	Y	77760 FQ	94400 MW	118900 TQ	USBLS	5/07
	District of Columbia	Y	81080 FQ	97290 MW	114470 TQ	USBLS	5/07
	Washington-Arlington-Alexandria MSA, DC-VA-MD-WV	Y	70510 FQ	90600 MW	110020 TQ	USBLS	5/07
	Florida	Y	57880 FQ	74630 MW	95660 TQ	USBLS	5/07
	Lakeland MSA, FL	Y	59180 FQ	71420 MW	84290 TQ	USBLS	5/07
	Miami-Fort Lauderdale-Miami Beach MSA, FL	Y	70230 FQ	87420 MW	98190 TQ	USBLS	5/07
	Tampa-St. Petersburg-Clearwater MSA, FL	Y	58510 FQ	85260 MW	96140 TQ	USBLS	5/07
	West Palm Beach-Boca Raton-Boynton Beach PMSA, FL	Y	76980 FQ	89770 MW	98950 TQ	USBLS	5/07
	Georgia	Y	50420 FQ	70520 MW	88010 TQ	USBLS	5/07
	Atlanta-Sandy Springs-Marietta MSA, GA	Y	47630 FQ	65590 MW	88470 TQ	USBLS	5/07
	Illinois	Y	60380 FQ	75420 MW	92180 TQ	USBLS	5/07
	Chicago-Naperville-Joliet MSA, IL-IN-WI	Y	60750 FQ	76320 MW	94150 TQ	USBLS	5/07
	Indiana	Y	61470 FQ	77830 MW	93650 TQ	USBLS	5/07
	Gary PMSA, IN	Y	65110 FQ	78030 MW	92350 TQ	USBLS	5/07
	Indianapolis-Carmel MSA, IN	Y	64490 FQ	84370 MW	98710 TQ	USBLS	5/07
	Iowa	Y	57370 FQ	71360 MW	92140 TQ	USBLS	5/07
	Kansas	Y	68930 FQ	81680 MW	95170 TQ	USBLS	5/07
	Wichita MSA, KS	Y	72260 FQ	84640 MW	98660 TQ	USBLS	5/07
	Kentucky	Y	69074 FQ	83901 MW	100791 TQ	KYBLS	2008
	Louisville-Jefferson County MSA, KY-IN	Y	64370 FQ	81480 MW	98760 TQ	USBLS	5/07
	Louisiana	H	33.07 FQ	41.58 MW	50.86 TQ	LABLS	1/08-3/08
	Baton Rouge MSA, LA	Y	71210 FQ	90720 MW	110950 TQ	USBLS	5/07

Chemical Engineer

Occupation/Type/Industry	Location	Per	Low	Mid	High	Source	Date
Chemical Engineer	New Orleans-Metairie-Kenner MSA, LA	Y	60060 FQ	80430 MW	101060 TQ	USBLS	5/07
	Maine	Y	69110 FQ	81330 MW	98410 TQ	USBLS	5/07
	Portland-South Portland-Biddeford MSA, ME	Y	72850 FQ	88690 MW	107610 TQ	USBLS	5/07
	Maryland	Y		87850 MW		MDBLS	3/08
	Baltimore-Towson MSA, MD	Y	69190 FQ	86320 MW	103190 TQ	USBLS	5/07
	Bethesda-Gaithersburg-Frederick PMSA, MD	Y	66430 FQ	84020 MW	102370 TQ	USBLS	5/07
	Massachusetts	Y	67190 FQ	82410 MW	108860 TQ	USBLS	5/07
	Boston-Cambridge-Quincy NECTA, MA	Y	66970 FQ	82360 MW	112140 TQ	USBLS	5/07
	Worcester MSA, MA-CT	Y	70350 FQ	84910 MW	98120 TQ	USBLS	5/07
	Michigan	Y	57200 FQ	74310 MW	94150 TQ	USBLS	5/07
	Detroit-Warren-Livonia MSA, MI	Y	53670 FQ	73970 MW	92580 TQ	USBLS	5/07
	Warren-Troy-Farmington Hills PMSA, MI	Y	54650 FQ	77000 MW	94050 TQ	USBLS	5/07
	Minnesota	Y	61423 FQ	75935 MW	87338 TQ	MNBLS	10/08-12/08
	Duluth-Superior MSA, MN-WI	Y	55690 FQ	70369 MW	82400 TQ	MNBLS	10/08-12/08
	Minneapolis-Saint Paul MSA, MN-WI	Y	65075 FQ	78205 MW	88259 TQ	MNBLS	10/08-12/08
	Mississippi	Y	66830 FQ	86300 MW	102500 TQ	USBLS	5/07
	Gulfport-Biloxi MSA, MS	Y	84250 FQ	96670 MW	111230 TQ	USBLS	5/07
	Missouri	Y	59720 FQ	76430 MW	103040 TQ	USBLS	5/07
	Kansas City MSA, MO-KS	Y	56980 FQ	74250 MW	90770 TQ	USBLS	5/07
	St. Louis MSA, MO-IL	Y	69400 FQ	86870 MW	121420 TQ	USBLS	5/07
	Montana	Y	46940 FQ	65340 MW	84730 TQ	USBLS	5/07
	Nebraska	Y	47030 FQ	56570 MW	73370 TQ	USBLS	5/07
	Omaha-Council Bluffs MSA, NE-IA	Y	49150 FQ	56380 MW	74640 TQ	USBLS	5/07
	Nevada	H	28.90 FQ	38.50 MW	46.58 TQ	NVBLS	5/08
	New Hampshire	H	23.34 AE	35.09 MW	42.45 AEX	NHBLS	6/08
	New Jersey	Y	71140 FQ	91380 MW	113820 TQ	USBLS	5/07
	Camden PMSA, NJ	Y	82150 FQ	109640 MW	128360 TQ	USBLS	5/07
	Edison PMSA, NJ	Y	69870 FQ	90120 MW	106200 TQ	USBLS	5/07
	Newark-Union PMSA, NJ-PA	Y	72780 FQ	92020 MW	116240 TQ	USBLS	5/07
	New Mexico	Y	72040 FQ	81540 MW	106140 TQ	USBLS	5/07
	Albuquerque MSA, NM	Y	71390 FQ	81000 MW	110280 TQ	USBLS	5/07
	New York	Y	64600 FQ	83330 MW	104730 TQ	USBLS	5/07
	Albany-Schenectady-Troy MSA, NY	Y	64300 FQ	83250 MW	109000 TQ	USBLS	5/07
	Buffalo-Niagara Falls MSA, NY	Y	78380 FQ	90270 MW	101230 TQ	USBLS	5/07
	Nassau-Suffolk PMSA, NY	Y	54430 FQ	67270 MW	87280 TQ	USBLS	5/07
	New York-Northern New Jersey-Long Island MSA, NY-NJ-PA	Y	65810 FQ	87540 MW	107940 TQ	USBLS	5/07
	North Carolina	Y	62890 FQ	78200 MW	94900 TQ	USBLS	5/07
	Charlotte-Gastonia-Concord MSA, NC-SC	Y	60950 FQ	76150 MW	93440 TQ	USBLS	5/07
	Raleigh-Cary MSA, NC	Y	58730 FQ	73850 MW	92670 TQ	USBLS	5/07
	North Dakota	Y	53610 FQ	68370 MW	85560 TQ	USBLS	5/07
	Ohio	Y	63290 FQ	78500 MW	97240 TQ	USBLS	5/07
	Cincinnati-Middletown MSA, OH-KY-IN	Y	70160 FQ	88140 MW	104660 TQ	USBLS	5/07
	Cleveland-Elyria-Mentor MSA, OH	Y	65000 FQ	81000 MW	105520 TQ	USBLS	5/07
	Columbus MSA, OH	Y	60850 FQ	73740 MW	88620 TQ	USBLS	5/07
	Dayton MSA, OH	Y	62390 FQ	75890 MW	94210 TQ	USBLS	5/07
	Oklahoma	Y	55620 FQ	68600 MW	84940 TQ	USBLS	5/07
	Oklahoma City MSA, OK	Y	60620 FQ	68270 MW	76090 TQ	USBLS	5/07
	Tulsa MSA, OK	Y	57330 FQ	71150 MW	85560 TQ	USBLS	5/07
	Oregon	H	33.49 FQ	41.59 MW	49.92 TQ	ORBLS	5/08
	Pennsylvania	Y	59290 FQ	74230 MW	90840 TQ	USBLS	5/07
	Allentown-Bethlehem-Easton MSA, PA-NJ	Y	57050 FQ	66160 MW	83600 TQ	USBLS	5/07
	Philadelphia-Camden-Wilmington MSA, PA-NJ-DE-MD	Y	68640 FQ	84680 MW	110700 TQ	USBLS	5/07
	Pittsburgh MSA, PA	Y	59070 FQ	75070 MW	92150 TQ	USBLS	5/07
	Rhode Island	Y	59790 FQ	73000 MW	92100 TQ	USBLS	5/07

AE	Average entry wage	AW	Average wage paid	FQ	First quartile wage
AER	Average entry range	AWR	Average wage range	H	Hourly
AEX	Average experienced wage	AXR	Average experienced range	HI	Highest wage paid
ATC	Average total compensation	D	Daily	HR	High end range

LO	Lowest wage paid	MTC	Median total compensation	TCC	Total cash compensation
LR	Low end range	MW	Median wage paid	TQ	Third quartile wage
M	Monthly	MWR	Median wage range	W	Weekly
MCC	Median cash compensation	S	See annotated source	Y	Yearly

Occupation/Type/Industry	Location	Per	Low	Mid	High	Source	Date
Chemical Engineer	Providence-Fall River-Warwick MSA, RI-MA	Y	61070 FQ	72730 MW	90850 TQ	USBLS	5/07
	South Carolina	Y	63760 FQ	77750 MW	93590 TQ	USBLS	5/07
	Columbia MSA, SC	Y	59490 FQ	74650 MW	89520 TQ	USBLS	5/07
	Florence MSA, SC	Y	65640 FQ	89050 MW	110590 TQ	USBLS	5/07
	Tennessee	Y	71100 FQ	82980 MW	98950 TQ	USBLS	5/07
	Memphis MSA, TN-MS-AR	Y	59560 FQ	76310 MW	91610 TQ	USBLS	5/07
	Texas	Y	66290 FQ	85050 MW	106710 TQ	USBLS	5/07
	Austin-Round Rock MSA, TX	Y	35460 FQ	41600 MW	65970 TQ	USBLS	5/07
	Dallas-Fort Worth-Arlington MSA, TX	Y	58710 FQ	67110 MW	89800 TQ	USBLS	5/07
	Houston-Sugar Land-Baytown MSA, TX	Y	75200 FQ	94160 MW	115570 TQ	USBLS	5/07
	Utah	Y	64700 FQ	79710 MW	104080 TQ	USBLS	5/07
	Salt Lake City MSA, UT	Y	65450 FQ	77250 MW	91080 TQ	USBLS	5/07
	Virginia	Y	67220 FQ	88360 MW	106750 TQ	USBLS	5/07
	Richmond MSA, VA	Y	69240 FQ	86630 MW	100650 TQ	USBLS	5/07
	Virginia Beach-Norfolk-Newport News MSA, VA-NC	Y	62260 FQ	81480 MW	105230 TQ	USBLS	5/07
	Washington	H	35.02 FQ	43.83 MW	53.34 TQ	WABLS	3/08
	Seattle-Tacoma-Bellevue MSA, WA	Y	68620 FQ	86090 MW	106470 TQ	USBLS	5/07
	West Virginia	Y	77931 FQ	92366 MW	107838 TQ	WVBLS	7/08-9/08
	Charleston MSA, WV	Y	79670 FQ	90360 MW	106920 TQ	USBLS	5/07
	Wisconsin	Y	61090 FQ	70990 MW	81670 TQ	USBLS	5/07
	Milwaukee-Waukesha-West Allis MSA, WI	Y	61310 FQ	68090 MW	75650 TQ	USBLS	5/07
	Wyoming	Y	58325 FQ	67816 MW	93808 TQ	WYBLS	9/08
	Puerto Rico	Y	63370 FQ	76700 MW	91580 TQ	USBLS	5/07
	San Juan-Caguas-Guaynabo MSA, PR	Y	63620 FQ	77360 MW	93040 TQ	USBLS	5/07
	Virgin Islands	Y	59540 FQ	80960 MW	97400 TQ	USBLS	5/07
Chemical Equipment Operator and Tender	Alabama	Y	30480 FQ	41340 MW	53260 TQ	USBLS	5/07
	Birmingham-Hoover MSA, AL	Y	27430 FQ	29650 MW	31580 TQ	USBLS	5/07
	Arizona	Y	25250 FQ	29720 MW	43130 TQ	USBLS	5/07
	Arkansas	Y	36540 FQ	42500 MW	47280 TQ	USBLS	5/07
	California	H	19.64 FQ	22.67 MW	26.51 TQ	CABLS	1/08-3/08
	Los Angeles-Long Beach-Glendale PMSA, CA	H	20.70 FQ	22.43 MW	24.46 TQ	CABLS	1/08-3/08
	Oakland-Fremont-Hayward MSA, CA	H	21.31 FQ	24.14 MW	27.91 TQ	CABLS	1/08-3/08
	Riverside-San Bernardino-Ontario MSA, CA	H	17.04 FQ	19.19 MW	23.91 TQ	CABLS	1/08-3/08
	Sacramento-Arden Arcade-Roseville MSA, CA	H	21.73 FQ	23.73 MW	26.26 TQ	CABLS	1/08-3/08
	San Diego-Carlsbad-San Marcos MSA, CA	H	17.39 FQ	19.07 MW	22.13 TQ	CABLS	1/08-3/08
	San Jose-Sunnyvale-Santa Clara MSA, CA	H	20.21 FQ	22.90 MW	26.89 TQ	CABLS	1/08-3/08
	Santa Ana-Anaheim-Irvine PMSA, CA	Y	28400 FQ	37270 MW	46320 TQ	USBLS	5/07
	Colorado	Y	27140 FQ	34070 MW	40870 TQ	USBLS	5/07
	Denver-Aurora MSA, CO	Y	30800 FQ	37150 MW	44560 TQ	USBLS	5/07
	Connecticut	H	14.50 AE	20.96 MW		CTBLS	1/08-3/08
	Bridgeport-Stamford-Norwalk MSA, CT	Y	38650 FQ	46080 MW	58910 TQ	USBLS	5/07
	Hartford-West Hartford-East Hartford MSA, CT	Y	26990 FQ	32880 MW	40310 TQ	USBLS	5/07
	Delaware	Y	41080 FQ	50300 MW	57600 TQ	USBLS	5/07
	Wilmington PMSA, DE-MD-NJ	Y	47630 FQ	54180 MW	59390 TQ	USBLS	5/07
	Washington-Arlington-Alexandria MSA, DC-VA-MD-WV	Y	36560 FQ	47820 MW	54320 TQ	USBLS	5/07
	Florida	Y	30590 FQ	39830 MW	47590 TQ	USBLS	5/07
	Miami-Fort Lauderdale-Miami Beach MSA, FL	Y	24570 FQ	28720 MW	35670 TQ	USBLS	5/07
	Tampa-St. Petersburg-Clearwater MSA, FL	Y	26140 FQ	33860 MW	43440 TQ	USBLS	5/07

AE Average entry wage	**AW** Average wage paid	**FQ** First quartile wage	**LO** Lowest wage paid	**MTC** Median total compensation	**TCC** Total cash compensation
AER Average entry range	**AWR** Average wage range	**H** Hourly	**LR** Low end range	**MW** Median wage paid	**TQ** Third quartile wage
AEX Average experienced wage	**AXR** Average experienced range	**HI** Highest wage paid	**M** Monthly	**MWR** Median wage range	**W** Weekly
ATC Average total compensation	**D** Daily	**HR** High end range	**MCC** Median cash compensation	**S** See annotated source	**Y** Yearly

Occupation/Type/Industry	Location	Per	Low	Mid	High	Source	Date
Chemical Equipment Operator and Tender							
	West Palm Beach-Boca Raton-Boynton Beach PMSA, FL	Y	23140 FQ	25100 MW	28340 TQ	USBLS	5/07
	Georgia	Y	30520 FQ	36790 MW	45430 TQ	USBLS	5/07
	Atlanta-Sandy Springs-Marietta MSA, GA	Y	31990 FQ	39840 MW	52180 TQ	USBLS	5/07
	Idaho	Y	42360 FQ	48140 MW	56140 TQ	USBLS	5/07
	Illinois	Y	25830 FQ	40650 MW	52300 TQ	USBLS	5/07
	Champaign-Urbana MSA, IL	Y	21580 FQ	30800 MW	41300 TQ	USBLS	5/07
	Chicago-Naperville-Joliet MSA, IL-IN-WI	Y	28300 FQ	40260 MW	52560 TQ	USBLS	5/07
	Indiana	Y	34500 FQ	45450 MW	54530 TQ	USBLS	5/07
	Gary PMSA, IN	Y	43000 FQ	49260 MW	54030 TQ	USBLS	5/07
	Iowa	Y	32340 FQ	37480 MW	46990 TQ	USBLS	5/07
	Des Moines-West Des Moines MSA, IA	Y	32070 FQ	34690 MW	37270 TQ	USBLS	5/07
	Kansas	Y	37650 FQ	43400 MW	48100 TQ	USBLS	5/07
	Wichita MSA, KS	Y	43620 FQ	46870 MW	50090 TQ	USBLS	5/07
	Kentucky	Y	44494 FQ	50705 MW	57040 TQ	KYBLS	2008
	Louisville-Jefferson County MSA, KY-IN	Y	46560 FQ	55130 MW	59920 TQ	USBLS	5/07
	Louisiana	H	20.68 FQ	25.22 MW	28.34 TQ	LABLS	1/08-3/08
	Baton Rouge MSA, LA	Y	44890 FQ	54140 MW	59970 TQ	USBLS	5/07
	New Orleans-Metairie-Kenner MSA, LA	Y	44000 FQ	53430 MW	58940 TQ	USBLS	5/07
	Maine	Y	35300 FQ	38790 MW	43330 TQ	USBLS	5/07
	Maryland	Y		40550 MW		MDBLS	3/08
	Baltimore-Towson MSA, MD	Y	33210 FQ	39520 MW	48630 TQ	USBLS	5/07
	Massachusetts	Y	35210 FQ	39460 MW	45170 TQ	USBLS	5/07
	Boston-Cambridge-Quincy NECTA, MA	Y	35850 FQ	39830 MW	45660 TQ	USBLS	5/07
	Worcester MSA, MA-CT	Y	33950 FQ	38200 MW	44760 TQ	USBLS	5/07
	Michigan	Y	37790 FQ	46350 MW	55850 TQ	USBLS	5/07
	Detroit-Warren-Livonia MSA, MI	Y	41730 FQ	48570 MW	56700 TQ	USBLS	5/07
	Warren-Troy-Farmington Hills PMSA, MI	Y	33200 FQ	39810 MW	46800 TQ	USBLS	5/07
	Minnesota	Y	28954 FQ	34220 MW	47873 TQ	MNBLS	10/08-12/08
	Minneapolis-Saint Paul MSA, MN-WI	Y	29607 FQ	37662 MW	54011 TQ	MNBLS	10/08-12/08
	Mississippi	Y	34770 FQ	42280 MW	49730 TQ	USBLS	5/07
	Missouri	Y	33450 FQ	42170 MW	49640 TQ	USBLS	5/07
	Kansas City MSA, MO-KS	Y	30620 FQ	42140 MW	49670 TQ	USBLS	5/07
	St. Louis MSA, MO-IL	Y	39540 FQ	45270 MW	50310 TQ	USBLS	5/07
	Nebraska	Y	27150 FQ	30110 MW	35190 TQ	USBLS	5/07
	Omaha-Council Bluffs MSA, NE-IA	Y	25720 FQ	29880 MW	36410 TQ	USBLS	5/07
	Nevada	H	18.33 FQ	20.91 MW	23.31 TQ	NVBLS	5/08
	New Hampshire	H	15.55 AE	18.24 MW	20.97 AEX	NHBLS	6/08
	New Jersey	Y	34400 FQ	43540 MW	51280 TQ	USBLS	5/07
	Camden PMSA, NJ	Y	35440 FQ	41610 MW	51140 TQ	USBLS	5/07
	Edison PMSA, NJ	Y	33500 FQ	43240 MW	50370 TQ	USBLS	5/07
	Newark-Union PMSA, NJ-PA	Y	34320 FQ	43700 MW	50920 TQ	USBLS	5/07
	New York	Y	34010 FQ	43140 MW	49080 TQ	USBLS	5/07
	Albany-Schenectady-Troy MSA, NY	Y	40690 FQ	46700 MW	55090 TQ	USBLS	5/07
	Buffalo-Niagara Falls MSA, NY	Y	29440 FQ	35470 MW	44220 TQ	USBLS	5/07
	Nassau-Suffolk PMSA, NY	Y	36180 FQ	44520 MW	49970 TQ	USBLS	5/07
	New York-Northern New Jersey-Long Island MSA, NY-NJ-PA	Y	33610 FQ	43210 MW	50080 TQ	USBLS	5/07
	North Carolina	Y	36050 FQ	42120 MW	48900 TQ	USBLS	5/07
	Charlotte-Gastonia-Concord MSA, NC-SC	Y	26360 FQ	34340 MW	41840 TQ	USBLS	5/07
	Ohio	Y	31490 FQ	41840 MW	50030 TQ	USBLS	5/07
	Cincinnati-Middletown MSA, OH-KY-IN	Y	38270 FQ	44300 MW	48570 TQ	USBLS	5/07
	Cleveland-Elyria-Mentor MSA, OH	Y	24050 FQ	30460 MW	37990 TQ	USBLS	5/07
	Columbus MSA, OH	Y	33900 FQ	40930 MW	47170 TQ	USBLS	5/07
	Dayton MSA, OH	Y	24240 FQ	31780 MW	47410 TQ	USBLS	5/07

AE Average entry wage	**AW** Average wage paid	**FQ** First quartile wage	**LO** Lowest wage paid	**MTC** Median total compensation	**TCC** Total cash compensation
AER Average entry range	**AWR** Average wage range	**H** Hourly	**LR** Low end range	**MW** Median wage paid	**TQ** Third quartile wage
AEX Average experienced wage	**AXR** Average experienced range	**HI** Highest wage paid	**M** Monthly	**MWR** Median wage range	**W** Weekly
ATC Average total compensation	**D** Daily	**HR** High end range	**MCC** Median cash compensation	**S** See annotated source	**Y** Yearly

Occupation/Type/Industry	Location	Per	Low	Mid	High	Source	Date
Chemical Equipment Operator and Tender	Oklahoma	Y	31430 FQ	39150 MW	45890 TQ	USBLS	5/07
	Tulsa MSA, OK	Y	32820 FQ	40320 MW	44740 TQ	USBLS	5/07
	Oregon	H	16.92 FQ	20.38 MW	24.57 TQ	ORBLS	5/08
	Portland-Vancouver-Beaverton MSA, OR-WA	Y	33130 FQ	45180 MW	53210 TQ	USBLS	5/07
	Pennsylvania	Y	34460 FQ	42720 MW	52230 TQ	USBLS	5/07
	Allentown-Bethlehem-Easton MSA, PA-NJ	Y	32720 FQ	38500 MW	51810 TQ	USBLS	5/07
	Philadelphia-Camden-Wilmington MSA, PA-NJ-DE-MD	Y	35620 FQ	44820 MW	54590 TQ	USBLS	5/07
	Pittsburgh MSA, PA	Y	36900 FQ	47670 MW	56850 TQ	USBLS	5/07
	Rhode Island	Y	35090 FQ	41210 MW	46980 TQ	USBLS	5/07
	Providence-Fall River-Warwick MSA, RI-MA	Y	34540 FQ	40620 MW	46650 TQ	USBLS	5/07
	South Carolina	Y	39020 FQ	49550 MW	67110 TQ	USBLS	5/07
	Charleston-North Charleston MSA, SC	Y	31670 FQ	37340 MW	47030 TQ	USBLS	5/07
	Columbia MSA, SC	Y	36040 FQ	40960 MW	46120 TQ	USBLS	5/07
	South Dakota	Y	25749 FQ	29345 MW	33996 TQ	SDBLS	7/08-9/08
	Sioux Falls MSA, SD	Y	26328 FQ	28732 MW	31156 TQ	SDBLS	7/08-9/08
	Tennessee	Y	30450 FQ	42850 MW	54130 TQ	USBLS	5/07
	Memphis MSA, TN-MS-AR	Y	38820 FQ	42650 MW	46030 TQ	USBLS	5/07
	Texas	Y	41420 FQ	52630 MW	60590 TQ	USBLS	5/07
	Austin-Round Rock MSA, TX	Y	42370 FQ	54920 MW	60140 TQ	USBLS	5/07
	Dallas-Fort Worth-Arlington MSA, TX	Y	32050 FQ	42330 MW	53860 TQ	USBLS	5/07
	Houston-Sugar Land-Baytown MSA, TX	Y	44030 FQ	54330 MW	61080 TQ	USBLS	5/07
	Utah	Y	27300 FQ	37060 MW	43470 TQ	USBLS	5/07
	Salt Lake City MSA, UT	Y	30870 FQ	36660 MW	42000 TQ	USBLS	5/07
	Virginia	Y	31900 FQ	38730 MW	46840 TQ	USBLS	5/07
	Richmond MSA, VA	Y	30620 FQ	39420 MW	50280 TQ	USBLS	5/07
	Washington	H	14.36 FQ	16.74 MW	22.02 TQ	WABLS	3/08
	Seattle-Tacoma-Bellevue MSA, WA	Y	34950 FQ	45960 MW	57140 TQ	USBLS	5/07
	West Virginia	Y	37626 FQ	45818 MW	55469 TQ	WVBLS	7/08-9/08
	Charleston MSA, WV	Y	31080 FQ	42280 MW	53590 TQ	USBLS	5/07
	Milwaukee-Waukesha-West Allis MSA, WI	Y	32520 FQ	38590 MW	44510 TQ	USBLS	5/07
	Puerto Rico	Y	22650 FQ	31640 MW	41050 TQ	USBLS	5/07
	San Juan-Caguas-Guaynabo MSA, PR	Y	21220 FQ	31120 MW	40160 TQ	USBLS	5/07
Chemical Plant and System Operator	Alabama	Y	48520 FQ	54170 MW	58960 TQ	USBLS	5/07
	Birmingham-Hoover MSA, AL	Y	36750 FQ	42930 MW	71100 TQ	USBLS	5/07
	Arizona	Y	33110 FQ	40330 MW	56830 TQ	USBLS	5/07
	Arkansas	Y	39870 FQ	47210 MW	54120 TQ	USBLS	5/07
	California	H	24.33 FQ	28.18 MW	31.84 TQ	CABLS	1/08-3/08
	Los Angeles-Long Beach-Glendale PMSA, CA	H	25.19 FQ	28.24 MW	31.70 TQ	CABLS	1/08-3/08
	Oakland-Fremont-Hayward MSA, CA	H	26.65 FQ	29.36 MW	33.40 TQ	CABLS	1/08-3/08
	Riverside-San Bernardino-Ontario MSA, CA	H	21.98 FQ	26.55 MW	29.64 TQ	CABLS	1/08-3/08
	San Diego-Carlsbad-San Marcos MSA, CA	H	21.00 FQ	22.88 MW	24.98 TQ	CABLS	1/08-3/08
	San Francisco-San Mateo-Redwood PMSA, CA	H	27.25 FQ	30.52 MW	35.24 TQ	CABLS	1/08-3/08
	Santa Ana-Anaheim-Irvine PMSA, CA	Y	25420 FQ	29780 MW	58310 TQ	USBLS	5/07
	Colorado	Y	33860 FQ	40060 MW	50080 TQ	USBLS	5/07
	Denver-Aurora MSA, CO	Y	31320 FQ	36910 MW	49210 TQ	USBLS	5/07
	Connecticut	H	20.64 AE	21.36 MW		CTBLS	1/08-3/08
	Delaware	Y	36290 FQ	39720 MW	53910 TQ	USBLS	5/07
	Wilmington PMSA, DE-MD-NJ	Y	36200 FQ	39540 MW	53390 TQ	USBLS	5/07

AE	Average entry wage	AW	Average wage paid	FQ	First quartile wage	LO	Lowest wage paid	MTC	Median total compensation	TCC	Total cash compensation
AER	Average entry range	AWR	Average wage range	H	Hourly	LR	Low end range	MW	Median wage paid	TQ	Third quartile wage
AEX	Average experienced wage	AXR	Average experienced range	HI	Highest wage paid	M	Monthly	MWR	Median wage range	W	Weekly
ATC	Average total compensation	D	Daily	HR	High end range	MCC	Median cash compensation	S	See annotated source	Y	Yearly

Occupation/Type/Industry	Location	Per	Low	Mid	High	Source	Date
Chemical Plant and System Operator	Washington-Arlington-Alexandria MSA, DC-VA-MD-WV	Y	39430 FQ	45650 MW	53660 TQ	USBLS	5/07
	Florida	Y	33550 FQ	39390 MW	45190 TQ	USBLS	5/07
	Tampa-St. Petersburg-Clearwater MSA, FL	Y	40820 FQ	44130 MW	47440 TQ	USBLS	5/07
	Georgia	Y	35620 FQ	43220 MW	50550 TQ	USBLS	5/07
	Atlanta-Sandy Springs-Marietta MSA, GA	Y	34570 FQ	38650 MW	44030 TQ	USBLS	5/07
	Idaho	Y	42240 FQ	47480 MW	52530 TQ	USBLS	5/07
	Illinois	Y	34000 FQ	44960 MW	53840 TQ	USBLS	5/07
	Chicago-Naperville-Joliet MSA, IL-IN-WI	Y	34640 FQ	44200 MW	52490 TQ	USBLS	5/07
	Indiana	Y	34070 FQ	43860 MW	53720 TQ	USBLS	5/07
	Gary PMSA, IN	Y	38950 FQ	45050 MW	50260 TQ	USBLS	5/07
	Iowa	Y	35900 FQ	44460 MW	57040 TQ	USBLS	5/07
	Kansas	Y	34010 FQ	44450 MW	51390 TQ	USBLS	5/07
	Kentucky	Y	45544 FQ	53084 MW	59740 TQ	KYBLS	2008
	Louisville-Jefferson County MSA, KY-IN	Y	42400 FQ	50250 MW	60440 TQ	USBLS	5/07
	Louisiana	H	25.12 FQ	28.10 MW	32.19 TQ	LABLS	1/08-3/08
	Baton Rouge MSA, LA	Y	52560 FQ	58420 MW	66700 TQ	USBLS	5/07
	Lake Charles MSA, LA	Y	52340 FQ	59160 MW	67850 TQ	USBLS	5/07
	New Orleans-Metairie-Kenner MSA, LA	Y	53210 FQ	59530 MW	69850 TQ	USBLS	5/07
	Maryland	Y		47650 MW		MDBLS	3/08
	Baltimore-Towson MSA, MD	Y	41140 FQ	46780 MW	55240 TQ	USBLS	5/07
	Massachusetts	Y	42040 FQ	48240 MW	54600 TQ	USBLS	5/07
	Boston-Cambridge-Quincy NECTA, MA	Y	38730 FQ	43330 MW	52570 TQ	USBLS	5/07
	Michigan	Y	41590 FQ	51020 MW	59770 TQ	USBLS	5/07
	Detroit-Warren-Livonia MSA, MI	Y	44090 FQ	56890 MW	63600 TQ	USBLS	5/07
	Warren-Troy-Farmington Hills PMSA, MI	Y	34630 FQ	45840 MW	59770 TQ	USBLS	5/07
	Minnesota	Y	37206 FQ	42006 MW	50652 TQ	MNBLS	10/08-12/08
	Minneapolis-Saint Paul MSA, MN-WI	Y	37133 FQ	41290 MW	47521 TQ	MNBLS	10/08-12/08
	Mississippi	Y	42400 FQ	48210 MW	54100 TQ	USBLS	5/07
	Missouri	Y	35140 FQ	39300 MW	49880 TQ	USBLS	5/07
	Kansas City MSA, MO-KS	Y	36480 FQ	40060 MW	56180 TQ	USBLS	5/07
	St. Louis MSA, MO-IL	Y	33870 FQ	38350 MW	47570 TQ	USBLS	5/07
	Nevada	H	24.15 FQ	25.74 MW	27.64 TQ	NVBLS	5/08
	New Jersey	Y	40770 FQ	47760 MW	57300 TQ	USBLS	5/07
	Camden PMSA, NJ	Y	47440 FQ	56640 MW	68650 TQ	USBLS	5/07
	Edison PMSA, NJ	Y	42270 FQ	52710 MW	60400 TQ	USBLS	5/07
	Newark-Union PMSA, NJ-PA	Y	40460 FQ	46130 MW	51810 TQ	USBLS	5/07
	New York	Y	43260 FQ	51560 MW	58450 TQ	USBLS	5/07
	Albany-Schenectady-Troy MSA, NY	Y	44670 FQ	55100 MW	61800 TQ	USBLS	5/07
	Buffalo-Niagara Falls MSA, NY	Y	48080 FQ	52380 MW	57350 TQ	USBLS	5/07
	New York-Northern New Jersey-Long Island MSA, NY-NJ-PA	Y	40880 FQ	47200 MW	56080 TQ	USBLS	5/07
	North Carolina	Y	36450 FQ	41830 MW	47260 TQ	USBLS	5/07
	Charlotte-Gastonia-Concord MSA, NC-SC	Y	34750 FQ	42900 MW	48430 TQ	USBLS	5/07
	Ohio	Y	39540 FQ	48600 MW	57470 TQ	USBLS	5/07
	Cincinnati-Middletown MSA, OH-KY-IN	Y	42170 FQ	50310 MW	59340 TQ	USBLS	5/07
	Cleveland-Elyria-Mentor MSA, OH	Y	32620 FQ	47290 MW	53410 TQ	USBLS	5/07
	Columbus MSA, OH	Y	40730 FQ	50530 MW	59130 TQ	USBLS	5/07
	Oklahoma	Y	37990 FQ	41890 MW	48320 TQ	USBLS	5/07
	Portland-Vancouver-Beaverton MSA, OR-WA	Y	38680 FQ	44920 MW	50030 TQ	USBLS	5/07
	Pennsylvania	Y	41820 FQ	49050 MW	60350 TQ	USBLS	5/07
	Allentown-Bethlehem-Easton MSA, PA-NJ	Y	41280 FQ	45800 MW	51130 TQ	USBLS	5/07
	Erie MSA, PA	Y	40260 FQ	43160 MW	46020 TQ	USBLS	5/07

AE Average entry wage	**AW** Average wage paid	**FQ** First quartile wage	**LO** Lowest wage paid	**MTC** Median total compensation	**TCC** Total cash compensation
AER Average entry range	**AWR** Average wage range	**H** Hourly	**LR** Low end range	**MW** Median wage paid	**TQ** Third quartile wage
AEX Average experienced wage	**AXR** Average experienced range	**HI** Highest wage paid	**M** Monthly	**MWR** Median wage range	**W** Weekly
ATC Average total compensation	**D** Daily	**HR** High end range	**MCC** Median cash compensation	**S** See annotated source	**Y** Yearly

Occupation/Type/Industry	Location	Per	Low	Mid	High	Source	Date
Chemical Plant and System Operator	Philadelphia-Camden-Wilmington MSA, PA-NJ-DE-MD	Y	38700 FQ	48980 MW	61760 TQ	USBLS	5/07
	Pittsburgh MSA, PA	Y	49000 FQ	55870 MW	60700 TQ	USBLS	5/07
	South Carolina	Y	34490 FQ	41150 MW	48740 TQ	USBLS	5/07
	Charleston-North Charleston MSA, SC	Y	37940 FQ	44690 MW	51980 TQ	USBLS	5/07
	Columbia MSA, SC	Y	36940 FQ	44640 MW	50710 TQ	USBLS	5/07'
	South Dakota	Y	42247 FQ	47129 MW	52198 TQ	SDBLS	7/08-9/08
	Tennessee	Y	36930 FQ	43720 MW	49920 TQ	USBLS	5/07
	Memphis MSA, TN-MS-AR	Y	42170 FQ	45570 MW	49250 TQ	USBLS	5/07
	Texas	Y	48780 FQ	58850 MW	68590 TQ	USBLS	5/07
	Beaumont-Port Arthur MSA, TX	Y	52390 FQ	59900 MW	71750 TQ	USBLS	5/07
	Dallas-Fort Worth-Arlington MSA, TX	Y	38740 FQ	55820 MW	68360 TQ	USBLS	5/07
	Houston-Sugar Land-Baytown MSA, TX	Y	48690 FQ	59470 MW	68390 TQ	USBLS	5/07
	Virginia	Y	40540 FQ	51500 MW	60370 TQ	USBLS	5/07
	Richmond MSA, VA	Y	43450 FQ	54130 MW	63390 TQ	USBLS	5/07
	Washington	H	17.41 FQ	22.96 MW	26.99 TQ	WABLS	3/08
	Seattle-Tacoma-Bellevue MSA, WA	Y	37230 FQ	46770 MW	55100 TQ	USBLS	5/07
	West Virginia	Y	47260 FQ	59176 MW	71391 TQ	WVBLS	7/08-9/08
	Charleston MSA, WV	Y	45290 FQ	56110 MW	77950 TQ	USBLS	5/07
	Wisconsin	Y	35320 FQ	41690 MW	48160 TQ	USBLS	5/07
	Wyoming	Y	51954 FQ	61758 MW	67433 TQ	WYBLS	9/08
	Puerto Rico	Y	21890 FQ	30100 MW	38040 TQ	USBLS	5/07
	San Juan-Caguas-Guaynabo MSA, PR	Y	21350 FQ	29850 MW	38240 TQ	USBLS	5/07
Chemical Stores Clerk							
State Government	Ohio	H	14.36 LO		15.41 HI	ODAS	2008
Chemical Technician	Alabama	Y	31150 FQ	39720 MW	49570 TQ	USBLS	5/07
	Birmingham-Hoover MSA, AL	Y	25260 FQ	36310 MW	44270 TQ	USBLS	5/07
	Mobile MSA, AL	Y	31400 FQ	43550 MW	56140 TQ	USBLS	5/07
	Tuscaloosa MSA, AL	Y	34180 FQ	39590 MW	52190 TQ	USBLS	5/07
	Arizona	Y	32230 FQ	40060 MW	54890 TQ	USBLS	5/07
	Phoenix-Mesa-Scottsdale MSA, AZ	Y	32950 FQ	42060 MW	58210 TQ	USBLS	5/07
	Tucson MSA, AZ	Y	27800 FQ	37760 MW	49280 TQ	USBLS	5/07
	Arkansas	Y	27510 FQ	34790 MW	43700 TQ	USBLS	5/07
	Little Rock-North Little Rock MSA, AR	Y	25950 FQ	31280 MW	38480 TQ	USBLS	5/07
	California	H	16.03 FQ	20.56 MW	25.86 TQ	CABLS	1/08-3/08
	Los Angeles-Long Beach-Glendale PMSA, CA	H	16.19 FQ	19.99 MW	24.31 TQ	CABLS	1/08-3/08
	Oakland-Fremont-Hayward MSA, CA	H	16.98 FQ	20.21 MW	23.78 TQ	CABLS	1/08-3/08
	Oxnard-Thousand Oaks-Ventura MSA, CA	H	21.35 FQ	24.97 MW	29.75 TQ	CABLS	1/08-3/08
	Riverside-San Bernardino-Ontario MSA, CA	H	15.36 FQ	17.81 MW	20.60 TQ	CABLS	1/08-3/08
	Sacramento-Arden Arcade-Roseville MSA, CA	H	11.69 FQ	16.43 MW	22.67 TQ	CABLS	1/08-3/08
	San Diego-Carlsbad-San Marcos MSA, CA	H	16.88 FQ	21.30 MW	26.09 TQ	CABLS	1/08-3/08
	San Francisco-San Mateo-Redwood PMSA, CA	H	21.77 FQ	26.70 MW	30.36 TQ	CABLS	1/08-3/08
	San Jose-Sunnyvale-Santa Clara MSA, CA	H	17.17 FQ	21.20 MW	27.80 TQ	CABLS	1/08-3/08
	Santa Ana-Anaheim-Irvine PMSA, CA	Y	24710 FQ	35970 MW	50100 TQ	USBLS	5/07
	Santa Rosa-Petaluma MSA, CA	H	16.23 FQ	18.13 MW	20.60 TQ	CABLS	1/08-3/08
	Colorado	Y	32240 FQ	41930 MW	50890 TQ	USBLS	5/07
	Denver-Aurora MSA, CO	Y	30220 FQ	38600 MW	47360 TQ	USBLS	5/07
	Connecticut	H	15.48 AE	20.12 MW		CTBLS	1/08-3/08
	Bridgeport-Stamford-Norwalk MSA, CT	Y	34360 FQ	39000 MW	51310 TQ	USBLS	5/07

AE	Average entry wage	AW	Average wage paid	FQ	First quartile wage	LO	Lowest wage paid	MTC	Median total compensation	TCC	Total cash compensation
AER	Average entry range	AWR	Average wage range	H	Hourly	LR	Low end range	MW	Median wage paid	TQ	Third quartile wage
AEX	Average experienced wage	AXR	Average experienced range	HI	Highest wage paid	M	Monthly	MWR	Median wage range	W	Weekly
ATC	Average total compensation	D	Daily	HR	High end range	MCC	Median cash compensation	S	See annotated source	Y	Yearly

193

Chemical Technician

Occupation/Type/Industry	Location	Per	Low	Mid	High	Source	Date
Chemical Technician	Hartford-West Hartford-East Hartford MSA, CT	Y	31170 FQ	36930 MW	42000 TQ	USBLS	5/07
	Delaware	Y	54980 FQ	59510 MW	64300 TQ	USBLS	5/07
	Wilmington PMSA, DE-MD-NJ	Y	54260 FQ	59010 MW	63990 TQ	USBLS	5/07
	Washington-Arlington-Alexandria MSA, DC-VA-MD-WV	Y	39860 FQ	48350 MW	56010 TQ	USBLS	5/07
	Florida	Y	27820 FQ	35260 MW	44880 TQ	USBLS	5/07
	Fort Lauderdale-Pompano Beach-Deerfield Beach PMSA, FL	Y	29290 FQ	35000 MW	40920 TQ	USBLS	5/07
	Jacksonville MSA, FL	Y	29220 FQ	33930 MW	46050 TQ	USBLS	5/07
	Miami-Fort Lauderdale-Miami Beach MSA, FL	Y	27820 FQ	33720 MW	41230 TQ	USBLS	5/07
	Orlando-Kissimmee MSA, FL	Y	26670 FQ	33390 MW	42560 TQ	USBLS	5/07
	Tallahassee MSA, FL	Y	34690 FQ	40790 MW	46510 TQ	USBLS	5/07
	Tampa-St. Petersburg-Clearwater MSA, FL	Y	25360 FQ	32160 MW	42610 TQ	USBLS	5/07
	West Palm Beach-Boca Raton-Boynton Beach PMSA, FL	Y	27350 FQ	31330 MW	38090 TQ	USBLS	5/07
	Georgia	Y	29430 FQ	37100 MW	46860 TQ	USBLS	5/07
	Atlanta-Sandy Springs-Marietta MSA, GA	Y	27310 FQ	33460 MW	40980 TQ	USBLS	5/07
	Hawaii	Y	42650 FQ	59390 MW	72540 TQ	USBLS	5/07
	Honolulu MSA, HI	Y	46900 FQ	60360 MW	73170 TQ	USBLS	5/07
	Idaho	Y	28960 FQ	35290 MW	42410 TQ	USBLS	5/07
	Boise City-Nampa MSA, ID	Y	31190 FQ	34400 MW	37410 TQ	USBLS	5/07
	Illinois	Y	31250 FQ	39220 MW	50860 TQ	USBLS	5/07
	Chicago-Naperville-Joliet MSA, IL-IN-WI	Y	32910 FQ	41850 MW	51520 TQ	USBLS	5/07
	Indiana	Y	27300 FQ	35020 MW	44490 TQ	USBLS	5/07
	Gary PMSA, IN	Y	35850 FQ	43810 MW	53650 TQ	USBLS	5/07
	Indianapolis-Carmel MSA, IN	Y	25640 FQ	32600 MW	42050 TQ	USBLS	5/07
	Iowa	Y	32160 FQ	38470 MW	47120 TQ	USBLS	5/07
	Des Moines-West Des Moines MSA, IA	Y	28170 FQ	33000 MW	36340 TQ	USBLS	5/07
	Kansas	Y	29750 FQ	39670 MW	51860 TQ	USBLS	5/07
	Wichita MSA, KS	Y	28300 FQ	38930 MW	52860 TQ	USBLS	5/07
	Kentucky	Y	32493 FQ	40209 MW	51448 TQ	KYBLS	2008
	Louisville-Jefferson County MSA, KY-IN	Y	30240 FQ	36560 MW	46720 TQ	USBLS	5/07
	Louisiana	H	19.96 FQ	24.37 MW	29.70 TQ	LABLS	1/08-3/08
	Baton Rouge MSA, LA	Y	43650 FQ	50250 MW	60480 TQ	USBLS	5/07
	New Orleans-Metairie-Kenner MSA, LA	Y	30940 FQ	41240 MW	59780 TQ	USBLS	5/07
	Maine	Y	27780 FQ	34890 MW	44790 TQ	USBLS	5/07
	Portland-South Portland-Biddeford MSA, ME	Y	25840 FQ	32030 MW	41820 TQ	USBLS	5/07
	Maryland	Y		47475 MW		MDBLS	3/08
	Baltimore-Towson MSA, MD	Y	31150 FQ	40140 MW	49630 TQ	USBLS	5/07
	Bethesda-Gaithersburg-Frederick PMSA, MD	Y	46300 FQ	51540 MW	58550 TQ	USBLS	5/07
	Massachusetts	Y	35160 FQ	42990 MW	53170 TQ	USBLS	5/07
	Boston-Cambridge-Quincy NECTA, MA	Y	34600 FQ	41300 MW	54940 TQ	USBLS	5/07
	Worcester MSA, MA-CT	Y	30490 FQ	37680 MW	47270 TQ	USBLS	5/07
	Michigan	Y	30460 FQ	37360 MW	45930 TQ	USBLS	5/07
	Ann Arbor MSA, MI	Y	22390 FQ	33440 MW	44110 TQ	USBLS	5/07
	Detroit-Warren-Livonia MSA, MI	Y	33010 FQ	39890 MW	46870 TQ	USBLS	5/07
	Warren-Troy-Farmington Hills PMSA, MI	Y	35780 FQ	43530 MW	50550 TQ	USBLS	5/07
	Minnesota	Y	34075 FQ	41242 MW	51547 TQ	MNBLS	10/08-12/08
	Duluth-Superior MSA, MN-WI	Y	44768 FQ	50072 MW	54769 TQ	MNBLS	10/08-12/08
	Minneapolis-Saint Paul MSA, MN-WI	Y	34860 FQ	42874 MW	52248 TQ	MNBLS	10/08-12/08
	Mississippi	Y	28310 FQ	34990 MW	43680 TQ	USBLS	5/07
	Gulfport-Biloxi MSA, MS	Y	26720 FQ	34700 MW	39410 TQ	USBLS	5/07
	Missouri	Y	30910 FQ	41080 MW	53110 TQ	USBLS	5/07
	Kansas City MSA, MO-KS	Y	30060 FQ	39310 MW	52490 TQ	USBLS	5/07
	St. Louis MSA, MO-IL	Y	29260 FQ	43000 MW	54020 TQ	USBLS	5/07

AE Average entry wage	AW Average wage paid	FQ First quartile wage	LO Lowest wage paid	MTC Median total compensation	TCC Total cash compensation
AER Average entry range	AWR Average wage range	H Hourly	LR Low end range	MW Median wage paid	TQ Third quartile wage
AEX Average experienced wage	AXR Average experienced range	HI Highest wage paid	M Monthly	MWR Median wage range	W Weekly
ATC Average total compensation	D Daily	HR High end range	MCC Median cash compensation	S See annotated source	Y Yearly

Occupation/Type/Industry	Location	Per	Low	Mid	High	Source	Date
Chemical Technician	Montana	Y	25940 FQ	35410 MW	42560 TQ	USBLS	5/07
	Billings MSA, MT	Y	19310 FQ	33760 MW	57780 TQ	USBLS	5/07
	Nebraska	Y	28000 FQ	34280 MW	40900 TQ	USBLS	5/07
	Omaha-Council Bluffs MSA, NE-IA	Y	33740 FQ	39940 MW	50880 TQ	USBLS	5/07
	Nevada	H	16.28 FQ	21.52 MW	26.85 TQ	NVBLS	5/08
	Las Vegas-Paradise MSA, NV	H	15.94 FQ	24.21 MW	31.46 TQ	NVBLS	5/08
	Reno-Sparks MSA, NV	H	11.66 FQ	14.85 MW	22.46 TQ	NVBLS	5/08
	New Hampshire	H	14.60 AE	19.13 MW	21.58 AEX	NHBLS	6/08
	New Jersey	Y	34440 FQ	42320 MW	52860 TQ	USBLS	5/07
	Camden PMSA, NJ	Y	34290 FQ	40000 MW	52390 TQ	USBLS	5/07
	Edison PMSA, NJ	Y	35480 FQ	44380 MW	56050 TQ	USBLS	5/07
	Newark-Union PMSA, NJ-PA	Y	31920 FQ	39790 MW	49130 TQ	USBLS	5/07
	New Mexico	Y	40590 FQ	59670 MW	72340 TQ	USBLS	5/07
	Albuquerque MSA, NM	Y	38980 FQ	60660 MW	73220 TQ	USBLS	5/07
	New York	Y	31660 FQ	40850 MW	49170 TQ	USBLS	5/07
	Albany-Schenectady-Troy MSA, NY	Y	30980 FQ	40530 MW	50390 TQ	USBLS	5/07
	Buffalo-Niagara Falls MSA, NY	Y	31470 FQ	41420 MW	49240 TQ	USBLS	5/07
	Nassau-Suffolk PMSA, NY	Y	29920 FQ	38500 MW	46320 TQ	USBLS	5/07
	New York-Northern New Jersey-Long Island MSA, NY-NJ-PA	Y	33840 FQ	42160 MW	52400 TQ	USBLS	5/07
	North Carolina	Y	30960 FQ	36620 MW	44220 TQ	USBLS	5/07
	Charlotte-Gastonia-Concord MSA, NC-SC	Y	34250 FQ	39740 MW	46540 TQ	USBLS	5/07
	Raleigh-Cary MSA, NC	Y	33880 FQ	38560 MW	44430 TQ	USBLS	5/07
	North Dakota	Y	27800 FQ	30930 MW	39720 TQ	USBLS	5/07
	Ohio	Y	31530 FQ	40010 MW	51090 TQ	USBLS	5/07
	Cincinnati-Middletown MSA, OH-KY-IN	Y	31430 FQ	39180 MW	47670 TQ	USBLS	5/07
	Cleveland-Elyria-Mentor MSA, OH	Y	33610 FQ	43990 MW	54630 TQ	USBLS	5/07
	Columbus MSA, OH	Y	30590 FQ	40520 MW	51440 TQ	USBLS	5/07
	Dayton MSA, OH	Y	27220 FQ	32430 MW	39200 TQ	USBLS	5/07
	Oklahoma	Y	24480 FQ	33200 MW	39710 TQ	USBLS	5/07
	Oklahoma City MSA, OK	Y	18330 FQ	25890 MW	35280 TQ	USBLS	5/07
	Tulsa MSA, OK	Y	29500 FQ	36890 MW	45870 TQ	USBLS	5/07
	Oregon	H	15.68 FQ	17.69 MW	20.06 TQ	ORBLS	5/08
	Portland-Vancouver-Beaverton MSA, OR-WA	Y	33130 FQ	37120 MW	43570 TQ	USBLS	5/07
	Pennsylvania	Y	33080 FQ	40350 MW	48040 TQ	USBLS	5/07
	Allentown-Bethlehem-Easton MSA, PA-NJ	Y	37640 FQ	43800 MW	49000 TQ	USBLS	5/07
	Erie MSA, PA	Y	32750 FQ	37730 MW	47870 TQ	USBLS	5/07
	Philadelphia-Camden-Wilmington MSA, PA-NJ-DE-MD	Y	37660 FQ	46820 MW	58150 TQ	USBLS	5/07
	Pittsburgh MSA, PA	Y	33160 FQ	37860 MW	46890 TQ	USBLS	5/07
	Rhode Island	Y	27850 FQ	35790 MW	45190 TQ	USBLS	5/07
	Providence-Fall River-Warwick MSA, RI-MA	Y	28400 FQ	36990 MW	46000 TQ	USBLS	5/07
	South Carolina	Y	34620 FQ	42600 MW	49300 TQ	USBLS	5/07
	Charleston-North Charleston MSA, SC	Y	31560 FQ	42020 MW	49830 TQ	USBLS	5/07
	Columbia MSA, SC	Y	40490 FQ	44970 MW	49730 TQ	USBLS	5/07
	South Dakota	Y	25755 FQ	29784 MW	34957 TQ	SDBLS	7/08-9/08
	Tennessee	Y	32550 FQ	44180 MW	54290 TQ	USBLS	5/07
	Knoxville MSA, TN	Y	33590 FQ	48520 MW	58100 TQ	USBLS	5/07
	Memphis MSA, TN-MS-AR	Y	28070 FQ	39690 MW	48110 TQ	USBLS	5/07
	Nashville-Davidson-Murfreesboro MSA, TN	Y	32740 FQ	43410 MW	51920 TQ	USBLS	5/07
	Texas	Y	31910 FQ	46130 MW	59930 TQ	USBLS	5/07
	Austin-Round Rock MSA, TX	Y	30970 FQ	39800 MW	50260 TQ	USBLS	5/07
	Dallas-Fort Worth-Arlington MSA, TX	Y	31100 FQ	39130 MW	51620 TQ	USBLS	5/07
	El Paso MSA, TX	Y	34290 FQ	45870 MW	58990 TQ	USBLS	5/07
	Houston-Sugar Land-Baytown MSA, TX	Y	35000 FQ	49620 MW	62400 TQ	USBLS	5/07
	San Antonio MSA, TX	Y	25430 FQ	30370 MW	37490 TQ	USBLS	5/07
	Utah	Y	29490 FQ	38340 MW	49320 TQ	USBLS	5/07

AE	Average entry wage	AW	Average wage paid	FQ	First quartile wage
AER	Average entry range	AWR	Average wage range	H	Hourly
AEX	Average experienced wage	AXR	Average experienced range	HI	Highest wage paid
ATC	Average total compensation	D	Daily	HR	High end range

LO	Lowest wage paid	MTC	Median total compensation	TCC	Total cash compensation
LR	Low end range	MW	Median wage paid	TQ	Third quartile wage
M	Monthly	MWR	Median wage range	W	Weekly
MCC	Median cash compensation	S	See annotated source	Y	Yearly

Occupation/Type/Industry	Location	Per	Low	Mid	High	Source	Date
Chemical Technician	Salt Lake City MSA, UT	Y	31170 FQ	44090 MW	56320 TQ	USBLS	5/07
	Vermont	Y	28630 FQ	36120 MW	48400 TQ	USBLS	5/07
	Burlington-South Burlington MSA, VT	Y	26200 FQ	32650 MW	38220 TQ	USBLS	5/07
	Virginia	Y	36540 FQ	44780 MW	54710 TQ	USBLS	5/07
	Richmond MSA, VA	Y	42230 FQ	50800 MW	66990 TQ	USBLS	5/07
	Virginia Beach-Norfolk-Newport News MSA, VA-NC	Y	40540 FQ	46970 MW	54950 TQ	USBLS	5/07
	Washington	H	14.93 FQ	19.51 MW	25.39 TQ	WABLS	3/08
	Seattle-Tacoma-Bellevue MSA, WA	Y	31980 FQ	40420 MW	49450 TQ	USBLS	5/07
	West Virginia	Y	22969 FQ	29651 MW	40862 TQ	WVBLS	7/08-9/08
	Charleston MSA, WV	Y	22180 FQ	33020 MW	54180 TQ	USBLS	5/07
	Wisconsin	Y	29310 FQ	36620 MW	46550 TQ	USBLS	5/07
	Milwaukee-Waukesha-West Allis MSA, WI	Y	27120 FQ	32500 MW	44370 TQ	USBLS	5/07
	Racine MSA, WI	Y	37080 FQ	43350 MW	49920 TQ	USBLS	5/07
	Puerto Rico	Y	26980 FQ	32820 MW	38090 TQ	USBLS	5/07
	San Juan-Caguas-Guaynabo MSA, PR	Y	26890 FQ	32760 MW	38040 TQ	USBLS	5/07
	Virgin Islands	Y	38270 FQ	43420 MW	52430 TQ	USBLS	5/07
Chemist	Alabama	Y	41440 FQ	54090 MW	70550 TQ	USBLS	5/07
	Birmingham-Hoover MSA, AL	Y	42020 FQ	56690 MW	71020 TQ	USBLS	5/07
	Alaska	Y	56700 FQ	74580 MW	86340 TQ	USBLS	5/07
	Anchorage MSA, AK	Y	58820 FQ	74020 MW	83370 TQ	USBLS	5/07
	Arizona	Y	43020 FQ	58200 MW	73600 TQ	USBLS	5/07
	Phoenix-Mesa-Scottsdale MSA, AZ	Y	43070 FQ	58870 MW	75320 TQ	USBLS	5/07
	Tucson MSA, AZ	Y	44780 FQ	56350 MW	63980 TQ	USBLS	5/07
	Arkansas	Y	49880 FQ	63370 MW	78590 TQ	USBLS	5/07
	Little Rock-North Little Rock MSA, AR	Y	37200 FQ	45070 MW	57990 TQ	USBLS	5/07
	California	H	26.76 FQ	35.96 MW	46.21 TQ	CABLS	1/08-3/08
	Los Angeles-Long Beach-Glendale PMSA, CA	H	23.41 FQ	33.32 MW	41.40 TQ	CABLS	1/08-3/08
	Oakland-Fremont-Hayward MSA, CA	H	23.67 FQ	32.67 MW	42.91 TQ	CABLS	1/08-3/08
	Riverside-San Bernardino-Ontario MSA, CA	H	26.33 FQ	33.89 MW	42.40 TQ	CABLS	1/08-3/08
	Sacramento-Arden Arcade-Roseville MSA, CA	H	24.66 FQ	31.92 MW	38.51 TQ	CABLS	1/08-3/08
	San Diego-Carlsbad-San Marcos MSA, CA	H	31.54 FQ	40.08 MW	51.30 TQ	CABLS	1/08-3/08
	San Francisco-San Mateo-Redwood PMSA, CA	H	26.30 FQ	38.01 MW	50.57 TQ	CABLS	1/08-3/08
	San Jose-Sunnyvale-Santa Clara MSA, CA	H	28.42 FQ	36.38 MW	47.29 TQ	CABLS	1/08-3/08
	Santa Ana-Anaheim-Irvine PMSA, CA	Y	56010 FQ	74330 MW	93820 TQ	USBLS	5/07
	Colorado	Y	49260 FQ	66170 MW	96750 TQ	USBLS	5/07
	Colorado Springs MSA, CO	Y	48670 FQ	62720 MW	87050 TQ	USBLS	5/07
	Denver-Aurora MSA, CO	Y	49300 FQ	63570 MW	88590 TQ	USBLS	5/07
	Fort Collins-Loveland MSA, CO	Y	37020 FQ	50870 MW	67740 TQ	USBLS	5/07
	Connecticut	H	21.03 AE	32.59 MW		CTBLS	1/08-3/08
	Bridgeport-Stamford-Norwalk MSA, CT	Y	51010 FQ	70880 MW	99240 TQ	USBLS	5/07
	Hartford-West Hartford-East Hartford MSA, CT	Y	46430 FQ	55930 MW	72150 TQ	USBLS	5/07
	Delaware	Y	57210 FQ	74640 MW	94810 TQ	USBLS	5/07
	Wilmington PMSA, DE-MD-NJ	Y	57230 FQ	74530 MW	94210 TQ	USBLS	5/07
	District of Columbia	Y	53100 FQ	91510 MW	114580 TQ	USBLS	5/07
	Washington-Arlington-Alexandria MSA, DC-VA-MD-WV	Y	72710 FQ	93700 MW	117300 TQ	USBLS	5/07
	Florida	Y	39590 FQ	49780 MW	68420 TQ	USBLS	5/07
	Fort Lauderdale-Pompano Beach-Deerfield Beach PMSA, FL	Y	38050 FQ	47250 MW	60110 TQ	USBLS	5/07
	Jacksonville MSA, FL	Y	38550 FQ	49560 MW	65550 TQ	USBLS	5/07

AE	Average entry wage	AW	Average wage paid	FQ	First quartile wage	LO	Lowest wage paid	MTC	Median total compensation	TCC	Total cash compensation
AER	Average entry range	AWR	Average wage range	H	Hourly	LR	Low end range	MW	Median wage paid	TQ	Third quartile wage
AEX	Average experienced wage	AXR	Average experienced range	HI	Highest wage paid	M	Monthly	MWR	Median wage range	W	Weekly
ATC	Average total compensation	D	Daily	HR	High end range	MCC	Median cash compensation	S	See annotated source	Y	Yearly

Chemist

Occupation/Type/Industry	Location	Per	Low	Mid	High	Source	Date
	Miami-Fort Lauderdale-Miami Beach MSA, FL	Y	39790 FQ	50440 MW	66390 TQ	USBLS	5/07
	Orlando-Kissimmee MSA, FL	Y	37900 FQ	46720 MW	62550 TQ	USBLS	5/07
	Sarasota-Bradenton-Venice MSA, FL	Y	39160 FQ	47640 MW	59900 TQ	USBLS	5/07
	Tallahassee MSA, FL	Y	35030 FQ	40390 MW	48270 TQ	USBLS	5/07
	Tampa-St. Petersburg-Clearwater MSA, FL	Y	44310 FQ	51780 MW	75290 TQ	USBLS	5/07
	West Palm Beach-Boca Raton-Boynton Beach PMSA, FL	Y	37460 FQ	49830 MW	66530 TQ	USBLS	5/07
	Georgia	Y	51470 FQ	67820 MW	85900 TQ	USBLS	5/07
	Atlanta-Sandy Springs-Marietta MSA, GA	Y	51770 FQ	67410 MW	86320 TQ	USBLS	5/07
	Hawaii	Y	44130 FQ	59870 MW	79470 TQ	USBLS	5/07
	Honolulu MSA, HI	Y	44310 FQ	58860 MW	77950 TQ	USBLS	5/07
	Idaho	Y	40200 FQ	78330 MW	93170 TQ	USBLS	5/07
	Boise City-Nampa MSA, ID	Y	33640 FQ	40980 MW	48890 TQ	USBLS	5/07
	Illinois	Y	49480 FQ	59820 MW	77390 TQ	USBLS	5/07
	Champaign-Urbana MSA, IL	Y	42070 FQ	49240 MW	67370 TQ	USBLS	5/07
	Chicago-Naperville-Joliet MSA, IL-IN-WI	Y	50280 FQ	60240 MW	79040 TQ	USBLS	5/07
	Indiana	Y	38710 FQ	51520 MW	68040 TQ	USBLS	5/07
	Elkhart-Goshen MSA, IN	Y	51320 FQ	58050 MW	65570 TQ	USBLS	5/07
	Gary PMSA, IN	Y	52540 FQ	62500 MW	85470 TQ	USBLS	5/07
	Indianapolis-Carmel MSA, IN	Y	35040 FQ	45700 MW	64890 TQ	USBLS	5/07
	Iowa	Y	42030 FQ	55560 MW	70150 TQ	USBLS	5/07
	Des Moines-West Des Moines MSA, IA	Y	47380 FQ	60370 MW	69220 TQ	USBLS	5/07
	Kansas	Y	43490 FQ	56180 MW	71040 TQ	USBLS	5/07
	Wichita MSA, KS	Y	38990 FQ	52950 MW	69330 TQ	USBLS	5/07
	Kentucky	Y	42615 FQ	54642 MW	74768 TQ	KYBLS	2008
	Louisville-Jefferson County MSA, KY-IN	Y	45200 FQ	55370 MW	74480 TQ	USBLS	5/07
	Louisiana	H	22.77 FQ	30.65 MW	37.60 TQ	LABLS	1/08-3/08
	Baton Rouge MSA, LA	Y	52190 FQ	65380 MW	76220 TQ	USBLS	5/07
	New Orleans-Metairie-Kenner MSA, LA	Y	46740 FQ	65700 MW	81440 TQ	USBLS	5/07
	Maine	Y	41670 FQ	49890 MW	60250 TQ	USBLS	5/07
	Portland-South Portland-Biddeford MSA, ME	Y	35040 FQ	41520 MW	51100 TQ	USBLS	5/07
	Maryland	Y		88000 MW		MDBLS	3/08
	Baltimore-Towson MSA, MD	Y	51320 FQ	69230 MW	93240 TQ	USBLS	5/07
	Bethesda-Gaithersburg-Frederick PMSA, MD	Y	74480 FQ	95310 MW	121120 TQ	USBLS	5/07
	Massachusetts	Y	57090 FQ	76100 MW	98950 TQ	USBLS	5/07
	Boston-Cambridge-Quincy NECTA, MA	Y	57760 FQ	77890 MW	100750 TQ	USBLS	5/07
	Worcester MSA, MA-CT	Y	51830 FQ	64830 MW	88130 TQ	USBLS	5/07
	Michigan	Y	41980 FQ	52330 MW	71510 TQ	USBLS	5/07
	Detroit-Warren-Livonia MSA, MI	Y	43710 FQ	53000 MW	67490 TQ	USBLS	5/07
	Grand Rapids-Wyoming MSA, MI	Y	42230 FQ	55780 MW	69970 TQ	USBLS	5/07
	Warren-Troy-Farmington Hills PMSA, MI	Y	44990 FQ	55490 MW	71360 TQ	USBLS	5/07
	Minnesota	Y	51233 FQ	66529 MW	86407 TQ	MNBLS	10/08-12/08
	Duluth-Superior MSA, MN-WI	Y	47676 FQ	54341 MW	77012 TQ	MNBLS	10/08-12/08
	Minneapolis-Saint Paul MSA, MN-WI	Y	52279 FQ	67042 MW	86606 TQ	MNBLS	10/08-12/08
	Rochester MSA, MN	Y	44193 FQ	49615 MW	63602 TQ	MNBLS	10/08-12/08
	Mississippi	Y	47140 FQ	63100 MW	82090 TQ	USBLS	5/07
	Jackson MSA, MS	Y	37400 FQ	43680 MW	56130 TQ	USBLS	5/07
	Missouri	Y	45440 FQ	59020 MW	77520 TQ	USBLS	5/07
	Kansas City MSA, MO-KS	Y	46020 FQ	61250 MW	77700 TQ	USBLS	5/07
	St. Louis MSA, MO-IL	Y	50500 FQ	61220 MW	81490 TQ	USBLS	5/07
	Montana	Y	28630 FQ	37380 MW	59980 TQ	USBLS	5/07
	Billings MSA, MT	Y	28740 FQ	32240 MW	39520 TQ	USBLS	5/07
	Nebraska	Y	39620 FQ	47660 MW	63000 TQ	USBLS	5/07
	Omaha-Council Bluffs MSA, NE-IA	Y	47920 FQ	60610 MW	81880 TQ	USBLS	5/07
	Nevada	H	25.90 FQ	33.16 MW	41.76 TQ	NVBLS	5/08
	Las Vegas-Paradise MSA, NV	H	27.74 FQ	40.64 MW	47.44 TQ	NVBLS	5/08

AE	Average entry wage	AW	Average wage paid	FQ	First quartile wage	LO	Lowest wage paid	MTC	Median total compensation	TCC	Total cash compensation
AER	Average entry range	AWR	Average wage range	H	Hourly	LR	Low end range	MW	Median wage paid	TQ	Third quartile wage
AEX	Average experienced wage	AXR	Average experienced range	HI	Highest wage paid	M	Monthly	MWR	Median wage range	W	Weekly
ATC	Average total compensation	D	Daily	HR	High end range	MCC	Median cash compensation	S	See annotated source	Y	Yearly

197

Occupation/Type/Industry	Location	Per	Low	Mid	High	Source	Date
Chemist	New Hampshire	H	26.31 AE	32.57 MW	40.97 AEX	NHBLS	6/08
	Nashua NECTA, NH-MA	Y	53050 FQ	58680 MW	73130 TQ	USBLS	5/07
	New Jersey	Y	52000 FQ	67780 MW	89490 TQ	USBLS	5/07
	Camden PMSA, NJ	Y	48230 FQ	61070 MW	82800 TQ	USBLS	5/07
	Edison PMSA, NJ	Y	55670 FQ	73090 MW	95880 TQ	USBLS	5/07
	Newark-Union PMSA, NJ-PA	Y	49320 FQ	61320 MW	82020 TQ	USBLS	5/07
	New Mexico	Y	35860 FQ	54990 MW	100940 TQ	USBLS	5/07
	Albuquerque MSA, NM	Y	39200 FQ	64540 MW	112460 TQ	USBLS	5/07
	New York	Y	50880 FQ	66450 MW	90060 TQ	USBLS	5/07
	Albany-Schenectady-Troy MSA, NY	Y	60500 FQ	79860 MW	98470 TQ	USBLS	5/07
	Buffalo-Niagara Falls MSA, NY	Y	49740 FQ	64290 MW	86530 TQ	USBLS	5/07
	Nassau-Suffolk PMSA, NY	Y	50970 FQ	65050 MW	85990 TQ	USBLS	5/07
	New York-Northern New Jersey-Long Island MSA, NY-NJ-PA	Y	52590 FQ	68650 MW	91110 TQ	USBLS	5/07
	North Carolina	Y	46200 FQ	58880 MW	77210 TQ	USBLS	5/07
	Charlotte-Gastonia-Concord MSA, NC-SC	Y	46440 FQ	59830 MW	74820 TQ	USBLS	5/07
	Raleigh-Cary MSA, NC	Y	45810 FQ	54690 MW	70020 TQ	USBLS	5/07
	North Dakota	Y	42030 FQ	53960 MW	71830 TQ	USBLS	5/07
	Fargo MSA, ND-MN	Y	37440 FQ	45140 MW	71450 TQ	USBLS	5/07
	Ohio	Y	45410 FQ	59530 MW	78190 TQ	USBLS	5/07
	Cincinnati-Middletown MSA, OH-KY-IN	Y	51570 FQ	64900 MW	84880 TQ	USBLS	5/07
	Cleveland-Elyria-Mentor MSA, OH	Y	42270 FQ	57230 MW	77380 TQ	USBLS	5/07
	Columbus MSA, OH	Y	49450 FQ	59370 MW	70910 TQ	USBLS	5/07
	Dayton MSA, OH	Y	47800 FQ	67670 MW	90990 TQ	USBLS	5/07
	Oklahoma	Y	46610 FQ	57810 MW	74340 TQ	USBLS	5/07
	Oklahoma City MSA, OK	Y	47880 FQ	57520 MW	74040 TQ	USBLS	5/07
	Tulsa MSA, OK	Y	48660 FQ	57100 MW	70130 TQ	USBLS	5/07
	Oregon	H	20.60 FQ	26.72 MW	34.07 TQ	ORBLS	5/08
	Portland-Vancouver-Beaverton MSA, OR-WA	Y	43150 FQ	53840 MW	66710 TQ	USBLS	5/07
	Pennsylvania	Y	46530 FQ	62650 MW	86140 TQ	USBLS	5/07
	Allentown-Bethlehem-Easton MSA, PA-NJ	Y	39830 FQ	46640 MW	58620 TQ	USBLS	5/07
	Philadelphia-Camden-Wilmington MSA, PA-NJ-DE-MD	Y	51330 FQ	70470 MW	94220 TQ	USBLS	5/07
	Pittsburgh MSA, PA	Y	52090 FQ	66960 MW	87900 TQ	USBLS	5/07
	Rhode Island	Y	46800 FQ	62670 MW	84300 TQ	USBLS	5/07
	Providence-Fall River-Warwick MSA, RI-MA	Y	50180 FQ	66760 MW	83520 TQ	USBLS	5/07
	South Carolina	Y	44920 FQ	61480 MW	86280 TQ	USBLS	5/07
	Charleston-North Charleston MSA, SC	Y	43790 FQ	58370 MW	80480 TQ	USBLS	5/07
	Columbia MSA, SC	Y	36470 FQ	48840 MW	65290 TQ	USBLS	5/07
	South Dakota	Y	40320 FQ	47068 MW	53928 TQ	SDBLS	7/08-9/08
	Sioux Falls MSA, SD	Y	41138 FQ	49775 MW	62638 TQ	SDBLS	7/08-9/08
	Tennessee	Y	42980 FQ	61090 MW	90010 TQ	USBLS	5/07
	Kingsport-Bristol-Bristol MSA, TN-VA	Y	36760 FQ	51480 MW	87770 TQ	USBLS	5/07
	Memphis MSA, TN-MS-AR	Y	42910 FQ	49810 MW	62050 TQ	USBLS	5/07
	Nashville-Davidson-Murfreesboro MSA, TN	Y	44140 FQ	57770 MW	84490 TQ	USBLS	5/07
	Texas	Y	39490 FQ	55860 MW	77710 TQ	USBLS	5/07
	Austin-Round Rock MSA, TX	Y	35810 FQ	42440 MW	56710 TQ	USBLS	5/07
	Dallas-Fort Worth-Arlington MSA, TX	Y	42290 FQ	61080 MW	75670 TQ	USBLS	5/07
	Houston-Sugar Land-Baytown MSA, TX	Y	41390 FQ	60770 MW	84730 TQ	USBLS	5/07
	San Antonio MSA, TX	Y	51070 FQ	61580 MW	80100 TQ	USBLS	5/07
	Utah	Y	42510 FQ	53610 MW	73120 TQ	USBLS	5/07
	Salt Lake City MSA, UT	Y	40660 FQ	50910 MW	72500 TQ	USBLS	5/07
	Vermont	Y	42730 FQ	50810 MW	65180 TQ	USBLS	5/07
	Burlington-South Burlington MSA, VT	Y	42100 FQ	48580 MW	57650 TQ	USBLS	5/07
	Virginia	Y	53940 FQ	72990 MW	96040 TQ	USBLS	5/07
	Richmond MSA, VA	Y	44880 FQ	59540 MW	82990 TQ	USBLS	5/07

AE	Average entry wage	AW	Average wage paid	FQ	First quartile wage	LO	Lowest wage paid	MTC Median total compensation TCC Total cash compensation
AER	Average entry range	AWR	Average wage range	H	Hourly	LR	Low end range	MW Median wage paid TQ Third quartile wage
AEX	Average experienced wage	AXR	Average experienced range	HI	Highest wage paid	M	Monthly	MWR Median wage range W Weekly
ATC	Average total compensation	D	Daily	HR	High end range	MCC	Median cash compensation	S See annotated source Y Yearly

Occupation/Type/Industry	Location	Per	Low	Mid	High	Source	Date
Chemist	Virginia Beach-Norfolk-						
	Newport News MSA, VA-NC	Y	57560 FQ	69540 MW	80130 TQ	USBLS	5/07
	Washington	H	24.92 FQ	33.68 MW	44.94 TQ	WABLS	3/08
	Olympia MSA, WA	Y	53990 FQ	66260 MW	79060 TQ	USBLS	5/07
	Seattle-Tacoma-Bellevue						
	MSA, WA	Y	49130 FQ	66460 MW	91360 TQ	USBLS	5/07
	West Virginia	Y	36661 FQ	45749 MW	70238 TQ	WVBLS	7/08-9/08
	Charleston MSA, WV	Y	35310 FQ	41970 MW	59730 TQ	USBLS	5/07
	Wisconsin	Y	41100 FQ	52350 MW	74460 TQ	USBLS	5/07
	Milwaukee-Waukesha-West						
	Allis MSA, WI	Y	43630 FQ	56120 MW	80770 TQ	USBLS	5/07
	Wyoming	Y	40445 FQ	53786 MW	72547 TQ	WYBLS	9/08
	Cheyenne MSA, WY	Y	46357 FQ	50209 MW	54062 TQ	WYBLS	9/08
	Puerto Rico	Y	35450 FQ	44360 MW	58050 TQ	USBLS	5/07
	San Juan-Caguas-Guaynabo						
	MSA, PR	Y	35430 FQ	44340 MW	57820 TQ	USBLS	5/07
Department of Environmental Quality	Oregon	M	3088 LO		5442 HI	ODEQSS	11/1/08
Chemistry Teacher							
Postsecondary	Alabama	Y	43160 FQ	53520 MW	64730 TQ	USBLS	5/07
Postsecondary	Birmingham-Hoover MSA, AL	Y	51290 FQ	58980 MW	66140 TQ	USBLS	5/07
Postsecondary	Arizona	Y	38650 FQ	53640 MW	102910 TQ	USBLS	5/07
Postsecondary	Phoenix-Mesa-Scottsdale						
	MSA, AZ	Y	36040 FQ	45600 MW	89800 TQ	USBLS	5/07
Postsecondary	Arkansas	Y	42940 FQ	50060 MW	64850 TQ	USBLS	5/07
Postsecondary	California	Y		84253 AW		CABLS	1/08-3/08
Postsecondary	Los Angeles-Long Beach-						
	Glendale PMSA, CA	Y		78705 AW		CABLS	1/08-3/08
Postsecondary	Oakland-Fremont-Hayward						
	MSA, CA	Y		83576 AW		CABLS	1/08-3/08
Postsecondary	Riverside-San Bernardino-						
	Ontario MSA, CA	Y		96005 AW		CABLS	1/08-3/08
Postsecondary	Sacramento-Arden Arcade-						
	Roseville MSA, CA	Y		80459 AW		CABLS	1/08-3/08
Postsecondary	San Diego-Carlsbad-San						
	Marcos MSA, CA	Y		74449 AW		CABLS	1/08-3/08
Postsecondary	San Francisco-San Mateo-						
	Redwood PMSA, CA	Y		95964 AW		CABLS	1/08-3/08
Postsecondary	Santa Ana-Anaheim-Irvine						
	PMSA, CA	Y	69950 FQ	81380 MW	110720 TQ	USBLS	5/07
Postsecondary	Colorado	Y	52530 FQ	73640 MW	116690 TQ	USBLS	5/07
Postsecondary	Denver-Aurora MSA, CO	Y	51970 FQ	70450 MW	112190 TQ	USBLS	5/07
Postsecondary	Delaware	Y	56490 FQ	76290 MW	108790 TQ	USBLS	5/07
Postsecondary	Wilmington PMSA, DE-MD-						
	NJ	Y	66840 FQ	82740 MW	123480 TQ	USBLS	5/07
Postsecondary	District of Columbia	Y	45970 FQ	61290 MW	82660 TQ	USBLS	5/07
Postsecondary	Washington-Arlington-						
	Alexandria MSA, DC-VA-						
	MD-WV	Y	49860 FQ	63950 MW	84220 TQ	USBLS	5/07
Postsecondary	Florida	Y	49540 FQ	65210 MW	79890 TQ	USBLS	5/07
Postsecondary	Miami-Fort Lauderdale-Miami						
	Beach MSA, FL	Y	53260 FQ	69040 MW	79820 TQ	USBLS	5/07
Postsecondary	Orlando-Kissimmee MSA, FL	Y	46740 FQ	68310 MW	79110 TQ	USBLS	5/07
Postsecondary	West Palm Beach-Boca Raton-						
	Boynton Beach PMSA, FL	Y	49950 FQ	59490 MW	72140 TQ	USBLS	5/07
Postsecondary	Georgia	Y	44170 FQ	58230 MW	76050 TQ	USBLS	5/07
Postsecondary	Atlanta-Sandy Springs-						
	Marietta MSA, GA	Y	41950 FQ	57050 MW	74410 TQ	USBLS	5/07
Postsecondary	Hawaii	Y	53920 FQ	64370 MW	90050 TQ	USBLS	5/07
Postsecondary	Honolulu MSA, HI	Y	57430 FQ	71620 MW	97680 TQ	USBLS	5/07
Postsecondary	Illinois	Y	50720 FQ	66590 MW	96710 TQ	USBLS	5/07
Postsecondary	Chicago-Naperville-Joliet						
	MSA, IL-IN-WI	Y	50840 FQ	70700 MW	102390 TQ	USBLS	5/07
Postsecondary	Indiana	Y	51050 FQ	64080 MW	99990 TQ	USBLS	5/07
Postsecondary	Gary PMSA, IN	Y	40350 FQ	55640 MW	69870 TQ	USBLS	5/07
Postsecondary	Iowa	Y	49220 FQ	67160 MW	83170 TQ	USBLS	5/07
Postsecondary	Des Moines-West Des Moines						
	MSA, IA	Y	44810 FQ	59460 MW	75290 TQ	USBLS	5/07
Postsecondary	Kansas	Y	39900 FQ	59970 MW	83960 TQ	USBLS	5/07
Postsecondary	Kentucky	Y	49494 FQ	61089 MW	76619 TQ	KYBLS	2008
Postsecondary	Louisiana	Y		66200 AW		LABLS	1/08-3/08
Postsecondary	Baton Rouge MSA, LA	Y	54440 FQ	65220 MW	83170 TQ	USBLS	5/07

AE	Average entry wage	**AW**	Average wage paid	**FQ**	First quartile wage	**LO**	Lowest wage paid	**MTC**	Median total compensation	**TCC**	Total cash compensation
AER	Average entry range	**AWR**	Average wage range	**H**	Hourly	**LR**	Low end range	**MW**	Median wage paid	**TQ**	Third quartile wage
AEX	Average experienced wage	**AXR**	Average experienced range	**HI**	Highest wage paid	**M**	Monthly	**MWR**	Median wage range	**W**	Weekly
ATC	Average total compensation	**D**	Daily	**HR**	High end range	**MCC**	Median cash compensation	**S**	See annotated source	**Y**	Yearly

Chemistry Teacher

Occupation/Type/Industry	Location	Per	Low	Mid	High	Source	Date
Postsecondary	New Orleans-Metairie-Kenner MSA, LA	Y	53310 FQ	62870 MW	80130 TQ	USBLS	5/07
Postsecondary	Maine	Y	52240 FQ	64760 MW	84460 TQ	USBLS	5/07
Postsecondary	Maryland	Y		70375 MW		MDBLS	3/08
Postsecondary	Baltimore-Towson MSA, MD	Y	56730 FQ	73360 MW	100450 TQ	USBLS	5/07
Postsecondary	Bethesda-Gaithersburg-Frederick PMSA, MD	Y	59550 FQ	70120 MW	95830 TQ	USBLS	5/07
Postsecondary	Massachusetts	Y	63380 FQ	77220 MW	102660 TQ	USBLS	5/07
Postsecondary	Boston-Cambridge-Quincy NECTA, MA	Y	60790 FQ	76610 MW	108590 TQ	USBLS	5/07
Postsecondary	Michigan	Y	49850 FQ	64040 MW	82540 TQ	USBLS·	5/07
Postsecondary	Detroit-Warren-Livonia MSA, MI	Y	48550 FQ	71420 MW	94430 TQ	USBLS	5/07
Postsecondary	Warren-Troy-Farmington Hills PMSA, MI	Y	38740 FQ	60920 MW	86690 TQ	USBLS	5/07
Postsecondary	Minnesota	Y	43271 FQ	53985 MW	68548 TQ	MNBLS	10/08-12/08
Postsecondary	Duluth-Superior MSA, MN-WI	Y	50490 FQ	62135 MW	75548 TQ	MNBLS	10/08-12/08
Postsecondary	Minneapolis-Saint Paul MSA, MN-WI	Y	43564 FQ	54456 MW	68726 TQ	MNBLS	10/08-12/08
Postsecondary	Mississippi	Y	52460 FQ	63320 MW	78020 TQ	USBLS	5/07
Postsecondary	Jackson MSA, MS	Y	53200 FQ	62910 MW	73370 TQ	USBLS	5/07
Postsecondary	Missouri	Y	42860 FQ	55460 MW	71250 TQ	USBLS	5/07
Postsecondary	Kansas City MSA, MO-KS	Y	47300 FQ	59150 MW	80100 TQ	USBLS	5/07
Postsecondary	St. Louis MSA, MO-IL	Y	41590 FQ	56520 MW	72900 TQ	USBLS	5/07
Postsecondary	Montana	Y	37350 FQ	52320 MW	63850 TQ	USBLS	5/07
Postsecondary	Nebraska	Y	40980 FQ	54830 MW	75630 TQ	USBLS	5/07
Postsecondary	Omaha-Council Bluffs MSA, NE-IA	Y	37450 FQ	55600 MW	74760 TQ	USBLS	5/07
Postsecondary	New Hampshire	Y	43796 AE	69812 MW	97127 AEX	NHBLS	6/08
Postsecondary	New Jersey	Y	49180 FQ	65690 MW	92770 TQ	USBLS	5/07
Postsecondary	Edison PMSA, NJ	Y	51400 FQ	65750 MW	89920 TQ	USBLS	5/07
Postsecondary	Newark-Union PMSA, NJ-PA	Y	47100 FQ	67200 MW	97360 TQ	USBLS	5/07
Postsecondary	New Mexico	Y	48310 FQ	56580 MW	67970 TQ	USBLS	5/07
Postsecondary	New York	Y	57640 FQ	74950 MW	98790 TQ	USBLS	5/07
Postsecondary	Nassau-Suffolk PMSA, NY	Y	49350 FQ	62300 MW	83250 TQ	USBLS	5/07
Postsecondary	New York-Northern New Jersey-Long Island MSA, NY-NJ-PA	Y	55660 FQ	72160 MW	94830 TQ	USBLS	5/07
Postsecondary	North Carolina	Y	48110 FQ	60490 MW	78650 TQ	USBLS	5/07
Postsecondary	Charlotte-Gastonia-Concord MSA, NC-SC	Y	52040 FQ	62660 MW	77570 TQ	USBLS	5/07
Postsecondary	North Dakota	Y	35820 FQ	55270 MW	72220 TQ	USBLS	5/07
Postsecondary	Fargo MSA, ND-MN	Y	38600 FQ	50570 MW	61190 TQ	USBLS	5/07
Postsecondary	Ohio	Y	49970 FQ	65070 MW	88700 TQ	USBLS	5/07
Postsecondary	Cincinnati-Middletown MSA, OH-KY-IN	Y	43800 FQ	61510 MW	87390 TQ	USBLS	5/07
Postsecondary	Cleveland-Elyria-Mentor MSA, OH	Y	45640 FQ	61330 MW	81880 TQ	USBLS	5/07
Postsecondary	Columbus MSA, OH	Y	69570 FQ	86860 MW	100820 TQ	USBLS	5/07
Postsecondary	Dayton MSA, OH	Y	45820 FQ	62440 MW	86660 TQ	USBLS	5/07
Postsecondary	Oklahoma	Y	35320 FQ	42960 MW	52050 TQ	USBLS	5/07
Postsecondary	Oklahoma City MSA, OK	Y	38480 FQ	53040 MW	68390 TQ	USBLS	5/07
Postsecondary	Tulsa MSA, OK	Y	35540 FQ	46160 MW	68740 TQ	USBLS	5/07
Postsecondary	Portland-Vancouver-Beaverton MSA, OR-WA	Y	52320 FQ	74760 MW	99400 TQ	USBLS	5/07
Postsecondary	Pennsylvania	Y	48830 FQ	61490 MW	81520 TQ	USBLS	5/07
Postsecondary	Allentown-Bethlehem-Easton MSA, PA-NJ	Y	48390 FQ	61020 MW	76570 TQ	USBLS	5/07
Postsecondary	Philadelphia-Camden-Wilmington MSA, PA-NJ-DE-MD	Y	52540 FQ	67540 MW	94470 TQ	USBLS	5/07
Postsecondary	Pittsburgh MSA, PA	Y	45620 FQ	57340 MW	74180 TQ	USBLS	5/07
Postsecondary	Rhode Island	Y	55300 FQ	71890 MW	95790 TQ	USBLS	5/07
Postsecondary	Providence-Fall River-Warwick MSA, RI-MA	Y	55660 FQ	72270 MW	95720 TQ	USBLS	5/07
Postsecondary	South Carolina	Y	42950 FQ	55540 MW	72190 TQ	USBLS	5/07
Postsecondary	Charleston-North Charleston MSA, SC	Y	46820 FQ	55660 MW	73780 TQ	USBLS	5/07
Postsecondary	Columbia MSA, SC	Y	41070 FQ	61320 MW	82550 TQ	USBLS	5/07
Postsecondary	South Dakota	Y	46375 FQ	57717 MW	68563 TQ	SDBLS	7/08-9/08
Postsecondary	Tennessee	Y	49390 FQ	66790 MW	107580 TQ	USBLS	5/07

AE	Average entry wage	AW	Average wage paid	FQ	First quartile wage	LO	Lowest wage paid	MTC	Median total compensation	TCC	Total cash compensation
AER	Average entry range	AWR	Average wage range	H	Hourly	LR	Low end range	MW	Median wage paid	TQ	Third quartile wage
AEX	Average experienced wage	AXR	Average experienced range	HI	Highest wage paid	M	Monthly	MWR	Median wage range	W	Weekly
ATC	Average total compensation	D	Daily	HR	High end range	MCC	Median cash compensation	S	See annotated source	Y	Yearly

Occupation/Type/Industry	Location	Per	Low	Mid	High	Source	Date
Chemistry Teacher							
Postsecondary	Memphis MSA, TN-MS-AR	Y	46510 FQ	61930 MW	83280 TQ	USBLS	5/07
Postsecondary	Nashville-Davidson-Murfreesboro MSA, TN	Y	51260 FQ	72870 MW	114310 TQ	USBLS	5/07
Postsecondary	Texas	Y	48050 FQ	66490 MW	98240 TQ	USBLS	5/07
Postsecondary	Austin-Round Rock MSA, TX	Y	50790 FQ	85340 MW	129180 TQ	USBLS	5/07
Postsecondary	Dallas-Fort Worth-Arlington MSA, TX	Y	46260 FQ	78940 MW	121120 TQ	USBLS	5/07
Postsecondary	El Paso MSA, TX	Y	55030 FQ	68740 MW	106490 TQ	USBLS	5/07
Postsecondary	Houston-Sugar Land-Baytown MSA, TX	Y	53280 FQ	80770 MW	123120 TQ	USBLS	5/07
Postsecondary	San Antonio MSA, TX	Y	47790 FQ	57890 MW	65820 TQ	USBLS	5/07
Postsecondary	Utah	Y	52380 FQ	68490 MW	97350 TQ	USBLS	5/07
Postsecondary	Vermont	Y	46760 FQ	56160 MW	69370 TQ	USBLS	5/07
Postsecondary	Virginia	Y	45410 FQ	58980 MW	75100 TQ	USBLS	5/07
Postsecondary	Richmond MSA, VA	Y	51040 FQ	62610 MW	84600 TQ	USBLS	5/07
Postsecondary	Virginia Beach-Norfolk-Newport News MSA, VA-NC	Y	50250 FQ	60410 MW	73170 TQ	USBLS	5/07
Postsecondary	Washington	Y		69679 AW		WABLS	3/08
Postsecondary	Seattle-Tacoma-Bellevue MSA, WA	Y	44840 FQ	58120 MW	87630 TQ	USBLS	5/07
Postsecondary	Spokane MSA, WA	Y	44040 FQ	57490 MW	80670 TQ	USBLS	5/07
Postsecondary	West Virginia	Y	44669 FQ	60243 MW	82264 TQ	WVBLS	7/08-9/08
Postsecondary	Wisconsin	Y	43210 FQ	54690 MW	70370 TQ	USBLS	5/07
Postsecondary	Milwaukee-Waukesha-West Allis MSA, WI	Y	43100 FQ	54470 MW	75430 TQ	USBLS	5/07
Postsecondary	Wyoming	Y	56117 FQ	69695 MW	87406 TQ	WYBLS	9/08
Postsecondary	Puerto Rico	Y	39200 FQ	58290 MW	75410 TQ	USBLS	5/07
Postsecondary	San Juan-Caguas-Guaynabo MSA, PR	Y	49910 FQ	69390 MW	78380 TQ	USBLS	5/07
Chestnut Harvester	Traverse City, MI	S			0.50 HI	MAG	10/08
Chief Administrative Officer							
United States House of Representatives	United States	Y			167800 HI	CRS01	1/08
Chief Air Pollution Technician							
Department of Environmental Services	New Hampshire	Y			44478 HI	NHUL03	2008
Chief Appraiser							
Municipal Government	Cincinnati, OH	Y	62598 LO		84507 HI	COHSS	10/08
Chief Bank Examiner							
Bank Commission, State Government	New Hampshire	Y		44632 AW		NHUL03	2008
Chief Counsel for the House Republican Caucus							
State Government	Pennsylvania	Y			197000 HI	STLEG2	2008
Chief Court Stenographer	Luzerne County, PA	Y			67150 HI	TLEAD01	2009
Chief Engineer							
Radio Station	United States	Y		58333 AW		RADM	2008
Chief Executive	Alabama	Y	93170 FQ	141750 MW		USBLS	5/07
	Birmingham-Hoover MSA, AL	Y	107020 FQ			USBLS	5/07
	Huntsville MSA, AL	Y	108630 FQ			USBLS	5/07
	Alaska	Y	74340 FQ	112740 MW		USBLS	5/07
	Anchorage MSA, AK	Y	90460 FQ	128520 MW		USBLS	5/07
	Arizona	Y	95810 FQ	139920 MW		USBLS	5/07
	Flagstaff MSA, AZ	Y	59140 FQ	89350 MW	115810 TQ	USBLS	5/07
	Phoenix-Mesa-Scottsdale MSA, AZ	Y	104810 FQ			USBLS	5/07
	Tucson MSA, AZ	Y	75590 FQ	121570 MW		USBLS	5/07
	Arkansas	Y	82960 FQ	108190 MW		USBLS	5/07
	Little Rock-North Little Rock MSA, AR	Y	92190 FQ	128800 MW		USBLS	5/07
	Pine Bluff MSA, AR	Y	80230 FQ	98750 MW	138450 TQ	USBLS	5/07
	California	H	68.49 FQ			CABLS	1/08-3/08
	Oakland-Fremont-Hayward MSA, CA	H	66.26 FQ			CABLS	1/08-3/08

Occupation/Type/Industry	Location	Per	Low	Mid	High	Source	Date
Chief Executive	Riverside-San Bernardino-Ontario MSA, CA	H	66.44 FQ			CABLS	1/08-3/08
	Sacramento-Arden Arcade-Roseville MSA, CA	H	48.87 FQ	60.91 MW		CABLS	1/08-3/08
	San Diego-Carlsbad-San Marcos MSA, CA	H	69.54 FQ			CABLS	1/08-3/08
	Colorado	Y	106400 FQ			USBLS	5/07
	Colorado Springs MSA, CO	Y	121340 FQ			USBLS	5/07
	Denver-Aurora MSA, CO	Y	117870 FQ			USBLS	5/07
	Connecticut	H	46.07 AE	81.59 AW		CTBLS	1/08-3/08
	Hartford-West Hartford-East Hartford MSA, CT	Y	123890 FQ			USBLS	5/07
	Delaware	Y	126470 FQ			USBLS	5/07
	Wilmington PMSA, DE-MD-NJ	Y	127720 FQ			USBLS	5/07
	District of Columbia	Y	140560 FQ			USBLS	5/07
	Washington-Arlington-Alexandria MSA, DC-VA-MD-WV	Y	137560 FQ			USBLS	5/07
	Florida	Y	114390 FQ			USBLS	5/07
	Fort Lauderdale-Pompano Beach-Deerfield Beach PMSA, FL	Y	120160 FQ			USBLS	5/07
	Jacksonville MSA, FL	Y	113860 FQ			USBLS	5/07
	Miami-Fort Lauderdale-Miami Beach MSA, FL	Y	125110 FQ			USBLS	5/07
	Orlando-Kissimmee MSA, FL	Y	120270 FQ			USBLS	5/07
	Pensacola-Ferry Pass-Brent MSA, FL	Y	108080 FQ			USBLS	5/07
	Tampa-St. Petersburg-Clearwater MSA, FL	Y	113870 FQ			USBLS	5/07
	West Palm Beach-Boca Raton-Boynton Beach PMSA, FL	Y	138950 FQ			USBLS	5/07
	Georgia	Y	97800 FQ			USBLS	5/07
	Atlanta-Sandy Springs-Marietta MSA, GA	Y	111470 FQ			USBLS	5/07
	Augusta-Richmond County MSA, GA-SC	Y	81520 FQ	123660 MW		USBLS	5/07
	Hawaii	Y	92870 FQ	126790 MW		USBLS	5/07
	Honolulu MSA, HI	Y	98940 FQ	132210 MW		USBLS	5/07
	Boise City-Nampa MSA, ID	Y	70260 FQ	104730 MW		USBLS	5/07
	Coeur d'Alene MSA, ID	Y	64840 FQ	87570 MW	127000 TQ	USBLS	5/07
	Illinois	Y	91170 FQ			USBLS	5/07
	Chicago-Naperville-Joliet MSA, IL-IN-WI	Y	108480 FQ			USBLS	5/07
	Indiana	Y	95080 FQ	143040 MW		USBLS	5/07
	Evansville MSA, IN-KY	Y	103380 FQ			USBLS	5/07
	Gary PMSA, IN	Y	88570 FQ	127820 MW		USBLS	5/07
	Indianapolis-Carmel MSA, IN	Y	112960 FQ			USBLS	5/07
	Iowa	Y	87000 FQ	120290 MW		USBLS	5/07
	Des Moines-West Des Moines MSA, IA	Y	112720 FQ			USBLS	5/07
	Kansas	Y	80270 FQ	110320 MW		USBLS	5/07
	Topeka MSA, KS	Y	75340 FQ	102720 MW		USBLS	5/07
	Wichita MSA, KS	Y	80350 FQ	114070 MW		USBLS	5/07
	Kentucky	Y	92658 FQ	134043 MW		KYBLS	2008
	Louisville-Jefferson County MSA, KY-IN	Y	106970 FQ			USBLS	5/07
	Owensboro MSA, KY	Y	111280 FQ			USBLS	5/07
	Louisiana	H	47.12 FQ	65.14 MW		LABLS	1/08-3/08
	Baton Rouge MSA, LA	Y	85110 FQ	127980 MW		USBLS	5/07
	New Orleans-Metairie-Kenner MSA, LA	Y	103330 FQ	139980 MW		USBLS	5/07
	Maine	Y	77340 FQ	102290 MW		USBLS	5/07
	Portland-South Portland-Biddeford MSA, ME	Y	89410 FQ	124940 MW		USBLS	5/07
	Maryland	Y		159300 AW		MDBLS	3/08
	Baltimore-Towson MSA, MD	Y	105760 FQ			USBLS	5/07
	Bethesda-Gaithersburg-Frederick PMSA, MD	Y	129030 FQ			USBLS	5/07
	Salisbury MSA, MD	Y	58150 FQ	91810 MW		USBLS	5/07
	Massachusetts	Y	104100 FQ			USBLS	5/07

AE	Average entry wage	AW	Average wage paid	FQ	First quartile wage	LO	Lowest wage paid	MTC	Median total compensation	TCC	Total cash compensation
AER	Average entry range	AWR	Average wage range	H	Hourly	LR	Low end range	MW	Median wage paid	TQ	Third quartile wage
AEX	Average experienced wage	AXR	Average experienced range	HI	Highest wage paid	M	Monthly	MWR	Median wage range	W	Weekly
ATC	Average total compensation	D	Daily	HR	High end range	MCC	Median cash compensation	S	See annotated source	Y	Yearly

202

Occupation/Type/Industry	Location	Per	Low	Mid	High	Source	Date
Chief Executive	Barnstable Town MSA, MA	Y	78270 FQ	140420 MW		USBLS	5/07
	Boston-Cambridge-Quincy NECTA, MA	Y	122600 FQ			USBLS	5/07
	Worcester MSA, MA-CT	Y	94880 FQ	127430 MW		USBLS	5/07
	Michigan	Y	93860 FQ	143440 MW		USBLS	5/07
	Ann Arbor MSA, MI	Y	119850 FQ			USBLS	5/07
	Detroit-Warren-Livonia MSA, MI	Y	107820 FQ			USBLS	5/07
	Grand Rapids-Wyoming MSA, MI	Y	90610 FQ			USBLS	5/07
	Lansing-East Lansing MSA, MI	Y	87380 FQ			USBLS	5/07
	Warren-Troy-Farmington Hills PMSA, MI	Y	110070 FQ			USBLS	5/07
	Minnesota	Y	119352 FQ	168743 AW		MNBLS	10/08-12/08
	Duluth-Superior MSA, MN-WI	Y	97727 FQ	128819 MW		MNBLS	10/08-12/08
	Minneapolis-Saint Paul MSA, MN-WI	Y	149068 FQ	189648 AW		MNBLS	10/08-12/08
	Rochester MSA, MN	Y	90856 FQ	141911 MW		MNBLS	10/08-12/08
	Mississippi	Y	63000 FQ	103750 MW		USBLS	5/07
	Gulfport-Biloxi MSA, MS	Y	62160 FQ	120030 MW		USBLS	5/07
	Jackson MSA, MS	Y	58750 FQ	88520 MW		USBLS	5/07
	Missouri	Y	88800 FQ	131710 MW		USBLS	5/07
	Joplin MSA, MO	Y	76160 FQ	110000 MW		USBLS	5/07
	Kansas City MSA, MO-KS	Y	98350 FQ	136260 MW		USBLS	5/07
	St. Louis MSA, MO-IL	Y	98360 FQ			USBLS	5/07
	Montana	Y	34080 FQ	73210 MW	106760 TQ	USBLS	5/07
	Billings MSA, MT	Y	87430 FQ	114740 MW		USBLS	5/07
	Missoula MSA, MT	Y	100670 FQ			USBLS	5/07
	Nebraska	Y	89610 FQ	134410 MW		USBLS	5/07
	Omaha-Council Bluffs MSA, NE-IA	Y	104330 FQ			USBLS	5/07
	Nevada	H	37.61 FQ	60.51 MW		NVBLS	5/08
	Las Vegas-Paradise MSA, NV	H	38.98 FQ	69.47 MW		NVBLS	5/08
	New Hampshire	H	36.34 AE	65.38 MW	85.07 AEX	NHBLS	6/08
	Manchester MSA, NH	Y	98840 FQ			USBLS	5/07
	Nashua NECTA, NH-MA	Y	96930 FQ	143990 MW		USBLS	5/07
	New Mexico	Y	82140 FQ	105520 MW		USBLS	5/07
	Albuquerque MSA, NM	Y	93520 FQ	121980 MW		USBLS	5/07
	New York	Y	114430 FQ			USBLS	5/07
	Albany-Schenectady-Troy MSA, NY	Y	89690 FQ	121500 MW		USBLS	5/07
	Buffalo-Niagara Falls MSA, NY	Y	98330 FQ	137100 MW		USBLS	5/07
	Nassau-Suffolk PMSA, NY	Y	120330 FQ			USBLS	5/07
	North Carolina	Y	127030 FQ			USBLS	5/07
	Asheville MSA, NC	Y	121190 FQ			USBLS	5/07
	Charlotte-Gastonia-Concord MSA, NC-SC	Y	122230 FQ			USBLS	5/07
	Durham MSA, NC	Y	138510 FQ			USBLS	5/07
	Raleigh-Cary MSA, NC	Y	120500 FQ			USBLS	5/07
	North Dakota	Y	84670 FQ	120930 MW		USBLS	5/07
	Fargo MSA, ND-MN	Y	92760 FQ	126730 MW		USBLS	5/07
	Grand Forks MSA, ND-MN	Y	78320 FQ			USBLS	5/07
	Ohio	Y	97440 FQ			USBLS	5/07
	Canton-Massillon MSA, OH	Y	81370 FQ	111520 MW		USBLS	5/07
	Cincinnati-Middletown MSA, OH-KY-IN	Y	111360 FQ			USBLS	5/07
	Cleveland-Elyria-Mentor MSA, OH	Y	111690 FQ			USBLS	5/07
	Columbus MSA, OH	Y	102450 FQ			USBLS	5/07
	Dayton MSA, OH	Y	94420 FQ	131560 MW		USBLS	5/07
	Oklahoma	Y	57680 FQ	91020 MW		USBLS	5/07
	Oklahoma City MSA, OK	Y	61040 FQ	101580 MW		USBLS	5/07
	Tulsa MSA, OK	Y	64250 FQ	96380 MW		USBLS	5/07
	Portland-Vancouver-Beaverton MSA, OR-WA	Y	122830 FQ			USBLS	5/07
	Pennsylvania	Y	91600 FQ	132460 MW		USBLS	5/07
	Allentown-Bethlehem-Easton MSA, PA-NJ	Y	92460 FQ			USBLS	5/07
	Philadelphia-Camden-Wilmington MSA, PA-NJ-DE-MD	Y	115000 FQ			USBLS	5/07

AE Average entry wage	**AW** Average wage paid	**FQ** First quartile wage	**LO** Lowest wage paid	**MTC** Median total compensation	**TCC** Total cash compensation
AER Average entry range	**AWR** Average wage range	**H** Hourly	**LR** Low end range	**MW** Median wage paid	**TQ** Third quartile wage
AEX Average experienced wage	**AXR** Average experienced range	**HI** Highest wage paid	**M** Monthly	**MWR** Median wage range	**W** Weekly
ATC Average total compensation	**D** Daily	**HR** High end range	**MCC** Median cash compensation	**S** See annotated source	**Y** Yearly

Occupation/Type/Industry	Location	Per	Low	Mid	High	Source	Date
Chief Executive	Pittsburgh MSA, PA	Y	92870 FQ	134280 MW		USBLS	5/07
	Rhode Island	Y	121940 FQ			USBLS	5/07
	Providence-Fall River-Warwick MSA, RI-MA	Y	108160 FQ			USBLS	5/07
	South Carolina	Y	102120 FQ			USBLS	5/07
	Charleston-North Charleston MSA, SC	Y	110940 FQ			USBLS	5/07
	Columbia MSA, SC	Y	103580 FQ			USBLS	5/07
	South Dakota	Y	40081 FQ	114812 MW		SDBLS	7/08-9/08
	Sioux Falls MSA, SD	Y	114566 FQ			SDBLS	7/08-9/08
	Tennessee	Y	81350 FQ	126910 MW		USBLS	5/07
	Johnson City MSA, TN	Y	65790 FQ	93660 MW		USBLS	5/07
	Memphis MSA, TN-MS-AR	Y	87090 FQ	130390 MW		USBLS	5/07
	Nashville-Davidson-Murfreesboro MSA, TN	Y	90560 FQ	140310 MW		USBLS	5/07
	Texas	Y	100000 FQ			USBLS	5/07
	Austin-Round Rock MSA, TX	Y	105530 FQ			USBLS	5/07
	Dallas-Fort Worth-Arlington MSA, TX	Y	130610 FQ			USBLS	5/07
	El Paso MSA, TX	Y	118320 FQ			USBLS	5/07
	Houston-Sugar Land-Baytown MSA, TX	Y	135520 FQ			USBLS	5/07
	San Antonio MSA, TX	Y	105690 FQ			USBLS	5/07
	Utah	Y	102410 FQ			USBLS	5/07
	Provo-Orem MSA, UT	Y	93140 FQ	134860 MW		USBLS	5/07
	Salt Lake City MSA, UT	Y	115540 FQ			USBLS	5/07
	Vermont	Y	80320 FQ	141480 MW		USBLS	5/07
	Burlington-South Burlington MSA, VT	Y	97380 FQ			USBLS	5/07
	Virginia	Y	103330 FQ			USBLS	5/07
	Richmond MSA, VA	Y	107230 FQ			USBLS	5/07
	Roanoke MSA, VA	Y	93590 FQ	131880 MW		USBLS	5/07
	Virginia Beach-Norfolk-Newport News MSA, VA-NC	Y	93180 FQ			USBLS	5/07
	Washington	Y		177477 AW		WABLS	3/08
	Olympia MSA, WA	Y	111610 FQ	126620 MW		USBLS	5/07
	West Virginia	Y	39732 FQ	76602 MW	119105 TQ	WVBLS	7/08-9/08
	Charleston MSA, WV	Y	51940 FQ	83640 MW	137390 TQ	USBLS	5/07
	Parkersburg-Marietta-Vienna MSA, WV-OH	Y	43520 FQ	87690 MW		USBLS	5/07
	Wisconsin	Y	103910 FQ	141190 MW		USBLS	5/07
	Appleton MSA, WI	Y	105240 FQ	121500 MW		USBLS	5/07
	Milwaukee-Waukesha-West Allis MSA, WI	Y	120710 FQ			USBLS	5/07
	Racine MSA, WI	Y	110460 FQ			USBLS	5/07
	Wyoming	Y	68940 FQ	94537 MW	127197 TQ	WYBLS	9/08
	Cheyenne MSA, WY	Y	74923 FQ	87452 MW	103773 TQ	WYBLS	9/08
	Puerto Rico	Y	59650 FQ	88710 MW		USBLS	5/07
	San Juan-Caguas-Guaynabo MSA, PR	Y	60030 FQ	91400 MW		USBLS	5/07
	Virgin Islands	Y	75700 FQ	104120 MW		USBLS	5/07
	Guam	Y	44360 FQ	62160 MW	100220 TQ	USBLS	5/07
Boy Scouts' Council	Orange County, CA	Y			283503 HI	OCREG	2008
Chief Executive Officer							
Bank	United States	Y		148100-542800 MCC		CUMGT	2008
Credit Union	United States	Y		103767-446499 MCC		CUMGT	2008
Dallas-Fort Worth International Airport	Dallas, TX	Y			344792 HI	FREEP06	2008
Detroit Metro Airport	Romulus, MI	Y			215759 HI	FREEP06	2008
Education Charity	United States	Y		240432 AW		CHNAV	2008
Free-Standing Hospital	United States	Y			497000 TCC	MHLTH01	2008
Philadelphia International Airport	Philadelphia, PA	Y			163894 HI	FREEP06	2008
Religious Charity	United States	Y		99708 AW		CHNAV	2008
System Hospital	United States	Y			395000 TCC	MHLTH01	2008
Tennessee Valley Authority	Knoxville, TN	Y			850000 HI	KNOXN	2008-2009
Chief Information Officer	San Antonio, TX	Y	119145-197400 LR			SABJ	2008
Chief Jailer/Jail Administrator	College Park, GA	Y	26534 LO		40375 HI	GACTY01	2008

AE Average entry wage AW Average wage paid FQ First quartile wage LO Lowest wage paid MTC Median total compensation TCC Total cash compensation
AER Average entry range AWR Average wage range H Hourly LR Low end range MW Median wage paid TQ Third quartile wage
AEX Average experienced wage AXR Average experienced range HI Highest wage paid M Monthly MWR Median wage range W Weekly
ATC Average total compensation D Daily HR High end range MCC Median cash compensation S See annotated source Y Yearly

Occupation/Type/Industry	Location	Per	Low	Mid	High	Source	Date
Chief Judge							
Magistrate Court	Fayette County, GA	Y			20194 HI	GACTY02	2008
Magistrate Court	Hall County, GA	Y			140285 HI	GACTY02	2008
State Court of Appeals	Arkansas	Y			137669 HI	ADGAZ	2008
Chief Justice							
State Supreme Court	Arkansas	Y			151049 HI	ADGAZ	2008
Chief Justice of the United States	United States	Y			217400 HI	CRS02	1/08
Chief Marketing Officer	United States	Y		1500000 ATC		ADAGE01	2007
Chief Master Sergeant							
U.S. Air Force, Active Duty, Pay Grade E-9	United States	M	4421 LO		6863 HI	DOD1	2009
Chief Medical Examiner							
State Government	Maryland	Y			227660 HI	BMAG	2009
Chief Medical Officer	United States	Y		435900 MTC		MODPHY	2008
Massachusetts Society for the Prevention of Cruelty to Animals	Massachusetts	Y			246337 HI	BGLOBE4	2009
Chief Museum Curator	United States	Y		87125 MW		WSJ08	2008
Chief of Staff							
For United States Representative	United States	Y			130000 HI	WPOST	2006
For United States Senator	United States	Y			157150 HI	WPOST	2006
Chief Operator							
Waste Water Treatment Facility	Ashfield, MA	Y			40267 HI	FRCOG	2009
Chief Petty Officer							
U.S. Navy, Active Duty, Pay Grade E-7	United States	M	2516 LO		4521 HI	DOD1	2009
Chief Plumbers Board Inspector							
Boards and Commissions, State Government	New Hampshire	Y			48324 HI	NHUL03	2008
Chief Probation Officer	Colorado Springs, CO	M	5182 LO			COSPRS	1/1/09
Chief Psychologist							
Department of Corrections	New Hampshire	Y			73621 HI	NHUL03	2008
Chief Toxicologist							
Sheriff's Office of Forensic Science Division	Washoe County, NV	W	7188 LO		9348 HI	CAC	2006-2007
Chief Water Poll Biologist							
Department of Environmental Services	New Hampshire	Y			84088 HI	NHUL03	2008
Child, Family, and School Social Worker	Alabama	Y	28640 FQ	35190 MW	44960 TQ	USBLS	5/07
	Birmingham-Hoover MSA, AL	Y	30660 FQ	36180 MW	44390 TQ	USBLS	5/07
	Alaska	Y	31930 FQ	42470 MW	50710 TQ	USBLS	5/07
	Anchorage MSA, AK	Y	34350 FQ	44320 MW	51050 TQ	USBLS	5/07
	Arizona	Y	29860 FQ	35810 MW	40850 TQ	USBLS	5/07
	Phoenix-Mesa-Scottsdale MSA, AZ	Y	31290 FQ	36110 MW	41510 TQ	USBLS	5/07
	Tucson MSA, AZ	Y	27250 FQ	35250 MW	40430 TQ	USBLS	5/07
	Arkansas	Y	25490 FQ	30030 MW	37610 TQ	USBLS	5/07
	Little Rock-North Little Rock MSA, AR	Y	25100 FQ	30110 MW	38240 TQ	USBLS	5/07
	Pine Bluff MSA, AR	Y	21760 FQ	27480 MW	43740 TQ	USBLS	5/07
	California	H	18.36 FQ	23.51 MW	31.18 TQ	CABLS	1/08-3/08
	Los Angeles-Long Beach-Glendale PMSA, CA	H	20.94 FQ	28.61 MW	35.95 TQ	CABLS	1/08-3/08
	Oakland-Fremont-Hayward MSA, CA	H	19.26 FQ	23.87 MW	34.15 TQ	CABLS	1/08-3/08
	Riverside-San Bernardino-Ontario MSA, CA	H	17.96 FQ	23.09 MW	29.52 TQ	CABLS	1/08-3/08
	Sacramento-Arden Arcade-Roseville MSA, CA	H	18.05 FQ	21.34 MW	24.75 TQ	CABLS	1/08-3/08

Occupation/Type/Industry	Location	Per	Low	Mid	High	Source	Date
Child, Family, and School Social Worker	San Diego-Carlsbad-San Marcos MSA, CA	H	21.02 FQ	26.63 MW	30.48 TQ	CABLS	1/08-3/08
	San Francisco-San Mateo-Redwood PMSA, CA	H	18.29 FQ	22.60 MW	30.10 TQ	CABLS	1/08-3/08
	San Jose-Sunnyvale-Santa Clara MSA, CA	H	17.60 FQ	22.56 MW	29.74 TQ	CABLS	1/08-3/08
	Santa Ana-Anaheim-Irvine PMSA, CA	Y	29890 FQ	41980 MW	48330 TQ	USBLS	5/07
	Colorado	Y	33430 FQ	43070 MW	56570 TQ	USBLS	5/07
	Denver-Aurora MSA, CO	Y	35070 FQ	44680 MW	59510 TQ	USBLS	5/07
	Connecticut	H	19.60 AE	29.66 MW		CTBLS	1/08-3/08
	Bridgeport-Stamford-Norwalk MSA, CT	Y	43030 FQ	55760 MW	71500 TQ	USBLS	5/07
	Danbury MSA, CT	Y	41310 FQ	51980 MW	70910 TQ	USBLS	5/07
	Hartford-West Hartford-East Hartford MSA, CT	Y	46060 FQ	61120 MW	72710 TQ	USBLS	5/07
	Norwich-New London MSA, CT-RI	Y	41280 FQ	54020 MW	71660 TQ	USBLS	5/07
	Delaware	Y	35590 FQ	43080 MW	50790 TQ	USBLS	5/07
	Wilmington PMSA, DE-MD-NJ	Y	36700 FQ	44130 MW	51710 TQ	USBLS	5/07
	District of Columbia	Y	39260 FQ	47030 MW	64850 TQ	USBLS	5/07
	Washington-Arlington-Alexandria MSA, DC-VA-MD-WV	Y	37180 FQ	49530 MW	66570 TQ	USBLS	5/07
	Florida	Y	28390 FQ	35280 MW	45270 TQ	USBLS	5/07
	Cape Coral-Fort Myers MSA, FL	Y	28170 FQ	34030 MW	41630 TQ	USBLS	5/07
	Fort Lauderdale-Pompano Beach-Deerfield Beach PMSA, FL	Y	30870 FQ	37360 MW	46040 TQ	USBLS	5/07
	Jacksonville MSA, FL	Y	29220 FQ	34440 MW	40110 TQ	USBLS	5/07
	Miami-Fort Lauderdale-Miami Beach MSA, FL	Y	29740 FQ	37250 MW	47300 TQ	USBLS	5/07
	Orlando-Kissimmee MSA, FL	Y	29640 FQ	35200 MW	47630 TQ	USBLS	5/07
	Tampa-St. Petersburg-Clearwater MSA, FL	Y	28570 FQ	36550 MW	48900 TQ	USBLS	5/07
	West Palm Beach-Boca Raton-Boynton Beach PMSA, FL	Y	27490 FQ	34630 MW	44240 TQ	USBLS	5/07
	Georgia	Y	26660 FQ	30870 MW	38750 TQ	USBLS	5/07
	Atlanta-Sandy Springs-Marietta MSA, GA	Y	25960 FQ	30320 MW	38130 TQ	USBLS	5/07
	Macon MSA, GA	Y	27640 FQ	32310 MW	39580 TQ	USBLS	5/07
	Hawaii	Y	36420 FQ	47390 MW	56320 TQ	USBLS	5/07
	Honolulu MSA, HI	Y	35710 FQ	47320 MW	56070 TQ	USBLS	5/07
	Idaho	Y	29190 FQ	35570 MW	43780 TQ	USBLS	5/07
	Boise City-Nampa MSA, ID	Y	27680 FQ	31680 MW	49990 TQ	USBLS	5/07
	Idaho Falls MSA, ID	Y	34750 FQ	38040 MW	41270 TQ	USBLS	5/07
	Illinois	Y	34790 FQ	47270 MW	61940 TQ	USBLS	5/07
	Chicago-Naperville-Joliet MSA, IL-IN-WI	Y	34570 FQ	46780 MW	63460 TQ	USBLS	5/07
	Peoria MSA, IL	Y	30600 FQ	41960 MW	59170 TQ	USBLS	5/07
	Indiana	Y	26660 FQ	32490 MW	37800 TQ	USBLS	5/07
	Evansville MSA, IN-KY	Y	28070 FQ	34240 MW	38690 TQ	USBLS	5/07
	Gary PMSA, IN	Y	25620 FQ	31630 MW	37520 TQ	USBLS	5/07
	Indianapolis-Carmel MSA, IN	Y	27650 FQ	33940 MW	39260 TQ	USBLS	5/07
	Iowa	Y	26000 FQ	35160 MW	46770 TQ	USBLS	5/07
	Des Moines-West Des Moines MSA, IA	Y	27500 FQ	39880 MW	51670 TQ	USBLS	5/07
	Kansas	Y	30040 FQ	36360 MW	44890 TQ	USBLS	5/07
	Wichita MSA, KS	Y	30290 FQ	39980 MW	47720 TQ	USBLS	5/07
	Kentucky	Y	30879 FQ	37140 MW	43981 TQ	KYBLS	2008
	Louisville-Jefferson County MSA, KY-IN	Y	30130 FQ	35690 MW	41650 TQ	USBLS	5/07
	Louisiana	H	14.41 FQ	19.45 MW	24.72 TQ	LABLS	1/08-3/08
	Baton Rouge MSA, LA	Y	32770 FQ	43270 MW	55540 TQ	USBLS	5/07
	New Orleans-Metairie-Kenner MSA, LA	Y	34120 FQ	42510 MW	51050 TQ	USBLS	5/07
	Maine	Y	31920 FQ	38710 MW	47250 TQ	USBLS	5/07
	Portland-South Portland-Biddeford MSA, ME	Y	37480 FQ	44110 MW	51590 TQ	USBLS	5/07

AE Average entry wage	**AW** Average wage paid	**FQ** First quartile wage	**LO** Lowest wage paid	**MTC** Median total compensation	**TCC** Total cash compensation
AER Average entry range	**AWR** Average wage range	**H** Hourly	**LR** Low end range	**MW** Median wage paid	**TQ** Third quartile wage
AEX Average experienced wage	**AXR** Average experienced range	**HI** Highest wage paid	**M** Monthly	**MWR** Median wage range	**W** Weekly
ATC Average total compensation	**D** Daily	**HR** High end range	**MCC** Median cash compensation	**S** See annotated source	**Y** Yearly

Occupation/Type/Industry	Location	Per	Low	Mid	High	Source	Date
Child, Family, and School Social Worker	Maryland	Y		48525 MW		MDBLS	3/08
	Baltimore-Towson MSA, MD	Y	39940 FQ	47880 MW	58080 TQ	USBLS	5/07
	Bethesda-Gaithersburg-Frederick PMSA, MD	Y	37460 FQ	47570 MW	61150 TQ	USBLS	5/07
	Massachusetts	Y	38470 FQ	48910 MW	59140 TQ	USBLS	5/07
	Boston-Cambridge-Quincy NECTA, MA	Y	38050 FQ	47200 MW	58020 TQ	USBLS	5/07
	Worcester MSA, MA-CT	Y	39010 FQ	49400 MW	58650 TQ	USBLS	5/07
	Michigan	Y	38700 FQ	46760 MW	56650 TQ	USBLS	5/07
	Detroit-Warren-Livonia MSA, MI	Y	39410 FQ	47480 MW	60920 TQ	USBLS	5/07
	Grand Rapids-Wyoming MSA, MI	Y	40380 FQ	48740 MW	65010 TQ	USBLS	5/07
	Warren-Troy-Farmington Hills PMSA, MI	Y	37450 FQ	46980 MW	62310 TQ	USBLS	5/07
	Minnesota	Y	42142 FQ	53294 MW	63851 TQ	MNBLS	10/08-12/08
	Duluth-Superior MSA, MN-WI	Y	53054 FQ	60858 MW	66927 TQ	MNBLS	10/08-12/08
	Minneapolis-Saint Paul MSA, MN-WI	Y	43659 FQ	56485 MW	66456 TQ	MNBLS	10/08-12/08
	Rochester MSA, MN	Y	38115 FQ	49839 MW	62550 TQ	MNBLS	10/08-12/08
	Mississippi	Y	26590 FQ	30860 MW	36400 TQ	USBLS	5/07
	Jackson MSA, MS	Y	26720 FQ	31380 MW	37560 TQ	USBLS	5/07
	Missouri	Y	26960 FQ	30890 MW	38290 TQ	USBLS	5/07
	Kansas City MSA, MO-KS	Y	27330 FQ	32600 MW	41530 TQ	USBLS	5/07
	St. Louis MSA, MO-IL	Y	28660 FQ	34490 MW	47740 TQ	USBLS	5/07
	Montana	Y	27060 FQ	34050 MW	40720 TQ	USBLS	5/07
	Billings MSA, MT	Y	23790 FQ	32550 MW	43210 TQ	USBLS	5/07
	Great Falls MSA, MT	Y	29710 FQ	35570 MW	40310 TQ	USBLS	5/07
	Nebraska	Y	27940 FQ	32200 MW	39750 TQ	USBLS	5/07
	Omaha-Council Bluffs MSA, NE-IA	Y	28290 FQ	33400 MW	42310 TQ	USBLS	5/07
	Nevada	H	19.09 FQ	23.30 MW	28.61 TQ	NVBLS	5/08
	Las Vegas-Paradise MSA, NV	H	19.30 FQ	23.49 MW	28.80 TQ	NVBLS	5/08
	New Hampshire	H	16.29 AE	20.30 MW	21.82 AEX	NHBLS	6/08
	Manchester MSA, NH	Y	31500 FQ	37340 MW	45840 TQ	USBLS	5/07
	Nashua NECTA, NH-MA	Y	39240 FQ	42510 MW	46030 TQ	USBLS	5/07
	New Jersey	Y	35700 FQ	49940 MW	68030 TQ	USBLS	5/07
	Camden PMSA, NJ	Y	30110 FQ	40130 MW	56800 TQ	USBLS	5/07
	Edison PMSA, NJ	Y	40390 FQ	51760 MW	65070 TQ	USBLS	5/07
	Newark-Union PMSA, NJ-PA	Y	34970 FQ	52090 MW	69490 TQ	USBLS	5/07
	Ocean City MSA, NJ	Y	34240 FQ	39630 MW	47810 TQ	USBLS	5/07
	New Mexico	Y	23200 FQ	30150 MW	38940 TQ	USBLS	5/07
	Albuquerque MSA, NM	Y	24680 FQ	32010 MW	43350 TQ	USBLS	5/07
	Las Cruces MSA, NM	Y	23810 FQ	30400 MW	37280 TQ	USBLS	5/07
	New York	Y	35940 FQ	44760 MW	57060 TQ	USBLS	5/07
	Albany-Schenectady-Troy MSA, NY	Y	34020 FQ	42320 MW	52770 TQ	USBLS	5/07
	Buffalo-Niagara Falls MSA, NY	Y	34280 FQ	46770 MW	59540 TQ	USBLS	5/07
	Nassau-Suffolk PMSA, NY	Y	41610 FQ	49950 MW	70660 TQ	USBLS	5/07
	New York-Northern New Jersey-Long Island MSA, NY-NJ-PA	Y	37550 FQ	47280 MW	62610 TQ	USBLS	5/07
	North Carolina	Y	33640 FQ	39360 MW	47270 TQ	USBLS	5/07
	Asheville MSA, NC	Y	32770 FQ	37130 MW	43220 TQ	USBLS	5/07
	Charlotte-Gastonia-Concord MSA, NC-SC	Y	33620 FQ	41250 MW	48750 TQ	USBLS	5/07
	Raleigh-Cary MSA, NC	Y	32530 FQ	42510 MW	55050 TQ	USBLS	5/07
	North Dakota	Y	31260 FQ	37450 MW	44580 TQ	USBLS	5/07
	Fargo MSA, ND-MN	Y	36420 FQ	42570 MW	50810 TQ	USBLS	5/07
	Ohio	Y	27370 FQ	33600 MW	40810 TQ	USBLS	5/07
	Cincinnati-Middletown MSA, OH-KY-IN	Y	27800 FQ	33670 MW	39560 TQ	USBLS	5/07
	Cleveland-Elyria-Mentor MSA, OH	Y	28290 FQ	35070 MW	41720 TQ	USBLS	5/07
	Columbus MSA, OH	Y	31060 FQ	37350 MW	44570 TQ	USBLS	5/07
	Dayton MSA, OH	Y	34510 FQ	41360 MW	50000 TQ	USBLS	5/07
	Oklahoma	Y	24340 FQ	29490 MW	35480 TQ	USBLS	5/07
	Oklahoma City MSA, OK	Y	23220 FQ	28440 MW	34070 TQ	USBLS	5/07
	Tulsa MSA, OK	Y	24320 FQ	30820 MW	35990 TQ	USBLS	5/07
	Oregon	H	14.84 FQ	18.03 MW	21.92 TQ	ORBLS	5/08

AE	Average entry wage	AW	Average wage paid	FQ	First quartile wage
AER	Average entry range	AWR	Average wage range	H	Hourly
AEX	Average experienced wage	AXR	Average experienced range	HI	Highest wage paid
ATC	Average total compensation	D	Daily	HR	High end range

LO	Lowest wage paid	MTC	Median total compensation	TCC	Total cash compensation
LR	Low end range	MW	Median wage paid	TQ	Third quartile wage
M	Monthly	MWR	Median wage range	W	Weekly
MCC	Median cash compensation	S	See annotated source	Y	Yearly

Occupation/Type/Industry	Location	Per	Low	Mid	High	Source	Date
Child, Family, and School Social Worker	Portland-Vancouver-Beaverton MSA, OR-WA	Y	31410 FQ	37100 MW	45020 TQ	USBLS	5/07
	Pennsylvania	Y	25830 FQ	30730 MW	38390 TQ	USBLS	5/07
	Allentown-Bethlehem-Easton MSA, PA-NJ	Y	27010 FQ	31820 MW	42680 TQ	USBLS	5/07
	Lancaster MSA, PA	Y	23110 FQ	27150 MW	31410 TQ	USBLS	5/07
	Philadelphia-Camden-Wilmington MSA, PA-NJ-DE-MD	Y	28770 FQ	35700 MW	46850 TQ	USBLS	5/07
	Pittsburgh MSA, PA	Y	26210 FQ	30560 MW	38290 TQ	USBLS	5/07
	Rhode Island	Y	37810 FQ	50280 MW	61980 TQ	USBLS	5/07
	Providence-Fall River-Warwick MSA, RI-MA	Y	39350 FQ	51270 MW	61830 TQ	USBLS	5/07
	South Carolina	Y	26820 FQ	30680 MW	36460 TQ	USBLS	5/07
	Charleston-North Charleston MSA, SC	Y	27360 FQ	31660 MW	38440 TQ	USBLS	5/07
	Columbia MSA, SC	Y	27750 FQ	31910 MW	37880 TQ	USBLS	5/07
	Florence MSA, SC	Y	26020 FQ	30750 MW	36020 TQ	USBLS	5/07
	South Dakota	Y	28960 FQ	33808 MW	39575 TQ	SDBLS	7/08-9/08
	Sioux Falls MSA, SD	Y	29705 FQ	35666 MW	40465 TQ	SDBLS	7/08-9/08
	Tennessee	Y	27020 FQ	34060 MW	38350 TQ	USBLS	5/07
	Memphis MSA, TN-MS-AR	Y	24300 FQ	33530 MW	38700 TQ	USBLS	5/07
	Nashville-Davidson-Murfreesboro MSA, TN	Y	30190 FQ	34830 MW	38550 TQ	USBLS	5/07
	Texas	Y	27700 FQ	31610 MW	38770 TQ	USBLS	5/07
	Austin-Round Rock MSA, TX	Y	28210 FQ	31940 MW	38450 TQ	USBLS	5/07
	Dallas-Fort Worth-Arlington MSA, TX	Y	28970 FQ	33690 MW	42120 TQ	USBLS	5/07
	El Paso MSA, TX	Y	26270 FQ	29420 MW	35260 TQ	USBLS	5/07
	Houston-Sugar Land-Baytown MSA, TX	Y	26960 FQ	32130 MW	38760 TQ	USBLS	5/07
	San Antonio MSA, TX	Y	27940 FQ	31160 MW	37680 TQ	USBLS	5/07
	Utah	Y	28070 FQ	32060 MW	39480 TQ	USBLS	5/07
	St. George MSA, UT	Y	24390 FQ	30930 MW	37910 TQ	USBLS	5/07
	Salt Lake City MSA, UT	Y	28710 FQ	32890 MW	40020 TQ	USBLS	5/07
	Vermont	Y	30430 FQ	37550 MW	47930 TQ	USBLS	5/07
	Burlington-South Burlington MSA, VT	Y	27590 FQ	34570 MW	44500 TQ	USBLS	5/07
	Virginia	Y	31060 FQ	40070 MW	52140 TQ	USBLS	5/07
	Charlottesville MSA, VA	Y	34170 FQ	41600 MW	48750 TQ	USBLS	5/07
	Richmond MSA, VA	Y	36620 FQ	45460 MW	54570 TQ	USBLS	5/07
	Virginia Beach-Norfolk-Newport News MSA, VA-NC	Y	33110 FQ	40190 MW	49500 TQ	USBLS	5/07
	Washington	H	18.13 FQ	21.81 MW	24.61 TQ	WABLS	3/08
	Seattle-Tacoma-Bellevue MSA, WA	Y	37040 FQ	44320 MW	50290 TQ	USBLS	5/07
	West Virginia	Y	24589 FQ	29037 MW	33173 TQ	WVBLS	7/08-9/08
	Charleston MSA, WV	Y	23280 FQ	27180 MW	31030 TQ	USBLS	5/07
	Wisconsin	Y	37440 FQ	46230 MW	55940 TQ	USBLS	5/07
	Appleton MSA, WI	Y	43050 FQ	50880 MW	56690 TQ	USBLS	5/07
	Milwaukee-Waukesha-West Allis MSA, WI	Y	35850 FQ	44300 MW	57730 TQ	USBLS	5/07
	Wyoming	Y	30291 FQ	37776 MW	45162 TQ	WYBLS	9/08
	Cheyenne MSA, WY	Y	39117 FQ	47261 MW	58634 TQ	WYBLS	9/08
	San Juan-Caguas-Guaynabo MSA, PR	Y	25840 FQ	30060 MW	34810 TQ	USBLS	5/07
	Virgin Islands	Y	34390 FQ	39500 MW	45610 TQ	USBLS	5/07
Child Care Worker	Alabama	Y	13010 FQ	14830 MW	17600 TQ	USBLS	5/07
	Birmingham-Hoover MSA, AL	Y	13620 FQ	15980 MW	18710 TQ	USBLS	5/07
	Huntsville MSA, AL	Y	12850 FQ	14510 MW	16700 TQ	USBLS	5/07
	Alaska	Y	18000 FQ	21440 MW	26960 TQ	USBLS	5/07
	Anchorage MSA, AK	Y	18080 FQ	21170 MW	26150 TQ	USBLS	5/07
	Arizona	Y	15200 FQ	17170 MW	20200 TQ	USBLS	5/07
	Flagstaff MSA, AZ	Y	15190 FQ	17470 MW	20650 TQ	USBLS	5/07
	Phoenix-Mesa-Scottsdale MSA, AZ	Y	15150 FQ	17070 MW	20350 TQ	USBLS	5/07
	Tucson MSA, AZ	Y	15810 FQ	17990 MW	20370 TQ	USBLS	5/07
	Yuma MSA, AZ	Y	14830 FQ	15620 MW	17410 TQ	USBLS	5/07
	Arkansas	Y	14240 FQ	15280 MW	17100 TQ	USBLS	5/07
	Jonesboro MSA, AR	Y	14140 FQ	15010 MW	16180 TQ	USBLS	5/07

AE	Average entry wage	AW	Average wage paid	FQ	First quartile wage	LO	Lowest wage paid	MTC	Median total compensation	TCC	Total cash compensation
AER	Average entry range	AWR	Average wage range	H	Hourly	LR	Low end range	MW	Median wage paid	TQ	Third quartile wage
AEX	Average experienced wage	AXR	Average experienced range	HI	Highest wage paid	M	Monthly	MWR	Median wage range	W	Weekly
ATC	Average total compensation	D	Daily	HR	High end range	MCC	Median cash compensation	S	See annotated source	Y	Yearly

Child Care Worker

Occupation/Type/Industry	Location	Per	Low	Mid	High	Source	Date
Child Care Worker	Little Rock-North Little Rock MSA, AR	Y	14190 FQ	15160 MW	16630 TQ	USBLS	5/07
	California	H	8.75 FQ	10.34 MW	12.56 TQ	CABLS	1/08-3/08
	Los Angeles-Long Beach-Glendale PMSA, CA	H	8.64 FQ	9.88 MW	12.01 TQ	CABLS	1/08-3/08
	Oakland-Fremont-Hayward MSA, CA	H	8.91 FQ	10.61 MW	13.25 TQ	CABLS	1/08-3/08
	Riverside-San Bernardino-Ontario MSA, CA	H	8.33 FQ	9.74 MW	11.85 TQ	CABLS	1/08-3/08
	Sacramento-Arden Arcade-Roseville MSA, CA	H	9.03 FQ	10.54 MW	12.19 TQ	CABLS	1/08-3/08
	San Diego-Carlsbad-San Marcos MSA, CA	H	9.07 FQ	10.47 MW	11.91 TQ	CABLS	1/08-3/08
	San Francisco-San Mateo-Redwood PMSA, CA	H	10.86 FQ	12.88 MW	14.97 TQ	CABLS	1/08-3/08
	San Jose-Sunnyvale-Santa Clara MSA, CA	H	8.89 FQ	11.34 MW	13.86 TQ	CABLS	1/08-3/08
	Santa Ana-Anaheim-Irvine PMSA, CA	Y	17630 FQ	21330 MW	27620 TQ	USBLS	5/07
	Colorado	Y	16990 FQ	20220 MW	24400 TQ	USBLS	5/07
	Denver-Aurora MSA, CO	Y	17530 FQ	20810 MW	24920 TQ	USBLS	5/07
	Connecticut	H	8.67 AE	10.18 MW		CTBLS	1/08-3/08
	Bridgeport-Stamford-Norwalk MSA, CT	Y	18490 FQ	21200 MW	24980 TQ	USBLS	5/07
	Hartford-West Hartford-East Hartford MSA, CT	Y	17880 FQ	20630 MW	26590 TQ	USBLS	5/07
	Delaware	Y	15930 FQ	18820 MW	23200 TQ	USBLS	5/07
	Wilmington PMSA, DE-MD-NJ	Y	16570 FQ	19700 MW	23190 TQ	USBLS	5/07
	District of Columbia	Y	21940 FQ	23760 MW	25640 TQ	USBLS	5/07
	Washington-Arlington-Alexandria MSA, DC-VA-MD-WV	Y	17130 FQ	21150 MW	25370 TQ	USBLS	5/07
	Florida	Y	15550 FQ	17740 MW	20380 TQ	USBLS	5/07
	Fort Lauderdale-Pompano Beach-Deerfield Beach PMSA, FL	Y	16270 FQ	18170 MW	21150 TQ	USBLS	5/07
	Jacksonville MSA, FL	Y	15640 FQ	18280 MW	21770 TQ	USBLS	5/07
	Miami-Fort Lauderdale-Miami Beach MSA, FL	Y	15370 FQ	17250 MW	19780 TQ	USBLS	5/07
	Orlando-Kissimmee MSA, FL	Y	15940 FQ	18090 MW	20660 TQ	USBLS	5/07
	Tampa-St. Petersburg-Clearwater MSA, FL	Y	15750 FQ	18070 MW	20810 TQ	USBLS	5/07
	West Palm Beach-Boca Raton-Boynton Beach PMSA, FL	Y	14980 FQ	16880 MW	19650 TQ	USBLS	5/07
	Georgia	Y	13320 FQ	15550 MW	18740 TQ	USBLS	5/07
	Atlanta-Sandy Springs-Marietta MSA, GA	Y	14460 FQ	17090 MW	19880 TQ	USBLS	5/07
	Savannah MSA, GA	Y	12520 FQ	14010 MW	15670 TQ	USBLS	5/07
	Hawaii	Y	15740 FQ	17210 MW	19460 TQ	USBLS	5/07
	Honolulu MSA, HI	Y	16180 FQ	18080 MW	20100 TQ	USBLS	5/07
	Idaho	Y	14510 FQ	17050 MW	19320 TQ	USBLS	5/07
	Boise City-Nampa MSA, ID	Y	15230 FQ	17470 MW	19540 TQ	USBLS	5/07
	Illinois	Y	16130 FQ	19150 MW	23820 TQ	USBLS	5/07
	Chicago-Naperville-Joliet MSA, IL-IN-WI	Y	16500 FQ	19960 MW	24730 TQ	USBLS	5/07
	Indiana	Y	14470 FQ	17520 MW	21070 TQ	USBLS	5/07
	Elkhart-Goshen MSA, IN	Y	15730 FQ	19760 MW	23200 TQ	USBLS	5/07
	Fort Wayne MSA, IN	Y	14420 FQ	17020 MW	19470 TQ	USBLS	5/07
	Gary PMSA, IN	Y	14170 FQ	17480 MW	21350 TQ	USBLS	5/07
	Indianapolis-Carmel MSA, IN	Y	16060 FQ	18970 MW	22790 TQ	USBLS	5/07
	Iowa	Y	14290 FQ	15920 MW	18850 TQ	USBLS	5/07
	Des Moines-West Des Moines MSA, IA	Y	15250 FQ	18090 MW	21420 TQ	USBLS	5/07
	Iowa City MSA, IA	Y	14510 FQ	16220 MW	18610 TQ	USBLS	5/07
	Kansas	Y	14400 FQ	16870 MW	19400 TQ	USBLS	5/07
	Topeka MSA, KS	Y	13660 FQ	16530 MW	19260 TQ	USBLS	5/07
	Wichita MSA, KS	Y	13900 FQ	16180 MW	18660 TQ	USBLS	5/07
	Kentucky	Y	13825 FQ	16244 MW	19975 TQ	KYBLS	2008
	Louisville-Jefferson County MSA, KY-IN	Y	13860 FQ	16420 MW	20770 TQ	USBLS	5/07
	Louisiana	H	6.25 FQ	7.11 MW	8.54 TQ	LABLS	1/08-3/08

AE Average entry wage	**AW** Average wage paid	**FQ** First quartile wage	**LO** Lowest wage paid	**MTC** Median total compensation	**TCC** Total cash compensation
AER Average entry range	**AWR** Average wage range	**H** Hourly	**LR** Low end range	**MW** Median wage paid	**TQ** Third quartile wage
AEX Average experienced wage	**AXR** Average experienced range	**HI** Highest wage paid	**M** Monthly	**MWR** Median wage range	**W** Weekly
ATC Average total compensation	**D** Daily	**HR** High end range	**MCC** Median cash compensation	**S** See annotated source	**Y** Yearly

Child Care Worker

Occupation/Type/Industry	Location	Per	Low	Mid	High	Source	Date
Child Care Worker	Baton Rouge MSA, LA	Y	13530 FQ	16120 MW	20790 TQ	USBLS	5/07
	Houma-Bayou Cane-Thibodaux MSA, LA	Y	13070 FQ	15060 MW	17600 TQ	USBLS	5/07
	Lake Charles MSA, LA	Y	12770 FQ	14300 MW	16140 TQ	USBLS	5/07
	New Orleans-Metairie-Kenner MSA, LA	Y	12990 FQ	14640 MW	17470 TQ	USBLS	5/07
	Maine	Y	18050 FQ	21510 MW	24650 TQ	USBLS	5/07
	Portland-South Portland-Biddeford MSA, ME	Y	20550 FQ	22750 MW	25100 TQ	USBLS	5/07
	Maryland	Y		20650 MW		MDBLS	3/08
	Baltimore-Towson MSA, MD	Y	16480 FQ	20200 MW	23090 TQ	USBLS	5/07
	Bethesda-Gaithersburg-Frederick PMSA, MD	Y	17530 FQ	22520 MW	28220 TQ	USBLS	5/07
	Hagerstown-Martinsburg MSA, MD-WV	Y	16820 FQ	19560 MW	23700 TQ	USBLS	5/07
	Salisbury MSA, MD	Y	14250 FQ	15340 MW	18100 TQ	USBLS	5/07
	Massachusetts	Y	18090 FQ	21440 MW	26050 TQ	USBLS	5/07
	Boston-Cambridge-Quincy NECTA, MA	Y	18380 FQ	22800 MW	27930 TQ	USBLS	5/07
	Worcester MSA, MA-CT	Y	19620 FQ	23200 MW	27410 TQ	USBLS	5/07
	Michigan	Y	16340 FQ	19510 MW	23580 TQ	USBLS	5/07
	Detroit-Warren-Livonia MSA, MI	Y	16860 FQ	19880 MW	23670 TQ	USBLS	5/07
	Grand Rapids-Wyoming MSA, MI	Y	17220 FQ	19640 MW	24210 TQ	USBLS	5/07
	Lansing-East Lansing MSA, MI	Y	15880 FQ	18420 MW	22770 TQ	USBLS	5/07
	Warren-Troy-Farmington Hills PMSA, MI	Y	16170 FQ	18990 MW	23630 TQ	USBLS	5/07
	Minnesota	Y	16614 FQ	19102 MW	23170 TQ	MNBLS	10/08-12/08
	Duluth-Superior MSA, MN-WI	Y	15077 FQ	16018 MW	17628 TQ	MNBLS	10/08-12/08
	Minneapolis-Saint Paul MSA, MN-WI	Y	17639 FQ	20158 MW	24351 TQ	MNBLS	10/08-12/08
	Rochester MSA, MN	Y	15039 FQ	16326 MW	19374 TQ	MNBLS	10/08-12/08
	Mississippi	Y	12870 FQ	14590 MW	17110 TQ	USBLS	5/07
	Jackson MSA, MS	Y	12980 FQ	14840 MW	17350 TQ	USBLS	5/07
	Missouri	Y	14940 FQ	17080 MW	20530 TQ	USBLS	5/07
	Kansas City MSA, MO-KS	Y	16200 FQ	18410 MW	21880 TQ	USBLS	5/07
	St. Louis MSA, MO-IL	Y	15130 FQ	17640 MW	21500 TQ	USBLS	5/07
	Montana	Y	14280 FQ	16190 MW	19000 TQ	USBLS	5/07
	Billings MSA, MT	Y	14010 FQ	15280 MW	17770 TQ	USBLS	5/07
	Nebraska	Y	14110 FQ	16900 MW	19770 TQ	USBLS	5/07
	Omaha-Council Bluffs MSA, NE-IA	Y	15230 FQ	17560 MW	20240 TQ	USBLS	5/07
	Carson City MSA, NV	H	6.72 FQ	7.99 MW	9.28 TQ	NVBLS	5/08
	Las Vegas-Paradise MSA, NV	H	6.90 FQ	8.19 MW	9.38 TQ	NVBLS	5/08
	New Hampshire	H	7.51 AE	9.33 MW	10.55 AEX	NHBLS	6/08
	Manchester MSA, NH	Y	15930 FQ	18780 MW	21830 TQ	USBLS	5/07
	Nashua NECTA, NH-MA	Y	15880 FQ	17860 MW	20590 TQ	USBLS	5/07
	New Jersey	Y	16770 FQ	20160 MW	24290 TQ	USBLS	5/07
	Camden PMSA, NJ	Y	15940 FQ	18020 MW	21720 TQ	USBLS	5/07
	Edison PMSA, NJ	Y	16650 FQ	19230 MW	23300 TQ	USBLS	5/07
	Newark-Union PMSA, NJ-PA	Y	17320 FQ	21250 MW	24730 TQ	USBLS	5/07
	New Mexico	Y	13360 FQ	15780 MW	19220 TQ	USBLS	5/07
	Albuquerque MSA, NM	Y	13590 FQ	16460 MW	18810 TQ	USBLS	5/07
	New York	Y	17510 FQ	22330 MW	27640 TQ	USBLS	5/07
	Albany-Schenectady-Troy MSA, NY	Y	16260 FQ	19810 MW	24670 TQ	USBLS	5/07
	Buffalo-Niagara Falls MSA, NY	Y	15630 FQ	17020 MW	19810 TQ	USBLS	5/07
	Glens Falls MSA, NY	Y	15130 FQ	17360 MW	21780 TQ	USBLS	5/07
	Kingston MSA, NY	Y	17620 FQ	21310 MW	23820 TQ	USBLS	5/07
	Nassau-Suffolk PMSA, NY	Y	18730 FQ	22370 MW	26220 TQ	USBLS	5/07
	New York-Northern New Jersey-Long Island MSA, NY-NJ-PA	Y	18670 FQ	23070 MW	27990 TQ	USBLS	5/07
	North Carolina	Y	15050 FQ	17890 MW	22070 TQ	USBLS	5/07
	Charlotte-Gastonia-Concord MSA, NC-SC	Y	15710 FQ	18470 MW	22020 TQ	USBLS	5/07
	Raleigh-Cary MSA, NC	Y	15450 FQ	20550 MW	26270 TQ	USBLS	5/07
	North Dakota	Y	13290 FQ	15510 MW	18860 TQ	USBLS	5/07
	Fargo MSA, ND-MN	Y	13480 FQ	15740 MW	18910 TQ	USBLS	5/07
	Ohio	Y	15610 FQ	19200 MW	24200 TQ	USBLS	5/07

Occupation/Type/Industry	Location	Per	Low	Mid	High	Source	Date
Child Care Worker	Cincinnati-Middletown MSA, OH-KY-IN	Y	15280 FQ	18330 MW	23090 TQ	USBLS	5/07
	Cleveland-Elyria-Mentor MSA, OH	Y	16940 FQ	20770 MW	26390 TQ	USBLS	5/07
	Columbus MSA, OH	Y	16010 FQ	19360 MW	23040 TQ	USBLS	5/07
	Dayton MSA, OH	Y	14930 FQ	16330 MW	22010 TQ	USBLS	5/07
	Oklahoma	Y	13630 FQ	15790 MW	17900 TQ	USBLS	5/07
	Oklahoma City MSA, OK	Y	12990 FQ	14870 MW	18100 TQ	USBLS	5/07
	Tulsa MSA, OK	Y	13250 FQ	15390 MW	18930 TQ	USBLS	5/07
	Oregon	H	8.64 FQ	9.33 MW	10.86 TQ	ORBLS	5/08
	Portland-Vancouver-Beaverton MSA, OR-WA	Y	17770 FQ	19500 MW	22730 TQ	USBLS	5/07
	Pennsylvania	Y	15350 FQ	17950 MW	21880 TQ	USBLS	5/07
	Allentown-Bethlehem-Easton MSA, PA-NJ	Y	14800 FQ	17090 MW	21890 TQ	USBLS	5/07
	Lancaster MSA, PA	Y	16210 FQ	18710 MW	22190 TQ	USBLS	5/07
	Philadelphia-Camden-Wilmington MSA, PA-NJ-DE-MD	Y	16140 FQ	18670 MW	22620 TQ	USBLS	5/07
	Pittsburgh MSA, PA	Y	14990 FQ	17030 MW	21010 TQ	USBLS	5/07
	York-Hanover MSA, PA	Y	15830 FQ	18160 MW	21460 TQ	USBLS	5/07
	Rhode Island	Y	17870 FQ	20480 MW	24060 TQ	USBLS	5/07
	Providence-Fall River-Warwick MSA, RI-MA	Y	17740 FQ	20240 MW	23690 TQ	USBLS	5/07
	South Carolina	Y	13400 FQ	15700 MW	18540 TQ	USBLS	5/07
	Charleston-North Charleston MSA, SC	Y	14440 FQ	17110 MW	19280 TQ	USBLS	5/07
	Columbia MSA, SC	Y	14170 FQ	16660 MW	19030 TQ	USBLS	5/07
	South Dakota	Y	15151 FQ	17705 MW	20326 TQ	SDBLS	7/08-9/08
	Sioux Falls MSA, SD	Y	15509 FQ	18864 MW	22124 TQ	SDBLS	7/08-9/08
	Tennessee	Y	13450 FQ	15760 MW	18440 TQ	USBLS	5/07
	Kingsport-Bristol-Bristol MSA, TN-VA	Y	12990 FQ	14770 MW	18110 TQ	USBLS	5/07
	Memphis MSA, TN-MS-AR	Y	13040 FQ	14730 MW	17200 TQ	USBLS	5/07
	Nashville-Davidson-Murfreesboro MSA, TN	Y	14370 FQ	17110 MW	19550 TQ	USBLS	5/07
	Texas	Y	13290 FQ	15470 MW	18470 TQ	USBLS	5/07
	Austin-Round Rock MSA, TX	Y	16640 FQ	19850 MW	22590 TQ	USBLS	5/07
	Dallas-Fort Worth-Arlington MSA, TX	Y	13890 FQ	16570 MW	18960 TQ	USBLS	5/07
	El Paso MSA, TX	Y	12810 FQ	14400 MW	16760 TQ	USBLS	5/07
	Houston-Sugar Land-Baytown MSA, TX	Y	13270 FQ	15340 MW	17870 TQ	USBLS	5/07
	San Antonio MSA, TX	Y	13820 FQ	16050 MW	18270 TQ	USBLS	5/07
	Utah	Y	14130 FQ	16600 MW	18850 TQ	USBLS	5/07
	Salt Lake City MSA, UT	Y	14480 FQ	16680 MW	18700 TQ	USBLS	5/07
	Vermont	Y	16720 FQ	18720 MW	21890 TQ	USBLS	5/07
	Burlington-South Burlington MSA, VT	Y	16720 FQ	18650 MW	21810 TQ	USBLS	5/07
	Virginia	Y	14800 FQ	17800 MW	21630 TQ	USBLS	5/07
	Richmond MSA, VA	Y	13930 FQ	16840 MW	20110 TQ	USBLS	5/07
	Virginia Beach-Norfolk-Newport News MSA, VA-NC	Y	14550 FQ	17470 MW	20340 TQ	USBLS	5/07
	Washington	H	8.77 FQ	9.61 MW	11.30 TQ	WABLS	3/08
	Seattle-Tacoma-Bellevue MSA, WA	Y	18390 FQ	20740 MW	24310 TQ	USBLS	5/07
	West Virginia	Y	14055 FQ	15175 MW	16490 TQ	WVBLS	7/08-9/08
	Charleston MSA, WV	Y	13610 FQ	14800 MW	16130 TQ	USBLS	5/07
	Wisconsin	Y	17150 FQ	20750 MW	26900 TQ	USBLS	5/07
	Milwaukee-Waukesha-West Allis MSA, WI	Y	18560 FQ	23960 MW	33760 TQ	USBLS	5/07
	Wyoming	Y	14315 FQ	17780 MW	22972 TQ	WYBLS	9/08
	Cheyenne MSA, WY	Y	13678 FQ	15713 MW	18398 TQ	WYBLS	9/08
	Puerto Rico	Y	12590 FQ	14020 MW	15580 TQ	USBLS	5/07
	San Juan-Caguas-Guaynabo MSA, PR	Y	12520 FQ	13870 MW	15310 TQ	USBLS	5/07
	Virgin Islands	Y	14640 FQ	17820 MW	31240 TQ	USBLS	5/07
Child Nutrition Assistant Public Schools	North Carolina	M	1835-1853 LR		2491-2943 HR	NCSS	2008-2009

AE	Average entry wage	AW	Average wage paid	FQ	First quartile wage	LO	Lowest wage paid	MTC Median total compensation	TCC Total cash compensation
AER	Average entry range	AWR	Average wage range	H	Hourly	LR	Low end range	MW Median wage paid	TQ Third quartile wage
AEX	Average experienced wage	AXR	Average experienced range	HI	Highest wage paid	M	Monthly	MWR Median wage range	W Weekly
ATC	Average total compensation	D	Daily	HR	High end range	MCC	Median cash compensation	S See annotated source	Y Yearly

Occupation/Type/Industry	Location	Per	Low	Mid	High	Source	Date
Child Nutrition Dietetic Supervisor							
Public Schools	Baldwin County, AL	Y	47636 LO		54424 HI	BCPSSS	2008-2009
Child Support Officer							
Department of Health and Human Services	New Hampshire	Y		39042 AW		NHUL03	2008
Child Welfare Services Deputy Director							
State Supreme Court	Michigan	Y			83812 HI	LSJ02	7/11/07
Children and Family Benefits Liason							
Public Schools	Chicago, IL	H			15.14 HI	CPSSS	7/1/06
Children's Home Superintendent							
State Government	Ohio	H	24.01 LO		54.04 HI	ODAS	2008
Children's Librarian	Deerfield, MA	H			13.94 HI	FRCOG	2009
	Montague, MA	Y			40833 HI	FRCOG	2009
Children's Services Assistant							
Library	Sunderland, MA	H			12.08 HI	FRCOG	2009
Chiropractic Board Enforcement Investigator							
State Government	Ohio	H	21.77 LO		31.86 HI	ODAS	2008
Chiropractor	United States	Y		136410 ATC		CHIRO	2008
	Alabama	Y	85030 FQ	111610 MW		USBLS	5/07
	Birmingham-Hoover MSA, AL	Y	91840 FQ	100480 MW		USBLS	5/07
	Alaska	Y	70730 FQ	83220 MW	102690 TQ	USBLS	5/07
	Arizona	Y	36670 FQ	53300 MW	86150 TQ	USBLS	5/07
	Phoenix-Mesa-Scottsdale MSA, AZ	Y	37090 FQ	53550 MW	89300 TQ	USBLS	5/07
	Tucson MSA, AZ	Y	34760 FQ	37270 MW	40080 TQ	USBLS	5/07
	Arkansas	Y	74110 FQ	90960 MW	118090 TQ	USBLS	5/07
	Little Rock-North Little Rock MSA, AR	Y	111770 FQ	124810 MW		USBLS	5/07
	California	H	22.07 FQ	27.67 MW	39.78 TQ	CABLS	1/08-3/08
	Los Angeles-Long Beach-Glendale PMSA, CA	H	19.21 FQ	23.50 MW	32.18 TQ	CABLS	1/08-3/08
	Riverside-San Bernardino-Ontario MSA, CA	H	24.42 FQ	28.35 MW	41.30 TQ	CABLS	1/08-3/08
	Sacramento-Arden Arcade-Roseville MSA, CA	H	18.31 FQ	22.55 MW	24.93 TQ	CABLS	1/08-3/08
	San Diego-Carlsbad-San Marcos MSA, CA	H	16.22 FQ	24.87 MW	41.71 TQ	CABLS	1/08-3/08
	San Jose-Sunnyvale-Santa Clara MSA, CA	H	26.24 FQ	32.09 MW	39.74 TQ	CABLS	1/08-3/08
	Santa Ana-Anaheim-Irvine PMSA, CA	Y	55960 FQ	63430 MW	97140 TQ	USBLS	5/07
	Colorado	Y	40620 FQ	48250 MW	75840 TQ	USBLS	5/07
	Connecticut	H	24.59 AE	39.56 MW		CTBLS	1/08-3/08
	Bridgeport-Stamford-Norwalk MSA, CT	Y	45900 FQ	67360 MW	84360 TQ	USBLS	5/07
	Delaware	Y	59310 FQ	66080 MW	90960 TQ	USBLS	5/07
	Wilmington PMSA, DE-MD-NJ	Y	59040 FQ	66240 MW	102370 TQ	USBLS	5/07
	Washington-Arlington-Alexandria MSA, DC-VA-MD-WV	Y	42750 FQ	72020 MW		USBLS	5/07
	Florida	Y	42980 FQ	58560 MW	96710 TQ	USBLS	5/07
	Fort Lauderdale-Pompano Beach-Deerfield Beach PMSA, FL	Y	44990 FQ	52310 MW	87660 TQ	USBLS	5/07
	Jacksonville MSA, FL	Y	30870 FQ	44100 MW	65400 TQ	USBLS	5/07
	Miami-Fort Lauderdale-Miami Beach MSA, FL	Y	43180 FQ	51820 MW	81730 TQ	USBLS	5/07
	Orlando-Kissimmee MSA, FL	Y	37710 FQ	108830 MW	122960 TQ	USBLS	5/07

AE	Average entry wage	AW	Average wage paid	FQ	First quartile wage
AER	Average entry range	AWR	Average wage range	H	Hourly
AEX	Average experienced wage	AXR	Average experienced range	HI	Highest wage paid
ATC	Average total compensation	D	Daily	HR	High end range

LO	Lowest wage paid	MTC	Median total compensation	TCC	Total cash compensation
LR	Low end range	MW	Median wage paid	TQ	Third quartile wage
M	Monthly	MWR	Median wage range	W	Weekly
MCC	Median cash compensation	S	See annotated source	Y	Yearly

Occupation/Type/Industry	Location	Per	Low	Mid	High	Source	Date
Chiropractor	Tampa-St. Petersburg-Clearwater MSA, FL	Y	52080 FQ	68920 MW	93620 TQ	USBLS	5/07
	West Palm Beach-Boca Raton-Boynton Beach PMSA, FL	Y	67580 FQ	77170 MW	119970 TQ	USBLS	5/07
	Georgia	Y	26090 FQ	47200 MW	64770 TQ	USBLS	5/07
	Atlanta-Sandy Springs-Marietta MSA, GA	Y	25040 FQ	45100 MW	61660 TQ	USBLS	5/07
	Hawaii	Y	35590 FQ	38540 MW	45890 TQ	USBLS	5/07
	Honolulu MSA, HI	Y	34930 FQ	37210 MW	39490 TQ	USBLS	5/07
	Idaho	Y	37130 FQ	50800 MW	83230 TQ	USBLS	5/07
	Illinois	Y	47590 FQ	77730 MW	106720 TQ	USBLS	5/07
	Chicago-Naperville-Joliet MSA, IL-IN-WI	Y	52290 FQ	79790 MW	137370 TQ	USBLS	5/07
	Indiana	Y	50650 FQ	77280 MW	100730 TQ	USBLS	5/07
	Gary PMSA, IN	Y	51180 FQ	59580 MW	93430 TQ	USBLS	5/07
	Indianapolis-Carmel MSA, IN	Y	86120 FQ	95240 MW	103860 TQ	USBLS	5/07
	Iowa	Y	25770 FQ	58210 MW	100930 TQ	USBLS	5/07
	Davenport-Moline-Rock Island MSA, IA-IL	Y	24410 FQ	62310 MW	86790 TQ	USBLS	5/07
	Kansas	Y	38180 FQ	61010 MW	115490 TQ	USBLS	5/07
	Wichita MSA, KS	Y	36670 FQ	40550 MW	101410 TQ	USBLS	5/07
	Kentucky	Y	71903 FQ	99946 MW	126076 TQ	KYBLS	2008
	Louisville-Jefferson County MSA, KY-IN	Y	58500 FQ	89700 MW	142540 TQ	USBLS	5/07
	Louisiana	H	17.82 FQ	25.23 MW	38.26 TQ	LABLS	1/08-3/08
	New Orleans-Metairie-Kenner MSA, LA	Y	35500 FQ	38540 MW	41700 TQ	USBLS	5/07
	Maine	Y	45570 FQ	64160 MW	84270 TQ	USBLS	5/07
	Portland-South Portland-Biddeford MSA, ME	Y	73130 FQ	82150 MW	97500 TQ	USBLS	5/07
	Maryland	Y		79275 MW		MDBLS	3/08
	Baltimore-Towson MSA, MD	Y	55900 FQ	62760 MW	79200 TQ	USBLS	5/07
	Bethesda-Gaithersburg-Frederick PMSA, MD	Y	63910 FQ			USBLS	5/07
	Massachusetts	Y	54020 FQ	79330 MW	96960 TQ	USBLS	5/07
	Boston-Cambridge-Quincy NECTA, MA	Y	56170 FQ	80370 MW	96700 TQ	USBLS	5/07
	New Bedford MSA, MA	Y	44400 FQ	50610 MW	62050 TQ	USBLS	5/07
	Worcester MSA, MA-CT	Y	77180 FQ	99870 MW	111880 TQ	USBLS	5/07
	Michigan	Y	53400 FQ	63600 MW	89250 TQ	USBLS	5/07
	Detroit-Warren-Livonia MSA, MI	Y	53980 FQ	63290 MW	81460 TQ	USBLS	5/07
	Grand Rapids-Wyoming MSA, MI	Y	91380 FQ	104560 MW	122940 TQ	USBLS	5/07
	Warren-Troy-Farmington Hills PMSA, MI	Y	52300 FQ	62030 MW	74450 TQ	USBLS	5/07
	Minnesota	Y	48796 FQ	78602 MW	91931 TQ	MNBLS	10/08-12/08
	Duluth-Superior MSA, MN-WI	Y	61957 FQ	78582 MW	90707 TQ	MNBLS	10/08-12/08
	Minneapolis-Saint Paul MSA, MN-WI	Y	51966 FQ	79994 MW	90080 TQ	MNBLS	10/08-12/08
	Mississippi	Y	39590 FQ	58620 MW	87180 TQ	USBLS	5/07
	Missouri	Y	43970 FQ	70220 MW	96160 TQ	USBLS	5/07
	Kansas City MSA, MO-KS	Y	42690 FQ	110890 MW	133300 TQ	USBLS	5/07
	St. Louis MSA, MO-IL	Y	47350 FQ	70480 MW	82950 TQ	USBLS	5/07
	Montana	Y	20510 FQ	39180 MW	50600 TQ	USBLS	5/07
	Billings MSA, MT	Y	29560 FQ	51420 MW	57840 TQ	USBLS	5/07
	Nebraska	Y	45360 FQ	106990 MW	135850 TQ	USBLS	5/07
	Omaha-Council Bluffs MSA, NE-IA	Y	46760 FQ	102640 MW	136390 TQ	USBLS	5/07
	Nevada	H	54.42 FQ	62.75 MW		NVBLS	5/08
	Las Vegas-Paradise MSA, NV	H	57.26 FQ	63.99 MW		NVBLS	5/08
	New Hampshire	H	20.84 AE	29.58 MW	51.83 AEX	NHBLS	6/08
	New Jersey	Y	58330 FQ	67050 MW	100180 TQ	USBLS	5/07
	Camden PMSA, NJ	Y	62440 FQ	86910 MW	105130 TQ	USBLS	5/07
	Edison PMSA, NJ	Y	56110 FQ	81840 MW	125330 TQ	USBLS	5/07
	Newark-Union PMSA, NJ-PA	Y	57730 FQ	63520 MW	73100 TQ	USBLS	5/07
	New Mexico	Y	49530 FQ	58130 MW	76670 TQ	USBLS	5/07
	Albuquerque MSA, NM	Y	50140 FQ	60610 MW	79240 TQ	USBLS	5/07
	New York	Y	64240 FQ	75020 MW	94110 TQ	USBLS	5/07
	Buffalo-Niagara Falls MSA, NY	Y	49040 FQ	56810 MW	62650 TQ	USBLS	5/07
	Nassau-Suffolk PMSA, NY	Y	74600 FQ	88800 MW	100720 TQ	USBLS	5/07

AE Average entry wage	AW Average wage paid	FQ First quartile wage	LO Lowest wage paid
AER Average entry range	AWR Average wage range	H Hourly	LR Low end range
AEX Average experienced wage	AXR Average experienced range	HI Highest wage paid	M Monthly
ATC Average total compensation	D Daily	HR High end range	MCC Median cash compensation

MTC Median total compensation	TCC Total cash compensation	
MW Median wage paid	TQ Third quartile wage	
MWR Median wage range	W Weekly	
S See annotated source	Y Yearly	

213

Occupation/Type/Industry	Location	Per	Low	Mid	High	Source	Date
Chiropractor	New York-Northern New Jersey-Long Island MSA, NY-NJ-PA	Y	62880 FQ	73450 MW	94900 TQ	USBLS	5/07
	North Carolina	Y	70550 FQ	91090 MW	134780 TQ	USBLS	5/07
	Charlotte-Gastonia-Concord MSA, NC-SC	Y	86490 FQ	118860 MW		USBLS	5/07
	North Dakota	Y	41210 FQ	56730 MW	68240 TQ	USBLS	5/07
	Fargo MSA, ND-MN	Y	42300 FQ	76330 MW	95240 TQ	USBLS	5/07
	Ohio	Y	71280 FQ	91250 MW	125210 TQ	USBLS	5/07
	Cincinnati-Middletown MSA, OH-KY-IN	Y	79860 FQ	105250 MW	131480 TQ	USBLS	5/07
	Cleveland-Elyria-Mentor MSA, OH	Y	69150 FQ	104760 MW	120570 TQ	USBLS	5/07
	Columbus MSA, OH	Y	70550 FQ	77220 MW	125650 TQ	USBLS	5/07
	Dayton MSA, OH	Y	56490 FQ	65470 MW	73490 TQ	USBLS	5/07
	Oklahoma	Y	28740 FQ	38470 MW	76590 TQ	USBLS	5/07
	Oregon	H	16.68 FQ	19.47 MW	30.76 TQ	ORBLS	5/08
	Portland-Vancouver-Beaverton MSA, OR-WA	Y	35330 FQ	40320 MW	65420 TQ	USBLS	5/07
	Pennsylvania	Y	38850 FQ	61410 MW	79510 TQ	USBLS	5/07
	Philadelphia-Camden-Wilmington MSA, PA-NJ-DE-MD	Y	51750 FQ	63650 MW	83280 TQ	USBLS	5/07
	Pittsburgh MSA, PA	Y	58260 FQ	75790 MW	102510 TQ	USBLS	5/07
	Rhode Island	Y	67720 FQ	76230 MW	108500 TQ	USBLS	5/07
	Providence-Fall River-Warwick MSA, RI-MA	Y	66200 FQ	79470 MW	94890 TQ	USBLS	5/07
	South Carolina	Y	46000 FQ	67650 MW	86460 TQ	USBLS	5/07
	Charleston-North Charleston MSA, SC	Y	84710 FQ	92650 MW	100710 TQ	USBLS	5/07
	Columbia MSA, SC	Y	62810 FQ	75180 MW	86760 TQ	USBLS	5/07
	South Dakota	Y	60855 FQ	67363 MW	105401 TQ	SDBLS	7/08-9/08
	Sioux Falls MSA, SD	Y	59976 FQ	64161 MW	68144 TQ	SDBLS	7/08-9/08
	Tennessee	Y	65860 FQ	84380 MW	118940 TQ	USBLS	5/07
	Memphis MSA, TN-MS-AR	Y	63360 FQ	70470 MW	81580 TQ	USBLS	5/07
	Nashville-Davidson-Murfreesboro MSA, TN	Y	61160 FQ	70900 MW	101040 TQ	USBLS	5/07
	Texas	Y	37630 FQ	50010 MW	81280 TQ	USBLS	5/07
	Austin-Round Rock MSA, TX	Y	59890 FQ	85700 MW		USBLS	5/07
	Dallas-Fort Worth-Arlington MSA, TX	Y	36240 FQ	42470 MW	56310 TQ	USBLS	5/07
	Houston-Sugar Land-Baytown MSA, TX	Y	33110 FQ	49880 MW	62240 TQ	USBLS	5/07
	San Antonio MSA, TX	Y	38710 FQ	50090 MW	74580 TQ	USBLS	5/07
	Utah	Y	48780 FQ	57800 MW	105790 TQ	USBLS	5/07
	Richmond MSA, VA	Y	52270 FQ	57020 MW	88130 TQ	USBLS	5/07
	Virginia Beach-Norfolk-Newport News MSA, VA-NC	Y	32560 FQ	50500 MW	60750 TQ	USBLS	5/07
	Washington	H	29.63 FQ	40.73 MW		WABLS	3/08
	Seattle-Tacoma-Bellevue MSA, WA	Y	62470 FQ	87740 MW		USBLS	5/07
	West Virginia	Y	56568 FQ	64459 MW	104966 TQ	WVBLS	7/08-9/08
	Wisconsin	Y	59220 FQ	89780 MW		USBLS	5/07
	Appleton MSA, WI	Y	71880 FQ	83630 MW	111210 TQ	USBLS	5/07
	Milwaukee-Waukesha-West Allis MSA, WI	Y	61780 FQ	115250 MW		USBLS	5/07
	Wyoming	Y	39632 FQ	58133 MW	84381 TQ	WYBLS	9/08
City	United States	Y		90000 MW		CHIRO	2008
Rural	United States	Y		75000 MW		CHIRO	2008
Suburb	United States	Y		80000 MW		CHIRO	2008
Choreographer	Alabama	Y	16090 FQ	32410 MW	45030 TQ	USBLS	5/07
	Arizona	Y	24030 FQ	32490 MW	49490 TQ	USBLS	5/07
	Phoenix-Mesa-Scottsdale MSA, AZ	Y	23930 FQ	31210 MW	51430 TQ	USBLS	5/07
	California	H	16.28 FQ	22.41 MW	28.83 TQ	CABLS	1/08-3/08
	Los Angeles-Long Beach-Glendale PMSA, CA	H	19.50 FQ	23.06 MW	27.96 TQ	CABLS	1/08-3/08
	Oakland-Fremont-Hayward MSA, CA	H	22.42 FQ	28.91 MW	36.22 TQ	CABLS	1/08-3/08
	Riverside-San Bernardino-Ontario MSA, CA	H	18.38 FQ	23.98 MW	30.39 TQ	CABLS	1/08-3/08

AE	Average entry wage	**AW**	Average wage paid	**FQ**	First quartile wage	**LO**	Lowest wage paid
AER	Average entry range	**AWR**	Average wage range	**H**	Hourly	**LR**	Low end range
AEX	Average experienced wage	**AXR**	Average experienced range	**HI**	Highest wage paid	**M**	Monthly
ATC	Average total compensation	**D**	Daily	**HR**	High end range	**MCC**	Median cash compensation

MTC	Median total compensation	**TCC**	Total cash compensation
MW	Median wage paid	**TQ**	Third quartile wage
MWR	Median wage range	**W**	Weekly
S	See annotated source	**Y**	Yearly

Occupation/Type/Industry	Location	Per	Low	Mid	High	Source	Date
Choreographer	San Diego-Carlsbad-San Marcos MSA, CA	H	17.04 FQ	20.98 MW	24.24 TQ	CABLS	1/08-3/08
	San Francisco-San Mateo-Redwood PMSA, CA	H	18.39 FQ	20.72 MW	23.00 TQ	CABLS	1/08-3/08
	San Jose-Sunnyvale-Santa Clara MSA, CA	H	22.26 FQ	25.86 MW	29.94 TQ	CABLS	1/08-3/08
	Santa Ana-Anaheim-Irvine PMSA, CA	Y	31210 FQ	48210 MW	59360 TQ	USBLS	5/07
	Connecticut	H	9.23 AE	16.31 MW		CTBLS	1/08-3/08
	Bridgeport-Stamford-Norwalk MSA, CT	Y	17350 FQ	18780 MW	23360 TQ	USBLS	5/07
	Hartford-West Hartford-East Hartford MSA, CT	Y	28520 FQ	33420 MW	40670 TQ	USBLS	5/07
	Washington-Arlington-Alexandria MSA, DC-VA-MD-WV	Y	28690 FQ	47880 MW	58710 TQ	USBLS	5/07
	Florida	Y	54820 FQ	63280 MW	73700 TQ	USBLS	5/07
	Georgia	Y	23750 FQ	54690 MW	60540 TQ	USBLS	5/07
	Atlanta-Sandy Springs-Marietta MSA, GA	Y	24840 FQ	55490 MW	60600 TQ	USBLS	5/07
	Illinois	Y	27070 FQ	36780 MW	50420 TQ	USBLS	5/07
	Chicago-Naperville-Joliet MSA, IL-IN-WI	Y	28230 FQ	36430 MW	50530 TQ	USBLS	5/07
	Indiana	Y	24520 FQ	30500 MW	40360 TQ	USBLS	5/07
	Indianapolis-Carmel MSA, IN	Y	28200 FQ	32780 MW	40650 TQ	USBLS	5/07
	Muncie MSA, IN	Y	25320 FQ	27140 MW	28960 TQ	USBLS	5/07
	Iowa	Y	17370 FQ	28140 MW	36720 TQ	USBLS	5/07
	Kansas	Y	16460 FQ	27050 MW	53850 TQ	USBLS	5/07
	Kentucky	Y	20465 FQ	23339 MW	27436 TQ	KYBLS	2008
	Louisville-Jefferson County MSA, KY-IN	Y	19250 FQ	22060 MW	24650 TQ	USBLS	5/07
	Louisiana	H	7.21 FQ	9.70 MW	11.10 TQ	LABLS	1/08-3/08
	Maine	Y	14850 FQ	15600 MW	36810 TQ	USBLS	5/07
	Maryland	Y		52675 MW		MDBLS	3/08
	Baltimore-Towson MSA, MD	Y	26800 FQ	53570 MW	66140 TQ	USBLS	5/07
	Massachusetts	Y	19300 FQ	36420 MW	47980 TQ	USBLS	5/07
	Michigan	Y	25000 FQ	33330 MW	46280 TQ	USBLS	5/07
	Detroit-Warren-Livonia MSA, MI	Y	27000 FQ	34600 MW	47890 TQ	USBLS	5/07
	Warren-Troy-Farmington Hills PMSA, MI	Y	28330 FQ	33400 MW	44030 TQ	USBLS	5/07
	Mississippi	Y	19970 FQ	22350 MW	25340 TQ	USBLS	5/07
	Jackson MSA, MS	Y	20240 FQ	21510 MW	22790 TQ	USBLS	5/07
	Missouri	Y	33460 FQ	57580 MW	66960 TQ	USBLS	5/07
	Kansas City MSA, MO-KS	Y	25440 FQ	49260 MW	60550 TQ	USBLS	5/07
	St. Louis MSA, MO-IL	Y	21610 FQ	58960 MW	73720 TQ	USBLS	5/07
	Nebraska	Y	18730 FQ	27600 MW	47190 TQ	USBLS	5/07
	Lincoln MSA, NE	Y	17090 FQ	18880 MW	24540 TQ	USBLS	5/07
	Omaha-Council Bluffs MSA, NE-IA	Y	33060 FQ	45920 MW	58350 TQ	USBLS	5/07
	Nevada	H	15.29 FQ	28.47 MW	35.58 TQ	NVBLS	5/08
	New Mexico	Y	32520 FQ	38650 MW	51840 TQ	USBLS	5/07
	New York	Y	42830 FQ	54050 MW	64950 TQ	USBLS	5/07
	New York-Northern New Jersey-Long Island MSA, NY-NJ-PA	Y	42910 FQ	53420 MW	64330 TQ	USBLS	5/07
	Charlotte-Gastonia-Concord MSA, NC-SC	Y	43400 FQ	61890 MW	73480 TQ	USBLS	5/07
	North Dakota	Y	27710 FQ	31190 MW	35620 TQ	USBLS	5/07
	Ohio	Y	20740 FQ	34610 MW	51930 TQ	USBLS	5/07
	Oklahoma	Y	14430 FQ	17660 MW	21230 TQ	USBLS	5/07
	Oklahoma City MSA, OK	Y	14440 FQ	17380 MW	20720 TQ	USBLS	5/07
	Oregon	H	11.65 FQ	17.88 MW	24.67 TQ	ORBLS	5/08
	Pennsylvania	Y	19420 FQ	25770 MW	40420 TQ	USBLS	5/07
	Philadelphia-Camden-Wilmington MSA, PA-NJ-DE-MD	Y	16310 FQ	17770 MW	22120 TQ	USBLS	5/07
	South Carolina	Y	26370 FQ	35890 MW	49250 TQ	USBLS	5/07
	Columbia MSA, SC	Y	30840 FQ	36420 MW	43450 TQ	USBLS	5/07
	South Dakota	Y	22560 FQ	27389 MW	32135 TQ	SDBLS	7/08-9/08
	Tennessee	Y	28910 FQ	44220 MW	58890 TQ	USBLS	5/07

AE	Average entry wage	AW	Average wage paid	FQ First quartile wage
AER	Average entry range	AWR	Average wage range	H Hourly
AEX	Average experienced wage	AXR	Average experienced range	HI Highest wage paid
ATC	Average total compensation	D	Daily	HR High end range

LO	Lowest wage paid	MTC	Median total compensation	TCC Total cash compensation
LR	Low end range	MW	Median wage paid	TQ Third quartile wage
M	Monthly	MWR	Median wage range	W Weekly
MCC	Median cash compensation	S	See annotated source	Y Yearly

Occupation/Type/Industry	Location	Per	Low	Mid	High	Source	Date
Choreographer	Nashville-Davidson-Murfreesboro MSA, TN	Y	23670 FQ	30000 MW	39920 TQ	USBLS	5/07
	Texas	Y	19820 FQ	32330 MW	47780 TQ	USBLS	5/07
	Brownsville-Harlingen MSA, TX	Y	22320 FQ	25410 MW	44020 TQ	USBLS	5/07
	Dallas-Fort Worth-Arlington MSA, TX	Y	28160 FQ	38440 MW	53590 TQ	USBLS	5/07
	Houston-Sugar Land-Baytown MSA, TX	Y	15920 FQ	41490 MW	49150 TQ	USBLS	5/07
	Utah	Y	24400 FQ	37870 MW	56700 TQ	USBLS	5/07
	Salt Lake City MSA, UT	Y	32860 FQ	39770 MW	59690 TQ	USBLS	5/07
	Virginia	Y	29810 FQ	46280 MW	57450 TQ	USBLS	5/07
	Washington	H	13.03 FQ	17.43 MW	21.26 TQ	WABLS	3/08
	Seattle-Tacoma-Bellevue MSA, WA	Y	25170 FQ	35050 MW	39950 TQ	USBLS	5/07
	Wisconsin	Y	21940 FQ	27580 MW	43850 TQ	USBLS	5/07
	Milwaukee-Waukesha-West Allis MSA, WI	Y	27360 FQ	33940 MW	44810 TQ	USBLS	5/07
	Wyoming	Y	18320 FQ	20781 MW	37006 TQ	WYBLS	9/08
Circulation Director							
Female	United States	Y		73300 ATC		AUDDEV	2008
Male	United States	Y		92100 ATC		AUDDEV	2008
Circulation Manager	Midwest	Y		47400 AW		FOLIO02	8/12/08-9/24/08
	Northeast	Y		62200 AW		FOLIO02	8/12/08-9/24/08
	South	Y		45100 AW		FOLIO02	8/12/08-9/24/08
	West	Y		44800 AW		FOLIO02	8/12/08-9/24/08
Association Publications	United States	Y		66600 AW		CIRMGT	2007
B-to-B Publications	United States	Y		55200 AW		CIRMGT	2007
Consumer Publications	United States	Y		64200 AW		CIRMGT	2007
Circulation Supervisor							
Municipal Government	Carlsbad, CA	S	1598 LO		1942 HI	CCSS01	8/5/08
Cisco Certified Internetwork Expert							
Routing & Switching	United States	Y		120330 AW		CERT03	2008
City Administrator	Bismarck, ND	M			9615 HI	NDLC01	2008
City Architect	Cincinnati, OH	Y	77518 LO		104649 HI	COHSS	10/08
City Assessor	Carrington, ND	M			250 HI	NDLC01	2008
	Fargo, ND	M	4439 LO		6118 HI	NDLC01	2008
City Attorney	Chula Vista, CA	Y			220667 HI	SDBJ02	2007-2008
	Seaside, CA	S	2077 LO		4846 HI	SSSS	8/08
	Ashley, ND	Y			500 HI	NDLC02	2008
City Clerk	Biloxi, MS	Y			60015 HI	MML	2008
	Monticello, MS	Y			29000 HI	MML	2008
	Tupelo, MS	Y			77250 HI	MML	2008
City Council Chairperson	Taylor, MI	Y			16306 HI	NHERLD4	2009
City Council Member	Hartford, CT	Y			15000 HI	HCOUR	2008
	Madison Heights, MI	Y			6086 HI	FREEP05	2007
	South Lyon, MI	M			180 HI	FREEP05	2007
	Cincinnati, OH	Y			65952 HI	COHSS	10/08
	Virginia Beach, VA	Y			28000 HI	VAPLT	2009
City Council President	Bethlehem, PA	Y			7600 HI	MORNC	2009
City Engineer	Cleveland, MS	Y			65564 HI	MML	2008
	Ridgeland, MS	Y			85426 HI	MML	2008
City Horticulturist	Colorado Springs, CO	M	4442 LO			COSPRS	1/1/09
City Letter Carrier	United States	Y	41166-42986 LR		52748-53882 HR	NALC	8/30/08
City Manager	Daly City, CA	M			25155 HI	BDPLAN	2009
	Hayward, CA	M			15833 HI	BDPLAN	2009

Occupation/Type/Industry	Location	Per	Low	Mid	High	Source	Date
City Manager	Groveland, FL	Y			101200 HI	OSENT	2008
	Marathon City, FL	Y			100000 HI	FLKK	2008
	Lincoln Park, MI	Y			102500 HI	NHERLD2	2009
	Laurel, MS	Y			59904 HI	MML	2008
	Pascagoula, MS	Y			97624 HI	MML	2008
	Cincinnati, OH	Y			223927 HI	COHSS	10/08
	Sunbury, PA	Y			66500 HI	TDI	2009
	Rock Hill, SC	Y			171683 HI	HERLD	2009
City Planner	D'Iberville, MS	Y			53076 HI	MML	2008
	Tunica, MS	Y			10368 HI	MML	2008
	Bismarck, ND	M			7375 HI	NDLC01	2008
	Cincinnati, OH	Y	45117 LO		60634 HI	COHSS	10/08
City Recorder	Gresham, OR	Y	42672 LO		55488 HI	GOSS01	7/1/08
City Solicitor	Cincinnati, OH	Y	114941 LO		155171 HI	COHSS	10/08
City Spokesman	Newton, MA	Y			100419 HI	BGLOBE2	2008
City Surveyor	Gresham, OR	Y	58224 LO		74376 HI	GOSS	1/1/09
City Traffic Engineer	Cincinnati, OH	Y	77518 LO		104649 HI	COHSS	10/08
Civil Engineer	Alabama	Y	50070 FQ	66550 MW	84760 TQ	USBLS	5/07
	Birmingham-Hoover MSA, AL	Y	52560 FQ	68500 MW	82980 TQ	USBLS	5/07
	Huntsville MSA, AL	Y	58590 FQ	79070 MW	98760 TQ	USBLS	5/07
	Tuscaloosa MSA, AL	Y	46470 FQ	57400 MW	72090 TQ	USBLS	5/07
	Alaska	Y	61870 FQ	75670 MW	90220 TQ	USBLS	5/07
	Anchorage MSA, AK	Y	61820 FQ	76420 MW	91350 TQ	USBLS	5/07
	Arizona	Y	54850 FQ	69740 MW	88100 TQ	USBLS	5/07
	Phoenix-Mesa-Scottsdale MSA, AZ	Y	55650 FQ	71580 MW	90600 TQ	USBLS	5/07
	Tucson MSA, AZ	Y	52130 FQ	68620 MW	83990 TQ	USBLS	5/07
	Arkansas	Y	49320 FQ	63360 MW	80030 TQ	USBLS	5/07
	Little Rock-North Little Rock MSA, AR	Y	49790 FQ	68130 MW	84330 TQ	USBLS	5/07
	California	H	32.05 FQ	38.41 MW	47.15 TQ	CABLS	1/08-3/08
	Los Angeles-Long Beach-Glendale PMSA, CA	H	32.37 FQ	39.13 MW	47.66 TQ	CABLS	1/08-3/08
	Oakland-Fremont-Hayward MSA, CA	H	33.44 FQ	38.43 MW	47.07 TQ	CABLS	1/08-3/08
	Riverside-San Bernardino-Ontario MSA, CA	H	29.87 FQ	37.13 MW	45.23 TQ	CABLS	1/08-3/08
	Sacramento-Arden Arcade-Roseville MSA, CA	H	32.56 FQ	38.34 MW	45.42 TQ	CABLS	1/08-3/08
	San Diego-Carlsbad-San Marcos MSA, CA	H	30.75 FQ	36.39 MW	43.18 TQ	CABLS	1/08-3/08
	San Francisco-San Mateo-Redwood PMSA, CA	H	35.20 FQ	44.77 MW	54.99 TQ	CABLS	1/08-3/08
	San Jose-Sunnyvale-Santa Clara MSA, CA	H	34.11 FQ	42.08 MW	53.44 TQ	CABLS	1/08-3/08
	Santa Ana-Anaheim-Irvine PMSA, CA	Y	62030 FQ	76730 MW	97820 TQ	USBLS	5/07
	Colorado	Y	56990 FQ	74950 MW	90930 TQ	USBLS	5/07
	Denver-Aurora MSA, CO	Y	58020 FQ	78760 MW	92780 TQ	USBLS	5/07
	Connecticut	H	26.56 AE	35.18 MW		CTBLS	1/08-3/08
	Bridgeport-Stamford-Norwalk MSA, CT	Y	61200 FQ	78210 MW	89990 TQ	USBLS	5/07
	Hartford-West Hartford-East Hartford MSA, CT	Y	59850 FQ	72680 MW	84900 TQ	USBLS	5/07
	Norwich-New London MSA, CT-RI	Y	62370 FQ	70100 MW	77720 TQ	USBLS	5/07
	Delaware	Y	61510 FQ	77980 MW	96070 TQ	USBLS	5/07
	Wilmington PMSA, DE-MD-NJ	Y	68130 FQ	85850 MW	102340 TQ	USBLS	5/07
	District of Columbia	Y	69950 FQ	82970 MW	103340 TQ	USBLS	5/07
	Washington-Arlington-Alexandria MSA, DC-VA-MD-WV	Y	62800 FQ	79710 MW	99240 TQ	USBLS	5/07
	Florida	Y	55570 FQ	71420 MW	92090 TQ	USBLS	5/07

AE	Average entry wage	AW	Average wage paid	FQ	First quartile wage
AER	Average entry range	AWR	Average wage range	H	Hourly
AEX	Average experienced wage	AXR	Average experienced range	HI	Highest wage paid
ATC	Average total compensation	D	Daily	HR	High end range

LO	Lowest wage paid	MTC	Median total compensation	TCC	Total cash compensation
LR	Low end range	MW	Median wage paid	TQ	Third quartile wage
M	Monthly	MWR	Median wage range	W	Weekly
MCC	Median cash compensation	S	See annotated source	Y	Yearly

Occupation/Type/Industry	Location	Per	Low	Mid	High	Source	Date
Civil Engineer	Fort Lauderdale-Pompano Beach-Deerfield Beach PMSA, FL	Y	55080 FQ	69230 MW	87690 TQ	USBLS	5/07
	Jacksonville MSA, FL	Y	58860 FQ	76140 MW	95450 TQ	USBLS	5/07
	Miami-Fort Lauderdale-Miami Beach MSA, FL	Y	56200 FQ	71550 MW	93860 TQ	USBLS	5/07
	Orlando-Kissimmee MSA, FL	Y	56120 FQ	71840 MW	91850 TQ	USBLS	5/07
	Sarasota-Bradenton-Venice MSA, FL	Y	54800 FQ	62290 MW	79120 TQ	USBLS	5/07
	Tampa-St. Petersburg-Clearwater MSA, FL	Y	54960 FQ	72650 MW	92090 TQ	USBLS	5/07
	West Palm Beach-Boca Raton-Boynton Beach PMSA, FL	Y	64550 FQ	82310 MW	103000 TQ	USBLS	5/07
	Georgia	Y	51070 FQ	65820 MW	86010 TQ	USBLS	5/07
	Atlanta-Sandy Springs-Marietta MSA, GA	Y	53120 FQ	68680 MW	89000 TQ	USBLS	5/07
	Macon MSA, GA	Y	52690 FQ	66440 MW	107310 TQ	USBLS	5/07
	Hawaii	Y	59320 FQ	72070 MW	83270 TQ	USBLS	5/07
	Honolulu MSA, HI	Y	60040 FQ	72500 MW	83710 TQ	USBLS	5/07
	Idaho	Y	54600 FQ	65120 MW	81360 TQ	USBLS	5/07
	Boise City-Nampa MSA, ID	Y	56830 FQ	70760 MW	84490 TQ	USBLS	5/07
	Illinois	Y	57570 FQ	72370 MW	92440 TQ	USBLS	5/07
	Chicago-Naperville-Joliet MSA, IL-IN-WI	Y	60010 FQ	74070 MW	94430 TQ	USBLS	5/07
	Indiana	Y	51280 FQ	63950 MW	79800 TQ	USBLS	5/07
	Evansville MSA, IN-KY	Y	49590 FQ	60920 MW	74390 TQ	USBLS	5/07
	Gary PMSA, IN	Y	69450 FQ	79100 MW	90760 TQ	USBLS	5/07
	Indianapolis-Carmel MSA, IN	Y	53590 FQ	65070 MW	81540 TQ	USBLS	5/07
	Iowa	Y	54140 FQ	70030 MW	84850 TQ	USBLS	5/07
	Des Moines-West Des Moines MSA, IA	Y	55590 FQ	70680 MW	82920 TQ	USBLS	5/07
	Kansas	Y	53970 FQ	67580 MW	83690 TQ	USBLS	5/07
	Wichita MSA, KS	Y	46250 FQ	54330 MW	67270 TQ	USBLS	5/07
	Kentucky	Y	56685 FQ	70446 MW	85556 TQ	KYBLS	2008
	Louisville-Jefferson County MSA, KY-IN	Y	54030 FQ	69940 MW	85560 TQ	USBLS	5/07
	Louisiana	H	29.48 FQ	35.58 MW	43.48 TQ	LABLS	1/08-3/08
	Baton Rouge MSA, LA	Y	62340 FQ	74780 MW	92260 TQ	USBLS	5/07
	New Orleans-Metairie-Kenner MSA, LA	Y	61270 FQ	73850 MW	90090 TQ	USBLS	5/07
	Maine	Y	50700 FQ	60480 MW	73660 TQ	USBLS	5/07
	Portland-South Portland-Biddeford MSA, ME	Y	52220 FQ	62400 MW	78750 TQ	USBLS	5/07
	Maryland	Y		71625 MW		MDBLS	3/08
	Baltimore-Towson MSA, MD	Y	53790 FQ	64280 MW	83210 TQ	USBLS	5/07
	Bethesda-Gaithersburg-Frederick PMSA, MD	Y	58240 FQ	77980 MW	106390 TQ	USBLS	5/07
	Salisbury MSA, MD	Y	53190 FQ	63800 MW	80090 TQ	USBLS	5/07
	Massachusetts	Y	60130 FQ	75160 MW	94390 TQ	USBLS	5/07
	Boston-Cambridge-Quincy NECTA, MA	Y	62760 FQ	79110 MW	98010 TQ	USBLS	5/07
	Lynn-Peabody-Salem NECTA, MA	Y	68410 FQ	75300 MW	82850 TQ	USBLS	5/07
	Springfield MSA, MA-CT	Y	57050 FQ	66230 MW	81160 TQ	USBLS	5/07
	Worcester MSA, MA-CT	Y	58490 FQ	67840 MW	77940 TQ	USBLS	5/07
	Michigan	Y	54370 FQ	64020 MW	78410 TQ	USBLS	5/07
	Detroit-Warren-Livonia MSA, MI	Y	55030 FQ	63970 MW	80560 TQ	USBLS	5/07
	Grand Rapids-Wyoming MSA, MI	Y	56060 FQ	65940 MW	76750 TQ	USBLS	5/07
	Warren-Troy-Farmington Hills PMSA, MI	Y	55450 FQ	62940 MW	77120 TQ	USBLS	5/07
	Minnesota	Y	57971 FQ	73445 MW	89546 TQ	MNBLS	10/08-12/08
	Duluth-Superior MSA, MN-WI	Y	58013 FQ	68527 MW	79356 TQ	MNBLS	10/08-12/08
	Minneapolis-Saint Paul MSA, MN-WI	Y	58494 FQ	74773 MW	93239 TQ	MNBLS	10/08-12/08
	Rochester MSA, MN	Y	58430 FQ	69151 MW	78893 TQ	MNBLS	10/08-12/08
	Mississippi	Y	55560 FQ	71280 MW	89110 TQ	USBLS	5/07
	Jackson MSA, MS	Y	49300 FQ	60790 MW	73870 TQ	USBLS	5/07
	Missouri	Y	54280 FQ	66410 MW	84460 TQ	USBLS	5/07
	Kansas City MSA, MO-KS	Y	56820 FQ	71960 MW	90760 TQ	USBLS	5/07
	St. Joseph MSA, MO-KS	Y	50890 FQ	56550 MW	63710 TQ	USBLS	5/07

AE	Average entry wage	AW	Average wage paid	FQ	First quartile wage	LO	Lowest wage paid	MTC	Median total compensation	TCC	Total cash compensation
AER	Average entry range	AWR	Average wage range	H	Hourly	LR	Low end range	MW	Median wage paid	TQ	Third quartile wage
AEX	Average experienced wage	AXR	Average experienced range	HI	Highest wage paid	M	Monthly	MWR	Median wage range	W	Weekly
ATC	Average total compensation	D	Daily	HR	High end range	MCC	Median cash compensation	S	See annotated source	Y	Yearly

Occupation/Type/Industry	Location	Per	Low	Mid	High	Source	Date
Civil Engineer	St. Louis MSA, MO-IL	Y	54340 FQ	66140 MW	84580 TQ	USBLS	5/07
	Montana	Y	49460 FQ	59810 MW	74350 TQ	USBLS	5/07
	Billings MSA, MT	Y	45220 FQ	63730 MW	82220 TQ	USBLS	5/07
	Nebraska	Y	51630 FQ	66420 MW	84680 TQ	USBLS	5/07
	Omaha-Council Bluffs MSA, NE-IA	Y	53320 FQ	71250 MW	92770 TQ	USBLS	5/07
	Nevada	H	31.02 FQ	38.31 MW	47.42 TQ	NVBLS	5/08
	Las Vegas-Paradise MSA, NV	H	32.39 FQ	39.72 MW	48.74 TQ	NVBLS	5/08
	New Hampshire	H	24.46 AE	32.00 MW	37.93 AEX	NHBLS	6/08
	Manchester MSA, NH	Y	57540 FQ	73700 MW	86670 TQ	USBLS	5/07
	Nashua NECTA, NH-MA	Y	54700 FQ	61560 MW	78210 TQ	USBLS	5/07
	Rochester-Dover MSA, NH-ME	Y	52770 FQ	64760 MW	96670 TQ	USBLS	5/07
	New Jersey	Y	63870 FQ	80510 MW	99670 TQ	USBLS	5/07
	Atlantic City MSA, NJ	Y	64270 FQ	81980 MW	104250 TQ	USBLS	5/07
	Camden PMSA, NJ	Y	61280 FQ	77770 MW	95450 TQ	USBLS	5/07
	Edison PMSA, NJ	Y	60590 FQ	82680 MW	102560 TQ	USBLS	5/07
	Newark-Union PMSA, NJ-PA	Y	67110 FQ	81490 MW	101820 TQ	USBLS	5/07
	New Mexico	Y	56780 FQ	71510 MW	89400 TQ	USBLS	5/07
	Albuquerque MSA, NM	Y	55820 FQ	73430 MW	93320 TQ	USBLS	5/07
	New York	Y	58830 FQ	71930 MW	90500 TQ	USBLS	5/07
	Albany-Schenectady-Troy MSA, NY	Y	59550 FQ	71150 MW	83310 TQ	USBLS	5/07
	Buffalo-Niagara Falls MSA, NY	Y	57700 FQ	70730 MW	90720 TQ	USBLS	5/07
	Glens Falls MSA, NY	Y	41710 FQ	54160 MW	63040 TQ	USBLS	5/07
	Ithaca MSA, NY	Y	53940 FQ	64720 MW	77240 TQ	USBLS	5/07
	Nassau-Suffolk PMSA, NY	Y	62770 FQ	76540 MW	96680 TQ	USBLS	5/07
	New York-Northern New Jersey-Long Island MSA, NY-NJ-PA	Y	62300 FQ	78230 MW	98820 TQ	USBLS	5/07
	North Carolina	Y	53260 FQ	65040 MW	79770 TQ	USBLS	5/07
	Charlotte-Gastonia-Concord MSA, NC-SC	Y	54540 FQ	67770 MW	87020 TQ	USBLS	5/07
	Durham MSA, NC	Y	52420 FQ	65790 MW	81020 TQ	USBLS	5/07
	Raleigh-Cary MSA, NC	Y	55320 FQ	65960 MW	78970 TQ	USBLS	5/07
	North Dakota	Y	49730 FQ	60090 MW	75310 TQ	USBLS	5/07
	Fargo MSA, ND-MN	Y	44510 FQ	55820 MW	72890 TQ	USBLS	5/07
	Ohio	Y	53860 FQ	66630 MW	81490 TQ	USBLS	5/07
	Cincinnati-Middletown MSA, OH-KY-IN	Y	56120 FQ	68930 MW	85110 TQ	USBLS	5/07
	Cleveland-Elyria-Mentor MSA, OH	Y	51530 FQ	64190 MW	77440 TQ	USBLS	5/07
	Columbus MSA, OH	Y	54690 FQ	68690 MW	85340 TQ	USBLS	5/07
	Dayton MSA, OH	Y	54990 FQ	72550 MW	84130 TQ	USBLS	5/07
	Oklahoma	Y	52880 FQ	69010 MW	87910 TQ	USBLS	5/07
	Oklahoma City MSA, OK	Y	57780 FQ	73560 MW	91630 TQ	USBLS	5/07
	Tulsa MSA, OK	Y	51750 FQ	67500 MW	88560 TQ	USBLS	5/07
	Oregon	H	26.75 FQ	33.82 MW	41.61 TQ	ORBLS	5/08
	Portland-Vancouver-Beaverton MSA, OR-WA	Y	55640 FQ	70800 MW	87690 TQ	USBLS	5/07
	Salem MSA, OR	Y	56990 FQ	67210 MW	78760 TQ	USBLS	5/07
	Pennsylvania	Y	53070 FQ	64920 MW	81880 TQ	USBLS	5/07
	Allentown-Bethlehem-Easton MSA, PA-NJ	Y	55090 FQ	66070 MW	80910 TQ	USBLS	5/07
	Philadelphia-Camden-Wilmington MSA, PA-NJ-DE-MD	Y	56630 FQ	71230 MW	91180 TQ	USBLS	5/07
	Pittsburgh MSA, PA	Y	53550 FQ	65380 MW	81320 TQ	USBLS	5/07
	Rhode Island	Y	64430 FQ	74620 MW	87290 TQ	USBLS	5/07
	Providence-Fall River-Warwick MSA, RI-MA	Y	63360 FQ	75170 MW	90480 TQ	USBLS	5/07
	South Carolina	Y	52650 FQ	66200 MW	84050 TQ	USBLS	5/07
	Charleston-North Charleston MSA, SC	Y	54330 FQ	68430 MW	83310 TQ	USBLS	5/07
	Columbia MSA, SC	Y	45640 FQ	57610 MW	71940 TQ	USBLS	5/07
	South Dakota	Y	51620 FQ	62044 MW	74771 TQ	SDBLS	7/08-9/08
	Sioux Falls MSA, SD	Y	50907 FQ	64136 MW	78144 TQ	SDBLS	7/08-9/08
	Tennessee	Y	51660 FQ	68420 MW	86140 TQ	USBLS	5/07
	Knoxville MSA, TN	Y	49870 FQ	61450 MW	81390 TQ	USBLS	5/07
	Memphis MSA, TN-MS-AR	Y	55610 FQ	73570 MW	91750 TQ	USBLS	5/07

AE Average entry wage	**AW** Average wage paid	**FQ** First quartile wage	**LO** Lowest wage paid	**MTC** Median total compensation	**TCC** Total cash compensation
AER Average entry range	**AWR** Average wage range	**H** Hourly	**LR** Low end range	**MW** Median wage paid	**TQ** Third quartile wage
AEX Average experienced wage	**AXR** Average experienced range	**HI** Highest wage paid	**M** Monthly	**MWR** Median wage range	**W** Weekly
ATC Average total compensation	**D** Daily	**HR** High end range	**MCC** Median cash compensation	**S** See annotated source	**Y** Yearly

Occupation/Type/Industry	Location	Per	Low	Mid	High	Source	Date
Civil Engineer	Nashville-Davidson- Murfreesboro MSA, TN	Y	53620 FQ	71470 MW	85530 TQ	USBLS	5/07
	Texas	Y	57510 FQ	76300 MW	101100 TQ	USBLS	5/07
	Austin-Round Rock MSA, TX	Y	55450 FQ	71960 MW	93770 TQ	USBLS	5/07
	Dallas-Fort Worth-Arlington MSA, TX	Y	57140 FQ	72910 MW	93880 TQ	USBLS	5/07
	El Paso MSA, TX	Y	47150 FQ	57790 MW	71160 TQ	USBLS	5/07
	Houston-Sugar Land-Baytown MSA, TX	Y	65140 FQ	86760 MW	114750 TQ	USBLS	5/07
	San Antonio MSA, TX	Y	53420 FQ	63480 MW	75480 TQ	USBLS	5/07
	Utah	Y	50390 FQ	62180 MW	77210 TQ	USBLS	5/07
	St. George MSA, UT	Y	49300 FQ	60370 MW	76170 TQ	USBLS	5/07
	Salt Lake City MSA, UT	Y	51640 FQ	63790 MW	79210 TQ	USBLS	5/07
	Vermont	Y	52640 FQ	63270 MW	76280 TQ	USBLS	5/07
	Burlington-South Burlington MSA, VT	Y	55300 FQ	68090 MW	79260 TQ	USBLS	5/07
	Virginia	Y	59190 FQ	74340 MW	92870 TQ	USBLS	5/07
	Charlottesville MSA, VA	Y	47270 FQ	61040 MW	79710 TQ	USBLS	5/07
	Richmond MSA, VA	Y	57620 FQ	69590 MW	85290 TQ	USBLS	5/07
	Virginia Beach-Norfolk- Newport News MSA, VA-NC	Y	58930 FQ	72380 MW	89250 TQ	USBLS	5/07
	Washington	H	29.57 FQ	35.81 MW	43.73 TQ	WABLS	3/08
	Seattle-Tacoma-Bellevue MSA, WA	Y	62520 FQ	75400 MW	91850 TQ	USBLS	5/07
	West Virginia	Y	49189 FQ	60759 MW	76429 TQ	WVBLS	7/08-9/08
	Charleston MSA, WV	Y	50730 FQ	61880 MW	75410 TQ	USBLS	5/07
	Wisconsin	Y	53530 FQ	62940 MW	75910 TQ	USBLS	5/07
	Milwaukee-Waukesha-West Allis MSA, WI	Y	54830 FQ	63260 MW	73770 TQ	USBLS	5/07
	Wyoming	Y	51535 FQ	61631 MW	71957 TQ	WYBLS	9/08
	Casper MSA, WY	Y	52185 FQ	64185 MW	75638 TQ	WYBLS	9/08
	Cheyenne MSA, WY	Y	54515 FQ	61037 MW	67322 TQ	WYBLS	9/08
	Puerto Rico	Y	38610 FQ	50420 MW	64940 TQ	USBLS	5/07
	Aguadilla-Isabela-San Sebastian MSA, PR	Y	32510 FQ	42370 MW	59710 TQ	USBLS	5/07
	San Juan-Caguas-Guaynabo MSA, PR	Y	39270 FQ	50830 MW	64540 TQ	USBLS	5/07
	Virgin Islands	Y	35950 FQ	42340 MW	68610 TQ	USBLS	5/07
	Guam	Y	36420 FQ	44670 MW	57020 TQ	USBLS	5/07
Small Organization	United States	Y	62294 FQ	70656 MW	79018 TQ	ALA06	2008
Civil Engineering Technician	Alabama	Y	24000 FQ	34000 MW	45200 TQ	USBLS	5/07
	Birmingham-Hoover MSA, AL	Y	26210 FQ	37610 MW	58130 TQ	USBLS	5/07
	Alaska	Y	42340 FQ	51140 MW	63780 TQ	USBLS	5/07
	Anchorage MSA, AK	Y	43700 FQ	54030 MW	65970 TQ	USBLS	5/07
	Arizona	Y	34410 FQ	43960 MW	54650 TQ	USBLS	5/07
	Phoenix-Mesa-Scottsdale MSA, AZ	Y	35350 FQ	44200 MW	54470 TQ	USBLS	5/07
	Tucson MSA, AZ	Y	30640 FQ	41570 MW	52780 TQ	USBLS	5/07
	Arkansas	Y	30300 FQ	38270 MW	51880 TQ	USBLS	5/07
	Little Rock-North Little Rock MSA, AR	Y	30300 FQ	36690 MW	55650 TQ	USBLS	5/07
	California	H	22.26 FQ	28.08 MW	32.82 TQ	CABLS	1/08-3/08
	Fresno MSA, CA	H	20.95 FQ	26.33 MW	29.58 TQ	CABLS	1/08-3/08
	Los Angeles-Long Beach- Glendale PMSA, CA	H	24.68 FQ	29.54 MW	34.65 TQ	CABLS	1/08-3/08
	Modesto MSA, CA	H	22.68 FQ	29.21 MW	37.20 TQ	CABLS	1/08-3/08
	Oakland-Fremont-Hayward MSA, CA	H	27.37 FQ	31.14 MW	37.86 TQ	CABLS	1/08-3/08
	Riverside-San Bernardino- Ontario MSA, CA	H	20.67 FQ	28.25 MW	35.75 TQ	CABLS	1/08-3/08
	Sacramento-Arden Arcade- Roseville MSA, CA	H	21.87 FQ	26.44 MW	31.06 TQ	CABLS	1/08-3/08
	San Diego-Carlsbad-San Marcos MSA, CA	H	20.77 FQ	26.17 MW	30.81 TQ	CABLS	1/08-3/08
	San Francisco-San Mateo- Redwood PMSA, CA	H	26.26 FQ	30.18 MW	35.22 TQ	CABLS	1/08-3/08
	San Jose-Sunnyvale-Santa Clara MSA, CA	H	23.99 FQ	32.70 MW	38.68 TQ	CABLS	1/08-3/08
	Santa Ana-Anaheim-Irvine PMSA, CA	Y	45640 FQ	57890 MW	67670 TQ	USBLS	5/07
	Colorado	Y	38200 FQ	49210 MW	59620 TQ	USBLS	5/07

AE	Average entry wage	AW	Average wage paid	FQ	First quartile wage
AER	Average entry range	AWR	Average wage range	H	Hourly
AEX	Average experienced wage	AXR	Average experienced range	HI	Highest wage paid
ATC	Average total compensation	D	Daily	HR	High end range

LO	Lowest wage paid	MTC	Median total compensation	TCC	Total cash compensation
LR	Low end range	MW	Median wage paid	TQ	Third quartile wage
M	Monthly	MWR	Median wage range	W	Weekly
MCC	Median cash compensation	S	See annotated source	Y	Yearly

Occupation/Type/Industry	Location	Per	Low	Mid	High	Source	Date
Civil Engineering Technician	Denver-Aurora MSA, CO	Y	37990 FQ	47990 MW	59320 TQ	USBLS	5/07
	Fort Collins-Loveland MSA, CO	Y	29480 FQ	42440 MW	55290 TQ	USBLS	5/07
	Connecticut	H	18.49 AE	26.63 MW		CTBLS	1/08-3/08
	Bridgeport-Stamford-Norwalk MSA, CT	Y	48200 FQ	54570 MW	62860 TQ	USBLS	5/07
	Hartford-West Hartford-East Hartford MSA, CT	Y	52260 FQ	62520 MW	74940 TQ	USBLS	5/07
	Delaware	Y	34290 FQ	41190 MW	48180 TQ	USBLS	5/07
	Dover MSA, DE	Y	35760 FQ	41640 MW	48010 TQ	USBLS	5/07
	Wilmington PMSA, DE-MD-NJ	Y	35130 FQ	41530 MW	49330 TQ	USBLS	5/07
	District of Columbia	Y	39780 FQ	52390 MW	60260 TQ	USBLS	5/07
	Washington-Arlington-Alexandria MSA, DC-VA-MD-WV	Y	37550 FQ	48730 MW	60270 TQ	USBLS	5/07
	Florida	Y	33680 FQ	42190 MW	53650 TQ	USBLS	5/07
	Fort Lauderdale-Pompano Beach-Deerfield Beach PMSA, FL	Y	34270 FQ	44620 MW	63060 TQ	USBLS	5/07
	Jacksonville MSA, FL	Y	38380 FQ	45760 MW	53740 TQ	USBLS	5/07
	Lakeland MSA, FL	Y	31490 FQ	39530 MW	49790 TQ	USBLS	5/07
	Miami-Fort Lauderdale-Miami Beach MSA, FL	Y	35190 FQ	45810 MW	59820 TQ	USBLS	5/07
	Orlando-Kissimmee MSA, FL	Y	31130 FQ	36840 MW	47280 TQ	USBLS	5/07
	Sarasota-Bradenton-Venice MSA, FL	Y	32940 FQ	40130 MW	47800 TQ	USBLS	5/07
	Tampa-St. Petersburg-Clearwater MSA, FL	Y	33390 FQ	42450 MW	54150 TQ	USBLS	5/07
	West Palm Beach-Boca Raton-Boynton Beach PMSA, FL	Y	37080 FQ	46860 MW	58750 TQ	USBLS	5/07
	Georgia	Y	29890 FQ	36220 MW	47490 TQ	USBLS	5/07
	Atlanta-Sandy Springs-Marietta MSA, GA	Y	30360 FQ	36480 MW	47780 TQ	USBLS	5/07
	Augusta-Richmond County MSA, GA-SC	Y	37450 FQ	53750 MW	66870 TQ	USBLS	5/07
	Hawaii	Y	36060 FQ	43360 MW	50590 TQ	USBLS	5/07
	Honolulu MSA, HI	Y	35370 FQ	42520 MW	51810 TQ	USBLS	5/07
	Idaho	Y	40070 FQ	45470 MW	50090 TQ	USBLS	5/07
	Boise City-Nampa MSA, ID	Y	42440 FQ	46790 MW	51130 TQ	USBLS	5/07
	Illinois	Y	36030 FQ	45400 MW	59130 TQ	USBLS	5/07
	Chicago-Naperville-Joliet MSA, IL-IN-WI	Y	36260 FQ	45730 MW	60200 TQ	USBLS	5/07
	Indiana	Y	29780 FQ	38610 MW	49560 TQ	USBLS	5/07
	Gary PMSA, IN	Y	39700 FQ	47050 MW	74510 TQ	USBLS	5/07
	Indianapolis-Carmel MSA, IN	Y	28610 FQ	37080 MW	50170 TQ	USBLS	5/07
	Iowa	Y	32680 FQ	39980 MW	50070 TQ	USBLS	5/07
	Cedar Rapids MSA, IA	Y	39420 FQ	45520 MW	55790 TQ	USBLS	5/07
	Des Moines-West Des Moines MSA, IA	Y	28630 FQ	34830 MW	49980 TQ	USBLS	5/07
	Kansas	Y	33590 FQ	41950 MW	51900 TQ	USBLS	5/07
	Wichita MSA, KS	Y	30860 FQ	36500 MW	43750 TQ	USBLS	5/07
	Kentucky	Y	36775 FQ	46949 MW	58227 TQ	KYBLS	2008
	Louisville-Jefferson County MSA, KY-IN	Y	35200 FQ	46670 MW	56780 TQ	USBLS	5/07
	Owensboro MSA, KY	Y	43770 FQ	58270 MW	70950 TQ	USBLS	5/07
	Louisiana	H	15.22 FQ	19.06 MW	23.58 TQ	LABLS	1/08-3/08
	Baton Rouge MSA, LA	Y	31050 FQ	40440 MW	50090 TQ	USBLS	5/07
	Lake Charles MSA, LA	Y	32100 FQ	40310 MW	53070 TQ	USBLS	5/07
	New Orleans-Metairie-Kenner MSA, LA	Y	31580 FQ	39290 MW	50980 TQ	USBLS	5/07
	Maine	Y	34780 FQ	41170 MW	48970 TQ	USBLS	5/07
	Portland-South Portland-Biddeford MSA, ME	Y	34460 FQ	39480 MW	46250 TQ	USBLS	5/07
	Maryland	Y		48775 MW		MDBLS	3/08
	Baltimore-Towson MSA, MD	Y	36500 FQ	45240 MW	51600 TQ	USBLS	5/07
	Bethesda-Gaithersburg-Frederick PMSA, MD	Y	44610 FQ	55620 MW	69170 TQ	USBLS	5/07
	Massachusetts	Y	40640 FQ	48770 MW	57100 TQ	USBLS	5/07
	Boston-Cambridge-Quincy NECTA, MA	Y	40300 FQ	51530 MW	59440 TQ	USBLS	5/07
	Worcester MSA, MA-CT	Y	28380 FQ	30790 MW	41290 TQ	USBLS	5/07

AE	Average entry wage	**AW**	Average wage paid	**FQ**	First quartile wage
AER	Average entry range	**AWR**	Average wage range	**H**	Hourly
AEX	Average experienced wage	**AXR**	Average experienced range	**HI**	Highest wage paid
ATC	Average total compensation	**D**	Daily	**HR**	High end range

LO	Lowest wage paid	**MTC**	Median total compensation	**TCC** Total cash compensation
LR	Low end range	**MW**	Median wage paid	**TQ** Third quartile wage
M	Monthly	**MWR**	Median wage range	**W** Weekly
MCC	Median cash compensation	**S**	See annotated source	**Y** Yearly

Occupation/Type/Industry	Location	Per	Low	Mid	High	Source	Date
Civil Engineering Technician	Michigan	Y	34660 FQ	43610 MW	49850 TQ	USBLS	5/07
	Detroit-Warren-Livonia MSA, MI	Y	35960 FQ	44360 MW	50060 TQ	USBLS	5/07
	Grand Rapids-Wyoming MSA, MI	Y	39390 FQ	45310 MW	51880 TQ	USBLS	5/07
	Warren-Troy-Farmington Hills PMSA, MI	Y	32890 FQ	44520 MW	49970 TQ	USBLS	5/07
	Minnesota	Y	43669 FQ	53566 MW	63066 TQ	MNBLS	10/08-12/08
	Duluth-Superior MSA, MN-WI	Y	46619 FQ	57270 MW	63987 TQ	MNBLS	10/08-12/08
	Minneapolis-Saint Paul MSA, MN-WI	Y	44401 FQ	54853 MW	64259 TQ	MNBLS	10/08-12/08
	Mississippi	Y	26130 FQ	30900 MW	36690 TQ	USBLS	5/07
	Jackson MSA, MS	Y	26330 FQ	30960 MW	36370 TQ	USBLS	5/07
	Missouri	Y	32210 FQ	40290 MW	50220 TQ	USBLS	5/07
	Kansas City MSA, MO-KS	Y	38240 FQ	48480 MW	60620 TQ	USBLS	5/07
	St. Louis MSA, MO-IL	Y	31110 FQ	40610 MW	51020 TQ	USBLS	5/07
	Montana	Y	32190 FQ	40450 MW	46360 TQ	USBLS	5/07
	Billings MSA, MT	Y	32850 FQ	39720 MW	45750 TQ	USBLS	5/07
	Nebraska	Y	28880 FQ	35100 MW	41530 TQ	USBLS	5/07
	Omaha-Council Bluffs MSA, NE-IA	Y	28910 FQ	35320 MW	42230 TQ	USBLS	5/07
	Nevada	H	19.21 FQ	24.13 MW	30.17 TQ	NVBLS	5/08
	Las Vegas-Paradise MSA, NV	H	18.82 FQ	25.28 MW	32.87 TQ	NVBLS	5/08
	New Hampshire	H	19.33 AE	23.56 MW	26.53 AEX	NHBLS	6/08
	Manchester MSA, NH	Y	41080 FQ	43970 MW	46850 TQ	USBLS	5/07
	New Jersey	Y	37060 FQ	45960 MW	57050 TQ	USBLS	5/07
	Camden PMSA, NJ	Y	33000 FQ	47200 MW	59110 TQ	USBLS	5/07
	Edison PMSA, NJ	Y	35860 FQ	43260 MW	52070 TQ	USBLS	5/07
	Newark-Union PMSA, NJ-PA	Y	37690 FQ	47380 MW	58140 TQ	USBLS	5/07
	New Mexico	Y	30110 FQ	38770 MW	49940 TQ	USBLS	5/07
	Albuquerque MSA, NM	Y	37910 FQ	49710 MW	60560 TQ	USBLS	5/07
	Santa Fe MSA, NM	Y	31250 FQ	41290 MW	47470 TQ	USBLS	5/07
	New York	Y	34260 FQ	48400 MW	61860 TQ	USBLS	5/07
	Albany-Schenectady-Troy MSA, NY	Y	28140 FQ	31040 MW	41450 TQ	USBLS	5/07
	Buffalo-Niagara Falls MSA, NY	Y	35980 FQ	43700 MW	56740 TQ	USBLS	5/07
	Ithaca MSA, NY	Y	41460 FQ	47910 MW	58050 TQ	USBLS	5/07
	Nassau-Suffolk PMSA, NY	Y	32750 FQ	58020 MW	72360 TQ	USBLS	5/07
	New York-Northern New Jersey-Long Island MSA, NY-NJ-PA	Y	39670 FQ	50920 MW	62920 TQ	USBLS	5/07
	North Carolina	Y	32910 FQ	40220 MW	48560 TQ	USBLS	5/07
	Charlotte-Gastonia-Concord MSA, NC-SC	Y	30330 FQ	38180 MW	49550 TQ	USBLS	5/07
	Raleigh-Cary MSA, NC	Y	33160 FQ	42540 MW	50530 TQ	USBLS	5/07
	North Dakota	Y	33230 FQ	39240 MW	46110 TQ	USBLS	5/07
	Fargo MSA, ND-MN	Y	33860 FQ	41490 MW	48510 TQ	USBLS	5/07
	Ohio	Y	35650 FQ	43760 MW	51680 TQ	USBLS	5/07
	Cincinnati-Middletown MSA, OH-KY-IN	Y	34490 FQ	44210 MW	52820 TQ	USBLS	5/07
	Cleveland-Elyria-Mentor MSA, OH	Y	37700 FQ	44930 MW	50880 TQ	USBLS	5/07
	Columbus MSA, OH	Y	33560 FQ	40260 MW	50380 TQ	USBLS	5/07
	Dayton MSA, OH	Y	36480 FQ	42380 MW	53340 TQ	USBLS	5/07
	Oklahoma	Y	30740 FQ	43110 MW	58920 TQ	USBLS	5/07
	Oklahoma City MSA, OK	Y	29700 FQ	42360 MW	60370 TQ	USBLS	5/07
	Tulsa MSA, OK	Y	29130 FQ	43130 MW	57870 TQ	USBLS	5/07
	Oregon	H	20.44 FQ	24.45 MW	28.78 TQ	ORBLS	5/08
	Portland-Vancouver-Beaverton MSA, OR-WA	Y	43580 FQ	52320 MW	59960 TQ	USBLS	5/07
	Pennsylvania	Y	27740 FQ	36270 MW	46510 TQ	USBLS	5/07
	Allentown-Bethlehem-Easton MSA, PA-NJ	Y	34660 FQ	45960 MW	54350 TQ	USBLS	5/07
	Philadelphia-Camden-Wilmington MSA, PA-NJ-DE-MD	Y	29500 FQ	36720 MW	46640 TQ	USBLS	5/07
	Pittsburgh MSA, PA	Y	27790 FQ	36050 MW	45910 TQ	USBLS	5/07
	York-Hanover MSA, PA	Y	40260 FQ	46270 MW	54520 TQ	USBLS	5/07
	Rhode Island	Y	41290 FQ	46500 MW	51670 TQ	USBLS	5/07
	Providence-Fall River-Warwick MSA, RI-MA	Y	41310 FQ	46530 MW	51740 TQ	USBLS	5/07

AE	Average entry wage	AW	Average wage paid	FQ	First quartile wage
AER	Average entry range	AWR	Average wage range	H	Hourly
AEX	Average experienced wage	AXR	Average experienced range	HI	Highest wage paid
ATC	Average total compensation	D	Daily	HR	High end range

LO	Lowest wage paid	MTC	Median total compensation	TCC	Total cash compensation
LR	Low end range	MW	Median wage paid	TQ	Third quartile wage
M	Monthly	MWR	Median wage range	W	Weekly
MCC	Median cash compensation	S	See annotated source	Y	Yearly

Occupation/Type/Industry	Location	Per	Low	Mid	High	Source	Date
Civil Engineering Technician	South Carolina	Y	30990 FQ	37890 MW	47170 TQ	USBLS	5/07
	Charleston-North Charleston MSA, SC	Y	32320 FQ	41620 MW	49050 TQ	USBLS	5/07
	Columbia MSA, SC	Y	32000 FQ	36640 MW	45040 TQ	USBLS	5/07
	South Dakota	Y	29272 FQ	34258 MW	39416 TQ	SDBLS	7/08-9/08
	Sioux Falls MSA, SD	Y	30700 FQ	36044 MW	41493 TQ	SDBLS	7/08-9/08
	Tennessee	Y	32350 FQ	42000 MW	53640 TQ	USBLS	5/07
	Knoxville MSA, TN	Y	30650 FQ	39130 MW	49350 TQ	USBLS	5/07
	Memphis MSA, TN-MS-AR	Y	32570 FQ	42830 MW	52680 TQ	USBLS	5/07
	Nashville-Davidson-Murfreesboro MSA, TN	Y	43580 FQ	50850 MW	62470 TQ	USBLS	5/07
	Texas	Y	23400 FQ	32770 MW	46100 TQ	USBLS	5/07
	Austin-Round Rock MSA, TX	Y	30570 FQ	38230 MW	55870 TQ	USBLS	5/07
	Dallas-Fort Worth-Arlington MSA, TX	Y	27940 FQ	39040 MW	52790 TQ	USBLS	5/07
	El Paso MSA, TX	Y	26190 FQ	36100 MW	46250 TQ	USBLS	5/07
	Houston-Sugar Land-Baytown MSA, TX	Y	28440 FQ	37780 MW	55550 TQ	USBLS	5/07
	San Antonio MSA, TX	Y	27750 FQ	34030 MW	43730 TQ	USBLS	5/07
	Utah	Y	32640 FQ	40730 MW	48340 TQ	USBLS	5/07
	Salt Lake City MSA, UT	Y	32160 FQ	39820 MW	48040 TQ	USBLS	5/07
	Vermont	Y	39480 FQ	46310 MW	53830 TQ	USBLS	5/07
	Burlington-South Burlington MSA, VT	Y	32530 FQ	43170 MW	50830 TQ	USBLS	5/07
	Virginia	Y	34720 FQ	44490 MW	55200 TQ	USBLS	5/07
	Richmond MSA, VA	Y	34690 FQ	45150 MW	55330 TQ	USBLS	5/07
	Virginia Beach-Norfolk-Newport News MSA, VA-NC	Y	35490 FQ	44740 MW	53440 TQ	USBLS	5/07
	Washington	H	20.73 FQ	24.09 MW	28.18 TQ	WABLS	3/08
	Seattle-Tacoma-Bellevue MSA, WA	Y	42860 FQ	50180 MW	59190 TQ	USBLS	5/07
	West Virginia	Y	31804 FQ	38322 MW	46363 TQ	WVBLS	7/08-9/08
	Charleston MSA, WV	Y	31120 FQ	38380 MW	46940 TQ	USBLS	5/07
	Wisconsin	Y	36420 FQ	42770 MW	50180 TQ	USBLS	5/07
	Milwaukee-Waukesha-West Allis MSA, WI	Y	36070 FQ	43980 MW	52600 TQ	USBLS	5/07
	Wyoming	Y	32021 FQ	40193 MW	46609 TQ	WYBLS	9/08
	Cheyenne MSA, WY	Y	33195 FQ	41157 MW	46037 TQ	WYBLS	9/08
	Puerto Rico	Y	17350 FQ	25910 MW	43830 TQ	USBLS	5/07
	San Juan-Caguas-Guaynabo MSA, PR	Y	19560 FQ	33000 MW	45960 TQ	USBLS	5/07
Civil Rights Compliance Coordinator							
State Government	Ohio	H	18.36 LO		23.87 HI	ODAS	2008
Civil Rights Representative	Wayne County, MI	Y			48400-58819 HR	LSJ01	6/07
Civil Rights Specialist							
State Government	Ohio	H	17.22 LO		21.77 HI	ODAS	2008
Civil Service Commissioner	Cincinnati, OH	Y			6000 HI	COHSS	10/08
Claims Adjuster, Examiner, and Investigator	Alabama	Y	39190 FQ	54890 MW	68410 TQ	USBLS	5/07
	Birmingham-Hoover MSA, AL	Y	40280 FQ	55700 MW	70700 TQ	USBLS	5/07
	Montgomery MSA, AL	Y	36590 FQ	52000 MW	64790 TQ	USBLS	5/07
	Tuscaloosa MSA, AL	Y	35290 FQ	40830 MW	58480 TQ	USBLS	5/07
	Alaska	Y	41420 FQ	55670 MW	70600 TQ	USBLS	5/07
	Anchorage MSA, AK	Y	42620 FQ	56970 MW	71420 TQ	USBLS	5/07
	Arizona	Y	36720 FQ	47490 MW	62850 TQ	USBLS	5/07
	Phoenix-Mesa-Scottsdale MSA, AZ	Y	36500 FQ	46880 MW	62480 TQ	USBLS	5/07
	Tucson MSA, AZ	Y	41660 FQ	55670 MW	64570 TQ	USBLS	5/07
	Arkansas	Y	39480 FQ	52580 MW	63870 TQ	USBLS	5/07
	Little Rock-North Little Rock MSA, AR	Y	39670 FQ	51230 MW	63070 TQ	USBLS	5/07
	California	H	22.00 FQ	28.32 MW	35.25 TQ	CABLS	1/08-3/08
	Los Angeles-Long Beach-Glendale PMSA, CA	H	20.78 FQ	27.09 MW	33.94 TQ	CABLS	1/08-3/08

AE	Average entry wage	AW	Average wage paid	FQ	First quartile wage	LO	Lowest wage paid	MTC	Median total compensation	TCC	Total cash compensation
AER	Average entry range	AWR	Average wage range	H	Hourly	LR	Low end range	MW	Median wage paid	TQ	Third quartile wage
AEX	Average experienced wage	AXR	Average experienced range	HI	Highest wage paid	M	Monthly	MWR	Median wage range	W	Weekly
ATC	Average total compensation	D	Daily	HR	High end range	MCC	Median cash compensation	S	See annotated source	Y	Yearly

Occupation/Type/Industry	Location	Per	Low	Mid	High	Source	Date
Claims Adjuster, Examiner, and Investigator							
	Oakland-Fremont-Hayward MSA, CA	H	24.05 FQ	30.92 MW	37.35 TQ	CABLS	1/08-3/08
	Riverside-San Bernardino-Ontario MSA, CA	H	22.37 FQ	28.37 MW	34.55 TQ	CABLS	1/08-3/08
	Sacramento-Arden Arcade-Roseville MSA, CA	H	21.18 FQ	27.54 MW	34.46 TQ	CABLS	1/08-3/08
	San Diego-Carlsbad-San Marcos MSA, CA	H	21.53 FQ	27.32 MW	34.17 TQ	CABLS	1/08-3/08
	San Francisco-San Mateo-Redwood PMSA, CA	H	22.70 FQ	30.31 MW	38.46 TQ	CABLS	1/08-3/08
	San Jose-Sunnyvale-Santa Clara MSA, CA	H	25.76 FQ	32.40 MW	39.20 TQ	CABLS	1/08-3/08
	Santa Ana-Anaheim-Irvine PMSA, CA	Y	44290 FQ	58470 MW	72050 TQ	USBLS	5/07
	Santa Rosa-Petaluma MSA, CA	H	23.82 FQ	29.26 MW	35.05 TQ	CABLS	1/08-3/08
	Colorado	Y	41190 FQ	53750 MW	68620 TQ	USBLS	5/07
	Denver-Aurora MSA, CO	Y	44530 FQ	55740 MW	69840 TQ	USBLS	5/07
	Connecticut	H	21.13 AE	28.98 MW		CTBLS	1/08-3/08
	Bridgeport-Stamford-Norwalk MSA, CT	Y	50810 FQ	62000 MW	73530 TQ	USBLS	5/07
	Hartford-West Hartford-East Hartford MSA, CT	Y	47180 FQ	57830 MW	68420 TQ	USBLS	5/07
	Delaware	Y	35210 FQ	44320 MW	58880 TQ	USBLS	5/07
	Wilmington PMSA, DE-MD-NJ	Y	34820 FQ	43320 MW	59000 TQ	USBLS	5/07
	District of Columbia	Y	44230 FQ	59100 MW	75610 TQ	USBLS	5/07
	Washington-Arlington-Alexandria MSA, DC-VA-MD-WV	Y	40800 FQ	52360 MW	66360 TQ	USBLS	5/07
	Florida	Y	38140 FQ	49700 MW	63350 TQ	USBLS	5/07
	Fort Lauderdale-Pompano Beach-Deerfield Beach PMSA, FL	Y	41080 FQ	51870 MW	66890 TQ	USBLS	5/07
	Jacksonville MSA, FL	Y	36540 FQ	51630 MW	68490 TQ	USBLS	5/07
	Miami-Fort Lauderdale-Miami Beach MSA, FL	Y	37510 FQ	48510 MW	63600 TQ	USBLS	5/07
	Orlando-Kissimmee MSA, FL	Y	38510 FQ	49210 MW	61640 TQ	USBLS	5/07
	Pensacola-Ferry Pass-Brent MSA, FL	Y	43950 FQ	55670 MW	64030 TQ	USBLS	5/07
	Tampa-St. Petersburg-Clearwater MSA, FL	Y	38430 FQ	49280 MW	62540 TQ	USBLS	5/07
	West Palm Beach-Boca Raton-Boynton Beach PMSA, FL	Y	34240 FQ	44060 MW	65280 TQ	USBLS	5/07
	Georgia	Y	40250 FQ	49950 MW	62790 TQ	USBLS	5/07
	Atlanta-Sandy Springs-Marietta MSA, GA	Y	40330 FQ	49700 MW	62580 TQ	USBLS	5/07
	Augusta-Richmond County MSA, GA-SC	Y	34920 FQ	44730 MW	62690 TQ	USBLS	5/07
	Hawaii	Y	45450 FQ	59450 MW	74080 TQ	USBLS	5/07
	Honolulu MSA, HI	Y	45010 FQ	58330 MW	73120 TQ	USBLS	5/07
	Idaho	Y	32520 FQ	50180 MW	65390 TQ	USBLS	5/07
	Boise City-Nampa MSA, ID	Y	30550 FQ	42250 MW	62030 TQ	USBLS	5/07
	Illinois	Y	42950 FQ	56290 MW	75130 TQ	USBLS	5/07
	Chicago-Naperville-Joliet MSA, IL-IN-WI	Y	44100 FQ	56970 MW	76660 TQ	USBLS	5/07
	Rockford MSA, IL	Y	33240 FQ	44940 MW	61620 TQ	USBLS	5/07
	Indiana	Y	39110 FQ	50930 MW	65050 TQ	USBLS	5/07
	Gary PMSA, IN	Y	51430 FQ	67700 MW	77560 TQ	USBLS	5/07
	Indianapolis-Carmel MSA, IN	Y	38330 FQ	48940 MW	63070 TQ	USBLS	5/07
	Iowa	Y	36080 FQ	44650 MW	58260 TQ	USBLS	5/07
	Cedar Rapids MSA, IA	Y	36850 FQ	46470 MW	58440 TQ	USBLS	5/07
	Des Moines-West Des Moines MSA, IA	Y	36120 FQ	42830 MW	57080 TQ	USBLS	5/07
	Kansas	Y	39500 FQ	50340 MW	64450 TQ	USBLS	5/07
	Wichita MSA, KS	Y	42760 FQ	55430 MW	66370 TQ	USBLS	5/07
	Kentucky	Y	37414 FQ	49821 MW	65497 TQ	KYBLS	2008
	Louisville-Jefferson County MSA, KY-IN	Y	35580 FQ	45120 MW	61470 TQ	USBLS	5/07
	Owensboro MSA, KY	Y	39000 FQ	58020 MW	68540 TQ	USBLS	5/07
	Louisiana	H	20.99 FQ	26.72 MW	33.30 TQ	LABLS	1/08-3/08
	Baton Rouge MSA, LA	Y	37040 FQ	44220 MW	52510 TQ	USBLS	5/07

AE	Average entry wage	AW	Average wage paid	FQ	First quartile wage	LO	Lowest wage paid	MTC	Median total compensation	TCC	Total cash compensation
AER	Average entry range	AWR	Average wage range	H	Hourly	LR	Low end range	MW	Median wage paid	TQ	Third quartile wage
AEX	Average experienced wage	AXR	Average experienced range	HI	Highest wage paid	M	Monthly	MWR	Median wage range	W	Weekly
ATC	Average total compensation	D	Daily	HR	High end range	MCC	Median cash compensation	S	See annotated source	Y	Yearly

224

Occupation/Type/Industry	Location	Per	Low	Mid	High	Source	Date
Claims Adjuster, Examiner, and Investigator	New Orleans-Metairie-Kenner MSA, LA	Y	45020 FQ	55280 MW	70840 TQ	USBLS	5/07
	Maine	Y	39850 FQ	49360 MW	60780 TQ	USBLS	5/07
	Portland-South Portland-Biddeford MSA, ME	Y	41440 FQ	49320 MW	59930 TQ	USBLS	5/07
	Maryland	Y		55325 MW		MDBLS	3/08
	Baltimore-Towson MSA, MD	Y	41920 FQ	55060 MW	73690 TQ	USBLS	5/07
	Bethesda-Gaithersburg-Frederick PMSA, MD	Y	38030 FQ	49070 MW	64010 TQ	USBLS	5/07
	Massachusetts	Y	42170 FQ	53850 MW	69820 TQ	USBLS	5/07
	Boston-Cambridge-Quincy NECTA, MA	Y	43250 FQ	57630 MW	74770 TQ	USBLS	5/07
	Worcester MSA, MA-CT	Y	41820 FQ	49110 MW	59610 TQ	USBLS	5/07
	Michigan	Y	44350 FQ	56890 MW	70510 TQ	USBLS	5/07
	Detroit-Warren-Livonia MSA, MI	Y	45340 FQ	57410 MW	71300 TQ	USBLS	5/07
	Grand Rapids-Wyoming MSA, MI	Y	40120 FQ	51110 MW	66230 TQ	USBLS	5/07
	Muskegon-Norton Shores MSA, MI	Y	51770 FQ	61730 MW	73150 TQ	USBLS	5/07
	Warren-Troy-Farmington Hills PMSA, MI	Y	44810 FQ	57050 MW	71000 TQ	USBLS	5/07
	Minnesota	Y	37222 FQ	47993 MW	61944 TQ	MNBLS	10/08-12/08
	Duluth-Superior MSA, MN-WI	Y	29392 FQ	32739 MW	40945 TQ	MNBLS	10/08-12/08
	Minneapolis-Saint Paul MSA, MN-WI	Y	38734 FQ	48942 MW	62163 TQ	MNBLS	10/08-12/08
	Rochester MSA, MN	Y	41077 FQ	51021 MW	73322 TQ	MNBLS	10/08-12/08
	Mississippi	Y	44290 FQ	57390 MW	69170 TQ	USBLS	5/07
	Jackson MSA, MS	Y	40510 FQ	53980 MW	65230 TQ	USBLS	5/07
	Missouri	Y	38180 FQ	52100 MW	65000 TQ	USBLS	5/07
	Kansas City MSA, MO-KS	Y	40620 FQ	54080 MW	69500 TQ	USBLS	5/07
	St. Louis MSA, MO-IL	Y	38960 FQ	51000 MW	62450 TQ	USBLS	5/07
	Montana	Y	29470 FQ	39880 MW	52660 TQ	USBLS	5/07
	Billings MSA, MT	Y	44910 FQ	59370 MW	71670 TQ	USBLS	5/07
	Nebraska	Y	35930 FQ	46190 MW	59120 TQ	USBLS	5/07
	Lincoln MSA, NE	Y	36990 FQ	46510 MW	61280 TQ	USBLS	5/07
	Omaha-Council Bluffs MSA, NE-IA	Y	34880 FQ	43920 MW	56110 TQ	USBLS	5/07
	Nevada	H	19.49 FQ	24.23 MW	29.59 TQ	NVBLS	5/08
	Las Vegas-Paradise MSA, NV	H	19.64 FQ	24.03 MW	29.29 TQ	NVBLS	5/08
	New Hampshire	H	21.82 AE	28.07 MW	32.36 AEX	NHBLS	6/08
	Manchester MSA, NH	Y	48820 FQ	55270 MW	62230 TQ	USBLS	5/07
	Nashua NECTA, NH-MA	Y	39830 FQ	52120 MW	64540 TQ	USBLS	5/07
	New Jersey	Y	47590 FQ	59820 MW	73670 TQ	USBLS	5/07
	Camden PMSA, NJ	Y	46160 FQ	59750 MW	73670 TQ	USBLS	5/07
	Edison PMSA, NJ	Y	51770 FQ	63690 MW	74450 TQ	USBLS	5/07
	Newark-Union PMSA, NJ-PA	Y	47420 FQ	59710 MW	74490 TQ	USBLS	5/07
	New Mexico	Y	43130 FQ	56000 MW	70250 TQ	USBLS	5/07
	Albuquerque MSA, NM	Y	41870 FQ	54620 MW	69970 TQ	USBLS	5/07
	New York	Y	44800 FQ	58740 MW	76180 TQ	USBLS	5/07
	Albany-Schenectady-Troy MSA, NY	Y	39530 FQ	52170 MW	66840 TQ	USBLS	5/07
	Buffalo-Niagara Falls MSA, NY	Y	35990 FQ	49030 MW	61830 TQ	USBLS	5/07
	Nassau-Suffolk PMSA, NY	Y	45060 FQ	59650 MW	74620 TQ	USBLS	5/07
	New York-Northern New Jersey-Long Island MSA, NY-NJ-PA	Y	48160 FQ	62060 MW	78460 TQ	USBLS	5/07
	North Carolina	Y	38150 FQ	51850 MW	64840 TQ	USBLS	5/07
	Charlotte-Gastonia-Concord MSA, NC-SC	Y	41750 FQ	54810 MW	66600 TQ	USBLS	5/07
	Greensboro-High Point MSA, NC	Y	38550 FQ	53260 MW	67280 TQ	USBLS	5/07
	Raleigh-Cary MSA, NC	Y	34900 FQ	51100 MW	66070 TQ	USBLS	5/07
	North Dakota	Y	34460 FQ	41950 MW	52020 TQ	USBLS	5/07
	Fargo MSA, ND-MN	Y	32920 FQ	41910 MW	52510 TQ	USBLS	5/07
	Ohio	Y	42210 FQ	55720 MW	69730 TQ	USBLS	5/07
	Cincinnati-Middletown MSA, OH-KY-IN	Y	42900 FQ	56100 MW	71250 TQ	USBLS	5/07
	Cleveland-Elyria-Mentor MSA, OH	Y	43460 FQ	58130 MW	72690 TQ	USBLS	5/07

AE Average entry wage	**AW** Average wage paid	**FQ** First quartile wage	**LO** Lowest wage paid	**MTC** Median total compensation	**TCC** Total cash compensation
AER Average entry range	**AWR** Average wage range	**H** Hourly	**LR** Low end range	**MW** Median wage paid	**TQ** Third quartile wage
AEX Average experienced wage	**AXR** Average experienced range	**HI** Highest wage paid	**M** Monthly	**MWR** Median wage range	**W** Weekly
ATC Average total compensation	**D** Daily	**HR** High end range	**MCC** Median cash compensation	**S** See annotated source	**Y** Yearly

Occupation/Type/Industry	Location	Per	Low	Mid	High	Source	Date
Claims Adjuster, Examiner, and Investigator	Columbus MSA, OH	Y	41310 FQ	53360 MW	67690 TQ	USBLS	5/07
	Dayton MSA, OH	Y	44270 FQ	56210 MW	65330 TQ	USBLS	5/07
	Oklahoma	Y	33070 FQ	42810 MW	56910 TQ	USBLS	5/07
	Lawton MSA, OK	Y	37710 FQ	49450 MW	59200 TQ	USBLS	5/07
	Oklahoma City MSA, OK	Y	33020 FQ	40210 MW	53840 TQ	USBLS	5/07
	Tulsa MSA, OK	Y	32690 FQ	44010 MW	57790 TQ	USBLS	5/07
	Oregon	H	21.89 FQ	26.24 MW	31.00 TQ	ORBLS	5/08
	Eugene-Springfield MSA, OR	Y	49020 FQ	60120 MW	72840 TQ	USBLS	5/07
	Portland-Vancouver-Beaverton MSA, OR-WA	Y	43710 FQ	52480 MW	62240 TQ	USBLS	5/07
	Pennsylvania	Y	38590 FQ	51850 MW	66620 TQ	USBLS	5/07
	Allentown-Bethlehem-Easton MSA, PA-NJ	Y	32330 FQ	48740 MW	63860 TQ	USBLS	5/07
	Philadelphia-Camden-Wilmington MSA, PA-NJ-DE-MD	Y	40840 FQ	53830 MW	68740 TQ	USBLS	5/07
	Pittsburgh MSA, PA	Y	42200 FQ	53870 MW	68080 TQ	USBLS	5/07
	Rhode Island	Y	37030 FQ	48810 MW	64610 TQ	USBLS	5/07
	Providence-Fall River-Warwick MSA, RI-MA	Y	37240 FQ	47690 MW	63560 TQ	USBLS	5/07
	South Carolina	Y	40030 FQ	53250 MW	63750 TQ	USBLS	5/07
	Charleston-North Charleston MSA, SC	Y	38110 FQ	50560 MW	66750 TQ	USBLS	5/07
	Columbia MSA, SC	Y	37190 FQ	49160 MW	61410 TQ	USBLS	5/07
	South Dakota	Y	43546 FQ	52813 MW	67639 TQ	SDBLS	7/08-9/08
	Sioux Falls MSA, SD	Y	47611 FQ	57209 MW	69752 TQ	SDBLS	7/08-9/08
	Tennessee	Y	37410 FQ	51310 MW	63930 TQ	USBLS	5/07
	Johnson City MSA, TN	Y	37060 FQ	46020 MW	60200 TQ	USBLS	5/07
	Knoxville MSA, TN	Y	42630 FQ	60050 MW	73950 TQ	USBLS	5/07
	Memphis MSA, TN-MS-AR	Y	46670 FQ	55910 MW	65680 TQ	USBLS	5/07
	Nashville-Davidson-Murfreesboro MSA, TN	Y	35180 FQ	46730 MW	59990 TQ	USBLS	5/07
	Texas	Y	38950 FQ	52540 MW	66740 TQ	USBLS	5/07
	Austin-Round Rock MSA, TX	Y	35000 FQ	45540 MW	59510 TQ	USBLS	5/07
	Dallas-Fort Worth-Arlington MSA, TX	Y	43040 FQ	55130 MW	69930 TQ	USBLS	5/07
	El Paso MSA, TX	Y	30260 FQ	45120 MW	59680 TQ	USBLS	5/07
	Houston-Sugar Land-Baytown MSA, TX	Y	45190 FQ	58330 MW	72760 TQ	USBLS	5/07
	San Antonio MSA, TX	Y	30120 FQ	40870 MW	57680 TQ	USBLS	5/07
	Utah	Y	41120 FQ	54670 MW	64340 TQ	USBLS	5/07
	Salt Lake City MSA, UT	Y	41080 FQ	55560 MW	64980 TQ	USBLS	5/07
	Vermont	Y	49040 FQ	58840 MW	73210 TQ	USBLS	5/07
	Burlington-South Burlington MSA, VT	Y	52330 FQ	59310 MW	73270 TQ	USBLS	5/07
	Virginia	Y	39360 FQ	52360 MW	65340 TQ	USBLS	5/07
	Richmond MSA, VA	Y	42020 FQ	54710 MW	69370 TQ	USBLS	5/07
	Virginia Beach-Norfolk-Newport News MSA, VA-NC	Y	35500 FQ	51530 MW	67210 TQ	USBLS	5/07
	Washington	H	20.71 FQ	25.61 MW	32.22 TQ	WABLS	3/08
	Olympia MSA, WA	Y	44260 FQ	52980 MW	60530 TQ	USBLS	5/07
	Seattle-Tacoma-Bellevue MSA, WA	Y	42950 FQ	53260 MW	70060 TQ	USBLS	5/07
	West Virginia	Y	34425 FQ	55330 MW	69723 TQ	WVBLS	7/08-9/08
	Charleston MSA, WV	Y	30930 FQ	51740 MW	67100 TQ	USBLS	5/07
	Wisconsin	Y	39190 FQ	48580 MW	61790 TQ	USBLS	5/07
	Green Bay MSA, WI	Y	37320 FQ	46330 MW	58430 TQ	USBLS	5/07
	Milwaukee-Waukesha-West Allis MSA, WI	Y	38080 FQ	52020 MW	65960 TQ	USBLS	5/07
	Wyoming	Y	32535 FQ	45075 MW	60676 TQ	WYBLS	9/08
	Cheyenne MSA, WY	Y	32298 FQ	48511 MW	64357 TQ	WYBLS	9/08
	Puerto Rico	Y	22700 FQ	29860 MW	45390 TQ	USBLS	5/07
	San Juan-Caguas-Guaynabo MSA, PR	Y	21860 FQ	27750 MW	35790 TQ	USBLS	5/07
	Virgin Islands	Y	35400 FQ	49370 MW	59720 TQ	USBLS	5/07
	Guam	Y	24200 FQ	30890 MW	44070 TQ	USBLS	5/07
Claims Analyst	United States	Y		51900 AW		RIMS	5/5/08-6/30/08
Claims Examiner Specialist State Government	Ohio	H	18.36 LO		23.87 HI	ODAS	2008

AE Average entry wage	**AW** Average wage paid	**FQ** First quartile wage	**LO** Lowest wage paid	**MTC** Median total compensation	**TCC** Total cash compensation
AER Average entry range	**AWR** Average wage range	**H** Hourly	**LR** Low end range	**MW** Median wage paid	**TQ** Third quartile wage
AEX Average experienced wage	**AXR** Average experienced range	**HI** Highest wage paid	**M** Monthly	**MWR** Median wage range	**W** Weekly
ATC Average total compensation	**D** Daily	**HR** High end range	**MCC** Median cash compensation	**S** See annotated source	**Y** Yearly

Occupation/Type/Industry	Location	Per	Low	Mid	High	Source	Date
Cleaner of Vehicles and Equipment							
	Alabama	Y	14870 FQ	18310 MW	22880 TQ	USBLS	5/07
	Birmingham-Hoover MSA, AL	Y	16010 FQ	18730 MW	23900 TQ	USBLS	5/07
	Alaska	Y	19500 FQ	22590 MW	27350 TQ	USBLS	5/07
	Anchorage MSA, AK	Y	19510 FQ	22840 MW	27700 TQ	USBLS	5/07
	Arizona	Y	15020 FQ	17530 MW	21570 TQ	USBLS	5/07
	Flagstaff MSA, AZ	Y	15960 FQ	18440 MW	20800 TQ	USBLS	5/07
	Phoenix-Mesa-Scottsdale MSA, AZ	Y	15020 FQ	17720 MW	22080 TQ	USBLS	5/07
	Tucson MSA, AZ	Y	14750 FQ	16260 MW	19030 TQ	USBLS	5/07
	Arkansas	Y	15770 FQ	19400 MW	22910 TQ	USBLS	5/07
	Little Rock-North Little Rock MSA, AR	Y	14530 FQ	16290 MW	18330 TQ	USBLS	5/07
	California	H	8.13 FQ	9.04 MW	11.26 TQ	CABLS	1/08-3/08
	Fresno MSA, CA	H	8.22 FQ	9.02 MW	10.42 TQ	CABLS	1/08-3/08
	Los Angeles-Long Beach-Glendale PMSA, CA	H	8.00 FQ	8.88 MW	10.68 TQ	CABLS	1/08-3/08
	Modesto MSA, CA	H	8.11 FQ	9.04 MW	13.24 TQ	CABLS	1/08-3/08
	Oakland-Fremont-Hayward MSA, CA	H	8.00 FQ	9.14 MW	12.06 TQ	CABLS	1/08-3/08
	Riverside-San Bernardino-Ontario MSA, CA	H	8.28 FQ	8.99 MW	10.79 TQ	CABLS	1/08-3/08
	Sacramento-Arden Arcade-Roseville MSA, CA	H	8.71 FQ	9.95 MW	12.29 TQ	CABLS	1/08-3/08
	San Diego-Carlsbad-San Marcos MSA, CA	H	8.23 FQ	9.11 MW	11.17 TQ	CABLS	1/08-3/08
	San Francisco-San Mateo-Redwood PMSA, CA	H	8.37 FQ	10.11 MW	13.07 TQ	CABLS	1/08-3/08
	San Jose-Sunnyvale-Santa Clara MSA, CA	H	8.22 FQ	10.02 MW	14.35 TQ	CABLS	1/08-3/08
	Santa Ana-Anaheim-Irvine PMSA, CA	Y	16520 FQ	17940 MW	20420 TQ	USBLS	5/07
	Colorado	Y	16600 FQ	20460 MW	25310 TQ	USBLS	5/07
	Denver-Aurora MSA, CO	Y	17480 FQ	21670 MW	26600 TQ	USBLS	5/07
	Connecticut	H	8.64 AE	10.70 MW		CTBLS	1/08-3/08
	Bridgeport-Stamford-Norwalk MSA, CT	Y	17820 FQ	20610 MW	25610 TQ	USBLS	5/07
	Hartford-West Hartford-East Hartford MSA, CT	Y	17710 FQ	20630 MW	24650 TQ	USBLS	5/07
	Delaware	Y	16550 FQ	20130 MW	23870 TQ	USBLS	5/07
	Wilmington PMSA, DE-MD-NJ	Y	16080 FQ	19050 MW	25370 TQ	USBLS	5/07
	District of Columbia	Y	15600 FQ	17520 MW	21240 TQ	USBLS	5/07
	Washington-Arlington-Alexandria MSA, DC-VA-MD-WV	Y	17240 FQ	20190 MW	24550 TQ	USBLS	5/07
	Florida	Y	16330 FQ	18940 MW	23040 TQ	USBLS	5/07
	Fort Lauderdale-Pompano Beach-Deerfield Beach PMSA, FL	Y	16460 FQ	18670 MW	22010 TQ	USBLS	5/07
	Jacksonville MSA, FL	Y	15350 FQ	18380 MW	22790 TQ	USBLS	5/07
	Miami-Fort Lauderdale-Miami Beach MSA, FL	Y	16290 FQ	18850 MW	22710 TQ	USBLS	5/07
	Orlando-Kissimmee MSA, FL	Y	17000 FQ	19320 MW	23450 TQ	USBLS	5/07
	Tallahassee MSA, FL	Y	15430 FQ	17680 MW	21980 TQ	USBLS	5/07
	Tampa-St. Petersburg-Clearwater MSA, FL	Y	15860 FQ	18620 MW	23730 TQ	USBLS	5/07
	West Palm Beach-Boca Raton-Boynton Beach PMSA, FL	Y	17710 FQ	20350 MW	23990 TQ	USBLS	5/07
	Georgia	Y	15260 FQ	18450 MW	22200 TQ	USBLS	5/07
	Atlanta-Sandy Springs-Marietta MSA, GA	Y	15300 FQ	18550 MW	22300 TQ	USBLS	5/07
	Hawaii	Y	17400 FQ	19700 MW	23610 TQ	USBLS	5/07
	Honolulu MSA, HI	Y	17310 FQ	19510 MW	23440 TQ	USBLS	5/07
	Idaho	Y	15180 FQ	17820 MW	20980 TQ	USBLS	5/07
	Boise City-Nampa MSA, ID	Y	15730 FQ	18090 MW	21220 TQ	USBLS	5/07
	Pocatello MSA, ID	Y	14680 FQ	18530 MW	21320 TQ	USBLS	5/07
	Illinois	Y	15310 FQ	17870 MW	22790 TQ	USBLS	5/07
	Chicago-Naperville-Joliet MSA, IL-IN-WI	Y	15240 FQ	18060 MW	23810 TQ	USBLS	5/07
	Rockford MSA, IL	Y	14720 FQ	17340 MW	22910 TQ	USBLS	5/07
	Indiana	Y	14740 FQ	18730 MW	25450 TQ	USBLS	5/07

AE Average entry wage	**AW** Average wage paid	**FQ** First quartile wage	**LO** Lowest wage paid	**MTC** Median total compensation	**TCC** Total cash compensation
AER Average entry range	**AWR** Average wage range	**H** Hourly	**LR** Low end range	**MW** Median wage paid	**TQ** Third quartile wage
AEX Average experienced wage	**AXR** Average experienced range	**HI** Highest wage paid	**M** Monthly	**MWR** Median wage range	**W** Weekly
ATC Average total compensation	**D** Daily	**HR** High end range	**MCC** Median cash compensation	**S** See annotated source	**Y** Yearly

Cleaner of Vehicles and Equipment

Occupation/Type/Industry	Location	Per	Low	Mid	High	Source	Date
	Gary PMSA, IN	Y	14200 FQ	20210 MW	28160 TQ	USBLS	5/07
	Indianapolis-Carmel MSA, IN	Y	16350 FQ	20670 MW	28410 TQ	USBLS	5/07
	Iowa	Y	15270 FQ	18630 MW	23720 TQ	USBLS	5/07
	Cedar Rapids MSA, IA	Y	17430 FQ	19760 MW	25400 TQ	USBLS	5/07
	Des Moines-West Des Moines MSA, IA	Y	17860 FQ	22260 MW	29200 TQ	USBLS	5/07
	Kansas	Y	14770 FQ	18200 MW	22100 TQ	USBLS	5/07
	Lawrence MSA, KS	Y	15390 FQ	20910 MW	23600 TQ	USBLS	5/07
	Wichita MSA, KS	Y	14830 AE	17460 MW	20250 TQ	USBLS	5/07
	Kentucky	Y	15434 FQ	19006 MW	23725 TQ	KYBLS	2008
	Bowling Green MSA, KY	Y	14580 FQ	16380 MW	18330 TQ	USBLS	5/07
	Elizabethtown MSA, KY	Y	12760 FQ	14390 MW	17730 TQ	USBLS	5/07
	Louisville-Jefferson County MSA, KY-IN	Y	16610 FQ	20490 MW	26030 TQ	USBLS	5/07
	Louisiana	H	6.62 FQ	8.09 MW	9.96 TQ	LABLS	1/08-3/08
	Baton Rouge MSA, LA	Y	15100 FQ	18110 MW	23050 TQ	USBLS	5/07
	Lake Charles MSA, LA	Y	13190 FQ	15420 MW	18750 TQ	USBLS	5/07
	New Orleans-Metairie-Kenner MSA, LA	Y	15060 FQ	18700 MW	22020 TQ	USBLS	5/07
	Maine	Y	16940 FQ	20080 MW	24560 TQ	USBLS	5/07
	Portland-South Portland-Biddeford MSA, ME	Y	16810 FQ	19360 MW	25140 TQ	USBLS	5/07
	Maryland	Y		20375 MW		MDBLS	3/08
	Baltimore-Towson MSA, MD	Y	16840 FQ	20660 MW	25540 TQ	USBLS	5/07
	Bethesda-Gaithersburg-Frederick PMSA, MD	Y	17740 FQ	20170 MW	27520 TQ	USBLS	5/07
	Massachusetts	Y	18610 FQ	22200 MW	28370 TQ	USBLS	5/07
	Boston-Cambridge-Quincy NECTA, MA	Y	18360 FQ	21730 MW	27940 TQ	USBLS	5/07
	Lynn-Peabody-Salem NECTA, MA	Y	18670 FQ	23580 MW	28900 TQ	USBLS	5/07
	New Bedford MSA, MA	Y	18790 FQ	21640 MW	25510 TQ	USBLS	5/07
	Worcester MSA, MA-CT	Y	17600 FQ	19620 MW	25660 TQ	USBLS	5/07
	Michigan	Y	15590 FQ	19650 MW	27850 TQ	USBLS	5/07
	Detroit-Warren-Livonia MSA, MI	Y	16060 FQ	23470 MW	49500 TQ	USBLS	5/07
	Grand Rapids-Wyoming MSA, MI	Y	16860 FQ	19740 MW	24650 TQ	USBLS	5/07
	Lansing-East Lansing MSA, MI	Y	16350 FQ	19640 MW	23210 TQ	USBLS	5/07
	Warren-Troy-Farmington Hills PMSA, MI	Y	15470 FQ	19530 MW	29130 TQ	USBLS	5/07
	Minnesota	Y	18091 FQ	22024 MW	27048 TQ	MNBLS	10/08-12/08
	Duluth-Superior MSA, MN-WI	Y	14928 FQ	16759 MW	20463 TQ	MNBLS	10/08-12/08
	Minneapolis-Saint Paul MSA, MN-WI	Y	18206 FQ	22128 MW	29088 TQ	MNBLS	10/08-12/08
	Rochester MSA, MN	Y	22272 FQ	26303 MW	30418 TQ	MNBLS	10/08-12/08
	Mississippi	Y	15450 FQ	18500 MW	21740 TQ	USBLS	5/07
	Jackson MSA, MS	Y	14500 FQ	17540 MW	21330 TQ	USBLS	5/07
	Missouri	Y	14710 FQ	17230 MW	21780 TQ	USBLS	5/07
	Joplin MSA, MO	Y	15300 FQ	18860 MW	22110 TQ	USBLS	5/07
	Kansas City MSA, MO-KS	Y	16230 FQ	20030 MW	25520 TQ	USBLS	5/07
	St. Louis MSA, MO-IL	Y	14380 FQ	15680 MW	20550 TQ	USBLS	5/07
	Montana	Y	14590 FQ	16570 MW	19400 TQ	USBLS	5/07
	Billings MSA, MT	Y	14860 FQ	16810 MW	19040 TQ	USBLS	5/07
	Nebraska	Y	15830 FQ	18920 MW	23320 TQ	USBLS	5/07
	Omaha-Council Bluffs MSA, NE-IA	Y	16030 FQ	18930 MW	23130 TQ	USBLS	5/07
	Nevada	H	7.06 FQ	8.93 MW	11.18 TQ	NVBLS	5/08
	Las Vegas-Paradise MSA, NV	H	6.87 FQ	8.67 MW	10.65 TQ	NVBLS	5/08
	New Hampshire	H	8.60 AE	11.25 MW	13.62 AEX	NHBLS	6/08
	Manchester MSA, NH	Y	20390 FQ	23180 MW	28130 TQ	USBLS	5/07
	Nashua NECTA, NH-MA	Y	21640 FQ	25190 MW	31410 TQ	USBLS	5/07
	New Jersey	Y	15540 FQ	18190 MW	24250 TQ	USBLS	5/07
	Camden PMSA, NJ	Y	15360 FQ	15940 MW	21330 TQ	USBLS	5/07
	Edison PMSA, NJ	Y	15500 FQ	18920 MW	26520 TQ	USBLS	5/07
	Newark-Union PMSA, NJ-PA	Y	15480 FQ	17170 MW	21110 TQ	USBLS	5/07
	Ocean City MSA, NJ	Y	15830 FQ	17420 MW	19610 TQ	USBLS	5/07
	New Mexico	Y	13740 FQ	17050 MW	21540 TQ	USBLS	5/07
	Albuquerque MSA, NM	Y	13810 FQ	17400 MW	22610 TQ	USBLS	5/07
	Las Cruces MSA, NM	Y	13910 FQ	16230 MW	18370 TQ	USBLS	5/07
	New York	Y	17170 FQ	21690 MW	33810 TQ	USBLS	5/07

AE	Average entry wage	AW	Average wage paid	FQ	First quartile wage	LO	Lowest wage paid	MTC	Median total compensation	TCC	Total cash compensation
AER	Average entry range	AWR	Average wage range	H	Hourly	LR	Low end range	MW	Median wage paid	TQ	Third quartile wage
AEX	Average experienced wage	AXR	Average experienced range	HI	Highest wage paid	M	Monthly	MWR	Median wage range	W	Weekly
ATC	Average total compensation	D	Daily	HR	High end range	MCC	Median cash compensation	S	See annotated source	Y	Yearly

228

Occupation/Type/Industry	Location	Per	Low	Mid	High	Source	Date
Cleaner of Vehicles and Equipment							
	Albany-Schenectady-Troy MSA, NY	Y	16690 FQ	21350 MW	26690 TQ	USBLS	5/07
	Buffalo-Niagara Falls MSA, NY	Y	14880 FQ	16090 MW	19610 TQ	USBLS	5/07
	Nassau-Suffolk PMSA, NY	Y	17580 FQ	21830 MW	28750 TQ	USBLS	5/07
	New York-Northern New Jersey-Long Island MSA, NY-NJ-PA	Y	17040 FQ	22050 MW	34190 TQ	USBLS	5/07
	North Carolina	Y	15370 FQ	18910 MW	23230 TQ	USBLS	5/07
	Charlotte-Gastonia-Concord MSA, NC-SC	Y	16290 FQ	21190 MW	29490 TQ	USBLS	5/07
	Raleigh-Cary MSA, NC	Y	20160 FQ	22050 MW	23960 TQ	USBLS	5/07
	North Dakota	Y	13580 FQ	15870 MW	18160 TQ	USBLS	5/07
	Bismarck MSA, ND	Y	14830 FQ	16780 MW	18560 TQ	USBLS	5/07
	Fargo MSA, ND-MN	Y	13690 FQ	16000 MW	18100 TQ	USBLS	5/07
	Ohio	Y	15510 FQ	19160 MW	24670 TQ	USBLS	5/07
	Cincinnati-Middletown MSA, OH-KY-IN	Y	16190 FQ	19500 MW	24020 TQ	USBLS	5/07
	Cleveland-Elyria-Mentor MSA, OH	Y	16640 FQ	20160 MW	25200 TQ	USBLS	5/07
	Columbus MSA, OH	Y	17810 FQ	21180 MW	25900 TQ	USBLS	5/07
	Dayton MSA, OH	Y	14990 FQ	18820 MW	27220 TQ	USBLS	5/07
	Mansfield MSA, OH	Y	15540 FQ	18060 MW	51100 TQ	USBLS	5/07
	Oklahoma	Y	15160 FQ	18600 MW	24420 TQ	USBLS	5/07
	Oklahoma City MSA, OK	Y	15000 FQ	17900 MW	26980 TQ	USBLS	5/07
	Tulsa MSA, OK	Y	16730 FQ	20930 MW	32980 TQ	USBLS	5/07
	Oregon	H	8.85 FQ	9.83 MW	11.96 TQ	ORBLS	5/08
	Portland-Vancouver-Beaverton MSA, OR-WA	Y	18070 FQ	20280 MW	24600 TQ	USBLS	5/07
	Pennsylvania	Y	15550 FQ	18560 MW	23010 TQ	USBLS	5/07
	Allentown-Bethlehem-Easton MSA, PA-NJ	Y	15690 FQ	19970 MW	23420 TQ	USBLS	5/07
	Philadelphia-Camden-Wilmington MSA, PA-NJ-DE-MD	Y	15640 FQ	18120 MW	22530 TQ	USBLS	5/07
	Pittsburgh MSA, PA	Y	14660 FQ	16510 MW	20790 TQ	USBLS	5/07
	Rhode Island	Y	17720 FQ	21500 MW	26510 TQ	USBLS	5/07
	Providence-Fall River-Warwick MSA, RI-MA	Y	18050 FQ	21650 MW	26300 TQ	USBLS	5/07
	South Carolina	Y	14190 FQ	17080 MW	21210 TQ	USBLS	5/07
	Charleston-North Charleston MSA, SC	Y	14320 FQ	17200 MW	21330 TQ	USBLS	5/07
	Columbia MSA, SC	Y	13600 FQ	16100 MW	20000 TQ	USBLS	5/07
	South Dakota	Y	14515 FQ	17251 MW	19981 TQ	SDBLS	7/08-9/08
	Sioux Falls MSA, SD	Y	14282 FQ	16778 MW	19144 TQ	SDBLS	7/08-9/08
	Tennessee	Y	14520 FQ	17390 MW	20670 TQ	USBLS	5/07
	Clarksville MSA, TN-KY	Y	13110 FQ	15190 MW	18370 TQ	USBLS	5/07
	Johnson City MSA, TN	Y	14790 FQ	16660 MW	18730 TQ	USBLS	5/07
	Memphis MSA, TN-MS-AR	Y	13740 FQ	16020 MW	19570 TQ	USBLS	5/07
	Nashville-Davidson-Murfreesboro MSA, TN	Y	15830 FQ	17880 MW	20820 TQ	USBLS	5/07
	Texas	Y	13820 FQ	16890 MW	20960 TQ	USBLS	5/07
	Austin-Round Rock MSA, TX	Y	16410 FQ	19270 MW	22900 TQ	USBLS	5/07
	Dallas-Fort Worth-Arlington MSA, TX	Y	14030 FQ	17500 MW	22560 TQ	USBLS	5/07
	El Paso MSA, TX	Y	12560 FQ	14170 MW	16210 TQ	USBLS	5/07
	Houston-Sugar Land-Baytown MSA, TX	Y	14570 FQ	18000 MW	22370 TQ	USBLS	5/07
	San Antonio MSA, TX	Y	13440 FQ	16030 MW	19830 TQ	USBLS	5/07
	Utah	Y	15490 FQ	18450 MW	22420 TQ	USBLS	5/07
	Ogden-Clearfield MSA, UT	Y	13560 FQ	17070 MW	21710 TQ	USBLS	5/07
	Salt Lake City MSA, UT	Y	16350 FQ	19030 MW	22940 TQ	USBLS	5/07
	Vermont	Y	19270 FQ	22930 MW	27930 TQ	USBLS	5/07
	Burlington-South Burlington MSA, VT	Y	19970 FQ	23460 MW	28350 TQ	USBLS	5/07
	Virginia	Y	16510 FQ	19870 MW	24310 TQ	USBLS	5/07
	Richmond MSA, VA	Y	15100 FQ	19050 MW	23390 TQ	USBLS	5/07
	Virginia Beach-Norfolk-Newport News MSA, VA-NC	Y	16460 FQ	20000 MW	26940 TQ	USBLS	5/07
	Washington	H	8.82 FQ	9.88 MW	12.27 TQ	WABLS	3/08

AE Average entry wage	**AW** Average wage paid	**FQ** First quartile wage	**LO** Lowest wage paid	**MTC** Median total compensation	**TCC** Total cash compensation
AER Average entry range	**AWR** Average wage range	**H** Hourly	**LR** Low end range	**MW** Median wage paid	**TQ** Third quartile wage
AEX Average experienced wage	**AXR** Average experienced range	**HI** Highest wage paid	**M** Monthly	**MWR** Median wage range	**W** Weekly
ATC Average total compensation	**D** Daily	**HR** High end range	**MCC** Median cash compensation	**S** See annotated source	**Y** Yearly

Occupation/Type/Industry	Location	Per	Low	Mid	High	Source	Date
Cleaner of Vehicles and Equipment	Seattle-Tacoma-Bellevue MSA, WA	Y	18390 FQ	21130 MW	27000 TQ	USBLS	5/07
	West Virginia	Y	14282 FQ	15890 MW	18844 TQ	WVBLS	7/08-9/08
	Charleston MSA, WV	Y	13930 FQ	15470 MW	18060 TQ	USBLS	5/07
	Wisconsin	Y	15700 FQ	19600 MW	25510 TQ	USBLS	5/07
	Green Bay MSA, WI	Y	15130 FQ	18100 MW	25030 TQ	USBLS	5/07
	Milwaukee-Waukesha-West Allis MSA, WI	Y	15860 FQ	18970 MW	24790 TQ	USBLS	5/07
	Wyoming	Y	16310 FQ	18799 MW	23195 TQ	WYBLS	9/08
	Cheyenne MSA, WY	Y	16383 FQ	17888 MW	20016 TQ	WYBLS	9/08
	Puerto Rico	Y	12320 FQ	13500 MW	14690 TQ	USBLS	5/07
	San Juan-Caguas-Guaynabo MSA, PR	Y	12330 FQ	13530 MW	14740 TQ	USBLS	5/07
	Virgin Islands	Y	14630 FQ	16720 MW	18500 TQ	USBLS	5/07
	Guam	Y	12550 FQ	13970 MW	15800 TQ	USBLS	5/07
Cleaning, Washing, and Metal Pickling Equipment Operator and Tender	Alabama	Y	19210 FQ	23640 MW	42880 TQ	USBLS	5/07
	Birmingham-Hoover MSA, AL	Y	20970 FQ	23450 MW	29930 TQ	USBLS	5/07
	Arizona	Y	17280 FQ	20130 MW	28800 TQ	USBLS	5/07
	Phoenix-Mesa-Scottsdale MSA, AZ	Y	17200 FQ	20840 MW	29290 TQ	USBLS	5/07
	Arkansas	Y	17530 FQ	20330 MW	23140 TQ	USBLS	5/07
	California	H	8.76 FQ	10.37 MW	14.71 TQ	CABLS	1/08-3/08
	Los Angeles-Long Beach-Glendale PMSA, CA	H	8.53 FQ	9.57 MW	12.37 TQ	CABLS	1/08-3/08
	Modesto MSA, CA	H	9.07 FQ	10.63 MW	13.59 TQ	CABLS	1/08-3/08
	Oakland-Fremont-Hayward MSA, CA	H	8.90 FQ	10.49 MW	15.88 TQ	CABLS	1/08-3/08
	Riverside-San Bernardino-Ontario MSA, CA	H	8.48 FQ	9.27 MW	10.72 TQ	CABLS	1/08-3/08
	San Diego-Carlsbad-San Marcos MSA, CA	H	12.20 FQ	17.47 MW	21.66 TQ	CABLS	1/08-3/08
	San Francisco-San Mateo-Redwood PMSA, CA	H	8.00 FQ	8.05 MW	12.76 TQ	CABLS	1/08-3/08
	San Jose-Sunnyvale-Santa Clara MSA, CA	H	13.33 FQ	15.41 MW	17.79 TQ	CABLS	1/08-3/08
	Santa Ana-Anaheim-Irvine PMSA, CA	Y	17160 FQ	18660 MW	22520 TQ	USBLS	5/07
	Colorado	Y	22820 FQ	27840 MW	31230 TQ	USBLS	5/07
	Connecticut	H	10.45 AE	14.13 MW		CTBLS	1/08-3/08
	Hartford-West Hartford-East Hartford MSA, CT	Y	25990 FQ	30900 MW	37780 TQ	USBLS	5/07
	Florida	Y	20450 FQ	24330 MW	29050 TQ	USBLS	5/07
	Miami-Fort Lauderdale-Miami Beach MSA, FL	Y	18980 FQ	23160 MW	29270 TQ	USBLS	5/07
	Tampa-St. Petersburg-Clearwater MSA, FL	Y	20460 FQ	23720 MW	31500 TQ	USBLS	5/07
	Georgia	Y	18330 FQ	22270 MW	28110 TQ	USBLS	5/07
	Atlanta-Sandy Springs-Marietta MSA, GA	Y	20900 FQ	24540 MW	28190 TQ	USBLS	5/07
	Idaho	Y	15090 FQ	18810 MW	27620 TQ	USBLS	5/07
	Illinois	Y	19000 FQ	22950 MW	32210 TQ	USBLS	5/07
	Chicago-Naperville-Joliet MSA, IL-IN-WI	Y	18740 FQ	22160 MW	29320 TQ	USBLS	5/07
	Indiana	Y	22000 FQ	26600 MW	30910 TQ	USBLS	5/07
	Elkhart-Goshen MSA, IN	Y	20590 FQ	23520 MW	28060 TQ	USBLS	5/07
	Indianapolis-Carmel MSA, IN	Y	21910 FQ	25030 MW	34950 TQ	USBLS	5/07
	Iowa	Y	20590 FQ	24760 MW	31240 TQ	USBLS	5/07
	Cedar Rapids MSA, IA	Y	23150 FQ	29710 MW	32390 TQ	USBLS	5/07
	Kansas	Y	19420 FQ	21820 MW	29240 TQ	USBLS	5/07
	Kentucky	Y	22854 FQ	26472 MW	32607 TQ	KYBLS	2008
	Louisiana	H	10.17 FQ	11.12 MW	12.12 TQ	LABLS	1/08-3/08
	Maine	Y	21270 FQ	22640 MW	24010 TQ	USBLS	5/07
	Maryland	Y		42350 MW		MDBLS	3/08
	Massachusetts	Y	15770 FQ	20690 MW	28470 TQ	USBLS	5/07
	Boston-Cambridge-Quincy NECTA, MA	Y	22510 FQ	27300 MW	32380 TQ	USBLS	5/07
	Worcester MSA, MA-CT	Y	26850 FQ	30410 MW	34610 TQ	USBLS	5/07

AE	Average entry wage	AW	Average wage paid	FQ	First quartile wage	LO	Lowest wage paid	MTC	Median total compensation	TCC Total cash compensation
AER	Average entry range	AWR	Average wage range	H	Hourly	LR	Low end range	MW	Median wage paid	TQ Third quartile wage
AEX	Average experienced wage	AXR	Average experienced range	HI	Highest wage paid	M	Monthly	MWR	Median wage range	W Weekly
ATC	Average total compensation	D	Daily	HR	High end range	MCC	Median cash compensation	S	See annotated source	Y Yearly

Occupation/Type/Industry	Location	Per	Low	Mid	High	Source	Date
Cleaning, Washing, and Metal Pickling Equipment Operator and Tender							
	Michigan	Y	19450 FQ	23080 MW	27680 TQ	USBLS	5/07
	Detroit-Warren-Livonia MSA, MI	Y	17320 FQ	21810 MW	27260 TQ	USBLS	5/07
	Grand Rapids-Wyoming MSA, MI	Y	18550 FQ	22710 MW	27460 TQ	USBLS	5/07
	Warren-Troy-Farmington Hills PMSA, MI	Y	17240 FQ	20190 MW	24090 TQ	USBLS	5/07
	Minnesota	Y	23771 FQ	29628 MW	36916 TQ	MNBLS	10/08-12/08
	Minneapolis-Saint Paul MSA, MN-WI	Y	27109 FQ	31100 MW	36542 TQ	MNBLS	10/08-12/08
	Mississippi	Y	20100 FQ	23870 MW	28620 TQ	USBLS	5/07
	Missouri	Y	20980 FQ	24700 MW	31910 TQ	USBLS	5/07
	Kansas City MSA, MO-KS	Y	20920 FQ	23520 MW	31910 TQ	USBLS	5/07
	St. Louis MSA, MO-IL	Y	23890 FQ	32710 MW	36900 TQ	USBLS	5/07
	Nebraska	Y	21990 FQ	25300 MW	28290 TQ	USBLS	5/07
	Nevada	H	9.90 FQ	11.26 MW	13.61 TQ	NVBLS	5/08
	Las Vegas-Paradise MSA, NV	H	9.90 FQ	11.26 MW	13.61 TQ	NVBLS	5/08
	New Hampshire	H	10.52 AE	14.43 MW	16.99 AEX	NHBLS	6/08
	New Jersey	Y	18630 FQ	22470 MW	29610 TQ	USBLS	5/07
	Camden PMSA, NJ	Y	18350 FQ	20320 MW	23120 TQ	USBLS	5/07
	Edison PMSA, NJ	Y	23630 FQ	29970 MW	39740 TQ	USBLS	5/07
	Newark-Union PMSA, NJ-PA	Y	17540 FQ	22830 MW	32500 TQ	USBLS	5/07
	New Mexico	Y	12920 FQ	14840 MW	17890 TQ	USBLS	5/07
	New York	Y	23250 FQ	30100 MW	35370 TQ	USBLS	5/07
	Nassau-Suffolk PMSA, NY	Y	22890 FQ	32440 MW	36210 TQ	USBLS	5/07
	New York-Northern New Jersey-Long Island MSA, NY-NJ-PA	Y	20730 FQ	25500 MW	34100 TQ	USBLS	5/07
	North Carolina	Y	17300 FQ	19470 MW	23290 TQ	USBLS	5/07
	Charlotte-Gastonia-Concord MSA, NC-SC	Y	19230 FQ	22880 MW	28820 TQ	USBLS	5/07
	Ohio	Y	20520 FQ	24030 MW	32250 TQ	USBLS	5/07
	Cincinnati-Middletown MSA, OH-KY-IN	Y	24110 FQ	29630 MW	36370 TQ	USBLS	5/07
	Cleveland-Elyria-Mentor MSA, OH	Y	17970 FQ	23300 MW	33870 TQ	USBLS	5/07
	Columbus MSA, OH	Y	19870 FQ	22130 MW	24420 TQ	USBLS	5/07
	Dayton MSA, OH	Y	21020 FQ	24510 MW	32710 TQ	USBLS	5/07
	Oklahoma	Y	18240 FQ	20920 MW	23540 TQ	USBLS	5/07
	Oregon	H	9.09 FQ	10.74 MW	13.84 TQ	ORBLS	5/08
	Portland-Vancouver-Beaverton MSA, OR-WA	Y	18990 FQ	22500 MW	30540 TQ	USBLS	5/07
	Pennsylvania	Y	17770 FQ	22200 MW	30460 TQ	USBLS	5/07
	Philadelphia-Camden-Wilmington MSA, PA-NJ-DE-MD	Y	21390 FQ	29670 MW	36090 TQ	USBLS	5/07
	Pittsburgh MSA, PA	Y	16310 FQ	19070 MW	23830 TQ	USBLS	5/07
	Providence-Fall River-Warwick MSA, RI-MA	Y	18830 FQ	23190 MW	30960 TQ	USBLS	5/07
	South Carolina	Y	19440 FQ	21470 MW	23410 TQ	USBLS	5/07
	South Dakota	Y	23810 FQ	26811 MW	29766 TQ	SDBLS	7/08-9/08
	Tennessee	Y	20940 FQ	23400 MW	27120 TQ	USBLS	5/07
	Memphis MSA, TN-MS-AR	Y	18590 FQ	26010 MW	30170 TQ	USBLS	5/07
	Nashville-Davidson-Murfreesboro MSA, TN	Y	25680 FQ	30460 MW	35750 TQ	USBLS	5/07
	Texas	Y	17260 FQ	20250 MW	23620 TQ	USBLS	5/07
	Dallas-Fort Worth-Arlington MSA, TX	Y	16670 FQ	19350 MW	24300 TQ	USBLS	5/07
	Houston-Sugar Land-Baytown MSA, TX	Y	17640 FQ	20440 MW	24110 TQ	USBLS	5/07
	San Antonio MSA, TX	Y	20870 FQ	25200 MW	28830 TQ	USBLS	5/07
	Utah	Y	16220 FQ	18330 MW	22350 TQ	USBLS	5/07
	Vermont	Y	24560 FQ	27570 MW	30950 TQ	USBLS	5/07
	Virginia	Y	19260 FQ	22780 MW	26390 TQ	USBLS	5/07
	Virginia Beach-Norfolk-Newport News MSA, VA-NC	Y	20740 FQ	23860 MW	27600 TQ	USBLS	5/07
	Washington	H	11.01 FQ	16.14 MW	20.97 TQ	WABLS	3/08
	Seattle-Tacoma-Bellevue MSA, WA	Y	36020 FQ	48400 MW	56120 TQ	USBLS	5/07

AE Average entry wage	**AW** Average wage paid	**FQ** First quartile wage	**LO** Lowest wage paid	**MTC** Median total compensation	**TCC** Total cash compensation
AER Average entry range	**AWR** Average wage range	**H** Hourly	**LR** Low end range	**MW** Median wage paid	**TQ** Third quartile wage
AEX Average experienced wage	**AXR** Average experienced range	**HI** Highest wage paid	**M** Monthly	**MWR** Median wage range	**W** Weekly
ATC Average total compensation	**D** Daily	**HR** High end range	**MCC** Median cash compensation	**S** See annotated source	**Y** Yearly

Occupation/Type/Industry	Location	Per	Low	Mid	High	Source	Date
Cleaning, Washing, and Metal Pickling Equipment Operator and Tender							
	West Virginia	Y	17846 FQ	21166 MW	25836 TQ	WVBLS	7/08-9/08
	Wheeling MSA, WV-OH	Y	30910 FQ	33230 MW	35520 TQ	USBLS	5/07
	Wisconsin	Y	24000 FQ	31530 MW	34990 TQ	USBLS	5/07
	Milwaukee-Waukesha-West Allis MSA, WI	Y	23210 FQ	30450 MW	33710 TQ	USBLS	5/07
	Puerto Rico	Y	12970 FQ	14710 MW	19690 TQ	USBLS	5/07
Cleaning Service Supervisor							
Municipal Government	Cincinnati, OH	Y	38340 LO		43264 HI	COHSS	10/08
Clearance Technician							
Department of Employment Security	New Hampshire	Y			39860 HI	NHUL03	2008
Clergy							
	Alabama	Y	30980 FQ	37410 MW	46090 TQ	USBLS	5/07
	Birmingham-Hoover MSA, AL	Y	39370 FQ	46060 MW	52460 TQ	USBLS	5/07
	Mobile MSA, AL	Y	27350 FQ	34500 MW	38750 TQ	USBLS	5/07
	Alaska	Y	22900 FQ	37610 MW	45280 TQ	USBLS	5/07
	Anchorage MSA, AK	Y	34870 FQ	38210 MW	42150 TQ	USBLS	5/07
	Arizona	Y	31230 FQ	37190 MW	44500 TQ	USBLS	5/07
	Phoenix-Mesa-Scottsdale MSA, AZ	Y	29950 FQ	35140 MW	42360 TQ	USBLS	5/07
	Tucson MSA, AZ	Y	37230 FQ	42200 MW	47480 TQ	USBLS	5/07
	Arkansas	Y	28500 FQ	34170 MW	45250 TQ	USBLS	5/07
	Little Rock-North Little Rock MSA, AR	Y	29070 FQ	37340 MW	49070 TQ	USBLS	5/07
	California	H	17.97 FQ	24.98 MW	32.39 TQ	CABLS	1/08-3/08
	Bakersfield MSA, CA	H	15.38 FQ	17.08 MW	19.59 TQ	CABLS	1/08-3/08
	Los Angeles-Long Beach-Glendale PMSA, CA	H	22.76 FQ	27.19 MW	35.26 TQ	CABLS	1/08-3/08
	Oakland-Fremont-Hayward MSA, CA	H	13.40 FQ	19.51 MW	34.91 TQ	CABLS	1/08-3/08
	Riverside-San Bernardino-Ontario MSA, CA	H	16.82 FQ	20.03 MW	27.73 TQ	CABLS	1/08-3/08
	Sacramento-Arden Arcade-Roseville MSA, CA	H	19.49 FQ	26.64 MW	31.62 TQ	CABLS	1/08-3/08
	San Diego-Carlsbad-San Marcos MSA, CA	H	18.33 FQ	23.69 MW	30.46 TQ	CABLS	1/08-3/08
	San Francisco-San Mateo-Redwood PMSA, CA	H	21.33 FQ	29.22 MW	37.34 TQ	CABLS	1/08-3/08
	San Jose-Sunnyvale-Santa Clara MSA, CA	H	20.71 FQ	29.37 MW	38.79 TQ	CABLS	1/08-3/08
	Santa Ana-Anaheim-Irvine PMSA, CA	Y	44830 FQ	59470 MW	77770 TQ	USBLS	5/07
	Colorado	Y	34940 FQ	45580 MW	58090 TQ	USBLS	5/07
	Denver-Aurora MSA, CO	Y	38700 FQ	48970 MW	63240 TQ	USBLS	5/07
	Connecticut	H	15.89 AE	27.72 MW		CTBLS	1/08-3/08
	Bridgeport-Stamford-Norwalk MSA, CT	Y	42970 FQ	55880 MW	68840 TQ	USBLS	5/07
	Hartford-West Hartford-East Hartford MSA, CT	Y	28790 FQ	52230 MW	62300 TQ	USBLS	5/07
	Delaware	Y	37450 FQ	46760 MW	58300 TQ	USBLS	5/07
	Wilmington PMSA, DE-MD-NJ	Y	35390 FQ	44950 MW	65360 TQ	USBLS	5/07
	District of Columbia	Y	40580 FQ	55730 MW	63050 TQ	USBLS	5/07
	Washington-Arlington-Alexandria MSA, DC-VA-MD-WV	Y	29480 FQ	43430 MW	58320 TQ	USBLS	5/07
	Florida	Y	26600 FQ	35570 MW	48120 TQ	USBLS	5/07
	Fort Lauderdale-Pompano Beach-Deerfield Beach PMSA, FL	Y	28430 FQ	41500 MW	49400 TQ	USBLS	5/07
	Jacksonville MSA, FL	Y	23780 FQ	33310 MW	40740 TQ	USBLS	5/07
	Lakeland MSA, FL	Y	30380 FQ	35250 MW	42950 TQ	USBLS	5/07
	Miami-Fort Lauderdale-Miami Beach MSA, FL	Y	27260 FQ	37130 MW	49010 TQ	USBLS	5/07
	Orlando-Kissimmee MSA, FL	Y	27030 FQ	32800 MW	47760 TQ	USBLS	5/07
	Tampa-St. Petersburg-Clearwater MSA, FL	Y	23880 FQ	40810 MW	55810 TQ	USBLS	5/07
	West Palm Beach-Boca Raton-Boynton Beach PMSA, FL	Y	35070 FQ	49850 MW	59820 TQ	USBLS	5/07

AE	Average entry wage	AW	Average wage paid	FQ	First quartile wage	LO	Lowest wage paid	MTC	Median total compensation	TCC	Total cash compensation
AER	Average entry range	AWR	Average wage range	H	Hourly	LR	Low end range	MW	Median wage paid	TQ	Third quartile wage
AEX	Average experienced wage	AXR	Average experienced range	HI	Highest wage paid	M	Monthly	MWR	Median wage range	W	Weekly
ATC	Average total compensation	D	Daily	HR	High end range	MCC	Median cash compensation	S	See annotated source	Y	Yearly

Occupation/Type/Industry	Location	Per	Low	Mid	High	Source	Date
Clergy	Georgia	Y	29540 FQ	39080 MW	55350 TQ	USBLS	5/07
	Atlanta-Sandy Springs-Marietta MSA, GA	Y	28620 FQ	37150 MW	56830 TQ	USBLS	5/07
	Hawaii	Y	23160 FQ	36040 MW	46990 TQ	USBLS	5/07
	Honolulu MSA, HI	Y	30910 FQ	37540 MW	48750 TQ	USBLS	5/07
	Idaho	Y	34480 FQ	40950 MW	46840 TQ	USBLS	5/07
	Illinois	Y	24960 FQ	38310 MW	50600 TQ	USBLS	5/07
	Chicago-Naperville-Joliet MSA, IL-IN-WI	Y	23860 FQ	36180 MW	48980 TQ	USBLS	5/07
	Indiana	Y	22300 FQ	35350 MW	46100 TQ	USBLS	5/07
	Gary PMSA, IN	Y	14190 FQ	18440 MW	32520 TQ	USBLS	5/07
	Indianapolis-Carmel MSA, IN	Y	35840 FQ	44620 MW	52810 TQ	USBLS	5/07
	South Bend-Mishawaka MSA, IN-MI	Y	39610 FQ	46430 MW	54050 TQ	USBLS	5/07
	Iowa	Y	30620 FQ	38040 MW	47280 TQ	USBLS	5/07
	Des Moines-West Des Moines MSA, IA	Y	31030 FQ	40020 MW	47390 TQ	USBLS	5/07
	Kansas	Y	32430 FQ	37550 MW	46300 TQ	USBLS	5/07
	Wichita MSA, KS	Y	27020 FQ	35700 MW	43470 TQ	USBLS	5/07
	Kentucky	Y	35282 FQ	42729 MW	52081 TQ	KYBLS	2008
	Louisville-Jefferson County MSA, KY-IN	Y	35770 FQ	41680 MW	49610 TQ	USBLS	5/07
	Louisiana	H	15.80 FQ	20.52 MW	24.26 TQ	LABLS	1/08-3/08
	New Orleans-Metairie-Kenner MSA, LA	Y	30710 FQ	41650 MW	48830 TQ	USBLS	5/07
	Maine	Y	36880 FQ	45670 MW	55370 TQ	USBLS	5/07
	Maryland	Y		45925 MW		MDBLS	3/08
	Baltimore-Towson MSA, MD	Y	34610 FQ	44080 MW	50060 TQ	USBLS	5/07
	Massachusetts	Y	38300 FQ	46880 MW	57680 TQ	USBLS	5/07
	Boston-Cambridge-Quincy NECTA, MA	Y	37630 FQ	45170 MW	53610 TQ	USBLS	5/07
	Michigan	Y	21460 FQ	28900 MW	42980 TQ	USBLS	5/07
	Ann Arbor MSA, MI	Y	25390 FQ	31170 MW	41440 TQ	USBLS	5/07
	Detroit-Warren-Livonia MSA, MI	Y	25610 FQ	37420 MW	50150 TQ	USBLS	5/07
	Grand Rapids-Wyoming MSA, MI	Y	26670 FQ	29340 MW	40880 TQ	USBLS	5/07
	Warren-Troy-Farmington Hills PMSA, MI	Y	24610 FQ	36500 MW	49390 TQ	USBLS	5/07
	Minnesota	Y	34431 FQ	46609 MW	57134 TQ	MNBLS	10/08-12/08
	Duluth-Superior MSA, MN-WI	Y	41325 FQ	47634 MW	54811 TQ	MNBLS	10/08-12/08
	Minneapolis-Saint Paul MSA, MN-WI	Y	39055 FQ	48712 MW	60126 TQ	MNBLS	10/08-12/08
	Rochester MSA, MN	Y	51083 FQ	55591 MW	60433 TQ	MNBLS	10/08-12/08
	Mississippi	Y	27150 FQ	31910 MW	41830 TQ	USBLS	5/07
	Jackson MSA, MS	Y	29250 FQ	35950 MW	50940 TQ	USBLS	5/07
	Missouri	Y	34460 FQ	40880 MW	48630 TQ	USBLS	5/07
	Kansas City MSA, MO-KS	Y	34090 FQ	42410 MW	50920 TQ	USBLS	5/07
	St. Louis MSA, MO-IL	Y	35120 FQ	42400 MW	52230 TQ	USBLS	5/07
	Montana	Y	22340 FQ	31260 MW	42530 TQ	USBLS	5/07
	Billings MSA, MT	Y	22180 FQ	26340 MW	43840 TQ	USBLS	5/07
	Great Falls MSA, MT	Y	43880 FQ	56360 MW	68070 TQ	USBLS	5/07
	Nebraska	Y	29440 FQ	39570 MW	48220 TQ	USBLS	5/07
	Omaha-Council Bluffs MSA, NE-IA	Y	30480 FQ	40030 MW	48890 TQ	USBLS	5/07
	Nevada	H	22.80 FQ	27.99 MW	31.80 TQ	NVBLS	5/08
	Las Vegas-Paradise MSA, NV	H	20.83 FQ	27.23 MW	33.56 TQ	NVBLS	5/08
	New Hampshire	H	16.02 AE	24.09 MW	26.78 AEX	NHBLS	6/08
	New Jersey	Y	30140 FQ	45760 MW	61790 TQ	USBLS	5/07
	Camden PMSA, NJ	Y	27460 FQ	40410 MW	49350 TQ	USBLS	5/07
	Edison PMSA, NJ	Y	29130 FQ	48650 MW	65830 TQ	USBLS	5/07
	Newark-Union PMSA, NJ-PA	Y	43580 FQ	52330 MW	63510 TQ	USBLS	5/07
	New Mexico	Y	31630 FQ	37670 MW	46980 TQ	USBLS	5/07
	Albuquerque MSA, NM	Y	36160 FQ	41340 MW	51460 TQ	USBLS	5/07
	New York	Y	28860 FQ	42110 MW	59240 TQ	USBLS	5/07
	Albany-Schenectady-Troy MSA, NY	Y	31650 FQ	41510 MW	63760 TQ	USBLS	5/07
	Buffalo-Niagara Falls MSA, NY	Y	32470 FQ	40170 MW	50920 TQ	USBLS	5/07
	Nassau-Suffolk PMSA, NY	Y	32500 FQ	53490 MW	78530 TQ	USBLS	5/07

AE Average entry wage	AW Average wage paid	FQ First quartile wage	LO Lowest wage paid
AER Average entry range	AWR Average wage range	HI Hourly	LR Low end range
AEX Average experienced wage	AXR Average experienced range	HI Highest wage paid	M Monthly
ATC Average total compensation	D Daily	HR High end range	MCC Median cash compensation

MTC Median total compensation	TCC Total cash compensation	
MW Median wage paid	TQ Third quartile wage	
MWR Median wage range	W Weekly	
S See annotated source	Y Yearly	

Occupation/Type/Industry	Location	Per	Low	Mid	High	Source	Date
Clergy	New York-Northern New Jersey-Long Island MSA, NY-NJ-PA	Y	29190 FQ	44990 MW	61520 TQ	USBLS	5/07
	North Carolina	Y	36600 FQ	45520 MW	56130 TQ	USBLS	5/07
	Charlotte-Gastonia-Concord MSA, NC-SC	Y	38770 FQ	47940 MW	59370 TQ	USBLS	5/07
	Raleigh-Cary MSA, NC	Y	37050 FQ	43650 MW	53250 TQ	USBLS	5/07
	North Dakota	Y	35480 FQ	43080 MW	50630 TQ	USBLS	5/07
	Fargo MSA, ND-MN	Y	33890 FQ	43320 MW	49910 TQ	USBLS	5/07
	Ohio	Y	26920 FQ	33340 MW	46190 TQ	USBLS	5/07
	Cincinnati-Middletown MSA, OH-KY-IN	Y	26750 FQ	31980 MW	43800 TQ	USBLS	5/07
	Cleveland-Elyria-Mentor MSA, OH	Y	36250 FQ	43270 MW	52430 TQ	USBLS	5/07
	Columbus MSA, OH	Y	33360 FQ	42780 MW	55830 TQ	USBLS	5/07
	Dayton MSA, OH	Y	29370 FQ	36390 MW	55950 TQ	USBLS	5/07
	Oklahoma	Y	27690 FQ	34680 MW	45640 TQ	USBLS	5/07
	Oklahoma City MSA, OK	Y	30180 FQ	43580 MW	56470 TQ	USBLS	5/07
	Tulsa MSA, OK	Y	26240 FQ	33620 MW	38340 TQ	USBLS	5/07
	Oregon	H	11.90 FQ	20.37 MW	26.42 TQ	ORBLS	5/08
	Portland-Vancouver-Beaverton MSA, OR-WA	Y	21580 FQ	40510 MW	56070 TQ	USBLS	5/07
	Salem MSA, OR	Y	23700 FQ	39430 MW	50910 TQ	USBLS	5/07
	Pennsylvania	Y	22600 FQ	32890 MW	45340 TQ	USBLS	5/07
	Allentown-Bethlehem-Easton MSA, PA-NJ	Y	25570 FQ	31410 MW	45680 TQ	USBLS	5/07
	Philadelphia-Camden-Wilmington MSA, PA-NJ-DE-MD	Y	23900 FQ	35970 MW	47290 TQ	USBLS	5/07
	Pittsburgh MSA, PA	Y	23460 FQ	34860 MW	41650 TQ	USBLS	5/07
	Rhode Island	Y	32800 FQ	38470 MW	57880 TQ	USBLS	5/07
	Providence-Fall River-Warwick MSA, RI-MA	Y	32640 FQ	38340 MW	58930 TQ	USBLS	5/07
	South Carolina	Y	29730 FQ	39040 MW	51430 TQ	USBLS	5/07
	Columbia MSA, SC	Y	28020 FQ	37780 MW	50080 TQ	USBLS	5/07
	South Dakota	Y	29205 FQ	38576 MW	47483 TQ	SDBLS	7/08-9/08
	Sioux Falls MSA, SD	Y	27793 FQ	38998 MW	47800 TQ	SDBLS	7/08-9/08
	Tennessee	Y	35960 FQ	44350 MW	53010 TQ	USBLS	5/07
	Memphis MSA, TN-MS-AR	Y	32250 FQ	42440 MW	51060 TQ	USBLS	5/07
	Nashville-Davidson-Murfreesboro MSA, TN	Y	34520 FQ	42500 MW	58330 TQ	USBLS	5/07
	Texas	Y	29610 FQ	37630 MW	47180 TQ	USBLS	5/07
	Austin-Round Rock MSA, TX	Y	34320 FQ	42030 MW	47160 TQ	USBLS	5/07
	Dallas-Fort Worth-Arlington MSA, TX	Y	29980 FQ	39960 MW	47930 TQ	USBLS	5/07
	Houston-Sugar Land-Baytown MSA, TX	Y	22900 FQ	35400 MW	46420 TQ	USBLS	5/07
	San Antonio MSA, TX	Y	32940 FQ	36770 MW	43790 TQ	USBLS	5/07
	Utah	Y	18230 FQ	34680 MW	47280 TQ	USBLS	5/07
	Salt Lake City MSA, UT	Y	16650 FQ	25830 MW	55290 TQ	USBLS	5/07
	Vermont	Y	26740 FQ	38490 MW	51970 TQ	USBLS	5/07
	Virginia	Y	24110 FQ	38150 MW	49230 TQ	USBLS	5/07
	Richmond MSA, VA	Y	22460 FQ	40550 MW	47240 TQ	USBLS	5/07
	Virginia Beach-Norfolk-Newport News MSA, VA-NC	Y	28320 FQ	42850 MW	52580 TQ	USBLS	5/07
	Washington	H	19.97 FQ	23.92 MW	28.51 TQ	WABLS	3/08
	Seattle-Tacoma-Bellevue MSA, WA	Y	41790 FQ	52410 MW	61310 TQ	USBLS	5/07
	West Virginia	Y	22956 FQ	37140 MW	65093 TQ	WVBLS	7/08-9/08
	Wisconsin	Y	37440 FQ	44190 MW	51620 TQ	USBLS	5/07
	Appleton MSA, WI	Y	41050 FQ	48580 MW	60020 TQ	USBLS	5/07
	Milwaukee-Waukesha-West Allis MSA, WI	Y	37410 FQ	44280 MW	52930 TQ	USBLS	5/07
	Wyoming	Y	43142 FQ	49334 MW	59499 TQ	WYBLS	9/08
	Puerto Rico	Y	14930 FQ	22740 MW	54430 TQ	USBLS	5/07
	San Juan-Caguas-Guaynabo MSA, PR	Y	14590 FQ	19240 MW	56390 TQ	USBLS	5/07
	Guam	Y	14740 FQ	23880 MW	30000 TQ	USBLS	5/07
Clerical Assistant State Government	Wisconsin	Y	23757 LO		36953 HI	AFT02	3/1/08

AE	Average entry wage	AW	Average wage paid	FQ	First quartile wage
AER	Average entry range	AWR	Average wage range	H	Hourly
AEX	Average experienced wage	AXR	Average experienced range	HI	Highest wage paid
ATC	Average total compensation	D	Daily	HR	High end range

LO	Lowest wage paid	MTC	Median total compensation	TCC Total cash compensation
LR	Low end range	MW	Median wage paid	TQ Third quartile wage
M	Monthly	MWR	Median wage range	W Weekly
MCC	Median cash compensation	S	See annotated source	Y Yearly

Occupation/Type/Industry	Location	Per	Low	Mid	High	Source	Date
Clerical Services Supervisor							
State Highway Patrol	Missouri	S	1153 LO		1613 HI	MSHPSS	7/1/08
Clerk							
Board of Health	Montague, MA	H			13.60 HI	FRCOG	2009
School District	Kiryas Joel, NY	Y			137000 HI	THREC3	2008
State Court	Thomas County, GA	Y			93686 HI	GACTY02	2008
Superior Court	Fulton County, GA	Y			146239 HI	GACTY02	2008
Clerk of the House							
United States House of Representatives	United States	Y			167800 HI	CRS01	1/08
Clerk of the Legislature	Nebraska	Y			149783 HI	NEST	2008
Client Advocate							
State Government	Ohio	H	17.58 LO		21.67 HI	ODAS	2008
Clinical, Counseling, and School Psychologist	Alabama	Y	43490 FQ	51550 MW	60920 TQ	USBLS	5/07
	Birmingham-Hoover MSA, AL	Y	45630 FQ	54240 MW	64500 TQ	USBLS	5/07
	Tuscaloosa MSA, AL	Y	46170 FQ	53350 MW	72940 TQ	USBLS	5/07
	Alaska	Y	46730 FQ	58460 MW	72400 TQ	USBLS	5/07
	Anchorage MSA, AK	Y	41270 FQ	56910 MW	71030 TQ	USBLS	5/07
	Arizona	Y	39320 FQ	46570 MW	58770 TQ	USBLS	5/07
	Phoenix-Mesa-Scottsdale MSA, AZ	Y	39260 FQ	45960 MW	58540 TQ	USBLS	5/07
	Tucson MSA, AZ	Y	39690 FQ	48380 MW	58460 TQ	USBLS	5/07
	Arkansas	Y	44900 FQ	55320 MW	70730 TQ	USBLS	5/07
	Little Rock-North Little Rock MSA, AR	Y	48190 FQ	59620 MW	76230 TQ	USBLS	5/07
	California	H	26.85 FQ	34.71 MW	44.28 TQ	CABLS	1/08-3/08
	Los Angeles-Long Beach-Glendale PMSA, CA	H	25.47 FQ	31.61 MW	42.67 TQ	CABLS	1/08-3/08
	Oakland-Fremont-Hayward MSA, CA	H	28.14 FQ	36.81 MW	42.80 TQ	CABLS	1/08-3/08
	Riverside-San Bernardino-Ontario MSA, CA	H	28.80 FQ	33.87 MW	46.38 TQ	CABLS	1/08-3/08
	Sacramento-Arden Arcade-Roseville MSA, CA	H	22.59 FQ	33.66 MW	41.40 TQ	CABLS	1/08-3/08
	San Diego-Carlsbad-San Marcos MSA, CA	H	24.08 FQ	34.58 MW	43.12 TQ	CABLS	1/08-3/08
	San Francisco-San Mateo-Redwood PMSA, CA	H	30.99 FQ	38.94 MW	45.74 TQ	CABLS	1/08-3/08
	San Jose-Sunnyvale-Santa Clara MSA, CA	H	26.52 FQ	37.62 MW	46.63 TQ	CABLS	1/08-3/08
	Santa Ana-Anaheim-Irvine PMSA, CA	Y	51710 FQ	74270 MW	94040 TQ	USBLS	5/07
	Colorado	Y	53650 FQ	66910 MW	82830 TQ	USBLS	5/07
	Denver-Aurora MSA, CO	Y	53660 FQ	66060 MW	81190 TQ	USBLS	5/07
	Fort Collins-Loveland MSA, CO	Y	59100 FQ	70950 MW	84860 TQ	USBLS	5/07
	Connecticut	H	22.53 AE	35.08 MW		CTBLS	1/08-3/08
	Bridgeport-Stamford-Norwalk MSA, CT	Y	53940 FQ	74460 MW	90110 TQ	USBLS	5/07
	Hartford-West Hartford-East Hartford MSA, CT	Y	54840 FQ	73840 MW	94050 TQ	USBLS	5/07
	New Haven MSA, CT	Y	52500 FQ	70000 MW	80400 TQ	USBLS	5/07
	Waterbury MSA, CT	Y	46900 FQ	62180 MW	82580 TQ	USBLS	5/07
	Delaware	Y	49690 FQ	66200 MW	77390 TQ	USBLS	5/07
	Wilmington PMSA, DE-MD-NJ	Y	48840 FQ	62320 MW	76540 TQ	USBLS	5/07
	District of Columbia	Y	45720 FQ	63770 MW	80160 TQ	USBLS	5/07
	Washington-Arlington-Alexandria MSA, DC-VA-MD-WV	Y	50930 FQ	68130 MW	84540 TQ	USBLS	5/07
	Florida	Y	46690 FQ	60100 MW	77090 TQ	USBLS	5/07
	Fort Lauderdale-Pompano Beach-Deerfield Beach PMSA, FL	Y	58700 FQ	80800 MW	127360 TQ	USBLS	5/07
	Jacksonville MSA, FL	Y	47210 FQ	56310 MW	68350 TQ	USBLS	5/07
	Miami-Fort Lauderdale-Miami Beach MSA, FL	Y	46420 FQ	60320 MW	84900 TQ	USBLS	5/07

235

Occupation/Type/Industry	Location	Per	Low	Mid	High	Source	Date
Clinical, Counseling, and School Psychologist	Orlando-Kissimmee MSA, FL	Y	45090 FQ	62180 MW	77800 TQ	USBLS	5/07
	Tallahassee MSA, FL	Y	46200 FQ	56090 MW	69780 TQ	USBLS	5/07
	Tampa-St. Petersburg-Clearwater MSA, FL	Y	47970 FQ	62990 MW	75290 TQ	USBLS	5/07
	West Palm Beach-Boca Raton-Boynton Beach PMSA, FL	Y	32260 FQ	53120 MW	67140 TQ	USBLS	5/07
	Georgia	Y	49290 FQ	60520 MW	70610 TQ	USBLS	5/07
	Atlanta-Sandy Springs-Marietta MSA, GA	Y	51730 FQ	61890 MW	70990 TQ	USBLS	5/07
	Hawaii	Y	50050 FQ	61490 MW	77240 TQ	USBLS	5/07
	Honolulu MSA, HI	Y	52720 FQ	65360 MW	80190 TQ	USBLS	5/07
	Idaho	Y	35650 FQ	51760 MW	65470 TQ	USBLS	5/07
	Boise City-Nampa MSA, ID	Y	42330 FQ	61950 MW	72740 TQ	USBLS	5/07
	Illinois	Y	43980 FQ	58860 MW	79310 TQ	USBLS	5/07
	Chicago-Naperville-Joliet MSA, IL-IN-WI	Y	45030 FQ	58990 MW	81200 TQ	USBLS	5/07
	Indiana	Y	43770 FQ	56050 MW	66390 TQ	USBLS	5/07
	Gary PMSA, IN	Y	42670 FQ	56540 MW	70050 TQ	USBLS	5/07
	Indianapolis-Carmel MSA, IN	Y	51050 FQ	59440 MW	71290 TQ	USBLS	5/07
	Iowa	Y	42650 FQ	52460 MW	63330 TQ	USBLS	5/07
	Des Moines-West Des Moines MSA, IA	Y	37380 FQ	51960 MW	71420 TQ	USBLS	5/07
	Iowa City MSA, IA	Y	55940 FQ	63260 MW	75770 TQ	USBLS	5/07
	Kansas	Y	42510 FQ	50980 MW	61270 TQ	USBLS	5/07
	Wichita MSA, KS	Y	40630 FQ	51250 MW	59380 TQ	USBLS	5/07
	Kentucky	Y	44818 FQ	53571 MW	63793 TQ	KYBLS	2008
	Bowling Green MSA, KY	Y	34560 FQ	39370 MW	47600 TQ	USBLS	5/07
	Louisville-Jefferson County MSA, KY-IN	Y	48070 FQ	57190 MW	67250 TQ	USBLS	5/07
	Louisiana	H	21.07 FQ	25.61 MW	34.35 TQ	LABLS	1/08-3/08
	Baton Rouge MSA, LA	Y	41210 FQ	57610 MW	73620 TQ	USBLS	5/07
	New Orleans-Metairie-Kenner MSA, LA	Y	45140 FQ	49480 MW	57710 TQ	USBLS	5/07
	Maine	Y	48170 FQ	61230 MW	80620 TQ	USBLS	5/07
	Portland-South Portland-Biddeford MSA, ME	Y	51480 FQ	61660 MW	83020 TQ	USBLS	5/07
	Maryland	Y		63475 MW		MDBLS	3/08
	Baltimore-Towson MSA, MD	Y	50520 FQ	60480 MW	76200 TQ	USBLS	5/07
	Bethesda-Gaithersburg-Frederick PMSA, MD	Y	44780 FQ	66330 MW	81570 TQ	USBLS	5/07
	Massachusetts	Y	50200 FQ	65640 MW	77810 TQ	USBLS	5/07
	Boston-Cambridge-Quincy NECTA, MA	Y	52220 FQ	66640 MW	80090 TQ	USBLS	5/07
	Worcester MSA, MA-CT	Y	50970 FQ	63000 MW	73490 TQ	USBLS	5/07
	Michigan	Y	48890 FQ	66170 MW	80170 TQ	USBLS	5/07
	Detroit-Warren-Livonia MSA, MI	Y	47990 FQ	65730 MW	80650 TQ	USBLS	5/07
	Grand Rapids-Wyoming MSA, MI	Y	54030 FQ	68210 MW	84630 TQ	USBLS	5/07
	Warren-Troy-Farmington Hills PMSA, MI	Y	53290 FQ	68320 MW	87470 TQ	USBLS	5/07
	Minnesota	Y	49455 FQ	61591 MW	75757 TQ	MNBLS	10/08-12/08
	Duluth-Superior MSA, MN-WI	Y	51014 FQ	63558 MW	76364 TQ	MNBLS	10/08-12/08
	Minneapolis-Saint Paul MSA, MN-WI	Y	49141 FQ	61518 MW	76050 TQ	MNBLS	10/08-12/08
	Rochester MSA, MN	Y	44867 FQ	57411 MW	70939 TQ	MNBLS	10/08-12/08
	Mississippi	Y	35940 FQ	43320 MW	54640 TQ	USBLS	5/07
	Jackson MSA, MS	Y	40040 FQ	50230 MW	64880 TQ	USBLS	5/07
	Missouri	Y	39400 FQ	49220 MW	69090 TQ	USBLS	5/07
	Kansas City MSA, MO-KS	Y	41140 FQ	50890 MW	69090 TQ	USBLS	5/07
	St. Louis MSA, MO-IL	Y	39250 FQ	49040 MW	69480 TQ	USBLS	5/07
	Montana	Y	30650 FQ	43860 MW	54280 TQ	USBLS	5/07
	Nebraska	Y	43500 FQ	53900 MW	63770 TQ	USBLS	5/07
	Omaha-Council Bluffs MSA, NE-IA	Y	42350 FQ	50720 MW	61920 TQ	USBLS	5/07
	Nevada	H	25.59 FQ	32.46 MW	38.27 TQ	NVBLS	5/08
	Las Vegas-Paradise MSA, NV	H	24.41 FQ	30.11 MW	37.18 TQ	NVBLS	5/08
	New Hampshire	H	21.22 AE	28.76 MW	34.85 AEX	NHBLS	6/08
	Manchester MSA, NH	Y	57030 FQ	65860 MW	73550 TQ	USBLS	5/07
	Nashua NECTA, NH-MA	Y	49960 FQ	59240 MW	67620 TQ	USBLS	5/07

AE	Average entry wage	AW	Average wage paid	FQ	First quartile wage	LO	Lowest wage paid	MTC Median total compensation	TCC Total cash compensation
AER	Average entry range	AWR	Average wage range	H	Hourly	LR	Low end range	MW Median wage paid	TQ Third quartile wage
AEX	Average experienced wage	AXR	Average experienced range	HI	Highest wage paid	M	Monthly	MWR Median wage range	W Weekly
ATC	Average total compensation	D	Daily	HR	High end range	MCC	Median cash compensation	S See annotated source	Y Yearly

Occupation/Type/Industry	Location	Per	Low	Mid	High	Source	Date
Clinical, Counseling, and School Psychologist	Rochester-Dover MSA, NH-ME	Y	40370 FQ	53130 MW	63720 TQ	USBLS	5/07
	New Jersey	Y	60500 FQ	81810 MW	127030 TQ	USBLS	5/07
	Camden PMSA, NJ	Y	60710 FQ	81340 MW	98310 TQ	USBLS	5/07
	Edison PMSA, NJ	Y	57220 FQ	72550 MW	95600 TQ	USBLS	5/07
	New Mexico	Y	42500 FQ	59810 MW	74890 TQ	USBLS	5/07
	Albuquerque MSA, NM	Y	43160 FQ	68950 MW	77770 TQ	USBLS	5/07
	New York	Y	58210 FQ	73930 MW	93880 TQ	USBLS	5/07
	Albany-Schenectady-Troy MSA, NY	Y	50440 FQ	64350 MW	98030 TQ	USBLS	5/07
	Buffalo-Niagara Falls MSA, NY	Y	53620 FQ	67560 MW	83470 TQ	USBLS	5/07
	Nassau-Suffolk PMSA, NY	Y	64610 FQ	82470 MW	105230 TQ	USBLS	5/07
	New York-Northern New Jersey-Long Island MSA, NY-NJ-PA	Y	63470 FQ	81460 MW	103990 TQ	USBLS	5/07
	North Carolina	Y	44650 FQ	54510 MW	66080 TQ	USBLS	5/07
	Charlotte-Gastonia-Concord MSA, NC-SC	Y	49510 FQ	58390 MW	69080 TQ	USBLS	5/07
	Raleigh-Cary MSA, NC	Y	54290 FQ	61940 MW	74430 TQ	USBLS	5/07
	Winston-Salem MSA, NC	Y	44880 FQ	53300 MW	68200 TQ	USBLS	5/07
	North Dakota	Y	42430 FQ	55320 MW	72240 TQ	USBLS	5/07
	Bismarck MSA, ND	Y	22200 FQ	24260 MW	69720 TQ	USBLS	5/07
	Fargo MSA, ND-MN	Y	47400 FQ	56650 MW	70920 TQ	USBLS	5/07
	Ohio	Y	58040 FQ	79420 MW	97180 TQ	USBLS	5/07
	Cincinnati-Middletown MSA, OH-KY-IN	Y	54330 FQ	78630 MW	98270 TQ	USBLS	5/07
	Cleveland-Elyria-Mentor MSA, OH	Y	61400 FQ	78490 MW	93380 TQ	USBLS	5/07
	Columbus MSA, OH	Y	55000 FQ	80290 MW	102310 TQ	USBLS	5/07
	Dayton MSA, OH	Y	70530 FQ	88620 MW	106330 TQ	USBLS	5/07
	Oklahoma	Y	36710 FQ	46610 MW	58370 TQ	USBLS	5/07
	Oklahoma City MSA, OK	Y	35440 FQ	45410 MW	56690 TQ	USBLS	5/07
	Tulsa MSA, OK	Y	33890 FQ	43070 MW	54620 TQ	USBLS	5/07
	Oregon	H	24.12 FQ	30.03 MW	36.09 TQ	ORBLS	5/08
	Portland-Vancouver-Beaverton MSA, OR-WA	Y	51020 FQ	66030 MW	80170 TQ	USBLS	5/07
	Pennsylvania	Y	44340 FQ	60450 MW	78830 TQ	USBLS	5/07
	Allentown-Bethlehem-Easton MSA, PA-NJ	Y	45850 FQ	56820 MW	86110 TQ	USBLS	5/07
	Philadelphia-Camden-Wilmington MSA, PA-NJ-DE-MD	Y	47290 FQ	63920 MW	85640 TQ	USBLS	5/07
	Pittsburgh MSA, PA	Y	44830 FQ	66010 MW	87880 TQ	USBLS	5/07
	Rhode Island	Y	58550 FQ	70310 MW	82080 TQ	USBLS	5/07
	Providence-Fall River-Warwick MSA, RI-MA	Y	57950 FQ	69810 MW	81380 TQ	USBLS	5/07
	South Carolina	Y	45620 FQ	55980 MW	65190 TQ	USBLS	5/07
	Charleston-North Charleston MSA, SC	Y	51920 FQ	60310 MW	69780 TQ	USBLS	5/07
	Columbia MSA, SC	Y	50860 FQ	58540 MW	67560 TQ	USBLS	5/07
	South Dakota	Y	55516 FQ	62622 MW	72469 TQ	SDBLS	7/08-9/08
	Sioux Falls MSA, SD	Y	58635 FQ	69806 MW	85964 TQ	SDBLS	7/08-9/08
	Tennessee	Y	42890 FQ	54220 MW	74720 TQ	USBLS	5/07
	Memphis MSA, TN-MS-AR	Y	49220 FQ	62520 MW	110140 TQ	USBLS	5/07
	Nashville-Davidson-Murfreesboro MSA, TN	Y	37740 FQ	48090 MW	60380 TQ	USBLS	5/07
	Texas	Y	42780 FQ	53080 MW	63820 TQ	USBLS	5/07
	Austin-Round Rock MSA, TX	Y	38310 FQ	47160 MW	57220 TQ	USBLS	5/07
	Dallas-Fort Worth-Arlington MSA, TX	Y	43440 FQ	55640 MW	63590 TQ	USBLS	5/07
	El Paso MSA, TX	Y	49300 FQ	66090 MW	78620 TQ	USBLS	5/07
	Houston-Sugar Land-Baytown MSA, TX	Y	46280 FQ	57050 MW	72330 TQ	USBLS	5/07
	San Antonio MSA, TX	Y	43150 FQ	55550 MW	68800 TQ	USBLS	5/07
	Utah	Y	45400 FQ	59030 MW	81500 TQ	USBLS	5/07
	Provo-Orem MSA, UT	Y	54830 FQ	72240 MW	112930 TQ	USBLS	5/07
	Salt Lake City MSA, UT	Y	44720 FQ	56570 MW	76840 TQ	USBLS	5/07
	Vermont	Y	44290 FQ	58380 MW	74500 TQ	USBLS	5/07
	Burlington-South Burlington MSA, VT	Y	47420 FQ	58680 MW	72480 TQ	USBLS	5/07

AE	Average entry wage	AW	Average wage paid	FQ	First quartile wage
AER	Average entry range	AWR	Average wage range	H	Hourly
AEX	Average experienced wage	AXR	Average experienced range	HI	Highest wage paid
ATC	Average total compensation	D	Daily	HR	High end range

LO	Lowest wage paid	MTC	Median total compensation
LR	Low end range	MW	Median wage paid
M	Monthly	MWR	Median wage range
MCC	Median cash compensation	S	See annotated source

TCC	Total cash compensation	
TQ	Third quartile wage	
W	Weekly	
Y	Yearly	

Occupation/Type/Industry	Location	Per	Low	Mid	High	Source	Date
Clinical, Counseling, and School Psychologist	Virginia	Y	50350 FQ	65160 MW	84530 TQ	USBLS	5/07
	Richmond MSA, VA	Y	55210 FQ	65630 MW	78400 TQ	USBLS	5/07
	Virginia Beach-Norfolk-Newport News MSA, VA-NC	Y	48320 FQ	66300 MW	91180 TQ	USBLS	5/07
	Washington	H	25.43 FQ	30.07 MW	36.19 TQ	WABLS	3/08
	Seattle-Tacoma-Bellevue MSA, WA	Y	54090 FQ	65310 MW	77590 TQ	USBLS	5/07
	West Virginia	Y	37918 FQ	48903 MW	63778 TQ	WVBLS	7/08-9/08
	Charleston MSA, WV	Y	35970 FQ	50400 MW	68710 TQ	USBLS	5/07
	Wisconsin	Y	46370 FQ	58670 MW	75270 TQ	USBLS	5/07
	Milwaukee-Waukesha-West Allis MSA, WI	Y	51890 FQ	64570 MW	78660 TQ	USBLS	5/07
	Racine MSA, WI	Y	33990 FQ	53610 MW	68990 TQ	USBLS	5/07
	Wyoming	Y	44824 FQ	56440 MW	67531 TQ	WYBLS	9/08
	Cheyenne MSA, WY	Y	46720 FQ	67941 MW	86448 TQ	WYBLS	9/08
	Puerto Rico	Y	35100 FQ	38990 MW	47460 TQ	USBLS	5/07
	San Juan-Caguas-Guaynabo MSA, PR	Y	35470 FQ	39090 MW	46440 TQ	USBLS	5/07
Clinical Medical Director							
Trenton Psychiatric Hospital	New Jersey	Y			214424 HI	APP	2008
Clinical Nurse Specialist							
Staff, Large Facility	United States	Y		82900 AW		AORN01	2007
Staff, Small Facility	United States	Y		80000 AW		AORN01	2007
State Government	Ohio	H	30.12 LO		42.25 HI	ODAS	2008
Clinical Psychologist							
State Government	Rhode Island	Y	45809 LO		50302 HI	AFT02	3/1/08
Clinical Psychology Intern							
New York Presbyterian Hospital - Weill Cornell Medical Center	New York, NY	Y			24000 HI	NYPH	2007-2008
Coach and Scout	Alabama	Y	17440 FQ	31230 MW	46370 TQ	USBLS	5/07
	Birmingham-Hoover MSA, AL	Y	19770 FQ	27430 MW	38590 TQ	USBLS	5/07
	Alaska	Y	16180 FQ	23400 MW	35140 TQ	USBLS	5/07
	Anchorage MSA, AK	Y	26850 FQ	31560 MW	40570 TQ	USBLS	5/07
	Arizona	Y	19390 FQ	25440 MW	33050 TQ	USBLS	5/07
	Phoenix-Mesa-Scottsdale MSA, AZ	Y	20520 FQ	24460 MW	30960 TQ	USBLS	5/07
	Tucson MSA, AZ	Y	25580 FQ	30320 MW	52910 TQ	USBLS	5/07
	Arkansas	Y	28340 FQ	40880 MW	52280 TQ	USBLS	5/07
	Fayetteville-Springdale-Rogers MSA, AR-MO	Y	25420 FQ	40680 MW	58360 TQ	USBLS	5/07
	Little Rock-North Little Rock MSA, AR	Y	27180 FQ	33250 MW	50550 TQ	USBLS	5/07
	California	Y		40783 AW		CABLS	1/08-3/08
	Los Angeles-Long Beach-Glendale PMSA, CA	Y		45787 AW		CABLS	1/08-3/08
	Oakland-Fremont-Hayward MSA, CA	Y		37758 AW		CABLS	1/08-3/08
	Riverside-San Bernardino-Ontario MSA, CA	Y		41388 AW		CABLS	1/08-3/08
	Sacramento-Arden Arcade-Roseville MSA, CA	Y		33830 MW		CABLS	1/08-3/08
	San Diego-Carlsbad-San Marcos MSA, CA	Y		41101 AW		CABLS	1/08-3/08
	San Francisco-San Mateo-Redwood PMSA, CA	Y		52699 AW		CABLS	1/08-3/08
	San Jose-Sunnyvale-Santa Clara MSA, CA	Y		44567 AW		CABLS	1/08-3/08
	Santa Ana-Anaheim-Irvine PMSA, CA	Y	20980 FQ	28740 MW	41260 TQ	USBLS	5/07
	Stockton MSA, CA	Y		37758 AW		CABLS	1/08-3/08
	Colorado	Y	20430 FQ	25900 MW	36810 TQ	USBLS	5/07
	Denver-Aurora MSA, CO	Y	18330 FQ	23710 MW	38790 TQ	USBLS	5/07
	Bridgeport-Stamford-Norwalk MSA, CT	Y	16520 FQ	25570 MW	44330 TQ	USBLS	5/07
	Hartford-West Hartford-East Hartford MSA, CT	Y	16350 FQ	18870 MW	36860 TQ	USBLS	5/07

AE	Average entry wage	AW	Average wage paid	FQ	First quartile wage	LO	Lowest wage paid	MTC	Median total compensation	TCC	Total cash compensation
AER	Average entry range	AWR	Average wage range	H	Hourly	LR	Low end range	MW	Median wage paid	TQ	Third quartile wage
AEX	Average experienced wage	AXR	Average experienced range	HI	Highest wage paid	M	Monthly	MWR	Median wage range	W	Weekly
ATC	Average total compensation	D	Daily	HR	High end range	MCC	Median cash compensation	S	See annotated source	Y	Yearly

238

Occupation/Type/Industry	Location	Per	Low	Mid	High	Source	Date
Coach and Scout	Norwich-New London MSA, CT-RI	Y	16060 FQ	19070 MW	24410 TQ	USBLS	5/07
	Waterbury MSA, CT	Y	19460 FQ	35080 MW	49150 TQ	USBLS	5/07
	Delaware	Y	19280 FQ	28720 MW	50930 TQ	USBLS	5/07
	Wilmington PMSA, DE-MD-NJ	Y	17470 FQ	25300 MW	46020 TQ	USBLS	5/07
	District of Columbia	Y	37520 FQ	46330 MW	61900 TQ	USBLS	5/07
	Washington-Arlington-Alexandria MSA, DC-VA-MD-WV	Y	26640 FQ	39310 MW	53600 TQ	USBLS	5/07
	Florida	Y	25980 FQ	32850 MW	51370 TQ	USBLS	5/07
	Fort Lauderdale-Pompano Beach-Deerfield Beach PMSA, FL	Y	22380 FQ	29240 MW	38340 TQ	USBLS	5/07
	Jacksonville MSA, FL	Y	28900 FQ	42990 MW	63130 TQ	USBLS	5/07
	Lakeland MSA, FL	Y	19530 FQ	30970 MW	39550 TQ	USBLS	5/07
	Miami-Fort Lauderdale-Miami Beach MSA, FL	Y	26190 FQ	31740 MW	51020 TQ	USBLS	5/07
	Orlando-Kissimmee MSA, FL	Y	22570 FQ	31170 MW	46240 TQ	USBLS	5/07
	Tampa-St. Petersburg-Clearwater MSA, FL	Y	27120 FQ	34230 MW	51460 TQ	USBLS	5/07
	West Palm Beach-Boca Raton-Boynton Beach PMSA, FL	Y	25610 FQ	32870 MW	53160 TQ	USBLS	5/07
	Georgia	Y	22980 FQ	32420 MW	47000 TQ	USBLS	5/07
	Atlanta-Sandy Springs-Marietta MSA, GA	Y	23470 FQ	30940 MW	43520 TQ	USBLS	5/07
	Savannah MSA, GA	Y	18370 FQ	34500 MW	53340 TQ	USBLS	5/07
	Hawaii	Y	26590 FQ	31620 MW	43090 TQ	USBLS	5/07
	Honolulu MSA, HI	Y	28460 FQ	36010 MW	47460 TQ	USBLS	5/07
	Idaho	Y	20850 FQ	23130 MW	25390 TQ	USBLS	5/07
	Boise City-Nampa MSA, ID	Y	21460 FQ	23200 MW	24930 TQ	USBLS	5/07
	Illinois	Y	14880 FQ	15970 MW	33950 TQ	USBLS	5/07
	Chicago-Naperville-Joliet MSA, IL-IN-WI	Y	14980 FQ	19040 MW	39290 TQ	USBLS	5/07
	Indiana	Y	13850 FQ	18230 MW	32240 TQ	USBLS	5/07
	Gary PMSA, IN	Y	13480 FQ	16100 MW	27400 TQ	USBLS	5/07
	Indianapolis-Carmel MSA, IN	Y	19800 FQ	26750 MW	44930 TQ	USBLS	5/07
	Iowa	Y	14600 FQ	17910 MW	30750 TQ	USBLS	5/07
	Des Moines-West Des Moines MSA, IA	Y	17480 FQ	31530 MW	42640 TQ	USBLS	5/07
	Kansas	Y	13450 FQ	15930 MW	24930 TQ	USBLS	5/07
	Wichita MSA, KS	Y	13490 FQ	15920 MW	26230 TQ	USBLS	5/07
	Kentucky	Y	17339 FQ	25267 MW	41369 TQ	KYBLS	2008
	Louisville-Jefferson County MSA, KY-IN	Y	13560 FQ	16740 MW	36460 TQ	USBLS	5/07
	Louisiana	Y		40084 AW		LABLS	1/08-3/08
	Baton Rouge MSA, LA	Y	24960 FQ	35360 MW	50460 TQ	USBLS	5/07
	New Orleans-Metairie-Kenner MSA, LA	Y	28020 FQ	36850 MW	49460 TQ	USBLS	5/07
	Maine	Y	14770 FQ	15380 MW	20920 TQ	USBLS	5/07
	Portland-South Portland-Biddeford MSA, ME	Y	14730 FQ	15260 MW	16180 TQ	USBLS	5/07
	Maryland	Y		38850 MW		MDBLS	3/08
	Baltimore-Towson MSA, MD	Y	26890 FQ	34370 MW	57400 TQ	USBLS	5/07
	Bethesda-Gaithersburg-Frederick PMSA, MD	Y	29150 FQ	45570 MW	62960 TQ	USBLS	5/07
	Massachusetts	Y	18650 FQ	33420 MW	51280 TQ	USBLS	5/07
	Boston-Cambridge-Quincy NECTA, MA	Y	20400 FQ	38360 MW	55590 TQ	USBLS	5/07
	Worcester MSA, MA-CT	Y	17230 FQ	33290 MW	50170 TQ	USBLS	5/07
	Michigan	Y	15540 FQ	23440 MW	45910 TQ	USBLS	5/07
	Detroit-Warren-Livonia MSA, MI	Y	15400 FQ	24700 MW	47830 TQ	USBLS	5/07
	Grand Rapids-Wyoming MSA, MI	Y	16400 FQ	20260 MW	41770 TQ	USBLS	5/07
	Warren-Troy-Farmington Hills PMSA, MI	Y	15260 FQ	24730 MW	44510 TQ	USBLS	5/07
	Minnesota	Y	20234 FQ	26961 MW	41577 TQ	MNBLS	10/08-12/08
	Duluth-Superior MSA, MN-WI	Y	19982 FQ	27086 MW	37308 TQ	MNBLS	10/08-12/08
	Minneapolis-Saint Paul MSA, MN-WI	Y	19438 FQ	26187 MW	42759 TQ	MNBLS	10/08-12/08
	Rochester MSA, MN	Y	19220 FQ	27318 MW	40345 TQ	MNBLS	10/08-12/08

AE	Average entry wage	AW	Average wage paid	FQ	First quartile wage	LO	Lowest wage paid	MTC	Median total compensation	TCC	Total cash compensation
AER	Average entry range	AWR	Average wage range	H	Hourly	LR	Low end range	MW	Median wage paid	TQ	Third quartile wage
AEX	Average experienced wage	AXR	Average experienced range	HI	Highest wage paid	M	Monthly	MWR	Median wage range	W	Weekly
ATC	Average total compensation	D	Daily	HR	High end range	MCC	Median cash compensation	S	See annotated source	Y	Yearly

239

Occupation/Type/Industry	Location	Per	Low	Mid	High	Source	Date
Coach and Scout	Mississippi	Y	28950 FQ	42470 MW	55050 TQ	USBLS	5/07
	Jackson MSA, MS	Y	24880 FQ	44560 MW	59470 TQ	USBLS	5/07
	Missouri	Y	19690 FQ	32310 MW	46230 TQ	USBLS	5/07
	Kansas City MSA, MO-KS	Y	18470 FQ	25420 MW	37020 TQ	USBLS	5/07
	St. Louis MSA, MO-IL	Y	16220 FQ	25400 MW	42670 TQ	USBLS	5/07
	Montana	Y	14090 FQ	15480 MW	20830 TQ	USBLS	5/07
	Billings MSA, MT	Y	13700 FQ	14600 MW	16220 TQ	USBLS	5/07
	Nebraska	Y	15970 FQ	23860 MW	35800 TQ	USBLS	5/07
	Omaha-Council Bluffs MSA, NE-IA	Y	16820 FQ	22750 MW	33140 TQ	USBLS	5/07
	Nevada	Y	21119 FQ	29466 MW	39423 TQ	NVBLS	5/08
	Las Vegas-Paradise MSA, NV	Y	24920 FQ	32403 MW	47735 TQ	NVBLS	5/08
	New Hampshire	Y	23291 AE	42367 MW	56941 AEX	NHBLS	6/08
	Manchester MSA, NH	Y	33860 FQ	39070 MW	57560 TQ	USBLS	5/07
	New Jersey	Y	17650 FQ	29970 MW	45890 TQ	USBLS	5/07
	Camden PMSA, NJ	Y	17280 FQ	28730 MW	41380 TQ	USBLS	5/07
	Edison PMSA, NJ	Y	20190 FQ	30160 MW	45400 TQ	USBLS	5/07
	Newark-Union PMSA, NJ-PA	Y	16710 FQ	25670 MW	44910 TQ	USBLS	5/07
	New Mexico	Y	13290 FQ	15180 MW	36930 TQ	USBLS	5/07
	Albuquerque MSA, NM	Y	14170 FQ	26980 MW	40210 TQ	USBLS	5/07
	New York	Y	21560 FQ	31060 MW	45320 TQ	USBLS	5/07
	Albany-Schenectady-Troy MSA, NY	Y	26570 FQ	35670 MW	53220 TQ	USBLS	5/07
	Buffalo-Niagara Falls MSA, NY	Y	21390 FQ	31840 MW	41610 TQ	USBLS	5/07
	Ithaca MSA, NY	Y	26910 FQ	41320 MW	57390 TQ	USBLS	5/07
	Nassau-Suffolk PMSA, NY	Y	20740 FQ	28600 MW	42360 TQ	USBLS	5/07
	New York-Northern New Jersey-Long Island MSA, NY-NJ-PA	Y	19030 FQ	30060 MW	47120 TQ	USBLS	5/07
	North Carolina	Y	21410 FQ	28650 MW	39980 TQ	USBLS	5/07
	Charlotte-Gastonia-Concord MSA, NC-SC	Y	18430 FQ	27400 MW	38140 TQ	USBLS	5/07
	Raleigh-Cary MSA, NC	Y	23360 FQ	29090 MW	42390 TQ	USBLS	5/07
	North Dakota	Y	16480 FQ	21900 MW	32360 TQ	USBLS	5/07
	Fargo MSA, ND-MN	Y	17850 FQ	25380 MW	35800 TQ	USBLS	5/07
	Ohio	Y	15470 FQ	20830 MW	32940 TQ	USBLS	5/07
	Cincinnati-Middletown MSA, OH-KY-IN	Y	15830 FQ	24120 MW	37010 TQ	USBLS	5/07
	Cleveland-Elyria-Mentor MSA, OH	Y	16160 FQ	25850 MW	38830 TQ	USBLS	5/07
	Columbus MSA, OH	Y	16260 FQ	25870 MW	40730 TQ	USBLS	5/07
	Dayton MSA, OH	Y	15550 FQ	20140 MW	24710 TQ	USBLS	5/07
	Oklahoma	Y	15670 FQ	25230 MW	35340 TQ	USBLS	5/07
	Oklahoma City MSA, OK	Y	14550 FQ	21240 MW	31580 TQ	USBLS	5/07
	Tulsa MSA, OK	Y	19450 FQ	26450 MW	32530 TQ	USBLS	5/07
	Oregon	Y	21422 FQ	31266 MW	48296 TQ	ORBLS	5/08
	Portland-Vancouver-Beaverton MSA, OR-WA	Y	21880 FQ	30330 MW	45700 TQ	USBLS	5/07
	Pennsylvania	Y	14630 FQ	16340 MW	32430 TQ	USBLS	5/07
	Allentown-Bethlehem-Easton MSA, PA-NJ	Y	16280 FQ	20040 MW	29100 TQ	USBLS	5/07
	Erie MSA, PA	Y	15600 FQ	26960 MW	38600 TQ	USBLS	5/07
	Philadelphia-Camden-Wilmington MSA, PA-NJ-DE-MD	Y	15070 FQ	22070 MW	39670 TQ	USBLS	5/07
	Pittsburgh MSA, PA	Y	14870 FQ	18610 MW	33690 TQ	USBLS	5/07
	Providence-Fall River-Warwick MSA, RI-MA	Y	18110 FQ	31820 MW	49440 TQ	USBLS	5/07
	South Carolina	Y	20470 FQ	33230 MW	50820 TQ	USBLS	5/07
	Charleston-North Charleston MSA, SC	Y	20610 FQ	27920 MW	42210 TQ	USBLS	5/07
	Columbia MSA, SC	Y	23720 FQ	38840 MW	60160 TQ	USBLS	5/07
	South Dakota	Y	24995 FQ	29038 MW	33823 TQ	SDBLS	7/08-9/08
	Sioux Falls MSA, SD	Y	25656 FQ	31239 MW	38691 TQ	SDBLS	7/08-9/08
	Tennessee	Y	16660 FQ	23450 MW	37760 TQ	USBLS	5/07
	Memphis MSA, TN-MS-AR	Y	19460 FQ	33290 MW	55900 TQ	USBLS	5/07
	Nashville-Davidson-Murfreesboro MSA, TN	Y	17950 FQ	23300 MW	37670 TQ	USBLS	5/07
	Texas	Y	18480 FQ	29170 MW	45040 TQ	USBLS	5/07
	Austin-Round Rock MSA, TX	Y	18210 FQ	26120 MW	45260 TQ	USBLS	5/07

AE	Average entry wage	**AW**	Average wage paid	**FQ**	First quartile wage
AER	Average entry range	**AWR**	Average wage range	**H**	Hourly
AEX	Average experienced wage	**AXR**	Average experienced range	**HI**	Highest wage paid
ATC	Average total compensation	**D**	Daily	**HR**	High end range

LO	Lowest wage paid	**MTC**	Median total compensation
LR	Low end range	**MW**	Median wage paid
M	Monthly	**MWR**	Median wage range
MCC	Median cash compensation	**S**	See annotated source

TCC	Total cash compensation
TQ	Third quartile wage
W	Weekly
Y	Yearly

Occupation/Type/Industry	Location	Per	Low	Mid	High	Source	Date
Coach and Scout	Dallas-Fort Worth-Arlington MSA, TX	Y	17920 FQ	26930 MW	40260 TQ	USBLS	5/07
	El Paso MSA, TX	Y	19890 FQ	37430 MW	54320 TQ	USBLS	5/07
	Houston-Sugar Land-Baytown MSA, TX	Y	20010 FQ	30970 MW	45450 TQ	USBLS	5/07
	San Antonio MSA, TX	Y	15580 FQ	25120 MW	33570 TQ	USBLS	5/07
	Utah	Y	21990 FQ	30140 MW	44200 TQ	USBLS	5/07
	Ogden-Clearfield MSA, UT	Y	16140 FQ	20990 MW	26200 TQ	USBLS	5/07
	Salt Lake City MSA, UT	Y	24260 FQ	33350 MW	47270 TQ	USBLS	5/07
	Vermont	Y	21030 FQ	28730 MW	39060 TQ	USBLS	5/07
	Burlington-South Burlington MSA, VT	Y	23320 FQ	31350 MW	43090 TQ	USBLS	5/07
	Virginia	Y	19540 FQ	30280 MW	43430 TQ	USBLS	5/07
	Richmond MSA, VA	Y	22320 FQ	30290 MW	40960 TQ	USBLS	5/07
	Roanoke MSA, VA	Y	26670 FQ	30290 MW	40730 TQ	USBLS	5/07
	Virginia Beach-Norfolk-Newport News MSA, VA-NC	Y	18450 FQ	24860 MW	36170 TQ	USBLS	5/07
	Washington	Y		38387 AW		WABLS	3/08
	Seattle-Tacoma-Bellevue MSA, WA	Y	23760 FQ	33530 MW	46230 TQ	USBLS	5/07
	West Virginia	Y	16633 FQ	27382 MW	44153 TQ	WVBLS	7/08-9/08
	Charleston MSA, WV	Y	28380 FQ	31190 MW	36320 TQ	USBLS	5/07
	Wisconsin	Y	16030 FQ	24940 MW	35570 TQ	USBLS	5/07
	Milwaukee-Waukesha-West Allis MSA, WI	Y	17860 FQ	26480 MW	35580 TQ	USBLS	5/07
	Wyoming	Y	13623 FQ	15748 MW	38213 TQ	WYBLS	9/08
	Cheyenne MSA, WY	Y	27045 FQ	31766 MW	38450 TQ	WYBLS	9/08
	Puerto Rico	Y	13430 FQ	15540 MW	22030 TQ	USBLS	5/07
	San Juan-Caguas-Guaynabo MSA, PR	Y	13460 FQ	15580 MW	23120 TQ	USBLS	5/07
	Virgin Islands	Y	32910 FQ	43820 MW	58210 TQ	USBLS	5/07
Coal Program Financial Analyst State Government	Ohio	H	21.77 LO		31.86 HI	ODAS	2008
Coating, Painting, and Spraying Machine Setter, Operator, and Tender	Alabama	Y	20320 FQ	26410 MW	31550 TQ	USBLS	5/07
	Birmingham-Hoover MSA, AL	Y	20160 FQ	27070 MW	31150 TQ	USBLS	5/07
	Arizona	Y	19580 FQ	24120 MW	32450 TQ	USBLS	5/07
	Phoenix-Mesa-Scottsdale MSA, AZ	Y	19540 FQ	24180 MW	32910 TQ	USBLS	5/07
	Tucson MSA, AZ	Y	21440 FQ	24720 MW	31480 TQ	USBLS	5/07
	Arkansas	Y	22250 FQ	26080 MW	31120 TQ	USBLS	5/07
	Little Rock-North Little Rock MSA, AR	Y	20050 FQ	23030 MW	29420 TQ	USBLS	5/07
	California	H	9.94 FQ	12.47 MW	16.70 TQ	CABLS	1/08-3/08
	Los Angeles-Long Beach-Glendale PMSA, CA	H	9.36 FQ	11.48 MW	14.94 TQ	CABLS	1/08-3/08
	Oakland-Fremont-Hayward MSA, CA	H	10.54 FQ	14.04 MW	19.69 TQ	CABLS	1/08-3/08
	Riverside-San Bernardino-Ontario MSA, CA	H	10.10 FQ	12.20 MW	15.01 TQ	CABLS	1/08-3/08
	Sacramento-Arden Arcade-Roseville MSA, CA	H	11.06 FQ	13.31 MW	17.29 TQ	CABLS	1/08-3/08
	San Diego-Carlsbad-San Marcos MSA, CA	H	10.72 FQ	13.84 MW	17.74 TQ	CABLS	1/08-3/08
	San Francisco-San Mateo-Redwood PMSA, CA	H	10.24 FQ	13.08 MW	17.76 TQ	CABLS	1/08-3/08
	San Jose-Sunnyvale-Santa Clara MSA, CA	H	12.65 FQ	17.02 MW	20.19 TQ	CABLS	1/08-3/08
	Santa Ana-Anaheim-Irvine PMSA, CA	Y	19920 FQ	23970 MW	31800 TQ	USBLS	5/07
	Colorado	Y	21070 FQ	26610 MW	32960 TQ	USBLS	5/07
	Denver-Aurora MSA, CO	Y	21540 FQ	29190 MW	34860 TQ	USBLS	5/07
	Connecticut	H	11.05 AE	14.72 MW		CTBLS	1/08-3/08
	Bridgeport-Stamford-Norwalk MSA, CT	Y	25520 FQ	31140 MW	36350 TQ	USBLS	5/07
	Hartford-West Hartford-East Hartford MSA, CT	Y	27880 FQ	33500 MW	39540 TQ	USBLS	5/07
	Delaware	Y	30430 FQ	33420 MW	36350 TQ	USBLS	5/07

AE Average entry wage	**AW** Average wage paid	**FQ** First quartile wage	**LO** Lowest wage paid	**MTC** Median total compensation	**TCC** Total cash compensation
AER Average entry range	**AWR** Average wage range	**H** Hourly	**LR** Low end range	**MW** Median wage paid	**TQ** Third quartile wage
AEX Average experienced wage	**AXR** Average experienced range	**HI** Highest wage paid	**M** Monthly	**MWR** Median wage range	**W** Weekly
ATC Average total compensation	**D** Daily	**HR** High end range	**MCC** Median cash compensation	**S** See annotated source	**Y** Yearly

Occupation/Type/Industry	Location	Per	Low	Mid	High	Source	Date
Coating, Painting, and Spraying Machine Setter, Operator, and Tender	Wilmington PMSA, DE-MD-NJ	Y	30170 FQ	32990 MW	35750 TQ	USBLS	5/07
	Washington-Arlington-Alexandria MSA, DC-VA-MD-WV	Y	23410 FQ	28240 MW	34460 TQ	USBLS	5/07
	Florida	Y	20800 FQ	25510 MW	30890 TQ	USBLS	5/07
	Fort Lauderdale-Pompano Beach-Deerfield Beach PMSA, FL	Y	19230 FQ	25100 MW	33730 TQ	USBLS	5/07
	Jacksonville MSA, FL	Y	22860 FQ	27140 MW	30960 TQ	USBLS	5/07
	Miami-Fort Lauderdale-Miami Beach MSA, FL	Y	18440 FQ	23400 MW	29830 TQ	USBLS	5/07
	Orlando-Kissimmee MSA, FL	Y	20810 FQ	23950 MW	29130 TQ	USBLS	5/07
	Tampa-St. Petersburg-Clearwater MSA, FL	Y	20170 FQ	25730 MW	30430 TQ	USBLS	5/07
	West Palm Beach-Boca Raton-Boynton Beach PMSA, FL	Y	22980 FQ	28040 MW	33400 TQ	USBLS	5/07
	Georgia	Y	21500 FQ	26310 MW	31630 TQ	USBLS	5/07
	Atlanta-Sandy Springs-Marietta MSA, GA	Y	21780 FQ	26950 MW	32090 TQ	USBLS	5/07
	Idaho	Y	21220 FQ	25860 MW	30440 TQ	USBLS	5/07
	Boise City-Nampa MSA, ID	Y	19790 FQ	23000 MW	29480 TQ	USBLS	5/07
	Illinois	Y	22090 FQ	27150 MW	36280 TQ	USBLS	5/07
	Chicago-Naperville-Joliet MSA, IL-IN-WI	Y	21790 FQ	27090 MW	38560 TQ	USBLS	5/07
	Indiana	Y	22970 FQ	28230 MW	35240 TQ	USBLS	5/07
	Gary PMSA, IN	Y	20820 FQ	27440 MW	36410 TQ	USBLS	5/07
	Indianapolis-Carmel MSA, IN	Y	23840 FQ	27750 MW	34030 TQ	USBLS	5/07
	Iowa	Y	23520 FQ	29520 MW	37130 TQ	USBLS	5/07
	Cedar Rapids MSA, IA	Y	25200 FQ	29370 MW	34180 TQ	USBLS	5/07
	Des Moines-West Des Moines MSA, IA	Y	24500 FQ	30230 MW	36960 TQ	USBLS	5/07
	Dubuque MSA, IA	Y	25260 FQ	28440 MW	35400 TQ	USBLS	5/07
	Kansas	Y	21610 FQ	25690 MW	31740 TQ	USBLS	5/07
	Wichita MSA, KS	Y	23090 FQ	28530 MW	36130 TQ	USBLS	5/07
	Kentucky	Y	20575 FQ	25755 MW	34189 TQ	KYBLS	2008
	Louisville-Jefferson County MSA, KY-IN	Y	21920 FQ	27620 MW	34430 TQ	USBLS	5/07
	Louisiana	H	10.55 FQ	13.73 MW	17.51 TQ	LABLS	1/08-3/08
	Baton Rouge MSA, LA	Y	22690 FQ	31360 MW	36380 TQ	USBLS	5/07
	New Orleans-Metairie-Kenner MSA, LA	Y	25410 FQ	31840 MW	36050 TQ	USBLS	5/07
	Maine	Y	27680 FQ	38860 MW	47830 TQ	USBLS	5/07
	Portland-South Portland-Biddeford MSA, ME	Y	24560 FQ	30490 MW	38260 TQ	USBLS	5/07
	Maryland	Y		32800 MW		MDBLS	3/08
	Baltimore-Towson MSA, MD	Y	26500 FQ	33860 MW	41200 TQ	USBLS	5/07
	Massachusetts	Y	24740 FQ	30360 MW	37260 TQ	USBLS	5/07
	Boston-Cambridge-Quincy NECTA, MA	Y	24230 FQ	31170 MW	39920 TQ	USBLS	5/07
	Worcester MSA, MA-CT	Y	21980 FQ	26650 MW	33610 TQ	USBLS	5/07
	Michigan	Y	24420 FQ	29860 MW	36460 TQ	USBLS	5/07
	Detroit-Warren-Livonia MSA, MI	Y	23900 FQ	28430 MW	37520 TQ	USBLS	5/07
	Grand Rapids-Wyoming MSA, MI	Y	24310 FQ	31440 MW	36350 TQ	USBLS	5/07
	Warren-Troy-Farmington Hills PMSA, MI	Y	23430 FQ	27750 MW	38880 TQ	USBLS	5/07
	Minnesota	Y	27845 FQ	34117 MW	42058 TQ	MNBLS	10/08-12/08
	Duluth-Superior MSA, MN-WI	Y	28570 FQ	33007 MW	38585 TQ	MNBLS	10/08-12/08
	Minneapolis-Saint Paul MSA, MN-WI	Y	29410 FQ	37621 MW	44701 TQ	MNBLS	10/08-12/08
	Rochester MSA, MN	Y	28097 FQ	30938 MW	34180 TQ	MNBLS	10/08-12/08
	Mississippi	Y	20950 FQ	25560 MW	30630 TQ	USBLS	5/07
	Jackson MSA, MS	Y	21010 FQ	25040 MW	29990 TQ	USBLS	5/07
	Missouri	Y	23450 FQ	28510 MW	34490 TQ	USBLS	5/07
	Kansas City MSA, MO-KS	Y	25260 FQ	31880 MW	39970 TQ	USBLS	5/07
	St. Louis MSA, MO-IL	Y	25030 FQ	28640 MW	33850 TQ	USBLS	5/07
	Montana	Y	20190 FQ	26110 MW	31520 TQ	USBLS	5/07

AE	Average entry wage	**AW**	Average wage paid	**FQ**	First quartile wage	**LO** Lowest wage paid	**MTC** Median total compensation	**TCC** Total cash compensation
AER	Average entry range	**AWR**	Average wage range	**H**	Hourly	**LR** Low end range	**MW** Median wage paid	**TQ** Third quartile wage
AEX	Average experienced wage	**AXR**	Average experienced range	**HI**	Highest wage paid	**M** Monthly	**MWR** Median wage range	**W** Weekly
ATC	Average total compensation	**D**	Daily	**HR**	High end range	**MCC** Median cash compensation	**S** See annotated source	**Y** Yearly

Occupation/Type/Industry	Location	Per	Low	Mid	High	Source	Date
Coating, Painting, and Spraying Machine Setter, Operator, and Tender							
	Nebraska	Y	22580 FQ	26310 MW	30280 TQ	USBLS	5/07
	Omaha-Council Bluffs MSA, NE-IA	Y	24570 FQ	27610 MW	31120 TQ	USBLS	5/07
	Nevada	H	10.66 FQ	13.09 MW	15.94 TQ	NVBLS	5/08
	Las Vegas-Paradise MSA, NV	H	10.11 FQ	13.65 MW	17.09 TQ	NVBLS	5/08
	New Hampshire	H	11.94 AE	14.70 MW	16.78 AEX	NHBLS	6/08
	Manchester MSA, NH	Y	25750 FQ	29850 MW	38280 TQ	USBLS	5/07
	New Jersey	Y	22700 FQ	28620 MW	37960 TQ	USBLS	5/07
	Camden PMSA, NJ	Y	24490 FQ	31260 MW	39030 TQ	USBLS	5/07
	Edison PMSA, NJ	Y	23980 FQ	31950 MW	40240 TQ	USBLS	5/07
	Newark-Union PMSA, NJ-PA	Y	23100 FQ	29640 MW	38510 TQ	USBLS	5/07
	Trenton-Ewing MSA, NJ	Y	23630 FQ	28380 MW	33860 TQ	USBLS	5/07
	New Mexico	Y	22300 FQ	27630 MW	34430 TQ	USBLS	5/07
	Albuquerque MSA, NM	Y	21850 FQ	26250 MW	31150 TQ	USBLS	5/07
	New York	Y	23490 FQ	29530 MW	36490 TQ	USBLS	5/07
	Albany-Schenectady-Troy MSA, NY	Y	22360 FQ	28810 MW	42260 TQ	USBLS	5/07
	Buffalo-Niagara Falls MSA, NY	Y	23830 FQ	27710 MW	41100 TQ	USBLS	5/07
	Nassau-Suffolk PMSA, NY	Y	20220 FQ	28300 MW	36280 TQ	USBLS	5/07
	New York-Northern New Jersey-Long Island MSA, NY-NJ-PA	Y	22490 FQ	29040 MW	37310 TQ	USBLS	5/07
	Utica-Rome MSA, NY	Y	23520 FQ	27780 MW	33570 TQ	USBLS	5/07
	North Carolina	Y	23470 FQ	27610 MW	31690 TQ	USBLS	5/07
	Charlotte-Gastonia-Concord MSA, NC-SC	Y	25600 FQ	32420 MW	38940 TQ	USBLS	5/07
	Raleigh-Cary MSA, NC	Y	25560 FQ	28840 MW	32020 TQ	USBLS	5/07
	Winston-Salem MSA, NC	Y	26640 FQ	30900 MW	37990 TQ	USBLS	5/07
	North Dakota	Y	23570 FQ	28550 MW	33620 TQ	USBLS	5/07
	Fargo MSA, ND-MN	Y	26110 FQ	31110 MW	36920 TQ	USBLS	5/07
	Ohio	Y	23750 FQ	29270 MW	36110 TQ	USBLS	5/07
	Cincinnati-Middletown MSA, OH-KY-IN	Y	23700 FQ	28670 MW	34900 TQ	USBLS	5/07
	Cleveland-Elyria-Mentor MSA, OH	Y	23950 FQ	30670 MW	40120 TQ	USBLS	5/07
	Columbus MSA, OH	Y	25010 FQ	30070 MW	35930 TQ	USBLS	5/07
	Dayton MSA, OH	Y	24320 FQ	28120 MW	33430 TQ	USBLS	5/07
	Oklahoma	Y	22120 FQ	27510 MW	32230 TQ	USBLS	5/07
	Oklahoma City MSA, OK	Y	22740 FQ	28220 MW	34640 TQ	USBLS	5/07
	Tulsa MSA, OK	Y	20690 FQ	27390 MW	32360 TQ	USBLS	5/07
	Oregon	H	10.99 FQ	13.31 MW	16.39 TQ	ORBLS	5/08
	Medford MSA, OR	Y	19360 FQ	26220 MW	29250 TQ	USBLS	5/07
	Portland-Vancouver-Beaverton MSA, OR-WA	Y	22800 FQ	28290 MW	36290 TQ	USBLS	5/07
	Pennsylvania	Y	24240 FQ	30360 MW	38470 TQ	USBLS	5/07
	Allentown-Bethlehem-Easton MSA, PA-NJ	Y	24760 FQ	31290 MW	37150 TQ	USBLS	5/07
	Philadelphia-Camden-Wilmington MSA, PA-NJ-DE-MD	Y	24930 FQ	32030 MW	38600 TQ	USBLS	5/07
	Pittsburgh MSA, PA	Y	27620 FQ	33050 MW	38830 TQ	USBLS	5/07
	Rhode Island	Y	18310 FQ	22540 MW	30780 TQ	USBLS	5/07
	Providence-Fall River-Warwick MSA, RI-MA	Y	18570 FQ	22850 MW	30580 TQ	USBLS	5/07
	South Carolina	Y	23940 FQ	28300 MW	32860 TQ	USBLS	5/07
	Charleston-North Charleston MSA, SC	Y	25450 FQ	29130 MW	36950 TQ	USBLS	5/07
	Columbia MSA, SC	Y	24250 FQ	29840 MW	35960 TQ	USBLS	5/07
	South Dakota	Y	22430 FQ	25925 MW	30191 TQ	SDBLS	7/08-9/08
	Sioux Falls MSA, SD	Y	21321 FQ	24228 MW	28148 TQ	SDBLS	7/08-9/08
	Tennessee	Y	20820 FQ	25840 MW	30270 TQ	USBLS	5/07
	Clarksville MSA, TN-KY	Y	20690 FQ	22990 MW	27980 TQ	USBLS	5/07
	Knoxville MSA, TN	Y	21550 FQ	26690 MW	30480 TQ	USBLS	5/07
	Memphis MSA, TN-MS-AR	Y	23790 FQ	27820 MW	35490 TQ	USBLS	5/07
	Nashville-Davidson-Murfreesboro MSA, TN	Y	24200 FQ	27460 MW	30400 TQ	USBLS	5/07
	Texas	Y	18690 FQ	23170 MW	28820 TQ	USBLS	5/07
	Austin-Round Rock MSA, TX	Y	20110 FQ	23960 MW	29110 TQ	USBLS	5/07

AE Average entry wage	**AW** Average wage paid	**FQ** First quartile wage	**LO** Lowest wage paid	**MTC** Median total compensation	**TCC** Total cash compensation
AER Average entry range	**AWR** Average wage range	**H** Hourly	**LR** Low end range	**MW** Median wage paid	**TQ** Third quartile wage
AEX Average experienced wage	**AXR** Average experienced range	**HI** Highest wage paid	**M** Monthly	**MWR** Median wage range	**W** Weekly
ATC Average total compensation	**D** Daily	**HR** High end range	**MCC** Median cash compensation	**S** See annotated source	**Y** Yearly

Occupation/Type/Industry	Location	Per	Low	Mid	High	Source	Date
Coating, Painting, and Spraying Machine Setter, Operator, and Tender							
	Beaumont-Port Arthur MSA, TX	Y	17170 FQ	23500 MW	30390 TQ	USBLS	5/07
	Dallas-Fort Worth-Arlington MSA, TX	Y	20390 FQ	24630 MW	29920 TQ	USBLS	5/07
	El Paso MSA, TX	Y	17370 FQ	19640 MW	23910 TQ	USBLS	5/07
	Houston-Sugar Land-Baytown MSA, TX	Y	17030 FQ	21650 MW	27230 TQ	USBLS	5/07
	San Antonio MSA, TX	Y	20130 FQ	23490 MW	27260 TQ	USBLS	5/07
	Utah	Y	21320 FQ	24570 MW	28840 TQ	USBLS	5/07
	Provo-Orem MSA, UT	Y	21330 FQ	23430 MW	25730 TQ	USBLS	5/07
	Salt Lake City MSA, UT	Y	23580 FQ	26990 MW	30780 TQ	USBLS	5/07
	Vermont	Y	22640 FQ	26640 MW	31090 TQ	USBLS	5/07
	Burlington-South Burlington MSA, VT	Y	24050 FQ	26350 MW	28770 TQ	USBLS	5/07
	Virginia	Y	23120 FQ	27140 MW	34690 TQ	USBLS	5/07
	Richmond MSA, VA	Y	23410 FQ	29430 MW	35740 TQ	USBLS	5/07
	Virginia Beach-Norfolk-Newport News MSA, VA-NC	Y	28600 FQ	36590 MW	47830 TQ	USBLS	5/07
	Washington	H	11.55 FQ	13.70 MW	16.89 TQ	WABLS	3/08
	Olympia MSA, WA	Y	23940 FQ	26090 MW	28270 TQ	USBLS	5/07
	Seattle-Tacoma-Bellevue MSA, WA	Y	23390 FQ	28060 MW	34450 TQ	USBLS	5/07
	West Virginia	Y	23237 FQ	30155 MW	36038 TQ	WVBLS	7/08-9/08
	Charleston MSA, WV	Y	13560 FQ	16200 MW	21260 TQ	USBLS	5/07
	Wisconsin	Y	25700 FQ	30980 MW	36670 TQ	USBLS	5/07
	Milwaukee-Waukesha-West Allis MSA, WI	Y	26010 FQ	30260 MW	35710 TQ	USBLS	5/07
	Racine MSA, WI	Y	28380 FQ	32520 MW	36530 TQ	USBLS	5/07
	Wyoming	Y	24182 FQ	27881 MW	34866 TQ	WYBLS	9/08
	Puerto Rico	Y	14940 FQ	16840 MW	18990 TQ	USBLS	5/07
	San Juan-Caguas-Guaynabo MSA, PR	Y	15030 FQ	16950 MW	19360 TQ	USBLS	5/07
Code Enforcement Officer	Walnut Creek, CA	Y	71429 LO		86207 HI	WCSWP	6/27/08
	Colorado Springs, CO	M	3488 LO			COSPRS	1/1/09
	Savannah, GA	Y	30907 LO		45431 HI	GACTY01	2008
	Gresham, OR	Y	47892 LO		60576 HI	GOSS	1/1/09
Coil Winder, Taper, and Finisher	Alabama	Y	21190 FQ	26280 MW	31830 TQ	USBLS	5/07
	Arizona	Y	17380 FQ	22380 MW	28520 TQ	USBLS	5/07
	Arkansas	Y	22470 FQ	26410 MW	33330 TQ	USBLS	5/07
	California	H	10.01 FQ	12.62 MW	14.78 TQ	CABLS	1/08-3/08
	Connecticut	H	9.99 AE	13.13 MW		CTBLS	1/08-3/08
	Florida	Y	17190 FQ	23230 MW	30700 TQ	USBLS	5/07
	Georgia	Y	20110 FQ	27660 MW	33970 TQ	USBLS	5/07
	Illinois	Y	19230 FQ	22550 MW	28030 TQ	USBLS	5/07
	Indiana	Y	18750 FQ	27350 MW	31300 TQ	USBLS	5/07
	Iowa	Y	15850 FQ	24190 MW	28330 TQ	USBLS	5/07
	Kansas	Y	20780 FQ	24560 MW	29120 TQ	USBLS	5/07
	Kentucky	Y	26823 FQ	32700 MW	36299 TQ	KYBLS	2008
	Louisiana	H	11.06 FQ	15.04 MW	18.07 TQ	LABLS	1/08-3/08
	Maine	Y	23020 FQ	31910 MW	34740 TQ	USBLS	5/07
	Maryland	Y		25075 MW		MDBLS	3/08
	Massachusetts	Y	21630 FQ	26860 MW	38650 TQ	USBLS	5/07
	Michigan	Y	26390 FQ	31730 MW	53230 TQ	USBLS	5/07
	Minnesota	Y	27233 FQ	36563 MW	40834 TQ	MNBLS	10/08-12/08
	Mississippi	Y	27830 FQ	30910 MW	35570 TQ	USBLS	5/07
	Missouri	Y	22630 FQ	29080 MW	38610 TQ	USBLS	5/07
	Nebraska	Y	21100 FQ	24440 MW	28040 TQ	USBLS	5/07
	Nevada	H	9.74 FQ	11.80 MW	14.92 TQ	NVBLS	5/08
	New Hampshire	H	11.78 AE	14.20 MW	14.89 AEX	NHBLS	6/08
	New Jersey	Y	21160 FQ	26070 MW	31930 TQ	USBLS	5/07
	New York	Y	19390 FQ	22720 MW	29510 TQ	USBLS	5/07
	North Carolina	Y	23260 FQ	27560 MW	34430 TQ	USBLS	5/07
	Ohio	Y	25120 FQ	31790 MW	37020 TQ	USBLS	5/07
	Oklahoma	Y	23830 FQ	27160 MW	30150 TQ	USBLS	5/07
	Oregon	H	8.92 FQ	11.68 MW	14.45 TQ	ORBLS	5/08
	Pennsylvania	Y	23770 FQ	28960 MW	34730 TQ	USBLS	5/07
	South Carolina	Y	23440 FQ	27590 MW	30950 TQ	USBLS	5/07
	South Dakota	Y	21441 FQ	23600 MW	27697 TQ	SDBLS	7/08-9/08

AE	Average entry wage	**AW**	Average wage paid	**FQ**	First quartile wage	**LO**	Lowest wage paid	**MTC** Median total compensation **TCC** Total cash compensation
AER	Average entry range	**AWR**	Average wage range	**H**	Hourly	**LR**	Low end range	**MW** Median wage paid **TQ** Third quartile wage
AEX	Average experienced wage	**AXR**	Average experienced range	**HI**	Highest wage paid	**M**	Monthly	**MWR** Median wage range **W** Weekly
ATC	Average total compensation	**D**	Daily	**HR**	High end range	**MCC**	Median cash compensation	**S** See annotated source **Y** Yearly

Occupation/Type/Industry	Location	Per	Low	Mid	High	Source	Date
Coil Winder, Taper, and Finisher	Tennessee	Y	25070 FQ	28160 MW	34780 TQ	USBLS	5/07
	Texas	Y	18580 FQ	25610 MW	34040 TQ	USBLS	5/07
	Utah	Y	27400 FQ	30900 MW	34630 TQ	USBLS	5/07
	Virginia	Y	23010 FQ	26840 MW	32620 TQ	USBLS	5/07
	Washington	H	10.04 FQ	11.35 MW	13.10 TQ	WABLS	3/08
	West Virginia	Y	31134 FQ	49789 MW	56053 TQ	WVBLS	7/08-9/08
	Wisconsin	Y	21350 FQ	24120 MW	28550 TQ	USBLS	5/07
	Puerto Rico	Y	16820 FQ	18790 MW	22930 TQ	USBLS	5/07
Coin, Vending, and Amusement Machine Servicer and Repairer	Alabama	Y	19730 FQ	24660 MW	31730 TQ	USBLS	5/07
	Birmingham-Hoover MSA, AL	Y	22890 FQ	29320 MW	36150 TQ	USBLS	5/07
	Montgomery MSA, AL	Y	17770 FQ	19290 MW	23830 TQ	USBLS	5/07
	Alaska	Y	21710 FQ	27740 MW	38580 TQ	USBLS	5/07
	Anchorage MSA, AK	Y	22450 FQ	29240 MW	40210 TQ	USBLS	5/07
	Arizona	Y	24410 FQ	31330 MW	36580 TQ	USBLS	5/07
	Phoenix-Mesa-Scottsdale MSA, AZ	Y	26100 FQ	33090 MW	37310 TQ	USBLS	5/07
	Tucson MSA, AZ	Y	22730 FQ	27320 MW	33100 TQ	USBLS	5/07
	Arkansas	Y	20210 FQ	24120 MW	31280 TQ	USBLS	5/07
	Little Rock-North Little Rock MSA, AR	Y	18690 FQ	22120 MW	31910 TQ	USBLS	5/07
	California	H	11.83 FQ	14.89 MW	18.46 TQ	CABLS	1/08-3/08
	Los Angeles-Long Beach-Glendale PMSA, CA	H	10.83 FQ	11.92 MW	15.16 TQ	CABLS	1/08-3/08
	Oakland-Fremont-Hayward MSA, CA	H	14.22 FQ	17.48 MW	19.78 TQ	CABLS	1/08-3/08
	Riverside-San Bernardino-Ontario MSA, CA	H	11.15 FQ	13.89 MW	19.23 TQ	CABLS	1/08-3/08
	Sacramento-Arden Arcade-Roseville MSA, CA	H	12.17 FQ	16.53 MW	18.67 TQ	CABLS	1/08-3/08
	San Diego-Carlsbad-San Marcos MSA, CA	H	11.58 FQ	14.79 MW	18.07 TQ	CABLS	1/08-3/08
	San Francisco-San Mateo-Redwood PMSA, CA	H	13.82 FQ	16.00 MW	18.52 TQ	CABLS	1/08-3/08
	San Jose-Sunnyvale-Santa Clara MSA, CA	H	13.12 FQ	14.83 MW	19.25 TQ	CABLS	1/08-3/08
	Santa Ana-Anaheim-Irvine PMSA, CA	Y	26340 FQ	32250 MW	43700 TQ	USBLS	5/07
	Colorado	Y	25830 FQ	34100 MW	43010 TQ	USBLS	5/07
	Denver-Aurora MSA, CO	Y	26940 FQ	34080 MW	40350 TQ	USBLS	5/07
	Connecticut	H	12.22 AE	14.91 MW		CTBLS	1/08-3/08
	Bridgeport-Stamford-Norwalk MSA, CT	Y	23790 FQ	26890 MW	29770 TQ	USBLS	5/07
	Hartford-West Hartford-East Hartford MSA, CT	Y	27070 FQ	31910 MW	42290 TQ	USBLS	5/07
	Norwich-New London MSA, CT-RI	Y	27650 FQ	31270 MW	43300 TQ	USBLS	5/07
	Delaware	Y	22580 FQ	27690 MW	31150 TQ	USBLS	5/07
	Wilmington PMSA, DE-MD-NJ	Y	19270 FQ	26070 MW	31130 TQ	USBLS	5/07
	Washington-Arlington-Alexandria MSA, DC-VA-MD-WV	Y	23090 FQ	33690 MW	50270 TQ	USBLS	5/07
	Florida	Y	18970 FQ	26700 MW	32070 TQ	USBLS	5/07
	Fort Lauderdale-Pompano Beach-Deerfield Beach PMSA, FL	Y	14950 FQ	16030 MW	33390 TQ	USBLS	5/07
	Jacksonville MSA, FL	Y	21140 FQ	24490 MW	28540 TQ	USBLS	5/07
	Miami-Fort Lauderdale-Miami Beach MSA, FL	Y	17020 FQ	27560 MW	34960 TQ	USBLS	5/07
	Orlando-Kissimmee MSA, FL	Y	15130 FQ	20040 MW	28270 TQ	USBLS	5/07
	Tampa-St. Petersburg-Clearwater MSA, FL	Y	16880 FQ	25080 MW	33660 TQ	USBLS	5/07
	West Palm Beach-Boca Raton-Boynton Beach PMSA, FL	Y	24100 FQ	32050 MW	37360 TQ	USBLS	5/07
	Georgia	Y	18360 FQ	24120 MW	32790 TQ	USBLS	5/07
	Atlanta-Sandy Springs-Marietta MSA, GA	Y	18030 FQ	24400 MW	34580 TQ	USBLS	5/07
	Hawaii	Y	22290 FQ	25220 MW	32380 TQ	USBLS	5/07
	Honolulu MSA, HI	Y	22160 FQ	24780 MW	30310 TQ	USBLS	5/07
	Idaho	Y	20060 FQ	26870 MW	32020 TQ	USBLS	5/07

AE	Average entry wage	AW	Average wage paid	FQ	First quartile wage
AER	Average entry range	AWR	Average wage range	H	Hourly
AEX	Average experienced wage	AXR	Average experienced range	HI	Highest wage paid
ATC	Average total compensation	D	Daily	HR	High end range

LO	Lowest wage paid	MTC	Median total compensation
LR	Low end range	MW	Median wage paid
M	Monthly	MWR	Median wage range
MCC	Median cash compensation	S	See annotated source

TCC	Total cash compensation
TQ	Third quartile wage
W	Weekly
Y	Yearly

Occupation/Type/Industry	Location	Per	Low	Mid	High	Source	Date
Coin, Vending, and Amusement Machine Servicer and Repairer	Boise City-Nampa MSA, ID	Y	12700 FQ	13940 MW	20930 TQ	USBLS	5/07
	Illinois	Y	22820 FQ	28410 MW	35640 TQ	USBLS	5/07
	Chicago-Naperville-Joliet MSA, IL-IN-WI	Y	23470 FQ	29920 MW	37690 TQ	USBLS	5/07
	Indiana	Y	22230 FQ	26110 MW	32930 TQ	USBLS	5/07
	Gary PMSA, IN	Y	22960 FQ	28420 MW	37950 TQ	USBLS	5/07
	Indianapolis-Carmel MSA, IN	Y	21860 FQ	23870 MW	29300 TQ	USBLS	5/07
	Terre Haute MSA, IN	Y	14680 FQ	27120 MW	35080 TQ	USBLS	5/07
	Iowa	Y	24400 FQ	29710 MW	35820 TQ	USBLS	5/07
	Cedar Rapids MSA, IA	Y	25400 FQ	30300 MW	34240 TQ	USBLS	5/07
	Des Moines-West Des Moines MSA, IA	Y	24170 FQ	34790 MW	49860 TQ	USBLS	5/07
	Kansas	Y	23750 FQ	29770 MW	34760 TQ	USBLS	5/07
	Wichita MSA, KS	Y	22470 FQ	29710 MW	36070 TQ	USBLS	5/07
	Kentucky	Y	22216 FQ	29028 MW	35574 TQ	KYBLS	2008
	Lexington-Fayette MSA, KY	Y	20950 FQ	24250 MW	31560 TQ	USBLS	5/07
	Louisville-Jefferson County MSA, KY-IN	Y	29670 FQ	34730 MW	37990 TQ	USBLS	5/07
	Louisiana	H	9.15 FQ	12.19 MW	15.58 TQ	LABLS	1/08-3/08
	Baton Rouge MSA, LA	Y	21290 FQ	26780 MW	31670 TQ	USBLS	5/07
	New Orleans-Metairie-Kenner MSA, LA	Y	14560 FQ	26910 MW	33720 TQ	USBLS	5/07
	Maine	Y	22310 FQ	27050 MW	32260 TQ	USBLS	5/07
	Maryland	Y		34825 MW		MDBLS	3/08
	Baltimore-Towson MSA, MD	Y	25710 FQ	31630 MW	37320 TQ	USBLS	5/07
	Bethesda-Gaithersburg-Frederick PMSA, MD	Y	31820 FQ	46000 MW	52500 TQ	USBLS	5/07
	Massachusetts	Y	31250 FQ	35390 MW	39430 TQ	USBLS	5/07
	Boston-Cambridge-Quincy NECTA, MA	Y	32980 FQ	35930 MW	39100 TQ	USBLS	5/07
	Worcester MSA, MA-CT	Y	30930 FQ	34600 MW	38790 TQ	USBLS	5/07
	Michigan	Y	22300 FQ	29360 MW	42070 TQ	USBLS	5/07
	Detroit-Warren-Livonia MSA, MI	Y	28450 FQ	41050 MW	54170 TQ	USBLS	5/07
	Grand Rapids-Wyoming MSA, MI	Y	26990 FQ	32050 MW	37980 TQ	USBLS	5/07
	Warren-Troy-Farmington Hills PMSA, MI	Y	25480 FQ	34230 MW	42410 TQ	USBLS	5/07
	Minnesota	Y	29926 FQ	36398 MW	43363 TQ	MNBLS	10/08-12/08
	Duluth-Superior MSA, MN-WI	Y	26234 FQ	32538 MW	37877 TQ	MNBLS	10/08-12/08
	Minneapolis-Saint Paul MSA, MN-WI	Y	32192 FQ	39807 MW	46258 TQ	MNBLS	10/08-12/08
	Mississippi	Y	23640 FQ	28110 MW	34570 TQ	USBLS	5/07
	Jackson MSA, MS	Y	26780 FQ	30170 MW	36000 TQ	USBLS	5/07
	Missouri	Y	21430 FQ	29090 MW	36930 TQ	USBLS	5/07
	Kansas City MSA, MO-KS	Y	22680 FQ	28250 MW	35240 TQ	USBLS	5/07
	St. Louis MSA, MO-IL	Y	25780 FQ	31690 MW	37340 TQ	USBLS	5/07
	Montana	Y	25390 FQ	29740 MW	35630 TQ	USBLS	5/07
	Nebraska	Y	19570 FQ	28820 MW	36710 TQ	USBLS	5/07
	Omaha-Council Bluffs MSA, NE-IA	Y	22910 FQ	29580 MW	37770 TQ	USBLS	5/07
	Nevada	H	14.37 FQ	18.02 MW	22.93 TQ	NVBLS	5/08
	Las Vegas-Paradise MSA, NV	H	15.35 FQ	19.22 MW	23.94 TQ	NVBLS	5/08
	New Hampshire	H	12.91 AE	16.43 MW	18.03 AEX	NHBLS	6/08
	New Jersey	Y	27040 FQ	34230 MW	41290 TQ	USBLS	5/07
	Camden PMSA, NJ	Y	15190 FQ	26170 MW	30120 TQ,	USBLS	5/07
	Edison PMSA, NJ	Y	29300 FQ	35850 MW	41040 TQ	USBLS	5/07
	Newark-Union PMSA, NJ-PA	Y	21540 FQ	27450 MW	35740 TQ	USBLS	5/07
	Ocean City MSA, NJ	Y	31350 FQ	40370 MW	47220 TQ	USBLS	5/07
	New Mexico	Y	24250 FQ	30170 MW	36680 TQ	USBLS	5/07
	Albuquerque MSA, NM	Y	30360 FQ	35220 MW	42030 TQ	USBLS	5/07
	New York	Y	20940 FQ	27360 MW	37690 TQ	USBLS	5/07
	Albany-Schenectady-Troy MSA, NY	Y	27880 FQ	34210 MW	44780 TQ	USBLS	5/07
	Buffalo-Niagara Falls MSA, NY	Y	23450 FQ	30140 MW	39510 TQ	USBLS	5/07
	Nassau-Suffolk PMSA, NY	Y	19700 FQ	24860 MW	45280 TQ	USBLS	5/07
	New York-Northern New Jersey-Long Island MSA, NY-NJ-PA	Y	22240 FQ	29670 MW	38620 TQ	USBLS	5/07
	North Carolina	Y	23320 FQ	30760 MW	36530 TQ	USBLS	5/07

AE	Average entry wage	AW	Average wage paid	FQ	First quartile wage	LO	Lowest wage paid	MTC Median total compensation
AER	Average entry range	AWR	Average wage range	H	Hourly	LR	Low end range	MW Median wage paid
AEX	Average experienced wage	AXR	Average experienced range	HI	Highest wage paid	M	Monthly	MWR Median wage range
ATC	Average total compensation	D	Daily	HR	High end range	MCC	Median cash compensation	S See annotated source

AE Average entry wage | AW Average wage paid | FQ First quartile wage | LO Lowest wage paid | MTC Median total compensation | TCC Total cash compensation
AER Average entry range | AWR Average wage range | H Hourly | LR Low end range | MW Median wage paid | TQ Third quartile wage
AEX Average experienced wage | AXR Average experienced range | HI Highest wage paid | M Monthly | MWR Median wage range | W Weekly
ATC Average total compensation | D Daily | HR High end range | MCC Median cash compensation | S See annotated source | Y Yearly

Occupation/Type/Industry	Location	Per	Low	Mid	High	Source	Date
Coin, Vending, and Amusement Machine Servicer and Repairer	Charlotte-Gastonia-Concord MSA, NC-SC	Y	19530 FQ	23640 MW	30650 TQ	USBLS	5/07
	Raleigh-Cary MSA, NC	Y	32570 FQ	36870 MW	41780 TQ	USBLS	5/07
	North Dakota	Y	27480 FQ	35050 MW	49840 TQ	USBLS	5/07
	Fargo MSA, ND-MN	Y	26530 FQ	30060 MW	37180 TQ	USBLS	5/07
	Ohio	Y	17200 FQ	24140 MW	32280 TQ	USBLS	5/07
	Cincinnati-Middletown MSA, OH-KY-IN	Y	21700 FQ	25060 MW	35000 TQ	USBLS	5/07
	Cleveland-Elyria-Mentor MSA, OH	Y	14830 FQ	26930 MW	33860 TQ	USBLS	5/07
	Columbus MSA, OH	Y	20540 FQ	25500 MW	32990 TQ	USBLS	5/07
	Dayton MSA, OH	Y	18230 FQ	20640 MW	23610 TQ	USBLS	5/07
	Mansfield MSA, OH	Y	14790 FQ	18420 MW	24800 TQ	USBLS	5/07
	Oklahoma	Y	19300 FQ	24500 MW	29100 TQ	USBLS	5/07
	Oklahoma City MSA, OK	Y	14000 FQ	20520 MW	24740 TQ	USBLS	5/07
	Tulsa MSA, OK	Y	24660 FQ	27450 MW	31120 TQ	USBLS	5/07
	Oregon	H	16.32 FQ	20.84 MW	23.18 TQ	ORBLS	5/08
	Portland-Vancouver-Beaverton MSA, OR-WA	Y	38120 FQ	43690 MW	47710 TQ	USBLS	5/07
	Pennsylvania	Y	24500 FQ	32530 MW	37660 TQ	USBLS	5/07
	Allentown-Bethlehem-Easton MSA, PA-NJ	Y	22960 FQ	34950 MW	38100 TQ	USBLS	5/07
	Erie MSA, PA	Y	27090 FQ	32490 MW	37460 TQ	USBLS	5/07
	Philadelphia-Camden-Wilmington MSA, PA-NJ-DE-MD	Y	25530 FQ	32010 MW	37610 TQ	USBLS	5/07
	Pittsburgh MSA, PA	Y	27690 FQ	34000 MW	37680 TQ	USBLS	5/07
	Reading MSA, PA	Y	24590 FQ	33780 MW	40180 TQ	USBLS	5/07
	Rhode Island	Y	21870 FQ	29540 MW	35290 TQ	USBLS	5/07
	Providence-Fall River-Warwick MSA, RI-MA	Y	22670 FQ	30000 MW	35850 TQ	USBLS	5/07
	South Carolina	Y	25870 FQ	29070 MW	33660 TQ	USBLS	5/07
	Charleston-North Charleston MSA, SC	Y	25770 FQ	28320 MW	30860 TQ	USBLS	5/07
	Columbia MSA, SC	Y	34620 FQ	39200 MW	44550 TQ	USBLS	5/07
	South Dakota	Y	23693 FQ	27081 MW	32214 TQ	SDBLS	7/08-9/08
	Sioux Falls MSA, SD	Y	23960 FQ	28301 MW	43925 TQ	SDBLS	7/08-9/08
	Tennessee	Y	22330 FQ	26140 MW	30310 TQ	USBLS	5/07
	Memphis MSA, TN-MS-AR	Y	23730 FQ	28560 MW	36570 TQ	USBLS	5/07
	Nashville-Davidson-Murfreesboro MSA, TN	Y	22730 FQ	25130 MW	31250 TQ	USBLS	5/07
	Texas	Y	19370 FQ	26330 MW	32990 TQ	USBLS	5/07
	Austin-Round Rock MSA, TX	Y	24920 FQ	30250 MW	34840 TQ	USBLS	5/07
	Dallas-Fort Worth-Arlington MSA, TX	Y	24700 FQ	30270 MW	37480 TQ	USBLS	5/07
	El Paso MSA, TX	Y	21870 FQ	27330 MW	31580 TQ	USBLS	5/07
	Houston-Sugar Land-Baytown MSA, TX	Y	17080 FQ	23030 MW	31020 TQ	USBLS	5/07
	San Antonio MSA, TX	Y	20400 FQ	25450 MW	33440 TQ	USBLS	5/07
	Vermont	Y	23730 FQ	33320 MW	38790 TQ	USBLS	5/07
	Virginia	Y	22650 FQ	28370 MW	34890 TQ	USBLS	5/07
	Richmond MSA, VA	Y	25310 FQ	28560 MW	37830 TQ	USBLS	5/07
	Roanoke MSA, VA	Y	27630 FQ	31390 MW	37380 TQ	USBLS	5/07
	Virginia Beach-Norfolk-Newport News MSA, VA-NC	Y	15490 FQ	27130 MW	31070 TQ	USBLS	5/07
	Washington	H	14.47 FQ	17.21 MW	19.64 TQ	WABLS	3/08
	Seattle-Tacoma-Bellevue MSA, WA	Y	30570 FQ	35530 MW	40230 TQ	USBLS	5/07
	West Virginia	Y	16297 FQ	22375 MW	28145 TQ	WVBLS	7/08-9/08
	Charleston MSA, WV	Y	14950 FQ	21190 MW	31070 TQ	USBLS	5/07
	Wisconsin	Y	26130 FQ	32330 MW	37530 TQ	USBLS	5/07
	Milwaukee-Waukesha-West Allis MSA, WI	Y	26500 FQ	32940 MW	39900 TQ	USBLS	5/07
	Wyoming	Y	15913 FQ	22811 MW	27134 TQ	WYBLS	9/08
	Puerto Rico	Y	14970 FQ	19050 MW	23440 TQ	USBLS	5/07
	San Juan-Caguas-Guaynabo MSA, PR	Y	15090 FQ	19360 MW	23490 TQ	USBLS	5/07
College Administrator	United States	Y		85870 AW		BBF	2009
	Western, NY	Y		96500 AW		BBF	2009

AE Average entry wage	**AW** Average wage paid	**FQ** First quartile wage	**LO** Lowest wage paid	**MTC** Median total compensation	**TCC** Total cash compensation
AER Average entry range	**AWR** Average wage range	**H** Hourly	**LR** Low end range	**MW** Median wage paid	**TQ** Third quartile wage
AEX Average experienced wage	**AXR** Average experienced range	**HI** Highest wage paid	**M** Monthly	**MWR** Median wage range	**W** Weekly
ATC Average total compensation	**D** Daily	**HR** High end range	**MCC** Median cash compensation	**S** See annotated source	**Y** Yearly

Occupation/Type/Industry	Location	Per	Low	Mid	High	Source	Date
College Tutor							
Public Schools	Chicago, IL	H	6.50 LO		15.00 HI	CPSSS	7/1/06
Combined Food Preparation and Serving Worker							
Including Fast Food	Alabama	Y	12490 FQ	13790 MW	15140 TQ	USBLS	5/07
Including Fast Food	Birmingham-Hoover MSA, AL	Y	12550 FQ	13920 MW	15450 TQ	USBLS	5/07
Including Fast Food	Huntsville MSA, AL	Y	12520 FQ	13920 MW	15410 TQ	USBLS	5/07
Including Fast Food	Alaska	Y	16200 FQ	17850 MW	20710 TQ	USBLS	5/07
Including Fast Food	Anchorage MSA, AK	Y	16160 FQ	17560 MW	19560 TQ	USBLS	5/07
Including Fast Food	Arizona	Y	14840 FQ	16180 MW	18910 TQ	USBLS	5/07
Including Fast Food	Phoenix-Mesa-Scottsdale MSA, AZ	Y	14960 FQ	16600 MW	19130 TQ	USBLS	5/07
Including Fast Food	Tucson MSA, AZ	Y	14580 FQ	15230 MW	17560 TQ	USBLS	5/07
Including Fast Food	Yuma MSA, AZ	Y	14810 FQ	16690 MW	20040 TQ	USBLS	5/07
Including Fast Food	Arkansas	Y	13930 FQ	14580 MW	15420 TQ	USBLS	5/07
Including Fast Food	Jonesboro MSA, AR	Y	13910 FQ	14570 MW	15340 TQ	USBLS	5/07
Including Fast Food	Little Rock-North Little Rock MSA, AR	Y	13970 FQ	14670 MW	15610 TQ	USBLS	5/07
Including Fast Food	California	H	8.00 FQ	8.56 MW	9.42 TQ	CABLS	1/08-3/08
Including Fast Food	Los Angeles-Long Beach-Glendale PMSA, CA	H	8.00 FQ	8.45 MW	9.25 TQ	CABLS	1/08-3/08
Including Fast Food	Oakland-Fremont-Hayward MSA, CA	H	8.00 FQ	8.73 MW	9.76 TQ	CABLS	1/08-3/08
Including Fast Food	Riverside-San Bernardino-Ontario MSA, CA	H	8.00 FQ	8.27 MW	9.12 TQ	CABLS	1/08-3/08
Including Fast Food	Sacramento-Arden Arcade-Roseville MSA, CA	H	8.00 FQ	8.47 MW	9.28 TQ	CABLS	1/08-3/08
Including Fast Food	San Diego-Carlsbad-San Marcos MSA, CA	H	8.00 FQ	8.71 MW	9.66 TQ	CABLS	1/08-3/08
Including Fast Food	San Francisco-San Mateo-Redwood PMSA, CA	H	8.42 FQ	9.43 MW	11.62 TQ	CABLS	1/08-3/08
Including Fast Food	San Jose-Sunnyvale-Santa Clara MSA, CA	H	8.19 FQ	8.87 MW	9.76 TQ	CABLS	1/08-3/08
Including Fast Food	Santa Ana-Anaheim-Irvine PMSA, CA	Y	16030 FQ	17270 MW	19060 TQ	USBLS	5/07
Including Fast Food	Colorado	Y	14960 FQ	16090 MW	18500 TQ	USBLS	5/07
Including Fast Food	Denver-Aurora MSA, CO	Y	15230 FQ	16730 MW	18960 TQ	USBLS	5/07
Including Fast Food	Fort Collins-Loveland MSA, CO	Y	14750 FQ	15370 MW	16420 TQ	USBLS	5/07
Including Fast Food	Connecticut	H	8.49 AE	9.04 MW		CTBLS	1/08-3/08
Including Fast Food	Bridgeport-Stamford-Norwalk MSA, CT	Y	16810 FQ	18410 MW	20810 TQ	USBLS	5/07
Including Fast Food	Hartford-West Hartford-East Hartford MSA, CT	Y	17050 FQ	18370 MW	20070 TQ	USBLS	5/07
Including Fast Food	Waterbury MSA, CT	Y	16960 FQ	18160 MW	19680 TQ	USBLS	5/07
Including Fast Food	Delaware	Y	14730 FQ	15740 MW	18490 TQ	USBLS	5/07
Including Fast Food	Wilmington PMSA, DE-MD-NJ	Y	14930 FQ	16080 MW	19170 TQ	USBLS	5/07
Including Fast Food	District of Columbia	Y	18940 FQ	21790 MW	26620 TQ	USBLS	5/07
Including Fast Food	Washington-Arlington-Alexandria MSA, DC-VA-MD-WV	Y	14660 FQ	17260 MW	20810 TQ	USBLS	5/07
Including Fast Food	Florida	Y	14620 FQ	15510 MW	17830 TQ	USBLS	5/07
Including Fast Food	Fort Lauderdale-Pompano Beach-Deerfield Beach PMSA, FL	Y	14650 FQ	15610 MW	17870 TQ	USBLS	5/07
Including Fast Food	Jacksonville MSA, FL	Y	14520 FQ	15210 MW	16930 TQ	USBLS	5/07
Including Fast Food	Miami-Fort Lauderdale-Miami Beach MSA, FL	Y	14610 FQ	15500 MW	17830 TQ	USBLS	5/07
Including Fast Food	Orlando-Kissimmee MSA, FL	Y	14760 FQ	15890 MW	18520 TQ	USBLS	5/07
Including Fast Food	Tampa-St. Petersburg-Clearwater MSA, FL	Y	14670 FQ	15630 MW	17800 TQ	USBLS	5/07
Including Fast Food	West Palm Beach-Boca Raton-Boynton Beach PMSA, FL	Y	14700 FQ	15750 MW	18710 TQ	USBLS	5/07
Including Fast Food	Georgia	Y	12770 FQ	14420 MW	16710 TQ	USBLS	5/07
Including Fast Food	Atlanta-Sandy Springs-Marietta MSA, GA	Y	12950 FQ	14810 MW	17810 TQ	USBLS	5/07
Including Fast Food	Hawaii	Y	15650 FQ	17180 MW	19760 TQ	USBLS	5/07
Including Fast Food	Honolulu MSA, HI	Y	15520 FQ	16620 MW	19400 TQ	USBLS	5/07
Including Fast Food	Idaho	Y	12890 FQ	14650 MW	17490 TQ	USBLS	5/07
Including Fast Food	Boise City-Nampa MSA, ID	Y	12840 FQ	14610 MW	17710 TQ	USBLS	5/07

AE	Average entry wage	AW	Average wage paid	FQ	First quartile wage	LO	Lowest wage paid	MTC	Median total compensation	TCC	Total cash compensation
AER	Average entry range	AWR	Average wage range	H	Hourly	LR	Low end range	MW	Median wage paid	TQ	Third quartile wage
AEX	Average experienced wage	AXR	Average experienced range	HI	Highest wage paid	M	Monthly	MWR	Median wage range	W	Weekly
ATC	Average total compensation	D	Daily	HR	High end range	MCC	Median cash compensation	S	See annotated source	Y	Yearly

Combined Food Preparation and Serving Worker

Occupation/Type/Industry	Location	Per	Low	Mid	High	Source	Date
Including Fast Food	Lewiston MSA, ID-WA	Y	13740 FQ	16540 MW	18830 TQ	USBLS	5/07
Including Fast Food	Illinois	Y	14820 FQ	15830 MW	18280 TQ	USBLS	5/07
Including Fast Food	Chicago-Naperville-Joliet MSA, IL-IN-WI	Y	14760 FQ	15930 MW	18530 TQ	USBLS	5/07
Including Fast Food	Indiana	Y	12890 FQ	14640 MW	17040 TQ	USBLS	5/07
Including Fast Food	Gary PMSA, IN	Y	12690 FQ	14210 MW	16030 TQ	USBLS	5/07
Including Fast Food	Indianapolis-Carmel MSA, IN	Y	13260 FQ	15360 MW	17740 TQ	USBLS	5/07
Including Fast Food	Iowa	Y	14000 FQ	15130 MW	17520 TQ	USBLS	5/07
Including Fast Food	Des Moines-West Des Moines MSA, IA	Y	14480 FQ	16380 MW	18880 TQ	USBLS	5/07
Including Fast Food	Sioux City MSA, IA-NE-SD	Y	13770 FQ	14820 MW	16300 TQ	USBLS	5/07
Including Fast Food	Waterloo-Cedar Falls MSA, IA	Y	13780 FQ	14660 MW	15780 TQ	USBLS	5/07
Including Fast Food	Kansas	Y	12780 FQ	14360 MW	16360 TQ	USBLS	5/07
Including Fast Food	Lawrence MSA, KS	Y	12970 FQ	14790 MW	17360 TQ	USBLS	5/07
Including Fast Food	Wichita MSA, KS	Y	12580 FQ	13940 MW	15450 TQ	USBLS	5/07
Including Fast Food	Kentucky	Y	13001 FQ	14423 MW	16000 TQ	KYBLS	2008
Including Fast Food	Louisville-Jefferson County MSA, KY-IN	Y	12720 FQ	14220 MW	16170 TQ	USBLS	5/07
Including Fast Food	Louisiana	H	6.08 FQ	6.77 MW	7.58 TQ	LABLS	1/08-3/08
Including Fast Food	Baton Rouge MSA, LA	Y	12820 FQ	14360 MW	16320 TQ	USBLS	5/07
Including Fast Food	New Orleans-Metairie-Kenner MSA, LA	Y	13060 FQ	14790 MW	17370 TQ	USBLS	5/07
Including Fast Food	Shreveport-Bossier City MSA, LA	Y	12640 FQ	14250 MW	16090 TQ	USBLS	5/07
Including Fast Food	Maine	Y	15060 FQ	16470 MW	18880 TQ	USBLS	5/07
Including Fast Food	Lewiston-Auburn MSA, ME	Y	14940 FQ	15910 MW	18190 TQ	USBLS	5/07
Including Fast Food	Portland-South Portland-Biddeford MSA, ME	Y	15880 FQ	17770 MW	19850 TQ	USBLS	5/07
Including Fast Food	Maryland	Y		16350 MW		MDBLS	3/08
Including Fast Food	Baltimore-Towson MSA, MD	Y	14590 FQ	16450 MW	19500 TQ	USBLS	5/07
Including Fast Food	Bethesda-Gaithersburg-Frederick PMSA, MD	Y	14700 FQ	16600 MW	19910 TQ	USBLS	5/07
Including Fast Food	Massachusetts	Y	16570 FQ	18090 MW	20060 TQ	USBLS	5/07
Including Fast Food	Boston-Cambridge-Quincy NECTA, MA	Y	16600 FQ	18220 MW	20410 TQ	USBLS	5/07
Including Fast Food	Worcester MSA, MA-CT	Y	16320 FQ	17890 MW	19540 TQ	USBLS	5/07
Including Fast Food	Michigan	Y	15040 FQ	15730 MW	18070 TQ	USBLS	5/07
Including Fast Food	Detroit-Warren-Livonia MSA, MI	Y	15080 FQ	15730 MW	18020 TQ	USBLS	5/07
Including Fast Food	Grand Rapids-Wyoming MSA, MI	Y	15060 FQ	15990 MW	18910 TQ	USBLS	5/07
Including Fast Food	Warren-Troy-Farmington Hills PMSA, MI	Y	15130 FQ	15830 MW	18390 TQ	USBLS	5/07
Including Fast Food	Minnesota	Y	15391 FQ	17346 MW	20106 TQ	MNBLS	10/08-12/08
Including Fast Food	Duluth-Superior MSA, MN-WI	Y	14983 FQ	16185 MW	18736 TQ	MNBLS	10/08-12/08
Including Fast Food	Minneapolis-Saint Paul MSA, MN-WI	Y	15673 FQ	17952 MW	20608 TQ	MNBLS	10/08-12/08
Including Fast Food	Rochester MSA, MN	Y	15342 FQ	16784 MW	19403 TQ	MNBLS	10/08-12/08
Including Fast Food	Mississippi	Y	12610 FQ	14090 MW	15760 TQ	USBLS	5/07
Including Fast Food	Hattiesburg MSA, MS	Y	12600 FQ	13960 MW	15500 TQ	USBLS	5/07
Including Fast Food	Jackson MSA, MS	Y	12600 FQ	14080 MW	15710 TQ	USBLS	5/07
Including Fast Food	Pascagoula MSA, MS	Y	12400 FQ	13530 MW	14660 TQ	USBLS	5/07
Including Fast Food	Missouri	Y	14400 FQ	15350 MW	17610 TQ	USBLS	5/07
Including Fast Food	Kansas City MSA, MO-KS	Y	14440 FQ	15800 MW	18420 TQ	USBLS	5/07
Including Fast Food	St. Louis MSA, MO-IL	Y	14520 FQ	15460 MW	17960 TQ	USBLS	5/07
Including Fast Food	Montana	Y	14030 FQ	15290 MW	17920 TQ	USBLS	5/07
Including Fast Food	Billings MSA, MT	Y	14060 FQ	15310 MW	16940 TQ	USBLS	5/07
Including Fast Food	Nebraska	Y	12980 FQ	14790 MW	17620 TQ	USBLS	5/07
Including Fast Food	Omaha-Council Bluffs MSA, NE-IA	Y	13610 FQ	15620 MW	18250 TQ	USBLS	5/07
Including Fast Food	Nevada	H	6.74 FQ	8.00 MW	9.41 TQ	NVBLS	5/08
Including Fast Food	Las Vegas-Paradise MSA, NV	H	6.66 FQ	7.87 MW	9.31 TQ	NVBLS	5/08
Including Fast Food	New Hampshire	H	6.85 AE	8.74 MW	10.06 AEX	NHBLS	6/08
Including Fast Food	Manchester MSA, NH	Y	13820 FQ	16530 MW	19180 TQ	USBLS	5/07
Including Fast Food	Nashua NECTA, NH-MA	Y	15640 FQ	17820 MW	20470 TQ	USBLS	5/07
Including Fast Food	New Jersey	Y	15490 FQ	16640 MW	19730 TQ	USBLS	5/07
Including Fast Food	Camden PMSA, NJ	Y	15420 FQ	16130 MW	18790 TQ	USBLS	5/07
Including Fast Food	Edison PMSA, NJ	Y	15500 FQ	16730 MW	19350 TQ	USBLS	5/07
Including Fast Food	Newark-Union PMSA, NJ-PA	Y	15530 FQ	16710 MW	20290 TQ	USBLS	5/07
Including Fast Food	Trenton-Ewing MSA, NJ	Y	15630 FQ	16800 MW	20190 TQ	USBLS	5/07

AE	Average entry wage	AW	Average wage paid	FQ	First quartile wage	LO	Lowest wage paid	MTC Median total compensation	TCC Total cash compensation
AER	Average entry range	AWR	Average wage range	H	Hourly	LR	Low end range	MW Median wage paid	TQ Third quartile wage
AEX	Average experienced wage	AXR	Average experienced range	HI	Highest wage paid	M	Monthly	MWR Median wage range	W Weekly
ATC	Average total compensation	D	Daily	HR	High end range	MCC	Median cash compensation	S See annotated source	Y Yearly

Occupation/Type/Industry	Location	Per	Low	Mid	High	Source	Date
Combined Food Preparation and Serving Worker							
Including Fast Food	New Mexico	Y	12580 FQ	14020 MW	15640 TQ	USBLS	5/07
Including Fast Food	Albuquerque MSA, NM	Y	12540 FQ	13960 MW	15520 TQ	USBLS	5/07
Including Fast Food	New York	Y	15070 FQ	15720 MW	18010 TQ	USBLS	5/07
Including Fast Food	Albany-Schenectady-Troy MSA, NY	Y	15190 FQ	15940 MW	18620 TQ	USBLS	5/07
Including Fast Food	Buffalo-Niagara Falls MSA, NY	Y	15050 FQ	15570 MW	16470 TQ	USBLS	5/07
Including Fast Food	Ithaca MSA, NY	Y	15120 FQ	15940 MW	18920 TQ	USBLS	5/07
Including Fast Food	Nassau-Suffolk PMSA, NY	Y	15090 FQ	15880 MW	18280 TQ	USBLS	5/07
Including Fast Food	New York-Northern New Jersey-Long Island MSA, NY-NJ-PA	Y	15290 FQ	16130 MW	19280 TQ	USBLS	5/07
Including Fast Food	North Carolina	Y	13840 FQ	14880 MW	16800 TQ	USBLS	5/07
Including Fast Food	Charlotte-Gastonia-Concord MSA, NC-SC	Y	13910 FQ	15110 MW	17630 TQ	USBLS	5/07
Including Fast Food	Raleigh-Cary MSA, NC	Y	13830 FQ	14860 MW	17030 TQ	USBLS	5/07
Including Fast Food	North Dakota	Y	13260 FQ	15390 MW	17930 TQ	USBLS	5/07
Including Fast Food	Fargo MSA, ND-MN	Y	14160 FQ	16250 MW	18500 TQ	USBLS	5/07
Including Fast Food	Ohio	Y	14720 FQ	15320 MW	16400 TQ	USBLS	5/07
Including Fast Food	Cincinnati-Middletown MSA, OH-KY-IN	Y	14600 FQ	15420 MW	17370 TQ	USBLS	5/07
Including Fast Food	Cleveland-Elyria-Mentor MSA, OH	Y	14740 FQ	15370 MW	16700 TQ	USBLS	5/07
Including Fast Food	Columbus MSA, OH	Y	14780 FQ	15490 MW	17420 TQ	USBLS	5/07
Including Fast Food	Dayton MSA, OH	Y	14690 FQ	15200 MW	16090 TQ	USBLS	5/07
Including Fast Food	Oklahoma	Y	12590 FQ	14000 MW	15530 TQ	USBLS	5/07
Including Fast Food	Oklahoma City MSA, OK	Y	12690 FQ	14200 MW	15960 TQ	USBLS	5/07
Including Fast Food	Tulsa MSA, OK	Y	12570 FQ	13970 MW	15460 TQ	USBLS	5/07
Including Fast Food	Oregon	H	8.46 FQ	8.99 MW	9.66 TQ	ORBLS	5/08
Including Fast Food	Medford MSA, OR	Y	17000 FQ	18040 MW	19210 TQ	USBLS	5/07
Including Fast Food	Portland-Vancouver-Beaverton MSA, OR-WA	Y	17170 FQ	18290 MW	19750 TQ	USBLS	5/07
Including Fast Food	Pennsylvania	Y	14600 FQ	15930 MW	19100 TQ	USBLS	5/07
Including Fast Food	Allentown-Bethlehem-Easton MSA, PA-NJ	Y	14760 FQ	15940 MW	18660 TQ	USBLS	5/07
Including Fast Food	Philadelphia-Camden-Wilmington MSA, PA-NJ-DE-MD	Y	15220 FQ	16600 MW	19870 TQ	USBLS	5/07
Including Fast Food	Pittsburgh MSA, PA	Y	14460 FQ	15540 MW	18630 TQ	USBLS	5/07
Including Fast Food	Reading MSA, PA	Y	14490 FQ	15580 MW	18640 TQ	USBLS	5/07
Including Fast Food	Rhode Island	Y	16350 FQ	18000 MW	19940 TQ	USBLS	5/07
Including Fast Food	Providence-Fall River-Warwick MSA, RI-MA	Y	16370 FQ	17890 MW	19640 TQ	USBLS	5/07
Including Fast Food	South Carolina	Y	12770 FQ	14390 MW	16530 TQ	USBLS	5/07
Including Fast Food	Charleston-North Charleston MSA, SC	Y	12830 FQ	14480 MW	16940 TQ	USBLS	5/07
Including Fast Food	Columbia MSA, SC	Y	12730 FQ	14410 MW	16310 TQ	USBLS	5/07
Including Fast Food	South Dakota	Y		15025 MW	17182 TQ	SDBLS	7/08-9/08
Including Fast Food	Rapid City MSA, SD	Y		14818 MW	16865 TQ	SDBLS	7/08-9/08
Including Fast Food	Sioux Falls MSA, SD	Y		15284 MW	17661 TQ	SDBLS	7/08-9/08
Including Fast Food	Tennessee	Y	12830 FQ	14530 MW	16920 TQ	USBLS	5/07
Including Fast Food	Clarksville MSA, TN-KY	Y	12570 FQ	14000 MW	15580 TQ	USBLS	5/07
Including Fast Food	Kingsport-Bristol-Bristol MSA, TN-VA	Y	12750 FQ	14340 MW	16190 TQ	USBLS	5/07
Including Fast Food	Memphis MSA, TN-MS-AR	Y	12970 FQ	14690 MW	17440 TQ	USBLS	5/07
Including Fast Food	Nashville-Davidson-Murfreesboro MSA, TN	Y	13100 FQ	15070 MW	18070 TQ	USBLS	5/07
Including Fast Food	Texas	Y	12770 FQ	14370 MW	16560 TQ	USBLS	5/07
Including Fast Food	Austin-Round Rock MSA, TX	Y	13450 FQ	15730 MW	18650 TQ	USBLS	5/07
Including Fast Food	Corpus Christi MSA, TX	Y	12490 FQ	13790 MW	15150 TQ	USBLS	5/07
Including Fast Food	Dallas-Fort Worth-Arlington MSA, TX	Y	12920 FQ	14690 MW	17550 TQ	USBLS	5/07
Including Fast Food	El Paso MSA, TX	Y	12610 FQ	14060 MW	15670 TQ	USBLS	5/07
Including Fast Food	Houston-Sugar Land-Baytown MSA, TX	Y	12790 FQ	14420 MW	16750 TQ	USBLS	5/07
Including Fast Food	San Antonio MSA, TX	Y	12770 FQ	14350 MW	16660 TQ	USBLS	5/07
Including Fast Food	Utah	Y	13160 FQ	15180 MW	17860 TQ	USBLS	5/07
Including Fast Food	Ogden-Clearfield MSA, UT	Y	12890 FQ	14660 MW	17030 TQ	USBLS	5/07
Including Fast Food	Salt Lake City MSA, UT	Y	13310 FQ	15480 MW	18280 TQ	USBLS	5/07
Including Fast Food	Vermont	Y	16940 FQ	18380 MW	20400 TQ	USBLS	5/07

AE	Average entry wage	AW	Average wage paid	FQ	First quartile wage
AER	Average entry range	AWR	Average wage range	H	Hourly
AEX	Average experienced wage	AXR	Average experienced range	HI	Highest wage paid
ATC	Average total compensation	D	Daily	HR	High end range

LO	Lowest wage paid	MTC	Median total compensation	TCC	Total cash compensation
LR	Low end range	MW	Median wage paid	TQ	Third quartile wage
M	Monthly	MWR	Median wage range	W	Weekly
MCC	Median cash compensation	S	See annotated source	Y	Yearly

Occupation/Type/Industry	Location	Per	Low	Mid	High	Source	Date
Combined Food Preparation and Serving Worker							
Including Fast Food	Burlington-South Burlington MSA, VT	Y	17110 FQ	18500 MW	20520 TQ	USBLS	5/07
Including Fast Food	Virginia	Y	13290 FQ	15480 MW	18670 TQ	USBLS	5/07
Including Fast Food	Richmond MSA, VA	Y	13130 FQ	15210 MW	18130 TQ	USBLS	5/07
Including Fast Food	Roanoke MSA, VA	Y	13270 FQ	15410 MW	18210 TQ	USBLS	5/07
Including Fast Food	Virginia Beach-Norfolk-Newport News MSA, VA-NC	Y	13150 FQ	15110 MW	18240 TQ	USBLS	5/07
Including Fast Food	Washington	H	8.55 FQ	9.13 MW	10.15 TQ	WABLS	3/08
Including Fast Food	Seattle-Tacoma-Bellevue MSA, WA	Y	17640 FQ	18940 MW	21940 TQ	USBLS	5/07
Including Fast Food	Spokane MSA, WA	Y	17390 FQ	18400 MW	19740 TQ	USBLS	5/07
Including Fast Food	West Virginia	Y	13898 FQ	14886 MW	15967 TQ	WVBLS	7/08-9/08
Including Fast Food	Charleston MSA, WV	Y	13330 FQ	14270 MW	15300 TQ	USBLS	5/07
Including Fast Food	Wheeling MSA, WV-OH	Y	13810 FQ	14660 MW	15320 TQ	USBLS	5/07
Including Fast Food	Wisconsin	Y	14650 FQ	15780 MW	18630 TQ	USBLS	5/07
Including Fast Food	Milwaukee-Waukesha-West Allis MSA, WI	Y	14770 FQ	16230 MW	19380 TQ	USBLS	5/07
Including Fast Food	Wyoming	Y	14060 FQ	16484 MW	19463 TQ	WYBLS	9/08
Including Fast Food	Cheyenne MSA, WY	Y	14694 FQ	17109 MW	20921 TQ	WYBLS	9/08
Including Fast Food	Puerto Rico	Y	12440 FQ	13660 MW	14890 TQ	USBLS	5/07
Including Fast Food	Aguadilla-Isabela-San Sebastian MSA, PR	Y	12330 FQ	13490 MW	14650 TQ	USBLS	5/07
Including Fast Food	San Juan-Caguas-Guaynabo MSA, PR	Y	12440 FQ	13680 MW	14910 TQ	USBLS	5/07
Including Fast Food	Virgin Islands	Y	14680 FQ	17240 MW	20950 TQ	USBLS	5/07
Including Fast Food	Guam	Y	12490 FQ	13790 MW	15130 TQ	USBLS	5/07
Comic Book Illustrator	United States	Y			250000 HI	CNASTP	2008
Command Sergeant Major							
U.S. Army, Active Duty, Pay Grade E-9	United States	M	4421 LO		6863 HI	DOD1	2009
Commercial and Industrial Designer							
	Alabama	Y	28970 FQ	38480 MW	58920 TQ	USBLS	5/07
	Birmingham-Hoover MSA, AL	Y	28450 FQ	38220 MW	60270 TQ	USBLS	5/07
	Arizona	Y	40320 FQ	53780 MW	67010 TQ	USBLS	5/07
	Phoenix-Mesa-Scottsdale MSA, AZ	Y	40760 FQ	53710 MW	65690 TQ	USBLS	5/07
	Arkansas	Y	28850 FQ	44300 MW	64130 TQ	USBLS	5/07
	California	H	23.62 FQ	32.23 MW	42.96 TQ	CABLS	1/08-3/08
	Los Angeles-Long Beach-Glendale PMSA, CA	H	22.08 FQ	30.52 MW	36.92 TQ	CABLS	1/08-3/08
	Oakland-Fremont-Hayward MSA, CA	H	24.21 FQ	29.14 MW	49.20 TQ	CABLS	1/08-3/08
	Riverside-San Bernardino-Ontario MSA, CA	H	20.68 FQ	24.68 MW	30.46 TQ	CABLS	1/08-3/08
	Sacramento-Arden Arcade-Roseville MSA, CA	H	25.03 FQ	30.56 MW	35.59 TQ	CABLS	1/08-3/08
	San Diego-Carlsbad-San Marcos MSA, CA	H	18.82 FQ	25.86 MW	35.55 TQ	CABLS	1/08-3/08
	San Francisco-San Mateo-Redwood PMSA, CA	H	28.21 FQ	38.21 MW	64.37 TQ	CABLS	1/08-3/08
	San Jose-Sunnyvale-Santa Clara MSA, CA	H	34.54 FQ	44.21 MW	59.44 TQ	CABLS	1/08-3/08
	Santa Ana-Anaheim-Irvine PMSA, CA	Y	51420 FQ	68290 MW	85430 TQ	USBLS	5/07
	Santa Rosa-Petaluma MSA, CA	H	27.99 FQ	32.37 MW	36.77 TQ	CABLS	1/08-3/08
	Colorado	Y	37160 FQ	47000 MW	60090 TQ	USBLS	5/07
	Denver-Aurora MSA, CO	Y	39010 FQ	47890 MW	60990 TQ	USBLS	5/07
	Connecticut	H	19.09 AE	28.56 MW		CTBLS	1/08-3/08
	Bridgeport-Stamford-Norwalk MSA, CT	Y	51010 FQ	65120 MW	95450 TQ	USBLS	5/07
	Hartford-West Hartford-East Hartford MSA, CT	Y	35530 FQ	46420 MW	54380 TQ	USBLS	5/07
	Washington-Arlington-Alexandria MSA, DC-VA-MD-WV	Y	35580 FQ	43770 MW	61150 TQ	USBLS	5/07
	Florida	Y	36920 FQ	51130 MW	66380 TQ	USBLS	5/07

AE	Average entry wage	AW	Average wage paid	FQ	First quartile wage
AER	Average entry range	AWR	Average wage range	H	Hourly
AEX	Average experienced wage	AXR	Average experienced range	HI	Highest wage paid
ATC	Average total compensation	D	Daily	HR	High end range

LO	Lowest wage paid	MTC	Median total compensation
LR	Low end range	MW	Median wage paid
M	Monthly	MWR	Median wage range
MCC	Median cash compensation	S	See annotated source

TCC	Total cash compensation
TQ	Third quartile wage
W	Weekly
Y	Yearly

Occupation/Type/Industry	Location	Per	Low	Mid	High	Source	Date
Commercial and Industrial Designer							
	Fort Lauderdale-Pompano Beach-Deerfield Beach PMSA, FL	Y	33120 FQ	36660 MW	55410 TQ	USBLS	5/07
	Jacksonville MSA, FL	Y	68460 FQ	76770 MW	89710 TQ	USBLS	5/07
	Miami-Fort Lauderdale-Miami Beach MSA, FL	Y	35050 FQ	39110 MW	53340 TQ	USBLS	5/07
	Tampa-St. Petersburg-Clearwater MSA, FL	Y	36090 FQ	50820 MW	59370 TQ	USBLS	5/07
	West Palm Beach-Boca Raton-Boynton Beach PMSA, FL	Y	36470 FQ	39510 MW	42190 TQ	USBLS	5/07
	Georgia	Y	38380 FQ	48530 MW	64230 TQ	USBLS	5/07
	Atlanta-Sandy Springs-Marietta MSA, GA	Y	39450 FQ	48920 MW	64820 TQ	USBLS	5/07
	Augusta-Richmond County MSA, GA-SC	Y	39240 FQ	51880 MW	69640 TQ	USBLS	5/07
	Idaho	Y	29160 FQ	33990 MW	43860 TQ	USBLS	5/07
	Illinois	Y	24350 FQ	43190 MW	60620 TQ	USBLS	5/07
	Chicago-Naperville-Joliet MSA, IL-IN-WI	Y	23350 FQ	42610 MW	60430 TQ	USBLS	5/07
	Indiana	Y	35820 FQ	46720 MW	66370 TQ	USBLS	5/07
	Elkhart-Goshen MSA, IN	Y	35120 FQ	42220 MW	51190 TQ	USBLS	5/07
	Gary PMSA, IN	Y	18520 FQ	32480 MW	53490 TQ	USBLS	5/07
	Indianapolis-Carmel MSA, IN	Y	37870 FQ	50450 MW	74850 TQ	USBLS	5/07
	Iowa	Y	35570 FQ	46270 MW	60420 TQ	USBLS	5/07
	Des Moines-West Des Moines MSA, IA	Y	33540 FQ	37740 MW	52350 TQ	USBLS	5/07
	Kansas	Y	31550 FQ	41920 MW	57760 TQ	USBLS	5/07
	Wichita MSA, KS	Y	50640 FQ	62990 MW	79670 TQ	USBLS	5/07
	Kentucky	Y	34491 FQ	46636 MW	59307 TQ	KYBLS	2008
	Louisville-Jefferson County MSA, KY-IN	Y	35780 FQ	42900 MW	53840 TQ	USBLS	5/07
	Louisiana	H	22.91 FQ	30.05 MW	37.57 TQ	LABLS	1/08-3/08
	Baton Rouge MSA, LA	Y	50160 FQ	64010 MW	80440 TQ	USBLS	5/07
	Maine	Y	35070 FQ	49170 MW	72210 TQ	USBLS	5/07
	Portland-South Portland-Biddeford MSA, ME	Y	58290 FQ	72830 MW	81180 TQ	USBLS	5/07
	Maryland	Y		37625 MW		MDBLS	3/08
	Baltimore-Towson MSA, MD	Y	28290 FQ	31490 MW	49370 TQ	USBLS	5/07
	Bethesda-Gaithersburg-Frederick PMSA, MD	Y	34830 FQ	38140 MW	55810 TQ	USBLS	5/07
	Massachusetts	Y	51840 FQ	70100 MW	89900 TQ	USBLS	5/07
	Boston-Cambridge-Quincy NECTA, MA	Y	47370 FQ	68440 MW	91180 TQ	USBLS	5/07
	Springfield MSA, MA-CT	Y	51680 FQ	67570 MW	89250 TQ	USBLS	5/07
	Worcester MSA, MA-CT	Y	46280 FQ	54290 MW	71910 TQ	USBLS	5/07
	Michigan	Y	55180 FQ	69880 MW	84870 TQ	USBLS	5/07
	Detroit-Warren-Livonia MSA, MI	Y	59210 FQ	74470 MW	89000 TQ	USBLS	5/07
	Grand Rapids-Wyoming MSA, MI	Y	49270 FQ	57810 MW	65100 TQ	USBLS	5/07
	Warren-Troy-Farmington Hills PMSA, MI	Y	58130 FQ	74020 MW	87540 TQ	USBLS	5/07
	Minnesota	Y	54121 FQ	76458 MW	106694 TQ	MNBLS	10/08-12/08
	Mississippi	Y	36000 FQ	47040 MW	63330 TQ	USBLS	5/07
	Missouri	Y	42400 FQ	54440 MW	70610 TQ	USBLS	5/07
	Kansas City MSA, MO-KS	Y	36390 FQ	46010 MW	59370 TQ	USBLS	5/07
	St. Louis MSA, MO-IL	Y	41810 FQ	58350 MW	74300 TQ	USBLS	5/07
	Nebraska	Y	28480 FQ	38010 MW	46680 TQ	USBLS	5/07
	Omaha-Council Bluffs MSA, NE-IA	Y	24740 FQ	32230 MW	44670 TQ	USBLS	5/07
	Nevada	H	27.07 FQ	35.73 MW	39.33 TQ	NVBLS	5/08
	Las Vegas-Paradise MSA, NV	H	33.13 FQ	36.34 MW	39.51 TQ	NVBLS	5/08
	New Hampshire	H	16.96 AE	24.34 MW	27.75 AEX	NHBLS	6/08
	Nashua NECTA, NH-MA	Y	37810 FQ	47400 MW	54600 TQ	USBLS	5/07
	New Jersey	Y	40320 FQ	59130 MW	77180 TQ	USBLS	5/07
	Camden PMSA, NJ	Y	34490 FQ	54580 MW	70170 TQ	USBLS	5/07
	Edison PMSA, NJ	Y	43350 FQ	57460 MW	68340 TQ	USBLS	5/07
	Newark-Union PMSA, NJ-PA	Y	53250 FQ	64870 MW	78450 TQ	USBLS	5/07
	New Mexico	Y	33360 FQ	49220 MW	81230 TQ	USBLS	5/07
	New York	Y	48190 FQ	60850 MW	78820 TQ	USBLS	5/07

AE Average entry wage	**AW** Average wage paid	**FQ** First quartile wage	**LO** Lowest wage paid	**MTC** Median total compensation	**TCC** Total cash compensation
AER Average entry range	**AWR** Average wage range	**H** Hourly	**LR** Low end range	**MW** Median wage paid	**TQ** Third quartile wage
AEX Average experienced wage	**AXR** Average experienced range	**HI** Highest wage paid	**M** Monthly	**MWR** Median wage range	**W** Weekly
ATC Average total compensation	**D** Daily	**HR** High end range	**MCC** Median cash compensation	**S** See annotated source	**Y** Yearly

Occupation/Type/Industry	Location	Per	Low	Mid	High	Source	Date
Commercial and Industrial Designer	Albany-Schenectady-Troy MSA, NY	Y	61680 FQ	68470 MW	74560 TQ	USBLS	5/07
	Buffalo-Niagara Falls MSA, NY	Y	40330 FQ	52670 MW	64620 TQ	USBLS	5/07
	Nassau-Suffolk PMSA, NY	Y	55410 FQ	60800 MW	66310 TQ	USBLS	5/07
	New York-Northern New Jersey-Long Island MSA, NY-NJ-PA	Y	47600 FQ	60330 MW	81040 TQ	USBLS	5/07
	Syracuse MSA, NY	Y	50000 FQ	63640 MW	75200 TQ	USBLS	5/07
	North Carolina	Y	34270 FQ	48490 MW	65970 TQ	USBLS	5/07
	Charlotte-Gastonia-Concord MSA, NC-SC	Y	32720 FQ	38930 MW	71790 TQ	USBLS	5/07
	Ohio	Y	40600 FQ	48840 MW	60840 TQ	USBLS	5/07
	Cincinnati-Middletown MSA, OH-KY-IN	Y	45230 FQ	59070 MW	70770 TQ	USBLS	5/07
	Cleveland-Elyria-Mentor MSA, OH	Y	41120 FQ	47450 MW	57230 TQ	USBLS	5/07
	Columbus MSA, OH	Y	41710 FQ	50680 MW	67080 TQ	USBLS	5/07
	Dayton MSA, OH	Y	44470 FQ	58880 MW	77160 TQ	USBLS	5/07
	Oklahoma	Y	27070 FQ	40390 MW	59100 TQ	USBLS	5/07
	Oklahoma City MSA, OK	Y	23410 FQ	36050 MW	54810 TQ	USBLS	5/07
	Tulsa MSA, OK	Y	35460 FQ	43240 MW	52790 TQ	USBLS	5/07
	Oregon	H	17.14 FQ	21.82 MW	26.87 TQ	ORBLS	5/08
	Eugene-Springfield MSA, OR	Y	32260 FQ	38060 MW	45410 TQ	USBLS	5/07
	Portland-Vancouver-Beaverton MSA, OR-WA	Y	40070 FQ	49560 MW	67780 TQ	USBLS	5/07
	Pennsylvania	Y	36160 FQ	49010 MW	62330 TQ	USBLS	5/07
	Allentown-Bethlehem-Easton MSA, PA-NJ	Y	40660 FQ	55190 MW	63720 TQ	USBLS	5/07
	Erie MSA, PA	Y	35160 FQ	42710 MW	48730 TQ	USBLS	5/07
	Philadelphia-Camden-Wilmington MSA, PA-NJ-DE-MD	Y	42640 FQ	53350 MW	65850 TQ	USBLS	5/07
	Pittsburgh MSA, PA	Y	26340 FQ	44000 MW	60450 TQ	USBLS	5/07
	Rhode Island	Y	44000 FQ	50840 MW	60020 TQ	USBLS	5/07
	Providence-Fall River-Warwick MSA, RI-MA	Y	44420 FQ	51910 MW	62550 TQ	USBLS	5/07
	South Carolina	Y	21430 FQ	38130 MW	53060 TQ	USBLS	5/07
	Columbia MSA, SC	Y	16620 FQ	20960 MW	24360 TQ	USBLS	5/07
	South Dakota	Y	28507 FQ	32363 MW	41762 TQ	SDBLS	7/08-9/08
	Sioux Falls MSA, SD	Y	27853 FQ	30728 MW	37690 TQ	SDBLS	7/08-9/08
	Tennessee	Y	34200 FQ	44440 MW	58560 TQ	USBLS	5/07
	Memphis MSA, TN-MS-AR	Y	24210 FQ	36180 MW	48860 TQ	USBLS	5/07
	Nashville-Davidson-Murfreesboro MSA, TN	Y	31830 FQ	39130 MW	56450 TQ	USBLS	5/07
	Texas	Y	34500 FQ	46900 MW	64230 TQ	USBLS	5/07
	Austin-Round Rock MSA, TX	Y	45990 FQ	58780 MW	71620 TQ	USBLS	5/07
	Dallas-Fort Worth-Arlington MSA, TX	Y	37250 FQ	55830 MW	71930 TQ	USBLS	5/07
	Houston-Sugar Land-Baytown MSA, TX	Y	34330 FQ	39900 MW	48550 TQ	USBLS	5/07
	San Antonio MSA, TX	Y	23080 FQ	30160 MW	52860 TQ	USBLS	5/07
	Utah	Y	45230 FQ	57610 MW	76650 TQ	USBLS	5/07
	Provo-Orem MSA, UT	Y	36000 FQ	46040 MW	62180 TQ	USBLS	5/07
	Salt Lake City MSA, UT	Y	47370 FQ	56920 MW	73950 TQ	USBLS	5/07
	Vermont	Y	32080 FQ	44150 MW	65500 TQ	USBLS	5/07
	Burlington-South Burlington MSA, VT	Y	37750 FQ	51770 MW	81710 TQ	USBLS	5/07
	Virginia	Y	37090 FQ	46590 MW	62970 TQ	USBLS	5/07
	Virginia Beach-Norfolk-Newport News MSA, VA-NC	Y	33570 FQ	41140 MW	55350 TQ	USBLS	5/07
	Washington	H	19.93 FQ	26.59 MW	32.58 TQ	WABLS	3/08
	Seattle-Tacoma-Bellevue MSA, WA	Y	39930 FQ	53500 MW	64190 TQ	USBLS	5/07
	West Virginia	Y	43772 FQ	50637 MW	67881 TQ	WVBLS	7/08-9/08
	Wisconsin	Y	43290 FQ	53980 MW	67480 TQ	USBLS	5/07
	Milwaukee-Waukesha-West Allis MSA, WI	Y	43380 FQ	52490 MW	65280 TQ	USBLS	5/07
	Wyoming	Y	35727 FQ	43230 MW	66575 TQ	WYBLS	9/08
Commercial Diver	Alaska	Y	47720 FQ	108480 MW	121470 TQ	USBLS	5/07

AE	Average entry wage	AW	Average wage paid	FQ	First quartile wage
AER	Average entry range	AWR	Average wage range	H	Hourly
AEX	Average experienced wage	AXR	Average experienced range	HI	Highest wage paid
ATC	Average total compensation	D	Daily	HR	High end range

LO	Lowest wage paid	MTC	Median total compensation	TCC	Total cash compensation
LR	Low end range	MW	Median wage paid	TQ	Third quartile wage
M	Monthly	MWR	Median wage range	W	Weekly
MCC	Median cash compensation	S	See annotated source	Y	Yearly

Occupation/Type/Industry	Location	Per	Low	Mid	High	Source	Date
Commercial Diver	California	H	29.25 FQ	35.25 MW	40.03 TQ	CABLS	1/08-3/08
	Florida	Y	36990 FQ	41200 MW	48830 TQ	USBLS	5/07
	Hawaii	Y	25040 FQ	37230 MW	45830 TQ	USBLS	5/07
	Maryland	Y		37075 MW		MDBLS	3/08
	Michigan	Y	20110 FQ	24490 MW	32180 TQ	USBLS	5/07
	Mississippi	Y	36750 FQ	43750 MW	48600 TQ	USBLS	5/07
	Missouri	Y	33120 FQ	36300 MW	44770 TQ	USBLS	5/07
	New York	Y	46320 FQ	53950 MW	92770 TQ	USBLS	5/07
	South Carolina	Y	37710 FQ	41370 MW	46230 TQ	USBLS	5/07
	Virginia	Y	31960 FQ	43480 MW	55140 TQ	USBLS	5/07
Commercial Lender							
1 to 3 Years Experience	Baltimore, MD	Y		50470-77507 AWR		BMAG	2009
Commercial Lines Manager							
Insurance Agency	United States	Y	64474 LO		144025 HI	INSJ01	2006
Commercial Pilot	United States	Y		57480 MW		FORB01	2007
	Alabama	Y	53180 FQ	69340 MW	81450 TQ	USBLS	5/07
	Birmingham-Hoover MSA, AL	Y	53960 FQ	76840 MW	94610 TQ	USBLS	5/07
	Alaska	Y	48330 FQ	61570 MW	82390 TQ	USBLS	5/07
	Anchorage MSA, AK	Y	55120 FQ	66850 MW	88150 TQ	USBLS	5/07
	Arizona	Y	41450 FQ	56550 MW	73580 TQ	USBLS	5/07
	Phoenix-Mesa-Scottsdale MSA, AZ	Y	39320 FQ	49090 MW	63500 TQ	USBLS	5/07
	Tucson MSA, AZ	Y	55840 FQ	71440 MW	82610 TQ	USBLS	5/07
	Arkansas	Y	43520 FQ	53880 MW	76670 TQ	USBLS	5/07
	Fayetteville-Springdale-Rogers MSA, AR-MO	Y	28590 FQ	67660 MW	93420 TQ	USBLS	5/07
	Little Rock-North Little Rock MSA, AR	Y	42340 FQ	49080 MW	73330 TQ	USBLS	5/07
	California	Y		76504 MW		CABLS	1/08-3/08
	Los Angeles-Long Beach-Glendale PMSA, CA	Y		79389 AW		CABLS	1/08-3/08
	Oakland-Fremont-Hayward MSA, CA	Y		73813 AW		CABLS	1/08-3/08
	Sacramento-Arden Arcade-Roseville MSA, CA	Y		62754 AW		CABLS	1/08-3/08
	San Diego-Carlsbad-San Marcos MSA, CA	Y		75819 AW		CABLS	1/08-3/08
	San Jose-Sunnyvale-Santa Clara MSA, CA	Y		61700 AW		CABLS	1/08-3/08
	Santa Ana-Anaheim-Irvine PMSA, CA	Y	43370 FQ	56240 MW	86510 TQ	USBLS	5/07
	Colorado	Y	43130 FQ	55140 MW	70190 TQ	USBLS	5/07
	Colorado Springs MSA, CO	Y	52220 FQ	57640 MW	63280 TQ	USBLS	5/07
	Denver-Aurora MSA, CO	Y	40100 FQ	55140 MW	83490 TQ	USBLS	5/07
	Bridgeport-Stamford-Norwalk MSA, CT	Y	48880 FQ	74050 MW	103590 TQ	USBLS	5/07
	Hartford-West Hartford-East Hartford MSA, CT	Y	69190 FQ	75760 MW	83190 TQ	USBLS	5/07
	Delaware	Y	49330 FQ	81840 MW	99300 TQ	USBLS	5/07
	Wilmington PMSA, DE-MD-NJ	Y	56830 FQ	85220 MW	102240 TQ	USBLS	5/07
	Washington-Arlington-Alexandria MSA, DC-VA-MD-WV	Y	36370 FQ	49350 MW	79170 TQ	USBLS	5/07
	Florida	Y	38870 FQ	55510 MW	82800 TQ	USBLS	5/07
	Cape Coral-Fort Myers MSA, FL	Y	66130 FQ	71290 MW	76470 TQ	USBLS	5/07
	Jacksonville MSA, FL	Y	35470 FQ	45400 MW	55530 TQ	USBLS	5/07
	Miami-Fort Lauderdale-Miami Beach MSA, FL	Y	54650 FQ	76020 MW	124160 TQ	USBLS	5/07
	Orlando-Kissimmee MSA, FL	Y	32350 FQ	40930 MW	57280 TQ	USBLS	5/07
	Tampa-St. Petersburg-Clearwater MSA, FL	Y	32310 FQ	52430 MW	59630 TQ	USBLS	5/07
	West Palm Beach-Boca Raton-Boynton Beach PMSA, FL	Y	49430 FQ	71430 MW	109220 TQ	USBLS	5/07
	Boise City-Nampa MSA, ID	Y	43390 FQ	52810 MW	76690 TQ	USBLS	5/07
	Illinois	Y	47560 FQ	66290 MW	82440 TQ	USBLS	5/07

AE	Average entry wage	**AW**	Average wage paid	**FQ**	First quartile wage
AER	Average entry range	**AWR**	Average wage range	**H**	Hourly
AEX	Average experienced wage	**AXR**	Average experienced range	**HI**	Highest wage paid
ATC	Average total compensation	**D**	Daily	**HR**	High end range

LO	Lowest wage paid	**MTC**	Median total compensation	**TCC**	Total cash compensation
LR	Low end range	**MW**	Median wage paid	**TQ**	Third quartile wage
M	Monthly	**MWR**	Median wage range	**W**	Weekly
MCC	Median cash compensation	**S**	See annotated source	**Y**	Yearly

Occupation/Type/Industry	Location	Per	Low	Mid	High	Source	Date
Commercial Pilot	Chicago-Naperville-Joliet MSA, IL-IN-WI	Y	48510 FQ	68320 MW	87930 TQ	USBLS	5/07
	Indiana	Y	37840 FQ	50870 MW	87090 TQ	USBLS	5/07
	Indianapolis-Carmel MSA, IN	Y	25980 FQ	41510 MW	56340 TQ	USBLS	5/07
	Iowa	Y	41700 FQ	63720 MW	76630 TQ	USBLS	5/07
	Des Moines-West Des Moines MSA, IA	Y	51600 FQ	66920 MW	75740 TQ	USBLS	5/07
	Kansas	Y	56630 FQ	70320 MW	98700 TQ	USBLS	5/07
	Wichita MSA, KS	Y	60470 FQ	78960 MW	103250 TQ	USBLS	5/07
	Kentucky	Y	52358 FQ	62557 MW	76083 TQ	KYBLS	2008
	Louisville-Jefferson County MSA, KY-IN	Y	40100 FQ	45150 MW	54760 TQ	USBLS	5/07
	Louisiana	Y		62099 AW		LABLS	1/08-3/08
	Baton Rouge MSA, LA	Y	58290 FQ	70720 MW	77930 TQ	USBLS	5/07
	New Orleans-Metairie-Kenner MSA, LA	Y	46580 FQ	71650 MW	97370 TQ	USBLS	5/07
	Maine	Y	28220 FQ	42040 MW	52090 TQ	USBLS	5/07
	Portland-South Portland-Biddeford MSA, ME	Y	25920 FQ	40530 MW	51120 TQ	USBLS	5/07
	Maryland	Y		56100 MW		MDBLS	3/08
	Baltimore-Towson MSA, MD	Y	51920 FQ	59540 MW	76050 TQ	USBLS	5/07
	Bethesda-Gaithersburg-Frederick PMSA, MD	Y	42810 FQ	47320 MW	51330 TQ	USBLS	5/07
	Massachusetts	Y	48610 FQ	69040 MW	81530 TQ	USBLS	5/07
	Boston-Cambridge-Quincy NECTA, MA	Y	53520 FQ	69140 MW	77480 TQ	USBLS	5/07
	Michigan	Y	51420 FQ	75310 MW	97390 TQ	USBLS	5/07
	Grand Rapids-Wyoming MSA, MI	Y	59010 FQ	79130 MW	126990 TQ	USBLS	5/07
	Minnesota	Y	30606 FQ	42727 MW	77297 TQ	MNBLS	10/08-12/08
	Duluth-Superior MSA, MN-WI	Y	44006 FQ	86952 MW	108216 TQ	MNBLS	10/08-12/08
	Minneapolis-Saint Paul MSA, MN-WI	Y	29785 FQ	34227 MW	68517 TQ	MNBLS	10/08-12/08
	Mississippi	Y	48160 FQ	68520 MW	89640 TQ	USBLS	5/07
	Jackson MSA, MS	Y	52350 FQ	69520 MW	79900 TQ	USBLS	5/07
	Missouri	Y	46000 FQ	55820 MW	68430 TQ	USBLS	5/07
	Kansas City MSA, MO-KS	Y	36370 FQ	50110 MW	64140 TQ	USBLS	5/07
	St. Louis MSA, MO-IL	Y	45910 FQ	57100 MW	71760 TQ	USBLS	5/07
	Montana	Y	42970 FQ	53750 MW	67120 TQ	USBLS	5/07
	Nebraska	Y	41800 FQ	54150 MW	71650 TQ	USBLS	5/07
	Omaha-Council Bluffs MSA, NE-IA	Y	47950 FQ	59120 MW	83420 TQ	USBLS	5/07
	Nevada	Y	39402 FQ	50785 MW	76368 TQ	NVBLS	5/08
	Las Vegas-Paradise MSA, NV	Y	37870 FQ	53061 MW	78775 TQ	NVBLS	5/08
	New Hampshire	Y	34420 AE	57504 MW	73075 AEX	NHBLS	6/08
	New Jersey	Y	43930 FQ	67530 MW	90750 TQ	USBLS	5/07
	Camden PMSA, NJ	Y	72900 FQ	84380 MW	94200 TQ	USBLS	5/07
	Newark-Union PMSA, NJ-PA	Y	36810 FQ	57200 MW	81690 TQ	USBLS	5/07
	New Mexico	Y	28350 FQ	39600 MW	53490 TQ	USBLS	5/07
	Albuquerque MSA, NM	Y	26590 FQ	30920 MW	65510 TQ	USBLS	5/07
	New York	Y	60640 FQ	74700 MW	84530 TQ	USBLS	5/07
	New York-Northern New Jersey-Long Island MSA, NY-NJ-PA	Y	43510 FQ	70190 MW	93060 TQ	USBLS	5/07
	North Carolina	Y	44810 FQ	59460 MW	75300 TQ	USBLS	5/07
	Charlotte-Gastonia-Concord MSA, NC-SC	Y	58650 FQ	88610 MW	105940 TQ	USBLS	5/07
	Raleigh-Cary MSA, NC	Y	47640 FQ	57680 MW	69470 TQ	USBLS	5/07
	North Dakota	Y	41350 FQ	51750 MW	64230 TQ	USBLS	5/07
	Fargo MSA, ND-MN	Y	25590 FQ	46420 MW	56630 TQ	USBLS	5/07
	Cincinnati-Middletown MSA, OH-KY-IN	Y	52930 FQ	61590 MW	75090 TQ	USBLS	5/07
	Cleveland-Elyria-Mentor MSA, OH	Y	43560 FQ	54520 MW	106350 TQ	USBLS	5/07
	Columbus MSA, OH	Y	29050 FQ	51130 MW	69470 TQ	USBLS	5/07
	Oklahoma	Y	46850 FQ	61010 MW	80690 TQ	USBLS	5/07
	Oklahoma City MSA, OK	Y	55540 FQ	66040 MW	93250 TQ	USBLS	5/07
	Tulsa MSA, OK	Y	62560 FQ	75500 MW	95510 TQ	USBLS	5/07
	Oregon	Y	31444 FQ	39865 MW	64200 TQ	ORBLS	5/08
	Portland-Vancouver-Beaverton MSA, OR-WA	Y	29240 FQ	35630 MW	62740 TQ	USBLS	5/07
	Pennsylvania	Y	41970 FQ	55730 MW	66390 TQ	USBLS	5/07

AE	Average entry wage	**AW**	Average wage paid	**FQ**	First quartile wage	**LO**	Lowest wage paid	**MTC** Median total compensation **TCC** Total cash compensation
AER	Average entry range	**AWR**	Average wage range	**H**	Hourly	**LR**	Low end range	**MW** Median wage paid **TQ** Third quartile wage
AEX	Average experienced wage	**AXR**	Average experienced range	**HI**	Highest wage paid	**M**	Monthly	**MWR** Median wage range **W** Weekly
ATC	Average total compensation	**D**	Daily	**HR**	High end range	**MCC**	Median cash compensation	**S** See annotated source **Y** Yearly

Occupation/Type/Industry	Location	Per	Low	Mid	High	Source	Date
Commercial Pilot	Allentown-Bethlehem-Easton MSA, PA-NJ	Y	36820 FQ	63550 MW	72020 TQ	USBLS	5/07
	Philadelphia-Camden-Wilmington MSA, PA-NJ-DE-MD	Y	45790 FQ	57140 MW	69780 TQ	USBLS	5/07
	Pittsburgh MSA, PA	Y	31790 FQ	52730 MW	74660 TQ	USBLS	5/07
	Rhode Island	Y	38090 FQ	42970 MW	57150 TQ	USBLS	5/07
	Providence-Fall River-Warwick MSA, RI-MA	Y	39030 FQ	44190 MW	59780 TQ	USBLS	5/07
	South Carolina	Y	34880 FQ	57360 MW	72750 TQ	USBLS	5/07
	South Dakota	Y	42729 FQ	51845 MW	60982 TQ	SDBLS	7/08-9/08
	Rapid City MSA, SD	Y	43344 FQ	48601 MW	60536 TQ	SDBLS	7/08-9/08
	Sioux Falls MSA, SD	Y	38592 FQ	55619 MW	67908 TQ	SDBLS	7/08-9/08
	Tennessee	Y	28550 FQ	48760 MW	76450 TQ	USBLS	5/07
	Memphis MSA, TN-MS-AR	Y	29180 FQ	35810 MW	61950 TQ	USBLS	5/07
	Nashville-Davidson-Murfreesboro MSA, TN	Y	27830 FQ	46000 MW	76550 TQ	USBLS	5/07
	Texas	Y	43130 FQ	61970 MW	85510 TQ	USBLS	5/07
	Austin-Round Rock MSA, TX	Y	42310 FQ	64050 MW	90300 TQ	USBLS	5/07
	Dallas-Fort Worth-Arlington MSA, TX	Y	47860 FQ	74290 MW	103930 TQ	USBLS	5/07
	El Paso MSA, TX	Y	51070 FQ	69950 MW	98050 TQ	USBLS	5/07
	Houston-Sugar Land-Baytown MSA, TX	Y	41850 FQ	58400 MW	72650 TQ	USBLS	5/07
	San Antonio MSA, TX	Y	46970 FQ	75560 MW	89050 TQ	USBLS	5/07
	Utah	Y	38370 FQ	60460 MW	82060 TQ	USBLS	5/07
	Vermont	Y	39370 FQ	46400 MW	70020 TQ	USBLS	5/07
	Virginia	Y	47270 FQ	72810 MW	92640 TQ	USBLS	5/07
	Richmond MSA, VA	Y	80590 FQ	87760 MW	94410 TQ	USBLS	5/07
	Virginia Beach-Norfolk-Newport News MSA, VA-NC	Y	39260 FQ	55460 MW	65440 TQ	USBLS	5/07
	Washington	Y		73202 AW		WABLS	3/08
	Seattle-Tacoma-Bellevue MSA, WA	Y	30870 FQ	79200 MW	114810 TQ	USBLS	5/07
	Spokane MSA, WA	Y	43860 FQ	60140 MW	70700 TQ	USBLS	5/07
	West Virginia	Y	51676 FQ	65933 MW	80226 TQ	WVBLS	7/08-9/08
	Wisconsin	Y	42960 FQ	59530 MW	86370 TQ	USBLS	5/07
	Milwaukee-Waukesha-West Allis MSA, WI	Y	47110 FQ	60050 MW	82410 TQ	USBLS	5/07
	Wyoming	Y	64714 FQ	69977 MW	75168 TQ	WYBLS	9/08
Commissioned Officer							
Military, Active Duty, Pay Grade 0-1	United States	M	2655 LO		3341 HI	DOD1	2009
Military, Active Duty, Pay Grade 0-10	United States	M	14689 LO		18061 HI	DOD1	2009
Military, Active Duty, Pay Grade 0-1E	United States	M	3339 LO		4148 HI	DOD1	2009
Military, Active Duty, Pay Grade 0-2	United States	M	3059 LO		4233 HI	DOD1	2009
Military, Active Duty, Pay Grade 0-2E	United States	M	4148 LO		4902 HI	DOD1	2009
Military, Active Duty, Pay Grade 0-3	United States	M	3540 LO		5760 HI	DOD1	2009
Military, Active Duty, Pay Grade 0-3E	United States	M	4722 LO		6147 HI	DOD1	2009
Military, Active Duty, Pay Grade 0-4	United States	M	4027 LO		6723 HI	DOD1	2009
Military, Active Duty, Pay Grade 0-5	United States	M	4667 LO		7929 HI	DOD1	2009
Military, Active Duty, Pay Grade 0-6	United States	M	5598 LO		9911 HI	DOD1	2009
Military, Active Duty, Pay Grade 0-7	United States	M	7553 LO		11285 HI	DOD1	2009
Military, Active Duty, Pay Grade 0-8	United States	M	9090 LO		13104 HI	DOD1	2009
Military, Active Duty, Pay Grade 0-9	United States	M	12847 LO		15936 HI	DOD1	2009
Military, Reserve, Pay Grade 0-1	United States	S	5488 LO		6904 HI	DOD2	2009
Military, Reserve, Pay Grade 0-10	United States	S	30356 LO		32244 HI	DOD2	2009
Military, Reserve, Pay Grade 0-1E	United States	S	6904 LO		8573 HI	DOD2	2009
Military, Reserve, Pay Grade 0-2	United States	S	6322 LO		8749 HI	DOD2	2009
Military, Reserve, Pay Grade 0-2E	United States	S	8573 LO		10131 HI	DOD2	2009
Military, Reserve, Pay Grade 0-3	United States	S	7317 LO		11903 HI	DOD2	2009
Military, Reserve, Pay Grade 0-3E	United States	S	9761 LO		12703 HI	DOD2	2009
Military, Reserve, Pay Grade 0-4	United States	S	8322 LO		13895 HI	DOD2	2009
Military, Reserve, Pay Grade 0-5	United States	S	9645 LO		16386 HI	DOD2	2009
Military, Reserve, Pay Grade 0-6	United States	S	11570 LO		20081 HI	DOD2	2009
Military, Reserve, Pay Grade 0-7	United States	S	15610 LO		22864 HI	DOD2	2009
Military, Reserve, Pay Grade 0-8	United States	S	18786 LO		25777 HI	DOD2	2009
Military, Reserve, Pay Grade 0-9	United States	S	26550 LO		28449 HI	DOD2	2009
Commissioner	Birmingham, MI	S			5.00 HI	FREEP05	2007
	Royal Oak, MI	S			20.00 HI	FREEP05	2007
Major League Baseball	United States	Y			18350000 HI	USATOD08	11/1/06-10/31/07

AE Average entry wage	**AW** Average wage paid	**FQ** First quartile wage	**LO** Lowest wage paid	**MTC** Median total compensation	**TCC** Total cash compensation
AER Average entry range	**AWR** Average wage range	**H** Hourly	**LR** Low end range	**MW** Median wage paid	**TQ** Third quartile wage
AEX Average experienced wage	**AXR** Average experienced range	**HI** Highest wage paid	**M** Monthly	**MWR** Median wage range	**W** Weekly
ATC Average total compensation	**D** Daily	**HR** High end range	**MCC** Median cash compensation	**S** See annotated source	**Y** Yearly

Occupation/Type/Industry	Location	Per	Low	Mid	High	Source	Date
Commissioner							
National Football League	United States	Y			11000000 HI	USATOD08	2009
National Hockey League	United States	Y			5590000 HI	USATOD08	2009
Commissioner of Public Lands							
State Government	Washington	Y			121608 HI	WCC	9/1/08
Communications Advisor							
White House Staff	United States	Y			50000 HI	WPOST02	2008
Communications Director	Douglasville, GA	Y	43096 LO		70157 HI	GACTY01	2008
	Stone Mountain, GA	Y	31782 LO		36340 HI	GACTY01	2008
Communications Teacher							
Postsecondary	Alabama	Y	37070 FQ	48680 MW	62220 TQ	USBLS	5/07
Postsecondary	Arizona	Y	38700 FQ	49320 MW	62380 TQ	USBLS	5/07
Postsecondary	Arkansas	Y	36600 FQ	47650 MW	61770 TQ	USBLS	5/07
Postsecondary	California	Y		78346 AW		CABLS	1/08-3/08
Postsecondary	Colorado	Y	35580 FQ	46980 MW	60290 TQ	USBLS	5/07
Postsecondary	District of Columbia	Y	50460 FQ	58570 MW	72590 TQ	USBLS	5/07
Postsecondary	Florida	Y	42920 FQ	55370 MW	72350 TQ	USBLS	5/07
Postsecondary	Georgia	Y	36060 FQ	50090 MW	67390 TQ	USBLS	5/07
Postsecondary	Hawaii	Y	45490 FQ	59400 MW	73180 TQ	USBLS	5/07
Postsecondary	Illinois	Y	37220 FQ	51900 MW	63870 TQ	USBLS	5/07
Postsecondary	Indiana	Y	46990 FQ	57590 MW	68880 TQ	USBLS	5/07
Postsecondary	Iowa	Y	44130 FQ	57520 MW	81030 TQ	USBLS	5/07
Postsecondary	Kansas	Y	38010 FQ	58570 MW	81640 TQ	USBLS	5/07
Postsecondary	Kentucky	Y	37278 FQ	51361 MW	67529 TQ	KYBLS	2008
Postsecondary	Louisiana	Y		41180 AW		LABLS	1/08-3/08
Postsecondary	Maine	Y	38640 FQ	50440 MW	59870 TQ	USBLS	5/07
Postsecondary	Maryland	Y		62050 MW		MDBLS	3/08
Postsecondary	Massachusetts	Y	46920 FQ	63590 MW	80770 TQ	USBLS	5/07
Postsecondary	Michigan	Y	31310 FQ	55020 MW	71970 TQ	USBLS	5/07
Postsecondary	Minnesota	Y	40028 FQ	52468 MW	64018 TQ	MNBLS	10/08-12/08
Postsecondary	Mississippi	Y	45230 FQ	56390 MW	68840 TQ	USBLS	5/07
Postsecondary	Missouri	Y	42460 FQ	57420 MW	79600 TQ	USBLS	5/07
Postsecondary	Montana	Y	30700 FQ	46410 MW	59130 TQ	USBLS	5/07
Postsecondary	Nebraska	Y	35880 FQ	47290 MW	59710 TQ	USBLS	5/07
Postsecondary	New Hampshire	Y	50680 AE	65561 MW	74115 AEX	NHBLS	6/08
Postsecondary	New Jersey	Y	44160 FQ	60030 MW	80920 TQ	USBLS	5/07
Postsecondary	New Mexico	Y	42180 FQ	47640 MW	60160 TQ	USBLS	5/07
Postsecondary	New York	Y	49720 FQ	66120 MW	87580 TQ	USBLS	5/07
Postsecondary	North Carolina	Y	39770 FQ	49920 MW	61410 TQ	USBLS	5/07
Postsecondary	North Dakota	Y	37750 FQ	51290 MW	61580 TQ	USBLS	5/07
Postsecondary	Ohio	Y	37560 FQ	52750 MW	71760 TQ	USBLS	5/07
Postsecondary	Oklahoma	Y	25740 FQ	40220 MW	57420 TQ	USBLS	5/07
Postsecondary	Pennsylvania	Y	42730 FQ	56540 MW	77290 TQ	USBLS	5/07
Postsecondary	Rhode Island	Y	48580 FQ	61760 MW	88700 TQ	USBLS	5/07
Postsecondary	South Carolina	Y	39400 FQ	53070 MW	64590 TQ	USBLS	5/07
Postsecondary	South Dakota	Y	40085 FQ	51677 MW	64364 TQ	SDBLS	7/08-9/08
Postsecondary	Tennessee	Y	35460 FQ	46520 MW	59150 TQ	USBLS	5/07
Postsecondary	Texas	Y	32030 FQ	47750 MW	63980 TQ	USBLS	5/07
Postsecondary	Utah	Y	37850 FQ	47880 MW	61640 TQ	USBLS	5/07
Postsecondary	Vermont	Y	41650 FQ	51150 MW	65560 TQ	USBLS	5/07
Postsecondary	Virginia	Y	43560 FQ	55020 MW	70610 TQ	USBLS	5/07
Postsecondary	Washington	Y		54950 AW		WABLS	3/08
Postsecondary	West Virginia	Y	44059 FQ	52230 MW	66997 TQ	WVBLS	7/08-9/08
Postsecondary	Wisconsin	Y	40950 FQ	56330 MW	72150 TQ	USBLS	5/07
Postsecondary	Wyoming	Y	40237 FQ	50037 MW	62619 TQ	WYBLS	9/08
Postsecondary	Puerto Rico	Y	41510 FQ	57950 MW	65490 TQ	USBLS	5/07
Community Arts Coordinator	Walnut Creek, CA	Y	69902 LO		84145 HI	WCSWP	7/11/08
Community Center Director	Cincinnati, OH	Y	30823 LO		41597 HI	COHSS	10/08
Community College Professor							
Department of Regional Community Technical Colleges	New Hampshire	Y		39988 AW		NHUL03	2008
Community Corrections Manager	Livingston County, MI	Y			62155 HI	LCPP	2009
Community Education Director							
Area Public Schools	Brighton, MI	Y			87348 HI	LCPP	2009

AE	Average entry wage	**AW**	Average wage paid	**FQ**	First quartile wage	**LO**	Lowest wage paid	**MTC**	Median total compensation
AER	Average entry range	**AWR**	Average wage range	**H**	Hourly	**LR**	Low end range	**MW**	Median wage paid
AEX	Average experienced wage	**AXR**	Average experienced range	**HI**	Highest wage paid	**M**	Monthly	**MWR**	Median wage range
ATC	Average total compensation	**D**	Daily	**HR**	High end range	**MCC**	Median cash compensation	**S**	See annotated source

TCC	Total cash compensation
TQ	Third quartile wage
W	Weekly
Y	Yearly

Occupation/Type/Industry	Location	Per	Low	Mid	High	Source	Date
Community Garden Coordinator	Seattle, WA	H	22.85 LO		26.59 HI	CSSS	2008
Community Relations Manager	Gresham, OR	Y	61068 LO		79380 HI	GOSS01	7/1/08
Community Relations Officer	Walnut Creek, CA	Y	86297 LO		104420 HI	WCSWP	7/11/08
Community Services Director	Washington County, MN	Y			126619 HI	MMTHLY	2008
Community Services Manager	Gresham, OR	Y	71208 LO		92544 HI	GOSS01	7/1/08
Companion Caregiver	United States	H	10.00 LO			ABCN02	2009
Compensation, Benefits, and Job Analysis Specialist	Alabama	Y	38280 FQ	45590 MW	55060 TQ	USBLS	5/07
	Birmingham-Hoover MSA, AL	Y	41700 FQ	48210 MW	57780 TQ	USBLS	5/07
	Mobile MSA, AL	Y	35140 FQ	42340 MW	49420 TQ	USBLS	5/07
	Alaska	Y	44250 FQ	51960 MW	60990 TQ	USBLS	5/07
	Anchorage MSA, AK	Y	40950 FQ	50060 MW	59340 TQ	USBLS	5/07
	Arizona	Y	38190 FQ	48500 MW	59020 TQ	USBLS	5/07
	Phoenix-Mesa-Scottsdale MSA, AZ	Y	39330 FQ	49660 MW	59730 TQ	USBLS	5/07
	Tucson MSA, AZ	Y	34450 FQ	43440 MW	54040 TQ	USBLS	5/07
	Arkansas	Y	31330 FQ	41120 MW	51130 TQ	USBLS	5/07
	Fayetteville-Springdale-Rogers MSA, AR-MO	Y	30670 FQ	41090 MW	52380 TQ	USBLS	5/07
	Little Rock-North Little Rock MSA, AR	Y	31790 FQ	42040 MW	52840 TQ	USBLS	5/07
	California	H	23.50 FQ	28.71 MW	35.19 TQ	CABLS	1/08-3/08
	Bakersfield MSA, CA	H	17.72 FQ	22.67 MW	28.78 TQ	CABLS	1/08-3/08
	Los Angeles-Long Beach-Glendale PMSA, CA	H	23.81 FQ	29.08 MW	36.09 TQ	CABLS	1/08-3/08
	Oakland-Fremont-Hayward MSA, CA	H	24.13 FQ	29.79 MW	36.79 TQ	CABLS	1/08-3/08
	Riverside-San Bernardino-Ontario MSA, CA	H	21.27 FQ	25.21 MW	29.14 TQ	CABLS	1/08-3/08
	Sacramento-Arden Arcade-Roseville MSA, CA	H	24.23 FQ	29.15 MW	34.29 TQ	CABLS	1/08-3/08
	San Diego-Carlsbad-San Marcos MSA, CA	H	23.42 FQ	28.10 MW	32.98 TQ	CABLS	1/08-3/08
	San Francisco-San Mateo-Redwood PMSA, CA	H	26.19 FQ	30.79 MW	38.77 TQ	CABLS	1/08-3/08
	San Jose-Sunnyvale-Santa Clara MSA, CA	H	28.22 FQ	35.67 MW	45.85 TQ	CABLS	1/08-3/08
	Santa Ana-Anaheim-Irvine PMSA, CA	Y	45230 FQ	54430 MW	64560 TQ	USBLS	5/07
	Colorado	Y	43800 FQ	56010 MW	71370 TQ	USBLS	5/07
	Colorado Springs MSA, CO	Y	39860 FQ	52410 MW	67300 TQ	USBLS	5/07
	Denver-Aurora MSA, CO	Y	45760 FQ	57840 MW	72750 TQ	USBLS	5/07
	Pueblo MSA, CO	Y	43250 FQ	54350 MW	71260 TQ	USBLS	5/07
	Connecticut	H	20.63 AE	30.30 MW		CTBLS	1/08-3/08
	Bridgeport-Stamford-Norwalk MSA, CT	Y	50320 FQ	63300 MW	81410 TQ	USBLS	5/07
	Hartford-West Hartford-East Hartford MSA, CT	Y	48450 FQ	62520 MW	78640 TQ	USBLS	5/07
	Delaware	Y	44110 FQ	53040 MW	66050 TQ	USBLS	5/07
	Wilmington PMSA, DE-MD-NJ	Y	45970 FQ	56780 MW	74950 TQ	USBLS	5/07
	District of Columbia	Y	51620 FQ	64040 MW	88930 TQ	USBLS	5/07
	Washington-Arlington-Alexandria MSA, DC-VA-MD-WV	Y	49400 FQ	62070 MW	80490 TQ	USBLS	5/07
	Florida	Y	36760 FQ	45490 MW	58190 TQ	USBLS	5/07
	Fort Lauderdale-Pompano Beach-Deerfield Beach PMSA, FL	Y	40880 FQ	48190 MW	62200 TQ	USBLS	5/07
	Jacksonville MSA, FL	Y	35970 FQ	45070 MW	59110 TQ	USBLS	5/07
	Miami-Fort Lauderdale-Miami Beach MSA, FL	Y	38570 FQ	48120 MW	62400 TQ	USBLS	5/07
	Orlando-Kissimmee MSA, FL	Y	35300 FQ	43170 MW	57550 TQ	USBLS	5/07
	Sarasota-Bradenton-Venice MSA, FL	Y	37590 FQ	45590 MW	58280 TQ	USBLS	5/07
	Tampa-St. Petersburg-Clearwater MSA, FL	Y	38120 FQ	47960 MW	59410 TQ	USBLS	5/07

AE	Average entry wage	AW	Average wage paid	FQ	First quartile wage
AER	Average entry range	AWR	Average wage range	H	Hourly
AEX	Average experienced wage	AXR	Average experienced range	HI	Highest wage paid
ATC	Average total compensation	D	Daily	HR	High end range

LO	Lowest wage paid	MTC	Median total compensation
LR	Low end range	MW	Median wage paid
M	Monthly	MWR	Median wage range
MCC	Median cash compensation	S	See annotated source

TCC	Total cash compensation
TQ	Third quartile wage
W	Weekly
Y	Yearly

Occupation/Type/Industry	Location	Per	Low	Mid	High	Source	Date
Compensation, Benefits, and Job Analysis Specialist	West Palm Beach-Boca Raton-Boynton Beach PMSA, FL	Y	41310 FQ	51420 MW	65740 TQ	USBLS	5/07
	Georgia	Y	38710 FQ	47860 MW	61130 TQ	USBLS	5/07
	Atlanta-Sandy Springs-Marietta MSA, GA	Y	39760 FQ	49010 MW	62210 TQ	USBLS	5/07
	Hawaii	Y	38760 FQ	44880 MW	55220 TQ	USBLS	5/07
	Honolulu MSA, HI	Y	38330 FQ	44700 MW	55430 TQ	USBLS	5/07
	Idaho	Y	36630 FQ	44640 MW	54640 TQ	USBLS	5/07
	Boise City-Nampa MSA, ID	Y	40760 FQ	47400 MW	55490 TQ	USBLS	5/07
	Illinois	Y	44290 FQ	55210 MW	71010 TQ	USBLS	5/07
	Chicago-Naperville-Joliet MSA, IL-IN-WI	Y	44850 FQ	55640 MW	70690 TQ	USBLS	5/07
	Indiana	Y	36190 FQ	46600 MW	61400 TQ	USBLS	5/07
	Fort Wayne MSA, IN	Y	36670 FQ	48650 MW	59150 TQ	USBLS	5/07
	Gary PMSA, IN	Y	41130 FQ	51850 MW	83590 TQ	USBLS	5/07
	Indianapolis-Carmel MSA, IN	Y	38690 FQ	48570 MW	65400 TQ	USBLS	5/07
	Iowa	Y	33430 FQ	41180 MW	51640 TQ	USBLS	5/07
	Des Moines-West Des Moines MSA, IA	Y	35070 FQ	41760 MW	53620 TQ	USBLS	5/07
	Kansas	Y	38160 FQ	47100 MW	62430 TQ	USBLS	5/07
	Wichita MSA, KS	Y	33550 FQ	43800 MW	53700 TQ	USBLS	5/07
	Kentucky	Y	36661 FQ	45979 MW	62346 TQ	KYBLS	2008
	Louisville-Jefferson County MSA, KY-IN	Y	37450 FQ	53580 MW	81060 TQ	USBLS	5/07
	Louisiana	H	15.12 FQ	17.95 MW	22.46 TQ	LABLS	1/08-3/08
	Baton Rouge MSA, LA	Y	32380 FQ	37880 MW	45800 TQ	USBLS	5/07
	New Orleans-Metairie-Kenner MSA, LA	Y	32490 FQ	38020 MW	47950 TQ	USBLS	5/07
	Maine	Y	35330 FQ	43900 MW	55780 TQ	USBLS	5/07
	Portland-South Portland-Biddeford MSA, ME	Y	39450 FQ	47900 MW	60830 TQ	USBLS	5/07
	Maryland	Y		55650 MW		MDBLS	3/08
	Baltimore-Towson MSA, MD	Y	37370 FQ	50730 MW	63400 TQ	USBLS	5/07
	Bethesda-Gaithersburg-Frederick PMSA, MD	Y	51250 FQ	64020 MW	79940 TQ	USBLS	5/07
	Massachusetts	Y	48520 FQ	58650 MW	72630 TQ	USBLS	5/07
	Boston-Cambridge-Quincy NECTA, MA	Y	50050 FQ	59570 MW	73400 TQ	USBLS	5/07
	Worcester MSA, MA-CT	Y	32710 FQ	51870 MW	63180 TQ	USBLS	5/07
	Michigan	Y	44180 FQ	56700 MW	72720 TQ	USBLS	5/07
	Detroit-Warren-Livonia MSA, MI	Y	47300 FQ	60010 MW	83440 TQ	USBLS	5/07
	Flint MSA, MI	Y	35860 FQ	44620 MW	84890 TQ	USBLS	5/07
	Grand Rapids-Wyoming MSA, MI	Y	39670 FQ	49890 MW	62360 TQ	USBLS	5/07
	Warren-Troy-Farmington Hills PMSA, MI	Y	44830 FQ	55300 MW	67030 TQ	USBLS	5/07
	Minnesota	Y	42759 FQ	53394 MW	66072 TQ	MNBLS	10/08-12/08
	Duluth-Superior MSA, MN-WI	Y	43030 FQ	48702 MW	60963 TQ	MNBLS	10/08-12/08
	Minneapolis-Saint Paul MSA, MN-WI	Y	43165 FQ	54030 MW	66458 TQ	MNBLS	10/08-12/08
	Rochester MSA, MN	Y	46991 FQ	63171 MW	78286 TQ	MNBLS	10/08-12/08
	Mississippi	Y	32410 FQ	38660 MW	49420 TQ	USBLS	5/07
	Hattiesburg MSA, MS	Y	34760 FQ	44810 MW	50130 TQ	USBLS	5/07
	Jackson MSA, MS	Y	29540 FQ	33850 MW	40200 TQ	USBLS	5/07
	Missouri	Y	35270 FQ	45090 MW	58530 TQ	USBLS	5/07
	Jefferson City MSA, MO	Y	29200 FQ	37160 MW	48700 TQ	USBLS	5/07
	Kansas City MSA, MO-KS	Y	38830 FQ	48800 MW	63640 TQ	USBLS	5/07
	St. Louis MSA, MO-IL	Y	37810 FQ	47320 MW	60730 TQ	USBLS	5/07
	Montana	Y	34400 FQ	39680 MW	50470 TQ	USBLS	5/07
	Billings MSA, MT	Y	35030 FQ	38420 MW	43850 TQ	USBLS	5/07
	Nebraska	Y	39430 FQ	51100 MW	64750 TQ	USBLS	5/07
	Omaha-Council Bluffs MSA, NE-IA	Y	41050 FQ	53530 MW	67560 TQ	USBLS	5/07
	Nevada	H	20.91 FQ	26.12 MW	31.80 TQ	NVBLS	5/08
	Las Vegas-Paradise MSA, NV	H	19.77 FQ	25.23 MW	32.06 TQ	NVBLS	5/08
	New Hampshire	H	18.60 AE	23.40 MW	27.96 AEX	NHBLS	6/08
	Manchester MSA, NH	Y	42740 FQ	54160 MW	63820 TQ	USBLS	5/07
	New Jersey	Y	48810 FQ	60020 MW	74510 TQ	USBLS	5/07
	Camden PMSA, NJ	Y	42340 FQ	50620 MW	63600 TQ	USBLS	5/07
	Edison PMSA, NJ	Y	47140 FQ	60180 MW	75530 TQ	USBLS	5/07

AE Average entry wage	**AW** Average wage paid	**FQ** First quartile wage	**LO** Lowest wage paid	**MTC** Median total compensation	**TCC** Total cash compensation
AER Average entry range	**AWR** Average wage range	**H** Hourly	**LR** Low end range	**MW** Median wage paid	**TQ** Third quartile wage
AEX Average experienced wage	**AXR** Average experienced range	**HI** Highest wage paid	**M** Monthly	**MWR** Median wage range	**W** Weekly
ATC Average total compensation	**D** Daily	**HR** High end range	**MCC** Median cash compensation	**S** See annotated source	**Y** Yearly

Occupation/Type/Industry	Location	Per	Low	Mid	High	Source	Date
Compensation, Benefits, and Job Analysis Specialist							
	Newark-Union PMSA, NJ-PA	Y	50900 FQ	61360 MW	74880 TQ	USBLS	5/07
	New Mexico	Y	36610 FQ	45190 MW	58440 TQ	USBLS	5/07
	Albuquerque MSA, NM	Y	38040 FQ	45760 MW	60540 TQ	USBLS	5/07
	New York	Y	48710 FQ	59750 MW	70490 TQ	USBLS	5/07
	Albany-Schenectady-Troy MSA, NY	Y	40360 FQ	50100 MW	60540 TQ	USBLS	5/07
	Buffalo-Niagara Falls MSA, NY	Y	39700 FQ	49080 MW	61470 TQ	USBLS	5/07
	Nassau-Suffolk PMSA, NY	Y	47760 FQ	58430 MW	70280 TQ	USBLS	5/07
	New York-Northern New Jersey-Long Island MSA, NY-NJ-PA	Y	51870 FQ	61710 MW	73330 TQ	USBLS	5/07
	North Carolina	Y	39690 FQ	48800 MW	60720 TQ	USBLS	5/07
	Charlotte-Gastonia-Concord MSA, NC-SC	Y	42960 FQ	51060 MW	63360 TQ	USBLS	5/07
	Raleigh-Cary MSA, NC	Y	37910 FQ	46060 MW	58800 TQ	USBLS	5/07
	North Dakota	Y	36230 FQ	46200 MW	59230 TQ	USBLS	5/07
	Bismarck MSA, ND	Y	42210 FQ	54440 MW	68830 TQ	USBLS	5/07
	Fargo MSA, ND-MN	Y	35820 FQ	40860 MW	51550 TQ	USBLS	5/07
	Ohio	Y	40340 FQ	49880 MW	64630 TQ	USBLS	5/07
	Cincinnati-Middletown MSA, OH-KY-IN	Y	41070 FQ	50090 MW	67970 TQ	USBLS	5/07
	Cleveland-Elyria-Mentor MSA, OH	Y	38950 FQ	49060 MW	63510 TQ	USBLS	5/07
	Columbus MSA, OH	Y	41210 FQ	50280 MW	64300 TQ	USBLS	5/07
	Dayton MSA, OH	Y	39280 FQ	49650 MW	60200 TQ	USBLS	5/07
	Oklahoma	Y	32170 FQ	39290 MW	52860 TQ	USBLS	5/07
	Oklahoma City MSA, OK	Y	30800 FQ	36160 MW	49360 TQ	USBLS	5/07
	Tulsa MSA, OK	Y	36680 FQ	48070 MW	56900 TQ	USBLS	5/07
	Oregon	H	17.85 FQ	22.10 MW	28.12 TQ	ORBLS	5/08
	Eugene-Springfield MSA, OR	Y	40300 FQ	48250 MW	64780 TQ	USBLS	5/07
	Portland-Vancouver-Beaverton MSA, OR-WA	Y	36300 FQ	45660 MW	57690 TQ	USBLS	5/07
	Pennsylvania	Y	38690 FQ	48090 MW	61160 TQ	USBLS	5/07
	Allentown-Bethlehem-Easton MSA, PA-NJ	Y	36670 FQ	45510 MW	66280 TQ	USBLS	5/07
	Philadelphia-Camden-Wilmington MSA, PA-NJ-DE-MD	Y	42160 FQ	50800 MW	64300 TQ	USBLS	5/07
	Pittsburgh MSA, PA	Y	36610 FQ	45760 MW	57640 TQ	USBLS	5/07
	York-Hanover MSA, PA	Y	36190 FQ	44440 MW	52960 TQ	USBLS	5/07
	Rhode Island	Y	42160 FQ	50940 MW	63260 TQ	USBLS	5/07
	Providence-Fall River-Warwick MSA, RI-MA	Y	43080 FQ	52300 MW	65220 TQ	USBLS	5/07
	South Carolina	Y	35650 FQ	43040 MW	51430 TQ	USBLS	5/07
	Charleston-North Charleston MSA, SC	Y	34990 FQ	39220 MW	48590 TQ	USBLS	5/07
	Columbia MSA, SC	Y	35580 FQ	42580 MW	55080 TQ	USBLS	5/07
	Spartanburg MSA, SC	Y	31850 FQ	37730 MW	49050 TQ	USBLS	5/07
	South Dakota	Y	35832 FQ	41623 MW	50732 TQ	SDBLS	7/08-9/08
	Sioux Falls MSA, SD	Y	36208 FQ	44093 MW	53432 TQ	SDBLS	7/08-9/08
	Tennessee	Y	35000 FQ	45860 MW	60320 TQ	USBLS	5/07
	Memphis MSA, TN-MS-AR	Y	40300 FQ	49490 MW	66080 TQ	USBLS	5/07
	Nashville-Davidson-Murfreesboro MSA, TN	Y	32600 FQ	43010 MW	58510 TQ	USBLS	5/07
	Texas	Y	39560 FQ	51090 MW	66320 TQ	USBLS	5/07
	Austin-Round Rock MSA, TX	Y	33770 FQ	46030 MW	66120 TQ	USBLS	5/07
	Dallas-Fort Worth-Arlington MSA, TX	Y	43900 FQ	54290 MW	67290 TQ	USBLS	5/07
	El Paso MSA, TX	Y	34930 FQ	46910 MW	65870 TQ	USBLS	5/07
	Houston-Sugar Land-Baytown MSA, TX	Y	41040 FQ	52590 MW	70060 TQ	USBLS	5/07
	San Antonio MSA, TX	Y	36370 FQ	48960 MW	63900 TQ	USBLS	5/07
	Utah	Y	36760 FQ	45660 MW	63290 TQ	USBLS	5/07
	Salt Lake City MSA, UT	Y	36730 FQ	44810 MW	58040 TQ	USBLS	5/07
	Vermont	Y	39940 FQ	47280 MW	57080 TQ	USBLS	5/07
	Burlington-South Burlington MSA, VT	Y	39740 FQ	47670 MW	58110 TQ	USBLS	5/07
	Virginia	Y	41740 FQ	53440 MW	71280 TQ	USBLS	5/07
	Richmond MSA, VA	Y	41980 FQ	49890 MW	66490 TQ	USBLS	5/07

AE Average entry wage	**AW** Average wage paid	**FQ** First quartile wage	**LO** Lowest wage paid	**MTC** Median total compensation	**TCC** Total cash compensation
AER Average entry range	**AWR** Average wage range	**H** Hourly	**LR** Low end range	**MW** Median wage paid	**TQ** Third quartile wage
AEX Average experienced wage	**AXR** Average experienced range	**HI** Highest wage paid	**M** Monthly	**MWR** Median wage range	**W** Weekly
ATC Average total compensation	**D** Daily	**HR** High end range	**MCC** Median cash compensation	**S** See annotated source	**Y** Yearly

Occupation/Type/Industry	Location	Per	Low	Mid	High	Source	Date
Compensation, Benefits, and Job Analysis Specialist	Virginia Beach-Norfolk-Newport News MSA, VA-NC	Y	37840 FQ	47600 MW	60260 TQ	USBLS	5/07
	Washington	H	21.78 FQ	27.65 MW	34.88 TQ	WABLS	3/08
	Seattle-Tacoma-Bellevue MSA, WA	Y	46310 FQ	60180 MW	74430 TQ	USBLS	5/07
	West Virginia	Y	31663 FQ	38541 MW	49750 TQ	WVBLS	7/08-9/08
	Charleston MSA, WV	Y	30960 FQ	38280 MW	48030 TQ	USBLS	5/07
	Huntington-Ashland MSA, WV-KY-OH	Y	37670 FQ	45280 MW	61420 TQ	USBLS	5/07
	Wisconsin	Y	37060 FQ	44790 MW	55390 TQ	USBLS	5/07
	Milwaukee-Waukesha-West Allis MSA, WI	Y	38780 FQ	46480 MW	59190 TQ	USBLS	5/07
	Wyoming	Y	39837 FQ	48534 MW	57375 TQ	WYBLS	9/08
	Cheyenne MSA, WY	Y	50825 FQ	59059 MW	64638 TQ	WYBLS	9/08
	Puerto Rico	Y	25030 FQ	31090 MW	40010 TQ	USBLS	5/07
	San Juan-Caguas-Guaynabo MSA, PR	Y	25570 FQ	31720 MW	40770 TQ	USBLS	5/07
Compensation and Benefits Manager	Alabama	Y	57140 FQ	73060 MW	92300 TQ	USBLS	5/07
	Birmingham-Hoover MSA, AL	Y	60890 FQ	75210 MW	97210 TQ	USBLS	5/07
	Alaska	Y	50810 FQ	63750 MW	82350 TQ	USBLS	5/07
	Anchorage MSA, AK	Y	54220 FQ	68890 MW	86450 TQ	USBLS	5/07
	Arizona	Y	44760 FQ	58600 MW	89520 TQ	USBLS	5/07
	Phoenix-Mesa-Scottsdale MSA, AZ	Y	44690 FQ	58520 MW	93260 TQ	USBLS	5/07
	Tucson MSA, AZ	Y	42430 FQ	60870 MW	78010 TQ	USBLS	5/07
	Arkansas	Y	49300 FQ	65330 MW	85630 TQ	USBLS	5/07
	Fayetteville-Springdale-Rogers MSA, AR-MO	Y	48180 FQ	62200 MW	85460 TQ	USBLS	5/07
	Little Rock-North Little Rock MSA, AR	Y	53400 FQ	65520 MW	88280 TQ	USBLS	5/07
	California	H	33.27 FQ	44.22 MW	57.14 TQ	CABLS	1/08-3/08
	Los Angeles-Long Beach-Glendale PMSA, CA	H	31.43 FQ	42.20 MW	53.52 TQ	CABLS	1/08-3/08
	Oakland-Fremont-Hayward MSA, CA	H	38.20 FQ	48.23 MW	57.34 TQ	CABLS	1/08-3/08
	Riverside-San Bernardino-Ontario MSA, CA	H	26.22 FQ	35.78 MW	46.97 TQ	CABLS	1/08-3/08
	Sacramento-Arden Arcade-Roseville MSA, CA	H	33.84 FQ	41.53 MW	48.71 TQ	CABLS	1/08-3/08
	San Diego-Carlsbad-San Marcos MSA, CA	H	36.58 FQ	46.19 MW	60.21 TQ	CABLS	1/08-3/08
	San Francisco-San Mateo-Redwood PMSA, CA	H	36.95 FQ	52.28 MW	66.04 TQ	CABLS	1/08-3/08
	San Jose-Sunnyvale-Santa Clara MSA, CA	H	45.12 FQ	61.36 MW		CABLS	1/08-3/08
	Santa Ana-Anaheim-Irvine PMSA, CA	Y	66550 FQ	85190 MW	103030 TQ	USBLS	5/07
	Colorado	Y	55900 FQ	76590 MW	111410 TQ	USBLS	5/07
	Boulder MSA, CO	Y	67720 FQ	87000 MW	117180 TQ	USBLS	5/07
	Denver-Aurora MSA, CO	Y	57060 FQ	79930 MW	117390 TQ	USBLS	5/07
	Connecticut	H	27.83 AE	39.46 MW		CTBLS	1/08-3/08
	Bridgeport-Stamford-Norwalk MSA, CT	Y	78060 FQ	96980 MW	129150 TQ	USBLS	5/07
	Hartford-West Hartford-East Hartford MSA, CT	Y	61620 FQ	77570 MW	99390 TQ	USBLS	5/07
	New Haven MSA, CT	Y	52990 FQ	69500 MW	80440 TQ	USBLS	5/07
	Delaware	Y	78770 FQ	93980 MW	136990 TQ	USBLS	5/07
	Wilmington PMSA, DE-MD-NJ	Y	80860 FQ	96700 MW		USBLS	5/07
	District of Columbia	Y	64580 FQ	82080 MW	108210 TQ	USBLS	5/07
	Washington-Arlington-Alexandria MSA, DC-VA-MD-WV	Y	67010 FQ	82990 MW	106270 TQ	USBLS	5/07
	Florida	Y	72850 FQ	93580 MW	117490 TQ	USBLS	5/07
	Fort Lauderdale-Pompano Beach-Deerfield Beach PMSA, FL	Y	77230 FQ	102400 MW	126810 TQ	USBLS	5/07
	Jacksonville MSA, FL	Y	69450 FQ	90110 MW	113540 TQ	USBLS	5/07

Occupation/Type/Industry	Location	Per	Low	Mid	High	Source	Date
Compensation and Benefits Manager							
	Miami-Fort Lauderdale-Miami Beach MSA, FL	Y	75630 FQ	99170 MW	124280 TQ	USBLS	5/07
	Orlando-Kissimmee MSA, FL	Y	72920 FQ	91790 MW	113180 TQ	USBLS	5/07
	Tampa-St. Petersburg-Clearwater MSA, FL	Y	77910 FQ	94130 MW	115750 TQ	USBLS	5/07
	West Palm Beach-Boca Raton-Boynton Beach PMSA, FL	Y	68260 FQ	96890 MW	122880 TQ	USBLS	5/07
	Georgia	Y	57770 FQ	75980 MW	100390 TQ	USBLS	5/07
	Atlanta-Sandy Springs-Marietta MSA, GA	Y	59020 FQ	78610 MW	103360 TQ	USBLS	5/07
	Augusta-Richmond County MSA, GA-SC	Y	57730 FQ	76960 MW	100610 TQ	USBLS	5/07
	Hawaii	Y	54740 FQ	69130 MW	82980 TQ	USBLS	5/07
	Honolulu MSA, HI	Y	59540 FQ	71970 MW	85760 TQ	USBLS	5/07
	Idaho	Y	47780 FQ	64070 MW	79460 TQ	USBLS	5/07
	Boise City-Nampa MSA, ID	Y	41950 FQ	64570 MW	82540 TQ	USBLS	5/07
	Illinois	Y	56110 FQ	74480 MW	92420 TQ	USBLS	5/07
	Chicago-Naperville-Joliet MSA, IL-IN-WI	Y	58580 FQ	76930 MW	93480 TQ	USBLS	5/07
	Indiana	Y	52290 FQ	66250 MW	88750 TQ	USBLS	5/07
	Gary PMSA, IN	Y	42810 FQ	57750 MW	83590 TQ	USBLS	5/07
	Indianapolis-Carmel MSA, IN	Y	58140 FQ	69660 MW	87700 TQ	USBLS	5/07
	Iowa	Y	50880 FQ	65410 MW	93370 TQ	USBLS	5/07
	Des Moines-West Des Moines MSA, IA	Y	54670 FQ	71820 MW	98650 TQ	USBLS	5/07
	Kansas	Y	61890 FQ	77150 MW	95350 TQ	USBLS	5/07
	Wichita MSA, KS	Y	62680 FQ	75250 MW	91920 TQ	USBLS	5/07
	Kentucky	Y	53760 FQ	64407 MW	84465 TQ	KYBLS	2008
	Lexington-Fayette MSA, KY	Y	49200 FQ	57440 MW	75970 TQ	USBLS	5/07
	Louisville-Jefferson County MSA, KY-IN	Y	52220 FQ	65830 MW	81820 TQ	USBLS	5/07
	Louisiana	H	23.42 FQ	29.64 MW	36.47 TQ	LABLS	1/08-3/08
	Baton Rouge MSA, LA	Y	53290 FQ	61500 MW	73490 TQ	USBLS	5/07
	New Orleans-Metairie-Kenner MSA, LA	Y	44080 FQ	61720 MW	79540 TQ	USBLS	5/07
	Maine	Y	56210 FQ	68560 MW	84930 TQ	USBLS	5/07
	Portland-South Portland-Biddeford MSA, ME	Y	60540 FQ	71560 MW	91470 TQ	USBLS	5/07
	Maryland	Y		79525 MW		MDBLS	3/08
	Baltimore-Towson MSA, MD	Y	61810 FQ	73800 MW	90400 TQ	USBLS	5/07
	Bethesda-Gaithersburg-Frederick PMSA, MD	Y	67490 FQ	86930 MW	112840 TQ	USBLS	5/07
	Massachusetts	Y	72940 FQ	97810 MW	130890 TQ	USBLS	5/07
	Boston-Cambridge-Quincy NECTA, MA	Y	77600 FQ	101540 MW	134780 TQ	USBLS	5/07
	Worcester MSA, MA-CT	Y	44800 FQ	86240 MW	110800 TQ	USBLS	5/07
	Michigan	Y	57700 FQ	79380 MW	106210 TQ	USBLS	5/07
	Detroit-Warren-Livonia MSA, MI	Y	61030 FQ	85960 MW	116250 TQ	USBLS	5/07
	Grand Rapids-Wyoming MSA, MI	Y	69560 FQ	85380 MW	102530 TQ	USBLS	5/07
	Warren-Troy-Farmington Hills PMSA, MI	Y	54860 FQ	78420 MW	105240 TQ	USBLS	5/07
	Minnesota	Y	90815 FQ	109165 MW	139872 TQ	MNBLS	10/08-12/08
	Minneapolis-Saint Paul MSA, MN-WI	Y	92587 FQ	110385 MW	142624 TQ	MNBLS	10/08-12/08
	Mississippi	Y	50860 FQ	60920 MW	76870 TQ	USBLS	5/07
	Jackson MSA, MS	Y	52370 FQ	63160 MW	80260 TQ	USBLS	5/07
	Missouri	Y	64820 FQ	81390 MW	101870 TQ	USBLS	5/07
	Kansas City MSA, MO-KS	Y	64070 FQ	80410 MW	97170 TQ	USBLS	5/07
	St. Louis MSA, MO-IL	Y	64600 FQ	82650 MW	106890 TQ	USBLS	5/07
	Montana	Y	46090 FQ	55470 MW	72890 TQ	USBLS	5/07
	Nebraska	Y	63720 FQ	80890 MW	102470 TQ	USBLS	5/07
	Omaha-Council Bluffs MSA, NE-IA	Y	68040 FQ	89580 MW	108090 TQ	USBLS	5/07
	Nevada	H	23.56 FQ	29.51 MW	36.97 TQ	NVBLS	5/08
	Las Vegas-Paradise MSA, NV	H	23.41 FQ	29.82 MW	40.37 TQ	NVBLS	5/08
	Reno-Sparks MSA, NV	H	26.53 FQ	30.57 MW	34.91 TQ	NVBLS	5/08
	New Hampshire	H	26.31 AE	39.73 MW	44.96 AEX	NHBLS	6/08
	New Jersey	Y	87420 FQ	110860 MW	140390 TQ	USBLS	5/07
	Camden PMSA, NJ	Y	78830 FQ	104130 MW	123760 TQ	USBLS	5/07

AE	Average entry wage	**AW**	Average wage paid	**FQ**	First quartile wage	**LO**	Lowest wage paid	**MTC**	Median total compensation	**TCC**	Total cash compensation
AER	Average entry range	**AWR**	Average wage range	**H**	Hourly	**LR**	Low end range	**MW**	Median wage paid	**TQ**	Third quartile wage
AEX	Average experienced wage	**AXR**	Average experienced range	**HI**	Highest wage paid	**M**	Monthly	**MWR**	Median wage range	**W**	Weekly
ATC	Average total compensation	**D**	Daily	**HR**	High end range	**MCC**	Median cash compensation	**S**	See annotated source	**Y**	Yearly

Occupation/Type/Industry	Location	Per	Low	Mid	High	Source	Date
Compensation and Benefits Manager	Edison PMSA, NJ	Y	88040 FQ	112690 MW	136740 TQ	USBLS	5/07
	Newark-Union PMSA, NJ-PA	Y	87490 FQ	108720 MW	137290 TQ	USBLS	5/07
	Trenton-Ewing MSA, NJ	Y	88310 FQ	109930 MW		USBLS	5/07
	New Mexico	Y	50170 FQ	62500 MW	78530 TQ	USBLS	5/07
	Albuquerque MSA, NM	Y	49970 FQ	67740 MW	82220 TQ	USBLS	5/07
	New York	Y	73500 FQ	100410 MW	130170 TQ	USBLS	5/07
	Albany-Schenectady-Troy MSA, NY	Y	69130 FQ	84250 MW	103540 TQ	USBLS	5/07
	Buffalo-Niagara Falls MSA, NY	Y	61020 FQ	83620 MW	116160 TQ	USBLS	5/07
	Nassau-Suffolk PMSA, NY	Y	75920 FQ	96750 MW	134360 TQ	USBLS	5/07
	New York-Northern New Jersey-Long Island MSA, NY-NJ-PA	Y	84250 FQ	109490 MW	138280 TQ	USBLS	5/07
	North Carolina	Y	65950 FQ	84260 MW	109620 TQ	USBLS	5/07
	Charlotte-Gastonia-Concord MSA, NC-SC	Y	71010 FQ	93190 MW	119520 TQ	USBLS	5/07
	Greensboro-High Point MSA, NC	Y	66440 FQ	80900 MW	112940 TQ	USBLS	5/07
	Raleigh-Cary MSA, NC	Y	74970 FQ	93450 MW	114360 TQ	USBLS	5/07
	North Dakota	Y	49590 FQ	67800 MW	98970 TQ	USBLS	5/07
	Fargo MSA, ND-MN	Y	56970 FQ	85190 MW	117050 TQ	USBLS	5/07
	Ohio	Y	61050 FQ	80180 MW	106860 TQ	USBLS	5/07
	Cincinnati-Middletown MSA, OH-KY-IN	Y	61840 FQ	82560 MW	114030 TQ	USBLS	5/07
	Cleveland-Elyria-Mentor MSA, OH	Y	66770 FQ	89380 MW	120560 TQ	USBLS	5/07
	Columbus MSA, OH	Y	67090 FQ	89960 MW	115910 TQ	USBLS	5/07
	Dayton MSA, OH	Y	61430 FQ	75450 MW	97250 TQ	USBLS	5/07
	Oklahoma	Y	44860 FQ	58700 MW	78640 TQ	USBLS	5/07
	Oklahoma City MSA, OK	Y	42420 FQ	57390 MW	77490 TQ	USBLS	5/07
	Tulsa MSA, OK	Y	45730 FQ	66490 MW	83110 TQ	USBLS	5/07
	Oregon	H	34.22 FQ	41.91 MW	50.97 TQ	ORBLS	5/08
	Portland-Vancouver-Beaverton MSA, OR-WA	Y	70630 FQ	86790 MW	107680 TQ	USBLS	5/07
	Pennsylvania	Y	57920 FQ	74830 MW	99920 TQ	USBLS	5/07
	Allentown-Bethlehem-Easton MSA, PA-NJ	Y	57750 FQ	73500 MW	101310 TQ	USBLS	5/07
	Philadelphia-Camden-Wilmington MSA, PA-NJ-DE-MD	Y	65910 FQ	85320 MW	112270 TQ	USBLS	5/07
	Pittsburgh MSA, PA	Y	57780 FQ	70660 MW	92790 TQ	USBLS	5/07
	York-Hanover MSA, PA	Y	62430 FQ	79470 MW	104840 TQ	USBLS	5/07
	Rhode Island	Y	65510 FQ	80010 MW	95910 TQ	USBLS	5/07
	Providence-Fall River-Warwick MSA, RI-MA	Y	63780 FQ	77940 MW	95580 TQ	USBLS	5/07
	South Carolina	Y	51040 FQ	68980 MW	85970 TQ	USBLS	5/07
	Charleston-North Charleston MSA, SC	Y	50160 FQ	64000 MW	73600 TQ	USBLS	5/07
	Columbia MSA, SC	Y	48930 FQ	63030 MW	81470 TQ	USBLS	5/07
	Myrtle Beach-Conway-North Myrtle Beach MSA, SC	Y	51940 FQ	78450 MW	94830 TQ	USBLS	5/07
	South Dakota	Y	69248 FQ	76637 MW	85731 TQ	SDBLS	7/08-9/08
	Sioux Falls MSA, SD	Y	66844 FQ	74992 MW	85961 TQ	SDBLS	7/08-9/08
	Tennessee	Y	43990 FQ	57530 MW	79060 TQ	USBLS	5/07
	Memphis MSA, TN-MS-AR	Y	46670 FQ	65580 MW	99040 TQ	USBLS	5/07
	Nashville-Davidson-Murfreesboro MSA, TN	Y	44850 FQ	55160 MW	72530 TQ	USBLS	5/07
	Texas	Y	69930 FQ	89830 MW	114200 TQ	USBLS	5/07
	Austin-Round Rock MSA, TX	Y	70470 FQ	92620 MW	138280 TQ	USBLS	5/07
	Dallas-Fort Worth-Arlington MSA, TX	Y	80800 FQ	98210 MW	121270 TQ	USBLS	5/07
	El Paso MSA, TX	Y	68940 FQ	81020 MW	94290 TQ	USBLS	5/07
	Houston-Sugar Land-Baytown MSA, TX	Y	72640 FQ	88280 MW	110180 TQ	USBLS	5/07
	San Antonio MSA, TX	Y	57690 FQ	81760 MW	108640 TQ	USBLS	5/07
	Utah	Y	61750 FQ	78760 MW	102830 TQ	USBLS	5/07
	Ogden-Clearfield MSA, UT	Y	57890 FQ	72000 MW	85860 TQ	USBLS	5/07
	Salt Lake City MSA, UT	Y	68280 FQ	87000 MW	114550 TQ	USBLS	5/07
	Vermont	Y	63050 FQ	75080 MW	93100 TQ	USBLS	5/07
	Virginia	Y	70960 FQ	90710 MW	120910 TQ	USBLS	5/07

AE	Average entry wage	AW	Average wage paid	FQ	First quartile wage
AER	Average entry range	AWR	Average wage range	H	Hourly
AEX	Average experienced wage	AXR	Average experienced range	HI	Highest wage paid
ATC	Average total compensation	D	Daily	HR	High end range

LO	Lowest wage paid	MTC	Median total compensation	TCC	Total cash compensation
LR	Low end range	MW	Median wage paid	TQ	Third quartile wage
M	Monthly	MWR	Median wage range	W	Weekly
MCC	Median cash compensation	S	See annotated source	Y	Yearly

Occupation/Type/Industry	Location	Per	Low	Mid	High	Source	Date
Compensation and Benefits Manager	Richmond MSA, VA	Y	70050 FQ	89270 MW	114680 TQ	USBLS	5/07
	Virginia Beach-Norfolk-Newport News MSA, VA-NC	Y	70250 FQ	89740 MW	115090 TQ	USBLS	5/07
	Washington	H	32.83 FQ	44.11 MW	56.43 TQ	WABLS	3/08
	Seattle-Tacoma-Bellevue MSA, WA	Y	71140 FQ	94790 MW	119790 TQ	USBLS	5/07
	West Virginia	Y	54384 FQ	82050 MW	106954 TQ	WVBLS	7/08-9/08
	Wisconsin	Y	57350 FQ	72400 MW	94790 TQ	USBLS	5/07
	Milwaukee-Waukesha-West Allis MSA, WI	Y	60420 FQ	72570 MW	97340 TQ	USBLS	5/07
	Wyoming	Y	49158 FQ	60910 MW	87986 TQ	WYBLS	9/08
	Puerto Rico	Y	37910 FQ	51120 MW	76140 TQ	USBLS	5/07
	San Juan-Caguas-Guaynabo MSA, PR	Y	37900 FQ	48130 MW	74870 TQ	USBLS	5/07
Complaint Investigator							
Municipal Government	Seattle, WA	H	24.16 LO		28.17 HI	CSSS	2008
Compliance Agent							
Pharmacy Board	Ohio	H	23.87 LO		35.02 HI	ODAS	2008
Compliance Officer							
Except Agriculture, Construction, Health and Safety, and Transportation	Alabama	Y	35750 FQ	46750 MW	59710 TQ	USBLS	5/07
Except Agriculture, Construction, Health and Safety, and Transportation	Birmingham-Hoover MSA, AL	Y	35120 FQ	46530 MW	62400 TQ	USBLS	5/07
Except Agriculture, Construction, Health and Safety, and Transportation	Montgomery MSA, AL	Y	41880 FQ	50680 MW	60950 TQ	USBLS	5/07
Except Agriculture, Construction, Health and Safety, and Transportation	Alaska	Y	27080 FQ	38750 MW	57740 TQ	USBLS	5/07
Except Agriculture, Construction, Health and Safety, and Transportation	Anchorage MSA, AK	Y	28340 FQ	40770 MW	60340 TQ	USBLS	5/07
Except Agriculture, Construction, Health and Safety, and Transportation	Arizona	Y	33070 FQ	44690 MW	59580 TQ	USBLS	5/07
Except Agriculture, Construction, Health and Safety, and Transportation	Phoenix-Mesa-Scottsdale MSA, AZ	Y	31840 FQ	41430 MW	58860 TQ	USBLS	5/07
Except Agriculture, Construction, Health and Safety, and Transportation	Tucson MSA, AZ	Y	31910 FQ	43740 MW	57470 TQ	USBLS	5/07
Except Agriculture, Construction, Health and Safety, and Transportation	Arkansas	Y	30660 FQ	40790 MW	54030 TQ	USBLS	5/07
Except Agriculture, Construction, Health and Safety, and Transportation	Little Rock-North Little Rock MSA, AR	Y	28930 FQ	35100 MW	47950 TQ	USBLS	5/07
Except Agriculture, Construction, Health and Safety, and Transportation	California	H	18.90 FQ	26.61 MW	34.92 TQ	CABLS	1/08-3/08
Except Agriculture, Construction, Health and Safety, and Transportation	Los Angeles-Long Beach-Glendale PMSA, CA	H	17.88 FQ	25.36 MW	34.15 TQ	CABLS	1/08-3/08
Except Agriculture, Construction, Health and Safety, and Transportation	Oakland-Fremont-Hayward MSA, CA	H	19.05 FQ	27.96 MW	38.20 TQ	CABLS	1/08-3/08
Except Agriculture, Construction, Health and Safety, and Transportation	Riverside-San Bernardino-Ontario MSA, CA	H	18.84 FQ	25.18 MW	32.06 TQ	CABLS	1/08-3/08
Except Agriculture, Construction, Health and Safety, and Transportation	Sacramento-Arden Arcade-Roseville MSA, CA	H	17.69 FQ	23.25 MW	31.59 TQ	CABLS	1/08-3/08
Except Agriculture, Construction, Health and Safety, and Transportation	San Diego-Carlsbad-San Marcos MSA, CA	H	18.86 FQ	26.60 MW	32.36 TQ	CABLS	1/08-3/08
Except Agriculture, Construction, Health and Safety, and Transportation	San Francisco-San Mateo-Redwood PMSA, CA	H	26.18 FQ	33.60 MW	42.82 TQ	CABLS	1/08-3/08
Except Agriculture, Construction, Health and Safety, and Transportation	San Jose-Sunnyvale-Santa Clara MSA, CA	H	18.70 FQ	27.65 MW	40.37 TQ	CABLS	1/08-3/08
Except Agriculture, Construction, Health and Safety, and Transportation	Santa Ana-Anaheim-Irvine PMSA, CA	Y	42380 FQ	56410 MW	73330 TQ	USBLS	5/07

Occupation/Type/Industry	Location	Per	Low	Mid	High	Source	Date
Compliance Officer							
Except Agriculture, Construction, Health and Safety, and Transportation	Colorado	Y	36460 FQ	49950 MW	66890 TQ	USBLS	5/07
Except Agriculture, Construction, Health and Safety, and Transportation	Denver-Aurora MSA, CO	Y	37190 FQ	51990 MW	69890 TQ	USBLS	5/07
Except Agriculture, Construction, Health and Safety, and Transportation	Fort Collins-Loveland MSA, CO	Y	38890 FQ	50970 MW	65640 TQ	USBLS	5/07
Except Agriculture, Construction, Health and Safety, and Transportation	Connecticut	H	20.28 AE	30.17 MW		CTBLS	1/08-3/08
Except Agriculture, Construction, Health and Safety, and Transportation	Bridgeport-Stamford-Norwalk MSA, CT	Y	55560 FQ	69240 MW	91400 TQ	USBLS	5/07
Except Agriculture, Construction, Health and Safety, and Transportation	Danbury MSA, CT	Y	52120 FQ	58840 MW	75940 TQ	USBLS	5/07
Except Agriculture, Construction, Health and Safety, and Transportation	Hartford-West Hartford-East Hartford MSA, CT	Y	54100 FQ	66330 MW	78950 TQ	USBLS	5/07
Except Agriculture, Construction, Health and Safety, and Transportation	Delaware	Y	38240 FQ	46700 MW	60540 TQ	USBLS	5/07
Except Agriculture, Construction, Health and Safety, and Transportation	Wilmington PMSA, DE-MD-NJ	Y	39000 FQ	48080 MW	64760 TQ	USBLS	5/07
Except Agriculture, Construction, Health and Safety, and Transportation	District of Columbia	Y	56120 FQ	71020 MW	87090 TQ	USBLS	5/07
Except Agriculture, Construction, Health and Safety, and Transportation	Washington-Arlington-Alexandria MSA, DC-VA-MD-WV	Y	45340 FQ	64090 MW	82060 TQ	USBLS	5/07
Except Agriculture, Construction, Health and Safety, and Transportation	Florida	Y	32970 FQ	40110 MW	57010 TQ	USBLS	5/07
Except Agriculture, Construction, Health and Safety, and Transportation	Fort Lauderdale-Pompano Beach-Deerfield Beach PMSA, FL	Y	33490 FQ	40180 MW	56820 TQ	USBLS	5/07
Except Agriculture, Construction, Health and Safety, and Transportation	Jacksonville MSA, FL	Y	33450 FQ	41010 MW	57990 TQ	USBLS	5/07
Except Agriculture, Construction, Health and Safety, and Transportation	Miami-Fort Lauderdale-Miami Beach MSA, FL	Y	35150 FQ	44050 MW	60550 TQ	USBLS	5/07
Except Agriculture, Construction, Health and Safety, and Transportation	Orlando-Kissimmee MSA, FL	Y	29510 FQ	37000 MW	53210 TQ	USBLS	5/07
Except Agriculture, Construction, Health and Safety, and Transportation	Tallahassee MSA, FL	Y	29720 FQ	34720 MW	40920 TQ	USBLS	5/07
Except Agriculture, Construction, Health and Safety, and Transportation	Tampa-St. Petersburg-Clearwater MSA, FL	Y	34000 FQ	43140 MW	59170 TQ	USBLS	5/07
Except Agriculture, Construction, Health and Safety, and Transportation	West Palm Beach-Boca Raton-Boynton Beach PMSA, FL	Y	33790 FQ	39710 MW	57560 TQ	USBLS	5/07
Except Agriculture, Construction, Health and Safety, and Transportation	Georgia	Y	35100 FQ	44680 MW	62910 TQ	USBLS	5/07
Except Agriculture, Construction, Health and Safety, and Transportation	Atlanta-Sandy Springs-Marietta MSA, GA	Y	35220 FQ	43320 MW	59730 TQ	USBLS	5/07
Except Agriculture, Construction, Health and Safety, and Transportation	Augusta-Richmond County MSA, GA-SC	Y	42050 FQ	60750 MW	112010 TQ	USBLS	5/07
Except Agriculture, Construction, Health and Safety, and Transportation	Hawaii	Y	28320 FQ	38700 MW	57810 TQ	USBLS	5/07
Except Agriculture, Construction, Health and Safety, and Transportation	Honolulu MSA, HI	Y	28740 FQ	44670 MW	63330 TQ	USBLS	5/07
Except Agriculture, Construction, Health and Safety, and Transportation	Idaho	Y	31020 FQ	39270 MW	52870 TQ	USBLS	5/07
Except Agriculture, Construction, Health and Safety, and Transportation	Boise City-Nampa MSA, ID	Y	33740 FQ	41350 MW	56210 TQ	USBLS	5/07
Except Agriculture, Construction, Health and Safety, and Transportation	Illinois	Y	34370 FQ	47320 MW	67830 TQ	USBLS	5/07
Except Agriculture, Construction, Health and Safety, and Transportation	Chicago-Naperville-Joliet MSA, IL-IN-WI	Y	35370 FQ	49110 MW	69990 TQ	USBLS	5/07

AE	Average entry wage	AW	Average wage paid	FQ	First quartile wage	LO	Lowest wage paid	MTC	Median total compensation	TCC	Total cash compensation
AER	Average entry range	AWR	Average wage range	H	Hourly	LR	Low end range	MW	Median wage paid	TQ	Third quartile wage
AEX	Average experienced wage	AXR	Average experienced range	HI	Highest wage paid	M	Monthly	MWR	Median wage range	W	Weekly
ATC	Average total compensation	D	Daily	HR	High end range	MCC	Median cash compensation	S	See annotated source	Y	Yearly

Compliance Officer

Occupation/Type/Industry	Location	Per	Low	Mid	High	Source	Date
Except Agriculture, Construction, Health and Safety, and Transportation	Indiana	Y	31120 FQ	42410 MW	58390 TQ	USBLS	5/07
Except Agriculture, Construction, Health and Safety, and Transportation	Gary PMSA, IN	Y	31020 FQ	44510 MW	65580 TQ	USBLS	5/07
Except Agriculture, Construction, Health and Safety, and Transportation	Indianapolis-Carmel MSA, IN	Y	31430 FQ	43050 MW	60710 TQ	USBLS	5/07
Except Agriculture, Construction, Health and Safety, and Transportation	Iowa	Y	35420 FQ	45000 MW	58220 TQ	USBLS	5/07
Except Agriculture, Construction, Health and Safety, and Transportation	Des Moines-West Des Moines MSA, IA	Y	37190 FQ	46480 MW	60110 TQ	USBLS	5/07
Except Agriculture, Construction, Health and Safety, and Transportation	Iowa City MSA, IA	Y	36440 FQ	51380 MW	66120 TQ	USBLS	5/07
Except Agriculture, Construction, Health and Safety, and Transportation	Waterloo-Cedar Falls MSA, IA	Y	32440 FQ	44530 MW	57540 TQ	USBLS	5/07
Except Agriculture, Construction, Health and Safety, and Transportation	Kansas	Y	37890 FQ	48260 MW	62340 TQ	USBLS	5/07
Except Agriculture, Construction, Health and Safety, and Transportation	Wichita MSA, KS	Y	33370 FQ	42540 MW	59250 TQ	USBLS	5/07
Except Agriculture, Construction, Health and Safety, and Transportation	Kentucky	Y	33457 FQ	41354 MW	54526 TQ	KYBLS	2008
Except Agriculture, Construction, Health and Safety, and Transportation	Louisville-Jefferson County MSA, KY-IN	Y	30820 FQ	39690 MW	55520 TQ	USBLS	5/07
Except Agriculture, Construction, Health and Safety, and Transportation	Louisiana	H	15.59 FQ	19.86 MW	25.92 TQ	LABLS	1/08-3/08
Except Agriculture, Construction, Health and Safety, and Transportation	Baton Rouge MSA, LA	Y	29970 FQ	37180 MW	47720 TQ	USBLS	5/07
Except Agriculture, Construction, Health and Safety, and Transportation	New Orleans-Metairie-Kenner MSA, LA	Y	34920 FQ	44100 MW	56990 TQ	USBLS	5/07
Except Agriculture, Construction, Health and Safety, and Transportation	Maine	Y	34460 FQ	44710 MW	57240 TQ	USBLS	5/07
Except Agriculture, Construction, Health and Safety, and Transportation	Portland-South Portland-Biddeford MSA, ME	Y	30900 FQ	39740 MW	52350 TQ	USBLS	5/07
Except Agriculture, Construction, Health and Safety, and Transportation	Maryland	Y		55025 MW		MDBLS	3/08
Except Agriculture, Construction, Health and Safety, and Transportation	Baltimore-Towson MSA, MD	Y	35950 FQ	46630 MW	64530 TQ	USBLS	5/07
Except Agriculture, Construction, Health and Safety, and Transportation	Bethesda-Gaithersburg-Frederick PMSA, MD	Y	53720 FQ	68870 MW	84020 TQ	USBLS	5/07
Except Agriculture, Construction, Health and Safety, and Transportation	Cumberland MSA, MD-WV	Y	50640 FQ	65730 MW	83610 TQ	USBLS	5/07
Except Agriculture, Construction, Health and Safety, and Transportation	Massachusetts	Y	42770 FQ	57420 MW	74710 TQ	USBLS	5/07
Except Agriculture, Construction, Health and Safety, and Transportation	Boston-Cambridge-Quincy NECTA, MA	Y	39880 FQ	57040 MW	76100 TQ	USBLS	5/07
Except Agriculture, Construction, Health and Safety, and Transportation	Worcester MSA, MA-CT	Y	53220 FQ	59230 MW	65530 TQ	USBLS	5/07
Except Agriculture, Construction, Health and Safety, and Transportation	Michigan	Y	36280 FQ	50580 MW	63520 TQ	USBLS	5/07
Except Agriculture, Construction, Health and Safety, and Transportation	Detroit-Warren-Livonia MSA, MI	Y	37780 FQ	53250 MW	65090 TQ	USBLS	5/07
Except Agriculture, Construction, Health and Safety, and Transportation	Grand Rapids-Wyoming MSA, MI	Y	31600 FQ	41100 MW	57320 TQ	USBLS	5/07
Except Agriculture, Construction, Health and Safety, and Transportation	Lansing-East Lansing MSA, MI	Y	35420 FQ	54690 MW	62790 TQ	USBLS	5/07
Except Agriculture, Construction, Health and Safety, and Transportation	Warren-Troy-Farmington Hills PMSA, MI	Y	49920 FQ	58910 MW	70500 TQ	USBLS	5/07
Except Agriculture, Construction, Health and Safety, and Transportation	Minnesota	Y	41591 FQ	55896 MW	70347 TQ	MNBLS	10/08-12/08
Except Agriculture, Construction, Health and Safety, and Transportation	Duluth-Superior MSA, MN-WI	Y	34053 FQ	51538 MW	66364 TQ	MNBLS	10/08-12/08

AE	Average entry wage	AW	Average wage paid	FQ	First quartile wage	LO	Lowest wage paid	MTC	Median total compensation	TCC	Total cash compensation
AER	Average entry range	AWR	Average wage range	H	Hourly	LR	Low end range	MW	Median wage paid	TQ	Third quartile wage
AEX	Average experienced wage	AXR	Average experienced range	HI	Highest wage paid	M	Monthly	MWR	Median wage range	W	Weekly
ATC	Average total compensation	D	Daily	HR	High end range	MCC	Median cash compensation	S	See annotated source	Y	Yearly

Compliance Officer

Occupation/Type/Industry	Location	Per	Low	Mid	High	Source	Date
Compliance Officer							
Except Agriculture, Construction, Health and Safety, and Transportation	Minneapolis-Saint Paul MSA, MN-WI	Y	41487 FQ	56000 MW	72745 TQ	MNBLS	10/08-12/08
Except Agriculture, Construction, Health and Safety, and Transportation	Rochester MSA, MN	Y	30668 FQ	40573 MW	59782 TQ	MNBLS	10/08-12/08
Except Agriculture, Construction, Health and Safety, and Transportation	Mississippi	Y	30240 FQ	37080 MW	47990 TQ	USBLS	5/07
Except Agriculture, Construction, Health and Safety, and Transportation	Jackson MSA, MS	Y	30860 FQ	37930 MW	50440 TQ	USBLS	5/07
Except Agriculture, Construction, Health and Safety, and Transportation	Missouri	Y	33830 FQ	45950 MW	61130 TQ	USBLS	5/07
Except Agriculture, Construction, Health and Safety, and Transportation	Jefferson City MSA, MO	Y	33230 FQ	39610 MW	50690 TQ	USBLS	5/07
Except Agriculture, Construction, Health and Safety, and Transportation	Kansas City MSA, MO-KS	Y	41880 FQ	52340 MW	67200 TQ	USBLS	5/07
Except Agriculture, Construction, Health and Safety, and Transportation	St. Louis MSA, MO-IL	Y	31780 FQ	46250 MW	63320 TQ	USBLS	5/07
Except Agriculture, Construction, Health and Safety, and Transportation	Montana	Y	32800 FQ	41100 MW	54810 TQ	USBLS	5/07
Except Agriculture, Construction, Health and Safety, and Transportation	Billings MSA, MT	Y	30800 FQ	35830 MW	49840 TQ	USBLS	5/07
Except Agriculture, Construction, Health and Safety, and Transportation	Nebraska	Y	34800 FQ	46690 MW	61690 TQ	USBLS	5/07
Except Agriculture, Construction, Health and Safety, and Transportation	Omaha-Council Bluffs MSA, NE-IA	Y	34350 FQ	45950 MW	60540 TQ	USBLS	5/07
Except Agriculture, Construction, Health and Safety, and Transportation	Nevada	H	14.57 FQ	18.79 MW	28.42 TQ	NVBLS	5/08
Except Agriculture, Construction, Health and Safety, and Transportation	Las Vegas-Paradise MSA, NV	H	14.44 FQ	18.01 MW	27.92 TQ	NVBLS	5/08
Except Agriculture, Construction, Health and Safety, and Transportation	Reno-Sparks MSA, NV	H	14.42 FQ	18.61 MW	27.75 TQ	NVBLS	5/08
Except Agriculture, Construction, Health and Safety, and Transportation	New Hampshire	H	16.16 AE	19.86 MW	25.26 AEX	NHBLS	6/08
Except Agriculture, Construction, Health and Safety, and Transportation	Manchester MSA, NH	Y	31580 FQ	36650 MW	46670 TQ	USBLS	5/07
Except Agriculture, Construction, Health and Safety, and Transportation	New Jersey	Y	42270 FQ	55780 MW	71100 TQ	USBLS	5/07
Except Agriculture, Construction, Health and Safety, and Transportation	Camden PMSA, NJ	Y	44650 FQ	56240 MW	68960 TQ	USBLS	5/07
Except Agriculture, Construction, Health and Safety, and Transportation	Edison PMSA, NJ	Y	46970 FQ	58760 MW	74220 TQ	USBLS	5/07
Except Agriculture, Construction, Health and Safety, and Transportation	Newark-Union PMSA, NJ-PA	Y	36750 FQ	49020 MW	65710 TQ	USBLS	5/07
Except Agriculture, Construction, Health and Safety, and Transportation	New Mexico	Y	32620 FQ	51170 MW	69750 TQ	USBLS	5/07
Except Agriculture, Construction, Health and Safety, and Transportation	Albuquerque MSA, NM	Y	29930 FQ	42500 MW	67950 TQ	USBLS	5/07
Except Agriculture, Construction, Health and Safety, and Transportation	New York	Y	37350 FQ	51940 MW	71990 TQ	USBLS	5/07
Except Agriculture, Construction, Health and Safety, and Transportation	Albany-Schenectady-Troy MSA, NY	Y	35320 FQ	46670 MW	61540 TQ	USBLS	5/07
Except Agriculture, Construction, Health and Safety, and Transportation	Binghamton MSA, NY	Y	34300 FQ	49210 MW	64010 TQ	USBLS	5/07
Except Agriculture, Construction, Health and Safety, and Transportation	Buffalo-Niagara Falls MSA, NY	Y	37240 FQ	51610 MW	60850 TQ	USBLS	5/07
Except Agriculture, Construction, Health and Safety, and Transportation	Ithaca MSA, NY	Y	33600 FQ	46210 MW	57340 TQ	USBLS	5/07
Except Agriculture, Construction, Health and Safety, and Transportation	Nassau-Suffolk PMSA, NY	Y	42120 FQ	58590 MW	77420 TQ	USBLS	5/07
Except Agriculture, Construction, Health and Safety, and Transportation	New York-Northern New Jersey-Long Island MSA, NY-NJ-PA	Y	38380 FQ	55100 MW	75860 TQ	USBLS	5/07
Except Agriculture, Construction, Health and Safety, and Transportation	North Carolina	Y	34700 FQ	43350 MW	59390 TQ	USBLS	5/07

AE	Average entry wage	AW	Average wage paid	FQ First quartile wage
AER	Average entry range	AWR	Average wage range	H Hourly
AEX	Average experienced wage	AXR	Average experienced range	HI Highest wage paid
ATC	Average total compensation	D	Daily	HR High end range

LO	Lowest wage paid	MTC Median total compensation	TCC Total cash compensation
LR	Low end range	MW Median wage paid	TQ Third quartile wage
M	Monthly	MWR Median wage range	W Weekly
MCC	Median cash compensation	S See annotated source	Y Yearly

Compliance Officer

Occupation/Type/Industry	Location	Per	Low	Mid	High	Source	Date
Except Agriculture, Construction, Health and Safety, and Transportation	Charlotte-Gastonia-Concord MSA, NC-SC	Y	32460 FQ	45890 MW	65010 TQ	USBLS	5/07
Except Agriculture, Construction, Health and Safety, and Transportation	Raleigh-Cary MSA, NC	Y	35640 FQ	44370 MW	64300 TQ	USBLS	5/07
Except Agriculture, Construction, Health and Safety, and Transportation	North Dakota	Y	37970 FQ	52310 MW	61550 TQ	USBLS	5/07
Except Agriculture, Construction, Health and Safety, and Transportation	Fargo MSA, ND-MN	Y	35980 FQ	52300 MW	71720 TQ	USBLS	5/07
Except Agriculture, Construction, Health and Safety, and Transportation	Ohio	Y	36510 FQ	50210 MW	65500 TQ	USBLS	5/07
Except Agriculture, Construction, Health and Safety, and Transportation	Canton-Massillon MSA, OH	Y	37790 FQ	54510 MW	67040 TQ	USBLS	5/07
Except Agriculture, Construction, Health and Safety, and Transportation	Cincinnati-Middletown MSA, OH-KY-IN	Y	35360 FQ	48550 MW	62440 TQ	USBLS	5/07
Except Agriculture, Construction, Health and Safety, and Transportation	Cleveland-Elyria-Mentor MSA, OH	Y	34810 FQ	44560 MW	62940 TQ	USBLS	5/07
Except Agriculture, Construction, Health and Safety, and Transportation	Columbus MSA, OH	Y	38060 FQ	53140 MW	70300 TQ	USBLS	5/07
Except Agriculture, Construction, Health and Safety, and Transportation	Dayton MSA, OH	Y	30800 FQ	42790 MW	61030 TQ	USBLS	5/07
Except Agriculture, Construction, Health and Safety, and Transportation	Oklahoma	Y	30020 FQ	37600 MW	49480 TQ	USBLS	5/07
Except Agriculture, Construction, Health and Safety, and Transportation	Oklahoma City MSA, OK	Y	29970 FQ	37430 MW	49030 TQ	USBLS	5/07
Except Agriculture, Construction, Health and Safety, and Transportation	Tulsa MSA, OK	Y	30270 FQ	37730 MW	51010 TQ	USBLS	5/07
Except Agriculture, Construction, Health and Safety, and Transportation	Oregon	H	18.03 FQ	22.65 MW	28.14 TQ	ORBLS	5/08
Except Agriculture, Construction, Health and Safety, and Transportation	Eugene-Springfield MSA, OR	Y	31450 FQ	43330 MW	54140 TQ	USBLS	5/07
Except Agriculture, Construction, Health and Safety, and Transportation	Portland-Vancouver-Beaverton MSA, OR-WA	Y	35820 FQ	45320 MW	59540 TQ	USBLS	5/07
Except Agriculture, Construction, Health and Safety, and Transportation	Pennsylvania	Y	33970 FQ	46750 MW	63480 TQ	USBLS	5/07
Except Agriculture, Construction, Health and Safety, and Transportation	Allentown-Bethlehem-Easton MSA, PA-NJ	Y	29340 FQ	41280 MW	55610 TQ	USBLS	5/07
Except Agriculture, Construction, Health and Safety, and Transportation	Lancaster MSA, PA	Y	35990 FQ	46890 MW	61990 TQ	USBLS	5/07
Except Agriculture, Construction, Health and Safety, and Transportation	Philadelphia-Camden-Wilmington MSA, PA-NJ-DE-MD	Y	36640 FQ	50000 MW	67090 TQ	USBLS	5/07
Except Agriculture, Construction, Health and Safety, and Transportation	Pittsburgh MSA, PA	Y	35250 FQ	48810 MW	65340 TQ	USBLS	5/07
Except Agriculture, Construction, Health and Safety, and Transportation	Rhode Island	Y	36200 FQ	49090 MW	68870 TQ	USBLS	5/07
Except Agriculture, Construction, Health and Safety, and Transportation	Providence-Fall River-Warwick MSA, RI-MA	Y	36260 FQ	49270 MW	68940 TQ	USBLS	5/07
Except Agriculture, Construction, Health and Safety, and Transportation	South Carolina	Y	31260 FQ	40180 MW	56420 TQ	USBLS	5/07
Except Agriculture, Construction, Health and Safety, and Transportation	Charleston-North Charleston MSA, SC	Y	33390 FQ	43620 MW	56760 TQ	USBLS	5/07
Except Agriculture, Construction, Health and Safety, and Transportation	Columbia MSA, SC	Y	33300 FQ	40050 MW	51060 TQ	USBLS	5/07
Except Agriculture, Construction, Health and Safety, and Transportation	South Dakota	Y	35522 FQ	42358 MW	51660 TQ	SDBLS	7/08-9/08
Except Agriculture, Construction, Health and Safety, and Transportation	Sioux Falls MSA, SD	Y	36422 FQ	44656 MW	57544 TQ	SDBLS	7/08-9/08
Except Agriculture, Construction, Health and Safety, and Transportation	Tennessee	Y	29080 FQ	39080 MW	55900 TQ	USBLS	5/07
Except Agriculture, Construction, Health and Safety, and Transportation	Memphis MSA, TN-MS-AR	Y	28910 FQ	37160 MW	54210 TQ	USBLS	5/07

AE	Average entry wage	AW	Average wage paid	FQ	First quartile wage	LO	Lowest wage paid	MTC	Median total compensation	TCC	Total cash compensation
AER	Average entry range	AWR	Average wage range	H	Hourly	LR	Low end range	MW	Median wage paid	TQ	Third quartile wage
AEX	Average experienced wage	AXR	Average experienced range	HI	Highest wage paid	M	Monthly	MWR	Median wage range	W	Weekly
ATC	Average total compensation	D	Daily	HR	High end range	MCC	Median cash compensation	S	See annotated source	Y	Yearly

Occupation/Type/Industry	Location	Per	Low	Mid	High	Source	Date
Compliance Officer							
Except Agriculture, Construction, Health and Safety, and Transportation	Nashville-Davidson-Murfreesboro MSA, TN	Y	28440 FQ	36960 MW	52500 TQ	USBLS	5/07
Except Agriculture, Construction, Health and Safety, and Transportation	Texas	Y	37520 FQ	51590 MW	64330 TQ	USBLS	5/07
Except Agriculture, Construction, Health and Safety, and Transportation	Austin-Round Rock MSA, TX	Y	31470 FQ	38940 MW	59560 TQ	USBLS	5/07
Except Agriculture, Construction, Health and Safety, and Transportation	Dallas-Fort Worth-Arlington MSA, TX	Y	37390 FQ	50180 MW	68890 TQ	USBLS	5/07
Except Agriculture, Construction, Health and Safety, and Transportation	El Paso MSA, TX	Y	45070 FQ	55910 MW	62930 TQ	USBLS	5/07
Except Agriculture, Construction, Health and Safety, and Transportation	Houston-Sugar Land-Baytown MSA, TX	Y	37080 FQ	49360 MW	68390 TQ	USBLS	5/07
Except Agriculture, Construction, Health and Safety, and Transportation	Midland MSA, TX	Y	33850 FQ	47220 MW	61160 TQ	USBLS	5/07
Except Agriculture, Construction, Health and Safety, and Transportation	San Antonio MSA, TX	Y	33730 FQ	48340 MW	65580 TQ	USBLS	5/07
Except Agriculture, Construction, Health and Safety, and Transportation	Utah	Y	30940 FQ	37770 MW	50560 TQ	USBLS	5/07
Except Agriculture, Construction, Health and Safety, and Transportation	Salt Lake City MSA, UT	Y	29700 FQ	35910 MW	48020 TQ	USBLS	5/07
Except Agriculture, Construction, Health and Safety, and Transportation	Vermont	Y	41190 FQ	52010 MW	67920 TQ	USBLS	5/07
Except Agriculture, Construction, Health and Safety, and Transportation	Burlington-South Burlington MSA, VT	Y	41190 FQ	50420 MW	70250 TQ	USBLS	5/07
Except Agriculture, Construction, Health and Safety, and Transportation	Virginia	Y	35440 FQ	48110 MW	67650 TQ	USBLS	5/07
Except Agriculture, Construction, Health and Safety, and Transportation	Richmond MSA, VA	Y	35470 FQ	46990 MW	61500 TQ	USBLS	5/07
Except Agriculture, Construction, Health and Safety, and Transportation	Virginia Beach-Norfolk-Newport News MSA, VA-NC	Y	34770 FQ	43800 MW	60170 TQ	USBLS	5/07
Except Agriculture, Construction, Health and Safety, and Transportation	Washington	H	19.04 FQ	26.06 MW	31.26 TQ	WABLS	3/08
Except Agriculture, Construction, Health and Safety, and Transportation	Seattle-Tacoma-Bellevue MSA, WA	Y	37400 FQ	51840 MW	64840 TQ	USBLS	5/07
Except Agriculture, Construction, Health and Safety, and Transportation	Charleston MSA, WV	Y	29380 FQ	37590 MW	47620 TQ	USBLS	5/07
Except Agriculture, Construction, Health and Safety, and Transportation	Wisconsin	Y	35770 FQ	45110 MW	56780 TQ	USBLS	5/07
Except Agriculture, Construction, Health and Safety, and Transportation	Milwaukee-Waukesha-West Allis MSA, WI	Y	36780 FQ	46400 MW	59730 TQ	USBLS	5/07
Except Agriculture, Construction, Health and Safety, and Transportation	Wyoming	Y	34140 FQ	46044 MW	55692 TQ	WYBLS	9/08
Except Agriculture, Construction, Health and Safety, and Transportation	Cheyenne MSA, WY	Y	45491 FQ	49921 MW	54353 TQ	WYBLS	9/08
Except Agriculture, Construction, Health and Safety, and Transportation	Puerto Rico	Y	25890 FQ	32700 MW	46850 TQ	USBLS	5/07
Except Agriculture, Construction, Health and Safety, and Transportation	San Juan-Caguas-Guaynabo MSA, PR	Y	25350 FQ	32370 MW	42860 TQ	USBLS	5/07
Except Agriculture, Construction, Health and Safety, and Transportation	Virgin Islands	Y	26730 FQ	36450 MW	51940 TQ	USBLS	5/07
Except Agriculture, Construction, Health and Safety, and Transportation	Guam	Y	28610 FQ	35860 MW	56420 TQ	USBLS	5/07
Comptroller	United States	Y		69800 MW		CNNM03	2007
Municipal Government	Baltimore, MD	Y			100450 HI	BMAG	2009
Comptroller General of the United States	United States	Y			172200 HI	CRS02	1/08
Computer, Automated Teller, and Office Machine Repairer	Alabama	Y	29010 FQ	38010 MW	51590 TQ	USBLS	5/07
	Birmingham-Hoover MSA, AL	Y	31420 FQ	41800 MW	54590 TQ	USBLS	5/07
	Alaska	Y	31450 FQ	41640 MW	51420 TQ	USBLS	5/07

AE	Average entry wage	AW	Average wage paid	FQ	First quartile wage	LO	Lowest wage paid	MTC	Median total compensation	TCC	Total cash compensation
AER	Average entry range	AWR	Average wage range	H	Hourly	LR	Low end range	MW	Median wage paid	TQ	Third quartile wage
AEX	Average experienced wage	AXR	Average experienced range	HI	Highest wage paid	M	Monthly	MWR	Median wage range	W	Weekly
ATC	Average total compensation	D	Daily	HR	High end range	MCC	Median cash compensation	S	See annotated source	Y	Yearly

Occupation/Type/Industry	Location	Per	Low	Mid	High	Source	Date
Computer, Automated Teller, and Office Machine Repairer							
	Anchorage MSA, AK	Y	30480 FQ	40390 MW	54150 TQ	USBLS	5/07
	Arizona	Y	28490 FQ	33930 MW	45500 TQ	USBLS	5/07
	Phoenix-Mesa-Scottsdale MSA, AZ	Y	28580 FQ	34220 MW	46390 TQ	USBLS	5/07
	Tucson MSA, AZ	Y	29000 FQ	33740 MW	40020 TQ	USBLS	5/07
	Arkansas	Y	26660 FQ	33010 MW	41880 TQ	USBLS	5/07
	Fayetteville-Springdale-Rogers MSA, AR-MO	Y	27020 FQ	34630 MW	48980 TQ	USBLS	5/07
	Little Rock-North Little Rock MSA, AR	Y	28010 FQ	33380 MW	43430 TQ	USBLS	5/07
	California	H	14.37 FQ	18.52 MW	23.68 TQ	CABLS	1/08-3/08
	Fresno MSA, CA	H	10.34 FQ	17.91 MW	23.48 TQ	CABLS	1/08-3/08
	Los Angeles-Long Beach-Glendale PMSA, CA	H	13.39 FQ	16.79 MW	22.30 TQ	CABLS	1/08-3/08
	Oakland-Fremont-Hayward MSA, CA	H	12.27 FQ	16.14 MW	23.24 TQ	CABLS	1/08-3/08
	Oxnard-Thousand Oaks-Ventura MSA, CA	H	18.47 FQ	21.49 MW	23.53 TQ	CABLS	1/08-3/08
	Riverside-San Bernardino-Ontario MSA, CA	H	13.37 FQ	16.60 MW	22.29 TQ	CABLS	1/08-3/08
	Sacramento-Arden Arcade-Roseville MSA, CA	H	15.06 FQ	18.12 MW	22.70 TQ	CABLS	1/08-3/08
	San Diego-Carlsbad-San Marcos MSA, CA	H	14.97 FQ	19.28 MW	23.81 TQ	CABLS	1/08-3/08
	San Francisco-San Mateo-Redwood PMSA, CA	H	16.81 FQ	22.85 MW	29.94 TQ	CABLS	1/08-3/08
	San Jose-Sunnyvale-Santa Clara MSA, CA	H	18.23 FQ	22.90 MW	28.21 TQ	CABLS	1/08-3/08
	Santa Ana-Anaheim-Irvine PMSA, CA	Y	33110 FQ	38830 MW	47040 TQ	USBLS	5/07
	Colorado	Y	31230 FQ	40680 MW	51410 TQ	USBLS	5/07
	Colorado Springs MSA, CO	Y	27150 FQ	36440 MW	43070 TQ	USBLS	5/07
	Denver-Aurora MSA, CO	Y	32330 FQ	42530 MW	54320 TQ	USBLS	5/07
	Connecticut	H	16.84 AE	22.59 MW		CTBLS	1/08-3/08
	Bridgeport-Stamford-Norwalk MSA, CT	Y	39880 FQ	47100 MW	56530 TQ	USBLS	5/07
	Hartford-West Hartford-East Hartford MSA, CT	Y	39280 FQ	47480 MW	57390 TQ	USBLS	5/07
	Delaware	Y	27450 FQ	35190 MW	44490 TQ	USBLS	5/07
	Wilmington PMSA, DE-MD-NJ	Y	27670 FQ	35680 MW	44960 TQ	USBLS	5/07
	District of Columbia	Y	46010 FQ	53600 MW	63850 TQ	USBLS	5/07
	Washington-Arlington-Alexandria MSA, DC-VA-MD-WV	Y	36840 FQ	45630 MW	56750 TQ	USBLS	5/07
	Florida	Y	28140 FQ	35670 MW	45130 TQ	USBLS	5/07
	Fort Lauderdale-Pompano Beach-Deerfield Beach PMSA, FL	Y	30090 FQ	37330 MW	48000 TQ	USBLS	5/07
	Jacksonville MSA, FL	Y	28030 FQ	35580 MW	49880 TQ	USBLS	5/07
	Miami-Fort Lauderdale-Miami Beach MSA, FL	Y	27750 FQ	35520 MW	44440 TQ	USBLS	5/07
	Orlando-Kissimmee MSA, FL	Y	30530 FQ	36720 MW	45370 TQ	USBLS	5/07
	Pensacola-Ferry Pass-Brent MSA, FL	Y	26150 FQ	31470 MW	38030 TQ	USBLS	5/07
	Tampa-St. Petersburg-Clearwater MSA, FL	Y	30440 FQ	39510 MW	47390 TQ	USBLS	5/07
	West Palm Beach-Boca Raton-Boynton Beach PMSA, FL	Y	29540 FQ	35300 MW	41770 TQ	USBLS	5/07
	Georgia	Y	29530 FQ	36760 MW	48150 TQ	USBLS	5/07
	Atlanta-Sandy Springs-Marietta MSA, GA	Y	29940 FQ	37230 MW	49020 TQ	USBLS	5/07
	Hawaii	Y	27940 FQ	34840 MW	45090 TQ	USBLS	5/07
	Honolulu MSA, HI	Y	28050 FQ	34430 MW	44730 TQ	USBLS	5/07
	Idaho	Y	25980 FQ	31010 MW	37290 TQ	USBLS	5/07
	Boise City-Nampa MSA, ID	Y	26150 FQ	30920 MW	36290 TQ	USBLS	5/07
	Illinois	Y	29800 FQ	39670 MW	48670 TQ	USBLS	5/07
	Chicago-Naperville-Joliet MSA, IL-IN-WI	Y	30490 FQ	40840 MW	49060 TQ	USBLS	5/07
	Indiana	Y	28070 FQ	37480 MW	46660 TQ	USBLS	5/07
	Elkhart-Goshen MSA, IN	Y	24920 FQ	31480 MW	36880 TQ	USBLS	5/07

AE Average entry wage	**AW** Average wage paid	**FQ** First quartile wage	**LO** Lowest wage paid	**MTC** Median total compensation	**TCC** Total cash compensation
AER Average entry range	**AWR** Average wage range	**H** Hourly	**LR** Low end range	**MW** Median wage paid	**TQ** Third quartile wage
AEX Average experienced wage	**AXR** Average experienced range	**HI** Highest wage paid	**M** Monthly	**MWR** Median wage range	**W** Weekly
ATC Average total compensation	**D** Daily	**HR** High end range	**MCC** Median cash compensation	**S** See annotated source	**Y** Yearly

Occupation/Type/Industry	Location	Per	Low	Mid	High	Source	Date
Computer, Automated Teller, and Office Machine Repairer	Evansville MSA, IN-KY	Y	27980 FQ	39410 MW	51820 TQ	USBLS	5/07
	Fort Wayne MSA, IN	Y	31270 FQ	43520 MW	51030 TQ	USBLS	5/07
	Gary PMSA, IN	Y	30120 FQ	40700 MW	51560 TQ	USBLS	5/07
	Indianapolis-Carmel MSA, IN	Y	27070 FQ	36720 MW	45540 TQ	USBLS	5/07
	Iowa	Y	26170 FQ	33360 MW	41400 TQ	USBLS	5/07
	Des Moines-West Des Moines MSA, IA	Y	28710 FQ	37160 MW	43890 TQ	USBLS	5/07
	Kansas	Y	27770 FQ	35520 MW	43850 TQ	USBLS	5/07
	Wichita MSA, KS	Y	22640 FQ	30180 MW	37190 TQ	USBLS	5/07
	Kentucky	Y	26637 FQ	33090 MW	42852 TQ	KYBLS	2008
	Louisville-Jefferson County MSA, KY-IN	Y	26200 FQ	34750 MW	45740 TQ	USBLS	5/07
	Louisiana	H	11.37 FQ	15.10 MW	19.45 TQ	LABLS	1/08-3/08
	Baton Rouge MSA, LA	Y	19070 FQ	22910 MW	33900 TQ	USBLS	5/07
	New Orleans-Metairie-Kenner MSA, LA	Y	26320 FQ	35200 MW	46180 TQ	USBLS	5/07
	Maine	Y	26610 FQ	32000 MW	38670 TQ	USBLS	5/07
	Portland-South Portland-Biddeford MSA, ME	Y	26700 FQ	31760 MW	38150 TQ	USBLS	5/07
	Maryland	Y		46150 MW		MDBLS	3/08
	Baltimore-Towson MSA, MD	Y	32640 FQ	43700 MW	51780 TQ	USBLS	5/07
	Bethesda-Gaithersburg-Frederick PMSA, MD	Y	36810 FQ	46200 MW	58490 TQ	USBLS	5/07
	Massachusetts	Y	31600 FQ	41790 MW	50930 TQ	USBLS	5/07
	Boston-Cambridge-Quincy NECTA, MA	Y	37250 FQ	46690 MW	56150 TQ	USBLS	5/07
	Springfield MSA, MA-CT	Y	32890 FQ	43060 MW	50610 TQ	USBLS	5/07
	Worcester MSA, MA-CT	Y	32070 FQ	35930 MW	39520 TQ	USBLS	5/07
	Michigan	Y	32630 FQ	41440 MW	49630 TQ	USBLS	5/07
	Detroit-Warren-Livonia MSA, MI	Y	35000 FQ	43500 MW	51140 TQ	USBLS	5/07
	Grand Rapids-Wyoming MSA, MI	Y	29210 FQ	40370 MW	48930 TQ	USBLS	5/07
	Warren-Troy-Farmington Hills PMSA, MI	Y	38290 FQ	46420 MW	55340 TQ	USBLS	5/07
	Minnesota	Y	32338 FQ	39566 MW	47989 TQ	MNBLS	10/08-12/08
	Duluth-Superior MSA, MN-WI	Y	28101 FQ	30681 MW	33251 TQ	MNBLS	10/08-12/08
	Minneapolis-Saint Paul MSA, MN-WI	Y	35223 FQ	42146 MW	49782 TQ	MNBLS	10/08-12/08
	Rochester MSA, MN	Y	29743 FQ	33484 MW	40144 TQ	MNBLS	10/08-12/08
	Mississippi	Y	24870 FQ	28740 MW	35340 TQ	USBLS	5/07
	Hattiesburg MSA, MS	Y	26370 FQ	31910 MW	35270 TQ	USBLS	5/07
	Jackson MSA, MS	Y	26360 FQ	29440 MW	52080 TQ	USBLS	5/07
	Missouri	Y	26280 FQ	32950 MW	42790 TQ	USBLS	5/07
	Kansas City MSA, MO-KS	Y	32580 FQ	39800 MW	47290 TQ	USBLS	5/07
	St. Louis MSA, MO-IL	Y	27890 FQ	33720 MW	43800 TQ	USBLS	5/07
	Springfield MSA, MO	Y	24580 FQ	32810 MW	38170 TQ	USBLS	5/07
	Montana	Y	27300 FQ	33060 MW	38350 TQ	USBLS	5/07
	Billings MSA, MT	Y	33050 FQ	36080 MW	39110 TQ	USBLS	5/07
	Nebraska	Y	30090 FQ	37170 MW	45780 TQ	USBLS	5/07
	Lincoln MSA, NE	Y	29550 FQ	33570 MW	38060 TQ	USBLS	5/07
	Omaha-Council Bluffs MSA, NE-IA	Y	32740 FQ	40090 MW	47720 TQ	USBLS	5/07
	Nevada	H	15.55 FQ	17.89 MW	20.65 TQ	NVBLS	5/08
	Las Vegas-Paradise MSA, NV	H	15.32 FQ	17.49 MW	19.44 TQ	NVBLS	5/08
	New Hampshire	H	13.49 AE	17.85 MW	21.44 AEX	NHBLS	6/08
	Manchester MSA, NH	Y	34560 FQ	42870 MW	50540 TQ	USBLS	5/07
	Nashua NECTA, NH-MA	Y	29290 FQ	35400 MW	43020 TQ	USBLS	5/07
	New Jersey	Y	34110 FQ	43570 MW	54040 TQ	USBLS	5/07
	Camden PMSA, NJ	Y	34020 FQ	40400 MW	49880 TQ	USBLS	5/07
	Edison PMSA, NJ	Y	35660 FQ	44820 MW	54810 TQ	USBLS	5/07
	Newark-Union PMSA, NJ-PA	Y	30240 FQ	43390 MW	55460 TQ	USBLS	5/07
	New Mexico	Y	28790 FQ	40930 MW	53340 TQ	USBLS	5/07
	Albuquerque MSA, NM	Y	27720 FQ	37680 MW	44970 TQ	USBLS	5/07
	New York	Y	33180 FQ	41820 MW	52880 TQ	USBLS	5/07
	Albany-Schenectady-Troy MSA, NY	Y	35150 FQ	39820 MW	49220 TQ	USBLS	5/07
	Buffalo-Niagara Falls MSA, NY	Y	29210 FQ	37030 MW	44350 TQ	USBLS	5/07
	Nassau-Suffolk PMSA, NY	Y	33370 FQ	44020 MW	54990 TQ	USBLS	5/07

AE	Average entry wage	AW	Average wage paid	FQ	First quartile wage	LO	Lowest wage paid	MTC	Median total compensation	TCC	Total cash compensation
AER	Average entry range	AWR	Average wage range	H	Hourly	LR	Low end range	MW	Median wage paid	TQ	Third quartile wage
AEX	Average experienced wage	AXR	Average experienced range	HI	Highest wage paid	M	Monthly	MWR	Median wage range	W	Weekly
ATC	Average total compensation	D	Daily	HR	High end range	MCC	Median cash compensation	S	See annotated source	Y	Yearly

Occupation/Type/Industry	Location	Per	Low	Mid	High	Source	Date
Computer, Automated Teller, and Office Machine Repairer	New York-Northern New Jersey-Long Island MSA, NY-NJ-PA	Y	34350 FQ	44020 MW	55200 TQ	USBLS	5/07
	North Carolina	Y	29140 FQ	36340 MW	47180 TQ	USBLS	5/07
	Charlotte-Gastonia-Concord MSA, NC-SC	Y	31710 FQ	37260 MW	45400 TQ	USBLS	5/07
	Greensboro-High Point MSA, NC	Y	36190 FQ	44340 MW	51230 TQ	USBLS	5/07
	Raleigh-Cary MSA, NC	Y	29770 FQ	35980 MW	46790 TQ	USBLS	5/07
	North Dakota	Y	28240 FQ	35180 MW	40410 TQ	USBLS	5/07
	Fargo MSA, ND-MN	Y	29210 FQ	35760 MW	41100 TQ	USBLS	5/07
	Ohio	Y	28940 FQ	36330 MW	45540 TQ	USBLS	5/07
	Cincinnati-Middletown MSA, OH-KY-IN	Y	30210 FQ	38420 MW	48410 TQ	USBLS	5/07
	Cleveland-Elyria-Mentor MSA, OH	Y	28880 FQ	35400 MW	45390 TQ	USBLS	5/07
	Columbus MSA, OH	Y	29230 FQ	37400 MW	45690 TQ	USBLS	5/07
	Dayton MSA, OH	Y	31670 FQ	35570 MW	40310 TQ	USBLS	5/07
	Oklahoma	Y	22410 FQ	32250 MW	44230 TQ	USBLS	5/07
	Oklahoma City MSA, OK	Y	26570 FQ	32870 MW	39370 TQ	USBLS	5/07
	Tulsa MSA, OK	Y	18980 FQ	34930 MW	51320 TQ	USBLS	5/07
	Oregon	H	14.77 FQ	17.97 MW	22.32 TQ	ORBLS	5/08
	Portland-Vancouver-Beaverton MSA, OR-WA	Y	31400 FQ	38090 MW	46900 TQ	USBLS	5/07
	Pennsylvania	Y	32700 FQ	40800 MW	49600 TQ	USBLS	5/07
	Allentown-Bethlehem-Easton MSA, PA-NJ	Y	28710 FQ	36080 MW	46900 TQ	USBLS	5/07
	Philadelphia-Camden-Wilmington MSA, PA-NJ-DE-MD	Y	34780 FQ	42740 MW	51480 TQ	USBLS	5/07
	Pittsburgh MSA, PA	Y	32280 FQ	38890 MW	46110 TQ	USBLS	5/07
	Rhode Island	Y	29840 FQ	36960 MW	45300 TQ	USBLS	5/07
	Providence-Fall River-Warwick MSA, RI-MA	Y	29390 FQ	36370 MW	45030 TQ	USBLS	5/07
	South Carolina	Y	28600 FQ	35210 MW	43440 TQ	USBLS	5/07
	Charleston-North Charleston MSA, SC	Y	32920 FQ	36980 MW	41560 TQ	USBLS	5/07
	Columbia MSA, SC	Y	30810 FQ	37230 MW	43370 TQ	USBLS	5/07
	South Dakota	Y	30738 FQ	36985 MW	43603 TQ	SDBLS	7/08-9/08
	Sioux Falls MSA, SD	Y	32592 FQ	40654 MW	48201 TQ	SDBLS	7/08-9/08
	Tennessee	Y	25550 FQ	31700 MW	40700 TQ	USBLS	5/07
	Memphis MSA, TN-MS-AR	Y	23870 FQ	30290 MW	36650 TQ	USBLS	5/07
	Nashville-Davidson-Murfreesboro MSA, TN	Y	28630 FQ	37770 MW	50140 TQ	USBLS	5/07
	Texas	Y	22300 FQ	29810 MW	39910 TQ	USBLS	5/07
	Austin-Round Rock MSA, TX	Y	25860 FQ	28980 MW	33230 TQ	USBLS	5/07
	Dallas-Fort Worth-Arlington MSA, TX	Y	21040 FQ	31430 MW	42850 TQ	USBLS	5/07
	El Paso MSA, TX	Y	18570 FQ	33010 MW	41320 TQ	USBLS	5/07
	Houston-Sugar Land-Baytown MSA, TX	Y	22110 FQ	28530 MW	38460 TQ	USBLS	5/07
	San Antonio MSA, TX	Y	23110 FQ	31950 MW	45320 TQ	USBLS	5/07
	Utah	Y	30060 FQ	37530 MW	46080 TQ	USBLS	5/07
	Salt Lake City MSA, UT	Y	34800 FQ	39830 MW	47890 TQ	USBLS	5/07
	Vermont	Y	37060 FQ	42640 MW	46760 TQ	USBLS	5/07
	Burlington-South Burlington MSA, VT	Y	39840 FQ	43990 MW	48020 TQ	USBLS	5/07
	Virginia	Y	32910 FQ	40780 MW	51160 TQ	USBLS	5/07
	Richmond MSA, VA	Y	33080 FQ	37740 MW	49730 TQ	USBLS	5/07
	Virginia Beach-Norfolk-Newport News MSA, VA-NC	Y	25510 FQ	38020 MW	47990 TQ	USBLS	5/07
	Washington	H	15.07 FQ	19.09 MW	24.49 TQ	WABLS	3/08
	Seattle-Tacoma-Bellevue MSA, WA	Y	33010 FQ	40770 MW	52880 TQ	USBLS	5/07
	West Virginia	Y	24030 FQ	35784 MW	45439 TQ	WVBLS	7/08-9/08
	Charleston MSA, WV	Y	26530 FQ	37870 MW	46400 TQ	USBLS	5/07
	Wisconsin	Y	27150 FQ	34710 MW	45300 TQ	USBLS	5/07
	Green Bay MSA, WI	Y	19780 FQ	26360 MW	29500 TQ	USBLS	5/07
	Milwaukee-Waukesha-West Allis MSA, WI	Y	28490 FQ	34970 MW	47600 TQ	USBLS	5/07
	Wyoming	Y	22767 FQ	27875 MW	36386 TQ	WYBLS	9/08

AE	Average entry wage	AW	Average wage paid	FQ	First quartile wage	LO	Lowest wage paid	MTC	Median total compensation	TCC	Total cash compensation
AER	Average entry range	AWR	Average wage range	H	Hourly	LR	Low end range	MW	Median wage paid	TQ	Third quartile wage
AEX	Average experienced wage	AXR	Average experienced range	HI	Highest wage paid	M	Monthly	MWR	Median wage range	W	Weekly
ATC	Average total compensation	D	Daily	HR	High end range	MCC	Median cash compensation	S	See annotated source	Y	Yearly

Occupation/Type/Industry	Location	Per	Low	Mid	High	Source	Date
Computer, Automated Teller, and Office Machine Repairer	Cheyenne MSA, WY	Y	28517 FQ	31828 MW	37543 TQ	WYBLS	9/08
	Puerto Rico	Y	16970 FQ	21240 MW	28340 TQ	USBLS	5/07
	San Juan-Caguas-Guaynabo MSA, PR	Y	17310 FQ	21710 MW	28700 TQ	USBLS	5/07
	Guam	Y	13390 FQ	15700 MW	17910 TQ	USBLS	5/07
Computer Acquisition Manager							
State Government	Ohio	H	41.08 LO		53.84 HI	ODAS	2008
Computer-Aided Design Drafter	Houston, TX	Y	50000 LO		80000 HI	HBJ	2008
Computer Analytical Laboratory Administrator							
State Government	Ohio	H	33.83 LO		44.38 HI	ODAS	2008
Computer and Information Scientist							
Research	Alabama	Y	79990 FQ	94230 MW	111890 TQ	USBLS	5/07
Research	Arizona	Y	67050 FQ	88340 MW	105240 TQ	USBLS	5/07
Research	Phoenix-Mesa-Scottsdale MSA, AZ	Y	57920 FQ	98670 MW	120400 TQ	USBLS	5/07
Research	Tucson MSA, AZ	Y	68940 FQ	86790 MW	98190 TQ	USBLS	5/07
Research	California	H	46.04 FQ	56.58 MW	69.08 TQ	CABLS	1/08-3/08
Research	Los Angeles-Long Beach-Glendale PMSA, CA	H	46.65 FQ	59.74 MW		CABLS	1/08-3/08
Research	Oakland-Fremont-Hayward MSA, CA	H	52.22 FQ	61.76 MW		CABLS	1/08-3/08
Research	Sacramento-Arden Arcade-Roseville MSA, CA	H	44.10 FQ	55.99 MW	68.73 TQ	CABLS	1/08-3/08
Research	San Diego-Carlsbad-San Marcos MSA, CA	H	41.69 FQ	48.20 MW	56.91 TQ	CABLS	1/08-3/08
Research	San Francisco-San Mateo-Redwood PMSA, CA	H	49.98 FQ	58.89 MW		CABLS	1/08-3/08
Research	San Jose-Sunnyvale-Santa Clara MSA, CA	H	50.54 FQ	62.49 MW		CABLS	1/08-3/08
Research	Santa Ana-Anaheim-Irvine PMSA, CA	Y	101010 FQ	118250 MW	138980 TQ	USBLS	5/07
Research	Colorado	Y	74410 FQ	93230 MW	119300 TQ	USBLS	5/07
Research	Boulder MSA, CO	Y	79790 FQ	109350 MW	133660 TQ	USBLS	5/07
Research	Denver-Aurora MSA, CO	Y	65380 FQ	78400 MW	97850 TQ	USBLS	5/07
Research	Connecticut	H	38.47 AE	56.14 MW		CTBLS	1/08-3/08
Research	Bridgeport-Stamford-Norwalk MSA, CT	Y	92130 FQ	127290 MW		USBLS	5/07
Research	Hartford-West Hartford-East Hartford MSA, CT	Y	71860 FQ	80260 MW	135980 TQ	USBLS	5/07
Research	Delaware	Y	74440 FQ	87000 MW	112520 TQ	USBLS	5/07
Research	Wilmington PMSA, DE-MD-NJ	Y	74440 FQ	87000 MW	112520 TQ	USBLS	5/07
Research	District of Columbia	Y	80500 FQ	98870 MW	121020 TQ	USBLS	5/07
Research	Washington-Arlington-Alexandria MSA, DC-VA-MD-WV	Y	82500 FQ	102920 MW	124600 TQ	USBLS	5/07
Research	Florida	Y	76810 FQ	95070 MW	118830 TQ	USBLS	5/07
Research	Miami-Fort Lauderdale-Miami Beach MSA, FL	Y	86420 FQ	102820 MW	135170 TQ	USBLS	5/07
Research	Orlando-Kissimmee MSA, FL	Y	88290 FQ	105060 MW	127450 TQ	USBLS	5/07
Research	Tampa-St. Petersburg-Clearwater MSA, FL	Y	82040 FQ	97990 MW	115800 TQ	USBLS	5/07
Research	West Palm Beach-Boca Raton-Boynton Beach PMSA, FL	Y	81710 FQ	90620 MW	100450 TQ	USBLS	5/07
Research	Georgia	Y	66510 FQ	91170 MW	123980 TQ	USBLS	5/07
Research	Atlanta-Sandy Springs-Marietta MSA, GA	Y	75650 FQ	107380 MW	133440 TQ	USBLS	5/07
Research	Idaho	Y	67020 FQ	84340 MW	101350 TQ	USBLS	5/07
Research	Illinois	Y	71520 FQ	92110 MW	117660 TQ	USBLS	5/07
Research	Chicago-Naperville-Joliet MSA, IL-IN-WI	Y	71940 FQ	92100 MW	118080 TQ	USBLS	5/07
Research	Indiana	Y	63240 FQ	80300 MW	99880 TQ	USBLS	5/07
Research	Indianapolis-Carmel MSA, IN	Y	66590 FQ	89770 MW	105320 TQ	USBLS	5/07
Research	Kansas	Y	60280 FQ	73350 MW	88490 TQ	USBLS	5/07

Computer and Information Scientist

Occupation/Type/Industry	Location	Per	Low	Mid	High	Source	Date
Research	Kentucky	Y	69795 FQ	93161 MW	125011 TQ	KYBLS	2008
Research	Louisiana	H	32.16 FQ	35.25 MW	38.34 TQ	LABLS	1/08-3/08
Research	Baton Rouge MSA, LA	Y	70040 FQ	75170 MW	80300 TQ	USBLS	5/07
Research	Maryland	Y		99800 MW		MDBLS	3/08
Research	Baltimore-Towson MSA, MD	Y	74040 FQ	93040 MW	113790 TQ	USBLS	5/07
Research	Bethesda-Gaithersburg-Frederick PMSA, MD	Y	81990 FQ	104440 MW	124960 TQ	USBLS	5/07
Research	Massachusetts	Y	97450 FQ	120460 MW	144790 TQ	USBLS	5/07
Research	Boston-Cambridge-Quincy NECTA, MA	Y	99660 FQ	121640 MW		USBLS	5/07
Research	Worcester MSA, MA-CT	Y	84590 FQ	116480 MW	137790 TQ	USBLS	5/07
Research	Michigan	Y	39400 FQ	69770 MW	97120 TQ	USBLS	5/07
Research	Detroit-Warren-Livonia MSA, MI	Y	39020 FQ	73500 MW	98010 TQ	USBLS	5/07
Research	Warren-Troy-Farmington Hills PMSA, MI	Y	38570 FQ	69840 MW	97210 TQ	USBLS	5/07
Research	Minnesota	Y	100197 FQ	122492 MW	143228 TQ	MNBLS	10/08-12/08
Research	Minneapolis-Saint Paul MSA, MN-WI	Y	99558 FQ	121937 MW	142956 TQ	MNBLS	10/08-12/08
Research	Mississippi	Y	64290 FQ	77440 MW	94810 TQ	USBLS	5/07
Research	Missouri	Y	58220 FQ	69140 MW	90040 TQ	USBLS	5/07
Research	Kansas City MSA, MO-KS	Y	57950 FQ	67400 MW	81580 TQ	USBLS	5/07
Research	St. Louis MSA, MO-IL	Y	67200 FQ	90010 MW	112480 TQ	USBLS	5/07
Research	Montana	Y	28580 FQ	42100 MW	59460 TQ	USBLS	5/07
Research	Nevada	H	39.80 FQ	51.76 MW	61.54 TQ	NVBLS	5/08
Research	Las Vegas-Paradise MSA, NV	H	38.43 FQ	53.87 MW	62.67 TQ	NVBLS	5/08
Research	New Hampshire	H	39.21 AE	52.37 MW	59.26 AEX	NHBLS	6/08
Research	Nashua NECTA, NH-MA	Y	89460 FQ	108220 MW	124230 TQ	USBLS	5/07
Research	New Jersey	Y	76740 FQ	100200 MW	125410 TQ	USBLS	5/07
Research	Edison PMSA, NJ	Y	80850 FQ	106630 MW	130950 TQ	USBLS	5/07
Research	Newark-Union PMSA, NJ-PA	Y	65890 FQ	83020 MW	102600 TQ	USBLS	5/07
Research	New Mexico	Y	62640 FQ	81370 MW	101960 TQ	USBLS	5/07
Research	Albuquerque MSA, NM	Y	69840 FQ	82530 MW	103360 TQ	USBLS	5/07
Research	New York	Y	75820 FQ	105040 MW	134860 TQ	USBLS	5/07
Research	Buffalo-Niagara Falls MSA, NY	Y	61930 FQ	86170 MW	119540 TQ	USBLS	5/07
Research	Nassau-Suffolk PMSA, NY	Y	66810 FQ	96230 MW	122260 TQ	USBLS	5/07
Research	New York-Northern New Jersey-Long Island MSA, NY-NJ-PA	Y	80190 FQ	107120 MW	135560 TQ	USBLS	5/07
Research	North Carolina	Y	59710 FQ	91430 MW	117790 TQ	USBLS	5/07
Research	Charlotte-Gastonia-Concord MSA, NC-SC	Y	84230 FQ	107040 MW	120740 TQ	USBLS	5/07
Research	Ohio	Y	74380 FQ	92960 MW	112590 TQ	USBLS	5/07
Research	Cincinnati-Middletown MSA, OH-KY-IN	Y	82220 FQ	98840 MW	117760 TQ	USBLS	5/07
Research	Cleveland-Elyria-Mentor MSA, OH	Y	62240 FQ	90490 MW	115990 TQ	USBLS	5/07
Research	Columbus MSA, OH	Y	74240 FQ	90150 MW	106320 TQ	USBLS	5/07
Research	Dayton MSA, OH	Y	83380 FQ	95370 MW	111490 TQ	USBLS	5/07
Research	Oklahoma	Y	66340 FQ	76430 MW	89200 TQ	USBLS	5/07
Research	Oklahoma City MSA, OK	Y	67410 FQ	76540 MW	88610 TQ	USBLS	5/07
Research	Tulsa MSA, OK	Y	71020 FQ	80970 MW	95590 TQ	USBLS	5/07
Research	Pennsylvania	Y	45800 FQ	70940 MW	98160 TQ	USBLS	5/07
Research	Philadelphia-Camden-Wilmington MSA, PA-NJ-DE-MD	Y	73410 FQ	93830 MW	124070 TQ	USBLS	5/07
Research	Pittsburgh MSA, PA	Y	37510 FQ	50890 MW	72810 TQ	USBLS	5/07
Research	Rhode Island	Y	84490 FQ	95620 MW	111800 TQ	USBLS	5/07
Research	Providence-Fall River-Warwick MSA, RI-MA	Y	84490 FQ	95620 MW	111800 TQ	USBLS	5/07
Research	South Carolina	Y	65890 FQ	80540 MW	104210 TQ	USBLS	5/07
Research	Columbia MSA, SC	Y	109170 FQ	116630 MW	124100 TQ	USBLS	5/07
Research	Tennessee	Y	73430 FQ	89650 MW	116200 TQ	USBLS	5/07
Research	Nashville-Davidson-Murfreesboro MSA, TN	Y	99390 FQ	116150 MW	135430 TQ	USBLS	5/07
Research	Texas	Y	61240 FQ	93340 MW	119200 TQ	USBLS	5/07
Research	Austin-Round Rock MSA, TX	Y	71270 FQ	105650 MW	126550 TQ	USBLS	5/07

AE	Average entry wage	AW	Average wage paid	FQ	First quartile wage	LO	Lowest wage paid	MTC	Median total compensation	TCC	Total cash compensation
AER	Average entry range	AWR	Average wage range	H	Hourly	LR	Low end range	MW	Median wage paid	TQ	Third quartile wage
AEX	Average experienced wage	AXR	Average experienced range	HI	Highest wage paid	M	Monthly	MWR	Median wage range	W	Weekly
ATC	Average total compensation	D	Daily	HR	High end range	MCC	Median cash compensation	S	See annotated source	Y	Yearly

Occupation/Type/Industry	Location	Per	Low	Mid	High	Source	Date
Computer and Information Scientist							
Research	Dallas-Fort Worth-Arlington MSA, TX	Y	49550 FQ	77970 MW	113990 TQ	USBLS	5/07
Research	Houston-Sugar Land-Baytown MSA, TX	Y	58710 FQ	86470 MW	108960 TQ	USBLS	5/07
Research	San Antonio MSA, TX	Y	66250 FQ	84270 MW	100490 TQ	USBLS	5/07
Research	Salt Lake City MSA, UT	Y	53500 FQ	71620 MW	93600 TQ	USBLS	5/07
Research	Virginia	Y	78270 FQ	95580 MW	117980 TQ	USBLS	5/07
Research	Richmond MSA, VA	Y	67880 FQ	75570 MW	90710 TQ	USBLS	5/07
Research	Virginia Beach-Norfolk-Newport News MSA, VA-NC	Y	72110 FQ	87010 MW	98130 TQ	USBLS	5/07
Research	Washington	H	40.22 FQ	47.58 MW	59.63 TQ	WABLS	3/08
Research	Seattle-Tacoma-Bellevue MSA, WA	Y	86610 FQ	101440 MW	127740 TQ	USBLS	5/07
Research	Wisconsin	Y	67180 FQ	85010 MW	109080 TQ	USBLS	5/07
Research	Milwaukee-Waukesha-West Allis MSA, WI	Y	63890 FQ	82620 MW	112790 TQ	USBLS	5/07
Computer and Information Systems Manager							
	Alabama	Y	76390 FQ	94330 MW	116010 TQ	USBLS	5/07
	Birmingham-Hoover MSA, AL	Y	79890 FQ	96340 MW	118050 TQ	USBLS	5/07
	Mobile MSA, AL	Y	68170 FQ	84810 MW	111180 TQ	USBLS	5/07
	Alaska	Y	68620 FQ	84990 MW	100230 TQ	USBLS	5/07
	Anchorage MSA, AK	Y	69820 FQ	87220 MW	102910 TQ	USBLS	5/07
	Arizona	Y	69960 FQ	94500 MW	121260 TQ	USBLS	5/07
	Phoenix-Mesa-Scottsdale MSA, AZ	Y	74420 FQ	97520 MW	123830 TQ	USBLS	5/07
	Tucson MSA, AZ	Y	58660 FQ	80350 MW	113090 TQ	USBLS	5/07
	Arkansas	Y	62870 FQ	80450 MW	104590 TQ	USBLS	5/07
	Little Rock-North Little Rock MSA, AR	Y	66180 FQ	88130 MW	114640 TQ	USBLS	5/07
	California	H	46.23 FQ	58.96 MW		CABLS	1/08-3/08
	Los Angeles-Long Beach-Glendale PMSA, CA	H	45.37 FQ	56.86 MW		CABLS	1/08-3/08
	Modesto MSA, CA	H	38.40 FQ	47.38 MW	59.93 TQ	CABLS	1/08-3/08
	Oakland-Fremont-Hayward MSA, CA	H	49.10 FQ	61.55 MW		CABLS	1/08-3/08
	Riverside-San Bernardino-Ontario MSA, CA	H	36.82 FQ	46.84 MW	58.33 TQ	CABLS	1/08-3/08
	Sacramento-Arden Arcade-Roseville MSA, CA	H	41.35 FQ	47.19 MW	54.81 TQ	CABLS	1/08-3/08
	San Diego-Carlsbad-San Marcos MSA, CA	H	40.53 FQ	51.07 MW	63.41 TQ	CABLS	1/08-3/08
	San Francisco-San Mateo-Redwood PMSA, CA	H	54.11 FQ	65.91 MW		CABLS	1/08-3/08
	San Jose-Sunnyvale-Santa Clara MSA, CA	H	55.69 FQ			CABLS	1/08-3/08
	Santa Ana-Anaheim-Irvine PMSA, CA	Y	89170 FQ	117570 MW		USBLS	5/07
	Colorado	Y	93250 FQ	112150 MW	133070 TQ	USBLS	5/07
	Denver-Aurora MSA, CO	Y	95190 FQ	113080 MW	133710 TQ	USBLS	5/07
	Connecticut	H	36.32 AE	52.31 MW		CTBLS	1/08-3/08
	Bridgeport-Stamford-Norwalk MSA, CT	Y	100630 FQ	124830 MW		USBLS	5/07
	Hartford-West Hartford-East Hartford MSA, CT	Y	83160 FQ	102050 MW	128540 TQ	USBLS	5/07
	Delaware	Y	92750 FQ	120830 MW		USBLS	5/07
	Wilmington PMSA, DE-MD-NJ	Y	97410 FQ	124940 MW		USBLS	5/07
	District of Columbia	Y	102110 FQ	119480 MW	138940 TQ	USBLS	5/07
	Washington-Arlington-Alexandria MSA, DC-VA-MD-WV	Y	104170 FQ	124210 MW		USBLS	5/07
	Florida	Y	84580 FQ	104810 MW	130490 TQ	USBLS	5/07
	Cape Coral-Fort Myers MSA, FL	Y	75840 FQ	95100 MW	120320 TQ	USBLS	5/07
	Fort Lauderdale-Pompano Beach-Deerfield Beach PMSA, FL	Y	88240 FQ	110510 MW	130880 TQ	USBLS	5/07
	Jacksonville MSA, FL	Y	89090 FQ	111110 MW	143700 TQ	USBLS	5/07

AE Average entry wage	**AW** Average wage paid	**FQ** First quartile wage	**LO** Lowest wage paid	**MTC** Median total compensation	**TCC** Total cash compensation
AER Average entry range	**AWR** Average wage range	**H** Hourly	**LR** Low end range	**MW** Median wage paid	**TQ** Third quartile wage
AEX Average experienced wage	**AXR** Average experienced range	**HI** Highest wage paid	**M** Monthly	**MWR** Median wage range	**W** Weekly
ATC Average total compensation	**D** Daily	**HR** High end range	**MCC** Median cash compensation	**S** See annotated source	**Y** Yearly

Computer and Information Systems Manager

Occupation/Type/Industry	Location	Per	Low	Mid	High	Source	Date
Computer and Information Systems Manager	Lakeland MSA, FL	Y	82520 FQ	105220 MW	126960 TQ	USBLS	5/07
	Miami-Fort Lauderdale-Miami Beach MSA, FL	Y	87570 FQ	109480 MW	133380 TQ	USBLS	5/07
	Orlando-Kissimmee MSA, FL	Y	86080 FQ	104030 MW	128830 TQ	USBLS	5/07
	Tallahassee MSA, FL	Y	76090 FQ	89720 MW	106010 TQ	USBLS	5/07
	Tampa-St. Petersburg-Clearwater MSA, FL	Y	82250 FQ	101300 MW	129760 TQ	USBLS	5/07
	West Palm Beach-Boca Raton-Boynton Beach PMSA, FL	Y	90160 FQ	113310 MW	141500 TQ	USBLS	5/07
	Georgia	Y	81320 FQ	101510 MW	128260 TQ	USBLS	5/07
	Atlanta-Sandy Springs-Marietta MSA, GA	Y	84710 FQ	103960 MW	131120 TQ	USBLS	5/07
	Augusta-Richmond County MSA, GA-SC	Y	69600 FQ	93530 MW	118600 TQ	USBLS	5/07
	Hawaii	Y	73150 FQ	93640 MW	114090 TQ	USBLS	5/07
	Honolulu MSA, HI	Y	75340 FQ	95040 MW	115630 TQ	USBLS	5/07
	Idaho	Y	54930 FQ	77010 MW	97950 TQ	USBLS	5/07
	Boise City-Nampa MSA, ID	Y	65170 FQ	83200 MW	103580 TQ	USBLS	5/07
	Idaho Falls MSA, ID	Y	55890 FQ	76580 MW	99130 TQ	USBLS	5/07
	Illinois	Y	79920 FQ	102260 MW	130920 TQ	USBLS	5/07
	Chicago-Naperville-Joliet MSA, IL-IN-WI	Y	83420 FQ	106060 MW	133940 TQ	USBLS	5/07
	Indiana	Y	65440 FQ	86290 MW	108800 TQ	USBLS	5/07
	Gary PMSA, IN	Y	68030 FQ	82870 MW	101660 TQ	USBLS	5/07
	Indianapolis-Carmel MSA, IN	Y	73430 FQ	93460 MW	115770 TQ	USBLS	5/07
	Iowa	Y	72300 FQ	91420 MW	112110 TQ	USBLS	5/07
	Davenport-Moline-Rock Island MSA, IA-IL	Y	58210 FQ	79010 MW	98820 TQ	USBLS	5/07
	Des Moines-West Des Moines MSA, IA	Y	80300 FQ	96440 MW	116510 TQ	USBLS	5/07
	Kansas	Y	71010 FQ	89110 MW	113540 TQ	USBLS	5/07
	Lawrence MSA, KS	Y	60560 FQ	73370 MW	85370 TQ	USBLS	5/07
	Wichita MSA, KS	Y	70080 FQ	88120 MW	105080 TQ	USBLS	5/07
	Kentucky	Y	69796 FQ	87964 MW	109328 TQ	KYBLS	2008
	Elizabethtown MSA, KY	Y	62710 FQ	85280 MW	105760 TQ	USBLS	5/07
	Louisville-Jefferson County MSA, KY-IN	Y	75080 FQ	91570 MW	110130 TQ	USBLS	5/07
	Louisiana	H	28.37 FQ	38.91 MW	47.82 TQ	LABLS	1/08-3/08
	Baton Rouge MSA, LA	Y	60100 FQ	80040 MW	97180 TQ	USBLS	5/07
	Lafayette MSA, LA	Y	56270 FQ	75080 MW	92370 TQ	USBLS	5/07
	New Orleans-Metairie-Kenner MSA, LA	Y	63570 FQ	86260 MW	101930 TQ	USBLS	5/07
	Maine	Y	66480 FQ	83130 MW	110520 TQ	USBLS	5/07
	Bangor MSA, ME	Y	57430 FQ	73080 MW	96150 TQ	USBLS	5/07
	Portland-South Portland-Biddeford MSA, ME	Y	75970 FQ	98210 MW	125740 TQ	USBLS	5/07
	Maryland	Y		119350 MW		MDBLS	3/08
	Baltimore-Towson MSA, MD	Y	88610 FQ	112940 MW	138580 TQ	USBLS	5/07
	Bethesda-Gaithersburg-Frederick PMSA, MD	Y	99730 FQ	123120 MW		USBLS	5/07
	Massachusetts	Y	93000 FQ	118220 MW		USBLS	5/07
	Boston-Cambridge-Quincy NECTA, MA	Y	94940 FQ	118840 MW		USBLS	5/07
	Lynn-Peabody-Salem NECTA, MA	Y	84890 FQ	118120 MW	143020 TQ	USBLS	5/07
	Worcester MSA, MA-CT	Y	75230 FQ	101590 MW	133720 TQ	USBLS	5/07
	Michigan	Y	76980 FQ	97830 MW	122050 TQ	USBLS	5/07
	Detroit-Warren-Livonia MSA, MI	Y	83280 FQ	105480 MW	130530 TQ	USBLS	5/07
	Grand Rapids-Wyoming MSA, MI	Y	68250 FQ	87830 MW	106740 TQ	USBLS	5/07
	Muskegon-Norton Shores MSA, MI	Y	82250 FQ	91860 MW	102300 TQ	USBLS	5/07
	Warren-Troy-Farmington Hills PMSA, MI	Y	78630 FQ	99750 MW	123860 TQ	USBLS	5/07
	Minnesota	Y	94120 FQ	114629 MW	137025 TQ	MNBLS	10/08-12/08
	Duluth-Superior MSA, MN-WI	Y	79398 FQ	94203 MW	107966 TQ	MNBLS	10/08-12/08
	Minneapolis-Saint Paul MSA, MN-WI	Y	96163 FQ	116287 MW	138089 TQ	MNBLS	10/08-12/08
	Rochester MSA, MN	Y	107190 FQ	129798 MW		MNBLS	10/08-12/08
	Mississippi	Y	56020 FQ	69600 MW	87970 TQ	USBLS	5/07

AE	Average entry wage	**AW**	Average wage paid	**FQ**	First quartile wage
AER	Average entry range	**AWR**	Average wage range	**H**	Hourly
AEX	Average experienced wage	**AXR**	Average experienced range	**HI**	Highest wage paid
ATC	Average total compensation	**D**	Daily	**HR**	High end range

LO	Lowest wage paid	**MTC**	Median total compensation	**TCC** Total cash compensation
LR	Low end range	**MW**	Median wage paid	**TQ** Third quartile wage
M	Monthly	**MWR**	Median wage range	**W** Weekly
MCC	Median cash compensation	**S**	See annotated source	**Y** Yearly

Occupation/Type/Industry	Location	Per	Low	Mid	High	Source	Date
Computer and Information Systems Manager	Jackson MSA, MS	Y	57930 FQ	69600 MW	83910 TQ	USBLS	5/07
	Missouri	Y	77840 FQ	94590 MW	114650 TQ	USBLS	5/07
	Kansas City MSA, MO-KS	Y	81230 FQ	97450 MW	120100 TQ	USBLS	5/07
	St. Louis MSA, MO-IL	Y	81040 FQ	97150 MW	117860 TQ	USBLS	5/07
	Montana	Y	62180 FQ	74960 MW	92720 TQ	USBLS	5/07
	Billings MSA, MT	Y	56560 FQ	65300 MW	79890 TQ	USBLS	5/07
	Nebraska	Y	76390 FQ	94650 MW	117750 TQ	USBLS	5/07
	Omaha-Council Bluffs MSA, NE-IA	Y	80820 FQ	99870 MW	122730 TQ	USBLS	5/07
	Nevada	H	36.08 FQ	45.20 MW	55.91 TQ	NVBLS	5/08
	Las Vegas-Paradise MSA, NV	H	34.61 FQ	44.67 MW	54.81 TQ	NVBLS	5/08
	Reno-Sparks MSA, NV	H	39.41 FQ	48.54 MW	63.23 TQ	NVBLS	5/08
	New Hampshire	H	37.26 AE	51.68 MW	63.10 AEX	NHBLS	6/08
	Manchester MSA, NH	Y	82580 FQ	104870 MW	139010 TQ	USBLS	5/07
	Nashua NECTA, NH-MA	Y	94920 FQ	115540 MW	139850 TQ	USBLS	5/07
	New Jersey	Y	101410 FQ	125910 MW		USBLS	5/07
	Camden PMSA, NJ	Y	96040 FQ	116350 MW	137990 TQ	USBLS	5/07
	Edison PMSA, NJ	Y	107440 FQ	130200 MW		USBLS	5/07
	Newark-Union PMSA, NJ-PA	Y	103900 FQ	128400 MW		USBLS	5/07
	New Mexico	Y	67420 FQ	85830 MW	109380 TQ	USBLS	5/07
	Albuquerque MSA, NM	Y	71930 FQ	86920 MW	106190 TQ	USBLS	5/07
	New York	Y	99140 FQ	127460 MW		USBLS	5/07
	Albany-Schenectady-Troy MSA, NY	Y	85940 FQ	98720 MW	116980 TQ	USBLS	5/07
	Buffalo-Niagara Falls MSA, NY	Y	78540 FQ	97560 MW	117760 TQ	USBLS	5/07
	Nassau-Suffolk PMSA, NY	Y	94110 FQ	119320 MW		USBLS	5/07
	New York-Northern New Jersey-Long Island MSA, NY-NJ-PA	Y	106920 FQ	133480 MW		USBLS	5/07
	Utica-Rome MSA, NY	Y	70280 FQ	87130 MW	103100 TQ	USBLS	5/07
	North Carolina	Y	85770 FQ	106690 MW	131440 TQ	USBLS	5/07
	Charlotte-Gastonia-Concord MSA, NC-SC	Y	91680 FQ	112950 MW	136270 TQ	USBLS	5/07
	Raleigh-Cary MSA, NC	Y	86620 FQ	103510 MW	125350 TQ	USBLS	5/07
	North Dakota	Y	59240 FQ	73850 MW	85680 TQ	USBLS	5/07
	Fargo MSA, ND-MN	Y	67650 FQ	75850 MW	85080 TQ	USBLS	5/07
	Ohio	Y	83370 FQ	102200 MW	125660 TQ	USBLS	5/07
	Cincinnati-Middletown MSA, OH-KY-IN	Y	83320 FQ	102790 MW	126780 TQ	USBLS	5/07
	Cleveland-Elyria-Mentor MSA, OH	Y	86120 FQ	103460 MW	125470 TQ	USBLS	5/07
	Columbus MSA, OH	Y	86590 FQ	105610 MW	130540 TQ	USBLS	5/07
	Dayton MSA, OH	Y	87280 FQ	104880 MW	124450 TQ	USBLS	5/07
	Oklahoma	Y	62540 FQ	80760 MW	101170 TQ	USBLS	5/07
	Oklahoma City MSA, OK	Y	68620 FQ	84110 MW	101050 TQ	USBLS	5/07
	Tulsa MSA, OK	Y	66650 FQ	87150 MW	108330 TQ	USBLS	5/07
	Oregon	H	39.48 FQ	48.39 MW	60.32 TQ	ORBLS	5/08
	Portland-Vancouver-Beaverton MSA, OR-WA	Y	85320 FQ	102290 MW	127660 TQ	USBLS	5/07
	Pennsylvania	Y	80370 FQ	105010 MW	137690 TQ	USBLS	5/07
	Allentown-Bethlehem-Easton MSA, PA-NJ	Y	81760 FQ	100660 MW	124530 TQ	USBLS	5/07
	Philadelphia-Camden-Wilmington MSA, PA-NJ-DE-MD	Y	93910 FQ	120470 MW		USBLS	5/07
	Pittsburgh MSA, PA	Y	71130 FQ	95520 MW	123270 TQ	USBLS	5/07
	Rhode Island	Y	90610 FQ	106700 MW	131950 TQ	USBLS	5/07
	Providence-Fall River-Warwick MSA, RI-MA	Y	90300 FQ	106800 MW	132810 TQ	USBLS	5/07
	South Carolina	Y	71100 FQ	89030 MW	110710 TQ	USBLS	5/07
	Charleston-North Charleston MSA, SC	Y	71520 FQ	87210 MW	103020 TQ	USBLS	5/07
	Columbia MSA, SC	Y	70670 FQ	87410 MW	105390 TQ	USBLS	5/07
	South Dakota	Y	79839 FQ	95055 MW	115683 TQ	SDBLS	7/08-9/08
	Rapid City MSA, SD	Y	87945 FQ	95207 MW	103141 TQ	SDBLS	7/08-9/08
	Sioux Falls MSA, SD	Y	79998 FQ	96801 MW	121861 TQ	SDBLS	7/08-9/08
	Tennessee	Y	57830 FQ	79720 MW	103360 TQ	USBLS	5/07
	Johnson City MSA, TN	Y	44080 FQ	80820 MW	98070 TQ	USBLS	5/07
	Memphis MSA, TN-MS-AR	Y	60610 FQ	79990 MW	98730 TQ	USBLS	5/07

AE Average entry wage	**AW** Average wage paid	**FQ** First quartile wage	**LO** Lowest wage paid	**MTC** Median total compensation	**TCC** Total cash compensation
AER Average entry range	**AWR** Average wage range	**H** Hourly	**LR** Low end range	**MW** Median wage paid	**TQ** Third quartile wage
AEX Average experienced wage	**AXR** Average experienced range	**HI** Highest wage paid	**M** Monthly	**MWR** Median wage range	**W** Weekly
ATC Average total compensation	**D** Daily	**HR** High end range	**MCC** Median cash compensation	**S** See annotated source	**Y** Yearly

Occupation/Type/Industry	Location	Per	Low	Mid	High	Source	Date
Computer and Information Systems Manager	Nashville-Davidson-Murfreesboro MSA, TN	Y	62760 FQ	84120 MW	110190 TQ	USBLS	5/07
	Texas	Y	86490 FQ	109140 MW	137250 TQ	USBLS	5/07
	Austin-Round Rock MSA, TX	Y	91570 FQ	117630 MW		USBLS	5/07
	Dallas-Fort Worth-Arlington MSA, TX	Y	89420 FQ	111270 MW	136310 TQ	USBLS	5/07
	El Paso MSA, TX	Y	83210 FQ	95650 MW	109230 TQ	USBLS	5/07
	Houston-Sugar Land-Baytown MSA, TX	Y	88800 FQ	113010 MW	141210 TQ	USBLS	5/07
	San Antonio MSA, TX	Y	78550 FQ	95310 MW	120420 TQ	USBLS	5/07
	Utah	Y	73000 FQ	90260 MW	107780 TQ	USBLS	5/07
	Ogden-Clearfield MSA, UT	Y	84410 FQ	95690 MW	115890 TQ	USBLS	5/07
	Salt Lake City MSA, UT	Y	69870 FQ	86610 MW	107920 TQ	USBLS	5/07
	Vermont	Y	76160 FQ	91100 MW	112850 TQ	USBLS	5/07
	Burlington-South Burlington MSA, VT	Y	85010 FQ	99080 MW	127420 TQ	USBLS	5/07
	Virginia	Y	100460 FQ	123000 MW		USBLS	5/07
	Richmond MSA, VA	Y	99230 FQ	118360 MW	137020 TQ	USBLS	5/07
	Virginia Beach-Norfolk-Newport News MSA, VA-NC	Y	84790 FQ	101590 MW	122680 TQ	USBLS	5/07
	Washington	H	46.12 FQ	57.47 MW		WABLS	3/08
	Bremerton-Silverdale MSA, WA	Y	78310 FQ	93050 MW	110530 TQ	USBLS	5/07
	Seattle-Tacoma-Bellevue MSA, WA	Y	100150 FQ	123700 MW		USBLS	5/07
	West Virginia	Y	63698 FQ	82716 MW	105807 TQ	WVBLS	7/08-9/08
	Charleston MSA, WV	Y	58100 FQ	67650 MW	78950 TQ	USBLS	5/07
	Wisconsin	Y	73700 FQ	91950 MW	113010 TQ	USBLS	5/07
	Milwaukee-Waukesha-West Allis MSA, WI	Y	76300 FQ	96940 MW	121460 TQ	USBLS	5/07
	Wyoming	Y	56944 FQ	64881 MW	75782 TQ	WYBLS	9/08
	Cheyenne MSA, WY	Y	60636 FQ	67298 MW	77400 TQ	WYBLS	9/08
	Puerto Rico	Y	53420 FQ	74270 MW	96050 TQ	USBLS	5/07
	San Juan-Caguas-Guaynabo MSA, PR	Y	55510 FQ	75120 MW	96670 TQ	USBLS	5/07
	Guam	Y	40060 FQ	51490 MW	65860 TQ	USBLS	5/07
Computer-Controlled Machine Tool Operator							
Metals and Plastics	Alabama	Y	21920 FQ	26950 MW	31770 TQ	USBLS	5/07
Metals and Plastics	Birmingham-Hoover MSA, AL	Y	21450 FQ	24630 MW	32270 TQ	USBLS	5/07
Metals and Plastics	Arizona	Y	26090 FQ	33130 MW	40060 TQ	USBLS	5/07
Metals and Plastics	Phoenix-Mesa-Scottsdale MSA, AZ	Y	27390 FQ	33640 MW	39920 TQ	USBLS	5/07
Metals and Plastics	Tucson MSA, AZ	Y	23210 FQ	32870 MW	42230 TQ	USBLS	5/07
Metals and Plastics	Arkansas	Y	27710 FQ	32440 MW	36430 TQ	USBLS	5/07
Metals and Plastics	Little Rock-North Little Rock MSA, AR	Y	35390 FQ	41660 MW	45730 TQ	USBLS	5/07
Metals and Plastics	California	H	11.73 FQ	15.02 MW	19.22 TQ	CABLS	1/08-3/08
Metals and Plastics	Los Angeles-Long Beach-Glendale PMSA, CA	H	10.88 FQ	14.46 MW	18.73 TQ	CABLS	1/08-3/08
Metals and Plastics	Oakland-Fremont-Hayward MSA, CA	H	12.32 FQ	15.59 MW	20.76 TQ	CABLS	1/08-3/08
Metals and Plastics	Riverside-San Bernardino-Ontario MSA, CA	H	11.77 FQ	14.07 MW	16.54 TQ	CABLS	1/08-3/08
Metals and Plastics	Sacramento-Arden Arcade-Roseville MSA, CA	H	14.03 FQ	17.40 MW	20.96 TQ	CABLS	1/08-3/08
Metals and Plastics	San Diego-Carlsbad-San Marcos MSA, CA	H	12.14 FQ	14.62 MW	18.60 TQ	CABLS	1/08-3/08
Metals and Plastics	San Francisco-San Mateo-Redwood PMSA, CA	H	13.81 FQ	17.10 MW	22.90 TQ	CABLS	1/08-3/08
Metals and Plastics	San Jose-Sunnyvale-Santa Clara MSA, CA	H	13.56 FQ	15.53 MW	21.73 TQ	CABLS	1/08-3/08
Metals and Plastics	Santa Ana-Anaheim-Irvine PMSA, CA	Y	23610 FQ	31800 MW	41370 TQ	USBLS	5/07
Metals and Plastics	Colorado	Y	25640 FQ	32170 MW	39350 TQ	USBLS	5/07
Metals and Plastics	Denver-Aurora MSA, CO	Y	24740 FQ	31080 MW	38040 TQ	USBLS	5/07
Metals and Plastics	Connecticut	H	14.04 AE	19.44 MW		CTBLS	1/08-3/08
Metals and Plastics	Bridgeport-Stamford-Norwalk MSA, CT	Y	30200 FQ	40420 MW	51730 TQ	USBLS	5/07

AE	Average entry wage	AW	Average wage paid	FQ	First quartile wage	LO Lowest wage paid	MTC Median total compensation	TCC Total cash compensation
AER	Average entry range	AWR	Average wage range	H	Hourly	LR Low end range	MW Median wage paid	TQ Third quartile wage
AEX	Average experienced wage	AXR	Average experienced range	HI	Highest wage paid	M Monthly	MWR Median wage range	W Weekly
ATC	Average total compensation	D	Daily	HR	High end range	MCC Median cash compensation	S See annotated source	Y Yearly

Occupation/Type/Industry	Location	Per	Low	Mid	High	Source	Date
Computer-Controlled Machine Tool Operator							
Metals and Plastics	Hartford-West Hartford-East Hartford MSA, CT	Y	33830 FQ	39910 MW	46130 TQ	USBLS	5/07
Metals and Plastics	Delaware	Y	26840 FQ	30540 MW	39090 TQ	USBLS	5/07
Metals and Plastics	Wilmington PMSA, DE-MD-NJ	Y	26940 FQ	31070 MW	40150 TQ	USBLS	5/07
Metals and Plastics	Washington-Arlington-Alexandria MSA, DC-VA-MD-WV	Y	30550 FQ	36890 MW	46340 TQ	USBLS	5/07
Metals and Plastics	Florida	Y	21800 FQ	28300 MW	36420 TQ	USBLS	5/07
Metals and Plastics	Fort Lauderdale-Pompano Beach-Deerfield Beach PMSA, FL	Y	28940 FQ	34870 MW	38820 TQ	USBLS	5/07
Metals and Plastics	Jacksonville MSA, FL	Y	22690 FQ	28190 MW	34480 TQ	USBLS	5/07
Metals and Plastics	Miami-Fort Lauderdale-Miami Beach MSA, FL	Y	19330 FQ	26010 MW	35580 TQ	USBLS	5/07
Metals and Plastics	Orlando-Kissimmee MSA, FL	Y	19670 FQ	23120 MW	37800 TQ	USBLS	5/07
Metals and Plastics	Tampa-St. Petersburg-Clearwater MSA, FL	Y	26310 FQ	31370 MW	37510 TQ	USBLS	5/07
Metals and Plastics	Georgia	Y	23340 FQ	29180 MW	35550 TQ	USBLS	5/07
Metals and Plastics	Atlanta-Sandy Springs-Marietta MSA, GA	Y	25380 FQ	30290 MW	37620 TQ	USBLS	5/07
Metals and Plastics	Idaho	Y	21550 FQ	26560 MW	34240 TQ	USBLS	5/07
Metals and Plastics	Boise City-Nampa MSA, ID	Y	21150 FQ	27510 MW	33700 TQ	USBLS	5/07
Metals and Plastics	Illinois	Y	26680 FQ	34690 MW	43610 TQ	USBLS	5/07
Metals and Plastics	Chicago-Naperville-Joliet MSA, IL-IN-WI	Y	27750 FQ	35800 MW	45400 TQ	USBLS	5/07
Metals and Plastics	Indiana	Y	25040 FQ	31280 MW	38470 TQ	USBLS	5/07
Metals and Plastics	Elkhart-Goshen MSA, IN	Y	24210 FQ	30310 MW	36660 TQ	USBLS	5/07
Metals and Plastics	Gary PMSA, IN	Y	28430 FQ	37130 MW	52900 TQ	USBLS	5/07
Metals and Plastics	Indianapolis-Carmel MSA, IN	Y	26610 FQ	32930 MW	40710 TQ	USBLS	5/07
Metals and Plastics	Iowa	Y	26810 FQ	32410 MW	38470 TQ	USBLS	5/07
Metals and Plastics	Des Moines-West Des Moines MSA, IA	Y	23360 FQ	27770 MW	32620 TQ	USBLS	5/07
Metals and Plastics	Kansas	Y	26650 FQ	32450 MW	40920 TQ	USBLS	5/07
Metals and Plastics	Wichita MSA, KS	Y	27340 FQ	36380 MW	49100 TQ	USBLS	5/07
Metals and Plastics	Kentucky	Y	24963 FQ	32127 MW	40333 TQ	KYBLS	2008
Metals and Plastics	Louisville-Jefferson County MSA, KY-IN	Y	24280 FQ	31320 MW	40310 TQ	USBLS	5/07
Metals and Plastics	Louisiana	H	12.88 FQ	15.73 MW	19.10 TQ	LABLS	1/08-3/08
Metals and Plastics	Baton Rouge MSA, LA	Y	32370 FQ	35840 MW	40000 TQ	USBLS	5/07
Metals and Plastics	Houma-Bayou Cane-Thibodaux MSA, LA	Y	32240 FQ	38250 MW	48170 TQ	USBLS	5/07
Metals and Plastics	New Orleans-Metairie-Kenner MSA, LA	Y	21230 FQ	27770 MW	34240 TQ	USBLS	5/07
Metals and Plastics	Maine	Y	33090 FQ	40490 MW	46540 TQ	USBLS	5/07
Metals and Plastics	Portland-South Portland-Biddeford MSA, ME	Y	29810 FQ	34150 MW	39340 TQ	USBLS	5/07
Metals and Plastics	Maryland	Y		34625 MW		MDBLS	3/08
Metals and Plastics	Baltimore-Towson MSA, MD	Y	26230 FQ	32860 MW	39670 TQ	USBLS	5/07
Metals and Plastics	Bethesda-Gaithersburg-Frederick PMSA, MD	Y	33090 FQ	35970 MW	38990 TQ	USBLS	5/07
Metals and Plastics	Massachusetts	Y	31120 FQ	37370 MW	45040 TQ	USBLS	5/07
Metals and Plastics	Boston-Cambridge-Quincy NECTA, MA	Y	33290 FQ	37570 MW	43130 TQ	USBLS	5/07
Metals and Plastics	Worcester MSA, MA-CT	Y	34170 FQ	38480 MW	47020 TQ	USBLS	5/07
Metals and Plastics	Michigan	Y	26770 FQ	33430 MW	41590 TQ	USBLS	5/07
Metals and Plastics	Detroit-Warren-Livonia MSA, MI	Y	27780 FQ	35280 MW	43270 TQ	USBLS	5/07
Metals and Plastics	Grand Rapids-Wyoming MSA, MI	Y	24210 FQ	34690 MW	44580 TQ	USBLS	5/07
Metals and Plastics	Lansing-East Lansing MSA, MI	Y	29580 FQ	37630 MW	44300 TQ	USBLS	5/07
Metals and Plastics	Muskegon-Norton Shores MSA, MI	Y	29040 FQ	34190 MW	44400 TQ	USBLS	5/07
Metals and Plastics	Warren-Troy-Farmington Hills PMSA, MI	Y	28220 FQ	35500 MW	42660 TQ	USBLS	5/07
Metals and Plastics	Minnesota	Y	30405 FQ	37175 MW	45116 TQ	MNBLS	10/08-12/08
Metals and Plastics	Duluth-Superior MSA, MN-WI	Y	30633 FQ	35599 MW	39684 TQ	MNBLS	10/08-12/08
Metals and Plastics	Minneapolis-Saint Paul MSA, MN-WI	Y	32717 FQ	40243 MW	48143 TQ	MNBLS	10/08-12/08
Metals and Plastics	Rochester MSA, MN	Y	35128 FQ	38521 MW	43079 TQ	MNBLS	10/08-12/08

AE Average entry wage	**AW** Average wage paid	**FQ** First quartile wage	**LO** Lowest wage paid	**MTC** Median total compensation **TCC** Total cash compensation
AER Average entry range	**AWR** Average wage range	**H** Hourly	**LR** Low end range	**MW** Median wage paid **TQ** Third quartile wage
AEX Average experienced wage	**AXR** Average experienced range	**HI** Highest wage paid	**M** Monthly	**MWR** Median wage range **W** Weekly
ATC Average total compensation	**D** Daily	**HR** High end range	**MCC** Median cash compensation **S** See annotated source	**Y** Yearly

Occupation/Type/Industry	Location	Per	Low	Mid	High	Source	Date
Computer-Controlled Machine Tool Operator							
Metals and Plastics	Mississippi	Y	20690 FQ	25350 MW	30670 TQ	USBLS	5/07
Metals and Plastics	Jackson MSA, MS	Y	21970 FQ	26240 MW	30460 TQ	USBLS	5/07
Metals and Plastics	Missouri	Y	24120 FQ	29110 MW	36910 TQ	USBLS	5/07
Metals and Plastics	Kansas City MSA, MO-KS	Y	26340 FQ	34940 MW	44250 TQ	USBLS	5/07
Metals and Plastics	St. Louis MSA, MO-IL	Y	28210 FQ	36710 MW	45460 TQ	USBLS	5/07
Metals and Plastics	Montana	Y	24500 FQ	29520 MW	36660 TQ	USBLS	5/07
Metals and Plastics	Billings MSA, MT	Y	27420 FQ	30880 MW	35710 TQ	USBLS	5/07
Metals and Plastics	Nebraska	Y	25280 FQ	31200 MW	36510 TQ	USBLS	5/07
Metals and Plastics	Omaha-Council Bluffs MSA, NE-IA	Y	19180 FQ	25250 MW	31840 TQ	USBLS	5/07
Metals and Plastics	Nevada	H	11.89 FQ	14.34 MW	17.88 TQ	NVBLS	5/08
Metals and Plastics	Carson City MSA, NV	H	12.54 FQ	14.66 MW	18.27 TQ	NVBLS	5/08
Metals and Plastics	Las Vegas-Paradise MSA, NV	H	11.00 FQ	13.68 MW	16.72 TQ	NVBLS	5/08
Metals and Plastics	New Hampshire	H	11.69 AE	15.34 MW	18.11 AEX	NHBLS	6/08
Metals and Plastics	Manchester MSA, NH	Y	25480 FQ	32270 MW	39380 TQ	USBLS	5/07
Metals and Plastics	Nashua NECTA, NH-MA	Y	24200 FQ	30890 MW	38890 TQ	USBLS	5/07
Metals and Plastics	New Jersey	Y	29340 FQ	38810 MW	50110 TQ	USBLS	5/07
Metals and Plastics	Camden PMSA, NJ	Y	28560 FQ	34310 MW	40660 TQ	USBLS	5/07
Metals and Plastics	Edison PMSA, NJ	Y	28460 FQ	35020 MW	44010 TQ	USBLS	5/07
Metals and Plastics	Newark-Union PMSA, NJ-PA	Y	26530 FQ	36760 MW	45860 TQ	USBLS	5/07
Metals and Plastics	New York	Y	24080 FQ	30820 MW	37580 TQ	USBLS	5/07
Metals and Plastics	Albany-Schenectady-Troy MSA, NY	Y	24830 FQ	34350 MW	46650 TQ	USBLS	5/07
Metals and Plastics	Buffalo-Niagara Falls MSA, NY	Y	23840 FQ	30530 MW	38160 TQ	USBLS	5/07
Metals and Plastics	Nassau-Suffolk PMSA, NY	Y	21950 FQ	26660 MW	35790 TQ	USBLS	5/07
Metals and Plastics	New York-Northern New Jersey-Long Island MSA, NY-NJ-PA	Y	24810 FQ	34570 MW	45500 TQ	USBLS	5/07
Metals and Plastics	North Carolina	Y	27130 FQ	31510 MW	37440 TQ	USBLS	5/07
Metals and Plastics	Asheville MSA, NC	Y	32180 FQ	36720 MW	45280 TQ	USBLS	5/07
Metals and Plastics	Charlotte-Gastonia-Concord MSA, NC-SC	Y	29400 FQ	34570 MW	39930 TQ	USBLS	5/07
Metals and Plastics	Raleigh-Cary MSA, NC	Y	24570 FQ	28660 MW	34460 TQ	USBLS	5/07
Metals and Plastics	North Dakota	Y	32250 FQ	36170 MW	41470 TQ	USBLS	5/07
Metals and Plastics	Fargo MSA, ND-MN	Y	33960 FQ	38060 MW	47810 TQ	USBLS	5/07
Metals and Plastics	Ohio	Y	25840 FQ	33050 MW	39720 TQ	USBLS	5/07
Metals and Plastics	Cincinnati-Middletown MSA, OH-KY-IN	Y	29550 FQ	35920 MW	43440 TQ	USBLS	5/07
Metals and Plastics	Cleveland-Elyria-Mentor MSA, OH	Y	28710 FQ	34740 MW	39620 TQ	USBLS	5/07
Metals and Plastics	Columbus MSA, OH	Y	24210 FQ	30050 MW	37790 TQ	USBLS	5/07
Metals and Plastics	Dayton MSA, OH	Y	27870 FQ	37610 MW	46010 TQ	USBLS	5/07
Metals and Plastics	Oklahoma	Y	24070 FQ	29230 MW	35130 TQ	USBLS	5/07
Metals and Plastics	Oklahoma City MSA, OK	Y	20550 FQ	25780 MW	35390 TQ	USBLS	5/07
Metals and Plastics	Tulsa MSA, OK	Y	28750 FQ	33840 MW	39550 TQ	USBLS	5/07
Metals and Plastics	Oregon	H	13.88 FQ	17.35 MW	21.10 TQ	ORBLS	5/08
Metals and Plastics	Portland-Vancouver-Beaverton MSA, OR-WA	Y	27780 FQ	35190 MW	43880 TQ	USBLS	5/07
Metals and Plastics	Salem MSA, OR	Y	31530 FQ	38220 MW	42730 TQ	USBLS	5/07
Metals and Plastics	Pennsylvania	Y	26740 FQ	32770 MW	39100 TQ	USBLS	5/07
Metals and Plastics	Allentown-Bethlehem-Easton MSA, PA-NJ	Y	27430 FQ	34910 MW	39740 TQ	USBLS	5/07
Metals and Plastics	Philadelphia-Camden-Wilmington MSA, PA-NJ-DE-MD	Y	30820 FQ	37500 MW	44680 TQ	USBLS	5/07
Metals and Plastics	Pittsburgh MSA, PA	Y	27290 FQ	31730 MW	37960 TQ	USBLS	5/07
Metals and Plastics	Rhode Island	Y	27030 FQ	32200 MW	38730 TQ	USBLS	5/07
Metals and Plastics	Providence-Fall River-Warwick MSA, RI-MA	Y	27280 FQ	33170 MW	39250 TQ	USBLS	5/07
Metals and Plastics	South Carolina	Y	27990 FQ	31660 MW	36720 TQ	USBLS	5/07
Metals and Plastics	Charleston-North Charleston MSA, SC	Y	25070 FQ	28700 MW	32870 TQ	USBLS	5/07
Metals and Plastics	Columbia MSA, SC	Y	28220 FQ	32440 MW	36990 TQ	USBLS	5/07
Metals and Plastics	South Dakota	Y	26313 FQ	29800 MW	34972 TQ	SDBLS	7/08-9/08
Metals and Plastics	Sioux Falls MSA, SD	Y	30421 FQ	35597 MW	42058 TQ	SDBLS	7/08-9/08
Metals and Plastics	Tennessee	Y	24220 FQ	32600 MW	38790 TQ	USBLS	5/07
Metals and Plastics	Memphis MSA, TN-MS-AR	Y	27850 FQ	32690 MW	42910 TQ	USBLS	5/07

AE	Average entry wage	AW	Average wage paid	FQ	First quartile wage	LO	Lowest wage paid	MTC	Median total compensation	TCC	Total cash compensation
AER	Average entry range	AWR	Average wage range	H	Hourly	LR	Low end range	MW	Median wage paid	TQ	Third quartile wage
AEX	Average experienced wage	AXR	Average experienced range	HI	Highest wage paid	M	Monthly	MWR	Median wage range	W	Weekly
ATC	Average total compensation	D	Daily	HR	High end range	MCC	Median cash compensation	S	See annotated source	Y	Yearly

280

Occupation/Type/Industry	Location	Per	Low	Mid	High	Source	Date
Computer-Controlled Machine Tool Operator							
Metals and Plastics	Nashville-Davidson-Murfreesboro MSA, TN	Y	32190 FQ	39240 MW	46740 TQ	USBLS	5/07
Metals and Plastics	Texas	Y	23540 FQ	31180 MW	38390 TQ	USBLS	5/07
Metals and Plastics	Austin-Round Rock MSA, TX	Y	22960 FQ	30710 MW	45600 TQ	USBLS	5/07
Metals and Plastics	Beaumont-Port Arthur MSA, TX	Y	32090 FQ	37580 MW	42790 TQ	USBLS	5/07
Metals and Plastics	Brownsville-Harlingen MSA, TX	Y	12950 FQ	14580 MW	20750 TQ	USBLS	5/07
Metals and Plastics	Dallas-Fort Worth-Arlington MSA, TX	Y	21830 FQ	28880 MW	35800 TQ	USBLS	5/07
Metals and Plastics	El Paso MSA, TX	Y	17830 FQ	22130 MW	30920 TQ	USBLS	5/07
Metals and Plastics	Houston-Sugar Land-Baytown MSA, TX	Y	25650 FQ	33760 MW	40630 TQ	USBLS	5/07
Metals and Plastics	San Antonio MSA, TX	Y	17570 FQ	24670 MW	33850 TQ	USBLS	5/07
Metals and Plastics	Utah	Y	23280 FQ	27740 MW	34050 TQ	USBLS	5/07
Metals and Plastics	Logan MSA, UT-ID	Y	25540 FQ	35360 MW	44900 TQ	USBLS	5/07
Metals and Plastics	Ogden-Clearfield MSA, UT	Y	22200 FQ	24480 MW	35000 TQ	USBLS	5/07
Metals and Plastics	Salt Lake City MSA, UT	Y	24750 FQ	28090 MW	31980 TQ	USBLS	5/07
Metals and Plastics	Vermont	Y	26070 FQ	30440 MW	35150 TQ	USBLS	5/07
Metals and Plastics	Burlington-South Burlington MSA, VT	Y	27520 FQ	32770 MW	38360 TQ	USBLS	5/07
Metals and Plastics	Virginia	Y	26640 FQ	33440 MW	39780 TQ	USBLS	5/07
Metals and Plastics	Richmond MSA, VA	Y	23350 FQ	26730 MW	31700 TQ	USBLS	5/07
Metals and Plastics	Virginia Beach-Norfolk-Newport News MSA, VA-NC	Y	35210 FQ	41110 MW	46420 TQ	USBLS	5/07
Metals and Plastics	Washington	H	14.62 FQ	19.44 MW	25.90 TQ	WABLS	3/08
Metals and Plastics	Seattle-Tacoma-Bellevue MSA, WA	Y	33660 FQ	44050 MW	63060 TQ	USBLS	5/07
Metals and Plastics	West Virginia	Y	27299 FQ	34798 MW	39182 TQ	WVBLS	7/08-9/08
Metals and Plastics	Huntington-Ashland MSA, WV-KY-OH	Y	28040 FQ	33850 MW	36660 TQ	USBLS	5/07
Metals and Plastics	Wisconsin	Y	27750 FQ	33500 MW	40230 TQ	USBLS	5/07
Metals and Plastics	Green Bay MSA, WI	Y	32870 FQ	36160 MW	39570 TQ	USBLS	5/07
Metals and Plastics	Milwaukee-Waukesha-West Allis MSA, WI	Y	27720 FQ	34110 MW	41580 TQ	USBLS	5/07
Metals and Plastics	Racine MSA, WI	Y	23920 FQ	28220 MW	32890 TQ	USBLS	5/07
Metals and Plastics	Wyoming	Y	28024 FQ	30171 MW	32483 TQ	WYBLS	9/08
Metals and Plastics	Cheyenne MSA, WY	Y	27891 FQ	29840 MW	31834 TQ	WYBLS	9/08
Metals and Plastics	Puerto Rico	Y	17000 FQ	19850 MW	23560 TQ	USBLS	5/07
Computer Forensic Professional	Alaska	Y		72000 AW		CFR	2009
	District of Columbia	Y		91000 AW		CFR	2009
	Iowa	Y		76000 AW		CFR	2009
	Maine	Y		56000 AW		CFR	2009
	Michigan	Y		78000 AW		CFR	2009
	New Mexico	Y		93000 AW		CFR	2009
	Texas	Y		74000 AW		CFR	2009
Computer Forensic Technician	Tech Valley, NY	Y		39700 MW		TVC07	2008
Computer Hardware Engineer	Alabama	Y	48400 FQ	78520 MW	96700 TQ	USBLS	5/07
	Birmingham-Hoover MSA, AL	Y	41450 FQ	46210 MW	66410 TQ	USBLS	5/07
	Arizona	Y	70290 FQ	84850 MW	100000 TQ	USBLS	5/07
	Phoenix-Mesa-Scottsdale MSA, AZ	Y	70490 FQ	84860 MW	99410 TQ	USBLS	5/07
	Arkansas	Y	61830 FQ	87310 MW	118140 TQ	USBLS	5/07
	Little Rock-North Little Rock MSA, AR	Y	59850 FQ	73410 MW	97960 TQ	USBLS	5/07
	California	H	39.44 FQ	49.84 MW	63.40 TQ	CABLS	1/08-3/08
	Los Angeles-Long Beach-Glendale PMSA, CA	H	34.44 FQ	45.40 MW	59.25 TQ	CABLS	1/08-3/08
	Oakland-Fremont-Hayward MSA, CA	H	40.65 FQ	47.64 MW	57.14 TQ	CABLS	1/08-3/08
	Riverside-San Bernardino-Ontario MSA, CA	H	33.33 FQ	39.56 MW	51.53 TQ	CABLS	1/08-3/08
	Sacramento-Arden Arcade-Roseville MSA, CA	H	36.33 FQ	46.25 MW	58.63 TQ	CABLS	1/08-3/08
	San Diego-Carlsbad-San Marcos MSA, CA	H	33.17 FQ	43.79 MW	54.07 TQ	CABLS	1/08-3/08

AE Average entry wage	**AW** Average wage paid	**FQ** First quartile wage	**LO** Lowest wage paid	**MTC** Median total compensation	**TCC** Total cash compensation
AER Average entry range	**AWR** Average wage range	**H** Hourly	**LR** Low end range	**MW** Median wage paid	**TQ** Third quartile wage
AEX Average experienced wage	**AXR** Average experienced range	**HI** Highest wage paid	**M** Monthly	**MWR** Median wage range	**W** Weekly
ATC Average total compensation	**D** Daily	**HR** High end range	**MCC** Median cash compensation	**S** See annotated source	**Y** Yearly

Occupation/Type/Industry	Location	Per	Low	Mid	High	Source	Date
Computer Hardware Engineer	San Francisco-San Mateo-Redwood PMSA, CA	H	35.75 FQ	50.26 MW	64.94 TQ	CABLS	1/08-3/08
	San Jose-Sunnyvale-Santa Clara MSA, CA	H	43.69 FQ	55.09 MW	68.96 TQ	CABLS	1/08-3/08
	Santa Ana-Anaheim-Irvine PMSA, CA	Y	79830 FQ	93230 MW	105440 TQ	USBLS	5/07
	Colorado	Y	80130 FQ	100580 MW	127410 TQ	USBLS	5/07
	Denver-Aurora MSA, CO	Y	66000 FQ	90820 MW	112390 TQ	USBLS	5/07
	Connecticut	H	23.61 AE	32.70 MW		CTBLS	1/08-3/08
	Bridgeport-Stamford-Norwalk MSA, CT	Y	58040 FQ	89300 MW	116460 TQ	USBLS	5/07
	Hartford-West Hartford-East Hartford MSA, CT	Y	53330 FQ	58520 MW	63730 TQ	USBLS	5/07
	Delaware	Y	70590 FQ	76150 MW	81860 TQ	USBLS	5/07
	Wilmington PMSA, DE-MD-NJ	Y	70450 FQ	76100 MW	81910 TQ	USBLS	5/07
	District of Columbia	Y	71420 FQ	90970 MW	118730 TQ	USBLS	5/07
	Washington-Arlington-Alexandria MSA, DC-VA-MD-WV	Y	81400 FQ	97340 MW	118090 TQ	USBLS	5/07
	Florida	Y	61710 FQ	79990 MW	96720 TQ	USBLS	5/07
	Fort Lauderdale-Pompano Beach-Deerfield Beach PMSA, FL	Y	53820 FQ	65340 MW	77150 TQ	USBLS	5/07
	Jacksonville MSA, FL	Y	65200 FQ	89630 MW	106350 TQ	USBLS	5/07
	Miami-Fort Lauderdale-Miami Beach MSA, FL	Y	54220 FQ	66950 MW	79690 TQ	USBLS	5/07
	Orlando-Kissimmee MSA, FL	Y	39400 FQ	82200 MW	99020 TQ	USBLS	5/07
	Tampa-St. Petersburg-Clearwater MSA, FL	Y	63670 FQ	91740 MW	108010 TQ	USBLS	5/07
	West Palm Beach-Boca Raton-Boynton Beach PMSA, FL	Y	74500 FQ	95180 MW	120910 TQ	USBLS	5/07
	Georgia	Y	61740 FQ	88230 MW	108380 TQ	USBLS	5/07
	Atlanta-Sandy Springs-Marietta MSA, GA	Y	62960 FQ	91190 MW	109890 TQ	USBLS	5/07
	Hawaii	Y	57450 FQ	71660 MW	84410 TQ	USBLS	5/07
	Honolulu MSA, HI	Y	60140 FQ	73780 MW	86880 TQ	USBLS	5/07
	Idaho	Y	64370 FQ	83870 MW	103070 TQ	USBLS	5/07
	Boise City-Nampa MSA, ID	Y	61270 FQ	80280 MW	100820 TQ	USBLS	5/07
	Illinois	Y	67980 FQ	84840 MW	101960 TQ	USBLS	5/07
	Chicago-Naperville-Joliet MSA, IL-IN-WI	Y	67640 FQ	84070 MW	101270 TQ	USBLS	5/07
	Indiana	Y	50270 FQ	70610 MW	84570 TQ	USBLS	5/07
	Indianapolis-Carmel MSA, IN	Y	50950 FQ	62990 MW	83960 TQ	USBLS	5/07
	Iowa	Y	54580 FQ	67080 MW	89620 TQ	USBLS	5/07
	Des Moines-West Des Moines MSA, IA	Y	60210 FQ	75530 MW	101110 TQ	USBLS	5/07
	Kansas	Y	46670 FQ	61090 MW	76670 TQ	USBLS	5/07
	Louisville-Jefferson County MSA, KY-IN	Y	47380 FQ	57030 MW	88360 TQ	USBLS	5/07
	Louisiana	H	15.72 FQ	23.55 MW	30.27 TQ	LABLS	1/08-3/08
	New Orleans-Metairie-Kenner MSA, LA	Y	29950 FQ	42940 MW	48850 TQ	USBLS	5/07
	Maryland	Y		97175 MW		MDBLS	3/08
	Baltimore-Towson MSA, MD	Y	66820 FQ	89050 MW	124820 TQ	USBLS	5/07
	Bethesda-Gaithersburg-Frederick PMSA, MD	Y	82820 FQ	97380 MW	114900 TQ	USBLS	5/07
	Massachusetts	Y	80500 FQ	99460 MW	121000 TQ	USBLS	5/07
	Boston-Cambridge-Quincy NECTA, MA	Y	78740 FQ	97250 MW	118920 TQ	USBLS	5/07
	Worcester MSA, MA-CT	Y	83720 FQ	105290 MW	123100 TQ	USBLS	5/07
	Michigan	Y	60560 FQ	73610 MW	88540 TQ	USBLS	5/07
	Detroit-Warren-Livonia MSA, MI	Y	62570 FQ	74070 MW	88420 TQ	USBLS	5/07
	Grand Rapids-Wyoming MSA, MI	Y	56750 FQ	66850 MW	80880 TQ	USBLS	5/07
	Warren-Troy-Farmington Hills PMSA, MI	Y	66790 FQ	76190 MW	92500 TQ	USBLS	5/07
	Minnesota	Y	76991 FQ	93522 MW	112029 TQ	MNBLS	10/08-12/08
	Minneapolis-Saint Paul MSA, MN-WI	Y	75704 FQ	90592 MW	107750 TQ	MNBLS	10/08-12/08
	Mississippi	Y	63920 FQ	84600 MW	104940 TQ	USBLS	5/07

AE Average entry wage	**AW** Average wage paid	**FQ** First quartile wage	**LO** Lowest wage paid	**MTC** Median total compensation	**TCC** Total cash compensation
AER Average entry range	**AWR** Average wage range	**H** Hourly	**LR** Low end range	**MW** Median wage paid	**TQ** Third quartile wage
AEX Average experienced wage	**AXR** Average experienced range	**HI** Highest wage paid	**M** Monthly	**MWR** Median wage range	**W** Weekly
ATC Average total compensation	**D** Daily	**HR** High end range	**MCC** Median cash compensation	**S** See annotated source	**Y** Yearly

Occupation/Type/Industry	Location	Per	Low	Mid	High	Source	Date
Computer Hardware Engineer	Missouri	Y	66090 FQ	79320 MW	116820 TQ	USBLS	5/07
	Kansas City MSA, MO-KS	Y	47610 FQ	63240 MW	76670 TQ	USBLS	5/07
	St. Louis MSA, MO-IL	Y	69790 FQ	87080 MW	108500 TQ	USBLS	5/07
	Nebraska	Y	44480 FQ	63720 MW	94810 TQ	USBLS	5/07
	Omaha-Council Bluffs MSA, NE-IA	Y	44940 FQ	62790 MW	92040 TQ	USBLS	5/07
	Nevada	H	24.04 FQ	34.52 MW	44.14 TQ	NVBLS	5/08
	Las Vegas-Paradise MSA, NV	H	23.26 FQ	32.40 MW	40.49 TQ	NVBLS	5/08
	New Hampshire	H	39.14 AE	53.95 MW	58.51 AEX	NHBLS	6/08
	Manchester MSA, NH	Y	68170 FQ	87350 MW	99750 TQ	USBLS	5/07
	New Jersey	Y	75900 FQ	97960 MW	117030 TQ	USBLS	5/07
	Camden PMSA, NJ	Y	87830 FQ	107410 MW	127240 TQ	USBLS	5/07
	Edison PMSA, NJ	Y	74830 FQ	97590 MW	120620 TQ	USBLS	5/07
	Newark-Union PMSA, NJ-PA	Y	76320 FQ	99170 MW	116500 TQ	USBLS	5/07
	New York	Y	72520 FQ	94710 MW	123230 TQ	USBLS	5/07
	Albany-Schenectady-Troy MSA, NY	Y	84560 FQ	100710 MW	121960 TQ	USBLS	5/07
	Buffalo-Niagara Falls MSA, NY	Y	49630 FQ	58980 MW	74390 TQ	USBLS	5/07
	Nassau-Suffolk PMSA, NY	Y	46010 FQ	64050 MW	94780 TQ	USBLS	5/07
	New York-Northern New Jersey-Long Island MSA, NY-NJ-PA	Y	73390 FQ	98500 MW	124040 TQ	USBLS	5/07
	North Carolina	Y	69730 FQ	90130 MW	113690 TQ	USBLS	5/07
	Charlotte-Gastonia-Concord MSA, NC-SC	Y	52370 FQ	71680 MW	98190 TQ	USBLS	5/07
	Durham MSA, NC	Y	79290 FQ	98040 MW	119580 TQ	USBLS	5/07
	Raleigh-Cary MSA, NC	Y	46950 FQ	67770 MW	92500 TQ	USBLS	5/07
	Ohio	Y	62290 FQ	86280 MW	100970 TQ	USBLS	5/07
	Cincinnati-Middletown MSA, OH-KY-IN	Y	29830 FQ	58560 MW	91100 TQ	USBLS	5/07
	Cleveland-Elyria-Mentor MSA, OH	Y	40120 FQ	63180 MW	99750 TQ	USBLS	5/07
	Columbus MSA, OH	Y	80820 FQ	91940 MW	103800 TQ	USBLS	5/07
	Dayton MSA, OH	Y	67960 FQ	85090 MW	98060 TQ	USBLS	5/07
	Oklahoma	Y	57770 FQ	82950 MW	99420 TQ	USBLS	5/07
	Oklahoma City MSA, OK	Y	75170 FQ	90530 MW	105510 TQ	USBLS	5/07
	Tulsa MSA, OK	Y	37570 FQ	47160 MW	93970 TQ	USBLS	5/07
	Oregon	H	36.06 FQ	42.56 MW	49.37 TQ	ORBLS	5/08
	Portland-Vancouver-Beaverton MSA, OR-WA	Y	72770 FQ	85860 MW	99450 TQ	USBLS	5/07
	Pennsylvania	Y	66240 FQ	85610 MW	108800 TQ	USBLS	5/07
	Allentown-Bethlehem-Easton MSA, PA-NJ	Y	110040 FQ	120350 MW	130660 TQ	USBLS	5/07
	Philadelphia-Camden-Wilmington MSA, PA-NJ-DE-MD	Y	70630 FQ	85780 MW	110090 TQ	USBLS	5/07
	Pittsburgh MSA, PA	Y	65490 FQ	81020 MW	97530 TQ	USBLS	5/07
	Rhode Island	Y	67670 FQ	81450 MW	103000 TQ	USBLS	5/07
	Providence-Fall River-Warwick MSA, RI-MA	Y	68170 FQ	82730 MW	107360 TQ	USBLS	5/07
	South Carolina	Y	45830 FQ	58710 MW	72630 TQ	USBLS	5/07
	Charleston-North Charleston MSA, SC	Y	55860 FQ	66490 MW	80610 TQ	USBLS	5/07
	Columbia MSA, SC	Y	45870 FQ	55720 MW	63200 TQ	USBLS	5/07
	South Dakota	Y	69589 FQ	76222 MW	83375 TQ	SDBLS	7/08-9/08
	Tennessee	Y	34200 FQ	55700 MW	77310 TQ	USBLS	5/07
	Johnson City MSA, TN	Y	19150 FQ	39720 MW	82590 TQ	USBLS	5/07
	Memphis MSA, TN-MS-AR	Y	38120 FQ	57170 MW	72750 TQ	USBLS	5/07
	Nashville-Davidson-Murfreesboro MSA, TN	Y	32630 FQ	52340 MW	69450 TQ	USBLS	5/07
	Texas	Y	77820 FQ	98140 MW	118810 TQ	USBLS	5/07
	Austin-Round Rock MSA, TX	Y	76330 FQ	95440 MW	120300 TQ	USBLS	5/07
	Dallas-Fort Worth-Arlington MSA, TX	Y	86540 FQ	103290 MW	119650 TQ	USBLS	5/07
	Houston-Sugar Land-Baytown MSA, TX	Y	76560 FQ	97880 MW	117020 TQ	USBLS	5/07
	San Antonio MSA, TX	Y	77380 FQ	88810 MW	101980 TQ	USBLS	5/07
	Utah	Y	68390 FQ	87040 MW	106920 TQ	USBLS	5/07
	Virginia	Y	74040 FQ	94790 MW	118120 TQ	USBLS	5/07
	Richmond MSA, VA	Y	58920 FQ	77880 MW	102030 TQ	USBLS	5/07

AE	Average entry wage	AW	Average wage paid	FQ	First quartile wage	LO	Lowest wage paid	MTC	Median total compensation	TCC	Total cash compensation
AER	Average entry range	AWR	Average wage range	H	Hourly	LR	Low end range	MW	Median wage paid	TQ	Third quartile wage
AEX	Average experienced wage	AXR	Average experienced range	HI	Highest wage paid	M	Monthly	MWR	Median wage range	W	Weekly
ATC	Average total compensation	D	Daily	HR	High end range	MCC	Median cash compensation	S	See annotated source	Y	Yearly

Occupation/Type/Industry	Location	Per	Low	Mid	High	Source	Date
Computer Hardware Engineer	Virginia Beach-Norfolk- Newport News MSA, VA-NC	Y	70090 FQ	87240 MW	103250 TQ	USBLS	5/07
	West Virginia	Y	65972 FQ	82453 MW	98731 TQ	WVBLS	7/08-9/08
	Wisconsin	Y	52830 FQ	76850 MW	96380 TQ	USBLS	5/07
	Milwaukee-Waukesha-West Allis MSA, WI	Y	72720 FQ	89590 MW	105300 TQ	USBLS	5/07
	Puerto Rico	Y	48360 FQ	61050 MW	80610 TQ	USBLS	5/07
	San Juan-Caguas-Guaynabo MSA, PR	Y	49960 FQ	63980 MW	85930 TQ	USBLS	5/07
Computer Numeric Control Machine Programmer	United States	Y	25000 AE			CCRUN02	2008
Computer Operator	Alabama	Y	23730 FQ	29160 MW	35870 TQ	USBLS	5/07
	Birmingham-Hoover MSA, AL	Y	25090 FQ	29760 MW	36870 TQ	USBLS	5/07
	Alaska	Y	31010 FQ	40490 MW	49630 TQ	USBLS	5/07
	Anchorage MSA, AK	Y	28200 FQ	37150 MW	46900 TQ	USBLS	5/07
	Arizona	Y	17500 FQ	29300 MW	38540 TQ	USBLS	5/07
	Phoenix-Mesa-Scottsdale MSA, AZ	Y	16070 FQ	29700 MW	40310 TQ	USBLS	5/07
	Tucson MSA, AZ	Y	26750 FQ	29730 MW	33360 TQ	USBLS	5/07
	Arkansas	Y	23140 FQ	26700 MW	32040 TQ	USBLS	5/07
	Fayetteville-Springdale-Rogers MSA, AR-MO	Y	24240 FQ	28630 MW	36120 TQ	USBLS	5/07
	Little Rock-North Little Rock MSA, AR	Y	23830 FQ	27980 MW	35730 TQ	USBLS	5/07
	Pine Bluff MSA, AR	Y	22450 FQ	24600 MW	30540 TQ	USBLS	5/07
	California	H	14.63 FQ	18.73 MW	23.32 TQ	CABLS	1/08-3/08
	Bakersfield MSA, CA	H	14.55 FQ	18.09 MW	22.01 TQ	CABLS	1/08-3/08
	Los Angeles-Long Beach- Glendale PMSA, CA	H	12.99 FQ	16.88 MW	21.49 TQ	CABLS	1/08-3/08
	Oakland-Fremont-Hayward MSA, CA	H	17.32 FQ	21.13 MW	28.23 TQ	CABLS	1/08-3/08
	Oxnard-Thousand Oaks- Ventura MSA, CA	H	16.61 FQ	19.27 MW	22.40 TQ	CABLS	1/08-3/08
	Riverside-San Bernardino- Ontario MSA, CA	H	12.55 FQ	17.50 MW	22.06 TQ	CABLS	1/08-3/08
	Sacramento-Arden Arcade- Roseville MSA, CA	H	14.69 FQ	18.95 MW	22.49 TQ	CABLS	1/08-3/08
	San Diego-Carlsbad-San Marcos MSA, CA	H	15.23 FQ	18.05 MW	22.79 TQ	CABLS	1/08-3/08
	San Francisco-San Mateo- Redwood PMSA, CA	H	18.51 FQ	22.36 MW	25.17 TQ	CABLS	1/08-3/08
	San Jose-Sunnyvale-Santa Clara MSA, CA	H	17.88 FQ	22.99 MW	27.48 TQ	CABLS	1/08-3/08
	Santa Ana-Anaheim-Irvine PMSA, CA	Y	30260 FQ	36740 MW	45660 TQ	USBLS	5/07
	Colorado	Y	31720 FQ	38360 MW	48890 TQ	USBLS	5/07
	Denver-Aurora MSA, CO	Y	32280 FQ	38550 MW	49510 TQ	USBLS	5/07
	Fort Collins-Loveland MSA, CO	Y	27300 FQ	32330 MW	40620 TQ	USBLS	5/07
	Connecticut	H	14.55 AE	20.36 MW		CTBLS	1/08-3/08
	Bridgeport-Stamford-Norwalk MSA, CT	Y	35940 FQ	42870 MW	49580 TQ	USBLS	5/07
	Hartford-West Hartford-East Hartford MSA, CT	Y	34780 FQ	41240 MW	50690 TQ	USBLS	5/07
	Delaware	Y	28920 FQ	36510 MW	46690 TQ	USBLS	5/07
	Wilmington PMSA, DE-MD- NJ	Y	29940 FQ	37440 MW	47660 TQ	USBLS	5/07
	District of Columbia	Y	38970 FQ	46160 MW	54900 TQ	USBLS	5/07

	Washington-Arlington-
	  Alexandria MSA, DC-VA-
	  MD-WV
		Y	29540 FQ	39420 MW	50690 TQ	USBLS	5/07

	Florida	Y	28130 FQ	35440 MW	43810 TQ	USBLS	5/07

	Fort Lauderdale-Pompano
	  Beach-Deerfield Beach
	  PMSA, FL
		Y	30030 FQ	39300 MW	44930 TQ	USBLS	5/07

	Jacksonville MSA, FL	Y	31650 FQ	39660 MW	45990 TQ	USBLS	5/07
	Miami-Fort Lauderdale-Miami Beach MSA, FL	Y	28560 FQ	36760 MW	44790 TQ	USBLS	5/07
	Orlando-Kissimmee MSA, FL	Y	29440 FQ	36350 MW	43490 TQ	USBLS	5/07

AE Average entry wage	**AW** Average wage paid	**FQ** First quartile wage	**LO** Lowest wage paid	**MTC** Median total compensation	**TCC** Total cash compensation
AER Average entry range	**AWR** Average wage range	**H** Hourly	**LR** Low end range	**MW** Median wage paid	**TQ** Third quartile wage
AEX Average experienced wage	**AXR** Average experienced range	**HI** Highest wage paid	**M** Monthly	**MWR** Median wage range	**W** Weekly
ATC Average total compensation	**D** Daily	**HR** High end range	**MCC** Median cash compensation	**S** See annotated source	**Y** Yearly

Occupation/Type/Industry	Location	Per	Low	Mid	High	Source	Date
Computer Operator	Pensacola-Ferry Pass-Brent MSA, FL	Y	19650 FQ	28970 MW	40250 TQ	USBLS	5/07
	Tampa-St. Petersburg-Clearwater MSA, FL	Y	28870 FQ	35060 MW	42640 TQ	USBLS	5/07
	West Palm Beach-Boca Raton-Boynton Beach PMSA, FL	Y	28310 FQ	36340 MW	47290 TQ	USBLS	5/07
	Georgia	Y	26170 FQ	32570 MW	40950 TQ	USBLS	5/07
	Atlanta-Sandy Springs-Marietta MSA, GA	Y	27960 FQ	34400 MW	43070 TQ	USBLS	5/07
	Hawaii	Y	24970 FQ	34220 MW	43490 TQ	USBLS	5/07
	Honolulu MSA, HI	Y	27270 FQ	35310 MW	43900 TQ	USBLS	5/07
	Idaho	Y	21710 FQ	26090 MW	36110 TQ	USBLS	5/07
	Boise City-Nampa MSA, ID	Y	21850 FQ	27770 MW	36420 TQ	USBLS	5/07
	Illinois	Y	28650 FQ	38510 MW	48750 TQ	USBLS	5/07
	Champaign-Urbana MSA, IL	Y	27070 FQ	34980 MW	55300 TQ	USBLS	5/07
	Chicago-Naperville-Joliet MSA, IL-IN-WI	Y	29760 FQ	40460 MW	50080 TQ	USBLS	5/07
	Indiana	Y	24620 FQ	30790 MW	39250 TQ	USBLS	5/07
	Gary PMSA, IN	Y	23360 FQ	27180 MW	36020 TQ	USBLS	5/07
	Indianapolis-Carmel MSA, IN	Y	27060 FQ	32870 MW	40810 TQ	USBLS	5/07
	South Bend-Mishawaka MSA, IN-MI	Y	19640 FQ	23120 MW	28570 TQ	USBLS	5/07
	Iowa	Y	21930 FQ	27330 MW	35120 TQ	USBLS	5/07
	Des Moines-West Des Moines MSA, IA	Y	25370 FQ	31110 MW	37950 TQ	USBLS	5/07
	Waterloo-Cedar Falls MSA, IA	Y	22020 FQ	30040 MW	37700 TQ	USBLS	5/07
	Kansas	Y	26020 FQ	32350 MW	41340 TQ	USBLS	5/07
	Wichita MSA, KS	Y	31350 FQ	36940 MW	45570 TQ	USBLS	5/07
	Kentucky	Y	27583 FQ	33577 MW	42669 TQ	KYBLS	2008
	Louisville-Jefferson County MSA, KY-IN	Y	28790 FQ	35150 MW	43190 TQ	USBLS	5/07
	Louisiana	H	11.05 FQ	14.13 MW	18.55 TQ	LABLS	1/08-3/08
	Baton Rouge MSA, LA	Y	21960 FQ	27960 MW	35470 TQ	USBLS	5/07
	New Orleans-Metairie-Kenner MSA, LA	Y	25910 FQ	33580 MW	43000 TQ	USBLS	5/07
	Maine	Y	27700 FQ	33120 MW	40520 TQ	USBLS	5/07
	Portland-South Portland-Biddeford MSA, ME	Y	28770 FQ	35000 MW	42050 TQ	USBLS	5/07
	Maryland	Y		38000 MW		MDBLS	3/08
	Baltimore-Towson MSA, MD	Y	29910 FQ	38290 MW	47400 TQ	USBLS	5/07
	Bethesda-Gaithersburg-Frederick PMSA, MD	Y	28970 FQ	38760 MW	50590 TQ	USBLS	5/07
	Massachusetts	Y	30690 FQ	38960 MW	46610 TQ	USBLS	5/07
	Boston-Cambridge-Quincy NECTA, MA	Y	31530 FQ	39730 MW	47110 TQ	USBLS	5/07
	Worcester MSA, MA-CT	Y	32480 FQ	41000 MW	48900 TQ	USBLS	5/07
	Michigan	Y	28000 FQ	36110 MW	44580 TQ	USBLS	5/07
	Detroit-Warren-Livonia MSA, MI	Y	32730 FQ	39370 MW	46640 TQ	USBLS	5/07
	Grand Rapids-Wyoming MSA, MI	Y	25030 FQ	34020 MW	45050 TQ	USBLS	5/07
	Warren-Troy-Farmington Hills PMSA, MI	Y	33020 FQ	39520 MW	47260 TQ	USBLS	5/07
	Minnesota	Y	30505 FQ	37551 MW	45545 TQ	MNBLS	10/08-12/08
	Duluth-Superior MSA, MN-WI	Y	28569 FQ	32910 MW	39508 TQ	MNBLS	10/08-12/08
	Minneapolis-Saint Paul MSA, MN-WI	Y	31692 FQ	38613 MW	46815 TQ	MNBLS	10/08-12/08
	Rochester MSA, MN	Y	32962 FQ	38638 MW	44698 TQ	MNBLS	10/08-12/08
	Mississippi	Y	23660 FQ	29610 MW	36250 TQ	USBLS	5/07
	Jackson MSA, MS	Y	30060 FQ	35220 MW	43050 TQ	USBLS	5/07
	Missouri	Y	27810 FQ	38380 MW	48210 TQ	USBLS	5/07
	Jefferson City MSA, MO	Y	24120 FQ	28790 MW	36530 TQ	USBLS	5/07
	Kansas City MSA, MO-KS	Y	28770 FQ	36360 MW	45420 TQ	USBLS	5/07
	St. Joseph MSA, MO-KS	Y	25480 FQ	30670 MW	37670 TQ	USBLS	5/07
	St. Louis MSA, MO-IL	Y	33060 FQ	43590 MW	53340 TQ	USBLS	5/07
	Montana	Y	23510 FQ	28940 MW	35890 TQ	USBLS	5/07
	Nebraska	Y	23170 FQ	27780 MW	33050 TQ	USBLS	5/07
	Omaha-Council Bluffs MSA, NE-IA	Y	23060 FQ	27950 MW	33340 TQ	USBLS	5/07
	Nevada	H	13.38 FQ	17.17 MW	22.42 TQ	NVBLS	5/08
	Las Vegas-Paradise MSA, NV	H	14.61 FQ	18.81 MW	23.28 TQ	NVBLS	5/08
	New Hampshire	H	10.06 AE	13.85 MW	17.96 AEX	NHBLS	6/08

AE	Average entry wage	AW	Average wage paid	FQ	First quartile wage
AER	Average entry range	AWR	Average wage range	H	Hourly
AEX	Average experienced wage	AXR	Average experienced range	HI	Highest wage paid
ATC	Average total compensation	D	Daily	HR	High end range

LO　Lowest wage paid　　MTC　Median total compensation　TCC　Total cash compensation
LR　Low end range　　　 MW　Median wage paid　　　　　 TQ　Third quartile wage
M　 Monthly　　　　　　 MWR　Median wage range　　　　 W　　Weekly
MCC　Median cash compensation　S　See annotated source　　 Y　　Yearly

Occupation/Type/Industry	Location	Per	Low	Mid	High	Source	Date
Computer Operator	Manchester MSA, NH	Y	19570 FQ	22940 MW	33470 TQ	USBLS	5/07
	Portsmouth MSA, NH-ME	Y	20290 FQ	23790 MW	30530 TQ	USBLS	5/07
	New Jersey	Y	30510 FQ	39540 MW	48270 TQ	USBLS	5/07
	Camden PMSA, NJ	Y	26990 FQ	35860 MW	43760 TQ	USBLS	5/07
	Edison PMSA, NJ	Y	29080 FQ	38600 MW	48640 TQ	USBLS	5/07
	Newark-Union PMSA, NJ-PA	Y	34190 FQ	42210 MW	48520 TQ	USBLS	5/07
	New Mexico	Y	26910 FQ	32420 MW	39220 TQ	USBLS	5/07
	Albuquerque MSA, NM	Y	27010 FQ	31100 MW	35720 TQ	USBLS	5/07
	New York	Y	26280 FQ	33280 MW	44200 TQ	USBLS	5/07
	Albany-Schenectady-Troy MSA, NY	Y	26800 FQ	31600 MW	41580 TQ	USBLS	5/07
	Buffalo-Niagara Falls MSA, NY	Y	20110 FQ	28400 MW	38400 TQ	USBLS	5/07
	Nassau-Suffolk PMSA, NY	Y	31820 FQ	40490 MW	49290 TQ	USBLS	5/07
	New York-Northern New Jersey-Long Island MSA, NY-NJ-PA	Y	29130 FQ	38100 MW	47940 TQ	USBLS	5/07
	North Carolina	Y	29030 FQ	34730 MW	40880 TQ	USBLS	5/07
	Charlotte-Gastonia-Concord MSA, NC-SC	Y	28450 FQ	36000 MW	45450 TQ	USBLS	5/07
	Greensboro-High Point MSA, NC	Y	29260 FQ	35580 MW	43490 TQ	USBLS	5/07
	Raleigh-Cary MSA, NC	Y	29840 FQ	34890 MW	39270 TQ	USBLS	5/07
	North Dakota	Y	22560 FQ	28890 MW	36420 TQ	USBLS	5/07
	Fargo MSA, ND-MN	Y	19980 FQ	28900 MW	37610 TQ	USBLS	5/07
	Ohio	Y	27630 FQ	35190 MW	43620 TQ	USBLS	5/07
	Cincinnati-Middletown MSA, OH-KY-IN	Y	28920 FQ	36230 MW	44820 TQ	USBLS	5/07
	Cleveland-Elyria-Mentor MSA, OH	Y	30910 FQ	37720 MW	44820 TQ	USBLS	5/07
	Columbus MSA, OH	Y	32990 FQ	40240 MW	46910 TQ	USBLS	5/07
	Dayton MSA, OH	Y	25590 FQ	29760 MW	36250 TQ	USBLS	5/07
	Oklahoma	Y	22930 FQ	28700 MW	36810 TQ	USBLS	5/07
	Oklahoma City MSA, OK	Y	22850 FQ	28460 MW	36580 TQ	USBLS	5/07
	Oregon	H	13.77 FQ	16.80 MW	20.38 TQ	ORBLS	5/08
	Eugene-Springfield MSA, OR	Y	33520 FQ	37250 MW	45840 TQ	USBLS	5/07
	Portland-Vancouver-Beaverton MSA, OR-WA	Y	27120 FQ	33930 MW	41060 TQ	USBLS	5/07
	Salem MSA, OR	Y	21580 FQ	36110 MW	45060 TQ	USBLS	5/07
	Pennsylvania	Y	26430 FQ	34190 MW	43100 TQ	USBLS	5/07
	Allentown-Bethlehem-Easton MSA, PA-NJ	Y	27020 FQ	34330 MW	40620 TQ	USBLS	5/07
	Philadelphia-Camden-Wilmington MSA, PA-NJ-DE-MD	Y	28710 FQ	36470 MW	45020 TQ	USBLS	5/07
	Pittsburgh MSA, PA	Y	25620 FQ	32930 MW	43380 TQ	USBLS	5/07
	Rhode Island	Y	28210 FQ	34710 MW	43100 TQ	USBLS	5/07
	Providence-Fall River-Warwick MSA, RI-MA	Y	28500 FQ	34850 MW	42910 TQ	USBLS	5/07
	South Carolina	Y	25890 FQ	32190 MW	39100 TQ	USBLS	5/07
	Charleston-North Charleston MSA, SC	Y	26040 FQ	34310 MW	39470 TQ	USBLS	5/07
	Columbia MSA, SC	Y	27370 FQ	33570 MW	39520 TQ	USBLS	5/07
	South Dakota	Y	24888 FQ	28883 MW	32990 TQ	SDBLS	7/08-9/08
	Sioux Falls MSA, SD	Y	26571 FQ	30221 MW	44631 TQ	SDBLS	7/08-9/08
	Tennessee	Y	24210 FQ	30740 MW	41210 TQ	USBLS	5/07
	Kingsport-Bristol-Bristol MSA, TN-VA	Y	28080 FQ	33420 MW	45670 TQ	USBLS	5/07
	Memphis MSA, TN-MS-AR	Y	29020 FQ	35540 MW	45970 TQ	USBLS	5/07
	Nashville-Davidson-Murfreesboro MSA, TN	Y	22310 FQ	29020 MW	43050 TQ	USBLS	5/07
	Texas	Y	25000 FQ	32280 MW	41070 TQ	USBLS	5/07
	Austin-Round Rock MSA, TX	Y	26650 FQ	32650 MW	43150 TQ	USBLS	5/07
	Corpus Christi MSA, TX	Y	22930 FQ	31300 MW	42740 TQ	USBLS	5/07
	Dallas-Fort Worth-Arlington MSA, TX	Y	27600 FQ	34410 MW	42300 TQ	USBLS	5/07
	El Paso MSA, TX	Y	18430 FQ	23730 MW	30760 TQ	USBLS	5/07
	Houston-Sugar Land-Baytown MSA, TX	Y	24210 FQ	33140 MW	42630 TQ	USBLS	5/07
	San Antonio MSA, TX	Y	28100 FQ	33800 MW	41040 TQ	USBLS	5/07
	Utah	Y	21360 FQ	27870 MW	37510 TQ	USBLS	5/07
	Salt Lake City MSA, UT	Y	18740 FQ	26120 MW	35120 TQ	USBLS	5/07

AE	Average entry wage	AW	Average wage paid	FQ	First quartile wage
AER	Average entry range	AWR	Average wage range	H	Hourly
AEX	Average experienced wage	AXR	Average experienced range	HI	Highest wage paid
ATC	Average total compensation	D	Daily	HR	High end range

LO	Lowest wage paid	MTC	Median total compensation	TCC	Total cash compensation
LR	Low end range	MW	Median wage paid	TQ	Third quartile wage
M	Monthly	MWR	Median wage range	W	Weekly
MCC	Median cash compensation	S	See annotated source	Y	Yearly

Occupation/Type/Industry	Location	Per	Low	Mid	High	Source	Date
Computer Operator	Vermont	Y	26630 FQ	31100 MW	37270 TQ	USBLS	5/07
	Burlington-South Burlington MSA, VT	Y	24670 FQ	28630 MW	32970 TQ	USBLS	5/07
	Virginia	Y	28020 FQ	35750 MW	46010 TQ	USBLS	5/07
	Richmond MSA, VA	Y	32270 FQ	39040 MW	46550 TQ	USBLS	5/07
	Virginia Beach-Norfolk-Newport News MSA, VA-NC	Y	23110 FQ	30050 MW	38430 TQ	USBLS	5/07
	Washington	H	14.58 FQ	18.66 MW	23.06 TQ	WABLS	3/08
	Olympia MSA, WA	Y	31160 FQ	36830 MW	48890 TQ	USBLS	5/07
	Seattle-Tacoma-Bellevue MSA, WA	Y	32230 FQ	40150 MW	48280 TQ	USBLS	5/07
	West Virginia	Y	20071 FQ	27195 MW	36565 TQ	WVBLS	7/08-9/08
	Charleston MSA, WV	Y	22210 FQ	26370 MW	32230 TQ	USBLS	5/07
	Wisconsin	Y	27700 FQ	34050 MW	41540 TQ	USBLS	5/07
	Milwaukee-Waukesha-West Allis MSA, WI	Y	27970 FQ	35080 MW	43450 TQ	USBLS	5/07
	Wyoming	Y	19300 FQ	25323 MW	34411 TQ	WYBLS	9/08
	Cheyenne MSA, WY	Y	32970 FQ	37108 MW	41018 TQ	WYBLS	9/08
	Puerto Rico	Y	15780 FQ	19060 MW	23860 TQ	USBLS	5/07
	San Juan-Caguas-Guaynabo MSA, PR	Y	15880 FQ	19350 MW	24030 TQ	USBLS	5/07
	Virgin Islands	Y	20460 FQ	26000 MW	30090 TQ	USBLS	5/07
	Guam	Y	19940 FQ	25720 MW	34540 TQ	USBLS	5/07
Computer Patternmaker Apparel Industry	United States	Y		72500 MW		247FASH	2009
Computer Programmer	Alabama	Y	45960 FQ	61660 MW	78030 TQ	USBLS	5/07
	Birmingham-Hoover MSA, AL	Y	55250 FQ	69360 MW	82150 TQ	USBLS	5/07
	Alaska	Y	55530 FQ	65530 MW	76720 TQ	USBLS	5/07
	Anchorage MSA, AK	Y	56980 FQ	66200 MW	77370 TQ	USBLS	5/07
	Arizona	Y	48040 FQ	65330 MW	81020 TQ	USBLS	5/07
	Phoenix-Mesa-Scottsdale MSA, AZ	Y	49710 FQ	66810 MW	83300 TQ	USBLS	5/07
	Prescott MSA, AZ	Y	53760 FQ	68630 MW	84710 TQ	USBLS	5/07
	Tucson MSA, AZ	Y	43030 FQ	60200 MW	75980 TQ	USBLS	5/07
	Arkansas	Y	50750 FQ	63140 MW	78410 TQ	USBLS	5/07
	Little Rock-North Little Rock MSA, AR	Y	55720 FQ	69260 MW	85410 TQ	USBLS	5/07
	California	H	28.45 FQ	37.54 MW	47.84 TQ	CABLS	1/08-3/08
	Fresno MSA, CA	H	24.17 FQ	27.94 MW	32.54 TQ	CABLS	1/08-3/08
	Los Angeles-Long Beach-Glendale PMSA, CA	H	27.46 FQ	36.20 MW	45.26 TQ	CABLS	1/08-3/08
	Modesto MSA, CA	H	25.78 FQ	29.87 MW	39.37 TQ	CABLS	1/08-3/08
	Oakland-Fremont-Hayward MSA, CA	H	28.28 FQ	36.27 MW	47.11 TQ	CABLS	1/08-3/08
	Riverside-San Bernardino-Ontario MSA, CA	H	20.16 FQ	25.55 MW	33.58 TQ	CABLS	1/08-3/08
	Sacramento-Arden Arcade-Roseville MSA, CA	H	26.75 FQ	33.37 MW	42.14 TQ	CABLS	1/08-3/08
	San Diego-Carlsbad-San Marcos MSA, CA	H	27.14 FQ	36.92 MW	45.66 TQ	CABLS	1/08-3/08
	San Francisco-San Mateo-Redwood PMSA, CA	H	33.05 FQ	42.40 MW	52.73 TQ	CABLS	1/08-3/08
	San Jose-Sunnyvale-Santa Clara MSA, CA	H	35.48 FQ	45.88 MW	59.25 TQ	CABLS	1/08-3/08
	Santa Ana-Anaheim-Irvine PMSA, CA	Y	58510 FQ	76140 MW	93940 TQ	USBLS	5/07
	Colorado	Y	56860 FQ	74770 MW	93190 TQ	USBLS	5/07
	Denver-Aurora MSA, CO	Y	57430 FQ	74130 MW	93320 TQ	USBLS	5/07
	Fort Collins-Loveland MSA, CO	Y	38610 FQ	60400 MW	87260 TQ	USBLS	5/07
	Connecticut	H	26.16 AE	40.41 MW		CTBLS	1/08-3/08
	Bridgeport-Stamford-Norwalk MSA, CT	Y	61790 FQ	78990 MW	104420 TQ	USBLS	5/07
	Hartford-West Hartford-East Hartford MSA, CT	Y	59640 FQ	73710 MW	91070 TQ	USBLS	5/07
	Norwich-New London MSA, CT-RI	Y	64160 FQ	77900 MW	97040 TQ	USBLS	5/07
	Delaware	Y	55830 FQ	71670 MW	90160 TQ	USBLS	5/07
	Wilmington PMSA, DE-MD-NJ	Y	56640 FQ	74280 MW	91670 TQ	USBLS	5/07

AE	Average entry wage	AW	Average wage paid	FQ	First quartile wage	LO	Lowest wage paid	MTC	Median total compensation	TCC	Total cash compensation
AER	Average entry range	AWR	Average wage range	H	Hourly	LR	Low end range	MW	Median wage paid	TQ	Third quartile wage
AEX	Average experienced wage	AXR	Average experienced range	HI	Highest wage paid	M	Monthly	MWR	Median wage range	W	Weekly
ATC	Average total compensation	D	Daily	HR	High end range	MCC	Median cash compensation	S	See annotated source	Y	Yearly

Occupation/Type/Industry	Location	Per	Low	Mid	High	Source	Date
Computer Programmer	District of Columbia Washington-Arlington-Alexandria MSA, DC-VA-MD-WV	Y	56130 FQ	69790 MW	86600 TQ	USBLS	5/07
		Y	61200 FQ	78600 MW	96980 TQ	USBLS	5/07
	Florida	Y	50400 FQ	64620 MW	81000 TQ	USBLS	5/07
	Cape Coral-Fort Myers MSA, FL	Y	55290 FQ	69830 MW	86980 TQ	USBLS	5/07
	Fort Lauderdale-Pompano Beach-Deerfield Beach PMSA, FL	Y	55430 FQ	69200 MW	84600 TQ	USBLS	5/07
	Jacksonville MSA, FL	Y	52970 FQ	66950 MW	83270 TQ	USBLS	5/07
	Miami-Fort Lauderdale-Miami Beach MSA, FL	Y	54550 FQ	69190 MW	85070 TQ	USBLS	5/07
	Orlando-Kissimmee MSA, FL	Y	52250 FQ	66800 MW	82520 TQ	USBLS	5/07
	Tampa-St. Petersburg-Clearwater MSA, FL	Y	47130 FQ	61420 MW	79010 TQ	USBLS	5/07
	West Palm Beach-Boca Raton-Boynton Beach PMSA, FL	Y	53490 FQ	68850 MW	87900 TQ	USBLS	5/07
	Georgia	Y	50990 FQ	69580 MW	89520 TQ	USBLS	5/07
	Atlanta-Sandy Springs-Marietta MSA, GA	Y	51350 FQ	69910 MW	92090 TQ	USBLS	5/07
	Macon MSA, GA	Y	45200 FQ	56960 MW	71350 TQ	USBLS	5/07
	Hawaii	Y	44090 FQ	58380 MW	73350 TQ	USBLS	5/07
	Honolulu MSA, HI	Y	44330 FQ	58740 MW	74020 TQ	USBLS	5/07
	Idaho	Y	39660 FQ	55270 MW	68230 TQ	USBLS	5/07
	Boise City-Nampa MSA, ID	Y	42610 FQ	57060 MW	71960 TQ	USBLS	5/07
	Illinois	Y	51340 FQ	69080 MW	91410 TQ	USBLS	5/07
	Champaign-Urbana MSA, IL	Y	33360 FQ	48600 MW	61260 TQ	USBLS	5/07
	Chicago-Naperville-Joliet MSA, IL-IN-WI	Y	53080 FQ	70980 MW	93760 TQ	USBLS	5/07
	Indiana	Y	45620 FQ	59620 MW	78990 TQ	USBLS	5/07
	Gary PMSA, IN	Y	39600 FQ	51390 MW	61190 TQ	USBLS	5/07
	Indianapolis-Carmel MSA, IN	Y	46690 FQ	62540 MW	86090 TQ	USBLS	5/07
	Iowa	Y	46390 FQ	57810 MW	70690 TQ	USBLS	5/07
	Des Moines-West Des Moines MSA, IA	Y	49120 FQ	61060 MW	74770 TQ	USBLS	5/07
	Kansas	Y	52090 FQ	63180 MW	77610 TQ	USBLS	5/07
	Wichita MSA, KS	Y	46060 FQ	60830 MW	77660 TQ	USBLS	5/07
	Kentucky	Y	50644 FQ	64692 MW	80548 TQ	KYBLS	2008
	Louisville-Jefferson County MSA, KY-IN	Y	51200 FQ	64010 MW	79780 TQ	USBLS	5/07
	Louisiana	H	18.81 FQ	24.41 MW	30.51 TQ	LABLS	1/08-3/08
	Baton Rouge MSA, LA	Y	40840 FQ	51170 MW	63200 TQ	USBLS	5/07
	New Orleans-Metairie-Kenner MSA, LA	Y	42180 FQ	55090 MW	66750 TQ	USBLS	5/07
	Maine	Y	46370 FQ	58240 MW	77420 TQ	USBLS	5/07
	Portland-South Portland-Biddeford MSA, ME	Y	49190 FQ	60310 MW	78630 TQ	USBLS	5/07
	Maryland	Y		74975 MW		MDBLS	3/08
	Baltimore-Towson MSA, MD	Y	54910 FQ	71590 MW	91350 TQ	USBLS	5/07
	Bethesda-Gaithersburg-Frederick PMSA, MD	Y	58310 FQ	76070 MW	96280 TQ	USBLS	5/07
	Massachusetts	Y	55550 FQ	73140 MW	94150 TQ	USBLS	5/07
	Boston-Cambridge-Quincy NECTA, MA	Y	56560 FQ	74380 MW	94230 TQ	USBLS	5/07
	Worcester MSA, MA-CT	Y	59680 FQ	79980 MW	104130 TQ	USBLS	5/07
	Michigan	Y	52480 FQ	67180 MW	80780 TQ	USBLS	5/07
	Detroit-Warren-Livonia MSA, MI	Y	57330 FQ	71300 MW	83590 TQ	USBLS	5/07
	Grand Rapids-Wyoming MSA, MI	Y	46720 FQ	55330 MW	66110 TQ	USBLS	5/07
	Lansing-East Lansing MSA, MI	Y	51660 FQ	64410 MW	75490 TQ	USBLS	5/07
	Muskegon-Norton Shores MSA, MI	Y	35370 FQ	40190 MW	49470 TQ	USBLS	5/07
	Warren-Troy-Farmington Hills PMSA, MI	Y	53810 FQ	69070 MW	83530 TQ	USBLS	5/07
	Minnesota	Y	53901 FQ	68297 MW	85842 TQ	MNBLS	10/08-12/08
	Duluth-Superior MSA, MN-WI	Y	43230 FQ	52206 MW	70955 TQ	MNBLS	10/08-12/08
	Minneapolis-Saint Paul MSA, MN-WI	Y	54968 FQ	69040 MW	85298 TQ	MNBLS	10/08-12/08
	Rochester MSA, MN	Y	67798 FQ	95296 MW	130456 TQ	MNBLS	10/08-12/08
	Mississippi	Y	36000 FQ	49070 MW	63010 TQ	USBLS	5/07

AE Average entry wage; AER Average entry range; AEX Average experienced wage; ATC Average total compensation; AW Average wage paid; AWR Average wage range; AXR Average experienced range; D Daily; FQ First quartile wage; H Hourly; HI Highest wage paid; HR High end range; LO Lowest wage paid; LR Low end range; M Monthly; MCC Median cash compensation; MTC Median total compensation; MW Median wage paid; MWR Median wage range; S See annotated source; TCC Total cash compensation; TQ Third quartile wage; W Weekly; Y Yearly

288

Occupation/Type/Industry	Location	Per	Low	Mid	High	Source	Date
Computer Programmer	Jackson MSA, MS	Y	31010 FQ	48310 MW	67460 TQ	USBLS	5/07
	Missouri	Y	48530 FQ	63650 MW	80380 TQ	USBLS	5/07
	Kansas City MSA, MO-KS	Y	55370 FQ	68020 MW	83170 TQ	USBLS	5/07
	St. Louis MSA, MO-IL	Y	47530 FQ	64690 MW	80980 TQ	USBLS	5/07
	Montana	Y	34890 FQ	44680 MW	61600 TQ	USBLS	5/07
	Billings MSA, MT	Y	39340 FQ	50370 MW	59400 TQ	USBLS	5/07
	Nebraska	Y	44350 FQ	58990 MW	79470 TQ	USBLS	5/07
	Omaha-Council Bluffs MSA, NE-IA	Y	47530 FQ	62740 MW	85350 TQ	USBLS	5/07
	Nevada	H	23.84 FQ	32.69 MW	39.26 TQ	NVBLS	5/08
	Las Vegas-Paradise MSA, NV	H	23.80 FQ	32.88 MW	39.14 TQ	NVBLS	5/08
	Reno-Sparks MSA, NV	H	21.23 FQ	27.19 MW	41.81 TQ	NVBLS	5/08
	New Hampshire	H	18.69 AE	25.37 MW	32.13 AEX	NHBLS	6/08
	Manchester MSA, NH	Y	35320 FQ	42090 MW	52960 TQ	USBLS	5/07
	Nashua NECTA, NH-MA	Y	48880 FQ	55220 MW	65460 TQ	USBLS	5/07
	New Jersey	Y	59460 FQ	78220 MW	102320 TQ	USBLS	5/07
	Atlantic City MSA, NJ	Y	58490 FQ	77630 MW	96430 TQ	USBLS	5/07
	Camden PMSA, NJ	Y	58940 FQ	76140 MW	95200 TQ	USBLS	5/07
	Edison PMSA, NJ	Y	58710 FQ	74850 MW	103260 TQ	USBLS	5/07
	Newark-Union PMSA, NJ-PA	Y	64340 FQ	84140 MW	120180 TQ	USBLS	5/07
	Vineland-Millville-Bridgeton MSA, NJ	Y	52090 FQ	65470 MW	76980 TQ	USBLS	5/07
	New Mexico	Y	50320 FQ	62340 MW	90490 TQ	USBLS	5/07
	Albuquerque MSA, NM	Y	51140 FQ	63660 MW	93600 TQ	USBLS	5/07
	New York	Y	52870 FQ	68680 MW	89260 TQ	USBLS	5/07
	Albany-Schenectady-Troy MSA, NY	Y	48310 FQ	59640 MW	72660 TQ	USBLS	5/07
	Buffalo-Niagara Falls MSA, NY	Y	44960 FQ	56470 MW	70220 TQ	USBLS	5/07
	Glens Falls MSA, NY	Y	34670 FQ	39950 MW	70610 TQ	USBLS	5/07
	Ithaca MSA, NY	Y	42050 FQ	50720 MW	61280 TQ	USBLS	5/07
	Nassau-Suffolk PMSA, NY	Y	57500 FQ	71540 MW	90620 TQ	USBLS	5/07
	New York-Northern New Jersey-Long Island MSA, NY-NJ-PA	Y	57840 FQ	75190 MW	98900 TQ	USBLS	5/07
	Utica-Rome MSA, NY	Y	41600 FQ	49240 MW	63730 TQ	USBLS	5/07
	North Carolina	Y	54690 FQ	71920 MW	90490 TQ	USBLS	5/07
	Charlotte-Gastonia-Concord MSA, NC-SC	Y	62770 FQ	77650 MW	94630 TQ	USBLS	5/07
	Raleigh-Cary MSA, NC	Y	52530 FQ	71130 MW	90020 TQ	USBLS	5/07
	North Dakota	Y	35790 FQ	43730 MW	53140 TQ	USBLS	5/07
	Fargo MSA, ND-MN	Y	39800 FQ	45890 MW	55040 TQ	USBLS	5/07
	Ohio	Y	46990 FQ	62750 MW	80180 TQ	USBLS	5/07
	Canton-Massillon MSA, OH	Y	47100 FQ	58810 MW	71900 TQ	USBLS	5/07
	Cincinnati-Middletown MSA, OH-KY-IN	Y	46640 FQ	61360 MW	75930 TQ	USBLS	5/07
	Cleveland-Elyria-Mentor MSA, OH	Y	43290 FQ	63510 MW	84490 TQ	USBLS	5/07
	Columbus MSA, OH	Y	51530 FQ	67520 MW	84960 TQ	USBLS	5/07
	Dayton MSA, OH	Y	52060 FQ	64520 MW	78630 TQ	USBLS	5/07
	Oklahoma	Y	39500 FQ	53840 MW	71370 TQ	USBLS	5/07
	Lawton MSA, OK	Y	37900 FQ	44770 MW	52400 TQ	USBLS	5/07
	Oklahoma City MSA, OK	Y	42450 FQ	55790 MW	74370 TQ	USBLS	5/07
	Tulsa MSA, OK	Y	37640 FQ	55730 MW	71710 TQ	USBLS	5/07
	Oregon	H	22.67 FQ	31.68 MW	40.26 TQ	ORBLS	5/08
	Medford MSA, OR	Y	34810 FQ	50340 MW	64150 TQ	USBLS	5/07
	Portland-Vancouver-Beaverton MSA, OR-WA	Y	48930 FQ	67920 MW	85510 TQ	USBLS	5/07
	Pennsylvania	Y	48180 FQ	65150 MW	84530 TQ	USBLS	5/07
	Allentown-Bethlehem-Easton MSA, PA-NJ	Y	47950 FQ	60580 MW	75200 TQ	USBLS	5/07
	Philadelphia-Camden-Wilmington MSA, PA-NJ-DE-MD	Y	52930 FQ	72090 MW	94680 TQ	USBLS	5/07
	Pittsburgh MSA, PA	Y	44920 FQ	61170 MW	78610 TQ	USBLS	5/07
	Rhode Island	Y	51660 FQ	67690 MW	82830 TQ	USBLS	5/07
	Providence-Fall River-Warwick MSA, RI-MA	Y	51370 FQ	67690 MW	82830 TQ	USBLS	5/07
	South Carolina	Y	44120 FQ	57330 MW	72820 TQ	USBLS	5/07
	Charleston-North Charleston MSA, SC	Y	39560 FQ	50040 MW	62060 TQ	USBLS	5/07
	Columbia MSA, SC	Y	43160 FQ	57990 MW	73940 TQ	USBLS	5/07

AE Average entry wage	**AW** Average wage paid	**FQ** First quartile wage	**LO** Lowest wage paid	**MTC** Median total compensation	**TCC** Total cash compensation
AER Average entry range	**AWR** Average wage range	**H** Hourly	**LR** Low end range	**MW** Median wage paid	**TQ** Third quartile wage
AEX Average experienced wage	**AXR** Average experienced range	**HI** Highest wage paid	**M** Monthly	**MWR** Median wage range	**W** Weekly
ATC Average total compensation	**D** Daily	**HR** High end range	**MCC** Median cash compensation	**S** See annotated source	**Y** Yearly

Occupation/Type/Industry	Location	Per	Low	Mid	High	Source	Date
Computer Programmer	Florence MSA, SC	Y	46000 FQ	56220 MW	68760 TQ	USBLS	5/07
	South Dakota	Y	38415 FQ	45391 MW	54387 TQ	SDBLS	7/08-9/08
	Sioux Falls MSA, SD	Y	37822 FQ	45135 MW	56949 TQ	SDBLS	7/08-9/08
	Tennessee	Y	45360 FQ	61360 MW	77540 TQ	USBLS	5/07
	Clarksville MSA, TN-KY	Y	42950 FQ	50890 MW	63140 TQ	USBLS	5/07
	Memphis MSA, TN-MS-AR	Y	56500 FQ	68580 MW	81200 TQ	USBLS	5/07
	Nashville-Davidson-Murfreesboro MSA, TN	Y	39220 FQ	53980 MW	77410 TQ	USBLS	5/07
	Texas	Y	53390 FQ	72740 MW	93510 TQ	USBLS	5/07
	Austin-Round Rock MSA, TX	Y	52470 FQ	68320 MW	89390 TQ	USBLS	5/07
	Dallas-Fort Worth-Arlington MSA, TX	Y	59900 FQ	78170 MW	96680 TQ	USBLS	5/07
	El Paso MSA, TX	Y	31320 FQ	40600 MW	51800 TQ	USBLS	5/07
	Houston-Sugar Land-Baytown MSA, TX	Y	54860 FQ	75850 MW	96480 TQ	USBLS	5/07
	San Antonio MSA, TX	Y	48700 FQ	64090 MW	80420 TQ	USBLS	5/07
	Utah	Y	49940 FQ	67200 MW	87650 TQ	USBLS	5/07
	Salt Lake City MSA, UT	Y	53570 FQ	71390 MW	98210 TQ	USBLS	5/07
	Vermont	Y	42720 FQ	57030 MW	75080 TQ	USBLS	5/07
	Burlington-South Burlington MSA, VT	Y	50720 FQ	64250 MW	82010 TQ	USBLS	5/07
	Virginia	Y	56860 FQ	76500 MW	96430 TQ	USBLS	5/07
	Charlottesville MSA, VA	Y	48440 FQ	60650 MW	80820 TQ	USBLS	5/07
	Lynchburg MSA, VA	Y	38170 FQ	47930 MW	66200 TQ	USBLS	5/07
	Richmond MSA, VA	Y	65820 FQ	79160 MW	99930 TQ	USBLS	5/07
	Virginia Beach-Norfolk-Newport News MSA, VA-NC	Y	42720 FQ	51670 MW	66500 TQ	USBLS	5/07
	Washington	H	30.14 FQ	39.07 MW	49.59 TQ	WABLS	3/08
	Seattle-Tacoma-Bellevue MSA, WA	Y	65390 FQ	83900 MW	104600 TQ	USBLS	5/07
	West Virginia	Y	38399 FQ	46074 MW	58402 TQ	WVBLS	7/08-9/08
	Charleston MSA, WV	Y	38640 FQ	46900 MW	58910 TQ	USBLS	5/07
	Wisconsin	Y	44800 FQ	56660 MW	72820 TQ	USBLS	5/07
	Milwaukee-Waukesha-West Allis MSA, WI	Y	46980 FQ	57560 MW	75020 TQ	USBLS	5/07
	Racine MSA, WI	Y	48240 FQ	58010 MW	67480 TQ	USBLS	5/07
	Wyoming	Y	31875 FQ	43805 MW	55730 TQ	WYBLS	9/08
	Cheyenne MSA, WY	Y	33288 FQ	46822 MW	55001 TQ	WYBLS	9/08
	Puerto Rico	Y	28220 FQ	36280 MW	47810 TQ	USBLS	5/07
	San Juan-Caguas-Guaynabo MSA, PR	Y	28920 FQ	36960 MW	48460 TQ	USBLS	5/07
	Virgin Islands	Y	36400 FQ	41030 MW	47320 TQ	USBLS	5/07
Computer Programmer/Analyst							
Municipal Government	Cincinnati, OH	Y	34657 LO		47722 HI	COHSS	10/08
State Government	Arkansas	Y	28182 LO		48960 HI	AFT02	3/1/08
Computer Science Teacher							
Postsecondary	Alabama	Y	43580 FQ	60820 MW	87810 TQ	USBLS	5/07
Postsecondary	Birmingham-Hoover MSA, AL	Y	45470 FQ	68980 MW	87680 TQ	USBLS	5/07
Postsecondary	Arizona	Y	45990 FQ	56780 MW	69170 TQ	USBLS	5/07
Postsecondary	Phoenix-Mesa-Scottsdale MSA, AZ	Y	48310 FQ	58090 MW	68100 TQ	USBLS	5/07
Postsecondary	Tucson MSA, AZ	Y	43620 FQ	51480 MW	89700 TQ	USBLS	5/07
Postsecondary	Arkansas	Y	36800 FQ	51420 MW	78710 TQ	USBLS	5/07
Postsecondary	California	Y		88673 AW		CABLS	1/08-3/08
Postsecondary	Los Angeles-Long Beach-Glendale PMSA, CA	Y		85914 AW		CABLS	1/08-3/08
Postsecondary	Oakland-Fremont-Hayward MSA, CA	Y		106372 AW		CABLS	1/08-3/08
Postsecondary	Riverside-San Bernardino-Ontario MSA, CA	Y		86211 AW		CABLS	1/08-3/08
Postsecondary	Sacramento-Arden Arcade-Roseville MSA, CA	Y		88560 AW		CABLS	1/08-3/08
Postsecondary	San Diego-Carlsbad-San Marcos MSA, CA	Y		78182 AW		CABLS	1/08-3/08
Postsecondary	San Francisco-San Mateo-Redwood PMSA, CA	Y		108362 AW		CABLS	1/08-3/08
Postsecondary	San Jose-Sunnyvale-Santa Clara MSA, CA	Y		72788 AW		CABLS	1/08-3/08
Postsecondary	Santa Ana-Anaheim-Irvine PMSA, CA	Y	65520 FQ	79300 MW	104760 TQ	USBLS	5/07

AE	Average entry wage	AW	Average wage paid	FQ	First quartile wage
AER	Average entry range	AWR	Average wage range	H	Hourly
AEX	Average experienced wage	AXR	Average experienced range	HI	Highest wage paid
ATC	Average total compensation	D	Daily	HR	High end range

LO	Lowest wage paid	MTC	Median total compensation
LR	Low end range	MW	Median wage paid
M	Monthly	MWR	Median wage range
MCC	Median cash compensation	S	See annotated source

TCC	Total cash compensation
TQ	Third quartile wage
W	Weekly
Y	Yearly

Computer Science Teacher

Occupation/Type/Industry	Location	Per	Low	Mid	High	Source	Date
Computer Science Teacher							
Postsecondary	Colorado	Y	42900 FQ	58460 MW	79850 TQ	USBLS	5/07
Postsecondary	Denver-Aurora MSA, CO	Y	42540 FQ	52420 MW	77660 TQ	USBLS	5/07
Postsecondary	Bridgeport-Stamford-Norwalk MSA, CT	Y	46750 FQ	65960 MW	100740 TQ	USBLS	5/07
Postsecondary	New Haven MSA, CT	Y	60190 FQ	79360 MW	103790 TQ	USBLS	5/07
Postsecondary	Delaware	Y	57700 FQ	74910 MW	100860 TQ	USBLS	5/07
Postsecondary	Wilmington PMSA, DE-MD-NJ	Y	55850 FQ	84010 MW	105280 TQ	USBLS	5/07
Postsecondary	District of Columbia	Y	45860 FQ	58980 MW	76670 TQ	USBLS	5/07
Postsecondary	Washington-Arlington-Alexandria MSA, DC-VA-MD-WV	Y	54980 FQ	73910 MW	89660 TQ	USBLS	5/07
Postsecondary	Florida	Y	43230 FQ	64530 MW	87170 TQ	USBLS	5/07
Postsecondary	Fort Lauderdale-Pompano Beach-Deerfield Beach PMSA, FL	Y	49690 FQ	70660 MW	93020 TQ	USBLS	5/07
Postsecondary	Miami-Fort Lauderdale-Miami Beach MSA, FL	Y	45920 FQ	68790 MW	94450 TQ	USBLS	5/07
Postsecondary	Orlando-Kissimmee MSA, FL	Y	33130 FQ	55140 MW	78890 TQ	USBLS	5/07
Postsecondary	Tampa-St. Petersburg-Clearwater MSA, FL	Y	51120 FQ	73690 MW	100920 TQ	USBLS	5/07
Postsecondary	West Palm Beach-Boca Raton-Boynton Beach PMSA, FL	Y	43780 FQ	72360 MW	102470 TQ	USBLS	5/07
Postsecondary	Georgia	Y	44870 FQ	56970 MW	80160 TQ	USBLS	5/07
Postsecondary	Atlanta-Sandy Springs-Marietta MSA, GA	Y	46710 FQ	63340 MW	83170 TQ	USBLS	5/07
Postsecondary	Hawaii	Y	44570 FQ	65590 MW	87220 TQ	USBLS	5/07
Postsecondary	Honolulu MSA, HI	Y	46400 FQ	66030 MW	86730 TQ	USBLS	5/07
Postsecondary	Illinois	Y	39580 FQ	56110 MW	80640 TQ	USBLS	5/07
Postsecondary	Chicago-Naperville-Joliet MSA, IL-IN-WI	Y	42380 FQ	58160 MW	79280 TQ	USBLS	5/07
Postsecondary	Indiana	Y	48420 FQ	60470 MW	81720 TQ	USBLS	5/07
Postsecondary	Gary PMSA, IN	Y	48010 FQ	59480 MW	71550 TQ	USBLS	5/07
Postsecondary	Indianapolis-Carmel MSA, IN	Y	43500 FQ	56210 MW	78630 TQ	USBLS	5/07
Postsecondary	Iowa	Y	44180 FQ	56670 MW	75340 TQ	USBLS	5/07
Postsecondary	Des Moines-West Des Moines MSA, IA	Y	48060 FQ	66840 MW	81330 TQ	USBLS	5/07
Postsecondary	Kansas	Y	40080 FQ	56120 MW	86740 TQ	USBLS	5/07
Postsecondary	Wichita MSA, KS	Y	41520 FQ	63200 MW	94060 TQ	USBLS	5/07
Postsecondary	Kentucky	Y	43289 FQ	55948 MW	79893 TQ	KYBLS	2008
Postsecondary	Louisville-Jefferson County MSA, KY-IN	Y	43570 FQ	57330 MW	99820 TQ	USBLS	5/07
Postsecondary	Louisiana	Y		61440 AW		LABLS	1/08-3/08
Postsecondary	Baton Rouge MSA, LA	Y	51410 FQ	64150 MW	81930 TQ	USBLS	5/07
Postsecondary	New Orleans-Metairie-Kenner MSA, LA	Y	36790 FQ	44080 MW	62800 TQ	USBLS	5/07
Postsecondary	Maine	Y	40800 FQ	52380 MW	78390 TQ	USBLS	5/07
Postsecondary	Maryland	Y		66775 MW		MDBLS	3/08
Postsecondary	Baltimore-Towson MSA, MD	Y	47370 FQ	61510 MW	92170 TQ	USBLS	5/07
Postsecondary	Bethesda-Gaithersburg-Frederick PMSA, MD	Y	57950 FQ	75270 MW	98040 TQ	USBLS	5/07
Postsecondary	Massachusetts	Y	59490 FQ	89150 MW	118630 TQ	USBLS	5/07
Postsecondary	Boston-Cambridge-Quincy NECTA, MA	Y	57900 FQ	93190 MW	122170 TQ	USBLS	5/07
Postsecondary	Worcester MSA, MA-CT	Y	57280 FQ	83200 MW	113070 TQ	USBLS	5/07
Postsecondary	Michigan	Y	45460 FQ	65190 MW	86280 TQ	USBLS	5/07
Postsecondary	Detroit-Warren-Livonia MSA, MI	Y	29310 FQ	55770 MW	77570 TQ	USBLS	5/07
Postsecondary	Warren-Troy-Farmington Hills PMSA, MI	Y	29550 FQ	63330 MW	95390 TQ	USBLS	5/07
Postsecondary	Minnesota	Y	49245 FQ	61183 MW	84231 TQ	MNBLS	10/08-12/08
Postsecondary	Duluth-Superior MSA, MN-WI	Y	49936 FQ	71112 MW	88876 TQ	MNBLS	10/08-12/08
Postsecondary	Minneapolis-Saint Paul MSA, MN-WI	Y	48816 FQ	60513 MW	85602 TQ	MNBLS	10/08-12/08
Postsecondary	Mississippi	Y	45610 FQ	56970 MW	74010 TQ	USBLS	5/07
Postsecondary	Jackson MSA, MS	Y	42940 FQ	50670 MW	58470 TQ	USBLS	5/07
Postsecondary	Missouri	Y	43900 FQ	65730 MW	86640 TQ	USBLS	5/07
Postsecondary	Kansas City MSA, MO-KS	Y	39490 FQ	57570 MW	82770 TQ	USBLS	5/07
Postsecondary	St. Louis MSA, MO-IL	Y	35260 FQ	58840 MW	85280 TQ	USBLS	5/07
Postsecondary	Montana	Y	35960 FQ	46170 MW	60910 TQ	USBLS	5/07
Postsecondary	Nebraska	Y	39380 FQ	51470 MW	71690 TQ	USBLS	5/07

AE	Average entry wage	AW	Average wage paid	FQ	First quartile wage
AER	Average entry range	AWR	Average wage range	H	Hourly
AEX	Average experienced wage	AXR	Average experienced range	HI	Highest wage paid
ATC	Average total compensation	D	Daily	HR	High end range

LO	Lowest wage paid	MTC	Median total compensation	TCC	Total cash compensation
LR	Low end range	MW	Median wage paid	TQ	Third quartile wage
M	Monthly	MWR	Median wage range	W	Weekly
MCC	Median cash compensation	S	See annotated source	Y	Yearly

Computer Science Teacher

Occupation/Type/Industry	Location	Per	Low	Mid	High	Source	Date
Postsecondary	Omaha-Council Bluffs MSA, NE-IA	Y	38050 FQ	52100 MW	76790 TQ	USBLS	5/07
Postsecondary	New Hampshire	Y	39803 AE	61415 MW	82388 AEX	NHBLS	6/08
Postsecondary	Nashua NECTA, NH-MA	Y	47210 FQ	67750 MW	78970 TQ	USBLS	5/07
Postsecondary	New Jersey	Y	52980 FQ	73330 MW	97320 TQ	USBLS	5/07
Postsecondary	Camden PMSA, NJ	Y	50750 FQ	75560 MW	99830 TQ	USBLS	5/07
Postsecondary	Edison PMSA, NJ	Y	54730 FQ	71860 MW	96930 TQ	USBLS	5/07
Postsecondary	Newark-Union PMSA, NJ-PA	Y	52640 FQ	72980 MW	94010 TQ	USBLS	5/07
Postsecondary	New Mexico	Y	45200 FQ	55500 MW	68200 TQ	USBLS	5/07
Postsecondary	Albuquerque MSA, NM	Y	40380 FQ	51340 MW	61770 TQ	USBLS	5/07
Postsecondary	New York	Y	55670 FQ	77690 MW	98120 TQ	USBLS	5/07
Postsecondary	Albany-Schenectady-Troy MSA, NY	Y	39850 FQ	50080 MW	75760 TQ	USBLS	5/07
Postsecondary	Buffalo-Niagara Falls MSA, NY	Y	38790 FQ	70320 MW	91400 TQ	USBLS	5/07
Postsecondary	New York-Northern New Jersey-Long Island MSA, NY-NJ-PA	Y	57470 FQ	77470 MW	98290 TQ	USBLS	5/07
Postsecondary	North Carolina	Y	44030 FQ	53140 MW	72090 TQ	USBLS	5/07
Postsecondary	Charlotte-Gastonia-Concord MSA, NC-SC	Y	41040 FQ	51280 MW	67920 TQ	USBLS	5/07
Postsecondary	Durham MSA, NC	Y	48730 FQ	67980 MW	110050 TQ	USBLS	5/07
Postsecondary	Greensboro-High Point MSA, NC	Y	42730 FQ	50780 MW	64300 TQ	USBLS	5/07
Postsecondary	Raleigh-Cary MSA, NC	Y	54800 FQ	83840 MW	97200 TQ	USBLS	5/07
Postsecondary	North Dakota	Y	38000 FQ	49900 MW	63500 TQ	USBLS	5/07
Postsecondary	Fargo MSA, ND-MN	Y	51370 FQ	57520 MW	66130 TQ	USBLS	5/07
Postsecondary	Ohio	Y	37050 FQ	56060 MW	85490 TQ	USBLS	5/07
Postsecondary	Cincinnati-Middletown MSA, OH-KY-IN	Y	47430 FQ	70760 MW	94850 TQ	USBLS	5/07
Postsecondary	Cleveland-Elyria-Mentor MSA, OH	Y	36210 FQ	55820 MW	78020 TQ	USBLS	5/07
Postsecondary	Columbus MSA, OH	Y	30050 FQ	66260 MW	97050 TQ	USBLS	5/07
Postsecondary	Dayton MSA, OH	Y	34820 FQ	51020 MW	84030 TQ	USBLS	5/07
Postsecondary	Oklahoma	Y	27430 FQ	34290 MW	44900 TQ	USBLS	5/07
Postsecondary	Oklahoma City MSA, OK	Y	31240 FQ	45770 MW	69810 TQ	USBLS	5/07
Postsecondary	Tulsa MSA, OK	Y	30980 FQ	36260 MW	45830 TQ	USBLS	5/07
Postsecondary	Portland-Vancouver-Beaverton MSA, OR-WA	Y	61180 FQ	96600 MW	119590 TQ	USBLS	5/07
Postsecondary	Pennsylvania	Y	49520 FQ	73420 MW	99900 TQ	USBLS	5/07
Postsecondary	Allentown-Bethlehem-Easton MSA, PA-NJ	Y	40720 FQ	90350 MW	118510 TQ	USBLS	5/07
Postsecondary	Philadelphia-Camden-Wilmington MSA, PA-NJ-DE-MD	Y	51480 FQ	74860 MW	96660 TQ	USBLS	5/07
Postsecondary	Pittsburgh MSA, PA	Y	53890 FQ	82920 MW	116450 TQ	USBLS	5/07
Postsecondary	Rhode Island	Y	68670 FQ	84040 MW	100680 TQ	USBLS	5/07
Postsecondary	Providence-Fall River-Warwick MSA, RI-MA	Y	66830 FQ	83110 MW	98920 TQ	USBLS	5/07
Postsecondary	South Carolina	Y	46790 FQ	58490 MW	74890 TQ	USBLS	5/07
Postsecondary	Charleston-North Charleston MSA, SC	Y	57130 FQ	63380 MW	75150 TQ	USBLS	5/07
Postsecondary	Columbia MSA, SC	Y	58250 FQ	73170 MW	92740 TQ	USBLS	5/07
Postsecondary	South Dakota	Y	42438 FQ	51189 MW	61853 TQ	SDBLS	7/08-9/08
Postsecondary	Sioux Falls MSA, SD	Y	38579 FQ	45087 MW	53280 TQ	SDBLS	7/08-9/08
Postsecondary	Tennessee	Y	44200 FQ	59430 MW	96080 TQ	USBLS	5/07
Postsecondary	Memphis MSA, TN-MS-AR	Y	36980 FQ	48730 MW	65650 TQ	USBLS	5/07
Postsecondary	Nashville-Davidson-Murfreesboro MSA, TN	Y	51700 FQ	79170 MW	119510 TQ	USBLS	5/07
Postsecondary	Texas	Y	41760 FQ	58500 MW	83420 TQ	USBLS	5/07
Postsecondary	Austin-Round Rock MSA, TX	Y	49590 FQ	82090 MW	115260 TQ	USBLS	5/07
Postsecondary	Dallas-Fort Worth-Arlington MSA, TX	Y	36010 FQ	57120 MW	81120 TQ	USBLS	5/07
Postsecondary	El Paso MSA, TX	Y	39780 FQ	58670 MW	88130 TQ	USBLS	5/07
Postsecondary	Houston-Sugar Land-Baytown MSA, TX	Y	46460 FQ	63810 MW	97140 TQ	USBLS	5/07
Postsecondary	San Antonio MSA, TX	Y	46590 FQ	59960 MW	78660 TQ	USBLS	5/07
Postsecondary	Utah	Y	51360 FQ	66750 MW	92430 TQ	USBLS	5/07
Postsecondary	Salt Lake City MSA, UT	Y	46240 FQ	64910 MW	112270 TQ	USBLS	5/07
Postsecondary	Vermont	Y	42950 FQ	51620 MW	63080 TQ	USBLS	5/07

AE	Average entry wage	AW	Average wage paid	FQ	First quartile wage	LO	Lowest wage paid	MTC	Median total compensation	TCC	Total cash compensation
AER	Average entry range	AWR	Average wage range	H	Hourly	LR	Low end range	MW	Median wage paid	TQ	Third quartile wage
AEX	Average experienced wage	AXR	Average experienced range	HI	Highest wage paid	M	Monthly	MWR	Median wage range	W	Weekly
ATC	Average total compensation	D	Daily	HR	High end range	MCC	Median cash compensation	S	See annotated source	Y	Yearly

Occupation/Type/Industry	Location	Per	Low	Mid	High	Source	Date
Computer Science Teacher							
Postsecondary	Burlington-South Burlington MSA, VT	Y	41360 FQ	52810 MW	66620 TQ	USBLS	5/07
Postsecondary	Virginia	Y	47210 FQ	68120 MW	87900 TQ	USBLS	5/07
Postsecondary	Richmond MSA, VA	Y	31330 FQ	50390 MW	69140 TQ	USBLS	5/07
Postsecondary	Virginia Beach-Norfolk-Newport News MSA, VA-NC	Y	46760 FQ	66190 MW	94700 TQ	USBLS	5/07
Postsecondary	Washington	Y		73861 AW		WABLS	3/08
Postsecondary	Seattle-Tacoma-Bellevue MSA, WA	Y	48590 FQ	60860 MW	88350 TQ	USBLS	5/07
Postsecondary	West Virginia	Y	40854 FQ	48710 MW	63499 TQ	WVBLS	7/08-9/08
Postsecondary	Wisconsin	Y	54020 FQ	70530 MW	92770 TQ	USBLS	5/07
Postsecondary	Milwaukee-Waukesha-West Allis MSA, WI	Y	52150 FQ	73550 MW	98560 TQ	USBLS	5/07
Postsecondary	Wyoming	Y	47193 FQ	58446 MW	77888 TQ	WYBLS	9/08
Postsecondary	Puerto Rico	Y	20990 FQ	26330 MW	40590 TQ	USBLS	5/07
Postsecondary	San Juan-Caguas-Guaynabo MSA, PR	Y	20720 FQ	26280 MW	42970 TQ	USBLS	5/07
Computer Security Specialist	United States	Y		59200 AW		GLKNO1	10/20/08-11/11/08
Computer Software Engineer							
Applications	Alabama	Y	54800 FQ	74140 MW	92040 TQ	USBLS	5/07
Applications	Birmingham-Hoover MSA, AL	Y	48870 FQ	63950 MW	80620 TQ	USBLS	5/07
Applications	Alaska	Y	54470 FQ	66840 MW	88580 TQ	USBLS	5/07
Applications	Anchorage MSA, AK	Y	58490 FQ	74360 MW	92320 TQ	USBLS	5/07
Applications	Arizona	Y	56410 FQ	73880 MW	92260 TQ	USBLS	5/07
Applications	Phoenix-Mesa-Scottsdale MSA, AZ	Y	55510 FQ	72600 MW	90720 TQ	USBLS	5/07
Applications	Prescott MSA, AZ	Y	51990 FQ	68590 MW	79350 TQ	USBLS	5/07
Applications	Tucson MSA, AZ	Y	64920 FQ	83050 MW	100400 TQ	USBLS	5/07
Applications	Arkansas	Y	48210 FQ	63590 MW	78590 TQ	USBLS	5/07
Applications	Little Rock-North Little Rock MSA, AR	Y	50150 FQ	65350 MW	81080 TQ	USBLS	5/07
Applications	California	H	36.01 FQ	46.38 MW	57.55 TQ	CABLS	1/08-3/08
Applications	Los Angeles-Long Beach-Glendale PMSA, CA	H	34.08 FQ	43.71 MW	53.81 TQ	CABLS	1/08-3/08
Applications	Modesto MSA, CA	H	35.15 FQ	43.08 MW	54.31 TQ	CABLS	1/08-3/08
Applications	Oakland-Fremont-Hayward MSA, CA	H	36.64 FQ	46.32 MW	58.14 TQ	CABLS	1/08-3/08
Applications	Oxnard-Thousand Oaks-Ventura MSA, CA	H	32.98 FQ	40.70 MW	49.95 TQ	CABLS	1/08-3/08
Applications	Riverside-San Bernardino-Ontario MSA, CA	H	32.74 FQ	41.69 MW	51.94 TQ	CABLS	1/08-3/08
Applications	Sacramento-Arden Arcade-Roseville MSA, CA	H	29.98 FQ	39.07 MW	48.46 TQ	CABLS	1/08-3/08
Applications	San Diego-Carlsbad-San Marcos MSA, CA	H	32.47 FQ	41.34 MW	51.72 TQ	CABLS	1/08-3/08
Applications	San Francisco-San Mateo-Redwood PMSA, CA	H	40.67 FQ	50.52 MW	60.50 TQ	CABLS	1/08-3/08
Applications	San Jose-Sunnyvale-Santa Clara MSA, CA	H	41.18 FQ	51.55 MW	61.61 TQ	CABLS	1/08-3/08
Applications	Santa Ana-Anaheim-Irvine PMSA, CA	Y	72580 FQ	92450 MW	114290 TQ	USBLS	5/07
Applications	Colorado	Y	70470 FQ	86950 MW	106770 TQ	USBLS	5/07
Applications	Denver-Aurora MSA, CO	Y	71380 FQ	87280 MW	107360 TQ	USBLS	5/07
Applications	Connecticut	H	30.65 AE	42.41 MW		CTBLS	1/08-3/08
Applications	Bridgeport-Stamford-Norwalk MSA, CT	Y	74420 FQ	92390 MW	112490 TQ	USBLS	5/07
Applications	Hartford-West Hartford-East Hartford MSA, CT	Y	66580 FQ	77210 MW	93520 TQ	USBLS	5/07
Applications	Delaware	Y	64370 FQ	83970 MW	100000 TQ	USBLS	5/07
Applications	Wilmington PMSA, DE-MD-NJ	Y	63270 FQ	82980 MW	99430 TQ	USBLS	5/07
Applications	District of Columbia	Y	59490 FQ	76390 MW	97840 TQ	USBLS	5/07
Applications	Washington-Arlington-Alexandria MSA, DC-VA-MD-WV	Y	69450 FQ	89000 MW	110500 TQ	USBLS	5/07
Applications	Florida	Y	53520 FQ	72830 MW	93710 TQ	USBLS	5/07
Applications	Fort Lauderdale-Pompano Beach-Deerfield Beach PMSA, FL	Y	62760 FQ	77220 MW	93990 TQ	USBLS	5/07

AE	Average entry wage	AW	Average wage paid	FQ	First quartile wage
AER	Average entry range	AWR	Average wage range	H	Hourly
AEX	Average experienced wage	AXR	Average experienced range	HI	Highest wage paid
ATC	Average total compensation	D	Daily	HR	High end range

LO	Lowest wage paid	MTC	Median total compensation	TCC	Total cash compensation
LR	Low end range	MW	Median wage paid	TQ	Third quartile wage
M	Monthly	MWR	Median wage range	W	Weekly
MCC	Median cash compensation	S	See annotated source	Y	Yearly

Computer Software Engineer

Occupation/Type/Industry	Location	Per	Low	Mid	High	Source	Date
Applications	Jacksonville MSA, FL	Y	67980 FQ	81680 MW	106040 TQ	USBLS	5/07
Applications	Miami-Fort Lauderdale-Miami Beach MSA, FL	Y	52860 FQ	68600 MW	87450 TQ	USBLS	5/07
Applications	Orlando-Kissimmee MSA, FL	Y	56100 FQ	74500 MW	94680 TQ	USBLS	5/07
Applications	Tampa-St. Petersburg-Clearwater MSA, FL	Y	48330 FQ	68820 MW	92470 TQ	USBLS	5/07
Applications	West Palm Beach-Boca Raton-Boynton Beach PMSA, FL	Y	50590 FQ	60460 MW	81650 TQ	USBLS	5/07
Applications	Georgia	Y	65400 FQ	81920 MW	98400 TQ	USBLS	5/07
Applications	Athens-Clarke County MSA, GA	Y	42790 FQ	49820 MW	58750 TQ	USBLS	5/07
Applications	Atlanta-Sandy Springs-Marietta MSA, GA	Y	67790 FQ	83790 MW	99920 TQ	USBLS	5/07
Applications	Hawaii	Y	60980 FQ	74520 MW	90440 TQ	USBLS	5/07
Applications	Honolulu MSA, HI	Y	61340 FQ	74510 MW	90680 TQ	USBLS	5/07
Applications	Idaho	Y	63620 FQ	78190 MW	97580 TQ	USBLS	5/07
Applications	Boise City-Nampa MSA, ID	Y	62830 FQ	75280 MW	93870 TQ	USBLS	5/07
Applications	Illinois	Y	66500 FQ	82870 MW	103360 TQ	USBLS	5/07
Applications	Chicago-Naperville-Joliet MSA, IL-IN-WI	Y	67110 FQ	83350 MW	103400 TQ	USBLS	5/07
Applications	Indiana	Y	55870 FQ	69350 MW	84710 TQ	USBLS	5/07
Applications	Gary PMSA, IN	Y	54790 FQ	62360 MW	78370 TQ	USBLS	5/07
Applications	Indianapolis-Carmel MSA, IN	Y	58500 FQ	70790 MW	84450 TQ	USBLS	5/07
Applications	Iowa	Y	57340 FQ	69100 MW	83100 TQ	USBLS	5/07
Applications	Des Moines-West Des Moines MSA, IA	Y	59760 FQ	71840 MW	85000 TQ	USBLS	5/07
Applications	Kansas	Y	61520 FQ	76270 MW	92640 TQ	USBLS	5/07
Applications	Wichita MSA, KS	Y	60940 FQ	75310 MW	91650 TQ	USBLS	5/07
Applications	Kentucky	Y	56197 FQ	72384 MW	89326 TQ	KYBLS	2008
Applications	Louisville-Jefferson County MSA, KY-IN	Y	53830 FQ	67410 MW	79580 TQ	USBLS	5/07
Applications	Louisiana	H	24.89 FQ	31.92 MW	41.76 TQ	LABLS	1/08-3/08
Applications	Baton Rouge MSA, LA	Y	50540 FQ	68110 MW	80750 TQ	USBLS	5/07
Applications	Lafayette MSA, LA	Y	49270 FQ	57770 MW	73710 TQ	USBLS	5/07
Applications	New Orleans-Metairie-Kenner MSA, LA	Y	57260 FQ	73390 MW	94790 TQ	USBLS	5/07
Applications	Maine	Y	49420 FQ	63750 MW	74900 TQ	USBLS	5/07
Applications	Portland-South Portland-Biddeford MSA, ME	Y	52660 FQ	66500 MW	76960 TQ	USBLS	5/07
Applications	Maryland	Y		92425 MW		MDBLS	3/08
Applications	Baltimore-Towson MSA, MD	Y	69700 FQ	93670 MW	125050 TQ	USBLS	5/07
Applications	Bethesda-Gaithersburg-Frederick PMSA, MD	Y	69950 FQ	90340 MW	112900 TQ	USBLS	5/07
Applications	Massachusetts	Y	75390 FQ	91900 MW	113040 TQ	USBLS	5/07
Applications	Boston-Cambridge-Quincy NECTA, MA	Y	75700 FQ	91260 MW	112180 TQ	USBLS	5/07
Applications	New Bedford MSA, MA	Y	58270 FQ	68360 MW	90640 TQ	USBLS	5/07
Applications	Worcester MSA, MA-CT	Y	69710 FQ	83660 MW	101190 TQ	USBLS	5/07
Applications	Michigan	Y	61030 FQ	74780 MW	90580 TQ	USBLS	5/07
Applications	Detroit-Warren-Livonia MSA, MI	Y	65230 FQ	79070 MW	94420 TQ	USBLS	5/07
Applications	Grand Rapids-Wyoming MSA, MI	Y	54180 FQ	68520 MW	81900 TQ	USBLS	5/07
Applications	Warren-Troy-Farmington Hills PMSA, MI	Y	62930 FQ	77140 MW	91760 TQ	USBLS	5/07
Applications	Minnesota	Y	69605 FQ	84660 MW	101431 TQ	MNBLS	10/08-12/08
Applications	Duluth-Superior MSA, MN-WI	Y	55073 FQ	71582 MW	84440 TQ	MNBLS	10/08-12/08
Applications	Minneapolis-Saint Paul MSA, MN-WI	Y	70996 FQ	86156 MW	102561 TQ	MNBLS	10/08-12/08
Applications	Rochester MSA, MN	Y	73688 FQ	87091 MW	101465 TQ	MNBLS	10/08-12/08
Applications	Mississippi	Y	47750 FQ	60650 MW	77030 TQ	USBLS	5/07
Applications	Jackson MSA, MS	Y	48430 FQ	59490 MW	73860 TQ	USBLS	5/07
Applications	Missouri	Y	55030 FQ	73700 MW	91150 TQ	USBLS	5/07
Applications	Joplin MSA, MO	Y	41370 FQ	48490 MW	58540 TQ	USBLS	5/07
Applications	Kansas City MSA, MO-KS	Y	62970 FQ	76200 MW	90980 TQ	USBLS	5/07
Applications	St. Louis MSA, MO-IL	Y	64070 FQ	80110 MW	96370 TQ	USBLS	5/07
Applications	Montana	Y	52810 FQ	65010 MW	77230 TQ	USBLS	5/07
Applications	Billings MSA, MT	Y	50950 FQ	58030 MW	68730 TQ	USBLS	5/07
Applications	Missoula MSA, MT	Y	50340 FQ	63010 MW	75960 TQ	USBLS	5/07
Applications	Nebraska	Y	55770 FQ	70470 MW	84370 TQ	USBLS	5/07

AE	Average entry wage	AW	Average wage paid	FQ	First quartile wage	LO	Lowest wage paid	MTC	Median total compensation	TCC	Total cash compensation
AER	Average entry range	AWR	Average wage range	H	Hourly	LR	Low end range	MW	Median wage paid	TQ	Third quartile wage
AEX	Average experienced wage	AXR	Average experienced range	HI	Highest wage paid	M	Monthly	MWR	Median wage range	W	Weekly
ATC	Average total compensation	D	Daily	HR	High end range	MCC	Median cash compensation	S	See annotated source	Y	Yearly

Occupation/Type/Industry	Location	Per	Low	Mid	High	Source	Date
Computer Software Engineer							
Applications	Omaha-Council Bluffs MSA, NE-IA	Y	60620 FQ	74960 MW	88830 TQ	USBLS	5/07
Applications	Nevada	H	28.15 FQ	36.59 MW	49.97 TQ	NVBLS	5/08
Applications	Las Vegas-Paradise MSA, NV	H	28.26 FQ	36.15 MW	47.74 TQ	NVBLS	5/08
Applications	Reno-Sparks MSA, NV	H	30.18 FQ	43.11 MW	56.46 TQ	NVBLS	5/08
Applications	New Hampshire	H	28.08 AE	40.77 MW	49.81 AEX	NHBLS	6/08
Applications	Manchester MSA, NH	Y	59670 FQ	80220 MW	96690 TQ	USBLS	5/07
Applications	Nashua NECTA, NH-MA	Y	64650 FQ	84060 MW	106460 TQ	USBLS	5/07
Applications	Rochester-Dover MSA, NH-ME	Y	59770 FQ	71000 MW	80490 TQ	USBLS	5/07
Applications	New Jersey	Y	69390 FQ	86570 MW	106170 TQ	USBLS	5/07
Applications	Camden PMSA, NJ	Y	68780 FQ	81940 MW	96320 TQ	USBLS	5/07
Applications	Edison PMSA, NJ	Y	70350 FQ	89430 MW	107810 TQ	USBLS	5/07
Applications	Newark-Union PMSA, NJ-PA	Y	68600 FQ	83640 MW	104750 TQ	USBLS	5/07
Applications	New Mexico	Y	66180 FQ	77230 MW	97140 TQ	USBLS	5/07
Applications	Albuquerque MSA, NM	Y	65880 FQ	75460 MW	92570 TQ	USBLS	5/07
Applications	New York	Y	68900 FQ	86480 MW	106850 TQ	USBLS	5/07
Applications	Albany-Schenectady-Troy MSA, NY	Y	61860 FQ	72280 MW	82530 TQ	USBLS	5/07
Applications	Buffalo-Niagara Falls MSA, NY	Y	51590 FQ	70300 MW	90330 TQ	USBLS	5/07
Applications	Glens Falls MSA, NY	Y	45780 FQ	55280 MW	68880 TQ	USBLS	5/07
Applications	Nassau-Suffolk PMSA, NY	Y	66520 FQ	88060 MW	103990 TQ	USBLS	5/07
Applications	New York-Northern New Jersey-Long Island MSA, NY-NJ-PA	Y	71390 FQ	90050 MW	110330 TQ	USBLS	5/07
Applications	North Carolina	Y	67330 FQ	84520 MW	101610 TQ	USBLS	5/07
Applications	Charlotte-Gastonia-Concord MSA, NC-SC	Y	64540 FQ	84800 MW	102270 TQ	USBLS	5/07
Applications	Raleigh-Cary MSA, NC	Y	70280 FQ	85880 MW	100950 TQ	USBLS	5/07
Applications	North Dakota	Y	48420 FQ	57900 MW	70690 TQ	USBLS	5/07
Applications	Fargo MSA, ND-MN	Y	46840 FQ	58120 MW	73930 TQ	USBLS	5/07
Applications	Ohio	Y	62660 FQ	76930 MW	92480 TQ	USBLS	5/07
Applications	Cincinnati-Middletown MSA, OH-KY-IN	Y	64750 FQ	78100 MW	93550 TQ	USBLS	5/07
Applications	Cleveland-Elyria-Mentor MSA, OH	Y	60760 FQ	75420 MW	91380 TQ	USBLS	5/07
Applications	Columbus MSA, OH	Y	63080 FQ	78190 MW	94970 TQ	USBLS	5/07
Applications	Dayton MSA, OH	Y	65200 FQ	77820 MW	91590 TQ	USBLS	5/07
Applications	Oklahoma	Y	44910 FQ	62690 MW	79160 TQ	USBLS	5/07
Applications	Oklahoma City MSA, OK	Y	45940 FQ	66170 MW	79040 TQ	USBLS	5/07
Applications	Tulsa MSA, OK	Y	45900 FQ	62210 MW	80290 TQ	USBLS	5/07
Applications	Oregon	H	33.09 FQ	41.13 MW	50.05 TQ	ORBLS	5/08
Applications	Portland-Vancouver-Beaverton MSA, OR-WA	Y	70160 FQ	86570 MW	103250 TQ	USBLS	5/07
Applications	Salem MSA, OR	Y	47770 FQ	65550 MW	77550 TQ	USBLS	5/07
Applications	Pennsylvania	Y	63060 FQ	79110 MW	98280 TQ	USBLS	5/07
Applications	Allentown-Bethlehem-Easton MSA, PA-NJ	Y	66590 FQ	83180 MW	99790 TQ	USBLS	5/07
Applications	Philadelphia-Camden-Wilmington MSA, PA-NJ-DE-MD	Y	68890 FQ	84310 MW	102820 TQ	USBLS	5/07
Applications	Pittsburgh MSA, PA	Y	57180 FQ	74810 MW	93240 TQ	USBLS	5/07
Applications	Rhode Island	Y	68020 FQ	81700 MW	96230 TQ	USBLS	5/07
Applications	Providence-Fall River-Warwick MSA, RI-MA	Y	66550 FQ	80660 MW	95920 TQ	USBLS	5/07
Applications	South Carolina	Y	59860 FQ	72830 MW	86930 TQ	USBLS	5/07
Applications	Charleston-North Charleston MSA, SC	Y	58750 FQ	72100 MW	90310 TQ	USBLS	5/07
Applications	Columbia MSA, SC	Y	62640 FQ	74020 MW	86350 TQ	USBLS	5/07
Applications	Florence MSA, SC	Y	41280 FQ	49210 MW	62260 TQ	USBLS	5/07
Applications	South Dakota	Y	55806 FQ	67978 MW	87468 TQ	SDBLS	7/08-9/08
Applications	Sioux Falls MSA, SD	Y	53156 FQ	66271 MW	83476 TQ	SDBLS	7/08-9/08
Applications	Tennessee	Y	56450 FQ	69930 MW	85610 TQ	USBLS	5/07
Applications	Clarksville MSA, TN-KY	Y	41240 FQ	45670 MW	59470 TQ	USBLS	5/07
Applications	Memphis MSA, TN-MS-AR	Y	59380 FQ	73680 MW	84840 TQ	USBLS	5/07
Applications	Nashville-Davidson-Murfreesboro MSA, TN	Y	57290 FQ	70100 MW	85380 TQ	USBLS	5/07
Applications	Texas	Y	68620 FQ	85210 MW	101830 TQ	USBLS	5/07
Applications	Austin-Round Rock MSA, TX	Y	74080 FQ	90780 MW	107620 TQ	USBLS	5/07
Applications	Corpus Christi MSA, TX	Y	56770 FQ	72060 MW	87900 TQ	USBLS	5/07

AE	Average entry wage	AW	Average wage paid	FQ	First quartile wage
AER	Average entry range	AWR	Average wage range	H	Hourly
AEX	Average experienced wage	AXR	Average experienced range	HI	Highest wage paid
ATC	Average total compensation	D	Daily	HR	High end range

LO	Lowest wage paid	MTC	Median total compensation
LR	Low end range	MW	Median wage paid
M	Monthly	MWR	Median wage range
MCC	Median cash compensation	S	See annotated source

TCC	Total cash compensation
TQ	Third quartile wage
W	Weekly
Y	Yearly

Occupation/Type/Industry	Location	Per	Low	Mid	High	Source	Date
Computer Software Engineer							
Applications	Dallas-Fort Worth-Arlington MSA, TX	Y	71240 FQ	87760 MW	103160 TQ	USBLS	5/07
Applications	El Paso MSA, TX	Y	47490 FQ	67170 MW	82280 TQ	USBLS	5/07
Applications	Houston-Sugar Land-Baytown MSA, TX	Y	69150 FQ	83910 MW	100190 TQ	USBLS	5/07
Applications	Midland MSA, TX	Y	67920 FQ	78940 MW	96480 TQ	USBLS	5/07
Applications	San Antonio MSA, TX	Y	57320 FQ	65620 MW	81760 TQ	USBLS	5/07
Applications	Utah	Y	58400 FQ	76460 MW	94150 TQ	USBLS	5/07
Applications	Salt Lake City MSA, UT	Y	57750 FQ	77480 MW	94430 TQ	USBLS	5/07
Applications	Vermont	Y	54300 FQ	63310 MW	76850 TQ	USBLS	5/07
Applications	Burlington-South Burlington MSA, VT	Y	54480 FQ	62520 MW	77770 TQ	USBLS	5/07
Applications	Virginia	Y	67780 FQ	87110 MW	107140 TQ	USBLS	5/07
Applications	Richmond MSA, VA	Y	68240 FQ	83800 MW	99580 TQ	USBLS	5/07
Applications	Virginia Beach-Norfolk-Newport News MSA, VA-NC	Y	50840 FQ	66120 MW	85590 TQ	USBLS	5/07
Applications	Washington	H	34.39 FQ	41.84 MW	49.49 TQ	WABLS	3/08
Applications	Olympia MSA, WA	Y	56200 FQ	62590 MW	72520 TQ	USBLS	5/07
Applications	Seattle-Tacoma-Bellevue MSA, WA	Y	74360 FQ	88930 MW	103380 TQ	USBLS	5/07
Applications	Spokane MSA, WA	Y	49490 FQ	59980 MW	71990 TQ	USBLS	5/07
Applications	West Virginia	Y	53185 FQ	68447 MW	82896 TQ	WVBLS	7/08-9/08
Applications	Charleston MSA, WV	Y	56680 FQ	69450 MW	78490 TQ	USBLS	5/07
Applications	Wisconsin	Y	56350 FQ	69070 MW	82240 TQ	USBLS	5/07
Applications	Green Bay MSA, WI	Y	59630 FQ	70940 MW	81780 TQ	USBLS	5/07
Applications	Milwaukee-Waukesha-West Allis MSA, WI	Y	57780 FQ	70560 MW	83610 TQ	USBLS	5/07
Applications	Wyoming	Y	51264 FQ	58643 MW	65059 TQ	WYBLS	9/08
Applications	Cheyenne MSA, WY	Y	51331 FQ	58910 MW	64654 TQ	WYBLS	9/08
Applications	Puerto Rico	Y	46210 FQ	56980 MW	79440 TQ	USBLS	5/07
Applications	San Juan-Caguas-Guaynabo MSA, PR	Y	47400 FQ	58120 MW	83210 TQ	USBLS	5/07
Systems Software	Alabama	Y	63620 FQ	82350 MW	99370 TQ	USBLS	5/07
Systems Software	Birmingham-Hoover MSA, AL	Y	52720 FQ	70500 MW	88140 TQ	USBLS	5/07
Systems Software	Alaska	Y	55080 FQ	81110 MW	95180 TQ	USBLS	5/07
Systems Software	Anchorage MSA, AK	Y	57210 FQ	81660 MW	95620 TQ	USBLS	5/07
Systems Software	Arizona	Y	63990 FQ	79470 MW	96710 TQ	USBLS	5/07
Systems Software	Phoenix-Mesa-Scottsdale MSA, AZ	Y	60110 FQ	79240 MW	98330 TQ	USBLS	5/07
Systems Software	Tucson MSA, AZ	Y	68560 FQ	79950 MW	94860 TQ	USBLS	5/07
Systems Software	Arkansas	Y	50400 FQ	70630 MW	91010 TQ	USBLS	5/07
Systems Software	Little Rock-North Little Rock MSA, AR	Y	51260 FQ	69120 MW	89540 TQ	USBLS	5/07
Systems Software	California	H	39.01 FQ	48.40 MW	59.59 TQ	CABLS	1/08-3/08
Systems Software	Los Angeles-Long Beach-Glendale PMSA, CA	H	36.47 FQ	45.13 MW	55.69 TQ	CABLS	1/08-3/08
Systems Software	Modesto MSA, CA	H	22.86 FQ	37.67 MW	47.89 TQ	CABLS	1/08-3/08
Systems Software	Oakland-Fremont-Hayward MSA, CA	H	37.48 FQ	46.68 MW	56.18 TQ	CABLS	1/08-3/08
Systems Software	Riverside-San Bernardino-Ontario MSA, CA	H	31.37 FQ	40.93 MW	51.27 TQ	CABLS	1/08-3/08
Systems Software	Sacramento-Arden Arcade-Roseville MSA, CA	H	33.37 FQ	39.55 MW	48.25 TQ	CABLS	1/08-3/08
Systems Software	San Diego-Carlsbad-San Marcos MSA, CA	H	38.16 FQ	46.35 MW	56.45 TQ	CABLS	1/08-3/08
Systems Software	San Francisco-San Mateo-Redwood PMSA, CA	H	43.18 FQ	50.79 MW	61.92 TQ	CABLS	1/08-3/08
Systems Software	San Jose-Sunnyvale-Santa Clara MSA, CA	H	43.93 FQ	53.90 MW	64.56 TQ	CABLS	1/08-3/08
Systems Software	Santa Ana-Anaheim-Irvine PMSA, CA	Y	71920 FQ	88400 MW	107820 TQ	USBLS	5/07
Systems Software	Colorado	Y	72380 FQ	89950 MW	111800 TQ	USBLS	5/07
Systems Software	Denver-Aurora MSA, CO	Y	71230 FQ	87560 MW	109100 TQ	USBLS	5/07
Systems Software	Connecticut	H	30.35 AE	42.56 MW		CTBLS	1/08-3/08
Systems Software	Bridgeport-Stamford-Norwalk MSA, CT	Y	71520 FQ	87410 MW	110380 TQ	USBLS	5/07
Systems Software	Danbury MSA, CT	Y	65770 FQ	85820 MW	107390 TQ	USBLS	5/07
Systems Software	Hartford-West Hartford-East Hartford MSA, CT	Y	66850 FQ	81490 MW	100890 TQ	USBLS	5/07
Systems Software	Delaware	Y	71420 FQ	86790 MW	105170 TQ	USBLS	5/07

AE	Average entry wage	AW	Average wage paid	FQ	First quartile wage
AER	Average entry range	AWR	Average wage range	H	Hourly
AEX	Average experienced wage	AXR	Average experienced range	HI	Highest wage paid
ATC	Average total compensation	D	Daily	HR	High end range

LO	Lowest wage paid	MTC	Median total compensation	TCC	Total cash compensation
LR	Low end range	MW	Median wage paid	TQ	Third quartile wage
M	Monthly	MWR	Median wage range	W	Weekly
MCC	Median cash compensation	S	See annotated source	Y	Yearly

Occupation/Type/Industry	Location	Per	Low	Mid	High	Source	Date
Computer Software Engineer							
Systems Software	Wilmington PMSA, DE-MD-NJ	Y	71950 FQ	86880 MW	104950 TQ	USBLS	5/07
Systems Software	District of Columbia	Y	68720 FQ	83260 MW	101890 TQ	USBLS	5/07
Systems Software	Washington-Arlington-Alexandria MSA, DC-VA-MD-WV	Y	78920 FQ	99300 MW	122560 TQ	USBLS	5/07
Systems Software	Florida	Y	63980 FQ	80430 MW	97800 TQ	USBLS	5/07
Systems Software	Fort Lauderdale-Pompano Beach-Deerfield Beach PMSA, FL	Y	58950 FQ	75950 MW	92160 TQ	USBLS	5/07
Systems Software	Jacksonville MSA, FL	Y	82620 FQ	93650 MW	105860 TQ	USBLS	5/07
Systems Software	Miami-Fort Lauderdale-Miami Beach MSA, FL	Y	64970 FQ	80680 MW	99230 TQ	USBLS	5/07
Systems Software	Orlando-Kissimmee MSA, FL	Y	65620 FQ	81440 MW	101070 TQ	USBLS	5/07
Systems Software	Tallahassee MSA, FL	Y	47860 FQ	71940 MW	89230 TQ	USBLS	5/07
Systems Software	Tampa-St. Petersburg-Clearwater MSA, FL	Y	61580 FQ	75010 MW	91580 TQ	USBLS	5/07
Systems Software	West Palm Beach-Boca Raton-Boynton Beach PMSA, FL	Y	63360 FQ	80820 MW	114530 TQ	USBLS	5/07
Systems Software	Georgia	Y	62260 FQ	78740 MW	96830 TQ	USBLS	5/07
Systems Software	Atlanta-Sandy Springs-Marietta MSA, GA	Y	62750 FQ	79430 MW	97670 TQ	USBLS	5/07
Systems Software	Hawaii	Y	70330 FQ	83800 MW	100960 TQ	USBLS	5/07
Systems Software	Honolulu MSA, HI	Y	70840 FQ	83480 MW	100510 TQ	USBLS	5/07
Systems Software	Idaho	Y	66750 FQ	82470 MW	101590 TQ	USBLS	5/07
Systems Software	Boise City-Nampa MSA, ID	Y	67670 FQ	84000 MW	102450 TQ	USBLS	5/07
Systems Software	Coeur d'Alene MSA, ID	Y	49640 FQ	74910 MW	89150 TQ	USBLS	5/07
Systems Software	Illinois	Y	68480 FQ	90140 MW	111540 TQ	USBLS	5/07
Systems Software	Chicago-Naperville-Joliet MSA, IL-IN-WI	Y	70080 FQ	92000 MW	112740 TQ	USBLS	5/07
Systems Software	Indiana	Y	61140 FQ	73960 MW	89690 TQ	USBLS	5/07
Systems Software	Indianapolis-Carmel MSA, IN	Y	65060 FQ	77920 MW	92700 TQ	USBLS	5/07
Systems Software	Iowa	Y	58600 FQ	71490 MW	87890 TQ	USBLS	5/07
Systems Software	Des Moines-West Des Moines MSA, IA	Y	62710 FQ	75830 MW	90750 TQ	USBLS	5/07
Systems Software	Kansas	Y	60840 FQ	74570 MW	94070 TQ	USBLS	5/07
Systems Software	Wichita MSA, KS	Y	62770 FQ	72210 MW	84460 TQ	USBLS	5/07
Systems Software	Kentucky	Y	56487 FQ	72426 MW	85688 TQ	KYBLS	2008
Systems Software	Bowling Green MSA, KY	Y	58390 FQ	72800 MW	82280 TQ	USBLS	5/07
Systems Software	Louisville-Jefferson County MSA, KY-IN	Y	52460 FQ	68010 MW	80820 TQ	USBLS	5/07
Systems Software	Louisiana	H	24.26 FQ	31.91 MW	43.34 TQ	LABLS	1/08-3/08
Systems Software	Baton Rouge MSA, LA	Y	48310 FQ	58460 MW	76580 TQ	USBLS	5/07
Systems Software	New Orleans-Metairie-Kenner MSA, LA	Y	68620 FQ	83150 MW	106860 TQ	USBLS	5/07
Systems Software	Maine	Y	61900 FQ	73410 MW	85280 TQ	USBLS	5/07
Systems Software	Portland-South Portland-Biddeford MSA, ME	Y	65640 FQ	76110 MW	88740 TQ	USBLS	5/07
Systems Software	Maryland	Y		96900 MW		MDBLS	3/08
Systems Software	Baltimore-Towson MSA, MD	Y	75240 FQ	95960 MW	122990 TQ	USBLS	5/07
Systems Software	Bethesda-Gaithersburg-Frederick PMSA, MD	Y	73760 FQ	93590 MW	114530 TQ	USBLS	5/07
Systems Software	Massachusetts	Y	75310 FQ	93350 MW	114660 TQ	USBLS	5/07
Systems Software	Boston-Cambridge-Quincy NECTA, MA	Y	74570 FQ	92000 MW	111760 TQ	USBLS	5/07
Systems Software	Worcester MSA, MA-CT	Y	72010 FQ	92230 MW	113120 TQ	USBLS	5/07
Systems Software	Michigan	Y	62670 FQ	79200 MW	95590 TQ	USBLS	5/07
Systems Software	Detroit-Warren-Livonia MSA, MI	Y	63770 FQ	80020 MW	96350 TQ	USBLS	5/07
Systems Software	Grand Rapids-Wyoming MSA, MI	Y	59430 FQ	76330 MW	96730 TQ	USBLS	5/07
Systems Software	Warren-Troy-Farmington Hills PMSA, MI	Y	63400 FQ	80150 MW	96560 TQ	USBLS	5/07
Systems Software	Minnesota	Y	76280 FQ	94746 MW	114927 TQ	MNBLS	10/08-12/08
Systems Software	Duluth-Superior MSA, MN-WI	Y	73120 FQ	94359 MW	108786 TQ	MNBLS	10/08-12/08
Systems Software	Minneapolis-Saint Paul MSA, MN-WI	Y	75725 FQ	94442 MW	114132 TQ	MNBLS	10/08-12/08
Systems Software	Mississippi	Y	54170 FQ	67010 MW	86400 TQ	USBLS	5/07
Systems Software	Jackson MSA, MS	Y	52130 FQ	64420 MW	82720 TQ	USBLS	5/07
Systems Software	Missouri	Y	64000 FQ	77200 MW	90220 TQ	USBLS	5/07
Systems Software	Kansas City MSA, MO-KS	Y	60390 FQ	74120 MW	90880 TQ	USBLS	5/07

AE	Average entry wage	AW	Average wage paid	FQ	First quartile wage	LO	Lowest wage paid	MTC	Median total compensation	TCC	Total cash compensation
AER	Average entry range	AWR	Average wage range	H	Hourly	LR	Low end range	MW	Median wage paid	TQ	Third quartile wage
AEX	Average experienced wage	AXR	Average experienced range	HI	Highest wage paid	M	Monthly	MWR	Median wage range	W	Weekly
ATC	Average total compensation	D	Daily	HR	High end range	MCC	Median cash compensation	S	See annotated source	Y	Yearly

Computer Software Engineer

Occupation/Type/Industry	Location	Per	Low	Mid	High	Source	Date
Systems Software	St. Joseph MSA, MO-KS	Y	40950 FQ	54940 MW	59710 TQ	USBLS	5/07
Systems Software	St. Louis MSA, MO-IL	Y	67630 FQ	79730 MW	91650 TQ	USBLS	5/07
Systems Software	Montana	Y	44880 FQ	63030 MW	79970 TQ	USBLS	5/07
Systems Software	Billings MSA, MT	Y	36480 FQ	48270 MW	72660 TQ	USBLS	5/07
Systems Software	Nebraska	Y	53210 FQ	72080 MW	89410 TQ	USBLS	5/07
Systems Software	Omaha-Council Bluffs MSA, NE-IA	Y	56630 FQ	73590 MW	91400 TQ	USBLS	5/07
Systems Software	Nevada	H	31.23 FQ	40.05 MW	49.43 TQ	NVBLS	5/08
Systems Software	Las Vegas-Paradise MSA, NV	H	34.96 FQ	42.81 MW	50.80 TQ	NVBLS	5/08
Systems Software	New Hampshire	H	31.61 AE	45.31 MW	54.21 AEX	NHBLS	6/08
Systems Software	Manchester MSA, NH	Y	50430 FQ	70580 MW	106360 TQ	USBLS	5/07
Systems Software	Nashua NECTA, NH-MA	Y	80360 FQ	99440 MW	122240 TQ	USBLS	5/07
Systems Software	Portsmouth MSA, NH-ME	Y	68410 FQ	78340 MW	95470 TQ	USBLS	5/07
Systems Software	New Jersey	Y	80080 FQ	99120 MW	117880 TQ	USBLS	5/07
Systems Software	Camden PMSA, NJ	Y	68800 FQ	85430 MW	105610 TQ	USBLS	5/07
Systems Software	Edison PMSA, NJ	Y	83900 FQ	101400 MW	119270 TQ	USBLS	5/07
Systems Software	Newark-Union PMSA, NJ-PA	Y	86680 FQ	103840 MW	119980 TQ	USBLS	5/07
Systems Software	New Mexico	Y	73800 FQ	93000 MW	113460 TQ	USBLS	5/07
Systems Software	Albuquerque MSA, NM	Y	76940 FQ	95520 MW	115680 TQ	USBLS	5/07
Systems Software	New York	Y	74720 FQ	94230 MW	116910 TQ	USBLS	5/07
Systems Software	Albany-Schenectady-Troy MSA, NY	Y	50960 FQ	65440 MW	87730 TQ	USBLS	5/07
Systems Software	Buffalo-Niagara Falls MSA, NY	Y	61430 FQ	75140 MW	91510 TQ	USBLS	5/07
Systems Software	Nassau-Suffolk PMSA, NY	Y	68780 FQ	88360 MW	110190 TQ	USBLS	5/07
Systems Software	New York-Northern New Jersey-Long Island MSA, NY-NJ-PA	Y	82550 FQ	100510 MW	120550 TQ	USBLS	5/07
Systems Software	North Carolina	Y	70730 FQ	88090 MW	107470 TQ	USBLS	5/07
Systems Software	Charlotte-Gastonia-Concord MSA, NC-SC	Y	71330 FQ	88440 MW	103270 TQ	USBLS	5/07
Systems Software	Raleigh-Cary MSA, NC	Y	68080 FQ	84190 MW	101600 TQ	USBLS	5/07
Systems Software	North Dakota	Y	48430 FQ	72130 MW	93240 TQ	USBLS	5/07
Systems Software	Fargo MSA, ND-MN	Y	48070 FQ	72910 MW	96770 TQ	USBLS	5/07
Systems Software	Ohio	Y	66660 FQ	81540 MW	97350 TQ	USBLS	5/07
Systems Software	Cincinnati-Middletown MSA, OH-KY-IN	Y	60920 FQ	79700 MW	97820 TQ	USBLS	5/07
Systems Software	Cleveland-Elyria-Mentor MSA, OH	Y	62650 FQ	74910 MW	88730 TQ	USBLS	5/07
Systems Software	Columbus MSA, OH	Y	70280 FQ	84530 MW	99130 TQ	USBLS	5/07
Systems Software	Dayton MSA, OH	Y	72280 FQ	86900 MW	102810 TQ	USBLS	5/07
Systems Software	Oklahoma	Y	56230 FQ	71050 MW	86180 TQ	USBLS	5/07
Systems Software	Oklahoma City MSA, OK	Y	56120 FQ	73690 MW	95230 TQ	USBLS	5/07
Systems Software	Tulsa MSA, OK	Y	59250 FQ	72070 MW	84470 TQ	USBLS	5/07
Systems Software	Oregon	H	37.39 FQ	45.16 MW	53.52 TQ	ORBLS	5/08
Systems Software	Portland-Vancouver-Beaverton MSA, OR-WA	Y	76470 FQ	91780 MW	109060 TQ	USBLS	5/07
Systems Software	Pennsylvania	Y	62540 FQ	80920 MW	101850 TQ	USBLS	5/07
Systems Software	Allentown-Bethlehem-Easton MSA, PA-NJ	Y	66370 FQ	83260 MW	102700 TQ	USBLS	5/07
Systems Software	Philadelphia-Camden-Wilmington MSA, PA-NJ-DE-MD	Y	69550 FQ	88300 MW	108310 TQ	USBLS	5/07
Systems Software	Pittsburgh MSA, PA	Y	61220 FQ	74860 MW	94440 TQ	USBLS	5/07
Systems Software	Reading MSA, PA	Y	46510 FQ	51800 MW	68760 TQ	USBLS	5/07
Systems Software	Rhode Island	Y	70350 FQ	84470 MW	101250 TQ	USBLS	5/07
Systems Software	Providence-Fall River-Warwick MSA, RI-MA	Y	69730 FQ	83850 MW	100300 TQ	USBLS	5/07
Systems Software	South Carolina	Y	50820 FQ	70840 MW	89580 TQ	USBLS	5/07
Systems Software	Charleston-North Charleston MSA, SC	Y	47120 FQ	61520 MW	81220 TQ	USBLS	5/07
Systems Software	Columbia MSA, SC	Y	61350 FQ	76470 MW	95760 TQ	USBLS	5/07
Systems Software	South Dakota	Y	62277 FQ	75954 MW	101070 TQ	SDBLS	7/08-9/08
Systems Software	Sioux Falls MSA, SD	Y	61495 FQ	72578 MW	88324 TQ	SDBLS	7/08-9/08
Systems Software	Tennessee	Y	57770 FQ	72340 MW	87120 TQ	USBLS	5/07
Systems Software	Knoxville MSA, TN	Y	55200 FQ	73790 MW	90420 TQ	USBLS	5/07
Systems Software	Memphis MSA, TN-MS-AR	Y	60370 FQ	74180 MW	87110 TQ	USBLS	5/07
Systems Software	Nashville-Davidson-Murfreesboro MSA, TN	Y	57900 FQ	71700 MW	86630 TQ	USBLS	5/07
Systems Software	Texas	Y	70550 FQ	89090 MW	107160 TQ	USBLS	5/07
Systems Software	Austin-Round Rock MSA, TX	Y	72510 FQ	89710 MW	112550 TQ	USBLS	5/07

AE	Average entry wage	AW	Average wage paid	FQ	First quartile wage	LO	Lowest wage paid	MTC	Median total compensation	TCC	Total cash compensation
AER	Average entry range	AWR	Average wage range	H	Hourly	LR	Low end range	MW	Median wage paid	TQ	Third quartile wage
AEX	Average experienced wage	AXR	Average experienced range	HI	Highest wage paid	M	Monthly	MWR	Median wage range	W	Weekly
ATC	Average total compensation	D	Daily	HR	High end range	MCC	Median cash compensation	S	See annotated source	Y	Yearly

Occupation/Type/Industry	Location	Per	Low	Mid	High	Source	Date
Computer Software Engineer							
Systems Software	Dallas-Fort Worth-Arlington MSA, TX	Y	72210 FQ	90790 MW	107400 TQ	USBLS	5/07
Systems Software	El Paso MSA, TX	Y	68970 FQ	83500 MW	106940 TQ	USBLS	5/07
Systems Software	Houston-Sugar Land-Baytown MSA, TX	Y	71480 FQ	89990 MW	107330 TQ	USBLS	5/07
Systems Software	San Antonio MSA, TX	Y	56030 FQ	66580 MW	85760 TQ	USBLS	5/07
Systems Software	Utah	Y	62990 FQ	78130 MW	94180 TQ	USBLS	5/07
Systems Software	Salt Lake City MSA, UT	Y	65020 FQ	80630 MW	95650 TQ	USBLS	5/07
Systems Software	Vermont	Y	65280 FQ	82110 MW	101680 TQ	USBLS	5/07
Systems Software	Burlington-South Burlington MSA, VT	Y	67790 FQ	84320 MW	104900 TQ	USBLS	5/07
Systems Software	Virginia	Y	79790 FQ	99810 MW	123320 TQ	USBLS	5/07
Systems Software	Richmond MSA, VA	Y	75660 FQ	91520 MW	109980 TQ	USBLS	5/07
Systems Software	Virginia Beach-Norfolk-Newport News MSA, VA-NC	Y	67110 FQ	82140 MW	97910 TQ	USBLS	5/07
Systems Software	Washington	H	37.22 FQ	44.18 MW	51.28 TQ	WABLS	3/08
Systems Software	Seattle-Tacoma-Bellevue MSA, WA	Y	77920 FQ	91950 MW	106590 TQ	USBLS	5/07
Systems Software	West Virginia	Y	43707 FQ	58989 MW	75839 TQ	WVBLS	7/08-9/08
Systems Software	Charleston MSA, W.V	Y	34070 FQ	43560 MW	60090 TQ	USBLS	5/07
Systems Software	Wisconsin	Y	62920 FQ	77460 MW	92630 TQ	USBLS	5/07
Systems Software	Green Bay MSA, WI	Y	60310 FQ	74820 MW	90800 TQ	USBLS	5/07
Systems Software	Milwaukee-Waukesha-West Allis MSA, WI	Y	63090 FQ	76930 MW	92350 TQ	USBLS	5/07
Systems Software	Wyoming	Y	57469 FQ	63996 MW	79972 TQ	WYBLS	9/08
Systems Software	Puerto Rico	Y	38030 FQ	51520 MW	67240 TQ	USBLS	5/07
Systems Software	San Juan-Caguas-Guaynabo MSA, PR	Y	38300 FQ	52210 MW	68330 TQ	USBLS	5/07
Computer Support Specialist	Alabama	Y	28530 FQ	36230 MW	46260 TQ	USBLS	5/07
	Birmingham-Hoover MSA, AL	Y	33480 FQ	40680 MW	49920 TQ	USBLS	5/07
	Tuscaloosa MSA, AL	Y	24760 FQ	37390 MW	46610 TQ	USBLS	5/07
	Alaska	Y	35930 FQ	44660 MW	55540 TQ	USBLS	5/07
	Anchorage MSA, AK	Y	35710 FQ	44540 MW	55410 TQ	USBLS	5/07
	Arizona	Y	34730 FQ	45090 MW	57890 TQ	USBLS	5/07
	Phoenix-Mesa-Scottsdale MSA, AZ	Y	35420 FQ	46080 MW	58610 TQ	USBLS	5/07
	Tucson MSA, AZ	Y	34420 FQ	41010 MW	50280 TQ	USBLS	5/07
	Arkansas	Y	27500 FQ	35230 MW	45050 TQ	USBLS	5/07
	Little Rock-North Little Rock MSA, AR	Y	29390 FQ	38470 MW	48570 TQ	USBLS	5/07
	California	H	18.01 FQ	23.26 MW	29.82 TQ	CABLS	1/08-3/08
	Los Angeles-Long Beach-Glendale PMSA, CA	H	16.04 FQ	21.34 MW	27.11 TQ	CABLS	1/08-3/08
	Oakland-Fremont-Hayward MSA, CA	H	20.97 FQ	25.52 MW	31.84 TQ	CABLS	1/08-3/08
	Riverside-San Bernardino-Ontario MSA, CA	H	16.62 FQ	21.72 MW	27.06 TQ	CABLS	1/08-3/08
	Sacramento-Arden Arcade-Roseville MSA, CA	H	18.43 FQ	23.01 MW	29.91 TQ	CABLS	1/08-3/08
	San Diego-Carlsbad-San Marcos MSA, CA	H	17.79 FQ	21.78 MW	27.03 TQ	CABLS	1/08-3/08
	San Francisco-San Mateo-Redwood PMSA, CA	H	22.84 FQ	28.60 MW	35.91 TQ	CABLS	1/08-3/08
	San Jose-Sunnyvale-Santa Clara MSA, CA	H	23.29 FQ	29.10 MW	38.00 TQ	CABLS	1/08-3/08
	Santa Ana-Anaheim-Irvine PMSA, CA	Y	35680 FQ	45040 MW	57570 TQ	USBLS	5/07
	Colorado	Y	37140 FQ	47860 MW	61550 TQ	USBLS	5/07
	Boulder MSA, CO	Y	36150 FQ	45960 MW	61430 TQ	USBLS	5/07
	Denver-Aurora MSA, CO	Y	38930 FQ	50290 MW	63250 TQ	USBLS	5/07
	Pueblo MSA, CO	Y	33750 FQ	40570 MW	47290 TQ	USBLS	5/07
	Connecticut	H	17.25 AE	25.22 MW		CTBLS	1/08-3/08
	Bridgeport-Stamford-Norwalk MSA, CT	Y	41690 FQ	52500 MW	64450 TQ	USBLS	5/07
	Hartford-West Hartford-East Hartford MSA, CT	Y	38880 FQ	46990 MW	58960 TQ	USBLS	5/07
	Delaware	Y	42530 FQ	52820 MW	66700 TQ	USBLS	5/07
	Wilmington PMSA, DE-MD-NJ	Y	42780 FQ	52790 MW	68250 TQ	USBLS	5/07
	District of Columbia	Y	42200 FQ	50860 MW	60120 TQ	USBLS	5/07

AE Average entry wage	**AW** Average wage paid	**FQ** First quartile wage	**LO** Lowest wage paid	**MTC** Median total compensation	**TCC** Total cash compensation
AER Average entry range	**AWR** Average wage range	**H** Hourly	**LR** Low end range	**MW** Median wage paid	**TQ** Third quartile wage
AEX Average experienced wage	**AXR** Average experienced range	**HI** Highest wage paid	**M** Monthly	**MWR** Median wage range	**W** Weekly
ATC Average total compensation	**D** Daily	**HR** High end range	**MCC** Median cash compensation	**S** See annotated source	**Y** Yearly

Occupation/Type/Industry	Location	Per	Low	Mid	High	Source	Date
Computer Support Specialist	Washington-Arlington-Alexandria MSA, DC-VA-MD-WV	Y	39730 FQ	50130 MW	62640 TQ	USBLS	5/07
	Florida	Y	28370 FQ	35470 MW	45310 TQ	USBLS	5/07
	Fort Lauderdale-Pompano Beach-Deerfield Beach PMSA, FL	Y	27360 FQ	30410 MW	40120 TQ	USBLS	5/07
	Jacksonville MSA, FL	Y	31180 FQ	38750 MW	47740 TQ	USBLS	5/07
	Miami-Fort Lauderdale-Miami Beach MSA, FL	Y	28130 FQ	33620 MW	44900 TQ	USBLS	5/07
	Orlando-Kissimmee MSA, FL	Y	27120 FQ	35880 MW	45540 TQ	USBLS	5/07
	Tampa-St. Petersburg-Clearwater MSA, FL	Y	27620 FQ	34900 MW	44660 TQ	USBLS	5/07
	West Palm Beach-Boca Raton-Boynton Beach PMSA, FL	Y	29420 FQ	37230 MW	47680 TQ	USBLS	5/07
	Georgia	Y	29980 FQ	39120 MW	51460 TQ	USBLS	5/07
	Atlanta-Sandy Springs-Marietta MSA, GA	Y	30950 FQ	41380 MW	54550 TQ	USBLS	5/07
	Hawaii	Y	32530 FQ	40810 MW	49700 TQ	USBLS	5/07
	Honolulu MSA, HI	Y	33130 FQ	41530 MW	50780 TQ	USBLS	5/07
	Idaho	Y	28760 FQ	35440 MW	47020 TQ	USBLS	5/07
	Boise City-Nampa MSA, ID	Y	28690 FQ	36050 MW	49410 TQ	USBLS	5/07
	Coeur d'Alene MSA, ID	Y	29880 FQ	35710 MW	41800 TQ	USBLS	5/07
	Idaho Falls MSA, ID	Y	28830 FQ	34840 MW	50010 TQ	USBLS	5/07
	Pocatello MSA, ID	Y	34240 FQ	41440 MW	46950 TQ	USBLS	5/07
	Illinois	Y	35300 FQ	46100 MW	60500 TQ	USBLS	5/07
	Chicago-Naperville-Joliet MSA, IL-IN-WI	Y	36880 FQ	47780 MW	62210 TQ	USBLS	5/07
	Indiana	Y	29220 FQ	37690 MW	48150 TQ	USBLS	5/07
	Gary PMSA, IN	Y	22820 FQ	29610 MW	42000 TQ	USBLS	5/07
	Indianapolis-Carmel MSA, IN	Y	31680 FQ	40220 MW	50860 TQ	USBLS	5/07
	Iowa	Y	32180 FQ	39600 MW	48750 TQ	USBLS	5/07
	Des Moines-West Des Moines MSA, IA	Y	34820 FQ	41500 MW	51330 TQ	USBLS	5/07
	Dubuque MSA, IA	Y	30610 FQ	38480 MW	48200 TQ	USBLS	5/07
	Sioux City MSA, IA-NE-SD	Y	28040 FQ	34450 MW	40900 TQ	USBLS	5/07
	Kansas	Y	30440 FQ	38820 MW	48420 TQ	USBLS	5/07
	Wichita MSA, KS	Y	30790 FQ	39180 MW	47960 TQ	USBLS	5/07
	Kentucky	Y	27910 FQ	35890 MW	46594 TQ	KYBLS	2008
	Louisville-Jefferson County MSA, KY-IN	Y	30860 FQ	37750 MW	48110 TQ	USBLS	5/07
	Louisiana	H	14.91 FQ	19.41 MW	24.55 TQ	LABLS	1/08-3/08
	Baton Rouge MSA, LA	Y	33180 FQ	45180 MW	57720 TQ	USBLS	5/07
	New Orleans-Metairie-Kenner MSA, LA	Y	31000 FQ	39120 MW	48450 TQ	USBLS	5/07
	Maine	Y	33090 FQ	40200 MW	47830 TQ	USBLS	5/07
	Portland-South Portland-Biddeford MSA, ME	Y	35480 FQ	42070 MW	48280 TQ	USBLS	5/07
	Maryland	Y		48075 MW		MDBLS	3/08
	Baltimore-Towson MSA, MD	Y	35940 FQ	45990 MW	58640 TQ	USBLS	5/07
	Bethesda-Gaithersburg-Frederick PMSA, MD	Y	40390 FQ	50060 MW	61550 TQ	USBLS	5/07
	Massachusetts	Y	41200 FQ	52490 MW	67580 TQ	USBLS	5/07
	Boston-Cambridge-Quincy NECTA, MA	Y	43970 FQ	55550 MW	71430 TQ	USBLS	5/07
	Worcester MSA, MA-CT	Y	39170 FQ	48650 MW	59190 TQ	USBLS	5/07
	Michigan	Y	32300 FQ	41440 MW	52920 TQ	USBLS	5/07
	Detroit-Warren-Livonia MSA, MI	Y	33850 FQ	43680 MW	55630 TQ	USBLS	5/07
	Grand Rapids-Wyoming MSA, MI	Y	32450 FQ	39380 MW	47880 TQ	USBLS	5/07
	Warren-Troy-Farmington Hills PMSA, MI	Y	33260 FQ	42650 MW	54770 TQ	USBLS	5/07
	Minnesota	Y	37831 FQ	46211 MW	55878 TQ	MNBLS	10/08-12/08
	Duluth-Superior MSA, MN-WI	Y	33583 FQ	40823 MW	48900 TQ	MNBLS	10/08-12/08
	Minneapolis-Saint Paul MSA, MN-WI	Y	39202 FQ	47634 MW	57845 TQ	MNBLS	10/08-12/08
	Rochester MSA, MN	Y	37030 FQ	44413 MW	53372 TQ	MNBLS	10/08-12/08
	Mississippi	Y	28210 FQ	35480 MW	45380 TQ	USBLS	5/07
	Jackson MSA, MS	Y	31870 FQ	38870 MW	48770 TQ	USBLS	5/07
	Missouri	Y	31950 FQ	39810 MW	49490 TQ	USBLS	5/07
	Kansas City MSA, MO-KS	Y	34370 FQ	41820 MW	50770 TQ	USBLS	5/07

AE	Average entry wage	AW	Average wage paid	FQ	First quartile wage	LO	Lowest wage paid	MTC	Median total compensation	TCC	Total cash compensation
AER	Average entry range	AWR	Average wage range	H	Hourly	LR	Low end range	MW	Median wage paid	TQ	Third quartile wage
AEX	Average experienced wage	AXR	Average experienced range	HI	Highest wage paid	M	Monthly	MWR	Median wage range	W	Weekly
ATC	Average total compensation	D	Daily	HR	High end range	MCC	Median cash compensation	S	See annotated source	Y	Yearly

Occupation/Type/Industry	Location	Per	Low	Mid	High	Source	Date
Computer Support Specialist	St. Louis MSA, MO-IL	Y	32650 FQ	39660 MW	50020 TQ	USBLS	5/07
	Montana	Y	26890 FQ	34490 MW	42830 TQ	USBLS	5/07
	Billings MSA, MT	Y	27790 FQ	34360 MW	40540 TQ	USBLS	5/07
	Missoula MSA, MT	Y	26100 FQ	31750 MW	42900 TQ	USBLS	5/07
	Nebraska	Y	29240 FQ	37480 MW	47090 TQ	USBLS	5/07
	Lincoln MSA, NE	Y	29390 FQ	37300 MW	47180 TQ	USBLS	5/07
	Omaha-Council Bluffs MSA, NE-IA	Y	29870 FQ	38250 MW	47910 TQ	USBLS	5/07
	Nevada	H	16.04 FQ	19.60 MW	24.83 TQ	NVBLS	5/08
	Las Vegas-Paradise MSA, NV	H	16.39 FQ	19.64 MW	25.13 TQ	NVBLS	5/08
	New Hampshire	H	15.54 AE	21.50 MW	26.46 AEX	NHBLS	6/08
	Manchester MSA, NH	Y	36260 FQ	45400 MW	56230 TQ	USBLS	5/07
	Nashua NECTA, NH-MA	Y	34820 FQ	44650 MW	61520 TQ	USBLS	5/07
	New Jersey	Y	38300 FQ	47960 MW	58550 TQ	USBLS	5/07
	Camden PMSA, NJ	Y	35350 FQ	43340 MW	52600 TQ	USBLS	5/07
	Edison PMSA, NJ	Y	38900 FQ	49630 MW	58980 TQ	USBLS	5/07
	Newark-Union PMSA, NJ-PA	Y	37180 FQ	46510 MW	57210 TQ	USBLS	5/07
	New Mexico	Y	32480 FQ	42300 MW	52340 TQ	USBLS	5/07
	Albuquerque MSA, NM	Y	33210 FQ	43280 MW	54480 TQ	USBLS	5/07
	Las Cruces MSA, NM	Y	33240 FQ	40600 MW	47470 TQ	USBLS	5/07
	Santa Fe MSA, NM	Y	31370 FQ	40850 MW	54110 TQ	USBLS	5/07
	New York	Y	37450 FQ	47750 MW	61040 TQ	USBLS	5/07
	Albany-Schenectady-Troy MSA, NY	Y	35430 FQ	43420 MW	50360 TQ	USBLS	5/07
	Buffalo-Niagara Falls MSA, NY	Y	29740 FQ	38900 MW	50300 TQ	USBLS	5/07
	Nassau-Suffolk PMSA, NY	Y	35200 FQ	45090 MW	56950 TQ	USBLS	5/07
	New York-Northern New Jersey-Long Island MSA, NY-NJ-PA	Y	40350 FQ	50480 MW	63400 TQ	USBLS	5/07
	North Carolina	Y	32950 FQ	41230 MW	51620 TQ	USBLS	5/07
	Charlotte-Gastonia-Concord MSA, NC-SC	Y	33060 FQ	42450 MW	54530 TQ	USBLS	5/07
	Greensboro-High Point MSA, NC	Y	33410 FQ	40280 MW	49390 TQ	USBLS	5/07
	Raleigh-Cary MSA, NC	Y	35180 FQ	43550 MW	55000 TQ	USBLS	5/07
	North Dakota	Y	22260 FQ	27050 MW	34980 TQ	USBLS	5/07
	Ohio	Y	30830 FQ	39360 MW	49910 TQ	USBLS	5/07
	Cincinnati-Middletown MSA, OH-KY-IN	Y	33140 FQ	41380 MW	53370 TQ	USBLS	5/07
	Cleveland-Elyria-Mentor MSA, OH	Y	33200 FQ	40160 MW	49550 TQ	USBLS	5/07
	Columbus MSA, OH	Y	24700 FQ	37400 MW	49450 TQ	USBLS	5/07
	Dayton MSA, OH	Y	33850 FQ	42550 MW	49720 TQ	USBLS	5/07
	Springfield MSA, OH	Y	27610 FQ	31020 MW	39840 TQ	USBLS	5/07
	Oklahoma	Y	23260 FQ	30270 MW	41900 TQ	USBLS	5/07
	Oklahoma City MSA, OK	Y	23490 FQ	30990 MW	44110 TQ	USBLS	5/07
	Tulsa MSA, OK	Y	22370 FQ	27360 MW	37510 TQ	USBLS	5/07
	Oregon	H	15.24 FQ	19.91 MW	25.62 TQ	ORBLS	5/08
	Portland-Vancouver-Beaverton MSA, OR-WA	Y	32710 FQ	42630 MW	54050 TQ	USBLS	5/07
	Pennsylvania	Y	31240 FQ	38180 MW	48490 TQ	USBLS	5/07
	Allentown-Bethlehem-Easton MSA, PA-NJ	Y	32090 FQ	38240 MW	51920 TQ	USBLS	5/07
	Philadelphia-Camden-Wilmington MSA, PA-NJ-DE-MD	Y	34400 FQ	41880 MW	53870 TQ	USBLS	5/07
	Pittsburgh MSA, PA	Y	30630 FQ	37480 MW	47150 TQ	USBLS	5/07
	Rhode Island	Y	35280 FQ	42650 MW	50050 TQ	USBLS	5/07
	Providence-Fall River-Warwick MSA, RI-MA	Y	33280 FQ	41450 MW	49480 TQ	USBLS	5/07
	South Carolina	Y	30240 FQ	38020 MW	48820 TQ	USBLS	5/07
	Charleston-North Charleston MSA, SC	Y	32950 FQ	40460 MW	51910 TQ	USBLS	5/07
	Columbia MSA, SC	Y	33070 FQ	38910 MW	49590 TQ	USBLS	5/07
	Myrtle Beach-Conway-North Myrtle Beach MSA, SC	Y	23640 FQ	29550 MW	37050 TQ	USBLS	5/07
	South Dakota	Y	29972 FQ	35180 MW	40796 TQ	SDBLS	7/08-9/08
	Sioux Falls MSA, SD	Y	31027 FQ	36441 MW	41350 TQ	SDBLS	7/08-9/08
	Tennessee	Y	32680 FQ	41040 MW	52390 TQ	USBLS	5/07
	Knoxville MSA, TN	Y	30760 FQ	38450 MW	49440 TQ	USBLS	5/07
	Memphis MSA, TN-MS-AR	Y	36330 FQ	47330 MW	56590 TQ	USBLS	5/07

AE Average entry wage	**AW** Average wage paid	**FQ** First quartile wage	**LO** Lowest wage paid	**MTC** Median total compensation	**TCC** Total cash compensation
AER Average entry range	**AWR** Average wage range	**H** Hourly	**LR** Low end range	**MW** Median wage paid	**TQ** Third quartile wage
AEX Average experienced wage	**AXR** Average experienced range	**HI** Highest wage paid	**M** Monthly	**MWR** Median wage range	**W** Weekly
ATC Average total compensation	**D** Daily	**HR** High end range	**MCC** Median cash compensation	**S** See annotated source	**Y** Yearly

Computer Support Specialist

Occupation/Type/Industry	Location	Per	Low	Mid	High	Source	Date
Computer Support Specialist	Nashville-Davidson-Murfreesboro MSA, TN	Y	33980 FQ	42860 MW	53050 TQ	USBLS	5/07
	Texas	Y	31280 FQ	40780 MW	53920 TQ	USBLS	5/07
	Austin-Round Rock MSA, TX	Y	31480 FQ	38320 MW	49990 TQ	USBLS	5/07
	Dallas-Fort Worth-Arlington MSA, TX	Y	30920 FQ	42620 MW	56250 TQ	USBLS	5/07
	El Paso MSA, TX	Y	29960 FQ	38540 MW	50270 TQ	USBLS	5/07
	Houston-Sugar Land-Baytown MSA, TX	Y	33660 FQ	42760 MW	56300 TQ	USBLS	5/07
	San Antonio MSA, TX	Y	33260 FQ	42250 MW	53830 TQ	USBLS	5/07
	Utah	Y	28040 FQ	36780 MW	49420 TQ	USBLS	5/07
	Salt Lake City MSA, UT	Y	30990 FQ	39060 MW	51760 TQ	USBLS	5/07
	Vermont	Y	33480 FQ	40080 MW	49760 TQ	USBLS	5/07
	Burlington-South Burlington MSA, VT	Y	33950 FQ	39820 MW	48440 TQ	USBLS	5/07
	Virginia	Y	33840 FQ	44070 MW	57980 TQ	USBLS	5/07
	Richmond MSA, VA	Y	31490 FQ	39700 MW	51490 TQ	USBLS	5/07
	Roanoke MSA, VA	Y	30450 FQ	36530 MW	44910 TQ	USBLS	5/07
	Virginia Beach-Norfolk-Newport News MSA, VA-NC	Y	32400 FQ	39710 MW	48850 TQ	USBLS	5/07
	Washington	H	17.71 FQ	22.09 MW	27.63 TQ	WABLS	3/08
	Seattle-Tacoma-Bellevue MSA, WA	Y	38070 FQ	47720 MW	60430 TQ	USBLS	5/07
	West Virginia	Y	27047 FQ	34460 MW	47758 TQ	WVBLS	7/08-9/08
	Charleston MSA, WV	Y	26660 FQ	33590 MW	44430 TQ	USBLS	5/07
	Wisconsin	Y	33360 FQ	40410 MW	48870 TQ	USBLS	5/07
	Milwaukee-Waukesha-West Allis MSA, WI	Y	35100 FQ	42550 MW	50720 TQ	USBLS	5/07
	Wyoming	Y	29350 FQ	38704 MW	47249 TQ	WYBLS	9/08
	Cheyenne MSA, WY	Y	31478 FQ	42780 MW	48305 TQ	WYBLS	9/08
	Puerto Rico	Y	21800 FQ	27150 MW	34150 TQ	USBLS	5/07
	Aguadilla-Isabela-San Sebastian MSA, PR	Y	20680 FQ	26310 MW	31370 TQ	USBLS	5/07
	San Juan-Caguas-Guaynabo MSA, PR	Y	22060 FQ	27500 MW	34430 TQ	USBLS	5/07
	Virgin Islands	Y	28770 FQ	34630 MW	40420 TQ	USBLS	5/07
	Guam	Y	25160 FQ	32430 MW	40690 TQ	USBLS	5/07
Computer Systems Analyst	Alabama	Y	52110 FQ	67140 MW	82070 TQ	USBLS	5/07
	Birmingham-Hoover MSA, AL	Y	52260 FQ	67350 MW	80550 TQ	USBLS	5/07
	Alaska	Y	61980 FQ	73350 MW	84340 TQ	USBLS	5/07
	Anchorage MSA, AK	Y	63840 FQ	74770 MW	84880 TQ	USBLS	5/07
	Arizona	Y	51030 FQ	67200 MW	85200 TQ	USBLS	5/07
	Phoenix-Mesa-Scottsdale MSA, AZ	Y	51820 FQ	68790 MW	88310 TQ	USBLS	5/07
	Tucson MSA, AZ	Y	49260 FQ	63110 MW	76390 TQ	USBLS	5/07
	Arkansas	Y	45500 FQ	58790 MW	73350 TQ	USBLS	5/07
	Little Rock-North Little Rock MSA, AR	Y	47360 FQ	59820 MW	74730 TQ	USBLS	5/07
	California	H	29.09 FQ	37.32 MW	47.12 TQ	CABLS	1/08-3/08
	Los Angeles-Long Beach-Glendale PMSA, CA	H	27.42 FQ	36.75 MW	47.01 TQ	CABLS	1/08-3/08
	Oakland-Fremont-Hayward MSA, CA	H	30.83 FQ	41.79 MW	55.07 TQ	CABLS	1/08-3/08
	Riverside-San Bernardino-Ontario MSA, CA	H	26.74 FQ	33.52 MW	40.74 TQ	CABLS	1/08-3/08
	Sacramento-Arden Arcade-Roseville MSA, CA	H	30.57 FQ	35.54 MW	39.40 TQ	CABLS	1/08-3/08
	San Diego-Carlsbad-San Marcos MSA, CA	H	28.33 FQ	35.29 MW	42.40 TQ	CABLS	1/08-3/08
	San Francisco-San Mateo-Redwood PMSA, CA	H	34.40 FQ	43.51 MW	54.20 TQ	CABLS	1/08-3/08
	San Jose-Sunnyvale-Santa Clara MSA, CA	H	27.22 FQ	39.20 MW	51.41 TQ	CABLS	1/08-3/08
	Santa Ana-Anaheim-Irvine PMSA, CA	Y	55960 FQ	72660 MW	90140 TQ	USBLS	5/07
	Colorado	Y	61400 FQ	77660 MW	96130 TQ	USBLS	5/07
	Denver-Aurora MSA, CO	Y	63840 FQ	79300 MW	97610 TQ	USBLS	5/07
	Connecticut	H	28.68 AE	40.15 MW		CTBLS	1/08-3/08
	Bridgeport-Stamford-Norwalk MSA, CT	Y	71440 FQ	89680 MW	111190 TQ	USBLS	5/07

Occupation/Type/Industry	Location	Per	Low	Mid	High	Source	Date
Computer Systems Analyst	Hartford-West Hartford-East Hartford MSA, CT	Y	65500 FQ	77300 MW	93510 TQ	USBLS	5/07
	Delaware	Y	57990 FQ	77640 MW	105970 TQ	USBLS	5/07
	Wilmington PMSA, DE-MD-NJ	Y	58520 FQ	78080 MW	108680 TQ	USBLS	5/07
	District of Columbia	Y	62930 FQ	79180 MW	97310 TQ	USBLS	5/07
	Washington-Arlington-Alexandria MSA, DC-VA-MD-WV	Y	66810 FQ	84710 MW	104060 TQ	USBLS	5/07
	Florida	Y	48570 FQ	63300 MW	79530 TQ	USBLS	5/07
	Fort Lauderdale-Pompano Beach-Deerfield Beach PMSA, FL	Y	37880 FQ	51650 MW	67530 TQ	USBLS	5/07
	Jacksonville MSA, FL	Y	48470 FQ	65350 MW	78870 TQ	USBLS	5/07
	Miami-Fort Lauderdale-Miami Beach MSA, FL	Y	44280 FQ	60720 MW	77820 TQ	USBLS	5/07
	Orlando-Kissimmee MSA, FL	Y	54730 FQ	68250 MW	84140 TQ	USBLS	5/07
	Tampa-St. Petersburg-Clearwater MSA, FL	Y	54100 FQ	69560 MW	86560 TQ	USBLS	5/07
	West Palm Beach-Boca Raton-Boynton Beach PMSA, FL	Y	54390 FQ	70280 MW	92230 TQ	USBLS	5/07
	Georgia	Y	57380 FQ	74930 MW	92120 TQ	USBLS	5/07
	Atlanta-Sandy Springs-Marietta MSA, GA	Y	60070 FQ	77760 MW	94940 TQ	USBLS	5/07
	Savannah MSA, GA	Y	48900 FQ	61620 MW	73550 TQ	USBLS	5/07
	Hawaii	Y	50260 FQ	63570 MW	80240 TQ	USBLS	5/07
	Honolulu MSA, HI	Y	51360 FQ	65580 MW	81760 TQ	USBLS	5/07
	Idaho	Y	46460 FQ	60000 MW	76930 TQ	USBLS	5/07
	Boise City-Nampa MSA, ID	Y	50080 FQ	63090 MW	79230 TQ	USBLS	5/07
	Illinois	Y	61650 FQ	78090 MW	97150 TQ	USBLS	5/07
	Chicago-Naperville-Joliet MSA, IL-IN-WI	Y	62370 FQ	79230 MW	98120 TQ	USBLS	5/07
	Rockford MSA, IL	Y	59600 FQ	68460 MW	80620 TQ	USBLS	5/07
	Indiana	Y	50940 FQ	65580 MW	80870 TQ	USBLS	5/07
	Gary PMSA, IN	Y	56680 FQ	72170 MW	84900 TQ	USBLS	5/07
	Indianapolis-Carmel MSA, IN	Y	55150 FQ	68730 MW	84010 TQ	USBLS	5/07
	Iowa	Y	50910 FQ	65050 MW	80420 TQ	USBLS	5/07
	Des Moines-West Des Moines MSA, IA	Y	54460 FQ	68750 MW	83780 TQ	USBLS	5/07
	Kansas	Y	50970 FQ	63640 MW	79960 TQ	USBLS	5/07
	Wichita MSA, KS	Y	52880 FQ	64970 MW	78250 TQ	USBLS	5/07
	Kentucky	Y	51674 FQ	66750 MW	85558 TQ	KYBLS	2008
	Louisville-Jefferson County MSA, KY-IN	Y	46270 FQ	62850 MW	80160 TQ	USBLS	5/07
	Louisiana	H	21.10 FQ	27.39 MW	34.83 TQ	LABLS	1/08-3/08
	Baton Rouge MSA, LA	Y	43170 FQ	54870 MW	68730 TQ	USBLS	5/07
	Lake Charles MSA, LA	Y	32470 FQ	47920 MW	73510 TQ	USBLS	5/07
	New Orleans-Metairie-Kenner MSA, LA	Y	48710 FQ	62710 MW	77620 TQ	USBLS	5/07
	Maine	Y	55820 FQ	69340 MW	82620 TQ	USBLS	5/07
	Portland-South Portland-Biddeford MSA, ME	Y	61130 FQ	75720 MW	90020 TQ	USBLS	5/07
	Maryland	Y		82725 MW		MDBLS	3/08
	Baltimore-Towson MSA, MD	Y	59790 FQ	78360 MW	97830 TQ	USBLS	5/07
	Bethesda-Gaithersburg-Frederick PMSA, MD	Y	67100 FQ	86730 MW	107740 TQ	USBLS	5/07
	Massachusetts	Y	65870 FQ	81520 MW	100250 TQ	USBLS	5/07
	Boston-Cambridge-Quincy NECTA, MA	Y	67550 FQ	82600 MW	101550 TQ	USBLS	5/07
	Worcester MSA, MA-CT	Y	59770 FQ	72790 MW	90290 TQ	USBLS	5/07
	Michigan	Y	61570 FQ	76350 MW	94100 TQ	USBLS	5/07
	Detroit-Warren-Livonia MSA, MI	Y	64970 FQ	80450 MW	98320 TQ	USBLS	5/07
	Grand Rapids-Wyoming MSA, MI	Y	52210 FQ	66490 MW	82240 TQ	USBLS	5/07
	Warren-Troy-Farmington Hills PMSA, MI	Y	58320 FQ	71860 MW	86080 TQ	USBLS	5/07
	Minnesota	Y	60450 FQ	74888 MW	89609 TQ	MNBLS	10/08-12/08
	Duluth-Superior MSA, MN-WI	Y	53995 FQ	63432 MW	73612 TQ	MNBLS	10/08-12/08
	Minneapolis-Saint Paul MSA, MN-WI	Y	61947 FQ	76384 MW	91670 TQ	MNBLS	10/08-12/08
	Rochester MSA, MN	Y	69325 FQ	79550 MW	97363 TQ	MNBLS	10/08-12/08

AE	Average entry wage	AW	Average wage paid	FQ	First quartile wage	LO	Lowest wage paid	MTC	Median total compensation	TCC	Total cash compensation
AER	Average entry range	AWR	Average wage range	H	Hourly	LR	Low end range	MW	Median wage paid	TQ	Third quartile wage
AEX	Average experienced wage	AXR	Average experienced range	HI	Highest wage paid	M	Monthly	MWR	Median wage range	W	Weekly
ATC	Average total compensation	D	Daily	HR	High end range	MCC	Median cash compensation	S	See annotated source	Y	Yearly

Occupation/Type/Industry	Location	Per	Low	Mid	High	Source	Date
Computer Systems Analyst	Mississippi	Y	43970 FQ	54040 MW	66300 TQ	USBLS	5/07
	Jackson MSA, MS	Y	46540 FQ	56070 MW	65910 TQ	USBLS	5/07
	Missouri	Y	54610 FQ	67000 MW	80560 TQ	USBLS	5/07
	Kansas City MSA, MO-KS	Y	53190 FQ	63770 MW	80260 TQ	USBLS	5/07
	St. Louis MSA, MO-IL	Y	57590 FQ	70780 MW	83040 TQ	USBLS	5/07
	Montana	Y	46030 FQ	58620 MW	73330 TQ	USBLS	5/07
	Billings MSA, MT	Y	51040 FQ	58780 MW	66070 TQ	USBLS	5/07
	Nebraska	Y	54270 FQ	67720 MW	82240 TQ	USBLS	5/07
	Omaha-Council Bluffs MSA, NE-IA	Y	56870 FQ	70630 MW	84560 TQ	USBLS	5/07
	Nevada	H	28.96 FQ	35.49 MW	41.44 TQ	NVBLS	5/08
	Las Vegas-Paradise MSA, NV	H	29.42 FQ	35.92 MW	42.22 TQ	NVBLS	5/08
	New Hampshire	H	24.66 AE	35.43 MW	43.49 AEX	NHBLS	6/08
	Manchester MSA, NH	Y	64130 FQ	86860 MW	111170 TQ	USBLS	5/07
	Nashua NECTA, NH-MA	Y	58330 FQ	75640 MW	97210 TQ	USBLS	5/07
	Rochester-Dover MSA, NH-ME	Y	56400 FQ	63390 MW	77280 TQ	USBLS	5/07
	New Jersey	Y	65760 FQ	82540 MW	101870 TQ	USBLS	5/07
	Camden PMSA, NJ	Y	56780 FQ	69860 MW	84970 TQ	USBLS	5/07
	Edison PMSA, NJ	Y	69030 FQ	86540 MW	105140 TQ	USBLS	5/07
	Newark-Union PMSA, NJ-PA	Y	68220 FQ	86470 MW	110570 TQ	USBLS	5/07
	Trenton-Ewing MSA, NJ	Y	59410 FQ	72430 MW	91420 TQ	USBLS	5/07
	New Mexico	Y	52310 FQ	68850 MW	90320 TQ	USBLS	5/07
	Albuquerque MSA, NM	Y	51300 FQ	67210 MW	88510 TQ	USBLS	5/07
	New York	Y	62110 FQ	80400 MW	103790 TQ	USBLS	5/07
	Albany-Schenectady-Troy MSA, NY	Y	51120 FQ	66300 MW	81660 TQ	USBLS	5/07
	Buffalo-Niagara Falls MSA, NY	Y	53540 FQ	69670 MW	82110 TQ	USBLS	5/07
	Nassau-Suffolk PMSA, NY	Y	60340 FQ	81590 MW	108870 TQ	USBLS	5/07
	New York-Northern New Jersey-Long Island MSA, NY-NJ-PA	Y	67210 FQ	85500 MW	107310 TQ	USBLS	5/07
	North Carolina	Y	56210 FQ	72490 MW	91410 TQ	USBLS	5/07
	Charlotte-Gastonia-Concord MSA, NC-SC	Y	58050 FQ	73150 MW	90370 TQ	USBLS	5/07
	Durham MSA, NC	Y	59840 FQ	77460 MW	99340 TQ	USBLS	5/07
	Raleigh-Cary MSA, NC	Y	58960 FQ	74880 MW	92470 TQ	USBLS	5/07
	North Dakota	Y	38880 FQ	46800 MW	60200 TQ	USBLS	5/07
	Fargo MSA, ND-MN	Y	38100 FQ	44100 MW	54680 TQ	USBLS	5/07
	Ohio	Y	56710 FQ	70830 MW	84710 TQ	USBLS	5/07
	Cincinnati-Middletown MSA, OH-KY-IN	Y	61080 FQ	74230 MW	88990 TQ	USBLS	5/07
	Cleveland-Elyria-Mentor MSA, OH	Y	54310 FQ	68330 MW	82510 TQ	USBLS	5/07
	Columbus MSA, OH	Y	61810 FQ	73760 MW	89810 TQ	USBLS	5/07
	Dayton MSA, OH	Y	58560 FQ	72210 MW	84840 TQ	USBLS	5/07
	Oklahoma	Y	46790 FQ	61030 MW	78950 TQ	USBLS	5/07
	Oklahoma City MSA, OK	Y	49020 FQ	60970 MW	79280 TQ	USBLS	5/07
	Tulsa MSA, OK	Y	46390 FQ	64870 MW	80750 TQ	USBLS	5/07
	Oregon	H	28.54 FQ	34.92 MW	41.25 TQ	ORBLS	5/08
	Eugene-Springfield MSA, OR	Y	49740 FQ	65460 MW	74510 TQ	USBLS	5/07
	Portland-Vancouver-Beaverton MSA, OR-WA	Y	60120 FQ	73120 MW	88160 TQ	USBLS	5/07
	Pennsylvania	Y	51140 FQ	66300 MW	84470 TQ	USBLS	5/07
	Allentown-Bethlehem-Easton MSA, PA-NJ	Y	47500 FQ	61340 MW	78070 TQ	USBLS	5/07
	Lancaster MSA, PA	Y	48770 FQ	62990 MW	77750 TQ	USBLS	5/07
	Philadelphia-Camden-Wilmington MSA, PA-NJ-DE-MD	Y	55860 FQ	72360 MW	95850 TQ	USBLS	5/07
	Pittsburgh MSA, PA	Y	50640 FQ	64970 MW	79690 TQ	USBLS	5/07
	Reading MSA, PA	Y	42630 FQ	63220 MW	75890 TQ	USBLS	5/07
	Rhode Island	Y	61320 FQ	77120 MW	95210 TQ	USBLS	5/07
	Providence-Fall River-Warwick MSA, RI-MA	Y	61400 FQ	76880 MW	94890 TQ	USBLS	5/07
	South Carolina	Y	47930 FQ	61670 MW	78010 TQ	USBLS	5/07
	Charleston-North Charleston MSA, SC	Y	46610 FQ	5?910 MW	77180 TQ	USBLS	5/07
	Columbia MSA, SC	Y	45940 FQ	5??70 MW	70950 TQ	USBLS	5/07
	Myrtle Beach-Conway-North Myrtle Beach MSA, SC	Y	42080 FQ	48800 MW	60470 TQ	USBLS	5/07

AE	Average entry wage	AW	Average wage paid	FQ	First quartile wage
AER	Average entry range	AWR	Average wage range	H	Hourly
AEX	Average experienced wage	AXR	Average experienced range	HI	Highest wage paid
ATC	Average total compensation	D	Daily	HR	High end range

LO	Lowest wage paid	MTC	Median total compensation	TCC	Total cash compensation
LR	Low end range	MW	Median wage paid	TQ	Third quartile wage
M	Monthly	MWR	Median wage range	W	Weekly
MCC	Median cash compensation	S	See annotated source	Y	Yearly

Occupation/Type/Industry	Location	Per	Low	Mid	High	Source	Date
Computer Systems Analyst	South Dakota	Y	51086 FQ	63136 MW	76003 TQ	SDBLS	7/08-9/08
	Sioux Falls MSA, SD	Y	53731 FQ	64596 MW	78336 TQ	SDBLS	7/08-9/08
	Tennessee	Y	44890 FQ	59300 MW	75730 TQ	USBLS	5/07
	Memphis MSA, TN-MS-AR	Y	48550 FQ	62660 MW	77480 TQ	USBLS	5/07
	Nashville-Davidson- Murfreesboro MSA, TN	Y	46500 FQ	60060 MW	75330 TQ	USBLS	5/07
	Texas	Y	53870 FQ	70870 MW	91740 TQ	USBLS	5/07
	Austin-Round Rock MSA, TX	Y	54900 FQ	65310 MW	89750 TQ	USBLS	5/07
	Brownsville-Harlingen MSA, TX	Y	29880 FQ	36820 MW	52580 TQ	USBLS	5/07
	Dallas-Fort Worth-Arlington MSA, TX	Y	59280 FQ	77800 MW	97120 TQ	USBLS	5/07
	El Paso MSA, TX	Y	52110 FQ	63570 MW	78190 TQ	USBLS	5/07
	Houston-Sugar Land-Baytown MSA, TX	Y	52040 FQ	71530 MW	91810 TQ	USBLS	5/07
	San Antonio MSA, TX	Y	48390 FQ	63030 MW	79300 TQ	USBLS	5/07
	Utah	Y	50080 FQ	64230 MW	82990 TQ	USBLS	5/07
	Salt Lake City MSA, UT	Y	51300 FQ	67310 MW	85440 TQ	USBLS	5/07
	Vermont	Y	55140 FQ	65650 MW	82190 TQ	USBLS	5/07
	Burlington-South Burlington MSA, VT	Y	56490 FQ	70610 MW	93910 TQ	USBLS	5/07
	Virginia	Y	63640 FQ	81390 MW	100450 TQ	USBLS	5/07
	Richmond MSA, VA	Y	61710 FQ	78610 MW	94900 TQ	USBLS	5/07
	Virginia Beach-Norfolk- Newport News MSA, VA-NC	Y	53930 FQ	65750 MW	81020 TQ	USBLS	5/07
	Washington	H	29.53 FQ	37.01 MW	46.36 TQ	WABLS	3/08
	Seattle-Tacoma-Bellevue MSA, WA	Y	62200 FQ	77810 MW	96640 TQ	USBLS	5/07
	West Virginia	Y	43393 FQ	59497 MW	77915 TQ	WVBLS	7/08-9/08
	Charleston MSA, WV	Y	42260 FQ	56710 MW	76040 TQ	USBLS	5/07
	Wheeling MSA, WV-OH	Y	44330 FQ	66250 MW	91260 TQ	USBLS	5/07
	Wisconsin	Y	50660 FQ	64000 MW	78080 TQ	USBLS	5/07
	Milwaukee-Waukesha-West Allis MSA, WI	Y	52090 FQ	67390 MW	81660 TQ	USBLS	5/07
	Racine MSA, WI	Y	54530 FQ	68830 MW	78900 TQ	USBLS	5/07
	Wyoming	Y	38117 FQ	45463 MW	62744 TQ	WYBLS	9/08
	Cheyenne MSA, WY	Y	37012 FQ	41676 MW	48548 TQ	WYBLS	9/08
	Puerto Rico	Y	32050 FQ	43970 MW	59110 TQ	USBLS	5/07
	San Juan-Caguas-Guaynabo MSA, PR	Y	32140 FQ	44110 MW	59310 TQ	USBLS	5/07
	Virgin Islands	Y	37080 FQ	43400 MW	50490 TQ	USBLS	5/07
	Guam	Y	34520 FQ	42740 MW	53010 TQ	USBLS	5/07
Computer Technician Municipal Government	Walnut Creek, CA	Y	49017 LO		59626 HI	WCSWP	6/27/08
Concierge	Alabama	Y	17580 FQ	20150 MW	25530 TQ	USBLS	5/07
	Alaska	Y	22590 FQ	25720 MW	31630 TQ	USBLS	5/07
	Arizona	Y	19830 FQ	22410 MW	25240 TQ	USBLS	5/07
	Phoenix-Mesa-Scottsdale MSA, AZ	Y	19860 FQ	22440 MW	25110 TQ	USBLS	5/07
	Tucson MSA, AZ	Y	18710 FQ	20840 MW	23310 TQ	USBLS	5/07
	California	H	10.45 FQ	12.97 MW	15.17 TQ	CABLS	1/08-3/08
	Los Angeles-Long Beach- Glendale PMSA, CA	H	8.00 FQ	10.96 MW	14.12 TQ	CABLS	1/08-3/08
	Oakland-Fremont-Hayward MSA, CA	H	10.65 FQ	12.38 MW	14.59 TQ	CABLS	1/08-3/08
	Riverside-San Bernardino- Ontario MSA, CA	H	10.56 FQ	12.05 MW	14.34 TQ	CABLS	1/08-3/08
	Sacramento-Arden Arcade- Roseville MSA, CA	H	11.06 FQ	12.90 MW	14.61 TQ	CABLS	1/08-3/08
	San Diego-Carlsbad-San Marcos MSA, CA	H	11.90 FQ	13.70 MW	15.07 TQ	CABLS	1/08-3/08
	San Francisco-San Mateo- Redwood PMSA, CA	H	13.24 FQ	17.00 MW	19.49 TQ	CABLS	1/08-3/08
	San Jose-Sunnyvale-Santa Clara MSA, CA	H	13.43 FQ	14.55 MW	15.82 TQ	CABLS	1/08-3/08
	Santa Ana-Anaheim-Irvine PMSA, CA	Y	22290 FQ	26440 MW	29800 TQ	USBLS	5/07
	Colorado	Y	21490 FQ	25650 MW	34110 TQ	USBLS	5/07
	Denver-Aurora MSA, CO	Y	20980 FQ	23670 MW	30340 TQ	USBLS	5/07
	Connecticut	H	10.00 AE	12.56 MW		CTBLS	1/08-3/08

AE	Average entry wage	AW	Average wage paid	FQ	First quartile wage	LO	Lowest wage paid	MTC	Median total compensation	TCC	Total cash compensation
AER	Average entry range	AWR	Average wage range	H	Hourly	LR	Low end range	MW	Median wage paid	TQ	Third quartile wage
AEX	Average experienced wage	AXR	Average experienced range	HI	Highest wage paid	M	Monthly	MWR	Median wage range	W	Weekly
ATC	Average total compensation	D	Daily	HR	High end range	MCC	Median cash compensation	S	See annotated source	Y	Yearly

Occupation/Type/Industry	Location	Per	Low	Mid	High	Source	Date
Concierge	Bridgeport-Stamford-Norwalk MSA, CT	Y	22760 FQ	26520 MW	32750 TQ	USBLS	5/07
	Hartford-West Hartford-East Hartford MSA, CT	Y	19380 FQ	23270 MW	28150 TQ	USBLS	5/07
	Delaware	Y	21610 FQ	24240 MW	29680 TQ	USBLS	5/07
	Wilmington PMSA, DE-MD-NJ	Y	22390 FQ	24650 MW	31420 TQ	USBLS	5/07
	District of Columbia	Y	26660 FQ	30380 MW	35520 TQ	USBLS	5/07
	Washington-Arlington-Alexandria MSA, DC-VA-MD-WV	Y	25750 FQ	29740 MW	34850 TQ	USBLS	5/07
	Florida	Y	18220 FQ	21720 MW	25660 TQ	USBLS	5/07
	Fort Lauderdale-Pompano Beach-Deerfield Beach PMSA, FL	Y	18920 FQ	23200 MW	30290 TQ	USBLS	5/07
	Jacksonville MSA, FL	Y	20790 FQ	22790 MW	24940 TQ	USBLS	5/07
	Miami-Fort Lauderdale-Miami Beach MSA, FL	Y	20580 FQ	23420 MW	27140 TQ	USBLS	5/07
	Orlando-Kissimmee MSA, FL	Y	16810 FQ	19280 MW	23480 TQ	USBLS	5/07
	Tampa-St. Petersburg-Clearwater MSA, FL	Y	18860 FQ	21750 MW	25350 TQ	USBLS	5/07
	West Palm Beach-Boca Raton-Boynton Beach PMSA, FL	Y	21560 FQ	23840 MW	26740 TQ	USBLS	5/07
	Georgia	Y	15460 FQ	21720 MW	26310 TQ	USBLS	5/07
	Atlanta-Sandy Springs-Marietta MSA, GA	Y	21350 FQ	23910 MW	28080 TQ	USBLS	5/07
	Hawaii	Y	30210 FQ	35010 MW	39540 TQ	USBLS	5/07
	Honolulu MSA, HI	Y	26990 FQ	33320 MW	39090 TQ	USBLS	5/07
	Illinois	Y	23540 FQ	27370 MW	30330 TQ	USBLS	5/07
	Chicago-Naperville-Joliet MSA, IL-IN-WI	Y	24240 FQ	27650 MW	30510 TQ	USBLS	5/07
	Indiana	Y	14890 FQ	21430 MW	28060 TQ	USBLS	5/07
	Kansas	Y	16640 FQ	18380 MW	22360 TQ	USBLS	5/07
	Kentucky	Y	17869 FQ	23429 MW	36097 TQ	KYBLS	2008
	Louisiana	H	9.98 FQ	11.88 MW	14.26 TQ	LABLS	1/08-3/08
	New Orleans-Metairie-Kenner MSA, LA	Y	21070 FQ	24090 MW	29050 TQ	USBLS	5/07
	Maryland	Y		26250 MW		MDBLS	3/08
	Baltimore-Towson MSA, MD	Y	19920 FQ	23970 MW	30860 TQ	USBLS	5/07
	Bethesda-Gaithersburg-Frederick PMSA, MD	Y	24450 FQ	28130 MW	30910 TQ	USBLS	5/07
	Massachusetts	Y	23780 FQ	28760 MW	32500 TQ	USBLS	5/07
	Boston-Cambridge-Quincy NECTA, MA	Y	25770 FQ	29340 MW	32750 TQ	USBLS	5/07
	Michigan	Y	19160 FQ	21610 MW	25520 TQ	USBLS	5/07
	Detroit-Warren-Livonia MSA, MI	Y	19330 FQ	22020 MW	27590 TQ	USBLS	5/07
	Warren-Troy-Farmington Hills PMSA, MI	Y	19410 FQ	22170 MW	30980 TQ	USBLS	5/07
	Minnesota	Y	22020 FQ	24623 MW	29318 TQ	MNBLS	10/08-12/08
	Minneapolis-Saint Paul MSA, MN-WI	Y	22020 FQ	24592 MW	29433 TQ	MNBLS	10/08-12/08
	Mississippi	Y	17050 FQ	19040 MW	23370 TQ	USBLS	5/07
	Missouri	Y	17870 FQ	20440 MW	23330 TQ	USBLS	5/07
	Kansas City MSA, MO-KS	Y	17540 FQ	20450 MW	23880 TQ	USBLS	5/07
	St. Louis MSA, MO-IL	Y	18050 FQ	20470 MW	23390 TQ	USBLS	5/07
	Nebraska	Y	19780 FQ	22460 MW	24460 TQ	USBLS	5/07
	Las Vegas-Paradise MSA, NV	H	12.13 FQ	15.32 MW	17.57 TQ	NVBLS	5/08
	New Hampshire	H	10.22 AE	12.85 MW	14.12 AEX	NHBLS	6/08
	New Jersey	Y	20910 FQ	24280 MW	28650 TQ	USBLS	5/07
	Atlantic City MSA, NJ	Y	20670 FQ	24170 MW	27570 TQ	USBLS	5/07
	Edison PMSA, NJ	Y	21010 FQ	24720 MW	29240 TQ	USBLS	5/07
	Newark-Union PMSA, NJ-PA	Y	18580 FQ	22880 MW	27820 TQ	USBLS	5/07
	New Mexico	Y	19710 FQ	23250 MW	26710 TQ	USBLS	5/07
	Albuquerque MSA, NM	Y	16910 FQ	20890 MW	26290 TQ	USBLS	5/07
	New York	Y	32600 FQ	37840 MW	43240 TQ	USBLS	5/07
	Buffalo-Niagara Falls MSA, NY	Y	17810 FQ	19480 MW	22770 TQ	USBLS	5/07
	Nassau-Suffolk PMSA, NY	Y	24050 FQ	28600 MW	36650 TQ	USBLS	5/07
	New York-Northern New Jersey-Long Island MSA, NY-NJ-PA	Y	29150 FQ	36530 MW	41920 TQ	USBLS	5/07

AE	Average entry wage	AW	Average wage paid	FQ	First quartile wage	LO	Lowest wage paid	MTC Median total compensation	TCC Total cash compensation
AER	Average entry range	AWR	Average wage range	H	Hourly	LR	Low end range	MW Median wage paid	TQ Third quartile wage
AEX	Average experienced wage	AXR	Average experienced range	HI	Highest wage paid	M	Monthly	MWR Median wage range	W Weekly
ATC	Average total compensation	D	Daily	HR	High end range	MCC	Median cash compensation	S See annotated source	Y Yearly

Occupation/Type/Industry	Location	Per	Low	Mid	High	Source	Date
Concierge	North Carolina	Y	17280 FQ	19750 MW	22700 TQ	USBLS	5/07
	Charlotte-Gastonia-Concord MSA, NC-SC	Y	16580 FQ	18980 MW	22560 TQ	USBLS	5/07
	Ohio	Y	19950 FQ	24490 MW	30120 TQ	USBLS	5/07
	Cleveland-Elyria-Mentor MSA, OH	Y	21250 FQ	25360 MW	28900 TQ	USBLS	5/07
	Columbus MSA, OH	Y	19850 FQ	24640 MW	31400 TQ	USBLS	5/07
	Oregon	H	9.22 FQ	11.12 MW	15.14 TQ	ORBLS	5/08
	Portland-Vancouver-Beaverton MSA, OR-WA	Y	21710 FQ	28160 MW	35660 TQ	USBLS	5/07
	Pennsylvania	Y	21690 FQ	26060 MW	29260 TQ	USBLS	5/07
	Philadelphia-Camden-Wilmington MSA, PA-NJ-DE-MD	Y	22600 FQ	26090 MW	29510 TQ	USBLS	5/07
	Pittsburgh MSA, PA	Y	23980 FQ	26760 MW	29280 TQ	USBLS	5/07
	Rhode Island	Y	20800 FQ	22930 MW	26990 TQ	USBLS	5/07
	Providence-Fall River-Warwick MSA, RI-MA	Y	20800 FQ	22930 MW	26990 TQ	USBLS	5/07
	South Carolina	Y	17150 FQ	19080 MW	23520 TQ	USBLS	5/07
	Charleston-North Charleston MSA, SC	Y	16390 FQ	17980 MW	22140 TQ	USBLS	5/07
	Tennessee	Y	18360 FQ	20930 MW	23450 TQ	USBLS	5/07
	Memphis MSA, TN-MS-AR	Y	15970 FQ	20070 MW	23500 TQ	USBLS	5/07
	Nashville-Davidson-Murfreesboro MSA, TN	Y	18870 FQ	21200 MW	23520 TQ	USBLS	5/07
	Texas	Y	20750 FQ	23560 MW	27700 TQ	USBLS	5/07
	Austin-Round Rock MSA, TX	Y	21470 FQ	23250 MW	25590 TQ	USBLS	5/07
	Dallas-Fort Worth-Arlington MSA, TX	Y	21230 FQ	24090 MW	27940 TQ	USBLS	5/07
	Houston-Sugar Land-Baytown MSA, TX	Y	18960 FQ	22910 MW	28500 TQ	USBLS	5/07
	San Antonio MSA, TX	Y	20030 FQ	22370 MW	24830 TQ	USBLS	5/07
	Utah	Y	18010 FQ	20430 MW	24150 TQ	USBLS	5/07
	Salt Lake City MSA, UT	Y	17780 FQ	19980 MW	23100 TQ	USBLS	5/07
	Virginia	Y	14330 FQ	20870 MW	28430 TQ	USBLS	5/07
	Virginia Beach-Norfolk-Newport News MSA, VA-NC	Y	13120 FQ	15160 MW	20920 TQ	USBLS	5/07
	Washington	H	11.52 FQ	13.82 MW	15.75 TQ	WABLS	3/08
	Seattle-Tacoma-Bellevue MSA, WA	Y	24530 FQ	28640 MW	32320 TQ	USBLS	5/07
	West Virginia	Y	17496 FQ	20972 MW	24242 TQ	WVBLS	7/08-9/08
	Wisconsin	Y	15800 FQ	18610 MW	22760 TQ	USBLS	5/07
	Milwaukee-Waukesha-West Allis MSA, WI	Y	15840 FQ	20080 MW	24340 TQ	USBLS	5/07
	Wyoming	Y	21308 FQ	24027 MW	29606 TQ	WYBLS	9/08
	Puerto Rico	Y	17270 FQ	19160 MW	25140 TQ	USBLS	5/07
	San Juan-Caguas-Guaynabo MSA, PR	Y	17420 FQ	19640 MW	26730 TQ	USBLS	5/07
	Virgin Islands	Y	20850 FQ	22820 MW	24830 TQ	USBLS	5/07
	Guam	Y	15340 FQ	20490 MW	25340 TQ	USBLS	5/07
Confidential Assistant White House Staff	United States	Y			35500 HI	WPOST02	2008
Conservation Aide State Government	Ohio	H	14.36 LO		15.41 HI	ODAS	2008
Conservation Officer Sergeant, Fish and Game Commission	New Hampshire	Y		66715 AW		NHUL03	2008
Conservation Scientist	Alabama	Y	45760 FQ	55990 MW	72210 TQ	USBLS	5/07
	Alaska	Y	60750 FQ	73230 MW	87440 TQ	USBLS	5/07
	Anchorage MSA, AK	Y	69260 FQ	79110 MW	99620 TQ	USBLS	5/07
	Arizona	Y	43930 FQ	56510 MW	67700 TQ	USBLS	5/07
	Phoenix-Mesa-Scottsdale MSA, AZ	Y	48390 FQ	59150 MW	70450 TQ	USBLS	5/07
	Arkansas	Y	54000 FQ	65030 MW	74290 TQ	USBLS	5/07
	California	H	27.28 FQ	31.37 MW	38.05 TQ	CABLS	1/08-3/08
	Los Angeles-Long Beach-Glendale PMSA, CA	H	29.93 FQ	39.08 MW	46.65 TQ	CABLS	1/08-3/08
	Oakland-Fremont-Hayward MSA, CA	H	28.41 FQ	30.65 MW	32.93 TQ	CABLS	1/08-3/08

Occupation/Type/Industry	Location	Per	Low	Mid	High	Source	Date
Conservation Scientist	Riverside-San Bernardino-Ontario MSA, CA	H	29.45 FQ	36.19 MW	45.93 TQ	CABLS	1/08-3/08
	San Diego-Carlsbad-San Marcos MSA, CA	H	31.87 FQ	37.28 MW	46.86 TQ	CABLS	1/08-3/08
	San Francisco-San Mateo-Redwood PMSA, CA	H	17.10 FQ	26.44 MW	37.90 TQ	CABLS	1/08-3/08
	Colorado	Y	45000 FQ	56030 MW	66400 TQ	USBLS	5/07
	Denver-Aurora MSA, CO	Y	42130 FQ	59550 MW	89400 TQ	USBLS	5/07
	Connecticut	H	24.39 AE	31.47 MW		CTBLS	1/08-3/08
	Hartford-West Hartford-East Hartford MSA, CT	Y	55160 FQ	61040 MW	69350 TQ	USBLS	5/07
	District of Columbia	Y	63100 FQ	77680 MW	107870 TQ	USBLS	5/07
	Washington-Arlington-Alexandria MSA, DC-VA-MD-WV	Y	54600 FQ	73520 MW	100450 TQ	USBLS	5/07
	Florida	Y	50800 FQ	64510 MW	77840 TQ	USBLS	5/07
	Miami-Fort Lauderdale-Miami Beach MSA, FL	Y	47310 FQ	70150 MW	84680 TQ	USBLS	5/07
	Georgia	Y	35120 FQ	60100 MW	75950 TQ	USBLS	5/07
	Atlanta-Sandy Springs-Marietta MSA, GA	Y	45750 FQ	69870 MW	87040 TQ	USBLS	5/07
	Hawaii	Y	51540 FQ	62450 MW	78460 TQ	USBLS	5/07
	Idaho	Y	43390 FQ	55700 MW	66140 TQ	USBLS	5/07
	Boise City-Nampa MSA, ID	Y	56300 FQ	67100 MW	76150 TQ	USBLS	5/07
	Illinois	Y	46230 FQ	60740 MW	73880 TQ	USBLS	5/07
	Chicago-Naperville-Joliet MSA, IL-IN-WI	Y	42900 FQ	57640 MW	78660 TQ	USBLS	5/07
	Indiana	Y	42130 FQ	60140 MW	73710 TQ	USBLS	5/07
	Indianapolis-Carmel MSA, IN	Y	30060 FQ	43690 MW	70900 TQ	USBLS	5/07
	Iowa	Y	36720 FQ	49550 MW	67720 TQ	USBLS	5/07
	Kentucky	Y	54222 FQ	61979 MW	71464 TQ	KYBLS	2008
	Louisville-Jefferson County MSA, KY-IN	Y	53610 FQ	58380 MW	63160 TQ	USBLS	5/07
	Louisiana	H	25.97 FQ	31.71 MW	37.53 TQ	LABLS	1/08-3/08
	Maine	Y	46690 FQ	58380 MW	70810 TQ	USBLS	5/07
	Maryland	Y		57675 MW		MDBLS	3/08
	Baltimore-Towson MSA, MD	Y	41640 FQ	49830 MW	63520 TQ	USBLS	5/07
	Bethesda-Gaithersburg-Frederick PMSA, MD	Y	53530 FQ	71910 MW	111740 TQ	USBLS	5/07
	Massachusetts	Y	45870 FQ	58680 MW	79300 TQ	USBLS	5/07
	Boston-Cambridge-Quincy NECTA, MA	Y	44600 FQ	60530 MW	80670 TQ	USBLS	5/07
	Michigan	Y	49910 FQ	62340 MW	76930 TQ	USBLS	5/07
	Detroit-Warren-Livonia MSA, MI	Y	54470 FQ	67420 MW	76710 TQ	USBLS	5/07
	Warren-Troy-Farmington Hills PMSA, MI	Y	55420 FQ	67350 MW	75860 TQ	USBLS	5/07
	Minnesota	Y	49036 FQ	58923 MW	69636 TQ	MNBLS	10/08-12/08
	Minneapolis-Saint Paul MSA, MN-WI	Y	45176 FQ	55491 MW	71268 TQ	MNBLS	10/08-12/08
	Mississippi	Y	34370 FQ	43580 MW	60800 TQ	USBLS	5/07
	Jackson MSA, MS	Y	40070 FQ	47570 MW	58160 TQ	USBLS	5/07
	Missouri	Y	23260 FQ	36450 MW	58350 TQ	USBLS	5/07
	Kansas City MSA, MO-KS	Y	28190 FQ	37380 MW	61550 TQ	USBLS	5/07
	St. Louis MSA, MO-IL	Y	30470 FQ	38060 MW	51160 TQ	USBLS	5/07
	Montana	Y	43130 FQ	53900 MW	64240 TQ	USBLS	5/07
	Nebraska	Y	42120 FQ	54480 MW	64730 TQ	USBLS	5/07
	Omaha-Council Bluffs MSA, NE-IA	Y	38570 FQ	53240 MW	67940 TQ	USBLS	5/07
	Nevada	H	24.09 FQ	28.54 MW	34.51 TQ	NVBLS	5/08
	Las Vegas-Paradise MSA, NV	H	28.43 FQ	33.77 MW	38.96 TQ	NVBLS	5/08
	New Hampshire	H	18.33 AE	28.88 MW	37.21 AEX	NHBLS	6/08
	New Jersey	Y	54260 FQ	69010 MW	79400 TQ	USBLS	5/07
	Camden PMSA, NJ	Y	61250 FQ	71760 MW	78320 TQ	USBLS	5/07
	Edison PMSA, NJ	Y	50570 FQ	63850 MW	78380 TQ	USBLS	5/07
	Newark-Union PMSA, NJ-PA	Y	52470 FQ	69000 MW	78760 TQ	USBLS	5/07
	New Mexico	Y	44950 FQ	57300 MW	69890 TQ	USBLS	5/07
	New York	Y	46180 FQ	55360 MW	63600 TQ	USBLS	5/07
	Albany-Schenectady-Troy MSA, NY	Y	43670 FQ	51220 MW	59040 TQ	USBLS	5/07
	Nassau-Suffolk PMSA, NY	Y	41330 FQ	52850 MW	62360 TQ	USBLS	5/07

AE	Average entry wage	AW	Average wage paid	FQ	First quartile wage	LO	Lowest wage paid	MTC	Median total compensation	TCC	Total cash compensation
AER	Average entry range	AWR	Average wage range	H	Hourly	LR	Low end range	MW	Median wage paid	TQ	Third quartile wage
AEX	Average experienced wage	AXR	Average experienced range	HI	Highest wage paid	M	Monthly	MWR	Median wage range	W	Weekly
ATC	Average total compensation	D	Daily	HR	High end range	MCC	Median cash compensation	S	See annotated source	Y	Yearly

Occupation/Type/Industry	Location	Per	Low	Mid	High	Source	Date
Conservation Scientist	New York-Northern New Jersey-Long Island MSA, NY-NJ-PA	Y	47380 FQ	59370 MW	74860 TQ	USBLS	5/07
	North Carolina	Y	37820 FQ	48840 MW	65160 TQ	USBLS	5/07
	Charlotte-Gastonia-Concord MSA, NC-SC	Y	39270 FQ	46300 MW	54670 TQ	USBLS	5/07
	Durham MSA, NC	Y	41460 FQ	53440 MW	74340 TQ	USBLS	5/07
	Raleigh-Cary MSA, NC	Y	47310 FQ	56190 MW	71420 TQ	USBLS	5/07
	North Dakota	Y	48460 FQ	59600 MW	71100 TQ	USBLS	5/07
	Ohio	Y	40620 FQ	53030 MW	72210 TQ	USBLS	5/07
	Cincinnati-Middletown MSA, OH-KY-IN	Y	53220 FQ	69760 MW	79650 TQ	USBLS	5/07
	Cleveland-Elyria-Mentor MSA, OH	Y	48370 FQ	65510 MW	86130 TQ	USBLS	5/07
	Columbus MSA, OH	Y	37360 FQ	46200 MW	55520 TQ	USBLS	5/07
	Oklahoma	Y	30170 FQ	48210 MW	64620 TQ	USBLS	5/07
	Oklahoma City MSA, OK	Y	29540 FQ	36020 MW	48440 TQ	USBLS	5/07
	Tulsa MSA, OK	Y	37330 FQ	51800 MW	68900 TQ	USBLS	5/07
	Oregon	H	21.92 FQ	28.06 MW	35.51 TQ	ORBLS	5/08
	Portland-Vancouver-Beaverton MSA, OR-WA	Y	46280 FQ	66500 MW	84750 TQ	USBLS	5/07
	Pennsylvania	Y	28620 FQ	36050 MW	51190 TQ	USBLS	5/07
	Philadelphia-Camden-Wilmington MSA, PA-NJ-DE-MD	Y	42980 FQ	62340 MW	76430 TQ	USBLS	5/07
	Pittsburgh MSA, PA	Y	32630 FQ	46010 MW	60380 TQ	USBLS	5/07
	Rhode Island	Y	42350 FQ	68590 MW	101820 TQ	USBLS	5/07
	Providence-Fall River-Warwick MSA, RI-MA	Y	37620 FQ	53310 MW	87070 TQ	USBLS	5/07
	South Carolina	Y	52190 FQ	61390 MW	74370 TQ	USBLS	5/07
	Charleston-North Charleston MSA, SC	Y	53340 FQ	61090 MW	75970 TQ	USBLS	5/07
	Columbia MSA, SC	Y	52370 FQ	63770 MW	73530 TQ	USBLS	5/07
	South Dakota	Y	37768 FQ	50423 MW	64188 TQ	SDBLS	7/08-9/08
	Tennessee	Y	51270 FQ	63190 MW	77130 TQ	USBLS	5/07
	Texas	Y	34300 FQ	43920 MW	59730 TQ	USBLS	5/07
	Austin-Round Rock MSA, TX	Y	33570 FQ	41530 MW	48580 TQ	USBLS	5/07
	Dallas-Fort Worth-Arlington MSA, TX	Y	29700 FQ	37710 MW	66870 TQ	USBLS	5/07
	Houston-Sugar Land-Baytown MSA, TX	Y	29700 FQ	35460 MW	45980 TQ	USBLS	5/07
	Utah	Y	48080 FQ	60860 MW	74130 TQ	USBLS	5/07
	Salt Lake City MSA, UT	Y	43290 FQ	53960 MW	70160 TQ	USBLS	5/07
	Vermont	Y	44510 FQ	50940 MW	64320 TQ	USBLS	5/07
	Burlington-South Burlington MSA, VT	Y	44450 FQ	48590 MW	56280 TQ	USBLS	5/07
	Virginia	Y	42790 FQ	59870 MW	77450 TQ	USBLS	5/07
	Virginia Beach-Norfolk-Newport News MSA, VA-NC	Y	44360 FQ	69770 MW	77890 TQ	USBLS	5/07
	Washington	H	22.27 FQ	26.80 MW	33.19 TQ	WABLS	3/08
	Seattle-Tacoma-Bellevue MSA, WA	Y	50290 FQ	66410 MW	84170 TQ	USBLS	5/07
	West Virginia	Y	52091 FQ	69268 MW	82809 TQ	WVBLS	7/08-9/08
	Wisconsin	Y	47730 FQ	58640 MW	70080 TQ	USBLS	5/07
	Milwaukee-Waukesha-West Allis MSA, WI	Y	49330 FQ	67440 MW	78310 TQ	USBLS	5/07
	Wyoming	Y	49321 FQ	60732 MW	71117 TQ	WYBLS	9/08
Construction and Building Inspector	Alabama	Y	32520 FQ	41510 MW	51570 TQ	USBLS	5/07
	Birmingham-Hoover MSA, AL	Y	40860 FQ	48350 MW	62040 TQ	USBLS	5/07
	Alaska	Y	59040 FQ	69220 MW	79630 TQ	USBLS	5/07
	Anchorage MSA, AK	Y	58600 FQ	67670 MW	77720 TQ	USBLS	5/07
	Arizona	Y	34780 FQ	44000 MW	55490 TQ	USBLS	5/07
	Phoenix-Mesa-Scottsdale MSA, AZ	Y	34140 FQ	45150 MW	56640 TQ	USBLS	5/07
	Prescott MSA, AZ	Y	36290 FQ	40820 MW	46240 TQ	USBLS	5/07
	Tucson MSA, AZ	Y	35980 FQ	47400 MW	59440 TQ	USBLS	5/07
	Arkansas	Y	32310 FQ	41180 MW	48410 TQ	USBLS	5/07
	Little Rock-North Little Rock MSA, AR	Y	32590 FQ	41030 MW	49680 TQ	USBLS	5/07
	California	H	24.31 FQ	31.72 MW	38.29 TQ	CABLS	1/08-3/08

AE	Average entry wage	AW	Average wage paid	FQ	First quartile wage
AER	Average entry range	AWR	Average wage range	H	Hourly
AEX	Average experienced wage	AXR	Average experienced range	HI	Highest wage paid
ATC	Average total compensation	D	Daily	HR	High end range

LO	Lowest wage paid	MTC	Median total compensation
LR	Low end range	MW	Median wage paid
M	Monthly	MWR	Median wage range
MCC	Median cash compensation	S	See annotated source

TCC	Total cash compensation
TQ	Third quartile wage
W	Weekly
Y	Yearly

Occupation/Type/Industry	Location	Per	Low	Mid	High	Source	Date
Construction and Building Inspector							
	Los Angeles-Long Beach-Glendale PMSA, CA	H	31.02 FQ	36.27 MW	41.30 TQ	CABLS	1/08-3/08
	Oakland-Fremont-Hayward MSA, CA	H	30.06 FQ	35.27 MW	40.00 TQ	CABLS	1/08-3/08
	Riverside-San Bernardino-Ontario MSA, CA	H	20.78 FQ	25.55 MW	30.58 TQ	CABLS	1/08-3/08
	Sacramento-Arden Arcade-Roseville MSA, CA	H	23.48 FQ	28.81 MW	34.97 TQ	CABLS	1/08-3/08
	San Diego-Carlsbad-San Marcos MSA, CA	H	26.54 FQ	31.83 MW	36.73 TQ	CABLS	1/08-3/08
	San Francisco-San Mateo-Redwood PMSA, CA	H	28.33 FQ	34.18 MW	39.09 TQ	CABLS	1/08-3/08
	San Jose-Sunnyvale-Santa Clara MSA, CA	H	27.75 FQ	36.91 MW	45.91 TQ	CABLS	1/08-3/08
	Santa Ana-Anaheim-Irvine PMSA, CA	Y	38680 FQ	58110 MW	73840 TQ	USBLS	5/07
	Colorado	Y	41110 FQ	50450 MW	59910 TQ	USBLS	5/07
	Denver-Aurora MSA, CO	Y	41520 FQ	50810 MW	60580 TQ	USBLS	5/07
	Connecticut	H	22.46 AE	30.14 MW		CTBLS	1/08-3/08
	Bridgeport-Stamford-Norwalk MSA, CT	Y	51610 FQ	61220 MW	70760 TQ	USBLS	5/07
	Hartford-West Hartford-East Hartford MSA, CT	Y	51810 FQ	61280 MW	71960 TQ	USBLS	5/07
	Delaware	Y	36930 FQ	43720 MW	54040 TQ	USBLS	5/07
	Wilmington PMSA, DE-MD-NJ	Y	37920 FQ	45070 MW	56810 TQ	USBLS	5/07
	District of Columbia	Y	54880 FQ	66680 MW	79960 TQ	USBLS	5/07
	Washington-Arlington-Alexandria MSA, DC-VA-MD-WV	Y	45940 FQ	56190 MW	67200 TQ	USBLS	5/07
	Florida	Y	40410 FQ	49030 MW	60010 TQ	USBLS	5/07
	Fort Lauderdale-Pompano Beach-Deerfield Beach PMSA, FL	Y	43990 FQ	57830 MW	69580 TQ	USBLS	5/07
	Jacksonville MSA, FL	Y	37830 FQ	47370 MW	58610 TQ	USBLS	5/07
	Lakeland MSA, FL	Y	39210 FQ	46520 MW	55270 TQ	USBLS	5/07
	Miami-Fort Lauderdale-Miami Beach MSA, FL	Y	44600 FQ	56150 MW	67680 TQ	USBLS	5/07
	Orlando-Kissimmee MSA, FL	Y	41920 FQ	49020 MW	59500 TQ	USBLS	5/07
	Tallahassee MSA, FL	Y	39860 FQ	46100 MW	57180 TQ	USBLS	5/07
	Tampa-St. Petersburg-Clearwater MSA, FL	Y	39740 FQ	47610 MW	57670 TQ	USBLS	5/07
	West Palm Beach-Boca Raton-Boynton Beach PMSA, FL	Y	44320 FQ	53270 MW	62090 TQ	USBLS	5/07
	Georgia	Y	32800 FQ	40680 MW	50430 TQ	USBLS	5/07
	Atlanta-Sandy Springs-Marietta MSA, GA	Y	33840 FQ	42800 MW	52110 TQ	USBLS	5/07
	Hawaii	Y	44390 FQ	54270 MW	64740 TQ	USBLS	5/07
	Honolulu MSA, HI	Y	44550 FQ	54040 MW	62850 TQ	USBLS	5/07
	Idaho	Y	36800 FQ	45080 MW	51090 TQ	USBLS	5/07
	Boise City-Nampa MSA, ID	Y	35820 FQ	43970 MW	50240 TQ	USBLS	5/07
	Illinois	Y	43780 FQ	57980 MW	73750 TQ	USBLS	5/07
	Chicago-Naperville-Joliet MSA, IL-IN-WI	Y	47740 FQ	60030 MW	77080 TQ	USBLS	5/07
	Peoria MSA, IL	Y	32220 FQ	45930 MW	61440 TQ	USBLS	5/07
	Indiana	Y	31180 FQ	38820 MW	50630 TQ	USBLS	5/07
	Elkhart-Goshen MSA, IN	Y	31950 FQ	35800 MW	39570 TQ	USBLS	5/07
	Fort Wayne MSA, IN	Y	34810 FQ	39600 MW	49110 TQ	USBLS	5/07
	Gary PMSA, IN	Y	28470 FQ	35250 MW	41440 TQ	USBLS	5/07
	Indianapolis-Carmel MSA, IN	Y	38370 FQ	49620 MW	57070 TQ	USBLS	5/07
	Iowa	Y	36940 FQ	47100 MW	57650 TQ	USBLS	5/07
	Des Moines-West Des Moines MSA, IA	Y	36600 FQ	48250 MW	57320 TQ	USBLS	5/07
	Kansas	Y	34070 FQ	41680 MW	53520 TQ	USBLS	5/07
	Wichita MSA, KS	Y	24000 FQ	45210 MW	58300 TQ	USBLS	5/07
	Kentucky	Y	36249 FQ	42007 MW	52005 TQ	KYBLS	2008
	Louisville-Jefferson County MSA, KY-IN	Y	34940 FQ	42440 MW	51670 TQ	USBLS	5/07
	Louisiana	H	17.91 FQ	21.43 MW	26.70 TQ	LABLS	1/08-3/08
	Baton Rouge MSA, LA	Y	38020 FQ	43160 MW	50650 TQ	USBLS	5/07

AE	Average entry wage	**AW**	Average wage paid	**FQ**	First quartile wage	**LO** Lowest wage paid
AER	Average entry range	**AWR**	Average wage range	**H**	Hourly	**LR** Low end range
AEX	Average experienced wage	**AXR**	Average experienced range	**HI**	Highest wage paid	**M** Monthly
ATC	Average total compensation	**D**	Daily	**HR**	High end range	**MCC** Median cash compensation

MTC Median total compensation	**TCC** Total cash compensation
MW Median wage paid	**TQ** Third quartile wage
MWR Median wage range	**W** Weekly
S See annotated source	**Y** Yearly

Occupation/Type/Industry	Location	Per	Low	Mid	High	Source	Date
Construction and Building Inspector	New Orleans-Metairie-Kenner MSA, LA	Y	39120 FQ	46400 MW	56320 TQ	USBLS	5/07
	Maine	Y	31910 FQ	42970 MW	48770 TQ	USBLS	5/07
	Portland-South Portland-Biddeford MSA, ME	Y	34870 FQ	44510 MW	49730 TQ	USBLS	5/07
	Maryland	Y		47650 MW		MDBLS	3/08
	Baltimore-Towson MSA, MD	Y	38430 FQ	44760 MW	52220 TQ	USBLS	5/07
	Bethesda-Gaithersburg-Frederick PMSA, MD	Y	46130 FQ	55980 MW	65540 TQ	USBLS	5/07
	Massachusetts	Y	37900 FQ	47370 MW	59010 TQ	USBLS	5/07
	Barnstable Town MSA, MA	Y	41870 FQ	48680 MW	57060 TQ	USBLS	5/07
	Boston-Cambridge-Quincy NECTA, MA	Y	36960 FQ	48020 MW	60610 TQ	USBLS	5/07
	Springfield MSA, MA-CT	Y	37650 FQ	47770 MW	59670 TQ	USBLS	5/07
	Worcester MSA, MA-CT	Y	37600 FQ	41230 MW	49130 TQ	USBLS	5/07
	Michigan	Y	41590 FQ	50290 MW	59100 TQ	USBLS	5/07
	Ann Arbor MSA, MI	Y	43700 FQ	56870 MW	71740 TQ	USBLS	5/07
	Detroit-Warren-Livonia MSA, MI	Y	43550 FQ	52570 MW	60120 TQ	USBLS	5/07
	Flint MSA, MI	Y	36530 FQ	45020 MW	51990 TQ	USBLS	5/07
	Grand Rapids-Wyoming MSA, MI	Y	47060 FQ	52650 MW	59100 TQ	USBLS	5/07
	Warren-Troy-Farmington Hills PMSA, MI	Y	42650 FQ	53330 MW	61720 TQ	USBLS	5/07
	Minnesota	Y	43957 FQ	56666 MW	66994 TQ	MNBLS	10/08-12/08
	Duluth-Superior MSA, MN-WI	Y	38782 FQ	45306 MW	54148 TQ	MNBLS	10/08-12/08
	Minneapolis-Saint Paul MSA, MN-WI	Y	46960 FQ	59522 MW	69070 TQ	MNBLS	10/08-12/08
	Rochester MSA, MN	Y	53294 FQ	61238 MW	67548 TQ	MNBLS	10/08-12/08
	Mississippi	Y	29250 FQ	37660 MW	48770 TQ	USBLS	5/07
	Jackson MSA, MS	Y	36600 FQ	44620 MW	54610 TQ	USBLS	5/07
	Missouri	Y	37430 FQ	45580 MW	53050 TQ	USBLS	5/07
	Kansas City MSA, MO-KS	Y	36660 FQ	43680 MW	51880 TQ	USBLS	5/07
	St. Louis MSA, MO-IL	Y	40400 FQ	47960 MW	56420 TQ	USBLS	5/07
	Montana	Y	34060 FQ	38720 MW	45330 TQ	USBLS	5/07
	Nebraska	Y	32390 FQ	41530 MW	49490 TQ	USBLS	5/07
	Omaha-Council Bluffs MSA, NE-IA	Y	31800 FQ	42770 MW	57370 TQ	USBLS	5/07
	Nevada	H	22.22 FQ	29.63 MW	36.30 TQ	NVBLS	5/08
	Las Vegas-Paradise MSA, NV	H	21.09 FQ	29.52 MW	36.40 TQ	NVBLS	5/08
	New Hampshire	H	15.55 AE	21.28 MW	26.37 AEX	NHBLS	6/08
	Manchester MSA, NH	Y	33490 FQ	41040 MW	53060 TQ	USBLS	5/07
	Nashua NECTA, NH-MA	Y	36170 FQ	47230 MW	57590 TQ	USBLS	5/07
	New Jersey	Y	45050 FQ	56510 MW	67720 TQ	USBLS	5/07
	Camden PMSA, NJ	Y	43340 FQ	53130 MW	64100 TQ	USBLS	5/07
	Edison PMSA, NJ	Y	43400 FQ	54730 MW	64520 TQ	USBLS	5/07
	Newark-Union PMSA, NJ-PA	Y	45680 FQ	58370 MW	70010 TQ	USBLS	5/07
	Ocean City MSA, NJ	Y	53380 FQ	68600 MW	87000 TQ	USBLS	5/07
	New Mexico	Y	34500 FQ	42720 MW	54190 TQ	USBLS	5/07
	Albuquerque MSA, NM	Y	33960 FQ	40900 MW	51520 TQ	USBLS	5/07
	Santa Fe MSA, NM	Y	49330 FQ	56320 MW	62200 TQ	USBLS	5/07
	New York	Y	39930 FQ	49490 MW	61100 TQ	USBLS	5/07
	Albany-Schenectady-Troy MSA, NY	Y	33790 FQ	43340 MW	54330 TQ	USBLS	5/07
	Buffalo-Niagara Falls MSA, NY	Y	39640 FQ	50010 MW	61730 TQ	USBLS	5/07
	Kingston MSA, NY	Y	37420 FQ	46230 MW	58090 TQ	USBLS	5/07
	Nassau-Suffolk PMSA, NY	Y	36820 FQ	53770 MW	65960 TQ	USBLS	5/07
	New York-Northern New Jersey-Long Island MSA, NY-NJ-PA	Y	44970 FQ	55030 MW	66990 TQ	USBLS	5/07
	North Carolina	Y	36740 FQ	43960 MW	51560 TQ	USBLS	5/07
	Charlotte-Gastonia-Concord MSA, NC-SC	Y	40340 FQ	45940 MW	52860 TQ	USBLS	5/07
	Raleigh-Cary MSA, NC	Y	42800 FQ	49940 MW	58980 TQ	USBLS	5/07
	North Dakota	Y	40150 FQ	49660 MW	57620 TQ	USBLS	5/07
	Fargo MSA, ND-MN	Y	42440 FQ	50120 MW	58160 TQ	USBLS	5/07
	Ohio	Y	33350 FQ	43300 MW	53960 TQ	USBLS	5/07
	Cincinnati-Middletown MSA, OH-KY-IN	Y	29310 FQ	45010 MW	52470 TQ	USBLS	5/07

AE Average entry wage	**AW** Average wage paid	**FQ** First quartile wage	**LO** Lowest wage paid	**MTC** Median total compensation	**TCC** Total cash compensation
AER Average entry range	**AWR** Average wage range	**H** Hourly	**LR** Low end range	**MW** Median wage paid	**TQ** Third quartile wage
AEX Average experienced wage	**AXR** Average experienced range	**HI** Highest wage paid	**M** Monthly	**MWR** Median wage range	**W** Weekly
ATC Average total compensation	**D** Daily	**HR** High end range	**MCC** Median cash compensation	**S** See annotated source	**Y** Yearly

Occupation/Type/Industry	Location	Per	Low	Mid	High	Source	Date
Construction and Building Inspector							
	Cleveland-Elyria-Mentor MSA, OH	Y	23870 FQ	39350 MW	49600 TQ	USBLS	5/07
	Columbus MSA, OH	Y	36080 FQ	45520 MW	59560 TQ	USBLS	5/07
	Dayton MSA, OH	Y	30760 FQ	41290 MW	52750 TQ	USBLS	5/07
	Oklahoma	Y	30390 FQ	38130 MW	49450 TQ	USBLS	5/07
	Oklahoma City MSA, OK	Y	34720 FQ	46260 MW	53040 TQ	USBLS	5/07
	Tulsa MSA, OK	Y	32210 FQ	36520 MW	44910 TQ	USBLS	5/07
	Oregon	H	23.78 FQ	27.59 MW	31.41 TQ	ORBLS	5/08
	Portland-Vancouver-Beaverton MSA, OR-WA	Y	49680 FQ	56890 MW	64000 TQ	USBLS	5/07
	Salem MSA, OR	Y	47750 FQ	54760 MW	61350 TQ	USBLS	5/07
	Pennsylvania	Y	35800 FQ	42410 MW	50680 TQ	USBLS	5/07
	Allentown-Bethlehem-Easton MSA, PA-NJ	Y	33590 FQ	40580 MW	54710 TQ	USBLS	5/07
	Philadelphia-Camden-Wilmington MSA, PA-NJ-DE-MD	Y	40150 FQ	48010 MW	59620 TQ	USBLS	5/07
	Pittsburgh MSA, PA	Y	35780 FQ	42600 MW	51360 TQ	USBLS	5/07
	Reading MSA, PA	Y	35850 FQ	40760 MW	48050 TQ	USBLS	5/07
	Rhode Island	Y	39400 FQ	46800 MW	53870 TQ	USBLS	5/07
	Providence-Fall River-Warwick MSA, RI-MA	Y	40250 FQ	47480 MW	55200 TQ	USBLS	5/07
	South Carolina	Y	33820 FQ	40510 MW	51520 TQ	USBLS	5/07
	Charleston-North Charleston MSA, SC	Y	31000 FQ	36640 MW	47480 TQ	USBLS	5/07
	Columbia MSA, SC	Y	42860 FQ	51570 MW	63950 TQ	USBLS	5/07
	South Dakota	Y	33510 FQ	40019 MW	51957 TQ	SDBLS	7/08-9/08
	Sioux Falls MSA, SD	Y	38306 FQ	47077 MW	56791 TQ	SDBLS	7/08-9/08
	Tennessee	Y	33320 FQ	40060 MW	48840 TQ	USBLS	5/07
	Memphis MSA, TN-MS-AR	Y	28120 FQ	36410 MW	42450 TQ	USBLS	5/07
	Nashville-Davidson-Murfreesboro MSA, TN	Y	36680 FQ	43780 MW	52640 TQ	USBLS	5/07
	Texas	Y	33810 FQ	41340 MW	53150 TQ	USBLS	5/07
	Austin-Round Rock MSA, TX	Y	35530 FQ	42620 MW	49250 TQ	USBLS	5/07
	Dallas-Fort Worth-Arlington MSA, TX	Y	38250 FQ	46340 MW	58040 TQ	USBLS	5/07
	El Paso MSA, TX	Y	29100 FQ	34400 MW	41990 TQ	USBLS	5/07
	Houston-Sugar Land-Baytown MSA, TX	Y	36900 FQ	46630 MW	65870 TQ	USBLS	5/07
	San Antonio MSA, TX	Y	31400 FQ	38050 MW	47550 TQ	USBLS	5/07
	Utah	Y	35500 FQ	43950 MW	52740 TQ	USBLS	5/07
	Salt Lake City MSA, UT	Y	35980 FQ	44140 MW	52780 TQ	USBLS	5/07
	Vermont	Y	34640 FQ	40330 MW	48130 TQ	USBLS	5/07
	Burlington-South Burlington MSA, VT	Y	35500 FQ	41560 MW	48760 TQ	USBLS	5/07
	Virginia	Y	39820 FQ	49680 MW	60620 TQ	USBLS	5/07
	Richmond MSA, VA	Y	38540 FQ	45930 MW	55540 TQ	USBLS	5/07
	Virginia Beach-Norfolk-Newport News MSA, VA-NC	Y	38930 FQ	46490 MW	55070 TQ	USBLS	5/07
	Washington	H	24.91 FQ	28.70 MW	32.43 TQ	WABLS	3/08
	Bremerton-Silverdale MSA, WA	Y	48750 FQ	54690 MW	59700 TQ	USBLS	5/07
	Seattle-Tacoma-Bellevue MSA, WA	Y	54370 FQ	61060 MW	70010 TQ	USBLS	5/07
	Spokane MSA, WA	Y	44200 FQ	49410 MW	56910 TQ	USBLS	5/07
	West Virginia	Y	31670 FQ	38666 MW	48350 TQ	WVBLS	7/08-9/08
	Charleston MSA, WV	Y	32290 FQ	38580 MW	45820 TQ	USBLS	5/07
	Wisconsin	Y	39460 FQ	50430 MW	62230 TQ	USBLS	5/07
	Milwaukee-Waukesha-West Allis MSA, WI	Y	50340 FQ	61820 MW	75980 TQ	USBLS	5/07
	Wyoming	Y	30796 FQ	44656 MW	55361 TQ	WYBLS	9/08
	Cheyenne MSA, WY	Y	35821 FQ	47334 MW	54800 TQ	WYBLS	9/08
	Puerto Rico	Y	18090 FQ	24030 MW	34510 TQ	USBLS	5/07
	San Juan-Caguas-Guaynabo MSA, PR	Y	18750 FQ	25160 MW	34830 TQ	USBLS	5/07
	Guam	Y	31460 FQ	38200 MW	45330 TQ	USBLS	5/07
Construction Cost Estimator	United States	Y			81800 TQ	FORB02	2009
Construction Laborer	Alabama	Y	17840 FQ	21480 MW	25390 TQ	USBLS	5/07
	Birmingham-Hoover MSA, AL	Y	18100 FQ	22060 MW	26270 TQ	USBLS	5/07

AE	Average entry wage	AW	Average wage paid	FQ First quartile wage
AER	Average entry range	AWR	Average wage range	H Hourly
AEX	Average experienced wage	AXR	Average experienced range	HI Highest wage paid
ATC	Average total compensation	D	Daily	HR High end range

LO Lowest wage paid   MTC Median total compensation   TCC Total cash compensation
LR Low end range   MW Median wage paid   TQ Third quartile wage
M Monthly   MWR Median wage range   W Weekly
MCC Median cash compensation   S See annotated source   Y Yearly

Occupation/Type/Industry	Location	Per	Low	Mid	High	Source	Date
Construction Laborer	Alaska	Y	31810 FQ	41040 MW	56200 TQ	USBLS	5/07
	Anchorage MSA, AK	Y	34290 FQ	48130 MW	59850 TQ	USBLS	5/07
	Arizona	Y	21260 FQ	26230 MW	32920 TQ	USBLS	5/07
	Phoenix-Mesa-Scottsdale MSA, AZ	Y	21790 FQ	27080 MW	33870 TQ	USBLS	5/07
	Tucson MSA, AZ	Y	20630 FQ	23940 MW	30420 TQ	USBLS	5/07
	Arkansas	Y	20210 FQ	23890 MW	28570 TQ	USBLS	5/07
	Fayetteville-Springdale-Rogers MSA, AR-MO	Y	19580 FQ	23380 MW	28990 TQ	USBLS	5/07
	Little Rock-North Little Rock MSA, AR	Y	19700 FQ	22830 MW	26660 TQ	USBLS	5/07
	California	H	12.68 FQ	16.36 MW	22.19 TQ	CABLS	1/08-3/08
	Los Angeles-Long Beach-Glendale PMSA, CA	H	12.63 FQ	16.75 MW	21.66 TQ	CABLS	1/08-3/08
	Oakland-Fremont-Hayward MSA, CA	H	14.91 FQ	21.07 MW	26.42 TQ	CABLS	1/08-3/08
	Riverside-San Bernardino-Ontario MSA, CA	H	12.11 FQ	14.82 MW	19.13 TQ	CABLS	1/08-3/08
	Sacramento-Arden Arcade-Roseville MSA, CA	H	12.73 FQ	16.69 MW	22.35 TQ	CABLS	1/08-3/08
	San Diego-Carlsbad-San Marcos MSA, CA	H	12.38 FQ	15.99 MW	21.73 TQ	CABLS	1/08-3/08
	San Francisco-San Mateo-Redwood PMSA, CA	H	19.82 FQ	24.10 MW	27.81 TQ	CABLS	1/08-3/08
	San Jose-Sunnyvale-Santa Clara MSA, CA	H	13.08 FQ	16.80 MW	22.23 TQ	CABLS	1/08-3/08
	Santa Ana-Anaheim-Irvine PMSA, CA	Y	24100 FQ	30550 MW	40360 TQ	USBLS	5/07
	Colorado	Y	22410 FQ	27090 MW	32320 TQ	USBLS	5/07
	Denver-Aurora MSA, CO	Y	23320 FQ	28230 MW	33160 TQ	USBLS	5/07
	Connecticut	H	12.63 AE	17.96 MW		CTBLS	1/08-3/08
	Bridgeport-Stamford-Norwalk MSA, CT	Y	27550 FQ	35000 MW	47730 TQ	USBLS	5/07
	Hartford-West Hartford-East Hartford MSA, CT	Y	28030 FQ	35590 MW	44310 TQ	USBLS	5/07
	Delaware	Y	22750 FQ	27600 MW	35140 TQ	USBLS	5/07
	Dover MSA, DE	Y	21220 FQ	24770 MW	30780 TQ	USBLS	5/07
	Wilmington PMSA, DE-MD-NJ	Y	23470 FQ	28880 MW	37540 TQ	USBLS	5/07
	District of Columbia	Y	27370 FQ	30850 MW	35530 TQ	USBLS	5/07
	Washington-Arlington-Alexandria MSA, DC-VA-MD-WV	Y	24160 FQ	28550 MW	33360 TQ	USBLS	5/07
	Florida	Y	19550 FQ	23350 MW	28250 TQ	USBLS	5/07
	Fort Lauderdale-Pompano Beach-Deerfield Beach PMSA, FL	Y	19540 FQ	23750 MW	29100 TQ	USBLS	5/07
	Jacksonville MSA, FL	Y	20670 FQ	23700 MW	27970 TQ	USBLS	5/07
	Miami-Fort Lauderdale-Miami Beach MSA, FL	Y	19400 FQ	23730 MW	28970 TQ	USBLS	5/07
	Orlando-Kissimmee MSA, FL	Y	19800 FQ	23570 MW	28620 TQ	USBLS	5/07
	Tallahassee MSA, FL	Y	17740 FQ	22520 MW	28010 TQ	USBLS	5/07
	Tampa-St. Petersburg-Clearwater MSA, FL	Y	19450 FQ	23410 MW	27960 TQ	USBLS	5/07
	West Palm Beach-Boca Raton-Boynton Beach PMSA, FL	Y	20170 FQ	24820 MW	29910 TQ	USBLS	5/07
	Georgia	Y	19870 FQ	23330 MW	28900 TQ	USBLS	5/07
	Atlanta-Sandy Springs-Marietta MSA, GA	Y	21110 FQ	24230 MW	30230 TQ	USBLS	5/07
	Hawaii	Y	31710 FQ	42830 MW	55440 TQ	USBLS	5/07
	Honolulu MSA, HI	Y	32130 FQ	45150 MW	57290 TQ	USBLS	5/07
	Idaho	Y	20700 FQ	26410 MW	31080 TQ	USBLS	5/07
	Boise City-Nampa MSA, ID	Y	22400 FQ	27370 MW	31870 TQ	USBLS	5/07
	Illinois	Y	21180 FQ	39080 MW	62720 TQ	USBLS	5/07
	Chicago-Naperville-Joliet MSA, IL-IN-WI	Y	16370 FQ	40110 MW	64960 TQ	USBLS	5/07
	Indiana	Y	25480 FQ	33990 MW	45120 TQ	USBLS	5/07
	Gary PMSA, IN	Y	25780 FQ	44630 MW	56920 TQ	USBLS	5/07
	Indianapolis-Carmel MSA, IN	Y	26470 FQ	36000 MW	45530 TQ	USBLS	5/07
	Iowa	Y	23680 FQ	29230 MW	36520 TQ	USBLS	5/07
	Des Moines-West Des Moines MSA, IA	Y	25880 FQ	33590 MW	40960 TQ	USBLS	5/07

AE	Average entry wage	AW	Average wage paid	FQ First quartile wage
AER	Average entry range	AWR	Average wage range	H Hourly
AEX	Average experienced wage	AXR	Average experienced range	HI Highest wage paid
ATC	Average total compensation	D	Daily	HR High end range

LO	Lowest wage paid	MTC Median total compensation	TCC Total cash compensation
LR	Low end range	MW Median wage paid	TQ Third quartile wage
M	Monthly	MWR Median wage range	W Weekly
MCC	Median cash compensation	S See annotated source	Y Yearly

Occupation/Type/Industry	Location	Per	Low	Mid	High	Source	Date
Construction Laborer	Kansas	Y	21260 FQ	25730 MW	32030 TQ	USBLS	5/07
	Wichita MSA, KS	Y	18010 FQ	21690 MW	26360 TQ	USBLS	5/07
	Kentucky	Y	21571 FQ	27571 MW	35256 TQ	KYBLS	2008
	Louisville-Jefferson County MSA, KY-IN	Y	22700 FQ	28470 MW	35590 TQ	USBLS	5/07
	Louisiana	H	9.36 FQ	11.29 MW	13.88 TQ	LABLS	1/08-3/08
	Baton Rouge MSA, LA	Y	19490 FQ	24620 MW	29580 TQ	USBLS	5/07
	Lake Charles MSA, LA	Y	18470 FQ	22990 MW	28800 TQ	USBLS	5/07
	New Orleans-Metairie-Kenner MSA, LA	Y	21810 FQ	25540 MW	32200 TQ	USBLS	5/07
	Maine	Y	22780 FQ	26660 MW	30710 TQ	USBLS	5/07
	Portland-South Portland-Biddeford MSA, ME	Y	24770 FQ	28250 MW	31930 TQ	USBLS	5/07
	Maryland	Y		29300 MW		MDBLS	3/08
	Baltimore-Towson MSA, MD	Y	23900 FQ	28630 MW	33560 TQ	USBLS	5/07
	Bethesda-Gaithersburg-Frederick PMSA, MD	Y	24550 FQ	28720 MW	34750 TQ	USBLS	5/07
	Massachusetts	Y	31340 FQ	41350 MW	53300 TQ	USBLS	5/07
	Boston-Cambridge-Quincy NECTA, MA	Y	38940 FQ	50120 MW	58260 TQ	USBLS	5/07
	New Bedford MSA, MA	Y	29450 FQ	36430 MW	46540 TQ	USBLS	5/07
	Worcester MSA, MA-CT	Y	27260 FQ	31650 MW	37370 TQ	USBLS	5/07
	Michigan	Y	26600 FQ	33750 MW	43300 TQ	USBLS	5/07
	Detroit-Warren-Livonia MSA, MI	Y	28570 FQ	38540 MW	47400 TQ	USBLS	5/07
	Grand Rapids-Wyoming MSA, MI	Y	22800 FQ	28800 MW	34520 TQ	USBLS	5/07
	Warren-Troy-Farmington Hills PMSA, MI	Y	28160 FQ	37140 MW	46210 TQ	USBLS	5/07
	Minnesota	Y	30425 FQ	40300 MW	54875 TQ	MNBLS	10/08-12/08
	Duluth-Superior MSA, MN-WI	Y	28401 FQ	37412 MW	46834 TQ	MNBLS	10/08-12/08
	Minneapolis-Saint Paul MSA, MN-WI	Y	34113 FQ	49742 MW	61019 TQ	MNBLS	10/08-12/08
	Rochester MSA, MN	Y	31389 FQ	37537 MW	47614 TQ	MNBLS	10/08-12/08
	Mississippi	Y	17910 FQ	21520 MW	25290 TQ	USBLS	5/07
	Jackson MSA, MS	Y	16730 FQ	20660 MW	25960 TQ	USBLS	5/07
	Missouri	Y	24980 FQ	34280 MW	51150 TQ	USBLS	5/07
	Kansas City MSA, MO-KS	Y	26390 FQ	34280 MW	48510 TQ	USBLS	5/07
	St. Louis MSA, MO-IL	Y	30120 FQ	46170 MW	55860 TQ	USBLS	5/07
	Montana	Y	23560 FQ	29810 MW	37860 TQ	USBLS	5/07
	Billings MSA, MT	Y	22580 FQ	28380 MW	37060 TQ	USBLS	5/07
	Great Falls MSA, MT	Y	24700 FQ	31900 MW	37310 TQ	USBLS	5/07
	Nebraska	Y	20600 FQ	23680 MW	28900 TQ	USBLS	5/07
	Omaha-Council Bluffs MSA, NE-IA	Y	22600 FQ	29070 MW	34820 TQ	USBLS	5/07
	Nevada	H	12.24 FQ	15.31 MW	20.75 TQ	NVBLS	5/08
	Las Vegas-Paradise MSA, NV	H	11.93 FQ	14.85 MW	21.40 TQ	NVBLS	5/08
	New Hampshire	H	11.47 AE	14.46 MW	16.31 AEX	NHBLS	6/08
	Manchester MSA, NH	Y	26790 FQ	30560 MW	35400 TQ	USBLS	5/07
	Nashua NECTA, NH-MA	Y	25780 FQ	28870 MW	34270 TQ	USBLS	5/07
	New Jersey	Y	29780 FQ	42280 MW	57530 TQ	USBLS	5/07
	Camden PMSA, NJ	Y	24720 FQ	29750 MW	42820 TQ	USBLS	5/07
	Edison PMSA, NJ	Y	33230 FQ	46180 MW	59390 TQ	USBLS	5/07
	Newark-Union PMSA, NJ-PA	Y	29990 FQ	42840 MW	57650 TQ	USBLS	5/07
	New Mexico	Y	16760 FQ	21150 MW	26830 TQ	USBLS	5/07
	Albuquerque MSA, NM	Y	15820 FQ	20740 MW	26550 TQ	USBLS	5/07
	New York	Y	28590 FQ	41020 MW	58830 TQ	USBLS	5/07
	Albany-Schenectady-Troy MSA, NY	Y	27640 FQ	35000 MW	46790 TQ	USBLS	5/07
	Buffalo-Niagara Falls MSA, NY	Y	27280 FQ	32590 MW	44280 TQ	USBLS	5/07
	Nassau-Suffolk PMSA, NY	Y	31530 FQ	44960 MW	63710 TQ	USBLS	5/07
	New York-Northern New Jersey-Long Island MSA, NY-NJ-PA	Y	32110 FQ	48400 MW	63030 TQ	USBLS	5/07
	North Carolina	Y	19860 FQ	23480 MW	28560 TQ	USBLS	5/07
	Charlotte-Gastonia-Concord MSA, NC-SC	Y	20390 FQ	24010 MW	29510 TQ	USBLS	5/07
	Raleigh-Cary MSA, NC	Y	20210 FQ	24130 MW	30290 TQ	USBLS	5/07
	North Dakota	Y	22470 FQ	25740 MW	29830 TQ	USBLS	5/07
	Bismarck MSA, ND	Y	22720 FQ	26010 MW	29080 TQ	USBLS	5/07
	Fargo MSA, ND-MN	Y	22950 FQ	26480 MW	30960 TQ	USBLS	5/07

AE	Average entry wage	AW	Average wage paid	FQ	First quartile wage	LO	Lowest wage paid	MTC	Median total compensation	TCC	Total cash compensation
AER	Average entry range	AWR	Average wage range	H	Hourly	LR	Low end range	MW	Median wage paid	TQ	Third quartile wage
AEX	Average experienced wage	AXR	Average experienced range	HI	Highest wage paid	M	Monthly	MWR	Median wage range	W	Weekly
ATC	Average total compensation	D	Daily	HR	High end range	MCC	Median cash compensation	S	See annotated source	Y	Yearly

Occupation/Type/Industry	Location	Per	Low	Mid	High	Source	Date
Construction Laborer	Ohio	Y	26170 FQ	33980 MW	47940 TQ	USBLS	5/07
	Canton-Massillon MSA, OH	Y	25310 FQ	32680 MW	39510 TQ	USBLS	5/07
	Cincinnati-Middletown MSA, OH-KY-IN	Y	24970 FQ	29580 MW	40100 TQ	USBLS	5/07
	Cleveland-Elyria-Mentor MSA, OH	Y	29600 FQ	43610 MW	54700 TQ	USBLS	5/07
	Columbus MSA, OH	Y	25590 FQ	32340 MW	46340 TQ	USBLS	5/07
	Dayton MSA, OH	Y	27520 FQ	33990 MW	46500 TQ	USBLS	5/07
	Oklahoma	Y	18480 FQ	22700 MW	28000 TQ	USBLS	5/07
	Lawton MSA, OK	Y	18130 FQ	21510 MW	25290 TQ	USBLS	5/07
	Oklahoma City MSA, OK	Y	18020 FQ	22410 MW	27600 TQ	USBLS	5/07
	Tulsa MSA, OK	Y	19460 FQ	23130 MW	28330 TQ	USBLS	5/07
	Oregon	H	11.82 FQ	14.60 MW	19.41 TQ	ORBLS	5/08
	Portland-Vancouver-Beaverton MSA, OR-WA	Y	24140 FQ	30880 MW	42810 TQ	USBLS	5/07
	Pennsylvania	Y	23750 FQ	30140 MW	41220 TQ	USBLS	5/07
	Allentown-Bethlehem-Easton MSA, PA-NJ	Y	23800 FQ	30210 MW	38620 TQ	USBLS	5/07
	Philadelphia-Camden-Wilmington MSA, PA-NJ-DE-MD	Y	26170 FQ	33690 MW	45740 TQ	USBLS	5/07
	Pittsburgh MSA, PA	Y	23820 FQ	33150 MW	44640 TQ	USBLS	5/07
	Rhode Island	Y	31150 FQ	41630 MW	50530 TQ	USBLS	5/07
	Providence-Fall River-Warwick MSA, RI-MA	Y	30950 FQ	41400 MW	50560 TQ	USBLS	5/07
	South Carolina	Y	19100 FQ	22840 MW	28230 TQ	USBLS	5/07
	Charleston-North Charleston MSA, SC	Y	18740 FQ	23050 MW	30970 TQ	USBLS	5/07
	Columbia MSA, SC	Y	19890 FQ	22630 MW	25750 TQ	USBLS	5/07
	South Dakota	Y	20336 FQ	23418 MW	26833 TQ	SDBLS	7/08-9/08
	Sioux Falls MSA, SD	Y	20892 FQ	24000 MW	27991 TQ	SDBLS	7/08-9/08
	Tennessee	Y	20920 FQ	24360 MW	28900 TQ	USBLS	5/07
	Clarksville MSA, TN-KY	Y	20350 FQ	24280 MW	29730 TQ	USBLS	5/07
	Memphis MSA, TN-MS-AR	Y	18960 FQ	22740 MW	27310 TQ	USBLS	5/07
	Nashville-Davidson-Murfreesboro MSA, TN	Y	22090 FQ	25590 MW	30150 TQ	USBLS	5/07
	Texas	Y	17610 FQ	20790 MW	24670 TQ	USBLS	5/07
	Austin-Round Rock MSA, TX	Y	18220 FQ	21080 MW	24400 TQ	USBLS	5/07
	Corpus Christi MSA, TX	Y	17270 FQ	20280 MW	24890 TQ	USBLS	5/07
	Dallas-Fort Worth-Arlington MSA, TX	Y	18790 FQ	21990 MW	25530 TQ	USBLS	5/07
	El Paso MSA, TX	Y	16150 FQ	18790 MW	22660 TQ	USBLS	5/07
	Houston-Sugar Land-Baytown MSA, TX	Y	17380 FQ	20440 MW	24830 TQ	USBLS	5/07
	San Antonio MSA, TX	Y	17830 FQ	20800 MW	24380 TQ	USBLS	5/07
	Utah	Y	18880 FQ	22990 MW	28180 TQ	USBLS	5/07
	Salt Lake City MSA, UT	Y	19100 FQ	23140 MW	28450 TQ	USBLS	5/07
	Vermont	Y	24180 FQ	28030 MW	31730 TQ	USBLS	5/07
	Burlington-South Burlington MSA, VT	Y	25430 FQ	28880 MW	33350 TQ	USBLS	5/07
	Virginia	Y	20680 FQ	24490 MW	29530 TQ	USBLS	5/07
	Richmond MSA, VA	Y	20210 FQ	23440 MW	27510 TQ	USBLS	5/07
	Virginia Beach-Norfolk-Newport News MSA, VA-NC	Y	19140 FQ	22440 MW	26520 TQ	USBLS	5/07
	Washington	H	12.41 FQ	15.03 MW	20.52 TQ	WABLS	3/08
	Seattle-Tacoma-Bellevue MSA, WA	Y	26560 FQ	32680 MW	51510 TQ	USBLS	5/07
	West Virginia	Y	20468 FQ	24929 MW	33782 TQ	WVBLS	7/08-9/08
	Charleston MSA, WV	Y	21370 FQ	28320 MW	44920 TQ	USBLS	5/07
	Wisconsin	Y	28350 FQ	37090 MW	46300 TQ	USBLS	5/07
	Green Bay MSA, WI	Y	31180 FQ	41600 MW	48250 TQ	USBLS	5/07
	Milwaukee-Waukesha-West Allis MSA, WI	Y	31640 FQ	42670 MW	50500 TQ	USBLS	5/07
	Wyoming	Y	24030 FQ	28198 MW	32389 TQ	WYBLS	9/08
	Cheyenne MSA, WY	Y	23135 FQ	26579 MW	30711 TQ	WYBLS	9/08
	Puerto Rico	Y	12650 FQ	14030 MW	15520 TQ	USBLS	5/07
	San Juan-Caguas-Guaynabo MSA, PR	Y	12720 FQ	14190 MW	15880 TQ	USBLS	5/07
	Virgin Islands	Y	21140 FQ	24160 MW	28690 TQ	USBLS	5/07
	Guam	Y	16420 FQ	18670 MW	21420 TQ	USBLS	5/07
Construction Manager	Alabama	Y	47680 FQ	61930 MW	83770 TQ	USBLS	5/07

AE Average entry wage	**AW** Average wage paid	**FQ** First quartile wage	**LO** Lowest wage paid	**MTC** Median total compensation	**TCC** Total cash compensation
AER Average entry range	**AWR** Average wage range	**H** Hourly	**LR** Low end range	**MW** Median wage paid	**TQ** Third quartile wage
AEX Average experienced wage	**AXR** Average experienced range	**HI** Highest wage paid	**M** Monthly	**MWR** Median wage range	**W** Weekly
ATC Average total compensation	**D** Daily	**HR** High end range	**MCC** Median cash compensation	**S** See annotated source	**Y** Yearly

Occupation/Type/Industry	Location	Per	Low	Mid	High	Source	Date
Construction Manager	Birmingham-Hoover MSA, AL	Y	49940 FQ	64140 MW	90740 TQ	USBLS	5/07
	Huntsville MSA, AL	Y	54090 FQ	63060 MW	87720 TQ	USBLS	5/07
	Tuscaloosa MSA, AL	Y	54820 FQ	61510 MW	77470 TQ	USBLS	5/07
	Alaska	Y	69840 FQ	86510 MW	108230 TQ	USBLS	5/07
	Anchorage MSA, AK	Y	68780 FQ	86890 MW	108150 TQ	USBLS	5/07
	Arizona	Y	57700 FQ	73480 MW	101270 TQ	USBLS	5/07
	Phoenix-Mesa-Scottsdale MSA, AZ	Y	60620 FQ	75920 MW	102140 TQ	USBLS	5/07
	Tucson MSA, AZ	Y	50950 FQ	63440 MW	92110 TQ	USBLS	5/07
	Arkansas	Y	41800 FQ	58410 MW	81540 TQ	USBLS	5/07
	Little Rock-North Little Rock MSA, AR	Y	37170 FQ	43050 MW	67270 TQ	USBLS	5/07
	California	H	37.75 FQ	46.95 MW	59.25 TQ	CABLS	1/08-3/08
	Los Angeles-Long Beach-Glendale PMSA, CA	H	37.05 FQ	47.36 MW	59.61 TQ	CABLS	1/08-3/08
	Oakland-Fremont-Hayward MSA, CA	H	40.08 FQ	48.94 MW	65.09 TQ	CABLS	1/08-3/08
	Riverside-San Bernardino-Ontario MSA, CA	H	35.76 FQ	44.27 MW	56.37 TQ	CABLS	1/08-3/08
	Sacramento-Arden Arcade-Roseville MSA, CA	H	39.69 FQ	47.34 MW	58.27 TQ	CABLS	1/08-3/08
	San Diego-Carlsbad-San Marcos MSA, CA	H	37.76 FQ	45.67 MW	55.03 TQ	CABLS	1/08-3/08
	San Francisco-San Mateo-Redwood PMSA, CA	H	44.79 FQ	53.81 MW	64.97 TQ	CABLS	1/08-3/08
	San Jose-Sunnyvale-Santa Clara MSA, CA	H	40.01 FQ	49.25 MW	59.68 TQ	CABLS	1/08-3/08
	Santa Ana-Anaheim-Irvine PMSA, CA	Y	80130 FQ	99940 MW	125200 TQ	USBLS	5/07
	Santa Rosa-Petaluma MSA, CA	H	37.84 FQ	45.82 MW	57.65 TQ	CABLS	1/08-3/08
	Colorado	Y	56650 FQ	73460 MW	94140 TQ	USBLS	5/07
	Boulder MSA, CO	Y	69550 FQ	86380 MW	113630 TQ	USBLS	5/07
	Colorado Springs MSA, CO	Y	60160 FQ	71700 MW	81830 TQ	USBLS	5/07
	Denver-Aurora MSA, CO	Y	60980 FQ	76050 MW	98750 TQ	USBLS	5/07
	Connecticut	H	30.40 AE	42.95 MW		CTBLS	1/08-3/08
	Bridgeport-Stamford-Norwalk MSA, CT	Y	78730 FQ	96820 MW		USBLS	5/07
	Danbury MSA, CT	Y	70140 FQ	103220 MW		USBLS	5/07
	Hartford-West Hartford-East Hartford MSA, CT	Y	68220 FQ	82870 MW	106820 TQ	USBLS	5/07
	Delaware	Y	61720 FQ	77200 MW	107090 TQ	USBLS	5/07
	Wilmington PMSA, DE-MD-NJ	Y	68500 FQ	84380 MW	119210 TQ	USBLS	5/07
	District of Columbia	Y	61590 FQ	79560 MW	96980 TQ	USBLS	5/07
	Washington-Arlington-Alexandria MSA, DC-VA-MD-WV	Y	68880 FQ	88250 MW	115880 TQ	USBLS	5/07
	Florida	Y	59300 FQ	77700 MW	103750 TQ	USBLS	5/07
	Fort Lauderdale-Pompano Beach-Deerfield Beach PMSA, FL	Y	62720 FQ	81320 MW	112750 TQ	USBLS	5/07
	Jacksonville MSA, FL	Y	55010 FQ	72360 MW	92060 TQ	USBLS	5/07
	Miami-Fort Lauderdale-Miami Beach MSA, FL	Y	62500 FQ	82410 MW	112440 TQ	USBLS	5/07
	Orlando-Kissimmee MSA, FL	Y	65020 FQ	78690 MW	99040 TQ	USBLS	5/07
	Sarasota-Bradenton-Venice MSA, FL	Y	58500 FQ	76680 MW	93630 TQ	USBLS	5/07
	Tampa-St. Petersburg-Clearwater MSA, FL	Y	57160 FQ	72610 MW	91650 TQ	USBLS	5/07
	West Palm Beach-Boca Raton-Boynton Beach PMSA, FL	Y	60200 FQ	76370 MW	101070 TQ	USBLS	5/07
	Georgia	Y	54020 FQ	67360 MW	90400 TQ	USBLS	5/07
	Atlanta-Sandy Springs-Marietta MSA, GA	Y	55300 FQ	68740 MW	91870 TQ	USBLS	5/07
	Hawaii	Y	69530 FQ	89430 MW	121340 TQ	USBLS	5/07
	Honolulu MSA, HI	Y	71800 FQ	93140 MW	127420 TQ	USBLS	5/07
	Idaho	Y	47150 FQ	59660 MW	71450 TQ	USBLS	5/07
	Boise City-Nampa MSA, ID	Y	48890 FQ	61920 MW	73280 TQ	USBLS	5/07
	Idaho Falls MSA, ID	Y	38990 FQ	47420 MW	61330 TQ	USBLS	5/07
	Illinois	Y	64840 FQ	82570 MW	107290 TQ	USBLS	5/07
	Chicago-Naperville-Joliet MSA, IL-IN-WI	Y	67480 FQ	85420 MW	110540 TQ	USBLS	5/07

AE	Average entry wage	**AW**	Average wage paid	**FQ**	First quartile wage	**LO**	Lowest wage paid	**MTC**	Median total compensation	**TCC**	Total cash compensation
AER	Average entry range	**AWR**	Average wage range	**H**	Hourly	**LR**	Low end range	**MW**	Median wage paid	**TQ**	Third quartile wage
AEX	Average experienced wage	**AXR**	Average experienced range	**HI**	Highest wage paid	**M**	Monthly	**MWR**	Median wage range	**W**	Weekly
ATC	Average total compensation	**D**	Daily	**HR**	High end range	**MCC**	Median cash compensation	**S**	See annotated source	**Y**	Yearly

Occupation/Type/Industry	Location	Per	Low	Mid	High	Source	Date
Construction Manager	Indiana	Y	61160 FQ	76350 MW	94780 TQ	USBLS	5/07
	Gary PMSA, IN	Y	70630 FQ	85600 MW	100890 TQ	USBLS	5/07
	Indianapolis-Carmel MSA, IN	Y	65070 FQ	80250 MW	98210 TQ	USBLS	5/07
	Iowa	Y	51030 FQ	68940 MW	93120 TQ	USBLS	5/07
	Davenport-Moline-Rock Island MSA, IA-IL	Y	33830 FQ	64080 MW	85560 TQ	USBLS	5/07
	Des Moines-West Des Moines MSA, IA	Y	63210 FQ	78170 MW	97330 TQ	USBLS	5/07
	Kansas	Y	50700 FQ	64410 MW	80390 TQ	USBLS	5/07
	Topeka MSA, KS	Y	50920 FQ	60330 MW	71760 TQ	USBLS	5/07
	Wichita MSA, KS	Y	46640 FQ	58160 MW	71450 TQ	USBLS	5/07
	Kentucky	Y	51006 FQ	62670 MW	77986 TQ	KYBLS	2008
	Elizabethtown MSA, KY	Y	50450 FQ	69250 MW	84290 TQ	USBLS	5/07
	Louisville-Jefferson County MSA, KY-IN	Y	50660 FQ	62720 MW	80280 TQ	USBLS	5/07
	Louisiana	H	23.93 FQ	29.17 MW	37.10 TQ	LABLS	1/08-3/08
	Baton Rouge MSA, LA	Y	52950 FQ	63880 MW	78020 TQ	USBLS	5/07
	Lafayette MSA, LA	Y	47860 FQ	59240 MW	76910 TQ	USBLS	5/07
	New Orleans-Metairie-Kenner MSA, LA	Y	49660 FQ	58230 MW	71270 TQ	USBLS	5/07
	Maine	Y	49960 FQ	72320 MW	93040 TQ	USBLS	5/07
	Portland-South Portland-Biddeford MSA, ME	Y	68800 FQ	79770 MW	95370 TQ	USBLS	5/07
	Maryland	Y		85150 MW		MDBLS	3/08
	Baltimore-Towson MSA, MD	Y	65360 FQ	84460 MW	121600 TQ	USBLS	5/07
	Bethesda-Gaithersburg-Frederick PMSA, MD	Y	65390 FQ	81150 MW	103670 TQ	USBLS	5/07
	Massachusetts	Y	73090 FQ	92380 MW	122730 TQ	USBLS	5/07
	Boston-Cambridge-Quincy NECTA, MA	Y	79600 FQ	99830 MW	132350 TQ	USBLS	5/07
	Worcester MSA, MA-CT	Y	53190 FQ	71570 MW	93690 TQ	USBLS	5/07
	Michigan	Y	62890 FQ	82020 MW	108940 TQ	USBLS	5/07
	Detroit-Warren-Livonia MSA, MI	Y	67120 FQ	91130 MW	118010 TQ	USBLS	5/07
	Grand Rapids-Wyoming MSA, MI	Y	68770 FQ	87190 MW	110100 TQ	USBLS	5/07
	Warren-Troy-Farmington Hills PMSA, MI	Y	63850 FQ	87980 MW	111560 TQ	USBLS	5/07
	Minnesota	Y	67219 FQ	86436 MW	109040 TQ	MNBLS	10/08-12/08
	Duluth-Superior MSA, MN-WI	Y	58586 FQ	75613 MW	93943 TQ	MNBLS	10/08-12/08
	Minneapolis-Saint Paul MSA, MN-WI	Y	75071 FQ	93661 MW	118977 TQ	MNBLS	10/08-12/08
	Rochester MSA, MN	Y	59849 FQ	72452 MW	86561 TQ	MNBLS	10/08-12/08
	Mississippi	Y	40390 FQ	51530 MW	65140 TQ	USBLS	5/07
	Jackson MSA, MS	Y	41480 FQ	53510 MW	69170 TQ	USBLS	5/07
	Missouri	Y	49780 FQ	68680 MW	88510 TQ	USBLS	5/07
	Jefferson City MSA, MO	Y	39020 FQ	52570 MW	63230 TQ	USBLS	5/07
	Joplin MSA, MO	Y	56500 FQ	69120 MW	86040 TQ	USBLS	5/07
	Kansas City MSA, MO-KS	Y	54730 FQ	71600 MW	89440 TQ	USBLS	5/07
	St. Louis MSA, MO-IL	Y	59080 FQ	73920 MW	93540 TQ	USBLS	5/07
	Montana	Y	46010 FQ	58660 MW	77590 TQ	USBLS	5/07
	Billings MSA, MT	Y	45090 FQ	63980 MW	97540 TQ	USBLS	5/07
	Nebraska	Y	46230 FQ	61310 MW	77650 TQ	USBLS	5/07
	Omaha-Council Bluffs MSA, NE-IA	Y	49010 FQ	62390 MW	78970 TQ	USBLS	5/07
	Nevada	H	31.47 FQ	41.39 MW	55.55 TQ	NVBLS	5/08
	Las Vegas-Paradise MSA, NV	H	31.21 FQ	41.32 MW	56.94 TQ	NVBLS	5/08
	Reno-Sparks MSA, NV	H	32.00 FQ	42.08 MW	52.17 TQ	NVBLS	5/08
	New Hampshire	H	25.99 AE	35.70 MW	43.67 AEX	NHBLS	6/08
	Manchester MSA, NH	Y	65910 FQ	75180 MW	105030 TQ	USBLS	5/07
	Nashua NECTA, NH-MA	Y	50980 FQ	63790 MW	80150 TQ	USBLS	5/07
	New Jersey	Y	74350 FQ	97240 MW	128730 TQ	USBLS	5/07
	Camden PMSA, NJ	Y	62390 FQ	77150 MW	100780 TQ	USBLS	5/07
	Edison PMSA, NJ	Y	76380 FQ	100280 MW	136960 TQ	USBLS	5/07
	Newark-Union PMSA, NJ-PA	Y	80720 FQ	101690 MW	129960 TQ	USBLS	5/07
	New Mexico	Y	53140 FQ	65960 MW	81400 TQ	USBLS	5/07
	Albuquerque MSA, NM	Y	56870 FQ	68450 MW	82350 TQ	USBLS	5/07
	New York	Y	75640 FQ	109690 MW		USBLS	5/07
	Albany-Schenectady-Troy MSA, NY	Y	75830 FQ	108350 MW		USBLS	5/07
	Buffalo-Niagara Falls MSA, NY	Y	74370 FQ	93060 MW		USBLS	5/07

AE Average entry wage	**AW** Average wage paid	**FQ** First quartile wage	**LO** Lowest wage paid	**MTC** Median total compensation	**TCC** Total cash compensation
AER Average entry range	**AWR** Average wage range	**H** Hourly	**LR** Low end range	**MW** Median wage paid	**TQ** Third quartile wage
AEX Average experienced wage	**AXR** Average experienced range	**HI** Highest wage paid	**M** Monthly	**MWR** Median wage range	**W** Weekly
ATC Average total compensation	**D** Daily	**HR** High end range	**MCC** Median cash compensation	**S** See annotated source	**Y** Yearly

317

Occupation/Type/Industry	Location	Per	Low	Mid	High	Source	Date
Construction Manager	Nassau-Suffolk PMSA, NY	Y	87620 FQ	126930 MW		USBLS	5/07
	New York-Northern New Jersey-Long Island MSA, NY-NJ-PA	Y	80260 FQ	113150 MW		USBLS	5/07
	North Carolina	Y	60720 FQ	71900 MW	90370 TQ	USBLS	5/07
	Charlotte-Gastonia-Concord MSA, NC-SC	Y	61480 FQ	75630 MW	94150 TQ	USBLS	5/07
	Raleigh-Cary MSA, NC	Y	63750 FQ	71270 MW	82270 TQ	USBLS	5/07
	North Dakota	Y	48940 FQ	60830 MW	78320 TQ	USBLS	5/07
	Fargo MSA, ND-MN	Y	56430 FQ	69890 MW	113090 TQ	USBLS	5/07
	Ohio	Y	63650 FQ	81560 MW	109690 TQ	USBLS	5/07
	Cincinnati-Middletown MSA, OH-KY-IN	Y	59950 FQ	78530 MW	101320 TQ	USBLS	5/07
	Cleveland-Elyria-Mentor MSA, OH	Y	65670 FQ	80780 MW	102160 TQ	USBLS	5/07
	Columbus MSA, OH	Y	65960 FQ	85420 MW	121070 TQ	USBLS	5/07
	Dayton MSA, OH	Y	63590 FQ	82030 MW	108290 TQ	USBLS	5/07
	Oklahoma	Y	43370 FQ	56950 MW	71310 TQ	USBLS	5/07
	Oklahoma City MSA, OK	Y	41530 FQ	54720 MW	70020 TQ	USBLS	5/07
	Tulsa MSA, OK	Y	45700 FQ	58430 MW	70630 TQ	USBLS	5/07
	Oregon	H	29.88 FQ	38.39 MW	46.63 TQ	ORBLS	5/08
	Portland-Vancouver-Beaverton MSA, OR-WA	Y	61190 FQ	77670 MW	94900 TQ	USBLS	5/07
	Pennsylvania	Y	61770 FQ	78170 MW	101900 TQ	USBLS	5/07
	Allentown-Bethlehem-Easton MSA, PA-NJ	Y	63710 FQ	78710 MW	93410 TQ	USBLS	5/07
	Philadelphia-Camden-Wilmington MSA, PA-NJ-DE-MD	Y	69920 FQ	89140 MW	118750 TQ	USBLS	5/07
	Pittsburgh MSA, PA	Y	60160 FQ	73980 MW	92380 TQ	USBLS	5/07
	Rhode Island	Y	68700 FQ	82110 MW	109610 TQ	USBLS	5/07
	Providence-Fall River-Warwick MSA, RI-MA	Y	71170 FQ	85460 MW	109850 TQ	USBLS	5/07
	South Carolina	Y	55980 FQ	69200 MW	85750 TQ	USBLS	5/07
	Charleston-North Charleston MSA, SC	Y	59710 FQ	73700 MW	93400 TQ	USBLS	5/07
	Columbia MSA, SC	Y	53670 FQ	62950 MW	85280 TQ	USBLS	5/07
	Florence MSA, SC	Y	49080 FQ	58620 MW	75840 TQ	USBLS	5/07
	South Dakota	Y	64298 FQ	73968 MW	83900 TQ	SDBLS	7/08-9/08
	Sioux Falls MSA, SD	Y	63470 FQ	72747 MW	82948 TQ	SDBLS	7/08-9/08
	Tennessee	Y	42980 FQ	55380 MW	71620 TQ	USBLS	5/07
	Memphis MSA, TN-MS-AR	Y	47300 FQ	61000 MW	78110 TQ	USBLS	5/07
	Nashville-Davidson-Murfreesboro MSA, TN	Y	44340 FQ	56290 MW	73330 TQ	USBLS	5/07
	Texas	Y	47000 FQ	60530 MW	79120 TQ	USBLS	5/07
	Austin-Round Rock MSA, TX	Y	50010 FQ	62380 MW	79360 TQ	USBLS	5/07
	Beaumont-Port Arthur MSA, TX	Y	44110 FQ	56570 MW	74770 TQ	USBLS	5/07
	Dallas-Fort Worth-Arlington MSA, TX	Y	47870 FQ	61120 MW	75930 TQ	USBLS	5/07
	El Paso MSA, TX	Y	44230 FQ	51560 MW	68720 TQ	USBLS	5/07
	Houston-Sugar Land-Baytown MSA, TX	Y	53830 FQ	66390 MW	91380 TQ	USBLS	5/07
	San Antonio MSA, TX	Y	41140 FQ	56350 MW	79510 TQ	USBLS	5/07
	Utah	Y	51550 FQ	69850 MW	86710 TQ	USBLS	5/07
	Logan MSA, UT-ID	Y	53520 FQ	62910 MW	75860 TQ	USBLS	5/07
	Salt Lake City MSA, UT	Y	64370 FQ	76740 MW	93120 TQ	USBLS	5/07
	Vermont	Y	60270 FQ	77900 MW	110990 TQ	USBLS	5/07
	Burlington-South Burlington MSA, VT	Y	58240 FQ	71700 MW	92970 TQ	USBLS	5/07
	Virginia	Y	62290 FQ	83100 MW	113700 TQ	USBLS	5/07
	Lynchburg MSA, VA	Y	61510 FQ	67920 MW	74900 TQ	USBLS	5/07
	Richmond MSA, VA	Y	56410 FQ	70610 MW	104730 TQ	USBLS	5/07
	Virginia Beach-Norfolk-Newport News MSA, VA-NC	Y	60150 FQ	81000 MW	101110 TQ	USBLS	5/07
	Washington	H	37.26 FQ	47.17 MW	61.69 TQ	WABLS	3/08
	Seattle-Tacoma-Bellevue MSA, WA	Y	80420 FQ	101130 MW	131140 TQ	USBLS	5/07
	Spokane MSA, WA	Y	66350 FQ	85420 MW	102750 TQ	USBLS	5/07
	West Virginia	Y	49895 FQ	61965 MW	75626 TQ	WVBLS	7/08-9/08
	Charleston MSA, WV	Y	45600 FQ	51580 MW	62140 TQ	USBLS	5/07
	Wisconsin	Y	62280 FQ	79870 MW	99610 TQ	USBLS	5/07

AE	Average entry wage	AW	Average wage paid	FQ	First quartile wage
AER	Average entry range	AWR	Average wage range	H	Hourly
AEX	Average experienced wage	AXR	Average experienced range	HI	Highest wage paid
ATC	Average total compensation	D	Daily	HR	High end range

LO	Lowest wage paid	MTC	Median total compensation
LR	Low end range	MW	Median wage paid
M	Monthly	MWR	Median wage range
MCC	Median cash compensation	S	See annotated source

TCC	Total cash compensation
TQ	Third quartile wage
W	Weekly
Y	Yearly

Occupation/Type/Industry	Location	Per	Low	Mid	High	Source	Date
Construction Manager	Milwaukee-Waukesha-West						
	Allis MSA, WI	Y	71060 FQ	89950 MW	104930 TQ	USBLS	5/07
	Racine MSA, WI	Y	49260 FQ	58430 MW	79910 TQ	USBLS	5/07
	Wyoming	Y	54435 FQ	67175 MW	83071 TQ	WYBLS	9/08
	Cheyenne MSA, WY	Y	59955 FQ	72722 MW	79533 TQ	WYBLS	9/08
	Puerto Rico	Y	40040 FQ	55270 MW	72370 TQ	USBLS	5/07
	San Juan-Caguas-Guaynabo						
	MSA, PR	Y	41670 FQ	57840 MW	74700 TQ	USBLS	5/07
	Virgin Islands	Y	61790 FQ	72800 MW	88760 TQ	USBLS	5/07
	Guam	Y	32920 FQ	46600 MW	72480 TQ	USBLS	5/07
Construction Superintendent							
Contractor Management	United States	Y		84540 ATC		ENR01	2007
General Contractor	United States	Y		83138 ATC		ENR01	2007
Consumer Loan Processor	United States	Y	22876 AE			CCRUN02	2008
Consumer Protection Inspector							
State Government	Maine	Y	29411 LO		39770 HI	AFT02	3/1/08
Continuous Mining Machine Operator	Alabama	Y	28280 FQ	39690 MW	45530 TQ	USBLS	5/07
	Alaska	Y	52770 FQ	68620 MW	84350 TQ	USBLS	5/07
	Arizona	Y	30420 FQ	36810 MW	42650 TQ	USBLS	5/07
	California	H	18.23 FQ	27.05 MW	31.12 TQ	CABLS	1/08-3/08
	Georgia	Y	33290 FQ	40930 MW	46390 TQ	USBLS	5/07
	Idaho	Y	34640 FQ	38700 MW	43940 TQ	USBLS	5/07
	Illinois	Y	34950 FQ	41820 MW	47480 TQ	USBLS	5/07
	Indiana	Y	41460 FQ	45400 MW	49040 TQ	USBLS	5/07
	Kentucky	Y	38615 FQ	42661 MW	48312 TQ	KYBLS	2008
	Louisiana	H	16.76 FQ	18.63 MW	20.91 TQ	LABLS	1/08-3/08
	Maryland	Y		34425 MW		MDBLS	3/08
	Michigan	Y	36730 FQ	41120 MW	46010 TQ	USBLS	5/07
	Minnesota	Y	45864 FQ	48857 MW	51850 TQ	MNBLS	10/08-12/08
	Missouri	Y	24200 FQ	31530 MW	40440 TQ	USBLS	5/07
	Montana	Y	40020 FQ	49880 MW	54840 TQ	USBLS	5/07
	Nevada	H	22.07 FQ	25.14 MW	28.91 TQ	NVBLS	5/08
	New Mexico	Y	33250 FQ	41800 MW	46270 TQ	USBLS	5/07
	New York	Y	24010 FQ	27760 MW	32200 TQ	USBLS	5/07
	Ohio	Y	42010 FQ	45980 MW	50040 TQ	USBLS	5/07
	Oklahoma	Y	23780 FQ	27270 MW	40530 TQ	USBLS	5/07
	Pennsylvania	Y	30660 FQ	42510 MW	49280 TQ	USBLS	5/07
	South Carolina	Y	26190 FQ	30640 MW	38450 TQ	USBLS	5/07
	Tennessee	Y	26180 FQ	28660 MW	31890 TQ	USBLS	5/07
	Texas	Y	20090 FQ	26380 MW	33440 TQ	USBLS	5/07
	Utah	Y	42730 FQ	46270 MW	50250 TQ	USBLS	5/07
	Virginia	Y	29560 FQ	35840 MW	45060 TQ	USBLS	5/07
	West Virginia	Y	42256 FQ	46218 MW	50241 TQ	WVBLS	7/08-9/08
	Wyoming	Y	45011 FQ	49637 MW	55685 TQ	WYBLS	9/08
Contract Analyst							
State Government	Connecticut	Y	56975 LO		71510 HI	AFT02	3/1/08
Contract Compliance Specialist							
Municipal Government	Cincinnati, OH	Y	45117 LO		60634 HI	COHSS	10/08
Contract Engineer							
Radio Station	United States	H		50.00-59.00 AW		RADM	2008
Contract Evaluator/Negotiator							
State Government	Ohio	H	18.36 LO		23.87 HI	ODAS	2008
Contract Specialist							
District Government	District of Columbia	Y	44603 LO		101467 HI	AFT02	3/1/08
Control and Valve Installer and Repairer							
Except Mechanical Door	Alabama	Y	30200 FQ	39750 MW	50410 TQ	USBLS	5/07
Except Mechanical Door	Birmingham-Hoover MSA, AL	Y	36340 FQ	51630 MW	64970 TQ	USBLS	5/07
Except Mechanical Door	Alaska	Y	51110 FQ	61450 MW	69490 TQ	USBLS	5/07
Except Mechanical Door	Arizona	Y	41710 FQ	55880 MW	72880 TQ	USBLS	5/07

AE	Average entry wage	AW	Average wage paid	FQ	First quartile wage	
AER	Average entry range	AWR	Average wage range	H	Hourly	
AEX	Average experienced wage	AXR	Average experienced range	HI	Highest wage paid	
ATC	Average total compensation	D	Daily	HR	High end range	

LO	Lowest wage paid	MTC	Median total compensation	TCC	Total cash compensation
LR	Low end range	MW	Median wage paid	TQ	Third quartile wage
M	Monthly	MWR	Median wage range	W	Weekly
MCC	Median cash compensation	S	See annotated source	Y	Yearly

Occupation/Type/Industry	Location	Per	Low	Mid	High	Source	Date
Control and Valve Installer and Repairer							
Except Mechanical Door	Phoenix-Mesa-Scottsdale MSA, AZ	Y	47720 FQ	67870 MW	76440 TQ	USBLS	5/07
Except Mechanical Door	Tucson MSA, AZ	Y	40200 FQ	44200 MW	50420 TQ	USBLS	5/07
Except Mechanical Door	Arkansas	Y	25600 FQ	33850 MW	45590 TQ	USBLS	5/07
Except Mechanical Door	Fort Smith MSA, AR-OK	Y	23460 FQ	33120 MW	37270 TQ	USBLS	5/07
Except Mechanical Door	Little Rock-North Little Rock MSA, AR	Y	25860 FQ	35490 MW	44410 TQ	USBLS	5/07
Except Mechanical Door	California	H	21.56 FQ	27.99 MW	32.53 TQ	CABLS	1/08-3/08
Except Mechanical Door	Los Angeles-Long Beach-Glendale PMSA, CA	H	18.88 FQ	28.13 MW	31.96 TQ	CABLS	1/08-3/08
Except Mechanical Door	Oakland-Fremont-Hayward MSA, CA	H	26.41 FQ	34.33 MW	38.05 TQ	CABLS	1/08-3/08
Except Mechanical Door	Riverside-San Bernardino-Ontario MSA, CA	H	26.12 FQ	29.31 MW	33.10 TQ	CABLS	1/08-3/08
Except Mechanical Door	Sacramento-Arden Arcade-Roseville MSA, CA	H	18.31 FQ	21.95 MW	28.53 TQ	CABLS	1/08-3/08
Except Mechanical Door	San Diego-Carlsbad-San Marcos MSA, CA	H	25.16 FQ	28.08 MW	31.02 TQ	CABLS	1/08-3/08
Except Mechanical Door	San Francisco-San Mateo-Redwood PMSA, CA	H	26.18 FQ	29.61 MW	32.65 TQ	CABLS	1/08-3/08
Except Mechanical Door	San Jose-Sunnyvale-Santa Clara MSA, CA	H	24.50 FQ	26.54 MW	28.57 TQ	CABLS	1/08-3/08
Except Mechanical Door	Santa Ana-Anaheim-Irvine PMSA, CA	Y	40570 FQ	57080 MW	67800 TQ	USBLS	5/07
Except Mechanical Door	Santa Rosa-Petaluma MSA, CA	H	15.75 FQ	18.15 MW	23.16 TQ	CABLS	1/08-3/08
Except Mechanical Door	Colorado	Y	37320 FQ	49250 MW	58510 TQ	USBLS	5/07
Except Mechanical Door	Denver-Aurora MSA, CO	Y	37980 FQ	48520 MW	57710 TQ	USBLS	5/07
Except Mechanical Door	Connecticut	H	19.89 AE	27.62 MW		CTBLS	1/08-3/08
Except Mechanical Door	Bridgeport-Stamford-Norwalk MSA, CT	Y	48880 FQ	56360 MW	63190 TQ	USBLS	5/07
Except Mechanical Door	Hartford-West Hartford-East Hartford MSA, CT	Y	53000 FQ	57520 MW	62090 TQ	USBLS	5/07
Except Mechanical Door	Delaware	Y	36400 FQ	57380 MW	71140 TQ	USBLS	5/07
Except Mechanical Door	Wilmington PMSA, DE-MD-NJ	Y	45120 FQ	58130 MW	70870 TQ	USBLS	5/07
Except Mechanical Door	Washington-Arlington-Alexandria MSA, DC-VA-MD-WV	Y	33890 FQ	43790 MW	54310 TQ	USBLS	5/07
Except Mechanical Door	Florida	Y	27660 FQ	34780 MW	46850 TQ	USBLS	5/07
Except Mechanical Door	Fort Lauderdale-Pompano Beach-Deerfield Beach PMSA, FL	Y	29850 FQ	35500 MW	45740 TQ	USBLS	5/07
Except Mechanical Door	Jacksonville MSA, FL	Y	43380 FQ	47270 MW	52370 TQ	USBLS	5/07
Except Mechanical Door	Miami-Fort Lauderdale-Miami Beach MSA, FL	Y	28550 FQ	33380 MW	47100 TQ	USBLS	5/07
Except Mechanical Door	Orlando-Kissimmee MSA, FL	Y	24260 FQ	40350 MW	46400 TQ	USBLS	5/07
Except Mechanical Door	Tampa-St. Petersburg-Clearwater MSA, FL	Y	26890 FQ	30870 MW	36460 TQ	USBLS	5/07
Except Mechanical Door	West Palm Beach-Boca Raton-Boynton Beach PMSA, FL	Y	27480 FQ	32590 MW	39970 TQ	USBLS	5/07
Except Mechanical Door	Georgia	Y	28310 FQ	34790 MW	43780 TQ	USBLS	5/07
Except Mechanical Door	Atlanta-Sandy Springs-Marietta MSA, GA	Y	33580 FQ	38370 MW	51460 TQ	USBLS	5/07
Except Mechanical Door	Hawaii	Y	37850 FQ	45680 MW	61180 TQ	USBLS	5/07
Except Mechanical Door	Idaho	Y	24310 FQ	30600 MW	48130 TQ	USBLS	5/07
Except Mechanical Door	Boise City-Nampa MSA, ID	Y	40500 FQ	52690 MW	64460 TQ	USBLS	5/07
Except Mechanical Door	Illinois	Y	38660 FQ	50850 MW	58260 TQ	USBLS	5/07
Except Mechanical Door	Chicago-Naperville-Joliet MSA, IL-IN-WI	Y	41560 FQ	52640 MW	59350 TQ	USBLS	5/07
Except Mechanical Door	Indiana	Y	36730 FQ	47570 MW	57130 TQ	USBLS	5/07
Except Mechanical Door	Gary PMSA, IN	Y	41340 FQ	54310 MW	59500 TQ	USBLS	5/07
Except Mechanical Door	Indianapolis-Carmel MSA, IN	Y	37890 FQ	45500 MW	56970 TQ	USBLS	5/07
Except Mechanical Door	South Bend-Mishawaka MSA, IN-MI	Y	29550 FQ	37300 MW	46970 TQ	USBLS	5/07
Except Mechanical Door	Iowa	Y	37220 FQ	44390 MW	52490 TQ	USBLS	5/07
Except Mechanical Door	Des Moines-West Des Moines MSA, IA	Y	45650 FQ	50410 MW	56440 TQ	USBLS	5/07
Except Mechanical Door	Kansas	Y	34770 FQ	46180 MW	54090 TQ	USBLS	5/07
Except Mechanical Door	Wichita MSA, KS	Y	21960 FQ	26110 MW	31570 TQ	USBLS	5/07
Except Mechanical Door	Kentucky	Y	25991 FQ	30803 MW	38733 TQ	KYBLS	2008

AE	Average entry wage	AW	Average wage paid	FQ First quartile wage
AER	Average entry range	AWR	Average wage range	H Hourly
AEX	Average experienced wage	AXR	Average experienced range	HI Highest wage paid
ATC	Average total compensation	D	Daily	HR High end range

LO	Lowest wage paid	MTC	Median total compensation
LR	Low end range	MW	Median wage paid
M	Monthly	MWR	Median wage range
MCC	Median cash compensation	S	See annotated source

TCC	Total cash compensation
TQ	Third quartile wage
W	Weekly
Y	Yearly

Occupation/Type/Industry	Location	Per	Low	Mid	High	Source	Date
Control and Valve Installer and Repairer							
Except Mechanical Door	Lexington-Fayette MSA, KY	Y	27920 FQ	35670 MW	53620 TQ	USBLS	5/07
Except Mechanical Door	Louisville-Jefferson County MSA, KY-IN	Y	31270 FQ	35110 MW	42260 TQ	USBLS	5/07
Except Mechanical Door	Louisiana	H	17.50 FQ	22.12 MW	27.17 TQ	LABLS	1/08-3/08
Except Mechanical Door	Baton Rouge MSA, LA	Y	37760 FQ	42690 MW	48330 TQ	USBLS	5/07
Except Mechanical Door	New Orleans-Metairie-Kenner MSA, LA	Y	34690 FQ	42590 MW	51130 TQ	USBLS	5/07
Except Mechanical Door	Maine	Y	37250 FQ	47860 MW	54430 TQ	USBLS	5/07
Except Mechanical Door	Portland-South Portland-Biddeford MSA, ME	Y	34260 FQ	38990 MW	47900 TQ	USBLS	5/07
Except Mechanical Door	Maryland	Y		50100 MW		MDBLS	3/08
Except Mechanical Door	Baltimore-Towson MSA, MD	Y	48910 FQ	54430 MW	58950 MW	USBLS	5/07
Except Mechanical Door	Bethesda-Gaithersburg-Frederick PMSA, MD	Y	33310 FQ	40340 MW	51720 TQ	USBLS	5/07
Except Mechanical Door	Massachusetts	Y	36510 FQ	49450 MW	64980 TQ	USBLS	5/07
Except Mechanical Door	Boston-Cambridge-Quincy NECTA, MA	Y	38970 FQ	50210 MW	59600 TQ	USBLS	5/07
Except Mechanical Door	Michigan	Y	42330 FQ	52050 MW	59920 TQ	USBLS	5/07
Except Mechanical Door	Detroit-Warren-Livonia MSA, MI	Y	42120 FQ	52210 MW	59540 TQ	USBLS	5/07
Except Mechanical Door	Grand Rapids-Wyoming MSA, MI	Y	38590 FQ	43930 MW	52570 TQ	USBLS	5/07
Except Mechanical Door	Warren-Troy-Farmington Hills PMSA, MI	Y	41860 FQ	51290 MW	58460 TQ	USBLS	5/07
Except Mechanical Door	Minnesota	Y	38496 FQ	49940 MW	60440 TQ	MNBLS	10/08-12/08
Except Mechanical Door	Duluth-Superior MSA, MN-WI	Y	44045 FQ	50590 MW	58184 TQ	MNBLS	10/08-12/08
Except Mechanical Door	Minneapolis-Saint Paul MSA, MN-WI	Y	38968 FQ	47139 MW	61583 TQ	MNBLS	10/08-12/08
Except Mechanical Door	Rochester MSA, MN	Y	29497 FQ	32813 MW	39632 TQ	MNBLS	10/08-12/08
Except Mechanical Door	Mississippi	Y	25930 FQ	35270 MW	44180 TQ	USBLS	5/07
Except Mechanical Door	Jackson MSA, MS	Y	21730 FQ	26620 MW	30210 TQ	USBLS	5/07
Except Mechanical Door	Missouri	Y	28900 FQ	42060 MW	55610 TQ	USBLS	5/07
Except Mechanical Door	Kansas City MSA, MO-KS	Y	44220 FQ	50120 MW	58050 TQ	USBLS	5/07
Except Mechanical Door	St. Louis MSA, MO-IL	Y	34640 FQ	47970 MW	57050 TQ	USBLS	5/07
Except Mechanical Door	Montana	Y	21330 FQ	46000 MW	62730 TQ	USBLS	5/07
Except Mechanical Door	Nebraska	Y	35590 FQ	48340 MW	58410 TQ	USBLS	5/07
Except Mechanical Door	Omaha-Council Bluffs MSA, NE-IA	Y	32100 FQ	45340 MW	50840 TQ	USBLS	5/07
Except Mechanical Door	Nevada	H	14.64 FQ	25.31 MW	31.45 TQ	NVBLS	5/08
Except Mechanical Door	Las Vegas-Paradise MSA, NV	H	13.27 FQ	14.76 MW	31.12 TQ	NVBLS	5/08
Except Mechanical Door	New Hampshire	H	14.32 AE	17.18 MW	19.84 AEX	NHBLS	6/08
Except Mechanical Door	New Jersey	Y	45260 FQ	54770 MW	62370 TQ	USBLS	5/07
Except Mechanical Door	Camden PMSA, NJ	Y	41240 FQ	52990 MW	60950 TQ	USBLS	5/07
Except Mechanical Door	Edison PMSA, NJ	Y	49010 FQ	54680 MW	59910 TQ	USBLS	5/07
Except Mechanical Door	Newark-Union PMSA, NJ-PA	Y	46070 FQ	54710 MW	62140 TQ	USBLS	5/07
Except Mechanical Door	New Mexico	Y	27120 FQ	41590 MW	50180 TQ	USBLS	5/07
Except Mechanical Door	Albuquerque MSA, NM	Y	39510 FQ	46040 MW	51210 TQ	USBLS	5/07
Except Mechanical Door	Farmington MSA, NM	Y	22770 FQ	25280 MW	32230 TQ	USBLS	5/07
Except Mechanical Door	New York	Y	53020 FQ	63150 MW	73580 TQ	USBLS	5/07
Except Mechanical Door	Albany-Schenectady-Troy MSA, NY	Y	38450 FQ	48160 MW	61340 TQ	USBLS	5/07
Except Mechanical Door	Buffalo-Niagara Falls MSA, NY	Y	41590 FQ	54130 MW	65410 TQ	USBLS	5/07
Except Mechanical Door	Nassau-Suffolk PMSA, NY	Y	54630 FQ	65340 MW	74080 TQ	USBLS	5/07
Except Mechanical Door	New York-Northern New Jersey-Long Island MSA, NY-NJ-PA	Y	53430 FQ	62290 MW	72850 TQ	USBLS	5/07
Except Mechanical Door	North Carolina	Y	32520 FQ	41040 MW	51550 TQ	USBLS	5/07
Except Mechanical Door	Charlotte-Gastonia-Concord MSA, NC-SC	Y	30260 FQ	37180 MW	45750 TQ	USBLS	5/07
Except Mechanical Door	Raleigh-Cary MSA, NC	Y	24720 FQ	32160 MW	39640 TQ	USBLS	5/07
Except Mechanical Door	Ohio	Y	39100 FQ	52330 MW	59470 TQ	USBLS	5/07
Except Mechanical Door	Cincinnati-Middletown MSA, OH-KY-IN	Y	41280 FQ	54680 MW	60340 TQ	USBLS	5/07
Except Mechanical Door	Cleveland-Elyria-Mentor MSA, OH	Y	45710 FQ	55410 MW	67830 TQ	USBLS	5/07
Except Mechanical Door	Columbus MSA, OH	Y	32290 FQ	46390 MW	57480 TQ	USBLS	5/07
Except Mechanical Door	Oklahoma	Y	39140 FQ	45040 MW	50220 TQ	USBLS	5/07
Except Mechanical Door	Oklahoma City MSA, OK	Y	41820 FQ	45630 MW	49410 TQ	USBLS	5/07
Except Mechanical Door	Tulsa MSA, OK	Y	25450 FQ	40980 MW	53130 TQ	USBLS	5/07

AE Average entry wage	AW Average wage paid	FQ First quartile wage	LO Lowest wage paid	MTC Median total compensation	TCC Total cash compensation
AER Average entry range	AWR Average wage range	H Hourly	LR Low end range	MW Median wage paid	TQ Third quartile wage
AEX Average experienced wage	AXR Average experienced range	HI Highest wage paid	M Monthly	MWR Median wage range	W Weekly
ATC Average total compensation	D Daily	HR High end range	MCC Median cash compensation	S See annotated source	Y Yearly

Occupation/Type/Industry	Location	Per	Low	Mid	High	Source	Date
Control and Valve Installer and Repairer							
Except Mechanical Door	Oregon	H	17.68 FQ	24.28 MW	28.56 TQ	ORBLS	5/08
Except Mechanical Door	Portland-Vancouver-Beaverton MSA, OR-WA	Y	41680 FQ	51320 MW	57400 TQ	USBLS	5/07
Except Mechanical Door	Pennsylvania	Y	39410 FQ	50450 MW	60420 TQ	USBLS	5/07
Except Mechanical Door	Allentown-Bethlehem-Easton MSA, PA-NJ	Y	37000 FQ	41720 MW	46780 TQ	USBLS	5/07
Except Mechanical Door	Philadelphia-Camden-Wilmington MSA, PA-NJ-DE-MD	Y	46590 FQ	57150 MW	66640 TQ	USBLS	5/07
Except Mechanical Door	Pittsburgh MSA, PA	Y	37050 FQ	47670 MW	56420 TQ	USBLS	5/07
Except Mechanical Door	Rhode Island	Y	38440 FQ	47280 MW	53910 TQ	USBLS	5/07
Except Mechanical Door	Providence-Fall River-Warwick MSA, RI-MA	Y	38580 FQ	47850 MW	54420 TQ	USBLS	5/07
Except Mechanical Door	South Carolina	Y	40320 FQ	47560 MW	58280 TQ	USBLS	5/07
Except Mechanical Door	Charleston-North Charleston MSA, SC	Y	38880 FQ	41970 MW	45040 TQ	USBLS	5/07
Except Mechanical Door	Columbia MSA, SC	Y	47700 FQ	54960 MW	60380 TQ	USBLS	5/07
Except Mechanical Door	South Dakota	Y	37944 FQ	48118 MW	56137 TQ	SDBLS	7/08-9/08
Except Mechanical Door	Sioux Falls MSA, SD	Y	41089 FQ	51068 MW	57275 TQ	SDBLS	7/08-9/08
Except Mechanical Door	Tennessee	Y	27640 FQ	35350 MW	48210 TQ	USBLS	5/07
Except Mechanical Door	Memphis MSA, TN-MS-AR	Y	27890 FQ	29900 MW	31840 TQ	USBLS	5/07
Except Mechanical Door	Nashville-Davidson-Murfreesboro MSA, TN	Y	48280 FQ	52380 MW	56740 TQ	USBLS	5/07
Except Mechanical Door	Texas	Y	27170 FQ	37040 MW	49730 TQ	USBLS	5/07
Except Mechanical Door	Austin-Round Rock MSA, TX	Y	27360 FQ	32000 MW	50340 TQ	USBLS	5/07
Except Mechanical Door	Dallas-Fort Worth-Arlington MSA, TX	Y	27050 FQ	35510 MW	42140 TQ	USBLS	5/07
Except Mechanical Door	El Paso MSA, TX	Y	28640 FQ	36450 MW	46270 TQ	USBLS	5/07
Except Mechanical Door	Houston-Sugar Land-Baytown MSA, TX	Y	28850 FQ	38940 MW	50700 TQ	USBLS	5/07
Except Mechanical Door	San Antonio MSA, TX	Y	20290 FQ	23670 MW	30570 TQ	USBLS	5/07
Except Mechanical Door	Utah	Y	43130 FQ	48900 MW	56810 TQ	USBLS	5/07
Except Mechanical Door	Ogden-Clearfield MSA, UT	Y	43230 FQ	47960 MW	55010 TQ	USBLS	5/07
Except Mechanical Door	Salt Lake City MSA, UT	Y	46200 FQ	53750 MW	62300 TQ	USBLS	5/07
Except Mechanical Door	Vermont	Y	30980 FQ	40690 MW	46470 TQ	USBLS	5/07
Except Mechanical Door	Burlington-South Burlington MSA, VT	Y	32350 FQ	39470 MW	44680 TQ	USBLS	5/07
Except Mechanical Door	Virginia	Y	30980 FQ	39170 MW	48120 TQ	USBLS	5/07
Except Mechanical Door	Richmond MSA, VA	Y	30210 FQ	39240 MW	45810 TQ	USBLS	5/07
Except Mechanical Door	Virginia Beach-Norfolk-Newport News MSA, VA-NC	Y	34670 FQ	40540 MW	48470 TQ	USBLS	5/07
Except Mechanical Door	Washington	H	17.16 FQ	22.45 MW	29.54 TQ	WABLS	3/08
Except Mechanical Door	Seattle-Tacoma-Bellevue MSA, WA	Y	41660 FQ	53150 MW	66670 TQ	USBLS	5/07
Except Mechanical Door	Spokane MSA, WA	Y	34550 FQ	39100 MW	45980 TQ	USBLS	5/07
Except Mechanical Door	West Virginia	Y	23561 FQ	35322 MW	54809 TQ	WVBLS	7/08-9/08
Except Mechanical Door	Charleston MSA, WV	Y	35820 FQ	49740 MW	54960 TQ	USBLS	5/07
Except Mechanical Door	Wisconsin	Y	36420 FQ	47610 MW	57230 TQ	USBLS	5/07
Except Mechanical Door	Milwaukee-Waukesha-West Allis MSA, WI	Y	34620 FQ	38700 MW	52130 TQ	USBLS	5/07
Except Mechanical Door	Wyoming	Y	30611 FQ	41010 MW	56131 TQ	WYBLS	9/08
Except Mechanical Door	Puerto Rico	Y	16950 FQ	26770 MW	31260 TQ	USBLS	5/07
Except Mechanical Door	San Juan-Caguas-Guaynabo MSA, PR	Y	17040 FQ	26500 MW	30580 TQ	USBLS	5/07
Except Mechanical Door	Virgin Islands	Y	37690 FQ	47860 MW	68830 TQ	USBLS	5/07
Control Bid Attorney							
State Government	Ohio	H	29.14 LO		64.45 HI	ODAS	2008
Controller	United States	Y	90000 FQ	110000 MW	135000 TQ	CTRLR01	2/08
	Great Lakes	Y		94644 AW		CTRLRPT	3/07
	Midwest	Y		78112 AW		CTRLRPT	3/07
	Southeast	Y		77056 AW		CTRLRPT	3/07
	Southwest	Y		81975 AW		CTRLRPT	3/07
Convention Hall Security Worker	Cincinnati, OH	Y	20555 LO		24474 HI	COHSS	10/08
Convention Hall Utility Worker	Cincinnati, OH	Y	28328 LO		33490 HI	COHSS	10/08
Conveyor Operator and Tender	Alabama	Y	19720 FQ	23890 MW	29240 TQ	USBLS	5/07

AE Average entry wage	**AW** Average wage paid	**FQ** First quartile wage	**LO** Lowest wage paid	**MTC** Median total compensation	**TCC** Total cash compensation
AER Average entry range	**AWR** Average wage range	**H** Hourly	**LR** Low end range	**MW** Median wage paid	**TQ** Third quartile wage
AEX Average experienced wage	**AXR** Average experienced range	**HI** Highest wage paid	**M** Monthly	**MWR** Median wage range	**W** Weekly
ATC Average total compensation	**D** Daily	**HR** High end range	**MCC** Median cash compensation	**S** See annotated source	**Y** Yearly

Occupation/Type/Industry	Location	Per	Low	Mid	High	Source	Date
Conveyor Operator and Tender	Birmingham-Hoover MSA, AL	Y	22200 FQ	24890 MW	29120 TQ	USBLS	5/07
	Montgomery MSA, AL	Y	32110 FQ	37630 MW	45960 TQ	USBLS	5/07
	Alaska	Y	28270 FQ	31310 MW	37300 TQ	USBLS	5/07
	Anchorage MSA, AK	Y	28100 FQ	30730 MW	35030 TQ	USBLS	5/07
	Arizona	Y	19420 FQ	25820 MW	31460 TQ	USBLS	5/07
	Phoenix-Mesa-Scottsdale MSA, AZ	Y	20250 FQ	25770 MW	30810 TQ	USBLS	5/07
	Tucson MSA, AZ	Y	23770 FQ	31940 MW	41360 TQ	USBLS	5/07
	Arkansas	Y	20540 FQ	24400 MW	31030 TQ	USBLS	5/07
	Little Rock-North Little Rock MSA, AR	Y	21620 FQ	24330 MW	28030 TQ	USBLS	5/07
	California	H	12.42 FQ	15.36 MW	19.02 TQ	CABLS	1/08-3/08
	Los Angeles-Long Beach-Glendale PMSA, CA	H	12.91 FQ	15.33 MW	17.82 TQ	CABLS	1/08-3/08
	Oakland-Fremont-Hayward MSA, CA	H	12.91 FQ	15.08 MW	17.67 TQ	CABLS	1/08-3/08
	Riverside-San Bernardino-Ontario MSA, CA	H	12.38 FQ	15.64 MW	20.54 TQ	CABLS	1/08-3/08
	Sacramento-Arden Arcade-Roseville MSA, CA	H	14.58 FQ	16.11 MW	18.75 TQ	CABLS	1/08-3/08
	San Diego-Carlsbad-San Marcos MSA, CA	H	13.70 FQ	15.32 MW	17.23 TQ	CABLS	1/08-3/08
	San Francisco-San Mateo-Redwood PMSA, CA	H	11.51 FQ	13.26 MW	15.87 TQ	CABLS	1/08-3/08
	San Jose-Sunnyvale-Santa Clara MSA, CA	H	15.46 FQ	17.41 MW	19.64 TQ	CABLS	1/08-3/08
	Santa Ana-Anaheim-Irvine PMSA, CA	Y	24080 FQ	34000 MW	43110 TQ	USBLS	5/07
	Colorado	Y	22870 FQ	26440 MW	37510 TQ	USBLS	5/07
	Denver-Aurora MSA, CO	Y	23060 FQ	26400 MW	33840 TQ	USBLS	5/07
	Connecticut	H	9.76 AE	12.78 MW		CTBLS	1/08-3/08
	Hartford-West Hartford-East Hartford MSA, CT	Y	24740 FQ	28800 MW	35570 TQ	USBLS	5/07
	Washington-Arlington-Alexandria MSA, DC-VA-MD-WV	Y	28600 FQ	34050 MW	39350 TQ	USBLS	5/07
	Florida	Y	24510 FQ	28790 MW	34040 TQ	USBLS	5/07
	Jacksonville MSA, FL	Y	25310 FQ	29580 MW	35340 TQ	USBLS	5/07
	Orlando-Kissimmee MSA, FL	Y	26680 FQ	28930 MW	31470 TQ	USBLS	5/07
	Tampa-St. Petersburg-Clearwater MSA, FL	Y	24200 FQ	27400 MW	31860 TQ	USBLS	5/07
	Georgia	Y	24060 FQ	28990 MW	33350 TQ	USBLS	5/07
	Atlanta-Sandy Springs-Marietta MSA, GA	Y	25410 FQ	29040 MW	32490 TQ	USBLS	5/07
	Hawaii	Y	26630 FQ	30420 MW	35630 TQ	USBLS	5/07
	Honolulu MSA, HI	Y	26840 FQ	30690 MW	35850 TQ	USBLS	5/07
	Idaho	Y	20900 FQ	24800 MW	30580 TQ	USBLS	5/07
	Illinois	Y	21450 FQ	29010 MW	39780 TQ	USBLS	5/07
	Chicago-Naperville-Joliet MSA, IL-IN-WI	Y	26070 FQ	32130 MW	39180 TQ	USBLS	5/07
	Peoria MSA, IL	Y	20550 FQ	24550 MW	28020 TQ	USBLS	5/07
	Indiana	Y	24920 FQ	28170 MW	33310 TQ	USBLS	5/07
	Fort Wayne MSA, IN	Y	24080 FQ	29790 MW	36160 TQ	USBLS	5/07
	Gary PMSA, IN	Y	34450 FQ	37800 MW	41250 TQ	USBLS	5/07
	Terre Haute MSA, IN	Y	20270 FQ	30390 MW	40700 TQ	USBLS	5/07
	Iowa	Y	20950 FQ	25480 MW	31850 TQ	USBLS	5/07
	Des Moines-West Des Moines MSA, IA	Y	20600 FQ	24760 MW	29790 TQ	USBLS	5/07
	Sioux City MSA, IA-NE-SD	Y	24810 FQ	27050 MW	29030 TQ	USBLS	5/07
	Kansas	Y	21510 FQ	29170 MW	35110 TQ	USBLS	5/07
	Wichita MSA, KS	Y	19290 FQ	26380 MW	30480 TQ	USBLS	5/07
	Kentucky	Y	25724 FQ	29370 MW	33418 TQ	KYBLS	2008
	Louisville-Jefferson County MSA, KY-IN	Y	25000 FQ	27410 MW	29700 TQ	USBLS	5/07
	Louisiana	H	9.78 FQ	12.62 MW	16.17 TQ	LABLS	1/08-3/08
	Baton Rouge MSA, LA	Y	24480 FQ	30710 MW	36140 TQ	USBLS	5/07
	New Orleans-Metairie-Kenner MSA, LA	Y	17060 FQ	20870 MW	28270 TQ	USBLS	5/07
	Maine	Y	24330 FQ	27890 MW	37610 TQ	USBLS	5/07
	Portland-South Portland-Biddeford MSA, ME	Y	24500 FQ	26380 MW	28380 TQ	USBLS	5/07
	Maryland	Y		29975 MW		MDBLS	3/08

Occupation/Type/Industry	Location	Per	Low	Mid	High	Source	Date
Conveyor Operator and Tender	Baltimore-Towson MSA, MD	Y	24120 FQ	27870 MW	32260 TQ	USBLS	5/07
	Massachusetts	Y	25030 FQ	31110 MW	35890 TQ	USBLS	5/07
	Boston-Cambridge-Quincy NECTA, MA	Y	23370 FQ	28980 MW	35470 TQ	USBLS	5/07
	Worcester MSA, MA-CT	Y	27990 FQ	33080 MW	38520 TQ	USBLS	5/07
	Michigan	Y	19770 FQ	26170 MW	33890 TQ	USBLS	5/07
	Detroit-Warren-Livonia MSA, MI	Y	18280 FQ	25070 MW	34410 TQ	USBLS	5/07
	Warren-Troy-Farmington Hills PMSA, MI	Y	19250 FQ	24190 MW	30350 TQ	USBLS	5/07
	Minnesota	Y	25571 FQ	31179 MW	38888 TQ	MNBLS	10/08-12/08
	Duluth-Superior MSA, MN-WI	Y	40084 FQ	45567 MW	49822 TQ	MNBLS	10/08-12/08
	Minneapolis-Saint Paul MSA, MN-WI	Y	26383 FQ	31127 MW	37702 TQ	MNBLS	10/08-12/08
	Rochester MSA, MN	Y	28815 FQ	34957 MW	38306 TQ	MNBLS	10/08-12/08
	Mississippi	Y	18690 FQ	23250 MW	28740 TQ	USBLS	5/07
	Jackson MSA, MS	Y	17690 FQ	22920 MW	28780 TQ	USBLS	5/07
	Missouri	Y	22560 FQ	27250 MW	34070 TQ	USBLS	5/07
	Kansas City MSA, MO-KS	Y	24960 FQ	31530 MW	36790 TQ	USBLS	5/07
	St. Louis MSA, MO-IL	Y	22870 FQ	27800 MW	33450 TQ	USBLS	5/07
	Montana	Y	24770 FQ	31820 MW	36910 TQ	USBLS	5/07
	Great Falls MSA, MT	Y	23470 FQ	32020 MW	45980 TQ	USBLS	5/07
	Nebraska	Y	20530 FQ	23910 MW	28770 TQ	USBLS	5/07
	Omaha-Council Bluffs MSA, NE-IA	Y	20380 FQ	23180 MW	28160 TQ	USBLS	5/07
	Nevada	H	11.71 FQ	14.88 MW	17.55 TQ	NVBLS	5/08
	Las Vegas-Paradise MSA, NV	H	12.93 FQ	16.47 MW	18.79 TQ	NVBLS	5/08
	Reno-Sparks MSA, NV	H	11.65 FQ	14.65 MW	17.31 TQ	NVBLS	5/08
	New Hampshire	H	12.24 AE	14.22 MW	15.70 AEX	NHBLS	6/08
	New Jersey	Y	18550 FQ	31160 MW	35870 TQ	USBLS	5/07
	Camden PMSA, NJ	Y	29370 FQ	32080 MW	35560 TQ	USBLS	5/07
	New York	Y	18780 FQ	25820 MW	33080 TQ	USBLS	5/07
	Albany-Schenectady-Troy MSA, NY	Y	31540 FQ	37650 MW	43810 TQ	USBLS	5/07
	New York-Northern New Jersey-Long Island MSA, NY-NJ-PA	Y	15720 FQ	27000 MW	34940 TQ	USBLS	5/07
	North Carolina	Y	16460 FQ	22010 MW	28690 TQ	USBLS	5/07
	Charlotte-Gastonia-Concord MSA, NC-SC	Y	23220 FQ	30230 MW	35630 TQ	USBLS	5/07
	Raleigh-Cary MSA, NC	Y	24360 FQ	27420 MW	30320 TQ	USBLS	5/07
	North Dakota	Y	22740 FQ	27110 MW	34470 TQ	USBLS	5/07
	Fargo MSA, ND-MN	Y	26810 FQ	31870 MW	37420 TQ	USBLS	5/07
	Ohio	Y	27820 FQ	33510 MW	38290 TQ	USBLS	5/07
	Cincinnati-Middletown MSA, OH-KY-IN	Y	23320 FQ	28050 MW	34950 TQ	USBLS	5/07
	Cleveland-Elyria-Mentor MSA, OH	Y	26650 FQ	32110 MW	39420 TQ	USBLS	5/07
	Columbus MSA, OH	Y	21250 FQ	25080 MW	32750 TQ	USBLS	5/07
	Oklahoma	Y	21390 FQ	26560 MW	30960 TQ	USBLS	5/07
	Oklahoma City MSA, OK	Y	22370 FQ	27230 MW	31760 TQ	USBLS	5/07
	Tulsa MSA, OK	Y	23170 FQ	30030 MW	34170 TQ	USBLS	5/07
	Oregon	H	12.34 FQ	15.23 MW	17.89 TQ	ORBLS	5/08
	Portland-Vancouver-Beaverton MSA, OR-WA	Y	25580 FQ	30380 MW	35320 TQ	USBLS	5/07
	Pennsylvania	Y	19840 FQ	28340 MW	34820 TQ	USBLS	5/07
	Allentown-Bethlehem-Easton MSA, PA-NJ	Y	19240 FQ	31130 MW	37070 TQ	USBLS	5/07
	Philadelphia-Camden-Wilmington MSA, PA-NJ-DE-MD	Y	21070 FQ	29050 MW	32620 TQ	USBLS	5/07
	Pittsburgh MSA, PA	Y	23560 FQ	31840 MW	43060 TQ	USBLS	5/07
	South Carolina	Y	20620 FQ	25220 MW	30540 TQ	USBLS	5/07
	Charleston-North Charleston MSA, SC	Y	17670 FQ	21640 MW	30370 TQ	USBLS	5/07
	Columbia MSA, SC	Y	24020 FQ	29350 MW	33140 TQ	USBLS	5/07
	South Dakota	Y	22081 FQ	24836 MW	28241 TQ	SDBLS	7/08-9/08
	Rapid City MSA, SD	Y	26241 FQ	29406 MW	33566 TQ	SDBLS	7/08-9/08
	Sioux Falls MSA, SD	Y	23406 FQ	26475 MW	29158 TQ	SDBLS	7/08-9/08
	Nashville-Davidson-Murfreesboro MSA, TN	Y	22810 FQ	32180 MW	54250 TQ	USBLS	5/07
	Texas	Y	19430 FQ	24600 MW	30380 TQ	USBLS	5/07

AE	Average entry wage	AW	Average wage paid	FQ	First quartile wage
AER	Average entry range	AWR	Average wage range	H	Hourly
AEX	Average experienced wage	AXR	Average experienced range	HI	Highest wage paid
ATC	Average total compensation	D	Daily	HR	High end range

LO	Lowest wage paid	MTC	Median total compensation	TCC Total cash compensation
LR	Low end range	MW	Median wage paid	TQ Third quartile wage
M	Monthly	MWR	Median wage range	W Weekly
MCC	Median cash compensation	S	See annotated source	Y Yearly

Occupation/Type/Industry	Location	Per	Low	Mid	High	Source	Date
Conveyor Operator and Tender	Austin-Round Rock MSA, TX	Y	21220 FQ	25510 MW	32780 TQ	USBLS	5/07
	Dallas-Fort Worth-Arlington MSA, TX	Y	20350 FQ	26470 MW	30750 TQ	USBLS	5/07
	El Paso MSA, TX	Y	17780 FQ	25780 MW	29090 TQ	USBLS	5/07
	Houston-Sugar Land-Baytown MSA, TX	Y	22640 FQ	29110 MW	33750 TQ	USBLS	5/07
	San Antonio MSA, TX	Y	21950 FQ	26650 MW	30360 TQ	USBLS	5/07
	Utah	Y	22080 FQ	28180 MW	46970 TQ	USBLS	5/07
	Salt Lake City MSA, UT	Y	21470 FQ	24200 MW	27630 TQ	USBLS	5/07
	Virginia	Y	22430 FQ	28030 MW	33960 TQ	USBLS	5/07
	Richmond MSA, VA	Y	24140 FQ	28870 MW	34300 TQ	USBLS	5/07
	Virginia Beach-Norfolk-Newport News MSA, VA-NC	Y	23400 FQ	27590 MW	32090 TQ	USBLS	5/07
	Washington	H	10.35 FQ	13.12 MW	16.04 TQ	WABLS	3/08
	Seattle-Tacoma-Bellevue MSA, WA	Y	22960 FQ	28310 MW	34110 TQ	USBLS	5/07
	West Virginia	Y	25560 FQ	42294 MW	47432 TQ	WVBLS	7/08-9/08
	Charleston MSA, WV	Y	36630 FQ	43180 MW	47460 TQ	USBLS	5/07
	Wisconsin	Y	23840 FQ	32520 MW	41660 TQ	USBLS	5/07
	Milwaukee-Waukesha-West Allis MSA, WI	Y	20260 FQ	27750 MW	31590 TQ	USBLS	5/07
	Wyoming	Y	41967 FQ	54089 MW	67372 TQ	WYBLS	9/08
	Puerto Rico	Y	16130 FQ	19090 MW	23120 TQ	USBLS	5/07
	San Juan-Caguas-Guaynabo MSA, PR	Y	16500 FQ	20020 MW	23710 TQ	USBLS	5/07
Cook							
Fast Food	Alabama	Y	12530 FQ	13880 MW	15300 TQ	USBLS	5/07
Fast Food	Birmingham-Hoover MSA, AL	Y	12630 FQ	14040 MW	15700 TQ	USBLS	5/07
Fast Food	Alaska	Y	16050 FQ	17450 MW	19110 TQ	USBLS	5/07
Fast Food	Anchorage MSA, AK	Y	16530 FQ	17850 MW	19310 TQ	USBLS	5/07
Fast Food	Arizona	Y	14900 FQ	16240 MW	18620 TQ	USBLS	5/07
Fast Food	Phoenix-Mesa-Scottsdale MSA, AZ	Y	15040 FQ	16430 MW	18720 TQ	USBLS	5/07
Fast Food	Tucson MSA, AZ	Y	14720 FQ	16370 MW	18900 TQ	USBLS	5/07
Fast Food	Arkansas	Y	13980 FQ	14700 MW	15640 TQ	USBLS	5/07
Fast Food	Jonesboro MSA, AR	Y	14050 FQ	14800 MW	15810 TQ	USBLS	5/07
Fast Food	Little Rock-North Little Rock MSA, AR	Y	13930 FQ	14610 MW	15480 TQ	USBLS	5/07
Fast Food	California	H	8.00 FQ	8.46 MW	9.21 TQ	CABLS	1/08-3/08
Fast Food	Los Angeles-Long Beach-Glendale PMSA, CA	H	8.00 FQ	8.38 MW	9.12 TQ	CABLS	1/08-3/08
Fast Food	Oakland-Fremont-Hayward MSA, CA	H	8.01 FQ	8.65 MW	9.30 TQ	CABLS	1/08-3/08
Fast Food	Riverside-San Bernardino-Ontario MSA, CA	H	8.00 FQ	8.32 MW	9.12 TQ	CABLS	1/08-3/08
Fast Food	Sacramento-Arden Arcade-Roseville MSA, CA	H	8.00 FQ	8.44 MW	9.17 TQ	CABLS	1/08-3/08
Fast Food	San Diego-Carlsbad-San Marcos MSA, CA	H	8.00 FQ	8.45 MW	9.15 TQ	CABLS	1/08-3/08
Fast Food	San Francisco-San Mateo-Redwood PMSA, CA	H	8.30 FQ	9.44 MW	10.93 TQ	CABLS	1/08-3/08
Fast Food	San Jose-Sunnyvale-Santa Clara MSA, CA	H	8.00 FQ	8.70 MW	9.48 TQ	CABLS	1/08-3/08
Fast Food	Santa Ana-Anaheim-Irvine PMSA, CA	Y	16060 FQ	17280 MW	18890 TQ	USBLS	5/07
Fast Food	Santa Rosa-Petaluma MSA, CA	H	8.00 FQ	8.55 MW	9.21 TQ	CABLS	1/08-3/08
Fast Food	Stockton MSA, CA	H	8.00 FQ	8.41 MW	9.20 TQ	CABLS	1/08-3/08
Fast Food	Colorado	Y	14970 FQ	16100 MW	20010 TQ	USBLS	5/07
Fast Food	Denver-Aurora MSA, CO	Y	15130 FQ	16860 MW	20790 TQ	USBLS	5/07
Fast Food	Fort Collins-Loveland MSA, CO	Y	14770 FQ	15710 MW	18380 TQ	USBLS	5/07
Fast Food	Pueblo MSA, CO	Y	14890 FQ	15740 MW	18040 TQ	USBLS	5/07
Fast Food	Connecticut	H	8.44 AE	9.51 MW		CTBLS	1/08-3/08
Fast Food	Bridgeport-Stamford-Norwalk MSA, CT	Y	17440 FQ	19910 MW	30140 TQ	USBLS	5/07
Fast Food	Hartford-West Hartford-East Hartford MSA, CT	Y	16420 FQ	18270 MW	20520 TQ	USBLS	5/07
Fast Food	New Haven MSA, CT	Y	17240 FQ	20150 MW	23580 TQ	USBLS	5/07
Fast Food	Delaware	Y	15220 FQ	17390 MW	20800 TQ	USBLS	5/07
Fast Food	Wilmington PMSA, DE-MD-NJ	Y	15110 FQ	17320 MW	20810 TQ	USBLS	5/07

AE	Average entry wage	AW	Average wage paid	FQ	First quartile wage
AER	Average entry range	AWR	Average wage range	H	Hourly
AEX	Average experienced wage	AXR	Average experienced range	HI	Highest wage paid
ATC	Average total compensation	D	Daily	HR	High end range

LO	Lowest wage paid	MTC	Median total compensation	TCC	Total cash compensation
LR	Low end range	MW	Median wage paid	TQ	Third quartile wage
M	Monthly	MWR	Median wage range	W	Weekly
MCC	Median cash compensation	S	See annotated source	Y	Yearly

Occupation/Type/Industry	Location	Per	Low	Mid	High	Source	Date
Cook							
Fast Food	District of Columbia	Y	18940 FQ	23520 MW	27910 TQ	USBLS	5/07
Fast Food	Washington-Arlington-Alexandria MSA, DC-VA-MD-WV	Y	15060 FQ	17910 MW	21510 TQ	USBLS	5/07
Fast Food	Florida	Y	14770 FQ	16040 MW	18730 TQ	USBLS	5/07
Fast Food	Fort Lauderdale-Pompano Beach-Deerfield Beach PMSA, FL	Y	14810 FQ	15800 MW	17860 TQ	USBLS	5/07
Fast Food	Jacksonville MSA, FL	Y	14620 FQ	15580 MW	17490 TQ	USBLS	5/07
Fast Food	Miami-Fort Lauderdale-Miami Beach MSA, FL	Y	15040 FQ	16740 MW	19380 TQ	USBLS	5/07
Fast Food	Orlando-Kissimmee MSA, FL	Y	14660 FQ	15850 MW	19810 TQ	USBLS	5/07
Fast Food	Tampa-St. Petersburg-Clearwater MSA, FL	Y	14760 FQ	15920 MW	18360 TQ	USBLS	5/07
Fast Food	West Palm Beach-Boca Raton-Boynton Beach PMSA, FL	Y	15260 FQ	18300 MW	22430 TQ	USBLS	5/07
Fast Food	Georgia	Y	13230 FQ	15200 MW	18250 TQ	USBLS	5/07
Fast Food	Atlanta-Sandy Springs-Marietta MSA, GA	Y	13530 FQ	16020 MW	18930 TQ	USBLS	5/07
Fast Food	Augusta-Richmond County MSA, GA-SC	Y	13170 FQ	15040 MW	18060 TQ	USBLS	5/07
Fast Food	Savannah MSA, GA	Y	13320 FQ	15300 MW	18540 TQ	USBLS	5/07
Fast Food	Hawaii	Y	15570 FQ	16460 MW	20060 TQ	USBLS	5/07
Fast Food	Honolulu MSA, HI	Y	15530 FQ	16140 MW	19040 TQ	USBLS	5/07
Fast Food	Idaho	Y	12680 FQ	14190 MW	16470 TQ	USBLS	5/07
Fast Food	Boise City-Nampa MSA, ID	Y	12950 FQ	14800 MW	17630 TQ	USBLS	5/07
Fast Food	Illinois	Y	14810 FQ	15950 MW	18850 TQ	USBLS	5/07
Fast Food	Chicago-Naperville-Joliet MSA, IL-IN-WI	Y	14770 FQ	16130 MW	19320 TQ	USBLS	5/07
Fast Food	Rockford MSA, IL	Y	14680 FQ	15500 MW	17770 TQ	USBLS	5/07
Fast Food	Indiana	Y	12940 FQ	14670 MW	17110 TQ	USBLS	5/07
Fast Food	Elkhart-Goshen MSA, IN	Y	12850 FQ	14470 MW	16050 TQ	USBLS	5/07
Fast Food	Evansville MSA, IN-KY	Y	13610 FQ	15630 MW	17480 TQ	USBLS	5/07
Fast Food	Gary PMSA, IN	Y	12760 FQ	14210 MW	16160 TQ	USBLS	5/07
Fast Food	Indianapolis-Carmel MSA, IN	Y	13340 FQ	15500 MW	18410 TQ	USBLS	5/07
Fast Food	Iowa	Y	13930 FQ	14980 MW	16880 TQ	USBLS	5/07
Fast Food	Cedar Rapids MSA, IA	Y	14180 FQ	15520 MW	18120 TQ	USBLS	5/07
Fast Food	Des Moines-West Des Moines MSA, IA	Y	14210 FQ	15440 MW	17330 TQ	USBLS	5/07
Fast Food	Kansas	Y	12830 FQ	14410 MW	16550 TQ	USBLS	5/07
Fast Food	Lawrence MSA, KS	Y	13100 FQ	14970 MW	17510 TQ	USBLS	5/07
Fast Food	Wichita MSA, KS	Y	12710 FQ	14240 MW	16180 TQ	USBLS	5/07
Fast Food	Kentucky	Y	13044 FQ	14558 MW	16299 TQ	KYBLS	2008
Fast Food	Elizabethtown MSA, KY	Y	12550 FQ	13960 MW	15460 TQ	USBLS	5/07
Fast Food	Louisville-Jefferson County MSA, KY-IN	Y	12980 FQ	14680 MW	17100 TQ	USBLS	5/07
Fast Food	Louisiana	H	6.07 FQ	6.74 MW	7.52 TQ	LABLS	1/08-3/08
Fast Food	Baton Rouge MSA, LA	Y	12660 FQ	14090 MW	15750 TQ	USBLS	5/07
Fast Food	Lafayette MSA, LA	Y	12450 FQ	13820 MW	15220 TQ	USBLS	5/07
Fast Food	New Orleans-Metairie-Kenner MSA, LA	Y	12900 FQ	14510 MW	17280 TQ	USBLS	5/07
Fast Food	Maine	Y	15610 FQ	17550 MW	19840 TQ	USBLS	5/07
Fast Food	Portland-South Portland-Biddeford MSA, ME	Y	16260 FQ	19330 MW	22860 TQ	USBLS	5/07
Fast Food	Maryland	Y		18500 MW		MDBLS	3/08
Fast Food	Baltimore-Towson MSA, MD	Y	14960 FQ	18460 MW	23360 TQ	USBLS	5/07
Fast Food	Bethesda-Gaithersburg-Frederick PMSA, MD	Y	15540 FQ	18130 MW	21880 TQ	USBLS	5/07
Fast Food	Cumberland MSA, MD-WV	Y	14150 FQ	15460 MW	17880 TQ	USBLS	5/07
Fast Food	Hagerstown-Martinsburg MSA, MD-WV	Y	13810 FQ	14700 MW	16280 TQ	USBLS	5/07
Fast Food	Massachusetts	Y	16970 FQ	18830 MW	22660 TQ	USBLS	5/07
Fast Food	Boston-Cambridge-Quincy NECTA, MA	Y	17200 FQ	19190 MW	22960 TQ	USBLS	5/07
Fast Food	Worcester MSA, MA-CT	Y	16290 FQ	18560 MW	24160 TQ	USBLS	5/07
Fast Food	Michigan	Y	15020 FQ	15750 MW	17760 TQ	USBLS	5/07
Fast Food	Detroit-Warren-Livonia MSA, MI	Y	15080 FQ	15850 MW	18140 TQ	USBLS	5/07
Fast Food	Grand Rapids-Wyoming MSA, MI	Y	15900 FQ	17750 MW	20310 TQ	USBLS	5/07

AE	Average entry wage	AW	Average wage paid	FQ	First quartile wage	LO	Lowest wage paid	MTC	Median total compensation	TCC	Total cash compensation
AER	Average entry range	AWR	Average wage range	H	Hourly	LR	Low end range	MW	Median wage paid	TQ	Third quartile wage
AEX	Average experienced wage	AXR	Average experienced range	HI	Highest wage paid	M	Monthly	MWR	Median wage range	W	Weekly
ATC	Average total compensation	D	Daily	HR	High end range	MCC	Median cash compensation	S	See annotated source	Y	Yearly

326

Cook

Occupation/Type/Industry	Location	Per	Low	Mid	High	Source	Date
Cook							
Fast Food	Warren-Troy-Farmington Hills PMSA, MI	Y	15240 FQ	16210 MW	19020 TQ	USBLS	5/07
Fast Food	Minnesota	Y	15715 FQ	17848 MW	20441 TQ	MNBLS	10/08-12/08
Fast Food	Duluth-Superior MSA, MN-WI	Y	15014 FQ	16122 MW	18402 TQ	MNBLS	10/08-12/08
Fast Food	Minneapolis-Saint Paul MSA, MN-WI	Y	15809 FQ	18004 MW	20524 TQ	MNBLS	10/08-12/08
Fast Food	Rochester MSA, MN	Y	16532 FQ	18276 MW	20131 TQ	MNBLS	10/08-12/08
Fast Food	Mississippi	Y	12830 FQ	14390 MW	16700 TQ	USBLS	5/07
Fast Food	Jackson MSA, MS	Y	12790 FQ	14370 MW	16940 TQ	USBLS	5/07
Fast Food	Pascagoula MSA, MS	Y	12620 FQ	13900 MW	15310 TQ	USBLS	5/07
Fast Food	Missouri	Y	14380 FQ	15360 MW	17590 TQ	USBLS	5/07
Fast Food	Joplin MSA, MO	Y	14380 FQ	15270 MW	17390 TQ	USBLS	5/07
Fast Food	Kansas City MSA, MO-KS	Y	14350 FQ	16020 MW	18100 TQ	USBLS	5/07
Fast Food	St. Louis MSA, MO-IL	Y	14630 FQ	15770 MW	18300 TQ	USBLS	5/07
Fast Food	Montana	Y	13910 FQ	15080 MW	18370 TQ	USBLS	5/07
Fast Food	Billings MSA, MT	Y	13530 FQ	14270 MW	15220 TQ	USBLS	5/07
Fast Food	Nebraska	Y	12920 FQ	14720 MW	17220 TQ	USBLS	5/07
Fast Food	Omaha-Council Bluffs MSA, NE-IA	Y	13500 FQ	15650 MW	18270 TQ	USBLS	5/07
Fast Food	Nevada	H	6.58 FQ	7.65 MW	9.06 TQ	NVBLS	5/08
Fast Food	Las Vegas-Paradise MSA, NV	H	6.67 FQ	7.85 MW	9.26 TQ	NVBLS	5/08
Fast Food	New Hampshire	H	7.78 AE	9.10 MW	10.42 AEX	NHBLS	6/08
Fast Food	Manchester MSA, NH	Y	15520 FQ	17920 MW	21270 TQ	USBLS	5/07
Fast Food	Nashua NECTA, NH-MA	Y	17760 FQ	20320 MW	24000 TQ	USBLS	5/07
Fast Food	Portsmouth MSA, NH-ME	Y	16320 FQ	18000 MW	22070 TQ	USBLS	5/07
Fast Food	New Jersey	Y	15460 FQ	17050 MW	22280 TQ	USBLS	5/07
Fast Food	Camden PMSA, NJ	Y	15230 FQ	16360 MW	20660 TQ	USBLS	5/07
Fast Food	Edison PMSA, NJ	Y	15650 FQ	19020 MW	24540 TQ	USBLS	5/07
Fast Food	Newark-Union PMSA, NJ-PA	Y	15560 FQ	16840 MW	20110 TQ	USBLS	5/07
Fast Food	New Mexico	Y	13290 FQ	15550 MW	18630 TQ	USBLS	5/07
Fast Food	Albuquerque MSA, NM	Y	13750 FQ	16350 MW	18860 TQ	USBLS	5/07
Fast Food	New York	Y	15370 FQ	16950 MW	19540 TQ	USBLS	5/07
Fast Food	Albany-Schenectady-Troy MSA, NY	Y	16030 FQ	18580 MW	22030 TQ	USBLS	5/07
Fast Food	Binghamton MSA, NY	Y	14970 FQ	15540 MW	18370 TQ	USBLS	5/07
Fast Food	Buffalo-Niagara Falls MSA, NY	Y	15070 FQ	16280 MW	19110 TQ	USBLS	5/07
Fast Food	Glens Falls MSA, NY	Y	15390 FQ	16860 MW	19040 TQ	USBLS	5/07
Fast Food	Kingston MSA, NY	Y	16200 FQ	18060 MW	20090 TQ	USBLS	5/07
Fast Food	Nassau-Suffolk PMSA, NY	Y	15890 FQ	17670 MW	20300 TQ	USBLS	5/07
Fast Food	New York-Northern New Jersey-Long Island MSA, NY-NJ-PA	Y	15560 FQ	17280 MW	20430 TQ	USBLS	5/07
Fast Food	Utica-Rome MSA, NY	Y	15060 FQ	15510 MW	18920 TQ	USBLS	5/07
Fast Food	North Carolina	Y	14300 FQ	15930 MW	18190 TQ	USBLS	5/07
Fast Food	Charlotte-Gastonia-Concord MSA, NC-SC	Y	14480 FQ	16670 MW	19090 TQ	USBLS	5/07
Fast Food	Raleigh-Cary MSA, NC	Y	14480 FQ	16060 MW	17820 TQ	USBLS	5/07
Fast Food	North Dakota	Y	13360 FQ	15750 MW	18560 TQ	USBLS	5/07
Fast Food	Fargo MSA, ND-MN	Y	15520 FQ	17460 MW	19650 TQ	USBLS	5/07
Fast Food	Ohio	Y	14910 FQ	16110 MW	18570 TQ	USBLS	5/07
Fast Food	Cincinnati-Middletown MSA, OH-KY-IN	Y	15220 FQ	16920 MW	18940 TQ	USBLS	5/07
Fast Food	Cleveland-Elyria-Mentor MSA, OH	Y	15130 FQ	16550 MW	18920 TQ	USBLS	5/07
Fast Food	Columbus MSA, OH	Y	15260 FQ	17290 MW	19490 TQ	USBLS	5/07
Fast Food	Dayton MSA, OH	Y	15500 FQ	17390 MW	19980 TQ	USBLS	5/07
Fast Food	Oklahoma	Y	12820 FQ	14480 MW	16920 TQ	USBLS	5/07
Fast Food	Oklahoma City MSA, OK	Y	13050 FQ	14980 MW	18080 TQ	USBLS	5/07
Fast Food	Tulsa MSA, OK	Y	13060 FQ	14950 MW	17310 TQ	USBLS	5/07
Fast Food	Oregon	H	8.48 FQ	8.99 MW	9.61 TQ	ORBLS	5/08
Fast Food	Portland-Vancouver-Beaverton MSA, OR-WA	Y	17250 FQ	18290 MW	19790 TQ	USBLS	5/07
Fast Food	Pennsylvania	Y	14380 FQ	15420 MW	18330 TQ	USBLS	5/07
Fast Food	Allentown-Bethlehem-Easton MSA, PA-NJ	Y	14480 FQ	15410 MW	18110 TQ	USBLS	5/07
Fast Food	Philadelphia-Camden-Wilmington MSA, PA-NJ-DE-MD	Y	14900 FQ	16090 MW	20480 TQ	USBLS	5/07
Fast Food	Pittsburgh MSA, PA	Y	14360 FQ	15420 MW	18030 TQ	USBLS	5/07
Fast Food	Rhode Island	Y	16000 FQ	17780 MW	20790 TQ	USBLS	5/07

AE Average entry wage	AW Average wage paid	FQ First quartile wage	LO Lowest wage paid	MTC Median total compensation	TCC Total cash compensation
AER Average entry range	AWR Average wage range	H Hourly	LR Low end range	MW Median wage paid	TQ Third quartile wage
AEX Average experienced wage	AXR Average experienced range	HI Highest wage paid	M Monthly	MWR Median wage range	W Weekly
ATC Average total compensation	D Daily	HR High end range	MCC Median cash compensation	S See annotated source	Y Yearly

Occupation/Type/Industry	Location	Per	Low	Mid	High	Source	Date
Cook							
Fast Food	Providence-Fall River-Warwick MSA, RI-MA	Y	16070 FQ	17570 MW	19970 TQ	USBLS	5/07
Fast Food	South Carolina	Y	12940 FQ	14660 MW	16970 TQ	USBLS	5/07
Fast Food	Charleston-North Charleston MSA, SC	Y	12940 FQ	14710 MW	17230 TQ	USBLS	5/07
Fast Food	Columbia MSA, SC	Y	13310 FQ	15390 MW	17760 TQ	USBLS	5/07
Fast Food	South Dakota	Y	13766 FQ	15928 MW	18341 TQ	SDBLS	7/08-9/08
Fast Food	Sioux Falls MSA, SD	Y	14133 FQ	16574 MW	18804 TQ	SDBLS	7/08-9/08
Fast Food	Tennessee	Y	12770 FQ	14260 MW	16120 TQ	USBLS	5/07
Fast Food	Memphis MSA, TN-MS-AR	Y	12900 FQ	14350 MW	16450 TQ	USBLS	5/07
Fast Food	Nashville-Davidson-Murfreesboro MSA, TN	Y	12960 FQ	14720 MW	16710 TQ	USBLS	5/07
Fast Food	Texas	Y	13040 FQ	14850 MW	17630 TQ	USBLS	5/07
Fast Food	Austin-Round Rock MSA, TX	Y	13900 FQ	16410 MW	18840 TQ	USBLS	5/07
Fast Food	Dallas-Fort Worth-Arlington MSA, TX	Y	13570 FQ	16030 MW	18500 TQ	USBLS	5/07
Fast Food	El Paso MSA, TX	Y	12660 FQ	14030 MW	15760 TQ	USBLS	5/07
Fast Food	Houston-Sugar Land-Baytown MSA, TX	Y	12850 FQ	14570 MW	17140 TQ	USBLS	5/07
Fast Food	San Antonio MSA, TX	Y	12820 FQ	14430 MW	16610 TQ	USBLS	5/07
Fast Food	Utah	Y	13250 FQ	15320 MW	18310 TQ	USBLS	5/07
Fast Food	Logan MSA, UT-ID	Y	14280 FQ	16870 MW	19440 TQ	USBLS	5/07
Fast Food	Salt Lake City MSA, UT	Y	13390 FQ	15860 MW	18890 TQ	USBLS	5/07
Fast Food	Vermont	Y	17240 FQ	18910 MW	22810 TQ	USBLS	5/07
Fast Food	Burlington-South Burlington MSA, VT	Y	17340 FQ	19720 MW	23810 TQ	USBLS	5/07
Fast Food	Virginia	Y	13150 FQ	15050 MW	18310 TQ	USBLS	5/07
Fast Food	Lynchburg MSA, VA	Y	12620 FQ	14010 MW	15530 TQ	USBLS	5/07
Fast Food	Richmond MSA, VA	Y	12880 FQ	14400 MW	17250 TQ	USBLS	5/07
Fast Food	Virginia Beach-Norfolk-Newport News MSA, VA-NC	Y	12940 FQ	14670 MW	17250 TQ	USBLS	5/07
Fast Food	Washington	H	8.46 FQ	8.99 MW	9.64 TQ	WABLS	3/08
Fast Food	Olympia MSA, WA	Y	17520 FQ	18590 MW	19630 TQ	USBLS	5/07
Fast Food	Seattle-Tacoma-Bellevue MSA, WA	Y	17410 FQ	18460 MW	19930 TQ	USBLS	5/07
Fast Food	West Virginia	Y	13882 FQ	14800 MW	15784 TQ	WVBLS	7/08-9/08
Fast Food	Charleston MSA, WV	Y	13230 FQ	14030 MW	14840 TQ	USBLS	5/07
Fast Food	Wisconsin	Y	15200 FQ	17060 MW	19460 TQ	USBLS	5/07
Fast Food	Appleton MSA, WI	Y	15000 FQ	16100 MW	18670 TQ	USBLS	5/07
Fast Food	Milwaukee-Waukesha-West Allis MSA, WI	Y	15550 FQ	17960 MW	21420 TQ	USBLS	5/07
Fast Food	Wyoming	Y	13358 FQ	14991 MW	17688 TQ	WYBLS	9/08
Fast Food	Casper MSA, WY	Y	13838 FQ	16011 MW	18659 TQ	WYBLS	9/08
Fast Food	Cheyenne MSA, WY	Y	13004 FQ	14368 MW	15758 TQ	WYBLS	9/08
Fast Food	Puerto Rico	Y	12280 FQ	13440 MW	14600 TQ	USBLS	5/07
Fast Food	San Juan-Caguas-Guaynabo MSA, PR	Y	12300 FQ	13450 MW	14600 TQ	USBLS	5/07
Fast Food	Virgin Islands	Y	14030 FQ	15290 MW	17820 TQ	USBLS	5/07
Fast Food	Guam	Y	12980 FQ	14670 MW	17900 TQ	USBLS	5/07
Institution and Cafeteria	Alabama	Y	13610 FQ	16150 MW	19000 TQ	USBLS	5/07
Institution and Cafeteria	Birmingham-Hoover MSA, AL	Y	15570 FQ	17790 MW	20130 TQ	USBLS	5/07
Institution and Cafeteria	Huntsville MSA, AL	Y	12950 FQ	14780 MW	19140 TQ	USBLS	5/07
Institution and Cafeteria	Alaska	Y	26540 FQ	31650 MW	41900 TQ	USBLS	5/07
Institution and Cafeteria	Anchorage MSA, AK	Y	26460 FQ	31850 MW	42800 TQ	USBLS	5/07
Institution and Cafeteria	Arizona	Y	19110 FQ	23080 MW	27670 TQ	USBLS	5/07
Institution and Cafeteria	Phoenix-Mesa-Scottsdale MSA, AZ	Y	19360 FQ	23460 MW	27600 TQ	USBLS	5/07
Institution and Cafeteria	Prescott MSA, AZ	Y	18620 FQ	21640 MW	26750 TQ	USBLS	5/07
Institution and Cafeteria	Tucson MSA, AZ	Y	19620 FQ	22530 MW	25850 TQ	USBLS	5/07
Institution and Cafeteria	Arkansas	Y	14540 FQ	16080 MW	19340 TQ	USBLS	5/07
Institution and Cafeteria	Little Rock-North Little Rock MSA, AR	Y	15540 FQ	18360 MW	22420 TQ	USBLS	5/07
Institution and Cafeteria	California	H	10.66 FQ	12.99 MW	15.96 TQ	CABLS	1/08-3/08
Institution and Cafeteria	Los Angeles-Long Beach-Glendale PMSA, CA	H	10.20 FQ	11.84 MW	14.14 TQ	CABLS	1/08-3/08
Institution and Cafeteria	Oakland-Fremont-Hayward MSA, CA	H	12.02 FQ	13.99 MW	16.51 TQ	CABLS	1/08-3/08
Institution and Cafeteria	Riverside-San Bernardino-Ontario MSA, CA	H	9.40 FQ	12.29 MW	15.31 TQ	CABLS	1/08-3/08
Institution and Cafeteria	Sacramento-Arden Arcade-Roseville MSA, CA	H	10.76 FQ	12.71 MW	15.22 TQ	CABLS	1/08-3/08

Occupation/Type/Industry	Location	Per	Low	Mid	High	Source	Date
Cook							
Institution and Cafeteria	San Diego-Carlsbad-San Marcos MSA, CA	H	10.81 FQ	12.91 MW	15.14 TQ	CABLS	1/08-3/08
Institution and Cafeteria	San Francisco-San Mateo-Redwood PMSA, CA	H	14.01 FQ	17.53 MW	20.42 TQ	CABLS	1/08-3/08
Institution and Cafeteria	San Jose-Sunnyvale-Santa Clara MSA, CA	H	11.97 FQ	15.05 MW	21.01 TQ	CABLS	1/08-3/08
Institution and Cafeteria	Santa Ana-Anaheim-Irvine PMSA, CA	Y	22670 FQ	26960 MW	32250 TQ	USBLS	5/07
Institution and Cafeteria	Stockton MSA, CA	H	10.84 FQ	12.97 MW	16.07 TQ	CABLS	1/08-3/08
Institution and Cafeteria	Colorado	Y	18350 FQ	23170 MW	28550 TQ	USBLS	5/07
Institution and Cafeteria	Denver-Aurora MSA, CO	Y	18500 FQ	23900 MW	29890 TQ	USBLS	5/07
Institution and Cafeteria	Pueblo MSA, CO	Y	19030 FQ	22610 MW	27560 TQ	USBLS	5/07
Institution and Cafeteria	Connecticut	H	10.39 AE	14.33 MW		CTBLS	1/08-3/08
Institution and Cafeteria	Bridgeport-Stamford-Norwalk MSA, CT	Y	23280 FQ	29310 MW	34810 TQ	USBLS	5/07
Institution and Cafeteria	Hartford-West Hartford-East Hartford MSA, CT	Y	24310 FQ	29740 MW	35720 TQ	USBLS	5/07
Institution and Cafeteria	Delaware	Y	20820 FQ	25110 MW	30030 TQ	USBLS	5/07
Institution and Cafeteria	Wilmington PMSA, DE-MD-NJ	Y	22860 FQ	26810 MW	32280 TQ	USBLS	5/07
Institution and Cafeteria	District of Columbia	Y	23050 FQ	27480 MW	32960 TQ	USBLS	5/07
Institution and Cafeteria	Washington-Arlington-Alexandria MSA, DC-VA-MD-WV	Y	22340 FQ	26270 MW	31400 TQ	USBLS	5/07
Institution and Cafeteria	Florida	Y	19230 FQ	22850 MW	27440 TQ	USBLS	5/07
Institution and Cafeteria	Cape Coral-Fort Myers MSA, FL	Y	21930 FQ	24980 MW	28950 TQ	USBLS	5/07
Institution and Cafeteria	Fort Lauderdale-Pompano Beach-Deerfield Beach PMSA, FL	Y	21730 FQ	24260 MW	28070 TQ	USBLS	5/07
Institution and Cafeteria	Jacksonville MSA, FL	Y	19090 FQ	22380 MW	25600 TQ	USBLS	5/07
Institution and Cafeteria	Miami-Fort Lauderdale-Miami Beach MSA, FL	Y	21070 FQ	24320 MW	29320 TQ	USBLS	5/07
Institution and Cafeteria	Orlando-Kissimmee MSA, FL	Y	16820 FQ	20220 MW	24260 TQ	USBLS	5/07
Institution and Cafeteria	Tampa-St. Petersburg-Clearwater MSA, FL	Y	19420 FQ	22630 MW	27160 TQ	USBLS	5/07
Institution and Cafeteria	West Palm Beach-Boca Raton-Boynton Beach PMSA, FL	Y	20880 FQ	25250 MW	29310 TQ	USBLS	5/07
Institution and Cafeteria	Georgia	Y	13590 FQ	16510 MW	21060 TQ	USBLS	5/07
Institution and Cafeteria	Athens-Clarke County MSA, GA	Y	14800 FQ	18050 MW	21080 TQ	USBLS	5/07
Institution and Cafeteria	Atlanta-Sandy Springs-Marietta MSA, GA	Y	13860 FQ	17260 MW	22150 TQ	USBLS	5/07
Institution and Cafeteria	Hawaii	Y	24740 FQ	30950 MW	35950 TQ	USBLS	5/07
Institution and Cafeteria	Honolulu MSA, HI	Y	23460 FQ	29590 MW	34740 TQ	USBLS	5/07
Institution and Cafeteria	Idaho	Y	17910 FQ	21460 MW	24530 TQ	USBLS	5/07
Institution and Cafeteria	Boise City-Nampa MSA, ID	Y	20590 FQ	22640 MW	24730 TQ	USBLS	5/07
Institution and Cafeteria	Illinois	Y	17860 FQ	21720 MW	26140 TQ	USBLS	5/07
Institution and Cafeteria	Chicago-Naperville-Joliet MSA, IL-IN-WI	Y	19740 FQ	23040 MW	27730 TQ	USBLS	5/07
Institution and Cafeteria	Indiana	Y	17680 FQ	20890 MW	24100 TQ	USBLS	5/07
Institution and Cafeteria	Gary PMSA, IN	Y	17520 FQ	20190 MW	23460 TQ	USBLS	5/07
Institution and Cafeteria	Indianapolis-Carmel MSA, IN	Y	18920 FQ	21960 MW	24880 TQ	USBLS	5/07
Institution and Cafeteria	Iowa	Y	17510 FQ	20550 MW	23910 TQ	USBLS	5/07
Institution and Cafeteria	Des Moines-West Des Moines MSA, IA	Y	19480 FQ	22590 MW	25920 TQ	USBLS	5/07
Institution and Cafeteria	Sioux City MSA, IA-NE-SD	Y	17220 FQ	19220 MW	22420 TQ	USBLS	5/07
Institution and Cafeteria	Kansas	Y	16570 FQ	19100 MW	22790 TQ	USBLS	5/07
Institution and Cafeteria	Lawrence MSA, KS	Y	16760 FQ	19570 MW	24270 TQ	USBLS	5/07
Institution and Cafeteria	Wichita MSA, KS	Y	15960 FQ	19320 MW	23620 TQ	USBLS	5/07
Institution and Cafeteria	Kentucky	Y	17870 FQ	20510 MW	23934 TQ	KYBLS	2008
Institution and Cafeteria	Elizabethtown MSA, KY	Y	17890 FQ	20480 MW	24950 TQ	USBLS	5/07
Institution and Cafeteria	Louisville-Jefferson County MSA, KY-IN	Y	18850 FQ	21610 MW	24310 TQ	USBLS	5/07
Institution and Cafeteria	Louisiana	H	6.28 FQ	7.20 MW	8.65 TQ	LABLS	1/08-3/08
Institution and Cafeteria	Baton Rouge MSA, LA	Y	13000 FQ	15010 MW	17830 TQ	USBLS	5/07
Institution and Cafeteria	Lake Charles MSA, LA	Y	12640 FQ	13840 MW	15060 TQ	USBLS	5/07
Institution and Cafeteria	New Orleans-Metairie-Kenner MSA, LA	Y	13910 FQ	16500 MW	19120 TQ	USBLS	5/07
Institution and Cafeteria	Maine	Y	20070 FQ	23190 MW	27250 TQ	USBLS	5/07

AE	Average entry wage	AW	Average wage paid	FQ	First quartile wage
AER	Average entry range	AWR	Average wage range	H	Hourly
AEX	Average experienced wage	AXR	Average experienced range	HI	Highest wage paid
ATC	Average total compensation	D	Daily	HR	High end range

LO	Lowest wage paid	MTC	Median total compensation	TCC	Total cash compensation
LR	Low end range	MW	Median wage paid	TQ	Third quartile wage
M	Monthly	MWR	Median wage range	W	Weekly
MCC	Median cash compensation	S	See annotated source	Y	Yearly

Occupation/Type/Industry	Location	Per	Low	Mid	High	Source	Date
Cook							
Institution and Cafeteria	Portland-South Portland-Biddeford MSA, ME	Y	21890 FQ	25430 MW	29550 TQ	USBLS	5/07
Institution and Cafeteria	Maryland	Y		25950 MW		MDBLS	3/08
Institution and Cafeteria	Baltimore-Towson MSA, MD	Y	21720 FQ	25440 MW	29760 TQ	USBLS	5/07
Institution and Cafeteria	Bethesda-Gaithersburg-Frederick PMSA, MD	Y	22920 FQ	26420 MW	32530 TQ	USBLS	5/07
Institution and Cafeteria	Massachusetts	Y	24240 FQ	28490 MW	33180 TQ	USBLS	5/07
Institution and Cafeteria	Boston-Cambridge-Quincy NECTA, MA	Y	25370 FQ	29320 MW	34620 TQ	USBLS	5/07
Institution and Cafeteria	Lynn-Peabody-Salem NECTA, MA	Y	27150 FQ	30380 MW	34860 TQ	USBLS	5/07
Institution and Cafeteria	Worcester MSA, MA-CT	Y	22040 FQ	26060 MW	30360 TQ	USBLS	5/07
Institution and Cafeteria	Michigan	Y	20060 FQ	23830 MW	28420 TQ	USBLS	5/07
Institution and Cafeteria	Ann Arbor MSA, MI	Y	22000 FQ	26760 MW	30470 TQ	USBLS	5/07
Institution and Cafeteria	Detroit-Warren-Livonia MSA, MI	Y	21010 FQ	25190 MW	29560 TQ	USBLS	5/07
Institution and Cafeteria	Flint MSA, MI	Y	20010 FQ	22290 MW	24700 TQ	USBLS	5/07
Institution and Cafeteria	Grand Rapids-Wyoming MSA, MI	Y	21710 FQ	25740 MW	29710 TQ	USBLS	5/07
Institution and Cafeteria	Muskegon-Norton Shores MSA, MI	Y	18370 FQ	22130 MW	26420 TQ	USBLS	5/07
Institution and Cafeteria	Warren-Troy-Farmington Hills PMSA, MI	Y	20350 FQ	25020 MW	29560 TQ	USBLS	5/07
Institution and Cafeteria	Minnesota	Y	22239 FQ	26265 MW	31179 TQ	MNBLS	10/08-12/08
Institution and Cafeteria	Duluth-Superior MSA, MN-WI	Y	15568 FQ	19876 MW	24780 TQ	MNBLS	10/08-12/08
Institution and Cafeteria	Minneapolis-Saint Paul MSA, MN-WI	Y	24445 FQ	28554 MW	32695 TQ	MNBLS	10/08-12/08
Institution and Cafeteria	Rochester MSA, MN	Y	22324 FQ	26290 MW	32217 TQ	MNBLS	10/08-12/08
Institution and Cafeteria	Mississippi	Y	13740 FQ	16450 MW	19750 TQ	USBLS	5/07
Institution and Cafeteria	Hattiesburg MSA, MS	Y	14970 FQ	17660 MW	20810 TQ	USBLS	5/07
Institution and Cafeteria	Jackson MSA, MS	Y	13630 FQ	16170 MW	19030 TQ	USBLS	5/07
Institution and Cafeteria	Missouri	Y	15980 FQ	19640 MW	23460 TQ	USBLS	5/07
Institution and Cafeteria	Kansas City MSA, MO-KS	Y	17550 FQ	21220 MW	25050 TQ	USBLS	5/07
Institution and Cafeteria	St. Joseph MSA, MO-KS	Y	15190 FQ	17680 MW	22760 TQ	USBLS	5/07
Institution and Cafeteria	St. Louis MSA, MO-IL	Y	16840 FQ	20630 MW	24500 TQ	USBLS	5/07
Institution and Cafeteria	Montana	Y	16610 FQ	18540 MW	22050 TQ	USBLS	5/07
Institution and Cafeteria	Billings MSA, MT	Y	17370 FQ	20040 MW	23670 TQ	USBLS	5/07
Institution and Cafeteria	Nebraska	Y	16700 FQ	19320 MW	23130 TQ	USBLS	5/07
Institution and Cafeteria	Omaha-Council Bluffs MSA, NE-IA	Y	17030 FQ	20530 MW	25230 TQ	USBLS	5/07
Institution and Cafeteria	Nevada	H	10.34 FQ	12.51 MW	15.35 TQ	NVBLS	5/08
Institution and Cafeteria	Las Vegas-Paradise MSA, NV	H	10.66 FQ	12.73 MW	15.39 TQ	NVBLS	5/08
Institution and Cafeteria	New Hampshire	H	9.97 AE	13.51 MW	15.16 AEX	NHBLS	6/08
Institution and Cafeteria	Manchester MSA, NH	Y	25350 FQ	28650 MW	32470 TQ	USBLS	5/07
Institution and Cafeteria	Nashua NECTA, NH-MA	Y	21390 FQ	26180 MW	30220 TQ	USBLS	5/07
Institution and Cafeteria	New Jersey	Y	23190 FQ	27860 MW	32370 TQ	USBLS	5/07
Institution and Cafeteria	Camden PMSA, NJ	Y	22540 FQ	27260 MW	31000 TQ	USBLS	5/07
Institution and Cafeteria	Edison PMSA, NJ	Y	23870 FQ	29150 MW	34070 TQ	USBLS	5/07
Institution and Cafeteria	Newark-Union PMSA, NJ-PA	Y	22400 FQ	27100 MW	31870 TQ	USBLS	5/07
Institution and Cafeteria	New Mexico	Y	14770 FQ	18310 MW	22840 TQ	USBLS	5/07
Institution and Cafeteria	Albuquerque MSA, NM	Y	15290 FQ	18500 MW	22650 TQ	USBLS	5/07
Institution and Cafeteria	Santa Fe MSA, NM	Y	18210 FQ	21310 MW	23770 TQ	USBLS	5/07
Institution and Cafeteria	New York	Y	21250 FQ	26620 MW	32980 TQ	USBLS	5/07
Institution and Cafeteria	Albany-Schenectady-Troy MSA, NY	Y	21010 FQ	25160 MW	30590 TQ	USBLS	5/07
Institution and Cafeteria	Buffalo-Niagara Falls MSA, NY	Y	17950 FQ	22790 MW	28790 TQ	USBLS	5/07
Institution and Cafeteria	Nassau-Suffolk PMSA, NY	Y	24640 FQ	30450 MW	37640 TQ	USBLS	5/07
Institution and Cafeteria	New York-Northern New Jersey-Long Island MSA, NY-NJ-PA	Y	23560 FQ	28740 MW	34730 TQ	USBLS	5/07
Institution and Cafeteria	North Carolina	Y	16690 FQ	19720 MW	23620 TQ	USBLS	5/07
Institution and Cafeteria	Charlotte-Gastonia-Concord MSA, NC-SC	Y	17440 FQ	20270 MW	23590 TQ	USBLS	5/07
Institution and Cafeteria	Durham MSA, NC	Y	16440 FQ	21960 MW	26920 TQ	USBLS	5/07
Institution and Cafeteria	Greensboro-High Point MSA, NC	Y	17580 FQ	20720 MW	24170 TQ	USBLS	5/07
Institution and Cafeteria	Raleigh-Cary MSA, NC	Y	18310 FQ	21740 MW	25200 TQ	USBLS	5/07
Institution and Cafeteria	North Dakota	Y	18390 FQ	21720 MW	24970 TQ	USBLS	5/07
Institution and Cafeteria	Fargo MSA, ND-MN	Y	20410 FQ	23070 MW	26680 TQ	USBLS	5/07
Institution and Cafeteria	Ohio	Y	20930 FQ	24630 MW	28930 TQ	USBLS	5/07

AE	Average entry wage	AW	Average wage paid	FQ	First quartile wage
AER	Average entry range	AWR	Average wage range	H	Hourly
AEX	Average experienced wage	AXR	Average experienced range	HI	Highest wage paid
ATC	Average total compensation	D	Daily	HR	High end range

LO	Lowest wage paid	MTC	Median total compensation	TCC	Total cash compensation
LR	Low end range	MW	Median wage paid	TQ	Third quartile wage
M	Monthly	MWR	Median wage range	W	Weekly
MCC	Median cash compensation	S	See annotated source	Y	Yearly

Cook

Occupation/Type/Industry	Location	Per	Low	Mid	High	Source	Date
Institution and Cafeteria	Cincinnati-Middletown MSA, OH-KY-IN	Y	21020 FQ	24580 MW	29020 TQ	USBLS	5/07
Institution and Cafeteria	Cleveland-Elyria-Mentor MSA, OH	Y	21330 FQ	25000 MW	29100 TQ	USBLS	5/07
Institution and Cafeteria	Columbus MSA, OH	Y	22170 FQ	26680 MW	31340 TQ	USBLS	5/07
Institution and Cafeteria	Dayton MSA, OH	Y	21120 FQ	24660 MW	29210 TQ	USBLS	5/07
Institution and Cafeteria	Oklahoma	Y	13660 FQ	16350 MW	19470 TQ	USBLS	5/07
Institution and Cafeteria	Oklahoma City MSA, OK	Y	13490 FQ	16090 MW	19680 TQ	USBLS	5/07
Institution and Cafeteria	Tulsa MSA, OK	Y	15260 FQ	17770 MW	20430 TQ	USBLS	5/07
Institution and Cafeteria	Oregon	H	9.63 FQ	11.18 MW	13.24 TQ	ORBLS	5/08
Institution and Cafeteria	Eugene-Springfield MSA, OR	Y	18910 FQ	22210 MW	26280 TQ	USBLS	5/07
Institution and Cafeteria	Portland-Vancouver-Beaverton MSA, OR-WA	Y	20330 FQ	23180 MW	27710 TQ	USBLS	5/07
Institution and Cafeteria	Pennsylvania	Y	18890 FQ	22640 MW	27250 TQ	USBLS	5/07
Institution and Cafeteria	Allentown-Bethlehem-Easton MSA, PA-NJ	Y	20090 FQ	23640 MW	28460 TQ	USBLS	5/07
Institution and Cafeteria	Philadelphia-Camden-Wilmington MSA, PA-NJ-DE-MD	Y	20680 FQ	24650 MW	29520 TQ	USBLS	5/07
Institution and Cafeteria	Pittsburgh MSA, PA	Y	18400 FQ	21790 MW	25640 TQ	USBLS	5/07
Institution and Cafeteria	Rhode Island	Y	25640 FQ	29520 MW	34810 TQ	USBLS	5/07
Institution and Cafeteria	Providence-Fall River-Warwick MSA, RI-MA	Y	25320 FQ	29310 MW	34570 TQ	USBLS	5/07
Institution and Cafeteria	South Carolina	Y	14050 FQ	17120 MW	21210 TQ	USBLS	5/07
Institution and Cafeteria	Charleston-North Charleston MSA, SC	Y	14720 FQ	17500 MW	21260 TQ	USBLS	5/07
Institution and Cafeteria	Columbia MSA, SC	Y	15240 FQ	20260 MW	23400 TQ	USBLS	5/07
Institution and Cafeteria	South Dakota	Y	18810 FQ	21520 MW	24523 TQ	SDBLS	7/08-9/08
Institution and Cafeteria	Sioux Falls MSA, SD	Y	19714 FQ	22849 MW	25947 TQ	SDBLS	7/08-9/08
Institution and Cafeteria	Tennessee	Y	14640 FQ	17370 MW	20280 TQ	USBLS	5/07
Institution and Cafeteria	Memphis MSA, TN-MS-AR	Y	13740 FQ	17180 MW	22700 TQ	USBLS	5/07
Institution and Cafeteria	Nashville-Davidson-Murfreesboro MSA, TN	Y	16290 FQ	18750 MW	22840 TQ	USBLS	5/07
Institution and Cafeteria	Texas	Y	14860 FQ	18290 MW	22360 TQ	USBLS	5/07
Institution and Cafeteria	Austin-Round Rock MSA, TX	Y	18630 FQ	21630 MW	24840 TQ	USBLS	5/07
Institution and Cafeteria	Brownsville-Harlingen MSA, TX	Y	15170 FQ	17700 MW	21600 TQ	USBLS	5/07
Institution and Cafeteria	Dallas-Fort Worth-Arlington MSA, TX	Y	14750 FQ	18720 MW	23370 TQ	USBLS	5/07
Institution and Cafeteria	El Paso MSA, TX	Y	14930 FQ	19370 MW	22900 TQ	USBLS	5/07
Institution and Cafeteria	Houston-Sugar Land-Baytown MSA, TX	Y	17150 FQ	20330 MW	24150 TQ	USBLS	5/07
Institution and Cafeteria	San Antonio MSA, TX	Y	15260 FQ	18920 MW	22560 TQ	USBLS	5/07
Institution and Cafeteria	Utah	Y	17720 FQ	20830 MW	24720 TQ	USBLS	5/07
Institution and Cafeteria	Salt Lake City MSA, UT	Y	18010 FQ	21680 MW	25350 TQ	USBLS	5/07
Institution and Cafeteria	Vermont	Y	21040 FQ	24430 MW	29040 TQ	USBLS	5/07
Institution and Cafeteria	Burlington-South Burlington MSA, VT	Y	22110 FQ	25740 MW	30500 TQ	USBLS	5/07
Institution and Cafeteria	Virginia	Y	17630 FQ	21860 MW	26500 TQ	USBLS	5/07
Institution and Cafeteria	Richmond MSA, VA	Y	17880 FQ	21650 MW	25610 TQ	USBLS	5/07
Institution and Cafeteria	Virginia Beach-Norfolk-Newport News MSA, VA-NC	Y	19410 FQ	22970 MW	28710 TQ	USBLS	5/07
Institution and Cafeteria	Washington	H	10.86 FQ	13.02 MW	15.44 TQ	WABLS	3/08
Institution and Cafeteria	Seattle-Tacoma-Bellevue MSA, WA	Y	23800 FQ	28220 MW	32800 TQ	USBLS	5/07
Institution and Cafeteria	West Virginia	Y	15920 FQ	18708 MW	22073 TQ	WVBLS	7/08-9/08
Institution and Cafeteria	Charleston MSA, WV	Y	16340 FQ	18740 MW	21550 TQ	USBLS	5/07
Institution and Cafeteria	Wheeling MSA, WV-OH	Y	15880 FQ	19120 MW	23070 TQ	USBLS	5/07
Institution and Cafeteria	Wisconsin	Y	20610 FQ	23580 MW	27370 TQ	USBLS	5/07
Institution and Cafeteria	Milwaukee-Waukesha-West Allis MSA, WI	Y	21000 FQ	24210 MW	28570 TQ	USBLS	5/07
Institution and Cafeteria	Wyoming	Y	17534 FQ	21619 MW	25983 TQ	WYBLS	9/08
Institution and Cafeteria	Cheyenne MSA, WY	Y	20239 FQ	23152 MW	25958 TQ	WYBLS	9/08
Institution and Cafeteria	Puerto Rico	Y	12570 FQ	13970 MW	15530 TQ	USBLS	5/07
Institution and Cafeteria	Guayama MSA, PR	Y	12220 FQ	13440 MW	14660 TQ	USBLS	5/07
Institution and Cafeteria	San Juan-Caguas-Guaynabo MSA, PR	Y	12610 FQ	14070 MW	15790 TQ	USBLS	5/07
Institution and Cafeteria	Virgin Islands	Y	18260 FQ	21640 MW	25180 TQ	USBLS	5/07
Private Household	California	H	11.63 FQ	21.87 MW	26.65 TQ	CABLS	1/08-3/08
Restaurant	Alabama	Y	14890 FQ	18460 MW	22490 TQ	USBLS	5/07
Restaurant	Birmingham-Hoover MSA, AL	Y	14150 FQ	17840 MW	22370 TQ	USBLS	5/07

AE	Average entry wage	AW	Average wage paid	FQ	First quartile wage	LO	Lowest wage paid	MTC Median total compensation	TCC Total cash compensation
AER	Average entry range	AWR	Average wage range	H	Hourly	LR	Low end range	MW Median wage paid	TQ Third quartile wage
AEX	Average experienced wage	AXR	Average experienced range	HI	Highest wage paid	M	Monthly	MWR Median wage range	W Weekly
ATC	Average total compensation	D	Daily	HR	High end range	MCC Median cash compensation	S See annotated source	Y Yearly

Occupation/Type/Industry	Location	Per	Low	Mid	High	Source	Date
Cook							
Restaurant	Alaska	Y	21550 FQ	24410 MW	29390 TQ	USBLS	5/07
Restaurant	Anchorage MSA, AK	Y	21890 FQ	24520 MW	29120 TQ	USBLS	5/07
Restaurant	Arizona	Y	17680 FQ	20590 MW	24150 TQ	USBLS	5/07
Restaurant	Phoenix-Mesa-Scottsdale MSA, AZ	Y	18110 FQ	21400 MW	24890 TQ	USBLS	5/07
Restaurant	Tucson MSA, AZ	Y	17230 FQ	19520 MW	22610 TQ	USBLS	5/07
Restaurant	Arkansas	Y	15630 FQ	17780 MW	20640 TQ	USBLS	5/07
Restaurant	Jonesboro MSA, AR	Y	16000 FQ	18190 MW	21570 TQ	USBLS	5/07
Restaurant	Little Rock-North Little Rock MSA, AR	Y	16780 FQ	18530 MW	21760 TQ	USBLS	5/07
Restaurant	California	H	9.91 FQ	11.28 MW	12.94 TQ	CABLS	1/08-3/08
Restaurant	Fresno MSA, CA	H	9.09 FQ	10.55 MW	11.86 TQ	CABLS	1/08-3/08
Restaurant	Los Angeles-Long Beach-Glendale PMSA, CA	H	9.66 FQ	11.01 MW	12.50 TQ	CABLS	1/08-3/08
Restaurant	Oakland-Fremont-Hayward MSA, CA	H	10.54 FQ	12.08 MW	14.03 TQ	CABLS	1/08-3/08
Restaurant	Riverside-San Bernardino-Ontario MSA, CA	H	9.83 FQ	11.19 MW	12.70 TQ	CABLS	1/08-3/08
Restaurant	Sacramento-Arden Arcade-Roseville MSA, CA	H	10.23 FQ	11.62 MW	13.27 TQ	CABLS	1/08-3/08
Restaurant	San Diego-Carlsbad-San Marcos MSA, CA	H	10.04 FQ	11.17 MW	12.50 TQ	CABLS	1/08-3/08
Restaurant	San Francisco-San Mateo-Redwood PMSA, CA	H	10.76 FQ	12.67 MW	15.14 TQ	CABLS	1/08-3/08
Restaurant	San Jose-Sunnyvale-Santa Clara MSA, CA	H	10.13 FQ	11.34 MW	12.81 TQ	CABLS	1/08-3/08
Restaurant	Santa Ana-Anaheim-Irvine PMSA, CA	Y	20230 FQ	22850 MW	26000 TQ	USBLS	5/07
Restaurant	Colorado	Y	18960 FQ	22000 MW	25440 TQ	USBLS	5/07
Restaurant	Denver-Aurora MSA, CO	Y	19260 FQ	21970 MW	24890 TQ	USBLS	5/07
Restaurant	Pueblo MSA, CO	Y	16990 FQ	19860 MW	22610 TQ	USBLS	5/07
Restaurant	Connecticut	H	10.07 AE	12.96 MW		CTBLS	1/08-3/08
Restaurant	Bridgeport-Stamford-Norwalk MSA, CT	Y	25170 FQ	29780 MW	35950 TQ	USBLS	5/07
Restaurant	Hartford-West Hartford-East Hartford MSA, CT	Y	20570 FQ	23800 MW	29230 TQ	USBLS	5/07
Restaurant	Norwich-New London MSA, CT-RI	Y	21810 FQ	25540 MW	29400 TQ	USBLS	5/07
Restaurant	Delaware	Y	20290 FQ	23440 MW	27380 TQ	USBLS	5/07
Restaurant	Wilmington PMSA, DE-MD-NJ	Y	20390 FQ	23420 MW	27520 TQ	USBLS	5/07
Restaurant	District of Columbia	Y	23170 FQ	28290 MW	33970 TQ	USBLS	5/07
Restaurant	Washington-Arlington-Alexandria MSA, DC-VA-MD-WV	Y	20070 FQ	24470 MW	29470 TQ	USBLS	5/07
Restaurant	Florida	Y	18850 FQ	22180 MW	25900 TQ	USBLS	5/07
Restaurant	Cape Coral-Fort Myers MSA, FL	Y	19280 FQ	22080 MW	25650 TQ	USBLS	5/07
Restaurant	Fort Lauderdale-Pompano Beach-Deerfield Beach PMSA, FL	Y	19500 FQ	22850 MW	26730 TQ	USBLS	5/07
Restaurant	Jacksonville MSA, FL	Y	18620 FQ	21200 MW	24030 TQ	USBLS	5/07
Restaurant	Lakeland MSA, FL	Y	17220 FQ	19950 MW	23160 TQ	USBLS	5/07
Restaurant	Miami-Fort Lauderdale-Miami Beach MSA, FL	Y	19610 FQ	23140 MW	27530 TQ	USBLS	5/07
Restaurant	Orlando-Kissimmee MSA, FL	Y	19050 FQ	22410 MW	26420 TQ	USBLS	5/07
Restaurant	Sarasota-Bradenton-Venice MSA, FL	Y	20290 FQ	23780 MW	27960 TQ	USBLS	5/07
Restaurant	Tampa-St. Petersburg-Clearwater MSA, FL	Y	18370 FQ	21490 MW	24750 TQ	USBLS	5/07
Restaurant	West Palm Beach-Boca Raton-Boynton Beach PMSA, FL	Y	20990 FQ	24780 MW	28970 TQ	USBLS	5/07
Restaurant	Georgia	Y	17370 FQ	20580 MW	24000 TQ	USBLS	5/07
Restaurant	Atlanta-Sandy Springs-Marietta MSA, GA	Y	18810 FQ	21800 MW	25100 TQ	USBLS	5/07
Restaurant	Hawaii	Y	20470 FQ	25440 MW	33260 TQ	USBLS	5/07
Restaurant	Honolulu MSA, HI	Y	20470 FQ	24220 MW	30340 TQ	USBLS	5/07
Restaurant	Idaho	Y	16440 FQ	19710 MW	24120 TQ	USBLS	5/07
Restaurant	Boise City-Nampa MSA, ID	Y	16830 FQ	20590 MW	24060 TQ	USBLS	5/07
Restaurant	Illinois	Y	15010 FQ	18550 MW	22970 TQ	USBLS	5/07

AE	Average entry wage	AW	Average wage paid	FQ	First quartile wage	LO	Lowest wage paid	MTC	Median total compensation	TCC	Total cash compensation
AER	Average entry range	AWR	Average wage range	H	Hourly	LR	Low end range	MW	Median wage paid	TQ	Third quartile wage
AEX	Average experienced wage	AXR	Average experienced range	HI	Highest wage paid	M	Monthly	MWR	Median wage range	W	Weekly
ATC	Average total compensation	D	Daily	HR	High end range	MCC	Median cash compensation	S	See annotated source	Y	Yearly

Occupation/Type/Industry	Location	Per	Low	Mid	High	Source	Date
Cook							
Restaurant	Chicago-Naperville-Joliet MSA, IL-IN-WI	Y	14920 FQ	18390 MW	23360 TQ	USBLS	5/07
Restaurant	Rockford MSA, IL	Y	14910 FQ	17160 MW	21530 TQ	USBLS	5/07
Restaurant	Indiana	Y	16940 FQ	19960 MW	23770 TQ	USBLS	5/07
Restaurant	Fort Wayne MSA, IN	Y	16910 FQ	19180 MW	22650 TQ	USBLS	5/07
Restaurant	Gary PMSA, IN	Y	16340 FQ	19340 MW	23420 TQ	USBLS	5/07
Restaurant	Indianapolis-Carmel MSA, IN	Y	18950 FQ	22190 MW	25560 TQ	USBLS	5/07
Restaurant	Iowa	Y	15430 FQ	18250 MW	21690 TQ	USBLS	5/07
Restaurant	Cedar Rapids MSA, IA	Y	16530 FQ	19050 MW	22570 TQ	USBLS	5/07
Restaurant	Des Moines-West Des Moines MSA, IA	Y	17380 FQ	20450 MW	24150 TQ	USBLS	5/07
Restaurant	Iowa City MSA, IA	Y	16900 FQ	19000 MW	21300 TQ	USBLS	5/07
Restaurant	Sioux City MSA, IA-NE-SD	Y	16900 FQ	19360 MW	22280 TQ	USBLS	5/07
Restaurant	Kansas	Y	15610 FQ	18770 MW	22960 TQ	USBLS	5/07
Restaurant	Wichita MSA, KS	Y	16290 FQ	18780 MW	22230 TQ	USBLS	5/07
Restaurant	Kentucky	Y	15995 FQ	18986 MW	22804 TQ	KYBLS	2008
Restaurant	Louisville-Jefferson County MSA, KY-IN	Y	17060 FQ	20000 MW	23170 TQ	USBLS	5/07
Restaurant	Louisiana	H	7.50 FQ	9.07 MW	11.03 TQ	LABLS	1/08-3/08
Restaurant	Baton Rouge MSA, LA	Y	16600 FQ	19360 MW	22860 TQ	USBLS	5/07
Restaurant	New Orleans-Metairie-Kenner MSA, LA	Y	16290 FQ	19750 MW	23930 TQ	USBLS	5/07
Restaurant	Maine	Y	18470 FQ	22460 MW	26750 TQ	USBLS	5/07
Restaurant	Portland-South Portland-Biddeford MSA, ME	Y	20930 FQ	23840 MW	27610 TQ	USBLS	5/07
Restaurant	Maryland	Y		24525 MW		MDBLS	3/08
Restaurant	Baltimore-Towson MSA, MD	Y	20300 FQ	24430 MW	28480 TQ	USBLS	5/07
Restaurant	Bethesda-Gaithersburg-Frederick PMSA, MD	Y	22020 FQ	25140 MW	29430 TQ	USBLS	5/07
Restaurant	Hagerstown-Martinsburg MSA, MD-WV	Y	18340 FQ	22290 MW	26690 TQ	USBLS	5/07
Restaurant	Massachusetts	Y	21430 FQ	25740 MW	30500 TQ	USBLS	5/07
Restaurant	Boston-Cambridge-Quincy NECTA, MA	Y	22280 FQ	26630 MW	31200 TQ	USBLS	5/07
Restaurant	Worcester MSA, MA-CT	Y	19810 FQ	23990 MW	28610 TQ	USBLS	5/07
Restaurant	Michigan	Y	17100 FQ	20520 MW	24720 TQ	USBLS	5/07
Restaurant	Detroit-Warren-Livonia MSA, MI	Y	19060 FQ	22930 MW	27380 TQ	USBLS	5/07
Restaurant	Grand Rapids-Wyoming MSA, MI	Y	16770 FQ	19370 MW	23070 TQ	USBLS	5/07
Restaurant	Warren-Troy-Farmington Hills PMSA, MI	Y	18740 FQ	23220 MW	28100 TQ	USBLS	5/07
Restaurant	Minnesota	Y	18977 FQ	22626 MW	26108 TQ	MNBLS	10/08-12/08
Restaurant	Duluth-Superior MSA, MN-WI	Y	16258 FQ	19217 MW	23159 TQ	MNBLS	10/08-12/08
Restaurant	Minneapolis-Saint Paul MSA, MN-WI	Y	20807 FQ	23692 MW	27080 TQ	MNBLS	10/08-12/08
Restaurant	Rochester MSA, MN	Y	19143 FQ	23056 MW	26689 TQ	MNBLS	10/08-12/08
Restaurant	Mississippi	Y	14520 FQ	17330 MW	20160 TQ	USBLS	5/07
Restaurant	Gulfport-Biloxi MSA, MS	Y	16230 FQ	19760 MW	23030 TQ	USBLS	5/07
Restaurant	Jackson MSA, MS	Y	15770 FQ	17510 MW	19440 TQ	USBLS	5/07
Restaurant	Missouri	Y	15970 FQ	19430 MW	23630 TQ	USBLS	5/07
Restaurant	Jefferson City MSA, MO	Y	15070 FQ	16970 MW	20100 TQ	USBLS	5/07
Restaurant	Kansas City MSA, MO-KS	Y	17520 FQ	20910 MW	24640 TQ	USBLS	5/07
Restaurant	St. Louis MSA, MO-IL	Y	17490 FQ	21210 MW	25170 TQ	USBLS	5/07
Restaurant	Montana	Y	15420 FQ	18120 MW	21720 TQ	USBLS	5/07
Restaurant	Billings MSA, MT	Y	14830 FQ	18100 MW	22710 TQ	USBLS	5/07
Restaurant	Nebraska	Y	16500 FQ	18980 MW	22690 TQ	USBLS	5/07
Restaurant	Omaha-Council Bluffs MSA, NE-IA	Y	17200 FQ	19670 MW	23300 TQ	USBLS	5/07
Restaurant	Nevada	H	10.68 FQ	12.92 MW	15.92 TQ	NVBLS	5/08
Restaurant	Las Vegas-Paradise MSA, NV	H	11.05 FQ	13.75 MW	16.57 TQ	NVBLS	5/08
Restaurant	New Hampshire	H	9.42 AE	11.81 MW	13.38 AEX	NHBLS	6/08
Restaurant	Manchester MSA, NH	Y	20990 FQ	23560 MW	27630 TQ	USBLS	5/07
Restaurant	Nashua NECTA, NH-MA	Y	19360 FQ	22960 MW	27500 TQ	USBLS	5/07
Restaurant	New Jersey	Y	19620 FQ	23810 MW	28750 TQ	USBLS	5/07
Restaurant	Camden PMSA, NJ	Y	17040 FQ	23360 MW	28250 TQ	USBLS	5/07
Restaurant	Edison PMSA, NJ	Y	20160 FQ	23940 MW	28710 TQ	USBLS	5/07
Restaurant	Newark-Union PMSA, NJ-PA	Y	19870 FQ	23980 MW	28890 TQ	USBLS	5/07
Restaurant	New Mexico	Y	15670 FQ	19100 MW	22960 TQ	USBLS	5/07
Restaurant	Albuquerque MSA, NM	Y	16710 FQ	20010 MW	23700 TQ	USBLS	5/07
Restaurant	Santa Fe MSA, NM	Y	19740 FQ	22390 MW	25310 TQ	USBLS	5/07

AE Average entry wage	**AW** Average wage paid	**FQ** First quartile wage	**LO** Lowest wage paid	**MTC** Median total compensation	**TCC** Total cash compensation
AER Average entry range	**AWR** Average wage range	**H** Hourly	**LR** Low end range	**MW** Median wage paid	**TQ** Third quartile wage
AEX Average experienced wage	**AXR** Average experienced range	**HI** Highest wage paid	**M** Monthly	**MWR** Median wage range	**W** Weekly
ATC Average total compensation	**D** Daily	**HR** High end range	**MCC** Median cash compensation	**S** See annotated source	**Y** Yearly

Cook

Occupation/Type/Industry	Location	Per	Low	Mid	High	Source	Date
Restaurant	New York	Y	20550 FQ	24590 MW	30740 TQ	USBLS	5/07
Restaurant	Albany-Schenectady-Troy MSA, NY	Y	20270 FQ	24060 MW	28170 TQ	USBLS	5/07
Restaurant	Buffalo-Niagara Falls MSA, NY	Y	18680 FQ	21520 MW	23970 TQ	USBLS	5/07
Restaurant	Nassau-Suffolk PMSA, NY	Y	22110 FQ	26720 MW	31810 TQ	USBLS	5/07
Restaurant	New York-Northern New Jersey-Long Island MSA, NY-NJ-PA	Y	21380 FQ	25870 MW	31720 TQ	USBLS	5/07
Restaurant	North Carolina	Y	16190 FQ	19740 MW	23590 TQ	USBLS	5/07
Restaurant	Charlotte-Gastonia-Concord MSA, NC-SC	Y	18410 FQ	21620 MW	24320 TQ	USBLS	5/07
Restaurant	Raleigh-Cary MSA, NC	Y	17820 FQ	21350 MW	25220 TQ	USBLS	5/07
Restaurant	Winston-Salem MSA, NC	Y	16170 FQ	20140 MW	24690 TQ	USBLS	5/07
Restaurant	North Dakota	Y	16290 FQ	18890 MW	21940 TQ	USBLS	5/07
Restaurant	Fargo MSA, ND-MN	Y	17980 FQ	20490 MW	23160 TQ	USBLS	5/07
Restaurant	Ohio	Y	17100 FQ	20130 MW	23730 TQ	USBLS	5/07
Restaurant	Cincinnati-Middletown MSA, OH-KY-IN	Y	17940 FQ	21360 MW	24850 TQ	USBLS	5/07
Restaurant	Cleveland-Elyria-Mentor MSA, OH	Y	18520 FQ	21500 MW	24450 TQ	USBLS	5/07
Restaurant	Columbus MSA, OH	Y	18270 FQ	21040 MW	24080 TQ	USBLS	5/07
Restaurant	Dayton MSA, OH	Y	15980 FQ	18680 MW	22560 TQ	USBLS	5/07
Restaurant	Oklahoma	Y	14810 FQ	17670 MW	20700 TQ	USBLS	5/07
Restaurant	Oklahoma City MSA, OK	Y	15100 FQ	18160 MW	21730 TQ	USBLS	5/07
Restaurant	Tulsa MSA, OK	Y	16250 FQ	18860 MW	22070 TQ	USBLS	5/07
Restaurant	Oregon	H	9.48 FQ	10.76 MW	12.06 TQ	ORBLS	5/08
Restaurant	Portland-Vancouver-Beaverton MSA, OR-WA	Y	20000 FQ	22240 MW	24640 TQ	USBLS	5/07
Restaurant	Pennsylvania	Y	17870 FQ	22160 MW	27460 TQ	USBLS	5/07
Restaurant	Allentown-Bethlehem-Easton MSA, PA-NJ	Y	19540 FQ	24070 MW	31690 TQ	USBLS	5/07
Restaurant	Philadelphia-Camden-Wilmington MSA, PA-NJ-DE-MD	Y	20680 FQ	25240 MW	30410 TQ	USBLS	5/07
Restaurant	Pittsburgh MSA, PA	Y	17910 FQ	21530 MW	25290 TQ	USBLS	5/07
Restaurant	Reading MSA, PA	Y	20540 FQ	24060 MW	28310 TQ	USBLS	5/07
Restaurant	Rhode Island	Y	20540 FQ	23900 MW	28400 TQ	USBLS	5/07
Restaurant	Providence-Fall River-Warwick MSA, RI-MA	Y	20650 FQ	24080 MW	28730 TQ	USBLS	5/07
Restaurant	South Carolina	Y	16720 FQ	19830 MW	24040 TQ	USBLS	5/07
Restaurant	Charleston-North Charleston MSA, SC	Y	17580 FQ	21230 MW	25180 TQ	USBLS	5/07
Restaurant	Columbia MSA, SC	Y	18100 FQ	21560 MW	25300 TQ	USBLS	5/07
Restaurant	South Dakota	Y	18555 FQ	21064 MW	23971 TQ	SDBLS	7/08-9/08
Restaurant	Sioux Falls MSA, SD	Y	19273 FQ	21973 MW	24404 TQ	SDBLS	7/08-9/08
Restaurant	Tennessee	Y	16760 FQ	19560 MW	23320 TQ	USBLS	5/07
Restaurant	Memphis MSA, TN-MS-AR	Y	16770 FQ	20570 MW	24210 TQ	USBLS	5/07
Restaurant	Nashville-Davidson-Murfreesboro MSA, TN	Y	17180 FQ	20200 MW	23930 TQ	USBLS	5/07
Restaurant	Texas	Y	15920 FQ	18540 MW	22470 TQ	USBLS	5/07
Restaurant	Austin-Round Rock MSA, TX	Y	16420 FQ	18450 MW	22570 TQ	USBLS	5/07
Restaurant	Corpus Christi MSA, TX	Y	14780 FQ	17280 MW	19460 TQ	USBLS	5/07
Restaurant	Dallas-Fort Worth-Arlington MSA, TX	Y	17100 FQ	20080 MW	24250 TQ	USBLS	5/07
Restaurant	El Paso MSA, TX	Y	13380 FQ	15650 MW	18980 TQ	USBLS	5/07
Restaurant	Houston-Sugar Land-Baytown MSA, TX	Y	16130 FQ	18540 MW	22020 TQ	USBLS	5/07
Restaurant	San Antonio MSA, TX	Y	16620 FQ	19800 MW	23310 TQ	USBLS	5/07
Restaurant	Utah	Y	17810 FQ	21170 MW	24540 TQ	USBLS	5/07
Restaurant	Logan MSA, UT-ID	Y	17740 FQ	19630 MW	23210 TQ	USBLS	5/07
Restaurant	Salt Lake City MSA, UT	Y	18450 FQ	21770 MW	24710 TQ	USBLS	5/07
Restaurant	Vermont	Y	20980 FQ	24570 MW	28940 TQ	USBLS	5/07
Restaurant	Burlington-South Burlington MSA, VT	Y	21280 FQ	24170 MW	28200 TQ	USBLS	5/07
Restaurant	Virginia	Y	17660 FQ	20810 MW	25160 TQ	USBLS	5/07
Restaurant	Richmond MSA, VA	Y	17720 FQ	20780 MW	24730 TQ	USBLS	5/07
Restaurant	Virginia Beach-Norfolk-Newport News MSA, VA-NC	Y	17730 FQ	20680 MW	23760 TQ	USBLS	5/07
Restaurant	Washington	H	9.55 FQ	11.27 MW	13.37 TQ	WABLS	3/08

AE	Average entry wage	AW	Average wage paid	FQ	First quartile wage	LO	Lowest wage paid	MTC	Median total compensation	TCC	Total cash compensation
AER	Average entry range	AWR	Average wage range	H	Hourly	LR	Low end range	MW	Median wage paid	TQ	Third quartile wage
AEX	Average experienced wage	AXR	Average experienced range	HI	Highest wage paid	M	Monthly	MWR	Median wage range	W	Weekly
ATC	Average total compensation	D	Daily	HR	High end range	MCC	Median cash compensation	S	See annotated source	Y	Yearly

Occupation/Type/Industry	Location	Per	Low	Mid	High	Source	Date
Cook							
Restaurant	Seattle-Tacoma-Bellevue MSA, WA	Y	19680 FQ	23830 MW	28350 TQ	USBLS	5/07
Restaurant	West Virginia	Y	15155 FQ	17724 MW	20962 TQ	WVBLS	7/08-9/08
Restaurant	Charleston MSA, WV	Y	15190 FQ	17680 MW	20290 TQ	USBLS	5/07
Restaurant	Parkersburg-Marietta-Vienna MSA, WV-OH	Y	14720 FQ	16710 MW	20190 TQ	USBLS	5/07
Restaurant	Wisconsin	Y	17570 FQ	20540 MW	23790 TQ	USBLS	5/07
Restaurant	Milwaukee-Waukesha-West Allis MSA, WI	Y	18470 FQ	21440 MW	24480 TQ	USBLS	5/07
Restaurant	Wyoming	Y	17456 FQ	20463 MW	25244 TQ	WYBLS	9/08
Restaurant	Cheyenne MSA, WY	Y	18904 FQ	22176 MW	25162 TQ	WYBLS	9/08
Restaurant	Puerto Rico	Y	13090 FQ	15040 MW	18050 TQ	USBLS	5/07
Restaurant	San Juan-Caguas-Guaynabo MSA, PR	Y	13250 FQ	15440 MW	18530 TQ	USBLS	5/07
Restaurant	Virgin Islands	Y	21490 FQ	24230 MW	27870 TQ	USBLS	5/07
Restaurant	Guam	Y	13640 FQ	15970 MW	18850 TQ	USBLS	5/07
Short Order	Alabama	Y	13130 FQ	14980 MW	17970 TQ	USBLS	5/07
Short Order	Birmingham-Hoover MSA, AL	Y	13290 FQ	15450 MW	18520 TQ	USBLS	5/07
Short Order	Montgomery MSA, AL	Y	12680 FQ	13890 MW	15460 TQ	USBLS	5/07
Short Order	Alaska	Y	21120 FQ	25250 MW	31000 TQ	USBLS	5/07
Short Order	Anchorage MSA, AK	Y	20910 FQ	25630 MW	31490 TQ	USBLS	5/07
Short Order	Fairbanks MSA, AK	Y	20960 FQ	23030 MW	26390 TQ	USBLS	5/07
Short Order	Arizona	Y	15770 FQ	18510 MW	23560 TQ	USBLS	5/07
Short Order	Phoenix-Mesa-Scottsdale MSA, AZ	Y	16670 FQ	19360 MW	26180 TQ	USBLS	5/07
Short Order	Prescott MSA, AZ	Y	17540 FQ	20030 MW	25580 TQ	USBLS	5/07
Short Order	Tucson MSA, AZ	Y	14880 FQ	16220 MW	20390 TQ	USBLS	5/07
Short Order	Arkansas	Y	15170 FQ	17310 MW	20050 TQ	USBLS	5/07
Short Order	Fayetteville-Springdale-Rogers MSA, AR-MO	Y	14550 FQ	15790 MW	18650 TQ	USBLS	5/07
Short Order	Little Rock-North Little Rock MSA, AR	Y	15290 FQ	18070 MW	21510 TQ	USBLS	5/07
Short Order	California	H	9.39 FQ	10.82 MW	12.41 TQ	CABLS	1/08-3/08
Short Order	Bakersfield MSA, CA	H	8.88 FQ	9.80 MW	11.21 TQ	CABLS	1/08-3/08
Short Order	Los Angeles-Long Beach-Glendale PMSA, CA	H	9.52 FQ	11.01 MW	12.70 TQ	CABLS	1/08-3/08
Short Order	Modesto MSA, CA	H	8.40 FQ	9.15 MW	10.07 TQ	CABLS	1/08-3/08
Short Order	Oakland-Fremont-Hayward MSA, CA	H	10.08 FQ	11.33 MW	13.02 TQ	CABLS	1/08-3/08
Short Order	Oxnard-Thousand Oaks-Ventura MSA, CA	H	8.88 FQ	10.22 MW	11.58 TQ	CABLS	1/08-3/08
Short Order	Riverside-San Bernardino-Ontario MSA, CA	H	9.07 FQ	10.13 MW	11.44 TQ	CABLS	1/08-3/08
Short Order	Sacramento-Arden Arcade-Roseville MSA, CA	H	9.25 FQ	10.65 MW	12.44 TQ	CABLS	1/08-3/08
Short Order	San Diego-Carlsbad-San Marcos MSA, CA	H	9.49 FQ	10.91 MW	12.50 TQ	CABLS	1/08-3/08
Short Order	San Francisco-San Mateo-Redwood PMSA, CA	H	10.65 FQ	12.32 MW	14.33 TQ	CABLS	1/08-3/08
Short Order	San Jose-Sunnyvale-Santa Clara MSA, CA	H	10.26 FQ	11.82 MW	13.50 TQ	CABLS	1/08-3/08
Short Order	Santa Ana-Anaheim-Irvine PMSA, CA	Y	18960 FQ	21930 MW	24940 TQ	USBLS	5/07
Short Order	Colorado	Y	17840 FQ	21190 MW	24580 TQ	USBLS	5/07
Short Order	Denver-Aurora MSA, CO	Y	18860 FQ	21870 MW	25290 TQ	USBLS	5/07
Short Order	Connecticut	H	8.85 AE	10.95 MW		CTBLS	1/08-3/08
Short Order	Bridgeport-Stamford-Norwalk MSA, CT	Y	17730 FQ	20580 MW	25010 TQ	USBLS	5/07
Short Order	Hartford-West Hartford-East Hartford MSA, CT	Y	20870 FQ	23250 MW	27710 TQ	USBLS	5/07
Short Order	Delaware	Y	16370 FQ	19700 MW	23860 TQ	USBLS	5/07
Short Order	Wilmington PMSA, DE-MD-NJ	Y	15350 FQ	18350 MW	22350 TQ	USBLS	5/07
Short Order	District of Columbia	Y	22250 FQ	25220 MW	28090 TQ	USBLS	5/07
Short Order	Washington-Arlington-Alexandria MSA, DC-VA-MD-WV	Y	17480 FQ	20840 MW	23920 TQ	USBLS	5/07
Short Order	Florida	Y	15740 FQ	18400 MW	22040 TQ	USBLS	5/07
Short Order	Fort Lauderdale-Pompano Beach-Deerfield Beach PMSA, FL	Y	17560 FQ	20530 MW	22970 TQ	USBLS	5/07

AE	Average entry wage	AW	Average wage paid	FQ	First quartile wage	LO	Lowest wage paid	MTC	Median total compensation	TCC	Total cash compensation
AER	Average entry range	AWR	Average wage range	H	Hourly	LR	Low end range	MW	Median wage paid	TQ	Third quartile wage
AEX	Average experienced wage	AXR	Average experienced range	HI	Highest wage paid	M	Monthly	MWR	Median wage range	W	Weekly
ATC	Average total compensation	D	Daily	HR	High end range	MCC	Median cash compensation	S	See annotated source	Y	Yearly

Occupation/Type/Industry	Location	Per	Low	Mid	High	Source	Date
Cook							
Short Order	Jacksonville MSA, FL	Y	14890 FQ	16760 MW	19980 TQ	USBLS	5/07
Short Order	Miami-Fort Lauderdale-Miami Beach MSA, FL	Y	16910 FQ	20330 MW	23620 TQ	USBLS	5/07
Short Order	Orlando-Kissimmee MSA, FL	Y	16660 FQ	19500 MW	23050 TQ	USBLS	5/07
Short Order	Pensacola-Ferry Pass-Brent MSA, FL	Y	14670 FQ	15930 MW	17990 TQ	USBLS	5/07
Short Order	Tallahassee MSA, FL	Y	14910 FQ	16740 MW	19590 TQ	USBLS	5/07
Short Order	Tampa-St. Petersburg-Clearwater MSA, FL	Y	16670 FQ	18900 MW	22800 TQ	USBLS	5/07
Short Order	West Palm Beach-Boca Raton-Boynton Beach PMSA, FL	Y	19340 FQ	21560 MW	24080 TQ	USBLS	5/07
Short Order	Georgia	Y	14580 FQ	17100 MW	20800 TQ	USBLS	5/07
Short Order	Atlanta-Sandy Springs-Marietta MSA, GA	Y	15380 FQ	17800 MW	22020 TQ	USBLS	5/07
Short Order	Hawaii	Y	17860 FQ	21800 MW	26140 TQ	USBLS	5/07
Short Order	Honolulu MSA, HI	Y	16600 FQ	19360 MW	23340 TQ	USBLS	5/07
Short Order	Idaho	Y	13560 FQ	15950 MW	19550 TQ	USBLS	5/07
Short Order	Boise City-Nampa MSA, ID	Y	17690 FQ	21620 MW	23680 TQ	USBLS	5/07
Short Order	Illinois	Y	15910 FQ	18590 MW	22480 TQ	USBLS	5/07
Short Order	Chicago-Naperville-Joliet MSA, IL-IN-WI	Y	16560 FQ	19370 MW	23180 TQ	USBLS	5/07
Short Order	Indiana	Y	14550 FQ	17470 MW	20450 TQ	USBLS	5/07
Short Order	Gary PMSA, IN	Y	15750 FQ	18420 MW	21440 TQ	USBLS	5/07
Short Order	Indianapolis-Carmel MSA, IN	Y	15230 FQ	18070 MW	22480 TQ	USBLS	5/07
Short Order	Iowa	Y	14360 FQ	16050 MW	19230 TQ	USBLS	5/07
Short Order	Des Moines-West Des Moines MSA, IA	Y	14960 FQ	17440 MW	20480 TQ	USBLS	5/07
Short Order	Waterloo-Cedar Falls MSA, IA	Y	13620 FQ	14330 MW	15390 TQ	USBLS	5/07
Short Order	Kansas	Y	13560 FQ	16260 MW	19660 TQ	USBLS	5/07
Short Order	Wichita MSA, KS	Y	14050 FQ	17160 MW	21960 TQ	USBLS	5/07
Short Order	Kentucky	Y	13470 FQ	15603 MW	18450 TQ	KYBLS	2008
Short Order	Louisville-Jefferson County MSA, KY-IN	Y	13140 FQ	15420 MW	18690 TQ	USBLS	5/07
Short Order	Louisiana	H	6.49 FQ	7.55 MW	8.71 TQ	LABLS	1/08-3/08
Short Order	Baton Rouge MSA, LA	Y	13110 FQ	15240 MW	18090 TQ	USBLS	5/07
Short Order	New Orleans-Metairie-Kenner MSA, LA	Y	13790 FQ	16160 MW	18720 TQ	USBLS	5/07
Short Order	Maine	Y	16160 FQ	18810 MW	22330 TQ	USBLS	5/07
Short Order	Portland-South Portland-Biddeford MSA, ME	Y	16930 FQ	20110 MW	23510 TQ	USBLS	5/07
Short Order	Maryland	Y		18475 MW		MDBLS	3/08
Short Order	Baltimore-Towson MSA, MD	Y	15270 FQ	18530 MW	23530 TQ	USBLS	5/07
Short Order	Bethesda-Gaithersburg-Frederick PMSA, MD	Y	17390 FQ	20870 MW	26270 TQ	USBLS	5/07
Short Order	Massachusetts	Y	19780 FQ	22860 MW	26980 TQ	USBLS	5/07
Short Order	Boston-Cambridge-Quincy NECTA, MA	Y	20230 FQ	23330 MW	27620 TQ	USBLS	5/07
Short Order	Worcester MSA, MA-CT	Y	19000 FQ	22390 MW	25920 TQ	USBLS	5/07
Short Order	Michigan	Y	16050 FQ	18360 MW	21990 TQ	USBLS	5/07
Short Order	Detroit-Warren-Livonia MSA, MI	Y	16170 FQ	18960 MW	23340 TQ	USBLS	5/07
Short Order	Grand Rapids-Wyoming MSA, MI	Y	16300 FQ	17960 MW	19820 TQ	USBLS	5/07
Short Order	Lansing-East Lansing MSA, MI	Y	15490 FQ	16300 MW	18990 TQ	USBLS	5/07
Short Order	Warren-Troy-Farmington Hills PMSA, MI	Y	16240 FQ	19220 MW	23700 TQ	USBLS	5/07
Short Order	Minnesota	Y	17283 FQ	20137 MW	24142 TQ	MNBLS	10/08-12/08
Short Order	Duluth-Superior MSA, MN-WI	Y	15338 FQ	17388 MW	20796 TQ	MNBLS	10/08-12/08
Short Order	Minneapolis-Saint Paul MSA, MN-WI	Y	18747 FQ	22396 MW	25982 TQ	MNBLS	10/08-12/08
Short Order	Rochester MSA, MN	Y	18283 FQ	20382 MW	24606 TQ	MNBLS	10/08-12/08
Short Order	Mississippi	Y	13160 FQ	15110 MW	17280 TQ	USBLS	5/07
Short Order	Jackson MSA, MS	Y	12670 FQ	14210 MW	15780 TQ	USBLS	5/07
Short Order	Missouri	Y	15280 FQ	17990 MW	21320 TQ	USBLS	5/07
Short Order	Kansas City MSA, MO-KS	Y	15470 FQ	18440 MW	22040 TQ	USBLS	5/07
Short Order	St. Louis MSA, MO-IL	Y	17170 FQ	19970 MW	23160 TQ	USBLS	5/07
Short Order	Montana	Y	14430 FQ	17250 MW	24550 TQ	USBLS	5/07
Short Order	Billings MSA, MT	Y	18210 FQ	27530 MW	30990 TQ	USBLS	5/07
Short Order	Nebraska	Y	15310 FQ	18200 MW	21940 TQ	USBLS	5/07
Short Order	Omaha-Council Bluffs MSA, NE-IA	Y	17410 FQ	20920 MW	23870 TQ	USBLS	5/07

AE Average entry wage	**AW** Average wage paid	**FQ** First quartile wage	**LO** Lowest wage paid	**MTC** Median total compensation	**TCC** Total cash compensation
AER Average entry range	**AWR** Average wage range	**H** Hourly	**LR** Low end range	**MW** Median wage paid	**TQ** Third quartile wage
AEX Average experienced wage	**AXR** Average experienced range	**HI** Highest wage paid	**M** Monthly	**MWR** Median wage range	**W** Weekly
ATC Average total compensation	**D** Daily	**HR** High end range	**MCC** Median cash compensation	**S** See annotated source	**Y** Yearly

Occupation/Type/Industry	Location	Per	Low	Mid	High	Source	Date
Cook							
Short Order	Nevada	H	10.15 FQ	11.55 MW	15.14 TQ	NVBLS	5/08
Short Order	Las Vegas-Paradise MSA, NV	H	10.30 FQ	11.70 MW	16.04 TQ	NVBLS	5/08
Short Order	New Hampshire	H	8.00 AE	9.86 MW	10.83 AEX	NHBLS	6/08
Short Order	Manchester MSA, NH	Y	14750 FQ	17980 MW	22250 TQ	USBLS	5/07
Short Order	Nashua NECTA, NH-MA	Y	16600 FQ	19630 MW	22660 TQ	USBLS	5/07
Short Order	New Jersey	Y	17180 FQ	21640 MW	25090 TQ	USBLS	5/07
Short Order	Camden PMSA, NJ	Y	16580 FQ	22410 MW	28200 TQ	USBLS	5/07
Short Order	Edison PMSA, NJ	Y	19940 FQ	22990 MW	26680 TQ	USBLS	5/07
Short Order	Newark-Union PMSA, NJ-PA	Y	16210 FQ	20510 MW	23520 TQ	USBLS	5/07
Short Order	New Mexico	Y	16290 FQ	18680 MW	21980 TQ	USBLS	5/07
Short Order	Albuquerque MSA, NM	Y	16590 FQ	18890 MW	22040 TQ	USBLS	5/07
Short Order	Las Cruces MSA, NM	Y	15030 FQ	17620 MW	20830 TQ	USBLS	5/07
Short Order	New York	Y	17280 FQ	20700 MW	24380 TQ	USBLS	5/07
Short Order	Albany-Schenectady-Troy MSA, NY	Y	16250 FQ	18360 MW	21340 TQ	USBLS	5/07
Short Order	Buffalo-Niagara Falls MSA, NY	Y	17110 FQ	19510 MW	22930 TQ	USBLS	5/07
Short Order	Kingston MSA, NY	Y	18480 FQ	21040 MW	23510 TQ	USBLS	5/07
Short Order	Nassau-Suffolk PMSA, NY	Y	19290 FQ	21580 MW	23830 TQ	USBLS	5/07
Short Order	New York-Northern New Jersey-Long Island MSA, NY-NJ-PA	Y	18400 FQ	21920 MW	25390 TQ	USBLS	5/07
Short Order	North Carolina	Y	14500 FQ	16570 MW	19520 TQ	USBLS	5/07
Short Order	Charlotte-Gastonia-Concord MSA, NC-SC	Y	15760 FQ	19090 MW	22610 TQ	USBLS	5/07
Short Order	Raleigh-Cary MSA, NC	Y	13990 FQ	15360 MW	18870 TQ	USBLS	5/07
Short Order	North Dakota	Y	14550 FQ	17670 MW	20480 TQ	USBLS	5/07
Short Order	Fargo MSA, ND-MN	Y	14120 FQ	17690 MW	21190 TQ	USBLS	5/07
Short Order	Ohio	Y	15640 FQ	17990 MW	21120 TQ	USBLS	5/07
Short Order	Cincinnati-Middletown MSA, OH-KY-IN	Y	15550 FQ	17530 MW	20170 TQ	USBLS	5/07
Short Order	Cleveland-Elyria-Mentor MSA, OH	Y	15720 FQ	19090 MW	21820 TQ	USBLS	5/07
Short Order	Columbus MSA, OH	Y	16560 FQ	18650 MW	22190 TQ	USBLS	5/07
Short Order	Dayton MSA, OH	Y	16540 FQ	18950 MW	22430 TQ	USBLS	5/07
Short Order	Oklahoma	Y	13270 FQ	15350 MW	18050 TQ	USBLS	5/07
Short Order	Oklahoma City MSA, OK	Y	14000 FQ	16480 MW	18760 TQ	USBLS	5/07
Short Order	Tulsa MSA, OK	Y	12910 FQ	14510 MW	17200 TQ	USBLS	5/07
Short Order	Oregon	H	8.84 FQ	9.71 MW	11.31 TQ	ORBLS	5/08
Short Order	Portland-Vancouver-Beaverton MSA, OR-WA	Y	17900 FQ	19750 MW	23210 TQ	USBLS	5/07
Short Order	Pennsylvania	Y	15610 FQ	18490 MW	22320 TQ	USBLS	5/07
Short Order	Allentown-Bethlehem-Easton MSA, PA-NJ	Y	16000 FQ	18410 MW	22880 TQ	USBLS	5/07
Short Order	Philadelphia-Camden-Wilmington MSA, PA-NJ-DE-MD	Y	17080 FQ	20350 MW	24580 TQ	USBLS	5/07
Short Order	Pittsburgh MSA, PA	Y	14770 FQ	17430 MW	20930 TQ	USBLS	5/07
Short Order	Rhode Island	Y	18000 FQ	21070 MW	24000 TQ	USBLS	5/07
Short Order	Providence-Fall River-Warwick MSA, RI-MA	Y	18090 FQ	21230 MW	24430 TQ	USBLS	5/07
Short Order	South Carolina	Y	14300 FQ	16590 MW	18890 TQ	USBLS	5/07
Short Order	Charleston-North Charleston MSA, SC	Y	15570 FQ	17980 MW	21130 TQ	USBLS	5/07
Short Order	Columbia MSA, SC	Y	13800 FQ	15970 MW	18350 TQ	USBLS	5/07
Short Order	South Dakota	Y	16754 FQ	19057 MW	21401 TQ	SDBLS	7/08-9/08
Short Order	Sioux Falls MSA, SD	Y	18295 FQ	20449 MW	22809 TQ	SDBLS	7/08-9/08
Short Order	Tennessee	Y	13640 FQ	16260 MW	18970 TQ	USBLS	5/07
Short Order	Memphis MSA, TN-MS-AR	Y	14920 FQ	17580 MW	19740 TQ	USBLS	5/07
Short Order	Nashville-Davidson-Murfreesboro MSA, TN	Y	13680 FQ	16210 MW	19800 TQ	USBLS	5/07
Short Order	Texas	Y	13810 FQ	16580 MW	20020 TQ	USBLS	5/07
Short Order	Austin-Round Rock MSA, TX	Y	14330 FQ	17410 MW	19960 TQ	USBLS	5/07
Short Order	Dallas-Fort Worth-Arlington MSA, TX	Y	17070 FQ	19490 MW	22860 TQ	USBLS	5/07
Short Order	El Paso MSA, TX	Y	12760 FQ	14060 MW	15860 TQ	USBLS	5/07
Short Order	Houston-Sugar Land-Baytown MSA, TX	Y	14340 FQ	17130 MW	20920 TQ	USBLS	5/07
Short Order	San Antonio MSA, TX	Y	13030 FQ	14570 MW	19720 TQ	USBLS	5/07
Short Order	Utah	Y	17770 FQ	20640 MW	23260 TQ	USBLS	5/07
Short Order	Salt Lake City MSA, UT	Y	18680 FQ	20830 MW	23230 TQ	USBLS	5/07

AE	Average entry wage	AW	Average wage paid	FQ	First quartile wage
AER	Average entry range	AWR	Average wage range	H	Hourly
AEX	Average experienced wage	AXR	Average experienced range	HI	Highest wage paid
ATC	Average total compensation	D	Daily	HR	High end range

LO Lowest wage paid   MTC Median total compensation   TCC Total cash compensation
LR Low end range   MW Median wage paid   TQ Third quartile wage
M Monthly   MWR Median wage range   W Weekly
MCC Median cash compensation   S See annotated source   Y Yearly

Occupation/Type/Industry	Location	Per	Low	Mid	High	Source	Date
Cook							
Short Order	Vermont	Y	17600 FQ	20810 MW	24340 TQ	USBLS	5/07
Short Order	Burlington-South Burlington MSA, VT	Y	17680 FQ	20880 MW	24640 TQ	USBLS	5/07
Short Order	Virginia	Y	16310 FQ	18950 MW	22480 TQ	USBLS	5/07
Short Order	Richmond MSA, VA	Y	14840 FQ	17740 MW	20990 TQ	USBLS	5/07
Short Order	Virginia Beach-Norfolk-Newport News MSA, VA-NC	Y	14920 FQ	17380 MW	20830 TQ	USBLS	5/07
Short Order	Washington	H	9.17 FQ	10.48 MW	12.13 TQ	WABLS	3/08
Short Order	Bremerton-Silverdale MSA, WA	Y	19010 FQ	21080 MW	23800 TQ	USBLS	5/07
Short Order	Seattle-Tacoma-Bellevue MSA, WA	Y	19710 FQ	22670 MW	26230 TQ	USBLS	5/07
Short Order	West Virginia	Y	15466 FQ	17978 MW	20842 TQ	WVBLS	7/08-9/08
Short Order	Charleston MSA, WV	Y	14480 FQ	17200 MW	21350 TQ	USBLS	5/07
Short Order	Wisconsin	Y	16150 FQ	18510 MW	21830 TQ	USBLS	5/07
Short Order	Milwaukee-Waukesha-West Allis MSA, WI	Y	17340 FQ	19440 MW	23350 TQ	USBLS	5/07
Short Order	Wyoming	Y	15097 FQ	18066 MW	20427 TQ	WYBLS	9/08
Short Order	Puerto Rico	Y	12770 FQ	14370 MW	16170 TQ	USBLS	5/07
Short Order	San Juan-Caguas-Guaynabo MSA, PR	Y	12880 FQ	14550 MW	16420 TQ	USBLS	5/07
Short Order	Virgin Islands	Y	17280 FQ	19270 MW	21330 TQ	USBLS	5/07
Short Order	Guam	Y	12710 FQ	14340 MW	16010 TQ	USBLS	5/07
Cooling and Freezing Equipment Operator and Tender	Alabama	Y	22030 FQ	31210 MW	35880 TQ	USBLS	5/07
	Alaska	Y	19560 FQ	23730 MW	31220 TQ	USBLS	5/07
	Arizona	Y	21160 FQ	24100 MW	28790 TQ	USBLS	5/07
	Arkansas	Y	19750 FQ	21900 MW	23970 TQ	USBLS	5/07
	California	H	10.41 FQ	13.69 MW	18.47 TQ	CABLS	1/08-3/08
	Colorado	Y	21930 FQ	26950 MW	35240 TQ	USBLS	5/07
	Connecticut	H	10.18 AE	10.74 MW		CTBLS	1/08-3/08
	Florida	Y	20060 FQ	22450 MW	25240 TQ	USBLS	5/07
	Georgia	Y	20860 FQ	23250 MW	27540 TQ	USBLS	5/07
	Idaho	Y	21770 FQ	25440 MW	29070 TQ	USBLS	5/07
	Illinois	Y	24760 FQ	29160 MW	35050 TQ	USBLS	5/07
	Indiana	Y	18990 FQ	25160 MW	32800 TQ	USBLS	5/07
	Iowa	Y	24530 FQ	33190 MW	36930 TQ	USBLS	5/07
	Kansas	Y	21400 FQ	23940 MW	26670 TQ	USBLS	5/07
	Kentucky	Y	17971 FQ	23006 MW	40216 TQ	KYBLS	2008
	Louisiana	H	12.77 FQ	14.50 MW	18.07 TQ	LABLS	1/08-3/08
	Maryland	Y		25825 MW		MDBLS	3/08
	Massachusetts	Y	20870 FQ	29450 MW	37670 TQ	USBLS	5/07
	Michigan	Y	19850 FQ	28900 MW	36220 TQ	USBLS	5/07
	Minnesota	Y	25720 FQ	29410 MW	35392 TQ	MNBLS	10/08-12/08
	Mississippi	Y	19350 FQ	21400 MW	23330 TQ	USBLS	5/07
	Missouri	Y	20350 FQ	25700 MW	33980 TQ	USBLS	5/07
	Nebraska	Y	26530 FQ	31650 MW	34650 TQ	USBLS	5/07
	Nevada	H	8.50 FQ	9.46 MW	10.94 TQ	NVBLS	5/08
	New Jersey	Y	17850 FQ	22290 MW	35230 TQ	USBLS	5/07
	New York	Y	19060 FQ	23230 MW	28630 TQ	USBLS	5/07
	North Carolina	Y	20970 FQ	23460 MW	28740 TQ	USBLS	5/07
	Ohio	Y	23670 FQ	28520 MW	35590 TQ	USBLS	5/07
	Oklahoma	Y	18680 FQ	21200 MW	25030 TQ	USBLS	5/07
	Oregon	H	9.21 FQ	11.40 MW	17.12 TQ	ORBLS	5/08
	Pennsylvania	Y	23480 FQ	28080 MW	36700 TQ	USBLS	5/07
	South Carolina	Y	21550 FQ	27430 MW	31270 TQ	USBLS	5/07
	South Dakota	Y	25008 FQ	26609 MW	28523 TQ	SDBLS	7/08-9/08
	Tennessee	Y	20660 FQ	24170 MW	30480 TQ	USBLS	5/07
	Texas	Y	17060 FQ	19660 MW	23120 TQ	USBLS	5/07
	Utah	Y	18730 FQ	21690 MW	25240 TQ	USBLS	5/07
	Vermont	Y	20010 FQ	23550 MW	29120 TQ	USBLS	5/07
	Virginia	Y	19570 FQ	21700 MW	23620 TQ	USBLS	5/07
	Washington	H	10.85 FQ	12.76 MW	17.11 TQ	WABLS	3/08
	Wisconsin	Y	17420 FQ	19060 MW	26540 TQ	USBLS	5/07
	Puerto Rico	Y	12240 FQ	13210 MW	14180 TQ	USBLS	5/07
Coordinator of Instruction Public Schools, Region 9	New York	Y		90269 AW		SAANYS	9/11/08

AE Average entry wage	**AW** Average wage paid	**FQ** First quartile wage	**LO** Lowest wage paid	**MTC** Median total compensation	**TCC** Total cash compensation
AER Average entry range	**AWR** Average wage range	**H** Hourly	**LR** Low end range	**MW** Median wage paid	**TQ** Third quartile wage
AEX Average experienced wage	**AXR** Average experienced range	**HI** Highest wage paid	**M** Monthly	**MWR** Median wage range	**W** Weekly
ATC Average total compensation	**D** Daily	**HR** High end range	**MCC** Median cash compensation	**S** See annotated source	**Y** Yearly

Occupation/Type/Industry	Location	Per	Low	Mid	High	Source	Date
Coordinator of Pupil Services							
Public Schools, Region 9	New York	Y		74487 AW		SAANYS	9/11/08
Copy Editor							
Small Organization	United States	Y	43032 FQ	49700 MW	56368 TQ	ALA04	2008
Copywriter	United States	Y	48000 FQ	60000 MW	75000 TQ	AIGA01	2008
Coroner	Bibb County, GA	Y			60551 HI	GACTY02	2008
	Dougherty County, GA	Y			125 HI	GACTY02	2008
Corporate Board Member							
Commercial Bank	United States	Y		37200 AW		PHBJ	2008
Energy Company	United States	Y		384000 AW		PHBJ	2008
Corporate Executive Chef	United States	Y		115000 AW		CLEAD	2008
Corporate Sales and Marketing Executive	United States	Y		242250 MCC		MANDP	2008
Correctional Officer and Jailer	Alabama	Y	25550 FQ	30330 MW	40730 TQ	USBLS	5/07
	Birmingham-Hoover MSA, AL	Y	25990 FQ	30240 MW	39260 TQ	USBLS	5/07
	Alaska	Y	41070 FQ	47520 MW	55650 TQ	USBLS	5/07
	Arizona	Y	33270 FQ	36320 MW	39420 TQ	USBLS	5/07
	Phoenix-Mesa-Scottsdale MSA, AZ	Y	33150 FQ	36280 MW	39430 TQ	USBLS	5/07
	Arkansas	Y	24490 FQ	28410 MW	31850 TQ	USBLS	5/07
	California	H	25.35 FQ	32.46 MW	36.83 TQ	CABLS	1/08-3/08
	Riverside-San Bernardino-Ontario MSA, CA	H	27.35 FQ	32.95 MW	37.01 TQ	CABLS	1/08-3/08
	Sacramento-Arden Arcade-Roseville MSA, CA	H	23.25 FQ	30.95 MW	36.68 TQ	CABLS	1/08-3/08
	San Diego-Carlsbad-San Marcos MSA, CA	H	22.88 FQ	27.12 MW	33.18 TQ	CABLS	1/08-3/08
	San Francisco-San Mateo-Redwood PMSA, CA	H	29.51 FQ	34.62 MW	37.95 TQ	CABLS	1/08-3/08
	Santa Ana-Anaheim-Irvine PMSA, CA	Y	43910 FQ	51370 MW	61090 TQ	USBLS	5/07
	Colorado	Y	35730 FQ	41950 MW	51550 TQ	USBLS	5/07
	Denver-Aurora MSA, CO	Y	38110 FQ	46300 MW	55610 TQ	USBLS	5/07
	Connecticut	H	19.82 AE	22.30 MW		CTBLS	1/08-3/08
	Delaware	Y	35830 FQ	40250 MW	46350 TQ	USBLS	5/07
	Washington-Arlington-Alexandria MSA, DC-VA-MD-WV	Y	40440 FQ	49230 MW	60340 TQ	USBLS	5/07
	Florida	Y	31970 FQ	36540 MW	41830 TQ	USBLS	5/07
	Jacksonville MSA, FL	Y	31860 FQ	36650 MW	41500 TQ	USBLS	5/07
	Miami-Fort Lauderdale-Miami Beach MSA, FL	Y	34470 FQ	42940 MW	56550 TQ	USBLS	5/07
	Orlando-Kissimmee MSA, FL	Y	31430 FQ	36090 MW	42300 TQ	USBLS	5/07
	Tampa-St. Petersburg-Clearwater MSA, FL	Y	34950 FQ	42310 MW	50720 TQ	USBLS	5/07
	Georgia	Y	26060 FQ	28750 MW	31490 TQ	USBLS	5/07
	Atlanta-Sandy Springs-Marietta MSA, GA	Y	27440 FQ	30510 MW	35200 TQ	USBLS	5/07
	Hawaii	Y	36340 FQ	40250 MW	46480 TQ	USBLS	5/07
	Honolulu MSA, HI	Y	36120 FQ	39830 MW	45890 TQ	USBLS	5/07
	Idaho	Y	26730 FQ	31280 MW	37770 TQ	USBLS	5/07
	Illinois	Y	42330 FQ	46180 MW	50050 TQ	USBLS	5/07
	Chicago-Naperville-Joliet MSA, IL-IN-WI	Y	39320 FQ	45730 MW	51010 TQ	USBLS	5/07
	Indiana	Y	25910 FQ	28740 MW	31680 TQ	USBLS	5/07
	Gary PMSA, IN	Y	25920 FQ	28340 MW	30790 TQ	USBLS	5/07
	Indianapolis-Carmel MSA, IN	Y	26060 FQ	28980 MW	32060 TQ	USBLS	5/07
	Iowa	Y	34040 FQ	41360 MW	47330 TQ	USBLS	5/07
	Kansas	Y	27380 FQ	31340 MW	37830 TQ	USBLS	5/07
	Topeka MSA, KS	Y	26840 FQ	29950 MW	34050 TQ	USBLS	5/07
	Wichita MSA, KS	Y	27610 FQ	30170 MW	33540 TQ	USBLS	5/07
	Kentucky	Y	23149 FQ	27969 MW	34789 TQ	KYBLS	2008
	Louisville-Jefferson County MSA, KY-IN	Y	23560 FQ	27340 MW	32120 TQ	USBLS	5/07
	Louisiana	H	10.30 FQ	12.30 MW	16.15 TQ	LABLS	1/08-3/08
	Baton Rouge MSA, LA	Y	22450 FQ	26140 MW	32660 TQ	USBLS	5/07

AE	Average entry wage	AW	Average wage paid	FQ	First quartile wage
AER	Average entry range	AWR	Average wage range	H	Hourly
AEX	Average experienced wage	AXR	Average experienced range	HI	Highest wage paid
ATC	Average total compensation	D	Daily	HR	High end range

LO	Lowest wage paid	MTC	Median total compensation
LR	Low end range	MW	Median wage paid
M	Monthly	MWR	Median wage range
MCC	Median cash compensation	S	See annotated source

TCC	Total cash compensation
TQ	Third quartile wage
W	Weekly
Y	Yearly

Occupation/Type/Industry	Location	Per	Low	Mid	High	Source	Date
Correctional Officer and Jailer	New Orleans-Metairie-Kenner MSA, LA	Y	20220 FQ	22930 MW	28100 TQ	USBLS	5/07
	Shreveport-Bossier City MSA, LA	Y	24890 FQ	34270 MW	39350 TQ	USBLS	5/07
	Maine	Y	27830 FQ	31330 MW	36150 TQ	USBLS	5/07
	Portland-South Portland-Biddeford MSA, ME	Y	30220 FQ	34830 MW	38550 TQ	USBLS	5/07
	Maryland	Y		42200 MW		MDBLS	3/08
	Baltimore-Towson MSA, MD	Y	36070 FQ	40330 MW	47600 TQ	USBLS	5/07
	Massachusetts	Y	46580 FQ	55570 MW	61240 TQ	USBLS	5/07
	Michigan	Y	41280 FQ	45060 MW	48880 TQ	USBLS	5/07
	Detroit-Warren-Livonia MSA, MI	Y	37070 FQ	44070 MW	48360 TQ	USBLS	5/07
	Warren-Troy-Farmington Hills PMSA, MI	Y	37610 FQ	43960 MW	48400 TQ	USBLS	5/07
	Minnesota	Y	36020 FQ	41394 MW	49131 TQ	MNBLS	10/08-12/08
	Duluth-Superior MSA, MN-WI	Y	39700 FQ	46141 MW	52091 TQ	MNBLS	10/08-12/08
	Minneapolis-Saint Paul MSA, MN-WI	Y	38101 FQ	43255 MW	50616 TQ	MNBLS	10/08-12/08
	Mississippi	Y	21110 FQ	23640 MW	27680 TQ	USBLS	5/07
	Jackson MSA, MS	Y	20890 FQ	23190 MW	25510 TQ	USBLS	5/07
	Missouri	Y	26450 FQ	28840 MW	31220 TQ	USBLS	5/07
	Kansas City MSA, MO-KS	Y	28100 FQ	31390 MW	37570 TQ	USBLS	5/07
	St. Louis MSA, MO-IL	Y	29360 FQ	34450 MW	44580 TQ	USBLS	5/07
	Montana	Y	24870 FQ	29110 MW	34250 TQ	USBLS	5/07
	Nebraska	Y	27410 FQ	30390 MW	35440 TQ	USBLS	5/07
	Omaha-Council Bluffs MSA, NE-IA	Y	28970 FQ	33870 MW	41040 TQ	USBLS	5/07
	Nevada	H	21.15 FQ	24.56 MW	30.37 TQ	NVBLS	5/08
	Las Vegas-Paradise MSA, NV	H	21.74 FQ	26.59 MW	32.85 TQ	NVBLS	5/08
	New Hampshire	H	15.24 AE	18.31 MW	20.15 AEX	NHBLS	6/08
	New Jersey	Y	49900 FQ	63610 MW	74410 TQ	USBLS	5/07
	Camden PMSA, NJ	Y	50930 FQ	61020 MW	73060 TQ	USBLS	5/07
	Edison PMSA, NJ	Y	55450 FQ	67990 MW	76440 TQ	USBLS	5/07
	Newark-Union PMSA, NJ-PA	Y	43940 FQ	62200 MW	73140 TQ	USBLS	5/07
	New Mexico	Y	25750 FQ	28550 MW	31330 TQ	USBLS	5/07
	Albuquerque MSA, NM	Y	26880 FQ	29240 MW	31600 TQ	USBLS	5/07
	New York	Y	44440 FQ	54040 MW	60810 TQ	USBLS	5/07
	Albany-Schenectady-Troy MSA, NY	Y	32090 FQ	42940 MW	51310 TQ	USBLS	5/07
	Buffalo-Niagara Falls MSA, NY	Y	47700 FQ	54730 MW	60470 TQ	USBLS	5/07
	New York-Northern New Jersey-Long Island MSA, NY-NJ-PA	Y	47210 FQ	58330 MW	65810 TQ	USBLS	5/07
	North Carolina	Y	27570 FQ	29970 MW	32310 TQ	USBLS	5/07
	Charlotte-Gastonia-Concord MSA, NC-SC	Y	28910 FQ	31520 MW	34700 TQ	USBLS	5/07
	Durham MSA, NC	Y	27460 FQ	30370 MW	34740 TQ	USBLS	5/07
	North Dakota	Y	27010 FQ	31150 MW	36330 TQ	USBLS	5/07
	Fargo MSA, ND-MN	Y	31870 FQ	36480 MW	44020 TQ	USBLS	5/07
	Ohio	Y	33750 FQ	37940 MW	43460 TQ	USBLS	5/07
	Cincinnati-Middletown MSA, OH-KY-IN	Y	29150 FQ	34240 MW	40800 TQ	USBLS	5/07
	Cleveland-Elyria-Mentor MSA, OH	Y	33310 FQ	37020 MW	40700 TQ	USBLS	5/07
	Oklahoma	Y	21280 FQ	25050 MW	31030 TQ	USBLS	5/07
	Oklahoma City MSA, OK	Y	24110 FQ	29300 MW	37260 TQ	USBLS	5/07
	Tulsa MSA, OK	Y	20570 FQ	27280 MW	31040 TQ	USBLS	5/07
	Oregon	H	18.36 FQ	21.80 MW	25.24 TQ	ORBLS	5/08
	Portland-Vancouver-Beaverton MSA, OR-WA	Y	39770 FQ	50090 MW	57180 TQ	USBLS	5/07
	Pennsylvania	Y	33810 FQ	39960 MW	50960 TQ	USBLS	5/07
	Allentown-Bethlehem-Easton MSA, PA-NJ	Y	30490 FQ	37610 MW	48720 TQ	USBLS	5/07
	Philadelphia-Camden-Wilmington MSA, PA-NJ-DE-MD	Y	37010 FQ	44530 MW	59830 TQ	USBLS	5/07
	Pittsburgh MSA, PA	Y	34540 FQ	42620 MW	54790 TQ	USBLS	5/07
	South Carolina	Y	25870 FQ	29150 MW	32570 TQ	USBLS	5/07
	Columbia MSA, SC	Y	24850 FQ	28200 MW	31370 TQ	USBLS	5/07
	South Dakota	Y	27349 FQ	30746 MW	34183 TQ	SDBLS	7/08-9/08

AE	Average entry wage	AW	Average wage paid	FQ	First quartile wage	LO	Lowest wage paid	MTC	Median total compensation	TCC	Total cash compensation
AER	Average entry range	AWR	Average wage range	H	Hourly	LR	Low end range	MW	Median wage paid	TQ	Third quartile wage
AEX	Average experienced wage	AXR	Average experienced range	HI	Highest wage paid	M	Monthly	MWR	Median wage range	W	Weekly
ATC	Average total compensation	D	Daily	HR	High end range	MCC	Median cash compensation	S	See annotated source	Y	Yearly

Occupation/Type/Industry	Location	Per	Low	Mid	High	Source	Date
Correctional Officer and Jailer	Tennessee	Y	23050 FQ	27700 MW	33400 TQ	USBLS	5/07
	Memphis MSA, TN-MS-AR	Y	31430 FQ	35020 MW	39610 TQ	USBLS	5/07
	Nashville-Davidson-Murfreesboro MSA, TN	Y	23330 FQ	27400 MW	31980 TQ	USBLS	5/07
	Texas	Y	25480 FQ	28560 MW	31540 TQ	USBLS	5/07
	Austin-Round Rock MSA, TX	Y	21700 FQ	24070 MW	30520 TQ	USBLS	5/07
	Dallas-Fort Worth-Arlington MSA, TX	Y	26910 FQ	30440 MW	35820 TQ	USBLS	5/07
	Houston-Sugar Land-Baytown MSA, TX	Y	25820 FQ	28770 MW	31660 TQ	USBLS	5/07
	San Antonio MSA, TX	Y	27300 FQ	31250 MW	36560 TQ	USBLS	5/07
	Utah	Y	30560 FQ	36100 MW	41270 TQ	USBLS	5/07
	Virginia	Y	30180 FQ	35070 MW	40190 TQ	USBLS	5/07
	Lynchburg MSA, VA	Y	27690 FQ	30070 MW	32450 TQ	USBLS	5/07
	Richmond MSA, VA	Y	30230 FQ	34740 MW	39580 TQ	USBLS	5/07
	Virginia Beach-Norfolk-Newport News MSA, VA-NC	Y	31860 FQ	36250 MW	40440 TQ	USBLS	5/07
	Washington	H	17.53 FQ	19.46 MW	23.27 TQ	WABLS	3/08
	Seattle-Tacoma-Bellevue MSA, WA	Y	37300 FQ	43390 MW	54430 TQ	USBLS	5/07
	West Virginia	Y	23566 FQ	26119 MW	35905 TQ	WVBLS	7/08-9/08
	Milwaukee-Waukesha-West Allis MSA, WI	Y	36970 FQ	42730 MW	53250 TQ	USBLS	5/07
	Wyoming	Y	31367 FQ	36826 MW	41936 TQ	WYBLS	9/08
	Puerto Rico	Y	21370 FQ	23020 MW	24670 TQ	USBLS	5/07
	San Juan-Caguas-Guaynabo MSA, PR	Y	21340 FQ	22950 MW	24570 TQ	USBLS	5/07
Correctional Printing Machine Coordinator	Ohio	H	16.78 LO		19.88 HI	ODAS	2008
Corrections Classification Specialist							
State Government	Ohio	H	17.58 LO		21.67 HI	ODAS	2008
Corrections Psychologist	Vermont	Y	42994 LO		67267 HI	AFT02	3/1/08
Corrections Specialist	Ohio	H	23.04 LO		30.13 HI	ODAS	2008
Correspondence Clerk	Alabama	Y	23120 FQ	27440 MW	35520 TQ	USBLS	5/07
	Birmingham-Hoover MSA, AL	Y	23420 FQ	29780 MW	39130 TQ	USBLS	5/07
	Arizona	Y	25210 FQ	27930 MW	31340 TQ	USBLS	5/07
	Phoenix-Mesa-Scottsdale MSA, AZ	Y	24570 FQ	27320 MW	29750 TQ	USBLS	5/07
	Arkansas	Y	20840 FQ	24440 MW	32750 TQ	USBLS	5/07
	California	H	12.69 FQ	16.40 MW	20.10 TQ	CABLS	1/08-3/08
	Los Angeles-Long Beach-Glendale PMSA, CA	H	16.06 FQ	19.09 MW	24.09 TQ	CABLS	1/08-3/08
	Oakland-Fremont-Hayward MSA, CA	H	15.53 FQ	18.11 MW	24.25 TQ	CABLS	1/08-3/08
	Riverside-San Bernardino-Ontario MSA, CA	H	9.21 FQ	12.03 MW	18.25 TQ	CABLS	1/08-3/08
	Sacramento-Arden Arcade-Roseville MSA, CA	H	10.38 FQ	11.78 MW	16.29 TQ	CABLS	1/08-3/08
	San Diego-Carlsbad-San Marcos MSA, CA	H	13.57 FQ	16.20 MW	19.26 TQ	CABLS	1/08-3/08
	San Francisco-San Mateo-Redwood PMSA, CA	H	13.90 FQ	18.53 MW	21.81 TQ	CABLS	1/08-3/08
	San Jose-Sunnyvale-Santa Clara MSA, CA	H	13.23 FQ	18.04 MW	19.85 TQ	CABLS	1/08-3/08
	Santa Ana-Anaheim-Irvine PMSA, CA	Y	25940 FQ	33700 MW	43580 TQ	USBLS	5/07
	Colorado	Y	24430 FQ	30410 MW	38490 TQ	USBLS	5/07
	Denver-Aurora MSA, CO	Y	29380 FQ	35720 MW	42920 TQ	USBLS	5/07
	Connecticut	H	12.33 AE	15.96 MW		CTBLS	1/08-3/08
	Hartford-West Hartford-East Hartford MSA, CT	Y	28340 FQ	33420 MW	39810 TQ	USBLS	5/07
	Delaware	Y	28160 FQ	32940 MW	37850 TQ	USBLS	5/07
	Wilmington PMSA, DE-MD-NJ	Y	28050 FQ	32850 MW	37860 TQ	USBLS	5/07
	District of Columbia	Y	37720 FQ	44980 MW	49950 TQ	USBLS	5/07

AE	Average entry wage	**AW**	Average wage paid	**FQ**	First quartile wage
AER	Average entry range	**AWR**	Average wage range	**H**	Hourly
AEX	Average experienced wage	**AXR**	Average experienced range	**HI**	Highest wage paid
ATC	Average total compensation	**D**	Daily	**HR**	High end range

LO	Lowest wage paid	**MTC**	Median total compensation
LR	Low end range	**MW**	Median wage paid
M	Monthly	**MWR**	Median wage range
MCC	Median cash compensation	**S**	See annotated source

TCC	Total cash compensation
TQ	Third quartile wage
W	Weekly
Y	Yearly

Occupation/Type/Industry	Location	Per	Low	Mid	High	Source	Date
Correspondence Clerk	Washington-Arlington-Alexandria MSA, DC-VA-MD-WV	Y	32900 FQ	40240 MW	47110 TQ	USBLS	5/07
	Florida	Y	21930 FQ	26080 MW	31710 TQ	USBLS	5/07
	Fort Lauderdale-Pompano Beach-Deerfield Beach PMSA, FL	Y	22180 FQ	26170 MW	31400 TQ	USBLS	5/07
	Jacksonville MSA, FL	Y	18340 FQ	21810 MW	24300 TQ	USBLS	5/07
	Miami-Fort Lauderdale-Miami Beach MSA, FL	Y	22570 FQ	25970 MW	30710 TQ	USBLS	5/07
	Orlando-Kissimmee MSA, FL	Y	26590 FQ	29660 MW	33050 TQ	USBLS	5/07
	Tampa-St. Petersburg-Clearwater MSA, FL	Y	27400 FQ	31900 MW	36530 TQ	USBLS	5/07
	Georgia	Y	28850 FQ	35140 MW	40620 TQ	USBLS	5/07
	Atlanta-Sandy Springs-Marietta MSA, GA	Y	29800 FQ	35720 MW	40980 TQ	USBLS	5/07
	Idaho	Y	23790 FQ	34260 MW	37960 TQ	USBLS	5/07
	Illinois	Y	27550 FQ	31420 MW	38970 TQ	USBLS	5/07
	Chicago-Naperville-Joliet MSA, IL-IN-WI	Y	27200 FQ	31090 MW	38970 TQ	USBLS	5/07
	Indiana	Y	23320 FQ	27650 MW	31370 TQ	USBLS	5/07
	Gary PMSA, IN	Y	19870 FQ	24990 MW	28660 TQ	USBLS	5/07
	Indianapolis-Carmel MSA, IN	Y	27270 FQ	30260 MW	35150 TQ	USBLS	5/07
	Iowa	Y	24250 FQ	27910 MW	32940 TQ	USBLS	5/07
	Des Moines-West Des Moines MSA, IA	Y	25900 FQ	29840 MW	34150 TQ	USBLS	5/07
	Kansas	Y	26060 FQ	29360 MW	34020 TQ	USBLS	5/07
	Wichita MSA, KS	Y	27300 FQ	29500 MW	31600 TQ	USBLS	5/07
	Kentucky	Y	28604 FQ	33958 MW	41577 TQ	KYBLS	2008
	Louisville-Jefferson County MSA, KY-IN	Y	25660 FQ	29470 MW	38060 TQ	USBLS	5/07
	Louisiana	H	13.46 FQ	15.61 MW	17.44 TQ	LABLS	1/08-3/08
	Maryland	Y		39425 MW		MDBLS	3/08
	Baltimore-Towson MSA, MD	Y	30930 FQ	36200 MW	41270 TQ	USBLS	5/07
	Massachusetts	Y	28120 FQ	35140 MW	40230 TQ	USBLS	5/07
	Boston-Cambridge-Quincy NECTA, MA	Y	28080 FQ	34950 MW	43060 TQ	USBLS	5/07
	Worcester MSA, MA-CT	Y	31710 FQ	35850 MW	39970 TQ	USBLS	5/07
	Michigan	Y	28880 FQ	33540 MW	37340 TQ	USBLS	5/07
	Detroit-Warren-Livonia MSA, MI	Y	27800 FQ	33160 MW	37210 TQ	USBLS	5/07
	Warren-Troy-Farmington Hills PMSA, MI	Y	29660 FQ	33160 MW	36690 TQ	USBLS	5/07
	Minnesota	Y	14914 FQ	16069 MW	27185 TQ	MNBLS	10/08-12/08
	Minneapolis-Saint Paul MSA, MN-WI	Y	26269 FQ	31785 MW	37749 TQ	MNBLS	10/08-12/08
	Missouri	Y	22470 FQ	24980 MW	29340 TQ	USBLS	5/07
	Kansas City MSA, MO-KS	Y	22290 FQ	24780 MW	28880 TQ	USBLS	5/07
	St. Louis MSA, MO-IL	Y	22710 FQ	25320 MW	30750 TQ	USBLS	5/07
	Nebraska	Y	25380 FQ	29830 MW	35010 TQ	USBLS	5/07
	Omaha-Council Bluffs MSA, NE-IA	Y	26290 FQ	30640 MW	35840 TQ	USBLS	5/07
	New Hampshire	H	13.77 AE	15.48 MW	16.61 AEX	NHBLS	6/08
	New Jersey	Y	29240 FQ	36690 MW	48750 TQ	USBLS	5/07
	Edison PMSA, NJ	Y	29800 FQ	39010 MW	51410 TQ	USBLS	5/07
	Newark-Union PMSA, NJ-PA	Y	29270 FQ	35160 MW	44620 TQ	USBLS	5/07
	New York	Y	28180 FQ	33970 MW	38150 TQ	USBLS	5/07
	Albany-Schenectady-Troy MSA, NY	Y	27140 FQ	32780 MW	36700 TQ	USBLS	5/07
	Buffalo-Niagara Falls MSA, NY	Y	23390 FQ	27130 MW	31980 TQ	USBLS	5/07
	Nassau-Suffolk PMSA, NY	Y	30120 FQ	35400 MW	39940 TQ	USBLS	5/07
	New York-Northern New Jersey-Long Island MSA, NY-NJ-PA	Y	31040 FQ	36020 MW	43310 TQ	USBLS	5/07
	North Carolina	Y	23410 FQ	28560 MW	32540 TQ	USBLS	5/07
	Charlotte-Gastonia-Concord MSA, NC-SC	Y	27240 FQ	29810 MW	35760 TQ	USBLS	5/07
	North Dakota	Y	21570 FQ	24650 MW	27560 TQ	USBLS	5/07
	Ohio	Y	26350 FQ	31930 MW	41660 TQ	USBLS	5/07
	Cincinnati-Middletown MSA, OH-KY-IN	Y	29070 FQ	37380 MW	43670 TQ	USBLS	5/07

AE	Average entry wage	**AW**	Average wage paid	**FQ**	First quartile wage
AER	Average entry range	**AWR**	Average wage range	**H**	Hourly
AEX	Average experienced wage	**AXR**	Average experienced range	**HI**	Highest wage paid
ATC	Average total compensation	**D**	Daily	**HR**	High end range

LO	Lowest wage paid	**MTC**	Median total compensation	**TCC** Total cash compensation
LR	Low end range	**MW**	Median wage paid	**TQ** Third quartile wage
M	Monthly	**MWR**	Median wage range	**W** Weekly
MCC	Median cash compensation	**S**	See annotated source	**Y** Yearly

Occupation/Type/Industry	Location	Per	Low	Mid	High	Source	Date
Correspondence Clerk	Cleveland-Elyria-Mentor						
	MSA, OH	Y	25740 FQ	31540 MW	39480 TQ	USBLS	5/07
	Columbus MSA, OH	Y	26650 FQ	30500 MW	41280 TQ	USBLS	5/07
	Oklahoma	Y	20790 FQ	25620 MW	31080 TQ	USBLS	5/07
	Oklahoma City MSA, OK	Y	17790 FQ	25390 MW	31750 TQ	USBLS	5/07
	Tulsa MSA, OK	Y	23580 FQ	26720 MW	31250 TQ	USBLS	5/07
	Oregon	H	13.94 FQ	16.22 MW	18.95 TQ	ORBLS	5/08
	Portland-Vancouver-Beaverton						
	MSA, OR-WA	Y	27820 FQ	32310 MW	37910 TQ	USBLS	5/07
	Pennsylvania	Y	24220 FQ	28620 MW	33560 TQ	USBLS	5/07
	Allentown-Bethlehem-Easton						
	MSA, PA-NJ	Y	19130 FQ	28620 MW	32570 TQ	USBLS	5/07
	Philadelphia-Camden-						
	Wilmington MSA, PA-NJ-DE-						
	MD	Y	27750 FQ	31510 MW	38280 TQ	USBLS	5/07
	Pittsburgh MSA, PA	Y	15900 FQ	23120 MW	32440 TQ	USBLS	5/07
	Rhode Island	Y	27380 FQ	30370 MW	35500 TQ	USBLS	5/07
	Providence-Fall River-						
	Warwick MSA, RI-MA	Y	27350 FQ	30300 MW	35420 TQ	USBLS	5/07
	South Carolina	Y	19460 FQ	22720 MW	26800 TQ	USBLS	5/07
	Columbia MSA, SC	Y	19880 FQ	22200 MW	24540 TQ	USBLS	5/07
	South Dakota	Y	23604 FQ	26901 MW	30653 TQ	SDBLS	7/08-9/08
	Sioux Falls MSA, SD	Y	24492 FQ	27881 MW	31614 TQ	SDBLS	7/08-9/08
	Tennessee	Y	23540 FQ	29240 MW	34970 TQ	USBLS	5/07
	Memphis MSA, TN-MS-AR	Y	22620 FQ	28140 MW	35460 TQ	USBLS	5/07
	Nashville-Davidson-						
	Murfreesboro MSA, TN	Y	24840 FQ	29190 MW	34570 TQ	USBLS	5/07
	Texas	Y	24340 FQ	30010 MW	35390 TQ	USBLS	5/07
	Austin-Round Rock MSA, TX	Y	22960 FQ	26830 MW	34980 TQ	USBLS	5/07
	Dallas-Fort Worth-Arlington						
	MSA, TX	Y	24820 FQ	29530 MW	36110 TQ	USBLS	5/07
	Houston-Sugar Land-Baytown						
	MSA, TX	Y	29040 FQ	32540 MW	36220 TQ	USBLS	5/07
	San Antonio MSA, TX	Y	19430 FQ	28460 MW	34560 TQ	USBLS	5/07
	Utah	Y	13620 FQ	15950 MW	26640 TQ	USBLS	5/07
	Salt Lake City MSA, UT	Y	25300 FQ	27760 MW	30740 TQ	USBLS	5/07
	Virginia	Y	26380 FQ	30330 MW	35740 TQ	USBLS	5/07
	Virginia Beach-Norfolk-						
	Newport News MSA, VA-NC	Y	23990 FQ	27490 MW	31480 TQ	USBLS	5/07
	Washington	H	15.35 FQ	17.75 MW	19.94 TQ	WABLS	3/08
	Seattle-Tacoma-Bellevue						
	MSA, WA	Y	34610 FQ	37610 MW	40720 TQ	USBLS	5/07
	Wisconsin	Y	24040 FQ	28870 MW	35910 TQ	USBLS	5/07
	Milwaukee-Waukesha-West						
	Allis MSA, WI	Y	23710 FQ	28160 MW	35280 TQ	USBLS	5/07
Cosmetologist							
Glencliff Home for the Elderly	New Hampshire	Y			28225 HI	NHUL03	2008
New Hampshire Hospital	New Hampshire	Y			27885 HI	NHUL03	2008
State Government	Ohio	H	14.85 LO		16.35 HI	ODAS	2008
Cosmetology Inspector							
State Government	Ohio	H	17.22 LO		21.77 HI	ODAS	2008
Cost Analyst							
Large Company	United States	Y	39750-49000 AER			IOMA07	2009
Midsize Company	United States	Y	37750-45500 AER			IOMA07	2009
Small Company	United States	Y	35500-42250 AER			IOMA07	2009
Cost Estimator	Alabama	Y	36550 FQ	48060 MW	61470 TQ	USBLS	5/07
	Birmingham-Hoover MSA, AL	Y	40880 FQ	54570 MW	67150 TQ	USBLS	5/07
	Montgomery MSA, AL	Y	39880 FQ	47170 MW	59380 TQ	USBLS	5/07
	Alaska	Y	48530 FQ	65350 MW	80780 TQ	USBLS	5/07
	Anchorage MSA, AK	Y	47750 FQ	60790 MW	80760 TQ	USBLS	5/07
	Arizona	Y	37760 FQ	50050 MW	64780 TQ	USBLS	5/07
	Phoenix-Mesa-Scottsdale						
	MSA, AZ	Y	39280 FQ	52220 MW	67560 TQ	USBLS	5/07
	Tucson MSA, AZ	Y	37750 FQ	47110 MW	60910 TQ	USBLS	5/07
	Arkansas	Y	36910 FQ	48010 MW	59640 TQ	USBLS	5/07

Cost Estimator

Occupation/Type/Industry	Location	Per	Low	Mid	High	Source	Date
Cost Estimator	Little Rock-North Little Rock MSA, AR	Y	39560 FQ	48130 MW	57100 TQ	USBLS	5/07
	California	H	22.68 FQ	30.20 MW	39.39 TQ	CABLS	1/08-3/08
	Fresno MSA, CA	H	20.53 FQ	25.47 MW	34.68 TQ	CABLS	1/08-3/08
	Los Angeles-Long Beach-Glendale PMSA, CA	H	21.14 FQ	28.97 MW	37.93 TQ	CABLS	1/08-3/08
	Oakland-Fremont-Hayward MSA, CA	H	25.23 FQ	33.83 MW	43.37 TQ	CABLS	1/08-3/08
	Riverside-San Bernardino-Ontario MSA, CA	H	21.20 FQ	28.28 MW	36.35 TQ	CABLS	1/08-3/08
	Sacramento-Arden Arcade-Roseville MSA, CA	H	21.55 FQ	29.97 MW	38.86 TQ	CABLS	1/08-3/08
	San Diego-Carlsbad-San Marcos MSA, CA	H	22.34 FQ	30.00 MW	39.37 TQ	CABLS	1/08-3/08
	San Francisco-San Mateo-Redwood PMSA, CA	H	28.33 FQ	36.35 MW	45.64 TQ	CABLS	1/08-3/08
	San Jose-Sunnyvale-Santa Clara MSA, CA	H	26.11 FQ	34.42 MW	41.69 TQ	CABLS	1/08-3/08
	Santa Ana-Anaheim-Irvine PMSA, CA	Y	48880 FQ	61210 MW	78360 TQ	USBLS	5/07
	Colorado	Y	42520 FQ	55290 MW	72510 TQ	USBLS	5/07
	Denver-Aurora MSA, CO	Y	41900 FQ	56030 MW	73960 TQ	USBLS	5/07
	Connecticut	H	20.44 AE	29.87 MW		CTBLS	1/08-3/08
	Bridgeport-Stamford-Norwalk MSA, CT	Y	48080 FQ	67960 MW	89280 TQ	USBLS	5/07
	Hartford-West Hartford-East Hartford MSA, CT	Y	45880 FQ	56900 MW	71360 TQ	USBLS	5/07
	Waterbury MSA, CT	Y	42050 FQ	53940 MW	75080 TQ	USBLS	5/07
	Delaware	Y	39860 FQ	51970 MW	73320 TQ	USBLS	5/07
	Wilmington PMSA, DE-MD-NJ	Y	44490 FQ	54710 MW	77190 TQ	USBLS	5/07
	District of Columbia	Y	64460 FQ	76850 MW	92910 TQ	USBLS	5/07
	Washington-Arlington-Alexandria MSA, DC-VA-MD-WV	Y	48230 FQ	62510 MW	79770 TQ	USBLS	5/07
	Florida	Y	37720 FQ	52020 MW	67880 TQ	USBLS	5/07
	Fort Lauderdale-Pompano Beach-Deerfield Beach PMSA, FL	Y	42820 FQ	55570 MW	74080 TQ	USBLS	5/07
	Jacksonville MSA, FL	Y	39690 FQ	53860 MW	72350 TQ	USBLS	5/07
	Miami-Fort Lauderdale-Miami Beach MSA, FL	Y	42190 FQ	55590 MW	72810 TQ	USBLS	5/07
	Orlando-Kissimmee MSA, FL	Y	35950 FQ	48820 MW	66150 TQ	USBLS	5/07
	Pensacola-Ferry Pass-Brent MSA, FL	Y	30980 FQ	44800 MW	59890 TQ	USBLS	5/07
	Tallahassee MSA, FL	Y	34020 FQ	47500 MW	69140 TQ	USBLS	5/07
	Tampa-St. Petersburg-Clearwater MSA, FL	Y	36820 FQ	50220 MW	65410 TQ	USBLS	5/07
	West Palm Beach-Boca Raton-Boynton Beach PMSA, FL	Y	43210 FQ	58050 MW	72750 TQ	USBLS	5/07
	Georgia	Y	44320 FQ	58230 MW	74600 TQ	USBLS	5/07
	Atlanta-Sandy Springs-Marietta MSA, GA	Y	47970 FQ	61030 MW	77750 TQ	USBLS	5/07
	Savannah MSA, GA	Y	39690 FQ	55610 MW	69590 TQ	USBLS	5/07
	Hawaii	Y	43620 FQ	60660 MW	79650 TQ	USBLS	5/07
	Honolulu MSA, HI	Y	46730 FQ	62470 MW	83910 TQ	USBLS	5/07
	Idaho	Y	30450 FQ	42310 MW	55790 TQ	USBLS	5/07
	Boise City-Nampa MSA, ID	Y	24830 FQ	41430 MW	59570 TQ	USBLS	5/07
	Illinois	Y	47470 FQ	63040 MW	80150 TQ	USBLS	5/07
	Chicago-Naperville-Joliet MSA, IL-IN-WI	Y	48900 FQ	65260 MW	81480 TQ	USBLS	5/07
	Rockford MSA, IL	Y	46110 FQ	55650 MW	65270 TQ	USBLS	5/07
	Indiana	Y	39960 FQ	51670 MW	67780 TQ	USBLS	5/07
	Gary PMSA, IN	Y	45600 FQ	62280 MW	81460 TQ	USBLS	5/07
	Indianapolis-Carmel MSA, IN	Y	44780 FQ	54650 MW	70930 TQ	USBLS	5/07
	Iowa	Y	38140 FQ	48190 MW	60720 TQ	USBLS	5/07
	Des Moines-West Des Moines MSA, IA	Y	45300 FQ	54820 MW	63620 TQ	USBLS	5/07
	Waterloo-Cedar Falls MSA, IA	Y	38550 FQ	48730 MW	59210 TQ	USBLS	5/07
	Kansas	Y	40640 FQ	50690 MW	66940 TQ	USBLS	5/07
	Topeka MSA, KS	Y	42110 FQ	56110 MW	80360 TQ	USBLS	5/07
	Wichita MSA, KS	Y	42490 FQ	50160 MW	63490 TQ	USBLS	5/07

AE	Average entry wage	AW	Average wage paid	FQ	First quartile wage	LO	Lowest wage paid	MTC	Median total compensation
AER	Average entry range	AWR	Average wage range	H	Hourly	LR	Low end range	MW	Median wage paid
AEX	Average experienced wage	AXR	Average experienced range	HI	Highest wage paid	M	Monthly	MWR	Median wage range
ATC	Average total compensation	D	Daily	HR	High end range	MCC	Median cash compensation	S	See annotated source

TCC	Total cash compensation
TQ	Third quartile wage
W	Weekly
Y	Yearly

344

Occupation/Type/Industry	Location	Per	Low	Mid	High	Source	Date
Cost Estimator	Kentucky	Y	37884 FQ	50322 MW	64540 TQ	KYBLS	2008
	Lexington-Fayette MSA, KY	Y	35740 FQ	47600 MW	65840 TQ	USBLS	5/07
	Louisville-Jefferson County MSA, KY-IN	Y	38960 FQ	49090 MW	62790 TQ	USBLS	5/07
	Louisiana	H	19.73 FQ	24.62 MW	31.02 TQ	LABLS	1/08-3/08
	Baton Rouge MSA, LA	Y	43510 FQ	53490 MW	69330 TQ	USBLS	5/07
	New Orleans-Metairie-Kenner MSA, LA	Y	43350 FQ	52660 MW	64020 TQ	USBLS	5/07
	Maine	Y	35920 FQ	44990 MW	58820 TQ	USBLS	5/07
	Lewiston-Auburn MSA, ME	Y	35940 FQ	42410 MW	51500 TQ	USBLS	5/07
	Portland-South Portland-Biddeford MSA, ME	Y	42270 FQ	51080 MW	63650 TQ	USBLS	5/07
	Maryland	Y		58525 MW		MDBLS	3/08
	Baltimore-Towson MSA, MD	Y	42510 FQ	56730 MW	68920 TQ	USBLS	5/07
	Bethesda-Gaithersburg-Frederick PMSA, MD	Y	46230 FQ	59040 MW	80470 TQ	USBLS	5/07
	Massachusetts	Y	48670 FQ	64000 MW	88910 TQ	USBLS	5/07
	Barnstable Town MSA, MA	Y	38150 FQ	46050 MW	65530 TQ	USBLS	5/07
	Boston-Cambridge-Quincy NECTA, MA	Y	51790 FQ	73760 MW	96820 TQ	USBLS	5/07
	Worcester MSA, MA-CT	Y	39530 FQ	51650 MW	69480 TQ	USBLS	5/07
	Michigan	Y	45010 FQ	58790 MW	75430 TQ	USBLS	5/07
	Detroit-Warren-Livonia MSA, MI	Y	49330 FQ	65580 MW	83100 TQ	USBLS	5/07
	Grand Rapids-Wyoming MSA, MI	Y	42460 FQ	53330 MW	64610 TQ	USBLS	5/07
	Lansing-East Lansing MSA, MI	Y	44020 FQ	56620 MW	74550 TQ	USBLS	5/07
	Warren-Troy-Farmington Hills PMSA, MI	Y	49250 FQ	64710 MW	82070 TQ	USBLS	5/07
	Minnesota	Y	44114 FQ	56939 MW	70671 TQ	MNBLS	10/08-12/08
	Duluth-Superior MSA, MN-WI	Y	42154 FQ	47743 MW	61172 TQ	MNBLS	10/08-12/08
	Minneapolis-Saint Paul MSA, MN-WI	Y	47805 FQ	60056 MW	73976 TQ	MNBLS	10/08-12/08
	Rochester MSA, MN	Y	43422 FQ	52794 MW	66445 TQ	MNBLS	10/08-12/08
	Mississippi	Y	36490 FQ	46920 MW	61800 TQ	USBLS	5/07
	Jackson MSA, MS	Y	40790 FQ	50190 MW	68050 TQ	USBLS	5/07
	Missouri	Y	40410 FQ	54170 MW	70660 TQ	USBLS	5/07
	Jefferson City MSA, MO	Y	29150 FQ	33460 MW	41170 TQ	USBLS	5/07
	Joplin MSA, MO	Y	36950 FQ	61520 MW	72820 TQ	USBLS	5/07
	Kansas City MSA, MO-KS	Y	43290 FQ	56110 MW	73110 TQ	USBLS	5/07
	St. Louis MSA, MO-IL	Y	44560 FQ	58960 MW	74030 TQ	USBLS	5/07
	Montana	Y	30800 FQ	47800 MW	66680 TQ	USBLS	5/07
	Billings MSA, MT	Y	14690 FQ	34810 MW	60740 TQ	USBLS	5/07
	Great Falls MSA, MT	Y	33400 FQ	42630 MW	67700 TQ	USBLS	5/07
	Nebraska	Y	36810 FQ	46360 MW	57530 TQ	USBLS	5/07
	Omaha-Council Bluffs MSA, NE-IA	Y	37830 FQ	47610 MW	60470 TQ	USBLS	5/07
	Nevada	H	23.31 FQ	29.80 MW	38.43 TQ	NVBLS	5/08
	Carson City MSA, NV	H	20.60 FQ	24.56 MW	31.33 TQ	NVBLS	5/08
	Las Vegas-Paradise MSA, NV	H	23.14 FQ	29.50 MW	38.92 TQ	NVBLS	5/08
	New Hampshire	H	19.13 AE	26.54 MW	32.09 AEX	NHBLS	6/08
	Manchester MSA, NH	Y	51090 FQ	56170 MW	64970 TQ	USBLS	5/07
	Nashua NECTA, NH-MA	Y	40210 FQ	51160 MW	68670 TQ	USBLS	5/07
	Portsmouth MSA, NH-ME	Y	42970 FQ	51110 MW	60700 TQ	USBLS	5/07
	New Jersey	Y	45890 FQ	62210 MW	82210 TQ	USBLS	5/07
	Atlantic City MSA, NJ	Y	59570 FQ	75740 MW	86000 TQ	USBLS	5/07
	Camden PMSA, NJ	Y	47610 FQ	61040 MW	78380 TQ	USBLS	5/07
	Edison PMSA, NJ	Y	49160 FQ	62690 MW	81230 TQ	USBLS	5/07
	Newark-Union PMSA, NJ-PA	Y	41870 FQ	59760 MW	85750 TQ	USBLS	5/07
	Vineland-Millville-Bridgeton MSA, NJ	Y	41690 FQ	62180 MW	88900 TQ	USBLS	5/07
	New Mexico	Y	36190 FQ	50140 MW	64010 TQ	USBLS	5/07
	Albuquerque MSA, NM	Y	35650 FQ	49440 MW	63710 TQ	USBLS	5/07
	New York	Y	43960 FQ	58790 MW	79800 TQ	USBLS	5/07
	Albany-Schenectady-Troy MSA, NY	Y	41480 FQ	49210 MW	64830 TQ	USBLS	5/07
	Buffalo-Niagara Falls MSA, NY	Y	41210 FQ	53470 MW	63890 TQ	USBLS	5/07
	Nassau-Suffolk PMSA, NY	Y	51680 FQ	67420 MW	83410 TQ	USBLS	5/07
	New York-Northern New Jersey-Long Island MSA, NY-NJ-PA	Y	48740 FQ	66400 MW	87470 TQ	USBLS	5/07

AE	Average entry wage	AW	Average wage paid	FQ	First quartile wage	LO	Lowest wage paid	MTC	Median total compensation	TCC Total cash compensation
AER	Average entry range	AWR	Average wage range	H	Hourly	LR	Low end range	MW	Median wage paid	TQ Third quartile wage
AEX	Average experienced wage	AXR	Average experienced range	HI	Highest wage paid	M	Monthly	MWR	Median wage range	W Weekly
ATC	Average total compensation	D	Daily	HR	High end range	MCC	Median cash compensation	S	See annotated source	Y Yearly

Occupation/Type/Industry	Location	Per	Low	Mid	High	Source	Date
Cost Estimator	North Carolina	Y	41020 FQ	50870 MW	61990 TQ	USBLS	5/07
	Charlotte-Gastonia-Concord MSA, NC-SC	Y	44220 FQ	53540 MW	65770 TQ	USBLS	5/07
	Raleigh-Cary MSA, NC	Y	38680 FQ	49590 MW	62180 TQ	USBLS	5/07
	North Dakota	Y	33920 FQ	40750 MW	55680 TQ	USBLS	5/07
	Fargo MSA, ND-MN	Y	32760 FQ	41710 MW	58010 TQ	USBLS	5/07
	Ohio	Y	40930 FQ	54150 MW	68890 TQ	USBLS	5/07
	Cincinnati-Middletown MSA, OH-KY-IN	Y	41720 FQ	54340 MW	70430 TQ	USBLS	5/07
	Cleveland-Elyria-Mentor MSA, OH	Y	44040 FQ	57690 MW	76330 TQ	USBLS	5/07
	Columbus MSA, OH	Y	41080 FQ	53080 MW	69640 TQ	USBLS	5/07
	Dayton MSA, OH	Y	43640 FQ	57550 MW	68380 TQ	USBLS	5/07
	Springfield MSA, OH	Y	21710 FQ	42250 MW	55520 TQ	USBLS	5/07
	Oklahoma	Y	36010 FQ	48230 MW	63420 TQ	USBLS	5/07
	Oklahoma City MSA, OK	Y	38600 FQ	49700 MW	66050 TQ	USBLS	5/07
	Tulsa MSA, OK	Y	35380 FQ	50650 MW	63010 TQ	USBLS	5/07
	Oregon	H	20.51 FQ	26.67 MW	34.16 TQ	ORBLS	5/08
	Portland-Vancouver-Beaverton MSA, OR-WA	Y	44190 FQ	56740 MW	71350 TQ	USBLS	5/07
	Pennsylvania	Y	39940 FQ	50260 MW	63830 TQ	USBLS	5/07
	Allentown-Bethlehem-Easton MSA, PA-NJ	Y	39810 FQ	50470 MW	68120 TQ	USBLS	5/07
	Philadelphia-Camden-Wilmington MSA, PA-NJ-DE-MD	Y	45590 FQ	57440 MW	72830 TQ	USBLS	5/07
	Pittsburgh MSA, PA	Y	40240 FQ	48340 MW	61250 TQ	USBLS	5/07
	Rhode Island	Y	46750 FQ	57790 MW	78860 TQ	USBLS	5/07
	Providence-Fall River-Warwick MSA, RI-MA	Y	47250 FQ	59230 MW	79520 TQ	USBLS	5/07
	South Carolina	Y	36740 FQ	46900 MW	59810 TQ	USBLS	5/07
	Charleston-North Charleston MSA, SC	Y	36830 FQ	44380 MW	57610 TQ	USBLS	5/07
	Columbia MSA, SC	Y	37290 FQ	48720 MW	59070 TQ	USBLS	5/07
	South Dakota	Y	37832 FQ	43760 MW	50670 TQ	SDBLS	7/08-9/08
	Rapid City MSA, SD	Y	38262 FQ	46227 MW	54975 TQ	SDBLS	7/08-9/08
	Sioux Falls MSA, SD	Y	40152 FQ	46160 MW	51918 TQ	SDBLS	7/08-9/08
	Tennessee	Y	38770 FQ	48470 MW	64830 TQ	USBLS	5/07
	Clarksville MSA, TN-KY	Y	35720 FQ	51320 MW	63760 TQ	USBLS	5/07
	Memphis MSA, TN-MS-AR	Y	41420 FQ	52170 MW	69330 TQ	USBLS	5/07
	Nashville-Davidson-Murfreesboro MSA, TN	Y	38160 FQ	46180 MW	61600 TQ	USBLS	5/07
	Texas	Y	39180 FQ	52380 MW	69070 TQ	USBLS	5/07
	Austin-Round Rock MSA, TX	Y	42960 FQ	52780 MW	68840 TQ	USBLS	5/07
	Dallas-Fort Worth-Arlington MSA, TX	Y	40090 FQ	54320 MW	69350 TQ	USBLS	5/07
	El Paso MSA, TX	Y	31830 FQ	40830 MW	57910 TQ	USBLS	5/07
	Houston-Sugar Land-Baytown MSA, TX	Y	43850 FQ	58390 MW	79210 TQ	USBLS	5/07
	Midland MSA, TX	Y	54700 FQ	61190 MW	71940 TQ	USBLS	5/07
	San Antonio MSA, TX	Y	38530 FQ	46320 MW	59080 TQ	USBLS	5/07
	Utah	Y	39810 FQ	50950 MW	66250 TQ	USBLS	5/07
	Salt Lake City MSA, UT	Y	40640 FQ	50640 MW	64540 TQ	USBLS	5/07
	Vermont	Y	43920 FQ	55540 MW	70780 TQ	USBLS	5/07
	Burlington-South Burlington MSA, VT	Y	43840 FQ	52510 MW	75460 TQ	USBLS	5/07
	Virginia	Y	42230 FQ	55000 MW	70230 TQ	USBLS	5/07
	Charlottesville MSA, VA	Y	43390 FQ	51620 MW	62750 TQ	USBLS	5/07
	Richmond MSA, VA	Y	39560 FQ	50750 MW	63020 TQ	USBLS	5/07
	Virginia Beach-Norfolk-Newport News MSA, VA-NC	Y	39990 FQ	51800 MW	64460 TQ	USBLS	5/07
	Washington	H	22.48 FQ	29.05 MW	38.43 TQ	WABLS	3/08
	Seattle-Tacoma-Bellevue MSA, WA	Y	50190 FQ	63750 MW	83040 TQ	USBLS	5/07
	Spokane MSA, WA	Y	33780 FQ	42200 MW	55290 TQ	USBLS	5/07
	West Virginia	Y	37329 FQ	49973 MW	63977 TQ	WVBLS	7/08-9/08
	Charleston MSA, WV	Y	36580 FQ	48260 MW	63690 TQ	USBLS	5/07
	Huntington-Ashland MSA, WV-KY-OH	Y	29740 FQ	42890 MW	58740 TQ	USBLS	5/07
	Wheeling MSA, WV-OH	Y	44730 FQ	52780 MW	60370 TQ	USBLS	5/07
	Wisconsin	Y	42410 FQ	53030 MW	67070 TQ	USBLS	5/07
	Appleton MSA, WI	Y	44080 FQ	50920 MW	62930 TQ	USBLS	5/07

AE	Average entry wage	**AW**	Average wage paid	**FQ**	First quartile wage	**LO**	Lowest wage paid	**MTC**	Median total compensation	**TCC** Total cash compensation
AER	Average entry range	**AWR**	Average wage range	**H**	Hourly	**LR**	Low end range	**MW**	Median wage paid	**TQ** Third quartile wage
AEX	Average experienced wage	**AXR**	Average experienced range	**HI**	Highest wage paid	**M**	Monthly	**MWR**	Median wage range	**W** Weekly
ATC	Average total compensation	**D**	Daily	**HR**	High end range	**MCC**	Median cash compensation	**S**	See annotated source	**Y** Yearly

Occupation/Type/Industry	Location	Per	Low	Mid	High	Source	Date
Cost Estimator	Milwaukee-Waukesha-West Allis MSA, WI	Y	47520 FQ	58030 MW	74020 TQ	USBLS	5/07
	Wyoming	Y	40660 FQ	50754 MW	64822 TQ	WYBLS	9/08
	Cheyenne MSA, WY	Y	39410 FQ	44935 MW	54686 TQ	WYBLS	9/08
	Puerto Rico	Y	24770 FQ	31750 MW	40670 TQ	USBLS	5/07
	San Juan-Caguas-Guaynabo MSA, PR	Y	24170 FQ	31090 MW	39870 TQ	USBLS	5/07
	Guam	Y	33650 FQ	41190 MW	49120 TQ	USBLS	5/07
Costume Attendant	Alabama	Y	22650 FQ	29200 MW	35100 TQ	USBLS	5/07
	Arizona	Y	25250 FQ	33260 MW	37490 TQ	USBLS	5/07
	California	H	9.22 FQ	14.54 MW	25.20 TQ	CABLS	1/08-3/08
	Colorado	Y	27260 FQ	30110 MW	35870 TQ	USBLS	5/07
	Florida	Y	15500 FQ	20900 MW	26890 TQ	USBLS	5/07
	Georgia	Y	16470 FQ	18330 MW	23570 TQ	USBLS	5/07
	Illinois	Y	18100 FQ	24130 MW	47160 TQ	USBLS	5/07
	Kentucky	Y	21030 FQ	24208 MW	30690 TQ	KYBLS	2008
	Louisiana	H	6.59 FQ	7.95 MW	9.78 TQ	LABLS	1/08-3/08
	Maryland	Y		25050 MW		MDBLS	3/08
	Massachusetts	Y	27190 FQ	36270 MW	54220 TQ	USBLS	5/07
	Michigan	Y	17390 FQ	26400 MW	35300 TQ	USBLS	5/07
	Minnesota	Y	27509 FQ	30938 MW	39899 TQ	MNBLS	10/08-12/08
	Missouri	Y	19250 FQ	24570 MW	29330 TQ	USBLS	5/07
	New York	Y	25780 FQ	47780 MW	58880 TQ	USBLS	5/07
	Ohio	Y	18140 FQ	26520 MW	37190 TQ	USBLS	5/07
	Oklahoma	Y	12890 FQ	14330 MW	16990 TQ	USBLS	5/07
	Oregon	H	10.79 FQ	15.16 MW	21.48 TQ	ORBLS	5/08
	Pennsylvania	Y	25330 FQ	32450 MW	37180 TQ	USBLS	5/07
	Texas	Y	15900 FQ	19830 MW	30020 TQ	USBLS	5/07
	Utah	Y	16980 FQ	20720 MW	25980 TQ	USBLS	5/07
	Virginia	Y	13770 FQ	16030 MW	20280 TQ	USBLS	5/07
	Washington	H	16.34 FQ	17.82 MW	19.31 TQ	WABLS	3/08
	Wisconsin	Y	16750 FQ	25460 MW	44300 TQ	USBLS	5/07
Counter and Rental Clerk	Alabama	Y	14140 FQ	18340 MW	24000 TQ	USBLS	5/07
	Birmingham-Hoover MSA, AL	Y	14930 FQ	19990 MW	26180 TQ	USBLS	5/07
	Mobile MSA, AL	Y	14800 FQ	17990 MW	22050 TQ	USBLS	5/07
	Alaska	Y	17360 FQ	20280 MW	26920 TQ	USBLS	5/07
	Anchorage MSA, AK	Y	16950 FQ	18730 MW	26940 TQ	USBLS	5/07
	Arizona	Y	15720 FQ	20290 MW	27300 TQ	USBLS	5/07
	Flagstaff MSA, AZ	Y	15260 FQ	18710 MW	22890 TQ	USBLS	5/07
	Phoenix-Mesa-Scottsdale MSA, AZ	Y	15940 FQ	20980 MW	28370 TQ	USBLS	5/07
	Tucson MSA, AZ	Y	15730 FQ	18900 MW	23560 TQ	USBLS	5/07
	Arkansas	Y	14750 FQ	17370 MW	23070 TQ	USBLS	5/07
	Little Rock-North Little Rock MSA, AR	Y	14790 FQ	17340 MW	23070 TQ	USBLS	5/07
	California	H	8.45 FQ	10.01 MW	14.11 TQ	CABLS	1/08-3/08
	Los Angeles-Long Beach-Glendale PMSA, CA	H	8.43 FQ	9.87 MW	14.03 TQ	CABLS	1/08-3/08
	Oakland-Fremont-Hayward MSA, CA	H	8.29 FQ	9.20 MW	12.14 TQ	CABLS	1/08-3/08
	Oxnard-Thousand Oaks-Ventura MSA, CA	H	8.00 FQ	9.88 MW	11.82 TQ	CABLS	1/08-3/08
	Riverside-San Bernardino-Ontario MSA, CA	H	8.19 FQ	9.77 MW	13.98 TQ	CABLS	1/08-3/08
	Sacramento-Arden Arcade-Roseville MSA, CA	H	8.40 FQ	10.34 MW	14.79 TQ	CABLS	1/08-3/08
	San Diego-Carlsbad-San Marcos MSA, CA	H	8.84 FQ	11.18 MW	16.71 TQ	CABLS	1/08-3/08
	San Francisco-San Mateo-Redwood PMSA, CA	H	9.79 FQ	11.84 MW	15.96 TQ	CABLS	1/08-3/08
	San Jose-Sunnyvale-Santa Clara MSA, CA	H	8.74 FQ	10.45 MW	13.86 TQ	CABLS	1/08-3/08
	Santa Ana-Anaheim-Irvine PMSA, CA	Y	18240 FQ	22910 MW	32400 TQ	USBLS	5/07
	Colorado	Y	17220 FQ	21560 MW	28930 TQ	USBLS	5/07
	Denver-Aurora MSA, CO	Y	17030 FQ	20930 MW	28600 TQ	USBLS	5/07
	Connecticut	H	8.62 AE	10.58 MW		CTBLS	1/08-3/08
	Bridgeport-Stamford-Norwalk MSA, CT	Y	19590 FQ	24240 MW	38010 TQ	USBLS	5/07
	Danbury MSA, CT	Y	18420 FQ	23290 MW	32910 TQ	USBLS	5/07

AE	Average entry wage	AW	Average wage paid	FQ	First quartile wage
AER	Average entry range	AWR	Average wage range	H	Hourly
AEX	Average experienced wage	AXR	Average experienced range	HI	Highest wage paid
ATC	Average total compensation	D	Daily	HR	High end range

LO	Lowest wage paid	MTC	Median total compensation	TCC	Total cash compensation
LR	Low end range	MW	Median wage paid	TQ	Third quartile wage
M	Monthly	MWR	Median wage range	W	Weekly
MCC	Median cash compensation	S	See annotated source	Y	Yearly

Occupation/Type/Industry	Location	Per	Low	Mid	High	Source	Date
Counter and Rental Clerk	Hartford-West Hartford-East Hartford MSA, CT	Y	17880 FQ	20000 MW	26050 TQ	USBLS	5/07
	Delaware	Y	15370 FQ	20920 MW	26980 TQ	USBLS	5/07
	Wilmington PMSA, DE-MD-NJ	Y	16010 FQ	22830 MW	28500 TQ	USBLS	5/07
	District of Columbia	Y	22580 FQ	25850 MW	30570 TQ	USBLS	5/07
	Washington-Arlington-Alexandria MSA, DC-VA-MD-WV	Y	17320 FQ	22930 MW	31250 TQ	USBLS	5/07
	Florida	Y	16550 FQ	20860 MW	27840 TQ	USBLS	5/07
	Fort Lauderdale-Pompano Beach-Deerfield Beach PMSA, FL	Y	17700 FQ	23650 MW	29350 TQ	USBLS	5/07
	Jacksonville MSA, FL	Y	17190 FQ	21220 MW	28220 TQ	USBLS	5/07
	Miami-Fort Lauderdale-Miami Beach MSA, FL	Y	17740 FQ	22370 MW	28780 TQ	USBLS	5/07
	Orlando-Kissimmee MSA, FL	Y	17440 FQ	21660 MW	27650 TQ	USBLS	5/07
	Pensacola-Ferry Pass-Brent MSA, FL	Y	14880 FQ	20820 MW	27800 TQ	USBLS	5/07
	Tampa-St. Petersburg-Clearwater MSA, FL	Y	15860 FQ	19210 MW	27030 TQ	USBLS	5/07
	West Palm Beach-Boca Raton-Boynton Beach PMSA, FL	Y	17240 FQ	21300 MW	27180 TQ	USBLS	5/07
	Georgia	Y	14840 FQ	19610 MW	27360 TQ	USBLS	5/07
	Athens-Clarke County MSA, GA	Y	16090 FQ	19670 MW	31930 TQ	USBLS	5/07
	Atlanta-Sandy Springs-Marietta MSA, GA	Y	17500 FQ	22660 MW	30630 TQ	USBLS	5/07
	Hawaii	Y	16450 FQ	18950 MW	24340 TQ	USBLS	5/07
	Honolulu MSA, HI	Y	16480 FQ	18600 MW	22690 TQ	USBLS	5/07
	Idaho	Y	15700 FQ	20590 MW	27850 TQ	USBLS	5/07
	Boise City-Nampa MSA, ID	Y	17500 FQ	21620 MW	28730 TQ	USBLS	5/07
	Illinois	Y	16130 FQ	19240 MW	24910 TQ	USBLS	5/07
	Chicago-Naperville-Joliet MSA, IL-IN-WI	Y	16630 FQ	19960 MW	25470 TQ	USBLS	5/07
	Indiana	Y	15060 FQ	19460 MW	26760 TQ	USBLS	5/07
	Gary PMSA, IN	Y	15400 FQ	20980 MW	25690 TQ	USBLS	5/07
	Indianapolis-Carmel MSA, IN	Y	18040 FQ	23450 MW	31540 TQ	USBLS	5/07
	Iowa	Y	15160 FQ	18960 MW	24400 TQ	USBLS	5/07
	Des Moines-West Des Moines MSA, IA	Y	17250 FQ	20370 MW	24870 TQ	USBLS	5/07
	Sioux City MSA, IA-NE-SD	Y	14360 FQ	17010 MW	21580 TQ	USBLS	5/07
	Kansas	Y	14860 FQ	18610 MW	26780 TQ	USBLS	5/07
	Wichita MSA, KS	Y	16860 FQ	23930 MW	33070 TQ	USBLS	5/07
	Kentucky	Y	13868 FQ	16659 MW	23803 TQ	KYBLS	2008
	Louisville-Jefferson County MSA, KY-IN	Y	14410 FQ	18510 MW	24270 TQ	USBLS	5/07
	Owensboro MSA, KY	Y	13020 FQ	15020 MW	25030 TQ	USBLS	5/07
	Louisiana	H	7.29 FQ	9.81 MW	13.81 TQ	LABLS	1/08-3/08
	Baton Rouge MSA, LA	Y	16900 FQ	23310 MW	29430 TQ	USBLS	5/07
	Lafayette MSA, LA	Y	15310 FQ	21820 MW	30590 TQ	USBLS	5/07
	New Orleans-Metairie-Kenner MSA, LA	Y	17240 FQ	22620 MW	30100 TQ	USBLS	5/07
	Maine	Y	15700 FQ	19640 MW	26200 TQ	USBLS	5/07
	Portland-South Portland-Biddeford MSA, ME	Y	18380 FQ	21580 MW	26440 TQ	USBLS	5/07
	Maryland	Y		23625 MW		MDBLS	3/08
	Baltimore-Towson MSA, MD	Y	17890 FQ	24980 MW	34550 TQ	USBLS	5/07
	Bethesda-Gaithersburg-Frederick PMSA, MD	Y	17300 FQ	23000 MW	36120 TQ	USBLS	5/07
	Massachusetts	Y	17940 FQ	23130 MW	32890 TQ	USBLS	5/07
	Boston-Cambridge-Quincy NECTA, MA	Y	17840 FQ	25360 MW	35970 TQ	USBLS	5/07
	Lynn-Peabody-Salem NECTA, MA	Y	22350 FQ	37380 MW	48470 TQ	USBLS	5/07
	Worcester MSA, MA-CT	Y	18360 FQ	23690 MW	33720 TQ	USBLS	5/07
	Michigan	Y	16300 FQ	19190 MW	24790 TQ	USBLS	5/07
	Ann Arbor MSA, MI	Y	15870 FQ	19180 MW	26080 TQ	USBLS	5/07
	Detroit-Warren-Livonia MSA, MI	Y	16700 FQ	19980 MW	26600 TQ	USBLS	5/07
	Grand Rapids-Wyoming MSA, MI	Y	18580 FQ	24130 MW	28780 TQ	USBLS	5/07

AE	Average entry wage	AW	Average wage paid	FQ	First quartile wage	LO	Lowest wage paid	MTC	Median total compensation	TCC	Total cash compensation
AER	Average entry range	AWR	Average wage range	H	Hourly	LR	Low end range	MW	Median wage paid	TQ	Third quartile wage
AEX	Average experienced wage	AXR	Average experienced range	HI	Highest wage paid	M	Monthly	MWR	Median wage range	W	Weekly
ATC	Average total compensation	D	Daily	HR	High end range	MCC	Median cash compensation	S	See annotated source	Y	Yearly

Occupation/Type/Industry	Location	Per	Low	Mid	High	Source	Date
Counter and Rental Clerk	Warren-Troy-Farmington Hills PMSA, MI	Y	16470 FQ	20030 MW	26590 TQ	USBLS	5/07
	Minnesota	Y	15621 FQ	18904 MW	24778 TQ	MNBLS	10/08-12/08
	Duluth-Superior MSA, MN-WI	Y	14858 FQ	17542 MW	25744 TQ	MNBLS	10/08-12/08
	Minneapolis-Saint Paul MSA, MN-WI	Y	16515 FQ	20011 MW	25815 TQ	MNBLS	10/08-12/08
	Rochester MSA, MN	Y	14970 FQ	17279 MW	20683 TQ	MNBLS	10/08-12/08
	Mississippi	Y	15350 FQ	19400 MW	27910 TQ	USBLS	5/07
	Jackson MSA, MS	Y	15440 FQ	23480 MW	31620 TQ	USBLS	5/07
	Missouri	Y	15230 FQ	18550 MW	26720 TQ	USBLS	5/07
	Kansas City MSA, MO-KS	Y	16420 FQ	19990 MW	30500 TQ	USBLS	5/07
	St. Louis MSA, MO-IL	Y	15300 FQ	18070 MW	25570 TQ	USBLS	5/07
	Montana	Y	15140 FQ	18450 MW	23630 TQ	USBLS	5/07
	Billings MSA, MT	Y	17560 FQ	21430 MW	26890 TQ	USBLS	5/07
	Nebraska	Y	14980 FQ	18990 MW	26760 TQ	USBLS	5/07
	Lincoln MSA, NE	Y	15090 FQ	19110 MW	27930 TQ	USBLS	5/07
	Omaha-Council Bluffs MSA, NE-IA	Y	16790 FQ	20300 MW	29790 TQ	USBLS	5/07
	Nevada	H	8.61 FQ	10.41 MW	13.47 TQ	NVBLS	5/08
	Las Vegas-Paradise MSA, NV	H	8.56 FQ	10.30 MW	13.38 TQ	NVBLS	5/08
	Reno-Sparks MSA, NV	H	10.21 FQ	11.60 MW	16.09 TQ	NVBLS	5/08
	New Hampshire	H	7.70 AE	10.97 MW	14.57 AEX	NHBLS	6/08
	Manchester MSA, NH	Y	18610 FQ	21840 MW	30540 TQ	USBLS	5/07
	Nashua NECTA, NH-MA	Y	18870 FQ	23540 MW	35560 TQ	USBLS	5/07
	New Jersey	Y	17080 FQ	22030 MW	33720 TQ	USBLS	5/07
	Camden PMSA, NJ	Y	17480 FQ	21850 MW	30350 TQ	USBLS	5/07
	Edison PMSA, NJ	Y	16520 FQ	22200 MW	35080 TQ	USBLS	5/07
	Newark-Union PMSA, NJ-PA	Y	18950 FQ	23670 MW	37940 TQ	USBLS	5/07
	New Mexico	Y	14850 FQ	19450 MW	25220 TQ	USBLS	5/07
	Albuquerque MSA, NM	Y	16520 FQ	21960 MW	30290 TQ	USBLS	5/07
	New York	Y	16800 FQ	22410 MW	31000 TQ	USBLS	5/07
	Albany-Schenectady-Troy MSA, NY	Y	17070 FQ	21270 MW	30880 TQ	USBLS	5/07
	Buffalo-Niagara Falls MSA, NY	Y	15350 FQ	22120 MW	29560 TQ	USBLS	5/07
	Nassau-Suffolk PMSA, NY	Y	17910 FQ	24720 MW	34510 TQ	USBLS	5/07
	New York-Northern New Jersey-Long Island MSA, NY-NJ-PA	Y	17540 FQ	23620 MW	33230 TQ	USBLS	5/07
	North Carolina	Y	15530 FQ	19220 MW	26790 TQ	USBLS	5/07
	Charlotte-Gastonia-Concord MSA, NC-SC	Y	16820 FQ	21990 MW	32100 TQ	USBLS	5/07
	Raleigh-Cary MSA, NC	Y	15460 FQ	18880 MW	27870 TQ	USBLS	5/07
	Winston-Salem MSA, NC	Y	14610 FQ	18870 MW	24540 TQ	USBLS	5/07
	North Dakota	Y	14070 FQ	17440 MW	21620 TQ	USBLS	5/07
	Fargo MSA, ND-MN	Y	15420 FQ	19110 MW	22600 TQ	USBLS	5/07
	Ohio	Y	16160 FQ	20160 MW	27430 TQ	USBLS	5/07
	Cincinnati-Middletown MSA, OH-KY-IN	Y	17340 FQ	22900 MW	32310 TQ	USBLS	5/07
	Cleveland-Elyria-Mentor MSA, OH	Y	16150 FQ	20290 MW	28970 TQ	USBLS	5/07
	Columbus MSA, OH	Y	17270 FQ	20980 MW	25930 TQ	USBLS	5/07
	Dayton MSA, OH	Y	17610 FQ	20150 MW	27790 TQ	USBLS	5/07
	Oklahoma	Y	14710 FQ	19350 MW	28170 TQ	USBLS	5/07
	Oklahoma City MSA, OK	Y	14910 FQ	19370 MW	29480 TQ	USBLS	5/07
	Tulsa MSA, OK	Y	18270 FQ	24920 MW	30380 TQ	USBLS	5/07
	Oregon	H	8.67 FQ	9.61 MW	12.43 TQ	ORBLS	5/08
	Eugene-Springfield MSA, OR	Y	17920 FQ	19730 MW	24070 TQ	USBLS	5/07
	Portland-Vancouver-Beaverton MSA, OR-WA	Y	18300 FQ	21870 MW	29760 TQ	USBLS	5/07
	Pennsylvania	Y	15720 FQ	19710 MW	26520 TQ	USBLS	5/07
	Allentown-Bethlehem-Easton MSA, PA-NJ	Y	16430 FQ	20020 MW	30110 TQ	USBLS	5/07
	Philadelphia-Camden-Wilmington MSA, PA-NJ-DE-MD	Y	16940 FQ	22250 MW	29800 TQ	USBLS	5/07
	Pittsburgh MSA, PA	Y	15730 FQ	18940 MW	24660 TQ	USBLS	5/07
	Reading MSA, PA	Y	15540 FQ	19950 MW	28230 TQ	USBLS	5/07
	Rhode Island	Y	18200 FQ	22190 MW	27970 TQ	USBLS	5/07
	Providence-Fall River-Warwick MSA, RI-MA	Y	18000 FQ	21950 MW	28190 TQ	USBLS	5/07
	South Carolina	Y	14840 FQ	19500 MW	26120 TQ	USBLS	5/07

AE	Average entry wage	AW	Average wage paid	FQ	First quartile wage
AER	Average entry range	AWR	Average wage range	H	Hourly
AEX	Average experienced wage	AXR	Average experienced range	HI	Highest wage paid
ATC	Average total compensation	D	Daily	HR	High end range

LO	Lowest wage paid	MTC	Median total compensation
LR	Low end range	MW	Median wage paid
M	Monthly	MWR	Median wage range
MCC	Median cash compensation	S	See annotated source

TCC	Total cash compensation
TQ	Third quartile wage
W	Weekly
Y	Yearly

Occupation/Type/Industry	Location	Per	Low	Mid	High	Source	Date
Counter and Rental Clerk	Charleston-North Charleston MSA, SC	Y	17990 FQ	21990 MW	27580 TQ	USBLS	5/07
	Columbia MSA, SC	Y	18160 FQ	22400 MW	28250 TQ	USBLS	5/07
	South Dakota	Y	14615 FQ	17635 MW	21593 TQ	SDBLS	7/08-9/08
	Sioux Falls MSA, SD	Y	15734 FQ	18648 MW	23698 TQ	SDBLS	7/08-9/08
	Tennessee	Y	14160 FQ	17840 MW	24070 TQ	USBLS	5/07
	Kingsport-Bristol-Bristol MSA, TN-VA	Y	13470 FQ	16710 MW	25690 TQ	USBLS	5/07
	Memphis MSA, TN-MS-AR	Y	14260 FQ	18610 MW	22960 TQ	USBLS	5/07
	Nashville-Davidson-Murfreesboro MSA, TN	Y	15280 FQ	18670 MW	29000 TQ	USBLS	5/07
	Texas	Y	14810 FQ	19410 MW	29860 TQ	USBLS	5/07
	Austin-Round Rock MSA, TX	Y	16940 FQ	22510 MW	32120 TQ	USBLS	5/07
	Dallas-Fort Worth-Arlington MSA, TX	Y	16260 FQ	21710 MW	34290 TQ	USBLS	5/07
	El Paso MSA, TX	Y	13810 FQ	17340 MW	26860 TQ	USBLS	5/07
	Houston-Sugar Land-Baytown MSA, TX	Y	15090 FQ	21250 MW	34220 TQ	USBLS	5/07
	San Antonio MSA, TX	Y	16130 FQ	18900 MW	25700 TQ	USBLS	5/07
	Utah	Y	15040 FQ	19780 MW	26540 TQ	USBLS	5/07
	Logan MSA, UT-ID	Y	16720 FQ	27060 MW	32490 TQ	USBLS	5/07
	Ogden-Clearfield MSA, UT	Y	14110 FQ	17830 MW	31540 TQ	USBLS	5/07
	Salt Lake City MSA, UT	Y	16240 FQ	20980 MW	25610 TQ	USBLS	5/07
	Vermont	Y	18250 FQ	23050 MW	29900 TQ	USBLS	5/07
	Burlington-South Burlington MSA, VT	Y	19490 FQ	25560 MW	31250 TQ	USBLS	5/07
	Virginia	Y	16040 FQ	21160 MW	29120 TQ	USBLS	5/07
	Richmond MSA, VA	Y	16970 FQ	22260 MW	31930 TQ	USBLS	5/07
	Virginia Beach-Norfolk-Newport News MSA, VA-NC	Y	16080 FQ	21600 MW	29190 TQ	USBLS	5/07
	Washington	H	9.13 FQ	11.21 MW	14.67 TQ	WABLS	3/08
	Seattle-Tacoma-Bellevue MSA, WA	Y	19010 FQ	23940 MW	31300 TQ	USBLS	5/07
	West Virginia	Y	14604 FQ	17635 MW	24298 TQ	WVBLS	7/08-9/08
	Charleston MSA, WV	Y	15320 FQ	19610 MW	28800 TQ	USBLS	5/07
	Huntington-Ashland MSA, WV-KY-OH	Y	13400 FQ	14940 MW	23240 TQ	USBLS	5/07
	Wisconsin	Y	15720 FQ	19380 MW	28980 TQ	USBLS	5/07
	Green Bay MSA, WI	Y	16870 FQ	21460 MW	35280 TQ	USBLS	5/07
	Milwaukee-Waukesha-West Allis MSA, WI	Y	16940 FQ	20800 MW	31330 TQ	USBLS	5/07
	Wyoming	Y	13355 FQ	15347 MW	19297 TQ	WYBLS	9/08
	Cheyenne MSA, WY	Y	13168 FQ	14976 MW	18818 TQ	WYBLS	9/08
	Puerto Rico	Y	12700 FQ	14300 MW	16390 TQ	USBLS	5/07
	San Juan-Caguas-Guaynabo MSA, PR	Y	12760 FQ	14440 MW	16780 TQ	USBLS	5/07
	Virgin Islands	Y	16810 FQ	18540 MW	20960 TQ	USBLS	5/07
	Guam	Y	13760 FQ	16620 MW	20230 TQ	USBLS	5/07
Counter Attendant							
Cafeteria, Food, Coffee Shop	Alabama	Y	13010 FQ	14870 MW	17810 TQ	USBLS	5/07
Cafeteria, Food, Coffee Shop	Birmingham-Hoover MSA, AL	Y	13750 FQ	16350 MW	19000 TQ	USBLS	5/07
Cafeteria, Food, Coffee Shop	Huntsville MSA, AL	Y	13110 FQ	14890 MW	17960 TQ	USBLS	5/07
Cafeteria, Food, Coffee Shop	Alaska	Y	17450 FQ	19530 MW	22870 TQ	USBLS	5/07
Cafeteria, Food, Coffee Shop	Anchorage MSA, AK	Y	17320 FQ	19260 MW	22700 TQ	USBLS	5/07
Cafeteria, Food, Coffee Shop	Arizona	Y	14810 FQ	16060 MW	18940 TQ	USBLS	5/07
Cafeteria, Food, Coffee Shop	Phoenix-Mesa-Scottsdale MSA, AZ	Y	14800 FQ	16110 MW	19000 TQ	USBLS	5/07
Cafeteria, Food, Coffee Shop	Tucson MSA, AZ	Y	14990 FQ	16080 MW	20160 TQ	USBLS	5/07
Cafeteria, Food, Coffee Shop	Arkansas	Y	14040 FQ	14800 MW	15890 TQ	USBLS	5/07
Cafeteria, Food, Coffee Shop	Little Rock-North Little Rock MSA, AR	Y	14110 FQ	14940 MW	16030 TQ	USBLS	5/07
Cafeteria, Food, Coffee Shop	California	H	8.02 FQ	8.80 MW	9.77 TQ	CABLS	1/08-3/08
Cafeteria, Food, Coffee Shop	Los Angeles-Long Beach-Glendale PMSA, CA	H	8.02 FQ	8.77 MW	9.66 TQ	CABLS	1/08-3/08
Cafeteria, Food, Coffee Shop	Oakland-Fremont-Hayward MSA, CA	H	8.05 FQ	8.79 MW	9.65 TQ	CABLS	1/08-3/08
Cafeteria, Food, Coffee Shop	Riverside-San Bernardino-Ontario MSA, CA	H	8.00 FQ	8.76 MW	9.89 TQ	CABLS	1/08-3/08
Cafeteria, Food, Coffee Shop	Sacramento-Arden Arcade-Roseville MSA, CA	H	8.00 FQ	8.56 MW	9.54 TQ	CABLS	1/08-3/08

AE Average entry wage	**AW** Average wage paid	**FQ** First quartile wage	**LO** Lowest wage paid	**MTC** Median total compensation	**TCC** Total cash compensation
AER Average entry range	**AWR** Average wage range	**H** Hourly	**LR** Low end range	**MW** Median wage paid	**TQ** Third quartile wage
AEX Average experienced wage	**AXR** Average experienced range	**HI** Highest wage paid	**M** Monthly	**MWR** Median wage range	**W** Weekly
ATC Average total compensation	**D** Daily	**HR** High end range	**MCC** Median cash compensation	**S** See annotated source	**Y** Yearly

Counter Attendant

Occupation/Type/Industry	Location	Per	Low	Mid	High	Source	Date
Cafeteria, Food, Coffee Shop	San Diego-Carlsbad-San Marcos MSA, CA	H	8.02 FQ	8.72 MW	9.58 TQ	CABLS	1/08-3/08
Cafeteria, Food, Coffee Shop	San Francisco-San Mateo-Redwood PMSA, CA	H	8.46 FQ	9.24 MW	10.57 TQ	CABLS	1/08-3/08
Cafeteria, Food, Coffee Shop	San Jose-Sunnyvale-Santa Clara MSA, CA	H	8.04 FQ	8.85 MW	9.74 TQ	CABLS	1/08-3/08
Cafeteria, Food, Coffee Shop	Santa Ana-Anaheim-Irvine PMSA, CA	Y	16350 FQ	18040 MW	20260 TQ	USBLS	5/07
Cafeteria, Food, Coffee Shop	Colorado	Y	14990 FQ	16690 MW	19610 TQ	USBLS	5/07
Cafeteria, Food, Coffee Shop	Denver-Aurora MSA, CO	Y	14900 FQ	16430 MW	20610 TQ	USBLS	5/07
Cafeteria, Food, Coffee Shop	Connecticut	H	8.59 AE	9.04 MW		CTBLS	1/08-3/08
Cafeteria, Food, Coffee Shop	Bridgeport-Stamford-Norwalk MSA, CT	Y	17460 FQ	19170 MW	23240 TQ	USBLS	5/07
Cafeteria, Food, Coffee Shop	Hartford-West Hartford-East Hartford MSA, CT	Y	17070 FQ	18220 MW	19850 TQ	USBLS	5/07
Cafeteria, Food, Coffee Shop	Norwich-New London MSA, CT-RI	Y	16860 FQ	18790 MW	22730 TQ	USBLS	5/07
Cafeteria, Food, Coffee Shop	Delaware	Y	16880 FQ	21790 MW	27560 TQ	USBLS	5/07
Cafeteria, Food, Coffee Shop	Dover MSA, DE	Y	16550 FQ	20220 MW	25620 TQ	USBLS	5/07
Cafeteria, Food, Coffee Shop	Wilmington PMSA, DE-MD-NJ	Y	16480 FQ	20310 MW	27100 TQ	USBLS	5/07
Cafeteria, Food, Coffee Shop	District of Columbia	Y	16600 FQ	18950 MW	22930 TQ	USBLS	5/07
Cafeteria, Food, Coffee Shop	Washington-Arlington-Alexandria MSA, DC-VA-MD-WV	Y	15240 FQ	17730 MW	20690 TQ	USBLS	5/07
Cafeteria, Food, Coffee Shop	Florida	Y	14870 FQ	16380 MW	19540 TQ	USBLS	5/07
Cafeteria, Food, Coffee Shop	Fort Lauderdale-Pompano Beach-Deerfield Beach PMSA, FL	Y	14750 FQ	16250 MW	19530 TQ	USBLS	5/07
Cafeteria, Food, Coffee Shop	Jacksonville MSA, FL	Y	14860 FQ	16440 MW	18560 TQ	USBLS	5/07
Cafeteria, Food, Coffee Shop	Miami-Fort Lauderdale-Miami Beach MSA, FL	Y	15010 FQ	16940 MW	20510 TQ	USBLS	5/07
Cafeteria, Food, Coffee Shop	Orlando-Kissimmee MSA, FL	Y	14630 FQ	15400 MW	18220 TQ	USBLS	5/07
Cafeteria, Food, Coffee Shop	Tampa-St. Petersburg-Clearwater MSA, FL	Y	14830 FQ	16290 MW	19050 TQ	USBLS	5/07
Cafeteria, Food, Coffee Shop	West Palm Beach-Boca Raton-Boynton Beach PMSA, FL	Y	14720 FQ	15740 MW	18560 TQ	USBLS	5/07
Cafeteria, Food, Coffee Shop	Georgia	Y	12760 FQ	14350 MW	17060 TQ	USBLS	5/07
Cafeteria, Food, Coffee Shop	Atlanta-Sandy Springs-Marietta MSA, GA	Y	12780 FQ	14400 MW	17570 TQ	USBLS	5/07
Cafeteria, Food, Coffee Shop	Hawaii	Y	15850 FQ	17950 MW	20720 TQ	USBLS	5/07
Cafeteria, Food, Coffee Shop	Honolulu MSA, HI	Y	15630 FQ	17270 MW	19470 TQ	USBLS	5/07
Cafeteria, Food, Coffee Shop	Idaho	Y	12820 FQ	14360 MW	16790 TQ	USBLS	5/07
Cafeteria, Food, Coffee Shop	Boise City-Nampa MSA, ID	Y	13080 FQ	14820 MW	17560 TQ	USBLS	5/07
Cafeteria, Food, Coffee Shop	Illinois	Y	14910 FQ	16360 MW	19640 TQ	USBLS	5/07
Cafeteria, Food, Coffee Shop	Chicago-Naperville-Joliet MSA, IL-IN-WI	Y	14970 FQ	16810 MW	20180 TQ	USBLS	5/07
Cafeteria, Food, Coffee Shop	Indiana	Y	13080 FQ	14960 MW	17910 TQ	USBLS	5/07
Cafeteria, Food, Coffee Shop	Evansville MSA, IN-KY	Y	12880 FQ	14570 MW	17190 TQ	USBLS	5/07
Cafeteria, Food, Coffee Shop	Gary PMSA, IN	Y	13180 FQ	15050 MW	18030 TQ	USBLS	5/07
Cafeteria, Food, Coffee Shop	Indianapolis-Carmel MSA, IN	Y	13870 FQ	16340 MW	19030 TQ	USBLS	5/07
Cafeteria, Food, Coffee Shop	Terre Haute MSA, IN	Y	12690 FQ	14000 MW	15860 TQ	USBLS	5/07
Cafeteria, Food, Coffee Shop	Iowa	Y	14220 FQ	15590 MW	17950 TQ	USBLS	5/07
Cafeteria, Food, Coffee Shop	Des Moines-West Des Moines MSA, IA	Y	14680 FQ	16620 MW	19050 TQ	USBLS	5/07
Cafeteria, Food, Coffee Shop	Kansas	Y	12720 FQ	14230 MW	16170 TQ	USBLS	5/07
Cafeteria, Food, Coffee Shop	Wichita MSA, KS	Y	12770 FQ	14480 MW	16800 TQ	USBLS	5/07
Cafeteria, Food, Coffee Shop	Kentucky	Y	13628 FQ	15785 MW	19140 TQ	KYBLS	2008
Cafeteria, Food, Coffee Shop	Louisville-Jefferson County MSA, KY-IN	Y	13240 FQ	15290 MW	18220 TQ	USBLS	5/07
Cafeteria, Food, Coffee Shop	Louisiana	H	6.17 FQ	6.97 MW	8.09 TQ	LABLS	1/08-3/08
Cafeteria, Food, Coffee Shop	Baton Rouge MSA, LA	Y	12590 FQ	14070 MW	15620 TQ	USBLS	5/07
Cafeteria, Food, Coffee Shop	Lake Charles MSA, LA	Y	12640 FQ	14090 MW	16450 TQ	USBLS	5/07
Cafeteria, Food, Coffee Shop	New Orleans-Metairie-Kenner MSA, LA	Y	13500 FQ	15750 MW	18230 TQ	USBLS	5/07
Cafeteria, Food, Coffee Shop	Maine	Y	15280 FQ	17050 MW	19280 TQ	USBLS	5/07
Cafeteria, Food, Coffee Shop	Portland-South Portland-Biddeford MSA, ME	Y	15670 FQ	17910 MW	20690 TQ	USBLS	5/07
Cafeteria, Food, Coffee Shop	Maryland	Y		18075 MW		MDBLS	3/08
Cafeteria, Food, Coffee Shop	Baltimore-Towson MSA, MD	Y	15080 FQ	17420 MW	20380 TQ	USBLS	5/07

AE	Average entry wage	AW	Average wage paid	FQ	First quartile wage	LO	Lowest wage paid	MTC	Median total compensation	TCC	Total cash compensation
AER	Average entry range	AWR	Average wage range	H	Hourly	LR	Low end range	MW	Median wage paid	TQ	Third quartile wage
AEX	Average experienced wage	AXR	Average experienced range	HI	Highest wage paid	M	Monthly	MWR	Median wage range	W	Weekly
ATC	Average total compensation	D	Daily	HR	High end range	MCC	Median cash compensation	S	See annotated source	Y	Yearly

Occupation/Type/Industry	Location	Per	Low	Mid	High	Source	Date
Counter Attendant							
Cafeteria, Food, Coffee Shop	Bethesda-Gaithersburg-Frederick PMSA, MD	Y	16580 FQ	19610 MW	22180 TQ	USBLS	5/07
Cafeteria, Food, Coffee Shop	Hagerstown-Martinsburg MSA, MD-WV	Y	13950 FQ	14800 MW	15720 TQ	USBLS	5/07
Cafeteria, Food, Coffee Shop	Salisbury MSA, MD	Y	14990 FQ	16680 MW	18550 TQ	USBLS	5/07
Cafeteria, Food, Coffee Shop	Massachusetts	Y	16710 FQ	18380 MW	21030 TQ	USBLS	5/07
Cafeteria, Food, Coffee Shop	Boston-Cambridge-Quincy NECTA, MA	Y	16970 FQ	18600 MW	21820 TQ	USBLS	5/07
Cafeteria, Food, Coffee Shop	Worcester MSA, MA-CT	Y	16610 FQ	18170 MW	20360 TQ	USBLS	5/07
Cafeteria, Food, Coffee Shop	Michigan	Y	15060 FQ	16070 MW	19020 TQ	USBLS	5/07
Cafeteria, Food, Coffee Shop	Detroit-Warren-Livonia MSA, MI	Y	15320 FQ	17040 MW	20500 TQ	USBLS	5/07
Cafeteria, Food, Coffee Shop	Grand Rapids-Wyoming MSA, MI	Y	15520 FQ	16850 MW	19940 TQ	USBLS	5/07
Cafeteria, Food, Coffee Shop	Lansing-East Lansing MSA, MI	Y	14890 FQ	15420 MW	18490 TQ	USBLS	5/07
Cafeteria, Food, Coffee Shop	Warren-Troy-Farmington Hills PMSA, MI	Y	15590 FQ	17690 MW	21110 TQ	USBLS	5/07
Cafeteria, Food, Coffee Shop	Minnesota	Y	15422 FQ	17733 MW	21497 TQ	MNBLS	10/08-12/08
Cafeteria, Food, Coffee Shop	Duluth-Superior MSA, MN-WI	Y	15056 FQ	16321 MW	19416 TQ	MNBLS	10/08-12/08
Cafeteria, Food, Coffee Shop	Minneapolis-Saint Paul MSA, MN-WI	Y	15756 FQ	18590 MW	22553 TQ	MNBLS	10/08-12/08
Cafeteria, Food, Coffee Shop	Rochester MSA, MN	Y	16584 FQ	19893 MW	23385 TQ	MNBLS	10/08-12/08
Cafeteria, Food, Coffee Shop	Mississippi	Y	12830 FQ	14550 MW	16800 TQ	USBLS	5/07
Cafeteria, Food, Coffee Shop	Jackson MSA, MS	Y	12690 FQ	14310 MW	16150 TQ	USBLS	5/07
Cafeteria, Food, Coffee Shop	Pascagoula MSA, MS	Y	12640 FQ	14020 MW	15840 TQ	USBLS	5/07
Cafeteria, Food, Coffee Shop	Missouri	Y	14730 FQ	16220 MW	19000 TQ	USBLS	5/07
Cafeteria, Food, Coffee Shop	Jefferson City MSA, MO	Y	14620 FQ	15870 MW	17700 TQ	USBLS	5/07
Cafeteria, Food, Coffee Shop	Kansas City MSA, MO-KS	Y	13830 FQ	15640 MW	18480 TQ	USBLS	5/07
Cafeteria, Food, Coffee Shop	St. Louis MSA, MO-IL	Y	14890 FQ	16460 MW	19020 TQ	USBLS	5/07
Cafeteria, Food, Coffee Shop	Springfield MSA, MO	Y	14280 FQ	15080 MW	16520 TQ	USBLS	5/07
Cafeteria, Food, Coffee Shop	Montana	Y	13720 FQ	14660 MW	16810 TQ	USBLS	5/07
Cafeteria, Food, Coffee Shop	Billings MSA, MT	Y	13540 FQ	14280 MW	15150 TQ	USBLS	5/07
Cafeteria, Food, Coffee Shop	Missoula MSA, MT	Y	14020 FQ	15220 MW	18400 TQ	USBLS	5/07
Cafeteria, Food, Coffee Shop	Nebraska	Y	12840 FQ	14510 MW	16770 TQ	USBLS	5/07
Cafeteria, Food, Coffee Shop	Omaha-Council Bluffs MSA, NE-IA	Y	13230 FQ	14960 MW	17630 TQ	USBLS	5/07
Cafeteria, Food, Coffee Shop	Nevada	H	6.88 FQ	8.90 MW	11.29 TQ	NVBLS	5/08
Cafeteria, Food, Coffee Shop	Las Vegas-Paradise MSA, NV	H	6.72 FQ	8.49 MW	11.24 TQ	NVBLS	5/08
Cafeteria, Food, Coffee Shop	New Hampshire	H	7.03 AE	8.62 MW	9.71 AEX	NHBLS	6/08
Cafeteria, Food, Coffee Shop	Manchester MSA, NH	Y	17220 FQ	18890 MW	20990 TQ	USBLS	5/07
Cafeteria, Food, Coffee Shop	Nashua NECTA, NH-MA	Y	15160 FQ	16810 MW	18470 TQ	USBLS	5/07
Cafeteria, Food, Coffee Shop	New Jersey	Y	15590 FQ	17650 MW	21400 TQ	USBLS	5/07
Cafeteria, Food, Coffee Shop	Atlantic City MSA, NJ	Y	16120 FQ	18280 MW	21880 TQ	USBLS	5/07
Cafeteria, Food, Coffee Shop	Camden PMSA, NJ	Y	15220 FQ	16700 MW	20800 TQ	USBLS	5/07
Cafeteria, Food, Coffee Shop	Edison PMSA, NJ	Y	15880 FQ	18210 MW	23630 TQ	USBLS	5/07
Cafeteria, Food, Coffee Shop	Newark-Union PMSA, NJ-PA	Y	15220 FQ	17500 MW	22170 TQ	USBLS	5/07
Cafeteria, Food, Coffee Shop	New Mexico	Y	12860 FQ	14500 MW	17640 TQ	USBLS	5/07
Cafeteria, Food, Coffee Shop	Albuquerque MSA, NM	Y	12730 FQ	14200 MW	17180 TQ	USBLS	5/07
Cafeteria, Food, Coffee Shop	New York	Y	15310 FQ	16510 MW	19420 TQ	USBLS	5/07
Cafeteria, Food, Coffee Shop	Albany-Schenectady-Troy MSA, NY	Y	15420 FQ	16440 MW	18710 TQ	USBLS	5/07
Cafeteria, Food, Coffee Shop	Buffalo-Niagara Falls MSA, NY	Y	15000 FQ	15560 MW	17580 TQ	USBLS	5/07
Cafeteria, Food, Coffee Shop	Nassau-Suffolk PMSA, NY	Y	15710 FQ	17500 MW	19710 TQ	USBLS	5/07
Cafeteria, Food, Coffee Shop	New York-Northern New Jersey-Long Island MSA, NY-NJ-PA	Y	15670 FQ	17800 MW	21250 TQ	USBLS	5/07
Cafeteria, Food, Coffee Shop	North Carolina	Y	14080 FQ	15440 MW	18090 TQ	USBLS	5/07
Cafeteria, Food, Coffee Shop	Charlotte-Gastonia-Concord MSA, NC-SC	Y	14070 FQ	15910 MW	18460 TQ	USBLS	5/07
Cafeteria, Food, Coffee Shop	Raleigh-Cary MSA, NC	Y	14870 FQ	17490 MW	21670 TQ	USBLS	5/07
Cafeteria, Food, Coffee Shop	North Dakota	Y	13600 FQ	16520 MW	21320 TQ	USBLS	5/07
Cafeteria, Food, Coffee Shop	Fargo MSA, ND-MN	Y	13680 FQ	16300 MW	23520 TQ	USBLS	5/07
Cafeteria, Food, Coffee Shop	Ohio	Y	14800 FQ	15800 MW	19260 TQ	USBLS	5/07
Cafeteria, Food, Coffee Shop	Cincinnati-Middletown MSA, OH-KY-IN	Y	14680 FQ	15760 MW	19610 TQ	USBLS	5/07
Cafeteria, Food, Coffee Shop	Cleveland-Elyria-Mentor MSA, OH	Y	14990 FQ	16290 MW	21190 TQ	USBLS	5/07
Cafeteria, Food, Coffee Shop	Columbus MSA, OH	Y	14920 FQ	16540 MW	20430 TQ	USBLS	5/07
Cafeteria, Food, Coffee Shop	Dayton MSA, OH	Y	14670 FQ	15140 MW	18380 TQ	USBLS	5/07
Cafeteria, Food, Coffee Shop	Oklahoma	Y	12810 FQ	14530 MW	17150 TQ	USBLS	5/07

AE Average entry wage	**AW** Average wage paid	**FQ** First quartile wage	**LO** Lowest wage paid	**MTC** Median total compensation	**TCC** Total cash compensation
AER Average entry range	**AWR** Average wage range	**H** Hourly	**LR** Low end range	**MW** Median wage paid	**TQ** Third quartile wage
AEX Average experienced wage	**AXR** Average experienced range	**HI** Highest wage paid	**M** Monthly	**MWR** Median wage range	**W** Weekly
ATC Average total compensation	**D** Daily	**HR** High end range	**MCC** Median cash compensation	**S** See annotated source	**Y** Yearly

Occupation/Type/Industry	Location	Per	Low	Mid	High	Source	Date
Counter Attendant							
Cafeteria, Food, Coffee Shop	Lawton MSA, OK	Y	12680 FQ	14100 MW	15900 TQ	USBLS	5/07
Cafeteria, Food, Coffee Shop	Oklahoma City MSA, OK	Y	13070 FQ	14990 MW	18680 TQ	USBLS	5/07
Cafeteria, Food, Coffee Shop	Tulsa MSA, OK	Y	12820 FQ	14620 MW	17030 TQ	USBLS	5/07
Cafeteria, Food, Coffee Shop	Oregon	H	8.59 FQ	9.14 MW	9.87 TQ	ORBLS	5/08
Cafeteria, Food, Coffee Shop	Medford MSA, OR	Y	17710 FQ	19170 MW	21390 TQ	USBLS	5/07
Cafeteria, Food, Coffee Shop	Portland-Vancouver-Beaverton MSA, OR-WA	Y	17530 FQ	18780 MW	20380 TQ	USBLS	5/07
Cafeteria, Food, Coffee Shop	Pennsylvania	Y	14360 FQ	15280 MW	17830 TQ	USBLS	5/07
Cafeteria, Food, Coffee Shop	Allentown-Bethlehem-Easton MSA, PA-NJ	Y	14320 FQ	15180 MW	17340 TQ	USBLS	5/07
Cafeteria, Food, Coffee Shop	Erie MSA, PA	Y	14050 FQ	14580 MW	15310 TQ	USBLS	5/07
Cafeteria, Food, Coffee Shop	Philadelphia-Camden-Wilmington MSA, PA-NJ-DE-MD	Y	14900 FQ	16060 MW	20990 TQ	USBLS	5/07
Cafeteria, Food, Coffee Shop	Pittsburgh MSA, PA	Y	14400 FQ	15430 MW	17950 TQ	USBLS	5/07
Cafeteria, Food, Coffee Shop	Rhode Island	Y	16420 FQ	18200 MW	21050 TQ	USBLS	5/07
Cafeteria, Food, Coffee Shop	Providence-Fall River-Warwick MSA, RI-MA	Y	16470 FQ	18250 MW	21090 TQ	USBLS	5/07
Cafeteria, Food, Coffee Shop	South Carolina	Y	12880 FQ	14670 MW	17140 TQ	USBLS	5/07
Cafeteria, Food, Coffee Shop	Charleston-North Charleston MSA, SC	Y	12990 FQ	14890 MW	17310 TQ	USBLS	5/07
Cafeteria, Food, Coffee Shop	Columbia MSA, SC	Y	12720 FQ	14240 MW	16180 TQ	USBLS	5/07
Cafeteria, Food, Coffee Shop	South Dakota	Y	14314 FQ	16843 MW	19359 TQ	SDBLS	7/08-9/08
Cafeteria, Food, Coffee Shop	Sioux Falls MSA, SD	Y	15406 FQ	17777 MW	20490 TQ	SDBLS	7/08-9/08
Cafeteria, Food, Coffee Shop	Tennessee	Y	13700 FQ	16350 MW	21070 TQ	USBLS	5/07
Cafeteria, Food, Coffee Shop	Memphis MSA, TN-MS-AR	Y	13060 FQ	14780 MW	17200 TQ	USBLS	5/07
Cafeteria, Food, Coffee Shop	Nashville-Davidson-Murfreesboro MSA, TN	Y	15930 FQ	20930 MW	23890 TQ	USBLS	5/07
Cafeteria, Food, Coffee Shop	Texas	Y	12960 FQ	14660 MW	17480 TQ	USBLS	5/07
Cafeteria, Food, Coffee Shop	Austin-Round Rock MSA, TX	Y	13700 FQ	16240 MW	18520 TQ	USBLS	5/07
Cafeteria, Food, Coffee Shop	Dallas-Fort Worth-Arlington MSA, TX	Y	13190 FQ	15180 MW	19200 TQ	USBLS	5/07
Cafeteria, Food, Coffee Shop	El Paso MSA, TX	Y	12750 FQ	14190 MW	15910 TQ	USBLS	5/07
Cafeteria, Food, Coffee Shop	Houston-Sugar Land-Baytown MSA, TX	Y	13020 FQ	14740 MW	17430 TQ	USBLS	5/07
Cafeteria, Food, Coffee Shop	San Antonio MSA, TX	Y	13110 FQ	15080 MW	17700 TQ	USBLS	5/07
Cafeteria, Food, Coffee Shop	Utah	Y	13140 FQ	15030 MW	17790 TQ	USBLS	5/07
Cafeteria, Food, Coffee Shop	Provo-Orem MSA, UT	Y	12700 FQ	14120 MW	16130 TQ	USBLS	5/07
Cafeteria, Food, Coffee Shop	Salt Lake City MSA, UT	Y	13830 FQ	16110 MW	18530 TQ	USBLS	5/07
Cafeteria, Food, Coffee Shop	Vermont	Y	17140 FQ	18740 MW	21390 TQ	USBLS	5/07
Cafeteria, Food, Coffee Shop	Burlington-South Burlington MSA, VT	Y	18020 FQ	20290 MW	22690 TQ	USBLS	5/07
Cafeteria, Food, Coffee Shop	Virginia	Y	13210 FQ	15230 MW	18380 TQ	USBLS	5/07
Cafeteria, Food, Coffee Shop	Richmond MSA, VA	Y	12650 FQ	14120 MW	15900 TQ	USBLS	5/07
Cafeteria, Food, Coffee Shop	Virginia Beach-Norfolk-Newport News MSA, VA-NC	Y	13360 FQ	15590 MW	18150 TQ	USBLS	5/07
Cafeteria, Food, Coffee Shop	Washington	H	8.60 FQ	9.23 MW	10.46 TQ	WABLS	3/08
Cafeteria, Food, Coffee Shop	Seattle-Tacoma-Bellevue MSA, WA	Y	17760 FQ	19280 MW	22480 TQ	USBLS	5/07
Cafeteria, Food, Coffee Shop	Spokane MSA, WA	Y	17590 FQ	18690 MW	20040 TQ	USBLS	5/07
Cafeteria, Food, Coffee Shop	West Virginia	Y	13883 FQ	14907 MW	15990 TQ	WVBLS	7/08-9/08
Cafeteria, Food, Coffee Shop	Charleston MSA, WV	Y	13380 FQ	14390 MW	15540 TQ	USBLS	5/07
Cafeteria, Food, Coffee Shop	Wisconsin	Y	14650 FQ	15730 MW	18550 TQ	USBLS	5/07
Cafeteria, Food, Coffee Shop	Appleton MSA, WI	Y	15140 FQ	18320 MW	23020 TQ	USBLS	5/07
Cafeteria, Food, Coffee Shop	Milwaukee-Waukesha-West Allis MSA, WI	Y	15100 FQ	16500 MW	19630 TQ	USBLS	5/07
Cafeteria, Food, Coffee Shop	Racine MSA, WI	Y	14470 FQ	15290 MW	17160 TQ	USBLS	5/07
Cafeteria, Food, Coffee Shop	Wyoming	Y	13036 FQ	14265 MW	15494 TQ	WYBLS	9/08
Cafeteria, Food, Coffee Shop	Cheyenne MSA, WY	Y	12980 FQ	14308 MW	15635 TQ	WYBLS	9/08
Cafeteria, Food, Coffee Shop	Puerto Rico	Y	12410 FQ	13490 MW	14560 TQ	USBLS	5/07
Cafeteria, Food, Coffee Shop	San Juan-Caguas-Guaynabo MSA, PR	Y	12420 FQ	13500 MW	14570 TQ	USBLS	5/07
Cafeteria, Food, Coffee Shop	Virgin Islands	Y	14700 FQ	16820 MW	18550 TQ	USBLS	5/07
Cafeteria, Food, Coffee Shop	Guam	Y	12460 FQ	13690 MW	14930 TQ	USBLS	5/07
County Administrator	Livingston County, MI	Y			152231 HI	LCPP	2009
County Attorney	DeKalb County, GA	Y	43464 LO		70632 HI	AREGC	2007
County Commission Chairperson							
Full-Time	Barrow County, GA	Y			63243 HI	GACTY02	2008

AE Average entry wage	**AW** Average wage paid	**FQ** First quartile wage	**LO** Lowest wage paid	**MTC** Median total compensation	**TCC** Total cash compensation
AER Average entry range	**AWR** Average wage range	**H** Hourly	**LR** Low end range	**MW** Median wage paid	**TQ** Third quartile wage
AEX Average experienced wage	**AXR** Average experienced range	**HI** Highest wage paid	**M** Monthly	**MWR** Median wage range	**W** Weekly
ATC Average total compensation	**D** Daily	**HR** High end range	**MCC** Median cash compensation	**S** See annotated source	**Y** Yearly

Occupation/Type/Industry	Location	Per	Low	Mid	High	Source	Date
County Commission Chairperson							
Full-Time	Clayton County, GA	Y			140694 HI	GACTY02	2008
Full-Time	Oconee County, GA	Y			92276 HI	GACTY02	2008
County Commissioner	Bryan County, GA	Y			3229 HI	GACTY02	2008
	Columbia County, GA	Y			8663 HI	GACTY02	2008
	Effingham County, GA	Y			17316 HI	GACTY02	2008
County Executive	Oakland County, MI	Y			178869 HI	SPO03	2008
County Manager	Northeast	Y		99832 AW		PMGT	2007
	South	Y		109327 AW		PMGT	2007
County Prosecutor	Oakland County, MI	Y			154583 HI	SPO03	2008
County Supervisor	Sutter County, CA	Y			41365 HI	APDEM	3/14/09
Courier and Messenger	Alabama	Y	14360 FQ	18080 MW	22460 TQ	USBLS	5/07
	Birmingham-Hoover MSA, AL	Y	14710 FQ	19710 MW	23290 TQ	USBLS	5/07
	Alaska	Y	23010 FQ	26150 MW	32290 TQ	USBLS	5/07
	Anchorage MSA, AK	Y	22950 FQ	26130 MW	33690 TQ	USBLS	5/07
	Arizona	Y	19740 FQ	22690 MW	25790 TQ	USBLS	5/07
	Phoenix-Mesa-Scottsdale MSA, AZ	Y	20480 FQ	22910 MW	25790 TQ	USBLS	5/07
	Tucson MSA, AZ	Y	17060 FQ	20490 MW	24930 TQ	USBLS	5/07
	Arkansas	Y	18120 FQ	21060 MW	24440 TQ	USBLS	5/07
	Little Rock-North Little Rock MSA, AR	Y	20380 FQ	23110 MW	26610 TQ	USBLS	5/07
	California	H	8.79 FQ	10.38 MW	13.26 TQ	CABLS	1/08-3/08
	Los Angeles-Long Beach-Glendale PMSA, CA	H	8.49 FQ	9.52 MW	11.98 TQ	CABLS	1/08-3/08
	Oakland-Fremont-Hayward MSA, CA	H	8.97 FQ	11.44 MW	15.09 TQ	CABLS	1/08-3/08
	Riverside-San Bernardino-Ontario MSA, CA	H	8.60 FQ	9.75 MW	12.55 TQ	CABLS	1/08-3/08
	Sacramento-Arden Arcade-Roseville MSA, CA	H	9.87 FQ	11.46 MW	13.86 TQ	CABLS	1/08-3/08
	San Diego-Carlsbad-San Marcos MSA, CA	H	9.84 FQ	11.46 MW	14.13 TQ	CABLS	1/08-3/08
	San Francisco-San Mateo-Redwood PMSA, CA	H	10.49 FQ	12.31 MW	16.21 TQ	CABLS	1/08-3/08
	San Jose-Sunnyvale-Santa Clara MSA, CA	H	8.99 FQ	10.55 MW	14.37 TQ	CABLS	1/08-3/08
	Santa Ana-Anaheim-Irvine PMSA, CA	Y	17540 FQ	20970 MW	29600 TQ	USBLS	5/07
	Colorado	Y	19310 FQ	23690 MW	29340 TQ	USBLS	5/07
	Denver-Aurora MSA, CO	Y	19420 FQ	24810 MW	31400 TQ	USBLS	5/07
	Connecticut	H	9.83 AE	13.64 MW		CTBLS	1/08-3/08
	Bridgeport-Stamford-Norwalk MSA, CT	Y	26740 FQ	31540 MW	36650 TQ	USBLS	5/07
	Hartford-West Hartford-East Hartford MSA, CT	Y	24530 FQ	28670 MW	35180 TQ	USBLS	5/07
	New Haven MSA, CT	Y	19900 FQ	25270 MW	29670 TQ	USBLS	5/07
	Delaware	Y	19820 FQ	23040 MW	28060 TQ	USBLS	5/07
	Wilmington PMSA, DE-MD-NJ	Y	19750 FQ	23440 MW	28620 TQ	USBLS	5/07
	District of Columbia	Y	22600 FQ	28160 MW	35600 TQ	USBLS	5/07
	Washington-Arlington-Alexandria MSA, DC-VA-MD-WV	Y	22600 FQ	28070 MW	34710 TQ	USBLS	5/07
	Florida	Y	18530 FQ	22500 MW	27460 TQ	USBLS	5/07
	Fort Lauderdale-Pompano Beach-Deerfield Beach PMSA, FL	Y	21120 FQ	25730 MW	31560 TQ	USBLS	5/07
	Jacksonville MSA, FL	Y	15850 FQ	20630 MW	25590 TQ	USBLS	5/07
	Lakeland MSA, FL	Y	17010 FQ	19240 MW	23250 TQ	USBLS	5/07
	Miami-Fort Lauderdale-Miami Beach MSA, FL	Y	19550 FQ	23570 MW	29960 TQ	USBLS	5/07
	Orlando-Kissimmee MSA, FL	Y	19030 FQ	22550 MW	27630 TQ	USBLS	5/07
	Pensacola-Ferry Pass-Brent MSA, FL	Y	18470 FQ	20900 MW	23420 TQ	USBLS	5/07
	Tallahassee MSA, FL	Y	16660 FQ	19250 MW	22770 TQ	USBLS	5/07

AE Average entry wage	**AW** Average wage paid	**FQ** First quartile wage	**LO** Lowest wage paid	**MTC** Median total compensation **TCC** Total cash compensation
AER Average entry range	**AWR** Average wage range	**H** Hourly	**LR** Low end range	**MW** Median wage paid **TQ** Third quartile wage
AEX Average experienced wage	**AXR** Average experienced range	**HI** Highest wage paid	**M** Monthly	**MWR** Median wage range **W** Weekly
ATC Average total compensation	**D** Daily	**HR** High end range	**MCC** Median cash compensation	**S** See annotated source **Y** Yearly

Occupation/Type/Industry	Location	Per	Low	Mid	High	Source	Date
Courier and Messenger	Tampa-St. Petersburg-Clearwater MSA, FL	Y	18950 FQ	23010 MW	27420 TQ	USBLS	5/07
	West Palm Beach-Boca Raton-Boynton Beach PMSA, FL	Y	18920 FQ	21950 MW	25550 TQ	USBLS	5/07
	Georgia	Y	18090 FQ	22620 MW	27840 TQ	USBLS	5/07
	Atlanta-Sandy Springs-Marietta MSA, GA	Y	21080 FQ	25800 MW	30540 TQ	USBLS	5/07
	Augusta-Richmond County MSA, GA-SC	Y	14910 FQ	19060 MW	28060 TQ	USBLS	5/07
	Hawaii	Y	18560 FQ	23570 MW	28850 TQ	USBLS	5/07
	Honolulu MSA, HI	Y	17930 FQ	22900 MW	27540 TQ	USBLS	5/07
	Idaho	Y	17380 FQ	20700 MW	23890 TQ	USBLS	5/07
	Boise City-Nampa MSA, ID	Y	18120 FQ	21340 MW	23780 TQ	USBLS	5/07
	Illinois	Y	18150 FQ	22330 MW	29680 TQ	USBLS	5/07
	Chicago-Naperville-Joliet MSA, IL-IN-WI	Y	18840 FQ	23200 MW	31900 TQ	USBLS	5/07
	Indiana	Y	17800 FQ	21820 MW	25960 TQ	USBLS	5/07
	Gary PMSA, IN	Y	19000 FQ	23360 MW	30420 TQ	USBLS	5/07
	Indianapolis-Carmel MSA, IN	Y	17470 FQ	22360 MW	28770 TQ	USBLS	5/07
	Terre Haute MSA, IN	Y	14470 FQ	17070 MW	20860 TQ	USBLS	5/07
	Iowa	Y	17730 FQ	20320 MW	23750 TQ	USBLS	5/07
	Des Moines-West Des Moines MSA, IA	Y	19160 FQ	23180 MW	28540 TQ	USBLS	5/07
	Kansas	Y	17610 FQ	21530 MW	27880 TQ	USBLS	5/07
	Wichita MSA, KS	Y	16920 FQ	18640 MW	26640 TQ	USBLS	5/07
	Kentucky	Y	16652 FQ	20516 MW	25378 TQ	KYBLS	2008
	Louisville-Jefferson County MSA, KY-IN	Y	14550 FQ	19820 MW	23980 TQ	USBLS	5/07
	Louisiana	H	7.01 FQ	8.85 MW	12.13 TQ	LABLS	1/08-3/08
	Baton Rouge MSA, LA	Y	13780 FQ	16800 MW	20660 TQ	USBLS	5/07
	New Orleans-Metairie-Kenner MSA, LA	Y	21250 FQ	25980 MW	31270 TQ	USBLS	5/07
	Maine	Y	20590 FQ	23920 MW	26970 TQ	USBLS	5/07
	Portland-South Portland-Biddeford MSA, ME	Y	22100 FQ	25300 MW	27820 TQ	USBLS	5/07
	Maryland	Y		27400 MW		MDBLS	3/08
	Baltimore-Towson MSA, MD	Y	21130 FQ	26670 MW	31560 TQ	USBLS	5/07
	Bethesda-Gaithersburg-Frederick PMSA, MD	Y	16210 FQ	27420 MW	35790 TQ	USBLS	5/07
	Cumberland MSA, MD-WV	Y	17460 FQ	21140 MW	23300 TQ	USBLS	5/07
	Hagerstown-Martinsburg MSA, MD-WV	Y	25170 FQ	28740 MW	33090 TQ	USBLS	5/07
	Massachusetts	Y	21280 FQ	25430 MW	31160 TQ	USBLS	5/07
	Boston-Cambridge-Quincy NECTA, MA	Y	21280 FQ	24770 MW	29890 TQ	USBLS	5/07
	Worcester MSA, MA-CT	Y	25380 FQ	32170 MW	52450 TQ	USBLS	5/07
	Michigan	Y	19130 FQ	22880 MW	27610 TQ	USBLS	5/07
	Detroit-Warren-Livonia MSA, MI	Y	19070 FQ	24000 MW	28470 TQ	USBLS	5/07
	Grand Rapids-Wyoming MSA, MI	Y	19980 FQ	22520 MW	25280 TQ	USBLS	5/07
	Warren-Troy-Farmington Hills PMSA, MI	Y	18050 FQ	24240 MW	28450 TQ	USBLS	5/07
	Minnesota	Y	22918 FQ	26425 MW	32878 TQ	MNBLS	10/08-12/08
	Minneapolis-Saint Paul MSA, MN-WI	Y	22741 FQ	25291 MW	29288 TQ	MNBLS	10/08-12/08
	Rochester MSA, MN	Y	29330 FQ	46600 MW	56913 TQ	MNBLS	10/08-12/08
	Mississippi	Y	14550 FQ	17500 MW	20860 TQ	USBLS	5/07
	Hattiesburg MSA, MS	Y	15740 FQ	18590 MW	22660 TQ	USBLS	5/07
	Jackson MSA, MS	Y	14350 FQ	17560 MW	22240 TQ	USBLS	5/07
	Missouri	Y	19160 FQ	22690 MW	27690 TQ	USBLS	5/07
	Joplin MSA, MO	Y	16790 FQ	20150 MW	23140 TQ	USBLS	5/07
	Kansas City MSA, MO-KS	Y	17830 FQ	21890 MW	26920 TQ	USBLS	5/07
	St. Louis MSA, MO-IL	Y	21000 FQ	24740 MW	31000 TQ	USBLS	5/07
	Montana	Y	16550 FQ	18300 MW	22600 TQ	USBLS	5/07
	Billings MSA, MT	Y	21100 FQ	23930 MW	28850 TQ	USBLS	5/07
	Nebraska	Y	17420 FQ	20390 MW	23680 TQ	USBLS	5/07
	Omaha-Council Bluffs MSA, NE-IA	Y	18640 FQ	21170 MW	23830 TQ	USBLS	5/07
	Nevada	H	9.28 FQ	10.78 MW	12.54 TQ	NVBLS	5/08
	Las Vegas-Paradise MSA, NV	H	9.12 FQ	10.60 MW	12.27 TQ	NVBLS	5/08
	New Hampshire	H	8.80 AE	11.74 MW	13.25 AEX	NHBLS	6/08

AE	Average entry wage	AW	Average wage paid	FQ	First quartile wage	LO	Lowest wage paid	MTC	Median total compensation	TCC	Total cash compensation
AER	Average entry range	AWR	Average wage range	H	Hourly	LR	Low end range	MW	Median wage paid	TQ	Third quartile wage
AEX	Average experienced wage	AXR	Average experienced range	HI	Highest wage paid	M	Monthly	MWR	Median wage range	W	Weekly
ATC	Average total compensation	D	Daily	HR	High end range	MCC	Median cash compensation	S	See annotated source	Y	Yearly

Occupation/Type/Industry	Location	Per	Low	Mid	High	Source	Date
Courier and Messenger	Manchester MSA, NH	Y	18630 FQ	22410 MW	25310 TQ	USBLS	5/07
	Nashua NECTA, NH-MA	Y	18560 FQ	23460 MW	28560 TQ	USBLS	5/07
	New Jersey	Y	19310 FQ	25300 MW	30900 TQ	USBLS	5/07
	Camden PMSA, NJ	Y	17400 FQ	20160 MW	27870 TQ	USBLS	5/07
	Edison PMSA, NJ	Y	20790 FQ	24360 MW	31030 TQ	USBLS	5/07
	Newark-Union PMSA, NJ-PA	Y	16020 FQ	25270 MW	29480 TQ	USBLS	5/07
	New Mexico	Y	16790 FQ	19050 MW	22360 TQ	USBLS	5/07
	Albuquerque MSA, NM	Y	16990 FQ	18880 MW	21650 TQ	USBLS	5/07
	New York	Y	16800 FQ	21450 MW	29880 TQ	USBLS	5/07
	Albany-Schenectady-Troy MSA, NY	Y	19480 FQ	22250 MW	25810 TQ	USBLS	5/07
	Buffalo-Niagara Falls MSA, NY	Y	19920 FQ	25850 MW	30830 TQ	USBLS	5/07
	Nassau-Suffolk PMSA, NY	Y	24430 FQ	33160 MW	39280 TQ	USBLS	5/07
	New York-Northern New Jersey-Long Island MSA, NY-NJ-PA	Y	16700 FQ	22090 MW	30400 TQ	USBLS	5/07
	North Carolina	Y	18620 FQ	22540 MW	26640 TQ	USBLS	5/07
	Charlotte-Gastonia-Concord MSA, NC-SC	Y	18560 FQ	22030 MW	26880 TQ	USBLS	5/07
	Raleigh-Cary MSA, NC	Y	23030 FQ	26380 MW	30300 TQ	USBLS	5/07
	North Dakota	Y	17630 FQ	19790 MW	22460 TQ	USBLS	5/07
	Bismarck MSA, ND	Y	17180 FQ	18560 MW	19940 TQ	USBLS	5/07
	Fargo MSA, ND-MN	Y	18340 FQ	20630 MW	22780 TQ	USBLS	5/07
	Ohio	Y	19330 FQ	22770 MW	27450 TQ	USBLS	5/07
	Cincinnati-Middletown MSA, OH-KY-IN	Y	20020 FQ	23350 MW	27770 TQ	USBLS	5/07
	Cleveland-Elyria-Mentor MSA, OH	Y	19880 FQ	23340 MW	28990 TQ	USBLS	5/07
	Columbus MSA, OH	Y	20730 FQ	25080 MW	29380 TQ	USBLS	5/07
	Dayton MSA, OH	Y	18680 FQ	21910 MW	27160 TQ	USBLS	5/07
	Oklahoma	Y	16440 FQ	20260 MW	24390 TQ	USBLS	5/07
	Oklahoma City MSA, OK	Y	14600 FQ	19490 MW	24050 TQ	USBLS	5/07
	Tulsa MSA, OK	Y	20110 FQ	22890 MW	28470 TQ	USBLS	5/07
	Oregon	H	10.66 FQ	13.27 MW	15.52 TQ	ORBLS	5/08
	Portland-Vancouver-Beaverton MSA, OR-WA	Y	22460 FQ	28050 MW	32880 TQ	USBLS	5/07
	Pennsylvania	Y	17600 FQ	21760 MW	26290 TQ	USBLS	5/07
	Allentown-Bethlehem-Easton MSA, PA-NJ	Y	17910 FQ	21970 MW	27420 TQ	USBLS	5/07
	Philadelphia-Camden-Wilmington MSA, PA-NJ-DE-MD	Y	19510 FQ	23350 MW	29010 TQ	USBLS	5/07
	Pittsburgh MSA, PA	Y	15260 FQ	20500 MW	25100 TQ	USBLS	5/07
	York-Hanover MSA, PA	Y	21410 FQ	23730 MW	27610 TQ	USBLS	5/07
	Providence-Fall River-Warwick MSA, RI-MA	Y	18780 FQ	25240 MW	33430 TQ	USBLS	5/07
	South Carolina	Y	15300 FQ	19830 MW	24150 TQ	USBLS	5/07
	Charleston-North Charleston MSA, SC	Y	17150 FQ	21070 MW	26350 TQ	USBLS	5/07
	Columbia MSA, SC	Y	16410 FQ	20470 MW	24060 TQ	USBLS	5/07
	Myrtle Beach-Conway-North Myrtle Beach MSA, SC	Y	20090 FQ	23100 MW	34700 TQ	USBLS	5/07
	South Dakota	Y	20373 FQ	22720 MW	25069 TQ	SDBLS	7/08-9/08
	Sioux Falls MSA, SD	Y	21836 FQ	23626 MW	25409 TQ	SDBLS	7/08-9/08
	Tennessee	Y	18140 FQ	21550 MW	26260 TQ	USBLS	5/07
	Memphis MSA, TN-MS-AR	Y	17990 FQ	20920 MW	25130 TQ	USBLS	5/07
	Nashville-Davidson-Murfreesboro MSA, TN	Y	17820 FQ	22330 MW	27560 TQ	USBLS	5/07
	Texas	Y	17890 FQ	22880 MW	28490 TQ	USBLS	5/07
	Austin-Round Rock MSA, TX	Y	20030 FQ	22570 MW	25240 TQ	USBLS	5/07
	Dallas-Fort Worth-Arlington MSA, TX	Y	20090 FQ	25110 MW	29650 TQ	USBLS	5/07
	El Paso MSA, TX	Y	14030 FQ	17030 MW	19880 TQ	USBLS	5/07
	Houston-Sugar Land-Baytown MSA, TX	Y	22790 FQ	26960 MW	36520 TQ	USBLS	5/07
	San Antonio MSA, TX	Y	15130 FQ	18800 MW	24120 TQ	USBLS	5/07
	Utah	Y	19160 FQ	22180 MW	25250 TQ	USBLS	5/07
	Provo-Orem MSA, UT	Y	17600 FQ	19390 MW	21960 TQ	USBLS	5/07
	Salt Lake City MSA, UT	Y	20250 FQ	22990 MW	26580 TQ	USBLS	5/07
	Burlington-South Burlington MSA, VT	Y	24260 FQ	30220 MW	42240 TQ	USBLS	5/07

AE Average entry wage	**AW** Average wage paid	**FQ** First quartile wage	**LO** Lowest wage paid	**MTC** Median total compensation	**TCC** Total cash compensation
AER Average entry range	**AWR** Average wage range	**H** Hourly	**LR** Low end range	**MW** Median wage paid	**TQ** Third quartile wage
AEX Average experienced wage	**AXR** Average experienced range	**HI** Highest wage paid	**M** Monthly	**MWR** Median wage range	**W** Weekly
ATC Average total compensation	**D** Daily	**HR** High end range	**MCC** Median cash compensation	**S** See annotated source	**Y** Yearly

Occupation/Type/Industry	Location	Per	Low	Mid	High	Source	Date
Courier and Messenger	Virginia	Y	20130 FQ	24140 MW	29960 TQ	USBLS	5/07
	Charlottesville MSA, VA	Y	22780 FQ	26150 MW	29680 TQ	USBLS	5/07
	Richmond MSA, VA	Y	19160 FQ	23660 MW	30110 TQ	USBLS	5/07
	Virginia Beach-Norfolk-Newport News MSA, VA-NC	Y	19880 FQ	22500 MW	26680 TQ	USBLS	5/07
	Washington	H	10.15 FQ	11.48 MW	13.84 TQ	WABLS	3/08
	Seattle-Tacoma-Bellevue MSA, WA	Y	22060 FQ	24900 MW	30250 TQ	USBLS	5/07
	West Virginia	Y	17340 FQ	21632 MW	25597 TQ	WVBLS	7/08-9/08
	Charleston MSA, WV	Y	16000 FQ	18940 MW	22980 TQ	USBLS	5/07
	Wisconsin	Y	20860 FQ	24490 MW	29610 TQ	USBLS	5/07
	Green Bay MSA, WI	Y	19870 FQ	23210 MW	33850 TQ	USBLS	5/07
	Milwaukee-Waukesha-West Allis MSA, WI	Y	22000 FQ	25440 MW	29100 TQ	USBLS	5/07
	Racine MSA, WI	Y	18730 FQ	22170 MW	24940 TQ	USBLS	5/07
	Wyoming	Y	18873 FQ	21823 MW	24165 TQ	WYBLS	9/08
	Cheyenne MSA, WY	Y	19873 FQ	22173 MW	24303 TQ	WYBLS	9/08
	Puerto Rico	Y	13180 FQ	15240 MW	19190 TQ	USBLS	5/07
	San Juan-Caguas-Guaynabo MSA, PR	Y	13320 FQ	15600 MW	19530 TQ	USBLS	5/07
	Virgin Islands	Y	16320 FQ	19940 MW	23910 TQ	USBLS	5/07
	Guam	Y	14550 FQ	17690 MW	23170 TQ	USBLS	5/07
Court, Municipal, and License Clerk	Alabama	Y	22370 FQ	26840 MW	33010 TQ	USBLS	5/07
	Birmingham-Hoover MSA, AL	Y	26010 FQ	30450 MW	37450 TQ	USBLS	5/07
	Alaska	Y	31300 FQ	36010 MW	40940 TQ	USBLS	5/07
	Anchorage MSA, AK	Y	29540 FQ	33990 MW	39060 TQ	USBLS	5/07
	Arizona	Y	27330 FQ	30700 MW	37310 TQ	USBLS	5/07
	Phoenix-Mesa-Scottsdale MSA, AZ	Y	28230 FQ	31740 MW	39200 TQ	USBLS	5/07
	Tucson MSA, AZ	Y	27480 FQ	30360 MW	36030 TQ	USBLS	5/07
	Arkansas	Y	19740 FQ	23410 MW	27950 TQ	USBLS	5/07
	Little Rock-North Little Rock MSA, AR	Y	21920 FQ	24520 MW	29510 TQ	USBLS	5/07
	Pine Bluff MSA, AR	Y	14970 FQ	17290 MW	22390 TQ	USBLS	5/07
	California	H	17.64 FQ	21.00 MW	25.53 TQ	CABLS	1/08-3/08
	Oakland-Fremont-Hayward MSA, CA	H	20.48 FQ	24.49 MW	28.86 TQ	CABLS	1/08-3/08
	Sacramento-Arden Arcade-Roseville MSA, CA	H	16.47 FQ	18.65 MW	22.18 TQ	CABLS	1/08-3/08
	San Diego-Carlsbad-San Marcos MSA, CA	H	17.05 FQ	19.08 MW	25.37 TQ	CABLS	1/08-3/08
	San Jose-Sunnyvale-Santa Clara MSA, CA	H	18.31 FQ	22.70 MW	27.34 TQ	CABLS	1/08-3/08
	Colorado	Y	28980 FQ	34600 MW	41220 TQ	USBLS	5/07
	Denver-Aurora MSA, CO	Y	30830 FQ	36720 MW	43720 TQ	USBLS	5/07
	Connecticut	H	13.39 AE	20.93 MW		CTBLS	1/08-3/08
	Bridgeport-Stamford-Norwalk MSA, CT	Y	35050 FQ	43320 MW	50160 TQ	USBLS	5/07
	Hartford-West Hartford-East Hartford MSA, CT	Y	35270 FQ	44620 MW	53440 TQ	USBLS	5/07
	Delaware	Y	27770 FQ	31950 MW	36770 TQ	USBLS	5/07
	Wilmington PMSA, DE-MD-NJ	Y	27590 FQ	31960 MW	37700 TQ	USBLS	5/07
	Washington-Arlington-Alexandria MSA, DC-VA-MD-WV	Y	33310 FQ	37830 MW	45440 TQ	USBLS	5/07
	Florida	Y	24650 FQ	29270 MW	35440 TQ	USBLS	5/07
	Fort Lauderdale-Pompano Beach-Deerfield Beach PMSA, FL	Y	25340 FQ	31220 MW	39010 TQ	USBLS	5/07
	Jacksonville MSA, FL	Y	26690 FQ	29990 MW	34300 TQ	USBLS	5/07
	Miami-Fort Lauderdale-Miami Beach MSA, FL	Y	26620 FQ	33050 MW	41530 TQ	USBLS	5/07
	Orlando-Kissimmee MSA, FL	Y	24390 FQ	28560 MW	33440 TQ	USBLS	5/07
	Pensacola-Ferry Pass-Brent MSA, FL	Y	25360 FQ	29850 MW	35190 TQ	USBLS	5/07
	Tampa-St. Petersburg-Clearwater MSA, FL	Y	26900 FQ	30620 MW	36010 TQ	USBLS	5/07
	West Palm Beach-Boca Raton-Boynton Beach PMSA, FL	Y	27100 FQ	32810 MW	41030 TQ	USBLS	5/07

AE Average entry wage	**AW** Average wage paid	**FQ** First quartile wage	**LO** Lowest wage paid	**MTC** Median total compensation	**TCC** Total cash compensation
AER Average entry range	**AWR** Average wage range	**H** Hourly	**LR** Low end range	**MW** Median wage paid	**TQ** Third quartile wage
AEX Average experienced wage	**AXR** Average experienced range	**HI** Highest wage paid	**M** Monthly	**MWR** Median wage range	**W** Weekly
ATC Average total compensation	**D** Daily	**HR** High end range	**MCC** Median cash compensation	**S** See annotated source	**Y** Yearly

Occupation/Type/Industry	Location	Per	Low	Mid	High	Source	Date
Court, Municipal, and License Clerk							
	Georgia	Y	22840 FQ	28350 MW	34770 TQ	USBLS	5/07
	Atlanta-Sandy Springs-Marietta MSA, GA	Y	26670 FQ	31350 MW	37850 TQ	USBLS	5/07
	Augusta-Richmond County MSA, GA-SC	Y	12820 FQ	14080 MW	26900 TQ	USBLS	5/07
	Hawaii	Y	32590 FQ	38260 MW	46070 TQ	USBLS	5/07
	Idaho	Y	24720 FQ	28820 MW	32920 TQ	USBLS	5/07
	Boise City-Nampa MSA, ID	Y	27570 FQ	30940 MW	36140 TQ	USBLS	5/07
	Illinois	Y	16380 FQ	28700 MW	36930 TQ	USBLS	5/07
	Chicago-Naperville-Joliet MSA, IL-IN-WI	Y	24750 FQ	32820 MW	38110 TQ	USBLS	5/07
	Indiana	Y	21520 FQ	24710 MW	28970 TQ	USBLS	5/07
	Gary PMSA, IN	Y	21750 FQ	23690 MW	26280 TQ	USBLS	5/07
	Indianapolis-Carmel MSA, IN	Y	19730 FQ	24500 MW	30100 TQ	USBLS	5/07
	Iowa	Y	25530 FQ	31750 MW	37410 TQ	USBLS	5/07
	Des Moines-West Des Moines MSA, IA	Y	27760 FQ	33860 MW	37840 TQ	USBLS	5/07
	Kansas	Y	23680 FQ	27990 MW	31790 TQ	USBLS	5/07
	Wichita MSA, KS	Y	25840 FQ	28710 MW	31590 TQ	USBLS	5/07
	Kentucky	Y	23077 FQ	27125 MW	32801 TQ	KYBLS	2008
	Louisiana	H	6.98 FQ	11.03 MW	15.04 TQ	LABLS	1/08-3/08
	Baton Rouge MSA, LA	Y	24040 FQ	28380 MW	32530 TQ	USBLS	5/07
	Maine	Y	23010 FQ	27650 MW	32310 TQ	USBLS	5/07
	Portland-South Portland-Biddeford MSA, ME	Y	26100 FQ	30260 MW	35470 TQ	USBLS	5/07
	Maryland	Y		36125 MW		MDBLS	3/08
	Massachusetts	Y	35550 FQ	44040 MW	53880 TQ	USBLS	5/07
	Boston-Cambridge-Quincy NECTA, MA	Y	36910 FQ	45030 MW	53310 TQ	USBLS	5/07
	Michigan	Y	30210 FQ	36290 MW	43040 TQ	USBLS	5/07
	Detroit-Warren-Livonia MSA, MI	Y	30890 FQ	37530 MW	44280 TQ	USBLS	5/07
	Grand Rapids-Wyoming MSA, MI	Y	34160 FQ	38740 MW	44890 TQ	USBLS	5/07
	Warren-Troy-Farmington Hills PMSA, MI	Y	34210 FQ	39690 MW	45880 TQ	USBLS	5/07
	Minnesota	Y	32691 FQ	38280 MW	44972 TQ	MNBLS	10/08-12/08
	Duluth-Superior MSA, MN-WI	Y	35439 FQ	40965 MW	47730 TQ	MNBLS	10/08-12/08
	Minneapolis-Saint Paul MSA, MN-WI	Y	32920 FQ	38103 MW	44525 TQ	MNBLS	10/08-12/08
	Rochester MSA, MN	Y	19032 FQ	35573 MW	46188 TQ	MNBLS	10/08-12/08
	Mississippi	Y	20620 FQ	24190 MW	29590 TQ	USBLS	5/07
	Jackson MSA, MS	Y	21760 FQ	25470 MW	30760 TQ	USBLS	5/07
	Missouri	Y	21040 FQ	24490 MW	29730 TQ	USBLS	5/07
	Kansas City MSA, MO-KS	Y	25850 FQ	28920 MW	31930 TQ	USBLS	5/07
	St. Louis MSA, MO-IL	Y	25150 FQ	32540 MW	41530 TQ	USBLS	5/07
	Montana	Y	21970 FQ	25690 MW	30480 TQ	USBLS	5/07
	Billings MSA, MT	Y	21540 FQ	24080 MW	27870 TQ	USBLS	5/07
	Nebraska	Y	25930 FQ	31120 MW	37670 TQ	USBLS	5/07
	Omaha-Council Bluffs MSA, NE-IA	Y	28520 FQ	33280 MW	39470 TQ	USBLS	5/07
	Nevada	H	16.22 FQ	19.30 MW	23.94 TQ	NVBLS	5/08
	Las Vegas-Paradise MSA, NV	H	16.90 FQ	19.92 MW	25.11 TQ	NVBLS	5/08
	New Hampshire	H	9.85 AE	13.92 MW	16.25 AEX	NHBLS	6/08
	Rochester-Dover MSA, NH-ME	Y	25380 FQ	29020 MW	33850 TQ	USBLS	5/07
	New Jersey	Y	30430 FQ	37220 MW	45900 TQ	USBLS	5/07
	Atlantic City MSA, NJ	Y	29950 FQ	37230 MW	45720 TQ	USBLS	5/07
	Camden PMSA, NJ	Y	29380 FQ	36410 MW	45440 TQ	USBLS	5/07
	Edison PMSA, NJ	Y	30810 FQ	37450 MW	45810 TQ	USBLS	5/07
	Newark-Union PMSA, NJ-PA	Y	31540 FQ	38670 MW	47020 TQ	USBLS	5/07
	Trenton-Ewing MSA, NJ	Y	29670 FQ	36100 MW	45540 TQ	USBLS	5/07
	New Mexico	Y	23790 FQ	28880 MW	34720 TQ	USBLS	5/07
	Albuquerque MSA, NM	Y	22960 FQ	27960 MW	33480 TQ	USBLS	5/07
	New York	Y	31280 FQ	40010 MW	63990 TQ	USBLS	5/07
	Albany-Schenectady-Troy MSA, NY	Y	29110 FQ	34070 MW	40140 TQ	USBLS	5/07
	Nassau-Suffolk PMSA, NY	Y	34930 FQ	47440 MW	71500 TQ	USBLS	5/07

AE	Average entry wage	AW	Average wage paid	FQ	First quartile wage
AER	Average entry range	AWR	Average wage range	H	Hourly
AEX	Average experienced wage	AXR	Average experienced range	HI	Highest wage paid
ATC	Average total compensation	D	Daily	HR	High end range

LO	Lowest wage paid	MTC	Median total compensation	TCC	Total cash compensation
LR	Low end range	MW	Median wage paid	TQ	Third quartile wage
M	Monthly	MWR	Median wage range	W	Weekly
MCC	Median cash compensation	S	See annotated source	Y	Yearly

Occupation/Type/Industry	Location	Per	Low	Mid	High	Source	Date
Court, Municipal, and License Clerk	New York-Northern New Jersey-Long Island MSA, NY-NJ-PA	Y	33870 FQ	43430 MW	62400 TQ	USBLS	5/07
	North Carolina	Y	24760 FQ	29490 MW	35530 TQ	USBLS	5/07
	Charlotte-Gastonia-Concord MSA, NC-SC	Y	25170 FQ	29340 MW	35230 TQ	USBLS	5/07
	Raleigh-Cary MSA, NC	Y	27220 FQ	30850 MW	36380 TQ	USBLS	5/07
	North Dakota	Y	23690 FQ	28880 MW	34050 TQ	USBLS	5/07
	Fargo MSA, ND-MN	Y	22110 FQ	31570 MW	39500 TQ	USBLS	5/07
	Ohio	Y	25850 FQ	31890 MW	38770 TQ	USBLS	5/07
	Cincinnati-Middletown MSA, OH-KY-IN	Y	24560 FQ	30170 MW	36620 TQ	USBLS	5/07
	Cleveland-Elyria-Mentor MSA, OH	Y	26860 FQ	32320 MW	39640 TQ	USBLS	5/07
	Columbus MSA, OH	Y	33040 FQ	36900 MW	40770 TQ	USBLS	5/07
	Dayton MSA, OH	Y	25950 FQ	29980 MW	35000 TQ	USBLS	5/07
	Oklahoma	Y	18870 FQ	22750 MW	28000 TQ	USBLS	5/07
	Oklahoma City MSA, OK	Y	19630 FQ	23840 MW	30490 TQ	USBLS	5/07
	Tulsa MSA, OK	Y	19100 FQ	23110 MW	29980 TQ	USBLS	5/07
	Oregon	H	14.29 FQ	16.53 MW	18.57 TQ	ORBLS	5/08
	Medford MSA, OR	Y	30550 FQ	34880 MW	38750 TQ	USBLS	5/07
	Portland-Vancouver-Beaverton MSA, OR-WA	Y	29950 FQ	34990 MW	39400 TQ	USBLS	5/07
	Pennsylvania	Y	23340 FQ	30540 MW	37780 TQ	USBLS	5/07
	Allentown-Bethlehem-Easton MSA, PA-NJ	Y	27780 FQ	32020 MW	38300 TQ	USBLS	5/07
	Lancaster MSA, PA	Y	16820 FQ	25700 MW	34870 TQ	USBLS	5/07
	Philadelphia-Camden-Wilmington MSA, PA-NJ-DE-MD	Y	28070 FQ	34390 MW	41770 TQ	USBLS	5/07
	Pittsburgh MSA, PA	Y	24160 FQ	30390 MW	36330 TQ	USBLS	5/07
	Rhode Island	Y	33940 FQ	40990 MW	48560 TQ	USBLS	5/07
	Providence-Fall River-Warwick MSA, RI-MA	Y	33700 FQ	40960 MW	48690 TQ	USBLS	5/07
	South Carolina	Y	22940 FQ	26570 MW	31180 TQ	USBLS	5/07
	Charleston-North Charleston MSA, SC	Y	23220 FQ	27180 MW	31960 TQ	USBLS	5/07
	Columbia MSA, SC	Y	22970 FQ	26450 MW	31320 TQ	USBLS	5/07
	South Dakota	Y	22076 FQ	25462 MW	30770 TQ	SDBLS	7/08-9/08
	Rapid City MSA, SD	Y	23552 FQ	26928 MW	30800 TQ	SDBLS	7/08-9/08
	Sioux Falls MSA, SD	Y	22951 FQ	28164 MW	32576 TQ	SDBLS	7/08-9/08
	Tennessee	Y	23260 FQ	29010 MW	36190 TQ	USBLS	5/07
	Memphis MSA, TN-MS-AR	Y	22480 FQ	30900 MW	37410 TQ	USBLS	5/07
	Nashville-Davidson-Murfreesboro MSA, TN	Y	26480 FQ	31410 MW	38510 TQ	USBLS	5/07
	Texas	Y	23220 FQ	27430 MW	32470 TQ	USBLS	5/07
	Austin-Round Rock MSA, TX	Y	25110 FQ	29870 MW	38730 TQ	USBLS	5/07
	Brownsville-Harlingen MSA, TX	Y	21590 FQ	27220 MW	43390 TQ	USBLS	5/07
	Dallas-Fort Worth-Arlington MSA, TX	Y	27000 FQ	31220 MW	36610 TQ	USBLS	5/07
	El Paso MSA, TX	Y	22590 FQ	24790 MW	29670 TQ	USBLS	5/07
	Houston-Sugar Land-Baytown MSA, TX	Y	24610 FQ	28500 MW	34160 TQ	USBLS	5/07
	San Antonio MSA, TX	Y	23740 FQ	27400 MW	32170 TQ	USBLS	5/07
	Utah	Y	23600 FQ	27540 MW	31830 TQ	USBLS	5/07
	Salt Lake City MSA, UT	Y	24650 FQ	28350 MW	32590 TQ	USBLS	5/07
	Vermont	Y	26870 FQ	30710 MW	36210 TQ	USBLS	5/07
	Burlington-South Burlington MSA, VT	Y	28890 FQ	32490 MW	38280 TQ	USBLS	5/07
	Virginia	Y	26280 FQ	31150 MW	37150 TQ	USBLS	5/07
	Richmond MSA, VA	Y	27590 FQ	31440 MW	37210 TQ	USBLS	5/07
	Virginia Beach-Norfolk-Newport News MSA, VA-NC	Y	26200 FQ	30110 MW	36220 TQ	USBLS	5/07
	Washington	H	16.02 FQ	18.38 MW	21.33 TQ	WABLS	3/08
	Seattle-Tacoma-Bellevue MSA, WA	Y	34060 FQ	40200 MW	46240 TQ	USBLS	5/07
	West Virginia	Y	22656 FQ	27451 MW	31215 TQ	WVBLS	7/08-9/08
	Charleston MSA, WV	Y	21230 FQ	25800 MW	29610 TQ	USBLS	5/07
	Wisconsin	Y	25540 FQ	33390 MW	38570 TQ	USBLS	5/07
	Appleton MSA, WI	Y	15720 FQ	34970 MW	40790 TQ	USBLS	5/07

AE	Average entry wage	AW	Average wage paid	FQ	First quartile wage
AER	Average entry range	AWR	Average wage range	H	Hourly
AEX	Average experienced wage	AXR	Average experienced range	HI	Highest wage paid
ATC	Average total compensation	D	Daily	HR	High end range

LO	Lowest wage paid	MTC	Median total compensation
LR	Low end range	MW	Median wage paid
M	Monthly	MWR	Median wage range
MCC	Median cash compensation	S	See annotated source

TCC	Total cash compensation
TQ	Third quartile wage
W	Weekly
Y	Yearly

Occupation/Type/Industry	Location	Per	Low	Mid	High	Source	Date
Court, Municipal, and License Clerk	Green Bay MSA, WI	Y	18050 FQ	26680 MW	34850 TQ	USBLS	5/07
	Milwaukee-Waukesha-West Allis MSA, WI	Y	34430 FQ	37380 MW	41060 TQ	USBLS	5/07
	Wyoming	Y	26469 FQ	31030 MW	37093 TQ	WYBLS	9/08
Court Administrator	Luzerne County, PA	Y			97050 HI	TLEAD	2009
Court Cashier	Seattle, WA	H	18.35 LO		21.29 HI	CSSS	2007
Court Clerk	Duluth, GA	Y	36598 LO		56702 HI	AREGC	2007
	Biloxi, MS	Y			35234 HI	MML	2008
	Pascagoula, MS	Y			41057 HI	MML	2008
Court Crier							
State Supreme Court	Michigan	Y			71410 HI	LSJ02	7/11/07
Court House Security Officer	Rhode Island	Y		41917 AW		RIM01	2009
Court Interpreter	Seattle, WA	H	24.63 LO		28.74 HI	CSSS	2008
Court Reporter	United States	Y	30000-50000 LR			WSJ12	2008
	Alabama	Y	14260 FQ	22160 MW	46970 TQ	USBLS	5/07
	Birmingham-Hoover MSA, AL	Y	13860 FQ	20480 MW	23010 TQ	USBLS	5/07
	Arizona	Y	42830 FQ	52530 MW	60160 TQ	USBLS	5/07
	Phoenix-Mesa-Scottsdale MSA, AZ	Y	50940 FQ	57820 MW	63410 TQ	USBLS	5/07
	Tucson MSA, AZ	Y	37670 FQ	43750 MW	54930 TQ	USBLS	5/07
	California	H	28.76 FQ	35.32 MW	39.74 TQ	CABLS	1/08-3/08
	Oakland-Fremont-Hayward MSA, CA	H	31.95 FQ	37.74 MW	44.10 TQ	CABLS	1/08-3/08
	Sacramento-Arden Arcade-Roseville MSA, CA	H	26.50 FQ	28.71 MW	30.92 TQ	CABLS	1/08-3/08
	San Jose-Sunnyvale-Santa Clara MSA, CA	H	26.96 FQ	29.52 MW	34.10 TQ	CABLS	1/08-3/08
	Colorado	Y	44210 FQ	54620 MW	64560 TQ	USBLS	5/07
	Denver-Aurora MSA, CO	Y	45600 FQ	55970 MW	67800 TQ	USBLS	5/07
	Delaware	Y	38550 FQ	59390 MW	70450 TQ	USBLS	5/07
	Wilmington PMSA, DE-MD-NJ	Y	32590 FQ	40250 MW	58520 TQ	USBLS	5/07
	District of Columbia	Y	42710 FQ	45630 MW	48800 TQ	USBLS	5/07
	Washington-Arlington-Alexandria MSA, DC-VA-MD-WV	Y	35540 FQ	41700 MW	47050 TQ	USBLS	5/07
	Florida	Y	25710 FQ	32910 MW	44550 TQ	USBLS	5/07
	Fort Lauderdale-Pompano Beach-Deerfield Beach PMSA, FL	Y	31460 FQ	35580 MW	47380 TQ	USBLS	5/07
	Jacksonville MSA, FL	Y	15270 FQ	21820 MW	24510 TQ	USBLS	5/07
	Miami-Fort Lauderdale-Miami Beach MSA, FL	Y	31240 FQ	37830 MW	47480 TQ	USBLS	5/07
	Orlando-Kissimmee MSA, FL	Y	15400 FQ	32500 MW	41650 TQ	USBLS	5/07
	Tampa-St. Petersburg-Clearwater MSA, FL	Y	21960 FQ	25230 MW	36400 TQ	USBLS	5/07
	West Palm Beach-Boca Raton-Boynton Beach PMSA, FL	Y	29200 FQ	40190 MW	44630 TQ	USBLS	5/07
	Georgia	Y	20850 FQ	39830 MW	55410 TQ	USBLS	5/07
	Atlanta-Sandy Springs-Marietta MSA, GA	Y	23300 FQ	43320 MW	64730 TQ	USBLS	5/07
	Idaho	Y	43060 FQ	46620 MW	50460 TQ	USBLS	5/07
	Illinois	Y	18280 FQ	46280 MW	52210 TQ	USBLS	5/07
	Chicago-Naperville-Joliet MSA, IL-IN-WI	Y	28930 FQ	43860 MW	50290 TQ	USBLS	5/07
	Indiana	Y	28100 FQ	32190 MW	37700 TQ	USBLS	5/07
	Gary PMSA, IN	Y	31470 FQ	34410 MW	37690 TQ	USBLS	5/07
	Indianapolis-Carmel MSA, IN	Y	28690 FQ	33290 MW	40350 TQ	USBLS	5/07
	Iowa	Y	52410 FQ	56820 MW	61260 TQ	USBLS	5/07
	Kansas	Y	46630 FQ	55550 MW	61390 TQ	USBLS	5/07
	Kentucky	Y	26776 FQ	37725 MW	52568 TQ	KYBLS	2008
	Louisville-Jefferson County MSA, KY-IN	Y	27120 FQ	30790 MW	52050 TQ	USBLS	5/07
	Louisiana	H	12.06 FQ	16.13 MW	21.21 TQ	LABLS	1/08-3/08

AE	Average entry wage	AW	Average wage paid	FQ First quartile wage
AER	Average entry range	AWR	Average wage range	H Hourly
AEX	Average experienced wage	AXR	Average experienced range	HI Highest wage paid
ATC	Average total compensation	D	Daily	HR High end range

LO	Lowest wage paid	MTC Median total compensation	TCC Total cash compensation
LR	Low end range	MW Median wage paid	TQ Third quartile wage
M	Monthly	MWR Median wage range	W Weekly
MCC	Median cash compensation	S See annotated source	Y Yearly

Occupation/Type/Industry	Location	Per	Low	Mid	High	Source	Date
Court Reporter	Baton Rouge MSA, LA	Y	15790 FQ	42690 MW	48990 TQ	USBLS	5/07
	New Orleans-Metairie-Kenner MSA, LA	Y	30060 FQ	33620 MW	42340 TQ	USBLS	5/07
	Maine	Y	31260 FQ	53640 MW	60450 TQ	USBLS	5/07
	Portland-South Portland-Biddeford MSA, ME	Y	29790 FQ	44050 MW	57360 TQ	USBLS	5/07
	Maryland	Y		36575 MW		MDBLS	3/08
	Baltimore-Towson MSA, MD	Y	29190 FQ	35420 MW	41170 TQ	USBLS	5/07
	Massachusetts	Y	56640 FQ	62920 MW	71340 TQ	USBLS	5/07
	Michigan	Y	38310 FQ	45390 MW	54410 TQ	USBLS	5/07
	Detroit-Warren-Livonia MSA, MI	Y	45900 FQ	54110 MW	60450 TQ	USBLS	5/07
	Grand Rapids-Wyoming MSA, MI	Y	40400 FQ	44830 MW	49730 TQ	USBLS	5/07
	Warren-Troy-Farmington Hills PMSA, MI	Y	43120 FQ	53530 MW	59900 TQ	USBLS	5/07
	Minnesota	Y	54937 FQ	60053 MW	65158 TQ	MNBLS	10/08-12/08
	Duluth-Superior MSA, MN-WI	Y	49549 FQ	57500 MW	63129 TQ	MNBLS	10/08-12/08
	Minneapolis-Saint Paul MSA, MN-WI	Y	55303 FQ	60524 MW	65744 TQ	MNBLS	10/08-12/08
	Mississippi	Y	27140 FQ	42760 MW	49160 TQ	USBLS	5/07
	Missouri	Y	41490 FQ	55280 MW	61140 TQ	USBLS	5/07
	Kansas City MSA, MO-KS	Y	40920 FQ	54270 MW	59930 TQ	USBLS	5/07
	St. Louis MSA, MO-IL	Y	45260 FQ	55940 MW	62060 TQ	USBLS	5/07
	Montana	Y	25050 FQ	35330 MW	41410 TQ	USBLS	5/07
	Nebraska	Y	30940 FQ	43710 MW	81550 TQ	USBLS	5/07
	Omaha-Council Bluffs MSA, NE-IA	Y	32700 FQ	49650 MW	81410 TQ	USBLS	5/07
	Nevada	H	18.55 FQ	22.61 MW	26.02 TQ	NVBLS	5/08
	Las Vegas-Paradise MSA, NV	H	21.23 FQ	24.11 MW	27.51 TQ	NVBLS	5/08
	New Jersey	Y	32750 FQ	47490 MW	75790 TQ	USBLS	5/07
	Camden PMSA, NJ	Y	28740 FQ	37760 MW	59560 TQ	USBLS	5/07
	Edison PMSA, NJ	Y	33120 FQ	39670 MW	74040 TQ	USBLS	5/07
	Newark-Union PMSA, NJ-PA	Y	68250 FQ	84740 MW	94850 TQ	USBLS	5/07
	New Mexico	Y	29930 FQ	53230 MW	73910 TQ	USBLS	5/07
	New York	Y	44010 FQ	70320 MW	91830 TQ	USBLS	5/07
	Buffalo-Niagara Falls MSA, NY	Y	38820 FQ	52630 MW	75000 TQ	USBLS	5/07
	Nassau-Suffolk PMSA, NY	Y	45910 FQ	67160 MW	88560 TQ	USBLS	5/07
	New York-Northern New Jersey-Long Island MSA, NY-NJ-PA	Y	40160 FQ	66480 MW	90420 TQ	USBLS	5/07
	North Carolina	Y	33120 FQ	41250 MW	51080 TQ	USBLS	5/07
	North Dakota	Y	19860 FQ	39870 MW	54630 TQ	USBLS	5/07
	Fargo MSA, ND-MN	Y	17650 FQ	19700 MW	24740 TQ	USBLS	5/07
	Ohio	Y	35050 FQ	44420 MW	52700 TQ	USBLS	5/07
	Cincinnati-Middletown MSA, OH-KY-IN	Y	26420 FQ	39630 MW	47680 TQ	USBLS	5/07
	Cleveland-Elyria-Mentor MSA, OH	Y	20530 FQ	37950 MW	56760 TQ	USBLS	5/07
	Columbus MSA, OH	Y	38630 FQ	48910 MW	59790 TQ	USBLS	5/07
	Dayton MSA, OH	Y	37740 FQ	43440 MW	50220 TQ	USBLS	5/07
	Oklahoma	Y	37010 FQ	44290 MW	51600 TQ	USBLS	5/07
	Oklahoma City MSA, OK	Y	36840 FQ	45520 MW	58280 TQ	USBLS	5/07
	Tulsa MSA, OK	Y	38180 FQ	45510 MW	52100 TQ	USBLS	5/07
	Portland-Vancouver-Beaverton MSA, OR-WA	Y	51860 FQ	87740 MW	118660 TQ	USBLS	5/07
	Pennsylvania	Y	37160 FQ	43670 MW	53660 TQ	USBLS	5/07
	Allentown-Bethlehem-Easton MSA, PA-NJ	Y	40310 FQ	43230 MW	46320 TQ	USBLS	5/07
	Philadelphia-Camden-Wilmington MSA, PA-NJ-DE-MD	Y	35730 FQ	46090 MW	61540 TQ	USBLS	5/07
	Pittsburgh MSA, PA	Y	39240 FQ	43430 MW	47190 TQ	USBLS	5/07
	South Carolina	Y	33930 FQ	37660 MW	41790 TQ	USBLS	5/07
	Columbia MSA, SC	Y	34090 FQ	37280 MW	40590 TQ	USBLS	5/07
	South Dakota	Y	43502 FQ	47231 MW	50961 TQ	SDBLS	7/08-9/08
	Tennessee	Y	23300 FQ	46400 MW	98610 TQ	USBLS	5/07
	Memphis MSA, TN-MS-AR	Y	23090 FQ	64250 MW	100420 TQ	USBLS	5/07
	Nashville-Davidson-Murfreesboro MSA, TN	Y	22990 FQ	45390 MW	102080 TQ	USBLS	5/07
	Texas	Y	28510 FQ	48760 MW	63750 TQ	USBLS	5/07

AE	Average entry wage	AW	Average wage paid	FQ	First quartile wage
AER	Average entry range	AWR	Average wage range	H	Hourly
AEX	Average experienced wage	AXR	Average experienced range	HI	Highest wage paid
ATC	Average total compensation	D	Daily	HR	High end range

LO	Lowest wage paid	MTC	Median total compensation	TCC	Total cash compensation
LR	Low end range	MW	Median wage paid	TQ	Third quartile wage
M	Monthly	MWR	Median wage range	W	Weekly
MCC	Median cash compensation	S	See annotated source	Y	Yearly

Occupation/Type/Industry	Location	Per	Low	Mid	High	Source	Date
Court Reporter	Austin-Round Rock MSA, TX	Y	26010 FQ	33780 MW	61020 TQ	USBLS	5/07
	Dallas-Fort Worth-Arlington MSA, TX	Y	31480 FQ *	51730 MW	71460 TQ	USBLS	5/07
	El Paso MSA, TX	Y	50650 FQ	58700 MW	66790 TQ	USBLS	5/07
	Houston-Sugar Land-Baytown MSA, TX	Y	22950 FQ	40990 MW	60300 TQ	USBLS	5/07
	San Antonio MSA, TX	Y	46520 FQ	53910 MW	67380 TQ	USBLS	5/07
	Virginia	Y	50760 FQ	54730 MW	58740 TQ	USBLS	5/07
	Washington	H	27.51 FQ	33.18 MW	36.76 TQ	WABLS	3/08
	West Virginia	Y	39810 FQ	46024 MW	50687 TQ	WVBLS	7/08-9/08
	Wisconsin	Y	30370 FQ	41980 MW	54970 TQ	USBLS	5/07
	Milwaukee-Waukesha-West Allis MSA, WI	Y	26050 FQ	38210 MW	44180 TQ	USBLS	5/07
	Puerto Rico	Y	26240 FQ	28680 MW	31110 TQ	USBLS	5/07
	San Juan-Caguas-Guaynabo MSA, PR	Y	26270 FQ	28700 MW	31120 TQ	USBLS	5/07
Court Security Officer State Court of Appeals	Michigan	Y		43414 AW		LSJ02	7/11/07
Courtroom Assistant	Colorado Springs, CO	M	3249 LO			COSPRS	1/1/09
Courtroom Clerk	New Hampshire	Y		31374 AW		NHUL03	2008
Craft Artist	Alabama	Y	17300 FQ	21430 MW	28610 TQ	USBLS	5/07
	Arizona	Y	21320 FQ	24000 MW	30670 TQ	USBLS	5/07
	Arkansas	Y	16450 FQ	17550 MW	18660 TQ	USBLS	5/07
	California	H	13.35 FQ	18.17 MW	23.70 TQ	CABLS	1/08-3/08
	Colorado	Y	17280 FQ	22940 MW	28860 TQ	USBLS	5/07
	Connecticut	H	10.49 AE	15.74 MW		CTBLS	1/08-3/08
	Florida	Y	19420 FQ	24950 MW	31270 TQ	USBLS	5/07
	Georgia	Y	24180 FQ	28710 MW	33390 TQ	USBLS	5/07
	Illinois	Y	29410 FQ	41150 MW	47220 TQ	USBLS	5/07
	Indiana	Y	22520 FQ	29820 MW	36700 TQ	USBLS	5/07
	Maine	Y	20980 FQ	23970 MW	36420 TQ	USBLS	5/07
	Maryland	Y		22750 MW		MDBLS	3/08
	Massachusetts	Y	26650 FQ	36720 MW	54440 TQ	USBLS	5/07
	Michigan	Y	14880 FQ	15040 MW	24750 TQ	USBLS	5/07
	Minnesota	Y	30079 FQ	49476 MW	72953 TQ	MNBLS	10/08-12/08
	Missouri	Y	23460 FQ	33510 MW	46260 TQ	USBLS	5/07
	Montana	Y	14210 FQ	15690 MW	34030 TQ	USBLS	5/07
	New Mexico	Y	16160 FQ	17770 MW	19740 TQ	USBLS	5/07
	New York	Y	30960 FQ	38030 MW	44880 TQ	USBLS	5/07
	North Carolina	Y	20490 FQ	23690 MW	27920 TQ	USBLS	5/07
	Ohio	Y	16190 FQ	19530 MW	25160 TQ	USBLS	5/07
	Oregon	H	11.28 FQ	12.72 MW	14.79 TQ	ORBLS	5/08
	Pennsylvania	Y	20180 FQ	22440 MW	26790 TQ	USBLS	5/07
	South Carolina	Y	16820 FQ	18300 MW	19950 TQ	USBLS	5/07
	South Dakota	Y	22411 FQ	26390 MW	30065 TQ	SDBLS	7/08-9/08
	Tennessee	Y	20290 FQ	23750 MW	54890 TQ	USBLS	5/07
	Texas	Y	14540 FQ	21590 MW	28950 TQ	USBLS	5/07
	Utah	Y	21340 FQ	27230 MW	30520 TQ	USBLS	5/07
	Washington	H	11.80 FQ	14.72 MW	17.95 TQ	WABLS	3/08
	West Virginia	Y	14416 FQ	15913 MW	19283 TQ	WVBLS	7/08-9/08
	Wisconsin	Y	18470 FQ	21310 MW	28060 TQ	USBLS	5/07
	Wyoming	Y	20569 FQ	28135 MW	36509 TQ	WYBLS	9/08
Crane and Tower Operator	Alabama	Y	18930 FQ	29410 MW	41750 TQ	USBLS	5/07
	Birmingham-Hoover MSA, AL	Y	31800 FQ	38260 MW	49490 TQ	USBLS	5/07
	Alaska	Y	61480 FQ	78190 MW	92280 TQ	USBLS	5/07
	Arizona	Y	35810 FQ	51950 MW	60750 TQ	USBLS	5/07
	Phoenix-Mesa-Scottsdale MSA, AZ	Y	30320 FQ	37480 MW	52120 TQ	USBLS	5/07
	Tucson MSA, AZ	Y	53570 FQ	60470 MW	69290 TQ	USBLS	5/07
	Arkansas	Y	27130 FQ	32230 MW	39330 TQ	USBLS	5/07
	Little Rock-North Little Rock MSA, AR	Y	28010 FQ	33100 MW	37730 TQ	USBLS	5/07
	California	H	15.99 FQ	22.89 MW	31.92 TQ	CABLS	1/08-3/08
	Los Angeles-Long Beach-Glendale PMSA, CA	H	14.09 FQ	16.91 MW	26.59 TQ	CABLS	1/08-3/08
	Oakland-Fremont-Hayward MSA, CA	H	18.25 FQ	31.25 MW	35.91 TQ	CABLS	1/08-3/08

AE	Average entry wage	**AW**	Average wage paid	**FQ** First quartile wage	**LO** Lowest wage paid	**MTC** Median total compensation	**TCC** Total cash compensation
AER	Average entry range	**AWR**	Average wage range	**H** Hourly	**LR** Low end range	**MW** Median wage paid	**TQ** Third quartile wage
AEX	Average experienced wage	**AXR**	Average experienced range	**HI** Highest wage paid	**M** Monthly	**MWR** Median wage range	**W** Weekly
ATC	Average total compensation	**D**	Daily	**HR** High end range	**MCC** Median cash compensation	**S** See annotated source	**Y** Yearly

Occupation/Type/Industry	Location	Per	Low	Mid	High	Source	Date
Crane and Tower Operator	Riverside-San Bernardino-Ontario MSA, CA	H	16.22 FQ	20.07 MW	25.33 TQ	CABLS	1/08-3/08
	Sacramento-Arden Arcade-Roseville MSA, CA	H	20.82 FQ	25.81 MW	32.25 TQ	CABLS	1/08-3/08
	San Diego-Carlsbad-San Marcos MSA, CA	H	26.18 FQ	31.00 MW	36.53 TQ	CABLS	1/08-3/08
	San Francisco-San Mateo-Redwood PMSA, CA	H	32.44 FQ	37.14 MW	42.14 TQ	CABLS	1/08-3/08
	San Jose-Sunnyvale-Santa Clara MSA, CA	H	14.29 FQ	16.01 MW	30.01 TQ	CABLS	1/08-3/08
	Santa Ana-Anaheim-Irvine PMSA, CA	Y	33980 FQ	48440 MW	60880 TQ	USBLS	5/07
	Colorado	Y	43190 FQ	53670 MW	59880 TQ	USBLS	5/07
	Denver-Aurora MSA, CO	Y	45070 FQ	56690 MW	62520 TQ	USBLS	5/07
	Pueblo MSA, CO	Y	42970 FQ	51090 MW	59570 TQ	USBLS	5/07
	Connecticut	H	19.21 AE	32.46 MW		CTBLS	1/08-3/08
	Bridgeport-Stamford-Norwalk MSA, CT	Y	47250 FQ	70510 MW	76610 TQ	USBLS	5/07
	Hartford-West Hartford-East Hartford MSA, CT	Y	43250 FQ	69320 MW	76430 TQ	USBLS	5/07
	Delaware	Y	33120 FQ	36500 MW	40010 TQ	USBLS	5/07
	Wilmington PMSA, DE-MD-NJ	Y	33140 FQ	36620 MW	40110 TQ	USBLS	5/07
	Washington-Arlington-Alexandria MSA, DC-VA-MD-WV	Y	43890 FQ	53800 MW	59440 TQ	USBLS	5/07
	Florida	Y	31480 FQ	42250 MW	53280 TQ	USBLS	5/07
	Fort Lauderdale-Pompano Beach-Deerfield Beach PMSA, FL	Y	38100 FQ	47590 MW	55000 TQ	USBLS	5/07
	Jacksonville MSA, FL	Y	33680 FQ	42260 MW	52110 TQ	USBLS	5/07
	Miami-Fort Lauderdale-Miami Beach MSA, FL	Y	32450 FQ	48900 MW	58080 TQ	USBLS	5/07
	Orlando-Kissimmee MSA, FL	Y	30430 FQ	40460 MW	48210 TQ	USBLS	5/07
	Tampa-St. Petersburg-Clearwater MSA, FL	Y	27390 FQ	35270 MW	44590 TQ	USBLS	5/07
	West Palm Beach-Boca Raton-Boynton Beach PMSA, FL	Y	30910 FQ	35330 MW	41460 TQ	USBLS	5/07
	Georgia	Y	32260 FQ	42160 MW	48350 TQ	USBLS	5/07
	Atlanta-Sandy Springs-Marietta MSA, GA	Y	36750 FQ	43250 MW	47660 TQ	USBLS	5/07
	Hawaii	Y	61350 FQ	66050 MW	71840 TQ	USBLS	5/07
	Honolulu MSA, HI	Y	61350 FQ	66050 MW	71840 TQ	USBLS	5/07
	Idaho	Y	29780 FQ	34010 MW	42980 TQ	USBLS	5/07
	Boise City-Nampa MSA, ID	Y	28960 FQ	32430 MW	41460 TQ	USBLS	5/07
	Illinois	Y	33980 FQ	42570 MW	60630 TQ	USBLS	5/07
	Chicago-Naperville-Joliet MSA, IL-IN-WI	Y	34680 FQ	38940 MW	48580 TQ	USBLS	5/07
	Indiana	Y	34650 FQ	38960 MW	47430 TQ	USBLS	5/07
	Gary PMSA, IN	Y	34850 FQ	38090 MW	41290 TQ	USBLS	5/07
	Indianapolis-Carmel MSA, IN	Y	41950 FQ	53410 MW	59200 TQ	USBLS	5/07
	Iowa	Y	32340 FQ	40670 MW	47280 TQ	USBLS	5/07
	Des Moines-West Des Moines MSA, IA	Y	37730 FQ	44590 MW	49750 TQ	USBLS	5/07
	Kansas	Y	27100 FQ	31760 MW	40480 TQ	USBLS	5/07
	Kentucky	Y	27525 FQ	36146 MW	48014 TQ	KYBLS	2008
	Louisville-Jefferson County MSA, KY-IN	Y	31490 FQ	47890 MW	54140 TQ	USBLS	5/07
	Louisiana	H	15.49 FQ	19.01 MW	23.45 TQ	LABLS	1/08-3/08
	Baton Rouge MSA, LA	Y	29770 FQ	36050 MW	41250 TQ	USBLS	5/07
	Lake Charles MSA, LA	Y	34560 FQ	42730 MW	47280 TQ	USBLS	5/07
	New Orleans-Metairie-Kenner MSA, LA	Y	31940 FQ	37320 MW	45330 TQ	USBLS	5/07
	Maine	Y	31710 FQ	41940 MW	47460 TQ	USBLS	5/07
	Portland-South Portland-Biddeford MSA, ME	Y	33740 FQ	39750 MW	49420 TQ	USBLS	5/07
	Maryland	Y		48000 MW		MDBLS	3/08
	Baltimore-Towson MSA, MD	Y	35620 FQ	43720 MW	50660 TQ	USBLS	5/07
	Bethesda-Gaithersburg-Frederick PMSA, MD	Y	40180 FQ	44430 MW	51800 TQ	USBLS	5/07
	Massachusetts	Y	39070 FQ	56440 MW	74650 TQ	USBLS	5/07

Occupation/Type/Industry	Location	Per	Low	Mid	High	Source	Date
Crane and Tower Operator	Boston-Cambridge-Quincy NECTA, MA	Y	48630 FQ	71380 MW	81730 TQ	USBLS	5/07
	Michigan	Y	35720 FQ	49160 MW	58380 TQ	USBLS	5/07
	Detroit-Warren-Livonia MSA, MI	Y	32810 FQ	37760 MW	56180 TQ	USBLS	5/07
	Grand Rapids-Wyoming MSA, MI	Y	34710 FQ	40710 MW	46510 TQ	USBLS	5/07
	Warren-Troy-Farmington Hills PMSA, MI	Y	36860 FQ	54840 MW	62030 TQ	USBLS	5/07
	Minnesota	Y	39980 FQ	47034 MW	55679 TQ	MNBLS	10/08-12/08
	Duluth-Superior MSA, MN-WI	Y	37442 FQ	44797 MW	50644 TQ	MNBLS	10/08-12/08
	Minneapolis-Saint Paul MSA, MN-WI	Y	41478 FQ	48407 MW	57853 TQ	MNBLS	10/08-12/08
	Mississippi	Y	27730 FQ	34390 MW	44020 TQ	USBLS	5/07
	Jackson MSA, MS	Y	27220 FQ	30720 MW	37360 TQ	USBLS	5/07
	Missouri	Y	33330 FQ	38260 MW	58000 TQ	USBLS	5/07
	Kansas City MSA, MO-KS	Y	41940 FQ	51500 MW	66520 TQ	USBLS	5/07
	St. Louis MSA, MO-IL	Y	33030 FQ	41640 MW	56400 TQ	USBLS	5/07
	Montana	Y	26100 FQ	38470 MW	49370 TQ	USBLS	5/07
	Nebraska	Y	35200 FQ	45290 MW	54940 TQ	USBLS	5/07
	Omaha-Council Bluffs MSA, NE-IA	Y	33040 FQ	38470 MW	46580 TQ	USBLS	5/07
	Nevada	H	18.99 FQ	34.54 MW	45.62 TQ	NVBLS	5/08
	Las Vegas-Paradise MSA, NV	H	18.47 FQ	40.42 MW	46.69 TQ	NVBLS	5/08
	New Hampshire	H	16.75 AE	24.20 MW	25.56 AEX	NHBLS	6/08
	New Jersey	Y	44680 FQ	56170 MW	68640 TQ	USBLS	5/07
	Camden PMSA, NJ	Y	36040 FQ	41140 MW	63460 TQ	USBLS	5/07
	Edison PMSA, NJ	Y	53580 FQ	58580 MW	63710 TQ	USBLS	5/07
	Newark-Union PMSA, NJ-PA	Y	48390 FQ	58720 MW	69670 TQ	USBLS	5/07
	New Mexico	Y	42680 FQ	46200 MW	49760 TQ	USBLS	5/07
	Albuquerque MSA, NM	Y	42480 FQ	46260 MW	50050 TQ	USBLS	5/07
	New York	Y	34860 FQ	43320 MW	59430 TQ	USBLS	5/07
	Albany-Schenectady-Troy MSA, NY	Y	35260 FQ	38350 MW	41390 TQ	USBLS	5/07
	Buffalo-Niagara Falls MSA, NY	Y	32930 FQ	36240 MW	51590 TQ	USBLS	5/07
	Nassau-Suffolk PMSA, NY	Y	47710 FQ	53520 MW	60350 TQ	USBLS	5/07
	New York-Northern New Jersey-Long Island MSA, NY-NJ-PA	Y	48090 FQ	58880 MW	71660 TQ	USBLS	5/07
	North Carolina	Y	30500 FQ	38080 MW	47370 TQ	USBLS	5/07
	Charlotte-Gastonia-Concord MSA, NC-SC	Y	31970 FQ	38790 MW	45610 TQ	USBLS	5/07
	Raleigh-Cary MSA, NC	Y	36880 FQ	53270 MW	59590 TQ	USBLS	5/07
	North Dakota	Y	29370 FQ	39670 MW	49560 TQ	USBLS	5/07
	Ohio	Y	28400 FQ	34010 MW	44680 TQ	USBLS	5/07
	Cincinnati-Middletown MSA, OH-KY-IN	Y	25950 FQ	32140 MW	42500 TQ	USBLS	5/07
	Cleveland-Elyria-Mentor MSA, OH	Y	29780 FQ	34770 MW	44850 TQ	USBLS	5/07
	Columbus MSA, OH	Y	32040 FQ	38560 MW	45800 TQ	USBLS	5/07
	Dayton MSA, OH	Y	32510 FQ	50450 MW	56030 TQ	USBLS	5/07
	Oklahoma	Y	29280 FQ	38870 MW	48510 TQ	USBLS	5/07
	Oklahoma City MSA, OK	Y	36030 FQ	42960 MW	49590 TQ	USBLS	5/07
	Tulsa MSA, OK	Y	27460 FQ	31930 MW	46950 TQ	USBLS	5/07
	Oregon	H	18.21 FQ	22.70 MW	31.76 TQ	ORBLS	5/08
	Portland-Vancouver-Beaverton MSA, OR-WA	Y	37030 FQ	46190 MW	64800 TQ	USBLS	5/07
	Pennsylvania	Y	32290 FQ	37620 MW	46900 TQ	USBLS	5/07
	Allentown-Bethlehem-Easton MSA, PA-NJ	Y	33350 FQ	36230 MW	39510 TQ	USBLS	5/07
	Philadelphia-Camden-Wilmington MSA, PA-NJ-DE-MD	Y	34180 FQ	39420 MW	52530 TQ	USBLS	5/07
	Pittsburgh MSA, PA	Y	32680 FQ	37100 MW	44910 TQ	USBLS	5/07
	Providence-Fall River-Warwick MSA, RI-MA	Y	39130 FQ	56290 MW	74410 TQ	USBLS	5/07
	South Carolina	Y	30430 FQ	40590 MW	50650 TQ	USBLS	5/07
	Charleston-North Charleston MSA, SC	Y	36840 FQ	45060 MW	62740 TQ	USBLS	5/07
	Columbia MSA, SC	Y	26760 FQ	29860 MW	33700 TQ	USBLS	5/07
	South Dakota	Y	34396 FQ	36894 MW	40288 TQ	SDBLS	7/08-9/08

AE	Average entry wage	**AW** Average wage paid	**FQ** First quartile wage	**LO** Lowest wage paid	**MTC** Median total compensation	**TCC** Total cash compensation
AER	Average entry range	**AWR** Average wage range	**H** Hourly	**LR** Low end range	**MW** Median wage paid	**TQ** Third quartile wage
AEX	Average experienced wage	**AXR** Average experienced range	**HI** Highest wage paid	**M** Monthly	**MWR** Median wage range	**W** Weekly
ATC	Average total compensation **D**	Daily	**HR** High end range	**MCC** Median cash compensation **S**	See annotated source	**Y** Yearly

Occupation/Type/Industry	Location	Per	Low	Mid	High	Source	Date
Crane and Tower Operator	Rapid City MSA, SD	Y	34208 FQ	37290 MW	44075 TQ	SDBLS	7/08-9/08
	Sioux Falls MSA, SD	Y	34788 FQ	37561 MW	41983 TQ	SDBLS	7/08-9/08
	Tennessee	Y	30290 FQ	38830 MW	47750 TQ	USBLS	5/07
	Memphis MSA, TN-MS-AR	Y	27500 FQ	32130 MW	43420 TQ	USBLS	5/07
	Nashville-Davidson-Murfreesboro MSA, TN	Y	28620 FQ	39400 MW	44840 TQ	USBLS	5/07
	Texas	Y	27420 FQ	34090 MW	43510 TQ	USBLS	5/07
	Austin-Round Rock MSA, TX	Y	26890 FQ	29030 MW	31100 TQ	USBLS	5/07
	Dallas-Fort Worth-Arlington MSA, TX	Y	26270 FQ	32540 MW	40620 TQ	USBLS	5/07
	El Paso MSA, TX	Y	22430 FQ	27440 MW	36240 TQ	USBLS	5/07
	Houston-Sugar Land-Baytown MSA, TX	Y	28230 FQ	36750 MW	45410 TQ	USBLS	5/07
	San Antonio MSA, TX	Y	34870 FQ	43360 MW	48770 TQ	USBLS	5/07
	Utah	Y	32280 FQ	47990 MW	55270 TQ	USBLS	5/07
	Salt Lake City MSA, UT	Y	48700 FQ	53360 MW	57340 TQ	USBLS	5/07
	Vermont	Y	28710 FQ	34200 MW	42200 TQ	USBLS	5/07
	Virginia	Y	29980 FQ	40650 MW	48400 TQ	USBLS	5/07
	Richmond MSA, VA	Y	31570 FQ	42330 MW	47320 TQ	USBLS	5/07
	Virginia Beach-Norfolk-Newport News MSA, VA-NC	Y	37990 FQ	43580 MW	48960 TQ	USBLS	5/07
	Washington	H	24.06 FQ	28.83 MW	33.25 TQ	WABLS	3/08
	Seattle-Tacoma-Bellevue MSA, WA	Y	51700 FQ	60710 MW	69900 TQ	USBLS	5/07
	West Virginia	Y	25225 FQ	31715 MW	39041 TQ	WVBLS	7/08-9/08
	Charleston MSA, WV	Y	26660 FQ	30970 MW	41290 TQ	USBLS	5/07
	Wisconsin	Y	31340 FQ	41160 MW	52150 TQ	USBLS	5/07
	Milwaukee-Waukesha-West Allis MSA, WI	Y	31470 FQ	39200 MW	48810 TQ	USBLS	5/07
	Wyoming	Y	37336 FQ	42751 MW	49623 TQ	WYBLS	9/08
	Cheyenne MSA, WY	Y	24950 FQ	42145 MW	50031 TQ	WYBLS	9/08
	Puerto Rico	Y	20900 FQ	24930 MW	29980 TQ	USBLS	5/07
	San Juan-Caguas-Guaynabo MSA, PR	Y	21620 FQ	25290 MW	29770 TQ	USBLS	5/07
	Guam	Y	26030 FQ	29500 MW	35870 TQ	USBLS	5/07
Creative Arts Therapist	United States	Y		36600 AW		HCC05	2009
Creative Director Online Media	United States	Y	80000 LO		120000 HI	PARD02	2008
Creative Services Director Apparel Industry	United States	Y		80000 MW		247FASH	2009
Credit Analyst	Alabama	Y	35380 FQ	47360 MW	67820 TQ	USBLS	5/07
	Birmingham-Hoover MSA, AL	Y	37410 FQ	51390 MW	67210 TQ	USBLS	5/07
	Alaska	Y	36670 FQ	48050 MW	71380 TQ	USBLS	5/07
	Arizona	Y	25390 FQ	30530 MW	39490 TQ	USBLS	5/07
	Phoenix-Mesa-Scottsdale MSA, AZ	Y	25270 FQ	30280 MW	38670 TQ	USBLS	5/07
	Tucson MSA, AZ	Y	33830 FQ	52940 MW	76030 TQ	USBLS	5/07
	Arkansas	Y	35900 FQ	45170 MW	59040 TQ	USBLS	5/07
	Little Rock-North Little Rock MSA, AR	Y	37920 FQ	47170 MW	59910 TQ	USBLS	5/07
	California	H	22.45 FQ	30.32 MW	41.79 TQ	CABLS	1/08-3/08
	Los Angeles-Long Beach-Glendale PMSA, CA	H	22.00 FQ	28.60 MW	39.13 TQ	CABLS	1/08-3/08
	Oakland-Fremont-Hayward MSA, CA	H	26.08 FQ	34.45 MW	42.67 TQ	CABLS	1/08-3/08
	Riverside-San Bernardino-Ontario MSA, CA	H	19.07 FQ	28.50 MW	42.09 TQ	CABLS	1/08-3/08
	Sacramento-Arden Arcade-Roseville MSA, CA	H	27.11 FQ	34.64 MW	46.12 TQ	CABLS	1/08-3/08
	San Diego-Carlsbad-San Marcos MSA, CA	H	21.92 FQ	28.84 MW	38.12 TQ	CABLS	1/08-3/08
	San Francisco-San Mateo-Redwood PMSA, CA	H	28.40 FQ	40.75 MW	53.59 TQ	CABLS	1/08-3/08
	San Jose-Sunnyvale-Santa Clara MSA, CA	H	25.81 FQ	32.37 MW	49.05 TQ	CABLS	1/08-3/08
	Santa Ana-Anaheim-Irvine PMSA, CA	Y	41060 FQ	57390 MW	76410 TQ	USBLS	5/07
	Colorado	Y	46090 FQ	66710 MW	87800 TQ	USBLS	5/07

AE	Average entry wage	AW	Average wage paid	FQ	First quartile wage
AER	Average entry range	AWR	Average wage range	H	Hourly
AEX	Average experienced wage	AXR	Average experienced range	HI	Highest wage paid
ATC	Average total compensation	D	Daily	HR	High end range

LO	Lowest wage paid	MTC	Median total compensation	TCC	Total cash compensation
LR	Low end range	MW	Median wage paid	TQ	Third quartile wage
M	Monthly	MWR	Median wage range	W	Weekly
MCC	Median cash compensation	S	See annotated source	Y	Yearly

Occupation/Type/Industry	Location	Per	Low	Mid	High	Source	Date
Credit Analyst	Denver-Aurora MSA, CO	Y	53360 FQ	72760 MW	95010 TQ	USBLS	5/07
	Connecticut	H	22.60 AE	30.46 MW		CTBLS	1/08-3/08
	Bridgeport-Stamford-Norwalk MSA, CT	Y-	55910 FQ	64520 MW	86150 TQ	USBLS	5/07
	Hartford-West Hartford-East Hartford MSA, CT	Y	46470 FQ	58760 MW	70420 TQ	USBLS	5/07
	Delaware	Y	36060 FQ	43840 MW	55930 TQ	USBLS	5/07
	Wilmington PMSA, DE-MD-NJ	Y	37000 FQ	45290 MW	58420 TQ	USBLS	5/07
	District of Columbia	Y	61450 FQ	72160 MW	105270 TQ	USBLS	5/07
	Washington-Arlington-Alexandria MSA, DC-VA-MD-WV	Y	46920 FQ	64860 MW	92580 TQ	USBLS	5/07
	Florida	Y	40450 FQ	53000 MW	70810 TQ	USBLS	5/07
	Fort Lauderdale-Pompano Beach-Deerfield Beach PMSA, FL	Y	41630 FQ	49780 MW	59260 TQ	USBLS	5/07
	Jacksonville MSA, FL	Y	44960 FQ	60580 MW	78150 TQ	USBLS	5/07
	Miami-Fort Lauderdale-Miami Beach MSA, FL	Y	41990 FQ	52090 MW	68460 TQ	USBLS	5/07
	Orlando-Kissimmee MSA, FL	Y	43080 FQ	57200 MW	75970 TQ	USBLS	5/07
	Tampa-St. Petersburg-Clearwater MSA, FL	Y	35470 FQ	47000 MW	60770 TQ	USBLS	5/07
	West Palm Beach-Boca Raton-Boynton Beach PMSA, FL	Y	47990 FQ	57630 MW	76440 TQ	USBLS	5/07
	Georgia	Y	46680 FQ	65700 MW	85170 TQ	USBLS	5/07
	Atlanta-Sandy Springs-Marietta MSA, GA	Y	50790 FQ	68950 MW	86790 TQ	USBLS	5/07
	Hawaii	Y	37040 FQ	42370 MW	59800 TQ	USBLS	5/07
	Honolulu MSA, HI	Y	37170 FQ	42650 MW	59510 TQ	USBLS	5/07
	Idaho	Y	42410 FQ	55980 MW	70640 TQ	USBLS	5/07
	Boise City-Nampa MSA, ID	Y	42640 FQ	58910 MW	71340 TQ	USBLS	5/07
	Illinois	Y	43060 FQ	55150 MW	73400 TQ	USBLS	5/07
	Chicago-Naperville-Joliet MSA, IL-IN-WI	Y	44990 FQ	56900 MW	74840 TQ	USBLS	5/07
	Indiana	Y	36080 FQ	48390 MW	72990 TQ	USBLS	5/07
	Gary PMSA, IN	Y	32060 FQ	44080 MW	88640 TQ	USBLS	5/07
	Indianapolis-Carmel MSA, IN	Y	38060 FQ	51470 MW	79960 TQ	USBLS	5/07
	Iowa	Y	38090 FQ	48850 MW	67180 TQ	USBLS	5/07
	Des Moines-West Des Moines MSA, IA	Y	41000 FQ	52380 MW	76770 TQ	USBLS	5/07
	Kansas	Y	38160 FQ	46780 MW	59300 TQ	USBLS	5/07
	Wichita MSA, KS	Y	45600 FQ	55190 MW	67030 TQ	USBLS	5/07
	Kentucky	Y	37424 FQ	49961 MW	66283 TQ	KYBLS	2008
	Lexington-Fayette MSA, KY	Y	51740 FQ	70270 MW	102060 TQ	USBLS	5/07
	Louisville-Jefferson County MSA, KY-IN	Y	34200 FQ	46620 MW	61670 TQ	USBLS	5/07
	Louisiana	H	15.79 FQ	20.05 MW	27.06 TQ	LABLS	1/08-3/08
	Baton Rouge MSA, LA	Y	35310 FQ	40290 MW	45290 TQ	USBLS	5/07
	New Orleans-Metairie-Kenner MSA, LA	Y	40320 FQ	49390 MW	63170 TQ	USBLS	5/07
	Maine	Y	33970 FQ	38740 MW	47740 TQ	USBLS	5/07
	Portland-South Portland-Biddeford MSA, ME	Y	36130 FQ	44360 MW	58930 TQ	USBLS	5/07
	Maryland	Y		62475 MW		MDBLS	3/08
	Baltimore-Towson MSA, MD	Y	39550 FQ	56190 MW	80960 TQ	USBLS	5/07
	Bethesda-Gaithersburg-Frederick PMSA, MD	Y	40500 FQ	58720 MW	88810 TQ	USBLS	5/07
	Massachusetts	Y	43530 FQ	55240 MW	72510 TQ	USBLS	5/07
	Boston-Cambridge-Quincy NECTA, MA	Y	45670 FQ	57920 MW	75530 TQ	USBLS	5/07
	New Bedford MSA, MA	Y	45890 FQ	57110 MW	75480 TQ	USBLS	5/07
	Worcester MSA, MA-CT	Y	41820 FQ	51480 MW	64250 TQ	USBLS	5/07
	Michigan	Y	36740 FQ	46760 MW	64370 TQ	USBLS	5/07
	Detroit-Warren-Livonia MSA, MI	Y	41380 FQ	53560 MW	73460 TQ	USBLS	5/07
	Grand Rapids-Wyoming MSA, MI	Y	27780 FQ	38530 MW	46990 TQ	USBLS	5/07
	Warren-Troy-Farmington Hills PMSA, MI	Y	43380 FQ	55880 MW	76260 TQ	USBLS	5/07
	Minnesota	Y	46366 FQ	57710 MW	71870 TQ	MNBLS	10/08-12/08
	Duluth-Superior MSA, MN-WI	Y	42071 FQ	47273 MW	53644 TQ	MNBLS	10/08-12/08

AE	Average entry wage	AW	Average wage paid	FQ	First quartile wage	LO	Lowest wage paid	MTC	Median total compensation	TCC	Total cash compensation
AER	Average entry range	AWR	Average wage range	H	Hourly	LR	Low end range	MW	Median wage paid	TQ	Third quartile wage
AEX	Average experienced wage	AXR	Average experienced range	HI	Highest wage paid	M	Monthly	MWR	Median wage range	W	Weekly
ATC	Average total compensation	D	Daily	HR	High end range	MCC	Median cash compensation	S	See annotated source	Y	Yearly

366

Credit Analyst

Occupation/Type/Industry	Location	Per	Low	Mid	High	Source	Date
Credit Analyst	Minneapolis-Saint Paul MSA, MN-WI	Y	47816 FQ	59243 MW	75290 TQ	MNBLS	10/08-12/08
	Rochester MSA, MN	Y	46634 FQ	51892 MW	58112 TQ	MNBLS	10/08-12/08
	Mississippi	Y	39210 FQ	45190 MW	52290 TQ	USBLS	5/07
	Jackson MSA, MS	Y	39700 FQ	44330 MW	49980 TQ	USBLS	5/07
	Missouri	Y	36120 FQ	47690 MW	65300 TQ	USBLS	5/07
	Kansas City MSA, MO-KS	Y	39930 FQ	48090 MW	61630 TQ	USBLS	5/07
	St. Louis MSA, MO-IL	Y	38300 FQ	49370 MW	69890 TQ	USBLS	5/07
	Montana	Y	30040 FQ	36880 MW	48900 TQ	USBLS	5/07
	Billings MSA, MT	Y	32110 FQ	41330 MW	69760 TQ	USBLS	5/07
	Nebraska	Y	33910 FQ	39460 MW	52610 TQ	USBLS	5/07
	Omaha-Council Bluffs MSA, NE-IA	Y	33240 FQ	37210 MW	47080 TQ	USBLS	5/07
	Nevada	H	18.28 FQ	27.19 MW	34.36 TQ	NVBLS	5/08
	Las Vegas-Paradise MSA, NV	H	17.85 FQ	27.07 MW	34.40 TQ	NVBLS	5/08
	New Hampshire	H	20.32 AE	27.19 MW	33.99 AEX	NHBLS	6/08
	New Jersey	Y	47380 FQ	60270 MW	73800 TQ	USBLS	5/07
	Camden PMSA, NJ	Y	42340 FQ	56450 MW	74210 TQ	USBLS	5/07
	Edison PMSA, NJ	Y	48350 FQ	60410 MW	72940 TQ	USBLS	5/07
	Newark-Union PMSA, NJ-PA	Y	47930 FQ	58090 MW	73390 TQ	USBLS	5/07
	Trenton-Ewing MSA, NJ	Y	50410 FQ	61790 MW	79060 TQ	USBLS	5/07
	New Mexico	Y	38680 FQ	45540 MW	58040 TQ	USBLS	5/07
	Albuquerque MSA, NM	Y	41310 FQ	47310 MW	61080 TQ	USBLS	5/07
	New York	Y	59380 FQ	82800 MW	121330 TQ	USBLS	5/07
	Albany-Schenectady-Troy MSA, NY	Y	45870 FQ	59890 MW	84000 TQ	USBLS	5/07
	Buffalo-Niagara Falls MSA, NY	Y	48470 FQ	68040 MW	84450 TQ	USBLS	5/07
	Nassau-Suffolk PMSA, NY	Y	48990 FQ	60730 MW	82100 TQ	USBLS	5/07
	New York-Northern New Jersey-Long Island MSA, NY-NJ-PA	Y	59210 FQ	79970 MW	118210 TQ	USBLS	5/07
	North Carolina	Y	43300 FQ	64950 MW	93010 TQ	USBLS	5/07
	Charlotte-Gastonia-Concord MSA, NC-SC	Y	49810 FQ	67110 MW	92020 TQ	USBLS	5/07
	Raleigh-Cary MSA, NC	Y	44910 FQ	57350 MW	76080 TQ	USBLS	5/07
	North Dakota	Y	48950 FQ	63810 MW	80460 TQ	USBLS	5/07
	Fargo MSA, ND-MN	Y	55000 FQ	70730 MW	89090 TQ	USBLS	5/07
	Ohio	Y	38770 FQ	49330 MW	63610 TQ	USBLS	5/07
	Cincinnati-Middletown MSA, OH-KY-IN	Y	40580 FQ	51410 MW	68160 TQ	USBLS	5/07
	Cleveland-Elyria-Mentor MSA, OH	Y	42930 FQ	52630 MW	64840 TQ	USBLS	5/07
	Columbus MSA, OH	Y	36430 FQ	45650 MW	62680 TQ	USBLS	5/07
	Dayton MSA, OH	Y	37810 FQ	46070 MW	57120 TQ	USBLS	5/07
	Oklahoma	Y	32300 FQ	42200 MW	57050 TQ	USBLS	5/07
	Oklahoma City MSA, OK	Y	26750 FQ	39960 MW	58750 TQ	USBLS	5/07
	Tulsa MSA, OK	Y	38530 FQ	46300 MW	58480 TQ	USBLS	5/07
	Oregon	H	21.73 FQ	26.84 MW	34.41 TQ	ORBLS	5/08
	Portland-Vancouver-Beaverton MSA, OR-WA	Y	44000 FQ	55830 MW	73130 TQ	USBLS	5/07
	Salem MSA, OR	Y	45450 FQ	52710 MW	73370 TQ	USBLS	5/07
	Pennsylvania	Y	35960 FQ	45780 MW	66120 TQ	USBLS	5/07
	Allentown-Bethlehem-Easton MSA, PA-NJ	Y	36470 FQ	43350 MW	58740 TQ	USBLS	5/07
	Philadelphia-Camden-Wilmington MSA, PA-NJ-DE-MD	Y	37190 FQ	46170 MW	62240 TQ	USBLS	5/07
	Pittsburgh MSA, PA	Y	35800 FQ	46730 MW	70350 TQ	USBLS	5/07
	Rhode Island	Y	49760 FQ	63900 MW	92510 TQ	USBLS	5/07
	Providence-Fall River-Warwick MSA, RI-MA	Y	47400 FQ	59560 MW	89890 TQ	USBLS	5/07
	South Carolina	Y	35140 FQ	47850 MW	64010 TQ	USBLS	5/07
	Charleston-North Charleston MSA, SC	Y	54750 FQ	60110 MW	65640 TQ	USBLS	5/07
	Columbia MSA, SC	Y	40580 FQ	51450 MW	68050 TQ	USBLS	5/07
	South Dakota	Y	39501 FQ	50053 MW	63726 TQ	SDBLS	7/08-9/08
	Sioux Falls MSA, SD	Y	44439 FQ	56576 MW	69428 TQ	SDBLS	7/08-9/08
	Tennessee	Y	31030 FQ	46550 MW	71820 TQ	USBLS	5/07
	Memphis MSA, TN-MS-AR	Y	35060 FQ	48890 MW	73230 TQ	USBLS	5/07
	Nashville-Davidson-Murfreesboro MSA, TN	Y	33730 FQ	52960 MW	74460 TQ	USBLS	5/07

AE	Average entry wage	AW	Average wage paid	FQ	First quartile wage	LO	Lowest wage paid	MTC	Median total compensation	TCC	Total cash compensation
AER	Average entry range	AWR	Average wage range	H	Hourly	LR	Low end range	MW	Median wage paid	TQ	Third quartile wage
AEX	Average experienced wage	AXR	Average experienced range	HI	Highest wage paid	M	Monthly	MWR	Median wage range	W	Weekly
ATC	Average total compensation	D	Daily	HR	High end range	MCC	Median cash compensation	S	See annotated source	Y	Yearly

Occupation/Type/Industry	Location	Per	Low	Mid	High	Source	Date
Credit Analyst	Texas	Y	41450 FQ	56430 MW	79590 TQ	USBLS	5/07
	Austin-Round Rock MSA, TX	Y	41970 FQ	59690 MW	80370 TQ	USBLS	5/07
	Corpus Christi MSA, TX	Y	34450 FQ	40850 MW	54390 TQ	USBLS	5/07
	Dallas-Fort Worth-Arlington MSA, TX	Y	44520 FQ	57210 MW	75880 TQ	USBLS	5/07
	El Paso MSA, TX	Y	42840 FQ	53830 MW	78470 TQ	USBLS	5/07
	Houston-Sugar Land-Baytown MSA, TX	Y	40070 FQ	56730 MW	91310 TQ	USBLS	5/07
	Midland MSA, TX	Y	67970 FQ	82550 MW	95690 TQ	USBLS	5/07
	San Antonio MSA, TX	Y	39880 FQ	63670 MW	85500 TQ	USBLS	5/07
	Utah	Y	34920 FQ	42770 MW	61860 TQ	USBLS	5/07
	Salt Lake City MSA, UT	Y	35750 FQ	42940 MW	67080 TQ	USBLS	5/07
	Vermont	Y	40650 FQ	49350 MW	60060 TQ	USBLS	5/07
	Burlington-South Burlington MSA, VT	Y	42050 FQ	50290 MW	62160 TQ	USBLS	5/07
	Virginia	Y	45760 FQ	64890 MW	95940 TQ	USBLS	5/07
	Lynchburg MSA, VA	Y	52720 FQ	59970 MW	74610 TQ	USBLS	5/07
	Richmond MSA, VA	Y	50400 FQ	78130 MW	106690 TQ	USBLS	5/07
	Virginia Beach-Norfolk-Newport News MSA, VA-NC	Y	38560 FQ	51570 MW	77280 TQ	USBLS	5/07
	Washington	H	20.14 FQ	25.97 MW	33.25 TQ	WABLS	3/08
	Seattle-Tacoma-Bellevue MSA, WA	Y	42700 FQ	57030 MW	72370 TQ	USBLS	5/07
	Spokane MSA, WA	Y	37270 FQ	45490 MW	56780 TQ	USBLS	5/07
	West Virginia	Y	34879 FQ	48321 MW	64110 TQ	WVBLS	7/08-9/08
	Charleston MSA, WV	Y	33280 FQ	42460 MW	58720 TQ	USBLS	5/07
	Wisconsin	Y	36120 FQ	44190 MW	57860 TQ	USBLS	5/07
	Appleton MSA, WI	Y	41310 FQ	48990 MW	65430 TQ	USBLS	5/07
	Milwaukee-Waukesha-West Allis MSA, WI	Y	39070 FQ	47200 MW	65350 TQ	USBLS	5/07
	Wyoming	Y	30690 FQ	38990 MW	47992 TQ	WYBLS	9/08
	Puerto Rico	Y	26550 FQ	30950 MW	39130 TQ	USBLS	5/07
	San Juan-Caguas-Guaynabo MSA, PR	Y	26450 FQ	30890 MW	39120 TQ	USBLS	5/07
State Lottery	Tennessee	Y			45121 HI	THETN	2008
Credit and Collections Clerk	United States	Y	26500-32750 LO		28000-34250 HI	WSJ02	2007
Credit and Collections Specialist Midsize Company	United States	Y	29250-37500 LR			PRN01	2009
Credit Authorizer, Checker, and Clerk	Alabama	Y	20680 FQ	24570 MW	29860 TQ	USBLS	5/07
	Birmingham-Hoover MSA, AL	Y	23230 FQ	28390 MW	32790 TQ	USBLS	5/07
	Mobile MSA, AL	Y	23830 FQ	27830 MW	32430 TQ	USBLS	5/07
	Alaska	Y	31790 FQ	37070 MW	42170 TQ	USBLS	5/07
	Arizona	Y	17020 FQ	18460 MW	20770 TQ	USBLS	5/07
	Phoenix-Mesa-Scottsdale MSA, AZ	Y	17010 FQ	18460 MW	20970 TQ	USBLS	5/07
	Arkansas	Y	22940 FQ	27690 MW	33950 TQ	USBLS	5/07
	Little Rock-North Little Rock MSA, AR	Y	23340 FQ	28400 MW	47660 TQ	USBLS	5/07
	California	H	13.79 FQ	17.17 MW	21.07 TQ	CABLS	1/08-3/08
	Los Angeles-Long Beach-Glendale PMSA, CA	H	12.28 FQ	16.79 MW	20.14 TQ	CABLS	1/08-3/08
	Oakland-Fremont-Hayward MSA, CA	H	14.65 FQ	17.16 MW	22.30 TQ	CABLS	1/08-3/08
	Riverside-San Bernardino-Ontario MSA, CA	H	13.21 FQ	15.92 MW	20.55 TQ	CABLS	1/08-3/08
	Sacramento-Arden Arcade-Roseville MSA, CA	H	16.43 FQ	20.46 MW	23.62 TQ	CABLS	1/08-3/08
	San Diego-Carlsbad-San Marcos MSA, CA	H	13.57 FQ	15.49 MW	19.10 TQ	CABLS	1/08-3/08
	San Francisco-San Mateo-Redwood PMSA, CA	H	16.46 FQ	18.02 MW	20.44 TQ	CABLS	1/08-3/08
	San Jose-Sunnyvale-Santa Clara MSA, CA	H	17.84 FQ	22.19 MW	24.88 TQ	CABLS	1/08-3/08
	Santa Ana-Anaheim-Irvine PMSA, CA	Y	27980 FQ	34580 MW	41930 TQ	USBLS	5/07
	Colorado	Y	27170 FQ	33180 MW	40610 TQ	USBLS	5/07

AE	Average entry wage	AW	Average wage paid	FQ First quartile wage	LO Lowest wage paid	MTC Median total compensation	TCC Total cash compensation
AER	Average entry range	AWR	Average wage range	H Hourly	LR Low end range	MW Median wage paid	TQ Third quartile wage
AEX	Average experienced wage	AXR	Average experienced range	HI Highest wage paid	M Monthly	MWR Median wage range	W Weekly
ATC	Average total compensation	D	Daily	HR High end range	MCC Median cash compensation	S See annotated source	Y Yearly

Occupation/Type/Industry	Location	Per	Low	Mid	High	Source	Date
Credit Authorizer, Checker, and Clerk	Denver-Aurora MSA, CO	Y	26860 FQ	32350 MW	39290 TQ	USBLS	5/07
	Connecticut	H	14.74 AE	18.31 MW		CTBLS	1/08-3/08
	Bridgeport-Stamford-Norwalk MSA, CT	Y	34100 FQ	39510 MW	48010 TQ	USBLS	5/07
	Hartford-West Hartford-East Hartford MSA, CT	Y	30510 FQ	35330 MW	40710 TQ	USBLS	5/07
	Delaware	Y	28730 FQ	34610 MW	40280 TQ	USBLS	5/07
	Wilmington PMSA, DE-MD-NJ	Y	28770 FQ	34530 MW	40200 TQ	USBLS	5/07
	District of Columbia	Y	28600 FQ	34530 MW	41090 TQ	USBLS	5/07
	Washington-Arlington-Alexandria MSA, DC-VA-MD-WV	Y	30630 FQ	36310 MW	44950 TQ	USBLS	5/07
	Florida	Y	26140 FQ	31590 MW	38650 TQ	USBLS	5/07
	Fort Lauderdale-Pompano Beach-Deerfield Beach PMSA, FL	Y	26640 FQ	33900 MW	40780 TQ	USBLS	5/07
	Jacksonville MSA, FL	Y	25490 FQ	30360 MW	36430 TQ	USBLS	5/07
	Miami-Fort Lauderdale-Miami Beach MSA, FL	Y	27500 FQ	34490 MW	41400 TQ	USBLS	5/07
	Orlando-Kissimmee MSA, FL	Y	25280 FQ	33170 MW	40930 TQ	USBLS	5/07
	Tampa-St. Petersburg-Clearwater MSA, FL	Y	25720 FQ	31740 MW	38540 TQ	USBLS	5/07
	West Palm Beach-Boca Raton-Boynton Beach PMSA, FL	Y	26380 FQ	29720 MW	33140 TQ	USBLS	5/07
	Georgia	Y	26260 FQ	31610 MW	37420 TQ	USBLS	5/07
	Atlanta-Sandy Springs-Marietta MSA, GA	Y	28400 FQ	32960 MW	38190 TQ	USBLS	5/07
	Hawaii	Y	25870 FQ	29200 MW	35710 TQ	USBLS	5/07
	Honolulu MSA, HI	Y	26130 FQ	29360 MW	36620 TQ	USBLS	5/07
	Idaho	Y	19520 FQ	26260 MW	30140 TQ	USBLS	5/07
	Boise City-Nampa MSA, ID	Y	19130 FQ	25320 MW	29150 TQ	USBLS	5/07
	Illinois	Y	27950 FQ	36780 MW	45600 TQ	USBLS	5/07
	Chicago-Naperville-Joliet MSA, IL-IN-WI	Y	28200 FQ	36950 MW	45590 TQ	USBLS	5/07
	Indiana	Y	22650 FQ	26120 MW	30750 TQ	USBLS	5/07
	Gary PMSA, IN	Y	22990 FQ	27500 MW	33320 TQ	USBLS	5/07
	Indianapolis-Carmel MSA, IN	Y	22330 FQ	24800 MW	30520 TQ	USBLS	5/07
	Iowa	Y	22860 FQ	26400 MW	31770 TQ	USBLS	5/07
	Des Moines-West Des Moines MSA, IA	Y	27670 FQ	31770 MW	36510 TQ	USBLS	5/07
	Kansas	Y	24260 FQ	30530 MW	37740 TQ	USBLS	5/07
	Wichita MSA, KS	Y	23850 FQ	28640 MW	36030 TQ	USBLS	5/07
	Kentucky	Y	25402 FQ	29761 MW	36779 TQ	KYBLS	2008
	Louisville-Jefferson County MSA, KY-IN	Y	24620 FQ	28860 MW	36840 TQ	USBLS	5/07
	Louisiana	H	10.34 FQ	12.18 MW	14.90 TQ	LABLS	1/08-3/08
	Baton Rouge MSA, LA	Y	26100 FQ	30440 MW	35650 TQ	USBLS	5/07
	New Orleans-Metairie-Kenner MSA, LA	Y	21230 FQ	24580 MW	29640 TQ	USBLS	5/07
	Maryland	Y		34300 MW		MDBLS	3/08
	Baltimore-Towson MSA, MD	Y	29930 FQ	38450 MW	47590 TQ	USBLS	5/07
	Bethesda-Gaithersburg-Frederick PMSA, MD	Y	32680 FQ	39040 MW	46020 TQ	USBLS	5/07
	Massachusetts	Y	30100 FQ	37030 MW	45070 TQ	USBLS	5/07
	Boston-Cambridge-Quincy NECTA, MA	Y	31260 FQ	37960 MW	45980 TQ	USBLS	5/07
	Worcester MSA, MA-CT	Y	29390 FQ	36210 MW	40490 TQ	USBLS	5/07
	Michigan	Y	29350 FQ	37010 MW	46250 TQ	USBLS	5/07
	Detroit-Warren-Livonia MSA, MI	Y	31720 FQ	38980 MW	47330 TQ	USBLS	5/07
	Grand Rapids-Wyoming MSA, MI	Y	25040 FQ	32970 MW	39460 TQ	USBLS	5/07
	Warren-Troy-Farmington Hills PMSA, MI	Y	32190 FQ	40400 MW	48230 TQ	USBLS	5/07
	Minnesota	Y	31400 FQ	36979 MW	44931 TQ	MNBLS	10/08-12/08
	Duluth-Superior MSA, MN-WI	Y	25520 FQ	28309 MW	31171 TQ	MNBLS	10/08-12/08
	Minneapolis-Saint Paul MSA, MN-WI	Y	33596 FQ	39487 MW	47023 TQ	MNBLS	10/08-12/08
	Mississippi	Y	19050 FQ	24260 MW	30170 TQ	USBLS	5/07
	Jackson MSA, MS	Y	23130 FQ	27990 MW	31470 TQ	USBLS	5/07

AE	Average entry wage	AW	Average wage paid	FQ	First quartile wage	LO	Lowest wage paid	MTC	Median total compensation	TCC	Total cash compensation
AER	Average entry range	AWR	Average wage range	H	Hourly	LR	Low end range	MW	Median wage paid	TQ	Third quartile wage
AEX	Average experienced wage	AXR	Average experienced range	HI	Highest wage paid	M	Monthly	MWR	Median wage range	W	Weekly
ATC	Average total compensation	D	Daily	HR	High end range	MCC	Median cash compensation	S	See annotated source	Y	Yearly

Occupation/Type/Industry	Location	Per	Low	Mid	High	Source	Date
Credit Authorizer, Checker, and Clerk							
	Missouri	Y	23910 FQ	30010 MW	36660 TQ	USBLS	5/07
	Kansas City MSA, MO-KS	Y	26660 FQ	33120 MW	38670 TQ	USBLS	5/07
	St. Louis MSA, MO-IL	Y	24870 FQ	31000 MW	37320 TQ	USBLS	5/07
	Springfield MSA, MO	Y	22820 FQ	29160 MW	36450 TQ	USBLS	5/07
	Montana	Y	25760 FQ	32690 MW	37930 TQ	USBLS	5/07
	Nebraska	Y	25710 FQ	29150 MW	33340 TQ	USBLS	5/07
	Omaha-Council Bluffs MSA, NE-IA	Y	26890 FQ	30030 MW	34400 TQ	USBLS	5/07
	Nevada	H	13.39 FQ	15.36 MW	18.18 TQ	NVBLS	5/08
	Las Vegas-Paradise MSA, NV	H	13.59 FQ	15.73 MW	18.51 TQ	NVBLS	5/08
	New Hampshire	H	13.59 AE	17.39 MW	21.85 AEX	NHBLS	6/08
	New Jersey	Y	27450 FQ	32670 MW	39610 TQ	USBLS	5/07
	Camden PMSA, NJ	Y	26920 FQ	32160 MW	39160 TQ	USBLS	5/07
	Edison PMSA, NJ	Y	26880 FQ	31030 MW	39310 TQ	USBLS	5/07
	Newark-Union PMSA, NJ-PA	Y	27630 FQ	32270 MW	39110 TQ	USBLS	5/07
	New Mexico	Y	19530 FQ	25040 MW	32850 TQ	USBLS	5/07
	Albuquerque MSA, NM	Y	18080 FQ	22490 MW	32880 TQ	USBLS	5/07
	New York	Y	32070 FQ	36690 MW	42750 TQ	USBLS	5/07
	Albany-Schenectady-Troy MSA, NY	Y	25280 FQ	28900 MW	36690 TQ	USBLS	5/07
	Buffalo-Niagara Falls MSA, NY	Y	27630 FQ	38240 MW	48020 TQ	USBLS	5/07
	Nassau-Suffolk PMSA, NY	Y	30920 FQ	37300 MW	47200 TQ	USBLS	5/07
	New York-Northern New Jersey-Long Island MSA, NY-NJ-PA	Y	30400 FQ	35880 MW	41410 TQ	USBLS	5/07
	Syracuse MSA, NY	Y	24200 FQ	32920 MW	38570 TQ	USBLS	5/07
	North Carolina	Y	26970 FQ	31550 MW	38430 TQ	USBLS	5/07
	Charlotte-Gastonia-Concord MSA, NC-SC	Y	27770 FQ	34540 MW	41820 TQ	USBLS	5/07
	Raleigh-Cary MSA, NC	Y	26590 FQ	30840 MW	35660 TQ	USBLS	5/07
	North Dakota	Y	23880 FQ	28940 MW	40830 TQ	USBLS	5/07
	Fargo MSA, ND-MN	Y	22840 FQ	26220 MW	32740 TQ	USBLS	5/07
	Ohio	Y	25440 FQ	29850 MW	35970 TQ	USBLS	5/07
	Cincinnati-Middletown MSA, OH-KY-IN	Y	26550 FQ	31820 MW	38520 TQ	USBLS	5/07
	Cleveland-Elyria-Mentor MSA, OH	Y	23800 FQ	28560 MW	34750 TQ	USBLS	5/07
	Columbus MSA, OH	Y	26430 FQ	30380 MW	36050 TQ	USBLS	5/07
	Dayton MSA, OH	Y	26400 FQ	29970 MW	35530 TQ	USBLS	5/07
	Oklahoma	Y	23030 FQ	27250 MW	32070 TQ	USBLS	5/07
	Oklahoma City MSA, OK	Y	22290 FQ	24590 MW	29080 TQ	USBLS	5/07
	Tulsa MSA, OK	Y	25580 FQ	28780 MW	35960 TQ	USBLS	5/07
	Oregon	H	14.01 FQ	17.08 MW	20.40 TQ	ORBLS	5/08
	Portland-Vancouver-Beaverton MSA, OR-WA	Y	30060 FQ	35560 MW	41930 TQ	USBLS	5/07
	Pennsylvania	Y	24970 FQ	30580 MW	37320 TQ	USBLS	5/07
	Allentown-Bethlehem-Easton MSA, PA-NJ	Y	28280 FQ	33780 MW	40920 TQ	USBLS	5/07
	Philadelphia-Camden-Wilmington MSA, PA-NJ-DE-MD	Y	27670 FQ	33440 MW	39430 TQ	USBLS	5/07
	Pittsburgh MSA, PA	Y	23330 FQ	28570 MW	35490 TQ	USBLS	5/07
	Rhode Island	Y	30640 FQ	40270 MW	47150 TQ	USBLS	5/07
	Providence-Fall River-Warwick MSA, RI-MA	Y	29990 FQ	39330 MW	47320 TQ	USBLS	5/07
	South Carolina	Y	22880 FQ	27660 MW	32400 TQ	USBLS	5/07
	Charleston-North Charleston MSA, SC	Y	30170 FQ	36640 MW	43320 TQ	USBLS	5/07
	Columbia MSA, SC	Y	24860 FQ	28190 MW	31390 TQ	USBLS	5/07
	South Dakota	Y	23267 FQ	26435 MW	30852 TQ	SDBLS	7/08-9/08
	Sioux Falls MSA, SD	Y	23990 FQ	28064 MW	31947 TQ	SDBLS	7/08-9/08
	Tennessee	Y	24180 FQ	29140 MW	36920 TQ	USBLS	5/07
	Memphis MSA, TN-MS-AR	Y	23800 FQ	30050 MW	38190 TQ	USBLS	5/07
	Nashville-Davidson-Murfreesboro MSA, TN	Y	28710 FQ	33640 MW	39830 TQ	USBLS	5/07
	Texas	Y	20360 FQ	28900 MW	37260 TQ	USBLS	5/07
	Dallas-Fort Worth-Arlington MSA, TX	Y	27390 FQ	34120 MW	40410 TQ	USBLS	5/07
	El Paso MSA, TX	Y	13920 FQ	21500 MW	32460 TQ	USBLS	5/07

AE	Average entry wage	AW	Average wage paid	FQ	First quartile wage
AER	Average entry range	AWR	Average wage range	H	Hourly
AEX	Average experienced wage	AXR	Average experienced range	HI	Highest wage paid
ATC	Average total compensation	D	Daily	HR	High end range

LO	Lowest wage paid	MTC	Median total compensation	TCC	Total cash compensation
LR	Low end range	MW	Median wage paid	TQ	Third quartile wage
M	Monthly	MWR	Median wage range	W	Weekly
MCC	Median cash compensation	S	See annotated source	Y	Yearly

Occupation/Type/Industry	Location	Per	Low	Mid	High	Source	Date
Credit Authorizer, Checker, and Clerk	Houston-Sugar Land-Baytown MSA, TX	Y	20100 FQ	32490 MW	41350 TQ	USBLS	5/07
	San Antonio MSA, TX	Y	22220 FQ	28130 MW	34090 TQ	USBLS	5/07
	Utah	Y	25280 FQ	32270 MW	39710 TQ	USBLS	5/07
	Salt Lake City MSA, UT	Y	25340 FQ	29420 MW	42250 TQ	USBLS	5/07
	Vermont	Y	23550 FQ	27370 MW	31240 TQ	USBLS	5/07
	Virginia	Y	25040 FQ	32060 MW	39970 TQ	USBLS	5/07
	Lynchburg MSA, VA	Y	25630 FQ	28770 MW	33310 TQ	USBLS	5/07
	Richmond MSA, VA	Y	22570 FQ	30080 MW	37790 TQ	USBLS	5/07
	Roanoke MSA, VA	Y	21830 FQ	24070 MW	28300 TQ	USBLS	5/07
	Virginia Beach-Norfolk-Newport News MSA, VA-NC	Y	22510 FQ	27000 MW	33950 TQ	USBLS	5/07
	Washington	H	14.50 FQ	17.41 MW	20.40 TQ	WABLS	3/08
	Seattle-Tacoma-Bellevue MSA, WA	Y	30920 FQ	36860 MW	43030 TQ	USBLS	5/07
	West Virginia	Y	21928 FQ	26396 MW	36878 TQ	WVBLS	7/08-9/08
	Wisconsin	Y	25990 FQ	30620 MW	36610 TQ	USBLS	5/07
	Milwaukee-Waukesha-West Allis MSA, WI	Y	25550 FQ	31490 MW	37030 TQ	USBLS	5/07
	Wyoming	Y	27474 FQ	30883 MW	34351 TQ	WYBLS	9/08
	Puerto Rico	Y	15110 FQ	19630 MW	24020 TQ	USBLS	5/07
	San Juan-Caguas-Guaynabo MSA, PR	Y	16160 FQ	21060 MW	24750 TQ	USBLS	5/07
Credit Union Employee	United States	Y		35000 MTC		CUMGT1	2008
Crew Leader							
County Government	Bartow County, GA	Y	33093 LO		39874 HI	GACTY03	2008
County Government	Pickens County, GA	Y	24000 LO		36519 HI	GACTY03	2008
Crew Scheduler	United States	Y		14757 AW		AVJOB02	2009
Crime Analyst							
Municipal Government	Cincinnati, OH	Y	34171 LO		45923 HI	COHSS	10/08
Municipal Government	Gresham, OR	Y	52584 LO		67152 HI	GOSS	1/1/09
Crime Laboratory Quality Assurance Administrator							
State Government	Ohio	H	33.83 LO		44.38 HI	ODAS	2008
Crime Laboratory Quality Assurance Coordinator							
State Highway Patrol	Missouri	S	1843 LO		2678 HI	MSHPSS	7/1/08
Crime Laboratory Supervisor	Colorado Springs, CO	M	5182 LO			COSPRS	1/1/09
Crime Prevention Specialist							
Municipal Government	Carlsbad, CA	S	1713 LO		2082 HI	CCSS01	8/5/08
Municipal Government	Gresham, OR	Y	45096 LO		57576 HI	GOSS	1/1/09
Crime-Scene Cleaner							
Working for a Contracting Company	United States	Y	35000 LO		80000 HI	ACONT	2009
Crime Scene Specialist Trainee							
Sheriff's Department Forensic Laboratory	San Bernardino, CA	W	2988 LO		3815 HI	CAC	2006-2007
Crime Scene Technician	Mesa, AZ	W	3056 LO		4115 HI	CAC	2006-2007
	Colorado Springs, CO	M	3488 LO			COSPRS	1/1/09
Criminal Justice and Law Enforcement Teacher							
Postsecondary	Alabama	Y	39740 FQ	48470 MW	60910 TQ	USBLS	5/07
Postsecondary	Arizona	Y	45490 FQ	50990 MW	56140 TQ	USBLS	5/07
Postsecondary	Phoenix-Mesa-Scottsdale MSA, AZ	Y	43200 FQ	46800 MW	50490 TQ	USBLS	5/07
Postsecondary	Arkansas	Y	39040 FQ	61830 MW	110910 TQ	USBLS	5/07
Postsecondary	California	Y		91718 AW		CABLS	1/08-3/08
Postsecondary	Los Angeles-Long Beach-Glendale PMSA, CA	Y		108167 AW		CABLS	1/08-3/08
Postsecondary	Oakland-Fremont-Hayward MSA, CA	Y		66861 AW		CABLS	1/08-3/08

AE Average entry wage	**AW** Average wage paid	**FQ** First quartile wage	**LO** Lowest wage paid	**MTC** Median total compensation	**TCC** Total cash compensation
AER Average entry range	**AWR** Average wage range	**H** Hourly	**LR** Low end range	**MW** Median wage paid	**TQ** Third quartile wage
AEX Average experienced wage	**AXR** Average experienced range	**HI** Highest wage paid	**M** Monthly	**MWR** Median wage range	**W** Weekly
ATC Average total compensation	**D** Daily	**HR** High end range	**MCC** Median cash compensation	**S** See annotated source	**Y** Yearly

Occupation/Type/Industry	Location	Per	Low	Mid	High	Source	Date
Criminal Justice and Law Enforcement Teacher							
Postsecondary	Riverside-San Bernardino-Ontario MSA, CA	Y		87421 AW		CABLS	1/08-3/08
Postsecondary	Colorado	Y	37720 FQ	43360 MW	52870 TQ	USBLS	5/07
Postsecondary	Denver-Aurora MSA, CO	Y	36550 FQ	39720 MW	45380 TQ	USBLS	5/07
Postsecondary	District of Columbia	Y	44940 FQ	52610 MW	61980 TQ	USBLS	5/07
Postsecondary	Washington-Arlington-Alexandria MSA, DC-VA-MD-WV	Y	42180 FQ	54120 MW	66370 TQ	USBLS	5/07
Postsecondary	Florida	Y	31100 FQ	50340 MW	64400 TQ	USBLS	5/07
Postsecondary	Pensacola-Ferry Pass-Brent MSA, FL	Y	50970 FQ	57530 MW	63700 TQ	USBLS	5/07
Postsecondary	Tampa-St. Petersburg-Clearwater MSA, FL	Y	33380 FQ	47970 MW	66690 TQ	USBLS	5/07
Postsecondary	Georgia	Y	30540 FQ	42610 MW	60800 TQ	USBLS	5/07
Postsecondary	Atlanta-Sandy Springs-Marietta MSA, GA	Y	35740 FQ	57240 MW	66940 TQ	USBLS	5/07
Postsecondary	Illinois	Y	39800 FQ	46090 MW	57740 TQ	USBLS	5/07
Postsecondary	Chicago-Naperville-Joliet MSA, IL-IN-WI	Y	36400 FQ	47370 MW	63320 TQ	USBLS	5/07
Postsecondary	Indiana	Y	44230 FQ	54410 MW	62930 TQ	USBLS	5/07
Postsecondary	Iowa	Y	42050 FQ	49610 MW	61410 TQ	USBLS	5/07
Postsecondary	Des Moines-West Des Moines MSA, IA	Y	48520 FQ	58100 MW	64220 TQ	USBLS	5/07
Postsecondary	Kansas	Y	28800 FQ	49190 MW	84270 TQ	USBLS	5/07
Postsecondary	Kentucky	Y	36960 FQ	47548 MW	59106 TQ	KYBLS	2008
Postsecondary	Louisiana	Y		52068 AW		LABLS	1/08-3/08
Postsecondary	Baton Rouge MSA, LA	Y	40800 FQ	48900 MW	58200 TQ	USBLS	5/07
Postsecondary	Maine	Y	41590 FQ	48880 MW	57610 TQ	USBLS	5/07
Postsecondary	Maryland	Y		56575 MW		MDBLS	3/08
Postsecondary	Baltimore-Towson MSA, MD	Y	45660 FQ	63140 MW	79930 TQ	USBLS	5/07
Postsecondary	Massachusetts	Y	49670 FQ	56120 MW	63140 TQ	USBLS	5/07
Postsecondary	Boston-Cambridge-Quincy NECTA, MA	Y	50880 FQ	56420 MW	62840 TQ	USBLS	5/07
Postsecondary	Michigan	Y	29600 FQ	54370 MW	75430 TQ	USBLS	5/07
Postsecondary	Detroit-Warren-Livonia MSA, MI	Y	27300 FQ	30050 MW	41080 TQ	USBLS	5/07
Postsecondary	Minnesota	Y	42884 FQ	54895 MW	63934 TQ	MNBLS	10/08-12/08
Postsecondary	Duluth-Superior MSA, MN-WI	Y	53441 FQ	60314 MW	66738 TQ	MNBLS	10/08-12/08
Postsecondary	Minneapolis-Saint Paul MSA, MN-WI	Y	40122 FQ	53681 MW	62825 TQ	MNBLS	10/08-12/08
Postsecondary	Mississippi	Y	46430 FQ	54690 MW	64870 TQ	USBLS	5/07
Postsecondary	Missouri	Y	35720 FQ	46150 MW	68670 TQ	USBLS	5/07
Postsecondary	Kansas City MSA, MO-KS	Y	35040 FQ	40810 MW	79640 TQ	USBLS	5/07
Postsecondary	St. Louis MSA, MO-IL	Y	31270 FQ	40350 MW	74760 TQ	USBLS	5/07
Postsecondary	Nebraska	Y	34740 FQ	44580 MW	60160 TQ	USBLS	5/07
Postsecondary	Omaha-Council Bluffs MSA, NE-IA	Y	29240 FQ	36910 MW	53040 TQ	USBLS	5/07
Postsecondary	New Jersey	Y	39760 FQ	54750 MW	71710 TQ	USBLS	5/07
Postsecondary	Edison PMSA, NJ	Y	49640 FQ	62420 MW	80780 TQ	USBLS	5/07
Postsecondary	Newark-Union PMSA, NJ-PA	Y	37060 FQ	48280 MW	68870 TQ	USBLS	5/07
Postsecondary	New York	Y	39460 FQ	48260 MW	64970 TQ	USBLS	5/07
Postsecondary	New York-Northern New Jersey-Long Island MSA, NY-NJ-PA	Y	43340 FQ	57420 MW	76080 TQ	USBLS	5/07
Postsecondary	North Carolina	Y	41140 FQ	47450 MW	54480 TQ	USBLS	5/07
Postsecondary	Asheville MSA, NC	Y	45240 FQ	52420 MW	59070 TQ	USBLS	5/07
Postsecondary	Charlotte-Gastonia-Concord MSA, NC-SC	Y	43110 FQ	47940 MW	54140 TQ	USBLS	5/07
Postsecondary	Durham MSA, NC	Y	45770 FQ	50730 MW	65880 TQ	USBLS	5/07
Postsecondary	Raleigh-Cary MSA, NC	Y	42420 FQ	48990 MW	56910 TQ	USBLS	5/07
Postsecondary	Ohio	Y	38590 FQ	53040 MW	72930 TQ	USBLS	5/07
Postsecondary	Cincinnati-Middletown MSA, OH-KY-IN	Y	39950 FQ	56540 MW	80750 TQ	USBLS	5/07
Postsecondary	Cleveland-Elyria-Mentor MSA, OH	Y	37640 FQ	53920 MW	65350 TQ	USBLS	5/07
Postsecondary	Oklahoma	Y	31070 FQ	39290 MW	51430 TQ	USBLS	5/07
Postsecondary	Oklahoma City MSA, OK	Y	31890 FQ	37890 MW	49040 TQ	USBLS	5/07
Postsecondary	Portland-Vancouver-Beaverton MSA, OR-WA	Y	44010 FQ	62270 MW	85290 TQ	USBLS	5/07
Postsecondary	Pennsylvania	Y	46390 FQ	63680 MW	97720 TQ	USBLS	5/07

AE	Average entry wage	**AW**	Average wage paid	**FQ**	First quartile wage	**LO**	Lowest wage paid	**MTC** Median total compensation **TCC** Total cash compensation
AER	Average entry range	**AWR**	Average wage range	**H**	Hourly	**LR**	Low end range	**MW** Median wage paid **TQ** Third quartile wage
AEX	Average experienced wage	**AXR**	Average experienced range	**HI**	Highest wage paid	**M**	Monthly	**MWR** Median wage range **W** Weekly
ATC	Average total compensation	**D**	Daily	**HR**	High end range	**MCC**	Median cash compensation	**S** See annotated source **Y** Yearly

Occupation/Type/Industry	Location	Per	Low	Mid	High	Source	Date
Criminal Justice and Law Enforcement Teacher							
Postsecondary	Philadelphia-Camden-Wilmington MSA, PA-NJ-DE-MD	Y	45050 FQ	59430 MW	85790 TQ	USBLS	5/07
Postsecondary	Pittsburgh MSA, PA	Y	50690 FQ	67520 MW	108420 TQ	USBLS	5/07
Postsecondary	South Carolina	Y	49080 FQ	59430 MW	72610 TQ	USBLS	5/07
Postsecondary	South Dakota	Y	42627 FQ	50319 MW	59150 TQ	SDBLS	7/08-9/08
Postsecondary	Tennessee	Y	40360 FQ	49610 MW	65130 TQ	USBLS	5/07
Postsecondary	Nashville-Davidson-Murfreesboro MSA, TN	Y	49210 FQ	59760 MW	76040 TQ	USBLS	5/07
Postsecondary	Texas	Y	35720 FQ	48650 MW	67130 TQ	USBLS	5/07
Postsecondary	El Paso MSA, TX	Y	27420 FQ	39710 MW	54340 TQ	USBLS	5/07
Postsecondary	Houston-Sugar Land-Baytown MSA, TX	Y	38090 FQ	56500 MW	67000 TQ	USBLS	5/07
Postsecondary	San Antonio MSA, TX	Y	34280 FQ	50110 MW	76620 TQ	USBLS	5/07
Postsecondary	Utah	Y	39690 FQ	49380 MW	57810 TQ	USBLS	5/07
Postsecondary	Vermont	Y	43320 FQ	50920 MW	59200 TQ	USBLS	5/07
Postsecondary	Burlington-South Burlington MSA, VT	Y	41700 FQ	51120 MW	60350 TQ	USBLS	5/07
Postsecondary	Virginia	Y	41570 FQ	50420 MW	64740 TQ	USBLS	5/07
Postsecondary	Washington	Y		57563 AW		WABLS	3/08
Postsecondary	West Virginia	Y	51492 FQ	70935 MW	100027 TQ	WVBLS	7/08-9/08
Postsecondary	Wisconsin	Y	35790 FQ	53170 MW	72290 TQ	USBLS	5/07
Postsecondary	Milwaukee-Waukesha-West Allis MSA, WI	Y	36030 FQ	40510 MW	63610 TQ	USBLS	5/07
Postsecondary	Wyoming	Y	45672 FQ	51266 MW	56766 TQ	WYBLS	9/08
Criminal Justice Investigator							
Department of Justice	New Hampshire	Y		65680 AW		NHUL03	2008
Criminal Justice Planner							
State Government	Ohio	H	19.88 LO		26.28 HI	ODAS	2008
Criminal Justice Policy Specialist							
State Government	Ohio	H	23.87 LO		35.02 HI	ODAS	2008
Criminalist Supervisor							
State Highway Patrol	Missouri	S	1843 LO		2678 HI	MSHPSS	7/1/08
Crop Assistant	United States	Y	26000 LO	32500 AW	40000 HI	AGRI	2008
Crossing Guard	Alabama	Y	13510 FQ	16080 MW	19220 TQ	USBLS	5/07
	Birmingham-Hoover MSA, AL	Y	13030 FQ	14860 MW	17620 TQ	USBLS	5/07
	Arizona	Y	14910 FQ	16320 MW	18450 TQ	USBLS	5/07
	Phoenix-Mesa-Scottsdale MSA, AZ	Y	14850 FQ	15960 MW	18030 TQ	USBLS	5/07
	Tucson MSA, AZ	Y	15910 FQ	17620 MW	19170 TQ	USBLS	5/07
	Arkansas	Y	14600 FQ	16170 MW	23400 TQ	USBLS	5/07
	Little Rock-North Little Rock MSA, AR	Y	13980 FQ	14930 MW	19040 TQ	USBLS	5/07
	California	H	8.73 FQ	10.00 MW	12.28 TQ	CABLS	1/08-3/08
	Los Angeles-Long Beach-Glendale PMSA, CA	H	8.47 FQ	9.17 MW	10.42 TQ	CABLS	1/08-3/08
	Oakland-Fremont-Hayward MSA, CA	H	10.62 FQ	12.09 MW	13.83 TQ	CABLS	1/08-3/08
	Riverside-San Bernardino-Ontario MSA, CA	H	8.93 FQ	10.33 MW	11.33 TQ	CABLS	1/08-3/08
	Sacramento-Arden Arcade-Roseville MSA, CA	H	8.91 FQ	11.50 MW	13.83 TQ	CABLS	1/08-3/08
	San Diego-Carlsbad-San Marcos MSA, CA	H	9.02 FQ	12.12 MW	20.29 TQ	CABLS	1/08-3/08
	San Francisco-San Mateo-Redwood PMSA, CA	H	9.67 FQ	11.39 MW	13.31 TQ	CABLS	1/08-3/08
	San Jose-Sunnyvale-Santa Clara MSA, CA	H	12.86 FQ	15.02 MW	17.01 TQ	CABLS	1/08-3/08
	Santa Ana-Anaheim-Irvine PMSA, CA	Y	18210 FQ	19860 MW	22130 TQ	USBLS	5/07
	Seaside, CA	S	500 LO		680 HI	SSSS	8/08
	Colorado	Y	19730 FQ	24330 MW	28490 TQ	USBLS	5/07
	Denver-Aurora MSA, CO	Y	19300 FQ	23790 MW	27930 TQ	USBLS	5/07
	Connecticut	H	9.12 AE	12.48 MW		CTBLS	1/08-3/08

AE	Average entry wage	AW	Average wage paid	FQ	First quartile wage
AER	Average entry range	AWR	Average wage range	H	Hourly
AEX	Average experienced wage	AXR	Average experienced range	HI	Highest wage paid
ATC	Average total compensation	D	Daily	HR	High end range

LO	Lowest wage paid	MTC	Median total compensation	TCC	Total cash compensation
LR	Low end range	MW	Median wage paid	TQ	Third quartile wage
M	Monthly	MWR	Median wage range	W	Weekly
MCC	Median cash compensation	S	See annotated source	Y	Yearly

Occupation/Type/Industry	Location	Per	Low	Mid	High	Source	Date
Crossing Guard	Bridgeport-Stamford-Norwalk MSA, CT	Y	18810 FQ	25240 MW	33400 TQ	USBLS	5/07
	Hartford-West Hartford-East Hartford MSA, CT	Y	22690 FQ	28590 MW	34600 TQ	USBLS	5/07
	Delaware	Y	27400 FQ	31450 MW	42390 TQ	USBLS	5/07
	Wilmington PMSA, DE-MD-NJ	Y	23670 FQ	27730 MW	31000 TQ	USBLS	5/07
	Washington-Arlington-Alexandria MSA, DC-VA-MD-WV	Y	21770 FQ	26570 MW	34120 TQ	USBLS	5/07
	Florida	Y	17110 FQ	19940 MW	23800 TQ	USBLS	5/07
	Fort Lauderdale-Pompano Beach-Deerfield Beach PMSA, FL	Y	21030 FQ	23590 MW	27000 TQ	USBLS	5/07
	Orlando-Kissimmee MSA, FL	Y	16900 FQ	18430 MW	19940 TQ	USBLS	5/07
	Tampa-St. Petersburg-Clearwater MSA, FL	Y	15430 FQ	17580 MW	20750 TQ	USBLS	5/07
	West Palm Beach-Boca Raton-Boynton Beach PMSA, FL	Y	21220 FQ	22820 MW	24430 TQ	USBLS	5/07
	Georgia	Y	14390 FQ	20850 MW	31860 TQ	USBLS	5/07
	Atlanta-Sandy Springs-Marietta MSA, GA	Y	18270 FQ	31420 MW	35330 TQ	USBLS	5/07
	Hawaii	Y	21120 FQ	23960 MW	27680 TQ	USBLS	5/07
	Hawai'i County, HI	H			10.95 HI	CHDHR02	1/09
	Idaho	Y	17360 FQ	19020 MW	21570 TQ	USBLS	5/07
	Boise City-Nampa MSA, ID	Y	17610 FQ	19260 MW	21450 TQ	USBLS	5/07
	Illinois	Y	19640 FQ	24570 MW	28890 TQ	USBLS	5/07
	Chicago-Naperville-Joliet MSA, IL-IN-WI	Y	21550 FQ	25580 MW	29370 TQ	USBLS	5/07
	Indiana	Y	13900 FQ	18970 MW	23390 TQ	USBLS	5/07
	Elkhart-Goshen MSA, IN	Y	13610 FQ	17130 MW	22650 TQ	USBLS	5/07
	Gary PMSA, IN	Y	14400 FQ	18250 MW	21970 TQ	USBLS	5/07
	Indianapolis-Carmel MSA, IN	Y	14860 FQ	21840 MW	34410 TQ	USBLS	5/07
	Iowa	Y	18690 FQ	23320 MW	28980 TQ	USBLS	5/07
	Des Moines-West Des Moines MSA, IA	Y	18400 FQ	24800 MW	28120 TQ	USBLS	5/07
	Kansas	Y	14270 FQ	17520 MW	24170 TQ	USBLS	5/07
	Wichita MSA, KS	Y	17350 FQ	20470 MW	23570 TQ	USBLS	5/07
	Kentucky	Y	18724 FQ	20652 MW	22644 TQ	KYBLS	2008
	Lexington-Fayette MSA, KY	Y	17560 FQ	18700 MW	19850 TQ	USBLS	5/07
	Louisville-Jefferson County MSA, KY-IN	Y	19230 FQ	20610 MW	22370 TQ	USBLS	5/07
	Louisiana	H	6.43 FQ	7.56 MW	10.24 TQ	LABLS	1/08-3/08
	Baton Rouge MSA, LA	Y	12910 FQ	14810 MW	18910 TQ	USBLS	5/07
	New Orleans-Metairie-Kenner MSA, LA	Y	13000 FQ	14810 MW	17860 TQ	USBLS	5/07
	Maine	Y	16890 FQ	18390 MW	20210 TQ	USBLS	5/07
	Portland-South Portland-Biddeford MSA, ME	Y	17690 FQ	19430 MW	21550 TQ	USBLS	5/07
	Maryland	Y		19350 MW		MDBLS	3/08
	Baltimore-Towson MSA, MD	Y	15000 FQ	16770 MW	20010 TQ	USBLS	5/07
	Bethesda-Gaithersburg-Frederick PMSA, MD	Y	22100 FQ	25170 MW	32200 TQ	USBLS	5/07
	Massachusetts	Y	18610 FQ	25880 MW	30680 TQ	USBLS	5/07
	Boston-Cambridge-Quincy NECTA, MA	Y	22210 FQ	27940 MW	31980 TQ	USBLS	5/07
	Worcester MSA, MA-CT	Y	16860 FQ	18380 MW	19910 TQ	USBLS	5/07
	Michigan	Y	16340 FQ	20470 MW	23880 TQ	USBLS	5/07
	Detroit-Warren-Livonia MSA, MI	Y	18000 FQ	21800 MW	24120 TQ	USBLS	5/07
	Grand Rapids-Wyoming MSA, MI	Y	17410 FQ	19630 MW	25470 TQ	USBLS	5/07
	Warren-Troy-Farmington Hills PMSA, MI	Y	19530 FQ	22020 MW	24040 TQ	USBLS	5/07
	Minnesota	Y	16248 FQ	20347 MW	24173 TQ	MNBLS	10/08-12/08
	Duluth-Superior MSA, MN-WI	Y	17241 FQ	19541 MW	22532 TQ	MNBLS	10/08-12/08
	Minneapolis-Saint Paul MSA, MN-WI	Y	16217 FQ	20200 MW	24466 TQ	MNBLS	10/08-12/08
	Rochester MSA, MN	Y	21179 FQ	42308 MW	51601 TQ	MNBLS	10/08-12/08
	Mississippi	Y	14050 FQ	20190 MW	24770 TQ	USBLS	5/07
	Jackson MSA, MS	Y	13040 FQ	15020 MW	19050 TQ	USBLS	5/07
	Missouri	Y	16500 FQ	20200 MW	22640 TQ	USBLS	5/07

Occupation/Type/Industry	Location	Per	Low	Mid	High	Source	Date
Crossing Guard	Kansas City MSA, MO-KS	Y	14300 FQ	19350 MW	27190 TQ	USBLS	5/07
	St. Louis MSA, MO-IL	Y	17710 FQ	20590 MW	22930 TQ	USBLS	5/07
	Montana	Y	19510 FQ	30260 MW	35860 TQ	USBLS	5/07
	Billings MSA, MT	Y	14430 FQ	16150 MW	34550 TQ	USBLS	5/07
	Nebraska	Y	13050 FQ	14680 MW	18420 TQ	USBLS	5/07
	Nevada	H	8.81 FQ	9.73 MW	11.08 TQ	NVBLS	5/08
	Las Vegas-Paradise MSA, NV	H	8.76 FQ	9.56 MW	10.86 TQ	NVBLS	5/08
	New Hampshire	H	8.83 AE	11.01 MW	12.13 AEX	NHBLS	6/08
	Manchester MSA, NH	Y	20560 FQ	21980 MW	23400 TQ	USBLS	5/07
	Nashua NECTA, NH-MA	Y	17920 FQ	23160 MW	27080 TQ	USBLS	5/07
	New Jersey	Y	20690 FQ	26530 MW	31830 TQ	USBLS	5/07
	Camden PMSA, NJ	Y	16790 FQ	20960 MW	26560 TQ	USBLS	5/07
	Edison PMSA, NJ	Y	21690 FQ	25970 MW	30300 TQ	USBLS	5/07
	Newark-Union PMSA, NJ-PA	Y	22450 FQ	28540 MW	33660 TQ	USBLS	5/07
	New Mexico	Y	21160 FQ	23510 MW	25870 TQ	USBLS	5/07
	New York	Y	22220 FQ	27360 MW	30990 TQ	USBLS	5/07
	Albany-Schenectady-Troy MSA, NY	Y	15690 FQ	18160 MW	22670 TQ	USBLS	5/07
	Binghamton MSA, NY	Y	16520 FQ	17610 MW	18690 TQ	USBLS	5/07
	Buffalo-Niagara Falls MSA, NY	Y	17610 FQ	19250 MW	21460 TQ	USBLS	5/07
	Nassau-Suffolk PMSA, NY	Y	29740 FQ	40190 MW	47050 TQ	USBLS	5/07
	New York-Northern New Jersey-Long Island MSA, NY-NJ-PA	Y	23810 FQ	28240 MW	31740 TQ	USBLS	5/07
	North Carolina	Y	17740 FQ	21800 MW	25980 TQ	USBLS	5/07
	Charlotte-Gastonia-Concord MSA, NC-SC	Y	15140 FQ	22310 MW	25740 TQ	USBLS	5/07
	Raleigh-Cary MSA, NC	Y	20130 FQ	23720 MW	30670 TQ	USBLS	5/07
	Ohio	Y	16230 FQ	19380 MW	23850 TQ	USBLS	5/07
	Cincinnati-Middletown MSA, OH-KY-IN	Y	14800 FQ	15420 MW	19320 TQ	USBLS	5/07
	Cleveland-Elyria-Mentor MSA, OH	Y	17540 FQ	19760 MW	22970 TQ	USBLS	5/07
	Columbus MSA, OH	Y	20240 FQ	27000 MW	31410 TQ	USBLS	5/07
	Cincinnati, OH	Y	19205 LO		20324 HI	COHSS	10/08
	Oklahoma	Y	13360 FQ	15850 MW	27700 TQ	USBLS	5/07
	Tulsa MSA, OK	Y	13160 FQ	15150 MW	18160 TQ	USBLS	5/07
	Oregon	H	10.79 FQ	13.13 MW	16.89 TQ	ORBLS	5/08
	Portland-Vancouver-Beaverton MSA, OR-WA	Y	21080 FQ	25620 MW	30680 TQ	USBLS	5/07
	Pennsylvania	Y	15190 FQ	18900 MW	23590 TQ	USBLS	5/07
	Allentown-Bethlehem-Easton MSA, PA-NJ	Y	15530 FQ	17540 MW	20850 TQ	USBLS	5/07
	Philadelphia-Camden-Wilmington MSA, PA-NJ-DE-MD	Y	15220 FQ	18870 MW	25390 TQ	USBLS	5/07
	Pittsburgh MSA, PA	Y	16380 FQ	20400 MW	23330 TQ	USBLS	5/07
	Rhode Island	Y	23210 FQ	33550 MW	38370 TQ	USBLS	5/07
	Providence-Fall River-Warwick MSA, RI-MA	Y	22530 FQ	31820 MW	37800 TQ	USBLS	5/07
	South Carolina	Y	15020 FQ	20560 MW	24050 TQ	USBLS	5/07
	Charleston-North Charleston MSA, SC	Y	14370 FQ	19490 MW	23190 TQ	USBLS	5/07
	Columbia MSA, SC	Y	14450 FQ	18890 MW	23870 TQ	USBLS	5/07
	South Dakota	Y	17994 FQ	20265 MW	23408 TQ	SDBLS	7/08-9/08
	Nashville-Davidson-Murfreesboro MSA, TN	Y	12300 FQ	13810 MW	15320 TQ	USBLS	5/07
	Texas	Y	14080 FQ	17670 MW	22120 TQ	USBLS	5/07
	Austin-Round Rock MSA, TX	Y	13570 FQ	15880 MW	21550 TQ	USBLS	5/07
	Beaumont-Port Arthur MSA, TX	Y	12650 FQ	14080 MW	15530 TQ	USBLS	5/07
	Dallas-Fort Worth-Arlington MSA, TX	Y	14020 FQ	18770 MW	22590 TQ	USBLS	5/07
	El Paso MSA, TX	Y	12660 FQ	14050 MW	15490 TQ	USBLS	5/07
	Houston-Sugar Land-Baytown MSA, TX	Y	17090 FQ	22020 MW	25310 TQ	USBLS	5/07
	Utah	Y	15280 FQ	17880 MW	20670 TQ	USBLS	5/07
	Salt Lake City MSA, UT	Y	15810 FQ	18780 MW	22590 TQ	USBLS	5/07
	Vermont	Y	20840 FQ	25240 MW	29460 TQ	USBLS	5/07
	Burlington-South Burlington MSA, VT	Y	26450 FQ	28620 MW	30790 TQ	USBLS	5/07

AE Average entry wage	**AW** Average wage paid	**FQ** First quartile wage	**LO** Lowest wage paid	**MTC** Median total compensation	**TCC** Total cash compensation
AER Average entry range	**AWR** Average wage range	**H** Hourly	**LR** Low end range	**MW** Median wage paid	**TQ** Third quartile wage
AEX Average experienced wage	**AXR** Average experienced range	**HI** Highest wage paid	**M** Monthly	**MWR** Median wage range	**W** Weekly
ATC Average total compensation	**D** Daily	**HR** High end range	**MCC** Median cash compensation	**S** See annotated source	**Y** Yearly

Occupation/Type/Industry	Location	Per	Low	Mid	High	Source	Date
Crossing Guard	Virginia	Y	19150 FQ	26500 MW	35030 TQ	USBLS	5/07
	Richmond MSA, VA	Y	20850 FQ	26380 MW	31400 TQ	USBLS	5/07
	Virginia Beach-Norfolk-Newport News MSA, VA-NC	Y	17420 FQ	19860 MW	36140 TQ	USBLS	5/07
	Washington	H	11.03 FQ	13.52 MW	19.75 TQ	WABLS	3/08
	Seattle-Tacoma-Bellevue MSA, WA	Y	23450 FQ	27780 MW	39550 TQ	USBLS	5/07
	Seattle, WA	H		12.86 HI		CSSS	2008
	West Virginia	Y	14413 FQ	16279 MW	21067 TQ	WVBLS	7/08-9/08
	Wisconsin	Y	18990 FQ	22400 MW	25360 TQ	USBLS	5/07
	Milwaukee-Waukesha-West Allis MSA, WI	Y	20490 FQ	22710 MW	25000 TQ	USBLS	5/07
	Wyoming	Y	20456 FQ	23619 MW	28967 TQ	WYBLS	9/08
Crushing, Grinding, and Polishing Machine Setter, Operator, and Tender	Alabama	Y	19520 FQ	25540 MW	35190 TQ	USBLS	5/07
	Birmingham-Hoover MSA, AL	Y	17730 FQ	19280 MW	21300 TQ	USBLS	5/07
	Alaska	Y	36800 FQ	60420 MW	71670 TQ	USBLS	5/07
	Arizona	Y	22010 FQ	30310 MW	36770 TQ	USBLS	5/07
	Phoenix-Mesa-Scottsdale MSA, AZ	Y	21740 FQ	26950 MW	34300 TQ	USBLS	5/07
	Tucson MSA, AZ	Y	16780 FQ	18640 MW	36010 TQ	USBLS	5/07
	Arkansas	Y	21780 FQ	27600 MW	32010 TQ	USBLS	5/07
	Jonesboro MSA, AR	Y	19580 FQ	24570 MW	28080 TQ	USBLS	5/07
	Little Rock-North Little Rock MSA, AR	Y	25130 FQ	28620 MW	32890 TQ	USBLS	5/07
	California	H	10.21 FQ	13.81 MW	18.86 TQ	CABLS	1/08-3/08
	Los Angeles-Long Beach-Glendale PMSA, CA	H	10.34 FQ	13.00 MW	17.39 TQ	CABLS	1/08-3/08
	Oakland-Fremont-Hayward MSA, CA	H	16.93 FQ	19.22 MW	22.69 TQ	CABLS	1/08-3/08
	Riverside-San Bernardino-Ontario MSA, CA	H	10.43 FQ	13.74 MW	20.08 TQ	CABLS	1/08-3/08
	Sacramento-Arden Arcade-Roseville MSA, CA	H	11.74 FQ	15.86 MW	18.28 TQ	CABLS	1/08-3/08
	San Diego-Carlsbad-San Marcos MSA, CA	H	8.27 FQ	8.88 MW	17.10 TQ	CABLS	1/08-3/08
	San Francisco-San Mateo-Redwood PMSA, CA	H	17.27 FQ	21.01 MW	25.12 TQ	CABLS	1/08-3/08
	San Jose-Sunnyvale-Santa Clara MSA, CA	H	17.72 FQ	21.34 MW	25.12 TQ	CABLS	1/08-3/08
	Santa Ana-Anaheim-Irvine PMSA, CA	Y	20210 FQ	23720 MW	29080 TQ	USBLS	5/07
	Colorado	Y	22360 FQ	27480 MW	37710 TQ	USBLS	5/07
	Boulder MSA, CO	Y	30720 FQ	35210 MW	40010 TQ	USBLS	5/07
	Denver-Aurora MSA, CO	Y	23080 FQ	27450 MW	36120 TQ	USBLS	5/07
	Connecticut	H	11.53 AE	14.05 MW		CTBLS	1/08-3/08
	Hartford-West Hartford-East Hartford MSA, CT	Y	27900 FQ	30370 MW	34040 TQ	USBLS	5/07
	Wilmington PMSA, DE-MD-NJ	Y	24860 FQ	33540 MW	37770 TQ	USBLS	5/07
	Washington-Arlington-Alexandria MSA, DC-VA-MD-WV	Y	23040 FQ	29210 MW	34770 TQ	USBLS	5/07
	Florida	Y	22390 FQ	28030 MW	34290 TQ	USBLS	5/07
	Cape Coral-Fort Myers MSA, FL	Y	18850 FQ	21900 MW	26980 TQ	USBLS	5/07
	Fort Lauderdale-Pompano Beach-Deerfield Beach PMSA, FL	Y	22710 FQ	34500 MW	41800 TQ	USBLS	5/07
	Jacksonville MSA, FL	Y	23550 FQ	32160 MW	36330 TQ	USBLS	5/07
	Miami-Fort Lauderdale-Miami Beach MSA, FL	Y	21430 FQ	26210 MW	30710 TQ	USBLS	5/07
	Orlando-Kissimmee MSA, FL	Y	22430 FQ	27280 MW	30850 TQ	USBLS	5/07
	Tampa-St. Petersburg-Clearwater MSA, FL	Y	23090 FQ	30500 MW	36190 TQ	USBLS	5/07
	West Palm Beach-Boca Raton-Boynton Beach PMSA, FL	Y	24390 FQ	27810 MW	31030 TQ	USBLS	5/07
	Georgia	Y	23570 FQ	32550 MW	40020 TQ	USBLS	5/07

AE	Average entry wage	AW	Average wage paid	FQ	First quartile wage	LO	Lowest wage paid	MTC	Median total compensation	TCC	Total cash compensation
AER	Average entry range	AWR	Average wage range	H	Hourly	LR	Low end range	MW	Median wage paid	TQ	Third quartile wage
AEX	Average experienced wage	AXR	Average experienced range	HI	Highest wage paid	M	Monthly	MWR	Median wage range	W	Weekly
ATC	Average total compensation	D	Daily	HR	High end range	MCC	Median cash compensation	S	See annotated source	Y	Yearly

Occupation/Type/Industry	Location	Per	Low	Mid	High	Source	Date
Crushing, Grinding, and Polishing Machine Setter, Operator, and Tender							
	Atlanta-Sandy Springs-Marietta MSA, GA	Y	26320 FQ	31340 MW	36160 TQ	USBLS	5/07
	Macon MSA, GA	Y	26420 FQ	39200 MW	43930 TQ	USBLS	5/07
	Idaho	Y	23760 FQ	29280 MW	34440 TQ	USBLS	5/07
	Boise City-Nampa MSA, ID	Y	19850 FQ	22830 MW	28540 TQ	USBLS	5/07
	Illinois	Y	24720 FQ	31420 MW	37340 TQ	USBLS	5/07
	Chicago-Naperville-Joliet MSA, IL-IN-WI	Y	27790 FQ	35200 MW	46160 TQ	USBLS	5/07
	Indiana	Y	27670 FQ	36000 MW	43190 TQ	USBLS	5/07
	Gary PMSA, IN	Y	41440 FQ	46740 MW	53630 TQ	USBLS	5/07
	Indianapolis-Carmel MSA, IN	Y	32550 FQ	35950 MW	39350 TQ	USBLS	5/07
	Iowa	Y	23480 FQ	27450 MW	31690 TQ	USBLS	5/07
	Des Moines-West Des Moines MSA, IA	Y	21460 FQ	24210 MW	30080 TQ	USBLS	5/07
	Kansas	Y	19990 FQ	23940 MW	28540 TQ	USBLS	5/07
	Wichita MSA, KS	Y	21630 FQ	23630 MW	28370 TQ	USBLS	5/07
	Kentucky	Y	21694 FQ	28412 MW	32527 TQ	KYBLS	2008
	Louisville-Jefferson County MSA, KY-IN	Y	19170 FQ	24070 MW	30080 TQ	USBLS	5/07
	Louisiana	H	11.54 FQ	16.38 MW	20.17 TQ	LABLS	1/08-3/08
	Baton Rouge MSA, LA	Y	34710 FQ	38670 MW	47910 TQ	USBLS	5/07
	New Orleans-Metairie-Kenner MSA, LA	Y	27330 FQ	38970 MW	45660 TQ	USBLS	5/07
	Maine	Y	23380 FQ	31320 MW	44360 TQ	USBLS	5/07
	Maryland	Y		27000 MW		MDBLS	3/08
	Baltimore-Towson MSA, MD	Y	20680 FQ	25550 MW	37880 TQ	USBLS	5/07
	Bethesda-Gaithersburg-Frederick PMSA, MD	Y	26690 FQ	32930 MW	37080 TQ	USBLS	5/07
	Massachusetts	Y	28540 FQ	34160 MW	43210 TQ	USBLS	5/07
	Boston-Cambridge-Quincy NECTA, MA	Y	26540 FQ	32200 MW	43040 TQ	USBLS	5/07
	Worcester MSA, MA-CT	Y	30090 FQ	34550 MW	40840 TQ	USBLS	5/07
	Michigan	Y	25640 FQ	30010 MW	36950 TQ	USBLS	5/07
	Detroit-Warren-Livonia MSA, MI	Y	29400 FQ	32780 MW	39380 TQ	USBLS	5/07
	Grand Rapids-Wyoming MSA, MI	Y	23700 FQ	27000 MW	30420 TQ	USBLS	5/07
	Warren-Troy-Farmington Hills PMSA, MI	Y	29110 FQ	33240 MW	40320 TQ	USBLS	5/07
	Minnesota	Y	28042 FQ	34469 MW	46619 TQ	MNBLS	10/08-12/08
	Duluth-Superior MSA, MN-WI	Y	44421 FQ	49439 MW	55949 TQ	MNBLS	10/08-12/08
	Minneapolis-Saint Paul MSA, MN-WI	Y	28819 FQ	33598 MW	46381 TQ	MNBLS	10/08-12/08
	Mississippi	Y	20340 FQ	23590 MW	33020 TQ	USBLS	5/07
	Missouri	Y	23640 FQ	30520 MW	35810 TQ	USBLS	5/07
	Jefferson City MSA, MO	Y	19320 FQ	27790 MW	37300 TQ	USBLS	5/07
	Joplin MSA, MO	Y	25030 FQ	27360 MW	29920 TQ	USBLS	5/07
	Kansas City MSA, MO-KS	Y	23370 FQ	29130 MW	35570 TQ	USBLS	5/07
	St. Louis MSA, MO-IL	Y	22080 FQ	26630 MW	33100 TQ	USBLS	5/07
	Montana	Y	22470 FQ	31050 MW	42940 TQ	USBLS	5/07
	Nebraska	Y	20030 FQ	23920 MW	31690 TQ	USBLS	5/07
	Omaha-Council Bluffs MSA, NE-IA	Y	18820 FQ	22230 MW	26290 TQ	USBLS	5/07
	Nevada	H	10.32 FQ	12.84 MW	17.03 TQ	NVBLS	5/08
	Las Vegas-Paradise MSA, NV	H	9.97 FQ	12.76 MW	16.16 TQ	NVBLS	5/08
	New Hampshire	H	13.54 AE	15.21 MW	16.60 AEX	NHBLS	6/08
	New Jersey	Y	25930 FQ	31360 MW	40140 TQ	USBLS	5/07
	Camden PMSA, NJ	Y	27730 FQ	30390 MW	33370 TQ	USBLS	5/07
	Edison PMSA, NJ	Y	36300 FQ	42710 MW	47120 TQ	USBLS	5/07
	Newark-Union PMSA, NJ-PA	Y	18370 FQ	24190 MW	37030 TQ	USBLS	5/07
	New Mexico	Y	19740 FQ	22760 MW	26780 TQ	USBLS	5/07
	New York	Y	23370 FQ	30620 MW	38770 TQ	USBLS	5/07
	Albany-Schenectady-Troy MSA, NY	Y	27340 FQ	30910 MW	38420 TQ	USBLS	5/07
	Buffalo-Niagara Falls MSA, NY	Y	17790 FQ	24790 MW	42840 TQ	USBLS	5/07
	Nassau-Suffolk PMSA, NY	Y	25140 FQ	30440 MW	39070 TQ	USBLS	5/07

AE	Average entry wage	AW	Average wage paid	FQ	First quartile wage
AER	Average entry range	AWR	Average wage range	H	Hourly
AEX	Average experienced wage	AXR	Average experienced range	HI	Highest wage paid
ATC	Average total compensation	D	Daily	HR	High end range

LO	Lowest wage paid	MTC	Median total compensation
LR	Low end range	MW	Median wage paid
M	Monthly	MWR	Median wage range
MCC	Median cash compensation	S	See annotated source

TCC	Total cash compensation
TQ	Third quartile wage
W	Weekly
Y	Yearly

Occupation/Type/Industry	Location	Per	Low	Mid	High	Source	Date
Crushing, Grinding, and Polishing Machine Setter, Operator, and Tender							
	New York-Northern New Jersey-Long Island MSA, NY-NJ-PA	Y	21370 FQ	28950 MW	41350 TQ	USBLS	5/07
	Syracuse MSA, NY	Y	22970 FQ	28540 MW	37540 TQ	USBLS	5/07
	Utica-Rome MSA, NY	Y	22080 FQ	24720 MW	27840 TQ	USBLS	5/07
	North Carolina	Y	21270 FQ	25550 MW	31730 TQ	USBLS	5/07
	Charlotte-Gastonia-Concord MSA, NC-SC	Y	29200 FQ	36020 MW	51940 TQ	USBLS	5/07
	Raleigh-Cary MSA, NC	Y	21960 FQ	26400 MW	31270 TQ	USBLS	5/07
	North Dakota	Y	32190 FQ	38080 MW	44350 TQ	USBLS	5/07
	Fargo MSA, ND-MN	Y	28250 FQ	33750 MW	37270 TQ	USBLS	5/07
	Grand Forks MSA, ND-MN	Y	27580 FQ	30590 MW	35420 TQ	USBLS	5/07
	Ohio	Y	23790 FQ	29160 MW	35830 TQ	USBLS	5/07
	Cincinnati-Middletown MSA, OH-KY-IN	Y	26180 FQ	29750 MW	33430 TQ	USBLS	5/07
	Cleveland-Elyria-Mentor MSA, OH	Y	22490 FQ	29200 MW	35480 TQ	USBLS	5/07
	Columbus MSA, OH	Y	22240 FQ	27400 MW	32690 TQ	USBLS	5/07
	Oklahoma	Y	18230 FQ	22340 MW	27300 TQ	USBLS	5/07
	Oklahoma City MSA, OK	Y	20860 FQ	27010 MW	31650 TQ	USBLS	5/07
	Tulsa MSA, OK	Y	20370 FQ	22850 MW	25300 TQ	USBLS	5/07
	Oregon	H	12.13 FQ	15.36 MW	19.43 TQ	ORBLS	5/08
	Portland-Vancouver-Beaverton MSA, OR-WA	Y	25400 FQ	30830 MW	38760 TQ	USBLS	5/07
	Pennsylvania	Y	25640 FQ	31200 MW	37530 TQ	USBLS	5/07
	Allentown-Bethlehem-Easton MSA, PA-NJ	Y	25900 FQ	31600 MW	40520 TQ	USBLS	5/07
	Philadelphia-Camden-Wilmington MSA, PA-NJ-DE-MD	Y	26770 FQ	30160 MW	35450 TQ	USBLS	5/07
	Pittsburgh MSA, PA	Y	26120 FQ	31610 MW	36390 TQ	USBLS	5/07
	Rhode Island	Y	18230 FQ	25870 MW	29330 TQ	USBLS	5/07
	Providence-Fall River-Warwick MSA, RI-MA	Y	18330 FQ	26100 MW	29670 TQ	USBLS	5/07
	South Carolina	Y	29270 FQ	36190 MW	47550 TQ	USBLS	5/07
	South Dakota	Y	24775 FQ	27975 MW	31585 TQ	SDBLS	7/08-9/08
	Rapid City MSA, SD	Y	28651 FQ	31356 MW	36866 TQ	SDBLS	7/08-9/08
	Sioux Falls MSA, SD	Y	25826 FQ	27872 MW	29977 TQ	SDBLS	7/08-9/08
	Tennessee	Y	21000 FQ	26140 MW	31980 TQ	USBLS	5/07
	Knoxville MSA, TN	Y	22060 FQ	24410 MW	37960 TQ	USBLS	5/07
	Memphis MSA, TN-MS-AR	Y	26310 FQ	32100 MW	36470 TQ	USBLS	5/07
	Nashville-Davidson-Murfreesboro MSA, TN	Y	18540 FQ	29210 MW	37360 TQ	USBLS	5/07
	Texas	Y	18960 FQ	23260 MW	29280 TQ	USBLS	5/07
	Austin-Round Rock MSA, TX	Y	18340 FQ	21010 MW	24540 TQ	USBLS	5/07
	Dallas-Fort Worth-Arlington MSA, TX	Y	18530 FQ	23080 MW	29450 TQ	USBLS	5/07
	El Paso MSA, TX	Y	13160 FQ	15340 MW	18710 TQ	USBLS	5/07
	Houston-Sugar Land-Baytown MSA, TX	Y	19820 FQ	24270 MW	29470 TQ	USBLS	5/07
	San Antonio MSA, TX	Y	17800 FQ	21950 MW	27370 TQ	USBLS	5/07
	Utah	Y	22120 FQ	27370 MW	33070 TQ	USBLS	5/07
	Salt Lake City MSA, UT	Y	24890 FQ	28510 MW	32790 TQ	USBLS	5/07
	Vermont	Y	27520 FQ	34950 MW	40980 TQ	USBLS	5/07
	Virginia	Y	22350 FQ	29610 MW	35950 TQ	USBLS	5/07
	Richmond MSA, VA	Y	19390 FQ	23940 MW	31690 TQ	USBLS	5/07
	Virginia Beach-Norfolk-Newport News MSA, VA-NC	Y	22440 FQ	33420 MW	42940 TQ	USBLS	5/07
	Washington	H	12.83 FQ	15.31 MW	19.76 TQ	WABLS	3/08
	Seattle-Tacoma-Bellevue MSA, WA	Y	26270 FQ	30270 MW	40610 TQ	USBLS	5/07
	West Virginia	Y	25821 FQ	32766 MW	45447 TQ	WVBLS	7/08-9/08
	Charleston MSA, WV	Y	23060 FQ	27630 MW	44510 TQ	USBLS	5/07
	Wisconsin	Y	24570 FQ	29620 MW	36200 TQ	USBLS	5/07
	Milwaukee-Waukesha-West Allis MSA, WI	Y	24940 FQ	28980 MW	34000 TQ	USBLS	5/07
	Wyoming	Y	30347 FQ	39330 MW	53128 TQ	WYBLS	9/08
	Cheyenne MSA, WY	Y	23663 FQ	29561 MW	32376 TQ	WYBLS	9/08
	Puerto Rico	Y	13430 FQ	16040 MW	20790 TQ	USBLS	5/07

AE	Average entry wage	AW	Average wage paid	FQ	First quartile wage
AER	Average entry range	AWR	Average wage range	H	Hourly
AEX	Average experienced wage	AXR	Average experienced range	HI	Highest wage paid
ATC	Average total compensation	D	Daily	HR	High end range

LO	Lowest wage paid	MTC	Median total compensation	TCC	Total cash compensation
LR	Low end range	MW	Median wage paid	TQ	Third quartile wage
M	Monthly	MWR	Median wage range	W	Weekly
MCC	Median cash compensation	S	See annotated source	Y	Yearly

Occupation/Type/Industry	Location	Per	Low	Mid	High	Source	Date
Crushing, Grinding, and Polishing Machine Setter, Operator, and Tender	San Juan-Caguas-Guaynabo MSA, PR	Y	13440 FQ	16090 MW	20900 TQ	USBLS	5/07
Cryptanalyst	United States	Y		66357 AW		CBUILD02	12/08
Cultural Services Manager							
Municipal Government	Colorado Springs, CO	M	6194 LO			COSPRS	1/1/09
Curator	United States	Y		46300 AW		CBUILD01	2008
	Alabama	Y	33080 FQ	37860 MW	45940 TQ	USBLS	5/07
	Birmingham-Hoover MSA, AL	Y	33710 FQ	37000 MW	40270 TQ	USBLS	5/07
	Alaska	Y	30800 FQ	44410 MW	61550 TQ	USBLS	5/07
	Arizona	Y	34700 FQ	44470 MW	60660 TQ	USBLS	5/07
	Phoenix-Mesa-Scottsdale MSA, AZ	Y	33710 FQ	42260 MW	61750 TQ	USBLS	5/07
	Arkansas	Y	23650 FQ	36460 MW	54600 TQ	USBLS	5/07
	California	H	19.89 FQ	27.72 MW	36.71 TQ	CABLS	1/08-3/08
	Los Angeles-Long Beach-Glendale PMSA, CA	H	23.38 FQ	29.50 MW	40.50 TQ	CABLS	1/08-3/08
	Oakland-Fremont-Hayward MSA, CA	H	15.21 FQ	26.05 MW	35.19 TQ	CABLS	1/08-3/08
	Riverside-San Bernardino-Ontario MSA, CA	H	24.31 FQ	29.58 MW	35.08 TQ	CABLS	1/08-3/08
	Sacramento-Arden Arcade-Roseville MSA, CA	H	14.33 FQ	20.28 MW	34.16 TQ	CABLS	1/08-3/08
	San Diego-Carlsbad-San Marcos MSA, CA	H	11.82 FQ	22.04 MW	34.46 TQ	CABLS	1/08-3/08
	San Francisco-San Mateo-Redwood PMSA, CA	H	26.09 FQ	32.22 MW	38.12 TQ	CABLS	1/08-3/08
	San Jose-Sunnyvale-Santa Clara MSA, CA	H	16.64 FQ	20.89 MW	30.33 TQ	CABLS	1/08-3/08
	Colorado	Y	41370 FQ	53360 MW	63230 TQ	USBLS	5/07
	Denver-Aurora MSA, CO	Y	43680 FQ	54030 MW	64730 TQ	USBLS	5/07
	Connecticut	H	15.67 AE	25.54 MW		CTBLS	1/08-3/08
	Hartford-West Hartford-East Hartford MSA, CT	Y	30490 FQ	42510 MW	53150 TQ	USBLS	5/07
	Delaware	Y	39580 FQ	47180 MW	57740 TQ	USBLS	5/07
	Wilmington PMSA, DE-MD-NJ	Y	40760 FQ	47620 MW	56970 TQ	USBLS	5/07
	District of Columbia	Y	57470 FQ	72220 MW	84850 TQ	USBLS	5/07
	Washington-Arlington-Alexandria MSA, DC-VA-MD-WV	Y	50070 FQ	65950 MW	78600 TQ	USBLS	5/07
	Florida	Y	34560 FQ	46340 MW	61750 TQ	USBLS	5/07
	Miami-Fort Lauderdale-Miami Beach MSA, FL	Y	37250 FQ	48650 MW	64490 TQ	USBLS	5/07
	Orlando-Kissimmee MSA, FL	Y	31990 FQ	53420 MW	75230 TQ	USBLS	5/07
	West Palm Beach-Boca Raton-Boynton Beach PMSA, FL	Y	40140 FQ	55300 MW	65080 TQ	USBLS	5/07
	Georgia	Y	30830 FQ	40760 MW	55340 TQ	USBLS	5/07
	Atlanta-Sandy Springs-Marietta MSA, GA	Y	42900 FQ	51950 MW	61830 TQ	USBLS	5/07
	Illinois	Y	35710 FQ	55210 MW	78860 TQ	USBLS	5/07
	Chicago-Naperville-Joliet MSA, IL-IN-WI	Y	38010 FQ	58290 MW	82750 TQ	USBLS	5/07
	Indiana	Y	34290 FQ	41730 MW	50920 TQ	USBLS	5/07
	Indianapolis-Carmel MSA, IN	Y	37370 FQ	46100 MW	61250 TQ	USBLS	5/07
	Iowa	Y	29370 FQ	45520 MW	61260 TQ	USBLS	5/07
	Kansas	Y	21560 FQ	33420 MW	41890 TQ	USBLS	5/07
	Kentucky	Y	32966 FQ	41995 MW	50675 TQ	KYBLS	2008
	Louisville-Jefferson County MSA, KY-IN	Y	33640 FQ	42580 MW	51900 TQ	USBLS	5/07
	Louisiana	H	13.45 FQ	16.84 MW	19.01 TQ	LABLS	1/08-3/08
	New Orleans-Metairie-Kenner MSA, LA	Y	34330 FQ	37530 MW	40910 TQ	USBLS	5/07
	Maine	Y	30680 FQ	44130 MW	51190 TQ	USBLS	5/07
	Maryland	Y		56300 MW		MDBLS	3/08
	Baltimore-Towson MSA, MD	Y	40980 FQ	65540 MW	74540 TQ	USBLS	5/07
	Bethesda-Gaithersburg-Frederick PMSA, MD	Y	43380 FQ	48900 MW	70500 TQ	USBLS	5/07

AE	Average entry wage	AW	Average wage paid	FQ	First quartile wage
AER	Average entry range	AWR	Average wage range	H	Hourly
AEX	Average experienced wage	AXR	Average experienced range	HI	Highest wage paid
ATC	Average total compensation	D	Daily	HR	High end range

LO	Lowest wage paid	MTC	Median total compensation	TCC	Total cash compensation
LR	Low end range	MW	Median wage paid	TQ	Third quartile wage
M	Monthly	MWR	Median wage range	W	Weekly
MCC	Median cash compensation	S	See annotated source	Y	Yearly

Occupation/Type/Industry	Location	Per	Low	Mid	High	Source	Date
Curator	Massachusetts	Y	41030 FQ	53320 MW	69540 TQ	USBLS	5/07
	Barnstable Town MSA, MA	Y	27530 FQ	30080 MW	36330 TQ	USBLS	5/07
	Boston-Cambridge-Quincy NECTA, MA	Y	49510 FQ	62150 MW	76550 TQ	USBLS	5/07
	Worcester MSA, MA-CT	Y	38790 FQ	45050 MW	62680 TQ	USBLS	5/07
	Michigan	Y	35150 FQ	45710 MW	64760 TQ	USBLS	5/07
	Detroit-Warren-Livonia MSA, MI	Y	46460 FQ	57860 MW	80130 TQ	USBLS	5/07
	Lansing-East Lansing MSA, MI	Y	36890 FQ	40330 MW	44720 TQ	USBLS	5/07
	Minnesota	Y	38417 FQ	54843 MW	67125 TQ	MNBLS	10/08-12/08
	Minneapolis-Saint Paul MSA, MN-WI	Y	49298 FQ	61026 MW	69835 TQ	MNBLS	10/08-12/08
	Missouri	Y	37250 FQ	45460 MW	57630 TQ	USBLS	5/07
	Kansas City MSA, MO-KS	Y	36810 FQ	47480 MW	71430 TQ	USBLS	5/07
	St. Louis MSA, MO-IL	Y	38130 FQ	46330 MW	56370 TQ	USBLS	5/07
	Montana	Y	25740 FQ	28760 MW	34050 TQ	USBLS	5/07
	Billings MSA, MT	Y	20120 FQ	29440 MW	45710 TQ	USBLS	5/07
	Nebraska	Y	35750 FQ	45630 MW	62480 TQ	USBLS	5/07
	Nevada	H	20.35 FQ	24.14 MW	30.63 TQ	NVBLS	5/08
	Las Vegas-Paradise MSA, NV	H	21.79 FQ	27.60 MW	36.02 TQ	NVBLS	5/08
	New Hampshire	H	16.38 AE	26.68 MW	30.04 AEX	NHBLS	6/08
	New Jersey	Y	28350 FQ	39250 MW	59140 TQ	USBLS	5/07
	Edison PMSA, NJ	Y	17300 FQ	24450 MW	46450 TQ	USBLS	5/07
	Newark-Union PMSA, NJ-PA	Y	28360 FQ	36590 MW	55730 TQ	USBLS	5/07
	New Mexico	Y	34340 FQ	46270 MW	54770 TQ	USBLS	5/07
	Albuquerque MSA, NM	Y	41130 FQ	48150 MW	63890 TQ	USBLS	5/07
	New York	Y	38780 FQ	54980 MW	74100 TQ	USBLS	5/07
	Albany-Schenectady-Troy MSA, NY	Y	29600 FQ	46530 MW	66610 TQ	USBLS	5/07
	Buffalo-Niagara Falls MSA, NY	Y	37670 FQ	41810 MW	59500 TQ	USBLS	5/07
	Nassau-Suffolk PMSA, NY	Y	61570 FQ	72200 MW	82980 TQ	USBLS	5/07
	New York-Northern New Jersey-Long Island MSA, NY-NJ-PA	Y	42260 FQ	59710 MW	79880 TQ	USBLS	5/07
	North Carolina	Y	28790 FQ	35770 MW	46980 TQ	USBLS	5/07
	Raleigh-Cary MSA, NC	Y	35090 FQ	41540 MW	50480 TQ	USBLS	5/07
	Ohio	Y	34370 FQ	46120 MW	60380 TQ	USBLS	5/07
	Cincinnati-Middletown MSA, OH-KY-IN	Y	36090 FQ	44510 MW	59410 TQ	USBLS	5/07
	Cleveland-Elyria-Mentor MSA, OH	Y	26570 FQ	53930 MW	64350 TQ	USBLS	5/07
	Columbus MSA, OH	Y	34340 FQ	40800 MW	53150 TQ	USBLS	5/07
	Oklahoma	Y	24110 FQ	38610 MW	46500 TQ	USBLS	5/07
	Oregon	H	16.23 FQ	18.43 MW	22.40 TQ	ORBLS	5/08
	Portland-Vancouver-Beaverton MSA, OR-WA	Y	38110 FQ	45360 MW	51360 TQ	USBLS	5/07
	Pennsylvania	Y	24260 FQ	41760 MW	55960 TQ	USBLS	5/07
	Philadelphia-Camden-Wilmington MSA, PA-NJ-DE-MD	Y	44550 FQ	51780 MW	68080 TQ	USBLS	5/07
	Pittsburgh MSA, PA	Y	28460 FQ	37020 MW	49850 TQ	USBLS	5/07
	Rhode Island	Y	35700 FQ	52720 MW	68270 TQ	USBLS	5/07
	Providence-Fall River-Warwick MSA, RI-MA	Y	33670 FQ	46080 MW	64400 TQ	USBLS	5/07
	South Carolina	Y	28820 FQ	39290 MW	50000 TQ	USBLS	5/07
	Columbia MSA, SC	Y	33630 FQ	39330 MW	47700 TQ	USBLS	5/07
	South Dakota	Y	36754 FQ	41033 MW	48018 TQ	SDBLS	7/08-9/08
	Tennessee	Y	34810 FQ	45180 MW	56760 TQ	USBLS	5/07
	Nashville-Davidson-Murfreesboro MSA, TN	Y	30330 FQ	40490 MW	49920 TQ	USBLS	5/07
	Texas	Y	36390 FQ	45750 MW	52820 TQ	USBLS	5/07
	Austin-Round Rock MSA, TX	Y	43650 FQ	48640 MW	55100 TQ	USBLS	5/07
	Dallas-Fort Worth-Arlington MSA, TX	Y	37930 FQ	46400 MW	51830 TQ	USBLS	5/07
	Houston-Sugar Land-Baytown MSA, TX	Y	36100 FQ	42060 MW	50970 TQ	USBLS	5/07
	San Antonio MSA, TX	Y	38590 FQ	47070 MW	67260 TQ	USBLS	5/07
	Utah	Y	37770 FQ	47470 MW	55620 TQ	USBLS	5/07
	Salt Lake City MSA, UT	Y	38540 FQ	49230 MW	57020 TQ	USBLS	5/07
	Vermont	Y	35200 FQ	44160 MW	52750 TQ	USBLS	5/07
	Virginia	Y	36900 FQ	46950 MW	63040 TQ	USBLS	5/07

Occupation/Type/Industry	Location	Per	Low	Mid	High	Source	Date
Curator	Richmond MSA, VA	Y	33910 FQ	40310 MW	51160 TQ	USBLS	5/07
	Virginia Beach-Norfolk-Newport News MSA, VA-NC	Y	38890 FQ	46160 MW	59390 TQ	USBLS	5/07
	Washington	H	17.08 FQ	24.28 MW	34.73 TQ	WABLS	3/08
	Seattle-Tacoma-Bellevue MSA, WA	Y	47460 FQ	67260 MW	78610 TQ	USBLS	5/07
	West Virginia	Y	80294 FQ	88963 MW	97306 TQ	WVBLS	7/08-9/08
	Wisconsin	Y	29010 FQ	40700 MW	51570 TQ	USBLS	5/07
	Milwaukee-Waukesha-West Allis MSA, WI	Y	29250 FQ	43240 MW	60000 TQ	USBLS	5/07
	Wyoming	Y	20802 FQ	29006 MW	37407 TQ	WYBLS	9/08
Custodial Attendant							
Municipal Government	Seaside, CA	S	1041 LO		1265 HI	SSSS	8/08
Custodian							
Department of Environmental Quality	Oregon	M	1847 LO		2381 HI	ODEQSS	11/1/08
Library	Gill, MA	H			12.36 HI	FRCOG	2009
Municipal Government	Colrain, MA	H			10.46 HI	FRCOG	2009
Waste Water Treatment Facility	Montague, MA	H			13.47 HI	FRCOG	2009
Customer Service Representative	Alabama	Y	21060 FQ	26360 MW	33200 TQ	USBLS	5/07
	Birmingham-Hoover MSA, AL	Y	23330 FQ	29170 MW	37050 TQ	USBLS	5/07
	Alaska	Y	26350 FQ	32880 MW	40830 TQ	USBLS	5/07
	Anchorage MSA, AK	Y	25700 FQ	32140 MW	40390 TQ	USBLS	5/07
	Arizona	Y	22200 FQ	27670 MW	35440 TQ	USBLS	5/07
	Flagstaff MSA, AZ	Y	21080 FQ	25720 MW	31300 TQ	USBLS	5/07
	Phoenix-Mesa-Scottsdale MSA, AZ	Y	23300 FQ	28930 MW	36930 TQ	USBLS	5/07
	Tucson MSA, AZ	Y	20360 FQ	23230 MW	29240 TQ	USBLS	5/07
	Yuma MSA, AZ	Y	22880 FQ	27530 MW	31590 TQ	USBLS	5/07
	Arkansas	Y	20640 FQ	25410 MW	32290 TQ	USBLS	5/07
	Little Rock-North Little Rock MSA, AR	Y	22200 FQ	27860 MW	35850 TQ	USBLS	5/07
	Pine Bluff MSA, AR	Y	19930 FQ	24460 MW	31190 TQ	USBLS	5/07
	California	H	12.93 FQ	16.05 MW	20.50 TQ	CABLS	1/08-3/08
	Los Angeles-Long Beach-Glendale PMSA, CA	H	12.57 FQ	15.62 MW	20.03 TQ	CABLS	1/08-3/08
	Oakland-Fremont-Hayward MSA, CA	H	14.86 FQ	18.05 MW	22.62 TQ	CABLS	1/08-3/08
	Riverside-San Bernardino-Ontario MSA, CA	H	11.90 FQ	14.71 MW	18.65 TQ	CABLS	1/08-3/08
	Sacramento-Arden Arcade-Roseville MSA, CA	H	13.22 FQ	15.91 MW	19.73 TQ	CABLS	1/08-3/08
	San Diego-Carlsbad-San Marcos MSA, CA	H	12.42 FQ	15.42 MW	19.24 TQ	CABLS	1/08-3/08
	San Francisco-San Mateo-Redwood PMSA, CA	H	15.18 FQ	18.57 MW	23.05 TQ	CABLS	1/08-3/08
	San Jose-Sunnyvale-Santa Clara MSA, CA	H	15.70 FQ	20.16 MW	25.45 TQ	CABLS	1/08-3/08
	Santa Ana-Anaheim-Irvine PMSA, CA	Y	27120 FQ	32840 MW	41250 TQ	USBLS	5/07
	Colorado	Y	24350 FQ	29880 MW	37500 TQ	USBLS	5/07
	Denver-Aurora MSA, CO	Y	26310 FQ	31520 MW	38960 TQ	USBLS	5/07
	Connecticut	H	12.13 AE	17.69 MW		CTBLS	1/08-3/08
	Bridgeport-Stamford-Norwalk MSA, CT	Y	29340 FQ	38040 MW	46700 TQ	USBLS	5/07
	Hartford-West Hartford-East Hartford MSA, CT	Y	28590 FQ	36070 MW	45530 TQ	USBLS	5/07
	Waterbury MSA, CT	Y	24490 FQ	31850 MW	39040 TQ	USBLS	5/07
	Delaware	Y	24270 FQ	29760 MW	37200 TQ	USBLS	5/07
	Wilmington PMSA, DE-MD-NJ	Y	25400 FQ	30860 MW	38440 TQ	USBLS	5/07
	District of Columbia	Y	28710 FQ	34790 MW	40850 TQ	USBLS	5/07
	Washington-Arlington-Alexandria MSA, DC-VA-MD-WV	Y	25790 FQ	32630 MW	40770 TQ	USBLS	5/07
	Florida	Y	22400 FQ	27350 MW	32510 TQ	USBLS	5/07
	Fort Lauderdale-Pompano Beach-Deerfield Beach PMSA, FL	Y	21720 FQ	27230 MW	33420 TQ	USBLS	5/07
	Jacksonville MSA, FL	Y	25370 FQ	29140 MW	32990 TQ	USBLS	5/07

AE	Average entry wage	AW	Average wage paid	FQ	First quartile wage	LO	Lowest wage paid	MTC	Median total compensation	TCC	Total cash compensation
AER	Average entry range	AWR	Average wage range	H	Hourly	LR	Low end range	MW	Median wage paid	TQ	Third quartile wage
AEX	Average experienced wage	AXR	Average experienced range	HI	Highest wage paid	M	Monthly	MWR	Median wage range	W	Weekly
ATC	Average total compensation	D	Daily	HR	High end range	MCC	Median cash compensation	S	See annotated source	Y	Yearly

Occupation/Type/Industry	Location	Per	Low	Mid	High	Source	Date
Customer Service Representative	Miami-Fort Lauderdale-Miami Beach MSA, FL	Y	22120 FQ	27580 MW	34140 TQ	USBLS	5/07
	Orlando-Kissimmee MSA, FL	Y	21720 FQ	26280 MW	32430 TQ	USBLS	5/07
	Pensacola-Ferry Pass-Brent MSA, FL	Y	19710 FQ	23920 MW	29590 TQ	USBLS	5/07
	Sarasota-Bradenton-Venice MSA, FL	Y	21200 FQ	25130 MW	30640 TQ	USBLS	5/07
	Tampa-St. Petersburg-Clearwater MSA, FL	Y	23920 FQ	28450 MW	33780 TQ	USBLS	5/07
	West Palm Beach-Boca Raton-Boynton Beach PMSA, FL	Y	23170 FQ	28130 MW	34660 TQ	USBLS	5/07
	Georgia	Y	23140 FQ	29350 MW	37360 TQ	USBLS	5/07
	Atlanta-Sandy Springs-Marietta MSA, GA	Y	25720 FQ	31170 MW	39640 TQ	USBLS	5/07
	Hawaii	Y	23260 FQ	29350 MW	36910 TQ	USBLS	5/07
	Honolulu MSA, HI	Y	23280 FQ	29320 MW	37160 TQ	USBLS	5/07
	Idaho	Y	19810 FQ	23660 MW	28850 TQ	USBLS	5/07
	Boise City-Nampa MSA, ID	Y	21140 FQ	24990 MW	29890 TQ	USBLS	5/07
	Illinois	Y	24900 FQ	31780 MW	41320 TQ	USBLS	5/07
	Chicago-Naperville-Joliet MSA, IL-IN-WI	Y	26060 FQ	32980 MW	43220 TQ	USBLS	5/07
	Indiana	Y	21960 FQ	27800 MW	35970 TQ	USBLS	5/07
	Gary PMSA, IN	Y	17000 FQ	21900 MW	33900 TQ	USBLS	5/07
	Indianapolis-Carmel MSA, IN	Y	23110 FQ	28780 MW	36330 TQ	USBLS	5/07
	Terre Haute MSA, IN	Y	21230 FQ	27190 MW	35340 TQ	USBLS	5/07
	Iowa	Y	21680 FQ	27340 MW	33220 TQ	USBLS	5/07
	Des Moines-West Des Moines MSA, IA	Y	24230 FQ	28990 MW	34490 TQ	USBLS	5/07
	Kansas	Y	21000 FQ	26370 MW	32640 TQ	USBLS	5/07
	Wichita MSA, KS	Y	18740 FQ	23920 MW	29400 TQ	USBLS	5/07
	Kentucky	Y	21490 FQ	27771 MW	35974 TQ	KYBLS	2008
	Louisville-Jefferson County MSA, KY-IN	Y	23220 FQ	28560 MW	35160 TQ	USBLS	5/07
	Louisiana	H	9.40 FQ	11.49 MW	14.19 TQ	LABLS	1/08-3/08
	Baton Rouge MSA, LA	Y	20170 FQ	23420 MW	28640 TQ	USBLS	5/07
	New Orleans-Metairie-Kenner MSA, LA	Y	19990 FQ	24560 MW	30820 TQ	USBLS	5/07
	Shreveport-Bossier City MSA, LA	Y	20730 FQ	27060 MW	30510 TQ	USBLS	5/07
	Maine	Y	21430 FQ	27330 MW	33680 TQ	USBLS	5/07
	Portland-South Portland-Biddeford MSA, ME	Y	24930 FQ	30010 MW	37160 TQ	USBLS	5/07
	Maryland	Y		31525 MW		MDBLS	3/08
	Baltimore-Towson MSA, MD	Y	25480 FQ	31310 MW	38860 TQ	USBLS	5/07
	Bethesda-Gaithersburg-Frederick PMSA, MD	Y	26540 FQ	32500 MW	43200 TQ	USBLS	5/07
	Hagerstown-Martinsburg MSA, MD-WV	Y	21560 FQ	24450 MW	30660 TQ	USBLS	5/07
	Massachusetts	Y	28010 FQ	35180 MW	45060 TQ	USBLS	5/07
	Boston-Cambridge-Quincy NECTA, MA	Y	29950 FQ	36850 MW	47590 TQ	USBLS	5/07
	Worcester MSA, MA-CT	Y	26640 FQ	32440 MW	39950 TQ	USBLS	5/07
	Michigan	Y	24560 FQ	31010 MW	39380 TQ	USBLS	5/07
	Detroit-Warren-Livonia MSA, MI	Y	26970 FQ	33960 MW	42880 TQ	USBLS	5/07
	Grand Rapids-Wyoming MSA, MI	Y	21410 FQ	26650 MW	34130 TQ	USBLS	5/07
	Muskegon-Norton Shores MSA, MI	Y	21720 FQ	27310 MW	36170 TQ	USBLS	5/07
	Warren-Troy-Farmington Hills PMSA, MI	Y	27510 FQ	34740 MW	43280 TQ	USBLS	5/07
	Minnesota	Y	28257 FQ	33940 MW	41257 TQ	MNBLS	10/08-12/08
	Duluth-Superior MSA, MN-WI	Y	27091 FQ	31432 MW	36812 TQ	MNBLS	10/08-12/08
	Minneapolis-Saint Paul MSA, MN-WI	Y	29392 FQ	35345 MW	42776 TQ	MNBLS	10/08-12/08
	Rochester MSA, MN	Y	24769 FQ	30888 MW	37407 TQ	MNBLS	10/08-12/08
	Mississippi	Y	20400 FQ	24350 MW	29810 TQ	USBLS	5/07
	Jackson MSA, MS	Y	21250 FQ	26070 MW	31310 TQ	USBLS	5/07
	Missouri	Y	21820 FQ	28330 MW	36960 TQ	USBLS	5/07
	Joplin MSA, MO	Y	20640 FQ	24250 MW	30370 TQ	USBLS	5/07
	Kansas City MSA, MO-KS	Y	23680 FQ	29090 MW	35850 TQ	USBLS	5/07
	St. Joseph MSA, MO-KS	Y	22410 FQ	27990 MW	33370 TQ	USBLS	5/07

AE Average entry wage · AW Average wage paid · FQ First quartile wage · LO Lowest wage paid · MTC Median total compensation · TCC Total cash compensation
AER Average entry range · AWR Average wage range · H Hourly · LR Low end range · MW Median wage paid · TQ Third quartile wage
AEX Average experienced wage · AXR Average experienced range · HI Highest wage paid · M Monthly · MWR Median wage range · W Weekly
ATC Average total compensation · D Daily · HR High end range · MCC Median cash compensation · S See annotated source · Y Yearly

382

Occupation/Type/Industry	Location	Per	Low	Mid	High	Source	Date
Customer Service Representative	St. Louis MSA, MO-IL	Y	22050 FQ	29180 MW	38020 TQ	USBLS	5/07
	Montana	Y	19880 FQ	25160 MW	32490 TQ	USBLS	5/07
	Billings MSA, MT	Y	21790 FQ	28510 MW	36270 TQ	USBLS	5/07
	Nebraska	Y	21430 FQ	26270 MW	32730 TQ	USBLS	5/07
	Lincoln MSA, NE	Y	21140 FQ	25410 MW	32600 TQ	USBLS	5/07
	Omaha-Council Bluffs MSA, NE-IA	Y	22310 FQ	27270 MW	33790 TQ	USBLS	5/07
	Nevada	H	11.26 FQ	13.84 MW	17.52 TQ	NVBLS	5/08
	Las Vegas-Paradise MSA, NV	H	11.11 FQ	13.61 MW	17.23 TQ	NVBLS	5/08
	New Hampshire	H	10.58 AE	14.91 MW	18.45 AEX	NHBLS	6/08
	Manchester MSA, NH	Y	22300 FQ	32640 MW	42660 TQ	USBLS	5/07
	Nashua NECTA, NH-MA	Y	26400 FQ	33570 MW	41510 TQ	USBLS	5/07
	New Jersey	Y	26220 FQ	32610 MW	40690 TQ	USBLS	5/07
	Camden PMSA, NJ	Y	24510 FQ	30250 MW	37390 TQ	USBLS	5/07
	Edison PMSA, NJ	Y	26730 FQ	33160 MW	42380 TQ	USBLS	5/07
	Newark-Union PMSA, NJ-PA	Y	25850 FQ	32710 MW	41210 TQ	USBLS	5/07
	New Mexico	Y	20980 FQ	25440 MW	30610 TQ	USBLS	5/07
	Albuquerque MSA, NM	Y	21740 FQ	25920 MW	30740 TQ	USBLS	5/07
	Las Cruces MSA, NM	Y	16240 FQ	18180 MW	24680 TQ	USBLS	5/07
	New York	Y	23720 FQ	30890 MW	40480 TQ	USBLS	5/07
	Albany-Schenectady-Troy MSA, NY	Y	22270 FQ	28820 MW	37290 TQ	USBLS	5/07
	Buffalo-Niagara Falls MSA, NY	Y	21180 FQ	27430 MW	34230 TQ	USBLS	5/07
	Glens Falls MSA, NY	Y	20350 FQ	27140 MW	34240 TQ	USBLS	5/07
	Nassau-Suffolk PMSA, NY	Y	26500 FQ	33300 MW	41280 TQ	USBLS	5/07
	New York-Northern New Jersey-Long Island MSA, NY-NJ-PA	Y	26020 FQ	33190 MW	43330 TQ	USBLS	5/07
	Syracuse MSA, NY	Y	22120 FQ	29140 MW	37580 TQ	USBLS	5/07
	North Carolina	Y	23090 FQ	28730 MW	35900 TQ	USBLS	5/07
	Charlotte-Gastonia-Concord MSA, NC-SC	Y	25450 FQ	31350 MW	38760 TQ	USBLS	5/07
	Raleigh-Cary MSA, NC	Y	22950 FQ	28390 MW	35990 TQ	USBLS	5/07
	North Dakota	Y	21290 FQ	24750 MW	29790 TQ	USBLS	5/07
	Fargo MSA, ND-MN	Y	21900 FQ	25060 MW	29780 TQ	USBLS	5/07
	Ohio	Y	23050 FQ	29460 MW	37110 TQ	USBLS	5/07
	Cincinnati-Middletown MSA, OH-KY-IN	Y	24310 FQ	30530 MW	37800 TQ	USBLS	5/07
	Cleveland-Elyria-Mentor MSA, OH	Y	24040 FQ	30240 MW	38010 TQ	USBLS	5/07
	Columbus MSA, OH	Y	23510 FQ	29570 MW	36850 TQ	USBLS	5/07
	Dayton MSA, OH	Y	23450 FQ	30540 MW	39060 TQ	USBLS	5/07
	Springfield MSA, OH	Y	21220 FQ	28140 MW	34820 TQ	USBLS	5/07
	Oklahoma	Y	20220 FQ	24490 MW	30750 TQ	USBLS	5/07
	Oklahoma City MSA, OK	Y	20580 FQ	24140 MW	29760 TQ	USBLS	5/07
	Tulsa MSA, OK	Y	22430 FQ	27100 MW	33540 TQ	USBLS	5/07
	Oregon	H	11.21 FQ	13.84 MW	17.43 TQ	ORBLS	5/08
	Portland-Vancouver-Beaverton MSA, OR-WA	Y	24530 FQ	29870 MW	37230 TQ	USBLS	5/07
	Pennsylvania	Y	22170 FQ	28500 MW	37230 TQ	USBLS	5/07
	Allentown-Bethlehem-Easton MSA, PA-NJ	Y	22570 FQ	28210 MW	34280 TQ	USBLS	5/07
	Erie MSA, PA	Y	21270 FQ	26750 MW	32160 TQ	USBLS	5/07
	Philadelphia-Camden-Wilmington MSA, PA-NJ-DE-MD	Y	24730 FQ	31820 MW	40760 TQ	USBLS	5/07
	Pittsburgh MSA, PA	Y	20980 FQ	27170 MW	34910 TQ	USBLS	5/07
	Rhode Island	Y	26360 FQ	30400 MW	37200 TQ	USBLS	5/07
	Providence-Fall River-Warwick MSA, RI-MA	Y	26070 FQ	30390 MW	37290 TQ	USBLS	5/07
	South Carolina	Y	22070 FQ	27330 MW	33100 TQ	USBLS	5/07
	Charleston-North Charleston MSA, SC	Y	22820 FQ	27640 MW	32920 TQ	USBLS	5/07
	Columbia MSA, SC	Y	22560 FQ	28150 MW	34130 TQ	USBLS	5/07
	South Dakota	Y	21479 FQ	24852 MW	30115 TQ	SDBLS	7/08-9/08
	Sioux Falls MSA, SD	Y	21966 FQ	25178 MW	29999 TQ	SDBLS	7/08-9/08
	Tennessee	Y	22040 FQ	27300 MW	34210 TQ	USBLS	5/07
	Knoxville MSA, TN	Y	21170 FQ	24710 MW	31030 TQ	USBLS	5/07
	Memphis MSA, TN-MS-AR	Y	23840 FQ	29530 MW	37500 TQ	USBLS	5/07
	Nashville-Davidson-Murfreesboro MSA, TN	Y	23890 FQ	28870 MW	35330 TQ	USBLS	5/07

AE	Average entry wage	AW	Average wage paid	FQ	First quartile wage	LO	Lowest wage paid	MTC	Median total compensation	TCC	Total cash compensation
AER	Average entry range	AWR	Average wage range	H	Hourly	LR	Low end range	MW	Median wage paid	TQ	Third quartile wage
AEX	Average experienced wage	AXR	Average experienced range	HI	Highest wage paid	M	Monthly	MWR	Median wage range	W	Weekly
ATC	Average total compensation	D	Daily	HR	High end range	MCC	Median cash compensation	S	See annotated source	Y	Yearly

Occupation/Type/Industry	Location	Per	Low	Mid	High	Source	Date
Customer Service Representative	Texas	Y	20640 FQ	26740 MW	33860 TQ	USBLS	5/07
	Austin-Round Rock MSA, TX	Y	21890 FQ	27690 MW	35100 TQ	USBLS	5/07
	Dallas-Fort Worth-Arlington MSA, TX	Y	24310 FQ	29610 MW	36770 TQ	USBLS	5/07
	El Paso MSA, TX	Y	18020 FQ	23210 MW	28900 TQ	USBLS	5/07
	Houston-Sugar Land-Baytown MSA, TX	Y	21210 FQ	28440 MW	36550 TQ	USBLS	5/07
	San Antonio MSA, TX	Y	19070 FQ	23710 MW	29750 TQ	USBLS	5/07
	Utah	Y	20720 FQ	25670 MW	31100 TQ	USBLS	5/07
	Salt Lake City MSA, UT	Y	22440 FQ	27300 MW	32220 TQ	USBLS	5/07
	Vermont	Y	21180 FQ	27380 MW	35780 TQ	USBLS	5/07
	Burlington-South Burlington MSA, VT	Y	22610 FQ	29040 MW	40540 TQ	USBLS	5/07
	Virginia	Y	22800 FQ	28570 MW	36230 TQ	USBLS	5/07
	Richmond MSA, VA	Y	25450 FQ	29530 MW	35920 TQ	USBLS	5/07
	Virginia Beach-Norfolk-Newport News MSA, VA-NC	Y	21660 FQ	26830 MW	32790 TQ	USBLS	5/07
	Washington	H	12.45 FQ	14.81 MW	18.13 TQ	WABLS	3/08
	Seattle-Tacoma-Bellevue MSA, WA	Y	27260 FQ	31880 MW	38770 TQ	USBLS	5/07
	Spokane MSA, WA	Y	23450 FQ	27630 MW	33410 TQ	USBLS	5/07
	West Virginia	Y	18206 FQ	22713 MW	27986 TQ	WVBLS	7/08-9/08
	Charleston MSA, WV	Y	17600 FQ	22450 MW	30250 TQ	USBLS	5/07
	Wisconsin	Y	25140 FQ	30230 MW	37740 TQ	USBLS	5/07
	Milwaukee-Waukesha-West Allis MSA, WI	Y	26560 FQ	32290 MW	40930 TQ	USBLS	5/07
	Wyoming	Y	20115 FQ	26183 MW	32566 TQ	WYBLS	9/08
	Cheyenne MSA, WY	Y	20827 FQ	26785 MW	32288 TQ	WYBLS	9/08
	Puerto Rico	Y	14610 FQ	18600 MW	25870 TQ	USBLS	5/07
	San Juan-Caguas-Guaynabo MSA, PR	Y	14830 FQ	18910 MW	26240 TQ	USBLS	5/07
	Virgin Islands	Y	19140 FQ	23480 MW	28410 TQ	USBLS	5/07
	Guam	Y	16270 FQ	22100 MW	31650 TQ	USBLS	5/07
Cutter and Trimmer							
Hand	Alabama	Y	18790 FQ	23570 MW	31630 TQ	USBLS	5/07
Hand	Arizona	Y	18100 FQ	24830 MW	29540 TQ	USBLS	5/07
Hand	Phoenix-Mesa-Scottsdale MSA, AZ	Y	23470 FQ	27530 MW	31060 TQ	USBLS	5/07
Hand	Arkansas	Y	21330 FQ	25400 MW	29630 TQ	USBLS	5/07
Hand	Little Rock-North Little Rock MSA, AR	Y	25110 FQ	27650 MW	30470 TQ	USBLS	5/07
Hand	California	H	8.53 FQ	9.52 MW	12.38 TQ	CABLS	1/08-3/08
Hand	Los Angeles-Long Beach-Glendale PMSA, CA	H	8.42 FQ	9.18 MW	11.44 TQ	CABLS	1/08-3/08
Hand	Oakland-Fremont-Hayward MSA, CA	H	11.36 FQ	12.77 MW	14.15 TQ	CABLS	1/08-3/08
Hand	Oxnard-Thousand Oaks-Ventura MSA, CA	H	8.53 FQ	9.53 MW	10.76 TQ	CABLS	1/08-3/08
Hand	Riverside-San Bernardino-Ontario MSA, CA	H	8.62 FQ	9.84 MW	11.74 TQ	CABLS	1/08-3/08
Hand	Sacramento-Arden Arcade-Roseville MSA, CA	H	9.79 FQ	15.86 MW	17.40 TQ	CABLS	1/08-3/08
Hand	San Diego-Carlsbad-San Marcos MSA, CA	H	10.14 FQ	12.71 MW	15.06 TQ	CABLS	1/08-3/08
Hand	San Francisco-San Mateo-Redwood PMSA, CA	H	8.62 FQ	9.86 MW	15.11 TQ	CABLS	1/08-3/08
Hand	San Jose-Sunnyvale-Santa Clara MSA, CA	H	9.80 FQ	15.08 MW	17.87 TQ	CABLS	1/08-3/08
Hand	Santa Ana-Anaheim-Irvine PMSA, CA	Y	17780 FQ	20290 MW	25950 TQ	USBLS	5/07
Hand	Colorado	Y	17750 FQ	22150 MW	26120 TQ	USBLS	5/07
Hand	Denver-Aurora MSA, CO	Y	18600 FQ	23380 MW	28300 TQ	USBLS	5/07
Hand	Connecticut	H	9.20 AE	12.74 MW		CTBLS	1/08-3/08
Hand	Bridgeport-Stamford-Norwalk MSA, CT	Y	18290 FQ	22340 MW	28740 TQ	USBLS	5/07
Hand	Delaware	Y	26980 FQ	29710 MW	34420 TQ	USBLS	5/07
Hand	Wilmington PMSA, DE-MD-NJ	Y	27100 FQ	29910 MW	34640 TQ	USBLS	5/07
Hand	Washington-Arlington-Alexandria MSA, DC-VA-MD-WV	Y	17190 FQ	18790 MW	25250 TQ	USBLS	5/07

AE	Average entry wage	AW	Average wage paid	FQ	First quartile wage	LO	Lowest wage paid	MTC	Median total compensation	TCC	Total cash compensation
AER	Average entry range	AWR	Average wage range	H	Hourly	LR	Low end range	MW	Median wage paid	TQ	Third quartile wage
AEX	Average experienced wage	AXR	Average experienced range	HI	Highest wage paid	M	Monthly	MWR	Median wage range	W	Weekly
ATC	Average total compensation	D	Daily	HR	High end range	MCC	Median cash compensation	S	See annotated source	Y	Yearly

384

Cutter and Trimmer

Occupation/Type/Industry	Location	Per	Low	Mid	High	Source	Date
Cutter and Trimmer							
Hand	Florida	Y	22060 FQ	26940 MW	35090 TQ	USBLS	5/07
Hand	Fort Lauderdale-Pompano Beach-Deerfield Beach PMSA, FL	Y	21730 FQ	27050 MW	34630 TQ	USBLS	5/07
Hand	Miami-Fort Lauderdale-Miami Beach MSA, FL	Y	22410 FQ	28010 MW	35140 TQ	USBLS	5/07
Hand	Tampa-St. Petersburg-Clearwater MSA, FL	Y	21150 FQ	23860 MW	29060 TQ	USBLS	5/07
Hand	West Palm Beach-Boca Raton-Boynton Beach PMSA, FL	Y	26050 FQ	31430 MW	36730 TQ	USBLS	5/07
Hand	Georgia	Y	17920 FQ	21820 MW	27670 TQ	USBLS	5/07
Hand	Atlanta-Sandy Springs-Marietta MSA, GA	Y	20260 FQ	24000 MW	30470 TQ	USBLS	5/07
Hand	Augusta-Richmond County MSA, GA-SC	Y	21180 FQ	22960 MW	24800 TQ	USBLS	5/07
Hand	Idaho	Y	16740 FQ	19210 MW	31850 TQ	USBLS	5/07
Hand	Boise City-Nampa MSA, ID	Y	17100 FQ	20450 MW	33030 TQ	USBLS	5/07
Hand	Illinois	Y	21310 FQ	27790 MW	32570 TQ	USBLS	5/07
Hand	Chicago-Naperville-Joliet MSA, IL-IN-WI	Y	22290 FQ	29420 MW	34380 TQ	USBLS	5/07
Hand	Indiana	Y	21120 FQ	24990 MW	31570 TQ	USBLS	5/07
Hand	Indianapolis-Carmel MSA, IN	Y	22450 FQ	26100 MW	31200 TQ	USBLS	5/07
Hand	Iowa	Y	24210 FQ	27610 MW	31680 TQ	USBLS	5/07
Hand	Kansas	Y	20480 FQ	25150 MW	32560 TQ	USBLS	5/07
Hand	Wichita MSA, KS	Y	15950 FQ	22650 MW	29140 TQ	USBLS	5/07
Hand	Kentucky	Y	19878 FQ	23121 MW	26803 TQ	KYBLS	2008
Hand	Louisiana	H	8.08 FQ	8.80 MW	9.94 TQ	LABLS	1/08-3/08
Hand	Maine	Y	18920 FQ	21810 MW	24600 TQ	USBLS	5/07
Hand	Maryland	Y		24425 MW		MDBLS	3/08
Hand	Baltimore-Towson MSA, MD	Y	21320 FQ	23630 MW	29940 TQ	USBLS	5/07
Hand	Massachusetts	Y	20390 FQ	23750 MW	29950 TQ	USBLS	5/07
Hand	Boston-Cambridge-Quincy NECTA, MA	Y	17840 FQ	24280 MW	35470 TQ	USBLS	5/07
Hand	Michigan	Y	19190 FQ	22630 MW	28670 TQ	USBLS	5/07
Hand	Detroit-Warren-Livonia MSA, MI	Y	17680 FQ	19720 MW	26430 TQ	USBLS	5/07
Hand	Grand Rapids-Wyoming MSA, MI	Y	19890 FQ	22480 MW	27640 TQ	USBLS	5/07
Hand	Warren-Troy-Farmington Hills PMSA, MI	Y	18900 FQ	23410 MW	30110 TQ	USBLS	5/07
Hand	Minnesota	Y	23242 FQ	27917 MW	41415 TQ	MNBLS	10/08-12/08
Hand	Minneapolis-Saint Paul MSA, MN-WI	Y	23729 FQ	28643 MW	40803 TQ	MNBLS	10/08-12/08
Hand	Mississippi	Y	18600 FQ	26220 MW	31730 TQ	USBLS	5/07
Hand	Missouri	Y	22510 FQ	29120 MW	53550 TQ	USBLS	5/07
Hand	St. Louis MSA, MO-IL	Y	22170 FQ	25770 MW	30510 TQ	USBLS	5/07
Hand	Montana	Y	22350 FQ	26040 MW	29000 TQ	USBLS	5/07
Hand	Nebraska	Y	20780 FQ	22910 MW	25550 TQ	USBLS	5/07
Hand	Lincoln MSA, NE	Y	21220 FQ	22990 MW	25140 TQ	USBLS	5/07
Hand	Nevada	H	8.67 FQ	10.99 MW	13.52 TQ	NVBLS	5/08
Hand	Las Vegas-Paradise MSA, NV	H	8.35 FQ	9.66 MW	12.38 TQ	NVBLS	5/08
Hand	New Hampshire	H	9.32 AE	10.31 MW	10.87 AEX	NHBLS	6/08
Hand	New Jersey	Y	16470 FQ	21450 MW	30320 TQ	USBLS	5/07
Hand	Camden PMSA, NJ	Y	16620 FQ	18090 MW	22720 TQ	USBLS	5/07
Hand	Edison PMSA, NJ	Y	22460 FQ	27880 MW	31100 TQ	USBLS	5/07
Hand	Newark-Union PMSA, NJ-PA	Y	15800 FQ	18930 MW	27620 TQ	USBLS	5/07
Hand	New York	Y	19620 FQ	30010 MW	41380 TQ	USBLS	5/07
Hand	Albany-Schenectady-Troy MSA, NY	Y	14900 FQ	17530 MW	24500 TQ	USBLS	5/07
Hand	Nassau-Suffolk PMSA, NY	Y	18780 FQ	24480 MW	34000 TQ	USBLS	5/07
Hand	New York-Northern New Jersey-Long Island MSA, NY-NJ-PA	Y	17610 FQ	25170 MW	34240 TQ	USBLS	5/07
Hand	North Carolina	Y	22320 FQ	28080 MW	35700 TQ	USBLS	5/07
Hand	Charlotte-Gastonia-Concord MSA, NC-SC	Y	17510 FQ	22450 MW	30860 TQ	USBLS	5/07
Hand	Durham MSA, NC	Y	20090 FQ	23550 MW	26880 TQ	USBLS	5/07
Hand	Ohio	Y	20640 FQ	24130 MW	30280 TQ	USBLS	5/07
Hand	Cincinnati-Middletown MSA, OH-KY-IN	Y	20050 FQ	22590 MW	27230 TQ	USBLS	5/07

AE	Average entry wage	AW	Average wage paid	FQ	First quartile wage	LO	Lowest wage paid	MTC	Median total compensation	TCC	Total cash compensation
AER	Average entry range	AWR	Average wage range	H	Hourly	LR	Low end range	MW	Median wage paid	TQ	Third quartile wage
AEX	Average experienced wage	AXR	Average experienced range	HI	Highest wage paid	M	Monthly	MWR	Median wage range	W	Weekly
ATC	Average total compensation	D	Daily	HR	High end range	MCC	Median cash compensation	S	See annotated source	Y	Yearly

Occupation/Type/Industry	Location	Per	Low	Mid	High	Source	Date
Cutter and Trimmer							
Hand	Cleveland-Elyria-Mentor MSA, OH	Y	20780 FQ	24420 MW	32750 TQ	USBLS	5/07
Hand	Columbus MSA, OH	Y	19330 FQ	23130 MW	32570 TQ	USBLS	5/07
Hand	Oklahoma	Y	18720 FQ	25100 MW	55900 TQ	USBLS	5/07
Hand	Oklahoma City MSA, OK	Y	17160 FQ	22050 MW	28360 TQ	USBLS	5/07
Hand	Tulsa MSA, OK	Y	21730 FQ	54710 MW	60040 TQ	USBLS	5/07
Hand	Oregon	H	9.35 FQ	10.81 MW	12.59 TQ	ORBLS	5/08
Hand	Portland-Vancouver-Beaverton MSA, OR-WA	Y	18950 FQ	22210 MW	25500 TQ	USBLS	5/07
Hand	Pennsylvania	Y	19860 FQ	23500 MW	28630 TQ	USBLS	5/07
Hand	Allentown-Bethlehem-Easton MSA, PA-NJ	Y	17060 FQ	21190 MW	25640 TQ	USBLS	5/07
Hand	Philadelphia-Camden-Wilmington MSA, PA-NJ-DE-MD	Y	17540 FQ	21650 MW	28560 TQ	USBLS	5/07
Hand	Pittsburgh MSA, PA	Y	21030 FQ	26980 MW	31470 TQ	USBLS	5/07
Hand	York-Hanover MSA, PA	Y	19780 FQ	22550 MW	25830 TQ	USBLS	5/07
Hand	Rhode Island	Y	19130 FQ	24060 MW	32700 TQ	USBLS	5/07
Hand	Providence-Fall River-Warwick MSA, RI-MA	Y	19450 FQ	25600 MW	31080 TQ	USBLS	5/07
Hand	South Carolina	Y	20460 FQ	24720 MW	32300 TQ	USBLS	5/07
Hand	Columbia MSA, SC	Y	26610 FQ	38930 MW	43150 TQ	USBLS	5/07
Hand	Spartanburg MSA, SC	Y	15440 FQ	26330 MW	32340 TQ	USBLS	5/07
Hand	South Dakota	Y	18069 FQ	21274 MW	24247 TQ	SDBLS	7/08-9/08
Hand	Tennessee	Y	19990 FQ	23570 MW	28020 TQ	USBLS	5/07
Hand	Knoxville MSA, TN	Y	20140 FQ	24480 MW	27980 TQ	USBLS	5/07
Hand	Memphis MSA, TN-MS-AR	Y	17100 FQ	19580 MW	25090 TQ	USBLS	5/07
Hand	Nashville-Davidson-Murfreesboro MSA, TN	Y	20180 FQ	26550 MW	31750 TQ	USBLS	5/07
Hand	Texas	Y	16250 FQ	19210 MW	24080 TQ	USBLS	5/07
Hand	Austin-Round Rock MSA, TX	Y	15720 FQ	25810 MW	29810 TQ	USBLS	5/07
Hand	Dallas-Fort Worth-Arlington MSA, TX	Y	17320 FQ	19920 MW	26250 TQ	USBLS	5/07
Hand	Houston-Sugar Land-Baytown MSA, TX	Y	17160 FQ	20010 MW	23790 TQ	USBLS	5/07
Hand	San Antonio MSA, TX	Y	13410 FQ	16040 MW	18890 TQ	USBLS	5/07
Hand	Utah	Y	18490 FQ	22990 MW	31380 TQ	USBLS	5/07
Hand	Salt Lake City MSA, UT	Y	22470 FQ	24940 MW	32110 TQ	USBLS	5/07
Hand	Vermont	Y	23730 FQ	27520 MW	30890 TQ	USBLS	5/07
Hand	Virginia	Y	18040 FQ	21010 MW	24930 TQ	USBLS	5/07
Hand	Richmond MSA, VA	Y	19930 FQ	21580 MW	23220 TQ	USBLS	5/07
Hand	Virginia Beach-Norfolk-Newport News MSA, VA-NC	Y	13890 FQ	16710 MW	20460 TQ	USBLS	5/07
Hand	Washington	H	9.87 FQ	12.08 MW	15.01 TQ	WABLS	3/08
Hand	Seattle-Tacoma-Bellevue MSA, WA	Y	20260 FQ	25050 MW	30180 TQ	USBLS	5/07
Hand	West Virginia	Y	15260 FQ	19106 MW	26569 TQ	WVBLS	7/08-9/08
Hand	Wisconsin	Y	20850 FQ	26370 MW	31450 TQ	USBLS	5/07
Hand	Milwaukee-Waukesha-West Allis MSA, WI	Y	19120 FQ	23540 MW	29030 TQ	USBLS	5/07
Hand	Puerto Rico	Y	12820 FQ	14450 MW	18970 TQ	USBLS	5/07
Hand	San Juan-Caguas-Guaynabo MSA, PR	Y	12850 FQ	14500 MW	19190 TQ	USBLS	5/07
Cutting, Punching, and Press Machine Setter, Operator, and Tender							
Metals and Plastics	Alabama	Y	21600 FQ	26620 MW	31650 TQ	USBLS	5/07
Metals and Plastics	Birmingham-Hoover MSA, AL	Y	23310 FQ	28180 MW	32630 TQ	USBLS	5/07
Metals and Plastics	Huntsville MSA, AL	Y	25090 FQ	29510 MW	34710 TQ	USBLS	5/07
Metals and Plastics	Mobile MSA, AL	Y	20560 FQ	23610 MW	29010 TQ	USBLS	5/07
Metals and Plastics	Alaska	Y	26380 FQ	29400 MW	41630 TQ	USBLS	5/07
Metals and Plastics	Arizona	Y	18850 FQ	23770 MW	31210 TQ	USBLS	5/07
Metals and Plastics	Phoenix-Mesa-Scottsdale MSA, AZ	Y	18570 FQ	23440 MW	31640 TQ	USBLS	5/07
Metals and Plastics	Tucson MSA, AZ	Y	22400 FQ	25950 MW	30010 TQ	USBLS	5/07
Metals and Plastics	Arkansas	Y	21620 FQ	25980 MW	29710 TQ	USBLS	5/07
Metals and Plastics	Fort Smith MSA, AR-OK	Y	21990 FQ	24960 MW	32210 TQ	USBLS	5/07
Metals and Plastics	Little Rock-North Little Rock MSA, AR	Y	21310 FQ	26110 MW	29510 TQ	USBLS	5/07

AE	Average entry wage	AW	Average wage paid	FQ	First quartile wage
AER	Average entry range	AWR	Average wage range	H	Hourly
AEX	Average experienced wage	AXR	Average experienced range	HI	Highest wage paid
ATC	Average total compensation	D	Daily	HR	High end range

LO	Lowest wage paid	MTC	Median total compensation
LR	Low end range	MW	Median wage paid
M	Monthly	MWR	Median wage range
MCC	Median cash compensation	S	See annotated source

TCC	Total cash compensation
TQ	Third quartile wage
W	Weekly
Y	Yearly

Occupation/Type/Industry	Location	Per	Low	Mid	High	Source	Date
Cutting, Punching, and Press Machine Setter, Operator, and Tender							
Metals and Plastics	California	H	10.17 FQ	12.77 MW	15.94 TQ	CABLS	1/08-3/08
Metals and Plastics	Los Angeles-Long Beach-Glendale PMSA, CA	H	9.49 FQ	11.93 MW	15.62 TQ	CABLS	1/08-3/08
Metals and Plastics	Oakland-Fremont-Hayward MSA, CA	H	11.32 FQ	14.33 MW	18.55 TQ	CABLS	1/08-3/08
Metals and Plastics	Riverside-San Bernardino-Ontario MSA, CA	H	9.99 FQ	12.23 MW	14.76 TQ	CABLS	1/08-3/08
Metals and Plastics	Sacramento-Arden Arcade-Roseville MSA, CA	H	11.20 FQ	13.43 MW	15.66 TQ	CABLS	1/08-3/08
Metals and Plastics	San Diego-Carlsbad-San Marcos MSA, CA	H	10.91 FQ	12.87 MW	15.82 TQ	CABLS	1/08-3/08
Metals and Plastics	San Francisco-San Mateo-Redwood PMSA, CA	H	11.31 FQ	15.04 MW	20.35 TQ	CABLS	1/08-3/08
Metals and Plastics	San Jose-Sunnyvale-Santa Clara MSA, CA	H	12.45 FQ	15.76 MW	19.48 TQ	CABLS	1/08-3/08
Metals and Plastics	Santa Ana-Anaheim-Irvine PMSA, CA	Y	20280 FQ	25360 MW	31170 TQ	USBLS	5/07
Metals and Plastics	Santa Rosa-Petaluma MSA, CA	H	10.34 FQ	12.92 MW	17.19 TQ	CABLS	1/08-3/08
Metals and Plastics	Colorado	Y	24170 FQ	28710 MW	34710 TQ	USBLS	5/07
Metals and Plastics	Boulder MSA, CO	Y	21420 FQ	24220 MW	31710 TQ	USBLS	5/07
Metals and Plastics	Denver-Aurora MSA, CO	Y	24910 FQ	29700 MW	35430 TQ	USBLS	5/07
Metals and Plastics	Fort Collins-Loveland MSA, CO	Y	26390 FQ	31170 MW	36610 TQ	USBLS	5/07
Metals and Plastics	Connecticut	H	10.15 AE	14.05 MW		CTBLS	1/08-3/08
Metals and Plastics	Bridgeport-Stamford-Norwalk MSA, CT	Y	20400 FQ	26210 MW	33980 TQ	USBLS	5/07
Metals and Plastics	Hartford-West Hartford-East Hartford MSA, CT	Y	25700 FQ	32470 MW	43120 TQ	USBLS	5/07
Metals and Plastics	Delaware	Y	24750 FQ	32330 MW	37460 TQ	USBLS	5/07
Metals and Plastics	Wilmington PMSA, DE-MD-NJ	Y	22310 FQ	25680 MW	33660 TQ	USBLS	5/07
Metals and Plastics	Washington-Arlington-Alexandria MSA, DC-VA-MD-WV	Y	21850 FQ	26490 MW	35090 TQ	USBLS	5/07
Metals and Plastics	Florida	Y	19000 FQ	23950 MW	30550 TQ	USBLS	5/07
Metals and Plastics	Fort Lauderdale-Pompano Beach-Deerfield Beach PMSA, FL	Y	20900 FQ	25170 MW	29370 TQ	USBLS	5/07
Metals and Plastics	Jacksonville MSA, FL	Y	22550 FQ	28880 MW	35000 TQ	USBLS	5/07
Metals and Plastics	Miami-Fort Lauderdale-Miami Beach MSA, FL	Y	18700 FQ	23630 MW	29210 TQ	USBLS	5/07
Metals and Plastics	Orlando-Kissimmee MSA, FL	Y	18120 FQ	23190 MW	30010 TQ	USBLS	5/07
Metals and Plastics	Tampa-St. Petersburg-Clearwater MSA, FL	Y	17990 FQ	22640 MW	29890 TQ	USBLS	5/07
Metals and Plastics	West Palm Beach-Boca Raton-Boynton Beach PMSA, FL	Y	19930 FQ	27100 MW	32410 TQ	USBLS	5/07
Metals and Plastics	Georgia	Y	21370 FQ	26170 MW	31340 TQ	USBLS	5/07
Metals and Plastics	Atlanta-Sandy Springs-Marietta MSA, GA	Y	21760 FQ	26040 MW	31340 TQ	USBLS	5/07
Metals and Plastics	Hawaii	Y	16530 FQ	19120 MW	23640 TQ	USBLS	5/07
Metals and Plastics	Honolulu MSA, HI	Y	15950 FQ	18340 MW	22080 TQ	USBLS	5/07
Metals and Plastics	Idaho	Y	20130 FQ	26600 MW	30430 TQ	USBLS	5/07
Metals and Plastics	Boise City-Nampa MSA, ID	Y	18310 FQ	22490 MW	27970 TQ	USBLS	5/07
Metals and Plastics	Illinois	Y	19560 FQ	26950 MW	34770 TQ	USBLS	5/07
Metals and Plastics	Chicago-Naperville-Joliet MSA, IL-IN-WI	Y	19150 FQ	26550 MW	34980 TQ	USBLS	5/07
Metals and Plastics	Peoria MSA, IL	Y	22150 FQ	28340 MW	35100 TQ	USBLS	5/07
Metals and Plastics	Indiana	Y	23220 FQ	27930 MW	35030 TQ	USBLS	5/07
Metals and Plastics	Gary PMSA, IN	Y	23530 FQ	29680 MW	38260 TQ	USBLS	5/07
Metals and Plastics	Indianapolis-Carmel MSA, IN	Y	23720 FQ	28870 MW	36840 TQ	USBLS	5/07
Metals and Plastics	South Bend-Mishawaka MSA, IN-MI	Y	21750 FQ	27450 MW	31700 TQ	USBLS	5/07
Metals and Plastics	Iowa	Y	23730 FQ	28550 MW	34400 TQ	USBLS	5/07
Metals and Plastics	Des Moines-West Des Moines MSA, IA	Y	29280 FQ	37440 MW	42520 TQ	USBLS	5/07
Metals and Plastics	Kansas	Y	20350 FQ	25230 MW	31670 TQ	USBLS	5/07
Metals and Plastics	Wichita MSA, KS	Y	20090 FQ	25840 MW	39340 TQ	USBLS	5/07
Metals and Plastics	Kentucky	Y	21130 FQ	27215 MW	32224 TQ	KYBLS	2008

AE	Average entry wage	AW	Average wage paid	FQ	First quartile wage
AER	Average entry range	AWR	Average wage range	H	Hourly
AEX	Average experienced wage	AXR	Average experienced range	HI	Highest wage paid
ATC	Average total compensation	D	Daily	HR	High end range

LO	Lowest wage paid	MTC	Median total compensation	TCC	Total cash compensation
LR	Low end range	MW	Median wage paid	TQ	Third quartile wage
M	Monthly	MWR	Median wage range	W	Weekly
MCC	Median cash compensation	S	See annotated source	Y	Yearly

Occupation/Type/Industry	Location	Per	Low	Mid	High	Source	Date
Cutting, Punching, and Press Machine Setter, Operator, and Tender							
Metals and Plastics	Lexington-Fayette MSA, KY	Y	23540 FQ	27410 MW	30720 TQ	USBLS	5/07
Metals and Plastics	Louisville-Jefferson County MSA, KY-IN	Y	23320 FQ	27650 MW	31920 TQ	USBLS	5/07
Metals and Plastics	Owensboro MSA, KY	Y	22360 FQ	26660 MW	30620 TQ	USBLS	5/07
Metals and Plastics	Louisiana	H	12.14 FQ	14.16 MW	17.37 TQ	LABLS	1/08-3/08
Metals and Plastics	Baton Rouge MSA, LA	Y	25920 FQ	28990 MW	32220 TQ	USBLS	5/07
Metals and Plastics	Houma-Bayou Cane-Thibodaux MSA, LA	Y	26450 FQ	33090 MW	37970 TQ	USBLS	5/07
Metals and Plastics	New Orleans-Metairie-Kenner MSA, LA	Y	25840 FQ	30010 MW	35520 TQ	USBLS	5/07
Metals and Plastics	Maine	Y	21840 FQ	27500 MW	31510 TQ	USBLS	5/07
Metals and Plastics	Portland-South Portland-Biddeford MSA, ME	Y	26680 FQ	29180 MW	31840 TQ	USBLS	5/07
Metals and Plastics	Maryland	Y		35150 MW		MDBLS	3/08
Metals and Plastics	Baltimore-Towson MSA, MD	Y	29180 FQ	36150 MW	41880 TQ	USBLS	5/07
Metals and Plastics	Bethesda-Gaithersburg-Frederick PMSA, MD	Y	27510 FQ	35580 MW	42500 TQ	USBLS	5/07
Metals and Plastics	Massachusetts	Y	24140 FQ	30730 MW	36880 TQ	USBLS	5/07
Metals and Plastics	Boston-Cambridge-Quincy NECTA, MA	Y	23140 FQ	30420 MW	36600 TQ	USBLS	5/07
Metals and Plastics	Worcester MSA, MA-CT	Y	27060 FQ	32500 MW	37580 TQ	USBLS	5/07
Metals and Plastics	Michigan	Y	23480 FQ	30020 MW	40260 TQ	USBLS	5/07
Metals and Plastics	Detroit-Warren-Livonia MSA, MI	Y	24180 FQ	31250 MW	43790 TQ	USBLS	5/07
Metals and Plastics	Grand Rapids-Wyoming MSA, MI	Y	23310 FQ	30390 MW	54050 TQ	USBLS	5/07
Metals and Plastics	Muskegon-Norton Shores MSA, MI	Y	23770 FQ	30120 MW	36510 TQ	USBLS	5/07
Metals and Plastics	Warren-Troy-Farmington Hills PMSA, MI	Y	22350 FQ	28650 MW	39140 TQ	USBLS	5/07
Metals and Plastics	Minnesota	Y	26673 FQ	32924 MW	39549 TQ	MNBLS	10/08-12/08
Metals and Plastics	Duluth-Superior MSA, MN-WI	Y	22444 FQ	27959 MW	33153 TQ	MNBLS	10/08-12/08
Metals and Plastics	Minneapolis-Saint Paul MSA, MN-WI	Y	27337 FQ	33775 MW	40160 TQ	MNBLS	10/08-12/08
Metals and Plastics	Rochester MSA, MN	Y	29969 FQ	33686 MW	37622 TQ	MNBLS	10/08-12/08
Metals and Plastics	Mississippi	Y	21730 FQ	25900 MW	30480 TQ	USBLS	5/07
Metals and Plastics	Jackson MSA, MS	Y	23710 FQ	29580 MW	33370 TQ	USBLS	5/07
Metals and Plastics	Missouri	Y	21110 FQ	25920 MW	31270 TQ	USBLS	5/07
Metals and Plastics	Kansas City MSA, MO-KS	Y	21240 FQ	27060 MW	32830 TQ	USBLS	5/07
Metals and Plastics	St. Joseph MSA, MO-KS	Y	22990 FQ	26620 MW	32270 TQ	USBLS	5/07
Metals and Plastics	St. Louis MSA, MO-IL	Y	21160 FQ	27240 MW	33360 TQ	USBLS	5/07
Metals and Plastics	Springfield MSA, MO	Y	22560 FQ	26830 MW	30940 TQ	USBLS	5/07
Metals and Plastics	Montana	Y	19740 FQ	25200 MW	30660 TQ	USBLS	5/07
Metals and Plastics	Billings MSA, MT	Y	20960 FQ	25890 MW	31720 TQ	USBLS	5/07
Metals and Plastics	Nebraska	Y	22420 FQ	27340 MW	33690 TQ	USBLS	5/07
Metals and Plastics	Omaha-Council Bluffs MSA, NE-IA	Y	22470 FQ	27430 MW	33600 TQ	USBLS	5/07
Metals and Plastics	Nevada	H	10.83 FQ	13.30 MW	16.85 TQ	NVBLS	5/08
Metals and Plastics	Las Vegas-Paradise MSA, NV	H	10.25 FQ	12.57 MW	15.84 TQ	NVBLS	5/08
Metals and Plastics	New Hampshire	H	9.71 AE	12.36 MW	15.14 AEX	NHBLS	6/08
Metals and Plastics	Manchester MSA, NH	Y	20030 FQ	25600 MW	32330 TQ	USBLS	5/07
Metals and Plastics	Nashua NECTA, NH-MA	Y	25200 FQ	31130 MW	37350 TQ	USBLS	5/07
Metals and Plastics	New Jersey	Y	21460 FQ	26730 MW	34640 TQ	USBLS	5/07
Metals and Plastics	Camden PMSA, NJ	Y	24460 FQ	31820 MW	38110 TQ	USBLS	5/07
Metals and Plastics	Edison PMSA, NJ	Y	19350 FQ	24050 MW	30220 TQ	USBLS	5/07
Metals and Plastics	Newark-Union PMSA, NJ-PA	Y	21660 FQ	26670 MW	36200 TQ	USBLS	5/07
Metals and Plastics	New Mexico	Y	20760 FQ	25540 MW	30210 TQ	USBLS	5/07
Metals and Plastics	Albuquerque MSA, NM	Y	22350 FQ	26420 MW	32870 TQ	USBLS	5/07
Metals and Plastics	Farmington MSA, NM	Y	24360 FQ	27300 MW	29940 TQ	USBLS	5/07
Metals and Plastics	New York	Y	21070 FQ	26560 MW	33800 TQ	USBLS	5/07
Metals and Plastics	Albany-Schenectady-Troy MSA, NY	Y	19870 FQ	23090 MW	28020 TQ	USBLS	5/07
Metals and Plastics	Buffalo-Niagara Falls MSA, NY	Y	27940 FQ	34590 MW	56270 TQ	USBLS	5/07
Metals and Plastics	Kingston MSA, NY	Y	27320 FQ	32450 MW	36680 TQ	USBLS	5/07
Metals and Plastics	Nassau-Suffolk PMSA, NY	Y	21220 FQ	25170 MW	33620 TQ	USBLS	5/07

AE	Average entry wage	AW	Average wage paid	FQ	First quartile wage	LO	Lowest wage paid	MTC Median total compensation TCC Total cash compensation
AER	Average entry range	AWR	Average wage range	H	Hourly	LR	Low end range	MW Median wage paid TQ Third quartile wage
AEX	Average experienced wage	AXR	Average experienced range	HI	Highest wage paid	M	Monthly	MWR Median wage range W Weekly
ATC	Average total compensation	D	Daily	HR	High end range	MCC	Median cash compensation	S See annotated source Y Yearly

Occupation/Type/Industry	Location	Per	Low	Mid	High	Source	Date
Cutting, Punching, and Press Machine Setter, Operator, and Tender							
Metals and Plastics	New York-Northern New Jersey-Long Island MSA, NY-NJ-PA	Y	20630 FQ	25450 MW	33290 TQ	USBLS	5/07
Metals and Plastics	North Carolina	Y	19490 FQ	25170 MW	32060 TQ	USBLS	5/07
Metals and Plastics	Charlotte-Gastonia-Concord MSA, NC-SC	Y	21540 FQ	26960 MW	33360 TQ	USBLS	5/07
Metals and Plastics	Raleigh-Cary MSA, NC	Y	20710 FQ	24560 MW	34910 TQ	USBLS	5/07
Metals and Plastics	North Dakota	Y	22940 FQ	28680 MW	37660 TQ	USBLS	5/07
Metals and Plastics	Fargo MSA, ND-MN	Y	21000 FQ	25530 MW	30620 TQ	USBLS	5/07
Metals and Plastics	Ohio	Y	22720 FQ	27840 MW	33780 TQ	USBLS	5/07
Metals and Plastics	Cincinnati-Middletown MSA, OH-KY-IN	Y	23040 FQ	27110 MW	31920 TQ	USBLS	5/07
Metals and Plastics	Cleveland-Elyria-Mentor MSA, OH	Y	22270 FQ	28480 MW	35140 TQ	USBLS	5/07
Metals and Plastics	Columbus MSA, OH	Y	20870 FQ	25760 MW	30610 TQ	USBLS	5/07
Metals and Plastics	Dayton MSA, OH	Y	23610 FQ	27700 MW	31620 TQ	USBLS	5/07
Metals and Plastics	Mansfield MSA, OH	Y	19760 FQ	34090 MW	58030 TQ	USBLS	5/07
Metals and Plastics	Oklahoma	Y	19790 FQ	24750 MW	30790 TQ	USBLS	5/07
Metals and Plastics	Oklahoma City MSA, OK	Y	19840 FQ	24570 MW	30810 TQ	USBLS	5/07
Metals and Plastics	Tulsa MSA, OK	Y	20030 FQ	25830 MW	31770 TQ	USBLS	5/07
Metals and Plastics	Oregon	H	11.19 FQ	13.77 MW	16.84 TQ	ORBLS	5/08
Metals and Plastics	Portland-Vancouver-Beaverton MSA, OR-WA	Y	23010 FQ	28480 MW	34670 TQ	USBLS	5/07
Metals and Plastics	Pennsylvania	Y	23760 FQ	29050 MW	35550 TQ	USBLS	5/07
Metals and Plastics	Allentown-Bethlehem-Easton MSA, PA-NJ	Y	24090 FQ	28890 MW	37280 TQ	USBLS	5/07
Metals and Plastics	Philadelphia-Camden-Wilmington MSA, PA-NJ-DE-MD	Y	23490 FQ	30880 MW	38390 TQ	USBLS	5/07
Metals and Plastics	Pittsburgh MSA, PA	Y	23850 FQ	28620 MW	34350 TQ	USBLS	5/07
Metals and Plastics	Rhode Island	Y	17720 FQ	21350 MW	28460 TQ	USBLS	5/07
Metals and Plastics	Providence-Fall River-Warwick MSA, RI-MA	Y	18210 FQ	23400 MW	31100 TQ	USBLS	5/07
Metals and Plastics	South Carolina	Y	21510 FQ	26220 MW	31240 TQ	USBLS	5/07
Metals and Plastics	Charleston-North Charleston MSA, SC	Y	23350 FQ	27420 MW	32140 TQ	USBLS	5/07
Metals and Plastics	Columbia MSA, SC	Y	22330 FQ	28640 MW	34280 TQ	USBLS	5/07
Metals and Plastics	South Dakota	Y	24878 FQ	28415 MW	32452 TQ	SDBLS	7/08-9/08
Metals and Plastics	Sioux Falls MSA, SD	Y	24888 FQ	28131 MW	31484 TQ	SDBLS	7/08-9/08
Metals and Plastics	Tennessee	Y	21790 FQ	26600 MW	32170 TQ	USBLS	5/07
Metals and Plastics	Kingsport-Bristol-Bristol MSA, TN-VA	Y	23350 FQ	26770 MW	30950 TQ	USBLS	5/07
Metals and Plastics	Memphis MSA, TN-MS-AR	Y	22570 FQ	27680 MW	35640 TQ	USBLS	5/07
Metals and Plastics	Nashville-Davidson-Murfreesboro MSA, TN	Y	21060 FQ	25590 MW	30810 TQ	USBLS	5/07
Metals and Plastics	Texas	Y	18780 FQ	23090 MW	29270 TQ	USBLS	5/07
Metals and Plastics	Austin-Round Rock MSA, TX	Y	17200 FQ	21660 MW	28430 TQ	USBLS	5/07
Metals and Plastics	Corpus Christi MSA, TX	Y	20760 FQ	23960 MW	28730 TQ	USBLS	5/07
Metals and Plastics	Dallas-Fort Worth-Arlington MSA, TX	Y	19170 FQ	23010 MW	29020 TQ	USBLS	5/07
Metals and Plastics	El Paso MSA, TX	Y	14930 FQ	18080 MW	25970 TQ	USBLS	5/07
Metals and Plastics	Houston-Sugar Land-Baytown MSA, TX	Y	19770 FQ	24880 MW	31170 TQ	USBLS	5/07
Metals and Plastics	San Antonio MSA, TX	Y	21090 FQ	26010 MW	30630 TQ	USBLS	5/07
Metals and Plastics	Utah	Y	21810 FQ	26290 MW	31720 TQ	USBLS	5/07
Metals and Plastics	Salt Lake City MSA, UT	Y	21180 FQ	25260 MW	32210 TQ	USBLS	5/07
Metals and Plastics	Vermont	Y	21610 FQ	24680 MW	31210 TQ	USBLS	5/07
Metals and Plastics	Burlington-South Burlington MSA, VT	Y	24380 FQ	34660 MW	44890 TQ	USBLS	5/07
Metals and Plastics	Virginia	Y	22170 FQ	27700 MW	33380 TQ	USBLS	5/07
Metals and Plastics	Richmond MSA, VA	Y	20610 FQ	27000 MW	34790 TQ	USBLS	5/07
Metals and Plastics	Virginia Beach-Norfolk-Newport News MSA, VA-NC	Y	20840 FQ	27170 MW	34000 TQ	USBLS	5/07
Metals and Plastics	Washington	H	11.70 FQ	14.71 MW	18.01 TQ	WABLS	3/08
Metals and Plastics	Seattle-Tacoma-Bellevue MSA, WA	Y	26120 FQ	32520 MW	40190 TQ	USBLS	5/07
Metals and Plastics	Spokane MSA, WA	Y	22270 FQ	24940 MW	32600 TQ	USBLS	5/07
Metals and Plastics	West Virginia	Y	23328 FQ	29201 MW	36826 TQ	WVBLS	7/08-9/08

AE Average entry wage	**AW** Average wage paid	**FQ** First quartile wage	**LO** Lowest wage paid	**MTC** Median total compensation **TCC** Total cash compensation
AER Average entry range	**AWR** Average wage range	**H** Hourly	**LR** Low end range	**MW** Median wage paid **TQ** Third quartile wage
AEX Average experienced wage	**AXR** Average experienced range	**HI** Highest wage paid	**M** Monthly	**MWR** Median wage range **W** Weekly
ATC Average total compensation	**D** Daily	**HR** High end range	**MCC** Median cash compensation	**S** See annotated source **Y** Yearly

Occupation/Type/Industry	Location	Per	Low	Mid	High	Source	Date
Cutting, Punching, and Press Machine Setter, Operator, and Tender							
Metals and Plastics	Charleston MSA, WV	Y	25820 FQ	28260 MW	30680 TQ	USBLS	5/07
Metals and Plastics	Huntington-Ashland MSA, WV-KY-OH	Y	26910 FQ	31590 MW	35790 TQ	USBLS	5/07
Metals and Plastics	Wisconsin	Y	24000 FQ	29670 MW	35620 TQ	USBLS	5/07
Metals and Plastics	Milwaukee-Waukesha-West Allis MSA, WI	Y	23890 FQ	29610 MW	36220 TQ	USBLS	5/07
Metals and Plastics	Wyoming	Y	22721 FQ	28978 MW	38686 TQ	WYBLS	9/08
Metals and Plastics	Cheyenne MSA, WY	Y	23405 FQ	26360 MW	31731 TQ	WYBLS	9/08
Metals and Plastics	Puerto Rico	Y	12960 FQ	14800 MW	19360 TQ	USBLS	5/07
Metals and Plastics	San Juan-Caguas-Guaynabo MSA, PR	Y	13390 FQ	16370 MW	20880 TQ	USBLS	5/07
Cutting and Slicing Machine Setter, Operator, and Tender	Alabama	Y	24300 FQ	36670 MW	43060 TQ	USBLS	5/07
	Alaska	Y	19850 FQ	25960 MW	38990 TQ	USBLS	5/07
	Arizona	Y	19920 FQ	26010 MW	31440 TQ	USBLS	5/07
	Phoenix-Mesa-Scottsdale MSA, AZ	Y	19340 FQ	25760 MW	31240 TQ	USBLS	5/07
	Tucson MSA, AZ	Y	21220 FQ	25840 MW	32120 TQ	USBLS	5/07
	Arkansas	Y	20880 FQ	25490 MW	35050 TQ	USBLS	5/07
	Little Rock-North Little Rock MSA, AR	Y	20650 FQ	22210 MW	23800 TQ	USBLS	5/07
	California	H	10.21 FQ	12.38 MW	17.04 TQ	CABLS	1/08-3/08
	Los Angeles-Long Beach-Glendale PMSA, CA	H	9.34 FQ	11.28 MW	14.25 TQ	CABLS	1/08-3/08
	Oakland-Fremont-Hayward MSA, CA	H	10.80 FQ	15.73 MW	19.35 TQ	CABLS	1/08-3/08
	Riverside-San Bernardino-Ontario MSA, CA	H	12.20 FQ	16.54 MW	21.43 TQ	CABLS	1/08-3/08
	Sacramento-Arden Arcade-Roseville MSA, CA	H	13.13 FQ	15.64 MW	19.35 TQ	CABLS	1/08-3/08
	San Diego-Carlsbad-San Marcos MSA, CA	H	9.38 FQ	12.34 MW	16.62 TQ	CABLS	1/08-3/08
	San Francisco-San Mateo-Redwood PMSA, CA	H	13.07 FQ	14.84 MW	19.93 TQ	CABLS	1/08-3/08
	San Jose-Sunnyvale-Santa Clara MSA, CA	H	10.31 FQ	13.89 MW	18.89 TQ	CABLS	1/08-3/08
	Santa Ana-Anaheim-Irvine PMSA, CA	Y	23220 FQ	29380 MW	37820 TQ	USBLS	5/07
	Stockton MSA, CA	H	9.64 FQ	12.52 MW	16.31 TQ	CABLS	1/08-3/08
	Colorado	Y	21080 FQ	26190 MW	33720 TQ	USBLS	5/07
	Denver-Aurora MSA, CO	Y	21720 FQ	26740 MW	35750 TQ	USBLS	5/07
	Connecticut	H	11.00 AE	16.41 MW		CTBLS	1/08-3/08
	Bridgeport-Stamford-Norwalk MSA, CT	Y	23780 FQ	32970 MW	37500 TQ	USBLS	5/07
	Hartford-West Hartford-East Hartford MSA, CT	Y	23840 FQ	35340 MW	44090 TQ	USBLS	5/07
	Delaware	Y	26590 FQ	33510 MW	40390 TQ	USBLS	5/07
	Washington-Arlington-Alexandria MSA, DC-VA-MD-WV	Y	26150 FQ	33910 MW	44630 TQ	USBLS	5/07
	Florida	Y	22570 FQ	28560 MW	37630 TQ	USBLS	5/07
	Fort Lauderdale-Pompano Beach-Deerfield Beach PMSA, FL	Y	21400 FQ	24940 MW	32890 TQ	USBLS	5/07
	Jacksonville MSA, FL	Y	24910 FQ	34970 MW	43690 TQ	USBLS	5/07
	Miami-Fort Lauderdale-Miami Beach MSA, FL	Y	20240 FQ	25410 MW	31960 TQ	USBLS	5/07
	Orlando-Kissimmee MSA, FL	Y	23360 FQ	29250 MW	42240 TQ	USBLS	5/07
	Tampa-St. Petersburg-Clearwater MSA, FL	Y	24110 FQ	27780 MW	31930 TQ	USBLS	5/07
	West Palm Beach-Boca Raton-Boynton Beach PMSA, FL	Y	28510 FQ	38680 MW	43850 TQ	USBLS	5/07
	Georgia	Y	21680 FQ	27230 MW	35640 TQ	USBLS	5/07
	Atlanta-Sandy Springs-Marietta MSA, GA	Y	23650 FQ	28990 MW	37940 TQ	USBLS	5/07
	Idaho	Y	17560 FQ	24190 MW	30930 TQ	USBLS	5/07
	Boise City-Nampa MSA, ID	Y	15220 FQ	17770 MW	23700 TQ	USBLS	5/07

AE	Average entry wage	AW	Average wage paid	FQ	First quartile wage	LO	Lowest wage paid	MTC	Median total compensation	TCC	Total cash compensation
AER	Average entry range	AWR	Average wage range	H	Hourly	LR	Low end range	MW	Median wage paid	TQ	Third quartile wage
AEX	Average experienced wage	AXR	Average experienced range	HI	Highest wage paid	M	Monthly	MWR	Median wage range	W	Weekly
ATC	Average total compensation	D	Daily	HR	High end range	MCC	Median cash compensation	S	See annotated source	Y	Yearly

Occupation/Type/Industry	Location	Per	Low	Mid	High	Source	Date
Cutting and Slicing Machine Setter, Operator, and Tender	Illinois	Y	24180 FQ	30520 MW	38590 TQ	USBLS	5/07
	Chicago-Naperville-Joliet MSA, IL-IN-WI	Y	24410 FQ	31520 MW	39230 TQ	USBLS	5/07
	Indiana	Y	22360 FQ	28140 MW	35440 TQ	USBLS	5/07
	Gary PMSA, IN	Y	26570 FQ	34390 MW	43230 TQ	USBLS	5/07
	Indianapolis-Carmel MSA, IN	Y	22720 FQ	29700 MW	36990 TQ	USBLS	5/07
	Iowa	Y	22800 FQ	29340 MW	36620 TQ	USBLS	5/07
	Des Moines-West Des Moines MSA, IA	Y	30380 FQ	33430 MW	36640 TQ	USBLS	5/07
	Iowa City MSA, IA	Y	27830 FQ	31560 MW	40480 TQ	USBLS	5/07
	Kansas	Y	21580 FQ	25450 MW	35270 TQ	USBLS	5/07
	Topeka MSA, KS	Y	17620 FQ	28460 MW	39150 TQ	USBLS	5/07
	Wichita MSA, KS	Y	23010 FQ	38490 MW	52600 TQ	USBLS	5/07
	Kentucky	Y	21768 FQ	25147 MW	31420 TQ	KYBLS	2008
	Lexington-Fayette MSA, KY	Y	25600 FQ	35240 MW	43130 TQ	USBLS	5/07
	Louisville-Jefferson County MSA, KY-IN	Y	22600 FQ	26950 MW	32560 TQ	USBLS	5/07
	Louisiana	H	11.31 FQ	15.82 MW	20.16 TQ	LABLS	1/08-3/08
	Baton Rouge MSA, LA	Y	35780 FQ	41820 MW	46940 TQ	USBLS	5/07
	New Orleans-Metairie-Kenner MSA, LA	Y	20500 FQ	22480 MW	27770 TQ	USBLS	5/07
	Maine	Y	26270 FQ	31350 MW	43790 TQ	USBLS	5/07
	Portland-South Portland-Biddeford MSA, ME	Y	24980 FQ	27100 MW	29190 TQ	USBLS	5/07
	Maryland	Y		30075 MW		MDBLS	3/08
	Baltimore-Towson MSA, MD	Y	23410 FQ	29570 MW	37570 TQ	USBLS	5/07
	Bethesda-Gaithersburg-Frederick PMSA, MD	Y	32490 FQ	43560 MW	49680 TQ	USBLS	5/07
	Massachusetts	Y	26900 FQ	31110 MW	36750 TQ	USBLS	5/07
	Boston-Cambridge-Quincy NECTA, MA	Y	27480 FQ	31010 MW	38240 TQ	USBLS	5/07
	New Bedford MSA, MA	Y	20590 FQ	27000 MW	32720 TQ	USBLS	5/07
	Worcester MSA, MA-CT	Y	26890 FQ	30370 MW	34630 TQ	USBLS	5/07
	Michigan	Y	25220 FQ	31810 MW	36990 TQ	USBLS	5/07
	Detroit-Warren-Livonia MSA, MI	Y	25690 FQ	32110 MW	37350 TQ	USBLS	5/07
	Grand Rapids-Wyoming MSA, MI	Y	29270 FQ	33920 MW	37220 TQ	USBLS	5/07
	Warren-Troy-Farmington Hills PMSA, MI	Y	25970 FQ	30910 MW	38990 TQ	USBLS	5/07
	Minnesota	Y	23470 FQ	31836 MW	39279 TQ	MNBLS	10/08-12/08
	Duluth-Superior MSA, MN-WI	Y	23594 FQ	26787 MW	33225 TQ	MNBLS	10/08-12/08
	Minneapolis-Saint Paul MSA, MN-WI	Y	29949 FQ	36936 MW	43882 TQ	MNBLS	10/08-12/08
	Rochester MSA, MN	Y	14397 FQ	15351 MW	16302 TQ	MNBLS	10/08-12/08
	Mississippi	Y	20630 FQ	24480 MW	29260 TQ	USBLS	5/07
	Jackson MSA, MS	Y	18890 FQ	26030 MW	29260 TQ	USBLS	5/07
	Missouri	Y	21290 FQ	27320 MW	32650 TQ	USBLS	5/07
	Kansas City MSA, MO-KS	Y	23260 FQ	28580 MW	34540 TQ	USBLS	5/07
	St. Louis MSA, MO-IL	Y	25710 FQ	31210 MW	36960 TQ	USBLS	5/07
	Montana	Y	25260 FQ	30280 MW	34500 TQ	USBLS	5/07
	Nebraska	Y	20770 FQ	25860 MW	30360 TQ	USBLS	5/07
	Omaha-Council Bluffs MSA, NE-IA	Y	23220 FQ	26950 MW	32360 TQ	USBLS	5/07
	Nevada	H	10.65 FQ	13.49 MW	16.78 TQ	NVBLS	5/08
	Las Vegas-Paradise MSA, NV	H	10.59 FQ	13.66 MW	17.01 TQ	NVBLS	5/08
	New Hampshire	H	12.06 AE	13.85 MW	15.76 AEX	NHBLS	6/08
	Nashua NECTA, NH-MA	Y	28340 FQ	32580 MW	36510 TQ	USBLS	5/07
	Portsmouth MSA, NH-ME	Y	23170 FQ	28960 MW	40280 TQ	USBLS	5/07
	New Jersey	Y	25940 FQ	35170 MW	42550 TQ	USBLS	5/07
	Camden PMSA, NJ	Y	23310 FQ	29580 MW	36050 TQ	USBLS	5/07
	Edison PMSA, NJ	Y	36800 FQ	40880 MW	44280 TQ	USBLS	5/07
	Newark-Union PMSA, NJ-PA	Y	23210 FQ	29250 MW	34260 TQ	USBLS	5/07
	New Mexico	Y	20600 FQ	22950 MW	25290 TQ	USBLS	5/07
	Albuquerque MSA, NM	Y	20530 FQ	22790 MW	25040 TQ	USBLS	5/07
	New York	Y	23920 FQ	30150 MW	37540 TQ	USBLS	5/07
	Albany-Schenectady-Troy MSA, NY	Y	26350 FQ	33200 MW	40590 TQ	USBLS	5/07
	Buffalo-Niagara Falls MSA, NY	Y	25090 FQ	32950 MW	41720 TQ	USBLS	5/07
	Nassau-Suffolk PMSA, NY	Y	20690 FQ	28300 MW	37390 TQ	USBLS	5/07

AE	Average entry wage	AW	Average wage paid	FQ	First quartile wage	LO	Lowest wage paid	MTC	Median total compensation	TCC Total cash compensation
AER	Average entry range	AWR	Average wage range	H	Hourly	LR	Low end range	MW	Median wage paid	TQ Third quartile wage
AEX	Average experienced wage	AXR	Average experienced range	HI	Highest wage paid	M	Monthly	MWR	Median wage range	W Weekly
ATC	Average total compensation	D	Daily	HR	High end range	MCC	Median cash compensation	S	See annotated source	Y Yearly

Occupation/Type/Industry	Location	Per	Low	Mid	High	Source	Date
Cutting and Slicing Machine Setter, Operator, and Tender	New York-Northern New Jersey-Long Island MSA, NY-NJ-PA	Y	24000 FQ	33570 MW	42390 TQ	USBLS	5/07
	North Carolina	Y	24720 FQ	33940 MW	54490 TQ	USBLS	5/07
	Charlotte-Gastonia-Concord MSA, NC-SC	Y	39630 FQ	56640 MW	66750 TQ	USBLS	5/07
	Raleigh-Cary MSA, NC	Y	26110 FQ	32020 MW	36140 TQ	USBLS	5/07
	North Dakota	Y	21900 FQ	26170 MW	30290 TQ	USBLS	5/07
	Fargo MSA, ND-MN	Y	24670 FQ	28660 MW	34090 TQ	USBLS	5/07
	Ohio	Y	23200 FQ	29350 MW	36800 TQ	USBLS	5/07
	Canton-Massillon MSA, OH	Y	20240 FQ	24510 MW	29460 TQ	USBLS	5/07
	Cincinnati-Middletown MSA, OH-KY-IN	Y	25200 FQ	30830 MW	36430 TQ	USBLS	5/07
	Cleveland-Elyria-Mentor MSA, OH	Y	20640 FQ	26470 MW	33780 TQ	USBLS	5/07
	Columbus MSA, OH	Y	21900 FQ	27460 MW	38070 TQ	USBLS	5/07
	Dayton MSA, OH	Y	30140 FQ	34810 MW	40000 TQ	USBLS	5/07
	Oklahoma	Y	21690 FQ	25960 MW	42460 TQ	USBLS	5/07
	Oklahoma City MSA, OK	Y	22670 FQ	26410 MW	30810 TQ	USBLS	5/07
	Tulsa MSA, OK	Y	20920 FQ	23420 MW	26770 TQ	USBLS	5/07
	Oregon	H	11.44 FQ	14.91 MW	20.21 TQ	ORBLS	5/08
	Portland-Vancouver-Beaverton MSA, OR-WA	Y	26460 FQ	32620 MW	42630 TQ	USBLS	5/07
	Salem MSA, OR	Y	17440 FQ	18650 MW	19830 TQ	USBLS	5/07
	Pennsylvania	Y	22940 FQ	28330 MW	34350 TQ	USBLS	5/07
	Allentown-Bethlehem-Easton MSA, PA-NJ	Y	20650 FQ	22770 MW	29260 TQ	USBLS	5/07
	Philadelphia-Camden-Wilmington MSA, PA-NJ-DE-MD	Y	25420 FQ	30550 MW	36680 TQ	USBLS	5/07
	Pittsburgh MSA, PA	Y	20810 FQ	25220 MW	33100 TQ	USBLS	5/07
	Rhode Island	Y	18160 FQ	21480 MW	31570 TQ	USBLS	5/07
	Providence-Fall River-Warwick MSA, RI-MA	Y	18600 FQ	24750 MW	32680 TQ	USBLS	5/07
	South Carolina	Y	23700 FQ	28860 MW	36710 TQ	USBLS	5/07
	Charleston-North Charleston MSA, SC	Y	23870 FQ	33870 MW	38800 TQ	USBLS	5/07
	Columbia MSA, SC	Y	22410 FQ	28220 MW	37280 TQ	USBLS	5/07
	Spartanburg MSA, SC	Y	22390 FQ	25430 MW	35260 TQ	USBLS	5/07
	South Dakota	Y	23564 FQ	28100 MW	33720 TQ	SDBLS	7/08-9/08
	Sioux Falls MSA, SD	Y	25895 FQ	28099 MW	30400 TQ	SDBLS	7/08-9/08
	Tennessee	Y	24500 FQ	30600 MW	38910 TQ	USBLS	5/07
	Knoxville MSA, TN	Y	24780 FQ	32750 MW	36660 TQ	USBLS	5/07
	Memphis MSA, TN-MS-AR	Y	26700 FQ	33470 MW	40010 TQ	USBLS	5/07
	Nashville-Davidson-Murfreesboro MSA, TN	Y	26590 FQ	31360 MW	37870 TQ	USBLS	5/07
	Texas	Y	17910 FQ	22020 MW	28480 TQ	USBLS	5/07
	Austin-Round Rock MSA, TX	Y	20440 FQ	24670 MW	32360 TQ	USBLS	5/07
	Dallas-Fort Worth-Arlington MSA, TX	Y	18530 FQ	22220 MW	27970 TQ	USBLS	5/07
	El Paso MSA, TX	Y	17880 FQ	20050 MW	23130 TQ	USBLS	5/07
	Houston-Sugar Land-Baytown MSA, TX	Y	17270 FQ	21080 MW	26230 TQ	USBLS	5/07
	San Antonio MSA, TX	Y	18780 FQ	23580 MW	30430 TQ	USBLS	5/07
	Utah	Y	21400 FQ	27110 MW	34740 TQ	USBLS	5/07
	Provo-Orem MSA, UT	Y	18730 FQ	23920 MW	31530 TQ	USBLS	5/07
	Salt Lake City MSA, UT	Y	23460 FQ	27510 MW	33520 TQ	USBLS	5/07
	Vermont	Y	22700 FQ	26460 MW	31290 TQ	USBLS	5/07
	Burlington-South Burlington MSA, VT	Y	23570 FQ	26880 MW	30330 TQ	USBLS	5/07
	Virginia	Y	25460 FQ	28400 MW	31350 TQ	USBLS	5/07
	Richmond MSA, VA	Y	25650 FQ	28140 MW	30630 TQ	USBLS	5/07
	Virginia Beach-Norfolk-Newport News MSA, VA-NC	Y	21780 FQ	28560 MW	40540 TQ	USBLS	5/07
	Washington	H	10.62 FQ	15.30 MW	21.97 TQ	WABLS	3/08
	Seattle-Tacoma-Bellevue MSA, WA	Y	27870 FQ	39530 MW	50200 TQ	USBLS	5/07
	West Virginia	Y	26353 FQ	29804 MW	35553 TQ	WVBLS	7/08-9/08
	Wisconsin	Y	26340 FQ	30860 MW	36690 TQ	USBLS	5/07
	Milwaukee-Waukesha-West Allis MSA, WI	Y	23770 FQ	31000 MW	37410 TQ	USBLS	5/07

AE Average entry wage	**AW** Average wage paid	**FQ** First quartile wage	**LO** Lowest wage paid	**MTC** Median total compensation	**TCC** Total cash compensation
AER Average entry range	**AWR** Average wage range	**H** Hourly	**LR** Low end range	**MW** Median wage paid	**TQ** Third quartile wage
AEX Average experienced wage	**AXR** Average experienced range	**HI** Highest wage paid	**M** Monthly	**MWR** Median wage range	**W** Weekly
ATC Average total compensation	**D** Daily	**HR** High end range	**MCC** Median cash compensation	**S** See annotated source	**Y** Yearly

Occupation/Type/Industry	Location	Per	Low	Mid	High	Source	Date
Cutting and Slicing Machine Setter, Operator, and Tender	Racine MSA, WI	Y	29520 FQ	33660 MW	37920 TQ	USBLS	5/07
	Wyoming	Y	33638 FQ	36370 MW	39102 TQ	WYBLS	9/08
	Puerto Rico	Y	14400 FQ	17460 MW	22380 TQ	USBLS	5/07
	San Juan-Caguas-Guaynabo MSA, PR	Y	14750 FQ	17750 MW	23390 TQ	USBLS	5/07
Cytogenetic Technologist	United States	Y		41900 AW		HCC03	2009
Dairy Processing Plant Operator							
Department of Corrections	Ohio	H	16.78 LO		19.88 HI	ODAS	2008
Dairy Worker							
State Government	Ohio	H	14.36 LO		17.03 HI	ODAS	2008
Dancer	Alabama	H	5.87 FQ	6.56 MW	7.26 TQ	USBLS	5/07
	California	H	8.35 FQ	9.29 MW	14.01 TQ	CABLS	1/08-3/08
	Colorado	H	7.05 FQ	7.26 MW	7.69 TQ	USBLS	5/07
	Connecticut	H	13.20 AE	14.99 MW		CTBLS	1/08-3/08
	District of Columbia	H	7.41 FQ	18.59 MW	54.74 TQ	USBLS	5/07
	Florida	H	6.99 FQ	7.46 MW	15.79 TQ	USBLS	5/07
	Georgia	H	6.49 FQ	7.64 MW	10.40 TQ	USBLS	5/07
	Hawaii	H	7.69 FQ	14.84 MW	25.30 TQ	USBLS	5/07
	Illinois	H	7.83 FQ	11.13 MW	15.90 TQ	USBLS	5/07
	Indiana	H	7.35 FQ	11.52 MW	14.14 TQ	USBLS	5/07
	Iowa	H	9.92 FQ	14.04 MW	19.73 TQ	USBLS	5/07
	Louisiana	H	7.48 FQ	9.55 MW	11.86 TQ	LABLS	1/08-3/08
	Maryland	H		34.50 MW		MDBLS	3/08
	Michigan	H	8.87 FQ	11.04 MW	13.57 TQ	USBLS	5/07
	Missouri	H	9.69 FQ	13.64 MW	17.06 TQ	USBLS	5/07
	Montana	H	6.76 FQ	7.36 MW	9.17 TQ	USBLS	5/07
	Nevada	H	17.01 FQ	22.46 MW	29.35 TQ	NVBLS	5/08
	New Jersey	H	12.12 FQ	18.26 MW	21.24 TQ	USBLS	5/07
	New York	H	8.00 FQ	14.03 MW	24.08 TQ	USBLS	5/07
	Ohio	H	8.03 FQ	11.90 MW	14.52 TQ	USBLS	5/07
	South Carolina	H	10.88 FQ	14.04 MW	15.98 TQ	USBLS	5/07
	Tennessee	H	7.03 FQ	8.62 MW	10.63 TQ	USBLS	5/07
	Texas	H	7.28 FQ	8.33 MW	10.50 TQ	USBLS	5/07
	Utah	H	9.19 FQ	10.63 MW	16.85 TQ	USBLS	5/07
	Virginia	H	7.83 FQ	8.32 MW	8.80 TQ	USBLS	5/07
	Washington	H	11.01 FQ	13.60 MW	27.52 TQ	WABLS	3/08
	West Virginia	H	7.57 FQ	12.34 MW	15.99 TQ	WVBLS	7/08-9/08
Data Entry Keyer	Alabama	Y	19700 FQ	23800 MW	29660 TQ	USBLS	5/07
	Birmingham-Hoover MSA, AL	Y	22510 FQ	27190 MW	34050 TQ	USBLS	5/07
	Mobile MSA, AL	Y	17230 FQ	19040 MW	23530 TQ	USBLS	5/07
	Alaska	Y	26490 FQ	30230 MW	42790 TQ	USBLS	5/07
	Anchorage MSA, AK	Y	25900 FQ	29010 MW	42290 TQ	USBLS	5/07
	Arizona	Y	23360 FQ	27590 MW	32000 TQ	USBLS	5/07
	Phoenix-Mesa-Scottsdale MSA, AZ	Y	24200 FQ	28100 MW	32780 TQ	USBLS	5/07
	Tucson MSA, AZ	Y	22410 FQ	25450 MW	29610 TQ	USBLS	5/07
	Arkansas	Y	19360 FQ	22730 MW	27510 TQ	USBLS	5/07
	Little Rock-North Little Rock MSA, AR	Y	20590 FQ	23550 MW	28130 TQ	USBLS	5/07
	California	H	10.96 FQ	13.37 MW	16.00 TQ	CABLS	1/08-3/08
	Fresno MSA, CA	H	11.66 FQ	13.79 MW	15.91 TQ	CABLS	1/08-3/08
	Los Angeles-Long Beach-Glendale PMSA, CA	H	10.69 FQ	12.80 MW	15.37 TQ	CABLS	1/08-3/08
	Oakland-Fremont-Hayward MSA, CA	H	13.08 FQ	15.19 MW	18.07 TQ	CABLS	1/08-3/08
	Riverside-San Bernardino-Ontario MSA, CA	H	10.70 FQ	12.52 MW	15.41 TQ	CABLS	1/08-3/08
	Sacramento-Arden Arcade-Roseville MSA, CA	H	12.42 FQ	14.55 MW	17.41 TQ	CABLS	1/08-3/08
	San Diego-Carlsbad-San Marcos MSA, CA	H	11.15 FQ	13.42 MW	15.73 TQ	CABLS	1/08-3/08
	San Francisco-San Mateo-Redwood PMSA, CA	H	11.86 FQ	14.36 MW	17.52 TQ	CABLS	1/08-3/08
	San Jose-Sunnyvale-Santa Clara MSA, CA	H	10.56 FQ	13.12 MW	16.57 TQ	CABLS	1/08-3/08

AE Average entry wage	AW Average wage paid	FQ First quartile wage	LO Lowest wage paid	MTC Median total compensation	TCC Total cash compensation
AER Average entry range	AWR Average wage range	H Hourly	LR Low end range	MW Median wage paid	TQ Third quartile wage
AEX Average experienced wage	AXR Average experienced range	HI Highest wage paid	M Monthly	MWR Median wage range	W Weekly
ATC Average total compensation	D Daily	HR High end range	MCC Median cash compensation	S See annotated source	Y Yearly

Data Entry Keyer

Occupation/Type/Industry	Location	Per	Low	Mid	High	Source	Date
Data Entry Keyer	Santa Ana-Anaheim-Irvine PMSA, CA	Y	21820 FQ	27480 MW	33550 TQ	USBLS	5/07
	Colorado	Y	21130 FQ	25470 MW	30100 TQ	USBLS	5/07
	Colorado Springs MSA, CO	Y	20660 FQ	23010 MW	26010 TQ	USBLS	5/07
	Denver-Aurora MSA, CO	Y	21670 FQ	26340 MW	30920 TQ	USBLS	5/07
	Connecticut	H	10.49 AE	14.08 MW		CTBLS	1/08-3/08
	Bridgeport-Stamford-Norwalk MSA, CT	Y	24910 FQ	28520 MW	33070 TQ	USBLS	5/07
	Hartford-West Hartford-East Hartford MSA, CT	Y	24050 FQ	29120 MW	37190 TQ	USBLS	5/07
	Delaware	Y	22030 FQ	25550 MW	30520 TQ	USBLS	5/07
	Wilmington PMSA, DE-MD-NJ	Y	22890 FQ	26300 MW	31340 TQ	USBLS	5/07
	District of Columbia	Y	27490 FQ	34450 MW	42230 TQ	USBLS	5/07
	Washington-Arlington-Alexandria MSA, DC-VA-MD-WV	Y	24140 FQ	29410 MW	36100 TQ	USBLS	5/07
	Florida	Y	20650 FQ	24330 MW	29410 TQ	USBLS	5/07
	Fort Lauderdale-Pompano Beach-Deerfield Beach PMSA, FL	Y	21070 FQ	26230 MW	31000 TQ	USBLS	5/07
	Jacksonville MSA, FL	Y	19290 FQ	23240 MW	28200 TQ	USBLS	5/07
	Miami-Fort Lauderdale-Miami Beach MSA, FL	Y	20650 FQ	24580 MW	29790 TQ	USBLS	5/07
	Orlando-Kissimmee MSA, FL	Y	18760 FQ	22760 MW	27400 TQ	USBLS	5/07
	Sarasota-Bradenton-Venice MSA, FL	Y	20810 FQ	26160 MW	30860 TQ	USBLS	5/07
	Tampa-St. Petersburg-Clearwater MSA, FL	Y	22860 FQ	27000 MW	31540 TQ	USBLS	5/07
	West Palm Beach-Boca Raton-Boynton Beach PMSA, FL	Y	21040 FQ	24180 MW	29550 TQ	USBLS	5/07
	Georgia	Y	21800 FQ	25640 MW	30670 TQ	USBLS	5/07
	Atlanta-Sandy Springs-Marietta MSA, GA	Y	22560 FQ	26510 MW	31600 TQ	USBLS	5/07
	Hawaii	Y	21290 FQ	26150 MW	30730 TQ	USBLS	5/07
	Honolulu MSA, HI	Y	20810 FQ	25790 MW	30760 TQ	USBLS	5/07
	Idaho	Y	18150 FQ	23690 MW	28610 TQ	USBLS	5/07
	Boise City-Nampa MSA, ID	Y	20310 FQ	26050 MW	30240 TQ	USBLS	5/07
	Pocatello MSA, ID	Y	16700 FQ	18690 MW	25410 TQ	USBLS	5/07
	Illinois	Y	19930 FQ	24740 MW	30070 TQ	USBLS	5/07
	Chicago-Naperville-Joliet MSA, IL-IN-WI	Y	20460 FQ	25240 MW	30220 TQ	USBLS	5/07
	Indiana	Y	20680 FQ	24970 MW	29130 TQ	USBLS	5/07
	Evansville MSA, IN-KY	Y	18550 FQ	21920 MW	26140 TQ	USBLS	5/07
	Gary PMSA, IN	Y	18110 FQ	22540 MW	27240 TQ	USBLS	5/07
	Indianapolis-Carmel MSA, IN	Y	21170 FQ	24960 MW	29050 TQ	USBLS	5/07
	Iowa	Y	19460 FQ	23060 MW	27920 TQ	USBLS	5/07
	Des Moines-West Des Moines MSA, IA	Y	21210 FQ	23730 MW	27980 TQ	USBLS	5/07
	Waterloo-Cedar Falls MSA, IA	Y	14400 FQ	15890 MW	22980 TQ	USBLS	5/07
	Kansas	Y	22610 FQ	26750 MW	30480 TQ	USBLS	5/07
	Wichita MSA, KS	Y	26150 FQ	28970 MW	32650 TQ	USBLS	5/07
	Kentucky	Y	20626 FQ	25029 MW	30371 TQ	KYBLS	2008
	Louisville-Jefferson County MSA, KY-IN	Y	22350 FQ	26550 MW	31310 TQ	USBLS	5/07
	Owensboro MSA, KY	Y	21280 FQ	23990 MW	28530 TQ	USBLS	5/07
	Louisiana	H	9.01 FQ	10.58 MW	12.35 TQ	LABLS	1/08-3/08
	Baton Rouge MSA, LA	Y	19620 FQ	22800 MW	26190 TQ	USBLS	5/07
	Lafayette MSA, LA	Y	18600 FQ	21650 MW	25000 TQ	USBLS	5/07
	New Orleans-Metairie-Kenner MSA, LA	Y	19680 FQ	22780 MW	26820 TQ	USBLS	5/07
	Maine	Y	20650 FQ	23900 MW	28760 TQ	USBLS	5/07
	Portland-South Portland-Biddeford MSA, ME	Y	22060 FQ	25860 MW	29600 TQ	USBLS	5/07
	Maryland	Y		27575 MW		MDBLS	3/08
	Baltimore-Towson MSA, MD	Y	22620 FQ	27770 MW	33500 TQ	USBLS	5/07
	Bethesda-Gaithersburg-Frederick PMSA, MD	Y	21460 FQ	27780 MW	33070 TQ	USBLS	5/07
	Hagerstown-Martinsburg MSA, MD-WV	Y	17420 FQ	19820 MW	23850 TQ	USBLS	5/07
	Massachusetts	Y	24050 FQ	29000 MW	35040 TQ	USBLS	5/07
	Barnstable Town MSA, MA	Y	31590 FQ	34030 MW	36500 TQ	USBLS	5/07

AE	Average entry wage	AW	Average wage paid	FQ	First quartile wage	LO	Lowest wage paid	MTC	Median total compensation	TCC	Total cash compensation
AER	Average entry range	AWR	Average wage range	H	Hourly	LR	Low end range	MW	Median wage paid	TQ	Third quartile wage
AEX	Average experienced wage	AXR	Average experienced range	HI	Highest wage paid	M	Monthly	MWR	Median wage range	W	Weekly
ATC	Average total compensation	D	Daily	HR	High end range	MCC	Median cash compensation	S	See annotated source	Y	Yearly

Data Entry Keyer

Occupation/Type/Industry	Location	Per	Low	Mid	High	Source	Date
Data Entry Keyer	Boston-Cambridge-Quincy NECTA, MA	Y	23680 FQ	28880 MW	35420 TQ	USBLS	5/07
	Worcester MSA, MA-CT	Y	25640 FQ	28600 MW	31590 TQ	USBLS	5/07
	Michigan	Y	22090 FQ	27040 MW	32340 TQ	USBLS	5/07
	Detroit-Warren-Livonia MSA, MI	Y	23120 FQ	28230 MW	33380 TQ	USBLS	5/07
	Grand Rapids-Wyoming MSA, MI	Y	22090 FQ	26840 MW	30230 TQ	USBLS	5/07
	Warren-Troy-Farmington Hills PMSA, MI	Y	23030 FQ	27890 MW	32750 TQ	USBLS	5/07
	Minnesota	Y	23959 FQ	28236 MW	32212 TQ	MNBLS	10/08-12/08
	Duluth-Superior MSA, MN-WI	Y	22314 FQ	25770 MW	29256 TQ	MNBLS	10/08-12/08
	Minneapolis-Saint Paul MSA, MN-WI	Y	25260 FQ	29027 MW	32930 TQ	MNBLS	10/08-12/08
	Rochester MSA, MN	Y	26229 FQ	31494 MW	38005 TQ	MNBLS	10/08-12/08
	Mississippi	Y	18110 FQ	21270 MW	25110 TQ	USBLS	5/07
	Jackson MSA, MS	Y	18250 FQ	20750 MW	25440 TQ	USBLS	5/07
	Missouri	Y	20570 FQ	24110 MW	29150 TQ	USBLS	5/07
	Jefferson City MSA, MO	Y	16810 FQ	19280 MW	22990 TQ	USBLS	5/07
	Kansas City MSA, MO-KS	Y	22720 FQ	26650 MW	31000 TQ	USBLS	5/07
	St. Joseph MSA, MO-KS	Y	20680 FQ	22310 MW	23930 TQ	USBLS	5/07
	St. Louis MSA, MO-IL*	Y	20650 FQ	24250 MW	28900 TQ	USBLS	5/07
	Montana	Y	18290 FQ	21670 MW	25680 TQ	USBLS	5/07
	Billings MSA, MT	Y	17700 FQ	20540 MW	24070 TQ	USBLS	5/07
	Nebraska	Y	19060 FQ	22300 MW	25540 TQ	USBLS	5/07
	Omaha-Council Bluffs MSA, NE-IA	Y	19800 FQ	23090 MW	27920 TQ	USBLS	5/07
	Nevada	H	10.33 FQ	12.18 MW	15.19 TQ	NVBLS	5/08
	Las Vegas-Paradise MSA, NV	H	10.68 FQ	12.74 MW	15.53 TQ	NVBLS	5/08
	New Hampshire	H	9.96 AE	13.01 MW	14.73 AEX	NHBLS	6/08
	Manchester MSA, NH	Y	23580 FQ	28260 MW	34500 TQ	USBLS	5/07
	Nashua NECTA, NH-MA	Y	25300 FQ	27680 MW	30360 TQ	USBLS	5/07
	Rochester-Dover MSA, NH-ME	Y	23240 FQ	26380 MW	29260 TQ	USBLS	5/07
	New Jersey	Y	22640 FQ	27500 MW	33570 TQ	USBLS	5/07
	Camden PMSA, NJ	Y	22620 FQ	26570 MW	32270 TQ	USBLS	5/07
	Edison PMSA, NJ	Y	22540 FQ	27810 MW	34030 TQ	USBLS	5/07
	Newark-Union PMSA, NJ-PA	Y	22490 FQ	27640 MW	34450 TQ	USBLS	5/07
	New Mexico	Y	16820 FQ	20920 MW	25740 TQ	USBLS	5/07
	Albuquerque MSA, NM	Y	17020 FQ	21830 MW	27480 TQ	USBLS	5/07
	Las Cruces MSA, NM	Y	16300 FQ	19140 MW	22720 TQ	USBLS	5/07
	New York	Y	21380 FQ	26210 MW	32320 TQ	USBLS	5/07
	Albany-Schenectady-Troy MSA, NY	Y	22100 FQ	25340 MW	31040 TQ	USBLS	5/07
	Binghamton MSA, NY	Y	17170 FQ	25610 MW	29640 TQ	USBLS	5/07
	Buffalo-Niagara Falls MSA, NY	Y	19590 FQ	23360 MW	30150 TQ	USBLS	5/07
	Kingston MSA, NY	Y	16120 FQ	17240 MW	18350 TQ	USBLS	5/07
	Nassau-Suffolk PMSA, NY	Y	22740 FQ	27530 MW	33590 TQ	USBLS	5/07
	New York-Northern New Jersey-Long Island MSA, NY-NJ-PA	Y	22360 FQ	27420 MW	33710 TQ	USBLS	5/07
	North Carolina	Y	21250 FQ	24830 MW	29310 TQ	USBLS	5/07
	Charlotte-Gastonia-Concord MSA, NC-SC	Y	22060 FQ	25860 MW	30320 TQ	USBLS	5/07
	Raleigh-Cary MSA, NC	Y	22400 FQ	25890 MW	30430 TQ	USBLS	5/07
	North Dakota	Y	18070 FQ	20870 MW	24370 TQ	USBLS	5/07
	Fargo MSA, ND-MN	Y	20980 FQ	24030 MW	27780 TQ	USBLS	5/07
	Ohio	Y	20360 FQ	24110 MW	29150 TQ	USBLS	5/07
	Cincinnati-Middletown MSA, OH-KY-IN	Y	22470 FQ	26310 MW	31300 TQ	USBLS	5/07
	Cleveland-Elyria-Mentor MSA, OH	Y	19360 FQ	23660 MW	28670 TQ	USBLS	5/07
	Columbus MSA, OH	Y	21350 FQ	25130 MW	29930 TQ	USBLS	5/07
	Dayton MSA, OH	Y	20590 FQ	23160 MW	26910 TQ	USBLS	5/07
	Springfield MSA, OH	Y	15860 FQ	20770 MW	25420 TQ	USBLS	5/07
	Oklahoma	Y	17920 FQ	21880 MW	26880 TQ	USBLS	5/07
	Oklahoma City MSA, OK	Y	18240 FQ	22270 MW	27060 TQ	USBLS	5/07
	Tulsa MSA, OK	Y	18560 FQ	22500 MW	28570 TQ	USBLS	5/07
	Oregon	H	10.84 FQ	12.69 MW	15.16 TQ	ORBLS	5/08
	Portland-Vancouver-Beaverton MSA, OR-WA	Y	22380 FQ	26480 MW	31570 TQ	USBLS	5/07

AE	Average entry wage	AW	Average wage paid	FQ	First quartile wage
AER	Average entry range	AWR	Average wage range	H	Hourly
AEX	Average experienced wage	AXR	Average experienced range	HI	Highest wage paid
ATC	Average total compensation	D	Daily	HR	High end range

LO	Lowest wage paid	MTC	Median total compensation
LR	Low end range	MW	Median wage paid
M	Monthly	MWR	Median wage range
MCC	Median cash compensation	S	See annotated source

TCC	Total cash compensation
TQ	Third quartile wage
W	Weekly
Y	Yearly

Occupation/Type/Industry	Location	Per	Low	Mid	High	Source	Date
Data Entry Keyer	Pennsylvania	Y	20850 FQ	24720 MW	30200 TQ	USBLS	5/07
	Allentown-Bethlehem-Easton MSA, PA-NJ	Y	20490 FQ	23970 MW	31860 TQ	USBLS	5/07
	Philadelphia-Camden-Wilmington MSA, PA-NJ-DE-MD	Y	22390 FQ	26830 MW	31940 TQ	USBLS	5/07
	Pittsburgh MSA, PA	Y	21390 FQ	24790 MW	30270 TQ	USBLS	5/07
	Rhode Island	Y	21640 FQ	27370 MW	33620 TQ	USBLS	5/07
	Providence-Fall River-Warwick MSA, RI-MA	Y	21630 FQ	27170 MW	33370 TQ	USBLS	5/07
	South Carolina	Y	19310 FQ	22790 MW	27260 TQ	USBLS	5/07
	Charleston-North Charleston MSA, SC	Y	20880 FQ	23340 MW	27410 TQ	USBLS	5/07
	Columbia MSA, SC	Y	18670 FQ	22180 MW	27240 TQ	USBLS	5/07
	South Dakota	Y	19289 FQ	24479 MW	28154 TQ	SDBLS	7/08-9/08
	Sioux Falls MSA, SD	Y	21822 FQ	25944 MW	29156 TQ	SDBLS	7/08-9/08
	Tennessee	Y	19550 FQ	23800 MW	28670 TQ	USBLS	5/07
	Clarksville MSA, TN-KY	Y	21760 FQ	26750 MW	33560 TQ	USBLS	5/07
	Memphis MSA, TN-MS-AR	Y	18840 FQ	23030 MW	26800 TQ	USBLS	5/07
	Nashville-Davidson-Murfreesboro MSA, TN	Y	21580 FQ	24800 MW	29850 TQ	USBLS	5/07
	Texas	Y	20320 FQ	24390 MW	29070 TQ	USBLS	5/07
	Austin-Round Rock MSA, TX	Y	22340 FQ	26360 MW	30540 TQ	USBLS	5/07
	Dallas-Fort Worth-Arlington MSA, TX	Y	21740 FQ	25850 MW	30140 TQ	USBLS	5/07
	El Paso MSA, TX	Y	14380 FQ	19570 MW	25540 TQ	USBLS	5/07
	Houston-Sugar Land-Baytown MSA, TX	Y	21090 FQ	24560 MW	28890 TQ	USBLS	5/07
	Midland MSA, TX	Y	16360 FQ	19600 MW	22620 TQ	USBLS	5/07
	San Antonio MSA, TX	Y	20080 FQ	22850 MW	26040 TQ	USBLS	5/07
	Utah	Y	22050 FQ	26870 MW	30350 TQ	USBLS	5/07
	Salt Lake City MSA, UT	Y	23430 FQ	27570 MW	30740 TQ	USBLS	5/07
	Vermont	Y	24190 FQ	27550 MW	30240 TQ	USBLS	5/07
	Burlington-South Burlington MSA, VT	Y	25550 FQ	28210 MW	30600 TQ	USBLS	5/07
	Virginia	Y	20830 FQ	24830 MW	30210 TQ	USBLS	5/07
	Richmond MSA, VA	Y	21140 FQ	23580 MW	27850 TQ	USBLS	5/07
	Virginia Beach-Norfolk-Newport News MSA, VA-NC	Y	18510 FQ	22260 MW	25780 TQ	USBLS	5/07
	Washington	H	11.10 FQ	13.39 MW	16.54 TQ	WABLS	3/08
	Seattle-Tacoma-Bellevue MSA, WA	Y	23570 FQ	28520 MW	35100 TQ	USBLS	5/07
	West Virginia	Y	20269 FQ	24795 MW	29842 TQ	WVBLS	7/08-9/08
	Charleston MSA, WV	Y	24540 FQ	27630 MW	30440 TQ	USBLS	5/07
	Wisconsin	Y	20940 FQ	23800 MW	28270 TQ	USBLS	5/07
	Green Bay MSA, WI	Y	19400 FQ	23940 MW	30060 TQ	USBLS	5/07
	Milwaukee-Waukesha-West Allis MSA, WI	Y	21130 FQ	24010 MW	28830 TQ	USBLS	5/07
	Wyoming	Y	18821 FQ	22785 MW	25253 TQ	WYBLS	9/08
	Cheyenne MSA, WY	Y	20154 FQ	23248 MW	25236 TQ	WYBLS	9/08
	Puerto Rico	Y	13580 FQ	16320 MW	21290 TQ	USBLS	5/07
	San Juan-Caguas-Guaynabo MSA, PR	Y	13710 FQ	16780 MW	21840 TQ	USBLS	5/07
	Virgin Islands	Y	18590 FQ	21710 MW	25210 TQ	USBLS	5/07
	Guam	Y	15980 FQ	19240 MW	23690 TQ	USBLS	5/07
Data Entry Technician							
State Government	Delaware	Y	23283 LO		34925 HI	AFT02	3/1/08
Data Librarian							
Department of Information Technology	New Hampshire	Y			36558 HI	NHUL03	2008
Database Administrator	Alabama	Y	41280 FQ	56260 MW	76330 TQ	USBLS	5/07
	Birmingham-Hoover MSA, AL	Y	42700 FQ	62130 MW	82100 TQ	USBLS	5/07
	Alaska	Y	53880 FQ	70180 MW	85500 TQ	USBLS	5/07
	Anchorage MSA, AK	Y	58360 FQ	75010 MW	91720 TQ	USBLS	5/07
	Arizona	Y	41780 FQ	60600 MW	78700 TQ	USBLS	5/07
	Phoenix-Mesa-Scottsdale MSA, AZ	Y	41560 FQ	60700 MW	79710 TQ	USBLS	5/07
	Tucson MSA, AZ	Y	46690 FQ	60780 MW	74850 TQ	USBLS	5/07
	Arkansas	Y	43740 FQ	57960 MW	76500 TQ	USBLS	5/07

AE	Average entry wage	AW	Average wage paid	FQ	First quartile wage	LO	Lowest wage paid	MTC	Median total compensation	TCC	Total cash compensation
AER	Average entry range	AWR	Average wage range	H	Hourly	LR	Low end range	MW	Median wage paid	TQ	Third quartile wage
AEX	Average experienced wage	AXR	Average experienced range	HI	Highest wage paid	M	Monthly	MWR	Median wage range	W	Weekly
ATC	Average total compensation	D	Daily	HR	High end range	MCC	Median cash compensation	S	See annotated source	Y	Yearly

Occupation/Type/Industry	Location	Per	Low	Mid	High	Source	Date
Database Administrator	Fayetteville-Springdale-Rogers MSA, AR-MO	Y	45040 FQ	55250 MW	66920 TQ	USBLS	5/07
	Little Rock-North Little Rock MSA, AR	Y	46750 FQ	62190 MW	87620 TQ	USBLS	5/07
	California	H	25.57 FQ	36.04 MW	47.76 TQ	CABLS	1/08-3/08
	Los Angeles-Long Beach-Glendale PMSA, CA	H	25.82 FQ	35.67 MW	46.48 TQ	CABLS	1/08-3/08
	Oakland-Fremont-Hayward MSA, CA	H	30.84 FQ	42.17 MW	51.66 TQ	CABLS	1/08-3/08
	Riverside-San Bernardino-Ontario MSA, CA	H	23.74 FQ	31.46 MW	42.36 TQ	CABLS	1/08-3/08
	Sacramento-Arden Arcade-Roseville MSA, CA	H	22.96 FQ	31.04 MW	41.82 TQ	CABLS	1/08-3/08
	San Diego-Carlsbad-San Marcos MSA, CA	H	19.37 FQ	29.87 MW	42.53 TQ	CABLS	1/08-3/08
	San Francisco-San Mateo-Redwood PMSA, CA	H	32.17 FQ	45.13 MW	56.61 TQ	CABLS	1/08-3/08
	San Jose-Sunnyvale-Santa Clara MSA, CA	H	31.43 FQ	42.97 MW	55.42 TQ	CABLS	1/08-3/08
	Santa Ana-Anaheim-Irvine PMSA, CA	Y	48930 FQ	69230 MW	91380 TQ	USBLS	5/07
	Colorado	Y	54670 FQ	70900 MW	89830 TQ	USBLS	5/07
	Denver-Aurora MSA, CO	Y	55100 FQ	73940 MW	93250 TQ	USBLS	5/07
	Connecticut	H	25.25 AE	37.26 MW		CTBLS	1/08-3/08
	Bridgeport-Stamford-Norwalk MSA, CT	Y	58470 FQ	72070 MW	92030 TQ	USBLS	5/07
	Hartford-West Hartford-East Hartford MSA, CT	Y	59150 FQ	76050 MW	94270 TQ	USBLS	5/07
	Delaware	Y	54790 FQ	69410 MW	95150 TQ	USBLS	5/07
	Wilmington PMSA, DE-MD-NJ	Y	56380 FQ	71390 MW	97210 TQ	USBLS	5/07
	District of Columbia	Y	50380 FQ	64300 MW	81820 TQ	USBLS	5/07
	Washington-Arlington-Alexandria MSA, DC-VA-MD-WV	Y	56080 FQ	75880 MW	98540 TQ	USBLS	5/07
	Florida	Y	47410 FQ	61410 MW	78200 TQ	USBLS	5/07
	Fort Lauderdale-Pompano Beach-Deerfield Beach PMSA, FL	Y	48350 FQ	58850 MW	71740 TQ	USBLS	5/07
	Jacksonville MSA, FL	Y	41430 FQ	54080 MW	75810 TQ	USBLS	5/07
	Miami-Fort Lauderdale-Miami Beach MSA, FL	Y	51760 FQ	62540 MW	79200 TQ	USBLS	5/07
	Orlando-Kissimmee MSA, FL	Y	46840 FQ	62810 MW	77990 TQ	USBLS	5/07
	Tampa-St. Petersburg-Clearwater MSA, FL	Y	47750 FQ	62210 MW	79740 TQ	USBLS	5/07
	West Palm Beach-Boca Raton-Boynton Beach PMSA, FL	Y	53020 FQ	70010 MW	87460 TQ	USBLS	5/07
	Georgia	Y	55190 FQ	71240 MW	88820 TQ	USBLS	5/07
	Atlanta-Sandy Springs-Marietta MSA, GA	Y	57230 FQ	73190 MW	90670 TQ	USBLS	5/07
	Hawaii	Y	46410 FQ	57580 MW	72840 TQ	USBLS	5/07
	Honolulu MSA, HI	Y	46380 FQ	57420 MW	72320 TQ	USBLS	5/07
	Idaho	Y	48640 FQ	61800 MW	85320 TQ	USBLS	5/07
	Boise City-Nampa MSA, ID	Y	50590 FQ	67050 MW	90400 TQ	USBLS	5/07
	Illinois	Y	53080 FQ	68840 MW	90780 TQ	USBLS	5/07
	Chicago-Naperville-Joliet MSA, IL-IN-WI	Y	53630 FQ	69910 MW	91320 TQ	USBLS	5/07
	Rockford MSA, IL	Y	41220 FQ	54560 MW	72350 TQ	USBLS	5/07
	Indiana	Y	43190 FQ	60300 MW	76650 TQ	USBLS	5/07
	Gary PMSA, IN	Y	31940 FQ	44290 MW	56030 TQ	USBLS	5/07
	Indianapolis-Carmel MSA, IN	Y	46330 FQ	64160 MW	79860 TQ	USBLS	5/07
	Iowa	Y	44210 FQ	58670 MW	75450 TQ	USBLS	5/07
	Des Moines-West Des Moines MSA, IA	Y	48580 FQ	68950 MW	88220 TQ	USBLS	5/07
	Kansas	Y	46950 FQ	58650 MW	74310 TQ	USBLS	5/07
	Lawrence MSA, KS	Y	30560 FQ	50280 MW	74290 TQ	USBLS	5/07
	Wichita MSA, KS	Y	45160 FQ	57010 MW	73170 TQ	USBLS	5/07
	Kentucky	Y	50688 FQ	63215 MW	78950 TQ	KYBLS	2008
	Louisville-Jefferson County MSA, KY-IN	Y	49170 FQ	61900 MW	81530 TQ	USBLS	5/07
	Louisiana	H	21.21 FQ	27.48 MW	36.85 TQ	LABLS	1/08-3/08
	Baton Rouge MSA, LA	Y	43330 FQ	52660 MW	67920 TQ	USBLS	5/07

AE	Average entry wage	AW	Average wage paid	FQ	First quartile wage	LO	Lowest wage paid	MTC	Median total compensation	TCC	Total cash compensation
AER	Average entry range	AWR	Average wage range	H	Hourly	LR	Low end range	MW	Median wage paid	TQ	Third quartile wage
AEX	Average experienced wage	AXR	Average experienced range	HI	Highest wage paid	M	Monthly	MWR	Median wage range	W	Weekly
ATC	Average total compensation	D	Daily	HR	High end range	MCC	Median cash compensation	S	See annotated source	Y	Yearly

Database Administrator

Occupation/Type/Industry	Location	Per	Low	Mid	High	Source	Date
Database Administrator	New Orleans-Metairie-Kenner MSA, LA	Y	49820 FQ	63190 MW	82500 TQ	USBLS	5/07
	Maine	Y	44390 FQ	60260 MW	77990 TQ	USBLS	5/07
	Portland-South Portland-Biddeford MSA, ME	Y	54710 FQ	69930 MW	87440 TQ	USBLS	5/07
	Maryland	Y		80100 MW		MDBLS	3/08
	Baltimore-Towson MSA, MD	Y	62570 FQ	83020 MW	108300 TQ	USBLS	5/07
	Bethesda-Gaithersburg-Frederick PMSA, MD	Y	52980 FQ	75620 MW	97450 TQ	USBLS	5/07
	Massachusetts	Y	54220 FQ	72950 MW	92980 TQ	USBLS	5/07
	Boston-Cambridge-Quincy NECTA, MA	Y	56080 FQ	75090 MW	95070 TQ	USBLS	5/07
	Worcester MSA, MA-CT	Y	48500 FQ	60070 MW	81210 TQ	USBLS	5/07
	Michigan	Y	48250 FQ	64130 MW	81680 TQ	USBLS	5/07
	Detroit-Warren-Livonia MSA, MI	Y	51900 FQ	68660 MW	84750 TQ	USBLS	5/07
	Flint MSA, MI	Y	43660 FQ	51340 MW	73470 TQ	USBLS	5/07
	Grand Rapids-Wyoming MSA, MI	Y	43500 FQ	63190 MW	84680 TQ	USBLS	5/07
	Warren-Troy-Farmington Hills PMSA, MI	Y	54010 FQ	69890 MW	85330 TQ	USBLS	5/07
	Minnesota	Y	54916 FQ	71540 MW	91502 TQ	MNBLS	10/08-12/08
	Duluth-Superior MSA, MN-WI	Y	55596 FQ	64824 MW	76468 TQ	MNBLS	10/08-12/08
	Minneapolis-Saint Paul MSA, MN-WI	Y	56234 FQ	72880 MW	92800 TQ	MNBLS	10/08-12/08
	Rochester MSA, MN	Y	49989 FQ	70367 MW	89241 TQ	MNBLS	10/08-12/08
	Mississippi	Y	40260 FQ	51330 MW	62730 TQ	USBLS	5/07
	Jackson MSA, MS	Y	44020 FQ	53360 MW	61980 TQ	USBLS	5/07
	Missouri	Y	39100 FQ	55200 MW	73070 TQ	USBLS	5/07
	Kansas City MSA, MO-KS	Y	49330 FQ	62110 MW	77200 TQ	USBLS	5/07
	St. Louis MSA, MO-IL	Y	38900 FQ	55340 MW	73780 TQ	USBLS	5/07
	Montana	Y	37860 FQ	47170 MW	58890 TQ	USBLS	5/07
	Nebraska	Y	47600 FQ	66940 MW	83700 TQ	USBLS	5/07
	Lincoln MSA, NE	Y	40670 FQ	54330 MW	67690 TQ	USBLS	5/07
	Omaha-Council Bluffs MSA, NE-IA	Y	52430 FQ	71530 MW	87000 TQ	USBLS	5/07
	Nevada	H	24.49 FQ	29.80 MW	39.16 TQ	NVBLS	5/08
	Las Vegas-Paradise MSA, NV	H	26.38 FQ	33.84 MW	44.45 TQ	NVBLS	5/08
	New Hampshire	H	19.31 AE	34.31 MW	39.01 AEX	NHBLS	6/08
	Manchester MSA, NH	Y	52430 FQ	60800 MW	76470 TQ	USBLS	5/07
	Nashua NECTA, NH-MA	Y	60360 FQ	74960 MW	86490 TQ	USBLS	5/07
	Portsmouth MSA, NH-ME	Y	59750 FQ	73670 MW	81930 TQ	USBLS	5/07
	New Jersey	Y	59490 FQ	77300 MW	96880 TQ	USBLS	5/07
	Camden PMSA, NJ	Y	63810 FQ	81410 MW	97390 TQ	USBLS	5/07
	Edison PMSA, NJ	Y	63660 FQ	78250 MW	94870 TQ	USBLS	5/07
	Newark-Union PMSA, NJ-PA	Y	57550 FQ	73770 MW	92850 TQ	USBLS	5/07
	Trenton-Ewing MSA, NJ	Y	57490 FQ	80510 MW	94830 TQ	USBLS	5/07
	New Mexico	Y	39910 FQ	51900 MW	68710 TQ	USBLS	5/07
	Albuquerque MSA, NM	Y	40760 FQ	52130 MW	69620 TQ	USBLS	5/07
	New York	Y	57570 FQ	74610 MW	99310 TQ	USBLS	5/07
	Albany-Schenectady-Troy MSA, NY	Y	62150 FQ	72420 MW	80770 TQ	USBLS	5/07
	Buffalo-Niagara Falls MSA, NY	Y	44310 FQ	58440 MW	75180 TQ	USBLS	5/07
	Nassau-Suffolk PMSA, NY	Y	55860 FQ	76590 MW	97690 TQ	USBLS	5/07
	New York-Northern New Jersey-Long Island MSA, NY-NJ-PA	Y	60020 FQ	78830 MW	103800 TQ	USBLS	5/07
	Utica-Rome MSA, NY	Y	43370 FQ	53430 MW	72330 TQ	USBLS	5/07
	North Carolina	Y	53440 FQ	66530 MW	84500 TQ	USBLS	5/07
	Charlotte-Gastonia-Concord MSA, NC-SC	Y	57420 FQ	73380 MW	93230 TQ	USBLS	5/07
	Raleigh-Cary MSA, NC	Y	52620 FQ	70640 MW	87980 TQ	USBLS	5/07
	North Dakota	Y	43560 FQ	56670 MW	73510 TQ	USBLS	5/07
	Ohio	Y	51460 FQ	67100 MW	84610 TQ	USBLS	5/07
	Cincinnati-Middletown MSA, OH-KY-IN	Y	53070 FQ	71050 MW	86960 TQ	USBLS	5/07
	Cleveland-Elyria-Mentor MSA, OH	Y	49930 FQ	64260 MW	80460 TQ	USBLS	5/07
	Columbus MSA, OH	Y	56470 FQ	73110 MW	90630 TQ	USBLS	5/07
	Dayton MSA, OH	Y	48000 FQ	62530 MW	81810 TQ	USBLS	5/07
	Oklahoma	Y	43040 FQ	56520 MW	70180 TQ	USBLS	5/07

AE Average entry wage	**AW** Average wage paid	**FQ** First quartile wage	**LO** Lowest wage paid	**MTC** Median total compensation	**TCC** Total cash compensation
AER Average entry range	**AWR** Average wage range	**H** Hourly	**LR** Low end range	**MW** Median wage paid	**TQ** Third quartile wage
AEX Average experienced wage	**AXR** Average experienced range	**HI** Highest wage paid	**M** Monthly	**MWR** Median wage range	**W** Weekly
ATC Average total compensation	**D** Daily	**HR** High end range	**MCC** Median cash compensation	**S** See annotated source	**Y** Yearly

Occupation/Type/Industry	Location	Per	Low	Mid	High	Source	Date
Database Administrator	Oklahoma City MSA, OK	Y	39340 FQ	52600 MW	66170 TQ	USBLS	5/07
	Tulsa MSA, OK	Y	49220 FQ	59580 MW	71750 TQ	USBLS	5/07
	Oregon	H	27.94 FQ	35.05 MW	42.08 TQ	ORBLS	5/08
	Portland-Vancouver-Beaverton MSA, OR-WA	Y	58240 FQ	72660 MW	87920 TQ	USBLS	5/07
	Pennsylvania	Y	50270 FQ	64200 MW	80460 TQ	USBLS	5/07
	Allentown-Bethlehem-Easton MSA, PA-NJ	Y	37740 FQ	58150 MW	75270 TQ	USBLS	5/07
	Philadelphia-Camden-Wilmington MSA, PA-NJ-DE-MD	Y	54800 FQ	70830 MW	92250 TQ	USBLS	5/07
	Pittsburgh MSA, PA	Y	41450 FQ	59500 MW	75310 TQ	USBLS	5/07
	Reading MSA, PA	Y	39530 FQ	53240 MW	70510 TQ	USBLS	5/07
	Rhode Island	Y	55990 FQ	73810 MW	96070 TQ	USBLS	5/07
	Providence-Fall River-Warwick MSA, RI-MA	Y	55320 FQ	73520 MW	95510 TQ	USBLS	5/07
	South Carolina	Y	43110 FQ	55310 MW	71770 TQ	USBLS	5/07
	Charleston-North Charleston MSA, SC	Y	39760 FQ	49320 MW	86950 TQ	USBLS	5/07
	Columbia MSA, SC	Y	43810 FQ	54850 MW	64380 TQ	USBLS	5/07
	South Dakota	Y	48108 FQ	57012 MW	71034 TQ	SDBLS	7/08-9/08
	Sioux Falls MSA, SD	Y	49226 FQ	59878 MW	77115 TQ	SDBLS	7/08-9/08
	Tennessee	Y	45130 FQ	64300 MW	80580 TQ	USBLS	5/07
	Memphis MSA, TN-MS-AR	Y	43580 FQ	69290 MW	87240 TQ	USBLS	5/07
	Nashville-Davidson-Murfreesboro MSA, TN	Y	55420 FQ	68270 MW	82010 TQ	USBLS	5/07
	Texas	Y	48600 FQ	64350 MW	84390 TQ	USBLS	5/07
	Austin-Round Rock MSA, TX	Y	51200 FQ	63560 MW	86470 TQ	USBLS	5/07
	Dallas-Fort Worth-Arlington MSA, TX	Y	51540 FQ	69240 MW	89600 TQ	USBLS	5/07
	El Paso MSA, TX	Y	39790 FQ	51320 MW	70320 TQ	USBLS	5/07
	Houston-Sugar Land-Baytown MSA, TX	Y	49240 FQ	64300 MW	83440 TQ	USBLS	5/07
	San Antonio MSA, TX	Y	44370 FQ	60930 MW	76310 TQ	USBLS	5/07
	Utah	Y	47210 FQ	66660 MW	85200 TQ	USBLS	5/07
	Salt Lake City MSA, UT	Y	47510 FQ	68500 MW	84170 TQ	USBLS	5/07
	Vermont	Y	45230 FQ	54530 MW	63990 TQ	USBLS	5/07
	Burlington-South Burlington MSA, VT	Y	45530 FQ	56030 MW	67150 TQ	USBLS	5/07
	Virginia	Y	54420 FQ	75590 MW	99840 TQ	USBLS	5/07
	Richmond MSA, VA	Y	48720 FQ	70900 MW	95900 TQ	USBLS	5/07
	Virginia Beach-Norfolk-Newport News MSA, VA-NC	Y	41190 FQ	55860 MW	71420 TQ	USBLS	5/07
	Washington	H	27.99 FQ	35.78 MW	45.53 TQ	WABLS	3/08
	Seattle-Tacoma-Bellevue MSA, WA	Y	59680 FQ	77660 MW	96270 TQ	USBLS	5/07
	West Virginia	Y	34264 FQ	46207 MW	60867 TQ	WVBLS	7/08-9/08
	Charleston MSA, WV	Y	40670 FQ	51270 MW	61580 TQ	USBLS	5/07
	Wisconsin	Y	49960 FQ	65060 MW	81660 TQ	USBLS	5/07
	Milwaukee-Waukesha-West Allis MSA, WI	Y	50080 FQ	68750 MW	84980 TQ	USBLS	5/07
	Wyoming	Y	31484 FQ	40738 MW	51313 TQ	WYBLS	9/08
	Puerto Rico	Y	41860 FQ	51840 MW	60700 TQ	USBLS	5/07
	San Juan-Caguas-Guaynabo MSA, PR	Y	42420 FQ	51790 MW	60880 TQ	USBLS	5/07
	Virgin Islands	Y	35960 FQ	39810 MW	54590 TQ	USBLS	5/07
Oracle, With Security Clearance	United States	Y		101905 AW		CLJOBS	3/20/07-2/20/08
Oracle, Without Security Clearance	United States	Y		75000 AW		CLJOBS	3/20/07-2/20/08
Database Administrator/ Developer	United States	Y		81495 AW		MCP	2008
Database Analyst	United States	Y		74163 AW		COWRLD	5/20/08-7/25/08
Defensive Coordinator and Linebackers Coach West Virginia University	Morgantown, WV	Y			295267 HI	TMC	2008
Delivery Technician	United States	Y		26954 AW		HOMECARE	8/25/08-9/24/08
Demographer State Government	Ohio	H	21.77 LO		31.86 HI	ODAS	2008

AE	Average entry wage	AW	Average wage paid	FQ	First quartile wage	LO	Lowest wage paid
AER	Average entry range	AWR	Average wage range	H	Hourly	LR	Low end range
AEX	Average experienced wage	AXR	Average experienced range	HI	Highest wage paid	M	Monthly
ATC	Average total compensation	D	Daily	HR	High end range	MCC	Median cash compensation

MTC Median total compensation TCC Total cash compensation
MW Median wage paid TQ Third quartile wage
MWR Median wage range W Weekly
S See annotated source Y Yearly

Occupation/Type/Industry	Location	Per	Low	Mid	High	Source	Date
Demonstrator and Product Promoter							
	Alabama	Y	17330 FQ	20330 MW	25620 TQ	USBLS	5/07
	Birmingham-Hoover MSA, AL	Y	18000 FQ	22420 MW	30060 TQ	USBLS	5/07
	Alaska	Y	19710 FQ	25120 MW	34360 TQ	USBLS	5/07
	Anchorage MSA, AK	Y	20760 FQ	27180 MW	35510 TQ	USBLS	5/07
	Arizona	Y	17690 FQ	22570 MW	33740 TQ	USBLS	5/07
	Phoenix-Mesa-Scottsdale MSA, AZ	Y	17810 FQ	23060 MW	36180 TQ	USBLS	5/07
	Tucson MSA, AZ	Y	17370 FQ	19730 MW	22810 TQ	USBLS	5/07
	Arkansas	Y	20490 FQ	26540 MW	40470 TQ	USBLS	5/07
	Little Rock-North Little Rock MSA, AR	Y	20950 FQ	23770 MW	32320 TQ	USBLS	5/07
	California	H	9.00 FQ	11.51 MW	14.84 TQ	CABLS	1/08-3/08
	Los Angeles-Long Beach-Glendale PMSA, CA	H	8.94 FQ	13.15 MW	16.22 TQ	CABLS	1/08-3/08
	Oakland-Fremont-Hayward MSA, CA	H	10.18 FQ	12.65 MW	14.41 TQ	CABLS	1/08-3/08
	Oxnard-Thousand Oaks-Ventura MSA, CA	H	8.61 FQ	9.37 MW	11.01 TQ	CABLS	1/08-3/08
	Riverside-San Bernardino-Ontario MSA, CA	H	8.67 FQ	9.86 MW	11.31 TQ	CABLS	1/08-3/08
	Sacramento-Arden Arcade-Roseville MSA, CA	H	9.14 FQ	10.94 MW	12.89 TQ	CABLS	1/08-3/08
	San Diego-Carlsbad-San Marcos MSA, CA	H	9.01 FQ	11.05 MW	16.98 TQ	CABLS	1/08-3/08
	San Francisco-San Mateo-Redwood PMSA, CA	H	12.82 FQ	14.00 MW	15.40 TQ	CABLS	1/08-3/08
	San Jose-Sunnyvale-Santa Clara MSA, CA	H	10.31 FQ	12.81 MW	15.13 TQ	CABLS	1/08-3/08
	Santa Ana-Anaheim-Irvine PMSA, CA	Y	18030 FQ	20920 MW	29840 TQ	USBLS	5/07
	Colorado	Y	18900 FQ	21850 MW	25890 TQ	USBLS	5/07
	Denver-Aurora MSA, CO	Y	21660 FQ	24450 MW	30890 TQ	USBLS	5/07
	Connecticut	H	9.12 AE	11.48 MW		CTBLS	1/08-3/08
	Bridgeport-Stamford-Norwalk MSA, CT	Y	23430 FQ	34370 MW	54220 TQ	USBLS	5/07
	Danbury MSA, CT	Y	22000 FQ	28620 MW	32240 TQ	USBLS	5/07
	Hartford-West Hartford-East Hartford MSA, CT	Y	19520 FQ	22530 MW	25910 TQ	USBLS	5/07
	Delaware	Y	17590 FQ	21120 MW	27490 TQ	USBLS	5/07
	Wilmington PMSA, DE-MD-NJ	Y	17360 FQ	22570 MW	34670 TQ	USBLS	5/07
	District of Columbia	Y	20740 FQ	28320 MW	44480 TQ	USBLS	5/07
	Washington-Arlington-Alexandria MSA, DC-VA-MD-WV	Y	19540 FQ	25580 MW	36910 TQ	USBLS	5/07
	Florida	Y	19630 FQ	23130 MW	29860 TQ	USBLS	5/07
	Fort Lauderdale-Pompano Beach-Deerfield Beach PMSA, FL	Y	20300 FQ	23970 MW	30840 TQ	USBLS	5/07
	Jacksonville MSA, FL	Y	18340 FQ	23300 MW	41330 TQ	USBLS	5/07
	Miami-Fort Lauderdale-Miami Beach MSA, FL	Y	20380 FQ	23360 MW	30240 TQ	USBLS	5/07
	Orlando-Kissimmee MSA, FL	Y	19930 FQ	22930 MW	26830 TQ	USBLS	5/07
	Tampa-St. Petersburg-Clearwater MSA, FL	Y	18610 FQ	22120 MW	30440 TQ	USBLS	5/07
	West Palm Beach-Boca Raton-Boynton Beach PMSA, FL	Y	23860 FQ	28850 MW	34680 TQ	USBLS	5/07
	Georgia	Y	19030 FQ	23060 MW	35630 TQ	USBLS	5/07
	Atlanta-Sandy Springs-Marietta MSA, GA	Y	18920 FQ	22870 MW	35740 TQ	USBLS	5/07
	Hawaii	Y	16540 FQ	18140 MW	19990 TQ	USBLS	5/07
	Honolulu MSA, HI	Y	16380 FQ	18080 MW	20180 TQ	USBLS	5/07
	Idaho	Y	16990 FQ	20950 MW	27940 TQ	USBLS	5/07
	Boise City-Nampa MSA, ID	Y	20460 FQ	24700 MW	37440 TQ	USBLS	5/07
	Illinois	Y	19120 FQ	23470 MW	32880 TQ	USBLS	5/07
	Chicago-Naperville-Joliet MSA, IL-IN-WI	Y	19310 FQ	23810 MW	33300 TQ	USBLS	5/07
	Rockford MSA, IL	Y	21530 FQ	44510 MW	55690 TQ	USBLS	5/07
	Indiana	Y	18980 FQ	23880 MW	31440 TQ	USBLS	5/07
	Fort Wayne MSA, IN	Y	20970 FQ	26360 MW	31200 TQ	USBLS	5/07
	Gary PMSA, IN	Y	21500 FQ	25220 MW	35260 TQ	USBLS	5/07

AE	Average entry wage	AW	Average wage paid	FQ	First quartile wage	LO	Lowest wage paid	MTC	Median total compensation	TCC	Total cash compensation
AER	Average entry range	AWR	Average wage range	H	Hourly	LR	Low end range	MW	Median wage paid	TQ	Third quartile wage
AEX	Average experienced wage	AXR	Average experienced range	HI	Highest wage paid	M	Monthly	MWR	Median wage range	W	Weekly
ATC	Average total compensation	D	Daily	HR	High end range	MCC	Median cash compensation	S	See annotated source	Y	Yearly

Demonstrator and Product Promoter

Occupation/Type/Industry	Location	Per	Low	Mid	High	Source	Date
Demonstrator and Product Promoter	Indianapolis-Carmel MSA, IN	Y	20100 FQ	23770 MW	29830 TQ	USBLS	5/07
	Iowa	Y	16790 FQ	18860 MW	23250 TQ	USBLS	5/07
	Des Moines-West Des Moines MSA, IA	Y	16670 FQ	18080 MW	19700 TQ	USBLS	5/07
	Kansas	Y	20010 FQ	24080 MW	29020 TQ	USBLS	5/07
	Wichita MSA, KS	Y	18860 FQ	22830 MW	28310 TQ	USBLS	5/07
	Kentucky	Y	18126 FQ	21378 MW	25338 TQ	KYBLS	2008
	Louisville-Jefferson County MSA, KY-IN	Y	18970 FQ	22910 MW	27760 TQ	USBLS	5/07
	Louisiana	H	7.95 FQ	10.27 MW	14.48 TQ	LABLS	1/08-3/08
	New Orleans-Metairie-Kenner MSA, LA	Y	15940 FQ	20060 MW	25330 TQ	USBLS	5/07
	Maine	Y	17460 FQ	19480 MW	22430 TQ	USBLS	5/07
	Portland-South Portland-Biddeford MSA, ME	Y	18010 FQ	19920 MW	23370 TQ	USBLS	5/07
	Maryland	Y		26475 MW		MDBLS	3/08
	Baltimore-Towson MSA, MD	Y	18280 FQ	23640 MW	35520 TQ	USBLS	5/07
	Bethesda-Gaithersburg-Frederick PMSA, MD	Y	19780 FQ	27040 MW	52770 TQ	USBLS	5/07
	Hagerstown-Martinsburg MSA, MD-WV	Y	17330 FQ	20910 MW	28600 TQ	USBLS	5/07
	Massachusetts	Y	20840 FQ	26010 MW	37610 TQ	USBLS	5/07
	Boston-Cambridge-Quincy NECTA, MA	Y	20970 FQ	27950 MW	39310 TQ	USBLS	5/07
	Springfield MSA, MA-CT	Y	20850 FQ	23460 MW	33090 TQ	USBLS	5/07
	Worcester MSA, MA-CT	Y	22100 FQ	27990 MW	37580 TQ	USBLS	5/07
	Michigan	Y	17700 FQ	20500 MW	24240 TQ	USBLS	5/07
	Detroit-Warren-Livonia MSA, MI	Y	18150 FQ	21490 MW	31950 TQ	USBLS	5/07
	Warren-Troy-Farmington Hills PMSA, MI	Y	18080 FQ	21070 MW	28010 TQ	USBLS	5/07
	Minnesota	Y	19076 FQ	22512 MW	26262 TQ	MNBLS	10/08-12/08
	Duluth-Superior MSA, MN-WI	Y	21770 FQ	24839 MW	29260 TQ	MNBLS	10/08-12/08
	Minneapolis-Saint Paul MSA, MN-WI	Y	21109 FQ	23894 MW	28599 TQ	MNBLS	10/08-12/08
	Mississippi	Y	17960 FQ	23270 MW	34180 TQ	USBLS	5/07
	Jackson MSA, MS	Y	18990 FQ	31330 MW	36890 TQ	USBLS	5/07
	Missouri	Y	19260 FQ	23390 MW	30620 TQ	USBLS	5/07
	Kansas City MSA, MO-KS	Y	18130 FQ	22030 MW	27370 TQ	USBLS	5/07
	St. Louis MSA, MO-IL	Y	18960 FQ	23350 MW	28980 TQ	USBLS	5/07
	Montana	Y	16930 FQ	18680 MW	24690 TQ	USBLS	5/07
	Billings MSA, MT	Y	16280 FQ	18160 MW	26790 TQ	USBLS	5/07
	Nebraska	Y	15210 FQ	18280 MW	23130 TQ	USBLS	5/07
	Omaha-Council Bluffs MSA, NE-IA	Y	14280 FQ	17880 MW	22460 TQ	USBLS	5/07
	Nevada	H	8.83 FQ	10.61 MW	13.29 TQ	NVBLS	5/08
	Las Vegas-Paradise MSA, NV	H	8.75 FQ	10.53 MW	13.45 TQ	NVBLS	5/08
	New Hampshire	H	8.97 AE	11.32 MW	13.79 AEX	NHBLS	6/08
	Nashua NECTA, NH-MA	Y	17240 FQ	18990 MW	21690 TQ	USBLS	5/07
	New Jersey	Y	18240 FQ	21810 MW	29650 TQ	USBLS	5/07
	Camden PMSA, NJ	Y	18530 FQ	22130 MW	27030 TQ	USBLS	5/07
	Edison PMSA, NJ	Y	17640 FQ	19540 MW	26210 TQ	USBLS	5/07
	Newark-Union PMSA, NJ-PA	Y	19630 FQ	24050 MW	36380 TQ	USBLS	5/07
	New Mexico	Y	19140 FQ	21890 MW	25520 TQ	USBLS	5/07
	Albuquerque MSA, NM	Y	19360 FQ	21780 MW	24330 TQ	USBLS	5/07
	New York	Y	18850 FQ	25030 MW	35560 TQ	USBLS	5/07
	Albany-Schenectady-Troy MSA, NY	Y	18570 FQ	21410 MW	25140 TQ	USBLS	5/07
	Buffalo-Niagara Falls MSA, NY	Y	15580 FQ	18310 MW	23080 TQ	USBLS	5/07
	Nassau-Suffolk PMSA, NY	Y	19770 FQ	24900 MW	30020 TQ	USBLS	5/07
	New York-Northern New Jersey-Long Island MSA, NY-NJ-PA	Y	19420 FQ	26110 MW	37230 TQ	USBLS	5/07
	North Carolina	Y	18600 FQ	24250 MW	32030 TQ	USBLS	5/07
	Charlotte-Gastonia-Concord MSA, NC-SC	Y	20290 FQ	25410 MW	29380 TQ	USBLS	5/07
	Raleigh-Cary MSA, NC	Y	15940 FQ	22010 MW	32320 TQ	USBLS	5/07
	North Dakota	Y	16790 FQ	18590 MW	24530 TQ	USBLS	5/07
	Bismarck MSA, ND	Y	16690 FQ	17930 MW	19220 TQ	USBLS	5/07
	Fargo MSA, ND-MN	Y	16140 FQ	18060 MW	23240 TQ	USBLS	5/07

AE	Average entry wage	AW	Average wage paid	FQ	First quartile wage	LO	Lowest wage paid	MTC	Median total compensation	TCC	Total cash compensation
AER	Average entry range	AWR	Average wage range	H	Hourly	LR	Low end range	MW	Median wage paid	TQ	Third quartile wage
AEX	Average experienced wage	AXR	Average experienced range	HI	Highest wage paid	M	Monthly	MWR	Median wage range	W	Weekly
ATC	Average total compensation	D	Daily	HR	High end range	MCC	Median cash compensation	S	See annotated source	Y	Yearly

Occupation/Type/Industry	Location	Per	Low	Mid	High	Source	Date
Demonstrator and Product Promoter	Ohio	Y	17670 FQ	20670 MW	25270 TQ	USBLS	5/07
	Cincinnati-Middletown MSA, OH-KY-IN	Y	17760 FQ	20140 MW	23770 TQ	USBLS	5/07
	Cleveland-Elyria-Mentor MSA, OH	Y	17410 FQ	19510 MW	24520 TQ	USBLS	5/07
	Columbus MSA, OH	Y	17890 FQ	23290 MW	30450 TQ	USBLS	5/07
	Dayton MSA, OH	Y	18140 FQ	20930 MW	25790 TQ	USBLS	5/07
	Oklahoma	Y	19940 FQ	23030 MW	28250 TQ	USBLS	5/07
	Oklahoma City MSA, OK	Y	19700 FQ	22710 MW	26680 TQ	USBLS	5/07
	Tulsa MSA, OK	Y	20050 FQ	22740 MW	25830 TQ	USBLS	5/07
	Oregon	H	8.62 FQ	9.39 MW	12.15 TQ	ORBLS	5/08
	Portland-Vancouver-Beaverton MSA, OR-WA	Y	17480 FQ	18710 MW	23160 TQ	USBLS	5/07
	Pennsylvania	Y	17090 FQ	19920 MW	29080 TQ	USBLS	5/07
	Allentown-Bethlehem-Easton MSA, PA-NJ	Y	15810 FQ	20110 MW	23510 TQ	USBLS	5/07
	Philadelphia-Camden-Wilmington MSA, PA-NJ-DE-MD	Y	19890 FQ	25620 MW	36640 TQ	USBLS	5/07
	Pittsburgh MSA, PA	Y	16170 FQ	18290 MW	21490 TQ	USBLS	5/07
	Rhode Island	Y	24090 FQ	31290 MW	39000 TQ	USBLS	5/07
	Providence-Fall River-Warwick MSA, RI-MA	Y	22890 FQ	30630 MW	38830 TQ	USBLS	5/07
	South Carolina	Y	20420 FQ	24260 MW	34580 TQ	USBLS	5/07
	Charleston-North Charleston MSA, SC	Y	30660 FQ	33400 MW	36130 TQ	USBLS	5/07
	Columbia MSA, SC	Y	22390 FQ	27660 MW	33730 TQ	USBLS	5/07
	South Dakota	Y	18040 FQ	20775 MW	23819 TQ	SDBLS	7/08-9/08
	Sioux Falls MSA, SD	Y	18356 FQ	21443 MW	24113 TQ	SDBLS	7/08-9/08
	Tennessee	Y	17980 FQ	22910 MW	31360 TQ	USBLS	5/07
	Memphis MSA, TN-MS-AR	Y	18450 FQ	25410 MW	32800 TQ	USBLS	5/07
	Nashville-Davidson-Murfreesboro MSA, TN	Y	20390 FQ	23080 MW	29420 TQ	USBLS	5/07
	Texas	Y	18860 FQ	23600 MW	29840 TQ	USBLS	5/07
	Austin-Round Rock MSA, TX	Y	23220 FQ	26680 MW	30130 TQ	USBLS	5/07
	Beaumont-Port Arthur MSA, TX	Y	16740 FQ	19010 MW	23730 TQ	USBLS	5/07
	Dallas-Fort Worth-Arlington MSA, TX	Y	17440 FQ	22120 MW	27370 TQ	USBLS	5/07
	El Paso MSA, TX	Y	15980 FQ	18930 MW	25530 TQ	USBLS	5/07
	Houston-Sugar Land-Baytown MSA, TX	Y	19820 FQ	24480 MW	31300 TQ	USBLS	5/07
	San Antonio MSA, TX	Y	21170 FQ	28450 MW	40070 TQ	USBLS	5/07
	Utah	Y	19810 FQ	28480 MW	34980 TQ	USBLS	5/07
	Provo-Orem MSA, UT	Y	16980 FQ	18440 MW	20250 TQ	USBLS	5/07
	Salt Lake City MSA, UT	Y	24790 FQ	30440 MW	36970 TQ	USBLS	5/07
	Vermont	Y	19810 FQ	21600 MW	23390 TQ	USBLS	5/07
	Burlington-South Burlington MSA, VT	Y	20020 FQ	21500 MW	23020 TQ	USBLS	5/07
	Virginia	Y	19350 FQ	24540 MW	29590 TQ	USBLS	5/07
	Richmond MSA, VA	Y	21140 FQ	24490 MW	33310 TQ	USBLS	5/07
	Virginia Beach-Norfolk-Newport News MSA, VA-NC	Y	19200 FQ	22870 MW	28080 TQ	USBLS	5/07
	Washington	H	8.78 FQ	9.53 MW	11.88 TQ	WABLS	3/08
	Bremerton-Silverdale MSA, WA	Y	21400 FQ	23160 MW	25330 TQ	USBLS	5/07
	Seattle-Tacoma-Bellevue MSA, WA	Y	18170 FQ	19800 MW	25470 TQ	USBLS	5/07
	West Virginia	Y	17201 FQ	19306 MW	23869 TQ	WVBLS	7/08-9/08
	Charleston MSA, WV	Y	16770 FQ	18520 MW	22320 TQ	USBLS	5/07
	Wisconsin	Y	18640 FQ	21720 MW	24730 TQ	USBLS	5/07
	Milwaukee-Waukesha-West Allis MSA, WI	Y	18960 FQ	21340 MW	23410 TQ	USBLS	5/07
	Wyoming	Y	17571 FQ	19431 MW	23509 TQ	WYBLS	9/08
	Puerto Rico	Y	14140 FQ	17250 MW	20390 TQ	USBLS	5/07
	San Juan-Caguas-Guaynabo MSA, PR	Y	14100 FQ	17180 MW	20140 TQ	USBLS	5/07
	Virgin Islands	Y	17130 FQ	20010 MW	22650 TQ	USBLS	5/07
	Guam	Y	13390 FQ	15740 MW	19940 TQ	USBLS	5/07
Dental Assistant	Alabama	Y	20240 FQ	25680 MW	31140 TQ	USBLS	5/07

AE	Average entry wage	AW	Average wage paid	FQ	First quartile wage	LO	Lowest wage paid	MTC	Median total compensation	TCC	Total cash compensation
AER	Average entry range	AWR	Average wage range	H	Hourly	LR	Low end range	MW	Median wage paid	TQ	Third quartile wage
AEX	Average experienced wage	AXR	Average experienced range	HI	Highest wage paid	M	Monthly	MWR	Median wage range	W	Weekly
ATC	Average total compensation	D	Daily	HR	High end range	MCC	Median cash compensation	S	See annotated source	Y	Yearly

Dental Assistant

Occupation/Type/Industry	Location	Per	Low	Mid	High	Source	Date
Dental Assistant	Birmingham-Hoover MSA, AL	Y	21510 FQ	27960 MW	31760 TQ	USBLS	5/07
	Tuscaloosa MSA, AL	Y	22090 FQ	24990 MW	29890 TQ	USBLS	5/07
	Alaska	Y	31990 FQ	40770 MW	47340 TQ	USBLS	5/07
	Anchorage MSA, AK	Y	34850 FQ	42430 MW	47610 TQ	USBLS	5/07
	Arizona	Y	27900 FQ	33610 MW	38300 TQ	USBLS	5/07
	Phoenix-Mesa-Scottsdale MSA, AZ	Y	28920 FQ	34250 MW	38610 TQ	USBLS	5/07
	Tucson MSA, AZ	Y	27340 FQ	32530 MW	38300 TQ	USBLS	5/07
	Yuma MSA, AZ	Y	26530 FQ	29910 MW	34640 TQ	USBLS	5/07
	Arkansas	Y	21390 FQ	26190 MW	30280 TQ	USBLS	5/07
	Little Rock-North Little Rock MSA, AR	Y	21720 FQ	27880 MW	33780 TQ	USBLS	5/07
	California	H	12.61 FQ	15.90 MW	19.70 TQ	CABLS	1/08-3/08
	Bakersfield MSA, CA	H	10.72 FQ	12.71 MW	16.56 TQ	CABLS	1/08-3/08
	Los Angeles-Long Beach-Glendale PMSA, CA	H	11.55 FQ	14.64 MW	18.57 TQ	CABLS	1/08-3/08
	Oakland-Fremont-Hayward MSA, CA	H	14.97 FQ	19.35 MW	22.73 TQ	CABLS	1/08-3/08
	Riverside-San Bernardino-Ontario MSA, CA	H	11.44 FQ	13.82 MW	17.32 TQ	CABLS	1/08-3/08
	Sacramento-Arden Arcade-Roseville MSA, CA	H	14.22 FQ	17.37 MW	21.23 TQ	CABLS	1/08-3/08
	San Diego-Carlsbad-San Marcos MSA, CA	H	14.02 FQ	16.50 MW	18.87 TQ	CABLS	1/08-3/08
	San Francisco-San Mateo-Redwood PMSA, CA	H	15.14 FQ	19.08 MW	26.93 TQ	CABLS	1/08-3/08
	San Jose-Sunnyvale-Santa Clara MSA, CA	H	14.20 FQ	19.50 MW	24.76 TQ	CABLS	1/08-3/08
	Santa Ana-Anaheim-Irvine PMSA, CA	Y	25390 FQ	32430 MW	39280 TQ	USBLS	5/07
	Colorado	Y	28290 FQ	34050 MW	40620 TQ	USBLS	5/07
	Denver-Aurora MSA, CO	Y	30330 FQ	36260 MW	41950 TQ	USBLS	5/07
	Connecticut	H	14.41 AE	18.45 MW		CTBLS	1/08-3/08
	Bridgeport-Stamford-Norwalk MSA, CT	Y	33050 FQ	38150 MW	44180 TQ	USBLS	5/07
	Hartford-West Hartford-East Hartford MSA, CT	Y	31050 FQ	36790 MW	43620 TQ	USBLS	5/07
	New Haven MSA, CT	Y	35380 FQ	42510 MW	47700 TQ	USBLS	5/07
	Delaware	Y	28820 FQ	34440 MW	39550 TQ	USBLS	5/07
	Wilmington PMSA, DE-MD-NJ	Y	28650 FQ	34510 MW	40300 TQ	USBLS	5/07
	District of Columbia	Y	34610 FQ	40460 MW	46190 TQ	USBLS	5/07
	Washington-Arlington-Alexandria MSA, DC-VA-MD-WV	Y	28800 FQ	34860 MW	42210 TQ	USBLS	5/07
	Florida	Y	26670 FQ	31420 MW	36890 TQ	USBLS	5/07
	Cape Coral-Fort Myers MSA, FL	Y	32390 FQ	37030 MW	41890 TQ	USBLS	5/07
	Fort Lauderdale-Pompano Beach-Deerfield Beach PMSA, FL	Y	25600 FQ	30410 MW	36650 TQ	USBLS	5/07
	Jacksonville MSA, FL	Y	27210 FQ	31850 MW	36950 TQ	USBLS	5/07
	Lakeland MSA, FL	Y	25770 FQ	30010 MW	34050 TQ	USBLS	5/07
	Miami-Fort Lauderdale-Miami Beach MSA, FL	Y	25850 FQ	30610 MW	36300 TQ	USBLS	5/07
	Orlando-Kissimmee MSA, FL	Y	27810 FQ	32930 MW	38100 TQ	USBLS	5/07
	Sarasota-Bradenton-Venice MSA, FL	Y	30390 FQ	33800 MW	37240 TQ	USBLS	5/07
	Tampa-St. Petersburg-Clearwater MSA, FL	Y	28080 FQ	32830 MW	38260 TQ	USBLS	5/07
	West Palm Beach-Boca Raton-Boynton Beach PMSA, FL	Y	29580 FQ	34550 MW	39310 TQ	USBLS	5/07
	Georgia	Y	26490 FQ	31480 MW	36860 TQ	USBLS	5/07
	Atlanta-Sandy Springs-Marietta MSA, GA	Y	28640 FQ	33570 MW	38210 TQ	USBLS	5/07
	Hawaii	Y	22160 FQ	28700 MW	34470 TQ	USBLS	5/07
	Honolulu MSA, HI	Y	23160 FQ	29090 MW	33620 TQ	USBLS	5/07
	Idaho	Y	23450 FQ	28100 MW	32730 TQ	USBLS	5/07
	Boise City-Nampa MSA, ID	Y	24900 FQ	30250 MW	35130 TQ	USBLS	5/07
	Illinois	Y	26050 FQ	30470 MW	35970 TQ	USBLS	5/07
	Chicago-Naperville-Joliet MSA, IL-IN-WI	Y	26760 FQ	31250 MW	36850 TQ	USBLS	5/07

AE	Average entry wage	AW	Average wage paid	FQ	First quartile wage
AER	Average entry range	AWR	Average wage range	H	Hourly
AEX	Average experienced wage	AXR	Average experienced range	HI	Highest wage paid
ATC	Average total compensation	D	Daily	HR	High end range

LO	Lowest wage paid	MTC	Median total compensation	TCC	Total cash compensation
LR	Low end range	MW	Median wage paid	TQ	Third quartile wage
M	Monthly	MWR	Median wage range	W	Weekly
MCC	Median cash compensation	S	See annotated source	Y	Yearly

Occupation/Type/Industry	Location	Per	Low	Mid	High	Source	Date
Dental Assistant	Peoria MSA, IL	Y	26840 FQ	28840 MW	31440 TQ	USBLS	5/07
	Indiana	Y	27280 FQ	32650 MW	38290 TQ	USBLS	5/07
	Elkhart-Goshen MSA, IN	Y	24090 FQ	32630 MW	36960 TQ	USBLS	5/07
	Gary PMSA, IN	Y	26550 FQ	31080 MW	36040 TQ	USBLS	5/07
	Indianapolis-Carmel MSA, IN	Y	31560 FQ	35980 MW	40930 TQ	USBLS	5/07
	Terre Haute MSA, IN	Y	23350 FQ	27190 MW	31270 TQ	USBLS	5/07
	Iowa	Y	26820 FQ	31120 MW	36580 TQ	USBLS	5/07
	Des Moines-West Des Moines MSA, IA	Y	30930 FQ	35540 MW	40120 TQ	USBLS	5/07
	Kansas	Y	25590 FQ	30130 MW	36300 TQ	USBLS	5/07
	Wichita MSA, KS	Y	26270 FQ	30080 MW	35910 TQ	USBLS	5/07
	Kentucky	Y	23249 FQ	28811 MW	34838 TQ	KYBLS	2008
	Bowling Green MSA, KY	Y	22310 FQ	26100 MW	30330 TQ	USBLS	5/07
	Louisville-Jefferson County MSA, KY-IN	Y	26510 FQ	31260 MW	36120 TQ	USBLS	5/07
	Louisiana	H	10.32 FQ	12.35 MW	14.37 TQ	LABLS	1/08-3/08
	Baton Rouge MSA, LA	Y	22020 FQ	26180 MW	29620 TQ	USBLS	5/07
	New Orleans-Metairie-Kenner MSA, LA	Y	22510 FQ	26660 MW	29950 TQ	USBLS	5/07
	Maine	Y	27330 FQ	32380 MW	39090 TQ	USBLS	5/07
	Portland-South Portland-Biddeford MSA, ME	Y	30400 FQ	36160 MW	41500 TQ	USBLS	5/07
	Maryland	Y		34375 MW		MDBLS	3/08
	Baltimore-Towson MSA, MD	Y	30440 FQ	34290 MW	37970 TQ	USBLS	5/07
	Bethesda-Gaithersburg-Frederick PMSA, MD	Y	26030 FQ	36420 MW	44430 TQ	USBLS	5/07
	Massachusetts	Y	31320 FQ	36920 MW	43930 TQ	USBLS	5/07
	Boston-Cambridge-Quincy NECTA, MA	Y	31290 FQ	36930 MW	43940 TQ	USBLS	5/07
	Worcester MSA, MA-CT	Y	34020 FQ	37520 MW	41760 TQ	USBLS	5/07
	Michigan	Y	28470 FQ	32790 MW	37900 TQ	USBLS	5/07
	Detroit-Warren-Livonia MSA, MI	Y	29160 FQ	33340 MW	38630 TQ	USBLS	5/07
	Grand Rapids-Wyoming MSA, MI	Y	29430 FQ	33210 MW	37520 TQ	USBLS	5/07
	Warren-Troy-Farmington Hills PMSA, MI	Y	29660 FQ	33890 MW	38770 TQ	USBLS	5/07
	Minnesota	Y	35403 FQ	40809 MW	46601 TQ	MNBLS	10/08-12/08
	Duluth-Superior MSA, MN-WI	Y	32643 FQ	38174 MW	44353 TQ	MNBLS	10/08-12/08
	Minneapolis-Saint Paul MSA, MN-WI	Y	36449 FQ	42011 MW	47699 TQ	MNBLS	10/08-12/08
	Rochester MSA, MN	Y	40781 FQ	44908 MW	48717 TQ	MNBLS	10/08-12/08
	Mississippi	Y	21750 FQ	25860 MW	30690 TQ	USBLS	5/07
	Jackson MSA, MS	Y	22830 FQ	27920 MW	33060 TQ	USBLS	5/07
	Missouri	Y	25480 FQ	29980 MW	36570 TQ	USBLS	5/07
	Kansas City MSA, MO-KS	Y	27230 FQ	32230 MW	39700 TQ	USBLS	5/07
	St. Louis MSA, MO-IL	Y	26440 FQ	30650 MW	37650 TQ	USBLS	5/07
	Montana	Y	23400 FQ	28330 MW	32960 TQ	USBLS	5/07
	Billings MSA, MT	Y	23060 FQ	28030 MW	31470 TQ	USBLS	5/07
	Nebraska	Y	26120 FQ	29080 MW	32400 TQ	USBLS	5/07
	Omaha-Council Bluffs MSA, NE-IA	Y	27410 FQ	30380 MW	35340 TQ	USBLS	5/07
	Nevada	H	14.30 FQ	17.27 MW	20.15 TQ	NVBLS	5/08
	Las Vegas-Paradise MSA, NV	H	13.80 FQ	16.54 MW	19.74 TQ	NVBLS	5/08
	New Hampshire	H	15.05 AE	19.39 MW	21.26 AEX	NHBLS	6/08
	Manchester MSA, NH	Y	40030 FQ	43450 MW	47020 TQ	USBLS	5/07
	Nashua NECTA, NH-MA	Y	33650 FQ	38070 MW	44620 TQ	USBLS	5/07
	New Jersey	Y	28140 FQ	35710 MW	43230 TQ	USBLS	5/07
	Camden PMSA, NJ	Y	29090 FQ	35670 MW	40200 TQ	USBLS	5/07
	Edison PMSA, NJ	Y	27800 FQ	34830 MW	41980 TQ	USBLS	5/07
	Newark-Union PMSA, NJ-PA	Y	29830 FQ	38940 MW	46730 TQ	USBLS	5/07
	New Mexico	Y	25160 FQ	29340 MW	34950 TQ	USBLS	5/07
	Albuquerque MSA, NM	Y	26630 FQ	29870 MW	35000 TQ	USBLS	5/07
	New York	Y	27350 FQ	31950 MW	37620 TQ	USBLS	5/07
	Albany-Schenectady-Troy MSA, NY	Y	27710 FQ	32370 MW	37230 TQ	USBLS	5/07
	Buffalo-Niagara Falls MSA, NY	Y	26110 FQ	28830 MW	32460 TQ	USBLS	5/07
	Nassau-Suffolk PMSA, NY	Y	30300 FQ	34730 MW	39210 TQ	USBLS	5/07
	New York-Northern New Jersey-Long Island MSA, NY-NJ-PA	Y	28230 FQ	34230 MW	40690 TQ	USBLS	5/07

AE	Average entry wage	AW	Average wage paid	FQ	First quartile wage	LO	Lowest wage paid	MTC	Median total compensation	TCC	Total cash compensation
AER	Average entry range	AWR	Average wage range	H	Hourly	LR	Low end range	MW	Median wage paid	TQ	Third quartile wage
AEX	Average experienced wage	AXR	Average experienced range	HI	Highest wage paid	M	Monthly	MWR	Median wage range	W	Weekly
ATC	Average total compensation	D	Daily	HR	High end range	MCC	Median cash compensation	S	See annotated source	Y	Yearly

Occupation/Type/Industry	Location	Per	Low	Mid	High	Source	Date
Dental Assistant	North Carolina	Y	28470 FQ	33450 MW	38790 TQ	USBLS	5/07
	Charlotte-Gastonia-Concord MSA, NC-SC	Y	32310 FQ	36900 MW	43410 TQ	USBLS	5/07
	Raleigh-Cary MSA, NC	Y	32810 FQ	36830 MW	42130 TQ	USBLS	5/07
	North Dakota	Y	25380 FQ	29240 MW	34860 TQ	USBLS	5/07
	Fargo MSA, ND-MN	Y	27510 FQ	31980 MW	37140 TQ	USBLS	5/07
	Ohio	Y	25790 FQ	30380 MW	35640 TQ	USBLS	5/07
	Cincinnati-Middletown MSA, OH-KY-IN	Y	27770 FQ	32470 MW	38820 TQ	USBLS	5/07
	Cleveland-Elyria-Mentor MSA, OH	Y	25550 FQ	30310 MW	35260 TQ	USBLS	5/07
	Columbus MSA, OH	Y	29040 FQ	32390 MW	37040 TQ	USBLS	5/07
	Dayton MSA, OH	Y	26800 FQ	32910 MW	37350 TQ	USBLS	5/07
	Mansfield MSA, OH	Y	27670 FQ	30390 MW	34480 TQ	USBLS	5/07
	Springfield MSA, OH	Y	26180 FQ	29770 MW	33910 TQ	USBLS	5/07
	Oklahoma	Y	22640 FQ	27140 MW	32430 TQ	USBLS	5/07
	Lawton MSA, OK	Y	20510 FQ	30870 MW	35960 TQ	USBLS	5/07
	Oklahoma City MSA, OK	Y	24090 FQ	28170 MW	32670 TQ	USBLS	5/07
	Tulsa MSA, OK	Y	23350 FQ	27010 MW	32350 TQ	USBLS	5/07
	Oregon	H	15.31 FQ	17.37 MW	19.39 TQ	ORBLS	5/08
	Portland-Vancouver-Beaverton MSA, OR-WA	Y	31900 FQ	36080 MW	40620 TQ	USBLS	5/07
	Pennsylvania	Y	24090 FQ	28730 MW	34850 TQ	USBLS	5/07
	Allentown-Bethlehem-Easton MSA, PA-NJ	Y	24570 FQ	28890 MW	34380 TQ	USBLS	5/07
	Philadelphia-Camden-Wilmington MSA, PA-NJ-DE-MD	Y	27270 FQ	33490 MW	39480 TQ	USBLS	5/07
	Pittsburgh MSA, PA	Y	23040 FQ	28010 MW	33240 TQ	USBLS	5/07
	Reading MSA, PA	Y	22780 FQ	26760 MW	34010 TQ	USBLS	5/07
	Rhode Island	Y	28300 FQ	34080 MW	40490 TQ	USBLS	5/07
	Providence-Fall River-Warwick MSA, RI-MA	Y	28720 FQ	34240 MW	40760 TQ	USBLS	5/07
	South Carolina	Y	26260 FQ	30630 MW	36410 TQ	USBLS	5/07
	Charleston-North Charleston MSA, SC	Y	25700 FQ	34260 MW	40570 TQ	USBLS	5/07
	Columbia MSA, SC	Y	27490 FQ	30970 MW	37300 TQ	USBLS	5/07
	South Dakota	Y	25787 FQ	30413 MW	35016 TQ	SDBLS	7/08-9/08
	Sioux Falls MSA, SD	Y	26856 FQ	32394 MW	37284 TQ	SDBLS	7/08-9/08
	Tennessee	Y	24390 FQ	30060 MW	35100 TQ	USBLS	5/07
	Memphis MSA, TN-MS-AR	Y	23660 FQ	29230 MW	34840 TQ	USBLS	5/07
	Nashville-Davidson-Murfreesboro MSA, TN	Y	23880 FQ	32210 MW	36660 TQ	USBLS	5/07
	Texas	Y	24620 FQ	29230 MW	34970 TQ	USBLS	5/07
	Austin-Round Rock MSA, TX	Y	27080 FQ	32330 MW	38810 TQ	USBLS	5/07
	Corpus Christi MSA, TX	Y	23070 FQ	27960 MW	31890 TQ	USBLS	5/07
	Dallas-Fort Worth-Arlington MSA, TX	Y	26200 FQ	30430 MW	36620 TQ	USBLS	5/07
	El Paso MSA, TX	Y	24130 FQ	26820 MW	29310 TQ	USBLS	5/07
	Houston-Sugar Land-Baytown MSA, TX	Y	25280 FQ	30200 MW	36190 TQ	USBLS	5/07
	San Antonio MSA, TX	Y	25750 FQ	29050 MW	32360 TQ	USBLS	5/07
	Utah	Y	23010 FQ	26890 MW	31070 TQ	USBLS	5/07
	Salt Lake City MSA, UT	Y	24920 FQ	28330 MW	32160 TQ	USBLS	5/07
	Vermont	Y	27780 FQ	33330 MW	38920 TQ	USBLS	5/07
	Burlington-South Burlington MSA, VT	Y	26930 FQ	33850 MW	39680 TQ	USBLS	5/07
	Virginia	Y	26180 FQ	31580 MW	37920 TQ	USBLS	5/07
	Richmond MSA, VA	Y	28320 FQ	33400 MW	37320 TQ	USBLS	5/07
	Roanoke MSA, VA	Y	26880 FQ	31530 MW	36760 TQ	USBLS	5/07
	Virginia Beach-Norfolk-Newport News MSA, VA-NC	Y	22690 FQ	29570 MW	35900 TQ	USBLS	5/07
	Washington	H	14.59 FQ	17.76 MW	21.03 TQ	WABLS	3/08
	Seattle-Tacoma-Bellevue MSA, WA	Y	31400 FQ	38240 MW	45970 TQ	USBLS	5/07
	West Virginia	Y	21182 FQ	24674 MW	30638 TQ	WVBLS	7/08-9/08
	Charleston MSA, WV	Y	20190 FQ	23470 MW	27740 TQ	USBLS	5/07
	Huntington-Ashland MSA, WV-KY-OH	Y	21200 FQ	24300 MW	30840 TQ	USBLS	5/07
	Wisconsin	Y	26660 FQ	30750 MW	35820 TQ	USBLS	5/07
	Milwaukee-Waukesha-West Allis MSA, WI	Y	27060 FQ	31020 MW	35540 TQ	USBLS	5/07

AE	Average entry wage	AW	Average wage paid	FQ	First quartile wage
AER	Average entry range	AWR	Average wage range	H	Hourly
AEX	Average experienced wage	AXR	Average experienced range	HI	Highest wage paid
ATC	Average total compensation	D	Daily	HR	High end range

LO	Lowest wage paid	MTC	Median total compensation	TCC	Total cash compensation
LR	Low end range	MW	Median wage paid	TQ	Third quartile wage
M	Monthly	MWR	Median wage range	W	Weekly
MCC	Median cash compensation	S	See annotated source	Y	Yearly

Occupation/Type/Industry	Location	Per	Low	Mid	High	Source	Date
Dental Assistant	Racine MSA, WI	Y	22200 FQ	29910 MW	35210 TQ	USBLS	5/07
	Wyoming	Y	20726 FQ	26335 MW	32749 TQ	WYBLS	9/08
	Cheyenne MSA, WY	Y	22409 FQ	30317 MW	34994 TQ	WYBLS	9/08
	Puerto Rico	Y	12740 FQ	14290 MW	16240 TQ	USBLS	5/07
	San Juan-Caguas-Guaynabo MSA, PR	Y	12790 FQ	14360 MW	16640 TQ	USBLS	5/07
	Virgin Islands	Y	20680 FQ	26260 MW	31670 TQ	USBLS	5/07
	Guam	Y	17830 FQ	23160 MW	32000 TQ	USBLS	5/07
Dental Hygienist	Alabama	Y	34160 FQ	40190 MW	47870 TQ	USBLS	5/07
	Birmingham-Hoover MSA, AL	Y	40250 FQ	47560 MW	53860 TQ	USBLS	5/07
	Alaska	Y	82540 FQ	92430 MW	103830 TQ	USBLS	5/07
	Anchorage MSA, AK	Y	82910 FQ	93260 MW	104810 TQ	USBLS	5/07
	Arizona	Y	66730 FQ	73400 MW	79780 TQ	USBLS	5/07
	Phoenix-Mesa-Scottsdale MSA, AZ	Y	65360 FQ	72400 MW	78680 TQ	USBLS	5/07
	Tucson MSA, AZ	Y	68970 FQ	74510 MW	80250 TQ	USBLS	5/07
	Arkansas	Y	42320 FQ	54470 MW	64870 TQ	USBLS	5/07
	Little Rock-North Little Rock MSA, AR	Y	42560 FQ	52910 MW	60480 TQ	USBLS	5/07
	California	H	31.08 FQ	41.71 MW	49.96 TQ	CABLS	1/08-3/08
	Bakersfield MSA, CA	H	41.32 FQ	44.27 MW	47.23 TQ	CABLS	1/08-3/08
	Los Angeles-Long Beach-Glendale PMSA, CA	H	32.17 FQ	40.13 MW	49.11 TQ	CABLS	1/08-3/08
	Oakland-Fremont-Hayward MSA, CA	H	40.87 FQ	48.49 MW	57.92 TQ	CABLS	1/08-3/08
	Oxnard-Thousand Oaks-Ventura MSA, CA	H	17.95 FQ	40.15 MW	47.88 TQ	CABLS	1/08-3/08
	Riverside-San Bernardino-Ontario MSA, CA	H	26.53 FQ	39.82 MW	46.79 TQ	CABLS	1/08-3/08
	Sacramento-Arden Arcade-Roseville MSA, CA	H	29.73 FQ	37.31 MW	47.52 TQ	CABLS	1/08-3/08
	San Diego-Carlsbad-San Marcos MSA, CA	H	35.45 FQ	42.48 MW	47.59 TQ	CABLS	1/08-3/08
	San Francisco-San Mateo-Redwood PMSA, CA	H	32.27 FQ	52.58 MW	58.72 TQ	CABLS	1/08-3/08
	San Jose-Sunnyvale-Santa Clara MSA, CA	H	21.36 FQ	30.77 MW	48.22 TQ	CABLS	1/08-3/08
	Santa Ana-Anaheim-Irvine PMSA, CA	Y	61260 FQ	80910 MW	93450 TQ	USBLS	5/07
	Colorado	Y	66750 FQ	74680 MW	83070 TQ	USBLS	5/07
	Denver-Aurora MSA, CO	Y	69020 FQ	77030 MW	86540 TQ	USBLS	5/07
	Connecticut	H	27.67 AE	35.45 MW		CTBLS	1/08-3/08
	Bridgeport-Stamford-Norwalk MSA, CT	Y	67480 FQ	75490 MW	83020 TQ	USBLS	5/07
	Danbury MSA, CT	Y	65110 FQ	72240 MW	77970 TQ	USBLS	5/07
	Hartford-West Hartford-East Hartford MSA, CT	Y	63300 FQ	70680 MW	76480 TQ	USBLS	5/07
	Norwich-New London MSA, CT-RI	Y	64790 FQ	70160 MW	75500 TQ	USBLS	5/07
	Delaware	Y	57700 FQ	68690 MW	75210 TQ	USBLS	5/07
	Dover MSA, DE	Y	55420 FQ	66330 MW	73890 TQ	USBLS	5/07
	Wilmington PMSA, DE-MD-NJ	Y	60740 FQ	69760 MW	75820 TQ	USBLS	5/07
	District of Columbia	Y	53280 FQ	68980 MW	77790 TQ	USBLS	5/07
	Washington-Arlington-Alexandria MSA, DC-VA-MD-WV	Y	53650 FQ	70650 MW	82160 TQ	USBLS	5/07
	Florida	Y	48860 FQ	57760 MW	65570 TQ	USBLS	5/07
	Fort Lauderdale-Pompano Beach-Deerfield Beach PMSA, FL	Y	52110 FQ	58930 MW	65910 TQ	USBLS	5/07
	Jacksonville MSA, FL	Y	50630 FQ	57350 MW	63040 TQ	USBLS	5/07
	Miami-Fort Lauderdale-Miami Beach MSA, FL	Y	46590 FQ	56040 MW	63900 TQ	USBLS	5/07
	Orlando-Kissimmee MSA, FL	Y	52990 FQ	59620 MW	66960 TQ	USBLS	5/07
	Tampa-St. Petersburg-Clearwater MSA, FL	Y	44650 FQ	58400 MW	65790 TQ	USBLS	5/07
	West Palm Beach-Boca Raton-Boynton Beach PMSA, FL	Y	40930 FQ	54760 MW	62520 TQ	USBLS	5/07
	Georgia	Y	51450 FQ	64120 MW	73230 TQ	USBLS	5/07

AE	Average entry wage	**AW**	Average wage paid	**FQ**	First quartile wage
AER	Average entry range	**AWR**	Average wage range	**H**	Hourly
AEX	Average experienced wage	**AXR**	Average experienced range	**HI**	Highest wage paid
ATC	Average total compensation	**D**	Daily	**HR**	High end range

LO	Lowest wage paid	**MTC**	Median total compensation	**TCC**	Total cash compensation
LR	Low end range	**MW**	Median wage paid	**TQ**	Third quartile wage
M	Monthly	**MWR**	Median wage range	**W**	Weekly
MCC	Median cash compensation	**S**	See annotated source	**Y**	Yearly

Dental Hygienist

Occupation/Type/Industry	Location	Per	Low	Mid	High	Source	Date
Dental Hygienist	Atlanta-Sandy Springs-Marietta MSA, GA	Y	62050 FQ	69850 MW	76090 TQ	USBLS	5/07
	Macon MSA, GA	Y	45070 FQ	52900 MW	58820 TQ	USBLS	5/07
	Savannah MSA, GA	Y	46840 FQ	60220 MW	72650 TQ	USBLS	5/07
	Hawaii	Y	54500 FQ	67060 MW	76660 TQ	USBLS	5/07
	Honolulu MSA, HI	Y	50540 FQ	65090 MW	74640 TQ	USBLS	5/07
	Idaho	Y	61160 FQ	70090 MW	78560 TQ	USBLS	5/07
	Boise City-Nampa MSA, ID	Y	66150 FQ	72420 MW	78380 TQ	USBLS	5/07
	Illinois	Y	52010 FQ	63740 MW	74760 TQ	USBLS	5/07
	Chicago-Naperville-Joliet MSA, IL-IN-WI	Y	56110 FQ	68480 MW	77660 TQ	USBLS	5/07
	Indiana	Y	55840 FQ	64680 MW	73590 TQ	USBLS	5/07
	Elkhart-Goshen MSA, IN	Y	52610 FQ	58300 MW	65060 TQ	USBLS	5/07
	Gary PMSA, IN	Y	50050 FQ	64290 MW	75740 TQ	USBLS	5/07
	Indianapolis-Carmel MSA, IN	Y	65860 FQ	71220 MW	76290 TQ	USBLS	5/07
	Iowa	Y	55330 FQ	61600 MW	68160 TQ	USBLS	5/07
	Des Moines-West Des Moines MSA, IA	Y	58690 FQ	65010 MW	71740 TQ	USBLS	5/07
	Dubuque MSA, IA	Y	49040 FQ	53420 MW	58410 TQ	USBLS	5/07
	Kansas	Y	57140 FQ	67760 MW	75870 TQ	USBLS	5/07
	Wichita MSA, KS	Y	53640 FQ	59970 MW	66910 TQ	USBLS	5/07
	Kentucky	Y	48731 FQ	56766 MW	64292 TQ	KYBLS	2008
	Bowling Green MSA, KY	Y	38630 FQ	45000 MW	55060 TQ	USBLS	5/07
	Louisville-Jefferson County MSA, KY-IN	Y	54380 FQ	59020 MW	63600 TQ	USBLS	5/07
	Louisiana	H	18.27 FQ	25.81 MW	32.45 TQ	LABLS	1/08-3/08
	Baton Rouge MSA, LA	Y	35100 FQ	46020 MW	61640 TQ	USBLS	5/07
	New Orleans-Metairie-Kenner MSA, LA	Y	39660 FQ	54390 MW	65800 TQ	USBLS	5/07
	Maine	Y	51870 FQ	58610 MW	64950 TQ	USBLS	5/07
	Portland-South Portland-Biddeford MSA, ME	Y	54730 FQ	61650 MW	67700 TQ	USBLS	5/07
	Maryland	Y		70600 MW		MDBLS	3/08
	Baltimore-Towson MSA, MD	Y	62580 FQ	71230 MW	79230 TQ	USBLS	5/07
	Bethesda-Gaithersburg-Frederick PMSA, MD	Y	60140 FQ	68010 MW	74710 TQ	USBLS	5/07
	Massachusetts	Y	64490 FQ	72690 MW	81190 TQ	USBLS	5/07
	Boston-Cambridge-Quincy NECTA, MA	Y	67870 FQ	77260 MW	87570 TQ	USBLS	5/07
	Lynn-Peabody-Salem NECTA, MA	Y	68390 FQ	73060 MW	78020 TQ	USBLS	5/07
	Worcester MSA, MA-CT	Y	62750 FQ	70620 MW	77520 TQ	USBLS	5/07
	Michigan	Y	54310 FQ	59860 MW	66250 TQ	USBLS	5/07
	Detroit-Warren-Livonia MSA, MI	Y	56080 FQ	62760 MW	70200 TQ	USBLS	5/07
	Grand Rapids-Wyoming MSA, MI	Y	54730 FQ	58190 MW	61890 TQ	USBLS	5/07
	Muskegon-Norton Shores MSA, MI	Y	32680 FQ	45190 MW	53240 TQ	USBLS	5/07
	Warren-Troy-Farmington Hills PMSA, MI	Y	55750 FQ	62760 MW	70590 TQ	USBLS	5/07
	Minnesota	Y	62710 FQ	71404 MW	79743 TQ	MNBLS	10/08-12/08
	Duluth-Superior MSA, MN-WI	Y	51505 FQ	57772 MW	64290 TQ	MNBLS	10/08-12/08
	Minneapolis-Saint Paul MSA, MN-WI	Y	66738 FQ	74041 MW	81103 TQ	MNBLS	10/08-12/08
	Rochester MSA, MN	Y	61800 FQ	69516 MW	76833 TQ	MNBLS	10/08-12/08
	Mississippi	Y	32880 FQ	43040 MW	54540 TQ	USBLS	5/07
	Jackson MSA, MS	Y	34010 FQ	43490 MW	52150 TQ	USBLS	5/07
	Missouri	Y	52500 FQ	62230 MW	73200 TQ	USBLS	5/07
	Kansas City MSA, MO-KS	Y	65390 FQ	71890 MW	77960 TQ	USBLS	5/07
	St. Louis MSA, MO-IL	Y	54080 FQ	59950 MW	66270 TQ	USBLS	5/07
	Springfield MSA, MO	Y	44170 FQ	61720 MW	72780 TQ	USBLS	5/07
	Montana	Y	55480 FQ	62930 MW	72180 TQ	USBLS	5/07
	Billings MSA, MT	Y	60280 FQ	68460 MW	75280 TQ	USBLS	5/07
	Nebraska	Y	52280 FQ	62520 MW	73360 TQ	USBLS	5/07
	Omaha-Council Bluffs MSA, NE-IA	Y	64010 FQ	70900 MW	77960 TQ	USBLS	5/07
	Nevada	H	33.45 FQ	38.80 MW	44.81 TQ	NVBLS	5/08
	Las Vegas-Paradise MSA, NV	H	32.87 FQ	37.17 MW	41.93 TQ	NVBLS	5/08
	New Hampshire	H	30.38 AE	36.07 MW	37.97 AEX	NHBLS	6/08
	Manchester MSA, NH	Y	69520 FQ	76470 MW	83340 TQ	USBLS	5/07
	Nashua NECTA, NH-MA	Y	70000 FQ	76220 MW	82940 TQ	USBLS	5/07

AE	Average entry wage	AW	Average wage paid	FQ	First quartile wage	LO	Lowest wage paid	MTC Median total compensation TCC Total cash compensation
AER	Average entry range	AWR	Average wage range	H	Hourly	LR	Low end range	MW Median wage paid TQ Third quartile wage
AEX	Average experienced wage	AXR	Average experienced range	HI	Highest wage paid	M	Monthly	MWR Median wage range W Weekly
ATC	Average total compensation	D	Daily	HR	High end range	MCC	Median cash compensation	S See annotated source Y Yearly

Occupation/Type/Industry	Location	Per	Low	Mid	High	Source	Date
Dental Hygienist	New Jersey	Y	67290 FQ	74160 MW	81330 TQ	USBLS	5/07
	Camden PMSA, NJ	Y	65140 FQ	72970 MW	79520 TQ	USBLS	5/07
	Edison PMSA, NJ	Y	65310 FQ	72720 MW	79450 TQ	USBLS	5/07
	Newark-Union PMSA, NJ-PA	Y	70660 FQ	78180 MW	85810 TQ	USBLS	5/07
	New Mexico	Y	66240 FQ	73320 MW	81140 TQ	USBLS	5/07
	Albuquerque MSA, NM	Y	68480 FQ	74620 MW	81600 TQ	USBLS	5/07
	New York	Y	51250 FQ	61090 MW	73900 TQ	USBLS	5/07
	Albany-Schenectady-Troy MSA, NY	Y	53620 FQ	58400 MW	63440 TQ	USBLS	5/07
	Buffalo-Niagara Falls MSA, NY	Y	43210 FQ	47170 MW	52200 TQ	USBLS	5/07
	Nassau-Suffolk PMSA, NY	Y	60480 FQ	69020 MW	76220 TQ	USBLS.	5/07
	New York-Northern New Jersey-Long Island MSA, NY-NJ-PA	Y	63300 FQ	72930 MW	81760 TQ	USBLS	5/07
	Syracuse MSA, NY	Y	45400 FQ	51070 MW	57800 TQ	USBLS	5/07
	North Carolina	Y	51980 FQ	60630 MW	70700 TQ	USBLS	5/07
	Charlotte-Gastonia-Concord MSA, NC-SC	Y	52430 FQ	62730 MW	72240 TQ	USBLS	5/07
	Raleigh-Cary MSA, NC	Y	57190 FQ	68460 MW	76610 TQ	USBLS	5/07
	North Dakota	Y	44720 FQ	53200 MW	60520 TQ	USBLS	5/07
	Fargo MSA, ND-MN	Y	46320 FQ	54090 MW	61210 TQ	USBLS	5/07
	Grand Forks MSA, ND-MN	Y	44630 FQ	53110 MW	58540 TQ	USBLS	5/07
	Ohio	Y	53940 FQ	61550 MW	70410 TQ	USBLS	5/07
	Cincinnati-Middletown MSA, OH-KY-IN	Y	56840 FQ	64490 MW	73130 TQ	USBLS	5/07
	Cleveland-Elyria-Mentor MSA, OH	Y	54860 FQ	62000 MW	69520 TQ	USBLS	5/07
	Columbus MSA, OH	Y	64340 FQ	71010 MW	76730 TQ	USBLS	5/07
	Dayton MSA, OH	Y	55980 FQ	62990 MW	70310 TQ	USBLS	5/07
	Oklahoma	Y	41340 FQ	58770 MW	74280 TQ	USBLS	5/07
	Oklahoma City MSA, OK	Y	37990 FQ	53520 MW	69440 TQ	USBLS	5/07
	Tulsa MSA, OK	Y	43030 FQ	61880 MW	78330 TQ	USBLS	5/07
	Oregon	H	34.24 FQ	37.02 MW	40.00 TQ	ORBLS	5/08
	Portland-Vancouver-Beaverton MSA, OR-WA	Y	70000 FQ	75840 MW	81970 TQ	USBLS	5/07
	Salem MSA, OR	Y	69630 FQ	74290 MW	79670 TQ	USBLS	5/07
	Pennsylvania	Y	45260 FQ	54530 MW	65060 TQ	USBLS	5/07
	Allentown-Bethlehem-Easton MSA, PA-NJ	Y	45690 FQ	55000 MW	63060 TQ	USBLS	5/07
	Erie MSA, PA	Y	40440 FQ	51230 MW	57980 TQ	USBLS	5/07
	Philadelphia-Camden-Wilmington MSA, PA-NJ-DE-MD	Y	54850 FQ	67720 MW	75570 TQ	USBLS	5/07
	Pittsburgh MSA, PA	Y	42670 FQ	47840 MW	52820 TQ	USBLS	5/07
	Rhode Island	Y	60590 FQ	67830 MW	74590 TQ	USBLS	5/07
	Providence-Fall River-Warwick MSA, RI-MA	Y	61270 FQ	68290 MW	74980 TQ	USBLS	5/07
	South Carolina	Y	43340 FQ	51510 MW	59800 TQ	USBLS	5/07
	Charleston-North Charleston MSA, SC	Y	41670 FQ	50750 MW	58710 TQ	USBLS	5/07
	Columbia MSA, SC	Y	44070 FQ	52030 MW	60920 TQ	USBLS	5/07
	South Dakota	Y	52589 FQ	58989 MW	64862 TQ	SDBLS	7/08-9/08
	Sioux Falls MSA, SD	Y	55809 FQ	61949 MW	69732 TQ	SDBLS	7/08-9/08
	Tennessee	Y	46440 FQ	56160 MW	64580 TQ	USBLS	5/07
	Memphis MSA, TN-MS-AR	Y	50930 FQ	58970 MW	66280 TQ	USBLS	5/07
	Nashville-Davidson-Murfreesboro MSA, TN	Y	43410 FQ	53950 MW	60700 TQ	USBLS	5/07
	Texas	Y	51830 FQ	66160 MW	76900 TQ	USBLS	5/07
	Austin-Round Rock MSA, TX	Y	67710 FQ	73850 MW	79950 TQ	USBLS	5/07
	Beaumont-Port Arthur MSA, TX	Y	53360 FQ	56850 MW	60290 TQ	USBLS	5/07
	Dallas-Fort Worth-Arlington MSA, TX	Y	58540 FQ	71080 MW	79670 TQ	USBLS	5/07
	El Paso MSA, TX	Y	45380 FQ	53360 MW	59470 TQ	USBLS	5/07
	Houston-Sugar Land-Baytown MSA, TX	Y	54270 FQ	69600 MW	80500 TQ	USBLS	5/07
	San Antonio MSA, TX	Y	45240 FQ	60050 MW	71840 TQ	USBLS	5/07
	Utah	Y	53410 FQ	63830 MW	73230 TQ	USBLS	5/07
	Salt Lake City MSA, UT	Y	47570 FQ	67620 MW	75690 TQ	USBLS	5/07
	Vermont	Y	50070 FQ	57930 MW	65120 TQ	USBLS	5/07

AE	Average entry wage	AW	Average wage paid	FQ	First quartile wage	LO	Lowest wage paid	MTC	Median total compensation	TCC	Total cash compensation
AER	Average entry range	AWR	Average wage range	H	Hourly	LR	Low end range	MW	Median wage paid	TQ	Third quartile wage
AEX	Average experienced wage	AXR	Average experienced range	HI	Highest wage paid	M	Monthly	MWR	Median wage range	W	Weekly
ATC	Average total compensation	D	Daily	HR	High end range	MCC	Median cash compensation	S	See annotated source	Y	Yearly

408

Occupation/Type/Industry	Location	Per	Low	Mid	High	Source	Date
Dental Hygienist	Burlington-South Burlington MSA, VT	Y	40650 FQ	55800 MW	62350 TQ	USBLS	5/07
	Virginia	Y	55170 FQ	68700 MW	80120 TQ	USBLS	5/07
	Richmond MSA, VA	Y	60260 FQ	69930 MW	78230 TQ	USBLS	5/07
	Virginia Beach-Norfolk-Newport News MSA, VA-NC	Y	56350 FQ	66080 MW	76360 TQ	USBLS	5/07
	Washington	H	38.95 FQ	43.39 MW	47.32 TQ	WABLS	3/08
	Seattle-Tacoma-Bellevue MSA, WA	Y	84470 FQ	91680 MW	98750 TQ	USBLS	5/07
	West Virginia	Y	36073 FQ	47444 MW	55687 TQ	WVBLS	7/08-9/08
	Charleston MSA, WV	Y	44760 FQ	49740 MW	56130 TQ	USBLS	5/07
	Wisconsin	Y	52400 FQ	57720 MW	63040 TQ	USBLS	5/07
	Milwaukee-Waukesha-West Allis MSA, WI	Y	52060 FQ	57220 MW	62290 TQ	USBLS	5/07
	Wyoming	Y	46073 FQ	54745 MW	64265 TQ	WYBLS	9/08
	Cheyenne MSA, WY	Y	58570 FQ	63381 MW	68895 TQ	WYBLS	9/08
	Puerto Rico	Y	20560 FQ	24740 MW	29520 TQ	USBLS	5/07
	San Juan-Caguas-Guaynabo MSA, PR	Y	20380 FQ	24640 MW	29120 TQ	USBLS	5/07
	Guam	Y	29780 FQ	36480 MW	42100 TQ	USBLS	5/07
Department of Corrections	New Hampshire	Y			27786 HI	NHUL03	2008
Dental Laboratory Technician	Alabama	Y	20050 FQ	29500 MW	37210 TQ	USBLS	5/07
	Alaska	Y	35050 FQ	43630 MW	51680 TQ	USBLS	5/07
	Anchorage MSA, AK	Y	40430 FQ	47160 MW	55100 TQ	USBLS	5/07
	Arizona	Y	21080 FQ	28240 MW	37470 TQ	USBLS	5/07
	Phoenix-Mesa-Scottsdale MSA, AZ	Y	23560 FQ	30460 MW	36690 TQ	USBLS	5/07
	Tucson MSA, AZ	Y	15930 FQ	20010 MW	41760 TQ	USBLS	5/07
	Arkansas	Y	24170 FQ	31570 MW	41410 TQ	USBLS	5/07
	Little Rock-North Little Rock MSA, AR	Y	27040 FQ	30570 MW	35720 TQ	USBLS	5/07
	California	H	13.53 FQ	17.76 MW	23.57 TQ	CABLS	1/08-3/08
	Los Angeles-Long Beach-Glendale PMSA, CA	H	12.13 FQ	16.84 MW	23.54 TQ	CABLS	1/08-3/08
	Oakland-Fremont-Hayward MSA, CA	H	13.76 FQ	18.73 MW	22.62 TQ	CABLS	1/08-3/08
	Oxnard-Thousand Oaks-Ventura MSA, CA	H	13.28 FQ	14.98 MW	29.28 TQ	CABLS	1/08-3/08
	Riverside-San Bernardino-Ontario MSA, CA	H	11.24 FQ	15.08 MW	17.95 TQ	CABLS	1/08-3/08
	Sacramento-Arden Arcade-Roseville MSA, CA	H	13.53 FQ	18.03 MW	25.79 TQ	CABLS	1/08-3/08
	San Diego-Carlsbad-San Marcos MSA, CA	H	13.25 FQ	15.47 MW	22.93 TQ	CABLS	1/08-3/08
	San Francisco-San Mateo-Redwood PMSA, CA	H	13.78 FQ	19.55 MW	25.67 TQ	CABLS	1/08-3/08
	San Jose-Sunnyvale-Santa Clara MSA, CA	H	12.46 FQ	16.34 MW	21.42 TQ	CABLS	1/08-3/08
	Santa Ana-Anaheim-Irvine PMSA, CA	Y	33830 FQ	40610 MW	51640 TQ	USBLS	5/07
	Colorado	Y	37940 FQ	41410 MW	45090 TQ	USBLS	5/07
	Denver-Aurora MSA, CO	Y	38960 FQ	42090 MW	45250 TQ	USBLS	5/07
	Connecticut	H	12.83 AE	17.06 MW		CTBLS	1/08-3/08
	Danbury MSA, CT	Y	25980 FQ	28240 MW	39900 TQ	USBLS	5/07
	Hartford-West Hartford-East Hartford MSA, CT	Y	29330 FQ	33460 MW	37010 TQ	USBLS	5/07
	Delaware	Y	18510 FQ	22440 MW	30950 TQ	USBLS	5/07
	Wilmington PMSA, DE-MD-NJ	Y	28200 FQ	39910 MW	46940 TQ	USBLS	5/07
	District of Columbia	Y	49130 FQ	62490 MW	72440 TQ	USBLS	5/07
	Washington-Arlington-Alexandria MSA, DC-VA-MD-WV	Y	24460 FQ	40540 MW	60660 TQ	USBLS	5/07
	Florida	Y	24240 FQ	33740 MW	46510 TQ	USBLS	5/07
	Fort Lauderdale-Pompano Beach-Deerfield Beach PMSA, FL	Y	22100 FQ	33210 MW	47160 TQ	USBLS	5/07
	Jacksonville MSA, FL	Y	29090 FQ	48610 MW	58330 TQ	USBLS	5/07
	Miami-Fort Lauderdale-Miami Beach MSA, FL	Y	24000 FQ	33950 MW	49180 TQ	USBLS	5/07
	Orlando-Kissimmee MSA, FL	Y	24040 FQ	35650 MW	42200 TQ	USBLS	5/07

AE	Average entry wage	AW	Average wage paid	FQ	First quartile wage
AER	Average entry range	AWR	Average wage range	H	Hourly
AEX	Average experienced wage	AXR	Average experienced range	HI	Highest wage paid
ATC	Average total compensation	D	Daily	HR	High end range

LO	Lowest wage paid	MTC	Median total compensation	TCC	Total cash compensation
LR	Low end range	MW	Median wage paid	TQ	Third quartile wage
M	Monthly	MWR	Median wage range	W	Weekly
MCC	Median cash compensation	S	See annotated source	Y	Yearly

Occupation/Type/Industry	Location	Per	Low	Mid	High	Source	Date
Dental Laboratory Technician	Tampa-St. Petersburg-Clearwater MSA, FL	Y	26520 FQ	34460 MW	44030 TQ	USBLS	5/07
	West Palm Beach-Boca Raton-Boynton Beach PMSA, FL	Y	33220 FQ	40130 MW	53680 TQ	USBLS	5/07
	Georgia	Y	24220 FQ	33900 MW	46570 TQ	USBLS	5/07
	Atlanta-Sandy Springs-Marietta MSA, GA	Y	24950 FQ	34890 MW	48770 TQ	USBLS	5/07
	Hawaii	Y	23360 FQ	28280 MW	42580 TQ	USBLS	5/07
	Honolulu MSA, HI	Y	24010 FQ	28770 MW	44150 TQ	USBLS	5/07
	Idaho	Y	15990 FQ	32610 MW	48430 TQ	USBLS	5/07
	Coeur d'Alene MSA, ID	Y	28510 FQ	42010 MW	50710 TQ	USBLS	5/07
	Illinois	Y	25070 FQ	30050 MW	39580 TQ	USBLS	5/07
	Chicago-Naperville-Joliet MSA, IL-IN-WI	Y	27040 FQ	32260 MW	39940 TQ	USBLS	5/07
	Indiana	Y	26250 FQ	32760 MW	40670 TQ	USBLS	5/07
	Gary PMSA, IN	Y	29180 FQ	34200 MW	39920 TQ	USBLS	5/07
	Indianapolis-Carmel MSA, IN	Y	28320 FQ	36020 MW	44940 TQ	USBLS	5/07
	Iowa	Y	24190 FQ	30890 MW	39070 TQ	USBLS	5/07
	Des Moines-West Des Moines MSA, IA	Y	28200 FQ	34290 MW	40990 TQ	USBLS	5/07
	Iowa City MSA, IA	Y	26600 FQ	30300 MW	51200 TQ	USBLS	5/07
	Waterloo-Cedar Falls MSA, IA	Y	31840 FQ	36790 MW	47180 TQ	USBLS	5/07
	Kansas	Y	25910 FQ	31910 MW	43450 TQ	USBLS	5/07
	Wichita MSA, KS	Y	16840 FQ	19710 MW	30040 TQ	USBLS	5/07
	Kentucky	Y	23071 FQ	29619 MW	41311 TQ	KYBLS	2008
	Louisville-Jefferson County MSA, KY-IN	Y	22510 FQ	29130 MW	38630 TQ	USBLS	5/07
	Louisiana	H	9.95 FQ	13.10 MW	16.73 TQ	LABLS	1/08-3/08
	Baton Rouge MSA, LA	Y	26100 FQ	29880 MW	35090 TQ	USBLS	5/07
	New Orleans-Metairie-Kenner MSA, LA	Y	15860 FQ	22220 MW	41010 TQ	USBLS	5/07
	Maine	Y	24210 FQ	29380 MW	33460 TQ	USBLS	5/07
	Portland-South Portland-Biddeford MSA, ME	Y	24580 FQ	30350 MW	33590 TQ	USBLS	5/07
	Maryland	Y		30075 MW		MDBLS	3/08
	Baltimore-Towson MSA, MD	Y	14900 FQ	28460 MW	38210 TQ	USBLS	5/07
	Bethesda-Gaithersburg-Frederick PMSA, MD	Y	14670 FQ	29070 MW	43640 TQ	USBLS	5/07
	Massachusetts	Y	28850 FQ	37340 MW	47010 TQ	USBLS	5/07
	Boston-Cambridge-Quincy NECTA, MA	Y	32320 FQ	40910 MW	53020 TQ	USBLS	5/07
	Michigan	Y	26070 FQ	33180 MW	38950 TQ	USBLS	5/07
	Detroit-Warren-Livonia MSA, MI	Y	29100 FQ	34020 MW	37640 TQ	USBLS	5/07
	Grand Rapids-Wyoming MSA, MI	Y	26520 FQ	37660 MW	44620 TQ	USBLS	5/07
	Warren-Troy-Farmington Hills PMSA, MI	Y	29390 FQ	33630 MW	37040 TQ	USBLS	5/07
	Minnesota	Y	33308 FQ	43333 MW	53192 TQ	MNBLS	10/08-12/08
	Duluth-Superior MSA, MN-WI	Y	25336 FQ	28912 MW	35661 TQ	MNBLS	10/08-12/08
	Minneapolis-Saint Paul MSA, MN-WI	Y	34459 FQ	43343 MW	54197 TQ	MNBLS	10/08-12/08
	Rochester MSA, MN	Y	44385 FQ	48212 MW	52041 TQ	MNBLS	10/08-12/08
	Mississippi	Y	20170 FQ	25130 MW	31180 TQ	USBLS	5/07
	Jackson MSA, MS	Y	21600 FQ	25310 MW	32120 TQ	USBLS	5/07
	Missouri	Y	24400 FQ	32330 MW	40500 TQ	USBLS	5/07
	Kansas City MSA, MO-KS	Y	25630 FQ	31700 MW	40190 TQ	USBLS	5/07
	St. Louis MSA, MO-IL	Y	24420 FQ	33180 MW	39310 TQ	USBLS	5/07
	Nebraska	Y	22880 FQ	29480 MW	39970 TQ	USBLS	5/07
	Omaha-Council Bluffs MSA, NE-IA	Y	24450 FQ	29360 MW	36480 TQ	USBLS	5/07
	Nevada	H	14.53 FQ	17.67 MW	20.53 TQ	NVBLS	5/08
	Las Vegas-Paradise MSA, NV	H	14.24 FQ	17.41 MW	19.88 TQ	NVBLS	5/08
	New Hampshire	H	14.02 AE	19.10 MW	22.20 AEX	NHBLS	6/08
	Manchester MSA, NH	Y	35570 FQ	39570 MW	43780 TQ	USBLS	5/07
	Nashua NECTA, NH-MA	Y	30790 FQ	37860 MW	45520 TQ	USBLS	5/07
	New Jersey	Y	28880 FQ	38010 MW	48010 TQ	USBLS	5/07
	Camden PMSA, NJ	Y	32410 FQ	38360 MW	45750 TQ	USBLS	5/07
	Edison PMSA, NJ	Y	31170 FQ	40750 MW	46320 TQ	USBLS	5/07
	Newark-Union PMSA, NJ-PA	Y	29490 FQ	41760 MW	61300 TQ	USBLS	5/07
	New Mexico	Y	21280 FQ	28570 MW	33830 TQ	USBLS	5/07
	Albuquerque MSA, NM	Y	22770 FQ	28770 MW	33090 TQ	USBLS	5/07

AE	Average entry wage	AW	Average wage paid	FQ	First quartile wage
AER	Average entry range	AWR	Average wage range	H	Hourly
AEX	Average experienced wage	AXR	Average experienced range	HI	Highest wage paid
ATC	Average total compensation	D	Daily	HR	High end range

LO	Lowest wage paid	MTC	Median total compensation
LR	Low end range	MW	Median wage paid
M	Monthly	MWR	Median wage range
MCC	Median cash compensation	S	See annotated source

TCC	Total cash compensation
TQ	Third quartile wage
W	Weekly
Y	Yearly

Occupation/Type/Industry	Location	Per	Low	Mid	High	Source	Date
Dental Laboratory Technician	New York	Y	25450 FQ	34320 MW	43790 TQ	USBLS	5/07
	Albany-Schenectady-Troy MSA, NY	Y	27030 FQ	31550 MW	37100 TQ	USBLS	5/07
	Buffalo-Niagara Falls MSA, NY	Y	20540 FQ	28050 MW	36060 TQ	USBLS	5/07
	Nassau-Suffolk PMSA, NY	Y	26550 FQ	37530 MW	44680 TQ	USBLS	5/07
	New York-Northern New Jersey-Long Island MSA, NY-NJ-PA	Y	27420 FQ	37290 MW	46170 TQ	USBLS	5/07
	North Carolina	Y	26150 FQ	31420 MW	40400 TQ	USBLS	5/07
	Charlotte-Gastonia-Concord MSA, NC-SC	Y	26870 FQ	32860 MW	45420 TQ	USBLS	5/07
	Raleigh-Cary MSA, NC	Y	26500 FQ	29250 MW	39560 TQ	USBLS	5/07
	North Dakota	Y	23340 FQ	28240 MW	32140 TQ	USBLS	5/07
	Ohio	Y	25330 FQ	33220 MW	41730 TQ	USBLS	5/07
	Cincinnati-Middletown MSA, OH-KY-IN	Y	26760 FQ	33870 MW	51410 TQ	USBLS	5/07
	Cleveland-Elyria-Mentor MSA, OH	Y	23440 FQ	32530 MW	37180 TQ	USBLS	5/07
	Columbus MSA, OH	Y	25540 FQ	34280 MW	48730 TQ	USBLS	5/07
	Dayton MSA, OH	Y	39960 FQ	44740 MW	51280 TQ	USBLS	5/07
	Oklahoma	Y	18880 FQ	27000 MW	33870 TQ	USBLS	5/07
	Oklahoma City MSA, OK	Y	19500 FQ	26640 MW	33000 TQ	USBLS	5/07
	Tulsa MSA, OK	Y	14530 FQ	26030 MW	31140 TQ	USBLS	5/07
	Oregon	H	14.31 FQ	18.11 MW	22.46 TQ	ORBLS	5/08
	Medford MSA, OR	Y	33250 FQ	36210 MW	40630 TQ	USBLS	5/07
	Portland-Vancouver-Beaverton MSA, OR-WA	Y	29300 FQ	37500 MW	46320 TQ	USBLS	5/07
	Pennsylvania	Y	25040 FQ	35340 MW	48510 TQ	USBLS	5/07
	Allentown-Bethlehem-Easton MSA, PA-NJ	Y	21490 FQ	28060 MW	35730 TQ	USBLS	5/07
	Lancaster MSA, PA	Y	22940 FQ	27750 MW	34180 TQ	USBLS	5/07
	Philadelphia-Camden-Wilmington MSA, PA-NJ-DE-MD	Y	31880 FQ	40730 MW	48070 TQ	USBLS	5/07
	South Carolina	Y	23230 FQ	31080 MW	47520 TQ	USBLS	5/07
	Charleston-North Charleston MSA, SC	Y	22170 FQ	26500 MW	31730 TQ	USBLS	5/07
	Columbia MSA, SC	Y	31290 FQ	43050 MW	51350 TQ	USBLS	5/07
	South Dakota	Y	22136 FQ	24495 MW	28651 TQ	SDBLS	7/08-9/08
	Sioux Falls MSA, SD	Y	23178 FQ	25693 MW	30391 TQ	SDBLS	7/08-9/08
	Tennessee	Y	26170 FQ	31120 MW	39710 TQ	USBLS	5/07
	Memphis MSA, TN-MS-AR	Y	27670 FQ	31420 MW	35160 TQ	USBLS	5/07
	Nashville-Davidson-Murfreesboro MSA, TN	Y	32240 FQ	41880 MW	53050 TQ	USBLS	5/07
	Texas	Y	24520 FQ	29730 MW	38190 TQ	USBLS	5/07
	Austin-Round Rock MSA, TX	Y	27670 FQ	33130 MW	38650 TQ	USBLS	5/07
	Dallas-Fort Worth-Arlington MSA, TX	Y	25500 FQ	32420 MW	40580 TQ	USBLS	5/07
	Houston-Sugar Land-Baytown MSA, TX	Y	20820 FQ	25640 MW	31970 TQ	USBLS	5/07
	San Antonio MSA, TX	Y	25550 FQ	29270 MW	36100 TQ	USBLS	5/07
	Utah	Y	20170 FQ	28950 MW	36750 TQ	USBLS	5/07
	Salt Lake City MSA, UT	Y	20330 FQ	28820 MW	36290 TQ	USBLS	5/07
	Vermont	Y	21930 FQ	26680 MW	32840 TQ	USBLS	5/07
	Virginia	Y	26320 FQ	33890 MW	50380 TQ	USBLS	5/07
	Richmond MSA, VA	Y	23380 FQ	28940 MW	32560 TQ	USBLS	5/07
	Virginia Beach-Norfolk-Newport News MSA, VA-NC	Y	29360 FQ	36210 MW	55680 TQ	USBLS	5/07
	Washington	H	15.38 FQ	18.41 MW	23.19 TQ	WABLS	3/08
	Seattle-Tacoma-Bellevue MSA, WA	Y	31120 FQ	37660 MW	47070 TQ	USBLS	5/07
	West Virginia	Y	21530 FQ	28755 MW	36352 TQ	WVBLS	7/08-9/08
	Charleston MSA, WV	Y	20450 FQ	23980 MW	32120 TQ	USBLS	5/07
	Wisconsin	Y	27060 FQ	33820 MW	42420 TQ	USBLS	5/07
	Milwaukee-Waukesha-West Allis MSA, WI	Y	29200 FQ	37600 MW	45510 TQ	USBLS	5/07
	Wyoming	Y	21630 FQ	27582 MW	32406 TQ	WYBLS	9/08
	Puerto Rico	Y	14090 FQ	16940 MW	24290 TQ	USBLS	5/07
	San Juan-Caguas-Guaynabo MSA, PR	Y	14980 FQ	17540 MW	25350 TQ	USBLS	5/07

AE Average entry wage	**AW** Average wage paid	**FQ** First quartile wage	**LO** Lowest wage paid	**MTC** Median total compensation	**TCC** Total cash compensation
AER Average entry range	**AWR** Average wage range	**H** Hourly	**LR** Low end range	**MW** Median wage paid	**TQ** Third quartile wage
AEX Average experienced wage	**AXR** Average experienced range	**HI** Highest wage paid	**M** Monthly	**MWR** Median wage range	**W** Weekly
ATC Average total compensation	**D** Daily	**HR** High end range	**MCC** Median cash compensation	**S** See annotated source	**Y** Yearly

Occupation/Type/Industry	Location	Per	Low	Mid	High	Source	Date
Dental Technician							
State Government	Ohio	H	15.62 LO		18.36 HI	ODAS	2008
Dentist	Alabama	Y	85310 FQ	136680 MW		USBLS	5/07
	Birmingham-Hoover MSA, AL	Y	76740 FQ			USBLS	5/07
	Alaska	Y	121090 FQ			USBLS	5/07
	Anchorage MSA, AK	Y	115770 FQ			USBLS	5/07
	Arizona	Y	96580 FQ	122180 MW		USBLS	5/07
	Phoenix-Mesa-Scottsdale MSA, AZ	Y	96290 FQ	116630 MW		USBLS	5/07
	Tucson MSA, AZ	Y	103570 FQ			USBLS	5/07
	Arkansas	Y	84130 FQ	116000 MW		USBLS	5/07
	Fort Smith MSA, AR-OK	Y	84220 FQ	107840 MW	125890 TQ	USBLS	5/07
	Little Rock-North Little Rock MSA, AR	Y	92360 FQ			USBLS	5/07
	California	H	47.22 FQ	61.28 MW		CABLS	1/08-3/08
	Los Angeles-Long Beach-Glendale PMSA, CA	H	36.78 FQ	52.87 MW		CABLS	1/08-3/08
	Oakland-Fremont-Hayward MSA, CA	H	60.71 FQ			CABLS	1/08-3/08
	Riverside-San Bernardino-Ontario MSA, CA	H	46.97 FQ	68.38 MW		CABLS	1/08-3/08
	Sacramento-Arden Arcade-Roseville MSA, CA	H	49.91 FQ	60.17 MW		CABLS	1/08-3/08
	San Diego-Carlsbad-San Marcos MSA, CA	H	43.83 FQ	56.36 MW		CABLS	1/08-3/08
	San Francisco-San Mateo-Redwood PMSA, CA	H	43.79 FQ	62.68 MW		CABLS	1/08-3/08
	San Jose-Sunnyvale-Santa Clara MSA, CA	H	52.10 FQ	68.29 MW		CABLS	1/08-3/08
	Santa Ana-Anaheim-Irvine PMSA, CA	Y	104640 FQ	119700 MW		USBLS	5/07
	Colorado	Y	108040 FQ			USBLS	5/07
	Denver-Aurora MSA, CO	Y	111260 FQ			USBLS	5/07
	Connecticut	H	50.42 AE	83.43 AW		CTBLS	1/08-3/08
	Bridgeport-Stamford-Norwalk MSA, CT	Y	112290 FQ	130950 MW		USBLS	5/07
	Delaware	Y	145410 FQ			USBLS	5/07
	Wilmington PMSA, DE-MD-NJ	Y	130780 FQ			USBLS	5/07
	District of Columbia	Y	103090 FQ	122630 MW		USBLS	5/07
	Washington-Arlington-Alexandria MSA, DC-VA-MD-WV	Y	97620 FQ			USBLS	5/07
	Florida	Y	90660 FQ	142510 MW		USBLS	5/07
	Cape Coral-Fort Myers MSA, FL	Y	98010 FQ			USBLS	5/07
	Fort Lauderdale-Pompano Beach-Deerfield Beach PMSA, FL	Y	69520 FQ			USBLS	5/07
	Jacksonville MSA, FL	Y	95340 FQ			USBLS	5/07
	Miami-Fort Lauderdale-Miami Beach MSA, FL	Y	83310 FQ	131690 MW		USBLS	5/07
	Orlando-Kissimmee MSA, FL	Y	91630 FQ			USBLS	5/07
	Tampa-St. Petersburg-Clearwater MSA, FL	Y	76540 FQ	113580 MW		USBLS	5/07
	West Palm Beach-Boca Raton-Boynton Beach PMSA, FL	Y	102740 FQ			USBLS	5/07
	Georgia	Y	106330 FQ			USBLS	5/07
	Atlanta-Sandy Springs-Marietta MSA, GA	Y	105680 FQ			USBLS	5/07
	Savannah MSA, GA	Y	126850 FQ			USBLS	5/07
	Hawaii	Y	104950 FQ	122370 MW		USBLS	5/07
	Honolulu MSA, HI	Y	101120 FQ	117780 MW		USBLS	5/07
	Boise City-Nampa MSA, ID	Y	51410 FQ			USBLS	5/07
	Illinois	Y	96730 FQ	138000 MW		USBLS	5/07
	Chicago-Naperville-Joliet MSA, IL-IN-WI	Y	98590 FQ	139430 MW		USBLS	5/07
	Indiana	Y	96630 FQ	130720 MW		USBLS	5/07
	Gary PMSA, IN	Y	135340 FQ			USBLS	5/07
	Indianapolis-Carmel MSA, IN	Y	89440 FQ	115500 MW	138850 TQ	USBLS	5/07
	Iowa	Y	109840 FQ	131160 MW		USBLS	5/07

AE	Average entry wage	AW	Average wage paid	FQ	First quartile wage	LO	Lowest wage paid	MTC	Median total compensation	TCC Total cash compensation
AER	Average entry range	AWR	Average wage range	H	Hourly	LR	Low end range	MW	Median wage paid	TQ Third quartile wage
AEX	Average experienced wage	AXR	Average experienced range	HI	Highest wage paid	M	Monthly	MWR	Median wage range	W Weekly
ATC	Average total compensation	D	Daily	HR	High end range	MCC	Median cash compensation	S	See annotated source	Y Yearly

Occupation/Type/Industry	Location	Per	Low	Mid	High	Source	Date
Dentist	Cedar Rapids MSA, IA	Y	94910 FQ	115040 MW		USBLS	5/07
	Des Moines-West Des Moines MSA, IA	Y	117940 FQ	131120 MW		USBLS	5/07
	Dubuque MSA, IA	Y	126140 FQ	141030 MW		USBLS	5/07
	Kansas	Y	96150 FQ	127380 MW		USBLS	5/07
	Wichita MSA, KS	Y	134300 FQ			USBLS	5/07
	Kentucky	Y	87295 FQ	123673 MW		KYBLS	2008
	Louisville-Jefferson County MSA, KY-IN	Y	92400 FQ	109310 MW		USBLS	5/07
	Louisiana	H	21.68 FQ	42.60 MW		LABLS	1/08-3/08
	Baton Rouge MSA, LA	Y	83010 FQ			USBLS	5/07
	Maine	Y	105080 FQ			USBLS	5/07
	Portland-South Portland-Biddeford MSA, ME	Y	97000 FQ			USBLS	5/07
	Maryland	Y		121025 MW		MDBLS	3/08
	Baltimore-Towson MSA, MD	Y	101350 FQ	117900 MW	142500 TQ	USBLS	5/07
	Bethesda-Gaithersburg-Frederick PMSA, MD	Y	82260 FQ	109800 MW		USBLS	5/07
	Massachusetts	Y	99960 FQ	143550 MW		USBLS	5/07
	Boston-Cambridge-Quincy NECTA, MA	Y	110160 FQ			USBLS	5/07
	Worcester MSA, MA-CT	Y	117740 FQ			USBLS	5/07
	Michigan	Y	108590 FQ			USBLS	5/07
	Detroit-Warren-Livonia MSA, MI	Y	104630 FQ	126020 MW		USBLS	5/07
	Grand Rapids-Wyoming MSA, MI	Y	139270 FQ			USBLS	5/07
	Warren-Troy-Farmington Hills PMSA, MI	Y	104450 FQ	121520 MW		USBLS	5/07
	Minnesota	Y	110805 FQ	161976 AW		MNBLS	10/08-12/08
	Duluth-Superior MSA, MN-WI	Y		189126 AW		MNBLS	10/08-12/08
	Minneapolis-Saint Paul MSA, MN-WI	Y	106934 FQ	158189 AW		MNBLS	10/08-12/08
	Rochester MSA, MN	Y	142901 FQ	169868 AW		MNBLS	10/08-12/08
	Mississippi	Y	77630 FQ	142600 MW		USBLS	5/07
	Jackson MSA, MS	Y	62370 FQ	105820 MW	142670 TQ	USBLS	5/07
	Missouri	Y	107870 FQ			USBLS	5/07
	Kansas City MSA, MO-KS	Y	99560 FQ			USBLS	5/07
	Montana	Y	74690 FQ	111510 MW	137450 TQ	USBLS	5/07
	Billings MSA, MT	Y	45480 FQ	86610 MW	117850 TQ	USBLS	5/07
	Nebraska	Y	98550 FQ			USBLS	5/07
	Omaha-Council Bluffs MSA, NE-IA	Y	129650 FQ			USBLS	5/07
	Nevada	H	59.12 FQ	80.97 AW		NVBLS	5/08
	Carson City MSA, NV	H	66.01 FQ			NVBLS	5/08
	Las Vegas-Paradise MSA, NV	H	57.25 FQ	67.38 MW		NVBLS	5/08
	New Hampshire	H	50.89 AE	70.53 MW	86.67 AEX	NHBLS	6/08
	Nashua NECTA, NH-MA	Y	116140 FQ	140260 MW		USBLS	5/07
	New Jersey	Y	92070 FQ	121790 MW		USBLS	5/07
	Camden PMSA, NJ	Y	104110 FQ	144690 MW		USBLS	5/07
	Edison PMSA, NJ	Y	86230 FQ	116160 MW		USBLS	5/07
	Newark-Union PMSA, NJ-PA	Y	101010 FQ			USBLS	5/07
	Trenton-Ewing MSA, NJ	Y	87650 FQ	105360 MW		USBLS	5/07
	New Mexico	Y	104870 FQ	136390 MW		USBLS	5/07
	Albuquerque MSA, NM	Y	126840 FQ			USBLS	5/07
	New York	Y	109780 FQ	134990 MW		USBLS	5/07
	Albany-Schenectady-Troy MSA, NY	Y	106710 FQ			USBLS	5/07
	Buffalo-Niagara Falls MSA, NY	Y	111510 FQ	128100 MW		USBLS	5/07
	Nassau-Suffolk PMSA, NY	Y	118640 FQ	141920 MW		USBLS	5/07
	New York-Northern New Jersey-Long Island MSA, NY-NJ-PA	Y	104440 FQ	132850 MW		USBLS	5/07
	Syracuse MSA, NY	Y	94170 FQ	110960 MW		USBLS	5/07
	North Carolina	Y	131630 FQ			USBLS	5/07
	Raleigh-Cary MSA, NC	Y	116330 FQ			USBLS	5/07
	North Dakota	Y	84280 FQ			USBLS	5/07
	Fargo MSA, ND-MN	Y	119810 FQ			USBLS	5/07
	Ohio	Y	112550 FQ			USBLS	5/07
	Cincinnati-Middletown MSA, OH-KY-IN	Y	136350 FQ			USBLS	5/07

AE	Average entry wage	AW	Average wage paid	FQ	First quartile wage
AER	Average entry range	AWR	Average wage range	H	Hourly
AEX	Average experienced wage	AXR	Average experienced range	HI	Highest wage paid
ATC	Average total compensation	D	Daily	HR	High end range

LO	Lowest wage paid	MTC	Median total compensation	TCC	Total cash compensation
LR	Low end range	MW	Median wage paid	TQ	Third quartile wage
M	Monthly	MWR	Median wage range	W	Weekly
MCC	Median cash compensation	S	See annotated source	Y	Yearly

Occupation/Type/Industry	Location	Per	Low	Mid	High	Source	Date
Dentist	Cleveland-Elyria-Mentor MSA, OH	Y	90730 FQ	124530 MW		USBLS	5/07
	Columbus MSA, OH	Y	125260 FQ			USBLS	5/07
	Dayton MSA, OH	Y	111650 FQ	134510 MW		USBLS	5/07
	Oklahoma	Y	71150 FQ	107950 MW		USBLS	5/07
	Oklahoma City MSA, OK	Y	79190 FQ	108350 MW		USBLS	5/07
	Tulsa MSA, OK	Y	64030 FQ	118270 MW		USBLS	5/07
	Portland-Vancouver-Beaverton MSA, OR-WA	Y	114050 FQ			USBLS	5/07
	Pennsylvania	Y	82150 FQ	116800 MW		USBLS	5/07
	Allentown-Bethlehem-Easton MSA, PA-NJ	Y	121740 FQ			USBLS	5/07
	Philadelphia-Camden-Wilmington MSA, PA-NJ-DE-MD	Y	96400 FQ	139330 MW		USBLS	5/07
	Pittsburgh MSA, PA	Y	75540 FQ	104480 MW	124230 TQ	USBLS	5/07
	Rhode Island	Y	103380 FQ			USBLS	5/07
	Providence-Fall River-Warwick MSA, RI-MA	Y	101470 FQ			USBLS	5/07
	South Carolina	Y	99430 FQ			USBLS	5/07
	Charleston-North Charleston MSA, SC	Y	70800 FQ	137400 MW		USBLS	5/07
	Columbia MSA, SC	Y	81560 FQ			USBLS	5/07
	South Dakota	Y	128457 FQ			SDBLS	7/08-9/08
	Sioux Falls MSA, SD	Y	133520 FQ			SDBLS	7/08-9/08
	Tennessee	Y	89870 FQ			USBLS	5/07
	Memphis MSA, TN-MS-AR	Y	95080 FQ			USBLS	5/07
	Nashville-Davidson-Murfreesboro MSA, TN	Y	72610 FQ	80840 MW		USBLS	5/07
	Texas	Y	92490 FQ			USBLS	5/07
	Austin-Round Rock MSA, TX	Y	97480 FQ	128470 MW		USBLS	5/07
	Dallas-Fort Worth-Arlington MSA, TX	Y	93130 FQ			USBLS	5/07
	El Paso MSA, TX	Y	122770 FQ			USBLS	5/07
	Houston-Sugar Land-Baytown MSA, TX	Y	91970 FQ			USBLS	5/07
	Midland MSA, TX	Y	68920 FQ	133090 MW		USBLS	5/07
	San Antonio MSA, TX	Y	92490 FQ	111490 MW		USBLS	5/07
	Utah	Y	79620 FQ	114680 MW		USBLS	5/07
	Provo-Orem MSA, UT	Y	58530 FQ	110060 MW	124200 TQ	USBLS	5/07
	Salt Lake City MSA, UT	Y	79510 FQ	104580 MW		USBLS	5/07
	Vermont	Y	106790 FQ			USBLS	5/07
	Burlington-South Burlington MSA, VT	Y	125940 FQ			USBLS	5/07
	Virginia	Y	109730 FQ			USBLS	5/07
	Richmond MSA, VA	Y	102890 FQ			USBLS	5/07
	Virginia Beach-Norfolk-Newport News MSA, VA-NC	Y	112570 FQ			USBLS	5/07
	Washington	Y		176112 AW		WABLS	3/08
	Seattle-Tacoma-Bellevue MSA, WA	Y	121830 FQ			USBLS	5/07
	West Virginia	Y	115985 FQ	161544 AW		WVBLS	7/08-9/08
	Wisconsin	Y	119210 FQ			USBLS	5/07
	Milwaukee-Waukesha-West Allis MSA, WI	Y	113790 FQ			USBLS	5/07
	Wyoming	Y	90837 FQ	112661 MW		WYBLS	9/08
	Casper MSA, WY	Y	64610 FQ	94264 MW	106879 TQ	WYBLS	9/08
	Cheyenne MSA, WY	Y	92061 FQ	106064 MW	119236 TQ	WYBLS	9/08
	Puerto Rico	Y	39460 FQ	52710 MW	97240 TQ	USBLS	5/07
	San Juan-Caguas-Guaynabo MSA, PR	Y	37870 FQ	49050 MW	95140 TQ	USBLS	5/07
Veterans Health Administration	United States	Y	93818 LO		137596 HI	OPM01	1/1/08
Deputy Administrator							
Municipal Government	Southfield, MI	Y			115000 HI	HLIFE	2008
Deputy Associate Director for Invitations and Correspondence							
White House Staff	United States	Y			38700 HI	WPOST02	2008

AE	Average entry wage	AW	Average wage paid	FQ	First quartile wage	LO	Lowest wage paid	MTC	Median total compensation	TCC Total cash compensation
AER	Average entry range	AWR	Average wage range	H	Hourly	LR	Low end range	MW	Median wage paid	TQ Third quartile wage
AEX	Average experienced wage	AXR	Average experienced range	HI	Highest wage paid	M	Monthly	MWR	Median wage range	W Weekly
ATC	Average total compensation	D	Daily	HR	High end range	MCC	Median cash compensation	S	See annotated source	Y Yearly

Occupation/Type/Industry	Location	Per	Low	Mid	High	Source	Date
Deputy Chief of Staff to the First Lady White House Staff	United States	Y			88500 ᴴᴵ	WPOST02	2008
Deputy City Attorney	Walnut Creek, CA	Y	105473 ʟᴏ		128200 ᴴᴵ	WCSWP	7/11/08
Deputy Comptroller General Federal Government	United States	Y			158500 ᴴᴵ	CRS02	1/08
Deputy Director of Proclamations White House Staff	United States	Y			44900 ᴴᴵ	WPOST02	2008
Deputy Director of the Gift Office White House Staff	United States	Y			37600 ᴴᴵ	WPOST02	2008
Deputy Legislative Fiscal Analyst	Nebraska	Y			102690 ᴴᴵ	NEST	2008
Deputy Library Director	United States	Y		74942 ᴬᵂ		AMLIB	2007
Deputy Mayor	Detroit, MI	Y			140000 ᴴᴵ	WXYZ	2008
Deputy Postmaster United States Postal Service	United States	Y			600026 ᴴᴵ	WATIME	2008
Deputy Registrar Field Representative State Government	Ohio	H	17.22 ʟᴏ		21.77 ᴴᴵ	ODAS	2008
Derrick Operator							
Oil and Gas	Alabama	Y	27810 ꜰQ	31330 ᴹᵂ	46030 ᵀQ	USBLS	5/07
Oil and Gas	Alaska	Y	35380 ꜰQ	49900 ᴹᵂ	65130 ᵀQ	USBLS	5/07
Oil and Gas	Arkansas	Y	28600 ꜰQ	31220 ᴹᵂ	34450 ᵀQ	USBLS	5/07
Oil and Gas	California	H	16.85 ꜰQ	19.57 ᴹᵂ	23.04 ᵀQ	CABLS	1/08-3/08
Oil and Gas	Colorado	Y	30270 ꜰQ	36780 ᴹᵂ	47440 ᵀQ	USBLS	5/07
Oil and Gas	Illinois	Y	32520 ꜰQ	36470 ᴹᵂ	39810 ᵀQ	USBLS	5/07
Oil and Gas	Kansas	Y	28180 ꜰQ	32780 ᴹᵂ	40870 ᵀQ	USBLS	5/07
Oil and Gas	Louisiana	H	14.97 ꜰQ	21.41 ᴹᵂ	25.86 ᵀQ	LABLS	1/08-3/08
Oil and Gas	Michigan	Y	26270 ꜰQ	28540 ᴹᵂ	30840 ᵀQ	USBLS	5/07
Oil and Gas	Mississippi	Y	28920 ꜰQ	32880 ᴹᵂ	46210 ᵀQ	USBLS	5/07
Oil and Gas	Montana	Y	32960 ꜰQ	45690 ᴹᵂ	58310 ᵀQ	USBLS	5/07
Oil and Gas	New Mexico	Y	27980 ꜰQ	43020 ᴹᵂ	54130 ᵀQ	USBLS	5/07
Oil and Gas	North Dakota	Y	34340 ꜰQ	42920 ᴹᵂ	50250 ᵀQ	USBLS	5/07
Oil and Gas	Ohio	Y	26740 ꜰQ	28880 ᴹᵂ	31010 ᵀQ	USBLS	5/07
Oil and Gas	Oklahoma	Y	37520 ꜰQ	45130 ᴹᵂ	50160 ᵀQ	USBLS	5/07
Oil and Gas	Pennsylvania	Y	30440 ꜰQ	33660 ᴹᵂ	37400 ᵀQ	USBLS	5/07
Oil and Gas	Texas	Y	28800 ꜰQ	34790 ᴹᵂ	42320 ᵀQ	USBLS	5/07
Oil and Gas	Utah	Y	33480 ꜰQ	38910 ᴹᵂ	50000 ᵀQ	USBLS	5/07
Oil and Gas	Wyoming	Y	35339 ꜰQ	42260 ᴹᵂ	53510 ᵀQ	WYBLS	9/08
Designer and Stylist Home Textiles Industry	United States	Y		86600 ᴬᵂ		HTT	2008
Desktop Publisher	Alabama	Y	22570 ꜰQ	28290 ᴹᵂ	33750 ᵀQ	USBLS	5/07
	Birmingham-Hoover MSA, AL	Y	23230 ꜰQ	28120 ᴹᵂ	34390 ᵀQ	USBLS	5/07
	Alaska	Y	35550 ꜰQ	41140 ᴹᵂ	50360 ᵀQ	USBLS	5/07
	Arizona	Y	28710 ꜰQ	35460 ᴹᵂ	46190 ᵀQ	USBLS	5/07
	Phoenix-Mesa-Scottsdale MSA, AZ	Y	27010 ꜰQ	33900 ᴹᵂ	44570 ᵀQ	USBLS	5/07
	Tucson MSA, AZ	Y	28150 ꜰQ	31870 ᴹᵂ	35320 ᵀQ	USBLS	5/07
	Arkansas	Y	18360 ꜰQ	23070 ᴹᵂ	31230 ᵀQ	USBLS	5/07
	Little Rock-North Little Rock MSA, AR	Y	22890 ꜰQ	27900 ᴹᵂ	32150 ᵀQ	USBLS	5/07
	California	H	14.74 ꜰQ	18.70 ᴹᵂ	24.06 ᵀQ	CABLS	1/08-3/08
	Los Angeles-Long Beach-Glendale PMSA, CA	H	13.96 ꜰQ	17.27 ᴹᵂ	23.92 ᵀQ	CABLS	1/08-3/08
	Oakland-Fremont-Hayward MSA, CA	H	18.07 ꜰQ	21.76 ᴹᵂ	27.68 ᵀQ	CABLS	1/08-3/08
	Riverside-San Bernardino-Ontario MSA, CA	H	15.19 ꜰQ	18.73 ᴹᵂ	22.96 ᵀQ	CABLS	1/08-3/08
	Sacramento-Arden Arcade-Roseville MSA, CA	H	15.45 ꜰQ	18.82 ᴹᵂ	22.30 ᵀQ	CABLS	1/08-3/08

Occupation/Type/Industry	Location	Per	Low	Mid	High	Source	Date
Desktop Publisher	San Diego-Carlsbad-San Marcos MSA, CA	H	14.42 FQ	19.40 MW	24.08 TQ	CABLS	1/08-3/08
	San Francisco-San Mateo-Redwood PMSA, CA	H	18.35 FQ	22.01 MW	28.63 TQ	CABLS	1/08-3/08
	San Jose-Sunnyvale-Santa Clara MSA, CA	H	16.20 FQ	22.29 MW	26.98 TQ	CABLS	1/08-3/08
	Santa Ana-Anaheim-Irvine PMSA, CA	Y	30920 FQ	37680 MW	48260 TQ	USBLS	5/07
	Colorado	Y	26090 FQ	40240 MW	50240 TQ	USBLS	5/07
	Boulder MSA, CO	Y	32710 FQ	48410 MW	59140 TQ	USBLS	5/07
	Denver-Aurora MSA, CO	Y	33080 FQ	43440 MW	50130 TQ	USBLS	5/07
	Connecticut	H	12.77 AE	18.73 MW		CTBLS	1/08-3/08
	Bridgeport-Stamford-Norwalk MSA, CT	Y	29600 FQ	37460 MW	45570 TQ	USBLS	5/07
	Hartford-West Hartford-East Hartford MSA, CT	Y	29190 FQ	41450 MW	51360 TQ	USBLS	5/07
	District of Columbia	Y	31620 FQ	43070 MW	51600 TQ	USBLS	5/07
	Washington-Arlington-Alexandria MSA, DC-VA-MD-WV	Y	31520 FQ	41260 MW	52240 TQ	USBLS	5/07
	Florida	Y	24430 FQ	32420 MW	44030 TQ	USBLS	5/07
	Fort Lauderdale-Pompano Beach-Deerfield Beach PMSA, FL	Y	26730 FQ	33590 MW	41690 TQ	USBLS	5/07
	Jacksonville MSA, FL	Y	24160 FQ	36950 MW	69290 TQ	USBLS	5/07
	Miami-Fort Lauderdale-Miami Beach MSA, FL	Y	22490 FQ	33770 MW	45860 TQ	USBLS	5/07
	Orlando-Kissimmee MSA, FL	Y	27880 FQ	37450 MW	47830 TQ	USBLS	5/07
	Tampa-St. Petersburg-Clearwater MSA, FL	Y	26970 FQ	32700 MW	37800 TQ	USBLS	5/07
	West Palm Beach-Boca Raton-Boynton Beach PMSA, FL	Y	19780 FQ	28640 MW	45550 TQ	USBLS	5/07
	Georgia	Y	27400 FQ	37320 MW	45320 TQ	USBLS	5/07
	Atlanta-Sandy Springs-Marietta MSA, GA	Y	34940 FQ	41260 MW	47800 TQ	USBLS	5/07
	Hawaii	Y	17600 FQ	30980 MW	37510 TQ	USBLS	5/07
	Honolulu MSA, HI	Y	16760 FQ	30330 MW	36570 TQ	USBLS	5/07
	Boise City-Nampa MSA, ID	Y	28470 FQ	32310 MW	39280 TQ	USBLS	5/07
	Illinois	Y	25750 FQ	34680 MW	46370 TQ	USBLS	5/07
	Chicago-Naperville-Joliet MSA, IL-IN-WI	Y	26440 FQ	36610 MW	47440 TQ	USBLS	5/07
	Indiana	Y	20830 FQ	28160 MW	36970 TQ	USBLS	5/07
	Indianapolis-Carmel MSA, IN	Y	26710 FQ	29790 MW	40340 TQ	USBLS	5/07
	Iowa	Y	23380 FQ	29780 MW	36710 TQ	USBLS	5/07
	Des Moines-West Des Moines MSA, IA	Y	27750 FQ	35220 MW	39450 TQ	USBLS	5/07
	Kansas	Y	23920 FQ	28140 MW	33010 TQ	USBLS	5/07
	Wichita MSA, KS	Y	26760 FQ	33860 MW	46900 TQ	USBLS	5/07
	Kentucky	Y	30346 FQ	36980 MW	48043 TQ	KYBLS	2008
	Louisville-Jefferson County MSA, KY-IN	Y	29030 FQ	33410 MW	38040 TQ	USBLS	5/07
	Louisiana	H	10.97 FQ	13.07 MW	15.63 TQ	LABLS	1/08-3/08
	Maine	Y	28370 FQ	32200 MW	37710 TQ	USBLS	5/07
	Portland-South Portland-Biddeford MSA, ME	Y	28550 FQ	31470 MW	36820 TQ	USBLS	5/07
	Maryland	Y		44400 MW		MDBLS	3/08
	Baltimore-Towson MSA, MD	Y	31040 FQ	39580 MW	51250 TQ	USBLS	5/07
	Bethesda-Gaithersburg-Frederick PMSA, MD	Y	33820 FQ	46630 MW	56980 TQ	USBLS	5/07
	Massachusetts	Y	37620 FQ	45010 MW	54660 TQ	USBLS	5/07
	Boston-Cambridge-Quincy NECTA, MA	Y	38660 FQ	45810 MW	55250 TQ	USBLS	5/07
	Worcester MSA, MA-CT	Y	32610 FQ	38880 MW	47800 TQ	USBLS	5/07
	Michigan	Y	26440 FQ	34550 MW	45060 TQ	USBLS	5/07
	Detroit-Warren-Livonia MSA, MI	Y	30300 FQ	41580 MW	47140 TQ	USBLS	5/07
	Grand Rapids-Wyoming MSA, MI	Y	25320 FQ	30330 MW	43320 TQ	USBLS	5/07
	Southeast, MI	Y		47944 AW		MIOAKL01	2008
	Warren-Troy-Farmington Hills PMSA, MI	Y	34600 FQ	43340 MW	47860 TQ	USBLS	5/07
	Minnesota	Y	29069 FQ	38519 MW	50072 TQ	MNBLS	10/08-12/08

AE	Average entry wage	AW	Average wage paid	FQ	First quartile wage	LO	Lowest wage paid	MTC	Median total compensation	TCC	Total cash compensation
AER	Average entry range	AWR	Average wage range	H	Hourly	LR	Low end range	MW	Median wage paid	TQ	Third quartile wage
AEX	Average experienced wage	AXR	Average experienced range	HI	Highest wage paid	M	Monthly	MWR	Median wage range	W	Weekly
ATC	Average total compensation	D	Daily	HR	High end range	MCC	Median cash compensation	S	See annotated source	Y	Yearly

416

Occupation/Type/Industry	Location	Per	Low	Mid	High	Source	Date
Desktop Publisher	Duluth-Superior MSA, MN-WI	Y	20524 FQ	24958 MW	35085 TQ	MNBLS	10/08-12/08
	Minneapolis-Saint Paul MSA, MN-WI	Y	37250 FQ	46700 MW	54464 TQ	MNBLS	10/08-12/08
	Rochester MSA, MN	Y	21967 FQ	24507 MW	27050 TQ	MNBLS	10/08-12/08
	Mississippi	Y	29400 FQ	37110 MW	43110 TQ	USBLS	5/07
	Missouri	Y	25650 FQ	37030 MW	48080 TQ	USBLS	5/07
	Kansas City MSA, MO-KS	Y	24150 FQ	29810 MW	39610 TQ	USBLS	5/07
	St. Louis MSA, MO-IL	Y	35070 FQ	44110 MW	51870 TQ	USBLS	5/07
	Montana	Y	25610 FQ	30580 MW	45420 TQ	USBLS	5/07
	Nebraska	Y	23900 FQ	29690 MW	38060 TQ	USBLS	5/07
	Omaha-Council Bluffs MSA, NE-IA	Y	28110 FQ	34770 MW	41400 TQ	USBLS	5/07
	Nevada	H	13.70 FQ	17.78 MW	22.03 TQ	NVBLS	5/08
	Las Vegas-Paradise MSA, NV	H	12.55 FQ	14.03 MW	16.66 TQ	NVBLS	5/08
	New Hampshire	H	12.96 AE	16.07 MW	20.42 AEX	NHBLS	6/08
	Nashua NECTA, NH-MA	Y	30420 FQ	45150 MW	53180 TQ	USBLS	5/07
	New Jersey	Y	33560 FQ	39920 MW	48080 TQ	USBLS	5/07
	Camden PMSA, NJ	Y	40340 FQ	48540 MW	55030 TQ	USBLS	5/07
	Edison PMSA, NJ	Y	28690 FQ	40460 MW	50190 TQ	USBLS	5/07
	Newark-Union PMSA, NJ-PA	Y	23180 FQ	28540 MW	41700 TQ	USBLS	5/07
	New Mexico	Y	15750 FQ	20330 MW	34270 TQ	USBLS	5/07
	Albuquerque MSA, NM	Y	15010 FQ	22140 MW	31650 TQ	USBLS	5/07
	New York	Y	32040 FQ	44520 MW	55840 TQ	USBLS	5/07
	Albany-Schenectady-Troy MSA, NY	Y	28980 FQ	35620 MW	46610 TQ	USBLS	5/07
	Buffalo-Niagara Falls MSA, NY	Y	24230 FQ	30280 MW	39470 TQ	USBLS	5/07
	Nassau-Suffolk PMSA, NY	Y	34750 FQ	41780 MW	53830 TQ	USBLS	5/07
	New York-Northern New Jersey-Long Island MSA, NY-NJ-PA	Y	33480 FQ	45800 MW	56620 TQ	USBLS	5/07
	North Carolina	Y	26300 FQ	30480 MW	38470 TQ	USBLS	5/07
	Charlotte-Gastonia-Concord MSA, NC-SC	Y	25180 FQ	33070 MW	45990 TQ	USBLS	5/07
	Raleigh-Cary MSA, NC	Y	29900 FQ	34850 MW	40400 TQ	USBLS	5/07
	North Dakota	Y	18400 FQ	24090 MW	31250 TQ	USBLS	5/07
	Ohio	Y	26450 FQ	32080 MW	37780 TQ	USBLS	5/07
	Cincinnati-Middletown MSA, OH-KY-IN	Y	26900 FQ	31710 MW	43990 TQ	USBLS	5/07
	Cleveland-Elyria-Mentor MSA, OH	Y	30520 FQ	35300 MW	39850 TQ	USBLS	5/07
	Columbus MSA, OH	Y	29450 FQ	34570 MW	39900 TQ	USBLS	5/07
	Dayton MSA, OH	Y	22780 FQ	27160 MW	32840 TQ	USBLS	5/07
	Oklahoma	Y	17650 FQ	19520 MW	27590 TQ	USBLS	5/07
	Oklahoma City MSA, OK	Y	17260 FQ	18660 MW	20080 TQ	USBLS	5/07
	Tulsa MSA, OK	Y	24830 FQ	28640 MW	36810 TQ	USBLS	5/07
	Oregon	H	12.42 FQ	16.53 MW	19.62 TQ	ORBLS	5/08
	Portland-Vancouver-Beaverton MSA, OR-WA	Y	29710 FQ	35620 MW	43570 TQ	USBLS	5/07
	Pennsylvania	Y	28170 FQ	39380 MW	49230 TQ	USBLS	5/07
	Allentown-Bethlehem-Easton MSA, PA-NJ	Y	23050 FQ	35670 MW	48240 TQ	USBLS	5/07
	Philadelphia-Camden-Wilmington MSA, PA-NJ-DE-MD	Y	36840 FQ	46210 MW	53620 TQ	USBLS	5/07
	Pittsburgh MSA, PA	Y	28320 FQ	39210 MW	48880 TQ	USBLS	5/07
	Providence-Fall River-Warwick MSA, RI-MA	Y	28380 FQ	34470 MW	43070 TQ	USBLS	5/07
	South Carolina	Y	28640 FQ	33310 MW	37470 TQ	USBLS	5/07
	Charleston-North Charleston MSA, SC	Y	31280 FQ	34140 MW	37410 TQ	USBLS	5/07
	South Dakota	Y	17358 FQ	20913 MW	24314 TQ	SDBLS	7/08-9/08
	Sioux Falls MSA, SD	Y	22799 FQ	24860 MW	27396 TQ	SDBLS	7/08-9/08
	Tennessee	Y	23800 FQ	29350 MW	36230 TQ	USBLS	5/07
	Nashville-Davidson-Murfreesboro MSA, TN	Y	29640 FQ	36640 MW	47030 TQ	USBLS	5/07
	Texas	Y	27190 FQ	35100 MW	44900 TQ	USBLS	5/07
	Austin-Round Rock MSA, TX	Y	33740 FQ	37750 MW	43510 TQ	USBLS	5/07
	Dallas-Fort Worth-Arlington MSA, TX	Y	27470 FQ	36480 MW	46700 TQ	USBLS	5/07
	El Paso MSA, TX	Y	17690 FQ	21900 MW	38040 TQ	USBLS	5/07

AE Average entry wage	**AW** Average wage paid	**FQ** First quartile wage	**LO** Lowest wage paid	**MTC** Median total compensation	**TCC** Total cash compensation
AER Average entry range	**AWR** Average wage range	**H** Hourly	**LR** Low end range	**MW** Median wage paid	**TQ** Third quartile wage
AEX Average experienced wage	**AXR** Average experienced range	**HI** Highest wage paid	**M** Monthly	**MWR** Median wage range	**W** Weekly
ATC Average total compensation	**D** Daily	**HR** High end range	**MCC** Median cash compensation	**S** See annotated source	**Y** Yearly

Occupation/Type/Industry	Location	Per	Low	Mid	High	Source	Date
Desktop Publisher	Houston-Sugar Land-Baytown MSA, TX	Y	30200 FQ	36930 MW	48180 TQ	USBLS	5/07
	San Antonio MSA, TX	Y	28790 FQ	34490 MW	39690 TQ	USBLS	5/07
	Utah	Y	25500 FQ	31330 MW	37890 TQ	USBLS	5/07
	Logan MSA, UT-ID	Y	22040 FQ	26670 MW	30220 TQ	USBLS	5/07
	Provo-Orem MSA, UT	Y	28850 FQ	33440 MW	37640 TQ	USBLS	5/07
	Salt Lake City MSA, UT	Y	26730 FQ	34270 MW	41570 TQ	USBLS	5/07
	Vermont	Y	28720 FQ	34900 MW	41520 TQ	USBLS	5/07
	Burlington-South Burlington MSA, VT	Y	33200 FQ	38720 MW	43990 TQ	USBLS	5/07
	Virginia	Y	26550 FQ	32140 MW	39140 TQ	USBLS	5/07
	Richmond MSA, VA	Y	25940 FQ	28880 MW	31630 TQ	USBLS	5/07
	Virginia Beach-Norfolk-Newport News MSA, VA-NC	Y	26360 FQ	32140 MW	38930 TQ	USBLS	5/07
	Washington	H	13.91 FQ	18.17 MW	24.03 TQ	WABLS	3/08
	Seattle-Tacoma-Bellevue MSA, WA	Y	30020 FQ	40960 MW	53040 TQ	USBLS	5/07
	West Virginia	Y	28842 FQ	34135 MW	41413 TQ	WVBLS	7/08-9/08
	Wisconsin	Y	29590 FQ	35700 MW	41260 TQ	USBLS	5/07
	Milwaukee-Waukesha-West Allis MSA, WI	Y	27950 FQ	37290 MW	42690 TQ	USBLS	5/07
	Wyoming	Y	23761 FQ	34851 MW	39784 TQ	WYBLS	9/08
Detective and Criminal Investigator	Alabama	Y	33220 FQ	42230 MW	61020 TQ	USBLS	5/07
	Birmingham-Hoover MSA, AL	Y	42330 FQ	60610 MW	76950 TQ	USBLS	5/07
	Alaska	Y	50280 FQ	73840 MW	90080 TQ	USBLS	5/07
	Arizona	Y	44780 FQ	53440 MW	61840 TQ	USBLS	5/07
	Flagstaff MSA, AZ	Y	53130 FQ	59190 MW	65520 TQ	USBLS	5/07
	Phoenix-Mesa-Scottsdale MSA, AZ	Y	44630 FQ	52990 MW	65170 TQ	USBLS	5/07
	Arkansas	Y	29230 FQ	35260 MW	51700 TQ	USBLS	5/07
	Fayetteville-Springdale-Rogers MSA, AR-MO	Y	35010 FQ	39910 MW	47060 TQ	USBLS	5/07
	Little Rock-North Little Rock MSA, AR	Y	32120 FQ	42510 MW	71790 TQ	USBLS	5/07
	California	H	28.15 FQ	37.27 MW	46.01 TQ	CABLS	1/08-3/08
	Fresno MSA, CA	H	28.37 FQ	35.04 MW	40.18 TQ	CABLS	1/08-3/08
	Oakland-Fremont-Hayward MSA, CA	H	37.41 FQ	44.87 MW	50.29 TQ	CABLS	1/08-3/08
	Riverside-San Bernardino-Ontario MSA, CA	H	26.64 FQ	35.21 MW	39.96 TQ	CABLS	1/08-3/08
	Sacramento-Arden Arcade-Roseville MSA, CA	H	23.76 FQ	30.06 MW	38.48 TQ	CABLS	1/08-3/08
	San Diego-Carlsbad-San Marcos MSA, CA	H	23.15 FQ	29.11 MW	36.85 TQ	CABLS	1/08-3/08
	San Jose-Sunnyvale-Santa Clara MSA, CA	H	34.98 FQ	43.63 MW	48.50 TQ	CABLS	1/08-3/08
	Santa Ana-Anaheim-Irvine PMSA, CA	Y	71590 FQ	86730 MW	97220 TQ	USBLS	5/07
	Colorado	Y	60570 FQ	72060 MW	81690 TQ	USBLS	5/07
	Denver-Aurora MSA, CO	Y	65700 FQ	74070 MW	82530 TQ	USBLS	5/07
	Connecticut	H	27.33 AE	31.99 MW		CTBLS	1/08-3/08
	Bridgeport-Stamford-Norwalk MSA, CT	Y	57950 FQ	64500 MW	77460 TQ	USBLS	5/07
	Hartford-West Hartford-East Hartford MSA, CT	Y	58140 FQ	65390 MW	78130 TQ	USBLS	5/07
	New Haven MSA, CT	Y	59760 FQ	74740 MW	92280 TQ	USBLS	5/07
	Delaware	Y	46540 FQ	63380 MW	75830 TQ	USBLS	5/07
	Wilmington PMSA, DE-MD-NJ	Y	57480 FQ	70960 MW	79780 TQ	USBLS	5/07
	District of Columbia	Y	72200 FQ	86530 MW	97340 TQ	USBLS	5/07
	Washington-Arlington-Alexandria MSA, DC-VA-MD-WV	Y	70730 FQ	86400 MW	98340 TQ	USBLS	5/07
	Florida	Y	45880 FQ	57120 MW	73800 TQ	USBLS	5/07
	Fort Lauderdale-Pompano Beach-Deerfield Beach PMSA, FL	Y	57490 FQ	71950 MW	88680 TQ	USBLS	5/07
	Miami-Fort Lauderdale-Miami Beach MSA, FL	Y	54540 FQ	66480 MW	84170 TQ	USBLS	5/07
	Orlando-Kissimmee MSA, FL	Y	41670 FQ	49710 MW	61720 TQ	USBLS	5/07

AE Average entry wage	**AW** Average wage paid	**FQ** First quartile wage	**LO** Lowest wage paid	**MTC** Median total compensation	**TCC** Total cash compensation
AER Average entry range	**AWR** Average wage range	**H** Hourly	**LR** Low end range	**MW** Median wage paid	**TQ** Third quartile wage
AEX Average experienced wage	**AXR** Average experienced range	**HI** Highest wage paid	**M** Monthly	**MWR** Median wage range	**W** Weekly
ATC Average total compensation	**D** Daily	**HR** High end range	**MCC** Median cash compensation	**S** See annotated source	**Y** Yearly

Occupation/Type/Industry	Location	Per	Low	Mid	High	Source	Date
Detective and Criminal Investigator	Sarasota-Bradenton-Venice MSA, FL	Y	43390 FQ	50710 MW	60760 TQ	USBLS	5/07
	Tampa-St. Petersburg-Clearwater MSA, FL	Y	47830 FQ	58210 MW	71790 TQ	USBLS	5/07
	West Palm Beach-Boca Raton-Boynton Beach PMSA, FL	Y	49580 FQ	61330 MW	75240 TQ	USBLS	5/07
	Georgia	Y	37150 FQ	45390 MW	62800 TQ	USBLS	5/07
	Atlanta-Sandy Springs-Marietta MSA, GA	Y	40280 FQ	48330 MW	65760 TQ	USBLS	5/07
	Hawaii	Y	59690 FQ	70980 MW	82800 TQ	USBLS	5/07
	Idaho	Y	43960 FQ	54530 MW	68780 TQ	USBLS	5/07
	Boise City-Nampa MSA, ID	Y	46520 FQ	60410 MW	79930 TQ	USBLS	5/07
	Illinois	Y	65150 FQ	80210 MW	89730 TQ	USBLS	5/07
	Chicago-Naperville-Joliet MSA, IL-IN-WI	Y	68200 FQ	81790 MW	90610 TQ	USBLS	5/07
	Indiana	Y	38600 FQ	46590 MW	56760 TQ	USBLS	5/07
	Gary PMSA, IN	Y	42610 FQ	47640 MW	63200 TQ	USBLS	5/07
	Indianapolis-Carmel MSA, IN	Y	39800 FQ	50370 MW	72830 TQ	USBLS	5/07
	Iowa	Y	47490 FQ	56790 MW	64530 TQ	USBLS	5/07
	Des Moines-West Des Moines MSA, IA	Y	49040 FQ	58630 MW	68080 TQ	USBLS	5/07
	Kansas	Y	41480 FQ	49840 MW	63600 TQ	USBLS	5/07
	Wichita MSA, KS	Y	42780 FQ	49180 MW	62830 TQ	USBLS	5/07
	Kentucky	Y	39816 FQ	49404 MW	76333 TQ	KYBLS	2008
	Louisville-Jefferson County MSA, KY-IN	Y	39260 FQ	64390 MW	84390 TQ	USBLS	5/07
	Louisiana	H	16.32 FQ	19.56 MW	31.33 TQ	LABLS	1/08-3/08
	Baton Rouge MSA, LA	Y	37450 FQ	45310 MW	68620 TQ	USBLS	5/07
	New Orleans-Metairie-Kenner MSA, LA	Y	41860 FQ	69150 MW	86320 TQ	USBLS	5/07
	Shreveport-Bossier City MSA, LA	Y	39350 FQ	49700 MW	69690 TQ	USBLS	5/07
	Maine	Y	44660 FQ	51560 MW	60960 TQ	USBLS	5/07
	Portland-South Portland-Biddeford MSA, ME	Y	46490 FQ	52070 MW	75140 TQ	USBLS	5/07
	Maryland	Y		76525 MW		MDBLS	3/08
	Baltimore-Towson MSA, MD	Y	53300 FQ	72470 MW	84780 TQ	USBLS	5/07
	Bethesda-Gaithersburg-Frederick PMSA, MD	Y	63700 FQ	77720 MW	98160 TQ	USBLS	5/07
	Massachusetts	Y	58220 FQ	67940 MW	86020 TQ	USBLS	5/07
	Boston-Cambridge-Quincy NECTA, MA	Y	58690 FQ	67930 MW	86930 TQ	USBLS	5/07
	Worcester MSA, MA-CT	Y	66590 FQ	82480 MW	96010 TQ	USBLS	5/07
	Michigan	Y	55160 FQ	65770 MW	77140 TQ	USBLS	5/07
	Detroit-Warren-Livonia MSA, MI	Y	60660 FQ	69520 MW	80640 TQ	USBLS	5/07
	Grand Rapids-Wyoming MSA, MI	Y	59590 FQ	72980 MW	85180 TQ	USBLS	5/07
	Warren-Troy-Farmington Hills PMSA, MI	Y	57570 FQ	64860 MW	74280 TQ	USBLS	5/07
	Minnesota	Y	55321 FQ	62902 MW	73703 TQ	MNBLS	10/08-12/08
	Duluth-Superior MSA, MN-WI	Y	55123 FQ	59796 MW	64648 TQ	MNBLS	10/08-12/08
	Minneapolis-Saint Paul MSA, MN-WI	Y	59075 FQ	67074 MW	79830 TQ	MNBLS	10/08-12/08
	Mississippi	Y	33220 FQ	41300 MW	54360 TQ	USBLS	5/07
	Jackson MSA, MS	Y	37870 FQ	51800 MW	74580 TQ	USBLS	5/07
	Pascagoula MSA, MS	Y	32800 FQ	36260 MW	39850 TQ	USBLS	5/07
	Missouri	Y	34230 FQ	44410 MW	58790 TQ	USBLS	5/07
	Kansas City MSA, MO-KS	Y	41440 FQ	52810 MW	63280 TQ	USBLS	5/07
	St. Louis MSA, MO-IL	Y	43210 FQ	55750 MW	74030 TQ	USBLS	5/07
	Montana	Y	46510 FQ	56870 MW	70520 TQ	USBLS	5/07
	Billings MSA, MT	Y	47160 FQ	64990 MW	82720 TQ	USBLS	5/07
	Nebraska	Y	43140 FQ	53090 MW	62660 TQ	USBLS	5/07
	Omaha-Council Bluffs MSA, NE-IA	Y	43860 FQ	54310 MW	67140 TQ	USBLS	5/07
	Nevada	H	27.59 FQ	32.70 MW	39.20 TQ	NVBLS	5/08
	Las Vegas-Paradise MSA, NV	H	27.82 FQ	33.24 MW	40.17 TQ	NVBLS	5/08
	New Hampshire	H	20.62 AE	25.97 MW	32.70 AEX	NHBLS	6/08
	Manchester MSA, NH	Y	50080 FQ	74200 MW	91990 TQ	USBLS	5/07
	Nashua NECTA, NH-MA	Y	50870 FQ	57610 MW	68060 TQ	USBLS	5/07
	New Jersey	Y	70940 FQ	86110 MW	98980 TQ	USBLS	5/07

AE	Average entry wage	AW	Average wage paid	FQ	First quartile wage	LO	Lowest wage paid	MTC	Median total compensation	TCC	Total cash compensation
AER	Average entry range	AWR	Average wage range	H	Hourly	LR	Low end range	MW	Median wage paid	TQ	Third quartile wage
AEX	Average experienced wage	AXR	Average experienced range	HI	Highest wage paid	M	Monthly	MWR	Median wage range	W	Weekly
ATC	Average total compensation	D	Daily	HR	High end range	MCC	Median cash compensation	S	See annotated source	Y	Yearly

Detective and Criminal Investigator

Occupation/Type/Industry	Location	Per	Low	Mid	High	Source	Date
Detective and Criminal Investigator	Atlantic City MSA, NJ	Y	68340 FQ	78840 MW	90950 TQ	USBLS	5/07
	Camden PMSA, NJ	Y	61610 FQ	73490 MW	84130 TQ	USBLS	5/07
	Edison PMSA, NJ	Y	78480 FQ	90480 MW	100090 TQ	USBLS	5/07
	Newark-Union PMSA, NJ-PA	Y	67860 FQ	82680 MW	94720 TQ	USBLS	5/07
	New Mexico	Y	42120 FQ	49440 MW	59450 TQ	USBLS	5/07
	Albuquerque MSA, NM	Y	51870 FQ	69430 MW	86510 TQ	USBLS	5/07
	New York	Y	46240 FQ	63390 MW	84730 TQ	USBLS	5/07
	Albany-Schenectady-Troy MSA, NY	Y	59780 FQ	70540 MW	77660 TQ	USBLS	5/07
	Buffalo-Niagara Falls MSA, NY	Y	53190 FQ	60730 MW	70980 TQ	USBLS	5/07
	New York-Northern New Jersey-Long Island MSA, NY-NJ-PA	Y	47640 FQ	77210 MW	94940 TQ	USBLS	5/07
	North Carolina	Y	35490 FQ	42200 MW	53410 TQ	USBLS	5/07
	Charlotte-Gastonia-Concord MSA, NC-SC	Y	37100 FQ	45990 MW	67530 TQ	USBLS	5/07
	Raleigh-Cary MSA, NC	Y	44240 FQ	55950 MW	70390 TQ	USBLS	5/07
	North Dakota	Y	41910 FQ	53800 MW	66980 TQ	USBLS	5/07
	Fargo MSA, ND-MN	Y	50770 FQ	59310 MW	82820 TQ	USBLS	5/07
	Ohio	Y	46840 FQ	58550 MW	73040 TQ	USBLS	5/07
	Cincinnati-Middletown MSA, OH-KY-IN	Y	52220 FQ	58430 MW	65170 TQ	USBLS	5/07
	Cleveland-Elyria-Mentor MSA, OH	Y	56290 FQ	66370 MW	81860 TQ	USBLS	5/07
	Columbus MSA, OH	Y	36470 FQ	56180 MW	72000 TQ	USBLS	5/07
	Dayton MSA, OH	Y	53370 FQ	65530 MW	85000 TQ	USBLS	5/07
	Oklahoma	Y	32510 FQ	42010 MW	54240 TQ	USBLS	5/07
	Oklahoma City MSA, OK	Y	33000 FQ	45440 MW	61900 TQ	USBLS	5/07
	Tulsa MSA, OK	Y	34720 FQ	43920 MW	57290 TQ	USBLS	5/07
	Oregon	H	26.14 FQ	31.29 MW	36.48 TQ	ORBLS	5/08
	Portland-Vancouver-Beaverton MSA, OR-WA	Y	56560 FQ	65340 MW	75160 TQ	USBLS	5/07
	Pennsylvania	Y	54120 FQ	62940 MW	76380 TQ	USBLS	5/07
	Allentown-Bethlehem-Easton MSA, PA-NJ	Y	56620 FQ	67540 MW	85330 TQ	USBLS	5/07
	Erie MSA, PA	Y	42570 FQ	56990 MW	68450 TQ	USBLS	5/07
	Philadelphia-Camden-Wilmington MSA, PA-NJ-DE-MD	Y	58440 FQ	67070 MW	81480 TQ	USBLS	5/07
	Pittsburgh MSA, PA	Y	44940 FQ	58760 MW	73030 TQ	USBLS	5/07
	Rhode Island	Y	50000 FQ	58410 MW	71940 TQ	USBLS	5/07
	Providence-Fall River-Warwick MSA, RI-MA	Y	49950 FQ	58210 MW	71350 TQ	USBLS	5/07
	South Carolina	Y	35600 FQ	42840 MW	58860 TQ	USBLS	5/07
	Charleston-North Charleston MSA, SC	Y	47280 FQ	69360 MW	86930 TQ	USBLS	5/07
	Columbia MSA, SC	Y	38660 FQ	51500 MW	66850 TQ	USBLS	5/07
	South Dakota	Y	39531 FQ	49898 MW	67094 TQ	SDBLS	7/08-9/08
	Tennessee	Y	35940 FQ	44540 MW	63580 TQ	USBLS	5/07
	Memphis MSA, TN-MS-AR	Y	36740 FQ	51490 MW	72620 TQ	USBLS	5/07
	Nashville-Davidson-Murfreesboro MSA, TN	Y	41070 FQ	49950 MW	65890 TQ	USBLS	5/07
	Texas	Y	40040 FQ	54060 MW	63450 TQ	USBLS	5/07
	Austin-Round Rock MSA, TX	Y	33010 FQ	40420 MW	68630 TQ	USBLS	5/07
	Beaumont-Port Arthur MSA, TX	Y	37780 FQ	48110 MW	63920 TQ	USBLS	5/07
	Dallas-Fort Worth-Arlington MSA, TX	Y	42020 FQ	58050 MW	82220 TQ	USBLS	5/07
	Houston-Sugar Land-Baytown MSA, TX	Y	42090 FQ	63510 MW	90990 TQ	USBLS	5/07
	San Antonio MSA, TX	Y	49260 FQ	59140 MW	66170 TQ	USBLS	5/07
	Utah	Y	42970 FQ	51110 MW	64340 TQ	USBLS	5/07
	Salt Lake City MSA, UT	Y	44380 FQ	52030 MW	66270 TQ	USBLS	5/07
	Vermont	Y	51110 FQ	59190 MW	73180 TQ	USBLS	5/07
	Burlington-South Burlington MSA, VT	Y	52110 FQ	73710 MW	89970 TQ	USBLS	5/07
	Virginia	Y	51040 FQ	70000 MW	89850 TQ	USBLS	5/07
	Lynchburg MSA, VA	Y	52930 FQ	65150 MW	79150 TQ	USBLS	5/07
	Virginia Beach-Norfolk-Newport News MSA, VA-NC	Y	49510 FQ	63950 MW	78550 TQ	USBLS	5/07

AE Average entry wage	**AW** Average wage paid	**FQ** First quartile wage	**LO** Lowest wage paid	**MTC** Median total compensation	**TCC** Total cash compensation
AER Average entry range	**AWR** Average wage range	**H** Hourly	**LR** Low end range	**MW** Median wage paid	**TQ** Third quartile wage
AEX Average experienced wage	**AXR** Average experienced range	**HI** Highest wage paid	**M** Monthly	**MWR** Median wage range	**W** Weekly
ATC Average total compensation	**D** Daily	**HR** High end range	**MCC** Median cash compensation	**S** See annotated source	**Y** Yearly

Occupation/Type/Industry	Location	Per	Low	Mid	High	Source	Date
Detective and Criminal Investigator	Washington	H	30.85 FQ	35.63 MW	40.10 TQ	WABLS	3/08
	Seattle-Tacoma-Bellevue MSA, WA	Y	68710 FQ	76070 MW	84660 TQ	USBLS	5/07
	West Virginia	Y	31511 FQ	38977 MW	72296 TQ	WVBLS	7/08-9/08
	Charleston MSA, WV	Y	29240 FQ	38500 MW	75750 TQ	USBLS	5/07
	Wisconsin	Y	53370 FQ	60710 MW	69180 TQ	USBLS	5/07
	Milwaukee-Waukesha-West Allis MSA, WI	Y	57940 FQ	64560 MW	73060 TQ	USBLS	5/07
	Wyoming	Y	45356 FQ	52636 MW	64792 TQ	WYBLS	9/08
	Puerto Rico	Y	30460 FQ	39790 MW	65160 TQ	USBLS	5/07
	San Juan-Caguas-Guaynabo MSA, PR	Y	27220 FQ	30940 MW	36010 TQ	USBLS	5/07
Detention Officer	Roswell, GA	Y	30607 LO		48971 HI	GACTY01	2008
	Caldwell County, NC	Y			28909 HI	NTOP	11/08
Development Engineering Specialist							
Municipal Government	Gresham, OR	Y	55356 LO		70656 HI	GOSS	1/1/09
Development Officer							
Municipal Government	Cincinnati, OH	Y	45117 LO		60634 HI	COHSS	10/08
Diabetes Educator	United States	Y		52143 AW		DIETCEN	2008
Diagnostic Medical Sonographer	Alabama	Y	42040 FQ	49260 MW	57620 TQ	USBLS	5/07
	Birmingham-Hoover MSA, AL	Y	42690 FQ	49830 MW	58020 TQ	USBLS	5/07
	Alaska	Y	65640 FQ	74140 MW	83270 TQ	USBLS	5/07
	Arizona	Y	58020 FQ	68430 MW	77490 TQ	USBLS	5/07
	Phoenix-Mesa-Scottsdale MSA, AZ	Y	60560 FQ	69980 MW	78080 TQ	USBLS	5/07
	Tucson MSA, AZ	Y	58020 FQ	67310 MW	77180 TQ	USBLS	5/07
	Arkansas	Y	36200 FQ	49430 MW	59020 TQ	USBLS	5/07
	Little Rock-North Little Rock MSA, AR	Y	25500 FQ	42870 MW	57780 TQ	USBLS	5/07
	California	H	27.55 FQ	33.75 MW	39.99 TQ	CABLS	1/08-3/08
	Los Angeles-Long Beach-Glendale PMSA, CA	H	24.54 FQ	29.62 MW	36.76 TQ	CABLS	1/08-3/08
	Oakland-Fremont-Hayward MSA, CA	H	29.44 FQ	40.24 MW	49.49 TQ	CABLS	1/08-3/08
	Riverside-San Bernardino-Ontario MSA, CA	H	28.44 FQ	33.18 MW	38.09 TQ	CABLS	1/08-3/08
	Sacramento-Arden Arcade-Roseville MSA, CA	H	31.49 FQ	36.38 MW	40.78 TQ	CABLS	1/08-3/08
	San Diego-Carlsbad-San Marcos MSA, CA	H	32.15 FQ	35.91 MW	39.82 TQ	CABLS	1/08-3/08
	San Francisco-San Mateo-Redwood PMSA, CA	H	32.00 FQ	38.58 MW	45.10 TQ	CABLS	1/08-3/08
	San Jose-Sunnyvale-Santa Clara MSA, CA	H	35.85 FQ	41.31 MW	47.17 TQ	CABLS	1/08-3/08
	Santa Ana-Anaheim-Irvine PMSA, CA	Y	58510 FQ	69110 MW	79060 TQ	USBLS	5/07
	Colorado	Y	58690 FQ	68750 MW	79440 TQ	USBLS	5/07
	Denver-Aurora MSA, CO	Y	62070 FQ	71330 MW	81470 TQ	USBLS	5/07
	Connecticut	H	28.04 AE	36.20 MW		CTBLS	1/08-3/08
	Bridgeport-Stamford-Norwalk MSA, CT	Y	67950 FQ	76630 MW	85230 TQ	USBLS	5/07
	Hartford-West Hartford-East Hartford MSA, CT	Y	67420 FQ	76390 MW	88140 TQ	USBLS	5/07
	Delaware	Y	33390 FQ	54770 MW	66470 TQ	USBLS	5/07
	Wilmington PMSA, DE-MD-NJ	Y	43530 FQ	56810 MW	67660 TQ	USBLS	5/07
	District of Columbia	Y	51700 FQ	60240 MW	70000 TQ	USBLS	5/07
	Washington-Arlington-Alexandria MSA, DC-VA-MD-WV	Y	61020 FQ	70900 MW	79700 TQ	USBLS	5/07
	Florida	Y	46770 FQ	55360 MW	62580 TQ	USBLS	5/07
	Cape Coral-Fort Myers MSA, FL	Y	50240 FQ	57590 MW	64890 TQ	USBLS	5/07

Occupation/Type/Industry	Location	Per	Low	Mid	High	Source	Date
Diagnostic Medical Sonographer	Fort Lauderdale-Pompano Beach-Deerfield Beach PMSA, FL	Y	49010 FQ	57200 MW	65350 TQ	USBLS	5/07
	Jacksonville MSA, FL	Y	48760 FQ	56880 MW	63170 TQ	USBLS	5/07
	Miami-Fort Lauderdale-Miami Beach MSA, FL	Y	49770 FQ	57510 MW	64880 TQ	USBLS	5/07
	Orlando-Kissimmee MSA, FL	Y	46380 FQ	54560 MW	61330 TQ	USBLS	5/07
	Tampa-St. Petersburg-Clearwater MSA, FL	Y	42850 FQ	52360 MW	61810 TQ	USBLS	5/07
	West Palm Beach-Boca Raton-Boynton Beach PMSA, FL	Y	51830 FQ	58550 MW	66020 TQ	USBLS	5/07
	Georgia	Y	51220 FQ	57710 MW	64520 TQ	USBLS	5/07
	Atlanta-Sandy Springs-Marietta MSA, GA	Y	53160 FQ	59000 MW	66050 TQ	USBLS	5/07
	Augusta-Richmond County MSA, GA-SC	Y	49190 FQ	55350 MW	62650 TQ	USBLS	5/07
	Hawaii	Y	67080 FQ	72480 MW	77810 TQ	USBLS	5/07
	Honolulu MSA, HI	Y	67820 FQ	73140 MW	78520 TQ	USBLS	5/07
	Idaho	Y	51260 FQ	58440 MW	66170 TQ	USBLS	5/07
	Boise City-Nampa MSA, ID	Y	52510 FQ	58310 MW	65670 TQ	USBLS	5/07
	Illinois	Y	52950 FQ	62470 MW	75550 TQ	USBLS	5/07
	Chicago-Naperville-Joliet MSA, IL-IN-WI	Y	55000 FQ	66640 MW	78030 TQ	USBLS	5/07
	Indiana	Y	47150 FQ	55870 MW	65640 TQ	USBLS	5/07
	Elkhart-Goshen MSA, IN	Y	50390 FQ	56890 MW	64020 TQ	USBLS	5/07
	Gary PMSA, IN	Y	60840 FQ	69290 MW	76470 TQ	USBLS	5/07
	Indianapolis-Carmel MSA, IN	Y	49520 FQ	58940 MW	70380 TQ	USBLS	5/07
	Iowa	Y	48330 FQ	55820 MW	62580 TQ	USBLS	5/07
	Des Moines-West Des Moines MSA, IA	Y	46360 FQ	53590 MW	59840 TQ	USBLS	5/07
	Kansas	Y	52040 FQ	59280 MW	68450 TQ	USBLS	5/07
	Topeka MSA, KS	Y	48430 FQ	54930 MW	61040 TQ	USBLS	5/07
	Wichita MSA, KS	Y	50350 FQ	59650 MW	71880 TQ	USBLS	5/07
	Kentucky	Y	46779 FQ	55224 MW	63014 TQ	KYBLS	2008
	Lexington-Fayette MSA, KY	Y	42790 FQ	50430 MW	59700 TQ	USBLS	5/07
	Louisville-Jefferson County MSA, KY-IN	Y	47780 FQ	55710 MW	62540 TQ	USBLS	5/07
	Louisiana	H	22.31 FQ	26.73 MW	30.76 TQ	LABLS	1/08-3/08
	Baton Rouge MSA, LA	Y	47930 FQ	55910 MW	64560 TQ	USBLS	5/07
	New Orleans-Metairie-Kenner MSA, LA	Y	50600 FQ	58720 MW	65640 TQ	USBLS	5/07
	Maine	Y	55530 FQ	63000 MW	72540 TQ	USBLS	5/07
	Portland-South Portland-Biddeford MSA, ME	Y	56030 FQ	62760 MW	72090 TQ	USBLS	5/07
	Maryland	Y		68750 MW		MDBLS	3/08
	Baltimore-Towson MSA, MD	Y	53490 FQ	62130 MW	73550 TQ	USBLS	5/07
	Bethesda-Gaithersburg-Frederick PMSA, MD	Y	67200 FQ	73770 MW	80610 TQ	USBLS	5/07
	Massachusetts	Y	60560 FQ	69570 MW	79200 TQ	USBLS	5/07
	Boston-Cambridge-Quincy NECTA, MA	Y	58940 FQ	68150 MW	78540 TQ	USBLS	5/07
	Michigan	Y	46570 FQ	54770 MW	62180 TQ	USBLS	5/07
	Ann Arbor MSA, MI	Y	49880 FQ	57090 MW	63240 TQ	USBLS	5/07
	Detroit-Warren-Livonia MSA, MI	Y	49000 FQ	57340 MW	65110 TQ	USBLS	5/07
	Grand Rapids-Wyoming MSA, MI	Y	49570 FQ	56770 MW	65770 TQ	USBLS	5/07
	Warren-Troy-Farmington Hills PMSA, MI	Y	48690 FQ	57010 MW	64360 TQ	USBLS	5/07
	Minnesota	Y	59415 FQ	67617 MW	77619 TQ	MNBLS	10/08-12/08
	Duluth-Superior MSA, MN-WI	Y	56851 FQ	64646 MW	74491 TQ	MNBLS	10/08-12/08
	Minneapolis-Saint Paul MSA, MN-WI	Y	60335 FQ	68590 MW	78184 TQ	MNBLS	10/08-12/08
	Rochester MSA, MN	Y	59613 FQ	66470 MW	76004 TQ	MNBLS	10/08-12/08
	Mississippi	Y	39630 FQ	47630 MW	58170 TQ	USBLS	5/07
	Jackson MSA, MS	Y	25210 FQ	52780 MW	61500 TQ	USBLS	5/07
	Missouri	Y	51370 FQ	58640 MW	67970 TQ	USBLS	5/07
	Kansas City MSA, MO-KS	Y	54160 FQ	60970 MW	69710 TQ	USBLS	5/07
	St. Louis MSA, MO-IL	Y	52380 FQ	58490 MW	66470 TQ	USBLS	5/07
	Montana	Y	50850 FQ	56210 MW	62880 TQ	USBLS	5/07
	Billings MSA, MT	Y	51800 FQ	55830 MW	59870 TQ	USBLS	5/07
	Nebraska	Y	48440 FQ	56930 MW	66400 TQ	USBLS	5/07

AE	Average entry wage	AW	Average wage paid	FQ	First quartile wage	LO	Lowest wage paid	MTC	Median total compensation	TCC	Total cash compensation
AER	Average entry range	AWR	Average wage range	H	Hourly	LR	Low end range	MW	Median wage paid	TQ	Third quartile wage
AEX	Average experienced wage	AXR	Average experienced range	HI	Highest wage paid	M	Monthly	MWR	Median wage range	W	Weekly
ATC	Average total compensation	D	Daily	HR	High end range	MCC	Median cash compensation	S	See annotated source	Y	Yearly

Occupation/Type/Industry	Location	Per	Low	Mid	High	Source	Date
Diagnostic Medical Sonographer	Lincoln MSA, NE	Y	48640 FQ	56550 MW	63570 TQ	USBLS	5/07
	Omaha-Council Bluffs MSA, NE-IA	Y	46740 FQ	54160 MW	61000 TQ	USBLS	5/07
	Nevada	H	27.89 FQ	31.72 MW	35.53 TQ	NVBLS	5/08
	Las Vegas-Paradise MSA, NV	H	27.94 FQ	31.15 MW	34.67 TQ	NVBLS	5/08
	New Hampshire	H	27.18 AE	33.51 MW	36.70 AEX	NHBLS	6/08
	Manchester MSA, NH	Y	58060 FQ	67460 MW	75720 TQ	USBLS	5/07
	Nashua NECTA, NH-MA	Y	64980 FQ	75380 MW	84290 TQ	USBLS	5/07
	New Jersey	Y	55720 FQ	66660 MW	77800 TQ	USBLS	5/07
	Camden PMSA, NJ	Y	56730 FQ	66630 MW	77550 TQ	USBLS	5/07
	Edison PMSA, NJ	Y	53660 FQ	62400 MW	73960 TQ	USBLS	5/07
	Newark-Union PMSA, NJ-PA	Y	53790 FQ	65570 MW	77710 TQ	USBLS	5/07
	Vineland-Millville-Bridgeton MSA, NJ	Y	52580 FQ	58310 MW	68390 TQ	USBLS	5/07
	New Mexico	Y	53400 FQ	60880 MW	70630 TQ	USBLS	5/07
	Albuquerque MSA, NM	Y	54230 FQ	61500 MW	70360 TQ	USBLS	5/07
	New York	Y	53100 FQ	61160 MW	71240 TQ	USBLS	5/07
	Albany-Schenectady-Troy MSA, NY	Y	54590 FQ	61270 MW	68200 TQ	USBLS	5/07
	Buffalo-Niagara Falls MSA, NY	Y	49920 FQ	55500 MW	60910 TQ	USBLS	5/07
	Nassau-Suffolk PMSA, NY	Y	54130 FQ	61320 MW	70070 TQ	USBLS	5/07
	New York-Northern New Jersey-Long Island MSA, NY-NJ-PA	Y	54500 FQ	63980 MW	75140 TQ	USBLS	5/07
	North Carolina	Y	51330 FQ	58510 MW	66150 TQ	USBLS	5/07
	Charlotte-Gastonia-Concord MSA, NC-SC	Y	55030 FQ	62240 MW	72710 TQ	USBLS	5/07
	Raleigh-Cary MSA, NC	Y	50930 FQ	56510 MW	62610 TQ	USBLS	5/07
	North Dakota	Y	54400 FQ	58920 MW	65240 TQ	USBLS	5/07
	Ohio	Y	48130 FQ	55360 MW	62250 TQ	USBLS	5/07
	Cincinnati-Middletown MSA, OH-KY-IN	Y	47950 FQ	56580 MW	66050 TQ	USBLS	5/07
	Cleveland-Elyria-Mentor MSA, OH	Y	48400 FQ	54780 MW	60700 TQ	USBLS	5/07
	Columbus MSA, OH	Y	54740 FQ	60680 MW	68420 TQ	USBLS	5/07
	Dayton MSA, OH	Y	48330 FQ	55360 MW	62400 TQ	USBLS	5/07
	Oklahoma	Y	49590 FQ	59200 MW	70690 TQ	USBLS	5/07
	Oklahoma City MSA, OK	Y	49460 FQ	62710 MW	73760 TQ	USBLS	5/07
	Tulsa MSA, OK	Y	51550 FQ	58290 MW	66680 TQ	USBLS	5/07
	Oregon	H	31.40 FQ	35.34 MW	39.05 TQ	ORBLS	5/08
	Medford MSA, OR	Y	58740 FQ	66040 MW	73790 TQ	USBLS	5/07
	Portland-Vancouver-Beaverton MSA, OR-WA	Y	65520 FQ	72760 MW	80510 TQ	USBLS	5/07
	Pennsylvania	Y	45440 FQ	53960 MW	62500 TQ	USBLS	5/07
	Allentown-Bethlehem-Easton MSA, PA-NJ	Y	49990 FQ	58070 MW	66650 TQ	USBLS	5/07
	Philadelphia-Camden-Wilmington MSA, PA-NJ-DE-MD	Y	50250 FQ	59130 MW	69570 TQ	USBLS	5/07
	Pittsburgh MSA, PA	Y	42460 FQ	48030 MW	55760 TQ	USBLS	5/07
	Rhode Island	Y	61540 FQ	69680 MW	76220 TQ	USBLS	5/07
	Providence-Fall River-Warwick MSA, RI-MA	Y	61290 FQ	69610 MW	76280 TQ	USBLS	5/07
	South Carolina	Y	45000 FQ	53450 MW	61390 TQ	USBLS	5/07
	Charleston-North Charleston MSA, SC	Y	42970 FQ	48600 MW	56740 TQ	USBLS	5/07
	Columbia MSA, SC	Y	43830 FQ	54290 MW	61030 TQ	USBLS	5/07
	Florence MSA, SC	Y	38950 FQ	49890 MW	63020 TQ	USBLS	5/07
	South Dakota	Y	42783 FQ	50429 MW	61401 TQ	SDBLS	7/08-9/08
	Rapid City MSA, SD	Y	55877 FQ	61520 MW	67126 TQ	SDBLS	7/08-9/08
	Sioux Falls MSA, SD	Y	42527 FQ	48578 MW	56906 TQ	SDBLS	7/08-9/08
	Tennessee	Y	43590 FQ	53980 MW	62970 TQ	USBLS	5/07
	Memphis MSA, TN-MS-AR	Y	45040 FQ	54470 MW	62480 TQ	USBLS	5/07
	Nashville-Davidson-Murfreesboro MSA, TN	Y	48140 FQ	59620 MW	70260 TQ	USBLS	5/07
	Texas	Y	52150 FQ	60020 MW	69150 TQ	USBLS	5/07
	Austin-Round Rock MSA, TX	Y	47330 FQ	60540 MW	72820 TQ	USBLS	5/07
	Dallas-Fort Worth-Arlington MSA, TX	Y	54570 FQ	62340 MW	72190 TQ	USBLS	5/07
	El Paso MSA, TX	Y	43930 FQ	54890 MW	63420 TQ	USBLS	5/07

AE Average entry wage	**AW** Average wage paid	**FQ** First quartile wage	**LO** Lowest wage paid	**MTC** Median total compensation	**TCC** Total cash compensation
AER Average entry range	**AWR** Average wage range	**H** Hourly	**LR** Low end range	**MW** Median wage paid	**TQ** Third quartile wage
AEX Average experienced wage	**AXR** Average experienced range	**HI** Highest wage paid	**M** Monthly	**MWR** Median wage range	**W** Weekly
ATC Average total compensation	**D** Daily	**HR** High end range	**MCC** Median cash compensation	**S** See annotated source	**Y** Yearly

Occupation/Type/Industry	Location	Per	Low	Mid	High	Source	Date
Diagnostic Medical Sonographer	Houston-Sugar Land-Baytown						
	MSA, TX	Y	50840 FQ	58180 MW	65410 TQ	USBLS	5/07
	San Antonio MSA, TX	Y	54240 FQ	60510 MW	68020 TQ	USBLS	5/07
	Utah	Y	48660 FQ	57710 MW	66290 TQ	USBLS	5/07
	Provo-Orem MSA, UT	Y	54600 FQ	64400 MW	72500 TQ	USBLS	5/07
	Salt Lake City MSA, UT	Y	47100 FQ	56940 MW	65130 TQ	USBLS	5/07
	Vermont	Y	51390 FQ	58550 MW	66850 TQ	USBLS	5/07
	Burlington-South Burlington						
	MSA, VT	Y	44700 FQ	58260 MW	69760 TQ	USBLS	5/07
	Virginia	Y	52880 FQ	60800 MW	72490 TQ	USBLS	5/07
	Lynchburg MSA, VA	Y	54490 FQ	60220 MW	69670 TQ	USBLS	5/07
	Richmond MSA, VA	Y	53770 FQ	60870 MW	71560 TQ	USBLS	5/07
	Virginia Beach-Norfolk-						
	Newport News MSA, VA-NC	Y	51260 FQ	56870 MW	62620 TQ	USBLS	5/07
	Washington	H	31.19 FQ	34.88 MW	38.72 TQ	WABLS	3/08
	Seattle-Tacoma-Bellevue						
	MSA, WA	Y	66210 FQ	73150 MW	81050 TQ	USBLS	5/07
	West Virginia	Y	39630 FQ	48245 MW	57156 TQ	WVBLS	7/08-9/08
	Charleston MSA, WV	Y	34870 FQ	43490 MW	52470 TQ	USBLS	5/07
	Wisconsin	Y	60630 FQ	69680 MW	79230 TQ	USBLS	5/07
	Milwaukee-Waukesha-West						
	Allis MSA, WI	Y	64680 FQ	74100 MW	84100 TQ	USBLS	5/07
	Wyoming	Y	42152 FQ	50909 MW	61255 TQ	WYBLS	9/08
	Puerto Rico	Y	18660 FQ	22510 MW	26810 TQ	USBLS	5/07
	San Juan-Caguas-Guaynabo						
	MSA, PR	Y	18310 FQ	22210 MW	27050 TQ	USBLS	5/07
Diesel Mechanic							
Municipal Government	Cincinnati, OH	Y	41597 LO		44936 HI	COHSS	10/08
Dietary Manager	United States	Y		42786 AW		DMA01	7/08-8/08
Dietetic Consultant							
State Government	Ohio	H	20.71 LO		26.11 HI	ODAS	2008
Dietetic Technician	Alabama	Y	19370 FQ	27320 MW	37100 TQ	USBLS	5/07
	Arizona	Y	15110 FQ	18900 MW	26890 TQ	USBLS	5/07
	Phoenix-Mesa-Scottsdale						
	MSA, AZ	Y	14920 FQ	17910 MW	26380 TQ	USBLS	5/07
	Tucson MSA, AZ	Y	19690 FQ	24020 MW	27790 TQ	USBLS	5/07
	Arkansas	Y	15480 FQ	18510 MW	23620 TQ	USBLS	5/07
	Little Rock-North Little Rock						
	MSA, AR	Y	17580 FQ	22050 MW	26660 TQ	USBLS	5/07
	California	H	11.31 FQ	13.94 MW	17.04 TQ	CABLS	1/08-3/08
	Bakersfield MSA, CA	H	11.77 FQ	15.05 MW	18.68 TQ	CABLS	1/08-3/08
	Los Angeles-Long Beach-						
	Glendale PMSA, CA	H	11.27 FQ	14.04 MW	17.74 TQ	CABLS	1/08-3/08
	Oakland-Fremont-Hayward						
	MSA, CA	H	10.41 FQ	13.04 MW	16.09 TQ	CABLS	1/08-3/08
	Riverside-San Bernardino-						
	Ontario MSA, CA	H	11.81 FQ	14.48 MW	17.27 TQ	CABLS	1/08-3/08
	Sacramento-Arden Arcade-						
	Roseville MSA, CA	H	11.79 FQ	13.91 MW	16.20 TQ	CABLS	1/08-3/08
	San Diego-Carlsbad-San						
	Marcos MSA, CA	H	9.37 FQ	11.25 MW	15.06 TQ	CABLS	1/08-3/08
	San Francisco-San Mateo-						
	Redwood PMSA, CA	H	15.51 FQ	17.52 MW	21.52 TQ	CABLS	1/08-3/08
	San Jose-Sunnyvale-Santa						
	Clara MSA, CA	H	12.35 FQ	15.51 MW	23.86 TQ	CABLS	1/08-3/08
	Santa Ana-Anaheim-Irvine						
	PMSA, CA	Y	25340 FQ	28590 MW	32080 TQ	USBLS	5/07
	Colorado	Y	19550 FQ	24370 MW	30000 TQ	USBLS	5/07
	Denver-Aurora MSA, CO	Y	18810 FQ	23110 MW	28700 TQ	USBLS	5/07
	Connecticut	H	10.94 AE	15.33 MW		CTBLS	1/08-3/08
	Bridgeport-Stamford-Norwalk						
	MSA, CT	Y	25650 FQ	33100 MW	39070 TQ	USBLS	5/07
	Hartford-West Hartford-East						
	Hartford MSA, CT	Y	23270 FQ	31310 MW	37810 TQ	USBLS	5/07
	Delaware	Y	15900 FQ	19510 MW	28680 TQ	USBLS	5/07
	Wilmington PMSA, DE-MD-						
	NJ	Y	16130 FQ	20360 MW	28330 TQ	USBLS	5/07
	District of Columbia	Y	18210 FQ	25850 MW	32230 TQ	USBLS	5/07

Occupation/Type/Industry	Location	Per	Low	Mid	High	Source	Date
Dietetic Technician	Washington-Arlington-Alexandria MSA, DC-VA-MD-WV	Y	25540 FQ	32270 MW	37010 TQ	USBLS	5/07
	Florida	Y	19640 FQ	25770 MW	31500 TQ	USBLS	5/07
	Fort Lauderdale-Pompano Beach-Deerfield Beach PMSA, FL	Y	17750 FQ	26400 MW	34350 TQ	USBLS	5/07
	Jacksonville MSA, FL	Y	18570 FQ	23130 MW	27040 TQ	USBLS	5/07
	Miami-Fort Lauderdale-Miami Beach MSA, FL	Y	18890 FQ	28020 MW	40840 TQ	USBLS	5/07
	Orlando-Kissimmee MSA, FL	Y	22990 FQ	28420 MW	32150 TQ	USBLS	5/07
	Tampa-St. Petersburg-Clearwater MSA, FL	Y	19960 FQ	27190 MW	32370 TQ	USBLS	5/07
	West Palm Beach-Boca Raton-Boynton Beach PMSA, FL	Y	30850 FQ	41820 MW	47110 TQ	USBLS	5/07
	Georgia	Y	16190 FQ	20220 MW	24970 TQ	USBLS	5/07
	Atlanta-Sandy Springs-Marietta MSA, GA	Y	18820 FQ	22300 MW	28720 TQ	USBLS	5/07
	Hawaii	Y	24730 FQ	27300 MW	30280 TQ	USBLS	5/07
	Honolulu MSA, HI	Y	24620 FQ	27300 MW	30950 TQ	USBLS	5/07
	Idaho	Y	18850 FQ	22760 MW	28330 TQ	USBLS	5/07
	Boise City-Nampa MSA, ID	Y	19770 FQ	24160 MW	30250 TQ	USBLS	5/07
	Illinois	Y	18160 FQ	21830 MW	26080 TQ	USBLS	5/07
	Chicago-Naperville-Joliet MSA, IL-IN-WI	Y	18470 FQ	22120 MW	26330 TQ	USBLS	5/07
	Indiana	Y	18270 FQ	21930 MW	27610 TQ	USBLS	5/07
	Gary PMSA, IN	Y	21930 FQ	26320 MW	31390 TQ	USBLS	5/07
	Indianapolis-Carmel MSA, IN	Y	17600 FQ	19960 MW	24040 TQ	USBLS	5/07
	Iowa	Y	19100 FQ	21980 MW	24980 TQ	USBLS	5/07
	Kansas	Y	17530 FQ	21660 MW	25540 TQ	USBLS	5/07
	Kentucky	Y	19273 FQ	22412 MW	26114 TQ	KYBLS	2008
	Louisville-Jefferson County MSA, KY-IN	Y	18660 FQ	21260 MW	24360 TQ	USBLS	5/07
	Louisiana	H	7.36 FQ	9.00 MW	11.20 TQ	LABLS	1/08-3/08
	Baton Rouge MSA, LA	Y	15800 FQ	18850 MW	23070 TQ	USBLS	5/07
	New Orleans-Metairie-Kenner MSA, LA	Y	13470 FQ	15440 MW	21370 TQ	USBLS	5/07
	Maine	Y	23410 FQ	27270 MW	31450 TQ	USBLS	5/07
	Portland-South Portland-Biddeford MSA, ME	Y	25240 FQ	29510 MW	33590 TQ	USBLS	5/07
	Maryland	Y		33550 MW		MDBLS	3/08
	Baltimore-Towson MSA, MD	Y	28540 FQ	32140 MW	36150 TQ	USBLS	5/07
	Bethesda-Gaithersburg-Frederick PMSA, MD	Y	27670 FQ	34450 MW	38020 TQ	USBLS	5/07
	Massachusetts	Y	19510 FQ	23590 MW	29780 TQ	USBLS	5/07
	Boston-Cambridge-Quincy NECTA, MA	Y	21310 FQ	24500 MW	30330 TQ	USBLS	5/07
	Worcester MSA, MA-CT	Y	17610 FQ	19110 MW	21630 TQ	USBLS	5/07
	Michigan	Y	20950 FQ	24550 MW	31200 TQ	USBLS	5/07
	Detroit-Warren-Livonia MSA, MI	Y	22130 FQ	28030 MW	33370 TQ	USBLS	5/07
	Warren-Troy-Farmington Hills PMSA, MI	Y	21080 FQ	25620 MW	31340 TQ	USBLS	5/07
	Minnesota	Y	31585 FQ	37549 MW	42100 TQ	MNBLS	10/08-12/08
	Minneapolis-Saint Paul MSA, MN-WI	Y	34044 FQ	38647 MW	42968 TQ	MNBLS	10/08-12/08
	Mississippi	Y	16090 FQ	19540 MW	23510 TQ	USBLS	5/07
	Jackson MSA, MS	Y	18140 FQ	20770 MW	23010 TQ	USBLS	5/07
	Missouri	Y	20270 FQ	27070 MW	37700 TQ	USBLS	5/07
	Kansas City MSA, MO-KS	Y	21510 FQ	26030 MW	33890 TQ	USBLS	5/07
	St. Louis MSA, MO-IL	Y	21570 FQ	28790 MW	39980 TQ	USBLS	5/07
	Montana	Y	17670 FQ	20620 MW	23380 TQ	USBLS	5/07
	Nebraska	Y	18060 FQ	24690 MW	30990 TQ	USBLS	5/07
	Omaha-Council Bluffs MSA, NE-IA	Y	22840 FQ	30210 MW	36210 TQ	USBLS	5/07
	Nevada	H	10.88 FQ	13.72 MW	17.54 TQ	NVBLS	5/08
	Las Vegas-Paradise MSA, NV	H	10.39 FQ	12.24 MW	16.51 TQ	NVBLS	5/08
	New Hampshire	H	12.44 AE	14.84 MW	18.06 AEX	NHBLS	6/08
	New Jersey	Y	25100 FQ	30580 MW	36000 TQ	USBLS	5/07
	Camden PMSA, NJ	Y	23970 FQ	28640 MW	33100 TQ	USBLS	5/07
	Edison PMSA, NJ	Y	24010 FQ	31590 MW	38060 TQ	USBLS	5/07
	Newark-Union PMSA, NJ-PA	Y	26300 FQ	31380 MW	36340 TQ	USBLS	5/07

AE	Average entry wage	AW	Average wage paid	FQ	First quartile wage
AER	Average entry range	AWR	Average wage range	H	Hourly
AEX	Average experienced wage	AXR	Average experienced range	HI	Highest wage paid
ATC	Average total compensation	D	Daily	HR	High end range

LO	Lowest wage paid	MTC	Median total compensation	TCC	Total cash compensation
LR	Low end range	MW	Median wage paid	TQ	Third quartile wage
M	Monthly	MWR	Median wage range	W	Weekly
MCC	Median cash compensation	S	See annotated source	Y	Yearly

Occupation/Type/Industry	Location	Per	Low	Mid	High	Source	Date
Dietetic Technician	New Mexico	Y	20640 FQ	22630 MW	24610 TQ	USBLS	5/07
	Albuquerque MSA, NM	Y	20930 FQ	22450 MW	23960 TQ	USBLS	5/07
	New York	Y	27030 FQ	33970 MW	38950 TQ	USBLS	5/07
	Albany-Schenectady-Troy MSA, NY	Y	22680 FQ	28240 MW	35470 TQ	USBLS	5/07
	Buffalo-Niagara Falls MSA, NY	Y	17720 FQ	22840 MW	34520 TQ	USBLS	5/07
	Nassau-Suffolk PMSA, NY	Y	35090 FQ	40670 MW	46910 TQ	USBLS	5/07
	New York-Northern New Jersey-Long Island MSA, NY-NJ-PA	Y	31240 FQ	35590 MW	40430 TQ	USBLS	5/07
	Syracuse MSA, NY	Y	28810 FQ	33660 MW	38640 TQ	USBLS	5/07
	North Carolina	Y	19560 FQ	23220 MW	28290 TQ	USBLS	5/07
	Charlotte-Gastonia-Concord MSA, NC-SC	Y	21630 FQ	24300 MW	29440 TQ	USBLS	5/07
	North Dakota	Y	18320 FQ	22750 MW	29460 TQ	USBLS	5/07
	Fargo MSA, ND-MN	Y	17730 FQ	19530 MW	27880 TQ	USBLS	5/07
	Ohio	Y	29280 FQ	34140 MW	38360 TQ	USBLS	5/07
	Cincinnati-Middletown MSA, OH-KY-IN	Y	26850 FQ	34860 MW	39730 TQ	USBLS	5/07
	Cleveland-Elyria-Mentor MSA, OH	Y	29070 FQ	33360 MW	37520 TQ	USBLS	5/07
	Columbus MSA, OH	Y	30410 FQ	34690 MW	38290 TQ	USBLS	5/07
	Dayton MSA, OH	Y	28770 FQ	32550 MW	36650 TQ	USBLS	5/07
	Oklahoma	Y	15620 FQ	18860 MW	26600 TQ	USBLS	5/07
	Oklahoma City MSA, OK	Y	16180 FQ	21420 MW	28630 TQ	USBLS	5/07
	Tulsa MSA, OK	Y	17510 FQ	22460 MW	28720 TQ	USBLS	5/07
	Oregon	H	14.72 FQ	17.94 MW	20.36 TQ	ORBLS	5/08
	Portland-Vancouver-Beaverton MSA, OR-WA	Y	34070 FQ	38060 MW	41790 TQ	USBLS	5/07
	Pennsylvania	Y	18130 FQ	21600 MW	28300 TQ	USBLS	5/07
	Philadelphia-Camden-Wilmington MSA, PA-NJ-DE-MD	Y	18010 FQ	21940 MW	28910 TQ	USBLS	5/07
	Pittsburgh MSA, PA	Y	18550 FQ	23080 MW	29210 TQ	USBLS	5/07
	Rhode Island	Y	22730 FQ	27960 MW	33370 TQ	USBLS	5/07
	Providence-Fall River-Warwick MSA, RI-MA	Y	22850 FQ	27900 MW	33160 TQ	USBLS	5/07
	South Carolina	Y	19640 FQ	23680 MW	34450 TQ	USBLS	5/07
	Charleston-North Charleston MSA, SC	Y	17870 FQ	19750 MW	22560 TQ	USBLS	5/07
	South Dakota	Y	27804 FQ	34785 MW	38832 TQ	SDBLS	7/08-9/08
	Tennessee	Y	18620 FQ	22450 MW	28140 TQ	USBLS	5/07
	Knoxville MSA, TN	Y	18010 FQ	23070 MW	28210 TQ	USBLS	5/07
	Memphis MSA, TN-MS-AR	Y	19050 FQ	29380 MW	43130 TQ	USBLS	5/07
	Nashville-Davidson-Murfreesboro MSA, TN	Y	19000 FQ	22350 MW	27060 TQ	USBLS	5/07
	Texas	Y	18260 FQ	21890 MW	27980 TQ	USBLS	5/07
	Dallas-Fort Worth-Arlington MSA, TX	Y	17380 FQ	20770 MW	27230 TQ	USBLS	5/07
	Houston-Sugar Land-Baytown MSA, TX	Y	20600 FQ	25090 MW	33570 TQ	USBLS	5/07
	San Antonio MSA, TX	Y	19120 FQ	22730 MW	27130 TQ	USBLS	5/07
	Utah	Y	19380 FQ	22270 MW	25520 TQ	USBLS	5/07
	Salt Lake City MSA, UT	Y	20560 FQ	22900 MW	26590 TQ	USBLS	5/07
	Vermont	Y	21490 FQ	25270 MW	31550 TQ	USBLS	5/07
	Burlington-South Burlington MSA, VT	Y	21280 FQ	24410 MW	31580 TQ	USBLS	5/07
	Virginia	Y	18820 FQ	23630 MW	29470 TQ	USBLS	5/07
	Lynchburg MSA, VA	Y	16680 FQ	18790 MW	22250 TQ	USBLS	5/07
	Richmond MSA, VA	Y	17720 FQ	21200 MW	26860 TQ	USBLS	5/07
	Virginia Beach-Norfolk-Newport News MSA, VA-NC	Y	25370 FQ	28100 MW	30850 TQ	USBLS	5/07
	Washington	H	15.36 FQ	17.47 MW	19.62 TQ	WABLS	3/08
	Seattle-Tacoma-Bellevue MSA, WA	Y	32070 FQ	36210 MW	40540 TQ	USBLS	5/07
	West Virginia	Y	18343 FQ	20764 MW	25597 TQ	WVBLS	7/08-9/08
	Wisconsin	Y	19170 FQ	25560 MW	32460 TQ	USBLS	5/07
	Milwaukee-Waukesha-West Allis MSA, WI	Y	28360 FQ	32790 MW	37670 TQ	USBLS	5/07
	Wyoming	Y	19129 FQ	22655 MW	28633 TQ	WYBLS	9/08
	Puerto Rico	Y	12730 FQ	14050 MW	16790 TQ	USBLS	5/07

AE Average entry wage	**AW** Average wage paid	**FQ** First quartile wage	**LO** Lowest wage paid	**MTC** Median total compensation	**TCC** Total cash compensation
AER Average entry range	**AWR** Average wage range	**H** Hourly	**LR** Low end range	**MW** Median wage paid	**TQ** Third quartile wage
AEX Average experienced wage	**AXR** Average experienced range	**HI** Highest wage paid	**M** Monthly	**MWR** Median wage range	**W** Weekly
ATC Average total compensation	**D** Daily	**HR** High end range	**MCC** Median cash compensation	**S** See annotated source	**Y** Yearly

Occupation/Type/Industry	Location	Per	Low	Mid	High	Source	Date
Dietetic Technician	San Juan-Caguas-Guaynabo MSA, PR	Y	12640 FQ	13900 MW	16200 TQ	USBLS	5/07
Dietitian and Nutritionist	Alabama	Y	38560 FQ	45690 MW	53380 TQ	USBLS	5/07
	Birmingham-Hoover MSA, AL	Y	37220 FQ	45110 MW	54130 TQ	USBLS	5/07
	Alaska	Y	43180 FQ	52730 MW	64190 TQ	USBLS	5/07
	Anchorage MSA, AK	Y	46170 FQ	54540 MW	66290 TQ	USBLS	5/07
	Arizona	Y	30600 FQ	44010 MW	54850 TQ	USBLS	5/07
	Phoenix-Mesa-Scottsdale MSA, AZ	Y	30140 FQ	43880 MW	53170 TQ	USBLS	5/07
	Tucson MSA, AZ	Y	33750 FQ	47030 MW	57920 TQ	USBLS	5/07
	Arkansas	Y	32640 FQ	41120 MW	53350 TQ	USBLS	5/07
	Little Rock-North Little Rock MSA, AR	Y	35430 FQ	43370 MW	55370 TQ	USBLS	5/07
	California	H	23.04 FQ	28.81 MW	34.57 TQ	CABLS	1/08-3/08
	Los Angeles-Long Beach-Glendale PMSA, CA	H	17.76 FQ	26.30 MW	31.64 TQ	CABLS	1/08-3/08
	Oakland-Fremont-Hayward MSA, CA	H	28.97 FQ	34.48 MW	38.50 TQ	CABLS	1/08-3/08
	Riverside-San Bernardino-Ontario MSA, CA	H	25.57 FQ	29.64 MW	33.49 TQ	CABLS	1/08-3/08
	Sacramento-Arden Arcade-Roseville MSA, CA	H	27.32 FQ	30.74 MW	35.51 TQ	CABLS	1/08-3/08
	San Diego-Carlsbad-San Marcos MSA, CA	H	20.52 FQ	25.30 MW	29.28 TQ	CABLS	1/08-3/08
	San Francisco-San Mateo-Redwood PMSA, CA	H	26.58 FQ	34.56 MW	39.47 TQ	CABLS	1/08-3/08
	San Jose-Sunnyvale-Santa Clara MSA, CA	H	31.68 FQ	36.94 MW	43.38 TQ	CABLS	1/08-3/08
	Santa Ana-Anaheim-Irvine PMSA, CA	Y	51390 FQ	57640 MW	64930 TQ	USBLS	5/07
	Colorado	Y	33400 FQ	41660 MW	53210 TQ	USBLS	5/07
	Denver-Aurora MSA, CO	Y	34160 FQ	39120 MW	51480 TQ	USBLS	5/07
	Connecticut	H	22.10 AE	28.89 MW		CTBLS	1/08-3/08
	Bridgeport-Stamford-Norwalk MSA, CT	Y	53740 FQ	62420 MW	73280 TQ	USBLS	5/07
	Hartford-West Hartford-East Hartford MSA, CT	Y	49960 FQ	57170 MW	64450 TQ	USBLS	5/07
	Delaware	Y	45680 FQ	51650 MW	57590 TQ	USBLS	5/07
	Wilmington PMSA, DE-MD-NJ	Y	46020 FQ	51970 MW	58210 TQ	USBLS	5/07
	District of Columbia	Y	44050 FQ	49870 MW	60700 TQ	USBLS	5/07
	Washington-Arlington-Alexandria MSA, DC-VA-MD-WV	Y	47390 FQ	56500 MW	68050 TQ	USBLS	5/07
	Florida	Y	42370 FQ	47880 MW	57760 TQ	USBLS	5/07
	Cape Coral-Fort Myers MSA, FL	Y	44240 FQ	49360 MW	58630 TQ	USBLS	5/07
	Fort Lauderdale-Pompano Beach-Deerfield Beach PMSA, FL	Y	44860 FQ	51070 MW	60820 TQ	USBLS	5/07
	Jacksonville MSA, FL	Y	31430 FQ	44460 MW	51400 TQ	USBLS	5/07
	Miami-Fort Lauderdale-Miami Beach MSA, FL	Y	45380 FQ	52530 MW	67290 TQ	USBLS	5/07
	Orlando-Kissimmee MSA, FL	Y	42070 FQ	47070 MW	53250 TQ	USBLS	5/07
	Tallahassee MSA, FL	Y	41360 FQ	46070 MW	50740 TQ	USBLS	5/07
	Tampa-St. Petersburg-Clearwater MSA, FL	Y	41390 FQ	45530 MW	51380 TQ	USBLS	5/07
	West Palm Beach-Boca Raton-Boynton Beach PMSA, FL	Y	42450 FQ	48360 MW	55520 TQ	USBLS	5/07
	Georgia	Y	34430 FQ	43880 MW	53490 TQ	USBLS	5/07
	Atlanta-Sandy Springs-Marietta MSA, GA	Y	37880 FQ	45780 MW	54250 TQ	USBLS	5/07
	Augusta-Richmond County MSA, GA-SC	Y	36260 FQ	42240 MW	48790 TQ	USBLS	5/07
	Hawaii	Y	44710 FQ	53120 MW	62790 TQ	USBLS	5/07
	Honolulu MSA, HI	Y	45240 FQ	53890 MW	63630 TQ	USBLS	5/07
	Idaho	Y	32240 FQ	46650 MW	55060 TQ	USBLS	5/07
	Boise City-Nampa MSA, ID	Y	41530 FQ	48520 MW	55750 TQ	USBLS	5/07
	Illinois	Y	37160 FQ	46220 MW	56860 TQ	USBLS	5/07
	Chicago-Naperville-Joliet MSA, IL-IN-WI	Y	37840 FQ	47020 MW	57850 TQ	USBLS	5/07

AE	Average entry wage	AW	Average wage paid	FQ	First quartile wage	LO	Lowest wage paid	MTC	Median total compensation	TCC	Total cash compensation
AER	Average entry range	AWR	Average wage range	H	Hourly	LR	Low end range	MW	Median wage paid	TQ	Third quartile wage
AEX	Average experienced wage	AXR	Average experienced range	HI	Highest wage paid	M	Monthly	MWR	Median wage range	W	Weekly
ATC	Average total compensation	D	Daily	HR	High end range	MCC	Median cash compensation	S	See annotated source	Y	Yearly

Dietitian and Nutritionist

Occupation/Type/Industry	Location	Per	Low	Mid	High	Source	Date
Dietitian and Nutritionist	Rockford MSA, IL	Y	36110 FQ	41880 MW	49690 TQ	USBLS	5/07
	Indiana	Y	37450 FQ	44760 MW	51740 TQ	USBLS	5/07
	Evansville MSA, IN-KY	Y	42820 FQ	47510 MW	52040 TQ	USBLS	5/07
	Gary PMSA, IN	Y	39570 FQ	44780 MW	50510 TQ	USBLS	5/07
	Indianapolis-Carmel MSA, IN	Y	41100 FQ	46410 MW	53960 TQ	USBLS	5/07
	Iowa	Y	36930 FQ	45290 MW	53080 TQ	USBLS	5/07
	Des Moines-West Des Moines MSA, IA	Y	40620 FQ	48850 MW	58060 TQ	USBLS	5/07
	Iowa City MSA, IA	Y	43420 FQ	50170 MW	59450 TQ	USBLS	5/07
	Kansas	Y	40610 FQ	47070 MW	55520 TQ	USBLS	5/07
	Wichita MSA, KS	Y	40620 FQ	52280 MW	60400 TQ	USBLS	5/07
	Kentucky	Y	41781 FQ	48668 MW	56448 TQ	KYBLS	2008
	Louisville-Jefferson County MSA, KY-IN	Y	42760 FQ	48080 MW	54400 TQ	USBLS	5/07
	Louisiana	H	14.80 FQ	19.35 MW	23.43 TQ	LABLS	1/08-3/08
	Baton Rouge MSA, LA	Y	36430 FQ	42030 MW	49960 TQ	USBLS	5/07
	Lake Charles MSA, LA	Y	17960 FQ	38610 MW	45350 TQ	USBLS	5/07
	New Orleans-Metairie-Kenner MSA, LA	Y	36040 FQ	44150 MW	51940 TQ	USBLS	5/07
	Maine	Y	34470 FQ	44360 MW	54480 TQ	USBLS	5/07
	Portland-South Portland-Biddeford MSA, ME	Y	35550 FQ	44550 MW	55230 TQ	USBLS	5/07
	Maryland	Y		57375 MW		MDBLS	3/08
	Baltimore-Towson MSA, MD	Y	44650 FQ	54910 MW	64180 TQ	USBLS	5/07
	Bethesda-Gaithersburg-Frederick PMSA, MD	Y	55070 FQ	60900 MW	73030 TQ	USBLS	5/07
	Massachusetts	Y	42070 FQ	51870 MW	64080 TQ	USBLS	5/07
	Boston-Cambridge-Quincy NECTA, MA	Y	44190 FQ	52920 MW	63700 TQ	USBLS	5/07
	Worcester MSA, MA-CT	Y	40300 FQ	48910 MW	59800 TQ	USBLS	5/07
	Michigan	Y	38920 FQ	45730 MW	55980 TQ	USBLS	5/07
	Detroit-Warren-Livonia MSA, MI	Y	37730 FQ	42020 MW	53160 TQ	USBLS	5/07
	Grand Rapids-Wyoming MSA, MI	Y	37540 FQ	41250 MW	49250 TQ	USBLS	5/07
	Warren-Troy-Farmington Hills PMSA, MI	Y	36870 FQ	40360 MW	49280 TQ	USBLS	5/07
	Minnesota	Y	47122 FQ	54477 MW	62721 TQ	MNBLS	10/08-12/08
	Duluth-Superior MSA, MN-WI	Y	46881 FQ	56527 MW	63108 TQ	MNBLS	10/08-12/08
	Minneapolis-Saint Paul MSA, MN-WI	Y	48021 FQ	55052 MW	63401 TQ	MNBLS	10/08-12/08
	Rochester MSA, MN	Y	49027 FQ	57525 MW	63142 TQ	MNBLS	10/08-12/08
	Mississippi	Y	34870 FQ	41890 MW	51670 TQ	USBLS	5/07
	Jackson MSA, MS	Y	37880 FQ	45390 MW	56110 TQ	USBLS	5/07
	Missouri	Y	31750 FQ	40880 MW	49830 TQ	USBLS	5/07
	Kansas City MSA, MO-KS	Y	20780 FQ	43810 MW	53420 TQ	USBLS	5/07
	St. Louis MSA, MO-IL	Y	37050 FQ	43990 MW	51440 TQ	USBLS	5/07
	Montana	Y	38910 FQ	45250 MW	51030 TQ	USBLS	5/07
	Billings MSA, MT	Y	38750 FQ	45130 MW	51300 TQ	USBLS	5/07
	Nebraska	Y	37530 FQ	46150 MW	57530 TQ	USBLS	5/07
	Omaha-Council Bluffs MSA, NE-IA	Y	41060 FQ	50500 MW	62490 TQ	USBLS	5/07
	Nevada	H	22.03 FQ	27.43 MW	31.82 TQ	NVBLS	5/08
	Las Vegas-Paradise MSA, NV	H	21.07 FQ	26.12 MW	30.45 TQ	NVBLS	5/08
	New Hampshire	H	15.14 AE	24.28 MW	27.15 AEX	NHBLS	6/08
	Nashua NECTA, NH-MA	Y	42230 FQ	48300 MW	57640 TQ	USBLS	5/07
	New Jersey	Y	50420 FQ	58210 MW	66440 TQ	USBLS	5/07
	Camden PMSA, NJ	Y	49890 FQ	57260 MW	64200 TQ	USBLS	5/07
	Edison PMSA, NJ	Y	50520 FQ	59180 MW	68360 TQ	USBLS	5/07
	Newark-Union PMSA, NJ-PA	Y	51370 FQ	58580 MW	66180 TQ	USBLS	5/07
	New Mexico	Y	38790 FQ	53260 MW	64280 TQ	USBLS	5/07
	Albuquerque MSA, NM	Y	46780 FQ	56160 MW	68380 TQ	USBLS	5/07
	New York	Y	45690 FQ	54010 MW	62580 TQ	USBLS	5/07
	Albany-Schenectady-Troy MSA, NY	Y	42510 FQ	52530 MW	65210 TQ	USBLS	5/07
	Buffalo-Niagara Falls MSA, NY	Y	43780 FQ	50740 MW	58290 TQ	USBLS	5/07
	Nassau-Suffolk PMSA, NY	Y	51770 FQ	58730 MW	65940 TQ	USBLS	5/07
	New York-Northern New Jersey-Long Island MSA, NY-NJ-PA	Y	48440 FQ	56520 MW	64870 TQ	USBLS	5/07
	North Carolina	Y	37990 FQ	45440 MW	53560 TQ	USBLS	5/07

AE	Average entry wage	AW	Average wage paid	FQ	First quartile wage
AER	Average entry range	AWR	Average wage range	H	Hourly
AEX	Average experienced wage	AXR	Average experienced range	HI	Highest wage paid
ATC	Average total compensation	D	Daily	HR	High end range

LO	Lowest wage paid	MTC	Median total compensation	TCC	Total cash compensation
LR	Low end range	MW	Median wage paid	TQ	Third quartile wage
M	Monthly	MWR	Median wage range	W	Weekly
MCC	Median cash compensation	S	See annotated source	Y	Yearly

Occupation/Type/Industry	Location	Per	Low	Mid	High	Source	Date
Dietitian and Nutritionist	Charlotte-Gastonia-Concord						
	MSA, NC-SC	Y	40520 FQ	46370 MW	53950 TQ	USBLS	5/07
	Raleigh-Cary MSA, NC	Y	41090 FQ	49470 MW	58480 TQ	USBLS	5/07
	North Dakota	Y	36180 FQ	44120 MW	52010 TQ	USBLS	5/07
	Fargo MSA, ND-MN	Y	38350 FQ	45990 MW	55190 TQ	USBLS	5/07
	Ohio	Y	42180 FQ	48480 MW	56820 TQ	USBLS	5/07
	Cincinnati-Middletown MSA,						
	OH-KY-IN	Y	44310 FQ	51830 MW	60470 TQ	USBLS	5/07
	Cleveland-Elyria-Mentor						
	MSA, OH	Y	42810 FQ	49290 MW	57910 TQ	USBLS	5/07
	Columbus MSA, OH	Y	43420 FQ	48810 MW	56160 TQ	USBLS	5/07
	Dayton MSA, OH	Y	43740 FQ	50320 MW	57570 TQ	USBLS	5/07
	Oklahoma	Y	30820 FQ	40630 MW	50890 TQ	USBLS	5/07
	Oklahoma City MSA, OK	Y	30840 FQ	39940 MW	49820 TQ	USBLS	5/07
	Tulsa MSA, OK	Y	36340 FQ	43760 MW	56440 TQ	USBLS	5/07
	Oregon	H	22.85 FQ	26.96 MW	30.98 TQ	ORBLS	5/08
	Portland-Vancouver-Beaverton						
	MSA, OR-WA	Y	47490 FQ	55010 MW	63370 TQ	USBLS	5/07
	Pennsylvania	Y	33540 FQ	42940 MW	52320 TQ	USBLS	5/07
	Allentown-Bethlehem-Easton						
	MSA, PA-NJ	Y	37080 FQ	47740 MW	56130 TQ	USBLS	5/07
	Lancaster MSA, PA	Y	28960 FQ	39190 MW	50440 TQ	USBLS	5/07
	Philadelphia-Camden-						
	Wilmington MSA, PA-NJ-DE-						
	MD	Y	41460 FQ	50390 MW	59550 TQ	USBLS	5/07
	Pittsburgh MSA, PA	Y	37590 FQ	43880 MW	50690 TQ	USBLS	5/07
	Rhode Island	Y	45320 FQ	54040 MW	62010 TQ	USBLS	5/07
	Providence-Fall River-						
	Warwick MSA, RI-MA	Y	44760 FQ	53600 MW	62360 TQ	USBLS	5/07
	South Carolina	Y	34210 FQ	44610 MW	54720 TQ	USBLS	5/07
	Charleston-North Charleston						
	MSA, SC	Y	35720 FQ	44380 MW	49950 TQ	USBLS	5/07
	Columbia MSA, SC	Y	42120 FQ	53420 MW	73720 TQ	USBLS	5/07
	Florence MSA, SC	Y	31760 FQ	39950 MW	51740 TQ	USBLS	5/07
	South Dakota	Y	39171 FQ	45426 MW	54180 TQ	SDBLS	7/08-9/08
	Sioux Falls MSA, SD	Y	40069 FQ	47262 MW	56686 TQ	SDBLS	7/08-9/08
	Tennessee	Y	36270 FQ	44080 MW	52840 TQ	USBLS	5/07
	Memphis MSA, TN-MS-AR	Y	37110 FQ	41790 MW	49380 TQ	USBLS	5/07
	Nashville-Davidson-						
	Murfreesboro MSA, TN	Y	40120 FQ	48210 MW	56900 TQ	USBLS	5/07
	Texas	Y	40070 FQ	47590 MW	56950 TQ	USBLS	5/07
	Austin-Round Rock MSA, TX	Y	36420 FQ	40710 MW	47050 TQ	USBLS	5/07
	Dallas-Fort Worth-Arlington						
	MSA, TX	Y	43910 FQ	49750 MW	58600 TQ	USBLS	5/07
	El Paso MSA, TX	Y	39600 FQ	45970 MW	53550 TQ	USBLS	5/07
	Houston-Sugar Land-Baytown						
	MSA, TX	Y	41200 FQ	48220 MW	57510 TQ	USBLS	5/07
	San Antonio MSA, TX	Y	40120 FQ	49580 MW	59220 TQ	USBLS	5/07
	Utah	Y	37140 FQ	44380 MW	53590 TQ	USBLS	5/07
	Provo-Orem MSA, UT	Y	35740 FQ	40250 MW	48850 TQ	USBLS	5/07
	Salt Lake City MSA, UT	Y	40730 FQ	48330 MW	56290 TQ	USBLS	5/07
	Vermont	Y	41270 FQ	48170 MW	57100 TQ	USBLS	5/07
	Burlington-South Burlington						
	MSA, VT	Y	41540 FQ	49080 MW	57110 TQ	USBLS	5/07
	Virginia	Y	42420 FQ	48810 MW	58560 TQ	USBLS	5/07
	Richmond MSA, VA	Y	42430 FQ	48340 MW	59560 TQ	USBLS	5/07
	Virginia Beach-Norfolk-						
	Newport News MSA, VA-NC	Y	42590 FQ	46960 MW	51860 TQ	USBLS	5/07
	Washington	H	23.06 FQ	26.70 MW	30.56 TQ	WABLS	3/08
	Seattle-Tacoma-Bellevue						
	MSA, WA	Y	48340 FQ	55930 MW	63800 TQ	USBLS	5/07
	Spokane MSA, WA	Y	44520 FQ	50380 MW	57590 TQ	USBLS	5/07
	West Virginia	Y	40455 FQ	48197 MW	61832 TQ	WVBLS	7/08-9/08
	Charleston MSA, WV	Y	37440 FQ	45210 MW	55010 TQ	USBLS	5/07
	Wisconsin	Y	42790 FQ	49900 MW	58530 TQ	USBLS	5/07
	Appleton MSA, WI	Y	43490 FQ	49810 MW	56640 TQ	USBLS	5/07
	Milwaukee-Waukesha-West						
	Allis MSA, WI	Y	43870 FQ	50620 MW	59480 TQ	USBLS	5/07
	Wyoming	Y	42096 FQ	49784 MW	57694 TQ	WYBLS	9/08
	Cheyenne MSA, WY	Y	43564 FQ	49853 MW	58284 TQ	WYBLS	9/08
	Puerto Rico	Y	26070 FQ	30330 MW	36300 TQ	USBLS	5/07

AE	Average entry wage	AW	Average wage paid	FQ	First quartile wage
AER	Average entry range	AWR	Average wage range	H	Hourly
AEX	Average experienced wage	AXR	Average experienced range	HI	Highest wage paid
ATC	Average total compensation	D	Daily	HR	High end range

LO	Lowest wage paid	MTC	Median total compensation	TCC	Total cash compensation
LR	Low end range	MW	Median wage paid	TQ	Third quartile wage
M	Monthly	MWR	Median wage range	W	Weekly
MCC	Median cash compensation	S	See annotated source	Y	Yearly

Occupation/Type/Industry	Location	Per	Low	Mid	High	Source	Date
Dietitian and Nutritionist	San Juan-Caguas-Guaynabo MSA, PR	Y	26280 FQ	30260 MW	35750 TQ	USBLS	5/07
	Guam	Y	22430 FQ	28350 MW	40510 TQ	USBLS	5/07
Digital Asset Manager							
Public Institutions	United States	Y		70000 AW		RORB	2009
Digital Asset Manager Consultant	United States	H			150.00 HI	RORB	2009
Digital Imaging Technician							
Municipal Government	Colorado Springs, CO	M	3249 LO			COSPRS	1/1/09
Digital Photo Technician							
State Government	Ohio	H	15.09 LO		17.03 HI	ODAS	2008
Digital Video Editor	United States	*Y		40000-60000 AW		ANISR	2006
Dining Room and Cafeteria Attendant and Bartender Helper	Alabama	Y	12800 FQ	14540 MW	16710 TQ	USBLS	5/07
	Birmingham-Hoover MSA, AL	Y	12790 FQ	14480 MW	16440 TQ	USBLS	5/07
	Alaska	Y	16140 FQ	18350 MW	23550 TQ	USBLS	5/07
	Anchorage MSA, AK	Y	15960 FQ	17470 MW	19690 TQ	USBLS	5/07
	Arizona	Y	14570 FQ	15190 MW	16750 TQ	USBLS	5/07
	Phoenix-Mesa-Scottsdale MSA, AZ	Y	14600 FQ	15290 MW	17420 TQ	USBLS	5/07
	Tucson MSA, AZ	Y	14530 FQ	15060 MW	16160 TQ	USBLS	5/07
	Arkansas	Y	14140 FQ	15060 MW	16600 TQ	USBLS	5/07
	Little Rock-North Little Rock MSA, AR	Y	14230 FQ	15260 MW	17160 TQ	USBLS	5/07
	California	H	8.00 FQ	8.40 MW	9.22 TQ	CABLS	1/08-3/08
	Los Angeles-Long Beach-Glendale PMSA, CA	H	8.00 FQ	8.29 MW	9.13 TQ	CABLS	1/08-3/08
	Oakland-Fremont-Hayward MSA, CA	H	8.00 FQ	8.37 MW	9.23 TQ	CABLS	1/08-3/08
	Riverside-San Bernardino-Ontario MSA, CA	H	8.00 FQ	8.36 MW	9.12 TQ	CABLS	1/08-3/08
	Sacramento-Arden Arcade-Roseville MSA, CA	H	8.00 FQ	8.45 MW	9.16 TQ	CABLS	1/08-3/08
	San Diego-Carlsbad-San Marcos MSA, CA	H	8.00 FQ	8.32 MW	9.13 TQ	CABLS	1/08-3/08
	San Francisco-San Mateo-Redwood PMSA, CA	H	8.47 FQ	9.43 MW	11.04 TQ	CABLS	1/08-3/08
	San Jose-Sunnyvale-Santa Clara MSA, CA	H	8.00 FQ	8.45 MW	9.44 TQ	CABLS	1/08-3/08
	Santa Ana-Anaheim-Irvine PMSA, CA	Y	15970 FQ	16850 MW	18450 TQ	USBLS	5/07
	Colorado	Y	14820 FQ	15710 MW	18480 TQ	USBLS	5/07
	Colorado Springs MSA, CO	Y	14690 FQ	15300 MW	17450 TQ	USBLS	5/07
	Denver-Aurora MSA, CO	Y	14860 FQ	15840 MW	18690 TQ	USBLS	5/07
	Connecticut	H	8.13 AE	8.82 MW		CTBLS	1/08-3/08
	Bridgeport-Stamford-Norwalk MSA, CT	Y	16630 FQ	18740 MW	24270 TQ	USBLS	5/07
	Hartford-West Hartford-East Hartford MSA, CT	Y	16850 FQ	18180 MW	19940 TQ	USBLS	5/07
	Delaware	Y	14710 FQ	16560 MW	20020 TQ	USBLS	5/07
	Wilmington PMSA, DE-MD-NJ	Y	15090 FQ	17280 MW	20870 TQ	USBLS	5/07
	District of Columbia	Y	16100 FQ	19220 MW	23830 TQ	USBLS	5/07
	Washington-Arlington-Alexandria MSA, DC-VA-MD-WV	Y	14630 FQ	17000 MW	22400 TQ	USBLS	5/07
	Florida	Y	14590 FQ	15480 MW	18400 TQ	USBLS	5/07
	Fort Lauderdale-Pompano Beach-Deerfield Beach PMSA, FL	Y	14540 FQ	15280 MW	17610 TQ	USBLS	5/07
	Jacksonville MSA, FL	Y	14730 FQ	15820 MW	17880 TQ	USBLS	5/07
	Miami-Fort Lauderdale-Miami Beach MSA, FL	Y	14540 FQ	15370 MW	18330 TQ	USBLS	5/07
	Orlando-Kissimmee MSA, FL	Y	14750 FQ	15850 MW	20010 TQ	USBLS	5/07
	Sarasota-Bradenton-Venice MSA, FL	Y	14930 FQ	17580 MW	21420 TQ	USBLS	5/07

AE	Average entry wage	AW	Average wage paid	FQ	First quartile wage	LO	Lowest wage paid	MTC Median total compensation TCC Total cash compensation
AER	Average entry range	AWR	Average wage range	H	Hourly	LR	Low end range	MW Median wage paid TQ Third quartile wage
AEX	Average experienced wage	AXR	Average experienced range	HI	Highest wage paid	M	Monthly	MWR Median wage range W Weekly
ATC	Average total compensation	D	Daily	HR	High end range	MCC	Median cash compensation	S See annotated source Y Yearly

Occupation/Type/Industry	Location	Per	Low	Mid	High	Source	Date
Dining Room and Cafeteria Attendant and Bartender Helper	Tampa-St. Petersburg-Clearwater MSA, FL	Y	14610 FQ	15470 MW	17710 TQ	USBLS	5/07
	West Palm Beach-Boca Raton-Boynton Beach PMSA, FL	Y	14570 FQ	15530 MW	18730 TQ	USBLS	5/07
	Georgia	Y	13290 FQ	15520 MW	20270 TQ	USBLS	5/07
	Atlanta-Sandy Springs-Marietta MSA, GA	Y	13290 FQ	15520 MW	19630 TQ	USBLS	5/07
	Hawaii	Y	16000 FQ	21100 MW	29830 TQ	USBLS	5/07
	Honolulu MSA, HI	Y	15840 FQ	19140 MW	27240 TQ	USBLS	5/07
	Idaho	Y	12850 FQ	14510 MW	16790 TQ	USBLS	5/07
	Boise City-Nampa MSA, ID	Y	13040 FQ	14820 MW	17500 TQ	USBLS	5/07
	Pocatello MSA, ID	Y	12680 FQ	14090 MW	16040 TQ	USBLS	5/07
	Illinois	Y	14840 FQ	15920 MW	19280 TQ	USBLS	5/07
	Chicago-Naperville-Joliet MSA, IL-IN-WI	Y	14870 FQ	16150 MW	19930 TQ	USBLS	5/07
	Indiana	Y	12950 FQ	14750 MW	17350 TQ	USBLS	5/07
	Gary PMSA, IN	Y	12710 FQ	14180 MW	15960 TQ	USBLS	5/07
	Indianapolis-Carmel MSA, IN	Y	13330 FQ	15520 MW	18600 TQ	USBLS	5/07
	Iowa	Y	14160 FQ	15500 MW	18040 TQ	USBLS	5/07
	Des Moines-West Des Moines MSA, IA	Y	14560 FQ	16090 MW	18380 TQ	USBLS	5/07
	Sioux City MSA, IA-NE-SD	Y	14130 FQ	16330 MW	18350 TQ	USBLS	5/07
	Kansas	Y	12680 FQ	14310 MW	16430 TQ	USBLS	5/07
	Wichita MSA, KS	Y	12430 FQ	13760 MW	15120 TQ	USBLS	5/07
	Kentucky	Y	13481 FQ	15489 MW	17864 TQ	KYBLS	2008
	Lexington-Fayette MSA, KY	Y	13690 FQ	16280 MW	18660 TQ	USBLS	5/07
	Louisville-Jefferson County MSA, KY-IN	Y	13650 FQ	15790 MW	18050 TQ	USBLS	5/07
	Louisiana	H	6.08 FQ	6.82 MW	7.70 TQ	LABLS	1/08-3/08
	Baton Rouge MSA, LA	Y	12660 FQ	14280 MW	16190 TQ	USBLS	5/07
	Houma-Bayou Cane-Thibodaux MSA, LA	Y	12920 FQ	14670 MW	17880 TQ	USBLS	5/07
	Lafayette MSA, LA	Y	12590 FQ	13890 MW	15310 TQ	USBLS	5/07
	New Orleans-Metairie-Kenner MSA, LA	Y	12640 FQ	14120 MW	15920 TQ	USBLS	5/07
	Maine	Y	14830 FQ	15960 MW	18430 TQ	USBLS	5/07
	Portland-South Portland-Biddeford MSA, ME	Y	14790 FQ	15690 MW	18260 TQ	USBLS	5/07
	Maryland	Y		15800 MW		MDBLS	3/08
	Baltimore-Towson MSA, MD	Y	14070 FQ	15020 MW	17320 TQ	USBLS	5/07
	Bethesda-Gaithersburg-Frederick PMSA, MD	Y	14890 FQ	18900 MW	25930 TQ	USBLS	5/07
	Massachusetts	Y	16530 FQ	19040 MW	23900 TQ	USBLS	5/07
	Boston-Cambridge-Quincy NECTA, MA	Y	17270 FQ	20590 MW	26220 TQ	USBLS	5/07
	Worcester MSA, MA-CT	Y	16810 FQ	19140 MW	23000 TQ	USBLS	5/07
	Michigan	Y	15140 FQ	15960 MW	20510 TQ	USBLS	5/07
	Detroit-Warren-Livonia MSA, MI	Y	15230 FQ	15950 MW	20420 TQ	USBLS	5/07
	Grand Rapids-Wyoming MSA, MI	Y	15270 FQ	16810 MW	21460 TQ	USBLS	5/07
	Warren-Troy-Farmington Hills PMSA, MI	Y	15170 FQ	15880 MW	18760 TQ	USBLS	5/07
	Minnesota	Y	15108 FQ	16582 MW	19751 TQ	MNBLS	10/08-12/08
	Duluth-Superior MSA, MN-WI	Y	14711 FQ	15589 MW	16802 TQ	MNBLS	10/08-12/08
	Minneapolis-Saint Paul MSA, MN-WI	Y	15192 FQ	16854 MW	20127 TQ	MNBLS	10/08-12/08
	Rochester MSA, MN	Y	15702 FQ	17250 MW	19055 TQ	MNBLS	10/08-12/08
	Mississippi	Y	12930 FQ	14690 MW	17380 TQ	USBLS	5/07
	Gulfport-Biloxi MSA, MS	Y	13220 FQ	15200 MW	18890 TQ	USBLS	5/07
	Jackson MSA, MS	Y	12630 FQ	14210 MW	15980 TQ	USBLS	5/07
	Missouri	Y	14360 FQ	15260 MW	17450 TQ	USBLS	5/07
	Kansas City MSA, MO-KS	Y	13920 FQ	14820 MW	16820 TQ	USBLS	5/07
	St. Louis MSA, MO-IL	Y	14520 FQ	15450 MW	17730 TQ	USBLS	5/07
	Montana	Y	13790 FQ	14780 MW	15950 TQ	USBLS	5/07
	Billings MSA, MT	Y	13870 FQ	14960 MW	16990 TQ	USBLS	5/07
	Nebraska	Y	13210 FQ	15260 MW	18250 TQ	USBLS	5/07
	Lincoln MSA, NE	Y	13130 FQ	15090 MW	18100 TQ	USBLS	5/07
	Omaha-Council Bluffs MSA, NE-IA	Y	13480 FQ	15570 MW	18670 TQ	USBLS	5/07
	Nevada	H	6.99 FQ	9.27 MW	11.63 TQ	NVBLS	5/08

AE	Average entry wage	AW	Average wage paid	FQ	First quartile wage	LO	Lowest wage paid	MTC	Median total compensation	TCC	Total cash compensation
AER	Average entry range	AWR	Average wage range	H	Hourly	LR	Low end range	MW	Median wage paid	TQ	Third quartile wage
AEX	Average experienced wage	AXR	Average experienced range	HI	Highest wage paid	M	Monthly	MWR	Median wage range	W	Weekly
ATC	Average total compensation	D	Daily	HR	High end range	MCC	Median cash compensation	S	See annotated source	Y	Yearly

Occupation/Type/Industry	Location	Per	Low	Mid	High	Source	Date
Dining Room and Cafeteria Attendant and Bartender Helper	Las Vegas-Paradise MSA, NV	H	7.43 FQ	10.08 MW	12.06 TQ	NVBLS	5/08
	New Hampshire	H	6.53 AE	7.70 MW	9.50 AEX	NHBLS	6/08
	Manchester MSA, NH	Y	14570 FQ	18340 MW	21650 TQ	USBLS	5/07
	Nashua NECTA, NH-MA	Y	14830 FQ	19400 MW	24070 TQ	USBLS	5/07
	New Jersey	Y	15470 FQ	16540 MW	19570 TQ	USBLS	5/07
	Camden PMSA, NJ	Y	15630 FQ	17420 MW	21810 TQ	USBLS	5/07
	Edison PMSA, NJ	Y	15360 FQ	15960 MW	18240 TQ	USBLS	5/07
	Newark-Union PMSA, NJ-PA	Y	15700 FQ	16920 MW	18810 TQ	USBLS	5/07
	Ocean City MSA, NJ	Y	15220 FQ	15840 MW	18600 TQ	USBLS	5/07
	New Mexico	Y	12670 FQ	14180 MW	15990 TQ	USBLS	5/07
	Albuquerque MSA, NM	Y	12570 FQ	14000 MW	15540 TQ	USBLS	5/07
	New York	Y	15410 FQ	17400 MW	22000 TQ	USBLS	5/07
	Albany-Schenectady-Troy MSA, NY	Y	15030 FQ	15830 MW	18480 TQ	USBLS	5/07
	Binghamton MSA, NY	Y	15300 FQ	16000 MW	19170 TQ	USBLS	5/07
	Buffalo-Niagara Falls MSA, NY	Y	15320 FQ	16290 MW	18780 TQ	USBLS	5/07
	Nassau-Suffolk PMSA, NY	Y	15630 FQ	17900 MW	21420 TQ	USBLS	5/07
	New York-Northern New Jersey-Long Island MSA, NY-NJ-PA	Y	15600 FQ	17780 MW	22320 TQ	USBLS	5/07
	North Carolina	Y	13910 FQ	15060 MW	17430 TQ	USBLS	5/07
	Charlotte-Gastonia-Concord MSA, NC-SC	Y	13900 FQ	15160 MW	17940 TQ	USBLS	5/07
	Durham MSA, NC	Y	13840 FQ	14880 MW	16850 TQ	USBLS	5/07
	Raleigh-Cary MSA, NC	Y	14310 FQ	15940 MW	19390 TQ	USBLS	5/07
	Winston-Salem MSA, NC	Y	13670 FQ	14550 MW	16100 TQ	USBLS	5/07
	North Dakota	Y	13220 FQ	15150 MW	18310 TQ	USBLS	5/07
	Fargo MSA, ND-MN	Y	13430 FQ	15320 MW	18760 TQ	USBLS	5/07
	Ohio	Y	14720 FQ	15320 MW	16980 TQ	USBLS	5/07
	Cincinnati-Middletown MSA, OH-KY-IN	Y	14510 FQ	15180 MW	16730 TQ	USBLS	5/07
	Cleveland-Elyria-Mentor MSA, OH	Y	14730 FQ	15360 MW	17230 TQ	USBLS	5/07
	Columbus MSA, OH	Y	14850 FQ	15800 MW	19110 TQ	USBLS	5/07
	Dayton MSA, OH	Y	14750 FQ	15410 MW	16920 TQ	USBLS	5/07
	Oklahoma	Y	12600 FQ	14140 MW	15920 TQ	USBLS	5/07
	Oklahoma City MSA, OK	Y	12610 FQ	14100 MW	15740 TQ	USBLS	5/07
	Tulsa MSA, OK	Y	12460 FQ	13970 MW	15520 TQ	USBLS	5/07
	Oregon	H	8.50 FQ	9.07 MW	9.78 TQ	ORBLS	5/08
	Portland-Vancouver-Beaverton MSA, OR-WA	Y	17340 FQ	18560 MW	20260 TQ	USBLS	5/07
	Pennsylvania	Y	14410 FQ	15430 MW	17920 TQ	USBLS	5/07
	Allentown-Bethlehem-Easton MSA, PA-NJ	Y	14370 FQ	15220 MW	17310 TQ	USBLS	5/07
	Philadelphia-Camden-Wilmington MSA, PA-NJ-DE-MD	Y	14760 FQ	15960 MW	19020 TQ	USBLS	5/07
	Pittsburgh MSA, PA	Y	14460 FQ	15520 MW	17720 TQ	USBLS	5/07
	York-Hanover MSA, PA	Y	14570 FQ	15750 MW	17730 TQ	USBLS	5/07
	Rhode Island	Y	15830 FQ	16950 MW	18740 TQ	USBLS	5/07
	Providence-Fall River-Warwick MSA, RI-MA	Y	15900 FQ	17150 MW	18910 TQ	USBLS	5/07
	South Carolina	Y	12960 FQ	14810 MW	17300 TQ	USBLS	5/07
	Charleston-North Charleston MSA, SC	Y	12710 FQ	14310 MW	16290 TQ	USBLS	5/07
	Columbia MSA, SC	Y	12970 FQ	14680 MW	17260 TQ	USBLS	5/07
	Spartanburg MSA, SC	Y	12620 FQ	14260 MW	16290 TQ	USBLS	5/07
	South Dakota	Y	14019 FQ	16380 MW	19080 TQ	SDBLS	7/08-9/08
	Sioux Falls MSA, SD	Y	14591 FQ	17099 MW	19658 TQ	SDBLS	7/08-9/08
	Tennessee	Y	13360 FQ	15590 MW	19290 TQ	USBLS	5/07
	Memphis MSA, TN-MS-AR	Y	13810 FQ	16600 MW	21120 TQ	USBLS	5/07
	Nashville-Davidson-Murfreesboro MSA, TN	Y	13720 FQ	16350 MW	20310 TQ	USBLS	5/07
	Texas	Y	12740 FQ	14310 MW	16220 TQ	USBLS	5/07
	Austin-Round Rock MSA, TX	Y	12720 FQ	14340 MW	16160 TQ	USBLS	5/07
	Beaumont-Port Arthur MSA, TX	Y	12520 FQ	13810 MW	15110 TQ	USBLS	5/07
	Dallas-Fort Worth-Arlington MSA, TX	Y	12990 FQ	14820 MW	17420 TQ	USBLS	5/07
	El Paso MSA, TX	Y	12450 FQ	13670 MW	14900 TQ	USBLS	5/07

AE	Average entry wage	AW	Average wage paid	FQ	First quartile wage	LO	Lowest wage paid	MTC	Median total compensation	TCC	Total cash compensation
AER	Average entry range	AWR	Average wage range	H	Hourly	LR	Low end range	MW	Median wage paid	TQ	Third quartile wage
AEX	Average experienced wage	AXR	Average experienced range	HI	Highest wage paid	M	Monthly	MWR	Median wage range	W	Weekly
ATC	Average total compensation	D	Daily	HR	High end range	MCC	Median cash compensation	S	See annotated source	Y	Yearly

Occupation/Type/Industry	Location	Per	Low	Mid	High	Source	Date
Dining Room and Cafeteria Attendant and Bartender Helper	Houston-Sugar Land-Baytown						
	MSA, TX	Y	12670 FQ	14220 MW	16020 TQ	USBLS	5/07
	San Antonio MSA, TX	Y	12890 FQ	14610 MW	16720 TQ	USBLS	5/07
	Utah	Y	13210 FQ	15290 MW	18650 TQ	USBLS	5/07
	Salt Lake City MSA, UT	Y	13440 FQ	15890 MW	18890 TQ	USBLS	5/07
	Vermont	Y	16150 FQ	17660 MW	19990 TQ	USBLS	5/07
	Burlington-South Burlington						
	MSA, VT	Y	16230 FQ	17960 MW	20700 TQ	USBLS	5/07
	Virginia	Y	13160 FQ	15150 MW	18490 TQ	USBLS	5/07
	Richmond MSA, VA	Y	15390 FQ	18230 MW	21830 TQ	USBLS	5/07
	Virginia Beach-Norfolk-						
	Newport News MSA, VA-NC	Y	12700 FQ	14210 MW	15890 TQ	USBLS	5/07
	Washington	H	8.48 FQ	9.06 MW	9.94 TQ	WABLS	3/08
	Seattle-Tacoma-Bellevue						
	MSA, WA	Y	17450 FQ	18740 MW	22010 TQ	USBLS	5/07
	West Virginia	Y	14033 FQ	15127 MW	16452 TQ	WVBLS	7/08-9/08
	Charleston MSA, WV	Y	13740 FQ	15070 MW	16880 TQ	USBLS	5/07
	Wisconsin	Y	14500 FQ	15340 MW	17600 TQ	USBLS	5/07
	Milwaukee-Waukesha-West						
	Allis MSA, WI	Y	14550 FQ	15530 MW	18200 TQ	USBLS	5/07
	Wyoming	Y	13551 FQ	15414 MW	19174 TQ	WYBLS	9/08
	Cheyenne MSA, WY	Y	13431 FQ	15133 MW	19395 TQ	WYBLS	9/08
	Puerto Rico	Y	12420 FQ	13610 MW	14800 TQ	USBLS	5/07
	San Juan-Caguas-Guaynabo						
	MSA, PR	Y	12400 FQ	13530 MW	14670 TQ	USBLS	5/07
	Virgin Islands	Y	14040 FQ	15580 MW	18130 TQ	USBLS	5/07
	Guam	Y	12410 FQ	13650 MW	14890 TQ	USBLS	5/07
Dining Room Attendant							
Municipal Government	Seattle, WA	H	12.16 LO		14.11 HI	CSSS	2007
Director							
Administrative Office of the U.S. Courts	United States	Y			169300 HI	CRS02	1/08
Congressional Budget Office	United States	Y			166800 HI	CRS02	1/08
Congressional Research Service	United States	Y			158500 HI	CRS02	1/08
Emergency Planning, Preparedness, and Operations, United States House of Representatives	United States	Y			167800 HI	CRS01	1/08
Interparliamentary Affairs, United States House of Representatives	United States	Y			167800 HI	CRS01	1/08
Religious Activities and Education	Arizona	Y	25890 FQ	39650 MW	48790 TQ	USBLS	5/07
Religious Activities and Education	Phoenix-Mesa-Scottsdale						
	MSA, AZ	Y	28830 FQ	40780 MW	49980 TQ	USBLS	5/07
Religious Activities and Education	California	H	15.47 FQ	18.95 MW	25.52 TQ	CABLS	1/08-3/08
Religious Activities and Education	Los Angeles-Long Beach-						
	Glendale PMSA, CA	H	16.86 FQ	19.37 MW	26.18 TQ	CABLS	1/08-3/08
Religious Activities and Education	Modesto MSA, CA	H	11.34 FQ	14.23 MW	20.35 TQ	CABLS	1/08-3/08
Religious Activities and Education	Oakland-Fremont-Hayward						
	MSA, CA	H	19.11 FQ	25.06 MW	29.23 TQ	CABLS	1/08-3/08
Religious Activities and Education	Riverside-San Bernardino-						
	Ontario MSA, CA	H	13.06 FQ	16.51 MW	21.98 TQ	CABLS	1/08-3/08
Religious Activities and Education	Sacramento-Arden Arcade-						
	Roseville MSA, CA	H	14.80 FQ	17.55 MW	19.37 TQ	CABLS	1/08-3/08
Religious Activities and Education	San Diego-Carlsbad-San						
	Marcos MSA, CA	H	15.52 FQ	17.28 MW	20.10 TQ	CABLS	1/08-3/08
Religious Activities and Education	San Francisco-San Mateo-						
	Redwood PMSA, CA	H	16.22 FQ	22.82 MW	30.51 TQ	CABLS	1/08-3/08
Religious Activities and Education	San Jose-Sunnyvale-Santa						
	Clara MSA, CA	H	17.53 FQ	21.22 MW	24.32 TQ	CABLS	1/08-3/08
Religious Activities and Education	Santa Ana-Anaheim-Irvine						
	PMSA, CA	Y	28030 FQ	36010 MW	46600 TQ	USBLS	5/07
Religious Activities and Education	Colorado	Y	34420 FQ	43450 MW	54290 TQ	USBLS	5/07
Religious Activities and Education	Denver-Aurora MSA, CO	Y	32940 FQ	41870 MW	51300 TQ	USBLS	5/07
Religious Activities and Education	Connecticut	H	16.55 AE	19.52 MW		CTBLS	1/08-3/08
Religious Activities and Education	Hartford-West Hartford-East						
	Hartford MSA, CT	Y	35720 FQ	39240 MW	42980 TQ	USBLS	5/07
Religious Activities and Education	District of Columbia	Y	25320 FQ	45850 MW	63850 TQ	USBLS	5/07
Religious Activities and Education	Washington-Arlington- Alexandria MSA, DC-VA-						
	MD-WV	Y	28420 FQ	39140 MW	56400 TQ	USBLS	5/07
Religious Activities and Education	Florida	Y	26580 FQ	33220 MW	41500 TQ	USBLS	5/07

AE Average entry wage	**AW** Average wage paid	**FQ** First quartile wage	**LO** Lowest wage paid	**MTC** Median total compensation **TCC** Total cash compensation
AER Average entry range	**AWR** Average wage range	**H** Hourly	**LR** Low end range	**MW** Median wage paid **TQ** Third quartile wage
AEX Average experienced wage	**AXR** Average experienced range	**HI** Highest wage paid	**M** Monthly	**MWR** Median wage range **W** Weekly
ATC Average total compensation	**D** Daily	**HR** High end range	**MCC** Median cash compensation	**S** See annotated source **Y** Yearly

Occupation/Type/Industry	Location	Per	Low	Mid	High	Source	Date
Director							
Religious Activities and Education	Fort Lauderdale-Pompano Beach-Deerfield Beach PMSA, FL	Y	27160 FQ	32020 MW	40170 TQ	USBLS	5/07
Religious Activities and Education	Jacksonville MSA, FL	Y	25470 FQ	33520 MW	39730 TQ	USBLS	5/07
Religious Activities and Education	Miami-Fort Lauderdale-Miami Beach MSA, FL	Y	28850 FQ	34730 MW	44460 TQ	USBLS	5/07
Religious Activities and Education	Orlando-Kissimmee MSA, FL	Y	29550 FQ	36230 MW	40520 TQ	USBLS	5/07
Religious Activities and Education	Tampa-St. Petersburg-Clearwater MSA, FL	Y	26850 FQ	31440 MW	39740 TQ	USBLS	5/07
Religious Activities and Education	West Palm Beach-Boca Raton-Boynton Beach PMSA, FL	Y	29980 FQ	35530 MW	40910 TQ	USBLS	5/07
Religious Activities and Education	Georgia	Y	27740 FQ	30310 MW	32850 TQ	USBLS	5/07
Religious Activities and Education	Atlanta-Sandy Springs-Marietta MSA, GA	Y	27740 FQ	30200 MW	32630 TQ	USBLS	5/07
Religious Activities and Education	Hawaii	Y	25670 FQ	33560 MW	45700 TQ	USBLS	5/07
Religious Activities and Education	Honolulu MSA, HI	Y	25170 FQ	36840 MW	47420 TQ	USBLS	5/07
Religious Activities and Education	Illinois	Y	27340 FQ	36230 MW	44670 TQ	USBLS	5/07
Religious Activities and Education	Chicago-Naperville-Joliet MSA, IL-IN-WI	Y	27370 FQ	35820 MW	44860 TQ	USBLS	5/07
Religious Activities and Education	Indiana	Y	24590 FQ	34900 MW	44370 TQ	USBLS	5/07
Religious Activities and Education	Gary PMSA, IN	Y	22580 FQ	25790 MW	31960 TQ	USBLS	5/07
Religious Activities and Education	Indianapolis-Carmel MSA, IN	Y	38410 FQ	45280 MW	50440 TQ	USBLS	5/07
Religious Activities and Education	Iowa	Y	28770 FQ	35570 MW	45330 TQ	USBLS	5/07
Religious Activities and Education	Louisiana	H	18.17 FQ	25.44 MW	39.37 TQ	LABLS	1/08-3/08
Religious Activities and Education	Maryland	Y		39275 MW		MDBLS	3/08
Religious Activities and Education	Baltimore-Towson MSA, MD	Y	24580 FQ	38400 MW	71220 TQ	USBLS	5/07
Religious Activities and Education	Bethesda-Gaithersburg-Frederick PMSA, MD	Y	27530 FQ	32250 MW	37800 TQ	USBLS	5/07
Religious Activities and Education	Massachusetts	Y	25750 FQ	35910 MW	44360 TQ	USBLS	5/07
Religious Activities and Education	Boston-Cambridge-Quincy NECTA, MA	Y	26990 FQ	36270 MW	41990 TQ	USBLS	5/07
Religious Activities and Education	Michigan	Y	25370 FQ	29870 MW	42850 TQ	USBLS	5/07
Religious Activities and Education	Detroit-Warren-Livonia MSA, MI	Y	25510 FQ	33630 MW	44250 TQ	USBLS	5/07
Religious Activities and Education	Flint MSA, MI	Y	25410 FQ	28320 MW	48480 TQ	USBLS	5/07
Religious Activities and Education	Grand Rapids-Wyoming MSA, MI	Y	25060 FQ	33750 MW	49210 TQ	USBLS	5/07
Religious Activities and Education	Warren-Troy-Farmington Hills PMSA, MI	Y	26500 FQ	33050 MW	41380 TQ	USBLS	5/07
Religious Activities and Education	Minnesota	Y	35351 FQ	54445 MW	77682 TQ	MNBLS	10/08-12/08
Religious Activities and Education	Minneapolis-Saint Paul MSA, MN-WI	Y	45981 FQ	58128 MW	78330 TQ	MNBLS	10/08-12/08
Religious Activities and Education	Mississippi	Y	24040 FQ	34680 MW	57760 TQ	USBLS	5/07
Religious Activities and Education	Montana	Y	20430 FQ	27130 MW	32950 TQ	USBLS	5/07
Religious Activities and Education	Billings MSA, MT	Y	19730 FQ	29980 MW	35970 TQ	USBLS	5/07
Religious Activities and Education	Missoula MSA, MT	Y	14690 FQ	26300 MW	29020 TQ	USBLS	5/07
Religious Activities and Education	New Jersey	Y	44770 FQ	51700 MW	68110 TQ	USBLS	5/07
Religious Activities and Education	Newark-Union PMSA, NJ-PA	Y	44570 FQ	62070 MW	74610 TQ	USBLS	5/07
Religious Activities and Education	New York	Y	25470 FQ	32880 MW	46770 TQ	USBLS	5/07
Religious Activities and Education	Albany-Schenectady-Troy MSA, NY	Y	20470 FQ	24700 MW	38830 TQ	USBLS	5/07
Religious Activities and Education	Buffalo-Niagara Falls MSA, NY	Y	23400 FQ	30170 MW	39980 TQ	USBLS	5/07
Religious Activities and Education	Nassau-Suffolk PMSA, NY	Y	30290 FQ	41460 MW	47950 TQ	USBLS	5/07
Religious Activities and Education	New York-Northern New Jersey-Long Island MSA, NY-NJ-PA	Y	28970 FQ	40850 MW	56310 TQ	USBLS	5/07
Religious Activities and Education	North Carolina	Y	37870 FQ	58310 MW	77630 TQ	USBLS	5/07
Religious Activities and Education	Charlotte-Gastonia-Concord MSA, NC-SC	Y	52720 FQ	67690 MW	98220 TQ	USBLS	5/07
Religious Activities and Education	Ohio	Y	28350 FQ	36060 MW	47980 TQ	USBLS	5/07
Religious Activities and Education	Cincinnati-Middletown MSA, OH-KY-IN	Y	31610 FQ	39730 MW	52110 TQ	USBLS	5/07
Religious Activities and Education	Columbus MSA, OH	Y	28620 FQ	38480 MW	47310 TQ	USBLS	5/07
Religious Activities and Education	Dayton MSA, OH	Y	31000 FQ	40480 MW	47670 TQ	USBLS	5/07
Religious Activities and Education	Oklahoma	Y	17260 FQ	21220 MW	39500 TQ	USBLS	5/07
Religious Activities and Education	Oregon	H	12.84 FQ	15.35 MW	19.34 TQ	ORBLS	5/08
Religious Activities and Education	Portland-Vancouver-Beaverton MSA, OR-WA	Y	24590 FQ	30970 MW	41470 TQ	USBLS	5/07
Religious Activities and Education	Salem MSA, OR	Y	25830 FQ	29470 MW	35040 TQ	USBLS	5/07
Religious Activities and Education	Pennsylvania	Y	20840 FQ	36160 MW	49860 TQ	USBLS	5/07

AE	Average entry wage	**AW**	Average wage paid	**FQ**	First quartile wage	**LO**	Lowest wage paid	**MTC**	Median total compensation	**TCC** Total cash compensation
AER	Average entry range	**AWR**	Average wage range	**H**	Hourly	**LR**	Low end range	**MW**	Median wage paid	**TQ** Third quartile wage
AEX	Average experienced wage	**AXR**	Average experienced range	**HI**	Highest wage paid	**M**	Monthly	**MWR**	Median wage range	**W** Weekly
ATC	Average total compensation	**D**	Daily	**HR**	High end range	**MCC**	Median cash compensation	**S**	See annotated source	**Y** Yearly

Occupation/Type/Industry	Location	Per	Low	Mid	High	Source	Date
Director							
Religious Activities and Education	Allentown-Bethlehem-Easton MSA, PA-NJ	Y	18930 FQ	27830 MW	57870 TQ	USBLS	5/07
Religious Activities and Education	Philadelphia-Camden-Wilmington MSA, PA-NJ-DE-MD	Y	38490 FQ	48980 MW	61770 TQ	USBLS	5/07
Religious Activities and Education	Pittsburgh MSA, PA	Y	14770 FQ	24340 MW	43930 TQ	USBLS	5/07
Religious Activities and Education	Rhode Island	Y	27920 FQ	34700 MW	43220 TQ	USBLS	5/07
Religious Activities and Education	Providence-Fall River-Warwick MSA, RI-MA	Y	28660 FQ	35370 MW	43650 TQ	USBLS	5/07
Religious Activities and Education	South Carolina	Y	26310 FQ	48140 MW	67860 TQ	USBLS	5/07
Religious Activities and Education	South Dakota	Y	33925 FQ	40520 MW	71605 TQ	SDBLS	7/08-9/08
Religious Activities and Education	Tennessee	Y	37730 FQ	59230 MW	81400 TQ	USBLS	5/07
Religious Activities and Education	Texas	Y	27770 FQ	43940 MW	69590 TQ	USBLS	5/07
Religious Activities and Education	Houston-Sugar Land-Baytown MSA, TX	Y	38380 FQ	57300 MW	73530 TQ	USBLS	5/07
Religious Activities and Education	Virginia	Y	30330 FQ	39250 MW	45760 TQ	USBLS	5/07
Religious Activities and Education	Richmond MSA, VA	Y	38850 FQ	42710 MW	46480 TQ	USBLS	5/07
Religious Activities and Education	Virginia Beach-Norfolk-Newport News MSA, VA-NC	Y	22970 FQ	25710 MW	38070 TQ	USBLS	5/07
Religious Activities and Education	Washington	H	16.11 FQ	19.79 MW	26.49 TQ	WABLS	3/08
Religious Activities and Education	Seattle-Tacoma-Bellevue MSA, WA	Y	31890 FQ	37530 MW	44510 TQ	USBLS	5/07
Director/Fire Chief							
Wayne County Airport Authority	Wayne County, MI	Y			122570 HI	FREEP06	2006
Director of Aeronautics							
Department of Transportation	New Hampshire	Y			79634 HI	NHUL03	2008
Director of Airfield Operations							
Wayne County Airport Authority	Wayne County, MI	Y			122521 HI	FREEP06	2006
Director of Airport Affairs	United States	Y		64238 AW		AVJOB04	2009
Director of Assessing							
Municipal Government	Montague, MA	Y			57374 HI	FRCOG	2009
Director of Athletics							
Public Schools, Region 9	New York	Y		80461 AW		SAANYS	9/11/08
Director of Aviation Security Policy							
White House Staff	United States	Y			88800 HI	WPOST02	2008
Director of Comment Line Greetings and Volunteers							
White House Staff	United States	Y			50000 HI	WPOST02	2008
Director of Cultural and Leisure Services							
Municipal Government	Seaside, CA	S	2554 LO		3339 HI	SSSS	8/08
Director of Curriculum							
Public Schools, Region 9	New York	Y		78493 AW		SAANYS	9/11/08
Director of Cyber-Security Policy							
White House Staff	United States	Y			91259 HI	WPOST02	2008
Director of Dining/Food Services							
Nursing Home	United States	Y		30342 MW		MLTCN03	2008-2009
Director of Environmental Services							
Municipal Government	Gresham, OR	Y	95772 LO		124524 HI	GOSS01	7/1/08
Director of Fact Checking							
White House Staff	United States	Y			60000 HI	WPOST02	2008
Director of Government Relations							
Wayne County Airport Authority	Wayne County, MI	Y			118450 HI	FREEP06	2006

AE Average entry wage	AW Average wage paid	FQ First quartile wage	LO Lowest wage paid	MTC Median total compensation	TCC Total cash compensation
AER Average entry range	AWR Average wage range	H Hourly	LR Low end range	MW Median wage paid	TQ Third quartile wage
AEX Average experienced wage	AXR Average experienced range	HI Highest wage paid	M Monthly	MWR Median wage range	W Weekly
ATC Average total compensation	D Daily	HR High end range	MCC Median cash compensation	S See annotated source	Y Yearly

Occupation/Type/Industry	Location	Per	Low	Mid	High	Source	Date
Director of Infrastructure Administration Wayne County Airport Authority	Wayne County, MI	Y			133090 HI	FREEP06	2006
Director of Mail Analysis White House Staff	United States	Y			81394 HI	WPOST02	2008
Director of Maintenance Wayne County Airport Authority	Wayne County, MI	Y			133596 HI	FREEP06	2006
Director of Nuclear Detection Policy White House Staff	United States	Y			94000 HI	WPOST02	2008
Director of Operations Nursing Home	United States	Y		105400 AW		ALTC	7/07-8/07
Director of Procurement Wayne County Airport Authority	Wayne County, MI	Y			112000 HI	FREEP06	2006
Director of Public Safety Dallas/Fort Worth International Airport	Dallas-Fort Worth, TX	Y			145600 HI	CBSTV	2008
Director of Public Safety Administration Wayne County Airport Authority	Wayne County, MI	Y			122570 HI	FREEP06	2006
Director of Sales	Illinois	Y		110000 MW		ZBB	2008
Director of Student Correspondence White House Staff	United States	Y			52268 HI	WPOST02	2008
Director of Technology Public Schools	Howell, MI	Y			95905 HI	LCPP	2009
Director of Treasury and Finance	United States	Y		123000 AW		AFP	2008
Director of Water and Wastewater	Tonawanda, NY	Y			99444 HI	BUFN	2009
Director/Police Chief Wayne County Airport Authority	Wayne County, MI	Y			108889 HI	FREEP06	2006
Director/Security Chief Wayne County Airport Authority	Wayne County, MI	Y			122570 HI	FREEP06	2006
Disability Examiner Department of Education	New Hampshire	Y		41324 AW		NHUL03	2008
Disability Insurance Claims Examiner State Government	Ohio	H	16.35 LO		19.88 HI	ODAS	2008
Disability Management Coordinator Municipal Government	Seattle, WA	H	24.63 LO		28.74 HI	CSSS	2008
Disabled Veterans Outreach Specialist State Government	Ohio	H	16.35 LO		19.88 HI	ODAS	2008
Disease Intervention Specialist State Government	Ohio	H	20.71 LO		26.11 HI	ODAS	2008
Disease Mapper	United States	Y	40000 LO		150000 HI	BUS202	2007
Dishwasher	Alabama	Y	13030 FQ	14850 MW	17510 TQ	USBLS	5/07
	Birmingham-Hoover MSA, AL	Y	13480 FQ	15860 MW	18520 TQ	USBLS	5/07
	Montgomery MSA, AL	Y	13010 FQ	14680 MW	17360 TQ	USBLS	5/07
	Alaska	Y	17130 FQ	18880 MW	23040 TQ	USBLS	5/07

AE Average entry wage	**AW** Average wage paid	**FQ** First quartile wage	**LO** Lowest wage paid	**MTC** Median total compensation	**TCC** Total cash compensation
AER Average entry range	**AWR** Average wage range	**H** Hourly	**LR** Low end range	**MW** Median wage paid	**TQ** Third quartile wage
AEX Average experienced wage	**AXR** Average experienced range	**HI** Highest wage paid	**M** Monthly	**MWR** Median wage range	**W** Weekly
ATC Average total compensation	**D** Daily	**HR** High end range	**MCC** Median cash compensation	**S** See annotated source	**Y** Yearly

Occupation/Type/Industry	Location	Per	Low	Mid	High	Source	Date
Dishwasher	Anchorage MSA, AK	Y	17190 FQ	18880 MW	23000 TQ	USBLS	5/07
	Arizona	Y	14770 FQ	15810 MW	17950 TQ	USBLS	5/07
	Phoenix-Mesa-Scottsdale MSA, AZ	Y	14830 FQ	15990 MW	18180 TQ	USBLS	5/07
	Tucson MSA, AZ	Y	14700 FQ	15490 MW	17190 TQ	USBLS	5/07
	Arkansas	Y	14260 FQ	15340 MW	17200 TQ	USBLS	5/07
	Little Rock-North Little Rock MSA, AR	Y	14680 FQ	16120 MW	17950 TQ	USBLS	5/07
	Pine Bluff MSA, AR	Y	14000 FQ	14730 MW	15590 TQ	USBLS	5/07
	California	H	8.00 FQ	8.61 MW	9.40 TQ	CABLS	1/08-3/08
	Bakersfield MSA, CA	H	8.00 FQ	8.30 MW	9.02 TQ	CABLS	1/08-3/08
	Los Angeles-Long Beach-Glendale PMSA, CA	H	8.00 FQ	8.44 MW	9.21 TQ	CABLS	1/08-3/08
	Modesto MSA, CA	H	8.00 FQ	8.54 MW	9.20 TQ	CABLS	1/08-3/08
	Oakland-Fremont-Hayward MSA, CA	H	8.11 FQ	8.81 MW	9.65 TQ	CABLS	1/08-3/08
	Riverside-San Bernardino-Ontario MSA, CA	H	8.00 FQ	8.50 MW	9.20 TQ	CABLS	1/08-3/08
	Sacramento-Arden Arcade-Roseville MSA, CA	H	8.00 FQ	8.58 MW	9.30 TQ	CABLS	1/08-3/08
	San Diego-Carlsbad-San Marcos MSA, CA	H	8.00 FQ	8.73 MW	9.59 TQ	CABLS	1/08-3/08
	San Francisco-San Mateo-Redwood PMSA, CA	H	8.60 FQ	9.56 MW	11.06 TQ	CABLS	1/08-3/08
	San Jose-Sunnyvale-Santa Clara MSA, CA	H	8.08 FQ	8.74 MW	9.47 TQ	CABLS	1/08-3/08
	Santa Ana-Anaheim-Irvine PMSA, CA	Y	16120 FQ	17420 MW	19060 TQ	USBLS	5/07
	Colorado	Y	15380 FQ	17210 MW	19510 TQ	USBLS	5/07
	Denver-Aurora MSA, CO	Y	15510 FQ	17270 MW	19390 TQ	USBLS	5/07
	Connecticut	H	8.59 AE	9.41 MW		CTBLS	1/08-3/08
	Bridgeport-Stamford-Norwalk MSA, CT	Y	17370 FQ	18860 MW	21290 TQ	USBLS	5/07
	Hartford-West Hartford-East Hartford MSA, CT	Y	17450 FQ	19700 MW	22600 TQ	USBLS	5/07
	Delaware	Y	15730 FQ	17540 MW	19380 TQ	USBLS	5/07
	Wilmington PMSA, DE-MD-NJ	Y	15980 FQ	17660 MW	19440 TQ	USBLS	5/07
	District of Columbia	Y	16590 FQ	19330 MW	23420 TQ	USBLS	5/07
	Washington-Arlington-Alexandria MSA, DC-VA-MD-WV	Y	14530 FQ	16950 MW	20020 TQ	USBLS	5/07
	Florida	Y	14780 FQ	16010 MW	18590 TQ	USBLS	5/07
	Cape Coral-Fort Myers MSA, FL	Y	15030 FQ	16470 MW	18630 TQ	USBLS	5/07
	Fort Lauderdale-Pompano Beach-Deerfield Beach PMSA, FL	Y	14750 FQ	15960 MW	18890 TQ	USBLS	5/07
	Jacksonville MSA, FL	Y	14870 FQ	16000 MW	18150 TQ	USBLS	5/07
	Miami-Fort Lauderdale-Miami Beach MSA, FL	Y	14710 FQ	15880 MW	18390 TQ	USBLS	5/07
	Orlando-Kissimmee MSA, FL	Y	14820 FQ	16090 MW	19580 TQ	USBLS	5/07
	Sarasota-Bradenton-Venice MSA, FL	Y	15200 FQ	17360 MW	20440 TQ	USBLS	5/07
	Tampa-St. Petersburg-Clearwater MSA, FL	Y	15120 FQ	16740 MW	18960 TQ	USBLS	5/07
	West Palm Beach-Boca Raton-Boynton Beach PMSA, FL	Y	14950 FQ	16490 MW	18800 TQ	USBLS	5/07
	Georgia	Y	13070 FQ	15010 MW	17720 TQ	USBLS	5/07
	Atlanta-Sandy Springs-Marietta MSA, GA	Y	13370 FQ	15630 MW	18460 TQ	USBLS	5/07
	Augusta-Richmond County MSA, GA-SC	Y	12910 FQ	14650 MW	16580 TQ	USBLS	5/07
	Savannah MSA, GA	Y	13560 FQ	15850 MW	19940 TQ	USBLS	5/07
	Hawaii	Y	15840 FQ	18260 MW	23920 TQ	USBLS	5/07
	Honolulu MSA, HI	Y	15580 FQ	17040 MW	20090 TQ	USBLS	5/07
	Idaho	Y	12890 FQ	14650 MW	17330 TQ	USBLS	5/07
	Boise City-Nampa MSA, ID	Y	13130 FQ	15250 MW	18020 TQ	USBLS	5/07
	Lewiston MSA, ID-WA	Y	13170 FQ	15310 MW	16930 TQ	USBLS	5/07
	Pocatello MSA, ID	Y	12950 FQ	14640 MW	17530 TQ	USBLS	5/07
	Illinois	Y	14890 FQ	16030 MW	18290 TQ	USBLS	5/07

AE	Average entry wage	AW	Average wage paid	FQ	First quartile wage
AER	Average entry range	AWR	Average wage range	H	Hourly
AEX	Average experienced wage	AXR	Average experienced range	HI	Highest wage paid
ATC	Average total compensation	D	Daily	HR	High end range

LO	Lowest wage paid	MTC	Median total compensation
LR	Low end range	MW	Median wage paid
M	Monthly	MWR	Median wage range
MCC	Median cash compensation	S	See annotated source

TCC	Total cash compensation
TQ	Third quartile wage
W	Weekly
Y	Yearly

Occupation/Type/Industry	Location	Per	Low	Mid	High	Source	Date
Dishwasher	Chicago-Naperville-Joliet						
	MSA, IL-IN-WI	Y	14890 FQ	16170 MW	18590 TQ	USBLS	5/07
	Indiana	Y	13320 FQ	15500 MW	18240 TQ	USBLS	5/07
	Gary PMSA, IN	Y	12770 FQ	14370 MW	16550 TQ	USBLS	5/07
	Indianapolis-Carmel MSA, IN	Y	14250 FQ	17030 MW	19460 TQ	USBLS	5/07
	Iowa	Y	14020 FQ	15180 MW	17480 TQ	USBLS	5/07
	Des Moines-West Des Moines						
	MSA, IA	Y	15110 FQ	17130 MW	19100 TQ	USBLS	5/07
	Kansas	Y	13270 FQ	15380 MW	17610 TQ	USBLS	5/07
	Wichita MSA, KS	Y	14720 FQ	16270 MW	17780 TQ	USBLS	5/07
	Kentucky	Y	14427 FQ	17193 MW	19639 TQ	KYBLS	2008
	Lexington-Fayette MSA, KY	Y	16240 FQ	18060 MW	19970 TQ	USBLS	5/07
	Louisville-Jefferson County						
	MSA, KY-IN	Y	14580 FQ	17250 MW	19570 TQ	USBLS	5/07
	Owensboro MSA, KY	Y	12920 FQ	14500 MW	16860 TQ	USBLS	5/07
	Louisiana	H	6.09 FQ	6.83 MW	7.78 TQ	LABLS	1/08-3/08
	Baton Rouge MSA, LA	Y	12860 FQ	14610 MW	16880 TQ	USBLS	5/07
	Houma-Bayou Cane-						
	Thibodaux MSA, LA	Y	12720 FQ	14300 MW	16220 TQ	USBLS	5/07
	New Orleans-Metairie-Kenner						
	MSA, LA	Y	12580 FQ	14090 MW	16080 TQ	USBLS	5/07
	Maine	Y	15550 FQ	17200 MW	19240 TQ	USBLS	5/07
	Bangor MSA, ME	Y	15380 FQ	16920 MW	18900 TQ	USBLS	5/07
	Portland-South Portland-						
	Biddeford MSA, ME	Y	15850 FQ	17850 MW	20200 TQ	USBLS	5/07
	Maryland	Y		16825 MW		MDBLS	3/08
	Baltimore-Towson MSA, MD	Y	14860 FQ	16750 MW	18960 TQ	USBLS	5/07
	Bethesda-Gaithersburg-						
	Frederick PMSA, MD	Y	14860 FQ	17210 MW	20150 TQ	USBLS	5/07
	Massachusetts	Y	16770 FQ	18430 MW	20800 TQ	USBLS	5/07
	Boston-Cambridge-Quincy						
	NECTA, MA	Y	16920 FQ	18570 MW	21290 TQ	USBLS	5/07
	Worcester MSA, MA-CT	Y	16470 FQ	18030 MW	19740 TQ	USBLS	5/07
	Michigan	Y	15110 FQ	15930 MW	18380 TQ	USBLS	5/07
	Detroit-Warren-Livonia MSA,						
	MI	Y	15280 FQ	16380 MW	19470 TQ	USBLS	5/07
	Grand Rapids-Wyoming MSA,						
	MI	Y	14960 FQ	15680 MW	17890 TQ	USBLS	5/07
	Lansing-East Lansing MSA, MI	Y	15250 FQ	16650 MW	18800 TQ	USBLS	5/07
	Warren-Troy-Farmington Hills						
	PMSA, MI	Y	15310 FQ	16210 MW	19280 TQ	USBLS	5/07
	Minnesota	Y	15401 FQ	17555 MW	20535 TQ	MNBLS	10/08-12/08
	Duluth-Superior MSA, MN-WI	Y	14993 FQ	16101 MW	18653 TQ	MNBLS	10/08-12/08
	Minneapolis-Saint Paul MSA,						
	MN-WI	Y	16352 FQ	18830 MW	21643 TQ	MNBLS	10/08-12/08
	Rochester MSA, MN	Y	15704 FQ	18110 MW	20590 TQ	MNBLS	10/08-12/08
	Mississippi	Y	12860 FQ	14600 MW	16690 TQ	USBLS	5/07
	Jackson MSA, MS	Y	12750 FQ	14430 MW	16170 TQ	USBLS	5/07
	Missouri	Y	14590 FQ	15830 MW	18160 TQ	USBLS	5/07
	Kansas City MSA, MO-KS	Y	14440 FQ	16180 MW	18680 TQ	USBLS	5/07
	St. Louis MSA, MO-IL	Y	15020 FQ	16500 MW	18460 TQ	USBLS	5/07
	Springfield MSA, MO	Y	14470 FQ	15440 MW	17650 TQ	USBLS	5/07
	Montana	Y	13950 FQ	15140 MW	17170 TQ	USBLS	5/07
	Billings MSA, MT	Y	14290 FQ	15940 MW	18160 TQ	USBLS	5/07
	Nebraska	Y	13230 FQ	15300 MW	17920 TQ	USBLS	5/07
	Omaha-Council Bluffs MSA,						
	NE-IA	Y	14410 FQ	16690 MW	18770 TQ	USBLS	5/07
	Nevada	H	7.74 FQ	9.58 MW	12.87 TQ	NVBLS	5/08
	Carson City MSA, NV	H	8.26 FQ	9.38 MW	10.48 TQ	NVBLS	5/08
	Las Vegas-Paradise MSA, NV	H	7.91 FQ	10.13 MW	13.41 TQ	NVBLS	5/08
	New Hampshire	H	7.21 AE	9.21 MW	10.17 AEX	NHBLS	6/08
	Manchester MSA, NH	Y	16180 FQ	18450 MW	20920 TQ	USBLS	5/07
	Nashua NECTA, NH-MA	Y	15970 FQ	18270 MW	21240 TQ	USBLS	5/07
	New Jersey	Y	15730 FQ	17360 MW	19510 TQ	USBLS	5/07
	Camden PMSA, NJ	Y	15470 FQ	16690 MW	18650 TQ	USBLS	5/07
	Edison PMSA, NJ	Y	15710 FQ	17430 MW	19640 TQ	USBLS	5/07
	Newark-Union PMSA, NJ-PA	Y	16000 FQ	17850 MW	20050 TQ	USBLS	5/07
	New Mexico	Y	12950 FQ	14690 MW	17340 TQ	USBLS	5/07
	Albuquerque MSA, NM	Y	13010 FQ	14820 MW	17430 TQ	USBLS	5/07
	New York	Y	15270 FQ	16090 MW	18570 TQ	USBLS	5/07
	Albany-Schenectady-Troy						
	MSA, NY	Y	15290 FQ	16240 MW	18340 TQ	USBLS	5/07

AE	Average entry wage	AW	Average wage paid	FQ	First quartile wage	LO	Lowest wage paid	MTC Median total compensation	TCC Total cash compensation
AER	Average entry range	AWR	Average wage range	H	Hourly	LR	Low end range	MW Median wage paid	TQ Third quartile wage
AEX	Average experienced wage	AXR	Average experienced range	HI	Highest wage paid	M	Monthly	MWR Median wage range	W Weekly
ATC	Average total compensation	D	Daily	HR	High end range	MCC	Median cash compensation	S See annotated source	Y Yearly

Occupation/Type/Industry	Location	Per	Low	Mid	High	Source	Date
Dishwasher	Buffalo-Niagara Falls MSA, NY	Y	15080 FQ	15590 MW	16570 TQ	USBLS	5/07
	Nassau-Suffolk PMSA, NY	Y	15510 FQ	16930 MW	18940 TQ	USBLS	5/07
	New York-Northern New Jersey-Long Island MSA, NY-NJ-PA	Y	15520 FQ	17040 MW	19540 TQ	USBLS	5/07
	North Carolina	Y	14260 FQ	15840 MW	18230 TQ	USBLS	5/07
	Charlotte-Gastonia-Concord MSA, NC-SC	Y	14870 FQ	16990 MW	19140 TQ	USBLS	5/07
	Greensboro-High Point MSA, NC	Y	14020 FQ	15250 MW	17570 TQ	USBLS	5/07
	Raleigh-Cary MSA, NC	Y	14670 FQ	16790 MW	19100 TQ	USBLS	5/07
	North Dakota	Y	13350 FQ	15530 MW	17960 TQ	USBLS	5/07
	Fargo MSA, ND-MN	Y	14300 FQ	16410 MW	18630 TQ	USBLS	5/07
	Ohio	Y	14910 FQ	16060 MW	18530 TQ	USBLS	5/07
	Cincinnati-Middletown MSA, OH-KY-IN	Y	15540 FQ	17450 MW	19540 TQ	USBLS	5/07
	Cleveland-Elyria-Mentor MSA, OH	Y	15160 FQ	16430 MW	18710 TQ	USBLS	5/07
	Columbus MSA, OH	Y	16200 FQ	18110 MW	20120 TQ	USBLS	5/07
	Dayton MSA, OH	Y	15330 FQ	16960 MW	18990 TQ	USBLS	5/07
	Oklahoma	Y	12750 FQ	14300 MW	16140 TQ	USBLS	5/07
	Oklahoma City MSA, OK	Y	12930 FQ	14580 MW	16880 TQ	USBLS	5/07
	Tulsa MSA, OK	Y	12800 FQ	14540 MW	16600 TQ	USBLS	5/07
	Oregon	H	8.49 FQ	9.01 MW	9.60 TQ	ORBLS	5/08
	Eugene-Springfield MSA, OR	Y	17140 FQ	18210 MW	19360 TQ	USBLS	5/07
	Portland-Vancouver-Beaverton MSA, OR-WA	Y	17240 FQ	18320 MW	19620 TQ	USBLS	5/07
	Pennsylvania	Y	14560 FQ	15890 MW	18460 TQ	USBLS	5/07
	Allentown-Bethlehem-Easton MSA, PA-NJ	Y	14710 FQ	15920 MW	18430 TQ	USBLS	5/07
	Erie MSA, PA	Y	14190 FQ	14850 MW	16270 TQ	USBLS	5/07
	Lancaster MSA, PA	Y	15320 FQ	17190 MW	19060 TQ	USBLS	5/07
	Philadelphia-Camden-Wilmington MSA, PA-NJ-DE-MD	Y	15220 FQ	17010 MW	19230 TQ	USBLS	5/07
	Pittsburgh MSA, PA	Y	14550 FQ	15700 MW	18090 TQ	USBLS	5/07
	Reading MSA, PA	Y	14620 FQ	15950 MW	19300 TQ	USBLS	5/07
	Rhode Island	Y	16240 FQ	17960 MW	20310 TQ	USBLS	5/07
	Providence-Fall River-Warwick MSA, RI-MA	Y	16220 FQ	17930 MW	20230 TQ	USBLS	5/07
	South Carolina	Y	13350 FQ	15600 MW	18040 TQ	USBLS	5/07
	Charleston-North Charleston MSA, SC	Y	13260 FQ	15400 MW	17880 TQ	USBLS	5/07
	Columbia MSA, SC	Y	15090 FQ	17130 MW	18700 TQ	USBLS	5/07
	South Dakota	Y		15198 MW	17796 TQ	SDBLS	7/08-9/08
	Sioux Falls MSA, SD	Y	14190 FQ	16790 MW	19572 TQ	SDBLS	7/08-9/08
	Tennessee	Y	13930 FQ	16450 MW	18790 TQ	USBLS	5/07
	Kingsport-Bristol-Bristol MSA, TN-VA	Y	12800 FQ	14480 MW	16370 TQ	USBLS	5/07
	Memphis MSA, TN-MS-AR	Y	15330 FQ	17340 MW	19350 TQ	USBLS	5/07
	Nashville-Davidson-Murfreesboro MSA, TN	Y	15100 FQ	17390 MW	19710 TQ	USBLS	5/07
	Texas	Y	12870 FQ	14590 MW	16950 TQ	USBLS	5/07
	Austin-Round Rock MSA, TX	Y	12980 FQ	14600 MW	17520 TQ	USBLS	5/07
	Dallas-Fort Worth-Arlington MSA, TX	Y	13230 FQ	15360 MW	17870 TQ	USBLS	5/07
	El Paso MSA, TX	Y	12440 FQ	13690 MW	14950 TQ	USBLS	5/07
	Houston-Sugar Land-Baytown MSA, TX	Y	12750 FQ	14430 MW	16600 TQ	USBLS	5/07
	Midland MSA, TX	Y	12950 FQ	14710 MW	16740 TQ	USBLS	5/07
	San Antonio MSA, TX	Y	13280 FQ	15430 MW	17730 TQ	USBLS	5/07
	Utah	Y	13700 FQ	16080 MW	18260 TQ	USBLS	5/07
	Ogden-Clearfield MSA, UT	Y	13290 FQ	15320 MW	17760 TQ	USBLS	5/07
	Salt Lake City MSA, UT	Y	14350 FQ	16620 MW	18470 TQ	USBLS	5/07
	Vermont	Y	16480 FQ	17860 MW	19440 TQ	USBLS	5/07
	Burlington-South Burlington MSA, VT	Y	16690 FQ	18460 MW	20980 TQ	USBLS	5/07
	Virginia	Y	13200 FQ	15290 MW	18310 TQ	USBLS	5/07
	Richmond MSA, VA	Y	13630 FQ	16070 MW	18670 TQ	USBLS	5/07
	Roanoke MSA, VA	Y	12940 FQ	14740 MW	17010 TQ	USBLS	5/07

AE Average entry wage	**AW** Average wage paid	**FQ** First quartile wage	**LO** Lowest wage paid	**MTC** Median total compensation **TCC** Total cash compensation
AER Average entry range	**AWR** Average wage range	**H** Hourly	**LR** Low end range	**MW** Median wage paid **TQ** Third quartile wage
AEX Average experienced wage	**AXR** Average experienced range	**HI** Highest wage paid	**M** Monthly	**MWR** Median wage range **W** Weekly
ATC Average total compensation	**D** Daily	**HR** High end range	**MCC** Median cash compensation	**S** See annotated source **Y** Yearly

Occupation/Type/Industry	Location	Per	Low	Mid	High	Source	Date
Dishwasher	Virginia Beach-Norfolk-						
	Newport News MSA, VA-NC	Y	13120 FQ	14990 MW	18150 TQ	USBLS	5/07
	Washington	H	8.53 FQ	9.08 MW	9.90 TQ	WABLS	3/08
	Seattle-Tacoma-Bellevue						
	MSA, WA	Y	17680 FQ	19050 MW	21810 TQ	USBLS	5/07
	West Virginia	Y	14192 FQ	15447 MW	17318 TQ	WVBLS	7/08-9/08
	Charleston MSA, WV	Y	13800 FQ	15220 MW	17610 TQ	USBLS	5/07
	Wheeling MSA, WV-OH	Y	14300 FQ	14870 MW	16010 TQ	USBLS	5/07
	Wisconsin	Y	14570 FQ	15530 MW	17620 TQ	USBLS	5/07
	Milwaukee-Waukesha-West						
	Allis MSA, WI	Y	14720 FQ	15910 MW	18160 TQ	USBLS	5/07
	Wyoming	Y	13688 FQ	15778 MW	18829 TQ	WYBLS	9/08
	Cheyenne MSA, WY	Y	14568 FQ	17345 MW	19458 TQ	WYBLS	9/08
	Puerto Rico	Y	12370 FQ	13590 MW	14810 TQ	USBLS	5/07
	San Juan-Caguas-Guaynabo						
	MSA, PR	Y	12390 FQ	13640 MW	14890 TQ	USBLS	5/07
	Virgin Islands	Y	15630 FQ	17470 MW	19270 TQ	USBLS	5/07
	Guam	Y	12380 FQ	13600 MW	14830 TQ	USBLS	5/07
Dispatcher							
Except Police, Fire, and Ambulance	Alabama	Y	23050 FQ	30140 MW	39500 TQ	USBLS	5/07
Except Police, Fire, and Ambulance	Birmingham-Hoover MSA, AL	Y	23540 FQ	30740 MW	42220 TQ	USBLS	5/07
Except Police, Fire, and Ambulance	Alaska	Y	28580 FQ	38090 MW	52360 TQ	USBLS	5/07
Except Police, Fire, and Ambulance	Anchorage MSA, AK	Y	26160 FQ	32670 MW	50220 TQ	USBLS	5/07
Except Police, Fire, and Ambulance	Arizona	Y	24880 FQ	31890 MW	41350 TQ	USBLS	5/07
Except Police, Fire, and Ambulance	Phoenix-Mesa-Scottsdale						
	MSA, AZ	Y	25080 FQ	32160 MW	41580 TQ	USBLS	5/07
Except Police, Fire, and Ambulance	Prescott MSA, AZ	Y	28070 FQ	33240 MW	42020 TQ	USBLS	5/07
Except Police, Fire, and Ambulance	Tucson MSA, AZ	Y	24300 FQ	32920 MW	42360 TQ	USBLS	5/07
Except Police, Fire, and Ambulance	Arkansas	Y	23820 FQ	29780 MW	37770 TQ	USBLS	5/07
Except Police, Fire, and Ambulance	Fort Smith MSA, AR-OK	Y	26830 FQ	29640 MW	34540 TQ	USBLS	5/07
Except Police, Fire, and Ambulance	Little Rock-North Little Rock						
	MSA, AR	Y	26870 FQ	31580 MW	39420 TQ	USBLS	5/07
Except Police, Fire, and Ambulance	California	H	13.49 FQ	17.26 MW	22.33 TQ	CABLS	1/08-3/08
Except Police, Fire, and Ambulance	Los Angeles-Long Beach-						
	Glendale PMSA, CA	H	13.18 FQ	15.97 MW	21.25 TQ	CABLS	1/08-3/08
Except Police, Fire, and Ambulance	Oakland-Fremont-Hayward						
	MSA, CA	H	16.53 FQ	20.67 MW	25.44 TQ	CABLS	1/08-3/08
Except Police, Fire, and Ambulance	Riverside-San Bernardino-						
	Ontario MSA, CA	H	13.13 FQ	17.89 MW	23.45 TQ	CABLS	1/08-3/08
Except Police, Fire, and Ambulance	Sacramento-Arden Arcade-						
	Roseville MSA, CA	H	14.27 FQ	17.59 MW	21.80 TQ	CABLS	1/08-3/08
Except Police, Fire, and Ambulance	San Diego-Carlsbad-San						
	Marcos MSA, CA	H	12.55 FQ	16.37 MW	19.49 TQ	CABLS	1/08-3/08
Except Police, Fire, and Ambulance	San Francisco-San Mateo-						
	Redwood PMSA, CA	H	15.11 FQ	17.43 MW	21.58 TQ	CABLS	1/08-3/08
Except Police, Fire, and Ambulance	San Jose-Sunnyvale-Santa						
	Clara MSA, CA	H	14.66 FQ	20.31 MW	27.64 TQ	CABLS	1/08-3/08
Except Police, Fire, and Ambulance	Santa Ana-Anaheim-Irvine						
	PMSA, CA	Y	28590 FQ	37870 MW	48680 TQ	USBLS	5/07
Except Police, Fire, and Ambulance	Colorado	Y	27410 FQ	34600 MW	43170 TQ	USBLS	5/07
Except Police, Fire, and Ambulance	Denver-Aurora MSA, CO	Y	29470 FQ	36460 MW	44860 TQ	USBLS	5/07
Except Police, Fire, and Ambulance	Connecticut	H	12.62 AE	17.37 MW		CTBLS	1/08-3/08
Except Police, Fire, and Ambulance	Bridgeport-Stamford-Norwalk						
	MSA, CT	Y	30330 FQ	37850 MW	47150 TQ	USBLS	5/07
Except Police, Fire, and Ambulance	Hartford-West Hartford-East						
	Hartford MSA, CT	Y	28810 FQ	34290 MW	42780 TQ	USBLS	5/07
Except Police, Fire, and Ambulance	Waterbury MSA, CT	Y	31710 FQ	36330 MW	43240 TQ	USBLS	5/07
Except Police, Fire, and Ambulance	Delaware	Y	27280 FQ	32190 MW	41430 TQ	USBLS	5/07
Except Police, Fire, and Ambulance	Dover MSA, DE	Y	23660 FQ	31330 MW	37620 TQ	USBLS	5/07
Except Police, Fire, and Ambulance	Wilmington PMSA, DE-MD-						
	NJ	Y	27360 FQ	33040 MW	43580 TQ	USBLS	5/07
Except Police, Fire, and Ambulance	District of Columbia	Y	32390 FQ	37180 MW	42610 TQ	USBLS	5/07
Except Police, Fire, and Ambulance	Washington-Arlington-						
	Alexandria MSA, DC-VA-						
	MD-WV	Y	28300 FQ	34660 MW	42180 TQ	USBLS	5/07
Except Police, Fire, and Ambulance	Florida	Y	24360 FQ	30850 MW	40800 TQ	USBLS	5/07
Except Police, Fire, and Ambulance	Fort Lauderdale-Pompano						
	Beach-Deerfield Beach						
	PMSA, FL	Y	22170 FQ	28810 MW	35630 TQ	USBLS	5/07
Except Police, Fire, and Ambulance	Jacksonville MSA, FL	Y	27040 FQ	32530 MW	40670 TQ	USBLS	5/07

AE Average entry wage	**AW** Average wage paid	**FQ** First quartile wage	**LO** Lowest wage paid	**MTC** Median total compensation	**TCC** Total cash compensation
AER Average entry range	**AWR** Average wage range	**H** Hourly	**LR** Low end range	**MW** Median wage paid	**TQ** Third quartile wage
AEX Average experienced wage	**AXR** Average experienced range	**HI** Highest wage paid	**M** Monthly	**MWR** Median wage range	**W** Weekly
ATC Average total compensation	**D** Daily	**HR** High end range	**MCC** Median cash compensation	**S** See annotated source	**Y** Yearly

Occupation/Type/Industry	Location	Per	Low	Mid	High	Source	Date
Dispatcher							
Except Police, Fire, and Ambulance	Miami-Fort Lauderdale-Miami Beach MSA, FL	Y	23410 FQ	29660 MW	38200 TQ	USBLS	5/07
Except Police, Fire, and Ambulance	Orlando-Kissimmee MSA, FL	Y	24470 FQ	31590 MW	41850 TQ	USBLS	5/07
Except Police, Fire, and Ambulance	Tampa-St. Petersburg-Clearwater MSA, FL	Y	24830 FQ	31610 MW	41400 TQ	USBLS	5/07
Except Police, Fire, and Ambulance	West Palm Beach-Boca Raton-Boynton Beach PMSA, FL	Y	23710 FQ	30680 MW	41320 TQ	USBLS	5/07
Except Police, Fire, and Ambulance	Georgia	Y	25960 FQ	33480 MW	42960 TQ	USBLS	5/07
Except Police, Fire, and Ambulance	Atlanta-Sandy Springs-Marietta MSA, GA	Y	27870 FQ	35130 MW	44310 TQ	USBLS	5/07
Except Police, Fire, and Ambulance	Hawaii	Y	22630 FQ	29680 MW	38550 TQ	USBLS	5/07
Except Police, Fire, and Ambulance	Honolulu MSA, HI	Y	21140 FQ	29130 MW	39140 TQ	USBLS	5/07
Except Police, Fire, and Ambulance	Idaho	Y	24200 FQ	31930 MW	45950 TQ	USBLS	5/07
Except Police, Fire, and Ambulance	Boise City-Nampa MSA, ID	Y	27320 FQ	35980 MW	51240 TQ	USBLS	5/07
Except Police, Fire, and Ambulance	Illinois	Y	27120 FQ	35520 MW	47150 TQ	USBLS	5/07
Except Police, Fire, and Ambulance	Champaign-Urbana MSA, IL	Y	21060 FQ	27610 MW	40110 TQ	USBLS	5/07
Except Police, Fire, and Ambulance	Chicago-Naperville-Joliet MSA, IL-IN-WI	Y	27870 FQ	36710 MW	48860 TQ	USBLS	5/07
Except Police, Fire, and Ambulance	Indiana	Y	25200 FQ	32720 MW	41080 TQ	USBLS	5/07
Except Police, Fire, and Ambulance	Gary PMSA, IN	Y	26840 FQ	34090 MW	41890 TQ	USBLS	5/07
Except Police, Fire, and Ambulance	Indianapolis-Carmel MSA, IN	Y	25040 FQ	33570 MW	42770 TQ	USBLS	5/07
Except Police, Fire, and Ambulance	Iowa	Y	26150 FQ	33170 MW	40190 TQ	USBLS	5/07
Except Police, Fire, and Ambulance	Des Moines-West Des Moines MSA, IA	Y	30400 FQ	37660 MW	45430 TQ	USBLS	5/07
Except Police, Fire, and Ambulance	Kansas	Y	23360 FQ	32170 MW	43340 TQ	USBLS	5/07
Except Police, Fire, and Ambulance	Wichita MSA, KS	Y	20600 FQ	31100 MW	40010 TQ	USBLS	5/07
Except Police, Fire, and Ambulance	Kentucky	Y	24371 FQ	31647 MW	41802 TQ	KYBLS	2008
Except Police, Fire, and Ambulance	Elizabethtown MSA, KY	Y	23730 FQ	30550 MW	40190 TQ	USBLS	5/07
Except Police, Fire, and Ambulance	Louisville-Jefferson County MSA, KY-IN	Y	26290 FQ	34070 MW	44520 TQ	USBLS	5/07
Except Police, Fire, and Ambulance	Louisiana	H	10.63 FQ	14.39 MW	19.52 TQ	LABLS	1/08-3/08
Except Police, Fire, and Ambulance	Baton Rouge MSA, LA	Y	23690 FQ	28500 MW	35280 TQ	USBLS	5/07
Except Police, Fire, and Ambulance	New Orleans-Metairie-Kenner MSA, LA	Y	21660 FQ	27890 MW	39580 TQ	USBLS	5/07
Except Police, Fire, and Ambulance	Maine	Y	26480 FQ	31480 MW	39050 TQ	USBLS	5/07
Except Police, Fire, and Ambulance	Portland-South Portland-Biddeford MSA, ME	Y	25870 FQ	31000 MW	37600 TQ	USBLS	5/07
Except Police, Fire, and Ambulance	Maryland	Y		35350 MW		MDBLS	3/08
Except Police, Fire, and Ambulance	Baltimore-Towson MSA, MD	Y	26320 FQ	35140 MW	45400 TQ	USBLS	5/07
Except Police, Fire, and Ambulance	Bethesda-Gaithersburg-Frederick PMSA, MD	Y	26100 FQ	31230 MW	37420 TQ	USBLS	5/07
Except Police, Fire, and Ambulance	Massachusetts	Y	29270 FQ	36460 MW	47190 TQ	USBLS	5/07
Except Police, Fire, and Ambulance	Boston-Cambridge-Quincy NECTA, MA	Y	30620 FQ	37570 MW	47500 TQ	USBLS	5/07
Except Police, Fire, and Ambulance	Worcester MSA, MA-CT	Y	26920 FQ	32960 MW	48530 TQ	USBLS	5/07
Except Police, Fire, and Ambulance	Michigan	Y	26400 FQ	34400 MW	44970 TQ	USBLS	5/07
Except Police, Fire, and Ambulance	Detroit-Warren-Livonia MSA, MI	Y	26350 FQ	34260 MW	46520 TQ	USBLS	5/07
Except Police, Fire, and Ambulance	Grand Rapids-Wyoming MSA, MI	Y	31960 FQ	39360 MW	46820 TQ	USBLS	5/07
Except Police, Fire, and Ambulance	Warren-Troy-Farmington Hills PMSA, MI	Y	26360 FQ	34120 MW	47280 TQ	USBLS	5/07
Except Police, Fire, and Ambulance	Minnesota	Y	30651 FQ	40726 MW	50718 TQ	MNBLS	10/08-12/08
Except Police, Fire, and Ambulance	Duluth-Superior MSA, MN-WI	Y	30099 FQ	39144 MW	48938 TQ	MNBLS	10/08-12/08
Except Police, Fire, and Ambulance	Minneapolis-Saint Paul MSA, MN-WI	Y	31983 FQ	41413 MW	51207 TQ	MNBLS	10/08-12/08
Except Police, Fire, and Ambulance	Rochester MSA, MN	Y	31510 FQ	41289 MW	49012 TQ	MNBLS	10/08-12/08
Except Police, Fire, and Ambulance	Mississippi	Y	21530 FQ	26930 MW	33410 TQ	USBLS	5/07
Except Police, Fire, and Ambulance	Jackson MSA, MS	Y	25600 FQ	28880 MW	32540 TQ	USBLS	5/07
Except Police, Fire, and Ambulance	Missouri	Y	24070 FQ	31770 MW	40540 TQ	USBLS	5/07
Except Police, Fire, and Ambulance	Kansas City MSA, MO-KS	Y	28310 FQ	36170 MW	45280 TQ	USBLS	5/07
Except Police, Fire, and Ambulance	St. Louis MSA, MO-IL	Y	26570 FQ	34240 MW	43180 TQ	USBLS	5/07
Except Police, Fire, and Ambulance	Montana	Y	25850 FQ	31010 MW	39960 TQ	USBLS	5/07
Except Police, Fire, and Ambulance	Billings MSA, MT	Y	26390 FQ	30390 MW	37880 TQ	USBLS	5/07
Except Police, Fire, and Ambulance	Nebraska	Y	27010 FQ	35290 MW	45350 TQ	USBLS	5/07
Except Police, Fire, and Ambulance	Omaha-Council Bluffs MSA, NE-IA	Y	28710 FQ	35820 MW	42690 TQ	USBLS	5/07
Except Police, Fire, and Ambulance	Nevada	H	12.21 FQ	14.72 MW	18.20 TQ	NVBLS	5/08
Except Police, Fire, and Ambulance	Carson City MSA, NV	H	11.45 FQ	14.96 MW	27.26 TQ	NVBLS	5/08
Except Police, Fire, and Ambulance	Las Vegas-Paradise MSA, NV	H	12.22 FQ	14.51 MW	17.48 TQ	NVBLS	5/08
Except Police, Fire, and Ambulance	New Hampshire	H	12.83 AE	16.73 MW	19.95 AEX	NHBLS	6/08

Dispatcher

Occupation/Type/Industry	Location	Per	Low	Mid	High	Source	Date
Except Police, Fire, and Ambulance	Manchester MSA, NH	Y	29880 FQ	34870 MW	38680 TQ	USBLS	5/07
Except Police, Fire, and Ambulance	Nashua NECTA, NH-MA	Y	30530 FQ	36520 MW	52210 TQ	USBLS	5/07
Except Police, Fire, and Ambulance	New Jersey	Y	27350 FQ	37030 MW	48770 TQ	USBLS	5/07
Except Police, Fire, and Ambulance	Atlantic City MSA, NJ	Y	17590 FQ	24310 MW	41510 TQ	USBLS	5/07
Except Police, Fire, and Ambulance	Camden PMSA, NJ	Y	22940 FQ	32230 MW	47840 TQ	USBLS	5/07
Except Police, Fire, and Ambulance	Edison PMSA, NJ	Y	29470 FQ	37820 MW	49400 TQ	USBLS	5/07
Except Police, Fire, and Ambulance	Newark-Union PMSA, NJ-PA	Y	28520 FQ	37990 MW	50470 TQ	USBLS	5/07
Except Police, Fire, and Ambulance	New Mexico	Y	22230 FQ	29140 MW	39380 TQ	USBLS	5/07
Except Police, Fire, and Ambulance	Albuquerque MSA, NM	Y	20850 FQ	27470 MW	36070 TQ	USBLS	5/07
Except Police, Fire, and Ambulance	Las Cruces MSA, NM	Y	26190 FQ	29230 MW	34920 TQ	USBLS	5/07
Except Police, Fire, and Ambulance	New York	Y	25350 FQ	31820 MW	41730 TQ	USBLS	5/07
Except Police, Fire, and Ambulance	Albany-Schenectady-Troy MSA, NY	Y	24090 FQ	32500 MW	38930 TQ	USBLS	5/07
Except Police, Fire, and Ambulance	Binghamton MSA, NY	Y	21230 FQ	26910 MW	32470 TQ	USBLS	5/07
Except Police, Fire, and Ambulance	Buffalo-Niagara Falls MSA, NY	Y	25070 FQ	30100 MW	39040 TQ	USBLS	5/07
Except Police, Fire, and Ambulance	Nassau-Suffolk PMSA, NY	Y	27020 FQ	33310 MW	47130 TQ	USBLS	5/07
Except Police, Fire, and Ambulance	New York-Northern New Jersey-Long Island MSA, NY-NJ-PA	Y	27150 FQ	34730 MW	47440 TQ	USBLS	5/07
Except Police, Fire, and Ambulance	Syracuse MSA, NY	Y	27000 FQ	33780 MW	44760 TQ	USBLS	5/07
Except Police, Fire, and Ambulance	North Carolina	Y	25550 FQ	31590 MW	39890 TQ	USBLS	5/07
Except Police, Fire, and Ambulance	Charlotte-Gastonia-Concord MSA, NC-SC	Y	27920 FQ	33290 MW	41640 TQ	USBLS	5/07
Except Police, Fire, and Ambulance	Raleigh-Cary MSA, NC	Y	26780 FQ	32050 MW	38300 TQ	USBLS	5/07
Except Police, Fire, and Ambulance	Winston-Salem MSA, NC	Y	27280 FQ	35770 MW	42870 TQ	USBLS	5/07
Except Police, Fire, and Ambulance	North Dakota	Y	24770 FQ	32460 MW	38670 TQ	USBLS	5/07
Except Police, Fire, and Ambulance	Fargo MSA, ND-MN	Y	25340 FQ	32090 MW	40200 TQ	USBLS	5/07
Except Police, Fire, and Ambulance	Ohio	Y	26080 FQ	34040 MW	44230 TQ	USBLS	5/07
Except Police, Fire, and Ambulance	Cincinnati-Middletown MSA, OH-KY-IN	Y	27590 FQ	35520 MW	44490 TQ	USBLS	5/07
Except Police, Fire, and Ambulance	Cleveland-Elyria-Mentor MSA, OH	Y	23480 FQ	31340 MW	44000 TQ	USBLS	5/07
Except Police, Fire, and Ambulance	Columbus MSA, OH	Y	30760 FQ	38570 MW	45880 TQ	USBLS	5/07
Except Police, Fire, and Ambulance	Dayton MSA, OH	Y	25490 FQ	31740 MW	38510 TQ	USBLS	5/07
Except Police, Fire, and Ambulance	Oklahoma	Y	21460 FQ	28810 MW	38980 TQ	USBLS	5/07
Except Police, Fire, and Ambulance	Oklahoma City MSA, OK	Y	24090 FQ	30780 MW	41360 TQ	USBLS	5/07
Except Police, Fire, and Ambulance	Tulsa MSA, OK	Y	21880 FQ	31350 MW	40480 TQ	USBLS	5/07
Except Police, Fire, and Ambulance	Oregon	H	12.33 FQ	16.41 MW	21.72 TQ	ORBLS	5/08
Except Police, Fire, and Ambulance	Portland-Vancouver-Beaverton MSA, OR-WA	Y	26260 FQ	35350 MW	46870 TQ	USBLS	5/07
Except Police, Fire, and Ambulance	Pennsylvania	Y	25140 FQ	32910 MW	42670 TQ	USBLS	5/07
Except Police, Fire, and Ambulance	Allentown-Bethlehem-Easton MSA, PA-NJ	Y	24980 FQ	32040 MW	39300 TQ	USBLS	5/07
Except Police, Fire, and Ambulance	Philadelphia-Camden-Wilmington MSA, PA-NJ-DE-MD	Y	25460 FQ	33990 MW	45590 TQ	USBLS	5/07
Except Police, Fire, and Ambulance	Pittsburgh MSA, PA	Y	26600 FQ	32770 MW	42420 TQ	USBLS	5/07
Except Police, Fire, and Ambulance	York-Hanover MSA, PA	Y	26060 FQ	31590 MW	40830 TQ	USBLS	5/07
Except Police, Fire, and Ambulance	Rhode Island	Y	26780 FQ	30700 MW	37610 TQ	USBLS	5/07
Except Police, Fire, and Ambulance	Providence-Fall River-Warwick MSA, RI-MA	Y	27060 FQ	31520 MW	39330 TQ	USBLS	5/07
Except Police, Fire, and Ambulance	South Carolina	Y	23880 FQ	30900 MW	41210 TQ	USBLS	5/07
Except Police, Fire, and Ambulance	Charleston-North Charleston MSA, SC	Y	24440 FQ	32090 MW	45070 TQ	USBLS	5/07
Except Police, Fire, and Ambulance	Columbia MSA, SC	Y	23980 FQ	29160 MW	37720 TQ	USBLS	5/07
Except Police, Fire, and Ambulance	South Dakota	Y	23844 FQ	28408 MW	33357 TQ	SDBLS	7/08-9/08
Except Police, Fire, and Ambulance	Sioux Falls MSA, SD	Y	25556 FQ	30613 MW	37649 TQ	SDBLS	7/08-9/08
Except Police, Fire, and Ambulance	Tennessee	Y	25490 FQ	33460 MW	42250 TQ	USBLS	5/07
Except Police, Fire, and Ambulance	Memphis MSA, TN-MS-AR	Y	27440 FQ	36620 MW	45280 TQ	USBLS	5/07
Except Police, Fire, and Ambulance	Nashville-Davidson-Murfreesboro MSA, TN	Y	26050 FQ	33310 MW	42750 TQ	USBLS	5/07
Except Police, Fire, and Ambulance	Texas	Y	26010 FQ	32900 MW	42460 TQ	USBLS	5/07
Except Police, Fire, and Ambulance	Austin-Round Rock MSA, TX	Y	27770 FQ	35410 MW	46010 TQ	USBLS	5/07
Except Police, Fire, and Ambulance	Beaumont-Port Arthur MSA, TX	Y	28800 FQ	33450 MW	39550 TQ	USBLS	5/07*
Except Police, Fire, and Ambulance	Dallas-Fort Worth-Arlington MSA, TX	Y	27620 FQ	33620 MW	41310 TQ	USBLS	5/07
Except Police, Fire, and Ambulance	El Paso MSA, TX	Y	20410 FQ	26620 MW	31360 TQ	USBLS	5/07
Except Police, Fire, and Ambulance	Houston-Sugar Land-Baytown MSA, TX	Y	27340 FQ	34320 MW	43220 TQ	USBLS	5/07

AE Average entry wage	**AW** Average wage paid	**FQ** First quartile wage	**LO** Lowest wage paid	**MTC** Median total compensation	**TCC** Total cash compensation
AER Average entry range	**AWR** Average wage range	**H** Hourly	**LR** Low end range	**MW** Median wage paid	**TQ** Third quartile wage
AEX Average experienced wage	**AXR** Average experienced range	**HI** Highest wage paid	**M** Monthly	**MWR** Median wage range	**W** Weekly
ATC Average total compensation	**D** Daily	**HR** High end range	**MCC** Median cash compensation	**S** See annotated source	**Y** Yearly

Occupation/Type/Industry	Location	Per	Low	Mid	High	Source	Date
Dispatcher							
Except Police, Fire, and Ambulance	San Antonio MSA, TX	Y	23620 FQ	30800 MW	39430 TQ	USBLS	5/07
Except Police, Fire, and Ambulance	Utah	Y	24450 FQ	30350 MW	41880 TQ	USBLS	5/07
Except Police, Fire, and Ambulance	Salt Lake City MSA, UT	Y	24260 FQ	31210 MW	44960 TQ	USBLS	5/07
Except Police, Fire, and Ambulance	Vermont	Y	27660 FQ	34010 MW	43770 TQ	USBLS	5/07
Except Police, Fire, and Ambulance	Burlington-South Burlington MSA, VT	Y	29640 FQ	37550 MW	50960 TQ	USBLS	5/07
Except Police, Fire, and Ambulance	Virginia	Y	26510 FQ	33510 MW	42250 TQ	USBLS	5/07
Except Police, Fire, and Ambulance	Charlottesville MSA, VA	Y	27660 FQ	32830 MW	40030 TQ	USBLS	5/07
Except Police, Fire, and Ambulance	Richmond MSA, VA	Y	27090 FQ	35980 MW	48800 TQ	USBLS	5/07
Except Police, Fire, and Ambulance	Virginia Beach-Norfolk-Newport News MSA, VA-NC	Y	24370 FQ	30100 MW	38740 TQ	USBLS	5/07
Except Police, Fire, and Ambulance	Washington	H	14.34 FQ	18.67 MW	23.61 TQ	WABLS	3/08
Except Police, Fire, and Ambulance	Seattle-Tacoma-Bellevue MSA, WA	Y	30110 FQ	39480 MW	50300 TQ	USBLS	5/07
Except Police, Fire, and Ambulance	West Virginia	Y	20003 FQ	26889 MW	34663 TQ	WVBLS	7/08-9/08
Except Police, Fire, and Ambulance	Charleston MSA, WV	Y	21280 FQ	30590 MW	37730 TQ	USBLS	5/07
Except Police, Fire, and Ambulance	Parkersburg-Marietta-Vienna MSA, WV-OH	Y	20930 FQ	25370 MW	29020 TQ	USBLS	5/07
Except Police, Fire, and Ambulance	Wheeling MSA, WV-OH	Y	24000 FQ	31730 MW	42930 TQ	USBLS	5/07
Except Police, Fire, and Ambulance	Wisconsin	Y	27120 FQ	32940 MW	40330 TQ	USBLS	5/07
Except Police, Fire, and Ambulance	Green Bay MSA, WI	Y	22010 FQ	30160 MW	37270 TQ	USBLS	5/07
Except Police, Fire, and Ambulance	Milwaukee-Waukesha-West Allis MSA, WI	Y	27070 FQ	32850 MW	41920 TQ	USBLS	5/07
Except Police, Fire, and Ambulance	Wyoming	Y	25887 FQ	34986 MW	41937 TQ	WYBLS	9/08
Except Police, Fire, and Ambulance	Cheyenne MSA, WY	Y	26695 FQ	34062 MW	38483 TQ	WYBLS	9/08
Except Police, Fire, and Ambulance	Puerto Rico	Y	13440 FQ	15940 MW	21360 TQ	USBLS	5/07
Except Police, Fire, and Ambulance	San Juan-Caguas-Guaynabo MSA, PR	Y	13370 FQ	15800 MW	21010 TQ	USBLS	5/07
Except Police, Fire, and Ambulance	Virgin Islands	Y	23120 FQ	26840 MW	31220 TQ	USBLS	5/07
Except Police, Fire, and Ambulance	Guam	Y	16580 FQ	21510 MW	29810 TQ	USBLS	5/07
Highway Patrol	Ohio	H	16.66 LO		19.78 HI	ODAS	2008
Dissemination Specialist							
Public Schools	Wake County, NC	Y		45418 MW		WCPS02	2008-2009
Distance Learning Instructional Assistant							
Public Schools	North Carolina	M	1835 LO		2849 HI	NCSS	2008-2009
Distance Learning Manager							
State Supreme Court	Michigan	Y			71243 HI	LSJ02	7/11/07
District Attorney	San Diego County, CA	Y			207953 HI	SDBJ01	2007
	Denver, CO	Y			176000 HI	DPOST	2009
	DeKalb County, GA	Y			145594 HI	GACTY02	2008
	Dougherty County, GA	Y			18000 HI	GACTY02	2008
District Preserve Manager							
State Government	Ohio	H	20.89 LO		26.11 HI	ODAS	2008
DNA Analyst							
Municipal Government	Colorado Springs, CO	M	4006 LO			COSPRS	1/1/09
Police Department Crime Lab	Oakland, CA	W			5848 HI	CAC	2006-2007
DNA Technical Leader							
Municipal Government	Colorado Springs, CO	M	5939 LO			COSPRS	1/1/09
Dock Master	Baltimore, MD	Y		31009 AW		BMAG	2009
Document Control Clerk	United States	Y	25250-31250 AER			IAAPHQ	2008
Document Delivery Technician							
State Government	Ohio	H	16.35 LO		19.88 HI	ODAS	2008
Dog Officer	Orange, MA	Y			6425 HI	FRCOG	2009
Doll Doctor	United States	Y		24413 AW		CBUILD03	2009
Domestic Commercial Officer							
State Government	Ohio	H	18.36 LO		23.87 HI	ODAS	2008

AE	Average entry wage	AW	Average wage paid	FQ	First quartile wage
AER	Average entry range	AWR	Average wage range	H	Hourly
AEX	Average experienced wage	AXR	Average experienced range	HI	Highest wage paid
ATC	Average total compensation	D	Daily	HR	High end range

LO	Lowest wage paid	MTC	Median total compensation	TCC	Total cash compensation
LR	Low end range	MW	Median wage paid	TQ	Third quartile wage
M	Monthly	MWR	Median wage range	W	Weekly
MCC	Median cash compensation	S	See annotated source	Y	Yearly

Occupation/Type/Industry	Location	Per	Low	Mid	High	Source	Date
Door-to-Door Sales Worker, News and Street Vendor, and Related Worker							
	Alabama	Y	31870 FQ	35400 MW	39140 TQ	USBLS	5/07
	Arkansas	Y	21430 FQ	26890 MW	35460 TQ	USBLS	5/07
	California	H	8.00 FQ	8.76 MW	11.41 TQ	CABLS	1/08-3/08
	Colorado	Y	17560 FQ	20410 MW	28390 TQ	USBLS	5/07
	Connecticut	H	10.27 AE	19.75 MW		CTBLS	1/08-3/08
	Florida	Y	15290 FQ	18330 MW	25180 TQ	USBLS	5/07
	Georgia	Y	16270 FQ	19630 MW	27380 TQ	USBLS	5/07
	Idaho	Y	16270 FQ	21210 MW	24890 TQ	USBLS	5/07
	Illinois	Y	14980 FQ	18570 MW	63270 TQ	USBLS	5/07
	Indiana	Y	14430 FQ	17720 MW	24240 TQ	USBLS	5/07
	Iowa	Y	14160 FQ	17990 MW	28960 TQ	USBLS	5/07
	Kansas	Y	14580 FQ	20480 MW	24000 TQ	USBLS	5/07
	Kentucky	Y	16129 FQ	18992 MW	22926 TQ	KYBLS	2008
	Louisiana	H	10.66 FQ	16.10 MW	24.68 TQ	LABLS	1/08-3/08
	Maine	Y	15530 FQ	18120 MW	28550 TQ	USBLS	5/07
	Maryland	Y		27725 MW		MDBLS	3/08
	Massachusetts	Y	18820 FQ	24560 MW	47820 TQ	USBLS	5/07
	Michigan	Y	22000 FQ	28720 MW	38220 TQ	USBLS	5/07
	Mississippi	Y	23580 FQ	32220 MW	56130 TQ	USBLS	5/07
	Missouri	Y	14230 FQ	14940 MW	20630 TQ	USBLS	5/07
	Montana	Y	19930 FQ	27360 MW	35590 TQ	USBLS	5/07
	Nevada	H	12.87 FQ	17.35 MW	23.82 TQ	NVBLS	5/08
	New Jersey	Y	20820 FQ	29830 MW	48540 TQ	USBLS	5/07
	North Carolina	Y	15810 FQ	21550 MW	35640 TQ	USBLS	5/07
	Ohio	Y	15860 FQ	22290 MW	34090 TQ	USBLS	5/07
	Oklahoma	Y	16270 FQ	22390 MW	25910 TQ	USBLS	5/07
	Oregon	H	9.06 FQ	15.39 MW	18.10 TQ	ORBLS	5/08
	Pennsylvania	Y	14470 FQ	18650 MW	25430 TQ	USBLS	5/07
	South Carolina	Y	18010 FQ	21370 MW	26190 TQ	USBLS	5/07
	Tennessee	Y	17580 FQ	22480 MW	34040 TQ	USBLS	5/07
	Texas	Y	18990 FQ	26300 MW	33350 TQ	USBLS	5/07
	Utah	Y	19490 FQ	43270 MW	47180 TQ	USBLS	5/07
	Virginia	Y	17650 FQ	19590 MW	22930 TQ	USBLS	5/07
	Wisconsin	Y	14510 FQ	15630 MW	25670 TQ	USBLS	5/07
	Wyoming	Y	13011 FQ	14370 MW	16767 TQ	WYBLS	9/08
	Puerto Rico	Y	12450 FQ	13930 MW	15410 TQ	USBLS	5/07
Doula	United States	S	500 LO			TWST	2008
Drawbridge Operator							
Department of Transportation	New Hampshire	Y		28814 AW		NHUL03	2008
Dredge Operator							
	Alabama	Y	20460 FQ	25910 MW	28940 TQ	USBLS	5/07
	Florida	Y	27560 FQ	32230 MW	40480 TQ	USBLS	5/07
	Illinois	Y	31660 FQ	36950 MW	42780 TQ	USBLS	5/07
	Indiana	Y	29000 FQ	35240 MW	53420 TQ	USBLS	5/07
	Iowa	Y	25580 FQ	30100 MW	33770 TQ	USBLS	5/07
	Kentucky	Y	28852 FQ	31701 MW	34342 TQ	KYBLS	2008
	Louisiana	H	13.41 FQ	17.41 MW	21.31 TQ	LABLS	1/08-3/08
	Maryland	Y		35575 MW		MDBLS	3/08
	Massachusetts	Y	29350 FQ	45740 MW	51690 TQ	USBLS	5/07
	Missouri	Y	40270 FQ	43910 MW	47350 TQ	USBLS	5/07
	Nebraska	Y	21350 FQ	28680 MW	34270 TQ	USBLS	5/07
	New Jersey	Y	35010 FQ	50000 MW	61030 TQ	USBLS	5/07
	North Carolina	Y	23910 FQ	27450 MW	31200 TQ	USBLS	5/07
	Ohio	Y	30650 FQ	33770 MW	36570 TQ	USBLS	5/07
	Oklahoma	Y	22930 FQ	26810 MW	31550 TQ	USBLS	5/07
	Texas	Y	25390 FQ	28880 MW	34780 TQ	USBLS	5/07
	Virginia	Y	42070 FQ	46640 MW	50930 TQ	USBLS	5/07
	Washington	H	20.71 FQ	30.89 MW	34.73 TQ	WABLS	3/08
Drilling and Boring Machine Tool Setter, Operator, and Tender							
Metals and Plastics	Alabama	Y	23130 FQ	27810 MW	32490 TQ	USBLS	5/07
Metals and Plastics	Birmingham-Hoover MSA, AL	Y	24280 FQ	29470 MW	40310 TQ	USBLS	5/07
Metals and Plastics	Arizona	Y	22640 FQ	30780 MW	36150 TQ	USBLS	5/07
Metals and Plastics	Phoenix-Mesa-Scottsdale MSA, AZ	Y	21410 FQ	32060 MW	37070 TQ	USBLS	5/07
Metals and Plastics	Tucson MSA, AZ	Y	23720 FQ	28140 MW	32630 TQ	USBLS	5/07

AE	Average entry wage	AW	Average wage paid	FQ	First quartile wage	LO	Lowest wage paid	MTC	Median total compensation	TCC	Total cash compensation
AER	Average entry range	AWR	Average wage range	H	Hourly	LR	Low end range	MW	Median wage paid	TQ	Third quartile wage
AEX	Average experienced wage	AXR	Average experienced range	HI	Highest wage paid	M	Monthly	MWR	Median wage range	W	Weekly
ATC	Average total compensation	D	Daily	HR	High end range	MCC	Median cash compensation	S	See annotated source	Y	Yearly

Occupation/Type/Industry	Location	Per	Low	Mid	High	Source	Date
Drilling and Boring Machine Tool Setter, Operator, and Tender							
Metals and Plastics	Arkansas	Y	24800 FQ	30190 MW	34870 TQ	USBLS	5/07
Metals and Plastics	Little Rock-North Little Rock MSA, AR	Y	31000 FQ	35310 MW	38360 TQ	USBLS	5/07
Metals and Plastics	California	H	10.66 FQ	13.79 MW	18.19 TQ	CABLS	1/08-3/08
Metals and Plastics	Los Angeles-Long Beach-Glendale PMSA, CA	H	9.65 FQ	12.81 MW	17.66 TQ	CABLS	1/08-3/08
Metals and Plastics	Oakland-Fremont-Hayward MSA, CA	H	12.29 FQ	15.75 MW	20.56 TQ	CABLS	1/08-3/08
Metals and Plastics	Riverside-San Bernardino-Ontario MSA, CA	H	11.07 FQ	13.37 MW	15.30 TQ	CABLS	1/08-3/08
Metals and Plastics	San Diego-Carlsbad-San Marcos MSA, CA	H	11.30 FQ	15.42 MW	20.26 TQ	CABLS	1/08-3/08
Metals and Plastics	San Jose-Sunnyvale-Santa Clara MSA, CA	H	13.98 FQ	18.24 MW	22.16 TQ	CABLS	1/08-3/08
Metals and Plastics	Santa Ana-Anaheim-Irvine PMSA, CA	Y	24240 FQ	31240 MW	37530 TQ	USBLS	5/07
Metals and Plastics	Colorado	Y	19980 FQ	23220 MW	27520 TQ	USBLS	5/07
Metals and Plastics	Denver-Aurora MSA, CO	Y	22360 FQ	26310 MW	30110 TQ	USBLS	5/07
Metals and Plastics	Connecticut	H	11.08 AE	14.56 MW		CTBLS	1/08-3/08
Metals and Plastics	Bridgeport-Stamford-Norwalk MSA, CT	Y	23720 FQ	28230 MW	34920 TQ	USBLS	5/07
Metals and Plastics	Hartford-West Hartford-East Hartford MSA, CT	Y	27100 FQ	34240 MW	39530 TQ	USBLS	5/07
Metals and Plastics	Wilmington PMSA, DE-MD-NJ	Y	26630 FQ	29130 MW	31620 TQ	USBLS	5/07
Metals and Plastics	Washington-Arlington-Alexandria MSA, DC-VA-MD-WV	Y	24650 FQ	28100 MW	31470 TQ	USBLS	5/07
Metals and Plastics	Florida	Y	20540 FQ	26320 MW	31010 TQ	USBLS	5/07
Metals and Plastics	Jacksonville MSA, FL	Y	23150 FQ	26910 MW	30330 TQ	USBLS	5/07
Metals and Plastics	Miami-Fort Lauderdale-Miami Beach MSA, FL	Y	20140 FQ	27860 MW	35270 TQ	USBLS	5/07
Metals and Plastics	Tampa-St. Petersburg-Clearwater MSA, FL	Y	18450 FQ	21160 MW	29770 TQ	USBLS	5/07
Metals and Plastics	Georgia	Y	20680 FQ	23160 MW	28640 TQ	USBLS	5/07
Metals and Plastics	Atlanta-Sandy Springs-Marietta MSA, GA	Y	23870 FQ	27200 MW	31370 TQ	USBLS	5/07
Metals and Plastics	Idaho	Y	31250 FQ	35780 MW	41280 TQ	USBLS	5/07
Metals and Plastics	Illinois	Y	23340 FQ	29580 MW	35970 TQ	USBLS	5/07
Metals and Plastics	Chicago-Naperville-Joliet MSA, IL-IN-WI	Y	23780 FQ	30260 MW	36910 TQ	USBLS	5/07
Metals and Plastics	Indiana	Y	26390 FQ	33980 MW	43180 TQ	USBLS	5/07
Metals and Plastics	Elkhart-Goshen MSA, IN	Y	27280 FQ	32460 MW	35750 TQ	USBLS	5/07
Metals and Plastics	Gary PMSA, IN	Y	35740 FQ	44850 MW	51890 TQ	USBLS	5/07
Metals and Plastics	Indianapolis-Carmel MSA, IN	Y	36170 FQ	41270 MW	51370 TQ	USBLS	5/07
Metals and Plastics	Iowa	Y	27630 FQ	31710 MW	37430 TQ	USBLS	5/07
Metals and Plastics	Kansas	Y	25640 FQ	30670 MW	39070 TQ	USBLS	5/07
Metals and Plastics	Wichita MSA, KS	Y	26040 FQ	31860 MW	44120 TQ	USBLS	5/07
Metals and Plastics	Kentucky	Y	24760 FQ	30658 MW	38154 TQ	KYBLS	2008
Metals and Plastics	Louisville-Jefferson County MSA, KY-IN	Y	25690 FQ	31940 MW	35500 TQ	USBLS	5/07
Metals and Plastics	Louisiana	H	10.26 FQ	14.15 MW	16.92 TQ	LABLS	1/08-3/08
Metals and Plastics	Maine	Y	27720 FQ	33030 MW	39630 TQ	USBLS	5/07
Metals and Plastics	Maryland	Y		41600 MW		MDBLS	3/08
Metals and Plastics	Baltimore-Towson MSA, MD	Y	30430 FQ	34290 MW	37520 TQ	USBLS	5/07
Metals and Plastics	Massachusetts	Y	28310 FQ	40900 MW	49820 TQ	USBLS	5/07
Metals and Plastics	Boston-Cambridge-Quincy NECTA, MA	Y	29590 FQ	42020 MW	48340 TQ	USBLS	5/07
Metals and Plastics	Worcester MSA, MA-CT	Y	20160 FQ	25150 MW	35600 TQ	USBLS	5/07
Metals and Plastics	Michigan	Y	28260 FQ	36540 MW	48780 TQ	USBLS	5/07
Metals and Plastics	Detroit-Warren-Livonia MSA, MI	Y	28560 FQ	40990 MW	53520 TQ	USBLS	5/07
Metals and Plastics	Flint MSA, MI	Y	34400 FQ	39820 MW	49320 TQ	USBLS	5/07
Metals and Plastics	Grand Rapids-Wyoming MSA, MI	Y	30060 FQ	33510 MW	38960 TQ	USBLS	5/07
Metals and Plastics	Muskegon-Norton Shores MSA, MI	Y	25270 FQ	29000 MW	37270 TQ	USBLS	5/07
Metals and Plastics	Warren-Troy-Farmington Hills PMSA, MI	Y	24780 FQ	34260 MW	45160 TQ	USBLS	5/07
Metals and Plastics	Minnesota	Y	29721 FQ	35817 MW	41830 TQ	MNBLS	10/08-12/08

AE   Average entry wage   AW   Average wage paid   FQ   First quartile wage   LO   Lowest wage paid   MTC   Median total compensation   TCC   Total cash compensation
AER   Average entry range   AWR   Average wage range   H   Hourly   LR   Low end range   MW   Median wage paid   TQ   Third quartile wage
AEX   Average experienced wage   AXR   Average experienced range   HI   Highest wage paid   M   Monthly   MWR   Median wage range   W   Weekly
ATC   Average total compensation   D   Daily   HR   High end range   MCC   Median cash compensation   S   See annotated source   Y   Yearly

Occupation/Type/Industry	Location	Per	Low	Mid	High	Source	Date
Drilling and Boring Machine Tool Setter, Operator, and Tender							
Metals and Plastics	Minneapolis-Saint Paul MSA, MN-WI	Y	30333 FQ	36905 MW	43830 TQ	MNBLS	10/08-12/08
Metals and Plastics	Mississippi	Y	16020 FQ	25050 MW	27610 TQ	USBLS	5/07
Metals and Plastics	Missouri	Y	22680 FQ	27370 MW	32190 TQ	USBLS	5/07
Metals and Plastics	Kansas City MSA, MO-KS	Y	28190 FQ	31600 MW	34980 TQ	USBLS	5/07
Metals and Plastics	St. Louis MSA, MO-IL	Y	23350 FQ	28190 MW	33220 TQ	USBLS	5/07
Metals and Plastics	Nebraska	Y	21700 FQ	26940 MW	34080 TQ	USBLS	5/07
Metals and Plastics	Omaha-Council Bluffs MSA, NE-IA	Y	18200 FQ	20750 MW	23960 TQ	USBLS	5/07
Metals and Plastics	Nevada	H	9.42 FQ	10.77 MW	13.56 TQ	NVBLS	5/08
Metals and Plastics	Carson City MSA, NV	H	8.97 FQ	10.72 MW	27.48 TQ	NVBLS	5/08
Metals and Plastics	New Hampshire	H	12.93 AE	15.61 MW	17.27 AEX	NHBLS	6/08
Metals and Plastics	New Jersey	Y	18540 FQ	22940 MW	31330 TQ	USBLS	5/07
Metals and Plastics	Camden PMSA, NJ	Y	22810 FQ	28430 MW	41880 TQ	USBLS	5/07
Metals and Plastics	Edison PMSA, NJ	Y	19330 FQ	28650 MW	36790 TQ	USBLS	5/07
Metals and Plastics	Newark-Union PMSA, NJ-PA	Y	16660 FQ	21530 MW	26690 TQ	USBLS	5/07
Metals and Plastics	New York	Y	24730 FQ	30040 MW	35930 TQ	USBLS	5/07
Metals and Plastics	Buffalo-Niagara Falls MSA, NY	Y	29620 FQ	34400 MW	38150 TQ	USBLS	5/07
Metals and Plastics	Nassau-Suffolk PMSA, NY	Y	21100 FQ	28480 MW	34620 TQ	USBLS	5/07
Metals and Plastics	New York-Northern New Jersey-Long Island MSA, NY-NJ-PA	Y	19030 FQ	25230 MW	33280 TQ	USBLS	5/07
Metals and Plastics	North Carolina	Y	26990 FQ	30880 MW	38160 TQ	USBLS	5/07
Metals and Plastics	Charlotte-Gastonia-Concord MSA, NC-SC	Y	28010 FQ	30750 MW	37910 TQ	USBLS	5/07
Metals and Plastics	North Dakota	Y	18870 FQ	29070 MW	39330 TQ	USBLS	5/07
Metals and Plastics	Fargo MSA, ND-MN	Y	17740 FQ	19690 MW	25500 TQ	USBLS	5/07
Metals and Plastics	Ohio	Y	29420 FQ	37320 MW	48290 TQ	USBLS	5/07
Metals and Plastics	Cincinnati-Middletown MSA, OH-KY-IN	Y	22380 FQ	28670 MW	37350 TQ	USBLS	5/07
Metals and Plastics	Cleveland-Elyria-Mentor MSA, OH	Y	30020 FQ	34710 MW	40630 TQ	USBLS	5/07
Metals and Plastics	Columbus MSA, OH	Y	23110 FQ	27580 MW	37220 TQ	USBLS	5/07
Metals and Plastics	Oklahoma	Y	22170 FQ	27720 MW	34630 TQ	USBLS	5/07
Metals and Plastics	Oklahoma City MSA, OK	Y	20340 FQ	24510 MW	34260 TQ	USBLS	5/07
Metals and Plastics	Tulsa MSA, OK	Y	24430 FQ	31140 MW	35720 TQ	USBLS	5/07
Metals and Plastics	Oregon	H	12.36 FQ	15.90 MW	23.87 TQ	ORBLS	5/08
Metals and Plastics	Portland-Vancouver-Beaverton MSA, OR-WA	Y	25460 FQ	33080 MW	59350 TQ	USBLS	5/07
Metals and Plastics	Pennsylvania	Y	25060 FQ	30910 MW	38180 TQ	USBLS	5/07
Metals and Plastics	Allentown-Bethlehem-Easton MSA, PA-NJ	Y	26220 FQ	30010 MW	34140 TQ	USBLS	5/07
Metals and Plastics	Philadelphia-Camden-Wilmington MSA, PA-NJ-DE-MD	Y	26350 FQ	31290 MW	39570 TQ	USBLS	5/07
Metals and Plastics	Pittsburgh MSA, PA	Y	25940 FQ	31150 MW	39140 TQ	USBLS	5/07
Metals and Plastics	Rhode Island	Y	20300 FQ	26510 MW	31460 TQ	USBLS	5/07
Metals and Plastics	Providence-Fall River-Warwick MSA, RI-MA	Y	21460 FQ	26790 MW	31600 TQ	USBLS	5/07
Metals and Plastics	South Carolina	Y	26540 FQ	30470 MW	34880 TQ	USBLS	5/07
Metals and Plastics	South Dakota	Y	25335 FQ	28442 MW	31511 TQ	SDBLS	7/08-9/08
Metals and Plastics	Sioux Falls MSA, SD	Y	25991 FQ	28305 MW	30645 TQ	SDBLS	7/08-9/08
Metals and Plastics	Tennessee	Y	23640 FQ	27490 MW	31480 TQ	USBLS	5/07
Metals and Plastics	Memphis MSA, TN-MS-AR	Y	22400 FQ	24950 MW	28500 TQ	USBLS	5/07
Metals and Plastics	Nashville-Davidson-Murfreesboro MSA, TN	Y	26470 FQ	29000 MW	31490 TQ	USBLS	5/07
Metals and Plastics	Texas	Y	18530 FQ	23160 MW	30240 TQ	USBLS	5/07
Metals and Plastics	Austin-Round Rock MSA, TX	Y	20330 FQ	28140 MW	32420 TQ	USBLS	5/07
Metals and Plastics	Dallas-Fort Worth-Arlington MSA, TX	Y	17550 FQ	21190 MW	26610 TQ	USBLS	5/07
Metals and Plastics	El Paso MSA, TX	Y	21630 FQ	26780 MW	30640 TQ	USBLS	5/07
Metals and Plastics	Houston-Sugar Land-Baytown MSA, TX	Y	20330 FQ	27140 MW	33040 TQ	USBLS	5/07
Metals and Plastics	San Antonio MSA, TX	Y	19350 FQ	24640 MW	30180 TQ	USBLS	5/07
Metals and Plastics	Utah	Y	23440 FQ	27460 MW	33630 TQ	USBLS	5/07
Metals and Plastics	Salt Lake City MSA, UT	Y	23300 FQ	27930 MW	32940 TQ	USBLS	5/07
Metals and Plastics	Vermont	Y	24360 FQ	29360 MW	34570 TQ	USBLS	5/07
Metals and Plastics	Virginia	Y	25970 FQ	29690 MW	36020 TQ	USBLS	5/07
Metals and Plastics	Richmond MSA, VA	Y	26640 FQ	31320 MW	43720 TQ	USBLS	5/07

AE	Average entry wage	AW	Average wage paid	FQ	First quartile wage	LO	Lowest wage paid	MTC	Median total compensation	TCC	Total cash compensation
AER	Average entry range	AWR	Average wage range	H	Hourly	LR	Low end range	MW	Median wage paid	TQ	Third quartile wage
AEX	Average experienced wage	AXR	Average experienced range	HI	Highest wage paid	M	Monthly	MWR	Median wage range	W	Weekly
ATC	Average total compensation	D	Daily	HR	High end range	MCC	Median cash compensation	S	See annotated source	Y	Yearly

Occupation/Type/Industry	Location	Per	Low	Mid	High	Source	Date
Drilling and Boring Machine Tool Setter, Operator, and Tender							
Metals and Plastics	Virginia Beach-Norfolk-Newport News MSA, VA-NC	Y	28650 FQ	33680 MW	38100 TQ	USBLS	5/07
Metals and Plastics	Washington	H	12.13 FQ	14.72 MW	18.74 TQ	WABLS	3/08
Metals and Plastics	Seattle-Tacoma-Bellevue MSA, WA	Y	24680 FQ	31430 MW	38610 TQ	USBLS	5/07
Metals and Plastics	Wisconsin	Y	25330 FQ	29570 MW	35330 TQ	USBLS	5/07
Metals and Plastics	Milwaukee-Waukesha-West Allis MSA, WI	Y	26040 FQ	31090 MW	37050 TQ	USBLS	5/07
Metals and Plastics	Wyoming	Y	35080 FQ	44037 MW	50623 TQ	WYBLS	9/08
Metals and Plastics	Puerto Rico	Y	19010 FQ	25790 MW	29440 TQ	USBLS	5/07
Metals and Plastics	San Juan-Caguas-Guaynabo MSA, PR	Y	19010 FQ	25790 MW	29440 TQ	USBLS	5/07
Driver/Sales Worker	Alabama	Y	13530 FQ	20070 MW	29760 TQ	USBLS	5/07
	Birmingham-Hoover MSA, AL	Y	13440 FQ	17400 MW	28710 TQ	USBLS	5/07
	Tuscaloosa MSA, AL	Y	20860 FQ	26910 MW	36860 TQ	USBLS	5/07
	Alaska	Y	19930 FQ	24250 MW	31640 TQ	USBLS	5/07
	Anchorage MSA, AK	Y	19010 FQ	24050 MW	30310 TQ	USBLS	5/07
	Fairbanks MSA, AK	Y	20690 FQ	23810 MW	38920 TQ	USBLS	5/07
	Arizona	Y	15100 FQ	21170 MW	29760 TQ	USBLS	5/07
	Phoenix-Mesa-Scottsdale MSA, AZ	Y	15240 FQ	21950 MW	30830 TQ	USBLS	5/07
	Tucson MSA, AZ	Y	15070 FQ	19010 MW	25730 TQ	USBLS	5/07
	Yuma MSA, AZ	Y	14660 FQ	17960 MW	32300 TQ	USBLS	5/07
	Arkansas	Y	14500 FQ	21650 MW	30660 TQ	USBLS	5/07
	Jonesboro MSA, AR	Y	13880 FQ	14570 MW	23760 TQ	USBLS	5/07
	Little Rock-North Little Rock MSA, AR	Y	14250 FQ	16030 MW	33590 TQ	USBLS	5/07
	California	H	8.00 FQ	8.99 MW	14.63 TQ	CABLS	1/08-3/08
	Los Angeles-Long Beach-Glendale PMSA, CA	H	8.00 FQ	9.12 MW	14.56 TQ	CABLS	1/08-3/08
	Oakland-Fremont-Hayward MSA, CA	H	8.01 FQ	12.61 MW	21.59 TQ	CABLS	1/08-3/08
	Riverside-San Bernardino-Ontario MSA, CA	H	8.00 FQ	8.48 MW	14.58 TQ	CABLS	1/08-3/08
	Sacramento-Arden Arcade-Roseville MSA, CA	H	8.00 FQ	9.79 MW	19.38 TQ	CABLS	1/08-3/08
	San Diego-Carlsbad-San Marcos MSA, CA	H	8.00 FQ	8.48 MW	11.54 TQ	CABLS	1/08-3/08
	San Francisco-San Mateo-Redwood PMSA, CA	H	8.87 FQ	10.52 MW	14.90 TQ	CABLS	1/08-3/08
	San Jose-Sunnyvale-Santa Clara MSA, CA	H	8.07 FQ	9.20 MW	12.40 TQ	CABLS	1/08-3/08
	Santa Ana-Anaheim-Irvine PMSA, CA	Y	15970 FQ	17530 MW	22720 TQ	USBLS	5/07
	Colorado	Y	14800 FQ	17560 MW	27850 TQ	USBLS	5/07
	Colorado Springs MSA, CO	Y	16570 FQ	19510 MW	25200 TQ	USBLS	5/07
	Denver-Aurora MSA, CO	Y	14770 FQ	17900 MW	29100 TQ	USBLS	5/07
	Pueblo MSA, CO	Y	14940 FQ	21450 MW	26990 TQ	USBLS	5/07
	Connecticut	H	9.88 AE	15.23 MW		CTBLS	1/08-3/08
	Bridgeport-Stamford-Norwalk MSA, CT	Y	22520 FQ	29570 MW	45680 TQ	USBLS	5/07
	Hartford-West Hartford-East Hartford MSA, CT	Y	26270 FQ	35440 MW	45230 TQ	USBLS	5/07
	Delaware	Y	15340 FQ	22490 MW	29470 TQ	USBLS	5/07
	Wilmington PMSA, DE-MD-NJ	Y	16710 FQ	22440 MW	29600 TQ	USBLS	5/07
	District of Columbia	Y	18700 FQ	22830 MW	26190 TQ	USBLS	5/07
	Washington-Arlington-Alexandria MSA, DC-VA-MD-WV	Y	18590 FQ	26210 MW	36230 TQ	USBLS	5/07
	Florida	Y	15420 FQ	22340 MW	33920 TQ	USBLS	5/07
	Fort Lauderdale-Pompano Beach-Deerfield Beach PMSA, FL	Y	15490 FQ	23720 MW	34860 TQ	USBLS	5/07
	Jacksonville MSA, FL	Y	16670 FQ	27650 MW	36480 TQ	USBLS	5/07
	Miami-Fort Lauderdale-Miami Beach MSA, FL	Y	15210 FQ	21810 MW	33890 TQ	USBLS	5/07
	Orlando-Kissimmee MSA, FL	Y	16670 FQ	22900 MW	32620 TQ	USBLS	5/07

Occupation/Type/Industry	Location	Per	Low	Mid	High	Source	Date
Driver/Sales Worker	Tampa-St. Petersburg-Clearwater MSA, FL	Y	15500 FQ	24630 MW	36520 TQ	USBLS	5/07
	West Palm Beach-Boca Raton-Boynton Beach PMSA, FL	Y	22360 FQ	25640 MW	41700 TQ	USBLS	5/07
	Georgia	Y	15410 FQ	22780 MW	30490 TQ	USBLS	5/07
	Atlanta-Sandy Springs-Marietta MSA, GA	Y	15340 FQ	23310 MW	30360 TQ	USBLS	5/07
	Hawaii	Y	20200 FQ	25860 MW	34590 TQ	USBLS	5/07
	Honolulu MSA, HI	Y	20730 FQ	27040 MW	35680 TQ	USBLS	5/07
	Idaho	Y	18450 FQ	27540 MW	40740 TQ	USBLS	5/07
	Boise City-Nampa MSA, ID	Y	18880 FQ	28950 MW	42420 TQ	USBLS	5/07
	Illinois	Y	16980 FQ	25330 MW	39280 TQ	USBLS	5/07
	Chicago-Naperville-Joliet MSA, IL-IN-WI	Y	19970 FQ	31650 MW	43270 TQ	USBLS	5/07
	Indiana	Y	14080 FQ	19870 MW	30230 TQ	USBLS	5/07
	Evansville MSA, IN-KY	Y	19470 FQ	22150 MW	30040 TQ	USBLS	5/07
	Gary PMSA, IN	Y	17730 FQ	30610 MW	36580 TQ	USBLS	5/07
	Indianapolis-Carmel MSA, IN	Y	14220 FQ	18220 MW	29880 TQ	USBLS	5/07
	Iowa	Y	14730 FQ	20740 MW	34160 TQ	USBLS	5/07
	Des Moines-West Des Moines MSA, IA	Y	14640 FQ	23560 MW	35500 TQ	USBLS	5/07
	Sioux City MSA, IA-NE-SD	Y	21940 FQ	30750 MW	36600 TQ	USBLS	5/07
	Kansas	Y	14480 FQ	20770 MW	32200 TQ	USBLS	5/07
	Lawrence MSA, KS	Y	13370 FQ	15480 MW	18020 TQ	USBLS	5/07
	Wichita MSA, KS	Y	13910 FQ	18420 MW	29320 TQ	USBLS	5/07
	Kentucky	Y	14613 FQ	22646 MW	33705 TQ	KYBLS	2008
	Bowling Green MSA, KY	Y	14340 FQ	19720 MW	28060 TQ	USBLS	5/07
	Lexington-Fayette MSA, KY	Y	19950 FQ	23910 MW	34560 TQ	USBLS	5/07
	Louisville-Jefferson County MSA, KY-IN	Y	13920 FQ	20650 MW	30140 TQ	USBLS	5/07
	Louisiana	H	7.83 FQ	10.88 MW	14.79 TQ	LABLS	1/08-3/08
	Baton Rouge MSA, LA	Y	21270 FQ	26360 MW	35830 TQ	USBLS	5/07
	New Orleans-Metairie-Kenner MSA, LA	Y	19220 FQ	23340 MW	32320 TQ	USBLS	5/07
	Maine	Y	16140 FQ	20580 MW	25050 TQ	USBLS	5/07
	Bangor MSA, ME	Y	18200 FQ	21460 MW	25560 TQ	USBLS	5/07
	Portland-South Portland-Biddeford MSA, ME	Y	15870 FQ	20750 MW	23630 TQ	USBLS	5/07
	Maryland	Y		25550 MW		MDBLS	3/08
	Baltimore-Towson MSA, MD	Y	15810 FQ	24870 MW	38610 TQ	USBLS	5/07
	Bethesda-Gaithersburg-Frederick PMSA, MD	Y	17530 FQ	21660 MW	32640 TQ	USBLS	5/07
	Cumberland MSA, MD-WV	Y	15330 FQ	21930 MW	28910 TQ	USBLS	5/07
	Hagerstown-Martinsburg MSA, MD-WV	Y	14120 FQ	18840 MW	36370 TQ	USBLS	5/07
	Massachusetts	Y	22020 FQ	32290 MW	43720 TQ	USBLS	5/07
	Boston-Cambridge-Quincy NECTA, MA	Y	24030 FQ	34820 MW	47360 TQ	USBLS	5/07
	Lynn-Peabody-Salem NECTA, MA	Y	18110 FQ	30140 MW	43310 TQ	USBLS	5/07
	Worcester MSA, MA-CT	Y	21000 FQ	25890 MW	37980 TQ	USBLS	5/07
	Michigan	Y	15790 FQ	21890 MW	34420 TQ	USBLS	5/07
	Detroit-Warren-Livonia MSA, MI	Y	16600 FQ	22700 MW	38450 TQ	USBLS	5/07
	Grand Rapids-Wyoming MSA, MI	Y	16280 FQ	20170 MW	31900 TQ	USBLS	5/07
	Lansing-East Lansing MSA, MI	Y	14800 FQ	18550 MW	33380 TQ	USBLS	5/07
	Muskegon-Norton Shores MSA, MI	Y	14730 FQ	17400 MW	24990 TQ	USBLS	5/07
	Warren-Troy-Farmington Hills PMSA, MI	Y	17550 FQ	21500 MW	27550 TQ	USBLS	5/07
	Minnesota	Y	15553 FQ	20078 MW	30242 TQ	MNBLS	10/08-12/08
	Duluth-Superior MSA, MN-WI	Y	16187 FQ	19828 MW	26476 TQ	MNBLS	10/08-12/08
	Minneapolis-Saint Paul MSA, MN-WI	Y	15261 FQ	19589 MW	29545 TQ	MNBLS	10/08-12/08
	Rochester MSA, MN	Y	15954 FQ	20953 MW	26558 TQ	MNBLS	10/08-12/08
	Mississippi	Y	18230 FQ	24080 MW	31990 TQ	USBLS	5/07
	Jackson MSA, MS	Y	19810 FQ	25280 MW	31970 TQ	USBLS	5/07
	Missouri	Y	14650 FQ	18720 MW	27670 TQ	USBLS	5/07
	Joplin MSA, MO	Y	14540 FQ	15560 MW	36660 TQ	USBLS	5/07
	Kansas City MSA, MO-KS	Y	16210 FQ	24740 MW	35750 TQ	USBLS	5/07
	St. Louis MSA, MO-IL	Y	14540 FQ	16500 MW	24820 TQ	USBLS	5/07

AE Average entry wage	**AW** Average wage paid	**FQ** First quartile wage	**LO** Lowest wage paid	**MTC** Median total compensation	**TCC** Total cash compensation
AER Average entry range	**AWR** Average wage range	**H** Hourly	**LR** Low end range	**MW** Median wage paid	**TQ** Third quartile wage
AEX Average experienced wage	**AXR** Average experienced range	**HI** Highest wage paid	**M** Monthly	**MWR** Median wage range	**W** Weekly
ATC Average total compensation	**D** Daily	**HR** High end range	**MCC** Median cash compensation	**S** See annotated source	**Y** Yearly

Occupation/Type/Industry	Location	Per	Low	Mid	High	Source	Date
Driver/Sales Worker	Montana	Y	15600 FQ	22820 MW	29110 TQ	USBLS	5/07
	Billings MSA, MT	Y	20720 FQ	27160 MW	31690 TQ	USBLS	5/07
	Nebraska	Y	14710 FQ	19950 MW	31950 TQ	USBLS	5/07
	Omaha-Council Bluffs MSA, NE-IA	Y	14660 FQ	19660 MW	28780 TQ	USBLS	5/07
	Nevada	H	8.39 FQ	11.80 MW	17.02 TQ	NVBLS	5/08
	Carson City MSA, NV	H	6.47 FQ	7.45 MW	12.63 TQ	NVBLS	5/08
	Las Vegas-Paradise MSA, NV	H	8.35 FQ	11.63 MW	16.04 TQ	NVBLS	5/08
	New Hampshire	H	6.42 AE	9.07 MW	12.62 AEX	NHBLS	6/08
	Manchester MSA, NH	Y	13430 FQ	19370 MW	34670 TQ	USBLS	5/07
	Nashua NECTA, NH-MA	Y	13230 FQ	15580 MW	21270 TQ	USBLS	5/07
	New Jersey	Y	19190 FQ	26720 MW	39760 TQ	USBLS	5/07
	Camden PMSA, NJ	Y	21170 FQ	24830 MW	37120 TQ	USBLS	5/07
	Edison PMSA, NJ	Y	16110 FQ	21490 MW	32010 TQ	USBLS	5/07
	Newark-Union PMSA, NJ-PA	Y	22160 FQ	29760 MW	38480 TQ	USBLS	5/07
	New Mexico	Y	18730 FQ	25400 MW	33560 TQ	USBLS	5/07
	Albuquerque MSA, NM	Y	22510 FQ	28020 MW	37040 TQ	USBLS	5/07
	New York	Y	17570 FQ	24440 MW	36950 TQ	USBLS	5/07
	Albany-Schenectady-Troy MSA, NY	Y	17520 FQ	23630 MW	31900 TQ	USBLS	5/07
	Buffalo-Niagara Falls MSA, NY	Y	16850 FQ	22240 MW	33750 TQ	USBLS	5/07
	Nassau-Suffolk PMSA, NY	Y	25170 FQ	37380 MW	45480 TQ	USBLS	5/07
	New York-Northern New Jersey-Long Island MSA, NY-NJ-PA	Y	18820 FQ	27980 MW	40180 TQ	USBLS	5/07
	North Carolina	Y	14540 FQ	20180 MW	30460 TQ	USBLS	5/07
	Charlotte-Gastonia-Concord MSA, NC-SC	Y	15180 FQ	24520 MW	37390 TQ	USBLS	5/07
	Raleigh-Cary MSA, NC	Y	14080 FQ	15720 MW	28690 TQ	USBLS	5/07
	North Dakota	Y	15260 FQ	19810 MW	28890 TQ	USBLS	5/07
	Fargo MSA, ND-MN	Y	18620 FQ	26240 MW	34640 TQ	USBLS	5/07
	Grand Forks MSA, ND-MN	Y	13120 FQ	14790 MW	21760 TQ	USBLS	5/07
	Ohio	Y	14830 FQ	16000 MW	28080 TQ	USBLS	5/07
	Cincinnati-Middletown MSA, OH-KY-IN	Y	14780 FQ	15970 MW	28180 TQ	USBLS	5/07
	Cleveland-Elyria-Mentor MSA, OH	Y	14780 FQ	17150 MW	29720 TQ	USBLS	5/07
	Columbus MSA, OH	Y	15200 FQ	19030 MW	29440 TQ	USBLS	5/07
	Dayton MSA, OH	Y	14750 FQ	15550 MW	25600 TQ	USBLS	5/07
	Oklahoma	Y	16740 FQ	23260 MW	32440 TQ	USBLS	5/07
	Oklahoma City MSA, OK	Y	15340 FQ	22120 MW	31430 TQ	USBLS	5/07
	Tulsa MSA, OK	Y	21510 FQ	26970 MW	36720 TQ	USBLS	5/07
	Oregon	H	9.31 FQ	11.46 MW	14.92 TQ	ORBLS	5/08
	Portland-Vancouver-Beaverton MSA, OR-WA	Y	21090 FQ	26280 MW	32930 TQ	USBLS	5/07
	Pennsylvania	Y	15330 FQ	19990 MW	31470 TQ	USBLS	5/07
	Allentown-Bethlehem-Easton MSA, PA-NJ	Y	15150 FQ	21880 MW	35550 TQ	USBLS	5/07
	Philadelphia-Camden-Wilmington MSA, PA-NJ-DE-MD	Y	17210 FQ	23980 MW	35940 TQ	USBLS	5/07
	Pittsburgh MSA, PA	Y	14750 FQ	16960 MW	23630 TQ	USBLS	5/07
	Rhode Island	Y	16650 FQ	20340 MW	30880 TQ	USBLS	5/07
	Providence-Fall River-Warwick MSA, RI-MA	Y	17100 FQ	21160 MW	31890 TQ	USBLS	5/07
	South Carolina	Y	14020 FQ	21120 MW	31600 TQ	USBLS	5/07
	Charleston-North Charleston MSA, SC	Y	13690 FQ	20670 MW	31070 TQ	USBLS	5/07
	Columbia MSA, SC	Y	19920 FQ	22680 MW	29140 TQ	USBLS	5/07
	South Dakota	Y	17591 FQ	23986 MW	36436 TQ	SDBLS	7/08-9/08
	Sioux Falls MSA, SD	Y	20130 FQ	29599 MW	38872 TQ	SDBLS	7/08-9/08
	Tennessee	Y	14950 FQ	22590 MW	33110 TQ	USBLS	5/07
	Johnson City MSA, TN	Y	13960 FQ	22370 MW	37420 TQ	USBLS	5/07
	Memphis MSA, TN-MS-AR	Y	14070 FQ	20720 MW	31240 TQ	USBLS	5/07
	Nashville-Davidson-Murfreesboro MSA, TN	Y	15330 FQ	20690 MW	30810 TQ	USBLS	5/07
	Texas	Y	13540 FQ	17720 MW	26500 TQ	USBLS	5/07
	Austin-Round Rock MSA, TX	Y	12960 FQ	14740 MW	24310 TQ	USBLS	5/07
	Dallas-Fort Worth-Arlington MSA, TX	Y	13630 FQ	18040 MW	26260 TQ	USBLS	5/07
	El Paso MSA, TX	Y	13700 FQ	18290 MW	27580 TQ	USBLS	5/07

AE Average entry wage	**AW** Average wage paid	**FQ** First quartile wage	**LO** Lowest wage paid	**MTC** Median total compensation	**TCC** Total cash compensation
AER Average entry range	**AWR** Average wage range	**H** Hourly	**LR** Low end range	**MW** Median wage paid	**TQ** Third quartile wage
AEX Average experienced wage	**AXR** Average experienced range	**HI** Highest wage paid	**M** Monthly	**MWR** Median wage range	**W** Weekly
ATC Average total compensation	**D** Daily	**HR** High end range	**MCC** Median cash compensation	**S** See annotated source	**Y** Yearly

Occupation/Type/Industry	Location	Per	Low	Mid	High	Source	Date
Driver/Sales Worker	Houston-Sugar Land-Baytown MSA, TX	Y	13340 FQ	16020 MW	26220 TQ	USBLS	5/07
	San Antonio MSA, TX	Y	14250 FQ	20950 MW	28590 TQ	USBLS	5/07
	Utah	Y	14490 FQ	22970 MW	33850 TQ	USBLS	5/07
	Salt Lake City MSA, UT	Y	17260 FQ	27730 MW	36700 TQ	USBLS	5/07
	Vermont	Y	20070 FQ	27200 MW	37120 TQ	USBLS	5/07
	Burlington-South Burlington MSA, VT	Y	18750 FQ	22460 MW	27610 TQ	USBLS	5/07
	Virginia	Y	16590 FQ	23840 MW	34190 TQ	USBLS	5/07
	Richmond MSA, VA	Y	16820 FQ	24120 MW	33800 TQ	USBLS	5/07
	Virginia Beach-Norfolk-Newport News MSA, VA-NC	Y	14760 FQ	19070 MW	28110 TQ	USBLS	5/07
	Washington	H	11.55 FQ	13.80 MW	15.82 TQ	WABLS	3/08
	Seattle-Tacoma-Bellevue MSA, WA	Y	23920 FQ	28510 MW	32770 TQ	USBLS	5/07
	West Virginia	Y	14062 FQ	15317 MW	25811 TQ	WVBLS	7/08-9/08
	Charleston MSA, WV	Y	14390 FQ	22340 MW	37650 TQ	USBLS	5/07
	Parkersburg-Marietta-Vienna MSA, WV-OH	Y	13450 FQ	14480 MW	19830 TQ	USBLS	5/07
	Wheeling MSA, WV-OH	Y	14430 FQ	17430 MW	38590 TQ	USBLS	5/07
	Wisconsin	Y	15370 FQ	20560 MW	31290 TQ	USBLS	5/07
	Milwaukee-Waukesha-West Allis MSA, WI	Y	15320 FQ	19090 MW	27290 TQ	USBLS	5/07
	Wyoming	Y	14058 FQ	20086 MW	28913 TQ	WYBLS	9/08
	Cheyenne MSA, WY	Y	14035 FQ	20740 MW	28282 TQ	WYBLS	9/08
	Puerto Rico	Y	13270 FQ	15580 MW	24370 TQ	USBLS	5/07
	San Juan-Caguas-Guaynabo MSA, PR	Y	13370 FQ	15790 MW	24290 TQ	USBLS	5/07
	Virgin Islands	Y	17270 FQ	19570 MW	29210 TQ	USBLS	5/07
	Guam	Y	12730 FQ	14400 MW	17940 TQ	USBLS	5/07
Drug Treatment Counselor							
State Government	Alabama	Y	28942 LO		43963 HI	AFT02	3/1/08
Drywall and Ceiling Tile Installer	Alabama	Y	25930 FQ	29770 MW	37150 TQ	USBLS	5/07
	Birmingham-Hoover MSA, AL	Y	26100 FQ	31890 MW	45000 TQ	USBLS	5/07
	Alaska	Y	37120 FQ	49760 MW	57250 TQ	USBLS	5/07
	Arizona	Y	25330 FQ	29990 MW	36660 TQ	USBLS	5/07
	Phoenix-Mesa-Scottsdale MSA, AZ	Y	25650 FQ	30130 MW	36620 TQ	USBLS	5/07
	Tucson MSA, AZ	Y	25030 FQ	28980 MW	35680 TQ	USBLS	5/07
	Arkansas	Y	22220 FQ	29260 MW	35280 TQ	USBLS	5/07
	Little Rock-North Little Rock MSA, AR	Y	28830 FQ	31420 MW	35570 TQ	USBLS	5/07
	California	H	18.88 FQ	22.75 MW	27.01 TQ	CABLS	1/08-3/08
	Los Angeles-Long Beach-Glendale PMSA, CA	H	20.11 FQ	22.46 MW	25.16 TQ	CABLS	1/08-3/08
	Modesto MSA, CA	H	19.81 FQ	22.70 MW	25.14 TQ	CABLS	1/08-3/08
	Oakland-Fremont-Hayward MSA, CA	H	21.53 FQ	24.09 MW	31.38 TQ	CABLS	1/08-3/08
	Riverside-San Bernardino-Ontario MSA, CA	H	16.57 FQ	20.84 MW	25.41 TQ	CABLS	1/08-3/08
	Sacramento-Arden Arcade-Roseville MSA, CA	H	16.76 FQ	21.91 MW	25.04 TQ	CABLS	1/08-3/08
	San Diego-Carlsbad-San Marcos MSA, CA	H	18.06 FQ	21.89 MW	26.95 TQ	CABLS	1/08-3/08
	San Francisco-San Mateo-Redwood PMSA, CA	H	27.07 FQ	30.62 MW	35.16 TQ	CABLS	1/08-3/08
	San Jose-Sunnyvale-Santa Clara MSA, CA	H	20.56 FQ	24.44 MW	31.70 TQ	CABLS	1/08-3/08
	Santa Ana-Anaheim-Irvine PMSA, CA	Y	37760 FQ	46680 MW	56250 TQ	USBLS	5/07
	Santa Rosa-Petaluma MSA, CA	H	21.91 FQ	24.98 MW	29.08 TQ	CABLS	1/08-3/08
	Colorado	Y	27160 FQ	33820 MW	40400 TQ	USBLS	5/07
	Denver-Aurora MSA, CO	Y	27350 FQ	33690 MW	40670 TQ	USBLS	5/07
	Connecticut	H	17.19 AE	24.70 MW		CTBLS	1/08-3/08
	Bridgeport-Stamford-Norwalk MSA, CT	Y	36590 FQ	46340 MW	54430 TQ	USBLS	5/07
	Hartford-West Hartford-East Hartford MSA, CT	Y	43760 FQ	51490 MW	58450 TQ	USBLS	5/07
	Delaware	Y	28640 FQ	39140 MW	48670 TQ	USBLS	5/07

AE Average entry wage	**AW** Average wage paid	**FQ** First quartile wage	**LO** Lowest wage paid	**MTC** Median total compensation	**TCC** Total cash compensation
AER Average entry range	**AWR** Average wage range	**H** Hourly	**LR** Low end range	**MW** Median wage paid	**TQ** Third quartile wage
AEX Average experienced wage	**AXR** Average experienced range	**HI** Highest wage paid	**M** Monthly	**MWR** Median wage range	**W** Weekly
ATC Average total compensation	**D** Daily	**HR** High end range	**MCC** Median cash compensation	**S** See annotated source	**Y** Yearly

Drywall and Ceiling Tile Installer

Occupation/Type/Industry	Location	Per	Low	Mid	High	Source	Date
Drywall and Ceiling Tile Installer	Wilmington PMSA, DE-MD-NJ	Y	30870 FQ	41250 MW	49510 TQ	USBLS	5/07
	District of Columbia	Y	33500 FQ	37380 MW	44340 TQ	USBLS	5/07
	Washington-Arlington-Alexandria MSA, DC-VA-MD-WV	Y	32210 FQ	37260 MW	45670 TQ	USBLS	5/07
	Florida	Y	26400 FQ	32260 MW	37690 TQ	USBLS	5/07
	Fort Lauderdale-Pompano Beach-Deerfield Beach PMSA, FL	Y	26770 FQ	30800 MW	38530 TQ	USBLS	5/07
	Jacksonville MSA, FL	Y	25980 FQ	31120 MW	36940 TQ	USBLS	5/07
	Miami-Fort Lauderdale-Miami Beach MSA, FL	Y	26310 FQ	30710 MW	38190 TQ	USBLS	5/07
	Orlando-Kissimmee MSA, FL	Y	26670 FQ	33540 MW	37480 TQ	USBLS	5/07
	Tampa-St. Petersburg-Clearwater MSA, FL	Y	28380 FQ	33660 MW	37790 TQ	USBLS	5/07
	West Palm Beach-Boca Raton-Boynton Beach PMSA, FL	Y	25480 FQ	32180 MW	41200 TQ	USBLS	5/07
	Georgia	Y	27510 FQ	32670 MW	37250 TQ	USBLS	5/07
	Atlanta-Sandy Springs-Marietta MSA, GA	Y	28180 FQ	33250 MW	37480 TQ	USBLS	5/07
	Hawaii	Y	36360 FQ	58200 MW	72960 TQ	USBLS	5/07
	Honolulu MSA, HI	Y	37310 FQ	62340 MW	73870 TQ	USBLS	5/07
	Idaho	Y	25320 FQ	31240 MW	37510 TQ	USBLS	5/07
	Boise City-Nampa MSA, ID	Y	27690 FQ	33410 MW	38320 TQ	USBLS	5/07
	Illinois	Y	35440 FQ	58520 MW	74700 TQ	USBLS	5/07
	Chicago-Naperville-Joliet MSA, IL-IN-WI	Y	36650 FQ	66030 MW	75710 TQ	USBLS	5/07
	Indiana	Y	27400 FQ	33420 MW	40550 TQ	USBLS	5/07
	Gary PMSA, IN	Y	33950 FQ	39500 MW	66440 TQ	USBLS	5/07
	Indianapolis-Carmel MSA, IN	Y	28980 FQ	35010 MW	42680 TQ	USBLS	5/07
	Iowa	Y	26030 FQ	32810 MW	43990 TQ	USBLS	5/07
	Des Moines-West Des Moines MSA, IA	Y	24710 FQ	34210 MW	49350 TQ	USBLS	5/07
	Kansas	Y	27840 FQ	33530 MW	39110 TQ	USBLS	5/07
	Topeka MSA, KS	Y	26010 FQ	33490 MW	37850 TQ	USBLS	5/07
	Wichita MSA, KS	Y	27180 FQ	32530 MW	38230 TQ	USBLS	5/07
	Kentucky	Y	26192 FQ	31825 MW	38234 TQ	KYBLS	2008
	Elizabethtown MSA, KY	Y	25190 FQ	27810 MW	30340 TQ	USBLS	5/07
	Louisville-Jefferson County MSA, KY-IN	Y	28130 FQ	33640 MW	41970 TQ	USBLS	5/07
	Louisiana	H	13.68 FQ	16.26 MW	19.25 TQ	LABLS	1/08-3/08
	New Orleans-Metairie-Kenner MSA, LA	Y	28230 FQ	33410 MW	38680 TQ	USBLS	5/07
	Maine	Y	30380 FQ	39090 MW	44880 TQ	USBLS	5/07
	Portland-South Portland-Biddeford MSA, ME	Y	35030 FQ	43040 MW	47160 TQ	USBLS	5/07
	Maryland	Y		40150 MW		MDBLS	3/08
	Baltimore-Towson MSA, MD	Y	31230 FQ	37170 MW	44150 TQ	USBLS	5/07
	Bethesda-Gaithersburg-Frederick PMSA, MD	Y	34650 FQ	42060 MW	53920 TQ	USBLS	5/07
	Massachusetts	Y	34850 FQ	52690 MW	62170 TQ	USBLS	5/07
	Boston-Cambridge-Quincy NECTA, MA	Y	26750 FQ	29470 MW	67590 TQ	USBLS	5/07
	Michigan	Y	29400 FQ	38710 MW	47410 TQ	USBLS	5/07
	Detroit-Warren-Livonia MSA, MI	Y	36400 FQ	45260 MW	50240 TQ	USBLS	5/07
	Grand Rapids-Wyoming MSA, MI	Y	34090 FQ	39740 MW	45980 TQ	USBLS	5/07
	Warren-Troy-Farmington Hills PMSA, MI	Y	43200 FQ	46980 MW	50520 TQ	USBLS	5/07
	Minnesota	Y	38097 FQ	55739 MW	68976 TQ	MNBLS	10/08-12/08
	Minneapolis-Saint Paul MSA, MN-WI	Y	55844 FQ	65445 MW	73160 TQ	MNBLS	10/08-12/08
	Rochester MSA, MN	Y	33646 FQ	39013 MW	55649 TQ	MNBLS	10/08-12/08
	Mississippi	Y	25450 FQ	30780 MW	34730 TQ	USBLS	5/07
	Jackson MSA, MS	Y	19550 FQ	26940 MW	31680 TQ	USBLS	5/07
	Missouri	Y	32860 FQ	45500 MW	58920 TQ	USBLS	5/07
	Kansas City MSA, MO-KS	Y	30740 FQ	35730 MW	41880 TQ	USBLS	5/07
	St. Louis MSA, MO-IL	Y	42590 FQ	54810 MW	65420 TQ	USBLS	5/07
	Montana	Y	19900 FQ	27480 MW	38640 TQ	USBLS	5/07
	Nebraska	Y	25850 FQ	30400 MW	36580 TQ	USBLS	5/07

AE Average entry wage	**AW** Average wage paid	**FQ** First quartile wage	**LO** Lowest wage paid	**MTC** Median total compensation	**TCC** Total cash compensation
AER Average entry range	**AWR** Average wage range	**H** Hourly	**LR** Low end range	**MW** Median wage paid	**TQ** Third quartile wage
AEX Average experienced wage	**AXR** Average experienced range	**HI** Highest wage paid	**M** Monthly	**MWR** Median wage range	**W** Weekly
ATC Average total compensation	**D** Daily	**HR** High end range	**MCC** Median cash compensation	**S** See annotated source	**Y** Yearly

Occupation/Type/Industry	Location	Per	Low	Mid	High	Source	Date
Drywall and Ceiling Tile Installer	Omaha-Council Bluffs MSA, NE-IA	Y	28350 FQ	33710 MW	39220 TQ	USBLS	5/07
	Nevada	H	16.71 FQ	19.90 MW	25.42 TQ	NVBLS	5/08
	Las Vegas-Paradise MSA, NV	H	17.12 FQ	20.43 MW	26.37 TQ	NVBLS	5/08
	New Hampshire	H	14.65 AE	20.11 MW	24.40 AEX	NHBLS	6/08
	Manchester MSA, NH	Y	35820 FQ	39280 MW	44710 TQ	USBLS	5/07
	New Jersey	Y	30650 FQ	38800 MW	68090 TQ	USBLS	5/07
	Camden PMSA, NJ	Y	36890 FQ	59840 MW	80010 TQ	USBLS	5/07
	Edison PMSA, NJ	Y	25440 FQ	37940 MW	50040 TQ	USBLS	5/07
	Newark-Union PMSA, NJ-PA	Y	30180 FQ	36800 MW	66580 TQ	USBLS	5/07
	New Mexico	Y	26420 FQ	31900 MW	44020 TQ	USBLS	5/07
	Albuquerque MSA, NM	Y	27270 FQ	34870 MW	47860 TQ	USBLS	5/07
	Las Cruces MSA, NM	Y	23620 FQ	26260 MW	29490 TQ	USBLS	5/07
	New York	Y	34140 FQ	47990 MW	68800 TQ	USBLS	5/07
	Albany-Schenectady-Troy MSA, NY	Y	43340 FQ	47890 MW	52800 TQ	USBLS	5/07
	Buffalo-Niagara Falls MSA, NY	Y	39500 FQ	45530 MW	55270 TQ	USBLS	5/07
	Nassau-Suffolk PMSA, NY	Y	35590 FQ	55920 MW	70590 TQ	USBLS	5/07
	New York-Northern New Jersey-Long Island MSA, NY-NJ-PA	Y	33720 FQ	49750 MW	71470 TQ	USBLS	5/07
	North Carolina	Y	25110 FQ	28670 MW	32610 TQ	USBLS	5/07
	Charlotte-Gastonia-Concord MSA, NC-SC	Y	26100 FQ	30400 MW	35370 TQ	USBLS	5/07
	Raleigh-Cary MSA, NC	Y	25290 FQ	27860 MW	30400 TQ	USBLS	5/07
	North Dakota	Y	27160 FQ	31150 MW	38090 TQ	USBLS	5/07
	Fargo MSA, ND-MN	Y	29600 FQ	33700 MW	41780 TQ	USBLS	5/07
	Ohio	Y	25080 FQ	31240 MW	38130 TQ	USBLS	5/07
	Cincinnati-Middletown MSA, OH-KY-IN	Y	27570 FQ	31600 MW	37580 TQ	USBLS	5/07
	Cleveland-Elyria-Mentor MSA, OH	Y	24200 FQ	29450 MW	34330 TQ	USBLS	5/07
	Columbus MSA, OH	Y	27200 FQ	31820 MW	39500 TQ	USBLS	5/07
	Dayton MSA, OH	Y	21780 FQ	25870 MW	34770 TQ	USBLS	5/07
	Oklahoma	Y	26540 FQ	29600 MW	32600 TQ	USBLS	5/07
	Oklahoma City MSA, OK	Y	27240 FQ	29390 MW	31650 TQ	USBLS	5/07
	Tulsa MSA, OK	Y	28220 FQ	32840 MW	37110 TQ	USBLS	5/07
	Oregon	H	14.90 FQ	20.87 MW	28.29 TQ	ORBLS	5/08
	Eugene-Springfield MSA, OR	Y	18170 FQ	20100 MW	39070 TQ	USBLS	5/07
	Portland-Vancouver-Beaverton MSA, OR-WA	Y	36370 FQ	52300 MW	60350 TQ	USBLS	5/07
	Pennsylvania	Y	29490 FQ	36820 MW	48230 TQ	USBLS	5/07
	Allentown-Bethlehem-Easton MSA, PA-NJ	Y	29880 FQ	37690 MW	51180 TQ	USBLS	5/07
	Erie MSA, PA	Y	24030 FQ	27580 MW	30760 TQ	USBLS	5/07
	Philadelphia-Camden-Wilmington MSA, PA-NJ-DE-MD	Y	31360 FQ	43200 MW	61120 TQ	USBLS	5/07
	Pittsburgh MSA, PA	Y	30850 FQ	38980 MW	52180 TQ	USBLS	5/07
	Reading MSA, PA	Y	33630 FQ	38840 MW	45030 TQ	USBLS	5/07
	Rhode Island	Y	29930 FQ	37430 MW	44110 TQ	USBLS	5/07
	Providence-Fall River-Warwick MSA, RI-MA	Y	29930 FQ	37430 MW	44110 TQ	USBLS	5/07
	South Carolina	Y	25590 FQ	29120 MW	32850 TQ	USBLS	5/07
	Charleston-North Charleston MSA, SC	Y	30010 FQ	33290 MW	37270 TQ	USBLS	5/07
	Columbia MSA, SC	Y	25650 FQ	28340 MW	30980 TQ	USBLS	5/07
	Spartanburg MSA, SC	Y	20230 FQ	28800 MW	36280 TQ	USBLS	5/07
	South Dakota	Y	27620 FQ	32201 MW	38949 TQ	SDBLS	7/08-9/08
	Sioux Falls MSA, SD	Y	29848 FQ	36515 MW	44302 TQ	SDBLS	7/08-9/08
	Tennessee	Y	25510 FQ	30900 MW	35970 TQ	USBLS	5/07
	Memphis MSA, TN-MS-AR	Y	27630 FQ	32740 MW	37530 TQ	USBLS	5/07
	Nashville-Davidson-Murfreesboro MSA, TN	Y	24730 FQ	31920 MW	36190 TQ	USBLS	5/07
	Texas	Y	26180 FQ	29150 MW	32520 TQ	USBLS	5/07
	Austin-Round Rock MSA, TX	Y	27130 FQ	30050 MW	34380 TQ	USBLS	5/07
	Beaumont-Port Arthur MSA, TX	Y	27280 FQ	31560 MW	36120 TQ	USBLS	5/07
	Dallas-Fort Worth-Arlington MSA, TX	Y	26600 FQ	29520 MW	32830 TQ	USBLS	5/07
	El Paso MSA, TX	Y	22620 FQ	26500 MW	29790 TQ	USBLS	5/07

AE	Average entry wage	**AW**	Average wage paid	**FQ**	First quartile wage	**LO**	Lowest wage paid	**MTC**	Median total compensation
AER	Average entry range	**AWR**	Average wage range	**H**	Hourly	**LR**	Low end range	**MW**	Median wage paid
AEX	Average experienced wage	**AXR**	Average experienced range	**HI**	Highest wage paid	**M**	Monthly	**MWR**	Median wage range
ATC	Average total compensation	**D**	Daily	**HR**	High end range	**MCC**	Median cash compensation	**S**	See annotated source

TCC Total cash compensation
TQ Third quartile wage
W Weekly
Y Yearly

Occupation/Type/Industry	Location	Per	Low	Mid	High	Source	Date
Drywall and Ceiling Tile Installer	Houston-Sugar Land-Baytown MSA, TX	Y	26530 FQ	29350 MW	33040 TQ	USBLS	5/07
	San Antonio MSA, TX	Y	25630 FQ	28290 MW	31020 TQ	USBLS	5/07
	Utah	Y	26010 FQ	34320 MW	39680 TQ	USBLS	5/07
	Salt Lake City MSA, UT	Y	23620 FQ	32140 MW	41340 TQ	USBLS	5/07
	Vermont	Y	30290 FQ	36100 MW	41020 TQ	USBLS	5/07
	Burlington-South Burlington MSA, VT	Y	33700 FQ	38130 MW	44340 TQ	USBLS	5/07
	Virginia	Y	29730 FQ	34780 MW	38850 TQ	USBLS	5/07
	Richmond MSA, VA	Y	30410 FQ	35430 MW	39090 TQ	USBLS	5/07
	Virginia Beach-Norfolk-Newport News MSA, VA-NC	Y	33140 FQ	36010 MW	39010 TQ	USBLS	5/07
	Washington	H	17.96 FQ	24.87 MW	30.78 TQ	WABLS	3/08
	Seattle-Tacoma-Bellevue MSA, WA	Y	38850 FQ	54170 MW	64490 TQ	USBLS	5/07
	West Virginia	Y	21996 FQ	26077 MW	37979 TQ	WVBLS	7/08-9/08
	Charleston MSA, WV	Y	35320 FQ	43900 MW	48380 TQ	USBLS	5/07
	Wisconsin	Y	33700 FQ	40050 MW	50970 TQ	USBLS	5/07
	Milwaukee-Waukesha-West Allis MSA, WI	Y	37160 FQ	46920 MW	55980 TQ	USBLS	5/07
	Wyoming	Y	29205 FQ	36500 MW	41490 TQ	WYBLS	9/08
	Cheyenne MSA, WY	Y	28224 FQ	36648 MW	40756 TQ	WYBLS	9/08
	Puerto Rico	Y	16600 FQ	18470 MW	21800 TQ	USBLS	5/07
	San Juan-Caguas-Guaynabo MSA, PR	Y	17260 FQ	18950 MW	22880 TQ	USBLS	5/07
Duplicating Equipment Operator Municipal Government	Walnut Creek, CA	Y	47473 LO		57088 HI	WCSWP	6/27/08
Duty Engineer	United States	Y		71950 AW		AVJOB02	2009
E-Business Specialist	United States	Y		77375 AW		GLKNO	10/11/07-10/26/07
E-Rate Support Analyst Public Schools	Wake County, NC	Y		65854 MW		WCPS02	2008-2009
Early Intervention Specialist State Government	Ohio	H	24.90 LO		34.83 HI	ODAS	2008
Earth Driller Except Oil and Gas	Alabama	Y	27200 FQ	31290 MW	41870 TQ	USBLS	5/07
Except Oil and Gas	Birmingham-Hoover MSA, AL	Y	29710 FQ	34640 MW	47110 TQ	USBLS	5/07
Except Oil and Gas	Mobile MSA, AL	Y	26880 FQ	30140 MW	36340 TQ	USBLS	5/07
Except Oil and Gas	Alaska	Y	43590 FQ	47880 MW	58410 TQ	USBLS	5/07
Except Oil and Gas	Arizona	Y	31770 FQ	35780 MW	39860 TQ	USBLS	5/07
Except Oil and Gas	Tucson MSA, AZ	Y	32570 FQ	35440 MW	39040 TQ	USBLS	5/07
Except Oil and Gas	Arkansas	Y	29490 FQ	33980 MW	40500 TQ	USBLS	5/07
Except Oil and Gas	California	H	20.16 FQ	24.90 MW	30.82 TQ	CABLS	1/08-3/08
Except Oil and Gas	Los Angeles-Long Beach-Glendale PMSA, CA	H	18.02 FQ	23.14 MW	27.22 TQ	CABLS	1/08-3/08
Except Oil and Gas	Riverside-San Bernardino-Ontario MSA, CA	H	26.13 FQ	31.55 MW	43.19 TQ	CABLS	1/08-3/08
Except Oil and Gas	Sacramento-Arden Arcade-Roseville MSA, CA	H	20.34 FQ	23.14 MW	27.29 TQ	CABLS	1/08-3/08
Except Oil and Gas	San Jose-Sunnyvale-Santa Clara MSA, CA	H	29.54 FQ	36.46 MW	40.94 TQ	CABLS	1/08-3/08
Except Oil and Gas	Colorado	Y	30120 FQ	36870 MW	44560 TQ	USBLS	5/07
Except Oil and Gas	Denver-Aurora MSA, CO	Y	28610 FQ	35840 MW	42930 TQ	USBLS	5/07
Except Oil and Gas	Connecticut	H	17.65 AE	20.98 MW		CTBLS	1/08-3/08
Except Oil and Gas	Washington-Arlington-Alexandria MSA, DC-VA-MD-WV	Y	33910 FQ	38780 MW	43860 TQ	USBLS	5/07
Except Oil and Gas	Florida	Y	26220 FQ	34160 MW	38660 TQ	USBLS	5/07
Except Oil and Gas	Miami-Fort Lauderdale-Miami Beach MSA, FL	Y	23600 FQ	32480 MW	38810 TQ	USBLS	5/07
Except Oil and Gas	Orlando-Kissimmee MSA, FL	Y	25330 FQ	31970 MW	37520 TQ	USBLS	5/07
Except Oil and Gas	Tampa-St. Petersburg-Clearwater MSA, FL	Y	27170 FQ	33550 MW	39190 TQ	USBLS	5/07
Except Oil and Gas	Georgia	Y	25390 FQ	31510 MW	38760 TQ	USBLS	5/07
Except Oil and Gas	Atlanta-Sandy Springs-Marietta MSA, GA	Y	31290 FQ	36130 MW	42710 TQ	USBLS	5/07
Except Oil and Gas	Hawaii	Y	41500 FQ	48800 MW	56780 TQ	USBLS	5/07
Except Oil and Gas	Honolulu MSA, HI	Y	43790 FQ	51440 MW	58840 TQ	USBLS	5/07

AE Average entry wage	AW Average wage paid	FQ First quartile wage	LO Lowest wage paid	MTC Median total compensation	TCC Total cash compensation
AER Average entry range	AWR Average wage range	H Hourly	LR Low end range	MW Median wage paid	TQ Third quartile wage
AEX Average experienced wage	AXR Average experienced range	HI Highest wage paid	M Monthly	MWR Median wage range	W Weekly
ATC Average total compensation	D Daily	HR High end range	MCC Median cash compensation	S See annotated source	Y Yearly

Earth Driller

Occupation/Type/Industry	Location	Per	Low	Mid	High	Source	Date
Earth Driller							
Except Oil and Gas	Idaho	Y	29410 FQ	35280 MW	40470 TQ	USBLS	5/07
Except Oil and Gas	Illinois	Y	31250 FQ	44930 MW	62100 TQ	USBLS	5/07
Except Oil and Gas	Chicago-Naperville-Joliet MSA, IL-IN-WI	Y	38460 FQ	60260 MW	71140 TQ	USBLS	5/07
Except Oil and Gas	Indiana	Y	25940 FQ	38050 MW	45120 TQ	USBLS	5/07
Except Oil and Gas	Gary PMSA, IN	Y	28520 FQ	33300 MW	38840 TQ	USBLS	5/07
Except Oil and Gas	Indianapolis-Carmel MSA, IN	Y	41120 FQ	44180 MW	47310 TQ	USBLS	5/07
Except Oil and Gas	Iowa	Y	32250 FQ	38540 MW	46790 TQ	USBLS	5/07
Except Oil and Gas	Kansas	Y	28830 FQ	40440 MW	45720 TQ	USBLS	5/07
Except Oil and Gas	Kentucky	Y	30216 FQ	34255 MW	39417 TQ	KYBLS	2008
Except Oil and Gas	Louisville-Jefferson County MSA, KY-IN	Y	23780 FQ	27780 MW	33250 TQ	USBLS	5/07
Except Oil and Gas	Louisiana	H	14.20 FQ	17.55 MW	24.85 TQ	LABLS	1/08-3/08
Except Oil and Gas	Maine	Y	32700 FQ	37470 MW	43920 TQ	USBLS	5/07
Except Oil and Gas	Portland-South Portland-Biddeford MSA, ME	Y	34370 FQ	38400 MW	54540 TQ	USBLS	5/07
Except Oil and Gas	Maryland	Y		41150 MW		MDBLS	3/08
Except Oil and Gas	Baltimore-Towson MSA, MD	Y	29620 FQ	35290 MW	51340 TQ	USBLS	5/07
Except Oil and Gas	Massachusetts	Y	32230 FQ	40770 MW	48440 TQ	USBLS	5/07
Except Oil and Gas	Boston-Cambridge-Quincy NECTA, MA	Y	36280 FQ	46190 MW	55450 TQ	USBLS	5/07
Except Oil and Gas	Michigan	Y	29510 FQ	35240 MW	45670 TQ	USBLS	5/07
Except Oil and Gas	Detroit-Warren-Livonia MSA, MI	Y	40520 FQ	46610 MW	51770 TQ	USBLS	5/07
Except Oil and Gas	Grand Rapids-Wyoming MSA, MI	Y	29360 FQ	33720 MW	41630 TQ	USBLS	5/07
Except Oil and Gas	Warren-Troy-Farmington Hills PMSA, MI	Y	41080 FQ	47050 MW	52380 TQ	USBLS	5/07
Except Oil and Gas	Minnesota	Y	36790 FQ	46813 MW	54590 TQ	MNBLS	10/08-12/08
Except Oil and Gas	Duluth-Superior MSA, MN-WI	Y	31352 FQ	43988 MW	49395 TQ	MNBLS	10/08-12/08
Except Oil and Gas	Minneapolis-Saint Paul MSA, MN-WI	Y	33776 FQ	47782 MW	58700 TQ	MNBLS	10/08-12/08
Except Oil and Gas	Mississippi	Y	29800 FQ	35010 MW	46520 TQ	USBLS	5/07
Except Oil and Gas	Missouri	Y	26680 FQ	32830 MW	37980 TQ	USBLS	5/07
Except Oil and Gas	Kansas City MSA, MO-KS	Y	28930 FQ	35870 MW	47690 TQ	USBLS	5/07
Except Oil and Gas	St. Louis MSA, MO-IL	Y	33200 FQ	36380 MW	39960 TQ	USBLS	5/07
Except Oil and Gas	Montana	Y	34370 FQ	44140 MW	50880 TQ	USBLS	5/07
Except Oil and Gas	Nebraska	Y	22140 FQ	26540 MW	35680 TQ	USBLS	5/07
Except Oil and Gas	Omaha-Council Bluffs MSA, NE-IA	Y	21820 FQ	29460 MW	43020 TQ	USBLS	5/07
Except Oil and Gas	Nevada	H	19.69 FQ	23.28 MW	27.66 TQ	NVBLS	5/08
Except Oil and Gas	New Hampshire	H	16.66 AE	19.00 MW	22.05 AEX	NHBLS	6/08
Except Oil and Gas	New Jersey	Y	36110 FQ	46720 MW	56500 TQ	USBLS	5/07
Except Oil and Gas	Camden PMSA, NJ	Y	32620 FQ	45060 MW	49670 TQ	USBLS	5/07
Except Oil and Gas	Edison PMSA, NJ	Y	44430 FQ	50620 MW	60640 TQ	USBLS	5/07
Except Oil and Gas	New Mexico	Y	30630 FQ	40530 MW	45210 TQ	USBLS	5/07
Except Oil and Gas	New York	Y	33770 FQ	40000 MW	52530 TQ	USBLS	5/07
Except Oil and Gas	Albany-Schenectady-Troy MSA, NY	Y	36870 FQ	44550 MW	56400 TQ	USBLS	5/07
Except Oil and Gas	Buffalo-Niagara Falls MSA, NY	Y	35380 FQ	46870 MW	59870 TQ	USBLS	5/07
Except Oil and Gas	Nassau-Suffolk PMSA, NY	Y	36160 FQ	43740 MW	54200 TQ	USBLS	5/07
Except Oil and Gas	New York-Northern New Jersey-Long Island MSA, NY-NJ-PA	Y	35100 FQ	44550 MW	57280 TQ	USBLS	5/07
Except Oil and Gas	North Carolina	Y	25370 FQ	33510 MW	40220 TQ	USBLS	5/07
Except Oil and Gas	Raleigh-Cary MSA, NC	Y	32150 FQ	41420 MW	66210 TQ	USBLS	5/07
Except Oil and Gas	North Dakota	Y	32560 FQ	38280 MW	42920 TQ	USBLS	5/07
Except Oil and Gas	Ohio	Y	28690 FQ	35580 MW	46960 TQ	USBLS	5/07
Except Oil and Gas	Columbus MSA, OH	Y	33450 FQ	43060 MW	66920 TQ	USBLS	5/07
Except Oil and Gas	Oklahoma	Y	24540 FQ	34100 MW	44100 TQ	USBLS	5/07
Except Oil and Gas	Tulsa MSA, OK	Y	19450 FQ	25070 MW	31160 TQ	USBLS	5/07
Except Oil and Gas	Portland-Vancouver-Beaverton MSA, OR-WA	Y	37560 FQ	46060 MW	80680 TQ	USBLS	5/07
Except Oil and Gas	Pennsylvania	Y	27000 FQ	34670 MW	43190 TQ	USBLS	5/07
Except Oil and Gas	Lancaster MSA, PA	Y	32910 FQ	37800 MW	43370 TQ	USBLS	5/07
Except Oil and Gas	Philadelphia-Camden-Wilmington MSA, PA-NJ-DE-MD	Y	36430 FQ	42050 MW	49600 TQ	USBLS	5/07
Except Oil and Gas	Pittsburgh MSA, PA	Y	29200 FQ	35320 MW	49430 TQ	USBLS	5/07
Except Oil and Gas	Rhode Island	Y	33960 FQ	39840 MW	50410 TQ	USBLS	5/07

Occupation/Type/Industry	Location	Per	Low	Mid	High	Source	Date
Earth Driller							
Except Oil and Gas	Providence-Fall River-Warwick MSA, RI-MA	Y	33960 FQ	39840 MW	50410 TQ	USBLS	5/07
Except Oil and Gas	South Carolina	Y	32130 FQ	36440 MW	49930 TQ	USBLS	5/07
Except Oil and Gas	South Dakota	Y	28502 FQ	33167 MW	38821 TQ	SDBLS	7/08-9/08
Except Oil and Gas	Tennessee	Y	26140 FQ	30560 MW	38510 TQ	USBLS	5/07
Except Oil and Gas	Memphis MSA, TN-MS-AR	Y	34070 FQ	39020 MW	88060 TQ	USBLS	5/07
Except Oil and Gas	Nashville-Davidson-Murfreesboro MSA, TN	Y	26450 FQ	28980 MW	32840 TQ	USBLS	5/07
Except Oil and Gas	Texas	Y	25510 FQ	30260 MW	40750 TQ	USBLS	5/07
Except Oil and Gas	Dallas-Fort Worth-Arlington MSA, TX	Y	26120 FQ	29740 MW	38220 TQ	USBLS	5/07
Except Oil and Gas	San Antonio MSA, TX	Y	27810 FQ	30250 MW	33600 TQ	USBLS	5/07
Except Oil and Gas	Utah	Y	29350 FQ	34080 MW	69920 TQ	USBLS	5/07
Except Oil and Gas	Vermont	Y	28150 FQ	30940 MW	35720 TQ	USBLS	5/07
Except Oil and Gas	Virginia	Y	29360 FQ	35250 MW	41220 TQ	USBLS	5/07
Except Oil and Gas	Richmond MSA, VA	Y	32250 FQ	49000 MW	67840 TQ	USBLS	5/07
Except Oil and Gas	Virginia Beach-Norfolk-Newport News MSA, VA-NC	Y	33910 FQ	41750 MW	49760 TQ	USBLS	5/07
Except Oil and Gas	Washington	H	17.18 FQ	25.34 MW	33.74 TQ	WABLS	3/08
Except Oil and Gas	Seattle-Tacoma-Bellevue MSA, WA	Y	64650 FQ	69730 MW	74610 TQ	USBLS	5/07
Except Oil and Gas	West Virginia	Y	28767 FQ	41825 MW	48552 TQ	WVBLS	7/08-9/08
Except Oil and Gas	Charleston MSA, WV	Y	27080 FQ	41010 MW	46400 TQ	USBLS	5/07
Except Oil and Gas	Wisconsin	Y	31680 FQ	37670 MW	45240 TQ	USBLS	5/07
Except Oil and Gas	Wyoming	Y	28751 FQ	33404 MW	40840 TQ	WYBLS	9/08
Except Oil and Gas	Puerto Rico	Y	18400 FQ	24450 MW	28980 TQ	USBLS	5/07
Except Oil and Gas	San Juan-Caguas-Guaynabo MSA, PR	Y	19010 FQ	25490 MW	29270 TQ	USBLS	5/07
Ecommerce/Intranet Manager	United States	Y		82254 AW		COWRLD1	5/20/08-7/25/08
Economic Development Director							
Municipal Government	Allen Park, MI	Y			69900 HI	NHERLD1	2009
Municipal Government	Cincinnati, OH	Y	98374 LO		132805 HI	COHSS	10/08
Economics Teacher							
Postsecondary	Alabama	Y	48040 FQ	65710 MW	86660 TQ	USBLS	5/07
Postsecondary	Arizona	Y	50140 FQ	72010 MW	125000 TQ	USBLS	5/07
Postsecondary	Arkansas	Y	44630 FQ	60820 MW	92440 TQ	USBLS	5/07
Postsecondary	California	Y		92251 AW		CABLS	1/08-3/08
Postsecondary	Los Angeles-Long Beach-Glendale PMSA, CA	Y		84468 AW		CABLS	1/08-3/08
Postsecondary	Oakland-Fremont-Hayward MSA, CA	Y		94518 AW		CABLS	1/08-3/08
Postsecondary	Riverside-San Bernardino-Ontario MSA, CA	Y		101070 AW		CABLS	1/08-3/08
Postsecondary	Sacramento-Arden Arcade-Roseville MSA, CA	Y		104055 AW		CABLS	1/08-3/08
Postsecondary	San Diego-Carlsbad-San Marcos MSA, CA	Y		102188 AW		CABLS	1/08-3/08
Postsecondary	San Francisco-San Mateo-Redwood PMSA, CA	Y		85586 AW		CABLS	1/08-3/08
Postsecondary	Santa Ana-Anaheim-Irvine PMSA, CA	Y	73900 FQ	87540 MW	104630 TQ	USBLS	5/07
Postsecondary	Colorado	Y	54120 FQ	70340 MW	83030 TQ	USBLS	5/07
Postsecondary	Denver-Aurora MSA, CO	Y	54560 FQ	67930 MW	84270 TQ	USBLS	5/07
Postsecondary	Fort Collins-Loveland MSA, CO	Y	36170 FQ	68510 MW	86040 TQ	USBLS	5/07
Postsecondary	Delaware	Y	66490 FQ	86960 MW	114650 TQ	USBLS	5/07
Postsecondary	Wilmington PMSA, DE-MD-NJ	Y	73810 FQ	93410 MW	123570 TQ	USBLS	5/07
Postsecondary	District of Columbia	Y	49190 FQ	60100 MW	75110 TQ	USBLS	5/07
Postsecondary	Washington-Arlington-Alexandria MSA, DC-VA-MD-WV	Y	53200 FQ	69950 MW	89680 TQ	USBLS	5/07
Postsecondary	Florida	Y	60350 FQ	76690 MW	96890 TQ	USBLS	5/07
Postsecondary	Miami-Fort Lauderdale-Miami Beach MSA, FL	Y	68300 FQ	76380 MW	85080 TQ	USBLS	5/07
Postsecondary	Orlando-Kissimmee MSA, FL	Y	48850 FQ	68610 MW	83830 TQ	USBLS	5/07
Postsecondary	Tampa-St. Petersburg-Clearwater MSA, FL	Y	62750 FQ	79880 MW	98990 TQ	USBLS	5/07

AE	Average entry wage	AW	Average wage paid	FQ	First quartile wage	LO	Lowest wage paid	MTC	Median total compensation	TCC	Total cash compensation
AER	Average entry range	AWR	Average wage range	H	Hourly	LR	Low end range	MW	Median wage paid	TQ	Third quartile wage
AEX	Average experienced wage	AXR	Average experienced range	HI	Highest wage paid	M	Monthly	MWR	Median wage range	W	Weekly
ATC	Average total compensation	D	Daily	HR	High end range	MCC	Median cash compensation	S	See annotated source	Y	Yearly

455

Economics Teacher

Occupation/Type/Industry	Location	Per	Low	Mid	High	Source	Date
Postsecondary	Georgia	Y	55920 FQ	74250 MW	93530 TQ	USBLS	5/07
Postsecondary	Atlanta-Sandy Springs-Marietta MSA, GA	Y	56430 FQ	74670 MW	94820 TQ	USBLS	5/07
Postsecondary	Illinois	Y	52000 FQ	67160 MW	90070 TQ	USBLS	5/07
Postsecondary	Chicago-Naperville-Joliet MSA, IL-IN-WI	Y	50160 FQ	61580 MW	82780 TQ	USBLS	5/07
Postsecondary	Indiana	Y	60540 FQ	77020 MW	104880 TQ	USBLS	5/07
Postsecondary	Iowa	Y	63710 FQ	93450 MW	131490 TQ	USBLS	5/07
Postsecondary	Kansas	Y	64390 FQ	97300 MW	126950 TQ	USBLS	5/07
Postsecondary	Kentucky	Y	55664 FQ	83036 MW	110911 TQ	KYBLS	2008
Postsecondary	Louisiana	Y		62047 AW		LABLS	1/08-3/08
Postsecondary	Baton Rouge MSA, LA	Y	44650 FQ	50380 MW	62460 TQ		5/07
Postsecondary	Maine	Y	58430 FQ	73830 MW	93640 TQ	USBLS	5/07
Postsecondary	Maryland	Y		76250 MW		MDBLS	3/08
Postsecondary	Baltimore-Towson MSA, MD	Y	55450 FQ	68360 MW	89960 TQ	USBLS	5/07
Postsecondary	Massachusetts	Y	67400 FQ	87290 MW	117930 TQ	USBLS	5/07
Postsecondary	Boston-Cambridge-Quincy NECTA, MA	Y	67970 FQ	95600 MW	135150 TQ	USBLS	5/07
Postsecondary	Michigan	Y	44730 FQ	73590 MW	93080 TQ	USBLS	5/07
Postsecondary	Detroit-Warren-Livonia MSA, MI	Y	36700 FQ	71560 MW	94470 TQ	USBLS	5/07
Postsecondary	Warren-Troy-Farmington Hills PMSA, MI	Y	62670 FQ	79330 MW	96870 TQ	USBLS	5/07
Postsecondary	Minnesota	Y	51359 FQ	72869 MW	101776 TQ	MNBLS	10/08-12/08
Postsecondary	Duluth-Superior MSA, MN-WI	Y	78676 FQ	96451 MW	116350 TQ	MNBLS	10/08-12/08
Postsecondary	Minneapolis-Saint Paul MSA, MN-WI	Y	53252 FQ	79167 MW	109801 TQ	MNBLS	10/08-12/08
Postsecondary	Mississippi	Y	54280 FQ	74650 MW	101640 TQ	USBLS	5/07
Postsecondary	Missouri	Y	58760 FQ	74920 MW	94460 TQ	USBLS	5/07
Postsecondary	Kansas City MSA, MO-KS	Y	57460 FQ	80570 MW	117790 TQ	USBLS	5/07
Postsecondary	St. Louis MSA, MO-IL	Y	54230 FQ	75470 MW	95030 TQ	USBLS	5/07
Postsecondary	New Jersey	Y	67150 FQ	89960 MW	121090 TQ	USBLS	5/07
Postsecondary	Edison PMSA, NJ	Y	66410 FQ	96850 MW	126720 TQ	USBLS	5/07
Postsecondary	Newark-Union PMSA, NJ-PA	Y	60770 FQ	85860 MW	118080 TQ	USBLS	5/07
Postsecondary	New Mexico	Y	53010 FQ	65000 MW	77960 TQ	USBLS	5/07
Postsecondary	Albuquerque MSA, NM	Y	61610 FQ	71370 MW	84800 TQ	USBLS	5/07
Postsecondary	New York	Y	60880 FQ	77720 MW	105380 TQ	USBLS	5/07
Postsecondary	New York-Northern New Jersey-Long Island MSA, NY-NJ-PA	Y	61180 FQ	82160 MW	110990 TQ	USBLS	5/07
Postsecondary	North Carolina	Y	53820 FQ	74310 MW	101750 TQ	USBLS	5/07
Postsecondary	Charlotte-Gastonia-Concord MSA, NC-SC	Y	50130 FQ	69640 MW	90310 TQ	USBLS	5/07
Postsecondary	Raleigh-Cary MSA, NC	Y	55640 FQ	82010 MW	104400 TQ	USBLS	5/07
Postsecondary	North Dakota	Y	45980 FQ	67460 MW	97310 TQ	USBLS	5/07
Postsecondary	Ohio	Y	53750 FQ	76760 MW	98540 TQ	USBLS	5/07
Postsecondary	Cincinnati-Middletown MSA, OH-KY-IN	Y	48200 FQ	77530 MW	99770 TQ	USBLS	5/07
Postsecondary	Cleveland-Elyria-Mentor MSA, OH	Y	45070 FQ	71100 MW	93510 TQ	USBLS	5/07
Postsecondary	Columbus MSA, OH	Y	75400 FQ	94780 MW	121240 TQ	USBLS	5/07
Postsecondary	Dayton MSA, OH	Y	47570 FQ	69760 MW	100200 TQ	USBLS	5/07
Postsecondary	Oklahoma	Y	27380 FQ	35980 MW	57820 TQ	USBLS	5/07
Postsecondary	Tulsa MSA, OK	Y	23030 FQ	35340 MW	57980 TQ	USBLS	5/07
Postsecondary	Portland-Vancouver-Beaverton MSA, OR-WA	Y	59060 FQ	79670 MW	113990 TQ	USBLS	5/07
Postsecondary	Pennsylvania	Y	54810 FQ	77170 MW	108950 TQ	USBLS	5/07
Postsecondary	Philadelphia-Camden-Wilmington MSA, PA-NJ-DE-MD	Y	62170 FQ	87790 MW	119310 TQ	USBLS	5/07
Postsecondary	Pittsburgh MSA, PA	Y	56470 FQ	70550 MW	97440 TQ	USBLS	5/07
Postsecondary	Rhode Island	Y	73430 FQ	93080 MW	121500 TQ	USBLS	5/07
Postsecondary	Providence-Fall River-Warwick MSA, RI-MA	Y	73430 FQ	93080 MW	121500 TQ	USBLS	5/07
Postsecondary	South Carolina	Y	55850 FQ	73010 MW	94120 TQ	USBLS	5/07
Postsecondary	South Dakota	Y	54177 FQ	69424 MW	81677 TQ	SDBLS	7/08-9/08
Postsecondary	Tennessee	Y	53790 FQ	80890 MW	127380 TQ	USBLS	5/07
Postsecondary	Nashville-Davidson-Murfreesboro MSA, TN	Y	55490 FQ	86280 MW	137680 TQ	USBLS	5/07
Postsecondary	Texas	Y	49710 FQ	71450 MW	98100 TQ	USBLS	5/07
Postsecondary	Austin-Round Rock MSA, TX	Y	53420 FQ	80350 MW	106360 TQ	USBLS	5/07

AE Average entry wage	**AW** Average wage paid	**FQ** First quartile wage	**LO** Lowest wage paid	**MTC** Median total compensation	**TCC** Total cash compensation
AER Average entry range	**AWR** Average wage range	**H** Hourly	**LR** Low end range	**MW** Median wage paid	**TQ** Third quartile wage
AEX Average experienced wage	**AXR** Average experienced range	**HI** Highest wage paid	**M** Monthly	**MWR** Median wage range	**W** Weekly
ATC Average total compensation	**D** Daily	**HR** High end range	**MCC** Median cash compensation	**S** See annotated source	**Y** Yearly

Occupation/Type/Industry	Location	Per	Low	Mid	High	Source	Date
Economics Teacher							
Postsecondary	Dallas-Fort Worth-Arlington MSA, TX	Y	54170 FQ	79270 MW	117610 TQ	USBLS	5/07
Postsecondary	El Paso MSA, TX	Y	45780 FQ	76020 MW	95420 TQ	USBLS	5/07
Postsecondary	Houston-Sugar Land-Baytown MSA, TX	Y	60280 FQ	83530 MW	145500 TQ	USBLS	5/07
Postsecondary	San Antonio MSA, TX	Y	46330 FQ	61080 MW	79130 TQ	USBLS	5/07
Postsecondary	Utah	Y	59250 FQ	78330 MW	103370 TQ	USBLS	5/07
Postsecondary	Vermont	Y	46170 FQ	57510 MW	70930 TQ	USBLS	5/07
Postsecondary	Burlington-South Burlington MSA, VT	Y	45460 FQ	57800 MW	69740 TQ	USBLS	5/07
Postsecondary	Virginia	Y	50900 FQ	72880 MW	96880 TQ	USBLS	5/07
Postsecondary	Richmond MSA, VA	Y	61770 FQ	80610 MW	102810 TQ	USBLS	5/07
Postsecondary	Virginia Beach-Norfolk-Newport News MSA, VA-NC	Y	54400 FQ	73970 MW	98300 TQ	USBLS	5/07
Postsecondary	Washington	Y		76825 AW		WABLS	3/08
Postsecondary	Seattle-Tacoma-Bellevue MSA, WA	Y	51580 FQ	61120 MW	92050 TQ	USBLS	5/07
Postsecondary	West Virginia	Y	63946 FQ	79431 MW	94903 TQ	WVBLS	7/08-9/08
Postsecondary	Wisconsin	Y	54800 FQ	68980 MW	88950 TQ	USBLS	5/07
Postsecondary	Milwaukee-Waukesha-West Allis MSA, WI	Y	55170 FQ	70180 MW	89980 TQ	USBLS	5/07
Postsecondary	Wyoming	Y	61489 FQ	74060 MW	89200 TQ	WYBLS	9/08
Postsecondary	Puerto Rico	Y	35750 FQ	45000 MW	70330 TQ	USBLS	5/07
Economist	Alaska	Y	58110 FQ	68970 MW	81920 TQ	USBLS	5/07
	Arizona	Y	49560 FQ	66640 MW	93810 TQ	USBLS	5/07
	Phoenix-Mesa-Scottsdale MSA, AZ	Y	53900 FQ	71500 MW	96810 TQ	USBLS	5/07
	Arkansas	Y	32740 FQ	41870 MW	55810 TQ	USBLS	5/07
	Little Rock-North Little Rock MSA, AR	Y	32180 FQ	41310 MW	57540 TQ	USBLS	5/07
	California	H	34.16 FQ	42.55 MW	56.32 TQ	CABLS	1/08-3/08
	Los Angeles-Long Beach-Glendale PMSA, CA	H	39.38 FQ	49.80 MW	63.11 TQ	CABLS	1/08-3/08
	Oakland-Fremont-Hayward MSA, CA	H	36.00 FQ	44.53 MW	65.58 TQ	CABLS	1/08-3/08
	Riverside-San Bernardino-Ontario MSA, CA	H	37.96 FQ	47.89 MW		CABLS	1/08-3/08
	Sacramento-Arden Arcade-Roseville MSA, CA	H	31.50 FQ	35.67 MW	39.19 TQ	CABLS	1/08-3/08
	San Diego-Carlsbad-San Marcos MSA, CA	H	17.99 FQ	19.51 MW	21.71 TQ	CABLS	1/08-3/08
	San Jose-Sunnyvale-Santa Clara MSA, CA	H	39.42 FQ	45.30 MW	51.90 TQ	CABLS	1/08-3/08
	Santa Ana-Anaheim-Irvine PMSA, CA	Y	50500 FQ	66450 MW	90310 TQ	USBLS	5/07
	Colorado	Y	73480 FQ	88230 MW	102790 TQ	USBLS	5/07
	Denver-Aurora MSA, CO	Y	71730 FQ	83710 MW	97320 TQ	USBLS	5/07
	Connecticut	H	30.90 AE	37.55 MW		CTBLS	1/08-3/08
	Hartford-West Hartford-East Hartford MSA, CT	Y	67760 FQ	75140 MW	82620 TQ	USBLS	5/07
	Delaware	Y	61870 FQ	74310 MW	93410 TQ	USBLS	5/07
	Wilmington PMSA, DE-MD-NJ	Y	65180 FQ	77500 MW	99250 TQ	USBLS	5/07
	District of Columbia	Y	75200 FQ	98820 MW	126690 TQ	USBLS	5/07
	Washington-Arlington-Alexandria MSA, DC-VA-MD-WV	Y	74770 FQ	99150 MW	127410 TQ	USBLS	5/07
	Florida	Y	57750 FQ	79540 MW	104690 TQ	USBLS	5/07
	Miami-Fort Lauderdale-Miami Beach MSA, FL	Y	64950 FQ	80200 MW	102000 TQ	USBLS	5/07
	Orlando-Kissimmee MSA, FL	Y	34870 FQ	46470 MW	75270 TQ	USBLS	5/07
	Tampa-St. Petersburg-Clearwater MSA, FL	Y	84830 FQ			USBLS	5/07
	Georgia	Y	61650 FQ	76810 MW	93410 TQ	USBLS	5/07
	Atlanta-Sandy Springs-Marietta MSA, GA	Y	68830 FQ	79550 MW	95820 TQ	USBLS	5/07
	Hawaii	Y	46680 FQ	59550 MW	79560 TQ	USBLS	5/07
	Honolulu MSA, HI	Y	45610 FQ	62600 MW	83870 TQ	USBLS	5/07
	Idaho	Y	47700 FQ	56770 MW	66440 TQ	USBLS	5/07
	Illinois	Y	63440 FQ	80140 MW	102700 TQ	USBLS	5/07

AE	Average entry wage	AW	Average wage paid	FQ	First quartile wage	LO	Lowest wage paid	MTC	Median total compensation	TCC	Total cash compensation
AER	Average entry range	AWR	Average wage range	H	Hourly	LR	Low end range	MW	Median wage paid	TQ	Third quartile wage
AEX	Average experienced wage	AXR	Average experienced range	HI	Highest wage paid	M	Monthly	MWR	Median wage range	W	Weekly
ATC	Average total compensation	D	Daily	HR	High end range	MCC	Median cash compensation	S	See annotated source	Y	Yearly

Occupation/Type/Industry	Location	Per	Low	Mid	High	Source	Date
Economist	Chicago-Naperville-Joliet MSA, IL-IN-WI	Y	64530 FQ	80640 MW	103770 TQ	USBLS	5/07
	Iowa	Y	50860 FQ	58580 MW	66220 TQ	USBLS	5/07
	Kentucky	Y	40616 FQ	51818 MW	66824 TQ	KYBLS	2008
	Louisville-Jefferson County MSA, KY-IN	Y	46120 FQ	56230 MW	78250 TQ	USBLS	5/07
	Louisiana	H	29.64 FQ	37.35 MW	44.06 TQ	LABLS	1/08-3/08
	Baton Rouge MSA, LA	Y	65700 FQ	80430 MW	92910 TQ	USBLS	5/07
	Maine	Y	42900 FQ	49150 MW	62640 TQ	USBLS	5/07
	Maryland	Y		105025 MW		MDBLS	3/08
	Baltimore-Towson MSA, MD	Y	83070 FQ	94960 MW	111480 TQ	USBLS	5/07
	Bethesda-Gaithersburg-Frederick PMSA, MD	Y	89900 FQ	109930 MW	127380 TQ	USBLS	5/07
	Massachusetts	Y	51240 FQ	65250 MW	93240 TQ	USBLS	5/07
	Boston-Cambridge-Quincy NECTA, MA	Y	52000 FQ	65780 MW	94240 TQ	USBLS	5/07
	Michigan	Y	62420 FQ	76210 MW	92760 TQ	USBLS	5/07
	Detroit-Warren-Livonia MSA, MI	Y	59760 FQ	74620 MW	93060 TQ	USBLS	5/07
	Warren-Troy-Farmington Hills PMSA, MI	Y	79400 FQ	89550 MW	98510 TQ	USBLS	5/07
	Minnesota	Y	44558 FQ	50773 MW	63777 TQ	MNBLS	10/08-12/08
	Minneapolis-Saint Paul MSA, MN-WI	Y	45060 FQ	52907 MW	64541 TQ	MNBLS	10/08-12/08
	Mississippi	Y	55880 FQ	66680 MW	94050 TQ	USBLS	5/07
	Jackson MSA, MS	Y	56580 FQ	65570 MW	95050 TQ	USBLS	5/07
	Missouri	Y	51040 FQ	73250 MW	99550 TQ	USBLS	5/07
	Kansas City MSA, MO-KS	Y	65680 FQ	81550 MW	105020 TQ	USBLS	5/07
	St. Louis MSA, MO-IL	Y	51970 FQ	73980 MW	115190 TQ	USBLS	5/07
	Montana	Y	34870 FQ	40870 MW	59500 TQ	USBLS	5/07
	Nebraska	Y	53700 FQ	85870 MW	98460 TQ	USBLS	5/07
	Lincoln MSA, NE	Y	89810 FQ	96430 MW	103060 TQ	USBLS	5/07
	Nevada	H	26.68 FQ	33.49 MW	40.54 TQ	NVBLS	5/08
	New Jersey	Y	74350 FQ	90560 MW	104760 TQ	USBLS	5/07
	New York	Y	69930 FQ	87260 MW	109820 TQ	USBLS	5/07
	Albany-Schenectady-Troy MSA, NY	Y	59480 FQ	74780 MW	91030 TQ	USBLS	5/07
	New York-Northern New Jersey-Long Island MSA, NY-NJ-PA	Y	83550 FQ	100010 MW	121690 TQ	USBLS	5/07
	North Carolina	Y	56950 FQ	73200 MW	87750 TQ	USBLS	5/07
	Charlotte-Gastonia-Concord MSA, NC-SC	Y	60940 FQ	73630 MW	88640 TQ	USBLS	5/07
	Raleigh-Cary MSA, NC	Y	52850 FQ	64910 MW	76320 TQ	USBLS	5/07
	Ohio	Y	47550 FQ	67690 MW	91050 TQ	USBLS	5/07
	Cleveland-Elyria-Mentor MSA, OH	Y	67830 FQ	84570 MW	99260 TQ	USBLS	5/07
	Oklahoma	Y	38010 FQ	46690 MW	57370 TQ	USBLS	5/07
	Oregon	H	30.28 FQ	36.81 MW	45.37 TQ	ORBLS	5/08
	Portland-Vancouver-Beaverton MSA, OR-WA	Y	65950 FQ	78900 MW	95220 TQ	USBLS	5/07
	Pennsylvania	Y	67050 FQ	82840 MW	101480 TQ	USBLS	5/07
	Philadelphia-Camden-Wilmington MSA, PA-NJ-DE-MD	Y	69880 FQ	84940 MW	105860 TQ	USBLS	5/07
	Pittsburgh MSA, PA	Y	63790 FQ	83330 MW	97690 TQ	USBLS	5/07
	South Carolina	Y	48680 FQ	60830 MW	76570 TQ	USBLS	5/07
	Columbia MSA, SC	Y	50020 FQ	60050 MW	73430 TQ	USBLS	5/07
	South Dakota	Y	32563 FQ	39697 MW	54749 TQ	SDBLS	7/08-9/08
	Tennessee	Y	50590 FQ	72990 MW	80670 TQ	USBLS	5/07
	Texas	Y	37810 FQ	56410 MW	96090 TQ	USBLS	5/07
	Austin-Round Rock MSA, TX	Y	33640 FQ	38200 MW	67240 TQ	USBLS	5/07
	Dallas-Fort Worth-Arlington MSA, TX	Y	47920 FQ	75430 MW	99170 TQ	USBLS	5/07
	Houston-Sugar Land-Baytown MSA, TX	Y	51950 FQ	81640 MW	103860 TQ	USBLS	5/07
	San Antonio MSA, TX	Y	36560 FQ	59410 MW	119970 TQ	USBLS	5/07
	Utah	Y	54320 FQ	64200 MW	80250 TQ	USBLS	5/07
	Salt Lake City MSA, UT	Y	54890 FQ	64560 MW	80040 TQ	USBLS	5/07
	Vermont	Y	57380 FQ	72080 MW	99150 TQ	USBLS	5/07
	Burlington-South Burlington MSA, VT	Y	47710 FQ	70680 MW	91380 TQ	USBLS	5/07

Occupation/Type/Industry	Location	Per	Low	Mid	High	Source	Date
Economist	Virginia	Y	62320 FQ	87380 MW	130770 TQ	USBLS	5/07
	Richmond MSA, VA	Y	65570 FQ	76870 MW	90560 TQ	USBLS	5/07
	Washington	H	28.44 FQ	32.95 MW	39.17 TQ	WABLS	3/08
	Seattle-Tacoma-Bellevue MSA, WA	Y	63060 FQ	74210 MW	84940 TQ	USBLS	5/07
	Wisconsin	Y	51120 FQ	65390 MW	95480 TQ	USBLS	5/07
Editor	Alabama	Y	29740 FQ	40950 MW	54520 TQ	USBLS	5/07
	Birmingham-Hoover MSA, AL	Y	37030 FQ	45330 MW	54230 TQ	USBLS	5/07
	Tuscaloosa MSA, AL	Y	23960 FQ	36810 MW	54130 TQ	USBLS	5/07
	Alaska	Y	38920 FQ	49360 MW	69330 TQ	USBLS	5/07
	Anchorage MSA, AK	Y	39020 FQ	52000 MW	75280 TQ	USBLS	5/07
	Arizona	Y	33720 FQ	41230 MW	55470 TQ	USBLS	5/07
	Phoenix-Mesa-Scottsdale MSA, AZ	Y	35580 FQ	43610 MW	58420 TQ	USBLS	5/07
	Tucson MSA, AZ	Y	31610 FQ	40210 MW	51160 TQ	USBLS	5/07
	Arkansas	Y	29470 FQ	36810 MW	50160 TQ	USBLS	5/07
	Little Rock-North Little Rock MSA, AR	Y	34500 FQ	45130 MW	64400 TQ	USBLS	5/07
	California	H	18.51 FQ	24.19 MW	34.05 TQ	CABLS	1/08-3/08
	Los Angeles-Long Beach-Glendale PMSA, CA	H	18.41 FQ	23.25 MW	33.00 TQ	CABLS	1/08-3/08
	Oakland-Fremont-Hayward MSA, CA	H	16.08 FQ	22.11 MW	30.90 TQ	CABLS	1/08-3/08
	Riverside-San Bernardino-Ontario MSA, CA	H	17.95 FQ	23.11 MW	29.18 TQ	CABLS	1/08-3/08
	Sacramento-Arden Arcade-Roseville MSA, CA	H	20.10 FQ	24.79 MW	30.83 TQ	CABLS	1/08-3/08
	San Diego-Carlsbad-San Marcos MSA, CA	H	16.85 FQ	19.86 MW	27.46 TQ	CABLS	1/08-3/08
	San Francisco-San Mateo-Redwood PMSA, CA	H	18.93 FQ	28.41 MW	39.61 TQ	CABLS	1/08-3/08
	San Jose-Sunnyvale-Santa Clara MSA, CA	H	22.90 FQ	29.40 MW	36.72 TQ	CABLS	1/08-3/08
	Santa Ana-Anaheim-Irvine PMSA, CA	Y	40230 FQ	58320 MW	74780 TQ	USBLS	5/07
	Colorado	Y	38220 FQ	48520 MW	64050 TQ	USBLS	5/07
	Denver-Aurora MSA, CO	Y	43090 FQ	53400 MW	68180 TQ	USBLS	5/07
	Connecticut	H	18.79 AE	28.34 MW		CTBLS	1/08-3/08
	Bridgeport-Stamford-Norwalk MSA, CT	Y	41940 FQ	57250 MW	73420 TQ	USBLS	5/07
	Hartford-West Hartford-East Hartford MSA, CT	Y	44450 FQ	58720 MW	73790 TQ	USBLS	5/07
	New Haven MSA, CT	Y	44970 FQ	58390 MW	76480 TQ	USBLS	5/07
	Delaware	Y	46780 FQ	56840 MW	81110 TQ	USBLS	5/07
	Wilmington PMSA, DE-MD-NJ	Y	49820 FQ	59230 MW	82630 TQ	USBLS	5/07
	District of Columbia	Y	44580 FQ	56730 MW	71980 TQ	USBLS	5/07
	Washington-Arlington-Alexandria MSA, DC-VA-MD-WV	Y	44370 FQ	57200 MW	72400 TQ	USBLS	5/07
	Florida	Y	33530 FQ	45890 MW	63280 TQ	USBLS	5/07
	Fort Lauderdale-Pompano Beach-Deerfield Beach PMSA, FL	Y	26050 FQ	39010 MW	56340 TQ	USBLS	5/07
	Jacksonville MSA, FL	Y	30840 FQ	45720 MW	58440 TQ	USBLS	5/07
	Miami-Fort Lauderdale-Miami Beach MSA, FL	Y	36230 FQ	47840 MW	67330 TQ	USBLS	5/07
	Orlando-Kissimmee MSA, FL	Y	36730 FQ	47810 MW	60100 TQ	USBLS	5/07
	Tallahassee MSA, FL	Y	31280 FQ	41850 MW	53020 TQ	USBLS	5/07
	Tampa-St. Petersburg-Clearwater MSA, FL	Y	39120 FQ	56530 MW	76230 TQ	USBLS	5/07
	West Palm Beach-Boca Raton-Boynton Beach PMSA, FL	Y	35570 FQ	44550 MW	58150 TQ	USBLS	5/07
	Georgia	Y	41890 FQ	51730 MW	63470 TQ	USBLS	5/07
	Atlanta-Sandy Springs-Marietta MSA, GA	Y	43960 FQ	52990 MW	62920 TQ	USBLS	5/07
	Hawaii	Y	28670 FQ	42820 MW	68090 TQ	USBLS	5/07
	Honolulu MSA, HI	Y	24950 FQ	45330 MW	69310 TQ	USBLS	5/07
	Idaho	Y	26260 FQ	39180 MW	53430 TQ	USBLS	5/07
	Boise City-Nampa MSA, ID	Y	36110 FQ	43820 MW	55230 TQ	USBLS	5/07
	Illinois	Y	38130 FQ	47780 MW	63160 TQ	USBLS	5/07

AE Average entry wage	**AW** Average wage paid	**FQ** First quartile wage	**LO** Lowest wage paid	**MTC** Median total compensation	**TCC** Total cash compensation
AER Average entry range	**AWR** Average wage range	**H** Hourly	**LR** Low end range	**MW** Median wage paid	**TQ** Third quartile wage
AEX Average experienced wage	**AXR** Average experienced range	**HI** Highest wage paid	**M** Monthly	**MWR** Median wage range	**W** Weekly
ATC Average total compensation	**D** Daily	**HR** High end range	**MCC** Median cash compensation	**S** See annotated source	**Y** Yearly

Occupation/Type/Industry	Location	Per	Low	Mid	High	Source	Date
Editor	Chicago-Naperville-Joliet MSA, IL-IN-WI	Y	40420 FQ	48780 MW	64140 TQ	USBLS	5/07
	Indiana	Y	31090 FQ	39510 MW	53460 TQ	USBLS	5/07
	Gary PMSA, IN	Y	34940 FQ	44230 MW	59350 TQ	USBLS	5/07
	Indianapolis-Carmel MSA, IN	Y	31090 FQ	39980 MW	58600 TQ	USBLS	5/07
	Iowa	Y	26550 FQ	36740 MW	49890 TQ	USBLS	5/07
	Des Moines-West Des Moines MSA, IA	Y	34090 FQ	47140 MW	61640 TQ	USBLS	5/07
	Kansas	Y	26690 FQ	35170 MW	47960 TQ	USBLS	5/07
	Wichita MSA, KS	Y	29420 FQ	40480 MW	53710 TQ	USBLS	5/07
	Kentucky	Y	29386 FQ	38812 MW	54914 TQ	KYBLS	2008
	Louisville-Jefferson County MSA, KY-IN	Y	33350 FQ	46120 MW	63650 TQ	USBLS	5/07
	Louisiana	H	15.25 FQ	20.24 MW	25.16 TQ	LABLS	1/08-3/08
	Baton Rouge MSA, LA	Y	34050 FQ	42690 MW	52740 TQ	USBLS	5/07
	New Orleans-Metairie-Kenner MSA, LA	Y	37410 FQ	46930 MW	69620 TQ	USBLS	5/07
	Shreveport-Bossier City MSA, LA	Y	24430 FQ	37520 MW	51060 TQ	USBLS	5/07
	Maine	Y	33010 FQ	42040 MW	58140 TQ	USBLS	5/07
	Lewiston-Auburn MSA, ME	Y	29290 FQ	41450 MW	62150 TQ	USBLS	5/07
	Portland-South Portland-Biddeford MSA, ME	Y	50260 FQ	58450 MW	65500 TQ	USBLS	5/07
	Maryland	Y		51350 MW		MDBLS	3/08
	Baltimore-Towson MSA, MD	Y	32380 FQ	44610 MW	63560 TQ	USBLS	5/07
	Bethesda-Gaithersburg-Frederick PMSA, MD	Y	48370 FQ	59270 MW	73420 TQ	USBLS	5/07
	Massachusetts	Y	43320 FQ	58060 MW	74400 TQ	USBLS	5/07
	Boston-Cambridge-Quincy NECTA, MA	Y	46110 FQ	59400 MW	75080 TQ	USBLS	5/07
	Springfield MSA, MA-CT	Y	31730 FQ	43690 MW	60110 TQ	USBLS	5/07
	Worcester MSA, MA-CT	Y	31490 FQ	41710 MW	52880 TQ	USBLS	5/07
	Michigan	Y	33710 FQ	43990 MW	60500 TQ	USBLS	5/07
	Detroit-Warren-Livonia MSA, MI	Y	38330 FQ	48030 MW	66040 TQ	USBLS	5/07
	Grand Rapids-Wyoming MSA, MI	Y	29720 FQ	39480 MW	58390 TQ	USBLS	5/07
	Lansing-East Lansing MSA, MI	Y	41080 FQ	52620 MW	60960 TQ	USBLS	5/07
	Warren-Troy-Farmington Hills PMSA, MI	Y	38440 FQ	49120 MW	63690 TQ	USBLS	5/07
	Minnesota	Y	36492 FQ	47038 MW	65242 TQ	MNBLS	10/08-12/08
	Duluth-Superior MSA, MN-WI	Y	29838 FQ	41765 MW	51819 TQ	MNBLS	10/08-12/08
	Minneapolis-Saint Paul MSA, MN-WI	Y	37779 FQ	48523 MW	68695 TQ	MNBLS	10/08-12/08
	Rochester MSA, MN	Y	29625 FQ	61052 MW	75829 TQ	MNBLS	10/08-12/08
	Mississippi	Y	28830 FQ	40420 MW	51510 TQ	USBLS	5/07
	Jackson MSA, MS	Y	34770 FQ	47590 MW	59940 TQ	USBLS	5/07
	Missouri	Y	27470 FQ	35880 MW	51680 TQ	USBLS	5/07
	Kansas City MSA, MO-KS	Y	30630 FQ	36370 MW	55980 TQ	USBLS	5/07
	St. Louis MSA, MO-IL	Y	37320 FQ	51990 MW	81100 TQ	USBLS	5/07
	Montana	Y	28470 FQ	34720 MW	41600 TQ	USBLS	5/07
	Nebraska	Y	28340 FQ	35020 MW	45970 TQ	USBLS	5/07
	Omaha-Council Bluffs MSA, NE-IA	Y	28930 FQ	38240 MW	47530 TQ	USBLS	5/07
	Nevada	H	15.84 FQ	23.60 MW	32.05 TQ	NVBLS	5/08
	Las Vegas-Paradise MSA, NV	H	19.28 FQ	28.55 MW	41.32 TQ	NVBLS	5/08
	New Hampshire	H	15.88 AE	21.79 MW	27.95 AEX	NHBLS	6/08
	Manchester MSA, NH	Y	48020 FQ	69800 MW	76940 TQ	USBLS	5/07
	Nashua NECTA, NH-MA	Y	35070 FQ	43700 MW	56570 TQ	USBLS	5/07
	New Jersey	Y	38250 FQ	51090 MW	67990 TQ	USBLS	5/07
	Camden PMSA, NJ	Y	33580 FQ	42290 MW	56280 TQ	USBLS	5/07
	Edison PMSA, NJ	Y	37050 FQ	48800 MW	64470 TQ	USBLS	5/07
	Newark-Union PMSA, NJ-PA	Y	38940 FQ	55340 MW	72140 TQ	USBLS	5/07
	New Mexico	Y	33210 FQ	43110 MW	57790 TQ	USBLS	5/07
	Albuquerque MSA, NM	Y	35870 FQ	47180 MW	59020 TQ	USBLS	5/07
	New York	Y	43340 FQ	61720 MW	92470 TQ	USBLS	5/07
	Albany-Schenectady-Troy MSA, NY	Y	37330 FQ	54960 MW	70750 TQ	USBLS	5/07
	Buffalo-Niagara Falls MSA, NY	Y	34150 FQ	45330 MW	72440 TQ	USBLS	5/07
	Nassau-Suffolk PMSA, NY	Y	43740 FQ	66630 MW	93650 TQ	USBLS	5/07

Editor

Occupation/Type/Industry	Location	Per	Low	Mid	High	Source	Date
Editor	New York-Northern New Jersey-Long Island MSA, NY-NJ-PA	Y	44310 FQ	61730 MW	90590 TQ	USBLS	5/07
	North Carolina	Y	34000 FQ	47270 MW	60500 TQ	USBLS	5/07
	Charlotte-Gastonia-Concord MSA, NC-SC	Y	33120 FQ	52980 MW	64350 TQ	USBLS	5/07
	Raleigh-Cary MSA, NC	Y	43920 FQ	53880 MW	62430 TQ	USBLS	5/07
	North Dakota	Y	24940 FQ	37380 MW	51290 TQ	USBLS	5/07
	Fargo MSA, ND-MN	Y	30550 FQ	41300 MW	52710 TQ	USBLS	5/07
	Ohio	Y	31780 FQ	42530 MW	57940 TQ	USBLS	5/07
	Cincinnati-Middletown MSA, OH-KY-IN	Y	30810 FQ	41710 MW	57470 TQ	USBLS	5/07
	Cleveland-Elyria-Mentor MSA, OH	Y	36050 FQ	47110 MW	65170 TQ	USBLS	5/07
	Columbus MSA, OH	Y	29710 FQ	36270 MW	47790 TQ	USBLS	5/07
	Dayton MSA, OH	Y	31940 FQ	42420 MW	58230 TQ	USBLS	5/07
	Oklahoma	Y	23680 FQ	30020 MW	39500 TQ	USBLS	5/07
	Oklahoma City MSA, OK	Y	23520 FQ	28230 MW	35050 TQ	USBLS	5/07
	Oregon	H	16.46 FQ	21.32 MW	27.46 TQ	ORBLS	5/08
	Portland-Vancouver-Beaverton MSA, OR-WA	Y	36900 FQ	47190 MW	60150 TQ	USBLS	5/07
	Pennsylvania	Y	33490 FQ	43370 MW	57610 TQ	USBLS	5/07
	Allentown-Bethlehem-Easton MSA, PA-NJ	Y	33250 FQ	42870 MW	52760 TQ	USBLS	5/07
	Philadelphia-Camden-Wilmington MSA, PA-NJ-DE-MD	Y	35380 FQ	46040 MW	62390 TQ	USBLS	5/07
	Pittsburgh MSA, PA	Y	35660 FQ	47150 MW	65340 TQ	USBLS	5/07
	Rhode Island	Y	50360 FQ	67010 MW	76450 TQ	USBLS	5/07
	Providence-Fall River-Warwick MSA, RI-MA	Y	50470 FQ	67080 MW	76480 TQ	USBLS	5/07
	South Carolina	Y	30400 FQ	44360 MW	62620 TQ	USBLS	5/07
	Charleston-North Charleston MSA, SC	Y	51750 FQ	63180 MW	76880 TQ	USBLS	5/07
	Columbia MSA, SC	Y	31880 FQ	38250 MW	57630 TQ	USBLS	5/07
	South Dakota	Y	30619 FQ	36880 MW	43799 TQ	SDBLS	7/08-9/08
	Rapid City MSA, SD	Y	31215 FQ	36262 MW	44004 TQ	SDBLS	7/08-9/08
	Sioux Falls MSA, SD	Y	34624 FQ	40554 MW	50611 TQ	SDBLS	7/08-9/08
	Tennessee	Y	24960 FQ	38750 MW	56700 TQ	USBLS	5/07
	Kingsport-Bristol-Bristol MSA, TN-VA	Y	24410 FQ	31530 MW	37890 TQ	USBLS	5/07
	Memphis MSA, TN-MS-AR	Y	38610 FQ	50080 MW	58990 TQ	USBLS	5/07
	Nashville-Davidson-Murfreesboro MSA, TN	Y	22210 FQ	32930 MW	56830 TQ	USBLS	5/07
	Texas	Y	33130 FQ	45220 MW	61400 TQ	USBLS	5/07
	Austin-Round Rock MSA, TX	Y	38900 FQ	47970 MW	62280 TQ	USBLS	5/07
	Dallas-Fort Worth-Arlington MSA, TX	Y	36920 FQ	50290 MW	69690 TQ	USBLS	5/07
	El Paso MSA, TX	Y	18050 FQ	26810 MW	44210 TQ	USBLS	5/07
	Houston-Sugar Land-Baytown MSA, TX	Y	39880 FQ	47610 MW	63740 TQ	USBLS	5/07
	San Antonio MSA, TX	Y	32010 FQ	44100 MW	59220 TQ	USBLS	5/07
	Utah	Y	32410 FQ	41920 MW	55630 TQ	USBLS	5/07
	Salt Lake City MSA, UT	Y	35270 FQ	44390 MW	56360 TQ	USBLS	5/07
	Vermont	Y	32970 FQ	40170 MW	52750 TQ	USBLS	5/07
	Burlington-South Burlington MSA, VT	Y	29860 FQ	40370 MW	51640 TQ	USBLS	5/07
	Virginia	Y	33010 FQ	47630 MW	64610 TQ	USBLS	5/07
	Richmond MSA, VA	Y	27730 FQ	38910 MW	53160 TQ	USBLS	5/07
	Virginia Beach-Norfolk-Newport News MSA, VA-NC	Y	30210 FQ	35000 MW	43500 TQ	USBLS	5/07
	Washington	H	20.89 FQ	28.68 MW	37.28 TQ	WABLS	3/08
	Bremerton-Silverdale MSA, WA	Y	33550 FQ	41030 MW	45650 TQ	USBLS	5/07
	Seattle-Tacoma-Bellevue MSA, WA	Y	51030 FQ	65490 MW	82750 TQ	USBLS	5/07
	West Virginia	Y	28261 FQ	37239 MW	48182 TQ	WVBLS	7/08-9/08
	Wisconsin	Y	30220 FQ	40060 MW	55990 TQ	USBLS	5/07
	Milwaukee-Waukesha-West Allis MSA, WI	Y	35570 FQ	50830 MW	63530 TQ	USBLS	5/07
	Wyoming	Y	32709 FQ	42807 MW	51560 TQ	WYBLS	9/08
	Cheyenne MSA, WY	Y	32804 FQ	38116 MW	46473 TQ	WYBLS	9/08

AE	Average entry wage	AW	Average wage paid	FQ	First quartile wage	LO	Lowest wage paid	MTC	Median total compensation	TCC	Total cash compensation
AER	Average entry range	AWR	Average wage range	H	Hourly	LR	Low end range	MW	Median wage paid	TQ	Third quartile wage
AEX	Average experienced wage	AXR	Average experienced range	HI	Highest wage paid	M	Monthly	MWR	Median wage range	W	Weekly
ATC	Average total compensation	D	Daily	HR	High end range	MCC	Median cash compensation	S	See annotated source	Y	Yearly

Occupation/Type/Industry	Location	Per	Low	Mid	High	Source	Date
Editor	Puerto Rico	Y	23970 FQ	32950 MW	47610 TQ	USBLS	5/07
	San Juan-Caguas-Guaynabo MSA, PR	Y	24030 FQ	33020 MW	47680 TQ	USBLS	5/07
Editorial Assistant							
State Supreme Court	Michigan	Y			32218 HI	LSJ02	7/11/07
Editorial Director	Midwest	Y		81600 AW		FOLIO	2008
	Northeast	Y		91600 AW		FOLIO	2008
	South	Y		81100 AW		FOLIO	2008
	West	Y		82500 AW		FOLIO	2008
Education Administrator							
Elementary and Secondary School	Alabama	Y	58760 FQ	69190 MW	79390 TQ	USBLS	5/07
Elementary and Secondary School	Birmingham-Hoover MSA, AL	Y	61330 FQ	73210 MW	85450 TQ	USBLS	5/07
Elementary and Secondary School	Tuscaloosa MSA, AL	Y	62440 FQ	72510 MW	85060 TQ	USBLS	5/07
Elementary and Secondary School	Alaska	Y	76850 FQ	88270 MW	99420 TQ	USBLS	5/07
Elementary and Secondary School	Arizona	Y	57480 FQ	71420 MW	86950 TQ	USBLS	5/07
Elementary and Secondary School	Phoenix-Mesa-Scottsdale MSA, AZ	Y	61190 FQ	75310 MW	90060 TQ	USBLS	5/07
Elementary and Secondary School	Prescott MSA, AZ	Y	45660 FQ	55560 MW	68920 TQ	USBLS	5/07
Elementary and Secondary School	Tucson MSA, AZ	Y	58030 FQ	69630 MW	84700 TQ	USBLS	5/07
Elementary and Secondary School	Arkansas	Y	59470 FQ	68130 MW	77440 TQ	USBLS	5/07
Elementary and Secondary School	Fort Smith MSA, AR-OK	Y	61040 FQ	68020 MW	75990 TQ	USBLS	5/07
Elementary and Secondary School	Little Rock-North Little Rock MSA, AR	Y	61450 FQ	71590 MW	80660 TQ	USBLS	5/07
Elementary and Secondary School	California	Y		99226 AW		CABLS	1/08-3/08
Elementary and Secondary School	Fresno MSA, CA	Y		101698 AW		CABLS	1/08-3/08
Elementary and Secondary School	Los Angeles-Long Beach-Glendale PMSA, CA	Y		103739 AW		CABLS	1/08-3/08
Elementary and Secondary School	Oakland-Fremont-Hayward MSA, CA	Y		98929 AW		CABLS	1/08-3/08
Elementary and Secondary School	Oxnard-Thousand Oaks-Ventura MSA, CA	Y		95831 AW		CABLS	1/08-3/08
Elementary and Secondary School	Riverside-San Bernardino-Ontario MSA, CA	Y		102703 AW		CABLS	1/08-3/08
Elementary and Secondary School	Sacramento-Arden Arcade-Roseville MSA, CA	Y		91011 AW		CABLS	1/08-3/08
Elementary and Secondary School	San Diego-Carlsbad-San Marcos MSA, CA	Y		110108 MW		CABLS	1/08-3/08
Elementary and Secondary School	San Francisco-San Mateo-Redwood PMSA, CA	Y		112077 AW		CABLS	1/08-3/08
Elementary and Secondary School	San Jose-Sunnyvale-Santa Clara MSA, CA	Y		101175 AW		CABLS	1/08-3/08
Elementary and Secondary School	Santa Ana-Anaheim-Irvine PMSA, CA	Y	86880 FQ	105810 MW	121400 TQ	USBLS	5/07
Elementary and Secondary School	Santa Rosa-Petaluma MSA, CA	Y		76325 AW		CABLS	1/08-3/08
Elementary and Secondary School	Colorado	Y	66100 FQ	76810 MW	89640 TQ	USBLS	5/07
Elementary and Secondary School	Denver-Aurora MSA, CO	Y	70620 FQ	81710 MW	94810 TQ	USBLS	5/07
Elementary and Secondary School	Bridgeport-Stamford-Norwalk MSA, CT	Y	97950 FQ	113680 MW	127870 TQ	USBLS	5/07
Elementary and Secondary School	Hartford-West Hartford-East Hartford MSA, CT	Y	97780 FQ	109390 MW	120800 TQ	USBLS	5/07
Elementary and Secondary School	Delaware	Y	86770 FQ	100350 MW	115640 TQ	USBLS	5/07
Elementary and Secondary School	Wilmington PMSA, DE-MD-NJ	Y	89080 FQ	103200 MW	118160 TQ	USBLS	5/07
Elementary and Secondary School	District of Columbia	Y	78610 FQ	91800 MW	101910 TQ	USBLS	5/07
Elementary and Secondary School	Washington-Arlington-Alexandria MSA, DC-VA-MD-WV	Y	79460 FQ	95060 MW	110270 TQ	USBLS	5/07
Elementary and Secondary School	Florida	Y	70060 FQ	82010 MW	95910 TQ	USBLS	5/07
Elementary and Secondary School	Jacksonville MSA, FL	Y	69320 FQ	78370 MW	91830 TQ	USBLS	5/07
Elementary and Secondary School	Miami-Fort Lauderdale-Miami Beach MSA, FL	Y	71310 FQ	87910 MW	101370 TQ	USBLS	5/07
Elementary and Secondary School	Orlando-Kissimmee MSA, FL	Y	76310 FQ	88240 MW	97740 TQ	USBLS	5/07
Elementary and Secondary School	Tampa-St. Petersburg-Clearwater MSA, FL	Y	71480 FQ	80730 MW	93120 TQ	USBLS	5/07
Elementary and Secondary School	West Palm Beach-Boca Raton-Boynton Beach PMSA, FL	Y	84640 FQ	93410 MW	102380 TQ	USBLS	5/07
Elementary and Secondary School	Georgia	Y	67510 FQ	79850 MW	93380 TQ	USBLS	5/07
Elementary and Secondary School	Atlanta-Sandy Springs-Marietta MSA, GA	Y	71340 FQ	82800 MW	95830 TQ	USBLS	5/07

AE	Average entry wage	AW	Average wage paid	FQ	First quartile wage
AER	Average entry range	AWR	Average wage range	H	Hourly
AEX	Average experienced wage	AXR	Average experienced range	HI	Highest wage paid
ATC	Average total compensation	D	Daily	HR	High end range

LO	Lowest wage paid	MTC	Median total compensation	TCC	Total cash compensation
LR	Low end range	MW	Median wage paid	TQ	Third quartile wage
M	Monthly	MWR	Median wage range	W	Weekly
MCC	Median cash compensation	S	See annotated source	Y	Yearly

Occupation/Type/Industry	Location	Per	Low	Mid	High	Source	Date
Education Administrator							
Elementary and Secondary School	Hawaii	Y	51720 FQ	68890 MW	92210 TQ	USBLS	5/07
Elementary and Secondary School	Honolulu MSA, HI	Y	40580 FQ	59310 MW	77900 TQ	USBLS	5/07
Elementary and Secondary School	Idaho	Y	67140 FQ	75040 MW	85030 TQ	USBLS	5/07
Elementary and Secondary School	Boise City-Nampa MSA, ID	Y	68970 FQ	78310 MW	89550 TQ	USBLS	5/07
Elementary and Secondary School	Illinois	Y	72210 FQ	94760 MW	117200 TQ	USBLS	5/07
Elementary and Secondary School	Chicago-Naperville-Joliet MSA, IL-IN-WI	Y	78310 FQ	101150 MW	121740 TQ	USBLS	5/07
Elementary and Secondary School	Indiana	Y	60590 FQ	73980 MW	85500 TQ	USBLS	5/07
Elementary and Secondary School	Gary PMSA, IN	Y	67230 FQ	76860 MW	87830 TQ	USBLS	5/07
Elementary and Secondary School	Indianapolis-Carmel MSA, IN	Y	53870 FQ	68470 MW	86590 TQ	USBLS	5/07
Elementary and Secondary School	Iowa	Y	61630 FQ	74490 MW	87250 TQ	USBLS	5/07
Elementary and Secondary School	Des Moines-West Des Moines MSA, IA	Y	64580 FQ	81950 MW	93770 TQ	USBLS	5/07
Elementary and Secondary School	Waterloo-Cedar Falls MSA, IA	Y	58550 FQ	75450 MW	86700 TQ	USBLS	5/07
Elementary and Secondary School	Kansas	Y	59990 FQ	67860 MW	76340 TQ	USBLS	5/07
Elementary and Secondary School	Wichita MSA, KS	Y	60930 FQ	67680 MW	75220 TQ	USBLS	5/07
Elementary and Secondary School	Kentucky	Y	64515 FQ	74871 MW	85979 TQ	KYBLS	2008
Elementary and Secondary School	Louisville-Jefferson County MSA, KY-IN	Y	70610 FQ	83420 MW	97410 TQ	USBLS	5/07
Elementary and Secondary School	Louisiana	Y		61027 AW		LABLS	1/08-3/08
Elementary and Secondary School	Baton Rouge MSA, LA	Y	55870 FQ	62760 MW	72090 TQ	USBLS	5/07
Elementary and Secondary School	New Orleans-Metairie-Kenner MSA, LA	Y	54530 FQ	63590 MW	73180 TQ	USBLS	5/07
Elementary and Secondary School	Maine	Y	56480 FQ	66870 MW	75950 TQ	USBLS	5/07
Elementary and Secondary School	Portland-South Portland-Biddeford MSA, ME	Y	62160 FQ	72070 MW	80950 TQ	USBLS	5/07
Elementary and Secondary School	Maryland	Y		91725 MW		MDBLS	3/08
Elementary and Secondary School	Baltimore-Towson MSA, MD	Y	75250 FQ	88090 MW	100340 TQ	USBLS	5/07
Elementary and Secondary School	Bethesda-Gaithersburg-Frederick PMSA, MD	Y	83490 FQ	99780 MW	115840 TQ	USBLS	5/07
Elementary and Secondary School	Salisbury MSA, MD	Y	68840 FQ	78040 MW	85290 TQ	USBLS	5/07
Elementary and Secondary School	Massachusetts	Y	74430 FQ	87820 MW	100690 TQ	USBLS	5/07
Elementary and Secondary School	Boston-Cambridge-Quincy NECTA, MA	Y	78640 FQ	91610 MW	105540 TQ	USBLS	5/07
Elementary and Secondary School	New Bedford MSA, MA	Y	71610 FQ	81680 MW	93570 TQ	USBLS	5/07
Elementary and Secondary School	Worcester MSA, MA-CT	Y	79680 FQ	90200 MW	99180 TQ	USBLS	5/07
Elementary and Secondary School	Michigan	Y	73580 FQ	87560 MW	102240 TQ	USBLS	5/07
Elementary and Secondary School	Ann Arbor MSA, MI	Y	85840 FQ	98510 MW	114740 TQ	USBLS	5/07
Elementary and Secondary School	Detroit-Warren-Livonia MSA, MI	Y	83320 FQ	97050 MW	112700 TQ	USBLS	5/07
Elementary and Secondary School	Grand Rapids-Wyoming MSA, MI	Y	70900 FQ	83090 MW	93860 TQ	USBLS	5/07
Elementary and Secondary School	Warren-Troy-Farmington Hills PMSA, MI	Y	85950 FQ	101940 MW	118230 TQ	USBLS	5/07
Elementary and Secondary School	Minnesota	Y	76562 FQ	91565 MW	105495 TQ	MNBLS	10/08-12/08
Elementary and Secondary School	Duluth-Superior MSA, MN-WI	Y	71734 FQ	82494 MW	91826 TQ	MNBLS	10/08-12/08
Elementary and Secondary School	Minneapolis-Saint Paul MSA, MN-WI	Y	83933 FQ	97717 MW	110229 TQ	MNBLS	10/08-12/08
Elementary and Secondary School	Rochester MSA, MN	Y	72240 FQ	84688 MW	99611 TQ	MNBLS	10/08-12/08
Elementary and Secondary School	Mississippi	Y	59040 FQ	68530 MW	77530 TQ	USBLS	5/07
Elementary and Secondary School	Jackson MSA, MS	Y	62470 FQ	71980 MW	81120 TQ	USBLS	5/07
Elementary and Secondary School	Missouri	Y	59430 FQ	72060 MW	87110 TQ	USBLS	5/07
Elementary and Secondary School	Jefferson City MSA, MO	Y	58000 FQ	65250 MW	71510 TQ	USBLS	5/07
Elementary and Secondary School	Kansas City MSA, MO-KS	Y	66020 FQ	75590 MW	88520 TQ	USBLS	5/07
Elementary and Secondary School	St. Louis MSA, MO-IL	Y	69380 FQ	82890 MW	96280 TQ	USBLS	5/07
Elementary and Secondary School	Springfield MSA, MO	Y	55570 FQ	65880 MW	78630 TQ	USBLS	5/07
Elementary and Secondary School	Montana	Y	54470 FQ	64360 MW	75150 TQ	USBLS	5/07
Elementary and Secondary School	Billings MSA, MT	Y	44570 FQ	66790 MW	77660 TQ	USBLS	5/07
Elementary and Secondary School	Nebraska	Y	62350 FQ	72840 MW	83770 TQ	USBLS	5/07
Elementary and Secondary School	Lincoln MSA, NE	Y	36730 FQ	76490 MW	93790 TQ	USBLS	5/07
Elementary and Secondary School	Omaha-Council Bluffs MSA, NE-IA	Y	64430 FQ	73450 MW	82520 TQ	USBLS	5/07
Elementary and Secondary School	Nevada	Y	69316 FQ	80470 MW	91383 TQ	NVBLS	5/08
Elementary and Secondary School	Las Vegas-Paradise MSA, NV	Y	69787 FQ	81998 MW	92071 TQ	NVBLS	5/08
Elementary and Secondary School	New Hampshire	Y	56371 AE	75600 MW	83316 AEX	NHBLS	6/08
Elementary and Secondary School	Manchester MSA, NH	Y	67020 FQ	74640 MW	83220 TQ	USBLS	5/07
Elementary and Secondary School	Nashua NECTA, NH-MA	Y	65920 FQ	76290 MW	88620 TQ	USBLS	5/07
Elementary and Secondary School	New Jersey	Y	85270 FQ	102860 MW	120160 TQ	USBLS	5/07
Elementary and Secondary School	Camden PMSA, NJ	Y	86990 FQ	100780 MW	116100 TQ	USBLS	5/07
Elementary and Secondary School	Edison PMSA, NJ	Y	82220 FQ	100630 MW	117660 TQ	USBLS	5/07
Elementary and Secondary School	Newark-Union PMSA, NJ-PA	Y	88090 FQ	105770 MW	123620 TQ	USBLS	5/07

AE	Average entry wage	AW	Average wage paid	FQ	First quartile wage	LO	Lowest wage paid	MTC Median total compensation	TCC Total cash compensation
AER	Average entry range	AWR	Average wage range	H	Hourly	LR	Low end range	MW Median wage paid	TQ Third quartile wage
AEX	Average experienced wage	AXR	Average experienced range	HI	Highest wage paid	M	Monthly	MWR Median wage range	W Weekly
ATC	Average total compensation	D	Daily	HR	High end range	MCC	Median cash compensation	S See annotated source	Y Yearly

Education Administrator

Occupation/Type/Industry	Location	Per	Low	Mid	High	Source	Date
Elementary and Secondary School	New Mexico	Y	60300 FQ	69550 MW	79800 TQ	USBLS	5/07
Elementary and Secondary School	Albuquerque MSA, NM	Y	59050 FQ	67930 MW	75210 TQ	USBLS	5/07
Elementary and Secondary School	New York	Y	81740 FQ	96060 MW	114690 TQ	USBLS	5/07
Elementary and Secondary School	Albany-Schenectady-Troy MSA, NY	Y	72150 FQ	88410 MW	102720 TQ	USBLS	5/07
Elementary and Secondary School	Binghamton MSA, NY	Y	74880 FQ	86020 MW	96960 TQ	USBLS	5/07
Elementary and Secondary School	Buffalo-Niagara Falls MSA, NY	Y	71890 FQ	87370 MW	101790 TQ	USBLS	5/07
Elementary and Secondary School	Nassau-Suffolk PMSA, NY	Y	106460 FQ	122350 MW	140360 TQ	USBLS	5/07
Elementary and Secondary School	New York-Northern New Jersey-Long Island MSA, NY-NJ-PA	Y	87120 FQ	102110 MW	121560 TQ	USBLS	5/07
Elementary and Secondary School	North Carolina	Y	52280 FQ	63710 MW	78220 TQ	USBLS	5/07
Elementary and Secondary School	Charlotte-Gastonia-Concord MSA, NC-SC	Y	53740 FQ	65890 MW	79730 TQ	USBLS	5/07
Elementary and Secondary School	Durham MSA, NC	Y	56360 FQ	72840 MW	94050 TQ	USBLS	5/07
Elementary and Secondary School	Raleigh-Cary MSA, NC	Y	56460 FQ	68080 MW	81220 TQ	USBLS	5/07
Elementary and Secondary School	Winston-Salem MSA, NC	Y	51380 FQ	62850 MW	78400 TQ	USBLS	5/07
Elementary and Secondary School	North Dakota	Y	55960 FQ	68190 MW	85280 TQ	USBLS	5/07
Elementary and Secondary School	Fargo MSA, ND-MN	Y	75910 FQ	88980 MW	99650 TQ	USBLS	5/07
Elementary and Secondary School	Ohio	Y	75110 FQ	89680 MW	104370 TQ	USBLS	5/07
Elementary and Secondary School	Cincinnati-Middletown MSA, OH-KY-IN	Y	76040 FQ	90380 MW	106020 TQ	USBLS	5/07
Elementary and Secondary School	Cleveland-Elyria-Mentor MSA, OH	Y	85390 FQ	99640 MW	116290 TQ	USBLS	5/07
Elementary and Secondary School	Columbus MSA, OH	Y	79630 FQ	92300 MW	104670 TQ	USBLS	5/07
Elementary and Secondary School	Dayton MSA, OH	Y	79240 FQ	95850 MW	116680 TQ	USBLS	5/07
Elementary and Secondary School	Oklahoma	Y	52300 FQ	60150 MW	69870 TQ	USBLS	5/07
Elementary and Secondary School	Oklahoma City MSA, OK	Y	54070 FQ	62410 MW	72910 TQ	USBLS	5/07
Elementary and Secondary School	Tulsa MSA, OK	Y	53280 FQ	62770 MW	74440 TQ	USBLS	5/07
Elementary and Secondary School	Oregon	Y	72328 FQ	86211 MW	97448 TQ	ORBLS	5/08
Elementary and Secondary School	Portland-Vancouver-Beaverton MSA, OR-WA	Y	77140 FQ	88650 MW	98410 TQ	USBLS	5/07
Elementary and Secondary School	Pennsylvania	Y	68760 FQ	84230 MW	100770 TQ	USBLS	5/07
Elementary and Secondary School	Allentown-Bethlehem-Easton MSA, PA-NJ	Y	68990 FQ	82820 MW	96280 TQ	USBLS	5/07
Elementary and Secondary School	Philadelphia-Camden-Wilmington MSA, PA-NJ-DE-MD	Y	82390 FQ	97920 MW	114940 TQ	USBLS	5/07
Elementary and Secondary School	Pittsburgh MSA, PA	Y	75880 FQ	90920 MW	106970 TQ	USBLS	5/07
Elementary and Secondary School	Rhode Island	Y	77770 FQ	89650 MW	101360 TQ	USBLS	5/07
Elementary and Secondary School	Providence-Fall River-Warwick MSA, RI-MA	Y	74710 FQ	87280 MW	99560 TQ	USBLS	5/07
Elementary and Secondary School	South Carolina	Y	58750 FQ	70690 MW	82320 TQ	USBLS	5/07
Elementary and Secondary School	Charleston-North Charleston MSA, SC	Y	60370 FQ	70650 MW	80250 TQ	USBLS	5/07
Elementary and Secondary School	Columbia MSA, SC	Y	58920 FQ	71090 MW	83900 TQ	USBLS	5/07
Elementary and Secondary School	Florence MSA, SC	Y	63230 FQ	71200 MW	79510 TQ	USBLS	5/07
Elementary and Secondary School	South Dakota	Y	53310 FQ	61909 MW	71455 TQ	SDBLS	7/08-9/08
Elementary and Secondary School	Tennessee	Y	56230 FQ	67220 MW	79830 TQ	USBLS	5/07
Elementary and Secondary School	Memphis MSA, TN-MS-AR	Y	49320 FQ	70010 MW	86910 TQ	USBLS	5/07
Elementary and Secondary School	Nashville-Davidson-Murfreesboro MSA, TN	Y	63480 FQ	73080 MW	82670 TQ	USBLS	5/07
Elementary and Secondary School	Texas	Y	57820 FQ	67120 MW	78280 TQ	USBLS	5/07
Elementary and Secondary School	Austin-Round Rock MSA, TX	Y	56250 FQ	66410 MW	77830 TQ	USBLS	5/07
Elementary and Secondary School	Beaumont-Port Arthur MSA, TX	Y	55530 FQ	64340 MW	73410 TQ	USBLS	5/07
Elementary and Secondary School	Dallas-Fort Worth-Arlington MSA, TX	Y	59850 FQ	70700 MW	81800 TQ	USBLS	5/07
Elementary and Secondary School	El Paso MSA, TX	Y	65450 FQ	75690 MW	85750 TQ	USBLS	5/07
Elementary and Secondary School	Houston-Sugar Land-Baytown MSA, TX	Y	60040 FQ	69900 MW	81190 TQ	USBLS	5/07
Elementary and Secondary School	Midland MSA, TX	Y	49480 FQ	59950 MW	69710 TQ	USBLS	5/07
Elementary and Secondary School	San Antonio MSA, TX	Y	60340 FQ	70250 MW	79440 TQ	USBLS	5/07
Elementary and Secondary School	Utah	Y	65000 FQ	73970 MW	83350 TQ	USBLS	5/07
Elementary and Secondary School	Provo-Orem MSA, UT	Y	67020 FQ	75210 MW	84690 TQ	USBLS	5/07
Elementary and Secondary School	Salt Lake City MSA, UT	Y	67010 FQ	75040 MW	83520 TQ	USBLS	5/07
Elementary and Secondary School	Vermont	Y	55300 FQ	69670 MW	85960 TQ	USBLS	5/07
Elementary and Secondary School	Burlington-South Burlington MSA, VT	Y	52250 FQ	70640 MW	89980 TQ	USBLS	5/07
Elementary and Secondary School	Virginia	Y	64640 FQ	78040 MW	95280 TQ	USBLS	5/07

AE	Average entry wage	AW	Average wage paid	FQ	First quartile wage	LO	Lowest wage paid	MTC	Median total compensation	TCC	Total cash compensation
AER	Average entry range	AWR	Average wage range	H	Hourly	LR	Low end range	MW	Median wage paid	TQ	Third quartile wage
AEX	Average experienced wage	AXR	Average experienced range	HI	Highest wage paid	M	Monthly	MWR	Median wage range	W	Weekly
ATC	Average total compensation	D	Daily	HR	High end range	MCC	Median cash compensation	S	See annotated source	Y	Yearly

464

Education Administrator

Occupation/Type/Industry	Location	Per	Low	Mid	High	Source	Date
Education Administrator							
Elementary and Secondary School	Richmond MSA, VA	Y	66430 FQ	79060 MW	91870 TQ	USBLS	5/07
Elementary and Secondary School	Virginia Beach-Norfolk-Newport News MSA, VA-NC	Y	60400 FQ	72520 MW	86420 TQ	USBLS	5/07
Elementary and Secondary School	Washington	Y		88803 AW		WABLS	3/08
Elementary and Secondary School	Seattle-Tacoma-Bellevue MSA, WA	Y	85260 FQ	94110 MW	103290 TQ	USBLS	5/07
Elementary and Secondary School	West Virginia	Y	50274 FQ	62000 MW	72068 TQ	WVBLS	7/08-9/08
Elementary and Secondary School	Charleston MSA, WV	Y	47980 FQ	61610 MW	71080 TQ	USBLS	5/07
Elementary and Secondary School	Wisconsin	Y	70450 FQ	80740 MW	93570 TQ	USBLS	5/07
Elementary and Secondary School	Milwaukee-Waukesha-West Allis MSA, WI	Y	80220 FQ	93880 MW	106330 TQ	USBLS	5/07
Elementary and Secondary School	Wyoming	Y	67176 FQ	78976 MW	91259 TQ	WYBLS	9/08
Elementary and Secondary School	Cheyenne MSA, WY	Y	75403 FQ	88069 MW	97835 TQ	WYBLS	9/08
Elementary and Secondary School	San Juan-Caguas-Guaynabo MSA, PR	Y	37240 FQ	41340 MW	45600 TQ	USBLS	5/07
Elementary and Secondary School	Virgin Islands	Y	59000 FQ	71460 MW	81110 TQ	USBLS	5/07
Elementary and Secondary School	Guam	Y	46310 FQ	65660 MW	77420 TQ	USBLS	5/07
Postsecondary	Alabama	Y	56540 FQ	78800 MW	102650 TQ	USBLS	5/07
Postsecondary	Tuscaloosa MSA, AL	Y	55810 FQ	72230 MW	95700 TQ	USBLS	5/07
Postsecondary	Alaska	Y	62960 FQ	88650 MW	120090 TQ	USBLS	5/07
Postsecondary	Anchorage MSA, AK	Y	57700 FQ	79640 MW	114280 TQ	USBLS	5/07
Postsecondary	Arizona	Y	55840 FQ	82630 MW	122490 TQ	USBLS	5/07
Postsecondary	Phoenix-Mesa-Scottsdale MSA, AZ	Y	52090 FQ	95200 MW	127190 TQ	USBLS	5/07
Postsecondary	Arkansas	Y	48510 FQ	67120 MW	95150 TQ	USBLS	5/07
Postsecondary	Little Rock-North Little Rock MSA, AR	Y	73230 FQ	102270 MW	127920 TQ	USBLS	5/07
Postsecondary	California	H	24.04 FQ	32.64 MW	47.20 TQ	CABLS	1/08-3/08
Postsecondary	Los Angeles-Long Beach-Glendale PMSA, CA	H	24.03 FQ	32.47 MW	48.23 TQ	CABLS	1/08-3/08
Postsecondary	Oakland-Fremont-Hayward MSA, CA	H	27.20 FQ	35.92 MW	45.80 TQ	CABLS	1/08-3/08
Postsecondary	Riverside-San Bernardino-Ontario MSA, CA	H	27.01 FQ	38.19 MW	52.62 TQ	CABLS	1/08-3/08
Postsecondary	Sacramento-Arden Arcade-Roseville MSA, CA	H	34.41 FQ	48.40 MW	59.80 TQ	CABLS	1/08-3/08
Postsecondary	San Diego-Carlsbad-San Marcos MSA, CA	H	21.55 FQ	25.72 MW	37.67 TQ	CABLS	1/08-3/08
Postsecondary	San Francisco-San Mateo-Redwood PMSA, CA	H	22.62 FQ	31.33 MW	42.98 TQ	CABLS	1/08-3/08
Postsecondary	San Jose-Sunnyvale-Santa Clara MSA, CA	H	26.47 FQ	33.00 MW	47.26 TQ	CABLS	1/08-3/08
Postsecondary	Santa Ana-Anaheim-Irvine PMSA, CA	Y	52940 FQ	63050 MW	97850 TQ	USBLS	5/07
Postsecondary	Santa Rosa-Petaluma MSA, CA	H	21.74 FQ	28.45 MW	38.59 TQ	CABLS	1/08-3/08
Postsecondary	Colorado	Y	54920 FQ	74820 MW	104860 TQ	USBLS	5/07
Postsecondary	Denver-Aurora MSA, CO	Y	57920 FQ	78560 MW	109680 TQ	USBLS	5/07
Postsecondary	Connecticut	H	26.51 AE	43.26 MW		CTBLS	1/08-3/08
Postsecondary	Bridgeport-Stamford-Norwalk MSA, CT	Y	53840 FQ	67350 MW	87310 TQ	USBLS	5/07
Postsecondary	Hartford-West Hartford-East Hartford MSA, CT	Y	70720 FQ	107620 MW		USBLS	5/07
Postsecondary	Waterbury MSA, CT	Y	49460 FQ	67830 MW	93980 TQ	USBLS	5/07
Postsecondary	Delaware	Y	61050 FQ	78630 MW	104760 TQ	USBLS	5/07
Postsecondary	Wilmington PMSA, DE-MD-NJ	Y	57000 FQ	76440 MW	102110 TQ	USBLS	5/07
Postsecondary	District of Columbia	Y	44240 FQ	70850 MW	112550 TQ	USBLS	5/07
Postsecondary	Washington-Arlington-Alexandria MSA, DC-VA-MD-WV	Y	63580 FQ	84220 MW	114740 TQ	USBLS	5/07
Postsecondary	Florida	Y	58640 FQ	75830 MW	96920 TQ	USBLS	5/07
Postsecondary	Fort Lauderdale-Pompano Beach-Deerfield Beach PMSA, FL	Y	71970 FQ	96820 MW	127910 TQ	USBLS	5/07
Postsecondary	Jacksonville MSA, FL	Y	54920 FQ	71230 MW	88650 TQ	USBLS	5/07
Postsecondary	Miami-Fort Lauderdale-Miami Beach MSA, FL	Y	70140 FQ	89050 MW	115870 TQ	USBLS	5/07
Postsecondary	Orlando-Kissimmee MSA, FL	Y	57670 FQ	70700 MW	83540 TQ	USBLS	5/07
Postsecondary	Tallahassee MSA, FL	Y	48790 FQ	63620 MW	83470 TQ	USBLS	5/07
Postsecondary	Tampa-St. Petersburg-Clearwater MSA, FL	Y	73350 FQ	88690 MW	110690 TQ	USBLS	5/07

AE	Average entry wage	AW	Average wage paid	FQ	First quartile wage
AER	Average entry range	AWR	Average wage range	H	Hourly
AEX	Average experienced wage	AXR	Average experienced range	HI	Highest wage paid
ATC	Average total compensation	D	Daily	HR	High end range

LO	Lowest wage paid	MTC	Median total compensation	TCC	Total cash compensation
LR	Low end range	MW	Median wage paid	TQ	Third quartile wage
M	Monthly	MWR	Median wage range	W	Weekly
MCC	Median cash compensation	S	See annotated source	Y	Yearly

Occupation/Type/Industry	Location	Per	Low	Mid	High	Source	Date

Education Administrator

Occupation/Type/Industry	Location	Per	Low	Mid	High	Source	Date
Postsecondary	West Palm Beach-Boca Raton-Boynton Beach PMSA, FL	Y	65410 FQ	84950 MW	99480 TQ	USBLS	5/07
Postsecondary	Georgia	Y	54520 FQ	73420 MW	101050 TQ	USBLS	5/07
Postsecondary	Atlanta-Sandy Springs-Marietta MSA, GA	Y	54980 FQ	72510 MW	97340 TQ	USBLS	5/07
Postsecondary	Hawaii	Y	72250 FQ	93310 MW	119640 TQ	USBLS	5/07
Postsecondary	Honolulu MSA, HI	Y	70430 FQ	92660 MW	120100 TQ	USBLS	5/07
Postsecondary	Idaho	Y	53970 FQ	69450 MW	95590 TQ	USBLS	5/07
Postsecondary	Boise City-Nampa MSA, ID	Y	52600 FQ	65540 MW	95120 TQ	USBLS	5/07
Postsecondary	Illinois	Y	48800 FQ	68270 MW	96400 TQ	USBLS	5/07
Postsecondary	Chicago-Naperville-Joliet MSA, IL-IN-WI	Y	53080 FQ	75920 MW	106270 TQ	USBLS	5/07
Postsecondary	Indiana	Y	46120 FQ	63770 MW	92910 TQ	USBLS	5/07
Postsecondary	Gary PMSA, IN	Y	60790 FQ	81450 MW	96070 TQ	USBLS	5/07
Postsecondary	Indianapolis-Carmel MSA, IN	Y	44800 FQ	60000 MW	92160 TQ	USBLS	5/07
Postsecondary	Iowa	Y	54000 FQ	71560 MW	95930 TQ	USBLS	5/07
Postsecondary	Des Moines-West Des Moines MSA, IA	Y	54170 FQ	69750 MW	86080 TQ	USBLS	5/07
Postsecondary	Kansas	Y	53900 FQ	76400 MW	111620 TQ	USBLS	5/07
Postsecondary	Wichita MSA, KS	Y	56700 FQ	87590 MW	123350 TQ	USBLS	5/07
Postsecondary	Kentucky	Y	47017 FQ	66486 MW	98595 TQ	KYBLS	2008
Postsecondary	Louisville-Jefferson County MSA, KY-IN	Y	50910 FQ	71450 MW	107110 TQ	USBLS	5/07
Postsecondary	Owensboro MSA, KY	Y	45680 FQ	69690 MW	86510 TQ	USBLS	5/07
Postsecondary	Louisiana	H	26.07 FQ	34.77 MW	48.20 TQ	LABLS	1/08-3/08
Postsecondary	Baton Rouge MSA, LA	Y	67240 FQ	81210 MW	125380 TQ	USBLS	5/07
Postsecondary	New Orleans-Metairie-Kenner MSA, LA	Y	51650 FQ	72030 MW	103740 TQ	USBLS	5/07
Postsecondary	Maine	Y	44310 FQ	58090 MW	79160 TQ	USBLS	5/07
Postsecondary	Portland-South Portland-Biddeford MSA, ME	Y	41740 FQ	55140 MW	68410 TQ	USBLS	5/07
Postsecondary	Maryland	Y		88225 MW		MDBLS	3/08
Postsecondary	Baltimore-Towson MSA, MD	Y	63450 FQ	81030 MW	115810 TQ	USBLS	5/07
Postsecondary	Bethesda-Gaithersburg-Frederick PMSA, MD	Y	69030 FQ	85010 MW	112990 TQ	USBLS	5/07
Postsecondary	Hagerstown-Martinsburg MSA, MD-WV	Y	58600 FQ	68810 MW	80020 TQ	USBLS	5/07
Postsecondary	Massachusetts	Y	63980 FQ	86300 MW	123890 TQ	USBLS	5/07
Postsecondary	Boston-Cambridge-Quincy NECTA, MA	Y	68090 FQ	93280 MW	134380 TQ	USBLS	5/07
Postsecondary	Worcester MSA, MA-CT	Y	52750 FQ	69190 MW	102070 TQ	USBLS	5/07
Postsecondary	Michigan	Y	57530 FQ	79250 MW	109930 TQ	USBLS	5/07
Postsecondary	Detroit-Warren-Livonia MSA, MI	Y	61370 FQ	82790 MW	113910 TQ	USBLS	5/07
Postsecondary	Grand Rapids-Wyoming MSA, MI	Y	48520 FQ	62590 MW	77900 TQ	USBLS	5/07
Postsecondary	Warren-Troy-Farmington Hills PMSA, MI	Y	50910 FQ	68560 MW	89570 TQ	USBLS	5/07
Postsecondary	Minnesota	Y	60317 FQ	78657 MW	103837 TQ	MNBLS	10/08-12/08
Postsecondary	Duluth-Superior MSA, MN-WI	Y	57387 FQ	79116 MW	107935 TQ	MNBLS	10/08-12/08
Postsecondary	Minneapolis-Saint Paul MSA, MN-WI	Y	60995 FQ	79669 MW	104609 TQ	MNBLS	10/08-12/08
Postsecondary	Rochester MSA, MN	Y	81203 FQ	95978 MW	110792 TQ	MNBLS	10/08-12/08
Postsecondary	Mississippi	Y	61240 FQ	78290 MW	96520 TQ	USBLS	5/07
Postsecondary	Jackson MSA, MS	Y	56320 FQ	74980 MW	91110 TQ	USBLS	5/07
Postsecondary	Missouri	Y	51490 FQ	69560 MW	96650 TQ	USBLS	5/07
Postsecondary	Kansas City MSA, MO-KS	Y	56680 FQ	76800 MW	100150 TQ	USBLS	5/07
Postsecondary	St. Louis MSA, MO-IL	Y	51060 FQ	68000 MW	92890 TQ	USBLS	5/07
Postsecondary	Billings MSA, MT	Y	48310 FQ	70140 MW	79720 TQ	USBLS	5/07
Postsecondary	Nebraska	Y	41290 FQ	56380 MW	80300 TQ	USBLS	5/07
Postsecondary	Omaha-Council Bluffs MSA, NE-IA	Y	46150 FQ	62720 MW	87300 TQ	USBLS	5/07
Postsecondary	New Hampshire	H	22.22 AE	34.55 MW	49.90 AEX	NHBLS	6/08
Postsecondary	Manchester MSA, NH	Y	41600 FQ	57990 MW	77250 TQ	USBLS	5/07
Postsecondary	New Jersey	Y	70800 FQ	91830 MW	118360 TQ	USBLS	5/07
Postsecondary	Camden PMSA, NJ	Y	74940 FQ	98060 MW	128970 TQ	USBLS	5/07
Postsecondary	Edison PMSA, NJ	Y	74120 FQ	91090 MW	114910 TQ	USBLS	5/07
Postsecondary	Newark-Union PMSA, NJ-PA	Y	67650 FQ	90670 MW	120190 TQ	USBLS	5/07
Postsecondary	New Mexico	Y	59770 FQ	78930 MW	107450 TQ	USBLS	5/07
Postsecondary	Albuquerque MSA, NM	Y	70460 FQ	102480 MW		USBLS	5/07
Postsecondary	New York	Y	71240 FQ	90470 MW	118140 TQ	USBLS	5/07

AE	Average entry wage	AW	Average wage paid	FQ	First quartile wage	LO	Lowest wage paid	MTC	Median total compensation	TCC	Total cash compensation
AER	Average entry range	AWR	Average wage range	H	Hourly	LR	Low end range	MW	Median wage paid	TQ	Third quartile wage
AEX	Average experienced wage	AXR	Average experienced range	HI	Highest wage paid	M	Monthly	MWR	Median wage range	W	Weekly
ATC	Average total compensation	D	Daily	HR	High end range	MCC	Median cash compensation	S	See annotated source	Y	Yearly

Occupation/Type/Industry	Location	Per	Low	Mid	High	Source	Date
Education Administrator							
Postsecondary	Albany-Schenectady-Troy MSA, NY	Y	71020 FQ	95160 MW	131420 TQ	USBLS	5/07
Postsecondary	Buffalo-Niagara Falls MSA, NY	Y	68450 FQ	87510 MW	114530 TQ	USBLS	5/07
Postsecondary	Nassau-Suffolk PMSA, NY	Y	73740 FQ	95900 MW	128570 TQ	USBLS	5/07
Postsecondary	New York-Northern New Jersey-Long Island MSA, NY-NJ-PA	Y	72270 FQ	91440 MW	117820 TQ	USBLS	5/07
Postsecondary	North Carolina	Y	49360 FQ	66910 MW	94470 TQ	USBLS	5/07
Postsecondary	Asheville MSA, NC	Y	42010 FQ	56840 MW	78730 TQ	USBLS	5/07
Postsecondary	Charlotte-Gastonia-Concord MSA, NC-SC	Y	46660 FQ	66460 MW	91760 TQ	USBLS	5/07
Postsecondary	Durham MSA, NC	Y	49500 FQ	66960 MW	99520 TQ	USBLS	5/07
Postsecondary	Winston-Salem MSA, NC	Y	50190 FQ	69440 MW	99120 TQ	USBLS	5/07
Postsecondary	North Dakota	Y	50880 FQ	83340 MW	112270 TQ	USBLS	5/07
Postsecondary	Fargo MSA, ND-MN	Y	59230 FQ	81280 MW	107220 TQ	USBLS	5/07
Postsecondary	Grand Forks MSA, ND-MN	Y	54380 FQ	78720 MW	142110 TQ	USBLS	5/07
Postsecondary	Ohio	Y	66110 FQ	87370 MW	123120 TQ	USBLS	5/07
Postsecondary	Cincinnati-Middletown MSA, OH-KY-IN	Y	72840 FQ	97880 MW	139260 TQ	USBLS	5/07
Postsecondary	Cleveland-Elyria-Mentor MSA, OH	Y	69310 FQ	87400 MW	114360 TQ	USBLS	5/07
Postsecondary	Columbus MSA, OH	Y	73000 FQ	104200 MW		USBLS	5/07
Postsecondary	Dayton MSA, OH	Y	67560 FQ	88450 MW	130360 TQ	USBLS	5/07
Postsecondary	Oklahoma	Y	45150 FQ	59060 MW	75670 TQ	USBLS	5/07
Postsecondary	Oklahoma City MSA, OK	Y	47260 FQ	60240 MW	88460 TQ	USBLS	5/07
Postsecondary	Tulsa MSA, OK	Y	36130 FQ	51660 MW	67680 TQ	USBLS	5/07
Postsecondary	Oregon	H	25.72 FQ	35.80 MW	48.98 TQ	ORBLS	5/08
Postsecondary	Portland-Vancouver-Beaverton MSA, OR-WA	Y	46320 FQ	67440 MW	94460 TQ	USBLS	5/07
Postsecondary	Pennsylvania	Y	53010 FQ	79520 MW	126680 TQ	USBLS	5/07
Postsecondary	Allentown-Bethlehem-Easton MSA, PA-NJ	Y	53650 FQ	69210 MW	106060 TQ	USBLS	5/07
Postsecondary	Philadelphia-Camden-Wilmington MSA, PA-NJ-DE-MD	Y	62300 FQ	92790 MW	141230 TQ	USBLS	5/07
Postsecondary	Pittsburgh MSA, PA	Y	44780 FQ	65730 MW	95860 TQ	USBLS	5/07
Postsecondary	Rhode Island	Y	71270 FQ	90510 MW	125790 TQ	USBLS	5/07
Postsecondary	Providence-Fall River-Warwick MSA, RI-MA	Y	69990 FQ	89110 MW	123580 TQ	USBLS	5/07
Postsecondary	South Carolina	Y	54860 FQ	73320 MW	102800 TQ	USBLS	5/07
Postsecondary	Charleston-North Charleston MSA, SC	Y	48390 FQ	66250 MW	111460 TQ	USBLS	5/07
Postsecondary	Columbia MSA, SC	Y	55340 FQ	74090 MW	116980 TQ	USBLS	5/07
Postsecondary	South Dakota	Y	65504 FQ	81978 MW	109178 TQ	SDBLS	7/08-9/08
Postsecondary	Rapid City MSA, SD	Y	61818 FQ	74704 MW	84729 TQ	SDBLS	7/08-9/08
Postsecondary	Sioux Falls MSA, SD	Y	68258 FQ	78778 MW	98147 TQ	SDBLS	7/08-9/08
Postsecondary	Tennessee	Y	45150 FQ	63610 MW	92860 TQ	USBLS	5/07
Postsecondary	Clarksville MSA, TN-KY	Y	49370 FQ	65640 MW	97360 TQ	USBLS	5/07
Postsecondary	Memphis MSA, TN-MS-AR	Y	45210 FQ	67140 MW	99220 TQ	USBLS	5/07
Postsecondary	Nashville-Davidson-Murfreesboro MSA, TN	Y	46440 FQ	69750 MW	99750 TQ	USBLS	5/07
Postsecondary	Texas	Y	55410 FQ	80170 MW	118590 TQ	USBLS	5/07
Postsecondary	Austin-Round Rock MSA, TX	Y	81490 FQ	118850 MW		USBLS	5/07
Postsecondary	Dallas-Fort Worth-Arlington MSA, TX	Y	59270 FQ	81560 MW	119900 TQ	USBLS	5/07
Postsecondary	El Paso MSA, TX	Y	55170 FQ	93090 MW	128260 TQ	USBLS	5/07
Postsecondary	Houston-Sugar Land-Baytown MSA, TX	Y	60120 FQ	88720 MW	131700 TQ	USBLS	5/07
Postsecondary	San Antonio MSA, TX	Y	47490 FQ	66150 MW	90870 TQ	USBLS	5/07
Postsecondary	Utah	Y	55450 FQ	74460 MW	104630 TQ	USBLS	5/07
Postsecondary	Salt Lake City MSA, UT	Y	52920 FQ	72530 MW	105630 TQ	USBLS	5/07
Postsecondary	Vermont	Y	52570 FQ	73890 MW	113170 TQ	USBLS	5/07
Postsecondary	Burlington-South Burlington MSA, VT	Y	57980 FQ	81020 MW	131640 TQ	USBLS	5/07
Postsecondary	Virginia	Y	60320 FQ	78570 MW	106190 TQ	USBLS	5/07
Postsecondary	Charlottesville MSA, VA	Y	62420 FQ	83640 MW	118990 TQ	USBLS	5/07
Postsecondary	Richmond MSA, VA	Y	58300 FQ	86450 MW	124350 TQ	USBLS	5/07
Postsecondary	Virginia Beach-Norfolk-Newport News MSA, VA-NC	Y	62890 FQ	80750 MW	112330 TQ	USBLS	5/07
Postsecondary	Washington	H	30.57 FQ	37.22 MW	49.05 TQ	WABLS	3/08

AE	Average entry wage	AW	Average wage paid	FQ	First quartile wage	LO	Lowest wage paid	MTC	Median total compensation	TCC	Total cash compensation
AER	Average entry range	AWR	Average wage range	H	Hourly	LR	Low end range	MW	Median wage paid	TQ	Third quartile wage
AEX	Average experienced wage	AXR	Average experienced range	HI	Highest wage paid	M	Monthly	MWR	Median wage range	W	Weekly
ATC	Average total compensation	D	Daily	HR	High end range	MCC	Median cash compensation	S	See annotated source	Y	Yearly

Occupation/Type/Industry	Location	Per	Low	Mid	High	Source	Date
Education Administrator							
Postsecondary	Seattle-Tacoma-Bellevue MSA, WA	Y	63490 FQ	76540 MW	98960 TQ	USBLS	5/07
Postsecondary	West Virginia	Y	50072 FQ	69109 MW	96143 TQ	WVBLS	7/08-9/08
Postsecondary	Charleston MSA, WV	Y	28960 FQ	51020 MW	74620 TQ	USBLS	5/07
Postsecondary	Wisconsin	Y	52660 FQ	67900 MW	91230 TQ	USBLS	5/07
Postsecondary	Milwaukee-Waukesha-West Allis MSA, WI	Y	46280 FQ	61730 MW	85730 TQ	USBLS	5/07
Postsecondary	Wyoming	Y	66873 FQ	84101 MW	109253 TQ	WYBLS	9/08
Postsecondary	Puerto Rico	Y	30460 FQ	44960 MW	60490 TQ	USBLS	5/07
Postsecondary	San Juan-Caguas-Guaynabo MSA, PR	Y	34620 FQ	48010 MW	63410 TQ	USBLS	5/07
Preschool and Child Care Center/Program	Alabama	Y	28420 FQ	36650 MW	59850 TQ	USBLS	5/07
Preschool and Child Care Center/Program	Birmingham-Hoover MSA, AL	Y	29520 FQ	37270 MW	50740 TQ	USBLS	5/07
Preschool and Child Care Center/Program	Huntsville MSA, AL	Y	27420 FQ	31360 MW	69210 TQ	USBLS	5/07
Preschool and Child Care Center/Program	Montgomery MSA, AL	Y	30920 FQ	40270 MW	55740 TQ	USBLS	5/07
Preschool and Child Care Center/Program	Alaska	Y	29540 FQ	38340 MW	48750 TQ	USBLS	5/07
Preschool and Child Care Center/Program	Anchorage MSA, AK	Y	29650 FQ	43820 MW	54150 TQ	USBLS	5/07
Preschool and Child Care Center/Program	Arizona	Y	29750 FQ	35980 MW	47070 TQ	USBLS	5/07
Preschool and Child Care Center/Program	Phoenix-Mesa-Scottsdale MSA, AZ	Y	29230 FQ	33730 MW	46750 TQ	USBLS	5/07
Preschool and Child Care Center/Program	Tucson MSA, AZ	Y	35260 FQ	40670 MW	54370 TQ	USBLS	5/07
Preschool and Child Care Center/Program	Arkansas	Y	28900 FQ	36100 MW	46950 TQ	USBLS	5/07
Preschool and Child Care Center/Program	Little Rock-North Little Rock MSA, AR	Y	23560 FQ	34950 MW	43490 TQ	USBLS	5/07
Preschool and Child Care Center/Program	California	H	17.65 FQ	22.34 MW	27.99 TQ	CABLS	1/08-3/08
Preschool and Child Care Center/Program	Los Angeles-Long Beach-Glendale PMSA, CA	H	17.01 FQ	20.57 MW	28.05 TQ	CABLS	1/08-3/08
Preschool and Child Care Center/Program	Modesto MSA, CA	H	22.82 FQ	27.28 MW	33.57 TQ	CABLS	1/08-3/08
Preschool and Child Care Center/Program	Oakland-Fremont-Hayward MSA, CA	H	21.22 FQ	25.09 MW	28.14 TQ	CABLS	1/08-3/08
Preschool and Child Care Center/Program	Riverside-San Bernardino-Ontario MSA, CA	H	12.81 FQ	18.29 MW	23.89 TQ	CABLS	1/08-3/08
Preschool and Child Care Center/Program	Sacramento-Arden Arcade-Roseville MSA, CA	H	13.13 FQ	17.42 MW	22.60 TQ	CABLS	1/08-3/08
Preschool and Child Care Center/Program	San Diego-Carlsbad-San Marcos MSA, CA	H	16.87 FQ	21.35 MW	29.36 TQ	CABLS	1/08-3/08
Preschool and Child Care Center/Program	San Francisco-San Mateo-Redwood PMSA, CA	H	23.35 FQ	27.08 MW	35.17 TQ	CABLS	1/08-3/08
Preschool and Child Care Center/Program	San Jose-Sunnyvale-Santa Clara MSA, CA	H	22.17 FQ	26.74 MW	30.42 TQ	CABLS	1/08-3/08
Preschool and Child Care Center/Program	Santa Ana-Anaheim-Irvine PMSA, CA	Y	38150 FQ	44250 MW	52040 TQ	USBLS	5/07
Preschool and Child Care Center/Program	Santa Rosa-Petaluma MSA, CA	H	18.22 FQ	20.71 MW	36.80 TQ	CABLS	1/08-3/08
Preschool and Child Care Center/Program	Colorado	Y	32330 FQ	41550 MW	55370 TQ	USBLS	5/07
Preschool and Child Care Center/Program	Denver-Aurora MSA, CO	Y	33970 FQ	44170 MW	62950 TQ	USBLS	5/07
Preschool and Child Care Center/Program	Connecticut	H	13.65 AE	20.43 MW		CTBLS	1/08-3/08
Preschool and Child Care Center/Program	Bridgeport-Stamford-Norwalk MSA, CT	Y	36000 FQ	43820 MW	57880 TQ	USBLS	5/07
Preschool and Child Care Center/Program	Hartford-West Hartford-East Hartford MSA, CT	Y	27030 FQ	39500 MW	54600 TQ	USBLS	5/07
Preschool and Child Care Center/Program	Waterbury MSA, CT	Y	28280 FQ	33380 MW	51590 TQ	USBLS	5/07
Preschool and Child Care Center/Program	Delaware	Y	31340 FQ	38150 MW	51290 TQ	USBLS	5/07
Preschool and Child Care Center/Program	Wilmington PMSA, DE-MD-NJ	Y	34030 FQ	41760 MW	57440 TQ	USBLS	5/07
Preschool and Child Care Center/Program	District of Columbia	Y	22720 FQ	29470 MW	46000 TQ	USBLS	5/07
Preschool and Child Care Center/Program	Washington-Arlington-Alexandria MSA, DC-VA-MD-WV	Y	29200 FQ	37940 MW	50490 TQ	USBLS	5/07
Preschool and Child Care Center/Program	Florida	Y	40370 FQ	58920 MW	76070 TQ	USBLS	5/07
Preschool and Child Care Center/Program	Fort Lauderdale-Pompano Beach-Deerfield Beach PMSA, FL	Y	49040 FQ	78500 MW	88210 TQ	USBLS	5/07
Preschool and Child Care Center/Program	Jacksonville MSA, FL	Y	36750 FQ	53470 MW	61530 TQ	USBLS	5/07
Preschool and Child Care Center/Program	Miami-Fort Lauderdale-Miami Beach MSA, FL	Y	49020 FQ	66900 MW	82080 TQ	USBLS	5/07
Preschool and Child Care Center/Program	Orlando-Kissimmee MSA, FL	Y	51130 FQ	67420 MW	87740 TQ	USBLS	5/07
Preschool and Child Care Center/Program	Tampa-St. Petersburg-Clearwater MSA, FL	Y	42600 FQ	55650 MW	62840 TQ	USBLS	5/07
Preschool and Child Care Center/Program	West Palm Beach-Boca Raton-Boynton Beach PMSA, FL	Y	61290 FQ	67900 MW	73870 TQ	USBLS	5/07
Preschool and Child Care Center/Program	Georgia	Y	30290 FQ	33490 MW	37290 TQ	USBLS	5/07

AE	Average entry wage	AW	Average wage paid	FQ	First quartile wage
AER	Average entry range	AWR	Average wage range	H	Hourly
AEX	Average experienced wage	AXR	Average experienced range	HI	Highest wage paid
ATC	Average total compensation	D	Daily	HR	High end range

LO	Lowest wage paid	MTC	Median total compensation
LR	Low end range	MW	Median wage paid
M	Monthly	MWR	Median wage range
MCC	Median cash compensation	S	See annotated source

TCC	Total cash compensation
TQ	Third quartile wage
W	Weekly
Y	Yearly

Occupation/Type/Industry	Location	Per	Low	Mid	High	Source	Date
Education Administrator							
Preschool and Child Care Center/Program	Atlanta-Sandy Springs-Marietta MSA, GA	Y	30970 FQ	33830 MW	36980 TQ	USBLS	5/07
Preschool and Child Care Center/Program	Hawaii	Y	36480 FQ	41720 MW	51150 TQ	USBLS	5/07
Preschool and Child Care Center/Program	Honolulu MSA, HI	Y	36990 FQ	42480 MW	51180 TQ	USBLS	5/07
Preschool and Child Care Center/Program	Idaho	Y	53230 FQ	83870 MW	99810 TQ	USBLS	5/07
Preschool and Child Care Center/Program	Boise City-Nampa MSA, ID	Y	28090 FQ	78190 MW	95120 TQ	USBLS	5/07
Preschool and Child Care Center/Program	Illinois	Y	32000 FQ	41740 MW	57870 TQ	USBLS	5/07
Preschool and Child Care Center/Program	Chicago-Naperville-Joliet MSA, IL-IN-WI	Y	34600 FQ	43350 MW	58080 TQ	USBLS	5/07
Preschool and Child Care Center/Program	Indiana	Y	27710 FQ	32820 MW	44490 TQ	USBLS	5/07
Preschool and Child Care Center/Program	Gary PMSA, IN	Y	25480 FQ	29030 MW	41490 TQ	USBLS	5/07
Preschool and Child Care Center/Program	Indianapolis-Carmel MSA, IN	Y	29010 FQ	35090 MW	46070 TQ	USBLS	5/07
Preschool and Child Care Center/Program	Iowa	Y	25620 FQ	30890 MW	37680 TQ	USBLS	5/07
Preschool and Child Care Center/Program	Des Moines-West Des Moines MSA, IA	Y	25570 FQ	33000 MW	37700 TQ	USBLS	5/07
Preschool and Child Care Center/Program	Kansas	Y	32360 FQ	40310 MW	54950 TQ	USBLS	5/07
Preschool and Child Care Center/Program	Wichita MSA, KS	Y	32720 FQ	36730 MW	43970 TQ	USBLS	5/07
Preschool and Child Care Center/Program	Kentucky	Y	26009 FQ	32663 MW	47067 TQ	KYBLS	2008
Preschool and Child Care Center/Program	Louisville-Jefferson County MSA, KY-IN	Y	27390 FQ	33900 MW	48290 TQ	USBLS	5/07
Preschool and Child Care Center/Program	Louisiana	H	11.70 FQ	16.87 MW	19.47 TQ	LABLS	1/08-3/08
Preschool and Child Care Center/Program	Baton Rouge MSA, LA	Y	34550 FQ	38560 MW	43120 TQ	USBLS	5/07
Preschool and Child Care Center/Program	New Orleans-Metairie-Kenner MSA, LA	Y	35540 FQ	41530 MW	47770 TQ	USBLS	5/07
Preschool and Child Care Center/Program	Maine	Y	33410 FQ	36840 MW	40610 TQ	USBLS	5/07
Preschool and Child Care Center/Program	Portland-South Portland-Biddeford MSA, ME	Y	33040 FQ	36070 MW	39260 TQ	USBLS	5/07
Preschool and Child Care Center/Program	Maryland	Y		42000 MW		MDBLS	3/08
Preschool and Child Care Center/Program	Baltimore-Towson MSA, MD	Y	34350 FQ	45400 MW	60360 TQ	USBLS	5/07
Preschool and Child Care Center/Program	Bethesda-Gaithersburg-Frederick PMSA, MD	Y	32010 FQ	39890 MW	52390 TQ	USBLS	5/07
Preschool and Child Care Center/Program	Massachusetts	Y	36460 FQ	45350 MW	58250 TQ	USBLS	5/07
Preschool and Child Care Center/Program	Boston-Cambridge-Quincy NECTA, MA	Y	37180 FQ	46710 MW	57810 TQ	USBLS	5/07
Preschool and Child Care Center/Program	Worcester MSA, MA-CT	Y	27490 FQ	36550 MW	50930 TQ	USBLS	5/07
Preschool and Child Care Center/Program	Michigan	Y	35050 FQ	45660 MW	61240 TQ	USBLS	5/07
Preschool and Child Care Center/Program	Detroit-Warren-Livonia MSA, MI	Y	39740 FQ	48340 MW	59760 TQ	USBLS	5/07
Preschool and Child Care Center/Program	Grand Rapids-Wyoming MSA, MI	Y	31120 FQ	70870 MW	82730 TQ	USBLS	5/07
Preschool and Child Care Center/Program	Warren-Troy-Farmington Hills PMSA, MI	Y	36620 FQ	44090 MW	54960 TQ	USBLS	5/07
Preschool and Child Care Center/Program	Minnesota	Y	35106 FQ	40256 MW	49036 TQ	MNBLS	10/08-12/08
Preschool and Child Care Center/Program	Duluth-Superior MSA, MN-WI	Y	35012 FQ	40454 MW	47409 TQ	MNBLS	10/08-12/08
Preschool and Child Care Center/Program	Minneapolis-Saint Paul MSA, MN-WI	Y	35940 FQ	41091 MW	50391 TQ	MNBLS	10/08-12/08
Preschool and Child Care Center/Program	Rochester MSA, MN	Y	35211 FQ	39778 MW	44128 TQ	MNBLS	10/08-12/08
Preschool and Child Care Center/Program	Mississippi	Y	25860 FQ	33940 MW	47240 TQ	USBLS	5/07
Preschool and Child Care Center/Program	Gulfport-Biloxi MSA, MS	Y	31290 FQ	45430 MW	82940 TQ	USBLS	5/07
Preschool and Child Care Center/Program	Jackson MSA, MS	Y	34470 FQ	41560 MW	49340 TQ	USBLS	5/07
Preschool and Child Care Center/Program	Missouri	Y	30610 FQ	36860 MW	48510 TQ	USBLS	5/07
Preschool and Child Care Center/Program	Joplin MSA, MO	Y	36300 FQ	41020 MW	44610 TQ	USBLS	5/07
Preschool and Child Care Center/Program	Kansas City MSA, MO-KS	Y	31800 FQ	37390 MW	52210 TQ	USBLS	5/07
Preschool and Child Care Center/Program	St. Louis MSA, MO-IL	Y	25190 FQ	34920 MW	52500 TQ	USBLS	5/07
Preschool and Child Care Center/Program	Montana	Y	24630 FQ	30720 MW	54990 TQ	USBLS	5/07
Preschool and Child Care Center/Program	Nebraska	Y	31810 FQ	36800 MW	50010 TQ	USBLS	5/07
Preschool and Child Care Center/Program	Omaha-Council Bluffs MSA, NE-IA	Y	31800 FQ	36730 MW	46630 TQ	USBLS	5/07
Preschool and Child Care Center/Program	Nevada	H	13.54 FQ	16.72 MW	20.19 TQ	NVBLS	5/08
Preschool and Child Care Center/Program	Las Vegas-Paradise MSA, NV	H	14.56 FQ	17.53 MW	21.48 TQ	NVBLS	5/08
Preschool and Child Care Center/Program	New Hampshire	H	14.27 AE	18.92 MW	22.32 AEX	NHBLS	6/08
Preschool and Child Care Center/Program	Manchester MSA, NH	Y	29990 FQ	32720 MW	41520 TQ	USBLS	5/07
Preschool and Child Care Center/Program	Nashua NECTA, NH-MA	Y	38270 FQ	44940 MW	53450 TQ	USBLS	5/07
Preschool and Child Care Center/Program	New Jersey	Y	36220 FQ	44600 MW	58470 TQ	USBLS	5/07
Preschool and Child Care Center/Program	Camden PMSA, NJ	Y	37020 FQ	43890 MW	56760 TQ	USBLS	5/07
Preschool and Child Care Center/Program	Edison PMSA, NJ	Y	33850 FQ	42810 MW	55420 TQ	USBLS	5/07
Preschool and Child Care Center/Program	Newark-Union PMSA, NJ-PA	Y	38260 FQ	46740 MW	58780 TQ	USBLS	5/07
Preschool and Child Care Center/Program	New Mexico	Y	34100 FQ	40380 MW	62970 TQ	USBLS	5/07
Preschool and Child Care Center/Program	Albuquerque MSA, NM	Y	33860 FQ	38040 MW	52890 TQ	USBLS	5/07
Preschool and Child Care Center/Program	New York	Y	39460 FQ	51120 MW	65560 TQ	USBLS	5/07

AE	Average entry wage	AW	Average wage paid	FQ	First quartile wage
AER	Average entry range	AWR	Average wage range	H	Hourly
AEX	Average experienced wage	AXR	Average experienced range	HI	Highest wage paid
ATC	Average total compensation	D	Daily	HR	High end range

LO	Lowest wage paid	MTC	Median total compensation	TCC	Total cash compensation
LR	Low end range	MW	Median wage paid	TQ	Third quartile wage
M	Monthly	MWR	Median wage range	W	Weekly
MCC	Median cash compensation	S	See annotated source	Y	Yearly

Education Administrator

Occupation/Type/Industry	Location	Per	Low	Mid	High	Source	Date
Preschool and Child Care Center/Program	Albany-Schenectady-Troy MSA, NY	Y	37980 FQ	46110 MW	53830 TQ	USBLS	5/07
Preschool and Child Care Center/Program	Buffalo-Niagara Falls MSA, NY	Y	31460 FQ	37110 MW	56130 TQ	USBLS	5/07
Preschool and Child Care Center/Program	Kingston MSA, NY	Y	28360 FQ	36100 MW	54080 TQ	USBLS	5/07
Preschool and Child Care Center/Program	Nassau-Suffolk PMSA, NY	Y	41120 FQ	46960 MW	63840 TQ	USBLS	5/07
Preschool and Child Care Center/Program	New York-Northern New Jersey-Long Island MSA, NY-NJ-PA	Y	39620 FQ	49850 MW	64770 TQ	USBLS	5/07
Preschool and Child Care Center/Program	North Carolina	Y	29920 FQ	35720 MW	44940 TQ	USBLS	5/07
Preschool and Child Care Center/Program	Charlotte-Gastonia-Concord MSA, NC-SC	Y	31280 FQ	36280 MW	42860 TQ	USBLS	5/07
Preschool and Child Care Center/Program	Greensboro-High Point MSA, NC	Y	31350 FQ	36370 MW	40600 TQ	USBLS	5/07
Preschool and Child Care Center/Program	Raleigh-Cary MSA, NC	Y	32540 FQ	36960 MW	45870 TQ	USBLS	5/07
Preschool and Child Care Center/Program	Winston-Salem MSA, NC	Y	24950 FQ	32240 MW	44680 TQ	USBLS	5/07
Preschool and Child Care Center/Program	North Dakota	Y	26210 FQ	33400 MW	37410 TQ	USBLS	5/07
Preschool and Child Care Center/Program	Ohio	Y	29100 FQ	34420 MW	42050 TQ	USBLS	5/07
Preschool and Child Care Center/Program	Cincinnati-Middletown MSA, OH-KY-IN	Y	27220 FQ	31950 MW	39570 TQ	USBLS	5/07
Preschool and Child Care Center/Program	Cleveland-Elyria-Mentor MSA, OH	Y	28050 FQ	33640 MW	40840 TQ	USBLS	5/07
Preschool and Child Care Center/Program	Columbus MSA, OH	Y	29650 FQ	36330 MW	50370 TQ	USBLS	5/07
Preschool and Child Care Center/Program	Dayton MSA, OH	Y	32780 FQ	35870 MW	39200 TQ	USBLS	5/07
Preschool and Child Care Center/Program	Oklahoma	Y	23040 FQ	30460 MW	39940 TQ	USBLS	5/07
Preschool and Child Care Center/Program	Oklahoma City MSA, OK	Y	21170 FQ	28950 MW	39730 TQ	USBLS	5/07
Preschool and Child Care Center/Program	Tulsa MSA, OK	Y	27500 FQ	31750 MW	39410 TQ	USBLS	5/07
Preschool and Child Care Center/Program	Oregon	H	13.69 FQ	17.17 MW	21.92 TQ	ORBLS	5/08
Preschool and Child Care Center/Program	Portland-Vancouver-Beaverton MSA, OR-WA	Y	28520 FQ	34710 MW	42960 TQ	USBLS	5/07
Preschool and Child Care Center/Program	Pennsylvania	Y	28380 FQ	36390 MW	48140 TQ	USBLS	5/07
Preschool and Child Care Center/Program	Allentown-Bethlehem-Easton MSA, PA-NJ	Y	26170 FQ	30150 MW	36030 TQ	USBLS	5/07
Preschool and Child Care Center/Program	Philadelphia-Camden-Wilmington MSA, PA-NJ-DE-MD	Y	33970 FQ	42670 MW	55210 TQ	USBLS	5/07
Preschool and Child Care Center/Program	Pittsburgh MSA, PA	Y	26810 FQ	35310 MW	45630 TQ	USBLS	5/07
Preschool and Child Care Center/Program	Rhode Island	Y	41630 FQ	48600 MW	60430 TQ	USBLS	5/07
Preschool and Child Care Center/Program	Providence-Fall River-Warwick MSA, RI-MA	Y	39770 FQ	47000 MW	57640 TQ	USBLS	5/07
Preschool and Child Care Center/Program	South Carolina	Y	27160 FQ	34630 MW	55710 TQ	USBLS	5/07
Preschool and Child Care Center/Program	Charleston-North Charleston MSA, SC	Y	25940 FQ	33920 MW	67610 TQ	USBLS	5/07
Preschool and Child Care Center/Program	Columbia MSA, SC	Y	27300 FQ	36510 MW	57570 TQ	USBLS	5/07
Preschool and Child Care Center/Program	South Dakota	Y	38775 FQ	45646 MW	54127 TQ	SDBLS	7/08-9/08
Preschool and Child Care Center/Program	Sioux Falls MSA, SD	Y	37067 FQ	41909 MW	48715 TQ	SDBLS	7/08-9/08
Preschool and Child Care Center/Program	Tennessee	Y	24190 FQ	29130 MW	38000 TQ	USBLS	5/07
Preschool and Child Care Center/Program	Knoxville MSA, TN	Y	21270 FQ	24590 MW	29910 TQ	USBLS	5/07
Preschool and Child Care Center/Program	Memphis MSA, TN-MS-AR	Y	26680 FQ	29720 MW	36480 TQ	USBLS	5/07
Preschool and Child Care Center/Program	Nashville-Davidson-Murfreesboro MSA, TN	Y	25630 FQ	31730 MW	39530 TQ	USBLS	5/07
Preschool and Child Care Center/Program	Texas	Y	25930 FQ	32340 MW	41080 TQ	USBLS	5/07
Preschool and Child Care Center/Program	Austin-Round Rock MSA, TX	Y	34790 FQ	41120 MW	46730 TQ	USBLS	5/07
Preschool and Child Care Center/Program	Dallas-Fort Worth-Arlington MSA, TX	Y	24000 FQ	30580 MW	40200 TQ	USBLS	5/07
Preschool and Child Care Center/Program	El Paso MSA, TX	Y	24020 FQ	32160 MW	41080 TQ	USBLS	5/07
Preschool and Child Care Center/Program	Houston-Sugar Land-Baytown MSA, TX	Y	27960 FQ	33100 MW	39100 TQ	USBLS	5/07
Preschool and Child Care Center/Program	San Antonio MSA, TX	Y	29760 FQ	33490 MW	37680 TQ	USBLS	5/07
Preschool and Child Care Center/Program	Utah	Y	29760 FQ	34170 MW	49490 TQ	USBLS	5/07
Preschool and Child Care Center/Program	Salt Lake City MSA, UT	Y	28950 FQ	31960 MW	38910 TQ	USBLS	5/07
Preschool and Child Care Center/Program	Vermont	Y	25810 FQ	33880 MW	42880 TQ	USBLS	5/07
Preschool and Child Care Center/Program	Burlington-South Burlington MSA, VT	Y	23850 FQ	30680 MW	40070 TQ	USBLS	5/07
Preschool and Child Care Center/Program	Virginia	Y	30660 FQ	37980 MW	51220 TQ	USBLS	5/07
Preschool and Child Care Center/Program	Richmond MSA, VA	Y	29250 FQ	37150 MW	51360 TQ	USBLS	5/07
Preschool and Child Care Center/Program	Roanoke MSA, VA	Y	33280 FQ	39730 MW	63880 TQ	USBLS	5/07
Preschool and Child Care Center/Program	Virginia Beach-Norfolk-Newport News MSA, VA-NC	Y	28000 FQ	32650 MW	42550 TQ	USBLS	5/07
Preschool and Child Care Center/Program	Washington	H	17.51 FQ	21.75 MW	27.08 TQ	WABLS	3/08

AE	Average entry wage	AW	Average wage paid	FQ	First quartile wage	LO	Lowest wage paid	MTC	Median total compensation	TCC	Total cash compensation
AER	Average entry range	AWR	Average wage range	H	Hourly	LR	Low end range	MW	Median wage paid	TQ	Third quartile wage
AEX	Average experienced wage	AXR	Average experienced range	HI	Highest wage paid	M	Monthly	MWR	Median wage range	W	Weekly
ATC	Average total compensation	D	Daily	HR	High end range	MCC	Median cash compensation	S	See annotated source	Y	Yearly

Occupation/Type/Industry	Location	Per	Low	Mid	High	Source	Date
Education Administrator							
Preschool and Child Care Center/Program	Seattle-Tacoma-Bellevue MSA, WA	Y	36620 FQ	44740 MW	56480 TQ	USBLS	5/07
Preschool and Child Care Center/Program	West Virginia	Y	25953 FQ	32666 MW	40431 TQ	WVBLS	7/08-9/08
Preschool and Child Care Center/Program	Wisconsin	Y	29000 FQ	36040 MW	51140 TQ	USBLS	5/07
Preschool and Child Care Center/Program	Milwaukee-Waukesha-West Allis MSA, WI	Y	30800 FQ	39880 MW	63520 TQ	USBLS	5/07
Preschool and Child Care Center/Program	Wyoming	Y	26763 FQ	35385 MW	41545 TQ	WYBLS	9/08
Preschool and Child Care Center/Program	Cheyenne MSA, WY	Y	25133 FQ	34282 MW	38545 TQ	WYBLS	9/08
Preschool and Child Care Center/Program	Puerto Rico	Y	21410 FQ	26890 MW	32970 TQ	USBLS	5/07
Preschool and Child Care Center/Program	San Juan-Caguas-Guaynabo MSA, PR	Y	21850 FQ	28020 MW	33080 TQ	USBLS	5/07
Preschool and Child Care Center/Program	Virgin Islands	Y	55380 FQ	69820 MW	79100 TQ	USBLS	5/07
Education Program Specialist							
State Government	Georgia	Y	47280 LO		82962 HI	AFT02	3/1/08
Education-Spiritual Formation Minister							
Church of Christ	United States	Y	57000-68000 LR	64750-76667 AWR	75000-82000 HR	ACU	2008
Education Teacher							
Postsecondary	Alabama	Y	41150 FQ	50510 MW	63920 TQ	USBLS	5/07
Postsecondary	Birmingham-Hoover MSA, AL	Y	30810 FQ	43890 MW	55940 TQ	USBLS	5/07
Postsecondary	Alaska	Y	55920 FQ	68780 MW	81820 TQ	USBLS	5/07
Postsecondary	Anchorage MSA, AK	Y	47630 FQ	65200 MW	80300 TQ	USBLS	5/07
Postsecondary	Arizona	Y	27250 FQ	29660 MW	36390 TQ	USBLS	5/07
Postsecondary	Phoenix-Mesa-Scottsdale MSA, AZ	Y	28160 FQ	31160 MW	44740 TQ	USBLS	5/07
Postsecondary	Arkansas	Y	34950 FQ	46400 MW	61960 TQ	USBLS	5/07
Postsecondary	Little Rock-North Little Rock MSA, AR	Y	31400 FQ	41860 MW	51990 TQ	USBLS	5/07
Postsecondary	California	Y		81976 AW		CABLS	1/08-3/08
Postsecondary	Los Angeles-Long Beach-Glendale PMSA, CA	Y		73106 AW		CABLS	1/08-3/08
Postsecondary	Oakland-Fremont-Hayward MSA, CA	Y		75259 AW		CABLS	1/08-3/08
Postsecondary	Riverside-San Bernardino-Ontario MSA, CA	Y		81053 AW		CABLS	1/08-3/08
Postsecondary	Sacramento-Arden Arcade-Roseville MSA, CA	Y		86232 AW		CABLS	1/08-3/08
Postsecondary	San Diego-Carlsbad-San Marcos MSA, CA	Y		82233 AW		CABLS	1/08-3/08
Postsecondary	San Francisco-San Mateo-Redwood PMSA, CA	Y		98415 AW		CABLS	1/08-3/08
Postsecondary	San Jose-Sunnyvale-Santa Clara MSA, CA	Y		76121 AW		CABLS	1/08-3/08
Postsecondary	Santa Ana-Anaheim-Irvine PMSA, CA	Y	51210 FQ	71960 MW	94190 TQ	USBLS	5/07
Postsecondary	Colorado	Y	39660 FQ	51360 MW	64410 TQ	USBLS	5/07
Postsecondary	Denver-Aurora MSA, CO	Y	48170 FQ	55100 MW	63130 TQ	USBLS	5/07
Postsecondary	Delaware	Y	41520 FQ	55370 MW	67070 TQ	USBLS	5/07
Postsecondary	Wilmington PMSA, DE-MD-NJ	Y	42890 FQ	56370 MW	68110 TQ	USBLS	5/07
Postsecondary	District of Columbia	Y	38720 FQ	50830 MW	65230 TQ	USBLS	5/07
Postsecondary	Washington-Arlington-Alexandria MSA, DC-VA-MD-WV	Y	44590 FQ	58660 MW	75270 TQ	USBLS	5/07
Postsecondary	Florida	Y	42600 FQ	58150 MW	73890 TQ	USBLS	5/07
Postsecondary	Fort Lauderdale-Pompano Beach-Deerfield Beach PMSA, FL	Y	60450 FQ	72190 MW	79790 TQ	USBLS	5/07
Postsecondary	Miami-Fort Lauderdale-Miami Beach MSA, FL	Y	53200 FQ	70120 MW	77990 TQ	USBLS	5/07
Postsecondary	Orlando-Kissimmee MSA, FL	Y	46980 FQ	59890 MW	74310 TQ	USBLS	5/07
Postsecondary	Tampa-St. Petersburg-Clearwater MSA, FL	Y	47180 FQ	60110 MW	74610 TQ	USBLS	5/07
Postsecondary	West Palm Beach-Boca Raton-Boynton Beach PMSA, FL	Y	43540 FQ	49680 MW	61790 TQ	USBLS	5/07
Postsecondary	Georgia	Y	40210 FQ	54960 MW	84610 TQ	USBLS	5/07

AE	Average entry wage	AW	Average wage paid	FQ	First quartile wage	LO	Lowest wage paid	MTC	Median total compensation	TCC	Total cash compensation
AER	Average entry range	AWR	Average wage range	H	Hourly	LR	Low end range	MW	Median wage paid	TQ	Third quartile wage
AEX	Average experienced wage	AXR	Average experienced range	HI	Highest wage paid	M	Monthly	MWR	Median wage range	W	Weekly
ATC	Average total compensation	D	Daily	HR	High end range	MCC	Median cash compensation	S	See annotated source	Y	Yearly

Education Teacher

Occupation/Type/Industry	Location	Per	Low	Mid	High	Source	Date
Postsecondary	Atlanta-Sandy Springs-Marietta MSA, GA	Y	38760 FQ	45680 MW	61370 TQ	USBLS	5/07
Postsecondary	Hawaii	Y	45860 FQ	57510 MW	72710 TQ	USBLS	5/07
Postsecondary	Honolulu MSA, HI	Y	47820 FQ	58710 MW	74070 TQ	USBLS	5/07
Postsecondary	Illinois	Y	29110 FQ	46810 MW	63940 TQ	USBLS	5/07
Postsecondary	Chicago-Naperville-Joliet MSA, IL-IN-WI	Y	29340 FQ	46600 MW	62060 TQ	USBLS	5/07
Postsecondary	Indiana	Y	35940 FQ	51310 MW	67460 TQ	USBLS	5/07
Postsecondary	Gary PMSA, IN	Y	45030 FQ	50960 MW	61310 TQ	USBLS	5/07
Postsecondary	Indianapolis-Carmel MSA, IN	Y	32260 FQ	50580 MW	67400 TQ	USBLS	5/07
Postsecondary	Iowa	Y	43850 FQ	57990 MW	76970 TQ	USBLS	5/07
Postsecondary	Des Moines-West Des Moines MSA, IA	Y	34950 FQ	40870 MW	57610 TQ	USBLS	5/07
Postsecondary	Kansas	Y	37240 FQ	52900 MW	69770 TQ	USBLS	5/07
Postsecondary	Kentucky	Y	39317 FQ	52013 MW	63643 TQ	KYBLS	2008
Postsecondary	Louisville-Jefferson County MSA, KY-IN	Y	36290 FQ	47170 MW	61230 TQ	USBLS	5/07
Postsecondary	Louisiana	Y		56490 AW		LABLS	1/08-3/08
Postsecondary	Baton Rouge MSA, LA	Y	41470 FQ	60810 MW	78140 TQ	USBLS	5/07
Postsecondary	Maine	Y	38320 FQ	48070 MW	62310 TQ	USBLS	5/07
Postsecondary	Portland-South Portland-Biddeford MSA, ME	Y	36960 FQ	50250 MW	64160 TQ	USBLS	5/07
Postsecondary	Maryland	Y		63250 MW		MDBLS	3/08
Postsecondary	Baltimore-Towson MSA, MD	Y	41500 FQ	57490 MW	74790 TQ	USBLS	5/07
Postsecondary	Bethesda-Gaithersburg-Frederick PMSA, MD	Y	54990 FQ	65720 MW	77330 TQ	USBLS	5/07
Postsecondary	Massachusetts	Y	51890 FQ	60950 MW	73690 TQ	USBLS	
Postsecondary	Boston-Cambridge-Quincy NECTA, MA	Y	53350 FQ	61070 MW	71820 TQ	USBLS	5/07
Postsecondary	Worcester MSA, MA-CT	Y	56110 FQ	64310 MW	75680 TQ	USBLS	5/07
Postsecondary	Michigan	Y	28940 FQ	41210 MW	58610 TQ	USBLS	5/07
Postsecondary	Detroit-Warren-Livonia MSA, MI	Y	26490 FQ	29940 MW	45280 TQ	USBLS	5/07
Postsecondary	Warren-Troy-Farmington Hills PMSA, MI	Y	42080 FQ	50360 MW	57190 TQ	USBLS	5/07
Postsecondary	Minnesota	Y	42916 FQ	53608 MW	69929 TQ	MNBLS	10/08-12/08
Postsecondary	Duluth-Superior MSA, MN-WI	Y	44370 FQ	55198 MW	66393 TQ	MNBLS	10/08-12/08
Postsecondary	Minneapolis-Saint Paul MSA, MN-WI	Y	42602 FQ	54801 MW	72806 TQ	MNBLS	10/08-12/08
Postsecondary	Mississippi	Y	43160 FQ	54710 MW	66990 TQ	USBLS	5/07
Postsecondary	Jackson MSA, MS	Y	42350 FQ	50990 MW	65310 TQ	USBLS	5/07
Postsecondary	Missouri	Y	40460 FQ	53610 MW	71220 TQ	USBLS	5/07
Postsecondary	Kansas City MSA, MO-KS	Y	39720 FQ	48700 MW	63840 TQ	USBLS	5/07
Postsecondary	St. Louis MSA, MO-IL	Y	35670 FQ	51660 MW	72900 TQ	USBLS	5/07
Postsecondary	Montana	Y	14520 FQ	36640 MW	51640 TQ	USBLS	5/07
Postsecondary	Nebraska	Y	34740 FQ	47420 MW	64490 TQ	USBLS	5/07
Postsecondary	Omaha-Council Bluffs MSA, NE-IA	Y	39310 FQ	54140 MW	72690 TQ	USBLS	5/07
Postsecondary	New Hampshire	Y	37190 AE	53969 MW	65093 AEX	NHBLS	6/08
Postsecondary	New Jersey	Y	46760 FQ	60730 MW	78730 TQ	USBLS	5/07
Postsecondary	Edison PMSA, NJ	Y	45070 FQ	56420 MW	77410 TQ	USBLS	5/07
Postsecondary	Newark-Union PMSA, NJ-PA	Y	49320 FQ	63320 MW	77570 TQ	USBLS	5/07
Postsecondary	New Mexico	Y	42810 FQ	50120 MW	64260 TQ	USBLS	5/07
Postsecondary	New York	Y	43240 FQ	56920 MW	78580 TQ	USBLS	5/07
Postsecondary	Buffalo-Niagara Falls MSA, NY	Y	45380 FQ	55960 MW	67170 TQ	USBLS	5/07
Postsecondary	Nassau-Suffolk PMSA, NY	Y	42310 FQ	47060 MW	57790 TQ	USBLS	5/07
Postsecondary	New York-Northern New Jersey-Long Island MSA, NY-NJ-PA	Y	46920 FQ	62950 MW	82290 TQ	USBLS	5/07
Postsecondary	Utica-Rome MSA, NY	Y	25930 FQ	44800 MW	48960 TQ	USBLS	5/07
Postsecondary	North Carolina	Y	42570 FQ	51660 MW	63070 TQ	USBLS	5/07
Postsecondary	Charlotte-Gastonia-Concord MSA, NC-SC	Y	41260 FQ	52650 MW	61810 TQ	USBLS	5/07
Postsecondary	Greensboro-High Point MSA, NC	Y	50420 FQ	59200 MW	76330 TQ	USBLS	5/07
Postsecondary	Raleigh-Cary MSA, NC	Y	40770 FQ	49750 MW	61730 TQ	USBLS	5/07
Postsecondary	North Dakota	Y	49830 FQ	61160 MW	78630 TQ	USBLS	5/07
Postsecondary	Fargo MSA, ND-MN	Y	41250 FQ	47710 MW	58730 TQ	USBLS	5/07
Postsecondary	Grand Forks MSA, ND-MN	Y	59920 FQ	72510 MW	89260 TQ	USBLS	5/07
Postsecondary	Ohio	Y	36710 FQ	52010 MW	67140 TQ	USBLS	5/07

AE	Average entry wage	AW	Average wage paid	FQ	First quartile wage
AER	Average entry range	AWR	Average wage range	H	Hourly
AEX	Average experienced wage	AXR	Average experienced range	HI	Highest wage paid
ATC	Average total compensation	D	Daily	HR	High end range

LO	Lowest wage paid	MTC	Median total compensation
LR	Low end range	MW	Median wage paid
M	Monthly	MWR	Median wage range
MCC	Median cash compensation	S	See annotated source

TCC	Total cash compensation
TQ	Third quartile wage
W	Weekly
Y	Yearly

Occupation/Type/Industry	Location	Per	Low	Mid	High	Source	Date
Education Teacher							
Postsecondary	Cincinnati-Middletown MSA, OH-KY-IN	Y	35320 FQ	47880 MW	64180 TQ	USBLS	5/07
Postsecondary	Cleveland-Elyria-Mentor MSA, OH	Y	32400 FQ	41280 MW	58250 TQ	USBLS	5/07
Postsecondary	Columbus MSA, OH	Y	56640 FQ	65120 MW	83630 TQ	USBLS	5/07
Postsecondary	Dayton MSA, OH	Y	36310 FQ	51480 MW	67640 TQ	USBLS	5/07
Postsecondary	Oklahoma	Y	30050 FQ	44520 MW	62200 TQ	USBLS	5/07
Postsecondary	Oklahoma City MSA, OK	Y	34990 FQ	50130 MW	67590 TQ	USBLS	5/07
Postsecondary	Tulsa MSA, OK	Y	25150 FQ	40860 MW	55610 TQ	USBLS	5/07
Postsecondary	Portland-Vancouver-Beaverton MSA, OR-WA	Y	43880 FQ	57360 MW	74340 TQ	USBLS	5/07
Postsecondary	Pennsylvania	Y	43550 FQ	59310 MW	79290 TQ	USBLS	5/07
Postsecondary	Allentown-Bethlehem-Easton MSA, PA-NJ	Y	48600 FQ	61080 MW	91180 TQ	USBLS	5/07
Postsecondary	Philadelphia-Camden-Wilmington MSA, PA-NJ-DE-MD	Y	44820 FQ	58710 MW	76940 TQ	USBLS	5/07
Postsecondary	Pittsburgh MSA, PA	Y	39330 FQ	56270 MW	76420 TQ	USBLS	5/07
Postsecondary	Rhode Island	Y	47360 FQ	56360 MW	74720 TQ	USBLS	5/07
Postsecondary	Providence-Fall River-Warwick MSA, RI-MA	Y	47310 FQ	56180 MW	74330 TQ	USBLS	5/07
Postsecondary	South Carolina	Y	37720 FQ	50660 MW	63590 TQ	USBLS	5/07
Postsecondary	Charleston-North Charleston MSA, SC	Y	54710 FQ	62200 MW	86180 TQ	USBLS	5/07
Postsecondary	Columbia MSA, SC	Y	42390 FQ	52570 MW	74870 TQ	USBLS	5/07
Postsecondary	South Dakota	Y	43800 FQ	53889 MW	65421 TQ	SDBLS	7/08-9/08
Postsecondary	Sioux Falls MSA, SD	Y	44658 FQ	54072 MW	61139 TQ	SDBLS	7/08-9/08
Postsecondary	Tennessee	Y	41990 FQ	55130 MW	76670 TQ	USBLS	5/07
Postsecondary	Nashville-Davidson-Murfreesboro MSA, TN	Y	45310 FQ	59030 MW	86930 TQ	USBLS	5/07
Postsecondary	Texas	Y	30850 FQ	51170 MW	69180 TQ	USBLS	5/07
Postsecondary	Austin-Round Rock MSA, TX	Y	38740 FQ	59220 MW	87420 TQ	USBLS	5/07
Postsecondary	Dallas-Fort Worth-Arlington MSA, TX	Y	16530 FQ	49800 MW	69250 TQ	USBLS	5/07
Postsecondary	El Paso MSA, TX	Y	27790 FQ	49810 MW	61040 TQ	USBLS	5/07
Postsecondary	Houston-Sugar Land-Baytown MSA, TX	Y	35180 FQ	52970 MW	72550 TQ	USBLS	5/07
Postsecondary	San Antonio MSA, TX	Y	43860 FQ	57600 MW	73570 TQ	USBLS	5/07
Postsecondary	Utah	Y	43680 FQ	52940 MW	64800 TQ	USBLS	5/07
Postsecondary	Salt Lake City MSA, UT	Y	43430 FQ	56640 MW	68480 TQ	USBLS	5/07
Postsecondary	Vermont	Y	40120 FQ	47680 MW	60780 TQ	USBLS	5/07
Postsecondary	Virginia	Y	44070 FQ	55860 MW	68680 TQ	USBLS	5/07
Postsecondary	Richmond MSA, VA	Y	42400 FQ	50980 MW	61120 TQ	USBLS	5/07
Postsecondary	Virginia Beach-Norfolk-Newport News MSA, VA-NC	Y	52940 FQ	61140 MW	77420 TQ	USBLS	5/07
Postsecondary	Washington	Y		60371 AW		WABLS	3/08
Postsecondary	Seattle-Tacoma-Bellevue MSA, WA	Y	45640 FQ	56060 MW	71330 TQ	USBLS	5/07
Postsecondary	West Virginia	Y	27520 FQ	49654 MW	63495 TQ	WVBLS	7/08-9/08
Postsecondary	Wisconsin	Y	36890 FQ	49120 MW	63730 TQ	USBLS	5/07
Postsecondary	Milwaukee-Waukesha-West Allis MSA, WI	Y	36150 FQ	47760 MW	64220 TQ	USBLS	5/07
Postsecondary	Wyoming	Y	43152 FQ	52004 MW	62886 TQ	WYBLS	9/08
Postsecondary	Puerto Rico	Y	47410 FQ	62350 MW	74000 TQ	USBLS	5/07
Postsecondary	San Juan-Caguas-Guaynabo MSA, PR	Y	54660 FQ	65780 MW	75790 TQ	USBLS	5/07
Educational, Vocational, and School Counselor							
	Alabama	Y	40140 FQ	47560 MW	55430 TQ	USBLS	5/07
	Birmingham-Hoover MSA, AL	Y	41480 FQ	50870 MW	58870 TQ	USBLS	5/07
	Mobile MSA, AL	Y	37610 FQ	46310 MW	53520 TQ	USBLS	5/07
	Alaska	Y	42720 FQ	54790 MW	66860 TQ	USBLS	5/07
	Anchorage MSA, AK	Y	41790 FQ	50800 MW	64430 TQ	USBLS	5/07
	Arizona	Y	32970 FQ	41630 MW	51220 TQ	USBLS	5/07
	Phoenix-Mesa-Scottsdale MSA, AZ	Y	32270 FQ	40850 MW	50220 TQ	USBLS	5/07
	Tucson MSA, AZ	Y	35540 FQ	43750 MW	55510 TQ	USBLS	5/07
	Arkansas	Y	40960 FQ	49470 MW	57990 TQ	USBLS	5/07
	Little Rock-North Little Rock MSA, AR	Y	45570 FQ	55980 MW	63230 TQ	USBLS	5/07
	California	H	19.39 FQ	26.45 MW	36.54 TQ	CABLS	1/08-3/08

AE	Average entry wage	AW	Average wage paid	FQ	First quartile wage	LO	Lowest wage paid	MTC	Median total compensation	TCC	Total cash compensation
AER	Average entry range	AWR	Average wage range	H	Hourly	LR	Low end range	MW	Median wage paid	TQ	Third quartile wage
AEX	Average experienced wage	AXR	Average experienced range	HI	Highest wage paid	M	Monthly	MWR	Median wage range	W	Weekly
ATC	Average total compensation	D	Daily	HR	High end range	MCC	Median cash compensation	S	See annotated source	Y	Yearly

473

Occupation/Type/Industry	Location	Per	Low	Mid	High	Source	Date
Educational, Vocational, and School Counselor	Fresno MSA, CA	H	14.55 FQ	21.51 MW	37.80 TQ	CABLS	1/08-3/08
	Los Angeles-Long Beach-Glendale PMSA, CA	H	19.38 FQ	23.20 MW	34.81 TQ	CABLS	1/08-3/08
	Oakland-Fremont-Hayward MSA, CA	H	20.65 FQ	28.37 MW	36.15 TQ	CABLS	1/08-3/08
	Riverside-San Bernardino-Ontario MSA, CA	H	21.17 FQ	28.37 MW	35.91 TQ	CABLS	1/08-3/08
	Sacramento-Arden Arcade-Roseville MSA, CA	H	16.37 FQ	24.77 MW	34.71 TQ	CABLS	1/08-3/08
	San Diego-Carlsbad-San Marcos MSA, CA	H	17.04 FQ	24.52 MW	35.53 TQ	CABLS	1/08-3/08
	San Francisco-San Mateo-Redwood PMSA, CA	H	20.70 FQ	29.68 MW	40.60 TQ	CABLS	1/08-3/08
	San Jose-Sunnyvale-Santa Clara MSA, CA	H	24.05 FQ	33.82 MW	39.83 TQ	CABLS	1/08-3/08
	Santa Ana-Anaheim-Irvine PMSA, CA	Y	39320 FQ	55620 MW	77930 TQ	USBLS	5/07
	Colorado	Y	36220 FQ	45100 MW	57920 TQ	USBLS	5/07
	Denver-Aurora MSA, CO	Y	37750 FQ	48230 MW	62660 TQ	USBLS	5/07
	Connecticut	H	16.69 AE	28.73 MW		CTBLS	1/08-3/08
	Bridgeport-Stamford-Norwalk MSA, CT	Y	43800 FQ	64030 MW	83590 TQ	USBLS	5/07
	Hartford-West Hartford-East Hartford MSA, CT	Y	35640 FQ	53560 MW	68290 TQ	USBLS	5/07
	Delaware	Y	36790 FQ	49700 MW	67190 TQ	USBLS	5/07
	Wilmington PMSA, DE-MD-NJ	Y	38870 FQ	52670 MW	71930 TQ	USBLS	5/07
	District of Columbia	Y	39150 FQ	47040 MW	56520 TQ	USBLS	5/07
	Washington-Arlington-Alexandria MSA, DC-VA-MD-WV	Y	45880 FQ	60630 MW	81520 TQ	USBLS	5/07
	Florida	Y	36510 FQ	50940 MW	67030 TQ	USBLS	5/07
	Fort Lauderdale-Pompano Beach-Deerfield Beach PMSA, FL	Y	23480 FQ	34770 MW	63600 TQ	USBLS	5/07
	Jacksonville MSA, FL	Y	31100 FQ	40520 MW	56710 TQ	USBLS	5/07
	Orlando-Kissimmee MSA, FL	Y	44520 FQ	56100 MW	68100 TQ	USBLS	5/07
	Pensacola-Ferry Pass-Brent MSA, FL	Y	34580 FQ	46910 MW	63060 TQ	USBLS	5/07
	Tampa-St. Petersburg-Clearwater MSA, FL	Y	42760 FQ	55050 MW	69550 TQ	USBLS	5/07
	West Palm Beach-Boca Raton-Boynton Beach PMSA, FL	Y	38030 FQ	47860 MW	63220 TQ	USBLS	5/07
	Georgia	Y	42490 FQ	54380 MW	64480 TQ	USBLS	5/07
	Atlanta-Sandy Springs-Marietta MSA, GA	Y	46640 FQ	56800 MW	67280 TQ	USBLS	5/07
	Macon MSA, GA	Y	33670 FQ	42640 MW	59110 TQ	USBLS	5/07
	Savannah MSA, GA	Y	38460 FQ	51380 MW	59440 TQ	USBLS	5/07
	Hawaii	Y	40920 FQ	50930 MW	61140 TQ	USBLS	5/07
	Honolulu MSA, HI	Y	36860 FQ	48480 MW	61750 TQ	USBLS	5/07
	Idaho	Y	38120 FQ	47220 MW	57450 TQ	USBLS	5/07
	Boise City-Nampa MSA, ID	Y	34560 FQ	43910 MW	56260 TQ	USBLS	5/07
	Illinois	Y	38940 FQ	59800 MW	83610 TQ	USBLS	5/07
	Chicago-Naperville-Joliet MSA, IL-IN-WI	Y	43560 FQ	66040 MW	88950 TQ	USBLS	5/07
	Indiana	Y	25230 FQ	32610 MW	48070 TQ	USBLS	5/07
	Gary PMSA, IN	Y	37430 FQ	48290 MW	62010 TQ	USBLS	5/07
	Indianapolis-Carmel MSA, IN	Y	23820 FQ	26900 MW	33510 TQ	USBLS	5/07
	Iowa	Y	32130 FQ	41650 MW	51930 TQ	USBLS	5/07
	Des Moines-West Des Moines MSA, IA	Y	36760 FQ	45460 MW	56330 TQ	USBLS	5/07
	Waterloo-Cedar Falls MSA, IA	Y	33030 FQ	41770 MW	49210 TQ	USBLS	5/07
	Kansas	Y	37330 FQ	45350 MW	53670 TQ	USBLS	5/07
	Lawrence MSA, KS	Y	33240 FQ	37230 MW	44900 TQ	USBLS	5/07
	Wichita MSA, KS	Y	39240 FQ	50280 MW	56780 TQ	USBLS	5/07
	Kentucky	Y	43997 FQ	55161 MW	64036 TQ	KYBLS	2008
	Louisville-Jefferson County MSA, KY-IN	Y	45090 FQ	60570 MW	74440 TQ	USBLS	5/07
	Louisiana	H	19.06 FQ	22.49 MW	26.03 TQ	LABLS	1/08-3/08
	Baton Rouge MSA, LA	Y	36870 FQ	46450 MW	54460 TQ	USBLS	5/07

AE	Average entry wage	AW	Average wage paid	FQ	First quartile wage	LO	Lowest wage paid	MTC	Median total compensation	TCC	Total cash compensation
AER	Average entry range	AWR	Average wage range	H	Hourly	LR	Low end range	MW	Median wage paid	TQ	Third quartile wage
AEX	Average experienced wage	AXR	Average experienced range	HI	Highest wage paid	M	Monthly	MWR	Median wage range	W	Weekly
ATC	Average total compensation	D	Daily	HR	High end range	MCC	Median cash compensation	S	See annotated source	Y	Yearly

474

Occupation/Type/Industry	Location	Per	Low	Mid	High	Source	Date
Educational, Vocational, and School Counselor	New Orleans-Metairie-Kenner MSA, LA	Y	41440 FQ	47550 MW	53730 TQ	USBLS	5/07
	Maine	Y	35650 FQ	44280 MW	54650 TQ	USBLS	5/07
	Lewiston-Auburn MSA, ME	Y	33740 FQ	41500 MW	53640 TQ	USBLS	5/07
	Portland-South Portland-Biddeford MSA, ME	Y	39530 FQ	49960 MW	58180 TQ	USBLS	5/07
	Maryland	Y		54475 MW		MDBLS	3/08
	Baltimore-Towson MSA, MD	Y	31050 FQ	47920 MW	66090 TQ	USBLS	5/07
	Bethesda-Gaithersburg-Frederick PMSA, MD	Y	44460 FQ	58130 MW	84480 TQ	USBLS	5/07
	Massachusetts	Y	38160 FQ	51630 MW	64350 TQ	USBLS	5/07
	Boston-Cambridge-Quincy NECTA, MA	Y	37630 FQ	50240 MW	65630 TQ	USBLS	5/07
	Worcester MSA, MA-CT	Y	40960 FQ	53430 MW	64140 TQ	USBLS	5/07
	Michigan	Y	38610 FQ	49560 MW	67190 TQ	USBLS	5/07
	Detroit-Warren-Livonia MSA, MI	Y	40510 FQ	49200 MW	72580 TQ	USBLS	5/07
	Grand Rapids-Wyoming MSA, MI	Y	26370 FQ	39380 MW	61480 TQ	USBLS	5/07
	Warren-Troy-Farmington Hills PMSA, MI	Y	42310 FQ	59190 MW	77880 TQ	USBLS	5/07
	Minnesota	Y	36617 FQ	47184 MW	60607 TQ	MNBLS	10/08-12/08
	Duluth-Superior MSA, MN-WI	Y	37297 FQ	49800 MW	60430 TQ	MNBLS	10/08-12/08
	Minneapolis-Saint Paul MSA, MN-WI	Y	37277 FQ	47917 MW	63150 TQ	MNBLS	10/08-12/08
	Rochester MSA, MN	Y	27041 FQ	32624 MW	41360 TQ	MNBLS	10/08-12/08
	Mississippi	Y	39010 FQ	48520 MW	57500 TQ	USBLS	5/07
	Jackson MSA, MS	Y	35070 FQ	44660 MW	55390 TQ	USBLS	5/07
	Missouri	Y	33980 FQ	42880 MW	56280 TQ	USBLS	5/07
	Kansas City MSA, MO-KS	Y	37140 FQ	47960 MW	59740 TQ	USBLS	5/07
	St. Louis MSA, MO-IL	Y	36690 FQ	48290 MW	63760 TQ	USBLS	5/07
	Montana	Y	24330 FQ	36970 MW	50010 TQ	USBLS	5/07
	Billings MSA, MT	Y	30220 FQ	39360 MW	53850 TQ	USBLS	5/07
	Missoula MSA, MT	Y	21610 FQ	24870 MW	41940 TQ	USBLS	5/07
	Nebraska	Y	34290 FQ	44550 MW	53820 TQ	USBLS	5/07
	Lincoln MSA, NE	Y	26280 FQ	44030 MW	55360 TQ	USBLS	5/07
	Omaha-Council Bluffs MSA, NE-IA	Y	33450 FQ	43400 MW	52410 TQ	USBLS	5/07
	Nevada	H	19.34 FQ	23.61 MW	28.34 TQ	NVBLS	5/08
	Las Vegas-Paradise MSA, NV	H	19.41 FQ	23.30 MW	27.57 TQ	NVBLS	5/08
	New Hampshire	H	18.85 AE	25.25 MW	28.54 AEX	NHBLS	6/08
	Manchester MSA, NH	Y	40000 FQ	51080 MW	59880 TQ	USBLS	5/07
	Nashua NECTA, NH-MA	Y	44310 FQ	55650 MW	64460 TQ	USBLS	5/07
	Rochester-Dover MSA, NH-ME	Y	39800 FQ	48970 MW	57920 TQ	USBLS	5/07
	New Jersey	Y	52240 FQ	66940 MW	83810 TQ	USBLS	5/07
	Camden PMSA, NJ	Y	54550 FQ	68500 MW	79750 TQ	USBLS	5/07
	Edison PMSA, NJ	Y	54170 FQ	66470 MW	80180 TQ	USBLS	5/07
	Newark-Union PMSA, NJ-PA	Y	49770 FQ	66880 MW	86250 TQ	USBLS	5/07
	Trenton-Ewing MSA, NJ	Y	45440 FQ	68080 MW	83780 TQ	USBLS	5/07
	New Mexico	Y	32950 FQ	44320 MW	57910 TQ	USBLS	5/07
	Albuquerque MSA, NM	Y	30640 FQ	39520 MW	55000 TQ	USBLS	5/07
	New York	Y	40760 FQ	54340 MW	71950 TQ	USBLS	5/07
	Albany-Schenectady-Troy MSA, NY	Y	36570 FQ	46960 MW	60860 TQ	USBLS	5/07
	Buffalo-Niagara Falls MSA, NY	Y	37820 FQ	48280 MW	60980 TQ	USBLS	5/07
	Nassau-Suffolk PMSA, NY	Y	51460 FQ	69400 MW	91020 TQ	USBLS	5/07
	New York-Northern New Jersey-Long Island MSA, NY-NJ-PA	Y	46230 FQ	62310 MW	80810 TQ	USBLS	5/07
	North Carolina	Y	36470 FQ	43990 MW	53000 TQ	USBLS	5/07
	Charlotte-Gastonia-Concord MSA, NC-SC	Y	35520 FQ	42600 MW	57090 TQ	USBLS	5/07
	Raleigh-Cary MSA, NC	Y	42030 FQ	49770 MW	59790 TQ	USBLS	5/07
	North Dakota	Y	34810 FQ	42720 MW	52380 TQ	USBLS	5/07
	Fargo MSA, ND-MN	Y	34140 FQ	40200 MW	55650 TQ	USBLS	5/07
	Ohio	Y	45730 FQ	59540 MW	71720 TQ	USBLS	5/07
	Cincinnati-Middletown MSA, OH-KY-IN	Y	46500 FQ	63630 MW	75420 TQ	USBLS	5/07

AE	Average entry wage	AW	Average wage paid	FQ	First quartile wage	LO	Lowest wage paid	MTC	Median total compensation	TCC	Total cash compensation
AER	Average entry range	AWR	Average wage range	H	Hourly	LR	Low end range	MW	Median wage paid	TQ	Third quartile wage
AEX	Average experienced wage	AXR	Average experienced range	HI	Highest wage paid	M	Monthly	MWR	Median wage range	W	Weekly
ATC	Average total compensation	D	Daily	HR	High end range	MCC	Median cash compensation	S	See annotated source	Y	Yearly

Occupation/Type/Industry	Location	Per	Low	Mid	High	Source	Date
Educational, Vocational, and School Counselor	Cleveland-Elyria-Mentor MSA, OH	Y	53930 FQ	65650 MW	77800 TQ	USBLS	5/07
	Columbus MSA, OH	Y	43810 FQ	58960 MW	73760 TQ	USBLS	5/07
	Dayton MSA, OH	Y	42590 FQ	56200 MW	67000 TQ	USBLS	5/07
	Oklahoma	Y	28560 FQ	38250 MW	47650 TQ	USBLS	5/07
	Oklahoma City MSA, OK	Y	34440 FQ	42110 MW	50860 TQ	USBLS	5/07
	Tulsa MSA, OK	Y	33250 FQ	41210 MW	50790 TQ	USBLS	5/07
	Oregon	H	19.03 FQ	24.01 MW	29.45 TQ	ORBLS	5/08
	Portland-Vancouver-Beaverton MSA, OR-WA	Y	38430 FQ	48320 MW	60930 TQ	USBLS	5/07
	Pennsylvania	Y	35410 FQ	45740 MW	59790 TQ	USBLS	5/07
	Allentown-Bethlehem-Easton MSA, PA-NJ	Y	41000 FQ	50600 MW	63130 TQ	USBLS	5/07
	Lancaster MSA, PA	Y	40570 FQ	48360 MW	61950 TQ	USBLS	5/07
	Philadelphia-Camden-Wilmington MSA, PA-NJ-DE-MD	Y	36660 FQ	49100 MW	66080 TQ	USBLS	5/07
	Pittsburgh MSA, PA	Y	35790 FQ	46360 MW	60160 TQ	USBLS	5/07
	Rhode Island	Y	40720 FQ	58210 MW	71680 TQ	USBLS	5/07
	Providence-Fall River-Warwick MSA, RI-MA	Y	40320 FQ	56540 MW	69890 TQ	USBLS	5/07
	South Carolina	Y	34490 FQ	45870 MW	57020 TQ	USBLS	5/07
	Charleston-North Charleston MSA, SC	Y	38510 FQ	47670 MW	60100 TQ	USBLS	5/07
	Columbia MSA, SC	Y	31400 FQ	42910 MW	54760 TQ	USBLS	5/07
	Myrtle Beach-Conway-North Myrtle Beach MSA, SC	Y	40250 FQ	51630 MW	63230 TQ	USBLS	5/07
	Spartanburg MSA, SC	Y	32330 FQ	44830 MW	56520 TQ	USBLS	5/07
	South Dakota	Y	32423 FQ	37435 MW	44529 TQ	SDBLS	7/08-9/08
	Sioux Falls MSA, SD	Y	34268 FQ	38090 MW	45149 TQ	SDBLS	7/08-9/08
	Tennessee	Y	32370 FQ	41600 MW	50910 TQ	USBLS	5/07
	Memphis MSA, TN-MS-AR	Y	36860 FQ	43820 MW	50550 TQ	USBLS	5/07
	Nashville-Davidson-Murfreesboro MSA, TN	Y	37630 FQ	47680 MW	60030 TQ	USBLS	5/07
	Texas	Y	42580 FQ	51820 MW	60750 TQ	USBLS	5/07
	Austin-Round Rock MSA, TX	Y	40670 FQ	48960 MW	58240 TQ	USBLS	5/07
	Dallas-Fort Worth-Arlington MSA, TX	Y	45210 FQ	54650 MW	62720 TQ	USBLS	5/07
	El Paso MSA, TX	Y	43450 FQ	55140 MW	64590 TQ	USBLS	5/07
	Houston-Sugar Land-Baytown MSA, TX	Y	43890 FQ	53740 MW	63070 TQ	USBLS	5/07
	San Antonio MSA, TX	Y	42530 FQ	52790 MW	62460 TQ	USBLS	5/07
	Utah	Y	33910 FQ	43700 MW	55230 TQ	USBLS	5/07
	Salt Lake City MSA, UT	Y	37270 FQ	48220 MW	62210 TQ	USBLS	5/07
	Vermont	Y	39860 FQ	46960 MW	56480 TQ	USBLS	5/07
	Burlington-South Burlington MSA, VT	Y	40940 FQ	51190 MW	62310 TQ	USBLS	5/07
	Virginia	Y	40670 FQ	53870 MW	69640 TQ	USBLS	5/07
	Richmond MSA, VA	Y	40250 FQ	52440 MW	64040 TQ	USBLS	5/07
	Virginia Beach-Norfolk-Newport News MSA, VA-NC	Y	38600 FQ	50140 MW	62340 TQ	USBLS	5/07
	Washington	H	21.40 FQ	24.88 MW	30.75 TQ	WABLS	3/08
	Olympia MSA, WA	Y	45460 FQ	52470 MW	62790 TQ	USBLS	5/07
	Seattle-Tacoma-Bellevue MSA, WA	Y	44580 FQ	51450 MW	64820 TQ	USBLS	5/07
	West Virginia	Y	29120 FQ	41217 MW	50393 TQ	WVBLS	7/08-9/08
	Charleston MSA, WV	Y	29870 FQ	43820 MW	54230 TQ	USBLS	5/07
	Wisconsin	Y	38060 FQ	48120 MW	59750 TQ	USBLS	5/07
	Milwaukee-Waukesha-West Allis MSA, WI	Y	35630 FQ'	48600 MW	64030 TQ	USBLS	5/07
	Wyoming	Y	39467 FQ	49770 MW	60268 TQ	WYBLS	9/08
	Casper MSA, WY	Y	43594 FQ	52661 MW	61773 TQ	WYBLS	9/08
	Cheyenne MSA, WY	Y	41225 FQ	52216 MW	65433 TQ	WYBLS	9/08
	Puerto Rico	Y	28210 FQ	33700 MW	37030 TQ	USBLS	5/07
	San Juan-Caguas-Guaynabo MSA, PR	Y	26910 FQ	33230 MW	36760 TQ	USBLS	5/07
	Virgin Islands	Y	41110 FQ	47370 MW	58280 TQ	USBLS	5/07
	Guam	Y	31670 FQ	43420 MW	53110 TQ	USBLS	5/07
Egg Products Inspector State Government	Ohio	H	16.35 LO		19.88 HI	ODAS	2008

AE	Average entry wage	AW	Average wage paid	FQ	First quartile wage	LO	Lowest wage paid	MTC	Median total compensation	TCC	Total cash compensation
AER	Average entry range	AWR	Average wage range	H	Hourly	LR	Low end range	MW	Median wage paid	TQ	Third quartile wage
AEX	Average experienced wage	AXR	Average experienced range	HI	Highest wage paid	M	Monthly	MWR	Median wage range	W	Weekly
ATC	Average total compensation	D	Daily	HR	High end range	MCC	Median cash compensation	S	See annotated source	Y	Yearly

Occupation/Type/Industry	Location	Per	Low	Mid	High	Source	Date
Elder Care Homemaker	Massachusetts	Y		16599 AW		MASS	2008
Election Chairperson	Michigan	D			175 HI	NHERLD3	2008
Election Worker	Michigan	D			135 HI	NHERLD3	2008
Electric Lineman	Walton County, GA	Y	28049 LO		50110 HI	GACTY03	2008
Electric Motor, Power Tool, and Related Repairer	Alabama	Y	26290 FQ	33570 MW	38800 TQ	USBLS	5/07
	Birmingham-Hoover MSA, AL	Y	28230 FQ	37230 MW	45020 TQ	USBLS	5/07
	Alaska	Y	28020 FQ	36290 MW	46820 TQ	USBLS	5/07
	Arizona	Y	15940 FQ	32800 MW	38300 TQ	USBLS	5/07
	Phoenix-Mesa-Scottsdale MSA, AZ	Y	15270 FQ	32670 MW	37540 TQ	USBLS	5/07
	Tucson MSA, AZ	Y	27780 FQ	34980 MW	42360 TQ	USBLS	5/07
	Arkansas	Y	21320 FQ	26380 MW	30820 TQ	USBLS	5/07
	Little Rock-North Little Rock MSA, AR	Y	21590 FQ	26640 MW	29760 TQ	USBLS	5/07
	California	H	14.10 FQ	18.81 MW	24.36 TQ	CABLS	1/08-3/08
	Bakersfield MSA, CA	H	17.74 FQ	19.71 MW	22.47 TQ	CABLS	1/08-3/08
	Los Angeles-Long Beach-Glendale PMSA, CA	H	14.53 FQ	20.23 MW	27.07 TQ	CABLS	1/08-3/08
	Oakland-Fremont-Hayward MSA, CA	H	18.99 FQ	23.89 MW	28.23 TQ	CABLS	1/08-3/08
	Riverside-San Bernardino-Ontario MSA, CA	H	14.10 FQ	18.11 MW	21.44 TQ	CABLS	1/08-3/08
	Sacramento-Arden Arcade-Roseville MSA, CA	H	13.81 FQ	16.28 MW	19.05 TQ	CABLS	1/08-3/08
	San Diego-Carlsbad-San Marcos MSA, CA	H	17.10 FQ	21.33 MW	24.80 TQ	CABLS	1/08-3/08
	Santa Ana-Anaheim-Irvine PMSA, CA	Y	25200 FQ	27720 MW	31280 TQ	USBLS	5/07
	Colorado	Y	26790 FQ	31400 MW	39760 TQ	USBLS	5/07
	Denver-Aurora MSA, CO	Y	26530 FQ	32300 MW	47140 TQ	USBLS	5/07
	Connecticut	H	16.10 AE	22.03 MW		CTBLS	1/08-3/08
	Bridgeport-Stamford-Norwalk MSA, CT	Y	37760 FQ	45760 MW	59380 TQ	USBLS	5/07
	Hartford-West Hartford-East Hartford MSA, CT	Y	37120 FQ	53750 MW	62210 TQ	USBLS	5/07
	Washington-Arlington-Alexandria MSA, DC-VA-MD-WV	Y	25400 FQ	29180 MW	35190 TQ	USBLS	5/07
	Florida	Y	25750 FQ	31330 MW	38260 TQ	USBLS	5/07
	Fort Lauderdale-Pompano Beach-Deerfield Beach PMSA, FL	Y	38000 FQ	43760 MW	52530 TQ	USBLS	5/07
	Jacksonville MSA, FL	Y	26250 FQ	32230 MW	37630 TQ	USBLS	5/07
	Miami-Fort Lauderdale-Miami Beach MSA, FL	Y	25450 FQ	35580 MW	45120 TQ	USBLS	5/07
	Orlando-Kissimmee MSA, FL	Y	26310 FQ	28930 MW	33180 TQ	USBLS	5/07
	Tampa-St. Petersburg-Clearwater MSA, FL	Y	26140 FQ	32300 MW	38360 TQ	USBLS	5/07
	West Palm Beach-Boca Raton-Boynton Beach PMSA, FL	Y	28180 FQ	32580 MW	35510 TQ	USBLS	5/07
	Georgia	Y	33350 FQ	41920 MW	47190 TQ	USBLS	5/07
	Atlanta-Sandy Springs-Marietta MSA, GA	Y	37330 FQ	44480 MW	49300 TQ	USBLS	5/07
	Augusta-Richmond County MSA, GA-SC	Y	28060 FQ	35450 MW	44290 TQ	USBLS	5/07
	Macon MSA, GA	Y	21050 FQ	32230 MW	39380 TQ	USBLS	5/07
	Hawaii	Y	25350 FQ	30830 MW	35050 TQ	USBLS	5/07
	Idaho	Y	27830 FQ	30670 MW	35680 TQ	USBLS	5/07
	Illinois	Y	29440 FQ	40980 MW	50860 TQ	USBLS	5/07
	Chicago-Naperville-Joliet MSA, IL-IN-WI	Y	31790 FQ	44130 MW	67970 TQ	USBLS	5/07
	Indiana	Y	25840 FQ	32870 MW	44180 TQ	USBLS	5/07
	Indianapolis-Carmel MSA, IN	Y	23410 FQ	26670 MW	33510 TQ	USBLS	5/07
	Iowa	Y	27280 FQ	34260 MW	39180 TQ	USBLS	5/07
	Sioux City MSA, IA-NE-SD	Y	26210 FQ	29980 MW	36270 TQ	USBLS	5/07
	Kansas	Y	27530 FQ	37870 MW	43640 TQ	USBLS	5/07
	Kentucky	Y	23223 FQ	28587 MW	32871 TQ	KYBLS	2008

AE Average entry wage	**AW** Average wage paid	**FQ** First quartile wage	**LO** Lowest wage paid	**MTC** Median total compensation	**TCC** Total cash compensation
AER Average entry range	**AWR** Average wage range	**H** Hourly	**LR** Low end range	**MW** Median wage paid	**TQ** Third quartile wage
AEX Average experienced wage	**AXR** Average experienced range	**HI** Highest wage paid	**M** Monthly	**MWR** Median wage range	**W** Weekly
ATC Average total compensation	**D** Daily	**HR** High end range	**MCC** Median cash compensation	**S** See annotated source	**Y** Yearly

Electric Motor, Power Tool, and Related Repairer

Occupation/Type/Industry	Location	Per	Low	Mid	High	Source	Date
	Lexington-Fayette MSA, KY	Y	26680 FQ	29100 MW	31780 TQ	USBLS	5/07
	Louisville-Jefferson County MSA, KY-IN	Y	26970 FQ	30180 MW	37910 TQ	USBLS	5/07
	Louisiana	H	13.88 FQ	17.50 MW	22.69 TQ	LABLS	1/08-3/08
	Baton Rouge MSA, LA	Y	28790 FQ	37950 MW	47790 TQ	USBLS	5/07
	New Orleans-Metairie-Kenner MSA, LA	Y	30260 FQ	35140 MW	43600 TQ	USBLS	5/07
	Maine	Y	26610 FQ	31210 MW	39540 TQ	USBLS	5/07
	Maryland	Y		29950 MW		MDBLS	3/08
	Baltimore-Towson MSA, MD	Y	26290 FQ	30210 MW	40270 TQ	USBLS	5/07
	Bethesda-Gaithersburg-Frederick PMSA, MD	Y	23520 FQ	26720 MW	29790 TQ	USBLS	5/07
	Massachusetts	Y	30680 FQ	39820 MW	49170 TQ	USBLS	5/07
	Boston-Cambridge-Quincy NECTA, MA	Y	41170 FQ	55410 MW	61240 TQ	USBLS	5/07
	Michigan	Y	29040 FQ	37130 MW	46770 TQ	USBLS	5/07
	Detroit-Warren-Livonia MSA, MI	Y	33600 FQ	40320 MW	57020 TQ	USBLS	5/07
	Grand Rapids-Wyoming MSA, MI	Y	26660 FQ	32090 MW	39190 TQ	USBLS	5/07
	Warren-Troy-Farmington Hills PMSA, MI	Y	33640 FQ	40580 MW	57140 TQ	USBLS	5/07
	Minnesota	Y	27828 FQ	39702 MW	50580 TQ	MNBLS	10/08-12/08
	Minneapolis-Saint Paul MSA, MN-WI	Y	36723 FQ	45272 MW	57345 TQ	MNBLS	10/08-12/08
	Mississippi	Y	23800 FQ	31150 MW	36120 TQ	USBLS	5/07
	Jackson MSA, MS	Y	17290 FQ	18850 MW	24570 TQ	USBLS	5/07
	Missouri	Y	23540 FQ	30400 MW	39940 TQ	USBLS	5/07
	Kansas City MSA, MO-KS	Y	28950 FQ	38530 MW	48350 TQ	USBLS	5/07
	St. Louis MSA, MO-IL	Y	33950 FQ	39240 MW	46140 TQ	USBLS	5/07
	Montana	Y	23310 FQ	38670 MW	49180 TQ	USBLS	5/07
	Billings MSA, MT	Y	28730 FQ	43710 MW	49150 TQ	USBLS	5/07
	Nebraska	Y	27520 FQ	33840 MW	43350 TQ	USBLS	5/07
	Omaha-Council Bluffs MSA, NE-IA	Y	30880 FQ	35460 MW	43630 TQ	USBLS	5/07
	Nevada	H	13.06 FQ	14.85 MW	18.68 TQ	NVBLS	5/08
	Las Vegas-Paradise MSA, NV	H	12.81 FQ	14.57 MW	17.27 TQ	NVBLS	5/08
	New Hampshire	H	15.99 AE	18.52 MW	24.70 AEX	NHBLS	6/08
	Manchester MSA, NH	Y	32610 FQ	36070 MW	43010 TQ	USBLS	5/07
	New Jersey	Y	33210 FQ	44210 MW	53010 TQ	USBLS	5/07
	Camden PMSA, NJ	Y	29520 FQ	41840 MW	50490 TQ	USBLS	5/07
	Edison PMSA, NJ	Y	40250 FQ	50890 MW	57970 TQ	USBLS	5/07
	Newark-Union PMSA, NJ-PA	Y	36190 FQ	45150 MW	54370 TQ	USBLS	5/07
	New Mexico	Y	23250 FQ	26670 MW	30460 TQ	USBLS	5/07
	Albuquerque MSA, NM	Y	22800 FQ	25740 MW	29760 TQ	USBLS	5/07
	New York	Y	25500 FQ	34180 MW	46220 TQ	USBLS	5/07
	Nassau-Suffolk PMSA, NY	Y	27320 FQ	35570 MW	44630 TQ	USBLS	5/07
	New York-Northern New Jersey-Long Island MSA, NY-NJ-PA	Y	33140 FQ	43560 MW	54150 TQ	USBLS	5/07
	North Carolina	Y	24820 FQ	28620 MW	37650 TQ	USBLS	5/07
	Charlotte-Gastonia-Concord MSA, NC-SC	Y	24080 FQ	32930 MW	38850 TQ	USBLS	5/07
	Raleigh-Cary MSA, NC	Y	27820 FQ	30270 MW	32770 TQ	USBLS	5/07
	Ohio	Y	31660 FQ	38490 MW	45780 TQ	USBLS	5/07
	Cincinnati-Middletown MSA, OH-KY-IN	Y	35590 FQ	40720 MW	46450 TQ	USBLS	5/07
	Cleveland-Elyria-Mentor MSA, OH	Y	20550 FQ	37370 MW	44220 TQ	USBLS	5/07
	Columbus MSA, OH	Y	35520 FQ	40820 MW	46030 TQ	USBLS	5/07
	Dayton MSA, OH	Y	42520 FQ	48010 MW	64930 TQ	USBLS	5/07
	Oklahoma	Y	24190 FQ	29430 MW	35920 TQ	USBLS	5/07
	Oklahoma City MSA, OK	Y	23190 FQ	27800 MW	35830 TQ	USBLS	5/07
	Tulsa MSA, OK	Y	28630 FQ	31920 MW	36720 TQ	USBLS	5/07
	Oregon	H	11.52 FQ	14.39 MW	21.10 TQ	ORBLS	5/08
	Portland-Vancouver-Beaverton MSA, OR-WA	Y	29240 FQ	40060 MW	56120 TQ	USBLS	5/07
	Pennsylvania	Y	30490 FQ	37100 MW	46530 TQ	USBLS	5/07
	Allentown-Bethlehem-Easton MSA, PA-NJ	Y	33630 FQ	37900 MW	43500 TQ	USBLS	5/07
	Lancaster MSA, PA	Y	31240 FQ	35160 MW	39440 TQ	USBLS	5/07

AE	Average entry wage	AW	Average wage paid	FQ	First quartile wage
AER	Average entry range	AWR	Average wage range	H	Hourly
AEX	Average experienced wage	AXR	Average experienced range	HI	Highest wage paid
ATC	Average total compensation	D	Daily	HR	High end range

LO	Lowest wage paid	MTC	Median total compensation
LR	Low end range	MW	Median wage paid
M	Monthly	MWR	Median wage range
MCC	Median cash compensation	S	See annotated source

TCC	Total cash compensation
TQ	Third quartile wage
W	Weekly
Y	Yearly

Occupation/Type/Industry	Location	Per	Low	Mid	High	Source	Date
Electric Motor, Power Tool, and Related Repairer	Philadelphia-Camden-Wilmington MSA, PA-NJ-DE-MD	Y	30860 FQ	41210 MW	50470 TQ	USBLS	5/07
	Pittsburgh MSA, PA	Y	28330 FQ	34300 MW	39740 TQ	USBLS	5/07
	Rhode Island	Y	28550 FQ	36460 MW	42890 TQ	USBLS	5/07
	Providence-Fall River-Warwick MSA, RI-MA	Y	26520 FQ	34070 MW	43820 TQ	USBLS	5/07
	South Carolina	Y	24240 FQ	31510 MW	37630 TQ	USBLS	5/07
	Charleston-North Charleston MSA, SC	Y	27860 FQ	33440 MW	38260 TQ	USBLS	5/07
	South Dakota	Y	18136 FQ	23505 MW	28944 TQ	SDBLS	7/08-9/08
	Tennessee	Y	28090 FQ	31200 MW	39900 TQ	USBLS	5/07
	Memphis MSA, TN-MS-AR	Y	27510 FQ	30270 MW	33020 TQ	USBLS	5/07
	Nashville-Davidson-Murfreesboro MSA, TN	Y	28190 FQ	30660 MW	37240 TQ	USBLS	5/07
	Texas	Y	21440 FQ	29460 MW	39090 TQ	USBLS	5/07
	Austin-Round Rock MSA, TX	Y	21500 FQ	29790 MW	46070 TQ	USBLS	5/07
	Dallas-Fort Worth-Arlington MSA, TX	Y	22830 FQ	29140 MW	37220 TQ	USBLS	5/07
	Houston-Sugar Land-Baytown MSA, TX	Y	18960 FQ	30990 MW	38650 TQ	USBLS	5/07
	San Antonio MSA, TX	Y	26070 FQ	32610 MW	51000 TQ	USBLS	5/07
	Utah	Y	25960 FQ	28450 MW	30910 TQ	USBLS	5/07
	Salt Lake City MSA, UT	Y	24530 FQ	27760 MW	30530 TQ	USBLS	5/07
	Vermont	Y	26000 FQ	33340 MW	37160 TQ	USBLS	5/07
	Virginia	Y	30170 FQ	35430 MW	41350 TQ	USBLS	5/07
	Richmond MSA, VA	Y	31810 FQ	35500 MW	39180 TQ	USBLS	5/07
	Roanoke MSA, VA	Y	34380 FQ	37470 MW	42120 TQ	USBLS	5/07
	Virginia Beach-Norfolk-Newport News MSA, VA-NC	Y	33100 FQ	39540 MW	49090 TQ	USBLS	5/07
	Washington	H	16.81 FQ	20.24 MW	26.10 TQ	WABLS	3/08
	Seattle-Tacoma-Bellevue MSA, WA	Y	35600 FQ	42810 MW	54330 TQ	USBLS	5/07
	West Virginia	Y	29341 FQ	39976 MW	47386 TQ	WVBLS	7/08-9/08
	Wisconsin	Y	30550 FQ	37130 MW	44420 TQ	USBLS	5/07
	Green Bay MSA, WI	Y	35040 FQ	40420 MW	44470 TQ	USBLS	5/07
	Milwaukee-Waukesha-West Allis MSA, WI	Y	30520 FQ	35910 MW	43750 TQ	USBLS	5/07
	Wyoming	Y	34210 FQ	42988 MW	49319 TQ	WYBLS	9/08
	Puerto Rico	Y	15650 FQ	18280 MW	34010 TQ	USBLS	5/07
	San Juan-Caguas-Guaynabo MSA, PR	Y	16440 FQ	26580 MW	39420 TQ	USBLS	5/07
Electric Superintendent/Manager	Walton County, GA	Y	38764 LO		68192 HI	GACTY03	2008
Electric Technician	Chatham County, GA	Y	35186 LO		55587 HI	GACTY03	2008
	Fulton County, GA	Y	23536 LO		45952 HI	GACTY03	2008
Electrical and Electronic Engineering Technician	Alabama	Y	35780 FQ	48980 MW	58400 TQ	USBLS	5/07
	Birmingham-Hoover MSA, AL	Y	35590 FQ	49870 MW	57630 TQ	USBLS	5/07
	Alaska	Y	43680 FQ	61810 MW	73720 TQ	USBLS	5/07
	Anchorage MSA, AK	Y	56630 FQ	66990 MW	76450 TQ	USBLS	5/07
	Arizona	Y	36940 FQ	49180 MW	61390 TQ	USBLS	5/07
	Phoenix-Mesa-Scottsdale MSA, AZ	Y	35830 FQ	48890 MW	61310 TQ	USBLS	5/07
	Tucson MSA, AZ	Y	41830 FQ	49500 MW	59290 TQ	USBLS	5/07
	Arkansas	Y	30990 FQ	42500 MW	56120 TQ	USBLS	5/07
	Little Rock-North Little Rock MSA, AR	Y	36350 FQ	50550 MW	59980 TQ	USBLS	5/07
	California	H	21.53 FQ	27.73 MW	34.49 TQ	CABLS	1/08-3/08
	Los Angeles-Long Beach-Glendale PMSA, CA	H	21.79 FQ	27.14 MW	32.52 TQ	CABLS	1/08-3/08
	Oakland-Fremont-Hayward MSA, CA	H	21.00 FQ	27.66 MW	34.21 TQ	CABLS	1/08-3/08
	Riverside-San Bernardino-Ontario MSA, CA	H	22.52 FQ	28.69 MW	33.94 TQ	CABLS	1/08-3/08
	Sacramento-Arden Arcade-Roseville MSA, CA	H	21.27 FQ	26.02 MW	30.54 TQ	CABLS	1/08-3/08
	San Diego-Carlsbad-San Marcos MSA, CA	H	19.96 FQ	26.28 MW	35.84 TQ	CABLS	1/08-3/08

AE	Average entry wage	AW	Average wage paid	FQ	First quartile wage
AER	Average entry range	AWR	Average wage range	H	Hourly
AEX	Average experienced wage	AXR	Average experienced range	HI	Highest wage paid
ATC	Average total compensation	D	Daily	HR	High end range

LO	Lowest wage paid	MTC	Median total compensation	TCC	Total cash compensation
LR	Low end range	MW	Median wage paid	TQ	Third quartile wage
M	Monthly	MWR	Median wage range	W	Weekly
MCC	Median cash compensation	S	See annotated source	Y	Yearly

Occupation/Type/Industry	Location	Per	Low	Mid	High	Source	Date
Electrical and Electronic Engineering Technician							
	San Francisco-San Mateo-Redwood PMSA, CA	H	26.20 FQ	30.57 MW	40.03 TQ	CABLS	1/08-3/08
	San Jose-Sunnyvale-Santa Clara MSA, CA	H	21.34 FQ	27.53 MW	34.78 TQ	CABLS	1/08-3/08
	Santa Ana-Anaheim-Irvine PMSA, CA	Y	40670 FQ	50120 MW	61860 TQ	USBLS	5/07
	Colorado	Y	43340 FQ	53510 MW	63650 TQ	USBLS	5/07
	Colorado Springs MSA, CO	Y	41610 FQ	52420 MW	64080 TQ	USBLS	5/07
	Denver-Aurora MSA, CO	Y	45840 FQ	55110 MW	64410 TQ	USBLS	5/07
	Connecticut	H	18.40 AE	25.21 MW		CTBLS	1/08-3/08
	Bridgeport-Stamford-Norwalk MSA, CT	Y	39000 FQ	46800 MW	59490 TQ	USBLS	5/07
	Hartford-West Hartford-East Hartford MSA, CT	Y	42830 FQ	52400 MW	60410 TQ	USBLS	5/07
	Delaware	Y	31380 FQ	55700 MW	65280 TQ	USBLS	5/07
	Wilmington PMSA, DE-MD-NJ	Y	36940 FQ	55850 MW	65000 TQ	USBLS	5/07
	District of Columbia	Y	51720 FQ	60750 MW	74890 TQ	USBLS	5/07
	Washington-Arlington-Alexandria MSA, DC-VA-MD-WV	Y	44310 FQ	55510 MW	67510 TQ	USBLS	5/07
	Florida	Y	38580 FQ	50660 MW	58730 TQ	USBLS	5/07
	Fort Lauderdale-Pompano Beach-Deerfield Beach PMSA, FL	Y	48810 FQ	54170 MW	59040 TQ	USBLS	5/07
	Jacksonville MSA, FL	Y	49220 FQ	55380 MW	61260 TQ	USBLS	5/07
	Miami-Fort Lauderdale-Miami Beach MSA, FL	Y	47000 FQ	54500 MW	60020 TQ	USBLS	5/07
	Orlando-Kissimmee MSA, FL	Y	36220 FQ	44910 MW	56550 TQ	USBLS	5/07
	Tampa-St. Petersburg-Clearwater MSA, FL	Y	30760 FQ	39250 MW	49770 TQ	USBLS	5/07
	West Palm Beach-Boca Raton-Boynton Beach PMSA, FL	Y	49380 FQ	55880 MW	61490 TQ	USBLS	5/07
	Georgia	Y	43360 FQ	53270 MW	60540 TQ	USBLS	5/07
	Athens-Clarke County MSA, GA	Y	37930 FQ	51190 MW	57500 TQ	USBLS	5/07
	Atlanta-Sandy Springs-Marietta MSA, GA	Y	43730 FQ	53570 MW	60440 TQ	USBLS	5/07
	Hawaii	Y	50090 FQ	59400 MW	72290 TQ	USBLS	5/07
	Honolulu MSA, HI	Y	49500 FQ	58520 MW	71920 TQ	USBLS	5/07
	Idaho	Y	34630 FQ	47070 MW	61320 TQ	USBLS	5/07
	Boise City-Nampa MSA, ID	Y	33500 FQ	46860 MW	63350 TQ	USBLS	5/07
	Pocatello MSA, ID	Y	37620 FQ	47230 MW	56430 TQ	USBLS	5/07
	Illinois	Y	42370 FQ	54560 MW	66450 TQ	USBLS	5/07
	Champaign-Urbana MSA, IL	Y	23400 FQ	51770 MW	58650 TQ	USBLS	5/07
	Chicago-Naperville-Joliet MSA, IL-IN-WI	Y	43070 FQ	55070 MW	67150 TQ	USBLS	5/07
	Rockford MSA, IL	Y	41080 FQ	50350 MW	62280 TQ	USBLS	5/07
	Indiana	Y	39000 FQ	50320 MW	60280 TQ	USBLS	5/07
	Gary PMSA, IN	Y	50030 FQ	54600 MW	58930 TQ	USBLS	5/07
	Indianapolis-Carmel MSA, IN	Y	40860 FQ	51020 MW	60260 TQ	USBLS	5/07
	South Bend-Mishawaka MSA, IN-MI	Y	50660 FQ	54590 MW	58530 TQ	USBLS	5/07
	Iowa	Y	42660 FQ	48890 MW	57260 TQ	USBLS	5/07
	Des Moines-West Des Moines MSA, IA	Y	41350 FQ	52750 MW	59680 TQ	USBLS	5/07
	Kansas	Y	40740 FQ	50480 MW	59090 TQ	USBLS	5/07
	Wichita MSA, KS	Y	43150 FQ	51240 MW	58160 TQ	USBLS	5/07
	Kentucky	Y	38822 FQ	52991 MW	61676 TQ	KYBLS	2008
	Louisville-Jefferson County MSA, KY-IN	Y	41410 FQ	53360 MW	61090 TQ	USBLS	5/07
	Louisiana	H	19.74 FQ	25.26 MW	28.90 TQ	LABLS	1/08-3/08
	Baton Rouge MSA, LA	Y	41210 FQ	52290 MW	62140 TQ	USBLS	5/07
	New Orleans-Metairie-Kenner MSA, LA	Y	43460 FQ	52800 MW	59330 TQ	USBLS	5/07
	Maine	Y	31610 FQ	45180 MW	61600 TQ	USBLS	5/07
	Portland-South Portland-Biddeford MSA, ME	Y	31460 FQ	40640 MW	53770 TQ	USBLS	5/07
	Maryland	Y		57900 MW		MDBLS	3/08
	Baltimore-Towson MSA, MD	Y	42040 FQ	55340 MW	64100 TQ	USBLS	5/07

AE	Average entry wage	AW	Average wage paid	FQ	First quartile wage	LO	Lowest wage paid	MTC	Median total compensation	TCC	Total cash compensation
AER	Average entry range	AWR	Average wage range	H	Hourly	LR	Low end range	MW	Median wage paid	TQ	Third quartile wage
AEX	Average experienced wage	AXR	Average experienced range	HI	Highest wage paid	M	Monthly	MWR	Median wage range	W	Weekly
ATC	Average total compensation	D	Daily	HR	High end range	MCC	Median cash compensation	S	See annotated source	Y	Yearly

480

Occupation/Type/Industry	Location	Per	Low	Mid	High	Source	Date
Electrical and Electronic Engineering Technician	Bethesda-Gaithersburg-Frederick PMSA, MD	Y	42090 FQ	52240 MW	64310 TQ	USBLS	5/07
	Massachusetts	Y	42570 FQ	51900 MW	61730 TQ	USBLS	5/07
	Boston-Cambridge-Quincy NECTA, MA	Y	44330 FQ	54680 MW	64360 TQ	USBLS	5/07
	Lynn-Peabody-Salem NECTA, MA	Y	37930 FQ	47240 MW	61470 TQ	USBLS	5/07
	Worcester MSA, MA-CT	Y	45670 FQ	54430 MW	63440 TQ	USBLS	5/07
	Michigan	Y	41130 FQ	51360 MW	59670 TQ	USBLS	5/07
	Detroit-Warren-Livonia MSA, MI	Y	39440 FQ	50920 MW	59490 TQ	USBLS	5/07
	Grand Rapids-Wyoming MSA, MI	Y	46330 FQ	53920 MW	60710 TQ	USBLS	5/07
	Lansing-East Lansing MSA, MI	Y	43490 FQ	52440 MW	57910 TQ	USBLS	5/07
	Warren-Troy-Farmington Hills PMSA, MI	Y	37150 FQ	47630 MW	56750 TQ	USBLS	5/07
	Minnesota	Y	40834 FQ	49800 MW	61685 TQ	MNBLS	10/08-12/08
	Duluth-Superior MSA, MN-WI	Y	30476 FQ	56548 MW	65922 TQ	MNBLS	10/08-12/08
	Minneapolis-Saint Paul MSA, MN-WI	Y	43230 FQ	52457 MW	63495 TQ	MNBLS	10/08-12/08
	Rochester MSA, MN	Y	37250 FQ	41636 MW	54686 TQ	MNBLS	10/08-12/08
	Mississippi	Y	42520 FQ	52640 MW	63710 TQ	USBLS	5/07
	Jackson MSA, MS	Y	39750 FQ	47630 MW	56740 TQ	USBLS	5/07
	Missouri	Y	40390 FQ	52080 MW	61570 TQ	USBLS	5/07
	Kansas City MSA, MO-KS	Y	43750 FQ	53740 MW	63600 TQ	USBLS	5/07
	St. Louis MSA, MO-IL	Y	38320 FQ	51290 MW	59570 TQ	USBLS	5/07
	Montana	Y	42380 FQ	55600 MW	65050 TQ	USBLS	5/07
	Billings MSA, MT	Y	49570 FQ	56430 MW	63470 TQ	USBLS	5/07
	Nebraska	Y	35260 FQ	45380 MW	56690 TQ	USBLS	5/07
	Omaha-Council Bluffs MSA, NE-IA	Y	36420 FQ	48070 MW	57960 TQ	USBLS	5/07
	Nevada	H	21.05 FQ	26.86 MW	31.03 TQ	NVBLS	5/08
	Las Vegas-Paradise MSA, NV	H	21.85 FQ	27.39 MW	31.34 TQ	NVBLS	5/08
	New Hampshire	H	17.48 AE	23.79 MW	26.63 AEX	NHBLS	6/08
	Manchester MSA, NH	Y	37980 FQ	51460 MW	58770 TQ	USBLS	5/07
	Nashua NECTA, NH-MA	Y	43070 FQ	51710 MW	58330 TQ	USBLS	5/07
	New Jersey	Y	41240 FQ	53940 MW	62510 TQ	USBLS	5/07
	Camden PMSA, NJ	Y	38990 FQ	52630 MW	61760 TQ	USBLS	5/07
	Edison PMSA, NJ	Y	40370 FQ	53300 MW	65560 TQ	USBLS	5/07
	Newark-Union PMSA, NJ-PA	Y	38210 FQ	50180 MW	60470 TQ	USBLS	5/07
	New Mexico	Y	46090 FQ	57960 MW	71520 TQ	USBLS	5/07
	Albuquerque MSA, NM	Y	47270 FQ	58810 MW	72700 TQ	USBLS	5/07
	New York	Y	38720 FQ	53770 MW	65580 TQ	USBLS	5/07
	Albany-Schenectady-Troy MSA, NY	Y	51460 FQ	61610 MW	69780 TQ	USBLS	5/07
	Buffalo-Niagara Falls MSA, NY	Y	32180 FQ	44760 MW	56800 TQ	USBLS	5/07
	Nassau-Suffolk PMSA, NY	Y	43600 FQ	55520 MW	65250 TQ	USBLS	5/07
	New York-Northern New Jersey-Long Island MSA, NY-NJ-PA	Y	45000 FQ	57180 MW	67320 TQ	USBLS	5/07
	North Carolina	Y	40230 FQ	50250 MW	58120 TQ	USBLS	5/07
	Charlotte-Gastonia-Concord MSA, NC-SC	Y	50390 FQ	55900 MW	60780 TQ	USBLS	5/07
	Raleigh-Cary MSA, NC	Y	36920 FQ	45760 MW	53940 TQ	USBLS	5/07
	North Dakota	Y	32730 FQ	42820 MW	54660 TQ	USBLS	5/07
	Ohio	Y	37530 FQ	50820 MW	59560 TQ	USBLS	5/07
	Canton-Massillon MSA, OH	Y	43190 FQ	54320 MW	60040 TQ	USBLS	5/07
	Cincinnati-Middletown MSA, OH-KY-IN	Y	37930 FQ	50930 MW	59410 TQ	USBLS	5/07
	Cleveland-Elyria-Mentor MSA, OH	Y	41130 FQ	52270 MW	60770 TQ	USBLS	5/07
	Columbus MSA, OH	Y	31700 FQ	48220 MW	60060 TQ	USBLS	5/07
	Dayton MSA, OH	Y	40530 FQ	50380 MW	58870 TQ	USBLS	5/07
	Oklahoma	Y	40470 FQ	50730 MW	66650 TQ	USBLS	5/07
	Oklahoma City MSA, OK	Y	44810 FQ	56140 MW	74960 TQ	USBLS	5/07
	Tulsa MSA, OK	Y	33070 FQ	42730 MW	54580 TQ	USBLS	5/07
	Oregon	H	19.88 FQ	24.48 MW	29.35 TQ	ORBLS	5/08
	Medford MSA, OR	Y	50160 FQ	61450 MW	72710 TQ	USBLS	5/07
	Portland-Vancouver-Beaverton MSA, OR-WA	Y	39460 FQ	48980 MW	59900 TQ	USBLS	5/07

AE Average entry wage	**AW** Average wage paid	**FQ** First quartile wage	**LO** Lowest wage paid	**MTC** Median total compensation **TCC** Total cash compensation
AER Average entry range	**AWR** Average wage range	**H** Hourly	**LR** Low end range	**MW** Median wage paid **TQ** Third quartile wage
AEX Average experienced wage	**AXR** Average experienced range	**HI** Highest wage paid	**M** Monthly	**MWR** Median wage range **W** Weekly
ATC Average total compensation	**D** Daily	**HR** High end range	**MCC** Median cash compensation **S** See annotated source	**Y** Yearly

Occupation/Type/Industry	Location	Per	Low	Mid	High	Source	Date
Electrical and Electronic Engineering Technician	Pennsylvania	Y	37240 FQ	48220 MW	58890 TQ	USBLS	5/07
	Allentown-Bethlehem-Easton MSA, PA-NJ	Y	39070 FQ	47850 MW	56860 TQ	USBLS	5/07
	Philadelphia-Camden-Wilmington MSA, PA-NJ-DE-MD	Y	37960 FQ	51210 MW	61600 TQ	USBLS	5/07
	Pittsburgh MSA, PA	Y	36350 FQ	45520 MW	57010 TQ	USBLS	5/07
	Rhode Island	Y	43450 FQ	54460 MW	64970 TQ	USBLS	5/07
	Providence-Fall River-Warwick MSA, RI-MA	Y	39980 FQ	50890 MW	60290 TQ	USBLS	5/07
	South Carolina	Y	38360 FQ	49870 MW	60340 TQ	USBLS	5/07
	Charleston-North Charleston MSA, SC	Y	44570 FQ	57520 MW	73730 TQ	USBLS	5/07
	Columbia MSA, SC	Y	39870 FQ	50790 MW	59100 TQ	USBLS	5/07
	Spartanburg MSA, SC	Y	40760 FQ	49650 MW	57230 TQ	USBLS	5/07
	South Dakota	Y	32016 FQ	38768 MW	47611 TQ	SDBLS	7/08-9/08
	Sioux Falls MSA, SD	Y	34274 FQ	41152 MW	54296 TQ	SDBLS	7/08-9/08
	Tennessee	Y	36610 FQ	48590 MW	57110 TQ	USBLS	5/07
	Clarksville MSA, TN-KY	Y	45680 FQ	53430 MW	60170 TQ	USBLS	5/07
	Memphis MSA, TN-MS-AR	Y	32170 FQ	47440 MW	56300 TQ	USBLS	5/07
	Nashville-Davidson-Murfreesboro MSA, TN	Y	39860 FQ	51580 MW	58340 TQ	USBLS	5/07
	Texas	Y	42190 FQ	54080 MW	63980 TQ	USBLS	5/07
	Austin-Round Rock MSA, TX	Y	30680 FQ	42860 MW	54420 TQ	USBLS	5/07
	Corpus Christi MSA, TX	Y	50070 FQ	59210 MW	69770 TQ	USBLS	5/07
	Dallas-Fort Worth-Arlington MSA, TX	Y	45270 FQ	56100 MW	66510 TQ	USBLS	5/07
	El Paso MSA, TX	Y	32720 FQ	46150 MW	58430 TQ	USBLS	5/07
	Houston-Sugar Land-Baytown MSA, TX	Y	44100 FQ	55270 MW	64150 TQ	USBLS	5/07
	San Antonio MSA, TX	Y	42990 FQ	54230 MW	63910 TQ	USBLS	5/07
	Utah	Y	33030 FQ	46230 MW	57190 TQ	USBLS	5/07
	Salt Lake City MSA, UT	Y	29150 FQ	43860 MW	53290 TQ	USBLS	5/07
	Vermont	Y	35570 FQ	45990 MW	55950 TQ	USBLS	5/07
	Burlington-South Burlington MSA, VT	Y	36390 FQ	46110 MW	55730 TQ	USBLS	5/07
	Virginia	Y	43480 FQ	54830 MW	66490 TQ	USBLS	5/07
	Richmond MSA, VA	Y	43860 FQ	55170 MW	65070 TQ	USBLS	5/07
	Virginia Beach-Norfolk-Newport News MSA, VA-NC	Y	50710 FQ	63490 MW	76510 TQ	USBLS	5/07
	Washington	H	21.44 FQ	28.02 MW	33.43 TQ	WABLS	3/08
	Bremerton-Silverdale MSA, WA	Y	65320 FQ	71790 MW	78300 TQ	USBLS	5/07
	Seattle-Tacoma-Bellevue MSA, WA	Y	41320 FQ	54650 MW	65030 TQ	USBLS	5/07
	West Virginia	Y	38297 FQ	55873 MW	64552 TQ	WVBLS	7/08-9/08
	Charleston MSA, WV	Y	35970 FQ	52000 MW	59250 TQ	USBLS	5/07
	Wisconsin	Y	37820 FQ	45840 MW	53690 TQ	USBLS	5/07
	Green Bay MSA, WI	Y	42470 FQ	50450 MW	58260 TQ	USBLS	5/07
	Milwaukee-Waukesha-West Allis MSA, WI	Y	38840 FQ	45880 MW	53140 TQ	USBLS	5/07
	Wyoming	Y	46409 FQ	57240 MW	67522 TQ	WYBLS	9/08
	Cheyenne MSA, WY	Y	50262 FQ	56961 MW	62609 TQ	WYBLS	9/08
	Puerto Rico	Y	23140 FQ	29210 MW	36920 TQ	USBLS	5/07
	San Juan-Caguas-Guaynabo MSA, PR	Y	22870 FQ	29170 MW	36740 TQ	USBLS	5/07
	Virgin Islands	Y	39560 FQ	49080 MW	62810 TQ	USBLS	5/07
	Guam	Y	23890 FQ	47110 MW	58810 TQ	USBLS	5/07
Electrical and Electronic Equipment Assembler	Alabama	Y	22630 FQ	31220 MW	37010 TQ	USBLS	5/07
	Birmingham-Hoover MSA, AL	Y	26420 FQ	33730 MW	39230 TQ	USBLS	5/07
	Mobile MSA, AL	Y	16680 FQ	33070 MW	42790 TQ	USBLS	5/07
	Arizona	Y	25090 FQ	34070 MW	45230 TQ	USBLS	5/07
	Phoenix-Mesa-Scottsdale MSA, AZ	Y	25660 FQ	34640 MW	45510 TQ	USBLS	5/07
	Tucson MSA, AZ	Y	18790 FQ	26390 MW	44120 TQ	USBLS	5/07
	Arkansas	Y	21550 FQ	27970 MW	34910 TQ	USBLS	5/07
	Little Rock-North Little Rock MSA, AR	Y	24330 FQ	28270 MW	34650 TQ	USBLS	5/07

AE Average entry wage	**AW** Average wage paid	**FQ** First quartile wage	**LO** Lowest wage paid	**MTC** Median total compensation	**TCC** Total cash compensation
AER Average entry range	**AWR** Average wage range	**H** Hourly	**LR** Low end range	**MW** Median wage paid	**TQ** Third quartile wage
AEX Average experienced wage	**AXR** Average experienced range	**HI** Highest wage paid	**M** Monthly	**MWR** Median wage range	**W** Weekly
ATC Average total compensation	**D** Daily	**HR** High end range	**MCC** Median cash compensation	**S** See annotated source	**Y** Yearly

Occupation/Type/Industry	Location	Per	Low	Mid	High	Source	Date
Electrical and Electronic Equipment Assembler	California	H	10.11 FQ	13.05 MW	17.21 TQ	CABLS	1/08-3/08
	Los Angeles-Long Beach-Glendale PMSA, CA	H	8.99 FQ	10.87 MW	14.75 TQ	CABLS	1/08-3/08
	Oakland-Fremont-Hayward MSA, CA	H	11.00 FQ	14.08 MW	18.83 TQ	CABLS	1/08-3/08
	Oxnard-Thousand Oaks-Ventura MSA, CA	H	10.79 FQ	13.95 MW	20.08 TQ	CABLS	1/08-3/08
	Riverside-San Bernardino-Ontario MSA, CA	H	8.93 FQ	11.73 MW	15.90 TQ	CABLS	1/08-3/08
	Sacramento-Arden Arcade-Roseville MSA, CA	H	9.00 FQ	10.55 MW	14.38 TQ	CABLS	1/08-3/08
	San Diego-Carlsbad-San Marcos MSA, CA	H	10.28 FQ	12.82 MW	16.51 TQ	CABLS	1/08-3/08
	San Francisco-San Mateo-Redwood PMSA, CA	H	10.21 FQ	14.40 MW	18.80 TQ	CABLS	1/08-3/08
	San Jose-Sunnyvale-Santa Clara MSA, CA	H	12.37 FQ	15.01 MW	21.13 TQ	CABLS	1/08-3/08
	Santa Ana-Anaheim-Irvine PMSA, CA	Y	20590 FQ	25770 MW	31550 TQ	USBLS	5/07
	Stockton MSA, CA	H	11.63 FQ	14.02 MW	16.12 TQ	CABLS	1/08-3/08
	Colorado	Y	21190 FQ	25450 MW	31270 TQ	USBLS	5/07
	Boulder MSA, CO	Y	20900 FQ	24280 MW	28630 TQ	USBLS	5/07
	Denver-Aurora MSA, CO	Y	20780 FQ	26350 MW	33340 TQ	USBLS	5/07
	Connecticut	H	9.72 AE	12.86 MW		CTBLS	1/08-3/08
	Bridgeport-Stamford-Norwalk MSA, CT	Y	22930 FQ	27480 MW	35970 TQ	USBLS	5/07
	Hartford-West Hartford-East Hartford MSA, CT	Y	21650 FQ	28000 MW	38990 TQ	USBLS	5/07
	Delaware	Y	27540 FQ	40470 MW	46510 TQ	USBLS	5/07
	Wilmington PMSA, DE-MD-NJ	Y	32860 FQ	42870 MW	47720 TQ	USBLS	5/07
	District of Columbia	Y	44880 FQ	50650 MW	55550 TQ	USBLS	5/07
	Washington-Arlington-Alexandria MSA, DC-VA-MD-WV	Y	25440 FQ	31810 MW	44730 TQ	USBLS	5/07
	Florida	Y	19810 FQ	24620 MW	30560 TQ	USBLS	5/07
	Fort Lauderdale-Pompano Beach-Deerfield Beach PMSA, FL	Y	19240 FQ	25070 MW	31520 TQ	USBLS	5/07
	Jacksonville MSA, FL	Y	24160 FQ	29550 MW	36340 TQ	USBLS	5/07
	Miami-Fort Lauderdale-Miami Beach MSA, FL	Y	18200 FQ	22940 MW	29640 TQ	USBLS	5/07
	Orlando-Kissimmee MSA, FL	Y	18740 FQ	24110 MW	30380 TQ	USBLS	5/07
	Tallahassee MSA, FL	Y	20450 FQ	23330 MW	28780 TQ	USBLS	5/07
	Tampa-St. Petersburg-Clearwater MSA, FL	Y	22950 FQ	26980 MW	31210 TQ	USBLS	5/07
	West Palm Beach-Boca Raton-Boynton Beach PMSA, FL	Y	20150 FQ	24400 MW	30310 TQ	USBLS	5/07
	Georgia	Y	21150 FQ	25160 MW	30510 TQ	USBLS	5/07
	Atlanta-Sandy Springs-Marietta MSA, GA	Y	23140 FQ	27250 MW	31880 TQ	USBLS	5/07
	Augusta-Richmond County MSA, GA-SC	Y	20640 FQ	22380 MW	24130 TQ	USBLS	5/07
	Idaho	Y	20170 FQ	23670 MW	27990 TQ	USBLS	5/07
	Boise City-Nampa MSA, ID	Y	21230 FQ	24370 MW	28610 TQ	USBLS	5/07
	Illinois	Y	18320 FQ	22680 MW	28590 TQ	USBLS	5/07
	Chicago-Naperville-Joliet MSA, IL-IN-WI	Y	17680 FQ	22160 MW	28260 TQ	USBLS	5/07
	Indiana	Y	19020 FQ	22290 MW	27820 TQ	USBLS	5/07
	Gary PMSA, IN	Y	22370 FQ	30910 MW	36690 TQ	USBLS	5/07
	Indianapolis-Carmel MSA, IN	Y	20820 FQ	24890 MW	31040 TQ	USBLS	5/07
	Iowa	Y	20690 FQ	23380 MW	29520 TQ	USBLS	5/07
	Des Moines-West Des Moines MSA, IA	Y	21090 FQ	22980 MW	30830 TQ	USBLS	5/07
	Kansas	Y	21650 FQ	29570 MW	41500 TQ	USBLS	5/07
	Wichita MSA, KS	Y	30320 FQ	40730 MW	47310 TQ	USBLS	5/07
	Kentucky	Y	24003 FQ	28894 MW	34727 TQ	KYBLS	2008
	Louisville-Jefferson County MSA, KY-IN	Y	21750 FQ	24780 MW	30930 TQ	USBLS	5/07
	Owensboro MSA, KY	Y	22890 FQ	30440 MW	34050 TQ	USBLS	5/07
	Louisiana	H	9.63 FQ	12.43 MW	16.23 TQ	LABLS	1/08-3/08

AE Average entry wage	**AW** Average wage paid	**FQ** First quartile wage	**LO** Lowest wage paid	**MTC** Median total compensation	**TCC** Total cash compensation
AER Average entry range	**AWR** Average wage range	**H** Hourly	**LR** Low end range	**MW** Median wage paid	**TQ** Third quartile wage
AEX Average experienced wage	**AXR** Average experienced range	**HI** Highest wage paid	**M** Monthly	**MWR** Median wage range	**W** Weekly
ATC Average total compensation	**D** Daily	**HR** High end range	**MCC** Median cash compensation	**S** See annotated source	**Y** Yearly

Occupation/Type/Industry	Location	Per	Low	Mid	High	Source	Date
Electrical and Electronic Equipment Assembler	Baton Rouge MSA, LA	Y	20310 FQ	24260 MW	29100 TQ	USBLS	5/07
	New Orleans-Metairie-Kenner MSA, LA	Y	23270 FQ	31590 MW	41950 TQ	USBLS	5/07
	Maine	Y	19770 FQ	22070 MW	25100 TQ	USBLS	5/07
	Portland-South Portland-Biddeford MSA, ME	Y	20520 FQ	22300 MW	24650 TQ	USBLS	5/07
	Maryland	Y		27775 MW		MDBLS	3/08
	Baltimore-Towson MSA, MD	Y	23880 FQ	29270 MW	41650 TQ	USBLS	5/07
	Bethesda-Gaithersburg-Frederick PMSA, MD	Y	22830 FQ	26550 MW	31580 TQ	USBLS	5/07
	Massachusetts	Y	25330 FQ	31070 MW	37660 TQ	USBLS	5/07
	Boston-Cambridge-Quincy NECTA, MA	Y	27330 FQ	33680 MW	40020 TQ	USBLS	5/07
	Worcester MSA, MA-CT	Y	22210 FQ	25360 MW	31150 TQ	USBLS	5/07
	Michigan	Y	22860 FQ	28110 MW	35000 TQ	USBLS	5/07
	Detroit-Warren-Livonia MSA, MI	Y	23480 FQ	28730 MW	35850 TQ	USBLS	5/07
	Grand Rapids-Wyoming MSA, MI	Y	24300 FQ	28300 MW	37310 TQ	USBLS	5/07
	Warren-Troy-Farmington Hills PMSA, MI	Y	23350 FQ	28420 MW	34530 TQ	USBLS	5/07
	Minnesota	Y	22641 FQ	27814 MW	34614 TQ	MNBLS	10/08-12/08
	Duluth-Superior MSA, MN-WI	Y	20080 FQ	22423 MW	24983 TQ	MNBLS	10/08-12/08
	Minneapolis-Saint Paul MSA, MN-WI	Y	25129 FQ	30177 MW	36812 TQ	MNBLS	10/08-12/08
	Mississippi	Y	19790 FQ	27490 MW	33400 TQ	USBLS	5/07
	Jackson MSA, MS	Y	26510 FQ	32780 MW	36150 TQ	USBLS	5/07
	Missouri	Y	21560 FQ	27380 MW	36260 TQ	USBLS	5/07
	Kansas City MSA, MO-KS	Y	21820 FQ	25920 MW	32030 TQ	USBLS	5/07
	St. Louis MSA, MO-IL	Y	24040 FQ	31860 MW	43910 TQ	USBLS	5/07
	Montana	Y	20940 FQ	23390 MW	27360 TQ	USBLS	5/07
	Nebraska	Y	20950 FQ	27050 MW	34370 TQ	USBLS	5/07
	Nevada	H	10.47 FQ	12.36 MW	15.09 TQ	NVBLS	5/08
	Las Vegas-Paradise MSA, NV	H	9.87 FQ	12.10 MW	14.42 TQ	NVBLS	5/08
	Reno-Sparks MSA, NV	H	11.23 FQ	13.17 MW	16.09 TQ	NVBLS	5/08
	New Hampshire	H	10.28 AE	13.69 MW	15.98 AEX	NHBLS	6/08
	Manchester MSA, NH	Y	24330 FQ	27730 MW	30910 TQ	USBLS	5/07
	Nashua NECTA, NH-MA	Y	27290 FQ	31560 MW	36900 TQ	USBLS	5/07
	Portsmouth MSA, NH-ME	Y	23610 FQ	26730 MW	29960 TQ	USBLS	5/07
	New Jersey	Y	22890 FQ	28730 MW	35990 TQ	USBLS	5/07
	Camden PMSA, NJ	Y	24170 FQ	28990 MW	38120 TQ	USBLS	5/07
	Edison PMSA, NJ	Y	22840 FQ	28660 MW	35420 TQ	USBLS	5/07
	Newark-Union PMSA, NJ-PA	Y	22080 FQ	27970 MW	34880 TQ	USBLS	5/07
	New Mexico	Y	20680 FQ	24830 MW	32770 TQ	USBLS	5/07
	Albuquerque MSA, NM	Y	20350 FQ	23210 MW	30440 TQ	USBLS	5/07
	New York	Y	19880 FQ	26490 MW	35990 TQ	USBLS	5/07
	Albany-Schenectady-Troy MSA, NY	Y	29780 FQ	36480 MW	54640 TQ	USBLS	5/07
	Buffalo-Niagara Falls MSA, NY	Y	19720 FQ	24600 MW	32960 TQ	USBLS	5/07
	Nassau-Suffolk PMSA, NY	Y	22230 FQ	28980 MW	36710 TQ	USBLS	5/07
	New York-Northern New Jersey-Long Island MSA, NY-NJ-PA	Y	21820 FQ	27720 MW	35410 TQ	USBLS	5/07
	Utica-Rome MSA, NY	Y	17380 FQ	19800 MW	23570 TQ	USBLS	5/07
	North Carolina	Y	22720 FQ	27920 MW	35740 TQ	USBLS	5/07
	Charlotte-Gastonia-Concord MSA, NC-SC	Y	24340 FQ	28510 MW	35710 TQ	USBLS	5/07
	Raleigh-Cary MSA, NC	Y	22400 FQ	26830 MW	32770 TQ	USBLS	5/07
	North Dakota	Y	19940 FQ	24960 MW	35510 TQ	USBLS	5/07
	Fargo MSA, ND-MN	Y	25740 FQ	35460 MW	39440 TQ	USBLS	5/07
	Ohio	Y	21490 FQ	26950 MW	34240 TQ	USBLS	5/07
	Cincinnati-Middletown MSA, OH-KY-IN	Y	21530 FQ	26320 MW	31890 TQ	USBLS	5/07
	Cleveland-Elyria-Mentor MSA, OH	Y	19990 FQ	24360 MW	32480 TQ	USBLS	5/07
	Columbus MSA, OH	Y	23100 FQ	27890 MW	34390 TQ	USBLS	5/07
	Dayton MSA, OH	Y	22050 FQ	26750 MW	34050 TQ	USBLS	5/07
	Oklahoma	Y	21680 FQ	26190 MW	33880 TQ	USBLS	5/07
	Oklahoma City MSA, OK	Y	20060 FQ	23740 MW	29700 TQ	USBLS	5/07
	Tulsa MSA, OK	Y	23050 FQ	28270 MW	35570 TQ	USBLS	5/07

AE Average entry wage	**AW** Average wage paid	**FQ** First quartile wage	**LO** Lowest wage paid	**MTC** Median total compensation	**TCC** Total cash compensation
AER Average entry range	**AWR** Average wage range	**H** Hourly	**LR** Low end range	**MW** Median wage paid	**TQ** Third quartile wage
AEX Average experienced wage	**AXR** Average experienced range	**HI** Highest wage paid	**M** Monthly	**MWR** Median wage range	**W** Weekly
ATC Average total compensation	**D** Daily	**HR** High end range	**MCC** Median cash compensation	**S** See annotated source	**Y** Yearly

Occupation/Type/Industry	Location	Per	Low	Mid	High	Source	Date
Electrical and Electronic Equipment Assembler	Oregon	H	10.96 FQ	13.20 MW	16.08 TQ	ORBLS	5/08
	Portland-Vancouver-Beaverton MSA, OR-WA	Y	21910 FQ	25770 MW	30980 TQ	USBLS	5/07
	Pennsylvania	Y	22100 FQ	28100 MW	37670 TQ	USBLS	5/07
	Philadelphia-Camden-Wilmington MSA, PA-NJ-DE-MD	Y	24040 FQ	29240 MW	37470 TQ	USBLS	5/07
	Pittsburgh MSA, PA	Y	22020 FQ	27760 MW	37360 TQ	USBLS	5/07
	Rhode Island	Y	21460 FQ	24610 MW	31470 TQ	USBLS	5/07
	Providence-Fall River-Warwick MSA, RI-MA	Y	22450 FQ	26310 MW	30860 TQ	USBLS	5/07
	South Carolina	Y	26540 FQ	31650 MW	37000 TQ	USBLS	5/07
	Columbia MSA, SC	Y	29950 FQ	33990 MW	37430 TQ	USBLS	5/07
	South Dakota	Y	19670 FQ	22792 MW	26215 TQ	SDBLS	7/08-9/08
	Sioux Falls MSA, SD	Y	22409 FQ	25639 MW	28194 TQ	SDBLS	7/08-9/08
	Tennessee	Y	19390 FQ	23590 MW	30360 TQ	USBLS	5/07
	Nashville-Davidson-Murfreesboro MSA, TN	Y	21060 FQ	28730 MW	35710 TQ	USBLS	5/07
	Texas	Y	19510 FQ	25360 MW	32220 TQ	USBLS	5/07
	Austin-Round Rock MSA, TX	Y	20690 FQ	26370 MW	32400 TQ	USBLS	5/07
	Dallas-Fort Worth-Arlington MSA, TX	Y	21540 FQ	27390 MW	39110 TQ	USBLS	5/07
	El Paso MSA, TX	Y	15450 FQ	18450 MW	22160 TQ	USBLS	5/07
	Houston-Sugar Land-Baytown MSA, TX	Y	18570 FQ	24110 MW	31390 TQ	USBLS	5/07
	San Antonio MSA, TX	Y	19370 FQ	26820 MW	30730 TQ	USBLS	5/07
	Utah	Y	19520 FQ	23560 MW	28970 TQ	USBLS	5/07
	Salt Lake City MSA, UT	Y	18790 FQ	22210 MW	28620 TQ	USBLS	5/07
	Vermont	Y	22200 FQ	31080 MW	40260 TQ	USBLS	5/07
	Virginia	Y	21720 FQ	26270 MW	34890 TQ	USBLS	5/07
	Richmond MSA, VA	Y	18150 FQ	21650 MW	27310 TQ	USBLS	5/07
	Virginia Beach-Norfolk-Newport News MSA, VA-NC	Y	18670 FQ	23590 MW	39000 TQ	USBLS	5/07
	Washington	H	11.30 FQ	13.70 MW	16.61 TQ	WABLS	3/08
	Seattle-Tacoma-Bellevue MSA, WA	Y	25240 FQ	29400 MW	35330 TQ	USBLS	5/07
	West Virginia	Y	17727 FQ	22373 MW	30324 TQ	WVBLS	7/08-9/08
	Wisconsin	Y	20950 FQ	25290 MW	30960 TQ	USBLS	5/07
	Milwaukee-Waukesha-West Allis MSA, WI	Y	21960 FQ	27310 MW	33650 TQ	USBLS	5/07
	Wyoming	Y	28102 FQ	34413 MW	57639 TQ	WYBLS	9/08
	Puerto Rico	Y	13110 FQ	14940 MW	17800 TQ	USBLS	5/07
	San Juan-Caguas-Guaynabo MSA, PR	Y	12910 FQ	14630 MW	16880 TQ	USBLS	5/07
Electrical and Electronics Drafter	Alabama	Y	33450 FQ	47580 MW	59950 TQ	USBLS	5/07
	Birmingham-Hoover MSA, AL	Y	32600 FQ	44800 MW	56360 TQ	USBLS	5/07
	Huntsville MSA, AL	Y	42000 FQ	55670 MW	65340 TQ	USBLS	5/07
	Alaska	Y	46930 FQ	79770 MW	102290 TQ	USBLS	5/07
	Anchorage MSA, AK	Y	50530 FQ	83770 MW	103830 TQ	USBLS	5/07
	Arizona	Y	42030 FQ	51820 MW	69920 TQ	USBLS	5/07
	Phoenix-Mesa-Scottsdale MSA, AZ	Y	41960 FQ	58690 MW	74280 TQ	USBLS	5/07
	Tucson MSA, AZ	Y	42560 FQ	48550 MW	54950 TQ	USBLS	5/07
	Arkansas	Y	34420 FQ	43390 MW	50860 TQ	USBLS	5/07
	Little Rock-North Little Rock MSA, AR	Y	39100 FQ	46740 MW	54280 TQ	USBLS	5/07
	California	H	19.80 FQ	25.17 MW	32.77 TQ	CABLS	1/08-3/08
	Fresno MSA, CA	H	15.25 FQ	19.06 MW	23.88 TQ	CABLS	1/08-3/08
	Los Angeles-Long Beach-Glendale PMSA, CA	H	17.73 FQ	22.07 MW	27.72 TQ	CABLS	1/08-3/08
	Oakland-Fremont-Hayward MSA, CA	H	21.34 FQ	27.71 MW	34.50 TQ	CABLS	1/08-3/08
	Riverside-San Bernardino-Ontario MSA, CA	H	16.11 FQ	22.05 MW	27.32 TQ	CABLS	1/08-3/08
	Sacramento-Arden Arcade-Roseville MSA, CA	H	19.13 FQ	25.79 MW	31.24 TQ	CABLS	1/08-3/08
	San Diego-Carlsbad-San Marcos MSA, CA	H	20.67 FQ	26.48 MW	32.57 TQ	CABLS	1/08-3/08
	San Francisco-San Mateo-Redwood PMSA, CA	H	24.44 FQ	27.84 MW	31.88 TQ	CABLS	1/08-3/08

Occupation/Type/Industry	Location	Per	Low	Mid	High	Source	Date
Electrical and Electronics Drafter	San Jose-Sunnyvale-Santa Clara MSA, CA	H	23.93 FQ	31.03 MW	39.75 TQ	CABLS	1/08-3/08
	Santa Ana-Anaheim-Irvine PMSA, CA	Y	40620 FQ	48560 MW	61640 TQ	USBLS	5/07
	Colorado	Y	41940 FQ	51560 MW	66050 TQ	USBLS	5/07
	Denver-Aurora MSA, CO	Y	42220 FQ	53370 MW	63320 TQ	USBLS	5/07
	Connecticut	H	18.87 AE	25.24 MW		CTBLS	1/08-3/08
	Bridgeport-Stamford-Norwalk MSA, CT	Y	41490 FQ	49620 MW	63090 TQ	USBLS	5/07
	Hartford-West Hartford-East Hartford MSA, CT	Y	43350 FQ	52240 MW	61250 TQ	USBLS	5/07
	Delaware	Y	37390 FQ	51750 MW	70300 TQ	USBLS	5/07
	Wilmington PMSA, DE-MD-NJ	Y	39540 FQ	47120 MW	65870 TQ	USBLS	5/07
	Washington-Arlington-Alexandria MSA, DC-VA-MD-WV	Y	43600 FQ	53890 MW	67290 TQ	USBLS	5/07
	Florida	Y	31250 FQ	42580 MW	56910 TQ	USBLS	5/07
	Fort Lauderdale-Pompano Beach-Deerfield Beach PMSA, FL	Y	34760 FQ	42710 MW	53080 TQ	USBLS	5/07
	Jacksonville MSA, FL	Y	24780 FQ	33390 MW	49960 TQ	USBLS	5/07
	Miami-Fort Lauderdale-Miami Beach MSA, FL	Y	35880 FQ	47180 MW	59950 TQ	USBLS	5/07
	Orlando-Kissimmee MSA, FL	Y	33900 FQ	44900 MW	57060 TQ	USBLS	5/07
	Tampa-St. Petersburg-Clearwater MSA, FL	Y	30430 FQ	42250 MW	56500 TQ	USBLS	5/07
	West Palm Beach-Boca Raton-Boynton Beach PMSA, FL	Y	35600 FQ	46300 MW	57600 TQ	USBLS	5/07
	Georgia	Y	42300 FQ	53580 MW	62600 TQ	USBLS	5/07
	Atlanta-Sandy Springs-Marietta MSA, GA	Y	43420 FQ	54060 MW	62930 TQ	USBLS	5/07
	Hawaii	Y	31790 FQ	40640 MW	55670 TQ	USBLS	5/07
	Honolulu MSA, HI	Y	31130 FQ	38760 MW	53390 TQ	USBLS	5/07
	Idaho	Y	32390 FQ	41910 MW	55400 TQ	USBLS	5/07
	Boise City-Nampa MSA, ID	Y	30630 FQ	40140 MW	48770 TQ	USBLS	5/07
	Illinois	Y	42490 FQ	52920 MW	74920 TQ	USBLS	5/07
	Chicago-Naperville-Joliet MSA, IL-IN-WI	Y	43460 FQ	57470 MW	87180 TQ	USBLS	5/07
	Indiana	Y	33610 FQ	40740 MW	56480 TQ	USBLS	5/07
	Indianapolis-Carmel MSA, IN	Y	33960 FQ	44750 MW	60160 TQ	USBLS	5/07
	Iowa	Y	30010 FQ	43110 MW	49520 TQ	USBLS	5/07
	Des Moines-West Des Moines MSA, IA	Y	28790 FQ	32270 MW	46260 TQ	USBLS	5/07
	Kansas	Y	42760 FQ	48800 MW	63180 TQ	USBLS	5/07
	Wichita MSA, KS	Y	43540 FQ	57160 MW	71580 TQ	USBLS	5/07
	Kentucky	Y	34523 FQ	40614 MW	57931 TQ	KYBLS	2008
	Louisville-Jefferson County MSA, KY-IN	Y	33800 FQ	39060 MW	46920 TQ	USBLS	5/07
	Louisiana	H	17.17 FQ	22.39 MW	29.71 TQ	LABLS	1/08-3/08
	Baton Rouge MSA, LA	Y	37460 FQ	50770 MW	64830 TQ	USBLS	5/07
	Lake Charles MSA, LA	Y	36810 FQ	49860 MW	68300 TQ	USBLS	5/07
	New Orleans-Metairie-Kenner MSA, LA	Y	37350 FQ	46250 MW	60960 TQ	USBLS	5/07
	Maine	Y	38660 FQ	44860 MW	52200 TQ	USBLS	5/07
	Portland-South Portland-Biddeford MSA, ME	Y	39330 FQ	44920 MW	52530 TQ	USBLS	5/07
	Maryland	Y		52775 MW		MDBLS	3/08
	Baltimore-Towson MSA, MD	Y	40170 FQ	52100 MW	63410 TQ	USBLS	5/07
	Bethesda-Gaithersburg-Frederick PMSA, MD	Y	43370 FQ	51000 MW	66730 TQ	USBLS	5/07
	Massachusetts	Y	43520 FQ	57300 MW	73410 TQ	USBLS	5/07
	Boston-Cambridge-Quincy NECTA, MA	Y	44270 FQ	57380 MW	73830 TQ	USBLS	5/07
	Worcester MSA, MA-CT	Y	42160 FQ	53230 MW	69010 TQ	USBLS	5/07
	Michigan	Y	41180 FQ	52790 MW	65970 TQ	USBLS	5/07
	Detroit-Warren-Livonia MSA, MI	Y	42040 FQ	53360 MW	66780 TQ	USBLS	5/07
	Grand Rapids-Wyoming MSA, MI	Y	50300 FQ	57060 MW	67130 TQ	USBLS	5/07
	Warren-Troy-Farmington Hills PMSA, MI	Y	40480 FQ	53890 MW	69890 TQ	USBLS	5/07

AE Average entry wage	**AW** Average wage paid	**FQ** First quartile wage	**LO** Lowest wage paid	**MTC** Median total compensation	**TCC** Total cash compensation
AER Average entry range	**AWR** Average wage range	**H** Hourly	**LR** Low end range	**MW** Median wage paid	**TQ** Third quartile wage
AEX Average experienced wage	**AXR** Average experienced range	**HI** Highest wage paid	**M** Monthly	**MWR** Median wage range	**W** Weekly
ATC Average total compensation	**D** Daily	**HR** High end range	**MCC** Median cash compensation	**S** See annotated source	**Y** Yearly

Occupation/Type/Industry	Location	Per	Low	Mid	High	Source	Date
Electrical and Electronics Drafter	Minnesota	Y	42424 FQ	51735 MW	63913 TQ	MNBLS	10/08-12/08
	Duluth-Superior MSA, MN-WI	Y	40760 FQ	48963 MW	58797 TQ	MNBLS	10/08-12/08
	Minneapolis-Saint Paul MSA, MN-WI	Y	42947 FQ	53022 MW	65368 TQ	MNBLS	10/08-12/08
	Rochester MSA, MN	Y	37046 FQ	41289 MW	55443 TQ	MNBLS	10/08-12/08
	Mississippi	Y	33240 FQ	40050 MW	47980 TQ	USBLS	5/07
	Jackson MSA, MS	Y	31100 FQ	42840 MW	49020 TQ	USBLS	5/07
	Missouri	Y	41950 FQ	49310 MW	62960 TQ	USBLS	5/07
	Kansas City MSA, MO-KS	Y	44070 FQ	49360 MW	62170 TQ	USBLS	5/07
	St. Louis MSA, MO-IL	Y	41880 FQ	47620 MW	58440 TQ	USBLS	5/07
	Montana	Y	34560 FQ	39530 MW	48150 TQ	USBLS	5/07
	Billings MSA, MT	Y	32370 FQ	36660 MW	42940 TQ	USBLS	5/07
	Nebraska	Y	35600 FQ	45840 MW	56880 TQ	USBLS	5/07
	Omaha-Council Bluffs MSA, NE-IA	Y	35000 FQ	44260 MW	61760 TQ	USBLS	5/07
	Nevada	H	18.84 FQ	22.54 MW	25.43 TQ	NVBLS	5/08
	Las Vegas-Paradise MSA, NV	H	20.09 FQ	22.98 MW	25.92 TQ	NVBLS	5/08
	New Hampshire	H	20.06 AE	27.36 MW	31.56 AEX	NHBLS	6/08
	Manchester MSA, NH	Y	39100 FQ	49670 MW	56240 TQ	USBLS	5/07
	Nashua NECTA, NH-MA	Y	49980 FQ	58770 MW	67890 TQ	USBLS	5/07
	New Jersey	Y	41770 FQ	54180 MW	69600 TQ	USBLS	5/07
	Camden PMSA, NJ	Y	39980 FQ	57450 MW	69530 TQ	USBLS	5/07
	Edison PMSA, NJ	Y	45210 FQ	56070 MW	67130 TQ	USBLS	5/07
	Newark-Union PMSA, NJ-PA	Y	42940 FQ	62610 MW	74390 TQ	USBLS	5/07
	New Mexico	Y	45020 FQ	55710 MW	63540 TQ	USBLS	5/07
	Albuquerque MSA, NM	Y	43230 FQ	54420 MW	61010 TQ	USBLS	5/07
	New York	Y	44790 FQ	60090 MW	73290 TQ	USBLS	5/07
	Albany-Schenectady-Troy MSA, NY	Y	37160 FQ	42090 MW	67670 TQ	USBLS	5/07
	Buffalo-Niagara Falls MSA, NY	Y	33510 FQ	44920 MW	56510 TQ	USBLS	5/07
	Nassau-Suffolk PMSA, NY	Y	54890 FQ	67330 MW	79580 TQ	USBLS	5/07
	New York-Northern New Jersey-Long Island MSA, NY-NJ-PA	Y	49010 FQ	61800 MW	73800 TQ	USBLS	5/07
	Syracuse MSA, NY	Y	42690 FQ	50500 MW	71120 TQ	USBLS	5/07
	North Carolina	Y	40020 FQ	51180 MW	59900 TQ	USBLS	5/07
	Charlotte-Gastonia-Concord MSA, NC-SC	Y	43500 FQ	53160 MW	60680 TQ	USBLS	5/07
	Durham MSA, NC	Y	43050 FQ	53390 MW	60850 TQ	USBLS	5/07
	Raleigh-Cary MSA, NC	Y	45380 FQ	53110 MW	62300 TQ	USBLS	5/07
	North Dakota	Y	31730 FQ	35730 MW	43870 TQ	USBLS	5/07
	Ohio	Y	31180 FQ	38930 MW	53350 TQ	USBLS	5/07
	Cincinnati-Middletown MSA, OH-KY-IN	Y	39170 FQ	61830 MW	73880 TQ	USBLS	5/07
	Cleveland-Elyria-Mentor MSA, OH	Y	33010 FQ	39220 MW	52030 TQ	USBLS	5/07
	Columbus MSA, OH	Y	24960 FQ	31440 MW	39390 TQ	USBLS	5/07
	Dayton MSA, OH	Y	30740 FQ	39610 MW	47890 TQ	USBLS	5/07
	Oklahoma	Y	36940 FQ	43820 MW	50100 TQ	USBLS	5/07
	Oklahoma City MSA, OK	Y	38190 FQ	46010 MW	57850 TQ	USBLS	5/07
	Tulsa MSA, OK	Y	33410 FQ	38940 MW	47020 TQ	USBLS	5/07
	Oregon	H	19.72 FQ	22.76 MW	28.37 TQ	ORBLS	5/08
	Portland-Vancouver-Beaverton MSA, OR-WA	Y	40390 FQ	46940 MW	59510 TQ	USBLS	5/07
	Pennsylvania	Y	39460 FQ	49610 MW	59570 TQ	USBLS	5/07
	Allentown-Bethlehem-Easton MSA, PA-NJ	Y	43290 FQ	54160 MW	69000 TQ	USBLS	5/07
	Philadelphia-Camden-Wilmington MSA, PA-NJ-DE-MD	Y	41880 FQ	51470 MW	64350 TQ	USBLS	5/07
	Pittsburgh MSA, PA	Y	36780 FQ	46950 MW	57390 TQ	USBLS	5/07
	Rhode Island	Y	43020 FQ	53450 MW	63620 TQ	USBLS	5/07
	Providence-Fall River-Warwick MSA, RI-MA	Y	43080 FQ	52590 MW	62580 TQ	USBLS	5/07
	South Carolina	Y	40830 FQ	48890 MW	60710 TQ	USBLS	5/07
	Charleston-North Charleston MSA, SC	Y	41180 FQ	47450 MW	57340 TQ	USBLS	5/07
	Columbia MSA, SC	Y	43700 FQ	48720 MW	53440 TQ	USBLS	5/07
	South Dakota	Y	32239 FQ	36988 MW	42269 TQ	SDBLS	7/08-9/08
	Tennessee	Y	36250 FQ	46970 MW	59810 TQ	USBLS	5/07
	Johnson City MSA, TN	Y	31570 FQ	43860 MW	48870 TQ	USBLS	5/07

AE	Average entry wage	AW	Average wage paid	FQ	First quartile wage
AER	Average entry range	AWR	Average wage range	H	Hourly
AEX	Average experienced wage	AXR	Average experienced range	HI	Highest wage paid
ATC	Average total compensation	D	Daily	HR	High end range

LO	Lowest wage paid	MTC	Median total compensation	TCC	Total cash compensation
LR	Low end range	MW	Median wage paid	TQ	Third quartile wage
M	Monthly	MWR	Median wage range	W	Weekly
MCC	Median cash compensation	S	See annotated source	Y	Yearly

Occupation/Type/Industry	Location	Per	Low	Mid	High	Source	Date
Electrical and Electronics Drafter	Memphis MSA, TN-MS-AR	Y	32190 FQ	48620 MW	61210 TQ	USBLS	5/07
	Nashville-Davidson-Murfreesboro MSA, TN	Y	39350 FQ	46780 MW	58460 TQ	USBLS	5/07
	Texas	Y	36800 FQ	48510 MW	65400 TQ	USBLS	5/07
	Austin-Round Rock MSA, TX	Y	29880 FQ	40100 MW	55290 TQ	USBLS	5/07
	Dallas-Fort Worth-Arlington MSA, TX	Y	44580 FQ	54750 MW	71460 TQ	USBLS	5/07
	El Paso MSA, TX	Y	18760 FQ	20930 MW	25590 TQ	USBLS	5/07
	Houston-Sugar Land-Baytown MSA, TX	Y	41810 FQ	56140 MW	76900 TQ	USBLS	5/07
	San Antonio MSA, TX	Y	31190 FQ	41100 MW	51440 TQ	USBLS	5/07
	Utah	Y	35570 FQ	44250 MW	53500 TQ	USBLS	5/07
	Salt Lake City MSA, UT	Y	40220 FQ	46660 MW	56960 TQ	USBLS	5/07
	Vermont	Y	34460 FQ	38130 MW	46720 TQ	USBLS	5/07
	Burlington-South Burlington MSA, VT	Y	35920 FQ	42000 MW	53340 TQ	USBLS	5/07
	Virginia	Y	38250 FQ	48070 MW	60100 TQ	USBLS	5/07
	Richmond MSA, VA	Y	30900 FQ	35990 MW	40290 TQ	USBLS	5/07
	Virginia Beach-Norfolk-Newport News MSA, VA-NC	Y	33270 FQ	39420 MW	50310 TQ	USBLS	5/07
	Washington	H	21.11 FQ	26.11 MW	31.76 TQ	WABLS	3/08
	Seattle-Tacoma-Bellevue MSA, WA	Y	45430 FQ	56160 MW	67530 TQ	USBLS	5/07
	West Virginia	Y	38701 FQ	48314 MW	60674 TQ	WVBLS	7/08-9/08
	Wisconsin	Y	37200 FQ	44220 MW	52670 TQ	USBLS	5/07
	Milwaukee-Waukesha-West Allis MSA, WI	Y	37910 FQ	44860 MW	53660 TQ	USBLS	5/07
	Wyoming	Y	25535 FQ	33657 MW	40374 TQ	WYBLS	9/08
	Puerto Rico	Y	29010 FQ	39180 MW	50220 TQ	USBLS	5/07
	San Juan-Caguas-Guaynabo MSA, PR	Y	28990 FQ	39250 MW	50220 TQ	USBLS	5/07
Electrical and Electronics Installer and Repairer							
Transportation Equipment	Alabama	Y	31960 FQ	43600 MW	47900 TQ	USBLS	5/07
Transportation Equipment	Arizona	Y	27150 FQ	33270 MW	41470 TQ	USBLS	5/07
Transportation Equipment	Phoenix-Mesa-Scottsdale MSA, AZ	Y	26260 FQ	32020 MW	36900 TQ	USBLS	5/07
Transportation Equipment	California	H	19.97 FQ	24.64 MW	29.20 TQ	CABLS	1/08-3/08
Transportation Equipment	Los Angeles-Long Beach-Glendale PMSA, CA	H	18.83 FQ	25.59 MW	29.53 TQ	CABLS	1/08-3/08
Transportation Equipment	Riverside-San Bernardino-Ontario MSA, CA	H	18.68 FQ	23.07 MW	27.27 TQ	CABLS	1/08-3/08
Transportation Equipment	Sacramento-Arden Arcade-Roseville MSA, CA	H	13.74 FQ	15.29 MW	22.34 TQ	CABLS	1/08-3/08
Transportation Equipment	San Diego-Carlsbad-San Marcos MSA, CA	H	17.89 FQ	20.70 MW	23.91 TQ	CABLS	1/08-3/08
Transportation Equipment	San Jose-Sunnyvale-Santa Clara MSA, CA	H	29.15 FQ	32.12 MW	35.58 TQ	CABLS	1/08-3/08
Transportation Equipment	Santa Ana-Anaheim-Irvine PMSA, CA	Y	31790 FQ	40970 MW	50110 TQ	USBLS	5/07
Transportation Equipment	Colorado	Y	34430 FQ	43460 MW	49660 TQ	USBLS	5/07
Transportation Equipment	Denver-Aurora MSA, CO	Y	36840 FQ	42460 MW	47530 TQ	USBLS	5/07
Transportation Equipment	Connecticut	H	19.55 AE	25.79 MW		CTBLS	1/08-3/08
Transportation Equipment	Hartford-West Hartford-East Hartford MSA, CT	Y	44500 FQ	51530 MW	61260 TQ	USBLS	5/07
Transportation Equipment	Delaware	Y	31100 FQ	42020 MW	53570 TQ	USBLS	5/07
Transportation Equipment	Florida	Y	30350 FQ	37840 MW	49640 TQ	USBLS	5/07
Transportation Equipment	Fort Lauderdale-Pompano Beach-Deerfield Beach PMSA, FL	Y	27640 FQ	30120 MW	32750 TQ	USBLS	5/07
Transportation Equipment	Jacksonville MSA, FL	Y	29830 FQ	38160 MW	47310 TQ	USBLS	5/07
Transportation Equipment	Miami-Fort Lauderdale-Miami Beach MSA, FL	Y	28490 FQ	33090 MW	54210 TQ	USBLS	5/07
Transportation Equipment	Orlando-Kissimmee MSA, FL	Y	32800 FQ	37430 MW	41680 TQ	USBLS	5/07
Transportation Equipment	Tampa-St. Petersburg-Clearwater MSA, FL	Y	30470 FQ	35090 MW	41970 TQ	USBLS	5/07
Transportation Equipment	West Palm Beach-Boca Raton-Boynton Beach PMSA, FL	Y	34950 FQ	44100 MW	55940 TQ	USBLS	5/07
Transportation Equipment	Georgia	Y	29890 FQ	35080 MW	39940 TQ	USBLS	5/07
Transportation Equipment	Atlanta-Sandy Springs-Marietta MSA, GA	Y	28820 FQ	36200 MW	45650 TQ	USBLS	5/07

AE Average entry wage	**AW** Average wage paid	**FQ** First quartile wage	**LO** Lowest wage paid	**MTC** Median total compensation	**TCC** Total cash compensation
AER Average entry range	**AWR** Average wage range	**H** Hourly	**LR** Low end range	**MW** Median wage paid	**TQ** Third quartile wage
AEX Average experienced wage	**AXR** Average experienced range	**HI** Highest wage paid	**M** Monthly	**MWR** Median wage range	**W** Weekly
ATC Average total compensation	**D** Daily	**HR** High end range	**MCC** Median cash compensation	**S** See annotated source	**Y** Yearly

Electrical and Electronics Installer and Repairer

Occupation/Type/Industry	Location	Per	Low	Mid	High	Source	Date
Electrical and Electronics Installer and Repairer							
Transportation Equipment	Hawaii	Y	44900 FQ	49880 MW	56570 TQ	USBLS	5/07
Transportation Equipment	Honolulu MSA, HI	Y	45490 FQ	50440 MW	57080 TQ	USBLS	5/07
Transportation Equipment	Idaho	Y	45310 FQ	60800 MW	72530 TQ	USBLS	5/07
Transportation Equipment	Illinois	Y	38250 FQ	45490 MW	55400 TQ	USBLS	5/07
Transportation Equipment	Chicago-Naperville-Joliet MSA, IL-IN-WI	Y	35050 FQ	39680 MW	48110 TQ	USBLS	5/07
Transportation Equipment	Indiana	Y	33770 FQ	42620 MW	48780 TQ	USBLS	5/07
Transportation Equipment	Indianapolis-Carmel MSA, IN	Y	27350 FQ	39200 MW	44030 TQ	USBLS	5/07
Transportation Equipment	Iowa	Y	36960 FQ	45250 MW	52840 TQ	USBLS	5/07
Transportation Equipment	Kansas	Y	31310 FQ	40490 MW	47950 TQ	USBLS	5/07
Transportation Equipment	Kentucky	Y	39459 FQ	46804 MW	55546 TQ	KYBLS	2008
Transportation Equipment	Louisiana	H	15.67 FQ	18.96 MW	23.07 TQ	LABLS	1/08-3/08
Transportation Equipment	Baton Rouge MSA, LA	Y	38800 FQ	43960 MW	50140 TQ	USBLS	5/07
Transportation Equipment	New Orleans-Metairie-Kenner MSA, LA	Y	29460 FQ	36640 MW	48260 TQ	USBLS	5/07
Transportation Equipment	Maine	Y	30190 FQ	35960 MW	44780 TQ	USBLS	5/07
Transportation Equipment	Maryland	Y		55875 MW		MDBLS	3/08
Transportation Equipment	Baltimore-Towson MSA, MD	Y	36420 FQ	45070 MW	51550 TQ	USBLS	5/07
Transportation Equipment	Massachusetts	Y	24990 FQ	29100 MW	37430 TQ	USBLS	5/07
Transportation Equipment	Worcester MSA, MA-CT	Y	23490 FQ	26770 MW	29760 TQ	USBLS	5/07
Transportation Equipment	Michigan	Y	42650 FQ	48900 MW	60260 TQ	USBLS	5/07
Transportation Equipment	Detroit-Warren-Livonia MSA, MI	Y	41750 FQ	48300 MW	64730 TQ	USBLS	5/07
Transportation Equipment	Warren-Troy-Farmington Hills PMSA, MI	Y	42090 FQ	50990 MW	66570 TQ	USBLS	5/07
Transportation Equipment	Minnesota	Y	53223 FQ	60681 MW	67992 TQ	MNBLS	10/08-12/08
Transportation Equipment	Minneapolis-Saint Paul MSA, MN-WI	Y	54209 FQ	58940 MW	63712 TQ	MNBLS	10/08-12/08
Transportation Equipment	Mississippi	Y	41080 FQ	48370 MW	57250 TQ	USBLS	5/07
Transportation Equipment	Missouri	Y	32970 FQ	39520 MW	44680 TQ	USBLS	5/07
Transportation Equipment	Kansas City MSA, MO-KS	Y	30040 FQ	36190 MW	42700 TQ	USBLS	5/07
Transportation Equipment	St. Louis MSA, MO-IL	Y	28710 FQ	37690 MW	51410 TQ	USBLS	5/07
Transportation Equipment	Montana	Y	34020 FQ	37910 MW	46710 TQ	USBLS	5/07
Transportation Equipment	Nebraska	Y	38370 FQ	42020 MW	45660 TQ	USBLS	5/07
Transportation Equipment	Nevada	H	18.87 FQ	22.65 MW	25.61 TQ	NVBLS	5/08
Transportation Equipment	New Hampshire	H	18.22 AE	21.58 MW	23.43 AEX	NHBLS	6/08
Transportation Equipment	New Jersey	Y	31850 FQ	42360 MW	55270 TQ	USBLS	5/07
Transportation Equipment	Camden PMSA, NJ	Y	19200 FQ	30510 MW	36950 TQ	USBLS	5/07
Transportation Equipment	Edison PMSA, NJ	Y	48280 FQ	56200 MW	61230 TQ	USBLS	5/07
Transportation Equipment	New Mexico	Y	33170 FQ	41440 MW	53980 TQ	USBLS	5/07
Transportation Equipment	Albuquerque MSA, NM	Y	48190 FQ	53080 MW	58650 TQ	USBLS	5/07
Transportation Equipment	Farmington MSA, NM	Y	28590 FQ	33670 MW	37980 TQ	USBLS	5/07
Transportation Equipment	New York-Northern New Jersey-Long Island MSA, NY-NJ-PA	Y	42220 FQ	48890 MW	55820 TQ	USBLS	5/07
Transportation Equipment	North Carolina	Y	31020 FQ	39190 MW	49720 TQ	USBLS	5/07
Transportation Equipment	Charlotte-Gastonia-Concord MSA, NC-SC	Y	28480 FQ	34970 MW	44070 TQ	USBLS	5/07
Transportation Equipment	Ohio	Y	31530 FQ	42980 MW	50050 TQ	USBLS	5/07
Transportation Equipment	Cleveland-Elyria-Mentor MSA, OH	Y	29660 FQ	41070 MW	47270 TQ	USBLS	5/07
Transportation Equipment	Columbus MSA, OH	Y	33240 FQ	38420 MW	44830 TQ	USBLS	5/07
Transportation Equipment	Dayton MSA, OH	Y	34530 FQ	42780 MW	48980 TQ	USBLS	5/07
Transportation Equipment	Oklahoma	Y	21520 FQ	31290 MW	41880 TQ	USBLS	5/07
Transportation Equipment	Tulsa MSA, OK	Y	21320 FQ	23740 MW	34750 TQ	USBLS	5/07
Transportation Equipment	Oregon	H	19.08 FQ	23.52 MW	32.40 TQ	ORBLS	5/08
Transportation Equipment	Portland-Vancouver-Beaverton MSA, OR-WA	Y	33600 FQ	43480 MW	55800 TQ	USBLS	5/07
Transportation Equipment	Pennsylvania	Y	35070 FQ	48700 MW	55090 TQ	USBLS	5/07
Transportation Equipment	Philadelphia-Camden-Wilmington MSA, PA-NJ-DE-MD	Y	26530 FQ	34550 MW	43100 TQ	USBLS	5/07
Transportation Equipment	South Carolina	Y	30790 FQ	36810 MW	45860 TQ	USBLS	5/07
Transportation Equipment	South Dakota	Y	24929 FQ	29231 MW	38660 TQ	SDBLS	7/08-9/08
Transportation Equipment	Tennessee	Y	32000 FQ	43130 MW	48390 TQ	USBLS	5/07
Transportation Equipment	Nashville-Davidson-Murfreesboro MSA, TN	Y	21610 FQ	26710 MW	32580 TQ	USBLS	5/07
Transportation Equipment	Texas	Y	37740 FQ	44170 MW	51810 TQ	USBLS	5/07

AE	Average entry wage	AW	Average wage paid	FQ	First quartile wage
AER	Average entry range	AWR	Average wage range	H	Hourly
AEX	Average experienced wage	AXR	Average experienced range	HI	Highest wage paid
ATC	Average total compensation	D	Daily	HR	High end range

LO	Lowest wage paid	MTC	Median total compensation	TCC	Total cash compensation
LR	Low end range	MW	Median wage paid	TQ	Third quartile wage
M	Monthly	MWR	Median wage range	W	Weekly
MCC	Median cash compensation	S	See annotated source	Y	Yearly

Occupation/Type/Industry	Location	Per	Low	Mid	High	Source	Date
Electrical and Electronics Installer and Repairer							
Transportation Equipment	Dallas-Fort Worth-Arlington MSA, TX	Y	36490 FQ	43470 MW	50420 TQ	USBLS	5/07
Transportation Equipment	Houston-Sugar Land-Baytown MSA, TX	Y	33530 FQ	42040 MW	51630 TQ	USBLS	5/07
Transportation Equipment	San Antonio MSA, TX	Y	27930 FQ	32480 MW	36740 TQ	USBLS	5/07
Transportation Equipment	Utah	Y	38380 FQ	42560 MW	47240 TQ	USBLS	5/07
Transportation Equipment	Salt Lake City MSA, UT	Y	37580 FQ	40590 MW	44410 TQ	USBLS	5/07
Transportation Equipment	Virginia	Y	37240 FQ	51990 MW	68350 TQ	USBLS	5/07
Transportation Equipment	Virginia Beach-Norfolk-Newport News MSA, VA-NC	Y	35180 FQ	42010 MW	54410 TQ	USBLS	5/07
Transportation Equipment	Washington	H	20.43 FQ	22.78 MW	25.04 TQ	WABLS	3/08
Transportation Equipment	Bremerton-Silverdale MSA, WA	Y	30910 FQ	41900 MW	45940 TQ	USBLS	5/07
Transportation Equipment	Seattle-Tacoma-Bellevue MSA, WA	Y	42190 FQ	46130 MW	49900 TQ	USBLS	5/07
Transportation Equipment	West Virginia	Y	32724 FQ	42505 MW	50573 TQ	WVBLS	7/08-9/08
Transportation Equipment	Wisconsin	Y	37600 FQ	42480 MW	47340 TQ	USBLS	5/07
Electrical and Electronics Repairer							
Commercial and Industrial Equipment	Alabama	Y	35830 FQ	45060 MW	51800 TQ	USBLS	5/07
Commercial and Industrial Equipment	Birmingham-Hoover MSA, AL	Y	43180 FQ	47850 MW	51750 TQ	USBLS	5/07
Commercial and Industrial Equipment	Alaska	Y	65320 FQ	72110 MW	78860 TQ	USBLS	5/07
Commercial and Industrial Equipment	Anchorage MSA, AK	Y	65240 FQ	71680 MW	78090 TQ	USBLS	5/07
Commercial and Industrial Equipment	Arizona	Y	36250 FQ	47200 MW	57380 TQ	USBLS	5/07
Commercial and Industrial Equipment	Phoenix-Mesa-Scottsdale MSA, AZ	Y	34430 FQ	44950 MW	55740 TQ	USBLS	5/07
Commercial and Industrial Equipment	Tucson MSA, AZ	Y	45760 FQ	54610 MW	60710 TQ	USBLS	5/07
Commercial and Industrial Equipment	Arkansas	Y	39620 FQ	44370 MW	49910 TQ	USBLS	5/07
Commercial and Industrial Equipment	Little Rock-North Little Rock MSA, AR	Y	41430 FQ	45190 MW	49370 TQ	USBLS	5/07
Commercial and Industrial Equipment	California	H	19.93 FQ	26.31 MW	31.60 TQ	CABLS	1/08-3/08
Commercial and Industrial Equipment	Los Angeles-Long Beach-Glendale PMSA, CA	H	17.78 FQ	23.93 MW	28.80 TQ	CABLS	1/08-3/08
Commercial and Industrial Equipment	Modesto MSA, CA	H	11.90 FQ	14.04 MW	22.91 TQ	CABLS	1/08-3/08
Commercial and Industrial Equipment	Oakland-Fremont-Hayward MSA, CA	H	19.91 FQ	31.37 MW	42.15 TQ	CABLS	1/08-3/08
Commercial and Industrial Equipment	Riverside-San Bernardino-Ontario MSA, CA	H	20.89 FQ	25.90 MW	28.88 TQ	CABLS	1/08-3/08
Commercial and Industrial Equipment	Sacramento-Arden Arcade-Roseville MSA, CA	H	28.94 FQ	53.78 MW	59.67 TQ	CABLS	1/08-3/08
Commercial and Industrial Equipment	San Diego-Carlsbad-San Marcos MSA, CA	H	16.93 FQ	22.61 MW	28.22 TQ	CABLS	1/08-3/08
Commercial and Industrial Equipment	San Francisco-San Mateo-Redwood PMSA, CA	H	24.65 FQ	32.54 MW	36.02 TQ	CABLS	1/08-3/08
Commercial and Industrial Equipment	San Jose-Sunnyvale-Santa Clara MSA, CA	H	23.31 FQ	29.29 MW	35.88 TQ	CABLS	1/08-3/08
Commercial and Industrial Equipment	Santa Ana-Anaheim-Irvine PMSA, CA	Y	35510 FQ	45940 MW	62300 TQ	USBLS	5/07
Commercial and Industrial Equipment	Stockton MSA, CA	H	26.27 FQ	28.92 MW	31.67 TQ	CABLS	1/08-3/08
Commercial and Industrial Equipment	Colorado	Y	37330 FQ	48100 MW	59300 TQ	USBLS	5/07
Commercial and Industrial Equipment	Denver-Aurora MSA, CO	Y	35160 FQ	46990 MW	59180 TQ	USBLS	5/07
Commercial and Industrial Equipment	Pueblo MSA, CO	Y	31930 FQ	39600 MW	45770 TQ	USBLS	5/07
Commercial and Industrial Equipment	Connecticut	H	17.37 AE	23.69 MW		CTBLS	1/08-3/08
Commercial and Industrial Equipment	Bridgeport-Stamford-Norwalk MSA, CT	Y	35470 FQ	44740 MW	51660 TQ	USBLS	5/07
Commercial and Industrial Equipment	Hartford-West Hartford-East Hartford MSA, CT	Y	43100 FQ	50460 MW	60710 TQ	USBLS	5/07
Commercial and Industrial Equipment	Norwich-New London MSA, CT-RI	Y	44630 FQ	51740 MW	57850 TQ	USBLS	5/07
Commercial and Industrial Equipment	Delaware	Y	40730 FQ	50730 MW	57660 TQ	USBLS	5/07
Commercial and Industrial Equipment	Wilmington PMSA, DE-MD-NJ	Y	42590 FQ	52660 MW	61400 TQ	USBLS	5/07
Commercial and Industrial Equipment	District of Columbia	Y	52290 FQ	61390 MW	88510 TQ	USBLS	5/07
Commercial and Industrial Equipment	Washington-Arlington-Alexandria MSA, DC-VA-MD-WV	Y	36020 FQ	48690 MW	59200 TQ	USBLS	5/07
Commercial and Industrial Equipment	Florida	Y	33550 FQ	42680 MW	51510 TQ	USBLS	5/07

AE	Average entry wage	AW	Average wage paid	FQ	First quartile wage
AER	Average entry range	AWR	Average wage range	H	Hourly
AEX	Average experienced wage	AXR	Average experienced range	HI	Highest wage paid
ATC	Average total compensation	D	Daily	HR	High end range

LO	Lowest wage paid	MTC	Median total compensation
LR	Low end range	MW	Median wage paid
M	Monthly	MWR	Median wage range
MCC	Median cash compensation	S	See annotated source

TCC	Total cash compensation		
TQ	Third quartile wage		
W	Weekly		
Y	Yearly		

Occupation/Type/Industry	Location	Per	Low	Mid	High	Source	Date
Electrical and Electronics Repairer							
Commercial and Industrial Equipment	Fort Lauderdale-Pompano Beach-Deerfield Beach PMSA, FL	Y	29430 FQ	38270 MW	50010 TQ	USBLS	5/07
Commercial and Industrial Equipment	Jacksonville MSA, FL	Y	42190 FQ	46800 MW	52860 TQ	USBLS	5/07
Commercial and Industrial Equipment	Miami-Fort Lauderdale-Miami Beach MSA, FL	Y	31570 FQ	42350 MW	54680 TQ	USBLS	5/07
Commercial and Industrial Equipment	Orlando-Kissimmee MSA, FL	Y	32920 FQ	40310 MW	46710 TQ	USBLS	5/07
Commercial and Industrial Equipment	Tampa-St. Petersburg-Clearwater MSA, FL	Y	32150 FQ	38450 MW	46970 TQ	USBLS	5/07
Commercial and Industrial Equipment	West Palm Beach-Boca Raton-Boynton Beach PMSA, FL	Y	22450 FQ	34880 MW	46460 TQ	USBLS	5/07
Commercial and Industrial Equipment	Georgia	Y	39620 FQ	49040 MW	56000 TQ	USBLS	5/07
Commercial and Industrial Equipment	Athens-Clarke County MSA, GA	Y	34810 FQ	39150 MW	44810 TQ	USBLS	5/07
Commercial and Industrial Equipment	Atlanta-Sandy Springs-Marietta MSA, GA	Y	47270 FQ	52880 MW	57770 TQ	USBLS	5/07
Commercial and Industrial Equipment	Hawaii	Y	52750 FQ	58740 MW	68610 TQ	USBLS	5/07
Commercial and Industrial Equipment	Honolulu MSA, HI	Y	55100 FQ	63310 MW	72470 TQ	USBLS	5/07
Commercial and Industrial Equipment	Idaho	Y	35530 FQ	45480 MW	56070 TQ	USBLS	5/07
Commercial and Industrial Equipment	Boise City-Nampa MSA, ID	Y	34760 FQ	45840 MW	56280 TQ	USBLS	5/07
Commercial and Industrial Equipment	Illinois	Y	35310 FQ	48840 MW	62590 TQ	USBLS	5/07
Commercial and Industrial Equipment	Chicago-Naperville-Joliet MSA, IL-IN-WI	Y	36840 FQ	51480 MW	64420 TQ	USBLS	5/07
Commercial and Industrial Equipment	Indiana	Y	30630 FQ	45940 MW	61790 TQ	USBLS	5/07
Commercial and Industrial Equipment	Gary PMSA, IN	Y	43850 FQ	51080 MW	57810 TQ	USBLS	5/07
Commercial and Industrial Equipment	Indianapolis-Carmel MSA, IN	Y	34390 FQ	44110 MW	57290 TQ	USBLS	5/07
Commercial and Industrial Equipment	Iowa	Y	39590 FQ	46600 MW	56780 TQ	USBLS	5/07
Commercial and Industrial Equipment	Des Moines-West Des Moines MSA, IA	Y	47730 FQ	55380 MW	60270 TQ	USBLS	5/07
Commercial and Industrial Equipment	Kansas	Y	36320 FQ	45360 MW	55360 TQ	USBLS	5/07
Commercial and Industrial Equipment	Wichita MSA, KS	Y	36970 FQ	48000 MW	57020 TQ	USBLS	5/07
Commercial and Industrial Equipment	Kentucky	Y	34509 FQ	44089 MW	57113 TQ	KYBLS	2008
Commercial and Industrial Equipment	Elizabethtown MSA, KY	Y	49500 FQ	55360 MW	60090 TQ	USBLS	5/07
Commercial and Industrial Equipment	Louisville-Jefferson County MSA, KY-IN	Y	31700 FQ	39170 MW	52720 TQ	USBLS	5/07
Commercial and Industrial Equipment	Louisiana	H	19.95 FQ	25.92 MW	29.57 TQ	LABLS	1/08-3/08
Commercial and Industrial Equipment	Baton Rouge MSA, LA	Y	37490 FQ	50850 MW	57700 TQ	USBLS	5/07
Commercial and Industrial Equipment	New Orleans-Metairie-Kenner MSA, LA	Y	48440 FQ	57320 MW	67330 TQ	USBLS	5/07
Commercial and Industrial Equipment	Maine	Y	43210 FQ	49450 MW	56600 TQ	USBLS	5/07
Commercial and Industrial Equipment	Portland-South Portland-Biddeford MSA, ME	Y	41970 FQ	47160 MW	51900 TQ	USBLS	5/07
Commercial and Industrial Equipment	Maryland	Y		53475 MW		MDBLS	3/08
Commercial and Industrial Equipment	Baltimore-Towson MSA, MD	Y	40900 FQ	51390 MW	62130 TQ	USBLS	5/07
Commercial and Industrial Equipment	Bethesda-Gaithersburg-Frederick PMSA, MD	Y	40690 FQ	53580 MW	62630 TQ	USBLS	5/07
Commercial and Industrial Equipment	Massachusetts	Y	43840 FQ	51880 MW	61530 TQ	USBLS	5/07
Commercial and Industrial Equipment	Boston-Cambridge-Quincy NECTA, MA	Y	43430 FQ	51160 MW	60530 TQ	USBLS	5/07
Commercial and Industrial Equipment	Worcester MSA, MA-CT	Y	42280 FQ	49260 MW	56950 TQ	USBLS	5/07
Commercial and Industrial Equipment	Michigan	Y	43430 FQ	48350 MW	56110 TQ	USBLS	5/07
Commercial and Industrial Equipment	Detroit-Warren-Livonia MSA, MI	Y	44460 FQ	48970 MW	57320 TQ	USBLS	5/07
Commercial and Industrial Equipment	Grand Rapids-Wyoming MSA, MI	Y	40520 FQ	45390 MW	50490 TQ	USBLS	5/07
Commercial and Industrial Equipment	Warren-Troy-Farmington Hills PMSA, MI	Y	49600 FQ	63820 MW	72600 TQ	USBLS	5/07
Commercial and Industrial Equipment	Minnesota	Y	42534 FQ	53055 MW	61992 TQ	MNBLS	10/08-12/08
Commercial and Industrial Equipment	Duluth-Superior MSA, MN-WI	Y	55499 FQ	59863 MW	64237 TQ	MNBLS	10/08-12/08
Commercial and Industrial Equipment	Minneapolis-Saint Paul MSA, MN-WI	Y	42020 FQ	51251 MW	61279 TQ	MNBLS	10/08-12/08
Commercial and Industrial Equipment	Rochester MSA, MN	Y	52732 FQ	57652 MW	62250 TQ	MNBLS	10/08-12/08
Commercial and Industrial Equipment	Mississippi	Y	27250 FQ	38280 MW	46240 TQ	USBLS	5/07
Commercial and Industrial Equipment	Gulfport-Biloxi MSA, MS	Y	41450 FQ	44880 MW	48380 TQ	USBLS	5/07
Commercial and Industrial Equipment	Jackson MSA, MS	Y	17580 FQ	22160 MW	38620 TQ	USBLS	5/07
Commercial and Industrial Equipment	Missouri	Y	32840 FQ	50360 MW	61230 TQ	USBLS	5/07
Commercial and Industrial Equipment	Kansas City MSA, MO-KS	Y	30780 FQ	40750 MW	54090 TQ	USBLS	5/07
Commercial and Industrial Equipment	St. Louis MSA, MO-IL	Y	38030 FQ	53720 MW	61780 TQ	USBLS	5/07
Commercial and Industrial Equipment	Montana	Y	44170 FQ	55950 MW	67170 TQ	USBLS	5/07
Commercial and Industrial Equipment	Missoula MSA, MT	Y	59010 FQ	68570 MW	75110 TQ	USBLS	5/07

AE	Average entry wage	**AW**	Average wage paid	**FQ**	First quartile wage	**LO**	Lowest wage paid	**MTC** Median total compensation	**TCC** Total cash compensation
AER	Average entry range	**AWR**	Average wage range	**H**	Hourly	**LR**	Low end range	**MW** Median wage paid	**TQ** Third quartile wage
AEX	Average experienced wage	**AXR**	Average experienced range	**HI**	Highest wage paid	**M**	Monthly	**MWR** Median wage range	**W** Weekly
ATC	Average total compensation	**D**	Daily	**HR**	High end range	**MCC**	Median cash compensation	**S** See annotated source	**Y** Yearly

Electrical and Electronics Repairer

Occupation/Type/Industry	Location	Per	Low	Mid	High	Source	Date
Commercial and Industrial Equipment	Nebraska	Y	28230 FQ	41190 MW	48240 TQ	USBLS	5/07
Commercial and Industrial Equipment	Omaha-Council Bluffs MSA, NE-IA	Y	33030 FQ	43060 MW	49900 TQ	USBLS	5/07
Commercial and Industrial Equipment	Nevada	H	20.71 FQ	25.65 MW	29.87 TQ	NVBLS	5/08
Commercial and Industrial Equipment	Las Vegas-Paradise MSA, NV	H	21.79 FQ	26.56 MW	30.42 TQ	NVBLS	5/08
Commercial and Industrial Equipment	New Hampshire	H	17.83 AE	23.86 MW	28.61 AEX	NHBLS	6/08
Commercial and Industrial Equipment	Manchester MSA, NH	Y	39840 FQ	43690 MW	48050 TQ	USBLS	5/07
Commercial and Industrial Equipment	Nashua NECTA, NH-MA	Y	39510 FQ	48070 MW	58110 TQ	USBLS	5/07
Commercial and Industrial Equipment	New Jersey	Y	39010 FQ	50420 MW	60810 TQ	USBLS	5/07
Commercial and Industrial Equipment	Camden PMSA, NJ	Y	37580 FQ	54680 MW	62060 TQ	USBLS	5/07
Commercial and Industrial Equipment	Edison PMSA, NJ	Y	40710 FQ	52260 MW	61400 TQ	USBLS	5/07
Commercial and Industrial Equipment	Newark-Union PMSA, NJ-PA	Y	35640 FQ	43580 MW	54870 TQ	USBLS	5/07
Commercial and Industrial Equipment	New Mexico	Y	50010 FQ	57790 MW	63380 TQ	USBLS	5/07
Commercial and Industrial Equipment	Albuquerque MSA, NM	Y	53780 FQ	59550 MW	64340 TQ	USBLS	5/07
Commercial and Industrial Equipment	New York	Y	29640 FQ	41210 MW	52840 TQ	USBLS	5/07
Commercial and Industrial Equipment	Albany-Schenectady-Troy MSA, NY	Y	36040 FQ	43570 MW	51360 TQ	USBLS	5/07
Commercial and Industrial Equipment	Buffalo-Niagara Falls MSA, NY	Y	35710 FQ	45700 MW	54430 TQ	USBLS	5/07
Commercial and Industrial Equipment	Nassau-Suffolk PMSA, NY	Y	34160 FQ	41870 MW	51700 TQ	USBLS	5/07
Commercial and Industrial Equipment	New York-Northern New Jersey-Long Island MSA, NY-NJ-PA	Y	37180 FQ	46830 MW	58050 TQ	USBLS	5/07
Commercial and Industrial Equipment	North Carolina	Y	36320 FQ	44330 MW	54240 TQ	USBLS	5/07
Commercial and Industrial Equipment	Charlotte-Gastonia-Concord MSA, NC-SC	Y	32130 FQ	40130 MW	48280 TQ	USBLS	5/07
Commercial and Industrial Equipment	Raleigh-Cary MSA, NC	Y	31740 FQ	39830 MW	50350 TQ	USBLS	5/07
Commercial and Industrial Equipment	North Dakota	Y	41110 FQ	50740 MW	59720 TQ	USBLS	5/07
Commercial and Industrial Equipment	Fargo MSA, ND-MN	Y	34470 FQ	44570 MW	55590 TQ	USBLS	5/07
Commercial and Industrial Equipment	Ohio	Y	34250 FQ	45510 MW	58320 TQ	USBLS	5/07
Commercial and Industrial Equipment	Cincinnati-Middletown MSA, OH-KY-IN	Y	38130 FQ	49960 MW	58750 TQ	USBLS	5/07
Commercial and Industrial Equipment	Cleveland-Elyria-Mentor MSA, OH	Y	31100 FQ	38380 MW	51630 TQ	USBLS	5/07
Commercial and Industrial Equipment	Columbus MSA, OH	Y	33490 FQ	41640 MW	53550 TQ	USBLS	5/07
Commercial and Industrial Equipment	Dayton MSA, OH	Y	37170 FQ	50660 MW	57520 TQ	USBLS	5/07
Commercial and Industrial Equipment	Oklahoma	Y	37270 FQ	47170 MW	56230 TQ	USBLS	5/07
Commercial and Industrial Equipment	Oklahoma City MSA, OK	Y	44480 FQ	50430 MW	58260 TQ	USBLS	5/07
Commercial and Industrial Equipment	Tulsa MSA, OK	Y	30180 FQ	37610 MW	53420 TQ	USBLS	5/07
Commercial and Industrial Equipment	Oregon	H	20.76 FQ	25.86 MW	30.64 TQ	ORBLS	5/08
Commercial and Industrial Equipment	Portland-Vancouver-Beaverton MSA, OR-WA	Y	44150 FQ	53840 MW	61660 TQ	USBLS	5/07
Commercial and Industrial Equipment	Pennsylvania	Y	40130 FQ	45460 MW	50930 TQ	USBLS	5/07
Commercial and Industrial Equipment	Allentown-Bethlehem-Easton MSA, PA-NJ	Y	38730 FQ	43840 MW	50190 TQ	USBLS	5/07
Commercial and Industrial Equipment	Philadelphia-Camden-Wilmington MSA, PA-NJ-DE-MD	Y	40360 FQ	53750 MW	61960 TQ	USBLS	5/07
Commercial and Industrial Equipment	Pittsburgh MSA, PA	Y	36740 FQ	44270 MW	54820 TQ	USBLS	5/07
Commercial and Industrial Equipment	Reading MSA, PA	Y	42030 FQ	45940 MW	49840 TQ	USBLS	5/07
Commercial and Industrial Equipment	Rhode Island	Y	41730 FQ	54460 MW	71420 TQ	USBLS	5/07
Commercial and Industrial Equipment	Providence-Fall River-Warwick MSA, RI-MA	Y	44490 FQ	53540 MW	67430 TQ	USBLS	5/07
Commercial and Industrial Equipment	South Carolina	Y	33070 FQ	42270 MW	50210 TQ	USBLS	5/07
Commercial and Industrial Equipment	Charleston-North Charleston MSA, SC	Y	38580 FQ	44450 MW	52130 TQ	USBLS	5/07
Commercial and Industrial Equipment	Columbia MSA, SC	Y	42120 FQ	47800 MW	55350 TQ	USBLS	5/07
Commercial and Industrial Equipment	Florence MSA, SC	Y	40420 FQ	45190 MW	49980 TQ	USBLS	5/07
Commercial and Industrial Equipment	South Dakota	Y	32346 FQ	44143 MW	61250 TQ	SDBLS	7/08-9/08
Commercial and Industrial Equipment	Sioux Falls MSA, SD	Y	32876 FQ	50682 MW	69348 TQ	SDBLS	7/08-9/08
Commercial and Industrial Equipment	Tennessee	Y	35090 FQ	42170 MW	50050 TQ	USBLS	5/07
Commercial and Industrial Equipment	Memphis MSA, TN-MS-AR	Y	31530 FQ	40410 MW	51130 TQ	USBLS	5/07
Commercial and Industrial Equipment	Nashville-Davidson-Murfreesboro MSA, TN	Y	41410 FQ	47650 MW	57170 TQ	USBLS	5/07
Commercial and Industrial Equipment	Texas	Y	37170 FQ	46640 MW	58680 TQ	USBLS	5/07
Commercial and Industrial Equipment	Austin-Round Rock MSA, TX	Y	27610 FQ	32520 MW	46460 TQ	USBLS	5/07
Commercial and Industrial Equipment	Dallas-Fort Worth-Arlington MSA, TX	Y	39360 FQ	47660 MW	60590 TQ	USBLS	5/07
Commercial and Industrial Equipment	El Paso MSA, TX	Y	29120 FQ	36180 MW	44550 TQ	USBLS	5/07

AE	Average entry wage	AW	Average wage paid	FQ	First quartile wage
AER	Average entry range	AWR	Average wage range	H	Hourly
AEX	Average experienced wage	AXR	Average experienced range	HI	Highest wage paid
ATC	Average total compensation	D	Daily	HR	High end range

LO	Lowest wage paid	MTC	Median total compensation	TCC	Total cash compensation
LR	Low end range	MW	Median wage paid	TQ	Third quartile wage
M	Monthly	MWR	Median wage range	W	Weekly
MCC	Median cash compensation	S	See annotated source	Y	Yearly

Occupation/Type/Industry	Location	Per	Low	Mid	High	Source	Date
Electrical and Electronics							
Repairer							
Commercial and Industrial Equipment	Houston-Sugar Land-Baytown MSA, TX	Y	37980 FQ	48810 MW	61730 TQ	USBLS	5/07
Commercial and Industrial Equipment	San Antonio MSA, TX	Y	40570 FQ	45180 MW	50040 TQ	USBLS	5/07
Commercial and Industrial Equipment	Utah	Y	36850 FQ	46060 MW	55230 TQ	USBLS	5/07
Commercial and Industrial Equipment	Provo-Orem MSA, UT	Y	35760 FQ	38830 MW	42820 TQ	USBLS	5/07
Commercial and Industrial Equipment	Salt Lake City MSA, UT	Y	28270 FQ	32090 MW	46740 TQ	USBLS	5/07
Commercial and Industrial Equipment	Vermont	Y	40320 FQ	47130 MW	56320 TQ	USBLS	5/07
Commercial and Industrial Equipment	Burlington-South Burlington MSA, VT	Y	44420 FQ	49860 MW	60460 TQ	USBLS	5/07
Commercial and Industrial Equipment	Virginia	Y	34290 FQ	44660 MW	55160 TQ	USBLS	5/07
Commercial and Industrial Equipment	Charlottesville MSA, VA	Y	33610 FQ	42750 MW	49470 TQ	USBLS	5/07
Commercial and Industrial Equipment	Richmond MSA, VA	Y	29150 FQ	43450 MW	62140 TQ	USBLS	5/07
Commercial and Industrial Equipment	Virginia Beach-Norfolk-Newport News MSA, VA-NC	Y	39980 FQ	45440 MW	50770 TQ	USBLS	5/07
Commercial and Industrial Equipment	Washington	H	21.77 FQ	28.62 MW	33.41 TQ	WABLS	3/08
Commercial and Industrial Equipment	Seattle-Tacoma-Bellevue MSA, WA	Y	43090 FQ	61080 MW	69890 TQ	USBLS	5/07
Commercial and Industrial Equipment	Spokane MSA, WA	Y	43090 FQ	48440 MW	56980 TQ	USBLS	5/07
Commercial and Industrial Equipment	West Virginia	Y	30814 FQ	44669 MW	56805 TQ	WVBLS	7/08-9/08
Commercial and Industrial Equipment	Charleston MSA, WV	Y	23820 FQ	35290 MW	55020 TQ	USBLS	5/07
Commercial and Industrial Equipment	Wisconsin	Y	40080 FQ	46880 MW	54620 TQ	USBLS	5/07
Commercial and Industrial Equipment	Appleton MSA, WI	Y	33070 FQ	38570 MW	52320 TQ	USBLS	5/07
Commercial and Industrial Equipment	Milwaukee-Waukesha-West Allis MSA, WI	Y	42990 FQ	49600 MW	57050 TQ	USBLS	5/07
Commercial and Industrial Equipment	Wyoming	Y	41619 FQ	53645 MW	62738 TQ	WYBLS	9/08
Commercial and Industrial Equipment	Puerto Rico	Y	18320 FQ	26010 MW	35830 TQ	USBLS	5/07
Commercial and Industrial Equipment	San Juan-Caguas-Guaynabo MSA, PR	Y	15920 FQ	21260 MW	30670 TQ	USBLS	5/07
Commercial and Industrial Equipment	Virgin Islands	Y	42140 FQ	66020 MW	74310 TQ	USBLS	5/07
Powerhouse, Substation, and Relay	Alabama	Y	44150 FQ	54760 MW	62080 TQ	USBLS	5/07
Powerhouse, Substation, and Relay	Birmingham-Hoover MSA, AL	Y	44160 FQ	55130 MW	63450 TQ	USBLS	5/07
Powerhouse, Substation, and Relay	Alaska	Y	49060 FQ	63940 MW	72760 TQ	USBLS	5/07
Powerhouse, Substation, and Relay	Arizona	Y	63760 FQ	69660 MW	75350 TQ	USBLS	5/07
Powerhouse, Substation, and Relay	Phoenix-Mesa-Scottsdale MSA, AZ	Y	62940 FQ	69660 MW	76040 TQ	USBLS	5/07
Powerhouse, Substation, and Relay	Arkansas	Y	41720 FQ	51080 MW	57930 TQ	USBLS	5/07
Powerhouse, Substation, and Relay	California	H	26.37 FQ	31.79 MW	36.13 TQ	CABLS	1/08-3/08
Powerhouse, Substation, and Relay	Oakland-Fremont-Hayward MSA, CA	H	30.43 FQ	34.41 MW	37.62 TQ	CABLS	1/08-3/08
Powerhouse, Substation, and Relay	Riverside-San Bernardino-Ontario MSA, CA	H	22.23 FQ	33.44 MW	37.39 TQ	CABLS	1/08-3/08
Powerhouse, Substation, and Relay	Sacramento-Arden Arcade-Roseville MSA, CA	H	32.13 FQ	35.20 MW	38.03 TQ	CABLS	1/08-3/08
Powerhouse, Substation, and Relay	San Jose-Sunnyvale-Santa Clara MSA, CA	H	31.88 FQ	35.79 MW	38.70 TQ	CABLS	1/08-3/08
Powerhouse, Substation, and Relay	Colorado	Y	51240 FQ	58110 MW	64090 TQ	USBLS	5/07
Powerhouse, Substation, and Relay	Denver-Aurora MSA, CO	Y	54670 FQ	59770 MW	64680 TQ	USBLS	5/07
Powerhouse, Substation, and Relay	Connecticut	H	23.17 AE	30.50 MW		CTBLS	1/08-3/08
Powerhouse, Substation, and Relay	Bridgeport-Stamford-Norwalk MSA, CT	Y	55360 FQ	61250 MW	68770 TQ	USBLS	5/07
Powerhouse, Substation, and Relay	Hartford-West Hartford-East Hartford MSA, CT	Y	43110 FQ	49340 MW	55920 TQ	USBLS	5/07
Powerhouse, Substation, and Relay	Delaware	Y	61090 FQ	68660 MW	74830 TQ	USBLS	5/07
Powerhouse, Substation, and Relay	Wilmington PMSA, DE-MD-NJ	Y	53220 FQ	62400 MW	71940 TQ	USBLS	5/07
Powerhouse, Substation, and Relay	Washington-Arlington-Alexandria MSA, DC-VA-MD-WV	Y	53370 FQ	60990 MW	69010 TQ	USBLS	5/07
Powerhouse, Substation, and Relay	Florida	Y	50760 FQ	57760 MW	63640 TQ	USBLS	5/07
Powerhouse, Substation, and Relay	Jacksonville MSA, FL	Y	54170 FQ	59170 MW	64190 TQ	USBLS	5/07
Powerhouse, Substation, and Relay	Miami-Fort Lauderdale-Miami Beach MSA, FL	Y	53140 FQ	59420 MW	66130 TQ	USBLS	5/07
Powerhouse, Substation, and Relay	Orlando-Kissimmee MSA, FL	Y	45750 FQ	56670 MW	62610 TQ	USBLS	5/07
Powerhouse, Substation, and Relay	Tampa-St. Petersburg-Clearwater MSA, FL	Y	53150 FQ	57820 MW	62570 TQ	USBLS	5/07
Powerhouse, Substation, and Relay	West Palm Beach-Boca Raton-Boynton Beach PMSA, FL	Y	52230 FQ	56480 MW	60720 TQ	USBLS	5/07
Powerhouse, Substation, and Relay	Georgia	Y	47210 FQ	54750 MW	61100 TQ	USBLS	5/07

Occupation/Type/Industry	Location	Per	Low	Mid	High	Source	Date
Electrical and Electronics Repairer							
Powerhouse, Substation, and Relay	Atlanta-Sandy Springs-Marietta MSA, GA	Y	47340 FQ	54790 MW	61880 TQ	USBLS	5/07
Powerhouse, Substation, and Relay	Hawaii	Y	60690 FQ	67100 MW	72800 TQ	USBLS	5/07
Powerhouse, Substation, and Relay	Idaho	Y	57190 FQ	63890 MW	72700 TQ	USBLS	5/07
Powerhouse, Substation, and Relay	Illinois	Y	48730 FQ	59300 MW	68680 TQ	USBLS	5/07
Powerhouse, Substation, and Relay	Chicago-Naperville-Joliet MSA, IL-IN-WI	Y	53930 FQ	60660 MW	70220 TQ	USBLS	5/07
Powerhouse, Substation, and Relay	Indiana	Y	48160 FQ	54900 MW	60050 TQ	USBLS	5/07
Powerhouse, Substation, and Relay	Indianapolis-Carmel MSA, IN	Y	44180 FQ	50540 MW	56460 TQ	USBLS	5/07
Powerhouse, Substation, and Relay	Iowa	Y	49130 FQ	57200 MW	65610 TQ	USBLS	5/07
Powerhouse, Substation, and Relay	Kansas	Y	57590 FQ	64010 MW	70130 TQ	USBLS	5/07
Powerhouse, Substation, and Relay	Wichita MSA, KS	Y	54290 FQ	60870 MW	67800 TQ	USBLS	5/07
Powerhouse, Substation, and Relay	Kentucky	Y	52495 FQ	58475 MW	68712 TQ	KYBLS	2008
Powerhouse, Substation, and Relay	Lexington-Fayette MSA, KY	Y	54630 FQ	59640 MW	68650 TQ	USBLS	5/07
Powerhouse, Substation, and Relay	Louisiana	H	22.92 FQ	28.11 MW	32.92 TQ	LABLS	1/08-3/08
Powerhouse, Substation, and Relay	Baton Rouge MSA, LA	Y	54090 FQ	62070 MW	71190 TQ	USBLS	5/07
Powerhouse, Substation, and Relay	New Orleans-Metairie-Kenner MSA, LA	Y	37000 FQ	54850 MW	65910 TQ	USBLS	5/07
Powerhouse, Substation, and Relay	Maryland	Y		69550 MW		MDBLS	3/08
Powerhouse, Substation, and Relay	Baltimore-Towson MSA, MD	Y	61540 FQ	69500 MW	75430 TQ	USBLS	5/07
Powerhouse, Substation, and Relay	Massachusetts	Y	53280 FQ	62560 MW	72040 TQ	USBLS	5/07
Powerhouse, Substation, and Relay	Michigan	Y	55900 FQ	62470 MW	69110 TQ	USBLS	5/07
Powerhouse, Substation, and Relay	Detroit-Warren-Livonia MSA, MI	Y	55020 FQ	60470 MW	65140 TQ	USBLS	5/07
Powerhouse, Substation, and Relay	Warren-Troy-Farmington Hills PMSA, MI	Y	54640 FQ	59190 MW	63660 TQ	USBLS	5/07
Powerhouse, Substation, and Relay	Minnesota	Y	54408 FQ	68443 MW	77516 TQ	MNBLS	10/08-12/08
Powerhouse, Substation, and Relay	Duluth-Superior MSA, MN-WI	Y	48136 FQ	59653 MW	67279 TQ	MNBLS	10/08-12/08
Powerhouse, Substation, and Relay	Minneapolis-Saint Paul MSA, MN-WI	Y	63230 FQ	72649 MW	79583 TQ	MNBLS	10/08-12/08
Powerhouse, Substation, and Relay	Mississippi	Y	42050 FQ	50800 MW	59090 TQ	USBLS	5/07
Powerhouse, Substation, and Relay	Missouri	Y	53860 FQ	61670 MW	69410 TQ	USBLS	5/07
Powerhouse, Substation, and Relay	Kansas City MSA, MO-KS	Y	51840 FQ	60450 MW	69990 TQ	USBLS	5/07
Powerhouse, Substation, and Relay	St. Louis MSA, MO-IL	Y	58310 FQ	65390 MW	71770 TQ	USBLS	5/07
Powerhouse, Substation, and Relay	Montana	Y	49030 FQ	58620 MW	65130 TQ	USBLS	5/07
Powerhouse, Substation, and Relay	Nebraska	Y	51050 FQ	59000 MW	69200 TQ	USBLS	5/07
Powerhouse, Substation, and Relay	Nevada	H	25.50 FQ	29.43 MW	34.00 TQ	NVBLS	5/08
Powerhouse, Substation, and Relay	New Hampshire	H	24.56 AE	30.50 MW	32.32 AEX	NHBLS	6/08
Powerhouse, Substation, and Relay	New Jersey	Y	53050 FQ	64100 MW	72310 TQ	USBLS	5/07
Powerhouse, Substation, and Relay	New Mexico	Y	40750 FQ	48300 MW	70500 TQ	USBLS	5/07
Powerhouse, Substation, and Relay	New York	Y	55420 FQ	62700 MW	73610 TQ	USBLS	5/07
Powerhouse, Substation, and Relay	Buffalo-Niagara Falls MSA, NY	Y	52090 FQ	60880 MW	68750 TQ	USBLS	5/07
Powerhouse, Substation, and Relay	New York-Northern New Jersey-Long Island MSA, NY-NJ-PA	Y	54810 FQ	60720 MW	71750 TQ	USBLS	5/07
Powerhouse, Substation, and Relay	North Carolina	Y	45540 FQ	54760 MW	61820 TQ	USBLS	5/07
Powerhouse, Substation, and Relay	Charlotte-Gastonia-Concord MSA, NC-SC	Y	50430 FQ	56570 MW	61910 TQ	USBLS	5/07
Powerhouse, Substation, and Relay	North Dakota	Y	61570 FQ	68700 MW	74150 TQ	USBLS	5/07
Powerhouse, Substation, and Relay	Ohio	Y	50080 FQ	56450 MW	62710 TQ	USBLS	5/07
Powerhouse, Substation, and Relay	Cincinnati-Middletown MSA, OH-KY-IN	Y	49700 FQ	57470 MW	64910 TQ	USBLS	5/07
Powerhouse, Substation, and Relay	Cleveland-Elyria-Mentor MSA, OH	Y	49880 FQ	55990 MW	62110 TQ	USBLS	5/07
Powerhouse, Substation, and Relay	Columbus MSA, OH	Y	50290 FQ	57660 MW	66440 TQ	USBLS	5/07
Powerhouse, Substation, and Relay	Oklahoma	Y	37320 FQ	49030 MW	58840 TQ	USBLS	5/07
Powerhouse, Substation, and Relay	Oklahoma City MSA, OK	Y	54110 FQ	60090 MW	65400 TQ	USBLS	5/07
Powerhouse, Substation, and Relay	Oregon	H	28.65 FQ	33.05 MW	37.69 TQ	ORBLS	5/08
Powerhouse, Substation, and Relay	Portland-Vancouver-Beaverton MSA, OR-WA	Y	58270 FQ	66940 MW	76240 TQ	USBLS	5/07
Powerhouse, Substation, and Relay	Pennsylvania	Y	50830 FQ	57840 MW	64430 TQ	USBLS	5/07
Powerhouse, Substation, and Relay	Allentown-Bethlehem-Easton MSA, PA-NJ	Y	64590 FQ	69610 MW	74550 TQ	USBLS	5/07
Powerhouse, Substation, and Relay	Philadelphia-Camden-Wilmington MSA, PA-NJ-DE-MD	Y	53470 FQ	61570 MW	71020 TQ	USBLS	5/07
Powerhouse, Substation, and Relay	Pittsburgh MSA, PA	Y	46960 FQ	53810 MW	61720 TQ	USBLS	5/07

AE	Average entry wage	AW	Average wage paid	FQ	First quartile wage
AER	Average entry range	AWR	Average wage range	H	Hourly
AEX	Average experienced wage	AXR	Average experienced range	HI	Highest wage paid
ATC	Average total compensation	D	Daily	HR	High end range

LO	Lowest wage paid	MTC	Median total compensation	TCC	Total cash compensation
LR	Low end range	MW	Median wage paid	TQ	Third quartile wage
M	Monthly	MWR	Median wage range	W	Weekly
MCC	Median cash compensation	S	See annotated source	Y	Yearly

Occupation/Type/Industry	Location	Per	Low	Mid	High	Source	Date
Electrical and Electronics Repairer							
Powerhouse, Substation, and Relay	Providence-Fall River-Warwick MSA, RI-MA	Y	54430 FQ	62980 MW	70720 TQ	USBLS	5/07
Powerhouse, Substation, and Relay	Charleston-North Charleston MSA, SC	Y	44480 FQ	49970 MW	57660 TQ	USBLS	5/07
Powerhouse, Substation, and Relay	South Dakota	Y	53137 FQ	59786 MW	66515 TQ	SDBLS	7/08-9/08
Powerhouse, Substation, and Relay	Tennessee	Y	39970 FQ	47470 MW	55630 TQ	USBLS	5/07
Powerhouse, Substation, and Relay	Nashville-Davidson-Murfreesboro MSA, TN	Y	41540 FQ	46090 MW	53970 TQ	USBLS	5/07
Powerhouse, Substation, and Relay	Texas	Y	46610 FQ	55970 MW	62440 TQ	USBLS	5/07
Powerhouse, Substation, and Relay	Austin-Round Rock MSA, TX	Y	36490 FQ	46020 MW	56510 TQ	USBLS	5/07
Powerhouse, Substation, and Relay	Dallas-Fort Worth-Arlington MSA, TX	Y	52110 FQ	58150 MW	64160 TQ	USBLS	5/07
Powerhouse, Substation, and Relay	Houston-Sugar Land-Baytown MSA, TX	Y	34700 FQ	47630 MW	58620 TQ	USBLS	5/07
Powerhouse, Substation, and Relay	Utah	Y	55720 FQ	63450 MW	70520 TQ	USBLS	5/07
Powerhouse, Substation, and Relay	Salt Lake City MSA, UT	Y	52880 FQ	60870 MW	67840 TQ	USBLS	5/07
Powerhouse, Substation, and Relay	Vermont	Y	44120 FQ	55890 MW	64530 TQ	USBLS	5/07
Powerhouse, Substation, and Relay	Burlington-South Burlington MSA, VT	Y	52130 FQ	56310 MW	60490 TQ	USBLS	5/07
Powerhouse, Substation, and Relay	Virginia	Y	53360 FQ	60990 MW	67590 TQ	USBLS	5/07
Powerhouse, Substation, and Relay	Richmond MSA, VA	Y	47480 FQ	56200 MW	62830 TQ	USBLS	5/07
Powerhouse, Substation, and Relay	Washington	H	26.71 FQ	30.58 MW	35.40 TQ	WABLS	3/08
Powerhouse, Substation, and Relay	Seattle-Tacoma-Bellevue MSA, WA	Y	52900 FQ	59290 MW	65750 TQ	USBLS	5/07
Powerhouse, Substation, and Relay	West Virginia	Y	42670 FQ	52881 MW	63502 TQ	WVBLS	7/08-9/08
Powerhouse, Substation, and Relay	Charleston MSA, WV	Y	49160 FQ	56140 MW	64850 TQ	USBLS	5/07
Powerhouse, Substation, and Relay	Wisconsin	Y	57060 FQ	67880 MW	75730 TQ	USBLS	5/07
Powerhouse, Substation, and Relay	Milwaukee-Waukesha-West Allis MSA, WI	Y	67200 FQ	72820 MW	78470 TQ	USBLS	5/07
Powerhouse, Substation, and Relay	Puerto Rico	Y	28640 FQ	32620 MW	36090 TQ	USBLS	5/07
Powerhouse, Substation, and Relay	San Juan-Caguas-Guaynabo MSA, PR	Y	28680 FQ	32630 MW	36080 TQ	USBLS	5/07
Electrical Construction Superintendent	United States	Y		66560 AW		EWHOL	2008
Electrical Design Engineer							
Texas Instruments	Dallas, TX	Y		126192 AW		CNNM01	2009
Electrical Engineer	Alabama	Y	62920 FQ	78050 MW	93520 TQ	USBLS	5/07
	Birmingham-Hoover MSA, AL	Y	65970 FQ	80160 MW	93160 TQ	USBLS	5/07
	Tuscaloosa MSA, AL	Y	57400 FQ	69280 MW	77870 TQ	USBLS	5/07
	Alaska	Y	70570 FQ	86260 MW	102030 TQ	USBLS	5/07
	Anchorage MSA, AK	Y	70880 FQ	87420 MW	103250 TQ	USBLS	5/07
	Arizona	Y	63570 FQ	78550 MW	97970 TQ	USBLS	5/07
	Phoenix-Mesa-Scottsdale MSA, AZ	Y	60890 FQ	77060 MW	96820 TQ	USBLS	5/07
	Arkansas	Y	54870 FQ	68270 MW	80810 TQ	USBLS	5/07
	Little Rock-North Little Rock MSA, AR	Y	62800 FQ	75400 MW	89730 TQ	USBLS	5/07
	California	H	34.89 FQ	43.97 MW	54.91 TQ	CABLS	1/08-3/08
	Los Angeles-Long Beach-Glendale PMSA, CA	H	32.34 FQ	41.53 MW	52.12 TQ	CABLS	1/08-3/08
	Oakland-Fremont-Hayward MSA, CA	H	34.55 FQ	40.93 MW	51.55 TQ	CABLS	1/08-3/08
	Riverside-San Bernardino-Ontario MSA, CA	H	33.65 FQ	38.88 MW	45.53 TQ	CABLS	1/08-3/08
	Sacramento-Arden Arcade-Roseville MSA, CA	H	34.13 FQ	39.39 MW	46.52 TQ	CABLS	1/08-3/08
	San Diego-Carlsbad-San Marcos MSA, CA	H	33.90 FQ	41.91 MW	51.34 TQ	CABLS	1/08-3/08
	San Francisco-San Mateo-Redwood PMSA, CA	H	39.58 FQ	47.24 MW	53.29 TQ	CABLS	1/08-3/08
	San Jose-Sunnyvale-Santa Clara MSA, CA	H	39.26 FQ	50.37 MW	62.21 TQ	CABLS	1/08-3/08
	Santa Ana-Anaheim-Irvine PMSA, CA	Y	68030 FQ	84120 MW	103130 TQ	USBLS	5/07
	Colorado	Y	64530 FQ	80740 MW	99540 TQ	USBLS	5/07
	Denver-Aurora MSA, CO	Y	62220 FQ	79300 MW	95820 TQ	USBLS	5/07
	Connecticut	H	28.82 AE	39.41 MW		CTBLS	1/08-3/08

AE	Average entry wage	AW	Average wage paid	FQ	First quartile wage
AER	Average entry range	AWR	Average wage range	H	Hourly
AEX	Average experienced wage	AXR	Average experienced range	HI	Highest wage paid
ATC	Average total compensation	D	Daily	HR	High end range

LO	Lowest wage paid	MTC	Median total compensation
LR	Low end range	MW	Median wage paid
M	Monthly	MWR	Median wage range
MCC	Median cash compensation	S	See annotated source

TCC	Total cash compensation		
TQ	Third quartile wage		
W	Weekly		
Y	Yearly		

Occupation/Type/Industry	Location	Per	Low	Mid	High	Source	Date
Electrical Engineer	Bridgeport-Stamford-Norwalk						
	MSA, CT	Y	67450 FQ	78050 MW	93930 TQ	USBLS	5/07
	Danbury MSA, CT	Y	63730 FQ	78750 MW	94100 TQ	USBLS	5/07
	Hartford-West Hartford-East						
	Hartford MSA, CT	Y	63250 FQ	80530 MW	97300 TQ	USBLS	5/07
	Waterbury MSA, CT	Y	57580 FQ	71640 MW	89270 TQ	USBLS	5/07
	Delaware	Y	66000 FQ	79060 MW	94910 TQ	USBLS	5/07
	Wilmington PMSA, DE-MD-						
	NJ	Y	61260 FQ	76790 MW	94810 TQ	USBLS	5/07
	District of Columbia	Y	69100 FQ	87260 MW	103350 TQ	USBLS	5/07
	Washington-Arlington-						
	Alexandria MSA, DC-VA-						
	MD-WV	Y	68910 FQ	88670 MW	107250 TQ	USBLS	5/07
	Florida	Y	58290 FQ	74890 MW	92690 TQ	USBLS	5/07
	Fort Lauderdale-Pompano						
	Beach-Deerfield Beach						
	PMSA, FL	Y	63320 FQ	79120 MW	99170 TQ	USBLS	5/07
	Jacksonville MSA, FL	Y	63360 FQ	75220 MW	88840 TQ	USBLS	5/07
	Miami-Fort Lauderdale-Miami						
	Beach MSA, FL	Y	54870 FQ	75190 MW	93340 TQ	USBLS	5/07
	Orlando-Kissimmee MSA, FL	Y	56710 FQ	70290 MW	86370 TQ	USBLS	5/07
	Sarasota-Bradenton-Venice						
	MSA, FL	Y	68810 FQ	77000 MW	84970 TQ	USBLS	5/07
	Tampa-St. Petersburg-						
	Clearwater MSA, FL	Y	54730 FQ	67480 MW	87480 TQ	USBLS	5/07
	West Palm Beach-Boca Raton-						
	Boynton Beach PMSA, FL	Y	48800 FQ	61630 MW	86840 TQ	USBLS	5/07
	Georgia	Y	59990 FQ	75390 MW	92010 TQ	USBLS	5/07
	Atlanta-Sandy Springs-						
	Marietta MSA, GA	Y	60750 FQ	77600 MW	93890 TQ	USBLS	5/07
	Augusta-Richmond County						
	MSA, GA-SC	Y	67150 FQ	77990 MW	91370 TQ	USBLS	5/07
	Savannah MSA, GA	Y	73820 FQ	90580 MW	100460 TQ	USBLS	5/07
	Hawaii	Y	58620 FQ	77370 MW	91300 TQ	USBLS	5/07
	Honolulu MSA, HI	Y	58170 FQ	75950 MW	89780 TQ	USBLS	5/07
	Idaho	Y	59480 FQ	75520 MW	91180 TQ	USBLS	5/07
	Boise City-Nampa MSA, ID	Y	57750 FQ	75290 MW	90680 TQ	USBLS	5/07
	Illinois	Y	63250 FQ	79300 MW	97360 TQ	USBLS	5/07
	Chicago-Naperville-Joliet						
	MSA, IL-IN-WI	Y	65800 FQ	81710 MW	98570 TQ	USBLS	5/07
	Indiana	Y	59360 FQ	72280 MW	86500 TQ	USBLS	5/07
	Evansville MSA, IN-KY	Y	57850 FQ	72850 MW	83630 TQ	USBLS	5/07
	Gary PMSA, IN	Y	65620 FQ	74640 MW	84930 TQ	USBLS	5/07
	Indianapolis-Carmel MSA, IN	Y	61570 FQ	73880 MW	89440 TQ	USBLS	5/07
	Iowa	Y	58790 FQ	73170 MW	93280 TQ	USBLS	5/07
	Des Moines-West Des Moines						
	MSA, IA	Y	48030 FQ	58570 MW	70540 TQ	USBLS	5/07
	Kansas	Y	55440 FQ	69980 MW	88550 TQ	USBLS	5/07
	Topeka MSA, KS	Y	50660 FQ	64070 MW	87250 TQ	USBLS	5/07
	Wichita MSA, KS	Y	57050 FQ	66600 MW	81760 TQ	USBLS	5/07
	Kentucky	Y	56039 FQ	71725 MW	88375 TQ	KYBLS	2008
	Louisville-Jefferson County						
	MSA, KY-IN	Y	57400 FQ	71940 MW	92040 TQ	USBLS	5/07
	Louisiana	H	26.36 FQ	35.33 MW	45.56 TQ	LABLS	1/08-3/08
	Baton Rouge MSA, LA	Y	59970 FQ	78910 MW	104500 TQ	USBLS	5/07
	New Orleans-Metairie-Kenner						
	MSA, LA	Y	61420 FQ	81570 MW	105740 TQ	USBLS	5/07
	Maine	Y	63740 FQ	73050 MW	85610 TQ	USBLS	5/07
	Portland-South Portland-						
	Biddeford MSA, ME	Y	62610 FQ	72020 MW	85850 TQ	USBLS	5/07
	Maryland	Y		90900 MW		MDBLS	3/08
	Baltimore-Towson MSA, MD	Y	66430 FQ	85720 MW	103460 TQ	USBLS	5/07
	Bethesda-Gaithersburg-						
	Frederick PMSA, MD	Y	72640 FQ	93160 MW	113270 TQ	USBLS	5/07
	Massachusetts	Y	73640 FQ	91270 MW	113930 TQ	USBLS	5/07
	Boston-Cambridge-Quincy						
	NECTA, MA	Y	76270 FQ	93970 MW	115420 TQ	USBLS	5/07
	Springfield MSA, MA-CT	Y	65010 FQ	75800 MW	89130 TQ	USBLS	5/07
	Worcester MSA, MA-CT	Y	65660 FQ	77610 MW	92980 TQ	USBLS	5/07
	Michigan	Y	59750 FQ	73790 MW	90610 TQ	USBLS	5/07
	Detroit-Warren-Livonia MSA,						
	MI	Y	64340 FQ	77330 MW	93590 TQ	USBLS	5/07

AE	Average entry wage	AW	Average wage paid	FQ	First quartile wage
AER	Average entry range	AWR	Average wage range	H	Hourly
AEX	Average experienced wage	AXR	Average experienced range	HI	Highest wage paid
ATC	Average total compensation	D	Daily	HR	High end range

LO	Lowest wage paid	MTC	Median total compensation
LR	Low end range	MW	Median wage paid
M	Monthly	MWR	Median wage range
MCC	Median cash compensation	S	See annotated source

TCC	Total cash compensation
TQ	Third quartile wage
W	Weekly
Y	Yearly

Occupation/Type/Industry	Location	Per	Low	Mid	High	Source	Date
Electrical Engineer	Grand Rapids-Wyoming MSA, MI	Y	52030 FQ	62150 MW	77340 TQ	USBLS	5/07
	Warren-Troy-Farmington Hills PMSA, MI	Y	62020 FQ	73450 MW	86450 TQ	USBLS	5/07
	Minnesota	Y	66895 FQ	82672 MW	100720 TQ	MNBLS	10/08-12/08
	Duluth-Superior MSA, MN-WI	Y	64771 FQ	80454 MW	95970 TQ	MNBLS	10/08-12/08
	Minneapolis-Saint Paul MSA, MN-WI	Y	68716 FQ	85298 MW	103283 TQ	MNBLS	10/08-12/08
	Rochester MSA, MN	Y	75905 FQ	98242 MW	122113 TQ	MNBLS	10/08-12/08
	Mississippi	Y	56230 FQ	70340 MW	85840 TQ	USBLS	5/07
	Jackson MSA, MS	Y	52470 FQ	68140 MW	84600 TQ	USBLS	5/07
	Missouri	Y	62130 FQ	76090 MW	93120 TQ	USBLS	5/07
	Kansas City MSA, MO-KS	Y	62550 FQ	81380 MW	96140 TQ	USBLS	5/07
	St. Louis MSA, MO-IL	Y	59450 FQ	71450 MW	86020 TQ	USBLS	5/07
	Montana	Y	54260 FQ	64800 MW	79270 TQ	USBLS	5/07
	Billings MSA, MT	Y	55910 FQ	65590 MW	79200 TQ	USBLS	5/07
	Nebraska	Y	57170 FQ	73360 MW	90590 TQ	USBLS	5/07
	Omaha-Council Bluffs MSA, NE-IA	Y	58420 FQ	78260 MW	92020 TQ	USBLS	5/07
	Nevada	H	31.01 FQ	37.14 MW	44.92 TQ	NVBLS	5/08
	Las Vegas-Paradise MSA, NV	H	31.49 FQ	37.10 MW	44.77 TQ	NVBLS	5/08
	New Hampshire	H	28.01 AE	36.31 MW	43.26 AEX	NHBLS	6/08
	Manchester MSA, NH	Y	58750 FQ	71900 MW	85300 TQ	USBLS	5/07
	Nashua NECTA, NH-MA	Y	64420 FQ	78140 MW	97610 TQ	USBLS	5/07
	New Jersey	Y	62190 FQ	79590 MW	100580 TQ	USBLS	5/07
	Camden PMSA, NJ	Y	68990 FQ	86200 MW	110240 TQ	USBLS	5/07
	Edison PMSA, NJ	Y	68410 FQ	89080 MW	111200 TQ	USBLS	5/07
	New Mexico	Y	61970 FQ	76530 MW	95650 TQ	USBLS	5/07
	Albuquerque MSA, NM	Y	67290 FQ	83180 MW	101140 TQ	USBLS	5/07
	New York	Y	61740 FQ	79970 MW	103880 TQ	USBLS	5/07
	Albany-Schenectady-Troy MSA, NY	Y	65830 FQ	87010 MW	106300 TQ	USBLS	5/07
	Buffalo-Niagara Falls MSA, NY	Y	59560 FQ	71240 MW	85320 TQ	USBLS	5/07
	Nassau-Suffolk PMSA, NY	Y	70100 FQ	91640 MW	111700 TQ	USBLS	5/07
	New York-Northern New Jersey-Long Island MSA, NY-NJ-PA	Y	64050 FQ	86120 MW	108630 TQ	USBLS	5/07
	North Carolina	Y	57710 FQ	73340 MW	93780 TQ	USBLS	5/07
	Charlotte-Gastonia-Concord MSA, NC-SC	Y	58460 FQ	74000 MW	95450 TQ	USBLS	5/07
	Durham MSA, NC	Y	60000 FQ	77790 MW	102330 TQ	USBLS	5/07
	Raleigh-Cary MSA, NC	Y	63770 FQ	80750 MW	100070 TQ	USBLS	5/07
	North Dakota	Y	57830 FQ	71400 MW	83820 TQ	USBLS	5/07
	Fargo MSA, ND-MN	Y	53390 FQ	71780 MW	80060 TQ	USBLS	5/07
	Ohio	Y	56010 FQ	67300 MW	83250 TQ	USBLS	5/07
	Cincinnati-Middletown MSA, OH-KY-IN	Y	48570 FQ	66470 MW	80980 TQ	USBLS	5/07
	Cleveland-Elyria-Mentor MSA, OH	Y	59670 FQ	73270 MW	89010 TQ	USBLS	5/07
	Columbus MSA, OH	Y	55660 FQ	70800 MW	84700 TQ	USBLS	5/07
	Dayton MSA, OH	Y	62240 FQ	74430 MW	90210 TQ	USBLS	5/07
	Oklahoma	Y	48980 FQ	68820 MW	83810 TQ	USBLS	5/07
	Oklahoma City MSA, OK	Y	29260 FQ	67770 MW	82870 TQ	USBLS	5/07
	Tulsa MSA, OK	Y	53050 FQ	69250 MW	81760 TQ	USBLS	5/07
	Oregon	H	29.40 FQ	37.76 MW	46.80 TQ	ORBLS	5/08
	Portland-Vancouver-Beaverton MSA, OR-WA	Y	63420 FQ	79690 MW	96850 TQ	USBLS	5/07
	Pennsylvania	Y	59560 FQ	75200 MW	94740 TQ	USBLS	5/07
	Allentown-Bethlehem-Easton MSA, PA-NJ	Y	60140 FQ	74290 MW	89300 TQ	USBLS	5/07
	Philadelphia-Camden-Wilmington MSA, PA-NJ-DE-MD	Y	64820 FQ	82320 MW	100450 TQ	USBLS	5/07
	Pittsburgh MSA, PA	Y	59310 FQ	74020 MW	94540 TQ	USBLS	5/07
	Rhode Island	Y	63360 FQ	78100 MW	101380 TQ	USBLS	5/07
	Providence-Fall River-Warwick MSA, RI-MA	Y	63470 FQ	77790 MW	101020 TQ	USBLS	5/07
	South Carolina	Y	62800 FQ	79860 MW	96000 TQ	USBLS	5/07
	Charleston-North Charleston MSA, SC	Y	60400 FQ	77330 MW	93580 TQ	USBLS	5/07
	Columbia MSA, SC	Y	65190 FQ	80390 MW	94210 TQ	USBLS	5/07

AE Average entry wage	**AW** Average wage paid	**FQ** First quartile wage	**LO** Lowest wage paid	**MTC** Median total compensation	**TCC** Total cash compensation
AER Average entry range	**AWR** Average wage range	**H** Hourly	**LR** Low end range	**MW** Median wage paid	**TQ** Third quartile wage
AEX Average experienced wage	**AXR** Average experienced range	**HI** Highest wage paid	**M** Monthly	**MWR** Median wage range	**W** Weekly
ATC Average total compensation	**D** Daily	**HR** High end range	**MCC** Median cash compensation	**S** See annotated source	**Y** Yearly

Occupation/Type/Industry	Location	Per	Low	Mid	High	Source	Date
Electrical Engineer	South Dakota	Y	54706 FQ	64350 MW	76706 TQ	SDBLS	7/08-9/08
	Sioux Falls MSA, SD	Y	59716 FQ	69644 MW	78541 TQ	SDBLS	7/08-9/08
	Tennessee	Y	59520 FQ	75660 MW	93520 TQ	USBLS	5/07
	Memphis MSA, TN-MS-AR	Y	56570 FQ	70770 MW	86320 TQ	USBLS	5/07
	Nashville-Davidson-Murfreesboro MSA, TN	Y	63140 FQ	76190 MW	92010 TQ	USBLS	5/07
	Texas	Y	67460 FQ	86570 MW	107520 TQ	USBLS	5/07
	Austin-Round Rock MSA, TX	Y	68440 FQ	91920 MW	117530 TQ	USBLS	5/07
	Brownsville-Harlingen MSA, TX	Y	56720 FQ	72560 MW	87150 TQ	USBLS	5/07
	Dallas-Fort Worth-Arlington MSA, TX	Y	70680 FQ	88360 MW	106770 TQ	USBLS	5/07
	El Paso MSA, TX	Y	48450 FQ	59170 MW	74420 TQ	USBLS	5/07
	Houston-Sugar Land-Baytown MSA, TX	Y	70870 FQ	90980 MW	112630 TQ	USBLS	5/07
	San Antonio MSA, TX	Y	58610 FQ	74810 MW	95070 TQ	USBLS	5/07
	Utah	Y	63260 FQ	78400 MW	93930 TQ	USBLS	5/07
	Logan MSA, UT-ID	Y	49770 FQ	58360 MW	67350 TQ	USBLS	5/07
	Salt Lake City MSA, UT	Y	70710 FQ	85350 MW	96970 TQ	USBLS	5/07
	Vermont	Y	57340 FQ	68070 MW	88800 TQ	USBLS	5/07
	Burlington-South Burlington MSA, VT	Y	56010 FQ	64590 MW	80640 TQ	USBLS	5/07
	Virginia	Y	62430 FQ	80490 MW	98260 TQ	USBLS	5/07
	Richmond MSA, VA	Y	67710 FQ	81450 MW	94550 TQ	USBLS	5/07
	Virginia Beach-Norfolk-Newport News MSA, VA-NC	Y	51710 FQ	66040 MW	84940 TQ	USBLS	5/07
	Washington	H	32.42 FQ	38.18 MW	45.78 TQ	WABLS	3/08
	Seattle-Tacoma-Bellevue MSA, WA	Y	65910 FQ	77690 MW	93820 TQ	USBLS	5/07
	West Virginia	Y	62559 FQ	78041 MW	94522 TQ	WVBLS	7/08-9/08
	Charleston MSA, WV	Y	55510 FQ	78860 MW	94170 TQ	USBLS	5/07
	Huntington-Ashland MSA, WV-KY-OH	Y	62440 FQ	73870 MW	89040 TQ	USBLS	5/07
	Wisconsin	Y	57540 FQ	72440 MW	89120 TQ	USBLS	5/07
	Appleton MSA, WI	Y	56150 FQ	63240 MW	75150 TQ	USBLS	5/07
	Milwaukee-Waukesha-West Allis MSA, WI	Y	60110 FQ	76060 MW	94300 TQ	USBLS	5/07
	Wyoming	Y	46131 FQ	57267 MW	83058 TQ	WYBLS	9/08
	Puerto Rico	Y	42480 FQ	49380 MW	65780 TQ	USBLS	5/07
	San Juan-Caguas-Guaynabo MSA, PR	Y	42440 FQ	48520 MW	62870 TQ	USBLS	5/07
	Guam	Y	36320 FQ	43320 MW	58800 TQ	USBLS	5/07
Electrical Inspector Department of Safety	New Hampshire	Y		34778 AW		NHUL03	2008
Electrical Power-Line Installer and Repairer	Alabama	Y	40940 FQ	51940 MW	57960 TQ	USBLS	5/07
	Birmingham-Hoover MSA, AL	Y	40380 FQ	52820 MW	58660 TQ	USBLS	5/07
	Huntsville MSA, AL	Y	29590 FQ	40080 MW	51180 TQ	USBLS	5/07
	Mobile MSA, AL	Y	50290 FQ	55380 MW	59850 TQ	USBLS	5/07
	Alaska	Y	51550 FQ	68590 MW	79950 TQ	USBLS	5/07
	Anchorage MSA, AK	Y	52040 FQ	67660 MW	76080 TQ	USBLS	5/07
	Arizona	Y	52680 FQ	63700 MW	72680 TQ	USBLS	5/07
	Phoenix-Mesa-Scottsdale MSA, AZ	Y	54980 FQ	64290 MW	73270 TQ	USBLS	5/07
	Tucson MSA, AZ	Y	40960 FQ	59660 MW	67980 TQ	USBLS	5/07
	Arkansas	Y	32550 FQ	43930 MW	54910 TQ	USBLS	5/07
	Fort Smith MSA, AR-OK	Y	24010 FQ	31230 MW	51290 TQ	USBLS	5/07
	Little Rock-North Little Rock MSA, AR	Y	31020 FQ	45530 MW	56410 TQ	USBLS	5/07
	California	H	26.64 FQ	33.10 MW	40.97 TQ	CABLS	1/08-3/08
	Fresno MSA, CA	H	36.03 FQ	44.35 MW	48.75 TQ	CABLS	1/08-3/08
	Los Angeles-Long Beach-Glendale PMSA, CA	H	26.94 FQ	30.32 MW	37.58 TQ	CABLS	1/08-3/08
	Riverside-San Bernardino-Ontario MSA, CA	H	23.38 FQ	29.59 MW	37.95 TQ	CABLS	1/08-3/08
	San Francisco-San Mateo-Redwood PMSA, CA	H	30.77 FQ	36.71 MW	42.83 TQ	CABLS	1/08-3/08
	Santa Ana-Anaheim-Irvine PMSA, CA	Y	50690 FQ	58830 MW	75800 TQ	USBLS	5/07
	Colorado	Y	52330 FQ	60230 MW	69540 TQ	USBLS	5/07

AE	Average entry wage	AW	Average wage paid	FQ	First quartile wage	LO	Lowest wage paid	MTC	Median total compensation	TCC	Total cash compensation
AER	Average entry range	AWR	Average wage range	H	Hourly	LR	Low end range	MW	Median wage paid	TQ	Third quartile wage
AEX	Average experienced wage	AXR	Average experienced range	HI	Highest wage paid	M	Monthly	MWR	Median wage range	W	Weekly
ATC	Average total compensation	D	Daily	HR	High end range	MCC	Median cash compensation	S	See annotated source	Y	Yearly

Occupation/Type/Industry	Location	Per	Low	Mid	High	Source	Date
Electrical Power-Line Installer and Repairer	Denver-Aurora MSA, CO	Y	56200 FQ	68540 MW	75670 TQ	USBLS	5/07
	Pueblo MSA, CO	Y	53370 FQ	58050 MW	62690 TQ	USBLS	5/07
	Connecticut	H	22.47 AE	32.45 MW		CTBLS	1/08-3/08
	Bridgeport-Stamford-Norwalk MSA, CT	Y	54650 FQ	66100 MW	73710 TQ	USBLS	5/07
	Hartford-West Hartford-East Hartford MSA, CT	Y	46420 FQ	62340 MW	72350 TQ	USBLS	5/07
	Delaware	Y	41020 FQ	57830 MW	70570 TQ	USBLS	5/07
	Wilmington PMSA, DE-MD-NJ	Y	42320 FQ	54990 MW	68660 TQ	USBLS	5/07
	District of Columbia	Y	45560 FQ	50960 MW	59520 TQ	USBLS	5/07
	Washington-Arlington-Alexandria MSA, DC-VA-MD-WV	Y	36520 FQ	49830 MW	58750 TQ	USBLS	5/07
	Florida	Y	41860 FQ	53140 MW	59240 TQ	USBLS	5/07
	Cape Coral-Fort Myers MSA, FL	Y	52110 FQ	57530 MW	62320 TQ	USBLS	5/07
	Fort Lauderdale-Pompano Beach-Deerfield Beach PMSA, FL	Y	48630 FQ	53010 MW	57410 TQ	USBLS	5/07
	Jacksonville MSA, FL	Y	37590 FQ	52400 MW	58780 TQ	USBLS	5/07
	Lakeland MSA, FL	Y	41750 FQ	53250 MW	62650 TQ	USBLS	5/07
	Miami-Fort Lauderdale-Miami Beach MSA, FL	Y	44850 FQ	53440 MW	58900 TQ	USBLS	5/07
	Orlando-Kissimmee MSA, FL	Y	44350 FQ	54080 MW	59670 TQ	USBLS	5/07
	Pensacola-Ferry Pass-Brent MSA, FL	Y	48960 FQ	53680 MW	58010 TQ	USBLS	5/07
	Tampa-St. Petersburg-Clearwater MSA, FL	Y	37770 FQ	49260 MW	57350 TQ	USBLS	5/07
	West Palm Beach-Boca Raton-Boynton Beach PMSA, FL	Y	48170 FQ	53700 MW	58350 TQ	USBLS	5/07
	Georgia	Y	35060 FQ	45890 MW	55130 TQ	USBLS	5/07
	Atlanta-Sandy Springs-Marietta MSA, GA	Y	32870 FQ	43390 MW	53920 TQ	USBLS	5/07
	Hawaii	Y	61100 FQ	67540 MW	72950 TQ	USBLS	5/07
	Honolulu MSA, HI	Y	60650 FQ	67530 MW	73170 TQ	USBLS	5/07
	Idaho	Y	39920 FQ	59080 MW	71030 TQ	USBLS	5/07
	Boise City-Nampa MSA, ID	Y	35150 FQ	47860 MW	64000 TQ	USBLS	5/07
	Illinois	Y	45920 FQ	56260 MW	69880 TQ	USBLS	5/07
	Chicago-Naperville-Joliet MSA, IL-IN-WI	Y	45510 FQ	56370 MW	70230 TQ	USBLS	5/07
	Indiana	Y	42170 FQ	53400 MW	60760 TQ	USBLS	5/07
	Indianapolis-Carmel MSA, IN	Y	36280 FQ	50000 MW	58380 TQ	USBLS	5/07
	Iowa	Y	43380 FQ	51370 MW	58310 TQ	USBLS	5/07
	Des Moines-West Des Moines MSA, IA	Y	34320 FQ	40710 MW	49080 TQ	USBLS	5/07
	Kansas	Y	41730 FQ	50040 MW	58010 TQ	USBLS	5/07
	Wichita MSA, KS	Y	42430 FQ	50100 MW	57530 TQ	USBLS	5/07
	Kentucky	Y	34141 FQ	46549 MW	56915 TQ	KYBLS	2008
	Louisville-Jefferson County MSA, KY-IN	Y	32290 FQ	48930 MW	56490 TQ	USBLS	5/07
	Louisiana	H	15.19 FQ	20.16 MW	24.86 TQ	LABLS	1/08-3/08
	Baton Rouge MSA, LA	Y	34050 FQ	42920 MW	51220 TQ	USBLS	5/07
	New Orleans-Metairie-Kenner MSA, LA	Y	34530 FQ	48760 MW	55040 TQ	USBLS	5/07
	Maine	Y	35500 FQ	47750 MW	53890 TQ	USBLS	5/07
	Portland-South Portland-Biddeford MSA, ME	Y	31540 FQ	33950 MW	36360 TQ	USBLS	5/07
	Maryland	Y		57200 MW		MDBLS	3/08
	Baltimore-Towson MSA, MD	Y	43180 FQ	57680 MW	68290 TQ	USBLS	5/07
	Bethesda-Gaithersburg-Frederick PMSA, MD	Y	27290 FQ	47920 MW	61690 TQ	USBLS	5/07
	Massachusetts	Y	54910 FQ	66320 MW	75710 TQ	USBLS	5/07
	Boston-Cambridge-Quincy NECTA, MA	Y	54560 FQ	66610 MW	76620 TQ	USBLS	5/07
	Worcester MSA, MA-CT	Y	39740 FQ	56250 MW	72500 TQ	USBLS	5/07
	Michigan	Y	46930 FQ	59040 MW	66840 TQ	USBLS	5/07
	Detroit-Warren-Livonia MSA, MI	Y	38570 FQ	55990 MW	64940 TQ	USBLS	5/07
	Grand Rapids-Wyoming MSA, MI	Y	52390 FQ	62660 MW	70020 TQ	USBLS	5/07

AE	Average entry wage	AW	Average wage paid	FQ	First quartile wage
AER	Average entry range	AWR	Average wage range	H	Hourly
AEX	Average experienced wage	AXR	Average experienced range	HI	Highest wage paid
ATC	Average total compensation	D	Daily	HR	High end range

LO	Lowest wage paid	MTC	Median total compensation	TCC	Total cash compensation
LR	Low end range	MW	Median wage paid	TQ	Third quartile wage
M	Monthly	MWR	Median wage range	W	Weekly
MCC	Median cash compensation	S	See annotated source	Y	Yearly

Occupation/Type/Industry	Location	Per	Low	Mid	High	Source	Date
Electrical Power-Line Installer and Repairer	Warren-Troy-Farmington Hills PMSA, MI	Y	36130 FQ	50890 MW	61750 TQ	USBLS	5/07
	Minnesota	Y	53359 FQ	61908 MW	72188 TQ	MNBLS	10/08-12/08
	Duluth-Superior MSA, MN-WI	Y	42870 FQ	52027 MW	61688 TQ	MNBLS	10/08-12/08
	Minneapolis-Saint Paul MSA, MN-WI	Y	59999 FQ	71674 MW	80191 TQ	MNBLS	10/08-12/08
	Mississippi	Y	33150 FQ	41490 MW	48510 TQ	USBLS	5/07
	Jackson MSA, MS	Y	31570 FQ	37710 MW	44900 TQ	USBLS	5/07
	Missouri	Y	42320 FQ	52640 MW	60010 TQ	USBLS	5/07
	Kansas City MSA, MO-KS	Y	45370 FQ	55710 MW	63170 TQ	USBLS	5/07
	St. Louis MSA, MO-IL	Y	37310 FQ	51250 MW	65030 TQ	USBLS	5/07
	Montana	Y	52630 FQ	61410 MW	70720 TQ	USBLS	5/07
	Billings MSA, MT	Y	56780 FQ	67240 MW	73350 TQ	USBLS	5/07
	Nebraska	Y	35420 FQ	46920 MW	57490 TQ	USBLS	5/07
	Omaha-Council Bluffs MSA, NE-IA	Y	41960 FQ	52150 MW	58450 TQ	USBLS	5/07
	Nevada	H	16.37 FQ	31.73 MW	36.29 TQ	NVBLS	5/08
	Las Vegas-Paradise MSA, NV	H	15.08 FQ	31.88 MW	36.48 TQ	NVBLS	5/08
	New Hampshire	H	20.47 AE	26.89 MW	29.25 AEX	NHBLS	6/08
	Nashua NECTA, NH-MA	Y	46750 FQ	55140 MW	61580 TQ	USBLS	5/07
	New Jersey	Y	47110 FQ	58870 MW	71240 TQ	USBLS	5/07
	Camden PMSA, NJ	Y	37720 FQ	46460 MW	59050 TQ	USBLS	5/07
	Edison PMSA, NJ	Y	54840 FQ	66660 MW	74320 TQ	USBLS	5/07
	Newark-Union PMSA, NJ-PA	Y	48710 FQ	58450 MW	71210 TQ	USBLS	5/07
	New Mexico	Y	31970 FQ	41190 MW	50500 TQ	USBLS	5/07
	Albuquerque MSA, NM	Y	30100 FQ	36710 MW	47020 TQ	USBLS	5/07
	New York	Y	54080 FQ	67710 MW	76760 TQ	USBLS	5/07
	Buffalo-Niagara Falls MSA, NY	Y	33110 FQ	40170 MW	68090 TQ	USBLS	5/07
	Nassau-Suffolk PMSA, NY	Y	67760 FQ	73180 MW	78840 TQ	USBLS	5/07
	New York-Northern New Jersey-Long Island MSA, NY-NJ-PA	Y	53950 FQ	67620 MW	76380 TQ	USBLS	5/07
	North Carolina	Y	36080 FQ	45690 MW	54280 TQ	USBLS	5/07
	Charlotte-Gastonia-Concord MSA, NC-SC	Y	39140 FQ	49750 MW	57150 TQ	USBLS	5/07
	Durham MSA, NC	Y	42070 FQ	50950 MW	58760 TQ	USBLS	5/07
	Raleigh-Cary MSA, NC	Y	37540 FQ	47350 MW	55090 TQ	USBLS	5/07
	North Dakota	Y	48160 FQ	53940 MW	59300 TQ	USBLS	5/07
	Fargo MSA, ND-MN	Y	41650 FQ	51450 MW	59320 TQ	USBLS	5/07
	Ohio	Y	46330 FQ	54090 MW	60060 TQ	USBLS	5/07
	Cincinnati-Middletown MSA, OH-KY-IN	Y	53220 FQ	58940 MW	64380 TQ	USBLS	5/07
	Cleveland-Elyria-Mentor MSA, OH	Y	49080 FQ	56160 MW	62690 TQ	USBLS	5/07
	Columbus MSA, OH	Y	43890 FQ	52300 MW	58150 TQ	USBLS	5/07
	Dayton MSA, OH	Y	43010 FQ	48080 MW	54130 TQ	USBLS	5/07
	Oklahoma	Y	28270 FQ	40560 MW	52890 TQ	USBLS	5/07
	Oklahoma City MSA, OK	Y	24740 FQ	43430 MW	57320 TQ	USBLS	5/07
	Tulsa MSA, OK	Y	22780 FQ	31760 MW	43830 TQ	USBLS	5/07
	Oregon	H	30.21 FQ	34.44 MW	37.66 TQ	ORBLS	5/08
	Portland-Vancouver-Beaverton MSA, OR-WA	Y	54150 FQ	69490 MW	77080 TQ	USBLS	5/07
	Salem MSA, OR	Y	32240 FQ	61980 MW	73650 TQ	USBLS	5/07
	Pennsylvania	Y	43560 FQ	55370 MW	63740 TQ	USBLS	5/07
	Allentown-Bethlehem-Easton MSA, PA-NJ	Y	51680 FQ	58330 MW	64990 TQ	USBLS	5/07
	Philadelphia-Camden-Wilmington MSA, PA-NJ-DE-MD	Y	43920 FQ	54440 MW	64670 TQ	USBLS	5/07
	Pittsburgh MSA, PA	Y	35550 FQ	54060 MW	64120 TQ	USBLS	5/07
	Providence-Fall River-Warwick MSA, RI-MA	Y	47960 FQ	64600 MW	72930 TQ	USBLS	5/07
	South Carolina	Y	33960 FQ	45390 MW	54870 TQ	USBLS	5/07
	Charleston-North Charleston MSA, SC	Y	44330 FQ	50290 MW	56470 TQ	USBLS	5/07
	Columbia MSA, SC	Y	29820 FQ	39880 MW	53690 TQ	USBLS	5/07
	South Dakota	Y	43563 FQ	51163 MW	58693 TQ	SDBLS	7/08-9/08
	Sioux Falls MSA, SD	Y	46303 FQ	55464 MW	61624 TQ	SDBLS	7/08-9/08
	Tennessee	Y	38770 FQ	50890 MW	58440 TQ	USBLS	5/07
	Johnson City MSA, TN	Y	45680 FQ	54060 MW	63080 TQ	USBLS	5/07

AE	Average entry wage	AW	Average wage paid	FQ	First quartile wage
AER	Average entry range	AWR	Average wage range	H	Hourly
AEX	Average experienced wage	AXR	Average experienced range	HI	Highest wage paid
ATC	Average total compensation	D	Daily	HR	High end range

LO	Lowest wage paid	MTC	Median total compensation
LR	Low end range	MW	Median wage paid
M	Monthly	MWR	Median wage range
MCC	Median cash compensation	S	See annotated source

TCC	Total cash compensation		
TQ	Third quartile wage		
W	Weekly		
Y	Yearly		

Occupation/Type/Industry	Location	Per	Low	Mid	High	Source	Date
Electrical Power-Line Installer and Repairer	Memphis MSA, TN-MS-AR	Y	34470 FQ	49840 MW	56320 TQ	USBLS	5/07
	Nashville-Davidson-Murfreesboro MSA, TN	Y	50250 FQ	56300 MW	64530 TQ	USBLS	5/07
	Texas	Y	31280 FQ	41330 MW	52490 TQ	USBLS	5/07
	Austin-Round Rock MSA, TX	Y	33070 FQ	41500 MW	50530 TQ	USBLS	5/07
	Dallas-Fort Worth-Arlington MSA, TX	Y	26570 FQ	34010 MW	43150 TQ	USBLS	5/07
	El Paso MSA, TX	Y	48020 FQ	52040 MW	56490 TQ	USBLS	5/07
	Houston-Sugar Land-Baytown MSA, TX	Y	37730 FQ	47450 MW	56200 TQ	USBLS	5/07
	San Antonio MSA, TX	Y	30680 FQ	39080 MW	45630 TQ	USBLS	5/07
	Utah	Y	35250 FQ	52610 MW	61970 TQ	USBLS	5/07
	St. George MSA, UT	Y	42650 FQ	51320 MW	59330 TQ	USBLS	5/07
	Salt Lake City MSA, UT	Y	41170 FQ	54380 MW	62750 TQ	USBLS	5/07
	Vermont	Y	44960 FQ	52170 MW	59190 TQ	USBLS	5/07
	Virginia	Y	34410 FQ	46620 MW	57870 TQ	USBLS	5/07
	Richmond MSA, VA	Y	30380 FQ	36960 MW	47870 TQ	USBLS	5/07
	Virginia Beach-Norfolk-Newport News MSA, VA-NC	Y	34410 FQ	50280 MW	60240 TQ	USBLS	5/07
	Washington	H	28.25 FQ	33.56 MW	37.52 TQ	WABLS	3/08
	Seattle-Tacoma-Bellevue MSA, WA	Y	51090 FQ	64580 MW	75220 TQ	USBLS	5/07
	West Virginia	Y	40391 FQ	53866 MW	62525 TQ	WVBLS	7/08-9/08
	Charleston MSA, WV	Y	44950 FQ	52850 MW	58710 TQ	USBLS	5/07
	Wisconsin	Y	45650 FQ	56210 MW	67320 TQ	USBLS	5/07
	Milwaukee-Waukesha-West Allis MSA, WI	Y	47060 FQ	60300 MW	71070 TQ	USBLS	5/07
	Wyoming	Y	39859 FQ	49722 MW	59824 TQ	WYBLS	9/08
	Cheyenne MSA, WY	Y	43781 FQ	50757 MW	59785 TQ	WYBLS	9/08
	Puerto Rico	Y	30670 FQ	34400 MW	37530 TQ	USBLS	5/07
	San Juan-Caguas-Guaynabo MSA, PR	Y	30650 FQ	34380 MW	37510 TQ	USBLS	5/07
Electrical Quality Assurance Specialist Municipal Government	Seattle, WA	H	30.68 LO		35.79 HI	CSSS	2008
Electrical Workload Supervisor Municipal Government	Seattle, WA	H	39.79 LO		43.00 HI	CSSS	2008
Electrician	Alabama	Y	29550 FQ	36400 MW	43890 TQ	USBLS	5/07
	Birmingham-Hoover MSA, AL	Y	34310 FQ	41600 MW	47010 TQ	USBLS	5/07
	Alaska	Y	54510 FQ	66670 MW	78330 TQ	USBLS	5/07
	Anchorage MSA, AK	Y	54510 FQ	68000 MW	79080 TQ	USBLS	5/07
	Fairbanks MSA, AK	Y	51840 FQ	66280 MW	77440 TQ	USBLS	5/07
	Arizona	Y	29620 FQ	38820 MW	48410 TQ	USBLS	5/07
	Flagstaff MSA, AZ	Y	26050 FQ	39290 MW	48880 TQ	USBLS	5/07
	Phoenix-Mesa-Scottsdale MSA, AZ	Y	29320 FQ	38510 MW	48760 TQ	USBLS	5/07
	Tucson MSA, AZ	Y	30060 FQ	38870 MW	46950 TQ	USBLS	5/07
	Arkansas	Y	31410 FQ	37900 MW	45400 TQ	USBLS	5/07
	Little Rock-North Little Rock MSA, AR	Y	29350 FQ	36500 MW	44050 TQ	USBLS	5/07
	California	H	18.43 FQ	24.69 MW	33.30 TQ	CABLS	1/08-3/08
	Los Angeles-Long Beach-Glendale PMSA, CA	H	16.92 FQ	22.63 MW	32.37 TQ	CABLS	1/08-3/08
	Oakland-Fremont-Hayward MSA, CA	H	23.74 FQ	31.23 MW	40.89 TQ	CABLS	1/08-3/08
	Riverside-San Bernardino-Ontario MSA, CA	H	18.20 FQ	21.98 MW	27.58 TQ	CABLS	1/08-3/08
	Sacramento-Arden Arcade-Roseville MSA, CA	H	18.93 FQ	22.74 MW	29.96 TQ	CABLS	1/08-3/08
	San Diego-Carlsbad-San Marcos MSA, CA	H	17.05 FQ	22.28 MW	30.50 TQ	CABLS	1/08-3/08
	San Francisco-San Mateo-Redwood PMSA, CA	H	31.16 FQ	39.82 MW	49.27 TQ	CABLS	1/08-3/08
	San Jose-Sunnyvale-Santa Clara MSA, CA	H	26.76 FQ	33.85 MW	44.61 TQ	CABLS	1/08-3/08
	Santa Ana-Anaheim-Irvine PMSA, CA	Y	30800 FQ	42110 MW	57030 TQ	USBLS	5/07
	Colorado	Y	34070 FQ	44840 MW	54850 TQ	USBLS	5/07

AE	Average entry wage	AW	Average wage paid	FQ	First quartile wage
AER	Average entry range	AWR	Average wage range	H	Hourly
AEX	Average experienced wage	AXR	Average experienced range	HI	Highest wage paid
ATC	Average total compensation	D	Daily	HR	High end range

LO	Lowest wage paid	MTC	Median total compensation	TCC	Total cash compensation
LR	Low end range	MW	Median wage paid	TQ	Third quartile wage
M	Monthly	MWR	Median wage range	W	Weekly
MCC	Median cash compensation	S	See annotated source	Y	Yearly

Occupation/Type/Industry	Location	Per	Low	Mid	High	Source	Date
Electrician	Boulder MSA, CO	Y	45950 FQ	56360 MW	64710 TQ	USBLS	5/07
	Denver-Aurora MSA, CO	Y	36350 FQ	46570 MW	56380 TQ	USBLS	5/07
	Connecticut	H	18.05 AE	25.55 MW		CTBLS	1/08-3/08
	Bridgeport-Stamford-Norwalk MSA, CT	Y	40820 FQ	51900 MW	63650 TQ	USBLS	5/07
	Hartford-West Hartford-East Hartford MSA, CT	Y	43160 FQ	53190 MW	64440 TQ	USBLS	5/07
	Delaware	Y	36440 FQ	45100 MW	58350 TQ	USBLS	5/07
	Wilmington PMSA, DE-MD-NJ	Y	39630 FQ	49860 MW	65250 TQ	USBLS	5/07
	District of Columbia	Y	50020 FQ	58860 MW	70620 TQ	USBLS	5/07
	Washington-Arlington-Alexandria MSA, DC-VA-MD-WV	Y	38910 FQ	50490 MW	64680 TQ	USBLS	5/07
	Florida	Y	30330 FQ	36420 MW	44130 TQ	USBLS	5/07
	Fort Lauderdale-Pompano Beach-Deerfield Beach PMSA, FL	Y	32170 FQ	37800 MW	47800 TQ	USBLS	5/07
	Jacksonville MSA, FL	Y	33730 FQ	38860 MW	45720 TQ	USBLS	5/07
	Miami-Fort Lauderdale-Miami Beach MSA, FL	Y	31630 FQ	37910 MW	47890 TQ	USBLS	5/07
	Orlando-Kissimmee MSA, FL	Y	28840 FQ	34570 MW	40190 TQ	USBLS	5/07
	Tallahassee MSA, FL	Y	27810 FQ	33700 MW	39180 TQ	USBLS	5/07
	Tampa-St. Petersburg-Clearwater MSA, FL	Y	30790 FQ	35810 MW	40690 TQ	USBLS	5/07
	West Palm Beach-Boca Raton-Boynton Beach PMSA, FL	Y	31590 FQ	38750 MW	48210 TQ	USBLS	5/07
	Georgia	Y	30680 FQ	37310 MW	47340 TQ	USBLS	5/07
	Atlanta-Sandy Springs-Marietta MSA, GA	Y	33080 FQ	39350 MW	50490 TQ	USBLS	5/07
	Augusta-Richmond County MSA, GA-SC	Y	31410 FQ	37020 MW	43760 TQ	USBLS	5/07
	Hawaii	Y	45820 FQ	60690 MW	73170 TQ	USBLS	5/07
	Honolulu MSA, HI	Y	46580 FQ	61330 MW	74260 TQ	USBLS	5/07
	Idaho	Y	29690 FQ	40530 MW	51540 TQ	USBLS	5/07
	Boise City-Nampa MSA, ID	Y	28170 FQ	43620 MW	55300 TQ	USBLS	5/07
	Illinois	Y	53130 FQ	68740 MW	78110 TQ	USBLS	5/07
	Champaign-Urbana MSA, IL	Y	41890 FQ	50110 MW	69560 TQ	USBLS	5/07
	Chicago-Naperville-Joliet MSA, IL-IN-WI	Y	55840 FQ	70390 MW	79310 TQ	USBLS	5/07
	Indiana	Y	37450 FQ	49650 MW	63410 TQ	USBLS	5/07
	Gary PMSA, IN	Y	49600 FQ	61740 MW	72540 TQ	USBLS	5/07
	Indianapolis-Carmel MSA, IN	Y	36210 FQ	47900 MW	62820 TQ	USBLS	5/07
	Iowa	Y	33550 FQ	42550 MW	53570 TQ	USBLS	5/07
	Des Moines-West Des Moines MSA, IA	Y	32520 FQ	42910 MW	58530 TQ	USBLS	5/07
	Kansas	Y	34130 FQ	43890 MW	57140 TQ	USBLS	5/07
	Wichita MSA, KS	Y	35580 FQ	43920 MW	52110 TQ	USBLS	5/07
	Kentucky	Y	31837 FQ	41000 MW	51885 TQ	KYBLS	2008
	Louisville-Jefferson County MSA, KY-IN	Y	30860 FQ	38490 MW	48650 TQ	USBLS	5/07
	Louisiana	H	15.75 FQ	19.78 MW	24.62 TQ	LABLS	1/08-3/08
	Baton Rouge MSA, LA	Y	32800 FQ	38510 MW	45780 TQ	USBLS	5/07
	New Orleans-Metairie-Kenner MSA, LA	Y	38100 FQ	47820 MW	55540 TQ	USBLS	5/07
	Maine	Y	36980 FQ	43650 MW	49050 TQ	USBLS	5/07
	Portland-South Portland-Biddeford MSA, ME	Y	40650 FQ	45380 MW	49810 TQ	USBLS	5/07
	Maryland	Y		48625 MW		MDBLS	3/08
	Baltimore-Towson MSA, MD	Y	34460 FQ	45590 MW	57090 TQ	USBLS	5/07
	Bethesda-Gaithersburg-Frederick PMSA, MD	Y	38580 FQ	47410 MW	58690 TQ	USBLS	5/07
	Salisbury MSA, MD	Y	30650 FQ	35260 MW	44070 TQ	USBLS	5/07
	Massachusetts	Y	41020 FQ	53470 MW	66050 TQ	USBLS	5/07
	Boston-Cambridge-Quincy NECTA, MA	Y	44490 FQ	57800 MW	78220 TQ	USBLS	5/07
	Worcester MSA, MA-CT	Y	42880 FQ	53790 MW	61630 TQ	USBLS	5/07
	Michigan	Y	41830 FQ	58220 MW	72890 TQ	USBLS	5/07
	Ann Arbor MSA, MI	Y	61320 FQ	71440 MW	78150 TQ	USBLS	5/07
	Detroit-Warren-Livonia MSA, MI	Y	49510 FQ	68130 MW	75990 TQ	USBLS	5/07

Occupation/Type/Industry	Location	Per	Low	Mid	High	Source	Date
Electrician	Grand Rapids-Wyoming MSA, MI	Y	37370 FQ	46360 MW	56880 TQ	USBLS	5/07
	Warren-Troy-Farmington Hills PMSA, MI	Y	48350 FQ	68080 MW	76230 TQ	USBLS	5/07
	Minnesota	Y	46022 FQ	60250 MW	73254 TQ	MNBLS	10/08-12/08
	Duluth-Superior MSA, MN-WI	Y	55096 FQ	60165 MW	65487 TQ	MNBLS	10/08-12/08
	Minneapolis-Saint Paul MSA, MN-WI	Y	52651 FQ	68364 MW	77733 TQ	MNBLS	10/08-12/08
	Rochester MSA, MN	Y	42535 FQ	56484 MW	63095 TQ	MNBLS	10/08-12/08
	Mississippi	Y	29650 FQ	36160 MW	46330 TQ	USBLS	5/07
	Hattiesburg MSA, MS	Y	29550 FQ	34170 MW	39460 TQ	USBLS	5/07
	Jackson MSA, MS	Y	31600 FQ	39140 MW	52760 TQ	USBLS	5/07
	Missouri	Y	35370 FQ	49450 MW	66490 TQ	USBLS	5/07
	Kansas City MSA, MO-KS	Y	37890 FQ	56240 MW	69590 TQ	USBLS	5/07
	St. Louis MSA, MO-IL	Y	45520 FQ	62020 MW	72290 TQ	USBLS	5/07
	Montana	Y	38120 FQ	46610 MW	55420 TQ	USBLS	5/07
	Billings MSA, MT	Y	28130 FQ	40270 MW	54070 TQ	USBLS	5/07
	Nebraska	Y	30630 FQ	39900 MW	53540 TQ	USBLS	5/07
	Omaha-Council Bluffs MSA, NE-IA	Y	32150 FQ	42890 MW	56860 TQ	USBLS	5/07
	Nevada	H	20.52 FQ	26.77 MW	33.72 TQ	NVBLS	5/08
	Las Vegas-Paradise MSA, NV	H	20.40 FQ	27.12 MW	35.34 TQ	NVBLS	5/08
	New Hampshire	H	16.46 AE	21.73 MW	25.52 AEX	NHBLS	6/08
	Manchester MSA, NH	Y	36090 FQ	43680 MW	52110 TQ	USBLS	5/07
	Nashua NECTA, NH-MA	Y	40230 FQ	50670 MW	58050 TQ	USBLS	5/07
	New Jersey	Y	42340 FQ	57340 MW	86440 TQ	USBLS	5/07
	Camden PMSA, NJ	Y	45000 FQ	65390 MW	91530 TQ	USBLS	5/07
	Edison PMSA, NJ	Y	39180 FQ	53010 MW	78780 TQ	USBLS	5/07
	Newark-Union PMSA, NJ-PA	Y	47700 FQ	60680 MW	88530 TQ	USBLS	5/07
	New Mexico	Y	32840 FQ	40540 MW	49720 TQ	USBLS	5/07
	Albuquerque MSA, NM	Y	30480 FQ	39330 MW	51330 TQ	USBLS	5/07
	New York	Y	41160 FQ	58630 MW	84220 TQ	USBLS	5/07
	Albany-Schenectady-Troy MSA, NY	Y	32900 FQ	40920 MW	54440 TQ	USBLS	5/07
	Buffalo-Niagara Falls MSA, NY	Y	32540 FQ	42960 MW	63780 TQ	USBLS	5/07
	Kingston MSA, NY	Y	42470 FQ	49660 MW	59590 TQ	USBLS	5/07
	Nassau-Suffolk PMSA, NY	Y	45040 FQ	59520 MW	79870 TQ	USBLS	5/07
	New York-Northern New Jersey-Long Island MSA, NY-NJ-PA	Y	46640 FQ	64250 MW	88780 TQ	USBLS	5/07
	North Carolina	Y	29780 FQ	35060 MW	40380 TQ	USBLS	5/07
	Charlotte-Gastonia-Concord MSA, NC-SC	Y	31300 FQ	35780 MW	41340 TQ	USBLS	5/07
	Greensboro-High Point MSA, NC	Y	30270 FQ	35100 MW	40000 TQ	USBLS	5/07
	Raleigh-Cary MSA, NC	Y	30220 FQ	34920 MW	39200 TQ	USBLS	5/07
	North Dakota	Y	32490 FQ	41710 MW	51860 TQ	USBLS	5/07
	Fargo MSA, ND-MN	Y	34710 FQ	43090 MW	48800 TQ	USBLS	5/07
	Ohio	Y	34220 FQ	46180 MW	60150 TQ	USBLS	5/07
	Cincinnati-Middletown MSA, OH-KY-IN	Y	33360 FQ	44970 MW	55800 TQ	USBLS	5/07
	Cleveland-Elyria-Mentor MSA, OH	Y	38650 FQ	57620 MW	73030 TQ	USBLS	5/07
	Columbus MSA, OH	Y	33660 FQ	46380 MW	56930 TQ	USBLS	5/07
	Dayton MSA, OH	Y	36530 FQ	46160 MW	60770 TQ	USBLS	5/07
	Oklahoma	Y	30710 FQ	40260 MW	48380 TQ	USBLS	5/07
	Oklahoma City MSA, OK	Y	25570 FQ	36850 MW	46140 TQ	USBLS	5/07
	Tulsa MSA, OK	Y	33590 FQ	41690 MW	49690 TQ	USBLS	5/07
	Oregon	H	23.71 FQ	29.08 MW	33.97 TQ	ORBLS	5/08
	Portland-Vancouver-Beaverton MSA, OR-WA	Y	47430 FQ	60070 MW	71640 TQ	USBLS	5/07
	Pennsylvania	Y	37270 FQ	49060 MW	67520 TQ	USBLS	5/07
	Allentown-Bethlehem-Easton MSA, PA-NJ	Y	41600 FQ	65530 MW	80150 TQ	USBLS	5/07
	Philadelphia-Camden-Wilmington MSA, PA-NJ-DE-MD	Y	42830 FQ	59390 MW	88790 TQ	USBLS	5/07
	Pittsburgh MSA, PA	Y	38020 FQ	51840 MW	63520 TQ	USBLS	5/07
	Rhode Island	Y	41060 FQ	52240 MW	60590 TQ	USBLS	5/07
	Providence-Fall River-Warwick MSA, RI-MA	Y	39700 FQ	50880 MW	59830 TQ	USBLS	5/07

AE	Average entry wage	AW	Average wage paid	FQ	First quartile wage
AER	Average entry range	AWR	Average wage range	H	Hourly
AEX	Average experienced wage	AXR	Average experienced range	HI	Highest wage paid
ATC	Average total compensation	D	Daily	HR	High end range

LO	Lowest wage paid
LR	Low end range
M	Monthly
MCC	Median cash compensation

MTC	Median total compensation
MW	Median wage paid
MWR	Median wage range
S	See annotated source

TCC	Total cash compensation
TQ	Third quartile wage
W	Weekly
Y	Yearly

Occupation/Type/Industry	Location	Per	Low	Mid	High	Source	Date
Electrician	South Carolina	Y	29460 FQ	34900 MW	41290 TQ	USBLS	5/07
	Charleston-North Charleston MSA, SC	Y	29790 FQ	36450 MW	43400 TQ	USBLS	5/07
	Columbia MSA, SC	Y	29810 FQ	35650 MW	42080 TQ	USBLS	5/07
	Florence MSA, SC	Y	22670 FQ	31780 MW	39070 TQ	USBLS	5/07
	South Dakota	Y	34194 FQ	39669 MW	47282 TQ	SDBLS	7/08-9/08
	Sioux Falls MSA, SD	Y	36399 FQ	40696 MW	47730 TQ	SDBLS	7/08-9/08
	Tennessee	Y	30990 FQ	39060 MW	48920 TQ	USBLS	5/07
	Memphis MSA, TN-MS-AR	Y	31940 FQ	41000 MW	51300 TQ	USBLS	5/07
	Nashville-Davidson-Murfreesboro MSA, TN	Y	30350 FQ	36320 MW	42330 TQ	USBLS	5/07
	Texas	Y	30930 FQ	38180 MW	46230 TQ	USBLS	5/07
	Austin-Round Rock MSA, TX	Y	28860 FQ	35650 MW	42740 TQ	USBLS	5/07
	Dallas-Fort Worth-Arlington MSA, TX	Y	33220 FQ	38910 MW	46650 TQ	USBLS	5/07
	El Paso MSA, TX	Y	26310 FQ	33430 MW	40720 TQ	USBLS	5/07
	Houston-Sugar Land-Baytown MSA, TX	Y	33680 FQ	41130 MW	48260 TQ	USBLS	5/07
	San Antonio MSA, TX	Y	26810 FQ	34920 MW	43270 TQ	USBLS	5/07
	Utah	Y	33060 FQ	42010 MW	49800 TQ	USBLS	5/07
	Provo-Orem MSA, UT	Y	37460 FQ	48030 MW	59310 TQ	USBLS	5/07
	Salt Lake City MSA, UT	Y	34680 FQ	42730 MW	49540 TQ	USBLS	5/07
	Vermont	Y	31720 FQ	37620 MW	45700 TQ	USBLS	5/07
	Burlington-South Burlington MSA, VT	Y	33000 FQ	37730 MW	47650 TQ	USBLS	5/07
	Virginia	Y	33220 FQ	41870 MW	50780 TQ	USBLS	5/07
	Richmond MSA, VA	Y	38140 FQ	45450 MW	52740 TQ	USBLS	5/07
	Virginia Beach-Norfolk-Newport News MSA, VA-NC	Y	32680 FQ	40710 MW	47930 TQ	USBLS	5/07
	Washington	H	19.84 FQ	25.49 MW	31.35 TQ	WABLS	3/08
	Seattle-Tacoma-Bellevue MSA, WA	Y	42980 FQ	55950 MW	67450 TQ	USBLS	5/07
	West Virginia	Y	33591 FQ	46287 MW	59750 TQ	WVBLS	7/08-9/08
	Charleston MSA, WV	Y	43000 FQ	53820 MW	63520 TQ	USBLS	5/07
	Wisconsin	Y	39640 FQ	50010 MW	59750 TQ	USBLS	5/07
	Milwaukee-Waukesha-West Allis MSA, WI	Y	45160 FQ	55620 MW	62860 TQ	USBLS	5/07
	Wyoming	Y	38438 FQ	47811 MW	57533 TQ	WYBLS	9/08
	Cheyenne MSA, WY	Y	35797 FQ	44540 MW	52804 TQ	WYBLS	9/08
	Puerto Rico	Y	17220 FQ	20750 MW	27770 TQ	USBLS	5/07
	San Juan-Caguas-Guaynabo MSA, PR	Y	17460 FQ	21400 MW	28460 TQ	USBLS	5/07
	Virgin Islands	Y	34880 FQ	41660 MW	46920 TQ	USBLS	5/07
	Guam	Y	26340 FQ	29860 MW	35430 TQ	USBLS	5/07
Electro-Mechanical Technician	Alabama	Y	37530 FQ	55100 MW	74450 TQ	USBLS	5/07
	Arizona	Y	35190 FQ	39400 MW	46150 TQ	USBLS	5/07
	Phoenix-Mesa-Scottsdale MSA, AZ	Y	34840 FQ	39310 MW	46150 TQ	USBLS	5/07
	Tucson MSA, AZ	Y	35680 FQ	38860 MW	44770 TQ	USBLS	5/07
	California	H	20.48 FQ	25.78 MW	30.83 TQ	CABLS	1/08-3/08
	Los Angeles-Long Beach-Glendale PMSA, CA	H	17.86 FQ	24.08 MW	28.65 TQ	CABLS	1/08-3/08
	Oakland-Fremont-Hayward MSA, CA	H	20.86 FQ	24.85 MW	34.80 TQ	CABLS	1/08-3/08
	Sacramento-Arden Arcade-Roseville MSA, CA	H	15.04 FQ	20.75 MW	24.41 TQ	CABLS	1/08-3/08
	San Diego-Carlsbad-San Marcos MSA, CA	H	18.45 FQ	23.37 MW	29.18 TQ	CABLS	1/08-3/08
	San Francisco-San Mateo-Redwood PMSA, CA	H	18.76 FQ	24.55 MW	31.17 TQ	CABLS	1/08-3/08
	San Jose-Sunnyvale-Santa Clara MSA, CA	H	22.96 FQ	27.68 MW	32.34 TQ	CABLS	1/08-3/08
	Santa Ana-Anaheim-Irvine PMSA, CA	Y	39890 FQ	52020 MW	59940 TQ	USBLS	5/07
	Colorado	Y	41540 FQ	52600 MW	63360 TQ	USBLS	5/07
	Denver-Aurora MSA, CO	Y	38240 FQ	44000 MW	52770 TQ	USBLS	5/07
	Connecticut	H	16.88 AE	23.87 MW		CTBLS	1/08-3/08
	Bridgeport-Stamford-Norwalk MSA, CT	Y	38710 FQ	49320 MW	58550 TQ	USBLS	5/07
	Hartford-West Hartford-East Hartford MSA, CT	Y	43870 FQ	54060 MW	61340 TQ	USBLS	5/07

AE	Average entry wage	AW	Average wage paid	FQ	First quartile wage	LO	Lowest wage paid	MTC	Median total compensation	TCC	Total cash compensation
AER	Average entry range	AWR	Average wage range	H	Hourly	LR	Low end range	MW	Median wage paid	TQ	Third quartile wage
AEX	Average experienced wage	AXR	Average experienced range	HI	Highest wage paid	M	Monthly	MWR	Median wage range	W	Weekly
ATC	Average total compensation	D	Daily	HR	High end range	MCC	Median cash compensation	S	See annotated source	Y	Yearly

Occupation/Type/Industry	Location	Per	Low	Mid	High	Source	Date
Electro-Mechanical Technician	Delaware	Y	31980 FQ	35080 MW	43200 TQ	USBLS	5/07
	Wilmington PMSA, DE-MD-NJ	Y	31980 FQ	35080 MW	43200 TQ	USBLS	5/07
	Washington-Arlington-Alexandria MSA, DC-VA-MD-WV	Y	43000 FQ	48750 MW	56840 TQ	USBLS	5/07
	Florida	Y	31520 FQ	36390 MW	42560 TQ	USBLS	5/07
	Fort Lauderdale-Pompano Beach-Deerfield Beach PMSA, FL	Y	34100 FQ	38390 MW	43710 TQ	USBLS	5/07
	Jacksonville MSA, FL	Y	29400 FQ	32750 MW	37470 TQ	USBLS	5/07
	Miami-Fort Lauderdale-Miami Beach MSA, FL	Y	33760 FQ	37860 MW	44040 TQ	USBLS	5/07
	Orlando-Kissimmee MSA, FL	Y	33700 FQ	39200 MW	52640 TQ	USBLS	5/07
	Tampa-St. Petersburg-Clearwater MSA, FL	Y	29820 FQ	34590 MW	40220 TQ	USBLS	5/07
	Georgia	Y	48770 FQ	59640 MW	71130 TQ	USBLS	5/07
	Atlanta-Sandy Springs-Marietta MSA, GA	Y	44800 FQ	51680 MW	59950 TQ	USBLS	5/07
	Idaho	Y	24240 FQ	37330 MW	51070 TQ	USBLS	5/07
	Boise City-Nampa MSA, ID	Y	24050 FQ	38370 MW	51780 TQ	USBLS	5/07
	Illinois	Y	30160 FQ	42870 MW	53230 TQ	USBLS	5/07
	Chicago-Naperville-Joliet MSA, IL-IN-WI	Y	24790 FQ	41630 MW	51120 TQ	USBLS	5/07
	Indiana	Y	35660 FQ	40000 MW	49730 TQ	USBLS	5/07
	Indianapolis-Carmel MSA, IN	Y	36430 FQ	44390 MW	51990 TQ	USBLS	5/07
	Iowa	Y	40560 FQ	44670 MW	48770 TQ	USBLS	5/07
	Kansas	Y	45030 FQ	49240 MW	53310 TQ	USBLS	5/07
	Kentucky	Y	36847 FQ	46597 MW	53237 TQ	KYBLS	2008
	Louisville-Jefferson County MSA, KY-IN	Y	43240 FQ	48530 MW	53690 TQ	USBLS	5/07
	Louisiana	H	21.27 FQ	24.69 MW	27.49 TQ	LABLS	1/08-3/08
	New Orleans-Metairie-Kenner MSA, LA	Y	50310 FQ	54420 MW	58540 TQ	USBLS	5/07
	Maryland	Y		44950 MW		MDBLS	3/08
	Baltimore-Towson MSA, MD	Y	37180 FQ	43920 MW	50330 TQ	USBLS	5/07
	Bethesda-Gaithersburg-Frederick PMSA, MD	Y	33770 FQ	41560 MW	51620 TQ	USBLS	5/07
	Massachusetts	Y	36560 FQ	44210 MW	54400 TQ	USBLS	5/07
	Boston-Cambridge-Quincy NECTA, MA	Y	41310 FQ	50350 MW	59580 TQ	USBLS	5/07
	Michigan	Y	46690 FQ	65340 MW	74490 TQ	USBLS	5/07
	Detroit-Warren-Livonia MSA, MI	Y	51170 FQ	67590 MW	75580 TQ	USBLS	5/07
	Warren-Troy-Farmington Hills PMSA, MI	Y	46810 FQ	68470 MW	76480 TQ	USBLS	5/07
	Minnesota	Y	43376 FQ	49632 MW	58044 TQ	MNBLS	10/08-12/08
	Minneapolis-Saint Paul MSA, MN-WI	Y	43407 FQ	49957 MW	58892 TQ	MNBLS	10/08-12/08
	Mississippi	Y	33900 FQ	38320 MW	47620 TQ	USBLS	5/07
	Missouri	Y	40780 FQ	46240 MW	54040 TQ	USBLS	5/07
	St. Louis MSA, MO-IL	Y	44580 FQ	50430 MW	58090 TQ	USBLS	5/07
	Nevada	H	18.68 FQ	22.29 MW	27.85 TQ	NVBLS	5/08
	Las Vegas-Paradise MSA, NV	H	21.37 FQ	25.10 MW	30.00 TQ	NVBLS	5/08
	New Hampshire	H	18.51 AE	22.90 MW	27.53 AEX	NHBLS	6/08
	New Jersey	Y	39220 FQ	48420 MW	60720 TQ	USBLS	5/07
	Camden PMSA, NJ	Y	38500 FQ	54540 MW	61750 TQ	USBLS	5/07
	Edison PMSA, NJ	Y	41280 FQ	47170 MW	55030 TQ	USBLS	5/07
	Newark-Union PMSA, NJ-PA	Y	36710 FQ	48860 MW	65270 TQ	USBLS	5/07
	New Mexico	Y	42360 FQ	51540 MW	63830 TQ	USBLS	5/07
	Albuquerque MSA, NM	Y	41500 FQ	52040 MW	64340 TQ	USBLS	5/07
	New York	Y	37280 FQ	47730 MW	60570 TQ	USBLS	5/07
	Albany-Schenectady-Troy MSA, NY	Y	39450 FQ	48840 MW	61230 TQ	USBLS	5/07
	Buffalo-Niagara Falls MSA, NY	Y	24530 FQ	34740 MW	46530 TQ	USBLS	5/07
	Nassau-Suffolk PMSA, NY	Y	44760 FQ	56020 MW	68760 TQ	USBLS	5/07
	New York-Northern New Jersey-Long Island MSA, NY-NJ-PA	Y	41550 FQ	50660 MW	63380 TQ	USBLS	5/07
	North Carolina	Y	36040 FQ	41400 MW	48030 TQ	USBLS	5/07

AE	Average entry wage	AW	Average wage paid	FQ	First quartile wage	LO	Lowest wage paid	MTC	Median total compensation	TCC	Total cash compensation
AER	Average entry range	AWR	Average wage range	H	Hourly	LR	Low end range	MW	Median wage paid	TQ	Third quartile wage
AEX	Average experienced wage	AXR	Average experienced range	HI	Highest wage paid	M	Monthly	MWR	Median wage range	W	Weekly
ATC	Average total compensation	D	Daily	HR	High end range	MCC	Median cash compensation	S	See annotated source	Y	Yearly

Occupation/Type/Industry	Location	Per	Low	Mid	High	Source	Date
Electro-Mechanical Technician	Charlotte-Gastonia-Concord MSA, NC-SC	Y	39370 FQ	44440 MW	50300 TQ	USBLS	5/07
	North Dakota	Y	40480 FQ	44260 MW	48220 TQ	USBLS	5/07
	Ohio	Y	37040 FQ	47430 MW	60700 TQ	USBLS	5/07
	Cincinnati-Middletown MSA, OH-KY-IN	Y	33940 FQ	40640 MW	53960 TQ	USBLS	5/07
	Cleveland-Elyria-Mentor MSA, OH	Y	45740 FQ	56820 MW	65270 TQ	USBLS	5/07
	Columbus MSA, OH	Y	35130 FQ	46870 MW	61840 TQ	USBLS	5/07
	Dayton MSA, OH	Y	37610 FQ	44560 MW	54070 TQ	USBLS	5/07
	Oklahoma	Y	32570 FQ	36900 MW	45150 TQ	USBLS	5/07
	Oklahoma City MSA, OK	Y	33910 FQ	40910 MW	62470 TQ	USBLS	5/07
	Tulsa MSA, OK	Y	32040 FQ	35290 MW	38490 TQ	USBLS	5/07
	Oregon	H	19.43 FQ	24.02 MW	32.66 TQ	ORBLS	5/08
	Portland-Vancouver-Beaverton MSA, OR-WA	Y	39540 FQ	48790 MW	67420 TQ	USBLS	5/07
	Pennsylvania	Y	33760 FQ	41130 MW	48060 TQ	USBLS	5/07
	Philadelphia-Camden-Wilmington MSA, PA-NJ-DE-MD	Y	35990 FQ	44340 MW	56370 TQ	USBLS	5/07
	Pittsburgh MSA, PA	Y	34210 FQ	43520 MW	52750 TQ	USBLS	5/07
	Rhode Island	Y	32770 FQ	36680 MW	44620 TQ	USBLS	5/07
	Providence-Fall River-Warwick MSA, RI-MA	Y	32770 FQ	36680 MW	44620 TQ	USBLS	5/07
	South Carolina	Y	52180 FQ	57110 MW	62150 TQ	USBLS	5/07
	Tennessee	Y	32130 FQ	38420 MW	46660 TQ	USBLS	5/07
	Memphis MSA, TN-MS-AR	Y	34670 FQ	38710 MW	47880 TQ	USBLS	5/07
	Texas	Y	36580 FQ	46060 MW	57950 TQ	USBLS	5/07
	Austin-Round Rock MSA, TX	Y	38210 FQ	43970 MW	51130 TQ	USBLS	5/07
	Dallas-Fort Worth-Arlington MSA, TX	Y	36680 FQ	46880 MW	58370 TQ	USBLS	5/07
	Houston-Sugar Land-Baytown MSA, TX	Y	36640 FQ	53110 MW	63500 TQ	USBLS	5/07
	Utah	Y	41950 FQ	46430 MW	51320 TQ	USBLS	5/07
	Salt Lake City MSA, UT	Y	41900 FQ	46160 MW	50470 TQ	USBLS	5/07
	Virginia	Y	43090 FQ	48570 MW	56700 TQ	USBLS	5/07
	Virginia Beach-Norfolk-Newport News MSA, VA-NC	Y	42990 FQ	50860 MW	63230 TQ	USBLS	5/07
	Washington	H	19.00 FQ	23.32 MW	28.12 TQ	WABLS	3/08
	Seattle-Tacoma-Bellevue MSA, WA	Y	38290 FQ	43270 MW	50500 TQ	USBLS	5/07
	West Virginia	Y	28522 FQ	38869 MW	56361 TQ	WVBLS	7/08-9/08
	Wisconsin	Y	34250 FQ	41160 MW	52550 TQ	USBLS	5/07
	Milwaukee-Waukesha-West Allis MSA, WI	Y	34780 FQ	44600 MW	59810 TQ	USBLS	5/07
Electrologist	United States	Y		25000-50000 AW		AEA	2008
Electromechanical Equipment Assembler	Alabama	Y	19720 FQ	25800 MW	32200 TQ	USBLS	5/07
	Birmingham-Hoover MSA, AL	Y	20540 FQ	28080 MW	35330 TQ	USBLS	5/07
	Arizona	Y	22820 FQ	32320 MW	37030 TQ	USBLS	5/07
	Phoenix-Mesa-Scottsdale MSA, AZ	Y	22800 FQ	29800 MW	36530 TQ	USBLS	5/07
	Tucson MSA, AZ	Y	26700 FQ	34700 MW	37980 TQ	USBLS	5/07
	Arkansas	Y	25430 FQ	32440 MW	39490 TQ	USBLS	5/07
	California	H	10.83 FQ	13.80 MW	17.73 TQ	CABLS	1/08-3/08
	Los Angeles-Long Beach-Glendale PMSA, CA	H	8.97 FQ	11.09 MW	14.36 TQ	CABLS	1/08-3/08
	Oakland-Fremont-Hayward MSA, CA	H	13.26 FQ	15.69 MW	18.62 TQ	CABLS	1/08-3/08
	Riverside-San Bernardino-Ontario MSA, CA	H	11.13 FQ	13.23 MW	16.09 TQ	CABLS	1/08-3/08
	Sacramento-Arden Arcade-Roseville MSA, CA	H	11.61 FQ	14.37 MW	18.04 TQ	CABLS	1/08-3/08
	San Diego-Carlsbad-San Marcos MSA, CA	H	11.56 FQ	14.26 MW	18.31 TQ	CABLS	1/08-3/08
	San Francisco-San Mateo-Redwood PMSA, CA	H	12.92 FQ	16.17 MW	19.50 TQ	CABLS	1/08-3/08
	San Jose-Sunnyvale-Santa Clara MSA, CA	H	12.53 FQ	15.73 MW	19.66 TQ	CABLS	1/08-3/08

Occupation/Type/Industry	Location	Per	Low	Mid	High	Source	Date
Electromechanical Equipment Assembler	Santa Ana-Anaheim-Irvine PMSA, CA	Y	22030 FQ	28090 MW	35920 TQ	USBLS	5/07
	Stockton MSA, CA	H	9.46 FQ	11.39 MW	14.34 TQ	CABLS	1/08-3/08
	Colorado	Y	25490 FQ	31010 MW	38210 TQ	USBLS	5/07
	Colorado Springs MSA, CO	Y	22270 FQ	26870 MW	33680 TQ	USBLS	5/07
	Denver-Aurora MSA, CO	Y	28050 FQ	32960 MW	40050 TQ	USBLS	5/07
	Connecticut	H	11.52 AE	15.04 MW		CTBLS	1/08-3/08
	Bridgeport-Stamford-Norwalk MSA, CT	Y	30470 FQ	36700 MW	42580 TQ	USBLS	5/07
	Hartford-West Hartford-East Hartford MSA, CT	Y	23970 FQ	29610 MW	36870 TQ	USBLS	5/07
	Washington-Arlington-Alexandria MSA, DC-VA-MD-WV	Y	26470 FQ	33520 MW	40740 TQ	USBLS	5/07
	Florida	Y	20110 FQ	23690 MW	28820 TQ	USBLS	5/07
	Fort Lauderdale-Pompano Beach-Deerfield Beach PMSA, FL	Y	17870 FQ	22320 MW	28230 TQ	USBLS	5/07
	Jacksonville MSA, FL	Y	18280 FQ	21350 MW	24420 TQ	USBLS	5/07
	Miami-Fort Lauderdale-Miami Beach MSA, FL	Y	19560 FQ	24320 MW	32880 TQ	USBLS	5/07
	Orlando-Kissimmee MSA, FL	Y	17740 FQ	22410 MW	28590 TQ	USBLS	5/07
	Tampa-St. Petersburg-Clearwater MSA, FL	Y	21660 FQ	24950 MW	29530 TQ	USBLS	5/07
	West Palm Beach-Boca Raton-Boynton Beach PMSA, FL	Y	21500 FQ	25020 MW	33830 TQ	USBLS	5/07
	Georgia	Y	22800 FQ	27410 MW	36390 TQ	USBLS	5/07
	Atlanta-Sandy Springs-Marietta MSA, GA	Y	22270 FQ	25430 MW	33000 TQ	USBLS	5/07
	Idaho	Y	23880 FQ	29240 MW	35950 TQ	USBLS	5/07
	Boise City-Nampa MSA, ID	Y	23680 FQ	28880 MW	35210 TQ	USBLS	5/07
	Illinois	Y	23070 FQ	28660 MW	35960 TQ	USBLS	5/07
	Chicago-Naperville-Joliet MSA, IL-IN-WI	Y	23120 FQ	28870 MW	36300 TQ	USBLS	5/07
	Indiana	Y	21270 FQ	27370 MW	31580 TQ	USBLS	5/07
	Indianapolis-Carmel MSA, IN	Y	26090 FQ	29890 MW	34020 TQ	USBLS	5/07
	Iowa	Y	19750 FQ	29840 MW	37200 TQ	USBLS	5/07
	Des Moines-West Des Moines MSA, IA	Y	15150 FQ	18260 MW	26740 TQ	USBLS	5/07
	Kansas	Y	19340 FQ	24590 MW	28850 TQ	USBLS	5/07
	Wichita MSA, KS	Y	20560 FQ	25760 MW	30800 TQ	USBLS	5/07
	Kentucky	Y	26840 FQ	31907 MW	38804 TQ	KYBLS	2008
	Louisiana	H	13.29 FQ	15.21 MW	16.88 TQ	LABLS	1/08-3/08
	Maine	Y	21810 FQ	26430 MW	32700 TQ	USBLS	5/07
	Maryland	Y		33900 MW		MDBLS	3/08
	Baltimore-Towson MSA, MD	Y	22710 FQ	35080 MW	42880 TQ	USBLS	5/07
	Bethesda-Gaithersburg-Frederick PMSA, MD	Y	21490 FQ	29980 MW	35770 TQ	USBLS	5/07
	Massachusetts	Y	26330 FQ	30900 MW	36640 TQ	USBLS	5/07
	Boston-Cambridge-Quincy NECTA, MA	Y	27670 FQ	31780 MW	37650 TQ	USBLS	5/07
	Lynn-Peabody-Salem NECTA, MA	Y	29250 FQ	33130 MW	36560 TQ	USBLS	5/07
	Worcester MSA, MA-CT	Y	24310 FQ	30180 MW	35370 TQ	USBLS	5/07
	Michigan	Y	22730 FQ	31680 MW	56500 TQ	USBLS	5/07
	Grand Rapids-Wyoming MSA, MI	Y	20590 FQ	23290 MW	33830 TQ	USBLS	5/07
	Warren-Troy-Farmington Hills PMSA, MI	Y	21260 FQ	24570 MW	28250 TQ	USBLS	5/07
	Minnesota	Y	28477 FQ	32271 MW	38212 TQ	MNBLS	10/08-12/08
	Minneapolis-Saint Paul MSA, MN-WI	Y	28830 FQ	32582 MW	38471 TQ	MNBLS	10/08-12/08
	Mississippi	Y	14140 FQ	29970 MW	34490 TQ	USBLS	5/07
	Missouri	Y	28830 FQ	35000 MW	38780 TQ	USBLS	5/07
	Kansas City MSA, MO-KS	Y	19420 FQ	22340 MW	28270 TQ	USBLS	5/07
	St. Louis MSA, MO-IL	Y	14610 FQ	23490 MW	30700 TQ	USBLS	5/07
	Nebraska	Y	21130 FQ	24700 MW	30560 TQ	USBLS	5/07
	Omaha-Council Bluffs MSA, NE-IA	Y	25620 FQ	28950 MW	37630 TQ	USBLS	5/07
	Nevada	H	11.75 FQ	13.25 MW	14.95 TQ	NVBLS	5/08
	Las Vegas-Paradise MSA, NV	H	12.29 FQ	13.60 MW	15.27 TQ	NVBLS	5/08

AE	Average entry wage	AW	Average wage paid	FQ	First quartile wage	LO	Lowest wage paid	MTC	Median total compensation	TCC	Total cash compensation
AER	Average entry range	AWR	Average wage range	H	Hourly	LR	Low end range	MW	Median wage paid	TQ	Third quartile wage
AEX	Average experienced wage	AXR	Average experienced range	HI	Highest wage paid	M	Monthly	MWR	Median wage range	W	Weekly
ATC	Average total compensation	D	Daily	HR	High end range	MCC	Median cash compensation	S	See annotated source	Y	Yearly

Occupation/Type/Industry	Location	Per	Low	Mid	High	Source	Date
Electromechanical Equipment Assembler							
	New Hampshire	H	11.63 AE	15.18 MW	17.20 AEX	NHBLS	6/08
	Manchester MSA, NH	Y	23490 FQ	26910 MW	30630 TQ	USBLS	5/07
	Nashua NECTA, NH-MA	Y	29700 FQ	33680 MW	38780 TQ	USBLS	5/07
	New Jersey	Y	24370 FQ	30320 MW	37720 TQ	USBLS	5/07
	Camden PMSA, NJ	Y	23080 FQ	29140 MW	36510 TQ	USBLS	5/07
	Edison PMSA, NJ	Y	25130 FQ	31560 MW	39450 TQ	USBLS	5/07
	Newark-Union PMSA, NJ-PA	Y	25640 FQ	31980 MW	40120 TQ	USBLS	5/07
	New Mexico	Y	26790 FQ	29190 MW	31660 TQ	USBLS	5/07
	Albuquerque MSA, NM	Y	26670 FQ	28960 MW	31300 TQ	USBLS	5/07
	New York	Y	23270 FQ	34330 MW	41260 TQ	USBLS	5/07
	Albany-Schenectady-Troy MSA, NY	Y	24590 FQ	27990 MW	31770 TQ	USBLS	5/07
	Buffalo-Niagara Falls MSA, NY	Y	19950 FQ	23210 MW	41000 TQ	USBLS	5/07
	Nassau-Suffolk PMSA, NY	Y	23950 FQ	29340 MW	36460 TQ	USBLS	5/07
	New York-Northern New Jersey-Long Island MSA, NY-NJ-PA	Y	24270 FQ	30300 MW	37630 TQ	USBLS	5/07
	North Carolina	Y	21310 FQ	25990 MW	30980 TQ	USBLS	5/07
	Charlotte-Gastonia-Concord MSA, NC-SC	Y	25620 FQ	28330 MW	31030 TQ	USBLS	5/07
	Raleigh-Cary MSA, NC	Y	24210 FQ	29710 MW	36560 TQ	USBLS	5/07
	Ohio	Y	23470 FQ	29870 MW	36410 TQ	USBLS	5/07
	Cincinnati-Middletown MSA, OH-KY-IN	Y	22370 FQ	29450 MW	35690 TQ	USBLS	5/07
	Cleveland-Elyria-Mentor MSA, OH	Y	26750 FQ	33250 MW	38220 TQ	USBLS	5/07
	Columbus MSA, OH	Y	28170 FQ	34560 MW	38200 TQ	USBLS	5/07
	Dayton MSA, OH	Y	21280 FQ	23690 MW	31860 TQ	USBLS	5/07
	Oklahoma	Y	25360 FQ	30660 MW	36460 TQ	USBLS	5/07
	Tulsa MSA, OK	Y	26780 FQ	31620 MW	35990 TQ	USBLS	5/07
	Oregon	H	11.69 FQ	13.78 MW	15.80 TQ	ORBLS	5/08
	Portland-Vancouver-Beaverton MSA, OR-WA	Y	24560 FQ	28480 MW	32550 TQ	USBLS	5/07
	Pennsylvania	Y	25500 FQ	31390 MW	37520 TQ	USBLS	5/07
	Allentown-Bethlehem-Easton MSA, PA-NJ	Y	29820 FQ	36720 MW	45570 TQ	USBLS	5/07
	Philadelphia-Camden-Wilmington MSA, PA-NJ-DE-MD	Y	24330 FQ	30370 MW	37480 TQ	USBLS	5/07
	Pittsburgh MSA, PA	Y	26960 FQ	31510 MW	35810 TQ	USBLS	5/07
	York-Hanover MSA, PA	Y	23960 FQ	29960 MW	36710 TQ	USBLS	5/07
	Rhode Island	Y	22750 FQ	28680 MW	36050 TQ	USBLS	5/07
	Providence-Fall River-Warwick MSA, RI-MA	Y	23820 FQ	29640 MW	36300 TQ	USBLS	5/07
	South Carolina	Y	22940 FQ	33680 MW	38620 TQ	USBLS	5/07
	Columbia MSA, SC	Y	32860 FQ	35250 MW	37640 TQ	USBLS	5/07
	Tennessee	Y	21990 FQ	26240 MW	30530 TQ	USBLS	5/07
	Knoxville MSA, TN	Y	25240 FQ	28590 MW	34500 TQ	USBLS	5/07
	Memphis MSA, TN-MS-AR	Y	14220 FQ	18040 MW	25450 TQ	USBLS	5/07
	Texas	Y	20330 FQ	24460 MW	30650 TQ	USBLS	5/07
	Austin-Round Rock MSA, TX	Y	20980 FQ	24240 MW	29270 TQ	USBLS	5/07
	Dallas-Fort Worth-Arlington MSA, TX	Y	19960 FQ	24020 MW	31230 TQ	USBLS	5/07
	Houston-Sugar Land-Baytown MSA, TX	Y	20280 FQ	25750 MW	32400 TQ	USBLS	5/07
	San Antonio MSA, TX	Y	22540 FQ	27080 MW	30270 TQ	USBLS	5/07
	Utah	Y	21120 FQ	26410 MW	31130 TQ	USBLS	5/07
	Salt Lake City MSA, UT	Y	20060 FQ	27420 MW	35770 TQ	USBLS	5/07
	Vermont	Y	26910 FQ	30940 MW	36280 TQ	USBLS	5/07
	Burlington-South Burlington MSA, VT	Y	27440 FQ	30780 MW	35630 TQ	USBLS	5/07
	Virginia	Y	24250 FQ	30820 MW	35810 TQ	USBLS	5/07
	Virginia Beach-Norfolk-Newport News MSA, VA-NC	Y	22070 FQ	25240 MW	29660 TQ	USBLS	5/07
	Washington	H	12.23 FQ	15.92 MW	19.51 TQ	WABLS	3/08
	Seattle-Tacoma-Bellevue MSA, WA	Y	24270 FQ	32180 MW	40650 TQ	USBLS	5/07
	West Virginia	Y	21824 FQ	25949 MW	30641 TQ	WVBLS	7/08-9/08
	Wisconsin	Y	23320 FQ	28770 MW	37100 TQ	USBLS	5/07

AE	Average entry wage	AW	Average wage paid	FQ	First quartile wage	LO	Lowest wage paid	MTC	Median total compensation	TCC	Total cash compensation
AER	Average entry range	AWR	Average wage range	H	Hourly	LR	Low end range	MW	Median wage paid	TQ	Third quartile wage
AEX	Average experienced wage	AXR	Average experienced range	HI	Highest wage paid	M	Monthly	MWR	Median wage range	W	Weekly
ATC	Average total compensation	D	Daily	HR	High end range	MCC	Median cash compensation	S	See annotated source	Y	Yearly

508

Occupation/Type/Industry	Location	Per	Low	Mid	High	Source	Date
Electromechanical Equipment Assembler	Milwaukee-Waukesha-West Allis MSA, WI	Y	24080 FQ	29480 MW	36510 TQ	USBLS	5/07
	Puerto Rico	Y	14030 FQ	17870 MW	28620 TQ	USBLS	5/07
	San Juan-Caguas-Guaynabo MSA, PR	Y	12890 FQ	14430 MW	16870 TQ	USBLS	5/07
Electroneurodiagnostic Technologist	United States	Y		47674 AW		OOSE02	2006
Electronic Equipment Installer and Repairer							
Motor Vehicles	Alabama	Y	20170 FQ	25260 MW	34100 TQ	USBLS	5/07
Motor Vehicles	Alaska	Y	24740 FQ	28560 MW	34480 TQ	USBLS	5/07
Motor Vehicles	Anchorage MSA, AK	Y	24400 FQ	27690 MW	32280 TQ	USBLS	5/07
Motor Vehicles	Arizona	Y	27200 FQ	32020 MW	39970 TQ	USBLS	5/07
Motor Vehicles	Phoenix-Mesa-Scottsdale MSA, AZ	Y	27500 FQ	33870 MW	41720 TQ	USBLS	5/07
Motor Vehicles	Arkansas	Y	20400 FQ	23380 MW	29570 TQ	USBLS	5/07
Motor Vehicles	Little Rock-North Little Rock MSA, AR	Y	21440 FQ	23440 MW	25920 TQ	USBLS	5/07
Motor Vehicles	California	H	11.58 FQ	13.98 MW	17.85 TQ	CABLS	1/08-3/08
Motor Vehicles	Fresno MSA, CA	H	10.07 FQ	10.74 MW	11.42 TQ	CABLS	1/08-3/08
Motor Vehicles	Los Angeles-Long Beach-Glendale PMSA, CA	H	11.89 FQ	13.84 MW	15.62 TQ	CABLS	1/08-3/08
Motor Vehicles	Oakland-Fremont-Hayward MSA, CA	H	12.22 FQ	14.51 MW	17.72 TQ	CABLS	1/08-3/08
Motor Vehicles	Riverside-San Bernardino-Ontario MSA, CA	H	12.48 FQ	15.05 MW	19.43 TQ	CABLS	1/08-3/08
Motor Vehicles	Sacramento-Arden Arcade-Roseville MSA, CA	H	11.36 FQ	13.24 MW	17.27 TQ	CABLS	1/08-3/08
Motor Vehicles	San Diego-Carlsbad-San Marcos MSA, CA	H	13.62 FQ	17.39 MW	24.37 TQ	CABLS	1/08-3/08
Motor Vehicles	San Francisco-San Mateo-Redwood PMSA, CA	H	12.98 FQ	15.61 MW	17.79 TQ	CABLS	1/08-3/08
Motor Vehicles	San Jose-Sunnyvale-Santa Clara MSA, CA	H	13.72 FQ	23.79 MW	34.06 TQ	CABLS	1/08-3/08
Motor Vehicles	Santa Ana-Anaheim-Irvine PMSA, CA	Y	22370 FQ	25770 MW	31260 TQ	USBLS	5/07
Motor Vehicles	Colorado	Y	23190 FQ	29310 MW	35070 TQ	USBLS	5/07
Motor Vehicles	Denver-Aurora MSA, CO	Y	24900 FQ	30590 MW	35840 TQ	USBLS	5/07
Motor Vehicles	Connecticut	H	11.23 AE	15.19 MW		CTBLS	1/08-3/08
Motor Vehicles	Hartford-West Hartford-East Hartford MSA, CT	Y	22330 FQ	27630 MW	33460 TQ	USBLS	5/07
Motor Vehicles	Delaware	Y	24010 FQ	27690 MW	32900 TQ	USBLS	5/07
Motor Vehicles	Wilmington PMSA, DE-MD-NJ	Y	23820 FQ	27500 MW	31690 TQ	USBLS	5/07
Motor Vehicles	Washington-Arlington-Alexandria MSA, DC-VA-MD-WV	Y	24630 FQ	30950 MW	38330 TQ	USBLS	5/07
Motor Vehicles	Florida	Y	20350 FQ	25300 MW	32520 TQ	USBLS	5/07
Motor Vehicles	Fort Lauderdale-Pompano Beach-Deerfield Beach PMSA, FL	Y	28270 FQ	42940 MW	47670 TQ	USBLS	5/07
Motor Vehicles	Jacksonville MSA, FL	Y	16150 FQ	19700 MW	28950 TQ	USBLS	5/07
Motor Vehicles	Miami-Fort Lauderdale-Miami Beach MSA, FL	Y	24030 FQ	32080 MW	42540 TQ	USBLS	5/07
Motor Vehicles	Orlando-Kissimmee MSA, FL	Y	22850 FQ	25290 MW	31360 TQ	USBLS	5/07
Motor Vehicles	Tampa-St. Petersburg-Clearwater MSA, FL	Y	15080 FQ	16870 MW	27710 TQ	USBLS	5/07
Motor Vehicles	West Palm Beach-Boca Raton-Boynton Beach PMSA, FL	Y	26660 FQ	32960 MW	38510 TQ	USBLS	5/07
Motor Vehicles	Georgia	Y	22890 FQ	28390 MW	33750 TQ	USBLS	5/07
Motor Vehicles	Atlanta-Sandy Springs-Marietta MSA, GA	Y	25830 FQ	30000 MW	35130 TQ	USBLS	5/07
Motor Vehicles	Hawaii	Y	26110 FQ	28600 MW	31310 TQ	USBLS	5/07
Motor Vehicles	Honolulu MSA, HI	Y	26170 FQ	28520 MW	31050 TQ	USBLS	5/07
Motor Vehicles	Idaho	Y	21710 FQ	25660 MW	30980 TQ	USBLS	5/07
Motor Vehicles	Illinois	Y	23020 FQ	28750 MW	35920 TQ	USBLS	5/07
Motor Vehicles	Indiana	Y	24670 FQ	29010 MW	35210 TQ	USBLS	5/07
Motor Vehicles	Gary PMSA, IN	Y	26120 FQ	30590 MW	36460 TQ	USBLS	5/07

AE	Average entry wage	AW	Average wage paid	FQ	First quartile wage	LO	Lowest wage paid	MTC	Median total compensation	TCC	Total cash compensation
AER	Average entry range	AWR	Average wage range	H	Hourly	LR	Low end range	MW	Median wage paid	TQ	Third quartile wage
AEX	Average experienced wage	AXR	Average experienced range	HI	Highest wage paid	M	Monthly	MWR	Median wage range	W	Weekly
ATC	Average total compensation	D	Daily	HR	High end range	MCC	Median cash compensation	S	See annotated source	Y	Yearly

Electronic Equipment Installer and Repairer

Occupation/Type/Industry	Location	Per	Low	Mid	High	Source	Date
Motor Vehicles	Indianapolis-Carmel MSA, IN	Y	23600 FQ	26800 MW	29690 TQ	USBLS	5/07
Motor Vehicles	Iowa	Y	20830 FQ	23680 MW	29480 TQ	USBLS	5/07
Motor Vehicles	Kansas	Y	21830 FQ	25570 MW	31580 TQ	USBLS	5/07
Motor Vehicles	Wichita MSA, KS	Y	21040 FQ	23360 MW	26880 TQ	USBLS	5/07
Motor Vehicles	Kentucky	Y	20538 FQ	24991 MW	33031 TQ	KYBLS	2008
Motor Vehicles	Louisville-Jefferson County MSA, KY-IN	Y	19590 FQ	26390 MW	32540 TQ	USBLS	5/07
Motor Vehicles	Louisiana	H	16.77 FQ	20.75 MW	23.24 TQ	LABLS	1/08-3/08
Motor Vehicles	Maine	Y	20880 FQ	25820 MW	28790 TQ	USBLS	5/07
Motor Vehicles	Maryland	Y		33425 MW		MDBLS	3/08
Motor Vehicles	Baltimore-Towson MSA, MD	Y	22830 FQ	28880 MW	46030 TQ	USBLS	5/07
Motor Vehicles	Bethesda-Gaithersburg-Frederick PMSA, MD	Y	28600 FQ	37800 MW	46400 TQ	USBLS	5/07
Motor Vehicles	Massachusetts	Y	25320 FQ	29640 MW	34300 TQ	USBLS	5/07
Motor Vehicles	Boston-Cambridge-Quincy NECTA, MA	Y	26100 FQ	30560 MW	34670 TQ	USBLS	5/07
Motor Vehicles	Michigan	Y	24800 FQ	32480 MW	36480 TQ	USBLS	5/07
Motor Vehicles	Detroit-Warren-Livonia MSA, MI	Y	22420 FQ	30520 MW	37840 TQ	USBLS	5/07
Motor Vehicles	Warren-Troy-Farmington Hills PMSA, MI	Y	21390 FQ	28820 MW	36450 TQ	USBLS	5/07
Motor Vehicles	Minnesota	Y	25038 FQ	31059 MW	37688 TQ	MNBLS	10/08-12/08
Motor Vehicles	Minneapolis-Saint Paul MSA, MN-WI	Y	25866 FQ	32370 MW	38664 TQ	MNBLS	10/08-12/08
Motor Vehicles	Mississippi	Y	15950 FQ	18810 MW	23490 TQ	USBLS	5/07
Motor Vehicles	Missouri	Y	22390 FQ	28110 MW	35230 TQ	USBLS	5/07
Motor Vehicles	Kansas City MSA, MO-KS	Y	25970 FQ	36910 MW	48290 TQ	USBLS	5/07
Motor Vehicles	St. Louis MSA, MO-IL	Y	22980 FQ	27080 MW	32390 TQ	USBLS	5/07
Motor Vehicles	Montana	Y	21190 FQ	24200 MW	34850 TQ	USBLS	5/07
Motor Vehicles	Nebraska	Y	21860 FQ	25150 MW	30000 TQ	USBLS	5/07
Motor Vehicles	Omaha-Council Bluffs MSA, NE-IA	Y	21470 FQ	25490 MW	29120 TQ	USBLS	5/07
Motor Vehicles	Nevada	H	11.80 FQ	13.88 MW	15.48 TQ	NVBLS	5/08
Motor Vehicles	Las Vegas-Paradise MSA, NV	H	12.48 FQ	13.95 MW	15.38 TQ	NVBLS	5/08
Motor Vehicles	New Hampshire	H	11.40 AE	13.91 MW	16.71 AEX	NHBLS	6/08
Motor Vehicles	New Jersey	Y	22910 FQ	30420 MW	37870 TQ	USBLS	5/07
Motor Vehicles	Camden PMSA, NJ	Y	21660 FQ	24540 MW	32740 TQ	USBLS	5/07
Motor Vehicles	Edison PMSA, NJ	Y	22910 FQ	29520 MW	36270 TQ	USBLS	5/07
Motor Vehicles	Newark-Union PMSA, NJ-PA	Y	28490 FQ	38310 MW	45780 TQ	USBLS	5/07
Motor Vehicles	Trenton-Ewing MSA, NJ	Y	24750 FQ	29750 MW	35950 TQ	USBLS	5/07
Motor Vehicles	New Mexico	Y	23580 FQ	31920 MW	52770 TQ	USBLS	5/07
Motor Vehicles	Albuquerque MSA, NM	Y	27910 FQ	36700 MW	72390 TQ	USBLS	5/07
Motor Vehicles	New York	Y	24720 FQ	30160 MW	49420 TQ	USBLS	5/07
Motor Vehicles	Buffalo-Niagara Falls MSA, NY	Y	23000 FQ	25720 MW	30580 TQ	USBLS	5/07
Motor Vehicles	Nassau-Suffolk PMSA, NY	Y	24030 FQ	28740 MW	40210 TQ	USBLS	5/07
Motor Vehicles	New York-Northern New Jersey-Long Island MSA, NY-NJ-PA	Y	24170 FQ	31570 MW	41050 TQ	USBLS	5/07
Motor Vehicles	North Carolina	Y	23290 FQ	28220 MW	34120 TQ	USBLS	5/07
Motor Vehicles	Charlotte-Gastonia-Concord MSA, NC-SC	Y	22820 FQ	27390 MW	32020 TQ	USBLS	5/07
Motor Vehicles	Raleigh-Cary MSA, NC	Y	23510 FQ	26870 MW	30360 TQ	USBLS	5/07
Motor Vehicles	North Dakota	Y	20230 FQ	22640 MW	26750 TQ	USBLS	5/07
Motor Vehicles	Bismarck MSA, ND	Y	17710 FQ	23050 MW	27280 TQ	USBLS	5/07
Motor Vehicles	Fargo MSA, ND-MN	Y	20700 FQ	22490 MW	24580 TQ	USBLS	5/07
Motor Vehicles	Ohio	Y	23540 FQ	30010 MW	39530 TQ	USBLS	5/07
Motor Vehicles	Cincinnati-Middletown MSA, OH-KY-IN	Y	21560 FQ	25120 MW	36580 TQ	USBLS	5/07
Motor Vehicles	Cleveland-Elyria-Mentor MSA, OH	Y	23330 FQ	30700 MW	38200 TQ	USBLS	5/07
Motor Vehicles	Columbus MSA, OH	Y	24540 FQ	30130 MW	37170 TQ	USBLS	5/07
Motor Vehicles	Dayton MSA, OH	Y	22590 FQ	26440 MW	30500 TQ	USBLS	5/07
Motor Vehicles	Oklahoma	Y	24710 FQ	27820 MW	30900 TQ	USBLS	5/07
Motor Vehicles	Oklahoma City MSA, OK	Y	25360 FQ	27740 MW	30140 TQ	USBLS	5/07
Motor Vehicles	Tulsa MSA, OK	Y	24560 FQ	29550 MW	34310 TQ	USBLS	5/07
Motor Vehicles	Oregon	H	11.10 FQ	12.63 MW	17.45 TQ	ORBLS	5/08
Motor Vehicles	Portland-Vancouver-Beaverton MSA, OR-WA	Y	22830 FQ	25570 MW	36910 TQ	USBLS	5/07
Motor Vehicles	Pennsylvania	Y	27480 FQ	36520 MW	46300 TQ	USBLS	5/07

Occupation/Type/Industry	Location	Per	Low	Mid	High	Source	Date
Electronic Equipment Installer and Repairer							
Motor Vehicles	Philadelphia-Camden-Wilmington MSA, PA-NJ-DE-MD	Y	24580 FQ	35390 MW	48900 TQ	USBLS	5/07
Motor Vehicles	Pittsburgh MSA, PA	Y	28610 FQ	35720 MW	42050 TQ	USBLS	5/07
Motor Vehicles	South Carolina	Y	18920 FQ	24560 MW	30740 TQ	USBLS	5/07
Motor Vehicles	Charleston-North Charleston MSA, SC	Y	19380 FQ	25840 MW	29790 TQ	USBLS	5/07
Motor Vehicles	South Dakota	Y	22124 FQ	24090 MW	26310 TQ	SDBLS	7/08-9/08
Motor Vehicles	Rapid City MSA, SD	Y	22478 FQ	24354 MW	26133 TQ	SDBLS	7/08-9/08
Motor Vehicles	Tennessee	Y	21470 FQ	26300 MW	33920 TQ	USBLS	5/07
Motor Vehicles	Memphis MSA, TN-MS-AR	Y	17170 FQ	21880 MW	29920 TQ	USBLS	5/07
Motor Vehicles	Nashville-Davidson-Murfreesboro MSA, TN	Y	23930 FQ	27510 MW	32820 TQ	USBLS	5/07
Motor Vehicles	Texas	Y	20400 FQ	24740 MW	31910 TQ	USBLS	5/07
Motor Vehicles	Austin-Round Rock MSA, TX	Y	20640 FQ	25090 MW	35520 TQ	USBLS	5/07
Motor Vehicles	Corpus Christi MSA, TX	Y	24100 FQ	26150 MW	28320 TQ	USBLS	5/07
Motor Vehicles	Dallas-Fort Worth-Arlington MSA, TX	Y	21720 FQ	25770 MW	33710 TQ	USBLS	5/07
Motor Vehicles	El Paso MSA, TX	Y	12960 FQ	15210 MW	32440 TQ	USBLS	5/07
Motor Vehicles	Houston-Sugar Land-Baytown MSA, TX	Y	22600 FQ	25190 MW	31120 TQ	USBLS	5/07
Motor Vehicles	San Antonio MSA, TX	Y	19630 FQ	24390 MW	33290 TQ	USBLS	5/07
Motor Vehicles	Utah	Y	21850 FQ	26240 MW	32180 TQ	USBLS	5/07
Motor Vehicles	Salt Lake City MSA, UT	Y	21840 FQ	24890 MW	30230 TQ	USBLS	5/07
Motor Vehicles	Virginia	Y	18530 FQ	26570 MW	33350 TQ	USBLS	5/07
Motor Vehicles	Richmond MSA, VA	Y	13260 FQ	15720 MW	26440 TQ	USBLS	5/07
Motor Vehicles	Virginia Beach-Norfolk-Newport News MSA, VA-NC	Y	16940 FQ	23850 MW	38130 TQ	USBLS	5/07
Motor Vehicles	Washington	H	13.51 FQ	18.25 MW	26.15 TQ	WABLS	3/08
Motor Vehicles	Seattle-Tacoma-Bellevue MSA, WA	Y	29880 FQ	40770 MW	57140 TQ	USBLS	5/07
Motor Vehicles	West Virginia	Y	13877 FQ	14936 MW	20458 TQ	WVBLS	7/08-9/08
Motor Vehicles	Wisconsin	Y	23520 FQ	27780 MW	34340 TQ	USBLS	5/07
Motor Vehicles	Milwaukee-Waukesha-West Allis MSA, WI	Y	23580 FQ	28110 MW	36220 TQ	USBLS	5/07
Motor Vehicles	Wyoming	Y	26140 FQ	34823 MW	38371 TQ	WYBLS	9/08
Motor Vehicles	Puerto Rico	Y	15400 FQ	16820 MW	18200 TQ	USBLS	5/07
Motor Vehicles	San Juan-Caguas-Guaynabo MSA, PR	Y	15630 FQ	16950 MW	18270 TQ	USBLS	5/07
Electronic Home Entertainment Equipment Installer and Repairer							
	Alabama	Y	21640 FQ	30450 MW	37190 TQ	USBLS	5/07
	Birmingham-Hoover MSA, AL	Y	20810 FQ	25510 MW	35730 TQ	USBLS	5/07
	Mobile MSA, AL	Y	22230 FQ	26890 MW	41540 TQ	USBLS	5/07
	Alaska	Y	27440 FQ	33220 MW	41600 TQ	USBLS	5/07
	Anchorage MSA, AK	Y	27430 FQ	31450 MW	42210 TQ	USBLS	5/07
	Arizona	Y	21940 FQ	30760 MW	41900 TQ	USBLS	5/07
	Phoenix-Mesa-Scottsdale MSA, AZ	Y	23330 FQ	32830 MW	45080 TQ	USBLS	5/07
	Tucson MSA, AZ	Y	16880 FQ	24580 MW	31340 TQ	USBLS	5/07
	Arkansas	Y	25720 FQ	29950 MW	35170 TQ	USBLS	5/07
	Little Rock-North Little Rock MSA, AR	Y	28830 FQ	32880 MW	37790 TQ	USBLS	5/07
	California	H	13.41 FQ	16.39 MW	21.14 TQ	CABLS	1/08-3/08
	Los Angeles-Long Beach-Glendale PMSA, CA	H	13.69 FQ	17.75 MW	24.12 TQ	CABLS	1/08-3/08
	Oakland-Fremont-Hayward MSA, CA	H	12.91 FQ	16.48 MW	20.06 TQ	CABLS	1/08-3/08
	Riverside-San Bernardino-Ontario MSA, CA	H	13.36 FQ	15.48 MW	18.51 TQ	CABLS	1/08-3/08
	Sacramento-Arden Arcade-Roseville MSA, CA	H	14.12 FQ	17.70 MW	21.33 TQ	CABLS	1/08-3/08
	San Diego-Carlsbad-San Marcos MSA, CA	H	13.98 FQ	17.24 MW	24.35 TQ	CABLS	1/08-3/08
	San Francisco-San Mateo-Redwood PMSA, CA	H	14.24 FQ	18.33 MW	25.39 TQ	CABLS	1/08-3/08
	San Jose-Sunnyvale-Santa Clara MSA, CA	H	12.62 FQ	16.16 MW	20.43 TQ	CABLS	1/08-3/08

AE	Average entry wage	AW	Average wage paid	FQ	First quartile wage	LO	Lowest wage paid	MTC	Median total compensation	TCC	Total cash compensation
AER	Average entry range	AWR	Average wage range	H	Hourly	LR	Low end range	MW	Median wage paid	TQ	Third quartile wage
AEX	Average experienced wage	AXR	Average experienced range	HI	Highest wage paid	M	Monthly	MWR	Median wage range	W	Weekly
ATC	Average total compensation	D	Daily	HR	High end range	MCC	Median cash compensation	S	See annotated source	Y	Yearly

Occupation/Type/Industry	Location	Per	Low	Mid	High	Source	Date
Electronic Home Entertainment Equipment Installer and Repairer							
	Santa Ana-Anaheim-Irvine PMSA, CA	Y	27600 FQ	32250 MW	37810 TQ	USBLS	5/07
	Colorado	Y	30730 FQ	38940 MW	48660 TQ	USBLS	5/07
	Denver-Aurora MSA, CO	Y	33320 FQ	38900 MW	46010 TQ	USBLS	5/07
	Connecticut	H	12.22 AE	17.30 MW		CTBLS	1/08-3/08
	Bridgeport-Stamford-Norwalk MSA, CT	Y	28020 FQ	34510 MW	40960 TQ	USBLS	5/07
	Delaware.	Y	25210 FQ	38600 MW	43530 TQ	USBLS	5/07
	Wilmington PMSA, DE-MD-NJ	Y	25210 FQ	38520 MW	43420 TQ	USBLS	5/07
	District of Columbia	Y	33770 FQ	37500 MW	46550 TQ	USBLS	5/07
	Washington-Arlington-Alexandria MSA, DC-VA-MD-WV	Y	30980 FQ	39870 MW	45870 TQ	USBLS	5/07
	Florida	Y	24250 FQ	29710 MW	37390 TQ	USBLS	5/07
	Fort Lauderdale-Pompano Beach-Deerfield Beach PMSA, FL	Y	22420 FQ	34140 MW	39290 TQ	USBLS	5/07
	Jacksonville MSA, FL	Y	28220 FQ	31540 MW	36360 TQ	USBLS	5/07
	Miami-Fort Lauderdale-Miami Beach MSA, FL	Y	25170 FQ	33420 MW	40850 TQ	USBLS	5/07
	Orlando-Kissimmee MSA, FL	Y	27920 FQ	34860 MW	46110 TQ	USBLS	5/07
	Pensacola-Ferry Pass-Brent MSA, FL	Y	25440 FQ	29670 MW	35540 TQ	USBLS	5/07
	Tampa-St. Petersburg-Clearwater MSA, FL	Y	20950 FQ	26200 MW	31660 TQ	USBLS	5/07
	West Palm Beach-Boca Raton-Boynton Beach PMSA, FL	Y	29090 FQ	34290 MW	41200 TQ	USBLS	5/07
	Georgia	Y	33150 FQ	42290 MW	47250 TQ	USBLS	5/07
	Atlanta-Sandy Springs-Marietta MSA, GA	Y	37990 FQ	43630 MW	47840 TQ	USBLS	5/07
	Hawaii	Y	27140 FQ	46110 MW	57600 TQ	USBLS	5/07
	Honolulu MSA, HI	Y	37840 FQ	47330 MW	58110 TQ	USBLS	5/07
	Idaho	Y	18200 FQ	24050 MW	28120 TQ	USBLS	5/07
	Illinois	Y	24510 FQ	29780 MW	42360 TQ	USBLS	5/07
	Chicago-Naperville-Joliet MSA, IL-IN-WI	Y	27600 FQ	31550 MW	45150 TQ	USBLS	5/07
	Indiana	Y	27620 FQ	33330 MW	37970 TQ	USBLS	5/07
	Gary PMSA, IN	Y	29940 FQ	32880 MW	35580 TQ	USBLS	5/07
	Indianapolis-Carmel MSA, IN	Y	29630 FQ	35180 MW	38970 TQ	USBLS	5/07
	Iowa	Y	24390 FQ	29880 MW	35530 TQ	USBLS	5/07
	Des Moines-West Des Moines MSA, IA	Y	23280 FQ	28620 MW	35250 TQ	USBLS	5/07
	Kansas	Y	25630 FQ	29730 MW	37050 TQ	USBLS	5/07
	Wichita MSA, KS	Y	29250 FQ	34500 MW	40970 TQ	USBLS	5/07
	Kentucky	Y	23652 FQ	29543 MW	37262 TQ	KYBLS	2008
	Louisville-Jefferson County MSA, KY-IN	Y	23690 FQ	30010 MW	37540 TQ	USBLS	5/07
	Louisiana	H	13.80 FQ	16.71 MW	18.76 TQ	LABLS	1/08-3/08
	New Orleans-Metairie-Kenner MSA, LA	Y	32810 FQ	36350 MW	40030 TQ	USBLS	5/07
	Maine	Y	22140 FQ	24850 MW	34450 TQ	USBLS	5/07
	Maryland	Y		37675 MW		MDBLS	3/08
	Baltimore-Towson MSA, MD	Y	34420 FQ	41650 MW	47900 TQ	USBLS	5/07
	Bethesda-Gaithersburg-Frederick PMSA, MD	Y	25700 FQ	31100 MW	37330 TQ	USBLS	5/07
	Massachusetts	Y	28650 FQ	35460 MW	44030 TQ	USBLS	5/07
	Boston-Cambridge-Quincy NECTA, MA	Y	33140 FQ	40000 MW	47030 TQ	USBLS	5/07
	Michigan	Y	25930 FQ	34940 MW	42810 TQ	USBLS	5/07
	Detroit-Warren-Livonia MSA, MI	Y	32220 FQ	39710 MW	45340 TQ	USBLS	5/07
	Grand Rapids-Wyoming MSA, MI	Y	20770 FQ	22620 MW	39540 TQ	USBLS	5/07
	Warren-Troy-Farmington Hills PMSA, MI	Y	32050 FQ	39750 MW	45370 TQ	USBLS	5/07
	Minnesota	Y	26706 FQ	33608 MW	44559 TQ	MNBLS	10/08-12/08
	Duluth-Superior MSA, MN-WI	Y	32695 FQ	37248 MW	41244 TQ	MNBLS	10/08-12/08

AE	Average entry wage	AW	Average wage paid
AER	Average entry range	AWR	Average wage range
AEX	Average experienced wage	AXR	Average experienced range
ATC	Average total compensation	D	Daily

FQ	First quartile wage	LO	Lowest wage paid	MTC	Median total compensation
H	Hourly	LR	Low end range	MW	Median wage paid
HI	Highest wage paid	M	Monthly	MWR	Median wage range
HR	High end range	MCC	Median cash compensation	S	See annotated source

TCC	Total cash compensation		
TQ	Third quartile wage		
W	Weekly		
Y	Yearly		

Electronic Home Entertainment Equipment Installer and Repairer

Occupation/Type/Industry	Location	Per	Low	Mid	High	Source	Date
	Minneapolis-Saint Paul MSA, MN-WI	Y	27807 FQ	35926 MW	46730 TQ	MNBLS	10/08-12/08
	Mississippi	Y	24300 FQ	28450 MW	31870 TQ	USBLS	5/07
	Missouri	Y	26090 FQ	31950 MW	42460 TQ	USBLS	5/07
	Jefferson City MSA, MO	Y	27530 FQ	32310 MW	46020 TQ	USBLS	5/07
	Kansas City MSA, MO-KS	Y	24080 FQ	31110 MW	40780 TQ	USBLS	5/07
	St. Louis MSA, MO-IL	Y	25850 FQ	31520 MW	40280 TQ	USBLS	5/07
	Montana	Y	31250 FQ	38070 MW	47840 TQ	USBLS	5/07
	Nebraska	Y	26060 FQ	29390 MW	36140 TQ	USBLS	5/07
	Lincoln MSA, NE	Y	25020 FQ	29130 MW	39580 TQ	USBLS	5/07
	Omaha-Council Bluffs MSA, NE-IA	Y	26380 FQ	29520 MW	35740 TQ	USBLS	5/07
	Nevada	H	11.91 FQ	14.64 MW	17.57 TQ	NVBLS	5/08
	Las Vegas-Paradise MSA, NV	H	12.17 FQ	15.50 MW	18.32 TQ	NVBLS	5/08
	New Hampshire	H	11.96 AE	16.04 MW	20.05 AEX	NHBLS	6/08
	Manchester MSA, NH	Y	36940 FQ	51700 MW	56310 TQ	USBLS	5/07
	Nashua NECTA, NH-MA	Y	22030 FQ	28620 MW	42830 TQ	USBLS	5/07
	New Jersey	Y	28380 FQ	33660 MW	41370 TQ	USBLS	5/07
	Camden PMSA, NJ	Y	27140 FQ	30080 MW	35810 TQ	USBLS	5/07
	Edison PMSA, NJ	Y	34170 FQ	38810 MW	45540 TQ	USBLS	5/07
	Newark-Union PMSA, NJ-PA	Y	29290 FQ	34110 MW	42830 TQ	USBLS	5/07
	New Mexico	Y	22000 FQ	27180 MW	36350 TQ	USBLS	5/07
	Albuquerque MSA, NM	Y	24850 FQ	31200 MW	50440 TQ	USBLS	5/07
	New York	Y	26810 FQ	31600 MW	37700 TQ	USBLS	5/07
	Albany-Schenectady-Troy MSA, NY	Y	28990 FQ	35050 MW	40830 TQ	USBLS	5/07
	Buffalo-Niagara Falls MSA, NY	Y	27570 FQ	31800 MW	39060 TQ	USBLS	5/07
	Nassau-Suffolk PMSA, NY	Y	25390 FQ	27950 MW	31770 TQ	USBLS	5/07
	New York-Northern New Jersey-Long Island MSA, NY-NJ-PA	Y	27300 FQ	33170 MW	39720 TQ	USBLS	5/07
	North Carolina	Y	23800 FQ	28250 MW	33380 TQ	USBLS	5/07
	Charlotte-Gastonia-Concord MSA, NC-SC	Y	22910 FQ	28170 MW	33100 TQ	USBLS	5/07
	Raleigh-Cary MSA, NC	Y	25800 FQ	28260 MW	31390 TQ	USBLS	5/07
	North Dakota	Y	25260 FQ	27950 MW	31540 TQ	USBLS	5/07
	Fargo MSA, ND-MN	Y	26180 FQ	28000 MW	29810 TQ	USBLS	5/07
	Ohio	Y	23480 FQ	29590 MW	39230 TQ	USBLS	5/07
	Canton-Massillon MSA, OH	Y	26740 FQ	29020 MW	31650 TQ	USBLS	5/07
	Cincinnati-Middletown MSA, OH-KY-IN	Y	24720 FQ	28360 MW	33600 TQ	USBLS	5/07
	Cleveland-Elyria-Mentor MSA, OH	Y	21000 FQ	28140 MW	40230 TQ	USBLS	5/07
	Columbus MSA, OH	Y	27250 FQ	32360 MW	43020 TQ	USBLS	5/07
	Dayton MSA, OH	Y	18070 FQ	21470 MW	27070 TQ	USBLS	5/07
	Oklahoma	Y	26300 FQ	32850 MW	39310 TQ	USBLS	5/07
	Oklahoma City MSA, OK	Y	30900 FQ	35980 MW	41400 TQ	USBLS	5/07
	Tulsa MSA, OK	Y	26060 FQ	29110 MW	34540 TQ	USBLS	5/07
	Oregon	H	13.01 FQ	17.02 MW	21.42 TQ	ORBLS	5/08
	Portland-Vancouver-Beaverton MSA, OR-WA	Y	27650 FQ	35390 MW	42850 TQ	USBLS	5/07
	Pennsylvania	Y	22880 FQ	29640 MW	37210 TQ	USBLS	5/07
	Philadelphia-Camden-Wilmington MSA, PA-NJ-DE-MD	Y	26280 FQ	30700 MW	38800 TQ	USBLS	5/07
	Pittsburgh MSA, PA	Y	25090 FQ	28670 MW	31930 TQ	USBLS	5/07
	Providence-Fall River-Warwick MSA, RI-MA	Y	24600 FQ	28610 MW	34580 TQ	USBLS	5/07
	South Carolina	Y	18870 FQ	30200 MW	37150 TQ	USBLS	5/07
	Charleston-North Charleston MSA, SC	Y	17600 FQ	26020 MW	30130 TQ	USBLS	5/07
	South Dakota	Y	25070 FQ	29633 MW	33615 TQ	SDBLS	7/08-9/08
	Sioux Falls MSA, SD	Y	25829 FQ	30016 MW	33612 TQ	SDBLS	7/08-9/08
	Tennessee	Y	22840 FQ	26980 MW	33100 TQ	USBLS	5/07
	Knoxville MSA, TN	Y	22230 FQ	24770 MW	32180 TQ	USBLS	5/07
	Memphis MSA, TN-MS-AR	Y	22180 FQ	24340 MW	28410 TQ	USBLS	5/07
	Nashville-Davidson-Murfreesboro MSA, TN	Y	26540 FQ	32580 MW	44740 TQ	USBLS	5/07

AE Average entry wage	**AW** Average wage paid	**FQ** First quartile wage	**LO** Lowest wage paid	**MTC** Median total compensation **TCC** Total cash compensation
AER Average entry range	**AWR** Average wage range	**H** Hourly	**LR** Low end range	**MW** Median wage paid **TQ** Third quartile wage
AEX Average experienced wage	**AXR** Average experienced range	**HI** Highest wage paid	**M** Monthly	**MWR** Median wage range **W** Weekly
ATC Average total compensation	**D** Daily	**HR** High end range	**MCC** Median cash compensation	**S** See annotated source **Y** Yearly

Occupation/Type/Industry	Location	Per	Low	Mid	High	Source	Date
Electronic Home Entertainment Equipment Installer and Repairer							
	Texas	Y	23460 FQ	27730 MW	34400 TQ	USBLS	5/07
	Austin-Round Rock MSA, TX	Y	22420 FQ	26770 MW	31570 TQ	USBLS	5/07
	Dallas-Fort Worth-Arlington MSA, TX	Y	25700 FQ	30350 MW	37770 TQ	USBLS	5/07
	El Paso MSA, TX	Y	12390 FQ	13930 MW	15480 TQ	USBLS	5/07
	Houston-Sugar Land-Baytown MSA, TX	Y	24400 FQ	27520 MW	32730 TQ	USBLS	5/07
	San Antonio MSA, TX	Y	25280 FQ	28520 MW	34140 TQ	USBLS	5/07
	Utah	Y	25680 FQ	28910 MW	36880 TQ	USBLS	5/07
	Salt Lake City MSA, UT	Y	25720 FQ	29040 MW	49850 TQ	USBLS	5/07
	Vermont	Y	26310 FQ	30390 MW	37620 TQ	USBLS	5/07
	Virginia	Y	26980 FQ	35620 MW	43900 TQ	USBLS	5/07
	Richmond MSA, VA	Y	23310 FQ	28830 MW	35400 TQ	USBLS	5/07
	Virginia Beach-Norfolk-Newport News MSA, VA-NC	Y	24090 FQ	29820 MW	35290 TQ	USBLS	5/07
	Washington	H	14.37 FQ	18.08 MW	22.67 TQ	WABLS	3/08
	Seattle-Tacoma-Bellevue MSA, WA	Y	32190 FQ	41310 MW	50830 TQ	USBLS	5/07
	West Virginia	Y	21577 FQ	27588 MW	32837 TQ	WVBLS	7/08-9/08
	Charleston MSA, WV	Y	24000 FQ	28490 MW	32820 TQ	USBLS	5/07
	Wisconsin	Y	27260 FQ	35910 MW	42700 TQ	USBLS	5/07
	Milwaukee-Waukesha-West Allis MSA, WI	Y	37190 FQ	42700 MW	47170 TQ	USBLS	5/07
	Wyoming	Y	21918 FQ	34876 MW	44586 TQ	WYBLS	9/08
	Puerto Rico	Y	19100 FQ	21880 MW	27510 TQ	USBLS	5/07
	San Juan-Caguas-Guaynabo MSA, PR	Y	19870 FQ	22360 MW	29600 TQ	USBLS	5/07
Electronics Engineer							
Except Computer	Alabama	Y	65380 FQ	85270 MW	99940 TQ	USBLS	5/07
Except Computer	Birmingham-Hoover MSA, AL	Y	68130 FQ	84790 MW	97850 TQ	USBLS	5/07
Except Computer	Mobile MSA, AL	Y	64200 FQ	81680 MW	95170 TQ	USBLS	5/07
Except Computer	Alaska	Y	64490 FQ	74890 MW	82970 TQ	USBLS	5/07
Except Computer	Anchorage MSA, AK	Y	63710 FQ	74580 MW	82620 TQ	USBLS	5/07
Except Computer	Arizona	Y	60260 FQ	76100 MW	97150 TQ	USBLS	5/07
Except Computer	Phoenix-Mesa-Scottsdale MSA, AZ	Y	59990 FQ	73080 MW	87600 TQ	USBLS	5/07
Except Computer	Tucson MSA, AZ	Y	61750 FQ	109210 MW	123850 TQ	USBLS	5/07
Except Computer	Arkansas	Y	54450 FQ	66590 MW	79740 TQ	USBLS	5/07
Except Computer	Fayetteville-Springdale-Rogers MSA, AR-MO	Y	38550 FQ	67480 MW	83230 TQ	USBLS	5/07
Except Computer	Fort Smith MSA, AR-OK	Y	53660 FQ	68890 MW	86630 TQ	USBLS	5/07
Except Computer	Little Rock-North Little Rock MSA, AR	Y	53660 FQ	64550 MW	78540 TQ	USBLS	5/07
Except Computer	California	H	36.08 FQ	45.41 MW	56.71 TQ	CABLS	1/08-3/08
Except Computer	Fresno MSA, CA	H	29.15 FQ	35.43 MW	43.85 TQ	CABLS	1/08-3/08
Except Computer	Los Angeles-Long Beach-Glendale PMSA, CA	H	34.79 FQ	44.60 MW	56.27 TQ	CABLS	1/08-3/08
Except Computer	Oakland-Fremont-Hayward MSA, CA	H	34.12 FQ	42.67 MW	51.69 TQ	CABLS	1/08-3/08
Except Computer	Riverside-San Bernardino-Ontario MSA, CA	H	34.05 FQ	41.63 MW	49.90 TQ	CABLS	1/08-3/08
Except Computer	San Diego-Carlsbad-San Marcos MSA, CA	H	36.74 FQ	46.04 MW	57.76 TQ	CABLS	1/08-3/08
Except Computer	San Francisco-San Mateo-Redwood PMSA, CA	H	38.41 FQ	47.02 MW	57.85 TQ	CABLS	1/08-3/08
Except Computer	San Jose-Sunnyvale-Santa Clara MSA, CA	H	40.53 FQ	49.99 MW	62.16 TQ	CABLS	1/08-3/08
Except Computer	Santa Ana-Anaheim-Irvine PMSA, CA	Y	71320 FQ	87960 MW	103240 TQ	USBLS	5/07
Except Computer	Colorado	Y	68560 FQ	84450 MW	105830 TQ	USBLS	5/07
Except Computer	Denver-Aurora MSA, CO	Y	66660 FQ	80750 MW	100280 TQ	USBLS	5/07
Except Computer	Connecticut	H	28.66 AE	40.37 MW		CTBLS	1/08-3/08
Except Computer	Bridgeport-Stamford-Norwalk MSA, CT	Y	67650 FQ	86660 MW	101920 TQ	USBLS	5/07
Except Computer	Hartford-West Hartford-East Hartford MSA, CT	Y	62570 FQ	82910 MW	93890 TQ	USBLS	5/07
Except Computer	Delaware	Y	56260 FQ	74880 MW	88330 TQ	USBLS	5/07

AE	Average entry wage	AW	Average wage paid	FQ	First quartile wage	LO	Lowest wage paid	MTC	Median total compensation	TCC	Total cash compensation
AER	Average entry range	AWR	Average wage range	H	Hourly	LR	Low end range	MW	Median wage paid	TQ	Third quartile wage
AEX	Average experienced wage	AXR	Average experienced range	HI	Highest wage paid	M	Monthly	MWR	Median wage range	W	Weekly
ATC	Average total compensation	D	Daily	HR	High end range	MCC	Median cash compensation	S	See annotated source	Y	Yearly

514

Electronics Engineer

Occupation/Type/Industry	Location	Per	Low	Mid	High	Source	Date
Electronics Engineer							
Except Computer	Wilmington PMSA, DE-MD-NJ	Y	60950 FQ	76630 MW	90740 TQ	USBLS	5/07
Except Computer	District of Columbia	Y	80850 FQ	93820 MW	117910 TQ	USBLS	5/07
Except Computer	Washington-Arlington-Alexandria MSA, DC-VA-MD-WV	Y	74310 FQ	92500 MW	113680 TQ	USBLS	5/07
Except Computer	Florida	Y	63490 FQ	78010 MW	93350 TQ	USBLS	5/07
Except Computer	Fort Lauderdale-Pompano Beach-Deerfield Beach PMSA, FL	Y	51490 FQ	69690 MW	80820 TQ	USBLS	5/07
Except Computer	Jacksonville MSA, FL	Y	69180 FQ	81720 MW	93850 TQ	USBLS	5/07
Except Computer	Miami-Fort Lauderdale-Miami Beach MSA, FL	Y	55030 FQ	72290 MW	86090 TQ	USBLS	5/07
Except Computer	Orlando-Kissimmee MSA, FL	Y	67850 FQ	85140 MW	97540 TQ	USBLS	5/07
Except Computer	Sarasota-Bradenton-Venice MSA, FL	Y	60390 FQ	77100 MW	89030 TQ	USBLS	5/07
Except Computer	Tampa-St. Petersburg-Clearwater MSA, FL	Y	65980 FQ	74860 MW	87300 TQ	USBLS	5/07
Except Computer	West Palm Beach-Boca Raton-Boynton Beach PMSA, FL	Y	51630 FQ	75170 MW	91990 TQ	USBLS	5/07
Except Computer	Georgia	Y	61840 FQ	77320 MW	94080 TQ	USBLS	5/07
Except Computer	Atlanta-Sandy Springs-Marietta MSA, GA	Y	63220 FQ	79440 MW	98370 TQ	USBLS	5/07
Except Computer	Hawaii	Y	65120 FQ	78760 MW	93570 TQ	USBLS	5/07
Except Computer	Honolulu MSA, HI	Y	65610 FQ	79380 MW	93570 TQ	USBLS	5/07
Except Computer	Idaho	Y	58320 FQ	67040 MW	97810 TQ	USBLS	5/07
Except Computer	Boise City-Nampa MSA, ID	Y	58540 FQ	68010 MW	100770 TQ	USBLS	5/07
Except Computer	Illinois	Y	61140 FQ	76870 MW	95380 TQ	USBLS	5/07
Except Computer	Chicago-Naperville-Joliet MSA, IL-IN-WI	Y	60350 FQ	76740 MW	95340 TQ	USBLS	5/07
Except Computer	Indiana	Y	59170 FQ	75700 MW	93950 TQ	USBLS	5/07
Except Computer	Gary PMSA, IN	Y	46520 FQ	52800 MW	76220 TQ	USBLS	5/07
Except Computer	Indianapolis-Carmel MSA, IN	Y	59650 FQ	79370 MW	95930 TQ	USBLS	5/07
Except Computer	Iowa	Y	58360 FQ	67670 MW	77190 TQ	USBLS	5/07
Except Computer	Cedar Rapids MSA, IA	Y	59830 FQ	70640 MW	84650 TQ	USBLS	5/07
Except Computer	Davenport-Moline-Rock Island MSA, IA-IL	Y	62810 FQ	77590 MW	95990 TQ	USBLS	5/07
Except Computer	Des Moines-West Des Moines MSA, IA	Y	60850 FQ	69740 MW	80590 TQ	USBLS	5/07
Except Computer	Kansas	Y	61530 FQ	76340 MW	92680 TQ	USBLS	5/07
Except Computer	Wichita MSA, KS	Y	61020 FQ	73070 MW	92120 TQ	USBLS	5/07
Except Computer	Kentucky	Y	59826 FQ	76667 MW	92523 TQ	KYBLS	2008
Except Computer	Louisville-Jefferson County MSA, KY-IN	Y	55340 FQ	73050 MW	88140 TQ	USBLS	5/07
Except Computer	Louisiana	H	28.18 FQ	35.48 MW	44.11 TQ	LABLS	1/08-3/08
Except Computer	Baton Rouge MSA, LA	Y	46630 FQ	57540 MW	78370 TQ	USBLS	5/07
Except Computer	New Orleans-Metairie-Kenner MSA, LA	Y	71710 FQ	84160 MW	97150 TQ	USBLS	5/07
Except Computer	Maine	Y	60640 FQ	76420 MW	93570 TQ	USBLS	5/07
Except Computer	Portland-South Portland-Biddeford MSA, ME	Y	63850 FQ	78660 MW	95800 TQ	USBLS	5/07
Except Computer	Maryland	Y		89600 MW		MDBLS	3/08
Except Computer	Baltimore-Towson MSA, MD	Y	62500 FQ	81500 MW	98970 TQ	USBLS	5/07
Except Computer	Bethesda-Gaithersburg-Frederick PMSA, MD	Y	72550 FQ	93210 MW	114390 TQ	USBLS	5/07
Except Computer	Massachusetts	Y	66180 FQ	86200 MW	112080 TQ	USBLS	5/07
Except Computer	Boston-Cambridge-Quincy NECTA, MA	Y	64150 FQ	85630 MW	112700 TQ	USBLS	5/07
Except Computer	Worcester MSA, MA-CT	Y	64530 FQ	78390 MW	101590 TQ	USBLS	5/07
Except Computer	Michigan	Y	63510 FQ	75490 MW	91190 TQ	USBLS	5/07
Except Computer	Detroit-Warren-Livonia MSA, MI	Y	65520 FQ	76730 MW	92990 TQ	USBLS	5/07
Except Computer	Grand Rapids-Wyoming MSA, MI	Y	53410 FQ	67310 MW	80500 TQ	USBLS	5/07
Except Computer	Warren-Troy-Farmington Hills PMSA, MI	Y	66100 FQ	76200 MW	92960 TQ	USBLS	5/07
Except Computer	Minnesota	Y	63453 FQ	80695 MW	106579 TQ	MNBLS	10/08-12/08
Except Computer	Minneapolis-Saint Paul MSA, MN-WI	Y	66247 FQ	84503 MW	109613 TQ	MNBLS	10/08-12/08
Except Computer	Mississippi	Y	66620 FQ	79540 MW	93030 TQ	USBLS	5/07
Except Computer	Jackson MSA, MS	Y	68170 FQ	74370 MW	80580 TQ	USBLS	5/07

AE	Average entry wage	AW	Average wage paid	FQ	First quartile wage
AER	Average entry range	AWR	Average wage range	H	Hourly
AEX	Average experienced wage	AXR	Average experienced range	HI	Highest wage paid
ATC	Average total compensation	D	Daily	HR	High end range

LO	Lowest wage paid	MTC	Median total compensation
LR	Low end range	MW	Median wage paid
M	Monthly	MWR	Median wage range
MCC	Median cash compensation	S	See annotated source

TCC	Total cash compensation	
TQ	Third quartile wage	
W	Weekly	
Y	Yearly	

Electronics Engineer

Occupation/Type/Industry	Location	Per	Low	Mid	High	Source	Date
Except Computer	Missouri	Y	63110 FQ	78390 MW	96790 TQ	USBLS	5/07
Except Computer	Kansas City MSA, MO-KS	Y	60590 FQ	74460 MW	91360 TQ	USBLS	5/07
Except Computer	St. Louis MSA, MO-IL	Y	67760 FQ	84740 MW	99620 TQ	USBLS	5/07
Except Computer	Montana	Y	50200 FQ	63410 MW	76430 TQ	USBLS	5/07
Except Computer	Nebraska	Y	57880 FQ	69120 MW	79240 TQ	USBLS	5/07
Except Computer	Omaha-Council Bluffs MSA, NE-IA	Y	57200 FQ	67960 MW	77780 TQ	USBLS	5/07
Except Computer	Nevada	H	30.97 FQ	38.24 MW	46.51 TQ	NVBLS	5/08
Except Computer	Las Vegas-Paradise MSA, NV	H	30.37 FQ	37.05 MW	45.64 TQ	NVBLS	5/08
Except Computer	New Hampshire	H	34.42 AE	48.97 MW	55.02 AEX	NHBLS	6/08
Except Computer	Manchester MSA, NH	Y	69270 FQ	85040 MW	94840 TQ	USBLS	5/07
Except Computer	Nashua NECTA, NH-MA	Y	85190 FQ	103620 MW	119970 TQ	USBLS	5/07
Except Computer	New Jersey	Y	73390 FQ	94590 MW	115350 TQ	USBLS	5/07
Except Computer	Camden PMSA, NJ	Y	74320 FQ	92220 MW	109860 TQ	USBLS	5/07
Except Computer	Edison PMSA, NJ	Y	83150 FQ	105250 MW	122940 TQ	USBLS	5/07
Except Computer	Newark-Union PMSA, NJ-PA	Y	69910 FQ	88880 MW	107490 TQ	USBLS	5/07
Except Computer	New Mexico	Y	73170 FQ	91600 MW	109670 TQ	USBLS	5/07
Except Computer	Albuquerque MSA, NM	Y	76410 FQ	95100 MW	114130 TQ	USBLS	5/07
Except Computer	New York	Y	64260 FQ	82570 MW	103950 TQ	USBLS	5/07
Except Computer	Albany-Schenectady-Troy MSA, NY	Y	72140 FQ	89800 MW	111250 TQ	USBLS	5/07
Except Computer	Binghamton MSA, NY	Y	80590 FQ	92670 MW	104330 TQ	USBLS	5/07
Except Computer	Buffalo-Niagara Falls MSA, NY	Y	50030 FQ	65890 MW	85710 TQ	USBLS	5/07
Except Computer	Nassau-Suffolk PMSA, NY	Y	68750 FQ	90540 MW	112050 TQ	USBLS	5/07
Except Computer	New York-Northern New Jersey-Long Island MSA, NY-NJ-PA	Y	70920 FQ	93870 MW	116090 TQ	USBLS	5/07
Except Computer	Syracuse MSA, NY	Y	48960 FQ	69220 MW	83790 TQ	USBLS	5/07
Except Computer	North Carolina	Y	63450 FQ	77640 MW	96360 TQ	USBLS	5/07
Except Computer	Asheville MSA, NC	Y	55880 FQ	67100 MW	83980 TQ	USBLS	5/07
Except Computer	Charlotte-Gastonia-Concord MSA, NC-SC	Y	62460 FQ	75450 MW	89360 TQ	USBLS	5/07
Except Computer	Raleigh-Cary MSA, NC	Y	62670 FQ	75170 MW	93890 TQ	USBLS	5/07
Except Computer	North Dakota	Y	56000 FQ	63020 MW	75640 TQ	USBLS	5/07
Except Computer	Fargo MSA, ND-MN	Y	60580 FQ	71720 MW	81320 TQ	USBLS	5/07
Except Computer	Ohio	Y	65460 FQ	82480 MW	99220 TQ	USBLS	5/07
Except Computer	Cincinnati-Middletown MSA, OH-KY-IN	Y	68830 FQ	82570 MW	97340 TQ	USBLS	5/07
Except Computer	Cleveland-Elyria-Mentor MSA, OH	Y	62990 FQ	75180 MW	89890 TQ	USBLS	5/07
Except Computer	Columbus MSA, OH	Y	58810 FQ	71650 MW	88020 TQ	USBLS	5/07
Except Computer	Dayton MSA, OH	Y	79360 FQ	93920 MW	111020 TQ	USBLS	5/07
Except Computer	Mansfield MSA, OH	Y	55320 FQ	64690 MW	81510 TQ	USBLS	5/07
Except Computer	Oklahoma	Y	66770 FQ	76630 MW	87920 TQ	USBLS	5/07
Except Computer	Oklahoma City MSA, OK	Y	70010 FQ	78260 MW	88390 TQ	USBLS	5/07
Except Computer	Tulsa MSA, OK	Y	52560 FQ	67450 MW	91420 TQ	USBLS	5/07
Except Computer	Oregon	H	31.93 FQ	39.85 MW	50.04 TQ	ORBLS	5/08
Except Computer	Portland-Vancouver-Beaverton MSA, OR-WA	Y	68390 FQ	84760 MW	107150 TQ	USBLS	5/07
Except Computer	Salem MSA, OR	Y	28500 FQ	31560 MW	83090 TQ	USBLS	5/07
Except Computer	Pennsylvania	Y	62040 FQ	79370 MW	100030 TQ	USBLS	5/07
Except Computer	Allentown-Bethlehem-Easton MSA, PA-NJ	Y	66630 FQ	89020 MW	117500 TQ	USBLS	5/07
Except Computer	Lancaster MSA, PA	Y	50070 FQ	69310 MW	83560 TQ	USBLS	5/07
Except Computer	Philadelphia-Camden-Wilmington MSA, PA-NJ-DE-MD	Y	71990 FQ	89800 MW	107800 TQ	USBLS	5/07
Except Computer	Pittsburgh MSA, PA	Y	58280 FQ	77410 MW	98570 TQ	USBLS	5/07
Except Computer	Rhode Island	Y	85830 FQ	98990 MW	117280 TQ	USBLS	5/07
Except Computer	Providence-Fall River-Warwick MSA, RI-MA	Y	84620 FQ	97760 MW	116130 TQ	USBLS	5/07
Except Computer	South Carolina	Y	58440 FQ	70790 MW	89580 TQ	USBLS	5/07
Except Computer	Charleston-North Charleston MSA, SC	Y	63710 FQ	82230 MW	95190 TQ	USBLS	5/07
Except Computer	Columbia MSA, SC	Y	62720 FQ	73460 MW	87560 TQ	USBLS	5/07
Except Computer	South Dakota	Y	59433 FQ	68741 MW	79360 TQ	SDBLS	7/08-9/08
Except Computer	Sioux Falls MSA, SD	Y	60748 FQ	69731 MW	79931 TQ	SDBLS	7/08-9/08
Except Computer	Tennessee	Y	58930 FQ	71180 MW	86070 TQ	USBLS	5/07
Except Computer	Memphis MSA, TN-MS-AR	Y	66390 FQ	77760 MW	95500 TQ	USBLS	5/07

AE	Average entry wage	AW	Average wage paid	FQ	First quartile wage
AER	Average entry range	AWR	Average wage range	H	Hourly
AEX	Average experienced wage	AXR	Average experienced range	HI	Highest wage paid
ATC	Average total compensation	D	Daily	HR	High end range

LO	Lowest wage paid	MTC	Median total compensation
LR	Low end range	MW	Median wage paid
M	Monthly	MWR	Median wage range
MCC	Median cash compensation	S	See annotated source

TCC	Total cash compensation	
TQ	Third quartile wage	
W	Weekly	
Y	Yearly	

Occupation/Type/Industry	Location	Per	Low	Mid	High	Source	Date
Electronics Engineer							
Except Computer	Nashville-Davidson-Murfreesboro MSA, TN	Y	56900 FQ	68160 MW	80170 TQ	USBLS	5/07
Except Computer	Texas	Y	66650 FQ	84120 MW	103230 TQ	USBLS	5/07
Except Computer	Austin-Round Rock MSA, TX	Y	56810 FQ	78430 MW	98850 TQ	USBLS	5/07
Except Computer	Dallas-Fort Worth-Arlington MSA, TX	Y	72520 FQ	89800 MW	107510 TQ	USBLS	5/07
Except Computer	El Paso MSA, TX	Y	54830 FQ	71040 MW	93800 TQ	USBLS	5/07
Except Computer	Houston-Sugar Land-Baytown MSA, TX	Y	64440 FQ	79880 MW	103400 TQ	USBLS	5/07
Except Computer	San Antonio MSA, TX	Y	62260 FQ	77200 MW	93290 TQ	USBLS	5/07
Except Computer	Utah	Y	67930 FQ	80000 MW	94450 TQ	USBLS	5/07
Except Computer	Salt Lake City MSA, UT	Y	64860 FQ	83150 MW	103070 TQ	USBLS	5/07
Except Computer	Vermont	Y	70950 FQ	87520 MW	101330 TQ	USBLS	5/07
Except Computer	Burlington-South Burlington MSA, VT	Y	72960 FQ	89970 MW	103160 TQ	USBLS	5/07
Except Computer	Virginia	Y	72550 FQ	90330 MW	107940 TQ	USBLS	5/07
Except Computer	Richmond MSA, VA	Y	59860 FQ	76030 MW	90230 TQ	USBLS	5/07
Except Computer	Virginia Beach-Norfolk-Newport News MSA, VA-NC	Y	66700 FQ	84680 MW	99250 TQ	USBLS	5/07
Except Computer	Washington	H	32.34 FQ	40.29 MW	49.53 TQ	WABLS	3/08
Except Computer	Seattle-Tacoma-Bellevue MSA, WA	Y	66950 FQ	82690 MW	101980 TQ	USBLS	5/07
Except Computer	Spokane MSA, WA	Y	57780 FQ	66690 MW	88340 TQ	USBLS	5/07
Except Computer	West Virginia	Y	41206 FQ	62131 MW	90861 TQ	WVBLS	7/08-9/08
Except Computer	Charleston MSA, WV	Y	37550 FQ	45260 MW	86320 TQ	USBLS	5/07
Except Computer	Wisconsin	Y	57040 FQ	67240 MW	84730 TQ	USBLS	5/07
Except Computer	Green Bay MSA, WI	Y	59470 FQ	69100 MW	79860 TQ	USBLS	5/07
Except Computer	Milwaukee-Waukesha-West Allis MSA, WI	Y	57940 FQ	68880 MW	86260 TQ	USBLS	5/07
Except Computer	Wyoming	Y	51433 FQ	62168 MW	77546 TQ	WYBLS	9/08
Except Computer	Puerto Rico	Y	45700 FQ	61800 MW	79520 TQ	USBLS	5/07
Except Computer	San Juan-Caguas-Guaynabo MSA, PR	Y	46380 FQ	63340 MW	80480 TQ	USBLS	5/07
Electrophysiology Resident							
Kaiser Permanente Los Angeles Medical Center	Los Angeles, CA	Y	46758 LO		56216 HI	KPSC	2008-2009
Elementary School Principal	Great Lakes	Y		83659 AW		PRINC	2007-2008
	Mideast	Y		99485 AW		PRINC	2007-2008
	New England	Y		93709 AW		PRINC	2007-2008
	Plains	Y		80059 AW		PRINC	2007-2008
	Southwest	Y		71995 AW		PRINC	2007-2008
Elementary School Teacher							
Except Special Education	Alabama	Y	36020 FQ	41710 MW	47220 TQ	USBLS	5/07
Except Special Education	Birmingham-Hoover MSA, AL	Y	36980 FQ	42690 MW	47980 TQ	USBLS	5/07
Except Special Education	Alaska	Y	48270 FQ	57210 MW	67420 TQ	USBLS	5/07
Except Special Education	Arizona	Y	28120 FQ	35170 MW	44730 TQ	USBLS	5/07
Except Special Education	Phoenix-Mesa-Scottsdale MSA, AZ	Y	27140 FQ	34260 MW	44440 TQ	USBLS	5/07
Except Special Education	Tucson MSA, AZ	Y	30720 FQ	37150 MW	50570 TQ	USBLS	5/07
Except Special Education	Arkansas	Y	34330 FQ	39420 MW	46170 TQ	USBLS	5/07
Except Special Education	Little Rock-North Little Rock MSA, AR	Y	34800 FQ	41280 MW	49880 TQ	USBLS	5/07
Except Special Education	California	Y		60349 AW		CABLS	1/08-3/08
Except Special Education	Los Angeles-Long Beach-Glendale PMSA, CA	Y		58462 AW		CABLS	1/08-3/08
Except Special Education	Oakland-Fremont-Hayward MSA, CA	Y		64195 AW		CABLS	1/08-3/08
Except Special Education	Riverside-San Bernardino-Ontario MSA, CA	Y		62902 AW		CABLS	1/08-3/08
Except Special Education	Sacramento-Arden Arcade-Roseville MSA, CA	Y		57170 MW		CABLS	1/08-3/08
Except Special Education	San Diego-Carlsbad-San Marcos MSA, CA	Y		67527 AW		CABLS	1/08-3/08
Except Special Education	San Francisco-San Mateo-Redwood PMSA, CA	Y		60216 AW		CABLS	1/08-3/08
Except Special Education	San Jose-Sunnyvale-Santa Clara MSA, CA	Y		60441 AW		CABLS	1/08-3/08

AE	Average entry wage	AW	Average wage paid	FQ	First quartile wage	LO	Lowest wage paid	MTC Median total compensation TCC Total cash compensation
AER	Average entry range	AWR	Average wage range	HI	Highest wage paid	LR	Low end range	MW Median wage paid TQ Third quartile wage
AEX	Average experienced wage	AXR	Average experienced range	H	Hourly	M	Monthly	MWR Median wage range W Weekly
ATC	Average total compensation	D	Daily	HR	High end range	MCC	Median cash compensation S	See annotated source Y Yearly

Elementary School Teacher

Occupation/Type/Industry	Location	Per	Low	Mid	High	Source	Date
Except Special Education	Santa Ana-Anaheim-Irvine PMSA, CA	Y	48170 FQ	63980 MW	79930 TQ	USBLS	5/07
Except Special Education	Colorado	Y	36450 FQ	44320 MW	55340 TQ	USBLS	5/07
Except Special Education	Denver-Aurora MSA, CO	Y	37930 FQ	47490 MW	59170 TQ	USBLS	5/07
Except Special Education	Bridgeport-Stamford-Norwalk MSA, CT	Y	50930 FQ	61420 MW	77020 TQ	USBLS	5/07
Except Special Education	Hartford-West Hartford-East Hartford MSA, CT	Y	48130 FQ	64450 MW	75460 TQ	USBLS	5/07
Except Special Education	Waterbury MSA, CT	Y	49120 FQ	61740 MW	76330 TQ	USBLS	5/07
Except Special Education	Delaware	Y	36410 FQ	48760 MW	63500 TQ	USBLS	5/07
Except Special Education	Wilmington PMSA, DE-MD-NJ	Y	42380 FQ	53420 MW	67580 TQ	USBLS	5/07
Except Special Education	District of Columbia	Y	44070 FQ	52660 MW	68310 TQ	USBLS	5/07
Except Special Education	Washington-Arlington-Alexandria MSA, DC-VA-MD-WV	Y	44850 FQ	57830 MW	76030 TQ	USBLS	5/07
Except Special Education	Florida	Y	38610 FQ	47250 MW	59960 TQ	USBLS	5/07
Except Special Education	Jacksonville MSA, FL	Y	35330 FQ	40090 MW	51660 TQ	USBLS	5/07
Except Special Education	Miami-Fort Lauderdale-Miami Beach MSA, FL	Y	40600 FQ	48920 MW	64550 TQ	USBLS	5/07
Except Special Education	Orlando-Kissimmee MSA, FL	Y	37530 FQ	44310 MW	54630 TQ	USBLS	5/07
Except Special Education	Sarasota-Bradenton-Venice MSA, FL	Y	33950 FQ	39570 MW	51980 TQ	USBLS	5/07
Except Special Education	Tampa-St. Petersburg-Clearwater MSA, FL	Y	43000 FQ	50470 MW	61620 TQ	USBLS	5/07
Except Special Education	West Palm Beach-Boca Raton-Boynton Beach PMSA, FL	Y	36490 FQ	43080 MW	53810 TQ	USBLS	5/07
Except Special Education	Georgia	Y	39110 FQ	48100 MW	57230 TQ	USBLS	5/07
Except Special Education	Atlanta-Sandy Springs-Marietta MSA, GA	Y	40330 FQ	49410 MW	58110 TQ	USBLS	5/07
Except Special Education	Hawaii	Y	34800 FQ	45300 MW	54030 TQ	USBLS	5/07
Except Special Education	Honolulu MSA, HI	Y	30010 FQ	37020 MW	47680 TQ	USBLS	5/07
Except Special Education	Idaho	Y	40060 FQ	47030 MW	53400 TQ	USBLS	5/07
Except Special Education	Boise City-Nampa MSA, ID	Y	41240 FQ	48570 MW	55990 TQ	USBLS	5/07
Except Special Education	Illinois	Y	40150 FQ	52230 MW	67890 TQ	USBLS	5/07
Except Special Education	Chicago-Naperville-Joliet MSA, IL-IN-WI	Y	42160 FQ	54980 MW	70450 TQ	USBLS	5/07
Except Special Education	Indiana	Y	35080 FQ	46280 MW	58520 TQ	USBLS	5/07
Except Special Education	Gary PMSA, IN	Y	34560 FQ	43150 MW	56790 TQ	USBLS	5/07
Except Special Education	Indianapolis-Carmel MSA, IN	Y	29760 FQ	41880 MW	59340 TQ	USBLS	5/07
Except Special Education	South Bend-Mishawaka MSA, IN-MI	Y	38510 FQ	48350 MW	63590 TQ	USBLS	5/07
Except Special Education	Iowa	Y	29270 FQ	36820 MW	44980 TQ	USBLS	5/07
Except Special Education	Des Moines-West Des Moines MSA, IA	Y	30030 FQ	37120 MW	45580 TQ	USBLS	5/07
Except Special Education	Dubuque MSA, IA	Y	25540 FQ	30540 MW	42960 TQ	USBLS	5/07
Except Special Education	Kansas	Y	32170 FQ	38050 MW	45420 TQ	USBLS	5/07
Except Special Education	Wichita MSA, KS	Y	33760 FQ	41270 MW	47490 TQ	USBLS	5/07
Except Special Education	Kentucky	Y	37960 FQ	45168 MW	52051 TQ	KYBLS	2008
Except Special Education	Elizabethtown MSA, KY	Y	36660 FQ	42640 MW	52510 TQ	USBLS	5/07
Except Special Education	Louisville-Jefferson County MSA, KY-IN	Y	38550 FQ	47740 MW	57930 TQ	USBLS	5/07
Except Special Education	Louisiana	Y		40962 AW		LABLS	1/08-3/08
Except Special Education	Baton Rouge MSA, LA	Y	36100 FQ	40370 MW	46350 TQ	USBLS	5/07
Except Special Education	New Orleans-Metairie-Kenner MSA, LA	Y	37090 FQ	42760 MW	48250 TQ	USBLS	5/07
Except Special Education	Maine	Y	35970 FQ	44740 MW	52310 TQ	USBLS	5/07
Except Special Education	Portland-South Portland-Biddeford MSA, ME	Y	40910 FQ	49110 MW	56680 TQ	USBLS	5/07
Except Special Education	Maryland	Y		54575 MW		MDBLS	3/08
Except Special Education	Baltimore-Towson MSA, MD	Y	42480 FQ	52090 MW	63830 TQ	USBLS	5/07
Except Special Education	Bethesda-Gaithersburg-Frederick PMSA, MD	Y	45270 FQ	59830 MW	78750 TQ	USBLS	5/07
Except Special Education	Massachusetts	Y	45860 FQ	57270 MW	67350 TQ	USBLS	5/07
Except Special Education	Boston-Cambridge-Quincy NECTA, MA	Y	47350 FQ	60440 MW	72550 TQ	USBLS	5/07
Except Special Education	Worcester MSA, MA-CT	Y	45980 FQ	55690 MW	63710 TQ	USBLS	5/07
Except Special Education	Michigan	Y	40610 FQ	52730 MW	68990 TQ	USBLS	5/07
Except Special Education	Detroit-Warren-Livonia MSA, MI	Y	42890 FQ	56320 MW	76180 TQ	USBLS	5/07

Occupation/Type/Industry	Location	Per	Low	Mid	High	Source	Date
Elementary School Teacher							
Except Special Education	Grand Rapids-Wyoming MSA, MI	Y	35700 FQ	43980 MW	56460 TQ	USBLS	5/07
Except Special Education	Warren-Troy-Farmington Hills PMSA, MI	Y	46510 FQ	65150 MW	81990 TQ	USBLS	5/07
Except Special Education	Minnesota	Y	39306 FQ	49287 MW	62407 TQ	MNBLS	10/08-12/08
Except Special Education	Duluth-Superior MSA, MN-WI	Y	40060 FQ	51317 MW	61204 TQ	MNBLS	10/08-12/08
Except Special Education	Minneapolis-Saint Paul MSA, MN-WI	Y	39944 FQ	50731 MW	65347 TQ	MNBLS	10/08-12/08
Except Special Education	Rochester MSA, MN	Y	39862 FQ	48932 MW	59298 TQ	MNBLS	10/08-12/08
Except Special Education	Mississippi	Y	33730 FQ	38980 MW	46510 TQ	USBLS	5/07
Except Special Education	Jackson MSA, MS	Y	35070 FQ	39110 MW	46090 TQ	USBLS	5/07
Except Special Education	Missouri	Y	33010 FQ	39440 MW	49560 TQ	USBLS	5/07
Except Special Education	Kansas City MSA, MO-KS	Y	34630 FQ	40650 MW	49910 TQ	USBLS	5/07
Except Special Education	St. Louis MSA, MO-IL	Y	37070 FQ	45780 MW	57200 TQ	USBLS	5/07
Except Special Education	Montana	Y	23830 FQ	34940 MW	47140 TQ	USBLS	5/07
Except Special Education	Billings MSA, MT	Y	33370 FQ	42190 MW	53530 TQ	USBLS	5/07
Except Special Education	Nebraska	Y	34410 FQ	41320 MW	49580 TQ	USBLS	5/07
Except Special Education	Omaha-Council Bluffs MSA, NE-IA	Y	34040 FQ	39640 MW	47350 TQ	USBLS	5/07
Except Special Education	Nevada	Y	29811 FQ	37691 MW	49837 TQ	NVBLS	5/08
Except Special Education	Las Vegas-Paradise MSA, NV	Y	29212 FQ	35764 MW	47027 TQ	NVBLS	5/08
Except Special Education	New Hampshire	Y	36455 AE	49453 MW	56163 AEX	NHBLS	6/08
Except Special Education	Manchester MSA, NH	Y	40300 FQ	48870 MW	58510 TQ	USBLS	5/07
Except Special Education	Nashua NECTA, NH-MA	Y	39980 FQ	49450 MW	57980 TQ	USBLS	5/07
Except Special Education	New Jersey	Y	45210 FQ	53210 MW	71230 TQ	USBLS	5/07
Except Special Education	Camden PMSA, NJ	Y	46500 FQ	56800 MW	71510 TQ	USBLS	5/07
Except Special Education	Edison PMSA, NJ	Y	45100 FQ	51790 MW	69960 TQ	USBLS	5/07
Except Special Education	Newark-Union PMSA, NJ-PA	Y	45450 FQ	53770 MW	70800 TQ	USBLS	5/07
Except Special Education	New Mexico	Y	35920 FQ	43100 MW	51540 TQ	USBLS	5/07
Except Special Education	Albuquerque MSA, NM	Y	35640 FQ	42530 MW	48920 TQ	USBLS	5/07
Except Special Education	New York	Y	46540 FQ	59900 MW	76330 TQ	USBLS	5/07
Except Special Education	Albany-Schenectady-Troy MSA, NY	Y	44470 FQ	55710 MW	72360 TQ	USBLS	5/07
Except Special Education	Buffalo-Niagara Falls MSA, NY	Y	39450 FQ	49480 MW	69850 TQ	USBLS	5/07
Except Special Education	Nassau-Suffolk PMSA, NY	Y	59820 FQ	76970 MW	96820 TQ	USBLS	5/07
Except Special Education	New York-Northern New Jersey-Long Island MSA, NY-NJ-PA	Y	47730 FQ	60770 MW	78240 TQ	USBLS	5/07
Except Special Education	North Carolina	Y	32420 FQ	38770 MW	46640 TQ	USBLS	5/07
Except Special Education	Charlotte-Gastonia-Concord MSA, NC-SC	Y	33070 FQ	39160 MW	47930 TQ	USBLS	5/07
Except Special Education	Raleigh-Cary MSA, NC	Y	32500 FQ	38620 MW	47020 TQ	USBLS	5/07
Except Special Education	North Dakota	Y	34040 FQ	40920 MW	48060 TQ	USBLS	5/07
Except Special Education	Fargo MSA, ND-MN	Y	33920 FQ	40650 MW	47620 TQ	USBLS	5/07
Except Special Education	Grand Forks MSA, ND-MN	Y	37790 FQ	45110 MW	52460 TQ	USBLS	5/07
Except Special Education	Ohio	Y	40810 FQ	51730 MW	63020 TQ	USBLS	5/07
Except Special Education	Cincinnati-Middletown MSA, OH-KY-IN	Y	41240 FQ	51880 MW	63700 TQ	USBLS	5/07
Except Special Education	Cleveland-Elyria-Mentor MSA, OH	Y	45860 FQ	60650 MW	73600 TQ	USBLS	5/07
Except Special Education	Columbus MSA, OH	Y	45110 FQ	56390 MW	69040 TQ	USBLS	5/07
Except Special Education	Dayton MSA, OH	Y	41170 FQ	52930 MW	62410 TQ	USBLS	5/07
Except Special Education	Oklahoma	Y	32170 FQ	36440 MW	41330 TQ	USBLS	5/07
Except Special Education	Oklahoma City MSA, OK	Y	31390 FQ	35690 MW	40210 TQ	USBLS	5/07
Except Special Education	Tulsa MSA, OK	Y	33080 FQ	38730 MW	47110 TQ	USBLS	5/07
Except Special Education	Oregon	Y	40018 FQ	48807 MW	59721 TQ	ORBLS	5/08
Except Special Education	Portland-Vancouver-Beaverton MSA, OR-WA	Y	40190 FQ	49200 MW	60950 TQ	USBLS	5/07
Except Special Education	Salem MSA, OR	Y	39590 FQ	47370 MW	56060 TQ	USBLS	5/07
Except Special Education	Pennsylvania	Y	37640 FQ	48150 MW	62470 TQ	USBLS	5/07
Except Special Education	Allentown-Bethlehem-Easton MSA, PA-NJ	Y	36890 FQ	47430 MW	64610 TQ	USBLS	5/07
Except Special Education	Philadelphia-Camden-Wilmington MSA, PA-NJ-DE-MD	Y	39550 FQ	49150 MW	65500 TQ	USBLS	5/07
Except Special Education	Pittsburgh MSA, PA	Y	39830 FQ	49620 MW	64810 TQ	USBLS	5/07
Except Special Education	Rhode Island	Y	51440 FQ	65040 MW	75190 TQ	USBLS	5/07
Except Special Education	Providence-Fall River-Warwick MSA, RI-MA	Y	47120 FQ	62110 MW	73330 TQ	USBLS	5/07
Except Special Education	South Carolina	Y	34780 FQ	42440 MW	51310 TQ	USBLS	5/07

AE	Average entry wage	AW	Average wage paid	FQ	First quartile wage
AER	Average entry range	AWR	Average wage range	H	Hourly
AEX	Average experienced wage	AXR	Average experienced range	HI	Highest wage paid
ATC	Average total compensation	D	Daily	HR	High end range

LO	Lowest wage paid	MTC	Median total compensation	TCC	Total cash compensation
LR	Low end range	MW	Median wage paid	TQ	Third quartile wage
M	Monthly	MWR	Median wage range	W	Weekly
MCC	Median cash compensation	S	See annotated source	Y	Yearly

Occupation/Type/Industry	Location	Per	Low	Mid	High	Source	Date
Elementary School Teacher							
Except Special Education	Charleston-North Charleston MSA, SC	Y	34520 FQ	41660 MW	51870 TQ	USBLS	5/07
Except Special Education	Columbia MSA, SC	Y	35650 FQ	43430 MW	52300 TQ	USBLS	5/07
Except Special Education	Spartanburg MSA, SC	Y	32980 FQ	42030 MW	51460 TQ	USBLS	5/07
Except Special Education	South Dakota	Y	30659 FQ	35669 MW	41618 TQ	SDBLS	7/08-9/08
Except Special Education	Sioux Falls MSA, SD	Y	29506 FQ	34400 MW	41524 TQ	SDBLS	7/08-9/08
Except Special Education	Tennessee	Y	36120 FQ	41980 MW	48780 TQ	USBLS	5/07
Except Special Education	Memphis MSA, TN-MS-AR	Y	35470 FQ	40480 MW	46840 TQ	USBLS	5/07
Except Special Education	Nashville-Davidson-Murfreesboro MSA, TN	Y	36890 FQ	44300 MW	52650 TQ	USBLS	5/07
Except Special Education	Texas	Y	38310 FQ	44210 MW	50050 TQ	USBLS	5/07
Except Special Education	Austin-Round Rock MSA, TX	Y	36730 FQ	40980 MW	48080 TQ	USBLS	5/07
Except Special Education	Dallas-Fort Worth-Arlington MSA, TX	Y	41490 FQ	46220 MW	51060 TQ	USBLS	5/07
Except Special Education	El Paso MSA, TX	Y	40790 FQ	45590 MW	50940 TQ	USBLS	5/07
Except Special Education	Houston-Sugar Land-Baytown MSA, TX	Y	40040 FQ	45410 MW	51230 TQ	USBLS	5/07
Except Special Education	San Antonio MSA, TX	Y	40170 FQ	45780 MW	51760 TQ	USBLS	5/07
Except Special Education	Utah	Y	34140 FQ	42870 MW	52520 TQ	USBLS	5/07
Except Special Education	Logan MSA, UT-ID	Y	33920 FQ	43020 MW	52470 TQ	USBLS	5/07
Except Special Education	Provo-Orem MSA, UT	Y	31560 FQ	40730 MW	55260 TQ	USBLS	5/07
Except Special Education	Salt Lake City MSA, UT	Y	36500 FQ	43970 MW	53900 TQ	USBLS	5/07
Except Special Education	Vermont	Y	35760 FQ	45470 MW	56450 TQ	USBLS	5/07
Except Special Education	Burlington-South Burlington MSA, VT	Y	40280 FQ	49280 MW	60860 TQ	USBLS	5/07
Except Special Education	Virginia	Y	39330 FQ	49900 MW	64450 TQ	USBLS	5/07
Except Special Education	Lynchburg MSA, VA	Y	34390 FQ	38420 MW	45160 TQ	USBLS	5/07
Except Special Education	Richmond MSA, VA	Y	42410 FQ	52860 MW	61620 TQ	USBLS	5/07
Except Special Education	Roanoke MSA, VA	Y	36420 FQ	44940 MW	53920 TQ	USBLS	5/07
Except Special Education	Virginia Beach-Norfolk-Newport News MSA, VA-NC	Y	39130 FQ	47820 MW	59860 TQ	USBLS	5/07
Except Special Education	Washington	Y		52146 AW		WABLS	3/08
Except Special Education	Seattle-Tacoma-Bellevue MSA, WA	Y	43190 FQ	52080 MW	62540 TQ	USBLS	5/07
Except Special Education	Spokane MSA, WA	Y	42720 FQ	52600 MW	59840 TQ	USBLS	5/07
Except Special Education	West Virginia	Y	37399 FQ	43236 MW	48625 TQ	WVBLS	7/08-9/08
Except Special Education	Charleston MSA, WV	Y	36690 FQ	41680 MW	46710 TQ	USBLS	5/07
Except Special Education	Parkersburg-Marietta-Vienna MSA, WV-OH	Y	38390 FQ	44500 MW	50320 TQ	USBLS	5/07
Except Special Education	Wisconsin	Y	37870 FQ	47690 MW	59090 TQ	USBLS	5/07
Except Special Education	Milwaukee-Waukesha-West Allis MSA, WI	Y	43620 FQ	57080 MW	72090 TQ	USBLS	5/07
Except Special Education	Wyoming	Y	43674 FQ	52090 MW	60090 TQ	WYBLS	9/08
Except Special Education	Virgin Islands	Y	34620 FQ	42820 MW	57340 TQ	USBLS	5/07
Elevator Constructor	United States	H		56.42 AW		ENR02	9/08
Elevator Inspector							
State Government	Ohio	H	21.77 LO		31.86 HI	ODAS	2008
Elevator Installer and Repairer	Alabama	Y	38750 FQ	59110 MW	71420 TQ	USBLS	5/07
	Arizona	Y	47850 FQ	66790 MW	74110 TQ	USBLS	5/07
	California	H	33.92 FQ	41.44 MW	51.77 TQ	CABLS	1/08-3/08
	Los Angeles-Long Beach-Glendale PMSA, CA	H	29.65 FQ	35.43 MW	41.29 TQ	CABLS	1/08-3/08
	Oakland-Fremont-Hayward MSA, CA	H	33.90 FQ	40.83 MW	49.15 TQ	CABLS	1/08-3/08
	Sacramento-Arden Arcade-Roseville MSA, CA	H	53.60 FQ	57.50 MW	61.39 TQ	CABLS	1/08-3/08
	San Jose-Sunnyvale-Santa Clara MSA, CA	H	19.92 FQ	21.83 MW	23.73 TQ	CABLS	1/08-3/08
	Colorado	Y	40080 FQ	56690 MW	69980 TQ	USBLS	5/07
	Denver-Aurora MSA, CO	Y	40180 FQ	58360 MW	69840 TQ	USBLS	5/07
	Connecticut	H	22.27 AE	34.56 MW		CTBLS	1/08-3/08
	Washington-Arlington-Alexandria MSA, DC-VA-MD-WV	Y	53620 FQ	67080 MW	74800 TQ	USBLS	5/07
	Florida	Y	38210 FQ	57670 MW	69630 TQ	USBLS	5/07
	Fort Lauderdale-Pompano Beach-Deerfield Beach PMSA, FL	Y	39420 FQ	56170 MW	65940 TQ	USBLS	5/07

AE	Average entry wage	AW	Average wage paid	FQ	First quartile wage	LO	Lowest wage paid	MTC	Median total compensation	TCC	Total cash compensation
AER	Average entry range	AWR	Average wage range	H	Hourly	LR	Low end range	MW	Median wage paid	TQ	Third quartile wage
AEX	Average experienced wage	AXR	Average experienced range	HI	Highest wage paid	M	Monthly	MWR	Median wage range	W	Weekly
ATC	Average total compensation	D	Daily	HR	High end range	MCC	Median cash compensation	S	See annotated source	Y	Yearly

Elevator Installer and Repairer

Occupation/Type/Industry	Location	Per	Low	Mid	High	Source	Date
Elevator Installer and Repairer	Miami-Fort Lauderdale-Miami Beach MSA, FL	Y	49170 FQ	63100 MW	70000 TQ	USBLS	5/07
	Orlando-Kissimmee MSA, FL	Y	63230 FQ	68060 MW	72890 TQ	USBLS	5/07
	Tampa-St. Petersburg-Clearwater MSA, FL	Y	35570 FQ	39510 MW	67350 TQ	USBLS	5/07
	Georgia	Y	49110 FQ	61400 MW	68540 TQ	USBLS	5/07
	Atlanta-Sandy Springs-Marietta MSA, GA	Y	46900 FQ	61050 MW	68460 TQ	USBLS	5/07
	Hawaii	Y	65870 FQ	85830 MW	96820 TQ	USBLS	5/07
	Honolulu MSA, HI	Y	65310 FQ	84970 MW	96720 TQ	USBLS	5/07
	Illinois	Y	45960 FQ	77720 MW	98300 TQ	USBLS	5/07
	Chicago-Naperville-Joliet MSA, IL-IN-WI	Y	74980 FQ	90220 MW	106210 TQ	USBLS	5/07
	Indiana	Y	60810 FQ	71710 MW	78970 TQ	USBLS	5/07
	Indianapolis-Carmel MSA, IN	Y	63860 FQ	71180 MW	77390 TQ	USBLS	5/07
	Iowa	Y	66690 FQ	71920 MW	76920 TQ	USBLS	5/07
	Des Moines-West Des Moines MSA, IA	Y	63770 FQ	69940 MW	75390 TQ	USBLS	5/07
	Kentucky	Y	55267 FQ	74079 MW	81101 TQ	KYBLS	2008
	Maryland	Y		72675 MW		MDBLS	3/08
	Baltimore-Towson MSA, MD	Y	57670 FQ	71300 MW	78070 TQ	USBLS	5/07
	Massachusetts	Y	59870 FQ	76000 MW	90950 TQ	USBLS	5/07
	Boston-Cambridge-Quincy NECTA, MA	Y	60690 FQ	76790 MW	91590 TQ	USBLS	5/07
	Michigan	Y	52040 FQ	61770 MW	73650 TQ	USBLS	5/07
	Detroit-Warren-Livonia MSA, MI	Y	47900 FQ	60610 MW	74480 TQ	USBLS	5/07
	Minnesota	Y	61019 FQ	74350 MW	83403 TQ	MNBLS	10/08-12/08
	Minneapolis-Saint Paul MSA, MN-WI	Y	62863 FQ	75510 MW	84236 TQ	MNBLS	10/08-12/08
	Missouri	Y	59030 FQ	67700 MW	74570 TQ	USBLS	5/07
	St. Louis MSA, MO-IL	Y	60140 FQ	69800 MW	77980 TQ	USBLS	5/07
	Nebraska	Y	61650 FQ	69380 MW	75720 TQ	USBLS	5/07
	Omaha-Council Bluffs MSA, NE-IA	Y	61650 FQ	69380 MW	75720 TQ	USBLS	5/07
	Nevada	H	39.92 FQ	44.51 MW	47.90 TQ	NVBLS	5/08
	New Hampshire	H	20.83 AE	40.19 MW	43.15 AEX	NHBLS	6/08
	New Jersey	Y	51990 FQ	66160 MW	76510 TQ	USBLS	5/07
	Camden PMSA, NJ	Y	60030 FQ	68590 MW	75860 TQ	USBLS	5/07
	Edison PMSA, NJ	Y	55540 FQ	69350 MW	80500 TQ	USBLS	5/07
	Newark-Union PMSA, NJ-PA	Y	24000 FQ	62090 MW	73920 TQ	USBLS	5/07
	New York	Y	59530 FQ	70290 MW	81060 TQ	USBLS	5/07
	New York-Northern New Jersey-Long Island MSA, NY-NJ-PA	Y	58100 FQ	69870 MW	81330 TQ	USBLS	5/07
	North Carolina	Y	39280 FQ	56500 MW	64100 TQ	USBLS	5/07
	Ohio	Y	60070 FQ	70740 MW	78890 TQ	USBLS	5/07
	Cincinnati-Middletown MSA, OH-KY-IN	Y	65720 FQ	72000 MW	78050 TQ	USBLS	5/07
	Cleveland-Elyria-Mentor MSA, OH	Y	74160 FQ	81030 MW	89220 TQ	USBLS	5/07
	Oklahoma	Y	37780 FQ	47700 MW	64750 TQ	USBLS	5/07
	Oklahoma City MSA, OK	Y	37780 FQ	47700 MW	64750 TQ	USBLS	5/07
	Oregon	H	32.03 FQ	43.93 MW	48.03 TQ	ORBLS	5/08
	Portland-Vancouver-Beaverton MSA, OR-WA	Y	64790 FQ	88620 MW	96830 TQ	USBLS	5/07
	Pennsylvania	Y	56520 FQ	72020 MW	81270 TQ	USBLS	5/07
	Philadelphia-Camden-Wilmington MSA, PA-NJ-DE-MD	Y	51670 FQ	68500 MW	81470 TQ	USBLS	5/07
	Pittsburgh MSA, PA	Y	48020 FQ	72090 MW	79580 TQ	USBLS	5/07
	South Carolina	Y	47240 FQ	55930 MW	66070 TQ	USBLS	5/07
	Tennessee	Y	45060 FQ	60740 MW	73260 TQ	USBLS	5/07
	Texas	Y	44540 FQ	58800 MW	69450 TQ	USBLS	5/07
	Dallas-Fort Worth-Arlington MSA, TX	Y	40090 FQ	60060 MW	70980 TQ	USBLS	5/07
	El Paso MSA, TX	Y	45390 FQ	61400 MW	70180 TQ	USBLS	5/07
	Houston-Sugar Land-Baytown MSA, TX	Y	45480 FQ	57710 MW	68220 TQ	USBLS	5/07
	San Antonio MSA, TX	Y	48040 FQ	56270 MW	66080 TQ	USBLS	5/07
	Virginia	Y	45820 FQ	51690 MW	61140 TQ	USBLS	5/07
	Richmond MSA, VA	Y	44900 FQ	49260 MW	55960 TQ	USBLS	5/07

AE	Average entry wage	AW	Average wage paid	FQ	First quartile wage	LO	Lowest wage paid	MTC	Median total compensation	TCC	Total cash compensation
AER	Average entry range	AWR	Average wage range	H	Hourly	LR	Low end range	MW	Median wage paid	TQ	Third quartile wage
AEX	Average experienced wage	AXR	Average experienced range	HI	Highest wage paid	M	Monthly	MWR	Median wage range	W	Weekly
ATC	Average total compensation	D	Daily	HR	High end range	MCC	Median cash compensation	S	See annotated source	Y	Yearly

Occupation/Type/Industry	Location	Per	Low	Mid	High	Source	Date
Elevator Installer and Repairer	Virginia Beach-Norfolk-Newport News MSA, VA-NC	Y	44560 FQ	50900 MW	59510 TQ	USBLS	5/07
	West Virginia	Y	64003 FQ	72526 MW	79012 TQ	WVBLS	7/08-9/08
	Puerto Rico	Y	20620 FQ	28790 MW	38140 TQ	USBLS	5/07
	San Juan-Caguas-Guaynabo MSA, PR	Y	20590 FQ	28730 MW	38150 TQ	USBLS	5/07
Eligibility Interviewer							
Government Programs	Alabama	Y	34620 FQ	41930 MW	47900 TQ	USBLS	5/07
Government Programs	Birmingham-Hoover MSA, AL	Y	37570 FQ	43470 MW	48670 TQ	USBLS	5/07
Government Programs	Mobile MSA, AL	Y	33920 FQ	40230 MW	46920 TQ	USBLS	5/07
Government Programs	Alaska	Y	34650 FQ	39220 MW	47090 TQ	USBLS	5/07
Government Programs	Anchorage MSA, AK	Y	33690 FQ	37230 MW	41080 TQ	USBLS	5/07
Government Programs	Arizona	Y	29420 FQ	34360 MW	39480 TQ	USBLS	5/07
Government Programs	Phoenix-Mesa-Scottsdale MSA, AZ	Y	29400 FQ	34350 MW	40100 TQ	USBLS	5/07
Government Programs	Tucson MSA, AZ	Y	30750 FQ	35260 MW	39170 TQ	USBLS	5/07
Government Programs	Arkansas	Y	24070 FQ	30610 MW	39950 TQ	USBLS	5/07
Government Programs	Fort Smith MSA, AR-OK	Y	21290 FQ	26150 MW	33580 TQ	USBLS	5/07
Government Programs	California	H	18.38 FQ	21.65 MW	24.39 TQ	CABLS	1/08-3/08
Government Programs	Oakland-Fremont-Hayward MSA, CA	H	21.82 FQ	24.79 MW	28.76 TQ	CABLS	1/08-3/08
Government Programs	Riverside-San Bernardino-Ontario MSA, CA	H	16.45 FQ	18.91 MW	22.64 TQ	CABLS	1/08-3/08
Government Programs	Sacramento-Arden Arcade-Roseville MSA, CA	H	16.75 FQ	18.87 MW	22.38 TQ	CABLS	1/08-3/08
Government Programs	San Diego-Carlsbad-San Marcos MSA, CA	H	16.51 FQ	20.26 MW	23.91 TQ	CABLS	1/08-3/08
Government Programs	Colorado	Y	34610 FQ	41920 MW	49670 TQ	USBLS	5/07
Government Programs	Denver-Aurora MSA, CO	Y	37730 FQ	44710 MW	52110 TQ	USBLS	5/07
Government Programs	Connecticut	H	20.56 AE	27.70 MW		CTBLS	1/08-3/08
Government Programs	Bridgeport-Stamford-Norwalk MSA, CT	Y	52690 FQ	57060 MW	61440 TQ	USBLS	5/07
Government Programs	Hartford-West Hartford-East Hartford MSA, CT	Y	44520 FQ	55730 MW	60750 TQ	USBLS	5/07
Government Programs	District of Columbia	Y	33860 FQ	39810 MW	48320 TQ	USBLS	5/07
Government Programs	Washington-Arlington-Alexandria MSA, DC-VA-MD-WV	Y	36180 FQ	43940 MW	53720 TQ	USBLS	5/07
Government Programs	Florida	Y	25490 FQ	34670 MW	43560 TQ	USBLS	5/07
Government Programs	Jacksonville MSA, FL	Y	32670 FQ	40510 MW	46590 TQ	USBLS	5/07
Government Programs	Miami-Fort Lauderdale-Miami Beach MSA, FL	Y	27910 FQ	36410 MW	45040 TQ	USBLS	5/07
Government Programs	Orlando-Kissimmee MSA, FL	Y	24370 FQ	30570 MW	39250 TQ	USBLS	5/07
Government Programs	Tampa-St. Petersburg-Clearwater MSA, FL	Y	27520 FQ	36420 MW	44490 TQ	USBLS	5/07
Government Programs	West Palm Beach-Boca Raton-Boynton Beach PMSA, FL	Y	26180 FQ	34260 MW	43900 TQ	USBLS	5/07
Government Programs	Georgia	Y	35790 FQ	44350 MW	50210 TQ	USBLS	5/07
Government Programs	Atlanta-Sandy Springs-Marietta MSA, GA	Y	41270 FQ	46420 MW	52360 TQ	USBLS	5/07
Government Programs	Hawaii	Y	34520 FQ	40210 MW	48110 TQ	USBLS	5/07
Government Programs	Honolulu MSA, HI	Y	34740 FQ	40570 MW	48760 TQ	USBLS	5/07
Government Programs	Idaho	Y	28150 FQ	34760 MW	40210 TQ	USBLS	5/07
Government Programs	Boise City-Nampa MSA, ID	Y	26840 FQ	32140 MW	39790 TQ	USBLS	5/07
Government Programs	Coeur d'Alene MSA, ID	Y	29770 FQ	34950 MW	39770 TQ	USBLS	5/07
Government Programs	Illinois	Y	35220 FQ	44710 MW	53170 TQ	USBLS	5/07
Government Programs	Chicago-Naperville-Joliet MSA, IL-IN-WI	Y	35940 FQ	45220 MW	53860 TQ	USBLS	5/07
Government Programs	Indiana	Y	24560 FQ	31070 MW	39430 TQ	USBLS	5/07
Government Programs	Gary PMSA, IN	Y	22730 FQ	30730 MW	37550 TQ	USBLS	5/07
Government Programs	Indianapolis-Carmel MSA, IN	Y	26830 FQ	33730 MW	43590 TQ	USBLS	5/07
Government Programs	Iowa	Y	36350 FQ	42640 MW	47700 TQ	USBLS	5/07
Government Programs	Kansas	Y	31700 FQ	36160 MW	40730 TQ	USBLS	5/07
Government Programs	Wichita MSA, KS	Y	35610 FQ	39530 MW	46220 TQ	USBLS	5/07
Government Programs	Kentucky	Y	35014 FQ	44221 MW	49556 TQ	KYBLS	2008
Government Programs	Louisville-Jefferson County MSA, KY-IN	Y	25360 FQ	33040 MW	41890 TQ	USBLS	5/07
Government Programs	Louisiana	H	14.63 FQ	17.59 MW	20.78 TQ	LABLS	1/08-3/08
Government Programs	New Orleans-Metairie-Kenner MSA, LA	Y	31820 FQ	37870 MW	44580 TQ	USBLS	5/07

Occupation/Type/Industry	Location	Per	Low	Mid	High	Source	Date
Eligibility Interviewer							
Government Programs	Shreveport-Bossier City MSA, LA	Y	29430 FQ	35450 MW	41200 TQ	USBLS	5/07
Government Programs	Maine	Y	29020 FQ	33440 MW	37900 TQ	USBLS	5/07
Government Programs	Portland-South Portland-Biddeford MSA, ME	Y	29770 FQ	34320 MW	38690 TQ	USBLS	5/07
Government Programs	Maryland	Y		44675 MW		MDBLS	3/08
Government Programs	Baltimore-Towson MSA, MD	Y	35270 FQ	43910 MW	49940 TQ	USBLS	5/07
Government Programs	Bethesda-Gaithersburg-Frederick PMSA, MD	Y	34420 FQ	43490 MW	50230 TQ	USBLS	5/07
Government Programs	Massachusetts	Y	37820 FQ	46380 MW	54660 TQ	USBLS	5/07
Government Programs	Boston-Cambridge-Quincy NECTA, MA	Y	38940 FQ	47440 MW	55640 TQ	USBLS	5/07
Government Programs	Worcester MSA, MA-CT	Y	44150 FQ	54360 MW	61270 TQ	USBLS	5/07
Government Programs	Michigan	Y	40430 FQ	44670 MW	48610 TQ	USBLS	5/07
Government Programs	Detroit-Warren-Livonia MSA, MI	Y	41660 FQ	45330 MW	49000 TQ	USBLS	5/07
Government Programs	Grand Rapids-Wyoming MSA, MI	Y	38430 FQ	43610 MW	48020 TQ	USBLS	5/07
Government Programs	Warren-Troy-Farmington Hills PMSA, MI	Y	41700 FQ	45120 MW	48590 TQ	USBLS	5/07
Government Programs	Minnesota	Y	36802 FQ	42964 MW	49302 TQ	MNBLS	10/08-12/08
Government Programs	Duluth-Superior MSA, MN-WI	Y	36511 FQ	42755 MW	49250 TQ	MNBLS	10/08-12/08
Government Programs	Minneapolis-Saint Paul MSA, MN-WI	Y	37812 FQ	44535 MW	50457 TQ	MNBLS	10/08-12/08
Government Programs	Mississippi	Y	24170 FQ	27760 MW	31260 TQ	USBLS	5/07
Government Programs	Jackson MSA, MS	Y	25390 FQ	29350 MW	34300 TQ	USBLS	5/07
Government Programs	Missouri	Y	28120 FQ	31040 MW	40700 TQ	USBLS	5/07
Government Programs	Kansas City MSA, MO-KS	Y	30880 FQ	39620 MW	46880 TQ	USBLS	5/07
Government Programs	St. Louis MSA, MO-IL	Y	28420 FQ	31490 MW	42240 TQ	USBLS	5/07
Government Programs	Springfield MSA, MO	Y	27520 FQ	29800 MW	32020 TQ	USBLS	5/07
Government Programs	Montana	Y	23040 FQ	28440 MW	34410 TQ	USBLS	5/07
Government Programs	Billings MSA, MT	Y	26700 FQ	30040 MW	35920 TQ	USBLS	5/07
Government Programs	Nebraska	Y	22400 FQ	29760 MW	38220 TQ	USBLS	5/07
Government Programs	Omaha-Council Bluffs MSA, NE-IA	Y	32580 FQ	39360 MW	45460 TQ	USBLS	5/07
Government Programs	Nevada	H	16.16 FQ	20.58 MW	23.99 TQ	NVBLS	5/08
Government Programs	Las Vegas-Paradise MSA, NV	H	15.39 FQ	20.30 MW	23.64 TQ	NVBLS	5/08
Government Programs	New Hampshire	H	13.64 AE	16.36 MW	17.96 AEX	NHBLS	6/08
Government Programs	Nashua NECTA, NH-MA	Y	27890 FQ	31800 MW	37670 TQ	USBLS	5/07
Government Programs	New Jersey	Y	38440 FQ	45250 MW	51570 TQ	USBLS	5/07
Government Programs	Camden PMSA, NJ	Y	38620 FQ	44870 MW	50730 TQ	USBLS	5/07
Government Programs	Edison PMSA, NJ	Y	38920 FQ	45390 MW	51890 TQ	USBLS	5/07
Government Programs	Newark-Union PMSA, NJ-PA	Y	41470 FQ	46170 MW	50920 TQ	USBLS	5/07
Government Programs	New Mexico	Y	28730 FQ	37270 MW	45090 TQ	USBLS	5/07
Government Programs	Albuquerque MSA, NM	Y	37210 FQ	43320 MW	47780 TQ	USBLS	5/07
Government Programs	New York	Y	32380 FQ	39650 MW	47700 TQ	USBLS	5/07
Government Programs	Albany-Schenectady-Troy MSA, NY	Y	33690 FQ	37880 MW	42520 TQ	USBLS	5/07
Government Programs	Buffalo-Niagara Falls MSA, NY	Y	40430 FQ	44410 MW	48500 TQ	USBLS	5/07
Government Programs	New York-Northern New Jersey-Long Island MSA, NY-NJ-PA	Y	32160 FQ	40970 MW	49650 TQ	USBLS	5/07
Government Programs	North Carolina	Y	27380 FQ	30870 MW	36210 TQ	USBLS	5/07
Government Programs	Charlotte-Gastonia-Concord MSA, NC-SC	Y	30040 FQ	33740 MW	38240 TQ	USBLS	5/07
Government Programs	Raleigh-Cary MSA, NC	Y	27920 FQ	31750 MW	37670 TQ	USBLS	5/07
Government Programs	North Dakota	Y	27070 FQ	32880 MW	38660 TQ	USBLS	5/07
Government Programs	Bismarck MSA, ND	Y	30940 FQ	35600 MW	40600 TQ	USBLS	5/07
Government Programs	Fargo MSA, ND-MN	Y	35540 FQ	40550 MW	45050 TQ	USBLS	5/07
Government Programs	Grand Forks MSA, ND-MN	Y	27430 FQ	31330 MW	37170 TQ	USBLS	5/07
Government Programs	Ohio	Y	31540 FQ	38540 MW	45600 TQ	USBLS	5/07
Government Programs	Cleveland-Elyria-Mentor MSA, OH	Y	36170 FQ	42850 MW	48130 TQ	USBLS	5/07
Government Programs	Dayton MSA, OH	Y	31040 FQ	36540 MW	44070 TQ	USBLS	5/07
Government Programs	Oklahoma	Y	25950 FQ	32080 MW	39020 TQ	USBLS	5/07
Government Programs	Oklahoma City MSA, OK	Y	21650 FQ	29080 MW	35710 TQ	USBLS	5/07
Government Programs	Tulsa MSA, OK	Y	24540 FQ	33620 MW	41930 TQ	USBLS	5/07
Government Programs	Oregon	H	14.18 FQ	16.97 MW	19.86 TQ	ORBLS	5/08
Government Programs	Portland-Vancouver-Beaverton MSA, OR-WA	Y	31950 FQ	37690 MW	44790 TQ	USBLS	5/07

Eligibility Interviewer

Occupation/Type/Industry	Location	Per	Low	Mid	High	Source	Date
Eligibility Interviewer							
Government Programs	Philadelphia-Camden-Wilmington MSA, PA-NJ-DE-MD	Y	37980 FQ	44350 MW	51040 TQ	USBLS	5/07
Government Programs	Rhode Island	Y	43290 FQ	50740 MW	58110 TQ	USBLS	5/07
Government Programs	Providence-Fall River-Warwick MSA, RI-MA	Y	42810 FQ	50390 MW	57980 TQ	USBLS	5/07
Government Programs	South Carolina	Y	27540 FQ	33850 MW	41480 TQ	USBLS	5/07
Government Programs	Charleston-North Charleston MSA, SC	Y	25010 FQ	30680 MW	40770 TQ	USBLS	5/07
Government Programs	South Dakota	Y	27019 FQ	30416 MW	34511 TQ	SDBLS	7/08-9/08
Government Programs	Tennessee	Y	26720 FQ	30700 MW	38660 TQ	USBLS	5/07
Government Programs	Johnson City MSA, TN	Y	26660 FQ	29840 MW	34370 TQ	USBLS	5/07
Government Programs	Kingsport-Bristol-Bristol MSA, TN-VA	Y	25870 FQ	29800 MW	36520 TQ	USBLS	5/07
Government Programs	Memphis MSA, TN-MS-AR	Y	26600 FQ	30920 MW	41440 TQ	USBLS	5/07
Government Programs	Nashville-Davidson-Murfreesboro MSA, TN	Y	26880 FQ	32440 MW	43400 TQ	USBLS	5/07
Government Programs	Texas	Y	28520 FQ	38750 MW	46630 TQ	USBLS	5/07
Government Programs	Austin-Round Rock MSA, TX	Y	35570 FQ	43170 MW	48580 TQ	USBLS	5/07
Government Programs	Corpus Christi MSA, TX	Y	24810 FQ	32500 MW	48900 TQ	USBLS	5/07
Government Programs	Dallas-Fort Worth-Arlington MSA, TX	Y	33760 FQ	43130 MW	48290 TQ	USBLS	5/07
Government Programs	El Paso MSA, TX	Y	23920 FQ	28850 MW	35980 TQ	USBLS	5/07
Government Programs	Houston-Sugar Land-Baytown MSA, TX	Y	32170 FQ	39090 MW	47860 TQ	USBLS	5/07
Government Programs	San Antonio MSA, TX	Y	26520 FQ	40930 MW	59230 TQ	USBLS	5/07
Government Programs	Utah	Y	34120 FQ	40450 MW	46530 TQ	USBLS	5/07
Government Programs	Salt Lake City MSA, UT	Y	31410 FQ	35520 MW	39420 TQ	USBLS	5/07
Government Programs	Vermont	Y	35480 FQ	38350 MW	41310 TQ	USBLS	5/07
Government Programs	Burlington-South Burlington MSA, VT	Y	35710 FQ	38340 MW	40980 TQ	USBLS	5/07
Government Programs	Virginia	Y	30330 FQ	37100 MW	45740 TQ	USBLS	5/07
Government Programs	Richmond MSA, VA	Y	30310 FQ	37130 MW	43870 TQ	USBLS	5/07
Government Programs	Virginia Beach-Norfolk-Newport News MSA, VA-NC	Y	30900 FQ	37220 MW	44980 TQ	USBLS	5/07
Government Programs	Washington	H	18.17 FQ	21.25 MW	23.46 TQ	WABLS	3/08
Government Programs	Seattle-Tacoma-Bellevue MSA, WA	Y	37430 FQ	43730 MW	48420 TQ	USBLS	5/07
Government Programs	West Virginia	Y	23431 FQ	27801 MW	32117 TQ	WVBLS	7/08-9/08
Government Programs	Charleston MSA, WV	Y	22830 FQ	27130 MW	31270 TQ	USBLS	5/07
Government Programs	Huntington-Ashland MSA, WV-KY-OH	Y	23520 FQ	29400 MW	37870 TQ	USBLS	5/07
Government Programs	Wisconsin	Y	31020 FQ	36780 MW	43630 TQ	USBLS	5/07
Government Programs	Milwaukee-Waukesha-West Allis MSA, WI	Y	30800 FQ	37320 MW	45810 TQ	USBLS	5/07
Government Programs	Wyoming	Y	33647 FQ	39892 MW	47067 TQ	WYBLS	9/08
Government Programs	Puerto Rico	Y	20540 FQ	28940 MW	41830 TQ	USBLS	5/07
Government Programs	San Juan-Caguas-Guaynabo MSA, PR	Y	17920 FQ	24010 MW	30640 TQ	USBLS	5/07
Embalmer	Alabama	Y	22170 FQ	31400 MW	39150 TQ	USBLS	5/07
	Arizona	Y	28650 FQ	36720 MW	48460 TQ	USBLS	5/07
	Phoenix-Mesa-Scottsdale MSA, AZ	Y	29050 FQ	37860 MW	50700 TQ	USBLS	5/07
	Arkansas	Y	26630 FQ	39520 MW	47850 TQ	USBLS	5/07
	California	H	15.52 FQ	19.79 MW	23.79 TQ	CABLS	1/08-3/08
	Los Angeles-Long Beach-Glendale PMSA, CA	H	14.30 FQ	17.30 MW	21.44 TQ	CABLS	1/08-3/08
	Oakland-Fremont-Hayward MSA, CA	H	11.84 FQ	20.14 MW	22.83 TQ	CABLS	1/08-3/08
	Riverside-San Bernardino-Ontario MSA, CA	H	17.03 FQ	19.10 MW	21.07 TQ	CABLS	1/08-3/08
	Sacramento-Arden Arcade-Roseville MSA, CA	H	20.40 FQ	22.86 MW	25.45 TQ	CABLS	1/08-3/08
	San Diego-Carlsbad-San Marcos MSA, CA	H	15.65 FQ	20.41 MW	23.96 TQ	CABLS	1/08-3/08
	San Francisco-San Mateo-Redwood PMSA, CA	H	20.56 FQ	23.02 MW	28.97 TQ	CABLS	1/08-3/08
	Santa Ana-Anaheim-Irvine PMSA, CA	Y	38650 FQ	52470 MW	59170 TQ	USBLS	5/07
	Colorado	Y	26470 FQ	30620 MW	40240 TQ	USBLS	5/07

AE   Average entry wage   AW   Average wage paid   FQ   First quartile wage   LO   Lowest wage paid   MTC   Median total compensation   TCC   Total cash compensation
AER   Average entry range   AWR   Average wage range   H   Hourly   LR   Low end range   MW   Median wage paid   TQ   Third quartile wage
AEX   Average experienced wage   AXR   Average experienced range   HI   Highest wage paid   M   Monthly   MWR   Median wage range   W   Weekly
ATC   Average total compensation D   Daily   HR   High end range   MCC   Median cash compensation S   See annotated source   Y   Yearly

524

Occupation/Type/Industry	Location	Per	Low	Mid	High	Source	Date
Embalmer	Connecticut	H	16.00 AE	25.16 MW		CTBLS	1/08-3/08
	Hartford-West Hartford-East Hartford MSA, CT	Y	30510 FQ	39400 MW	50610 TQ	USBLS	5/07
	Washington-Arlington-Alexandria MSA, DC-VA-MD-WV	Y	32990 FQ	40780 MW	51640 TQ	USBLS	5/07
	Florida	Y	28650 FQ	38640 MW	47180 TQ	USBLS	5/07
	Fort Lauderdale-Pompano Beach-Deerfield Beach PMSA, FL	Y	14860 FQ	48090 MW	54190 TQ	USBLS	5/07
	Miami-Fort Lauderdale-Miami Beach MSA, FL	Y	30360 FQ	38740 MW	50110 TQ	USBLS	5/07
	Tampa-St. Petersburg-Clearwater MSA, FL	Y	27350 FQ	39250 MW	44930 TQ	USBLS	5/07
	Illinois	Y	34220 FQ	39610 MW	56350 TQ	USBLS	5/07
	Chicago-Naperville-Joliet MSA, IL-IN-WI	Y	36690 FQ	52480 MW	69580 TQ	USBLS	5/07
	Indiana	Y	31880 FQ	43310 MW	50280 TQ	USBLS	5/07
	Kansas	Y	19570 FQ	24180 MW	32740 TQ	USBLS	5/07
	Kentucky	Y	27861 FQ	35635 MW	45498 TQ	KYBLS	2008
	Louisville-Jefferson County MSA, KY-IN	Y	38220 FQ	42960 MW	46340 TQ	USBLS	5/07
	Louisiana	H	12.40 FQ	16.57 MW	20.03 TQ	LABLS	1/08-3/08
	New Orleans-Metairie-Kenner MSA, LA	Y	21060 FQ	23390 MW	35350 TQ	USBLS	5/07
	Maryland	Y		36450 MW		MDBLS	3/08
	Baltimore-Towson MSA, MD	Y	28650 FQ	38850 MW	56130 TQ	USBLS	5/07
	Massachusetts	Y	37940 FQ	48060 MW	64150 TQ	USBLS	5/07
	Boston-Cambridge-Quincy NECTA, MA	Y	36110 FQ	52220 MW	67460 TQ	USBLS	5/07
	Michigan	Y	29180 FQ	37620 MW	46110 TQ	USBLS	5/07
	Minnesota	Y		50000 AW		MMTHLY	2008
	Mississippi	Y	27270 FQ	32020 MW	36710 TQ	USBLS	5/07
	Jackson MSA, MS	Y	23740 FQ	29640 MW	35770 TQ	USBLS	5/07
	Missouri	Y	33870 FQ	41390 MW	50590 TQ	USBLS	5/07
	Kansas City MSA, MO-KS	Y	19050 FQ	33110 MW	38810 TQ	USBLS	5/07
	St. Louis MSA, MO-IL	Y	36640 FQ	47640 MW	56090 TQ	USBLS	5/07
	New Jersey	Y	30520 FQ	49820 MW	68910 TQ	USBLS	5/07
	New York	Y	34620 FQ	44260 MW	50890 TQ	USBLS	5/07
	Albany-Schenectady-Troy MSA, NY	Y	44430 FQ	47560 MW	50560 TQ	USBLS	5/07
	Nassau-Suffolk PMSA, NY	Y	42330 FQ	45920 MW	49580 TQ	USBLS	5/07
	New York-Northern New Jersey-Long Island MSA, NY-NJ-PA	Y	34940 FQ	45520 MW	52830 TQ	USBLS	5/07
	North Carolina	Y	30170 FQ	41990 MW	52330 TQ	USBLS	5/07
	Ohio	Y	30180 FQ	36560 MW	49500 TQ	USBLS	5/07
	Cincinnati-Middletown MSA, OH-KY-IN	Y	27360 FQ	33730 MW	44920 TQ	USBLS	5/07
	Cleveland-Elyria-Mentor MSA, OH	Y	31590 FQ	35900 MW	61080 TQ	USBLS	5/07
	Oklahoma	Y	18380 FQ	26950 MW	38230 TQ	USBLS	5/07
	Oklahoma City MSA, OK	Y	18690 FQ	21920 MW	27670 TQ	USBLS	5/07
	Pennsylvania	Y	25990 FQ	31970 MW	39610 TQ	USBLS	5/07
	Pittsburgh MSA, PA	Y	25350 FQ	30430 MW	38060 TQ	USBLS	5/07
	Rhode Island	Y	40730 FQ	54000 MW	64220 TQ	USBLS	5/07
	Providence-Fall River-Warwick MSA, RI-MA	Y	40370 FQ	53010 MW	63830 TQ	USBLS	5/07
	South Carolina	Y	28950 FQ	38650 MW	47370 TQ	USBLS	5/07
	Columbia MSA, SC	Y	23560 FQ	31000 MW	37680 TQ	USBLS	5/07
	Tennessee	Y	28770 FQ	33640 MW	44560 TQ	USBLS	5/07
	Texas	Y	27200 FQ	31850 MW	37890 TQ	USBLS	5/07
	Austin-Round Rock MSA, TX	Y	31480 FQ	35030 MW	38360 TQ	USBLS	5/07
	Dallas-Fort Worth-Arlington MSA, TX	Y	28900 FQ	32650 MW	37360 TQ	USBLS	5/07
	Houston-Sugar Land-Baytown MSA, TX	Y	27460 FQ	30390 MW	35470 TQ	USBLS	5/07
	San Antonio MSA, TX	Y	15780 FQ	32330 MW	37600 TQ	USBLS	5/07
	Utah	Y	33240 FQ	39810 MW	55840 TQ	USBLS	5/07
	Virginia	Y	32960 FQ	40420 MW	51960 TQ	USBLS	5/07
	Richmond MSA, VA	Y	36640 FQ	53900 MW	62170 TQ	USBLS	5/07
	Roanoke MSA, VA	Y	31890 FQ	37650 MW	45360 TQ	USBLS	5/07

AE	Average entry wage	AW	Average wage paid	FQ	First quartile wage
AER	Average entry range	AWR	Average wage range	H	Hourly
AEX	Average experienced wage	AXR	Average experienced range	HI	Highest wage paid
ATC	Average total compensation	D	Daily	HR	High end range

LO	Lowest wage paid	MTC	Median total compensation	TCC	Total cash compensation
LR	Low end range	MW	Median wage paid	TQ	Third quartile wage
M	Monthly	MWR	Median wage range	W	Weekly
MCC	Median cash compensation	S	See annotated source	Y	Yearly

Occupation/Type/Industry	Location	Per	Low	Mid	High	Source	Date
Embalmer	Virginia Beach-Norfolk-Newport News MSA, VA-NC	Y	29740 FQ	42290 MW	57850 TQ	USBLS	5/07
	Washington	H	14.67 FQ	19.39 MW	24.99 TQ	WABLS	3/08
	Seattle-Tacoma-Bellevue MSA, WA	Y	28430 FQ	37010 MW	46790 TQ	USBLS	5/07
	West Virginia	Y	32622 FQ	39254 MW	51640 TQ	WVBLS	7/08-9/08
	Wisconsin	Y	32720 FQ	35690 MW	38900 TQ	USBLS	5/07
	Wyoming	Y	22478 FQ	32837 MW	37938 TQ	WYBLS	9/08
Emergency Management Coordinator							
Municipal Government	Gresham, OR	Y	61068 LO		79380 HI	GOSS01	7/1/08
Emergency Management Director	Savannah, GA	Y	58732 LO		88232 HI	GACTY01	2008
	Montague, MA	Y			5490 HI	FRCOG	2009
Emergency Management Service Coordinator							
Fire Department	Orange, MA	Y			1000 HI	FRCOG	2009
Emergency Management Specialist	Alabama	Y	33560 FQ	41850 MW	58850 TQ	USBLS	5/07
	Birmingham-Hoover MSA, AL	Y	36110 FQ	46060 MW	73180 TQ	USBLS	5/07
	Arizona	Y	44940 FQ	54560 MW	75720 TQ	USBLS	5/07
	Phoenix-Mesa-Scottsdale MSA, AZ	Y	46550 FQ	60810 MW	81070 TQ	USBLS	5/07
	Arkansas	Y	24620 FQ	33840 MW	47380 TQ	USBLS	5/07
	Little Rock-North Little Rock MSA, AR	Y	37070 FQ	44590 MW	54850 TQ	USBLS	5/07
	California	H	27.98 FQ	34.50 MW	41.80 TQ	CABLS	1/08-3/08
	Los Angeles-Long Beach-Glendale PMSA, CA	H	30.07 FQ	39.45 MW	47.82 TQ	CABLS	1/08-3/08
	Oakland-Fremont-Hayward MSA, CA	H	34.23 FQ	39.73 MW	48.07 TQ	CABLS	1/08-3/08
	Riverside-San Bernardino-Ontario MSA, CA	H	26.57 FQ	30.55 MW	34.93 TQ	CABLS	1/08-3/08
	Sacramento-Arden Arcade-Roseville MSA, CA	H	25.76 FQ	30.29 MW	36.03 TQ	CABLS	1/08-3/08
	San Diego-Carlsbad-San Marcos MSA, CA	H	29.80 FQ	33.14 MW	36.50 TQ	CABLS	1/08-3/08
	San Francisco-San Mateo-Redwood PMSA, CA	H	32.33 FQ	37.42 MW	42.46 TQ	CABLS	1/08-3/08
	San Jose-Sunnyvale-Santa Clara MSA, CA	H	35.67 FQ	43.55 MW	51.32 TQ	CABLS	1/08-3/08
	Santa Ana-Anaheim-Irvine PMSA, CA	Y	57000 FQ	65120 MW	85170 TQ	USBLS	5/07
	Colorado	Y	40920 FQ	53550 MW	69330 TQ	USBLS	5/07
	Denver-Aurora MSA, CO	Y	42980 FQ	54440 MW	72540 TQ	USBLS	5/07
	Connecticut	H	20.60 AE	30.45 MW		CTBLS	1/08-3/08
	Bridgeport-Stamford-Norwalk MSA, CT	Y	49830 FQ	58790 MW	68260 TQ	USBLS	5/07
	Hartford-West Hartford-East Hartford MSA, CT	Y	54070 FQ	60600 MW	69460 TQ	USBLS	5/07
	Wilmington PMSA, DE-MD-NJ	Y	35320 FQ	47100 MW	60860 TQ	USBLS	5/07
	District of Columbia	Y	50690 FQ	62380 MW	74680 TQ	USBLS	5/07
	Washington-Arlington-Alexandria MSA, DC-VA-MD-WV	Y	49310 FQ	63320 MW	82150 TQ	USBLS	5/07
	Florida	Y	37870 FQ	49870 MW	68090 TQ	USBLS	5/07
	Miami-Fort Lauderdale-Miami Beach MSA, FL	Y	32380 FQ	43880 MW	65830 TQ	USBLS	5/07
	Orlando-Kissimmee MSA, FL	Y	54750 FQ	64500 MW	71420 TQ	USBLS	5/07
	West Palm Beach-Boca Raton-Boynton Beach PMSA, FL	Y	29300 FQ	35300 MW	43980 TQ	USBLS	5/07
	Georgia	Y	33370 FQ	44850 MW	57970 TQ	USBLS	5/07
	Atlanta-Sandy Springs-Marietta MSA, GA	Y	45620 FQ	55280 MW	65990 TQ	USBLS	5/07
	Augusta-Richmond County MSA, GA-SC	Y	37930 FQ	48160 MW	68820 TQ	USBLS	5/07
	Idaho	Y	44320 FQ	54450 MW	61370 TQ	USBLS	5/07

AE Average entry wage	**AW** Average wage paid	**FQ** First quartile wage	**LO** Lowest wage paid	**MTC** Median total compensation	**TCC** Total cash compensation
AER Average entry range	**AWR** Average wage range	**H** Hourly	**LR** Low end range	**MW** Median wage paid	**TQ** Third quartile wage
AEX Average experienced wage	**AXR** Average experienced range	**HI** Highest wage paid	**M** Monthly	**MWR** Median wage range	**W** Weekly
ATC Average total compensation	**D** Daily	**HR** High end range	**MCC** Median cash compensation	**S** See annotated source	**Y** Yearly

Occupation/Type/Industry	Location	Per	Low	Mid	High	Source	Date
Emergency Management Specialist	Boise City-Nampa MSA, ID	Y	45640 FQ	54600 MW	64520 TQ	USBLS	5/07
	Illinois	Y	15060 FQ	33520 MW	50430 TQ	USBLS	5/07
	Chicago-Naperville-Joliet MSA, IL-IN-WI	Y	30650 FQ	40110 MW	55730 TQ	USBLS	5/07
	Indiana	Y	26280 FQ	34980 MW	44400 TQ	USBLS	5/07
	Indianapolis-Carmel MSA, IN	Y	29960 FQ	45550 MW	58990 TQ	USBLS	5/07
	Iowa	Y	25340 FQ	36620 MW	47800 TQ	USBLS	5/07
	Des Moines-West Des Moines MSA, IA	Y	22430 FQ	25010 MW	50490 TQ	USBLS	5/07
	Kansas	Y	29420 FQ	39280 MW	51540 TQ	USBLS	5/07
	Kentucky	Y	29916 FQ	36594 MW	47737 TQ	KYBLS	2008
	Louisiana	H	17.53 FQ	23.31 MW	27.33 TQ	LABLS	1/08-3/08
	Maine	Y	34620 FQ	41790 MW	60970 TQ	USBLS	5/07
	Portland-South Portland-Biddeford MSA, ME	Y	38710 FQ	46280 MW	60900 TQ	USBLS	5/07
	Maryland	Y		58875 MW		MDBLS	3/08
	Baltimore-Towson MSA, MD	Y	44120 FQ	55820 MW	64650 TQ	USBLS	5/07
	Bethesda-Gaithersburg-Frederick PMSA, MD	Y	56110 FQ	67850 MW	94790 TQ	USBLS	5/07
	Massachusetts	Y	47260 FQ	62150 MW	81690 TQ	USBLS	5/07
	Boston-Cambridge-Quincy NECTA, MA	Y	47860 FQ	63760 MW	83030 TQ	USBLS	5/07
	Michigan	Y	43310 FQ	52580 MW	68830 TQ	USBLS	5/07
	Detroit-Warren-Livonia MSA, MI	Y	47980 FQ	59000 MW	75740 TQ	USBLS	5/07
	Warren-Troy-Farmington Hills PMSA, MI	Y	40860 FQ	67770 MW	96840 TQ	USBLS	5/07
	Minnesota	Y	45313 FQ	52977 MW	75571 TQ	MNBLS	10/08-12/08
	Duluth-Superior MSA, MN-WI	Y	46606 FQ	53300 MW	84173 TQ	MNBLS	10/08-12/08
	Minneapolis-Saint Paul MSA, MN-WI	Y	50370 FQ	65249 MW	86519 TQ	MNBLS	10/08-12/08
	Mississippi	Y	24390 FQ	33460 MW	39140 TQ	USBLS	5/07
	Jackson MSA, MS	Y	33270 FQ	36360 MW	39450 TQ	USBLS	5/07
	Missouri	Y	35150 FQ	43020 MW	55150 TQ	USBLS	5/07
	Kansas City MSA, MO-KS	Y	45240 FQ	57830 MW	72020 TQ	USBLS	5/07
	St. Louis MSA, MO-IL	Y	34930 FQ	42310 MW	53830 TQ	USBLS	5/07
	Montana	Y	28360 FQ	36070 MW	45120 TQ	USBLS	5/07
	Nebraska	Y	30640 FQ	37450 MW	49570 TQ	USBLS	5/07
	Nevada	H	19.08 FQ	25.08 MW	31.58 TQ	NVBLS	5/08
	Las Vegas-Paradise MSA, NV	H	18.32 FQ	21.02 MW	31.43 TQ	NVBLS	5/08
	New Hampshire	H	13.79 AE	21.95 MW	25.40 AEX	NHBLS	6/08
	New Jersey	Y	35030 FQ	49140 MW	64350 TQ	USBLS	5/07
	Camden PMSA, NJ	Y	40080 FQ	53730 MW	64890 TQ	USBLS	5/07
	Edison PMSA, NJ	Y	35540 FQ	47780 MW	62750 TQ	USBLS	5/07
	Newark-Union PMSA, NJ-PA	Y	36440 FQ	50630 MW	64740 TQ	USBLS	5/07
	New Mexico	Y	35390 FQ	50140 MW	65010 TQ	USBLS	5/07
	New York	Y	44710 FQ	53020 MW	66610 TQ	USBLS	5/07
	Buffalo-Niagara Falls MSA, NY	Y	42990 FQ	52350 MW	65760 TQ	USBLS	5/07
	New York-Northern New Jersey-Long Island MSA, NY-NJ-PA	Y	38800 FQ	51000 MW	64880 TQ	USBLS	5/07
	North Carolina	Y	35920 FQ	42130 MW	52370 TQ	USBLS	5/07
	Charlotte-Gastonia-Concord MSA, NC-SC	Y	48590 FQ	61690 MW	76820 TQ	USBLS	5/07
	Raleigh-Cary MSA, NC	Y	32010 FQ	36970 MW	42570 TQ	USBLS	5/07
	North Dakota	Y	28940 FQ	40580 MW	50060 TQ	USBLS	5/07
	Ohio	Y	43000 FQ	55500 MW	68670 TQ	USBLS	5/07
	Cincinnati-Middletown MSA, OH-KY-IN	Y	28260 FQ	41530 MW	49850 TQ	USBLS	5/07
	Columbus MSA, OH	Y	50160 FQ	60500 MW	71800 TQ	USBLS	5/07
	Oklahoma	Y	25810 FQ	39990 MW	60300 TQ	USBLS	5/07
	Tulsa MSA, OK	Y	42300 FQ	54720 MW	64330 TQ	USBLS	5/07
	Oregon	H	22.99 FQ	28.08 MW	36.78 TQ	ORBLS	5/08
	Portland-Vancouver-Beaverton MSA, OR-WA	Y	60970 FQ	73420 MW	87990 TQ	USBLS	5/07
	Pennsylvania	Y	32020 FQ	43310 MW	54060 TQ	USBLS	5/07
	Allentown-Bethlehem-Easton MSA, PA-NJ	Y	21510 FQ	36320 MW	51850 TQ	USBLS	5/07

AE	Average entry wage	**AW**	Average wage paid	**FQ**	First quartile wage	**LO**	Lowest wage paid	**MTC**	Median total compensation
AER	Average entry range	**AWR**	Average wage range	**H**	Hourly	**LR**	Low end range	**MW**	Median wage paid
AEX	Average experienced wage	**AXR**	Average experienced range	**HI**	Highest wage paid	**M**	Monthly	**MWR**	Median wage range
ATC	Average total compensation	**D**	Daily	**HR**	High end range	**MCC**	Median cash compensation	**S**	See annotated source

TCC	Total cash compensation
TQ	Third quartile wage
W	Weekly
Y	Yearly

Occupation/Type/Industry	Location	Per	Low	Mid	High	Source	Date
Emergency Management Specialist							
	Philadelphia-Camden-Wilmington MSA, PA-NJ-DE-MD	Y	34310 FQ	48860 MW	64290 TQ	USBLS	5/07
	Pittsburgh MSA, PA	Y	30670 FQ	46760 MW	63780 TQ	USBLS	5/07
	Rhode Island	Y	46290 FQ	55850 MW	67650 TQ	USBLS	5/07
	Providence-Fall River-Warwick MSA, RI-MA	Y	47360 FQ	57700 MW	69800 TQ	USBLS	5/07
	South Carolina	Y	38710 FQ	47530 MW	62740 TQ	USBLS	5/07
	Charleston-North Charleston MSA, SC	Y	27950 FQ	51200 MW	76650 TQ	USBLS	5/07
	Columbia MSA, SC	Y	35250 FQ	39430 MW	45050 TQ	USBLS	5/07
	South Dakota	Y	29326 FQ	33755 MW	43829 TQ	SDBLS	7/08-9/08
	Sioux Falls MSA, SD	Y	40736 FQ	46436 MW	53826 TQ	SDBLS	7/08-9/08
	Tennessee	Y	35400 FQ	53310 MW	74350 TQ	USBLS	5/07
	Nashville-Davidson-Murfreesboro MSA, TN	Y	34870 FQ	48970 MW	64190 TQ	USBLS	5/07
	Texas	Y	33620 FQ	46870 MW	64030 TQ	USBLS	5/07
	Dallas-Fort Worth-Arlington MSA, TX	Y	45810 FQ	58500 MW	67430 TQ	USBLS	5/07
	Houston-Sugar Land-Baytown MSA, TX	Y	44580 FQ	57210 MW	73470 TQ	USBLS	5/07
	Utah	Y	30890 FQ	42460 MW	55910 TQ	USBLS	5/07
	Salt Lake City MSA, UT	Y	30920 FQ	41070 MW	52270 TQ	USBLS	5/07
	Vermont	Y	44210 FQ	52390 MW	63970 TQ	USBLS	5/07
	Virginia	Y	44540 FQ	60000 MW	78120 TQ	USBLS	5/07
	Richmond MSA, VA	Y	53540 FQ	68580 MW	80060 TQ	USBLS	5/07
	Virginia Beach-Norfolk-Newport News MSA, VA-NC	Y	44310 FQ	55440 MW	76160 TQ	USBLS	5/07
	Washington	H	22.11 FQ	27.88 MW	32.84 TQ	WABLS	3/08
	Seattle-Tacoma-Bellevue MSA, WA	Y	43730 FQ	56000 MW	65640 TQ	USBLS	5/07
	West Virginia	Y	26841 FQ	31949 MW	40085 TQ	WVBLS	7/08-9/08
	Charleston MSA, WV	Y	27530 FQ	31240 MW	37500 TQ	USBLS	5/07
	Wisconsin	Y	42280 FQ	52490 MW	61540 TQ	USBLS	5/07
	Milwaukee-Waukesha-West Allis MSA, WI	Y	42000 FQ	56930 MW	64650 TQ	USBLS	5/07
	Wyoming	Y	32019 FQ	44951 MW	54138 TQ	WYBLS	9/08
	Puerto Rico	Y	15600 FQ	21870 MW	29970 TQ	USBLS	5/07
	San Juan-Caguas-Guaynabo MSA, PR	Y	15540 FQ	22630 MW	32180 TQ	USBLS	5/07
Emergency Management Technician	Whately, MA	H			11.77 HI	FRCOG	2009
Emergency Management Technician Director	Whately, MA	Y			3177 HI	FRCOG	2009
Emergency Medical Technician							
Basic	United States	Y		20280-35556 MW		JEMS	2008
Intermediate	United States	Y		23978-31114 MW		JEMS	2008
Emergency Medical Technician and Paramedic							
	Alabama	Y	20430 FQ	24860 MW	31290 TQ	USBLS	5/07
	Birmingham-Hoover MSA, AL	Y	24140 FQ	28840 MW	35330 TQ	USBLS	5/07
	Alaska	Y	44500 FQ	51910 MW	58210 TQ	USBLS	5/07
	Arizona	Y	21630 FQ	24300 MW	30970 TQ	USBLS	5/07
	Phoenix-Mesa-Scottsdale MSA, AZ	Y	21610 FQ	23930 MW	29870 TQ	USBLS	5/07
	Tucson MSA, AZ	Y	23480 FQ	33830 MW	44500 TQ	USBLS	5/07
	Arkansas	Y	17110 FQ	22840 MW	30430 TQ	USBLS	5/07
	Fayetteville-Springdale-Rogers MSA, AR-MO	Y	22040 FQ	26160 MW	30960 TQ	USBLS	5/07
	Little Rock-North Little Rock MSA, AR	Y	14730 FQ	16270 MW	23490 TQ	USBLS	5/07
	California	H	10.93 FQ	13.13 MW	17.86 TQ	CABLS	1/08-3/08
	Los Angeles-Long Beach-Glendale PMSA, CA	H	10.89 FQ	12.59 MW	16.13 TQ	CABLS	1/08-3/08

AE	Average entry wage	AW	Average wage paid	FQ	First quartile wage	LO Lowest wage paid	MTC Median total compensation	TCC Total cash compensation
AER	Average entry range	AWR	Average wage range	H	Hourly	LR Low end range	MW Median wage paid	TQ Third quartile wage
AEX	Average experienced wage	AXR	Average experienced range	HI	Highest wage paid	M Monthly	MWR Median wage range	W Weekly
ATC	Average total compensation	D	Daily	HR	High end range	MCC Median cash compensation	S See annotated source	Y Yearly

Occupation/Type/Industry	Location	Per	Low	Mid	High	Source	Date
Emergency Medical Technician and Paramedic							
	Oakland-Fremont-Hayward MSA, CA	H	10.51 FQ	11.48 MW	14.10 TQ	CABLS	1/08-3/08
	Riverside-San Bernardino-Ontario MSA, CA	H	11.63 FQ	13.72 MW	16.39 TQ	CABLS	1/08-3/08
	Sacramento-Arden Arcade-Roseville MSA, CA	H	10.55 FQ	12.00 MW	16.99 TQ	CABLS	1/08-3/08
	San Diego-Carlsbad-San Marcos MSA, CA	H	11.87 FQ	14.56 MW	19.70 TQ	CABLS	1/08-3/08
	San Francisco-San Mateo-Redwood PMSA, CA	H	15.05 FQ	21.41 MW	26.14 TQ	CABLS	1/08-3/08
	San Jose-Sunnyvale-Santa Clara MSA, CA	H	10.73 FQ	11.94 MW	16.09 TQ	CABLS	1/08-3/08
	Santa Ana-Anaheim-Irvine PMSA, CA	Y	21810 FQ	27390 MW	33010 TQ	USBLS	5/07
	Santa Rosa-Petaluma MSA, CA	H	13.09 FQ	19.29 MW	23.62 TQ	CABLS	1/08-3/08
	Colorado	Y	24460 FQ	31210 MW	42140 TQ	USBLS	5/07
	Denver-Aurora MSA, CO	Y	22890 FQ	30410 MW	45880 TQ	USBLS	5/07
	Connecticut	H	13.15 AE	16.93 MW		CTBLS	1/08-3/08
	Bridgeport-Stamford-Norwalk MSA, CT	Y	28550 FQ	36230 MW	46300 TQ	USBLS	5/07
	Hartford-West Hartford-East Hartford MSA, CT	Y	26840 FQ	31380 MW	40640 TQ	USBLS	5/07
	New Haven MSA, CT	Y	27860 FQ	32440 MW	40400 TQ	USBLS	5/07
	Delaware	Y	27210 FQ	32890 MW	43730 TQ	USBLS	5/07
	Wilmington PMSA, DE-MD-NJ	Y	30120 FQ	35940 MW	46410 TQ	USBLS	5/07
	District of Columbia	Y	32820 FQ	44770 MW	50350 TQ	USBLS	5/07
	Washington-Arlington-Alexandria MSA, DC-VA-MD-WV	Y	31630 FQ	43750 MW	51780 TQ	USBLS	5/07
	Florida	Y	24450 FQ	29170 MW	35050 TQ	USBLS	5/07
	Fort Lauderdale-Pompano Beach-Deerfield Beach PMSA, FL	Y	23840 FQ	28290 MW	31680 TQ	USBLS	5/07
	Jacksonville MSA, FL	Y	27790 FQ	32320 MW	35850 TQ	USBLS	5/07
	Miami-Fort Lauderdale-Miami Beach MSA, FL	Y	25580 FQ	29220 MW	33410 TQ	USBLS	5/07
	Orlando-Kissimmee MSA, FL	Y	25870 FQ	29410 MW	34150 TQ	USBLS	5/07
	Pensacola-Ferry Pass-Brent MSA, FL	Y	25430 FQ	31280 MW	41140 TQ	USBLS	5/07
	Tampa-St. Petersburg-Clearwater MSA, FL	Y	23500 FQ	28590 MW	34610 TQ	USBLS	5/07
	West Palm Beach-Boca Raton-Boynton Beach PMSA, FL	Y	27040 FQ	30590 MW	37470 TQ	USBLS	5/07
	Georgia	Y	23030 FQ	29400 MW	36930 TQ	USBLS	5/07
	Atlanta-Sandy Springs-Marietta MSA, GA	Y	27760 FQ	34970 MW	40390 TQ	USBLS	5/07
	Hawaii	Y	35070 FQ	40940 MW	47740 TQ	USBLS	5/07
	Honolulu MSA, HI	Y	34960 FQ	40790 MW	47830 TQ	USBLS	5/07
	Idaho	Y	25390 FQ	35680 MW	40930 TQ	USBLS	5/07
	Boise City-Nampa MSA, ID	Y	34600 FQ	37850 MW	41040 TQ	USBLS	5/07
	Lewiston MSA, ID-WA	Y	34580 FQ	50320 MW	61170 TQ	USBLS	5/07
	Illinois	Y	21700 FQ	28150 MW	39900 TQ	USBLS	5/07
	Champaign-Urbana MSA, IL	Y	22490 FQ	26260 MW	35170 TQ	USBLS	5/07
	Chicago-Naperville-Joliet MSA, IL-IN-WI	Y	24100 FQ	30390 MW	42430 TQ	USBLS	5/07
	Indiana	Y	22090 FQ	28130 MW	35680 TQ	USBLS	5/07
	Gary PMSA, IN	Y	22910 FQ	28460 MW	37010 TQ	USBLS	5/07
	Indianapolis-Carmel MSA, IN	Y	24060 FQ	32030 MW	37960 TQ	USBLS	5/07
	Terre Haute MSA, IN	Y	21230 FQ	24100 MW	31260 TQ	USBLS	5/07
	Iowa	Y	18810 FQ	25030 MW	31900 TQ	USBLS	5/07
	Des Moines-West Des Moines MSA, IA	Y	17840 FQ	24590 MW	33420 TQ	USBLS	5/07
	Iowa City MSA, IA	Y	23280 FQ	32120 MW	37920 TQ	USBLS	5/07
	Kansas	Y	18970 FQ	24610 MW	33050 TQ	USBLS	5/07
	Wichita MSA, KS	Y	28020 FQ	35580 MW	40010 TQ	USBLS	5/07
	Kentucky	Y	18878 FQ	25068 MW	32831 TQ	KYBLS	2008
	Louisville-Jefferson County MSA, KY-IN	Y	19450 FQ	26680 MW	33780 TQ	USBLS	5/07
	Louisiana	H	9.02 FQ	11.79 MW	14.37 TQ	LABLS	1/08-3/08
	Baton Rouge MSA, LA	Y	22630 FQ	29430 MW	38730 TQ	USBLS	5/07

AE	Average entry wage	AW	Average wage paid	FQ	First quartile wage	LO	Lowest wage paid	MTC	Median total compensation	TCC	Total cash compensation
AER	Average entry range	AWR	Average wage range	H	Hourly	LR	Low end range	MW	Median wage paid	TQ	Third quartile wage
AEX	Average experienced wage	AXR	Average experienced range	HI	Highest wage paid	M	Monthly	MWR	Median wage range	W	Weekly
ATC	Average total compensation	D	Daily	HR	High end range	MCC	Median cash compensation	S	See annotated source	Y	Yearly

Occupation/Type/Industry	Location	Per	Low	Mid	High	Source	Date
Emergency Medical Technician and Paramedic	New Orleans-Metairie-Kenner MSA, LA	Y	22770 FQ	29480 MW	39450 TQ	USBLS	5/07
	Maine	Y	21940 FQ	26590 MW	32610 TQ	USBLS	5/07
	Portland-South Portland-Biddeford MSA, ME	Y	22700 FQ	28410 MW	35850 TQ	USBLS	5/07
	Maryland	Y		40050 MW		MDBLS	3/08
	Baltimore-Towson MSA, MD	Y	28530 FQ	35410 MW	48300 TQ	USBLS	5/07
	Bethesda-Gaithersburg-Frederick PMSA, MD	Y	28990 FQ	38990 MW	51190 TQ	USBLS	5/07
	Salisbury MSA, MD	Y	27480 FQ	30960 MW	36530 TQ	USBLS	5/07
	Massachusetts	Y	28900 FQ	35260 MW	44120 TQ	USBLS	5/07
	Boston-Cambridge-Quincy NECTA, MA	Y	30080 FQ	37760 MW	47170 TQ	USBLS	5/07
	Worcester MSA, MA-CT	Y	27890 FQ	34590 MW	44020 TQ	USBLS	5/07
	Michigan	Y	22630 FQ	29050 MW	36330 TQ	USBLS	5/07
	Detroit-Warren-Livonia MSA, MI	Y	24620 FQ	31010 MW	37470 TQ	USBLS	5/07
	Grand Rapids-Wyoming MSA, MI	Y	21000 FQ	25110 MW	30890 TQ	USBLS	5/07
	Lansing-East Lansing MSA, MI	Y	23400 FQ	31230 MW	48200 TQ	USBLS	5/07
	Warren-Troy-Farmington Hills PMSA, MI	Y	24150 FQ	29170 MW	36540 TQ	USBLS	5/07
	Minnesota	Y	23152 FQ	29806 MW	37664 TQ	MNBLS	10/08-12/08
	Duluth-Superior MSA, MN-WI	Y	21646 FQ	27892 MW	34734 TQ	MNBLS	10/08-12/08
	Minneapolis-Saint Paul MSA, MN-WI	Y	28467 FQ	35571 MW	42026 TQ	MNBLS	10/08-12/08
	Mississippi	Y	19760 FQ	24430 MW	31890 TQ	USBLS	5/07
	Jackson MSA, MS	Y	12610 FQ	14510 MW	18130 TQ	USBLS	5/07
	Missouri	Y	21670 FQ	28590 MW	37820 TQ	USBLS	5/07
	Joplin MSA, MO	Y	20180 FQ	30190 MW	40540 TQ	USBLS	5/07
	Kansas City MSA, MO-KS	Y	23280 FQ	29180 MW	38120 TQ	USBLS	5/07
	St. Louis MSA, MO-IL	Y	23030 FQ	33890 MW	50190 TQ	USBLS	5/07
	Montana	Y	15600 FQ	22220 MW	29380 TQ	USBLS	5/07
	Billings MSA, MT	Y	13760 FQ	14720 MW	22800 TQ	USBLS	5/07
	Nebraska	Y	24170 FQ	29920 MW	35240 TQ	USBLS	5/07
	Omaha-Council Bluffs MSA, NE-IA	Y	23560 FQ	28470 MW	34780 TQ	USBLS	5/07
	Nevada	H	13.41 FQ	17.58 MW	28.28 TQ	NVBLS	5/08
	Las Vegas-Paradise MSA, NV	H	13.44 FQ	17.47 MW	26.64 TQ	NVBLS	5/08
	New Hampshire	H	12.64 AE	17.08 MW	20.17 AEX	NHBLS	6/08
	Nashua NECTA, NH-MA	Y	29190 FQ	32310 MW	45200 TQ	USBLS	5/07
	New Jersey	Y	26390 FQ	30310 MW	39470 TQ	USBLS	5/07
	Camden PMSA, NJ	Y	23600 FQ	27480 MW	33080 TQ	USBLS	5/07
	Edison PMSA, NJ	Y	27590 FQ	31070 MW	39570 TQ	USBLS	5/07
	Newark-Union PMSA, NJ-PA	Y	28730 FQ	33240 MW	45610 TQ	USBLS	5/07
	Ocean City MSA, NJ	Y	24080 FQ	27190 MW	31030 TQ	USBLS	5/07
	New Mexico	Y	22370 FQ	28010 MW	36500 TQ	USBLS	5/07
	Albuquerque MSA, NM	Y	22930 FQ	28230 MW	37020 TQ	USBLS	5/07
	New York	Y	27720 FQ	36120 MW	45740 TQ	USBLS	5/07
	Albany-Schenectady-Troy MSA, NY	Y	22980 FQ	27990 MW	34680 TQ	USBLS	5/07
	Binghamton MSA, NY	Y	20860 FQ	24630 MW	29330 TQ	USBLS	5/07
	Buffalo-Niagara Falls MSA, NY	Y	19230 FQ	24050 MW	32290 TQ	USBLS	5/07
	Nassau-Suffolk PMSA, NY	Y	28960 FQ	34530 MW	43960 TQ	USBLS	5/07
	New York-Northern New Jersey-Long Island MSA, NY-NJ-PA	Y	29680 FQ	37420 MW	47790 TQ	USBLS	5/07
	Syracuse MSA, NY	Y	22980 FQ	27250 MW	30910 TQ	USBLS	5/07
	North Carolina	Y	23530 FQ	28430 MW	34660 TQ	USBLS	5/07
	Asheville MSA, NC	Y	26480 FQ	31560 MW	36790 TQ	USBLS	5/07
	Charlotte-Gastonia-Concord MSA, NC-SC	Y	25360 FQ	30600 MW	38290 TQ	USBLS	5/07
	Raleigh-Cary MSA, NC	Y	22340 FQ	25340 MW	29620 TQ	USBLS	5/07
	North Dakota	Y	18790 FQ	24580 MW	32750 TQ	USBLS	5/07
	Ohio	Y	20590 FQ	25310 MW	32010 TQ	USBLS	5/07
	Cincinnati-Middletown MSA, OH-KY-IN	Y	21640 FQ	25930 MW	30610 TQ	USBLS	5/07
	Cleveland-Elyria-Mentor MSA, OH	Y	25280 FQ	30550 MW	36080 TQ	USBLS	5/07
	Columbus MSA, OH	Y	20300 FQ	26000 MW	35420 TQ	USBLS	5/07

AE	Average entry wage	AW	Average wage paid	FQ	First quartile wage	LO	Lowest wage paid	MTC	Median total compensation	TCC	Total cash compensation
AER	Average entry range	AWR	Average wage range	H	Hourly	LR	Low end range	MW	Median wage paid	TQ	Third quartile wage
AEX	Average experienced wage	AXR	Average experienced range	HI	Highest wage paid	M	Monthly	MWR	Median wage range	W	Weekly
ATC	Average total compensation	D	Daily	HR	High end range	MCC	Median cash compensation	S	See annotated source	Y	Yearly

530

Occupation/Type/Industry	Location	Per	Low	Mid	High	Source	Date
Emergency Medical Technician and Paramedic	Dayton MSA, OH	Y	21800 FQ	24240 MW	30060 TQ	USBLS	5/07
	Oklahoma	Y	17570 FQ	21290 MW	27090 TQ	USBLS	5/07
	Oklahoma City MSA, OK	Y	19240 FQ	24800 MW	30400 TQ	USBLS	5/07
	Tulsa MSA, OK	Y	19040 FQ	23180 MW	29810 TQ	USBLS	5/07
	Oregon	H	14.41 FQ	18.94 MW	22.08 TQ	ORBLS	5/08
	Portland-Vancouver-Beaverton MSA, OR-WA	Y	33810 FQ	41260 MW	46520 TQ	USBLS	5/07
	Pennsylvania	Y	20860 FQ	25900 MW	33460 TQ	USBLS	5/07
	Allentown-Bethlehem-Easton MSA, PA-NJ	Y	23540 FQ	31440 MW	38470 TQ	USBLS	5/07
	Philadelphia-Camden-Wilmington MSA, PA-NJ-DE-MD	Y	26350 FQ	31520 MW	40620 TQ	USBLS	5/07
	Pittsburgh MSA, PA	Y	21460 FQ	25470 MW	31100 TQ	USBLS	5/07
	Rhode Island	Y	27040 FQ	31320 MW	37410 TQ	USBLS	5/07
	Providence-Fall River-Warwick MSA, RI-MA	Y	27620 FQ	32240 MW	38320 TQ	USBLS	5/07
	South Carolina	Y	23590 FQ	28750 MW	35580 TQ	USBLS	5/07
	Charleston-North Charleston MSA, SC	Y	28540 FQ	35120 MW	39520 TQ	USBLS	5/07
	Columbia MSA, SC	Y	23450 FQ	28770 MW	36350 TQ	USBLS	5/07
	South Dakota	Y	22359 FQ	25142 MW	30454 TQ	SDBLS	7/08-9/08
	Sioux Falls MSA, SD	Y	21264 FQ	23474 MW	25766 TQ	SDBLS	7/08-9/08
	Tennessee	Y	22950 FQ	28430 MW	36630 TQ	USBLS	5/07
	Memphis MSA, TN-MS-AR	Y	26790 FQ	35420 MW	54810 TQ	USBLS	5/07
	Nashville-Davidson-Murfreesboro MSA, TN	Y	23310 FQ	28680 MW	45160 TQ	USBLS	5/07
	Texas	Y	21500 FQ	26710 MW	31690 TQ	USBLS	5/07
	Austin-Round Rock MSA, TX	Y	20100 FQ	25230 MW	29930 TQ	USBLS	5/07
	Dallas-Fort Worth-Arlington MSA, TX	Y	23960 FQ	29520 MW	35660 TQ	USBLS	5/07
	El Paso MSA, TX	Y	20880 FQ	26790 MW	31980 TQ	USBLS	5/07
	Houston-Sugar Land-Baytown MSA, TX	Y	25580 FQ	28880 MW	33040 TQ	USBLS	5/07
	San Antonio MSA, TX	Y	21650 FQ	25360 MW	30390 TQ	USBLS	5/07
	Utah	Y	21670 FQ	27680 MW	37300 TQ	USBLS	5/07
	Salt Lake City MSA, UT	Y	23850 FQ	32920 MW	40090 TQ	USBLS	5/07
	Vermont	Y	25180 FQ	29180 MW	34000 TQ	USBLS	5/07
	Burlington-South Burlington MSA, VT	Y	18240 FQ	27730 MW	32500 TQ	USBLS	5/07
	Virginia	Y	23020 FQ	29030 MW	36750 TQ	USBLS	5/07
	Lynchburg MSA, VA	Y	22460 FQ	25850 MW	30890 TQ	USBLS	5/07
	Richmond MSA, VA	Y	27330 FQ	32560 MW	39850 TQ	USBLS	5/07
	Virginia Beach-Norfolk-Newport News MSA, VA-NC	Y	29140 FQ	35140 MW	40400 TQ	USBLS	5/07
	Washington	H	9.94 FQ	15.31 MW	25.70 TQ	WABLS	3/08
	Seattle-Tacoma-Bellevue MSA, WA	Y	19990 FQ	31360 MW	51830 TQ	USBLS	5/07
	West Virginia	Y	17234 FQ	22425 MW	29556 TQ	WVBLS	7/08-9/08
	Charleston MSA, WV	Y	17600 FQ	22980 MW	34890 TQ	USBLS	5/07
	Wisconsin	Y	16200 FQ	25800 MW	33510 TQ	USBLS	5/07
	Milwaukee-Waukesha-West Allis MSA, WI	Y	22060 FQ	28640 MW	40870 TQ	USBLS	5/07
	Wyoming	Y	21057 FQ	28521 MW	38323 TQ	WYBLS	9/08
	Puerto Rico	Y	14420 FQ	17470 MW	20440 TQ	USBLS	5/07
	San Juan-Caguas-Guaynabo MSA, PR	Y	16110 FQ	18490 MW	21600 TQ	USBLS	5/07
	Virgin Islands	Y	30430 FQ	36450 MW	43280 TQ	USBLS	5/07
Emergency Medicine Doctor	Baltimore, MD	Y		240000 AW		BMAG	2009
Emergency Room Physician	United States	Y	178000 AE			USATOD02	2007
Employee Benefits Administrator State Government	Vermont	Y	38314 LO		59800 HI	AFT02	3/1/08
Employee Benefits Specialist State Government	Idaho	Y	30472 LO		50793 HI	AFT02	3/1/08
Employee Health Nurse State Government	Ohio	H	22.60 LO		31.62 HI	ODAS	2008

AE	Average entry wage	AW	Average wage paid	FQ	First quartile wage	LO	Lowest wage paid	MTC	Median total compensation	TCC	Total cash compensation
AER	Average entry range	AWR	Average wage range	H	Hourly	LR	Low end range	MW	Median wage paid	TQ	Third quartile wage
AEX	Average experienced wage	AXR	Average experienced range	HI	Highest wage paid	M	Monthly	MWR	Median wage range	W	Weekly
ATC	Average total compensation	D	Daily	HR	High end range	MCC	Median cash compensation	S	See annotated source	Y	Yearly

Occupation/Type/Industry	Location	Per	Low	Mid	High	Source	Date
Employee Relations Manager							
Municipal Government	Colorado Springs, CO	M	5606 LO			COSPRS	1/1/09
Employment, Recruitment, and Placement Specialist							
	Alabama	Y	29100 FQ	37610 MW	50530 TQ	USBLS	5/07
	Birmingham-Hoover MSA, AL	Y	33710 FQ	43700 MW	61180 TQ	USBLS	5/07
	Alaska	Y	37840 FQ	45420 MW	54420 TQ	USBLS	5/07
	Anchorage MSA, AK	Y	38410 FQ	46670 MW	57410 TQ	USBLS	5/07
	Arizona	Y	32280 FQ	41500 MW	52120 TQ	USBLS	5/07
	Phoenix-Mesa-Scottsdale MSA, AZ	Y	32520 FQ	42310 MW	52840 TQ	USBLS	5/07
	Tucson MSA, AZ	Y	28760 FQ	36570 MW	44130 TQ	USBLS	5/07
	Arkansas	Y	26770 FQ	33370 MW	41660 TQ	USBLS	5/07
	Fort Smith MSA, AR-OK	Y	28320 FQ	36420 MW	52530 TQ	USBLS	5/07
	Little Rock-North Little Rock MSA, AR	Y	28910 FQ	35910 MW	46230 TQ	USBLS	5/07
	California	H	18.77 FQ	25.81 MW	36.63 TQ	CABLS	1/08-3/08
	Los Angeles-Long Beach-Glendale PMSA, CA	H	18.88 FQ	25.64 MW	37.32 TQ	CABLS	1/08-3/08
	Oakland-Fremont-Hayward MSA, CA	H	19.37 FQ	26.39 MW	33.09 TQ	CABLS	1/08-3/08
	Riverside-San Bernardino-Ontario MSA, CA	H	16.58 FQ	19.37 MW	25.51 TQ	CABLS	1/08-3/08
	Sacramento-Arden Arcade-Roseville MSA, CA	H	19.67 FQ	27.22 MW	34.87 TQ	CABLS	1/08-3/08
	San Diego-Carlsbad-San Marcos MSA, CA	H	19.15 FQ	24.86 MW	34.94 TQ	CABLS	1/08-3/08
	San Francisco-San Mateo-Redwood PMSA, CA	H	22.79 FQ	31.45 MW	48.07 TQ	CABLS	1/08-3/08
	San Jose-Sunnyvale-Santa Clara MSA, CA	H	26.01 FQ	32.31 MW	58.42 TQ	CABLS	1/08-3/08
	Santa Ana-Anaheim-Irvine PMSA, CA	Y	34810 FQ	44980 MW	60440 TQ	USBLS	5/07
	Colorado	Y	33620 FQ	44800 MW	59520 TQ	USBLS	5/07
	Boulder MSA, CO	Y	33080 FQ	39400 MW	65320 TQ	USBLS	5/07
	Colorado Springs MSA, CO	Y	30930 FQ	38820 MW	57030 TQ	USBLS	5/07
	Denver-Aurora MSA, CO	Y	37010 FQ	46960 MW	61780 TQ	USBLS	5/07
	Connecticut	H	16.22 AE	25.73 MW		CTBLS	1/08-3/08
	Bridgeport-Stamford-Norwalk MSA, CT	Y	45460 FQ	59230 MW	80380 TQ	USBLS	5/07
	Hartford-West Hartford-East Hartford MSA, CT	Y	37920 FQ	53840 MW	72470 TQ	USBLS	5/07
	Delaware	Y	39270 FQ	49130 MW	59070 TQ	USBLS	5/07
	Dover MSA, DE	Y	41050 FQ	44410 MW	47880 TQ	USBLS	5/07
	Wilmington PMSA, DE-MD-NJ	Y	38650 FQ	50810 MW	60700 TQ	USBLS	5/07
	District of Columbia	Y	41520 FQ	55000 MW	74650 TQ	USBLS	5/07
	Washington-Arlington-Alexandria MSA, DC-VA-MD-WV	Y	41200 FQ	56240 MW	75980 TQ	USBLS	5/07
	Florida	Y	31460 FQ	38510 MW	52490 TQ	USBLS	5/07
	Fort Lauderdale-Pompano Beach-Deerfield Beach PMSA, FL	Y	32670 FQ	41510 MW	54520 TQ	USBLS	5/07
	Jacksonville MSA, FL	Y	33800 FQ	40540 MW	53640 TQ	USBLS	5/07
	Miami-Fort Lauderdale-Miami Beach MSA, FL	Y	31710 FQ	39740 MW	54660 TQ	USBLS	5/07
	Orlando-Kissimmee MSA, FL	Y	31130 FQ	39120 MW	56890 TQ	USBLS	5/07
	Tallahassee MSA, FL	Y	27140 FQ	31560 MW	40000 TQ	USBLS	5/07
	Tampa-St. Petersburg-Clearwater MSA, FL	Y	31020 FQ	35420 MW	43790 TQ	USBLS	5/07
	West Palm Beach-Boca Raton-Boynton Beach PMSA, FL	Y	29280 FQ	36310 MW	56160 TQ	USBLS	5/07
	Georgia	Y	33630 FQ	44680 MW	63270 TQ	USBLS	5/07
	Atlanta-Sandy Springs-Marietta MSA, GA	Y	36600 FQ	50320 MW	66770 TQ	USBLS	5/07
	Hawaii	Y	37450 FQ	46930 MW	59430 TQ	USBLS	5/07
	Honolulu MSA, HI	Y	37340 FQ	46810 MW	59680 TQ	USBLS	5/07
	Idaho	Y	32190 FQ	45310 MW	59860 TQ	USBLS	5/07
	Boise City-Nampa MSA, ID	Y	35360 FQ	48550 MW	60860 TQ	USBLS	5/07
	Illinois	Y	34110 FQ	44710 MW	60720 TQ	USBLS	5/07

AE	Average entry wage	AW	Average wage paid	FQ	First quartile wage	LO	Lowest wage paid	MTC	Median total compensation	TCC	Total cash compensation
AER	Average entry range	AWR	Average wage range	H	Hourly	LR	Low end range	MW	Median wage paid	TQ	Third quartile wage
AEX	Average experienced wage	AXR	Average experienced range	HI	Highest wage paid	M	Monthly	MWR	Median wage range	W	Weekly
ATC	Average total compensation	D	Daily	HR	High end range	MCC	Median cash compensation	S	See annotated source	Y	Yearly

532

Occupation/Type/Industry	Location	Per	Low	Mid	High	Source	Date
Employment, Recruitment, and Placement Specialist	Chicago-Naperville-Joliet						
	MSA, IL-IN-WI	Y	34980 FQ	45510 MW	61100 TQ	USBLS	5/07
	Indiana	Y	30110 FQ	37720 MW	53380 TQ	USBLS	5/07
	Gary PMSA, IN	Y	28330 FQ	36170 MW	56090 TQ	USBLS	5/07
	Indianapolis-Carmel MSA, IN	Y	32340 FQ	40080 MW	53970 TQ	USBLS	5/07
	Terre Haute MSA, IN	Y	27860 FQ	31020 MW	35660 TQ	USBLS	5/07
	Iowa	Y	34400 FQ	43850 MW	50570 TQ	USBLS	5/07
	Des Moines-West Des Moines						
	MSA, IA	Y	37960 FQ	45530 MW	53700 TQ	USBLS	5/07
	Kansas	Y	29700 FQ	37430 MW	47850 TQ	USBLS	5/07
	Wichita MSA, KS	Y	25110 FQ	32220 MW	41540 TQ	USBLS	5/07
	Kentucky	Y	27327 FQ	34084 MW	43216 TQ	KYBLS	2008
	Louisville-Jefferson County						
	MSA, KY-IN	Y	28600 FQ	35680 MW	47080 TQ	USBLS	5/07
	Louisiana	H	13.12 FQ	16.69 MW	21.99 TQ	LABLS	1/08-3/08
	Baton Rouge MSA, LA	Y	28150 FQ	36290 MW	47480 TQ	USBLS	5/07
	New Orleans-Metairie-Kenner						
	MSA, LA	Y	30720 FQ	36930 MW	50270 TQ	USBLS	5/07
	Maine	Y	34040 FQ	41200 MW	52290 TQ	USBLS	5/07
	Portland-South Portland-						
	Biddeford MSA, ME	Y	33000 FQ	44770 MW	62240 TQ	USBLS	5/07
	Maryland	Y		50875 MW		MDBLS	3/08
	Baltimore-Towson MSA, MD	Y	38430 FQ	50910 MW	76160 TQ	USBLS	5/07
	Bethesda-Gaithersburg-						
	Frederick PMSA, MD	Y	40960 FQ	54060 MW	75550 TQ	USBLS	5/07
	Massachusetts	Y	39670 FQ	51350 MW	70090 TQ	USBLS	5/07
	Boston-Cambridge-Quincy						
	NECTA, MA	Y	41070 FQ	53220 MW	73410 TQ	USBLS	5/07
	Springfield MSA, MA-CT	Y	35050 FQ	40780 MW	52080 TQ	USBLS	5/07
	Worcester MSA, MA-CT	Y	44070 FQ	60130 MW	74990 TQ	USBLS	5/07
	Michigan	Y	36260 FQ	47350 MW	63900 TQ	USBLS	5/07
	Detroit-Warren-Livonia MSA,						
	MI	Y	36210 FQ	46950 MW	73650 TQ	USBLS	5/07
	Grand Rapids-Wyoming MSA,						
	MI	Y	41730 FQ	48980 MW	58310 TQ	USBLS	5/07
	Muskegon-Norton Shores						
	MSA, MI	Y	31670 FQ	47360 MW	57680 TQ	USBLS	5/07
	Warren-Troy-Farmington Hills						
	PMSA, MI	Y	33790 FQ	43650 MW	63720 TQ	USBLS	5/07
	Minnesota	Y	38734 FQ	49067 MW	67063 TQ	MNBLS	10/08-12/08
	Duluth-Superior MSA, MN-WI	Y	41111 FQ	48441 MW	62319 TQ	MNBLS	10/08-12/08
	Minneapolis-Saint Paul MSA,						
	MN-WI	Y	39318 FQ	50485 MW	69044 TQ	MNBLS	10/08-12/08
	Rochester MSA, MN	Y	37102 FQ	47184 MW	64032 TQ	MNBLS	10/08-12/08
	Mississippi	Y	27520 FQ	31840 MW	40360 TQ	USBLS	5/07
	Hattiesburg MSA, MS	Y	27550 FQ	31200 MW	39120 TQ	USBLS	5/07
	Jackson MSA, MS	Y	27050 FQ	31840 MW	40390 TQ	USBLS	5/07
	Missouri	Y	31100 FQ	39930 MW	53040 TQ	USBLS	5/07
	Kansas City MSA, MO-KS	Y	32000 FQ	38790 MW	49270 TQ	USBLS	5/07
	St. Louis MSA, MO-IL	Y	33840 FQ	44140 MW	59740 TQ	USBLS	5/07
	Montana	Y	28480 FQ	34790 MW	39540 TQ	USBLS	5/07
	Billings MSA, MT	Y	26260 FQ	30730 MW	37600 TQ	USBLS	5/07
	Nebraska	Y	36840 FQ	49140 MW	71440 TQ	USBLS	5/07
	Omaha-Council Bluffs MSA,						
	NE-IA	Y	38340 FQ	52080 MW	74150 TQ	USBLS	5/07
	Nevada	H	14.15 FQ	18.83 MW	24.50 TQ	NVBLS	5/08
	Las Vegas-Paradise MSA, NV	H	13.90 FQ	18.26 MW	23.65 TQ	NVBLS	5/08
	New Hampshire	H	15.43 AE	21.68 MW	30.09 AEX	NHBLS	6/08
	Manchester MSA, NH	Y	30960 FQ	45690 MW	64210 TQ	USBLS	5/07
	Nashua NECTA, NH-MA	Y	36490 FQ	42090 MW	55120 TQ	USBLS	5/07
	New Jersey	Y	38860 FQ	51630 MW	69270 TQ	USBLS	5/07
	Camden PMSA, NJ	Y	36780 FQ	46300 MW	59370 TQ	USBLS	5/07
	Edison PMSA, NJ	Y	37460 FQ	50900 MW	71750 TQ	USBLS	5/07
	Newark-Union PMSA, NJ-PA	Y	41660 FQ	53410 MW	73600 TQ	USBLS	5/07
	New Mexico	Y	29420 FQ	36110 MW	44910 TQ	USBLS	5/07
	Albuquerque MSA, NM	Y	30150 FQ	36500 MW	45460 TQ	USBLS	5/07
	New York	Y	39050 FQ	49210 MW	72060 TQ	USBLS	5/07
	Albany-Schenectady-Troy						
	MSA, NY	Y	35780 FQ	46660 MW	58070 TQ	USBLS	5/07
	Binghamton MSA, NY	Y	36190 FQ	40540 MW	55650 TQ	USBLS	5/07

AE	Average entry wage	**AW**	Average wage paid	**FQ**	First quartile wage	
AER	Average entry range	**AWR**	Average wage range	**H**	Hourly	
AEX	Average experienced wage	**AXR**	Average experienced range	**HI**	Highest wage paid	
ATC	Average total compensation	**D**	Daily	**HR**	High end range	

LO	Lowest wage paid	**MTC**	Median total compensation	**TCC**	Total cash compensation
LR	Low end range	**MW**	Median wage paid	**TQ**	Third quartile wage
M	Monthly	**MWR**	Median wage range	**W**	Weekly
MCC	Median cash compensation	**S**	See annotated source	**Y**	Yearly

Occupation/Type/Industry	Location	Per	Low	Mid	High	Source	Date
Employment, Recruitment, and Placement Specialist	Buffalo-Niagara Falls MSA, NY	Y	36440 FQ	44810 MW	55220 TQ	USBLS	5/07
	Nassau-Suffolk PMSA, NY	Y	42100 FQ	53130 MW	75670 TQ	USBLS	5/07
	New York-Northern New Jersey-Long Island MSA, NY-NJ-PA	Y	39800 FQ	51200 MW	75320 TQ	USBLS	5/07
	North Carolina	Y	32800 FQ	41120 MW	56380 TQ	USBLS	5/07
	Charlotte-Gastonia-Concord MSA, NC-SC	Y	34210 FQ	44050 MW	60520 TQ	USBLS	5/07
	Raleigh-Cary MSA, NC	Y	37080 FQ	45370 MW	60580 TQ	USBLS	5/07
	North Dakota	Y	30670 FQ	37740 MW	46930 TQ	USBLS	5/07
	Fargo MSA, ND-MN	Y	32610 FQ	38560 MW	44980 TQ	USBLS	5/07
	Ohio	Y	34280 FQ	43020 MW	56280 TQ	USBLS	5/07
	Cincinnati-Middletown MSA, OH-KY-IN	Y	36020 FQ	45750 MW	63120 TQ	USBLS	5/07
	Cleveland-Elyria-Mentor MSA, OH	Y	33000 FQ	41640 MW	55420 TQ	USBLS	5/07
	Columbus MSA, OH	Y	35840 FQ	43400 MW	60200 TQ	USBLS	5/07
	Dayton MSA, OH	Y	35460 FQ	43370 MW	52900 TQ	USBLS	5/07
	Oklahoma	Y	26170 FQ	33390 MW	44760 TQ	USBLS	5/07
	Oklahoma City MSA, OK	Y	28690 FQ	36320 MW	49680 TQ	USBLS	5/07
	Tulsa MSA, OK	Y	27250 FQ	33610 MW	42920 TQ	USBLS	5/07
	Oregon	H	16.24 FQ	19.63 MW	24.49 TQ	ORBLS	5/08
	Portland-Vancouver-Beaverton MSA, OR-WA	Y	33250 FQ	40190 MW	54190 TQ	USBLS	5/07
	Salem MSA, OR	Y	29700 FQ	36870 MW	46180 TQ	USBLS	5/07
	Pennsylvania	Y	34150 FQ	43780 MW	58020 TQ	USBLS	5/07
	Allentown-Bethlehem-Easton MSA, PA-NJ	Y	34230 FQ	44220 MW	62190 TQ	USBLS	5/07
	Erie MSA, PA	Y	32920 FQ	40700 MW	53370 TQ	USBLS	5/07
	Philadelphia-Camden-Wilmington MSA, PA-NJ-DE-MD	Y	37440 FQ	47110 MW	61550 TQ	USBLS	5/07
	Pittsburgh MSA, PA	Y	31330 FQ	41420 MW	60280 TQ	USBLS	5/07
	York-Hanover MSA, PA	Y	29520 FQ	36970 MW	48020 TQ	USBLS	5/07
	Rhode Island	Y	39490 FQ	46310 MW	57420 TQ	USBLS	5/07
	Providence-Fall River-Warwick MSA, RI-MA	Y	38930 FQ	46160 MW	57380 TQ	USBLS	5/07
	South Carolina	Y	28280 FQ	34520 MW	44500 TQ	USBLS	5/07
	Charleston-North Charleston MSA, SC	Y	27210 FQ	32750 MW	43010 TQ	USBLS	5/07
	Columbia MSA, SC	Y	29230 FQ	36860 MW	48040 TQ	USBLS	5/07
	South Dakota	Y	35803 FQ	40468 MW	47474 TQ	SDBLS	7/08-9/08
	Sioux Falls MSA, SD	Y	36070 FQ	40853 MW	48286 TQ	SDBLS	7/08-9/08
	Tennessee	Y	29850 FQ	40220 MW	53870 TQ	USBLS	5/07
	Knoxville MSA, TN	Y	28440 FQ	37200 MW	52390 TQ	USBLS	5/07
	Memphis MSA, TN-MS-AR	Y	31190 FQ	39920 MW	52030 TQ	USBLS	5/07
	Nashville-Davidson-Murfreesboro MSA, TN	Y	36680 FQ	47860 MW	59090 TQ	USBLS	5/07
	Texas	Y	31510 FQ	41830 MW	59070 TQ	USBLS	5/07
	Austin-Round Rock MSA, TX	Y	31630 FQ	38970 MW	53760 TQ	USBLS	5/07
	Dallas-Fort Worth-Arlington MSA, TX	Y	33460 FQ	43480 MW	60770 TQ	USBLS	5/07
	El Paso MSA, TX	Y	23170 FQ	31430 MW	42220 TQ	USBLS	5/07
	Houston-Sugar Land-Baytown MSA, TX	Y	37890 FQ	51500 MW	67190 TQ	USBLS	5/07
	San Antonio MSA, TX	Y	24210 FQ	34400 MW	48770 TQ	USBLS	5/07
	Utah	Y	30570 FQ	37910 MW	50990 TQ	USBLS	5/07
	Salt Lake City MSA, UT	Y	30620 FQ	38780 MW	54330 TQ	USBLS	5/07
	Vermont	Y	30340 FQ	38850 MW	54200 TQ	USBLS	5/07
	Burlington-South Burlington MSA, VT	Y	34060 FQ	43780 MW	58040 TQ	USBLS	5/07
	Virginia	Y	34370 FQ	45750 MW	67680 TQ	USBLS	5/07
	Lynchburg MSA, VA	Y	27760 FQ	31300 MW	40400 TQ	USBLS	5/07
	Richmond MSA, VA	Y	30190 FQ	38270 MW	52460 TQ	USBLS	5/07
	Virginia Beach-Norfolk-Newport News MSA, VA-NC	Y	24800 FQ	34230 MW	44700 TQ	USBLS	5/07
	Washington	H	18.46 FQ	25.17 MW	35.30 TQ	WABLS	3/08
	Seattle-Tacoma-Bellevue MSA, WA	Y	41260 FQ	55160 MW	76830 TQ	USBLS	5/07
	West Virginia	Y	30653 FQ	35964 MW	43054 TQ	WVBLS	7/08-9/08

AE	Average entry wage	AW	Average wage paid	FQ	First quartile wage	LO	Lowest wage paid
AER	Average entry range	AWR	Average wage range	H	Hourly	LR	Low end range
AEX	Average experienced wage	AXR	Average experienced range	HI	Highest wage paid	M	Monthly
ATC	Average total compensation	D	Daily	HR	High end range	MCC	Median cash compensation

MTC	Median total compensation	TCC Total cash compensation
MW	Median wage paid	TQ Third quartile wage
MWR	Median wage range	W Weekly
S	See annotated source	Y Yearly

Occupation/Type/Industry	Location	Per	Low	Mid	High	Source	Date
Employment, Recruitment, and Placement Specialist	Charleston MSA, WV	Y	34110 FQ	39150 MW	45590 TQ	USBLS	5/07
	Wisconsin	Y	36550 FQ	59210 MW	85930 TQ	USBLS	5/07
	Milwaukee-Waukesha-West Allis MSA, WI	Y	50110 FQ	81060 MW	89700 TQ	USBLS	5/07
	Wyoming	Y	32340 FQ	37924 MW	45054 TQ	WYBLS	9/08
	Cheyenne MSA, WY	Y	33492 FQ	40773 MW	48466 TQ	WYBLS	9/08
	Puerto Rico	Y	18910 FQ	23470 MW	30020 TQ	USBLS	5/07
	San Juan-Caguas-Guaynabo MSA, PR	Y	18570 FQ	23410 MW	30490 TQ	USBLS	5/07
	Guam	Y	32910 FQ	39120 MW	47610 TQ	USBLS	5/07
Employment and Training Supervisor							
Municipal Government	Cincinnati, OH	Y	62598 LO		84507 HI	COHSS	10/08
Employment Counselor							
Department of Employment Security	New Hampshire	Y		33565 AW		NHUL03	2008
State Government	Alaska	Y	41400 LO		79948 HI	AFT02	3/1/08
Employment Services Interviewer							
State Government	Ohio	H	15.62 LO		18.36 HI	ODAS	2008
EMS Director	Cedartown, GA	Y	38000 LO		46000 HI	GACTY01	2008
	Livingston County, MI	Y			93060 HI	LCPP	2009
EMS Training Coordinator							
Department of Safety	New Hampshire	Y		44399 AW		NHUL03	2008
Endocrinologist	United States	Y		205497 AW		CEJ01	2008
Energy Conservation Representative							
Municipal Government	Seattle, WA	H	21.43 LO		24.82 HI	CSSS	2007
Energy Management Analyst							
Municipal Government	Seattle, WA	H	28.39 LO		33.16 HI	CSSS	2008
Energy Manager							
Dallas/Fort Worth International Airport	Dallas-Fort Worth, TX	Y			102576 HI	CBSTV	2008
Energy Program Developer							
State Government	Ohio	H	23.87 LO		35.02 HI	ODAS	2008
Engine and Other Machine Assembler	Alabama	Y	21680 FQ	34150 MW	40720 TQ	USBLS	5/07
	Arizona	Y	27410 FQ	34570 MW	45890 TQ	USBLS	5/07
	Phoenix-Mesa-Scottsdale MSA, AZ	Y	29970 FQ	40950 MW	46600 TQ	USBLS	5/07
	Arkansas	Y	21630 FQ	24330 MW	27980 TQ	USBLS	5/07
	California	H	11.77 FQ	15.35 MW	22.61 TQ	CABLS	1/08-3/08
	Los Angeles-Long Beach-Glendale PMSA, CA	H	11.11 FQ	13.79 MW	21.20 TQ	CABLS	1/08-3/08
	Oakland-Fremont-Hayward MSA, CA	H	17.28 FQ	23.08 MW	25.44 TQ	CABLS	1/08-3/08
	Riverside-San Bernardino-Ontario, CA	H	8.51 FQ	10.66 MW	16.56 TQ	CABLS	1/08-3/08
	San Diego-Carlsbad-San Marcos MSA, CA	H	15.91 FQ	24.11 MW	26.78 TQ	CABLS	1/08-3/08
	San Jose-Sunnyvale-Santa Clara MSA, CA	H	10.68 FQ	11.57 MW	12.76 TQ	CABLS	1/08-3/08
	Santa Ana-Anaheim-Irvine PMSA, CA	Y	32470 FQ	38340 MW	44260 TQ	USBLS	5/07
	Colorado	Y	24340 FQ	28390 MW	34450 TQ	USBLS	5/07
	Denver-Aurora MSA, CO	Y	24250 FQ	27460 MW	30950 TQ	USBLS	5/07
	Connecticut	H	13.16 AE	17.14 MW		CTBLS	1/08-3/08
	Hartford-West Hartford-East Hartford MSA, CT	Y	32390 FQ	36970 MW	43060 TQ	USBLS	5/07
	Washington-Arlington-Alexandria MSA, DC-VA-MD-WV	Y	24970 FQ	34790 MW	38810 TQ	USBLS	5/07
	Florida	Y	20010 FQ	25870 MW	32990 TQ	USBLS	5/07

AE Average entry wage	**AW** Average wage paid	**FQ** First quartile wage	**LO** Lowest wage paid	**MTC** Median total compensation **TCC** Total cash compensation
AER Average entry range	**AWR** Average wage range	**H** Hourly	**LR** Low end range	**MW** Median wage paid **TQ** Third quartile wage
AEX Average experienced wage	**AXR** Average experienced range **HI** Highest wage paid		**M** Monthly	**MWR** Median wage range **W** Weekly
ATC Average total compensation **D** Daily		**HR** High end range	**MCC** Median cash compensation **S** See annotated source	**Y** Yearly

Occupation/Type/Industry	Location	Per	Low	Mid	High	Source	Date
Engine and Other Machine Assembler							
	Fort Lauderdale-Pompano Beach-Deerfield Beach PMSA, FL	Y	23020 FQ	31980 MW	41340 TQ	USBLS	5/07
	Jacksonville MSA, FL	Y	22460 FQ	26200 MW	30250 TQ	USBLS	5/07
	Miami-Fort Lauderdale-Miami Beach MSA, FL	Y	21180 FQ	25710 MW	35410 TQ	USBLS	5/07
	Orlando-Kissimmee MSA, FL	Y	17570 FQ	19170 MW	26610 TQ	USBLS	5/07
	Georgia	Y	22210 FQ	24890 MW	36410 TQ	USBLS	5/07
	Atlanta-Sandy Springs-Marietta MSA, GA	Y	25330 FQ	35470 MW	40520 TQ	USBLS	5/07
	Illinois	Y	21820 FQ	25700 MW	30820 TQ	USBLS	5/07
	Chicago-Naperville-Joliet MSA, IL-IN-WI	Y	20770 FQ	25790 MW	33540 TQ	USBLS	5/07
	Indiana	Y	24050 FQ	30790 MW	44500 TQ	USBLS	5/07
	Gary PMSA, IN	Y	26320 FQ	28840 MW	31410 TQ	USBLS	5/07
	Indianapolis-Carmel MSA, IN	Y	29960 FQ	34640 MW	42380 TQ	USBLS	5/07
	Iowa	Y	29010 FQ	32990 MW	37870 TQ	USBLS	5/07
	Des Moines-West Des Moines MSA, IA	Y	29030 FQ	33390 MW	37520 TQ	USBLS	5/07
	Kansas	Y	19390 FQ	25920 MW	35460 TQ	USBLS	5/07
	Wichita MSA, KS	Y	25850 FQ	40870 MW	46580 TQ	USBLS	5/07
	Kentucky	Y	33554 FQ	38642 MW	50042 TQ	KYBLS	2008
	Louisville-Jefferson County MSA, KY-IN	Y	22180 FQ	32920 MW	38360 TQ	USBLS	5/07
	Louisiana	H	12.94 FQ	15.99 MW	17.81 TQ	LABLS	1/08-3/08
	Maryland	Y		41000 MW		MDBLS	3/08
	Baltimore-Towson MSA, MD	Y	31120 FQ	36420 MW	42320 TQ	USBLS	5/07
	Massachusetts	Y	25490 FQ	29760 MW	50480 TQ	USBLS	5/07
	Worcester MSA, MA-CT	Y	37200 FQ	43450 MW	47810 TQ	USBLS	5/07
	Michigan	Y	32040 FQ	40290 MW	55770 TQ	USBLS	5/07
	Grand Rapids-Wyoming MSA, MI	Y	32110 FQ	38340 MW	43150 TQ	USBLS	5/07
	Minnesota	Y	24465 FQ	36128 MW	43405 TQ	MNBLS	10/08-12/08
	Minneapolis-Saint Paul MSA, MN-WI	Y	30094 FQ	39331 MW	44214 TQ	MNBLS	10/08-12/08
	Mississippi	Y	24600 FQ	28490 MW	32830 TQ	USBLS	5/07
	Missouri	Y	21280 FQ	26610 MW	33060 TQ	USBLS	5/07
	Kansas City MSA, MO-KS	Y	17700 FQ	19740 MW	29690 TQ	USBLS	5/07
	St. Louis MSA, MO-IL	Y	21900 FQ	27960 MW	34630 TQ	USBLS	5/07
	Springfield MSA, MO	Y	25790 FQ	28130 MW	30520 TQ	USBLS	5/07
	Nebraska	Y	21700 FQ	24570 MW	29140 TQ	USBLS	5/07
	Omaha-Council Bluffs MSA, NE-IA	Y	24790 FQ	30140 MW	36700 TQ	USBLS	5/07
	Nevada	H	13.84 FQ	15.75 MW	18.18 TQ	NVBLS	5/08
	New Hampshire	H	8.74 AE	11.55 MW	15.85 AEX	NHBLS	6/08
	New Jersey	Y	27620 FQ	34160 MW	44120 TQ	USBLS	5/07
	Camden PMSA, NJ	Y	27890 FQ	33160 MW	44130 TQ	USBLS	5/07
	Edison PMSA, NJ	Y	29810 FQ	36440 MW	44030 TQ	USBLS	5/07
	Newark-Union PMSA, NJ-PA	Y	31640 FQ	38440 MW	43650 TQ	USBLS	5/07
	New Mexico	Y	23620 FQ	30580 MW	44460 TQ	USBLS	5/07
	New York	Y	27040 FQ	32940 MW	45160 TQ	USBLS	5/07
	Buffalo-Niagara Falls MSA, NY	Y	28740 FQ	35420 MW	43880 TQ	USBLS	5/07
	New York-Northern New Jersey-Long Island MSA, NY-NJ-PA	Y	26620 FQ	34110 MW	42420 TQ	USBLS	5/07
	North Carolina	Y	25900 FQ	31460 MW	41410 TQ	USBLS	5/07
	Charlotte-Gastonia-Concord MSA, NC-SC	Y	32340 FQ	37080 MW	50060 TQ	USBLS	5/07
	Ohio	Y	30860 FQ	36180 MW	53140 TQ	USBLS	5/07
	Cincinnati-Middletown MSA, OH-KY-IN	Y	35560 FQ	55500 MW	61140 TQ	USBLS	5/07
	Columbus MSA, OH	Y	25650 FQ	31410 MW	37530 TQ	USBLS	5/07
	Dayton MSA, OH	Y	26580 FQ	32490 MW	38920 TQ	USBLS	5/07
	Oklahoma	Y	24340 FQ	31200 MW	38690 TQ	USBLS	5/07
	Oklahoma City MSA, OK	Y	24260 FQ	29750 MW	33970 TQ	USBLS	5/07
	Tulsa MSA, OK	Y	22020 FQ	25570 MW	30080 TQ	USBLS	5/07
	Oregon	H	11.81 FQ	15.68 MW	19.73 TQ	ORBLS	5/08
	Eugene-Springfield MSA, OR	Y	30550 FQ	37360 MW	43450 TQ	USBLS	5/07
	Portland-Vancouver-Beaverton MSA, OR-WA	Y	22610 FQ	31390 MW	40180 TQ	USBLS	5/07

AE	Average entry wage	**AW**	Average wage paid	**FQ**	First quartile wage
AER	Average entry range	**AWR**	Average wage range	**H**	Hourly
AEX	Average experienced wage	**AXR**	Average experienced range	**HI**	Highest wage paid
ATC	Average total compensation	**D**	Daily	**HR**	High end range

LO	Lowest wage paid	**MTC**	Median total compensation
LR	Low end range	**MW**	Median wage paid
M	Monthly	**MWR**	Median wage range
MCC	Median cash compensation	**S**	See annotated source

TCC	Total cash compensation
TQ	Third quartile wage
W	Weekly
Y	Yearly

Occupation/Type/Industry	Location	Per	Low	Mid	High	Source	Date
Engine and Other Machine Assembler	Pennsylvania	Y	25820 FQ	35190 MW	43960 TQ	USBLS	5/07
	Allentown-Bethlehem-Easton MSA, PA-NJ	Y	27420 FQ	31040 MW	34970 TQ	USBLS	5/07
	Philadelphia-Camden-Wilmington MSA, PA-NJ-DE-MD	Y	28010 FQ	34010 MW	44500 TQ	USBLS	5/07
	Pittsburgh MSA, PA	Y	29170 FQ	35670 MW	41610 TQ	USBLS	5/07
	York-Hanover MSA, PA	Y	23430 FQ	30100 MW	38230 TQ	USBLS	5/07
	South Carolina	Y	20820 FQ	27680 MW	33100 TQ	USBLS	5/07
	Charleston-North Charleston MSA, SC	Y	23280 FQ	26980 MW	31100 TQ	USBLS	5/07
	South Dakota	Y	23319 FQ	26340 MW	29260 TQ	SDBLS	7/08-9/08
	Tennessee	Y	21110 FQ	25240 MW	27960 TQ	USBLS	5/07
	Nashville-Davidson-Murfreesboro MSA, TN	Y	23990 FQ	28590 MW	33800 TQ	USBLS	5/07
	Texas	Y	21720 FQ	30750 MW	37970 TQ	USBLS	5/07
	Dallas-Fort Worth-Arlington MSA, TX	Y	20710 FQ	28040 MW	39130 TQ	USBLS	5/07
	Houston-Sugar Land-Baytown MSA, TX	Y	18850 FQ	23360 MW	36230 TQ	USBLS	5/07
	San Antonio MSA, TX	Y	31810 FQ	34770 MW	37820 TQ	USBLS	5/07
	Utah	Y	22460 FQ	27690 MW	37060 TQ	USBLS	5/07
	Virginia	Y	26010 FQ	31410 MW	36450 TQ	USBLS	5/07
	Richmond MSA, VA	Y	26740 FQ	31430 MW	40260 TQ	USBLS	5/07
	Virginia Beach-Norfolk-Newport News MSA, VA-NC	Y	23130 FQ	28960 MW	36700 TQ	USBLS	5/07
	Washington	H	14.22 FQ	17.41 MW	20.03 TQ	WABLS	3/08
	Seattle-Tacoma-Bellevue MSA, WA	Y	30340 FQ	36570 MW	42100 TQ	USBLS	5/07
	West Virginia	Y	25406 FQ	29165 MW	40256 TQ	WVBLS	7/08-9/08
	Wisconsin	Y	29360 FQ	34770 MW	42780 TQ	USBLS	5/07
	Green Bay MSA, WI	Y	42590 FQ	45690 MW	48800 TQ	USBLS	5/07
	Milwaukee-Waukesha-West Allis MSA, WI	Y	28770 FQ	34400 MW	42310 TQ	USBLS	5/07
	Wyoming	Y	35402 FQ	39324 MW	42454 TQ	WYBLS	9/08
	Puerto Rico	Y	15330 FQ	17190 MW	18710 TQ	USBLS	5/07
Engineer							
Computer	United States	Y	91890 FQ	117300 MW	145000 TQ	IOMA02	2005
Metal	United States	Y	64270 FQ	87680 MW	108430 TQ	IOMA02	2005
Military Software, With Security Clearance	United States	Y		82821 AW		CLJOBS	3/20/07-2/20/08
Military Software, Without Security Clearance	United States	Y		66060 AW		CLJOBS	3/20/07-2/20/08
Petroleum/Chemical	United States	Y	82770 FQ	102170 MW	124380 TQ	IOMA02	2005
Engineer Intern							
Municipal Government	Cincinnati, OH	Y	45117 LO		60634 HI	COHSS	10/08
Engineering Geologist							
Municipal Government	Cincinnati, OH	Y	57719 LO		77569 HI	COHSS	10/08
State Government	Idaho	Y	41932 LO		69888 HI	AFT02	3/1/08
Engineering Inspector							
Municipal Government	Walnut Creek, CA	Y	71429 LO		86207 HI	WCSWP	6/27/08
Engineering Manager	Alabama	Y	75510 FQ	97610 MW	123750 TQ	USBLS	5/07
	Birmingham-Hoover MSA, AL	Y	84630 FQ	99630 MW	118800 TQ	USBLS	5/07
	Huntsville MSA, AL	Y	88460 FQ	115350 MW	133100 TQ	USBLS	5/07
	Alaska	Y	84260 FQ	99420 MW	118930 TQ	USBLS	5/07
	Anchorage MSA, AK	Y	86370 FQ	101940 MW	124660 TQ	USBLS	5/07
	Arizona	Y	89910 FQ	109610 MW	129540 TQ	USBLS	5/07
	Phoenix-Mesa-Scottsdale MSA, AZ	Y	92040 FQ	111000 MW	129430 TQ	USBLS	5/07
	Tucson MSA, AZ	Y	84270 FQ	107970 MW	138430 TQ	USBLS	5/07
	Arkansas	Y	74690 FQ	89460 MW	103010 TQ	USBLS	5/07
	Little Rock-North Little Rock MSA, AR	Y	81710 FQ	94360 MW	111020 TQ	USBLS	5/07
	California	H	48.63 FQ	60.97 MW		CABLS	1/08-3/08
	Fresno MSA, CA	H	33.66 FQ	41.36 MW	54.51 TQ	CABLS	1/08-3/08
	Los Angeles-Long Beach-Glendale PMSA, CA	H	47.30 FQ	59.75 MW		CABLS	1/08-3/08

AE	Average entry wage	AW	Average wage paid	FQ	First quartile wage	LO	Lowest wage paid	MTC	Median total compensation	TCC	Total cash compensation
AER	Average entry range	AWR	Average wage range	H	Hourly	LR	Low end range	MW	Median wage paid	TQ	Third quartile wage
AEX	Average experienced wage	AXR	Average experienced range	HI	Highest wage paid	M	Monthly	MWR	Median wage range	W	Weekly
ATC	Average total compensation	D	Daily	HR	High end range	MCC	Median cash compensation	S	See annotated source	Y	Yearly

Occupation/Type/Industry	Location	Per	Low	Mid	High	Source	Date
Engineering Manager	Modesto MSA, CA	H	35.72 FQ	45.73 MW	61.10 TQ	CABLS	1/08-3/08
	Oakland-Fremont-Hayward MSA, CA	H	50.33 FQ	61.25 MW		CABLS	1/08-3/08
	Riverside-San Bernardino-Ontario MSA, CA	H	41.97 FQ	49.54 MW	61.32 TQ	CABLS	1/08-3/08
	Sacramento-Arden Arcade-Roseville MSA, CA	H	45.80 FQ	55.15 MW	65.68 TQ	CABLS	1/08-3/08
	San Diego-Carlsbad-San Marcos MSA, CA	H	45.29 FQ	57.58 MW		CABLS	1/08-3/08
	San Francisco-San Mateo-Redwood PMSA, CA	H	52.09 FQ	62.42 MW		CABLS	1/08-3/08
	San Jose-Sunnyvale-Santa Clara MSA, CA	H	58.88 FQ			CABLS	1/08-3/08
	Santa Ana-Anaheim-Irvine PMSA, CA	Y	96810 FQ	117590 MW	144700 TQ	USBLS	5/07
	Santa Rosa-Petaluma MSA, CA	H	43.21 FQ	57.68 MW		CABLS	1/08-3/08
	Colorado	Y	97000 FQ	116600 MW	140560 TQ	USBLS	5/07
	Colorado Springs MSA, CO	Y	89430 FQ	107210 MW	127300 TQ	USBLS	5/07
	Denver-Aurora MSA, CO	Y	98690 FQ	116080 MW	135460 TQ	USBLS	5/07
	Connecticut	H	39.59 AE	52.29 MW		CTBLS	1/08-3/08
	Bridgeport-Stamford-Norwalk MSA, CT	Y	96420 FQ	118530 MW	142330 TQ	USBLS	5/07
	Hartford-West Hartford-East Hartford MSA, CT	Y	89890 FQ	106340 MW	126660 TQ	USBLS	5/07
	Waterbury MSA, CT	Y	79480 FQ	111330 MW	129750 TQ	USBLS	5/07
	Delaware	Y	97580 FQ	116410 MW	141430 TQ	USBLS	5/07
	Wilmington PMSA, DE-MD-NJ	Y	101830 FQ	120690 MW		USBLS	5/07
	District of Columbia	Y	105620 FQ	119160 MW	135170 TQ	USBLS	5/07
	Washington-Arlington-Alexandria MSA, DC-VA-MD-WV	Y	107130 FQ	123030 MW	144790 TQ	USBLS	5/07
	Florida	Y	86350 FQ	106960 MW	130370 TQ	USBLS	5/07
	Fort Lauderdale-Pompano Beach-Deerfield Beach PMSA, FL	Y	82740 FQ	105910 MW	129810 TQ	USBLS	5/07
	Jacksonville MSA, FL	Y	76480 FQ	104650 MW	128460 TQ	USBLS	5/07
	Miami-Fort Lauderdale-Miami Beach MSA, FL	Y	89180 FQ	110840 MW	134320 TQ	USBLS	5/07
	Orlando-Kissimmee MSA, FL	Y	83520 FQ	103750 MW	136780 TQ	USBLS	5/07
	Sarasota-Bradenton-Venice MSA, FL	Y	74010 FQ	91380 MW	128920 TQ	USBLS	5/07
	Tallahassee MSA, FL	Y	97070 FQ	115830 MW	128850 TQ	USBLS	5/07
	Tampa-St. Petersburg-Clearwater MSA, FL	Y	85420 FQ	103060 MW	128440 TQ	USBLS	5/07
	West Palm Beach-Boca Raton-Boynton Beach PMSA, FL	Y	96280 FQ	118050 MW	140340 TQ	USBLS	5/07
	Georgia	Y	80100 FQ	99600 MW	120820 TQ	USBLS	5/07
	Atlanta-Sandy Springs-Marietta MSA, GA	Y	81460 FQ	101750 MW	122810 TQ	USBLS	5/07
	Macon MSA, GA	Y	77760 FQ	100340 MW	120370 TQ	USBLS	5/07
	Hawaii	Y	90020 FQ	103730 MW	118530 TQ	USBLS	5/07
	Honolulu MSA, HI	Y	90760 FQ	104220 MW	118310 TQ	USBLS	5/07
	Idaho	Y	70570 FQ	91370 MW	117250 TQ	USBLS	5/07
	Boise City-Nampa MSA, ID	Y	72880 FQ	94130 MW	120910 TQ	USBLS	5/07
	Illinois	Y	83070 FQ	105080 MW	130900 TQ	USBLS	5/07
	Chicago-Naperville-Joliet MSA, IL-IN-WI	Y	84990 FQ	107370 MW	131470 TQ	USBLS	5/07
	Indiana	Y	73640 FQ	89840 MW	107600 TQ	USBLS	5/07
	Evansville MSA, IN-KY	Y	77220 FQ	90780 MW	108010 TQ	USBLS	5/07
	Gary PMSA, IN	Y	85020 FQ	97360 MW	124120 TQ	USBLS	5/07
	Indianapolis-Carmel MSA, IN	Y	72920 FQ	89510 MW	108390 TQ	USBLS	5/07
	Iowa	Y	77830 FQ	95920 MW	116730 TQ	USBLS	5/07
	Des Moines-West Des Moines MSA, IA	Y	76740 FQ	91150 MW	106280 TQ	USBLS	5/07
	Kansas	Y	83230 FQ	101470 MW	123450 TQ	USBLS	5/07
	Wichita MSA, KS	Y	83000 FQ	103710 MW	129490 TQ	USBLS	5/07
	Kentucky	Y	80114 FQ	96003 MW	118397 TQ	KYBLS	2008
	Lexington-Fayette MSA, KY	Y	82600 FQ	102790 MW	145280 TQ	USBLS	5/07
	Louisville-Jefferson County MSA, KY-IN	Y	80250 FQ	95930 MW	117200 TQ	USBLS	5/07
	Louisiana	H	38.82 FQ	50.99 MW	64.55 TQ	LABLS	1/08-3/08

Occupation/Type/Industry	Location	Per	Low	Mid	High	Source	Date
Engineering Manager	Baton Rouge MSA, LA	Y	93450 FQ	130770 MW		USBLS	5/07
	New Orleans-Metairie-Kenner MSA, LA	Y	80060 FQ	101150 MW	122080 TQ	USBLS	5/07
	Maine	Y	73720 FQ	91030 MW	115430 TQ	USBLS	5/07
	Portland-South Portland-Biddeford MSA, ME	Y	86130 FQ	110240 MW	132220 TQ	USBLS	5/07
	Maryland	Y		117075 MW		MDBLS	3/08
	Baltimore-Towson MSA, MD	Y	86390 FQ	106870 MW	125250 TQ	USBLS	5/07
	Bethesda-Gaithersburg-Frederick PMSA, MD	Y	108780 FQ	126800 MW		USBLS	5/07
	Massachusetts	Y	102500 FQ	125940 MW		USBLS	5/07
	Boston-Cambridge-Quincy NECTA, MA	Y	107560 FQ	129690 MW		USBLS	5/07
	Worcester MSA, MA-CT	Y	86530 FQ	103170 MW	123700 TQ	USBLS	5/07
	Michigan	Y	86980 FQ	106910 MW	130560 TQ	USBLS	5/07
	Detroit-Warren-Livonia MSA, MI	Y	94490 FQ	114040 MW	134780 TQ	USBLS	5/07
	Grand Rapids-Wyoming MSA, MI	Y	73140 FQ	85940 MW	102640 TQ	USBLS	5/07
	Warren-Troy-Farmington Hills PMSA, MI	Y	92320 FQ	110130 MW	129090 TQ	USBLS	5/07
	Minnesota	Y	91169 FQ	110469 MW	134554 TQ	MNBLS	10/08-12/08
	Duluth-Superior MSA, MN-WI	Y	78355 FQ	92274 MW	105964 TQ	MNBLS	10/08-12/08
	Minneapolis-Saint Paul MSA, MN-WI	Y	94203 FQ	114316 MW	137234 TQ	MNBLS	10/08-12/08
	Rochester MSA, MN	Y	99243 FQ	126303 MW		MNBLS	10/08-12/08
	Mississippi	Y	85880 FQ	110560 MW	123500 TQ	USBLS	5/07
	Jackson MSA, MS	Y	74220 FQ	90350 MW	109930 TQ	USBLS	5/07
	Missouri	Y	82460 FQ	96050 MW	113480 TQ	USBLS	5/07
	Kansas City MSA, MO-KS	Y	87370 FQ	103620 MW	122970 TQ	USBLS	5/07
	St. Louis MSA, MO-IL	Y	85310 FQ	98190 MW	115260 TQ	USBLS	5/07
	Montana	Y	72250 FQ	88520 MW	103360 TQ	USBLS	5/07
	Billings MSA, MT	Y	72680 FQ	90750 MW	102220 TQ	USBLS	5/07
	Nebraska	Y	78630 FQ	95590 MW	116370 TQ	USBLS	5/07
	Lincoln MSA, NE	Y	78990 FQ	93900 MW	109560 TQ	USBLS	5/07
	Omaha-Council Bluffs MSA, NE-IA	Y	82800 FQ	103690 MW	124840 TQ	USBLS	5/07
	Nevada	H	43.36 FQ	53.68 MW	69.46 TQ	NVBLS	5/08
	Las Vegas-Paradise MSA, NV	H	47.50 FQ	60.62 MW		NVBLS	5/08
	New Hampshire	H	38.39 AE	56.48 MW	69.91 AEX	NHBLS	6/08
	Manchester MSA, NH	Y	84660 FQ	105620 MW	129960 TQ	USBLS	5/07
	Nashua NECTA, NH-MA	Y	103940 FQ	129670 MW		USBLS	5/07
	New Jersey	Y	102040 FQ	121720 MW		USBLS	5/07
	Camden PMSA, NJ	Y	102810 FQ	125590 MW		USBLS	5/07
	Edison PMSA, NJ	Y	105000 FQ	120940 MW	141920 TQ	USBLS	5/07
	Newark-Union PMSA, NJ-PA	Y	101990 FQ	124560 MW		USBLS	5/07
	New Mexico	Y	96480 FQ	119950 MW	144400 TQ	USBLS	5/07
	Albuquerque MSA, NM	Y	106710 FQ	125470 MW		USBLS	5/07
	New York	Y	95030 FQ	118880 MW		USBLS	5/07
	Albany-Schenectady-Troy MSA, NY	Y	96520 FQ	122940 MW	145330 TQ	USBLS	5/07
	Buffalo-Niagara Falls MSA, NY	Y	84110 FQ	97510 MW	118770 TQ	USBLS	5/07
	Glens Falls MSA, NY	Y	93740 FQ	112060 MW	135260 TQ	USBLS	5/07
	Nassau-Suffolk PMSA, NY	Y	110610 FQ	128990 MW		USBLS	5/07
	New York-Northern New Jersey-Long Island MSA, NY-NJ-PA	Y	101110 FQ	123490 MW		USBLS	5/07
	Utica-Rome MSA, NY	Y	68430 FQ	94160 MW	122260 TQ	USBLS	5/07
	North Carolina	Y	86740 FQ	108950 MW	136230 TQ	USBLS	5/07
	Charlotte-Gastonia-Concord MSA, NC-SC	Y	76870 FQ	95380 MW	118320 TQ	USBLS	5/07
	Greensboro-High Point MSA, NC	Y	84660 FQ	99370 MW	126490 TQ	USBLS	5/07
	Raleigh-Cary MSA, NC	Y	86840 FQ	103160 MW	123480 TQ	USBLS	5/07
	North Dakota	Y	73290 FQ	88430 MW	102380 TQ	USBLS	5/07
	Fargo MSA, ND-MN	Y	72520 FQ	85840 MW	96260 TQ	USBLS	5/07
	Ohio	Y	78980 FQ	98910 MW	121110 TQ	USBLS	5/07
	Canton-Massillon MSA, OH	Y	76480 FQ	95480 MW	116770 TQ	USBLS	5/07
	Cincinnati-Middletown MSA, OH-KY-IN	Y	91500 FQ	112180 MW	134470 TQ	USBLS	5/07

AE Average entry wage	**AW** Average wage paid	**FQ** First quartile wage	**LO** Lowest wage paid	**MTC** Median total compensation	**TCC** Total cash compensation
AER Average entry range	**AWR** Average wage range	**H** Hourly	**LR** Low end range	**MW** Median wage paid	**TQ** Third quartile wage
AEX Average experienced wage	**AXR** Average experienced range	**HI** Highest wage paid	**M** Monthly	**MWR** Median wage range	**W** Weekly
ATC Average total compensation	**D** Daily	**HR** High end range	**MCC** Median cash compensation	**S** See annotated source	**Y** Yearly

Occupation/Type/Industry	Location	Per	Low	Mid	High	Source	Date
Engineering Manager	Cleveland-Elyria-Mentor						
	MSA, OH	Y	82810 FQ	101380 MW	121980 TQ	USBLS	5/07
	Columbus MSA, OH	Y	69480 FQ	87230 MW	109530 TQ	USBLS	5/07
	Dayton MSA, OH	Y	89740 FQ	106930 MW	123480 TQ	USBLS	5/07
	Oklahoma	Y	71350 FQ	90490 MW	114540 TQ	USBLS	5/07
	Oklahoma City MSA, OK	Y	74300 FQ	95430 MW	118320 TQ	USBLS	5/07
	Tulsa MSA, OK	Y	76860 FQ	92370 MW	114370 TQ	USBLS	5/07
	Pennsylvania	Y	78370 FQ	100000 MW	130430 TQ	USBLS	5/07
	Allentown-Bethlehem-Easton						
	MSA, PA-NJ	Y	81250 FQ	102870 MW	124800 TQ	USBLS	5/07
	Philadelphia-Camden-						
	Wilmington MSA, PA-NJ-DE-						
	MD	Y	93730 FQ	117810 MW		USBLS	5/07
	Pittsburgh MSA, PA	Y	75750 FQ	95040 MW	125760 TQ	USBLS	5/07
	Rhode Island	Y	83910 FQ	104910 MW	128080 TQ	USBLS	5/07
	Providence-Fall River-						
	Warwick MSA, RI-MA	Y	86270 FQ	109360 MW	134820 TQ	USBLS	5/07
	South Carolina	Y	77180 FQ	95440 MW	118880 TQ	USBLS	5/07
	Charleston-North Charleston						
	MSA, SC	Y	75440 FQ	92900 MW	113060 TQ	USBLS	5/07
	Columbia MSA, SC	Y	72180 FQ	90650 MW	116870 TQ	USBLS	5/07
	South Dakota	Y	78242 FQ	90826 MW	109297 TQ	SDBLS	7/08-9/08
	Sioux Falls MSA, SD	Y	75986 FQ	91165 MW	104180 TQ	SDBLS	7/08-9/08
	Tennessee	Y	63820 FQ	84070 MW	108000 TQ	USBLS	5/07
	Clarksville MSA, TN-KY	Y	40610 FQ	74730 MW	91660 TQ	USBLS	5/07
	Memphis MSA, TN-MS-AR	Y	66500 FQ	82500 MW	108200 TQ	USBLS	5/07
	Nashville-Davidson-						
	Murfreesboro MSA, TN	Y	61020 FQ	84260 MW	107290 TQ	USBLS	5/07
	Texas	Y	96370 FQ	119250 MW		USBLS	5/07
	Austin-Round Rock MSA, TX	Y	96890 FQ	122380 MW		USBLS	5/07
	Dallas-Fort Worth-Arlington						
	MSA, TX	Y	102000 FQ	123380 MW		USBLS	5/07
	El Paso MSA, TX	Y	91370 FQ	107940 MW	122460 TQ	USBLS	5/07
	Houston-Sugar Land-Baytown						
	MSA, TX	Y	100010 FQ	120890 MW		USBLS	5/07
	San Antonio MSA, TX	Y	83420 FQ	102790 MW	124930 TQ	USBLS	5/07
	Utah	Y	80900 FQ	100680 MW	123610 TQ	USBLS	5/07
	Logan MSA, UT-ID	Y	69620 FQ	84120 MW	102780 TQ	USBLS	5/07
	Salt Lake City MSA, UT	Y	83220 FQ	104600 MW	131950 TQ	USBLS	5/07
	Vermont	Y	98930 FQ	127480 MW		USBLS	5/07
	Burlington-South Burlington						
	MSA, VT	Y	114050 FQ	137740 MW		USBLS	5/07
	Virginia	Y	95050 FQ	116080 MW	137290 TQ	USBLS	5/07
	Richmond MSA, VA	Y	71760 FQ	92390 MW	118820 TQ	USBLS	5/07
	Roanoke MSA, VA	Y	73180 FQ	90430 MW	103780 TQ	USBLS	5/07
	Virginia Beach-Norfolk-						
	Newport News MSA, VA-NC	Y	91160 FQ	108150 MW	123960 TQ	USBLS	5/07
	Washington	H	49.05 FQ	59.78 MW	69.57 TQ	WABLS	3/08
	Seattle-Tacoma-Bellevue						
	MSA, WA	Y	104060 FQ	127330 MW		USBLS	5/07
	West Virginia	Y	84131 FQ	101033 MW	123163 TQ	WVBLS	7/08-9/08
	Charleston MSA, WV	Y	80960 FQ	97750 MW	118360 TQ	USBLS	5/07
	Wisconsin	Y	75490 FQ	91040 MW	110080 TQ	USBLS	5/07
	Milwaukee-Waukesha-West						
	Allis MSA, WI	Y	78250 FQ	93200 MW	111170 TQ	USBLS	5/07
	Wyoming	Y	74289 FQ	86002 MW	105438 TQ	WYBLS	9/08
	Cheyenne MSA, WY	Y	74017 FQ	84309 MW	102177 TQ	WYBLS	9/08
	Puerto Rico	Y	67700 FQ	86540 MW	109600 TQ	USBLS	5/07
	San Juan-Caguas-Guaynabo						
	MSA, PR	Y	65920 FQ	85090 MW	109380 TQ	USBLS	5/07
	Guam	Y	42800 FQ	51300 MW	73880 TQ	USBLS	5/07
Engineering Teacher							
Postsecondary	Alabama	Y	40510 FQ	65270 MW	87390 TQ	USBLS	5/07
Postsecondary	Alaska	Y	71630 FQ	92550 MW	111270 TQ	USBLS	5/07
Postsecondary	California	Y		95718 AW		CABLS	1/08-3/08
Postsecondary	Colorado	Y	55910 FQ	77510 MW	98740 TQ	USBLS	5/07
Postsecondary	Delaware	Y	57220 FQ	84720 MW	117950 TQ	USBLS	5/07
Postsecondary	District of Columbia	Y	57500 FQ	71530 MW	107360 TQ	USBLS	5/07
Postsecondary	Florida	Y	62660 FQ	77330 MW	97660 TQ	USBLS	5/07
Postsecondary	Georgia	Y	60600 FQ	73200 MW	92100 TQ	USBLS	5/07
Postsecondary	Illinois	Y	51820 FQ	76240 MW	101240 TQ	USBLS	5/07

Occupation/Type/Industry	Location	Per	Low	Mid	High	Source	Date
Engineering Teacher							
Postsecondary	Indiana	Y	73180 FQ	105510 MW	116590 TQ	USBLS	5/07
Postsecondary	Iowa	Y	88380 FQ	114190 MW	138580 TQ	USBLS	5/07
Postsecondary	Kansas	Y	68250 FQ	88910 MW	112030 TQ	USBLS	5/07
Postsecondary	Kentucky	Y	70668 FQ	90374 MW	117277 TQ	KYBLS	2008
Postsecondary	Louisiana	Y		86072 AW		LABLS	1/08-3/08
Postsecondary	Maine	Y	58020 FQ	75970 MW	96360 TQ	USBLS	5/07
Postsecondary	Maryland	Y		99350 MW		MDBLS	3/08
Postsecondary	Massachusetts	Y	77940 FQ	99710 MW	122920 TQ	USBLS	5/07
Postsecondary	Michigan	Y	62830 FQ	80160 MW	98680 TQ	USBLS	5/07
Postsecondary	Minnesota	Y	56632 FQ	76897 MW	100856 TQ	MNBLS	10/08-12/08
Postsecondary	Mississippi	Y	59390 FQ	72710 MW	88600 TQ	USBLS	5/07
Postsecondary	Missouri	Y	57610 FQ	77450 MW	101580 TQ	USBLS	5/07
Postsecondary	Montana	Y	49490 FQ	64720 MW	80330 TQ	USBLS	5/07
Postsecondary	New Hampshire	Y	66263 AE	108561 MW	124389 AEX	NHBLS	6/08
Postsecondary	New Jersey	Y	63640 FQ	82710 MW	112720 TQ	USBLS	5/07
Postsecondary	New Mexico	Y	61350 FQ	74270 MW	93070 TQ	USBLS	5/07
Postsecondary	New York	Y	62360 FQ	77570 MW	102740 TQ	USBLS	5/07
Postsecondary	North Carolina	Y	59920 FQ	79180 MW	101320 TQ	USBLS	5/07
Postsecondary	North Dakota	Y	65290 FQ	84290 MW	98730 TQ	USBLS	5/07
Postsecondary	Ohio	Y	56330 FQ	78710 MW	102490 TQ	USBLS	5/07
Postsecondary	Oklahoma	Y	44600 FQ	52990 MW	58950 TQ	USBLS	5/07
Postsecondary	Pennsylvania	Y	67800 FQ	95270 MW	123800 TQ	USBLS	5/07
Postsecondary	Rhode Island	Y	74740 FQ	91820 MW	119140 TQ	USBLS	5/07
Postsecondary	South Carolina	Y	54070 FQ	69360 MW	82900 TQ	USBLS	5/07
Postsecondary	Tennessee	Y	51300 FQ	61040 MW	76980 TQ	USBLS	5/07
Postsecondary	Texas	Y	62140 FQ	83020 MW	108320 TQ	USBLS	5/07
Postsecondary	Utah	Y	67670 FQ	90610 MW	121840 TQ	USBLS	5/07
Postsecondary	Vermont	Y	53690 FQ	61390 MW	76560 TQ	USBLS	5/07
Postsecondary	Virginia	Y	54800 FQ	75130 MW	94840 TQ	USBLS	5/07
Postsecondary	Washington	Y		94265 AW		WABLS	3/08
Postsecondary	Wisconsin	Y	62510 FQ	78530 MW	104010 TQ	USBLS	5/07
Postsecondary	Wyoming	Y	69907 FQ	79887 MW	88949 TQ	WYBLS	9/08
Postsecondary	Puerto Rico	Y	41220 FQ	44600 MW	47970 TQ	USBLS	5/07
English Language and Literature Teacher							
Postsecondary	Alabama	Y	33770 FQ	44860 MW	60830 TQ	USBLS	5/07
Postsecondary	Birmingham-Hoover MSA, AL	Y	36170 FQ	46730 MW	65950 TQ	USBLS	5/07
Postsecondary	Montgomery MSA, AL	Y	40530 FQ	51350 MW	63450 TQ	USBLS	5/07
Postsecondary	Alaska	Y	50970 FQ	70960 MW	84860 TQ	USBLS	5/07
Postsecondary	Anchorage MSA, AK	Y	55560 FQ	75260 MW	90680 TQ	USBLS	5/07
Postsecondary	Arizona	Y	33670 FQ	44730 MW	56330 TQ	USBLS	5/07
Postsecondary	Phoenix-Mesa-Scottsdale MSA, AZ	Y	30370 FQ	37880 MW	48130 TQ	USBLS	5/07
Postsecondary	Tucson MSA, AZ	Y	47700 FQ	56770 MW	73620 TQ	USBLS	5/07
Postsecondary	Arkansas	Y	32540 FQ	41870 MW	54380 TQ	USBLS	5/07
Postsecondary	Little Rock-North Little Rock MSA, AR	Y	34560 FQ	41690 MW	52620 TQ	USBLS	5/07
Postsecondary	California	Y		86273 AW		CABLS	1/08-3/08
Postsecondary	Los Angeles-Long Beach-Glendale PMSA, CA	Y		84581 AW		CABLS	1/08-3/08
Postsecondary	Oakland-Fremont-Hayward MSA, CA	Y		80940 AW		CABLS	1/08-3/08
Postsecondary	Riverside-San Bernardino-Ontario MSA, CA	Y		79659 AW		CABLS	1/08-3/08
Postsecondary	Sacramento-Arden Arcade-Roseville MSA, CA	Y		78992 AW		CABLS	1/08-3/08
Postsecondary	San Diego-Carlsbad-San Marcos MSA, CA	Y		96312 AW		CABLS	1/08-3/08
Postsecondary	San Francisco-San Mateo-Redwood PMSA, CA	Y		100301 AW		CABLS	1/08-3/08
Postsecondary	Santa Ana-Anaheim-Irvine PMSA, CA	Y	50260 FQ	74170 MW	95960 TQ	USBLS	5/07
Postsecondary	Colorado	Y	35520 FQ	46330 MW	65090 TQ	USBLS	5/07
Postsecondary	Denver-Aurora MSA, CO	Y	38430 FQ	46160 MW	64040 TQ	USBLS	5/07
Postsecondary	Delaware	Y	45700 FQ	59090 MW	76980 TQ	USBLS	5/07
Postsecondary	Wilmington PMSA, DE-MD-NJ	Y	47160 FQ	60350 MW	86360 TQ	USBLS	5/07
Postsecondary	District of Columbia	Y	45140 FQ	62940 MW	80360 TQ	USBLS	5/07

AE	Average entry wage	AW	Average wage paid	FQ	First quartile wage
AER	Average entry range	AWR	Average wage range	H	Hourly
AEX	Average experienced wage	AXR	Average experienced range	HI	Highest wage paid
ATC	Average total compensation	D	Daily	HR	High end range

LO	Lowest wage paid	MTC	Median total compensation	TCC	Total cash compensation
LR	Low end range	MW	Median wage paid	TQ	Third quartile wage
M	Monthly	MWR	Median wage range	W	Weekly
MCC	Median cash compensation	S	See annotated source	Y	Yearly

Occupation/Type/Industry	Location	Per	Low	Mid	High	Source	Date
English Language and Literature Teacher							
Postsecondary	Washington-Arlington-Alexandria MSA, DC-VA-MD-WV	Y	43980 FQ	59760 MW	77970 TQ	USBLS	5/07
Postsecondary	Florida	Y	35590 FQ	49190 MW	68790 TQ	USBLS	5/07
Postsecondary	Jacksonville MSA, FL	Y	35790 FQ	43520 MW	55370 TQ	USBLS	5/07
Postsecondary	Lakeland MSA, FL	Y	36820 FQ	50060 MW	70710 TQ	USBLS	5/07
Postsecondary	Miami-Fort Lauderdale-Miami Beach MSA, FL	Y	32280 FQ	51450 MW	73250 TQ	USBLS	5/07
Postsecondary	Orlando-Kissimmee MSA, FL	Y	30680 FQ	45490 MW	65600 TQ	USBLS	5/07
Postsecondary	Tampa-St. Petersburg-Clearwater MSA, FL	Y	41230 FQ	54300 MW	79120 TQ	USBLS	5/07
Postsecondary	West Palm Beach-Boca Raton-Boynton Beach PMSA, FL	Y	32860 FQ	42810 MW	58790 TQ	USBLS	5/07
Postsecondary	Georgia	Y	36670 FQ	48720 MW	64510 TQ	USBLS	5/07
Postsecondary	Atlanta-Sandy Springs-Marietta MSA, GA	Y	39600 FQ	53450 MW	72090 TQ	USBLS	5/07
Postsecondary	Hawaii	Y	42490 FQ	52560 MW	68740 TQ	USBLS	5/07
Postsecondary	Honolulu MSA, HI	Y	42690 FQ	53720 MW	69990 TQ	USBLS	5/07
Postsecondary	Boise City-Nampa MSA, ID	Y	25380 FQ	37300 MW	44360 TQ	USBLS	5/07
Postsecondary	Illinois	Y	33470 FQ	49620 MW	64770 TQ	USBLS	5/07
Postsecondary	Chicago-Naperville-Joliet MSA, IL-IN-WI	Y	35800 FQ	50370 MW	66640 TQ	USBLS	5/07
Postsecondary	Indiana	Y	38400 FQ	50670 MW	63250 TQ	USBLS	5/07
Postsecondary	Evansville MSA, IN-KY	Y	30120 FQ	42540 MW	61930 TQ	USBLS	5/07
Postsecondary	Gary PMSA, IN	Y	36430 FQ	45360 MW	53790 TQ	USBLS	5/07
Postsecondary	Indianapolis-Carmel MSA, IN	Y	37910 FQ	45070 MW	61020 TQ	USBLS	5/07
Postsecondary	Iowa	Y	45810 FQ	58960 MW	76440 TQ	USBLS	5/07
Postsecondary	Davenport-Moline-Rock Island MSA, IA-IL	Y	42010 FQ	56150 MW	68670 TQ	USBLS	5/07
Postsecondary	Des Moines-West Des Moines MSA, IA	Y	47330 FQ	63590 MW	86010 TQ	USBLS	5/07
Postsecondary	Kansas	Y	34320 FQ	46010 MW	63250 TQ	USBLS	5/07
Postsecondary	Wichita MSA, KS	Y	43740 FQ	55910 MW	73660 TQ	USBLS	5/07
Postsecondary	Kentucky	Y	37221 FQ	49377 MW	63370 TQ	KYBLS	2008
Postsecondary	Louisville-Jefferson County MSA, KY-IN	Y	37560 FQ	47810 MW	60260 TQ	USBLS	5/07
Postsecondary	Louisiana	Y		53713 AW		LABLS	1/08-3/08
Postsecondary	Baton Rouge MSA, LA	Y	43960 FQ	49020 MW	56770 TQ	USBLS	5/07
Postsecondary	New Orleans-Metairie-Kenner MSA, LA	Y	36550 FQ	44050 MW	55840 TQ	USBLS	5/07
Postsecondary	Shreveport-Bossier City MSA, LA	Y	14260 FQ	32500 MW	48730 TQ	USBLS	5/07
Postsecondary	Maine	Y	41860 FQ	51000 MW	63140 TQ	USBLS	5/07
Postsecondary	Portland-South Portland-Biddeford MSA, ME	Y	43880 FQ	51940 MW	62760 TQ	USBLS	5/07
Postsecondary	Maryland	Y		63325 MW		MDBLS	3/08
Postsecondary	Baltimore-Towson MSA, MD	Y	49010 FQ	62520 MW	89060 TQ	USBLS	5/07
Postsecondary	Bethesda-Gaithersburg-Frederick PMSA, MD	Y	60080 FQ	76170 MW	102160 TQ	USBLS	5/07
Postsecondary	Massachusetts	Y	47130 FQ	60200 MW	81100 TQ	USBLS	5/07
Postsecondary	Boston-Cambridge-Quincy NECTA, MA	Y	45120 FQ	57700 MW	74290 TQ	USBLS	5/07
Postsecondary	Worcester MSA, MA-CT	Y	50960 FQ	63910 MW	87550 TQ	USBLS	5/07
Postsecondary	Michigan	Y	43860 FQ	60120 MW	78290 TQ	USBLS	5/07
Postsecondary	Detroit-Warren-Livonia MSA, MI	Y	44170 FQ	60880 MW	89450 TQ	USBLS	5/07
Postsecondary	Warren-Troy-Farmington Hills PMSA, MI	Y	39520 FQ	58790 MW	92450 TQ	USBLS	5/07
Postsecondary	Minnesota	Y	44485 FQ	57500 MW	74616 TQ	MNBLS	10/08-12/08
Postsecondary	Duluth-Superior MSA, MN-WI	Y	47299 FQ	56789 MW	65420 TQ	MNBLS	10/08-12/08
Postsecondary	Minneapolis-Saint Paul MSA, MN-WI	Y	44496 FQ	57469 MW	75056 TQ	MNBLS	10/08-12/08
Postsecondary	Mississippi	Y	41850 FQ	52480 MW	63630 TQ	USBLS	5/07
Postsecondary	Jackson MSA, MS	Y	42350 FQ	54560 MW	63210 TQ	USBLS	5/07
Postsecondary	Missouri	Y	39350 FQ	54730 MW	79920 TQ	USBLS	5/07
Postsecondary	Kansas City MSA, MO-KS	Y	36590 FQ	47230 MW	63890 TQ	USBLS	5/07
Postsecondary	St. Louis MSA, MO-IL	Y	35960 FQ	55690 MW	82960 TQ	USBLS	5/07
Postsecondary	Montana	Y	33500 FQ	45670 MW	56140 TQ	USBLS	5/07
Postsecondary	Nebraska	Y	35250 FQ	47400 MW	62040 TQ	USBLS	5/07

AE	Average entry wage	AW	Average wage paid	FQ	First quartile wage
AER	Average entry range	AWR	Average wage range	H	Hourly
AEX	Average experienced wage	AXR	Average experienced range	HI	Highest wage paid
ATC	Average total compensation	D	Daily	HR	High end range

LO	Lowest wage paid	MTC	Median total compensation	TCC	Total cash compensation
LR	Low end range	MW	Median wage paid	TQ	Third quartile wage
M	Monthly	MWR	Median wage range	W	Weekly
MCC	Median cash compensation	S	See annotated source	Y	Yearly

Occupation/Type/Industry	Location	Per	Low	Mid	High	Source	Date
English Language and Literature Teacher							
Postsecondary	Omaha-Council Bluffs MSA, NE-IA	Y	30220 FQ	40230 MW	59060 TQ	USBLS	5/07
Postsecondary	New Hampshire	Y	39250 AE	55037 MW	65770 AEX	NHBLS	6/08
Postsecondary	Manchester MSA, NH	Y	44400 FQ	49670 MW	64450 TQ	USBLS	5/07
Postsecondary	New Jersey	Y	46340 FQ	67540 MW	93550 TQ	USBLS	5/07
Postsecondary	Camden PMSA, NJ	Y	41040 FQ	61870 MW	91600 TQ	USBLS	5/07
Postsecondary	Edison PMSA, NJ	Y	53130 FQ	71160 MW	98280 TQ	USBLS	5/07
Postsecondary	Newark-Union PMSA, NJ-PA	Y	45500 FQ	67330 MW	91670 TQ	USBLS	5/07
Postsecondary	New Mexico	Y	39750 FQ	46740 MW	55770 TQ	USBLS	5/07
Postsecondary	Albuquerque MSA, NM	Y	40140 FQ	47160 MW	56230 TQ	USBLS	5/07
Postsecondary	New York	Y	46360 FQ	61200 MW	84930 TQ	USBLS	5/07
Postsecondary	Buffalo-Niagara Falls MSA, NY	Y	40720 FQ	56350 MW	81580 TQ	USBLS	5/07
Postsecondary	Nassau-Suffolk PMSA, NY	Y	47840 FQ	60430 MW	77590 TQ	USBLS	5/07
Postsecondary	New York-Northern New Jersey-Long Island MSA, NY-NJ-PA	Y	48440 FQ	67200 MW	92310 TQ	USBLS	5/07
Postsecondary	North Carolina	Y	38810 FQ	48060 MW	59800 TQ	USBLS	5/07
Postsecondary	Charlotte-Gastonia-Concord MSA, NC-SC	Y	35340 FQ	40660 MW	54140 TQ	USBLS	5/07
Postsecondary	Raleigh-Cary MSA, NC	Y	32960 FQ	40430 MW	55400 TQ	USBLS	5/07
Postsecondary	North Dakota	Y	28920 FQ	41180 MW	51360 TQ	USBLS	5/07
Postsecondary	Fargo MSA, ND-MN	Y	30700 FQ	46610 MW	61770 TQ	USBLS	5/07
Postsecondary	Ohio	Y	38400 FQ	53810 MW	75630 TQ	USBLS	5/07
Postsecondary	Cincinnati-Middletown MSA, OH-KY-IN	Y	36160 FQ	48760 MW	64590 TQ	USBLS	5/07
Postsecondary	Cleveland-Elyria-Mentor MSA, OH	Y	37080 FQ	51840 MW	70780 TQ	USBLS	5/07
Postsecondary	Columbus MSA, OH	Y	56400 FQ	75120 MW	94510 TQ	USBLS	5/07
Postsecondary	Dayton MSA, OH	Y	31160 FQ	47650 MW	67520 TQ	USBLS	5/07
Postsecondary	Oklahoma	Y	24650 FQ	36550 MW	48030 TQ	USBLS	5/07
Postsecondary	Oklahoma City MSA, OK	Y	28950 FQ	42750 MW	62710 TQ	USBLS	5/07
Postsecondary	Tulsa MSA, OK	Y	24110 FQ	35790 MW	44680 TQ	USBLS	5/07
Postsecondary	Portland-Vancouver-Beaverton MSA, OR-WA	Y	47100 FQ	74950 MW	106980 TQ	USBLS	5/07
Postsecondary	Pennsylvania	Y	43690 FQ	56360 MW	75330 TQ	USBLS	5/07
Postsecondary	Allentown-Bethlehem-Easton MSA, PA-NJ	Y	53780 FQ	62830 MW	83540 TQ	USBLS	5/07
Postsecondary	Erie MSA, PA	Y	48700 FQ	58060 MW	73510 TQ	USBLS	5/07
Postsecondary	Philadelphia-Camden-Wilmington MSA, PA-NJ-DE-MD	Y	43240 FQ	56200 MW	75240 TQ	USBLS	5/07
Postsecondary	Pittsburgh MSA, PA	Y	48770 FQ	67710 MW	89840 TQ	USBLS	5/07
Postsecondary	Rhode Island	Y	49310 FQ	63530 MW	85340 TQ	USBLS	5/07
Postsecondary	Providence-Fall River-Warwick MSA, RI-MA	Y	49350 FQ	63410 MW	84620 TQ	USBLS	5/07
Postsecondary	South Carolina	Y	42920 FQ	51810 MW	64020 TQ	USBLS	5/07
Postsecondary	Charleston-North Charleston MSA, SC	Y	44690 FQ	51220 MW	68440 TQ	USBLS	5/07
Postsecondary	Columbia MSA, SC	Y	45380 FQ	55940 MW	66520 TQ	USBLS	5/07
Postsecondary	Spartanburg MSA, SC	Y	32930 FQ	43650 MW	51420 TQ	USBLS	5/07
Postsecondary	South Dakota	Y	40139 FQ	48736 MW	62273 TQ	SDBLS	7/08-9/08
Postsecondary	Sioux Falls MSA, SD	Y	38421 FQ	45887 MW	53586 TQ	SDBLS	7/08-9/08
Postsecondary	Tennessee	Y	40220 FQ	48130 MW	68870 TQ	USBLS	5/07
Postsecondary	Kingsport-Bristol-Bristol MSA, TN-VA	Y	35320 FQ	43940 MW	54190 TQ	USBLS	5/07
Postsecondary	Knoxville MSA, TN	Y	41120 FQ	48000 MW	93180 TQ	USBLS	5/07
Postsecondary	Memphis MSA, TN-MS-AR	Y	41710 FQ	50790 MW	75790 TQ	USBLS	5/07
Postsecondary	Nashville-Davidson-Murfreesboro MSA, TN	Y	42010 FQ	51130 MW	85680 TQ	USBLS	5/07
Postsecondary	Texas	Y	34100 FQ	50470 MW	69840 TQ	USBLS	5/07
Postsecondary	Austin-Round Rock MSA, TX	Y	28240 FQ	51410 MW	76940 TQ	USBLS	5/07
Postsecondary	Dallas-Fort Worth-Arlington MSA, TX	Y	38730 FQ	52660 MW	75210 TQ	USBLS	5/07
Postsecondary	El Paso MSA, TX	Y	30910 FQ	49400 MW	64960 TQ	USBLS	5/07
Postsecondary	Houston-Sugar Land-Baytown MSA, TX	Y	45440 FQ	64010 MW	83610 TQ	USBLS	5/07
Postsecondary	San Antonio MSA, TX	Y	39410 FQ	49440 MW	61210 TQ	USBLS	5/07
Postsecondary	Utah	Y	41990 FQ	51800 MW	60370 TQ	USBLS	5/07
Postsecondary	Salt Lake City MSA, UT	Y	41380 FQ	54050 MW	69130 TQ	USBLS	5/07

AE Average entry wage	**AW** Average wage paid	**FQ** First quartile wage	**LO** Lowest wage paid	**MTC** Median total compensation	**TCC** Total cash compensation
AER Average entry range	**AWR** Average wage range	**H** Hourly	**LR** Low end range	**MW** Median wage paid	**TQ** Third quartile wage
AEX Average experienced wage	**AXR** Average experienced range	**HI** Highest wage paid	**M** Monthly	**MWR** Median wage range	**W** Weekly
ATC Average total compensation	**D** Daily	**HR** High end range	**MCC** Median cash compensation	**S** See annotated source	**Y** Yearly

Occupation/Type/Industry	Location	Per	Low	Mid	High	Source	Date
English Language and Literature Teacher							
Postsecondary	Vermont	Y	42700 FQ	52680 MW	64240 TQ	USBLS	5/07
Postsecondary	Burlington-South Burlington MSA, VT	Y	40540 FQ	53000 MW	66080 TQ	USBLS	5/07
Postsecondary	Virginia	Y	35900 FQ	48250 MW	62720 TQ	USBLS	5/07
Postsecondary	Lynchburg MSA, VA	Y	26540 FQ	42660 MW	55050 TQ	USBLS	5/07
Postsecondary	Richmond MSA, VA	Y	35140 FQ	47950 MW	64010 TQ	USBLS	5/07
Postsecondary	Virginia Beach-Norfolk-Newport News MSA, VA-NC	Y	35870 FQ	46590 MW	62430 TQ	USBLS	5/07
Postsecondary	Washington	Y		52588 AW		WABLS	3/08
Postsecondary	Seattle-Tacoma-Bellevue MSA, WA	Y	40890 FQ	50190 MW	61840 TQ	USBLS	5/07
Postsecondary	West Virginia	Y	40753 FQ	51246 MW	62118 TQ	WVBLS	7/08-9/08
Postsecondary	Wisconsin	Y	39470 FQ	49900 MW	68220 TQ	USBLS	5/07
Postsecondary	Milwaukee-Waukesha-West Allis MSA, WI	Y	37480 FQ	45670 MW	62900 TQ	USBLS	5/07
Postsecondary	Wyoming	Y	41492 FQ	49604 MW	63010 TQ	WYBLS	9/08
Postsecondary	Puerto Rico	Y	37410 FQ	47640 MW	61840 TQ	USBLS	5/07
Postsecondary	San Juan-Caguas-Guaynabo MSA, PR	Y	41710 FQ	54480 MW	64250 TQ	USBLS	5/07
Enlisted Member							
Military, Active Duty, Pay Grade E-1 < 4 Months	United States	M		1295 AW		DOD1	2009
Military, Active Duty, Pay Grade E-1 > 4 Months	United States	M		1400 AW		DOD1	2009
Military, Active Duty, Pay Grade E-2	United States	M		1569 AW		DOD1	2009
Military, Active Duty, Pay Grade E-3	United States	M	1650 LO		1860 HI	DOD1	2009
Military, Active Duty, Pay Grade E-4	United States	M	1827 LO		2219 HI	DOD1	2009
Military, Active Duty, Pay Grade E-5	United States	M	1994 LO		2828 HI	DOD1	2009
Military, Active Duty, Pay Grade E-6	United States	M	2176 LO		3370 HI	DOD1	2009
Military, Active Duty, Pay Grade E-7	United States	M	2516 LO		4521 HI	DOD1	2009
Military, Active Duty, Pay Grade E-8	United States	M	3619 LO		5161 HI	DOD1	2009
Military, Active Duty, Pay Grade E-9	United States	M	4421 LO		6863 HI	DOD1	2009
Military, Reserve, Pay Grade E-1	United States	S		2892 AW		DOD2	2009
Military, Reserve, Pay Grade E-2	United States	S		3242 AW		DOD2	2009
Military, Reserve, Pay Grade E-3	United States	S	3409 LO		3843 HI	DOD2	2009
Military, Reserve, Pay Grade E-4	United States	S	3777 LO		4585 HI	DOD2	2009
Military, Reserve, Pay Grade E-5	United States	S	4120 LO		5845 HI	DOD2	2009
Military, Reserve, Pay Grade E-6	United States	S	4496 LO		6964 HI	DOD2	2009
Military, Reserve, Pay Grade E-7	United States	S	5199 LO		9343 HI	DOD2	2009
Military, Reserve, Pay Grade E-8	United States	S	7478 LO		10456 HI	DOD2	2009
Military, Reserve, Pay Grade E-9	United States	S	9136 LO		12252 HI	DOD2	2009
Entomologist							
Public Health	Ohio	H	21.77 LO		31.86 HI	ODAS	2008
Environmental Analyst							
State Government	Wyoming	Y	39540 LO		52272 HI	AFT02	3/1/08
Environmental Compliance Inspector							
	Virginia	Y	31352-40959 LR		64347-84062 HR	VACG01	11/25/07
Environmental Engineer							
	Alabama	Y	52730 FQ	67360 MW	82740 TQ	USBLS	5/07
	Birmingham-Hoover MSA, AL	Y	52150 FQ	64860 MW	76300 TQ	USBLS	5/07
	Montgomery MSA, AL	Y	50120 FQ	66670 MW	81770 TQ	USBLS	5/07
	Alaska	Y	47040 FQ	66230 MW	81030 TQ	USBLS	5/07
	Anchorage MSA, AK	Y	52810 FQ	69160 MW	82700 TQ	USBLS	5/07
	Arizona	Y	46910 FQ	62580 MW	87150 TQ	USBLS	5/07
	Phoenix-Mesa-Scottsdale MSA, AZ	Y	46940 FQ	62570 MW	88950 TQ	USBLS	5/07
	Tucson MSA, AZ	Y	51660 FQ	65410 MW	86730 TQ	USBLS	5/07
	Yuma MSA, AZ	Y	45120 FQ	81850 MW	91570 TQ	USBLS	5/07
	Arkansas	Y	48200 FQ	62490 MW	77480 TQ	USBLS	5/07
	Little Rock-North Little Rock MSA, AR	Y	45650 FQ	60590 MW	76680 TQ	USBLS	5/07
	California	H	31.08 FQ	38.59 MW	47.27 TQ	CABLS	1/08-3/08
	Fresno MSA, CA	H	27.91 FQ	33.08 MW	37.55 TQ	CABLS	1/08-3/08
	Los Angeles-Long Beach-Glendale PMSA, CA	H	33.57 FQ	40.66 MW	47.40 TQ	CABLS	1/08-3/08

AE Average entry wage	**AW** Average wage paid	**FQ** First quartile wage	**LO** Lowest wage paid	**MTC** Median total compensation	**TCC** Total cash compensation
AER Average entry range	**AWR** Average wage range	**H** Hourly	**LR** Low end range	**MW** Median wage paid	**TQ** Third quartile wage
AEX Average experienced wage	**AXR** Average experienced range	**HI** Highest wage paid	**M** Monthly	**MWR** Median wage range	**W** Weekly
ATC Average total compensation	**D** Daily	**HR** High end range	**MCC** Median cash compensation	**S** See annotated source	**Y** Yearly

Occupation/Type/Industry	Location	Per	Low	Mid	High	Source	Date
Environmental Engineer	Oakland-Fremont-Hayward MSA, CA	H	32.11 FQ	38.02 MW	47.41 TQ	CABLS	1/08-3/08
	Riverside-San Bernardino-Ontario MSA, CA	H	38.14 FQ	44.92 MW	49.54 TQ	CABLS	1/08-3/08
	Sacramento-Arden Arcade-Roseville MSA, CA	H	29.60 FQ	35.60 MW	41.01 TQ	CABLS	1/08-3/08
	San Diego-Carlsbad-San Marcos MSA, CA	H	30.37 FQ	36.82 MW	45.75 TQ	CABLS	1/08-3/08
	San Francisco-San Mateo-Redwood PMSA, CA	H	42.69 FQ	49.10 MW	57.25 TQ	CABLS	1/08-3/08
	San Jose-Sunnyvale-Santa Clara MSA, CA	H	32.12 FQ	38.08 MW	46.61 TQ	CABLS	1/08-3/08
	Santa Ana-Anaheim-Irvine PMSA, CA	Y	57550 FQ	64860 MW	88340 TQ	USBLS	5/07
	Colorado	Y	53640 FQ	72990 MW	93960 TQ	USBLS	5/07
	Denver-Aurora MSA, CO	Y	55120 FQ	77420 MW	96010 TQ	USBLS	5/07
	Connecticut	H	27.79 AE	38.14 MW		CTBLS	1/08-3/08
	Bridgeport-Stamford-Norwalk MSA, CT	Y	57890 FQ	66990 MW	88180 TQ	USBLS	5/07
	Hartford-West Hartford-East Hartford MSA, CT	Y	68110 FQ	81030 MW	93810 TQ	USBLS	5/07
	Delaware	Y	54270 FQ	69020 MW	84500 TQ	USBLS	5/07
	Wilmington PMSA, DE-MD-NJ	Y	51000 FQ	66050 MW	86920 TQ	USBLS	5/07
	District of Columbia	Y	65530 FQ	86570 MW	104580 TQ	USBLS	5/07
	Washington-Arlington-Alexandria MSA, DC-VA-MD-WV	Y	64680 FQ	85090 MW	101970 TQ	USBLS	5/07
	Florida	Y	51290 FQ	65210 MW	83520 TQ	USBLS	5/07
	Fort Lauderdale-Pompano Beach-Deerfield Beach PMSA, FL	Y	60780 FQ	76470 MW		USBLS	5/07
	Jacksonville MSA, FL	Y	46960 FQ	66950 MW	84310 TQ	USBLS	5/07
	Miami-Fort Lauderdale-Miami Beach MSA, FL	Y	56230 FQ	69920 MW	97380 TQ	USBLS	5/07
	Orlando-Kissimmee MSA, FL	Y	50990 FQ	57880 MW	69450 TQ	USBLS	5/07
	Tampa-St. Petersburg-Clearwater MSA, FL	Y	50810 FQ	62090 MW	78520 TQ	USBLS	5/07
	West Palm Beach-Boca Raton-Boynton Beach PMSA, FL	Y	54180 FQ	65870 MW	80540 TQ	USBLS	5/07
	Georgia	Y	51620 FQ	63550 MW	86580 TQ	USBLS	5/07
	Atlanta-Sandy Springs-Marietta MSA, GA	Y	53330 FQ	64430 MW	88230 TQ	USBLS	5/07
	Hawaii	Y	68020 FQ	81730 MW	93010 TQ	USBLS	5/07
	Honolulu MSA, HI	Y	67890 FQ	82450 MW	93500 TQ	USBLS	5/07
	Idaho	Y	43450 FQ	51450 MW	71780 TQ	USBLS	5/07
	Boise City-Nampa MSA, ID	Y	46880 FQ	56460 MW	68820 TQ	USBLS	5/07
	Idaho Falls MSA, ID	Y	37240 FQ	47180 MW	63890 TQ	USBLS	5/07
	Illinois	Y	61300 FQ	80950 MW	95990 TQ	USBLS	5/07
	Chicago-Naperville-Joliet MSA, IL-IN-WI	Y	59300 FQ	84730 MW	97280 TQ	USBLS	5/07
	Indiana	Y	49550 FQ	65730 MW	81850 TQ	USBLS	5/07
	Gary PMSA, IN	Y	53130 FQ	63470 MW	81240 TQ	USBLS	5/07
	Indianapolis-Carmel MSA, IN	Y	49760 FQ	63100 MW	78540 TQ	USBLS	5/07
	Iowa	Y	57970 FQ	68870 MW	79250 TQ	USBLS	5/07
	Kansas	Y	62230 FQ	75830 MW	91030 TQ	USBLS	5/07
	Wichita MSA, KS	Y	63050 FQ	73100 MW	86630 TQ	USBLS	5/07
	Kentucky	Y	53659 FQ	69667 MW	83187 TQ	KYBLS	2008
	Lexington-Fayette MSA, KY	Y	45720 FQ	50170 MW	58840 TQ	USBLS	5/07
	Louisville-Jefferson County MSA, KY-IN	Y	42350 FQ	52520 MW	73220 TQ	USBLS	5/07
	Louisiana	H	25.40 FQ	32.34 MW	42.03 TQ	LABLS	1/08-3/08
	Baton Rouge MSA, LA	Y	53370 FQ	64200 MW	84510 TQ	USBLS	5/07
	New Orleans-Metairie-Kenner MSA, LA	Y	59260 FQ	80670 MW	94600 TQ	USBLS	5/07
	Maine	Y	49970 FQ	62340 MW	76680 TQ	USBLS	5/07
	Portland-South Portland-Biddeford MSA, ME	Y	57250 FQ	69900 MW	82190 TQ	USBLS	5/07
	Maryland	Y		86175 MW		MDBLS	3/08
	Baltimore-Towson MSA, MD	Y	60170 FQ	76960 MW	95310 TQ	USBLS	5/07
	Bethesda-Gaithersburg-Frederick PMSA, MD	Y	70060 FQ	87970 MW	101250 TQ	USBLS	5/07

Occupation/Type/Industry	Location	Per	Low	Mid	High	Source	Date
Environmental Engineer	Massachusetts	Y	62500 FQ	76120 MW	91740 TQ	USBLS	5/07
	Boston-Cambridge-Quincy NECTA, MA	Y	64140 FQ	77240 MW	92210 TQ	USBLS	5/07
	Worcester MSA, MA-CT	Y	63530 FQ	72550 MW	79920 TQ	USBLS	5/07
	Michigan	Y	58710 FQ	74070 MW	88700 TQ	USBLS	5/07
	Detroit-Warren-Livonia MSA, MI	Y	66250 FQ	79870 MW	96760 TQ	USBLS	5/07
	Grand Rapids-Wyoming MSA, MI	Y	57100 FQ	77380 MW	102770 TQ	USBLS	5/07
	Warren-Troy-Farmington Hills PMSA, MI	Y	62260 FQ	75200 MW	88940 TQ	USBLS	5/07
	Minnesota	Y	63014 FQ	77054 MW	91806 TQ	MNBLS	10/08-12/08
	Duluth-Superior MSA, MN-WI	Y	49664 FQ	72901 MW	92130 TQ	MNBLS	10/08-12/08
	Minneapolis-Saint Paul MSA, MN-WI	Y	64730 FQ	77891 MW	92643 TQ	MNBLS	10/08-12/08
	Mississippi	Y	49280 FQ	59470 MW	72750 TQ	USBLS	5/07
	Jackson MSA, MS	Y	48330 FQ	56590 MW	66600 TQ	USBLS	5/07
	Missouri	Y	51460 FQ	68290 MW	88700 TQ	USBLS	5/07
	Kansas City MSA, MO-KS	Y	63670 FQ	78710 MW	95460 TQ	USBLS	5/07
	St. Louis MSA, MO-IL	Y	53340 FQ	70730 MW	90600 TQ	USBLS	5/07
	Montana	Y	42300 FQ	56600 MW	65380 TQ	USBLS	5/07
	Nebraska	Y	55760 FQ	69080 MW	82090 TQ	USBLS	5/07
	Omaha-Council Bluffs MSA, NE-IA	Y	56360 FQ	71950 MW	88430 TQ	USBLS	5/07
	Nevada	H	30.41 FQ	36.54 MW	44.27 TQ	NVBLS	5/08
	Carson City MSA, NV	H	30.09 FQ	35.13 MW	39.31 TQ	NVBLS	5/08
	Las Vegas-Paradise MSA, NV	H	31.76 FQ	38.64 MW	47.93 TQ	NVBLS	5/08
	New Hampshire	H	22.33 AE	28.95 MW	37.37 AEX	NHBLS	6/08
	Manchester MSA, NH	Y	44000 FQ	50330 MW	57660 TQ	USBLS	5/07
	New Jersey	Y	62440 FQ	80280 MW	96150 TQ	USBLS	5/07
	Atlantic City MSA, NJ	Y	66370 FQ	84230 MW	92560 TQ	USBLS	5/07
	Camden PMSA, NJ	Y	57850 FQ	71580 MW	92180 TQ	USBLS	5/07
	Edison PMSA, NJ	Y	57010 FQ	85500 MW	101770 TQ	USBLS	5/07
	Newark-Union PMSA, NJ-PA	Y	66640 FQ	81430 MW	95150 TQ	USBLS	5/07
	Trenton-Ewing MSA, NJ	Y	63790 FQ	74580 MW	86000 TQ	USBLS	5/07
	New Mexico	Y	57520 FQ	73010 MW	98190 TQ	USBLS	5/07
	Albuquerque MSA, NM	Y	57110 FQ	75800 MW	107840 TQ	USBLS	5/07
	New York	Y	54530 FQ	74120 MW	94170 TQ	USBLS	5/07
	Albany-Schenectady-Troy MSA, NY	Y	50520 FQ	66910 MW	79700 TQ	USBLS	5/07
	Buffalo-Niagara Falls MSA, NY	Y	64630 FQ	79220 MW	92230 TQ	USBLS	5/07
	Nassau-Suffolk PMSA, NY	Y	48400 FQ	69720 MW	86530 TQ	USBLS	5/07
	New York-Northern New Jersey-Long Island MSA, NY-NJ-PA	Y	59040 FQ	81280 MW	98970 TQ	USBLS	5/07
	North Carolina	Y	54590 FQ	66670 MW	82850 TQ	USBLS	5/07
	Charlotte-Gastonia-Concord MSA, NC-SC	Y	53410 FQ	68900 MW	88730 TQ	USBLS	5/07
	Raleigh-Cary MSA, NC	Y	55650 FQ	65500 MW	76250 TQ	USBLS	5/07
	North Dakota	Y	49250 FQ	59320 MW	72490 TQ	USBLS	5/07
	Ohio	Y	59320 FQ	73730 MW	92630 TQ	USBLS	5/07
	Cincinnati-Middletown MSA, OH-KY-IN	Y	67690 FQ	76750 MW	89040 TQ	USBLS	5/07
	Cleveland-Elyria-Mentor MSA, OH	Y	61070 FQ	75170 MW	97590 TQ	USBLS	5/07
	Columbus MSA, OH	Y	55960 FQ	77000 MW	107320 TQ	USBLS	5/07
	Dayton MSA, OH	Y	60310 FQ	76970 MW	94780 TQ	USBLS	5/07
	Oklahoma	Y	47890 FQ	69550 MW	88510 TQ	USBLS	5/07
	Oklahoma City MSA, OK	Y	68100 FQ	77850 MW	90900 TQ	USBLS	5/07
	Tulsa MSA, OK	Y	44970 FQ	60580 MW	89430 TQ	USBLS	5/07
	Oregon	H	30.03 FQ	36.00 MW	42.69 TQ	ORBLS	5/08
	Portland-Vancouver-Beaverton MSA, OR-WA	Y	53470 FQ	67210 MW	84700 TQ	USBLS	5/07
	Pennsylvania	Y	56880 FQ	75920 MW	97650 TQ	USBLS	5/07
	Allentown-Bethlehem-Easton MSA, PA-NJ	Y	74270 FQ	90590 MW	116720 TQ	USBLS	5/07
	Philadelphia-Camden-Wilmington MSA, PA-NJ-DE-MD	Y	63720 FQ	83680 MW	104380 TQ	USBLS	5/07
	Pittsburgh MSA, PA	Y	52140 FQ	71110 MW	88710 TQ	USBLS	5/07
	Rhode Island	Y	58980 FQ	67950 MW	80720 TQ	USBLS	5/07

AE	Average entry wage	AW	Average wage paid	FQ	First quartile wage	LO	Lowest wage paid	MTC	Median total compensation	TCC	Total cash compensation
AER	Average entry range	AWR	Average wage range	H	Hourly	LR	Low end range	MW	Median wage paid	TQ	Third quartile wage
AEX	Average experienced wage	AXR	Average experienced range	HI	Highest wage paid	M	Monthly	MWR	Median wage range	W	Weekly
ATC	Average total compensation	D	Daily	HR	High end range	MCC	Median cash compensation	S	See annotated source	Y	Yearly

546

Occupation/Type/Industry	Location	Per	Low	Mid	High	Source	Date
Environmental Engineer	Providence-Fall River-Warwick MSA, RI-MA	Y	58730 FQ	67720 MW	80080 TQ	USBLS	5/07
	South Carolina	Y	48970 FQ	62240 MW	81970 TQ	USBLS	5/07
	Charleston-North Charleston MSA, SC	Y	57820 FQ	78220 MW	91070 TQ	USBLS	5/07
	Columbia MSA, SC	Y	43270 FQ	52700 MW	64850 TQ	USBLS	5/07
	Florence MSA, SC	Y	55830 FQ	66900 MW	79750 TQ	USBLS	5/07
	South Dakota	Y	47097 FQ	55624 MW	67832 TQ	SDBLS	7/08-9/08
	Sioux Falls MSA, SD	Y	42584 FQ	51773 MW	63825 TQ	SDBLS	7/08-9/08
	Tennessee	Y	56080 FQ	77380 MW	97780 TQ	USBLS	5/07
	Memphis MSA, TN-MS-AR	Y	42120 FQ	50060 MW	70980 TQ	USBLS	5/07
	Nashville-Davidson-Murfreesboro MSA, TN	Y	35780 FQ	60590 MW	79110 TQ	USBLS	5/07
	Texas	Y	44990 FQ	67150 MW	90790 TQ	USBLS	5/07
	Austin-Round Rock MSA, TX	Y	41360 FQ	57270 MW	76820 TQ	USBLS	5/07
	Dallas-Fort Worth-Arlington MSA, TX	Y	44490 FQ	74700 MW	100080 TQ	USBLS	5/07
	El Paso MSA, TX	Y	30730 FQ	42780 MW	68720 TQ	USBLS	5/07
	Houston-Sugar Land-Baytown MSA, TX	Y	49700 FQ	71980 MW	96260 TQ	USBLS	5/07
	San Antonio MSA, TX	Y	63450 FQ	83940 MW	96640 TQ	USBLS	5/07
	Utah	Y	54770 FQ	69090 MW	125140 TQ	USBLS	5/07
	Salt Lake City MSA, UT	Y	56410 FQ	71340 MW	132850 TQ	USBLS	5/07
	Vermont	Y	56460 FQ	62800 MW	71190 TQ	USBLS	5/07
	Burlington-South Burlington MSA, VT	Y	58900 FQ	65030 MW	73160 TQ	USBLS	5/07
	Virginia	Y	56160 FQ	70200 MW	86120 TQ	USBLS	5/07
	Richmond MSA, VA	Y	53890 FQ	66260 MW	78150 TQ	USBLS	5/07
	Virginia Beach-Norfolk-Newport News MSA, VA-NC	Y	63000 FQ	79080 MW	94420 TQ	USBLS	5/07
	Washington	H	30.63 FQ	37.78 MW	45.84 TQ	WABLS	3/08
	Seattle-Tacoma-Bellevue MSA, WA	Y	62040 FQ	79810 MW	97170 TQ	USBLS	5/07
	West Virginia	Y	53939 FQ	72117 MW	86312 TQ	WVBLS	7/08-9/08
	Charleston MSA, WV	Y	38560 FQ	62250 MW	74120 TQ	USBLS	5/07
	Wisconsin	Y	55990 FQ	69630 MW	80910 TQ	USBLS	5/07
	Milwaukee-Waukesha-West Allis MSA, WI	Y	51640 FQ	69190 MW	85060 TQ	USBLS	5/07
	Wyoming	Y	49219 FQ	62261 MW	82528 TQ	WYBLS	9/08
	Puerto Rico	Y	52220 FQ	71600 MW	81740 TQ	USBLS	5/07
	San Juan-Caguas-Guaynabo MSA, PR	Y	53950 FQ	72100 MW	81110 TQ	USBLS	5/07
	Guam	Y	36930 FQ	46500 MW	67130 TQ	USBLS	5/07
Environmental Engineering Technician	Alabama	Y	27490 FQ	33310 MW	40000 TQ	USBLS	5/07
	Birmingham-Hoover MSA, AL	Y	27760 FQ	33120 MW	40640 TQ	USBLS	5/07
	Mobile MSA, AL	Y	22510 FQ	25970 MW	32890 TQ	USBLS	5/07
	Alaska	Y	42790 FQ	48860 MW	57230 TQ	USBLS	5/07
	Arizona	Y	31540 FQ	38740 MW	49320 TQ	USBLS	5/07
	Phoenix-Mesa-Scottsdale MSA, AZ	Y	30110 FQ	37230 MW	47790 TQ	USBLS	5/07
	Tucson MSA, AZ	Y	41050 FQ	47350 MW	59850 TQ	USBLS	5/07
	Arkansas	Y	32330 FQ	40400 MW	58300 TQ	USBLS	5/07
	Little Rock-North Little Rock MSA, AR	Y	26590 FQ	36150 MW	57570 TQ	USBLS	5/07
	California	H	17.34 FQ	23.74 MW	30.75 TQ	CABLS	1/08-3/08
	Los Angeles-Long Beach-Glendale PMSA, CA	H	26.71 FQ	31.81 MW	37.47 TQ	CABLS	1/08-3/08
	Oakland-Fremont-Hayward MSA, CA	H	20.75 FQ	25.76 MW	35.18 TQ	CABLS	1/08-3/08
	Oxnard-Thousand Oaks-Ventura MSA, CA	H	16.43 FQ	21.58 MW	25.92 TQ	CABLS	1/08-3/08
	Riverside-San Bernardino-Ontario MSA, CA	H	14.17 FQ	16.46 MW	24.82 TQ	CABLS	1/08-3/08
	Sacramento-Arden Arcade-Roseville MSA, CA	H	19.83 FQ	22.16 MW	24.87 TQ	CABLS	1/08-3/08
	San Diego-Carlsbad-San Marcos MSA, CA	H	19.37 FQ	25.86 MW	31.06 TQ	CABLS	1/08-3/08
	San Francisco-San Mateo-Redwood PMSA, CA	H	21.68 FQ	25.27 MW	31.44 TQ	CABLS	1/08-3/08

AE	Average entry wage	AW	Average wage paid	FQ	First quartile wage
AER	Average entry range	AWR	Average wage range	H	Hourly
AEX	Average experienced wage	AXR	Average experienced range	HI	Highest wage paid
ATC	Average total compensation	D	Daily	HR	High end range

LO	Lowest wage paid	MTC	Median total compensation	TCC	Total cash compensation
LR	Low end range	MW	Median wage paid	TQ	Third quartile wage
M	Monthly	MWR	Median wage range	W	Weekly
MCC	Median cash compensation	S	See annotated source	Y	Yearly

Occupation/Type/Industry	Location	Per	Low	Mid	High	Source	Date
Environmental Engineering Technician	San Jose-Sunnyvale-Santa Clara MSA, CA	H	22.27 FQ	28.64 MW	34.69 TQ	CABLS	1/08-3/08
	Santa Ana-Anaheim-Irvine PMSA, CA	Y	31170 FQ	44960 MW	54950 TQ	USBLS	5/07
	Colorado	Y	29760 FQ	40710 MW	53250 TQ	USBLS	5/07
	Denver-Aurora MSA, CO	Y	28820 FQ	39940 MW	54300 TQ	USBLS	5/07
	Connecticut	H	15.73 AE	21.36 MW		CTBLS	1/08-3/08
	Hartford-West Hartford-East Hartford MSA, CT	Y	36300 FQ	44330 MW	57810 TQ	USBLS	5/07
	Delaware	Y	29450 FQ	35180 MW	42690 TQ	USBLS	5/07
	District of Columbia	Y	36630 FQ	43400 MW	50700 TQ	USBLS	5/07
	Washington-Arlington-Alexandria MSA, DC-VA-MD-WV	Y	37050 FQ	47000 MW	65290 TQ	USBLS	5/07
	Florida	Y	25720 FQ	33200 MW	42930 TQ	USBLS	5/07
	Jacksonville MSA, FL	Y	27540 FQ	35630 MW	44880 TQ	USBLS	5/07
	Miami-Fort Lauderdale-Miami Beach MSA, FL	Y	26540 FQ	31120 MW	55780 TQ	USBLS	5/07
	Orlando-Kissimmee MSA, FL	Y	23100 FQ	25590 MW	30850 TQ	USBLS	5/07
	Tampa-St. Petersburg-Clearwater MSA, FL	Y	24930 FQ	34840 MW	40020 TQ	USBLS	5/07
	West Palm Beach-Boca Raton-Boynton Beach PMSA, FL	Y	33250 FQ	58570 MW	80040 TQ	USBLS	5/07
	Georgia	Y	30970 FQ	33640 MW	36740 TQ	USBLS	5/07
	Atlanta-Sandy Springs-Marietta MSA, GA	Y	30910 FQ	33480 MW	36500 TQ	USBLS	5/07
	Idaho	Y	39960 FQ	46910 MW	58410 TQ	USBLS	5/07
	Illinois	Y	40830 FQ	46190 MW	51690 TQ	USBLS	5/07
	Chicago-Naperville-Joliet MSA, IL-IN-WI	Y	41610 FQ	46330 MW	51010 TQ	USBLS	5/07
	Indiana	Y	32850 FQ	39320 MW	47830 TQ	USBLS	5/07
	Gary PMSA, IN	Y	33560 FQ	37930 MW	44710 TQ	USBLS	5/07
	Indianapolis-Carmel MSA, IN	Y	33290 FQ	40260 MW	47540 TQ	USBLS	5/07
	Iowa	Y	32110 FQ	40140 MW	47750 TQ	USBLS	5/07
	Kansas	Y	39310 FQ	45910 MW	58360 TQ	USBLS	5/07
	Kentucky	Y	35414 FQ	44474 MW	52399 TQ	KYBLS	2008
	Louisville-Jefferson County MSA, KY-IN	Y	31130 FQ	34860 MW	42150 TQ	USBLS	5/07
	Louisiana	H	15.29 FQ	20.06 MW	24.29 TQ	LABLS	1/08-3/08
	Baton Rouge MSA, LA	Y	40870 FQ	47080 MW	59080 TQ	USBLS	5/07
	New Orleans-Metairie-Kenner MSA, LA	Y	27550 FQ	30510 MW	35160 TQ	USBLS	5/07
	Maine	Y	31300 FQ	41630 MW	47480 TQ	USBLS	5/07
	Portland-South Portland-Biddeford MSA, ME	Y	35490 FQ	44220 MW	48920 TQ	USBLS	5/07
	Maryland	Y		54125 MW		MDBLS	3/08
	Baltimore-Towson MSA, MD	Y	36350 FQ	42640 MW	47340 TQ	USBLS	5/07
	Bethesda-Gaithersburg-Frederick PMSA, MD	Y	49500 FQ	63290 MW	72220 TQ	USBLS	5/07
	Massachusetts	Y	37380 FQ	45390 MW	52980 TQ	USBLS	5/07
	Boston-Cambridge-Quincy NECTA, MA	Y	38860 FQ	45900 MW	53150 TQ	USBLS	5/07
	Michigan	Y	36280 FQ	43240 MW	50350 TQ	USBLS	5/07
	Detroit-Warren-Livonia MSA, MI	Y	37080 FQ	42890 MW	48320 TQ	USBLS	5/07
	Grand Rapids-Wyoming MSA, MI	Y	37850 FQ	48960 MW	62290 TQ	USBLS	5/07
	Warren-Troy-Farmington Hills PMSA, MI	Y	37160 FQ	42700 MW	47350 TQ	USBLS	5/07
	Minnesota	Y	39735 FQ	52248 MW	66623 TQ	MNBLS	10/08-12/08
	Duluth-Superior MSA, MN-WI	Y	34002 FQ	43052 MW	57385 TQ	MNBLS	10/08-12/08
	Minneapolis-Saint Paul MSA, MN-WI	Y	41723 FQ	56715 MW	68590 TQ	MNBLS	10/08-12/08
	Mississippi	Y	28020 FQ	35450 MW	42120 TQ	USBLS	5/07
	Jackson MSA, MS	Y	28320 FQ	34460 MW	37990 TQ	USBLS	5/07
	Missouri	Y	33540 FQ	54470 MW	70730 TQ	USBLS	5/07
	Kansas City MSA, MO-KS	Y	39820 FQ	47450 MW	58710 TQ	USBLS	5/07
	St. Louis MSA, MO-IL	Y	39390 FQ	50960 MW	66640 TQ	USBLS	5/07
	Nebraska	Y	23160 FQ	29450 MW	39420 TQ	USBLS	5/07
	Omaha-Council Bluffs MSA, NE-IA	Y	36780 FQ	44120 MW	49730 TQ	USBLS	5/07

AE Average entry wage	**AW** Average wage paid	**FQ** First quartile wage	**LO** Lowest wage paid	**MTC** Median total compensation	**TCC** Total cash compensation
AER Average entry range	**AWR** Average wage range	**LR** Low end range		**MW** Median wage paid	**TQ** Third quartile wage
AEX Average experienced wage	**AXR** Average experienced range	**HI** Highest wage paid	**M** Monthly	**MWR** Median wage range	**W** Weekly
ATC Average total compensation	**D** Daily	**HR** High end range	**MCC** Median cash compensation	**S** See annotated source	**Y** Yearly

Occupation/Type/Industry	Location	Per	Low	Mid	High	Source	Date
Environmental Engineering Technician							
	Nevada	H	21.05 FQ	24.39 MW	29.85 TQ	NVBLS	5/08
	Las Vegas-Paradise MSA, NV	H	22.02 FQ	25.09 MW	30.68 TQ	NVBLS	5/08
	New Hampshire	H	18.82 AE	24.52 MW	28.64 AEX	NHBLS	6/08
	New Jersey	Y	31400 FQ	38820 MW	50470 TQ	USBLS	5/07
	Camden PMSA, NJ	Y	27880 FQ	31680 MW	43120 TQ	USBLS	5/07
	Edison PMSA, NJ	Y	34100 FQ	41090 MW	47620 TQ	USBLS	5/07
	Newark-Union PMSA, NJ-PA	Y	28760 FQ	36010 MW	46580 TQ	USBLS	5/07
	New Mexico	Y	28310 FQ	36740 MW	52180 TQ	USBLS	5/07
	Albuquerque MSA, NM	Y	28440 FQ	33340 MW	49090 TQ	USBLS	5/07
	New York	Y	32980 FQ	40430 MW	51060 TQ	USBLS	5/07
	Albany-Schenectady-Troy MSA, NY	Y	36380 FQ	43920 MW	49850 TQ	USBLS	5/07
	Buffalo-Niagara Falls MSA, NY	Y	35370 FQ	40440 MW	45720 TQ	USBLS	5/07
	Nassau-Suffolk PMSA, NY	Y	47830 FQ	67770 MW	74990 TQ	USBLS	5/07
	New York-Northern New Jersey-Long Island MSA, NY-NJ-PA	Y	32390 FQ	40320 MW	53530 TQ	USBLS	5/07
	North Carolina	Y	33300 FQ	38710 MW	46120 TQ	USBLS	5/07
	Charlotte-Gastonia-Concord MSA, NC-SC	Y	28650 FQ	34670 MW	40180 TQ	USBLS	5/07
	Raleigh-Cary MSA, NC	Y	34700 FQ	42790 MW	52060 TQ	USBLS	5/07
	North Dakota	Y	35150 FQ	41790 MW	48100 TQ	USBLS	5/07
	Ohio	Y	31830 FQ	41130 MW	55200 TQ	USBLS	5/07
	Cincinnati-Middletown MSA, OH-KY-IN	Y	29490 FQ	34900 MW	47900 TQ	USBLS	5/07
	Cleveland-Elyria-Mentor MSA, OH	Y	32990 FQ	37940 MW	55330 TQ	USBLS	5/07
	Columbus MSA, OH	Y	38840 FQ	53250 MW	67470 TQ	USBLS	5/07
	Dayton MSA, OH	Y	34690 FQ	43360 MW	51300 TQ	USBLS	5/07
	Oklahoma	Y	30180 FQ	37730 MW	52270 TQ	USBLS	5/07
	Oklahoma City MSA, OK	Y	36590 FQ	48230 MW	57300 TQ	USBLS	5/07
	Oregon	H	18.21 FQ	22.96 MW	27.37 TQ	ORBLS	5/08
	Portland-Vancouver-Beaverton MSA, OR-WA	Y	36830 FQ	48970 MW	56990 TQ	USBLS	5/07
	Pennsylvania	Y	27720 FQ	35040 MW	44140 TQ	USBLS	5/07
	Philadelphia-Camden-Wilmington MSA, PA-NJ-DE-MD	Y	29970 FQ	36900 MW	45170 TQ	USBLS	5/07
	Pittsburgh MSA, PA	Y	28690 FQ	35230 MW	40990 TQ	USBLS	5/07
	Providence-Fall River-Warwick MSA, RI-MA	Y	28620 FQ	31940 MW	44770 TQ	USBLS	5/07
	South Carolina	Y	32570 FQ	42440 MW	54040 TQ	USBLS	5/07
	Charleston-North Charleston MSA, SC	Y	29870 FQ	38940 MW	48750 TQ	USBLS	5/07
	Columbia MSA, SC	Y	31850 FQ	39650 MW	52840 TQ	USBLS	5/07
	South Dakota	Y	31285 FQ	38899 MW	44991 TQ	SDBLS	7/08-9/08
	Tennessee	Y	41730 FQ	49130 MW	57860 TQ	USBLS	5/07
	Knoxville MSA, TN	Y	38400 FQ	45840 MW	55400 TQ	USBLS	5/07
	Memphis MSA, TN-MS-AR	Y	43150 FQ	54790 MW	63730 TQ	USBLS	5/07
	Nashville-Davidson-Murfreesboro MSA, TN	Y	41810 FQ	47560 MW	55100 TQ	USBLS	5/07
	Texas	Y	23930 FQ	34240 MW	55970 TQ	USBLS	5/07
	Austin-Round Rock MSA, TX	Y	43490 FQ	54560 MW	64610 TQ	USBLS	5/07
	Dallas-Fort Worth-Arlington MSA, TX	Y	29800 FQ	37550 MW	52670 TQ	USBLS	5/07
	El Paso MSA, TX	Y	24310 FQ	33130 MW	71040 TQ	USBLS	5/07
	Houston-Sugar Land-Baytown MSA, TX	Y	23390 FQ	31650 MW	57680 TQ	USBLS	5/07
	San Antonio MSA, TX	Y	32630 FQ	41240 MW	51970 TQ	USBLS	5/07
	Utah	Y	26450 FQ	29770 MW	43240 TQ	USBLS	5/07
	Salt Lake City MSA, UT	Y	26460 FQ	29610 MW	43190 TQ	USBLS	5/07
	Vermont	Y	32620 FQ	37380 MW	44320 TQ	USBLS	5/07
	Burlington-South Burlington MSA, VT	Y	31350 FQ	38550 MW	46390 TQ	USBLS	5/07
	Virginia	Y	31450 FQ	38170 MW	49480 TQ	USBLS	5/07
	Richmond MSA, VA	Y	32420 FQ	38400 MW	46010 TQ	USBLS	5/07
	Virginia Beach-Norfolk-Newport News MSA, VA-NC	Y	23810 FQ	31850 MW	39360 TQ	USBLS	5/07
	Washington	H	18.15 FQ	23.09 MW	32.97 TQ	WABLS	3/08

AE	Average entry wage	AW	Average wage paid	FQ	First quartile wage	LO	Lowest wage paid
AER	Average entry range	AWR	Average wage range	H	Hourly	LR	Low end range
AEX	Average experienced wage	AXR	Average experienced range	HI	Highest wage paid	M	Monthly
ATC	Average total compensation	D	Daily	HR	High end range	MCC	Median cash compensation

MTC	Median total compensation	TCC Total cash compensation
MW	Median wage paid	TQ Third quartile wage
MWR	Median wage range	W Weekly
S	See annotated source	Y Yearly

Occupation/Type/Industry	Location	Per	Low	Mid	High	Source	Date
Environmental Engineering Technician	Seattle-Tacoma-Bellevue						
	MSA, WA	Y	40680 FQ	53690 MW	73610 TQ	USBLS	5/07
	West Virginia	Y	33312 FQ	40277 MW	48461 TQ	WVBLS	7/08-9/08
	Charleston MSA, WV	Y	33160 FQ	38240 MW	45420 TQ	USBLS	5/07
	Wisconsin	Y	35480 FQ	43960 MW	55940 TQ	USBLS	5/07
	Milwaukee-Waukesha-West						
	Allis MSA, WI	Y	36380 FQ	44890 MW	56170 TQ	USBLS	5/07
	Wyoming	Y	29982 FQ	37787 MW	51026 TQ	WYBLS	9/08
	Puerto Rico	Y	13680 FQ	16230 MW	19670 TQ	USBLS	5/07
	San Juan-Caguas-Guaynabo						
	MSA, PR	Y	14220 FQ	17120 MW	21580 TQ	USBLS	5/07
Environmental Grant Analyst							
State Government	Ohio	H	21.77 LO		31.86 HI	ODAS	2008
Environmental Law Specialist							
Department of Environmental Quality	Oregon	M	4090 LO		5986 HI	ODEQSS	11/1/08
Environmental Lawyer	United States	Y	40000-71000 LR	103130 MW		OPOL	2008
Environmental Program Coordinator							
Municipal Government	Gresham, OR	Y	61296 LO		78252 HI	GOSS	1/1/09
Environmental Quality Specialist							
Department of Transportation	Michigan	H	23.02 LO		40.32 HI	MDOT	10/1/07
Environmental Science and Protection Technician							
Including Health	Alabama	Y	29220 FQ	36370 MW	51020 TQ	USBLS	5/07
Including Health	Birmingham-Hoover MSA, AL	Y	30590 FQ	39020 MW	50300 TQ	USBLS	5/07
Including Health	Alaska	Y	33550 FQ	40420 MW	48170 TQ	USBLS	5/07
Including Health	Anchorage MSA, AK	Y	33270 FQ	37080 MW	46720 TQ	USBLS	5/07
Including Health	Arizona	Y	36850 FQ	43890 MW	50670 TQ	USBLS	5/07
Including Health	Phoenix-Mesa-Scottsdale						
	MSA, AZ	Y	34950 FQ	44050 MW	50180 TQ	USBLS	5/07
Including Health	Arkansas	Y	29740 FQ	35370 MW	39890 TQ	USBLS	5/07
Including Health	Little Rock-North Little Rock						
	MSA, AR	Y	29590 FQ	34630 MW	38650 TQ	USBLS	5/07
Including Health	California	H	16.93 FQ	21.96 MW	29.62 TQ	CABLS	1/08-3/08
Including Health	Los Angeles-Long Beach-						
	Glendale PMSA, CA	H	20.77 FQ	24.87 MW	29.18 TQ	CABLS	1/08-3/08
Including Health	Oakland-Fremont-Hayward						
	MSA, CA	H	19.59 FQ	27.28 MW	35.62 TQ	CABLS	1/08-3/08
Including Health	Riverside-San Bernardino-						
	Ontario MSA, CA	H	24.37 FQ	28.71 MW	31.94 TQ	CABLS	1/08-3/08
Including Health	Sacramento-Arden Arcade-						
	Roseville MSA, CA	H	18.56 FQ	22.76 MW	28.33 TQ	CABLS	1/08-3/08
Including Health	San Diego-Carlsbad-San						
	Marcos MSA, CA	H	16.80 FQ	19.69 MW	26.63 TQ	CABLS	1/08-3/08
Including Health	San Francisco-San Mateo-						
	Redwood PMSA, CA	H	18.91 FQ	26.63 MW	32.70 TQ	CABLS	1/08-3/08
Including Health	San Jose-Sunnyvale-Santa						
	Clara MSA, CA	H	17.69 FQ	23.91 MW	31.18 TQ	CABLS	1/08-3/08
Including Health	Santa Ana-Anaheim-Irvine						
	PMSA, CA	Y	37990 FQ	49220 MW	60680 TQ	USBLS	5/07
Including Health	Colorado	Y	30420 FQ	39850 MW	51570 TQ	USBLS	5/07
Including Health	Denver-Aurora MSA, CO	Y	28940 FQ	33940 MW	49210 TQ	USBLS	5/07
Including Health	Connecticut	H	13.21 AE	18.81 MW		CTBLS	1/08-3/08
Including Health	Bridgeport-Stamford-Norwalk						
	MSA, CT	Y	41620 FQ	55610 MW	64820 TQ	USBLS	5/07
Including Health	Hartford-West Hartford-East						
	Hartford MSA, CT	Y	27920 FQ	35980 MW	42540 TQ	USBLS	5/07
Including Health	Delaware	Y	27940 FQ	31630 MW	41510 TQ	USBLS	5/07
Including Health	Wilmington PMSA, DE-MD-NJ	Y	27440 FQ	30630 MW	35150 TQ	USBLS	5/07
Including Health	District of Columbia	Y	37430 FQ	47890 MW	64210 TQ	USBLS	5/07

Occupation/Type/Industry	Location	Per	Low	Mid	High	Source	Date
Environmental Science and Protection Technician							
Including Health	Washington-Arlington- Alexandria MSA, DC-VA- MD-WV	Y	39770 FQ	48120 MW	60820 TQ	USBLS	5/07
Including Health	Florida	Y	28520 FQ	35360 MW	41780 TQ	USBLS	5/07
Including Health	Fort Lauderdale-Pompano Beach-Deerfield Beach PMSA, FL	Y	27050 FQ	31430 MW	38120 TQ	USBLS	5/07
Including Health	Jacksonville MSA, FL	Y	33560 FQ	38800 MW	49030 TQ	USBLS	5/07
Including Health	Miami-Fort Lauderdale-Miami Beach MSA, FL	Y	30970 FQ	37180 MW	47700 TQ	USBLS	5/07
Including Health	Orlando-Kissimmee MSA, FL	Y	27500 FQ	33770 MW	38950 TQ	USBLS	5/07
Including Health	Tampa-St. Petersburg- Clearwater MSA, FL	Y	26110 FQ	34650 MW	42120 TQ	USBLS	5/07
Including Health	West Palm Beach-Boca Raton- Boynton Beach PMSA, FL	Y	35830 FQ	41780 MW	59440 TQ	USBLS	5/07
Including Health	Georgia	Y	27220 FQ	32540 MW	40080 TQ	USBLS	5/07
Including Health	Atlanta-Sandy Springs- Marietta MSA, GA	Y	29340 FQ	33910 MW	40370 TQ	USBLS	5/07
Including Health	Hawaii	Y	35800 FQ	42120 MW	50290 TQ	USBLS	5/07
Including Health	Honolulu MSA, HI	Y	36970 FQ	45010 MW	54210 TQ	USBLS	5/07
Including Health	Boise City-Nampa MSA, ID	Y	17440 FQ	18970 MW	23860 TQ	USBLS	5/07
Including Health	Illinois	Y	32630 FQ	48020 MW	59990 TQ	USBLS	5/07
Including Health	Chicago-Naperville-Joliet MSA, IL-IN-WI	Y	33130 FQ	48330 MW	60610 TQ	USBLS	5/07
Including Health	Indiana	Y	30750 FQ	36740 MW	45610 TQ	USBLS	5/07
Including Health	Gary PMSA, IN	Y	29430 FQ	33820 MW	38340 TQ	USBLS	5/07
Including Health	Indianapolis-Carmel MSA, IN	Y	34110 FQ	38850 MW	50770 TQ	USBLS	5/07
Including Health	Iowa	Y	34750 FQ	46300 MW	57170 TQ	USBLS	5/07
Including Health	Kansas	Y	31130 FQ	37730 MW	45280 TQ	USBLS	5/07
Including Health	Kentucky	Y	30961 FQ	40090 MW	51017 TQ	KYBLS	2008
Including Health	Louisville-Jefferson County MSA, KY-IN	Y	25040 FQ	34580 MW	49820 TQ	USBLS	5/07
Including Health	Louisiana	H	13.92 FQ	17.00 MW	21.79 TQ	LABLS	1/08-3/08
Including Health	Baton Rouge MSA, LA	Y	26760 FQ	31560 MW	38510 TQ	USBLS	5/07
Including Health	New Orleans-Metairie-Kenner MSA, LA	Y	29840 FQ	37320 MW	50450 TQ	USBLS	5/07
Including Health	Maine	Y	25980 FQ	30600 MW	36670 TQ	USBLS	5/07
Including Health	Maryland	Y		47050 MW		MDBLS	3/08
Including Health	Baltimore-Towson MSA, MD	Y	34280 FQ	44460 MW	53880 TQ	USBLS	5/07
Including Health	Bethesda-Gaithersburg- Frederick PMSA, MD	Y	43300 FQ	48640 MW	55510 TQ	USBLS	5/07
Including Health	Massachusetts	Y	33270 FQ	41860 MW	50930 TQ	USBLS	5/07
Including Health	Boston-Cambridge-Quincy NECTA, MA	Y	31770 FQ	42120 MW	50910 TQ	USBLS	5/07
Including Health	Worcester MSA, MA-CT	Y	32250 FQ	36400 MW	43860 TQ	USBLS	5/07
Including Health	Michigan	Y	28510 FQ	39570 MW	49070 TQ	USBLS	5/07
Including Health	Detroit-Warren-Livonia MSA, MI	Y	32370 FQ	43320 MW	50930 TQ	USBLS	5/07
Including Health	Lansing-East Lansing MSA, MI	Y	26070 FQ	28120 MW	30610 TQ	USBLS	5/07
Including Health	Warren-Troy-Farmington Hills PMSA, MI	Y	28630 FQ	42380 MW	53770 TQ	USBLS	5/07
Including Health	Minnesota	Y	36617 FQ	44956 MW	52708 TQ	MNBLS	10/08-12/08
Including Health	Duluth-Superior MSA, MN-WI	Y	36387 FQ	46410 MW	52897 TQ	MNBLS	10/08-12/08
Including Health	Minneapolis-Saint Paul MSA, MN-WI	Y	39139 FQ	46640 MW	54916 TQ	MNBLS	10/08-12/08
Including Health	Mississippi	Y	26460 FQ	29250 MW	49140 TQ	USBLS	5/07
Including Health	Missouri	Y	32230 FQ	36970 MW	43080 TQ	USBLS	5/07
Including Health	Kansas City MSA, MO-KS	Y	30250 FQ	36430 MW	44880 TQ	USBLS	5/07
Including Health	St. Louis MSA, MO-IL	Y	34370 FQ	40210 MW	51860 TQ	USBLS	5/07
Including Health	Montana	Y	26120 FQ	33780 MW	38890 TQ	USBLS	5/07
Including Health	Billings MSA, MT	Y	24580 FQ	29780 MW	35520 TQ	USBLS	5/07
Including Health	Nebraska	Y	36260 FQ	41560 MW	49110 TQ	USBLS	5/07
Including Health	Omaha-Council Bluffs MSA, NE-IA	Y	37460 FQ	43140 MW	51340 TQ	USBLS	5/07
Including Health	Nevada	H	14.87 FQ	23.67 MW	32.07 TQ	NVBLS	5/08
Including Health	Las Vegas-Paradise MSA, NV	H	15.61 FQ	23.16 MW	30.24 TQ	NVBLS	5/08
Including Health	Reno-Sparks MSA, NV	H	22.24 FQ	31.61 MW	37.11 TQ	NVBLS	5/08
Including Health	New Hampshire	H	14.37 AE	18.35 MW	20.54 AEX	NHBLS	6/08
Including Health	Manchester MSA, NH	Y	32940 FQ	36310 MW	39760 TQ	USBLS	5/07
Including Health	Nashua NECTA, NH-MA	Y	25210 FQ	32920 MW	39470 TQ	USBLS	5/07

AE	Average entry wage	AW	Average wage paid	FQ	First quartile wage	LO	Lowest wage paid	MTC	Median total compensation	TCC	Total cash compensation
AER	Average entry range	AWR	Average wage range	H	Hourly	LR	Low end range	MW	Median wage paid	TQ	Third quartile wage
AEX	Average experienced wage	AXR	Average experienced range	HI	Highest wage paid	M	Monthly	MWR	Median wage range	W	Weekly
ATC	Average total compensation	D	Daily	HR	High end range	MCC	Median cash compensation	S	See annotated source	Y	Yearly

Occupation/Type/Industry	Location	Per	Low	Mid	High	Source	Date
Environmental Science and Protection Technician							
Including Health	New Jersey	Y	32150 FQ	38610 MW	48770 TQ	USBLS	5/07
Including Health	Camden PMSA, NJ	Y	27940 FQ	36390 MW	44980 TQ	USBLS	5/07
Including Health	Edison PMSA, NJ	Y	33870 FQ	39400 MW	50710 TQ	USBLS	5/07
Including Health	Newark-Union PMSA, NJ-PA	Y	32510 FQ	38900 MW	49220 TQ	USBLS	5/07
Including Health	New Mexico	Y	26790 FQ	37390 MW	51990 TQ	USBLS	5/07
Including Health	Albuquerque MSA, NM	Y	24170 FQ	33970 MW	52040 TQ	USBLS	5/07
Including Health	New York	Y	30230 FQ	39150 MW	51010 TQ	USBLS	5/07
Including Health	Albany-Schenectady-Troy MSA, NY	Y	38620 FQ	51250 MW	59460 TQ	USBLS	5/07
Including Health	Buffalo-Niagara Falls MSA, NY	Y	23410 FQ	29430 MW	39340 TQ	USBLS	5/07
Including Health	Nassau-Suffolk PMSA, NY	Y	34500 FQ	42480 MW	51150 TQ	USBLS	5/07
Including Health	New York-Northern New Jersey-Long Island MSA, NY-NJ-PA	Y	32070 FQ	39090 MW	49940 TQ	USBLS	5/07
Including Health	North Carolina	Y	32040 FQ	38440 MW	47620 TQ	USBLS	5/07
Including Health	Charlotte-Gastonia-Concord MSA, NC-SC	Y	27970 FQ	33940 MW	38100 TQ	USBLS	5/07
Including Health	Raleigh-Cary MSA, NC	Y	37220 FQ	45700 MW	56410 TQ	USBLS	5/07
Including Health	North Dakota	Y	22850 FQ	28060 MW	31600 TQ	USBLS	5/07
Including Health	Ohio	Y	27360 FQ	33600 MW	43800 TQ	USBLS	5/07
Including Health	Cincinnati-Middletown MSA, OH-KY-IN	Y	28430 FQ	33350 MW	44280 TQ	USBLS	5/07
Including Health	Cleveland-Elyria-Mentor MSA, OH	Y	26570 FQ	32610 MW	43100 TQ	USBLS	5/07
Including Health	Columbus MSA, OH	Y	28160 FQ	37060 MW	51340 TQ	USBLS	5/07
Including Health	Dayton MSA, OH	Y	24630 FQ	29680 MW	40160 TQ	USBLS	5/07
Including Health	Oklahoma	Y	27090 FQ	35110 MW	46160 TQ	USBLS	5/07
Including Health	Oklahoma City MSA, OK	Y	35320 FQ	43740 MW	53640 TQ	USBLS	5/07
Including Health	Tulsa MSA, OK	Y	29480 FQ	32550 MW	37600 TQ	USBLS	5/07
Including Health	Oregon	H	17.03 FQ	20.72 MW	25.00 TQ	ORBLS	5/08
Including Health	Portland-Vancouver-Beaverton MSA, OR-WA	Y	35430 FQ	43540 MW	53430 TQ	USBLS	5/07
Including Health	Pennsylvania	Y	28950 FQ	37420 MW	49370 TQ	USBLS	5/07
Including Health	Allentown-Bethlehem-Easton MSA, PA-NJ	Y	28640 FQ	36230 MW	40780 TQ	USBLS	5/07
Including Health	Philadelphia-Camden-Wilmington MSA, PA-NJ-DE-MD	Y	29730 FQ	36100 MW	45840 TQ	USBLS	5/07
Including Health	Pittsburgh MSA, PA	Y	30630 FQ	42950 MW	57860 TQ	USBLS	5/07
Including Health	York-Hanover MSA, PA	Y	23710 FQ	28460 MW	41650 TQ	USBLS	5/07
Including Health	Rhode Island	Y	31910 FQ	38160 MW	47700 TQ	USBLS	5/07
Including Health	Providence-Fall River-Warwick MSA, RI-MA	Y	32400 FQ	37870 MW	46820 TQ	USBLS	5/07
Including Health	South Carolina	Y	31240 FQ	53560 MW	60610 TQ	USBLS	5/07
Including Health	Charleston-North Charleston MSA, SC	Y	26630 FQ	34900 MW	41480 TQ	USBLS	5/07
Including Health	South Dakota	Y	21902 FQ	24080 MW	27113 TQ	SDBLS	7/08-9/08
Including Health	Tennessee	Y	37520 FQ	51360 MW	63330 TQ	USBLS	5/07
Including Health	Memphis MSA, TN-MS-AR	Y	32930 FQ	39370 MW	49780 TQ	USBLS	5/07
Including Health	Nashville-Davidson-Murfreesboro MSA, TN	Y	24130 FQ	41110 MW	57340 TQ	USBLS	5/07
Including Health	Texas	Y	30180 FQ	38240 MW	55500 TQ	USBLS	5/07
Including Health	Austin-Round Rock MSA, TX	Y	32550 FQ	38020 MW	57120 TQ	USBLS	5/07
Including Health	Dallas-Fort Worth-Arlington MSA, TX	Y	38990 FQ	51150 MW	65340 TQ	USBLS	5/07
Including Health	El Paso MSA, TX	Y	33740 FQ	37560 MW	45250 TQ	USBLS	5/07
Including Health	Houston-Sugar Land-Baytown MSA, TX	Y	25240 FQ	36220 MW	51920 TQ	USBLS	5/07
Including Health	Midland MSA, TX	Y	31640 FQ	38110 MW	56200 TQ	USBLS	5/07
Including Health	San Antonio MSA, TX	Y	28810 FQ	32450 MW	43030 TQ	USBLS	5/07
Including Health	Utah	Y	35930 FQ	42450 MW	48350 TQ	USBLS	5/07
Including Health	Salt Lake City MSA, UT	Y	40570 FQ	45170 MW	51350 TQ	USBLS	5/07
Including Health	Vermont	Y	27940 FQ	32810 MW	37550 TQ	USBLS	5/07
Including Health	Burlington-South Burlington MSA, VT	Y	27030 FQ	30500 MW	35280 TQ	USBLS	5/07
Including Health	Virginia	Y	30070 FQ	39580 MW	50690 TQ	USBLS	5/07
Including Health	Richmond MSA, VA	Y	32020 FQ	39150 MW	47100 TQ	USBLS	5/07

AE	Average entry wage	**AW**	Average wage paid	**FQ**	First quartile wage
AER	Average entry range	**AWR**	Average wage range	**H**	Hourly
AEX	Average experienced wage	**AXR**	Average experienced range	**HI**	Highest wage paid
ATC	Average total compensation	**D**	Daily	**HR**	High end range

LO	Lowest wage paid	**MTC**	Median total compensation	**TCC**	Total cash compensation
LR	Low end range	**MW**	Median wage paid	**TQ**	Third quartile wage
M	Monthly	**MWR**	Median wage range	**W**	Weekly
MCC	Median cash compensation	**S**	See annotated source	**Y**	Yearly

Occupation/Type/Industry	Location	Per	Low	Mid	High	Source	Date
Environmental Science and Protection Technician							
Including Health	Virginia Beach-Norfolk-Newport News MSA, VA-NC	Y	30240 FQ	39510 MW	50690 TQ	USBLS	5/07
Including Health	Washington	H	18.40 FQ	24.10 MW	31.93 TQ	WABLS	3/08
Including Health	Seattle-Tacoma-Bellevue MSA, WA	Y	34650 FQ	41320 MW	50870 TQ	USBLS	5/07
Including Health	West Virginia	Y	21318 FQ	26011 MW	33513 TQ	WVBLS	7/08-9/08
Including Health	Charleston MSA, WV	Y	18990 FQ	23260 MW	29430 TQ	USBLS	5/07
Including Health	Wisconsin	Y	30050 FQ	36400 MW	44580 TQ	USBLS	5/07
Including Health	Milwaukee-Waukesha-West Allis MSA, WI	Y	27980 FQ	37160 MW	45350 TQ	USBLS	5/07
Including Health	Wyoming	Y	31930 FQ	34875 MW	38144 TQ	WYBLS	9/08
Including Health	Puerto Rico	Y	17620 FQ	21440 MW	25880 TQ	USBLS	5/07
Including Health	San Juan-Caguas-Guaynabo MSA, PR	Y	17270 FQ	20670 MW	24700 TQ	USBLS	5/07
Environmental Science Teacher							
Postsecondary	Arizona	Y	31360 FQ	48100 MW	93960 TQ	USBLS	5/07
Postsecondary	California	Y		104557 AW		CABLS	1/08-3/08
Postsecondary	District of Columbia	Y	45770 FQ	64950 MW	84040 TQ	USBLS	5/07
Postsecondary	Florida	Y	42740 FQ	58610 MW	73890 TQ	USBLS	5/07
Postsecondary	Georgia	Y	42790 FQ	55610 MW	66330 TQ	USBLS	5/07
Postsecondary	Illinois	Y	42490 FQ	53950 MW	73590 TQ	USBLS	5/07
Postsecondary	Indiana	Y	51400 FQ	69310 MW	105030 TQ	USBLS	5/07
Postsecondary	Iowa	Y	46520 FQ	74460 MW	100610 TQ	USBLS	5/07
Postsecondary	Louisiana	Y		53237 AW		LABLS	1/08-3/08
Postsecondary	Maine	Y	38280 FQ	52760 MW	66080 TQ	USBLS	5/07
Postsecondary	Maryland	Y		68750 MW		MDBLS	3/08
Postsecondary	Massachusetts	Y	54660 FQ	70910 MW	93810 TQ	USBLS	5/07
Postsecondary	Michigan	Y	51850 FQ	60980 MW	76180 TQ	USBLS	5/07
Postsecondary	Minnesota	Y	44998 FQ	58609 MW	99328 TQ	MNBLS	10/08-12/08
Postsecondary	Mississippi	Y	61550 FQ	87840 MW	104620 TQ	USBLS	5/07
Postsecondary	Montana	Y	38440 FQ	50410 MW	61560 TQ	USBLS	5/07
Postsecondary	New Hampshire	Y	56707 AE	75573 MW	100838 AEX	NHBLS	6/08
Postsecondary	New Jersey	Y	54060 FQ	72300 MW	94970 TQ	USBLS	5/07
Postsecondary	New York	Y	52610 FQ	70640 MW	95900 TQ	USBLS	5/07
Postsecondary	North Carolina	Y	44510 FQ	57700 MW	78590 TQ	USBLS	5/07
Postsecondary	Ohio	Y	46680 FQ	57000 MW	72220 TQ	USBLS	5/07
Postsecondary	Oklahoma	Y	30640 FQ	47930 MW	61310 TQ	USBLS	5/07
Postsecondary	Pennsylvania	Y	47830 FQ	69180 MW	92810 TQ	USBLS	5/07
Postsecondary	South Carolina	Y	54360 FQ	71470 MW	83180 TQ	USBLS	5/07
Postsecondary	South Dakota	Y	43048 FQ	51479 MW	64888 TQ	SDBLS	7/08-9/08
Postsecondary	Tennessee	Y	41000 FQ	58410 MW	71450 TQ	USBLS	5/07
Postsecondary	Texas	Y	54970 FQ	72160 MW	87660 TQ	USBLS	5/07
Postsecondary	Utah	Y	46410 FQ	62850 MW	78400 TQ	USBLS	5/07
Postsecondary	Vermont	Y	44240 FQ	50740 MW	58310 TQ	USBLS	5/07
Postsecondary	Virginia	Y	43800 FQ	62940 MW	88980 TQ	USBLS	5/07
Postsecondary	Washington	Y		85673 AW		WABLS	3/08
Postsecondary	West Virginia	Y	43435 FQ	85034 MW	120258 TQ	WVBLS	7/08-9/08
Postsecondary	Wisconsin	Y	25520 FQ	41810 MW	60120 TQ	USBLS	5/07
Environmental Scientist and Specialist							
Including Health	Alabama	Y	39980 FQ	53600 MW	68590 TQ	USBLS	5/07
Including Health	Birmingham-Hoover MSA, AL	Y	46810 FQ	60830 MW	79460 TQ	USBLS	5/07
Including Health	Mobile MSA, AL	Y	39620 FQ	50330 MW	65610 TQ	USBLS	5/07
Including Health	Alaska	Y	48440 FQ	60600 MW	76200 TQ	USBLS	5/07
Including Health	Anchorage MSA, AK	Y	50820 FQ	60800 MW	76120 TQ	USBLS	5/07
Including Health	Fairbanks MSA, AK	Y	43770 FQ	54760 MW	68010 TQ	USBLS	5/07
Including Health	Arizona	Y	38920 FQ	47920 MW	59230 TQ	USBLS	5/07
Including Health	Phoenix-Mesa-Scottsdale MSA, AZ	Y	39040 FQ	47860 MW	58430 TQ	USBLS	5/07
Including Health	Tucson MSA, AZ	Y	36430 FQ	46240 MW	58180 TQ	USBLS	5/07
Including Health	Arkansas	Y	32750 FQ	44110 MW	57730 TQ	USBLS	5/07
Including Health	Little Rock-North Little Rock MSA, AR	Y	34240 FQ	47560 MW	60710 TQ	USBLS	5/07
Including Health	California	H	25.88 FQ	32.37 MW	40.07 TQ	CABLS	1/08-3/08
Including Health	Bakersfield MSA, CA	H	17.74 FQ	24.31 MW	35.16 TQ	CABLS	1/08-3/08
Including Health	Fresno MSA, CA	H	22.40 FQ	26.24 MW	30.18 TQ	CABLS	1/08-3/08

AE	Average entry wage	AW	Average wage paid	FQ	First quartile wage	LO	Lowest wage paid	MTC	Median total compensation	TCC	Total cash compensation
AER	Average entry range	AWR	Average wage range	H	Hourly	LR	Low end range	MW	Median wage paid	TQ	Third quartile wage
AEX	Average experienced wage	AXR	Average experienced range	HI	Highest wage paid	M	Monthly	MWR	Median wage range	W	Weekly
ATC	Average total compensation	D	Daily	HR	High end range	MCC	Median cash compensation	S	See annotated source	Y	Yearly

Occupation/Type/Industry	Location	Per	Low	Mid	High	Source	Date
Environmental Scientist and Specialist							
Including Health	Los Angeles-Long Beach-Glendale PMSA, CA	H	23.18 FQ	32.48 MW	43.35 TQ	CABLS	1/08-3/08
Including Health	Oakland-Fremont-Hayward MSA, CA	H	26.02 FQ	31.94 MW	42.37 TQ	CABLS	1/08-3/08
Including Health	Oxnard-Thousand Oaks-Ventura MSA, CA	H	28.28 FQ	31.92 MW	38.38 TQ	CABLS	1/08-3/08
Including Health	Riverside-San Bernardino-Ontario MSA, CA	H	23.07 FQ	30.05 MW	36.07 TQ	CABLS	1/08-3/08
Including Health	Sacramento-Arden Arcade-Roseville MSA, CA	H	27.73 FQ	33.76 MW	38.41 TQ	CABLS	1/08-3/08
Including Health	San Diego-Carlsbad-San Marcos MSA, CA	H	21.26 FQ	26.91 MW	33.76 TQ	CABLS	1/08-3/08
Including Health	San Francisco-San Mateo-Redwood PMSA, CA	H	33.31 FQ	39.14 MW	49.51 TQ	CABLS	1/08-3/08
Including Health	San Jose-Sunnyvale-Santa Clara MSA, CA	H	29.92 FQ	37.01 MW	45.78 TQ	CABLS	1/08-3/08
Including Health	Santa Ana-Anaheim-Irvine PMSA, CA	Y	47780 FQ	61970 MW	80590 TQ	USBLS	5/07
Including Health	Colorado	Y	52510 FQ	65920 MW	88890 TQ	USBLS	5/07
Including Health	Denver-Aurora MSA, CO	Y	52770 FQ	66460 MW	90250 TQ	USBLS	5/07
Including Health	Connecticut	H	20.02 AE	31.19 MW		CTBLS	1/08-3/08
Including Health	Bridgeport-Stamford-Norwalk MSA, CT	Y	55140 FQ	64660 MW	81900 TQ	USBLS	5/07
Including Health	Hartford-West Hartford-East Hartford MSA, CT	Y	47620 FQ	64140 MW	75690 TQ	USBLS	5/07
Including Health	Delaware	Y	42600 FQ	49280 MW	62870 TQ	USBLS	5/07
Including Health	Wilmington PMSA, DE-MD-NJ	Y	42860 FQ	50710 MW	73330 TQ	USBLS	5/07
Including Health	District of Columbia	Y	71210 FQ	95480 MW	118790 TQ	USBLS	5/07
Including Health	Washington-Arlington-Alexandria MSA, DC-VA-MD-WV	Y	65770 FQ	87310 MW	102580 TQ	USBLS	5/07
Including Health	Florida	Y	39930 FQ	49050 MW	61990 TQ	USBLS	5/07
Including Health	Fort Lauderdale-Pompano Beach-Deerfield Beach PMSA, FL	Y	42230 FQ	52620 MW	62160 TQ	USBLS	5/07
Including Health	Jacksonville MSA, FL	Y	39240 FQ	48120 MW	58940 TQ	USBLS	5/07
Including Health	Lakeland MSA, FL	Y	36780 FQ	42990 MW	54230 TQ	USBLS	5/07
Including Health	Miami-Fort Lauderdale-Miami Beach MSA, FL	Y	43320 FQ	54550 MW	64930 TQ	USBLS	5/07
Including Health	Orlando-Kissimmee MSA, FL	Y	38430 FQ	47750 MW	61750 TQ	USBLS	5/07
Including Health	Tampa-St. Petersburg-Clearwater MSA, FL	Y	39850 FQ	48340 MW	62790 TQ	USBLS	5/07
Including Health	West Palm Beach-Boca Raton-Boynton Beach PMSA, FL	Y	43500 FQ	53580 MW	65630 TQ	USBLS	5/07
Including Health	Georgia	Y	42200 FQ	54190 MW	70530 TQ	USBLS	5/07
Including Health	Atlanta-Sandy Springs-Marietta MSA, GA	Y	42940 FQ	55110 MW	74080 TQ	USBLS	5/07
Including Health	Hawaii	Y	46080 FQ	60100 MW	77020 TQ	USBLS	5/07
Including Health	Honolulu MSA, HI	Y	46310 FQ	61380 MW	78220 TQ	USBLS	5/07
Including Health	Idaho	Y	44850 FQ	53000 MW	60490 TQ	USBLS	5/07
Including Health	Boise City-Nampa MSA, ID	Y	46820 FQ	56410 MW	64020 TQ	USBLS	5/07
Including Health	Illinois	Y	48300 FQ	61630 MW	83850 TQ	USBLS	5/07
Including Health	Chicago-Naperville-Joliet MSA, IL-IN-WI	Y	46340 FQ	63880 MW	88960 TQ	USBLS	5/07
Including Health	Rockford MSA, IL	Y	52890 FQ	60030 MW	71120 TQ	USBLS	5/07
Including Health	Indiana	Y	35920 FQ	49740 MW	72280 TQ	USBLS	5/07
Including Health	Gary PMSA, IN	Y	34590 FQ	43930 MW	67030 TQ	USBLS	5/07
Including Health	Indianapolis-Carmel MSA, IN	Y	38980 FQ	61200 MW	79030 TQ	USBLS	5/07
Including Health	Iowa	Y	42570 FQ	54460 MW	67770 TQ	USBLS	5/07
Including Health	Des Moines-West Des Moines MSA, IA	Y	42500 FQ	58920 MW	71920 TQ	USBLS	5/07
Including Health	Kansas	Y	45140 FQ	56080 MW	65250 TQ	USBLS	5/07
Including Health	Wichita MSA, KS	Y	37920 FQ	46810 MW	60440 TQ	USBLS	5/07
Including Health	Kentucky	Y	42897 FQ	52147 MW	64336 TQ	KYBLS	2008
Including Health	Louisville-Jefferson County MSA, KY-IN	Y	39620 FQ	51160 MW	65120 TQ	USBLS	5/07
Including Health	Louisiana	H	18.33 FQ	23.15 MW	30.81 TQ	LABLS	1/08-3/08
Including Health	Baton Rouge MSA, LA	Y	37380 FQ	47400 MW	63420 TQ	USBLS	5/07

AE Average entry wage	**AW** Average wage paid	**FQ** First quartile wage	**LO** Lowest wage paid	**MTC** Median total compensation **TCC** Total cash compensation
AER Average entry range	**AWR** Average wage range	**H** Hourly	**LR** Low end range	**MW** Median wage paid **TQ** Third quartile wage
AEX Average experienced wage	**AXR** Average experienced range	**HI** Highest wage paid	**M** Monthly	**MWR** Median wage range **W** Weekly
ATC Average total compensation	**D** Daily	**HR** High end range	**MCC** Median cash compensation	**S** See annotated source **Y** Yearly

Occupation/Type/Industry	Location	Per	Low	Mid	High	Source	Date
Environmental Scientist and Specialist							
Including Health	New Orleans-Metairie-Kenner MSA, LA	Y	41700 FQ	49100 MW	63320 TQ	USBLS	5/07
Including Health	Maine	Y	39820 FQ	46890 MW	58070 TQ	USBLS	5/07
Including Health	Portland-South Portland-Biddeford MSA, ME	Y	37770 FQ	43200 MW	61960 TQ	USBLS	5/07
Including Health	Maryland	Y		63425 MW		MDBLS	3/08
Including Health	Baltimore-Towson MSA, MD	Y	43700 FQ	54280 MW	74550 TQ	USBLS	5/07
Including Health	Bethesda-Gaithersburg-Frederick PMSA, MD	Y	58150 FQ	81980 MW	103360 TQ	USBLS	5/07
Including Health	Massachusetts	Y	62450 FQ	81480 MW	108090 TQ	USBLS	5/07
Including Health	Boston-Cambridge-Quincy NECTA, MA	Y	70030 FQ	90040 MW	113650 TQ	USBLS	5/07
Including Health	Michigan	Y	49420 FQ	58780 MW	69280 TQ	USBLS	5/07
Including Health	Detroit-Warren-Livonia MSA, MI	Y	45200 FQ	54760 MW	63650 TQ	USBLS	5/07
Including Health	Grand Rapids-Wyoming MSA, MI	Y	54310 FQ	59690 MW	65370 TQ	USBLS	5/07
Including Health	Warren-Troy-Farmington Hills PMSA, MI	Y	43650 FQ	52830 MW	62620 TQ	USBLS	5/07
Including Health	Minnesota	Y	50532 FQ	59593 MW	70411 TQ	MNBLS	10/08-12/08
Including Health	Duluth-Superior MSA, MN-WI	Y	50585 FQ	60105 MW	69971 TQ	MNBLS	10/08-12/08
Including Health	Minneapolis-Saint Paul MSA, MN-WI	Y	52123 FQ	60545 MW	72681 TQ	MNBLS	10/08-12/08
Including Health	Rochester MSA, MN	Y	50408 FQ	59562 MW	66128 TQ	MNBLS	10/08-12/08
Including Health	Mississippi	Y	32590 FQ	38420 MW	48920 TQ	USBLS	5/07
Including Health	Jackson MSA, MS	Y	31550 FQ	37040 MW	43960 TQ	USBLS	5/07
Including Health	Pascagoula MSA, MS	Y	44510 FQ	59480 MW	73280 TQ	USBLS	5/07
Including Health	Missouri	Y	35470 FQ	41790 MW	51830 TQ	USBLS	5/07
Including Health	Kansas City MSA, MO-KS	Y	37940 FQ	49210 MW	69840 TQ	USBLS	5/07
Including Health	St. Louis MSA, MO-IL	Y	39680 FQ	49630 MW	62090 TQ	USBLS	5/07
Including Health	Montana	Y	35340 FQ	41960 MW	49730 TQ	USBLS	5/07
Including Health	Billings MSA, MT	Y	33300 FQ	37310 MW	48050 TQ	USBLS	5/07
Including Health	Nebraska	Y	37330 FQ	44050 MW	53020 TQ	USBLS	5/07
Including Health	Omaha-Council Bluffs MSA, NE-IA	Y	34540 FQ	41330 MW	52780 TQ	USBLS	5/07
Including Health	Nevada	H	26.50 FQ	32.85 MW	41.45 TQ	NVBLS	5/08
Including Health	Las Vegas-Paradise MSA, NV	H	26.79 FQ	34.00 MW	43.33 TQ	NVBLS	5/08
Including Health	New Hampshire	H	20.59 AE	26.72 MW	37.03 AEX	NHBLS	6/08
Including Health	New Jersey	Y	51730 FQ	65140 MW	81710 TQ	USBLS	5/07
Including Health	Camden PMSA, NJ	Y	42870 FQ	56550 MW	73680 TQ	USBLS	5/07
Including Health	Edison PMSA, NJ	Y	55330 FQ	65540 MW	86060 TQ	USBLS	5/07
Including Health	Newark-Union PMSA, NJ-PA	Y	44930 FQ	56560 MW	70000 TQ	USBLS	5/07
Including Health	New Mexico	Y	45050 FQ	60050 MW	88170 TQ	USBLS	5/07
Including Health	Albuquerque MSA, NM	Y	46420 FQ	66690 MW	103900 TQ	USBLS	5/07
Including Health	New York	Y	52000 FQ	66580 MW	86470 TQ	USBLS	5/07
Including Health	Albany-Schenectady-Troy MSA, NY	Y	49280 FQ	59100 MW	69210 TQ	USBLS	5/07
Including Health	Buffalo-Niagara Falls MSA, NY	Y	50530 FQ	62930 MW	76020 TQ	USBLS	5/07
Including Health	Nassau-Suffolk PMSA, NY	Y	51000 FQ	69700 MW	84620 TQ	USBLS	5/07
Including Health	New York-Northern New Jersey-Long Island MSA, NY-NJ-PA	Y	52560 FQ	67950 MW	88750 TQ	USBLS	5/07
Including Health	North Carolina	Y	39600 FQ	47990 MW	63410 TQ	USBLS	5/07
Including Health	Charlotte-Gastonia-Concord MSA, NC-SC	Y	38400 FQ	45870 MW	58240 TQ	USBLS	5/07
Including Health	Raleigh-Cary MSA, NC	Y	42640 FQ	52660 MW	74070 TQ	USBLS	5/07
Including Health	North Dakota	Y	45990 FQ	59520 MW	75960 TQ	USBLS	5/07
Including Health	Ohio	Y	45600 FQ	57530 MW	71530 TQ	USBLS	5/07
Including Health	Cincinnati-Middletown MSA, OH-KY-IN	Y	50680 FQ	61860 MW	78700 TQ	USBLS	5/07
Including Health	Cleveland-Elyria-Mentor MSA, OH	Y	42790 FQ	52040 MW	67080 TQ	USBLS	5/07
Including Health	Columbus MSA, OH	Y	46860 FQ	57560 MW	71170 TQ	USBLS	5/07
Including Health	Dayton MSA, OH	Y	58490 FQ	67480 MW	76430 TQ	USBLS	5/07
Including Health	Oklahoma	Y	32700 FQ	41180 MW	50030 TQ	USBLS	5/07
Including Health	Oklahoma City MSA, OK	Y	30710 FQ	41100 MW	48450 TQ	USBLS	5/07
Including Health	Tulsa MSA, OK	Y	38260 FQ	50750 MW	62630 TQ	USBLS	5/07
Including Health	Oregon	H	24.80 FQ	29.58 MW	35.80 TQ	ORBLS	5/08
Including Health	Eugene-Springfield MSA, OR	Y	41810 FQ	54700 MW	63570 TQ	USBLS	5/07

AE	Average entry wage	AW	Average wage paid	FQ	First quartile wage	LO	Lowest wage paid	MTC	Median total compensation	TCC	Total cash compensation
AER	Average entry range	AWR	Average wage range	H	Hourly	LR	Low end range	MW	Median wage paid	TQ	Third quartile wage
AEX	Average experienced wage	AXR	Average experienced range	HI	Highest wage paid	M	Monthly	MWR	Median wage range	W	Weekly
ATC	Average total compensation	D	Daily	HR	High end range	MCC	Median cash compensation	S	See annotated source	Y	Yearly

Occupation/Type/Industry	Location	Per	Low	Mid	High	Source	Date
Environmental Scientist and Specialist							
Including Health	Portland-Vancouver-Beaverton MSA, OR-WA	Y	50020 FQ	61430 MW	76370 TQ	USBLS	5/07
Including Health	Pennsylvania	Y	43360 FQ	58400 MW	77800 TQ	USBLS	5/07
Including Health	Allentown-Bethlehem-Easton MSA, PA-NJ	Y	34980 FQ	52420 MW	66110 TQ	USBLS	5/07
Including Health	Philadelphia-Camden-Wilmington MSA, PA-NJ-DE-MD	Y	47410 FQ	62730 MW	84040 TQ	USBLS	5/07
Including Health	Pittsburgh MSA, PA	Y	35970 FQ	48370 MW	61960 TQ	USBLS	5/07
Including Health	Rhode Island	Y	55160 FQ	64910 MW	76610 TQ	USBLS	5/07
Including Health	Providence-Fall River-Warwick MSA, RI-MA	Y	55220 FQ	64920 MW	76750 TQ	USBLS	5/07
Including Health	South Carolina	Y	33280 FQ	43240 MW	59440 TQ	USBLS	5/07
Including Health	Charleston-North Charleston MSA, SC	Y	47560 FQ	58050 MW	66130 TQ	USBLS	5/07
Including Health	Columbia MSA, SC	Y	29800 FQ	36270 MW	46800 TQ	USBLS	5/07
Including Health	South Dakota	Y	43343 FQ	52710 MW	70181 TQ	SDBLS	7/08-9/08
Including Health	Sioux Falls MSA, SD	Y	61047 FQ	72473 MW	79976 TQ	SDBLS	7/08-9/08
Including Health	Tennessee	Y	35400 FQ	46200 MW	61700 TQ	USBLS	5/07
Including Health	Memphis MSA, TN-MS-AR	Y	36210 FQ	46060 MW	53600 TQ	USBLS	5/07
Including Health	Nashville-Davidson-Murfreesboro MSA, TN	Y	39700 FQ	50060 MW	62020 TQ	USBLS	5/07
Including Health	Texas	Y	37570 FQ	51930 MW	76720 TQ	USBLS	5/07
Including Health	Austin-Round Rock MSA, TX	Y	38980 FQ	50690 MW	63630 TQ	USBLS	5/07
Including Health	Dallas-Fort Worth-Arlington MSA, TX	Y	51590 FQ	62530 MW	81700 TQ	USBLS	5/07
Including Health	El Paso MSA, TX	Y	36580 FQ	43570 MW	58140 TQ	USBLS	5/07
Including Health	Houston-Sugar Land-Baytown MSA, TX	Y	39250 FQ	54620 MW	95800 TQ	USBLS	5/07
Including Health	Midland MSA, TX	Y	54530 FQ	79020 MW	98660 TQ	USBLS	5/07
Including Health	San Antonio MSA, TX	Y	42370 FQ	50700 MW	70630 TQ	USBLS	5/07
Including Health	Utah	Y	47560 FQ	64080 MW	83420 TQ	USBLS	5/07
Including Health	Salt Lake City MSA, UT	Y	42830 FQ	55860 MW	69040 TQ	USBLS	5/07
Including Health	Vermont	Y	43980 FQ	51730 MW	60850 TQ	USBLS	5/07
Including Health	Burlington-South Burlington MSA, VT	Y	44890 FQ	54850 MW	68020 TQ	USBLS	5/07
Including Health	Virginia	Y	54210 FQ	75770 MW	91870 TQ	USBLS	5/07
Including Health	Richmond MSA, VA	Y	48950 FQ	60560 MW	79450 TQ	USBLS	5/07
Including Health	Virginia Beach-Norfolk-Newport News MSA, VA-NC	Y	45220 FQ	58050 MW	72330 TQ	USBLS	5/07
Including Health	Washington	H	24.81 FQ	30.52 MW	39.19 TQ	WABLS	3/08
Including Health	Seattle-Tacoma-Bellevue MSA, WA	Y	51370 FQ	65220 MW	83320 TQ	USBLS	5/07
Including Health	West Virginia	Y	34179 FQ	41993 MW	55181 TQ	WVBLS	7/08-9/08 *
Including Health	Charleston MSA, WV	Y	33630 FQ	40760 MW	50900 TQ	USBLS	5/07
Including Health	Wisconsin	Y	45440 FQ	55990 MW	70830 TQ	USBLS	5/07
Including Health	Green Bay MSA, WI	Y	47340 FQ	55440 MW	62080 TQ	USBLS	5/07
Including Health	Milwaukee-Waukesha-West Allis MSA, WI	Y	49200 FQ	68040 MW	95810 TQ	USBLS	5/07
Including Health	Wyoming	Y	42866 FQ	49522 MW	60750 TQ	WYBLS	9/08
Including Health	Cheyenne MSA, WY	Y	46349 FQ	54724 MW	61660 TQ	WYBLS	9/08
Including Health	Puerto Rico	Y	23570 FQ	33480 MW	43860 TQ	USBLS	5/07
Including Health	San Juan-Caguas-Guaynabo MSA, PR	Y	23220 FQ	33040 MW	42930 TQ	USBLS	5/07
Including Health	Guam	Y	28150 FQ	33570 MW	44210 TQ	USBLS	5/07
Epidemiologist	Arizona	Y	41910 FQ	46830 MW	51930 TQ	USBLS	5/07
	Arkansas	Y	46050 FQ	55540 MW	63080 TQ	USBLS	5/07
	California	H	29.56 FQ	35.86 MW	40.69 TQ	CABLS	1/08-3/08
	Colorado	Y	55510 FQ	65140 MW	72580 TQ	USBLS	5/07
	Connecticut	H	25.31 AE	34.25 MW		CTBLS	1/08-3/08
	District of Columbia	Y	56870 FQ	66870 MW	81320 TQ	USBLS	5/07
	Georgia	Y	45580 FQ	55190 MW	63760 TQ	USBLS	5/07
	Illinois	Y	44090 FQ	54170 MW	68380 TQ	USBLS	5/07
	Kansas	Y	50370 FQ	60860 MW	114080 TQ	USBLS	5/07
	Kentucky	Y	42447 FQ	48911 MW	58727 TQ	KYBLS	2008
	Louisiana	H	19.44 FQ	22.99 MW	28.17 TQ	LABLS	1/08-3/08
	Maryland	Y		59625 MW		MDBLS	3/08
	Massachusetts	Y	54650 FQ	64240 MW	79090 TQ	USBLS	5/07
	Michigan	Y	54150 FQ	61900 MW	74570 TQ	USBLS	5/07

AE   Average entry wage
AER Average entry range
AEX Average experienced wage
ATC Average total compensation
AW   Average wage paid
AWR Average wage range
AXR Average experienced range
D   Daily
FQ   First quartile wage
H   Hourly
HI   Highest wage paid
HR   High end range
LO   Lowest wage paid
LR   Low end range
M   Monthly
MCC Median cash compensation
MTC Median total compensation
MW   Median wage paid
MWR Median wage range
S   See annotated source
TCC Total cash compensation
TQ   Third quartile wage
W   Weekly
Y   Yearly

556

Occupation/Type/Industry	Location	Per	Low	Mid	High	Source	Date
Epidemiologist	Minnesota	Y	57197 FQ	68946 MW	79879 TQ	MNBLS	10/08-12/08
	Mississippi	Y	30070 FQ	35060 MW	39480 TQ	USBLS	5/07
	Missouri	Y	42150 FQ	49240 MW	62590 TQ	USBLS	5/07
	Nebraska	Y	44780 FQ	53260 MW	69650 TQ	USBLS	5/07
	Nevada	H	21.78 FQ	26.67 MW	35.55 TQ	NVBLS	5/08
	New Jersey	Y	53170 FQ	66990 MW	75860 TQ	USBLS	5/07
	New York	Y	53930 FQ	80010 MW	110240 TQ	USBLS	5/07
	North Carolina	Y	55690 FQ	64740 MW	81010 TQ	USBLS	5/07
	Ohio	Y	45530 FQ	53910 MW	69460 TQ	USBLS	5/07
	Oklahoma	Y	49480 FQ	60550 MW	79520 TQ	USBLS	5/07
	Oregon	H	23.36 FQ	29.28 MW	34.71 TQ	ORBLS	5/08
	Pennsylvania	Y	54750 FQ	63140 MW	81330 TQ	USBLS	5/07
	South Carolina	Y	45150 FQ	58240 MW	75700 TQ	USBLS	5/07
	Tennessee	Y	54190 FQ	60180 MW	68090 TQ	USBLS	5/07
	Texas	Y	42950 FQ	49320 MW	57330 TQ	USBLS	5/07
	Utah	Y	42630 FQ	49070 MW	58130 TQ	USBLS	5/07
	Virginia	Y	55120 FQ	62600 MW	72940 TQ	USBLS	5/07
	Washington	H	27.29 FQ	32.91 MW	38.24 TQ	WABLS	3/08
	West Virginia	Y	37580 FQ	43232 MW	56365 TQ	WVBLS	7/08-9/08
	Wisconsin	Y	55240 FQ	60580 MW	66500 TQ	USBLS	5/07
	Wyoming	Y	45758 FQ	49596 MW	55737 TQ	WYBLS	9/08
	Puerto Rico	Y	24100 FQ	30060 MW	40650 TQ	USBLS	5/07
Ergonomist State Government	Ohio	H	19.88 LO		38.57 HI	ODAS	2008
Esthetician	United States	Y		27113 AW		CSENET	2008
Estimator/Planner Printing Industry	United States	Y		48153 AW		GRAM	2006
Estimator/Scheduler/Planner Converting Industry	United States	Y		53336 ATC		CVERT	2007
Etcher and Engraver	Alabama	Y	19840 FQ	24710 MW	30930 TQ	USBLS	5/07
	Arizona	Y	22120 FQ	24650 MW	36850 TQ	USBLS	5/07
	Arkansas	Y	21550 FQ	25030 MW	32540 TQ	USBLS	5/07
	California	H	10.33 FQ	13.14 MW	16.81 TQ	CABLS	1/08-3/08
	Los Angeles-Long Beach-Glendale PMSA, CA	H	9.42 FQ	12.26 MW	16.96 TQ	CABLS	1/08-3/08
	Oakland-Fremont-Hayward MSA, CA	H	9.94 FQ	13.79 MW	17.59 TQ	CABLS	1/08-3/08
	Riverside-San Bernardino-Ontario MSA, CA	H	21.06 FQ	22.74 MW	24.42 TQ	CABLS	1/08-3/08
	Sacramento-Arden Arcade-Roseville MSA, CA	H	12.98 FQ	14.85 MW	18.66 TQ	CABLS	1/08-3/08
	San Diego-Carlsbad-San Marcos MSA, CA	H	10.09 FQ	11.69 MW	13.50 TQ	CABLS	1/08-3/08
	San Francisco-San Mateo-Redwood PMSA, CA	H	16.34 FQ	17.59 MW	18.84 TQ	CABLS	1/08-3/08
	San Jose-Sunnyvale-Santa Clara MSA, CA	H	15.95 FQ	18.49 MW	23.79 TQ	CABLS	1/08-3/08
	Santa Ana-Anaheim-Irvine PMSA, CA	Y	21210 FQ	26310 MW	31030 TQ	USBLS	5/07
	Colorado	Y	21990 FQ	27310 MW	32110 TQ	USBLS	5/07
	Denver-Aurora MSA, CO	Y	22610 FQ	28470 MW	34460 TQ	USBLS	5/07
	Connecticut	H	10.99 AE	16.99 MW		CTBLS	1/08-3/08
	Bridgeport-Stamford-Norwalk MSA, CT	Y	25920 FQ	34560 MW	48800 TQ	USBLS	5/07
	Hartford-West Hartford-East Hartford MSA, CT	Y	30150 FQ	38040 MW	46010 TQ	USBLS	5/07
	Washington-Arlington-Alexandria MSA, DC-VA-MD-WV	Y	23150 FQ	28190 MW	32920 TQ	USBLS	5/07
	Florida	Y	17390 FQ	21280 MW	24360 TQ	USBLS	5/07
	Jacksonville MSA, FL	Y	21790 FQ	23570 MW	25290 TQ	USBLS	5/07
	Miami-Fort Lauderdale-Miami Beach MSA, FL	Y	16230 FQ	17770 MW	21960 TQ	USBLS	5/07
	Tampa-St. Petersburg-Clearwater MSA, FL	Y	26640 FQ	31410 MW	37470 TQ	USBLS	5/07
	Georgia	Y	15850 FQ	18070 MW	20060 TQ	USBLS	5/07

AE Average entry wage	**AW** Average wage paid	**FQ** First quartile wage	**LO** Lowest wage paid	**MTC** Median total compensation	**TCC** Total cash compensation
AER Average entry range	**AWR** Average wage range	**H** Hourly	**LR** Low end range	**MW** Median wage paid	**TQ** Third quartile wage
AEX Average experienced wage	**AXR** Average experienced range	**HI** Highest wage paid	**M** Monthly	**MWR** Median wage range	**W** Weekly
ATC Average total compensation	**D** Daily	**HR** High end range	**MCC** Median cash compensation	**S** See annotated source	**Y** Yearly

Occupation/Type/Industry	Location	Per	Low	Mid	High	Source	Date
Etcher and Engraver	Atlanta-Sandy Springs-Marietta MSA, GA	Y	16920 FQ	18390 MW	19840 TQ	USBLS	5/07
	Hawaii	Y	21610 FQ	25130 MW	45670 TQ	USBLS	5/07
	Honolulu MSA, HI	Y	21610 FQ	25130 MW	45670 TQ	USBLS	5/07
	Idaho	Y	16530 FQ	21690 MW	27830 TQ	USBLS	5/07
	Illinois	Y	23960 FQ	30550 MW	37230 TQ	USBLS	5/07
	Chicago-Naperville-Joliet MSA, IL-IN-WI	Y	26850 FQ	34920 MW	40790 TQ	USBLS	5/07
	Indiana	Y	21200 FQ	26880 MW	36330 TQ	USBLS	5/07
	Gary PMSA, IN	Y	40000 FQ	45830 MW	52790 TQ	USBLS	5/07
	Indianapolis-Carmel MSA, IN	Y	13670 FQ	21300 MW	27440 TQ	USBLS	5/07
	Iowa	Y	17760 FQ	21470 MW	37310 TQ	USBLS	5/07
	Kansas	Y	22430 FQ	30330 MW	38900 TQ	USBLS	5/07
	Kentucky	Y	19485 FQ	23561 MW	30780 TQ	KYBLS	2008
	Louisville-Jefferson County MSA, KY-IN	Y	21000 FQ	24670 MW	33680 TQ	USBLS	5/07
	Louisiana	H	10.25 FQ	11.63 MW	13.32 TQ	LABLS	1/08-3/08
	New Orleans-Metairie-Kenner MSA, LA	Y	26350 FQ	28820 MW	38390 TQ	USBLS	5/07
	Maine	Y	17960 FQ	19700 MW	25820 TQ	USBLS	5/07
	Maryland	Y		27700 MW		MDBLS	3/08
	Baltimore-Towson MSA, MD	Y	25030 FQ	28390 MW	32020 TQ	USBLS	5/07
	Massachusetts	Y	24190 FQ	32180 MW	39720 TQ	USBLS	5/07
	Boston-Cambridge-Quincy NECTA, MA	Y	33490 FQ	39480 MW	45720 TQ	USBLS	5/07
	Michigan	Y	22290 FQ	27960 MW	36440 TQ	USBLS	5/07
	Detroit-Warren-Livonia MSA, MI	Y	23290 FQ	36530 MW	39980 TQ	USBLS	5/07
	Warren-Troy-Farmington Hills PMSA, MI	Y	23560 FQ	36820 MW	40120 TQ	USBLS	5/07
	Minnesota	Y	27347 FQ	33360 MW	38212 TQ	MNBLS	10/08-12/08
	Minneapolis-Saint Paul MSA, MN-WI	Y	25491 FQ	32354 MW	37206 TQ	MNBLS	10/08-12/08
	Mississippi	Y	14490 FQ	17390 MW	19780 TQ	USBLS	5/07
	Missouri	Y	15360 FQ	21170 MW	25200 TQ	USBLS	5/07
	Kansas City MSA, MO-KS	Y	20960 FQ	33850 MW	40120 TQ	USBLS	5/07
	St. Louis MSA, MO-IL	Y	23200 FQ	27180 MW	30880 TQ	USBLS	5/07
	Montana	Y	18340 FQ	24360 MW	31450 TQ	USBLS	5/07
	Nebraska	Y	20540 FQ	23070 MW	29590 TQ	USBLS	5/07
	Nevada	H	13.25 FQ	15.60 MW	19.99 TQ	NVBLS	5/08
	New Jersey	Y	24210 FQ	29530 MW	40020 TQ	USBLS	5/07
	Edison PMSA, NJ	Y	23920 FQ	39810 MW	48090 TQ	USBLS	5/07
	Newark-Union PMSA, NJ-PA	Y	25910 FQ	29240 MW	41540 TQ	USBLS	5/07
	New York	Y	26080 FQ	30230 MW	36540 TQ	USBLS	5/07
	Nassau-Suffolk PMSA, NY	Y	27050 FQ	30900 MW	36350 TQ	USBLS	5/07
	New York-Northern New Jersey-Long Island MSA, NY-NJ-PA	Y	25130 FQ	29700 MW	38540 TQ	USBLS	5/07
	Syracuse MSA, NY	Y	26840 FQ	29110 MW	31340 TQ	USBLS	5/07
	North Carolina	Y	21060 FQ	24940 MW	33530 TQ	USBLS	5/07
	Charlotte-Gastonia-Concord MSA, NC-SC	Y	20690 FQ	22810 MW	36540 TQ	USBLS	5/07
	Raleigh-Cary MSA, NC	Y	22780 FQ	26550 MW	31940 TQ	USBLS	5/07
	Ohio	Y	24450 FQ	27990 MW	33130 TQ	USBLS	5/07
	Cincinnati-Middletown MSA, OH-KY-IN	Y	25600 FQ	33880 MW	37470 TQ	USBLS	5/07
	Cleveland-Elyria-Mentor MSA, OH	Y	31680 FQ	38080 MW	44380 TQ	USBLS	5/07
	Columbus MSA, OH	Y	20640 FQ	22700 MW	32640 TQ	USBLS	5/07
	Oklahoma	Y	16670 FQ	19460 MW	25510 TQ	USBLS	5/07
	Portland-Vancouver-Beaverton MSA, OR-WA	Y	23460 FQ	32970 MW	38260 TQ	USBLS	5/07
	Pennsylvania	Y	19610 FQ	27030 MW	33660 TQ	USBLS	5/07
	Philadelphia-Camden-Wilmington MSA, PA-NJ-DE-MD	Y	18150 FQ	25840 MW	33850 TQ	USBLS	5/07
	Rhode Island	Y	23630 FQ	29640 MW	42280 TQ	USBLS	5/07
	Providence-Fall River-Warwick MSA, RI-MA	Y	23820 FQ	29010 MW	40520 TQ	USBLS	5/07
	South Carolina	Y	27290 FQ	31300 MW	37620 TQ	USBLS	5/07
	South Dakota	Y	16149 FQ	20645 MW	24877 TQ	SDBLS	7/08-9/08
	Sioux Falls MSA, SD	Y	22690 FQ	35122 MW	38768 TQ	SDBLS	7/08-9/08

AE	Average entry wage	**AW**	Average wage paid	**FQ**	First quartile wage
AER	Average entry range	**AWR**	Average wage range	**H**	Hourly
AEX	Average experienced wage	**AXR**	Average experienced range	**HI**	Highest wage paid
ATC	Average total compensation	**D**	Daily	**HR**	High end range

LO Lowest wage paid   **MTC** Median total compensation   **TCC** Total cash compensation
LR Low end range   **MW** Median wage paid   **TQ** Third quartile wage
M Monthly   **MWR** Median wage range   **W** Weekly
MCC Median cash compensation   **S** See annotated source   **Y** Yearly

Occupation/Type/Industry	Location	Per	Low	Mid	High	Source	Date
Etcher and Engraver	Tennessee	Y	20640 FQ	23890 MW	29010 TQ	USBLS	5/07
	Memphis MSA, TN-MS-AR	Y	23330 FQ	26870 MW	30340 TQ	USBLS	5/07
	Texas	Y	19670 FQ	25070 MW	31970 TQ	USBLS	5/07
	Austin-Round Rock MSA, TX	Y	22070 FQ	24870 MW	27370 TQ	USBLS	5/07
	Dallas-Fort Worth-Arlington MSA, TX	Y	25620 FQ	33160 MW	38480 TQ	USBLS	5/07
	El Paso MSA, TX	Y	16790 FQ	17930 MW	19070 TQ	USBLS	5/07
	Houston-Sugar Land-Baytown MSA, TX	Y	23790 FQ	26040 MW	28110 TQ	USBLS	5/07
	San Antonio MSA, TX	Y	17880 FQ	19870 MW	27830 TQ	USBLS	5/07
	Utah	Y	19470 FQ	23880 MW	31000 TQ	USBLS	5/07
	Salt Lake City MSA, UT	Y	20460 FQ	26910 MW	36980 TQ	USBLS	5/07
	Virginia	Y	26550 FQ	30330 MW	42070 TQ	USBLS	5/07
	Richmond MSA, VA	Y	31230 FQ	41660 MW	50050 TQ	USBLS	5/07
	Virginia Beach-Norfolk-Newport News MSA, VA-NC	Y	27530 FQ	30180 MW	42620 TQ	USBLS	5/07
	Washington	H	12.71 FQ	14.03 MW	17.89 TQ	WABLS	3/08
	Seattle-Tacoma-Bellevue MSA, WA	Y	25890 FQ	27910 MW	30790 TQ	USBLS	5/07
	West Virginia	Y	17825 FQ	20358 MW	30033 TQ	WVBLS	7/08-9/08
	Wisconsin	Y	22390 FQ	31800 MW	44400 TQ	USBLS	5/07
	Milwaukee-Waukesha-West Allis MSA, WI	Y	23750 FQ	31600 MW	65780 TQ	USBLS	5/07
	Wyoming	Y	17604 FQ	18930 MW	20255 TQ	WYBLS	9/08
Ethics Advisor White House Staff	United States	Y			58206-130694 HR	WPOST02	2008
Ethics Commission Special Investigator State Government	Ohio	H	21.77 LO		31.86 HI	ODAS	2008
Evaluation Engineer	Central	Y		76000 MW		EE01	2008
	Mountain	Y		85000 MW		EE01	2008
	Northeast	Y		80000 MW		EE01	2008
	Pacific	Y		97000 MW		EE01	2008
	Southeast	Y		78000 MW		EE01	2008
Event Coordinator Municipal Government	Cincinnati, OH	Y	45117 LO		60634 HI	COHSS	10/08
Events Booking Representative Municipal Government	Seattle, WA	H	24.63 LO		28.74 HI	CSSS	2008
Evidence Technician	Colorado Springs, CO	M	3249 LO			COSPRS	1/1/09
Excavating and Loading Machine and Dragline Operator	Alabama	Y	25430 FQ	30010 MW	35390 TQ	USBLS	5/07
	Birmingham-Hoover MSA, AL	Y	27790 FQ	32960 MW	39170 TQ	USBLS	5/07
	Alaska	Y	41930 FQ	52370 MW	67320 TQ	USBLS	5/07
	Anchorage MSA, AK	Y	47330 FQ	51840 MW	56710 TQ	USBLS	5/07
	Arizona	Y	32540 FQ	38770 MW	45300 TQ	USBLS	5/07
	Phoenix-Mesa-Scottsdale MSA, AZ	Y	34640 FQ	40170 MW	46620 TQ	USBLS	5/07
	Tucson MSA, AZ	Y	30460 FQ	34240 MW	41060 TQ	USBLS	5/07
	Arkansas	Y	24990 FQ	28540 MW	31850 TQ	USBLS	5/07
	Little Rock-North Little Rock MSA, AR	Y	22930 FQ	27420 MW	31130 TQ	USBLS	5/07
	California	H	19.54 FQ	26.77 MW	33.27 TQ	CABLS	1/08-3/08
	Bakersfield MSA, CA	H	17.74 FQ	20.93 MW	24.42 TQ	CABLS	1/08-3/08
	Los Angeles-Long Beach-Glendale PMSA, CA	H	16.07 FQ	21.23 MW	27.07 TQ	CABLS	1/08-3/08
	Oakland-Fremont-Hayward MSA, CA	H	20.33 FQ	25.85 MW	33.72 TQ	CABLS	1/08-3/08
	Riverside-San Bernardino-Ontario MSA, CA	H	25.98 FQ	30.44 MW	33.75 TQ	CABLS	1/08-3/08
	Sacramento-Arden Arcade-Roseville MSA, CA	H	23.27 FQ	26.47 MW	30.80 TQ	CABLS	1/08-3/08
	San Diego-Carlsbad-San Marcos MSA, CA	H	18.48 FQ	26.00 MW	29.26 TQ	CABLS	1/08-3/08

AE	Average entry wage	AW	Average wage paid	FQ	First quartile wage
AER	Average entry range	AWR	Average wage range	H	Hourly
AEX	Average experienced wage	AXR	Average experienced range	HI	Highest wage paid
ATC	Average total compensation	D	Daily	HR	High end range

LO Lowest wage paid   MTC Median total compensation   TCC Total cash compensation
LR Low end range   MW Median wage paid   TQ Third quartile wage
M Monthly   MWR Median wage range   W Weekly
MCC Median cash compensation   S See annotated source   Y Yearly

Occupation/Type/Industry	Location	Per	Low	Mid	High	Source	Date
Excavating and Loading Machine and Dragline Operator							
	San Francisco-San Mateo-Redwood PMSA, CA	H	31.75 FQ	34.79 MW	38.46 TQ	CABLS	1/08-3/08
	San Jose-Sunnyvale-Santa Clara MSA, CA	H	15.14 FQ	18.07 MW	31.97 TQ	CABLS	1/08-3/08
	Santa Ana-Anaheim-Irvine PMSA, CA	Y	52970 FQ	67670 MW	77960 TQ	USBLS	5/07
	Colorado	Y	30840 FQ	37940 MW	45920 TQ	USBLS	5/07
	Denver-Aurora MSA, CO	Y	38790 FQ	43600 MW	48680 TQ	USBLS	5/07
	Connecticut	H	15.14 AE	19.42 MW		CTBLS	1/08-3/08
	Bridgeport-Stamford-Norwalk MSA, CT	Y	35500 FQ	51330 MW	63310 TQ	USBLS	5/07
	Hartford-West Hartford-East Hartford MSA, CT	Y	31680 FQ	37960 MW	44070 TQ	USBLS	5/07
	Delaware	Y	37830 FQ	41840 MW	46790 TQ	USBLS	5/07
	Wilmington PMSA, DE-MD-NJ	Y	37680 FQ	43760 MW	49710 TQ	USBLS	5/07
	Washington-Arlington-Alexandria MSA, DC-VA-MD-WV	Y	31850 FQ	38380 MW	45930 TQ	USBLS	5/07
	Florida	Y	24640 FQ	29150 MW	35170 TQ	USBLS	5/07
	Fort Lauderdale-Pompano Beach-Deerfield Beach PMSA, FL	Y	17610 FQ	22710 MW	35030 TQ	USBLS	5/07
	Jacksonville MSA, FL	Y	25960 FQ	29940 MW	35280 TQ	USBLS	5/07
	Miami-Fort Lauderdale-Miami Beach MSA, FL	Y	20070 FQ	29720 MW	37860 TQ	USBLS	5/07
	Orlando-Kissimmee MSA, FL	Y	26750 FQ	29520 MW	32710 TQ	USBLS	5/07
	Tampa-St. Petersburg-Clearwater MSA, FL	Y	24470 FQ	28200 MW	32000 TQ	USBLS	5/07
	West Palm Beach-Boca Raton-Boynton Beach PMSA, FL	Y	28610 FQ	33850 MW	42960 TQ	USBLS	5/07
	Georgia	Y	26920 FQ	31010 MW	37200 TQ	USBLS	5/07
	Atlanta-Sandy Springs-Marietta MSA, GA	Y	29180 FQ	33240 MW	38380 TQ	USBLS	5/07
	Augusta-Richmond County MSA, GA-SC	Y	23210 FQ	34530 MW	53960 TQ	USBLS	5/07
	Hawaii	Y	34380 FQ	38970 MW	46600 TQ	USBLS	5/07
	Honolulu MSA, HI	Y	33490 FQ	37680 MW	45120 TQ	USBLS	5/07
	Idaho	Y	30430 FQ	36200 MW	43100 TQ	USBLS	5/07
	Boise City-Nampa MSA, ID	Y	28420 FQ	34300 MW	38950 TQ	USBLS	5/07
	Illinois	Y	35000 FQ	41660 MW	69780 TQ	USBLS	5/07
	Chicago-Naperville-Joliet MSA, IL-IN-WI	Y	36360 FQ	49510 MW	72960 TQ	USBLS	5/07
	Indiana	Y	29960 FQ	36590 MW	45960 TQ	USBLS	5/07
	Elkhart-Goshen MSA, IN	Y	31740 FQ	35640 MW	38830 TQ	USBLS	5/07
	Gary PMSA, IN	Y	42890 FQ	50270 MW	57710 TQ	USBLS	5/07
	Indianapolis-Carmel MSA, IN	Y	33560 FQ	38350 MW	43070 TQ	USBLS	5/07
	Iowa	Y	26790 FQ	30750 MW	37140 TQ	USBLS	5/07
	Des Moines-West Des Moines MSA, IA	Y	29650 FQ	40920 MW	51120 TQ	USBLS	5/07
	Kansas	Y	27710 FQ	32540 MW	37850 TQ	USBLS	5/07
	Wichita MSA, KS	Y	25500 FQ	30440 MW	36830 TQ	USBLS	5/07
	Kentucky	Y	30543 FQ	34835 MW	38851 TQ	KYBLS	2008
	Lexington-Fayette MSA, KY	Y	34380 FQ	54660 MW	63000 TQ	USBLS	5/07
	Louisville-Jefferson County MSA, KY-IN	Y	26710 FQ	30830 MW	35690 TQ	USBLS	5/07
	Louisiana	H	11.78 FQ	13.93 MW	16.50 TQ	LABLS	1/08-3/08
	Baton Rouge MSA, LA	Y	26550 FQ	30520 MW	34610 TQ	USBLS	5/07
	New Orleans-Metairie-Kenner MSA, LA	Y	21230 FQ	25210 MW	30960 TQ	USBLS	5/07
	Shreveport-Bossier City MSA, LA	Y	29550 FQ	32920 MW	35900 TQ	USBLS	5/07
	Maine	Y	28120 FQ	32160 MW	36860 TQ	USBLS	5/07
	Portland-South Portland-Biddeford MSA, ME	Y	30690 FQ	33850 MW	37290 TQ	USBLS	5/07
	Maryland	Y		38275 MW		MDBLS	3/08
	Baltimore-Towson MSA, MD	Y	33900 FQ	39370 MW	48290 TQ	USBLS	5/07
	Bethesda-Gaithersburg-Frederick PMSA, MD	Y	32780 FQ	36170 MW	40490 TQ	USBLS	5/07
	Massachusetts	Y	35290 FQ	46240 MW	59110 TQ	USBLS	5/07

Occupation/Type/Industry	Location	Per	Low	Mid	High	Source	Date
Excavating and Loading Machine and Dragline Operator	Boston-Cambridge-Quincy NECTA, MA	Y	39780 FQ	48000 MW	59590 TQ	USBLS	5/07
	Worcester MSA, MA-CT	Y	19580 FQ	28830 MW	32850 TQ	USBLS	5/07
	Michigan	Y	32350 FQ	38490 MW	48350 TQ	USBLS	5/07
	Detroit-Warren-Livonia MSA, MI	Y	39760 FQ	49690 MW	57640 TQ	USBLS	5/07
	Grand Rapids-Wyoming MSA, MI	Y	35550 FQ	39260 MW	43830 TQ	USBLS	5/07
	Warren-Troy-Farmington Hills PMSA, MI	Y	39340 FQ	48800 MW	57550 TQ	USBLS	5/07
	Minnesota	Y	31366 FQ	40105 MW	54607 TQ	MNBLS	10/08-12/08
	Minneapolis-Saint Paul MSA, MN-WI	Y	45764 FQ	58571 MW	68194 TQ	MNBLS	10/08-12/08
	Rochester MSA, MN	Y	39455 FQ	43829 MW	50187 TQ	MNBLS	10/08-12/08
	Mississippi	Y	25180 FQ	28370 MW	32920 TQ	USBLS	5/07
	Jackson MSA, MS	Y	21780 FQ	28090 MW	35070 TQ	USBLS	5/07
	Missouri	Y	34400 FQ	44050 MW	56760 TQ	USBLS	5/07
	Kansas City MSA, MO-KS	Y	34100 FQ	42760 MW	52390 TQ	USBLS	5/07
	St. Louis MSA, MO-IL	Y	44340 FQ	54510 MW	60960 TQ	USBLS	5/07
	Montana	Y	32190 FQ	38490 MW	45840 TQ	USBLS	5/07
	Billings MSA, MT	Y	33800 FQ	37960 MW	54030 TQ	USBLS	5/07
	Nebraska	Y	24220 FQ	31040 MW	38960 TQ	USBLS	5/07
	Omaha-Council Bluffs MSA, NE-IA	Y	34050 FQ	44480 MW	52020 TQ	USBLS	5/07
	Nevada	H	16.03 FQ	19.47 MW	23.31 TQ	NVBLS	5/08
	Las Vegas-Paradise MSA, NV	H	15.56 FQ	18.23 MW	23.05 TQ	NVBLS	5/08
	New Hampshire	H	15.47 AE	18.86 MW	21.66 AEX	NHBLS	6/08
	Manchester MSA, NH	Y	33620 FQ	38380 MW	44060 TQ	USBLS	5/07
	Nashua NECTA, NH-MA	Y	31520 FQ	41080 MW	50250 TQ	USBLS	5/07
	New Jersey	Y	38020 FQ	45750 MW	55900 TQ	USBLS	5/07
	Camden PMSA, NJ	Y	49760 FQ	66820 MW	75210 TQ	USBLS	5/07
	Edison PMSA, NJ	Y	38770 FQ	46140 MW	55640 TQ	USBLS	5/07
	Newark-Union PMSA, NJ-PA	Y	38990 FQ	44920 MW	50940 TQ	USBLS	5/07
	New Mexico	Y	30310 FQ	37540 MW	50380 TQ	USBLS	5/07
	Albuquerque MSA, NM	Y	26870 FQ	42550 MW	63260 TQ	USBLS	5/07
	New York	Y	31050 FQ	38930 MW	48730 TQ	USBLS	5/07
	Albany-Schenectady-Troy MSA, NY	Y	26790 FQ	30260 MW	37330 TQ	USBLS	5/07
	Buffalo-Niagara Falls MSA, NY	Y	26390 FQ	36740 MW	44930 TQ	USBLS	5/07
	Nassau-Suffolk PMSA, NY	Y	34580 FQ	47910 MW	79920 TQ	USBLS	5/07
	New York-Northern New Jersey-Long Island MSA, NY-NJ-PA	Y	37890 FQ	44680 MW	54870 TQ	USBLS	5/07
	Syracuse MSA, NY	Y	27560 FQ	30450 MW	32830 TQ	USBLS	5/07
	North Carolina	Y	25680 FQ	30090 MW	35780 TQ	USBLS	5/07
	Charlotte-Gastonia-Concord MSA, NC-SC	Y	23610 FQ	29710 MW	35770 TQ	USBLS	5/07
	Raleigh-Cary MSA, NC	Y	27760 FQ	31600 MW	35990 TQ	USBLS	5/07
	North Dakota	Y	28880 FQ	36230 MW	58160 TQ	USBLS	5/07
	Fargo MSA, ND-MN	Y	27220 FQ	29540 MW	31930 TQ	USBLS	5/07
	Ohio	Y	27960 FQ	34880 MW	44770 TQ	USBLS	5/07
	Cincinnati-Middletown MSA, OH-KY-IN	Y	31820 FQ	36850 MW	44890 TQ	USBLS	5/07
	Cleveland-Elyria-Mentor MSA, OH	Y	39850 FQ	54040 MW	60820 TQ	USBLS	5/07
	Columbus MSA, OH	Y	28620 FQ	34720 MW	41510 TQ	USBLS	5/07
	Dayton MSA, OH	Y	30250 FQ	35590 MW	43630 TQ	USBLS	5/07
	Oklahoma	Y	26330 FQ	30000 MW	36350 TQ	USBLS	5/07
	Oklahoma City MSA, OK	Y	24600 FQ	28600 MW	39470 TQ	USBLS	5/07
	Tulsa MSA, OK	Y	28340 FQ	33230 MW	38600 TQ	USBLS	5/07
	Oregon	H	14.72 FQ	17.21 MW	20.93 TQ	ORBLS	5/08
	Portland-Vancouver-Beaverton MSA, OR-WA	Y	33990 FQ	41850 MW	55340 TQ	USBLS	5/07
	Pennsylvania	Y	27610 FQ	33680 MW	40360 TQ	USBLS	5/07
	Allentown-Bethlehem-Easton MSA, PA-NJ	Y	31280 FQ	35590 MW	40220 TQ	USBLS	5/07
	Pittsburgh MSA, PA	Y	28100 FQ	34210 MW	39790 TQ	USBLS	5/07
	Rhode Island	Y	34210 FQ	40630 MW	46760 TQ	USBLS	5/07
	Providence-Fall River-Warwick MSA, RI-MA	Y	34240 FQ	40290 MW	46530 TQ	USBLS	5/07

Occupation/Type/Industry	Location	Per	Low	Mid	High	Source	Date
Excavating and Loading Machine and Dragline Operator	South Carolina	Y	25600 FQ	29060 MW	34380 TQ	USBLS	5/07
	Charleston-North Charleston MSA, SC	Y	26820 FQ	30260 MW	40250 TQ	USBLS	5/07
	Columbia MSA, SC	Y	23860 FQ	27160 MW	30410 TQ	USBLS	5/07
	Myrtle Beach-Conway-North Myrtle Beach MSA, SC	Y	25780 FQ	28760 MW	34800 TQ	USBLS	5/07
	South Dakota	Y	24898 FQ	31154 MW	36930 TQ	SDBLS	7/08-9/08
	Sioux Falls MSA, SD	Y	27312 FQ	34654 MW	44325 TQ	SDBLS	7/08-9/08
	Tennessee	Y	24530 FQ	28040 MW	31970 TQ	USBLS	5/07
	Knoxville MSA, TN	Y	27260 FQ	29740 MW	32670 TQ	USBLS	5/07
	Memphis MSA, TN-MS-AR	Y	24600 FQ	28010 MW	31420 TQ	USBLS	5/07
	Nashville-Davidson-Murfreesboro MSA, TN	Y	23730 FQ	28860 MW	34240 TQ	USBLS	5/07
	Texas	Y	23330 FQ	28200 MW	33740 TQ	USBLS	5/07
	Austin-Round Rock MSA, TX	Y	23050 FQ	26760 MW	30800 TQ	USBLS	5/07
	Corpus Christi MSA, TX	Y	20370 FQ	30210 MW	36040 TQ	USBLS	5/07
	Dallas-Fort Worth-Arlington MSA, TX	Y	24890 FQ	29370 MW	34760 TQ	USBLS	5/07
	El Paso MSA, TX	Y	19430 FQ	24630 MW	33320 TQ	USBLS	5/07
	Houston-Sugar Land-Baytown MSA, TX	Y	24400 FQ	28310 MW	32750 TQ	USBLS	5/07
	San Antonio MSA, TX	Y	20620 FQ	26820 MW	32460 TQ	USBLS	5/07
	Utah	Y	30400 FQ	34000 MW	37730 TQ	USBLS	5/07
	Ogden-Clearfield MSA, UT	Y	31400 FQ	33340 MW	35280 TQ	USBLS	5/07
	Salt Lake City MSA, UT	Y	28860 FQ	32890 MW	36300 TQ	USBLS	5/07
	Vermont	Y	29690 FQ	34480 MW	39420 TQ	USBLS	5/07
	Burlington-South Burlington MSA, VT	Y	27530 FQ	31390 MW	35790 TQ	USBLS	5/07
	Virginia	Y	26350 FQ	32030 MW	39580 TQ	USBLS	5/07
	Charlottesville MSA, VA	Y	27770 FQ	30270 MW	33110 TQ	USBLS	5/07
	Richmond MSA, VA	Y	24110 FQ	30410 MW	38630 TQ	USBLS	5/07
	Roanoke MSA, VA	Y	20430 FQ	29540 MW	33820 TQ	USBLS	5/07
	Virginia Beach-Norfolk-Newport News MSA, VA-NC	Y	24760 FQ	30170 MW	37660 TQ	USBLS	5/07
	Washington	H	20.85 FQ	24.11 MW	28.04 TQ	WABLS	3/08
	Seattle-Tacoma-Bellevue MSA, WA	Y	45310 FQ	51580 MW	58960 TQ	USBLS	5/07
	West Virginia	Y	33944 FQ	43655 MW	49602 TQ	WVBLS	7/08-9/08
	Charleston MSA, WV	Y	36630 FQ	44090 MW	48080 TQ	USBLS	5/07
	Wisconsin	Y	30120 FQ	35580 MW	43360 TQ	USBLS	5/07
	Green Bay MSA, WI	Y	27760 FQ	34010 MW	67230 TQ	USBLS	5/07
	Milwaukee-Waukesha-West Allis MSA, WI	Y	30850 FQ	37150 MW	44130 TQ	USBLS	5/07
	Wyoming	Y	32194 FQ	36415 MW	40896 TQ	WYBLS	9/08
	Cheyenne MSA, WY	Y	33069 FQ	36903 MW	40547 TQ	WYBLS	9/08
	Puerto Rico	Y	16240 FQ	17920 MW	20660 TQ	USBLS	5/07
	San Juan-Caguas-Guaynabo MSA, PR	Y	16370 FQ	17910 MW	20170 TQ	USBLS	5/07
	Virgin Islands	Y	25680 FQ	28720 MW	31760 TQ	USBLS	5/07
Executive Assistant Municipal Government	Walnut Creek, CA	Y	56055 LO		67587 HI	WCSWP	7/11/08
Executive Coach	United States	H	125.00 LO		500.00 HI	NYT01	2007
Executive Director Board of Alcohol, Drug Addiction and Mental Health Services	Summit County, OH	Y			110000 HI	ABJ	2008
Executive Director for Curriculum Instruction Area Public Schools	Brighton, MI	Y			113380 HI	LCPP	2009
Executive Manager County Emergency Management Office	Fort Bend County, TX	Y			90014 HI	HCHRON	2009
Executive Secretary and Administrative Assistant	Alabama	Y	33380 FQ	38310 MW	46700 TQ	USBLS	5/07
	Birmingham-Hoover MSA, AL	Y	33940 FQ	38950 MW	47360 TQ	USBLS	5/07
	Alaska	Y	32720 FQ	38680 MW	47540 TQ	USBLS	5/07
	Anchorage MSA, AK	Y	33140 FQ	38700 MW	47790 TQ	USBLS	5/07

Occupation/Type/Industry	Location	Per	Low	Mid	High	Source	Date
Executive Secretary and Administrative Assistant	Fairbanks MSA, AK	Y	30220 FQ	36570 MW	46080 TQ	USBLS	5/07
	Arizona	Y	27920 FQ	33460 MW	41070 TQ	USBLS	5/07
	Phoenix-Mesa-Scottsdale MSA, AZ	Y	28310 FQ	34230 MW	41910 TQ	USBLS	5/07
	Tucson MSA, AZ	Y	28220 FQ	33960 MW	42020 TQ	USBLS	5/07
	Yuma MSA, AZ	Y	25900 FQ	29350 MW	33720 TQ	USBLS	5/07
	Arkansas	Y	24380 FQ	29750 MW	36920 TQ	USBLS	5/07
	Little Rock-North Little Rock MSA, AR	Y	24800 FQ	30760 MW	37830 TQ	USBLS	5/07
	California	H	16.92 FQ	20.98 MW	25.89 TQ	CABLS	1/08-3/08
	Los Angeles-Long Beach-Glendale PMSA, CA	H	16.77 FQ	20.67 MW	25.40 TQ	CABLS	1/08-3/08
	Oakland-Fremont-Hayward MSA, CA	H	18.20 FQ	22.50 MW	27.36 TQ	CABLS	1/08-3/08
	Oxnard-Thousand Oaks-Ventura MSA, CA	H	16.39 FQ	20.35 MW	25.36 TQ	CABLS	1/08-3/08
	Riverside-San Bernardino-Ontario MSA, CA	H	15.41 FQ	18.91 MW	23.33 TQ	CABLS	1/08-3/08
	Sacramento-Arden Arcade-Roseville MSA, CA	H	16.59 FQ	20.19 MW	23.99 TQ	CABLS	1/08-3/08
	San Diego-Carlsbad-San Marcos MSA, CA	H	16.39 FQ	19.84 MW	24.66 TQ	CABLS	1/08-3/08
	San Francisco-San Mateo-Redwood PMSA, CA	H	19.35 FQ	24.05 MW	29.54 TQ	CABLS	1/08-3/08
	San Jose-Sunnyvale-Santa Clara MSA, CA	H	19.72 FQ	24.85 MW	30.41 TQ	CABLS	1/08-3/08
	Santa Ana-Anaheim-Irvine PMSA, CA	Y	35330 FQ	43840 MW	53260 TQ	USBLS	5/07
	Colorado	Y	33680 FQ	40570 MW	49260 TQ	USBLS	5/07
	Denver-Aurora MSA, CO	Y	34860 FQ	41810 MW	49800 TQ	USBLS	5/07
	Connecticut	H	15.44 AE	21.32 MW		CTBLS	1/08-3/08
	Bridgeport-Stamford-Norwalk MSA, CT	Y	35950 FQ	44970 MW	56040 TQ	USBLS	5/07
	Hartford-West Hartford-East Hartford MSA, CT	Y	35690 FQ	44150 MW	53510 TQ	USBLS	5/07
	Waterbury MSA, CT	Y	29220 FQ	35530 MW	45550 TQ	USBLS	5/07
	Delaware	Y	31910 FQ	39420 MW	49000 TQ	USBLS	5/07
	Wilmington PMSA, DE-MD-NJ	Y	32250 FQ	40120 MW	49460 TQ	USBLS	5/07
	District of Columbia	Y	36840 FQ	46240 MW	56990 TQ	USBLS	5/07
	Washington-Arlington-Alexandria MSA, DC-VA-MD-WV	Y	38340 FQ	47130 MW	57870 TQ	USBLS	5/07
	Florida	Y	29080 FQ	35440 MW	43650 TQ	USBLS	5/07
	Fort Lauderdale-Pompano Beach-Deerfield Beach PMSA, FL	Y	29130 FQ	36220 MW	45530 TQ	USBLS	5/07
	Jacksonville MSA, FL	Y	28310 FQ	34720 MW	42620 TQ	USBLS	5/07
	Miami-Fort Lauderdale-Miami Beach MSA, FL	Y	30400 FQ	37410 MW	46610 TQ	USBLS	5/07
	Orlando-Kissimmee MSA, FL	Y	29350 FQ	35520 MW	43740 TQ	USBLS	5/07
	Sarasota-Bradenton-Venice MSA, FL	Y	29610 FQ	34760 MW	40900 TQ	USBLS	5/07
	Tallahassee MSA, FL	Y	28700 FQ	34140 MW	41480 TQ	USBLS	5/07
	Tampa-St. Petersburg-Clearwater MSA, FL	Y	28960 FQ	35200 MW	42570 TQ	USBLS	5/07
	West Palm Beach-Boca Raton-Boynton Beach PMSA, FL	Y	31220 FQ	38070 MW	46810 TQ	USBLS	5/07
	Georgia	Y	29810 FQ	36640 MW	45960 TQ	USBLS	5/07
	Atlanta-Sandy Springs-Marietta MSA, GA	Y	31290 FQ	38700 MW	48320 TQ	USBLS	5/07
	Hawaii	Y	33220 FQ	40070 MW	49950 TQ	USBLS	5/07
	Honolulu MSA, HI	Y	33210 FQ	40430 MW	50330 TQ	USBLS	5/07
	Idaho	Y	27230 FQ	31770 MW	38880 TQ	USBLS	5/07
	Boise City-Nampa MSA, ID	Y	28210 FQ	32800 MW	40090 TQ	USBLS	5/07
	Illinois	Y	32270 FQ	40520 MW	51360 TQ	USBLS	5/07
	Chicago-Naperville-Joliet MSA, IL-IN-WI	Y	33540 FQ	42000 MW	52860 TQ	USBLS	5/07
	Indiana	Y	28110 FQ	33990 MW	40800 TQ	USBLS	5/07
	Elkhart-Goshen MSA, IN	Y	27790 FQ	33610 MW	40340 TQ	USBLS	5/07
	Evansville MSA, IN-KY	Y	25280 FQ	29970 MW	36300 TQ	USBLS	5/07

AE	Average entry wage	AW	Average wage paid	FQ	First quartile wage	LO	Lowest wage paid	MTC	Median total compensation	TCC	Total cash compensation
AER	Average entry range	AWR	Average wage range	H	Hourly	LR	Low end range	MW	Median wage paid	TQ	Third quartile wage
AEX	Average experienced wage	AXR	Average experienced range	HI	Highest wage paid	M	Monthly	MWR	Median wage range	W	Weekly
ATC	Average total compensation	D	Daily	HR	High end range	MCC	Median cash compensation	S	See annotated source	Y	Yearly

Executive Secretary and Administrative Assistant

Occupation/Type/Industry	Location	Per	Low	Mid	High	Source	Date
	Gary PMSA, IN	Y	27860 FQ	34170 MW	43670 TQ	USBLS	5/07
	Indianapolis-Carmel MSA, IN	Y	29850 FQ	36010 MW	43630 TQ	USBLS	5/07
	Iowa	Y	27840 FQ	34160 MW	40970 TQ	USBLS	5/07
	Des Moines-West Des Moines MSA, IA	Y	31360 FQ	37280 MW	44290 TQ	USBLS	5/07
	Kansas	Y	28900 FQ	33810 MW	39600 TQ	USBLS	5/07
	Topeka MSA, KS	Y	27840 FQ	32410 MW	38210 TQ	USBLS	5/07
	Wichita MSA, KS	Y	28840 FQ	33420 MW	39430 TQ	USBLS	5/07
	Kentucky	Y	27577 FQ	32642 MW	39993 TQ	KYBLS	2008
	Louisville-Jefferson County MSA, KY-IN	Y	27260 FQ	32600 MW	39830 TQ	USBLS	5/07
	Louisiana	H	12.76 FQ	15.17 MW	18.40 TQ	LABLS	1/08-3/08
	Baton Rouge MSA, LA	Y	26810 FQ	33000 MW	40670 TQ	USBLS	5/07
	New Orleans-Metairie-Kenner MSA, LA	Y	27210 FQ	32050 MW	38350 TQ	USBLS	5/07
	Shreveport-Bossier City MSA, LA	Y	25710 FQ	31170 MW	37500 TQ	USBLS	5/07
	Maine	Y	33280 FQ	38830 MW	46250 TQ	USBLS	5/07
	Portland-South Portland-Biddeford MSA, ME	Y	34150 FQ	39430 MW	47400 TQ	USBLS	5/07
	Maryland	Y		43500 MW		MDBLS	3/08
	Baltimore-Towson MSA, MD	Y	35100 FQ	41220 MW	50340 TQ	USBLS	5/07
	Bethesda-Gaithersburg-Frederick PMSA, MD	Y	38690 FQ	46540 MW	57150 TQ	USBLS	5/07
	Massachusetts	Y	37260 FQ	45120 MW	53410 TQ	USBLS	5/07
	Boston-Cambridge-Quincy NECTA, MA	Y	38520 FQ	46270 MW	54980 TQ	USBLS	5/07
	Springfield MSA, MA-CT	Y	32720 FQ	38720 MW	46420 TQ	USBLS	5/07
	Worcester MSA, MA-CT	Y	34580 FQ	41670 MW	48910 TQ	USBLS	5/07
	Michigan	Y	32620 FQ	39930 MW	47790 TQ	USBLS	5/07
	Detroit-Warren-Livonia MSA, MI	Y	34370 FQ	41710 MW	49180 TQ	USBLS	5/07
	Flint MSA, MI	Y	30500 FQ	39340 MW	49310 TQ	USBLS	5/07
	Grand Rapids-Wyoming MSA, MI	Y	29600 FQ	36880 MW	44690 TQ	USBLS	5/07
	Muskegon-Norton Shores MSA, MI	Y	30480 FQ	36320 MW	44990 TQ	USBLS	5/07
	Warren-Troy-Farmington Hills PMSA, MI	Y	33680 FQ	41070 MW	48550 TQ	USBLS	5/07
	Minnesota	Y	35938 FQ	42121 MW	49375 TQ	MNBLS	10/08-12/08
	Duluth-Superior MSA, MN-WI	Y	31380 FQ	37895 MW	44358 TQ	MNBLS	10/08-12/08
	Minneapolis-Saint Paul MSA, MN-WI	Y	37073 FQ	43474 MW	50489 TQ	MNBLS	10/08-12/08
	Rochester MSA, MN	Y	34888 FQ	39915 MW	45693 TQ	MNBLS	10/08-12/08
	Mississippi	Y	25600 FQ	31020 MW	38380 TQ	USBLS	5/07
	Hattiesburg MSA, MS	Y	25300 FQ	30420 MW	38740 TQ	USBLS	5/07
	Jackson MSA, MS	Y	25430 FQ	30670 MW	38550 TQ	USBLS	5/07
	Missouri	Y	30950 FQ	37770 MW	46790 TQ	USBLS	5/07
	Kansas City MSA, MO-KS	Y	31740 FQ	37340 MW	45250 TQ	USBLS	5/07
	St. Louis MSA, MO-IL	Y	32630 FQ	39430 MW	48710 TQ	USBLS	5/07
	Montana	Y	23990 FQ	28850 MW	35380 TQ	USBLS	5/07
	Billings MSA, MT	Y	24150 FQ	28780 MW	35680 TQ	USBLS	5/07
	Nebraska	Y	26740 FQ	31670 MW	38130 TQ	USBLS	5/07
	Omaha-Council Bluffs MSA, NE-IA	Y	27990 FQ	33170 MW	39310 TQ	USBLS	5/07
	Nevada	H	14.80 FQ	18.21 MW	22.84 TQ	NVBLS	5/08
	Las Vegas-Paradise MSA, NV	H	14.91 FQ	18.27 MW	23.09 TQ	NVBLS	5/08
	New Hampshire	H	14.61 AE	18.57 MW	21.63 AEX	NHBLS	6/08
	Manchester MSA, NH	Y	35270 FQ	41870 MW	49830 TQ	USBLS	5/07
	Nashua NECTA, NH-MA	Y	31820 FQ	39290 MW	48900 TQ	USBLS	5/07
	New Jersey	Y	42750 FQ	50330 MW	59260 TQ	USBLS	5/07
	Camden PMSA, NJ	Y	39330 FQ	46250 MW	53390 TQ	USBLS	5/07
	Edison PMSA, NJ	Y	43200 FQ	50560 MW	59460 TQ	USBLS	5/07
	Newark-Union PMSA, NJ-PA	Y	43490 FQ	50630 MW	59870 TQ	USBLS	5/07
	New Mexico	Y	29780 FQ	35650 MW	43660 TQ	USBLS	5/07
	Albuquerque MSA, NM	Y	29710 FQ	35270 MW	43000 TQ	USBLS	5/07
	Las Cruces MSA, NM	Y	30200 FQ	35000 MW	42460 TQ	USBLS	5/07
	New York	Y	36380 FQ	44690 MW	55740 TQ	USBLS	5/07
	Albany-Schenectady-Troy MSA, NY	Y	33880 FQ	40090 MW	47800 TQ	USBLS	5/07

AE	Average entry wage	AW	Average wage paid	FQ	First quartile wage
AER	Average entry range	AWR	Average wage range	H	Hourly
AEX	Average experienced wage	AXR	Average experienced range	HI	Highest wage paid
ATC	Average total compensation	D	Daily	HR	High end range

LO	Lowest wage paid	MTC	Median total compensation	TCC	Total cash compensation
LR	Low end range	MW	Median wage paid	TQ	Third quartile wage
M	Monthly	MWR	Median wage range	W	Weekly
MCC	Median cash compensation	S	See annotated source	Y	Yearly

Occupation/Type/Industry	Location	Per	Low	Mid	High	Source	Date
Executive Secretary and Administrative Assistant	Buffalo-Niagara Falls MSA, NY	Y	32550 FQ	38860 MW	46670 TQ	USBLS	5/07
	Nassau-Suffolk PMSA, NY	Y	37220 FQ	45570 MW	55970 TQ	USBLS	5/07
	New York-Northern New Jersey-Long Island MSA, NY-NJ-PA	Y	39310 FQ	47830 MW	58910 TQ	USBLS	5/07
	North Carolina	Y	29020 FQ	34880 MW	41510 TQ	USBLS	5/07
	Asheville MSA, NC	Y	27450 FQ	32200 MW	38910 TQ	USBLS	5/07
	Charlotte-Gastonia-Concord MSA, NC-SC	Y	30270 FQ	36350 MW	43780 TQ	USBLS	5/07
	Greensboro-High Point MSA, NC	Y	29330 FQ	34730 MW	40460 TQ	USBLS	5/07
	Raleigh-Cary MSA, NC	Y	29720 FQ	35650 MW	42690 TQ	USBLS	5/07
	North Dakota	Y	27260 FQ	32380 MW	39970 TQ	USBLS	5/07
	Fargo MSA, ND-MN	Y	28270 FQ	33740 MW	41190 TQ	USBLS	5/07
	Ohio	Y	30920 FQ	37300 MW	45530 TQ	USBLS	5/07
	Canton-Massillon MSA, OH	Y	28860 FQ	34220 MW	39560 TQ	USBLS	5/07
	Cincinnati-Middletown MSA, OH-KY-IN	Y	30800 FQ	37130 MW	45130 TQ	USBLS	5/07
	Cleveland-Elyria-Mentor MSA, OH	Y	31990 FQ	38170 MW	45620 TQ	USBLS	5/07
	Columbus MSA, OH	Y	32220 FQ	39720 MW	48580 TQ	USBLS	5/07
	Dayton MSA, OH	Y	30400 FQ	36060 MW	43630 TQ	USBLS	5/07
	Mansfield MSA, OH	Y	27690 FQ	33350 MW	39200 TQ	USBLS	5/07
	Oklahoma	Y	26100 FQ	31350 MW	38330 TQ	USBLS	5/07
	Oklahoma City MSA, OK	Y	26820 FQ	32150 MW	39320 TQ	USBLS	5/07
	Tulsa MSA, OK	Y	27320 FQ	33620 MW	39880 TQ	USBLS	5/07
	Oregon	H	15.23 FQ	18.53 MW	22.19 TQ	ORBLS	5/08
	Portland-Vancouver-Beaverton MSA, OR-WA	Y	33290 FQ	40150 MW	46970 TQ	USBLS	5/07
	Pennsylvania	Y	29950 FQ	37330 MW	46560 TQ	USBLS	5/07
	Allentown-Bethlehem-Easton MSA, PA-NJ	Y	30170 FQ	36390 MW	44400 TQ	USBLS	5/07
	Erie MSA, PA	Y	28220 FQ	33740 MW	40280 TQ	USBLS	5/07
	Philadelphia-Camden-Wilmington MSA, PA-NJ-DE-MD	Y	34460 FQ	41960 MW	51010 TQ	USBLS	5/07
	Pittsburgh MSA, PA	Y	28330 FQ	35370 MW	43170 TQ	USBLS	5/07
	Rhode Island	Y	36370 FQ	42810 MW	49590 TQ	USBLS	5/07
	Providence-Fall River-Warwick MSA, RI-MA	Y	35540 FQ	42310 MW	49580 TQ	USBLS	5/07
	South Carolina	Y	28690 FQ	34560 MW	41260 TQ	USBLS	5/07
	Charleston-North Charleston MSA, SC	Y	29540 FQ	35500 MW	43920 TQ	USBLS	5/07
	Columbia MSA, SC	Y	29430 FQ	35150 MW	41720 TQ	USBLS	5/07
	Myrtle Beach-Conway-North Myrtle Beach MSA, SC	Y	27650 FQ	32700 MW	37820 TQ	USBLS	5/07
	South Dakota	Y	27440 FQ	30651 MW	35339 TQ	SDBLS	7/08-9/08
	Rapid City MSA, SD	Y	27266 FQ	30741 MW	35550 TQ	SDBLS	7/08-9/08
	Sioux Falls MSA, SD	Y	28686 FQ	32354 MW	37518 TQ	SDBLS	7/08-9/08
	Tennessee	Y	26830 FQ	32630 MW	39860 TQ	USBLS	5/07
	Johnson City MSA, TN	Y	24180 FQ	28330 MW	32760 TQ	USBLS	5/07
	Memphis MSA, TN-MS-AR	Y	28030 FQ	33850 MW	41060 TQ	USBLS	5/07
	Nashville-Davidson-Murfreesboro MSA, TN	Y	28790 FQ	34940 MW	41440 TQ	USBLS	5/07
	Texas	Y	29820 FQ	36970 MW	45790 TQ	USBLS	5/07
	Austin-Round Rock MSA, TX	Y	29040 FQ	36270 MW	45260 TQ	USBLS	5/07
	Beaumont-Port Arthur MSA, TX	Y	27500 FQ	33500 MW	39990 TQ	USBLS	5/07
	Brownsville-Harlingen MSA, TX	Y	25130 FQ	32050 MW	41440 TQ	USBLS	5/07
	Dallas-Fort Worth-Arlington MSA, TX	Y	32300 FQ	38820 MW	47020 TQ	USBLS	5/07
	El Paso MSA, TX	Y	25280 FQ	31700 MW	39150 TQ	USBLS	5/07
	Houston-Sugar Land-Baytown MSA, TX	Y	32410 FQ	39420 MW	48290 TQ	USBLS	5/07
	San Antonio MSA, TX	Y	27860 FQ	34410 MW	42750 TQ	USBLS	5/07
	Utah	Y	30940 FQ	36550 MW	43380 TQ	USBLS	5/07
	St. George MSA, UT	Y	27530 FQ	32510 MW	40420 TQ	USBLS	5/07
	Salt Lake City MSA, UT	Y	31040 FQ	36750 MW	43850 TQ	USBLS	5/07
	Vermont	Y	32580 FQ	38150 MW	44890 TQ	USBLS	5/07

AE Average entry wage	**AW** Average wage paid	**FQ** First quartile wage	**LO** Lowest wage paid	**MTC** Median total compensation	**TCC** Total cash compensation
AER Average entry range	**AWR** Average wage range	**H** Hourly	**LR** Low end range	**MW** Median wage paid	**TQ** Third quartile wage
AEX Average experienced wage	**AXR** Average experienced range	**HI** Highest wage paid	**M** Monthly	**MWR** Median wage range	**W** Weekly
ATC Average total compensation	**D** Daily	**HR** High end range	**MCC** Median cash compensation	**S** See annotated source	**Y** Yearly

Occupation/Type/Industry	Location	Per	Low	Mid	High	Source	Date
Executive Secretary and Administrative Assistant	Burlington-South Burlington MSA, VT	Y	32790 FQ	38520 MW	44710 TQ	USBLS	5/07
	Virginia	Y	34480 FQ	43000 MW	53290 TQ	USBLS	5/07
	Richmond MSA, VA	Y	32970 FQ	38920 MW	47040 TQ	USBLS	5/07
	Virginia Beach-Norfolk-Newport News MSA, VA-NC	Y	29750 FQ	36530 MW	44500 TQ	USBLS	5/07
	Washington	H	18.14 FQ	21.33 MW	24.80 TQ	WABLS	3/08
	Seattle-Tacoma-Bellevue MSA, WA	Y	38170 FQ	44580 MW	51840 TQ	USBLS	5/07
	Spokane MSA, WA	Y	33980 FQ	39600 MW	46210 TQ	USBLS	5/07
	West Virginia	Y	26127 FQ	31077 MW	37864 TQ	WVBLS	7/08-9/08
	Charleston MSA, WV	Y	27430 FQ	33340 MW	39160 TQ	USBLS	5/07
	Wisconsin	Y	28830 FQ	34980 MW	41750 TQ	USBLS	5/07
	Milwaukee-Waukesha-West Allis MSA, WI	Y	31600 FQ	37370 MW	44680 TQ	USBLS	5/07
	Wyoming	Y	29051 FQ	34548 MW	40858 TQ	WYBLS	9/08
	Cheyenne MSA, WY	Y	28009 FQ	32007 MW	37663 TQ	WYBLS	9/08
	Puerto Rico	Y	20210 FQ	25150 MW	31630 TQ	USBLS	5/07
	San German-Cabo Rojo MSA, PR	Y	14680 FQ	19060 MW	24960 TQ	USBLS	5/07
	San Juan-Caguas-Guaynabo MSA, PR	Y	20800 FQ	25750 MW	32070 TQ	USBLS	5/07
	Virgin Islands	Y	27640 FQ	30940 MW	36210 TQ	USBLS	5/07
	Guam	Y	21700 FQ	28140 MW	35180 TQ	USBLS	5/07
Executive Sous Chef							
Fine Dining Restaurant	United States	Y		60118 AW		STARC	2007
Hotel Restaurant	United States	Y		58333 AW		STARC	2007
Upscale Casual Restaurant	United States	Y		46100 AW		STARC	2007
Exercise Physiologist Assistant							
State Government	Ohio	H	15.62 LO		18.36 HI	ODAS	2008
Exhibit Designer	Northern Virginia, VA	Y	23999-31352 LR		64032-83651 HR	VACG02	11/25/07
Exhibits Design Coordinator							
Municipal Government	Seattle, WA	H	23.94 LO		27.96 HI	CSSS	2007
Expert Dog Handler	United States	Y	100000 LO			ABCN01	2009
Explosives Worker, Ordnance Handling Expert, and Blaster	Alabama	Y	40630 FQ	45620 MW	50170 TQ	USBLS	5/07
	Alaska	Y	46160 FQ	52630 MW	84260 TQ	USBLS	5/07
	Arizona	Y	40710 FQ	44010 MW	47510 TQ	USBLS	5/07
	Arkansas	Y	27990 FQ	30990 MW	40160 TQ	USBLS	5/07
	California	H	20.51 FQ	22.67 MW	25.37 TQ	CABLS	1/08-3/08
	Colorado	Y	40680 FQ	53080 MW	59020 TQ	USBLS	5/07
	Connecticut	H	24.91 AE	29.68 MW		CTBLS	1/08-3/08
	Florida	Y	41580 FQ	45530 MW	50130 TQ	USBLS	5/07
	Georgia	Y	27350 FQ	30280 MW	36500 TQ	USBLS	5/07
	Hawaii	Y	46510 FQ	53400 MW	58980 TQ	USBLS	5/07
	Illinois	Y	33050 FQ	38220 MW	49130 TQ	USBLS	5/07
	Indiana	Y	34220 FQ	36850 MW	39580 TQ	USBLS	5/07
	Kansas	Y	33860 FQ	37670 MW	42870 TQ	USBLS	5/07
	Kentucky	Y	34262 FQ	37846 MW	41527 TQ	KYBLS	2008
	Louisiana	H	15.78 FQ	17.11 MW	18.43 TQ	LABLS	1/08-3/08
	Maine	Y	39090 FQ	44240 MW	49560 TQ	USBLS	5/07
	Maryland	Y		48500 MW		MDBLS	3/08
	Michigan	Y	34970 FQ	40860 MW	47390 TQ	USBLS	5/07
	Minnesota	Y	45580 FQ	48710 MW	52019 TQ	MNBLS	10/08-12/08
	Missouri	Y	36450 FQ	46840 MW	56490 TQ	USBLS	5/07
	Nevada	H	14.11 FQ	15.59 MW	22.72 TQ	NVBLS	5/08
	New Mexico	Y	31680 FQ	45560 MW	53260 TQ	USBLS	5/07
	New York	Y	34920 FQ	42530 MW	50020 TQ	USBLS	5/07
	North Carolina	Y	36270 FQ	40490 MW	50240 TQ	USBLS	5/07
	Ohio	Y	35940 FQ	43560 MW	47440 TQ	USBLS	5/07
	Oklahoma	Y	33270 FQ	37040 MW	42290 TQ	USBLS	5/07
	Oregon	H	13.78 FQ	15.22 MW	19.90 TQ	ORBLS	5/08
	Pennsylvania	Y	32620 FQ	37560 MW	48380 TQ	USBLS	5/07
	South Dakota	Y	42651 FQ	47648 MW	52445 TQ	SDBLS	7/08-9/08

Occupation/Type/Industry	Location	Per	Low	Mid	High	Source	Date
Explosives Worker, Ordnance Handling Expert, and Blaster	Tennessee	Y	39310 FQ	47350 MW	55880 TQ	USBLS	5/07
	Texas	Y	33780 FQ	40990 MW	59780 TQ	USBLS	5/07
	Virginia	Y	33100 FQ	40880 MW	48570 TQ	USBLS	5/07
	Washington	H	19.18 FQ	22.51 MW	27.58 TQ	WABLS	3/08
	West Virginia	Y	36298 FQ	42622 MW	50107 TQ	WVBLS	7/08-9/08
	Wisconsin	Y	47420 FQ	55950 MW	62150 TQ	USBLS	5/07
	Wyoming	Y	38873 FQ	46943 MW	55556 TQ	WYBLS	9/08
	Puerto Rico	Y	23020 FQ	34900 MW	49400 TQ	USBLS	5/07
External Pre-Auditor Department of Administrative Services	New Hampshire	Y			56142 HI	NHUL03	2008
Extruding, Forming, Pressing, and Compacting Machine Setter, Operator, and Tender	Alabama	Y	24660 FQ	34130 MW	43670 TQ	USBLS	5/07
	Birmingham-Hoover MSA, AL	Y	20150 FQ	24650 MW	30520 TQ	USBLS	5/07
	Arizona	Y	22410 FQ	27990 MW	35750 TQ	USBLS	5/07
	Phoenix-Mesa-Scottsdale MSA, AZ	Y	22240 FQ	26880 MW	34580 TQ	USBLS	5/07
	Tucson MSA, AZ	Y	22470 FQ	31970 MW	41820 TQ	USBLS	5/07
	Arkansas	Y	23170 FQ	28570 MW	34980 TQ	USBLS	5/07
	Little Rock-North Little Rock MSA, AR	Y	26160 FQ	28250 MW	30840 TQ	USBLS	5/07
	California	H	9.61 FQ	11.59 MW	14.89 TQ	CABLS	1/08-3/08
	Los Angeles-Long Beach-Glendale PMSA, CA	H	8.94 FQ	10.71 MW	13.68 TQ	CABLS	1/08-3/08
	Oakland-Fremont-Hayward MSA, CA	H	11.43 FQ	13.11 MW	17.61 TQ	CABLS	1/08-3/08
	Riverside-San Bernardino-Ontario MSA, CA	H	9.20 FQ	10.68 MW	12.89 TQ	CABLS	1/08-3/08
	Sacramento-Arden Arcade-Roseville MSA, CA	H	11.25 FQ	13.95 MW	16.79 TQ	CABLS	1/08-3/08
	San Diego-Carlsbad-San Marcos MSA, CA	H	10.84 FQ	15.12 MW	18.90 TQ	CABLS	1/08-3/08
	San Francisco-San Mateo-Redwood PMSA, CA	H	12.04 FQ	16.66 MW	18.32 TQ	CABLS	1/08-3/08
	San Jose-Sunnyvale-Santa Clara MSA, CA	H	10.65 FQ	13.69 MW	18.49 TQ	CABLS	1/08-3/08
	Santa Ana-Anaheim-Irvine PMSA, CA	Y	19250 FQ	23030 MW	27920 TQ	USBLS	5/07
	Colorado	Y	19770 FQ	25230 MW	35240 TQ	USBLS	5/07
	Denver-Aurora MSA, CO	Y	15590 FQ	24830 MW	42730 TQ	USBLS	5/07
	Connecticut	H	10.71 AE	13.96 MW		CTBLS	1/08-3/08
	Bridgeport-Stamford-Norwalk MSA, CT	Y	23690 FQ	27280 MW	30960 TQ	USBLS	5/07
	Hartford-West Hartford-East Hartford MSA, CT	Y	24800 FQ	29640 MW	35110 TQ	USBLS	5/07
	Delaware	Y	23720 FQ	28100 MW	35190 TQ	USBLS	5/07
	Wilmington PMSA, DE-MD-NJ	Y	28920 FQ	35430 MW	40540 TQ	USBLS	5/07
	Washington-Arlington-Alexandria MSA, DC-VA-MD-WV	Y	23870 FQ	29930 MW	35170 TQ	USBLS	5/07
	Florida	Y	22160 FQ	27830 MW	33930 TQ	USBLS	5/07
	Fort Lauderdale-Pompano Beach-Deerfield Beach PMSA, FL	Y	15640 FQ	20090 MW	26270 TQ	USBLS	5/07
	Jacksonville MSA, FL	Y	26140 FQ	31480 MW	34270 TQ	USBLS	5/07
	Miami-Fort Lauderdale-Miami Beach MSA, FL	Y	19880 FQ	24380 MW	30310 TQ	USBLS	5/07
	Orlando-Kissimmee MSA, FL	Y	17930 FQ	22160 MW	28120 TQ	USBLS	5/07
	Tampa-St. Petersburg-Clearwater MSA, FL	Y	22310 FQ	28410 MW	37320 TQ	USBLS	5/07
	West Palm Beach-Boca Raton-Boynton Beach PMSA, FL	Y	15450 FQ	20900 MW	28140 TQ	USBLS	5/07
	Georgia	Y	22800 FQ	28880 MW	37200 TQ	USBLS	5/07
	Atlanta-Sandy Springs-Marietta MSA, GA	Y	21860 FQ	28310 MW	35610 TQ	USBLS	5/07
	Macon MSA, GA	Y	22140 FQ	24850 MW	28040 TQ	USBLS	5/07
	Hawaii	Y	21730 FQ	25250 MW	30630 TQ	USBLS	5/07

Extruding, Forming, Pressing, and Compacting Machine Setter, Operator, and Tender

Occupation/Type/Industry	Location	Per	Low	Mid	High	Source	Date
	Honolulu MSA, HI	Y	20820 FQ	23140 MW	26320 TQ	USBLS	5/07
	Idaho	Y	24390 FQ	28340 MW	34600 TQ	USBLS	5/07
	Illinois	Y	24690 FQ	31070 MW	41260 TQ	USBLS	5/07
	Chicago-Naperville-Joliet MSA, IL-IN-WI	Y	24600 FQ	31020 MW	41870 TQ	USBLS	5/07
	Indiana	Y	23760 FQ	29880 MW	38300 TQ	USBLS	5/07
	Evansville MSA, IN-KY	Y	24670 FQ	43160 MW	47730 TQ	USBLS	5/07
	Gary PMSA, IN	Y	24850 FQ	30050 MW	39230 TQ	USBLS	5/07
	Indianapolis-Carmel MSA, IN	Y	24100 FQ	33150 MW	39840 TQ	USBLS	5/07
	Iowa	Y	23170 FQ	27580 MW	33130 TQ	USBLS	5/07
	Des Moines-West Des Moines MSA, IA	Y	27030 FQ	29460 MW	31430 TQ	USBLS	5/07
	Kansas	Y	24730 FQ	28300 MW	32150 TQ	USBLS	5/07
	Kentucky	Y	23488 FQ	27653 MW	32570 TQ	KYBLS	2008
	Louisville-Jefferson County MSA, KY-IN	Y	20700 FQ	22990 MW	26300 TQ	USBLS	5/07
	Louisiana	H	9.44 FQ	11.18 MW	14.69 TQ	LABLS	1/08-3/08
	Baton Rouge MSA, LA	Y	19520 FQ	24710 MW	30630 TQ	USBLS	5/07
	New Orleans-Metairie-Kenner MSA, LA	Y	21650 FQ	25790 MW	31140 TQ	USBLS	5/07
	Maine	Y	21160 FQ	28330 MW	35290 TQ	USBLS	5/07
	Portland-South Portland-Biddeford MSA, ME	Y	20080 FQ	25700 MW	31540 TQ	USBLS	5/07
	Maryland	Y		27700 MW		MDBLS	3/08
	Baltimore-Towson MSA, MD	Y	24000 FQ	27570 MW	31370 TQ	USBLS	5/07
	Bethesda-Gaithersburg-Frederick PMSA, MD	Y	21710 FQ	24630 MW	31020 TQ	USBLS	5/07
	Massachusetts	Y	25370 FQ	29570 MW	35010 TQ	USBLS	5/07
	Boston-Cambridge-Quincy NECTA, MA	Y	25140 FQ	30110 MW	35520 TQ	USBLS	5/07
	Worcester MSA, MA-CT	Y	26820 FQ	31820 MW	40820 TQ	USBLS	5/07
	Michigan	Y	22880 FQ	27050 MW	31890 TQ	USBLS	5/07
	Detroit-Warren-Livonia MSA, MI	Y	21430 FQ	26300 MW	33180 TQ	USBLS	5/07
	Grand Rapids-Wyoming MSA, MI	Y	23980 FQ	26570 MW	29310 TQ	USBLS	5/07
	Warren-Troy-Farmington Hills PMSA, MI	Y	22040 FQ	27130 MW	34150 TQ	USBLS	5/07
	Minnesota	Y	29016 FQ	35081 MW	41342 TQ	MNBLS	10/08-12/08
	Duluth-Superior MSA, MN-WI	Y	25357 FQ	34614 MW	40295 TQ	MNBLS	10/08-12/08
	Minneapolis-Saint Paul MSA, MN-WI	Y	29535 FQ	36138 MW	44266 TQ	MNBLS	10/08-12/08
	Rochester MSA, MN	Y	29361 FQ	33335 MW	41677 TQ	MNBLS	10/08-12/08
	Mississippi	Y	18670 FQ	24960 MW	31670 TQ	USBLS	5/07
	Jackson MSA, MS	Y	21350 FQ	23730 MW	27290 TQ	USBLS	5/07
	Missouri	Y	23980 FQ	29410 MW	34440 TQ	USBLS	5/07
	Kansas City MSA, MO-KS	Y	22250 FQ	27660 MW	33310 TQ	USBLS	5/07
	St. Louis MSA, MO-IL	Y	24870 FQ	31020 MW	36160 TQ	USBLS	5/07
	Montana	Y	18020 FQ	23380 MW	32300 TQ	USBLS	5/07
	Billings MSA, MT	Y	20910 FQ	26230 MW	31500 TQ	USBLS	5/07
	Nebraska	Y	19830 FQ	25570 MW	33770 TQ	USBLS	5/07
	Omaha-Council Bluffs MSA, NE-IA	Y	26610 FQ	33850 MW	48220 TQ	USBLS	5/07
	Nevada	H	11.59 FQ	14.19 MW	17.35 TQ	NVBLS	5/08
	Las Vegas-Paradise MSA, NV	H	11.33 FQ	13.86 MW	17.37 TQ	NVBLS	5/08
	New Hampshire	H	10.17 AE	13.80 MW	16.46 AEX	NHBLS	6/08
	Nashua NECTA, NH-MA	Y	23010 FQ	26950 MW	31280 TQ	USBLS	5/07
	New Jersey	Y	22440 FQ	28140 MW	35160 TQ	USBLS	5/07
	Camden PMSA, NJ	Y	22600 FQ	28600 MW	38110 TQ	USBLS	5/07
	Edison PMSA, NJ	Y	23150 FQ	28210 MW	34920 TQ	USBLS	5/07
	Newark-Union PMSA, NJ-PA	Y	21050 FQ	25070 MW	30100 TQ	USBLS	5/07
	New Mexico	Y	20700 FQ	23140 MW	29590 TQ	USBLS	5/07
	Albuquerque MSA, NM	Y	20820 FQ	23260 MW	29840 TQ	USBLS	5/07
	New York	Y	23010 FQ	30660 MW	39100 TQ	USBLS	5/07
	Albany-Schenectady-Troy MSA, NY	Y	33540 FQ	39160 MW	43260 TQ	USBLS	5/07
	Buffalo-Niagara Falls MSA, NY	Y	40910 FQ	46690 MW	50770 TQ	USBLS	5/07
	Nassau-Suffolk PMSA, NY	Y	19180 FQ	22650 MW	29930 TQ	USBLS	5/07

AE	Average entry wage	AW	Average wage paid	FQ	First quartile wage
AER	Average entry range	AWR	Average wage range	H	Hourly
AEX	Average experienced wage	AXR	Average experienced range	HI	Highest wage paid
ATC	Average total compensation	D	Daily	HR	High end range

LO	Lowest wage paid	MTC	Median total compensation	TCC	Total cash compensation
LR	Low end range	MW	Median wage paid	TQ	Third quartile wage
M	Monthly	MWR	Median wage range	W	Weekly
MCC	Median cash compensation	S	See annotated source	Y	Yearly

Occupation/Type/Industry	Location	Per	Low	Mid	High	Source	Date
Extruding, Forming, Pressing, and Compacting Machine Setter, Operator, and Tender	New York-Northern New Jersey-Long Island MSA, NY-NJ-PA	Y	20530 FQ	25440 MW	32130 TQ	USBLS	5/07
	North Carolina	Y	23230 FQ	28820 MW	36480 TQ	USBLS	5/07
	Asheville MSA, NC	Y	20340 FQ	22980 MW	28330 TQ	USBLS	5/07
	Charlotte-Gastonia-Concord MSA, NC-SC	Y	25880 FQ	29200 MW	34980 TQ	USBLS	5/07
	Durham MSA, NC	Y	33420 FQ	36430 MW	39480 TQ	USBLS	5/07
	Raleigh-Cary MSA, NC	Y	28840 FQ	37680 MW	45390 TQ	USBLS	5/07
	North Dakota	Y	23790 FQ	27530 MW	30200 TQ	USBLS	5/07
	Fargo MSA, ND-MN	Y	26520 FQ	28680 MW	30830 TQ	USBLS	5/07
	Ohio	Y	22920 FQ	27390 MW	33730 TQ	USBLS	5/07
	Cincinnati-Middletown MSA, OH-KY-IN	Y	24980 FQ	28490 MW	34430 TQ	USBLS	5/07
	Cleveland-Elyria-Mentor MSA, OH	Y	22410 FQ	26880 MW	32570 TQ	USBLS	5/07
	Columbus MSA, OH	Y	25340 FQ	29830 MW	37470 TQ	USBLS	5/07
	Dayton MSA, OH	Y	21630 FQ	27020 MW	39820 TQ	USBLS	5/07
	Oklahoma	Y	19620 FQ	24330 MW	40870 TQ	USBLS	5/07
	Oklahoma City MSA, OK	Y	19480 FQ	42000 MW	49260 TQ	USBLS	5/07
	Tulsa MSA, OK	Y	24690 FQ	32500 MW	42770 TQ	USBLS	5/07
	Oregon	H	11.68 FQ	14.86 MW	18.17 TQ	ORBLS	5/08
	Portland-Vancouver-Beaverton MSA, OR-WA	Y	22830 FQ	30470 MW	40530 TQ	USBLS	5/07
	Pennsylvania	Y	25430 FQ	31190 MW	37950 TQ	USBLS	5/07
	Allentown-Bethlehem-Easton MSA, PA-NJ	Y	25410 FQ	32720 MW	39650 TQ	USBLS	5/07
	Philadelphia-Camden-Wilmington MSA, PA-NJ-DE-MD	Y	25680 FQ	32000 MW	38270 TQ	USBLS	5/07
	Pittsburgh MSA, PA	Y	27010 FQ	33000 MW	37810 TQ	USBLS	5/07
	Rhode Island	Y	27320 FQ	30860 MW	35680 TQ	USBLS	5/07
	Providence-Fall River-Warwick MSA, RI-MA	Y	27230 FQ	30860 MW	35870 TQ	USBLS	5/07
	South Carolina	Y	26110 FQ	30450 MW	38450 TQ	USBLS	5/07
	Charleston-North Charleston MSA, SC	Y	28550 FQ	32660 MW	36750 TQ	USBLS	5/07
	Columbia MSA, SC	Y	35130 FQ	40240 MW	43920 TQ	USBLS	5/07
	South Dakota	Y	25673 FQ	29969 MW	33923 TQ	SDBLS	7/08-9/08
	Sioux Falls MSA, SD	Y	25390 FQ	28055 MW	30501 TQ	SDBLS	7/08-9/08
	Tennessee	Y	22890 FQ	26700 MW	31110 TQ	USBLS	5/07
	Knoxville MSA, TN	Y	27910 FQ	35250 MW	55200 TQ	USBLS	5/07
	Memphis MSA, TN-MS-AR	Y	19850 FQ	28890 MW	36860 TQ	USBLS	5/07
	Nashville-Davidson-Murfreesboro MSA, TN	Y	22810 FQ	31870 MW	38920 TQ	USBLS	5/07
	Texas	Y	18270 FQ	23070 MW	29560 TQ	USBLS	5/07
	Austin-Round Rock MSA, TX	Y	20300 FQ	22510 MW	24780 TQ	USBLS	5/07
	Beaumont-Port Arthur MSA, TX	Y	20530 FQ	30200 MW	45720 TQ	USBLS	5/07
	Brownsville-Harlingen MSA, TX	Y	13410 FQ	16720 MW	22810 TQ	USBLS	5/07
	Dallas-Fort Worth-Arlington MSA, TX	Y	19860 FQ	23970 MW	29380 TQ	USBLS	5/07
	El Paso MSA, TX	Y	17340 FQ	20630 MW	23970 TQ	USBLS	5/07
	Houston-Sugar Land-Baytown MSA, TX	Y	17720 FQ	21660 MW	28040 TQ	USBLS	5/07
	San Antonio MSA, TX	Y	17230 FQ	20300 MW	23470 TQ	USBLS	5/07
	Utah	Y	20830 FQ	25130 MW	31920 TQ	USBLS	5/07
	Ogden-Clearfield MSA, UT	Y	19780 FQ	21590 MW	23380 TQ	USBLS	5/07
	Salt Lake City MSA, UT	Y	20570 FQ	25160 MW	32660 TQ	USBLS	5/07
	Vermont	Y	22630 FQ	28370 MW	35970 TQ	USBLS	5/07
	Burlington-South Burlington MSA, VT	Y	21750 FQ	26200 MW	37280 TQ	USBLS	5/07
	Virginia	Y	25230 FQ	32710 MW	46750 TQ	USBLS	5/07
	Roanoke MSA, VA	Y	26530 FQ	30800 MW	38150 TQ	USBLS	5/07
	Virginia Beach-Norfolk-Newport News MSA, VA-NC	Y	21390 FQ	24050 MW	28950 TQ	USBLS	5/07
	Washington	H	11.83 FQ	14.83 MW	18.03 TQ	WABLS	3/08

AE	Average entry wage	AW	Average wage paid	FQ	First quartile wage
AER	Average entry range	AWR	Average wage range	H	Hourly
AEX	Average experienced wage	AXR	Average experienced range	HI	Highest wage paid
ATC	Average total compensation	D	Daily	HR	High end range

LO	Lowest wage paid	MTC	Median total compensation
LR	Low end range	MW	Median wage paid
M	Monthly	MWR	Median wage range
MCC	Median cash compensation	S	See annotated source

TCC	Total cash compensation
TQ	Third quartile wage
W	Weekly
Y	Yearly

Occupation/Type/Industry	Location	Per	Low	Mid	High	Source	Date
Extruding, Forming, Pressing, and Compacting Machine Setter, Operator, and Tender	Seattle-Tacoma-Bellevue MSA, WA	Y	25830 FQ	31100 MW	38700 TQ	USBLS	5/07
	West Virginia	Y	21359 FQ	26082 MW	34166 TQ	WVBLS	7/08-9/08
	Wisconsin	Y	21890 FQ	27650 MW	34750 TQ	USBLS	5/07
	Milwaukee-Waukesha-West Allis MSA, WI	Y	20630 FQ	23440 MW	27260 TQ	USBLS	5/07
	Wyoming	Y	29255 FQ	34124 MW	37528 TQ	WYBLS	9/08
	Puerto Rico	Y	12640 FQ	14330 MW	16330 TQ	USBLS	5/07
	San Juan-Caguas-Guaynabo MSA, PR	Y	12660 FQ	14350 MW	16310 TQ	USBLS	5/07
Extruding and Drawing Machine Setter, Operator, and Tender							
Metals and Plastics	Alabama	Y	21460 FQ	26520 MW	31300 TQ	USBLS	5/07
Metals and Plastics	Birmingham-Hoover MSA, AL	Y	20100 FQ	22370 MW	26650 TQ	USBLS	5/07
Metals and Plastics	Arizona	Y	22870 FQ	28260 MW	33150 TQ	USBLS	5/07
Metals and Plastics	Phoenix-Mesa-Scottsdale MSA, AZ	Y	25080 FQ	30320 MW	35550 TQ	USBLS	5/07
Metals and Plastics	Arkansas	Y	26370 FQ	30540 MW	34620 TQ	USBLS	5/07
Metals and Plastics	Little Rock-North Little Rock MSA, AR	Y	28520 FQ	32520 MW	35500 TQ	USBLS	5/07
Metals and Plastics	California	H	10.24 FQ	13.32 MW	17.54 TQ	CABLS	1/08-3/08
Metals and Plastics	Los Angeles-Long Beach-Glendale PMSA, CA	H	10.73 FQ	12.95 MW	15.13 TQ	CABLS	1/08-3/08
Metals and Plastics	Oakland-Fremont-Hayward MSA, CA	H	11.57 FQ	14.07 MW	17.25 TQ	CABLS	1/08-3/08
Metals and Plastics	Riverside-San Bernardino-Ontario MSA, CA	H	10.90 FQ	15.42 MW	19.50 TQ	CABLS	1/08-3/08
Metals and Plastics	Sacramento-Arden Arcade-Roseville MSA, CA	H	9.57 FQ	16.69 MW	35.30 TQ	CABLS	1/08-3/08
Metals and Plastics	San Diego-Carlsbad-San Marcos MSA, CA	H	10.54 FQ	12.99 MW	15.57 TQ	CABLS	1/08-3/08
Metals and Plastics	San Jose-Sunnyvale-Santa Clara MSA, CA	H	12.76 FQ	20.43 MW	24.08 TQ	CABLS	1/08-3/08
Metals and Plastics	Santa Ana-Anaheim-Irvine PMSA, CA	Y	20810 FQ	23710 MW	29550 TQ	USBLS	5/07
Metals and Plastics	Colorado	Y	22900 FQ	29560 MW	35180 TQ	USBLS	5/07
Metals and Plastics	Denver-Aurora MSA, CO	Y	20120 FQ	29620 MW	36410 TQ	USBLS	5/07
Metals and Plastics	Connecticut	H	12.08 AE	16.56 MW		CTBLS	1/08-3/08
Metals and Plastics	Bridgeport-Stamford-Norwalk MSA, CT	Y	31730 FQ	37290 MW	42910 TQ	USBLS	5/07
Metals and Plastics	Hartford-West Hartford-East Hartford MSA, CT	Y	26980 FQ	32860 MW	37950 TQ	USBLS	5/07
Metals and Plastics	Delaware	Y	30050 FQ	34250 MW	38780 TQ	USBLS	5/07
Metals and Plastics	Wilmington PMSA, DE-MD-NJ	Y	24370 FQ	30260 MW	35670 TQ	USBLS	5/07
Metals and Plastics	Florida	Y	21090 FQ	26410 MW	32800 TQ	USBLS	5/07
Metals and Plastics	Fort Lauderdale-Pompano Beach-Deerfield Beach PMSA, FL	Y	25880 FQ	35860 MW	42630 TQ	USBLS	5/07
Metals and Plastics	Jacksonville MSA, FL	Y	19180 FQ	21440 MW	24040 TQ	USBLS	5/07
Metals and Plastics	Miami-Fort Lauderdale-Miami Beach MSA, FL	Y	21060 FQ	28750 MW	36310 TQ	USBLS	5/07
Metals and Plastics	Orlando-Kissimmee MSA, FL	Y	21270 FQ	27150 MW	41100 TQ	USBLS	5/07
Metals and Plastics	Tampa-St. Petersburg-Clearwater MSA, FL	Y	23100 FQ	27790 MW	33380 TQ	USBLS	5/07
Metals and Plastics	Georgia	Y	24360 FQ	28820 MW	34130 TQ	USBLS	5/07
Metals and Plastics	Atlanta-Sandy Springs-Marietta MSA, GA	Y	24820 FQ	28940 MW	33740 TQ	USBLS	5/07
Metals and Plastics	Illinois	Y	18940 FQ	24850 MW	32140 TQ	USBLS	5/07
Metals and Plastics	Chicago-Naperville-Joliet MSA, IL-IN-WI	Y	18780 FQ	24630 MW	34060 TQ	USBLS	5/07
Metals and Plastics	Indiana	Y	25520 FQ	32330 MW	40520 TQ	USBLS	5/07
Metals and Plastics	Fort Wayne MSA, IN	Y	25880 FQ	32360 MW	41460 TQ	USBLS	5/07
Metals and Plastics	Gary PMSA, IN	Y	24970 FQ	35280 MW	53490 TQ	USBLS	5/07
Metals and Plastics	Indianapolis-Carmel MSA, IN	Y	23400 FQ	27840 MW	32790 TQ	USBLS	5/07
Metals and Plastics	Iowa	Y	23070 FQ	28430 MW	34470 TQ	USBLS	5/07
Metals and Plastics	Des Moines-West Des Moines MSA, IA	Y	20880 FQ	24460 MW	41870 TQ	USBLS	5/07

AE	Average entry wage	AW	Average wage paid	FQ	First quartile wage	LO	Lowest wage paid	MTC	Median total compensation	TCC	Total cash compensation
AER	Average entry range	AWR	Average wage range	H	Hourly	LR	Low end range	MW	Median wage paid	TQ	Third quartile wage
AEX	Average experienced wage	AXR	Average experienced range	HI	Highest wage paid	M	Monthly	MWR	Median wage range	W	Weekly
ATC	Average total compensation	D	Daily	HR	High end range	MCC	Median cash compensation	S	See annotated source	Y	Yearly

570

Extruding and Drawing Machine Setter, Operator, and Tender

Occupation/Type/Industry	Location	Per	Low	Mid	High	Source	Date
Metals and Plastics	Kansas	Y	21160 FQ	27230 MW	33900 TQ	USBLS	5/07
Metals and Plastics	Wichita MSA, KS	Y	27390 FQ	31980 MW	38640 TQ	USBLS	5/07
Metals and Plastics	Kentucky	Y	25358 FQ	33296 MW	38008 TQ	KYBLS	2008
Metals and Plastics	Louisville-Jefferson County MSA, KY-IN	Y	25840 FQ	30330 MW	36190 TQ	USBLS	5/07
Metals and Plastics	Louisiana	H	10.47 FQ	12.02 MW	14.23 TQ	LABLS	1/08-3/08
Metals and Plastics	New Orleans-Metairie-Kenner MSA, LA	Y	20370 FQ	23490 MW	31070 TQ	USBLS	5/07
Metals and Plastics	Maine	Y	22590 FQ	26190 MW	32730 TQ	USBLS	5/07
Metals and Plastics	Massachusetts	Y	26380 FQ	31240 MW	37180 TQ	USBLS	5/07
Metals and Plastics	Boston-Cambridge-Quincy NECTA, MA	Y	27810 FQ	33310 MW	41330 TQ	USBLS	5/07
Metals and Plastics	New Bedford MSA, MA	Y	21180 FQ	23920 MW	28830 TQ	USBLS	5/07
Metals and Plastics	Worcester MSA, MA-CT	Y	25540 FQ	29270 MW	33920 TQ	USBLS	5/07
Metals and Plastics	Michigan	Y	22410 FQ	27410 MW	33720 TQ	USBLS	5/07
Metals and Plastics	Detroit-Warren-Livonia MSA, MI	Y	22590 FQ	27740 MW	34030 TQ	USBLS	5/07
Metals and Plastics	Grand Rapids-Wyoming MSA, MI	Y	21400 FQ	25260 MW	33290 TQ	USBLS	5/07
Metals and Plastics	Warren-Troy-Farmington Hills PMSA, MI	Y	22420 FQ	27450 MW	33620 TQ	USBLS	5/07
Metals and Plastics	Minnesota	Y	27161 FQ	34044 MW	42763 TQ	MNBLS	10/08-12/08
Metals and Plastics	Minneapolis-Saint Paul MSA, MN-WI	Y	26767 FQ	35330 MW	45178 TQ	MNBLS	10/08-12/08
Metals and Plastics	Rochester MSA, MN	Y	30164 FQ	34969 MW	40039 TQ	MNBLS	10/08-12/08
Metals and Plastics	Mississippi	Y	24580 FQ	27680 MW	31320 TQ	USBLS	5/07
Metals and Plastics	Jackson MSA, MS	Y	25970 FQ	30800 MW	38520 TQ	USBLS	5/07
Metals and Plastics	Missouri	Y	26640 FQ	32300 MW	41680 TQ	USBLS	5/07
Metals and Plastics	Kansas City MSA, MO-KS	Y	19590 FQ	24490 MW	36380 TQ	USBLS	5/07
Metals and Plastics	St. Louis MSA, MO-IL	Y	18700 FQ	35700 MW	45160 TQ	USBLS	5/07
Metals and Plastics	Nebraska	Y	26230 FQ	28980 MW	33220 TQ	USBLS	5/07
Metals and Plastics	Lincoln MSA, NE	Y	27990 FQ	34430 MW	37670 TQ	USBLS	5/07
Metals and Plastics	Omaha-Council Bluffs MSA, NE-IA	Y	26000 FQ	28680 MW	34550 TQ	USBLS	5/07
Metals and Plastics	Nevada	H	12.38 FQ	14.48 MW	17.32 TQ	NVBLS	5/08
Metals and Plastics	Las Vegas-Paradise MSA, NV	H	13.89 FQ	16.82 MW	18.90 TQ	NVBLS	5/08
Metals and Plastics	New Hampshire	H	10.47 AE	12.98 MW	15.21 AEX	NHBLS	6/08
Metals and Plastics	Manchester MSA, NH	Y	22430 FQ	26290 MW	31400 TQ	USBLS	5/07
Metals and Plastics	Nashua NECTA, NH-MA	Y	31080 FQ	35890 MW	42230 TQ	USBLS	5/07
Metals and Plastics	New Jersey	Y	21920 FQ	27090 MW	33560 TQ	USBLS	5/07
Metals and Plastics	Camden PMSA, NJ	Y	31510 FQ	35480 MW	42100 TQ	USBLS	5/07
Metals and Plastics	Edison PMSA, NJ	Y	21580 FQ	26070 MW	31370 TQ	USBLS	5/07
Metals and Plastics	Newark-Union PMSA, NJ-PA	Y	20880 FQ	26760 MW	33680 TQ	USBLS	5/07
Metals and Plastics	New Mexico	Y	19820 FQ	28750 MW	40190 TQ	USBLS	5/07
Metals and Plastics	Albuquerque MSA, NM	Y	20790 FQ	29390 MW	40610 TQ	USBLS	5/07
Metals and Plastics	New York	Y	23020 FQ	30100 MW	39370 TQ	USBLS	5/07
Metals and Plastics	Buffalo-Niagara Falls MSA, NY	Y	32080 FQ	71260 MW	91680 TQ	USBLS	5/07
Metals and Plastics	Nassau-Suffolk PMSA, NY	Y	20780 FQ	25690 MW	31070 TQ	USBLS	5/07
Metals and Plastics	New York-Northern New Jersey-Long Island MSA, NY-NJ-PA	Y	21190 FQ	26410 MW	33670 TQ	USBLS	5/07
Metals and Plastics	North Carolina	Y	23790 FQ	29550 MW	34170 TQ	USBLS	5/07
Metals and Plastics	Charlotte-Gastonia-Concord MSA, NC-SC	Y	23620 FQ	29560 MW	36600 TQ	USBLS	5/07
Metals and Plastics	Raleigh-Cary MSA, NC	Y	21010 FQ	25980 MW	30920 TQ	USBLS	5/07
Metals and Plastics	Ohio	Y	23410 FQ	28400 MW	36370 TQ	USBLS	5/07
Metals and Plastics	Canton-Massillon MSA, OH	Y	22960 FQ	26900 MW	30970 TQ	USBLS	5/07
Metals and Plastics	Cincinnati-Middletown MSA, OH-KY-IN	Y	24050 FQ	28430 MW	32920 TQ	USBLS	5/07
Metals and Plastics	Cleveland-Elyria-Mentor MSA, OH	Y	26130 FQ	33790 MW	57640 TQ	USBLS	5/07
Metals and Plastics	Columbus MSA, OH	Y	21700 FQ	24160 MW	30880 TQ	USBLS	5/07
Metals and Plastics	Dayton MSA, OH	Y	23910 FQ	28350 MW	33000 TQ	USBLS	5/07
Metals and Plastics	Oklahoma	Y	22190 FQ	28670 MW	36420 TQ	USBLS	5/07
Metals and Plastics	Tulsa MSA, OK	Y	21300 FQ	26440 MW	32750 TQ	USBLS	5/07
Metals and Plastics	Oregon	H	11.33 FQ	14.80 MW	20.02 TQ	ORBLS	5/08
Metals and Plastics	Portland-Vancouver-Beaverton MSA, OR-WA	Y	22720 FQ	29950 MW	41090 TQ	USBLS	5/07
Metals and Plastics	Pennsylvania	Y	28090 FQ	33220 MW	38870 TQ	USBLS	5/07

AE	Average entry wage	AW	Average wage paid	FQ	First quartile wage
AER	Average entry range	AWR	Average wage range	H	Hourly
AEX	Average experienced wage	AXR	Average experienced range	HI	Highest wage paid
ATC	Average total compensation	D	Daily	HR	High end range

LO	Lowest wage paid	MTC	Median total compensation	TCC	Total cash compensation
LR	Low end range	MW	Median wage paid	TQ	Third quartile wage
M	Monthly	MWR	Median wage range	W	Weekly
MCC	Median cash compensation	S	See annotated source	Y	Yearly

Occupation/Type/Industry	Location	Per	Low	Mid	High	Source	Date
Extruding and Drawing Machine							
Setter, Operator, and Tender							
Metals and Plastics	Allentown-Bethlehem-Easton MSA, PA-NJ	Y	31410 FQ	34860 MW	38660 TQ	USBLS	5/07
Metals and Plastics	Philadelphia-Camden-Wilmington MSA, PA-NJ-DE-MD	Y	27480 FQ	32570 MW	37450 TQ	USBLS	5/07
Metals and Plastics	Pittsburgh MSA, PA	Y	28110 FQ	34070 MW	43640 TQ	USBLS	5/07
Metals and Plastics	Rhode Island	Y	29530 FQ	34530 MW	38480 TQ	USBLS	5/07
Metals and Plastics	Providence-Fall River-Warwick MSA, RI-MA	Y	29470 FQ	34130 MW	38010 TQ	USBLS	5/07
Metals and Plastics	South Carolina	Y	24200 FQ	28150 MW	34780 TQ	USBLS	5/07
Metals and Plastics	Charleston-North Charleston MSA, SC	Y	35280 FQ	39100 MW	51330 TQ	USBLS	5/07
Metals and Plastics	Columbia MSA, SC	Y	24850 FQ	33020 MW	37360 TQ	USBLS	5/07
Metals and Plastics	South Dakota	Y	23249 FQ	26467 MW	30853 TQ	SDBLS	7/08-9/08
Metals and Plastics	Sioux Falls MSA, SD	Y	24330 FQ	27794 MW	30921 TQ	SDBLS	7/08-9/08
Metals and Plastics	Tennessee	Y	23010 FQ	28570 MW	36810 TQ	USBLS	5/07
Metals and Plastics	Memphis MSA, TN-MS-AR	Y	24990 FQ	27650 MW	30870 TQ	USBLS	5/07
Metals and Plastics	Nashville-Davidson-Murfreesboro MSA, TN	Y	20200 FQ	24370 MW	34540 TQ	USBLS	5/07
Metals and Plastics	Texas	Y	20170 FQ	24660 MW	31720 TQ	USBLS	5/07
Metals and Plastics	Dallas-Fort Worth-Arlington MSA, TX	Y	20820 FQ	24030 MW	29640 TQ	USBLS	5/07
Metals and Plastics	El Paso MSA, TX	Y	17400 FQ	23600 MW	27100 TQ	USBLS	5/07
Metals and Plastics	Houston-Sugar Land-Baytown MSA, TX	Y	21560 FQ	28100 MW	36500 TQ	USBLS	5/07
Metals and Plastics	San Antonio MSA, TX	Y	18360 FQ	21170 MW	23520 TQ	USBLS	5/07
Metals and Plastics	Utah	Y	23200 FQ	28640 MW	33330 TQ	USBLS	5/07
Metals and Plastics	Logan MSA, UT-ID	Y	19460 FQ	22260 MW	24820 TQ	USBLS	5/07
Metals and Plastics	Salt Lake City MSA, UT	Y	24370 FQ	28950 MW	33840 TQ	USBLS	5/07
Metals and Plastics	Vermont	Y	26690 FQ	31130 MW	37080 TQ	USBLS	5/07
Metals and Plastics	Burlington-South Burlington MSA, VT	Y	26340 FQ	29180 MW	33870 TQ	USBLS	5/07
Metals and Plastics	Virginia	Y	23510 FQ	27770 MW	32900 TQ	USBLS	5/07
Metals and Plastics	Richmond MSA, VA	Y	24730 FQ	31080 MW	37250 TQ	USBLS	5/07
Metals and Plastics	Virginia Beach-Norfolk-Newport News MSA, VA-NC	Y	26090 FQ	31400 MW	36300 TQ	USBLS	5/07
Metals and Plastics	Washington	H	10.90 FQ	13.56 MW	17.40 TQ	WABLS	3/08
Metals and Plastics	Seattle-Tacoma-Bellevue MSA, WA	Y	24330 FQ	32470 MW	36560 TQ	USBLS	5/07
Metals and Plastics	West Virginia	Y	24601 FQ	29059 MW	33911 TQ	WVBLS	7/08-9/08
Metals and Plastics	Parkersburg-Marietta-Vienna MSA, WV-OH	Y	18940 FQ	22300 MW	27680 TQ	USBLS	5/07
Metals and Plastics	Wisconsin	Y	23800 FQ	29220 MW	35510 TQ	USBLS	5/07
Metals and Plastics	Milwaukee-Waukesha-West Allis MSA, WI	Y	24850 FQ	30880 MW	37360 TQ	USBLS	5/07
Metals and Plastics	Puerto Rico	Y	18540 FQ	27160 MW	34830 TQ	USBLS	5/07
Metals and Plastics	San Juan-Caguas-Guaynabo MSA, PR	Y	21340 FQ	29090 MW	36900 TQ	USBLS	5/07
Extruding and Forming Machine							
Setter, Operator, and Tender							
Synthetic and Glass Fibers	Alabama	Y	27280 FQ	29640 MW	32010 TQ	USBLS	5/07
Synthetic and Glass Fibers	Arkansas	Y	27870 FQ	34060 MW	37140 TQ	USBLS	5/07
Synthetic and Glass Fibers	California	H	8.99 FQ	11.12 MW	13.39 TQ	CABLS	1/08-3/08
Synthetic and Glass Fibers	Los Angeles-Long Beach-Glendale PMSA, CA	H	10.28 FQ	11.39 MW	12.87 TQ	CABLS	1/08-3/08
Synthetic and Glass Fibers	Oakland-Fremont-Hayward MSA, CA	H	10.24 FQ	11.17 MW	12.21 TQ	CABLS	1/08-3/08
Synthetic and Glass Fibers	Riverside-San Bernardino-Ontario MSA, CA	H	8.91 FQ	11.68 MW	13.93 TQ	CABLS	1/08-3/08
Synthetic and Glass Fibers	Santa Ana-Anaheim-Irvine PMSA, CA	Y	17950 FQ	26260 MW	35500 TQ	USBLS	5/07
Synthetic and Glass Fibers	Connecticut	H	10.23 AE	12.32 MW		CTBLS	1/08-3/08
Synthetic and Glass Fibers	Florida	Y	24070 FQ	30540 MW	40670 TQ	USBLS	5/07
Synthetic and Glass Fibers	Georgia	Y	25080 FQ	27850 MW	30710 TQ	USBLS	5/07
Synthetic and Glass Fibers	Atlanta-Sandy Springs-Marietta MSA, GA	Y	25530 FQ	28960 MW	32110 TQ	USBLS	5/07
Synthetic and Glass Fibers	Illinois	Y	26910 FQ	32120 MW	37200 TQ	USBLS	5/07

AE Average entry wage	**AW** Average wage paid	**FQ** First quartile wage	**LO** Lowest wage paid	**MTC** Median total compensation	**TCC** Total cash compensation
AER Average entry range	**AWR** Average wage range	**H** Hourly	**LR** Low end range	**MW** Median wage paid	**TQ** Third quartile wage
AEX Average experienced wage	**AXR** Average experienced range	**HI** Highest wage paid	**M** Monthly	**MWR** Median wage range	**W** Weekly
ATC Average total compensation	**D** Daily	**HR** High end range	**MCC** Median cash compensation	**S** See annotated source	**Y** Yearly

Occupation/Type/Industry	Location	Per	Low	Mid	High	Source	Date
Extruding and Forming Machine Setter, Operator, and Tender							
Synthetic and Glass Fibers	Chicago-Naperville-Joliet MSA, IL-IN-WI	Y	25940 FQ	30870 MW	35800 TQ	USBLS	5/07
Synthetic and Glass Fibers	Indiana	Y	25750 FQ	28500 MW	31550 TQ	USBLS	5/07
Synthetic and Glass Fibers	Kansas	Y	22650 FQ	27700 MW	31720 TQ	USBLS	5/07
Synthetic and Glass Fibers	Kentucky	Y	23128 FQ	27681 MW	35523 TQ	KYBLS	2008
Synthetic and Glass Fibers	Louisville-Jefferson County MSA, KY-IN	Y	18780 FQ	23040 MW	28330 TQ	USBLS	5/07
Synthetic and Glass Fibers	Louisiana	H	10.30 FQ	13.33 MW	17.23 TQ	LABLS	1/08-3/08
Synthetic and Glass Fibers	Maryland	Y		39475 MW		MDBLS	3/08
Synthetic and Glass Fibers	Baltimore-Towson MSA, MD	Y	20530 FQ	23310 MW	28240 TQ	USBLS	5/07
Synthetic and Glass Fibers	Massachusetts	Y	25820 FQ	34020 MW	45010 TQ	USBLS	5/07
Synthetic and Glass Fibers	Boston-Cambridge-Quincy NECTA, MA	Y	24720 FQ	39520 MW	51720 TQ	USBLS	5/07
Synthetic and Glass Fibers	Michigan	Y	22540 FQ	30060 MW	36740 TQ	USBLS	5/07
Synthetic and Glass Fibers	Detroit-Warren-Livonia MSA, MI	Y	22280 FQ	24810 MW	36530 TQ	USBLS	5/07
Synthetic and Glass Fibers	Minnesota	Y	23511 FQ	27907 MW	35070 TQ	MNBLS	10/08-12/08
Synthetic and Glass Fibers	Minneapolis-Saint Paul MSA, MN-WI	Y	24279 FQ	28384 MW	35672 TQ	MNBLS	10/08-12/08
Synthetic and Glass Fibers	Mississippi	Y	31040 FQ	39720 MW	43680 TQ	USBLS	5/07
Synthetic and Glass Fibers	Missouri	Y	31800 FQ	38980 MW	44770 TQ	USBLS	5/07
Synthetic and Glass Fibers	Kansas City MSA, MO-KS	Y	28530 FQ	36370 MW	40290 TQ	USBLS	5/07
Synthetic and Glass Fibers	St. Louis MSA, MO-IL	Y	25520 FQ	36910 MW	54320 TQ	USBLS	5/07
Synthetic and Glass Fibers	Nevada	H	10.57 FQ	11.94 MW	14.26 TQ	NVBLS	5/08
Synthetic and Glass Fibers	New Jersey	Y	24180 FQ	26950 MW	30930 TQ	USBLS	5/07
Synthetic and Glass Fibers	New York	Y	27780 FQ	37990 MW	44790 TQ	USBLS	5/07
Synthetic and Glass Fibers	Albany-Schenectady-Troy MSA, NY	Y	41580 FQ	44900 MW	48230 TQ	USBLS	5/07
Synthetic and Glass Fibers	New York-Northern New Jersey-Long Island MSA, NY-NJ-PA	Y	23580 FQ	26710 MW	30510 TQ	USBLS	5/07
Synthetic and Glass Fibers	North Carolina	Y	23660 FQ	29160 MW	37900 TQ	USBLS	5/07
Synthetic and Glass Fibers	Charlotte-Gastonia-Concord MSA, NC-SC	Y	27050 FQ	30340 MW	34740 TQ	USBLS	5/07
Synthetic and Glass Fibers	Greensboro-High Point MSA, NC	Y	21750 FQ	27060 MW	30030 TQ	USBLS	5/07
Synthetic and Glass Fibers	Ohio	Y	24890 FQ	29820 MW	37790 TQ	USBLS	5/07
Synthetic and Glass Fibers	Cincinnati-Middletown MSA, OH-KY-IN	Y	25190 FQ	27310 MW	29510 TQ	USBLS	5/07
Synthetic and Glass Fibers	Cleveland-Elyria-Mentor MSA, OH	Y	21610 FQ	29290 MW	36280 TQ	USBLS	5/07
Synthetic and Glass Fibers	Columbus MSA, OH	Y	23620 FQ	30740 MW	39580 TQ	USBLS	5/07
Synthetic and Glass Fibers	Oklahoma	Y	22050 FQ	28080 MW	32570 TQ	USBLS	5/07
Synthetic and Glass Fibers	Pennsylvania	Y	25630 FQ	30340 MW	35450 TQ	USBLS	5/07
Synthetic and Glass Fibers	Philadelphia-Camden-Wilmington MSA, PA-NJ-DE-MD	Y	29120 FQ	36300 MW	42320 TQ	USBLS	5/07
Synthetic and Glass Fibers	South Carolina	Y	26860 FQ	31960 MW	36200 TQ	USBLS	5/07
Synthetic and Glass Fibers	Columbia MSA, SC	Y	31050 FQ	33800 MW	36740 TQ	USBLS	5/07
Synthetic and Glass Fibers	Tennessee	Y	22970 FQ	38320 MW	45380 TQ	USBLS	5/07
Synthetic and Glass Fibers	Nashville-Davidson-Murfreesboro MSA, TN	Y	42810 FQ	45890 MW	49000 TQ	USBLS	5/07
Synthetic and Glass Fibers	Texas	Y	19050 FQ	23640 MW	34440 TQ	USBLS	5/07
Synthetic and Glass Fibers	Dallas-Fort Worth-Arlington MSA, TX	Y	20150 FQ	21820 MW	23570 TQ	USBLS	5/07
Synthetic and Glass Fibers	San Antonio MSA, TX	Y	13620 FQ	16320 MW	20930 TQ	USBLS	5/07
Synthetic and Glass Fibers	Utah	Y	21700 FQ	25000 MW	30140 TQ	USBLS	5/07
Synthetic and Glass Fibers	Virginia	Y	23470 FQ	28170 MW	34330 TQ	USBLS	5/07
Synthetic and Glass Fibers	Washington	H	11.90 FQ	14.31 MW	16.90 TQ	WABLS	3/08
Synthetic and Glass Fibers	Seattle-Tacoma-Bellevue MSA, WA	Y	24610 FQ	29520 MW	34770 TQ	USBLS	5/07
Synthetic and Glass Fibers	Wisconsin	Y	27380 FQ	33390 MW	40520 TQ	USBLS	5/07
Fabric and Apparel Patternmaker	Alabama	Y	20690 FQ	22630 MW	26480 TQ	USBLS	5/07
	Arizona	Y	18050 FQ	19880 MW	25160 TQ	USBLS	5/07
	California	H	15.61 FQ	24.03 MW	30.85 TQ	CABLS	1/08-3/08
	Colorado	Y	17370 FQ	28190 MW	37810 TQ	USBLS	5/07
	Florida	Y	28190 FQ	35140 MW	49560 TQ	USBLS	5/07
	Georgia	Y	24250 FQ	27920 MW	31190 TQ	USBLS	5/07
	Idaho	Y	17280 FQ	18590 MW	19820 TQ	USBLS	5/07

AE	Average entry wage	AW	Average wage paid	FQ	First quartile wage	LO	Lowest wage paid	MTC	Median total compensation	TCC	Total cash compensation
AER	Average entry range	AWR	Average wage range	H	Hourly	LR	Low end range	MW	Median wage paid	TQ	Third quartile wage
AEX	Average experienced wage	AXR	Average experienced range	HI	Highest wage paid	M	Monthly	MWR	Median wage range	W	Weekly
ATC	Average total compensation	D	Daily	HR	High end range	MCC	Median cash compensation	S	See annotated source	Y	Yearly

Occupation/Type/Industry	Location	Per	Low	Mid	High	Source	Date
Fabric and Apparel Patternmaker	Illinois	Y	20180 FQ	23300 MW	33950 TQ	USBLS	5/07
	Indiana	Y	26190 FQ	30550 MW	37170 TQ	USBLS	5/07
	Iowa	Y	15990 FQ	30120 MW	37560 TQ	USBLS	5/07
	Kansas	Y	16970 FQ	18660 MW	29360 TQ	USBLS	5/07
	Louisiana	H	8.27 FQ	9.12 MW	11.62 TQ	LABLS	1/08-3/08
	Maryland	Y		24375 MW		MDBLS	3/08
	Massachusetts	Y	27040 FQ	35940 MW	51920 TQ	USBLS	5/07
	Michigan	Y	25440 FQ	28990 MW	33540 TQ	USBLS	5/07
	Minnesota	Y	23553 FQ	27129 MW	32924 TQ	MNBLS	10/08-12/08
	Mississippi	Y	22900 FQ	29990 MW	34170 TQ	USBLS	5/07
	Missouri	Y	20590 FQ	25190 MW	35120 TQ	USBLS	5/07
	New Jersey	Y	25540 FQ	38020 MW	50160 TQ	USBLS	5/07
	New York	Y	40730 FQ	58490 MW	74160 TQ	USBLS	5/07
	North Carolina	Y	24700 FQ	29810 MW	37860 TQ	USBLS	5/07
	Ohio	Y	28050 FQ	37790 MW	43370 TQ	USBLS	5/07
	Oklahoma	Y	20140 FQ	23810 MW	28840 TQ	USBLS	5/07
	Oregon	H	14.99 FQ	18.27 MW	24.71 TQ	ORBLS	5/08
	Pennsylvania	Y	24570 FQ	35350 MW	46160 TQ	USBLS	5/07
	South Carolina	Y	22050 FQ	26520 MW	30120 TQ	USBLS	5/07
	Tennessee	Y	18910 FQ	22630 MW	27630 TQ	USBLS	5/07
	Texas	Y	15060 FQ	19590 MW	26100 TQ	USBLS	5/07
	Virginia	Y	19060 FQ	24100 MW	29840 TQ	USBLS	5/07
	Washington	H	13.26 FQ	15.10 MW	19.61 TQ	WABLS	3/08
	Wisconsin	Y	28660 FQ	34580 MW	38820 TQ	USBLS	5/07
Fabric Mender							
Except Garment	California	H	12.59 FQ	14.98 MW	20.12 TQ	CABLS	1/08-3/08
Except Garment	Colorado	Y	27200 FQ	30870 MW	35960 TQ	USBLS	5/07
Except Garment	Georgia	Y	25500 FQ	28260 MW	30910 TQ	USBLS	5/07
Except Garment	Illinois	Y	26660 FQ	28450 MW	30250 TQ	USBLS	5/07
Except Garment	Massachusetts	Y	25640 FQ	28480 MW	31360 TQ	USBLS	5/07
Except Garment	North Carolina	Y	16520 FQ	18080 MW	19590 TQ	USBLS	5/07
Except Garment	South Carolina	Y	21740 FQ	23680 MW	27630 TQ	USBLS	5/07
Fabric Worker							
State Government	Ohio	H	14.36 LO		15.41 HI	ODAS	2008
Fabrics and Trim Buyer	United States	Y		97000 MW		247FASH	2009
Facilities Coordinator/Supervisor							
Higher Education	United States	Y		59400 MW		BOM	5/08-7/08
Medical	United States	Y		61500 MW		BOM	5/08-7/08
Faculty Member							
University of Califonia System	California	Y		97369 AW		UCSC1	2008
Faller	Alabama	Y	23140 FQ	29300 MW	34360 TQ	USBLS	5/07
	Arizona	Y	29230 FQ	34740 MW	38260 TQ	USBLS	5/07
	Arkansas	Y	21490 FQ	27290 MW	35690 TQ	USBLS	5/07
	Colorado	Y	16040 FQ	31930 MW	36100 TQ	USBLS	5/07
	Connecticut	H	11.54 AE	15.64 MW		CTBLS	1/08-3/08
	Florida	Y	24200 FQ	32270 MW	36990 TQ	USBLS	5/07
	Georgia	Y	26820 FQ	34380 MW	39450 TQ	USBLS	5/07
	Idaho	Y	32430 FQ	35820 MW	39460 TQ	USBLS	5/07
	Indiana	Y	27850 FQ	31590 MW	35360 TQ	USBLS	5/07
	Kentucky	Y	20656 FQ	24811 MW	28038 TQ	KYBLS	2008
	Louisiana	H	12.54 FQ	14.43 MW	17.36 TQ	LABLS	1/08-3/08
	Maryland	Y		28700 MW		MDBLS	3/08
	Michigan	Y	19480 FQ	23180 MW	27230 TQ	USBLS	5/07
	Minnesota	Y	24333 FQ	33460 MW	39762 TQ	MNBLS	10/08-12/08
	Mississippi	Y	24150 FQ	29460 MW	34690 TQ	USBLS	5/07
	Missouri	Y	25510 FQ	27830 MW	29980 TQ	USBLS	5/07
	New Jersey	Y	26560 FQ	34520 MW	51960 TQ	USBLS	5/07
	New York	Y	26460 FQ	34510 MW	53870 TQ	USBLS	5/07
	North Carolina	Y	26010 FQ	29100 MW	32790 TQ	USBLS	5/07
	Ohio	Y	18100 FQ	23000 MW	29390 TQ	USBLS	5/07
	Oklahoma	Y	30340 FQ	35050 MW	52780 TQ	USBLS	5/07
	Oregon	H	23.88 FQ	30.75 MW	34.50 TQ	ORBLS	5/08
	Pennsylvania	Y	20700 FQ	25350 MW	29230 TQ	USBLS	5/07
	South Carolina	Y	20740 FQ	23480 MW	27480 TQ	USBLS	5/07
	Tennessee	Y	19540 FQ	24580 MW	30780 TQ	USBLS	5/07
	Texas	Y	30570 FQ	34670 MW	37630 TQ	USBLS	5/07
	Virginia	Y	23570 FQ	29610 MW	36560 TQ	USBLS	5/07

AE	Average entry wage	AW	Average wage paid	FQ	First quartile wage	LO	Lowest wage paid	MTC	Median total compensation	TCC	Total cash compensation
AER	Average entry range	AWR	Average wage range	H	Hourly	LR	Low end range	MW	Median wage paid	TQ	Third quartile wage
AEX	Average experienced wage	AXR	Average experienced range	HI	Highest wage paid	M	Monthly	MWR	Median wage range	W	Weekly
ATC	Average total compensation	D	Daily	HR	High end range	MCC	Median cash compensation	S	See annotated source	Y	Yearly

Occupation/Type/Industry	Location	Per	Low	Mid	High	Source	Date
Faller	Washington	H	16.88 FQ	19.61 MW	28.31 TQ	WABLS	3/08
	West Virginia	Y	22009 FQ	23991 MW	25957 TQ	WVBLS	7/08-9/08
	Wisconsin	Y	20910 FQ	24950 MW	31500 TQ	USBLS	5/07
Family and General Practitioner	Alabama	Y	99030 FQ			USBLS	5/07
	Birmingham-Hoover MSA, AL	Y	104830 FQ	143570 MW		USBLS	5/07
	Alaska	Y	78910 FQ	137870 MW		USBLS	5/07
	Anchorage MSA, AK	Y	50520 FQ	124080 MW		USBLS	5/07
	Fairbanks MSA, AK	Y	88380 FQ	138340 MW		USBLS	5/07
	Arizona	Y	108840 FQ	132320 MW		USBLS	5/07
	Flagstaff MSA, AZ	Y	113430 FQ	126170 MW		USBLS	5/07
	Phoenix-Mesa-Scottsdale MSA, AZ	Y	104100 FQ	131270 MW		USBLS	5/07
	Tucson MSA, AZ	Y	114260 FQ	130970 MW		USBLS	5/07
	Arkansas	Y	139020 FQ			USBLS	5/07
	Fort Smith MSA, AR-OK	Y	67430 FQ			USBLS	5/07
	Little Rock-North Little Rock MSA, AR	Y	126700 FQ			USBLS	5/07
	California	H	44.35 FQ	69.28 MW		CABLS	1/08-3/08
	Los Angeles-Long Beach-Glendale PMSA, CA	H	27.90 FQ	57.56 MW		CABLS	1/08-3/08
	Oakland-Fremont-Hayward MSA, CA	H	58.94 FQ			CABLS	1/08-3/08
	Riverside-San Bernardino-Ontario MSA, CA	H	38.15 FQ	67.53 MW		CABLS	1/08-3/08
	Sacramento-Arden Arcade-Roseville MSA, CA	H	45.57 FQ	67.51 MW		CABLS	1/08-3/08
	San Diego-Carlsbad-San Marcos MSA, CA	H	60.00 FQ			CABLS	1/08-3/08
	Santa Ana-Anaheim-Irvine PMSA, CA	Y	95230 FQ	128120 MW		USBLS	5/07
	Colorado	Y	103980 FQ	131310 MW		USBLS	5/07
	Colorado Springs MSA, CO	Y	101180 FQ	138070 MW		USBLS	5/07
	Denver-Aurora MSA, CO	Y	108750 FQ	132520 MW		USBLS	5/07
	Fort Collins-Loveland MSA, CO	Y	74740 FQ	100570 MW	126710 TQ	USBLS	5/07
	Connecticut	H	46.19 AE	76.57 AW		CTBLS	1/08-3/08
	Bridgeport-Stamford-Norwalk MSA, CT	Y	129980 FQ			USBLS	5/07
	Hartford-West Hartford-East Hartford MSA, CT	Y	94780 FQ			USBLS	5/07
	Delaware	Y	129380 FQ			USBLS	5/07
	Wilmington PMSA, DE-MD-NJ	Y	128930 FQ	144820 MW		USBLS	5/07
	District of Columbia	Y	39960 FQ	45060 MW	136190 TQ	USBLS	5/07
	Washington-Arlington-Alexandria MSA, DC-VA-MD-WV	Y	45560 FQ	131080 MW		USBLS	5/07
	Florida	Y	110450 FQ			USBLS	5/07
	Jacksonville MSA, FL	Y	111780 FQ			USBLS	5/07
	Miami-Fort Lauderdale-Miami Beach MSA, FL	Y	118860 FQ			USBLS	5/07
	Orlando-Kissimmee MSA, FL	Y	80080 FQ	97030 MW		USBLS	5/07
	Sarasota-Bradenton-Venice MSA, FL	Y	101580 FQ			USBLS	5/07
	Tampa-St. Petersburg-Clearwater MSA, FL	Y	84500 FQ	129600 MW		USBLS	5/07
	West Palm Beach-Boca Raton-Boynton Beach PMSA, FL	Y	135060 FQ			USBLS	5/07
	Georgia	Y	137370 FQ			USBLS	5/07
	Atlanta-Sandy Springs-Marietta MSA, GA	Y	142390 FQ			USBLS	5/07
	Savannah MSA, GA	Y	126960 FQ			USBLS	5/07
	Hawaii	Y	93190 FQ	139570 MW		USBLS	5/07
	Honolulu MSA, HI	Y	96630 FQ			USBLS	5/07
	Idaho	Y	117220 FQ			USBLS	5/07
	Boise City-Nampa MSA, ID	Y	113180 FQ	139330 MW		USBLS	5/07
	Illinois	Y	88750 FQ			USBLS	5/07
	Chicago-Naperville-Joliet MSA, IL-IN-WI	Y	63930 FQ	141730 MW		USBLS	5/07
	Indiana	Y	110110 FQ			USBLS	5/07
	Gary PMSA, IN	Y	113010 FQ			USBLS	5/07

AE	Average entry wage	AW	Average wage paid	FQ	First quartile wage
AER	Average entry range	AWR	Average wage range	H	Hourly
AEX	Average experienced wage	AXR	Average experienced range	HI	Highest wage paid
ATC	Average total compensation	D	Daily	HR	High end range

LO	Lowest wage paid	MTC	Median total compensation
LR	Low end range	MW	Median wage paid
M	Monthly	MWR	Median wage range
MCC	Median cash compensation	S	See annotated source

TCC	Total cash compensation
TQ	Third quartile wage
W	Weekly
Y	Yearly

Occupation/Type/Industry	Location	Per	Low	Mid	High	Source	Date
Family and General Practitioner	Indianapolis-Carmel MSA, IN	Y	76650 FQ	129490 MW		USBLS	5/07
	Iowa	Y	131380 FQ			USBLS	5/07
	Des Moines-West Des Moines MSA, IA	Y	112090 FQ	133450 MW		USBLS	5/07
	Kansas	Y	145400 FQ			USBLS	5/07
	Kentucky	Y	123904 FQ			KYBLS	2008
	Louisville-Jefferson County MSA, KY-IN	Y	135930 FQ			USBLS	5/07
	Louisiana	Y		164451 AW		LABLS	1/08-3/08
	Baton Rouge MSA, LA	Y	110800 FQ			USBLS	5/07
	New Orleans-Metairie-Kenner MSA, LA	Y	129430 FQ			USBLS	5/07
	Maine	Y	113470 FQ	138550 MW		USBLS	5/07
	Portland-South Portland-Biddeford MSA, ME	Y	121630 FQ			USBLS	5/07
	Maryland	Y		161700 AW		MDBLS	3/08
	Baltimore-Towson MSA, MD	Y	103480 FQ			USBLS	5/07
	Bethesda-Gaithersburg-Frederick PMSA, MD	Y	130450 FQ			USBLS	5/07
	Massachusetts	Y	134580 FQ			USBLS	5/07
	Boston-Cambridge-Quincy NECTA, MA	Y	145080 FQ			USBLS	5/07
	Michigan	Y	112540 FQ			USBLS	5/07
	Detroit-Warren-Livonia MSA, MI	Y	109230 FQ			USBLS	5/07
	Grand Rapids-Wyoming MSA, MI	Y	115840 FQ	129480 MW		USBLS	5/07
	Warren-Troy-Farmington Hills PMSA, MI	Y	110790 FQ			USBLS	5/07
	Minnesota	Y	132368 FQ	169028 AW		MNBLS	10/08-12/08
	Duluth-Superior MSA, MN-WI	Y	143312 FQ	162070 AW		MNBLS	10/08-12/08
	Minneapolis-Saint Paul MSA, MN-WI	Y	129889 FQ	168159 AW		MNBLS	10/08-12/08
	Rochester MSA, MN	Y	135220 FQ	147728 MW		MNBLS	10/08-12/08
	Mississippi	Y	130500 FQ			USBLS	5/07
	Jackson MSA, MS	Y	145330 FQ			USBLS	5/07
	Missouri	Y	84880 FQ			USBLS	5/07
	St. Louis MSA, MO-IL	Y	48740 FQ	118180 MW		USBLS	5/07
	Montana	Y	113130 FQ	138140 MW		USBLS	5/07
	Nebraska	Y	123030 FQ			USBLS	5/07
	Omaha-Council Bluffs MSA, NE-IA	Y	128150 FQ			USBLS	5/07
	Nevada	H	54.30 FQ	77.08 AW		NVBLS	5/08
	Las Vegas-Paradise MSA, NV	H	48.16 FQ	63.96 MW		NVBLS	5/08
	New Hampshire	H	48.68 AE	70.39 MW	83.84 AEX	NHBLS	6/08
	Manchester MSA, NH	Y	118200 FQ	140640 MW		USBLS	5/07
	Nashua NECTA, NH-MA	Y	126140 FQ			USBLS	5/07
	New Jersey	Y	123340 FQ			USBLS	5/07
	Camden PMSA, NJ	Y	105070 FQ	132120 MW		USBLS	5/07
	Edison PMSA, NJ	Y	116340 FQ	139650 MW		USBLS	5/07
	Newark-Union PMSA, NJ-PA	Y	140760 FQ			USBLS	5/07
	Trenton-Ewing MSA, NJ	Y	123780 FQ			USBLS	5/07
	New Mexico	Y	126790 FQ			USBLS	5/07
	Albuquerque MSA, NM	Y	137560 FQ			USBLS	5/07
	New York	Y	118250 FQ			USBLS	5/07
	Albany-Schenectady-Troy MSA, NY	Y	107200 FQ	128970 MW		USBLS	5/07
	Buffalo-Niagara Falls MSA, NY	Y	109550 FQ			USBLS	5/07
	Nassau-Suffolk PMSA, NY	Y	144980 FQ			USBLS	5/07
	New York-Northern New Jersey-Long Island MSA, NY-NJ-PA	Y	125290 FQ			USBLS	5/07
	North Carolina	Y	132140 FQ			USBLS	5/07
	Charlotte-Gastonia-Concord MSA, NC-SC	Y	140190 FQ			USBLS	5/07
	Raleigh-Cary MSA, NC	Y	124410 FQ			USBLS	5/07
	North Dakota	Y	123400 FQ	143120 MW		USBLS	5/07
	Fargo MSA, ND-MN	Y	135440 FQ			USBLS	5/07
	Ohio	Y	120580 FQ			USBLS	5/07
	Cincinnati-Middletown MSA, OH-KY-IN	Y	114080 FQ	143050 MW		USBLS	5/07

AE	Average entry wage	AW	Average wage paid	FQ	First quartile wage
AER	Average entry range	AWR	Average wage range	H	Hourly
AEX	Average experienced wage	AXR	Average experienced range	HI	Highest wage paid
ATC	Average total compensation	D	Daily	HR	High end range

LO Lowest wage paid MTC Median total compensation TCC Total cash compensation
LR Low end range MW Median wage paid TQ Third quartile wage
M Monthly MWR Median wage range W Weekly
MCC Median cash compensation S See annotated source Y Yearly

Occupation/Type/Industry	Location	Per	Low	Mid	High	Source	Date
Family and General Practitioner	Cleveland-Elyria-Mentor						
	MSA, OH	Y	114050 FQ			USBLS	5/07
	Dayton MSA, OH	Y	96920 FQ	137940 MW		USBLS	5/07
	Oklahoma	Y	125310 FQ			USBLS	5/07
	Oklahoma City MSA, OK	Y	116510 FQ			USBLS	5/07
	Medford MSA, OR	Y	61590 FQ	119950 MW	133250 TQ	USBLS	5/07
	Portland-Vancouver-Beaverton						
	MSA, OR-WA	Y	118600 FQ			USBLS	5/07
	Pennsylvania	Y	109670 FQ			USBLS	5/07
	Allentown-Bethlehem-Easton						
	MSA, PA-NJ	Y	121260 FQ			USBLS	5/07
	Erie MSA, PA	Y	137090 FQ			USBLS	5/07
	Lancaster MSA, PA	Y	96810 FQ	115110 MW	141790 TQ	USBLS	5/07
	Philadelphia-Camden-						
	Wilmington MSA, PA-NJ-DE-						
	MD	Y	107510 FQ	140210 MW		USBLS	5/07
	Pittsburgh MSA, PA	Y	137930 FQ			USBLS	5/07
	Rhode Island	Y	137700 FQ			USBLS	5/07
	Providence-Fall River-						
	Warwick MSA, RI-MA	Y	132850 FQ			USBLS	5/07
	South Carolina	Y	112550 FQ			USBLS	5/07
	Charleston-North Charleston						
	MSA, SC	Y	76580 FQ	134520 MW		USBLS	5/07
	Columbia MSA, SC	Y	118660 FQ			USBLS	5/07
	South Dakota	Y	110548 FQ			SDBLS	7/08-9/08
	Sioux Falls MSA, SD	Y	50509 FQ	134843 MW		SDBLS	7/08-9/08
	Tennessee	Y	105980 FQ	138710 MW		USBLS	5/07
	Knoxville MSA, TN	Y	113890 FQ	125570 MW	143620 TQ	USBLS	5/07
	Memphis MSA, TN-MS-AR	Y	133800 FQ			USBLS	5/07
	Nashville-Davidson-						
	Murfreesboro MSA, TN	Y	82860 FQ	111270 MW		USBLS	5/07
	Texas	Y	81930 FQ	136560 MW		USBLS	5/07
	Austin-Round Rock MSA, TX	Y	90120 FQ	117880 MW		USBLS	5/07
	Dallas-Fort Worth-Arlington						
	MSA, TX	Y	123200 FQ			USBLS	5/07
	Houston-Sugar Land-Baytown						
	MSA, TX	Y	81390 FQ	120560 MW		USBLS	5/07
	San Antonio MSA, TX	Y	76840 FQ	115990 MW		USBLS	5/07
	Utah	Y	118770 FQ			USBLS	5/07
	Provo-Orem MSA, UT	Y	78290 FQ			USBLS	5/07
	Salt Lake City MSA, UT	Y	126400 FQ			USBLS	5/07
	Vermont	Y	107310 FQ	128610 MW		USBLS	5/07
	Burlington-South Burlington						
	MSA, VT	Y	49720 FQ	102740 MW	132360 TQ	USBLS	5/07
	Virginia	Y	123990 FQ			USBLS	5/07
	Richmond MSA, VA	Y	123020 FQ			USBLS	5/07
	Virginia Beach-Norfolk-						
	Newport News MSA, VA-NC	Y	116080 FQ	139820 MW		USBLS	5/07
	Washington	H	58.01 FQ	70.96 MW		WABLS	3/08
	Seattle-Tacoma-Bellevue						
	MSA, WA	Y	120320 FQ			USBLS	5/07
	West Virginia	Y	135207 FQ	178967 AW		WVBLS	7/08-9/08
	Charleston MSA, WV	Y	115150 FQ			USBLS	5/07
	Wyoming	Y	134656 FQ	181362 AW		WYBLS	9/08
	Puerto Rico	Y	52790 FQ	70350 MW	95290 TQ	USBLS	5/07
	San Juan-Caguas-Guaynabo						
	MSA, PR	Y	53310 FQ	72830 MW	99130 TQ	USBLS	5/07
	Guam	Y	109360 FQ	137960 MW		USBLS	5/07
Family Crisis Therapist							
State Government	Delaware	Y	42801 LO		64201 HI	AFT02	3/1/08
Family Independence Specialist							
State Government	Maine	Y	27206 LO		36421 HI	AFT02	3/1/08
Family Services Division Deputy							
Director							
State Supreme Court	Michigan	Y			92060 HI	LSJ02	7/11/07
Farm, Ranch, and Other							
Agricultural Manager	Arizona	Y	45400 FQ	58530 MW	92590 TQ	USBLS	5/07
	Arkansas	Y	41900 FQ	55920 MW	65710 TQ	USBLS	5/07

AE	Average entry wage	**AW**	Average wage paid	**FQ**	First quartile wage	**LO** Lowest wage paid	**MTC** Median total compensation **TCC** Total cash compensation
AER	Average entry range	**AWR**	Average wage range	**H**	Hourly	**LR** Low end range	**MW** Median wage paid **TQ** Third quartile wage
AEX	Average experienced wage	**AXR**	Average experienced range	**HI**	Highest wage paid	**M** Monthly	**MWR** Median wage range **W** Weekly
ATC	Average total compensation	**D**	Daily	**HR**	High end range	**MCC** Median cash compensation **S** See annotated source	**Y** Yearly

Occupation/Type/Industry	Location	Per	Low	Mid	High	Source	Date
Farm, Ranch, and Other Agricultural Manager	California	H	23.51 FQ	30.52 MW	41.43 TQ	CABLS	1/08-3/08
	Colorado	Y	41860 FQ	71490 MW	83120 TQ	USBLS	5/07
	Florida	Y	62990 FQ	94600 MW	118780 TQ	USBLS	5/07
	Idaho	Y	37050 FQ	53530 MW	64630 TQ	USBLS	5/07
	Illinois	Y	17580 FQ	49530 MW	57120 TQ	USBLS	5/07
	Indiana	Y	40330 FQ	51030 MW	61460 TQ	USBLS	5/07
	Iowa	Y	34340 FQ	40310 MW	66260 TQ	USBLS	5/07
	Kansas	Y	43540 FQ	52420 MW	62890 TQ	USBLS	5/07
	Kentucky	Y	35941 FQ	40355 MW	56854 TQ	KYBLS	2008
	Louisiana	H	18.93 FQ	26.41 MW	30.20 TQ	LABLS	1/08-3/08
	Maryland	Y		123775 MW		MDBLS	3/08
	Massachusetts	Y	31220 FQ	38240 MW	47590 TQ	USBLS	5/07
	Michigan	Y	46530 FQ	53570 MW	59910 TQ	USBLS	5/07
	Mississippi	Y	30430 FQ	42410 MW	49190 TQ	USBLS	5/07
	Missouri	Y	40030 FQ	55770 MW	83710 TQ	USBLS	5/07
	Nebraska	Y	41950 FQ	45550 MW	53270 TQ	USBLS	5/07
	New Jersey	Y	30260 FQ	50220 MW	75070 TQ	USBLS	5/07
	New Mexico	Y	40200 FQ	53610 MW	62600 TQ	USBLS	5/07
	New York	Y	50680 FQ	66360 MW	88280 TQ	USBLS	5/07
	Ohio	Y	43140 FQ	51860 MW	66320 TQ	USBLS	5/07
	Oklahoma	Y	49480 FQ	68330 MW	75720 TQ	USBLS	5/07
	Pennsylvania	Y	43200 FQ	48240 MW	55930 TQ	USBLS	5/07
	South Dakota	Y	37564 FQ	40888 MW	52049 TQ	SDBLS	7/08-9/08
	Tennessee	Y	41630 FQ	56150 MW	107070 TQ	USBLS	5/07
	Texas	Y	32490 FQ	48020 MW	61820 TQ	USBLS	5/07
	Utah	Y	46910 FQ	63170 MW	76120 TQ	USBLS	5/07
	Washington	H	25.41 FQ	34.83 MW	55.04 TQ	WABLS	3/08
	Wisconsin	Y	44290 FQ	60550 MW	69830 TQ	USBLS	5/07
Farm and Home Management Advisor	Alabama	Y	27340 FQ	42670 MW	58920 TQ	USBLS	5/07
	Arkansas	Y	38220 FQ	55520 MW	75500 TQ	USBLS	5/07
	California	H	20.09 FQ	26.15 MW	38.55 TQ	CABLS	1/08-3/08
	Florida	Y	26640 FQ	37360 MW	54540 TQ	USBLS	5/07
	Georgia	Y	13870 FQ	18810 MW	24640 TQ	USBLS	5/07
	Idaho	Y	23760 FQ	33270 MW	39920 TQ	USBLS	5/07
	Illinois	Y	21430 FQ	25050 MW	45900 TQ	USBLS	5/07
	Indiana	Y	29850 FQ	49090 MW	58210 TQ	USBLS	5/07
	Iowa	Y	23140 FQ	40040 MW	57130 TQ	USBLS	5/07
	Kansas	Y	35000 FQ	42550 MW	52120 TQ	USBLS	5/07
	Maryland	Y		66625 MW		MDBLS	3/08
	Minnesota	Y	35676 FQ	39474 MW	44370 TQ	MNBLS	10/08-12/08
	Mississippi	Y	15760 FQ	28020 MW	40790 TQ	USBLS	5/07
	Montana	Y	30440 FQ	40330 MW	47560 TQ	USBLS	5/07
	Nebraska	Y	41580 FQ	50740 MW	65450 TQ	USBLS	5/07
	New Jersey	Y	25350 FQ	46930 MW	65240 TQ	USBLS	5/07
	New York	Y	21830 FQ	41330 MW	55810 TQ	USBLS	5/07
	North Carolina	Y	33740 FQ	43690 MW	53280 TQ	USBLS	5/07
	North Dakota	Y	34240 FQ	40520 MW	48660 TQ	USBLS	5/07
	Ohio	Y	23340 FQ	31800 MW	44970 TQ	USBLS	5/07
	Oklahoma	Y	32930 FQ	35900 MW	38830 TQ	USBLS	5/07
	Tennessee	Y	33910 FQ	44750 MW	56490 TQ	USBLS	5/07
	Texas	Y	15500 FQ	23940 MW	31260 TQ	USBLS	5/07
	Utah	Y	30290 FQ	91390 MW	99570 TQ	USBLS	5/07
	Virginia	Y	34900 FQ	45100 MW	53640 TQ	USBLS	5/07
	Washington	H	15.96 FQ	19.92 MW	27.21 TQ	WABLS	3/08
	West Virginia	Y	34875 FQ	42977 MW	57569 TQ	WVBLS	7/08-9/08
	Wisconsin	Y	38200 FQ	45940 MW	56970 TQ	USBLS	5/07
	Wyoming	Y	40547 FQ	54436 MW	68725 TQ	WYBLS	9/08
	Puerto Rico	Y	18400 FQ	22100 MW	25480 TQ	USBLS	5/07
Farm Coordinator State Government	Ohio	H	16.78 LO		19.88 HI	ODAS	2008
Farm Equipment Mechanic	Alabama	Y	19200 FQ	26350 MW	34150 TQ	USBLS	5/07
	Birmingham-Hoover MSA, AL	Y	25840 FQ	30140 MW	35890 TQ	USBLS	5/07
	Arizona	Y	22420 FQ	28030 MW	34780 TQ	USBLS	5/07
	Phoenix-Mesa-Scottsdale MSA, AZ	Y	22150 FQ	27270 MW	34040 TQ	USBLS	5/07
	Tucson MSA, AZ	Y	22230 FQ	28180 MW	34740 TQ	USBLS	5/07
	Arkansas	Y	19870 FQ	24400 MW	30950 TQ	USBLS	5/07

AE	Average entry wage	AW	Average wage paid	FQ	First quartile wage
AER	Average entry range	AWR	Average wage range	H	Hourly
AEX	Average experienced wage	AXR	Average experienced range	HI	Highest wage paid
ATC	Average total compensation	D	Daily	HR	High end range

LO	Lowest wage paid
LR	Low end range
M	Monthly
MCC	Median cash compensation

MTC	Median total compensation
MW	Median wage paid
MWR	Median wage range
S	See annotated source

TCC	Total cash compensation
TQ	Third quartile wage
W	Weekly
Y	Yearly

Occupation/Type/Industry	Location	Per	Low	Mid	High	Source	Date
Farm Equipment Mechanic	Little Rock-North Little Rock MSA, AR	Y	22850 FQ	25340 MW	31400 TQ	USBLS	5/07
	California	H	13.17 FQ	17.63 MW	21.62 TQ	CABLS	1/08-3/08
	Los Angeles-Long Beach-Glendale PMSA, CA	H	15.76 FQ	19.00 MW	26.62 TQ	CABLS	1/08-3/08
	Riverside-San Bernardino-Ontario MSA, CA	H	13.96 FQ	16.54 MW	19.99 TQ	CABLS	1/08-3/08
	Sacramento-Arden Arcade-Roseville MSA, CA	H	19.14 FQ	23.02 MW	26.47 TQ	CABLS	1/08-3/08
	San Diego-Carlsbad-San Marcos MSA, CA	H	14.92 FQ	18.13 MW	22.29 TQ	CABLS	1/08-3/08
	San Jose-Sunnyvale-Santa Clara MSA, CA	H	15.42 FQ	19.24 MW	23.17 TQ	CABLS	1/08-3/08
	Santa Ana-Anaheim-Irvine PMSA, CA	Y	32290 FQ	37350 MW	44580 TQ	USBLS	5/07
	Colorado	Y	27080 FQ	32740 MW	37900 TQ	USBLS	5/07
	Connecticut	H	9.43 AE	11.89 MW		CTBLS	1/08-3/08
	Delaware	Y	31760 FQ	38230 MW	42950 TQ	USBLS	5/07
	Washington-Arlington-Alexandria MSA, DC-VA-MD-WV	Y	27230 FQ	34500 MW	40460 TQ	USBLS	5/07
	Florida	Y	20930 FQ	27320 MW	33860 TQ	USBLS	5/07
	Miami-Fort Lauderdale-Miami Beach MSA, FL	Y	19090 FQ	29090 MW	40370 TQ	USBLS	5/07
	Orlando-Kissimmee MSA, FL	Y	26830 FQ	29120 MW	31400 TQ	USBLS	5/07
	West Palm Beach-Boca Raton-Boynton Beach PMSA, FL	Y	26330 FQ	35400 MW	43530 TQ	USBLS	5/07
	Georgia	Y	24500 FQ	28640 MW	34780 TQ	USBLS	5/07
	Atlanta-Sandy Springs-Marietta MSA, GA	Y	26040 FQ	29560 MW	45050 TQ	USBLS	5/07
	Idaho	Y	24130 FQ	31260 MW	37420 TQ	USBLS	5/07
	Illinois	Y	25870 FQ	31800 MW	38890 TQ	USBLS	5/07
	Chicago-Naperville-Joliet MSA, IL-IN-WI	Y	29850 FQ	35660 MW	43830 TQ	USBLS	5/07
	Indiana	Y	25180 FQ	31260 MW	36580 TQ	USBLS	5/07
	Gary PMSA, IN	Y	27680 FQ	35120 MW	46270 TQ	USBLS	5/07
	Indianapolis-Carmel MSA, IN	Y	22990 FQ	28900 MW	36580 TQ	USBLS	5/07
	Iowa	Y	24090 FQ	31210 MW	37730 TQ	USBLS	5/07
	Des Moines-West Des Moines MSA, IA	Y	28640 FQ	35630 MW	45720 TQ	USBLS	5/07
	Kansas	Y	26080 FQ	32840 MW	39620 TQ	USBLS	5/07
	Wichita MSA, KS	Y	22860 FQ	29830 MW	36470 TQ	USBLS	5/07
	Kentucky	Y	21687 FQ	25121 MW	30874 TQ	KYBLS	2008
	Louisville-Jefferson County MSA, KY-IN	Y	21880 FQ	27080 MW	31570 TQ	USBLS	5/07
	Louisiana	H	12.12 FQ	14.01 MW	16.18 TQ	LABLS	1/08-3/08
	Maine	Y	22550 FQ	28580 MW	34540 TQ	USBLS	5/07
	Maryland	Y		35275 MW		MDBLS	3/08
	Baltimore-Towson MSA, MD	Y	28570 FQ	34110 MW	37270 TQ	USBLS	5/07
	Massachusetts	Y	22560 FQ	27230 MW	34070 TQ	USBLS	5/07
	Michigan	Y	24740 FQ	30960 MW	40050 TQ	USBLS	5/07
	Warren-Troy-Farmington Hills PMSA, MI	Y	28020 FQ	41180 MW	55050 TQ	USBLS	5/07
	Minnesota	Y	32873 FQ	38234 MW	44380 TQ	MNBLS	10/08-12/08
	Minneapolis-Saint Paul MSA, MN-WI	Y	36503 FQ	40384 MW	46101 TQ	MNBLS	10/08-12/08
	Rochester MSA, MN	Y	31867 FQ	37428 MW	44078 TQ	MNBLS	10/08-12/08
	Mississippi	Y	22710 FQ	27810 MW	34730 TQ	USBLS	5/07
	Jackson MSA, MS	Y	21310 FQ	25800 MW	35660 TQ	USBLS	5/07
	Missouri	Y	23070 FQ	28900 MW	35940 TQ	USBLS	5/07
	Kansas City MSA, MO-KS	Y	23740 FQ	28640 MW	34250 TQ	USBLS	5/07
	St. Louis MSA, MO-IL	Y	24400 FQ	30880 MW	38430 TQ	USBLS	5/07
	Montana	Y	26480 FQ	30500 MW	36620 TQ	USBLS	5/07
	Nebraska	Y	22840 FQ	28000 MW	34640 TQ	USBLS	5/07
	Omaha-Council Bluffs MSA, NE-IA	Y	30140 FQ	34700 MW	39030 TQ	USBLS	5/07
	Nevada	H	14.92 FQ	17.69 MW	21.79 TQ	NVBLS	5/08
	Las Vegas-Paradise MSA, NV	H	15.26 FQ	17.40 MW	20.36 TQ	NVBLS	5/08
	New Hampshire	H	13.35 AE	17.00 MW	18.65 AEX	NHBLS	6/08
	New Jersey	Y	29960 FQ	33660 MW	37090 TQ	USBLS	5/07
	New Mexico	Y	26790 FQ	32950 MW	39310 TQ	USBLS	5/07
	Albuquerque MSA, NM	Y	30330 FQ	34730 MW	38560 TQ	USBLS	5/07

AE	Average entry wage	AW	Average wage paid	FQ	First quartile wage	LO	Lowest wage paid	MTC	Median total compensation	TCC	Total cash compensation
AER	Average entry range	AWR	Average wage range	H	Hourly	LR	Low end range	MW	Median wage paid	TQ	Third quartile wage
AEX	Average experienced wage	AXR	Average experienced range	HI	Highest wage paid	M	Monthly	MWR	Median wage range	W	Weekly
ATC	Average total compensation	D	Daily	HR	High end range	MCC	Median cash compensation	S	See annotated source	Y	Yearly

Occupation/Type/Industry	Location	Per	Low	Mid	High	Source	Date
Farm Equipment Mechanic	New York New York-Northern New Jersey-Long Island MSA, NY-NJ-PA	Y	24320 FQ	29450 MW	36590 TQ	USBLS	5/07
		Y	31010 FQ	34010 MW	36850 TQ	USBLS	5/07
	Utica-Rome MSA, NY	Y	26370 FQ	29110 MW	32880 TQ	USBLS	5/07
	North Carolina	Y	28190 FQ	33320 MW	37850 TQ	USBLS	5/07
	Charlotte-Gastonia-Concord MSA, NC-SC	Y	28630 FQ	34240 MW	39240 TQ	USBLS	5/07
	North Dakota	Y	26420 FQ	31180 MW	36900 TQ	USBLS	5/07
	Fargo MSA, ND-MN	Y	27910 FQ	35540 MW	45900 TQ	USBLS	5/07
	Grand Forks MSA, ND-MN	Y	27810 FQ	32260 MW	37950 TQ	USBLS	5/07
	Ohio	Y	25860 FQ	29870 MW	35600 TQ	USBLS	5/07
	Cincinnati-Middletown MSA, OH-KY-IN	Y	25280 FQ	31020 MW	41270 TQ	USBLS	5/07
	Cleveland-Elyria-Mentor MSA, OH	Y	28870 FQ	31760 MW	35060 TQ	USBLS	5/07
	Columbus MSA, OH	Y	26250 FQ	29510 MW	34680 TQ	USBLS	5/07
	Dayton MSA, OH	Y	22220 FQ	27550 MW	31180 TQ	USBLS	5/07
	Oklahoma	Y	20650 FQ	28250 MW	35610 TQ	USBLS	5/07
	Oklahoma City MSA, OK	Y	26320 FQ	31560 MW	39950 TQ	USBLS	5/07
	Tulsa MSA, OK	Y	23880 FQ	29830 MW	37210 TQ	USBLS	5/07
	Oregon	H	14.79 FQ	17.94 MW	20.67 TQ	ORBLS	5/08
	Portland-Vancouver-Beaverton MSA, OR-WA	Y	28420 FQ	35510 MW	43000 TQ	USBLS	5/07
	Pennsylvania	Y	24160 FQ	32060 MW	39010 TQ	USBLS	5/07
	Philadelphia-Camden-Wilmington MSA, PA-NJ-DE-MD	Y	25920 FQ	33040 MW	41440 TQ	USBLS	5/07
	Pittsburgh MSA, PA	Y	23500 FQ	31680 MW	37970 TQ	USBLS	5/07
	South Carolina	Y	24190 FQ	28960 MW	34110 TQ	USBLS	5/07
	South Dakota	Y	25471 FQ	30133 MW	35857 TQ	SDBLS	7/08-9/08
	Tennessee	Y	20950 FQ	26510 MW	32890 TQ	USBLS	5/07
	Memphis MSA, TN-MS-AR	Y	22630 FQ	32400 MW	53940 TQ	USBLS	5/07
	Nashville-Davidson-Murfreesboro MSA, TN	Y	25310 FQ	29530 MW	36240 TQ	USBLS	5/07
	Texas	Y	24780 FQ	29570 MW	36420 TQ	USBLS	5/07
	Dallas-Fort Worth-Arlington MSA, TX	Y	27560 FQ	30760 MW	36110 TQ	USBLS	5/07
	Houston-Sugar Land-Baytown MSA, TX	Y	26090 FQ	29300 MW	33830 TQ	USBLS	5/07
	San Antonio MSA, TX	Y	21780 FQ	28550 MW	35070 TQ	USBLS	5/07
	Utah	Y	26210 FQ	30990 MW	38310 TQ	USBLS	5/07
	Salt Lake City MSA, UT	Y	26940 FQ	34300 MW	40700 TQ	USBLS	5/07
	Vermont	Y	28850 FQ	33500 MW	37670 TQ	USBLS	5/07
	Burlington-South Burlington MSA, VT	Y	32910 FQ	35540 MW	38200 TQ	USBLS	5/07
	Virginia	Y	25650 FQ	30110 MW	35550 TQ	USBLS	5/07
	Richmond MSA, VA	Y	22210 FQ	26090 MW	32590 TQ	USBLS	5/07
	Washington	H	14.64 FQ	17.73 MW	20.61 TQ	WABLS	3/08
	Seattle-Tacoma-Bellevue MSA, WA	Y	36180 FQ	43520 MW	57880 TQ	USBLS	5/07
	West Virginia	Y	19083 FQ	21802 MW	24603 TQ	WVBLS	7/08-9/08
	Wisconsin	Y	26020 FQ	30060 MW	35690 TQ	USBLS	5/07
	Wyoming	Y	28201 FQ	32460 MW	36955 TQ	WYBLS	9/08
Farm Labor Contractor	Arizona	Y	14630 FQ	15220 MW	36640 TQ	USBLS	5/07
	California	H	11.18 FQ	15.28 MW	19.80 TQ	CABLS	1/08-3/08
	Florida	Y	26010 FQ	34260 MW	43590 TQ	USBLS	5/07
	Indiana	Y	21860 FQ	29290 MW	45840 TQ	USBLS	5/07
	Oregon	H	17.19 FQ	21.66 MW	24.46 TQ	ORBLS	5/08
	Tennessee	Y	25430 FQ	27550 MW	29680 TQ	USBLS	5/07
Farm Laborer Department of Corrections	Ohio	H	14.36 LO		15.41 HI	ODAS	2008
Farmer and Rancher	Oklahoma	Y	21950 FQ	23670 MW	25370 TQ	USBLS	5/07
	Tennessee	Y	31740 FQ	33760 MW	35780 TQ	USBLS	5/07
Farmworker Farm and Ranch Animals	Alabama	Y	17010 FQ	23950 MW	29920 TQ	USBLS	5/07
Farm and Ranch Animals	Birmingham-Hoover MSA, AL	Y	16330 FQ	20790 MW	23910 TQ	USBLS	5/07
Farm and Ranch Animals	Arizona	Y	17850 FQ	21610 MW	31600 TQ	USBLS	5/07

AE Average entry wage	**AW** Average wage paid	**FQ** First quartile wage	**LO** Lowest wage paid	**MTC** Median total compensation	**TCC** Total cash compensation
AER Average entry range	**AWR** Average wage range	**H** Hourly	**LR** Low end range	**MW** Median wage paid	**TQ** Third quartile wage
AEX Average experienced wage	**AXR** Average experienced range	**HI** Highest wage paid	**M** Monthly	**MWR** Median wage range	**W** Weekly
ATC Average total compensation	**D** Daily	**HR** High end range	**MCC** Median cash compensation	**S** See annotated source	**Y** Yearly

Occupation/Type/Industry	Location	Per	Low	Mid	High	Source	Date
Farmworker							
Farm and Ranch Animals	Phoenix-Mesa-Scottsdale MSA, AZ	Y	18970 FQ	24330 MW	34910 TQ	USBLS	5/07
Farm and Ranch Animals	Tucson MSA, AZ	Y	18290 FQ	24150 MW	30010 TQ	USBLS	5/07
Farm and Ranch Animals	Arkansas	Y	15760 FQ	20420 MW	25010 TQ	USBLS	5/07
Farm and Ranch Animals	Fayetteville-Springdale-Rogers MSA, AR-MO	Y	15610 FQ	18690 MW	24570 TQ	USBLS	5/07
Farm and Ranch Animals	Little Rock-North Little Rock MSA, AR	Y	14560 FQ	15960 MW	18870 TQ	USBLS	5/07
Farm and Ranch Animals	California	H	8.93 FQ	10.74 MW	13.10 TQ	CABLS	1/08-3/08
Farm and Ranch Animals	Los Angeles-Long Beach-Glendale PMSA, CA	H	8.82 FQ	11.21 MW	14.55 TQ	CABLS	1/08-3/08
Farm and Ranch Animals	Oakland-Fremont-Hayward MSA, CA	H	8.00 FQ	11.54 MW	15.10 TQ	CABLS	1/08-3/08
Farm and Ranch Animals	Riverside-San Bernardino-Ontario MSA, CA	H	8.21 FQ	9.40 MW	11.70 TQ	CABLS	1/08-3/08
Farm and Ranch Animals	Sacramento-Arden Arcade-Roseville MSA, CA	H	9.06 FQ	10.78 MW	12.95 TQ	CABLS	1/08-3/08
Farm and Ranch Animals	San Diego-Carlsbad-San Marcos MSA, CA	H	11.37 FQ	12.92 MW	14.04 TQ	CABLS	1/08-3/08
Farm and Ranch Animals	San Francisco-San Mateo-Redwood PMSA, CA	H	10.30 FQ	12.34 MW	13.95 TQ	CABLS	1/08-3/08
Farm and Ranch Animals	San Jose-Sunnyvale-Santa Clara MSA, CA	H	11.00 FQ	11.81 MW	12.63 TQ	CABLS	1/08-3/08
Farm and Ranch Animals	Santa Ana-Anaheim-Irvine PMSA, CA	Y	20840 FQ	22800 MW	25380 TQ	USBLS	5/07
Farm and Ranch Animals	Colorado	Y	15210 FQ	17610 MW	23490 TQ	USBLS	5/07
Farm and Ranch Animals	Denver-Aurora MSA, CO	Y	14930 FQ	15950 MW	18550 TQ	USBLS	5/07
Farm and Ranch Animals	Fort Collins-Loveland MSA, CO	Y	20260 FQ	22520 MW	24790 TQ	USBLS	5/07
Farm and Ranch Animals	Connecticut	H	8.61 AE	9.57 MW		CTBLS	1/08-3/08
Farm and Ranch Animals	Hartford-West Hartford-East Hartford MSA, CT	Y	17030 FQ	18510 MW	19990 TQ	USBLS	5/07
Farm and Ranch Animals	Delaware	Y	23810 FQ	29230 MW	33530 TQ	USBLS	5/07
Farm and Ranch Animals	Wilmington PMSA, DE-MD-NJ	Y	22410 FQ	25770 MW	32610 TQ	USBLS	5/07
Farm and Ranch Animals	Washington-Arlington-Alexandria MSA, DC-VA-MD-WV	Y	20010 FQ	24370 MW	32340 TQ	USBLS	5/07
Farm and Ranch Animals	Florida	Y	18990 FQ	22240 MW	28360 TQ	USBLS	5/07
Farm and Ranch Animals	Tampa-St. Petersburg-Clearwater MSA, FL	Y	16050 FQ	20660 MW	25420 TQ	USBLS	5/07
Farm and Ranch Animals	Georgia	Y	18020 FQ	23700 MW	27710 TQ	USBLS	5/07
Farm and Ranch Animals	Atlanta-Sandy Springs-Marietta MSA, GA	Y	20580 FQ	24260 MW	26790 TQ	USBLS	5/07
Farm and Ranch Animals	Hawaii	Y	16950 FQ	21680 MW	25510 TQ	USBLS	5/07
Farm and Ranch Animals	Honolulu MSA, HI	Y	16700 FQ	21120 MW	25150 TQ	USBLS	5/07
Farm and Ranch Animals	Idaho	Y	13010 FQ	15230 MW	18790 TQ	USBLS	5/07
Farm and Ranch Animals	Boise City-Nampa MSA, ID	Y	12360 FQ	13960 MW	15520 TQ	USBLS	5/07
Farm and Ranch Animals	Illinois	Y	15870 FQ	18800 MW	24070 TQ	USBLS	5/07
Farm and Ranch Animals	Chicago-Naperville-Joliet MSA, IL-IN-WI	Y	15440 FQ	16610 MW	24140 TQ	USBLS	5/07
Farm and Ranch Animals	Indiana	Y	15310 FQ	20770 MW	25840 TQ	USBLS	5/07
Farm and Ranch Animals	Indianapolis-Carmel MSA, IN	Y	13860 FQ	21110 MW	24350 TQ	USBLS	5/07
Farm and Ranch Animals	Iowa	Y	19120 FQ	23520 MW	29480 TQ	USBLS	5/07
Farm and Ranch Animals	Des Moines-West Des Moines MSA, IA	Y	14640 FQ	16300 MW	18150 TQ	USBLS	5/07
Farm and Ranch Animals	Kansas	Y	16680 FQ	20970 MW	28520 TQ	USBLS	5/07
Farm and Ranch Animals	Kentucky	Y	17332 FQ	20670 MW	23938 TQ	KYBLS	2008
Farm and Ranch Animals	Louisville-Jefferson County MSA, KY-IN	Y	17680 FQ	20790 MW	24210 TQ	USBLS	5/07
Farm and Ranch Animals	Louisiana	H	7.55 FQ	8.67 MW	11.27 TQ	LABLS	1/08-3/08
Farm and Ranch Animals	Baton Rouge MSA, LA	Y	15270 FQ	16860 MW	18450 TQ	USBLS	5/07
Farm and Ranch Animals	New Orleans-Metairie-Kenner MSA, LA	Y	23220 FQ	26310 MW	29690 TQ	USBLS	5/07
Farm and Ranch Animals	Maine	Y	16840 FQ	20000 MW	26310 TQ	USBLS	5/07
Farm and Ranch Animals	Portland-South Portland-Biddeford MSA, ME	Y	16940 FQ	19900 MW	27900 TQ	USBLS	5/07
Farm and Ranch Animals	Maryland	Y		22650 MW		MDBLS	3/08
Farm and Ranch Animals	Baltimore-Towson MSA, MD	Y	17590 FQ	19520 MW	28330 TQ	USBLS	5/07
Farm and Ranch Animals	Bethesda-Gaithersburg-Frederick PMSA, MD	Y	18290 FQ	26230 MW	29570 TQ	USBLS	5/07

AE	Average entry wage	AW	Average wage paid	FQ	First quartile wage	LO	Lowest wage paid	MTC	Median total compensation	TCC	Total cash compensation
AER	Average entry range	AWR	Average wage range	H	Hourly	LR	Low end range	MW	Median wage paid	TQ	Third quartile wage
AEX	Average experienced wage	AXR	Average experienced range	HI	Highest wage paid	M	Monthly	MWR	Median wage range	W	Weekly
ATC	Average total compensation	D	Daily	HR	High end range	MCC	Median cash compensation	S	See annotated source	Y	Yearly

Occupation/Type/Industry	Location	Per	Low	Mid	High	Source	Date
Farmworker							
Farm and Ranch Animals	Massachusetts	Y	17740 FQ	19330 MW	21680 TQ	USBLS	5/07
Farm and Ranch Animals	Michigan	Y	15100 FQ	19900 MW	23130 TQ	USBLS	5/07
Farm and Ranch Animals	Minnesota	Y	19707 FQ	23374 MW	27769 TQ	MNBLS	10/08-12/08
Farm and Ranch Animals	Minneapolis-Saint Paul MSA, MN-WI	Y	22089 FQ	24607 MW	27632 TQ	MNBLS	10/08-12/08
Farm and Ranch Animals	Rochester MSA, MN	Y	16126 FQ	22817 MW	26981 TQ	MNBLS	10/08-12/08
Farm and Ranch Animals	Mississippi	Y	15310 FQ	17160 MW	18950 TQ	USBLS	5/07
Farm and Ranch Animals	Jackson MSA, MS	Y	13030 FQ	15260 MW	19270 TQ	USBLS	5/07
Farm and Ranch Animals	Missouri	Y	15080 FQ	19560 MW	24520 TQ	USBLS	5/07
Farm and Ranch Animals	Jefferson City MSA, MO	Y	17020 FQ	18860 MW	21770 TQ	USBLS	5/07
Farm and Ranch Animals	Kansas City MSA, MO-KS	Y	14270 FQ	15050 MW	19560 TQ	USBLS	5/07
Farm and Ranch Animals	St. Joseph MSA, MO-KS	Y	25730 FQ	27830 MW	29920 TQ	USBLS	5/07
Farm and Ranch Animals	St. Louis MSA, MO-IL	Y	16770 FQ	20900 MW	24120 TQ	USBLS	5/07
Farm and Ranch Animals	Montana	Y	15520 FQ	19160 MW	26280 TQ	USBLS	5/07
Farm and Ranch Animals	Billings MSA, MT	Y	19980 FQ	21880 MW	23590 TQ	USBLS	5/07
Farm and Ranch Animals	Nebraska	Y	15030 FQ	18780 MW	23990 TQ	USBLS	5/07
Farm and Ranch Animals	Omaha-Council Bluffs MSA, NE-IA	Y	13060 FQ	15040 MW	18140 TQ	USBLS	5/07
Farm and Ranch Animals	Nevada	H	6.59 FQ	7.64 MW	9.27 TQ	NVBLS	5/08
Farm and Ranch Animals	New Hampshire	H	8.09 AE	12.20 MW	14.67 AEX	NHBLS	6/08
Farm and Ranch Animals	New Jersey	Y	16300 FQ	24550 MW	28780 TQ	USBLS	5/07
Farm and Ranch Animals	Camden PMSA, NJ	Y	15830 FQ	21240 MW	24980 TQ	USBLS	5/07
Farm and Ranch Animals	Edison PMSA, NJ	Y	25290 FQ	27520 MW	29880 TQ	USBLS	5/07
Farm and Ranch Animals	Newark-Union PMSA, NJ-PA	Y	15430 FQ	15720 MW	17790 TQ	USBLS	5/07
Farm and Ranch Animals	New Mexico	Y	13350 FQ	15530 MW	20070 TQ	USBLS	5/07
Farm and Ranch Animals	New York	Y	16720 FQ	21710 MW	28080 TQ	USBLS	5/07
Farm and Ranch Animals	Albany-Schenectady-Troy MSA, NY	Y	21990 FQ	25140 MW	30800 TQ	USBLS	5/07
Farm and Ranch Animals	Buffalo-Niagara Falls MSA, NY	Y	15040 FQ	15220 MW	22980 TQ	USBLS	5/07
Farm and Ranch Animals	Nassau-Suffolk PMSA, NY	Y	15970 FQ	20000 MW	23580 TQ	USBLS	5/07
Farm and Ranch Animals	New York-Northern New Jersey-Long Island MSA, NY-NJ-PA	Y	18080 FQ	24710 MW	30920 TQ	USBLS	5/07
Farm and Ranch Animals	North Carolina	Y	17520 FQ	20280 MW	23570 TQ	USBLS	5/07
Farm and Ranch Animals	Raleigh-Cary MSA, NC	Y	17590 FQ	23190 MW	28320 TQ	USBLS	5/07
Farm and Ranch Animals	North Dakota	Y	14600 FQ	17620 MW	19790 TQ	USBLS	5/07
Farm and Ranch Animals	Ohio	Y	16220 FQ	20510 MW	26880 TQ	USBLS	5/07
Farm and Ranch Animals	Cincinnati-Middletown MSA, OH-KY-IN	Y	17740 FQ	22480 MW	28930 TQ	USBLS	5/07
Farm and Ranch Animals	Cleveland-Elyria-Mentor MSA, OH	Y	15880 FQ	17790 MW	19650 TQ	USBLS	5/07
Farm and Ranch Animals	Columbus MSA, OH	Y	20770 FQ	25160 MW	32300 TQ	USBLS	5/07
Farm and Ranch Animals	Oklahoma	Y	15480 FQ	18770 MW	22400 TQ	USBLS	5/07
Farm and Ranch Animals	Oklahoma City MSA, OK	Y	14860 FQ	17570 MW	19890 TQ	USBLS	5/07
Farm and Ranch Animals	Tulsa MSA, OK	Y	13650 FQ	17370 MW	26290 TQ	USBLS	5/07
Farm and Ranch Animals	Oregon	H	8.97 FQ	10.58 MW	13.26 TQ	ORBLS	5/08
Farm and Ranch Animals	Portland-Vancouver-Beaverton MSA, OR-WA	Y	18430 FQ	22420 MW	25810 TQ	USBLS	5/07
Farm and Ranch Animals	Pennsylvania	Y	16850 FQ	19990 MW	24840 TQ	USBLS	5/07
Farm and Ranch Animals	Allentown-Bethlehem-Easton MSA, PA-NJ	Y	19740 FQ	24530 MW	33960 TQ	USBLS	5/07
Farm and Ranch Animals	Philadelphia-Camden-Wilmington MSA, PA-NJ-DE-MD	Y	16680 FQ	20610 MW	24650 TQ	USBLS	5/07
Farm and Ranch Animals	Pittsburgh MSA, PA	Y	17530 FQ	20990 MW	24780 TQ	USBLS	5/07
Farm and Ranch Animals	South Carolina	Y	18070 FQ	23880 MW	34610 TQ	USBLS	5/07
Farm and Ranch Animals	South Dakota	Y	19372 FQ	22580 MW	25745 TQ	SDBLS	7/08-9/08
Farm and Ranch Animals	Tennessee	Y	15500 FQ	18530 MW	22810 TQ	USBLS	5/07
Farm and Ranch Animals	Nashville-Davidson-Murfreesboro MSA, TN	Y	16610 FQ	18980 MW	22190 TQ	USBLS	5/07
Farm and Ranch Animals	Texas	Y	13120 FQ	14960 MW	18970 TQ	USBLS	5/07
Farm and Ranch Animals	Dallas-Fort Worth-Arlington MSA, TX	Y	13910 FQ	16860 MW	21610 TQ	USBLS	5/07
Farm and Ranch Animals	Houston-Sugar Land-Baytown MSA, TX	Y	13520 FQ	15710 MW	21250 TQ	USBLS	5/07
Farm and Ranch Animals	San Antonio MSA, TX	Y	12450 FQ	13770 MW	15090 TQ	USBLS	5/07
Farm and Ranch Animals	Utah	Y	12890 FQ	14820 MW	19150 TQ	USBLS	5/07
Farm and Ranch Animals	Vermont	Y	20380 FQ	26770 MW	29860 TQ	USBLS	5/07
Farm and Ranch Animals	Virginia	Y	18480 FQ	22070 MW	24880 TQ	USBLS	5/07
Farm and Ranch Animals	Richmond MSA, VA	Y	15220 FQ	21980 MW	26530 TQ	USBLS	5/07

AE Average entry wage	**AW** Average wage paid	**FQ** First quartile wage	**LO** Lowest wage paid	**MTC** Median total compensation	**TCC** Total cash compensation
AER Average entry range	**AWR** Average wage range	**H** Hourly	**LR** Low end range	**MW** Median wage paid	**TQ** Third quartile wage
AEX Average experienced wage	**AXR** Average experienced range	**HI** Highest wage paid	**M** Monthly	**MWR** Median wage range	**W** Weekly
ATC Average total compensation	**D** Daily	**HR** High end range	**MCC** Median cash compensation	**S** See annotated source	**Y** Yearly

Occupation/Type/Industry	Location	Per	Low	Mid	High	Source	Date
Farmworker							
Farm and Ranch Animals	Virginia Beach-Norfolk-Newport News MSA, VA-NC	Y	16960 FQ	18870 MW	21790 TQ	USBLS	5/07
Farm and Ranch Animals	Washington	H	9.34 FQ	13.16 MW	16.31 TQ	WABLS	3/08
Farm and Ranch Animals	Seattle-Tacoma-Bellevue MSA, WA	Y	28240 FQ	32290 MW	37950 TQ	USBLS	5/07
Farm and Ranch Animals	West Virginia	Y	14970 FQ	18045 MW	24861 TQ	WVBLS	7/08-9/08
Farm and Ranch Animals	Charleston MSA, WV	Y	19790 FQ	23200 MW	28000 TQ	USBLS	5/07
Farm and Ranch Animals	Wisconsin	Y	18700 FQ	22100 MW	25060 TQ	USBLS	5/07
Farm and Ranch Animals	Milwaukee-Waukesha-West Allis MSA, WI	Y	21520 FQ	23330 MW	25160 TQ	USBLS	5/07
Farm and Ranch Animals	Wyoming	Y	26241 FQ	29954 MW	39452 TQ	WYBLS	9/08
Farm and Ranch Animals	Puerto Rico	Y	12570 FQ	13680 MW	14790 TQ	USBLS	5/07
Farm and Ranch Animals	San Juan-Caguas-Guaynabo MSA, PR	Y	13190 FQ	15080 MW	18200 TQ	USBLS	5/07
Farmworker and Laborer							
Crop, Nursery, and Greenhouse	Alabama	Y	13670 FQ	16650 MW	20400 TQ	USBLS	5/07
Crop, Nursery, and Greenhouse	Birmingham-Hoover MSA, AL	Y	12420 FQ	14120 MW	17420 TQ	USBLS	5/07
Crop, Nursery, and Greenhouse	Arizona	Y	14990 FQ	16360 MW	18450 TQ	USBLS	5/07
Crop, Nursery, and Greenhouse	Phoenix-Mesa-Scottsdale MSA, AZ	Y	14760 FQ	15630 MW	20080 TQ	USBLS	5/07
Crop, Nursery, and Greenhouse	Tucson MSA, AZ	Y	15440 FQ	18600 MW	22920 TQ	USBLS	5/07
Crop, Nursery, and Greenhouse	Arkansas	Y	14870 FQ	17270 MW	22960 TQ	USBLS	5/07
Crop, Nursery, and Greenhouse	Little Rock-North Little Rock MSA, AR	Y	15190 FQ	24730 MW	45380 TQ	USBLS	5/07
Crop, Nursery, and Greenhouse	California	H	8.00 FQ	8.36 MW	9.21 TQ	CABLS	1/08-3/08
Crop, Nursery, and Greenhouse	Fresno MSA, CA	H	8.00 FQ	8.24 MW	9.00 TQ	CABLS	1/08-3/08
Crop, Nursery, and Greenhouse	Los Angeles-Long Beach-Glendale PMSA, CA	H	8.54 FQ	9.87 MW	11.60 TQ	CABLS	1/08-3/08
Crop, Nursery, and Greenhouse	Oakland-Fremont-Hayward MSA, CA	H	8.30 FQ	9.25 MW	11.55 TQ	CABLS	1/08-3/08
Crop, Nursery, and Greenhouse	Oxnard-Thousand Oaks-Ventura MSA, CA	H	8.15 FQ	8.97 MW	9.94 TQ	CABLS	1/08-3/08
Crop, Nursery, and Greenhouse	Riverside-San Bernardino-Ontario MSA, CA	H	8.00 FQ	8.61 MW	9.45 TQ	CABLS	1/08-3/08
Crop, Nursery, and Greenhouse	Sacramento-Arden Arcade-Roseville MSA, CA	H	8.00 FQ	8.42 MW	9.17 TQ	CABLS	1/08-3/08
Crop, Nursery, and Greenhouse	San Diego-Carlsbad-San Marcos MSA, CA	H	8.27 FQ	9.18 MW	10.91 TQ	CABLS	1/08-3/08
Crop, Nursery, and Greenhouse	San Francisco-San Mateo-Redwood PMSA, CA	H	10.54 FQ	12.38 MW	14.12 TQ	CABLS	1/08-3/08
Crop, Nursery, and Greenhouse	San Jose-Sunnyvale-Santa Clara MSA, CA	H	8.00 FQ	8.00 MW	9.16 TQ	CABLS	1/08-3/08
Crop, Nursery, and Greenhouse	Santa Ana-Anaheim-Irvine PMSA, CA	Y	17350 FQ	19030 MW	20930 TQ	USBLS	5/07
Crop, Nursery, and Greenhouse	Colorado	Y	16070 FQ	18540 MW	24290 TQ	USBLS	5/07
Crop, Nursery, and Greenhouse	Denver-Aurora MSA, CO	Y	16460 FQ	19230 MW	25260 TQ	USBLS	5/07
Crop, Nursery, and Greenhouse	Connecticut	H	8.87 AE	11.54 MW		CTBLS	1/08-3/08
Crop, Nursery, and Greenhouse	Bridgeport-Stamford-Norwalk MSA, CT	Y	21690 FQ	26920 MW	34470 TQ	USBLS	5/07
Crop, Nursery, and Greenhouse	Hartford-West Hartford-East Hartford MSA, CT	Y	17270 FQ	18510 MW	22240 TQ	USBLS	5/07
Crop, Nursery, and Greenhouse	Delaware	Y	17310 FQ	18680 MW	20040 TQ	USBLS	5/07
Crop, Nursery, and Greenhouse	Wilmington PMSA, DE-MD-NJ	Y	17100 FQ	19810 MW	24290 TQ	USBLS	5/07
Crop, Nursery, and Greenhouse	Washington-Arlington-Alexandria MSA, DC-VA-MD-WV	Y	17190 FQ	20090 MW	27500 TQ	USBLS	5/07
Crop, Nursery, and Greenhouse	Florida	Y	14910 FQ	16360 MW	21050 TQ	USBLS	5/07
Crop, Nursery, and Greenhouse	Fort Lauderdale-Pompano Beach-Deerfield Beach PMSA, FL	Y	14640 FQ	15480 MW	17440 TQ	USBLS	5/07
Crop, Nursery, and Greenhouse	Jacksonville MSA, FL	Y	16390 FQ	19470 MW	24590 TQ	USBLS	5/07
Crop, Nursery, and Greenhouse	Miami-Fort Lauderdale-Miami Beach MSA, FL	Y	14700 FQ	15640 MW	18410 TQ	USBLS	5/07
Crop, Nursery, and Greenhouse	Orlando-Kissimmee MSA, FL	Y	17040 FQ	20590 MW	29490 TQ	USBLS	5/07
Crop, Nursery, and Greenhouse	Pensacola-Ferry Pass-Brent MSA, FL	Y	19220 FQ	22690 MW	26840 TQ	USBLS	5/07
Crop, Nursery, and Greenhouse	Tampa-St. Petersburg-Clearwater MSA, FL	Y	14740 FQ	15580 MW	17680 TQ	USBLS	5/07

AE Average entry wage	**AW** Average wage paid	**FQ** First quartile wage	**LO** Lowest wage paid	**MTC** Median total compensation	**TCC** Total cash compensation
AER Average entry range	**AWR** Average wage range	**H** Hourly	**LR** Low end range	**MW** Median wage paid	**TQ** Third quartile wage
AEX Average experienced wage	**AXR** Average experienced range	**HI** Highest wage paid	**M** Monthly	**MWR** Median wage range	**W** Weekly
ATC Average total compensation	**D** Daily	**HR** High end range	**MCC** Median cash compensation	**S** See annotated source	**Y** Yearly

Occupation/Type/Industry	Location	Per	Low	Mid	High	Source	Date
Farmworker and Laborer							
Crop, Nursery, and Greenhouse	West Palm Beach-Boca Raton-Boynton Beach PMSA, FL	Y	14650 FQ	15470 MW	16500 TQ	USBLS	5/07
Crop, Nursery, and Greenhouse	Georgia	Y	13380 FQ	15430 MW	18740 TQ	USBLS	5/07
Crop, Nursery, and Greenhouse	Atlanta-Sandy Springs-Marietta MSA, GA	Y	13530 FQ	15820 MW	22480 TQ	USBLS	5/07
Crop, Nursery, and Greenhouse	Hawaii	Y	16150 FQ	18340 MW	22650 TQ	USBLS	5/07
Crop, Nursery, and Greenhouse	Honolulu MSA, HI	Y	15770 FQ	17040 MW	22620 TQ	USBLS	5/07
Crop, Nursery, and Greenhouse	Idaho	Y	15790 FQ	18860 MW	26690 TQ	USBLS	5/07
Crop, Nursery, and Greenhouse	Boise City-Nampa MSA, ID	Y	15110 FQ	17790 MW	21940 TQ	USBLS	5/07
Crop, Nursery, and Greenhouse	Illinois	Y	17330 FQ	19550 MW	25480 TQ	USBLS	5/07
Crop, Nursery, and Greenhouse	Chicago-Naperville-Joliet MSA, IL-IN-WI	Y	17090 FQ	18860 MW	21730 TQ	USBLS	5/07
Crop, Nursery, and Greenhouse	Indiana	Y	17260 FQ	22460 MW	33920 TQ	USBLS	5/07
Crop, Nursery, and Greenhouse	Elkhart-Goshen MSA, IN	Y	17340 FQ	20210 MW	27850 TQ	USBLS	5/07
Crop, Nursery, and Greenhouse	Evansville MSA, IN-KY	Y	13950 FQ	16630 MW	19270 TQ	USBLS	5/07
Crop, Nursery, and Greenhouse	Gary PMSA, IN	Y	17430 FQ	24100 MW	30300 TQ	USBLS	5/07
Crop, Nursery, and Greenhouse	Indianapolis-Carmel MSA, IN	Y	17250 FQ	20990 MW	36010 TQ	USBLS	5/07
Crop, Nursery, and Greenhouse	South Bend-Mishawaka MSA, IN-MI	Y	15500 FQ	17580 MW	24340 TQ	USBLS	5/07
Crop, Nursery, and Greenhouse	Iowa	Y	17400 FQ	21610 MW	26780 TQ	USBLS	5/07
Crop, Nursery, and Greenhouse	Des Moines-West Des Moines MSA, IA	Y	17820 FQ	20860 MW	23810 TQ	USBLS	5/07
Crop, Nursery, and Greenhouse	Kansas	Y	17470 FQ	19410 MW	23410 TQ	USBLS	5/07
Crop, Nursery, and Greenhouse	Kentucky	Y	16676 FQ	20291 MW	26914 TQ	KYBLS	2008
Crop, Nursery, and Greenhouse	Louisville-Jefferson County MSA, KY-IN	Y	15680 FQ	17770 MW	20910 TQ	USBLS	5/07
Crop, Nursery, and Greenhouse	Louisiana	H	7.54 FQ	8.91 MW	10.83 TQ	LABLS	1/08-3/08
Crop, Nursery, and Greenhouse	Baton Rouge MSA, LA	Y	13910 FQ	16570 MW	20020 TQ	USBLS	5/07
Crop, Nursery, and Greenhouse	New Orleans-Metairie-Kenner MSA, LA	Y	15830 FQ	19460 MW	25490 TQ	USBLS	5/07
Crop, Nursery, and Greenhouse	Maine	Y	16940 FQ	19720 MW	26560 TQ	USBLS	5/07
Crop, Nursery, and Greenhouse	Portland-South Portland-Biddeford MSA, ME	Y	17100 FQ	18820 MW	22040 TQ	USBLS	5/07
Crop, Nursery, and Greenhouse	Maryland	Y		20850 MW		MDBLS	3/08
Crop, Nursery, and Greenhouse	Baltimore-Towson MSA, MD	Y	16270 FQ	20930 MW	25660 TQ	USBLS	5/07
Crop, Nursery, and Greenhouse	Bethesda-Gaithersburg-Frederick PMSA, MD	Y	17440 FQ	20740 MW	27850 TQ	USBLS	5/07
Crop, Nursery, and Greenhouse	Salisbury MSA, MD	Y	16210 FQ	17940 MW	19700 TQ	USBLS	5/07
Crop, Nursery, and Greenhouse	Massachusetts	Y	19150 FQ	22520 MW	27530 TQ	USBLS	5/07
Crop, Nursery, and Greenhouse	Boston-Cambridge-Quincy NECTA, MA	Y	18960 FQ	21440 MW	23790 TQ	USBLS	5/07
Crop, Nursery, and Greenhouse	Worcester MSA, MA-CT	Y	20780 FQ	24290 MW	28710 TQ	USBLS	5/07
Crop, Nursery, and Greenhouse	Michigan	Y	15620 FQ	18780 MW	23540 TQ	USBLS	5/07
Crop, Nursery, and Greenhouse	Detroit-Warren-Livonia MSA, MI	Y	15400 FQ	18330 MW	25260 TQ	USBLS	5/07
Crop, Nursery, and Greenhouse	Grand Rapids-Wyoming MSA, MI	Y	15180 FQ	15760 MW	17020 TQ	USBLS	5/07
Crop, Nursery, and Greenhouse	Warren-Troy-Farmington Hills PMSA, MI	Y	15390 FQ	18380 MW	24830 TQ	USBLS	5/07
Crop, Nursery, and Greenhouse	Minnesota	Y	16008 FQ	19328 MW	28106 TQ	MNBLS	10/08-12/08
Crop, Nursery, and Greenhouse	Duluth-Superior MSA, MN-WI	Y	15175 FQ	16261 MW	17410 TQ	MNBLS	10/08-12/08
Crop, Nursery, and Greenhouse	Minneapolis-Saint Paul MSA, MN-WI	Y	18516 FQ	22163 MW	24924 TQ	MNBLS	10/08-12/08
Crop, Nursery, and Greenhouse	Mississippi	Y	13770 FQ	16310 MW	18470 TQ	USBLS	5/07
Crop, Nursery, and Greenhouse	Jackson MSA, MS	Y	17180 FQ	18680 MW	20180 TQ	USBLS	5/07
Crop, Nursery, and Greenhouse	Missouri	Y	16210 FQ	18520 MW	22330 TQ	USBLS	5/07
Crop, Nursery, and Greenhouse	Kansas City MSA, MO-KS	Y	14990 FQ	16950 MW	20680 TQ	USBLS	5/07
Crop, Nursery, and Greenhouse	St. Louis MSA, MO-IL	Y	18040 FQ	24400 MW	32120 TQ	USBLS	5/07
Crop, Nursery, and Greenhouse	Montana	Y	15280 FQ	19730 MW	25710 TQ	USBLS	5/07
Crop, Nursery, and Greenhouse	Billings MSA, MT	Y	16120 FQ	18340 MW	21370 TQ	USBLS	5/07
Crop, Nursery, and Greenhouse	Nebraska	Y	19240 FQ	25230 MW	33150 TQ	USBLS	5/07
Crop, Nursery, and Greenhouse	Omaha-Council Bluffs MSA, NE-IA	Y	19190 FQ	23950 MW	33160 TQ	USBLS	5/07
Crop, Nursery, and Greenhouse	Nevada	H	8.89 FQ	11.41 MW	15.31 TQ	NVBLS	5/08
Crop, Nursery, and Greenhouse	Las Vegas-Paradise MSA, NV	H	9.24 FQ	11.66 MW	15.07 TQ	NVBLS	5/08
Crop, Nursery, and Greenhouse	New Hampshire	H	7.58 AE	9.43 MW	10.96 AEX	NHBLS	6/08
Crop, Nursery, and Greenhouse	New Jersey	Y	15220 FQ	18340 MW	23060 TQ	USBLS	5/07
Crop, Nursery, and Greenhouse	Camden PMSA, NJ	Y	15200 FQ	15220 MW	18830 TQ	USBLS	5/07
Crop, Nursery, and Greenhouse	Edison PMSA, NJ	Y	17990 FQ	19960 MW	22450 TQ	USBLS	5/07
Crop, Nursery, and Greenhouse	Newark-Union PMSA, NJ-PA	Y	20690 FQ	23830 MW	32040 TQ	USBLS	5/07
Crop, Nursery, and Greenhouse	Trenton-Ewing MSA, NJ	Y	15240 FQ	16340 MW	19270 TQ	USBLS	5/07

AE	Average entry wage	AW	Average wage paid	FQ	First quartile wage
AER	Average entry range	AWR	Average wage range	H	Hourly
AEX	Average experienced wage	AXR	Average experienced range	HI	Highest wage paid
ATC	Average total compensation	D	Daily	HR	High end range

LO	Lowest wage paid	MTC	Median total compensation	TCC	Total cash compensation
LR	Low end range	MW	Median wage paid	TQ	Third quartile wage
		MWR	Median wage range	W	Weekly
M	Monthly				
MCC	Median cash compensation	S	See annotated source	Y	Yearly

Occupation/Type/Industry	Location	Per	Low	Mid	High	Source	Date
Farmworker and Laborer							
Crop, Nursery, and Greenhouse	New Mexico	Y	12670 FQ	13950 MW	15310 TQ	USBLS	5/07
Crop, Nursery, and Greenhouse	Albuquerque MSA, NM	Y	12660 FQ	14050 MW	15530 TQ	USBLS	5/07
Crop, Nursery, and Greenhouse	New York	Y	17250 FQ	20450 MW	24490 TQ	USBLS	5/07
Crop, Nursery, and Greenhouse	Albany-Schenectady-Troy MSA, NY	Y	20240 FQ	22220 MW	25460 TQ	USBLS	5/07
Crop, Nursery, and Greenhouse	Binghamton MSA, NY	Y	14980 FQ	15480 MW	20580 TQ	USBLS	5/07
Crop, Nursery, and Greenhouse	Buffalo-Niagara Falls MSA, NY	Y	18510 FQ	21130 MW	23760 TQ	USBLS	5/07
Crop, Nursery, and Greenhouse	Nassau-Suffolk PMSA, NY	Y	18320 FQ	22570 MW	28720 TQ	USBLS	5/07
Crop, Nursery, and Greenhouse	New York-Northern New Jersey-Long Island MSA, NY-NJ-PA	Y	18150 FQ	21790 MW	27070 TQ	USBLS	5/07
Crop, Nursery, and Greenhouse	North Carolina	Y	14440 FQ	16650 MW	20220 TQ	USBLS	5/07
Crop, Nursery, and Greenhouse	Charlotte-Gastonia-Concord MSA, NC-SC	Y	16070 FQ	18780 MW	23220 TQ	USBLS	5/07
Crop, Nursery, and Greenhouse	Raleigh-Cary MSA, NC	Y	17020 FQ	18790 MW	22410 TQ	USBLS	5/07
Crop, Nursery, and Greenhouse	Winston-Salem MSA, NC	Y	14340 FQ	16080 MW	17920 TQ	USBLS	5/07
Crop, Nursery, and Greenhouse	North Dakota	Y	18410 FQ	21980 MW	26460 TQ	USBLS	5/07
Crop, Nursery, and Greenhouse	Fargo MSA, ND-MN	Y	17080 FQ	18240 MW	19400 TQ	USBLS	5/07
Crop, Nursery, and Greenhouse	Ohio	Y	17700 FQ	20250 MW	24410 TQ	USBLS	5/07
Crop, Nursery, and Greenhouse	Canton-Massillon MSA, OH	Y	17630 FQ	19280 MW	22280 TQ	USBLS	5/07
Crop, Nursery, and Greenhouse	Cincinnati-Middletown MSA, OH-KY-IN	Y	17650 FQ	20230 MW	26090 TQ	USBLS	5/07
Crop, Nursery, and Greenhouse	Cleveland-Elyria-Mentor MSA, OH	Y	20950 FQ	23110 MW	25680 TQ	USBLS	5/07
Crop, Nursery, and Greenhouse	Columbus MSA, OH	Y	18540 FQ	21140 MW	24720 TQ	USBLS	5/07
Crop, Nursery, and Greenhouse	Dayton MSA, OH	Y	17730 FQ	19700 MW	23180 TQ	USBLS	5/07
Crop, Nursery, and Greenhouse	Oklahoma	Y	13390 FQ	15410 MW	20180 TQ	USBLS	5/07
Crop, Nursery, and Greenhouse	Oklahoma City MSA, OK	Y	17040 FQ	19990 MW	26980 TQ	USBLS	5/07
Crop, Nursery, and Greenhouse	Oregon	H	8.59 FQ	9.10 MW	9.70 TQ	ORBLS	5/08
Crop, Nursery, and Greenhouse	Eugene-Springfield MSA, OR	Y	17170 FQ	18110 MW	19250 TQ	USBLS	5/07
Crop, Nursery, and Greenhouse	Portland-Vancouver-Beaverton MSA, OR-WA	Y	17310 FQ	18500 MW	20270 TQ	USBLS	5/07
Crop, Nursery, and Greenhouse	Pennsylvania	Y	17040 FQ	21080 MW	26860 TQ	USBLS	5/07
Crop, Nursery, and Greenhouse	Allentown-Bethlehem-Easton MSA, PA-NJ	Y	18980 FQ	22270 MW	26740 TQ	USBLS	5/07
Crop, Nursery, and Greenhouse	Philadelphia-Camden-Wilmington MSA, PA-NJ-DE-MD	Y	15230 FQ	18770 MW	25740 TQ	USBLS	5/07
Crop, Nursery, and Greenhouse	Pittsburgh MSA, PA	Y	14900 FQ	19530 MW	23520 TQ	USBLS	5/07
Crop, Nursery, and Greenhouse	Rhode Island	Y	16740 FQ	18890 MW	22540 TQ	USBLS	5/07
Crop, Nursery, and Greenhouse	Providence-Fall River-Warwick MSA, RI-MA	Y	16760 FQ	18930 MW	22640 TQ	USBLS	5/07
Crop, Nursery, and Greenhouse	South Carolina	Y	14780 FQ	17740 MW	22290 TQ	USBLS	5/07
Crop, Nursery, and Greenhouse	Charleston-North Charleston MSA, SC	Y	15040 FQ	17800 MW	19790 TQ	USBLS	5/07
Crop, Nursery, and Greenhouse	Columbia MSA, SC	Y	12890 FQ	14590 MW	18120 TQ	USBLS	5/07
Crop, Nursery, and Greenhouse	Florence MSA, SC	Y	16300 FQ	17500 MW	18710 TQ	USBLS	5/07
Crop, Nursery, and Greenhouse	South Dakota	Y	18014 FQ	20339 MW	24148 TQ	SDBLS	7/08-9/08
Crop, Nursery, and Greenhouse	Sioux Falls MSA, SD	Y	18010 FQ	19757 MW	22785 TQ	SDBLS	7/08-9/08
Crop, Nursery, and Greenhouse	Tennessee	Y	15140 FQ	17850 MW	21160 TQ	USBLS	5/07
Crop, Nursery, and Greenhouse	Memphis MSA, TN-MS-AR	Y	14420 FQ	17130 MW	24370 TQ	USBLS	5/07
Crop, Nursery, and Greenhouse	Nashville-Davidson-Murfreesboro MSA, TN	Y	13850 FQ	17170 MW	23610 TQ	USBLS	5/07
Crop, Nursery, and Greenhouse	Texas	Y	12970 FQ	14790 MW	17650 TQ	USBLS	5/07
Crop, Nursery, and Greenhouse	Austin-Round Rock MSA, TX	Y	13840 FQ	16290 MW	20080 TQ	USBLS	5/07
Crop, Nursery, and Greenhouse	Dallas-Fort Worth-Arlington MSA, TX	Y	13970 FQ	16710 MW	20610 TQ	USBLS	5/07
Crop, Nursery, and Greenhouse	Houston-Sugar Land-Baytown MSA, TX	Y	13450 FQ	15470 MW	18620 TQ	USBLS	5/07
Crop, Nursery, and Greenhouse	San Antonio MSA, TX	Y	14170 FQ	17850 MW	26390 TQ	USBLS	5/07
Crop, Nursery, and Greenhouse	Utah	Y	17650 FQ	21220 MW	25710 TQ	USBLS	5/07
Crop, Nursery, and Greenhouse	Logan MSA, UT-ID	Y	17160 FQ	18990 MW	22770 TQ	USBLS	5/07
Crop, Nursery, and Greenhouse	Salt Lake City MSA, UT	Y	18240 FQ	21320 MW	24300 TQ	USBLS	5/07
Crop, Nursery, and Greenhouse	Vermont	Y	19500 FQ	23140 MW	28250 TQ	USBLS	5/07
Crop, Nursery, and Greenhouse	Burlington-South Burlington MSA, VT	Y	20920 FQ	24510 MW	29340 TQ	USBLS	5/07
Crop, Nursery, and Greenhouse	Virginia	Y	15420 FQ	17910 MW	22310 TQ	USBLS	5/07
Crop, Nursery, and Greenhouse	Richmond MSA, VA	Y	13620 FQ	17620 MW	23620 TQ	USBLS	5/07
Crop, Nursery, and Greenhouse	Virginia Beach-Norfolk-Newport News MSA, VA-NC	Y	13400 FQ	15590 MW	19040 TQ	USBLS	5/07

AE	Average entry wage	AW	Average wage paid	FQ	First quartile wage	LO	Lowest wage paid	MTC Median total compensation TCC Total cash compensation
AER	Average entry range	AWR	Average wage range	H	Hourly	LR	Low end range	MW Median wage paid TQ Third quartile wage
AEX	Average experienced wage	AXR	Average experienced range	HI	Highest wage paid	M	Monthly	MWR Median wage range W Weekly
ATC	Average total compensation	D	Daily	HR	High end range	MCC	Median cash compensation	S See annotated source Y Yearly

Occupation/Type/Industry	Location	Per	Low	Mid	High	Source	Date
Farmworker and Laborer							
Crop, Nursery, and Greenhouse	Washington	H	8.83 FQ	9.89 MW	12.05 TQ	WABLS	3/08
Crop, Nursery, and Greenhouse	Seattle-Tacoma-Bellevue MSA, WA	Y	18310 FQ	22440 MW	28950 TQ	USBLS	5/07
Crop, Nursery, and Greenhouse	Spokane MSA, WA	Y	19970 FQ	21800 MW	23600 TQ	USBLS	5/07
Crop, Nursery, and Greenhouse	West Virginia	Y	16787 FQ	19561 MW	24044 TQ	WVBLS	7/08-9/08
Crop, Nursery, and Greenhouse	Wisconsin	Y	15450 FQ	19030 MW	22900 TQ	USBLS	5/07
Crop, Nursery, and Greenhouse	Milwaukee-Waukesha-West Allis MSA, WI	Y	17480 FQ	20340 MW	24010 TQ	USBLS	5/07
Crop, Nursery, and Greenhouse	Wyoming	Y	14498 FQ	19926 MW	33025 TQ	WYBLS	9/08
Crop, Nursery, and Greenhouse	San Juan-Caguas-Guaynabo MSA, PR	Y	15440 FQ	21430 MW	24670 TQ	USBLS	5/07
Fashion Designer	United States	Y			150000-300000 AXR	WSJ05	2007
	California	H	20.47 FQ	29.80 MW	43.35 TQ	CABLS	1/08-3/08
	Los Angeles-Long Beach-Glendale PMSA, CA	H	20.60 FQ	29.08 MW	45.83 TQ	CABLS	1/08-3/08
	Oakland-Fremont-Hayward MSA, CA	H	22.55 FQ	35.39 MW	50.95 TQ	CABLS	1/08-3/08
	Oxnard-Thousand Oaks-Ventura MSA, CA	H	18.39 FQ	22.86 MW	43.80 TQ	CABLS	1/08-3/08
	Riverside-San Bernardino-Ontario MSA, CA	H	16.53 FQ	18.68 MW	27.43 TQ	CABLS	1/08-3/08
	San Diego-Carlsbad-San Marcos MSA, CA	H	15.40 FQ	27.00 MW	34.27 TQ	CABLS	1/08-3/08
	San Francisco-San Mateo-Redwood PMSA, CA	H	30.86 FQ	37.54 MW	45.99 TQ	CABLS	1/08-3/08
	San Jose-Sunnyvale-Santa Clara MSA, CA	H	26.86 FQ	39.39 MW	44.75 TQ	CABLS	1/08-3/08
	Santa Ana-Anaheim-Irvine PMSA, CA	Y	42440 FQ	62830 MW	81900 TQ	USBLS	5/07
	Colorado	Y	35940 FQ	44740 MW	68280 TQ	USBLS	5/07
	Denver-Aurora MSA, CO	Y	35210 FQ	38730 MW	57710 TQ	USBLS	5/07
	Connecticut	H	20.82 AE	26.79 MW		CTBLS	1/08-3/08
	Bridgeport-Stamford-Norwalk MSA, CT	Y	45300 FQ	52320 MW	79980 TQ	USBLS	5/07
	Florida	Y	31960 FQ	46660 MW	71790 TQ	USBLS	5/07
	Miami-Fort Lauderdale-Miami Beach MSA, FL	Y	37040 FQ	51930 MW	58510 TQ	USBLS	5/07
	Orlando-Kissimmee MSA, FL	Y	30770 FQ	45090 MW	88840 TQ	USBLS	5/07
	Georgia	Y	38570 FQ	48650 MW	66510 TQ	USBLS	5/07
	Atlanta-Sandy Springs-Marietta MSA, GA	Y	35920 FQ	45430 MW	55700 TQ	USBLS	5/07
	Hawaii	Y	22820 FQ	38400 MW	52970 TQ	USBLS	5/07
	Indiana	Y	32350 FQ	36820 MW	47500 TQ	USBLS	5/07
	Kansas	Y	46580 FQ	61010 MW	77480 TQ	USBLS	5/07
	Maine	Y	43760 FQ	71370 MW	90380 TQ	USBLS	5/07
	Portland-South Portland-Biddeford MSA, ME	Y	60720 FQ	78080 MW	92500 TQ	USBLS	5/07
	Maryland	Y		32400 MW		MDBLS	3/08
	Baltimore-Towson MSA, MD	Y	55570 FQ	59570 MW	63660 TQ	USBLS	5/07
	Massachusetts	Y	30450 FQ	47770 MW	70820 TQ	USBLS	5/07
	Boston-Cambridge-Quincy NECTA, MA	Y	39240 FQ	46330 MW	64290 TQ	USBLS	5/07
	Michigan	Y	34730 FQ	45210 MW	59210 TQ	USBLS	5/07
	Detroit-Warren-Livonia MSA, MI	Y	41180 FQ	49650 MW	71620 TQ	USBLS	5/07
	Minnesota	Y	40572 FQ	52750 MW	73371 TQ	MNBLS	10/08-12/08
	Minneapolis-Saint Paul MSA, MN-WI	Y	41692 FQ	53577 MW	74867 TQ	MNBLS	10/08-12/08
	Missouri	Y	43740 FQ	55310 MW	78680 TQ	USBLS	5/07
	St. Louis MSA, MO-IL	Y	44730 FQ	55850 MW	79520 TQ	USBLS	5/07
	New Jersey	Y	40300 FQ	62170 MW	83120 TQ	USBLS	5/07
	Camden PMSA, NJ	Y	42360 FQ	67690 MW	100470 TQ	USBLS	5/07
	Edison PMSA, NJ	Y	39410 FQ	64710 MW	79860 TQ	USBLS	5/07
	Newark-Union PMSA, NJ-PA	Y	58600 FQ	75740 MW	85890 TQ	USBLS	5/07
	New York	Y	52780 FQ	74060 MW	99740 TQ	USBLS	5/07
	Nassau-Suffolk PMSA, NY	Y	48590 FQ	74250 MW	101010 TQ	USBLS	5/07
	New York-Northern New Jersey-Long Island MSA, NY-NJ-PA	Y	52250 FQ	73650 MW	99540 TQ	USBLS	5/07

AE Average entry wage	**AW** Average wage paid	**FQ** First quartile wage	**LO** Lowest wage paid	**MTC** Median total compensation	**TCC** Total cash compensation
AER Average entry range	**AWR** Average wage range	**H** Hourly	**LR** Low end range	**MW** Median wage paid	**TQ** Third quartile wage
AEX Average experienced wage	**AXR** Average experienced range	**HI** Highest wage paid	**M** Monthly	**MWR** Median wage range	**W** Weekly
ATC Average total compensation	**D** Daily	**HR** High end range	**MCC** Median cash compensation	**S** See annotated source	**Y** Yearly

Occupation/Type/Industry	Location	Per	Low	Mid	High	Source	Date
Fashion Designer	North Carolina	Y	32680 FQ	54980 MW	75960 TQ	USBLS	5/07
	Ohio	Y	38260 FQ	50010 MW	70550 TQ	USBLS	5/07
	Columbus MSA, OH	Y	40380 FQ	51530 MW	71730 TQ	USBLS	5/07
	Portland-Vancouver-Beaverton MSA, OR-WA	Y	39370 FQ	47440 MW	59800 TQ	USBLS	5/07
	Pennsylvania	Y	34680 FQ	45920 MW	64570 TQ	USBLS	5/07
	Allentown-Bethlehem-Easton MSA, PA-NJ	Y	41970 FQ	52370 MW	71490 TQ	USBLS	5/07
	Philadelphia-Camden-Wilmington MSA, PA-NJ-DE-MD	Y	35770 FQ	53350 MW	75610 TQ	USBLS	5/07
	Dallas-Fort Worth-Arlington MSA, TX	Y	44690 FQ	73630 MW	98440 TQ	USBLS	5/07
	Virginia	Y	34610 FQ	45530 MW	65460 TQ	USBLS	5/07
	Washington	H	25.04 FQ	32.12 MW	36.00 TQ	WABLS	3/08
	Seattle-Tacoma-Bellevue MSA, WA	Y	51320 FQ	65940 MW	73680 TQ	USBLS	5/07
	Wisconsin	Y	34770 FQ	56990 MW	93690 TQ	USBLS	5/07
Fashion Director	United States	Y		124000 MW		247FASH	2009
Fashion Model							
Top Female	United States	D		10000 AW		ASKM	2008
Top Male	United States	D		2500 AW		ASKM	2008
Feature Animation Editor	West Coast	W			1578 HI	MPEG03	8/3/08-7/31/09
Fence Erector	Alabama	Y	18750 FQ	21250 MW	24170 TQ	USBLS	5/07
	Alaska	Y	25550 FQ	29910 MW	40620 TQ	USBLS	5/07
	Arizona	Y	20340 FQ	25320 MW	30350 TQ	USBLS	5/07
	Arkansas	Y	17900 FQ	24100 MW	32660 TQ	USBLS	5/07
	California	H	12.65 FQ	15.70 MW	20.96 TQ	CABLS	1/08-3/08
	Colorado	Y	27660 FQ	31400 MW	39580 TQ	USBLS	5/07
	Connecticut	H	12.07 AE	15.01 MW		CTBLS	1/08-3/08
	Florida	Y	21950 FQ	27140 MW	32250 TQ	USBLS	5/07
	Georgia	Y	20280 FQ	22410 MW	24660 TQ	USBLS	5/07
	Hawaii	Y	20780 FQ	22370 MW	23970 TQ	USBLS	5/07
	Idaho	Y	17310 FQ	21600 MW	28900 TQ	USBLS	5/07
	Illinois	Y	20280 FQ	29350 MW	54250 TQ	USBLS	5/07
	Indiana	Y	21430 FQ	24230 MW	29130 TQ	USBLS	5/07
	Iowa	Y	23470 FQ	28290 MW	34380 TQ	USBLS	5/07
	Kansas	Y	19140 FQ	24510 MW	29490 TQ	USBLS	5/07
	Kentucky	Y	21998 FQ	25300 MW	30049 TQ	KYBLS	2008
	Louisiana	H	8.46 FQ	10.66 MW	12.88 TQ	LABLS	1/08-3/08
	Maine	Y	26150 FQ	30280 MW	35910 TQ	USBLS	5/07
	Maryland	Y		31425 MW		MDBLS	3/08
	Massachusetts	Y	23860 FQ	32310 MW	39630 TQ	USBLS	5/07
	Michigan	Y	23370 FQ	28730 MW	36880 TQ	USBLS	5/07
	Minnesota	Y	26504 FQ	30267 MW	38845 TQ	MNBLS	10/08-12/08
	Mississippi	Y	15990 FQ	19690 MW	23900 TQ	USBLS	5/07
	Missouri	Y	22450 FQ	26600 MW	31950 TQ	USBLS	5/07
	Montana	Y	22520 FQ	25490 MW	29030 TQ	USBLS	5/07
	Nebraska	Y	20770 FQ	27740 MW	33340 TQ	USBLS	5/07
	Nevada	H	11.09 FQ	13.52 MW	15.35 TQ	NVBLS	5/08
	New Hampshire	H	11.30 AE	13.92 MW	15.39 AEX	NHBLS	6/08
	New Jersey	Y	22670 FQ	27030 MW	36610 TQ	USBLS	5/07
	New Mexico	Y	16660 FQ	18190 MW	25110 TQ	USBLS	5/07
	New York	Y	23200 FQ	28730 MW	37700 TQ	USBLS	5/07
	North Carolina	Y	21180 FQ	23780 MW	27680 TQ	USBLS	5/07
	North Dakota	Y	23080 FQ	27710 MW	35740 TQ	USBLS	5/07
	Ohio	Y	22720 FQ	27020 MW	31670 TQ	USBLS	5/07
	Oklahoma	Y	20570 FQ	22360 MW	24210 TQ	USBLS	5/07
	Oregon	H	12.12 FQ	14.58 MW	17.36 TQ	ORBLS	5/08
	Pennsylvania	Y	27100 FQ	31470 MW	38620 TQ	USBLS	5/07
	Rhode Island	Y	19420 FQ	24040 MW	29760 TQ	USBLS	5/07
	South Carolina	Y	20220 FQ	23780 MW	28390 TQ	USBLS	5/07
	South Dakota	Y	26763 FQ	30604 MW	33364 TQ	SDBLS	7/08-9/08
	Tennessee	Y	20540 FQ	24460 MW	30280 TQ	USBLS	5/07
	Texas	Y	17020 FQ	20430 MW	24790 TQ	USBLS	5/07
	Utah	Y	19340 FQ	23660 MW	28280 TQ	USBLS	5/07
	Vermont	Y	24300 FQ	28130 MW	31540 TQ	USBLS	5/07
	Virginia	Y	21400 FQ	26420 MW	30160 TQ	USBLS	5/07
	Washington	H	11.41 FQ	15.40 MW	19.20 TQ	WABLS	3/08

Occupation/Type/Industry	Location	Per	Low	Mid	High	Source	Date
Fence Erector	West Virginia	Y	24860 FQ	28565 MW	31452 TQ	WVBLS	7/08-9/08
	Wisconsin	Y	22500 FQ	27110 MW	33900 TQ	USBLS	5/07
	Wyoming	Y	27535 FQ	29844 MW	32162 TQ	WYBLS	9/08
Fiberglass Boat Builder	Rhode Island	H		15.09 MW		RIM01	2009
Fiberglass Laminator and Fabricator	Alabama	Y	20550 FQ	25630 MW	34480 TQ	USBLS	5/07
	Birmingham-Hoover MSA, AL	Y	18560 FQ	33720 MW	37170 TQ	USBLS	5/07
	Alaska	Y	26660 FQ	42820 MW	52590 TQ	USBLS	5/07
	Arizona	Y	18480 FQ	23420 MW	32620 TQ	USBLS	5/07
	Phoenix-Mesa-Scottsdale MSA, AZ	Y	18140 FQ	23040 MW	32430 TQ	USBLS	5/07
	Arkansas	Y	19700 FQ	22570 MW	25710 TQ	USBLS	5/07
	Little Rock-North Little Rock MSA, AR	Y	21610 FQ	24530 MW	28180 TQ	USBLS	5/07
	California	H	11.01 FQ	13.41 MW	16.00 TQ	CABLS	1/08-3/08
	Los Angeles-Long Beach-Glendale PMSA, CA	H	10.81 FQ	12.21 MW	15.33 TQ	CABLS	1/08-3/08
	Riverside-San Bernardino-Ontario MSA, CA	H	10.38 FQ	11.63 MW	13.82 TQ	CABLS	1/08-3/08
	Sacramento-Arden Arcade-Roseville MSA, CA	H	10.10 FQ	13.23 MW	16.00 TQ	CABLS	1/08-3/08
	San Diego-Carlsbad-San Marcos MSA, CA	H	13.22 FQ	15.16 MW	17.58 TQ	CABLS	1/08-3/08
	San Jose-Sunnyvale-Santa Clara MSA, CA	H	11.33 FQ	13.27 MW	14.88 TQ	CABLS	1/08-3/08
	Santa Ana-Anaheim-Irvine PMSA, CA	Y	21230 FQ	26680 MW	30340 TQ	USBLS	5/07
	Connecticut	H	10.84 AE	13.33 MW		CTBLS	1/08-3/08
	Wilmington PMSA, DE-MD-NJ	Y	26970 FQ	30640 MW	37820 TQ	USBLS	5/07
	Washington-Arlington-Alexandria MSA, DC-VA-MD-WV	Y	30660 FQ	33550 MW	36500 TQ	USBLS	5/07
	Florida	Y	22560 FQ	27880 MW	33450 TQ	USBLS	5/07
	Fort Lauderdale-Pompano Beach-Deerfield Beach PMSA, FL	Y	26650 FQ	30740 MW	35460 TQ	USBLS	5/07
	Jacksonville MSA, FL	Y	22380 FQ	24560 MW	28050 TQ	USBLS	5/07
	Lakeland MSA, FL	Y	25740 FQ	30460 MW	35770 TQ	USBLS	5/07
	Miami-Fort Lauderdale-Miami Beach MSA, FL	Y	21740 FQ	27150 MW	33870 TQ	USBLS	5/07
	Orlando-Kissimmee MSA, FL	Y	25420 FQ	29440 MW	34390 TQ	USBLS	5/07
	Tampa-St. Petersburg-Clearwater MSA, FL	Y	20170 FQ	26280 MW	31390 TQ	USBLS	5/07
	West Palm Beach-Boca Raton-Boynton Beach PMSA, FL	Y	26640 FQ	34370 MW	43080 TQ	USBLS	5/07
	Georgia	Y	20180 FQ	25720 MW	32150 TQ	USBLS	5/07
	Atlanta-Sandy Springs-Marietta MSA, GA	Y	26190 FQ	29920 MW	34940 TQ	USBLS	5/07
	Idaho	Y	19460 FQ	22170 MW	25990 TQ	USBLS	5/07
	Illinois	Y	22770 FQ	28500 MW	35300 TQ	USBLS	5/07
	Indiana	Y	23130 FQ	27610 MW	34090 TQ	USBLS	5/07
	Elkhart-Goshen MSA, IN	Y	20580 FQ	25660 MW	31520 TQ	USBLS	5/07
	Indianapolis-Carmel MSA, IN	Y	24800 FQ	28990 MW	34860 TQ	USBLS	5/07
	Iowa	Y	19150 FQ	24560 MW	28610 TQ	USBLS	5/07
	Des Moines-West Des Moines MSA, IA	Y	23470 FQ	25430 MW	28480 TQ	USBLS	5/07
	Kansas	Y	24240 FQ	28500 MW	35300 TQ	USBLS	5/07
	Wichita MSA, KS	Y	31840 FQ	37980 MW	45070 TQ	USBLS	5/07
	Kentucky	Y	22982 FQ	28097 MW	33467 TQ	KYBLS	2008
	Louisville-Jefferson County MSA, KY-IN	Y	25320 FQ	27810 MW	32940 TQ	USBLS	5/07
	Louisiana	H	11.51 FQ	13.15 MW	14.67 TQ	LABLS	1/08-3/08
	Baton Rouge MSA, LA	Y	22630 FQ	28050 MW	31600 TQ	USBLS	5/07
	New Orleans-Metairie-Kenner MSA, LA	Y	23270 FQ	27300 MW	30680 TQ	USBLS	5/07
	Maine	Y	28310 FQ	33960 MW	37560 TQ	USBLS	5/07
	Portland-South Portland-Biddeford MSA, ME	Y	26600 FQ	29050 MW	31490 TQ	USBLS	5/07
	Maryland	Y		24100 MW		MDBLS	3/08

AE	Average entry wage	**AW**	Average wage paid	**FQ**	First quartile wage	**LO** Lowest wage paid	**MTC** Median total compensation	**TCC** Total cash compensation
AER	Average entry range	**AWR**	Average wage range	**H**	Hourly	**LR** Low end range	**MW** Median wage paid	**TQ** Third quartile wage
AEX	Average experienced wage	**AXR**	Average experienced range	**HI**	Highest wage paid	**M** Monthly	**MWR** Median wage range	**W** Weekly
ATC	Average total compensation	**D**	Daily	**HR**	High end range	**MCC** Median cash compensation	**S** See annotated source	**Y** Yearly

Occupation/Type/Industry	Location	Per	Low	Mid	High	Source	Date
Fiberglass Laminator and Fabricator							
	Massachusetts	Y	27260 FQ	30540 MW	35180 TQ	USBLS	5/07
	Michigan	Y	25620 FQ	28070 MW	30860 TQ	USBLS	5/07
	Detroit-Warren-Livonia MSA, MI	Y	23670 FQ	26560 MW	30370 TQ	USBLS	5/07
	Grand Rapids-Wyoming MSA, MI	Y	26530 FQ	29510 MW	35360 TQ	USBLS	5/07
	Warren-Troy-Farmington Hills PMSA, MI	Y	23730 FQ	26470 MW	29980 TQ	USBLS	5/07
	Minnesota	Y	22464 FQ	27223 MW	32282 TQ	MNBLS	10/08-12/08
	Minneapolis-Saint Paul MSA, MN-WI	Y	21003 FQ	24320 MW	30094 TQ	MNBLS	10/08-12/08
	Mississippi	Y	18750 FQ	22230 MW	26970 TQ	USBLS	5/07
	Missouri	Y	18240 FQ	21420 MW	25430 TQ	USBLS	5/07
	Kansas City MSA, MO-KS	Y	17940 FQ	19830 MW	33170 TQ	USBLS	5/07
	St. Louis MSA, MO-IL	Y	19750 FQ	22830 MW	28100 TQ	USBLS	5/07
	Nebraska	Y	24310 FQ	27170 MW	30330 TQ	USBLS	5/07
	Omaha-Council Bluffs MSA, NE-IA	Y	25130 FQ	27300 MW	29650 TQ	USBLS	5/07
	Nevada	H	12.14 FQ	14.92 MW	17.80 TQ	NVBLS	5/08
	Las Vegas-Paradise MSA, NV	H	11.95 FQ	15.72 MW	17.92 TQ	NVBLS	5/08
	New Hampshire	H	15.24 AE	16.33 MW	16.51 AEX	NHBLS	6/08
	New Jersey	Y	25100 FQ	32210 MW	37150 TQ	USBLS	5/07
	Edison PMSA, NJ	Y	22530 FQ	26670 MW	33840 TQ	USBLS	5/07
	New Mexico	Y	28650 FQ	38050 MW	42280 TQ	USBLS	5/07
	New York	Y	19180 FQ	23130 MW	27540 TQ	USBLS	5/07
	Buffalo-Niagara Falls MSA, NY	Y	19310 FQ	22990 MW	27490 TQ	USBLS	5/07
	Nassau-Suffolk PMSA, NY	Y	16880 FQ	21160 MW	25880 TQ	USBLS	5/07
	New York-Northern New Jersey-Long Island MSA, NY-NJ-PA	Y	19580 FQ	24200 MW	31020 TQ	USBLS	5/07
	North Carolina	Y	20910 FQ	25270 MW	29720 TQ	USBLS	5/07
	North Dakota	Y	25920 FQ	28260 MW	30620 TQ	USBLS	5/07
	Ohio	Y	22610 FQ	26590 MW	30380 TQ	USBLS	5/07
	Cincinnati-Middletown MSA, OH-KY-IN	Y	24260 FQ	27170 MW	31020 TQ	USBLS	5/07
	Cleveland-Elyria-Mentor MSA, OH	Y	21450 FQ	25820 MW	29940 TQ	USBLS	5/07
	Oklahoma	Y	17390 FQ	21740 MW	28280 TQ	USBLS	5/07
	Oklahoma City MSA, OK	Y	20080 FQ	26360 MW	31730 TQ	USBLS	5/07
	Tulsa MSA, OK	Y	21290 FQ	24200 MW	36470 TQ	USBLS	5/07
	Oregon	H	10.96 FQ	13.01 MW	15.03 TQ	ORBLS	5/08
	Portland-Vancouver-Beaverton MSA, OR-WA	Y	23250 FQ	28140 MW	34710 TQ	USBLS	5/07
	Pennsylvania	Y	21090 FQ	25050 MW	30580 TQ	USBLS	5/07
	Philadelphia-Camden-Wilmington MSA, PA-NJ-DE-MD	Y	28290 FQ	33800 MW	38110 TQ	USBLS	5/07
	Pittsburgh MSA, PA	Y	20260 FQ	24050 MW	28320 TQ	USBLS	5/07
	Rhode Island	Y	26290 FQ	31390 MW	38680 TQ	USBLS	5/07
	Providence-Fall River-Warwick MSA, RI-MA	Y	26830 FQ	30160 MW	35560 TQ	USBLS	5/07
	South Carolina	Y	22270 FQ	25990 MW	29900 TQ	USBLS	5/07
	Charleston-North Charleston MSA, SC	Y	21070 FQ	23830 MW	28220 TQ	USBLS	5/07
	Columbia MSA, SC	Y	22640 FQ	26830 MW	30560 TQ	USBLS	5/07
	Tennessee	Y	24040 FQ	26670 MW	29040 TQ	USBLS	5/07
	Memphis MSA, TN-MS-AR	Y	19030 FQ	23430 MW	31480 TQ	USBLS	5/07
	Nashville-Davidson-Murfreesboro MSA, TN	Y	23230 FQ	26590 MW	30010 TQ	USBLS	5/07
	Texas	Y	20660 FQ	24660 MW	32580 TQ	USBLS	5/07
	Houston-Sugar Land-Baytown MSA, TX	Y	22170 FQ	25460 MW	30260 TQ	USBLS	5/07
	San Antonio MSA, TX	Y	20110 FQ	22430 MW	24700 TQ	USBLS	5/07
	Utah	Y	14330 FQ	21590 MW	28580 TQ	USBLS	5/07
	Salt Lake City MSA, UT	Y	21760 FQ	24960 MW	31060 TQ	USBLS	5/07
	Washington	H	12.45 FQ	14.51 MW	16.89 TQ	WABLS	3/08
	Seattle-Tacoma-Bellevue MSA, WA	Y	25960 FQ	30050 MW	34950 TQ	USBLS	5/07
	Wisconsin	Y	23250 FQ	27510 MW	33680 TQ	USBLS	5/07

AE	Average entry wage	AW	Average wage paid	FQ	First quartile wage	LO	Lowest wage paid
AER	Average entry range	AWR	Average wage range	H	Hourly	LR	Low end range
AEX	Average experienced wage	AXR	Average experienced range	HI	Highest wage paid	M	Monthly
ATC	Average total compensation	D	Daily	HR	High end range	MCC	Median cash compensation

MTC	Median total compensation	TCC	Total cash compensation
MW	Median wage paid	TQ	Third quartile wage
MWR	Median wage range	W	Weekly
S	See annotated source	Y	Yearly

Occupation/Type/Industry	Location	Per	Low	Mid	High	Source	Date
Fiberglass Laminator and Fabricator	Milwaukee-Waukesha-West Allis MSA, WI	Y	22160 FQ	24500 MW	29560 TQ	USBLS	5/07
Field Support Technician	United States	Y		60000 MW		ASP01	2008
File Clerk	Alabama	Y	14840 FQ	18770 MW	24140 TQ	USBLS	5/07
	Birmingham-Hoover MSA, AL	Y	16300 FQ	21720 MW	28360 TQ	USBLS	5/07
	Alaska	Y	23810 FQ	27930 MW	31530 TQ	USBLS	5/07
	Anchorage MSA, AK	Y	24650 FQ	28370 MW	32000 TQ	USBLS	5/07
	Fairbanks MSA, AK	Y	21200 FQ	23810 MW	33240 TQ	USBLS	5/07
	Arizona	Y	16950 FQ	19450 MW	24910 TQ	USBLS	5/07
	Phoenix-Mesa-Scottsdale MSA, AZ	Y	16940 FQ	19400 MW	24960 TQ	USBLS	5/07
	Tucson MSA, AZ	Y	18520 FQ	22970 MW	32690 TQ	USBLS	5/07
	Arkansas	Y	16420 FQ	18540 MW	21810 TQ	USBLS	5/07
	Little Rock-North Little Rock MSA, AR	Y	16660 FQ	18760 MW	22490 TQ	USBLS	5/07
	California	H	9.78 FQ	12.18 MW	15.27 TQ	CABLS	1/08-3/08
	Los Angeles-Long Beach-Glendale PMSA, CA	H	10.04 FQ	12.26 MW	15.07 TQ	CABLS	1/08-3/08
	Oakland-Fremont-Hayward MSA, CA	H	11.57 FQ	14.20 MW	18.13 TQ	CABLS	1/08-3/08
	Riverside-San Bernardino-Ontario MSA, CA	H	8.37 FQ	9.76 MW	12.01 TQ	CABLS	1/08-3/08
	Sacramento-Arden Arcade-Roseville MSA, CA	H	10.43 FQ	12.96 MW	16.52 TQ	CABLS	1/08-3/08
	San Diego-Carlsbad-San Marcos MSA, CA	H	10.21 FQ	12.77 MW	15.04 TQ	CABLS	1/08-3/08
	San Francisco-San Mateo-Redwood PMSA, CA	H	12.80 FQ	15.85 MW	19.14 TQ	CABLS	1/08-3/08
	San Jose-Sunnyvale-Santa Clara MSA, CA	H	12.07 FQ	14.80 MW	18.77 TQ	CABLS	1/08-3/08
	Santa Ana-Anaheim-Irvine PMSA, CA	Y	19340 FQ	23280 MW	28370 TQ	USBLS	5/07
	Colorado	Y	21810 FQ	26810 MW	32150 TQ	USBLS	5/07
	Boulder MSA, CO	Y	22450 FQ	25940 MW	35200 TQ	USBLS	5/07
	Denver-Aurora MSA, CO	Y	23330 FQ	28290 MW	33400 TQ	USBLS	5/07
	Connecticut	H	9.03 AE	12.22 MW		CTBLS	1/08-3/08
	Bridgeport-Stamford-Norwalk MSA, CT	Y	20050 FQ	26430 MW	32410 TQ	USBLS	5/07
	Hartford-West Hartford-East Hartford MSA, CT	Y	19250 FQ	23850 MW	29740 TQ	USBLS	5/07
	Delaware	Y	21270 FQ	26330 MW	31510 TQ	USBLS	5/07
	Dover MSA, DE	Y	20360 FQ	25540 MW	29970 TQ	USBLS	5/07
	Wilmington PMSA, DE-MD-NJ	Y	21350 FQ	26390 MW	31620 TQ	USBLS	5/07
	District of Columbia	Y	27250 FQ	33660 MW	38720 TQ	USBLS	5/07
	Washington-Arlington-Alexandria MSA, DC-VA-MD-WV	Y	22010 FQ	27370 MW	34750 TQ	USBLS	5/07
	Florida	Y	19790 FQ	23300 MW	28510 TQ	USBLS	5/07
	Fort Lauderdale-Pompano Beach-Deerfield Beach PMSA, FL	Y	19840 FQ	23000 MW	28280 TQ	USBLS	5/07
	Jacksonville MSA, FL	Y	20640 FQ	23610 MW	27600 TQ	USBLS	5/07
	Miami-Fort Lauderdale-Miami Beach MSA, FL	Y	20530 FQ	24390 MW	31210 TQ	USBLS	5/07
	Orlando-Kissimmee MSA, FL	Y	19880 FQ	23100 MW	27570 TQ	USBLS	5/07
	Tampa-St. Petersburg-Clearwater MSA, FL	Y	19370 FQ	23470 MW	29170 TQ	USBLS	5/07
	West Palm Beach-Boca Raton-Boynton Beach PMSA, FL	Y	20120 FQ	23540 MW	29100 TQ	USBLS	5/07
	Georgia	Y	17880 FQ	22210 MW	27150 TQ	USBLS	5/07
	Atlanta-Sandy Springs-Marietta MSA, GA	Y	21280 FQ	24710 MW	29610 TQ	USBLS	5/07
	Hawaii	Y	18040 FQ	22500 MW	28420 TQ	USBLS	5/07
	Honolulu MSA, HI	Y	18000 FQ	22380 MW	28600 TQ	USBLS	5/07
	Idaho	Y	21340 FQ	26850 MW	32050 TQ	USBLS	5/07
	Boise City-Nampa MSA, ID	Y	24070 FQ	29220 MW	34320 TQ	USBLS	5/07
	Lewiston MSA, ID-WA	Y	18670 FQ	26960 MW	30560 TQ	USBLS	5/07
	Illinois	Y	18380 FQ	22650 MW	28650 TQ	USBLS	5/07

AE Average entry wage	**AW** Average wage paid	**FQ** First quartile wage	**LO** Lowest wage paid	**MTC** Median total compensation	**TCC** Total cash compensation
AER Average entry range	**AWR** Average wage range	**H** Hourly	**LR** Low end range	**MW** Median wage paid	**TQ** Third quartile wage
AEX Average experienced wage	**AXR** Average experienced range	**HI** Highest wage paid	**M** Monthly	**MWR** Median wage range	**W** Weekly
ATC Average total compensation	**D** Daily	**HR** High end range	**MCC** Median cash compensation	**S** See annotated source	**Y** Yearly

Occupation/Type/Industry	Location	Per	Low	Mid	High	Source	Date
File Clerk	Chicago-Naperville-Joliet MSA, IL-IN-WI	Y	19530 FQ	23980 MW	30320 TQ	USBLS	5/07
	Indiana	Y	18080 FQ	22100 MW	26210 TQ	USBLS	5/07
	Gary PMSA, IN	Y	14590 FQ	18950 MW	23850 TQ	USBLS	5/07
	Indianapolis-Carmel MSA, IN	Y	21130 FQ	23840 MW	27780 TQ	USBLS	5/07
	Iowa	Y	18050 FQ	21980 MW	26850 TQ	USBLS	5/07
	Des Moines-West Des Moines MSA, IA	Y	19730 FQ	22790 MW	26340 TQ	USBLS	5/07
	Kansas	Y	17250 FQ	21180 MW	25860 TQ	USBLS	5/07
	Wichita MSA, KS	Y	16750 FQ	20150 MW	24200 TQ	USBLS	5/07
	Kentucky	Y	17223 FQ	21109 MW	25836 TQ	KYBLS	2008
	Louisville-Jefferson County MSA, KY-IN	Y	16920 FQ	20750 MW	25520 TQ	USBLS	5/07
	Louisiana	H	7.41 FQ	8.84 MW	10.72 TQ	LABLS	1/08-3/08
	Baton Rouge MSA, LA	Y	15570 FQ	17720 MW	19950 TQ	USBLS	5/07
	Lafayette MSA, LA	Y	13530 FQ	15970 MW	19060 TQ	USBLS	5/07
	New Orleans-Metairie-Kenner MSA, LA	Y	17460 FQ	20840 MW	24420 TQ	USBLS	5/07
	Maine	Y	20000 FQ	23030 MW	27030 TQ	USBLS	5/07
	Portland-South Portland-Biddeford MSA, ME	Y	21350 FQ	24830 MW	29290 TQ	USBLS	5/07
	Maryland	Y		27375 MW		MDBLS	3/08
	Baltimore-Towson MSA, MD	Y	22230 FQ	28610 MW	35210 TQ	USBLS	5/07
	Bethesda-Gaithersburg-Frederick PMSA, MD	Y	23600 FQ	29980 MW	36680 TQ	USBLS	5/07
	Cumberland MSA, MD-WV	Y	16400 FQ	19420 MW	22640 TQ	USBLS	5/07
	Massachusetts	Y	19910 FQ	24170 MW	29740 TQ	USBLS	5/07
	Boston-Cambridge-Quincy NECTA, MA	Y	20830 FQ	24390 MW	29650 TQ	USBLS	5/07
	Worcester MSA, MA-CT	Y	22430 FQ	27530 MW	33950 TQ	USBLS	5/07
	Michigan	Y	18550 FQ	22190 MW	26770 TQ	USBLS	5/07
	Detroit-Warren-Livonia MSA, MI	Y	18900 FQ	22830 MW	27590 TQ	USBLS	5/07
	Grand Rapids-Wyoming MSA, MI	Y	20200 FQ	23140 MW	27100 TQ	USBLS	5/07
	Warren-Troy-Farmington Hills PMSA, MI	Y	18230 FQ	22090 MW	26650 TQ	USBLS	5/07
	Minnesota	Y	22189 FQ	26457 MW	31327 TQ	MNBLS	10/08-12/08
	Duluth-Superior MSA, MN-WI	Y	22158 FQ	25426 MW	31109 TQ	MNBLS	10/08-12/08
	Minneapolis-Saint Paul MSA, MN-WI	Y	22887 FQ	26987 MW	31962 TQ	MNBLS	10/08-12/08
	Rochester MSA, MN	Y	26896 FQ	29612 MW	32429 TQ	MNBLS	10/08-12/08
	Mississippi	Y	15240 FQ	18750 MW	22650 TQ	USBLS	5/07
	Jackson MSA, MS	Y	16270 FQ	20540 MW	24020 TQ	USBLS	5/07
	Missouri	Y	19450 FQ	23800 MW	31380 TQ	USBLS	5/07
	Kansas City MSA, MO-KS	Y	21940 FQ	26420 MW	32090 TQ	USBLS	5/07
	St. Louis MSA, MO-IL	Y	20040 FQ	24400 MW	33410 TQ	USBLS	5/07
	Montana	Y	15120 FQ	18730 MW	23230 TQ	USBLS	5/07
	Billings MSA, MT	Y	20070 FQ	21850 MW	23520 TQ	USBLS	5/07
	Nebraska	Y	18480 FQ	21670 MW	25940 TQ	USBLS	5/07
	Omaha-Council Bluffs MSA, NE-IA	Y	19110 FQ	22760 MW	27790 TQ	USBLS	5/07
	Nevada	H	9.40 FQ	11.34 MW	13.62 TQ	NVBLS	5/08
	Las Vegas-Paradise MSA, NV	H	9.61 FQ	11.31 MW	13.20 TQ	NVBLS	5/08
	Reno-Sparks MSA, NV	H	9.89 FQ	12.06 MW	17.21 TQ	NVBLS	5/08
	New Hampshire	H	8.80 AE	10.96 MW	12.71 AEX	NHBLS	6/08
	Manchester MSA, NH	Y	18270 FQ	20640 MW	23630 TQ	USBLS	5/07
	Nashua NECTA, NH-MA	Y	21250 FQ	23920 MW	27970 TQ	USBLS	5/07
	New Jersey	Y	18990 FQ	23370 MW	28870 TQ	USBLS	5/07
	Camden PMSA, NJ	Y	20130 FQ	23570 MW	27830 TQ	USBLS	5/07
	Edison PMSA, NJ	Y	19380 FQ	23260 MW	29190 TQ	USBLS	5/07
	Newark-Union PMSA, NJ-PA	Y	19510 FQ	23590 MW	28770 TQ	USBLS	5/07
	New Mexico	Y	16950 FQ	20910 MW	24530 TQ	USBLS	5/07
	Albuquerque MSA, NM	Y	17100 FQ	21630 MW	24960 TQ	USBLS	5/07
	New York	Y	19630 FQ	24480 MW	31360 TQ	USBLS	5/07
	Albany-Schenectady-Troy MSA, NY	Y	16920 FQ	20930 MW	26530 TQ	USBLS	5/07
	Buffalo-Niagara Falls MSA, NY	Y	19310 FQ	23110 MW	28660 TQ	USBLS	5/07
	Glens Falls MSA, NY	Y	18630 FQ	20930 MW	23490 TQ	USBLS	5/07
	Nassau-Suffolk PMSA, NY	Y	19020 FQ	22890 MW	27620 TQ	USBLS	5/07

AE	Average entry wage	AW	Average wage paid	FQ	First quartile wage	LO	Lowest wage paid	MTC	Median total compensation	TCC	Total cash compensation
AER	Average entry range	AWR	Average wage range	H	Hourly	LR	Low end range	MW	Median wage paid	TQ	Third quartile wage
AEX	Average experienced wage	AXR	Average experienced range	HI	Highest wage paid	M	Monthly	MWR	Median wage range	W	Weekly
ATC	Average total compensation	D	Daily	HR	High end range	MCC	Median cash compensation	S	See annotated source	Y	Yearly

Occupation/Type/Industry	Location	Per	Low	Mid	High	Source	Date
File Clerk	New York-Northern New Jersey-Long Island MSA, NY-NJ-PA	Y	19950 FQ	24960 MW	31470 TQ	USBLS	5/07
	Syracuse MSA, NY	Y	17540 FQ	21770 MW	26460 TQ	USBLS	5/07
	North Carolina	Y	18030 FQ	22140 MW	26080 TQ	USBLS	5/07
	Charlotte-Gastonia-Concord MSA, NC-SC	Y	18220 FQ	23070 MW	28090 TQ	USBLS	5/07
	Raleigh-Cary MSA, NC	Y	20600 FQ	23460 MW	28090 TQ	USBLS	5/07
	North Dakota	Y	17620 FQ	20650 MW	24360 TQ	USBLS	5/07
	Fargo MSA, ND-MN	Y	19920 FQ	23720 MW	28400 TQ	USBLS	5/07
	Ohio	Y	18740 FQ	23040 MW	28550 TQ	USBLS	5/07
	Cincinnati-Middletown MSA, OH-KY-IN	Y	19910 FQ	25090 MW	30280 TQ	USBLS	5/07
	Cleveland-Elyria-Mentor MSA, OH	Y	20510 FQ	23690 MW	28430 TQ	USBLS	5/07
	Columbus MSA, OH	Y	20980 FQ	24740 MW	30160 TQ	USBLS	5/07
	Dayton MSA, OH	Y	19380 FQ	23220 MW	29040 TQ	USBLS	5/07
	Mansfield MSA, OH	Y	16270 FQ	20950 MW	27510 TQ	USBLS	5/07
	Oklahoma	Y	16360 FQ	19830 MW	24450 TQ	USBLS	5/07
	Oklahoma City MSA, OK	Y	16100 FQ	21060 MW	26170 TQ	USBLS	5/07
	Tulsa MSA, OK	Y	18070 FQ	21490 MW	25070 TQ	USBLS	5/07
	Oregon	H	10.06 FQ	12.18 MW	14.89 TQ	ORBLS	5/08
	Portland-Vancouver-Beaverton MSA, OR-WA	Y	22020 FQ	26470 MW	31520 TQ	USBLS	5/07
	Pennsylvania	Y	18400 FQ	22370 MW	27370 TQ	USBLS	5/07
	Allentown-Bethlehem-Easton MSA, PA-NJ	Y	17890 FQ	21380 MW	24540 TQ	USBLS	5/07
	Philadelphia-Camden-Wilmington MSA, PA-NJ-DE-MD	Y	19330 FQ	23380 MW	28430 TQ	USBLS	5/07
	Pittsburgh MSA, PA	Y	19390 FQ	22870 MW	27270 TQ	USBLS	5/07
	Rhode Island	Y	22270 FQ	26870 MW	35380 TQ	USBLS	5/07
	Providence-Fall River-Warwick MSA, RI-MA	Y	19300 FQ	24780 MW	32040 TQ	USBLS	5/07
	South Carolina	Y	14090 FQ	17580 MW	22340 TQ	USBLS	5/07
	Charleston-North Charleston MSA, SC	Y	12770 FQ	14010 MW	15680 TQ	USBLS	5/07
	Columbia MSA, SC	Y	17090 FQ	20070 MW	24240 TQ	USBLS	5/07
	South Dakota	Y	18540 FQ	21524 MW	24457 TQ	SDBLS	7/08-9/08
	Sioux Falls MSA, SD	Y	19465 FQ	22758 MW	25168 TQ	SDBLS	7/08-9/08
	Tennessee	Y	17280 FQ	20570 MW	24510 TQ	USBLS	5/07
	Memphis MSA, TN-MS-AR	Y	17670 FQ	20630 MW	24450 TQ	USBLS	5/07
	Nashville-Davidson-Murfreesboro MSA, TN	Y	19310 FQ	22470 MW	25900 TQ	USBLS	5/07
	Texas	Y	17710 FQ	22170 MW	28020 TQ	USBLS	5/07
	Austin-Round Rock MSA, TX	Y	18780 FQ	23080 MW	28600 TQ	USBLS	5/07
	Brownsville-Harlingen MSA, TX	Y	13960 FQ	17140 MW	21000 TQ	USBLS	5/07
	Dallas-Fort Worth-Arlington MSA, TX	Y	20310 FQ	25000 MW	32250 TQ	USBLS	5/07
	El Paso MSA, TX	Y	15040 FQ	18310 MW	23590 TQ	USBLS	5/07
	Houston-Sugar Land-Baytown MSA, TX	Y	18830 FQ	22130 MW	27660 TQ	USBLS	5/07
	San Antonio MSA, TX	Y	18040 FQ	22050 MW	28600 TQ	USBLS	5/07
	Utah	Y	19580 FQ	23230 MW	27790 TQ	USBLS	5/07
	St. George MSA, UT	Y	21880 FQ	26140 MW	29380 TQ	USBLS	5/07
	Salt Lake City MSA, UT	Y	21300 FQ	24480 MW	29490 TQ	USBLS	5/07
	Vermont	Y	19640 FQ	23420 MW	27810 TQ	USBLS	5/07
	Burlington-South Burlington MSA, VT	Y	21410 FQ	25080 MW	28500 TQ	USBLS	5/07
	Virginia	Y	19710 FQ	23570 MW	28910 TQ	USBLS	5/07
	Richmond MSA, VA	Y	22050 FQ	25710 MW	30130 TQ	USBLS	5/07
	Virginia Beach-Norfolk-Newport News MSA, VA-NC	Y	18280 FQ	21600 MW	24680 TQ	USBLS	5/07
	Washington	H	10.13 FQ	11.95 MW	14.27 TQ	WABLS	3/08
	Seattle-Tacoma-Bellevue MSA, WA	Y	22450 FQ	26510 MW	30820 TQ	USBLS	5/07
	West Virginia	Y	16961 FQ	19918 MW	26925 TQ	WVBLS	7/08-9/08
	Charleston MSA, WV	Y	17130 FQ	19940 MW	24850 TQ	USBLS	5/07
	Wisconsin	Y	20650 FQ	24260 MW	28930 TQ	USBLS	5/07
	Milwaukee-Waukesha-West Allis MSA, WI	Y	20970 FQ	24310 MW	28880 TQ	USBLS	5/07

AE Average entry wage	**AW** Average wage paid	**FQ** First quartile wage	**LO** Lowest wage paid	**MTC** Median total compensation	**TCC** Total cash compensation
AER Average entry range	**AWR** Average wage range	**H** Hourly	**LR** Low end range	**MW** Median wage paid	**TQ** Third quartile wage
AEX Average experienced wage	**AXR** Average experienced range	**HI** Highest wage paid	**M** Monthly	**MWR** Median wage range	**W** Weekly
ATC Average total compensation	**D** Daily	**HR** High end range	**MCC** Median cash compensation	**S** See annotated source	**Y** Yearly

Occupation/Type/Industry	Location	Per	Low	Mid	High	Source	Date
File Clerk	Wyoming	Y	16380 FQ	18367 MW	21422 TQ	WYBLS	9/08
	Casper MSA, WY	Y	17887 FQ	20205 MW	23199 TQ	WYBLS	9/08
	Cheyenne MSA, WY	Y	16425 FQ	17847 MW	19278 TQ	WYBLS	9/08
	Puerto Rico	Y	13330 FQ	15530 MW	18970 TQ	USBLS	5/07
	San Juan-Caguas-Guaynabo MSA, PR	Y	13430 FQ	15780 MW	19350 TQ	USBLS	5/07
	Virgin Islands	Y	16460 FQ	18480 MW	21950 TQ	USBLS	5/07
	Guam	Y	15670 FQ	17970 MW	20910 TQ	USBLS	5/07
Film and Video Editor	Alabama	Y	18900 FQ	31670 MW	43960 TQ	USBLS	5/07
	Birmingham-Hoover MSA, AL	Y	17650 FQ	31480 MW	49590 TQ	USBLS	5/07
	Arizona	Y	26960 FQ	34150 MW	47150 TQ	USBLS	5/07
	Phoenix-Mesa-Scottsdale MSA, AZ	Y	26520 FQ	31550 MW	45040 TQ	USBLS	5/07
	Arkansas	Y	21840 FQ	27580 MW	35330 TQ	USBLS	5/07
	Little Rock-North Little Rock MSA, AR	Y	18070 FQ	28110 MW	35430 TQ	USBLS	5/07
	California	H	19.32 FQ	31.62 MW	51.09 TQ	CABLS	1/08-3/08
	Los Angeles-Long Beach-Glendale PMSA, CA	H	21.01 FQ	34.08 MW	53.26 TQ	CABLS	1/08-3/08
	Sacramento-Arden Arcade-Roseville MSA, CA	H	12.06 FQ	17.50 MW	33.41 TQ	CABLS	1/08-3/08
	San Diego-Carlsbad-San Marcos MSA, CA	H	10.55 FQ	17.48 MW	29.64 TQ	CABLS	1/08-3/08
	San Francisco-San Mateo-Redwood PMSA, CA	H	18.93 FQ	21.96 MW	36.64 TQ	CABLS	1/08-3/08
	Santa Ana-Anaheim-Irvine PMSA, CA	Y	47260 FQ	79350 MW	109740 TQ	USBLS	5/07
	Colorado	Y	38830 FQ	55530 MW	83710 TQ	USBLS	5/07
	Denver-Aurora MSA, CO	Y	42260 FQ	58060 MW	89930 TQ	USBLS	5/07
	Connecticut	H	14.11 AE	15.57 MW		CTBLS	1/08-3/08
	Hartford-West Hartford-East Hartford MSA, CT	Y	34490 FQ	41210 MW	45230 TQ	USBLS	5/07
	District of Columbia	Y	22160 FQ	26830 MW	45570 TQ	USBLS	5/07
	Washington-Arlington-Alexandria MSA, DC-VA-MD-WV	Y	26570 FQ	37340 MW	61700 TQ	USBLS	5/07
	Florida	Y	28770 FQ	36030 MW	51790 TQ	USBLS	5/07
	Fort Lauderdale-Pompano Beach-Deerfield Beach PMSA, FL	Y	34710 FQ	46720 MW	68150 TQ	USBLS	5/07
	Miami-Fort Lauderdale-Miami Beach MSA, FL	Y	29220 FQ	35650 MW	53000 TQ	USBLS	5/07
	Orlando-Kissimmee MSA, FL	Y	25690 FQ	35730 MW	53410 TQ	USBLS	5/07
	Tampa-St. Petersburg-Clearwater MSA, FL	Y	29380 FQ	40150 MW	50460 TQ	USBLS	5/07
	Georgia	Y	41390 FQ	56720 MW	80830 TQ	USBLS	5/07
	Atlanta-Sandy Springs-Marietta MSA, GA	Y	45170 FQ	60560 MW	81160 TQ	USBLS	5/07
	Hawaii	Y	27240 FQ	37050 MW	47180 TQ	USBLS	5/07
	Honolulu MSA, HI	Y	28140 FQ	38960 MW	48570 TQ	USBLS	5/07
	Illinois	Y	34770 FQ	50780 MW	65380 TQ	USBLS	5/07
	Chicago-Naperville-Joliet MSA, IL-IN-WI	Y	39070 FQ	54700 MW	66960 TQ	USBLS	5/07
	Indiana	Y	26130 FQ	29010 MW	35630 TQ	USBLS	5/07
	Iowa	Y	25870 FQ	29410 MW	52080 TQ	USBLS	5/07
	Kansas	Y	15120 FQ	25140 MW	45020 TQ	USBLS	5/07
	Kentucky	Y	29411 FQ	36727 MW	41736 TQ	KYBLS	2008
	Louisville-Jefferson County MSA, KY-IN	Y	29480 FQ	35580 MW	39720 TQ	USBLS	5/07
	Louisiana	H	11.44 FQ	12.97 MW	14.73 TQ	LABLS	1/08-3/08
	Maine	Y	25880 FQ	30810 MW	43630 TQ	USBLS	5/07
	Portland-South Portland-Biddeford MSA, ME	Y	28670 FQ	41200 MW	46440 TQ	USBLS	5/07
	Maryland	Y		49600 MW		MDBLS	3/08
	Baltimore-Towson MSA, MD	Y	43190 FQ	48970 MW	56120 TQ	USBLS	5/07
	Bethesda-Gaithersburg-Frederick PMSA, MD	Y	36650 FQ	41620 MW	72570 TQ	USBLS	5/07
	Massachusetts	Y	34360 FQ	55810 MW	84270 TQ	USBLS	5/07
	Boston-Cambridge-Quincy NECTA, MA	Y	36860 FQ	68530 MW	105360 TQ	USBLS	5/07
	Michigan	Y	33550 FQ	46960 MW	66610 TQ	USBLS	5/07

Occupation/Type/Industry	Location	Per	Low	Mid	High	Source	Date
Film and Video Editor	Detroit-Warren-Livonia MSA, MI	Y	35300 FQ	50950 MW	76140 TQ	USBLS	5/07
	Warren-Troy-Farmington Hills PMSA, MI	Y	34190 FQ	47050 MW	79120 TQ	USBLS	5/07
	Minnesota	Y	28959 FQ	33678 MW	52395 TQ	MNBLS	10/08-12/08
	Duluth-Superior MSA, MN-WI	Y	29817 FQ	33018 MW	37706 TQ	MNBLS	10/08-12/08
	Minneapolis-Saint Paul MSA, MN-WI	Y	29430 FQ	33803 MW	55648 TQ	MNBLS	10/08-12/08
	Missouri	Y	26560 FQ	35400 MW	47060 TQ	USBLS	5/07
	Kansas City MSA, MO-KS	Y	33200 FQ	42080 MW	55170 TQ	USBLS	5/07
	St. Louis MSA, MO-IL	Y	26450 FQ	34670 MW	44090 TQ	USBLS	5/07
	Nevada	H	12.45 FQ	15.47 MW	26.43 TQ	NVBLS	5/08
	Las Vegas-Paradise MSA, NV	H	12.89 FQ	17.30 MW	27.21 TQ	NVBLS	5/08
	New Jersey	Y	37030 FQ	44800 MW	62760 TQ	USBLS	5/07
	New York	Y	41320 FQ	59400 MW	87770 TQ	USBLS	5/07
	Nassau-Suffolk PMSA, NY	Y	46490 FQ	64490 MW	92000 TQ	USBLS	5/07
	New York-Northern New Jersey-Long Island MSA, NY-NJ-PA	Y	41370 FQ	58200 MW	86210 TQ	USBLS	5/07
	North Carolina	Y	29510 FQ	38610 MW	47480 TQ	USBLS	5/07
	Charlotte-Gastonia-Concord MSA, NC-SC	Y	32640 FQ	41510 MW	54850 TQ	USBLS	5/07
	Raleigh-Cary MSA, NC	Y	29240 FQ	38450 MW	47980 TQ	USBLS	5/07
	Ohio	Y	24850 FQ	34470 MW	48130 TQ	USBLS	5/07
	Cincinnati-Middletown MSA, OH-KY-IN	Y	28950 FQ	37880 MW	52830 TQ	USBLS	5/07
	Cleveland-Elyria-Mentor MSA, OH	Y	34640 FQ	44010 MW	56490 TQ	USBLS	5/07
	Dayton MSA, OH	Y	23340 FQ	27920 MW	37210 TQ	USBLS	5/07
	Oklahoma	Y	22660 FQ	25590 MW	34000 TQ	USBLS	5/07
	Oklahoma City MSA, OK	Y	22300 FQ	24450 MW	29080 TQ	USBLS	5/07
	Tulsa MSA, OK	Y	23050 FQ	27190 MW	37460 TQ	USBLS	5/07
	Oregon	H	18.99 FQ	22.62 MW	31.25 TQ	ORBLS	5/08
	Portland-Vancouver-Beaverton MSA, OR-WA	Y	40810 FQ	47340 MW	66230 TQ	USBLS	5/07
	Pennsylvania	Y	35270 FQ	47540 MW	70010 TQ	USBLS	5/07
	Philadelphia-Camden-Wilmington MSA, PA-NJ-DE-MD	Y	39440 FQ	54550 MW	75520 TQ	USBLS	5/07
	Pittsburgh MSA, PA	Y	34940 FQ	49430 MW	84060 TQ	USBLS	5/07
	South Carolina	Y	20670 FQ	44720 MW	50790 TQ	USBLS	5/07
	South Dakota	Y	27561 FQ	29908 MW	32497 TQ	SDBLS	7/08-9/08
	Sioux Falls MSA, SD	Y	28409 FQ	30445 MW	32923 TQ	SDBLS	7/08-9/08
	Tennessee	Y	32120 FQ	44940 MW	55770 TQ	USBLS	5/07
	Memphis MSA, TN-MS-AR	Y	25620 FQ	33560 MW	38260 TQ	USBLS	5/07
	Nashville-Davidson-Murfreesboro MSA, TN	Y	43870 FQ	50770 MW	59520 TQ	USBLS	5/07
	Texas	Y	29390 FQ	37920 MW	59480 TQ	USBLS	5/07
	Austin-Round Rock MSA, TX	Y	27420 FQ	39470 MW	81050 TQ	USBLS	5/07
	Dallas-Fort Worth-Arlington MSA, TX	Y	33540 FQ	44600 MW	71760 TQ	USBLS	5/07
	Houston-Sugar Land-Baytown MSA, TX	Y	26750 FQ	36400 MW	44690 TQ	USBLS	5/07
	San Antonio MSA, TX	Y	34580 FQ	44860 MW	83760 TQ	USBLS	5/07
	Utah	Y	28430 FQ	35840 MW	56810 TQ	USBLS	5/07
	Salt Lake City MSA, UT	Y	29270 FQ	36590 MW	56310 TQ	USBLS	5/07
	Virginia	Y	24890 FQ	33100 MW	54490 TQ	USBLS	5/07
	Richmond MSA, VA	Y	22370 FQ	28220 MW	45240 TQ	USBLS	5/07
	Virginia Beach-Norfolk-Newport News MSA, VA-NC	Y	22840 FQ	29480 MW	49740 TQ	USBLS	5/07
	Washington	H	14.49 FQ	19.85 MW	33.58 TQ	WABLS	3/08
	Seattle-Tacoma-Bellevue MSA, WA	Y	30230 FQ	42840 MW	66390 TQ	USBLS	5/07
	West Virginia	Y	14654 FQ	18740 MW	22771 TQ	WVBLS	7/08-9/08
	Wisconsin	Y	27240 FQ	36640 MW	46960 TQ	USBLS	5/07
	Puerto Rico	Y	18330 FQ	28860 MW	37060 TQ	USBLS	5/07
	San Juan-Caguas-Guaynabo MSA, PR	Y	18330 FQ	28860 MW	37060 TQ	USBLS	5/07
Finance Director	Bismarck, ND	M			7886 HI	NDLC01	2008
Finance Executive	United States	Y		236000 AW		USATOD03	2008

AE	Average entry wage	**AW**	Average wage paid	**FQ**	First quartile wage	**LO** Lowest wage paid	**MTC** Median total compensation	**TCC** Total cash compensation
AER	Average entry range	**AWR**	Average wage range	**H**	Hourly	**LR** Low end range	**MW** Median wage paid	**TQ** Third quartile wage
AEX	Average experienced wage	**AXR**	Average experienced range	**HI**	Highest wage paid	**M** Monthly	**MWR** Median wage range	**W** Weekly
ATC	Average total compensation	**D**	Daily	**HR**	High end range	**MCC** Median cash compensation	**S** See annotated source	**Y** Yearly

Occupation/Type/Industry	Location	Per	Low	Mid	High	Source	Date
Finance Manager							
Municipal Government	Walnut Creek, CA	Y	90947 LO		127312 HI	WCSWP	7/11/08
Financial Aid Officer							
Department of Regional Community Technical Colleges	New Hampshire	Y		68548 AW		NHUL03	2008
Financial Analysis Manager	Southeast, MI	Y		105862 AW		MIOAKL01	2008
Financial Analyst	Alabama	Y	43940 FQ	57340 MW	82650 TQ	USBLS	5/07
	Birmingham-Hoover MSA, AL	Y	44060 FQ	56740 MW	81090 TQ	USBLS	5/07
	Montgomery MSA, AL	Y	38510 FQ	50410 MW	71310 TQ	USBLS	5/07
	Alaska	Y	54740 FQ	67690 MW	79760 TQ	USBLS	5/07
	Anchorage MSA, AK	Y	52850 FQ	65260 MW	75540 TQ	USBLS	5/07
	Arizona	Y	44270 FQ	59650 MW	78940 TQ	USBLS	5/07
	Phoenix-Mesa-Scottsdale MSA, AZ	Y	43910 FQ	60020 MW	79530 TQ	USBLS	5/07
	Tucson MSA, AZ	Y	46990 FQ	59710 MW	76850 TQ	USBLS	5/07
	Arkansas	Y	43690 FQ	56900 MW	67330 TQ	USBLS	5/07
	Little Rock-North Little Rock MSA, AR	Y	43310 FQ	53070 MW	75480 TQ	USBLS	5/07
	California	H	28.84 FQ	37.73 MW	50.92 TQ	CABLS	1/08-3/08
	Los Angeles-Long Beach-Glendale PMSA, CA	H	27.40 FQ	35.77 MW	48.92 TQ	CABLS	1/08-3/08
	Oakland-Fremont-Hayward MSA, CA	H	32.64 FQ	42.52 MW	57.93 TQ	CABLS	1/08-3/08
	Riverside-San Bernardino-Ontario MSA, CA	H	21.08 FQ	25.51 MW	31.57 TQ	CABLS	1/08-3/08
	Sacramento-Arden Arcade-Roseville MSA, CA	H	27.12 FQ	33.29 MW	39.76 TQ	CABLS	1/08-3/08
	San Diego-Carlsbad-San Marcos MSA, CA	H	28.46 FQ	37.23 MW	52.69 TQ	CABLS	1/08-3/08
	San Francisco-San Mateo-Redwood PMSA, CA	H	35.19 FQ	45.82 MW	69.82 TQ	CABLS	1/08-3/08
	San Jose-Sunnyvale-Santa Clara MSA, CA	H	31.64 FQ	41.72 MW	52.39 TQ	CABLS	1/08-3/08
	Santa Ana-Anaheim-Irvine PMSA, CA	Y	53700 FQ	68540 MW	91420 TQ	USBLS	5/07
	Colorado	Y	44900 FQ	63340 MW	91050 TQ	USBLS	5/07
	Boulder MSA, CO	Y	46000 FQ	70620 MW	95770 TQ	USBLS	5/07
	Colorado Springs MSA, CO	Y	41930 FQ	51390 MW	69250 TQ	USBLS	5/07
	Denver-Aurora MSA, CO	Y	44800 FQ	62810 MW	91530 TQ	USBLS	5/07
	Connecticut	H	26.10 AE	40.41 MW		CTBLS	1/08-3/08
	Bridgeport-Stamford-Norwalk MSA, CT	Y	75350 FQ	110600 MW		USBLS	5/07
	Hartford-West Hartford-East Hartford MSA, CT	Y	52550 FQ	66170 MW	82320 TQ	USBLS	5/07
	New Haven MSA, CT	Y	56130 FQ	66660 MW	82480 TQ	USBLS	5/07
	Delaware	Y	53300 FQ	70060 MW	90270 TQ	USBLS	5/07
	Wilmington PMSA, DE-MD-NJ	Y	53760 FQ	70610 MW	91240 TQ	USBLS	5/07
	District of Columbia	Y	50870 FQ	70850 MW	104280 TQ	USBLS	5/07
	Washington-Arlington-Alexandria MSA, DC-VA-MD-WV	Y	53950 FQ	72640 MW	100810 TQ	USBLS	5/07
	Florida	Y	46030 FQ	59080 MW	78420 TQ	USBLS	5/07
	Fort Lauderdale-Pompano Beach-Deerfield Beach PMSA, FL	Y	49800 FQ	66670 MW	91070 TQ	USBLS	5/07
	Jacksonville MSA, FL	Y	45840 FQ	65010 MW	91210 TQ	USBLS	5/07
	Miami-Fort Lauderdale-Miami Beach MSA, FL	Y	50300 FQ	65720 MW	86740 TQ	USBLS	5/07
	Orlando-Kissimmee MSA, FL	Y	44940 FQ	54330 MW	64380 TQ	USBLS	5/07
	Tampa-St. Petersburg-Clearwater MSA, FL	Y	42940 FQ	51930 MW	68390 TQ	USBLS	5/07
	West Palm Beach-Boca Raton-Boynton Beach PMSA, FL	Y	52530 FQ	65420 MW	84260 TQ	USBLS	5/07
	Georgia	Y	51660 FQ	65610 MW	85230 TQ	USBLS	5/07
	Atlanta-Sandy Springs-Marietta MSA, GA	Y	53030 FQ	66390 MW	85940 TQ	USBLS	5/07
	Hawaii	Y	49060 FQ	67320 MW	94300 TQ	USBLS	5/07
	Honolulu MSA, HI	Y	50900 FQ	68360 MW	97090 TQ	USBLS	5/07

AE	Average entry wage	AW	Average wage paid	FQ First quartile wage
AER	Average entry range	AWR	Average wage range	H Hourly
AEX	Average experienced wage	AXR	Average experienced range	HI Highest wage paid
ATC	Average total compensation	D	Daily	HR High end range

LO Lowest wage paid
LR Low end range
M Monthly
MCC Median cash compensation

MTC Median total compensation
MW Median wage paid
MWR Median wage range
S See annotated source

TCC Total cash compensation
TQ Third quartile wage
W Weekly
Y Yearly

Occupation/Type/Industry	Location	Per	Low	Mid	High	Source	Date
Financial Analyst	Idaho	Y	50250 FQ	62480 MW	76120 TQ	USBLS	5/07
	Boise City-Nampa MSA, ID	Y	50060 FQ	60540 MW	73280 TQ	USBLS	5/07
	Illinois	Y	55390 FQ	72140 MW	101230 TQ	USBLS	5/07
	Chicago-Naperville-Joliet MSA, IL-IN-WI	Y	56230 FQ	73460 MW	103730 TQ	USBLS	5/07
	Indiana	Y	38640 FQ	54180 MW	73890 TQ	USBLS	5/07
	Gary PMSA, IN	Y	47560 FQ	61330 MW	69720 TQ	USBLS	5/07
	Indianapolis-Carmel MSA, IN	Y	39880 FQ	55000 MW	75110 TQ	USBLS	5/07
	Iowa	Y	45350 FQ	58340 MW	74810 TQ	USBLS	5/07
	Cedar Rapids MSA, IA	Y	45880 FQ	58600 MW	73520 TQ	USBLS	5/07
	Davenport-Moline-Rock Island MSA, IA-IL	Y	52430 FQ	82800 MW	109700 TQ	USBLS	5/07
	Des Moines-West Des Moines MSA, IA	Y	46890 FQ	60010 MW	76070 TQ	USBLS	5/07
	Iowa City MSA, IA	Y	41590 FQ	54520 MW	66180 TQ	USBLS	5/07
	Kansas	Y	49020 FQ	61060 MW	76410 TQ	USBLS	5/07
	Wichita MSA, KS	Y	47350 FQ	58230 MW	70220 TQ	USBLS	5/07
	Kentucky	Y	50060 FQ	60855 MW	77301 TQ	KYBLS	2008
	Louisville-Jefferson County MSA, KY-IN	Y	42260 FQ	54890 MW	70260 TQ	USBLS	5/07
	Louisiana	H	21.29 FQ	26.84 MW	34.81 TQ	LABLS	1/08-3/08
	Baton Rouge MSA, LA	Y	43060 FQ	53670 MW	63110 TQ	USBLS	5/07
	New Orleans-Metairie-Kenner MSA, LA	Y	46890 FQ	56130 MW	74530 TQ	USBLS	5/07
	Maine	Y	56320 FQ	71380 MW	86220 TQ	USBLS	5/07
	Portland-South Portland-Biddeford MSA, ME	Y	60890 FQ	74610 MW	94880 TQ	USBLS	5/07
	Maryland	Y		67025 MW		MDBLS	3/08
	Baltimore-Towson MSA, MD	Y	48860 FQ	64140 MW	88790 TQ	USBLS	5/07
	Bethesda-Gaithersburg-Frederick PMSA, MD	Y	51820 FQ	69120 MW	89900 TQ	USBLS	5/07
	Massachusetts	Y	57480 FQ	76480 MW	105680 TQ	USBLS	5/07
	Barnstable Town MSA, MA	Y	57270 FQ	68960 MW	96070 TQ	USBLS	5/07
	Boston-Cambridge-Quincy NECTA, MA	Y	58100 FQ	78140 MW	109460 TQ	USBLS	5/07
	Worcester MSA, MA-CT	Y	55350 FQ	65800 MW	82320 TQ	USBLS	5/07
	Michigan	Y	53590 FQ	72460 MW	92970 TQ	USBLS	5/07
	Detroit-Warren-Livonia MSA, MI	Y	59470 FQ	78690 MW	97600 TQ	USBLS	5/07
	Flint MSA, MI	Y	59320 FQ	69670 MW	79360 TQ	USBLS	5/07
	Grand Rapids-Wyoming MSA, MI	Y	45140 FQ	58110 MW	71900 TQ	USBLS	5/07
	Warren-Troy-Farmington Hills PMSA, MI	Y	55440 FQ	70860 MW	87120 TQ	USBLS	5/07
	Minnesota	Y	54395 FQ	70045 MW	85382 TQ	MNBLS	10/08-12/08
	Duluth-Superior MSA, MN-WI	Y	56960 FQ	64884 MW	79439 TQ	MNBLS	10/08-12/08
	Minneapolis-Saint Paul MSA, MN-WI	Y	53915 FQ	70097 MW	85622 TQ	MNBLS	10/08-12/08
	Rochester MSA, MN	Y	54838 FQ	74311 MW	87189 TQ	MNBLS	10/08-12/08
	Mississippi	Y	41280 FQ	54110 MW	71640 TQ	USBLS	5/07
	Jackson MSA, MS	Y	50020 FQ	63640 MW	84430 TQ	USBLS	5/07
	Missouri	Y	49430 FQ	63690 MW	81380 TQ	USBLS	5/07
	Kansas City MSA, MO-KS	Y	49350 FQ	62170 MW	80270 TQ	USBLS	5/07
	St. Louis MSA, MO-IL	Y	53830 FQ	67040 MW	83310 TQ	USBLS	5/07
	Montana	Y	53480 FQ	67210 MW	88580 TQ	USBLS	5/07
	Nebraska	Y	41010 FQ	52790 MW	68500 TQ	USBLS	5/07
	Lincoln MSA, NE	Y	39050 FQ	51150 MW	64400 TQ	USBLS	5/07
	Omaha-Council Bluffs MSA, NE-IA	Y	40850 FQ	52280 MW	66740 TQ	USBLS	5/07
	Nevada	H	27.59 FQ	35.54 MW	43.74 TQ	NVBLS	5/08
	Las Vegas-Paradise MSA, NV	H	26.83 FQ	34.08 MW	44.38 TQ	NVBLS	5/08
	New Hampshire	H	22.72 AE	32.89 MW	39.20 AEX	NHBLS	6/08
	Manchester MSA, NH	Y	54490 FQ	70060 MW	79220 TQ	USBLS	5/07
	Nashua NECTA, NH-MA	Y	48510 FQ	61650 MW	85960 TQ	USBLS	5/07
	New Jersey	Y	60040 FQ	78520 MW	104110 TQ	USBLS	5/07
	Camden PMSA, NJ	Y	55190 FQ	70490 MW	89470 TQ	USBLS	5/07
	Edison PMSA, NJ	Y	59700 FQ	75820 MW	96580 TQ	USBLS	5/07
	Newark-Union PMSA, NJ-PA	Y	56910 FQ	75550 MW	97170 TQ	USBLS	5/07
	New Mexico	Y	46310 FQ	54380 MW	69970 TQ	USBLS	5/07
	Albuquerque MSA, NM	Y	49210 FQ	57680 MW	71040 TQ	USBLS	5/07
	New York	Y	62960 FQ	84440 MW	121740 TQ	USBLS	5/07

AE	Average entry wage	AW	Average wage paid	FQ First quartile wage
AER	Average entry range	AWR	Average wage range	H Hourly
AEX	Average experienced wage	AXR	Average experienced range	HI Highest wage paid
ATC	Average total compensation	D	Daily	HR High end range

LO Lowest wage paid
LR Low end range
M Monthly
MCC Median cash compensation

MTC Median total compensation
MW Median wage paid
MWR Median wage range
S See annotated source

TCC Total cash compensation
TQ Third quartile wage
W Weekly
Y Yearly

Occupation/Type/Industry	Location	Per	Low	Mid	High	Source	Date
Financial Analyst	Albany-Schenectady-Troy MSA, NY	Y	49780 FQ	62910 MW	79860 TQ	USBLS	5/07
	Buffalo-Niagara Falls MSA, NY	Y	46110 FQ	61210 MW	77020 TQ	USBLS	5/07
	Nassau-Suffolk PMSA, NY	Y	53410 FQ	69620 MW	91020 TQ	USBLS	5/07
	New York-Northern New Jersey-Long Island MSA, NY-NJ-PA	Y	65120 FQ	87010 MW	123330 TQ	USBLS	5/07
	North Carolina	Y	54490 FQ	68730 MW	84210 TQ	USBLS	5/07
	Charlotte-Gastonia-Concord MSA, NC-SC	Y	56830 FQ	71970 MW	89420 TQ	USBLS	5/07
	Greensboro-High Point MSA, NC	Y	56990 FQ	68530 MW	79600 TQ	USBLS	5/07
	Raleigh-Cary MSA, NC	Y	53140 FQ	67110 MW	81070 TQ	USBLS	5/07
	North Dakota	Y	50980 FQ	68850 MW	84610 TQ	USBLS	5/07
	Fargo MSA, ND-MN	Y	59700 FQ	76740 MW	98740 TQ	USBLS	5/07
	Ohio	Y	47840 FQ	62070 MW	80590 TQ	USBLS	5/07
	Cincinnati-Middletown MSA, OH-KY-IN	Y	52080 FQ	65820 MW	83640 TQ	USBLS	5/07
	Cleveland-Elyria-Mentor MSA, OH	Y	47050 FQ	59270 MW	75840 TQ	USBLS	5/07
	Columbus MSA, OH	Y	46960 FQ	60990 MW	82840 TQ	USBLS	5/07
	Dayton MSA, OH	Y	49750 FQ	62600 MW	77280 TQ	USBLS	5/07
	Oklahoma	Y	39970 FQ	53550 MW	72970 TQ	USBLS	5/07
	Oklahoma City MSA, OK	Y	40260 FQ	50210 MW	69100 TQ	USBLS	5/07
	Tulsa MSA, OK	Y	41330 FQ	58440 MW	74510 TQ	USBLS	5/07
	Oregon	H	26.80 FQ	34.63 MW	44.78 TQ	ORBLS	5/08
	Portland-Vancouver-Beaverton MSA, OR-WA	Y	54370 FQ	70090 MW	90280 TQ	USBLS	5/07
	Pennsylvania	Y	47710 FQ	62170 MW	81240 TQ	USBLS	5/07
	Allentown-Bethlehem-Easton MSA, PA-NJ	Y	47650 FQ	61270 MW	74930 TQ	USBLS	5/07
	Philadelphia-Camden-Wilmington MSA, PA-NJ-DE-MD	Y	50640 FQ	65870 MW	85460 TQ	USBLS	5/07
	Pittsburgh MSA, PA	Y	44150 FQ	56810 MW	75270 TQ	USBLS	5/07
	Rhode Island	Y	48310 FQ	59080 MW	73130 TQ	USBLS	5/07
	Providence-Fall River-Warwick MSA, RI-MA	Y	48730 FQ	59680 MW	73770 TQ	USBLS	5/07
	South Carolina	Y	41460 FQ	49130 MW	60740 TQ	USBLS	5/07
	Charleston-North Charleston MSA, SC	Y	36530 FQ	44920 MW	54350 TQ	USBLS	5/07
	Columbia MSA, SC	Y	42130 FQ	48560 MW	57570 TQ	USBLS	5/07
	South Dakota	Y	41007 FQ	50840 MW	64761 TQ	SDBLS	7/08-9/08
	Sioux Falls MSA, SD	Y	40165 FQ	48706 MW	62197 TQ	SDBLS	7/08-9/08
	Tennessee	Y	44150 FQ	59070 MW	75400 TQ	USBLS	5/07
	Memphis MSA, TN-MS-AR	Y	52190 FQ	66870 MW	76960 TQ	USBLS	5/07
	Nashville-Davidson-Murfreesboro MSA, TN	Y	41730 FQ	55910 MW	78860 TQ	USBLS	5/07
	Texas	Y	52120 FQ	67550 MW	89790 TQ	USBLS	5/07
	Austin-Round Rock MSA, TX	Y	57240 FQ	71520 MW	104280 TQ	USBLS	5/07
	Dallas-Fort Worth-Arlington MSA, TX	Y	55120 FQ	70520 MW	94600 TQ	USBLS	5/07
	El Paso MSA, TX	Y	45000 FQ	54450 MW	68160 TQ	USBLS	5/07
	Houston-Sugar Land-Baytown MSA, TX	Y	50450 FQ	64740 MW	83830 TQ	USBLS	5/07
	San Antonio MSA, TX	Y	33100 FQ	40710 MW	60000 TQ	USBLS	5/07
	Utah	Y	45310 FQ	57380 MW	71680 TQ	USBLS	5/07
	Ogden-Clearfield MSA, UT	Y	38320 FQ	42850 MW	53030 TQ	USBLS	5/07
	Salt Lake City MSA, UT	Y	47230 FQ	58780 MW	72230 TQ	USBLS	5/07
	Vermont	Y	46760 FQ	60740 MW	80070 TQ	USBLS	5/07
	Burlington-South Burlington MSA, VT	Y	50480 FQ	65880 MW	84630 TQ	USBLS	5/07
	Virginia	Y	52180 FQ	69340 MW	92920 TQ	USBLS	5/07
	Richmond MSA, VA	Y	50640 FQ	65260 MW	85690 TQ	USBLS	5/07
	Virginia Beach-Norfolk-Newport News MSA, VA-NC	Y	44570 FQ	56330 MW	72440 TQ	USBLS	5/07
	Washington	H	28.73 FQ	37.22 MW	48.28 TQ	WABLS	3/08
	Spokane MSA, WA	Y	51440 FQ	67200 MW	92110 TQ	USBLS	5/07
	West Virginia	Y	42321 FQ	57360 MW	70650 TQ	WVBLS	7/08-9/08
	Charleston MSA, WV	Y	47540 FQ	58810 MW	70700 TQ	USBLS	5/07

AE Average entry wage	**AW** Average wage paid	**FQ** First quartile wage	**LO** Lowest wage paid	**MTC** Median total compensation	**TCC** Total cash compensation
AER Average entry range	**AWR** Average wage range	**H** Hourly	**LR** Low end range	**MW** Median wage paid	**TQ** Third quartile wage
AEX Average experienced wage	**AXR** Average experienced range	**HI** Highest wage paid	**M** Monthly	**MWR** Median wage range	**W** Weekly
ATC Average total compensation	**D** Daily	**HR** High end range	**MCC** Median cash compensation	**S** See annotated source	**Y** Yearly

Occupation/Type/Industry	Location	Per	Low	Mid	High	Source	Date
Financial Analyst	Huntington-Ashland MSA,						
	WV-KY-OH	Y	45200 FQ	58600 MW	73850 TQ	USBLS	5/07
	Wisconsin	Y	44840 FQ	60990 MW	81770 TQ	USBLS	5/07
	Green Bay MSA, WI	Y	42180 FQ	61390 MW	82940 TQ	USBLS	5/07
	Milwaukee-Waukesha-West						
	Allis MSA, WI	Y	50850 FQ	65220 MW	87100 TQ	USBLS	5/07
	Wyoming	Y	49893 FQ	56417 MW	118127 TQ	WYBLS	9/08
	Cheyenne MSA, WY	Y	62562 FQ	121323 MW	132822 TQ	WYBLS	9/08
	Puerto Rico	Y	34410 FQ	47300 MW	63110 TQ	USBLS	5/07
	San Juan-Caguas-Guaynabo						
	MSA, PR	Y	33920 FQ	46280 MW	62820 TQ	USBLS	5/07
	Virgin Islands	Y	41990 FQ	48640 MW	59870 TQ	USBLS	5/07
Financial Examiner	Alabama	Y	34770 FQ	41510 MW	59900 TQ	USBLS	5/07
	Birmingham-Hoover MSA, AL	Y	35570 FQ	41430 MW	54760 TQ	USBLS	5/07
	Arizona	Y	30050 FQ	37250 MW	47580 TQ	USBLS	5/07
	Phoenix-Mesa-Scottsdale						
	MSA, AZ	Y	29960 FQ	36960 MW	47250 TQ	USBLS	5/07
	Arkansas	Y	43770 FQ	61330 MW	79550 TQ	USBLS	5/07
	Little Rock-North Little Rock						
	MSA, AR	Y	51650 FQ	66950 MW	86480 TQ	USBLS	5/07
	California	H	25.18 FQ	34.69 MW	47.21 TQ	CABLS	1/08-3/08
	Fresno MSA, CA	H	24.36 FQ	27.79 MW	31.31 TQ	CABLS	1/08-3/08
	Los Angeles-Long Beach-						
	Glendale PMSA, CA	H	27.70 FQ	36.20 MW	47.71 TQ	CABLS	1/08-3/08
	Oakland-Fremont-Hayward						
	MSA, CA	H	29.43 FQ	38.83 MW	47.28 TQ	CABLS	1/08-3/08
	Riverside-San Bernardino-						
	Ontario MSA, CA	H	24.62 FQ	30.34 MW	43.37 TQ	CABLS	1/08-3/08
	Sacramento-Arden Arcade-						
	Roseville MSA, CA	H	25.94 FQ	33.85 MW	39.43 TQ	CABLS	1/08-3/08
	San Diego-Carlsbad-San						
	Marcos MSA, CA	H	20.58 FQ	33.79 MW	39.50 TQ	CABLS	1/08-3/08
	San Francisco-San Mateo-						
	Redwood PMSA, CA	H	30.06 FQ	45.21 MW	63.37 TQ	CABLS	1/08-3/08
	San Jose-Sunnyvale-Santa						
	Clara MSA, CA	H	32.70 FQ	38.78 MW	47.50 TQ	CABLS	1/08-3/08
	Santa Ana-Anaheim-Irvine						
	PMSA, CA	Y	37340 FQ	52550 MW	76610 TQ	USBLS	5/07
	Colorado	Y	59260 FQ	77040 MW	101220 TQ	USBLS	5/07
	Denver-Aurora MSA, CO	Y	59790 FQ	78350 MW	104810 TQ	USBLS	5/07
	Connecticut	H	30.15 AE	40.05 MW		CTBLS	1/08-3/08
	Bridgeport-Stamford-Norwalk						
	MSA, CT	Y	67200 FQ	82350 MW	103880 TQ	USBLS	5/07
	Hartford-West Hartford-East						
	Hartford MSA, CT	Y	68390 FQ	80860 MW	98660 TQ	USBLS	5/07
	Delaware	Y	55790 FQ	76450 MW	104280 TQ	USBLS	5/07
	Wilmington PMSA, DE-MD-						
	NJ	Y	56390 FQ	80070 MW	114370 TQ	USBLS	5/07
	District of Columbia	Y	65200 FQ	113840 MW	142840 TQ	USBLS	5/07
	Washington-Arlington-						
	Alexandria MSA, DC-VA-						
	MD-WV	Y	57290 FQ	99860 MW	132360 TQ	USBLS	5/07
	Florida	Y	52350 FQ	65510 MW	90530 TQ	USBLS	5/07
	Fort Lauderdale-Pompano						
	Beach-Deerfield Beach						
	PMSA, FL	Y	51350 FQ	55140 MW	58940 TQ	USBLS	5/07
	Jacksonville MSA, FL	Y	49500 FQ	67660 MW	89360 TQ	USBLS	5/07
	Miami-Fort Lauderdale-Miami						
	Beach MSA, FL	Y	51540 FQ	58710 MW	85760 TQ	USBLS	5/07
	Tampa-St. Petersburg-						
	Clearwater MSA, FL	Y	65390 FQ	84970 MW	102620 TQ	USBLS	5/07
	West Palm Beach-Boca Raton-						
	Boynton Beach PMSA, FL	Y	47700 FQ	68360 MW	83300 TQ	USBLS	5/07
	Georgia	Y	45130 FQ	61940 MW	92670 TQ	USBLS	5/07
	Atlanta-Sandy Springs-						
	Marietta MSA, GA	Y	45680 FQ	61520 MW	92280 TQ	USBLS	5/07
	Hawaii	Y	48720 FQ	61380 MW	78550 TQ	USBLS	5/07
	Honolulu MSA, HI	Y	48720 FQ	61380 MW	78550 TQ	USBLS	5/07
	Idaho	Y	47290 FQ	56620 MW	65120 TQ	USBLS	5/07
	Boise City-Nampa MSA, ID	Y	47290 FQ	56620 MW	65120 TQ	USBLS	5/07
	Illinois	Y	51230 FQ	75300 MW	104700 TQ	USBLS	5/07

AE	Average entry wage	AW	Average wage paid	FQ	First quartile wage	LO	Lowest wage paid	MTC	Median total compensation	TCC	Total cash compensation
AER	Average entry range	AWR	Average wage range	H	Hourly	LR	Low end range	MW	Median wage paid	TQ	Third quartile wage
AEX	Average experienced wage	AXR	Average experienced range	HI	Highest wage paid	M	Monthly	MWR	Median wage range	W	Weekly
ATC	Average total compensation	D	Daily	HR	High end range	MCC	Median cash compensation	S	See annotated source	Y	Yearly

Occupation/Type/Industry	Location	Per	Low	Mid	High	Source	Date
Financial Examiner	Chicago-Naperville-Joliet						
	MSA, IL-IN-WI	Y	51050 FQ	73790 MW	106690 TQ	USBLS	5/07
	Indiana	Y	44900 FQ	58450 MW	80930 TQ	USBLS	5/07
	Gary PMSA, IN	Y	55680 FQ	61540 MW	76460 TQ	USBLS	5/07
	Indianapolis-Carmel MSA, IN	Y	44830 FQ	62680 MW	90830 TQ	USBLS	5/07
	Iowa	Y	51600 FQ	71240 MW	91930 TQ	USBLS	5/07
	Des Moines-West Des Moines						
	MSA, IA	Y	57200 FQ	74930 MW	93820 TQ	USBLS	5/07
	Kansas	Y	50390 FQ	67800 MW	97300 TQ	USBLS	5/07
	Wichita MSA, KS	Y	48630 FQ	68690 MW	93830 TQ	USBLS	5/07
	Kentucky	Y	46550 FQ	60369 MW	85457 TQ	KYBLS	2008
	Louisville-Jefferson County						
	MSA, KY-IN	Y	42590 FQ	53540 MW	66890 TQ	USBLS	5/07
	Louisiana	H	24.20 FQ	39.55 MW	47.94 TQ	LABLS	1/08-3/08
	Baton Rouge MSA, LA	Y	72330 FQ	89580 MW	104650 TQ	USBLS	5/07
	New Orleans-Metairie-Kenner						
	MSA, LA	Y	47640 FQ	82190 MW	100660 TQ	USBLS	5/07
	Maine	Y	43420 FQ	55110 MW	71670 TQ	USBLS	5/07
	Portland-South Portland-						
	Biddeford MSA, ME	Y	42310 FQ	50090 MW	75010 TQ	USBLS	5/07
	Maryland	Y		59775 MW		MDBLS	3/08
	Baltimore-Towson MSA, MD	Y	49050 FQ	60310 MW	74190 TQ	USBLS	5/07
	Bethesda-Gaithersburg-						
	Frederick PMSA, MD	Y	38920 FQ	49260 MW	60930 TQ	USBLS	5/07
	Massachusetts	Y	55720 FQ	70920 MW	95070 TQ	USBLS	5/07
	Boston-Cambridge-Quincy						
	NECTA, MA	Y	55610 FQ	70410 MW	93320 TQ	USBLS	5/07
	Worcester MSA, MA-CT	Y	47900 FQ	64230 MW	92140 TQ	USBLS	5/07
	Michigan	Y	47630 FQ	64280 MW	80130 TQ	USBLS	5/07
	Detroit-Warren-Livonia MSA,						
	MI	Y	48510 FQ	67620 MW	92390 TQ	USBLS	5/07
	Minnesota	Y	49390 FQ	63643 MW	88761 TQ	MNBLS	10/08-12/08
	Duluth-Superior MSA, MN-WI	Y	49526 FQ	70055 MW	79794 TQ	MNBLS	10/08-12/08
	Minneapolis-Saint Paul MSA,						
	MN-WI	Y	50516 FQ	65103 MW	91232 TQ	MNBLS	10/08-12/08
	Mississippi	Y	39780 FQ	57220 MW	83830 TQ	USBLS	5/07
	Jackson MSA, MS	Y	44110 FQ	63240 MW	90100 TQ	USBLS	5/07
	Missouri	Y	49880 FQ	72990 MW	102290 TQ	USBLS	5/07
	Kansas City MSA, MO-KS	Y	57450 FQ	82840 MW	107940 TQ	USBLS	5/07
	St. Louis MSA, MO-IL	Y	53130 FQ	74700 MW	107020 TQ	USBLS	5/07
	Montana	Y	31740 FQ	45470 MW	72050 TQ	USBLS	5/07
	Billings MSA, MT	Y	33970 FQ	57560 MW	88600 TQ	USBLS	5/07
	Nebraska	Y	45680 FQ	60610 MW	88320 TQ	USBLS	5/07
	Omaha-Council Bluffs MSA,						
	NE-IA	Y	45210 FQ	60530 MW	88820 TQ	USBLS	5/07
	Nevada	H	22.41 FQ	28.78 MW	37.60 TQ	NVBLS	5/08
	Las Vegas-Paradise MSA, NV	H	22.21 FQ	28.94 MW	37.86 TQ	NVBLS	5/08
	New Hampshire	H	23.55 AE	35.55 MW	44.88 AEX	NHBLS	6/08
	New Jersey	Y	55290 FQ	71000 MW	95880 TQ	USBLS	5/07
	Camden PMSA, NJ	Y	56660 FQ	69400 MW	87760 TQ	USBLS	5/07
	Edison PMSA, NJ	Y	48010 FQ	73730 MW	121840 TQ	USBLS	5/07
	Newark-Union PMSA, NJ-PA	Y	54620 FQ	65610 MW	78150 TQ	USBLS	5/07
	New Mexico	Y	50810 FQ	77250 MW	102560 TQ	USBLS	5/07
	Albuquerque MSA, NM	Y	52510 FQ	78250 MW	101160 TQ	USBLS	5/07
	New York	Y	44520 FQ	69980 MW	102970 TQ	USBLS	5/07
	Buffalo-Niagara Falls MSA,						
	NY	Y	71280 FQ	83760 MW	95640 TQ	USBLS	5/07
	Nassau-Suffolk PMSA, NY	Y	43380 FQ	50940 MW	84670 TQ	USBLS	5/07
	New York-Northern New						
	Jersey-Long Island MSA, NY-						
	NJ-PA	Y	54870 FQ	74940 MW	106280 TQ	USBLS	5/07
	Syracuse MSA, NY	Y	58630 FQ	80420 MW	104440 TQ	USBLS	5/07
	North Carolina	Y	61550 FQ	83350 MW	109290 TQ	USBLS	5/07
	Charlotte-Gastonia-Concord						
	MSA, NC-SC	Y	67910 FQ	92290 MW	117220 TQ	USBLS	5/07
	Raleigh-Cary MSA, NC	Y	55230 FQ	67290 MW	84340 TQ	USBLS	5/07
	North Dakota	Y	48140 FQ	61440 MW	80290 TQ	USBLS	5/07
	Ohio	Y	47500 FQ	66120 MW	88360 TQ	USBLS	5/07
	Cincinnati-Middletown MSA,						
	OH-KY-IN	Y	52400 FQ	68730 MW	91890 TQ	USBLS	5/07
	Cleveland-Elyria-Mentor						
	MSA, OH	Y	48400 FQ	70670 MW	97950 TQ	USBLS	5/07

AE	Average entry wage	AW	Average wage paid	FQ	First quartile wage
AER	Average entry range	AWR	Average wage range	H	Hourly
AEX	Average experienced wage	AXR	Average experienced range	HI	Highest wage paid
ATC	Average total compensation	D	Daily	HR	High end range

LO	Lowest wage paid	MTC	Median total compensation
LR	Low end range	MW	Median wage paid
M	Monthly	MWR	Median wage range
MCC	Median cash compensation	S	See annotated source

TCC	Total cash compensation
TQ	Third quartile wage
W	Weekly
Y	Yearly

Occupation/Type/Industry	Location	Per	Low	Mid	High	Source	Date
Financial Examiner	Columbus MSA, OH	Y	48190 FQ	68810 MW	87530 TQ	USBLS	5/07
	Oklahoma	Y	50110 FQ	71330 MW	95240 TQ	USBLS	5/07
	Oklahoma City MSA, OK	Y	60920 FQ	81930 MW	100380 TQ	USBLS	5/07
	Tulsa MSA, OK	Y	45740 FQ	67000 MW	93110 TQ	USBLS	5/07
	Oregon	H	24.16 FQ	29.31 MW	39.68 TQ	ORBLS	5/08
	Portland-Vancouver-Beaverton MSA, OR-WA	Y	53170 FQ	67830 MW	92190 TQ	USBLS	5/07
	Pennsylvania	Y	56210 FQ	76590 MW	96360 TQ	USBLS	5/07
	Allentown-Bethlehem-Easton MSA, PA-NJ	Y	54590 FQ	75130 MW	95550 TQ	USBLS	5/07
	Philadelphia-Camden-Wilmington MSA, PA-NJ-DE-MD	Y	61240 FQ	82170 MW	102920 TQ	USBLS	5/07
	Pittsburgh MSA, PA	Y	56250 FQ	72990 MW	97370 TQ	USBLS	5/07
	Rhode Island	Y	49390 FQ	64920 MW	104820 TQ	USBLS	5/07
	Providence-Fall River-Warwick MSA, RI-MA	Y	49220 FQ	65070 MW	108230 TQ	USBLS	5/07
	South Carolina	Y	46650 FQ	67570 MW	91690 TQ	USBLS	5/07
	Columbia MSA, SC	Y	44830 FQ	78350 MW	96460 TQ	USBLS	5/07
	South Dakota	Y	42249 FQ	62690 MW	84245 TQ	SDBLS	7/08-9/08
	Sioux Falls MSA, SD	Y	54612 FQ	69856 MW	91270 TQ	SDBLS	7/08-9/08
	Tennessee	Y	44510 FQ	68800 MW	107850 TQ	USBLS	5/07
	Memphis MSA, TN-MS-AR	Y	46720 FQ	77880 MW	125400 TQ	USBLS	5/07
	Nashville-Davidson-Murfreesboro MSA, TN	Y	44050 FQ	57640 MW	87550 TQ	USBLS	5/07
	Texas	Y	54500 FQ	71940 MW	99620 TQ	USBLS	5/07
	Austin-Round Rock MSA, TX	Y	53420 FQ	62840 MW	77620 TQ	USBLS	5/07
	Dallas-Fort Worth-Arlington MSA, TX	Y	56910 FQ	77530 MW	106970 TQ	USBLS	5/07
	Houston-Sugar Land-Baytown MSA, TX	Y	58780 FQ	82410 MW	109820 TQ	USBLS	5/07
	San Antonio MSA, TX	Y	47680 FQ	63980 MW	86080 TQ	USBLS	5/07
	Utah	Y	42160 FQ	56770 MW	88670 TQ	USBLS	5/07
	Salt Lake City MSA, UT	Y	42010 FQ	57000 MW	88760 TQ	USBLS	5/07
	Vermont	Y	47660 FQ	56080 MW	66710 TQ	USBLS	5/07
	Virginia	Y	57960 FQ	87110 MW	110030 TQ	USBLS	5/07
	Richmond MSA, VA	Y	78320 FQ	98090 MW	116920 TQ	USBLS	5/07
	Virginia Beach-Norfolk-Newport News MSA, VA-NC	Y	37380 FQ	53100 MW	61970 TQ	USBLS	5/07
	Washington	H	25.65 FQ	31.09 MW	39.84 TQ	WABLS	3/08
	Seattle-Tacoma-Bellevue MSA, WA	Y	50710 FQ	65690 MW	90520 TQ	USBLS	5/07
	West Virginia	Y	49248 FQ	63269 MW	85272 TQ	WVBLS	7/08-9/08
	Charleston MSA, WV	Y	48080 FQ	68220 MW	92490 TQ	USBLS	5/07
	Wisconsin	Y	47090 FQ	57990 MW	81340 TQ	USBLS	5/07
	Milwaukee-Waukesha-West Allis MSA, WI	Y	48220 FQ	58240 MW	80080 TQ	USBLS	5/07
	Wyoming	Y	39768 FQ	44124 MW	90958 TQ	WYBLS	9/08
	Puerto Rico	Y	22090 FQ	35600 MW	55390 TQ	USBLS	5/07
	San Juan-Caguas-Guaynabo MSA, PR	Y	19270 FQ	34370 MW	53340 TQ	USBLS	5/07
Financial Institution Examiner State Government	Minnesota	Y	39087 LO		57336 HI	AFT02	3/1/08
Financial Manager	Alabama	Y	60900 FQ	82140 MW	106210 TQ	USBLS	5/07
	Birmingham-Hoover MSA, AL	Y	70460 FQ	91090 MW	116520 TQ	USBLS	5/07
	Alaska	Y	55500 FQ	77180 MW	99680 TQ	USBLS	5/07
	Anchorage MSA, AK	Y	59380 FQ	81540 MW	101330 TQ	USBLS	5/07
	Arizona	Y	56650 FQ	75330 MW	102490 TQ	USBLS	5/07
	Phoenix-Mesa-Scottsdale MSA, AZ	Y	58680 FQ	79440 MW	105800 TQ	USBLS	5/07
	Tucson MSA, AZ	Y	50890 FQ	65110 MW	89910 TQ	USBLS	5/07
	Arkansas	Y	51560 FQ	69910 MW	93220 TQ	USBLS	5/07
	Little Rock-North Little Rock MSA, AR	Y	55490 FQ	74230 MW	98080 TQ	USBLS	5/07
	Pine Bluff MSA, AR	Y	56400 FQ	69130 MW	86090 TQ	USBLS	5/07
	California	H	38.10 FQ	50.90 MW		CABLS	1/08-3/08
	Los Angeles-Long Beach-Glendale PMSA, CA	H	39.55 FQ	51.38 MW	68.75 TQ	CABLS	1/08-3/08
	Oakland-Fremont-Hayward MSA, CA	H	40.79 FQ	51.62 MW		CABLS	1/08-3/08

AE	Average entry wage	AW	Average wage paid	FQ	First quartile wage	LO	Lowest wage paid	MTC	Median total compensation	TCC	Total cash compensation
AER	Average entry range	AWR	Average wage range	H	Hourly	LR	Low end range	MW	Median wage paid	TQ	Third quartile wage
AEX	Average experienced wage	AXR	Average experienced range	HI	Highest wage paid	M	Monthly	MWR	Median wage range	W	Weekly
ATC	Average total compensation	D	Daily	HR	High end range	MCC	Median cash compensation	S	See annotated source	Y	Yearly

600

Financial Manager

Occupation/Type/Industry	Location	Per	Low	Mid	High	Source	Date
Financial Manager	Riverside-San Bernardino-Ontario MSA, CA	H	34.03 FQ	45.11 MW	59.46 TQ	CABLS	1/08-3/08
	Sacramento-Arden Arcade-Roseville MSA, CA	H	33.96 FQ	42.52 MW	55.21 TQ	CABLS	1/08-3/08
	San Diego-Carlsbad-San Marcos MSA, CA	H	34.83 FQ	49.20 MW	67.98 TQ	CABLS	1/08-3/08
	San Francisco-San Mateo-Redwood PMSA, CA	H	46.31 FQ	62.95 MW		CABLS	1/08-3/08
	San Jose-Sunnyvale-Santa Clara MSA, CA	H	47.86 FQ	63.75 MW		CABLS	1/08-3/08
	Santa Ana-Anaheim-Irvine PMSA, CA	Y	79730 FQ	104060 MW	138130 TQ	USBLS	5/07
	Colorado	Y	78230 FQ	98740 MW	130320 TQ	USBLS	5/07
	Denver-Aurora MSA, CO	Y	81620 FQ	101480 MW	133870 TQ	USBLS	5/07
	Connecticut	H	30.56 AE	48.92 MW		CTBLS	1/08-3/08
	Bridgeport-Stamford-Norwalk MSA, CT	Y	82920 FQ	118010 MW		USBLS	5/07
	Hartford-West Hartford-East Hartford MSA, CT	Y	77130 FQ	99980 MW	129750 TQ	USBLS	5/07
	Waterbury MSA, CT	Y	55790 FQ	76870 MW	108190 TQ	USBLS	5/07
	Delaware	Y	82330 FQ	107550 MW		USBLS	5/07
	Wilmington PMSA, DE-MD-NJ	Y	86610 FQ	111820 MW		USBLS	5/07
	District of Columbia	Y	90780 FQ	111930 MW	131050 TQ	USBLS	5/07
	Washington-Arlington-Alexandria MSA, DC-VA-MD-WV	Y	86320 FQ	109990 MW	135400 TQ	USBLS	5/07
	Florida	Y	68860 FQ	93950 MW	124410 TQ	USBLS	5/07
	Fort Lauderdale-Pompano Beach-Deerfield Beach PMSA, FL	Y	61020 FQ	85720 MW	120810 TQ	USBLS	5/07
	Jacksonville MSA, FL	Y	73350 FQ	99670 MW	133790 TQ	USBLS	5/07
	Miami-Fort Lauderdale-Miami Beach MSA, FL	Y	66170 FQ	96080 MW	129600 TQ	USBLS	5/07
	Orlando-Kissimmee MSA, FL	Y	71540 FQ	92560 MW	122990 TQ	USBLS	5/07
	Tampa-St. Petersburg-Clearwater MSA, FL	Y	74010 FQ	95510 MW	120390 TQ	USBLS	5/07
	West Palm Beach-Boca Raton-Boynton Beach PMSA, FL	Y	71690 FQ	98200 MW	130020 TQ	USBLS	5/07
	Georgia	Y	67460 FQ	89510 MW	121950 TQ	USBLS	5/07
	Atlanta-Sandy Springs-Marietta MSA, GA	Y	71960 FQ	94670 MW	128890 TQ	USBLS	5/07
	Hawaii	Y	59570 FQ	77160 MW	100190 TQ	USBLS	5/07
	Honolulu MSA, HI	Y	60430 FQ	77310 MW	101360 TQ	USBLS	5/07
	Idaho	Y	45130 FQ	61330 MW	81080 TQ	USBLS	5/07
	Boise City-Nampa MSA, ID	Y	50050 FQ	71350 MW	91750 TQ	USBLS	5/07
	Illinois	Y	74040 FQ	101570 MW	135120 TQ	USBLS	5/07
	Chicago-Naperville-Joliet MSA, IL-IN-WI	Y	79810 FQ	106280 MW	142350 TQ	USBLS	5/07
	Indiana	Y	64100 FQ	87030 MW	115670 TQ	USBLS	5/07
	Gary PMSA, IN	Y	55910 FQ	73170 MW	95870 TQ	USBLS	5/07
	Indianapolis-Carmel MSA, IN	Y	74350 FQ	96180 MW	130690 TQ	USBLS	5/07
	Iowa	Y	61820 FQ	83840 MW	108150 TQ	USBLS	5/07
	Des Moines-West Des Moines MSA, IA	Y	67340 FQ	91530 MW	118850 TQ	USBLS	5/07
	Kansas	Y	54310 FQ	73200 MW	100840 TQ	USBLS	5/07
	Wichita MSA, KS	Y	55110 FQ	76540 MW	102660 TQ	USBLS	5/07
	Kentucky	Y	57457 FQ	78083 MW	103107 TQ	KYBLS	2008
	Louisville-Jefferson County MSA, KY-IN	Y	61710 FQ	80700 MW	110730 TQ	USBLS	5/07
	Louisiana	H	25.04 FQ	32.94 MW	43.33 TQ	LABLS	1/08-3/08
	Baton Rouge MSA, LA	Y	52930 FQ	67660 MW	82400 TQ	USBLS	5/07
	New Orleans-Metairie-Kenner MSA, LA	Y	57440 FQ	74820 MW	102670 TQ	USBLS	5/07
	Maine	Y	51360 FQ	67670 MW	89670 TQ	USBLS	5/07
	Portland-South Portland-Biddeford MSA, ME	Y	57540 FQ	74700 MW	99830 TQ	USBLS	5/07
	Maryland	Y		98550 MW		MDBLS	3/08
	Baltimore-Towson MSA, MD	Y	63560 FQ	92960 MW	125310 TQ	USBLS	5/07
	Bethesda-Gaithersburg-Frederick PMSA, MD	Y	79740 FQ	104440 MW	137560 TQ	USBLS	5/07
	Massachusetts	Y	72350 FQ	99510 MW	134780 TQ	USBLS	5/07

Occupation/Type/Industry	Location	Per	Low	Mid	High	Source	Date
Financial Manager	Boston-Cambridge-Quincy NECTA, MA	Y	80660 FQ	107900 MW		USBLS	5/07
	Lynn-Peabody-Salem NECTA, MA	Y	76280 FQ	92900 MW	124080 TQ	USBLS	5/07
	Worcester MSA, MA-CT	Y	55510 FQ	76570 MW	112590 TQ	USBLS	5/07
	Michigan	Y	68030 FQ	89030 MW	116830 TQ	USBLS	5/07
	Detroit-Warren-Livonia MSA, MI	Y	75550 FQ	95470 MW	124950 TQ	USBLS	5/07
	Grand Rapids-Wyoming MSA, MI	Y	65200 FQ	82260 MW	102770 TQ	USBLS	5/07
	Warren-Troy-Farmington Hills PMSA, MI	Y	74500 FQ	92040 MW	119590 TQ	USBLS	5/07
	Minnesota	Y	86477 FQ	107382 MW	139402 TQ	MNBLS	10/08-12/08
	Duluth-Superior MSA, MN-WI	Y	64905 FQ	82254 MW	100501 TQ	MNBLS	10/08-12/08
	Minneapolis-Saint Paul MSA, MN-WI	Y	90210 FQ	111949 MW	146419 TQ	MNBLS	10/08-12/08
	Rochester MSA, MN	Y	68290 FQ	98044 MW	117841 TQ	MNBLS	10/08-12/08
	Mississippi	Y	51290 FQ	64920 MW	83250 TQ	USBLS	5/07
	Jackson MSA, MS	Y	54930 FQ	70360 MW	91410 TQ	USBLS	5/07
	Missouri	Y	73300 FQ	93710 MW	124320 TQ	USBLS	5/07
	Jefferson City MSA, MO	Y	66290 FQ	93030 MW	136470 TQ	USBLS	5/07
	Kansas City MSA, MO-KS	Y	66060 FQ	88610 MW	116340 TQ	USBLS	5/07
	St. Louis MSA, MO-IL	Y	74610 FQ	97630 MW	132280 TQ	USBLS	5/07
	Springfield MSA, MO	Y	69880 FQ	92080 MW	118620 TQ	USBLS	5/07
	Montana	Y	43290 FQ	63910 MW	86690 TQ	USBLS	5/07
	Billings MSA, MT	Y	57840 FQ	77200 MW	102330 TQ	USBLS	5/07
	Nebraska	Y	65260 FQ	86590 MW	117350 TQ	USBLS	5/07
	Lincoln MSA, NE	Y	65440 FQ	84590 MW	114290 TQ	USBLS	5/07
	Omaha-Council Bluffs MSA, NE-IA	Y	68380 FQ	90100 MW	120800 TQ	USBLS	5/07
	Nevada	H	27.31 FQ	38.09 MW	51.41 TQ	NVBLS	5/08
	Las Vegas-Paradise MSA, NV	H	27.43 FQ	39.04 MW	53.02 TQ	NVBLS	5/08
	New Hampshire	H	25.39 AE	39.33 MW	55.78 AEX	NHBLS	6/08
	Manchester MSA, NH	Y	62240 FQ	78870 MW	98820 TQ	USBLS	5/07
	Nashua NECTA, NH-MA	Y	56240 FQ	88420 MW	134840 TQ	USBLS	5/07
	New Jersey	Y	89190 FQ	115220 MW		USBLS	5/07
	Camden PMSA, NJ	Y	80160 FQ	101310 MW	129340 TQ	USBLS	5/07
	Edison PMSA, NJ	Y	92560 FQ	116310 MW		USBLS	5/07
	Newark-Union PMSA, NJ-PA	Y	89390 FQ	117830 MW		USBLS	5/07
	New Mexico	Y	48380 FQ	68030 MW	95380 TQ	USBLS	5/07
	Albuquerque MSA, NM	Y	49110 FQ	72310 MW	99730 TQ	USBLS	5/07
	Santa Fe MSA, NM	Y	57970 FQ	79060 MW	114470 TQ	USBLS	5/07
	New York	Y	89470 FQ	128500 MW		USBLS	5/07
	Albany-Schenectady-Troy MSA, NY	Y	74400 FQ	94440 MW	123030 TQ	USBLS	5/07
	Buffalo-Niagara Falls MSA, NY	Y	70600 FQ	91440 MW	125220 TQ	USBLS	5/07
	Nassau-Suffolk PMSA, NY	Y	78710 FQ	105900 MW		USBLS	5/07
	New York-Northern New Jersey-Long Island MSA, NY-NJ-PA	Y	97530 FQ	132290 MW		USBLS	5/07
	Syracuse MSA, NY	Y	71090 FQ	89030 MW	124340 TQ	USBLS	5/07
	North Carolina	Y	67110 FQ	89640 MW	122710 TQ	USBLS	5/07
	Charlotte-Gastonia-Concord MSA, NC-SC	Y	79410 FQ	108140 MW	143630 TQ	USBLS	5/07
	Raleigh-Cary MSA, NC	Y	67240 FQ	82540 MW	105790 TQ	USBLS	5/07
	Winston-Salem MSA, NC	Y	66140 FQ	90630 MW	126930 TQ	USBLS	5/07
	North Dakota	Y	55390 FQ	74430 MW	97600 TQ	USBLS	5/07
	Fargo MSA, ND-MN	Y	57230 FQ	76650 MW	106310 TQ	USBLS	5/07
	Ohio	Y	71280 FQ	93440 MW	123200 TQ	USBLS	5/07
	Cincinnati-Middletown MSA, OH-KY-IN	Y	73210 FQ	97850 MW	127530 TQ	USBLS	5/07
	Cleveland-Elyria-Mentor MSA, OH	Y	77910 FQ	100020 MW	129930 TQ	USBLS	5/07
	Columbus MSA, OH	Y	76750 FQ	99440 MW	129210 TQ	USBLS	5/07
	Dayton MSA, OH	Y	66950 FQ	86350 MW	111900 TQ	USBLS	5/07
	Springfield MSA, OH	Y	60080 FQ	74710 MW	94160 TQ	USBLS	5/07
	Oklahoma	Y	49200 FQ	66280 MW	91290 TQ	USBLS	5/07
	Oklahoma City MSA, OK	Y	49440 FQ	66460 MW	92820 TQ	USBLS	5/07
	Tulsa MSA, OK	Y	56620 FQ	74070 MW	98360 TQ	USBLS	5/07
	Oregon	H	35.52 FQ	45.70 MW	59.38 TQ	ORBLS	5/08
	Eugene-Springfield MSA, OR	Y	59910 FQ	81570 MW	102140 TQ	USBLS	5/07

Occupation/Type/Industry	Location	Per	Low	Mid	High	Source	Date
Financial Manager	Medford MSA, OR	Y	61070 FQ	71310 MW	86280 TQ	USBLS	5/07
	Portland-Vancouver-Beaverton MSA, OR-WA	Y	76920 FQ	96490 MW	124960 TQ	USBLS	5/07
	Pennsylvania	Y	60860 FQ	86430 MW	122180 TQ	USBLS	5/07
	Allentown-Bethlehem-Easton MSA, PA-NJ	Y	61320 FQ	81640 MW	109110 TQ	USBLS	5/07
	Philadelphia-Camden-Wilmington MSA, PA-NJ-DE-MD	Y	76630 FQ	104660 MW	144040 TQ	USBLS	5/07
	Pittsburgh MSA, PA	Y	53980 FQ	77710 MW	111630 TQ	USBLS	5/07
	Rhode Island	Y	74470 FQ	96460 MW	125800 TQ	USBLS	5/07
	Providence-Fall River-Warwick MSA, RI-MA	Y	70240 FQ	94090 MW	124000 TQ	USBLS	5/07
	South Carolina	Y	59590 FQ	81260 MW	108460 TQ	USBLS	5/07
	Charleston-North Charleston MSA, SC	Y	57190 FQ	76980 MW	101180 TQ	USBLS	5/07
	Columbia MSA, SC	Y	61920 FQ	81340 MW	104620 TQ	USBLS	5/07
	Spartanburg MSA, SC	Y	62090 FQ	84390 MW	113750 TQ	USBLS	5/07
	South Dakota	Y	79828 FQ	94688 MW	114060 TQ	SDBLS	7/08-9/08
	Sioux Falls MSA, SD	Y	85792 FQ	98492 MW	120199 TQ	SDBLS	7/08-9/08
	Tennessee	Y	48600 FQ	66370 MW	92940 TQ	USBLS	5/07
	Memphis MSA, TN-MS-AR	Y	52050 FQ	72440 MW	105930 TQ	USBLS	5/07
	Nashville-Davidson-Murfreesboro MSA, TN	Y	52340 FQ	72350 MW	99780 TQ	USBLS	5/07
	Texas	Y	72410 FQ	98920 MW	132030 TQ	USBLS	5/07
	Austin-Round Rock MSA, TX	Y	73650 FQ	100560 MW	128430 TQ	USBLS	5/07
	Beaumont-Port Arthur MSA, TX	Y	55810 FQ	74760 MW	97740 TQ	USBLS	5/07
	Dallas-Fort Worth-Arlington MSA, TX	Y	81420 FQ	104130 MW	135090 TQ	USBLS	5/07
	El Paso MSA, TX	Y	47600 FQ	66520 MW	93600 TQ	USBLS	5/07
	Houston-Sugar Land-Baytown MSA, TX	Y	81260 FQ	108600 MW	143630 TQ	USBLS	5/07
	San Antonio MSA, TX	Y	69660 FQ	98450 MW		USBLS	5/07
	Utah	Y	65060 FQ	81910 MW	102600 TQ	USBLS	5/07
	Salt Lake City MSA, UT	Y	67870 FQ	85510 MW	106170 TQ	USBLS	5/07
	Vermont	Y	67380 FQ	89420 MW	130280 TQ	USBLS	5/07
	Burlington-South Burlington MSA, VT	Y	75400 FQ	100390 MW	135670 TQ	USBLS	5/07
	Virginia	Y	71330 FQ	101320 MW	132760 TQ	USBLS	5/07
	Charlottesville MSA, VA	Y	61010 FQ	82380 MW	103580 TQ	USBLS	5/07
	Richmond MSA, VA	Y	72590 FQ	101750 MW	132040 TQ	USBLS	5/07
	Virginia Beach-Norfolk-Newport News MSA, VA-NC	Y	70100 FQ	91910 MW	117030 TQ	USBLS	5/07
	Washington	H	36.03 FQ	46.77 MW	61.67 TQ	WABLS	3/08
	Seattle-Tacoma-Bellevue MSA, WA	Y	79180 FQ	103960 MW	137780 TQ	USBLS	5/07
	Spokane MSA, WA	Y	64950 FQ	87820 MW	106450 TQ	USBLS	5/07
	West Virginia	Y	43107 FQ	62942 MW	86603 TQ	WVBLS	7/08-9/08
	Charleston MSA, WV	Y	43690 FQ	64260 MW	86800 TQ	USBLS	5/07
	Wisconsin	Y	67920 FQ	88460 MW	116230 TQ	USBLS	5/07
	Appleton MSA, WI	Y	66890 FQ	83180 MW	109140 TQ	USBLS	5/07
	Milwaukee-Waukesha-West Allis MSA, WI	Y	73300 FQ	95230 MW	124630 TQ	USBLS	5/07
	Wyoming	Y	56738 FQ	73705 MW	96557 TQ	WYBLS	9/08
	Cheyenne MSA, WY	Y	61403 FQ	79770 MW	96596 TQ	WYBLS	9/08
	Puerto Rico	Y	41220 FQ	56120 MW	76910 TQ	USBLS	5/07
	San German-Cabo Rojo MSA, PR	Y	29640 FQ	39130 MW	49560 TQ	USBLS	5/07
	San Juan-Caguas-Guaynabo MSA, PR	Y	42660 FQ	58070 MW	78710 TQ	USBLS	5/07
	Virgin Islands	Y	49830 FQ	67750 MW	85930 TQ	USBLS	5/07
	Guam	Y	41930 FQ	55420 MW	75210 TQ	USBLS	5/07
Detroit Public Schools	Detroit, MI	Y			260000 HI	FREEP07	2009
Financial Research Analyst							
Secretary of State	New Hampshire	Y			64079 HI	NHUL03	2008
Financial Specialist							
State Government	Idaho	Y	32385 LO		53996 HI	AFT02	3/1/08

Occupation/Type/Industry	Location	Per	Low	Mid	High	Source	Date
Fine Artist, Including Painter, Sculptor, and Illustrator	Alabama	Y	29540 FQ	50310 MW	56940 TQ	USBLS	5/07
	Arizona	Y	22950 FQ	47230 MW	62450 TQ	USBLS	5/07
	Phoenix-Mesa-Scottsdale MSA, AZ	Y	32300 FQ	52250 MW	62530 TQ	USBLS	5/07
	California	H	19.82 FQ	29.74 MW	42.62 TQ	CABLS	1/08-3/08
	Los Angeles-Long Beach-Glendale PMSA, CA	H	22.65 FQ	33.49 MW	50.27 TQ	CABLS	1/08-3/08
	Oakland-Fremont-Hayward MSA, CA	H	14.01 FQ	16.67 MW	21.32 TQ	CABLS	1/08-3/08
	Riverside-San Bernardino-Ontario MSA, CA	H	19.76 FQ	28.00 MW	35.64 TQ	CABLS	1/08-3/08
	Sacramento-Arden Arcade-Roseville MSA, CA	H	26.12 FQ	28.82 MW	31.54 TQ	CABLS	1/08-3/08
	San Diego-Carlsbad-San Marcos MSA, CA	H	12.19 FQ	25.54 MW	36.04 TQ	CABLS	1/08-3/08
	Santa Ana-Anaheim-Irvine PMSA, CA	Y	27650 FQ	30830 MW	47960 TQ	USBLS	5/07
	Colorado	Y	14740 FQ	15240 MW	40370 TQ	USBLS	5/07
	Denver-Aurora MSA, CO	Y	15540 FQ	30430 MW	59120 TQ	USBLS	5/07
	Pueblo MSA, CO	Y	14520 FQ	14790 MW	15060 TQ	USBLS	5/07
	Hartford-West Hartford-East Hartford MSA, CT	Y	19740 FQ	36310 MW	51820 TQ	USBLS	5/07
	Washington-Arlington-Alexandria MSA, DC-VA-MD-WV	Y	35250 FQ	52550 MW	68820 TQ	USBLS	5/07
	Florida	Y	27490 FQ	38880 MW	51790 TQ	USBLS	5/07
	Fort Lauderdale-Pompano Beach-Deerfield Beach PMSA, FL	Y	27980 FQ	34860 MW	56600 TQ	USBLS	5/07
	Miami-Fort Lauderdale-Miami Beach MSA, FL	Y	26590 FQ	36320 MW	50950 TQ	USBLS	5/07
	Orlando-Kissimmee MSA, FL	Y	33290 FQ	43330 MW	59430 TQ	USBLS	5/07
	Tampa-St. Petersburg-Clearwater MSA, FL	Y	21610 FQ	35140 MW	47110 TQ	USBLS	5/07
	Georgia	Y	33990 FQ	46350 MW	59720 TQ	USBLS	5/07
	Atlanta-Sandy Springs-Marietta MSA, GA	Y	31820 FQ	53080 MW	61690 TQ	USBLS	5/07
	Hawaii	Y	15880 FQ	18970 MW	38370 TQ	USBLS	5/07
	Idaho	Y	26170 FQ	29340 MW	35370 TQ	USBLS	5/07
	Boise City-Nampa MSA, ID	Y	26590 FQ	30080 MW	37170 TQ	USBLS	5/07
	Illinois	Y	26880 FQ	32980 MW	39570 TQ	USBLS	5/07
	Chicago-Naperville-Joliet MSA, IL-IN-WI	Y	25200 FQ	31050 MW	39540 TQ	USBLS	5/07
	Indiana	Y	28050 FQ	35820 MW	49080 TQ	USBLS	5/07
	Iowa	Y	24930 FQ	32320 MW	40990 TQ	USBLS	5/07
	Kansas	Y	12970 FQ	14580 MW	16190 TQ	USBLS	5/07
	Kentucky	Y	27916 FQ	32055 MW	57012 TQ	KYBLS	2008
	Louisville-Jefferson County MSA, KY-IN	Y	28210 FQ	31290 MW	58180 TQ	USBLS	5/07
	Louisiana	H	10.97 FQ	14.29 MW	18.55 TQ	LABLS	1/08-3/08
	Maine	Y	18920 FQ	22690 MW	26210 TQ	USBLS	5/07
	Portland-South Portland-Biddeford MSA, ME	Y	19670 FQ	23250 MW	26300 TQ	USBLS	5/07
	Maryland	Y		39775 MW		MDBLS	3/08
	Baltimore-Towson MSA, MD	Y	28730 FQ	31470 MW	52050 TQ	USBLS	5/07
	Bethesda-Gaithersburg-Frederick PMSA, MD	Y	48340 FQ	58370 MW	69950 TQ	USBLS	5/07
	Massachusetts	Y	21580 FQ	41700 MW	59590 TQ	USBLS	5/07
	Boston-Cambridge-Quincy NECTA, MA	Y	21180 FQ	45430 MW	62120 TQ	USBLS	5/07
	Michigan	Y	48400 FQ	71810 MW	98660 TQ	USBLS	5/07
	Detroit-Warren-Livonia MSA, MI	Y	61510 FQ	77590 MW	102790 TQ	USBLS	5/07
	Warren-Troy-Farmington Hills PMSA, MI	Y	62220 FQ	77180 MW	105650 TQ	USBLS	5/07
	Minnesota	Y	28834 FQ	42665 MW	58620 TQ	MNBLS	10/08-12/08
	Duluth-Superior MSA, MN-WI	Y	22535 FQ	24125 MW	25862 TQ	MNBLS	10/08-12/08
	Minneapolis-Saint Paul MSA, MN-WI	Y	32757 FQ	47435 MW	61926 TQ	MNBLS	10/08-12/08
	Missouri	Y	28960 FQ	43270 MW	55770 TQ	USBLS	5/07
	Kansas City MSA, MO-KS	Y	13420 FQ	14850 MW	18130 TQ	USBLS	5/07

AE Average entry wage	**AW** Average wage paid	**FQ** First quartile wage	**LO** Lowest wage paid	**MTC** Median total compensation	**TCC** Total cash compensation
AER Average entry range	**AWR** Average wage range	**H** Hourly	**LR** Low end range	**MW** Median wage paid	**TQ** Third quartile wage
AEX Average experienced wage	**AXR** Average experienced range	**HI** Highest wage paid	**M** Monthly	**MWR** Median wage range	**W** Weekly
ATC Average total compensation	**D** Daily	**HR** High end range	**MCC** Median cash compensation	**S** See annotated source	**Y** Yearly

Occupation/Type/Industry	Location	Per	Low	Mid	High	Source	Date
Fine Artist, Including Painter, Sculptor, and Illustrator	St. Louis MSA, MO-IL	Y	40980 FQ	46830 MW	62010 TQ	USBLS	5/07
	Nebraska	Y	22990 FQ	35520 MW	44090 TQ	USBLS	5/07
	Nevada	H	11.29 FQ	12.77 MW	14.91 TQ	NVBLS	5/08
	Las Vegas-Paradise MSA, NV	H	11.24 FQ	12.65 MW	14.68 TQ	NVBLS	5/08
	New Jersey	Y	33580 FQ	52190 MW	61880 TQ	USBLS	5/07
	Camden PMSA, NJ	Y	29840 FQ	45760 MW	60220 TQ	USBLS	5/07
	Edison PMSA, NJ	Y	27010 FQ	38340 MW	54960 TQ	USBLS	5/07
	New Mexico	Y	16880 FQ	18830 MW	52000 TQ	USBLS	5/07
	Albuquerque MSA, NM	Y	16570 FQ	18210 MW	41440 TQ	USBLS	5/07
	New York	Y	40130 FQ	48890 MW	60410 TQ	USBLS	5/07
	Nassau-Suffolk PMSA, NY	Y	23360 FQ	54380 MW	74220 TQ	USBLS	5/07
	New York-Northern New Jersey-Long Island MSA, NY-NJ-PA	Y	40060 FQ	49310 MW	60570 TQ	USBLS	5/07
	North Carolina	Y	24240 FQ	34600 MW	41240 TQ	USBLS	5/07
	Charlotte-Gastonia-Concord MSA, NC-SC	Y	35890 FQ	47980 MW	58610 TQ	USBLS	5/07
	Raleigh-Cary MSA, NC	Y	33360 FQ	37820 MW	44520 TQ	USBLS	5/07
	Ohio	Y	16240 FQ	35560 MW	54480 TQ	USBLS	5/07
	Cincinnati-Middletown MSA, OH-KY-IN	Y	38950 FQ	53110 MW	60480 TQ	USBLS	5/07
	Dayton MSA, OH	Y	32630 FQ	39140 MW	45160 TQ	USBLS	5/07
	Oklahoma	Y	34970 FQ	54080 MW	64420 TQ	USBLS	5/07
	Oregon	H	18.17 FQ	23.93 MW	31.80 TQ	ORBLS	5/08
	Portland-Vancouver-Beaverton MSA, OR-WA	Y	37490 FQ	54220 MW	74140 TQ	USBLS	5/07
	Pennsylvania	Y	17600 FQ	24380 MW	38060 TQ	USBLS	5/07
	Philadelphia-Camden-Wilmington MSA, PA-NJ-DE-MD	Y	32600 FQ	45950 MW	68580 TQ	USBLS	5/07
	Pittsburgh MSA, PA	Y	21140 FQ	23630 MW	26920 TQ	USBLS	5/07
	Rhode Island	Y	31230 FQ	37720 MW	50330 TQ	USBLS	5/07
	Providence-Fall River-Warwick MSA, RI-MA	Y	22220 FQ	27630 MW	37570 TQ	USBLS	5/07
	South Carolina	Y	36900 FQ	71960 MW	79160 TQ	USBLS	5/07
	Tennessee	Y	39440 FQ	42760 MW	46400 TQ	USBLS	5/07
	Nashville-Davidson-Murfreesboro MSA, TN	Y	40990 FQ	43630 MW	46280 TQ	USBLS	5/07
	Texas	Y	31780 FQ	43660 MW	57730 TQ	USBLS	5/07
	Dallas-Fort Worth-Arlington MSA, TX	Y	31420 FQ	51550 MW	60150 TQ	USBLS	5/07
	Houston-Sugar Land-Baytown MSA, TX	Y	33610 FQ	38940 MW	53420 TQ	USBLS	5/07
	San Antonio MSA, TX	Y	42520 FQ	46680 MW	57240 TQ	USBLS	5/07
	Utah	Y	26760 FQ	42540 MW	57130 TQ	USBLS	5/07
	Salt Lake City MSA, UT	Y	27990 FQ	45070 MW	59330 TQ	USBLS	5/07
	Vermont	Y	39780 FQ	91600 MW	106620 TQ	USBLS	5/07
	Virginia	Y	17570 FQ	38320 MW	60110 TQ	USBLS	5/07
	Virginia Beach-Norfolk-Newport News MSA, VA-NC	Y	13790 FQ	27640 MW	57550 TQ	USBLS	5/07
	Washington	H	18.61 FQ	22.37 MW	30.38 TQ	WABLS	3/08
	Seattle-Tacoma-Bellevue MSA, WA	Y	38930 FQ	46440 MW	62540 TQ	USBLS	5/07
	Wisconsin	Y	23360 FQ	26110 MW	36980 TQ	USBLS	5/07
	Milwaukee-Waukesha-West Allis MSA, WI	Y	22760 FQ	24760 MW	39820 TQ	USBLS	5/07
	Wyoming	Y	23142 FQ	28462 MW	32886 TQ	WYBLS	9/08
Fine Arts Administrator State Government	Ohio	H	27.93 LO		36.59 HI	ODAS	2008
Fingerprint Clerk Department of Safety	New Hampshire	Y		26985 AW		NHUL03	2008
Fire Alarm Operator and Dispatcher Municipal Government	Cincinnati, OH	Y	45777 LO		50908 HI	COHSS	10/08
Fire and Life Safety Educator Municipal Government	Colorado Springs, CO	M	4006 LO			COSPRS	1/1/09

AE	Average entry wage	AW	Average wage paid	FQ	First quartile wage	LO	Lowest wage paid	MTC	Median total compensation	TCC	Total cash compensation
AER	Average entry range	AWR	Average wage range	H	Hourly	LR	Low end range	MW	Median wage paid	TQ	Third quartile wage
AEX	Average experienced wage	AXR	Average experienced range	HI	Highest wage paid	M	Monthly	MWR	Median wage range	W	Weekly
ATC	Average total compensation	D	Daily	HR	High end range	MCC	Median cash compensation	S	See annotated source	Y	Yearly

Occupation/Type/Industry	Location	Per	Low	Mid	High	Source	Date
Fire Chief	Eastman, GA	Y	21788 LO		45941 HI	GACTY01	2008
	Valdosta, GA	Y	62062 LO		109517 HI	GACTY01	2008
	Charlemont, MA	Y			6135 HI	FRCOG	2009
	Conway, MA	Y			4752 HI	FRCOG	2009
	Biloxi, MS	Y			83542 HI	MML	2008
	Carthage, MS	Y			41695 HI	MML	2008
	Macon, MS	Y			12978 HI	MML	2008
	Christine, ND	Y			800 HI	NDLC02	2008
	Devils Lake, ND	M	3355 LO		4841 HI	NDLC01	2008
	Fargo, ND	M	5902 LO		8155 HI	NDLC01	2008
Fire Code Examiner	Colorado Springs, CO	M	4025 LO			COSPRS	1/1/09
Fire Engine Operator/Driver	Atlanta, GA	Y	38641 LO		55532 HI	GACTY01	2008
	Rome, GA	Y	29500 LO		47700 HI	GACTY01	2008
Fire Fighter	Alabama	Y	27250 FQ	33990 MW	43190 TQ	USBLS	5/07
	Birmingham-Hoover MSA, AL	Y	27350 FQ	34440 MW	49910 TQ	USBLS	5/07
	Arizona	Y	28460 FQ	37090 MW	48940 TQ	USBLS	5/07
	Phoenix-Mesa-Scottsdale MSA, AZ	Y	32840 FQ	43840 MW	57380 TQ	USBLS	5/07
	Tucson MSA, AZ	Y	33520 FQ	39020 MW	45920 TQ	USBLS	5/07
	Arkansas	Y	22630 FQ	32140 MW	42730 TQ	USBLS	5/07
	Fort Smith MSA, AR-OK	Y	27040 FQ	30950 MW	37530 TQ	USBLS	5/07
	Little Rock-North Little Rock MSA, AR	Y	26210 FQ	38160 MW	46800 TQ	USBLS	5/07
	Pine Bluff MSA, AR	Y	28530 FQ	37950 MW	44180 TQ	USBLS	5/07
	California	H	21.25 FQ	30.54 MW	39.07 TQ	CABLS	1/08-3/08
	Bakersfield MSA, CA	H	18.97 FQ	22.17 MW	25.09 TQ	CABLS	1/08-3/08
	Los Angeles-Long Beach-Glendale PMSA, CA	H	29.91 FQ	37.13 MW	45.01 TQ	CABLS	1/08-3/08
	Oakland-Fremont-Hayward MSA, CA	H	34.33 FQ	43.94 MW	49.78 TQ	CABLS	1/08-3/08
	Riverside-San Bernardino-Ontario MSA, CA	H	11.84 FQ	19.53 MW	27.96 TQ	CABLS	1/08-3/08
	Sacramento-Arden Arcade-Roseville MSA, CA	H	18.67 FQ	24.70 MW	31.19 TQ	CABLS	1/08-3/08
	San Diego-Carlsbad-San Marcos MSA, CA	H	21.32 FQ	26.60 MW	33.87 TQ	CABLS	1/08-3/08
	San Jose-Sunnyvale-Santa Clara MSA, CA	H	30.77 FQ	37.00 MW	45.04 TQ	CABLS	1/08-3/08
	Santa Ana-Anaheim-Irvine PMSA, CA	Y	40980 FQ	55800 MW	71480 TQ	USBLS	5/07
	Santa Rosa-Petaluma MSA, CA	H	13.08 FQ	18.43 MW	27.91 TQ	CABLS	1/08-3/08
	Colorado	Y	38420 FQ	47970 MW	62820 TQ	USBLS	5/07
	Boulder MSA, CO	Y	38340 FQ	46200 MW	59650 TQ	USBLS	5/07
	Denver-Aurora MSA, CO	Y	44920 FQ	58700 MW	71650 TQ	USBLS	5/07
	Connecticut	H	16.90 AE	25.36 MW		CTBLS	1/08-3/08
	Bridgeport-Stamford-Norwalk MSA, CT	Y	49010 FQ	58380 MW	64260 TQ	USBLS	5/07
	Hartford-West Hartford-East Hartford MSA, CT	Y	50790 FQ	57320 MW	62560 TQ	USBLS	5/07
	Norwich-New London MSA, CT-RI	Y	37520 FQ	42190 MW	48810 TQ	USBLS	5/07
	Danbury, CT	Y	44944 LO		55461 HI	FIREH	2006
	Delaware	Y	50330 FQ	57230 MW	62870 TQ	USBLS	5/07
	Wilmington PMSA, DE-MD-NJ	Y	47080 FQ	56380 MW	62560 TQ	USBLS	5/07
	Florida	Y	32770 FQ	42180 MW	55090 TQ	USBLS	5/07
	Fort Lauderdale-Pompano Beach-Deerfield Beach PMSA, FL	Y	44050 FQ	52910 MW	62650 TQ	USBLS	5/07
	Jacksonville MSA, FL	Y	34370 FQ	42830 MW	55880 TQ	USBLS	5/07
	Miami-Fort Lauderdale-Miami Beach MSA, FL	Y	42920 FQ	53090 MW	63640 TQ	USBLS	5/07
	Orlando-Kissimmee MSA, FL	Y	28100 FQ	34640 MW	44350 TQ	USBLS	5/07
	Tallahassee MSA, FL	Y	33170 FQ	41980 MW	53530 TQ	USBLS	5/07
	Tampa-St. Petersburg-Clearwater MSA, FL	Y	28600 FQ	37530 MW	52110 TQ	USBLS	5/07
	West Palm Beach-Boca Raton-Boynton Beach PMSA, FL	Y	43780 FQ	55860 MW	69410 TQ	USBLS	5/07
	Isle of Capri, FL	Y	32280 LO		48191 HI	FIREH	2006
	Georgia	Y	26960 FQ	33300 MW	41000 TQ	USBLS	5/07

AE Average entry wage	**AW** Average wage paid	**FQ** First quartile wage	**LO** Lowest wage paid	**MTC** Median total compensation	**TCC** Total cash compensation
AER Average entry range	**AWR** Average wage range	**H** Hourly	**LR** Low end range	**MW** Median wage paid	**TQ** Third quartile wage
AEX Average experienced wage	**AXR** Average experienced range	**HI** Highest wage paid	**M** Monthly	**MWR** Median wage range	**W** Weekly
ATC Average total compensation	**D** Daily	**HR** High end range	**MCC** Median cash compensation	**S** See annotated source	**Y** Yearly

Occupation/Type/Industry	Location	Per	Low	Mid	High	Source	Date
Fire Fighter	Atlanta-Sandy Springs-Marietta MSA, GA	Y	30020 FQ	37500 MW	45910 TQ	USBLS	5/07
	Savannah MSA, GA	Y	30340 FQ	34640 MW	38680 TQ	USBLS	5/07
	Americus, GA	Y	25111 LO		35156 HI	GACTY01	2008
	Cedartown, GA	Y	29994 LO		34100 HI	GACTY01	2008
	Gainesville, GA	Y	27312 LO		40982 HI	GACTY01	2008
	Hawaii	Y	39760 FQ	45780 MW	51780 TQ	USBLS	5/07
	Honolulu MSA, HI	Y	41420 FQ	47080 MW	53750 TQ	USBLS	5/07
	Idaho	Y	21670 FQ	33960 MW	50770 TQ	USBLS	5/07
	Boise City-Nampa MSA, ID	Y	40570 FQ	52600 MW	59710 TQ	USBLS	5/07
	Illinois	Y	25010 FQ	50550 MW	67080 TQ	USBLS	5/07
	Chicago-Naperville-Joliet MSA, IL-IN-WI	Y	32100 FQ	57280 MW	69380 TQ	USBLS	5/07
	East Peoria, IL	Y	29000 LO		55897 HI	FIREH	2006
	Indiana	Y	34600 FQ	40950 MW	47390 TQ	USBLS	5/07
	Gary PMSA, IN	Y	23960 FQ	39880 MW	44670 TQ	USBLS	5/07
	Indianapolis-Carmel MSA, IN	Y	37340 FQ	45810 MW	54490 TQ	USBLS	5/07
	Iowa	Y	23810 FQ	34180 MW	41470 TQ	USBLS	5/07
	Des Moines-West Des Moines MSA, IA	Y	22220 FQ	30800 MW	39370 TQ	USBLS	5/07
	Kansas	Y	24190 FQ	33110 MW	48700 TQ	USBLS	5/07
	Wichita MSA, KS	Y	26670 FQ	31710 MW	38200 TQ	USBLS	5/07
	Overland Park, KS	Y	35568 LO		61116 HI	FIREH	2006
	Kentucky	Y	23182 FQ	31086 MW	40635 TQ	KYBLS	2008
	Elizabethtown MSA, KY	Y	20810 FQ	30530 MW	37320 TQ	USBLS	5/07
	Louisville-Jefferson County MSA, KY-IN	Y	26850 FQ	38930 MW	45980 TQ	USBLS	5/07
	Louisiana	H	9.74 FQ	13.11 MW	17.09 TQ	LABLS	1/08-3/08
	Baton Rouge MSA, LA	Y	22990 FQ	29660 MW	35460 TQ	USBLS	5/07
	New Orleans-Metairie-Kenner MSA, LA	Y	19770 FQ	25410 MW	33000 TQ	USBLS	5/07
	Maine	Y	25560 FQ	35680 MW	41270 TQ	USBLS	5/07
	Portland-South Portland-Biddeford MSA, ME	Y	28290 FQ	36830 MW	41310 TQ	USBLS	5/07
	Maryland	Y		48525 MW		MDBLS	3/08
	Baltimore-Towson MSA, MD	Y	41750 FQ	46770 MW	51820 TQ	USBLS	5/07
	Massachusetts	Y	40970 FQ	48280 MW	57290 TQ	USBLS	5/07
	Boston-Cambridge-Quincy NECTA, MA	Y	45470 FQ	52600 MW	65220 TQ	USBLS	5/07
	Worcester MSA, MA-CT	Y	18420 FQ	37770 MW	53870 TQ	USBLS	5/07
	Conway, MA	H			8.83 HI	FRCOG	2009
	Michigan	Y	29760 FQ	43310 MW	52940 TQ	USBLS	5/07
	Detroit-Warren-Livonia MSA, MI	Y	39460 FQ	49050 MW	56940 TQ	USBLS	5/07
	Warren-Troy-Farmington Hills PMSA, MI	Y	34350 FQ	45960 MW	54980 TQ	USBLS	5/07
	Royal Oak, MI	Y	38661 LO		55225 HI	FIREH	2006
	Minnesota	Y	22427 FQ	29244 MW	42523 TQ	MNBLS	10/08-12/08
	Duluth-Superior MSA, MN-WI	Y	27049 FQ	33646 MW	39627 TQ	MNBLS	10/08-12/08
	Minneapolis-Saint Paul MSA, MN-WI	Y	21915 FQ	28502 MW	50407 TQ	MNBLS	10/08-12/08
	Mississippi	Y	22430 FQ	29290 MW	35700 TQ	USBLS	5/07
	Jackson MSA, MS	Y	28410 FQ	33680 MW	39890 TQ	USBLS	5/07
	Missouri	Y	27480 FQ	42170 MW	54540 TQ	USBLS	5/07
	Joplin MSA, MO	Y	22540 FQ	26050 MW	31820 TQ	USBLS	5/07
	Kansas City MSA, MO-KS	Y	36600 FQ	47790 MW	60440 TQ	USBLS	5/07
	St. Louis MSA, MO-IL	Y	35200 FQ	48320 MW	61910 TQ	USBLS	5/07
	Montana	Y	33890 FQ	39680 MW	46330 TQ	USBLS	5/07
	Missoula, MT	Y	33396 LO		46224 HI	FIREH	2006
	Nebraska	Y	31960 FQ	40450 MW	56800 TQ	USBLS	5/07
	Omaha-Council Bluffs MSA, NE-IA	Y	40350 FQ	55270 MW	61170 TQ	USBLS	5/07
	Nevada	H	19.39 FQ	23.43 MW	27.63 TQ	NVBLS	5/08
	Las Vegas-Paradise MSA, NV	H	21.78 FQ	25.67 MW	29.34 TQ	NVBLS	5/08
	New Hampshire	H	13.85 AE	19.98 MW	22.11 AEX	NHBLS	6/08
	Nashua NECTA, NH-MA	Y	42320 FQ	46910 MW	52590 TQ	USBLS	5/07
	New Jersey	Y	44410 FQ	61230 MW	73230 TQ	USBLS	5/07
	Camden PMSA, NJ	Y	49250 FQ	55900 MW	62420 TQ	USBLS	5/07
	Edison PMSA, NJ	Y	31050 FQ	46030 MW	67690 TQ	USBLS	5/07
	Newark-Union PMSA, NJ-PA	Y	57990 FQ	67960 MW	74850 TQ	USBLS	5/07
	Teaneck, NJ	Y	27334 LO		79682 HI	FIREH	2006
	Vineland, NJ	Y	31083 LO		63455 HI	FIREH	2006

AE	Average entry wage	AW	Average wage paid	FQ	First quartile wage	LO	Lowest wage paid	MTC	Median total compensation	TCC	Total cash compensation
AER	Average entry range	AWR	Average wage range	H	Hourly	LR	Low end range	MW	Median wage paid	TQ	Third quartile wage
AEX	Average experienced wage	AXR	Average experienced range	HI	Highest wage paid	M	Monthly	MWR	Median wage range	W	Weekly
ATC	Average total compensation	D	Daily	HR	High end range	MCC	Median cash compensation	S	See annotated source	Y	Yearly

Fire Fighter

Occupation/Type/Industry	Location	Per	Low	Mid	High	Source	Date
Fire Fighter	New Mexico	Y	26560 FQ	30620 MW	36630 TQ	USBLS	5/07
	Espanola, NM	Y	24000 LO		36000 HI	FIREH	2006
	New York	Y	48690 FQ	56100 MW	62390 TQ	USBLS	5/07
	Albany-Schenectady-Troy MSA, NY	Y	42590 FQ	47720 MW	54400 TQ	USBLS	5/07
	Nassau-Suffolk PMSA, NY	Y	45620 FQ	52720 MW	69640 TQ	USBLS	5/07
	New York-Northern New Jersey-Long Island MSA, NY-NJ-PA	Y	49630 FQ	58630 MW	66000 TQ	USBLS	5/07
	North Carolina	Y	25330 FQ	31800 MW	39510 TQ	USBLS	5/07
	Charlotte-Gastonia-Concord MSA, NC-SC	Y	27010 FQ	37540 MW	47030 TQ	USBLS	5/07
	Raleigh-Cary MSA, NC	Y	26590 FQ	34910 MW	43240 TQ	USBLS	5/07
	North Dakota	Y	33970 FQ	39480 MW	46300 TQ	USBLS	5/07
	Fargo MSA, ND-MN	Y	36060 FQ	39200 MW	43860 TQ	USBLS	5/07
	Ohio	Y	25840 FQ	38890 MW	53710 TQ	USBLS	5/07
	Cincinnati-Middletown MSA, OH-KY-IN	Y	26460 FQ	39010 MW	53620 TQ	USBLS	5/07
	Cleveland-Elyria-Mentor MSA, OH	Y	28390 FQ	43740 MW	56720 TQ	USBLS	5/07
	Columbus MSA, OH	Y	28580 FQ	50540 MW	60000 TQ	USBLS	5/07
	Dayton MSA, OH	Y	21070 FQ	28360 MW	45020 TQ	USBLS	5/07
	Oklahoma	Y	27610 FQ	38000 MW	49600 TQ	USBLS	5/07
	Oklahoma City MSA, OK	Y	41130 FQ	49870 MW	59390 TQ	USBLS	5/07
	Tulsa MSA, OK	Y	29180 FQ	40590 MW	49960 TQ	USBLS	5/07
	Oregon	H	18.95 FQ	24.02 MW	29.57 TQ	ORBLS	5/08
	Portland-Vancouver-Beaverton MSA, OR-WA	Y	45390 FQ	54980 MW	65520 TQ	USBLS	5/07
	Pennsylvania	Y	37100 FQ	47290 MW	57540 TQ	USBLS	5/07
	Allentown-Bethlehem-Easton MSA, PA-NJ	Y	28290 FQ	44070 MW	52370 TQ	USBLS	5/07
	Philadelphia-Camden-Wilmington MSA, PA-NJ-DE-MD	Y	43840 FQ	55660 MW	61460 TQ	USBLS	5/07
	Pittsburgh MSA, PA	Y	40930 FQ	46060 MW	50790 TQ	USBLS	5/07
	Rhode Island	Y	42730 FQ	46440 MW	50840 TQ	USBLS	5/07
	Providence-Fall River-Warwick MSA, RI-MA	Y	42810 FQ	46530 MW	50750 TQ	USBLS	5/07
	South Carolina	Y	23030 FQ	28920 MW	36660 TQ	USBLS	5/07
	Charleston-North Charleston MSA, SC	Y	21240 FQ	25920 MW	33560 TQ	USBLS	5/07
	Columbia MSA, SC	Y	28470 FQ	34530 MW	40590 TQ	USBLS	5/07
	Myrtle Beach-Conway-North Myrtle Beach MSA, SC	Y	22600 FQ	25380 MW	30840 TQ	USBLS	5/07
	South Dakota	Y	31541 FQ	38149 MW	47303 TQ	SDBLS	7/08-9/08
	Tennessee	Y	29390 FQ	37600 MW	49500 TQ	USBLS	5/07
	Memphis MSA, TN-MS-AR	Y	33700 FQ	43020 MW	49380 TQ	USBLS	5/07
	Nashville-Davidson-Murfreesboro MSA, TN	Y	34820 FQ	50560 MW	57670 TQ	USBLS	5/07
	Texas	Y	34900 FQ	43890 MW	52960 TQ	USBLS	5/07
	Austin-Round Rock MSA, TX	Y	32450 FQ	41410 MW	51690 TQ	USBLS	5/07
	Dallas-Fort Worth-Arlington MSA, TX	Y	38430 FQ	50700 MW	62020 TQ	USBLS	5/07
	Houston-Sugar Land-Baytown MSA, TX	Y	35980 FQ	43290 MW	50400 TQ	USBLS	5/07
	San Antonio MSA, TX	Y	38650 FQ	46150 MW	51260 TQ	USBLS	5/07
	Utah	Y	23620 FQ	34490 MW	46580 TQ	USBLS	5/07
	Provo-Orem MSA, UT	Y	24950 FQ	31240 MW	46100 TQ	USBLS	5/07
	Salt Lake City MSA, UT	Y	29040 FQ	41470 MW	51120 TQ	USBLS	5/07
	Vermont	Y	18150 FQ	28920 MW	40750 TQ	USBLS	5/07
	Virginia	Y	34890 FQ	41190 MW	49950 TQ	USBLS	5/07
	Richmond MSA, VA	Y	36450 FQ	42610 MW	51710 TQ	USBLS	5/07
	Virginia Beach-Norfolk-Newport News MSA, VA-NC	Y	34450 FQ	39870 MW	47110 TQ	USBLS	5/07
	Washington	H	22.42 FQ	28.48 MW	32.73 TQ	WABLS	3/08
	Seattle-Tacoma-Bellevue MSA, WA	Y	55820 FQ	62620 MW	70900 TQ	USBLS	5/07
	West Virginia	Y	22135 FQ	27379 MW	37736 TQ	WVBLS	7/08-9/08
	Wisconsin	Y	15520 FQ	27680 MW	45360 TQ	USBLS	5/07
	Appleton MSA, WI	Y	29060 FQ	35600 MW	51690 TQ	USBLS	5/07
	Milwaukee-Waukesha-West Allis MSA, WI	Y	14600 FQ	25070 MW	54080 TQ	USBLS	5/07

AE Average entry wage	**AW** Average wage paid	**FQ** First quartile wage	**LO** Lowest wage paid	**MTC** Median total compensation	**TCC** Total cash compensation
AER Average entry range	**AWR** Average wage range	**H** Hourly	**LR** Low end range	**MW** Median wage paid	**TQ** Third quartile wage
AEX Average experienced wage	**AXR** Average experienced range	**HI** Highest wage paid	**M** Monthly	**MWR** Median wage range	**W** Weekly
ATC Average total compensation	**D** Daily	**HR** High end range	**MCC** Median cash compensation	**S** See annotated source	**Y** Yearly

Occupation/Type/Industry	Location	Per	Low	Mid	High	Source	Date
Fire Fighter	Wyoming	Y	39245 FQ	48371 MW	57824 TQ	WYBLS	9/08
	Puerto Rico	Y	20570 FQ	22410 MW	24250 TQ	USBLS	5/07
	San Juan-Caguas-Guaynabo MSA, PR	Y	20570 FQ	22370 MW	24180 TQ	USBLS	5/07
Department of Corrections	Ohio	H	16.35 LO		19.88 HI	ODAS	2008
Fire Fighter/Emergency Medical Technician	Gainesville, GA	Y	28690 LO		43049 HI	GACTY01	2008
	McDonough, GA	Y	34497 LO		55420 HI	GACTY01	2008
Fire Inspector and Investigator	Alabama	Y	37850 FQ	46660 MW	65300 TQ	USBLS	5/07
	Birmingham-Hoover MSA, AL	Y	39600 FQ	58860 MW	73890 TQ	USBLS	5/07
	Arizona	Y	51570 FQ	58680 MW	65660 TQ	USBLS	5/07
	Phoenix-Mesa-Scottsdale MSA, AZ	Y	48980 FQ	62380 MW	81600 TQ	USBLS	5/07
	Arkansas	Y	34920 FQ	38860 MW	48690 TQ	USBLS	5/07
	California	H	30.41 FQ	38.78 MW	47.50 TQ	CABLS	1/08-3/08
	Los Angeles-Long Beach-Glendale PMSA, CA	H	40.48 FQ	45.79 MW	50.37 TQ	CABLS	1/08-3/08
	Oakland-Fremont-Hayward MSA, CA	H	34.36 FQ	43.88 MW	49.43 TQ	CABLS	1/08-3/08
	Riverside-San Bernardino-Ontario MSA, CA	H	24.46 FQ	28.81 MW	32.23 TQ	CABLS	1/08-3/08
	Sacramento-Arden Arcade-Roseville MSA, CA	H	30.29 FQ	35.00 MW	39.47 TQ	CABLS	1/08-3/08
	San Diego-Carlsbad-San Marcos MSA, CA	H	31.84 FQ	37.54 MW	51.09 TQ	CABLS	1/08-3/08
	San Francisco-San Mateo-Redwood PMSA, CA	H	38.16 FQ	43.79 MW	56.22 TQ	CABLS	1/08-3/08
	Santa Ana-Anaheim-Irvine PMSA, CA	Y	54040 FQ	61090 MW	70290 TQ	USBLS	5/07
	Colorado	Y	53210 FQ	59810 MW	66410 TQ	USBLS	5/07
	Denver-Aurora MSA, CO	Y	55830 FQ	61070 MW	66010 TQ	USBLS	5/07
	Connecticut	H	16.67 AE	28.10 MW		CTBLS	1/08-3/08
	Bridgeport-Stamford-Norwalk MSA, CT	Y	45910 FQ	57750 MW	72140 TQ	USBLS	5/07
	Hartford-West Hartford-East Hartford MSA, CT	Y	44460 FQ	56670 MW	68440 TQ	USBLS	5/07
	Delaware	Y	39060 FQ	48010 MW	58330 TQ	USBLS	5/07
	Wilmington PMSA, DE-MD-NJ	Y	36200 FQ	45300 MW	58000 TQ	USBLS	5/07
	Washington-Arlington-Alexandria MSA, DC-VA-MD-WV	Y	51030 FQ	64250 MW	75150 TQ	USBLS	5/07
	Florida	Y	41540 FQ	51580 MW	65180 TQ	USBLS	5/07
	Fort Lauderdale-Pompano Beach-Deerfield Beach PMSA, FL	Y	56100 FQ	67080 MW	78600 TQ	USBLS	5/07
	Miami-Fort Lauderdale-Miami Beach MSA, FL	Y	48500 FQ	60990 MW	75500 TQ	USBLS	5/07
	Orlando-Kissimmee MSA, FL	Y	37430 FQ	44100 MW	54780 TQ	USBLS	5/07
	Tampa-St. Petersburg-Clearwater MSA, FL	Y	41750 FQ	48530 MW	58740 TQ	USBLS	5/07
	West Palm Beach-Boca Raton-Boynton Beach PMSA, FL	Y	54240 FQ	68890 MW	82780 TQ	USBLS	5/07
	Georgia	Y	33940 FQ	37680 MW	49090 TQ	USBLS	5/07
	Atlanta-Sandy Springs-Marietta MSA, GA	Y	35440 FQ	42490 MW	55790 TQ	USBLS	5/07
	Illinois	Y	47100 FQ	59060 MW	71680 TQ	USBLS	5/07
	Chicago-Naperville-Joliet MSA, IL-IN-WI	Y	45640 FQ	59490 MW	73480 TQ	USBLS	5/07
	Indiana	Y	35410 FQ	41740 MW	48730 TQ	USBLS	5/07
	Indianapolis-Carmel MSA, IN	Y	31230 FQ	37350 MW	45660 TQ	USBLS	5/07
	Iowa	Y	45680 FQ	57250 MW	66220 TQ	USBLS	5/07
	Kansas	Y	44390 FQ	54260 MW	61860 TQ	USBLS	5/07
	Kentucky	Y	39225 FQ	45913 MW	51154 TQ	KYBLS	2008
	Louisville-Jefferson County MSA, KY-IN	Y	43340 FQ	47020 MW	50910 TQ	USBLS	5/07
	Louisiana	H	14.47 FQ	18.89 MW	24.00 TQ	LABLS	1/08-3/08
	New Orleans-Metairie-Kenner MSA, LA	Y	35820 FQ	45380 MW	51430 TQ	USBLS	5/07
	Maine	Y	34030 FQ	37800 MW	41410 TQ	USBLS	5/07

AE	Average entry wage	AW	Average wage paid	FQ	First quartile wage
AER	Average entry range	AWR	Average wage range	H	Hourly
AEX	Average experienced wage	AXR	Average experienced range	HI	Highest wage paid
ATC	Average total compensation	D	Daily	HR	High end range

LO	Lowest wage paid	MTC	Median total compensation
LR	Low end range	MW	Median wage paid
M	Monthly	MWR	Median wage range
MCC	Median cash compensation	S	See annotated source

TCC	Total cash compensation
TQ	Third quartile wage
W	Weekly
Y	Yearly

609

Occupation/Type/Industry	Location	Per	Low	Mid	High	Source	Date
Fire Inspector and Investigator	Maryland	Y		48200 MW		MDBLS	3/08
	Baltimore-Towson MSA, MD	Y	30770 FQ	43140 MW	58290 TQ	USBLS	5/07
	Massachusetts	Y	51560 FQ	61340 MW	71170 TQ	USBLS	5/07
	Boston-Cambridge-Quincy NECTA, MA	Y	59170 FQ	65450 MW	74230 TQ	USBLS	5/07
	Worcester MSA, MA-CT	Y	40100 FQ	48420 MW	75460 TQ	USBLS	5/07
	Michigan	Y	39100 FQ	49650 MW	63280 TQ	USBLS	5/07
	Detroit-Warren-Livonia MSA, MI	Y	53440 FQ	63160 MW	71680 TQ	USBLS	5/07
	Warren-Troy-Farmington Hills PMSA, MI	Y	53860 FQ	60900 MW	69550 TQ	USBLS	5/07
	Minnesota	Y	53094 FQ	61773 MW	69426 TQ	MNBLS	10/08-12/08
	Minneapolis-Saint Paul MSA, MN-WI	Y	54464 FQ	62369 MW	70043 TQ	MNBLS	10/08-12/08
	Mississippi	Y	29650 FQ	38840 MW	47220 TQ	USBLS	5/07
	Missouri	Y	38040 FQ	49020 MW	60950 TQ	USBLS	5/07
	Kansas City MSA, MO-KS	Y	49740 FQ	56500 MW	63350 TQ	USBLS	5/07
	St. Louis MSA, MO-IL	Y	44690 FQ	55970 MW	72120 TQ	USBLS	5/07
	Nebraska	Y	39650 FQ	52830 MW	61700 TQ	USBLS	5/07
	Nevada	H	28.25 FQ	32.46 MW	39.23 TQ	NVBLS	5/08
	Las Vegas-Paradise MSA, NV	H	28.46 FQ	33.30 MW	40.19 TQ	NVBLS	5/08
	New Hampshire	H	14.09 AE	20.62 MW	22.42 AEX	NHBLS	6/08
	New Jersey	Y	35540 FQ	49470 MW	66330 TQ	USBLS	5/07
	Camden PMSA, NJ	Y	34020 FQ	46270 MW	61580 TQ	USBLS	5/07
	Edison PMSA, NJ	Y	45230 FQ	63260 MW	76690 TQ	USBLS	5/07
	Newark-Union PMSA, NJ-PA	Y	30490 FQ	39320 MW	56150 TQ	USBLS	5/07
	New Mexico	Y	38860 FQ	45880 MW	51610 TQ	USBLS	5/07
	Albuquerque MSA, NM	Y	43480 FQ	47540 MW	51590 TQ	USBLS	5/07
	New York	Y	39700 FQ	49470 MW	66200 TQ	USBLS	5/07
	Albany-Schenectady-Troy MSA, NY	Y	43590 FQ	50660 MW	61910 TQ	USBLS	5/07
	Nassau-Suffolk PMSA, NY	Y	39040 FQ	48310 MW	59410 TQ	USBLS	5/07
	New York-Northern New Jersey-Long Island MSA, NY-NJ-PA	Y	38080 FQ	51130 MW	68990 TQ	USBLS	5/07
	North Carolina	Y	36990 FQ	44150 MW	50660 TQ	USBLS	5/07
	Charlotte-Gastonia-Concord MSA, NC-SC	Y	42690 FQ	46930 MW	51140 TQ	USBLS	5/07
	Raleigh-Cary MSA, NC	Y	36460 FQ	47850 MW	60200 TQ	USBLS	5/07
	Ohio	Y	37810 FQ	49510 MW	59110 TQ	USBLS	5/07
	Cincinnati-Middletown MSA, OH-KY-IN	Y	38480 FQ	53480 MW	61010 TQ	USBLS	5/07
	Cleveland-Elyria-Mentor MSA, OH	Y	37950 FQ	52880 MW	59980 TQ	USBLS	5/07
	Columbus MSA, OH	Y	50750 FQ	58230 MW	64180 TQ	USBLS	5/07
	Oklahoma	Y	37910 FQ	54480 MW	71290 TQ	USBLS	5/07
	Oklahoma City MSA, OK	Y	57900 FQ	64060 MW	71760 TQ	USBLS	5/07
	Oregon	H	29.24 FQ	34.79 MW	39.48 TQ	ORBLS	5/08
	Portland-Vancouver-Beaverton MSA, OR-WA	Y	66240 FQ	76820 MW	86580 TQ	USBLS	5/07
	Pennsylvania	Y	30930 FQ	40480 MW	51030 TQ	USBLS	5/07
	Philadelphia-Camden-Wilmington MSA, PA-NJ-DE-MD	Y	32850 FQ	43310 MW	56980 TQ	USBLS	5/07
	Pittsburgh MSA, PA	Y	15710 FQ	32140 MW	49300 TQ	USBLS	5/07
	Rhode Island	Y	40910 FQ	50920 MW	62490 TQ	USBLS	5/07
	Providence-Fall River-Warwick MSA, RI-MA	Y	41500 FQ	52920 MW	64850 TQ	USBLS	5/07
	South Carolina	Y	33030 FQ	37240 MW	43750 TQ	USBLS	5/07
	Columbia MSA, SC	Y	33050 FQ	36330 MW	41630 TQ	USBLS	5/07
	South Dakota	Y	38325 FQ	48607 MW	61335 TQ	SDBLS	7/08-9/08
	Tennessee	Y	33830 FQ	45100 MW	55600 TQ	USBLS	5/07
	Memphis MSA, TN-MS-AR	Y	28400 FQ	53590 MW	61020 TQ	USBLS	5/07
	Nashville-Davidson-Murfreesboro MSA, TN	Y	36720 FQ	51600 MW	58260 TQ	USBLS	5/07
	Texas	Y	38930 FQ	49090 MW	61050 TQ	USBLS	5/07
	Austin-Round Rock MSA, TX	Y	26980 FQ	40630 MW	52650 TQ	USBLS	5/07
	Dallas-Fort Worth-Arlington MSA, TX	Y	50910 FQ	63310 MW	74940 TQ	USBLS	5/07
	Houston-Sugar Land-Baytown MSA, TX	Y	40650 FQ	49150 MW	58630 TQ	USBLS	5/07
	San Antonio MSA, TX	Y	34160 FQ	39510 MW	47580 TQ	USBLS	5/07

AE	Average entry wage	AW	Average wage paid	FQ	First quartile wage	LO	Lowest wage paid	MTC	Median total compensation	TCC	Total cash compensation
AER	Average entry range	AWR	Average wage range	H	Hourly	LR	Low end range	MW	Median wage paid	TQ	Third quartile wage
AEX	Average experienced wage	AXR	Average experienced range	HI	Highest wage paid	M	Monthly	MWR	Median wage range	W	Weekly
ATC	Average total compensation	D	Daily	HR	High end range	MCC	Median cash compensation	S	See annotated source	Y	Yearly

Occupation/Type/Industry	Location	Per	Low	Mid	High	Source	Date
Fire Inspector and Investigator	Utah	Y	38740 FQ	47820 MW	58430 TQ	USBLS	5/07
	Virginia	Y	38580 FQ	46980 MW	56350 TQ	USBLS	5/07
	Washington	H	28.74 FQ	34.16 MW	38.58 TQ	WABLS	3/08
	Seattle-Tacoma-Bellevue MSA, WA	Y	65190 FQ	73430 MW	81520 TQ	USBLS	5/07
	Wisconsin	Y	25030 FQ	44790 MW	61230 TQ	USBLS	5/07
	Milwaukee-Waukesha-West Allis MSA, WI	Y	31100 FQ	55870 MW	61530 TQ	USBLS	5/07
	Wyoming	Y	38766 FQ	42940 MW	53240 TQ	WYBLS	9/08
Fire Marshal	Colorado Springs, CO	M	7937 LO			COSPRS	1/1/09
	Peachtree City, GA	Y	54334 LO		87496 HI	GACTY01	2008
	Thomasville, GA	Y	30118 LO		43368 HI	GACTY01	2008
	Maryland	Y			96501 HI	BMAG	2009
	Nebraska	Y			67981 HI	NEST	2008
Fire Prevention Bureau Chief	Ohio	H	27.93 LO		36.59 HI	ODAS	2008
Fire Protection Engineer							
6 to 8 Years Experience	United States	Y		72500 MW		FCHF	2006
Less Than 2 Years Experience	United States	Y		55000 MW		FCHF	2006
Fire Recruit	Cincinnati, OH	Y			35050 HI	COHSS	10/08
Fire Safety Inspector	Ohio	H	18.36 LO		23.87 HI	ODAS	2008
Fire Specialist							
Municipal Government	Cincinnati, OH	Y			63158 HI	COHSS	10/08
Fire Station Captain	Ohio	H	19.19 LO		23.76 HI	ODAS	2008
Firearms Technical Leader							
Sheriff's Department Crime Lab	San Mateo County, CA	W	6788 LO		8484 HI	CAC	2006-2007
First-Line Supervisor/Manager							
Construction Trade and Extraction Worker	Alabama	Y	36470 FQ	45420 MW	58340 TQ	USBLS	5/07
Construction Trade and Extraction Worker	Birmingham-Hoover MSA, AL	Y	40610 FQ	50980 MW	69410 TQ	USBLS	5/07
Construction Trade and Extraction Worker	Tuscaloosa MSA, AL	Y	38870 FQ	47340 MW	59120 TQ	USBLS	5/07
Construction Trade and Extraction Worker	Alaska	Y	66290 FQ	80950 MW	105960 TQ	USBLS	5/07
Construction Trade and Extraction Worker	Anchorage MSA, AK	Y	65240 FQ	77760 MW	99770 TQ	USBLS	5/07
Construction Trade and Extraction Worker	Fairbanks MSA, AK	Y	60050 FQ	70250 MW	84600 TQ	USBLS	5/07
Construction Trade and Extraction Worker	Arizona	Y	43210 FQ	53630 MW	66590 TQ	USBLS	5/07
Construction Trade and Extraction Worker	Phoenix-Mesa-Scottsdale MSA, AZ	Y	44660 FQ	55270 MW	68790 TQ	USBLS	5/07
Construction Trade and Extraction Worker	Tucson MSA, AZ	Y	41210 FQ	51400 MW	63660 TQ	USBLS	5/07
Construction Trade and Extraction Worker	Arkansas	Y	35210 FQ	44340 MW	55630 TQ	USBLS	5/07
Construction Trade and Extraction Worker	Little Rock-North Little Rock MSA, AR	Y	38530 FQ	47470 MW	57270 TQ	USBLS	5/07
Construction Trade and Extraction Worker	California	H	27.10 FQ	33.40 MW	41.31 TQ	CABLS	1/08-3/08
Construction Trade and Extraction Worker	Los Angeles-Long Beach-Glendale PMSA, CA	H	26.01 FQ	32.07 MW	39.63 TQ	CABLS	1/08-3/08
Construction Trade and Extraction Worker	Oakland-Fremont-Hayward MSA, CA	H	32.10 FQ	39.20 MW	47.97 TQ	CABLS	1/08-3/08
Construction Trade and Extraction Worker	Riverside-San Bernardino-Ontario MSA, CA	H	25.06 FQ	31.03 MW	39.29 TQ	CABLS	1/08-3/08
Construction Trade and Extraction Worker	Sacramento-Arden Arcade-Roseville MSA, CA	H	28.11 FQ	34.04 MW	41.38 TQ	CABLS	1/08-3/08
Construction Trade and Extraction Worker	San Diego-Carlsbad-San Marcos MSA, CA	H	28.64 FQ	34.58 MW	41.11 TQ	CABLS	1/08-3/08
Construction Trade and Extraction Worker	San Francisco-San Mateo-Redwood PMSA, CA	H	32.88 FQ	40.78 MW	49.68 TQ	CABLS	1/08-3/08
Construction Trade and Extraction Worker	San Jose-Sunnyvale-Santa Clara MSA, CA	H	31.76 FQ	39.52 MW	49.99 TQ	CABLS	1/08-3/08
Construction Trade and Extraction Worker	Santa Ana-Anaheim-Irvine PMSA, CA	Y	53710 FQ	64280 MW	80240 TQ	USBLS	5/07
Construction Trade and Extraction Worker	Colorado	Y	44220 FQ	55930 MW	69380 TQ	USBLS	5/07
Construction Trade and Extraction Worker	Denver-Aurora MSA, CO	Y	45750 FQ	56500 MW	68670 TQ	USBLS	5/07
Construction Trade and Extraction Worker	Connecticut	H	23.51 AE	31.82 MW		CTBLS	1/08-3/08
Construction Trade and Extraction Worker	Bridgeport-Stamford-Norwalk MSA, CT	Y	58910 FQ	72960 MW	85020 TQ	USBLS	5/07
Construction Trade and Extraction Worker	Hartford-West Hartford-East Hartford MSA, CT	Y	51770 FQ	64850 MW	76020 TQ	USBLS	5/07
Construction Trade and Extraction Worker	Delaware	Y	47900 FQ	59390 MW	73290 TQ	USBLS	5/07

Occupation/Type/Industry	Location	Per	Low	Mid	High	Source	Date
First-Line Supervisor/Manager							
Construction Trade and Extraction Worker	Wilmington PMSA, DE-MD-NJ	Y	50700 FQ	61100 MW	74580 TQ	USBLS	5/07
Construction Trade and Extraction Worker	District of Columbia	Y	60200 FQ	70050 MW	79270 TQ	USBLS	5/07
Construction Trade and Extraction Worker	Washington-Arlington-Alexandria MSA, DC-VA-MD-WV	Y	50250 FQ	63030 MW	77410 TQ	USBLS	5/07
Construction Trade and Extraction Worker	Florida	Y	41810 FQ	52600 MW	66290 TQ	USBLS	5/07
Construction Trade and Extraction Worker	Fort Lauderdale-Pompano Beach-Deerfield Beach PMSA, FL	Y	45230 FQ	56720 MW	71110 TQ	USBLS	5/07
Construction Trade and Extraction Worker	Jacksonville MSA, FL	Y	42460 FQ	51260 MW	65970 TQ	USBLS	5/07
Construction Trade and Extraction Worker	Miami-Fort Lauderdale-Miami Beach MSA, FL	Y	44570 FQ	56440 MW	71050 TQ	USBLS	5/07
Construction Trade and Extraction Worker	Orlando-Kissimmee MSA, FL	Y	43040 FQ	53290 MW	67030 TQ	USBLS	5/07
Construction Trade and Extraction Worker	Tampa-St. Petersburg-Clearwater MSA, FL	Y	40000 FQ	50450 MW	63860 TQ	USBLS	5/07
Construction Trade and Extraction Worker	West Palm Beach-Boca Raton-Boynton Beach PMSA, FL	Y	45380 FQ	57730 MW	71700 TQ	USBLS	5/07
Construction Trade and Extraction Worker	Georgia	Y	39560 FQ	48970 MW	61710 TQ	USBLS	5/07
Construction Trade and Extraction Worker	Atlanta-Sandy Springs-Marietta MSA, GA	Y	43150 FQ	52570 MW	65690 TQ	USBLS	5/07
Construction Trade and Extraction Worker	Hawaii	Y	54600 FQ	72880 MW	92040 TQ	USBLS	5/07
Construction Trade and Extraction Worker	Honolulu MSA, HI	Y	62930 FQ	77850 MW	97130 TQ	USBLS	5/07
Construction Trade and Extraction Worker	Idaho	Y	34510 FQ	43290 MW	55110 TQ	USBLS	5/07
Construction Trade and Extraction Worker	Boise City-Nampa MSA, ID	Y	37170 FQ	45420 MW	55540 TQ	USBLS	5/07
Construction Trade and Extraction Worker	Illinois	Y	58580 FQ	73670 MW	89270 TQ	USBLS	5/07
Construction Trade and Extraction Worker	Chicago-Naperville-Joliet MSA, IL-IN-WI	Y	61940 FQ	75740 MW	90960 TQ	USBLS	5/07
Construction Trade and Extraction Worker	Indiana	Y	41480 FQ	54080 MW	66580 TQ	USBLS	5/07
Construction Trade and Extraction Worker	Gary PMSA, IN	Y	47150 FQ	65000 MW	81300 TQ	USBLS	5/07
Construction Trade and Extraction Worker	Indianapolis-Carmel MSA, IN	Y	45320 FQ	56890 MW	67420 TQ	USBLS	5/07
Construction Trade and Extraction Worker	Terre Haute MSA, IN	Y	40660 FQ	54240 MW	62670 TQ	USBLS	5/07
Construction Trade and Extraction Worker	Iowa	Y	44120 FQ	54320 MW	68190 TQ	USBLS	5/07
Construction Trade and Extraction Worker	Des Moines-West Des Moines MSA, IA	Y	46080 FQ	55110 MW	67070 TQ	USBLS	5/07
Construction Trade and Extraction Worker	Kansas	Y	40070 FQ	50590 MW	63290 TQ	USBLS	5/07
Construction Trade and Extraction Worker	Wichita MSA, KS	Y	36040 FQ	46160 MW	59980 TQ	USBLS	5/07
Construction Trade and Extraction Worker	Kentucky	Y	39356 FQ	49007 MW	62246 TQ	KYBLS	2008
Construction Trade and Extraction Worker	Lexington-Fayette MSA, KY	Y	35230 FQ	45270 MW	58580 TQ	USBLS	5/07
Construction Trade and Extraction Worker	Louisville-Jefferson County MSA, KY-IN	Y	39700 FQ	48760 MW	59890 TQ	USBLS	5/07
Construction Trade and Extraction Worker	Louisiana	H	19.29 FQ	23.73 MW	29.72 TQ	LABLS	1/08-3/08
Construction Trade and Extraction Worker	Baton Rouge MSA, LA	Y	41070 FQ	48800 MW	58430 TQ	USBLS	5/07
Construction Trade and Extraction Worker	New Orleans-Metairie-Kenner MSA, LA	Y	42780 FQ	51640 MW	63030 TQ	USBLS	5/07
Construction Trade and Extraction Worker	Maine	Y	38550 FQ	46630 MW	57710 TQ	USBLS	5/07
Construction Trade and Extraction Worker	Portland-South Portland-Biddeford MSA, ME	Y	43060 FQ	53170 MW	63780 TQ	USBLS	5/07
Construction Trade and Extraction Worker	Maryland	Y		59875 MW		MDBLS	3/08
Construction Trade and Extraction Worker	Baltimore-Towson MSA, MD	Y	45680 FQ	56110 MW	69760 TQ	USBLS	5/07
Construction Trade and Extraction Worker	Bethesda-Gaithersburg-Frederick PMSA, MD	Y	49070 FQ	60630 MW	75930 TQ	USBLS	5/07
Construction Trade and Extraction Worker	Hagerstown-Martinsburg MSA, MD-WV	Y	52480 FQ	59050 MW	75710 TQ	USBLS	5/07
Construction Trade and Extraction Worker	Massachusetts	Y	55450 FQ	68840 MW	82920 TQ	USBLS	5/07
Construction Trade and Extraction Worker	Boston-Cambridge-Quincy NECTA, MA	Y	61020 FQ	72780 MW	86430 TQ	USBLS	5/07
Construction Trade and Extraction Worker	Worcester MSA, MA-CT	Y	41240 FQ	58920 MW	74730 TQ	USBLS	5/07
Construction Trade and Extraction Worker	Michigan	Y	49590 FQ	60740 MW	76420 TQ	USBLS	5/07
Construction Trade and Extraction Worker	Detroit-Warren-Livonia MSA, MI	Y	55550 FQ	66780 MW	81550 TQ	USBLS	5/07
Construction Trade and Extraction Worker	Flint MSA, MI	Y	55220 FQ	72930 MW		USBLS	5/07
Construction Trade and Extraction Worker	Grand Rapids-Wyoming MSA, MI	Y	42220 FQ	53830 MW	68320 TQ	USBLS	5/07
Construction Trade and Extraction Worker	Muskegon-Norton Shores MSA, MI	Y	42240 FQ	57760 MW	87140 TQ	USBLS	5/07
Construction Trade and Extraction Worker	Warren-Troy-Farmington Hills PMSA, MI	Y	54480 FQ	64660 MW	80120 TQ	USBLS	5/07
Construction Trade and Extraction Worker	Minnesota	Y	52915 FQ	64634 MW	78840 TQ	MNBLS	10/08-12/08
Construction Trade and Extraction Worker	Duluth-Superior MSA, MN-WI	Y	50986 FQ	65245 MW	77480 TQ	MNBLS	10/08-12/08

AE	Average entry wage	AW	Average wage paid	FQ	First quartile wage	LO	Lowest wage paid
AER	Average entry range	AWR	Average wage range	H	Hourly	LR	Low end range
AEX	Average experienced wage	AXR	Average experienced range	HI	Highest wage paid	M	Monthly
ATC	Average total compensation	D	Daily	HR	High end range	MCC	Median cash compensation

MTC	Median total compensation	TCC	Total cash compensation
MW	Median wage paid	TQ	Third quartile wage
MWR	Median wage range	W	Weekly
S	See annotated source	Y	Yearly

Occupation/Type/Industry	Location	Per	Low	Mid	High	Source	Date

First-Line Supervisor/Manager

Occupation/Type/Industry	Location	Per	Low	Mid	High	Source	Date
Construction Trade and Extraction Worker	Minneapolis-Saint Paul MSA, MN-WI	Y	57541 FQ	69629 MW	82655 TQ	MNBLS	10/08-12/08
Construction Trade and Extraction Worker	Rochester MSA, MN	Y	47507 FQ	59127 MW	69413 TQ	MNBLS	10/08-12/08
Construction Trade and Extraction Worker	Mississippi	Y	35830 FQ	45040 MW	55420 TQ	USBLS	5/07
Construction Trade and Extraction Worker	Jackson MSA, MS	Y	33200 FQ	42840 MW	55400 TQ	USBLS	5/07
Construction Trade and Extraction Worker	Missouri	Y	46880 FQ	59740 MW	74290 TQ	USBLS	5/07
Construction Trade and Extraction Worker	Kansas City MSA, MO-KS	Y	49360 FQ	60370 MW	73420 TQ	USBLS	5/07
Construction Trade and Extraction Worker	St. Louis MSA, MO-IL	Y	55720 FQ	68550 MW	81340 TQ	USBLS	5/07
Construction Trade and Extraction Worker	Montana	Y	40520 FQ	50910 MW	63060 TQ	USBLS	5/07
Construction Trade and Extraction Worker	Billings MSA, MT	Y	45430 FQ	56260 MW	69870 TQ	USBLS	5/07
Construction Trade and Extraction Worker	Nebraska	Y	39560 FQ	49680 MW	63340 TQ	USBLS	5/07
Construction Trade and Extraction Worker	Omaha-Council Bluffs MSA, NE-IA	Y	43590 FQ	54020 MW	68950 TQ	USBLS	5/07
Construction Trade and Extraction Worker	Nevada	H	24.87 FQ	31.18 MW	38.73 TQ	NVBLS	5/08
Construction Trade and Extraction Worker	Las Vegas-Paradise MSA, NV	H	24.44 FQ	30.91 MW	38.77 TQ	NVBLS	5/08
Construction Trade and Extraction Worker	New Hampshire	H	18.55 AE	25.30 MW	30.61 AEX	NHBLS	6/08
Construction Trade and Extraction Worker	Manchester MSA, NH	Y	47550 FQ	60190 MW	74470 TQ	USBLS	5/07
Construction Trade and Extraction Worker	Nashua NECTA, NH-MA	Y	45920 FQ	59780 MW	77440 TQ	USBLS	5/07
Construction Trade and Extraction Worker	New Jersey	Y	53750 FQ	67590 MW	88400 TQ	USBLS	5/07
Construction Trade and Extraction Worker	Atlantic City MSA, NJ	Y	51650 FQ	61520 MW	84590 TQ	USBLS	5/07
Construction Trade and Extraction Worker	Camden PMSA, NJ	Y	53300 FQ	64050 MW	84890 TQ	USBLS	5/07
Construction Trade and Extraction Worker	Edison PMSA, NJ	Y	51100 FQ	65080 MW	85190 TQ	USBLS	5/07
Construction Trade and Extraction Worker	Newark-Union PMSA, NJ-PA	Y	57680 FQ	73570 MW	94880 TQ	USBLS	5/07
Construction Trade and Extraction Worker	New Mexico	Y	36580 FQ	48170 MW	63320 TQ	USBLS	5/07
Construction Trade and Extraction Worker	Albuquerque MSA, NM	Y	37340 FQ	49540 MW	63890 TQ	USBLS	5/07
Construction Trade and Extraction Worker	New York	Y	51710 FQ	68180 MW	88990 TQ	USBLS	5/07
Construction Trade and Extraction Worker	Albany-Schenectady-Troy MSA, NY	Y	45090 FQ	57410 MW	71050 TQ	USBLS	5/07
Construction Trade and Extraction Worker	Buffalo-Niagara Falls MSA, NY	Y	47040 FQ	58580 MW	72360 TQ	USBLS	5/07
Construction Trade and Extraction Worker	Nassau-Suffolk PMSA, NY	Y	56600 FQ	72700 MW	91050 TQ	USBLS	5/07
Construction Trade and Extraction Worker	New York-Northern New Jersey-Long Island MSA, NY-NJ-PA	Y	57930 FQ	74910 MW	95570 TQ	USBLS	5/07
Construction Trade and Extraction Worker	North Carolina	Y	38060 FQ	46660 MW	57630 TQ	USBLS	5/07
Construction Trade and Extraction Worker	Charlotte-Gastonia-Concord MSA, NC-SC	Y	41900 FQ	50610 MW	61620 TQ	USBLS	5/07
Construction Trade and Extraction Worker	Raleigh-Cary MSA, NC	Y	38990 FQ	48200 MW	61480 TQ	USBLS	5/07
Construction Trade and Extraction Worker	North Dakota	Y	39110 FQ	48460 MW	62880 TQ	USBLS	5/07
Construction Trade and Extraction Worker	Bismarck MSA, ND	Y	35590 FQ	41980 MW	52320 TQ	USBLS	5/07
Construction Trade and Extraction Worker	Fargo MSA, ND-MN	Y	37040 FQ	44730 MW	56090 TQ	USBLS	5/07
Construction Trade and Extraction Worker	Ohio	Y	45120 FQ	56550 MW	69810 TQ	USBLS	5/07
Construction Trade and Extraction Worker	Cincinnati-Middletown MSA, OH-KY-IN	Y	44180 FQ	54660 MW	69180 TQ	USBLS	5/07
Construction Trade and Extraction Worker	Cleveland-Elyria-Mentor MSA, OH	Y	49470 FQ	60260 MW	73380 TQ	USBLS	5/07
Construction Trade and Extraction Worker	Columbus MSA, OH	Y	47510 FQ	57710 MW	70210 TQ	USBLS	5/07
Construction Trade and Extraction Worker	Dayton MSA, OH	Y	44350 FQ	55030 MW	66000 TQ	USBLS	5/07
Construction Trade and Extraction Worker	Oklahoma	Y	36530 FQ	48900 MW	63170 TQ	USBLS	5/07
Construction Trade and Extraction Worker	Oklahoma City MSA, OK	Y	41270 FQ	53370 MW	69690 TQ	USBLS	5/07
Construction Trade and Extraction Worker	Tulsa MSA, OK	Y	36270 FQ	47010 MW	60930 TQ	USBLS	5/07
Construction Trade and Extraction Worker	Oregon	H	22.54 FQ	28.16 MW	34.46 TQ	ORBLS	5/08
Construction Trade and Extraction Worker	Portland-Vancouver-Beaverton MSA, OR-WA	Y	47140 FQ	59400 MW	73050 TQ	USBLS	5/07
Construction Trade and Extraction Worker	Pennsylvania	Y	45600 FQ	58000 MW	74090 TQ	USBLS	5/07
Construction Trade and Extraction Worker	Allentown-Bethlehem-Easton MSA, PA-NJ	Y	48320 FQ	58290 MW	72010 TQ	USBLS	5/07
Construction Trade and Extraction Worker	Philadelphia-Camden-Wilmington MSA, PA-NJ-DE-MD	Y	52890 FQ	64580 MW	82450 TQ	USBLS	5/07
Construction Trade and Extraction Worker	Pittsburgh MSA, PA	Y	47390 FQ	59860 MW	74060 TQ	USBLS	5/07
Construction Trade and Extraction Worker	Rhode Island	Y	51210 FQ	63540 MW	75560 TQ	USBLS	5/07
Construction Trade and Extraction Worker	Providence-Fall River-Warwick MSA, RI-MA	Y	50980 FQ	64030 MW	76070 TQ	USBLS	5/07
Construction Trade and Extraction Worker	South Carolina	Y	39240 FQ	46690 MW	57340 TQ	USBLS	5/07
Construction Trade and Extraction Worker	Charleston-North Charleston MSA, SC	Y	40730 FQ	46980 MW	57440 TQ	USBLS	5/07
Construction Trade and Extraction Worker	Columbia MSA, SC	Y	38110 FQ	44900 MW	52560 TQ	USBLS	5/07
Construction Trade and Extraction Worker	South Dakota	Y	43898 FQ	50247 MW	59786 TQ	SDBLS	7/08-9/08
Construction Trade and Extraction Worker	Sioux Falls MSA, SD	Y	43649 FQ	50571 MW	60213 TQ	SDBLS	7/08-9/08
Construction Trade and Extraction Worker	Tennessee	Y	34720 FQ	44100 MW	56800 TQ	USBLS	5/07

AE	Average entry wage	AW	Average wage paid	FQ	First quartile wage	LO	Lowest wage paid	MTC	Median total compensation	TCC	Total cash compensation
AER	Average entry range	AWR	Average wage range	H	Hourly	LR	Low end range	MW	Median wage paid	TQ	Third quartile wage
AEX	Average experienced wage	AXR	Average experienced range	HI	Highest wage paid	M	Monthly	MWR	Median wage range	W	Weekly
ATC	Average total compensation	D	Daily	HR	High end range	MCC	Median cash compensation	S	See annotated source	Y	Yearly

First-Line Supervisor/Manager

Occupation/Type/Industry	Location	Per	Low	Mid	High	Source	Date
Construction Trade and Extraction Worker	Memphis MSA, TN-MS-AR	Y	38730 FQ	47280 MW	60090 TQ	USBLS	5/07
Construction Trade and Extraction Worker	Nashville-Davidson-Murfreesboro MSA, TN	Y	36400 FQ	48320 MW	62060 TQ	USBLS	5/07
Construction Trade and Extraction Worker	Texas	Y	37850 FQ	48460 MW	61980 TQ	USBLS	5/07
Construction Trade and Extraction Worker	Austin-Round Rock MSA, TX	Y	35360 FQ	45960 MW	60130 TQ	USBLS	5/07
Construction Trade and Extraction Worker	Beaumont-Port Arthur MSA, TX	Y	37080 FQ	45030 MW	52960 TQ	USBLS	5/07
Construction Trade and Extraction Worker	Dallas-Fort Worth-Arlington MSA, TX	Y	39840 FQ	51350 MW	63950 TQ	USBLS	5/07
Construction Trade and Extraction Worker	El Paso MSA, TX	Y	28360 FQ	38370 MW	46240 TQ	USBLS	5/07
Construction Trade and Extraction Worker	Houston-Sugar Land-Baytown MSA, TX	Y	41170 FQ	50560 MW	63250 TQ	USBLS	5/07
Construction Trade and Extraction Worker	San Antonio MSA, TX	Y	38200 FQ	47190 MW	58430 TQ	USBLS	5/07
Construction Trade and Extraction Worker	Utah	Y	41970 FQ	49340 MW	60550 TQ	USBLS	5/07
Construction Trade and Extraction Worker	Salt Lake City MSA, UT	Y	43090 FQ	50220 MW	63760 TQ	USBLS	5/07
Construction Trade and Extraction Worker	Vermont	Y	46130 FQ	55570 MW	68290 TQ	USBLS	5/07
Construction Trade and Extraction Worker	Burlington-South Burlington MSA, VT	Y	49160 FQ	58680 MW	72950 TQ	USBLS	5/07
Construction Trade and Extraction Worker	Virginia	Y	44450 FQ	56480 MW	72070 TQ	USBLS	5/07
Construction Trade and Extraction Worker	Richmond MSA, VA	Y	44380 FQ	54410 MW	69410 TQ	USBLS	5/07
Construction Trade and Extraction Worker	Virginia Beach-Norfolk-Newport News MSA, VA-NC	Y	45570 FQ	55210 MW	65030 TQ	USBLS	5/07
Construction Trade and Extraction Worker	Washington	H	25.97 FQ	32.87 MW	39.84 TQ	WABLS	3/08
Construction Trade and Extraction Worker	Seattle-Tacoma-Bellevue MSA, WA	Y	58190 FQ	72450 MW	88560 TQ	USBLS	5/07
Construction Trade and Extraction Worker	West Virginia	Y	46143 FQ	66482 MW	81178 TQ	WVBLS	7/08-9/08
Construction Trade and Extraction Worker	Charleston MSA, WV	Y	59030 FQ	71290 MW	79990 TQ	USBLS	5/07
Construction Trade and Extraction Worker	Wisconsin	Y	46780 FQ	58250 MW	71770 TQ	USBLS	5/07
Construction Trade and Extraction Worker	Milwaukee-Waukesha-West Allis MSA, WI	Y	50950 FQ	65530 MW	79730 TQ	USBLS	5/07
Construction Trade and Extraction Worker	Racine MSA, WI	Y	53070 FQ	59600 MW	69730 TQ	USBLS	5/07
Construction Trade and Extraction Worker	Wyoming	Y	43721 FQ	53420 MW	70354 TQ	WYBLS	9/08
Construction Trade and Extraction Worker	Cheyenne MSA, WY	Y	41419 FQ	48518 MW	59631 TQ	WYBLS	9/08
Construction Trade and Extraction Worker	Puerto Rico	Y	20930 FQ	25430 MW	32690 TQ	USBLS	5/07
Construction Trade and Extraction Worker	San Juan-Caguas-Guaynabo MSA, PR	Y	21630 FQ	26160 MW	33870 TQ	USBLS	5/07
Construction Trade and Extraction Worker	Virgin Islands	Y	46720 FQ	55410 MW	63290 TQ	USBLS	5/07
Construction Trade and Extraction Worker	Guam	Y	31940 FQ	38630 MW	47830 TQ	USBLS	5/07
Correctional Officers	Alabama	Y	37390 FQ	46890 MW	57770 TQ	USBLS	5/07
Correctional Officers	Birmingham-Hoover MSA, AL	Y	42140 FQ	49780 MW	59720 TQ	USBLS	5/07
Correctional Officers	Alaska	Y	54670 FQ	64710 MW	75980 TQ	USBLS	5/07
Correctional Officers	Arizona	Y	41210 FQ	48380 MW	57790 TQ	USBLS	5/07
Correctional Officers	Phoenix-Mesa-Scottsdale MSA, AZ	Y	40970 FQ	50340 MW	60110 TQ	USBLS	5/07
Correctional Officers	Arkansas	Y	32460 FQ	48930 MW	62010 TQ	USBLS	5/07
Correctional Officers	California	H	35.27 FQ	39.01 MW	44.94 TQ	CABLS	1/08-3/08
Correctional Officers	Los Angeles-Long Beach-Glendale PMSA, CA	H	35.17 FQ	38.51 MW	43.33 TQ	CABLS	1/08-3/08
Correctional Officers	Oakland-Fremont-Hayward MSA, CA	H	34.98 FQ	38.48 MW	42.46 TQ	CABLS	1/08-3/08
Correctional Officers	Riverside-San Bernardino-Ontario MSA, CA	H	35.65 FQ	39.10 MW	44.82 TQ	CABLS	1/08-3/08
Correctional Officers	San Diego-Carlsbad-San Marcos MSA, CA	H	34.20 FQ	37.88 MW	43.27 TQ	CABLS	1/08-3/08
Correctional Officers	San Francisco-San Mateo-Redwood PMSA, CA	H	36.06 FQ	39.98 MW	46.07 TQ	CABLS	1/08-3/08
Correctional Officers	Santa Ana-Anaheim-Irvine PMSA, CA	Y	58450 FQ	64130 MW	77130 TQ	USBLS	5/07
Correctional Officers	Colorado	Y	54930 FQ	61610 MW	71540 TQ	USBLS	5/07
Correctional Officers	Connecticut	H	27.79 AE	30.71 MW		CTBLS	1/08-3/08
Correctional Officers	Delaware	Y	47490 FQ	54430 MW	62480 TQ	USBLS	5/07
Correctional Officers	Washington-Arlington-Alexandria MSA, DC-VA-MD-WV	Y	50540 FQ	65970 MW	83810 TQ	USBLS	5/07
Correctional Officers	Florida	Y	45810 FQ	52650 MW	64720 TQ	USBLS	5/07
Correctional Officers	Fort Lauderdale-Pompano Beach-Deerfield Beach PMSA, FL	Y	52860 FQ	70310 MW	95470 TQ	USBLS	5/07
Correctional Officers	Miami-Fort Lauderdale-Miami Beach MSA, FL	Y	50210 FQ	68860 MW	89840 TQ	USBLS	5/07
Correctional Officers	Orlando-Kissimmee MSA, FL	Y	47580 FQ	58600 MW	74810 TQ	USBLS	5/07

AE	Average entry wage	AW	Average wage paid	FQ	First quartile wage
AER	Average entry range	AWR	Average wage range	H	Hourly
AEX	Average experienced wage	AXR	Average experienced range	HI	Highest wage paid
ATC	Average total compensation	D	Daily	HR	High end range

LO	Lowest wage paid
LR	Low end range
M	Monthly
MCC	Median cash compensation

MTC	Median total compensation
MW	Median wage paid
MWR	Median wage range
S	See annotated source

TCC	Total cash compensation
TQ	Third quartile wage
W	Weekly
Y	Yearly

Occupation/Type/Industry	Location	Per	Low	Mid	High	Source	Date
First-Line Supervisor/Manager							
Correctional Officers	Tampa-St. Petersburg-Clearwater MSA, FL	Y	47210 FQ	65920 MW	83030 TQ	USBLS	5/07
Correctional Officers	Georgia	Y	33980 FQ	41550 MW	51250 TQ	USBLS	5/07
Correctional Officers	Atlanta-Sandy Springs-Marietta MSA, GA	Y	36410 FQ	46470 MW	61030 TQ	USBLS	5/07
Correctional Officers	Hawaii	Y	55070 FQ	66830 MW	77080 TQ	USBLS	5/07
Correctional Officers	Idaho	Y	35190 FQ	40260 MW	50770 TQ	USBLS	5/07
Correctional Officers	Illinois	Y	58180 FQ	65650 MW	74840 TQ	USBLS	5/07
Correctional Officers	Chicago-Naperville-Joliet MSA, IL-IN-WI	Y	57200 FQ	63070 MW	71890 TQ	USBLS	5/07
Correctional Officers	Indiana	Y	30130 FQ	34860 MW	39630 TQ	USBLS	5/07
Correctional Officers	Indianapolis-Carmel MSA, IN	Y	29890 FQ	34900 MW	39410 TQ	USBLS	5/07
Correctional Officers	Iowa	Y	51280 FQ	58470 MW	65360 TQ	USBLS	5/07
Correctional Officers	Kansas	Y	35000 FQ	41860 MW	53380 TQ	USBLS	5/07
Correctional Officers	Wichita MSA, KS	Y	35130 FQ	40770 MW	49100 TQ	USBLS	5/07
Correctional Officers	Kentucky	Y	32758 FQ	41814 MW	51976 TQ	KYBLS	2008
Correctional Officers	Louisiana	H	16.23 FQ	20.20 MW	24.43 TQ	LABLS	1/08-3/08
Correctional Officers	Baton Rouge MSA, LA	Y	36990 FQ	45000 MW	52730 TQ	USBLS	5/07
Correctional Officers	New Orleans-Metairie-Kenner MSA, LA	Y	27250 FQ	32530 MW	42720 TQ	USBLS	5/07
Correctional Officers	Maine	Y	40540 FQ	45620 MW	50610 TQ	USBLS	5/07
Correctional Officers	Maryland	Y		53650 MW		MDBLS	3/08
Correctional Officers	Baltimore-Towson MSA, MD	Y	46580 FQ	54510 MW	73600 TQ	USBLS	5/07
Correctional Officers	Massachusetts	Y	43400 FQ	50190 MW	65390 TQ	USBLS	5/07
Correctional Officers	Boston-Cambridge-Quincy NECTA, MA	Y	58930 FQ	74210 MW	104460 TQ	USBLS	5/07
Correctional Officers	Michigan	Y	53680 FQ	57920 MW	62190 TQ	USBLS	5/07
Correctional Officers	Detroit-Warren-Livonia MSA, MI	Y	53410 FQ	58190 MW	63060 TQ	USBLS	5/07
Correctional Officers	Grand Rapids-Wyoming MSA, MI	Y	54020 FQ	58030 MW	62040 TQ	USBLS	5/07
Correctional Officers	Warren-Troy-Farmington Hills PMSA, MI	Y	55130 FQ	59910 MW	64690 TQ	USBLS	5/07
Correctional Officers	Minnesota	Y	52781 FQ	64481 MW	76630 TQ	MNBLS	10/08-12/08
Correctional Officers	Duluth-Superior MSA, MN-WI	Y	51641 FQ	59127 MW	70650 TQ	MNBLS	10/08-12/08
Correctional Officers	Minneapolis-Saint Paul MSA, MN-WI	Y	59253 FQ	70095 MW	79453 TQ	MNBLS	10/08-12/08
Correctional Officers	Mississippi	Y	30890 FQ	35720 MW	40440 TQ	USBLS	5/07
Correctional Officers	Jackson MSA, MS	Y	29400 FQ	34050 MW	40460 TQ	USBLS	5/07
Correctional Officers	Missouri	Y	34990 FQ	39250 MW	49060 TQ	USBLS	5/07
Correctional Officers	Kansas City MSA, MO-KS	Y	39510 FQ	45810 MW	59120 TQ	USBLS	5/07
Correctional Officers	St. Louis MSA, MO-IL	Y	50750 FQ	61270 MW	72620 TQ	USBLS	5/07
Correctional Officers	Montana	Y	30460 FQ	37780 MW	47240 TQ	USBLS	5/07
Correctional Officers	Nebraska	Y	36300 FQ	40570 MW	49680 TQ	USBLS	5/07
Correctional Officers	Omaha-Council Bluffs MSA, NE-IA	Y	40730 FQ	49630 MW	70110 TQ	USBLS	5/07
Correctional Officers	Nevada	H	27.41 FQ	31.01 MW	36.15 TQ	NVBLS	5/08
Correctional Officers	Las Vegas-Paradise MSA, NV	H	27.58 FQ	32.00 MW	38.31 TQ	NVBLS	5/08
Correctional Officers	New Hampshire	H	22.63 AE	27.84 MW	30.25 AEX	NHBLS	6/08
Correctional Officers	New Jersey	Y	77070 FQ	90070 MW	98240 TQ	USBLS	5/07
Correctional Officers	Camden PMSA, NJ	Y	76220 FQ	89360 MW	97440 TQ	USBLS	5/07
Correctional Officers	Edison PMSA, NJ	Y	88240 FQ	96030 MW	103590 TQ	USBLS	5/07
Correctional Officers	Newark-Union PMSA, NJ-PA	Y	68140 FQ	87760 MW	95710 TQ	USBLS	5/07
Correctional Officers	New Mexico	Y	29210 FQ	33870 MW	49520 TQ	USBLS	5/07
Correctional Officers	Albuquerque MSA, NM	Y	28630 FQ	31710 MW	50080 TQ	USBLS	5/07
Correctional Officers	New York	Y	60110 FQ	69600 MW	77940 TQ	USBLS	5/07
Correctional Officers	Albany-Schenectady-Troy MSA, NY	Y	56520 FQ	63200 MW	71960 TQ	USBLS	5/07
Correctional Officers	Buffalo-Niagara Falls MSA, NY	Y	62430 FQ*	70000 MW	76890 TQ	USBLS	5/07
Correctional Officers	New York-Northern New Jersey-Long Island MSA, NY-NJ-PA	Y	63640 FQ	74260 MW	84900 TQ	USBLS	5/07
Correctional Officers	North Carolina	Y	35290 FQ	40990 MW	50010 TQ	USBLS	5/07
Correctional Officers	Charlotte-Gastonia-Concord MSA, NC-SC	Y	37140 FQ	42240 MW	47160 TQ	USBLS	5/07
Correctional Officers	North Dakota	Y	39180 FQ	45730 MW	55640 TQ	USBLS	5/07
Correctional Officers	Ohio	Y	43250 FQ	51490 MW	59730 TQ	USBLS	5/07
Correctional Officers	Cincinnati-Middletown MSA, OH-KY-IN	Y	44630 FQ	51050 MW	59760 TQ	USBLS	5/07

AE	Average entry wage	AW	Average wage paid	FQ	First quartile wage
AER	Average entry range	AWR	Average wage range	H	Hourly
AEX	Average experienced wage	AXR	Average experienced range	HI	Highest wage paid
ATC	Average total compensation	D	Daily	HR	High end range

LO	Lowest wage paid	MTC	Median total compensation	TCC	Total cash compensation
LR	Low end range	MW	Median wage paid	TQ	Third quartile wage
M	Monthly	MWR	Median wage range	W	Weekly
MCC	Median cash compensation	S	See annotated source	Y	Yearly

Occupation/Type/Industry	Location	Per	Low	Mid	High	Source	Date
First-Line Supervisor/Manager							
Correctional Officers	Cleveland-Elyria-Mentor MSA, OH	Y	41010 FQ	52550 MW	63480 TQ	USBLS	5/07
Correctional Officers	Oklahoma	Y	35610 FQ	44630 MW	64940 TQ	USBLS	5/07
Correctional Officers	Tulsa MSA, OK	Y	32700 FQ	38350 MW	47720 TQ	USBLS	5/07
Correctional Officers	Oregon	H	27.00 FQ	30.17 MW	33.99 TQ	ORBLS	5/08
Correctional Officers	Portland-Vancouver-Beaverton MSA, OR-WA	Y	58440 FQ	67850 MW	75530 TQ	USBLS	5/07
Correctional Officers	Pennsylvania	Y	41630 FQ	54820 MW	68910 TQ	USBLS	5/07
Correctional Officers	Allentown-Bethlehem-Easton MSA, PA-NJ	Y	43490 FQ	59100 MW	74950 TQ	USBLS	5/07
Correctional Officers	Philadelphia-Camden-Wilmington MSA, PA-NJ-DE-MD	Y	59040 FQ	75000 MW	92460 TQ	USBLS	5/07
Correctional Officers	Pittsburgh MSA, PA	Y	40240 FQ	48750 MW	60550 TQ	USBLS	5/07
Correctional Officers	South Carolina	Y	37320 FQ	47350 MW	60770 TQ	USBLS	5/07
Correctional Officers	South Dakota	Y	42648 FQ	50578 MW	60189 TQ	SDBLS	7/08-9/08
Correctional Officers	Tennessee	Y	33800 FQ	42320 MW	50070 TQ	USBLS	5/07
Correctional Officers	Memphis MSA, TN-MS-AR	Y	26620 FQ	42270 MW	49880 TQ	USBLS	5/07
Correctional Officers	Nashville-Davidson-Murfreesboro MSA, TN	Y	35460 FQ	43640 MW	51000 TQ	USBLS	5/07
Correctional Officers	Texas	Y	28970 FQ	32450 MW	38310 TQ	USBLS	5/07
Correctional Officers	Austin-Round Rock MSA, TX	Y	29420 FQ	37840 MW	68040 TQ	USBLS	5/07
Correctional Officers	Dallas-Fort Worth-Arlington MSA, TX	Y	35720 FQ	58240 MW	71060 TQ	USBLS	5/07
Correctional Officers	Houston-Sugar Land-Baytown MSA, TX	Y	29110 FQ	32770 MW	38710 TQ	USBLS	5/07
Correctional Officers	San Antonio MSA, TX	Y	29760 FQ	34250 MW	39080 TQ	USBLS	5/07
Correctional Officers	Utah	Y	37590 FQ	49360 MW	58850 TQ	USBLS	5/07
Correctional Officers	Virginia	Y	41430 FQ	48990 MW	62790 TQ	USBLS	5/07
Correctional Officers	Virginia Beach-Norfolk-Newport News MSA, VA-NC	Y	43630 FQ	50130 MW	72170 TQ	USBLS	5/07
Correctional Officers	Washington	H	27.54 FQ	32.39 MW	38.36 TQ	WABLS	3/08
Correctional Officers	Seattle-Tacoma-Bellevue MSA, WA	Y	60760 FQ	70570 MW	80500 TQ	USBLS	5/07
Correctional Officers	Green Bay MSA, WI	Y	56160 FQ	60170 MW	64180 TQ	USBLS	5/07
Correctional Officers	Milwaukee-Waukesha-West Allis MSA, WI	Y	53240 FQ	58680 MW	64260 TQ	USBLS	5/07
Correctional Officers	Wyoming	Y	45008 FQ	52832 MW	62636 TQ	WYBLS	9/08
Correctional Officers	Puerto Rico	Y	37470 FQ	43190 MW	49050 TQ	USBLS	5/07
Farming, Fishing, and Forestry Workers	Alabama	Y	33210 FQ	45630 MW	56360 TQ	USBLS	5/07
Farming, Fishing, and Forestry Workers	Birmingham-Hoover MSA, AL	Y	21780 FQ	23760 MW	33030 TQ	USBLS	5/07
Farming, Fishing, and Forestry Workers	Arizona	Y	29220 FQ	39750 MW	50990 TQ	USBLS	5/07
Farming, Fishing, and Forestry Workers	Phoenix-Mesa-Scottsdale MSA, AZ	Y	29240 FQ	36880 MW	65060 TQ	USBLS	5/07
Farming, Fishing, and Forestry Workers	Arkansas	Y	32060 FQ	39640 MW	54760 TQ	USBLS	5/07
Farming, Fishing, and Forestry Workers	Little Rock-North Little Rock MSA, AR	Y	35650 FQ	40200 MW	68490 TQ	USBLS	5/07
Farming, Fishing, and Forestry Workers	California	H	10.42 FQ	14.69 MW	21.75 TQ	CABLS	1/08-3/08
Farming, Fishing, and Forestry Workers	Los Angeles-Long Beach-Glendale PMSA, CA	H	18.61 FQ	23.85 MW	30.08 TQ	CABLS	1/08-3/08
Farming, Fishing, and Forestry Workers	Oakland-Fremont-Hayward MSA, CA	H	11.65 FQ	18.23 MW	42.10 TQ	CABLS	1/08-3/08
Farming, Fishing, and Forestry Workers	Oxnard-Thousand Oaks-Ventura MSA, CA	H	12.78 FQ	16.64 MW	20.38 TQ	CABLS	1/08-3/08
Farming, Fishing, and Forestry Workers	Riverside-San Bernardino-Ontario MSA, CA	H	11.18 FQ	14.59 MW	20.02 TQ	CABLS	1/08-3/08
Farming, Fishing, and Forestry Workers	Sacramento-Arden Arcade-Roseville MSA, CA	H	12.41 FQ	24.40 MW	36.50 TQ	CABLS	1/08-3/08
Farming, Fishing, and Forestry Workers	San Diego-Carlsbad-San Marcos MSA, CA	H	13.44 FQ	16.79 MW	22.11 TQ	CABLS	1/08-3/08
Farming, Fishing, and Forestry Workers	San Francisco-San Mateo-Redwood PMSA, CA	H	21.14 FQ	27.48 MW	34.84 TQ	CABLS	1/08-3/08
Farming, Fishing, and Forestry Workers	San Jose-Sunnyvale-Santa Clara MSA, CA	H	13.81 FQ	15.99 MW	23.63 TQ	CABLS	1/08-3/08
Farming, Fishing, and Forestry Workers	Santa Ana-Anaheim-Irvine PMSA, CA	Y	30680 FQ	39090 MW	56520 TQ	USBLS	5/07
Farming, Fishing, and Forestry Workers	Stockton MSA, CA	H	11.66 FQ	15.70 MW	22.87 TQ	CABLS	1/08-3/08
Farming, Fishing, and Forestry Workers	Colorado	Y	33080 FQ	37060 MW	45700 TQ	USBLS	5/07
Farming, Fishing, and Forestry Workers	Connecticut	H	13.50 AE	22.76 MW		CTBLS	1/08-3/08
Farming, Fishing, and Forestry Workers	Bridgeport-Stamford-Norwalk MSA, CT	Y	43140 FQ	48420 MW	58550 TQ	USBLS	5/07

AE	Average entry wage	AW	Average wage paid	FQ	First quartile wage	LO	Lowest wage paid	MTC	Median total compensation	TCC	Total cash compensation
AER	Average entry range	AWR	Average wage range	H	Hourly	LR	Low end range	MW	Median wage paid	TQ	Third quartile wage
AEX	Average experienced wage	AXR	Average experienced range	HI	Highest wage paid	M	Monthly	MWR	Median wage range	W	Weekly
ATC	Average total compensation	D	Daily	HR	High end range	MCC	Median cash compensation	S	See annotated source	Y	Yearly

616

First-Line Supervisor/Manager

Occupation/Type/Industry	Location	Per	Low	Mid	High	Source	Date
First-Line Supervisor/Manager							
Farming, Fishing, and Forestry Workers	Delaware	Y	41790 FQ	48220 MW	57270 TQ	USBLS	5/07
Farming, Fishing, and Forestry Workers	Wilmington PMSA, DE-MD-NJ	Y	41770 FQ	47130 MW	54020 TQ	USBLS	5/07
Farming, Fishing, and Forestry Workers	Washington-Arlington-Alexandria MSA, DC-VA-MD-WV	Y	34470 FQ	39150 MW	50160 TQ	USBLS	5/07
Farming, Fishing, and Forestry Workers	Florida	Y	30930 FQ	40660 MW	52210 TQ	USBLS	5/07
Farming, Fishing, and Forestry Workers	Jacksonville MSA, FL	Y	43560 FQ	57500 MW	68100 TQ	USBLS	5/07
Farming, Fishing, and Forestry Workers	Lakeland MSA, FL	Y	39460 FQ	48180 MW	58700 TQ	USBLS	5/07
Farming, Fishing, and Forestry Workers	Miami-Fort Lauderdale-Miami Beach MSA, FL	Y	29660 FQ	37870 MW	47690 TQ	USBLS	5/07
Farming, Fishing, and Forestry Workers	Orlando-Kissimmee MSA, FL	Y	30380 FQ	42910 MW	53240 TQ	USBLS	5/07
Farming, Fishing, and Forestry Workers	Tampa-St. Petersburg-Clearwater MSA, FL	Y	29140 FQ	36890 MW	48290 TQ	USBLS	5/07
Farming, Fishing, and Forestry Workers	West Palm Beach-Boca Raton-Boynton Beach PMSA, FL	Y	33670 FQ	39380 MW	46270 TQ	USBLS	5/07
Farming, Fishing, and Forestry Workers	Georgia	Y	33800 FQ	41540 MW	51610 TQ	USBLS	5/07
Farming, Fishing, and Forestry Workers	Atlanta-Sandy Springs-Marietta MSA, GA	Y	41300 FQ	51100 MW	57920 TQ	USBLS	5/07
Farming, Fishing, and Forestry Workers	Hawaii	Y	29710 FQ	36320 MW	49160 TQ	USBLS	5/07
Farming, Fishing, and Forestry Workers	Honolulu MSA, HI	Y	33670 FQ	39330 MW	55330 TQ	USBLS	5/07
Farming, Fishing, and Forestry Workers	Idaho	Y	27720 FQ	37410 MW	47640 TQ	USBLS	5/07
Farming, Fishing, and Forestry Workers	Boise City-Nampa MSA, ID	Y	26510 FQ	31780 MW	45420 TQ	USBLS	5/07
Farming, Fishing, and Forestry Workers	Illinois	Y	35270 FQ	39920 MW	60700 TQ	USBLS	5/07
Farming, Fishing, and Forestry Workers	Chicago-Naperville-Joliet MSA, IL-IN-WI	Y	34440 FQ	37260 MW	41500 TQ	USBLS	5/07
Farming, Fishing, and Forestry Workers	Indiana	Y	32110 FQ	37720 MW	51090 TQ	USBLS	5/07
Farming, Fishing, and Forestry Workers	Indianapolis-Carmel MSA, IN	Y	28800 FQ	39160 MW	55370 TQ	USBLS	5/07
Farming, Fishing, and Forestry Workers	Iowa	Y	42060 FQ	50100 MW	61800 TQ	USBLS	5/07
Farming, Fishing, and Forestry Workers	Kansas	Y	34570 FQ	42700 MW	53410 TQ	USBLS	5/07
Farming, Fishing, and Forestry Workers	Kentucky	Y	28817 FQ	36050 MW	45298 TQ	KYBLS	2008
Farming, Fishing, and Forestry Workers	Louisville-Jefferson County MSA, KY-IN	Y	26340 FQ	29730 MW	36460 TQ	USBLS	5/07
Farming, Fishing, and Forestry Workers	Louisiana	H	13.90 FQ	17.08 MW	22.80 TQ	LABLS	1/08-3/08
Farming, Fishing, and Forestry Workers	Maine	Y	35360 FQ	41590 MW	59280 TQ	USBLS	5/07
Farming, Fishing, and Forestry Workers	Maryland	Y		44175 MW		MDBLS	3/08
Farming, Fishing, and Forestry Workers	Baltimore-Towson MSA, MD	Y	36990 FQ	44370 MW	52800 TQ	USBLS	5/07
Farming, Fishing, and Forestry Workers	Bethesda-Gaithersburg-Frederick PMSA, MD	Y	37600 FQ	41080 MW	46360 TQ	USBLS	5/07
Farming, Fishing, and Forestry Workers	Massachusetts	Y	24690 FQ	30940 MW	50950 TQ	USBLS	5/07
Farming, Fishing, and Forestry Workers	Boston-Cambridge-Quincy NECTA, MA	Y	23460 FQ	27760 MW	49830 TQ	USBLS	5/07
Farming, Fishing, and Forestry Workers	Michigan	Y	39230 FQ	52370 MW	62770 TQ	USBLS	5/07
Farming, Fishing, and Forestry Workers	Detroit-Warren-Livonia MSA, MI	Y	34660 FQ	51180 MW	63070 TQ	USBLS	5/07
Farming, Fishing, and Forestry Workers	Grand Rapids-Wyoming MSA, MI	Y	41800 FQ	54190 MW	61090 TQ	USBLS	5/07
Farming, Fishing, and Forestry Workers	Warren-Troy-Farmington Hills PMSA, MI	Y	33780 FQ	47220 MW	62150 TQ	USBLS	5/07
Farming, Fishing, and Forestry Workers	Minnesota	Y	34029 FQ	44968 MW	58648 TQ	MNBLS	10/08-12/08
Farming, Fishing, and Forestry Workers	Duluth-Superior MSA, MN-WI	Y	29308 FQ	31331 MW	33344 TQ	MNBLS	10/08-12/08
Farming, Fishing, and Forestry Workers	Minneapolis-Saint Paul MSA, MN-WI	Y	36000 FQ	41343 MW	49648 TQ	MNBLS	10/08-12/08
Farming, Fishing, and Forestry Workers	Rochester MSA, MN	Y	36201 FQ	42205 MW	47470 TQ	MNBLS	10/08-12/08
Farming, Fishing, and Forestry Workers	Mississippi	Y	34620 FQ	41490 MW	53270 TQ	USBLS	5/07
Farming, Fishing, and Forestry Workers	Jackson MSA, MS	Y	39600 FQ	43430 MW	47350 TQ	USBLS	5/07
Farming, Fishing, and Forestry Workers	Missouri	Y	37130 FQ	45400 MW	58360 TQ	USBLS	5/07
Farming, Fishing, and Forestry Workers	St. Louis MSA, MO-IL	Y	27920 FQ	41910 MW	54270 TQ	USBLS	5/07
Farming, Fishing, and Forestry Workers	Montana	Y	30100 FQ	37620 MW	52950 TQ	USBLS	5/07
Farming, Fishing, and Forestry Workers	Nebraska	Y	32430 FQ	38850 MW	47000 TQ	USBLS	5/07
Farming, Fishing, and Forestry Workers	Omaha-Council Bluffs MSA, NE-IA	Y	41070 FQ	44560 MW	48060 TQ	USBLS	5/07
Farming, Fishing, and Forestry Workers	Nevada	H	20.57 FQ	23.15 MW	26.17 TQ	NVBLS	5/08
Farming, Fishing, and Forestry Workers	Las Vegas-Paradise MSA, NV	H	21.32 FQ	23.24 MW	25.70 TQ	NVBLS	5/08
Farming, Fishing, and Forestry Workers	New Hampshire	H	17.10 AE	23.30 MW	25.23 AEX	NHBLS	6/08
Farming, Fishing, and Forestry Workers	New Jersey	Y	42120 FQ	50140 MW	59050 TQ	USBLS	5/07
Farming, Fishing, and Forestry Workers	Camden PMSA, NJ	Y	42310 FQ	47230 MW	51740 TQ	USBLS	5/07
Farming, Fishing, and Forestry Workers	Newark-Union PMSA, NJ-PA	Y	51790 FQ	57630 MW	65100 TQ	USBLS	5/07
Farming, Fishing, and Forestry Workers	New Mexico	Y	24920 FQ	33420 MW	40340 TQ	USBLS	5/07
Farming, Fishing, and Forestry Workers	New York	Y	31500 FQ	40140 MW	49470 TQ	USBLS	5/07
Farming, Fishing, and Forestry Workers	Nassau-Suffolk PMSA, NY	Y	33330 FQ	39190 MW	48070 TQ	USBLS	5/07

AE Average entry wage	**AW** Average wage paid	**FQ** First quartile wage	**LO** Lowest wage paid	**MTC** Median total compensation	**TCC** Total cash compensation
AER Average entry range	**AWR** Average wage range	**H** Hourly	**LR** Low end range	**MW** Median wage paid	**TQ** Third quartile wage
AEX Average experienced wage	**AXR** Average experienced range	**HI** Highest wage paid	**M** Monthly	**MWR** Median wage range	**W** Weekly
ATC Average total compensation	**D** Daily	**HR** High end range	**MCC** Median cash compensation	**S** See annotated source	**Y** Yearly

Occupation/Type/Industry	Location	Per	Low	Mid	High	Source	Date
First-Line Supervisor/Manager							
Farming, Fishing, and Forestry Workers	New York-Northern New Jersey-Long Island MSA, NY-NJ-PA	Y	37490 FQ	48860 MW	60230 TQ	USBLS	5/07
Farming, Fishing, and Forestry Workers	North Carolina	Y	30560 FQ	37480 MW	51990 TQ	USBLS	5/07
Farming, Fishing, and Forestry Workers	Charlotte-Gastonia-Concord MSA, NC-SC	Y	28450 FQ	33120 MW	39700 TQ	USBLS	5/07
Farming, Fishing, and Forestry Workers	Greensboro-High Point MSA, NC	Y	31300 FQ	36410 MW	41880 TQ	USBLS	5/07
Farming, Fishing, and Forestry Workers	Raleigh-Cary MSA, NC	Y	33420 FQ	38640 MW	48700 TQ	USBLS	5/07
Farming, Fishing, and Forestry Workers	North Dakota	Y	33570 FQ	37990 MW	47810 TQ	USBLS	5/07
Farming, Fishing, and Forestry Workers	Ohio	Y	34260 FQ	43730 MW	53880 TQ	USBLS	5/07
Farming, Fishing, and Forestry Workers	Cincinnati-Middletown MSA, OH-KY-IN	Y	37130 FQ	44400 MW	51980 TQ	USBLS	5/07
Farming, Fishing, and Forestry Workers	Columbus MSA, OH	Y	33510 FQ	40860 MW	50450 TQ	USBLS	5/07
Farming, Fishing, and Forestry Workers	Oklahoma	Y	32210 FQ	39260 MW	47590 TQ	USBLS	5/07
Farming, Fishing, and Forestry Workers	Oklahoma City MSA, OK	Y	44020 FQ	47880 MW	51680 TQ	USBLS	5/07
Farming, Fishing, and Forestry Workers	Oregon	H	17.12 FQ	20.82 MW	26.61 TQ	ORBLS	5/08
Farming, Fishing, and Forestry Workers	Portland-Vancouver-Beaverton MSA, OR-WA	Y	36210 FQ	42870 MW	56750 TQ	USBLS	5/07
Farming, Fishing, and Forestry Workers	Pennsylvania	Y	39420 FQ	48490 MW	60870 TQ	USBLS	5/07
Farming, Fishing, and Forestry Workers	Philadelphia-Camden-Wilmington MSA, PA-NJ-DE-MD	Y	42200 FQ	47870 MW	55550 TQ	USBLS	5/07
Farming, Fishing, and Forestry Workers	Pittsburgh MSA, PA	Y	29420 FQ	46990 MW	58720 TQ	USBLS	5/07
Farming, Fishing, and Forestry Workers	South Carolina	Y	36050 FQ	44680 MW	52970 TQ	USBLS	5/07
Farming, Fishing, and Forestry Workers	Columbia MSA, SC	Y	37680 FQ	49650 MW	60410 TQ	USBLS	5/07
Farming, Fishing, and Forestry Workers	South Dakota	Y	30940 FQ	38046 MW	47069 TQ	SDBLS	7/08-9/08
Farming, Fishing, and Forestry Workers	Tennessee	Y	24200 FQ	33920 MW	51650 TQ	USBLS	5/07
Farming, Fishing, and Forestry Workers	Memphis MSA, TN-MS-AR	Y	30670 FQ	40640 MW	51910 TQ	USBLS	5/07
Farming, Fishing, and Forestry Workers	Texas	Y	20520 FQ	27890 MW	38400 TQ	USBLS	5/07
Farming, Fishing, and Forestry Workers	Dallas-Fort Worth-Arlington MSA, TX	Y	18410 FQ	24000 MW	39050 TQ	USBLS	5/07
Farming, Fishing, and Forestry Workers	Houston-Sugar Land-Baytown MSA, TX	Y	19830 FQ	23470 MW	30000 TQ	USBLS	5/07
Farming, Fishing, and Forestry Workers	San Antonio MSA, TX	Y	25260 FQ	27840 MW	30320 TQ	USBLS	5/07
Farming, Fishing, and Forestry Workers	Utah	Y	30430 FQ	39690 MW	49270 TQ	USBLS	5/07
Farming, Fishing, and Forestry Workers	Vermont	Y	37670 FQ	43020 MW	48320 TQ	USBLS	5/07
Farming, Fishing, and Forestry Workers	Virginia	Y	36140 FQ	45280 MW	59270 TQ	USBLS	5/07
Farming, Fishing, and Forestry Workers	Richmond MSA, VA	Y	39450 FQ	55740 MW	69590 TQ	USBLS	5/07
Farming, Fishing, and Forestry Workers	Virginia Beach-Norfolk-Newport News MSA, VA-NC	Y	42580 FQ	49370 MW	57720 TQ	USBLS	5/07
Farming, Fishing, and Forestry Workers	Washington	H	16.43 FQ	20.87 MW	29.57 TQ	WABLS	3/08
Farming, Fishing, and Forestry Workers	Seattle-Tacoma-Bellevue MSA, WA	Y	34830 FQ	46750 MW	64700 TQ	USBLS	5/07
Farming, Fishing, and Forestry Workers	West Virginia	Y	28252 FQ	31817 MW	39229 TQ	WVBLS	7/08-9/08
Farming, Fishing, and Forestry Workers	Wisconsin	Y	37420 FQ	46000 MW	54880 TQ	USBLS	5/07
Farming, Fishing, and Forestry Workers	Wisconsin	H	17.99 FQ	22.11 MW	26.39 TQ	USBLS	5/07
Farming, Fishing, and Forestry Workers	Wyoming	Y	37699 FQ	47967 MW	56709 TQ	WYBLS	9/08
Farming, Fishing, and Forestry Workers	Puerto Rico	Y	20560 FQ	22940 MW	25290 TQ	USBLS	5/07
Farming, Fishing, and Forestry Workers	San Juan-Caguas-Guaynabo MSA, PR	Y	20920 FQ	23080 MW	25210 TQ	USBLS	5/07
Fire Fighting and Prevention Workers	Alabama	Y	41340 FQ	49760 MW	59990 TQ	USBLS	5/07
Fire Fighting and Prevention Workers	Birmingham-Hoover MSA, AL	Y	47390 FQ	60050 MW	74290 TQ	USBLS	5/07
Fire Fighting and Prevention Workers	Alaska	Y	58090 FQ	64840 MW	75170 TQ	USBLS	5/07
Fire Fighting and Prevention Workers	Anchorage MSA, AK	Y	58060 FQ	63420 MW	73700 TQ	USBLS	5/07
Fire Fighting and Prevention Workers	Phoenix-Mesa-Scottsdale MSA, AZ	Y	68280 FQ	76120 MW	84620 TQ	USBLS	5/07
Fire Fighting and Prevention Workers	Tucson MSA, AZ	Y	53280 FQ	67170 MW	85740 TQ	USBLS	5/07
Fire Fighting and Prevention Workers	Arkansas	Y	45550 FQ	55670 MW	61990 TQ	USBLS	5/07
Fire Fighting and Prevention Workers	California	H	30.11 FQ	43.92 MW	53.98 TQ	CABLS	1/08-3/08
Fire Fighting and Prevention Workers	Bakersfield MSA, CA	H	27.98 FQ	31.59 MW	41.14 TQ	CABLS	1/08-3/08
Fire Fighting and Prevention Workers	Oakland-Fremont-Hayward MSA, CA	H	44.30 FQ	53.26 MW	62.93 TQ	CABLS	1/08-3/08
Fire Fighting and Prevention Workers	Riverside-San Bernardino-Ontario MSA, CA	H	26.83 FQ	29.74 MW	37.74 TQ	CABLS	1/08-3/08
Fire Fighting and Prevention Workers	Sacramento-Arden Arcade-Roseville MSA, CA	H	28.60 FQ	36.11 MW	52.15 TQ	CABLS	1/08-3/08
Fire Fighting and Prevention Workers	San Diego-Carlsbad-San Marcos MSA, CA	H	28.59 FQ	31.76 MW	45.51 TQ	CABLS	1/08-3/08
Fire Fighting and Prevention Workers	San Francisco-San Mateo-Redwood PMSA, CA	H	48.33 FQ	59.88 MW		CABLS	1/08-3/08

AE	Average entry wage	**AW**	Average wage paid	**FQ**	First quartile wage	**LO**	Lowest wage paid	**MTC**	Median total compensation	**TCC** Total cash compensation
AER	Average entry range	**AWR**	Average wage range	**H**	Hourly	**LR**	Low end range	**MW**	Median wage paid	**TQ** Third quartile wage
AEX	Average experienced wage	**AXR**	Average experienced range	**HI**	Highest wage paid	**M**	Monthly	**MWR**	Median wage range	**W** Weekly
ATC	Average total compensation	**D**	Daily	**HR**	High end range	**MCC**	Median cash compensation	**S**	See annotated source	**Y** Yearly

Occupation/Type/Industry	Location	Per	Low	Mid	High	Source	Date

First-Line Supervisor/Manager

Occupation/Type/Industry	Location	Per	Low	Mid	High	Source	Date
Fire Fighting and Prevention Workers	San Jose-Sunnyvale-Santa Clara MSA, CA	H	29.87 FQ	51.46 MW	66.49 TQ	CABLS	1/08-3/08
Fire Fighting and Prevention Workers	Santa Ana-Anaheim-Irvine PMSA, CA	Y	62720 FQ	76290 MW	95150 TQ	USBLS	5/07
Fire Fighting and Prevention Workers	Santa Rosa-Petaluma MSA, CA	H	20.39 FQ	30.96 MW	47.59 TQ	CABLS	1/08-3/08
Fire Fighting and Prevention Workers	Colorado	Y	50670 FQ	63340 MW	81260 TQ	USBLS	5/07
Fire Fighting and Prevention Workers	Denver-Aurora MSA, CO	Y	67820 FQ	80200 MW	93240 TQ	USBLS	5/07
Fire Fighting and Prevention Workers	Connecticut	H	27.52 AE	35.42 MW		CTBLS	1/08-3/08
Fire Fighting and Prevention Workers	Bridgeport-Stamford-Norwalk MSA, CT	Y	61680 FQ	72310 MW	81250 TQ	USBLS	5/07
Fire Fighting and Prevention Workers	Hartford-West Hartford-East Hartford MSA, CT	Y	64420 FQ	72810 MW	80350 TQ	USBLS	5/07
Fire Fighting and Prevention Workers	Washington-Arlington-Alexandria MSA, DC-VA-MD-WV	Y	72190 FQ	84790 MW	99810 TQ	USBLS	5/07
Fire Fighting and Prevention Workers	Florida	Y	58080 FQ	72450 MW	88860 TQ	USBLS	5/07
Fire Fighting and Prevention Workers	Fort Lauderdale-Pompano Beach-Deerfield Beach PMSA, FL	Y	70400 FQ	82900 MW	99020 TQ	USBLS	5/07
Fire Fighting and Prevention Workers	Jacksonville MSA, FL	Y	48900 FQ	66600 MW	89660 TQ	USBLS	5/07
Fire Fighting and Prevention Workers	Miami-Fort Lauderdale-Miami Beach MSA, FL	Y	68120 FQ	81870 MW	100350 TQ	USBLS	5/07
Fire Fighting and Prevention Workers	Orlando-Kissimmee MSA, FL	Y	58500 FQ	69200 MW	80040 TQ	USBLS	5/07
Fire Fighting and Prevention Workers	Tampa-St. Petersburg-Clearwater MSA, FL	Y	41300 FQ	62620 MW	78050 TQ	USBLS	5/07
Fire Fighting and Prevention Workers	West Palm Beach-Boca Raton-Boynton Beach PMSA, FL	Y	77840 FQ	92630 MW	105040 TQ	USBLS	5/07
Fire Fighting and Prevention Workers	Georgia	Y	46300 FQ	57210 MW	66980 TQ	USBLS	5/07
Fire Fighting and Prevention Workers	Atlanta-Sandy Springs-Marietta MSA, GA	Y	52500 FQ	61230 MW	71170 TQ	USBLS	5/07
Fire Fighting and Prevention Workers	Augusta-Richmond County MSA, GA-SC	Y	48620 FQ	53730 MW	58400 TQ	USBLS	5/07
Fire Fighting and Prevention Workers	Hawaii	Y	59930 FQ	69040 MW	77170 TQ	USBLS	5/07
Fire Fighting and Prevention Workers	Honolulu MSA, HI	Y	62640 FQ	71180 MW	78380 TQ	USBLS	5/07
Fire Fighting and Prevention Workers	Idaho	Y	42300 FQ	52870 MW	68740 TQ	USBLS	5/07
Fire Fighting and Prevention Workers	Boise City-Nampa MSA, ID	Y	52150 FQ	59120 MW	71000 TQ	USBLS	5/07
Fire Fighting and Prevention Workers	Illinois	Y	72320 FQ	86240 MW	98200 TQ	USBLS	5/07
Fire Fighting and Prevention Workers	Chicago-Naperville-Joliet MSA, IL-IN-WI	Y	78020 FQ	88650 MW	100300 TQ	USBLS	5/07
Fire Fighting and Prevention Workers	Indiana	Y	44960 FQ	54940 MW	64610 TQ	USBLS	5/07
Fire Fighting and Prevention Workers	Gary PMSA, IN	Y	44560 FQ	51790 MW	58370 TQ	USBLS	5/07
Fire Fighting and Prevention Workers	Indianapolis-Carmel MSA, IN	Y	54550 FQ	66750 MW	74250 TQ	USBLS	5/07
Fire Fighting and Prevention Workers	Iowa	Y	39170 FQ	55680 MW	70790 TQ	USBLS	5/07
Fire Fighting and Prevention Workers	Davenport-Moline-Rock Island MSA, IA-IL	Y	44620 FQ	65080 MW	86950 TQ	USBLS	5/07
Fire Fighting and Prevention Workers	Des Moines-West Des Moines MSA, IA	Y	50000 FQ	59910 MW	80330 TQ	USBLS	5/07
Fire Fighting and Prevention Workers	Kansas	Y	40210 FQ	51720 MW	64140 TQ	USBLS	5/07
Fire Fighting and Prevention Workers	Wichita MSA, KS	Y	40710 FQ	57730 MW	64130 TQ	USBLS	5/07
Fire Fighting and Prevention Workers	Kentucky	Y	40227 FQ	50182 MW	59510 TQ	KYBLS	2008
Fire Fighting and Prevention Workers	Louisville-Jefferson County MSA, KY-IN	Y	48070 FQ	52280 MW	58220 TQ	USBLS	5/07
Fire Fighting and Prevention Workers	Louisiana	H	17.26 FQ	21.27 MW	27.23 TQ	LABLS	1/08-3/08
Fire Fighting and Prevention Workers	Lake Charles MSA, LA	Y	33570 FQ	36450 MW	39380 TQ	USBLS	5/07
Fire Fighting and Prevention Workers	New Orleans-Metairie-Kenner MSA, LA	Y	32720 FQ	36950 MW	47970 TQ	USBLS	5/07
Fire Fighting and Prevention Workers	Portland-South Portland-Biddeford MSA, ME	Y	44670 FQ	52400 MW	60990 TQ	USBLS	5/07
Fire Fighting and Prevention Workers	Maryland	Y		67600 MW		MDBLS	3/08
Fire Fighting and Prevention Workers	Baltimore-Towson MSA, MD	Y	56440 FQ	62100 MW	69320 TQ	USBLS	5/07
Fire Fighting and Prevention Workers	Massachusetts	Y	57950 FQ	66880 MW	84930 TQ	USBLS	5/07
Fire Fighting and Prevention Workers	Boston-Cambridge-Quincy NECTA, MA	Y	64040 FQ	78110 MW	95420 TQ	USBLS	5/07
Fire Fighting and Prevention Workers	Worcester MSA, MA-CT	Y	59410 FQ	70210 MW	81010 TQ	USBLS	5/07
Fire Fighting and Prevention Workers	Michigan	Y	59050 FQ	66440 MW	74600 TQ	USBLS	5/07
Fire Fighting and Prevention Workers	Detroit-Warren-Livonia MSA, MI	Y	62630 FQ	68870 MW	75450 TQ	USBLS	5/07
Fire Fighting and Prevention Workers	Grand Rapids-Wyoming MSA, MI	Y	59860 FQ	70980 MW	87080 TQ	USBLS	5/07
Fire Fighting and Prevention Workers	Warren-Troy-Farmington Hills PMSA, MI	Y	59470 FQ	68800 MW	79800 TQ	USBLS	5/07

AE	Average entry wage	AW	Average wage paid	FQ	First quartile wage	LO	Lowest wage paid	MTC	Median total compensation	TCC	Total cash compensation
AER	Average entry range	AWR	Average wage range	H	Hourly	LR	Low end range	MW	Median wage paid	TQ	Third quartile wage
AEX	Average experienced wage	AXR	Average experienced range	HI	Highest wage paid	M	Monthly	MWR	Median wage range	W	Weekly
ATC	Average total compensation	D	Daily	HR	High end range	MCC	Median cash compensation	S	See annotated source	Y	Yearly

First-Line Supervisor/Manager

Occupation/Type/Industry	Location	Per	Low	Mid	High	Source	Date
Fire Fighting and Prevention Workers	Minnesota	Y	43381 FQ	61375 MW	77059 TQ	MNBLS	10/08-12/08
Fire Fighting and Prevention Workers	Duluth-Superior MSA, MN-WI	Y	35142 FQ	38352 MW	41561 TQ	MNBLS	10/08-12/08
Fire Fighting and Prevention Workers	Minneapolis-Saint Paul MSA, MN-WI	Y	51306 FQ	67021 MW	84221 TQ	MNBLS	10/08-12/08
Fire Fighting and Prevention Workers	Mississippi	Y	32170 FQ	39030 MW	48200 TQ	USBLS	5/07
Fire Fighting and Prevention Workers	Jackson MSA, MS	Y	40120 FQ	46410 MW	51920 TQ	USBLS	5/07
Fire Fighting and Prevention Workers	Missouri	Y	50490 FQ	70410 MW	94490 TQ	USBLS	5/07
Fire Fighting and Prevention Workers	Kansas City MSA, MO-KS	Y	51110 FQ	63670 MW	76180 TQ	USBLS	5/07
Fire Fighting and Prevention Workers	St. Louis MSA, MO-IL	Y	69720 FQ	91750 MW	104260 TQ	USBLS	5/07
Fire Fighting and Prevention Workers	Montana	Y	43780 FQ	50950 MW	59700 TQ	USBLS	5/07
Fire Fighting and Prevention Workers	Great Falls MSA, MT	Y	45200 FQ	49360 MW	54680 TQ	USBLS	5/07
Fire Fighting and Prevention Workers	Nebraska	Y	46090 FQ	69310 MW	77140 TQ	USBLS	5/07
Fire Fighting and Prevention Workers	Omaha-Council Bluffs MSA, NE-IA	Y	69220 FQ	74510 MW	79860 TQ	USBLS	5/07
Fire Fighting and Prevention Workers	Nevada	H	28.28 FQ	32.04 MW	41.87 TQ	NVBLS	5/08
Fire Fighting and Prevention Workers	Las Vegas-Paradise MSA, NV	H	29.50 FQ	35.14 MW	44.07 TQ	NVBLS	5/08
Fire Fighting and Prevention Workers	New Hampshire	H	21.97 AE	28.45 MW	31.76 AEX	NHBLS	6/08
Fire Fighting and Prevention Workers	Nashua NECTA, NH-MA	Y	54490 FQ	59840 MW	66500 TQ	USBLS	5/07
Fire Fighting and Prevention Workers	New Jersey	Y	74110 FQ	89460 MW	106630 TQ	USBLS	5/07
Fire Fighting and Prevention Workers	Atlantic City MSA, NJ	Y	78360 FQ	92150 MW	105770 TQ	USBLS	5/07
Fire Fighting and Prevention Workers	Camden PMSA, NJ	Y	67320 FQ	72760 MW	79240 TQ	USBLS	5/07
Fire Fighting and Prevention Workers	Edison PMSA, NJ	Y	62730 FQ	70380 MW	82890 TQ	USBLS	5/07
Fire Fighting and Prevention Workers	Newark-Union PMSA, NJ-PA	Y	84790 FQ	93520 MW	106850 TQ	USBLS	5/07
Fire Fighting and Prevention Workers	New Mexico	Y	37710 FQ	43880 MW	53570 TQ	USBLS	5/07
Fire Fighting and Prevention Workers	Albuquerque MSA, NM	Y	44130 FQ	53580 MW	63060 TQ	USBLS	5/07
Fire Fighting and Prevention Workers	New York	Y	64880 FQ	74670 MW	83730 TQ	USBLS	5/07
Fire Fighting and Prevention Workers	Albany-Schenectady-Troy MSA, NY	Y	56980 FQ	61860 MW	67220 TQ	USBLS	5/07
Fire Fighting and Prevention Workers	Nassau-Suffolk PMSA, NY	Y	64460 FQ	75360 MW	87480 TQ	USBLS	5/07
Fire Fighting and Prevention Workers	New York-Northern New Jersey-Long Island MSA, NY-NJ-PA	Y	71690 FQ	80620 MW	96010 TQ	USBLS	5/07
Fire Fighting and Prevention Workers	North Carolina	Y	43470 FQ	52440 MW	66220 TQ	USBLS	5/07
Fire Fighting and Prevention Workers	Charlotte-Gastonia-Concord MSA, NC-SC	Y	56750 FQ	69820 MW	77300 TQ	USBLS	5/07
Fire Fighting and Prevention Workers	Greensboro-High Point MSA, NC	Y	41440 FQ	47090 MW	55090 TQ	USBLS	5/07
Fire Fighting and Prevention Workers	North Dakota	Y	43800 FQ	52980 MW	63870 TQ	USBLS	5/07
Fire Fighting and Prevention Workers	Fargo MSA, ND-MN	Y	45060 FQ	50580 MW	60080 TQ	USBLS	5/07
Fire Fighting and Prevention Workers	Ohio	Y	47000 FQ	59310 MW	70100 TQ	USBLS	5/07
Fire Fighting and Prevention Workers	Cincinnati-Middletown MSA, OH-KY-IN	Y	32610 FQ	63010 MW	75370 TQ	USBLS	5/07
Fire Fighting and Prevention Workers	Cleveland-Elyria-Mentor MSA, OH	Y	53020 FQ	63240 MW	74820 TQ	USBLS	5/07
Fire Fighting and Prevention Workers	Columbus MSA, OH	Y	57320 FQ	63700 MW	75170 TQ	USBLS	5/07
Fire Fighting and Prevention Workers	Dayton MSA, OH	Y	42220 FQ	60070 MW	72570 TQ	USBLS	5/07
Fire Fighting and Prevention Workers	Oklahoma	Y	45230 FQ	62660 MW	74840 TQ	USBLS	5/07
Fire Fighting and Prevention Workers	Oklahoma City MSA, OK	Y	67970 FQ	74430 MW	81360 TQ	USBLS	5/07
Fire Fighting and Prevention Workers	Oregon	H	27.45 FQ	32.74 MW	39.71 TQ	ORBLS	5/08
Fire Fighting and Prevention Workers	Portland-Vancouver-Beaverton MSA, OR-WA	Y	59450 FQ	72900 MW	86320 TQ	USBLS	5/07
Fire Fighting and Prevention Workers	Pennsylvania	Y	55050 FQ	61240 MW	69490 TQ	USBLS	5/07
Fire Fighting and Prevention Workers	Allentown-Bethlehem-Easton MSA, PA-NJ	Y	47040 FQ	56530 MW	66060 TQ	USBLS	5/07
Fire Fighting and Prevention Workers	Philadelphia-Camden-Wilmington MSA, PA-NJ-DE-MD	Y	59130 FQ	66130 MW	75730 TQ	USBLS	5/07
Fire Fighting and Prevention Workers	Pittsburgh MSA, PA	Y	54650 FQ	59100 MW	63790 TQ	USBLS	5/07
Fire Fighting and Prevention Workers	Rhode Island	Y	51980 FQ	58380 MW	66290 TQ	USBLS	5/07
Fire Fighting and Prevention Workers	Providence-Fall River-Warwick MSA, RI-MA	Y	52330 FQ	58610 MW	66370 TQ	USBLS	5/07
Fire Fighting and Prevention Workers	South Carolina	Y	35250 FQ	44650 MW	54650 TQ	USBLS	5/07
Fire Fighting and Prevention Workers	Charleston-North Charleston MSA, SC	Y	34150 FQ	41310 MW	53960 TQ	USBLS	5/07
Fire Fighting and Prevention Workers	Columbia MSA, SC	Y	36100 FQ	43180 MW	51960 TQ	USBLS	5/07
Fire Fighting and Prevention Workers	South Dakota	Y	56806 FQ	63004 MW	69581 TQ	SDBLS	7/08-9/08
Fire Fighting and Prevention Workers	Tennessee	Y	43440 FQ	55130 MW	70650 TQ	USBLS	5/07
Fire Fighting and Prevention Workers	Memphis MSA, TN-MS-AR	Y	52290 FQ	62870 MW	76490 TQ	USBLS	5/07
Fire Fighting and Prevention Workers	Nashville-Davidson-Murfreesboro MSA, TN	Y	64750 FQ	70480 MW	76250 TQ	USBLS	5/07
Fire Fighting and Prevention Workers	Texas	Y	45990 FQ	64760 MW	83190 TQ	USBLS	5/07

AE Average entry wage	AW Average wage paid	FQ First quartile wage	LO Lowest wage paid	MTC Median total compensation	TCC Total cash compensation
AER Average entry range	AWR Average wage range	H Hourly	LR Low end range	MW Median wage paid	TQ Third quartile wage
AEX Average experienced wage	AXR Average experienced range	HI Highest wage paid	M Monthly	MWR Median wage range	W Weekly
ATC Average total compensation	D Daily	HR High end range	MCC Median cash compensation	S See annotated source	Y Yearly

First-Line Supervisor/Manager

Occupation/Type/Industry	Location	Per	Low	Mid	High	Source	Date
First-Line Supervisor/Manager							
Fire Fighting and Prevention Workers	Austin-Round Rock MSA, TX	Y	43440 FQ	54560 MW	81050 TQ	USBLS	5/07
Fire Fighting and Prevention Workers	Dallas-Fort Worth-Arlington MSA, TX	Y	64790 FQ	77650 MW	92360 TQ	USBLS	5/07
Fire Fighting and Prevention Workers	Houston-Sugar Land-Baytown MSA, TX	Y	50540 FQ	70340 MW	84790 TQ	USBLS	5/07
Fire Fighting and Prevention Workers	San Antonio MSA, TX	Y	51700 FQ	62500 MW	72770 TQ	USBLS	5/07
Fire Fighting and Prevention Workers	Utah	Y	56720 FQ	70250 MW	80880 TQ	USBLS	5/07
Fire Fighting and Prevention Workers	Salt Lake City MSA, UT	Y	63250 FQ	74420 MW	82920 TQ	USBLS	5/07
Fire Fighting and Prevention Workers	Vermont	Y	49430 FQ	56650 MW	62140 TQ	USBLS	5/07
Fire Fighting and Prevention Workers	Virginia	Y	53860 FQ	67800 MW	81540 TQ	USBLS	5/07
Fire Fighting and Prevention Workers	Richmond MSA, VA	Y	55560 FQ	67490 MW	81060 TQ	USBLS	5/07
Fire Fighting and Prevention Workers	Virginia Beach-Norfolk-Newport News MSA, VA-NC	Y	50100 FQ	60640 MW	72930 TQ	USBLS	5/07
Fire Fighting and Prevention Workers	Washington	H	34.07 FQ	37.80 MW	41.96 TQ	WABLS	3/08
Fire Fighting and Prevention Workers	Seattle-Tacoma-Bellevue MSA, WA	Y	71840 FQ	79280 MW	89330 TQ	USBLS	5/07
Fire Fighting and Prevention Workers	West Virginia	Y	27232 FQ	39136 MW	52241 TQ	WVBLS	7/08-9/08
Fire Fighting and Prevention Workers	Wisconsin	Y	43830 FQ	63430 MW	76400 TQ	USBLS	5/07
Fire Fighting and Prevention Workers	Milwaukee-Waukesha-West Allis MSA, WI	Y	60030 FQ	73360 MW	83460 TQ	USBLS	5/07
Fire Fighting and Prevention Workers	Puerto Rico	Y	24230 FQ	27720 MW	30930 TQ	USBLS	5/07
Fire Fighting and Prevention Workers	San Juan-Caguas-Guaynabo MSA, PR	Y	24280 FQ	27720 MW	30900 TQ	USBLS	5/07
Food Preparation and Serving Workers	Alabama	Y	19340 FQ	24050 MW	30270 TQ	USBLS	5/07
Food Preparation and Serving Workers	Birmingham-Hoover MSA, AL	Y	20520 FQ	25840 MW	31690 TQ	USBLS	5/07
Food Preparation and Serving Workers	Mobile MSA, AL	Y	19610 FQ	24000 MW	29660 TQ	USBLS	5/07
Food Preparation and Serving Workers	Alaska	Y	25270 FQ	31030 MW	39730 TQ	USBLS	5/07
Food Preparation and Serving Workers	Anchorage MSA, AK	Y	25280 FQ	30600 MW	38590 TQ	USBLS	5/07
Food Preparation and Serving Workers	Fairbanks MSA, AK	Y	25270 FQ	30460 MW	37490 TQ	USBLS	5/07
Food Preparation and Serving Workers	Arizona	Y	22650 FQ	29200 MW	37210 TQ	USBLS	5/07
Food Preparation and Serving Workers	Phoenix-Mesa-Scottsdale MSA, AZ	Y	23980 FQ	29780 MW	38430 TQ	USBLS	5/07
Food Preparation and Serving Workers	Tucson MSA, AZ	Y	20530 FQ	29140 MW	36100 TQ	USBLS	5/07
Food Preparation and Serving Workers	Arkansas	Y	18480 FQ	22700 MW	28940 TQ	USBLS	5/07
Food Preparation and Serving Workers	Little Rock-North Little Rock MSA, AR	Y	19040 FQ	23050 MW	29800 TQ	USBLS	5/07
Food Preparation and Serving Workers	California	H	10.48 FQ	12.81 MW	16.82 TQ	CABLS	1/08-3/08
Food Preparation and Serving Workers	Los Angeles-Long Beach-Glendale PMSA, CA	H	10.48 FQ	12.80 MW	16.37 TQ	CABLS	1/08-3/08
Food Preparation and Serving Workers	Oakland-Fremont-Hayward MSA, CA	H	10.50 FQ	12.60 MW	17.12 TQ	CABLS	1/08-3/08
Food Preparation and Serving Workers	Riverside-San Bernardino-Ontario MSA, CA	H	10.18 FQ	11.91 MW	15.33 TQ	CABLS	1/08-3/08
Food Preparation and Serving Workers	Sacramento-Arden Arcade-Roseville MSA, CA	H	10.39 FQ	12.73 MW	16.93 TQ	CABLS	1/08-3/08
Food Preparation and Serving Workers	San Diego-Carlsbad-San Marcos MSA, CA	H	10.41 FQ	12.53 MW	17.69 TQ	CABLS	1/08-3/08
Food Preparation and Serving Workers	San Francisco-San Mateo-Redwood PMSA, CA	H	11.97 FQ	15.18 MW	19.10 TQ	CABLS	1/08-3/08
Food Preparation and Serving Workers	San Jose-Sunnyvale-Santa Clara MSA, CA	H	11.16 FQ	13.92 MW	17.69 TQ	CABLS	1/08-3/08
Food Preparation and Serving Workers	Santa Ana-Anaheim-Irvine PMSA, CA	Y	21620 FQ	26720 MW	35430 TQ	USBLS	5/07
Food Preparation and Serving Workers	Stockton MSA, CA	H	10.02 FQ	11.80 MW	15.10 TQ	CABLS	1/08-3/08
Food Preparation and Serving Workers	Colorado	Y	22500 FQ	29840 MW	38490 TQ	USBLS	5/07
Food Preparation and Serving Workers	Denver-Aurora MSA, CO	Y	22640 FQ	30130 MW	39230 TQ	USBLS	5/07
Food Preparation and Serving Workers	Pueblo MSA, CO	Y	21250 FQ	30630 MW	39540 TQ	USBLS	5/07
Food Preparation and Serving Workers	Connecticut	H	11.63 AE	15.63 MW		CTBLS	1/08-3/08
Food Preparation and Serving Workers	Bridgeport-Stamford-Norwalk MSA, CT	Y	28230 FQ	36280 MW	47850 TQ	USBLS	5/07
Food Preparation and Serving Workers	Hartford-West Hartford-East Hartford MSA, CT	Y	24680 FQ	29810 MW	38660 TQ	USBLS	5/07
Food Preparation and Serving Workers	New Haven MSA, CT	Y	24810 FQ	32020 MW	40960 TQ	USBLS	5/07
Food Preparation and Serving Workers	Delaware	Y	26640 FQ	32990 MW	40910 TQ	USBLS	5/07
Food Preparation and Serving Workers	Wilmington PMSA, DE-MD-NJ	Y	27380 FQ	34920 MW	42700 TQ	USBLS	5/07
Food Preparation and Serving Workers	District of Columbia	Y	27730 FQ	36450 MW	46590 TQ	USBLS	5/07
Food Preparation and Serving Workers	Washington-Arlington-Alexandria MSA, DC-VA-MD-WV	Y	27320 FQ	34640 MW	44170 TQ	USBLS	5/07
Food Preparation and Serving Workers	Florida	Y	24810 FQ	30660 MW	38820 TQ	USBLS	5/07

AE	Average entry wage	AW	Average wage paid	FQ	First quartile wage	LO	Lowest wage paid	MTC	Median total compensation	TCC	Total cash compensation
AER	Average entry range	AWR	Average wage range	H	Hourly	LR	Low end range	MW	Median wage paid	TQ	Third quartile wage
AEX	Average experienced wage	AXR	Average experienced range	HI	Highest wage paid	M	Monthly	MWR	Median wage range	W	Weekly
ATC	Average total compensation	D	Daily	HR	High end range	MCC	Median cash compensation	S	See annotated source	Y	Yearly

First-Line Supervisor/Manager

Occupation/Type/Industry	Location	Per	Low	Mid	High	Source	Date
Food Preparation and Serving Workers	Fort Lauderdale-Pompano Beach-Deerfield Beach PMSA, FL	Y	24770 FQ	30990 MW	40630 TQ	USBLS	5/07
Food Preparation and Serving Workers	Jacksonville MSA, FL	Y	23370 FQ	29250 MW	36430 TQ	USBLS	5/07
Food Preparation and Serving Workers	Miami-Fort Lauderdale-Miami Beach MSA, FL	Y	25280 FQ	31110 MW	39020 TQ	USBLS	5/07
Food Preparation and Serving Workers	Orlando-Kissimmee MSA, FL	Y	25460 FQ	31060 MW	39310 TQ	USBLS	5/07
Food Preparation and Serving Workers	Tampa-St. Petersburg-Clearwater MSA, FL	Y	25250 FQ	31280 MW	39570 TQ	USBLS	5/07
Food Preparation and Serving Workers	West Palm Beach-Boca Raton-Boynton Beach PMSA, FL	Y	25380 FQ	31420 MW	38450 TQ	USBLS	5/07
Food Preparation and Serving Workers	Georgia	Y	22470 FQ	27950 MW	34670 TQ	USBLS	5/07
Food Preparation and Serving Workers	Atlanta-Sandy Springs-Marietta MSA, GA	Y	23780 FQ	29050 MW	36260 TQ	USBLS	5/07
Food Preparation and Serving Workers	Hawaii	Y	24270 FQ	30770 MW	41710 TQ	USBLS	5/07
Food Preparation and Serving Workers	Honolulu MSA, HI	Y	23850 FQ	29460 MW	39210 TQ	USBLS	5/07
Food Preparation and Serving Workers	Idaho	Y	18020 FQ	22380 MW	30740 TQ	USBLS	5/07
Food Preparation and Serving Workers	Boise City-Nampa MSA, ID	Y	19550 FQ	26390 MW	36110 TQ	USBLS	5/07
Food Preparation and Serving Workers	Illinois	Y	23360 FQ	30190 MW	39060 TQ	USBLS	5/07
Food Preparation and Serving Workers	Chicago-Naperville-Joliet MSA, IL-IN-WI	Y	24760 FQ	31270 MW	39970 TQ	USBLS	5/07
Food Preparation and Serving Workers	Indiana	Y	22250 FQ	27700 MW	34630 TQ	USBLS	5/07
Food Preparation and Serving Workers	Fort Wayne MSA, IN	Y	22610 FQ	27480 MW	32830 TQ	USBLS	5/07
Food Preparation and Serving Workers	Gary PMSA, IN	Y	21640 FQ	26370 MW	34790 TQ	USBLS	5/07
Food Preparation and Serving Workers	Indianapolis-Carmel MSA, IN	Y	24750 FQ	30290 MW	37430 TQ	USBLS	5/07
Food Preparation and Serving Workers	Terre Haute MSA, IN	Y	19960 FQ	25900 MW	34460 TQ	USBLS	5/07
Food Preparation and Serving Workers	Iowa	Y	20980 FQ	26530 MW	34120 TQ	USBLS	5/07
Food Preparation and Serving Workers	Cedar Rapids MSA, IA	Y	21230 FQ	26690 MW	32590 TQ	USBLS	5/07
Food Preparation and Serving Workers	Davenport-Moline-Rock Island MSA, IA-IL	Y	19080 FQ	24440 MW	33860 TQ	USBLS	5/07
Food Preparation and Serving Workers	Des Moines-West Des Moines MSA, IA	Y	22750 FQ	28860 MW	36680 TQ	USBLS	5/07
Food Preparation and Serving Workers	Sioux City MSA, IA-NE-SD	Y	23090 FQ	27340 MW	32180 TQ	USBLS	5/07
Food Preparation and Serving Workers	Kansas	Y	19450 FQ	24680 MW	31740 TQ	USBLS	5/07
Food Preparation and Serving Workers	Wichita MSA, KS	Y	19600 FQ	25430 MW	32040 TQ	USBLS	5/07
Food Preparation and Serving Workers	Kentucky	Y	19652 FQ	24082 MW	29870 TQ	KYBLS	2008
Food Preparation and Serving Workers	Louisville-Jefferson County MSA, KY-IN	Y	20570 FQ	25260 MW	31500 TQ	USBLS	5/07
Food Preparation and Serving Workers	Louisiana	H	9.76 FQ	12.22 MW	15.08 TQ	LABLS	1/08-3/08
Food Preparation and Serving Workers	Baton Rouge MSA, LA	Y	21210 FQ	25880 MW	31340 TQ	USBLS	5/07
Food Preparation and Serving Workers	New Orleans-Metairie-Kenner MSA, LA	Y	21140 FQ	26290 MW	32090 TQ	USBLS	5/07
Food Preparation and Serving Workers	Maine	Y	22220 FQ	27520 MW	33230 TQ	USBLS	5/07
Food Preparation and Serving Workers	Bangor MSA, ME	Y	21370 FQ	26490 MW	32860 TQ	USBLS	5/07
Food Preparation and Serving Workers	Portland-South Portland-Biddeford MSA, ME	Y	24580 FQ	29390 MW	36250 TQ	USBLS	5/07
Food Preparation and Serving Workers	Maryland	Y		33975 MW		MDBLS	3/08
Food Preparation and Serving Workers	Baltimore-Towson MSA, MD	Y	26150 FQ	33080 MW	41460 TQ	USBLS	5/07
Food Preparation and Serving Workers	Bethesda-Gaithersburg-Frederick PMSA, MD	Y	28360 FQ	35980 MW	44670 TQ	USBLS	5/07
Food Preparation and Serving Workers	Hagerstown-Martinsburg MSA, MD-WV	Y	20230 FQ	28600 MW	37860 TQ	USBLS	5/07
Food Preparation and Serving Workers	Massachusetts	Y	26720 FQ	33200 MW	40180 TQ	USBLS	5/07
Food Preparation and Serving Workers	Boston-Cambridge-Quincy NECTA, MA	Y	28340 FQ	34950 MW	40920 TQ	USBLS	5/07
Food Preparation and Serving Workers	Worcester MSA, MA-CT	Y	25300 FQ	31350 MW	39350 TQ	USBLS	5/07
Food Preparation and Serving Workers	Michigan	Y	21630 FQ	28790 MW	38020 TQ	USBLS	5/07
Food Preparation and Serving Workers	Detroit-Warren-Livonia MSA, MI	Y	22530 FQ	30720 MW	39550 TQ	USBLS	5/07
Food Preparation and Serving Workers	Grand Rapids-Wyoming MSA, MI	Y	20380 FQ	27210 MW	36650 TQ	USBLS	5/07
Food Preparation and Serving Workers	Warren-Troy-Farmington Hills PMSA, MI	Y	22860 FQ	30630 MW	38410 TQ	USBLS	5/07
Food Preparation and Serving Workers	Minnesota	Y	21810 FQ	26526 MW	33845 TQ	MNBLS	10/08-12/08
Food Preparation and Serving Workers	Duluth-Superior MSA, MN-WI	Y	19207 FQ	23504 MW	29579 TQ	MNBLS	10/08-12/08
Food Preparation and Serving Workers	Minneapolis-Saint Paul MSA, MN-WI	Y	23107 FQ	28084 MW	35623 TQ	MNBLS	10/08-12/08
Food Preparation and Serving Workers	Rochester MSA, MN	Y	20423 FQ	26159 MW	36984 TQ	MNBLS	10/08-12/08
Food Preparation and Serving Workers	Mississippi	Y	20260 FQ	24280 MW	30330 TQ	USBLS	5/07
Food Preparation and Serving Workers	Jackson MSA, MS	Y	21150 FQ	24050 MW	29650 TQ	USBLS	5/07
Food Preparation and Serving Workers	Missouri	Y	26020 FQ	32180 MW	39730 TQ	USBLS	5/07

AE	Average entry wage	AW	Average wage paid	FQ	First quartile wage	LO	Lowest wage paid	MTC	Median total compensation	TCC	Total cash compensation
AER	Average entry range	AWR	Average wage range	H	Hourly	LR	Low end range	MW	Median wage paid	TQ	Third quartile wage
AEX	Average experienced wage	AXR	Average experienced range	HI	Highest wage paid	M	Monthly	MWR	Median wage range	W	Weekly
ATC	Average total compensation	D	Daily	HR	High end range	MCC	Median cash compensation	S	See annotated source	Y	Yearly

Occupation/Type/Industry	Location	Per	Low	Mid	High	Source	Date
First-Line Supervisor/Manager							
Food Preparation and Serving Workers	Kansas City MSA, MO-KS	Y	24120 FQ	30590 MW	37570 TQ	USBLS	5/07
Food Preparation and Serving Workers	St. Louis MSA, MO-IL	Y	25900 FQ	32440 MW	40720 TQ	USBLS	5/07
Food Preparation and Serving Workers	Montana	Y	20910 FQ	26650 MW	33210 TQ	USBLS	5/07
Food Preparation and Serving Workers	Billings MSA, MT	Y	21160 FQ	24210 MW	30200 TQ	USBLS	5/07
Food Preparation and Serving Workers	Nebraska	Y	21540 FQ	26970 MW	32790 TQ	USBLS	5/07
Food Preparation and Serving Workers	Omaha-Council Bluffs MSA, NE-IA	Y	22130 FQ	28060 MW	35820 TQ	USBLS	5/07
Food Preparation and Serving Workers	Nevada	H	11.64 FQ	14.96 MW	18.96 TQ	NVBLS	5/08
Food Preparation and Serving Workers	Las Vegas-Paradise MSA, NV	H	11.92 FQ	15.29 MW	19.35 TQ	NVBLS	5/08
Food Preparation and Serving Workers	Manchester MSA, NH	Y	24700 FQ	31590 MW	37370 TQ	USBLS	5/07
Food Preparation and Serving Workers	Nashua NECTA, NH-MA	Y	27850 FQ	34100 MW	41370 TQ	USBLS	5/07
Food Preparation and Serving Workers	New Jersey	Y	26950 FQ	34680 MW	44650 TQ	USBLS	5/07
Food Preparation and Serving Workers	Atlantic City MSA, NJ	Y	25460 FQ	31990 MW	41370 TQ	USBLS	5/07
Food Preparation and Serving Workers	Camden PMSA, NJ	Y	25270 FQ	33130 MW	42910 TQ	USBLS	5/07
Food Preparation and Serving Workers	Edison PMSA, NJ	Y	28170 FQ	36280 MW	45610 TQ	USBLS	5/07
Food Preparation and Serving Workers	Newark-Union PMSA, NJ-PA	Y	27210 FQ	33770 MW	45350 TQ	USBLS	5/07
Food Preparation and Serving Workers	Trenton-Ewing MSA, NJ	Y	27340 FQ	35250 MW	43370 TQ	USBLS	5/07
Food Preparation and Serving Workers	New Mexico	Y	19100 FQ	24530 MW	31200 TQ	USBLS	5/07
Food Preparation and Serving Workers	Albuquerque MSA, NM	Y	18910 FQ	23840 MW	30440 TQ	USBLS	5/07
Food Preparation and Serving Workers	New York	Y	22040 FQ	28310 MW	37160 TQ	USBLS	5/07
Food Preparation and Serving Workers	Albany-Schenectady-Troy MSA, NY	Y	22420 FQ	27860 MW	35020 TQ	USBLS	5/07
Food Preparation and Serving Workers	Buffalo-Niagara Falls MSA, NY	Y	19580 FQ	23230 MW	30630 TQ	USBLS	5/07
Food Preparation and Serving Workers	Glens Falls MSA, NY	Y	21930 FQ	27050 MW	36580 TQ	USBLS	5/07
Food Preparation and Serving Workers	Nassau-Suffolk PMSA, NY	Y	22460 FQ	28860 MW	40160 TQ	USBLS	5/07
Food Preparation and Serving Workers	New York-Northern New Jersey-Long Island MSA, NY-NJ-PA	Y	24890 FQ	31810 MW	42310 TQ	USBLS	5/07
Food Preparation and Serving Workers	North Carolina	Y	21250 FQ	26940 MW	34580 TQ	USBLS	5/07
Food Preparation and Serving Workers	Charlotte-Gastonia-Concord MSA, NC-SC	Y	21580 FQ	28770 MW	36140 TQ	USBLS	5/07
Food Preparation and Serving Workers	Raleigh-Cary MSA, NC	Y	21860 FQ	28340 MW	37170 TQ	USBLS	5/07
Food Preparation and Serving Workers	North Dakota	Y	21890 FQ	26620 MW	32140 TQ	USBLS	5/07
Food Preparation and Serving Workers	Fargo MSA, ND-MN	Y	22420 FQ	27790 MW	33210 TQ	USBLS	5/07
Food Preparation and Serving Workers	Ohio	Y	21700 FQ	27650 MW	35360 TQ	USBLS	5/07
Food Preparation and Serving Workers	Cincinnati-Middletown MSA, OH-KY-IN	Y	22550 FQ	28560 MW	35930 TQ	USBLS	5/07
Food Preparation and Serving Workers	Cleveland-Elyria-Mentor MSA, OH	Y	22240 FQ	28230 MW	36580 TQ	USBLS	5/07
Food Preparation and Serving Workers	Columbus MSA, OH	Y	23750 FQ	29760 MW	37500 TQ	USBLS	5/07
Food Preparation and Serving Workers	Dayton MSA, OH	Y	21490 FQ	26100 MW	33690 TQ	USBLS	5/07
Food Preparation and Serving Workers	Oklahoma	Y	18320 FQ	23010 MW	29530 TQ	USBLS	5/07
Food Preparation and Serving Workers	Lawton MSA, OK	Y	17590 FQ	22410 MW	27400 TQ	USBLS	5/07
Food Preparation and Serving Workers	Oklahoma City MSA, OK	Y	18030 FQ	22940 MW	30000 TQ	USBLS	5/07
Food Preparation and Serving Workers	Tulsa MSA, OK	Y	20010 FQ	24550 MW	31380 TQ	USBLS	5/07
Food Preparation and Serving Workers	Oregon	H	11.78 FQ	14.53 MW	18.43 TQ	ORBLS	5/08
Food Preparation and Serving Workers	Portland-Vancouver-Beaverton MSA, OR-WA	Y	25650 FQ	31210 MW	39900 TQ	USBLS	5/07
Food Preparation and Serving Workers	Pennsylvania	Y	22840 FQ	30590 MW	38960 TQ	USBLS	5/07
Food Preparation and Serving Workers	Allentown-Bethlehem-Easton MSA, PA-NJ	Y	22190 FQ	29540 MW	37560 TQ	USBLS	5/07
Food Preparation and Serving Workers	Philadelphia-Camden-Wilmington MSA, PA-NJ-DE-MD	Y	27230 FQ	34810 MW	43550 TQ	USBLS	5/07
Food Preparation and Serving Workers	Pittsburgh MSA, PA	Y	22590 FQ	29810 MW	37750 TQ	USBLS	5/07
Food Preparation and Serving Workers	Rhode Island	Y	27830 FQ	33300 MW	39790 TQ	USBLS	5/07
Food Preparation and Serving Workers	Providence-Fall River-Warwick MSA, RI-MA	Y	27420 FQ	32870 MW	39790 TQ	USBLS	5/07
Food Preparation and Serving Workers	South Carolina	Y	22130 FQ	27580 MW	35110 TQ	USBLS	5/07
Food Preparation and Serving Workers	Charleston-North Charleston MSA, SC	Y	22100 FQ	28140 MW	34700 TQ	USBLS	5/07
Food Preparation and Serving Workers	Columbia MSA, SC	Y	24020 FQ	29020 MW	36950 TQ	USBLS	5/07
Food Preparation and Serving Workers	South Dakota	Y	25089 FQ	28273 MW	31395 TQ	SDBLS	7/08-9/08
Food Preparation and Serving Workers	Sioux Falls MSA, SD	Y	25110 FQ	28348 MW	31478 TQ	SDBLS	7/08-9/08
Food Preparation and Serving Workers	Tennessee	Y	18740 FQ	24510 MW	31590 TQ	USBLS	5/07
Food Preparation and Serving Workers	Knoxville MSA, TN	Y	18820 FQ	23910 MW	30670 TQ	USBLS	5/07
Food Preparation and Serving Workers	Memphis MSA, TN-MS-AR	Y	22290 FQ	28350 MW	34570 TQ	USBLS	5/07
Food Preparation and Serving Workers	Nashville-Davidson-Murfreesboro MSA, TN	Y	19620 FQ	25050 MW	32910 TQ	USBLS	5/07
Food Preparation and Serving Workers	Texas	Y	19120 FQ	25010 MW	33150 TQ	USBLS	5/07

AE	Average entry wage	AW	Average wage paid	FQ	First quartile wage
AER	Average entry range	AWR	Average wage range	H	Hourly
AEX	Average experienced wage	AXR	Average experienced range	HI	Highest wage paid
ATC	Average total compensation	D	Daily	HR	High end range

LO　Lowest wage paid　　MTC Median total compensation　TCC Total cash compensation
LR　Low end range　　　MW　Median wage paid　　　TQ　Third quartile wage
M　Monthly　　　　　　MWR Median wage range　　W　Weekly
MCC Median cash compensation S　See annotated source　　Y　Yearly

Occupation/Type/Industry	Location	Per	Low	Mid	High	Source	Date
First-Line Supervisor/Manager							
Food Preparation and Serving Workers	Austin-Round Rock MSA, TX	Y	20570 FQ	27480 MW	36360 TQ	USBLS	5/07
Food Preparation and Serving Workers	Dallas-Fort Worth-Arlington MSA, TX	Y	20150 FQ	26040 MW	34690 TQ	USBLS	5/07
Food Preparation and Serving Workers	El Paso MSA, TX	Y	17230 FQ	22570 MW	31880 TQ	USBLS	5/07
Food Preparation and Serving Workers	Houston-Sugar Land-Baytown MSA, TX	Y	20270 FQ	26260 MW	35670 TQ	USBLS	5/07
Food Preparation and Serving Workers	Midland MSA, TX	Y	19390 FQ	25660 MW	33570 TQ	USBLS	5/07
Food Preparation and Serving Workers	San Antonio MSA, TX	Y	18440 FQ	24240 MW	31970 TQ	USBLS	5/07
Food Preparation and Serving Workers	Utah	Y	23270 FQ	28840 MW	35290 TQ	USBLS	5/07
Food Preparation and Serving Workers	Provo-Orem MSA, UT	Y	21110 FQ	25810 MW	30970 TQ	USBLS	5/07
Food Preparation and Serving Workers	Salt Lake City MSA, UT	Y	24720 FQ	30330 MW	36510 TQ	USBLS	5/07
Food Preparation and Serving Workers	Vermont	Y	27410 FQ	32480 MW	39860 TQ	USBLS	5/07
Food Preparation and Serving Workers	Burlington-South Burlington MSA, VT	Y	27600 FQ	32520 MW	39650 TQ	USBLS	5/07
Food Preparation and Serving Workers	Virginia	Y	24290 FQ	30630 MW	38930 TQ	USBLS	5/07
Food Preparation and Serving Workers	Lynchburg MSA, VA	Y	23700 FQ	30400 MW	36930 TQ	USBLS	5/07
Food Preparation and Serving Workers	Richmond MSA, VA	Y	23440 FQ	31260 MW	38430 TQ	USBLS	5/07
Food Preparation and Serving Workers	Virginia Beach-Norfolk-Newport News MSA, VA-NC	Y	24830 FQ	29990 MW	37390 TQ	USBLS	5/07
Food Preparation and Serving Workers	Washington	H	14.49 FQ	17.61 MW	21.04 TQ	WABLS	3/08
Food Preparation and Serving Workers	Seattle-Tacoma-Bellevue MSA, WA	Y	30390 FQ	37470 MW	44570 TQ	USBLS	5/07
Food Preparation and Serving Workers	West Virginia	Y	18729 FQ	22939 MW	29504 TQ	WVBLS	7/08-9/08
Food Preparation and Serving Workers	Charleston MSA, WV	Y	19460 FQ	23360 MW	29560 TQ	USBLS	5/07
Food Preparation and Serving Workers	Wisconsin	Y	23270 FQ	29240 MW	36490 TQ	USBLS	5/07
Food Preparation and Serving Workers	Milwaukee-Waukesha-West Allis MSA, WI	Y	25800 FQ	31060 MW	37420 TQ	USBLS	5/07
Food Preparation and Serving Workers	Wyoming	Y	20113 FQ	25419 MW	32119 TQ	WYBLS	9/08
Food Preparation and Serving Workers	Cheyenne MSA, WY	Y	19727 FQ	25099 MW	33322 TQ	WYBLS	9/08
Food Preparation and Serving Workers	Puerto Rico	Y	15760 FQ	20030 MW	24620 TQ	USBLS	5/07
Food Preparation and Serving Workers	San German-Cabo Rojo MSA, PR	Y	16930 FQ	20520 MW	25550 TQ	USBLS	5/07
Food Preparation and Serving Workers	San Juan-Caguas-Guaynabo MSA, PR	Y	16020 FQ	20240 MW	24720 TQ	USBLS	5/07
Food Preparation and Serving Workers	Virgin Islands	Y	27980 FQ	31150 MW	36160 TQ	USBLS	5/07
Food Preparation and Serving Workers	Guam	Y	17460 FQ	20530 MW	25390 TQ	USBLS	5/07
Helpers, Laborers, and Material Movers	Alabama	Y	29010 FQ	36650 MW	45840 TQ	USBLS	5/07
Helpers, Laborers, and Material Movers	Birmingham-Hoover MSA, AL	Y	32250 FQ	38420 MW	46680 TQ	USBLS	5/07
Helpers, Laborers, and Material Movers	Alaska	Y	33860 FQ	42910 MW	63600 TQ	USBLS	5/07
Helpers, Laborers, and Material Movers	Anchorage MSA, AK	Y	34320 FQ	42850 MW	67550 TQ	USBLS	5/07
Helpers, Laborers, and Material Movers	Arizona	Y	31460 FQ	39290 MW	49840 TQ	USBLS	5/07
Helpers, Laborers, and Material Movers	Phoenix-Mesa-Scottsdale MSA, AZ	Y	32190 FQ	40150 MW	49530 TQ	USBLS	5/07
Helpers, Laborers, and Material Movers	Tucson MSA, AZ	Y	28510 FQ	33950 MW	44520 TQ	USBLS	5/07
Helpers, Laborers, and Material Movers	Arkansas	Y	27430 FQ	35670 MW	47420 TQ	USBLS	5/07
Helpers, Laborers, and Material Movers	Little Rock-North Little Rock MSA, AR	Y	26070 FQ	34660 MW	52920 TQ	USBLS	5/07
Helpers, Laborers, and Material Movers	California	H	16.30 FQ	20.62 MW	25.80 TQ	CABLS	1/08-3/08
Helpers, Laborers, and Material Movers	Bakersfield MSA, CA	H	16.12 FQ	18.91 MW	22.62 TQ	CABLS	1/08-3/08
Helpers, Laborers, and Material Movers	Los Angeles-Long Beach-Glendale PMSA, CA	H	15.86 FQ	20.15 MW	25.24 TQ	CABLS	1/08-3/08
Helpers, Laborers, and Material Movers	Oakland-Fremont-Hayward MSA, CA	H	17.30 FQ	21.98 MW	27.61 TQ	CABLS	1/08-3/08
Helpers, Laborers, and Material Movers	Riverside-San Bernardino-Ontario MSA, CA	H	16.22 FQ	21.40 MW	28.51 TQ	CABLS	1/08-3/08
Helpers, Laborers, and Material Movers	Sacramento-Arden Arcade-Roseville MSA, CA	H	18.17 FQ	22.33 MW	26.51 TQ	CABLS	1/08-3/08
Helpers, Laborers, and Material Movers	San Diego-Carlsbad-San Marcos MSA, CA	H	15.79 FQ	19.78 MW	24.37 TQ	CABLS	1/08-3/08
Helpers, Laborers, and Material Movers	San Francisco-San Mateo-Redwood PMSA, CA	H	18.36 FQ	22.31 MW	27.44 TQ	CABLS	1/08-3/08
Helpers, Laborers, and Material Movers	San Jose-Sunnyvale-Santa Clara MSA, CA	H	17.17 FQ	21.48 MW	27.37 TQ	CABLS	1/08-3/08
Helpers, Laborers, and Material Movers	Santa Ana-Anaheim-Irvine PMSA, CA	Y	34850 FQ	42650 MW	52860 TQ	USBLS	5/07
Helpers, Laborers, and Material Movers	Stockton MSA, CA	H	16.11 FQ	21.48 MW	28.60 TQ	CABLS	1/08-3/08
Helpers, Laborers, and Material Movers	Colorado	Y	32570 FQ	41880 MW	57290 TQ	USBLS	5/07
Helpers, Laborers, and Material Movers	Boulder MSA, CO	Y	32720 FQ	37460 MW	47290 TQ	USBLS	5/07
Helpers, Laborers, and Material Movers	Denver-Aurora MSA, CO	Y	32890 FQ	44110 MW	61260 TQ	USBLS	5/07
Helpers, Laborers, and Material Movers	Connecticut	H	14.49 AE	21.49 MW		CTBLS	1/08-3/08

AE	Average entry wage	AW	Average wage paid	FQ	First quartile wage	LO	Lowest wage paid	MTC	Median total compensation	TCC	Total cash compensation
AER	Average entry range	AWR	Average wage range	H	Hourly	LR	Low end range	MW	Median wage paid	TQ	Third quartile wage
AEX	Average experienced wage	AXR	Average experienced range	HI	Highest wage paid	M	Monthly	MWR	Median wage range	W	Weekly
ATC	Average total compensation	D	Daily	HR	High end range	MCC	Median cash compensation	S	See annotated source	Y	Yearly

Occupation/Type/Industry	Location	Per	Low	Mid	High	Source	Date
First-Line Supervisor/Manager							
Helpers, Laborers, and Material Movers	Bridgeport-Stamford-Norwalk MSA, CT	Y	34890 FQ	45520 MW	58340 TQ	USBLS	5/07
Helpers, Laborers, and Material Movers	Hartford-West Hartford-East Hartford MSA, CT	Y	30750 FQ	40560 MW	52760 TQ	USBLS	5/07
Helpers, Laborers, and Material Movers	Delaware	Y	35870 FQ	44990 MW	56060 TQ	USBLS	5/07
Helpers, Laborers, and Material Movers	Wilmington PMSA, DE-MD-NJ	Y	34960 FQ	45540 MW	57190 TQ	USBLS	5/07
Helpers, Laborers, and Material Movers	District of Columbia	Y	47770 FQ	55730 MW	63140 TQ	USBLS	5/07
Helpers, Laborers, and Material Movers	Washington-Arlington-Alexandria MSA, DC-VA-MD-WV	Y	36890 FQ	46830 MW	58360 TQ	USBLS	5/07
Helpers, Laborers, and Material Movers	Florida	Y	31410 FQ	40210 MW	51040 TQ	USBLS	5/07
Helpers, Laborers, and Material Movers	Fort Lauderdale-Pompano Beach-Deerfield Beach PMSA, FL	Y	34970 FQ	40160 MW	48190 TQ	USBLS	5/07
Helpers, Laborers, and Material Movers	Jacksonville MSA, FL	Y	33990 FQ	39520 MW	48990 TQ	USBLS	5/07
Helpers, Laborers, and Material Movers	Lakeland MSA, FL	Y	28220 FQ	35110 MW	44750 TQ	USBLS	5/07
Helpers, Laborers, and Material Movers	Miami-Fort Lauderdale-Miami Beach MSA, FL	Y	32750 FQ	40600 MW	52270 TQ	USBLS	5/07
Helpers, Laborers, and Material Movers	Orlando-Kissimmee MSA, FL	Y	29590 FQ	40660 MW	57090 TQ	USBLS	5/07
Helpers, Laborers, and Material Movers	Pensacola-Ferry Pass-Brent MSA, FL	Y	29700 FQ	45570 MW	59610 TQ	USBLS	5/07
Helpers, Laborers, and Material Movers	Tampa-St. Petersburg-Clearwater MSA, FL	Y	30060 FQ	41770 MW	49900 TQ	USBLS	5/07
Helpers, Laborers, and Material Movers	West Palm Beach-Boca Raton-Boynton Beach PMSA, FL	Y	29450 FQ	39830 MW	54940 TQ	USBLS	5/07
Helpers, Laborers, and Material Movers	Georgia	Y	30510 FQ	39090 MW	50280 TQ	USBLS	5/07
Helpers, Laborers, and Material Movers	Atlanta-Sandy Springs-Marietta MSA, GA	Y	31220 FQ	39660 MW	49960 TQ	USBLS	5/07
Helpers, Laborers, and Material Movers	Hawaii	Y	28880 FQ	39050 MW	48250 TQ	USBLS	5/07
Helpers, Laborers, and Material Movers	Honolulu MSA, HI	Y	29250 FQ	39930 MW	48430 TQ	USBLS	5/07
Helpers, Laborers, and Material Movers	Idaho	Y	25180 FQ	37330 MW	46880 TQ	USBLS	5/07
Helpers, Laborers, and Material Movers	Boise City-Nampa MSA, ID	Y	22620 FQ	34270 MW	44990 TQ	USBLS	5/07
Helpers, Laborers, and Material Movers	Lewiston MSA, ID-WA	Y	33070 FQ	42050 MW	51260 TQ	USBLS	5/07
Helpers, Laborers, and Material Movers	Illinois	Y	28860 FQ	40780 MW	54610 TQ	USBLS	5/07
Helpers, Laborers, and Material Movers	Chicago-Naperville-Joliet MSA, IL-IN-WI	Y	28050 FQ	40920 MW	55590 TQ	USBLS	5/07
Helpers, Laborers, and Material Movers	Indiana	Y	33310 FQ	41460 MW	50680 TQ	USBLS	5/07
Helpers, Laborers, and Material Movers	Elkhart-Goshen MSA, IN	Y	36320 FQ	42630 MW	50410 TQ	USBLS	5/07
Helpers, Laborers, and Material Movers	Gary PMSA, IN	Y	29610 FQ	42420 MW	59580 TQ	USBLS	5/07
Helpers, Laborers, and Material Movers	Indianapolis-Carmel MSA, IN	Y	35450 FQ	42690 MW	51530 TQ	USBLS	5/07
Helpers, Laborers, and Material Movers	Iowa	Y	31850 FQ	41120 MW	50370 TQ	USBLS	5/07
Helpers, Laborers, and Material Movers	Cedar Rapids MSA, IA	Y	29870 FQ	38250 MW	50130 TQ	USBLS	5/07
Helpers, Laborers, and Material Movers	Des Moines-West Des Moines MSA, IA	Y	29470 FQ	39180 MW	45560 TQ	USBLS	5/07
Helpers, Laborers, and Material Movers	Sioux City MSA, IA-NE-SD	Y	32920 FQ	45750 MW	52730 TQ	USBLS	5/07
Helpers, Laborers, and Material Movers	Kansas	Y	30490 FQ	38930 MW	47530 TQ	USBLS	5/07
Helpers, Laborers, and Material Movers	Wichita MSA, KS	Y	30860 FQ	39240 MW	46230 TQ	USBLS	5/07
Helpers, Laborers, and Material Movers	Kentucky	Y	27566 FQ	37610 MW	49672 TQ	KYBLS	2008
Helpers, Laborers, and Material Movers	Louisville-Jefferson County MSA, KY-IN	Y	22480 FQ	35000 MW	46770 TQ	USBLS	5/07
Helpers, Laborers, and Material Movers	Louisiana	H	14.20 FQ	17.34 MW	21.70 TQ	LABLS	1/08-3/08
Helpers, Laborers, and Material Movers	Baton Rouge MSA, LA	Y	28280 FQ	34520 MW	40840 TQ	USBLS	5/07
Helpers, Laborers, and Material Movers	New Orleans-Metairie-Kenner MSA, LA	Y	31710 FQ	36930 MW	44540 TQ	USBLS	5/07
Helpers, Laborers, and Material Movers	Shreveport-Bossier City MSA, LA	Y	30910 FQ	35540 MW	39830 TQ	USBLS	5/07
Helpers, Laborers, and Material Movers	Maine	Y	25180 FQ	34540 MW	43730 TQ	USBLS	5/07
Helpers, Laborers, and Material Movers	Portland-South Portland-Biddeford MSA, ME	Y	24730 FQ	33380 MW	42120 TQ	USBLS	5/07
Helpers, Laborers, and Material Movers	Maryland	Y		46275 MW		MDBLS	3/08
Helpers, Laborers, and Material Movers	Baltimore-Towson MSA, MD	Y	34250 FQ	44980 MW	58220 TQ	USBLS	5/07
Helpers, Laborers, and Material Movers	Bethesda-Gaithersburg-Frederick PMSA, MD	Y	36520 FQ	46310 MW	56720 TQ	USBLS	5/07
Helpers, Laborers, and Material Movers	Salisbury MSA, MD	Y	31920 FQ	39410 MW	62270 TQ	USBLS	5/07
Helpers, Laborers, and Material Movers	Massachusetts	Y	35680 FQ	43900 MW	55450 TQ	USBLS	5/07
Helpers, Laborers, and Material Movers	Boston-Cambridge-Quincy NECTA, MA	Y	35820 FQ	44290 MW	55960 TQ	USBLS	5/07
Helpers, Laborers, and Material Movers	Springfield MSA, MA-CT	Y	34090 FQ	44450 MW	53930 TQ	USBLS	5/07
Helpers, Laborers, and Material Movers	Worcester MSA, MA-CT	Y	39350 FQ	44240 MW	54290 TQ	USBLS	5/07
Helpers, Laborers, and Material Movers	Michigan	Y	34010 FQ	47840 MW	65380 TQ	USBLS	5/07

AE Average entry wage	**AW** Average wage paid	**FQ** First quartile wage	**LO** Lowest wage paid	**MTC** Median total compensation	**TCC** Total cash compensation
AER Average entry range	**AWR** Average wage range	**H** Hourly	**LR** Low end range	**MW** Median wage paid	**TQ** Third quartile wage
AEX Average experienced wage	**AXR** Average experienced range	**HI** Highest wage paid	**M** Monthly	**MWR** Median wage range	**W** Weekly
ATC Average total compensation	**D** Daily	**HR** High end range	**MCC** Median cash compensation	**S** See annotated source	**Y** Yearly

Occupation/Type/Industry	Location	Per	Low	Mid	High	Source	Date
First-Line Supervisor/Manager							
Helpers, Laborers, and Material Movers	Detroit-Warren-Livonia MSA, MI	Y	36600 FQ	50710 MW	67590 TQ	USBLS	5/07
Helpers, Laborers, and Material Movers	Grand Rapids-Wyoming MSA, MI	Y	31820 FQ	48800 MW	61430 TQ	USBLS	5/07
Helpers, Laborers, and Material Movers	Lansing-East Lansing MSA, MI	Y	33340 FQ	51110 MW	69710 TQ	USBLS	5/07
Helpers, Laborers, and Material Movers	Warren-Troy-Farmington Hills PMSA, MI	Y	35540 FQ	52740 MW	69110 TQ	USBLS	5/07
Helpers, Laborers, and Material Movers	Minnesota	Y	34019 FQ	42342 MW	54826 TQ	MNBLS	10/08-12/08
Helpers, Laborers, and Material Movers	Duluth-Superior MSA, MN-WI	Y	31980 FQ	41873 MW	55918 TQ	MNBLS	10/08-12/08
Helpers, Laborers, and Material Movers	Minneapolis-Saint Paul MSA, MN-WI	Y	35819 FQ	45473 MW	58373 TQ	MNBLS	10/08-12/08
Helpers, Laborers, and Material Movers	Rochester MSA, MN	Y	31576 FQ	38022 MW	46469 TQ	MNBLS	10/08-12/08
Helpers, Laborers, and Material Movers	Mississippi	Y	28390 FQ	35940 MW	46030 TQ	USBLS	5/07
Helpers, Laborers, and Material Movers	Jackson MSA, MS	Y	30980 FQ	36740 MW	47810 TQ	USBLS	5/07
Helpers, Laborers, and Material Movers	Missouri	Y	32460 FQ	40500 MW	51720 TQ	USBLS	5/07
Helpers, Laborers, and Material Movers	Jefferson City MSA, MO	Y	24710 FQ	28150 MW	40130 TQ	USBLS	5/07
Helpers, Laborers, and Material Movers	Kansas City MSA, MO-KS	Y	34240 FQ	41750 MW	50680 TQ	USBLS	5/07
Helpers, Laborers, and Material Movers	St. Louis MSA, MO-IL	Y	33750 FQ	43660 MW	58050 TQ	USBLS	5/07
Helpers, Laborers, and Material Movers	Montana	Y	25430 FQ	34340 MW	48020 TQ	USBLS	5/07
Helpers, Laborers, and Material Movers	Billings MSA, MT	Y	22110 FQ	30420 MW	46970 TQ	USBLS	5/07
Helpers, Laborers, and Material Movers	Nebraska	Y	32630 FQ	41330 MW	52860 TQ	USBLS	5/07
Helpers, Laborers, and Material Movers	Omaha-Council Bluffs MSA, NE-IA	Y	32800 FQ	41840 MW	54020 TQ	USBLS	5/07
Helpers, Laborers, and Material Movers	Nevada	H	15.81 FQ	19.09 MW	24.23 TQ	NVBLS	5/08
Helpers, Laborers, and Material Movers	Las Vegas-Paradise MSA, NV	H	15.41 FQ	19.10 MW	24.67 TQ	NVBLS	5/08
Helpers, Laborers, and Material Movers	New Hampshire	H	14.69 AE	19.53 MW	22.69 AEX	NHBLS	6/08
Helpers, Laborers, and Material Movers	Manchester MSA, NH	Y	30290 FQ	38630 MW	46690 TQ	USBLS	5/07
Helpers, Laborers, and Material Movers	Nashua NECTA, NH-MA	Y	37770 FQ	44550 MW	53140 TQ	USBLS	5/07
Helpers, Laborers, and Material Movers	New Jersey	Y	34210 FQ	44380 MW	56790 TQ	USBLS	5/07
Helpers, Laborers, and Material Movers	Camden PMSA, NJ	Y	33330 FQ	43410 MW	52660 TQ	USBLS	5/07
Helpers, Laborers, and Material Movers	Edison PMSA, NJ	Y	36950 FQ	47220 MW	58120 TQ	USBLS	5/07
Helpers, Laborers, and Material Movers	Newark-Union PMSA, NJ-PA	Y	33090 FQ	43370 MW	57660 TQ	USBLS	5/07
Helpers, Laborers, and Material Movers	New Mexico	Y	27840 FQ	34130 MW	45030 TQ	USBLS	5/07
Helpers, Laborers, and Material Movers	Albuquerque MSA, NM	Y	29510 FQ	37260 MW	47800 TQ	USBLS	5/07
Helpers, Laborers, and Material Movers	Santa Fe MSA, NM	Y	32990 FQ	36710 MW	40530 TQ	USBLS	5/07
Helpers, Laborers, and Material Movers	New York	Y	34670 FQ	45650 MW	57950 TQ	USBLS	5/07
Helpers, Laborers, and Material Movers	Albany-Schenectady-Troy MSA, NY	Y	36310 FQ	46840 MW	56570 TQ	USBLS	5/07
Helpers, Laborers, and Material Movers	Binghamton MSA, NY	Y	33870 FQ	41590 MW	54370 TQ	USBLS	5/07
Helpers, Laborers, and Material Movers	Buffalo-Niagara Falls MSA, NY	Y	34840 FQ	45880 MW	58240 TQ	USBLS	5/07
Helpers, Laborers, and Material Movers	Glens Falls MSA, NY	Y	43010 FQ	48240 MW	56410 TQ	USBLS	5/07
Helpers, Laborers, and Material Movers	Nassau-Suffolk PMSA, NY	Y	38080 FQ	51410 MW	62380 TQ	USBLS	5/07
Helpers, Laborers, and Material Movers	New York-Northern New Jersey-Long Island MSA, NY-NJ-PA	Y	35090 FQ	46510 MW	59090 TQ	USBLS	5/07
Helpers, Laborers, and Material Movers	North Carolina	Y	30160 FQ	37380 MW	46580 TQ	USBLS	5/07
Helpers, Laborers, and Material Movers	Asheville MSA, NC	Y	30760 FQ	36830 MW	47440 TQ	USBLS	5/07
Helpers, Laborers, and Material Movers	Charlotte-Gastonia-Concord MSA, NC-SC	Y	32260 FQ	39290 MW	49080 TQ	USBLS	5/07
Helpers, Laborers, and Material Movers	Raleigh-Cary MSA, NC	Y	28850 FQ	36170 MW	43870 TQ	USBLS	5/07
Helpers, Laborers, and Material Movers	North Dakota	Y	29820 FQ	36810 MW	45890 TQ	USBLS	5/07
Helpers, Laborers, and Material Movers	Fargo MSA, ND-MN	Y	26690 FQ	34160 MW	45960 TQ	USBLS	5/07
Helpers, Laborers, and Material Movers	Ohio	Y	33030 FQ	42030 MW	52990 TQ	USBLS	5/07
Helpers, Laborers, and Material Movers	Cincinnati-Middletown MSA, OH-KY-IN	Y	34660 FQ	43860 MW	56900 TQ	USBLS	5/07
Helpers, Laborers, and Material Movers	Cleveland-Elyria-Mentor MSA, OH	Y	36850 FQ	45430 MW	57740 TQ	USBLS	5/07
Helpers, Laborers, and Material Movers	Columbus MSA, OH	Y	32330 FQ	41390 MW	51600 TQ	USBLS	5/07
Helpers, Laborers, and Material Movers	Dayton MSA, OH	Y	33290 FQ	43820 MW	58120 TQ	USBLS	5/07
Helpers, Laborers, and Material Movers	Oklahoma	Y	25670 FQ	35050 MW	46980 TQ	USBLS	5/07
Helpers, Laborers, and Material Movers	Oklahoma City MSA, OK	Y	26340 FQ	37120 MW	49400 TQ	USBLS	5/07
Helpers, Laborers, and Material Movers	Tulsa MSA, OK	Y	24840 FQ	31300 MW	44720 TQ	USBLS	5/07
Helpers, Laborers, and Material Movers	Oregon	H	15.52 FQ	18.40 MW	22.61 TQ	ORBLS	5/08
Helpers, Laborers, and Material Movers	Portland-Vancouver-Beaverton MSA, OR-WA	Y	32320 FQ	39210 MW	47620 TQ	USBLS	5/07
Helpers, Laborers, and Material Movers	Pennsylvania	Y	33370 FQ	43560 MW	55820 TQ	USBLS	5/07
Helpers, Laborers, and Material Movers	Allentown-Bethlehem-Easton MSA, PA-NJ	Y	36520 FQ	44810 MW	57700 TQ	USBLS	5/07

AE	Average entry wage	AW	Average wage paid	FQ	First quartile wage
AER	Average entry range	AWR	Average wage range	H	Hourly
AEX	Average experienced wage	AXR	Average experienced range	HI	Highest wage paid
ATC	Average total compensation	D	Daily	HR	High end range

LO	Lowest wage paid	MTC	Median total compensation
LR	Low end range	MW	Median wage paid
M	Monthly	MWR	Median wage range
MCC	Median cash compensation	S	See annotated source

TCC	Total cash compensation
TQ	Third quartile wage
W	Weekly
Y	Yearly

Occupation/Type/Industry	Location	Per	Low	Mid	High	Source	Date
First-Line Supervisor/Manager							
Helpers, Laborers, and Material Movers	Philadelphia-Camden-Wilmington MSA, PA-NJ-DE-MD	Y	33870 FQ	44650 MW	56830 TQ	USBLS	5/07
Helpers, Laborers, and Material Movers	Pittsburgh MSA, PA	Y	32520 FQ	43270 MW	54120 TQ	USBLS	5/07
Helpers, Laborers, and Material Movers	Rhode Island	Y	33030 FQ	40820 MW	50860 TQ	USBLS	5/07
Helpers, Laborers, and Material Movers	Providence-Fall River-Warwick MSA, RI-MA	Y	33860 FQ	42150 MW	52100 TQ	USBLS	5/07
Helpers, Laborers, and Material Movers	South Carolina	Y	31180 FQ	39640 MW	49960 TQ	USBLS	5/07
Helpers, Laborers, and Material Movers	Charleston-North Charleston MSA, SC	Y	32430 FQ	42650 MW	55520 TQ	USBLS	5/07
Helpers, Laborers, and Material Movers	Columbia MSA, SC	Y	28430 FQ	36520 MW	47590 TQ	USBLS	5/07
Helpers, Laborers, and Material Movers	Spartanburg MSA, SC	Y	30420 FQ	38190 MW	46310 TQ	USBLS	5/07
Helpers, Laborers, and Material Movers	South Dakota	Y	35526 FQ	42766 MW	50909 TQ	SDBLS	7/08-9/08
Helpers, Laborers, and Material Movers	Sioux Falls MSA, SD	Y	35730 FQ	42222 MW	49658 TQ	SDBLS	7/08-9/08
Helpers, Laborers, and Material Movers	Tennessee	Y	31800 FQ	40720 MW	50720 TQ	USBLS	5/07
Helpers, Laborers, and Material Movers	Memphis MSA, TN-MS-AR	Y	33720 FQ	42940 MW	52970 TQ	USBLS	5/07
Helpers, Laborers, and Material Movers	Nashville-Davidson-Murfreesboro MSA, TN	Y	30330 FQ	37150 MW	49300 TQ	USBLS	5/07
Helpers, Laborers, and Material Movers	Texas	Y	29140 FQ	37600 MW	47550 TQ	USBLS	5/07
Helpers, Laborers, and Material Movers	Austin-Round Rock MSA, TX	Y	27530 FQ	35030 MW	45190 TQ	USBLS	5/07
Helpers, Laborers, and Material Movers	Brownsville-Harlingen MSA, TX	Y	21780 FQ	25510 MW	38640 TQ	USBLS	5/07
Helpers, Laborers, and Material Movers	Dallas-Fort Worth-Arlington MSA, TX	Y	30760 FQ	39920 MW	49900 TQ	USBLS	5/07
Helpers, Laborers, and Material Movers	El Paso MSA, TX	Y	26830 FQ	33450 MW	42100 TQ	USBLS	5/07
Helpers, Laborers, and Material Movers	Houston-Sugar Land-Baytown MSA, TX	Y	30770 FQ	39190 MW	48690 TQ	USBLS	5/07
Helpers, Laborers, and Material Movers	San Antonio MSA, TX	Y	31260 FQ	38930 MW	49010 TQ	USBLS	5/07
Helpers, Laborers, and Material Movers	Utah	Y	31710 FQ	36970 MW	45470 TQ	USBLS	5/07
Helpers, Laborers, and Material Movers	Salt Lake City MSA, UT	Y	32180 FQ	37100 MW	45730 TQ	USBLS	5/07
Helpers, Laborers, and Material Movers	Vermont	Y	32810 FQ	40950 MW	49680 TQ	USBLS	5/07
Helpers, Laborers, and Material Movers	Burlington-South Burlington MSA, VT	Y	30430 FQ	37180 MW	44400 TQ	USBLS	5/07
Helpers, Laborers, and Material Movers	Virginia	Y	33270 FQ	42240 MW	54020 TQ	USBLS	5/07
Helpers, Laborers, and Material Movers	Richmond MSA, VA	Y	32480 FQ	40890 MW	52180 TQ	USBLS	5/07
Helpers, Laborers, and Material Movers	Roanoke MSA, VA	Y	33680 FQ	43740 MW	60450 TQ	USBLS	5/07
Helpers, Laborers, and Material Movers	Virginia Beach-Norfolk-Newport News MSA, VA-NC	Y	35780 FQ	44010 MW	54060 TQ	USBLS	5/07
Helpers, Laborers, and Material Movers	Washington	H	17.54 FQ	21.66 MW	27.14 TQ	WABLS	3/08
Helpers, Laborers, and Material Movers	Seattle-Tacoma-Bellevue MSA, WA	Y	37150 FQ	46110 MW	58300 TQ	USBLS	5/07
Helpers, Laborers, and Material Movers	West Virginia	Y	28028 FQ	38876 MW	60064 TQ	WVBLS	7/08-9/08
Helpers, Laborers, and Material Movers	Charleston MSA, WV	Y	26170 FQ	35100 MW	67200 TQ	USBLS	5/07
Helpers, Laborers, and Material Movers	Wisconsin	Y	33400 FQ	42140 MW	52020 TQ	USBLS	5/07
Helpers, Laborers, and Material Movers	Milwaukee-Waukesha-West Allis MSA, WI	Y	35350 FQ	44860 MW	54090 TQ	USBLS	5/07
Helpers, Laborers, and Material Movers	Racine MSA, WI	Y	32610 FQ	40990 MW	51580 TQ	USBLS	5/07
Helpers, Laborers, and Material Movers	Wyoming	Y	30043 FQ	37154 MW	52211 TQ	WYBLS	9/08
Helpers, Laborers, and Material Movers	Cheyenne MSA, WY	Y	29494 FQ	35477 MW	42015 TQ	WYBLS	9/08
Helpers, Laborers, and Material Movers	Puerto Rico	Y	19670 FQ	24660 MW	32130 TQ	USBLS	5/07
Helpers, Laborers, and Material Movers	San Juan-Caguas-Guaynabo MSA, PR	Y	20300 FQ	24850 MW	32340 TQ	USBLS	5/07
Helpers, Laborers, and Material Movers	Guam	Y	24390 FQ	30210 MW	41550 TQ	USBLS	5/07
Housekeeping and Janitorial Workers	Alabama	Y	20880 FQ	27010 MW	35090 TQ	USBLS	5/07
Housekeeping and Janitorial Workers	Birmingham-Hoover MSA, AL	Y	22180 FQ	29150 MW	37500 TQ	USBLS	5/07
Housekeeping and Janitorial Workers	Huntsville MSA, AL	Y	21080 FQ	26100 MW	31770 TQ	USBLS	5/07
Housekeeping and Janitorial Workers	Mobile MSA, AL	Y	19820 FQ	24780 MW	30990 TQ	USBLS	5/07
Housekeeping and Janitorial Workers	Alaska	Y	30780 FQ	37110 MW	47200 TQ	USBLS	5/07
Housekeeping and Janitorial Workers	Anchorage MSA, AK	Y	29460 FQ	34960 MW	46080 TQ	USBLS	5/07
Housekeeping and Janitorial Workers	Arizona	Y	23330 FQ	29720 MW	37610 TQ	USBLS	5/07
Housekeeping and Janitorial Workers	Phoenix-Mesa-Scottsdale MSA, AZ	Y	24470 FQ	31020 MW	38910 TQ	USBLS	5/07
Housekeeping and Janitorial Workers	Tucson MSA, AZ	Y	23200 FQ	28660 MW	34390 TQ	USBLS	5/07
Housekeeping and Janitorial Workers	Arkansas	Y	19830 FQ	24530 MW	31940 TQ	USBLS	5/07
Housekeeping and Janitorial Workers	Little Rock-North Little Rock MSA, AR	Y	19600 FQ	24320 MW	32590 TQ	USBLS	5/07
Housekeeping and Janitorial Workers	California	H	13.67 FQ	17.54 MW	22.47 TQ	CABLS	1/08-3/08
Housekeeping and Janitorial Workers	Los Angeles-Long Beach-Glendale PMSA, CA	H	13.41 FQ	17.43 MW	22.34 TQ	CABLS	1/08-3/08
Housekeeping and Janitorial Workers	Modesto MSA, CA	H	16.38 FQ	21.21 MW	23.89 TQ	CABLS	1/08-3/08

AE Average entry wage	**AW** Average wage paid	**FQ** First quartile wage	**LO** Lowest wage paid	**MTC** Median total compensation	**TCC** Total cash compensation
AER Average entry range	**AWR** Average wage range	**H** Hourly	**LR** Low end range	**MW** Median wage paid	**TQ** Third quartile wage
AEX Average experienced wage	**AXR** Average experienced range	**HI** Highest wage paid	**M** Monthly	**MWR** Median wage range	**W** Weekly
ATC Average total compensation	**D** Daily	**HR** High end range	**MCC** Median cash compensation	**S** See annotated source	**Y** Yearly

Occupation/Type/Industry	Location	Per	Low	Mid	High	Source	Date
First-Line Supervisor/Manager							
Housekeeping and Janitorial Workers	Oakland-Fremont-Hayward MSA, CA	H	16.02 FQ	19.27 MW	25.46 TQ	CABLS	1/08-3/08
Housekeeping and Janitorial Workers	Riverside-San Bernardino-Ontario MSA, CA	H	14.22 FQ	17.99 MW	23.04 TQ	CABLS	1/08-3/08
Housekeeping and Janitorial Workers	Sacramento-Arden Arcade-Roseville MSA, CA	H	12.92 FQ	17.43 MW	21.78 TQ	CABLS	1/08-3/08
Housekeeping and Janitorial Workers	San Diego-Carlsbad-San Marcos MSA, CA	H	13.47 FQ	16.73 MW	21.10 TQ	CABLS	1/08-3/08
Housekeeping and Janitorial Workers	San Francisco-San Mateo-Redwood PMSA, CA	H	15.17 FQ	19.72 MW	25.09 TQ	CABLS	1/08-3/08
Housekeeping and Janitorial Workers	San Jose-Sunnyvale-Santa Clara MSA, CA	H	14.52 FQ	17.52 MW	23.96 TQ	CABLS	1/08-3/08
Housekeeping and Janitorial Workers	Santa Ana-Anaheim-Irvine PMSA, CA	Y	27510 FQ	35500 MW	44470 TQ	USBLS	5/07
Housekeeping and Janitorial Workers	Stockton MSA, CA	H	14.53 FQ	17.52 MW	20.18 TQ	CABLS	1/08-3/08
Housekeeping and Janitorial Workers	Colorado	Y	26050 FQ	33030 MW	44000 TQ	USBLS	5/07
Housekeeping and Janitorial Workers	Denver-Aurora MSA, CO	Y	25790 FQ	32500 MW	44960 TQ	USBLS	5/07
Housekeeping and Janitorial Workers	Fort Collins-Loveland MSA, CO	Y	17840 FQ	26140 MW	35690 TQ	USBLS	5/07
Housekeeping and Janitorial Workers	Connecticut	H	14.88 AE	21.13 MW		CTBLS	1/08-3/08
Housekeeping and Janitorial Workers	Bridgeport-Stamford-Norwalk MSA, CT	Y	31580 FQ	43020 MW	52720 TQ	USBLS	5/07
Housekeeping and Janitorial Workers	Hartford-West Hartford-East Hartford MSA, CT	Y	34420 FQ	42540 MW	53240 TQ	USBLS	5/07
Housekeeping and Janitorial Workers	Delaware	Y	28050 FQ	33870 MW	40110 TQ	USBLS	5/07
Housekeeping and Janitorial Workers	Wilmington PMSA, DE-MD-NJ	Y	29610 FQ	36490 MW	42790 TQ	USBLS	5/07
Housekeeping and Janitorial Workers	District of Columbia	Y	31800 FQ	36680 MW	44590 TQ	USBLS	5/07
Housekeeping and Janitorial Workers	Washington-Arlington-Alexandria MSA, DC-VA-MD-WV	Y	28810 FQ	35300 MW	44300 TQ	USBLS	5/07
Housekeeping and Janitorial Workers	Florida	Y	24630 FQ	30840 MW	39330 TQ	USBLS	5/07
Housekeeping and Janitorial Workers	Fort Lauderdale-Pompano Beach-Deerfield Beach PMSA, FL	Y	24820 FQ	29570 MW	35820 TQ	USBLS	5/07
Housekeeping and Janitorial Workers	Jacksonville MSA, FL	Y	24190 FQ	29720 MW	37180 TQ	USBLS	5/07
Housekeeping and Janitorial Workers	Miami-Fort Lauderdale-Miami Beach MSA, FL	Y	24100 FQ	29920 MW	38390 TQ	USBLS	5/07
Housekeeping and Janitorial Workers	Orlando-Kissimmee MSA, FL	Y	25900 FQ	32200 MW	39600 TQ	USBLS	5/07
Housekeeping and Janitorial Workers	Tampa-St. Petersburg-Clearwater MSA, FL	Y	25280 FQ	34000 MW	42370 TQ	USBLS	5/07
Housekeeping and Janitorial Workers	West Palm Beach-Boca Raton-Boynton Beach PMSA, FL	Y	23710 FQ	29760 MW	40280 TQ	USBLS	5/07
Housekeeping and Janitorial Workers	Georgia	Y	24520 FQ	30290 MW	37410 TQ	USBLS	5/07
Housekeeping and Janitorial Workers	Atlanta-Sandy Springs-Marietta MSA, GA	Y	26280 FQ	32000 MW	39030 TQ	USBLS	5/07
Housekeeping and Janitorial Workers	Savannah MSA, GA	Y	23910 FQ	29710 MW	38010 TQ	USBLS	5/07
Housekeeping and Janitorial Workers	Hawaii	Y	30420 FQ	35700 MW	41810 TQ	USBLS	5/07
Housekeeping and Janitorial Workers	Honolulu MSA, HI	Y	30590 FQ	35910 MW	42290 TQ	USBLS	5/07
Housekeeping and Janitorial Workers	Idaho	Y	21990 FQ	27770 MW	37530 TQ	USBLS	5/07
Housekeeping and Janitorial Workers	Boise City-Nampa MSA, ID	Y	21900 FQ	26170 MW	36430 TQ	USBLS	5/07
Housekeeping and Janitorial Workers	Illinois	Y	27320 FQ	35540 MW	47350 TQ	USBLS	5/07
Housekeeping and Janitorial Workers	Chicago-Naperville-Joliet MSA, IL-IN-WI	Y	28480 FQ	36540 MW	48290 TQ	USBLS	5/07
Housekeeping and Janitorial Workers	Rockford MSA, IL	Y	27700 FQ	35100 MW	45180 TQ	USBLS	5/07
Housekeeping and Janitorial Workers	Indiana	Y	25780 FQ	32550 MW	39550 TQ	USBLS	5/07
Housekeeping and Janitorial Workers	Gary PMSA, IN	Y	26500 FQ	31920 MW	38740 TQ	USBLS	5/07
Housekeeping and Janitorial Workers	Indianapolis-Carmel MSA, IN	Y	26480 FQ	33030 MW	40170 TQ	USBLS	5/07
Housekeeping and Janitorial Workers	Iowa	Y	25640 FQ	32020 MW	40260 TQ	USBLS	5/07
Housekeeping and Janitorial Workers	Des Moines-West Des Moines MSA, IA	Y	24420 FQ	29990 MW	40210 TQ	USBLS	5/07
Housekeeping and Janitorial Workers	Dubuque MSA, IA	Y	27170 FQ	32410 MW	41930 TQ	USBLS	5/07
Housekeeping and Janitorial Workers	Iowa City MSA, IA	Y	28460 FQ	33510 MW	38430 TQ	USBLS	5/07
Housekeeping and Janitorial Workers	Kansas	Y	24070 FQ	29540 MW	36090 TQ	USBLS	5/07
Housekeeping and Janitorial Workers	Lawrence MSA, KS	Y	28460 FQ	34040 MW	42940 TQ	USBLS	5/07
Housekeeping and Janitorial Workers	Wichita MSA, KS	Y	23260 FQ	28680 MW	34550 TQ	USBLS	5/07
Housekeeping and Janitorial Workers	Kentucky	Y	22571 FQ	27611 MW	34548 TQ	KYBLS	2008
Housekeeping and Janitorial Workers	Louisville-Jefferson County MSA, KY-IN	Y	21640 FQ	28040 MW	36810 TQ	USBLS	5/07
Housekeeping and Janitorial Workers	Louisiana	H	10.23 FQ	12.57 MW	16.24 TQ	LABLS	1/08-3/08
Housekeeping and Janitorial Workers	Baton Rouge MSA, LA	Y	20320 FQ	25190 MW	33130 TQ	USBLS	5/07

AE	Average entry wage	AW	Average wage paid	FQ	First quartile wage	LO	Lowest wage paid	MTC	Median total compensation	TCC Total cash compensation
AER	Average entry range	AWR	Average wage range	H	Hourly	LR	Low end range	MW	Median wage paid	TQ Third quartile wage
AEX	Average experienced wage	AXR	Average experienced range	HI	Highest wage paid	M	Monthly	MWR	Median wage range	W Weekly
ATC	Average total compensation	D	Daily	HR	High end range	MCC	Median cash compensation	S	See annotated source	Y Yearly

Occupation/Type/Industry	Location	Per	Low	Mid	High	Source	Date
First-Line Supervisor/Manager							
Housekeeping and Janitorial Workers	New Orleans-Metairie-Kenner MSA, LA	Y	22730 FQ	28910 MW	36450 TQ	USBLS	5/07
Housekeeping and Janitorial Workers	Maine	Y	26540 FQ	33840 MW	41770 TQ	USBLS	5/07
Housekeeping and Janitorial Workers	Portland-South Portland-Biddeford MSA, ME	Y	24600 FQ	31690 MW	46840 TQ	USBLS	5/07
Housekeeping and Janitorial Workers	Maryland	Y		33150 MW		MDBLS	3/08
Housekeeping and Janitorial Workers	Baltimore-Towson MSA, MD	Y	25810 FQ	32600 MW	41120 TQ	USBLS	5/07
Housekeeping and Janitorial Workers	Bethesda-Gaithersburg-Frederick PMSA, MD	Y	24660 FQ	30670 MW	37260 TQ	USBLS	5/07
Housekeeping and Janitorial Workers	Massachusetts	Y	30930 FQ	39090 MW	49690 TQ	USBLS	5/07
Housekeeping and Janitorial Workers	Barnstable Town MSA, MA	Y	28540 FQ	39400 MW	50970 TQ	USBLS	5/07
Housekeeping and Janitorial Workers	Boston-Cambridge-Quincy NECTA, MA	Y	31400 FQ	39470 MW	51250 TQ	USBLS	5/07
Housekeeping and Janitorial Workers	Worcester MSA, MA-CT	Y	32300 FQ	39670 MW	48270 TQ	USBLS	5/07
Housekeeping and Janitorial Workers	Michigan	Y	27210 FQ	35190 MW	46760 TQ	USBLS	5/07
Housekeeping and Janitorial Workers	Detroit-Warren-Livonia MSA, MI	Y	27530 FQ	35500 MW	48690 TQ	USBLS	5/07
Housekeeping and Janitorial Workers	Grand Rapids-Wyoming MSA, MI	Y	28600 FQ	35680 MW	50560 TQ	USBLS	5/07
Housekeeping and Janitorial Workers	Warren-Troy-Farmington Hills PMSA, MI	Y	26270 FQ	32860 MW	45990 TQ	USBLS	5/07
Housekeeping and Janitorial Workers	Minnesota	Y	30217 FQ	37003 MW	45252 TQ	MNBLS	10/08-12/08
Housekeeping and Janitorial Workers	Duluth-Superior MSA, MN-WI	Y	29945 FQ	36459 MW	42743 TQ	MNBLS	10/08-12/08
Housekeeping and Janitorial Workers	Minneapolis-Saint Paul MSA, MN-WI	Y	30614 FQ	37411 MW	46308 TQ	MNBLS	10/08-12/08
Housekeeping and Janitorial Workers	Rochester MSA, MN	Y	28377 FQ	40189 MW	48589 TQ	MNBLS	10/08-12/08
Housekeeping and Janitorial Workers	Mississippi	Y	21880 FQ	26920 MW	34110 TQ	USBLS	5/07
Housekeeping and Janitorial Workers	Gulfport-Biloxi MSA, MS	Y	26030 FQ	31210 MW	35680 TQ	USBLS	5/07
Housekeeping and Janitorial Workers	Jackson MSA, MS	Y	23180 FQ	27340 MW	35320 TQ	USBLS	5/07
Housekeeping and Janitorial Workers	Missouri	Y	25710 FQ	31710 MW	40240 TQ	USBLS	5/07
Housekeeping and Janitorial Workers	Jefferson City MSA, MO	Y	23340 FQ	28750 MW	39090 TQ	USBLS	5/07
Housekeeping and Janitorial Workers	Kansas City MSA, MO-KS	Y	25210 FQ	31140 MW	39190 TQ	USBLS	5/07
Housekeeping and Janitorial Workers	St. Louis MSA, MO-IL	Y	27500 FQ	35040 MW	43910 TQ	USBLS	5/07
Housekeeping and Janitorial Workers	Montana	Y	26540 FQ	32900 MW	42430 TQ	USBLS	5/07
Housekeeping and Janitorial Workers	Billings MSA, MT	Y	24480 FQ	31740 MW	37560 TQ	USBLS	5/07
Housekeeping and Janitorial Workers	Great Falls MSA, MT	Y	24910 FQ	34020 MW	38200 TQ	USBLS	5/07
Housekeeping and Janitorial Workers	Nebraska	Y	25260 FQ	32290 MW	38690 TQ	USBLS	5/07
Housekeeping and Janitorial Workers	Omaha-Council Bluffs MSA, NE-IA	Y	27920 FQ	34370 MW	39380 TQ	USBLS	5/07
Housekeeping and Janitorial Workers	Nevada	H	12.61 FQ	15.70 MW	18.82 TQ	NVBLS	5/08
Housekeeping and Janitorial Workers	Las Vegas-Paradise MSA, NV	H	13.16 FQ	16.03 MW	18.81 TQ	NVBLS	5/08
Housekeeping and Janitorial Workers	New Hampshire	H	12.25 AE	17.49 MW	20.39 AEX	NHBLS	6/08
Housekeeping and Janitorial Workers	Manchester MSA, NH	Y	32050 FQ	37480 MW	43930 TQ	USBLS	5/07
Housekeeping and Janitorial Workers	Nashua NECTA, NH-MA	Y	23640 FQ	34940 MW	41120 TQ	USBLS	5/07
Housekeeping and Janitorial Workers	New Jersey	Y	32340 FQ	42010 MW	52480 TQ	USBLS	5/07
Housekeeping and Janitorial Workers	Camden PMSA, NJ	Y	32520 FQ	42230 MW	54780 TQ	USBLS	5/07
Housekeeping and Janitorial Workers	Edison PMSA, NJ	Y	33380 FQ	44470 MW	53940 TQ	USBLS	5/07
Housekeeping and Janitorial Workers	Newark-Union PMSA, NJ-PA	Y	32350 FQ	39770 MW	51930 TQ	USBLS	5/07
Housekeeping and Janitorial Workers	Trenton-Ewing MSA, NJ	Y	34490 FQ	42150 MW	50140 TQ	USBLS	5/07
Housekeeping and Janitorial Workers	Vineland-Millville-Bridgeton MSA, NJ	Y	35700 FQ	43910 MW	53740 TQ	USBLS	5/07
Housekeeping and Janitorial Workers	New Mexico	Y	20360 FQ	26100 MW	33360 TQ	USBLS	5/07
Housekeeping and Janitorial Workers	Albuquerque MSA, NM	Y	22590 FQ	28170 MW	35920 TQ	USBLS	5/07
Housekeeping and Janitorial Workers	New York	Y	32830 FQ	42160 MW	51400 TQ	USBLS	5/07
Housekeeping and Janitorial Workers	Albany-Schenectady-Troy MSA, NY	Y	30480 FQ	39340 MW	49010 TQ	USBLS	5/07
Housekeeping and Janitorial Workers	Buffalo-Niagara Falls MSA, NY	Y	30450 FQ	37740 MW	44580 TQ	USBLS	5/07
Housekeeping and Janitorial Workers	Nassau-Suffolk PMSA, NY	Y	38250 FQ	49840 MW	59080 TQ	USBLS	5/07
Housekeeping and Janitorial Workers	New York-Northern New Jersey-Long Island MSA, NY-NJ-PA	Y	34590 FQ	44690 MW	53890 TQ	USBLS	5/07
Housekeeping and Janitorial Workers	North Carolina	Y	22960 FQ	28580 MW	37370 TQ	USBLS	5/07
Housekeeping and Janitorial Workers	Charlotte-Gastonia-Concord MSA, NC-SC	Y	25110 FQ	32900 MW	44620 TQ	USBLS	5/07
Housekeeping and Janitorial Workers	Raleigh-Cary MSA, NC	Y	24860 FQ	29020 MW	36390 TQ	USBLS	5/07
Housekeeping and Janitorial Workers	North Dakota	Y	24760 FQ	29140 MW	36370 TQ	USBLS	5/07
Housekeeping and Janitorial Workers	Bismarck MSA, ND	Y	26520 FQ	31250 MW	40070 TQ	USBLS	5/07
Housekeeping and Janitorial Workers	Fargo MSA, ND-MN	Y	25620 FQ	29860 MW	38160 TQ	USBLS	5/07
Housekeeping and Janitorial Workers	Ohio	Y	25620 FQ	32570 MW	39850 TQ	USBLS	5/07
Housekeeping and Janitorial Workers	Canton-Massillon MSA, OH	Y	23100 FQ	29030 MW	37930 TQ	USBLS	5/07

AE	Average entry wage	AW	Average wage paid	FQ	First quartile wage	LO	Lowest wage paid	MTC	Median total compensation	TCC	Total cash compensation
AER	Average entry range	AWR	Average wage range	H	Hourly	LR	Low end range	MW	Median wage paid	TQ	Third quartile wage
AEX	Average experienced wage	AXR	Average experienced range	HI	Highest wage paid	M	Monthly	MWR	Median wage range	W	Weekly
ATC	Average total compensation	D	Daily	HR	High end range	MCC	Median cash compensation	S	See annotated source	Y	Yearly

Occupation/Type/Industry	Location	Per	Low	Mid	High	Source	Date
First-Line Supervisor/Manager							
Housekeeping and Janitorial Workers	Cincinnati-Middletown MSA, OH-KY-IN	Y	24790 FQ	32430 MW	39130 TQ	USBLS	5/07
Housekeeping and Janitorial Workers	Cleveland-Elyria-Mentor MSA, OH	Y	26200 FQ	32740 MW	40410 TQ	USBLS	5/07
Housekeeping and Janitorial Workers	Columbus MSA, OH	Y	27200 FQ	33850 MW	40880 TQ	USBLS	5/07
Housekeeping and Janitorial Workers	Dayton MSA, OH	Y	24900 FQ	33510 MW	41840 TQ	USBLS	5/07
Housekeeping and Janitorial Workers	Oklahoma	Y	20660 FQ	26940 MW	35620 TQ	USBLS	5/07
Housekeeping and Janitorial Workers	Lawton MSA, OK	Y	20120 FQ	27290 MW	39520 TQ	USBLS	5/07
Housekeeping and Janitorial Workers	Oklahoma City MSA, OK	Y	22610 FQ	28510 MW	37980 TQ	USBLS	5/07
Housekeeping and Janitorial Workers	Tulsa MSA, OK	Y	18500 FQ	26650 MW	35930 TQ	USBLS	5/07
Housekeeping and Janitorial Workers	Oregon	H	11.82 FQ	15.62 MW	20.48 TQ	ORBLS	5/08
Housekeeping and Janitorial Workers	Portland-Vancouver-Beaverton MSA, OR-WA	Y	26030 FQ	33830 MW	43060 TQ	USBLS	5/07
Housekeeping and Janitorial Workers	Pennsylvania	Y	27940 FQ	35630 MW	46440 TQ	USBLS	5/07
Housekeeping and Janitorial Workers	Allentown-Bethlehem-Easton MSA, PA-NJ	Y	24630 FQ	33570 MW	48190 TQ	USBLS	5/07
Housekeeping and Janitorial Workers	Philadelphia-Camden-Wilmington MSA, PA-NJ-DE-MD	Y	31040 FQ	39660 MW	51210 TQ	USBLS	5/07
Housekeeping and Janitorial Workers	Pittsburgh MSA, PA	Y	26760 FQ	33280 MW	40910 TQ	USBLS	5/07
Housekeeping and Janitorial Workers	Rhode Island	Y	32120 FQ	39630 MW	49360 TQ	USBLS	5/07
Housekeeping and Janitorial Workers	Providence-Fall River-Warwick MSA, RI-MA	Y	31390 FQ	38630 MW	49260 TQ	USBLS	5/07
Housekeeping and Janitorial Workers	South Carolina	Y	22850 FQ	27720 MW	35220 TQ	USBLS	5/07
Housekeeping and Janitorial Workers	Charleston-North Charleston MSA, SC	Y	23950 FQ	28930 MW	36640 TQ	USBLS	5/07
Housekeeping and Janitorial Workers	Columbia MSA, SC	Y	24820 FQ	29850 MW	37430 TQ	USBLS	5/07
Housekeeping and Janitorial Workers	South Dakota	Y	26389 FQ	31613 MW	37611 TQ	SDBLS	7/08-9/08
Housekeeping and Janitorial Workers	Sioux Falls MSA, SD	Y	28069 FQ	32971 MW	39544 TQ	SDBLS	7/08-9/08
Housekeeping and Janitorial Workers	Tennessee	Y	22850 FQ	28600 MW	35310 TQ	USBLS	5/07
Housekeeping and Janitorial Workers	Johnson City MSA, TN	Y	23420 FQ	27840 MW	32090 TQ	USBLS	5/07
Housekeeping and Janitorial Workers	Kingsport-Bristol-Bristol MSA, TN-VA	Y	22090 FQ	26480 MW	31010 TQ	USBLS	5/07
Housekeeping and Janitorial Workers	Knoxville MSA, TN	Y	22690 FQ	27250 MW	32980 TQ	USBLS	5/07
Housekeeping and Janitorial Workers	Memphis MSA, TN-MS-AR	Y	24980 FQ	29920 MW	34520 TQ	USBLS	5/07
Housekeeping and Janitorial Workers	Nashville-Davidson-Murfreesboro MSA, TN	Y	23970 FQ	30380 MW	37770 TQ	USBLS	5/07
Housekeeping and Janitorial Workers	Texas	Y	20980 FQ	27470 MW	37030 TQ	USBLS	5/07
Housekeeping and Janitorial Workers	Austin-Round Rock MSA, TX	Y	19200 FQ	23500 MW	33140 TQ	USBLS	5/07
Housekeeping and Janitorial Workers	Dallas-Fort Worth-Arlington MSA, TX	Y	22930 FQ	30570 MW	39490 TQ	USBLS	5/07
Housekeeping and Janitorial Workers	El Paso MSA, TX	Y	19490 FQ	26130 MW	31590 TQ	USBLS	5/07
Housekeeping and Janitorial Workers	Houston-Sugar Land-Baytown MSA, TX	Y	20550 FQ	27090 MW	37560 TQ	USBLS	5/07
Housekeeping and Janitorial Workers	San Antonio MSA, TX	Y	20890 FQ	27880 MW	36640 TQ	USBLS	5/07
Housekeeping and Janitorial Workers	Utah	Y	26480 FQ	32560 MW	38760 TQ	USBLS	5/07
Housekeeping and Janitorial Workers	Salt Lake City MSA, UT	Y	26780 FQ	33740 MW	39090 TQ	USBLS	5/07
Housekeeping and Janitorial Workers	Vermont	Y	31410 FQ	36950 MW	44200 TQ	USBLS	5/07
Housekeeping and Janitorial Workers	Burlington-South Burlington MSA, VT	Y	31290 FQ	38020 MW	46050 TQ	USBLS	5/07
Housekeeping and Janitorial Workers	Virginia	Y	25370 FQ	32050 MW	41870 TQ	USBLS	5/07
Housekeeping and Janitorial Workers	Charlottesville MSA, VA	Y	26170 FQ	32030 MW	39540 TQ	USBLS	5/07
Housekeeping and Janitorial Workers	Richmond MSA, VA	Y	23570 FQ	28820 MW	38080 TQ	USBLS	5/07
Housekeeping and Janitorial Workers	Virginia Beach-Norfolk-Newport News MSA, VA-NC	Y	23980 FQ	31480 MW	38660 TQ	USBLS	5/07
Housekeeping and Janitorial Workers	Washington	H	14.48 FQ	17.61 MW	22.22 TQ	WABLS	3/08
Housekeeping and Janitorial Workers	Seattle-Tacoma-Bellevue MSA, WA	Y	31000 FQ	37180 MW	47190 TQ	USBLS	5/07
Housekeeping and Janitorial Workers	West Virginia	Y	20450 FQ	25296 MW	32684 TQ	WVBLS	7/08-9/08
Housekeeping and Janitorial Workers	Charleston MSA, WV	Y	16350 FQ	21570 MW	27680 TQ	USBLS	5/07
Housekeeping and Janitorial Workers	Parkersburg-Marietta-Vienna MSA, WV-OH	Y	22340 FQ	27770 MW	31440 TQ	USBLS	5/07
Housekeeping and Janitorial Workers	Wisconsin	Y	27320 FQ	34880 MW	45100 TQ	USBLS	5/07
Housekeeping and Janitorial Workers	Milwaukee-Waukesha-West Allis MSA, WI	Y	29430 FQ	38120 MW	48310 TQ	USBLS	5/07
Housekeeping and Janitorial Workers	Wyoming	Y	24785 FQ	30229 MW	37690 TQ	WYBLS	9/08
Housekeeping and Janitorial Workers	Cheyenne MSA, WY	Y	27220 FQ	31089 MW	40785 TQ	WYBLS	9/08
Housekeeping and Janitorial Workers	Puerto Rico	Y	14920 FQ	19930 MW	24340 TQ	USBLS	5/07
Housekeeping and Janitorial Workers	San Juan-Caguas-Guaynabo MSA, PR	Y	15510 FQ	20180 MW	25240 TQ	USBLS	5/07
Housekeeping and Janitorial Workers	Virgin Islands	Y	27720 FQ	30360 MW	34580 TQ	USBLS	5/07

AE	Average entry wage	AW	Average wage paid	FQ	First quartile wage	LO	Lowest wage paid	MTC	Median total compensation	TCC	Total cash compensation
AER	Average entry range	AWR	Average wage range	H	Hourly	LR	Low end range	MW	Median wage paid	TQ	Third quartile wage
AEX	Average experienced wage	AXR	Average experienced range	HI	Highest wage paid	M	Monthly	MWR	Median wage range	W	Weekly
ATC	Average total compensation	D	Daily	HR	High end range	MCC	Median cash compensation	S	See annotated source	Y	Yearly

630

Occupation/Type/Industry	Location	Per	Low	Mid	High	Source	Date
First-Line Supervisor/Manager							
Housekeeping and Janitorial Workers	Guam	Y	16940 FQ	22310 MW	34200 TQ	USBLS	5/07
Landscaping, Lawn, Grounds	Alabama	Y	27560 FQ	32870 MW	42020 TQ	USBLS	5/07
Landscaping, Lawn, Grounds	Birmingham-Hoover MSA, AL	Y	30430 FQ	37450 MW	45140 TQ	USBLS	5/07
Landscaping, Lawn, Grounds	Montgomery MSA, AL	Y	30380 FQ	41330 MW	47430 TQ	USBLS	5/07
Landscaping, Lawn, Grounds	Tuscaloosa MSA, AL	Y	22070 FQ	35320 MW	44270 TQ	USBLS	5/07
Landscaping, Lawn, Grounds	Alaska	Y	24880 FQ	36400 MW	45580 TQ	USBLS	5/07
Landscaping, Lawn, Grounds	Anchorage MSA, AK	Y	32540 FQ	38820 MW	45280 TQ	USBLS	5/07
Landscaping, Lawn, Grounds	Arizona	Y	29450 FQ	36800 MW	47560 TQ	USBLS	5/07
Landscaping, Lawn, Grounds	Phoenix-Mesa-Scottsdale MSA, AZ	Y	29680 FQ	37510 MW	48270 TQ	USBLS	5/07
Landscaping, Lawn, Grounds	Tucson MSA, AZ	Y	29100 FQ	34980 MW	44550 TQ	USBLS	5/07
Landscaping, Lawn, Grounds	Arkansas	Y	28300 FQ	33550 MW	40720 TQ	USBLS	5/07
Landscaping, Lawn, Grounds	Little Rock-North Little Rock MSA, AR	Y	30130 FQ	34850 MW	40890 TQ	USBLS	5/07
Landscaping, Lawn, Grounds	California	H	16.36 FQ	21.06 MW	27.10 TQ	CABLS	1/08-3/08
Landscaping, Lawn, Grounds	Los Angeles-Long Beach-Glendale PMSA, CA	H	17.35 FQ	22.02 MW	28.47 TQ	CABLS	1/08-3/08
Landscaping, Lawn, Grounds	Oakland-Fremont-Hayward MSA, CA	H	19.56 FQ	24.34 MW	33.44 TQ	CABLS	1/08-3/08
Landscaping, Lawn, Grounds	Riverside-San Bernardino-Ontario MSA, CA	H	15.60 FQ	19.15 MW	25.18 TQ	CABLS	1/08-3/08
Landscaping, Lawn, Grounds	Sacramento-Arden Arcade-Roseville MSA, CA	H	16.98 FQ	20.52 MW	24.96 TQ	CABLS	1/08-3/08
Landscaping, Lawn, Grounds	San Diego-Carlsbad-San Marcos MSA, CA	H	15.94 FQ	19.85 MW	26.14 TQ	CABLS	1/08-3/08
Landscaping, Lawn, Grounds	San Francisco-San Mateo-Redwood PMSA, CA	H	22.50 FQ	27.32 MW	31.70 TQ	CABLS	1/08-3/08
Landscaping, Lawn, Grounds	San Jose-Sunnyvale-Santa Clara MSA, CA	H	13.81 FQ	21.43 MW	30.75 TQ	CABLS	1/08-3/08
Landscaping, Lawn, Grounds	Santa Ana-Anaheim-Irvine PMSA, CA	Y	27750 FQ	35540 MW	49370 TQ	USBLS	5/07
Landscaping, Lawn, Grounds	Colorado	Y	35100 FQ	42810 MW	52980 TQ	USBLS	5/07
Landscaping, Lawn, Grounds	Denver-Aurora MSA, CO	Y	36260 FQ	44300 MW	55080 TQ	USBLS	5/07
Landscaping, Lawn, Grounds	Connecticut	H	16.31 AE	24.47 MW		CTBLS	1/08-3/08
Landscaping, Lawn, Grounds	Bridgeport-Stamford-Norwalk MSA, CT	Y	35140 FQ	50110 MW	71090 TQ	USBLS	5/07
Landscaping, Lawn, Grounds	Hartford-West Hartford-East Hartford MSA, CT	Y	36170 FQ	48270 MW	62820 TQ	USBLS	5/07
Landscaping, Lawn, Grounds	New Haven MSA, CT	Y	45260 FQ	55850 MW	65340 TQ	USBLS	5/07
Landscaping, Lawn, Grounds	Delaware	Y	37190 FQ	52160 MW	64770 TQ	USBLS	5/07
Landscaping, Lawn, Grounds	Wilmington PMSA, DE-MD-NJ	Y	37570 FQ	49720 MW	61630 TQ	USBLS	5/07
Landscaping, Lawn, Grounds	District of Columbia	Y	36120 FQ	49930 MW	66260 TQ	USBLS	5/07
Landscaping, Lawn, Grounds	Washington-Arlington-Alexandria MSA, DC-VA-MD-WV	Y	34710 FQ	42700 MW	56600 TQ	USBLS	5/07
Landscaping, Lawn, Grounds	Florida	Y	30020 FQ	38620 MW	50020 TQ	USBLS	5/07
Landscaping, Lawn, Grounds	Cape Coral-Fort Myers MSA, FL	Y	36420 FQ	43960 MW	51780 TQ	USBLS	5/07
Landscaping, Lawn, Grounds	Fort Lauderdale-Pompano Beach-Deerfield Beach PMSA, FL	Y	35150 FQ	43150 MW	55670 TQ	USBLS	5/07
Landscaping, Lawn, Grounds	Jacksonville MSA, FL	Y	27410 FQ	32020 MW	42270 TQ	USBLS	5/07
Landscaping, Lawn, Grounds	Miami-Fort Lauderdale-Miami Beach MSA, FL	Y	31700 FQ	39120 MW	50270 TQ	USBLS	5/07
Landscaping, Lawn, Grounds	Orlando-Kissimmee MSA, FL	Y	31810 FQ	44420 MW	56950 TQ	USBLS	5/07
Landscaping, Lawn, Grounds	Tampa-St. Petersburg-Clearwater MSA, FL	Y	29490 FQ	37430 MW	47450 TQ	USBLS	5/07
Landscaping, Lawn, Grounds	West Palm Beach-Boca Raton-Boynton Beach PMSA, FL	Y	33950 FQ	40400 MW	50890 TQ	USBLS	5/07
Landscaping, Lawn, Grounds	Georgia	Y	30550 FQ	36600 MW	45920 TQ	USBLS	5/07
Landscaping, Lawn, Grounds	Atlanta-Sandy Springs-Marietta MSA, GA	Y	31850 FQ	37890 MW	48630 TQ	USBLS	5/07
Landscaping, Lawn, Grounds	Augusta-Richmond County MSA, GA-SC	Y	31870 FQ	37300 MW	46370 TQ	USBLS	5/07
Landscaping, Lawn, Grounds	Macon MSA, GA	Y	31690 FQ	35950 MW	41520 TQ	USBLS	5/07
Landscaping, Lawn, Grounds	Hawaii	Y	35020 FQ	44120 MW	54010 TQ	USBLS	5/07
Landscaping, Lawn, Grounds	Honolulu MSA, HI	Y	33540 FQ	42700 MW	52430 TQ	USBLS	5/07
Landscaping, Lawn, Grounds	Idaho	Y	25700 FQ	29740 MW	36050 TQ	USBLS	5/07
Landscaping, Lawn, Grounds	Boise City-Nampa MSA, ID	Y	26080 FQ	30260 MW	37740 TQ	USBLS	5/07
Landscaping, Lawn, Grounds	Illinois	Y	30250 FQ	39680 MW	52730 TQ	USBLS	5/07

AE	Average entry wage	AW	Average wage paid	FQ	First quartile wage	LO	Lowest wage paid	MTC	Median total compensation	TCC	Total cash compensation
AER	Average entry range	AWR	Average wage range	H	Hourly	LR	Low end range	MW	Median wage paid	TQ	Third quartile wage
AEX	Average experienced wage	AXR	Average experienced range	HI	Highest wage paid	M	Monthly	MWR	Median wage range	W	Weekly
ATC	Average total compensation	D	Daily	HR	High end range	MCC	Median cash compensation	S	See annotated source	Y	Yearly

Occupation/Type/Industry	Location	Per	Low	Mid	High	Source	Date
First-Line Supervisor/Manager							
Landscaping, Lawn, Grounds	Chicago-Naperville-Joliet MSA, IL-IN-WI	Y	31870 FQ	40810 MW	54500 TQ	USBLS	5/07
Landscaping, Lawn, Grounds	Peoria MSA, IL	Y	33010 FQ	37520 MW	53740 TQ	USBLS	5/07
Landscaping, Lawn, Grounds	Indiana	Y	30030 FQ	36660 MW	48140 TQ	USBLS	5/07
Landscaping, Lawn, Grounds	Gary PMSA, IN	Y	33100 FQ	40950 MW	52010 TQ	USBLS	5/07
Landscaping, Lawn, Grounds	Indianapolis-Carmel MSA, IN	Y	30280 FQ	40640 MW	58380 TQ	USBLS	5/07
Landscaping, Lawn, Grounds	Iowa	Y	30650 FQ	38410 MW	49390 TQ	USBLS	5/07
Landscaping, Lawn, Grounds	Davenport-Moline-Rock Island MSA, IA-IL	Y	25120 FQ	34610 MW	44280 TQ	USBLS	5/07
Landscaping, Lawn, Grounds	Des Moines-West Des Moines MSA, IA	Y	32480 FQ	41720 MW	59250 TQ	USBLS	5/07
Landscaping, Lawn, Grounds	Kansas	Y	27950 FQ	34640 MW	41970 TQ	USBLS	5/07
Landscaping, Lawn, Grounds	Wichita MSA, KS	Y	21260 FQ	27980 MW	36930 TQ	USBLS	5/07
Landscaping, Lawn, Grounds	Kentucky	Y	27379 FQ	32588 MW	41508 TQ	KYBLS	2008
Landscaping, Lawn, Grounds	Louisville-Jefferson County MSA, KY-IN	Y	29200 FQ	34130 MW	42130 TQ	USBLS	5/07
Landscaping, Lawn, Grounds	Louisiana	H	12.64 FQ	15.43 MW	19.22 TQ	LABLS	1/08-3/08
Landscaping, Lawn, Grounds	Baton Rouge MSA, LA	Y	23680 FQ	29270 MW	37530 TQ	USBLS	5/07
Landscaping, Lawn, Grounds	Houma-Bayou Cane-Thibodaux MSA, LA	Y	26250 FQ	29710 MW	32610 TQ	USBLS	5/07
Landscaping, Lawn, Grounds	New Orleans-Metairie-Kenner MSA, LA	Y	28070 FQ	32490 MW	42990 TQ	USBLS	5/07
Landscaping, Lawn, Grounds	Maine	Y	27100 FQ	33470 MW	43570 TQ	USBLS	5/07
Landscaping, Lawn, Grounds	Portland-South Portland-Biddeford MSA, ME	Y	31320 FQ	38230 MW	46420 TQ	USBLS	5/07
Landscaping, Lawn, Grounds	Maryland	Y		41400 MW		MDBLS	3/08
Landscaping, Lawn, Grounds	Baltimore-Towson MSA, MD	Y	34620 FQ	39380 MW	49570 TQ	USBLS	5/07
Landscaping, Lawn, Grounds	Bethesda-Gaithersburg-Frederick PMSA, MD	Y	36250 FQ	45130 MW	59460 TQ	USBLS	5/07
Landscaping, Lawn, Grounds	Hagerstown-Martinsburg MSA, MD-WV	Y	30280 FQ	43530 MW	49130 TQ	USBLS	5/07
Landscaping, Lawn, Grounds	Massachusetts	Y	36260 FQ	46120 MW	56640 TQ	USBLS	5/07
Landscaping, Lawn, Grounds	Boston-Cambridge-Quincy NECTA, MA	Y	42040 FQ	50250 MW	58990 TQ	USBLS	5/07
Landscaping, Lawn, Grounds	Worcester MSA, MA-CT	Y	35030 FQ	39060 MW	49720 TQ	USBLS	5/07
Landscaping, Lawn, Grounds	Michigan	Y	33030 FQ	40300 MW	53300 TQ	USBLS	5/07
Landscaping, Lawn, Grounds	Detroit-Warren-Livonia MSA, MI	Y	33860 FQ	41520 MW	56220 TQ	USBLS	5/07
Landscaping, Lawn, Grounds	Flint MSA, MI	Y	35490 FQ	42270 MW	50200 TQ	USBLS	5/07
Landscaping, Lawn, Grounds	Grand Rapids-Wyoming MSA, MI	Y	33200 FQ	40280 MW	49080 TQ	USBLS	5/07
Landscaping, Lawn, Grounds	Lansing-East Lansing MSA, MI	Y	32710 FQ	41920 MW	54920 TQ	USBLS	5/07
Landscaping, Lawn, Grounds	Warren-Troy-Farmington Hills PMSA, MI	Y	34480 FQ	40750 MW	56260 TQ	USBLS	5/07
Landscaping, Lawn, Grounds	Minnesota	Y	35204 FQ	41886 MW	50763 TQ	MNBLS	10/08-12/08
Landscaping, Lawn, Grounds	Duluth-Superior MSA, MN-WI	Y	35413 FQ	40861 MW	54704 TQ	MNBLS	10/08-12/08
Landscaping, Lawn, Grounds	Minneapolis-Saint Paul MSA, MN-WI	Y	36731 FQ	42837 MW	51777 TQ	MNBLS	10/08-12/08
Landscaping, Lawn, Grounds	Rochester MSA, MN	Y	26199 FQ	39251 MW	45978 TQ	MNBLS	10/08-12/08
Landscaping, Lawn, Grounds	Mississippi	Y	26640 FQ	33290 MW	40850 TQ	USBLS	5/07
Landscaping, Lawn, Grounds	Gulfport-Biloxi MSA, MS	Y	27210 FQ	34190 MW	41460 TQ	USBLS	5/07
Landscaping, Lawn, Grounds	Jackson MSA, MS	Y	28410 FQ	33650 MW	46780 TQ	USBLS	5/07
Landscaping, Lawn, Grounds	Missouri	Y	33200 FQ	42010 MW	50000 TQ	USBLS	5/07
Landscaping, Lawn, Grounds	Kansas City MSA, MO-KS	Y	30370 FQ	38510 MW	47920 TQ	USBLS	5/07
Landscaping, Lawn, Grounds	St. Louis MSA, MO-IL	Y	32300 FQ	42850 MW	52030 TQ	USBLS	5/07
Landscaping, Lawn, Grounds	Montana	Y	27030 FQ	30730 MW	41200 TQ	USBLS	5/07
Landscaping, Lawn, Grounds	Billings MSA, MT	Y	26830 FQ	40390 MW	52690 TQ	USBLS	5/07
Landscaping, Lawn, Grounds	Missoula MSA, MT	Y	27750 FQ	30000 MW	32710 TQ	USBLS	5/07
Landscaping, Lawn, Grounds	Nebraska	Y	33410 FQ	43030 MW	52730 TQ	USBLS	5/07
Landscaping, Lawn, Grounds	Omaha-Council Bluffs MSA, NE-IA	Y	34960 FQ	45120 MW	53710 TQ	USBLS	5/07
Landscaping, Lawn, Grounds	Nevada	H	15.64 FQ	19.63 MW	25.25 TQ	NVBLS	5/08
Landscaping, Lawn, Grounds	Las Vegas-Paradise MSA, NV	H	15.10 FQ	19.17 MW	25.30 TQ	NVBLS	5/08
Landscaping, Lawn, Grounds	New Hampshire	H	15.78 AE	20.17 MW	23.53 AEX	NHBLS	6/08
Landscaping, Lawn, Grounds	Manchester MSA, NH	Y	29530 FQ	35180 MW	41920 TQ	USBLS	5/07
Landscaping, Lawn, Grounds	Nashua NECTA, NH-MA	Y	40490 FQ	44010 MW	47690 TQ	USBLS	5/07
Landscaping, Lawn, Grounds	New Jersey	Y	36510 FQ	44220 MW	56590 TQ	USBLS	5/07
Landscaping, Lawn, Grounds	Atlantic City MSA, NJ	Y	34540 FQ	41600 MW	48960 TQ	USBLS	5/07
Landscaping, Lawn, Grounds	Camden PMSA, NJ	Y	35390 FQ	43100 MW	51900 TQ	USBLS	5/07
Landscaping, Lawn, Grounds	Edison PMSA, NJ	Y	39170 FQ	47230 MW	61270 TQ	USBLS	5/07
Landscaping, Lawn, Grounds	Newark-Union PMSA, NJ-PA	Y	35760 FQ	43190 MW	57660 TQ	USBLS	5/07

AE	Average entry wage	AW	Average wage paid	FQ	First quartile wage
AER	Average entry range	AWR	Average wage range	H	Hourly
AEX	Average experienced wage	AXR	Average experienced range	HI	Highest wage paid
ATC	Average total compensation	D	Daily	HR	High end range

LO	Lowest wage paid	MTC	Median total compensation	TCC	Total cash compensation
LR	Low end range	MW	Median wage paid	TQ	Third quartile wage
M	Monthly	MWR	Median wage range	W	Weekly
MCC	Median cash compensation	S	See annotated source	Y	Yearly

First-Line Supervisor/Manager

Occupation/Type/Industry	Location	Per	Low	Mid	High	Source	Date
Landscaping, Lawn, Grounds	New Mexico	Y	29830 FQ	35910 MW	43800 TQ	USBLS	5/07
Landscaping, Lawn, Grounds	Albuquerque MSA, NM	Y	30990 FQ	36580 MW	43900 TQ	USBLS	5/07
Landscaping, Lawn, Grounds	Santa Fe MSA, NM	Y	34730 FQ	40050 MW	51620 TQ	USBLS	5/07
Landscaping, Lawn, Grounds	New York	Y	36780 FQ	46980 MW	59200 TQ	USBLS	5/07
Landscaping, Lawn, Grounds	Albany-Schenectady-Troy MSA, NY	Y	35650 FQ	39460 MW	45890 TQ	USBLS	5/07
Landscaping, Lawn, Grounds	Binghamton MSA, NY	Y	30710 FQ	38960 MW	47910 TQ	USBLS	5/07
Landscaping, Lawn, Grounds	Buffalo-Niagara Falls MSA, NY	Y	31940 FQ	39240 MW	47820 TQ	USBLS	5/07
Landscaping, Lawn, Grounds	Nassau-Suffolk PMSA, NY	Y	40170 FQ	51300 MW	66180 TQ	USBLS	5/07
Landscaping, Lawn, Grounds	New York-Northern New Jersey-Long Island MSA, NY-NJ-PA	Y	38800 FQ	49580 MW	62360 TQ	USBLS	5/07
Landscaping, Lawn, Grounds	North Carolina	Y	29580 FQ	36690 MW	45550 TQ	USBLS	5/07
Landscaping, Lawn, Grounds	Charlotte-Gastonia-Concord MSA, NC-SC	Y	29920 FQ	38720 MW	46640 TQ	USBLS	5/07
Landscaping, Lawn, Grounds	Greensboro-High Point MSA, NC	Y	32340 FQ	36390 MW	42490 TQ	USBLS	5/07
Landscaping, Lawn, Grounds	Raleigh-Cary MSA, NC	Y	31080 FQ	37590 MW	46830 TQ	USBLS	5/07
Landscaping, Lawn, Grounds	North Dakota	Y	28330 FQ	35130 MW	45700 TQ	USBLS	5/07
Landscaping, Lawn, Grounds	Fargo MSA, ND-MN	Y	30560 FQ	35430 MW	43950 TQ	USBLS	5/07
Landscaping, Lawn, Grounds	Ohio	Y	29110 FQ	37730 MW	48420 TQ	USBLS	5/07
Landscaping, Lawn, Grounds	Cincinnati-Middletown MSA, OH-KY-IN	Y	29470 FQ	38880 MW	48560 TQ	USBLS	5/07
Landscaping, Lawn, Grounds	Cleveland-Elyria-Mentor MSA, OH	Y	25990 FQ	37280 MW	49720 TQ	USBLS	5/07
Landscaping, Lawn, Grounds	Columbus MSA, OH	Y	33280 FQ	38940 MW	47910 TQ	USBLS	5/07
Landscaping, Lawn, Grounds	Dayton MSA, OH	Y	30740 FQ	40150 MW	51570 TQ	USBLS	5/07
Landscaping, Lawn, Grounds	Oklahoma	Y	24370 FQ	31070 MW	39770 TQ	USBLS	5/07
Landscaping, Lawn, Grounds	Oklahoma City MSA, OK	Y	21260 FQ	29540 MW	37200 TQ	USBLS	5/07
Landscaping, Lawn, Grounds	Tulsa MSA, OK	Y	29210 FQ	36710 MW	45170 TQ	USBLS	5/07
Landscaping, Lawn, Grounds	Oregon	H	16.20 FQ	20.36 MW	25.69 TQ	ORBLS	5/08
Landscaping, Lawn, Grounds	Eugene-Springfield MSA, OR	Y	32650 FQ	39090 MW	50230 TQ	USBLS	5/07
Landscaping, Lawn, Grounds	Medford MSA, OR	Y	31490 FQ	42880 MW	48620 TQ	USBLS	5/07
Landscaping, Lawn, Grounds	Portland-Vancouver-Beaverton MSA, OR-WA	Y	33300 FQ	43140 MW	54730 TQ	USBLS	5/07
Landscaping, Lawn, Grounds	Pennsylvania	Y	34160 FQ	42120 MW	53360 TQ	USBLS	5/07
Landscaping, Lawn, Grounds	Allentown-Bethlehem-Easton MSA, PA-NJ	Y	34820 FQ	40760 MW	48820 TQ	USBLS	5/07
Landscaping, Lawn, Grounds	Erie MSA, PA	Y	26540 FQ	29520 MW	37020 TQ	USBLS	5/07
Landscaping, Lawn, Grounds	Philadelphia-Camden-Wilmington MSA, PA-NJ-DE-MD	Y	35640 FQ	44440 MW	56420 TQ	USBLS	5/07
Landscaping, Lawn, Grounds	Pittsburgh MSA, PA	Y	29810 FQ	39990 MW	52090 TQ	USBLS	5/07
Landscaping, Lawn, Grounds	Rhode Island	Y	39050 FQ	46300 MW	57440 TQ	USBLS	5/07
Landscaping, Lawn, Grounds	Providence-Fall River-Warwick MSA, RI-MA	Y	37360 FQ	46000 MW	58160 TQ	USBLS	5/07
Landscaping, Lawn, Grounds	South Carolina	Y	28970 FQ	35630 MW	43670 TQ	USBLS	5/07
Landscaping, Lawn, Grounds	Charleston-North Charleston MSA, SC	Y	29080 FQ	35550 MW	42770 TQ	USBLS	5/07
Landscaping, Lawn, Grounds	Columbia MSA, SC	Y	32900 FQ	37080 MW	41180 TQ	USBLS	5/07
Landscaping, Lawn, Grounds	Spartanburg MSA, SC	Y	27050 FQ	30790 MW	39980 TQ	USBLS	5/07
Landscaping, Lawn, Grounds	South Dakota	Y	32270 FQ	37503 MW	44082 TQ	SDBLS	7/08-9/08
Landscaping, Lawn, Grounds	Sioux Falls MSA, SD	Y	33702 FQ	39879 MW	47110 TQ	SDBLS	7/08-9/08
Landscaping, Lawn, Grounds	Tennessee	Y	26410 FQ	32890 MW	40610 TQ	USBLS	5/07
Landscaping, Lawn, Grounds	Kingsport-Bristol-Bristol MSA, TN-VA	Y	23560 FQ	29840 MW	38490 TQ	USBLS	5/07
Landscaping, Lawn, Grounds	Knoxville MSA, TN	Y	25940 FQ	31640 MW	41270 TQ	USBLS	5/07
Landscaping, Lawn, Grounds	Memphis MSA, TN-MS-AR	Y	31460 FQ	36750 MW	44440 TQ	USBLS	5/07
Landscaping, Lawn, Grounds	Nashville-Davidson-Murfreesboro MSA, TN	Y	27310 FQ	32830 MW	39040 TQ	USBLS	5/07
Landscaping, Lawn, Grounds	Texas	Y	24560 FQ	30350 MW	39830 TQ	USBLS	5/07
Landscaping, Lawn, Grounds	Austin-Round Rock MSA, TX	Y	26320 FQ	29890 MW	37100 TQ	USBLS	5/07
Landscaping, Lawn, Grounds	Dallas-Fort Worth-Arlington MSA, TX	Y	27400 FQ	35360 MW	46260 TQ	USBLS	5/07
Landscaping, Lawn, Grounds	El Paso MSA, TX	Y	18930 FQ	22730 MW	27920 TQ	USBLS	5/07
Landscaping, Lawn, Grounds	Houston-Sugar Land-Baytown MSA, TX	Y	23250 FQ	27260 MW	35750 TQ	USBLS	5/07
Landscaping, Lawn, Grounds	San Antonio MSA, TX	Y	24250 FQ	28860 MW	36240 TQ	USBLS	5/07
Landscaping, Lawn, Grounds	Utah	Y	28400 FQ	34010 MW	41150 TQ	USBLS	5/07
Landscaping, Lawn, Grounds	Salt Lake City MSA, UT	Y	27470 FQ	31030 MW	38760 TQ	USBLS	5/07

Occupation/Type/Industry	Location	Per	Low	Mid	High	Source	Date
First-Line Supervisor/Manager							
Landscaping, Lawn, Grounds	Vermont	Y	33880 FQ	41320 MW	50240 TQ	USBLS	5/07
Landscaping, Lawn, Grounds	Burlington-South Burlington MSA, VT	Y	34460 FQ	40710 MW	47140 TQ	USBLS	5/07
Landscaping, Lawn, Grounds	Virginia	Y	33220 FQ	40880 MW	54480 TQ	USBLS	5/07
Landscaping, Lawn, Grounds	Richmond MSA, VA	Y	29890 FQ	36830 MW	45910 TQ	USBLS	5/07
Landscaping, Lawn, Grounds	Virginia Beach-Norfolk-Newport News MSA, VA-NC	Y	38110 FQ	47430 MW	64280 TQ	USBLS	5/07
Landscaping, Lawn, Grounds	Washington	H	17.84 FQ	21.32 MW	27.24 TQ	WABLS	3/08
Landscaping, Lawn, Grounds	Seattle-Tacoma-Bellevue MSA, WA	Y	36720 FQ	43770 MW	56200 TQ	USBLS	5/07
Landscaping, Lawn, Grounds	West Virginia	Y	26704 FQ	34687 MW	42058 TQ	WVBLS	7/08-9/08
Landscaping, Lawn, Grounds	Charleston MSA, WV	Y	25930 FQ	36450 MW	43230 TQ	USBLS	5/07
Landscaping, Lawn, Grounds	Wisconsin	Y	32630 FQ	42570 MW	53870 TQ	USBLS	5/07
Landscaping, Lawn, Grounds	Green Bay MSA, WI	Y	33970 FQ	44770 MW	51920 TQ	USBLS	5/07
Landscaping, Lawn, Grounds	Milwaukee-Waukesha-West Allis MSA, WI	Y	32910 FQ	45640 MW	57200 TQ	USBLS	5/07
Landscaping, Lawn, Grounds	Wyoming	Y	32845 FQ	39161 MW	49420 TQ	WYBLS	9/08
Landscaping, Lawn, Grounds	Cheyenne MSA, WY	Y	29304 FQ	34858 MW	46328 TQ	WYBLS	9/08
Landscaping, Lawn, Grounds	Puerto Rico	Y	15670 FQ	20280 MW	29160 TQ	USBLS	5/07
Landscaping, Lawn, Grounds	San Juan-Caguas-Guaynabo MSA, PR	Y	17210 FQ	22140 MW	30690 TQ	USBLS	5/07
Landscaping, Lawn, Grounds	Virgin Islands	Y	32000 FQ	36040 MW	40860 TQ	USBLS	5/07
Landscaping, Lawn, Grounds	Guam	Y	16150 FQ	22340 MW	37610 TQ	USBLS	5/07
Mechanics, Installers, and Repairers	Alabama	Y	37340 FQ	48960 MW	62450 TQ	USBLS	5/07
Mechanics, Installers, and Repairers	Birmingham-Hoover MSA, AL	Y	41540 FQ	53920 MW	66370 TQ	USBLS	5/07
Mechanics, Installers, and Repairers	Tuscaloosa MSA, AL	Y	40040 FQ	52040 MW	76300 TQ	USBLS	5/07
Mechanics, Installers, and Repairers	Alaska	Y	51950 FQ	68420 MW	84140 TQ	USBLS	5/07
Mechanics, Installers, and Repairers	Anchorage MSA, AK	Y	51880 FQ	67810 MW	81410 TQ	USBLS	5/07
Mechanics, Installers, and Repairers	Arizona	Y	41230 FQ	54730 MW	71410 TQ	USBLS	5/07
Mechanics, Installers, and Repairers	Phoenix-Mesa-Scottsdale MSA, AZ	Y	41050 FQ	55850 MW	75140 TQ	USBLS	5/07
Mechanics, Installers, and Repairers	Tucson MSA, AZ	Y	41730 FQ	52520 MW	62810 TQ	USBLS	5/07
Mechanics, Installers, and Repairers	Yuma MSA, AZ	Y	42070 FQ	58140 MW	72070 TQ	USBLS	5/07
Mechanics, Installers, and Repairers	Arkansas	Y	34890 FQ	44620 MW	57760 TQ	USBLS	5/07
Mechanics, Installers, and Repairers	Fayetteville-Springdale-Rogers MSA, AR-MO	Y	36320 FQ	46670 MW	58750 TQ	USBLS	5/07
Mechanics, Installers, and Repairers	Little Rock-North Little Rock MSA, AR	Y	36280 FQ	48520 MW	60130 TQ	USBLS	5/07
Mechanics, Installers, and Repairers	California	H	23.27 FQ	30.08 MW	37.85 TQ	CABLS	1/08-3/08
Mechanics, Installers, and Repairers	Los Angeles-Long Beach-Glendale PMSA, CA	H	22.30 FQ	29.95 MW	37.65 TQ	CABLS	1/08-3/08
Mechanics, Installers, and Repairers	Oakland-Fremont-Hayward MSA, CA	H	26.46 FQ	32.33 MW	41.22 TQ	CABLS	1/08-3/08
Mechanics, Installers, and Repairers	Riverside-San Bernardino-Ontario MSA, CA	H	23.03 FQ	28.11 MW	35.07 TQ	CABLS	1/08-3/08
Mechanics, Installers, and Repairers	Sacramento-Arden Arcade-Roseville MSA, CA	H	24.50 FQ	30.11 MW	37.18 TQ	CABLS	1/08-3/08
Mechanics, Installers, and Repairers	San Diego-Carlsbad-San Marcos MSA, CA	H	23.27 FQ	30.47 MW	37.51 TQ	CABLS	1/08-3/08
Mechanics, Installers, and Repairers	San Francisco-San Mateo-Redwood PMSA, CA	H	28.83 FQ	35.08 MW	41.35 TQ	CABLS	1/08-3/08
Mechanics, Installers, and Repairers	San Jose-Sunnyvale-Santa Clara MSA, CA	H	25.64 FQ	34.72 MW	44.51 TQ	CABLS	1/08-3/08
Mechanics, Installers, and Repairers	Santa Ana-Anaheim-Irvine PMSA, CA	Y	42920 FQ	61100 MW	77840 TQ	USBLS	5/07
Mechanics, Installers, and Repairers	Stockton MSA, CA	H	24.78 FQ	29.13 MW	34.92 TQ	CABLS	1/08-3/08
Mechanics, Installers, and Repairers	Colorado	Y	43880 FQ	56100 MW	69460 TQ	USBLS	5/07
Mechanics, Installers, and Repairers	Denver-Aurora MSA, CO	Y	44560 FQ	57120 MW	70320 TQ	USBLS	5/07
Mechanics, Installers, and Repairers	Connecticut	H	22.20 AE	31.11 MW		CTBLS	1/08-3/08
Mechanics, Installers, and Repairers	Bridgeport-Stamford-Norwalk MSA, CT	Y	57060 FQ	68940 MW	81070 TQ	USBLS	5/07
Mechanics, Installers, and Repairers	Hartford-West Hartford-East Hartford MSA, CT	Y	50010 FQ	61560 MW	78820 TQ	USBLS	5/07
Mechanics, Installers, and Repairers	Delaware	Y	46220 FQ	58940 MW	74270 TQ	USBLS	5/07
Mechanics, Installers, and Repairers	Wilmington PMSA, DE-MD-NJ	Y	48060 FQ	60790 MW	75340 TQ	USBLS	5/07
Mechanics, Installers, and Repairers	District of Columbia	Y	47350 FQ	58790 MW	72470 TQ	USBLS	5/07
Mechanics, Installers, and Repairers	Washington-Arlington-Alexandria MSA, DC-VA-MD-WV	Y	48540 FQ	61790 MW	77430 TQ	USBLS	5/07
Mechanics, Installers, and Repairers	Florida	Y	41400 FQ	52810 MW	66700 TQ	USBLS	5/07

AE	Average entry wage	AW	Average wage paid	FQ	First quartile wage
AER	Average entry range	AWR	Average wage range	H	Hourly
AEX	Average experienced wage	AXR	Average experienced range	HI	Highest wage paid
ATC	Average total compensation	D	Daily	HR	High end range

LO	Lowest wage paid	MTC	Median total compensation	TCC	Total cash compensation
LR	Low end range	MW	Median wage paid	TQ	Third quartile wage
M	Monthly	MWR	Median wage range	W	Weekly
MCC	Median cash compensation	S	See annotated source	Y	Yearly

Occupation/Type/Industry	Location	Per	Low	Mid	High	Source	Date
First-Line Supervisor/Manager							
Mechanics, Installers, and Repairers	Fort Lauderdale-Pompano Beach-Deerfield Beach PMSA, FL	Y	45380 FQ	58660 MW	74390 TQ	USBLS	5/07
Mechanics, Installers, and Repairers	Jacksonville MSA, FL	Y	43440 FQ	55230 MW	69960 TQ	USBLS	5/07
Mechanics, Installers, and Repairers	Miami-Fort Lauderdale-Miami Beach MSA, FL	Y	41830 FQ	54500 MW	70790 TQ	USBLS	5/07
Mechanics, Installers, and Repairers	Orlando-Kissimmee MSA, FL	Y	41720 FQ	52990 MW	66620 TQ	USBLS	5/07
Mechanics, Installers, and Repairers	Tampa-St. Petersburg-Clearwater MSA, FL	Y	38370 FQ	48080 MW	62080 TQ	USBLS	5/07
Mechanics, Installers, and Repairers	West Palm Beach-Boca Raton-Boynton Beach PMSA, FL	Y	42860 FQ	53320 MW	68490 TQ	USBLS	5/07
Mechanics, Installers, and Repairers	Georgia	Y	39240 FQ	51090 MW	64680 TQ	USBLS	5/07
Mechanics, Installers, and Repairers	Atlanta-Sandy Springs-Marietta MSA, GA	Y	41850 FQ	53630 MW	67150 TQ	USBLS	5/07
Mechanics, Installers, and Repairers	Macon MSA, GA	Y	37260 FQ	45820 MW	63110 TQ	USBLS	5/07
Mechanics, Installers, and Repairers	Hawaii	Y	45540 FQ	59720 MW	77930 TQ	USBLS	5/07
Mechanics, Installers, and Repairers	Honolulu MSA, HI	Y	46950 FQ	63250 MW	81490 TQ	USBLS	5/07
Mechanics, Installers, and Repairers	Idaho	Y	35060 FQ	44490 MW	56970 TQ	USBLS	5/07
Mechanics, Installers, and Repairers	Boise City-Nampa MSA, ID	Y	33830 FQ	45250 MW	60450 TQ	USBLS	5/07
Mechanics, Installers, and Repairers	Illinois	Y	47680 FQ	61850 MW	76560 TQ	USBLS	5/07
Mechanics, Installers, and Repairers	Chicago-Naperville-Joliet MSA, IL-IN-WI	Y	50790 FQ	64690 MW	79030 TQ	USBLS	5/07
Mechanics, Installers, and Repairers	Indiana	Y	41630 FQ	52490 MW	66180 TQ	USBLS	5/07
Mechanics, Installers, and Repairers	Gary PMSA, IN	Y	44170 FQ	54140 MW	68170 TQ	USBLS	5/07
Mechanics, Installers, and Repairers	Indianapolis-Carmel MSA, IN	Y	43050 FQ	54610 MW	68530 TQ	USBLS	5/07
Mechanics, Installers, and Repairers	Iowa	Y	41850 FQ	53700 MW	66920 TQ	USBLS	5/07
Mechanics, Installers, and Repairers	Cedar Rapids MSA, IA	Y	38300 FQ	57840 MW	70290 TQ	USBLS	5/07
Mechanics, Installers, and Repairers	Des Moines-West Des Moines MSA, IA	Y	48840 FQ	58030 MW	70030 TQ	USBLS	5/07
Mechanics, Installers, and Repairers	Iowa City MSA, IA	Y	40740 FQ	49570 MW	61310 TQ	USBLS	5/07
Mechanics, Installers, and Repairers	Kansas	Y	39450 FQ	51250 MW	65440 TQ	USBLS	5/07
Mechanics, Installers, and Repairers	Wichita MSA, KS	Y	43450 FQ	55230 MW	67570 TQ	USBLS	5/07
Mechanics, Installers, and Repairers	Kentucky	Y	38840 FQ	49643 MW	64532 TQ	KYBLS	2008
Mechanics, Installers, and Repairers	Louisville-Jefferson County MSA, KY-IN	Y	41010 FQ	50230 MW	64740 TQ	USBLS	5/07
Mechanics, Installers, and Repairers	Louisiana	H	18.21 FQ	23.42 MW	30.04 TQ	LABLS	1/08-3/08
Mechanics, Installers, and Repairers	Baton Rouge MSA, LA	Y	37470 FQ	47080 MW	61140 TQ	USBLS	5/07
Mechanics, Installers, and Repairers	New Orleans-Metairie-Kenner MSA, LA	Y	39180 FQ	49780 MW	63000 TQ	USBLS	5/07
Mechanics, Installers, and Repairers	Maine	Y	37540 FQ	46810 MW	59530 TQ	USBLS	5/07
Mechanics, Installers, and Repairers	Portland-South Portland-Biddeford MSA, ME	Y	36370 FQ	46340 MW	58960 TQ	USBLS	5/07
Mechanics, Installers, and Repairers	Maryland	Y		58750 MW		MDBLS	3/08
Mechanics, Installers, and Repairers	Baltimore-Towson MSA, MD	Y	46120 FQ	58510 MW	72500 TQ	USBLS	5/07
Mechanics, Installers, and Repairers	Bethesda-Gaithersburg-Frederick PMSA, MD	Y	44170 FQ	54820 MW	70370 TQ	USBLS	5/07
Mechanics, Installers, and Repairers	Cumberland MSA, MD-WV	Y	29960 FQ	37560 MW	52930 TQ	USBLS	5/07
Mechanics, Installers, and Repairers	Massachusetts	Y	49080 FQ	60750 MW	74890 TQ	USBLS	5/07
Mechanics, Installers, and Repairers	Boston-Cambridge-Quincy NECTA, MA	Y	52790 FQ	63720 MW	77810 TQ	USBLS	5/07
Mechanics, Installers, and Repairers	Worcester MSA, MA-CT	Y	45320 FQ	55610 MW	65160 TQ	USBLS	5/07
Mechanics, Installers, and Repairers	Michigan	Y	47080 FQ	61030 MW	76020 TQ	USBLS	5/07
Mechanics, Installers, and Repairers	Detroit-Warren-Livonia MSA, MI	Y	53170 FQ	66060 MW	80430 TQ	USBLS	5/07
Mechanics, Installers, and Repairers	Grand Rapids-Wyoming MSA, MI	Y	43960 FQ	57380 MW	69730 TQ	USBLS	5/07
Mechanics, Installers, and Repairers	Warren-Troy-Farmington Hills PMSA, MI	Y	52180 FQ	66770 MW	80290 TQ	USBLS	5/07
Mechanics, Installers, and Repairers	Minnesota	Y	46678 FQ	57712 MW	69628 TQ	MNBLS	10/08-12/08
Mechanics, Installers, and Repairers	Duluth-Superior MSA, MN-WI	Y	41863 FQ	52657 MW	67489 TQ	MNBLS	10/08-12/08
Mechanics, Installers, and Repairers	Minneapolis-Saint Paul MSA, MN-WI	Y	49940 FQ	59863 MW	72324 TQ	MNBLS	10/08-12/08
Mechanics, Installers, and Repairers	Rochester MSA, MN	Y	47796 FQ	60206 MW	73275 TQ	MNBLS	10/08-12/08
Mechanics, Installers, and Repairers	Mississippi	Y	36460 FQ	46860 MW	58920 TQ	USBLS	5/07
Mechanics, Installers, and Repairers	Jackson MSA, MS	Y	33880 FQ	46710 MW	60290 TQ	USBLS	5/07
Mechanics, Installers, and Repairers	Missouri	Y	42440 FQ	55280 MW	70120 TQ	USBLS	5/07
Mechanics, Installers, and Repairers	Kansas City MSA, MO-KS	Y	44140 FQ	57780 MW	72050 TQ	USBLS	5/07
Mechanics, Installers, and Repairers	St. Louis MSA, MO-IL	Y	46200 FQ	57370 MW	71010 TQ	USBLS	5/07
Mechanics, Installers, and Repairers	Montana	Y	39950 FQ	51990 MW	67440 TQ	USBLS	5/07
Mechanics, Installers, and Repairers	Billings MSA, MT	Y	42290 FQ	52020 MW	68930 TQ	USBLS	5/07
Mechanics, Installers, and Repairers	Nebraska	Y	44170 FQ	54900 MW	68000 TQ	USBLS	5/07

AE	Average entry wage	AW	Average wage paid	FQ	First quartile wage
AER	Average entry range	AWR	Average wage range	H	Hourly
AEX	Average experienced wage	AXR	Average experienced range	HI	Highest wage paid
ATC	Average total compensation	D	Daily	HR	High end range

LO	Lowest wage paid	MTC	Median total compensation	TCC	Total cash compensation
LR	Low end range	MW	Median wage paid	TQ	Third quartile wage
M	Monthly	MWR	Median wage range	W	Weekly
MCC	Median cash compensation	S	See annotated source	Y	Yearly

Occupation/Type/Industry	Location	Per	Low	Mid	High	Source	Date
First-Line Supervisor/Manager							
Mechanics, Installers, and Repairers	Omaha-Council Bluffs MSA, NE-IA	Y	44850 FQ	55300 MW	70390 TQ	USBLS	5/07
Mechanics, Installers, and Repairers	Nevada	H	21.93 FQ	27.65 MW	34.69 TQ	NVBLS	5/08
Mechanics, Installers, and Repairers	Las Vegas-Paradise MSA, NV	H	21.75 FQ	27.34 MW	33.98 TQ	NVBLS	5/08
Mechanics, Installers, and Repairers	New Hampshire	H	19.50 AE	28.03 MW	33.62 AEX	NHBLS	6/08
Mechanics, Installers, and Repairers	Manchester MSA, NH	Y	50570 FQ	58840 MW	75080 TQ	USBLS	5/07
Mechanics, Installers, and Repairers	Nashua NECTA, NH-MA	Y	46860 FQ	61620 MW	75060 TQ	USBLS	5/07
Mechanics, Installers, and Repairers	New Jersey	Y	51740 FQ	63850 MW	77480 TQ	USBLS	5/07
Mechanics, Installers, and Repairers	Camden PMSA, NJ	Y	51220 FQ	62460 MW	74040 TQ	USBLS	5/07
Mechanics, Installers, and Repairers	Edison PMSA, NJ	Y	49290 FQ	63980 MW	78650 TQ	USBLS	5/07
Mechanics, Installers, and Repairers	Newark-Union PMSA, NJ-PA	Y	53220 FQ	65560 MW	78780 TQ	USBLS	5/07
Mechanics, Installers, and Repairers	Ocean City MSA, NJ	Y	46910 FQ	56720 MW	70240 TQ	USBLS	5/07
Mechanics, Installers, and Repairers	New Mexico	Y	35350 FQ	47110 MW	61150 TQ	USBLS	5/07
Mechanics, Installers, and Repairers	Albuquerque MSA, NM	Y	38940 FQ	49600 MW	63350 TQ	USBLS	5/07
Mechanics, Installers, and Repairers	New York	Y	48990 FQ	62610 MW	79700 TQ	USBLS	5/07
Mechanics, Installers, and Repairers	Albany-Schenectady-Troy MSA, NY	Y	41930 FQ	56140 MW	71460 TQ	USBLS	5/07
Mechanics, Installers, and Repairers	Binghamton MSA, NY	Y	40120 FQ	49400 MW	61410 TQ	USBLS	5/07
Mechanics, Installers, and Repairers	Buffalo-Niagara Falls MSA, NY	Y	43540 FQ	55140 MW	68840 TQ	USBLS	5/07
Mechanics, Installers, and Repairers	Nassau-Suffolk PMSA, NY	Y	55690 FQ	71380 MW	87630 TQ	USBLS	5/07
Mechanics, Installers, and Repairers	New York-Northern New Jersey-Long Island MSA, NY-NJ-PA	Y	54290 FQ	67990 MW	83470 TQ	USBLS	5/07
Mechanics, Installers, and Repairers	North Carolina	Y	41710 FQ	51990 MW	64270 TQ	USBLS	5/07
Mechanics, Installers, and Repairers	Charlotte-Gastonia-Concord MSA, NC-SC	Y	44500 FQ	54950 MW	68510 TQ	USBLS	5/07
Mechanics, Installers, and Repairers	Raleigh-Cary MSA, NC	Y	42250 FQ	52700 MW	65970 TQ	USBLS	5/07
Mechanics, Installers, and Repairers	North Dakota	Y	40530 FQ	52890 MW	66850 TQ	USBLS	5/07
Mechanics, Installers, and Repairers	Fargo MSA, ND-MN	Y	43600 FQ	53540 MW	62900 TQ	USBLS	5/07
Mechanics, Installers, and Repairers	Ohio	Y	42530 FQ	54600 MW	68080 TQ	USBLS	5/07
Mechanics, Installers, and Repairers	Cincinnati-Middletown MSA, OH-KY-IN	Y	43110 FQ	54470 MW	68180 TQ	USBLS	5/07
Mechanics, Installers, and Repairers	Cleveland-Elyria-Mentor MSA, OH	Y	47520 FQ	58840 MW	72310 TQ	USBLS	5/07
Mechanics, Installers, and Repairers	Columbus MSA, OH	Y	42100 FQ	54300 MW	65850 TQ	USBLS	5/07
Mechanics, Installers, and Repairers	Dayton MSA, OH	Y	42340 FQ	55300 MW	72270 TQ	USBLS	5/07
Mechanics, Installers, and Repairers	Oklahoma	Y	37500 FQ	51530 MW	64820 TQ	USBLS	5/07
Mechanics, Installers, and Repairers	Oklahoma City MSA, OK	Y	37330 FQ	52020 MW	65410 TQ	USBLS	5/07
Mechanics, Installers, and Repairers	Tulsa MSA, OK	Y	42070 FQ	54900 MW	67190 TQ	USBLS	5/07
Mechanics, Installers, and Repairers	Oregon	H	21.82 FQ	27.40 MW	34.05 TQ	ORBLS	5/08
Mechanics, Installers, and Repairers	Portland-Vancouver-Beaverton MSA, OR-WA	Y	47570 FQ	59230 MW	73680 TQ	USBLS	5/07
Mechanics, Installers, and Repairers	Pennsylvania	Y	45250 FQ	57110 MW	71650 TQ	USBLS	5/07
Mechanics, Installers, and Repairers	Allentown-Bethlehem-Easton MSA, PA-NJ	Y	43190 FQ	57430 MW	74630 TQ	USBLS	5/07
Mechanics, Installers, and Repairers	Erie MSA, PA	Y	39640 FQ	48480 MW	59710 TQ	USBLS	5/07
Mechanics, Installers, and Repairers	Lancaster MSA, PA	Y	42200 FQ	55440 MW	72130 TQ	USBLS	5/07
Mechanics, Installers, and Repairers	Philadelphia-Camden-Wilmington MSA, PA-NJ-DE-MD	Y	49930 FQ	61700 MW	76140 TQ	USBLS	5/07
Mechanics, Installers, and Repairers	Pittsburgh MSA, PA	Y	45200 FQ	58010 MW	71520 TQ	USBLS	5/07
Mechanics, Installers, and Repairers	Rhode Island	Y	44630 FQ	56770 MW	68820 TQ	USBLS	5/07
Mechanics, Installers, and Repairers	Providence-Fall River-Warwick MSA, RI-MA	Y	45110 FQ	56880 MW	69050 TQ	USBLS	5/07
Mechanics, Installers, and Repairers	South Carolina	Y	38710 FQ	48420 MW	60650 TQ	USBLS	5/07
Mechanics, Installers, and Repairers	Charleston-North Charleston MSA, SC	Y	40850 FQ	49970 MW	59740 TQ	USBLS	5/07
Mechanics, Installers, and Repairers	Columbia MSA, SC	Y	40090 FQ	48830 MW	60440 TQ	USBLS	5/07
Mechanics, Installers, and Repairers	Myrtle Beach-Conway-North Myrtle Beach MSA, SC	Y	35360 FQ	43050 MW	53950 TQ	USBLS	5/07
Mechanics, Installers, and Repairers	South Dakota	Y	46591 FQ	56605 MW	66690 TQ	SDBLS	7/08-9/08
Mechanics, Installers, and Repairers	Sioux Falls MSA, SD	Y	47687 FQ	55602 MW	66286 TQ	SDBLS	7/08-9/08
Mechanics, Installers, and Repairers	Tennessee	Y	35370 FQ	46330 MW	60690 TQ	USBLS	5/07
Mechanics, Installers, and Repairers	Memphis MSA, TN-MS-AR	Y	38530 FQ	52310 MW	66040 TQ	USBLS	5/07
Mechanics, Installers, and Repairers	Nashville-Davidson-Murfreesboro MSA, TN	Y	37910 FQ	48090 MW	61510 TQ	USBLS	5/07
Mechanics, Installers, and Repairers	Texas	Y	37620 FQ	50840 MW	65830 TQ	USBLS	5/07
Mechanics, Installers, and Repairers	Austin-Round Rock MSA, TX	Y	39440 FQ	49710 MW	63880 TQ	USBLS	5/07
Mechanics, Installers, and Repairers	Dallas-Fort Worth-Arlington MSA, TX	Y	39150 FQ	52490 MW	67740 TQ	USBLS	5/07

AE	Average entry wage	AW	Average wage paid	FQ	First quartile wage
AER	Average entry range	AWR	Average wage range	H	Hourly
AEX	Average experienced wage	AXR	Average experienced range	HI	Highest wage paid
ATC	Average total compensation	D	Daily	HR	High end range

LO	Lowest wage paid	MTC	Median total compensation	TCC	Total cash compensation
LR	Low end range	MW	Median wage paid	TQ	Third quartile wage
M	Monthly	MWR	Median wage range	W	Weekly
MCC	Median cash compensation	S	See annotated source	Y	Yearly

Occupation/Type/Industry	Location	Per	Low	Mid	High	Source	Date
First-Line Supervisor/Manager							
Mechanics, Installers, and Repairers	El Paso MSA, TX	Y	34500 FQ	45650 MW	58380 TQ	USBLS	5/07
Mechanics, Installers, and Repairers	Houston-Sugar Land-Baytown MSA, TX	Y	40420 FQ	54660 MW	71180 TQ	USBLS	5/07
Mechanics, Installers, and Repairers	San Antonio MSA, TX	Y	36270 FQ	50040 MW	64010 TQ	USBLS	5/07
Mechanics, Installers, and Repairers	Utah	Y	44620 FQ	56070 MW	68770 TQ	USBLS	5/07
Mechanics, Installers, and Repairers	Salt Lake City MSA, UT	Y	47480 FQ	58310 MW	71510 TQ	USBLS	5/07
Mechanics, Installers, and Repairers	Vermont	Y	44320 FQ	53580 MW	66370 TQ	USBLS	5/07
Mechanics, Installers, and Repairers	Burlington-South Burlington MSA, VT	Y	46390 FQ	56980 MW	68320 TQ	USBLS	5/07
Mechanics, Installers, and Repairers	Virginia	Y	45970 FQ	58300 MW	73720 TQ	USBLS	5/07
Mechanics, Installers, and Repairers	Richmond MSA, VA	Y	44690 FQ	57610 MW	72330 TQ	USBLS	5/07
Mechanics, Installers, and Repairers	Virginia Beach-Norfolk-Newport News MSA, VA-NC	Y	47250 FQ	56970 MW	68120 TQ	USBLS	5/07
Mechanics, Installers, and Repairers	Washington	H	25.20 FQ	31.18 MW	37.38 TQ	WABLS	3/08
Mechanics, Installers, and Repairers	Olympia MSA, WA	Y	46160 FQ	58000 MW	72270 TQ	USBLS	5/07
Mechanics, Installers, and Repairers	Seattle-Tacoma-Bellevue MSA, WA	Y	54630 FQ	66450 MW	78840 TQ	USBLS	5/07
Mechanics, Installers, and Repairers	West Virginia	Y	37361 FQ	55708 MW	73808 TQ	WVBLS	7/08-9/08
Mechanics, Installers, and Repairers	Charleston MSA, WV	Y	48610 FQ	63560 MW	75350 TQ	USBLS	5/07
Mechanics, Installers, and Repairers	Wisconsin	Y	44070 FQ	55230 MW	67820 TQ	USBLS	5/07
Mechanics, Installers, and Repairers	Wisconsin	H	21.19 FQ	26.55 MW	32.61 TQ	USBLS	5/07
Mechanics, Installers, and Repairers	Milwaukee-Waukesha-West Allis MSA, WI	Y	47640 FQ	59720 MW	74310 TQ	USBLS	5/07
Mechanics, Installers, and Repairers	Wyoming	Y	42843 FQ	58327 MW	74395 TQ	WYBLS	9/08
Mechanics, Installers, and Repairers	Cheyenne MSA, WY	Y	44534 FQ	57289 MW	72622 TQ	WYBLS	9/08
Mechanics, Installers, and Repairers	Puerto Rico	Y	24380 FQ	33290 MW	48950 TQ	USBLS	5/07
Mechanics, Installers, and Repairers	San Juan-Caguas-Guaynabo MSA, PR	Y	25140 FQ	34190 MW	48940 TQ	USBLS	5/07
Mechanics, Installers, and Repairers	Virgin Islands	Y	40960 FQ	54560 MW	63650 TQ	USBLS	5/07
Mechanics, Installers, and Repairers	Guam	Y	30310 FQ	39210 MW	48440 TQ	USBLS	5/07
Non-Retail Sales Workers	Alabama	Y	42130 FQ	56330 MW	81560 TQ	USBLS	5/07
Non-Retail Sales Workers	Birmingham-Hoover MSA, AL	Y	44880 FQ	59800 MW	85550 TQ	USBLS	5/07
Non-Retail Sales Workers	Alaska	Y	38120 FQ	52260 MW	61760 TQ	USBLS	5/07
Non-Retail Sales Workers	Anchorage MSA, AK	Y	38840 FQ	52060 MW	61740 TQ	USBLS	5/07
Non-Retail Sales Workers	Arizona	Y	37600 FQ	55800 MW	74770 TQ	USBLS	5/07
Non-Retail Sales Workers	Flagstaff MSA, AZ	Y	30700 FQ	46890 MW	56900 TQ	USBLS	5/07
Non-Retail Sales Workers	Phoenix-Mesa-Scottsdale MSA, AZ	Y	38500 FQ	56740 MW	78110 TQ	USBLS	5/07
Non-Retail Sales Workers	Tucson MSA, AZ	Y	32540 FQ	54200 MW	64110 TQ	USBLS	5/07
Non-Retail Sales Workers	Arkansas	Y	40970 FQ	54670 MW	72750 TQ	USBLS	5/07
Non-Retail Sales Workers	Fort Smith MSA, AR-OK	Y	48700 FQ	59580 MW	81560 TQ	USBLS	5/07
Non-Retail Sales Workers	Jonesboro MSA, AR	Y	27180 FQ	48560 MW	63750 TQ	USBLS	5/07
Non-Retail Sales Workers	Little Rock-North Little Rock MSA, AR	Y	39520 FQ	54740 MW	81280 TQ	USBLS	5/07
Non-Retail Sales Workers	California	H	25.26 FQ	33.16 MW	45.94 TQ	CABLS	1/08-3/08
Non-Retail Sales Workers	Fresno MSA, CA	H	20.97 FQ	27.08 MW	34.54 TQ	CABLS	1/08-3/08
Non-Retail Sales Workers	Los Angeles-Long Beach-Glendale PMSA, CA	H	25.00 FQ	32.45 MW	43.72 TQ	CABLS	1/08-3/08
Non-Retail Sales Workers	Oakland-Fremont-Hayward MSA, CA	H	27.37 FQ	35.14 MW	45.65 TQ	CABLS	1/08-3/08
Non-Retail Sales Workers	Riverside-San Bernardino-Ontario MSA, CA	H	23.91 FQ	30.45 MW	42.05 TQ	CABLS	1/08-3/08
Non-Retail Sales Workers	Sacramento-Arden Arcade-Roseville MSA, CA	H	25.27 FQ	31.14 MW	40.21 TQ	CABLS	1/08-3/08
Non-Retail Sales Workers	San Diego-Carlsbad-San Marcos MSA, CA	H	24.35 FQ	31.92 MW	41.43 TQ	CABLS	1/08-3/08
Non-Retail Sales Workers	San Francisco-San Mateo-Redwood PMSA, CA	H	27.97 FQ	38.22 MW	52.25 TQ	CABLS	1/08-3/08
Non-Retail Sales Workers	San Jose-Sunnyvale-Santa Clara MSA, CA	H	29.24 FQ	42.98 MW	60.94 TQ	CABLS	1/08-3/08
Non-Retail Sales Workers	Santa Ana-Anaheim-Irvine PMSA, CA	Y	53170 FQ	72940 MW	101900 TQ	USBLS	5/07
Non-Retail Sales Workers	Colorado	Y	52720 FQ	68770 MW	98850 TQ	USBLS	5/07
Non-Retail Sales Workers	Colorado Springs MSA, CO	Y	40510 FQ	54600 MW	73230 TQ	USBLS	5/07
Non-Retail Sales Workers	Denver-Aurora MSA, CO	Y	56890 FQ	74010 MW	104960 TQ	USBLS	5/07
Non-Retail Sales Workers	Connecticut	H	24.13 AE	33.73 MW		CTBLS	1/08-3/08
Non-Retail Sales Workers	Bridgeport-Stamford-Norwalk MSA, CT	Y	56170 FQ	67600 MW	93850 TQ	USBLS	5/07
Non-Retail Sales Workers	Danbury MSA, CT	Y	61960 FQ	76660 MW	93010 TQ	USBLS	5/07
Non-Retail Sales Workers	Hartford-West Hartford-East Hartford MSA, CT	Y	60320 FQ	78310 MW	96290 TQ	USBLS	5/07

AE Average entry wage	**AW** Average wage paid	**FQ** First quartile wage	**LO** Lowest wage paid	**MTC** Median total compensation	**TCC** Total cash compensation
AER Average entry range	**AWR** Average wage range	**H** Hourly	**LR** Low end range	**MW** Median wage paid	**TQ** Third quartile wage
AEX Average experienced wage	**AXR** Average experienced range	**HI** Highest wage paid	**M** Monthly	**MWR** Median wage range	**W** Weekly
ATC Average total compensation	**D** Daily	**HR** High end range	**MCC** Median cash compensation	**S** See annotated source	**Y** Yearly

First-Line Supervisor/Manager

Occupation/Type/Industry	Location	Per	Low	Mid	High	Source	Date
Non-Retail Sales Workers	Delaware	Y	53330 FQ	71260 MW	96130 TQ	USBLS	5/07
Non-Retail Sales Workers	Wilmington PMSA, DE-MD-NJ	Y	54950 FQ	72850 MW	96520 TQ	USBLS	5/07
Non-Retail Sales Workers	District of Columbia	Y	51030 FQ	62580 MW	80580 TQ	USBLS	5/07
Non-Retail Sales Workers	Washington-Arlington-Alexandria MSA; DC-VA-MD-WV	Y	55790 FQ	75620 MW	110520 TQ	USBLS	5/07
Non-Retail Sales Workers	Florida	Y	49690 FQ	65130 MW	89050 TQ	USBLS	5/07
Non-Retail Sales Workers	Cape Coral-Fort Myers MSA, FL	Y	43600 FQ	56250 MW	74500 TQ	USBLS	5/07
Non-Retail Sales Workers	Fort Lauderdale-Pompano Beach-Deerfield Beach PMSA, FL	Y	52930 FQ	66340 MW	90830 TQ	USBLS	5/07
Non-Retail Sales Workers	Jacksonville MSA, FL	Y	44960 FQ	61620 MW	86530 TQ	USBLS	5/07
Non-Retail Sales Workers	Miami-Fort Lauderdale-Miami Beach MSA, FL	Y	51940 FQ	67490 MW	94190 TQ	USBLS	5/07
Non-Retail Sales Workers	Orlando-Kissimmee MSA, FL	Y	49590 FQ	68970 MW	92120 TQ	USBLS	5/07
Non-Retail Sales Workers	Pensacola-Ferry Pass-Brent MSA, FL	Y	52550 FQ	60890 MW	76470 TQ	USBLS	5/07
Non-Retail Sales Workers	Tampa-St. Petersburg-Clearwater MSA, FL	Y	50190 FQ	67090 MW	86740 TQ	USBLS	5/07
Non-Retail Sales Workers	West Palm Beach-Boca Raton-Boynton Beach PMSA, FL	Y	50890 FQ	62170 MW	91820 TQ	USBLS	5/07
Non-Retail Sales Workers	Georgia	Y	45290 FQ	58850 MW	86160 TQ	USBLS	5/07
Non-Retail Sales Workers	Atlanta-Sandy Springs-Marietta MSA, GA	Y	47230 FQ	62100 MW	91580 TQ	USBLS	5/07
Non-Retail Sales Workers	Hawaii	Y	33500 FQ	55750 MW	75130 TQ	USBLS	5/07
Non-Retail Sales Workers	Honolulu MSA, HI	Y	34180 FQ	55540 MW	74990 TQ	USBLS	5/07
Non-Retail Sales Workers	Idaho	Y	41230 FQ	49080 MW	61380 TQ	USBLS	5/07
Non-Retail Sales Workers	Boise City-Nampa MSA, ID	Y	39960 FQ	45740 MW	54930 TQ	USBLS	5/07
Non-Retail Sales Workers	Idaho Falls MSA, ID	Y	42570 FQ	50380 MW	61240 TQ	USBLS	5/07
Non-Retail Sales Workers	Illinois	Y	53580 FQ	74900 MW	109190 TQ	USBLS	5/07
Non-Retail Sales Workers	Chicago-Naperville-Joliet MSA, IL-IN-WI	Y	55660 FQ	80610 MW	117210 TQ	USBLS	5/07
Non-Retail Sales Workers	Indiana	Y	49050 FQ	63180 MW	93130 TQ	USBLS	5/07
Non-Retail Sales Workers	Elkhart-Goshen MSA, IN	Y	37960 FQ	58620 MW	93490 TQ	USBLS	5/07
Non-Retail Sales Workers	Gary PMSA, IN	Y	45450 FQ	57620 MW	95510 TQ	USBLS	5/07
Non-Retail Sales Workers	Indianapolis-Carmel MSA, IN	Y	54310 FQ	69910 MW	100560 TQ	USBLS	5/07
Non-Retail Sales Workers	Iowa	Y	48520 FQ	61460 MW	83220 TQ	USBLS	5/07
Non-Retail Sales Workers	Des Moines-West Des Moines MSA, IA	Y	55740 FQ	78170 MW	127390 TQ	USBLS	5/07
Non-Retail Sales Workers	Dubuque MSA, IA	Y	44450 FQ	56640 MW	68030 TQ	USBLS	5/07
Non-Retail Sales Workers	Kansas	Y	44090 FQ	58920 MW	86090 TQ	USBLS	5/07
First-Line Supervisor/Manager	Topeka MSA, KS	Y	43170 FQ	60300 MW	86600 TQ	USBLS	5/07
Non-Retail Sales Workers	Wichita MSA, KS	Y	43270 FQ	55270 MW	74650 TQ	USBLS	5/07
Non-Retail Sales Workers	Kentucky	Y	35553 FQ	52559 MW	69831 TQ	KYBLS	2008
Non-Retail Sales Workers	Bowling Green MSA, KY	Y	27730 FQ	37150 MW	55590 TQ	USBLS	5/07
Non-Retail Sales Workers	Lexington-Fayette MSA, KY	Y	43570 FQ	55640 MW	65160 TQ	USBLS	5/07
Non-Retail Sales Workers	Louisville-Jefferson County MSA, KY-IN	Y	41050 FQ	54820 MW	75770 TQ	USBLS	5/07
Non-Retail Sales Workers	Louisiana	H	18.35 FQ	26.14 MW	32.94 TQ	LABLS	1/08-3/08
Non-Retail Sales Workers	Baton Rouge MSA, LA	Y	35310 FQ	52380 MW	65250 TQ	USBLS	5/07
Non-Retail Sales Workers	Lake Charles MSA, LA	Y	38400 FQ	46520 MW	58600 TQ	USBLS	5/07
Non-Retail Sales Workers	New Orleans-Metairie-Kenner MSA, LA	Y	41210 FQ	59650 MW	78410 TQ	USBLS	5/07
Non-Retail Sales Workers	Maine	Y	36620 FQ	55220 MW	72480 TQ	USBLS	5/07
Non-Retail Sales Workers	Lewiston-Auburn MSA, ME	Y	39230 FQ	46510 MW	58930 TQ	USBLS	5/07
Non-Retail Sales Workers	Portland-South Portland-Biddeford MSA, ME	Y	45300 FQ	60590 MW	82840 TQ	USBLS	5/07
Non-Retail Sales Workers	Maryland	Y		70875 MW		MDBLS	3/08
Non-Retail Sales Workers	Baltimore-Towson MSA, MD	Y	55230 FQ	71760 MW	97860 TQ	USBLS	5/07
Non-Retail Sales Workers	Bethesda-Gaithersburg-Frederick PMSA, MD	Y	52810 FQ	66840 MW	109370 TQ	USBLS	5/07
Non-Retail Sales Workers	Cumberland MSA, MD-WV	Y	53110 FQ	62360 MW	75950 TQ	USBLS	5/07
Non-Retail Sales Workers	Massachusetts	Y	55580 FQ	74110 MW	102920 TQ	USBLS	5/07
Non-Retail Sales Workers	Boston-Cambridge-Quincy NECTA, MA	Y	59500 FQ	81130 MW	108880 TQ	USBLS	5/07
Non-Retail Sales Workers	Worcester MSA, MA-CT	Y	49600 FQ	64880 MW	88410 TQ	USBLS	5/07
Non-Retail Sales Workers	Michigan	Y	53200 FQ	68180 MW	94910 TQ	USBLS	5/07
Non-Retail Sales Workers	Detroit-Warren-Livonia MSA, MI	Y	56280 FQ	74380 MW	102650 TQ	USBLS	5/07

AE Average entry wage	**AW** Average wage paid	**FQ** First quartile wage	**LO** Lowest wage paid	**MTC** Median total compensation	**TCC** Total cash compensation
AER Average entry range	**AWR** Average wage range	**H** Hourly	**LR** Low end range	**MW** Median wage paid	**TQ** Third quartile wage
AEX Average experienced wage	**AXR** Average experienced range	**HI** Highest wage paid	**M** Monthly	**MWR** Median wage range	**W** Weekly
ATC Average total compensation	**D** Daily	**HR** High end range	**MCC** Median cash compensation	**S** See annotated source	**Y** Yearly

Occupation/Type/Industry	Location	Per	Low	Mid	High	Source	Date
First-Line Supervisor/Manager							
Non-Retail Sales Workers	Grand Rapids-Wyoming MSA, MI	Y	50480 FQ	66700 MW	84530 TQ	USBLS	5/07
Non-Retail Sales Workers	Warren-Troy-Farmington Hills PMSA, MI	Y	56830 FQ	75870 MW	106770 TQ	USBLS	5/07
Non-Retail Sales Workers	Minnesota	Y	57535 FQ	76988 MW	105039 TQ	MNBLS	10/08-12/08
Non-Retail Sales Workers	Duluth-Superior MSA, MN-WI	Y	45308 FQ	57870 MW	77872 TQ	MNBLS	10/08-12/08
Non-Retail Sales Workers	Minneapolis-Saint Paul MSA, MN-WI	Y	60564 FQ	80687 MW	109297 TQ	MNBLS	10/08-12/08
Non-Retail Sales Workers	Rochester MSA, MN	Y	56820 FQ	65981 MW	89392 TQ	MNBLS	10/08-12/08
Non-Retail Sales Workers	Mississippi	Y	43590 FQ	56540 MW	72000 TQ	USBLS	5/07
Non-Retail Sales Workers	Jackson MSA, MS	Y	49340 FQ	58420 MW	78220 TQ	USBLS	5/07
Non-Retail Sales Workers	Missouri	Y	49290 FQ	62910 MW	90040 TQ	USBLS	5/07
Non-Retail Sales Workers	Jefferson City MSA, MO	Y	48140 FQ	63710 MW	107940 TQ	USBLS	5/07
Non-Retail Sales Workers	Kansas City MSA, MO-KS	Y	52030 FQ	71110 MW	100610 TQ	USBLS	5/07
Non-Retail Sales Workers	St. Louis MSA, MO-IL	Y	52060 FQ	64270 MW	90460 TQ	USBLS	5/07
Non-Retail Sales Workers	Montana	Y	38820 FQ	53270 MW	62700 TQ	USBLS	5/07
Non-Retail Sales Workers	Billings MSA, MT	Y	39930 FQ	52560 MW	61750 TQ	USBLS	5/07
Non-Retail Sales Workers	Great Falls MSA, MT	Y	26600 FQ	31260 MW	39900 TQ	USBLS	5/07
Non-Retail Sales Workers	Nebraska	Y	46020 FQ	61800 MW	85040 TQ	USBLS	5/07
Non-Retail Sales Workers	Omaha-Council Bluffs MSA, NE-IA	Y	49850 FQ	63740 MW	85890 TQ	USBLS	5/07
Non-Retail Sales Workers	Nevada	H	20.62 FQ	29.54 MW	43.69 TQ	NVBLS	5/08
Non-Retail Sales Workers	Las Vegas-Paradise MSA, NV	H	20.83 FQ	30.48 MW	46.48 TQ	NVBLS	5/08
Non-Retail Sales Workers	New Hampshire	H	22.16 AE	33.45 MW	43.79 AEX	NHBLS	6/08
Non-Retail Sales Workers	Manchester MSA, NH	Y	54000 FQ	63310 MW	72490 TQ	USBLS	5/07
Non-Retail Sales Workers	Nashua NECTA, NH-MA	Y	56880 FQ	74080 MW	94150 TQ	USBLS	5/07
Non-Retail Sales Workers	New Jersey	Y	63680 FQ	85720 MW	119370 TQ	USBLS	5/07
Non-Retail Sales Workers	Camden PMSA, NJ	Y	59920 FQ	80280 MW	117510 TQ	USBLS	5/07
Non-Retail Sales Workers	Edison PMSA, NJ	Y	66020 FQ	91090 MW	120770 TQ	USBLS	5/07
Non-Retail Sales Workers	Newark-Union PMSA, NJ-PA	Y	65170 FQ	89500 MW	126670 TQ	USBLS	5/07
Non-Retail Sales Workers	New Mexico	Y	36580 FQ	52050 MW	60620 TQ	USBLS	5/07
Non-Retail Sales Workers	Albuquerque MSA, NM	Y	40460 FQ	52610 MW	60780 TQ	USBLS	5/07
Non-Retail Sales Workers	New York	Y	61490 FQ	85540 MW	125020 TQ	USBLS	5/07
Non-Retail Sales Workers	Albany-Schenectady-Troy MSA, NY	Y	51520 FQ	67660 MW	94550 TQ	USBLS	5/07
Non-Retail Sales Workers	Binghamton MSA, NY	Y	45970 FQ	68460 MW	115230 TQ	USBLS	5/07
Non-Retail Sales Workers	Buffalo-Niagara Falls MSA, NY	Y	52410 FQ	66110 MW	97090 TQ	USBLS	5/07
Non-Retail Sales Workers	Nassau-Suffolk PMSA, NY	Y	60700 FQ	85700 MW	120900 TQ	USBLS	5/07
Non-Retail Sales Workers	New York-Northern New Jersey-Long Island MSA, NY-NJ-PA	Y	66240 FQ	91640 MW	128560 TQ	USBLS	5/07
Non-Retail Sales Workers	North Carolina	Y	43320 FQ	61200 MW	90360 TQ	USBLS	5/07
Non-Retail Sales Workers	Charlotte-Gastonia-Concord MSA, NC-SC	Y	47520 FQ	68750 MW	95730 TQ	USBLS	5/07
Non-Retail Sales Workers	Raleigh-Cary MSA, NC	Y	43530 FQ	67670 MW	103370 TQ	USBLS	5/07
Non-Retail Sales Workers	North Dakota	Y	32330 FQ	46980 MW	61360 TQ	USBLS	5/07
Non-Retail Sales Workers	Fargo MSA, ND-MN	Y	44090 FQ	50880 MW	72710 TQ	USBLS	5/07
Non-Retail Sales Workers	Ohio	Y	53200 FQ	68140 MW	95050 TQ	USBLS	5/07
Non-Retail Sales Workers	Cincinnati-Middletown MSA, OH-KY-IN	Y	56530 FQ	73590 MW	102080 TQ	USBLS	5/07
Non-Retail Sales Workers	Cleveland-Elyria-Mentor MSA, OH	Y	52040 FQ	70260 MW	98990 TQ	USBLS	5/07
Non-Retail Sales Workers	Columbus MSA, OH	Y	53110 FQ	69610 MW	92620 TQ	USBLS	5/07
Non-Retail Sales Workers	Dayton MSA, OH	Y	51380 FQ	67660 MW	92750 TQ	USBLS	5/07
Non-Retail Sales Workers	Oklahoma	Y	32080 FQ	48180 MW	67900 TQ	USBLS	5/07
Non-Retail Sales Workers	Oklahoma City MSA, OK	Y	34140 FQ	51670 MW	77860 TQ	USBLS	5/07
Non-Retail Sales Workers	Tulsa MSA, OK	Y	31660 FQ	45640 MW	61250 TQ	USBLS	5/07
Non-Retail Sales Workers	Oregon	H	22.86 FQ	30.95 MW	45.61 TQ	ORBLS	5/08
Non-Retail Sales Workers	Portland-Vancouver-Beaverton MSA, OR-WA	Y	49720 FQ	66800 MW	100100 TQ	USBLS	5/07
Non-Retail Sales Workers	Pennsylvania	Y	53820 FQ	72960 MW	106360 TQ	USBLS	5/07
Non-Retail Sales Workers	Allentown-Bethlehem-Easton MSA, PA-NJ	Y	44850 FQ	65190 MW	98220 TQ	USBLS	5/07
Non-Retail Sales Workers	Erie MSA, PA	Y	55100 FQ	69720 MW	100990 TQ	USBLS	5/07
Non-Retail Sales Workers	Philadelphia-Camden-Wilmington MSA, PA-NJ-DE-MD	Y	58390 FQ	80800 MW	119910 TQ	USBLS	5/07
Non-Retail Sales Workers	Pittsburgh MSA, PA	Y	52520 FQ	71300 MW	96910 TQ	USBLS	5/07
Non-Retail Sales Workers	Rhode Island	Y	60030 FQ	76630 MW	103270 TQ	USBLS	5/07

AE Average entry wage	**AW** Average wage paid	**FQ** First quartile wage	**LO** Lowest wage paid	**MTC** Median total compensation	**TCC** Total cash compensation
AER Average entry range	**AWR** Average wage range	**H** Hourly	**LR** Low end range	**MW** Median wage paid	**TQ** Third quartile wage
AEX Average experienced wage	**AXR** Average experienced range	**HI** Highest wage paid	**M** Monthly	**MWR** Median wage range	**W** Weekly
ATC Average total compensation	**D** Daily	**HR** High end range	**MCC** Median cash compensation	**S** See annotated source	**Y** Yearly

Occupation/Type/Industry	Location	Per	Low	Mid	High	Source	Date
First-Line Supervisor/Manager							
Non-Retail Sales Workers	Providence-Fall River-Warwick MSA, RI-MA	Y	54590 FQ	70120 MW	97740 TQ	USBLS	5/07
Non-Retail Sales Workers	South Carolina	Y	41920 FQ	56860 MW	77980 TQ	USBLS	5/07
Non-Retail Sales Workers	Charleston-North Charleston MSA, SC	Y	43270 FQ	59250 MW	80320 TQ	USBLS	5/07
Non-Retail Sales Workers	Columbia MSA, SC	Y	41840 FQ	56790 MW	78160 TQ	USBLS	5/07
Non-Retail Sales Workers	South Dakota	Y	54855 FQ	69467 MW	90925 TQ	SDBLS	7/08-9/08
Non-Retail Sales Workers	Sioux Falls MSA, SD	Y	58998 FQ	76060 MW	98235 TQ	SDBLS	7/08-9/08
Non-Retail Sales Workers	Tennessee	Y	43900 FQ	61030 MW	87900 TQ	USBLS	5/07
Non-Retail Sales Workers	Memphis MSA, TN-MS-AR	Y	38530 FQ	61960 MW	80740 TQ	USBLS	5/07
Non-Retail Sales Workers	Nashville-Davidson-Murfreesboro MSA, TN	Y	48690 FQ	66360 MW	98320 TQ	USBLS	5/07
Non-Retail Sales Workers	Texas	Y	48280 FQ	64600 MW	92320 TQ	USBLS	5/07
Non-Retail Sales Workers	Austin-Round Rock MSA, TX	Y	52970 FQ	69610 MW	101670 TQ	USBLS	5/07
Non-Retail Sales Workers	Beaumont-Port Arthur MSA, TX	Y	51450 FQ	60860 MW	82180 TQ	USBLS	5/07
Non-Retail Sales Workers	Corpus Christi MSA, TX	Y	43760 FQ	54550 MW	64240 TQ	USBLS	5/07
Non-Retail Sales Workers	Dallas-Fort Worth-Arlington MSA, TX	Y	51300 FQ	72460 MW	101550 TQ	USBLS	5/07
Non-Retail Sales Workers	El Paso MSA, TX	Y	34350 FQ	51010 MW	65030 TQ	USBLS	5/07
Non-Retail Sales Workers	Houston-Sugar Land-Baytown MSA, TX	Y	52210 FQ	68440 MW	92310 TQ	USBLS	5/07
Non-Retail Sales Workers	San Antonio MSA, TX	Y	44240 FQ	59960 MW	85700 TQ	USBLS	5/07
Non-Retail Sales Workers	Utah	Y	41010 FQ	55140 MW	77650 TQ	USBLS	5/07
Non-Retail Sales Workers	Salt Lake City MSA, UT	Y	42320 FQ	58560 MW	85890 TQ	USBLS	5/07
Non-Retail Sales Workers	Vermont	Y	40320 FQ	59060 MW	79670 TQ	USBLS	5/07
Non-Retail Sales Workers	Burlington-South Burlington MSA, VT	Y	46270 FQ	62530 MW	89610 TQ	USBLS	5/07
Non-Retail Sales Workers	Virginia	Y	55220 FQ	76020 MW	107780 TQ	USBLS	5/07
Non-Retail Sales Workers	Richmond MSA, VA	Y	54550 FQ	77010 MW	103450 TQ	USBLS	5/07
Non-Retail Sales Workers	Virginia Beach-Norfolk-Newport News MSA, VA-NC	Y	55750 FQ	71960 MW	107830 TQ	USBLS	5/07
Non-Retail Sales Workers	Washington	H	26.43 FQ	34.67 MW	48.79 TQ	WABLS	3/08
Non-Retail Sales Workers	Olympia MSA, WA	Y	48010 FQ	57400 MW	69760 TQ	USBLS	5/07
Non-Retail Sales Workers	Seattle-Tacoma-Bellevue MSA, WA	Y	56830 FQ	76820 MW	106130 TQ	USBLS	5/07
Non-Retail Sales Workers	Spokane MSA, WA	Y	53790 FQ	64680 MW	86230 TQ	USBLS	5/07
Non-Retail Sales Workers	West Virginia	Y	47373 FQ	60020 MW	80240 TQ	WVBLS	7/08-9/08
Non-Retail Sales Workers	Charleston MSA, WV	Y	32770 FQ	55230 MW	75290 TQ	USBLS	5/07
Non-Retail Sales Workers	Wisconsin	Y	51980 FQ	67430 MW	92550 TQ	USBLS	5/07
Non-Retail Sales Workers	Appleton MSA, WI	Y	53610 FQ	73310 MW	101550 TQ	USBLS	5/07
Non-Retail Sales Workers	Green Bay MSA, WI	Y	52710 FQ	64020 MW	81330 TQ	USBLS	5/07
Non-Retail Sales Workers	Milwaukee-Waukesha-West Allis MSA, WI	Y	59460 FQ	76450 MW	111070 TQ	USBLS	5/07
Non-Retail Sales Workers	Wyoming	Y	33833 FQ	44487 MW	58254 TQ	WYBLS	9/08
Non-Retail Sales Workers	Cheyenne MSA, WY	Y	40388 FQ	45090 MW	49912 TQ	WYBLS	9/08
Non-Retail Sales Workers	Puerto Rico	Y	27980 FQ	36040 MW	55120 TQ	USBLS	
Non-Retail Sales Workers	San Juan-Caguas-Guaynabo MSA, PR	Y	28060 FQ	36140 MW	56150 TQ	USBLS	5/07
Non-Retail Sales Workers	Virgin Islands	Y	34510 FQ	43360 MW	54380 TQ	USBLS	5/07
Non-Retail Sales Workers	Guam	Y	23360 FQ	31470 MW	41540 TQ	USBLS	5/07
Office and Administrative Support Workers	Alabama	Y	30850 FQ	39500 MW	51090 TQ	USBLS	5/07
Office and Administrative Support Workers	Birmingham-Hoover MSA, AL	Y	33160 FQ	42480 MW	54170 TQ	USBLS	5/07
Office and Administrative Support Workers	Alaska	Y	35640 FQ	44790 MW	56830 TQ	USBLS	5/07
Office and Administrative Support Workers	Anchorage MSA, AK	Y	35200 FQ	43620 MW	55250 TQ	USBLS	5/07
Office and Administrative Support Workers	Arizona	Y	34100 FQ	42860 MW	54690 TQ	USBLS	5/07
Office and Administrative Support Workers	Phoenix-Mesa-Scottsdale MSA, AZ	Y	35010 FQ	44380 MW	56800 TQ	USBLS	5/07
Office and Administrative Support Workers	Tucson MSA, AZ	Y	33170 FQ	40100 MW	49650 TQ	USBLS	5/07
Office and Administrative Support Workers	Arkansas	Y	28210 FQ	36030 MW	46720 TQ	USBLS	5/07
Office and Administrative Support Workers	Jonesboro MSA, AR	Y	25120 FQ	31440 MW	42920 TQ	USBLS	5/07
Office and Administrative Support Workers	Little Rock-North Little Rock MSA, AR	Y	30930 FQ	39650 MW	50180 TQ	USBLS	5/07
Office and Administrative Support Workers	California	H	18.77 FQ	23.94 MW	30.45 TQ	CABLS	1/08-3/08
Office and Administrative Support Workers	Los Angeles-Long Beach-Glendale PMSA, CA	H	18.58 FQ	23.84 MW	30.39 TQ	CABLS	1/08-3/08
Office and Administrative Support Workers	Oakland-Fremont-Hayward MSA, CA	H	20.41 FQ	26.26 MW	32.38 TQ	CABLS	1/08-3/08
Office and Administrative Support Workers	Riverside-San Bernardino-Ontario MSA, CA	H	17.68 FQ	22.26 MW	27.30 TQ	CABLS	1/08-3/08

AE	Average entry wage	AW	Average wage paid	FQ	First quartile wage	LO	Lowest wage paid	MTC	Median total compensation	TCC	Total cash compensation
AER	Average entry range	AWR	Average wage range	H	Hourly	LR	Low end range	MW	Median wage paid	TQ	Third quartile wage
AEX	Average experienced wage	AXR	Average experienced range	HI	Highest wage paid	M	Monthly	MWR	Median wage range	W	Weekly
ATC	Average total compensation	D	Daily	HR	High end range	MCC	Median cash compensation	S	See annotated source	Y	Yearly

First-Line Supervisor/Manager

Occupation/Type/Industry	Location	Per	Low	Mid	High	Source	Date
Office and Administrative Support Workers	Sacramento-Arden Arcade-Roseville MSA, CA	H	20.18 FQ	26.23 MW	33.78 TQ	CABLS	1/08-3/08
Office and Administrative Support Workers	San Diego-Carlsbad-San Marcos MSA, CA	H	18.40 FQ	23.11 MW	29.23 TQ	CABLS	1/08-3/08
Office and Administrative Support Workers	San Francisco-San Mateo-Redwood PMSA, CA	H	20.98 FQ	26.49 MW	33.78 TQ	CABLS	1/08-3/08
Office and Administrative Support Workers	San Jose-Sunnyvale-Santa Clara MSA, CA	H	20.31 FQ	26.68 MW	34.26 TQ	CABLS	1/08-3/08
Office and Administrative Support Workers	Santa Ana-Anaheim-Irvine PMSA, CA	Y	40180 FQ	50720 MW	62600 TQ	USBLS	5/07
Office and Administrative Support Workers	Santa Rosa-Petaluma MSA, CA	H	18.35 FQ	22.26 MW	28.22 TQ	CABLS	1/08-3/08
Office and Administrative Support Workers	Stockton MSA, CA	H	17.63 FQ	22.04 MW	27.55 TQ	CABLS	1/08-3/08
Office and Administrative Support Workers	Colorado	Y	35860 FQ	46560 MW	60310 TQ	USBLS	5/07
Office and Administrative Support Workers	Denver-Aurora MSA, CO	Y	38690 FQ	49510 MW	62800 TQ	USBLS	5/07
Office and Administrative Support Workers	Connecticut	H	17.24 AE	23.92 MW		CTBLS	1/08-3/08
Office and Administrative Support Workers	Bridgeport-Stamford-Norwalk MSA, CT	Y	42370 FQ	50680 MW	64070 TQ	USBLS	5/07
Office and Administrative Support Workers	Hartford-West Hartford-East Hartford MSA, CT	Y	39220 FQ	48450 MW	58940 TQ	USBLS	5/07
Office and Administrative Support Workers	Norwich-New London MSA, CT-RI	Y	34460 FQ	41280 MW	51530 TQ	USBLS	5/07
Office and Administrative Support Workers	Waterbury MSA, CT	Y	35480 FQ	44620 MW	57110 TQ	USBLS	5/07
Office and Administrative Support Workers	Delaware	Y	37520 FQ	47070 MW	60670 TQ	USBLS	5/07
Office and Administrative Support Workers	Wilmington PMSA, DE-MD-NJ	Y	39160 FQ	48390 MW	61470 TQ	USBLS	5/07
Office and Administrative Support Workers	District of Columbia	Y	46490 FQ	58390 MW	73260 TQ	USBLS	5/07
Office and Administrative Support Workers	Washington-Arlington-Alexandria MSA, DC-VA-MD-WV	Y	41370 FQ	53400 MW	67850 TQ	USBLS	5/07
Office and Administrative Support Workers	Florida	Y	32690 FQ	42570 MW	55050 TQ	USBLS	5/07
Office and Administrative Support Workers	Fort Lauderdale-Pompano Beach-Deerfield Beach PMSA, FL	Y	35730 FQ	45130 MW	57520 TQ	USBLS	5/07
Office and Administrative Support Workers	Jacksonville MSA, FL	Y	35340 FQ	45620 MW	57370 TQ	USBLS	5/07
Office and Administrative Support Workers	Miami-Fort Lauderdale-Miami Beach MSA, FL	Y	34960 FQ	44550 MW	57050 TQ	USBLS	5/07
Office and Administrative Support Workers	Orlando-Kissimmee MSA, FL	Y	31180 FQ	40860 MW	53800 TQ	USBLS	5/07
Office and Administrative Support Workers	Tampa-St. Petersburg-Clearwater MSA, FL	Y	32800 FQ	42710 MW	54900 TQ	USBLS	5/07
Office and Administrative Support Workers	West Palm Beach-Boca Raton-Boynton Beach PMSA, FL	Y	33970 FQ	43870 MW	57100 TQ	USBLS	5/07
Office and Administrative Support Workers	Georgia	Y	33810 FQ	43020 MW	55860 TQ	USBLS	5/07
Office and Administrative Support Workers	Atlanta-Sandy Springs-Marietta MSA, GA	Y	35750 FQ	45100 MW	58140 TQ	USBLS	5/07
Office and Administrative Support Workers	Augusta-Richmond County MSA, GA-SC	Y	29150 FQ	38810 MW	48410 TQ	USBLS	5/07
Office and Administrative Support Workers	Hawaii	Y	34150 FQ	42470 MW	55300 TQ	USBLS	5/07
Office and Administrative Support Workers	Honolulu MSA, HI	Y	34450 FQ	44070 MW	57560 TQ	USBLS	5/07
Office and Administrative Support Workers	Idaho	Y	29970 FQ	37320 MW	48220 TQ	USBLS	5/07
Office and Administrative Support Workers	Boise City-Nampa MSA, ID	Y	31040 FQ	37750 MW	48680 TQ	USBLS	5/07
Office and Administrative Support Workers	Illinois	Y	35370 FQ	46930 MW	61760 TQ	USBLS	5/07
Office and Administrative Support Workers	Chicago-Naperville-Joliet MSA, IL-IN-WI	Y	37510 FQ	48780 MW	63560 TQ	USBLS	5/07
Office and Administrative Support Workers	Rockford MSA, IL	Y	30010 FQ	40150 MW	55300 TQ	USBLS	5/07
Office and Administrative Support Workers	Indiana	Y	32310 FQ	41070 MW	53170 TQ	USBLS	5/07
Office and Administrative Support Workers	Gary PMSA, IN	Y	30990 FQ	38850 MW	52910 TQ	USBLS	5/07
Office and Administrative Support Workers	Indianapolis-Carmel MSA, IN	Y	34860 FQ	44420 MW	56860 TQ	USBLS	5/07
Office and Administrative Support Workers	Terre Haute MSA, IN	Y	31480 FQ	40490 MW	55930 TQ	USBLS	5/07
Office and Administrative Support Workers	Iowa	Y	33610 FQ	42600 MW	52670 TQ	USBLS	5/07
Office and Administrative Support Workers	Des Moines-West Des Moines MSA, IA	Y	36770 FQ	44770 MW	53580 TQ	USBLS	5/07
Office and Administrative Support Workers	Kansas	Y	29370 FQ	38140 MW	49000 TQ	USBLS	5/07
Office and Administrative Support Workers	Wichita MSA, KS	Y	29150 FQ	36810 MW	49310 TQ	USBLS	5/07
Office and Administrative Support Workers	Kentucky	Y	30753 FQ	39072 MW	49658 TQ	KYBLS	2008
Office and Administrative Support Workers	Lexington-Fayette MSA, KY	Y	30630 FQ	37900 MW	48150 TQ	USBLS	5/07
Office and Administrative Support Workers	Louisville-Jefferson County MSA, KY-IN	Y	32180 FQ	39720 MW	50270 TQ	USBLS	5/07
Office and Administrative Support Workers	Louisiana	H	13.53 FQ	17.26 MW	22.02 TQ	LABLS	1/08-3/08
Office and Administrative Support Workers	Baton Rouge MSA, LA	Y	28210 FQ	35290 MW	44200 TQ	USBLS	5/07
Office and Administrative Support Workers	Lake Charles MSA, LA	Y	25360 FQ	32210 MW	43090 TQ	USBLS	5/07

AE	Average entry wage	AW	Average wage paid	FQ	First quartile wage
AER	Average entry range	AWR	Average wage range	H	Hourly
AEX	Average experienced wage	AXR	Average experienced range	HI	Highest wage paid
ATC	Average total compensation	D	Daily	HR	High end range

LO	Lowest wage paid	MTC	Median total compensation
LR	Low end range	MW	Median wage paid
M	Monthly	MWR	Median wage range
MCC	Median cash compensation	S	See annotated source

TCC	Total cash compensation		
TQ	Third quartile wage		
W	Weekly		
Y	Yearly		

Occupation/Type/Industry	Location	Per	Low	Mid	High	Source	Date
First-Line Supervisor/Manager							
Office and Administrative Support Workers	New Orleans-Metairie-Kenner MSA, LA	Y	29110 FQ	37930 MW	47800 TQ	USBLS	5/07
Office and Administrative Support Workers	Maine	Y	30940 FQ	38420 MW	47860 TQ	USBLS	5/07
Office and Administrative Support Workers	Portland-South Portland-Biddeford MSA, ME	Y	33440 FQ	42040 MW	52320 TQ	USBLS	5/07
Office and Administrative Support Workers	Maryland	Y		48275 MW		MDBLS	3/08
Office and Administrative Support Workers	Baltimore-Towson MSA, MD	Y	37620 FQ	47350 MW	59790 TQ	USBLS	5/07
Office and Administrative Support Workers	Bethesda-Gaithersburg-Frederick PMSA, MD	Y	40470 FQ	50800 MW	63420 TQ	USBLS	5/07
Office and Administrative Support Workers	Massachusetts	Y	39770 FQ	50250 MW	62690 TQ	USBLS	5/07
Office and Administrative Support Workers	Boston-Cambridge-Quincy NECTA, MA	Y	43580 FQ	54300 MW	66510 TQ	USBLS	5/07
Office and Administrative Support Workers	New Bedford MSA, MA	Y	32910 FQ	40280 MW	54670 TQ	USBLS	5/07
Office and Administrative Support Workers	Worcester MSA, MA-CT	Y	36060 FQ	45050 MW	54470 TQ	USBLS	5/07
Office and Administrative Support Workers	Michigan	Y	35740 FQ	46050 MW	59690 TQ	USBLS	5/07
Office and Administrative Support Workers	Detroit-Warren-Livonia MSA, MI	Y	38970 FQ	49640 MW	63570 TQ	USBLS	5/07
Office and Administrative Support Workers	Grand Rapids-Wyoming MSA, MI	Y	35610 FQ	45180 MW	59670 TQ	USBLS	5/07
Office and Administrative Support Workers	Warren-Troy-Farmington Hills PMSA, MI	Y	39300 FQ	50440 MW	64450 TQ	USBLS	5/07
Office and Administrative Support Workers	Minnesota	Y	37041 FQ	46908 MW	59054 TQ	MNBLS	10/08-12/08
Office and Administrative Support Workers	Duluth-Superior MSA, MN-WI	Y	31494 FQ	39071 MW	49677 TQ	MNBLS	10/08-12/08
Office and Administrative Support Workers	Minneapolis-Saint Paul MSA, MN-WI	Y	39852 FQ	49406 MW	61594 TQ	MNBLS	10/08-12/08
Office and Administrative Support Workers	Rochester MSA, MN	Y	34708 FQ	40744 MW	51035 TQ	MNBLS	10/08-12/08
Office and Administrative Support Workers	Mississippi	Y	31730 FQ	40040 MW	50950 TQ	USBLS	5/07
Office and Administrative Support Workers	Jackson MSA, MS	Y	34990 FQ	43620 MW	55010 TQ	USBLS	5/07
Office and Administrative Support Workers	Missouri	Y	33990 FQ	44580 MW	58310 TQ	USBLS	5/07
Office and Administrative Support Workers	Joplin MSA, MO	Y	28950 FQ	38730 MW	49710 TQ	USBLS	5/07
Office and Administrative Support Workers	Kansas City MSA, MO-KS	Y	34980 FQ	44870 MW	57140 TQ	USBLS	5/07
Office and Administrative Support Workers	St. Louis MSA, MO-IL	Y	35920 FQ	46620 MW	60270 TQ	USBLS	5/07
Office and Administrative Support Workers	Montana	Y	30200 FQ	38290 MW	52380 TQ	USBLS	5/07
Office and Administrative Support Workers	Nebraska	Y	33090 FQ	41430 MW	52130 TQ	USBLS	5/07
Office and Administrative Support Workers	Lincoln MSA, NE	Y	34970 FQ	42990 MW	51230 TQ	USBLS	5/07
Office and Administrative Support Workers	Omaha-Council Bluffs MSA, NE-IA	Y	34400 FQ	44190 MW	56090 TQ	USBLS	5/07
Office and Administrative Support Workers	Nevada	H	16.08 FQ	19.86 MW	25.33 TQ	NVBLS	5/08
Office and Administrative Support Workers	Las Vegas-Paradise MSA, NV	H	16.19 FQ	19.69 MW	24.76 TQ	NVBLS	5/08
Office and Administrative Support Workers	New Hampshire	H	15.85 AE	21.77 MW	26.09 AEX	NHBLS	6/08
Office and Administrative Support Workers	Manchester MSA, NH	Y	37270 FQ	49310 MW	61530 TQ	USBLS	5/07
Office and Administrative Support Workers	Nashua NECTA, NH-MA	Y	37390 FQ	46380 MW	56210 TQ	USBLS	5/07
Office and Administrative Support Workers	New Jersey	Y	40120 FQ	49650 MW	61530 TQ	USBLS	5/07
Office and Administrative Support Workers	Camden PMSA, NJ	Y	37880 FQ	47450 MW	59100 TQ	USBLS	5/07
Office and Administrative Support Workers	Edison PMSA, NJ	Y	40180 FQ	49430 MW	61070 TQ	USBLS	5/07
Office and Administrative Support Workers	Newark-Union PMSA, NJ-PA	Y	41130 FQ	50850 MW	63130 TQ	USBLS	5/07
Office and Administrative Support Workers	New Mexico	Y	28840 FQ	36820 MW	47300 TQ	USBLS	5/07
Office and Administrative Support Workers	Albuquerque MSA, NM	Y	30100 FQ	38830 MW	49550 TQ	USBLS	5/07
Office and Administrative Support Workers	New York	Y	40210 FQ	50180 MW	63480 TQ	USBLS	5/07
Office and Administrative Support Workers	Albany-Schenectady-Troy MSA, NY	Y	36380 FQ	45350 MW	58900 TQ	USBLS	5/07
Office and Administrative Support Workers	Buffalo-Niagara Falls MSA, NY	Y	34710 FQ	43050 MW	52490 TQ	USBLS	5/07
Office and Administrative Support Workers	Glens Falls MSA, NY	Y	32780 FQ	38050 MW	50080 TQ	USBLS	5/07
Office and Administrative Support Workers	Nassau-Suffolk PMSA, NY	Y	42880 FQ	51740 MW	62430 TQ	USBLS	5/07
Office and Administrative Support Workers	New York-Northern New Jersey-Long Island MSA, NY-NJ-PA	Y	42810 FQ	52920 MW	65760 TQ	USBLS	5/07
Office and Administrative Support Workers	Syracuse MSA, NY	Y	36880 FQ	45470 MW	56920 TQ	USBLS	5/07
Office and Administrative Support Workers	North Carolina	Y	33190 FQ	41250 MW	51510 TQ	USBLS	5/07
Office and Administrative Support Workers	Charlotte-Gastonia-Concord MSA, NC-SC	Y	34700 FQ	43500 MW	54390 TQ	USBLS	5/07
Office and Administrative Support Workers	Raleigh-Cary MSA, NC	Y	34520 FQ	42660 MW	53050 TQ	USBLS	5/07
Office and Administrative Support Workers	North Dakota	Y	29700 FQ	37280 MW	46880 TQ	USBLS	5/07
Office and Administrative Support Workers	Fargo MSA, ND-MN	Y	30370 FQ	37500 MW	47000 TQ	USBLS	5/07
Office and Administrative Support Workers	Ohio	Y	33510 FQ	42830 MW	54130 TQ	USBLS	5/07
Office and Administrative Support Workers	Cincinnati-Middletown MSA, OH-KY-IN	Y	34290 FQ	43640 MW	55160 TQ	USBLS	5/07
Office and Administrative Support Workers	Cleveland-Elyria-Mentor MSA, OH	Y	34550 FQ	44650 MW	57040 TQ	USBLS	5/07
Office and Administrative Support Workers	Columbus MSA, OH	Y	36450 FQ	45280 MW	56550 TQ	USBLS	5/07

AE Average entry wage	**AW** Average wage paid	**FQ** First quartile wage	**LO** Lowest wage paid	**MTC** Median total compensation	**TCC** Total cash compensation
AER Average entry range	**AWR** Average wage range	**H** Hourly	**LR** Low end range	**MW** Median wage paid	**TQ** Third quartile wage
AEX Average experienced wage	**AXR** Average experienced range	**HI** Highest wage paid	**M** Monthly	**MWR** Median wage range	**W** Weekly
ATC Average total compensation	**D** Daily	**HR** High end range	**MCC** Median cash compensation	**S** See annotated source	**Y** Yearly

First-Line Supervisor/Manager

Occupation/Type/Industry	Location	Per	Low	Mid	High	Source	Date
First-Line Supervisor/Manager							
Office and Administrative Support Workers	Dayton MSA, OH	Y	34640 FQ	43680 MW	54170 TQ	USBLS	5/07
Office and Administrative Support Workers	Oklahoma	Y	27580 FQ	35880 MW	46540 TQ	USBLS	5/07
Office and Administrative Support Workers	Oklahoma City MSA, OK	Y	28770 FQ	37100 MW	47950 TQ	USBLS	5/07
Office and Administrative Support Workers	Tulsa MSA, OK	Y	29820 FQ	38110 MW	48820 TQ	USBLS	5/07
Office and Administrative Support Workers	Oregon	H	17.43 FQ	21.75 MW	27.28 TQ	ORBLS	5/08
Office and Administrative Support Workers	Portland-Vancouver-Beaverton MSA, OR-WA	Y	37790 FQ	46840 MW	58640 TQ	USBLS	5/07
Office and Administrative Support Workers	Pennsylvania	Y	34650 FQ	45190 MW	58920 TQ	USBLS	5/07
Office and Administrative Support Workers	Allentown-Bethlehem-Easton MSA, PA-NJ	Y	36620 FQ	46090 MW	58000 TQ	USBLS	5/07
Office and Administrative Support Workers	Philadelphia-Camden-Wilmington MSA, PA-NJ-DE-MD	Y	38250 FQ	48740 MW	61650 TQ	USBLS	5/07
Office and Administrative Support Workers	Pittsburgh MSA, PA	Y	34180 FQ	44110 MW	58900 TQ	USBLS	5/07
Office and Administrative Support Workers	York-Hanover MSA, PA	Y	31450 FQ	38180 MW	50540 TQ	USBLS	5/07
Office and Administrative Support Workers	Rhode Island	Y	40710 FQ	48250 MW	58090 TQ	USBLS	5/07
Office and Administrative Support Workers	Providence-Fall River-Warwick MSA, RI-MA	Y	39600 FQ	47750 MW	57860 TQ	USBLS	5/07
Office and Administrative Support Workers	South Carolina	Y	31500 FQ	38910 MW	49110 TQ	USBLS	5/07
Office and Administrative Support Workers	Charleston-North Charleston MSA, SC	Y	32540 FQ	40210 MW	51390 TQ	USBLS	5/07
Office and Administrative Support Workers	Columbia MSA, SC	Y	33190 FQ	40010 MW	48950 TQ	USBLS	5/07
Office and Administrative Support Workers	South Dakota	Y	35441 FQ	42179 MW	49922 TQ	SDBLS	7/08-9/08
Office and Administrative Support Workers	Rapid City MSA, SD	Y	34399 FQ	40847 MW	48328 TQ	SDBLS	7/08-9/08
Office and Administrative Support Workers	Sioux Falls MSA, SD	Y	37745 FQ	44612 MW	52068 TQ	SDBLS	7/08-9/08
Office and Administrative Support Workers	Tennessee	Y	29900 FQ	39030 MW	51150 TQ	USBLS	5/07
Office and Administrative Support Workers	Johnson City MSA, TN	Y	29190 FQ	36040 MW	45270 TQ	USBLS	5/07
Office and Administrative Support Workers	Kingsport-Bristol-Bristol MSA, TN-VA	Y	26250 FQ	35050 MW	45930 TQ	USBLS	5/07
Office and Administrative Support Workers	Memphis MSA, TN-MS-AR	Y	31310 FQ	39440 MW	52310 TQ	USBLS	5/07
Office and Administrative Support Workers	Nashville-Davidson-Murfreesboro MSA, TN	Y	33400 FQ	44230 MW	58560 TQ	USBLS	5/07
Office and Administrative Support Workers	Texas	Y	32130 FQ	42680 MW	56620 TQ	USBLS	5/07
Office and Administrative Support Workers	Austin-Round Rock MSA, TX	Y	34130 FQ	46520 MW	61230 TQ	USBLS	5/07
Office and Administrative Support Workers	Dallas-Fort Worth-Arlington MSA, TX	Y	34900 FQ	45770 MW	58510 TQ	USBLS	5/07
Office and Administrative Support Workers	El Paso MSA, TX	Y	28500 FQ	36870 MW	51500 TQ	USBLS	5/07
Office and Administrative Support Workers	Houston-Sugar Land-Baytown MSA, TX	Y	34530 FQ	45330 MW	59620 TQ	USBLS	5/07
Office and Administrative Support Workers	San Antonio MSA, TX	Y	32140 FQ	40800 MW	54230 TQ	USBLS	5/07
Office and Administrative Support Workers	Utah	Y	32260 FQ	39420 MW	49790 TQ	USBLS	5/07
Office and Administrative Support Workers	Salt Lake City MSA, UT	Y	33260 FQ	40380 MW	51080 TQ	USBLS	5/07
Office and Administrative Support Workers	Vermont	Y	37790 FQ	45460 MW	55500 TQ	USBLS	5/07
Office and Administrative Support Workers	Burlington-South Burlington MSA, VT	Y	39660 FQ	47380 MW	57630 TQ	USBLS	5/07
Office and Administrative Support Workers	Virginia	Y	36420 FQ	47660 MW	62940 TQ	USBLS	5/07
Office and Administrative Support Workers	Richmond MSA, VA	Y	39570 FQ	49040 MW	62120 TQ	USBLS	5/07
Office and Administrative Support Workers	Virginia Beach-Norfolk-Newport News MSA, VA-NC	Y	34220 FQ	43650 MW	56560 TQ	USBLS	5/07
Office and Administrative Support Workers	Washington	H	19.09 FQ	23.76 MW	29.57 TQ	WABLS	3/08
Office and Administrative Support Workers	Seattle-Tacoma-Bellevue MSA, WA	Y	41210 FQ	50880 MW	63000 TQ	USBLS	5/07
Office and Administrative Support Workers	West Virginia	Y	27182 FQ	35267 MW	47829 TQ	WVBLS	7/08-9/08
Office and Administrative Support Workers	Charleston MSA, WV	Y	28730 FQ	38230 MW	50900 TQ	USBLS	5/07
Office and Administrative Support Workers	Wisconsin	Y	33750 FQ	43380 MW	54890 TQ	USBLS	5/07
Office and Administrative Support Workers	Milwaukee-Waukesha-West Allis MSA, WI	Y	35800 FQ	45670 MW	57830 TQ	USBLS	5/07
Office and Administrative Support Workers	Wyoming	Y	30135 FQ	39273 MW	51156 TQ	WYBLS	9/08
Office and Administrative Support Workers	Cheyenne MSA, WY	Y	32979 FQ	39907 MW	52799 TQ	WYBLS	9/08
Office and Administrative Support Workers	Puerto Rico	Y	23270 FQ	29420 MW	38580 TQ	USBLS	5/07
Office and Administrative Support Workers	San Juan-Caguas-Guaynabo MSA, PR	Y	24260 FQ	30380 MW	39700 TQ	USBLS	5/07
Office and Administrative Support Workers	Virgin Islands	Y	33640 FQ	38950 MW	47120 TQ	USBLS	5/07
Office and Administrative Support Workers	Guam	Y	27770 FQ	36610 MW	46750 TQ	USBLS	5/07
Personal Service Workers	Alabama	Y	20650 FQ	27990 MW	40880 TQ	USBLS	5/07
Personal Service Workers	Birmingham-Hoover MSA, AL	Y	20570 FQ	34250 MW	45820 TQ	USBLS	5/07
Personal Service Workers	Arizona	Y	27120 FQ	34450 MW	45980 TQ	USBLS	5/07
Personal Service Workers	Phoenix-Mesa-Scottsdale MSA, AZ	Y	27030 FQ	32610 MW	44150 TQ	USBLS	5/07
Personal Service Workers	Tucson MSA, AZ	Y	27460 FQ	42590 MW	48480 TQ	USBLS	5/07
Personal Service Workers	Arkansas	Y	20610 FQ	24320 MW	33880 TQ	USBLS	5/07

AE	Average entry wage	AW	Average wage paid	FQ	First quartile wage
AER	Average entry range	AWR	Average wage range	H	Hourly
AEX	Average experienced wage	AXR	Average experienced range	HI	Highest wage paid
ATC	Average total compensation	D	Daily	HR	High end range

LO	Lowest wage paid	MTC	Median total compensation	TCC	Total cash compensation
LR	Low end range	MW	Median wage paid	TQ	Third quartile wage
M	Monthly	MWR	Median wage range	W	Weekly
MCC	Median cash compensation	S	See annotated source	Y	Yearly

First-Line Supervisor/Manager

Occupation/Type/Industry	Location	Per	Low	Mid	High	Source	Date
Personal Service Workers	Little Rock-North Little Rock MSA, AR	Y	20380 FQ	23680 MW	34090 TQ	USBLS	5/07
Personal Service Workers	California	H	13.72 FQ	17.85 MW	23.68 TQ	CABLS	1/08-3/08
Personal Service Workers	Bakersfield MSA, CA	H	13.76 FQ	15.94 MW	21.61 TQ	CABLS	1/08-3/08
Personal Service Workers	Los Angeles-Long Beach-Glendale PMSA, CA	H	14.63 FQ	18.97 MW	24.48 TQ	CABLS	1/08-3/08
Personal Service Workers	Oakland-Fremont-Hayward MSA, CA	H	14.09 FQ	18.12 MW	25.04 TQ	CABLS	1/08-3/08
Personal Service Workers	Riverside-San Bernardino-Ontario MSA, CA	H	12.78 FQ	15.21 MW	19.72 TQ	CABLS	1/08-3/08
Personal Service Workers	Sacramento-Arden Arcade-Roseville MSA, CA	H	12.44 FQ	16.20 MW	20.25 TQ	CABLS	1/08-3/08
Personal Service Workers	San Diego-Carlsbad-San Marcos MSA, CA	H	14.60 FQ	18.85 MW	23.79 TQ	CABLS	1/08-3/08
Personal Service Workers	San Francisco-San Mateo-Redwood PMSA, CA	H	16.32 FQ	21.35 MW	29.60 TQ	CABLS	1/08-3/08
Personal Service Workers	San Jose-Sunnyvale-Santa Clara MSA, CA	H	12.54 FQ	16.57 MW	23.25 TQ	CABLS	1/08-3/08
Personal Service Workers	Santa Ana-Anaheim-Irvine PMSA, CA	Y	25950 FQ	37420 MW	47860 TQ	USBLS	5/07
Personal Service Workers	Santa Rosa-Petaluma MSA, CA	H	13.75 FQ	19.05 MW	25.65 TQ	CABLS	1/08-3/08
Personal Service Workers	Stockton MSA, CA	H	14.71 FQ	17.93 MW	21.65 TQ	CABLS	1/08-3/08
Personal Service Workers	Colorado	Y	26610 FQ	33340 MW	46760 TQ	USBLS	5/07
Personal Service Workers	Denver-Aurora MSA, CO	Y	26400 FQ	33250 MW	47590 TQ	USBLS	5/07
Personal Service Workers	Connecticut	H	13.39 AE	19.37 MW		CTBLS	1/08-3/08
Personal Service Workers	Bridgeport-Stamford-Norwalk MSA, CT	Y	34080 FQ	42470 MW	50280 TQ	USBLS	5/07
Personal Service Workers	Hartford-West Hartford-East Hartford MSA, CT	Y	27670 FQ	37160 MW	45690 TQ	USBLS	5/07
Personal Service Workers	Delaware	Y	26920 FQ	35090 MW	47350 TQ	USBLS	5/07
Personal Service Workers	Wilmington PMSA, DE-MD-NJ	Y	28080 FQ	35240 MW	46750 TQ	USBLS	5/07
Personal Service Workers	District of Columbia	Y	36550 FQ	50940 MW	64290 TQ	USBLS	5/07
Personal Service Workers	Washington-Arlington-Alexandria MSA, DC-VA-MD-WV	Y	30210 FQ	39360 MW	56430 TQ	USBLS	5/07
Personal Service Workers	Florida	Y	29990 FQ	39010 MW	52220 TQ	USBLS	5/07
Personal Service Workers	Cape Coral-Fort Myers MSA, FL	Y	33140 FQ	39990 MW	52850 TQ	USBLS	5/07
Personal Service Workers	Fort Lauderdale-Pompano Beach-Deerfield Beach PMSA, FL	Y	34250 FQ	44020 MW	54020 TQ	USBLS	5/07
Personal Service Workers	Jacksonville MSA, FL	Y	27710 FQ	35080 MW	48320 TQ	USBLS	5/07
Personal Service Workers	Miami-Fort Lauderdale-Miami Beach MSA, FL	Y	31860 FQ	43970 MW	59050 TQ	USBLS	5/07
Personal Service Workers	Orlando-Kissimmee MSA, FL	Y	34180 FQ	41290 MW	54160 TQ	USBLS	5/07
Personal Service Workers	Sarasota-Bradenton-Venice MSA, FL	Y	31790 FQ	37300 MW	44290 TQ	USBLS	5/07
Personal Service Workers	Tampa-St. Petersburg-Clearwater MSA, FL	Y	27240 FQ	33180 MW	42400 TQ	USBLS	5/07
Personal Service Workers	West Palm Beach-Boca Raton-Boynton Beach PMSA, FL	Y	31200 FQ	40330 MW	56400 TQ	USBLS	5/07
Personal Service Workers	Georgia	Y	23330 FQ	32640 MW	44340 TQ	USBLS	5/07
Personal Service Workers	Atlanta-Sandy Springs-Marietta MSA, GA	Y	24480 FQ	33690 MW	43990 TQ	USBLS	5/07
Personal Service Workers	Augusta-Richmond County MSA, GA-SC	Y	24320 FQ	29130 MW	38810 TQ	USBLS	5/07
Personal Service Workers	Savannah MSA, GA	Y	25770 FQ	43940 MW	51020 TQ	USBLS	5/07
Personal Service Workers	Hawaii	Y	27090 FQ	32990 MW	42130 TQ	USBLS	5/07
Personal Service Workers	Honolulu MSA, HI	Y	26260 FQ	31020 MW	38100 TQ	USBLS	5/07
Personal Service Workers	Idaho	Y	21020 FQ	25370 MW	30370 TQ	USBLS	5/07
Personal Service Workers	Boise City-Nampa MSA, ID	Y	20840 FQ	25880 MW	31430 TQ	USBLS	5/07
Personal Service Workers	Illinois	Y	26060 FQ	33730 MW	46450 TQ	USBLS	5/07
Personal Service Workers	Chicago-Naperville-Joliet MSA, IL-IN-WI	Y	26870 FQ	34680 MW	47120 TQ	USBLS	5/07
Personal Service Workers	Indiana	Y	22720 FQ	28460 MW	35910 TQ	USBLS	5/07
Personal Service Workers	Gary PMSA, IN	Y	21050 FQ	24860 MW	31700 TQ	USBLS	5/07
Personal Service Workers	Indianapolis-Carmel MSA, IN	Y	25220 FQ	30980 MW	41320 TQ	USBLS	5/07
Personal Service Workers	Iowa	Y	25430 FQ	30220 MW	38370 TQ	USBLS	5/07
Personal Service Workers	Des Moines-West Des Moines MSA, IA	Y	27820 FQ	34200 MW	45910 TQ	USBLS	5/07

Occupation/Type/Industry	Location	Per	Low	Mid	High	Source	Date
First-Line Supervisor/Manager							
Personal Service Workers	Waterloo-Cedar Falls MSA, IA	Y	27000 FQ	33310 MW	50790 TQ	USBLS	5/07
Personal Service Workers	Kansas	Y	23540 FQ	28720 MW	37110 TQ	USBLS	5/07
Personal Service Workers	Wichita MSA, KS	Y	22280 FQ	26960 MW	32530 TQ	USBLS	5/07
Personal Service Workers	Kentucky	Y	21113 FQ	26285 MW	33119 TQ	KYBLS	2008
Personal Service Workers	Bowling Green MSA, KY	Y	17750 FQ	26280 MW	37180 TQ	USBLS	5/07
Personal Service Workers	Louisville-Jefferson County MSA, KY-IN	Y	21720 FQ	27050 MW	36170 TQ	USBLS	5/07
Personal Service Workers	Louisiana	H	11.06 FQ	13.87 MW	17.77 TQ	LABLS	1/08-3/08
Personal Service Workers	Baton Rouge MSA, LA	Y	25840 FQ	32510 MW	47850 TQ	USBLS	5/07
Personal Service Workers	Lake Charles MSA, LA	Y	23620 FQ	29270 MW	39160 TQ	USBLS	5/07
Personal Service Workers	New Orleans-Metairie-Kenner MSA, LA	Y	22250 FQ	28060 MW	35760 TQ	USBLS	5/07
Personal Service Workers	Maine	Y	25260 FQ	29290 MW	34530 TQ	USBLS	5/07
Personal Service Workers	Portland-South Portland-Biddeford MSA, ME	Y	26950 FQ	30380 MW	37650 TQ	USBLS	5/07
Personal Service Workers	Maryland	Y		35775 MW		MDBLS	3/08
Personal Service Workers	Baltimore-Towson MSA, MD	Y	28040 FQ	34590 MW	42840 TQ	USBLS	5/07
Personal Service Workers	Bethesda-Gaithersburg-Frederick PMSA, MD	Y	29640 FQ	38760 MW	50680 TQ	USBLS	5/07
Personal Service Workers	Hagerstown-Martinsburg MSA, MD-WV	Y	26250 FQ	32900 MW	44530 TQ	USBLS	5/07
Personal Service Workers	Massachusetts	Y	29260 FQ	35610 MW	45350 TQ	USBLS	5/07
Personal Service Workers	Boston-Cambridge-Quincy NECTA, MA	Y	29820 FQ	37050 MW	50100 TQ	USBLS	5/07
Personal Service Workers	Worcester MSA, MA-CT	Y	28990 FQ	34180 MW	39390 TQ	USBLS	5/07
Personal Service Workers	Michigan	Y	27410 FQ	34260 MW	45620 TQ	USBLS	5/07
Personal Service Workers	Detroit-Warren-Livonia MSA, MI	Y	28250 FQ	34910 MW	45280 TQ	USBLS	5/07
Personal Service Workers	Grand Rapids-Wyoming MSA, MI	Y	25490 FQ	31890 MW	44040 TQ	USBLS	5/07
Personal Service Workers	Warren-Troy-Farmington Hills PMSA, MI	Y	28900 FQ	36550 MW	46650 TQ	USBLS	5/07
Personal Service Workers	Minnesota	Y	27080 FQ	33082 MW	41143 TQ	MNBLS	10/08-12/08
Personal Service Workers	Duluth-Superior MSA, MN-WI	Y	19207 FQ	24257 MW	29297 TQ	MNBLS	10/08-12/08
Personal Service Workers	Minneapolis-Saint Paul MSA, MN-WI	Y	29746 FQ	35926 MW	44374 TQ	MNBLS	10/08-12/08
Personal Service Workers	Rochester MSA, MN	Y	25619 FQ	35008 MW	46708 TQ	MNBLS	10/08-12/08
Personal Service Workers	Mississippi	Y	22570 FQ	26930 MW	31590 TQ	USBLS	5/07
Personal Service Workers	Jackson MSA, MS	Y	23650 FQ	27280 MW	32210 TQ	USBLS	5/07
Personal Service Workers	Missouri	Y	27440 FQ	33710 MW	42430 TQ	USBLS	5/07
Personal Service Workers	Kansas City MSA, MO-KS	Y	24990 FQ	31520 MW	40920 TQ	USBLS	5/07
Personal Service Workers	St. Louis MSA, MO-IL	Y	29790 FQ	35080 MW	43950 TQ	USBLS	5/07
Personal Service Workers	Montana	Y	21860 FQ	25760 MW	32370 TQ	USBLS	5/07
Personal Service Workers	Billings MSA, MT	Y	23870 FQ	29070 MW	34490 TQ	USBLS	5/07
Personal Service Workers	Nebraska	Y	24490 FQ	31240 MW	38910 TQ	USBLS	5/07
Personal Service Workers	Omaha-Council Bluffs MSA, NE-IA	Y	28390 FQ	33540 MW	45300 TQ	USBLS	5/07
Personal Service Workers	Carson City MSA, NV	H	12.05 FQ	16.35 MW	18.57 TQ	NVBLS	5/08
Personal Service Workers	Las Vegas-Paradise MSA, NV	H	13.33 FQ	16.86 MW	22.27 TQ	NVBLS	5/08
Personal Service Workers	New Hampshire	H	12.64 AE	16.20 MW	19.04 AEX	NHBLS	6/08
Personal Service Workers	Manchester MSA, NH	Y	31880 FQ	35210 MW	39300 TQ	USBLS	5/07
Personal Service Workers	Nashua NECTA, NH-MA	Y	27560 FQ	32540 MW	39750 TQ	USBLS	5/07
Personal Service Workers	Portsmouth MSA, NH-ME	Y	24390 FQ	30840 MW	36560 TQ	USBLS	5/07
Personal Service Workers	New Jersey	Y	33430 FQ	41130 MW	50410 TQ	USBLS	5/07
Personal Service Workers	Camden PMSA, NJ	Y	32460 FQ	42140 MW	50090 TQ	USBLS	5/07
Personal Service Workers	Edison PMSA, NJ	Y	32820 FQ	38990 MW	49120 TQ	USBLS	5/07
Personal Service Workers	Newark-Union PMSA, NJ-PA	Y	34490 FQ	42230 MW	50460 TQ	USBLS	5/07
Personal Service Workers	Ocean City MSA, NJ	Y	36260 FQ	44440 MW	49710 TQ	USBLS	5/07
Personal Service Workers	New Mexico	Y	22990 FQ	29580 MW	36360 TQ	USBLS	5/07
Personal Service Workers	Albuquerque MSA, NM	Y	24850 FQ	33190 MW	39130 TQ	USBLS	5/07
Personal Service Workers	New York	Y	30650 FQ	37100 MW	48190 TQ	USBLS	5/07
Personal Service Workers	Albany-Schenectady-Troy MSA, NY	Y	29270 FQ	34900 MW	52080 TQ	USBLS	5/07
Personal Service Workers	Binghamton MSA, NY	Y	27880 FQ	32870 MW	43030 TQ	USBLS	5/07
Personal Service Workers	Buffalo-Niagara Falls MSA, NY	Y	29470 FQ	35680 MW	45170 TQ	USBLS	5/07
Personal Service Workers	Nassau-Suffolk PMSA, NY	Y	29780 FQ	38190 MW	50300 TQ	USBLS	5/07
Personal Service Workers	New York-Northern New Jersey-Long Island MSA, NY-NJ-PA	Y	32990 FQ	39360 MW	51470 TQ	USBLS	5/07
Personal Service Workers	North Carolina	Y	22180 FQ	29680 MW	39900 TQ	USBLS	5/07

AE	Average entry wage	AW	Average wage paid	FQ	First quartile wage
AER	Average entry range	AWR	Average wage range	H	Hourly
AEX	Average experienced wage	AXR	Average experienced range	HI	Highest wage paid
ATC	Average total compensation	D	Daily	HR	High end range

LO	Lowest wage paid	MTC	Median total compensation
LR	Low end range	MW	Median wage paid
M	Monthly	MWR	Median wage range
MCC	Median cash compensation	S	See annotated source

TCC	Total cash compensation
TQ	Third quartile wage
W	Weekly
Y	Yearly

First-Line Supervisor/Manager

Occupation/Type/Industry	Location	Per	Low	Mid	High	Source	Date
First-Line Supervisor/Manager							
Personal Service Workers	Charlotte-Gastonia-Concord MSA, NC-SC	Y	23400 FQ	32080 MW	41020 TQ	USBLS	5/07
Personal Service Workers	Greensboro-High Point MSA, NC	Y	17490 FQ	20260 MW	34270 TQ	USBLS	5/07
Personal Service Workers	Raleigh-Cary MSA, NC	Y	24550 FQ	28630 MW	39410 TQ	USBLS	5/07
Personal Service Workers	Winston-Salem MSA, NC	Y	21090 FQ	27420 MW	38560 TQ	USBLS	5/07
Personal Service Workers	North Dakota	Y	26050 FQ	30730 MW	37470 TQ	USBLS	5/07
Personal Service Workers	Fargo MSA, ND-MN	Y	26070 FQ	30180 MW	37730 TQ	USBLS	5/07
Personal Service Workers	Ohio	Y	25700 FQ	31910 MW	40840 TQ	USBLS	5/07
Personal Service Workers	Cincinnati-Middletown MSA, OH-KY-IN	Y	26050 FQ	31540 MW	43800 TQ	USBLS	5/07
Personal Service Workers	Cleveland-Elyria-Mentor MSA, OH	Y	25580 FQ	34320 MW	45250 TQ	USBLS	5/07
Personal Service Workers	Columbus MSA, OH	Y	28080 FQ	33350 MW	40700 TQ	USBLS	5/07
Personal Service Workers	Dayton MSA, OH	Y	26480 FQ	31460 MW	42490 TQ	USBLS	5/07
Personal Service Workers	Oklahoma	Y	19410 FQ	24640 MW	34340 TQ	USBLS	5/07
Personal Service Workers	Oklahoma City MSA, OK	Y	21440 FQ	30870 MW	35720 TQ	USBLS	5/07
Personal Service Workers	Tulsa MSA, OK	Y	18010 FQ	20040 MW	24530 TQ	USBLS	5/07
Personal Service Workers	Oregon	H	12.71 FQ	15.71 MW	20.65 TQ	ORBLS	5/08
Personal Service Workers	Portland-Vancouver-Beaverton MSA, OR-WA	Y	29050 FQ	37340 MW	48620 TQ	USBLS	5/07
Personal Service Workers	Pennsylvania	Y	29390 FQ	38740 MW	51730 TQ	USBLS	5/07
Personal Service Workers	Allentown-Bethlehem-Easton MSA, PA-NJ	Y	32470 FQ	37680 MW	51530 TQ	USBLS	5/07
Personal Service Workers	Philadelphia-Camden-Wilmington MSA, PA-NJ-DE-MD	Y	32440 FQ	42800 MW	53460 TQ	USBLS	5/07
Personal Service Workers	Pittsburgh MSA, PA	Y	29560 FQ	37310 MW	46380 TQ	USBLS	5/07
Personal Service Workers	York-Hanover MSA, PA	Y	29570 FQ	35150 MW	40410 TQ	USBLS	5/07
Personal Service Workers	Rhode Island	Y	32070 FQ	40320 MW	50130 TQ	USBLS	5/07
Personal Service Workers	Providence-Fall River-Warwick MSA, RI-MA	Y	30410 FQ	38100 MW	47540 TQ	USBLS	5/07
Personal Service Workers	South Carolina	Y	23660 FQ	30530 MW	38730 TQ	USBLS	5/07
Personal Service Workers	Charleston-North Charleston MSA, SC	Y	23330 FQ	33480 MW	47470 TQ	USBLS	5/07
Personal Service Workers	Columbia MSA, SC	Y	23480 FQ	28050 MW	34410 TQ	USBLS	5/07
Personal Service Workers	Myrtle Beach-Conway-North Myrtle Beach MSA, SC	Y	24950 FQ	34920 MW	38860 TQ	USBLS	5/07
Personal Service Workers	South Dakota	Y	27647 FQ	32188 MW	37870 TQ	SDBLS	7/08-9/08
Personal Service Workers	Sioux Falls MSA, SD	Y	30566 FQ	35357 MW	41049 TQ	SDBLS	7/08-9/08
Personal Service Workers	Tennessee	Y	21090 FQ	26990 MW	34530 TQ	USBLS	5/07
Personal Service Workers	Memphis MSA, TN-MS-AR	Y	25780 FQ	33460 MW	53410 TQ	USBLS	5/07
Personal Service Workers	Nashville-Davidson-Murfreesboro MSA, TN	Y	22670 FQ	27070 MW	34680 TQ	USBLS	5/07
First-Line Supervisor/Manager	Texas	Y	21550 FQ	28920 MW	39610 TQ	USBLS	5/07
Personal Service Workers	Austin-Round Rock MSA, TX	Y	24060 FQ	30180 MW	47240 TQ	USBLS	5/07
Personal Service Workers	Dallas-Fort Worth-Arlington MSA, TX	Y	24680 FQ	33880 MW	44250 TQ	USBLS	5/07
Personal Service Workers	El Paso MSA, TX	Y	18200 FQ	22000 MW	33420 TQ	USBLS	5/07
Personal Service Workers	Houston-Sugar Land-Baytown MSA, TX	Y	22930 FQ	30650 MW	42010 TQ	USBLS	5/07
Personal Service Workers	San Antonio MSA, TX	Y	19940 FQ	24200 MW	31620 TQ	USBLS	5/07
Personal Service Workers	Utah	Y	22560 FQ	29950 MW	38170 TQ	USBLS	5/07
Personal Service Workers	St. George MSA, UT	Y	25550 FQ	31700 MW	38480 TQ	USBLS	5/07
Personal Service Workers	Salt Lake City MSA, UT	Y	22110 FQ	30060 MW	38160 TQ	USBLS	5/07
Personal Service Workers	Vermont	Y	26050 FQ	34920 MW	45950 TQ	USBLS	5/07
Personal Service Workers	Burlington-South Burlington MSA, VT	Y	24510 FQ	32920 MW	45430 TQ	USBLS	5/07
Personal Service Workers	Virginia	Y	27300 FQ	35990 MW	49430 TQ	USBLS	5/07
Personal Service Workers	Richmond MSA, VA	Y	25740 FQ	33700 MW	43440 TQ	USBLS	5/07
Personal Service Workers	Virginia Beach-Norfolk-Newport News MSA, VA-NC	Y	22740 FQ	32500 MW	46080 TQ	USBLS	5/07
Personal Service Workers	Washington	H	15.87 FQ	20.27 MW	25.79 TQ	WABLS	3/08
Personal Service Workers	Seattle-Tacoma-Bellevue MSA, WA	Y	34150 FQ	43450 MW	55310 TQ	USBLS	5/07
Personal Service Workers	West Virginia	Y	23537 FQ	29671 MW	40494 TQ	WVBLS	7/08-9/08
Personal Service Workers	Charleston MSA, WV	Y	28690 FQ	39050 MW	55120 TQ	USBLS	5/07
Personal Service Workers	Huntington-Ashland MSA, WV-KY-OH	Y	18620 FQ	23990 MW	30370 TQ	USBLS	5/07
Personal Service Workers	Wheeling MSA, WV-OH	Y	21690 FQ	28180 MW	36620 TQ	USBLS	5/07
Personal Service Workers	Wisconsin	Y	27350 FQ	32150 MW	40240 TQ	USBLS	5/07

AE	Average entry wage	AW	Average wage paid	FQ	First quartile wage
AER	Average entry range	AWR	Average wage range	H	Hourly
AEX	Average experienced wage	AXR	Average experienced range	HI	Highest wage paid
ATC	Average total compensation	D	Daily	HR	High end range

LO Lowest wage paid   MTC Median total compensation   TCC Total cash compensation
LR Low end range   MW Median wage paid   TQ Third quartile wage
M Monthly   MWR Median wage range   W Weekly
MCC Median cash compensation   S See annotated source   Y Yearly

Occupation/Type/Industry	Location	Per	Low	Mid	High	Source	Date
First-Line Supervisor/Manager							
Personal Service Workers	Milwaukee-Waukesha-West Allis MSA, WI	Y	29780 FQ	36490 MW	49370 TQ	USBLS	5/07
Personal Service Workers	Wyoming	Y	23920 FQ	28745 MW	34176 TQ	WYBLS	9/08
Personal Service Workers	Cheyenne MSA, WY	Y	22096 FQ	24639 MW	29838 TQ	WYBLS	9/08
Personal Service Workers	Puerto Rico	Y	18110 FQ	23820 MW	28850 TQ	USBLS	5/07
Personal Service Workers	San Juan-Caguas-Guaynabo MSA, PR	Y	18050 FQ	23840 MW	28440 TQ	USBLS	5/07
Personal Service Workers	Virgin Islands	Y	27650 FQ	30350 MW	36410 TQ	USBLS	5/07
Personal Service Workers	Guam	Y	17960 FQ	22670 MW	30010 TQ	USBLS	5/07
Police and Detectives	Alabama	Y	40190 FQ	49850 MW	63820 TQ	USBLS	5/07
Police and Detectives	Birmingham-Hoover MSA, AL	Y	44840 FQ	60350 MW	80660 TQ	USBLS	5/07
Police and Detectives	Montgomery MSA, AL	Y	48110 FQ	63870 MW	76280 TQ	USBLS	5/07
Police and Detectives	Alaska	Y	70800 FQ	79310 MW	91840 TQ	USBLS	5/07
Police and Detectives	Anchorage MSA, AK	Y	73810 FQ	83440 MW	95920 TQ	USBLS	5/07
Police and Detectives	Arizona	Y	65250 FQ	75460 MW	87890 TQ	USBLS	5/07
Police and Detectives	Phoenix-Mesa-Scottsdale MSA, AZ	Y	69450 FQ	78690 MW	91120 TQ	USBLS	5/07
Police and Detectives	Tucson MSA, AZ	Y	60900 FQ	70930 MW	90840 TQ	USBLS	5/07
Police and Detectives	Arkansas	Y	35770 FQ	46340 MW	62350 TQ	USBLS	5/07
Police and Detectives	Little Rock-North Little Rock MSA, AR	Y	47630 FQ	59080 MW	70770 TQ	USBLS	5/07
Police and Detectives	California	H	40.44 FQ	47.97 MW	57.26 TQ	CABLS	1/08-3/08
Police and Detectives	Oakland-Fremont-Hayward MSA, CA	H	45.01 FQ	50.06 MW	59.57 TQ	CABLS	1/08-3/08
Police and Detectives	Riverside-San Bernardino-Ontario MSA, CA	H	39.43 FQ	46.82 MW	56.10 TQ	CABLS	1/08-3/08
Police and Detectives	Sacramento-Arden Arcade-Roseville MSA, CA	H	36.52 FQ	41.73 MW	48.77 TQ	CABLS	1/08-3/08
Police and Detectives	San Diego-Carlsbad-San Marcos MSA, CA	H	35.96 FQ	40.49 MW	48.17 TQ	CABLS	1/08-3/08
Police and Detectives	San Francisco-San Mateo-Redwood PMSA, CA	H	45.24 FQ	52.20 MW	60.68 TQ	CABLS	1/08-3/08
Police and Detectives	San Jose-Sunnyvale-Santa Clara MSA, CA	H	44.16 FQ	56.25 MW	68.56 TQ	CABLS	1/08-3/08
Police and Detectives	Santa Ana-Anaheim-Irvine PMSA, CA	Y	92530 FQ	103190 MW	122610 TQ	USBLS	5/07
Police and Detectives	Colorado	Y	72600 FQ	85830 MW	97650 TQ	USBLS	5/07
Police and Detectives	Denver-Aurora MSA, CO	Y	79710 FQ	90910 MW	101510 TQ	USBLS	5/07
Police and Detectives	Fort Collins-Loveland MSA, CO	Y	74800 FQ	82110 MW	93270 TQ	USBLS	5/07
Police and Detectives	Connecticut	H	31.70 AE	37.18 MW		CTBLS	1/08-3/08
Police and Detectives	Bridgeport-Stamford-Norwalk MSA, CT	Y	69630 FQ	77300 MW	85760 TQ	USBLS	5/07
Police and Detectives	Hartford-West Hartford-East Hartford MSA, CT	Y	69590 FQ	76240 MW	83050 TQ	USBLS	5/07
Police and Detectives	Delaware	Y	74370 FQ	87650 MW	98550 TQ	USBLS	5/07
Police and Detectives	Wilmington PMSA, DE-MD-NJ	Y	62130 FQ	80670 MW	94020 TQ	USBLS	5/07
Police and Detectives	District of Columbia	Y	86000 FQ	97450 MW	113960 TQ	USBLS	5/07
Police and Detectives	Washington-Arlington-Alexandria MSA, DC-VA-MD-WV	Y	76480 FQ	92670 MW	109540 TQ	USBLS	5/07
Police and Detectives	Florida	Y	62290 FQ	78160 MW	95980 TQ	USBLS	5/07
Police and Detectives	Fort Lauderdale-Pompano Beach-Deerfield Beach PMSA, FL	Y	87580 FQ	99360 MW	113330 TQ	USBLS	5/07
Police and Detectives	Miami-Fort Lauderdale-Miami Beach MSA, FL	Y	83210 FQ	96560 MW	112180 TQ	USBLS	5/07
Police and Detectives	Orlando-Kissimmee MSA, FL	Y	66530 FQ	75920 MW	87360 TQ	USBLS	5/07
Police and Detectives	Tampa-St. Petersburg-Clearwater MSA, FL	Y	65380 FQ	83530 MW	98360 TQ	USBLS	5/07
Police and Detectives	West Palm Beach-Boca Raton-Boynton Beach PMSA, FL	Y	74470 FQ	90150 MW	103570 TQ	USBLS	5/07
Police and Detectives	Georgia	Y	41360 FQ	52150 MW	63600 TQ	USBLS	5/07
Police and Detectives	Atlanta-Sandy Springs-Marietta MSA, GA	Y	48330 FQ	57810 MW	68670 TQ	USBLS	5/07
Police and Detectives	Hawaii	Y	58700 FQ	65310 MW	75740 TQ	USBLS	5/07
Police and Detectives	Idaho	Y	45720 FQ	58120 MW	76300 TQ	USBLS	5/07
Police and Detectives	Boise City-Nampa MSA, ID	Y	58240 FQ	76130 MW	91860 TQ	USBLS	5/07
Police and Detectives	Coeur d'Alene MSA, ID	Y	44860 FQ	52340 MW	63790 TQ	USBLS	5/07
Police and Detectives	Illinois	Y	71070 FQ	86370 MW	100630 TQ	USBLS	5/07

AE	Average entry wage	AW	Average wage paid	FQ	First quartile wage	LO	Lowest wage paid
AER	Average entry range	AWR	Average wage range	H	Hourly	LR	Low end range
AEX	Average experienced wage	AXR	Average experienced range	HI	Highest wage paid	M	Monthly
ATC	Average total compensation	D	Daily	HR	High end range	MCC	Median cash compensation

MTC	Median total compensation	TCC	Total cash compensation			
MW	Median wage paid	TQ	Third quartile wage			
MWR	Median wage range	W	Weekly			
S	See annotated source	Y	Yearly			

Occupation/Type/Industry	Location	Per	Low	Mid	High	Source	Date
First-Line Supervisor/Manager							
Police and Detectives	Chicago-Naperville-Joliet MSA, IL-IN-WI	Y	72800 FQ	86290 MW	101270 TQ	USBLS	5/07
Police and Detectives	Indiana	Y	51040 FQ	57340 MW	63810 TQ	USBLS	5/07
Police and Detectives	Gary PMSA, IN	Y	44820 FQ	54550 MW	62710 TQ	USBLS	5/07
Police and Detectives	Indianapolis-Carmel MSA, IN	Y	55160 FQ	60580 MW	68210 TQ	USBLS	5/07
Police and Detectives	Iowa	Y	49740 FQ	60020 MW	72340 TQ	USBLS	5/07
Police and Detectives	Des Moines-West Des Moines MSA, IA	Y	64430 FQ	74240 MW	83710 TQ	USBLS	5/07
Police and Detectives	Kansas	Y	44180 FQ	56380 MW	69460 TQ	USBLS	5/07
Police and Detectives	Wichita MSA, KS	Y	44340 FQ	54310 MW	63930 TQ	USBLS	5/07
Police and Detectives	Kentucky	Y	50040 FQ	59130 MW	69260 TQ	KYBLS	2008
Police and Detectives	Louisville-Jefferson County MSA, KY-IN	Y	49960 FQ	56580 MW	68570 TQ	USBLS	5/07
Police and Detectives	Louisiana	H	19.61 FQ	23.50 MW	29.85 TQ	LABLS	1/08-3/08
Police and Detectives	Baton Rouge MSA, LA	Y	39360 FQ	50510 MW	63650 TQ	USBLS	5/07
Police and Detectives	New Orleans-Metairie-Kenner MSA, LA	Y	44560 FQ	51380 MW	84690 TQ	USBLS	5/07
Police and Detectives	Maine	Y	46480 FQ	52720 MW	62570 TQ	USBLS	5/07
Police and Detectives	Bangor MSA, ME	Y	47030 FQ	54240 MW	69140 TQ	USBLS	5/07
Police and Detectives	Portland-South Portland-Biddeford MSA, ME	Y	50000 FQ	57380 MW	67000 TQ	USBLS	5/07
Police and Detectives	Maryland	Y		74150 MW		MDBLS	3/08
Police and Detectives	Baltimore-Towson MSA, MD	Y	63600 FQ	73260 MW	94380 TQ	USBLS	5/07
Police and Detectives	Bethesda-Gaithersburg-Frederick PMSA, MD	Y	66270 FQ	82460 MW	102150 TQ	USBLS	5/07
Police and Detectives	Massachusetts	Y	66400 FQ	77800 MW	92580 TQ	USBLS	5/07
Police and Detectives	Boston-Cambridge-Quincy NECTA, MA	Y	70090 FQ	81900 MW	98240 TQ	USBLS	5/07
Police and Detectives	Worcester MSA, MA-CT	Y	62410 FQ	73260 MW	86200 TQ	USBLS	5/07
Police and Detectives	Michigan	Y	61480 FQ	70140 MW	78850 TQ	USBLS	5/07
Police and Detectives	Ann Arbor MSA, MI	Y	73310 FQ	82050 MW	94520 TQ	USBLS	5/07
Police and Detectives	Detroit-Warren-Livonia MSA, MI	Y	66880 FQ	72850 MW	81500 TQ	USBLS	5/07
Police and Detectives	Grand Rapids-Wyoming MSA, MI	Y	68330 FQ	74330 MW	80450 TQ	USBLS	5/07
Police and Detectives	Warren-Troy-Farmington Hills PMSA, MI	Y	68530 FQ	74990 MW	82630 TQ	USBLS	5/07
Police and Detectives	Minnesota	Y	62463 FQ	74111 MW	83500 TQ	MNBLS	10/08-12/08
Police and Detectives	Duluth-Superior MSA, MN-WI	Y	57507 FQ	63226 MW	70284 TQ	MNBLS	10/08-12/08
Police and Detectives	Minneapolis-Saint Paul MSA, MN-WI	Y	72804 FQ	79767 MW	86867 TQ	MNBLS	10/08-12/08
Police and Detectives	Mississippi	Y	34500 FQ	42970 MW	52090 TQ	USBLS	5/07
Police and Detectives	Gulfport-Biloxi MSA, MS	Y	36060 FQ	46520 MW	70310 TQ	USBLS	5/07
Police and Detectives	Jackson MSA, MS	Y	41830 FQ	49570 MW	62890 TQ	USBLS	5/07
Police and Detectives	Missouri	Y	52720 FQ	62790 MW	76080 TQ	USBLS	5/07
Police and Detectives	Kansas City MSA, MO-KS	Y	55540 FQ	67660 MW	81670 TQ	USBLS	5/07
Police and Detectives	St. Louis MSA, MO-IL	Y	56070 FQ	66340 MW	81290 TQ	USBLS	5/07
Police and Detectives	Montana	Y	47380 FQ	58920 MW	72460 TQ	USBLS	5/07
Police and Detectives	Nebraska	Y	41180 FQ	57920 MW	75560 TQ	USBLS	5/07
Police and Detectives	Omaha-Council Bluffs MSA, NE-IA	Y	58090 FQ	70850 MW	87300 TQ	USBLS	5/07
Police and Detectives	Nevada	H	37.20 FQ	43.93 MW	49.07 TQ	NVBLS	5/08
Police and Detectives	Las Vegas-Paradise MSA, NV	H	42.86 FQ	46.62 MW	50.43 TQ	NVBLS	5/08
Police and Detectives	New Hampshire	H	23.08 AE	31.54 MW	35.37 AEX	NHBLS	6/08
Police and Detectives	Manchester MSA, NH	Y	68720 FQ	78490 MW	93020 TQ	USBLS	5/07
Police and Detectives	Nashua NECTA, NH-MA	Y	61880 FQ	70770 MW	79040 TQ	USBLS	5/07
Police and Detectives	Rochester-Dover MSA, NH-ME	Y	61490 FQ	68340 MW	75280 TQ	USBLS	5/07
Police and Detectives	New Jersey	Y	89310 FQ	102290 MW	118250 TQ	USBLS	5/07
Police and Detectives	Camden PMSA, NJ	Y	78080 FQ	89880 MW	100310 TQ	USBLS	5/07
Police and Detectives	Edison PMSA, NJ	Y	92780 FQ	105680 MW	120410 TQ	USBLS	5/07
Police and Detectives	Newark-Union PMSA, NJ-PA	Y	83920 FQ	94760 MW	108060 TQ	USBLS	5/07
Police and Detectives	New Mexico	Y	45560 FQ	57680 MW	70280 TQ	USBLS	5/07
Police and Detectives	Albuquerque MSA, NM	Y	40220 FQ	56890 MW	76230 TQ	USBLS	5/07
Police and Detectives	New York	Y	70360 FQ	78220 MW	88690 TQ	USBLS	5/07
Police and Detectives	Albany-Schenectady-Troy MSA, NY	Y	56920 FQ	62750 MW	72300 TQ	USBLS	5/07
Police and Detectives	Buffalo-Niagara Falls MSA, NY	Y	65040 FQ	73210 MW	81210 TQ	USBLS	5/07
Police and Detectives	Nassau-Suffolk PMSA, NY	Y	110270 FQ	120480 MW	130620 TQ	USBLS	5/07

AE Average entry wage	**AW** Average wage paid	**FQ** First quartile wage	**LO** Lowest wage paid	**MTC** Median total compensation	**TCC** Total cash compensation
AER Average entry range	**AWR** Average wage range	**H** Hourly	**LR** Low end range	**MW** Median wage paid	**TQ** Third quartile wage
AEX Average experienced wage	**AXR** Average experienced range	**HI** Highest wage paid	**M** Monthly	**MWR** Median wage range	**W** Weekly
ATC Average total compensation	**D** Daily	**HR** High end range	**MCC** Median cash compensation	**S** See annotated source	**Y** Yearly

Occupation/Type/Industry	Location	Per	Low	Mid	High	Source	Date
First-Line Supervisor/Manager							
Police and Detectives	New York-Northern New Jersey-Long Island MSA, NY-NJ-PA	Y	75340 FQ	83640 MW	110190 TQ	USBLS	5/07
Police and Detectives	North Carolina	Y	43960 FQ	53760 MW	66830 TQ	USBLS	5/07
Police and Detectives	Charlotte-Gastonia-Concord MSA, NC-SC	Y	51540 FQ	64940 MW	74860 TQ	USBLS	5/07
Police and Detectives	Raleigh-Cary MSA, NC	Y	53640 FQ	65150 MW	74210 TQ	USBLS	5/07
Police and Detectives	North Dakota	Y	44740 FQ	60680 MW	73180 TQ	USBLS	5/07
Police and Detectives	Fargo MSA, ND-MN	Y	58050 FQ	64450 MW	74340 TQ	USBLS	5/07
Police and Detectives	Ohio	Y	53800 FQ	65200 MW	77700 TQ	USBLS	5/07
Police and Detectives	Cincinnati-Middletown MSA, OH-KY-IN	Y	62010 FQ	72770 MW	83550 TQ	USBLS	5/07
Police and Detectives	Cleveland-Elyria-Mentor MSA, OH	Y	60990 FQ	70940 MW	79740 TQ	USBLS	5/07
Police and Detectives	Columbus MSA, OH	Y	63750 FQ	74800 MW	83130 TQ	USBLS	5/07
Police and Detectives	Dayton MSA, OH	Y	55320 FQ	62830 MW	76270 TQ	USBLS	5/07
Police and Detectives	Oklahoma	Y	32310 FQ	53780 MW	70150 TQ	USBLS	5/07
Police and Detectives	Oklahoma City MSA, OK	Y	34750 FQ	65220 MW	77230 TQ	USBLS	5/07
Police and Detectives	Tulsa MSA, OK	Y	43790 FQ	59240 MW	68550 TQ	USBLS	5/07
Police and Detectives	Oregon	H	31.69 FQ	35.88 MW	40.84 TQ	ORBLS	5/08
Police and Detectives	Portland-Vancouver-Beaverton MSA, OR-WA	Y	67790 FQ	75020 MW	85190 TQ	USBLS	5/07
Police and Detectives	Pennsylvania	Y	66220 FQ	74800 MW	83460 TQ	USBLS	5/07
Police and Detectives	Allentown-Bethlehem-Easton MSA, PA-NJ	Y	59040 FQ	74590 MW	86450 TQ	USBLS	5/07
Police and Detectives	Philadelphia-Camden-Wilmington MSA, PA-NJ-DE-MD	Y	71350 FQ	80170 MW	92560 TQ	USBLS	5/07
Police and Detectives	Pittsburgh MSA, PA	Y	61320 FQ	75480 MW	89100 TQ	USBLS	5/07
Police and Detectives	Rhode Island	Y	58130 FQ	66560 MW	79620 TQ	USBLS	5/07
Police and Detectives	Providence-Fall River-Warwick MSA, RI-MA	Y	58200 FQ	66880 MW	80170 TQ	USBLS	5/07
Police and Detectives	South Carolina	Y	37990 FQ	46640 MW	57620 TQ	USBLS	5/07
Police and Detectives	Charleston-North Charleston MSA, SC	Y	42000 FQ	49430 MW	63570 TQ	USBLS	5/07
Police and Detectives	Columbia MSA, SC	Y	41890 FQ	47320 MW	59870 TQ	USBLS	5/07
Police and Detectives	South Dakota	Y	44748 FQ	56039 MW	66428 TQ	SDBLS	7/08-9/08
Police and Detectives	Rapid City MSA, SD	Y	52560 FQ	64667 MW	75308 TQ	SDBLS	7/08-9/08
Police and Detectives	Sioux Falls MSA, SD	Y	56237 FQ	69734 MW	99189 TQ	SDBLS	7/08-9/08
Police and Detectives	Tennessee	Y	40440 FQ	53420 MW	66140 TQ	USBLS	5/07
Police and Detectives	Memphis MSA, TN-MS-AR	Y	48090 FQ	58840 MW	73610 TQ	USBLS	5/07
Police and Detectives	Nashville-Davidson-Murfreesboro MSA, TN	Y	35320 FQ	59720 MW	74120 TQ	USBLS	5/07
Police and Detectives	Texas	Y	53530 FQ	67600 MW	81110 TQ	USBLS	5/07
Police and Detectives	Austin-Round Rock MSA, TX	Y	57810 FQ	67730 MW	80710 TQ	USBLS	5/07
Police and Detectives	Dallas-Fort Worth-Arlington MSA, TX	Y	60170 FQ	79540 MW	96290 TQ	USBLS	5/07
Police and Detectives	El Paso MSA, TX	Y	66780 FQ	75240 MW	87640 TQ	USBLS	5/07
Police and Detectives	Houston-Sugar Land-Baytown MSA, TX	Y	62000 FQ	74840 MW	106550 TQ	USBLS	5/07
Police and Detectives	San Antonio MSA, TX	Y	54930 FQ	65780 MW	84120 TQ	USBLS	5/07
Police and Detectives	Utah	Y	51710 FQ	61660 MW	73350 TQ	USBLS	5/07
Police and Detectives	Salt Lake City MSA, UT	Y	53560 FQ	63510 MW	75220 TQ	USBLS	5/07
Police and Detectives	Vermont	Y	53860 FQ	68390 MW	77360 TQ	USBLS	5/07
Police and Detectives	Burlington-South Burlington MSA, VT	Y	62740 FQ	75820 MW	96750 TQ	USBLS	5/07
Police and Detectives	Virginia	Y	58350 FQ	73520 MW	92520 TQ	USBLS	5/07
Police and Detectives	Lynchburg MSA, VA	Y	57280 FQ	66690 MW	84000 TQ	USBLS	5/07
Police and Detectives	Richmond MSA, VA	Y	56590 FQ	65950 MW	82920 TQ	USBLS	5/07
Police and Detectives	Virginia Beach-Norfolk-Newport News MSA, VA-NC	Y	56400 FQ	70730 MW	88550 TQ	USBLS	5/07
Police and Detectives	Washington	H	34.13 FQ	38.46 MW	44.70 TQ	WABLS	3/08
Police and Detectives	Bremerton-Silverdale MSA, WA	Y	62240 FQ	75430 MW	84540 TQ	USBLS	5/07
Police and Detectives	Seattle-Tacoma-Bellevue MSA, WA	Y	73710 FQ	83300 MW	95620 TQ	USBLS	5/07
Police and Detectives	West Virginia	Y	46119 FQ	56670 MW	64114 TQ	WVBLS	7/08-9/08
Police and Detectives	Charleston MSA, WV	Y	45770 FQ	56440 MW	64420 TQ	USBLS	5/07
Police and Detectives	Huntington-Ashland MSA, WV-KY-OH	Y	28380 FQ	52510 MW	61300 TQ	USBLS	5/07
Police and Detectives	Wisconsin	Y	56570 FQ	68660 MW	78630 TQ	USBLS	5/07

AE	Average entry wage	AW	Average wage paid	FQ	First quartile wage
AER	Average entry range	AWR	Average wage range	H	Hourly
AEX	Average experienced wage	AXR	Average experienced range	HI	Highest wage paid
ATC	Average total compensation	D	Daily	HR	High end range

LO	Lowest wage paid	MTC	Median total compensation
LR	Low end range	MW	Median wage paid
M	Monthly	MWR	Median wage range
MCC	Median cash compensation	S	See annotated source

TCC	Total cash compensation
TQ	Third quartile wage
W	Weekly
Y	Yearly

Occupation/Type/Industry	Location	Per	Low	Mid	High	Source	Date
First-Line Supervisor/Manager							
Police and Detectives	Milwaukee-Waukesha-West Allis MSA, WI	Y	70070 FQ	77200 MW	84360 TQ	USBLS	5/07
Police and Detectives	Wyoming	Y	47859 FQ	58005 MW	69091 TQ	WYBLS	9/08
Police and Detectives	Cheyenne MSA, WY	Y	57304 FQ	69230 MW	83732 TQ	WYBLS	9/08
Police and Detectives	Puerto Rico	Y	27170 FQ	31110 MW	36280 TQ	USBLS	5/07
Police and Detectives	San Juan-Caguas-Guaynabo MSA, PR	Y	28030 FQ	31610 MW	36440 TQ	USBLS	5/07
Production and Operating Workers	Alabama	Y	34130 FQ	44610 MW	59040 TQ	USBLS	5/07
Production and Operating Workers	Birmingham-Hoover MSA, AL	Y	37070 FQ	48550 MW	63170 TQ	USBLS	5/07
Production and Operating Workers	Alaska	Y	40360 FQ	63590 MW	90440 TQ	USBLS	5/07
Production and Operating Workers	Anchorage MSA, AK	Y	40590 FQ	57180 MW	77780 TQ	USBLS	5/07
Production and Operating Workers	Arizona	Y	34880 FQ	44330 MW	58220 TQ	USBLS	5/07
Production and Operating Workers	Phoenix-Mesa-Scottsdale MSA, AZ	Y	35170 FQ	44160 MW	58270 TQ	USBLS	5/07
Production and Operating Workers	Tucson MSA, AZ	Y	35090 FQ	46320 MW	58640 TQ	USBLS	5/07
Production and Operating Workers	Yuma MSA, AZ	Y	23540 FQ	37240 MW	54400 TQ	USBLS	5/07
Production and Operating Workers	Arkansas	Y	33130 FQ	41560 MW	51580 TQ	USBLS	5/07
Production and Operating Workers	Little Rock-North Little Rock MSA, AR	Y	34870 FQ	43030 MW	51850 TQ	USBLS	5/07
Production and Operating Workers	Pine Bluff MSA, AR	Y	38830 FQ	45610 MW	51420 TQ	USBLS	5/07
Production and Operating Workers	California	H	18.66 FQ	24.45 MW	31.84 TQ	CABLS	1/08-3/08
Production and Operating Workers	Los Angeles-Long Beach-Glendale PMSA, CA	H	17.07 FQ	22.78 MW	30.34 TQ	CABLS	1/08-3/08
Production and Operating Workers	Oakland-Fremont-Hayward MSA, CA	H	21.28 FQ	27.35 MW	35.70 TQ	CABLS	1/08-3/08
Production and Operating Workers	Riverside-San Bernardino-Ontario MSA, CA	H	18.03 FQ	22.49 MW	29.28 TQ	CABLS	1/08-3/08
Production and Operating Workers	Sacramento-Arden Arcade-Roseville MSA, CA	H	19.96 FQ	25.29 MW	31.43 TQ	CABLS	1/08-3/08
Production and Operating Workers	San Diego-Carlsbad-San Marcos MSA, CA	H	19.74 FQ	25.74 MW	32.20 TQ	CABLS	1/08-3/08
Production and Operating Workers	San Francisco-San Mateo-Redwood PMSA, CA	H	21.81 FQ	30.45 MW	40.56 TQ	CABLS	1/08-3/08
Production and Operating Workers	San Jose-Sunnyvale-Santa Clara MSA, CA	H	23.37 FQ	30.15 MW	38.58 TQ	CABLS	1/08-3/08
Production and Operating Workers	Santa Ana-Anaheim-Irvine PMSA, CA	Y	38380 FQ	50270 MW	63610 TQ	USBLS	5/07
Production and Operating Workers	Colorado	Y	38270 FQ	49120 MW	62690 TQ	USBLS	5/07
Production and Operating Workers	Denver-Aurora MSA, CO	Y	38380 FQ	48550 MW	61430 TQ	USBLS	5/07
Production and Operating Workers	Connecticut	H	18.89 AE	27.41 MW		CTBLS	1/08-3/08
Production and Operating Workers	Bridgeport-Stamford-Norwalk MSA, CT	Y	46960 FQ	60050 MW	74180 TQ	USBLS	5/07
Production and Operating Workers	Hartford-West Hartford-East Hartford MSA, CT	Y	45070 FQ	56790 MW	70480 TQ	USBLS	5/07
Production and Operating Workers	Delaware	Y	38800 FQ	53560 MW	70800 TQ	USBLS	5/07
Production and Operating Workers	Dover MSA, DE	Y	36570 FQ	48990 MW	69850 TQ	USBLS	5/07
Production and Operating Workers	Wilmington PMSA, DE-MD-NJ	Y	48240 FQ	63200 MW	76310 TQ	USBLS	5/07
Production and Operating Workers	District of Columbia	Y	45880 FQ	60160 MW	72150 TQ	USBLS	5/07
Production and Operating Workers	Washington-Arlington-Alexandria MSA, DC-VA-MD-WV	Y	44030 FQ	55750 MW	73200 TQ	USBLS	5/07
Production and Operating Workers	Florida	Y	36950 FQ	49110 MW	63110 TQ	USBLS	5/07
Production and Operating Workers	Cape Coral-Fort Myers MSA, FL	Y	33980 FQ	49990 MW	65360 TQ	USBLS	5/07
Production and Operating Workers	Fort Lauderdale-Pompano Beach-Deerfield Beach PMSA, FL	Y	38040 FQ	47950 MW	62330 TQ	USBLS	5/07
Production and Operating Workers	Jacksonville MSA, FL	Y	38850 FQ	50730 MW	63040 TQ	USBLS	5/07
Production and Operating Workers	Miami-Fort Lauderdale-Miami Beach MSA, FL	Y	36850 FQ	49000 MW	62990 TQ	USBLS	5/07
Production and Operating Workers	Orlando-Kissimmee MSA, FL	Y	35440 FQ	46830 MW	62130 TQ	USBLS	5/07
Production and Operating Workers	Tampa-St. Petersburg-Clearwater MSA, FL	Y	37810 FQ	49010 MW	62460 TQ	USBLS	5/07
Production and Operating Workers	West Palm Beach-Boca Raton-Boynton Beach PMSA, FL	Y	38980 FQ	51070 MW	66170 TQ	USBLS	5/07
Production and Operating Workers	Georgia	Y	34810 FQ	44780 MW	57340 TQ	USBLS	5/07
Production and Operating Workers	Atlanta-Sandy Springs-Marietta MSA, GA	Y	35890 FQ	46620 MW	58610 TQ	USBLS	5/07
Production and Operating Workers	Savannah MSA, GA	Y	43430 FQ	54810 MW	63370 TQ	USBLS	5/07
Production and Operating Workers	Hawaii	Y	35150 FQ	46650 MW	64750 TQ	USBLS	5/07

AE	Average entry wage	AW	Average wage paid	FQ	First quartile wage
AER	Average entry range	AWR	Average wage range	H	Hourly
AEX	Average experienced wage	AXR	Average experienced range	HI	Highest wage paid
ATC	Average total compensation	D	Daily	HR	High end range

LO	Lowest wage paid	MTC	Median total compensation	TCC	Total cash compensation
LR	Low end range	MW	Median wage paid	TQ	Third quartile wage
M	Monthly	MWR	Median wage range	W	Weekly
MCC	Median cash compensation	S	See annotated source	Y	Yearly

Occupation/Type/Industry	Location	Per	Low	Mid	High	Source	Date
First-Line Supervisor/Manager							
Production and Operating Workers	Honolulu MSA, HI	Y	35020 FQ	48260 MW	66510 TQ	USBLS	5/07
Production and Operating Workers	Idaho	Y	32060 FQ	41400 MW	55340 TQ	USBLS	5/07
Production and Operating Workers	Boise City-Nampa MSA, ID	Y	33570 FQ	44810 MW	57400 TQ	USBLS	5/07
Production and Operating Workers	Coeur d'Alene MSA, ID	Y	31760 FQ	43820 MW	57090 TQ	USBLS	5/07
Production and Operating Workers	Illinois	Y	38460 FQ	51060 MW	66240 TQ	USBLS	5/07
Production and Operating Workers	Chicago-Naperville-Joliet MSA, IL-IN-WI	Y	38750 FQ	52320 MW	67890 TQ	USBLS	5/07
Production and Operating Workers	Indiana	Y	37030 FQ	47100 MW	60790 TQ	USBLS	5/07
Production and Operating Workers	Gary PMSA, IN	Y	42600 FQ	55640 MW	70130 TQ	USBLS	5/07
Production and Operating Workers	Indianapolis-Carmel MSA, IN	Y	37910 FQ	48030 MW	61400 TQ	USBLS	5/07
Production and Operating Workers	South Bend-Mishawaka MSA, IN-MI	Y	38710 FQ	45720 MW	55670 TQ	USBLS	5/07
Production and Operating Workers	Iowa	Y	37140 FQ	47030 MW	58980 TQ	USBLS	5/07
Production and Operating Workers	Des Moines-West Des Moines MSA, IA	Y	41830 FQ	53100 MW	63490 TQ	USBLS	5/07
Production and Operating Workers	Sioux City MSA, IA-NE-SD	Y	42290 FQ	48890 MW	56940 TQ	USBLS	5/07
Production and Operating Workers	Kansas	Y	36360 FQ	46290 MW	57690 TQ	USBLS	5/07
Production and Operating Workers	Wichita MSA, KS	Y	40150 FQ	50930 MW	63420 TQ	USBLS	5/07
Production and Operating Workers	Kentucky	Y	36726 FQ	47550 MW	60840 TQ	KYBLS	2008
Production and Operating Workers	Elizabethtown MSA, KY	Y	35530 FQ	48240 MW	58790 TQ	USBLS	5/07
Production and Operating Workers	Louisville-Jefferson County MSA, KY-IN	Y	37370 FQ	47410 MW	60530 TQ	USBLS	5/07
Production and Operating Workers	Owensboro MSA, KY	Y	34240 FQ	48960 MW	65710 TQ	USBLS	5/07
Production and Operating Workers	Louisiana	H	17.56 FQ	22.75 MW	31.38 TQ	LABLS	1/08-3/08
Production and Operating Workers	Baton Rouge MSA, LA	Y	41930 FQ	59800 MW	79400 TQ	USBLS	5/07
Production and Operating Workers	Lafayette MSA, LA	Y	34890 FQ	48170 MW	65150 TQ	USBLS	5/07
Production and Operating Workers	New Orleans-Metairie-Kenner MSA, LA	Y	39020 FQ	47230 MW	67200 TQ	USBLS	5/07
Production and Operating Workers	Maine	Y	34780 FQ	45510 MW	58890 TQ	USBLS	5/07
Production and Operating Workers	Portland-South Portland-Biddeford MSA, ME	Y	37160 FQ	44700 MW	55060 TQ	USBLS	5/07
Production and Operating Workers	Maryland	Y		53900 MW		MDBLS	3/08
Production and Operating Workers	Baltimore-Towson MSA, MD	Y	41700 FQ	54280 MW	68570 TQ	USBLS	5/07
Production and Operating Workers	Bethesda-Gaithersburg-Frederick PMSA, MD	Y	44430 FQ	53060 MW	68940 TQ	USBLS	5/07
Production and Operating Workers	Massachusetts	Y	42530 FQ	53790 MW	66430 TQ	USBLS	5/07
Production and Operating Workers	Boston-Cambridge-Quincy NECTA, MA	Y	43120 FQ	54140 MW	67890 TQ	USBLS	5/07
Production and Operating Workers	New Bedford MSA, MA	Y	39900 FQ	54650 MW	63500 TQ	USBLS	5/07
Production and Operating Workers	Worcester MSA, MA-CT	Y	42200 FQ	53370 MW	65070 TQ	USBLS	5/07
Production and Operating Workers	Michigan	Y	42430 FQ	56190 MW	73640 TQ	USBLS	5/07
Production and Operating Workers	Detroit-Warren-Livonia MSA, MI	Y	47370 FQ	62970 MW	79470 TQ	USBLS	5/07
Production and Operating Workers	Grand Rapids-Wyoming MSA, MI	Y	39220 FQ	49390 MW	63200 TQ	USBLS	5/07
Production and Operating Workers	Lansing-East Lansing MSA, MI	Y	45450 FQ	60550 MW	76880 TQ	USBLS	5/07
Production and Operating Workers	Warren-Troy-Farmington Hills PMSA, MI	Y	46770 FQ	60910 MW	78040 TQ	USBLS	5/07
Production and Operating Workers	Minnesota	Y	41508 FQ	51440 MW	64118 TQ	MNBLS	10/08-12/08
Production and Operating Workers	Duluth-Superior MSA, MN-WI	Y	36470 FQ	47345 MW	60314 TQ	MNBLS	10/08-12/08
Production and Operating Workers	Minneapolis-Saint Paul MSA, MN-WI	Y	44815 FQ	55783 MW	67985 TQ	MNBLS	10/08-12/08
Production and Operating Workers	Rochester MSA, MN	Y	39989 FQ	47117 MW	56409 TQ	MNBLS	10/08-12/08
Production and Operating Workers	Mississippi	Y	33500 FQ	42330 MW	52940 TQ	USBLS	5/07
Production and Operating Workers	Jackson MSA, MS	Y	30820 FQ	40520 MW	50520 TQ	USBLS	5/07
Production and Operating Workers	Missouri	Y	36030 FQ	47610 MW	61960 TQ	USBLS	5/07
Production and Operating Workers	Kansas City MSA, MO-KS	Y	39990 FQ	50830 MW	64160 TQ	USBLS	5/07
Production and Operating Workers	St. Joseph MSA, MO-KS	Y	40800 FQ	49660 MW	59280 TQ	USBLS	5/07
Production and Operating Workers	St. Louis MSA, MO-IL	Y	42690 FQ	54190 MW	70530 TQ	USBLS	5/07
Production and Operating Workers	Montana	Y	35250 FQ	45270 MW	60600 TQ	USBLS	5/07
Production and Operating Workers	Billings MSA, MT	Y	31680 FQ	42870 MW	54550 TQ	USBLS	5/07
Production and Operating Workers	Nebraska	Y	37720 FQ	46500 MW	57840 TQ	USBLS	5/07
Production and Operating Workers	Omaha-Council Bluffs MSA, NE-IA	Y	36630 FQ	46370 MW	58080 TQ	USBLS	5/07
Production and Operating Workers	Nevada	H	16.60 FQ	22.56 MW	29.26 TQ	NVBLS	5/08
Production and Operating Workers	Las Vegas-Paradise MSA, NV	H	16.29 FQ	22.45 MW	29.42 TQ	NVBLS	5/08
Production and Operating Workers	New Hampshire	H	17.59 AE	24.77 MW	29.25 AEX	NHBLS	6/08
Production and Operating Workers	Manchester MSA, NH	Y	39000 FQ	51060 MW	62290 TQ	USBLS	5/07
Production and Operating Workers	Nashua NECTA, NH-MA	Y	43540 FQ	53370 MW	65030 TQ	USBLS	5/07
Production and Operating Workers	New Jersey	Y	43150 FQ	54800 MW	68920 TQ	USBLS	5/07
Production and Operating Workers	Camden PMSA, NJ	Y	44170 FQ	56280 MW	69800 TQ	USBLS	5/07

AE	Average entry wage	AW	Average wage paid	FQ	First quartile wage
AER	Average entry range	AWR	Average wage range	H	Hourly
AEX	Average experienced wage	AXR	Average experienced range	HI	Highest wage paid
ATC	Average total compensation	D	Daily	HR	High end range

LO	Lowest wage paid	MTC	Median total compensation	TCC	Total cash compensation
LR	Low end range	MW	Median wage paid	TQ	Third quartile wage
M	Monthly	MWR	Median wage range	W	Weekly
MCC	Median cash compensation	S	See annotated source	Y	Yearly

Occupation/Type/Industry	Location	Per	Low	Mid	High	Source	Date
First-Line Supervisor/Manager							
Production and Operating Workers	Edison PMSA, NJ	Y	42680 FQ	54400 MW	68650 TQ	USBLS	5/07
Production and Operating Workers	Newark-Union PMSA, NJ-PA	Y	44800 FQ	56220 MW	70300 TQ	USBLS	5/07
Production and Operating Workers	New Mexico	Y	32530 FQ	45570 MW	64650 TQ	USBLS	5/07
Production and Operating Workers	Albuquerque MSA, NM	Y	34870 FQ	48220 MW	69700 TQ	USBLS	5/07
Production and Operating Workers	New York	Y	39940 FQ	51470 MW	65370 TQ	USBLS	5/07
Production and Operating Workers	Albany-Schenectady-Troy MSA, NY	Y	43460 FQ	53450 MW	65300 TQ	USBLS	5/07
Production and Operating Workers	Buffalo-Niagara Falls MSA, NY	Y	40630 FQ	53050 MW	65720 TQ	USBLS	5/07
Production and Operating Workers	Nassau-Suffolk PMSA, NY	Y	46130 FQ	58110 MW	73000 TQ	USBLS	5/07
Production and Operating Workers	New York-Northern New Jersey-Long Island MSA, NY-NJ-PA	Y	42790 FQ	55560 MW	70860 TQ	USBLS	5/07
Production and Operating Workers	North Carolina	Y	35810 FQ	45280 MW	57460 TQ	USBLS	5/07
Production and Operating Workers	Charlotte-Gastonia-Concord MSA, NC-SC	Y	39420 FQ	48310 MW	62660 TQ	USBLS	5/07
Production and Operating Workers	Raleigh-Cary MSA, NC	Y	37720 FQ	47370 MW	61410 TQ	USBLS	5/07
Production and Operating Workers	Winston-Salem MSA, NC	Y	36300 FQ	46650 MW	59810 TQ	USBLS	5/07
Production and Operating Workers	North Dakota	Y	35410 FQ	45250 MW	59170 TQ	USBLS	5/07
Production and Operating Workers	Fargo MSA, ND-MN	Y	33020 FQ	39520 MW	50420 TQ	USBLS	5/07
Production and Operating Workers	Grand Forks MSA, ND-MN	Y	38070 FQ	45300 MW	54300 TQ	USBLS	5/07
Production and Operating Workers	Ohio	Y	38010 FQ	48320 MW	60640 TQ	USBLS	5/07
Production and Operating Workers	Cincinnati-Middletown MSA, OH-KY-IN	Y	41730 FQ	51870 MW	63220 TQ	USBLS	5/07
Production and Operating Workers	Cleveland-Elyria-Mentor MSA, OH	Y	40220 FQ	50880 MW	63380 TQ	USBLS	5/07
Production and Operating Workers	Columbus MSA, OH	Y	37390 FQ	47390 MW	60210 TQ	USBLS	5/07
Production and Operating Workers	Dayton MSA, OH	Y	38840 FQ	51100 MW	65210 TQ	USBLS	5/07
Production and Operating Workers	Oklahoma	Y	33730 FQ	43750 MW	57630 TQ	USBLS	5/07
Production and Operating Workers	Lawton MSA, OK	Y	31980 FQ	44130 MW	54150 TQ	USBLS	5/07
Production and Operating Workers	Oklahoma City MSA, OK	Y	31430 FQ	42060 MW	55850 TQ	USBLS	5/07
Production and Operating Workers	Tulsa MSA, OK	Y	36590 FQ	46160 MW	58130 TQ	USBLS	5/07
Production and Operating Workers	Oregon	H	18.05 FQ	23.58 MW	30.10 TQ	ORBLS	5/08
Production and Operating Workers	Portland-Vancouver-Beaverton MSA, OR-WA	Y	39790 FQ	51760 MW	64150 TQ	USBLS	5/07
Production and Operating Workers	Pennsylvania	Y	39710 FQ	50710 MW	63640 TQ	USBLS	5/07
Production and Operating Workers	Allentown-Bethlehem-Easton MSA, PA-NJ	Y	42200 FQ	53750 MW	64730 TQ	USBLS	5/07
Production and Operating Workers	Philadelphia-Camden-Wilmington MSA, PA-NJ-DE-MD	Y	46380 FQ	58480 MW	73140 TQ	USBLS	5/07
Production and Operating Workers	Pittsburgh MSA, PA	Y	39060 FQ	49770 MW	62870 TQ	USBLS	5/07
Production and Operating Workers	Rhode Island	Y	40750 FQ	51440 MW	63020 TQ	USBLS	5/07
Production and Operating Workers	Providence-Fall River-Warwick MSA, RI-MA	Y	40330 FQ	50850 MW	62870 TQ	USBLS	5/07
Production and Operating Workers	South Carolina	Y	38840 FQ	49960 MW	63210 TQ	USBLS	5/07
Production and Operating Workers	Charleston-North Charleston MSA, SC	Y	37560 FQ	51460 MW	65140 TQ	USBLS	5/07
Production and Operating Workers	Columbia MSA, SC	Y	38260 FQ	52240 MW	64150 TQ	USBLS	5/07
Production and Operating Workers	Florence MSA, SC	Y	42550 FQ	51740 MW	68100 TQ	USBLS	5/07
Production and Operating Workers	South Dakota	Y	39386 FQ	46935 MW	55893 TQ	SDBLS	7/08-9/08
Production and Operating Workers	Rapid City MSA, SD	Y	37223 FQ	45904 MW	53846 TQ	SDBLS	7/08-9/08
Production and Operating Workers	Sioux Falls MSA, SD	Y	42372 FQ	48746 MW	56668 TQ	SDBLS	7/08-9/08
Production and Operating Workers	Tennessee	Y	33190 FQ	42770 MW	55460 TQ	USBLS	5/07
Production and Operating Workers	Memphis MSA, TN-MS-AR	Y	30290 FQ	43380 MW	57820 TQ	USBLS	5/07
Production and Operating Workers	Nashville-Davidson-Murfreesboro MSA, TN	Y	37270 FQ	46470 MW	59040 TQ	USBLS	5/07
Production and Operating Workers	Texas	Y	36030 FQ	47100 MW	61430 TQ	USBLS	5/07
Production and Operating Workers	Austin-Round Rock MSA, TX	Y	35930 FQ	49970 MW	62550 TQ	USBLS	5/07
Production and Operating Workers	Dallas-Fort Worth-Arlington MSA, TX	Y	37790 FQ	48340 MW	60710 TQ	USBLS	5/07
Production and Operating Workers	El Paso MSA, TX	Y	29190 FQ	37360 MW	48740 TQ	USBLS	5/07
Production and Operating Workers	Houston-Sugar Land-Baytown MSA, TX	Y	39810 FQ	51750 MW	69020 TQ	USBLS	5/07
Production and Operating Workers	San Antonio MSA, TX	Y	32010 FQ	41030 MW	54670 TQ	USBLS	5/07
Production and Operating Workers	Utah	Y	34650 FQ	46420 MW	60460 TQ	USBLS	5/07
Production and Operating Workers	Logan MSA, UT-ID	Y	32660 FQ	39270 MW	48920 TQ	USBLS	5/07
Production and Operating Workers	Salt Lake City MSA, UT	Y	36410 FQ	49460 MW	62490 TQ	USBLS	5/07
Production and Operating Workers	Vermont	Y	39190 FQ	49580 MW	60410 TQ	USBLS	5/07
Production and Operating Workers	Burlington-South Burlington MSA, VT	Y	43890 FQ	53720 MW	62290 TQ	USBLS	5/07

AE	Average entry wage	AW	Average wage paid	FQ	First quartile wage
AER	Average entry range	AWR	Average wage range	H	Hourly
AEX	Average experienced wage	AXR	Average experienced range	HI	Highest wage paid
ATC	Average total compensation	D	Daily	HR	High end range

LO	Lowest wage paid	MTC	Median total compensation	TCC	Total cash compensation
LR	Low end range	MW	Median wage paid	TQ	Third quartile wage
M	Monthly	MWR	Median wage range	W	Weekly
MCC	Median cash compensation	S	See annotated source	Y	Yearly

Occupation/Type/Industry	Location	Per	Low	Mid	High	Source	Date
First-Line Supervisor/Manager							
Production and Operating Workers	Virginia	Y	38730 FQ	48960 MW	63380 TQ	USBLS	5/07
Production and Operating Workers	Richmond MSA, VA	Y	40330 FQ	50160 MW	66600 TQ	USBLS	5/07
Production and Operating Workers	Roanoke MSA, VA	Y	37680 FQ	45180 MW	56780 TQ	USBLS	5/07
Production and Operating Workers	Virginia Beach-Norfolk-Newport News MSA, VA-NC	Y	41980 FQ	51790 MW	64080 TQ	USBLS	5/07
Production and Operating Workers	Washington	H	21.69 FQ	27.64 MW	35.99 TQ	WABLS	3/08
Production and Operating Workers	Olympia MSA, WA	Y	41950 FQ	51090 MW	60240 TQ	USBLS	5/07
Production and Operating Workers	Seattle-Tacoma-Bellevue MSA, WA	Y	46610 FQ	59320 MW	76860 TQ	USBLS	5/07
Production and Operating Workers	West Virginia	Y	36271 FQ	47994 MW	62450 TQ	WVBLS	7/08-9/08
Production and Operating Workers	Charleston MSA, WV	Y	37520 FQ	56300 MW	72130 TQ	USBLS	5/07
Production and Operating Workers	Wisconsin	Y	39380 FQ	49020 MW	61110 TQ	USBLS	5/07
Production and Operating Workers	Milwaukee-Waukesha-West Allis MSA, WI	Y	42450 FQ	52340 MW	64800 TQ	USBLS	5/07
Production and Operating Workers	Wyoming	Y	41523 FQ	56276 MW	75833 TQ	WYBLS	9/08
Production and Operating Workers	Cheyenne MSA, WY	Y	36301 FQ	43797 MW	58077 TQ	WYBLS	9/08
Production and Operating Workers	Puerto Rico	Y	23320 FQ	32590 MW	48540 TQ	USBLS	5/07
Production and Operating Workers	Aguadilla-Isabela-San Sebastian MSA, PR	Y	19510 FQ	30990 MW	45820 TQ	USBLS	5/07
Production and Operating Workers	San Juan-Caguas-Guaynabo MSA, PR	Y	25000 FQ	34840 MW	50620 TQ	USBLS	5/07
Production and Operating Workers	Virgin Islands	Y	50760 FQ	65970 MW	79460 TQ	USBLS	5/07
Production and Operating Workers	Guam	Y	33690 FQ	38580 MW	47820 TQ	USBLS	5/07
Retail Sales Workers	Alabama	Y	24560 FQ	30570 MW	38920 TQ	USBLS	5/07
Retail Sales Workers	Birmingham-Hoover MSA, AL	Y	26180 FQ	32760 MW	41810 TQ	USBLS	5/07
Retail Sales Workers	Alaska	Y	27880 FQ	35590 MW	45800 TQ	USBLS	5/07
Retail Sales Workers	Anchorage MSA, AK	Y	27120 FQ	35500 MW	47700 TQ	USBLS	5/07
Retail Sales Workers	Fairbanks MSA, AK	Y	30170 FQ	38330 MW	45530 TQ	USBLS	5/07
Retail Sales Workers	Arizona	Y	27940 FQ	35490 MW	46730 TQ	USBLS	5/07
Retail Sales Workers	Phoenix-Mesa-Scottsdale MSA, AZ	Y	28480 FQ	36380 MW	48280 TQ	USBLS	5/07
Retail Sales Workers	Tucson MSA, AZ	Y	27510 FQ	34190 MW	44510 TQ	USBLS	5/07
Retail Sales Workers	Arkansas	Y	22850 FQ	29000 MW	37980 TQ	USBLS	5/07
Retail Sales Workers	Jonesboro MSA, AR	Y	21410 FQ	27460 MW	35610 TQ	USBLS	5/07
Retail Sales Workers	Little Rock-North Little Rock MSA, AR	Y	24260 FQ	30670 MW	40680 TQ	USBLS	5/07
Retail Sales Workers	California	H	13.81 FQ	17.63 MW	22.86 TQ	CABLS	1/08-3/08
Retail Sales Workers	Los Angeles-Long Beach-Glendale PMSA, CA	H	13.68 FQ	17.63 MW	22.84 TQ	CABLS	1/08-3/08
Retail Sales Workers	Oakland-Fremont-Hayward MSA, CA	H	14.69 FQ	18.43 MW	23.74 TQ	CABLS	1/08-3/08
Retail Sales Workers	Riverside-San Bernardino-Ontario MSA, CA	H	13.32 FQ	16.87 MW	21.76 TQ	CABLS	1/08-3/08
Retail Sales Workers	Sacramento-Arden Arcade-Roseville MSA, CA	H	13.62 FQ	17.88 MW	23.37 TQ	CABLS	1/08-3/08
Retail Sales Workers	San Diego-Carlsbad-San Marcos MSA, CA	H	13.68 FQ	17.61 MW	22.73 TQ	CABLS	1/08-3/08
Retail Sales Workers	San Francisco-San Mateo-Redwood PMSA, CA	H	16.13 FQ	20.59 MW	26.20 TQ	CABLS	1/08-3/08
Retail Sales Workers	San Jose-Sunnyvale-Santa Clara MSA, CA	H	14.70 FQ	19.02 MW	24.04 TQ	CABLS	1/08-3/08
Retail Sales Workers	Santa Ana-Anaheim-Irvine PMSA, CA	Y	28830 FQ	36200 MW	47140 TQ	USBLS	5/07
Retail Sales Workers	Santa Rosa-Petaluma MSA, CA	H	15.41 FQ	18.67 MW	23.65 TQ	CABLS	1/08-3/08
Retail Sales Workers	Colorado	Y	28270 FQ	36050 MW	48150 TQ	USBLS	5/07
Retail Sales Workers	Denver-Aurora MSA, CO	Y	29300 FQ	37160 MW	49520 TQ	USBLS	5/07
Retail Sales Workers	Fort Collins-Loveland MSA, CO	Y	28450 FQ	36120 MW	47040 TQ	USBLS	5/07
Retail Sales Workers	Connecticut	H	12.64 AE	18.07 MW		CTBLS	1/08-3/08
Retail Sales Workers	Bridgeport-Stamford-Norwalk MSA, CT	Y	31250 FQ	40190 MW	55130 TQ	USBLS	5/07
Retail Sales Workers	Danbury MSA, CT	Y	32700 FQ	40150 MW	49720 TQ	USBLS	5/07
Retail Sales Workers	Hartford-West Hartford-East Hartford MSA, CT	Y	28740 FQ	36410 MW	45670 TQ	USBLS	5/07
Retail Sales Workers	Delaware	Y	29170 FQ	37610 MW	49100 TQ	USBLS	5/07
Retail Sales Workers	Dover MSA, DE	Y	26280 FQ	32470 MW	43990 TQ	USBLS	5/07
Retail Sales Workers	Wilmington PMSA, DE-MD-NJ	Y	30150 FQ	39110 MW	49770 TQ	USBLS	5/07
Retail Sales Workers	District of Columbia	Y	32230 FQ	39280 MW	47770 TQ	USBLS	5/07

AE Average entry wage	**AW** Average wage paid	**FQ** First quartile wage	**LO** Lowest wage paid	**MTC** Median total compensation	**TCC** Total cash compensation
AER Average entry range	**AWR** Average wage range	**H** Hourly	**LR** Low end range	**MW** Median wage paid	**TQ** Third quartile wage
AEX Average experienced wage	**AXR** Average experienced range	**HI** Highest wage paid	**M** Monthly	**MWR** Median wage range	**W** Weekly
ATC Average total compensation	**D** Daily	**HR** High end range	**MCC** Median cash compensation	**S** See annotated source	**Y** Yearly

Occupation/Type/Industry	Location	Per	Low	Mid	High	Source	Date
First-Line Supervisor/Manager							
Retail Sales Workers	Washington-Arlington-Alexandria MSA, DC-VA-MD-WV	Y	30420 FQ	38570 MW	49660 TQ	USBLS	5/07
Retail Sales Workers	Florida	Y	30280 FQ	37580 MW	49310 TQ	USBLS	5/07
Retail Sales Workers	Fort Lauderdale-Pompano Beach-Deerfield Beach PMSA, FL	Y	32600 FQ	38920 MW	51070 TQ	USBLS	5/07
Retail Sales Workers	Jacksonville MSA, FL	Y	30230 FQ	38440 MW	49200 TQ	USBLS	5/07
Retail Sales Workers	Miami-Fort Lauderdale-Miami Beach MSA, FL	Y	31940 FQ	38710 MW	50990 TQ	USBLS	5/07
Retail Sales Workers	Orlando-Kissimmee MSA, FL	Y	30430 FQ	39540 MW	51480 TQ	USBLS	5/07
Retail Sales Workers	Tampa-St. Petersburg-Clearwater MSA, FL	Y	30010 FQ	36870 MW	48290 TQ	USBLS	5/07
Retail Sales Workers	West Palm Beach-Boca Raton-Boynton Beach PMSA, FL	Y	32750 FQ	39750 MW	53040 TQ	USBLS	5/07
Retail Sales Workers	Georgia	Y	24930 FQ	30640 MW	39250 TQ	USBLS	5/07
Retail Sales Workers	Athens-Clarke County MSA, GA	Y	23430 FQ	28890 MW	36790 TQ	USBLS	5/07
Retail Sales Workers	Atlanta-Sandy Springs-Marietta MSA, GA	Y	25940 FQ	31840 MW	41590 TQ	USBLS	5/07
Retail Sales Workers	Hawaii	Y	28680 FQ	36310 MW	46830 TQ	USBLS	5/07
Retail Sales Workers	Honolulu MSA, HI	Y	28400 FQ	36340 MW	47890 TQ	USBLS	5/07
Retail Sales Workers	Idaho	Y	25380 FQ	31310 MW	41630 TQ	USBLS	5/07
Retail Sales Workers	Boise City-Nampa MSA, ID	Y	25730 FQ	30990 MW	40480 TQ	USBLS	5/07
Retail Sales Workers	Illinois	Y	27060 FQ	35080 MW	46520 TQ	USBLS	5/07
Retail Sales Workers	Champaign-Urbana MSA, IL	Y	25220 FQ	31620 MW	39930 TQ	USBLS	5/07
Retail Sales Workers	Chicago-Naperville-Joliet MSA, IL-IN-WI	Y	28140 FQ	36610 MW	48040 TQ	USBLS	5/07
Retail Sales Workers	Indiana	Y	26470 FQ	33110 MW	43490 TQ	USBLS	5/07
Retail Sales Workers	Gary PMSA, IN	Y	26980 FQ	33990 MW	45580 TQ	USBLS	5/07
Retail Sales Workers	Indianapolis-Carmel MSA, IN	Y	27960 FQ	35120 MW	46660 TQ	USBLS	5/07
Retail Sales Workers	Iowa	Y	26160 FQ	32360 MW	41990 TQ	USBLS	5/07
Retail Sales Workers	Cedar Rapids MSA, IA	Y	27810 FQ	33820 MW	40520 TQ	USBLS	5/07
Retail Sales Workers	Des Moines-West Des Moines MSA, IA	Y	28090 FQ	35060 MW	45740 TQ	USBLS	5/07
Retail Sales Workers	Kansas	Y	23750 FQ	30850 MW	39690 TQ	USBLS	5/07
Retail Sales Workers	Wichita MSA, KS	Y	24420 FQ	31700 MW	41360 TQ	USBLS	5/07
Retail Sales Workers	Kentucky	Y	23101 FQ	30008 MW	38882 TQ	KYBLS	2008
Retail Sales Workers	Bowling Green MSA, KY	Y	22180 FQ	29650 MW	37790 TQ	USBLS	5/07
Retail Sales Workers	Louisville-Jefferson County MSA, KY-IN	Y	25870 FQ	33130 MW	42790 TQ	USBLS	5/07
Retail Sales Workers	Louisiana	H	12.00 FQ	14.50 MW	18.12 TQ	LABLS	1/08-3/08
Retail Sales Workers	Baton Rouge MSA, LA	Y	25030 FQ	30080 MW	37810 TQ	USBLS	5/07
Retail Sales Workers	Lake Charles MSA, LA	Y	24000 FQ	29900 MW	38100 TQ	USBLS	5/07
Retail Sales Workers	New Orleans-Metairie-Kenner MSA, LA	Y	26260 FQ	32360 MW	39950 TQ	USBLS	5/07
Retail Sales Workers	Maine	Y	25130 FQ	31720 MW	40480 TQ	USBLS	5/07
Retail Sales Workers	Portland-South Portland-Biddeford MSA, ME	Y	26580 FQ	34320 MW	45470 TQ	USBLS	5/07
Retail Sales Workers	Maryland	Y		38125 MW		MDBLS	3/08
Retail Sales Workers	Baltimore-Towson MSA, MD	Y	29930 FQ	38350 MW	50670 TQ	USBLS	5/07
Retail Sales Workers	Bethesda-Gaithersburg-Frederick PMSA, MD	Y	31360 FQ	39020 MW	49600 TQ	USBLS	5/07
Retail Sales Workers	Massachusetts	Y	29290 FQ	37210 MW	48470 TQ	USBLS	5/07
Retail Sales Workers	Boston-Cambridge-Quincy NECTA, MA	Y	30770 FQ	38910 MW	49910 TQ	USBLS	5/07
Retail Sales Workers	Lynn-Peabody-Salem NECTA, MA	Y	26840 FQ	34000 MW	47290 TQ	USBLS	5/07
Retail Sales Workers	Worcester MSA, MA-CT	Y	26530 FQ	35240 MW	45330 TQ	USBLS	5/07
Retail Sales Workers	Michigan	Y	28530 FQ	36530 MW	47220 TQ	USBLS	5/07
Retail Sales Workers	Detroit-Warren-Livonia MSA, MI	Y	30280 FQ	38200 MW	49990 TQ	USBLS	5/07
Retail Sales Workers	Grand Rapids-Wyoming MSA, MI	Y	28870 FQ	36420 MW	46830 TQ	USBLS	5/07
Retail Sales Workers	Warren-Troy-Farmington Hills PMSA, MI	Y	30350 FQ	39320 MW	52200 TQ	USBLS	5/07
Retail Sales Workers	Minnesota	Y	25683 FQ	33143 MW	43072 TQ	MNBLS	10/08-12/08
Retail Sales Workers	Duluth-Superior MSA, MN-WI	Y	24067 FQ	30175 MW	38468 TQ	MNBLS	10/08-12/08
Retail Sales Workers	Minneapolis-Saint Paul MSA, MN-WI	Y	27207 FQ	34799 MW	44770 TQ	MNBLS	10/08-12/08
Retail Sales Workers	Rochester MSA, MN	Y	25522 FQ	30892 MW	39226 TQ	MNBLS	10/08-12/08

AE   Average entry wage   AW   Average wage paid   FQ   First quartile wage   LO   Lowest wage paid   MTC   Median total compensation   TCC   Total cash compensation
AER   Average entry range   AWR   Average wage range   H   Hourly   LR   Low end range   MW   Median wage paid   TQ   Third quartile wage
AEX   Average experienced wage   AXR   Average experienced range HI   Highest wage paid   M   Monthly   MWR   Median wage range   W   Weekly
ATC   Average total compensation D   Daily   HR   High end range   MCC   Median cash compensation S See annotated source   Y   Yearly

654

Occupation/Type/Industry	Location	Per	Low	Mid	High	Source	Date
First-Line Supervisor/Manager							
Retail Sales Workers	Mississippi	Y	23220 FQ	28920 MW	37840 TQ	USBLS	5/07
Retail Sales Workers	Jackson MSA, MS	Y	24640 FQ	31230 MW	41390 TQ	USBLS	5/07
Retail Sales Workers	Missouri	Y	26970 FQ	33950 MW	44280 TQ	USBLS	5/07
Retail Sales Workers	Joplin MSA, MO	Y	25280 FQ	30390 MW	38940 TQ	USBLS	5/07
Retail Sales Workers	Kansas City MSA, MO-KS	Y	27840 FQ	34820 MW	45040 TQ	USBLS	5/07
Retail Sales Workers	St. Louis MSA, MO-IL	Y	28420 FQ	35730 MW	46710 TQ	USBLS	5/07
Retail Sales Workers	Springfield MSA, MO	Y	25270 FQ	33760 MW	43500 TQ	USBLS	5/07
Retail Sales Workers	Montana	Y	23210 FQ	29030 MW	37750 TQ	USBLS	5/07
Retail Sales Workers	Billings MSA, MT	Y	24300 FQ	30090 MW	37350 TQ	USBLS	5/07
Retail Sales Workers	Great Falls MSA, MT	Y	23650 FQ	29410 MW	36700 TQ	USBLS	5/07
Retail Sales Workers	Nebraska	Y	26500 FQ	32370 MW	42540 TQ	USBLS	5/07
Retail Sales Workers	Omaha-Council Bluffs MSA, NE-IA	Y	28470 FQ	35550 MW	47010 TQ	USBLS	5/07
Retail Sales Workers	Nevada	H	12.90 FQ	16.78 MW	21.77 TQ	NVBLS	5/08
Retail Sales Workers	Las Vegas-Paradise MSA, NV	H	13.03 FQ	16.86 MW	21.75 TQ	NVBLS	5/08
Retail Sales Workers	New Hampshire	H	12.19 AE	17.13 MW	21.80 AEX	NHBLS	6/08
Retail Sales Workers	Manchester MSA, NH	Y	28200 FQ	35830 MW	46330 TQ	USBLS	5/07
Retail Sales Workers	Nashua NECTA, NH-MA	Y	29770 FQ	37490 MW	45600 TQ	USBLS	5/07
Retail Sales Workers	New Jersey	Y	30720 FQ	39010 MW	51630 TQ	USBLS	5/07
Retail Sales Workers	Camden PMSA, NJ	Y	29380 FQ	37110 MW	48500 TQ	USBLS	5/07
Retail Sales Workers	Edison PMSA, NJ	Y	30810 FQ	38750 MW	51970 TQ	USBLS	5/07
Retail Sales Workers	Newark-Union PMSA, NJ-PA	Y	32270 FQ	39770 MW	54140 TQ	USBLS	5/07
Retail Sales Workers	New Mexico	Y	23290 FQ	30490 MW	39670 TQ	USBLS	5/07
Retail Sales Workers	Albuquerque MSA, NM	Y	24640 FQ	31360 MW	41080 TQ	USBLS	5/07
Retail Sales Workers	New York	Y	29580 FQ	38360 MW	51320 TQ	USBLS	5/07
Retail Sales Workers	Albany-Schenectady-Troy MSA, NY	Y	27770 FQ	34880 MW	46100 TQ	USBLS	5/07
Retail Sales Workers	Binghamton MSA, NY	Y	27160 FQ	34140 MW	42800 TQ	USBLS	5/07
Retail Sales Workers	Buffalo-Niagara Falls MSA, NY	Y	27060 FQ	34580 MW	43760 TQ	USBLS	5/07
Retail Sales Workers	Kingston MSA, NY	Y	27760 FQ	35940 MW	46390 TQ	USBLS	5/07
Retail Sales Workers	Nassau-Suffolk PMSA, NY	Y	33030 FQ	42170 MW	56440 TQ	USBLS	5/07
Retail Sales Workers	New York-Northern New Jersey-Long Island MSA, NY-NJ-PA	Y	32120 FQ	40740 MW	54830 TQ	USBLS	5/07
Retail Sales Workers	North Carolina	Y	24450 FQ	31160 MW	40360 TQ	USBLS	5/07
Retail Sales Workers	Charlotte-Gastonia-Concord MSA, NC-SC	Y	25150 FQ	32930 MW	42720 TQ	USBLS	5/07
Retail Sales Workers	Raleigh-Cary MSA, NC	Y	25520 FQ	31500 MW	41320 TQ	USBLS	5/07
Retail Sales Workers	North Dakota	Y	25290 FQ	31410 MW	39720 TQ	USBLS	5/07
Retail Sales Workers	Fargo MSA, ND-MN	Y	26620 FQ	33570 MW	43600 TQ	USBLS	5/07
Retail Sales Workers	Ohio	Y	26390 FQ	33690 MW	43690 TQ	USBLS	5/07
Retail Sales Workers	Cincinnati-Middletown MSA, OH-KY-IN	Y	27320 FQ	34410 MW	44580 TQ	USBLS	5/07
Retail Sales Workers	Cleveland-Elyria-Mentor MSA, OH	Y	27110 FQ	34030 MW	44680 TQ	USBLS	5/07
Retail Sales Workers	Columbus MSA, OH	Y	28000 FQ	35430 MW	45870 TQ	USBLS	5/07
Retail Sales Workers	Dayton MSA, OH	Y	26510 FQ	33830 MW	43880 TQ	USBLS	5/07
Retail Sales Workers	Oklahoma	Y	23020 FQ	29560 MW	38050 TQ	USBLS	5/07
Retail Sales Workers	Oklahoma City MSA, OK	Y	24080 FQ	30540 MW	40070 TQ	USBLS	5/07
Retail Sales Workers	Tulsa MSA, OK	Y	24580 FQ	30750 MW	38410 TQ	USBLS	5/07
Retail Sales Workers	Oregon	H	13.40 FQ	16.92 MW	22.03 TQ	ORBLS	5/08
Retail Sales Workers	Portland-Vancouver-Beaverton MSA, OR-WA	Y	28990 FQ	36700 MW	46810 TQ	USBLS	5/07
Retail Sales Workers	Pennsylvania	Y	28730 FQ	36830 MW	47300 TQ	USBLS	5/07
Retail Sales Workers	Allentown-Bethlehem-Easton MSA, PA-NJ	Y	29480 FQ	36850 MW	48220 TQ	USBLS	5/07
Retail Sales Workers	Philadelphia-Camden-Wilmington MSA, PA-NJ-DE-MD	Y	31300 FQ	39460 MW	50590 TQ	USBLS	5/07
Retail Sales Workers	Pittsburgh MSA, PA	Y	28330 FQ	36290 MW	46530 TQ	USBLS	5/07
Retail Sales Workers	Reading MSA, PA	Y	28900 FQ	36180 MW	46330 TQ	USBLS	5/07
Retail Sales Workers	Rhode Island	Y	30770 FQ	36970 MW	46810 TQ	USBLS	5/07
Retail Sales Workers	Providence-Fall River-Warwick MSA, RI-MA	Y	29930 FQ	36570 MW	47010 TQ	USBLS	5/07
Retail Sales Workers	South Carolina	Y	26880 FQ	33600 MW	41660 TQ	USBLS	5/07
Retail Sales Workers	Charleston-North Charleston MSA, SC	Y	26870 FQ	33660 MW	43380 TQ	USBLS	5/07
Retail Sales Workers	Columbia MSA, SC	Y	28630 FQ	35090 MW	43360 TQ	USBLS	5/07
Retail Sales Workers	South Dakota	Y	29317 FQ	35790 MW	46265 TQ	SDBLS	7/08-9/08
Retail Sales Workers	Sioux Falls MSA, SD	Y	31308 FQ	38090 MW	49899 TQ	SDBLS	7/08-9/08

AE	Average entry wage	AW	Average wage paid	FQ	First quartile wage	LO	Lowest wage paid	MTC	Median total compensation	TCC	Total cash compensation
AER	Average entry range	AWR	Average wage range	H	Hourly	LR	Low end range	MW	Median wage paid	TQ	Third quartile wage
AEX	Average experienced wage	AXR	Average experienced range	HI	Highest wage paid	M	Monthly	MWR	Median wage range	W	Weekly
ATC	Average total compensation	D	Daily	HR	High end range	MCC	Median cash compensation	S	See annotated source	Y	Yearly

First-Line Supervisor/Manager

Occupation/Type/Industry	Location	Per	Low	Mid	High	Source	Date
Retail Sales Workers	Tennessee	Y	25500 FQ	31960 MW	41740 TQ	USBLS	5/07
Retail Sales Workers	Memphis MSA, TN-MS-AR	Y	26280 FQ	32550 MW	43620 TQ	USBLS	5/07
Retail Sales Workers	Nashville-Davidson-Murfreesboro MSA, TN	Y	26530 FQ	33530 MW	43540 TQ	USBLS	5/07
Retail Sales Workers	Texas	Y	26310 FQ	33120 MW	43260 TQ	USBLS	5/07
Retail Sales Workers	Austin-Round Rock MSA, TX	Y	27950 FQ	35290 MW	46280 TQ	USBLS	5/07
Retail Sales Workers	Dallas-Fort Worth-Arlington MSA, TX	Y	28040 FQ	34790 MW	44680 TQ	USBLS	5/07
Retail Sales Workers	El Paso MSA, TX	Y	25500 FQ	30940 MW	39900 TQ	USBLS	5/07
Retail Sales Workers	Houston-Sugar Land-Baytown MSA, TX	Y	27310 FQ	35320 MW	46230 TQ	USBLS	5/07
Retail Sales Workers	San Antonio MSA, TX	Y	26260 FQ	32820 MW	42890 TQ	USBLS	5/07
Retail Sales Workers	Utah	Y	26100 FQ	31810 MW	41050 TQ	USBLS	5/07
Retail Sales Workers	Provo-Orem MSA, UT	Y	26010 FQ	31610 MW	39560 TQ	USBLS	5/07
Retail Sales Workers	Salt Lake City MSA, UT	Y	26890 FQ	33070 MW	43830 TQ	USBLS	5/07
Retail Sales Workers	Vermont	Y	29040 FQ	36160 MW	47260 TQ	USBLS	5/07
Retail Sales Workers	Burlington-South Burlington MSA, VT	Y	30030 FQ	37400 MW	48610 TQ	USBLS	5/07
Retail Sales Workers	Virginia	Y	28180 FQ	35560 MW	46510 TQ	USBLS	5/07
Retail Sales Workers	Lynchburg MSA, VA	Y	26450 FQ	30990 MW	37850 TQ	USBLS	5/07
Retail Sales Workers	Richmond MSA, VA	Y	29570 FQ	36720 MW	47640 TQ	USBLS	5/07
Retail Sales Workers	Roanoke MSA, VA	Y	26320 FQ	31740 MW	42020 TQ	USBLS	5/07
Retail Sales Workers	Virginia Beach-Norfolk-Newport News MSA, VA-NC	Y	27500 FQ	33950 MW	44780 TQ	USBLS	5/07
Retail Sales Workers	Washington	H	15.93 FQ	19.69 MW	26.21 TQ	WABLS	3/08
Retail Sales Workers	Seattle-Tacoma-Bellevue MSA, WA	Y	33940 FQ	42140 MW	56050 TQ	USBLS	5/07
Retail Sales Workers	West Virginia	Y	23984 FQ	30150 MW	40241 TQ	WVBLS	7/08-9/08
Retail Sales Workers	Charleston MSA, WV	Y	24520 FQ	29980 MW	39050 TQ	USBLS	5/07
Retail Sales Workers	Wisconsin	Y	26850 FQ	33970 MW	44560 TQ	USBLS	5/07
Retail Sales Workers	Milwaukee-Waukesha-West Allis MSA, WI	Y	27770 FQ	34840 MW	46130 TQ	USBLS	5/07
Retail Sales Workers	Wyoming	Y	23787 FQ	30225 MW	39351 TQ	WYBLS	9/08
Retail Sales Workers	Casper MSA, WY	Y	23899 FQ	32257 MW	44122 TQ	WYBLS	9/08
Retail Sales Workers	Cheyenne MSA, WY	Y	24247 FQ	31427 MW	39160 TQ	WYBLS	9/08
Retail Sales Workers	Puerto Rico	Y	19660 FQ	24270 MW	30770 TQ	USBLS	5/07
Retail Sales Workers	San Juan-Caguas-Guaynabo MSA, PR	Y	20220 FQ	24680 MW	31650 TQ	USBLS	5/07
Retail Sales Workers	Virgin Islands	Y	29330 FQ	34240 MW	41130 TQ	USBLS	5/07
Retail Sales Workers	Guam	Y	19060 FQ	26440 MW	35200 TQ	USBLS	5/07
Transportation, Movers, Drivers	Alabama	Y	34640 FQ	44480 MW	57060 TQ	USBLS	5/07
Transportation, Movers, Drivers	Birmingham-Hoover MSA, AL	Y	36880 FQ	47200 MW	58420 TQ	USBLS	5/07
Transportation, Movers, Drivers	Alaska	Y	49680 FQ	63830 MW	80910 TQ	USBLS	5/07
Transportation, Movers, Drivers	Anchorage MSA, AK	Y	49570 FQ	65130 MW	77910 TQ	USBLS	5/07
Transportation, Movers, Drivers	Arizona	Y	37080 FQ	48940 MW	62370 TQ	USBLS	5/07
Transportation, Movers, Drivers	Phoenix-Mesa-Scottsdale MSA, AZ	Y	38230 FQ	51300 MW	64900 TQ	USBLS	5/07
Transportation, Movers, Drivers	Tucson MSA, AZ	Y	39600 FQ	47830 MW	57800 TQ	USBLS	5/07
Transportation, Movers, Drivers	Yuma MSA, AZ	Y	34300 FQ	42740 MW	49670 TQ	USBLS	5/07
Transportation, Movers, Drivers	Arkansas	Y	33150 FQ	43270 MW	55100 TQ	USBLS	5/07
Transportation, Movers, Drivers	Little Rock-North Little Rock MSA, AR	Y	37460 FQ	46030 MW	56240 TQ	USBLS	5/07
Transportation, Movers, Drivers	California	H	20.65 FQ	26.75 MW	33.79 TQ	CABLS	1/08-3/08
Transportation, Movers, Drivers	Los Angeles-Long Beach-Glendale PMSA, CA	H	20.65 FQ	27.67 MW	35.49 TQ	CABLS	1/08-3/08
Transportation, Movers, Drivers	Oakland-Fremont-Hayward MSA, CA	H	23.81 FQ	30.59 MW	38.26 TQ	CABLS	1/08-3/08
Transportation, Movers, Drivers	Riverside-San Bernardino-Ontario MSA, CA	H	20.52 FQ	25.30 MW	31.14 TQ	CABLS	1/08-3/08
Transportation, Movers, Drivers	Sacramento-Arden Arcade-Roseville MSA, CA	H	21.65 FQ	26.77 MW	31.80 TQ	CABLS	1/08-3/08
Transportation, Movers, Drivers	San Diego-Carlsbad-San Marcos MSA, CA	H	19.48 FQ	25.16 MW	31.95 TQ	CABLS	1/08-3/08
Transportation, Movers, Drivers	San Francisco-San Mateo-Redwood PMSA, CA	H	20.89 FQ	27.68 MW	32.50 TQ	CABLS	1/08-3/08
Transportation, Movers, Drivers	San Jose-Sunnyvale-Santa Clara MSA, CA	H	19.70 FQ	25.86 MW	33.12 TQ	CABLS	1/08-3/08
Transportation, Movers, Drivers	Santa Ana-Anaheim-Irvine PMSA, CA	Y	42910 FQ	53510 MW	65080 TQ	USBLS	5/07
Transportation, Movers, Drivers	Colorado	Y	37670 FQ	49560 MW	62260 TQ	USBLS	5/07
Transportation, Movers, Drivers	Denver-Aurora MSA, CO	Y	37660 FQ	49560 MW	61300 TQ	USBLS	5/07

AE	Average entry wage	AW	Average wage paid	FQ	First quartile wage
AER	Average entry range	AWR	Average wage range	H	Hourly
AEX	Average experienced wage	AXR	Average experienced range	HI	Highest wage paid
ATC	Average total compensation	D	Daily	HR	High end range

LO	Lowest wage paid	MTC	Median total compensation
LR	Low end range	MW	Median wage paid
M	Monthly	MWR	Median wage range
MCC	Median cash compensation	S	See annotated source

TCC	Total cash compensation
TQ	Third quartile wage
W	Weekly
Y	Yearly

Occupation/Type/Industry	Location	Per	Low	Mid	High	Source	Date
First-Line Supervisor/Manager							
Transportation, Movers, Drivers	Fort Collins-Loveland MSA, CO	Y	36320 FQ	47530 MW	61730 TQ	USBLS	5/07
Transportation, Movers, Drivers	Connecticut	H	17.36 AE	26.16 MW		CTBLS	1/08-3/08
Transportation, Movers, Drivers	Bridgeport-Stamford-Norwalk MSA, CT	Y	38590 FQ	52310 MW	66590 TQ	USBLS	5/07
Transportation, Movers, Drivers	Hartford-West Hartford-East Hartford MSA, CT	Y	44890 FQ	56710 MW	67260 TQ	USBLS	5/07
Transportation, Movers, Drivers	Norwich-New London MSA, CT-RI	Y	34470 FQ	40620 MW	50580 TQ	USBLS	5/07
Transportation, Movers, Drivers	Delaware	Y	41210 FQ	52470 MW	64140 TQ	USBLS	5/07
Transportation, Movers, Drivers	Wilmington PMSA, DE-MD-NJ	Y	43230 FQ	52950 MW	65130 TQ	USBLS	5/07
Transportation, Movers, Drivers	District of Columbia	Y	29490 FQ	39600 MW	63560 TQ	USBLS	5/07
Transportation, Movers, Drivers	Washington-Arlington-Alexandria MSA, DC-VA-MD-WV	Y	40040 FQ	54110 MW	70080 TQ	USBLS	5/07
Transportation, Movers, Drivers	Florida	Y	38310 FQ	49190 MW	62400 TQ	USBLS	5/07
Transportation, Movers, Drivers	Fort Lauderdale-Pompano Beach-Deerfield Beach PMSA, FL	Y	32960 FQ	48080 MW	63470 TQ	USBLS	5/07
Transportation, Movers, Drivers	Jacksonville MSA, FL	Y	37110 FQ	49430 MW	61440 TQ	USBLS	5/07
Transportation, Movers, Drivers	Lakeland MSA, FL	Y	42200 FQ	49880 MW	65020 TQ	USBLS	5/07
Transportation, Movers, Drivers	Miami-Fort Lauderdale-Miami Beach MSA, FL	Y	38530 FQ	50740 MW	65950 TQ	USBLS	5/07
Transportation, Movers, Drivers	Orlando-Kissimmee MSA, FL	Y	37250 FQ	48120 MW	60960 TQ	USBLS	5/07
Transportation, Movers, Drivers	Sarasota-Bradenton-Venice MSA, FL	Y	39330 FQ	52380 MW	61290 TQ	USBLS	5/07
Transportation, Movers, Drivers	Tallahassee MSA, FL	Y	33250 FQ	42670 MW	57720 TQ	USBLS	5/07
Transportation, Movers, Drivers	Tampa-St. Petersburg-Clearwater MSA, FL	Y	38470 FQ	49010 MW	62090 TQ	USBLS	5/07
Transportation, Movers, Drivers	West Palm Beach-Boca Raton-Boynton Beach PMSA, FL	Y	41790 FQ	52860 MW	67350 TQ	USBLS	5/07
Transportation, Movers, Drivers	Georgia	Y	34000 FQ	44400 MW	57780 TQ	USBLS	5/07
Transportation, Movers, Drivers	Atlanta-Sandy Springs-Marietta MSA, GA	Y	34760 FQ	46360 MW	59880 TQ	USBLS	5/07
Transportation, Movers, Drivers	Hawaii	Y	36600 FQ	48940 MW	65550 TQ	USBLS	5/07
Transportation, Movers, Drivers	Honolulu MSA, HI	Y	36100 FQ	50050 MW	65400 TQ	USBLS	5/07
Transportation, Movers, Drivers	Idaho	Y	32830 FQ	39230 MW	50390 TQ	USBLS	5/07
Transportation, Movers, Drivers	Boise City-Nampa MSA, ID	Y	32610 FQ	37860 MW	45780 TQ	USBLS	5/07
Transportation, Movers, Drivers	Pocatello MSA, ID	Y	35090 FQ	49510 MW	60560 TQ	USBLS	5/07
Transportation, Movers, Drivers	Illinois	Y	41330 FQ	53960 MW	66530 TQ	USBLS	5/07
Transportation, Movers, Drivers	Chicago-Naperville-Joliet MSA, IL-IN-WI	Y	42020 FQ	54770 MW	67180 TQ	USBLS	5/07
Transportation, Movers, Drivers	Indiana	Y	37580 FQ	48280 MW	60450 TQ	USBLS	5/07
Transportation, Movers, Drivers	Gary PMSA, IN	Y	37570 FQ	50230 MW	64400 TQ	USBLS	5/07
Transportation, Movers, Drivers	Indianapolis-Carmel MSA, IN	Y	40630 FQ	48940 MW	59350 TQ	USBLS	5/07
Transportation, Movers, Drivers	Iowa	Y	36400 FQ	47200 MW	58980 TQ	USBLS	5/07
Transportation, Movers, Drivers	Cedar Rapids MSA, IA	Y	40250 FQ	51210 MW	59620 TQ	USBLS	5/07
Transportation, Movers, Drivers	Des Moines-West Des Moines MSA, IA	Y	40500 FQ	52770 MW	62400 TQ	USBLS	5/07
Transportation, Movers, Drivers	Kansas	Y	34760 FQ	45110 MW	58090 TQ	USBLS	5/07
Transportation, Movers, Drivers	Wichita MSA, KS	Y	35600 FQ	47940 MW	60320 TQ	USBLS	5/07
Transportation, Movers, Drivers	Kentucky	Y	35014 FQ	45502 MW	59212 TQ	KYBLS	2008
Transportation, Movers, Drivers	Lexington-Fayette MSA, KY	Y	36180 FQ	47660 MW	58150 TQ	USBLS	5/07
Transportation, Movers, Drivers	Louisville-Jefferson County MSA, KY-IN	Y	36150 FQ	47090 MW	58920 TQ	USBLS	5/07
Transportation, Movers, Drivers	Louisiana	H	18.30 FQ	22.94 MW	30.10 TQ	LABLS	1/08-3/08
Transportation, Movers, Drivers	Baton Rouge MSA, LA	Y	37090 FQ	46700 MW	62130 TQ	USBLS	5/07
Transportation, Movers, Drivers	New Orleans-Metairie-Kenner MSA, LA	Y	40550 FQ	49090 MW	62600 TQ	USBLS	5/07
Transportation, Movers, Drivers	Maine	Y	36350 FQ	48690 MW	60710 TQ	USBLS	5/07
Transportation, Movers, Drivers	Lewiston-Auburn MSA, ME	Y	31390 FQ	42160 MW	48890 TQ	USBLS	5/07
Transportation, Movers, Drivers	Portland-South Portland-Biddeford MSA, ME	Y	39590 FQ	50860 MW	59900 TQ	USBLS	5/07
Transportation, Movers, Drivers	Maryland	Y		49875 MW		MDBLS	3/08
Transportation, Movers, Drivers	Baltimore-Towson MSA, MD	Y	35930 FQ	47210 MW	59960 TQ	USBLS	5/07
Transportation, Movers, Drivers	Bethesda-Gaithersburg-Frederick PMSA, MD	Y	41960 FQ	54280 MW	64460 TQ	USBLS	5/07
Transportation, Movers, Drivers	Massachusetts	Y	44190 FQ	55430 MW	66130 TQ	USBLS	5/07
Transportation, Movers, Drivers	Boston-Cambridge-Quincy NECTA, MA	Y	43720 FQ	55480 MW	65640 TQ	USBLS	5/07

AE	Average entry wage	AW	Average wage paid	FQ	First quartile wage
AER	Average entry range	AWR	Average wage range	H	Hourly
AEX	Average experienced wage	AXR	Average experienced range	HI	Highest wage paid
ATC	Average total compensation	D	Daily	HR	High end range

LO	Lowest wage paid	MTC	Median total compensation	TCC	Total cash compensation
LR	Low end range	MW	Median wage paid	TQ	Third quartile wage
M	Monthly	MWR	Median wage range	W	Weekly
MCC	Median cash compensation	S	See annotated source	Y	Yearly

First-Line Supervisor/Manager

Occupation/Type/Industry	Location	Per	Low	Mid	High	Source	Date
First-Line Supervisor/Manager							
Transportation, Movers, Drivers	Worcester MSA, MA-CT	Y	44750 FQ	53250 MW	62790 TQ	USBLS	5/07
Transportation, Movers, Drivers	Michigan	Y	39870 FQ	52270 MW	64640 TQ	USBLS	5/07
Transportation, Movers, Drivers	Detroit-Warren-Livonia MSA, MI	Y	43540 FQ	55500 MW	70350 TQ	USBLS	5/07
Transportation, Movers, Drivers	Grand Rapids-Wyoming MSA, MI	Y	41400 FQ	51730 MW	61200 TQ	USBLS	5/07
Transportation, Movers, Drivers	Warren-Troy-Farmington Hills PMSA, MI	Y	45900 FQ	57410 MW	69650 TQ	USBLS	5/07
Transportation, Movers, Drivers	Minnesota	Y	36745 FQ	48386 MW	60423 TQ	MNBLS	10/08-12/08
Transportation, Movers, Drivers	Duluth-Superior MSA, MN-WI	Y	38648 FQ	49000 MW	59445 TQ	MNBLS	10/08-12/08
Transportation, Movers, Drivers	Minneapolis-Saint Paul MSA, MN-WI	Y	41676 FQ	53234 MW	63461 TQ	MNBLS	10/08-12/08
Transportation, Movers, Drivers	Rochester MSA, MN	Y	26638 FQ	45310 MW	57552 TQ	MNBLS	10/08-12/08
Transportation, Movers, Drivers	Mississippi	Y	33950 FQ	42850 MW	56450 TQ	USBLS	5/07
Transportation, Movers, Drivers	Hattiesburg MSA, MS	Y	36220 FQ	49380 MW	62730 TQ	USBLS	5/07
Transportation, Movers, Drivers	Jackson MSA, MS	Y	34780 FQ	43270 MW	57060 TQ	USBLS	5/07
Transportation, Movers, Drivers	Pascagoula MSA, MS	Y	33350 FQ	44290 MW	56870 TQ	USBLS	5/07
Transportation, Movers, Drivers	Missouri	Y	39780 FQ	51280 MW	61460 TQ	USBLS	5/07
Transportation, Movers, Drivers	Kansas City MSA, MO-KS	Y	42430 FQ	52560 MW	61180 TQ	USBLS	5/07
Transportation, Movers, Drivers	St. Louis MSA, MO-IL	Y	43620 FQ	54030 MW	65630 TQ	USBLS	5/07
Transportation, Movers, Drivers	Montana	Y	32280 FQ	43940 MW	58990 TQ	USBLS	5/07
Transportation, Movers, Drivers	Billings MSA, MT	Y	32570 FQ	40260 MW	53840 TQ	USBLS	5/07
Transportation, Movers, Drivers	Nebraska	Y	36510 FQ	48700 MW	63530 TQ	USBLS	5/07
Transportation, Movers, Drivers	Omaha-Council Bluffs MSA, NE-IA	Y	37790 FQ	46780 MW	58620 TQ	USBLS	5/07
Transportation, Movers, Drivers	Nevada	H	17.92 FQ	23.60 MW	30.74 TQ	NVBLS	5/08
Transportation, Movers, Drivers	Las Vegas-Paradise MSA, NV	H	17.73 FQ	23.95 MW	31.38 TQ	NVBLS	5/08
Transportation, Movers, Drivers	New Hampshire	H	16.43 AE	23.67 MW	29.24 AEX	NHBLS	6/08
Transportation, Movers, Drivers	Manchester MSA, NH	Y	39810 FQ	53490 MW	62460 TQ	USBLS	5/07
Transportation, Movers, Drivers	Nashua NECTA, NH-MA	Y	36320 FQ	46970 MW	61220 TQ	USBLS	5/07
Transportation, Movers, Drivers	New Jersey	Y	43180 FQ	56350 MW	69870 TQ	USBLS	5/07
Transportation, Movers, Drivers	Camden PMSA, NJ	Y	42130 FQ	52920 MW	63420 TQ	USBLS	5/07
Transportation, Movers, Drivers	Edison PMSA, NJ	Y	44590 FQ	57270 MW	70090 TQ	USBLS	5/07
Transportation, Movers, Drivers	Newark-Union PMSA, NJ-PA	Y	42560 FQ	56260 MW	69540 TQ	USBLS	5/07
Transportation, Movers, Drivers	New Mexico	Y	36900 FQ	51590 MW	65520 TQ	USBLS	5/07
Transportation, Movers, Drivers	Albuquerque MSA, NM	Y	40390 FQ	54290 MW	64720 TQ	USBLS	5/07
Transportation, Movers, Drivers	New York	Y	42780 FQ	55320 MW	68370 TQ	USBLS	5/07
Transportation, Movers, Drivers	Albany-Schenectady-Troy MSA, NY	Y	36700 FQ	48990 MW	59960 TQ	USBLS	5/07
Transportation, Movers, Drivers	Buffalo-Niagara Falls MSA, NY	Y	36770 FQ	44110 MW	56080 TQ	USBLS	5/07
Transportation, Movers, Drivers	Glens Falls MSA, NY	Y	35860 FQ	41170 MW	47450 TQ	USBLS	5/07
Transportation, Movers, Drivers	Nassau-Suffolk PMSA, NY	Y	49060 FQ	60250 MW	71680 TQ	USBLS	5/07
Transportation, Movers, Drivers	New York-Northern New Jersey-Long Island MSA, NY-NJ-PA	Y	46400 FQ	59210 MW	72850 TQ	USBLS	5/07
Transportation, Movers, Drivers	North Carolina	Y	35650 FQ	44510 MW	56350 TQ	USBLS	5/07
Transportation, Movers, Drivers	Charlotte-Gastonia-Concord MSA, NC-SC	Y	35240 FQ	45820 MW	57690 TQ	USBLS	5/07
Transportation, Movers, Drivers	Raleigh-Cary MSA, NC	Y	35440 FQ	42700 MW	53510 TQ	USBLS	5/07
Transportation, Movers, Drivers	North Dakota	Y	36860 FQ	49330 MW	63080 TQ	USBLS	5/07
Transportation, Movers, Drivers	Bismarck MSA, ND	Y	34820 FQ	48690 MW	59530 TQ	USBLS	5/07
Transportation, Movers, Drivers	Fargo MSA, ND-MN	Y	34600 FQ	46600 MW	61150 TQ	USBLS	5/07
Transportation, Movers, Drivers	Ohio	Y	38590 FQ	49200 MW	61320 TQ	USBLS	5/07
Transportation, Movers, Drivers	Cincinnati-Middletown MSA, OH-KY-IN	Y	37070 FQ	50700 MW	63070 TQ	USBLS	5/07
Transportation, Movers, Drivers	Cleveland-Elyria-Mentor MSA, OH	Y	39760 FQ	50960 MW	64350 TQ	USBLS	5/07
Transportation, Movers, Drivers	Columbus MSA, OH	Y	40980 FQ	50430 MW	62540 TQ	USBLS	5/07
Transportation, Movers, Drivers	Dayton MSA, OH	Y	42010 FQ	54400 MW	64130 TQ	USBLS	5/07
Transportation, Movers, Drivers	Mansfield MSA, OH	Y	22870 FQ	41480 MW	55120 TQ	USBLS	5/07
Transportation, Movers, Drivers	Oklahoma	Y	37220 FQ	50030 MW	59720 TQ	USBLS	5/07
Transportation, Movers, Drivers	Oklahoma City MSA, OK	Y	37270 FQ	45380 MW	59530 TQ	USBLS	5/07
Transportation, Movers, Drivers	Tulsa MSA, OK	Y	50480 FQ	56430 MW	61250 TQ	USBLS	5/07
Transportation, Movers, Drivers	Oregon	H	16.78 FQ	22.32 MW	29.32 TQ	ORBLS	5/08
Transportation, Movers, Drivers	Portland-Vancouver-Beaverton MSA, OR-WA	Y	38360 FQ	50070 MW	64700 TQ	USBLS	5/07
Transportation, Movers, Drivers	Pennsylvania	Y	38000 FQ	50100 MW	62740 TQ	USBLS	5/07
Transportation, Movers, Drivers	Allentown-Bethlehem-Easton MSA, PA-NJ	Y	42460 FQ	52660 MW	65070 TQ	USBLS	5/07

AE	Average entry wage	AW	Average wage paid	FQ	First quartile wage	LO	Lowest wage paid	MTC	Median total compensation	TCC	Total cash compensation
AER	Average entry range	AWR	Average wage range	H	Hourly	LR	Low end range	MW	Median wage paid	TQ	Third quartile wage
AEX	Average experienced wage	AXR	Average experienced range	HI	Highest wage paid	M	Monthly	MWR	Median wage range	W	Weekly
ATC	Average total compensation	D	Daily	HR	High end range	MCC	Median cash compensation	S	See annotated source	Y	Yearly

Occupation/Type/Industry	Location	Per	Low	Mid	High	Source	Date
First-Line Supervisor/Manager							
Transportation, Movers, Drivers	Philadelphia-Camden-Wilmington MSA, PA-NJ-DE-MD	Y	40180 FQ	51290 MW	63910 TQ	USBLS	5/07
Transportation, Movers, Drivers	Pittsburgh MSA, PA	Y	32590 FQ	47940 MW	61530 TQ	USBLS	5/07
Transportation, Movers, Drivers	Rhode Island	Y	39750 FQ	51760 MW	62240 TQ	USBLS	5/07
Transportation, Movers, Drivers	Providence-Fall River-Warwick MSA, RI-MA	Y	39170 FQ	50630 MW	61270 TQ	USBLS	5/07
Transportation, Movers, Drivers	South Carolina	Y	35320 FQ	46110 MW	58360 TQ	USBLS	5/07
Transportation, Movers, Drivers	Charleston-North Charleston MSA, SC	Y	34980 FQ	47380 MW	57140 TQ	USBLS	5/07
Transportation, Movers, Drivers	Columbia MSA, SC	Y	36860 FQ	47080 MW	59090 TQ	USBLS	5/07
Transportation, Movers, Drivers	South Dakota	Y	42282 FQ	50425 MW	59737 TQ	SDBLS	7/08-9/08
Transportation, Movers, Drivers	Sioux Falls MSA, SD	Y	44348 FQ	51871 MW	65022 TQ	SDBLS	7/08-9/08
Transportation, Movers, Drivers	Tennessee	Y	33430 FQ	44170 MW	59240 TQ	USBLS	5/07
Transportation, Movers, Drivers	Memphis MSA, TN-MS-AR	Y	37780 FQ	53710 MW	71540 TQ	USBLS	5/07
Transportation, Movers, Drivers	Nashville-Davidson-Murfreesboro MSA, TN	Y	30380 FQ	44430 MW	58720 TQ	USBLS	5/07
Transportation, Movers, Drivers	Texas	Y	36080 FQ	47980 MW	61480 TQ	USBLS	5/07
Transportation, Movers, Drivers	Austin-Round Rock MSA, TX	Y	35320 FQ	45270 MW	57480 TQ	USBLS	5/07
Transportation, Movers, Drivers	Beaumont-Port Arthur MSA, TX	Y	30730 FQ	41880 MW	58980 TQ	USBLS	5/07
Transportation, Movers, Drivers	Dallas-Fort Worth-Arlington MSA, TX	Y	38800 FQ	50300 MW	62360 TQ	USBLS	5/07
Transportation, Movers, Drivers	El Paso MSA, TX	Y	32750 FQ	42940 MW	58390 TQ	USBLS	5/07
Transportation, Movers, Drivers	Houston-Sugar Land-Baytown MSA, TX	Y	37660 FQ	50280 MW	63090 TQ	USBLS	5/07
Transportation, Movers, Drivers	San Antonio MSA, TX	Y	34310 FQ	45760 MW	56980 TQ	USBLS	5/07
Transportation, Movers, Drivers	Utah	Y	34950 FQ	48730 MW	61110 TQ	USBLS	5/07
Transportation, Movers, Drivers	Salt Lake City MSA, UT	Y	37270 FQ	51490 MW	63090 TQ	USBLS	5/07
Transportation, Movers, Drivers	Vermont	Y	41090 FQ	51230 MW	61930 TQ	USBLS	5/07
Transportation, Movers, Drivers	Burlington-South Burlington MSA, VT	Y	41080 FQ	50320 MW	59170 TQ	USBLS	5/07
Transportation, Movers, Drivers	Virginia	Y	40350 FQ	50890 MW	65340 TQ	USBLS	5/07
Transportation, Movers, Drivers	Charlottesville MSA, VA	Y	39700 FQ	53700 MW	61250 TQ	USBLS	5/07
Transportation, Movers, Drivers	Richmond MSA, VA	Y	40670 FQ	50610 MW	64630 TQ	USBLS	5/07
Transportation, Movers, Drivers	Virginia Beach-Norfolk-Newport News MSA, VA-NC	Y	38750 FQ	47330 MW	59590 TQ	USBLS	5/07
Transportation, Movers, Drivers	Washington	H	22.29 FQ	28.21 MW	35.29 TQ	WABLS	3/08
Transportation, Movers, Drivers	Seattle-Tacoma-Bellevue MSA, WA	Y	48020 FQ	60620 MW	75250 TQ	USBLS	5/07
Transportation, Movers, Drivers	West Virginia	Y	34328 FQ	46029 MW	62912 TQ	WVBLS	7/08-9/08
Transportation, Movers, Drivers	Charleston MSA, WV	Y	33920 FQ	47240 MW	62520 TQ	USBLS	5/07
Transportation, Movers, Drivers	Wisconsin	Y	39870 FQ	50020 MW	62840 TQ	USBLS	5/07
Transportation, Movers, Drivers	Milwaukee-Waukesha-West Allis MSA, WI	Y	44480 FQ	56760 MW	71850 TQ	USBLS	5/07
Transportation, Movers, Drivers	Wyoming	Y	40576 FQ	48212 MW	68883 TQ	WYBLS	9/08
Transportation, Movers, Drivers	Casper MSA, WY	Y	36861 FQ	44527 MW	50542 TQ	WYBLS	9/08
Transportation, Movers, Drivers	Cheyenne MSA, WY	Y	42554 FQ	47356 MW	52236 TQ	WYBLS	9/08
Transportation, Movers, Drivers	Puerto Rico	Y	19410 FQ	24240 MW	31100 TQ	USBLS	5/07
Transportation, Movers, Drivers	San Juan-Caguas-Guaynabo MSA, PR	Y	20640 FQ	24850 MW	31020 TQ	USBLS	5/07
Transportation, Movers, Drivers	Virgin Islands	Y	40120 FQ	48680 MW	62820 TQ	USBLS	5/07
Transportation, Movers, Drivers	Guam	Y	23960 FQ	30190 MW	39020 TQ	USBLS	5/07
Fish and Game Warden	Alabama	Y	34470 FQ	43610 MW	51890 TQ	USBLS	5/07
	Arizona	Y	43070 FQ	49150 MW	57470 TQ	USBLS	5/07
	Arkansas	Y	33410 FQ	38940 MW	48640 TQ	USBLS	5/07
	Colorado	Y	45920 FQ	52720 MW	59680 TQ	USBLS	5/07
	Connecticut	H	18.19 AE	23.67 MW		CTBLS	1/08-3/08
	Florida	Y	35180 FQ	37910 MW	40630 TQ	USBLS	5/07
	Georgia	Y	27590 FQ	30040 MW	32590 TQ	USBLS	5/07
	Hawaii	Y	45390 FQ	50470 MW	57630 TQ	USBLS	5/07
	Idaho	Y	42960 FQ	48930 MW	58070 TQ	USBLS	5/07
	Indiana	Y	42350 FQ	45660 MW	48980 TQ	USBLS	5/07
	Iowa	Y	45540 FQ	54170 MW	60080 TQ	USBLS	5/07
	Kansas	Y	44510 FQ	48180 MW	51870 TQ	USBLS	5/07
	Louisiana	H	18.64 FQ	21.74 MW	24.15 TQ	LABLS	1/08-3/08
	Maine	Y	38110 FQ	44230 MW	48370 TQ	USBLS	5/07
	Massachusetts	Y	38150 FQ	52570 MW	59460 TQ	USBLS	5/07
	Mississippi	Y	30810 FQ	36430 MW	42410 TQ	USBLS	5/07
	Missouri	Y	37450 FQ	43680 MW	52020 TQ	USBLS	5/07

AE	Average entry wage	AW	Average wage paid	FQ	First quartile wage	LO	Lowest wage paid	MTC	Median total compensation
AER	Average entry range	AWR	Average wage range	H	Hourly	LR	Low end range	MW	Median wage paid
AEX	Average experienced wage	AXR	Average experienced range	HI	Highest wage paid	M	Monthly	MWR	Median wage range
ATC	Average total compensation	D	Daily	HR	High end range	MCC	Median cash compensation	S	See annotated source

TCC   Total cash compensation
TQ   Third quartile wage
W   Weekly
Y   Yearly

Occupation/Type/Industry	Location	Per	Low	Mid	High	Source	Date
Fish and Game Warden	Montana	Y	34030 FQ	39100 MW	45360 TQ	USBLS	5/07
	Nevada	H	23.07 FQ	27.38 MW	31.01 TQ	NVBLS	5/08
	North Dakota	Y	37350 FQ	48660 MW	60890 TQ	USBLS	5/07
	Oklahoma	Y	32240 FQ	42110 MW	47460 TQ	USBLS	5/07
	South Carolina	Y	45670 FQ	53830 MW	61510 TQ	USBLS	5/07
	South Dakota	Y	30551 FQ	36558 MW	40158 TQ	SDBLS	7/08-9/08
	Virginia	Y	38700 FQ	47180 MW	59150 TQ	USBLS	5/07
	Washington	H	25.55 FQ	27.82 MW	30.14 TQ	WABLS	3/08
	West Virginia	Y	36303 FQ	39989 MW	46688 TQ	WVBLS	7/08-9/08
	Wisconsin	Y	32890 FQ	47230 MW	56530 TQ	USBLS	5/07
Fish Hatchery Coordinator							
State Government	Ohio	H	17.22 LO		21.77 HI	ODAS	2008
Fisher and Related Fishing Worker							
	California	H	11.55 FQ	13.27 MW	16.43 TQ	CABLS	1/08-3/08
	Louisiana	H	9.75 FQ	13.76 MW	15.19 TQ	LABLS	1/08-3/08
	Massachusetts	Y	22480 FQ	24790 MW	43750 TQ	USBLS	5/07
	New Jersey	Y	17280 FQ	23260 MW	44670 TQ	USBLS	5/07
	Washington	H	13.18 FQ	14.50 MW	17.13 TQ	WABLS	3/08
	West Virginia	Y	23197 FQ	27873 MW	32086 TQ	WVBLS	7/08-9/08
Fisheries Biologist							
State Government	Ohio	H	18.36 LO		26.28 HI	ODAS	2008
Fitness Trainer and Aerobics Instructor							
	Alabama	Y	16590 FQ	20780 MW	35650 TQ	USBLS	5/07
	Birmingham-Hoover MSA, AL	Y	19200 FQ	30580 MW	39180 TQ	USBLS	5/07
	Alaska	Y	21240 FQ	31760 MW	41800 TQ	USBLS	5/07
	Anchorage MSA, AK	Y	22250 FQ	33580 MW	42950 TQ	USBLS	5/07
	Arizona	Y	17220 FQ	23020 MW	37250 TQ	USBLS	5/07
	Phoenix-Mesa-Scottsdale MSA, AZ	Y	18200 FQ	26440 MW	40760 TQ	USBLS	5/07
	Tucson MSA, AZ	Y	15730 FQ	18690 MW	30500 TQ	USBLS	5/07
	Arkansas	Y	16040 FQ	19190 MW	26130 TQ	USBLS	5/07
	Little Rock-North Little Rock MSA, AR	Y	15400 FQ	17530 MW	22520 TQ	USBLS	5/07
	California	H	11.81 FQ	18.14 MW	24.36 TQ	CABLS	1/08-3/08
	Los Angeles-Long Beach-Glendale PMSA, CA	H	11.40 FQ	19.05 MW	26.49 TQ	CABLS	1/08-3/08
	Oakland-Fremont-Hayward MSA, CA	H	11.88 FQ	17.29 MW	23.42 TQ	CABLS	1/08-3/08
	Riverside-San Bernardino-Ontario MSA, CA	H	9.70 FQ	13.10 MW	17.05 TQ	CABLS	1/08-3/08
	Sacramento-Arden Arcade-Roseville MSA, CA	H	16.22 FQ	22.13 MW	27.97 TQ	CABLS	1/08-3/08
	San Diego-Carlsbad-San Marcos MSA, CA	H	10.89 FQ	16.61 MW	23.02 TQ	CABLS	1/08-3/08
	San Francisco-San Mateo-Redwood PMSA, CA	H	15.22 FQ	19.08 MW	26.06 TQ	CABLS	1/08-3/08
	San Jose-Sunnyvale-Santa Clara MSA, CA	H	16.10 FQ	22.97 MW	32.78 TQ	CABLS	1/08-3/08
	Santa Ana-Anaheim-Irvine PMSA, CA	Y	26470 FQ	37970 MW	44910 TQ	USBLS	5/07
	Colorado	Y	21220 FQ	30940 MW	44110 TQ	USBLS	5/07
	Denver-Aurora MSA, CO	Y	23340 FQ	32040 MW	45870 TQ	USBLS	5/07
	Connecticut	H	10.31 AE	17.84 MW		CTBLS	1/08-3/08
	Bridgeport-Stamford-Norwalk MSA, CT	Y	26200 FQ	38470 MW	76820 TQ	USBLS	5/07
	Hartford-West Hartford-East Hartford MSA, CT	Y	22530 FQ	32270 MW	46520 TQ	USBLS	5/07
	Delaware	Y	18160 FQ	21760 MW	28480 TQ	USBLS	5/07
	Wilmington PMSA, DE-MD-NJ	Y	18230 FQ	21360 MW	27910 TQ	USBLS	5/07
	District of Columbia	Y	23570 FQ	32850 MW	38280 TQ	USBLS	5/07
	Washington-Arlington-Alexandria MSA, DC-VA-MD-WV	Y	21430 FQ	33580 MW	53420 TQ	USBLS	5/07
	Florida	Y	19520 FQ	30470 MW	41780 TQ	USBLS	5/07
	Cape Coral-Fort Myers MSA, FL	Y	24150 FQ	46960 MW	62760 TQ	USBLS	5/07

AE	Average entry wage	**AW**	Average wage paid	**FQ**	First quartile wage
AER	Average entry range	**AWR**	Average wage range	**H**	Hourly
AEX	Average experienced wage	**AXR**	Average experienced range	**HI**	Highest wage paid
ATC	Average total compensation	**D**	Daily	**HR**	High end range

LO	Lowest wage paid	**MTC**	Median total compensation	**TCC**	Total cash compensation
LR	Low end range	**MW**	Median wage paid	**TQ**	Third quartile wage
M	Monthly	**MWR**	Median wage range	**W**	Weekly
MCC	Median cash compensation	**S**	See annotated source	**Y**	Yearly

Occupation/Type/Industry	Location	Per	Low	Mid	High	Source	Date
Fitness Trainer and Aerobics Instructor	Fort Lauderdale-Pompano Beach-Deerfield Beach PMSA, FL	Y	26830 FQ	30910 MW	39520 TQ	USBLS	5/07
	Jacksonville MSA, FL	Y	19550 FQ	35890 MW	42150 TQ	USBLS	5/07
	Miami-Fort Lauderdale-Miami Beach MSA, FL	Y	20890 FQ	31190 MW	46770 TQ	USBLS	5/07
	Orlando-Kissimmee MSA, FL	Y	26230 FQ	33010 MW	39410 TQ	USBLS	5/07
	Tampa-St. Petersburg-Clearwater MSA, FL	Y	15890 FQ	27680 MW	39670 TQ	USBLS	5/07
	West Palm Beach-Boca Raton-Boynton Beach PMSA, FL	Y	23300 FQ	45220 MW	59780 TQ	USBLS	5/07
	Georgia	Y	18360 FQ	28170 MW	40420 TQ	USBLS	5/07
	Atlanta-Sandy Springs-Marietta MSA, GA	Y	18940 FQ	29840 MW	41450 TQ	USBLS	5/07
	Augusta-Richmond County MSA, GA-SC	Y	18270 FQ	24580 MW	38220 TQ	USBLS	5/07
	Hawaii	Y	19320 FQ	26850 MW	35490 TQ	USBLS	5/07
	Honolulu MSA, HI	Y	18690 FQ	24000 MW	31190 TQ	USBLS	5/07
	Idaho	Y	16060 FQ	26890 MW	38940 TQ	USBLS	5/07
	Boise City-Nampa MSA, ID	Y	18450 FQ	34390 MW	41480 TQ	USBLS	5/07
	Pocatello MSA, ID	Y	19680 FQ	25740 MW	35260 TQ	USBLS	5/07
	Illinois	Y	18010 FQ	24650 MW	44730 TQ	USBLS	5/07
	Champaign-Urbana MSA, IL	Y	20030 FQ	33110 MW	47580 TQ	USBLS	5/07
	Chicago-Naperville-Joliet MSA, IL-IN-WI	Y	18330 FQ	25660 MW	47510 TQ	USBLS	5/07
	Indiana	Y	16500 FQ	19590 MW	28130 TQ	USBLS	5/07
	Gary PMSA, IN	Y	14270 FQ	17640 MW	23330 TQ	USBLS	5/07
	Indianapolis-Carmel MSA, IN	Y	17690 FQ	20810 MW	50410 TQ	USBLS	5/07
	Iowa	Y	15600 FQ	20590 MW	28490 TQ	USBLS	5/07
	Des Moines-West Des Moines MSA, IA	Y	17320 FQ	23460 MW	29770 TQ	USBLS	5/07
	Kansas	Y	15510 FQ	24570 MW	33000 TQ	USBLS	5/07
	Wichita MSA, KS	Y	15200 FQ	24570 MW	32200 TQ	USBLS	5/07
	Kentucky	Y	16823 FQ	28666 MW	39195 TQ	KYBLS	2008
	Louisville-Jefferson County MSA, KY-IN	Y	20250 FQ	29630 MW	43870 TQ	USBLS	5/07
	Louisiana	H	7.24 FQ	9.93 MW	19.36 TQ	LABLS	1/08-3/08
	Baton Rouge MSA, LA	Y	14400 FQ	34850 MW	45060 TQ	USBLS	5/07
	New Orleans-Metairie-Kenner MSA, LA	Y	15710 FQ	18270 MW	33910 TQ	USBLS	5/07
	Maine	Y	16190 FQ	20280 MW	28300 TQ	USBLS	5/07
	Portland-South Portland-Biddeford MSA, ME	Y	18650 FQ	23510 MW	38000 TQ	USBLS	5/07
	Maryland	Y		25600 MW		MDBLS	3/08
	Baltimore-Towson MSA, MD	Y	18350 FQ	24910 MW	38220 TQ	USBLS	5/07
	Bethesda-Gaithersburg-Frederick PMSA, MD	Y	20980 FQ	29070 MW	48060 TQ	USBLS	5/07
	Massachusetts	Y	22750 FQ	36810 MW	59280 TQ	USBLS	5/07
	Boston-Cambridge-Quincy NECTA, MA	Y	27390 FQ	49920 MW	65650 TQ	USBLS	5/07
	New Bedford MSA, MA	Y	20490 FQ	22360 MW	25060 TQ	USBLS	5/07
	Worcester MSA, MA-CT	Y	19910 FQ	26300 MW	33200 TQ	USBLS	5/07
	Michigan	Y	15810 FQ	19550 MW	29330 TQ	USBLS	5/07
	Detroit-Warren-Livonia MSA, MI	Y	15570 FQ	19910 MW	29430 TQ	USBLS	5/07
	Flint MSA, MI	Y	17290 FQ	18930 MW	20350 TQ	USBLS	5/07
	Grand Rapids-Wyoming MSA, MI	Y	15930 FQ	18330 MW	29160 TQ	USBLS	5/07
	Warren-Troy-Farmington Hills PMSA, MI	Y	15300 FQ	19050 MW	27660 TQ	USBLS	5/07
	Minnesota	Y	19688 FQ	25554 MW	34629 TQ	MNBLS	10/08-12/08
	Duluth-Superior MSA, MN-WI	Y	20503 FQ	24215 MW	27300 TQ	MNBLS	10/08-12/08
	Minneapolis-Saint Paul MSA, MN-WI	Y	20807 FQ	27017 MW	36292 TQ	MNBLS	10/08-12/08
	Rochester MSA, MN	Y	19570 FQ	31205 MW	41885 TQ	MNBLS	10/08-12/08
	Mississippi	Y	18460 FQ	25350 MW	36210 TQ	USBLS	5/07
	Jackson MSA, MS	Y	18380 FQ	33950 MW	40120 TQ	USBLS	5/07
	Missouri	Y	16250 FQ	22020 MW	31200 TQ	USBLS	5/07
	Kansas City MSA, MO-KS	Y	21310 FQ	29800 MW	38620 TQ	USBLS	5/07
	St. Joseph MSA, MO-KS	Y	14600 FQ	16600 MW	21020 TQ	USBLS	5/07
	St. Louis MSA, MO-IL	Y	18080 FQ	23330 MW	35150 TQ	USBLS	5/07

AE	Average entry wage	AW	Average wage paid	FQ	First quartile wage	LO	Lowest wage paid	MTC Median total compensation	TCC Total cash compensation
AER	Average entry range	AWR	Average wage range	H	Hourly	LR	Low end range	MW Median wage paid	TQ Third quartile wage
AEX	Average experienced wage	AXR	Average experienced range	HI	Highest wage paid	M	Monthly	MWR Median wage range	W Weekly
ATC	Average total compensation	D	Daily	HR	High end range	MCC	Median cash compensation	S See annotated source	Y Yearly

661

Occupation/Type/Industry	Location	Per	Low	Mid	High	Source	Date
Fitness Trainer and Aerobics Instructor	Montana	Y	18170 FQ	26520 MW	35490 TQ	USBLS	5/07
	Billings MSA, MT	Y	16870 FQ	20360 MW	37090 TQ	USBLS	5/07
	Nebraska	Y	17430 FQ	25040 MW	37550 TQ	USBLS	5/07
	Omaha-Council Bluffs MSA, NE-IA	Y	17710 FQ	28480 MW	41950 TQ	USBLS	5/07
	Las Vegas-Paradise MSA, NV	H	10.68 FQ	15.32 MW	20.34 TQ	NVBLS	5/08
	New Hampshire	H	9.02 AE	12.97 MW	16.45 AEX	NHBLS	6/06
	Manchester MSA, NH	Y	20010 FQ	25910 MW	29010 TQ	USBLS	5/07
	Nashua NECTA, NH-MA	Y	21910 FQ	27180 MW	33750 TQ	USBLS	5/07
	Portsmouth MSA, NH-ME	Y	19320 FQ	32430 MW	46450 TQ	USBLS	5/07
	New Jersey	Y	21520 FQ	37080 MW	55200 TQ	USBLS	5/07
	Camden PMSA, NJ	Y	25870 FQ	40700 MW	52140 TQ	USBLS	5/07
	Edison PMSA, NJ	Y	18010 FQ	26150 MW	51040 TQ	USBLS	5/07
	Newark-Union PMSA, NJ-PA	Y	24470 FQ	36320 MW	52440 TQ	USBLS	5/07
	New Mexico	Y	17360 FQ	23350 MW	33250 TQ	USBLS	5/07
	Albuquerque MSA, NM	Y	19250 FQ	24460 MW	33710 TQ	USBLS	5/07
	New York	Y	22580 FQ	37150 MW	55960 TQ	USBLS	5/07
	Albany-Schenectady-Troy MSA, NY	Y	18370 FQ	22600 MW	29100 TQ	USBLS	5/07
	Buffalo-Niagara Falls MSA, NY	Y	17430 FQ	23470 MW	32890 TQ	USBLS	5/07
	Nassau-Suffolk PMSA, NY	Y	31020 FQ	51400 MW	69460 TQ	USBLS	5/07
	New York-Northern New Jersey-Long Island MSA, NY-NJ-PA	Y	24780 FQ	41330 MW	59260 TQ	USBLS	5/07
	North Carolina	Y	19350 FQ	26530 MW	37360 TQ	USBLS	5/07
	Asheville MSA, NC	Y	22040 FQ	33610 MW	41930 TQ	USBLS	5/07
	Charlotte-Gastonia-Concord MSA, NC-SC	Y	20840 FQ	28130 MW	35770 TQ	USBLS	5/07
	Raleigh-Cary MSA, NC	Y	35100 FQ	39570 MW	46220 TQ	USBLS	5/07
	North Dakota	Y	14550 FQ	17430 MW	22840 TQ	USBLS	5/07
	Fargo MSA, ND-MN	Y	15230 FQ	18540 MW	23960 TQ	USBLS	5/07
	Grand Forks MSA, ND-MN	Y	15090 FQ	16760 MW	18670 TQ	USBLS	5/07
	Ohio	Y	15990 FQ	20420 MW	30180 TQ	USBLS	5/07
	Cincinnati-Middletown MSA, OH-KY-IN	Y	15840 FQ	22360 MW	31300 TQ	USBLS	5/07
	Cleveland-Elyria-Mentor MSA, OH	Y	16120 FQ	20020 MW	30680 TQ	USBLS	5/07
	Columbus MSA, OH	Y	19190 FQ	29460 MW	42220 TQ	USBLS	5/07
	Dayton MSA, OH	Y	16500 FQ	21660 MW	30480 TQ	USBLS	5/07
	Mansfield MSA, OH	Y	16110 FQ	22570 MW	32560 TQ	USBLS	5/07
	Oklahoma	Y	14770 FQ	21920 MW	34950 TQ	USBLS	5/07
	Oklahoma City MSA, OK	Y	15480 FQ	22740 MW	35430 TQ	USBLS	5/07
	Tulsa MSA, OK	Y	15210 FQ	25300 MW	37410 TQ	USBLS	5/07
	Oregon	H	10.44 FQ	15.60 MW	22.92 TQ	ORBLS	5/08
	Portland-Vancouver-Beaverton MSA, OR-WA	Y	22130 FQ	37880 MW	53620 TQ	USBLS	5/07
	Pennsylvania	Y	17640 FQ	22480 MW	29730 TQ	USBLS	5/07
	Allentown-Bethlehem-Easton MSA, PA-NJ	Y	17280 FQ	22560 MW	34410 TQ	USBLS	5/07
	Philadelphia-Camden-Wilmington MSA, PA-NJ-DE-MD	Y	19350 FQ	24080 MW	33040 TQ	USBLS	5/07
	Pittsburgh MSA, PA	Y	16680 FQ	20980 MW	27820 TQ	USBLS	5/07
	Rhode Island	Y	20490 FQ	25150 MW	35730 TQ	USBLS	5/07
	Providence-Fall River-Warwick MSA, RI-MA	Y	20280 FQ	25340 MW	35670 TQ	USBLS	5/07
	South Carolina	Y	19870 FQ	29720 MW	37400 TQ	USBLS	5/07
	Charleston-North Charleston MSA, SC	Y	20230 FQ	27160 MW	41760 TQ	USBLS	5/07
	Columbia MSA, SC	Y	31900 FQ	35230 MW	38550 TQ	USBLS	5/07
	Florence MSA, SC	Y	14940 FQ	21130 MW	33140 TQ	USBLS	5/07
	South Dakota	Y	18521 FQ	21955 MW	25629 TQ	SDBLS	7/08-9/08
	Rapid City MSA, SD	Y	18215 FQ	22381 MW	26001 TQ	SDBLS	7/08-9/08
	Sioux Falls MSA, SD	Y	20259 FQ	23330 MW	28003 TQ	SDBLS	7/08-9/08
	Tennessee	Y	19610 FQ	30450 MW	39010 TQ	USBLS	5/07
	Memphis MSA, TN-MS-AR	Y	17920 FQ	30710 MW	38040 TQ	USBLS	5/07
	Nashville-Davidson-Murfreesboro MSA, TN	Y	22120 FQ	31490 MW	42580 TQ	USBLS	5/07
	Texas	Y	17400 FQ	25780 MW	42080 TQ	USBLS	5/07
	Austin-Round Rock MSA, TX	Y	14170 FQ	25080 MW	43670 TQ	USBLS	5/07

AE	Average entry wage	AW	Average wage paid	FQ	First quartile wage
AER	Average entry range	AWR	Average wage range	H	Hourly
AEX	Average experienced wage	AXR	Average experienced range	HI	Highest wage paid
ATC	Average total compensation	D	Daily	HR	High end range

LO	Lowest wage paid	MTC	Median total compensation	TCC	Total cash compensation
LR	Low end range	MW	Median wage paid	TQ	Third quartile wage
HI	Highest wage paid	MWR	Median wage range	W	Weekly
M	Monthly	S	See annotated source	Y	Yearly
MCC	Median cash compensation			

Occupation/Type/Industry	Location	Per	Low	Mid	High	Source	Date
Fitness Trainer and Aerobics Instructor	Dallas-Fort Worth-Arlington MSA, TX	Y	21740 FQ	31120 MW	49580 TQ	USBLS	5/07
	El Paso MSA, TX	Y	20610 FQ	25440 MW	32930 TQ	USBLS	5/07
	Houston-Sugar Land-Baytown MSA, TX	Y	15940 FQ	24220 MW	39200 TQ	USBLS	5/07
	San Antonio MSA, TX	Y	16940 FQ	21410 MW	36980 TQ	USBLS	5/07
	Utah	Y	31000 FQ	43230 MW	54890 TQ	USBLS	5/07
	St. George MSA, UT	Y	24400 FQ	40380 MW	49840 TQ	USBLS	5/07
	Salt Lake City MSA, UT	Y	31900 FQ	42840 MW	55680 TQ	USBLS	5/07
	Vermont	Y	17710 FQ	24090 MW	35590 TQ	USBLS	5/07
	Burlington-South Burlington MSA, VT	Y	18450 FQ	24980 MW	36130 TQ	USBLS	5/07
	Virginia	Y	18450 FQ	29300 MW	48340 TQ	USBLS	5/07
	Richmond MSA, VA	Y	16250 FQ	22350 MW	36490 TQ	USBLS	5/07
	Virginia Beach-Norfolk-Newport News MSA, VA-NC	Y	18740 FQ	24560 MW	32460 TQ	USBLS	5/07
	Washington	H	10.87 FQ	16.60 MW	26.27 TQ	WABLS	3/08
	Seattle-Tacoma-Bellevue MSA, WA	Y	22630 FQ	36150 MW	57570 TQ	USBLS	5/07
	West Virginia	Y	14565 FQ	16791 MW	24360 TQ	WVBLS	7/08-9/08
	Charleston MSA, WV	Y	20270 FQ	23270 MW	26000 TQ	USBLS	5/07
	Wisconsin	Y	16640 FQ	19380 MW	24970 TQ	USBLS	5/07
	Milwaukee-Waukesha-West Allis MSA, WI	Y	16070 FQ	18540 MW	22390 TQ	USBLS	5/07
	Wyoming	Y	15314 FQ	19223 MW	23851 TQ	WYBLS	9/08
	Cheyenne MSA, WY	Y	15424 FQ	20761 MW	23616 TQ	WYBLS	9/08
	Puerto Rico	Y	12620 FQ	14040 MW	15650 TQ	USBLS	5/07
	San Juan-Caguas-Guaynabo MSA, PR	Y	12610 FQ	14000 MW	15590 TQ	USBLS	5/07
	Virgin Islands	Y	19440 FQ	24010 MW	29440 TQ	USBLS	5/07
Fleet Control Coordinator State Highway Patrol	Missouri	S	1192 LO		1676 HI	MSHPSS	7/1/08
Fleet Supervisor Public Schools	Howell, MI	Y			61992 HI	LCPP	2009
Flight Attendant	Colorado	Y	52320 FQ	57600 MW	62820 TQ	USBLS	5/07
	Florida	Y	56370 FQ	82440 MW	101430 TQ	USBLS	5/07
	Georgia	Y	31520 FQ	54170 MW	80030 TQ	USBLS	5/07
	Hawaii	Y	51740 FQ	59160 MW	71560 TQ	USBLS	5/07
	Illinois	Y	55050 FQ	62180 MW	80960 TQ	USBLS	5/07
	Massachusetts	Y	52490 FQ	61540 MW	85550 TQ	USBLS	5/07
	Michigan	Y	53210 FQ	61160 MW	76860 TQ	USBLS	5/07
	Minnesota	Y	53460 FQ	58584 MW	63602 TQ	MNBLS	10/08-12/08
	Missouri	Y	61080 FQ	74620 MW	89530 TQ	USBLS	5/07
	New Jersey	Y	66820 FQ	72280 MW	77760 TQ	USBLS	5/07
	New York	Y	52550 FQ	65400 MW	92920 TQ	USBLS	5/07
	Ohio	Y	43070 FQ	57780 MW	86810 TQ	USBLS	5/07
	Texas	Y	15540 FQ	58210 MW	94530 TQ	USBLS	5/07
	Utah	Y	32450 FQ	39450 MW	48560 TQ	USBLS	5/07
	Wisconsin	Y	48620 FQ	57960 MW	68920 TQ	USBLS	5/07
Flight Line Mechanic	United States	H		20.00 AW		AVJOB07	2009
Floor Layer Except Carpet, Wood, and Hard Tiles	Alabama	Y	28180 FQ	31290 MW	35750 TQ	USBLS	5/07
Except Carpet, Wood, and Hard Tiles	Arizona	Y	24170 FQ	30010 MW	46050 TQ	USBLS	5/07
Except Carpet, Wood, and Hard Tiles	Phoenix-Mesa-Scottsdale MSA, AZ	Y	24010 FQ	29440 MW	41070 TQ	USBLS	5/07
Except Carpet, Wood, and Hard Tiles	Tucson MSA, AZ	Y	21730 FQ	29700 MW	58320 TQ	USBLS	5/07
Except Carpet, Wood, and Hard Tiles	Arkansas	Y	21330 FQ	26600 MW	34210 TQ	USBLS	5/07
Except Carpet, Wood, and Hard Tiles	California	H	13.72 FQ	18.72 MW	24.58 TQ	CABLS	1/08-3/08
Except Carpet, Wood, and Hard Tiles	Los Angeles-Long Beach-Glendale PMSA, CA	H	14.74 FQ	18.58 MW	24.22 TQ	CABLS	1/08-3/08
Except Carpet, Wood, and Hard Tiles	Oakland-Fremont-Hayward MSA, CA	H	14.94 FQ	21.15 MW	30.39 TQ	CABLS	1/08-3/08
Except Carpet, Wood, and Hard Tiles	Riverside-San Bernardino-Ontario MSA, CA	H	12.66 FQ	17.37 MW	25.49 TQ	CABLS	1/08-3/08
Except Carpet, Wood, and Hard Tiles	Sacramento-Arden Arcade-Roseville MSA, CA	H	17.09 FQ	20.59 MW	23.59 TQ	CABLS	1/08-3/08

AE	Average entry wage	**AW**	Average wage paid	**FQ**	First quartile wage	**LO**	Lowest wage paid	**MTC** Median total compensation	**TCC** Total cash compensation
AER	Average entry range	**AWR**	Average wage range	**H**	Hourly	**LR**	Low end range	**MW** Median wage paid	**TQ** Third quartile wage
AEX	Average experienced wage	**AXR**	Average experienced range	**HI**	Highest wage paid	**M**	Monthly	**MWR** Median wage range	**W** Weekly
ATC	Average total compensation	**D**	Daily	**HR**	High end range	**MCC**	Median cash compensation	**S** See annotated source	**Y** Yearly

Occupation/Type/Industry	Location	Per	Low	Mid	High	Source	Date
Floor Layer							
Except Carpet, Wood, and Hard Tiles	San Diego-Carlsbad-San Marcos MSA, CA	H	12.86 FQ	18.08 MW	23.70 TQ	CABLS	1/08-3/08
Except Carpet, Wood, and Hard Tiles	San Jose-Sunnyvale-Santa Clara MSA, CA	H	16.34 FQ	23.75 MW	31.91 TQ	CABLS	1/08-3/08
Except Carpet, Wood, and Hard Tiles	Santa Ana-Anaheim-Irvine PMSA, CA	Y	25720 FQ	34430 MW	40100 TQ	USBLS	5/07
Except Carpet, Wood, and Hard Tiles	Colorado	Y	24300 FQ	33190 MW	46130 TQ	USBLS	5/07
Except Carpet, Wood, and Hard Tiles	Connecticut	H	16.55 AE	23.11 MW		CTBLS	1/08-3/08
Except Carpet, Wood, and Hard Tiles	Delaware	Y	24850 FQ	32580 MW	38650 TQ	USBLS	5/07
Except Carpet, Wood, and Hard Tiles	Wilmington PMSA, DE-MD-NJ	Y	22890 FQ	32780 MW	38400 TQ	USBLS	5/07
Except Carpet, Wood, and Hard Tiles	Washington-Arlington-Alexandria MSA, DC-VA-MD-WV	Y	22060 FQ	25140 MW	32050 TQ	USBLS	5/07
Except Carpet, Wood, and Hard Tiles	Florida	Y	23140 FQ	29830 MW	41930 TQ	USBLS	5/07
Except Carpet, Wood, and Hard Tiles	Miami-Fort Lauderdale-Miami Beach MSA, FL	Y	22910 FQ	26030 MW	33190 TQ	USBLS	5/07
Except Carpet, Wood, and Hard Tiles	Orlando-Kissimmee MSA, FL	Y	33170 FQ	43230 MW	49310 TQ	USBLS	5/07
Except Carpet, Wood, and Hard Tiles	Tampa-St. Petersburg-Clearwater MSA, FL	Y	20800 FQ	24160 MW	28130 TQ	USBLS	5/07
Except Carpet, Wood, and Hard Tiles	West Palm Beach-Boca Raton-Boynton Beach PMSA, FL	Y	22090 FQ	24520 MW	36410 TQ	USBLS	5/07
Except Carpet, Wood, and Hard Tiles	Georgia	Y	25750 FQ	33560 MW	39560 TQ	USBLS	5/07
Except Carpet, Wood, and Hard Tiles	Atlanta-Sandy Springs-Marietta MSA, GA	Y	29920 FQ	33840 MW	37880 TQ	USBLS	5/07
Except Carpet, Wood, and Hard Tiles	Hawaii	Y	37520 FQ	53280 MW	60450 TQ	USBLS	5/07
Except Carpet, Wood, and Hard Tiles	Honolulu MSA, HI	Y	36440 FQ	52740 MW	59530 TQ	USBLS	5/07
Except Carpet, Wood, and Hard Tiles	Idaho	Y	28280 FQ	30320 MW	32410 TQ	USBLS	5/07
Except Carpet, Wood, and Hard Tiles	Illinois	Y	36320 FQ	41250 MW	72080 TQ	USBLS	5/07
Except Carpet, Wood, and Hard Tiles	Chicago-Naperville-Joliet MSA, IL-IN-WI	Y	36550 FQ	41640 MW	72930 TQ	USBLS	5/07
Except Carpet, Wood, and Hard Tiles	Indiana	Y	18540 FQ	23710 MW	38150 TQ	USBLS	5/07
Except Carpet, Wood, and Hard Tiles	Indianapolis-Carmel MSA, IN	Y	19500 FQ	26440 MW	46390 TQ	USBLS	5/07
Except Carpet, Wood, and Hard Tiles	Iowa	Y	23140 FQ	29080 MW	54210 TQ	USBLS	5/07
Except Carpet, Wood, and Hard Tiles	Kansas	Y	27310 FQ	31610 MW	39830 TQ	USBLS	5/07
Except Carpet, Wood, and Hard Tiles	Kentucky	Y	20472 FQ	29525 MW	36777 TQ	KYBLS	2008
Except Carpet, Wood, and Hard Tiles	Louisiana	H	12.71 FQ	16.49 MW	18.07 TQ	LABLS	1/08-3/08
Except Carpet, Wood, and Hard Tiles	Baltimore-Towson MSA, MD	Y	44470 FQ	55930 MW	61450 TQ	USBLS	5/07
Except Carpet, Wood, and Hard Tiles	Bethesda-Gaithersburg-Frederick PMSA, MD	Y	21060 FQ	24590 MW	28870 TQ	USBLS	5/07
Except Carpet, Wood, and Hard Tiles	Massachusetts	Y	29740 FQ	38730 MW	73360 TQ	USBLS	5/07
Except Carpet, Wood, and Hard Tiles	Boston-Cambridge-Quincy NECTA, MA	Y	40570 FQ	69820 MW	77660 TQ	USBLS	5/07
Except Carpet, Wood, and Hard Tiles	Michigan	Y	28290 FQ	31180 MW	34850 TQ	USBLS	5/07
Except Carpet, Wood, and Hard Tiles	Grand Rapids-Wyoming MSA, MI	Y	33060 FQ	35390 MW	37710 TQ	USBLS	5/07
Except Carpet, Wood, and Hard Tiles	Minnesota	Y	39541 FQ	55634 MW	61820 TQ	MNBLS	10/08-12/08
Except Carpet, Wood, and Hard Tiles	Mississippi	Y	21520 FQ	28570 MW	37250 TQ	USBLS	5/07
Except Carpet, Wood, and Hard Tiles	Missouri	Y	34630 FQ	42430 MW	57900 TQ	USBLS	5/07
Except Carpet, Wood, and Hard Tiles	Kansas City MSA, MO-KS	Y	30350 FQ	40990 MW	51160 TQ	USBLS	5/07
Except Carpet, Wood, and Hard Tiles	St. Louis MSA, MO-IL	Y	34510 FQ	40930 MW	59650 TQ	USBLS	5/07
Except Carpet, Wood, and Hard Tiles	Omaha-Council Bluffs MSA, NE-IA	Y	34850 FQ	42840 MW	47130 TQ	USBLS	5/07
Except Carpet, Wood, and Hard Tiles	Nevada	H	18.14 FQ	22.47 MW	26.98 TQ	NVBLS	5/08
Except Carpet, Wood, and Hard Tiles	Las Vegas-Paradise MSA, NV	H	20.92 FQ	23.47 MW	28.73 TQ	NVBLS	5/08
Except Carpet, Wood, and Hard Tiles	New Jersey	Y	26020 FQ	30940 MW	38340 TQ	USBLS	5/07
Except Carpet, Wood, and Hard Tiles	Edison PMSA, NJ	Y	27560 FQ	30740 MW	36130 TQ	USBLS	5/07
Except Carpet, Wood, and Hard Tiles	New York	Y	21180 FQ	30310 MW	48390 TQ	USBLS	5/07
Except Carpet, Wood, and Hard Tiles	Nassau-Suffolk PMSA, NY	Y	30820 FQ	44530 MW	62910 TQ	USBLS	5/07
Except Carpet, Wood, and Hard Tiles	New York-Northern New Jersey-Long Island MSA, NY-NJ-PA	Y	21290 FQ	30550 MW	46980 TQ	USBLS	5/07
Except Carpet, Wood, and Hard Tiles	North Carolina	Y	19990 FQ	23100 MW	34560 TQ	USBLS	5/07
Except Carpet, Wood, and Hard Tiles	Ohio	Y	33580 FQ	38180 MW	47920 TQ	USBLS	5/07
Except Carpet, Wood, and Hard Tiles	Cincinnati-Middletown MSA, OH-KY-IN	Y	33220 FQ	44990 MW	50320 TQ	USBLS	5/07
Except Carpet, Wood, and Hard Tiles	Oklahoma	Y	28630 FQ	34430 MW	38160 TQ	USBLS	5/07
Except Carpet, Wood, and Hard Tiles	Portland-Vancouver-Beaverton MSA, OR-WA	Y	28260 FQ	35260 MW	40140 TQ	USBLS	5/07
Except Carpet, Wood, and Hard Tiles	Pennsylvania	Y	29460 FQ	36250 MW	46730 TQ	USBLS	5/07

AE	Average entry wage	**AW**	Average wage paid	**FQ**	First quartile wage	**LO**	Lowest wage paid	**MTC**	Median total compensation	**TCC**	Total cash compensation
AER	Average entry range	**AWR**	Average wage range	**H**	Hourly	**LR**	Low end range	**MW**	Median wage paid	**TQ**	Third quartile wage
AEX	Average experienced wage	**AXR**	Average experienced range	**HI**	Highest wage paid	**M**	Monthly	**MWR**	Median wage range	**W**	Weekly
ATC	Average total compensation	**D**	Daily	**HR**	High end range	**MCC**	Median cash compensation	**S**	See annotated source	**Y**	Yearly

Occupation/Type/Industry	Location	Per	Low	Mid	High	Source	Date
Floor Layer							
Except Carpet, Wood, and Hard Tiles	Philadelphia-Camden-Wilmington MSA, PA-NJ-DE-MD	Y	33290 FQ	42050 MW	50520 TQ	USBLS	5/07
Except Carpet, Wood, and Hard Tiles	Rhode Island	Y	28250 FQ	31530 MW	47710 TQ	USBLS	5/07
Except Carpet, Wood, and Hard Tiles	Providence-Fall River-Warwick MSA, RI-MA	Y	28880 FQ	43400 MW	69500 TQ	USBLS	5/07
Except Carpet, Wood, and Hard Tiles	South Carolina	Y	25550 FQ	29660 MW	34650 TQ	USBLS	5/07
Except Carpet, Wood, and Hard Tiles	South Dakota	Y	27938 FQ	31284 MW	34602 TQ	SDBLS	7/08-9/08
Except Carpet, Wood, and Hard Tiles	Tennessee	Y	24770 FQ	28620 MW	32570 TQ	USBLS	5/07
Except Carpet, Wood, and Hard Tiles	Texas	Y	22730 FQ	27720 MW	35790 TQ	USBLS	5/07
Except Carpet, Wood, and Hard Tiles	Dallas-Fort Worth-Arlington MSA, TX	Y	23170 FQ	28580 MW	38050 TQ	USBLS	5/07
Except Carpet, Wood, and Hard Tiles	Utah	Y	23530 FQ	27970 MW	36860 TQ	USBLS	5/07
Except Carpet, Wood, and Hard Tiles	Salt Lake City MSA, UT	Y	27850 FQ	33180 MW	46810 TQ	USBLS	5/07
Except Carpet, Wood, and Hard Tiles	Vermont	Y	27310 FQ	34930 MW	38720 TQ	USBLS	5/07
Except Carpet, Wood, and Hard Tiles	Virginia	Y	28180 FQ	32240 MW	37840 TQ	USBLS	5/07
Except Carpet, Wood, and Hard Tiles	Washington	H	14.52 FQ	21.85 MW	33.19 TQ	WABLS	3/08
Except Carpet, Wood, and Hard Tiles	Seattle-Tacoma-Bellevue MSA, WA	Y	36410 FQ	53440 MW	68650 TQ	USBLS	5/07
Except Carpet, Wood, and Hard Tiles	Spokane MSA, WA	Y	26970 FQ	29950 MW	40250 TQ	USBLS	5/07
Except Carpet, Wood, and Hard Tiles	West Virginia	Y	17676 FQ	38296 MW	44560 TQ	WVBLS	7/08-9/08
Except Carpet, Wood, and Hard Tiles	Wisconsin	Y	29660 FQ	37650 MW	55240 TQ	USBLS	5/07
Except Carpet, Wood, and Hard Tiles	Milwaukee-Waukesha-West Allis MSA, WI	Y	33020 FQ	56500 MW	65810 TQ	USBLS	5/07
Floor Sander and Finisher	Alabama	Y	26190 FQ	31110 MW	35340 TQ	USBLS	5/07
	Arizona	Y	23480 FQ	35960 MW	40560 TQ	USBLS	5/07
	Arkansas	Y	19370 FQ	26000 MW	29270 TQ	USBLS	5/07
	California	H	16.08 FQ	20.30 MW	23.60 TQ	CABLS	1/08-3/08
	Colorado	Y	27540 FQ	31360 MW	39800 TQ	USBLS	5/07
	Connecticut	H	16.33 AE	17.94 MW		CTBLS	1/08-3/08
	Georgia	Y	20560 FQ	27380 MW	33870 TQ	USBLS	5/07
	Illinois	Y	27800 FQ	47100 MW	62180 TQ	USBLS	5/07
	Indiana	Y	25750 FQ	32910 MW	39900 TQ	USBLS	5/07
	Kansas	Y	26440 FQ	29940 MW	40020 TQ	USBLS	5/07
	Kentucky	Y	26408 FQ	31361 MW	40703 TQ	KYBLS	2008
	Louisiana	H	9.50 FQ	11.44 MW	14.36 TQ	LABLS	1/08-3/08
	Maryland	Y		33500 MW		MDBLS	3/08
	Michigan	Y	28360 FQ	30850 MW	33620 TQ	USBLS	5/07
	Minnesota	Y	29497 FQ	35894 MW	47898 TQ	MNBLS	10/08-12/08
	Mississippi	Y	19990 FQ	25540 MW	29740 TQ	USBLS	5/07
	Missouri	Y	27710 FQ	30650 MW	45500 TQ	USBLS	5/07
	Nevada	H	15.43 FQ	18.78 MW	21.12 TQ	NVBLS	5/08
	New Jersey	Y	20980 FQ	22900 MW	29210 TQ	USBLS	5/07
	New York	Y	27010 FQ	31660 MW	38600 TQ	USBLS	5/07
	North Carolina	Y	22360 FQ	26660 MW	30550 TQ	USBLS	5/07
	Ohio	Y	26190 FQ	30150 MW	36350 TQ	USBLS	5/07
	Oklahoma	Y	25080 FQ	29060 MW	33670 TQ	USBLS	5/07
	Pennsylvania	Y	22590 FQ	27640 MW	33330 TQ	USBLS	5/07
	South Carolina	Y	22280 FQ	25360 MW	34430 TQ	USBLS	5/07
	Tennessee	Y	24580 FQ	27770 MW	30260 TQ	USBLS	5/07
	Texas	Y	22330 FQ	27190 MW	31160 TQ	USBLS	5/07
	Utah	Y	28580 FQ	35730 MW	44370 TQ	USBLS	5/07
	Virginia	Y	25250 FQ	30480 MW	36470 TQ	USBLS	5/07
	West Virginia	Y	18125 FQ	20630 MW	24008 TQ	WVBLS	7/08-9/08
	Wisconsin	Y	27030 FQ	30130 MW	35070 TQ	USBLS	5/07
Floral Designer	Alabama	Y	16890 FQ	19940 MW	24380 TQ	USBLS	5/07
	Birmingham-Hoover MSA, AL	Y	21610 FQ	25300 MW	28880 TQ	USBLS	5/07
	Mobile MSA, AL	Y	15170 FQ	18860 MW	24810 TQ	USBLS	5/07
	Alaska	Y	20690 FQ	25130 MW	30270 TQ	USBLS	5/07
	Anchorage MSA, AK	Y	21830 FQ	26520 MW	30610 TQ	USBLS	5/07
	Arizona	Y	19640 FQ	24110 MW	28920 TQ	USBLS	5/07
	Phoenix-Mesa-Scottsdale MSA, AZ	Y	19790 FQ	23710 MW	28890 TQ	USBLS	5/07
	Tucson MSA, AZ	Y	21330 FQ	26190 MW	29270 TQ	USBLS	5/07
	Arkansas	Y	16930 FQ	19250 MW	22840 TQ	USBLS	5/07
	Little Rock-North Little Rock MSA, AR	Y	19730 FQ	22990 MW	27680 TQ	USBLS	5/07
	California	H	10.17 FQ	13.05 MW	16.27 TQ	CABLS	1/08-3/08

AE	Average entry wage	AW	Average wage paid	FQ	First quartile wage
AER	Average entry range	AWR	Average wage range	H	Hourly
AEX	Average experienced wage	AXR	Average experienced range	HI	Highest wage paid
ATC	Average total compensation	D	Daily	HR	High end range

LO	Lowest wage paid	MTC	Median total compensation	TCC	Total cash compensation
LR	Low end range	MW	Median wage paid	TQ	Third quartile wage
M	Monthly	MWR	Median wage range	W	Weekly
MCC	Median cash compensation	S	See annotated source	Y	Yearly

Occupation/Type/Industry	Location	Per	Low	Mid	High	Source	Date
Floral Designer	Los Angeles-Long Beach-Glendale PMSA, CA	H	9.39 FQ	13.19 MW	14.98 TQ	CABLS	1/08-3/08
	Oakland-Fremont-Hayward MSA, CA	H	13.88 FQ	17.57 MW	20.99 TQ	CABLS	1/08-3/08
	Riverside-San Bernardino-Ontario MSA, CA	H	10.54 FQ	11.36 MW	12.26 TQ	CABLS	1/08-3/08
	Sacramento-Arden Arcade-Roseville MSA, CA	H	11.26 FQ	13.32 MW	16.91 TQ	CABLS	1/08-3/08
	San Diego-Carlsbad-San Marcos MSA, CA	H	9.85 FQ	12.91 MW	15.49 TQ	CABLS	1/08-3/08
	San Francisco-San Mateo-Redwood PMSA, CA	H	10.61 FQ	19.64 MW	24.30 TQ	CABLS	1/08-3/08
	San Jose-Sunnyvale-Santa Clara MSA, CA	H	17.06 FQ	19.43 MW	22.27 TQ	CABLS	1/08-3/08
	Santa Ana-Anaheim-Irvine PMSA, CA	Y	20990 FQ	26990 MW	33540 TQ	USBLS	5/07
	Colorado	Y	19540 FQ	23660 MW	29080 TQ	USBLS	5/07
	Denver-Aurora MSA, CO	Y	20430 FQ	24440 MW	28980 TQ	USBLS	5/07
	Connecticut	H	10.33 AE	13.91 MW		CTBLS	1/08-3/08
	Bridgeport-Stamford-Norwalk MSA, CT	Y	26610 FQ	30630 MW	38050 TQ	USBLS	5/07
	Hartford-West Hartford-East Hartford MSA, CT	Y	22470 FQ	25840 MW	30800 TQ	USBLS	5/07
	Delaware	Y	20170 FQ	23030 MW	28250 TQ	USBLS	5/07
	Wilmington PMSA, DE-MD-NJ	Y	20830 FQ	23410 MW	29280 TQ	USBLS	5/07
	District of Columbia	Y	26690 FQ	29770 MW	33130 TQ	USBLS	5/07
	Washington-Arlington-Alexandria MSA, DC-VA-MD-WV	Y	16590 FQ	26970 MW	31530 TQ	USBLS	5/07
	Florida	Y	19660 FQ	24090 MW	28720 TQ	USBLS	5/07
	Fort Lauderdale-Pompano Beach-Deerfield Beach PMSA, FL	Y	21640 FQ	26240 MW	29600 TQ	USBLS	5/07
	Jacksonville MSA, FL	Y	16930 FQ	20190 MW	26340 TQ	USBLS	5/07
	Miami-Fort Lauderdale-Miami Beach MSA, FL	Y	21690 FQ	26620 MW	30980 TQ	USBLS	5/07
	Orlando-Kissimmee MSA, FL	Y	18130 FQ	22480 MW	26440 TQ	USBLS	5/07
	Pensacola-Ferry Pass-Brent MSA, FL	Y	18960 FQ	21880 MW	24590 TQ	USBLS	5/07
	Tampa-St. Petersburg-Clearwater MSA, FL	Y	19060 FQ	22400 MW	27160 TQ	USBLS	5/07
	West Palm Beach-Boca Raton-Boynton Beach PMSA, FL	Y	27070 FQ	31490 MW	42230 TQ	USBLS	5/07
	Georgia	Y	17890 FQ	21210 MW	25390 TQ	USBLS	5/07
	Atlanta-Sandy Springs-Marietta MSA, GA	Y	18860 FQ	21950 MW	27140 TQ	USBLS	5/07
	Hawaii	Y	19350 FQ	24200 MW	28890 TQ	USBLS	5/07
	Honolulu MSA, HI	Y	19600 FQ	24020 MW	28870 TQ	USBLS	5/07
	Idaho	Y	15990 FQ	18620 MW	21700 TQ	USBLS	5/07
	Boise City-Nampa MSA, ID	Y	17820 FQ	20110 MW	22950 TQ	USBLS	5/07
	Pocatello MSA, ID	Y	13750 FQ	16150 MW	20200 TQ	USBLS	5/07
	Illinois	Y	17720 FQ	21830 MW	28870 TQ	USBLS	5/07
	Chicago-Naperville-Joliet MSA, IL-IN-WI	Y	20170 FQ	24830 MW	31860 TQ	USBLS	5/07
	Indiana	Y	18060 FQ	21580 MW	25160 TQ	USBLS	5/07
	Gary PMSA, IN	Y	18510 FQ	22060 MW	25540 TQ	USBLS	5/07
	Indianapolis-Carmel MSA, IN	Y	20650 FQ	22850 MW	25450 TQ	USBLS	5/07
	Iowa	Y	17190 FQ	19580 MW	23490 TQ	USBLS	5/07
	Des Moines-West Des Moines MSA, IA	Y	17880 FQ	21950 MW	27680 TQ	USBLS	5/07
	Waterloo-Cedar Falls MSA, IA	Y	17880 FQ	20750 MW	23530 TQ	USBLS	5/07
	Kansas	Y	16880 FQ	21190 MW	25410 TQ	USBLS	5/07
	Wichita MSA, KS	Y	17630 FQ	20540 MW	29460 TQ	USBLS	5/07
	Kentucky	Y	17093 FQ	20164 MW	24796 TQ	KYBLS	2008
	Lexington-Fayette MSA, KY	Y	19210 FQ	22620 MW	29330 TQ	USBLS	5/07
	Louisville-Jefferson County MSA, KY-IN	Y	18310 FQ	20480 MW	24250 TQ	USBLS	5/07
	Louisiana	H	8.95 FQ	10.81 MW	12.84 TQ	LABLS	1/08-3/08
	Baton Rouge MSA, LA	Y	22690 FQ	26270 MW	29770 TQ	USBLS	5/07
	Lafayette MSA, LA	Y	19350 FQ	22690 MW	25500 TQ	USBLS	5/07
	Lake Charles MSA, LA	Y	16350 FQ	20320 MW	23320 TQ	USBLS	5/07

Occupation/Type/Industry	Location	Per	Low	Mid	High	Source	Date
Floral Designer	New Orleans-Metairie-Kenner MSA, LA	Y	20780 FQ	23270 MW	27620 TQ	USBLS	5/07
	Maine	Y	16120 FQ	21150 MW	25630 TQ	USBLS	5/07
	Portland-South Portland-Biddeford MSA, ME	Y	21110 FQ	23540 MW	25930 TQ	USBLS	5/07
	Maryland	Y		25500 MW		MDBLS	3/08
	Baltimore-Towson MSA, MD	Y	23060 FQ	28980 MW	33490 TQ	USBLS	5/07
	Bethesda-Gaithersburg-Frederick PMSA, MD	Y	14710 FQ	20920 MW	28370 TQ	USBLS	5/07
	Hagerstown-Martinsburg MSA, MD-WV	Y	14580 FQ	17730 MW	22300 TQ	USBLS	5/07
	Massachusetts	Y	23250 FQ	29170 MW	34750 TQ	USBLS	5/07
	Boston-Cambridge-Quincy NECTA, MA	Y	25450 FQ	31030 MW	36170 TQ	USBLS	5/07
	Worcester MSA, MA-CT	Y	20420 FQ	25400 MW	35210 TQ	USBLS	5/07
	Michigan	Y	18370 FQ	22410 MW	27850 TQ	USBLS	5/07
	Detroit-Warren-Livonia MSA, MI	Y	18540 FQ	24080 MW	30180 TQ	USBLS	5/07
	Grand Rapids-Wyoming MSA, MI	Y	18740 FQ	22290 MW	29150 TQ	USBLS	5/07
	Lansing-East Lansing MSA, MI	Y	24820 FQ	26730 MW	28670 TQ	USBLS	5/07
	Warren-Troy-Farmington Hills PMSA, MI	Y	18980 FQ	26020 MW	31050 TQ	USBLS	5/07
	Minnesota	Y	19627 FQ	23822 MW	29733 TQ	MNBLS	10/08-12/08
	Duluth-Superior MSA, MN-WI	Y	17335 FQ	19250 MW	21562 TQ	MNBLS	10/08-12/08
	Minneapolis-Saint Paul MSA, MN-WI	Y	22839 FQ	27243 MW	32359 TQ	MNBLS	10/08-12/08
	Rochester MSA, MN	Y	18957 FQ	23983 MW	29293 TQ	MNBLS	10/08-12/08
	Mississippi	Y	15750 FQ	18700 MW	22640 TQ	USBLS	5/07
	Jackson MSA, MS	Y	17330 FQ	20590 MW	26460 TQ	USBLS	5/07
	Missouri	Y	15860 FQ	18630 MW	23120 TQ	USBLS	5/07
	Kansas City MSA, MO-KS	Y	20050 FQ	23350 MW	27740 TQ	USBLS	5/07
	St. Louis MSA, MO-IL	Y	16070 FQ	19070 MW	26390 TQ	USBLS	5/07
	Montana	Y	15900 FQ	18420 MW	22200 TQ	USBLS	5/07
	Billings MSA, MT	Y	18140 FQ	19980 MW	23530 TQ	USBLS	5/07
	Nebraska	Y	17560 FQ	21370 MW	25980 TQ	USBLS	5/07
	Omaha-Council Bluffs MSA, NE-IA	Y	21010 FQ	23760 MW	28160 TQ	USBLS	5/07
	Nevada	H	11.29 FQ	14.33 MW	17.28 TQ	NVBLS	5/08
	Las Vegas-Paradise MSA, NV	H	12.87 FQ	14.96 MW	17.42 TQ	NVBLS	5/08
	New Hampshire	H	9.76 AE	11.77 MW	13.75 AEX	NHBLS	6/08
	Manchester MSA, NH	Y	20710 FQ	26560 MW	30130 TQ	USBLS	5/07
	Nashua NECTA, NH-MA	Y	24460 FQ	28130 MW	33100 TQ	USBLS	5/07
	New Jersey	Y	22900 FQ	28720 MW	36370 TQ	USBLS	5/07
	Atlantic City MSA, NJ	Y	23180 FQ	25820 MW	31650 TQ	USBLS	5/07
	Camden PMSA, NJ	Y	19180 FQ	24020 MW	29190 TQ	USBLS	5/07
	Edison PMSA, NJ	Y	24780 FQ	31090 MW	36700 TQ	USBLS	5/07
	Newark-Union PMSA, NJ-PA	Y	27280 FQ	34710 MW	41670 TQ	USBLS	5/07
	New Mexico	Y	16620 FQ	20050 MW	23270 TQ	USBLS	5/07
	Albuquerque MSA, NM	Y	17230 FQ	20160 MW	23350 TQ	USBLS	5/07
	New York	Y	19110 FQ	25340 MW	33480 TQ	USBLS	5/07
	Albany-Schenectady-Troy MSA, NY	Y	20110 FQ	24880 MW	31080 TQ	USBLS	5/07
	Binghamton MSA, NY	Y	17830 FQ	22770 MW	27400 TQ	USBLS	5/07
	Buffalo-Niagara Falls MSA, NY	Y	20340 FQ	24260 MW	29910 TQ	USBLS	5/07
	Glens Falls MSA, NY	Y	18170 FQ	21690 MW	25340 TQ	USBLS	5/07
	Kingston MSA, NY	Y	19230 FQ	21560 MW	26310 TQ	USBLS	5/07
	Nassau-Suffolk PMSA, NY	Y	20520 FQ	30930 MW	36800 TQ	USBLS	5/07
	New York-Northern New Jersey-Long Island MSA, NY-NJ-PA	Y	22340 FQ	30870 MW	36720 TQ	USBLS	5/07
	Syracuse MSA, NY	Y	20690 FQ	28080 MW	34480 TQ	USBLS	5/07
	North Carolina	Y	17100 FQ	22380 MW	27510 TQ	USBLS	5/07
	Charlotte-Gastonia-Concord MSA, NC-SC	Y	19050 FQ	23340 MW	30930 TQ	USBLS	5/07
	Raleigh-Cary MSA, NC	Y	18950 FQ	23510 MW	27880 TQ	USBLS	5/07
	North Dakota	Y	17320 FQ	19710 MW	25520 TQ	USBLS	5/07
	Fargo MSA, ND-MN	Y	17620 FQ	21450 MW	26690 TQ	USBLS	5/07
	Ohio	Y	16740 FQ	19470 MW	23930 TQ	USBLS	5/07
	Cincinnati-Middletown MSA, OH-KY-IN	Y	16340 FQ	19440 MW	26730 TQ	USBLS	5/07

AE	Average entry wage	AW	Average wage paid	FQ	First quartile wage
AER	Average entry range	AWR	Average wage range	H	Hourly
AEX	Average experienced wage	AXR	Average experienced range	HI	Highest wage paid
ATC	Average total compensation	D	Daily	HR	High end range

LO	Lowest wage paid	MTC	Median total compensation	TCC	Total cash compensation
LR	Low end range	MW	Median wage paid	TQ	Third quartile wage
M	Monthly	MWR	Median wage range	W	Weekly
MCC	Median cash compensation	S	See annotated source	Y	Yearly

Floral Designer

Occupation/Type/Industry	Location	Per	Low	Mid	High	Source	Date
Floral Designer	Cleveland-Elyria-Mentor MSA, OH	Y	18080 FQ	20780 MW	27290 TQ	USBLS	5/07
	Columbus MSA, OH	Y	15760 FQ	21090 MW	28290 TQ	USBLS	5/07
	Dayton MSA, OH	Y	16650 FQ	19020 MW	22190 TQ	USBLS	5/07
	Oklahoma	Y	16140 FQ	18870 MW	23670 TQ	USBLS	5/07
	Oklahoma City MSA, OK	Y	15480 FQ	23840 MW	29270 TQ	USBLS	5/07
	Tulsa MSA, OK	Y	17120 FQ	18590 MW	21310 TQ	USBLS	5/07
	Oregon	H	9.28 FQ	10.68 MW	12.70 TQ	ORBLS	5/08
	Eugene-Springfield MSA, OR	Y	17980 FQ	19720 MW	22570 TQ	USBLS	5/07
	Portland-Vancouver-Beaverton MSA, OR-WA	Y	19890 FQ	24010 MW	28970 TQ	USBLS	5/07
	Pennsylvania	Y	18250 FQ	21710 MW	26020 TQ	USBLS	5/07
	Allentown-Bethlehem-Easton MSA, PA-NJ	Y	21360 FQ	23790 MW	29250 TQ	USBLS	5/07
	Philadelphia-Camden-Wilmington MSA, PA-NJ-DE-MD	Y	19690 FQ	23160 MW	29910 TQ	USBLS	5/07
	Pittsburgh MSA, PA	Y	15330 FQ	19490 MW	23580 TQ	USBLS	5/07
	Rhode Island	Y	21960 FQ	28610 MW	35540 TQ	USBLS	5/07
	Providence-Fall River-Warwick MSA, RI-MA	Y	23000 FQ	29040 MW	35310 TQ	USBLS	5/07
	South Carolina	Y	16810 FQ	19970 MW	23990 TQ	USBLS	5/07
	Charleston-North Charleston MSA, SC	Y	17420 FQ	19760 MW	23170 TQ	USBLS	5/07
	Columbia MSA, SC	Y	15430 FQ	18820 MW	22210 TQ	USBLS	5/07
	South Dakota	Y	18947 FQ	22003 MW	24647 TQ	SDBLS	7/08-9/08
	Sioux Falls MSA, SD	Y	21883 FQ	23889 MW	26137 TQ	SDBLS	7/08-9/08
	Tennessee	Y	16870 FQ	21130 MW	26950 TQ	USBLS	5/07
	Memphis MSA, TN-MS-AR	Y	16950 FQ	20500 MW	32410 TQ	USBLS	5/07
	Nashville-Davidson-Murfreesboro MSA, TN	Y	21980 FQ	27380 MW	31940 TQ	USBLS	5/07
	Texas	Y	17310 FQ	20790 MW	25390 TQ	USBLS	5/07
	Austin-Round Rock MSA, TX	Y	20040 FQ	23590 MW	27390 TQ	USBLS	5/07
	Beaumont-Port Arthur MSA, TX	Y	15210 FQ	18100 MW	21580 TQ	USBLS	5/07
	Corpus Christi MSA, TX	Y	17570 FQ	19580 MW	24770 TQ	USBLS	5/07
	Dallas-Fort Worth-Arlington MSA, TX	Y	18130 FQ	21690 MW	26260 TQ	USBLS	5/07
	El Paso MSA, TX	Y	17750 FQ	19820 MW	21860 TQ	USBLS	5/07
	Houston-Sugar Land-Baytown MSA, TX	Y	20000 FQ	23870 MW	28480 TQ	USBLS	5/07
	San Antonio MSA, TX	Y	18310 FQ	20610 MW	23620 TQ	USBLS	5/07
	Utah	Y	17090 FQ	19760 MW	24960 TQ	USBLS	5/07
	Salt Lake City MSA, UT	Y	20120 FQ	25900 MW	30600 TQ	USBLS	5/07
	Vermont	Y	22950 FQ	28670 MW	33540 TQ	USBLS	5/07
	Burlington-South Burlington MSA, VT	Y	27780 FQ	30090 MW	32480 TQ	USBLS	5/07
	Virginia	Y	18930 FQ	24040 MW	29670 TQ	USBLS	5/07
	Richmond MSA, VA	Y	20120 FQ	24280 MW	30690 TQ	USBLS	5/07
	Virginia Beach-Norfolk-Newport News MSA, VA-NC	Y	19500 FQ	23420 MW	27580 TQ	USBLS	5/07
	Washington	H	10.59 FQ	13.00 MW	15.93 TQ	WABLS	3/08
	Seattle-Tacoma-Bellevue MSA, WA	Y	25500 FQ	30310 MW	36140 TQ	USBLS	5/07
	West Virginia	Y	15657 FQ	18309 MW	21083 TQ	WVBLS	7/08-9/08
	Charleston MSA, WV	Y	17430 FQ	18850 MW	20530 TQ	USBLS	5/07
	Wisconsin	Y	18820 FQ	22970 MW	28480 TQ	USBLS	5/07
	Milwaukee-Waukesha-West Allis MSA, WI	Y	18580 FQ	22410 MW	28020 TQ	USBLS	5/07
	Wyoming	Y	15879 FQ	18784 MW	22503 TQ	WYBLS	9/08
	Cheyenne MSA, WY	Y	17417 FQ	18567 MW	19718 TQ	WYBLS	9/08
	Puerto Rico	Y	12560 FQ	13840 MW	15130 TQ	USBLS	5/07
	San Juan-Caguas-Guaynabo MSA, PR	Y	12560 FQ	13830 MW	15100 TQ	USBLS	5/07

Florist

Occupation/Type/Industry	Location	Per	Low	Mid	High	Source	Date
Municipal Government	Cincinnati, OH	Y	37647 LO		40748 HI	COHSS	10/08

Foley Artist

Occupation/Type/Industry	Location	Per	Low	Mid	High	Source	Date
Independent Motion Picture	East Coast	W			2333 HI	MPEG05	8/1/08-7/31/09
Major Motion Picture	East Coast	W			2189 HI	MPEG04	8/3/08-7/31/09

AE	Average entry wage	AW	Average wage paid	FQ	First quartile wage
AER	Average entry range	AWR	Average wage range	H	Hourly
AEX	Average experienced wage	AXR	Average experienced range	HI	Highest wage paid
ATC	Average total compensation	D	Daily	HR	High end range

LO	Lowest wage paid	MTC	Median total compensation	TCC	Total cash compensation
LR	Low end range	MW	Median wage paid	TQ	Third quartile wage
M	Monthly	MWR	Median wage range	W	Weekly
MCC	Median cash compensation	S	See annotated source	Y	Yearly

Occupation/Type/Industry	Location	Per	Low	Mid	High	Source	Date
Food and Tobacco Roasting, Baking, and Drying Machine Operator and Tender	Alabama	Y	24050 FQ	30500 MW	34000 TQ	USBLS	5/07
	Arizona	Y	19870 FQ	23930 MW	28280 TQ	USBLS	5/07
	Phoenix-Mesa-Scottsdale MSA, AZ	Y	20550 FQ	24840 MW	28900 TQ	USBLS	5/07
	Arkansas	Y	23310 FQ	28110 MW	32120 TQ	USBLS	5/07
	Fayetteville-Springdale-Rogers MSA, AR-MO	Y	21710 FQ	29380 MW	35710 TQ	USBLS	5/07
	California	H	8.70 FQ	11.05 MW	17.23 TQ	.CABLS	1/08-3/08
	Los Angeles-Long Beach-Glendale PMSA, CA	H	9.96 FQ	16.64 MW	21.27 TQ	CABLS	1/08-3/08
	Oakland-Fremont-Hayward MSA, CA	H	9.52 FQ	15.79 MW	18.76 TQ	CABLS	1/08-3/08
	Riverside-San Bernardino-Ontario MSA, CA	H	8.00 FQ	9.44 MW	18.82 TQ	CABLS	1/08-3/08
	San Diego-Carlsbad-San Marcos MSA, CA	H	8.09 FQ	8.61 MW	9.23 TQ	CABLS	1/08-3/08
	San Francisco-San Mateo-Redwood PMSA, CA	H	10.81 FQ	16.02 MW	17.36 TQ	CABLS	1/08-3/08
	Santa Ana-Anaheim-Irvine PMSA, CA	Y	21050 FQ	22980 MW	25960 TQ	USBLS	5/07
	Colorado	Y	18060 FQ	22350 MW	27540 TQ	USBLS	5/07
	Denver-Aurora MSA, CO	Y	17490 FQ	22210 MW	27680 TQ	USBLS	5/07
	Connecticut	H	8.74 AE	11.22 MW		CTBLS	1/08-3/08
	Washington-Arlington-Alexandria MSA, DC-VA-MD-WV	Y	21840 FQ	25470 MW	34940 TQ	USBLS	5/07
	Florida	Y	20650 FQ	23540 MW	27610 TQ	USBLS	5/07
	Miami-Fort Lauderdale-Miami Beach MSA, FL	Y	18130 FQ	20010 MW	25010 TQ	USBLS	5/07
	Tampa-St. Petersburg-Clearwater MSA, FL	Y	18920 FQ	21520 MW	23950 TQ	USBLS	5/07
	Georgia	Y	32230 FQ	35290 MW	38400 TQ	USBLS	5/07
	Atlanta-Sandy Springs-Marietta MSA, GA	Y	25920 FQ	30600 MW	35110 TQ	USBLS	5/07
	Hawaii	Y	15330 FQ	18090 MW	25660 TQ	USBLS	5/07
	Honolulu MSA, HI	Y	15080 FQ	17460 MW	22040 TQ	USBLS	5/07
	Idaho	Y	25680 FQ	30550 MW	34790 TQ	USBLS	5/07
	Illinois	Y	22620 FQ	27410 MW	34420 TQ	USBLS	5/07
	Chicago-Naperville-Joliet MSA, IL-IN-WI	Y	22310 FQ	26130 MW	33090 TQ	USBLS	5/07
	Indiana	Y	18290 FQ	22820 MW	28790 TQ	USBLS	5/07
	Iowa	Y	22520 FQ	27400 MW	33500 TQ	USBLS	5/07
	Kansas	Y	20660 FQ	27050 MW	34130 TQ	USBLS	5/07
	Kentucky	Y	18650 FQ	26357 MW	32967 TQ	KYBLS	2008
	Lexington-Fayette MSA, KY	Y	38230 FQ	41810 MW	45390 TQ	USBLS	5/07
	Louisville-Jefferson County MSA, KY-IN	Y	22340 FQ	27550 MW	35170 TQ	USBLS	5/07
	Louisiana	H	6.22 FQ	7.14 MW	10.48 TQ	LABLS	1/08-3/08
	Baton Rouge MSA, LA	Y	18780 FQ	21790 MW	25300 TQ	USBLS	5/07
	New Orleans-Metairie-Kenner MSA, LA	Y	19170 FQ	27400 MW	33590 TQ	USBLS	5/07
	Maine	Y	24520 FQ	27600 MW	33690 TQ	USBLS	5/07
	Maryland	Y		26150 MW		MDBLS	3/08
	Baltimore-Towson MSA, MD	Y	22080 FQ	26280 MW	30380 TQ	USBLS	5/07
	Massachusetts	Y	22790 FQ	29630 MW	35180 TQ	USBLS	5/07
	Boston-Cambridge-Quincy NECTA, MA	Y	28320 FQ	32580 MW	36310 TQ	USBLS	5/07
	Michigan	Y	21170 FQ	26700 MW	29890 TQ	USBLS	5/07
	Detroit-Warren-Livonia MSA, MI	Y	17460 FQ	19690 MW	26420 TQ	USBLS	5/07
	Grand Rapids-Wyoming MSA, MI	Y	17670 FQ	20420 MW	28000 TQ	USBLS	5/07
	Warren-Troy-Farmington Hills PMSA, MI	Y	16680 FQ	17960 MW	19560 TQ	USBLS	5/07
	Minnesota	Y	22734 FQ	25409 MW	32199 TQ	MNBLS	10/08-12/08
	Minneapolis-Saint Paul MSA, MN-WI	Y	24621 FQ	29617 MW	35288 TQ	MNBLS	10/08-12/08
	Missouri	Y	19130 FQ	23400 MW	29640 TQ	USBLS	5/07
	Kansas City MSA, MO-KS	Y	25360 FQ	27700 MW	30030 TQ	USBLS	5/07

AE	Average entry wage	AW	Average wage paid	FQ	First quartile wage
AER	Average entry range	AWR	Average wage range	H	Hourly
AEX	Average experienced wage	AXR	Average experienced range	HI	Highest wage paid
ATC	Average total compensation	D	Daily	HR	High end range

LO	Lowest wage paid	MTC	Median total compensation
LR	Low end range	MW	Median wage paid
M	Monthly	MWR	Median wage range
MCC	Median cash compensation	S	See annotated source

TCC	Total cash compensation
TQ	Third quartile wage
W	Weekly
Y	Yearly

Occupation/Type/Industry	Location	Per	Low	Mid	High	Source	Date
Food and Tobacco Roasting, Baking, and Drying Machine Operator and Tender	St. Louis MSA, MO-IL	Y	18450 FQ	21560 MW	30830 TQ	USBLS	5/07
	Montana	Y	20230 FQ	22670 MW	25760 TQ	USBLS	5/07
	Nebraska	Y	21150 FQ	23980 MW	28340 TQ	USBLS	5/07
	Omaha-Council Bluffs MSA, NE-IA	Y	21330 FQ	24820 MW	32970 TQ	USBLS	5/07
	Nevada	H	11.02 FQ	14.10 MW	18.29 TQ	NVBLS	5/08
	Las Vegas-Paradise MSA, NV	H	10.11 FQ	10.95 MW	11.78 TQ	NVBLS	5/08
	New Hampshire	H	9.40 AE	11.20 MW	13.60 AEX	NHBLS	6/08
	New Jersey	Y	16000 FQ	18920 MW	26500 TQ	USBLS	5/07
	Camden PMSA, NJ	Y	20130 FQ	30830 MW	37480 TQ	USBLS	5/07
	Edison PMSA, NJ	Y	20290 FQ	23710 MW	30880 TQ	USBLS	5/07
	New Mexico	Y	16910 FQ	19880 MW	26910 TQ	USBLS	5/07
	New York	Y	16590 FQ	23950 MW	35930 TQ	USBLS	5/07
	Buffalo-Niagara Falls MSA, NY	Y	23450 FQ	39080 MW	45360 TQ	USBLS	5/07
	Nassau-Suffolk PMSA, NY	Y	19490 FQ	29550 MW	41420 TQ	USBLS	5/07
	New York-Northern New Jersey-Long Island MSA, NY-NJ-PA	Y	15620 FQ	19240 MW	32080 TQ	USBLS	5/07
	North Carolina	Y	20290 FQ	29280 MW	47920 TQ	USBLS	5/07
	North Dakota	Y	23050 FQ	30600 MW	36860 TQ	USBLS	5/07
	Grand Forks MSA, ND-MN	Y	23770 FQ	26880 MW	31100 TQ	USBLS	5/07
	Ohio	Y	20700 FQ	27320 MW	35280 TQ	USBLS	5/07
	Cincinnati-Middletown MSA, OH-KY-IN	Y	19580 FQ	23700 MW	32440 TQ	USBLS	5/07
	Cleveland-Elyria-Mentor MSA, OH	Y	21240 FQ	23910 MW	26640 TQ	USBLS	5/07
	Columbus MSA, OH	Y	21280 FQ	23450 MW	29180 TQ	USBLS	5/07
	Oklahoma	Y	31020 FQ	34800 MW	37830 TQ	USBLS	5/07
	Oregon	H	8.86 FQ	10.29 MW	13.07 TQ	ORBLS	5/08
	Portland-Vancouver-Beaverton MSA, OR-WA	Y	18800 FQ	21470 MW	25770 TQ	USBLS	5/07
	Pennsylvania	Y	21440 FQ	26740 MW	36220 TQ	USBLS	5/07
	Lancaster MSA, PA	Y	22760 FQ	25830 MW	29330 TQ	USBLS	5/07
	Philadelphia-Camden-Wilmington MSA, PA-NJ-DE-MD	Y	23590 FQ	31880 MW	39800 TQ	USBLS	5/07
	Pittsburgh MSA, PA	Y	14180 FQ	14890 MW	15870 TQ	USBLS	5/07
	South Carolina	Y	17730 FQ	19740 MW	27240 TQ	USBLS	5/07
	South Dakota	Y	21420 FQ	24816 MW	30541 TQ	SDBLS	7/08-9/08
	Sioux Falls MSA, SD	Y	24039 FQ	28531 MW	32539 TQ	SDBLS	7/08-9/08
	Tennessee	Y	26300 FQ	31730 MW	35480 TQ	USBLS	5/07
	Nashville-Davidson-Murfreesboro MSA, TN	Y	27510 FQ	32810 MW	35980 TQ	USBLS	5/07
	Texas	Y	17790 FQ	21140 MW	24100 TQ	USBLS	5/07
	Dallas-Fort Worth-Arlington MSA, TX	Y	21350 FQ	24540 MW	29020 TQ	USBLS	5/07
	Houston-Sugar Land-Baytown MSA, TX	Y	17980 FQ	21220 MW	23510 TQ	USBLS	5/07
	San Antonio MSA, TX	Y	13450 FQ	18140 MW	27680 TQ	USBLS	5/07
	Utah	Y	22680 FQ	27660 MW	33970 TQ	USBLS	5/07
	Virginia	Y	20840 FQ	29060 MW	34470 TQ	USBLS	5/07
	Richmond MSA, VA	Y	20130 FQ	22850 MW	27570 TQ	USBLS	5/07
	Virginia Beach-Norfolk-Newport News MSA, VA-NC	Y	25310 FQ	32950 MW	35900 TQ	USBLS	5/07
	Washington	H	11.88 FQ	16.68 MW	20.46 TQ	WABLS	3/08
	West Virginia	Y	16695 FQ	19049 MW	34575 TQ	WVBLS	7/08-9/08
	Wisconsin	Y	23110 FQ	30140 MW	37050 TQ	USBLS	5/07
	Milwaukee-Waukesha-West Allis MSA, WI	Y	18990 FQ	20690 MW	22630 TQ	USBLS	5/07
	Wyoming	Y	25358 FQ	31631 MW	45406 TQ	WYBLS	9/08
	Puerto Rico	Y	12440 FQ	14060 MW	16250 TQ	USBLS	5/07
	San Juan-Caguas-Guaynabo MSA, PR	Y	12280 FQ	13740 MW	15270 TQ	USBLS	5/07
Food Batchmaker	Alabama	Y	16720 FQ	20340 MW	23000 TQ	USBLS	5/07
	Birmingham-Hoover MSA, AL	Y	18250 FQ	21400 MW	24570 TQ	USBLS	5/07
	Mobile MSA, AL	Y	12830 FQ	14670 MW	18050 TQ	USBLS	5/07
	Alaska	Y	19140 FQ	21990 MW	26410 TQ	USBLS	5/07

AE	Average entry wage	AW	Average wage paid	FQ	First quartile wage	LO	Lowest wage paid	MTC	Median total compensation	TCC	Total cash compensation
AER	Average entry range	AWR	Average wage range	H	Hourly	LR	Low end range	MW	Median wage paid	TQ	Third quartile wage
AEX	Average experienced wage	AXR	Average experienced range	HI	Highest wage paid	M	Monthly	MWR	Median wage range	W	Weekly
ATC	Average total compensation	D	Daily	HR	High end range	MCC	Median cash compensation	S	See annotated source	Y	Yearly

Food Batchmaker

Occupation/Type/Industry	Location	Per	Low	Mid	High	Source	Date
Food Batchmaker	Arizona	Y	15530 FQ	18960 MW	24340 TQ	USBLS	5/07
	Phoenix-Mesa-Scottsdale MSA, AZ	Y	15210 FQ	18580 MW	24260 TQ	USBLS	5/07
	Tucson MSA, AZ	Y	17190 FQ	19480 MW	25080 TQ	USBLS	5/07
	Arkansas	Y	20220 FQ	25500 MW	29810 TQ	USBLS	5/07
	Little Rock-North Little Rock MSA, AR	Y	19370 FQ	22310 MW	25090 TQ	USBLS	5/07
	California	H	9.46 FQ	12.33 MW	16.67 TQ	CABLS	1/08-3/08
	Los Angeles-Long Beach-Glendale PMSA, CA	H	8.52 FQ	9.75 MW	16.49 TQ	CABLS	1/08-3/08
	Oakland-Fremont-Hayward MSA, CA	H	10.20 FQ	11.27 MW	12.50 TQ	CABLS	1/08-3/08
	Riverside-San Bernardino-Ontario MSA, CA	H	9.23 FQ	11.28 MW	16.01 TQ	CABLS	1/08-3/08
	Sacramento-Arden Arcade-Roseville MSA, CA	H	11.07 FQ	13.93 MW	16.38 TQ	CABLS	1/08-3/08
	San Diego-Carlsbad-San Marcos MSA, CA	H	9.25 FQ	11.00 MW	12.78 TQ	CABLS	1/08-3/08
	San Francisco-San Mateo-Redwood PMSA, CA	H	12.60 FQ	13.83 MW	15.04 TQ	CABLS	1/08-3/08
	San Jose-Sunnyvale-Santa Clara MSA, CA	H	8.80 FQ	11.26 MW	14.65 TQ	CABLS	1/08-3/08
	Santa Ana-Anaheim-Irvine PMSA, CA	Y	18110 FQ	22760 MW	27630 TQ	USBLS	5/07
	Stockton MSA, CA	H	13.30 FQ	14.44 MW	15.60 TQ	CABLS	1/08-3/08
	Colorado	Y	18170 FQ	22580 MW	32810 TQ	USBLS	5/07
	Denver-Aurora MSA, CO	Y	17390 FQ	21180 MW	29920 TQ	USBLS	5/07
	Connecticut	H	8.50 AE	11.85 MW		CTBLS	1/08-3/08
	Bridgeport-Stamford-Norwalk MSA, CT	Y	16350 FQ	19560 MW	28310 TQ	USBLS	5/07
	Hartford-West Hartford-East Hartford MSA, CT	Y	17840 FQ	22380 MW	28910 TQ	USBLS	5/07
	Delaware	Y	16760 FQ	19150 MW	24730 TQ	USBLS	5/07
	Washington-Arlington-Alexandria MSA, DC-VA-MD-WV	Y	20800 FQ	26630 MW	30880 TQ	USBLS	5/07
	Florida	Y	15900 FQ	20070 MW	26750 TQ	USBLS	5/07
	Fort Lauderdale-Pompano Beach-Deerfield Beach PMSA, FL	Y	15400 FQ	17790 MW	22480 TQ	USBLS	5/07
	Jacksonville MSA, FL	Y	20960 FQ	26070 MW	29980 TQ	USBLS	5/07
	Miami-Fort Lauderdale-Miami Beach MSA, FL	Y	15500 FQ	19460 MW	24810 TQ	USBLS	5/07
	Orlando-Kissimmee MSA, FL	Y	17090 FQ	21960 MW	28240 TQ	USBLS	5/07
	Tampa-St. Petersburg-Clearwater MSA, FL	Y	15070 FQ	18590 MW	25880 TQ	USBLS	5/07
	West Palm Beach-Boca Raton-Boynton Beach PMSA, FL	Y	14780 FQ	15660 MW	18120 TQ	USBLS	5/07
	Georgia	Y	17530 FQ	21990 MW	28470 TQ	USBLS	5/07
	Atlanta-Sandy Springs-Marietta MSA, GA	Y	18040 FQ	23170 MW	29200 TQ	USBLS	5/07
	Hawaii	Y	15880 FQ	21030 MW	24460 TQ	USBLS	5/07
	Honolulu MSA, HI	Y	15080 FQ	20280 MW	23470 TQ	USBLS	5/07
	Idaho	Y	25370 FQ	31400 MW	36410 TQ	USBLS	5/07
	Boise City-Nampa MSA, ID	Y	25540 FQ	29700 MW	34650 TQ	USBLS	5/07
	Illinois	Y	18400 FQ	24750 MW	32440 TQ	USBLS	5/07
	Chicago-Naperville-Joliet MSA, IL-IN-WI	Y	18150 FQ	24840 MW	32650 TQ	USBLS	5/07
	Indiana	Y	21810 FQ	30790 MW	37520 TQ	USBLS	5/07
	Gary PMSA, IN	Y	18680 FQ	25910 MW	38680 TQ	USBLS	5/07
	Indianapolis-Carmel MSA, IN	Y	21770 FQ	26310 MW	33190 TQ	USBLS	5/07
	Iowa	Y	19960 FQ	27050 MW	35570 TQ	USBLS	5/07
	Des Moines-West Des Moines MSA, IA	Y	22900 FQ	33960 MW	37210 TQ	USBLS	5/07
	Kansas	Y	19590 FQ	23620 MW	29120 TQ	USBLS	5/07
	Wichita MSA, KS	Y	20210 FQ	23610 MW	28390 TQ	USBLS	5/07
	Kentucky	Y	21790 FQ	24759 MW	29414 TQ	KYBLS	2008
	Louisville-Jefferson County MSA, KY-IN	Y	21290 FQ	23350 MW	30040 TQ	USBLS	5/07
	Louisiana	H	7.33 FQ	8.48 MW	10.63 TQ	LABLS	1/08-3/08
	Baton Rouge MSA, LA	Y	15180 FQ	17320 MW	19670 TQ	USBLS	5/07

AE	Average entry wage	AW	Average wage paid	FQ	First quartile wage	LO	Lowest wage paid	MTC Median total compensation TCC Total cash compensation
AER	Average entry range	AWR	Average wage range	H	Hourly	LR	Low end range	MW Median wage paid TQ Third quartile wage
AEX	Average experienced wage	AXR	Average experienced range	HI	Highest wage paid	M	Monthly	MWR Median wage range W Weekly
ATC	Average total compensation	D	Daily	HR	High end range	MCC	Median cash compensation	S See annotated source Y Yearly

Occupation/Type/Industry	Location	Per	Low	Mid	High	Source	Date
Food Batchmaker	New Orleans-Metairie-Kenner MSA, LA	Y	16920 FQ	18990 MW	23230 TQ	USBLS	5/07
	Maine	Y	19680 FQ	25410 MW	29620 TQ	USBLS	5/07
	Portland-South Portland-Biddeford MSA, ME	Y	22630 FQ	27160 MW	30290 TQ	USBLS	5/07
	Maryland	Y		27825 MW		MDBLS	3/08
	Baltimore-Towson MSA, MD	Y	24100 FQ	27030 MW	30480 TQ	USBLS	5/07
	Bethesda-Gaithersburg-Frederick PMSA, MD	Y	27270 FQ	30060 MW	34490 TQ	USBLS	5/07
	Massachusetts	Y	21450 FQ	27000 MW	33620 TQ	USBLS	5/07
	Boston-Cambridge-Quincy NECTA, MA	Y	20690 FQ	26540 MW	31330 TQ	USBLS	5/07
	Worcester MSA, MA-CT	Y	22670 FQ	25800 MW	34150 TQ	USBLS	5/07
	Michigan	Y	18720 FQ	24550 MW	37200 TQ	USBLS	5/07
	Detroit-Warren-Livonia MSA, MI	Y	18320 FQ	23040 MW	32620 TQ	USBLS	5/07
	Grand Rapids-Wyoming MSA, MI	Y	18300 FQ	23830 MW	53890 TQ	USBLS	5/07
	Minnesota	Y	23802 FQ	30157 MW	38533 TQ	MNBLS	10/08-12/08
	Duluth-Superior MSA, MN-WI	Y	25035 FQ	29503 MW	34780 TQ	MNBLS	10/08-12/08
	Minneapolis-Saint Paul MSA, MN-WI	Y	26103 FQ	33277 MW	39176 TQ	MNBLS	10/08-12/08
	Rochester MSA, MN	Y	21619 FQ	24178 MW	27794 TQ	MNBLS	10/08-12/08
	Mississippi	Y	14370 FQ	20820 MW	25100 TQ	USBLS	5/07
	Jackson MSA, MS	Y	19260 FQ	20940 MW	22580 TQ	USBLS	5/07
	Missouri	Y	18550 FQ	25110 MW	32170 TQ	USBLS	5/07
	Kansas City MSA, MO-KS	Y	20930 FQ	25260 MW	32140 TQ	USBLS	5/07
	St. Louis MSA, MO-IL	Y	18030 FQ	24850 MW	30130 TQ	USBLS	5/07
	Montana	Y	17970 FQ	22310 MW	30110 TQ	USBLS	5/07
	Billings MSA, MT	Y	20770 FQ	23880 MW	29550 TQ	USBLS	5/07
	Nebraska	Y	18740 FQ	21980 MW	29550 TQ	USBLS	5/07
	Omaha-Council Bluffs MSA, NE-IA	Y	19830 FQ	24500 MW	31850 TQ	USBLS	5/07
	Nevada	H	6.86 FQ	8.66 MW	13.07 TQ	NVBLS	5/08
	Las Vegas-Paradise MSA, NV	H	6.57 FQ	8.32 MW	14.15 TQ	NVBLS	5/08
	New Hampshire	H	12.46 AE	17.31 MW	19.64 AEX	NHBLS	6/08
	New Jersey	Y	19250 FQ	24530 MW	32640 TQ	USBLS	5/07
	Camden PMSA, NJ	Y	22430 FQ	27060 MW	33400 TQ	USBLS	5/07
	Edison PMSA, NJ	Y	18580 FQ	22510 MW	31790 TQ	USBLS	5/07
	Newark-Union PMSA, NJ-PA	Y	19100 FQ	23820 MW	31280 TQ	USBLS	5/07
	New Mexico	Y	15460 FQ	20650 MW	24300 TQ	USBLS	5/07
	Albuquerque MSA, NM	Y	17110 FQ	20050 MW	23930 TQ	USBLS	5/07
	New York	Y	16030 FQ	19650 MW	27290 TQ	USBLS	5/07
	Albany-Schenectady-Troy MSA, NY	Y	16960 FQ	18970 MW	21820 TQ	USBLS	5/07
	Buffalo-Niagara Falls MSA, NY	Y	16120 FQ	22560 MW	34580 TQ	USBLS	5/07
	Nassau-Suffolk PMSA, NY	Y	17050 FQ	21090 MW	36030 TQ	USBLS	5/07
	New York-Northern New Jersey-Long Island MSA, NY-NJ-PA	Y	16230 FQ	19930 MW	25580 TQ	USBLS	5/07
	North Carolina	Y	18100 FQ	22880 MW	29040 TQ	USBLS	5/07
	Asheville MSA, NC	Y	13490 FQ	14180 MW	14880 TQ	USBLS	5/07
	Charlotte-Gastonia-Concord MSA, NC-SC	Y	21740 FQ	26030 MW	34860 TQ	USBLS	5/07
	Raleigh-Cary MSA, NC	Y	18100 FQ	24650 MW	28720 TQ	USBLS	5/07
	North Dakota	Y	17870 FQ	20660 MW	24350 TQ	USBLS	5/07
	Fargo MSA, ND-MN	Y	16970 FQ	18280 MW	19680 TQ	USBLS	5/07
	Ohio	Y	19930 FQ	28190 MW	35370 TQ	USBLS	5/07
	Cincinnati-Middletown MSA, OH-KY-IN	Y	23470 FQ	31000 MW	41740 TQ	USBLS	5/07
	Cleveland-Elyria-Mentor MSA, OH	Y	16080 FQ	20600 MW	27960 TQ	USBLS	5/07
	Columbus MSA, OH	Y	27480 FQ	33500 MW	42160 TQ	USBLS	5/07
	Dayton MSA, OH	Y	17190 FQ	20360 MW	24230 TQ	USBLS	5/07
	Oklahoma	Y	17860 FQ	22790 MW	26820 TQ	USBLS	5/07
	Oklahoma City MSA, OK	Y	18180 FQ	24240 MW	27260 TQ	USBLS	5/07
	Tulsa MSA, OK	Y	17240 FQ	19870 MW	26260 TQ	USBLS	5/07
	Oregon	H	9.36 FQ	11.27 MW	14.17 TQ	ORBLS	5/08
	Portland-Vancouver-Beaverton MSA, OR-WA	Y	18930 FQ	23500 MW	30200 TQ	USBLS	5/07
	Pennsylvania	Y	20410 FQ	24870 MW	30810 TQ	USBLS	5/07

AE	Average entry wage	**AW**	Average wage paid	**FQ**	First quartile wage	**LO**	Lowest wage paid	**MTC**	Median total compensation	**TCC**	Total cash compensation
AER	Average entry range	**AWR**	Average wage range	**H**	Hourly	**LR**	Low end range	**MW**	Median wage paid	**TQ**	Third quartile wage
AEX	Average experienced wage	**AXR**	Average experienced range	**HI**	Highest wage paid	**M**	Monthly	**MWR**	Median wage range	**W**	Weekly
ATC	Average total compensation	**D**	Daily	**HR**	High end range	**MCC**	Median cash compensation	**S**	See annotated source	**Y**	Yearly

Occupation/Type/Industry	Location	Per	Low	Mid	High	Source	Date
Food Batchmaker	Allentown-Bethlehem-Easton MSA, PA-NJ	Y	22860 FQ	26620 MW	33010 TQ	USBLS	5/07
	Philadelphia-Camden-Wilmington MSA, PA-NJ-DE-MD	Y	21810 FQ	25860 MW	30940 TQ	USBLS	5/07
	Pittsburgh MSA, PA	Y	17440 FQ	21530 MW	27740 TQ	USBLS	5/07
	Rhode Island	Y	20260 FQ	22500 MW	26880 TQ	USBLS	5/07
	Providence-Fall River-Warwick MSA, RI-MA	Y	21270 FQ	24660 MW	28010 TQ	USBLS	5/07
	South Carolina	Y	18610 FQ	22120 MW	29160 TQ	USBLS	5/07
	Charleston-North Charleston MSA, SC	Y	19830 FQ	21710 MW	23510 TQ	USBLS	5/07
	Columbia MSA, SC	Y	19010 FQ	21460 MW	23760 TQ	USBLS	5/07
	South Dakota	Y	21295 FQ	24340 MW	27709 TQ	SDBLS	7/08-9/08
	Rapid City MSA, SD	Y	19956 FQ	22529 MW	25282 TQ	SDBLS	7/08-9/08
	Sioux Falls MSA, SD	Y	18902 FQ	23197 MW	26953 TQ	SDBLS	7/08-9/08
	Tennessee	Y	17500 FQ	25600 MW	38450 TQ	USBLS	5/07
	Memphis MSA, TN-MS-AR	Y	30790 FQ	38310 MW	42530 TQ	USBLS	5/07
	Nashville-Davidson-Murfreesboro MSA, TN	Y	20580 FQ	33190 MW	41400 TQ	USBLS	5/07
	Texas	Y	14240 FQ	17480 MW	22160 TQ	USBLS	5/07
	Austin-Round Rock MSA, TX	Y	16290 FQ	17900 MW	20090 TQ	USBLS	5/07
	Dallas-Fort Worth-Arlington MSA, TX	Y	14780 FQ	18240 MW	23960 TQ	USBLS	5/07
	El Paso MSA, TX	Y	12620 FQ	14110 MW	15850 TQ	USBLS	5/07
	Houston-Sugar Land-Baytown MSA, TX	Y	13460 FQ	16410 MW	21380 TQ	USBLS	5/07
	San Antonio MSA, TX	Y	15000 FQ	17660 MW	21710 TQ	USBLS	5/07
	Utah	Y	17820 FQ	22220 MW	28780 TQ	USBLS	5/07
	Provo-Orem MSA, UT	Y	24390 FQ	31780 MW	34450 TQ	USBLS	5/07
	Salt Lake City MSA, UT	Y	16610 FQ	18260 MW	20960 TQ	USBLS	5/07
	Vermont	Y	20810 FQ	24940 MW	29910 TQ	USBLS	5/07
	Burlington-South Burlington MSA, VT	Y	21740 FQ	27460 MW	31970 TQ	USBLS	5/07
	Virginia	Y	19780 FQ	25160 MW	31160 TQ	USBLS	5/07
	Richmond MSA, VA	Y	18380 FQ	25950 MW	31990 TQ	USBLS	5/07
	Virginia Beach-Norfolk-Newport News MSA, VA-NC	Y	17690 FQ	20410 MW	24910 TQ	USBLS	5/07
	Washington	H	9.12 FQ	10.64 MW	13.85 TQ	WABLS	3/08
	Seattle-Tacoma-Bellevue MSA, WA	Y	18630 FQ	20690 MW	28540 TQ	USBLS	5/07
	Spokane MSA, WA	Y	18190 FQ	25250 MW	28720 TQ	USBLS	5/07
	West Virginia	Y	16598 FQ	19030 MW	23165 TQ	WVBLS	7/08-9/08
	Wisconsin	Y	22160 FQ	28490 MW	35710 TQ	USBLS	5/07
	Milwaukee-Waukesha-West Allis MSA, WI	Y	22620 FQ	31100 MW	39400 TQ	USBLS	5/07
	Wyoming	Y	18151 FQ	26307 MW	30002 TQ	WYBLS	9/08
	Puerto Rico	Y	12850 FQ	14620 MW	17230 TQ	USBLS	5/07
	San Juan-Caguas-Guaynabo MSA, PR	Y	13100 FQ	15260 MW	17700 TQ	USBLS	5/07
Food Chemist Small Organization	United States	Y	55040 FQ	64451 MW	73862 TQ	ALA02	2008
Food Cooking Machine Operator and Tender	Alabama	Y	17600 FQ	20280 MW	22670 TQ	USBLS	5/07
	Birmingham-Hoover MSA, AL	Y	18600 FQ	21150 MW	23570 TQ	USBLS	5/07
	Alaska	Y	18530 FQ	24110 MW	27260 TQ	USBLS	5/07
	Arizona	Y	18310 FQ	22130 MW	27320 TQ	USBLS	5/07
	Phoenix-Mesa-Scottsdale MSA, AZ	Y	18060 FQ	21510 MW	26210 TQ	USBLS	5/07
	Tucson MSA, AZ	Y	17220 FQ	24490 MW	27230 TQ	USBLS	5/07
	Arkansas	Y	17900 FQ	21950 MW	25620 TQ	USBLS	5/07
	Little Rock-North Little Rock MSA, AR	Y	15930 FQ	17700 MW	19990 TQ	USBLS	5/07
	California	H	9.26 FQ	11.89 MW	14.56 TQ	CABLS	1/08-3/08
	Los Angeles-Long Beach-Glendale PMSA, CA	H	8.66 FQ	10.01 MW	12.45 TQ	CABLS	1/08-3/08
	Oakland-Fremont-Hayward MSA, CA	H	8.48 FQ	9.44 MW	13.12 TQ	CABLS	1/08-3/08
	Riverside-San Bernardino-Ontario MSA, CA	H	8.06 FQ	9.12 MW	10.98 TQ	CABLS	1/08-3/08

AE	Average entry wage	AW	Average wage paid	FQ	First quartile wage
AER	Average entry range	AWR	Average wage range	H	Hourly
AEX	Average experienced wage	AXR	Average experienced range	HI	Highest wage paid
ATC	Average total compensation	D	Daily	HR	High end range

LO	Lowest wage paid	MTC	Median total compensation	TCC	Total cash compensation
LR	Low end range	MW	Median wage paid	TQ	Third quartile wage
M	Monthly	MWR	Median wage range	W	Weekly
MCC	Median cash compensation	S	See annotated source	Y	Yearly

673

Occupation/Type/Industry	Location	Per	Low	Mid	High	Source	Date
Food Cooking Machine Operator and Tender							
	Sacramento-Arden Arcade-Roseville MSA, CA	H	9.31 FQ	14.70 MW	20.34 TQ	CABLS	1/08-3/08
	San Diego-Carlsbad-San Marcos MSA, CA	H	8.64 FQ	9.98 MW	11.75 TQ	CABLS	1/08-3/08
	San Francisco-San Mateo-Redwood PMSA, CA	H	9.02 FQ	10.60 MW	12.35 TQ	CABLS	1/08-3/08
	San Jose-Sunnyvale-Santa Clara MSA, CA	H	10.87 FQ	14.51 MW	17.81 TQ	CABLS	1/08-3/08
	Santa Ana-Anaheim-Irvine PMSA, CA	Y	17750 FQ	19710 MW	28250 TQ	USBLS	5/07
	Colorado	Y	18310 FQ	21610 MW	24660 TQ	USBLS	5/07
	Denver-Aurora MSA, CO	Y	18350 FQ	21740 MW	26310 TQ	USBLS	5/07
	Connecticut	H	8.84 AE	12.45 MW		CTBLS	1/08-3/08
	Bridgeport-Stamford-Norwalk MSA, CT	Y	19170 FQ	25690 MW	30810 TQ	USBLS	5/07
	Hartford-West Hartford-East Hartford MSA, CT	Y	18320 FQ	22480 MW	26680 TQ	USBLS	5/07
	Delaware	Y	16650 FQ	19200 MW	22890 TQ	USBLS	5/07
	Wilmington PMSA, DE-MD-NJ	Y	16670 FQ	18380 MW	22340 TQ	USBLS	5/07
	Washington-Arlington-Alexandria MSA, DC-VA-MD-WV	Y	17990 FQ	22630 MW	28280 TQ	USBLS	5/07
	Florida	Y	18870 FQ	22500 MW	27840 TQ	USBLS	5/07
	Jacksonville MSA, FL	Y	30690 FQ	34700 MW	37480 TQ	USBLS	5/07
	Miami-Fort Lauderdale-Miami Beach MSA, FL	Y	18250 FQ	20730 MW	24620 TQ	USBLS	5/07
	Orlando-Kissimmee MSA, FL	Y	20460 FQ	23950 MW	34470 TQ	USBLS	5/07
	Tampa-St. Petersburg-Clearwater MSA, FL	Y	17110 FQ	18840 MW	21590 TQ	USBLS	5/07
	Georgia	Y	18340 FQ	23270 MW	34540 TQ	USBLS	5/07
	Atlanta-Sandy Springs-Marietta MSA, GA	Y	17890 FQ	21600 MW	26670 TQ	USBLS	5/07
	Hawaii	Y	16690 FQ	18820 MW	22840 TQ	USBLS	5/07
	Honolulu MSA, HI	Y	16960 FQ	19330 MW	23430 TQ	USBLS	5/07
	Idaho	Y	18040 FQ	22080 MW	28150 TQ	USBLS	5/07
	Illinois	Y	20080 FQ	23050 MW	27780 TQ	USBLS	5/07
	Chicago-Naperville-Joliet MSA, IL-IN-WI	Y	20380 FQ	23130 MW	27920 TQ	USBLS	5/07
	Indiana	Y	16830 FQ	21290 MW	28900 TQ	USBLS	5/07
	Gary PMSA, IN	Y	16190 FQ	19550 MW	24620 TQ	USBLS	5/07
	Indianapolis-Carmel MSA, IN	Y	18390 FQ	22100 MW	28310 TQ	USBLS	5/07
	Iowa	Y	19310 FQ	24450 MW	31310 TQ	USBLS	5/07
	Des Moines-West Des Moines MSA, IA	Y	17330 FQ	18700 MW	20040 TQ	USBLS	5/07
	Kansas	Y	14830 FQ	19190 MW	26950 TQ	USBLS	5/07
	Wichita MSA, KS	Y	19300 FQ	22150 MW	26780 TQ	USBLS	5/07
	Kentucky	Y	19135 FQ	26668 MW	32756 TQ	KYBLS	2008
	Louisville-Jefferson County MSA, KY-IN	Y	25260 FQ	31120 MW	34610 TQ	USBLS	5/07
	Louisiana	H	7.56 FQ	9.30 MW	11.03 TQ	LABLS	1/08-3/08
	Baton Rouge MSA, LA	Y	16760 FQ	18810 MW	21530 TQ	USBLS	5/07
	New Orleans-Metairie-Kenner MSA, LA	Y	17150 FQ	20850 MW	24190 TQ	USBLS	5/07
	Maine	Y	18770 FQ	22970 MW	27770 TQ	USBLS	5/07
	Maryland	Y		20275 MW		MDBLS	3/08
	Baltimore-Towson MSA, MD	Y	16060 FQ	18220 MW	22660 TQ	USBLS	5/07
	Massachusetts	Y	19500 FQ	23960 MW	29060 TQ	USBLS	5/07
	Boston-Cambridge-Quincy NECTA, MA	Y	20750 FQ	24540 MW	28690 TQ	USBLS	5/07
	Springfield MSA, MA-CT	Y	21070 FQ	29750 MW	33530 TQ	USBLS	5/07
	Michigan	Y	16860 FQ	20680 MW	27590 TQ	USBLS	5/07
	Detroit-Warren-Livonia MSA, MI	Y	16770 FQ	20820 MW	31650 TQ	USBLS	5/07
	Grand Rapids-Wyoming MSA, MI	Y	23790 FQ	32250 MW	38270 TQ	USBLS	5/07
	Warren-Troy-Farmington Hills PMSA, MI	Y	16390 FQ	19680 MW	28110 TQ	USBLS	5/07
	Minnesota	Y	21956 FQ	26041 MW	30747 TQ	MNBLS	10/08-12/08
	Duluth-Superior MSA, MN-WI	Y	19012 FQ	25077 MW	27710 TQ	MNBLS	10/08-12/08

AE	Average entry wage	AW	Average wage paid	FQ	First quartile wage	LO Lowest wage paid	MTC Median total compensation	TCC Total cash compensation
AER	Average entry range	AWR	Average wage range	H	Hourly	LR Low end range	MW Median wage paid	TQ Third quartile wage
AEX	Average experienced wage	AXR	Average experienced range	HI	Highest wage paid	M Monthly	MWR Median wage range	W Weekly
ATC	Average total compensation	D	Daily	HR	High end range	MCC Median cash compensation	S See annotated source	Y Yearly

Occupation/Type/Industry	Location	Per	Low	Mid	High	Source	Date
Food Cooking Machine Operator and Tender	Minneapolis-Saint Paul MSA, MN-WI	Y	21780 FQ	26673 MW	30664 TQ	MNBLS	10/08-12/08
	Rochester MSA, MN	Y	22957 FQ	27902 MW	31251 TQ	MNBLS	10/08-12/08
	Mississippi	Y	17510 FQ	19380 MW	21840 TQ	USBLS	5/07
	Jackson MSA, MS	Y	17230 FQ	18790 MW	20680 TQ	USBLS	5/07
	Missouri	Y	15570 FQ	20970 MW	26000 TQ	USBLS	5/07
	Kansas City MSA, MO-KS	Y	18440 FQ	21630 MW	25350 TQ	USBLS	5/07
	St. Louis MSA, MO-IL	Y	19090 FQ	23650 MW	28640 TQ	USBLS	5/07
	Montana	Y	17670 FQ	20320 MW	22740 TQ	USBLS	5/07
	Nebraska	Y	19280 FQ	24060 MW	34950 TQ	USBLS	5/07
	Omaha-Council Bluffs MSA, NE-IA	Y	19390 FQ	29720 MW	52470 TQ	USBLS	5/07
	Nevada	H	9.21 FQ	11.01 MW	12.90 TQ	NVBLS	5/08
	Las Vegas-Paradise MSA, NV	H	8.68 FQ	10.11 MW	12.67 TQ	NVBLS	5/08
	New Hampshire	H	8.25 AE	11.27 MW	12.55 AEX	NHBLS	6/08
	New Jersey	Y	24120 FQ	27400 MW	31360 TQ	USBLS	5/07
	Camden PMSA, NJ	Y	21000 FQ	26620 MW	30360 TQ	USBLS	5/07
	Edison PMSA, NJ	Y	24680 FQ	26800 MW	28900 TQ	USBLS	5/07
	New Mexico	Y	15850 FQ	18120 MW	21450 TQ	USBLS	5/07
	Albuquerque MSA, NM	Y	17850 FQ	20190 MW	23220 TQ	USBLS	5/07
	New York	Y	16420 FQ	22100 MW	28300 TQ	USBLS	5/07
	Albany-Schenectady-Troy MSA, NY	Y	17390 FQ	19840 MW	22540 TQ	USBLS	5/07
	Buffalo-Niagara Falls MSA, NY	Y	16490 FQ	19040 MW	25880 TQ	USBLS	5/07
	Nassau-Suffolk PMSA, NY	Y	15590 FQ	20970 MW	34250 TQ	USBLS	5/07
	New York-Northern New Jersey-Long Island MSA, NY-NJ-PA	Y	17400 FQ	24440 MW	28550 TQ	USBLS	5/07
	North Carolina	Y	17910 FQ	21230 MW	25470 TQ	USBLS	5/07
	Charlotte-Gastonia-Concord MSA, NC-SC	Y	19220 FQ	21870 MW	24410 TQ	USBLS	5/07
	North Dakota	Y	18450 FQ	24660 MW	29390 TQ	USBLS	5/07
	Ohio	Y	15930 FQ	19540 MW	26480 TQ	USBLS	5/07
	Canton-Massillon MSA, OH	Y	21190 FQ	23630 MW	27630 TQ	USBLS	5/07
	Cincinnati-Middletown MSA, OH-KY-IN	Y	17460 FQ	21460 MW	28280 TQ	USBLS	5/07
	Cleveland-Elyria-Mentor MSA, OH	Y	15180 FQ	16240 MW	21420 TQ	USBLS	5/07
	Columbus MSA, OH	Y	19490 FQ	24530 MW	27650 TQ	USBLS	5/07
	Dayton MSA, OH	Y	17590 FQ	21100 MW	28380 TQ	USBLS	5/07
	Oklahoma	Y	14190 FQ	17370 MW	22270 TQ	USBLS	5/07
	Oklahoma City MSA, OK	Y	14240 FQ	17420 MW	22480 TQ	USBLS	5/07
	Tulsa MSA, OK	Y	15530 FQ	19170 MW	23500 TQ	USBLS	5/07
	Oregon	H	9.84 FQ	11.49 MW	15.10 TQ	ORBLS	5/08
	Portland-Vancouver-Beaverton MSA, OR-WA	Y	20960 FQ	23020 MW	25270 TQ	USBLS	5/07
	Pennsylvania	Y	18260 FQ	23690 MW	28720 TQ	USBLS	5/07
	Allentown-Bethlehem-Easton MSA, PA-NJ	Y	21610 FQ	23970 MW	28170 TQ	USBLS	5/07
	Philadelphia-Camden-Wilmington MSA, PA-NJ-DE-MD	Y	24110 FQ	27410 MW	31900 TQ	USBLS	5/07
	Pittsburgh MSA, PA	Y	17730 FQ	20670 MW	24180 TQ	USBLS	5/07
	Rhode Island	Y	22150 FQ	25820 MW	29000 TQ	USBLS	5/07
	South Carolina	Y	19810 FQ	23750 MW	37910 TQ	USBLS	5/07
	Columbia MSA, SC	Y	19410 FQ	23110 MW	27360 TQ	USBLS	5/07
	South Dakota	Y	22072 FQ	27486 MW	34019 TQ	SDBLS	7/08-9/08
	Tennessee	Y	15230 FQ	18830 MW	24580 TQ	USBLS	5/07
	Memphis MSA, TN-MS-AR	Y	21540 FQ	25830 MW	30630 TQ	USBLS	5/07
	Nashville-Davidson-Murfreesboro MSA, TN	Y	19210 FQ	23210 MW	35380 TQ	USBLS	5/07
	Texas	Y	16450 FQ	19410 MW	23630 TQ	USBLS	5/07
	Austin-Round Rock MSA, TX	Y	17020 FQ	18330 MW	19630 TQ	USBLS	5/07
	Dallas-Fort Worth-Arlington MSA, TX	Y	17040 FQ	20710 MW	26460 TQ	USBLS	5/07
	El Paso MSA, TX	Y	16970 FQ	18390 MW	20220 TQ	USBLS	5/07
	Houston-Sugar Land-Baytown MSA, TX	Y	14680 FQ	17480 MW	20500 TQ	USBLS	5/07
	San Antonio MSA, TX	Y	20040 FQ	22110 MW	23980 TQ	USBLS	5/07
	Utah	Y	18240 FQ	22690 MW	32400 TQ	USBLS	5/07

AE	Average entry wage	AW	Average wage paid	FQ	First quartile wage	LO	Lowest wage paid	MTC	Median total compensation	TCC	Total cash compensation
AER	Average entry range	AWR	Average wage range	H	Hourly	LR	Low end range	MW	Median wage paid	TQ	Third quartile wage
AEX	Average experienced wage	AXR	Average experienced range	HI	Highest wage paid	M	Monthly	MWR	Median wage range	W	Weekly
ATC	Average total compensation	D	Daily	HR	High end range	MCC	Median cash compensation	S	See annotated source	Y	Yearly

Food Cooking Machine Operator and Tender

Occupation/Type/Industry	Location	Per	Low	Mid	High	Source	Date
Food Cooking Machine Operator and Tender	Salt Lake City MSA, UT	Y	20280 FQ	27760 MW	35560 TQ	USBLS	5/07
	Vermont	Y	17560 FQ	20380 MW	23710 TQ	USBLS	5/07
	Virginia	Y	21110 FQ	26010 MW	29750 TQ	USBLS	5/07
	Lynchburg MSA, VA	Y	16120 FQ	18070 MW	19960 TQ	USBLS	5/07
	Richmond MSA, VA	Y	25810 FQ	28100 MW	30900 TQ	USBLS	5/07
	Virginia Beach-Norfolk-Newport News MSA, VA-NC	Y	19540 FQ	22550 MW	26510 TQ	USBLS	5/07
	Washington	H	10.64 FQ	13.39 MW	15.62 TQ	WABLS	3/08
	Seattle-Tacoma-Bellevue MSA, WA	Y	20570 FQ	25570 MW	31680 TQ	USBLS	5/07
	West Virginia	Y	15391 FQ	18047 MW	21865 TQ	WVBLS	7/08-9/08
	Wisconsin	Y	19180 FQ	23490 MW	30300 TQ	USBLS	5/07
	Green Bay MSA, WI	Y	30050 FQ	32460 MW	35020 TQ	USBLS	5/07
	Milwaukee-Waukesha-West Allis MSA, WI	Y	18280 FQ	21780 MW	25890 TQ	USBLS	5/07
	Wyoming	Y	18820 FQ	23215 MW	29244 TQ	WYBLS	9/08
	Puerto Rico	Y	14220 FQ	19230 MW	22760 TQ	USBLS	5/07
	San Juan-Caguas-Guaynabo MSA, PR	Y	15410 FQ	20560 MW	23320 TQ	USBLS	5/07
Food Industry Specialist	Ingham County, MI	Y			61638-74730 HR	LSJ01	6/07
Food Inspection Supervisor							
State Government	Ohio	H	20.89 LO		26.11 HI	ODAS	2008
Food Preparation Worker	Alabama	Y	13040 FQ	14900 MW	18040 TQ	USBLS	5/07
	Birmingham-Hoover MSA, AL	Y	13340 FQ	15580 MW	19300 TQ	USBLS	5/07
	Alaska	Y	19830 FQ	23840 MW	29250 TQ	USBLS	5/07
	Anchorage MSA, AK	Y	20340 FQ	24340 MW	29850 TQ	USBLS	5/07
	Arizona	Y	15900 FQ	18890 MW	26100 TQ	USBLS	5/07
	Phoenix-Mesa-Scottsdale MSA, AZ	Y	16030 FQ	19120 MW	26870 TQ	USBLS	5/07
	Tucson MSA, AZ	Y	15780 FQ	18860 MW	26290 TQ	USBLS	5/07
	Arkansas	Y	14270 FQ	15400 MW	18170 TQ	USBLS	5/07
	Fayetteville-Springdale-Rogers MSA, AR-MO	Y	14310 FQ	15510 MW	18230 TQ	USBLS	5/07
	Jonesboro MSA, AR	Y	14610 FQ	16150 MW	18480 TQ	USBLS	5/07
	Little Rock-North Little Rock MSA, AR	Y	14470 FQ	15830 MW	19270 TQ	USBLS	5/07
	California	H	8.25 FQ	9.18 MW	11.08 TQ	CABLS	1/08-3/08
	Bakersfield MSA, CA	H	8.01 FQ	8.69 MW	9.54 TQ	CABLS	1/08-3/08
	Los Angeles-Long Beach-Glendale PMSA, CA	H	8.05 FQ	8.93 MW	10.21 TQ	CABLS	1/08-3/08
	Oakland-Fremont-Hayward MSA, CA	H	8.52 FQ	9.57 MW	12.23 TQ	CABLS	1/08-3/08
	Riverside-San Bernardino-Ontario MSA, CA	H	8.30 FQ	9.24 MW	11.20 TQ	CABLS	1/08-3/08
	Sacramento-Arden Arcade-Roseville MSA, CA	H	8.38 FQ	9.26 MW	11.08 TQ	CABLS	1/08-3/08
	San Diego-Carlsbad-San Marcos MSA, CA	H	8.20 FQ	9.00 MW	10.43 TQ	CABLS	1/08-3/08
	San Francisco-San Mateo-Redwood PMSA, CA	H	9.40 FQ	10.79 MW	12.42 TQ	CABLS	1/08-3/08
	San Jose-Sunnyvale-Santa Clara MSA, CA	H	8.43 FQ	9.40 MW	11.74 TQ	CABLS	1/08-3/08
	Santa Ana-Anaheim-Irvine PMSA, CA	Y	16510 FQ	18250 MW	21300 TQ	USBLS	5/07
	Colorado	Y	16300 FQ	19090 MW	23110 TQ	USBLS	5/07
	Denver-Aurora MSA, CO	Y	16300 FQ	18960 MW	23370 TQ	USBLS	5/07
	Connecticut	H	8.73 AE	10.36 MW		CTBLS	1/08-3/08
	Bridgeport-Stamford-Norwalk MSA, CT	Y	18290 FQ	21500 MW	25640 TQ	USBLS	5/07
	Hartford-West Hartford-East Hartford MSA, CT	Y	18250 FQ	20610 MW	24000 TQ	USBLS	5/07
	Delaware	Y	16070 FQ	19060 MW	22760 TQ	USBLS	5/07
	Wilmington PMSA, DE-MD-NJ	Y	15990 FQ	19000 MW	22450 TQ	USBLS	5/07
	District of Columbia	Y	18350 FQ	21740 MW	24980 TQ	USBLS	5/07

AE	Average entry wage	AW	Average wage paid	FQ	First quartile wage	LO Lowest wage paid	MTC Median total compensation	TCC Total cash compensation
AER	Average entry range	AWR	Average wage range	H	Hourly	LR Low end range	MW Median wage paid	TQ Third quartile wage
AEX	Average experienced wage	AXR	Average experienced range	HI	Highest wage paid	M Monthly	MWR Median wage range	W Weekly
ATC	Average total compensation	D	Daily	HR	High end range	MCC Median cash compensation	S See annotated source	Y Yearly

Occupation/Type/Industry	Location	Per	Low	Mid	High	Source	Date
Food Preparation Worker	Washington-Arlington-Alexandria MSA, DC-VA-MD-WV	Y	16830 FQ	20230 MW	24150 TQ	USBLS	5/07
	Florida	Y	15540 FQ	18370 MW	22720 TQ	USBLS	5/07
	Fort Lauderdale-Pompano Beach-Deerfield Beach PMSA, FL	Y	15660 FQ	19300 MW	23700 TQ	USBLS	5/07
	Jacksonville MSA, FL	Y	15000 FQ	16640 MW	19860 TQ	USBLS	5/07
	Miami-Fort Lauderdale-Miami Beach MSA, FL	Y	15600 FQ	18640 MW	23130 TQ	USBLS	5/07
	Orlando-Kissimmee MSA, FL	Y	15170 FQ	17760 MW	22480 TQ	USBLS	5/07
	Tampa-St. Petersburg-Clearwater MSA, FL	Y	16270 FQ	19110 MW	23470 TQ	USBLS	5/07
	West Palm Beach-Boca Raton-Boynton Beach PMSA, FL	Y	16840 FQ	20500 MW	25380 TQ	USBLS	5/07
	Georgia	Y	15400 FQ	18600 MW	22650 TQ	USBLS	5/07
	Atlanta-Sandy Springs-Marietta MSA, GA	Y	16420 FQ	19760 MW	23550 TQ	USBLS	5/07
	Hawaii	Y	16890 FQ	19450 MW	25390 TQ	USBLS	5/07
	Honolulu MSA, HI	Y	16310 FQ	18420 MW	22120 TQ	USBLS	5/07
	Idaho	Y	14800 FQ	17630 MW	20170 TQ	USBLS	5/07
	Boise City-Nampa MSA, ID	Y	15020 FQ	17800 MW	20760 TQ	USBLS	5/07
	Illinois	Y	15320 FQ	17830 MW	21480 TQ	USBLS	5/07
	Chicago-Naperville-Joliet MSA, IL-IN-WI	Y	15530 FQ	18420 MW	22230 TQ	USBLS	5/07
	Indiana	Y	14440 FQ	17390 MW	20560 TQ	USBLS	5/07
	Elkhart-Goshen MSA, IN	Y	14330 FQ	16880 MW	19370 TQ	USBLS	5/07
	Gary PMSA, IN	Y	14660 FQ	17950 MW	21920 TQ	USBLS	5/07
	Indianapolis-Carmel MSA, IN	Y	15490 FQ	18380 MW	21560 TQ	USBLS	5/07
	Iowa	Y	14950 FQ	17250 MW	20130 TQ	USBLS	5/07
	Des Moines-West Des Moines MSA, IA	Y	15700 FQ	18090 MW	21550 TQ	USBLS	5/07
	Kansas	Y	14060 FQ	16740 MW	19530 TQ	USBLS	5/07
	Wichita MSA, KS	Y	14450 FQ	16580 MW	18610 TQ	USBLS	5/07
	Kentucky	Y	15445 FQ	18608 MW	22480 TQ	KYBLS	2008
	Louisville-Jefferson County MSA, KY-IN	Y	16580 FQ	19170 MW	23200 TQ	USBLS	5/07
	Louisiana	H	6.14 FQ	6.90 MW	7.90 TQ	LABLS	1/08-3/08
	Baton Rouge MSA, LA	Y	12780 FQ	14370 MW	16470 TQ	USBLS	5/07
	New Orleans-Metairie-Kenner MSA, LA	Y	12940 FQ	14800 MW	17770 TQ	USBLS	5/07
	Maine	Y	17310 FQ	20040 MW	23200 TQ	USBLS	5/07
	Portland-South Portland-Biddeford MSA, ME	Y	17860 FQ	20730 MW	23690 TQ	USBLS	5/07
	Maryland	Y		19350 MW		MDBLS	3/08
	Baltimore-Towson MSA, MD	Y	16070 FQ	19190 MW	22800 TQ	USBLS	5/07
	Bethesda-Gaithersburg-Frederick PMSA, MD	Y	16710 FQ	19620 MW	23520 TQ	USBLS	5/07
	Massachusetts	Y	17590 FQ	20210 MW	24510 TQ	USBLS	5/07
	Boston-Cambridge-Quincy NECTA, MA	Y	17650 FQ	20290 MW	24870 TQ	USBLS	5/07
	New Bedford MSA, MA	Y	17360 FQ	19630 MW	23950 TQ	USBLS	5/07
	Springfield MSA, MA-CT	Y	17620 FQ	20130 MW	23900 TQ	USBLS	5/07
	Worcester MSA, MA-CT	Y	18650 FQ	21660 MW	25180 TQ	USBLS	5/07
	Michigan	Y	15690 FQ	18640 MW	23200 TQ	USBLS	5/07
	Detroit-Warren-Livonia MSA, MI	Y	16720 FQ	20390 MW	24750 TQ	USBLS	5/07
	Flint MSA, MI	Y	15520 FQ	17590 MW	21070 TQ	USBLS	5/07
	Grand Rapids-Wyoming MSA, MI	Y	15520 FQ	17810 MW	22060 TQ	USBLS	5/07
	Warren-Troy-Farmington Hills PMSA, MI	Y	16790 FQ	19910 MW	24820 TQ	USBLS	5/07
	Minnesota	Y	17701 FQ	21131 MW	25324 TQ	MNBLS	10/08-12/08
	Duluth-Superior MSA, MN-WI	Y	18611 FQ	22971 MW	28073 TQ	MNBLS	10/08-12/08
	Minneapolis-Saint Paul MSA, MN-WI	Y	17994 FQ	21539 MW	25376 TQ	MNBLS	10/08-12/08
	Rochester MSA, MN	Y	18389 FQ	21719 MW	28961 TQ	MNBLS	10/08-12/08
	Mississippi	Y	12880 FQ	14590 MW	17150 TQ	USBLS	5/07
	Jackson MSA, MS	Y	12780 FQ	14370 MW	16780 TQ	USBLS	5/07
	Missouri	Y	15280 FQ	17600 MW	20570 TQ	USBLS	5/07
	Jefferson City MSA, MO	Y	14750 FQ	16450 MW	18970 TQ	USBLS	5/07
	Kansas City MSA, MO-KS	Y	15760 FQ	18450 MW	21780 TQ	USBLS	5/07

AE Average entry wage	**AW** Average wage paid	**FQ** First quartile wage	**LO** Lowest wage paid	**MTC** Median total compensation	**TCC** Total cash compensation
AER Average entry range	**AWR** Average wage range	**H** Hourly	**LR** Low end range	**MW** Median wage paid	**TQ** Third quartile wage
AEX Average experienced wage	**AXR** Average experienced range	**HI** Highest wage paid	**M** Monthly	**MWR** Median wage range	**W** Weekly
ATC Average total compensation	**D** Daily	**HR** High end range	**MCC** Median cash compensation	**S** See annotated source	**Y** Yearly

Occupation/Type/Industry	Location	Per	Low	Mid	High	Source	Date
Food Preparation Worker	St. Louis MSA, MO-IL	Y	15390 FQ	17420 MW	19960 TQ	USBLS	5/07
	Montana	Y	15540 FQ	18030 MW	20730 TQ	USBLS	5/07
	Billings MSA, MT	Y	16410 FQ	18600 MW	21700 TQ	USBLS	5/07
	Nebraska	Y	13800 FQ	16440 MW	19410 TQ	USBLS	5/07
	Lincoln MSA, NE	Y	13750 FQ	16410 MW	19350 TQ	USBLS	5/07
	Omaha-Council Bluffs MSA, NE-IA	Y	15160 FQ	17830 MW	20710 TQ	USBLS	5/07
	Nevada	H	8.53 FQ	10.32 MW	13.63 TQ	NVBLS	5/08
	Las Vegas-Paradise MSA, NV	H	8.96 FQ	11.33 MW	14.45 TQ	NVBLS	5/08
	New Hampshire	H	7.20 AE	9.45 MW	11.00 AEX	NHBLS	6/08
	Manchester MSA, NH	Y	16510 FQ	19010 MW	22400 TQ	USBLS	5/07
	Nashua NECTA, NH-MA	Y	13790 FQ	17620 MW	21770 TQ	USBLS	5/07
	Portsmouth MSA, NH-ME	Y	19440 FQ	22920 MW	26850 TQ	USBLS	5/07
	Rochester-Dover MSA, NH-ME	Y	16830 FQ	20100 MW	25280 TQ	USBLS	5/07
	New Jersey	Y	16510 FQ	18930 MW	23150 TQ	USBLS	5/07
	Camden PMSA, NJ	Y	16260 FQ	18700 MW	22690 TQ	USBLS	5/07
	Edison PMSA, NJ	Y	16970 FQ	19450 MW	23510 TQ	USBLS	5/07
	Newark-Union PMSA, NJ-PA	Y	16450 FQ	18920 MW	23290 TQ	USBLS	5/07
	New Mexico	Y	14440 FQ	17460 MW	20590 TQ	USBLS	5/07
	Albuquerque MSA, NM	Y	15790 FQ	17990 MW	20430 TQ	USBLS	5/07
	New York	Y	16050 FQ	19230 MW	24960 TQ	USBLS	5/07
	Albany-Schenectady-Troy MSA, NY	Y	16350 FQ	18440 MW	21750 TQ	USBLS	5/07
	Buffalo-Niagara Falls MSA, NY	Y	15470 FQ	17340 MW	20100 TQ	USBLS	5/07
	Glens Falls MSA, NY	Y	15840 FQ	17740 MW	20990 TQ	USBLS	5/07
	Nassau-Suffolk PMSA, NY	Y	17680 FQ	21050 MW	26790 TQ	USBLS	5/07
	New York-Northern New Jersey-Long Island MSA, NY-NJ-PA	Y	16770 FQ	20520 MW	26880 TQ	USBLS	5/07
	North Carolina	Y	14440 FQ	16290 MW	19210 TQ	USBLS	5/07
	Charlotte-Gastonia-Concord MSA, NC-SC	Y	14540 FQ	16580 MW	19710 TQ	USBLS	5/07
	Durham MSA, NC	Y	14800 FQ	17010 MW	20930 TQ	USBLS	5/07
	Raleigh-Cary MSA, NC	Y	14960 FQ	17380 MW	20150 TQ	USBLS	5/07
	Winston-Salem MSA, NC	Y	14400 FQ	16270 MW	19440 TQ	USBLS	5/07
	North Dakota	Y	16130 FQ	18840 MW	22870 TQ	USBLS	5/07
	Fargo MSA, ND-MN	Y	15820 FQ	18720 MW	26060 TQ	USBLS	5/07
	Ohio	Y	15170 FQ	17270 MW	21200 TQ	USBLS	5/07
	Cincinnati-Middletown MSA, OH-KY-IN	Y	15560 FQ	18490 MW	23380 TQ	USBLS	5/07
	Cleveland-Elyria-Mentor MSA, OH	Y	15180 FQ	17650 MW	21340 TQ	USBLS	5/07
	Columbus MSA, OH	Y	15480 FQ	17870 MW	22190 TQ	USBLS	5/07
	Dayton MSA, OH	Y	14860 FQ	15800 MW	20700 TQ	USBLS	5/07
	Oklahoma	Y	13030 FQ	14870 MW	17610 TQ	USBLS	5/07
	Oklahoma City MSA, OK	Y	13070 FQ	14890 MW	17970 TQ	USBLS	5/07
	Tulsa MSA, OK	Y	13000 FQ	14850 MW	17370 TQ	USBLS	5/07
	Oregon	H	8.78 FQ	9.58 MW	11.32 TQ	ORBLS	5/08
	Portland-Vancouver-Beaverton MSA, OR-WA	Y	18030 FQ	20180 MW	24580 TQ	USBLS	5/07
	Pennsylvania	Y	15690 FQ	18550 MW	22260 TQ	USBLS	5/07
	Allentown-Bethlehem-Easton MSA, PA-NJ	Y	16130 FQ	18510 MW	22000 TQ	USBLS	5/07
	Lancaster MSA, PA	Y	16360 FQ	18770 MW	22160 TQ	USBLS	5/07
	Philadelphia-Camden-Wilmington MSA, PA-NJ-DE-MD	Y	16500 FQ	19630 MW	23220 TQ	USBLS	5/07
	Pittsburgh MSA, PA	Y	15200 FQ	18000 MW	21880 TQ	USBLS	5/07
	York-Hanover MSA, PA	Y	15650 FQ	18330 MW	21690 TQ	USBLS	5/07
	Rhode Island	Y	16800 FQ	19090 MW	23160 TQ	USBLS	5/07
	Providence-Fall River-Warwick MSA, RI-MA	Y	16720 FQ	19000 MW	23090 TQ	USBLS	5/07
	South Carolina	Y	13660 FQ	16320 MW	19290 TQ	USBLS	5/07
	Charleston-North Charleston MSA, SC	Y	13370 FQ	15710 MW	18840 TQ	USBLS	5/07
	Columbia MSA, SC	Y	13230 FQ	15480 MW	18620 TQ	USBLS	5/07
	South Dakota	Y	14762 FQ	17473 MW	19803 TQ	SDBLS	7/08-9/08
	Sioux Falls MSA, SD	Y	16456 FQ	18730 MW	21676 TQ	SDBLS	7/08-9/08
	Tennessee	Y	14700 FQ	17640 MW	21050 TQ	USBLS	5/07

Occupation/Type/Industry	Location	Per	Low	Mid	High	Source	Date
Food Preparation Worker	Kingsport-Bristol-Bristol						
	MSA, TN-VA	Y	13050 FQ	14950 MW	18290 TQ	USBLS	5/07
	Memphis MSA, TN-MS-AR	Y	14570 FQ	17660 MW	21860 TQ	USBLS	5/07
	Nashville-Davidson-						
	Murfreesboro MSA, TN	Y	15180 FQ	18240 MW	22490 TQ	USBLS	5/07
	Texas	Y	13760 FQ	16300 MW	19170 TQ	USBLS	5/07
	Austin-Round Rock MSA, TX	Y	15960 FQ	19800 MW	23040 TQ	USBLS	5/07
	Corpus Christi MSA, TX	Y	12930 FQ	14480 MW	18040 TQ	USBLS	5/07
	Dallas-Fort Worth-Arlington						
	MSA, TX	Y	14670 FQ	17410 MW	20220 TQ	USBLS	5/07
	El Paso MSA, TX	Y	13170 FQ	15120 MW	17480 TQ	USBLS	5/07
	Houston-Sugar Land-Baytown						
	MSA, TX	Y	14340 FQ	16870 MW	19380 TQ	USBLS	5/07
	San Antonio MSA, TX	Y	13900 FQ	16230 MW	18630 TQ	USBLS	5/07
	Utah	Y	14110 FQ	16730 MW	19400 TQ	USBLS	5/07
	Logan MSA, UT-ID	Y	12850 FQ	14400 MW	15950 TQ	USBLS	5/07
	Salt Lake City MSA, UT	Y	15010 FQ	17470 MW	19880 TQ	USBLS	5/07
	Vermont	Y	17490 FQ	19440 MW	22410 TQ	USBLS	5/07
	Burlington-South Burlington						
	MSA, VT	Y	17930 FQ	20070 MW	23040 TQ	USBLS	5/07
	Virginia	Y	15430 FQ	18300 MW	22140 TQ	USBLS	5/07
	Richmond MSA, VA	Y	16130 FQ	18530 MW	22130 TQ	USBLS	5/07
	Virginia Beach-Norfolk-						
	Newport News MSA, VA-NC	Y	16100 FQ	18330 MW	21510 TQ	USBLS	5/07
	Washington	H	8.92 FQ	10.15 MW	12.74 TQ	WABLS	3/08
	Seattle-Tacoma-Bellevue						
	MSA, WA	Y	18990 FQ	22830 MW	27710 TQ	USBLS	5/07
	West Virginia	Y	14702 FQ	16741 MW	20609 TQ	WVBLS	7/08-9/08
	Charleston MSA, WV	Y	13910 FQ	15750 MW	20310 TQ	USBLS	5/07
	Wisconsin	Y	15820 FQ	18390 MW	21910 TQ	USBLS	5/07
	Milwaukee-Waukesha-West						
	Allis MSA, WI	Y	16490 FQ	18850 MW	22200 TQ	USBLS	5/07
	Wyoming	Y	16295 FQ	18914 MW	22668 TQ	WYBLS	9/08
	Cheyenne MSA, WY	Y	17841 FQ	19799 MW	22745 TQ	WYBLS	9/08
	Puerto Rico	Y	12660 FQ	14270 MW	16180 TQ	USBLS	5/07
	Guayama MSA, PR	Y	12370 FQ	13600 MW	14830 TQ	USBLS	5/07
	San German-Cabo Rojo MSA,						
	PR	Y	12290 FQ	13520 MW	14740 TQ	USBLS	5/07
	San Juan-Caguas-Guaynabo						
	MSA, PR	Y	12740 FQ	14440 MW	16630 TQ	USBLS	5/07
	Virgin Islands	Y	14790 FQ	16930 MW	18920 TQ	USBLS	5/07
	Guam	Y	12650 FQ	14040 MW	15700 TQ	USBLS	5/07
Food Scientist and Technologist	Alabama	Y	36700 FQ	47830 MW	60290 TQ	USBLS	5/07
	Arizona	Y	32040 FQ	37980 MW	65140 TQ	USBLS	5/07
	Phoenix-Mesa-Scottsdale						
	MSA, AZ	Y	32290 FQ	37960 MW	64560 TQ	USBLS	5/07
	Arkansas	Y	27950 FQ	31810 MW	69680 TQ	USBLS	5/07
	California	H	24.45 FQ	32.09 MW	42.35 TQ	CABLS	1/08-3/08
	Los Angeles-Long Beach-						
	Glendale PMSA, CA	H	27.02 FQ	33.57 MW	44.19 TQ	CABLS	1/08-3/08
	Oakland-Fremont-Hayward						
	MSA, CA	H	23.82 FQ	31.08 MW	39.11 TQ	CABLS	1/08-3/08
	Oxnard-Thousand Oaks-						
	Ventura MSA, CA	H	21.63 FQ	23.91 MW	26.61 TQ	CABLS	1/08-3/08
	Riverside-San Bernardino-						
	Ontario MSA, CA	H	21.77 FQ	24.69 MW	34.70 TQ	CABLS	1/08-3/08
	Sacramento-Arden Arcade-						
	Roseville MSA, CA	H	26.34 FQ	36.19 MW	44.88 TQ	CABLS	1/08-3/08
	San Diego-Carlsbad-San						
	Marcos MSA, CA	H	34.14 FQ	40.11 MW	50.45 TQ	CABLS	1/08-3/08
	San Francisco-San Mateo-						
	Redwood PMSA, CA	H	30.57 FQ	36.59 MW	45.73 TQ	CABLS	1/08-3/08
	Santa Ana-Anaheim-Irvine						
	PMSA, CA	Y	54400 FQ	80800 MW	109470 TQ	USBLS	5/07
	Colorado	Y	45780 FQ	58510 MW	77460 TQ	USBLS	5/07
	Denver-Aurora MSA, CO	Y	49830 FQ	63220 MW	82110 TQ	USBLS	5/07
	Bridgeport-Stamford-Norwalk						
	MSA, CT	Y	52640 FQ	66950 MW	83880 TQ	USBLS	5/07
	Hartford-West Hartford-East						
	Hartford MSA, CT	Y	44100 FQ	58650 MW	78650 TQ	USBLS	5/07
	District of Columbia	Y	84580 FQ	92420 MW	99990 TQ	USBLS	5/07

AE	Average entry wage	**AW**	Average wage paid	**FQ**	First quartile wage	**LO** Lowest wage paid	**MTC** Median total compensation	**TCC** Total cash compensation
AER	Average entry range	**AWR**	Average wage range	**H**	Hourly	**LR** Low end range	**MW** Median wage paid	**TQ** Third quartile wage
AEX	Average experienced wage	**AXR**	Average experienced range	**HI**	Highest wage paid	**M** Monthly	**MWR** Median wage range	**W** Weekly
ATC	Average total compensation	**D**	Daily	**HR**	High end range	**MCC** Median cash compensation	**S** See annotated source	**Y** Yearly

Occupation/Type/Industry	Location	Per	Low	Mid	High	Source	Date
Food Scientist and Technologist	Washington-Arlington-Alexandria MSA, DC-VA-MD-WV	Y	81850 FQ	91410 MW	99960 TQ	USBLS	5/07
	Florida	Y	27300 FQ	37380 MW	49230 TQ	USBLS	5/07
	Georgia	Y	41650 FQ	55530 MW	64480 TQ	USBLS	5/07
	Atlanta-Sandy Springs-Marietta MSA, GA	Y	44980 FQ	56040 MW	64200 TQ	USBLS	5/07
	Hawaii	Y	45730 FQ	70230 MW	86770 TQ	USBLS	5/07
	Honolulu MSA, HI	Y	57540 FQ	74990 MW	89120 TQ	USBLS	5/07
	Idaho	Y	35120 FQ	40830 MW	65220 TQ	USBLS	5/07
	Illinois	Y	42000 FQ	55700 MW	70640 TQ	USBLS	5/07
	Chicago-Naperville-Joliet MSA, IL-IN-WI	Y	47690 FQ	67680 MW	86240 TQ	USBLS	5/07
	Indiana	Y	31420 FQ	42000 MW	60640 TQ	USBLS	5/07
	Indianapolis-Carmel MSA, IN	Y	40650 FQ	61070 MW	70810 TQ	USBLS	5/07
	Iowa	Y	40190 FQ	52500 MW	64940 TQ	USBLS	5/07
	Kansas	Y	40110 FQ	67770 MW	93410 TQ	USBLS	5/07
	Kentucky	Y	47141 FQ	61099 MW	81630 TQ	KYBLS	2008
	Louisiana	H	16.03 FQ	26.58 MW	33.59 TQ	LABLS	1/08-3/08
	Maryland	Y		61075 MW		MDBLS	3/08
	Baltimore-Towson MSA, MD	Y	40840 FQ	56540 MW	88320 TQ	USBLS	5/07
	Massachusetts	Y	52220 FQ	63860 MW	80130 TQ	USBLS	5/07
	Boston-Cambridge-Quincy NECTA, MA	Y	53180 FQ	62530 MW	78500 TQ	USBLS	5/07
	Michigan	Y	53600 FQ	76290 MW	106800 TQ	USBLS	5/07
	Minnesota	Y	61026 FQ	78006 MW	100657 TQ	MNBLS	10/08-12/08
	Minneapolis-Saint Paul MSA, MN-WI	Y	65431 FQ	85058 MW	105689 TQ	MNBLS	10/08-12/08
	Rochester MSA, MN	Y	43038 FQ	50446 MW	60405 TQ	MNBLS	10/08-12/08
	Mississippi	Y	41200 FQ	49170 MW	59930 TQ	USBLS	5/07
	Missouri	Y	36130 FQ	54740 MW	78730 TQ	USBLS	5/07
	Kansas City MSA, MO-KS	Y	37830 FQ	58230 MW	77550 TQ	USBLS	5/07
	St. Louis MSA, MO-IL	Y	41070 FQ	63100 MW	74680 TQ	USBLS	5/07
	Nebraska	Y	27460 FQ	31440 MW	51310 TQ	USBLS	5/07
	Nevada	H	19.83 FQ	23.13 MW	31.61 TQ	NVBLS	5/08
	New Jersey	Y	54360 FQ	66870 MW	84110 TQ	USBLS	5/07
	Edison PMSA, NJ	Y	52470 FQ	66740 MW	78330 TQ	USBLS	5/07
	Newark-Union PMSA, NJ-PA	Y	54900 FQ	61140 MW	72600 TQ	USBLS	5/07
	New York	Y	35730 FQ	56290 MW	81680 TQ	USBLS	5/07
	Nassau-Suffolk PMSA, NY	Y	34270 FQ	46050 MW	85140 TQ	USBLS	5/07
	New York-Northern New Jersey-Long Island MSA, NY-NJ-PA	Y	51540 FQ	63270 MW	81460 TQ	USBLS	5/07
	North Carolina	Y	35380 FQ	50190 MW	70830 TQ	USBLS	5/07
	North Dakota	Y	36340 FQ	53050 MW	71840 TQ	USBLS	5/07
	Ohio	Y	42710 FQ	67050 MW	90010 TQ	USBLS	5/07
	Cincinnati-Middletown MSA, OH-KY-IN	Y	47110 FQ	61350 MW	91870 TQ	USBLS	5/07
	Columbus MSA, OH	Y	48080 FQ	76380 MW	93080 TQ	USBLS	5/07
	Oklahoma	Y	34410 FQ	38300 MW	64140 TQ	USBLS	5/07
	Oklahoma City MSA, OK	Y	33530 FQ	36160 MW	40180 TQ	USBLS	5/07
	Oregon	H	15.78 FQ	19.98 MW	23.80 TQ	ORBLS	5/08
	Portland-Vancouver-Beaverton MSA, OR-WA	Y	35310 FQ	42440 MW	50160 TQ	USBLS	5/07
	Pennsylvania	Y	39730 FQ	57830 MW	79540 TQ	USBLS	5/07
	Philadelphia-Camden-Wilmington MSA, PA-NJ-DE-MD	Y	54910 FQ	71250 MW	90440 TQ	USBLS	5/07
	Pittsburgh MSA, PA	Y	57360 FQ	66350 MW	117650 TQ	USBLS	5/07
	South Carolina	Y	37720 FQ	45520 MW	63200 TQ	USBLS	5/07
	South Dakota	Y	37582 FQ	45015 MW	54785 TQ	SDBLS	7/08-9/08
	Tennessee	Y	29970 FQ	32750 MW	45170 TQ	USBLS	5/07
	Memphis MSA, TN-MS-AR	Y	29130 FQ	31910 MW	56860 TQ	USBLS	5/07
	Texas	Y	41210 FQ	67890 MW	93790 TQ	USBLS	5/07
	Dallas-Fort Worth-Arlington MSA, TX	Y	41190 FQ	70300 MW	90880 TQ	USBLS	5/07
	Houston-Sugar Land-Baytown MSA, TX	Y	37880 FQ	50570 MW	72980 TQ	USBLS	5/07
	San Antonio MSA, TX	Y	46310 FQ	57730 MW	78970 TQ	USBLS	5/07
	Utah	Y	42540 FQ	53510 MW	75090 TQ	USBLS	5/07
	Vermont	Y	35640 FQ	45320 MW	63010 TQ	USBLS	5/07

AE	Average entry wage	AW	Average wage paid	FQ	First quartile wage	LO	Lowest wage paid	MTC Median total compensation · TCC Total cash compensation
AER	Average entry range	AWR	Average wage range	H	Hourly	LR	Low end range	MW Median wage paid · TQ Third quartile wage
AEX	Average experienced wage	AXR	Average experienced range	HI	Highest wage paid	M	Monthly	MWR Median wage range · W Weekly
ATC	Average total compensation	D	Daily	HR	High end range	MCC	Median cash compensation	S See annotated source · Y Yearly

Occupation/Type/Industry	Location	Per	Low	Mid	High	Source	Date
Food Scientist and Technologist	Burlington-South Burlington MSA, VT	Y	36750 FQ	48000 MW	66740 TQ	USBLS	5/07
	Virginia	Y	45580 FQ	63060 MW	79980 TQ	USBLS	5/07
	Washington	H	21.49 FQ	30.27 MW	39.77 TQ	WABLS	3/08
	Seattle-Tacoma-Bellevue MSA, WA	Y	41600 FQ	66260 MW	85440 TQ	USBLS	5/07
	Wisconsin	Y	36760 FQ	46630 MW	61370 TQ	USBLS	5/07
	Milwaukee-Waukesha-West Allis MSA, WI	Y	41550 FQ	56780 MW	80570 TQ	USBLS	5/07
	San Juan-Caguas-Guaynabo MSA, PR	Y	18480 FQ	21750 MW	32490 TQ	USBLS	5/07
Food Server							
Nonrestaurant	Alabama	Y	13520 FQ	16230 MW	18930 TQ	USBLS	5/07
Nonrestaurant	Birmingham-Hoover MSA, AL	Y	14100 FQ	17050 MW	19420 TQ	USBLS	5/07
Nonrestaurant	Alaska	Y	25150 FQ	42230 MW	47760 TQ	USBLS	5/07
Nonrestaurant	Anchorage MSA, AK	Y	32520 FQ	45290 MW	49380 TQ	USBLS	5/07
Nonrestaurant	Arizona	Y	14980 FQ	16470 MW	21510 TQ	USBLS	5/07
Nonrestaurant	Phoenix-Mesa-Scottsdale MSA, AZ	Y	14830 FQ	15990 MW	22200 TQ	USBLS	5/07
	Tucson MSA, AZ	Y	16350 FQ	18780 MW	22040 TQ	USBLS	5/07
	Arkansas	Y	13960 FQ	14680 MW	15550 TQ	USBLS	5/07
	Fort Smith MSA, AR-OK	Y	13850 FQ	14460 MW	15160 TQ	USBLS	5/07
	Jonesboro MSA, AR	Y	13970 FQ	14630 MW	15690 TQ	USBLS	5/07
Nonrestaurant	Little Rock-North Little Rock MSA, AR	Y	14150 FQ	15030 MW	16570 TQ	USBLS	5/07
Nonrestaurant	California	H	8.38 FQ	9.83 MW	13.35 TQ	CABLS	1/08-3/08
Nonrestaurant	Los Angeles-Long Beach-Glendale PMSA, CA	H	8.16 FQ	9.58 MW	12.58 TQ	CABLS	1/08-3/08
Nonrestaurant	Oakland-Fremont-Hayward MSA, CA	H	8.71 FQ	10.53 MW	13.38 TQ	CABLS	1/08-3/08
Nonrestaurant	Riverside-San Bernardino-Ontario MSA, CA	H	8.74 FQ	10.43 MW	13.44 TQ	CABLS	1/08-3/08
Nonrestaurant	Sacramento-Arden Arcade-Roseville MSA, CA	H	8.00 FQ	11.23 MW	14.43 TQ	CABLS	1/08-3/08
Nonrestaurant	San Diego-Carlsbad-San Marcos MSA, CA	H	8.29 FQ	9.22 MW	11.51 TQ	CABLS	1/08-3/08
Nonrestaurant	San Francisco-San Mateo-Redwood PMSA, CA	H	9.72 FQ	12.04 MW	16.86 TQ	CABLS	1/08-3/08
Nonrestaurant	San Jose-Sunnyvale-Santa Clara MSA, CA	H	8.78 FQ	11.06 MW	15.28 TQ	CABLS	1/08-3/08
Nonrestaurant	Santa Ana-Anaheim-Irvine PMSA, CA	Y	16720 FQ	18680 MW	26630 TQ	USBLS	5/07
Nonrestaurant	Colorado	Y	16770 FQ	20180 MW	24440 TQ	USBLS	5/07
Nonrestaurant	Denver-Aurora MSA, CO	Y	18240 FQ	21580 MW	25040 TQ	USBLS	5/07
Nonrestaurant	Connecticut	H	9.26 AE	11.39 MW		CTBLS	1/08-3/08
Nonrestaurant	Bridgeport-Stamford-Norwalk MSA, CT	Y	20150 FQ	23820 MW	30450 TQ	USBLS	5/07
Nonrestaurant	Hartford-West Hartford-East Hartford MSA, CT	Y	19620 FQ	23620 MW	29500 TQ	USBLS	5/07
Nonrestaurant	Delaware	Y	17270 FQ	21190 MW	25060 TQ	USBLS	5/07
Nonrestaurant	Wilmington PMSA, DE-MD-NJ	Y	18220 FQ	22130 MW	25810 TQ	USBLS	5/07
Nonrestaurant	District of Columbia	Y	17600 FQ	24470 MW	31400 TQ	USBLS	5/07
Nonrestaurant	Washington-Arlington-Alexandria MSA, DC-VA-MD-WV	Y	17280 FQ	21400 MW	28440 TQ	USBLS	5/07
Nonrestaurant	Florida	Y	15450 FQ	18020 MW	21820 TQ	USBLS	5/07
Nonrestaurant	Fort Lauderdale-Pompano Beach-Deerfield Beach PMSA, FL	Y	15370 FQ	17990 MW	23990 TQ	USBLS	5/07
Nonrestaurant	Jacksonville MSA, FL	Y	15140 FQ	17110 MW	19700 TQ	USBLS	5/07
Nonrestaurant	Miami-Fort Lauderdale-Miami Beach MSA, FL	Y	16020 FQ	18590 MW	22570 TQ	USBLS	5/07
Nonrestaurant	Orlando-Kissimmee MSA, FL	Y	14730 FQ	17170 MW	21830 TQ	USBLS	5/07
Nonrestaurant	Tampa-St. Petersburg-Clearwater MSA, FL	Y	15050 FQ	16690 MW	20100 TQ	USBLS	5/07
Nonrestaurant	West Palm Beach-Boca Raton-Boynton Beach PMSA, FL	Y	16880 FQ	19210 MW	22530 TQ	USBLS	5/07
Nonrestaurant	Georgia	Y	15410 FQ	20080 MW	25340 TQ	USBLS	5/07
Nonrestaurant	Atlanta-Sandy Springs-Marietta MSA, GA	Y	18860 FQ	23560 MW	28290 TQ	USBLS	5/07

AE	Average entry wage	AW	Average wage paid	FQ	First quartile wage
AER	Average entry range	AWR	Average wage range	H	Hourly
AEX	Average experienced wage	AXR	Average experienced range	HI	Highest wage paid
ATC	Average total compensation	D	Daily	HR	High end range

LO	Lowest wage paid	MTC	Median total compensation	TCC	Total cash compensation
LR	Low end range	MW	Median wage paid	TQ	Third quartile wage
M	Monthly	MWR	Median wage range	W	Weekly
MCC	Median cash compensation	S	See annotated source	Y	Yearly

Occupation/Type/Industry	Location	Per	Low	Mid	High	Source	Date
Food Server							
Nonrestaurant	Augusta-Richmond County MSA, GA-SC	Y	14510 FQ	16180 MW	17980 TQ	USBLS	5/07
Nonrestaurant	Hawaii	Y	17460 FQ	25940 MW	31220 TQ	USBLS	5/07
Nonrestaurant	Honolulu MSA, HI	Y	18360 FQ	27870 MW	34390 TQ	USBLS	5/07
Nonrestaurant	Idaho	Y	13990 FQ	17860 MW	22550 TQ	USBLS	5/07
Nonrestaurant	Boise City-Nampa MSA, ID	Y	14970 FQ	18200 MW	20850 TQ	USBLS	5/07
Nonrestaurant	Illinois	Y	15090 FQ	17330 MW	21590 TQ	USBLS	5/07
Nonrestaurant	Chicago-Naperville-Joliet MSA, IL-IN-WI	Y	15030 FQ	17490 MW	22900 TQ	USBLS	5/07
Nonrestaurant	Indiana	Y	15380 FQ	18270 MW	21270 TQ	USBLS	5/07
Nonrestaurant	Gary PMSA, IN	Y	14880 FQ	17700 MW	20980 TQ	USBLS	5/07
Nonrestaurant	Indianapolis-Carmel MSA, IN	Y	15890 FQ	18730 MW	21890 TQ	USBLS	5/07
Nonrestaurant	Iowa	Y	15730 FQ	18500 MW	21700 TQ	USBLS	5/07
Nonrestaurant	Des Moines-West Des Moines MSA, IA	Y	17290 FQ	20390 MW	23780 TQ	USBLS	5/07
Nonrestaurant	Kansas	Y	13290 FQ	15380 MW	18370 TQ	USBLS	5/07
Nonrestaurant	Wichita MSA, KS	Y	14550 FQ	16700 MW	18740 TQ	USBLS	5/07
Nonrestaurant	Kentucky	Y	14975 FQ	18010 MW	21115 TQ	KYBLS	2008
Nonrestaurant	Lexington-Fayette MSA, KY	Y	16350 FQ	18410 MW	21620 TQ	USBLS	5/07
Nonrestaurant	Louisville-Jefferson County MSA, KY-IN	Y	14440 FQ	17600 MW	20630 TQ	USBLS	5/07
Nonrestaurant	Louisiana	H	6.38 FQ	7.37 MW	9.17 TQ	LABLS	1/08-3/08
Nonrestaurant	Baton Rouge MSA, LA	Y	13930 FQ	16120 MW	20050 TQ	USBLS	5/07
Nonrestaurant	New Orleans-Metairie-Kenner MSA, LA	Y	13460 FQ	15830 MW	19960 TQ	USBLS	5/07
Nonrestaurant	Maine	Y	15040 FQ	18050 MW	22080 TQ	USBLS	5/07
Nonrestaurant	Portland-South Portland-Biddeford MSA, ME	Y	14940 FQ	18090 MW	22500 TQ	USBLS	5/07
Nonrestaurant	Maryland	Y		20150 MW		MDBLS	3/08
Nonrestaurant	Baltimore-Towson MSA, MD	Y	17030 FQ	19880 MW	23190 TQ	USBLS	5/07
Nonrestaurant	Bethesda-Gaithersburg-Frederick PMSA, MD	Y	17080 FQ	19660 MW	23960 TQ	USBLS	5/07
Nonrestaurant	Massachusetts	Y	18100 FQ	21030 MW	25250 TQ	USBLS	5/07
Nonrestaurant	Boston-Cambridge-Quincy NECTA, MA	Y	18470 FQ	22010 MW	25970 TQ	USBLS	5/07
Nonrestaurant	Worcester MSA, MA-CT	Y	17590 FQ	19950 MW	23800 TQ	USBLS	5/07
Nonrestaurant	Michigan	Y	16660 FQ	20570 MW	25140 TQ	USBLS	5/07
Nonrestaurant	Detroit-Warren-Livonia MSA, MI	Y	17930 FQ	22940 MW	27890 TQ	USBLS	5/07
Nonrestaurant	Flint MSA, MI	Y	16420 FQ	19480 MW	23810 TQ	USBLS	5/07
Nonrestaurant	Grand Rapids-Wyoming MSA, MI	Y	16090 FQ	19410 MW	22400 TQ	USBLS	5/07
Nonrestaurant	Warren-Troy-Farmington Hills PMSA, MI	Y	18920 FQ	23320 MW	27950 TQ	USBLS	5/07
Nonrestaurant	Minnesota	Y	19040 FQ	22500 MW	27289 TQ	MNBLS	10/08-12/08
Nonrestaurant	Duluth-Superior MSA, MN-WI	Y	17105 FQ	19907 MW	24843 TQ	MNBLS	10/08-12/08
Nonrestaurant	Minneapolis-Saint Paul MSA, MN-WI	Y	19510 FQ	23295 MW	28774 TQ	MNBLS	10/08-12/08
Nonrestaurant	Rochester MSA, MN	Y	18745 FQ	22227 MW	25801 TQ	MNBLS	10/08-12/08
Nonrestaurant	Mississippi	Y	12700 FQ	14270 MW	15970 TQ	USBLS	5/07
Nonrestaurant	Gulfport-Biloxi MSA, MS	Y	13420 FQ	15910 MW	20090 TQ	USBLS	5/07
Nonrestaurant	Jackson MSA, MS	Y	12850 FQ	14550 MW	16700 TQ	USBLS	5/07
Nonrestaurant	Missouri	Y	14600 FQ	16330 MW	20280 TQ	USBLS	5/07
Nonrestaurant	Joplin MSA, MO	Y	16300 FQ	17580 MW	18870 TQ	USBLS	5/07
Nonrestaurant	Kansas City MSA, MO-KS	Y	14760 FQ	17390 MW	21860 TQ	USBLS	5/07
Nonrestaurant	St. Louis MSA, MO-IL	Y	14700 FQ	16750 MW	20220 TQ	USBLS	5/07
Nonrestaurant	Montana	Y	14730 FQ	16950 MW	19760 TQ	USBLS	5/07
Nonrestaurant	Billings MSA, MT	Y	13840 FQ	14900 MW	17460 TQ	USBLS	5/07
Nonrestaurant	Nebraska	Y	14540 FQ	17550 MW	20530 TQ	USBLS	5/07
Nonrestaurant	Omaha-Council Bluffs MSA, NE-IA	Y	15230 FQ	19140 MW	22220 TQ	USBLS	5/07
Nonrestaurant	Nevada	H	7.29 FQ	9.71 MW	11.65 TQ	NVBLS	5/08
Nonrestaurant	Las Vegas-Paradise MSA, NV	H	7.57 FQ	10.14 MW	11.86 TQ	NVBLS	5/08
Nonrestaurant	New Hampshire	H	7.86 AE	9.37 MW	10.87 AEX	NHBLS	6/08
Nonrestaurant	Manchester MSA, NH	Y	17120 FQ	19350 MW	22980 TQ	USBLS	5/07
Nonrestaurant	Nashua NECTA, NH-MA	Y	15840 FQ	17800 MW	19600 TQ	USBLS	5/07
Nonrestaurant	New Jersey	Y	17770 FQ	20570 MW	24120 TQ	USBLS	5/07
Nonrestaurant	Camden PMSA, NJ	Y	16770 FQ	19140 MW	22740 TQ	USBLS	5/07
Nonrestaurant	Edison PMSA, NJ	Y	17410 FQ	19530 MW	23170 TQ	USBLS	5/07
Nonrestaurant	Newark-Union PMSA, NJ-PA	Y	18300 FQ	21200 MW	24420 TQ	USBLS	5/07
Nonrestaurant	New Mexico	Y	13040 FQ	14900 MW	18590 TQ	USBLS	5/07

AE	Average entry wage	AW	Average wage paid	FQ	First quartile wage	LO	Lowest wage paid	MTC	Median total compensation	TCC	Total cash compensation
AER	Average entry range	AWR	Average wage range	H	Hourly	LR	Low end range	MW	Median wage paid	TQ	Third quartile wage
AEX	Average experienced wage	AXR	Average experienced range	HI	Highest wage paid	M	Monthly	MWR	Median wage range	W	Weekly
ATC	Average total compensation	D	Daily	HR	High end range	MCC	Median cash compensation	S	See annotated source	Y	Yearly

682

Occupation/Type/Industry	Location	Per	Low	Mid	High	Source	Date
Food Server							
Nonrestaurant	Albuquerque MSA, NM	Y	12850 FQ	14520 MW	16820 TQ	USBLS	5/07
Nonrestaurant	New York	Y	20630 FQ	27800 MW	34460 TQ	USBLS	5/07
Nonrestaurant	Albany-Schenectady-Troy MSA, NY	Y	17340 FQ	19440 MW	24360 TQ	USBLS	5/07
Nonrestaurant	Buffalo-Niagara Falls MSA, NY	Y	16820 FQ	21440 MW	25210 TQ	USBLS	5/07
Nonrestaurant	Nassau-Suffolk PMSA, NY	Y	21460 FQ	28710 MW	35510 TQ	USBLS	5/07
Nonrestaurant	New York-Northern New Jersey-Long Island MSA, NY-NJ-PA	Y	19510 FQ	24570 MW	31640 TQ	USBLS	5/07
Nonrestaurant	Utica-Rome MSA, NY	Y	15890 FQ	17680 MW	22050 TQ	USBLS	5/07
Nonrestaurant	North Carolina	Y	15620 FQ	18330 MW	21900 TQ	USBLS	5/07
Nonrestaurant	Charlotte-Gastonia-Concord MSA, NC-SC	Y	15810 FQ	19240 MW	22970 TQ	USBLS	5/07
Nonrestaurant	Durham MSA, NC	Y	16340 FQ	18860 MW	23240 TQ	USBLS	5/07
Nonrestaurant	Raleigh-Cary MSA, NC	Y	16870 FQ	19230 MW	22240 TQ	USBLS	5/07
Nonrestaurant	Winston-Salem MSA, NC	Y	17530 FQ	19480 MW	22480 TQ	USBLS	5/07
Nonrestaurant	North Dakota	Y	16870 FQ	18790 MW	21610 TQ	USBLS	5/07
Nonrestaurant	Fargo MSA, ND-MN	Y	16970 FQ	18700 MW	21020 TQ	USBLS	5/07
Nonrestaurant	Ohio	Y	15710 FQ	18080 MW	21090 TQ	USBLS	5/07
Nonrestaurant	Cincinnati-Middletown MSA, OH-KY-IN	Y	16740 FQ	19280 MW	22860 TQ	USBLS	5/07
Nonrestaurant	Cleveland-Elyria-Mentor MSA, OH	Y	16320 FQ	18740 MW	22780 TQ	USBLS	5/07
Nonrestaurant	Columbus MSA, OH	Y	15600 FQ	17610 MW	19900 TQ	USBLS	5/07
Nonrestaurant	Dayton MSA, OH	Y	15520 FQ	17620 MW	20610 TQ	USBLS	5/07
Nonrestaurant	Springfield MSA, OH	Y	15930 FQ	18130 MW	20210 TQ	USBLS	5/07
Nonrestaurant	Oklahoma	Y	12730 FQ	14220 MW	16120 TQ	USBLS	5/07
Nonrestaurant	Oklahoma City MSA, OK	Y	13040 FQ	14910 MW	18070 TQ	USBLS	5/07
Nonrestaurant	Tulsa MSA, OK	Y	12980 FQ	14660 MW	17910 TQ	USBLS	5/07
Nonrestaurant	Oregon	H	8.59 FQ	9.19 MW	10.32 TQ	ORBLS	5/08
Nonrestaurant	Portland-Vancouver-Beaverton MSA, OR-WA	Y	17420 FQ	18710 MW	21270 TQ	USBLS	5/07
Nonrestaurant	Pennsylvania	Y	15300 FQ	18080 MW	22440 TQ	USBLS	5/07
Nonrestaurant	Allentown-Bethlehem-Easton MSA, PA-NJ	Y	15690 FQ	17900 MW	20180 TQ	USBLS	5/07
Nonrestaurant	Lancaster MSA, PA	Y	17220 FQ	19140 MW	22140 TQ	USBLS	5/07
Nonrestaurant	Philadelphia-Camden-Wilmington MSA, PA-NJ-DE-MD	Y	16870 FQ	19890 MW	23960 TQ	USBLS	5/07
Nonrestaurant	Pittsburgh MSA, PA	Y	14490 FQ	15470 MW	19370 TQ	USBLS	5/07
Nonrestaurant	Rhode Island	Y	17250 FQ	19850 MW	23240 TQ	USBLS	5/07
Nonrestaurant	Providence-Fall River-Warwick MSA, RI-MA	Y	17250 FQ	19620 MW	23080 TQ	USBLS	5/07
Nonrestaurant	South Carolina	Y	14240 FQ	16550 MW	18890 TQ	USBLS	5/07
Nonrestaurant	Charleston-North Charleston MSA, SC	Y	15880 FQ	17500 MW	19110 TQ	USBLS	5/07
Nonrestaurant	Columbia MSA, SC	Y	13220 FQ	15450 MW	18140 TQ	USBLS	5/07
Nonrestaurant	Florence MSA, SC	Y	14580 FQ	17230 MW	20010 TQ	USBLS	5/07
Nonrestaurant	South Dakota	Y	18170 FQ	21417 MW	24058 TQ	SDBLS	7/08-9/08
Nonrestaurant	Sioux Falls MSA, SD	Y	21989 FQ	23592 MW	25234 TQ	SDBLS	7/08-9/08
Nonrestaurant	Tennessee	Y	14020 FQ	17130 MW	22420 TQ	USBLS	5/07
Nonrestaurant	Memphis MSA, TN-MS-AR	Y	13540 FQ	15540 MW	19120 TQ	USBLS	5/07
Nonrestaurant	Nashville-Davidson-Murfreesboro MSA, TN	Y	15370 FQ	19900 MW	25840 TQ	USBLS	5/07
Nonrestaurant	Texas	Y	14370 FQ	17160 MW	20140 TQ	USBLS	5/07
Nonrestaurant	Austin-Round Rock MSA, TX	Y	14260 FQ	17350 MW	21840 TQ	USBLS	5/07
Nonrestaurant	Corpus Christi MSA, TX	Y	16310 FQ	18090 MW	19880 TQ	USBLS	5/07
Nonrestaurant	Dallas-Fort Worth-Arlington MSA, TX	Y	14950 FQ	17150 MW	19250 TQ	USBLS	5/07
Nonrestaurant	Houston-Sugar Land-Baytown MSA, TX	Y	14830 FQ	18270 MW	22880 TQ	USBLS	5/07
Nonrestaurant	San Antonio MSA, TX	Y	14130 FQ	17100 MW	20020 TQ	USBLS	5/07
Nonrestaurant	Utah	Y	13680 FQ	16540 MW	19290 TQ	USBLS	5/07
Nonrestaurant	Ogden-Clearfield MSA, UT	Y	14150 FQ	16800 MW	19960 TQ	USBLS	5/07
Nonrestaurant	Salt Lake City MSA, UT	Y	14110 FQ	17090 MW	19380 TQ	USBLS	5/07
Nonrestaurant	Vermont	Y	18330 FQ	21620 MW	25250 TQ	USBLS	5/07
Nonrestaurant	Burlington-South Burlington MSA, VT	Y	19430 FQ	22240 MW	25240 TQ	USBLS	5/07
Nonrestaurant	Virginia	Y	15560 FQ	18210 MW	22230 TQ	USBLS	5/07
Nonrestaurant	Lynchburg MSA, VA	Y	12520 FQ	13890 MW	15390 TQ	USBLS	5/07

AE Average entry wage	**AW** Average wage paid	**FQ** First quartile wage	**LO** Lowest wage paid	**MTC** Median total compensation	**TCC** Total cash compensation
AER Average entry range	**AWR** Average wage range	**H** Hourly	**LR** Low end range	**MW** Median wage paid	**TQ** Third quartile wage
AEX Average experienced wage	**AXR** Average experienced range	**HI** Highest wage paid	**M** Monthly	**MWR** Median wage range	**W** Weekly
ATC Average total compensation	**D** Daily	**HR** High end range	**MCC** Median cash compensation	**S** See annotated source	**Y** Yearly

Occupation/Type/Industry	Location	Per	Low	Mid	High	Source	Date
Food Server							
Nonrestaurant	Richmond MSA, VA	Y	16450 FQ	18510 MW	22160 TQ	USBLS	5/07
Nonrestaurant	Virginia Beach-Norfolk-						
	Newport News MSA, VA-NC	Y	14850 FQ	17320 MW	19660 TQ	USBLS	5/07
Nonrestaurant	Washington	H	9.05 FQ	10.82 MW	14.01 TQ	WABLS	3/08
Nonrestaurant	Olympia MSA, WA	Y	18570 FQ	20530 MW	26080 TQ	USBLS	5/07
Nonrestaurant	Seattle-Tacoma-Bellevue						
	MSA, WA	Y	19310 FQ	24440 MW	30830 TQ	USBLS	5/07
Nonrestaurant	West Virginia	Y	14765 FQ	16652 MW	19565 TQ	WVBLS	7/08-9/08
Nonrestaurant	Charleston MSA, WV	Y	13420 FQ	14620 MW	16500 TQ	USBLS	5/07
Nonrestaurant	Wisconsin	Y	17260 FQ	20280 MW	24090 TQ	USBLS	5/07
Nonrestaurant	Milwaukee-Waukesha-West						
	Allis MSA, WI	Y	17540 FQ	20520 MW	24250 TQ	USBLS	5/07
Nonrestaurant	Wyoming	Y	16319 FQ	18868 MW	22902 TQ	WYBLS	9/08
Nonrestaurant	Puerto Rico	Y	12720 FQ	14180 MW	16150 TQ	USBLS	5/07
Nonrestaurant	San Juan-Caguas-Guaynabo						
	MSA, PR	Y	12750 FQ	14280 MW	16570 TQ	USBLS.	5/07
Nonrestaurant	Virgin Islands	Y	14620 FQ	17080 MW	20650 TQ	USBLS	5/07
Nonrestaurant	Guam	Y	12250 FQ	13390 MW	14530 TQ	USBLS	5/07
Food Service Manager	Alabama	Y	32400 FQ	39780 MW	50570 TQ	USBLS	5/07
	Birmingham-Hoover MSA, AL	Y	33240 FQ	40580 MW	52050 TQ	USBLS	5/07
	Alaska	Y	24370 FQ	33460 MW	46940 TQ	USBLS	5/07
	Anchorage MSA, AK	Y	24180 FQ	34030 MW	47610 TQ	USBLS	5/07
	Arizona	Y	32190 FQ	41230 MW	52670 TQ	USBLS	5/07
	Phoenix-Mesa-Scottsdale						
	MSA, AZ	Y	33300 FQ	41800 MW	53140 TQ	USBLS	5/07
	Tucson MSA, AZ	Y	28250 FQ	36980 MW	49610 TQ	USBLS	5/07
	Yuma MSA, AZ	Y	32000 FQ	45120 MW	61640 TQ	USBLS	5/07
	Arkansas	Y	31600 FQ	37610 MW	46160 TQ	USBLS	5/07
	Little Rock-North Little Rock						
	MSA, AR	Y	33700 FQ	41090 MW	48870 TQ	USBLS	5/07
	California	H	18.90 FQ	22.33 MW	26.71 TQ	CABLS	1/08-3/08
	Los Angeles-Long Beach-						
	Glendale PMSA, CA	H	18.89 FQ	22.09 MW	25.80 TQ	CABLS	1/08-3/08
	Oakland-Fremont-Hayward						
	MSA, CA	H	18.22 FQ	21.99 MW	26.72 TQ	CABLS	1/08-3/08
	Riverside-San Bernardino-						
	Ontario MSA, CA	H	18.76 FQ	22.18 MW	25.48 TQ	CABLS	1/08-3/08
	Sacramento-Arden Arcade-						
	Roseville MSA, CA	H	18.93 FQ	21.79 MW	25.60 TQ	CABLS	1/08-3/08
	San Diego-Carlsbad-San						
	Marcos MSA, CA	H	19.35 FQ	22.80 MW	28.40 TQ	CABLS	1/08-3/08
	San Francisco-San Mateo-						
	Redwood PMSA, CA	H	21.58 FQ	25.37 MW	31.20 TQ	CABLS	1/08-3/08
	San Jose-Sunnyvale-Santa						
	Clara MSA, CA	H	19.81 FQ	22.93 MW	27.91 TQ	CABLS	1/08-3/08
	Santa Ana-Anaheim-Irvine						
	PMSA, CA	Y	38410 FQ	46340 MW	56840 TQ	USBLS	5/07
	Colorado	Y	38020 FQ	46990 MW	61560 TQ	USBLS	5/07
	Denver-Aurora MSA, CO	Y	40570 FQ	48220 MW	64120 TQ	USBLS	5/07
	Pueblo MSA, CO	Y	33590 FQ	41040 MW	57560 TQ	USBLS	5/07
	Connecticut	H	16.42 AE	23.72 MW		CTBLS	1/08-3/08
	Bridgeport-Stamford-Norwalk						
	MSA, CT	Y	45220 FQ	57000 MW	79300 TQ	USBLS	5/07
	Hartford-West Hartford-East						
	Hartford MSA, CT	Y	35730 FQ	44870 MW	56190 TQ	USBLS	5/07
	Delaware	Y	46940 FQ	56450 MW	73350 TQ	USBLS	5/07
	Wilmington PMSA, DE-MD-						
	NJ	Y	47080 FQ	57300 MW	73990 TQ	USBLS	5/07
	District of Columbia	Y	33360 FQ	45430 MW	63390 TQ	USBLS	5/07
	Washington-Arlington-						
	Alexandria MSA, DC-VA-						
	MD-WV	Y	39530 FQ	50350 MW	67280 TQ	USBLS	5/07
	Florida	Y	38160 FQ	48190 MW	62480 TQ	USBLS	5/07
	Fort Lauderdale-Pompano						
	Beach-Deerfield Beach						
	PMSA, FL	Y	31460 FQ	45480 MW	60980 TQ	USBLS	5/07
	Jacksonville MSA, FL	Y	33040 FQ	43710 MW	55790 TQ	USBLS	5/07
	Miami-Fort Lauderdale-Miami						
	Beach MSA, FL	Y	38500 FQ	49110 MW	63460 TQ	USBLS	5/07
	Orlando-Kissimmee MSA, FL	Y	38750 FQ	47220 MW	60630 TQ	USBLS	5/07

AE	Average entry wage	AW	Average wage paid	FQ	First quartile wage
AER	Average entry range	AWR	Average wage range	H	Hourly
AEX	Average experienced wage	AXR	Average experienced range	HI	Highest wage paid
ATC	Average total compensation	D	Daily	HR	High end range

LO	Lowest wage paid	MTC	Median total compensation	TCC	Total cash compensation
LR	Low end range	MW	Median wage paid	TQ	Third quartile wage
M	Monthly	MWR	Median wage range	W	Weekly
MCC	Median cash compensation	S	See annotated source	Y	Yearly

Food Service Manager

Occupation/Type/Industry	Location	Per	Low	Mid	High	Source	Date
Food Service Manager	Tampa-St. Petersburg-Clearwater MSA, FL	Y	42450 FQ	54880 MW	69250 TQ	USBLS	5/07
	West Palm Beach-Boca Raton-Boynton Beach PMSA, FL	Y	43250 FQ	52030 MW	68850 TQ	USBLS	5/07
	Georgia	Y	38810 FQ	50840 MW	68290 TQ	USBLS	5/07
	Atlanta-Sandy Springs-Marietta MSA, GA	Y	40510 FQ	54480 MW	79370 TQ	USBLS	5/07
	Savannah MSA, GA	Y	40930 FQ	49700 MW	64710 TQ	USBLS	5/07
	Hawaii	Y	37460 FQ	45620 MW	57170 TQ	USBLS	5/07
	Honolulu MSA, HI	Y	36150 FQ	43900 MW	55010 TQ	USBLS	5/07
	Idaho	Y	26350 FQ	32990 MW	41810 TQ	USBLS	5/07
	Boise City-Nampa MSA, ID	Y	28000 FQ	34680 MW	41880 TQ	USBLS	5/07
	Pocatello MSA, ID	Y	22020 FQ	28140 MW	36920 TQ	USBLS	5/07
	Illinois	Y	30250 FQ	40980 MW	53900 TQ	USBLS	5/07
	Chicago-Naperville-Joliet MSA, IL-IN-WI	Y	34060 FQ	45140 MW	59720 TQ	USBLS	5/07
	Indiana	Y	33850 FQ	42170 MW	53390 TQ	USBLS	5/07
	Gary PMSA, IN	Y	33500 FQ	45150 MW	64330 TQ	USBLS	5/07
	Indianapolis-Carmel MSA, IN	Y	35190 FQ	43740 MW	54520 TQ	USBLS	5/07
	Iowa	Y	31260 FQ	40800 MW	52780 TQ	USBLS	5/07
	Des Moines-West Des Moines MSA, IA	Y	37350 FQ	44520 MW	53340 TQ	USBLS	5/07
	Dubuque MSA, IA	Y	28870 FQ	35600 MW	48440 TQ	USBLS	5/07
	Kansas	Y	30690 FQ	38700 MW	49560 TQ	USBLS	5/07
	Wichita MSA, KS	Y	29930 FQ	39620 MW	49380 TQ	USBLS	5/07
	Kentucky	Y	35107 FQ	40067 MW	48549 TQ	KYBLS	2008
	Louisville-Jefferson County MSA, KY-IN	Y	34120 FQ	39510 MW	47640 TQ	USBLS	5/07
	Louisiana	H	13.25 FQ	17.90 MW	24.46 TQ	LABLS	1/08-3/08
	Baton Rouge MSA, LA	Y	30810 FQ	40520 MW	52210 TQ	USBLS	5/07
	New Orleans-Metairie-Kenner MSA, LA	Y	29090 FQ	40630 MW	52520 TQ	USBLS	5/07
	Maine	Y	34500 FQ	43490 MW	57460 TQ	USBLS	5/07
	Portland-South Portland-Biddeford MSA, ME	Y	36870 FQ	44580 MW	57600 TQ	USBLS	5/07
	Maryland	Y		51325 MW		MDBLS	3/08
	Baltimore-Towson MSA, MD	Y	39380 FQ	52510 MW	64570 TQ	USBLS	5/07
	Bethesda-Gaithersburg-Frederick PMSA, MD	Y	39050 FQ	48100 MW	65170 TQ	USBLS	5/07
	Massachusetts	Y	40100 FQ	49600 MW	59980 TQ	USBLS	5/07
	Boston-Cambridge-Quincy NECTA, MA	Y	43410 FQ	51540 MW	61390 TQ	USBLS	5/07
	Lynn-Peabody-Salem NECTA, MA	Y	43920 FQ	56050 MW	88060 TQ	USBLS	5/07
	Worcester MSA, MA-CT	Y	26600 FQ	41890 MW	51940 TQ	USBLS	5/07
	Michigan	Y	32130 FQ	41250 MW	55510 TQ	USBLS	5/07
	Detroit-Warren-Livonia MSA, MI	Y	34870 FQ	45390 MW	59070 TQ	USBLS	5/07
	Grand Rapids-Wyoming MSA, MI	Y	31100 FQ	37350 MW	51700 TQ	USBLS	5/07
	Warren-Troy-Farmington Hills PMSA, MI	Y	35890 FQ	45510 MW	59300 TQ	USBLS	5/07
	Minnesota	Y	33479 FQ	40079 MW	50141 TQ	MNBLS	10/08-12/08
	Duluth-Superior MSA, MN-WI	Y	33656 FQ	38473 MW	45407 TQ	MNBLS	10/08-12/08
	Minneapolis-Saint Paul MSA, MN-WI	Y	35200 FQ	41695 MW	52737 TQ	MNBLS	10/08-12/08
	Rochester MSA, MN	Y	31470 FQ	39145 MW	47100 TQ	MNBLS	10/08-12/08
	Mississippi	Y	33650 FQ	42360 MW	55050 TQ	USBLS	5/07
	Jackson MSA, MS	Y	33590 FQ	41680 MW	56550 TQ	USBLS	5/07
	Missouri	Y	41870 FQ	51610 MW	68860 TQ	USBLS	5/07
	Kansas City MSA, MO-KS	Y	38010 FQ	48010 MW	59290 TQ	USBLS	5/07
	St. Louis MSA, MO-IL	Y	37710 FQ	46370 MW	56830 TQ	USBLS	5/07
	Montana	Y	21440 FQ	31040 MW	46930 TQ	USBLS	5/07
	Billings MSA, MT	Y	28560 FQ	35420 MW	47690 TQ	USBLS	5/07
	Nebraska	Y	34910 FQ	41650 MW	51210 TQ	USBLS	5/07
	Omaha-Council Bluffs MSA, NE-IA	Y	35910 FQ	42450 MW	53000 TQ	USBLS	5/07
	Nevada	H	18.60 FQ	23.12 MW	31.17 TQ	NVBLS	5/08
	Las Vegas-Paradise MSA, NV	H	18.77 FQ	23.26 MW	32.39 TQ	NVBLS	5/08
	New Hampshire	H	16.88 AE	21.99 MW	27.58 AEX	NHBLS	6/08
	Manchester MSA, NH	Y	37060 FQ	44590 MW	58970 TQ	USBLS	5/07
	Nashua NECTA, NH-MA	Y	38790 FQ	50340 MW	63150 TQ	USBLS	5/07

AE Average entry wage	**AW** Average wage paid	**FQ** First quartile wage	**LO** Lowest wage paid	**MTC** Median total compensation	**TCC** Total cash compensation
AER Average entry range	**AWR** Average wage range	**H** Hourly	**LR** Low end range	**MW** Median wage paid	**TQ** Third quartile wage
AEX Average experienced wage	**AXR** Average experienced range	**HI** Highest wage paid	**M** Monthly	**MWR** Median wage range	**W** Weekly
ATC Average total compensation	**D** Daily	**HR** High end range	**MCC** Median cash compensation	**S** See annotated source	**Y** Yearly

Occupation/Type/Industry	Location	Per	Low	Mid	High	Source	Date
Food Service Manager	New Jersey	Y	50120 FQ	62140 MW	76380 TQ	USBLS	5/07
	Camden PMSA, NJ	Y	47440 FQ	62580 MW	77990 TQ	USBLS	5/07
	Edison PMSA, NJ	Y	50670 FQ	65640 MW	78060 TQ	USBLS	5/07
	Newark-Union PMSA, NJ-PA	Y	54410 FQ	63780 MW	78130 TQ	USBLS	5/07
	New Mexico	Y	32470 FQ	39380 MW	51180 TQ	USBLS	5/07
	Albuquerque MSA, NM	Y	33270 FQ	38110 MW	47900 TQ	USBLS	5/07
	New York	Y	37600 FQ	48160 MW	63330 TQ	USBLS	5/07
	Albany-Schenectady-Troy MSA, NY	Y	35570 FQ	43100 MW	54980 TQ	USBLS	5/07
	Buffalo-Niagara Falls MSA, NY	Y	33070 FQ	41720 MW	52050 TQ	USBLS	5/07
	Nassau-Suffolk PMSA, NY	Y	43770 FQ	54320 MW	69580 TQ	USBLS	5/07
	New York-Northern New Jersey-Long Island MSA, NY-NJ-PA	Y	43640 FQ	56990 MW	72750 TQ	USBLS	5/07
	Utica-Rome MSA, NY	Y	35210 FQ	43150 MW	55880 TQ	USBLS	5/07
	North Carolina	Y	37180 FQ	47390 MW	60700 TQ	USBLS	5/07
	Charlotte-Gastonia-Concord MSA, NC-SC	Y	36670 FQ	45540 MW	56800 TQ	USBLS	5/07
	Raleigh-Cary MSA, NC	Y	38930 FQ	50710 MW	68830 TQ	USBLS	5/07
	North Dakota	Y	35950 FQ	46120 MW	55370 TQ	USBLS	5/07
	Bismarck MSA, ND	Y	37940 FQ	46320 MW	51940 TQ	USBLS	5/07
	Fargo MSA, ND-MN	Y	32260 FQ	45920 MW	59330 TQ	USBLS	5/07
	Ohio	Y	33360 FQ	40690 MW	51480 TQ	USBLS	5/07
	Cincinnati-Middletown MSA, OH-KY-IN	Y	34290 FQ	41270 MW	51820 TQ	USBLS	5/07
	Cleveland-Elyria-Mentor MSA, OH	Y	34560 FQ	41620 MW	52750 TQ	USBLS	5/07
	Columbus MSA, OH	Y	36440 FQ	44340 MW	52770 TQ	USBLS	5/07
	Dayton MSA, OH	Y	34540 FQ	41540 MW	52480 TQ	USBLS	5/07
	Oklahoma	Y	25170 FQ	33040 MW	40140 TQ	USBLS	5/07
	Oklahoma City MSA, OK	Y	28610 FQ	35080 MW	41420 TQ	USBLS	5/07
	Tulsa MSA, OK	Y	25480 FQ	33970 MW	42130 TQ	USBLS	5/07
	Oregon	H	17.78 FQ	21.79 MW	27.52 TQ	ORBLS	5/08
	Portland-Vancouver-Beaverton MSA, OR-WA	Y	38120 FQ	47020 MW	59250 TQ	USBLS	5/07
	Pennsylvania	Y	35910 FQ	48050 MW	62180 TQ	USBLS	5/07
	Allentown-Bethlehem-Easton MSA, PA-NJ	Y	34580 FQ	44090 MW	60410 TQ	USBLS	5/07
	Lancaster MSA, PA	Y	38290 FQ	49950 MW	57670 TQ	USBLS	5/07
	Philadelphia-Camden-Wilmington MSA, PA-NJ-DE-MD	Y	43560 FQ	57180 MW	72950 TQ	USBLS	5/07
	Pittsburgh MSA, PA	Y	37210 FQ	48970 MW	60810 TQ	USBLS	5/07
	Rhode Island	Y	48330 FQ	58050 MW	65450 TQ	USBLS	5/07
	Providence-Fall River-Warwick MSA, RI-MA	Y	45860 FQ	56870 MW	64170 TQ	USBLS	5/07
	South Carolina	Y	33640 FQ	41290 MW	51540 TQ	USBLS	5/07
	Charleston-North Charleston MSA, SC	Y	34740 FQ	42190 MW	56020 TQ	USBLS	5/07
	Columbia MSA, SC	Y	32280 FQ	41500 MW	49910 TQ	USBLS	5/07
	Florence MSA, SC	Y	30300 FQ	39070 MW	48190 TQ	USBLS	5/07
	South Dakota	Y	39863 FQ	45249 MW	51026 TQ	SDBLS	7/08-9/08
	Sioux Falls MSA, SD	Y	40090 FQ	45805 MW	51849 TQ	SDBLS	7/08-9/08
	Tennessee	Y	28020 FQ	35720 MW	45720 TQ	USBLS	5/07
	Memphis MSA, TN-MS-AR	Y	30860 FQ	38300 MW	49750 TQ	USBLS	5/07
	Nashville-Davidson-Murfreesboro MSA, TN	Y	29740 FQ	36890 MW	46060 TQ	USBLS	5/07
	Texas	Y	38700 FQ	48280 MW	61390 TQ	USBLS	5/07
	Austin-Round Rock MSA, TX	Y	34520 FQ	45700 MW	61030 TQ	USBLS	5/07
	Dallas-Fort Worth-Arlington MSA, TX	Y	40570 FQ	50340 MW	64980 TQ	USBLS	5/07
	El Paso MSA, TX	Y	38060 FQ	49260 MW	58030 TQ	USBLS	5/07
	Houston-Sugar Land-Baytown MSA, TX	Y	42810 FQ	52370 MW	63170 TQ	USBLS	5/07
	San Antonio MSA, TX	Y	39750 FQ	46470 MW	58300 TQ	USBLS	5/07
	Utah	Y	36830 FQ	46770 MW	57530 TQ	USBLS	5/07
	Provo-Orem MSA, UT	Y	36230 FQ	44830 MW	51850 TQ	USBLS	5/07
	Salt Lake City MSA, UT	Y	35900 FQ	46050 MW	62270 TQ	USBLS	5/07
	Vermont	Y	34540 FQ	46770 MW	59280 TQ	USBLS	5/07
	Burlington-South Burlington MSA, VT	Y	33920 FQ	45900 MW	58010 TQ	USBLS	5/07

AE Average entry wage	**AW** Average wage paid	**FQ** First quartile wage	**LO** Lowest wage paid	**MTC** Median total compensation	**TCC** Total cash compensation
AER Average entry range	**AWR** Average wage range	**H** Hourly	**LR** Low end range	**MW** Median wage paid	**TQ** Third quartile wage
AEX Average experienced wage	**AXR** Average experienced range	**HI** Highest wage paid	**M** Monthly	**MWR** Median wage range	**W** Weekly
ATC Average total compensation	**D** Daily	**HR** High end range	**MCC** Median cash compensation	**S** See annotated source	**Y** Yearly

Occupation/Type/Industry	Location	Per	Low	Mid	High	Source	Date
Food Service Manager	Virginia	Y	37650 FQ	48510 MW	62550 TQ	USBLS	5/07
	Richmond MSA, VA	Y	35370 FQ	43510 MW	59240 TQ	USBLS	5/07
	Virginia Beach-Norfolk- Newport News MSA, VA-NC	Y	37200 FQ	46540 MW	58380 TQ	USBLS	5/07
	Washington	H	28.17 FQ	33.69 MW	43.93 TQ	WABLS	3/08
	Seattle-Tacoma-Bellevue MSA, WA	Y	59980 FQ	72840 MW	95480 TQ	USBLS	5/07
	West Virginia	Y	31451 FQ	37144 MW	46896 TQ	WVBLS	7/08-9/08
	Charleston MSA, WV	Y	30960 FQ	38530 MW	47030 TQ	USBLS	5/07
	Wisconsin	Y	30810 FQ	40100 MW	50730 TQ	USBLS	5/07
	Appleton MSA, WI	Y	29650 FQ	36750 MW	48710 TQ	USBLS	5/07
	Milwaukee-Waukesha-West Allis MSA, WI	Y	39680 FQ	47180 MW	61500 TQ	USBLS	5/07
	Wyoming	Y	29532 FQ	38992 MW	50505 TQ	WYBLS	9/08
	Cheyenne MSA, WY	Y	29542 FQ	33272 MW	52131 TQ	WYBLS	9/08
	Puerto Rico	Y	25600 FQ	29350 MW	36400 TQ	USBLS	5/07
	San Juan-Caguas-Guaynabo MSA, PR	Y	25630 FQ	29600 MW	37410 TQ	USBLS	5/07
	Virgin Islands	Y	36170 FQ	46320 MW	56690 TQ	USBLS	5/07
	Guam	Y	21920 FQ	25530 MW	33650 TQ	USBLS	5/07
Food Services Director							
Public Schools	Howell, MI	Y			64816 HI	LCPP	2009
Football Coach							
Ohio State University	Columbus, OH	Y			3500000 HI	UPI02	2008
University of Arkansas	Fayetteville, AR	Y			2850000 HI	CSM01	2008
University of Iowa	Iowa City, IA	Y			2870000 HI	DREG	2008
University of Notre Dame	Notre Dame, IN	Y			4200000 HI	CSM01	2008
University of Oklahoma	Norman, OK	Y			6500000 HI	CSM01	2008
Football Player							
Arena Football League	United States	S	31000 LO	80000 AW		NYDN01	2008
National Football League	United States	Y		440520-1102880 MW		USATOD05	2007
Foreign Language and Literature Teacher							
Postsecondary	Alabama	Y	36720 FQ	47880 MW	63630 TQ	USBLS	5/07
Postsecondary	Birmingham-Hoover MSA, AL	Y	40890 FQ	56060 MW	65340 TQ	USBLS	5/07
Postsecondary	Arizona	Y	43560 FQ	53750 MW	65460 TQ	USBLS	5/07
Postsecondary	Phoenix-Mesa-Scottsdale MSA, AZ	Y	40160 FQ	51120 MW	67080 TQ	USBLS	5/07
Postsecondary	Tucson MSA, AZ	Y	50320 FQ	56130 MW	66140 TQ	USBLS	5/07
Postsecondary	Arkansas	Y	39400 FQ	49290 MW	61250 TQ	USBLS	5/07
Postsecondary	Little Rock-North Little Rock MSA, AR	Y	34070 FQ	45910 MW	59560 TQ	USBLS	5/07
Postsecondary	California	Y		80038 AW		CABLS	1/08-3/08
Postsecondary	Los Angeles-Long Beach- Glendale PMSA, CA	Y		80582 AW		CABLS	1/08-3/08
Postsecondary	Oakland-Fremont-Hayward MSA, CA	Y		78736 AW		CABLS	1/08-3/08
Postsecondary	Riverside-San Bernardino- Ontario MSA, CA	Y		85596 AW		CABLS	1/08-3/08
Postsecondary	Sacramento-Arden Arcade- Roseville MSA, CA	Y		104813 AW		CABLS	1/08-3/08
Postsecondary	San Diego-Carlsbad-San Marcos MSA, CA	Y		80602 AW		CABLS	1/08-3/08
Postsecondary	San Francisco-San Mateo- Redwood PMSA, CA	Y		67425 AW		CABLS	1/08-3/08
Postsecondary	Santa Ana-Anaheim-Irvine PMSA, CA	Y	47530 FQ	75340 MW	120200 TQ	USBLS	5/07
Postsecondary	Colorado	Y	39210 FQ	52350 MW	67350 TQ	USBLS	5/07
Postsecondary	Denver-Aurora MSA, CO	Y	39060 FQ	55670 MW	70250 TQ	USBLS	5/07
Postsecondary	Delaware	Y	32530 FQ	42900 MW	59390 TQ	USBLS	5/07
Postsecondary	Wilmington PMSA, DE-MD-NJ	Y	31780 FQ	41120 MW	58220 TQ	USBLS	5/07
Postsecondary	District of Columbia	Y	51820 FQ	64580 MW	77470 TQ	USBLS	5/07
Postsecondary	Washington-Arlington- Alexandria MSA, DC-VA-MD-WV	Y	42710 FQ	57600 MW	71390 TQ	USBLS	5/07
Postsecondary	Florida	Y	42400 FQ	56960 MW	72820 TQ	USBLS	5/07

AE	Average entry wage	AW	Average wage paid	FQ	First quartile wage	LO	Lowest wage paid	MTC	Median total compensation	TCC	Total cash compensation
AER	Average entry range	AWR	Average wage range	H	Hourly	LR	Low end range	MW	Median wage paid	TQ	Third quartile wage
AEX	Average experienced wage	AXR	Average experienced range	HI	Highest wage paid	M	Monthly	MWR	Median wage range	W	Weekly
ATC	Average total compensation	D	Daily	HR	High end range	MCC	Median cash compensation	S	See annotated source	Y	Yearly

Occupation/Type/Industry	Location	Per	Low	Mid	High	Source	Date
Foreign Language and Literature Teacher							
Postsecondary	Orlando-Kissimmee MSA, FL	Y	35220 FQ	43560 MW	56530 TQ	USBLS	5/07
Postsecondary	Georgia	Y	40200 FQ	48600 MW	58230 TQ	USBLS	5/07
Postsecondary	Atlanta-Sandy Springs-Marietta MSA, GA	Y	40120 FQ	47910 MW	56880 TQ	USBLS	5/07
Postsecondary	Hawaii	Y	46620 FQ	55680 MW	68250 TQ	USBLS	5/07
Postsecondary	Honolulu MSA, HI	Y	47340 FQ	56420 MW	69380 TQ	USBLS	5/07
Postsecondary	Boise City-Nampa MSA, ID	Y	23250 FQ	26830 MW	29590 TQ	USBLS	5/07
Postsecondary	Illinois	Y	33280 FQ	45150 MW	60740 TQ	USBLS	5/07
Postsecondary	Chicago-Naperville-Joliet MSA, IL-IN-WI	Y	32910 FQ	43500 MW	58870 TQ	USBLS	5/07
Postsecondary	Indiana	Y	40080 FQ	53210 MW	70070 TQ	USBLS	5/07
Postsecondary	Gary PMSA, IN	Y	44030 FQ	51390 MW	63120 TQ	USBLS	5/07
Postsecondary	Indianapolis-Carmel MSA, IN	Y	41030 FQ	52470 MW	71050 TQ	USBLS	5/07
Postsecondary	South Bend-Mishawaka MSA, IN-MI	Y	41710 FQ	49750 MW	73380 TQ	USBLS	5/07
Postsecondary	Iowa	Y	45000 FQ	59250 MW	76460 TQ	USBLS	5/07
Postsecondary	Kansas	Y	34170 FQ	44210 MW	63990 TQ	USBLS	5/07
Postsecondary	Kentucky	Y	36479 FQ	47202 MW	61643 TQ	KYBLS	2008
Postsecondary	Louisiana	Y		53863 AW		LABLS	1/08-3/08
Postsecondary	New Orleans-Metairie-Kenner MSA, LA	Y	35250 FQ	40540 MW	58450 TQ	USBLS	5/07
Postsecondary	Maine	Y	42520 FQ	54370 MW	69200 TQ	USBLS	5/07
Postsecondary	Maryland	Y		64400 MW		MDBLS	3/08
Postsecondary	Baltimore-Towson MSA, MD	Y	53820 FQ	65920 MW	86090 TQ	USBLS	5/07
Postsecondary	Bethesda-Gaithersburg-Frederick PMSA, MD	Y	54110 FQ	65340 MW	83650 TQ	USBLS	5/07
Postsecondary	Massachusetts	Y	51120 FQ	66850 MW	93280 TQ	USBLS	5/07
Postsecondary	Boston-Cambridge-Quincy NECTA, MA	Y	49610 FQ	64620 MW	89520 TQ	USBLS	5/07
Postsecondary	Michigan	Y	42500 FQ	55170 MW	73330 TQ	USBLS	5/07
Postsecondary	Detroit-Warren-Livonia MSA, MI	Y	35720 FQ	54690 MW	76380 TQ	USBLS	5/07
Postsecondary	Warren-Troy-Farmington Hills PMSA, MI	Y	29850 FQ	52620 MW	69180 TQ	USBLS	5/07
Postsecondary	Minnesota	Y	37402 FQ	51819 MW	69542 TQ	MNBLS	10/08-12/08
Postsecondary	Duluth-Superior MSA, MN-WI	Y	44098 FQ	51045 MW	68485 TQ	MNBLS	10/08-12/08
Postsecondary	Minneapolis-Saint Paul MSA, MN-WI	Y	33730 FQ	49151 MW	70400 TQ	MNBLS	10/08-12/08
Postsecondary	Mississippi	Y	45310 FQ	57420 MW	70160 TQ	USBLS	5/07
Postsecondary	Jackson MSA, MS	Y	45320 FQ	56510 MW	64750 TQ	USBLS	5/07
Postsecondary	Missouri	Y	37530 FQ	48070 MW	61630 TQ	USBLS	5/07
Postsecondary	Kansas City MSA, MO-KS	Y	37920 FQ	49420 MW	63550 TQ	USBLS	5/07
Postsecondary	St. Louis MSA, MO-IL	Y	39900 FQ	52560 MW	65150 TQ	USBLS	5/07
Postsecondary	Springfield MSA, MO	Y	40100 FQ	54870 MW	70410 TQ	USBLS	5/07
Postsecondary	Nebraska	Y	36790 FQ	48960 MW	62170 TQ	USBLS	5/07
Postsecondary	Omaha-Council Bluffs MSA, NE-IA	Y	46490 FQ	57510 MW	69680 TQ	USBLS	5/07
Postsecondary	New Hampshire	Y	38464 AE	60145 MW	73187 AEX	NHBLS	6/08
Postsecondary	Manchester MSA, NH	Y	46980 FQ	60120 MW	76020 TQ	USBLS	5/07
Postsecondary	New Jersey	Y	53160 FQ	69630 MW	86260 TQ	USBLS	5/07
Postsecondary	Edison PMSA, NJ	Y	54850 FQ	76000 MW	98330 TQ	USBLS	5/07
Postsecondary	Newark-Union PMSA, NJ-PA	Y	54760 FQ	70620 MW	83850 TQ	USBLS	5/07
Postsecondary	New Mexico	Y	45550 FQ	56190 MW	70730 TQ	USBLS	5/07
Postsecondary	New York	Y	45370 FQ	57400 MW	81930 TQ	USBLS	5/07
Postsecondary	Nassau-Suffolk PMSA, NY	Y	47420 FQ	58450 MW	72650 TQ	USBLS	5/07
Postsecondary	New York-Northern New Jersey-Long Island MSA, NY-NJ-PA	Y	49020 FQ	64650 MW	85740 TQ	USBLS	5/07
Postsecondary	North Carolina	Y	37680 FQ	46280 MW	58840 TQ	USBLS	5/07
Postsecondary	Charlotte-Gastonia-Concord MSA, NC-SC	Y	24380 FQ	35130 MW	53420 TQ	USBLS	5/07
Postsecondary	Raleigh-Cary MSA, NC	Y	31610 FQ	37870 MW	51570 TQ	USBLS	5/07
Postsecondary	North Dakota	Y	31380 FQ	43570 MW	55390 TQ	USBLS	5/07
Postsecondary	Fargo MSA, ND-MN	Y	35800 FQ	44080 MW	53680 TQ	USBLS	5/07
Postsecondary	Ohio	Y	38520 FQ	55020 MW	76670 TQ	USBLS	5/07
Postsecondary	Cincinnati-Middletown MSA, OH-KY-IN	Y	28440 FQ	37210 MW	51580 TQ	USBLS	5/07
Postsecondary	Cleveland-Elyria-Mentor MSA, OH	Y	38440 FQ	52950 MW	74920 TQ	USBLS	5/07
Postsecondary	Columbus MSA, OH	Y	54900 FQ	66420 MW	90580 TQ	USBLS	5/07

AE	Average entry wage	AW	Average wage paid	FQ	First quartile wage	LO	Lowest wage paid	MTC	Median total compensation	TCC	Total cash compensation
AER	Average entry range	AWR	Average wage range	H	Hourly	LR	Low end range	MW	Median wage paid	TQ	Third quartile wage
AEX	Average experienced wage	AXR	Average experienced range	HI	Highest wage paid	M	Monthly	MWR	Median wage range	W	Weekly
ATC	Average total compensation	D	Daily	HR	High end range	MCC	Median cash compensation	S	See annotated source	Y	Yearly

Occupation/Type/Industry	Location	Per	Low	Mid	High	Source	Date
Foreign Language and Literature Teacher							
Postsecondary	Dayton MSA, OH	Y	40880 FQ	53770 MW	70490 TQ	USBLS	5/07
Postsecondary	Oklahoma	Y	25910 FQ	35530 MW	45470 TQ	USBLS	5/07
Postsecondary	Oklahoma City MSA, OK	Y	30050 FQ	37640 MW	51960 TQ	USBLS	5/07
Postsecondary	Tulsa MSA, OK	Y	22980 FQ	29800 MW	43040 TQ	USBLS	5/07
Postsecondary	Portland-Vancouver-Beaverton MSA, OR-WA	Y	42280 FQ	60650 MW	91140 TQ	USBLS	5/07
Postsecondary	Pennsylvania	Y	45300 FQ	57600 MW	76550 TQ	USBLS	5/07
Postsecondary	Allentown-Bethlehem-Easton MSA, PA-NJ	Y	43940 FQ	56180 MW	66770 TQ	USBLS	5/07
Postsecondary	Philadelphia-Camden-Wilmington MSA, PA-NJ-DE-MD	Y	44790 FQ	57480 MW	76280 TQ	USBLS	5/07
Postsecondary	Pittsburgh MSA, PA	Y	34430 FQ	53700 MW	72900 TQ	USBLS	5/07
Postsecondary	Rhode Island	Y	50960 FQ	64920 MW	85390 TQ	USBLS	5/07
Postsecondary	Providence-Fall River-Warwick MSA, RI-MA	Y	50860 FQ	64610 MW	85010 TQ	USBLS	5/07
Postsecondary	South Carolina	Y	41820 FQ	52080 MW	65720 TQ	USBLS	5/07
Postsecondary	Charleston-North Charleston MSA, SC	Y	45270 FQ	52820 MW	61240 TQ	USBLS	5/07
Postsecondary	Columbia MSA, SC	Y	40660 FQ	47720 MW	54120 TQ	USBLS	5/07
Postsecondary	South Dakota	Y	37882 FQ	42189 MW	52444 TQ	SDBLS	7/08-9/08
Postsecondary	Sioux Falls MSA, SD	Y	39007 FQ	42649 MW	48402 TQ	SDBLS	7/08-9/08
Postsecondary	Tennessee	Y	35930 FQ	46060 MW	56780 TQ	USBLS	5/07
Postsecondary	Knoxville MSA, TN	Y	35950 FQ	44860 MW	53700 TQ	USBLS	5/07
Postsecondary	Memphis MSA, TN-MS-AR	Y	40960 FQ	51800 MW	63070 TQ	USBLS	5/07
Postsecondary	Nashville-Davidson-Murfreesboro MSA, TN	Y	37090 FQ	45500 MW	54930 TQ	USBLS	5/07
Postsecondary	Texas	Y	33350 FQ	51040 MW	69230 TQ	USBLS	5/07
Postsecondary	Austin-Round Rock MSA, TX	Y	28370 FQ	32930 MW	62450 TQ	USBLS	5/07
Postsecondary	Dallas-Fort Worth-Arlington MSA, TX	Y	43350 FQ	59220 MW	74760 TQ	USBLS	5/07
Postsecondary	El Paso MSA, TX	Y	20060 FQ	37860 MW	59800 TQ	USBLS	5/07
Postsecondary	Houston-Sugar Land-Baytown MSA, TX	Y	40910 FQ	59190 MW	85800 TQ	USBLS	5/07
Postsecondary	San Antonio MSA, TX	Y	39440 FQ	53930 MW	64680 TQ	USBLS	5/07
Postsecondary	Utah	Y	41460 FQ	51340 MW	59960 TQ	USBLS	5/07
Postsecondary	Vermont	Y	45500 FQ	58040 MW	72730 TQ	USBLS	5/07
Postsecondary	Virginia	Y	39500 FQ	50700 MW	64670 TQ	USBLS	5/07
Postsecondary	Richmond MSA, VA	Y	42550 FQ	51980 MW	64270 TQ	USBLS	5/07
Postsecondary	Virginia Beach-Norfolk-Newport News MSA, VA-NC	Y	43390 FQ	55660 MW	66300 TQ	USBLS	5/07
Postsecondary	Washington	Y		53659 AW		WABLS	3/08
Postsecondary	Seattle-Tacoma-Bellevue MSA, WA	Y	39550 FQ	48430 MW	61660 TQ	USBLS	5/07
Postsecondary	West Virginia	Y	40357 FQ	49744 MW	66949 TQ	WVBLS	7/08-9/08
Postsecondary	Wisconsin	Y	39600 FQ	50490 MW	70650 TQ	USBLS	5/07
Postsecondary	Milwaukee-Waukesha-West Allis MSA, WI	Y	37690 FQ	49640 MW	74880 TQ	USBLS	5/07
Postsecondary	Wyoming	Y	35001 FQ	49599 MW	62170 TQ	WYBLS	9/08
Postsecondary	Puerto Rico	Y	30210 FQ	45940 MW	61700 TQ	USBLS	5/07
Postsecondary	San Juan-Caguas-Guaynabo MSA, PR	Y	31750 FQ	49300 MW	65500 TQ	USBLS	5/07
Forensic Autopsy Assistant	United States	H		24.04-29.08 AW		INPRIS	2006
Forensic Chemist	Colorado Springs, CO	M	3741 LO			COSPRS	1/1/09
	Maine	Y	35214 LO		48256 HI	AFT02	3/1/08
Forensic Document Examiner							
Sheriff's Department Crime Lab	San Diego County, CA	W	6184 LO		7515 HI	CAC	2006-2007
Forensic Evidence Technician	Wyoming	Y	30912 LO		39648 HI	AFT02	3/1/08
Forensic Science Technician	Alabama	Y	31520 FQ	41040 MW	49930 TQ	USBLS	5/07
	Alaska	Y	45720 FQ	56340 MW	67040 TQ	USBLS	5/07
	Arizona	Y	39690 FQ	48040 MW	61370 TQ	USBLS	5/07
	Phoenix-Mesa-Scottsdale MSA, AZ	Y	39880 FQ	48490 MW	62740 TQ	USBLS	5/07
	Tucson MSA, AZ	Y	36940 FQ	45970 MW	54540 TQ	USBLS	5/07

AE	Average entry wage	AW	Average wage paid	FQ	First quartile wage
AER	Average entry range	AWR	Average wage range	H	Hourly
AEX	Average experienced wage	AXR	Average experienced range	HI	Highest wage paid
ATC	Average total compensation	D	Daily	HR	High end range

LO	Lowest wage paid	MTC	Median total compensation	TCC	Total cash compensation
LR	Low end range	MW	Median wage paid	TQ	Third quartile wage
M	Monthly	MWR	Median wage range	W	Weekly
MCC	Median cash compensation	S	See annotated source	Y	Yearly

Occupation/Type/Industry	Location	Per	Low	Mid	High	Source	Date
Forensic Science Technician	Arkansas	Y	25560 FQ	31970 MW	41680 TQ	USBLS	5/07
	California	H	22.94 FQ	29.57 MW	37.40 TQ	CABLS	1/08-3/08
	Los Angeles-Long Beach-Glendale PMSA, CA	H	27.86 FQ	33.70 MW	40.74 TQ	CABLS	1/08-3/08
	Oakland-Fremont-Hayward MSA, CA	H	25.76 FQ	31.93 MW	38.47 TQ	CABLS	1/08-3/08
	Riverside-San Bernardino-Ontario MSA, CA	H	22.16 FQ	24.92 MW	28.17 TQ	CABLS	1/08-3/08
	Sacramento-Arden Arcade-Roseville MSA, CA	H	19.21 FQ	27.64 MW	33.34 TQ	CABLS	1/08-3/08
	San Diego-Carlsbad-San Marcos MSA, CA	H	21.57 FQ	29.09 MW	39.43 TQ	CABLS	1/08-3/08
	Santa Ana-Anaheim-Irvine PMSA, CA	Y	29270 FQ	55810 MW	80350 TQ	USBLS	5/07
	Colorado	Y	41500 FQ	50040 MW	59610 TQ	USBLS	5/07
	Denver-Aurora MSA, CO	Y	44730 FQ	53780 MW	62800 TQ	USBLS	5/07
	Connecticut	H	25.09 AE	33.90 MW		CTBLS	1/08-3/08
	Washington-Arlington-Alexandria MSA, DC-VA-MD-WV	Y	52380 FQ	62520 MW	86210 TQ	USBLS	5/07
	Florida	Y	32190 FQ	40780 MW	50630 TQ	USBLS	5/07
	Fort Lauderdale-Pompano Beach-Deerfield Beach PMSA, FL	Y	40080 FQ	47190 MW	57510 TQ	USBLS	5/07
	Miami-Fort Lauderdale-Miami Beach MSA, FL	Y	37300 FQ	46330 MW	58080 TQ	USBLS	5/07
	Orlando-Kissimmee MSA, FL	Y	31800 FQ	40260 MW	49470 TQ	USBLS	5/07
	Tampa-St. Petersburg-Clearwater MSA, FL	Y	36080 FQ	44250 MW	52290 TQ	USBLS	5/07
	West Palm Beach-Boca Raton-Boynton Beach PMSA, FL	Y	37020 FQ	44520 MW	52220 TQ	USBLS	5/07
	Georgia	Y	32170 FQ	37480 MW	48980 TQ	USBLS	5/07
	Atlanta-Sandy Springs-Marietta MSA, GA	Y	30320 FQ	37720 MW	56510 TQ	USBLS	5/07
	Hawaii	Y	37710 FQ	44150 MW	51400 TQ	USBLS	5/07
	Idaho	Y	34260 FQ	39060 MW	51830 TQ	USBLS	5/07
	Illinois	Y	45460 FQ	56130 MW	70960 TQ	USBLS	5/07
	Chicago-Naperville-Joliet MSA, IL-IN-WI	Y	44250 FQ	53050 MW	68560 TQ	USBLS	5/07
	Indiana	Y	36120 FQ	44660 MW	53120 TQ	USBLS	5/07
	Kansas	Y	51150 FQ	57040 MW	63650 TQ	USBLS	5/07
	Kentucky	Y	28946 FQ	35917 MW	42776 TQ	KYBLS	2008
	Louisville-Jefferson County MSA, KY-IN	Y	26740 FQ	30000 MW	40460 TQ	USBLS	5/07
	Louisiana	H	19.80 FQ	25.85 MW	33.07 TQ	LABLS	1/08-3/08
	Maryland	Y		54400 MW		MDBLS	3/08
	Baltimore-Towson MSA, MD	Y	33300 FQ	48250 MW	60020 TQ	USBLS	5/07
	Boston-Cambridge-Quincy NECTA, MA	Y	41640 FQ	60050 MW	108810 TQ	USBLS	5/07
	Michigan	Y	40220 FQ	49500 MW	58210 TQ	USBLS	5/07
	Detroit-Warren-Livonia MSA, MI	Y	39250 FQ	47370 MW	54550 TQ	USBLS	5/07
	Warren-Troy-Farmington Hills PMSA, MI	Y	39700 FQ	47150 MW	53600 TQ	USBLS	5/07
	Minnesota	Y	34054 FQ	39379 MW	44904 TQ	MNBLS	10/08-12/08
	Minneapolis-Saint Paul MSA, MN-WI	Y	34044 FQ	39087 MW	44108 TQ	MNBLS	10/08-12/08
	Mississippi	Y	34450 FQ	44700 MW	56020 TQ	USBLS	5/07
	Missouri	Y	37430 FQ	44890 MW	53510 TQ	USBLS	5/07
	St. Louis MSA, MO-IL	Y	41370 FQ	48770 MW	61780 TQ	USBLS	5/07
	Nebraska	Y	25680 FQ	33840 MW	40520 TQ	USBLS	5/07
	New Hampshire	H	22.32 AE	25.36 MW	28.28 AEX	NHBLS	6/08
	New Jersey	Y	29320 FQ	37100 MW	49060 TQ	USBLS	5/07
	New York	Y	48000 FQ	57700 MW	66900 TQ	USBLS	5/07
	New York-Northern New Jersey-Long Island MSA, NY-NJ-PA	Y	41220 FQ	54650 MW	65910 TQ	USBLS	5/07
	North Carolina	Y	29890 FQ	35450 MW	43890 TQ	USBLS	5/07
	Charlotte-Gastonia-Concord MSA, NC-SC	Y	35220 FQ	39980 MW	54220 TQ	USBLS	5/07
	Raleigh-Cary MSA, NC	Y	27940 FQ	32450 MW	41550 TQ	USBLS	5/07
	Ohio	Y	36910 FQ	43970 MW	55690 TQ	USBLS	5/07

AE	Average entry wage	AW	Average wage paid	FQ	First quartile wage
AER	Average entry range	AWR	Average wage range	H	Hourly
AEX	Average experienced wage	AXR	Average experienced range	HI	Highest wage paid
ATC	Average total compensation	D	Daily	HR	High end range

LO	Lowest wage paid	MTC	Median total compensation	TCC	Total cash compensation
LR	Low end range	MW	Median wage paid	TQ	Third quartile wage
M	Monthly	MWR	Median wage range	W	Weekly
MCC	Median cash compensation	S	See annotated source	Y	Yearly

Occupation/Type/Industry	Location	Per	Low	Mid	High	Source	Date
Forensic Science Technician	Columbus MSA, OH	Y	35810 FQ	40550 MW	48710 TQ	USBLS	5/07
	Oklahoma	Y	40530 FQ	47680 MW	58650 TQ	USBLS	5/07
	Oregon	H	22.23 FQ	28.14 MW	33.01 TQ	ORBLS	5/08
	Portland-Vancouver-Beaverton MSA, OR-WA	Y	50680 FQ	60480 MW	68740 TQ	USBLS	5/07
	Pennsylvania	Y	40000 FQ	49260 MW	59710 TQ	USBLS	5/07
	South Carolina	Y	28810 FQ	35400 MW	46070 TQ	USBLS	5/07
	Tennessee	Y	31960 FQ	39700 MW	56490 TQ	USBLS	5/07
	Texas	Y	31580 FQ	39130 MW	50830 TQ	USBLS	5/07
	Austin-Round Rock MSA, TX	Y	28240 FQ	35710 MW	54440 TQ	USBLS	5/07
	Dallas-Fort Worth-Arlington MSA, TX	Y	36650 FQ	44070 MW	51490 TQ	USBLS	5/07
	Houston-Sugar Land-Baytown MSA, TX	Y	37420 FQ	45740 MW	56020 TQ	USBLS	5/07
	San Antonio MSA, TX	Y	27590 FQ	34530 MW	39670 TQ	USBLS	5/07
	Utah	Y	32330 FQ	36670 MW	41140 TQ	USBLS	5/07
	Salt Lake City MSA, UT	Y	32180 FQ	36440 MW	40820 TQ	USBLS	5/07
	Virginia	Y	36250 FQ	60030 MW	81680 TQ	USBLS	5/07
	Richmond MSA, VA	Y	23060 FQ	40120 MW	69450 TQ	USBLS	5/07
	Virginia Beach-Norfolk-Newport News MSA, VA-NC	Y	34690 FQ	44610 MW	71470 TQ	USBLS	5/07
	Washington	H	22.35 FQ	26.51 MW	30.65 TQ	WABLS	3/08
	Wyoming	Y	36913 FQ	41519 MW	49277 TQ	WYBLS	9/08
Forensic Scientist Trainee Metropolitan Police Department	Las Vegas, NV	W	4146 LO		6137 HI	CAC	2006-2007
Forensic Toxicologist	District of Columbia	Y	52134 LO		96013 HI	AFT02	3/1/08
	Ohio	H	30.68 LO		40.22 HI	ODAS	2008
Forest and Conservation Technician	Alabama	Y	28180 FQ	36950 MW	45300 TQ	USBLS	5/07
	Alaska	Y	33980 FQ	39700 MW	49050 TQ	USBLS	5/07
	Anchorage MSA, AK	Y	31900 FQ	36450 MW	43610 TQ	USBLS	5/07
	Arizona	Y	26690 FQ	31190 MW	39480 TQ	USBLS	5/07
	Phoenix-Mesa-Scottsdale MSA, AZ	Y	26890 FQ	32640 MW	43160 TQ	USBLS	5/07
	Arkansas	Y	31790 FQ	37550 MW	45020 TQ	USBLS	5/07
	California	H	13.66 FQ	15.76 MW	21.40 TQ	CABLS	1/08-3/08
	Riverside-San Bernardino-Ontario MSA, CA	H	14.17 FQ	16.94 MW	22.94 TQ	CABLS	1/08-3/08
	Sacramento-Arden Arcade-Roseville MSA, CA	H	13.47 FQ	15.54 MW	22.27 TQ	CABLS	1/08-3/08
	San Diego-Carlsbad-San Marcos MSA, CA	H	14.33 FQ	17.68 MW	22.94 TQ	CABLS	1/08-3/08
	San Francisco-San Mateo-Redwood PMSA, CA	H	14.45 FQ	15.89 MW	18.68 TQ	CABLS	1/08-3/08
	San Jose-Sunnyvale-Santa Clara MSA, CA	H	14.13 FQ	15.82 MW	22.77 TQ	CABLS	1/08-3/08
	Colorado	Y	27170 FQ	31270 MW	39670 TQ	USBLS	5/07
	Denver-Aurora MSA, CO	Y	29240 FQ	36140 MW	45880 TQ	USBLS	5/07
	Fort Collins-Loveland MSA, CO	Y	27730 FQ	31680 MW	42540 TQ	USBLS	5/07
	Connecticut	H	20.77 AE	32.87 MW		CTBLS	1/08-3/08
	Florida	Y	33010 FQ	38610 MW	46540 TQ	USBLS	5/07
	Georgia	Y	29240 FQ	36110 MW	46820 TQ	USBLS	5/07
	Atlanta-Sandy Springs-Marietta MSA, GA	Y	24240 FQ	40260 MW	58710 TQ	USBLS	5/07
	Hawaii	Y	29460 FQ	34990 MW	39710 TQ	USBLS	5/07
	Idaho	Y	26670 FQ	31760 MW	40840 TQ	USBLS	5/07
	Boise City-Nampa MSA, ID	Y	28000 FQ	34250 MW	43260 TQ	USBLS	5/07
	Illinois	Y	29750 FQ	37790 MW	48670 TQ	USBLS	5/07
	Chicago-Naperville-Joliet MSA, IL-IN-WI	Y	29490 FQ	37400 MW	52780 TQ	USBLS	5/07
	Indiana	Y	25200 FQ	31070 MW	39990 TQ	USBLS	5/07
	Iowa	Y	31230 FQ	38850 MW	45370 TQ	USBLS	5/07
	Kansas	Y	32910 FQ	40990 MW	46020 TQ	USBLS	5/07
	Kentucky	Y	27141 FQ	34869 MW	44518 TQ	KYBLS	2008
	Louisiana	H	16.52 FQ	19.17 MW	22.47 TQ	LABLS	1/08-3/08
	Maine	Y	30160 FQ	35710 MW	40640 TQ	USBLS	5/07
	Maryland	Y		38175 MW		MDBLS	3/08
	Baltimore-Towson MSA, MD	Y	28170 FQ	36290 MW	43980 TQ	USBLS	5/07

AE	Average entry wage	AW	Average wage paid	FQ	First quartile wage
AER	Average entry range	AWR	Average wage range	H	Hourly
AEX	Average experienced wage	AXR	Average experienced range	HI	Highest wage paid
ATC	Average total compensation	D	Daily	HR	High end range

LO	Lowest wage paid	MTC	Median total compensation
LR	Low end range	MW	Median wage paid
M	Monthly	MWR	Median wage range
MCC	Median cash compensation	S	See annotated source

TCC	Total cash compensation		
TQ	Third quartile wage		
W	Weekly		
Y	Yearly		

Occupation/Type/Industry	Location	Per	Low	Mid	High	Source	Date
Forest and Conservation Technician	Massachusetts	Y	28370 FQ	39670 MW	48660 TQ	USBLS	5/07
	Michigan	Y	34530 FQ	42300 MW	48240 TQ	USBLS	5/07
	Minnesota	Y	29357 FQ	37318 MW	46714 TQ	MNBLS	10/08-12/08
	Duluth-Superior MSA, MN-WI	Y	34347 FQ	40509 MW	48126 TQ	MNBLS	10/08-12/08
	Minneapolis-Saint Paul MSA, MN-WI	Y	28331 FQ	33385 MW	43345 TQ	MNBLS	10/08-12/08
	Mississippi	Y	28670 FQ	36410 MW	45080 TQ	USBLS	5/07
	Jackson MSA, MS	Y	25550 FQ	30060 MW	40070 TQ	USBLS	5/07
	Missouri	Y	19830 FQ	25700 MW	32850 TQ	USBLS	5/07
	Kansas City MSA, MO-KS	Y	19870 FQ	24240 MW	40650 TQ	USBLS	5/07
	Billings MSA, MT	Y	25620 FQ	30410 MW	37470 TQ	USBLS	5/07
	Nebraska	Y	21110 FQ	23070 MW	28660 TQ	USBLS	5/07
	Nevada	H	13.64 FQ	17.26 MW	21.89 TQ	NVBLS	5/08
	Las Vegas-Paradise MSA, NV	H	14.12 FQ	18.01 MW	22.59 TQ	NVBLS	5/08
	New Hampshire	H	13.84 AE	17.72 MW	19.94 AEX	NHBLS	6/08
	New Jersey	Y	39660 FQ	44910 MW	49210 TQ	USBLS	5/07
	Newark-Union PMSA, NJ-PA	Y	38490 FQ	44190 MW	48730 TQ	USBLS	5/07
	New Mexico	Y	27920 FQ	33670 MW	40860 TQ	USBLS	5/07
	Albuquerque MSA, NM	Y	27640 FQ	33280 MW	39990 TQ	USBLS	5/07
	New York	Y	29410 FQ	35080 MW	43740 TQ	USBLS	5/07
	New York-Northern New Jersey-Long Island MSA, NY-NJ-PA	Y	37880 FQ	44870 MW	50990 TQ	USBLS	5/07
	North Carolina	Y	30500 FQ	36680 MW	44160 TQ	USBLS	5/07
	Charlotte-Gastonia-Concord MSA, NC-SC	Y	31830 FQ	35760 MW	40720 TQ	USBLS	5/07
	North Dakota	Y	30040 FQ	35910 MW	42950 TQ	USBLS	5/07
	Ohio	Y	30180 FQ	35520 MW	39620 TQ	USBLS	5/07
	Oklahoma City MSA, OK	Y	29110 FQ	33980 MW	39630 TQ	USBLS	5/07
	Oregon	H	13.69 FQ	17.14 MW	22.42 TQ	ORBLS	5/08
	Portland-Vancouver-Beaverton MSA, OR-WA	Y	28360 FQ	35580 MW	48460 TQ	USBLS	5/07
	Salem MSA, OR	Y	29130 FQ	37380 MW	48370 TQ	USBLS	5/07
	Pennsylvania	Y	29230 FQ	35350 MW	41940 TQ	USBLS	5/07
	Philadelphia-Camden-Wilmington MSA, PA-NJ-DE-MD	Y	37180 FQ	44760 MW	51530 TQ	USBLS	5/07
	South Carolina	Y	26940 FQ	32270 MW	41300 TQ	USBLS	5/07
	Charleston-North Charleston MSA, SC	Y	27320 FQ	35690 MW	50280 TQ	USBLS	5/07
	South Dakota	Y	27994 FQ	32654 MW	39707 TQ	SDBLS	7/08-9/08
	Tennessee	Y	26730 FQ	30920 MW	36820 TQ	USBLS	5/07
	Texas	Y	29500 FQ	37080 MW	45740 TQ	USBLS	5/07
	Utah	Y	25720 FQ	30160 MW	37810 TQ	USBLS	5/07
	Salt Lake City MSA, UT	Y	24430 FQ	28840 MW	35260 TQ	USBLS	5/07
	Vermont	Y	27710 FQ	31920 MW	43000 TQ	USBLS	5/07
	Virginia	Y	26850 FQ	35810 MW	45110 TQ	USBLS	5/07
	Washington	H	13.30 FQ	16.50 MW	21.72 TQ	WABLS	3/08
	Olympia MSA, WA	Y	31570 FQ	38140 MW	44560 TQ	USBLS	5/07
	Seattle-Tacoma-Bellevue MSA, WA	Y	29590 FQ	37810 MW	49920 TQ	USBLS	5/07
	West Virginia	Y	28186 FQ	34786 MW	42239 TQ	WVBLS	7/08-9/08
	Wyoming	Y	27782 FQ	32022 MW	39242 TQ	WYBLS	9/08
	Cheyenne MSA, WY	Y	29405 FQ	32846 MW	42089 TQ	WYBLS	9/08
Forest and Conservation Worker	Alabama	Y	12910 FQ	14860 MW	29580 TQ	USBLS	5/07
	Arkansas	Y	21190 FQ	28930 MW	36320 TQ	USBLS	5/07
	California	H	9.00 FQ	10.32 MW	11.81 TQ	CABLS	1/08-3/08
	Colorado	Y	27510 FQ	35920 MW	42860 TQ	USBLS	5/07
	Delaware	Y	30080 FQ	34660 MW	38050 TQ	USBLS	5/07
	Georgia	Y	13110 FQ	14590 MW	17040 TQ	USBLS	5/07
	Hawaii	Y	26950 FQ	31750 MW	35910 TQ	USBLS	5/07
	Idaho	Y	21970 FQ	34280 MW	39350 TQ	USBLS	5/07
	Illinois	Y	38530 FQ	46450 MW	52570 TQ	USBLS	5/07
	Iowa	Y	19140 FQ	22490 MW	26940 TQ	USBLS	5/07
	Maryland	Y		19125 MW		MDBLS	3/08
	Massachusetts	Y	34010 FQ	42660 MW	47570 TQ	USBLS	5/07
	Michigan	Y	16990 FQ	18950 MW	29280 TQ	USBLS	5/07
	Minnesota	Y	18284 FQ	19559 MW	20824 TQ	MNBLS	10/08-12/08
	Mississippi	Y	21550 FQ	24070 MW	31040 TQ	USBLS	5/07
	Nevada	H	10.65 FQ	11.62 MW	12.62 TQ	NVBLS	5/08

AE	Average entry wage	AW	Average wage paid	FQ	First quartile wage	LO	Lowest wage paid	MTC	Median total compensation	TCC	Total cash compensation
AER	Average entry range	AWR	Average wage range	H	Hourly	LR	Low end range	MW	Median wage paid	TQ	Third quartile wage
AEX	Average experienced wage	AXR	Average experienced range	HI	Highest wage paid	M	Monthly	MWR	Median wage range	W	Weekly
ATC	Average total compensation	D	Daily	HR	High end range	MCC	Median cash compensation	S	See annotated source	Y	Yearly

692

Occupation/Type/Industry	Location	Per	Low	Mid	High	Source	Date
Forest and Conservation Worker	New Mexico	Y	27220 FQ	29690 MW	32280 TQ	USBLS	5/07
	New York	Y	26850 FQ	33020 MW	38550 TQ	USBLS	5/07
	North Dakota	Y	19320 FQ	23740 MW	28500 TQ	USBLS	5/07
	Oregon	H	9.81 FQ	11.97 MW	16.03 TQ	ORBLS	5/08
	South Carolina	Y	19280 FQ	22060 MW	24640 TQ	USBLS	5/07
	South Dakota	Y	20290 FQ	23442 MW	27203 TQ	SDBLS	7/08-9/08
	Tennessee	Y	18770 FQ	21580 MW	24480 TQ	USBLS	5/07
	Virginia	Y	25500 FQ	30660 MW	35910 TQ	USBLS	5/07
	Washington	H	8.77 FQ	9.55 MW	13.77 TQ	WABLS	3/08
	Wisconsin	Y	22470 FQ	33670 MW	38630 TQ	USBLS	5/07
Forest Entomologist/Pathologist Department of Resources and Economic Development	New Hampshire	Y			50538 HI	NHUL03	2008
Forest Fire Inspector and Prevention Specialist	California	H	22.18 FQ	29.71 MW	36.33 TQ	CABLS	1/08-3/08
	Georgia	Y	31550 FQ	35850 MW	39890 TQ	USBLS	5/07
	Maryland	Y		61575 MW		MDBLS	3/08
	Mississippi	Y	18760 FQ	21640 MW	24630 TQ	USBLS	5/07
	New Jersey	Y	37730 FQ	45660 MW	56490 TQ	USBLS	5/07
	New York	Y	41660 FQ	46030 MW	50430 TQ	USBLS	5/07
	Oregon	H	16.18 FQ	17.99 MW	19.78 TQ	ORBLS	5/08
	Wyoming	Y	25572 FQ	30091 MW	41759 TQ	WYBLS	9/08
Forest Maintenance Worker	Seattle, WA	H	21.87 LO		23.56 HI	CSSS	2007
Forester	Alabama	Y	42750 FQ	54800 MW	63810 TQ	USBLS	5/07
	Birmingham-Hoover MSA, AL	Y	30150 FQ	37010 MW	54320 TQ	USBLS	5/07
	Alaska	Y	50420 FQ	58810 MW	68860 TQ	USBLS	5/07
	Arkansas	Y	37970 FQ	51370 MW	61720 TQ	USBLS	5/07
	Little Rock-North Little Rock MSA, AR	Y	34220 FQ	39760 MW	56070 TQ	USBLS	5/07
	California	H	22.43 FQ	29.07 MW	34.61 TQ	CABLS	1/08-3/08
	Fresno MSA, CA	H	27.36 FQ	30.16 MW	32.97 TQ	CABLS	1/08-3/08
	Riverside-San Bernardino-Ontario MSA, CA	H	30.68 FQ	36.19 MW	41.47 TQ	CABLS	1/08-3/08
	Sacramento-Arden Arcade-Roseville MSA, CA	H	29.49 FQ	34.90 MW	40.02 TQ	CABLS	1/08-3/08
	San Francisco-San Mateo-Redwood PMSA, CA	H	28.36 FQ	33.28 MW	40.17 TQ	CABLS	1/08-3/08
	Colorado	Y	48790 FQ	56420 MW	63540 TQ	USBLS	5/07
	Denver-Aurora MSA, CO	Y	45390 FQ	52210 MW	65270 TQ	USBLS	5/07
	Connecticut	H	21.18 AE	31.10 MW		CTBLS	1/08-3/08
	Washington-Arlington-Alexandria MSA, DC-VA-MD-WV	Y	57900 FQ	74830 MW	107910 TQ	USBLS	5/07
	Florida	Y	37780 FQ	44890 MW	54800 TQ	USBLS	5/07
	Jacksonville MSA, FL	Y	36430 FQ	40340 MW	52350 TQ	USBLS	5/07
	Tampa-St. Petersburg-Clearwater MSA, FL	Y	39870 FQ	50460 MW	61070 TQ	USBLS	5/07
	Georgia	Y	39280 FQ	51970 MW	68850 TQ	USBLS	5/07
	Idaho	Y	51730 FQ	58850 MW	66660 TQ	USBLS	5/07
	Illinois	Y	46270 FQ	53220 MW	63920 TQ	USBLS	5/07
	Chicago-Naperville-Joliet MSA, IL-IN-WI	Y	47830 FQ	56100 MW	65430 TQ	USBLS	5/07
	Indiana	Y	36160 FQ	43510 MW	51550 TQ	USBLS	5/07
	Iowa	Y	34070 FQ	48650 MW	59180 TQ	USBLS	5/07
	Louisiana	H	20.01 FQ	25.69 MW	32.99 TQ	LABLS	1/08-3/08
	Maine	Y	38270 FQ	45880 MW	53260 TQ	USBLS	5/07
	Maryland	Y		53900 MW		MDBLS	3/08
	Massachusetts	Y	45890 FQ	54780 MW	61100 TQ	USBLS	5/07
	Boston-Cambridge-Quincy NECTA, MA	Y	45730 FQ	53880 MW	60050 TQ	USBLS	5/07
	Michigan	Y	47080 FQ	56460 MW	63730 TQ	USBLS	5/07
	Minnesota	Y	43271 FQ	55387 MW	65064 TQ	MNBLS	10/08-12/08
	Duluth-Superior MSA, MN-WI	Y	47697 FQ	58745 MW	67418 TQ	MNBLS	10/08-12/08
	Minneapolis-Saint Paul MSA, MN-WI	Y	47142 FQ	58076 MW	66278 TQ	MNBLS	10/08-12/08
	Mississippi	Y	38550 FQ	48770 MW	67800 TQ	USBLS	5/07
	Missouri	Y	38610 FQ	46890 MW	57990 TQ	USBLS	5/07
	Montana	Y	41660 FQ	49350 MW	59390 TQ	USBLS	5/07

AE Average entry wage	**AW** Average wage paid	**FQ** First quartile wage	**LO** Lowest wage paid	**MTC** Median total compensation	**TCC** Total cash compensation
AER Average entry range	**AWR** Average wage range	**H** Hourly	**LR** Low end range	**MW** Median wage paid	**TQ** Third quartile wage
AEX Average experienced wage	**AXR** Average experienced range	**HI** Highest wage paid	**M** Monthly	**MWR** Median wage range	**W** Weekly
ATC Average total compensation	**D** Daily	**HR** High end range	**MCC** Median cash compensation	**S** See annotated source	**Y** Yearly

Occupation/Type/Industry	Location	Per	Low	Mid	High	Source	Date
Forester	Nebraska	Y	37140 FQ	45500 MW	58080 TQ	USBLS	5/07
	Nevada	H	21.98 FQ	25.84 MW	30.04 TQ	NVBLS	5/08
	New Hampshire	H	19.78 AE	25.32 MW	28.33 AEX	NHBLS	6/08
	New Jersey	Y	45170 FQ	51480 MW	60220 TQ	USBLS	5/07
	New Mexico	Y	51640 FQ	57440 MW	63170 TQ	USBLS	5/07
	New York	Y	41380 FQ	49720 MW	58740 TQ	USBLS	5/07
	New York-Northern New Jersey-Long Island MSA, NY-NJ-PA	Y	40740 FQ	47060 MW	53410 TQ	USBLS	5/07
	North Carolina	Y	45030 FQ	56750 MW	68900 TQ	USBLS	5/07
	Charlotte-Gastonia-Concord MSA, NC-SC	Y	47350 FQ	68100 MW	76660 TQ	USBLS	5/07
	Raleigh-Cary MSA, NC	Y	52920 FQ	64440 MW	71380 TQ	USBLS	5/07
	Ohio	Y	42820 FQ	48360 MW	55580 TQ	USBLS	5/07
	Oklahoma	Y	36100 FQ	43660 MW	54810 TQ	USBLS	5/07
	Oregon	H	24.51 FQ	28.58 MW	32.69 TQ	ORBLS	5/08
	Eugene-Springfield MSA, OR	Y	52020 FQ	59060 MW	66360 TQ	USBLS	5/07
	Portland-Vancouver-Beaverton MSA, OR-WA	Y	47650 FQ	57640 MW	70860 TQ	USBLS	5/07
	Pennsylvania	Y	36910 FQ	45120 MW	57830 TQ	USBLS	5/07
	Philadelphia-Camden-Wilmington MSA, PA-NJ-DE-MD	Y	45580 FQ	58810 MW	71900 TQ	USBLS	5/07
	Pittsburgh MSA, PA	Y	36510 FQ	50040 MW	59750 TQ	USBLS	5/07
	South Carolina	Y	42050 FQ	53660 MW	71110 TQ	USBLS	5/07
	Charleston-North Charleston MSA, SC	Y	48990 FQ	73760 MW	112270 TQ	USBLS	5/07
	South Dakota	Y	37496 FQ	46633 MW	58736 TQ	SDBLS	7/08-9/08
	Tennessee	Y	35440 FQ	41640 MW	50690 TQ	USBLS	5/07
	Texas	Y	49490 FQ	58540 MW	68700 TQ	USBLS	5/07
	Utah	Y	39040 FQ	48500 MW	59680 TQ	USBLS	5/07
	Salt Lake City MSA, UT	Y	35010 FQ	41130 MW	49080 TQ	USBLS	5/07
	Vermont	Y	41900 FQ	50600 MW	59050 TQ	USBLS	5/07
	Virginia	Y	46160 FQ	60720 MW	73220 TQ	USBLS	5/07
	Richmond MSA, VA	Y	43590 FQ	56430 MW	63940 TQ	USBLS	5/07
	Washington	H	24.86 FQ	28.97 MW	34.11 TQ	WABLS	3/08
	Seattle-Tacoma-Bellevue MSA, WA	Y	46520 FQ	56820 MW	66820 TQ	USBLS	5/07
	West Virginia	Y	35732 FQ	45430 MW	65953 TQ	WVBLS	7/08-9/08
	Wisconsin	Y	43840 FQ	47750 MW	52520 TQ	USBLS	5/07
	Milwaukee-Waukesha-West Allis MSA, WI	Y	44410 FQ	47660 MW	50900 TQ	USBLS	5/07
Forestry Aide							
Department of Resources and Economic Development	New Hampshire	Y		14578 AW		NHUL03	2008
Forestry and Conservation Science Teacher							
Postsecondary	Alabama	Y	45990 FQ	56880 MW	76360 TQ	USBLS	5/07
Postsecondary	Arizona	Y	33080 FQ	36500 MW	39920 TQ	USBLS	5/07
Postsecondary	California	Y		73701 AW		CABLS	1/08-3/08
Postsecondary	Florida	Y	58910 FQ	75730 MW	91650 TQ	USBLS	5/07
Postsecondary	Maine	Y	54880 FQ	70700 MW	91040 TQ	USBLS	5/07
Postsecondary	Maryland	Y		40825 MW		MDBLS	3/08
Postsecondary	Massachusetts	Y	48300 FQ	62250 MW	92280 TQ	USBLS	5/07
Postsecondary	Mississippi	Y	84130 FQ	95330 MW	108120 TQ	USBLS	5/07
Postsecondary	New York	Y	46890 FQ	60640 MW	79570 TQ	USBLS	5/07
Postsecondary	North Carolina	Y	43580 FQ	58320 MW	81660 TQ	USBLS	5/07
Postsecondary	Pennsylvania	Y	54860 FQ	72480 MW	93770 TQ	USBLS	5/07
Postsecondary	South Dakota	Y	42213 FQ	51441 MW	67254 TQ	SDBLS	7/08-9/08
Postsecondary	West Virginia	Y	45175 FQ	52713 MW	66973 TQ	WVBLS	7/08-9/08
Postsecondary	Wisconsin	Y	48420 FQ	72740 MW	103670 TQ	USBLS	5/07
Forging Machine Setter, Operator, and Tender							
Metals and Plastics	Alabama	Y	22340 FQ	27980 MW	36460 TQ	USBLS	5/07
Metals and Plastics	Birmingham-Hoover MSA, AL	Y	18900 FQ	25700 MW	42420 TQ	USBLS	5/07
Metals and Plastics	Montgomery MSA, AL	Y	22550 FQ	31710 MW	35910 TQ	USBLS	5/07
Metals and Plastics	Arizona	Y	21960 FQ	27030 MW	35310 TQ	USBLS	5/07

AE Average entry wage	**AW** Average wage paid	**FQ** First quartile wage	**LO** Lowest wage paid	**MTC** Median total compensation	**TCC** Total cash compensation
AER Average entry range	**AWR** Average wage range		**LR** Low end range	**MW** Median wage paid	**TQ** Third quartile wage
AEX Average experienced wage	**AXR** Average experienced range	**HI** Hourly	**M** Monthly	**MWR** Median wage range	**W** Weekly
ATC Average total compensation	**D** Daily	**HI** Highest wage paid	**MCC** Median cash compensation	**S** See annotated source	**Y** Yearly
		HR High end range			

Forging Machine Setter, Operator, and Tender

Occupation/Type/Industry	Location	Per	Low	Mid	High	Source	Date
Forging Machine Setter, Operator, and Tender							
Metals and Plastics	Phoenix-Mesa-Scottsdale MSA, AZ	Y	21980 FQ	27320 MW	35580 TQ	USBLS	5/07
Metals and Plastics	Arkansas	Y	24570 FQ	31640 MW	35430 TQ	USBLS	5/07
Metals and Plastics	California	H	12.09 FQ	16.03 MW	19.85 TQ	CABLS	1/08-3/08
Metals and Plastics	Los Angeles-Long Beach-Glendale PMSA, CA	H	13.25 FQ	17.80 MW	21.64 TQ	CABLS	1/08-3/08
Metals and Plastics	Oakland-Fremont-Hayward MSA, CA	H	14.79 FQ	17.65 MW	21.36 TQ	CABLS	1/08-3/08
Metals and Plastics	Riverside-San Bernardino-Ontario MSA, CA	H	10.40 FQ	13.69 MW	17.38 TQ	CABLS	1/08-3/08
Metals and Plastics	San Diego-Carlsbad-San Marcos MSA, CA	H	13.15 FQ	17.28 MW	20.77 TQ	CABLS	1/08-3/08
Metals and Plastics	San Jose-Sunnyvale-Santa Clara MSA, CA	H	11.64 FQ	16.55 MW	20.38 TQ	CABLS	1/08-3/08
Metals and Plastics	Santa Ana-Anaheim-Irvine PMSA, CA	Y	19160 FQ	28420 MW	35850 TQ	USBLS	5/07
Metals and Plastics	Denver-Aurora MSA, CO	Y	34260 FQ	41850 MW	46490 TQ	USBLS	5/07
Metals and Plastics	Connecticut	H	11.02 AE	15.21 MW		CTBLS	1/08-3/08
Metals and Plastics	Bridgeport-Stamford-Norwalk MSA, CT	Y	27060 FQ	31580 MW	36840 TQ	USBLS	5/07
Metals and Plastics	Hartford-West Hartford-East Hartford MSA, CT	Y	27290 FQ	32480 MW	36130 TQ	USBLS	5/07
Metals and Plastics	Washington-Arlington-Alexandria MSA, DC-VA-MD-WV	Y	20890 FQ	23030 MW	27530 TQ	USBLS	5/07
Metals and Plastics	Florida	Y	18540 FQ	22190 MW	28170 TQ	USBLS	5/07
Metals and Plastics	Tampa-St. Petersburg-Clearwater MSA, FL	Y	17260 FQ	19270 MW	22730 TQ	USBLS	5/07
Metals and Plastics	Georgia	Y	21940 FQ	26450 MW	29590 TQ	USBLS	5/07
Metals and Plastics	Atlanta-Sandy Springs-Marietta MSA, GA	Y	18440 FQ	24140 MW	30620 TQ	USBLS	5/07
Metals and Plastics	Illinois	Y	23670 FQ	28100 MW	34370 TQ	USBLS	5/07
Metals and Plastics	Chicago-Naperville-Joliet MSA, IL-IN-WI	Y	20780 FQ	31200 MW	39540 TQ	USBLS	5/07
Metals and Plastics	Indiana	Y	25390 FQ	29700 MW	40090 TQ	USBLS	5/07
Metals and Plastics	Iowa	Y	24820 FQ	34890 MW	39730 TQ	USBLS	5/07
Metals and Plastics	Kansas	Y	23210 FQ	29300 MW	36140 TQ	USBLS	5/07
Metals and Plastics	Wichita MSA, KS	Y	34720 FQ	42860 MW	52340 TQ	USBLS	5/07
Metals and Plastics	Kentucky	Y	27466 FQ	33798 MW	38022 TQ	KYBLS	2008
Metals and Plastics	Louisville-Jefferson County MSA, KY-IN	Y	19130 FQ	26630 MW	33030 TQ	USBLS	5/07
Metals and Plastics	Louisiana	H	10.60 FQ	11.83 MW	13.78 TQ	LABLS	1/08-3/08
Metals and Plastics	Maryland	Y		30925 MW		MDBLS	3/08
Metals and Plastics	Massachusetts	Y	26030 FQ	32960 MW	37500 TQ	USBLS	5/07
Metals and Plastics	Boston-Cambridge-Quincy NECTA, MA	Y	24390 FQ	31820 MW	36630 TQ	USBLS	5/07
Metals and Plastics	Worcester MSA, MA-CT	Y	34080 FQ	37330 MW	53170 TQ	USBLS	5/07
Metals and Plastics	Michigan	Y	23590 FQ	31450 MW	38020 TQ	USBLS	5/07
Metals and Plastics	Detroit-Warren-Livonia MSA, MI	Y	26870 FQ	33630 MW	39100 TQ	USBLS	5/07
Metals and Plastics	Grand Rapids-Wyoming MSA, MI	Y	26420 FQ	32420 MW	36090 TQ	USBLS	5/07
Metals and Plastics	Warren-Troy-Farmington Hills PMSA, MI	Y	26840 FQ	33420 MW	38640 TQ	USBLS	5/07
Metals and Plastics	Minnesota	Y	30561 FQ	33961 MW	37776 TQ	MNBLS	10/08-12/08
Metals and Plastics	Minneapolis-Saint Paul MSA, MN-WI	Y	31297 FQ	34179 MW	37279 TQ	MNBLS	10/08-12/08
Metals and Plastics	Mississippi	Y	21460 FQ	28440 MW	34610 TQ	USBLS	5/07
Metals and Plastics	Missouri	Y	25170 FQ	35460 MW	47320 TQ	USBLS	5/07
Metals and Plastics	St. Louis MSA, MO-IL	Y	19400 FQ	46980 MW	79380 TQ	USBLS	5/07
Metals and Plastics	Montana	Y	16790 FQ	20680 MW	23590 TQ	USBLS	5/07
Metals and Plastics	Nebraska	Y	29970 FQ	32660 MW	36310 TQ	USBLS	5/07
Metals and Plastics	Omaha-Council Bluffs MSA, NE-IA	Y	26260 FQ	30260 MW	34490 TQ	USBLS	5/07
Metals and Plastics	Nevada	H	11.40 FQ	14.29 MW	18.41 TQ	NVBLS	5/08
Metals and Plastics	New Hampshire	H	9.99 AE	12.11 MW	14.95 AEX	NHBLS	6/08
Metals and Plastics	New Jersey	Y	21140 FQ	27560 MW	35540 TQ	USBLS	5/07
Metals and Plastics	Camden PMSA, NJ	Y	20580 FQ	22620 MW	33420 TQ	USBLS	5/07
Metals and Plastics	Newark-Union PMSA, NJ-PA	Y	23730 FQ	31270 MW	37930 TQ	USBLS	5/07
Metals and Plastics	New York	Y	27030 FQ	34750 MW	42770 TQ	USBLS	5/07

Occupation/Type/Industry	Location	Per	Low	Mid	High	Source	Date
Forging Machine Setter, Operator, and Tender							
Metals and Plastics	Buffalo-Niagara Falls MSA, NY	Y	28330 FQ	36300 MW	47550 TQ	USBLS	5/07
Metals and Plastics	Nassau-Suffolk PMSA, NY	Y	34720 FQ	39110 MW	48200 TQ	USBLS	5/07
Metals and Plastics	New York-Northern New Jersey-Long Island MSA, NY-NJ-PA	Y	23890 FQ	31220 MW	39720 TQ	USBLS	5/07
Metals and Plastics	North Carolina	Y	25850 FQ	31270 MW	36980 TQ	USBLS	5/07
Metals and Plastics	Charlotte-Gastonia-Concord MSA, NC-SC	Y	27170 FQ	33760 MW	38950 TQ	USBLS	5/07
Metals and Plastics	Ohio	Y	28580 FQ	35020 MW	40730 TQ	USBLS	5/07
Metals and Plastics	Cincinnati-Middletown MSA, OH-KY-IN	Y	23150 FQ	27550 MW	33860 TQ	USBLS	5/07
Metals and Plastics	Cleveland-Elyria-Mentor MSA, OH	Y	34360 FQ	40530 MW	47690 TQ	USBLS	5/07
Metals and Plastics	Columbus MSA, OH	Y	26490 FQ	31620 MW	36590 TQ	USBLS	5/07
Metals and Plastics	Dayton MSA, OH	Y	25170 FQ	30540 MW	35640 TQ	USBLS	5/07
Metals and Plastics	Oklahoma	Y	15320 FQ	18070 MW	23520 TQ	USBLS	5/07
Metals and Plastics	Oregon	H	13.23 FQ	15.35 MW	19.18 TQ	ORBLS	5/08
Metals and Plastics	Portland-Vancouver-Beaverton MSA, OR-WA	Y	21850 FQ	27580 MW	34420 TQ	USBLS	5/07
Metals and Plastics	Pennsylvania	Y	25930 FQ	31430 MW	37010 TQ	USBLS	5/07
Metals and Plastics	Philadelphia-Camden-Wilmington MSA, PA-NJ-DE-MD	Y	26370 FQ	34780 MW	42410 TQ	USBLS	5/07
Metals and Plastics	Pittsburgh MSA, PA	Y	25760 FQ	30240 MW	34100 TQ	USBLS	5/07
Metals and Plastics	Providence-Fall River-Warwick MSA, RI-MA	Y	24080 FQ	28580 MW	34420 TQ	USBLS	5/07
Metals and Plastics	South Carolina	Y	23120 FQ	27350 MW	33700 TQ	USBLS	5/07
Metals and Plastics	South Dakota	Y	27021 FQ	31194 MW	34861 TQ	SDBLS	7/08-9/08
Metals and Plastics	Tennessee	Y	26580 FQ	30720 MW	34540 TQ	USBLS	5/07
Metals and Plastics	Knoxville MSA, TN	Y	23330 FQ	28360 MW	33060 TQ	USBLS	5/07
Metals and Plastics	Memphis MSA, TN-MS-AR	Y	17520 FQ	19070 MW	23720 TQ	USBLS	5/07
Metals and Plastics	Nashville-Davidson-Murfreesboro MSA, TN	Y	24610 FQ	27730 MW	32040 TQ	USBLS	5/07
Metals and Plastics	Texas	Y	19780 FQ	26120 MW	34930 TQ	USBLS	5/07
Metals and Plastics	Dallas-Fort Worth-Arlington MSA, TX	Y	21650 FQ	27220 MW	32650 TQ	USBLS	5/07
Metals and Plastics	Houston-Sugar Land-Baytown MSA, TX	Y	18420 FQ	23750 MW	33520 TQ	USBLS	5/07
Metals and Plastics	Utah	Y	23810 FQ	28140 MW	32380 TQ	USBLS	5/07
Metals and Plastics	Salt Lake City MSA, UT	Y	26710 FQ	28970 MW	31220 TQ	USBLS	5/07
Metals and Plastics	Vermont	Y	22890 FQ	26620 MW	30750 TQ	USBLS	5/07
Metals and Plastics	Virginia	Y	25970 FQ	28010 MW	30110 TQ	USBLS	5/07
Metals and Plastics	Richmond MSA, VA	Y	26840 FQ	28640 MW	30460 TQ	USBLS	5/07
Metals and Plastics	Washington	H	12.46 FQ	15.34 MW	19.33 TQ	WABLS	3/08
Metals and Plastics	West Virginia	Y	23213 FQ	25870 MW	33156 TQ	WVBLS	7/08-9/08
Metals and Plastics	Wisconsin	Y	27570 FQ	33550 MW	39150 TQ	USBLS	5/07
Metals and Plastics	Milwaukee-Waukesha-West Allis MSA, WI	Y	37590 FQ	40780 MW	44160 TQ	USBLS	5/07
Forklift Operator							
Small Organization	United States	Y	25385 FQ	27875 MW	30365 TQ	ALA05	2008
Forms and Manuals Analyst							
State Supreme Court	Michigan	Y			46270 HI	LSJ02	7/11/07
Foundry Mold and Coremaker	Alabama	Y	22790 FQ	27480 MW	33980 TQ	USBLS	5/07
	Birmingham-Hoover MSA, AL	Y	23830 FQ	30080 MW	36210 TQ	USBLS	5/07
	Arizona	Y	24310 FQ	29230 MW	33280 TQ	USBLS	5/07
	Phoenix-Mesa-Scottsdale MSA, AZ	Y	24900 FQ	29660 MW	33520 TQ	USBLS	5/07
	Arkansas	Y	21810 FQ	25770 MW	28690 TQ	USBLS	5/07
	California	H	9.74 FQ	12.02 MW	15.41 TQ	CABLS	1/08-3/08
	Los Angeles-Long Beach-Glendale PMSA, CA	H	9.59 FQ	11.38 MW	14.39 TQ	CABLS	1/08-3/08
	Oakland-Fremont-Hayward MSA, CA	H	10.24 FQ	16.28 MW	18.29 TQ	CABLS	1/08-3/08
	San Diego-Carlsbad-San Marcos MSA, CA	H	10.35 FQ	12.32 MW	13.62 TQ	CABLS	1/08-3/08
	Colorado	Y	24830 FQ	27930 MW	31040 TQ	USBLS	5/07

AE Average entry wage	**AW** Average wage paid	**FQ** First quartile wage	**LO** Lowest wage paid	**MTC** Median total compensation	**TCC** Total cash compensation
AER Average entry range	**AWR** Average wage range	**H** Hourly	**LR** Low end range	**MW** Median wage paid	**TQ** Third quartile wage
AEX Average experienced wage	**AXR** Average experienced range	**HI** Highest wage paid	**M** Monthly	**MWR** Median wage range	**W** Weekly
ATC Average total compensation	**D** Daily	**HR** High end range	**MCC** Median cash compensation	**S** See annotated source	**Y** Yearly

Occupation/Type/Industry	Location	Per	Low	Mid	High	Source	Date
Foundry Mold and Coremaker	Connecticut	H	11.08 AE	13.85 MW		CTBLS	1/08-3/08
	Hartford-West Hartford-East Hartford MSA, CT	Y	23580 FQ	26930 MW	30170 TQ	USBLS	5/07
	Florida	Y	21860 FQ	25380 MW	30370 TQ	USBLS	5/07
	Jacksonville MSA, FL	Y	23630 FQ	26540 MW	30100 TQ	USBLS	5/07
	Tampa-St. Petersburg-Clearwater MSA, FL	Y	22600 FQ	26070 MW	31390 TQ	USBLS	5/07
	Georgia	Y	22940 FQ	28270 MW	32900 TQ	USBLS	5/07
	Atlanta-Sandy Springs-Marietta MSA, GA	Y	20950 FQ	24540 MW	30590 TQ	USBLS	5/07
	Idaho	Y	23060 FQ	33020 MW	46900 TQ	USBLS	5/07
	Illinois	Y	23300 FQ	29540 MW	35310 TQ	USBLS	5/07
	Chicago-Naperville-Joliet MSA, IL-IN-WI	Y	22930 FQ	26300 MW	34560 TQ	USBLS	5/07
	Indiana	Y	25900 FQ	31230 MW	40830 TQ	USBLS	5/07
	Iowa	Y	25880 FQ	28700 MW	34420 TQ	USBLS	5/07
	Kansas	Y	22470 FQ	26050 MW	28790 TQ	USBLS	5/07
	Wichita MSA, KS	Y	20830 FQ	23300 MW	25790 TQ	USBLS	5/07
	Kentucky	Y	27863 FQ	31462 MW	39487 TQ	KYBLS	2008
	Louisiana	H	7.34 FQ	9.45 MW	11.02 TQ	LABLS	1/08-3/08
	Massachusetts	Y	31230 FQ	36930 MW	41190 TQ	USBLS	5/07
	Boston-Cambridge-Quincy NECTA, MA	Y	36740 FQ	40570 MW	44570 TQ	USBLS	5/07
	Michigan	Y	30200 FQ	36030 MW	40400 TQ	USBLS	5/07
	Detroit-Warren-Livonia MSA, MI	Y	29510 FQ	40240 MW	45280 TQ	USBLS	5/07
	Grand Rapids-Wyoming MSA, MI	Y	26880 FQ	29770 MW	37510 TQ	USBLS	5/07
	Warren-Troy-Farmington Hills PMSA, MI	Y	30920 FQ	41160 MW	45750 TQ	USBLS	5/07
	Minnesota	Y	30499 FQ	36263 MW	42286 TQ	MNBLS	10/08-12/08
	Minneapolis-Saint Paul MSA, MN-WI	Y	32738 FQ	38906 MW	46277 TQ	MNBLS	10/08-12/08
	Mississippi	Y	26930 FQ	29100 MW	31260 TQ	USBLS	5/07
	Missouri	Y	22340 FQ	28490 MW	33410 TQ	USBLS	5/07
	Kansas City MSA, MO-KS	Y	30270 FQ	34210 MW	37610 TQ	USBLS	5/07
	St. Louis MSA, MO-IL	Y	27340 FQ	30790 MW	34290 TQ	USBLS	5/07
	Nebraska	Y	23790 FQ	28600 MW	33780 TQ	USBLS	5/07
	New Hampshire	H	12.45 AE	13.74 MW	14.91 AEX	NHBLS	6/08
	New Jersey	Y	21440 FQ	28800 MW	38620 TQ	USBLS	5/07
	New Mexico	Y	21820 FQ	28820 MW	34150 TQ	USBLS	5/07
	New York	Y	25000 FQ	31880 MW	39920 TQ	USBLS	5/07
	New York-Northern New Jersey-Long Island MSA, NY-NJ-PA	Y	22170 FQ	29540 MW	38450 TQ	USBLS	5/07
	North Carolina	Y	22670 FQ	27400 MW	50070 TQ	USBLS	5/07
	Ohio	Y	24300 FQ	28760 MW	35480 TQ	USBLS	5/07
	Cincinnati-Middletown MSA, OH-KY-IN	Y	25020 FQ	29030 MW	38000 TQ	USBLS	5/07
	Cleveland-Elyria-Mentor MSA, OH	Y	24520 FQ	27830 MW	31620 TQ	USBLS	5/07
	Dayton MSA, OH	Y	24200 FQ	27930 MW	32330 TQ	USBLS	5/07
	Oklahoma	Y	21820 FQ	26270 MW	29610 TQ	USBLS	5/07
	Oregon	H	12.18 FQ	14.69 MW	18.14 TQ	ORBLS	5/08
	Portland-Vancouver-Beaverton MSA, OR-WA	Y	24220 FQ	29650 MW	37780 TQ	USBLS	5/07
	Pennsylvania	Y	26830 FQ	30130 MW	35190 TQ	USBLS	5/07
	Allentown-Bethlehem-Easton MSA, PA-NJ	Y	27380 FQ	29940 MW	32400 TQ	USBLS	5/07
	Philadelphia-Camden-Wilmington MSA, PA-NJ-DE-MD	Y	30870 FQ	37430 MW	51320 TQ	USBLS	5/07
	Pittsburgh MSA, PA	Y	28170 FQ	32440 MW	38140 TQ	USBLS	5/07
	South Carolina	Y	28760 FQ	33220 MW	41900 TQ	USBLS	5/07
	Charleston-North Charleston MSA, SC	Y	33260 FQ	36680 MW	48310 TQ	USBLS	5/07
	Tennessee	Y	26890 FQ	32620 MW	37260 TQ	USBLS	5/07
	Texas	Y	17920 FQ	22390 MW	28510 TQ	USBLS	5/07
	Dallas-Fort Worth-Arlington MSA, TX	Y	17840 FQ	22780 MW	28400 TQ	USBLS	5/07
	Houston-Sugar Land-Baytown MSA, TX	Y	17950 FQ	20560 MW	24300 TQ	USBLS	5/07

AE Average entry wage	**AW** Average wage paid	**FQ** First quartile wage	**LO** Lowest wage paid	**MTC** Median total compensation	**TCC** Total cash compensation
AER Average entry range	**AWR** Average wage range	**H** Hourly	**LR** Low end range	**MW** Median wage paid	**TQ** Third quartile wage
AEX Average experienced wage	**AXR** Average experienced range	**HI** Highest wage paid	**M** Monthly	**MWR** Median wage range	**W** Weekly
ATC Average total compensation	**D** Daily	**HR** High end range	**MCC** Median cash compensation	**S** See annotated source	**Y** Yearly

Occupation/Type/Industry	Location	Per	Low	Mid	High	Source	Date
Foundry Mold and Coremaker	Utah	Y	21520 FQ	26480 MW	32020 TQ	USBLS	5/07
	Provo-Orem MSA, UT	Y	19520 FQ	22970 MW	27190 TQ	USBLS	5/07
	Salt Lake City MSA, UT	Y	25570 FQ	30080 MW	36360 TQ	USBLS	5/07
	Vermont	Y	23800 FQ	28490 MW	34610 TQ	USBLS	5/07
	Virginia	Y	23260 FQ	27050 MW	30220 TQ	USBLS	5/07
	Washington	H	12.74 FQ	14.41 MW	16.79 TQ	WABLS	3/08
	Seattle-Tacoma-Bellevue MSA, WA	Y	28420 FQ	32450 MW	36290 TQ	USBLS	5/07
	West Virginia	Y	24389 FQ	29021 MW	42283 TQ	WVBLS	7/08-9/08
	Wisconsin	Y	23870 FQ	29100 MW	35570 TQ	USBLS	5/07
	Milwaukee-Waukesha-West Allis MSA, WI	Y	20060 FQ	26250 MW	32250 TQ	USBLS	5/07
Franchiser Manager							
Site Selection and Pre-Opening Activities	United States	Y		130690 AW		WSJ11	8/07-7/08
Fraud Investigator							
Department of Health and Human Services, Transitional Assistance	New Hampshire	Y		44144 AW		NHUL03	2008
Freelance Writer	Rhode Island	Y		38000-55000 AWR		RIM01	2009
Friend of the Court	Livingston County, MI	Y			95633 HI	LCPP	2009
Fruit and Vegetable Inspector							
State Government	Ohio	H	17.22 LO		21.77 HI	ODAS	2008
Fuel Cell Engineer							
With Bachelor's Degree	Tech Valley, NY	Y	40000-60000 LR			TVC02	2008
Functional Specialist							
University Libraries	East North Central	Y		53447 AW		ARL	2007-2008
University Libraries	East South Central	Y		54994 AW		ARL	2007-2008
University Libraries	Mountain	Y		58614 AW		ARL	2007-2008
University Libraries	New England	Y		69418 AW		ARL	2007-2008
University Libraries	Pacific	Y		66141 AW		ARL	2007-2008
University Libraries	West North Central	Y		59721 AW		ARL	2007-2008
University Libraries	West South Central	Y		55500 AW		ARL	2007-2008
Fund Raiser							
Civic and Public Affairs Groups	United States	Y		59000 AW		CPHIL	2007
Scientific and Research Organizations	United States	Y		83000 AW		CPHIL	2007
Funeral Attendant	Alabama	Y	13480 FQ	15980 MW	22110 TQ	USBLS	5/07
	Birmingham-Hoover MSA, AL	Y	13350 FQ	15550 MW	20210 TQ	USBLS	5/07
	Arizona	Y	21120 FQ	25770 MW	35190 TQ	USBLS	5/07
	Phoenix-Mesa-Scottsdale MSA, AZ	Y	21840 FQ	26070 MW	34520 TQ	USBLS	5/07
	Tucson MSA, AZ	Y	19000 FQ	23240 MW	31080 TQ	USBLS	5/07
	Arkansas	Y	15900 FQ	19810 MW	25060 TQ	USBLS	5/07
	Little Rock-North Little Rock MSA, AR	Y	19900 FQ	27990 MW	30480 TQ	USBLS	5/07
	California	H	10.63 FQ	12.47 MW	15.25 TQ	CABLS	1/08-3/08
	Fresno MSA, CA	H	9.17 FQ	11.80 MW	14.81 TQ	CABLS	1/08-3/08
	Los Angeles-Long Beach-Glendale PMSA, CA	H	11.31 FQ	13.76 MW	18.06 TQ	CABLS	1/08-3/08
	Oakland-Fremont-Hayward MSA, CA	H	10.11 FQ	11.94 MW	13.99 TQ	CABLS	1/08-3/08
	Riverside-San Bernardino-Ontario MSA, CA	H	10.40 FQ	11.79 MW	13.65 TQ	CABLS	1/08-3/08
	Sacramento-Arden Arcade-Roseville MSA, CA	H	11.46 FQ	12.73 MW	14.71 TQ	CABLS	1/08-3/08
	San Diego-Carlsbad-San Marcos MSA, CA	H	10.52 FQ	11.73 MW	14.08 TQ	CABLS	1/08-3/08
	San Francisco-San Mateo-Redwood PMSA, CA	H	10.92 FQ	11.90 MW	13.14 TQ	CABLS	1/08-3/08
	San Jose-Sunnyvale-Santa Clara MSA, CA	H	9.30 FQ	12.69 MW	17.11 TQ	CABLS	1/08-3/08
	Santa Ana-Anaheim-Irvine PMSA, CA	Y	20100 FQ	23360 MW	26900 TQ	USBLS	5/07
	Colorado	Y	20310 FQ	26530 MW	31350 TQ	USBLS	5/07

Funeral Attendant

Occupation/Type/Industry	Location	Per	Low	Mid	High	Source	Date
Funeral Attendant	Denver-Aurora MSA, CO	Y	24780 FQ	28440 MW	31880 TQ	USBLS	5/07
	Connecticut	H	9.00 AE	12.99 MW		CTBLS	1/08-3/08
	Bridgeport-Stamford-Norwalk MSA, CT	Y	24070 FQ	28260 MW	36440 TQ	USBLS	5/07
	Hartford-West Hartford-East Hartford MSA, CT	Y	21750 FQ	27460 MW	30550 TQ	USBLS	5/07
	Delaware	Y	20910 FQ	23440 MW	34300 TQ	USBLS	5/07
	Wilmington PMSA, DE-MD-NJ	Y	19710 FQ	22450 MW	26000 TQ	USBLS	5/07
	Washington-Arlington-Alexandria MSA, DC-VA-MD-WV	Y	21300 FQ	23980 MW	27690 TQ	USBLS	5/07
	Florida	Y	16440 FQ	18480 MW	21510 TQ	USBLS	5/07
	Fort Lauderdale-Pompano Beach-Deerfield Beach PMSA, FL	Y	15270 FQ	17350 MW	22080 TQ	USBLS	5/07
	Jacksonville MSA, FL	Y	16430 FQ	18210 MW	21420 TQ	USBLS	5/07
	Miami-Fort Lauderdale-Miami Beach MSA, FL	Y	15320 FQ	17010 MW	19520 TQ	USBLS	5/07
	Orlando-Kissimmee MSA, FL	Y	15640 FQ	17310 MW	19330 TQ	USBLS	5/07
	Sarasota-Bradenton-Venice MSA, FL	Y	17360 FQ	18750 MW	20200 TQ	USBLS	5/07
	Tampa-St. Petersburg-Clearwater MSA, FL	Y	17880 FQ	19610 MW	22140 TQ	USBLS	5/07
	Georgia	Y	16460 FQ	20910 MW	27100 TQ	USBLS	5/07
	Atlanta-Sandy Springs-Marietta MSA, GA	Y	20510 FQ	24390 MW	29150 TQ	USBLS	5/07
	Hawaii	Y	19900 FQ	23260 MW	28060 TQ	USBLS	5/07
	Idaho	Y	17190 FQ	20520 MW	25140 TQ	USBLS	5/07
	Illinois	Y	20240 FQ	22700 MW	25530 TQ	USBLS	5/07
	Chicago-Naperville-Joliet MSA, IL-IN-WI	Y	20760 FQ	22720 MW	24940 TQ	USBLS	5/07
	Indiana	Y	16710 FQ	19220 MW	22910 TQ	USBLS	5/07
	Gary PMSA, IN	Y	14060 FQ	21740 MW	24910 TQ	USBLS	5/07
	Indianapolis-Carmel MSA, IN	Y	17580 FQ	19850 MW	24110 TQ	USBLS	5/07
	Iowa	Y	17680 FQ	19720 MW	23280 TQ	USBLS	5/07
	Des Moines-West Des Moines MSA, IA	Y	17990 FQ	20110 MW	23530 TQ	USBLS	5/07
	Kansas	Y	13790 FQ	17210 MW	20820 TQ	USBLS	5/07
	Wichita MSA, KS	Y	13930 FQ	16570 MW	19370 TQ	USBLS	5/07
	Kentucky	Y	15013 FQ	17957 MW	20597 TQ	KYBLS	2008
	Louisville-Jefferson County MSA, KY-IN	Y	14640 FQ	17650 MW	20170 TQ	USBLS	5/07
	Louisiana	H	7.81 FQ	9.53 MW	11.33 TQ	LABLS	1/08-3/08
	New Orleans-Metairie-Kenner MSA, LA	Y	15670 FQ	19660 MW	23390 TQ	USBLS	5/07
	Maine	Y	19980 FQ	27710 MW	34150 TQ	USBLS	5/07
	Maryland	Y		23700 MW		MDBLS	3/08
	Baltimore-Towson MSA, MD	Y	21100 FQ	23330 MW	25900 TQ	USBLS	5/07
	Bethesda-Gaithersburg-Frederick PMSA, MD	Y	14540 FQ	23370 MW	30410 TQ	USBLS	5/07
	Massachusetts	Y	20380 FQ	27670 MW	36110 TQ	USBLS	5/07
	Boston-Cambridge-Quincy NECTA, MA	Y	27800 FQ	33050 MW	37220 TQ	USBLS	5/07
	Worcester MSA, MA-CT	Y	19430 FQ	23490 MW	41010 TQ	USBLS	5/07
	Michigan	Y	16460 FQ	21540 MW	27360 TQ	USBLS	5/07
	Detroit-Warren-Livonia MSA, MI	Y	16630 FQ	22010 MW	28290 TQ	USBLS	5/07
	Grand Rapids-Wyoming MSA, MI	Y	20790 FQ	27740 MW	31430 TQ	USBLS	5/07
	Warren-Troy-Farmington Hills PMSA, MI	Y	15730 FQ	20990 MW	27730 TQ	USBLS	5/07
	Minnesota	Y	20200 FQ	24686 MW	30342 TQ	MNBLS	10/08-12/08
	Duluth-Superior MSA, MN-WI	Y	22061 FQ	24184 MW	26285 TQ	MNBLS	10/08-12/08
	Minneapolis-Saint Paul MSA, MN-WI	Y	20022 FQ	26233 MW	30175 TQ	MNBLS	10/08-12/08
	Rochester MSA, MN	Y	30541 FQ	34027 MW	36884 TQ	MNBLS	10/08-12/08
	Mississippi	Y	17200 FQ	21170 MW	25690 TQ	USBLS	5/07
	Jackson MSA, MS	Y	14710 FQ	21670 MW	25570 TQ	USBLS	5/07
	Missouri	Y	17050 FQ	19720 MW	23040 TQ	USBLS	5/07
	Kansas City MSA, MO-KS	Y	19340 FQ	23750 MW	31710 TQ	USBLS	5/07
	St. Louis MSA, MO-IL	Y	18120 FQ	20940 MW	25160 TQ	USBLS	5/07

AE Average entry wage	**AW** Average wage paid	**FQ** First quartile wage	**LO** Lowest wage paid	**MTC** Median total compensation	**TCC** Total cash compensation
AER Average entry range	**AWR** Average wage range	**H** Hourly	**LR** Low end range	**MW** Median wage paid	**TQ** Third quartile wage
AEX Average experienced wage	**AXR** Average experienced range	**HI** Highest wage paid	**M** Monthly	**MWR** Median wage range	**W** Weekly
ATC Average total compensation	**D** Daily	**HR** High end range	**MCC** Median cash compensation	**S** See annotated source	**Y** Yearly

Occupation/Type/Industry	Location	Per	Low	Mid	High	Source	Date
Funeral Attendant	Springfield MSA, MO	Y	15810 FQ	20410 MW	35200 TQ	USBLS	5/07
	Montana	Y	17330 FQ	20970 MW	25850 TQ	USBLS	5/07
	Nebraska	Y	15410 FQ	18560 MW	22000 TQ	USBLS	5/07
	Omaha-Council Bluffs MSA, NE-IA	Y	14590 FQ	18160 MW	20480 TQ	USBLS	5/07
	Las Vegas-Paradise MSA, NV	H	8.65 FQ	10.12 MW	13.01 TQ	NVBLS	5/08
	New Hampshire	H	9.39 AE	12.56 MW	13.53 AEX	NHBLS	6/08
	New Jersey	Y	23240 FQ	30680 MW	47250 TQ	USBLS	5/07
	Edison PMSA, NJ	Y	20570 FQ	42440 MW	48590 TQ	USBLS	5/07
	Newark-Union PMSA, NJ-PA	Y	44550 FQ	48260 MW	51740 TQ	USBLS	5/07
	New Mexico	Y	18010 FQ	22430 MW	25490 TQ	USBLS	5/07
	Albuquerque MSA, NM	Y	17700 FQ	21320 MW	23400 TQ	USBLS	5/07
	New York	Y	21070 FQ	23270 MW	27020 TQ	USBLS	5/07
	Albany-Schenectady-Troy MSA, NY	Y	21040 FQ	22540 MW	24110 TQ	USBLS	5/07
	Buffalo-Niagara Falls MSA, NY	Y	21390 FQ	23470 MW	38620 TQ	USBLS	5/07
	Nassau-Suffolk PMSA, NY	Y	22180 FQ	24800 MW	31640 TQ	USBLS	5/07
	New York-Northern New Jersey-Long Island MSA, NY-NJ-PA	Y	21610 FQ	24330 MW	31640 TQ	USBLS	5/07
	North Carolina	Y	16650 FQ	20130 MW	24020 TQ	USBLS	5/07
	Asheville MSA, NC	Y	15300 FQ	19560 MW	22870 TQ	USBLS	5/07
	Charlotte-Gastonia-Concord MSA, NC-SC	Y	16600 FQ	18500 MW	20910 TQ	USBLS	5/07
	Raleigh-Cary MSA, NC	Y	21660 FQ	24880 MW	31220 TQ	USBLS	5/07
	North Dakota	Y	14370 FQ	20550 MW	24280 TQ	USBLS	5/07
	Ohio	Y	16540 FQ	20390 MW	24820 TQ	USBLS	5/07
	Cincinnati-Middletown MSA, OH-KY-IN	Y	18080 FQ	21220 MW	25250 TQ	USBLS	5/07
	Cleveland-Elyria-Mentor MSA, OH	Y	17440 FQ	20100 MW	24320 TQ	USBLS	5/07
	Columbus MSA, OH	Y	20500 FQ	23110 MW	27430 TQ	USBLS	5/07
	Dayton MSA, OH	Y	15770 FQ	21390 MW	28250 TQ	USBLS	5/07
	Mansfield MSA, OH	Y	14990 FQ	15710 MW	16970 TQ	USBLS	5/07
	Oklahoma	Y	15310 FQ	17970 MW	21230 TQ	USBLS	5/07
	Oklahoma City MSA, OK	Y	17760 FQ	19590 MW	22070 TQ	USBLS	5/07
	Tulsa MSA, OK	Y	15420 FQ	20990 MW	24450 TQ	USBLS	5/07
	Oregon	H	10.29 FQ	11.38 MW	13.19 TQ	ORBLS	5/08
	Portland-Vancouver-Beaverton MSA, OR-WA	Y	25240 FQ	39080 MW	43590 TQ	USBLS	5/07
	Pennsylvania	Y	17770 FQ	21280 MW	24750 TQ	USBLS	5/07
	Allentown-Bethlehem-Easton MSA, PA-NJ	Y	18330 FQ	26100 MW	28910 TQ	USBLS	5/07
	Lancaster MSA, PA	Y	23620 FQ	26630 MW	29700 TQ	USBLS	5/07
	Philadelphia-Camden-Wilmington MSA, PA-NJ-DE-MD	Y	19620 FQ	22610 MW	26390 TQ	USBLS	5/07
	Pittsburgh MSA, PA	Y	17150 FQ	19340 MW	22460 TQ	USBLS	5/07
	Rhode Island	Y	18650 FQ	24090 MW	29790 TQ	USBLS	5/07
	Providence-Fall River-Warwick MSA, RI-MA	Y	19700 FQ	24970 MW	28870 TQ	USBLS	5/07
	South Carolina	Y	14970 FQ	19100 MW	24210 TQ	USBLS	5/07
	Charleston-North Charleston MSA, SC	Y	14920 FQ	18410 MW	23210 TQ	USBLS	5/07
	Columbia MSA, SC	Y	13760 FQ	16700 MW	21660 TQ	USBLS	5/07
	Florence MSA, SC	Y	13090 FQ	14660 MW	18740 TQ	USBLS	5/07
	South Dakota	Y	16789 FQ	19158 MW	22412 TQ	SDBLS	7/08-9/08
	Tennessee	Y	16620 FQ	18920 MW	22700 TQ	USBLS	5/07
	Kingsport-Bristol-Bristol MSA, TN-VA	Y	16230 FQ	17810 MW	19710 TQ	USBLS	5/07
	Memphis MSA, TN-MS-AR	Y	17450 FQ	18830 MW	20170 TQ	USBLS	5/07
	Nashville-Davidson-Murfreesboro MSA, TN	Y	16920 FQ	18590 MW	20190 TQ	USBLS	5/07
	Texas	Y	14480 FQ	17700 MW	23040 TQ	USBLS	5/07
	Austin-Round Rock MSA, TX	Y	17570 FQ	19570 MW	22400 TQ	USBLS	5/07
	Brownsville-Harlingen MSA, TX	Y	15230 FQ	18510 MW	33190 TQ	USBLS	5/07
	Dallas-Fort Worth-Arlington MSA, TX	Y	17150 FQ	19950 MW	26200 TQ	USBLS	5/07
	El Paso MSA, TX	Y	16470 FQ	17850 MW	19610 TQ	USBLS	5/07

AE Average entry wage	**AW** Average wage paid	**FQ** First quartile wage	**LO** Lowest wage paid	**MTC** Median total compensation **TCC** Total cash compensation
AER Average entry range	**AWR** Average wage range	**H** Hourly	**LR** Low end range	**MW** Median wage paid **TQ** Third quartile wage
AEX Average experienced wage	**AXR** Average experienced range	**HI** Highest wage paid	**M** Monthly	**MWR** Median wage range **W** Weekly
ATC Average total compensation	**D** Daily	**HR** High end range	**MCC** Median cash compensation	**S** See annotated source **Y** Yearly

Occupation/Type/Industry	Location	Per	Low	Mid	High	Source	Date
Funeral Attendant	Houston-Sugar Land-Baytown MSA, TX	Y	15940 FQ	19620 MW	26170 TQ	USBLS	5/07
	San Antonio MSA, TX	Y	13170 FQ	15200 MW	18150 TQ	USBLS	5/07
	Utah	Y	22450 FQ	29850 MW	39930 TQ	USBLS	5/07
	Salt Lake City MSA, UT	Y	22120 FQ	28700 MW	40830 TQ	USBLS	5/07
	Vermont	Y	20280 FQ	31350 MW	42160 TQ	USBLS	5/07
	Virginia	Y	15760 FQ	19170 MW	23950 TQ	USBLS	5/07
	Richmond MSA, VA	Y	15910 FQ	18100 MW	21170 TQ	USBLS	5/07
	Virginia Beach-Norfolk-Newport News MSA, VA-NC	Y	13630 FQ	16150 MW	22550 TQ	USBLS	5/07
	Washington	H	9.38 FQ	12.66 MW	21.23 TQ	WABLS	3/08
	West Virginia	Y	16890 FQ	19651 MW	22738 TQ	WVBLS	7/08-9/08
	Charleston MSA, WV	Y	15440 FQ	19310 MW	22120 TQ	USBLS	5/07
	Wisconsin	Y	21210 FQ	25390 MW	29460 TQ	USBLS	5/07
	Milwaukee-Waukesha-West Allis MSA, WI	Y	24280 FQ	27220 MW	29700 TQ	USBLS	5/07
	Wyoming	Y	18411 FQ	22084 MW	26152 TQ	WYBLS	9/08
	Puerto Rico	Y	12930 FQ	14710 MW	17700 TQ	USBLS	5/07
	San Juan-Caguas-Guaynabo MSA, PR	Y	12990 FQ	14810 MW	17950 TQ	USBLS	5/07
Funeral Director	Alabama	Y	31280 FQ	37550 MW	47840 TQ	USBLS	5/07
	Arizona	Y	33110 FQ	49580 MW	69260 TQ	USBLS	
	Phoenix-Mesa-Scottsdale MSA, AZ	Y	34200 FQ	51600 MW	72030 TQ	USBLS	5/07
	Tucson MSA, AZ	Y	24200 FQ	35190 MW	59020 TQ	USBLS	5/07
	Arkansas	Y	31800 FQ	40100 MW	52120 TQ	USBLS	5/07
	California	H	20.39 FQ	24.60 MW	33.93 TQ	CABLS	1/08-3/08
	Los Angeles-Long Beach-Glendale PMSA, CA	H	19.18 FQ	23.93 MW	37.96 TQ	CABLS	1/08-3/08
	Modesto MSA, CA	H	20.59 FQ	22.38 MW	26.07 TQ	CABLS	1/08-3/08
	Oakland-Fremont-Hayward MSA, CA	H	27.23 FQ	33.05 MW	37.10 TQ	CABLS	1/08-3/08
	Riverside-San Bernardino-Ontario MSA, CA	H	19.70 FQ	24.14 MW	29.61 TQ	CABLS	1/08-3/08
	Sacramento-Arden Arcade-Roseville MSA, CA	H	21.16 FQ	23.52 MW	25.88 TQ	CABLS	1/08-3/08
	San Diego-Carlsbad-San Marcos MSA, CA	H	17.74 FQ	20.89 MW	23.20 TQ	CABLS	1/08-3/08
	San Francisco-San Mateo-Redwood PMSA, CA	H	20.18 FQ	22.89 MW	34.02 TQ	CABLS	1/08-3/08
	San Jose-Sunnyvale-Santa Clara MSA, CA	H	22.86 FQ	25.80 MW	30.84 TQ	CABLS	1/08-3/08
	Santa Ana-Anaheim-Irvine PMSA, CA	Y	55720 FQ	71080 MW	77330 TQ	USBLS	5/07
	Colorado	Y	39720 FQ	46820 MW	58400 TQ	USBLS	5/07
	Denver-Aurora MSA, CO	Y	42470 FQ	48200 MW	60560 TQ	USBLS	5/07
	Connecticut	H	24.16 AE	37.23 MW		CTBLS	1/08-3/08
	Hartford-West Hartford-East Hartford MSA, CT	Y	54960 FQ	68160 MW	90810 TQ	USBLS	5/07
	Delaware	Y	54760 FQ	70780 MW	78550 TQ	USBLS	5/07
	Wilmington PMSA, DE-MD-NJ	Y	45010 FQ	67530 MW	77150 TQ	USBLS	5/07
	District of Columbia	Y	36310 FQ	49750 MW	62320 TQ	USBLS	5/07
	Washington-Arlington-Alexandria MSA, DC-VA-MD-WV	Y	45240 FQ	59380 MW	75270 TQ	USBLS	5/07
	Florida	Y	39160 FQ	47250 MW	57070 TQ	USBLS	5/07
	Fort Lauderdale-Pompano Beach-Deerfield Beach PMSA, FL	Y	43270 FQ	48920 MW	56690 TQ	USBLS	5/07
	Jacksonville MSA, FL	Y	40810 FQ	49590 MW	60500 TQ	USBLS	5/07
	Miami-Fort Lauderdale-Miami Beach MSA, FL	Y	37480 FQ	45060 MW	53210 TQ	USBLS	5/07
	Orlando-Kissimmee MSA, FL	Y	40090 FQ	48000 MW	53610 TQ	USBLS	5/07
	Tampa-St. Petersburg-Clearwater MSA, FL	Y	44280 FQ	51650 MW	60470 TQ	USBLS	5/07
	West Palm Beach-Boca Raton-Boynton Beach PMSA, FL	Y	36130 FQ	39500 MW	47450 TQ	USBLS	5/07
	Georgia	Y	37750 FQ	49150 MW	71600 TQ	USBLS	5/07
	Atlanta-Sandy Springs-Marietta MSA, GA	Y	36880 FQ	41290 MW	67570 TQ	USBLS	5/07

AE	Average entry wage	AW	Average wage paid	FQ	First quartile wage
AER	Average entry range	AWR	Average wage range	H	Hourly
AEX	Average experienced wage	AXR	Average experienced range	HI	Highest wage paid
ATC	Average total compensation	D	Daily	HR	High end range

LO	Lowest wage paid	MTC	Median total compensation
LR	Low end range	MW	Median wage paid
M	Monthly	MWR	Median wage range
MCC	Median cash compensation	S	See annotated source

TCC	Total cash compensation
TQ	Third quartile wage
W	Weekly
Y	Yearly

Occupation/Type/Industry	Location	Per	Low	Mid	High	Source	Date
Funeral Director	Idaho	Y	28970 FQ	45310 MW	59310 TQ	USBLS	5/07
	Boise City-Nampa MSA, ID	Y	54990 FQ	59150 MW	63210 TQ	USBLS	5/07
	Illinois	Y	51990 FQ	62030 MW	76030 TQ	USBLS	5/07
	Chicago-Naperville-Joliet MSA, IL-IN-WI	Y	56170 FQ	65170 MW	77380 TQ	USBLS	5/07
	Indiana	Y	37660 FQ	48030 MW	59350 TQ	USBLS	5/07
	Indianapolis-Carmel MSA, IN	Y	40950 FQ	48110 MW	61860 TQ	USBLS	5/07
	Iowa	Y	43200 FQ	54920 MW	77470 TQ	USBLS	5/07
	Des Moines-West Des Moines MSA, IA	Y	53970 FQ	65960 MW	78740 TQ	USBLS	5/07
	Kansas	Y	35860 FQ	45090 MW	58340 TQ	USBLS	5/07
	Wichita MSA, KS	Y	27980 FQ	36000 MW	45210 TQ	USBLS	5/07
	Kentucky	Y	30433 FQ	39806 MW	57057 TQ	KYBLS	2008
	Lexington-Fayette MSA, KY	Y	24600 FQ	52320 MW	64460 TQ	USBLS	5/07
	Louisville-Jefferson County MSA, KY-IN	Y	32820 FQ	38960 MW	49930 TQ	USBLS	5/07
	Louisiana	H	14.17 FQ	17.45 MW	24.22 TQ	LABLS	1/08-3/08
	New Orleans-Metairie-Kenner MSA, LA	Y	30280 FQ	42470 MW	58630 TQ	USBLS	5/07
	Maine	Y	39340 FQ	47880 MW	59670 TQ	USBLS	5/07
	Portland-South Portland-Biddeford MSA, ME	Y	29340 FQ	39010 MW	62290 TQ	USBLS	5/07
	Maryland	Y		59150 MW		MDBLS	3/08
	Baltimore-Towson MSA, MD	Y	45050 FQ	57770 MW	67990 TQ	USBLS	5/07
	Bethesda-Gaithersburg-Frederick PMSA, MD	Y	52710 FQ	65290 MW	87090 TQ	USBLS	5/07
	Hagerstown-Martinsburg MSA, MD-WV	Y	47590 FQ	54770 MW	89870 TQ	USBLS	5/07
	Massachusetts	Y	49330 FQ	68310 MW	82360 TQ	USBLS	5/07
	Boston-Cambridge-Quincy NECTA, MA	Y	61720 FQ	73330 MW	82340 TQ	USBLS	5/07
	Worcester MSA, MA-CT	Y	57710 FQ	83710 MW	107620 TQ	USBLS	5/07
	Michigan	Y	45670 FQ	56750 MW	73040 TQ	USBLS	5/07
	Detroit-Warren-Livonia MSA, MI	Y	44500 FQ	55520 MW	71700 TQ	USBLS	5/07
	Grand Rapids-Wyoming MSA, MI	Y	42410 FQ	48810 MW	62610 TQ	USBLS	5/07
	Warren-Troy-Farmington Hills PMSA, MI	Y	42180 FQ	53430 MW	62750 TQ	USBLS	5/07
	Minnesota	Y	47503 FQ	58836 MW	79377 TQ	MNBLS	10/08-12/08
	Duluth-Superior MSA, MN-WI	Y	47346 FQ	63414 MW	75654 TQ	MNBLS	10/08-12/08
	Minneapolis-Saint Paul MSA, MN-WI	Y	50141 FQ	63727 MW	99385 TQ	MNBLS	10/08-12/08
	Rochester MSA, MN	Y	52297 FQ	58228 MW	71117 TQ	MNBLS	10/08-12/08
	Mississippi	Y	29160 FQ	35700 MW	47400 TQ	USBLS	5/07
	Jackson MSA, MS	Y	26850 FQ	33190 MW	44590 TQ	USBLS	5/07
	Missouri	Y	33000 FQ	45110 MW	67510 TQ	USBLS	5/07
	Kansas City MSA, MO-KS	Y	37630 FQ	58250 MW	89850 TQ	USBLS	5/07
	St. Joseph MSA, MO-KS	Y	60260 FQ	84190 MW	94000 TQ	USBLS	5/07
	St. Louis MSA, MO-IL	Y	36700 FQ	53680 MW	68030 TQ	USBLS	5/07
	Montana	Y	29590 FQ	43370 MW	58740 TQ	USBLS	5/07
	Nebraska	Y	33290 FQ	46480 MW	65180 TQ	USBLS	5/07
	Omaha-Council Bluffs MSA, NE-IA	Y	42960 FQ	61120 MW	87750 TQ	USBLS	5/07
	Nevada	H	15.11 FQ	28.50 MW	32.81 TQ	NVBLS	5/08
	Las Vegas-Paradise MSA, NV	H	30.57 FQ	32.50 MW	34.86 TQ	NVBLS	5/08
	New Hampshire	H	16.86 AE	25.81 MW	32.42 AEX	NHBLS	6/08
	New Jersey	Y	48660 FQ	60670 MW	79160 TQ	USBLS	5/07
	Camden PMSA, NJ	Y	41470 FQ	46540 MW	51780 TQ	USBLS	5/07
	Edison PMSA, NJ	Y	55550 FQ	64450 MW	77320 TQ	USBLS	5/07
	Newark-Union PMSA, NJ-PA	Y	45630 FQ	56410 MW	71870 TQ	USBLS	5/07
	New Mexico	Y	33380 FQ	42910 MW	51510 TQ	USBLS	5/07
	Albuquerque MSA, NM	Y	34060 FQ	39880 MW	49340 TQ	USBLS	5/07
	New York	Y	52660 FQ	61370 MW	77060 TQ	USBLS	5/07
	Albany-Schenectady-Troy MSA, NY	Y	54290 FQ	59380 MW	64500 TQ	USBLS	5/07
	Nassau-Suffolk PMSA, NY	Y	59360 FQ	72420 MW	83150 TQ	USBLS	5/07
	New York-Northern New Jersey-Long Island MSA, NY-NJ-PA	Y	54340 FQ	63140 MW	80290 TQ	USBLS	5/07
	North Carolina	Y	31940 FQ	44380 MW	58980 TQ	USBLS	5/07

AE	Average entry wage	AW	Average wage paid	FQ	First quartile wage
AER	Average entry range	AWR	Average wage range	H	Hourly
AEX	Average experienced wage	AXR	Average experienced range	HI	Highest wage paid
ATC	Average total compensation	D	Daily	HR	High end range

LO	Lowest wage paid	MTC	Median total compensation
LR	Low end range	MW	Median wage paid
M	Monthly	MWR	Median wage range
MCC	Median cash compensation	S	See annotated source

TCC	Total cash compensation
TQ	Third quartile wage
W	Weekly
Y	Yearly

Occupation/Type/Industry	Location	Per	Low	Mid	High	Source	Date
Funeral Director	Charlotte-Gastonia-Concord MSA, NC-SC	Y	38700 FQ	51690 MW	61580 TQ	USBLS	5/07
	Raleigh-Cary MSA, NC	Y	54260 FQ	74410 MW		USBLS	5/07
	North Dakota	Y	40550 FQ	54250 MW	73140 TQ	USBLS	5/07
	Ohio	Y	40050 FQ	53250 MW	68360 TQ	USBLS	5/07
	Cincinnati-Middletown MSA, OH-KY-IN	Y	42740 FQ	53680 MW	71570 TQ	USBLS	5/07
	Cleveland-Elyria-Mentor MSA, OH	Y	43310 FQ	57650 MW	75540 TQ	USBLS	5/07
	Columbus MSA, OH	Y	34670 FQ	38980 MW	62870 TQ	USBLS	5/07
	Dayton MSA, OH	Y	47160 FQ	62430 MW	77590 TQ	USBLS	5/07
	Oklahoma	Y	32440 FQ	45370 MW	61660 TQ	USBLS	5/07
	Oklahoma City MSA, OK	Y	30810 FQ	39840 MW	59590 TQ	USBLS	5/07
	Oregon	H	21.52 FQ	25.43 MW	29.15 TQ	ORBLS	5/08
	Portland-Vancouver-Beaverton MSA, OR-WA	Y	48580 FQ	54510 MW	60940 TQ	USBLS	5/07
	Pennsylvania	Y	41880 FQ	54720 MW	71130 TQ	USBLS	5/07
	Allentown-Bethlehem-Easton MSA, PA-NJ	Y	60650 FQ	74480 MW	110860 TQ	USBLS	5/07
	Philadelphia-Camden-Wilmington MSA, PA-NJ-DE-MD	Y	44240 FQ	53070 MW	65180 TQ	USBLS	5/07
	Pittsburgh MSA, PA	Y	47420 FQ	56170 MW	83660 TQ	USBLS	5/07
	York-Hanover MSA, PA	Y	47830 FQ	76540 MW	100740 TQ	USBLS	5/07
	Rhode Island	Y	58110 FQ	89660 MW	103090 TQ	USBLS	5/07
	Providence-Fall River-Warwick MSA, RI-MA	Y	56680 FQ	87870 MW	103160 TQ	USBLS	5/07
	South Carolina	Y	38670 FQ	48230 MW	74630 TQ	USBLS	5/07
	Charleston-North Charleston MSA, SC	Y	46470 FQ	56700 MW	80240 TQ	USBLS	5/07
	South Dakota	Y	43756 FQ	53384 MW	60535 TQ	SDBLS	7/08-9/08
	Sioux Falls MSA, SD	Y	40406 FQ	48017 MW	61440 TQ	SDBLS	7/08-9/08
	Tennessee	Y	27690 FQ	33900 MW	45620 TQ	USBLS	5/07
	Memphis MSA, TN-MS-AR	Y	30470 FQ	38080 MW	60180 TQ	USBLS	5/07
	Nashville-Davidson-Murfreesboro MSA, TN	Y	28810 FQ	42970 MW	57290 TQ	USBLS	5/07
	Texas	Y	33470 FQ	41080 MW	51480 TQ	USBLS	5/07
	Austin-Round Rock MSA, TX	Y	38580 FQ	45320 MW	52100 TQ	USBLS	5/07
	Dallas-Fort Worth-Arlington MSA, TX	Y	35180 FQ	42030 MW	50100 TQ	USBLS	5/07
	Houston-Sugar Land-Baytown MSA, TX	Y	34010 FQ	38770 MW	50640 TQ	USBLS	5/07
	San Antonio MSA, TX	Y	26370 FQ	31790 MW	37150 TQ	USBLS	5/07
	Utah	Y	53750 FQ	63800 MW	84470 TQ	USBLS	5/07
	Salt Lake City MSA, UT	Y	58760 FQ	77630 MW	90630 TQ	USBLS	5/07
	Vermont	Y	43730 FQ	57200 MW	71620 TQ	USBLS	5/07
	Washington	H	29.31 FQ	42.61 MW	51.35 TQ	WABLS	3/08
	West Virginia	Y	50317 FQ	66828 MW	77367 TQ	WVBLS	7/08-9/08
	Wheeling MSA, WV-OH	Y	44630 FQ	50040 MW	54630 TQ	USBLS	5/07
	Wisconsin	Y	41340 FQ	48260 MW	61680 TQ	USBLS	5/07
	Milwaukee-Waukesha-West Allis MSA, WI	Y	41730 FQ	46250 MW	51380 TQ	USBLS	5/07
	Wyoming	Y	39057 FQ	47566 MW	58134 TQ	WYBLS	9/08
Funeral Home Owner	United States	Y		75737 MW		NFDA	2006
Furnace, Kiln, Oven, Drier, and Kettle Operator and Tender	Alabama	Y	25020 FQ	32100 MW	41400 TQ	USBLS	5/07
	Birmingham-Hoover MSA, AL	Y	25810 FQ	30270 MW	35190 TQ	USBLS	5/07
	Arizona	Y	23460 FQ	27350 MW	30700 TQ	USBLS	5/07
	Phoenix-Mesa-Scottsdale MSA, AZ	Y	24800 FQ	27830 MW	30570 TQ	USBLS	5/07
	Arkansas	Y	26170 FQ	29850 MW	35500 TQ	USBLS	5/07
	California	H	11.26 FQ	13.64 MW	17.55 TQ	CABLS	1/08-3/08
	Los Angeles-Long Beach-Glendale PMSA, CA	H	11.19 FQ	13.79 MW	17.64 TQ	CABLS	1/08-3/08
	Oakland-Fremont-Hayward MSA, CA	H	13.42 FQ	18.49 MW	23.46 TQ	CABLS	1/08-3/08
	Riverside-San Bernardino-Ontario MSA, CA	H	11.79 FQ	13.29 MW	15.60 TQ	CABLS	1/08-3/08
	San Diego-Carlsbad-San Marcos MSA, CA	H	9.19 FQ	10.63 MW	12.84 TQ	CABLS	1/08-3/08

AE	Average entry wage	**AW**	Average wage paid	**FQ**	First quartile wage	**LO**	Lowest wage paid	**MTC**	Median total compensation	**TCC**	Total cash compensation
AER	Average entry range	**AWR**	Average wage range	**H**	Hourly	**LR**	Low end range	**MW**	Median wage paid	**TQ**	Third quartile wage
AEX	Average experienced wage	**AXR**	Average experienced range	**HI**	Highest wage paid	**M**	Monthly	**MWR**	Median wage range	**W**	Weekly
ATC	Average total compensation	**D**	Daily	**HR**	High end range	**MCC**	Median cash compensation	**S**	See annotated source	**Y**	Yearly

Occupation/Type/Industry	Location	Per	Low	Mid	High	Source	Date
Furnace, Kiln, Oven, Drier, and Kettle Operator and Tender							
	San Francisco-San Mateo-Redwood PMSA, CA	H	25.40 FQ	27.47 MW	29.53 TQ	CABLS	1/08-3/08
	San Jose-Sunnyvale-Santa Clara MSA, CA	H	11.76 FQ	13.89 MW	17.56 TQ	CABLS	1/08-3/08
	Santa Ana-Anaheim-Irvine PMSA, CA	Y	22490 FQ	27460 MW	33380 TQ	USBLS	5/07
	Colorado	Y	31680 FQ	37140 MW	42880 TQ	USBLS	5/07
	Denver-Aurora MSA, CO	Y	29920 FQ	35680 MW	42190 TQ	USBLS	5/07
	Connecticut	H	13.52 AE	18.05 MW		CTBLS	1/08-3/08
	Washington-Arlington-Alexandria MSA, DC-VA-MD-WV	Y	26920 FQ	30240 MW	35990 TQ	USBLS	5/07
	Florida	Y	24160 FQ	30590 MW	43580 TQ	USBLS	5/07
	Jacksonville MSA, FL	Y	21140 FQ	23510 MW	45820 TQ	USBLS	5/07
	Miami-Fort Lauderdale-Miami Beach MSA, FL	Y	23560 FQ	28960 MW	38140 TQ	USBLS	5/07
	Tampa-St. Petersburg-Clearwater MSA, FL	Y	21990 FQ	25770 MW	31440 TQ	USBLS	5/07
	Georgia	Y	24260 FQ	28990 MW	34900 TQ	USBLS	5/07
	Atlanta-Sandy Springs-Marietta MSA, GA	Y	27360 FQ	31090 MW	34740 TQ	USBLS	5/07
	Idaho	Y	29010 FQ	33610 MW	37790 TQ	USBLS	5/07
	Illinois	Y	25320 FQ	30730 MW	40200 TQ	USBLS	5/07
	Chicago-Naperville-Joliet MSA, IL-IN-WI	Y	26160 FQ	34800 MW	45120 TQ	USBLS	5/07
	Indiana	Y	24490 FQ	28260 MW	36240 TQ	USBLS	5/07
	Evansville MSA, IN-KY	Y	25700 FQ	30330 MW	35930 TQ	USBLS	5/07
	Gary PMSA, IN	Y	30950 FQ	40890 MW	51330 TQ	USBLS	5/07
	Indianapolis-Carmel MSA, IN	Y	24330 FQ	33810 MW	39290 TQ	USBLS	5/07
	South Bend-Mishawaka MSA, IN-MI	Y	21520 FQ	23000 MW	24410 TQ	USBLS	5/07
	Iowa	Y	26400 FQ	31690 MW	35790 TQ	USBLS	5/07
	Kansas	Y	23270 FQ	28780 MW	41810 TQ	USBLS	5/07
	Kentucky	Y	23385 FQ	29534 MW	38497 TQ	KYBLS	2008
	Louisville-Jefferson County MSA, KY-IN	Y	24370 FQ	28370 MW	36290 TQ	USBLS	5/07
	Louisiana	H	11.93 FQ	17.20 MW	22.31 TQ	LABLS	1/08-3/08
	Baton Rouge MSA, LA	Y	20220 FQ	39300 MW	45900 TQ	USBLS	5/07
	Maine	Y	27670 FQ	32980 MW	37570 TQ	USBLS	5/07
	Maryland	Y		39125 MW		MDBLS	3/08
	Baltimore-Towson MSA, MD	Y	34030 FQ	40030 MW	44060 TQ	USBLS	5/07
	Massachusetts	Y	30500 FQ	36080 MW	42550 TQ	USBLS	5/07
	Worcester MSA, MA-CT	Y	32170 FQ	37370 MW	43780 TQ	USBLS	5/07
	Michigan	Y	27150 FQ	31860 MW	36870 TQ	USBLS	5/07
	Detroit-Warren-Livonia MSA, MI	Y	27340 FQ	33300 MW	37620 TQ	USBLS	5/07
	Grand Rapids-Wyoming MSA, MI	Y	31540 FQ	33900 MW	36250 TQ	USBLS	5/07
	Warren-Troy-Farmington Hills PMSA, MI	Y	29490 FQ	34700 MW	38960 TQ	USBLS	5/07
	Minnesota	Y	35008 FQ	40140 MW	45251 TQ	MNBLS	10/08-12/08
	Duluth-Superior MSA, MN-WI	Y	33204 FQ	41363 MW	47904 TQ	MNBLS	10/08-12/08
	Minneapolis-Saint Paul MSA, MN-WI	Y	34127 FQ	38481 MW	43115 TQ	MNBLS	10/08-12/08
	Mississippi	Y	25180 FQ	29140 MW	35120 TQ	USBLS	5/07
	Missouri	Y	20930 FQ	24580 MW	32160 TQ	USBLS	5/07
	Kansas City MSA, MO-KS	Y	20680 FQ	27740 MW	36360 TQ	USBLS	5/07
	St. Louis MSA, MO-IL	Y	26960 FQ	32780 MW	36760 TQ	USBLS	5/07
	Montana	Y	27060 FQ	33510 MW	39920 TQ	USBLS	5/07
	Nebraska	Y	26450 FQ	31130 MW	41780 TQ	USBLS	5/07
	Omaha-Council Bluffs MSA, NE-IA	Y	26460 FQ	33190 MW	36730 TQ	USBLS	5/07
	Nevada	H	18.04 FQ	19.42 MW	21.40 TQ	NVBLS	5/08
	Las Vegas-Paradise MSA, NV	H	17.61 FQ	19.05 MW	20.63 TQ	NVBLS	5/08
	New Hampshire	H	10.68 AE	13.43 MW	16.12 AEX	NHBLS	6/08
	New Jersey	Y	25520 FQ	32730 MW	40260 TQ	USBLS	5/07
	Camden PMSA, NJ	Y	23170 FQ	30480 MW	40500 TQ	USBLS	5/07
	Edison PMSA, NJ	Y	27550 FQ	38240 MW	43120 TQ	USBLS	5/07
	Newark-Union PMSA, NJ-PA	Y	18370 FQ	22290 MW	29970 TQ	USBLS	5/07
	New York	Y	21790 FQ	31110 MW	38850 TQ	USBLS	5/07

AE Average entry wage	**AW** Average wage paid	**FQ** First quartile wage	**LO** Lowest wage paid	**MTC** Median total compensation	**TCC** Total cash compensation
AER Average entry range	**AWR** Average wage range	**H** Hourly	**LR** Low end range	**MW** Median wage paid	**TQ** Third quartile wage
AEX Average experienced wage	**AXR** Average experienced range	**HI** Highest wage paid	**M** Monthly	**MWR** Median wage range	**W** Weekly
ATC Average total compensation	**D** Daily	**HR** High end range	**MCC** Median cash compensation	**S** See annotated source	**Y** Yearly

Occupation/Type/Industry	Location	Per	Low	Mid	High	Source	Date
Furnace, Kiln, Oven, Drier, and Kettle Operator and Tender	Albany-Schenectady-Troy MSA, NY	Y	33440 FQ	41970 MW	47120 TQ	USBLS	5/07
	Buffalo-Niagara Falls MSA, NY	Y	18400 FQ	22000 MW	29830 TQ	USBLS	5/07
	New York-Northern New Jersey-Long Island MSA, NY-NJ-PA	Y	20220 FQ	24670 MW	38100 TQ	USBLS	5/07
	North Carolina	Y	23560 FQ	30590 MW	37060 TQ	USBLS	5/07
	Charlotte-Gastonia-Concord MSA, NC-SC	Y	25990 FQ	31070 MW	35500 TQ	USBLS	5/07
	North Dakota	Y	23570 FQ	33280 MW	43560 TQ	USBLS	5/07
	Ohio	Y	25140 FQ	31870 MW	40930 TQ	USBLS	5/07
	Cincinnati-Middletown MSA, OH-KY-IN	Y	23440 FQ	26870 MW	31540 TQ	USBLS	5/07
	Cleveland-Elyria-Mentor MSA, OH	Y	22220 FQ	26070 MW	32530 TQ	USBLS	5/07
	Oklahoma	Y	28280 FQ	36710 MW	46930 TQ	USBLS	5/07
	Tulsa MSA, OK	Y	26210 FQ	31280 MW	42710 TQ	USBLS	5/07
	Oregon	H	14.36 FQ	16.97 MW	21.07 TQ	ORBLS	5/08
	Portland-Vancouver-Beaverton MSA, OR-WA	Y	27360 FQ	31020 MW	35880 TQ	USBLS	5/07
	Pennsylvania	Y	25290 FQ	31170 MW	37940 TQ	USBLS	5/07
	Allentown-Bethlehem-Easton MSA, PA-NJ	Y	27180 FQ	31260 MW	36130 TQ	USBLS	5/07
	Philadelphia-Camden-Wilmington MSA, PA-NJ-DE-MD	Y	24020 FQ	30940 MW	36810 TQ	USBLS	5/07
	Pittsburgh MSA, PA	Y	24710 FQ	30590 MW	37800 TQ	USBLS	5/07
	South Carolina	Y	24820 FQ	30770 MW	38140 TQ	USBLS	5/07
	Charleston-North Charleston MSA, SC	Y	42750 FQ	47800 MW	51920 TQ	USBLS	5/07
	Columbia MSA, SC	Y	28890 FQ	37230 MW	42320 TQ	USBLS	5/07
	South Dakota	Y	29451 FQ	34443 MW	40173 TQ	SDBLS	7/08-9/08
	Rapid City MSA, SD	Y	28528 FQ	31727 MW	39615 TQ	SDBLS	7/08-9/08
	Tennessee	Y	24960 FQ	33900 MW	39610 TQ	USBLS	5/07
	Nashville-Davidson-Murfreesboro MSA, TN	Y	35860 FQ	42470 MW	50380 TQ	USBLS	5/07
	Texas	Y	21550 FQ	26470 MW	33660 TQ	USBLS	5/07
	Austin-Round Rock MSA, TX	Y	23010 FQ	31860 MW	41680 TQ	USBLS	5/07
	Dallas-Fort Worth-Arlington MSA, TX	Y	20240 FQ	24750 MW	30900 TQ	USBLS	5/07
	El Paso MSA, TX	Y	20580 FQ	27520 MW	33170 TQ	USBLS	5/07
	Houston-Sugar Land-Baytown MSA, TX	Y	18800 FQ	23930 MW	30360 TQ	USBLS	5/07
	San Antonio MSA, TX	Y	22270 FQ	24810 MW	31220 TQ	USBLS	5/07
	Utah	Y	29270 FQ	33840 MW	39270 TQ	USBLS	5/07
	Salt Lake City MSA, UT	Y	32050 FQ	38460 MW	43180 TQ	USBLS	5/07
	Vermont	Y	23340 FQ	28420 MW	34890 TQ	USBLS	5/07
	Virginia	Y	23480 FQ	27010 MW	32990 TQ	USBLS	5/07
	Richmond MSA, VA	Y	18430 FQ	23320 MW	44150 TQ	USBLS	5/07
	Virginia Beach-Norfolk-Newport News MSA, VA-NC	Y	18140 FQ	24070 MW	31480 TQ	USBLS	5/07
	Washington	H	15.51 FQ	18.24 MW	21.28 TQ	WABLS	3/08
	Seattle-Tacoma-Bellevue MSA, WA	Y	33600 FQ	39210 MW	45620 TQ	USBLS	5/07
	West Virginia	Y	22963 FQ	28084 MW	35568 TQ	WVBLS	7/08-9/08
	Wisconsin	Y	22000 FQ	30560 MW	42360 TQ	USBLS	5/07
	Milwaukee-Waukesha-West Allis MSA, WI	Y	14610 FQ	18650 MW	26170 TQ	USBLS	5/07
	Wyoming	Y	35136 FQ	40331 MW	64111 TQ	WYBLS	9/08
Furniture Finisher	Alabama	Y	20340 FQ	23250 MW	27260 TQ	USBLS	5/07
	Arizona	Y	20780 FQ	29120 MW	37590 TQ	USBLS	5/07
	Phoenix-Mesa-Scottsdale MSA, AZ	Y	21100 FQ	29560 MW	38190 TQ	USBLS	5/07
	Prescott MSA, AZ	Y	21370 FQ	30810 MW	37330 TQ	USBLS	5/07
	Arkansas	Y	19650 FQ	22170 MW	24690 TQ	USBLS	5/07
	Little Rock-North Little Rock MSA, AR	Y	18890 FQ	21730 MW	23750 TQ	USBLS	5/07
	California	H	8.98 FQ	11.00 MW	15.13 TQ	CABLS	1/08-3/08

AE	Average entry wage	**AW**	Average wage paid	**FQ**	First quartile wage	**LO**	Lowest wage paid	**MTC**	Median total compensation	**TCC** Total cash compensation
AER	Average entry range	**AWR**	Average wage range	**H**	Hourly	**LR**	Low end range	**MW**	Median wage paid	**TQ** Third quartile wage
AEX	Average experienced wage	**AXR**	Average experienced range	**HI**	Highest wage paid	**M**	Monthly	**MWR**	Median wage range	**W** Weekly
ATC	Average total compensation	**D**	Daily	**HR**	High end range	**MCC**	Median cash compensation	**S**	See annotated source	**Y** Yearly

Occupation/Type/Industry	Location	Per	Low	Mid	High	Source	Date
Furniture Finisher	Los Angeles-Long Beach-Glendale PMSA, CA	H	8.81 FQ	10.85 MW	14.32 TQ	CABLS	1/08-3/08
	Modesto MSA, CA	H	10.69 FQ	11.58 MW	12.80 TQ	CABLS	1/08-3/08
	Oakland-Fremont-Hayward MSA, CA	H	10.01 FQ	12.97 MW	17.03 TQ	CABLS	1/08-3/08
	Riverside-San Bernardino-Ontario MSA, CA	H	8.58 FQ	9.68 MW	11.72 TQ	CABLS	1/08-3/08
	Sacramento-Arden Arcade-Roseville MSA, CA	H	11.82 FQ	15.29 MW	19.03 TQ	CABLS	1/08-3/08
	San Diego-Carlsbad-San Marcos MSA, CA	H	10.07 FQ	12.97 MW	17.62 TQ	CABLS	1/08-3/08
	San Francisco-San Mateo-Redwood PMSA, CA	H	11.60 FQ	14.99 MW	18.29 TQ	CABLS	1/08-3/08
	San Jose-Sunnyvale-Santa Clara MSA, CA	H	16.65 FQ	18.34 MW	20.32 TQ	CABLS	1/08-3/08
	Santa Ana-Anaheim-Irvine PMSA, CA	Y	17780 FQ	19570 MW	23110 TQ	USBLS	5/07
	Colorado	Y	22680 FQ	29310 MW	35710 TQ	USBLS	5/07
	Denver-Aurora MSA, CO	Y	22190 FQ	28850 MW	35000 TQ	USBLS	5/07
	Connecticut	H	11.38 AE	15.94 MW		CTBLS	1/08-3/08
	Hartford-West Hartford-East Hartford MSA, CT	Y	25930 FQ	31400 MW	37510 TQ	USBLS	5/07
	Washington-Arlington-Alexandria MSA, DC-VA-MD-WV	Y	29690 FQ	36830 MW	45100 TQ	USBLS	5/07
	Florida	Y	20840 FQ	25390 MW	34690 TQ	USBLS	5/07
	Fort Lauderdale-Pompano Beach-Deerfield Beach PMSA, FL	Y	26180 FQ	33160 MW	42520 TQ	USBLS	5/07
	Jacksonville MSA, FL	Y	22880 FQ	27240 MW	31970 TQ	USBLS	5/07
	Miami-Fort Lauderdale-Miami Beach MSA, FL	Y	22090 FQ	30340 MW	36590 TQ	USBLS	5/07
	Orlando-Kissimmee MSA, FL	Y	16890 FQ	19120 MW	28680 TQ	USBLS	5/07
	Tampa-St. Petersburg-Clearwater MSA, FL	Y	19070 FQ	21680 MW	36250 TQ	USBLS	5/07
	West Palm Beach-Boca Raton-Boynton Beach PMSA, FL	Y	25910 FQ	34910 MW	40280 TQ	USBLS	5/07
	Georgia	Y	19630 FQ	25530 MW	30580 TQ	USBLS	5/07
	Atlanta-Sandy Springs-Marietta MSA, GA	Y	25340 FQ	28740 MW	32110 TQ	USBLS	5/07
	Idaho	Y	20140 FQ	24040 MW	29320 TQ	USBLS	5/07
	Boise City-Nampa MSA, ID	Y	20600 FQ	24410 MW	29650 TQ	USBLS	5/07
	Illinois	Y	25500 FQ	33240 MW	46470 TQ	USBLS	5/07
	Chicago-Naperville-Joliet MSA, IL-IN-WI	Y	26160 FQ	35390 MW	48930 TQ	USBLS	5/07
	Indiana	Y	22290 FQ	25900 MW	29300 TQ	USBLS	5/07
	Indianapolis-Carmel MSA, IN	Y	21830 FQ	25750 MW	29670 TQ	USBLS	5/07
	Iowa	Y	19830 FQ	25500 MW	29110 TQ	USBLS	5/07
	Kansas	Y	21290 FQ	26740 MW	32170 TQ	USBLS	5/07
	Kentucky	Y	19037 FQ	27371 MW	35685 TQ	KYBLS	2008
	Louisville-Jefferson County MSA, KY-IN	Y	18110 FQ	26560 MW	29490 TQ	USBLS	5/07
	Louisiana	H	10.35 FQ	11.69 MW	13.64 TQ	LABLS	1/08-3/08
	Maine	Y	25830 FQ	28550 MW	31370 TQ	USBLS	5/07
	Maryland	Y		30900 MW		MDBLS	3/08
	Baltimore-Towson MSA, MD	Y	21520 FQ	25230 MW	32010 TQ	USBLS	5/07
	Bethesda-Gaithersburg-Frederick PMSA, MD	Y	34930 FQ	42430 MW	46960 TQ	USBLS	5/07
	Hagerstown-Martinsburg MSA, MD-WV	Y	21580 FQ	23460 MW	25670 TQ	USBLS	5/07
	Massachusetts	Y	25330 FQ	29320 MW	37630 TQ	USBLS	5/07
	Boston-Cambridge-Quincy NECTA, MA	Y	28670 FQ	34860 MW	42430 TQ	USBLS	5/07
	Michigan	Y	23110 FQ	29050 MW	35460 TQ	USBLS	5/07
	Detroit-Warren-Livonia MSA, MI	Y	29740 FQ	37340 MW	50480 TQ	USBLS	5/07
	Warren-Troy-Farmington Hills PMSA, MI	Y	33040 FQ	40530 MW	53590 TQ	USBLS	5/07
	Minnesota	Y	26932 FQ	30302 MW	36501 TQ	MNBLS	10/08-12/08
	Minneapolis-Saint Paul MSA, MN-WI	Y	27979 FQ	32282 MW	40679 TQ	MNBLS	10/08-12/08
	Mississippi	Y	19490 FQ	23870 MW	30270 TQ	USBLS	5/07

Furniture Finisher

Occupation/Type/Industry	Location	Per	Low	Mid	High	Source	Date
Furniture Finisher	Missouri	Y	20890 FQ	24980 MW	34900 TQ	USBLS	5/07
	Kansas City MSA, MO-KS	Y	20610 FQ	23200 MW	27790 TQ	USBLS	5/07
	St. Louis MSA, MO-IL	Y	29160 FQ	35070 MW	39650 TQ	USBLS	5/07
	Montana	Y	20730 FQ	25580 MW	30980 TQ	USBLS	5/07
	Nevada	H	11.55 FQ	13.58 MW	15.36 TQ	NVBLS	5/08
	Las Vegas-Paradise MSA, NV	H	9.43 FQ	12.36 MW	14.38 TQ	NVBLS	5/08
	New Hampshire	H	11.05 AE	14.38 MW	16.93 AEX	NHBLS	6/08
	Nashua NECTA, NH-MA	Y	25880 FQ	30020 MW	34570 TQ	USBLS	5/07
	New Jersey	Y	24660 FQ	31460 MW	39230 TQ	USBLS	5/07
	Edison PMSA, NJ	Y	22810 FQ	28240 MW	40850 TQ	USBLS	5/07
	Newark-Union PMSA, NJ-PA	Y	24260 FQ	31730 MW	39270 TQ	USBLS	5/07
	New York	Y	20300 FQ	26980 MW	36950 TQ	USBLS	5/07
	Nassau-Suffolk PMSA, NY	Y	27290 FQ	36100 MW	44050 TQ	USBLS	5/07
	New York-Northern New Jersey-Long Island MSA, NY-NJ-PA	Y	24140 FQ	32920 MW	42840 TQ	USBLS	5/07
	North Carolina	Y	21350 FQ	25050 MW	29310 TQ	USBLS	5/07
	Charlotte-Gastonia-Concord MSA, NC-SC	Y	19890 FQ	24630 MW	29420 TQ	USBLS	5/07
	Ohio	Y	19000 FQ	23830 MW	30090 TQ	USBLS	5/07
	Cincinnati-Middletown MSA, OH-KY-IN	Y	27070 FQ	32210 MW	37110 TQ	USBLS	5/07
	Cleveland-Elyria-Mentor MSA, OH	Y	18290 FQ	22840 MW	34340 TQ	USBLS	5/07
	Columbus MSA, OH	Y	22480 FQ	26470 MW	33190 TQ	USBLS	5/07
	Oklahoma	Y	17440 FQ	20770 MW	26430 TQ	USBLS	5/07
	Oklahoma City MSA, OK	Y	17560 FQ	20660 MW	26860 TQ	USBLS	5/07
	Oregon	H	11.85 FQ	14.22 MW	18.67 TQ	ORBLS	5/08
	Portland-Vancouver-Beaverton MSA, OR-WA	Y	29040 FQ	36060 MW	42420 TQ	USBLS	5/07
	Pennsylvania	Y	22850 FQ	28170 MW	34530 TQ	USBLS	5/07
	Allentown-Bethlehem-Easton MSA, PA-NJ	Y	22820 FQ	26510 MW	29760 TQ	USBLS	5/07
	Philadelphia-Camden-Wilmington MSA, PA-NJ-DE-MD	Y	37590 FQ	53090 MW	59400 TQ	USBLS	5/07
	Pittsburgh MSA, PA	Y	21180 FQ	26460 MW	38410 TQ	USBLS	5/07
	Rhode Island	Y	21680 FQ	24130 MW	31220 TQ	USBLS	5/07
	Providence-Fall River-Warwick MSA, RI-MA	Y	22720 FQ	25660 MW	32790 TQ	USBLS	5/07
	South Carolina	Y	22670 FQ	26730 MW	30700 TQ	USBLS	5/07
	Charleston-North Charleston MSA, SC	Y	22840 FQ	27250 MW	31300 TQ	USBLS	5/07
	Columbia MSA, SC	Y	26050 FQ	28670 MW	31470 TQ	USBLS	5/07
	South Dakota	Y	20169 FQ	23898 MW	28331 TQ	SDBLS	7/08-9/08
	Tennessee	Y	20240 FQ	26890 MW	32900 TQ	USBLS	5/07
	Memphis MSA, TN-MS-AR	Y	28230 FQ	32980 MW	40570 TQ	USBLS	5/07
	Nashville-Davidson-Murfreesboro MSA, TN	Y	27540 FQ	30830 MW	37970 TQ	USBLS	5/07
	Texas	Y	18820 FQ	23060 MW	28850 TQ	USBLS	5/07
	Dallas-Fort Worth-Arlington MSA, TX	Y	19190 FQ	22960 MW	29390 TQ	USBLS	5/07
	Houston-Sugar Land-Baytown MSA, TX	Y	22440 FQ	27030 MW	30130 TQ	USBLS	5/07
	San Antonio MSA, TX	Y	16330 FQ	20950 MW	27800 TQ	USBLS	5/07
	Utah	Y	24530 FQ	31640 MW	40650 TQ	USBLS	5/07
	Salt Lake City MSA, UT	Y	31320 FQ	38500 MW	58530 TQ	USBLS	5/07
	Vermont	Y	24510 FQ	27550 MW	30350 TQ	USBLS	5/07
	Virginia	Y	19830 FQ	23910 MW	29680 TQ	USBLS	5/07
	Richmond MSA, VA	Y	19880 FQ	22120 MW	30920 TQ	USBLS	5/07
	Virginia Beach-Norfolk-Newport News MSA, VA-NC	Y	19160 FQ	22610 MW	26100 TQ	USBLS	5/07
	Washington	H	11.77 FQ	14.38 MW	18.22 TQ	WABLS	3/08
	Seattle-Tacoma-Bellevue MSA, WA	Y	24840 FQ	31490 MW	40360 TQ	USBLS	5/07
	West Virginia	Y	15911 FQ	22932 MW	25680 TQ	WVBLS	7/08-9/08
	Wisconsin	Y	21860 FQ	27220 MW	34050 TQ	USBLS	5/07
	Milwaukee-Waukesha-West Allis MSA, WI	Y	29010 FQ	35820 MW	43860 TQ	USBLS	5/07
	Wyoming	Y	22409 FQ	25705 MW	29998 TQ	WYBLS	9/08
	Puerto Rico	Y	12440 FQ	13800 MW	15240 TQ	USBLS	5/07

AE	Average entry wage	AW	Average wage paid	FQ	First quartile wage
AER	Average entry range	AWR	Average wage range	H	Hourly
AEX	Average experienced wage	AXR	Average experienced range	HI	Highest wage paid
ATC	Average total compensation	D	Daily	HR	High end range

LO Lowest wage paid
LR Low end range
M Monthly
MCC Median cash compensation

MTC Median total compensation
MW Median wage paid
MWR Median wage range
S See annotated source

TCC Total cash compensation
TQ Third quartile wage
W Weekly
Y Yearly

Occupation/Type/Industry	Location	Per	Low	Mid	High	Source	Date
Furniture Finisher	San Juan-Caguas-Guaynabo MSA, PR	Y	12500 FQ	13950 MW	15450 TQ	USBLS	5/07
Furniture Salesperson	United States	Y		25000-50000 MWR		FURNT	2007
Games Analyst							
State Lottery	Tennessee	Y			37380 HI	THETN	2008
Games and Quality Assurance Manager							
State Lottery	Tennessee	Y			58610 HI	THETN	2008
Games Manager							
Lottery Commission	New Hampshire	Y			51159 HI	NHUL03	2008
Gaming and Sports Book Writer and Runner	Alabama	Y	20440 FQ	24410 MW	28410 TQ	USBLS	5/07
	Arizona	Y	16710 FQ	19960 MW	23120 TQ	USBLS	5/07
	California	H	9.81 FQ	14.68 MW	20.57 TQ	CABLS	1/08-3/08
	Colorado	Y	18420 FQ	21330 MW	25370 TQ	USBLS	5/07
	Connecticut	H	8.36 AE	10.09 MW		CTBLS	1/08-3/08
	Delaware	Y	22380 FQ	28170 MW	43190 TQ	USBLS	5/07
	Florida	Y	15870 FQ	19930 MW	26170 TQ	USBLS	5/07
	Illinois	Y	25740 FQ	34580 MW	38200 TQ	USBLS	5/07
	Indiana	Y	17180 FQ	23850 MW	28070 TQ	USBLS	5/07
	Iowa	Y	19870 FQ	25410 MW	29850 TQ	USBLS	5/07
	Kentucky	Y	34162 FQ	36887 MW	39611 TQ	KYBLS	2008
	Louisiana	H	6.45 FQ	7.66 MW	9.03 TQ	LABLS	1/08-3/08
	Maine	Y	15770 FQ	17330 MW	19720 TQ	USBLS	5/07
	Massachusetts	Y	19000 FQ	26320 MW	39200 TQ	USBLS	5/07
	Michigan	Y	17580 FQ	23580 MW	39900 TQ	USBLS	5/07
	Minnesota	Y	15673 FQ	20535 MW	25595 TQ	MNBLS	10/08-12/08
	Mississippi	Y	13360 FQ	15690 MW	20660 TQ	USBLS	5/07
	Montana	Y	13970 FQ	15120 MW	16160 TQ	USBLS	5/07
	Nebraska	Y	15780 FQ	17990 MW	20440 TQ	USBLS	5/07
	New Mexico	Y	13470 FQ	15730 MW	18000 TQ	USBLS	5/07
	North Carolina	Y	13670 FQ	14550 MW	15450 TQ	USBLS	5/07
	North Dakota	Y	15420 FQ	19370 MW	24580 TQ	USBLS	5/07
	Oklahoma	Y	13900 FQ	17430 MW	22220 TQ	USBLS	5/07
	Oregon	H	8.79 FQ	9.55 MW	11.91 TQ	ORBLS	5/08
	Pennsylvania	Y	14640 FQ	16060 MW	18600 TQ	USBLS	5/07
	South Carolina	Y	15940 FQ	17450 MW	18970 TQ	USBLS	5/07
	South Dakota	Y	17455 FQ	19089 MW	21294 TQ	SDBLS	7/08-9/08
	Texas	Y	14120 FQ	18420 MW	23800 TQ	USBLS	5/07
	Washington	H	8.77 FQ	9.84 MW	11.70 TQ	WABLS	3/08
	West Virginia	Y	14496 FQ	16138 MW	23209 TQ	WVBLS	7/08-9/08
	Wisconsin	Y	17660 FQ	20830 MW	25390 TQ	USBLS	5/07
Gaming Cage Worker	Alabama	Y	18170 FQ	19950 MW	25120 TQ	USBLS	5/07
	Arizona	Y	20450 FQ	23190 MW	26930 TQ	USBLS	5/07
	California	H	10.39 FQ	12.26 MW	14.60 TQ	CABLS	1/08-3/08
	Colorado	Y	22880 FQ	26950 MW	31080 TQ	USBLS	5/07
	Florida	Y	19300 FQ	21950 MW	24470 TQ	USBLS	5/07
	Illinois	Y	21540 FQ	25140 MW	30570 TQ	USBLS	5/07
	Indiana	Y	20860 FQ	23400 MW	26770 TQ	USBLS	5/07
	Iowa	Y	17860 FQ	19870 MW	23550 TQ	USBLS	5/07
	Kansas	Y	18710 FQ	21220 MW	25180 TQ	USBLS	5/07
	Louisiana	H	9.77 FQ	10.83 MW	12.00 TQ	LABLS	1/08-3/08
	Michigan	Y	20830 FQ	25250 MW	35000 TQ	USBLS	5/07
	Minnesota	Y	19920 FQ	25104 MW	34283 TQ	MNBLS	10/08-12/08
	Mississippi	Y	20870 FQ	23440 MW	28400 TQ	USBLS	5/07
	Missouri	Y	20860 FQ	23360 MW	26680 TQ	USBLS	5/07
	Montana	Y	14270 FQ	15870 MW	25890 TQ	USBLS	5/07
	Nevada	H	10.27 FQ	12.45 MW	15.09 TQ	NVBLS	5/08
	New Mexico	Y	18090 FQ	21340 MW	24650 TQ	USBLS	5/07
	New York	Y	20580 FQ	22090 MW	23590 TQ	USBLS	5/07
	North Dakota	Y	17510 FQ	19290 MW	22890 TQ	USBLS	5/07
	Oklahoma	Y	16590 FQ	19860 MW	24100 TQ	USBLS	5/07
	Oregon	H	10.59 FQ	11.92 MW	13.67 TQ	ORBLS	5/08
	Pennsylvania	Y	17930 FQ	22040 MW	35210 TQ	USBLS	5/07
	South Dakota	Y	17746 FQ	19238 MW	21033 TQ	SDBLS	7/08-9/08

AE Average entry wage	**AW** Average wage paid	**FQ** First quartile wage	**LO** Lowest wage paid	**MTC** Median total compensation	**TCC** Total cash compensation
AER Average entry range	**AWR** Average wage range	**H** Hourly	**LR** Low end range	**MW** Median wage paid	**TQ** Third quartile wage
AEX Average experienced wage	**AXR** Average experienced range	**HI** Highest wage paid	**M** Monthly	**MWR** Median wage range	**W** Weekly
ATC Average total compensation	**D** Daily	**HR** High end range	**MCC** Median cash compensation	**S** See annotated source	**Y** Yearly

Occupation/Type/Industry	Location	Per	Low	Mid	High	Source	Date
Gaming Cage Worker	Texas	Y	20230 FQ	22750 MW	25100 TQ	USBLS	5/07
	Washington	H	9.82 FQ	11.22 MW	13.56 TQ	WABLS	3/08
	Wisconsin	Y	20910 FQ	23560 MW	27840 TQ	USBLS	5/07
	Puerto Rico	Y	14680 FQ	18920 MW	26680 TQ	USBLS	5/07
Gaming Change Person and Booth Cashier	Alabama	Y	16790 FQ	19090 MW	22440 TQ	USBLS	5/07
	Alaska	Y	15570 FQ	18290 MW	21970 TQ	USBLS	5/07
	Arizona	Y	16850 FQ	18520 MW	21520 TQ	USBLS	5/07
	California	H	8.86 FQ	10.33 MW	11.91 TQ	CABLS	1/08-3/08
	Colorado	Y	19450 FQ	24840 MW	31090 TQ	USBLS	5/07
	Delaware	Y	14830 FQ	18290 MW	22170 TQ	USBLS	5/07
	Florida	Y	17180 FQ	20500 MW	24230 TQ	USBLS	5/07
	Illinois	Y	18970 FQ	21920 MW	25980 TQ	USBLS	5/07
	Indiana	Y	19840 FQ	23150 MW	27760 TQ	USBLS	5/07
	Iowa	Y	18610 FQ	21400 MW	24800 TQ	USBLS	5/07
	Kansas	Y	18290 FQ	21350 MW	23530 TQ	USBLS	5/07
	Louisiana	H	8.45 FQ	10.06 MW	11.84 TQ	LABLS	1/08-3/08
	Michigan	Y	20090 FQ	25700 MW	31210 TQ	USBLS	5/07
	Minnesota	Y	19473 FQ	22024 MW	24067 TQ	MNBLS	10/08-12/08
	Mississippi	Y	19300 FQ	22290 MW	25500 TQ	USBLS	5/07
	Missouri	Y	19930 FQ	25900 MW	29020 TQ	USBLS	5/07
	Montana	Y	14330 FQ	16500 MW	19740 TQ	USBLS	5/07
	Nebraska	Y	15850 FQ	16990 MW	18110 TQ	USBLS	5/07
	Nevada	H	8.22 FQ	11.37 MW	14.15 TQ	NVBLS	5/08
	New Jersey	Y	20250 FQ	25660 MW	30760 TQ	USBLS	5/07
	New Mexico	Y	16400 FQ	17930 MW	20120 TQ	USBLS	5/07
	New York	Y	19980 FQ	22060 MW	24170 TQ	USBLS	5/07
	North Dakota	Y	17570 FQ	21260 MW	24190 TQ	USBLS	5/07
	Ohio	Y	21750 FQ	26780 MW	30100 TQ	USBLS	5/07
	Oklahoma	Y	15480 FQ	17670 MW	19950 TQ	USBLS	5/07
	Oregon	H	9.03 FQ	10.03 MW	11.36 TQ	ORBLS	5/08
	Pennsylvania	Y	16010 FQ	18590 MW	23710 TQ	USBLS	5/07
	South Carolina	Y	14970 FQ	19340 MW	22410 TQ	USBLS	5/07
	South Dakota	Y	17210 FQ	18955 MW	21474 TQ	SDBLS	7/08-9/08
	Washington	H	8.85 FQ	9.91 MW	11.51 TQ	WABLS	3/08
	West Virginia	Y	15268 FQ	17724 MW	21623 TQ	WVBLS	7/08-9/08
	Wisconsin	Y	16930 FQ	19070 MW	22060 TQ	USBLS	5/07
	Puerto Rico	Y	13330 FQ	15570 MW	19930 TQ	USBLS	5/07
Gaming Dealer	Alaska	Y	26150 FQ	29510 MW	33060 TQ	USBLS	5/07
	Arizona	Y	14470 FQ	14890 MW	20860 TQ	USBLS	5/07
	California	H	8.15 FQ	8.97 MW	10.82 TQ	CABLS	1/08-3/08
	Colorado	Y	14670 FQ	15180 MW	17760 TQ	USBLS	5/07
	Florida	Y	14630 FQ	15530 MW	21780 TQ	USBLS	5/07
	Idaho	Y	13080 FQ	15170 MW	19190 TQ	USBLS	5/07
	Illinois	Y	14870 FQ	17180 MW	23500 TQ	USBLS	5/07
	Indiana	Y	12440 FQ	13850 MW	15300 TQ	USBLS	5/07
	Iowa	Y	13970 FQ	15050 MW	21740 TQ	USBLS	5/07
	Kansas	Y	14400 FQ	27670 MW	37830 TQ	USBLS	5/07
	Louisiana	H	6.03 FQ	6.71 MW	7.41 TQ	LABLS	1/08-3/08
	Maryland	Y		31650 MW		MDBLS	3/08
	Michigan	Y	15400 FQ	17180 MW	22260 TQ	USBLS	5/07
	Mississippi	Y	12840 FQ	14340 MW	17350 TQ	USBLS	5/07
	Missouri	Y	14200 FQ	14890 MW	15850 TQ	USBLS	5/07
	Montana	Y	15400 FQ	17990 MW	21070 TQ	USBLS	5/07
	New Mexico	Y	12480 FQ	13780 MW	15120 TQ	USBLS	5/07
	New York	Y	15040 FQ	15380 MW	17440 TQ	USBLS	5/07
	North Dakota	Y	13430 FQ	15700 MW	18640 TQ	USBLS	5/07
	Oklahoma	Y	13830 FQ	16220 MW	18920 TQ	USBLS	5/07
	Oregon	H	9.09 FQ	10.53 MW	12.03 TQ	ORBLS	5/08
	South Carolina	Y	13580 FQ	21710 MW	28750 TQ	USBLS	5/07
	South Dakota	Y	20136 FQ	23697 MW	28020 TQ	SDBLS	7/08-9/08
	Texas	Y	16790 FQ	19260 MW	21540 TQ	USBLS	5/07
	Washington	H	11.16 FQ	14.01 MW	16.62 TQ	WABLS	3/08
	Wisconsin	Y	14930 FQ	16820 MW	20260 TQ	USBLS	5/07
	Puerto Rico	Y	12550 FQ	13800 MW	15150 TQ	USBLS	5/07
Gaming Enforcement Investigator Racing and Charitable Gaming Commission	New Hampshire	Y		61655 AW		NHUL03	2008

AE	Average entry wage	AW	Average wage paid	FQ	First quartile wage
AER	Average entry range	AWR	Average wage range	H	Hourly
AEX	Average experienced wage	AXR	Average experienced range	HI	Highest wage paid
ATC	Average total compensation	D	Daily	HR	High end range

LO	Lowest wage paid	MTC	Median total compensation	TCC	Total cash compensation
LR	Low end range	MW	Median wage paid	TQ	Third quartile wage
M	Monthly	MWR	Median wage range	W	Weekly
MCC	Median cash compensation	S	See annotated source	Y	Yearly

Occupation/Type/Industry	Location	Per	Low	Mid	High	Source	Date
Gaming Manager	Arizona	Y	47300 FQ	64070 MW	82350 TQ	USBLS	5/07
	California	H	31.56 FQ	37.89 MW	45.86 TQ	CABLS	1/08-3/08
	Florida	Y	52310 FQ	60540 MW	75310 TQ	USBLS	5/07
	Idaho	Y	37350 FQ	47220 MW	65620 TQ	USBLS	5/07
	Illinois	Y	51460 FQ	63000 MW	78970 TQ	USBLS	5/07
	Indiana	Y	54650 FQ	63790 MW	79960 TQ	USBLS	5/07
	Iowa	Y	46490 FQ	56320 MW	65670 TQ	USBLS	5/07
	Louisiana	H	25.64 FQ	32.44 MW	43.01 TQ	LABLS	1/08-3/08
	Michigan	Y	66840 FQ	73840 MW	81530 TQ	USBLS	5/07
	Minnesota	Y	42342 FQ	60015 MW	75748 TQ	MNBLS	10/08-12/08
	Mississippi	Y	64140 FQ	78270 MW	93810 TQ	USBLS	5/07
	Missouri	Y	44680 FQ	55430 MW	70340 TQ	USBLS	5/07
	Montana	Y	30750 FQ	33460 MW	36820 TQ	USBLS	5/07
	Nevada	H	27.76 FQ	36.86 MW	48.40 TQ	NVBLS	5/08
	New Mexico	Y	52700 FQ	59880 MW	68280 TQ	USBLS	5/07
	New York	Y	54020 FQ	61780 MW	73000 TQ	USBLS	5/07
	Oklahoma	Y	34470 FQ	43800 MW	57150 TQ	USBLS	5/07
	Oregon	H	24.50 FQ	30.23 MW	36.12 TQ	ORBLS	5/08
	South Dakota	Y	48692 FQ	59027 MW	69175 TQ	SDBLS	7/08-9/08
	Washington	H	25.99 FQ	32.37 MW	39.80 TQ	WABLS	3/08
	Puerto Rico	Y	31540 FQ	40790 MW	70510 TQ	USBLS	5/07
Gaming Supervisor	Alabama	Y	28740 FQ	33010 MW	46760 TQ	USBLS	5/07
	Alaska	Y	38360 FQ	46180 MW	51800 TQ	USBLS	5/07
	Arizona	Y	33940 FQ	40280 MW	47110 TQ	USBLS	5/07
	California	H	18.08 FQ	22.83 MW	29.20 TQ	CABLS	1/08-3/08
	Colorado	Y	35220 FQ	43610 MW	52870 TQ	USBLS	5/07
	Florida	Y	40290 FQ	45190 MW	50730 TQ	USBLS	5/07
	Illinois	Y	38030 FQ	53500 MW	69240 TQ	USBLS	5/07
	Indiana	Y	40960 FQ	46880 MW	56740 TQ	USBLS	5/07
	Iowa	Y	36660 FQ	42800 MW	49430 TQ	USBLS	5/07
	Kansas	Y	33520 FQ	38130 MW	44940 TQ	USBLS	5/07
	Kentucky	Y	31968 FQ	46289 MW	51596 TQ	KYBLS	2008
	Louisiana	H	17.93 FQ	21.44 MW	24.17 TQ	LABLS	1/08-3/08
	Michigan	Y	37930 FQ	53730 MW	70150 TQ	USBLS	5/07
	Minnesota	Y	29642 FQ	36511 MW	45744 TQ	MNBLS	10/08-12/08
	Mississippi	Y	35600 FQ	42750 MW	48960 TQ	USBLS	5/07
	Missouri	Y	34850 FQ	40930 MW	47490 TQ	USBLS	5/07
	Montana	Y	20460 FQ	22790 MW	25090 TQ	USBLS	5/07
	Nebraska	Y	24930 FQ	30970 MW	43140 TQ	USBLS	5/07
	New Jersey	Y	35120 FQ	44800 MW	56030 TQ	USBLS	5/07
	New Mexico	Y	23160 FQ	32820 MW	40680 TQ	USBLS	5/07
	New York	Y	34290 FQ	39740 MW	46710 TQ	USBLS	5/07
	North Dakota	Y	21690 FQ	25560 MW	34610 TQ	USBLS	5/07
	Oklahoma	Y	29220 FQ	37060 MW	46130 TQ	USBLS	5/07
	Oregon	H	18.82 FQ	21.75 MW	24.83 TQ	ORBLS	5/08
	South Carolina	Y	15640 FQ	22040 MW	24570 TQ	USBLS	5/07
	South Dakota	Y	28040 FQ	30841 MW	34596 TQ	SDBLS	7/08-9/08
	Texas	Y	23830 FQ	36360 MW	44860 TQ	USBLS	5/07
	Washington	H	18.20 FQ	20.83 MW	24.15 TQ	WABLS	3/08
	West Virginia	Y	27905 FQ	35439 MW	45140 TQ	WVBLS	7/08-9/08
	Puerto Rico	Y	24040 FQ	28840 MW	40350 TQ	USBLS	5/07
Gaming Surveillance Officer and Gaming Investigator	Alabama	Y	19600 FQ	23110 MW	27840 TQ	USBLS	5/07
	Arizona	Y	22950 FQ	27390 MW	35550 TQ	USBLS	5/07
	California	H	11.79 FQ	15.55 MW	21.34 TQ	CABLS	1/08-3/08
	Colorado	Y	28730 FQ	33030 MW	37470 TQ	USBLS	5/07
	Connecticut	H	10.61 AE	14.95 MW		CTBLS	1/08-3/08
	Delaware	Y	23210 FQ	26110 MW	30400 TQ	USBLS	5/07
	Florida	Y	20320 FQ	23270 MW	29910 TQ	USBLS	5/07
	Illinois	Y	17220 FQ	23230 MW	31530 TQ	USBLS	5/07
	Indiana	Y	23880 FQ	34830 MW	44910 TQ	USBLS	5/07
	Iowa	Y	21310 FQ	24900 MW	30160 TQ	USBLS	5/07
	Louisiana	H	9.19 FQ	12.02 MW	16.52 TQ	LABLS	1/08-3/08
	Michigan	Y	24770 FQ	31550 MW	38380 TQ	USBLS	5/07
	Minnesota	Y	20085 FQ	24393 MW	30332 TQ	MNBLS	10/08-12/08
	Mississippi	Y	25070 FQ	30170 MW	36460 TQ	USBLS	5/07
	Missouri	Y	21580 FQ	26700 MW	31720 TQ	USBLS	5/07
	Nevada	H	14.05 FQ	16.85 MW	19.24 TQ	NVBLS	5/08
	New Mexico	Y	20930 FQ	25500 MW	32750 TQ	USBLS	5/07
	New York	Y	21600 FQ	23530 MW	27620 TQ	USBLS	5/07

AE	Average entry wage	AW	Average wage paid	FQ	First quartile wage	LO	Lowest wage paid	MTC	Median total compensation	TCC	Total cash compensation
AER	Average entry range	AWR	Average wage range	H	Hourly	LR	Low end range	MW	Median wage paid	TQ	Third quartile wage
AEX	Average experienced wage	AXR	Average experienced range	HI	Highest wage paid	M	Monthly	MWR	Median wage range	W	Weekly
ATC	Average total compensation	D	Daily	HR	High end range	MCC	Median cash compensation	S	See annotated source	Y	Yearly

710

Occupation/Type/Industry	Location	Per	Low	Mid	High	Source	Date
Gaming Surveillance Officer and Gaming Investigator	Oklahoma	Y	19620 FQ	22180 MW	24900 TQ	USBLS	5/07
	Oregon	H	10.91 FQ	12.53 MW	14.64 TQ	ORBLS	5/08
	South Dakota	Y	19607 FQ	22695 MW	25908 TQ	SDBLS	7/08-9/08
	Texas	Y	21830 FQ	24630 MW	30520 TQ	USBLS	5/07
	Washington	H	10.96 FQ	12.90 MW	16.25 TQ	WABLS	3/08
	West Virginia	Y	22352 FQ	24933 MW	34337 TQ	WVBLS	7/08-9/08
	Wisconsin	Y	23470 FQ	31070 MW	42570 TQ	USBLS	5/07
	Puerto Rico	Y	16640 FQ	18450 MW	24060 TQ	USBLS	5/07
Garage Superintendent State Highway Patrol	Missouri	S	1554 LO		2221 HI	MSHPSS	7/1/08
Gardener Municipal Government	Seattle, WA	H	19.27 LO		20.80 HI	CSSS	2007
Gas Compressor and Gas Pumping Station Operator	Alabama	Y	34600 FQ	49890 MW	54990 TQ	USBLS	5/07
	Arizona	Y	29410 FQ	43890 MW	51220 TQ	USBLS	5/07
	Arkansas	Y	46800 FQ	52720 MW	58170 TQ	USBLS	5/07
	California	H	12.87 FQ	15.08 MW	24.58 TQ	CABLS	1/08-3/08
	Colorado	Y	40750 FQ	51500 MW	60870 TQ	USBLS	5/07
	Kansas	Y	37450 FQ	50400 MW	56650 TQ	USBLS	5/07
	Louisiana	H	22.57 FQ	26.07 MW	29.80 TQ	LABLS	1/08-3/08
	Massachusetts	Y	43690 FQ	47090 MW	50850 TQ	USBLS	5/07
	Michigan	Y	31910 FQ	39100 MW	55320 TQ	USBLS	5/07
	Minnesota	Y	30367 FQ	35038 MW	47523 TQ	MNBLS	10/08-12/08
	Mississippi	Y	52030 FQ	57890 MW	63670 TQ	USBLS	5/07
	New York	Y	29580 FQ	35880 MW	49870 TQ	USBLS	5/07
	Ohio	Y	35470 FQ	44640 MW	51540 TQ	USBLS	5/07
	Oklahoma	Y	33470 FQ	37700 MW	46560 TQ	USBLS	5/07
	Pennsylvania	Y	38360 FQ	49000 MW	56060 TQ	USBLS	5/07
	Tennessee	Y	40670 FQ	44240 MW	48320 TQ	USBLS	5/07
	Texas	Y	34710 FQ	43130 MW	51520 TQ	USBLS	5/07
	Virginia	Y	27920 FQ	41700 MW	64870 TQ	USBLS	5/07
	West Virginia	Y	31462 FQ	44525 MW	49120 TQ	WVBLS	7/08-9/08
	Wyoming	Y	40299 FQ	46660 MW	56117 TQ	WYBLS	9/08
Gas Pipeline Safety Compliance Inspector Public Utilities	Ohio	H	23.87 LO		35.02 HI	ODAS	2008
Gas Plant Operator	Alabama	Y	42340 FQ	49080 MW	58180 TQ	USBLS	5/07
	Arkansas	Y	39630 FQ	52050 MW	58590 TQ	USBLS	5/07
	California	H	29.40 FQ	34.43 MW	39.31 TQ	CABLS	1/08-3/08
	Colorado	Y	45120 FQ	53940 MW	60350 TQ	USBLS	5/07
	Connecticut	H	19.45 AE	26.79 MW		CTBLS	1/08-3/08
	Florida	Y	27250 FQ	32800 MW	44860 TQ	USBLS	5/07
	Georgia	Y	30470 FQ	34900 MW	39270 TQ	USBLS	5/07
	Illinois	Y	47390 FQ	55340 MW	66680 TQ	USBLS	5/07
	Indiana	Y	41040 FQ	46660 MW	56250 TQ	USBLS	5/07
	Iowa	Y	43920 FQ	52080 MW	59730 TQ	USBLS	5/07
	Kansas	Y	44030 FQ	52160 MW	59190 TQ	USBLS	5/07
	Kentucky	Y	42713 FQ	50741 MW	58904 TQ	KYBLS	2008
	Louisiana	H	21.41 FQ	26.67 MW	30.09 TQ	LABLS	1/08-3/08
	Maryland	Y		56150 MW		MDBLS	3/08
	Massachusetts	Y	48510 FQ	59560 MW	74290 TQ	USBLS	5/07
	Michigan	Y	49790 FQ	54320 MW	58360 TQ	USBLS	5/07
	Minnesota	Y	33349 FQ	43602 MW	56924 TQ	MNBLS	10/08-12/08
	Mississippi	Y	41240 FQ	49570 MW	55870 TQ	USBLS	5/07
	Missouri	Y	42190 FQ	46050 MW	49840 TQ	USBLS	5/07
	New Hampshire	H	13.88 AE	16.55 MW	18.20 AEX	NHBLS	6/08
	New Jersey	Y	53310 FQ	62270 MW	78370 TQ	USBLS	5/07
	New Mexico	Y	45970 FQ	53280 MW	61290 TQ	USBLS	5/07
	New York	Y	62450 FQ	71320 MW	81550 TQ	USBLS	5/07
	North Carolina	Y	38610 FQ	44380 MW	48920 TQ	USBLS	5/07
	Ohio	Y	50270 FQ	57010 MW	65040 TQ	USBLS	5/07
	Oklahoma	Y	40850 FQ	48330 MW	57000 TQ	USBLS	5/07
	Pennsylvania	Y	40410 FQ	51420 MW	59380 TQ	USBLS	5/07
	South Carolina	Y	38520 FQ	45540 MW	51160 TQ	USBLS	5/07
	Tennessee	Y	41090 FQ	47770 MW	53750 TQ	USBLS	5/07
	Texas	Y	45100 FQ	53510 MW	59760 TQ	USBLS	5/07

AE	Average entry wage	AW	Average wage paid	FQ	First quartile wage	LO	Lowest wage paid	MTC Median total compensation	TCC Total cash compensation
AER	Average entry range	AWR	Average wage range	H	Hourly	LR	Low end range	MW Median wage paid	TQ Third quartile wage
AEX	Average experienced wage	AXR	Average experienced range	HI	Highest wage paid	M	Monthly	MWR Median wage range	W Weekly
ATC	Average total compensation	D	Daily	HR	High end range	MCC	Median cash compensation	S See annotated source	Y Yearly

Occupation/Type/Industry	Location	Per	Low	Mid	High	Source	Date
Gas Plant Operator	Virginia	Y	49510 FQ	57260 MW	66260 TQ	USBLS	5/07
	Washington	H	21.88 FQ	28.28 MW	33.77 TQ	WABLS	3/08
	West Virginia	Y	49716 FQ	58123 MW	63967 TQ	WVBLS	7/08-9/08
	Wisconsin	Y	61580 FQ	66670 MW	71920 TQ	USBLS	5/07
	Wyoming	Y	43307 FQ	55343 MW	62840 TQ	WYBLS	9/08
Gas Superintendent/Manager	Pickens County, GA	Y	27833 LO		42351 HI	GACTY03	2008
Gas Supply Manager	United States	Y	91000 AE			CCRUN02	2008
Gate Operator							
Department of Transportation	New Hampshire	Y		16321 AW		NHUL03	2008
Gem Cutter	United States	Y		26260 AW		SUSA03	2008
Gemologist/Appraiser	United States	Y		39970 AW		JEWEL	2008
General and Operations Manager	Alabama	Y	53340 FQ	75660 MW	114410 TQ	USBLS	5/07
	Birmingham-Hoover MSA, AL	Y	57800 FQ	82070 MW	126220 TQ	USBLS	5/07
	Alaska	Y	43910 FQ	66640 MW	93720 TQ	USBLS	5/07
	Anchorage MSA, AK	Y	46860 FQ	71060 MW	97660 TQ	USBLS	5/07
	Arizona	Y	56180 FQ	80340 MW	120180 TQ	USBLS	5/07
	Phoenix-Mesa-Scottsdale MSA, AZ	Y	59350 FQ	84540 MW	125120 TQ	USBLS	5/07
	Tucson MSA, AZ	Y	52280 FQ	75470 MW	116980 TQ	USBLS	5/07
	Arkansas	Y	55610 FQ	75990 MW	106930 TQ	USBLS	5/07
	Little Rock-North Little Rock MSA, AR	Y	60510 FQ	83320 MW	118450 TQ	USBLS	5/07
	California	H	34.85 FQ	50.50 MW		CABLS	1/08-3/08
	Los Angeles-Long Beach-Glendale PMSA, CA	H	35.61 FQ	51.51 MW		CABLS	1/08-3/08
	Oakland-Fremont-Hayward MSA, CA	H	37.97 FQ	54.09 MW		CABLS	1/08-3/08
	Oxnard-Thousand Oaks-Ventura MSA, CA	H	35.53 FQ	52.56 MW		CABLS	1/08-3/08
	Riverside-San Bernardino-Ontario MSA, CA	H	32.98 FQ	45.55 MW	65.30 TQ	CABLS	1/08-3/08
	Sacramento-Arden Arcade-Roseville MSA, CA	H	33.52 FQ	46.46 MW	65.82 TQ	CABLS	1/08-3/08
	San Diego-Carlsbad-San Marcos MSA, CA	H	34.10 FQ	49.82 MW		CABLS	1/08-3/08
	San Francisco-San Mateo-Redwood PMSA, CA	H	38.45 FQ	56.87 MW		CABLS	1/08-3/08
	San Jose-Sunnyvale-Santa Clara MSA, CA	H	41.16 FQ	63.77 MW		CABLS	1/08-3/08
	Santa Ana-Anaheim-Irvine PMSA, CA	Y	75610 FQ	112160 MW		USBLS	5/07
	Colorado	Y	56870 FQ	84640 MW	130310 TQ	USBLS	5/07
	Denver-Aurora MSA, CO	Y	62390 FQ	93300 MW	142490 TQ	USBLS	5/07
	Connecticut	H	28.59 AE	50.82 MW		CTBLS	1/08-3/08
	Bridgeport-Stamford-Norwalk MSA, CT	Y	94940 FQ	143570 MW		USBLS	5/07
	Hartford-West Hartford-East Hartford MSA, CT	Y	62100 FQ	91330 MW	131550 TQ	USBLS	5/07
	Delaware	Y	71330 FQ	99610 MW	143950 TQ	USBLS	5/07
	Wilmington PMSA, DE-MD-NJ	Y	72490 FQ	100280 MW		USBLS	5/07
	District of Columbia	Y	89810 FQ	117260 MW		USBLS	5/07
	Washington-Arlington-Alexandria MSA, DC-VA-MD-WV	Y	84920 FQ	117400 MW		USBLS	5/07
	Florida	Y	60250 FQ	86350 MW	126210 TQ	USBLS	5/07
	Fort Lauderdale-Pompano Beach-Deerfield Beach PMSA, FL	Y	66410 FQ	92910 MW	133090 TQ	USBLS	5/07
	Jacksonville MSA, FL	Y	59880 FQ	82100 MW	118910 TQ	USBLS	5/07
	Miami-Fort Lauderdale-Miami Beach MSA, FL	Y	66480 FQ	94400 MW	136010 TQ	USBLS	5/07
	Orlando-Kissimmee MSA, FL	Y	59990 FQ	82760 MW	122360 TQ	USBLS	5/07
	Tampa-St. Petersburg-Clearwater MSA, FL	Y	59800 FQ	86620 MW	128840 TQ	USBLS	5/07
	West Palm Beach-Boca Raton-Boynton Beach PMSA, FL	Y	64760 FQ	94180 MW	131180 TQ	USBLS	5/07

AE	Average entry wage	AW	Average wage paid	FQ	First quartile wage	LO	Lowest wage paid	MTC	Median total compensation	TCC	Total cash compensation
AER	Average entry range	AWR	Average wage range	H	Hourly	LR	Low end range	MW	Median wage paid	TQ	Third quartile wage
AEX	Average experienced wage	AXR	Average experienced range	HI	Highest wage paid	M	Monthly	MWR	Median wage range	W	Weekly
ATC	Average total compensation	D	Daily	HR	High end range	MCC	Median cash compensation	S	See annotated source	Y	Yearly

Occupation/Type/Industry	Location	Per	Low	Mid	High	Source	Date
General and Operations Manager	Georgia	Y	52600 FQ	73890 MW	108740 TQ	USBLS	5/07
	Athens-Clarke County MSA, GA	Y	48100 FQ	64410 MW	93810 TQ	USBLS	5/07
	Atlanta-Sandy Springs-Marietta MSA, GA	Y	55750 FQ	79450 MW	119450 TQ	USBLS	5/07
	Hawaii	Y	58320 FQ	83500 MW	121720 TQ	USBLS	5/07
	Honolulu MSA, HI	Y	61200 FQ	89230 MW	127420 TQ	USBLS	5/07
	Idaho	Y	41470 FQ	58250 MW	81980 TQ	USBLS	5/07
	Boise City-Nampa MSA, ID	Y	47090 FQ	64540 MW	90350 TQ	USBLS	5/07
	Coeur d'Alene MSA, ID	Y	42670 FQ	59640 MW	78180 TQ	USBLS	5/07
	Illinois	Y	64750 FQ	92390 MW	143470 TQ	USBLS	5/07
	Champaign-Urbana MSA, IL	Y	56090 FQ	71950 MW	94750 TQ	USBLS	5/07
	Chicago-Naperville-Joliet MSA, IL-IN-WI	Y	71160 FQ	102810 MW		USBLS	5/07
	Indiana	Y	62930 FQ	87230 MW	124360 TQ	USBLS	5/07
	Gary PMSA, IN	Y	58230 FQ	82310 MW	124970 TQ	USBLS	5/07
	Indianapolis-Carmel MSA, IN	Y	68640 FQ	94540 MW	133760 TQ	USBLS	5/07
	South Bend-Mishawaka MSA, IN-MI	Y	61700 FQ	83610 MW	120980 TQ	USBLS	5/07
	Terre Haute MSA, IN	Y	62590 FQ	80420 MW	106320 TQ	USBLS	5/07
	Iowa	Y	59830 FQ	83070 MW	114750 TQ	USBLS	5/07
	Des Moines-West Des Moines MSA, IA	Y	68140 FQ	93530 MW	122670 TQ	USBLS	5/07
	Iowa City MSA, IA	Y	65770 FQ	84290 MW	110120 TQ	USBLS	5/07
	Kansas	Y	51740 FQ	70490 MW	96850 TQ	USBLS	5/07
	Wichita MSA, KS	Y	49860 FQ	66960 MW	96460 TQ	USBLS	5/07
	Kentucky	Y	53814 FQ	74930 MW	106546 TQ	KYBLS	2008
	Louisville-Jefferson County MSA, KY-IN	Y	57810 FQ	79990 MW	108470 TQ	USBLS	5/07
	Louisiana	H	24.86 FQ	34.88 MW	51.65 TQ	LABLS	1/08-3/08
	Baton Rouge MSA, LA	Y	52840 FQ	77620 MW	112560 TQ	USBLS	5/07
	New Orleans-Metairie-Kenner MSA, LA	Y	52970 FQ	75040 MW	114330 TQ	USBLS	5/07
	Maine	Y	55190 FQ	77050 MW	108800 TQ	USBLS	5/07
	Portland-South Portland-Biddeford MSA, ME	Y	60590 FQ	83710 MW	123140 TQ	USBLS	5/07
	Maryland	Y		101825 MW		MDBLS	3/08
	Baltimore-Towson MSA, MD	Y	66750 FQ	96900 MW	145120 TQ	USBLS	5/07
	Bethesda-Gaithersburg-Frederick PMSA, MD	Y	78630 FQ	114120 MW		USBLS	5/07
	Cumberland MSA, MD-WV	Y	50900 FQ	70880 MW	103920 TQ	USBLS	5/07
	Massachusetts	Y	71610 FQ	98830 MW	145540 TQ	USBLS	5/07
	Boston-Cambridge-Quincy NECTA, MA	Y	77850 FQ	106650 MW		USBLS	5/07
	Lynn-Peabody-Salem NECTA, MA	Y	70960 FQ	97040 MW	143280 TQ	USBLS	5/07
	Worcester MSA, MA-CT	Y	67480 FQ	90680 MW	124860 TQ	USBLS	5/07
	Michigan	Y	62640 FQ	87480 MW	124540 TQ	USBLS	5/07
	Ann Arbor MSA, MI	Y	60120 FQ	96680 MW	141100 TQ	USBLS	5/07
	Detroit-Warren-Livonia MSA, MI	Y	70600 FQ	96970 MW	143950 TQ	USBLS	5/07
	Grand Rapids-Wyoming MSA, MI	Y	57440 FQ	80880 MW	111020 TQ	USBLS	5/07
	Warren-Troy-Farmington Hills PMSA, MI	Y	72640 FQ	99120 MW	145580 TQ	USBLS	5/07
	Minnesota	Y	63706 FQ	91638 MW	142614 TQ	MNBLS	10/08-12/08
	Duluth-Superior MSA, MN-WI	Y	58419 FQ	76416 MW	104432 TQ	MNBLS	10/08-12/08
	Minneapolis-Saint Paul MSA, MN-WI	Y	70108 FQ	101106 MW		MNBLS	10/08-12/08
	Rochester MSA, MN	Y	58498 FQ	75763 MW	108359 TQ	MNBLS	10/08-12/08
	Mississippi	Y	53160 FQ	74230 MW	107540 TQ	USBLS	5/07
	Jackson MSA, MS	Y	54710 FQ	80220 MW	119530 TQ	USBLS	5/07
	Missouri	Y	58490 FQ	85000 MW	123940 TQ	USBLS	5/07
	Kansas City MSA, MO-KS	Y	60000 FQ	83440 MW	119180 TQ	USBLS	5/07
	St. Louis MSA, MO-IL	Y	65690 FQ	95060 MW	135870 TQ	USBLS	5/07
	Montana	Y	43700 FQ	62390 MW	89350 TQ	USBLS	5/07
	Billings MSA, MT	Y	49820 FQ	71740 MW	97730 TQ	USBLS	5/07
	Nebraska	Y	61400 FQ	85090 MW	119660 TQ	USBLS	5/07
	Omaha-Council Bluffs MSA, NE-IA	Y	63700 FQ	87660 MW	123120 TQ	USBLS	5/07
	Nevada	H	29.32 FQ	41.45 MW	64.67 TQ	NVBLS	5/08
	Las Vegas-Paradise MSA, NV	H	29.96 FQ	42.60 MW	66.52 TQ	NVBLS	5/08

AE	Average entry wage	AW	Average wage paid	FQ	First quartile wage
AER	Average entry range	AWR	Average wage range	H	Hourly
AEX	Average experienced wage	AXR	Average experienced range	HI	Highest wage paid
ATC	Average total compensation	D	Daily	HR	High end range

LO	Lowest wage paid	MTC	Median total compensation	TCC	Total cash compensation
LR	Low end range	MW	Median wage paid	TQ	Third quartile wage
M	Monthly	MWR	Median wage range	W	Weekly
MCC	Median cash compensation	S	See annotated source	Y	Yearly

Occupation/Type/Industry	Location	Per	Low	Mid	High	Source	Date
General and Operations Manager	New Hampshire	H	26.16 AE	39.03 MW	57.61 AEX	NHBLS	6/08
	Manchester MSA, NH	Y	63980 FQ	83840 MW	129350 TQ	USBLS	5/07
	Nashua NECTA, NH-MA	Y	67860 FQ	90460 MW	133340 TQ	USBLS	5/07
	New Jersey	Y	91740 FQ	137080 MW		USBLS	5/07
	Camden PMSA, NJ	Y	84310 FQ	119540 MW		USBLS	5/07
	Edison PMSA, NJ	Y	92650 FQ	138600 MW		USBLS	5/07
	Newark-Union PMSA, NJ-PA	Y	91980 FQ	137350 MW		USBLS	5/07
	New Mexico	Y	53140 FQ	75460 MW	106410 TQ	USBLS	5/07
	Albuquerque MSA, NM	Y	59340 FQ	80080 MW	112770 TQ	USBLS	5/07
	New York	Y	73180 FQ	111820 MW		USBLS	5/07
	Albany-Schenectady-Troy MSA, NY	Y	66290 FQ	90970 MW	132090 TQ	USBLS	5/07
	Buffalo-Niagara Falls MSA, NY	Y	59530 FQ	81450 MW	122840 TQ	USBLS	5/07
	Nassau-Suffolk PMSA, NY	Y	74140 FQ	108710 MW		USBLS	5/07
	New York-Northern New Jersey-Long Island MSA, NY-NJ-PA	Y	86610 FQ	132590 MW		USBLS	5/07
	North Carolina	Y	65710 FQ	93700 MW	140220 TQ	USBLS	5/07
	Charlotte-Gastonia-Concord MSA, NC-SC	Y	71270 FQ	103260 MW		USBLS	5/07
	Durham MSA, NC	Y	76350 FQ	109360 MW		USBLS	5/07
	Raleigh-Cary MSA, NC	Y	73100 FQ	103860 MW		USBLS	5/07
	North Dakota	Y	56750 FQ	75360 MW	106180 TQ	USBLS	5/07
	Fargo MSA, ND-MN	Y	58710 FQ	83510 MW	119800 TQ	USBLS	5/07
	Ohio	Y	61430 FQ	85900 MW	121930 TQ	USBLS	5/07
	Cincinnati-Middletown MSA, OH-KY-IN	Y	61630 FQ	89210 MW	126110 TQ	USBLS	5/07
	Cleveland-Elyria-Mentor MSA, OH	Y	64920 FQ	92830 MW	133140 TQ	USBLS	5/07
	Columbus MSA, OH	Y	66120 FQ	91310 MW	131490 TQ	USBLS	5/07
	Dayton MSA, OH	Y	68350 FQ	92250 MW	122900 TQ	USBLS	5/07
	Oklahoma	Y	42360 FQ	61690 MW	91310 TQ	USBLS	5/07
	Oklahoma City MSA, OK	Y	44820 FQ	65460 MW	94830 TQ	USBLS	5/07
	Tulsa MSA, OK	Y	44310 FQ	63930 MW	96390 TQ	USBLS	5/07
	Oregon	H	30.25 FQ	42.50 MW	61.41 TQ	ORBLS	5/08
	Portland-Vancouver-Beaverton MSA, OR-WA	Y	67680 FQ	95420 MW	136450 TQ	USBLS	5/07
	Pennsylvania	Y	59290 FQ	84380 MW	122740 TQ	USBLS	5/07
	Allentown-Bethlehem-Easton MSA, PA-NJ	Y	61150 FQ	86750 MW	123670 TQ	USBLS	5/07
	Philadelphia-Camden-Wilmington MSA, PA-NJ-DE-MD	Y	73790 FQ	104330 MW		USBLS	5/07
	Pittsburgh MSA, PA	Y	57960 FQ	80410 MW	115270 TQ	USBLS	5/07
	York-Hanover MSA, PA	Y	55360 FQ	75280 MW	107530 TQ	USBLS	5/07
	Rhode Island	Y	73420 FQ	96960 MW	133970 TQ	USBLS	5/07
	Providence-Fall River-Warwick MSA, RI-MA	Y	72280 FQ	96680 MW	135040 TQ	USBLS	5/07
	South Carolina	Y	54200 FQ	76010 MW	106190 TQ	USBLS	5/07
	Charleston-North Charleston MSA, SC	Y	55990 FQ	76400 MW	104990 TQ	USBLS	5/07
	Columbia MSA, SC	Y	55540 FQ	77820 MW	104680 TQ	USBLS	5/07
	South Dakota	Y	74306 FQ	92782 MW	120297 TQ	SDBLS	7/08-9/08
	Sioux Falls MSA, SD	Y	77948 FQ	98228 MW	128384 TQ	SDBLS	7/08-9/08
	Tennessee	Y	49260 FQ	71280 MW	104820 TQ	USBLS	5/07
	Clarksville MSA, TN-KY	Y	40220 FQ	59020 MW	87680 TQ	USBLS	5/07
	Kingsport-Bristol-Bristol MSA, TN-VA	Y	46050 FQ	61360 MW	92570 TQ	USBLS	5/07
	Memphis MSA, TN-MS-AR	Y	53450 FQ	75960 MW	116270 TQ	USBLS	5/07
	Nashville-Davidson-Murfreesboro MSA, TN	Y	54110 FQ	78480 MW	114150 TQ	USBLS	5/07
	Texas	Y	58040 FQ	85030 MW	133290 TQ	USBLS	5/07
	Austin-Round Rock MSA, TX	Y	59610 FQ	89650 MW	137720 TQ	USBLS	5/07
	Dallas-Fort Worth-Arlington MSA, TX	Y	65120 FQ	95450 MW		USBLS	5/07
	El Paso MSA, TX	Y	45720 FQ	65420 MW	102950 TQ	USBLS	5/07
	Houston-Sugar Land-Baytown MSA, TX	Y	64070 FQ	95640 MW		USBLS	5/07
	Midland MSA, TX	Y	54720 FQ	77160 MW	123610 TQ	USBLS	5/07
	San Antonio MSA, TX	Y	55490 FQ	81770 MW	121070 TQ	USBLS	5/07
	Utah	Y	51600 FQ	73850 MW	107880 TQ	USBLS	5/07

AE	Average entry wage	**AW**	Average wage paid	**FQ**	First quartile wage	**LO**	Lowest wage paid	**MTC**	Median total compensation	**TCC**	Total cash compensation
AER	Average entry range	**AWR**	Average wage range	**H**	Hourly	**LR**	Low end range	**MW**	Median wage paid	**TQ**	Third quartile wage
AEX	Average experienced wage	**AXR**	Average experienced range	**HI**	Highest wage paid	**M**	Monthly	**MWR**	Median wage range	**W**	Weekly
ATC	Average total compensation	**D**	Daily	**HR**	High end range	**MCC**	Median cash compensation	**S**	See annotated source	**Y**	Yearly

Occupation/Type/Industry	Location	Per	Low	Mid	High	Source	Date
General and Operations Manager	Logan MSA, UT-ID	Y	44540 FQ	62060 MW	92080 TQ	USBLS	5/07
	St. George MSA, UT	Y	38410 FQ	59030 MW	80910 TQ	USBLS	5/07
	Salt Lake City MSA, UT	Y	56110 FQ	79870 MW	119570 TQ	USBLS	5/07
	Vermont	Y	59670 FQ	84750 MW	123010 TQ	USBLS	5/07
	Burlington-South Burlington MSA, VT	Y	62040 FQ	93570 MW	143280 TQ	USBLS	5/07
	Virginia	Y	72840 FQ	106380 MW		USBLS	5/07
	Richmond MSA, VA	Y	66910 FQ	93960 MW	130140 TQ	USBLS	5/07
	Virginia Beach-Norfolk-Newport News MSA, VA-NC	Y	74020 FQ	101090 MW		USBLS	5/07
	Washington	H	40.91 FQ	54.58 MW		WABLS	3/08
	Seattle-Tacoma-Bellevue MSA, WA	Y	89030 FQ	124250 MW		USBLS	5/07
	West Virginia	Y	43886 FQ	67180 MW	95802 TQ	WVBLS	7/08-9/08
	Charleston MSA, WV	Y	46090 FQ	68760 MW	98680 TQ	USBLS	5/07
	Wisconsin	Y	62160 FQ	87020 MW	124790 TQ	USBLS	5/07
	Green Bay MSA, WI	Y	70290 FQ	90970 MW	127750 TQ	USBLS	5/07
	Milwaukee-Waukesha-West Allis MSA, WI	Y	68480 FQ	98170 MW		USBLS	5/07
	Wyoming	Y	51461 FQ	69412 MW	96963 TQ	WYBLS	9/08
	Casper MSA, WY	Y	50873 FQ	71842 MW	99981 TQ	WYBLS	9/08
	Cheyenne MSA, WY	Y	49650 FQ	66825 MW	88956 TQ	WYBLS	9/08
	Puerto Rico	Y	46210 FQ	67420 MW	101860 TQ	USBLS	5/07
	San German-Cabo Rojo MSA, PR	Y	44880 FQ	62790 MW	89100 TQ	USBLS	5/07
	San Juan-Caguas-Guaynabo MSA, PR	Y	47570 FQ	69740 MW	105650 TQ	USBLS	5/07
	Virgin Islands	Y	58030 FQ	74580 MW	92680 TQ	USBLS	5/07
	Guam	Y	32900 FQ	46660 MW	65810 TQ	USBLS	5/07
General Counsel to the House United States House of Representatives	United States	Y			167800 HI	CRS01	1/08
General Manager Board of Public Works	Gaffney, SC	Y			147950 HI	GOUPS	2009
Genetic Counselor	United States	Y		67200 MW		USNEWS06	2008
Geneticist	United States	Y		91470 AW		OOH03	2007
Geochemical Technician	United States	Y		37440 AW		SUSA05	2009
Geodetic Technician	United States	Y		54081 AW		OOH01	2007
Geographer	California	H	26.48 FQ	32.08 MW	38.28 TQ	CABLS	1/08-3/08
	Florida	Y	55740 FQ	65560 MW	75960 TQ	USBLS	5/07
	Louisiana	H	27.05 FQ	34.32 MW	47.76 TQ	LABLS	1/08-3/08
	Maryland	Y		73100 MW		MDBLS	3/08
	Mississippi	Y	39960 FQ	45350 MW	50430 TQ	USBLS	5/07
	New York	Y	50770 FQ	69220 MW	77180 TQ	USBLS	5/07
	Oregon	H	23.25 FQ	28.72 MW	39.69 TQ	ORBLS	5/08
	Pennsylvania	Y	35840 FQ	46720 MW	63880 TQ	USBLS	5/07
	Texas	Y	43860 FQ	58580 MW	88090 TQ	USBLS	5/07
	Virginia	Y	74280 FQ	87930 MW	99650 TQ	USBLS	5/07
Geography Teacher							
Postsecondary	Alabama	Y	42360 FQ	54690 MW	68580 TQ	USBLS	5/07
Postsecondary	Arizona	Y	48920 FQ	65050 MW	76550 TQ	USBLS	5/07
Postsecondary	Arkansas	Y	47190 FQ	57960 MW	65380 TQ	USBLS	5/07
Postsecondary	California	Y		72214 AW		CABLS	1/08-3/08
Postsecondary	Colorado	Y	51960 FQ	59960 MW	71910 TQ	USBLS	5/07
Postsecondary	District of Columbia	Y	45120 FQ	54480 MW	63580 TQ	USBLS	5/07
Postsecondary	Florida	Y	56060 FQ	65030 MW	82500 TQ	USBLS	5/07
Postsecondary	Georgia	Y	51930 FQ	72980 MW	93050 TQ	USBLS	5/07
Postsecondary	Hawaii	Y	51070 FQ	64980 MW	80900 TQ	USBLS	5/07
Postsecondary	Illinois	Y	49260 FQ	58560 MW	73870 TQ	USBLS	5/07
Postsecondary	Indiana	Y	48880 FQ	58820 MW	76810 TQ	USBLS	5/07
Postsecondary	Iowa	Y	54280 FQ	68350 MW	90400 TQ	USBLS	5/07
Postsecondary	Kansas	Y	28890 FQ	54340 MW	69220 TQ	USBLS	5/07
Postsecondary	Kentucky	Y	30302 FQ	50828 MW	65834 TQ	KYBLS	2008
Postsecondary	Louisiana	Y		46899 AW		LABLS	1/08-3/08
Postsecondary	Maryland	Y		70400 MW		MDBLS	3/08
Postsecondary	Massachusetts	Y	55960 FQ	72420 MW	90870 TQ	USBLS	5/07

AE	Average entry wage	AW	Average wage paid	FQ	First quartile wage
AER	Average entry range	AWR	Average wage range	H	Hourly
AEX	Average experienced wage	AXR	Average experienced range	HI	Highest wage paid
ATC	Average total compensation	D	Daily	HR	High end range

LO	Lowest wage paid	MTC	Median total compensation	TCC	Total cash compensation
LR	Low end range	MW	Median wage paid	TQ	Third quartile wage
M	Monthly	MWR	Median wage range	W	Weekly
MCC	Median cash compensation	S	See annotated source	Y	Yearly

Occupation/Type/Industry	Location	Per	Low	Mid	High	Source	Date
Geography Teacher							
Postsecondary	Michigan	Y	52110 FQ	60840 MW	81430 TQ	USBLS	5/07
Postsecondary	Minnesota	Y	45877 FQ	59990 MW	78728 TQ	MNBLS	10/08-12/08
Postsecondary	Missouri	Y	45590 FQ	53960 MW	65120 TQ	USBLS	5/07
Postsecondary	New Jersey	Y	54790 FQ	66710 MW	89640 TQ	USBLS	5/07
Postsecondary	New Mexico	Y	57810 FQ	66550 MW	76110 TQ	USBLS	5/07
Postsecondary	New York	Y	43370 FQ	65030 MW	77720 TQ	USBLS	5/07
Postsecondary	North Carolina	Y	49990 FQ	59910 MW	73470 TQ	USBLS	5/07
Postsecondary	Ohio	Y	50890 FQ	60920 MW	77740 TQ	USBLS	5/07
Postsecondary	Pennsylvania	Y	53790 FQ	67950 MW	89670 TQ	USBLS	5/07
Postsecondary	South Carolina	Y	48170 FQ	59740 MW	72720 TQ	USBLS	5/07
Postsecondary	Tennessee	Y	43830 FQ	57700 MW	80080 TQ	USBLS	5/07
Postsecondary	Texas	Y	42920 FQ	57280 MW	77620 TQ	USBLS	5/07
Postsecondary	Virginia	Y	39980 FQ	53050 MW	61010 TQ	USBLS	5/07
Postsecondary	Washington	Y		57259 AW		WABLS	3/08
Postsecondary	Wisconsin	Y	44400 FQ	54150 MW	64140 TQ	USBLS	5/07
Geological and Petroleum Technician	Alabama	Y	32700 FQ	35130 MW	37530 TQ	USBLS	5/07
	Arizona	Y	30210 FQ	36250 MW	40720 TQ	USBLS	5/07
	California	H	27.85 FQ	36.30 MW	51.58 TQ	CABLS	1/08-3/08
	Colorado	Y	37100 FQ	53940 MW	68220 TQ	USBLS	5/07
	Florida	Y	25810 FQ	31320 MW	38710 TQ	USBLS	5/07
	Idaho	Y	28550 FQ	34490 MW	43310 TQ	USBLS	5/07
	Illinois	Y	32850 FQ	46350 MW	56500 TQ	USBLS	5/07
	Kansas	Y	21910 FQ	25290 MW	33460 TQ	USBLS	5/07
	Kentucky	Y	31503 FQ	39726 MW	65700 TQ	KYBLS	2008
	Louisiana	H	17.09 FQ	26.61 MW	33.17 TQ	LABLS	1/08-3/08
	Maryland	Y		45175 MW		MDBLS	3/08
	Massachusetts	Y	31210 FQ	40690 MW	58620 TQ	USBLS	5/07
	Mississippi	Y	62430 FQ	67920 MW	73420 TQ	USBLS	5/07
	Missouri	Y	20790 FQ	31510 MW	37900 TQ	USBLS	5/07
	Montana	Y	34220 FQ	44820 MW	50720 TQ	USBLS	5/07
	Nevada	H	21.79 FQ	25.70 MW	29.92 TQ	NVBLS	5/08
	New Jersey	Y	36080 FQ	48030 MW	61200 TQ	USBLS	5/07
	New Mexico	Y	15540 FQ	37300 MW	51870 TQ	USBLS	5/07
	New York	Y	24750 FQ	39020 MW	48390 TQ	USBLS	5/07
	Ohio	Y	28390 FQ	35850 MW	51460 TQ	USBLS	5/07
	Oklahoma	Y	34820 FQ	44530 MW	56850 TQ	USBLS	5/07
	Oregon	H	15.58 FQ	19.10 MW	24.84 TQ	ORBLS	5/08
	Pennsylvania	Y	31230 FQ	38250 MW	47510 TQ	USBLS	5/07
	South Carolina	Y	34020 FQ	36540 MW	39060 TQ	USBLS	5/07
	Texas	Y	31860 FQ	49390 MW	64400 TQ	USBLS	5/07
	Utah	Y	29540 FQ	38340 MW	61910 TQ	USBLS	5/07
	Virginia	Y	28150 FQ	32990 MW	39160 TQ	USBLS	5/07
	Washington	H	16.01 FQ	18.11 MW	20.95 TQ	WABLS	3/08
	West Virginia	Y	19431 FQ	28809 MW	36810 TQ	WVBLS	7/08-9/08
	Wyoming	Y	32701 FQ	41924 MW	60319 TQ	WYBLS	9/08
Geological Project Analyst							
State Government	Wyoming	Y	48468 LO		66804 HI	AFT02	3/1/08
Geologist							
State Government	Maine	Y	33384 LO		45739 HI	AFT02	3/1/08
Geophysicist							
Small Organization	United States	Y	63083 FQ	74557 MW	86031 TQ	ALA08	2008
With Bachelor's Degree	Tech Valley, NY	Y	40000-60000 LR			TVC04	2008
Geoscientist							
Except Hydrologists and Geographers	Alabama	Y	41000 FQ	52370 MW	64160 TQ	USBLS	5/07
Except Hydrologists and Geographers	Birmingham-Hoover MSA, AL	Y	38560 FQ	44670 MW	55100 TQ	USBLS	5/07
Except Hydrologists and Geographers	Alaska	Y	61460 FQ	79390 MW	96030 TQ	USBLS	5/07
Except Hydrologists and Geographers	Anchorage MSA, AK	Y	58620 FQ	84540 MW	101850 TQ	USBLS	5/07
Except Hydrologists and Geographers	Arizona	Y	47370 FQ	62280 MW	83970 TQ	USBLS	5/07
Except Hydrologists and Geographers	Phoenix-Mesa-Scottsdale MSA, AZ	Y	45530 FQ	56900 MW	74630 TQ	USBLS	5/07
Except Hydrologists and Geographers	Tucson MSA, AZ	Y	48950 FQ	69090 MW	94550 TQ	USBLS	5/07
Except Hydrologists and Geographers	Arkansas	Y	45150 FQ	51500 MW	72010 TQ	USBLS	5/07
Except Hydrologists and Geographers	California	H	30.05 FQ	37.39 MW	46.84 TQ	CABLS	1/08-3/08

AE Average entry wage	AW Average wage paid	FQ First quartile wage	LO Lowest wage paid	MTC Median total compensation	TCC Total cash compensation
AER Average entry range	AWR Average wage range	H Hourly	LR Low end range	MW Median wage paid	TQ Third quartile wage
AEX Average experienced wage	AXR Average experienced range	HI Highest wage paid	M Monthly	MWR Median wage range	W Weekly
ATC Average total compensation	D Daily	HR High end range	MCC Median cash compensation	S See annotated source	Y Yearly

Occupation/Type/Industry	Location	Per	Low	Mid	High	Source	Date
Geoscientist							
Except Hydrologists and Geographers	Los Angeles-Long Beach-Glendale PMSA, CA	H	31.63 FQ	37.52 MW	45.33 TQ	CABLS	1/08-3/08
Except Hydrologists and Geographers	Oakland-Fremont-Hayward MSA, CA	H	28.84 FQ	37.27 MW	51.47 TQ	CABLS	1/08-3/08
Except Hydrologists and Geographers	Riverside-San Bernardino-Ontario MSA, CA	H	25.54 FQ	29.85 MW	39.20 TQ	CABLS	1/08-3/08
Except Hydrologists and Geographers	Sacramento-Arden Arcade-Roseville MSA, CA	H	32.54 FQ	36.21 MW	39.81 TQ	CABLS	1/08-3/08
Except Hydrologists and Geographers	San Diego-Carlsbad-San Marcos MSA, CA	H	27.84 FQ	37.30 MW	44.35 TQ	CABLS	1/08-3/08
Except Hydrologists and Geographers	San Francisco-San Mateo-Redwood PMSA, CA	H	39.88 FQ	47.73 MW	61.11 TQ	CABLS	1/08-3/08
Except Hydrologists and Geographers	San Jose-Sunnyvale-Santa Clara MSA, CA	H	24.91 FQ	30.14 MW	48.14 TQ	CABLS	1/08-3/08
Except Hydrologists and Geographers	Santa Ana-Anaheim-Irvine PMSA, CA	Y	55150 FQ	72210 MW	94470 TQ	USBLS	5/07
Except Hydrologists and Geographers	Colorado	Y	57370 FQ	85850 MW	121510 TQ	USBLS	5/07
Except Hydrologists and Geographers	Denver-Aurora MSA, CO	Y	75310 FQ	102270 MW	137830 TQ	USBLS	5/07
Except Hydrologists and Geographers	Connecticut	H	23.69 AE	42.09 MW		CTBLS	1/08-3/08
Except Hydrologists and Geographers	Hartford-West Hartford-East Hartford MSA, CT	Y	43590 FQ	51100 MW	77880 TQ	USBLS	5/07
Except Hydrologists and Geographers	Delaware	Y	43600 FQ	59010 MW	84480 TQ	USBLS	5/07
Except Hydrologists and Geographers	District of Columbia	Y	68500 FQ	90220 MW	126170 TQ	USBLS	5/07
Except Hydrologists and Geographers	Washington-Arlington-Alexandria MSA, DC-VA-MD-WV	Y	67920 FQ	90610 MW	120230 TQ	USBLS	5/07
Except Hydrologists and Geographers	Florida	Y	43170 FQ	57030 MW	77140 TQ	USBLS	5/07
Except Hydrologists and Geographers	Fort Lauderdale-Pompano Beach-Deerfield Beach PMSA, FL	Y	44000 FQ	62540 MW	83730 TQ	USBLS	5/07
Except Hydrologists and Geographers	Jacksonville MSA, FL	Y	48050 FQ	55820 MW	65880 TQ	USBLS	5/07
Except Hydrologists and Geographers	Miami-Fort Lauderdale-Miami Beach MSA, FL	Y	46760 FQ	66750 MW	89960 TQ	USBLS	5/07
Except Hydrologists and Geographers	Orlando-Kissimmee MSA, FL	Y	50390 FQ	60980 MW	80710 TQ	USBLS	5/07
Except Hydrologists and Geographers	Tampa-St. Petersburg-Clearwater MSA, FL	Y	51620 FQ	59970 MW	76510 TQ	USBLS	5/07
Except Hydrologists and Geographers	West Palm Beach-Boca Raton-Boynton Beach PMSA, FL	Y	42650 FQ	53850 MW	65210 TQ	USBLS	5/07
Except Hydrologists and Geographers	Georgia	Y	42950 FQ	53720 MW	65550 TQ	USBLS	5/07
Except Hydrologists and Geographers	Atlanta-Sandy Springs-Marietta MSA, GA	Y	43870 FQ	52840 MW	62230 TQ	USBLS	5/07
Except Hydrologists and Geographers	Hawaii	Y	64460 FQ	82810 MW	104270 TQ	USBLS	5/07
Except Hydrologists and Geographers	Honolulu MSA, HI	Y	64670 FQ	82980 MW	104490 TQ	USBLS	5/07
Except Hydrologists and Geographers	Idaho	Y	50860 FQ	59030 MW	72350 TQ	USBLS	5/07
Except Hydrologists and Geographers	Illinois	Y	47690 FQ	65250 MW	89000 TQ	USBLS	5/07
Except Hydrologists and Geographers	Chicago-Naperville-Joliet MSA, IL-IN-WI	Y	46610 FQ	65340 MW	90550 TQ	USBLS	5/07
Except Hydrologists and Geographers	Indiana	Y	39540 FQ	49970 MW	85720 TQ	USBLS	5/07
Except Hydrologists and Geographers	Indianapolis-Carmel MSA, IN	Y	36120 FQ	43320 MW	56010 TQ	USBLS	5/07
Except Hydrologists and Geographers	Iowa	Y	52810 FQ	61220 MW	71650 TQ	USBLS	5/07
Except Hydrologists and Geographers	Kansas	Y	48880 FQ	58630 MW	68200 TQ	USBLS	5/07
Except Hydrologists and Geographers	Wichita MSA, KS	Y	53270 FQ	60610 MW	67820 TQ	USBLS	5/07
Except Hydrologists and Geographers	Kentucky	Y	45392 FQ	60215 MW	81827 TQ	KYBLS	2008
Except Hydrologists and Geographers	Louisiana	H	29.65 FQ	42.86 MW	64.27 TQ	LABLS	1/08-3/08
Except Hydrologists and Geographers	Baton Rouge MSA, LA	Y	37940 FQ	56700 MW	71400 TQ	USBLS	5/07
Except Hydrologists and Geographers	New Orleans-Metairie-Kenner MSA, LA	Y	80780 FQ	92930 MW	105290 TQ	USBLS	5/07
Except Hydrologists and Geographers	Maine	Y	42960 FQ	48770 MW	56870 TQ	USBLS	5/07
Except Hydrologists and Geographers	Portland-South Portland-Biddeford MSA, ME	Y	42180 FQ	46010 MW	49840 TQ	USBLS	5/07
Except Hydrologists and Geographers	Maryland	Y		82625 MW		MDBLS	3/08
Except Hydrologists and Geographers	Baltimore-Towson MSA, MD	Y	49320 FQ	58390 MW	69000 TQ	USBLS	5/07
Except Hydrologists and Geographers	Bethesda-Gaithersburg-Frederick PMSA, MD	Y	77380 FQ	97240 MW	117640 TQ	USBLS	5/07
Except Hydrologists and Geographers	Massachusetts	Y	49210 FQ	65740 MW	95120 TQ	USBLS	5/07
Except Hydrologists and Geographers	Boston-Cambridge-Quincy NECTA, MA	Y	44590 FQ	52960 MW	68270 TQ	USBLS	5/07
Except Hydrologists and Geographers	Michigan	Y	49120 FQ	58850 MW	69410 TQ	USBLS	5/07
Except Hydrologists and Geographers	Detroit-Warren-Livonia MSA, MI	Y	45910 FQ	57800 MW	73500 TQ	USBLS	5/07

AE	Average entry wage	AW	Average wage paid	FQ	First quartile wage
AER	Average entry range	AWR	Average wage range	H	Hourly
AEX	Average experienced wage	AXR	Average experienced range	HI	Highest wage paid
ATC	Average total compensation D	Daily		HR	High end range

LO	Lowest wage paid	MTC	Median total compensation	TCC	Total cash compensation
LR	Low end range	MW	Median wage paid	TQ	Third quartile wage
M	Monthly	MWR	Median wage range	W	Weekly
MCC	Median cash compensation	S	See annotated source	Y	Yearly

Geoscientist

Occupation/Type/Industry	Location	Per	Low	Mid	High	Source	Date
Geoscientist							
Except Hydrologists and Geographers	Warren-Troy-Farmington Hills PMSA, MI	Y	44290 FQ	56720 MW	75660 TQ	USBLS	5/07
Except Hydrologists and Geographers	Minnesota	Y	49277 FQ	59404 MW	72890 TQ	MNBLS	10/08-12/08
Except Hydrologists and Geographers	Minneapolis-Saint Paul MSA, MN-WI	Y	49758 FQ	59749 MW	73204 TQ	MNBLS	10/08-12/08
Except Hydrologists and Geographers	Mississippi	Y	66790 FQ	83010 MW	97200 TQ	USBLS	5/07
Except Hydrologists and Geographers	Gulfport-Biloxi MSA, MS	Y	75710 FQ	88850 MW	99920 TQ	USBLS	5/07
Except Hydrologists and Geographers	Jackson MSA, MS	Y	55240 FQ	64870 MW	74200 TQ	USBLS	5/07
Except Hydrologists and Geographers	Missouri	Y	50130 FQ	69160 MW	88900 TQ	USBLS	5/07
Except Hydrologists and Geographers	Kansas City MSA, MO-KS	Y	47020 FQ	60590 MW	86500 TQ	USBLS	5/07
Except Hydrologists and Geographers	Montana	Y	55970 FQ	71590 MW	83850 TQ	USBLS	5/07
Except Hydrologists and Geographers	Billings MSA, MT	Y	53560 FQ	73370 MW	95800 TQ	USBLS	5/07
Except Hydrologists and Geographers	Nebraska	Y	37720 FQ	45780 MW	69490 TQ	USBLS	5/07
Except Hydrologists and Geographers	Omaha-Council Bluffs MSA, NE-IA	Y	37700 FQ	45370 MW	70730 TQ	USBLS	5/07
Except Hydrologists and Geographers	Nevada	H	28.25 FQ	37.79 MW	46.24 TQ	NVBLS	5/08
Except Hydrologists and Geographers	Las Vegas-Paradise MSA, NV	H	26.02 FQ	34.94 MW	47.92 TQ	NVBLS	5/08
Except Hydrologists and Geographers	Reno-Sparks MSA, NV	H	40.95 FQ	44.97 MW	48.68 TQ	NVBLS	5/08
Except Hydrologists and Geographers	New Hampshire	H	22.12 AE	28.57 MW	36.35 AEX	NHBLS	6/08
Except Hydrologists and Geographers	Manchester MSA, NH	Y	45050 FQ	53720 MW	64110 TQ	USBLS	5/07
Except Hydrologists and Geographers	New Jersey	Y	56060 FQ	75660 MW	100150 TQ	USBLS	5/07
Except Hydrologists and Geographers	Camden PMSA, NJ	Y	63140 FQ	81620 MW	116090 TQ	USBLS	5/07
Except Hydrologists and Geographers	Edison PMSA, NJ	Y	89600 FQ	103810 MW	121740 TQ	USBLS	5/07
Except Hydrologists and Geographers	Newark-Union PMSA, NJ-PA	Y	57630 FQ	74540 MW	96560 TQ	USBLS	5/07
Except Hydrologists and Geographers	New Mexico	Y	56090 FQ	71240 MW	84210 TQ	USBLS	5/07
Except Hydrologists and Geographers	Albuquerque MSA, NM	Y	61730 FQ	77290 MW	96420 TQ	USBLS	5/07
Except Hydrologists and Geographers	New York	Y	42170 FQ	57550 MW	75190 TQ	USBLS	5/07
Except Hydrologists and Geographers	Albany-Schenectady-Troy MSA, NY	Y	45490 FQ	62370 MW	75520 TQ	USBLS	5/07
Except Hydrologists and Geographers	Buffalo-Niagara Falls MSA, NY	Y	46190 FQ	60740 MW	73010 TQ	USBLS	5/07
Except Hydrologists and Geographers	New York-Northern New Jersey-Long Island MSA, NY-NJ-PA	Y	46020 FQ	65940 MW	93850 TQ	USBLS	5/07
Except Hydrologists and Geographers	North Carolina	Y	40000 FQ	58930 MW	78020 TQ	USBLS	5/07
Except Hydrologists and Geographers	Charlotte-Gastonia-Concord MSA, NC-SC	Y	47480 FQ	60450 MW	75450 TQ	USBLS	5/07
Except Hydrologists and Geographers	Raleigh-Cary MSA, NC	Y	47490 FQ	69630 MW	81380 TQ	USBLS	5/07
Except Hydrologists and Geographers	Ohio	Y	47590 FQ	61710 MW	76880 TQ	USBLS	5/07
Except Hydrologists and Geographers	Cincinnati-Middletown MSA, OH-KY-IN	Y	60750 FQ	73520 MW	89110 TQ	USBLS	5/07
Except Hydrologists and Geographers	Columbus MSA, OH	Y	44990 FQ	58420 MW	73540 TQ	USBLS	5/07
Except Hydrologists and Geographers	Oklahoma	Y	52890 FQ	76680 MW	114610 TQ	USBLS	5/07
Except Hydrologists and Geographers	Oklahoma City MSA, OK	Y	43270 FQ	82770 MW	125040 TQ	USBLS	5/07
Except Hydrologists and Geographers	Tulsa MSA, OK	Y	52140 FQ	63420 MW	111250 TQ	USBLS	5/07
Except Hydrologists and Geographers	Oregon	H	25.28 FQ	32.87 MW	40.81 TQ	ORBLS	5/08
Except Hydrologists and Geographers	Portland-Vancouver-Beaverton MSA, OR-WA	Y	51860 FQ	70940 MW	87320 TQ	USBLS	5/07
Except Hydrologists and Geographers	Pennsylvania	Y	46940 FQ	63890 MW	82780 TQ	USBLS	5/07
Except Hydrologists and Geographers	Philadelphia-Camden-Wilmington MSA, PA-NJ-DE-MD	Y	45140 FQ	63900 MW	86560 TQ	USBLS	5/07
Except Hydrologists and Geographers	Pittsburgh MSA, PA	Y	51580 FQ	74740 MW	106350 TQ	USBLS	5/07
Except Hydrologists and Geographers	South Carolina	Y	28080 FQ	33710 MW	40160 TQ	USBLS	5/07
Except Hydrologists and Geographers	Charleston-North Charleston MSA, SC	Y	30540 FQ	37630 MW	50540 TQ	USBLS	5/07
Except Hydrologists and Geographers	Columbia MSA, SC	Y	29550 FQ	35320 MW	40980 TQ	USBLS	5/07
Except Hydrologists and Geographers	South Dakota	Y	40813 FQ	46849 MW	55444 TQ	SDBLS	7/08-9/08
Except Hydrologists and Geographers	Tennessee	Y	42000 FQ	48500 MW	65710 TQ	USBLS	5/07
Except Hydrologists and Geographers	Nashville-Davidson-Murfreesboro MSA, TN	Y	44010 FQ	48260 MW	52640 TQ	USBLS	5/07
Except Hydrologists and Geographers	Texas	Y	71080 FQ	103710 MW	141370 TQ	USBLS	5/07
Except Hydrologists and Geographers	Austin-Round Rock MSA, TX	Y	49960 FQ	62600 MW	96560 TQ	USBLS	5/07
Except Hydrologists and Geographers	Dallas-Fort Worth-Arlington MSA, TX	Y	48310 FQ	82490 MW	116420 TQ	USBLS	5/07
Except Hydrologists and Geographers	Houston-Sugar Land-Baytown MSA, TX	Y	81340 FQ	116160 MW		USBLS	5/07
Except Hydrologists and Geographers	San Antonio MSA, TX	Y	45250 FQ	73840 MW	128130 TQ	USBLS	5/07
Except Hydrologists and Geographers	Utah	Y	48650 FQ	61450 MW	75580 TQ	USBLS	5/07
Except Hydrologists and Geographers	Salt Lake City MSA, UT	Y	45600 FQ	57300 MW	71650 TQ	USBLS	5/07
Except Hydrologists and Geographers	Vermont	Y	63200 FQ	72120 MW	78980 TQ	USBLS	5/07

AE	Average entry wage	AW	Average wage paid	FQ	First quartile wage
AER	Average entry range	AWR	Average wage range	H	Hourly
AEX	Average experienced wage	AXR	Average experienced range	HI	Highest wage paid
ATC	Average total compensation	D	Daily	HR	High end range

LO	Lowest wage paid	MTC	Median total compensation	TCC	Total cash compensation
LR	Low end range	MW	Median wage paid	TQ	Third quartile wage
M	Monthly	MWR	Median wage range	W	Weekly
		MCC	Median cash compensation	S	See annotated source
				Y	Yearly

Occupation/Type/Industry	Location	Per	Low	Mid	High	Source	Date
Geoscientist							
Except Hydrologists and Geographers	Virginia	Y	53820 FQ	71680 MW	97650 TQ	USBLS	5/07
Except Hydrologists and Geographers	Richmond MSA, VA	Y	52710 FQ	61200 MW	75920 TQ	USBLS	5/07
Except Hydrologists and Geographers	Virginia Beach-Norfolk-Newport News MSA, VA-NC	Y	48190 FQ	58630 MW	79530 TQ	USBLS	5/07
Except Hydrologists and Geographers	Washington	H	25.39 FQ	31.60 MW	43.40 TQ	WABLS	3/08
Except Hydrologists and Geographers	Seattle-Tacoma-Bellevue MSA, WA	Y	46150 FQ	65310 MW	94710 TQ	USBLS	5/07
Except Hydrologists and Geographers	West Virginia	Y	40744 FQ	62166 MW	82011 TQ	WVBLS	7/08-9/08
Except Hydrologists and Geographers	Charleston MSA, WV	Y	37280 FQ	58590 MW	80010 TQ	USBLS	5/07
Except Hydrologists and Geographers	Wisconsin	Y	45250 FQ	66190 MW	92810 TQ	USBLS	5/07
Except Hydrologists and Geographers	Milwaukee-Waukesha-West Allis MSA, WI	Y	44530 FQ	69430 MW	90430 TQ	USBLS	5/07
Except Hydrologists and Geographers	Wyoming	Y	43235 FQ	66087 MW	86913 TQ	WYBLS	9/08
Except Hydrologists and Geographers	Puerto Rico	Y	39620 FQ	56300 MW	64510 TQ	USBLS	5/07
Except Hydrologists and Geographers	San Juan-Caguas-Guaynabo MSA, PR	Y	39320 FQ	55780 MW	63730 TQ	USBLS	5/07
Geotechnical Engineer							
Municipal Government	Cincinnati, OH	Y	62598 LO		84507 HI	COHSS	10/08
Geothermal Senior Reservoir Engineer							
With Bachelor's Degree, Experience, Licensure	Tech Valley, NY	Y	60000-80000 LR			TVC03	2008
Gerontologist	United States	Y		149433 AW		CBUILD02	12/08
Ghostwriter	United States	Y		61000 MW		USNEWS02	2008
Gift Analyst							
White House Staff	United States	Y			34000-35500 HR	WPOST02	2008
GIS Mapping Supervisor							
County Government	Livingston County, MI	Y			49435 HI	LCPP	2009
Glazier	Alabama	Y	24080 FQ	27770 MW	32910 TQ	USBLS	5/07
	Birmingham-Hoover MSA, AL	Y	22940 FQ	27260 MW	34500 TQ	USBLS	5/07
	Alaska	Y	53310 FQ	57670 MW	61990 TQ	USBLS	5/07
	Arizona	Y	23980 FQ	31210 MW	40880 TQ	USBLS	5/07
	Phoenix-Mesa-Scottsdale MSA, AZ	Y	25390 FQ	32310 MW	41720 TQ	USBLS	5/07
	Tucson MSA, AZ	Y	22560 FQ	31460 MW	42640 TQ	USBLS	5/07
	Arkansas	Y	20560 FQ	26510 MW	30300 TQ	USBLS	5/07
	Fayetteville-Springdale-Rogers MSA, AR-MO	Y	21620 FQ	23930 MW	29100 TQ	USBLS	5/07
	Little Rock-North Little Rock MSA, AR	Y	25540 FQ	30250 MW	41910 TQ	USBLS	5/07
	California	H	15.88 FQ	22.29 MW	32.56 TQ	CABLS	1/08-3/08
	Los Angeles-Long Beach-Glendale PMSA, CA	H	15.37 FQ	24.47 MW	40.98 TQ	CABLS	1/08-3/08
	Oakland-Fremont-Hayward MSA, CA	H	16.71 FQ	26.46 MW	39.16 TQ	CABLS	1/08-3/08
	Riverside-San Bernardino-Ontario MSA, CA	H	17.19 FQ	22.40 MW	29.21 TQ	CABLS	1/08-3/08
	Sacramento-Arden Arcade-Roseville MSA, CA	H	16.32 FQ	19.51 MW	24.61 TQ	CABLS	1/08-3/08
	San Diego-Carlsbad-San Marcos MSA, CA	H	23.37 FQ	33.21 MW	36.47 TQ	CABLS	1/08-3/08
	San Francisco-San Mateo-Redwood PMSA, CA	H	21.64 FQ	27.76 MW	38.28 TQ	CABLS	1/08-3/08
	San Jose-Sunnyvale-Santa Clara MSA, CA	H	20.03 FQ	23.31 MW	28.00 TQ	CABLS	1/08-3/08
	Santa Ana-Anaheim-Irvine PMSA, CA	Y	30510 FQ	40670 MW	50900 TQ	USBLS	5/07
	Stockton MSA, CA	H	15.36 FQ	18.44 MW	22.27 TQ	CABLS	1/08-3/08
	Colorado	Y	31990 FQ	39530 MW	49480 TQ	USBLS	5/07
	Denver-Aurora MSA, CO	Y	33930 FQ	42190 MW	52440 TQ	USBLS	5/07
	Connecticut	H	14.86 AE	22.12 MW		CTBLS	1/08-3/08

AE	Average entry wage	**AW**	Average wage paid	**FQ**	First quartile wage	**LO**	Lowest wage paid
AER	Average entry range	**AWR**	Average wage range	**H**	Hourly	**LR**	Low end range
AEX	Average experienced wage	**AXR**	Average experienced range	**HI**	Highest wage paid	**M**	Monthly
ATC	Average total compensation	**D**	Daily	**HR**	High end range	**MCC**	Median cash compensation

MTC	Median total compensation	**TCC**	Total cash compensation
MW	Median wage paid	**TQ**	Third quartile wage
MWR	Median wage range	**W**	Weekly
S	See annotated source	**Y**	Yearly

Glazier

Occupation/Type/Industry	Location	Per	Low	Mid	High	Source	Date
Glazier	Bridgeport-Stamford-Norwalk MSA, CT	Y	39310 FQ	51560 MW	61850 TQ	USBLS	5/07
	Hartford-West Hartford-East Hartford MSA, CT	Y	30530 FQ	37440 MW	50650 TQ	USBLS	5/07
	Delaware	Y	27250 FQ	30250 MW	33770 TQ	USBLS	5/07
	Washington-Arlington-Alexandria MSA, DC-VA-MD-WV	Y	32650 FQ	40430 MW	48810 TQ	USBLS	5/07
	Florida	Y	26620 FQ	32110 MW	37590 TQ	USBLS	5/07
	Cape Coral-Fort Myers MSA, FL	Y	30220 FQ	36000 MW	42950 TQ	USBLS	5/07
	Fort Lauderdale-Pompano Beach-Deerfield Beach PMSA, FL	Y	33440 FQ	37070 MW	43440 TQ	USBLS	5/07
	Jacksonville MSA, FL	Y	32400 FQ	38740 MW	45060 TQ	USBLS	5/07
	Miami-Fort Lauderdale-Miami Beach MSA, FL	Y	26810 FQ	34060 MW	39580 TQ	USBLS	5/07
	Orlando-Kissimmee MSA, FL	Y	25790 FQ	31980 MW	36830 TQ	USBLS	5/07
	Pensacola-Ferry Pass-Brent MSA, FL	Y	24500 FQ	29590 MW	34280 TQ	USBLS	5/07
	Tampa-St. Petersburg-Clearwater MSA, FL	Y	27820 FQ	32510 MW	37200 TQ	USBLS	5/07
	West Palm Beach-Boca Raton-Boynton Beach PMSA, FL	Y	25650 FQ	33710 MW	38470 TQ	USBLS	5/07
	Georgia	Y	28710 FQ	33760 MW	39910 TQ	USBLS	5/07
	Atlanta-Sandy Springs-Marietta MSA, GA	Y	30830 FQ	35200 MW	42160 TQ	USBLS	5/07
	Hawaii	Y	34390 FQ	40830 MW	51510 TQ	USBLS	5/07
	Honolulu MSA, HI	Y	34950 FQ	39980 MW	54360 TQ	USBLS	5/07
	Idaho	Y	22260 FQ	32630 MW	42610 TQ	USBLS	5/07
	Illinois	Y	50250 FQ	67720 MW	75300 TQ	USBLS	5/07
	Chicago-Naperville-Joliet MSA, IL-IN-WI	Y	52210 FQ	70570 MW	77150 TQ	USBLS	5/07
	Indiana	Y	27580 FQ	35300 MW	44930 TQ	USBLS	5/07
	Indianapolis-Carmel MSA, IN	Y	29850 FQ	40850 MW	47700 TQ	USBLS	5/07
	Iowa	Y	28410 FQ	35610 MW	41690 TQ	USBLS	5/07
	Des Moines-West Des Moines MSA, IA	Y	31790 FQ	40220 MW	47930 TQ	USBLS	5/07
	Kansas	Y	28870 FQ	33960 MW	41930 TQ	USBLS	5/07
	Wichita MSA, KS	Y	30180 FQ	35720 MW	54500 TQ	USBLS	5/07
	Kentucky	Y	24449 FQ	30798 MW	40086 TQ	KYBLS	2008
	Louisville-Jefferson County MSA, KY-IN	Y	25930 FQ	29870 MW	39120 TQ	USBLS	5/07
	Louisiana	H	12.56 FQ	14.47 MW	17.54 TQ	LABLS	1/08-3/08
	Baton Rouge MSA, LA	Y	25710 FQ	28200 MW	30710 TQ	USBLS	5/07
	New Orleans-Metairie-Kenner MSA, LA	Y	27330 FQ	33500 MW	40740 TQ	USBLS	5/07
	Maine	Y	27050 FQ	29640 MW	32460 TQ	USBLS	5/07
	Maryland	Y		39125 MW		MDBLS	3/08
	Baltimore-Towson MSA, MD	Y	29330 FQ	37900 MW	47040 TQ	USBLS	5/07
	Bethesda-Gaithersburg-Frederick PMSA, MD	Y	34000 FQ	38110 MW	44620 TQ	USBLS	5/07
	Massachusetts	Y	29690 FQ	37250 MW	47530 TQ	USBLS	5/07
	Boston-Cambridge-Quincy NECTA, MA	Y	29930 FQ	36910 MW	48990 TQ	USBLS	5/07
	Worcester MSA, MA-CT	Y	27710 FQ	30180 MW	36760 TQ	USBLS	5/07
	Michigan	Y	31970 FQ	43120 MW	51160 TQ	USBLS	5/07
	Detroit-Warren-Livonia MSA, MI	Y	33450 FQ	43080 MW	51900 TQ	USBLS	5/07
	Grand Rapids-Wyoming MSA, MI	Y	41930 FQ	46100 MW	50270 TQ	USBLS	5/07
	Warren-Troy-Farmington Hills PMSA, MI	Y	31710 FQ	40040 MW	52780 TQ	USBLS	5/07
	Minnesota	Y	36843 FQ	46265 MW	53968 TQ	MNBLS	10/08-12/08
	Minneapolis-Saint Paul MSA, MN-WI	Y	40458 FQ	49331 MW	64939 TQ	MNBLS	10/08-12/08
	Mississippi	Y	25500 FQ	30420 MW	38280 TQ	USBLS	5/07
	Jackson MSA, MS	Y	23940 FQ	31830 MW	41070 TQ	USBLS	5/07
	Missouri	Y	31280 FQ	44350 MW	62520 TQ	USBLS	5/07
	Kansas City MSA, MO-KS	Y	33270 FQ	42940 MW	55070 TQ	USBLS	5/07
	St. Louis MSA, MO-IL	Y	35880 FQ	55570 MW	70640 TQ	USBLS	5/07
	Montana	Y	27480 FQ	31840 MW	37240 TQ	USBLS	5/07

Glazier

Occupation/Type/Industry	Location	Per	Low	Mid	High	Source	Date
Glazier	Nebraska	Y	25680 FQ	31530 MW	38780 TQ	USBLS	5/07
	Omaha-Council Bluffs MSA, NE-IA	Y	24360 FQ	31630 MW	39460 TQ	USBLS	5/07
	Nevada	H	15.51 FQ	22.18 MW	33.57 TQ	NVBLS	5/08
	Carson City MSA, NV	H	10.78 FQ	15.32 MW	21.55 TQ	NVBLS	5/08
	Las Vegas-Paradise MSA, NV	H	17.69 FQ	27.04 MW	35.51 TQ	NVBLS	5/08
	New Hampshire	H	13.58 AE	18.55 MW	22.23 AEX	NHBLS	6/08
	New Jersey	Y	39720 FQ	46000 MW	61970 TQ	USBLS	5/07
	Camden PMSA, NJ	Y	39740 FQ	42630 MW	45540 TQ	USBLS	5/07
	Edison PMSA, NJ	Y	27060 FQ	63510 MW	70900 TQ	USBLS	5/07
	Newark-Union PMSA, NJ-PA	Y	50880 FQ	64450 MW	72290 TQ	USBLS	5/07
	New Mexico	Y	22450 FQ	28800 MW	36040 TQ	USBLS	5/07
	Albuquerque MSA, NM	Y	21670 FQ	26510 MW	32050 TQ	USBLS	5/07
	New York	Y	32990 FQ	44900 MW	69340 TQ	USBLS	5/07
	Buffalo-Niagara Falls MSA, NY	Y	33570 FQ	38210 MW	43850 TQ	USBLS	5/07
	New York-Northern New Jersey-Long Island MSA, NY-NJ-PA	Y	35370 FQ	47780 MW	70160 TQ	USBLS	5/07
	North Carolina	Y	26190 FQ	30100 MW	35480 TQ	USBLS	5/07
	Charlotte-Gastonia-Concord MSA, NC-SC	Y	27100 FQ	31740 MW	37170 TQ	USBLS	5/07
	Raleigh-Cary MSA, NC	Y	26650 FQ	29800 MW	36080 TQ	USBLS	5/07
	North Dakota	Y	25180 FQ	30370 MW	42800 TQ	USBLS	5/07
	Ohio	Y	26500 FQ	35050 MW	52190 TQ	USBLS	5/07
	Cincinnati-Middletown MSA, OH-KY-IN	Y	26340 FQ	37280 MW	48460 TQ	USBLS	5/07
	Cleveland-Elyria-Mentor MSA, OH	Y	37850 FQ	54720 MW	60800 TQ	USBLS	5/07
	Columbus MSA, OH	Y	25930 FQ	31770 MW	41960 TQ	USBLS	5/07
	Dayton MSA, OH	Y	28890 FQ	54140 MW	60040 TQ	USBLS	5/07
	Oklahoma	Y	21930 FQ	25120 MW	30110 TQ	USBLS	5/07
	Oklahoma City MSA, OK	Y	22120 FQ	27710 MW	33910 TQ	USBLS	5/07
	Tulsa MSA, OK	Y	22360 FQ	24920 MW	29230 TQ	USBLS	5/07
	Oregon	H	12.66 FQ	16.94 MW	24.12 TQ	ORBLS	5/08
	Portland-Vancouver-Beaverton MSA, OR-WA	Y	31160 FQ	40000 MW	57020 TQ	USBLS	5/07
	Pennsylvania	Y	21170 FQ	31560 MW	46840 TQ	USBLS	5/07
	Allentown-Bethlehem-Easton MSA, PA-NJ	Y	31740 FQ	38990 MW	61900 TQ	USBLS	5/07
	Philadelphia-Camden-Wilmington MSA, PA-NJ-DE-MD	Y	26550 FQ	39520 MW	48160 TQ	USBLS	5/07
	Pittsburgh MSA, PA	Y	14980 FQ	16410 MW	29250 TQ	USBLS	5/07
	Providence-Fall River-Warwick MSA, RI-MA	Y	34230 FQ	44100 MW	58340 TQ	USBLS	5/07
	South Carolina	Y	23900 FQ	27640 MW	31300 TQ	USBLS	5/07
	Charleston-North Charleston MSA, SC	Y	22660 FQ	25930 MW	35260 TQ	USBLS	5/07
	Columbia MSA, SC	Y	25830 FQ	29240 MW	32800 TQ	USBLS	5/07
	South Dakota	Y	24452 FQ	28162 MW	34067 TQ	SDBLS	7/08-9/08
	Tennessee	Y	21520 FQ	26190 MW	31940 TQ	USBLS	5/07
	Memphis MSA, TN-MS-AR	Y	27000 FQ	30190 MW	34800 TQ	USBLS	5/07
	Nashville-Davidson-Murfreesboro MSA, TN	Y	22970 FQ	28780 MW	35910 TQ	USBLS	5/07
	Texas	Y	23680 FQ	29580 MW	36500 TQ	USBLS	5/07
	Beaumont-Port Arthur MSA, TX	Y	24800 FQ	30660 MW	39140 TQ	USBLS	5/07
	Brownsville-Harlingen MSA, TX	Y	16700 FQ	17930 MW	19190 TQ	USBLS	5/07
	Dallas-Fort Worth-Arlington MSA, TX	Y	28140 FQ	33790 MW	39730 TQ	USBLS	5/07
	El Paso MSA, TX	Y	22620 FQ	25250 MW	29790 TQ	USBLS	5/07
	Houston-Sugar Land-Baytown MSA, TX	Y	28270 FQ	35060 MW	40290 TQ	USBLS	5/07
	San Antonio MSA, TX	Y	19930 FQ	24970 MW	29450 TQ	USBLS	5/07
	Utah	Y	27190 FQ	34380 MW	42330 TQ	USBLS	5/07
	Salt Lake City MSA, UT	Y	28060 FQ	34770 MW	42180 TQ	USBLS	5/07
	Vermont	Y	27350 FQ	35250 MW	40570 TQ	USBLS	5/07
	Burlington-South Burlington MSA, VT	Y	25360 FQ	34510 MW	38920 TQ	USBLS	5/07
	Virginia	Y	27610 FQ	34300 MW	44570 TQ	USBLS	5/07

AE	Average entry wage	AW	Average wage paid	FQ	First quartile wage
AER	Average entry range	AWR	Average wage range	H	Hourly
AEX	Average experienced wage	AXR	Average experienced range	HI	Highest wage paid
ATC	Average total compensation	D	Daily	HR	High end range

LO	Lowest wage paid	MTC	Median total compensation	TCC	Total cash compensation
LR	Low end range	MW	Median wage paid	TQ	Third quartile wage
M	Monthly	MWR	Median wage range	W	Weekly
MCC	Median cash compensation	S	See annotated source	Y	Yearly

Occupation/Type/Industry	Location	Per	Low	Mid	High	Source	Date
Glazier	Richmond MSA, VA	Y	33780 FQ	38330 MW	45110 TQ	USBLS	5/07
	Roanoke MSA, VA	Y	23100 FQ	28540 MW	33260 TQ	USBLS	5/07
	Virginia Beach-Norfolk- Newport News MSA, VA-NC	Y	24980 FQ	30180 MW	38170 TQ	USBLS	5/07
	Washington	H	15.97 FQ	19.55 MW	24.33 TQ	WABLS	3/08
	Seattle-Tacoma-Bellevue MSA, WA	Y	34160 FQ	42280 MW	52670 TQ	USBLS	5/07
	West Virginia	Y	26959 FQ	37916 MW	55469 TQ	WVBLS	7/08-9/08
	Wisconsin	Y	33970 FQ	41170 MW	56670 TQ	USBLS	5/07
	Milwaukee-Waukesha-West Allis MSA, WI	Y	36000 FQ	44750 MW	57850 TQ	USBLS	5/07
	Wyoming	Y	28041 FQ	34298 MW	39760 TQ	WYBLS	9/08
	Puerto Rico	Y	12810 FQ	14880 MW	17550 TQ	USBLS	5/07
	San Juan-Caguas-Guaynabo MSA, PR	Y	12960 FQ	15160 MW	17850 TQ	USBLS	5/07
Global Practice Leader Disaster Recovery	United States	Y		176900 AW		DRJ01	2006-2007
Goal Ball Head Coach Montana State School for the Deaf and Blind	Montana	S			1000 HI	MTSDB	10/08-6/09
Golf Coach Public High School	Baldwin County, AL	S	1685 LO		2809 HI	BCPSSS	2008-2009
Golf Course Technician Municipal Government	Seattle, WA	H	17.43 LO		20.80 HI	CSSS	2007
Governor	Alaska	Y			125000 HI	PARD01	2008
	Louisiana	Y			130000 HI	STLEG1	2008
	Maine	Y			70000 HI	PARD01	2008
	Michigan	Y			177000 HI	LSJ01	6/07
	Nebraska	Y			105000 HI	NEST	2008
	Nevada	Y			141000 HI	LVSUN	2008
	Pennsylvania	Y			170000 HI	STLEG2	2008
	Rhode Island	Y			119818 HI	RIM01	2009
Grader and Sorter							
Agricultural Products	Alabama	Y	16800 FQ	20700 MW	23180 TQ	USBLS	5/07
Agricultural Products	Birmingham-Hoover MSA, AL	Y	18220 FQ	21850 MW	23910 TQ	USBLS	5/07
Agricultural Products	Arizona	Y	15900 FQ	17300 MW	18750 TQ	USBLS	5/07
Agricultural Products	Phoenix-Mesa-Scottsdale MSA, AZ	Y	16320 FQ	17730 MW	19140 TQ	USBLS	5/07
Agricultural Products	Arkansas	Y	19800 FQ	22100 MW	24340 TQ	USBLS	5/07
Agricultural Products	Little Rock-North Little Rock MSA, AR	Y	24050 FQ	28870 MW	40270 TQ	USBLS	5/07
Agricultural Products	California	H	8.08 FQ	8.75 MW	9.48 TQ	CABLS	1/08-3/08
Agricultural Products	Los Angeles-Long Beach- Glendale PMSA, CA	H	8.00 FQ	8.00 MW	8.87 TQ	CABLS	1/08-3/08
Agricultural Products	Oakland-Fremont-Hayward MSA, CA	H	8.28 FQ	8.94 MW	10.31 TQ	CABLS	1/08-3/08
Agricultural Products	Oxnard-Thousand Oaks- Ventura MSA, CA	H	8.53 FQ	9.17 MW	9.83 TQ	CABLS	1/08-3/08
Agricultural Products	Riverside-San Bernardino- Ontario MSA, CA	H	8.06 FQ	8.61 MW	9.25 TQ	CABLS	1/08-3/08
Agricultural Products	Sacramento-Arden Arcade- Roseville MSA, CA	H	9.49 FQ	10.20 MW	11.26 TQ	CABLS	1/08-3/08
Agricultural Products	San Diego-Carlsbad-San Marcos MSA, CA	H	8.22 FQ	8.75 MW	9.28 TQ	CABLS	1/08-3/08
Agricultural Products	San Jose-Sunnyvale-Santa Clara MSA, CA	H	8.00 FQ	8.00 MW	8.02 TQ	CABLS	1/08-3/08
Agricultural Products	Colorado	Y	14690 FQ	15160 MW	15830 TQ	USBLS	5/07
Agricultural Products	Denver-Aurora MSA, CO	Y	15630 FQ	22600 MW	31750 TQ	USBLS	5/07
Agricultural Products	Connecticut	H	8.60 AE	10.14 MW		CTBLS	1/08-3/08
Agricultural Products	Florida	Y	14740 FQ	15690 MW	17500 TQ	USBLS	5/07
Agricultural Products	Lakeland MSA, FL	Y	14670 FQ	15500 MW	17380 TQ	USBLS	5/07
Agricultural Products	Miami-Fort Lauderdale-Miami Beach MSA, FL	Y	15530 FQ	16750 MW	18050 TQ	USBLS	5/07
Agricultural Products	Tampa-St. Petersburg- Clearwater MSA, FL	Y	14480 FQ	15080 MW	16370 TQ	USBLS	5/07

AE	Average entry wage	**AW**	Average wage paid	**FQ**	First quartile wage	**LO** Lowest wage paid
AER	Average entry range	**AWR**	Average wage range	**H**	Hourly	**LR** Low end range
AEX	Average experienced wage	**AXR**	Average experienced range	**HI**	Highest wage paid	**M** Monthly
ATC	Average total compensation	**D**	Daily	**HR**	High end range	**MCC** Median cash compensation

MTC Median total compensation **TCC** Total cash compensation
MW Median wage paid **TQ** Third quartile wage
MWR Median wage range **W** Weekly
S See annotated source **Y** Yearly

Occupation/Type/Industry	Location	Per	Low	Mid	High	Source	Date
Grader and Sorter							
Agricultural Products	West Palm Beach-Boca Raton-Boynton Beach PMSA, FL	Y	16740 FQ	17950 MW	19150 TQ	USBLS	5/07
Agricultural Products	Georgia	Y	13460 FQ	15750 MW	23770 TQ	USBLS	5/07
Agricultural Products	Atlanta-Sandy Springs-Marietta MSA, GA	Y	16530 FQ	19670 MW	23330 TQ	USBLS	5/07
Agricultural Products	Idaho	Y	12810 FQ	14360 MW	16360 TQ	USBLS	5/07
Agricultural Products	Boise City-Nampa MSA, ID	Y	13470 FQ	15660 MW	19320 TQ	USBLS	5/07
Agricultural Products	Idaho Falls MSA, ID	Y	12720 FQ	13980 MW	15240 TQ	USBLS	5/07
Agricultural Products	Illinois	Y	16340 FQ	19830 MW	24870 TQ	USBLS	5/07
Agricultural Products	Chicago-Naperville-Joliet MSA, IL-IN-WI	Y	15760 FQ	18690 MW	23240 TQ	USBLS	5/07
Agricultural Products	Indiana	Y	18200 FQ	22410 MW	27360 TQ	USBLS	5/07
Agricultural Products	Iowa	Y	22640 FQ	26820 MW	31820 TQ	USBLS	5/07
Agricultural Products	Sioux City MSA, IA-NE-SD	Y	19670 FQ	22110 MW	24290 TQ	USBLS	5/07
Agricultural Products	Kansas	Y	18870 FQ	26590 MW	33870 TQ	USBLS	5/07
Agricultural Products	Kentucky	Y	19354 FQ	23950 MW	30959 TQ	KYBLS	2008
Agricultural Products	Louisville-Jefferson County MSA, KY-IN	Y	21310 FQ	24490 MW	31000 TQ	USBLS	5/07
Agricultural Products	Louisiana	H	7.48 FQ	10.28 MW	11.92 TQ	LABLS	1/08-3/08
Agricultural Products	New Orleans-Metairie-Kenner MSA, LA	Y	22420 FQ	25520 MW	33580 TQ	USBLS	5/07
Agricultural Products	Maine	Y	15160 FQ	17170 MW	19150 TQ	USBLS	5/07
Agricultural Products	Maryland	Y		18100 MW		MDBLS	3/08
Agricultural Products	Massachusetts	Y	16040 FQ	18150 MW	22990 TQ	USBLS	5/07
Agricultural Products	Boston-Cambridge-Quincy NECTA, MA	Y	15890 FQ	16270 MW	21700 TQ	USBLS	5/07
Agricultural Products	Springfield MSA, MA-CT	Y	16640 FQ	18770 MW	21600 TQ	USBLS	5/07
Agricultural Products	Michigan	Y	15060 FQ	15800 MW	28370 TQ	USBLS	5/07
Agricultural Products	Grand Rapids-Wyoming MSA, MI	Y	14910 FQ	15250 MW	17800 TQ	USBLS	5/07
Agricultural Products	Minnesota	Y	20961 FQ	27611 MW	36253 TQ	MNBLS	10/08-12/08
Agricultural Products	Mississippi	Y	16940 FQ	20400 MW	23050 TQ	USBLS	5/07
Agricultural Products	Missouri	Y	15840 FQ	22940 MW	32810 TQ	USBLS	5/07
Agricultural Products	Nebraska	Y	20640 FQ	23220 MW	26320 TQ	USBLS	5/07
Agricultural Products	Nevada	H	7.24 FQ	8.55 MW	9.91 TQ	NVBLS	5/08
Agricultural Products	Las Vegas-Paradise MSA, NV	H	6.87 FQ	8.00 MW	8.95 TQ	NVBLS	5/08
Agricultural Products	New Jersey	Y	16530 FQ	18010 MW	19790 TQ	USBLS	5/07
Agricultural Products	New Mexico	Y	12500 FQ	13530 MW	14550 TQ	USBLS	5/07
Agricultural Products	New York	Y	16160 FQ	18640 MW	23170 TQ	USBLS	5/07
Agricultural Products	Buffalo-Niagara Falls MSA, NY	Y	17070 FQ	19110 MW	22600 TQ	USBLS	5/07
Agricultural Products	North Carolina	Y	14000 FQ	15220 MW	18770 TQ	USBLS	5/07
Agricultural Products	North Dakota	Y	16820 FQ	21310 MW	25740 TQ	USBLS	5/07
Agricultural Products	Ohio	Y	18010 FQ	20480 MW	28950 TQ	USBLS	5/07
Agricultural Products	Oklahoma	Y	17510 FQ	21210 MW	23870 TQ	USBLS	5/07
Agricultural Products	Oregon	H	8.65 FQ	9.34 MW	10.82 TQ	ORBLS	5/08
Agricultural Products	Portland-Vancouver-Beaverton MSA, OR-WA	Y	17680 FQ	19170 MW	23860 TQ	USBLS	5/07
Agricultural Products	Pennsylvania	Y	17180 FQ	22390 MW	30380 TQ	USBLS	5/07
Agricultural Products	Philadelphia-Camden-Wilmington MSA, PA-NJ-DE-MD	Y	15900 FQ	17690 MW	19700 TQ	USBLS	5/07
Agricultural Products	South Carolina	Y	12580 FQ	14220 MW	15860 TQ	USBLS	5/07
Agricultural Products	South Dakota	Y	21471 FQ	23780 MW	26192 TQ	SDBLS	7/08-9/08
Agricultural Products	Rapid City MSA, SD	Y	27577 FQ	29273 MW	30967 TQ	SDBLS	7/08-9/08
Agricultural Products	Sioux Falls MSA, SD	Y	22436 FQ	24478 MW	27044 TQ	SDBLS	7/08-9/08
Agricultural Products	Tennessee	Y	20750 FQ	22640 MW	24550 TQ	USBLS	5/07
Agricultural Products	Memphis MSA, TN-MS-AR	Y	21090 FQ	22690 MW	24290 TQ	USBLS	5/07
Agricultural Products	Texas	Y	13910 FQ	17150 MW	22260 TQ	USBLS	5/07
Agricultural Products	Dallas-Fort Worth-Arlington MSA, TX	Y	23370 FQ	40930 MW	44720 TQ	USBLS	5/07
Agricultural Products	Houston-Sugar Land-Baytown MSA, TX	Y	15310 FQ	17250 MW	18960 TQ	USBLS	5/07
Agricultural Products	San Antonio MSA, TX	Y	13830 FQ	15930 MW	18080 TQ	USBLS	5/07
Agricultural Products	Utah	Y	16750 FQ	20640 MW	24520 TQ	USBLS	5/07
Agricultural Products	Salt Lake City MSA, UT	Y	20820 FQ	22410 MW	24000 TQ	USBLS	5/07
Agricultural Products	Vermont	Y	17650 FQ	19840 MW	24300 TQ	USBLS	5/07
Agricultural Products	Virginia	Y	20340 FQ	22260 MW	24130 TQ	USBLS	5/07
Agricultural Products	Washington	H	8.63 FQ	9.37 MW	11.21 TQ	WABLS	3/08
Agricultural Products	Seattle-Tacoma-Bellevue MSA, WA	Y	18320 FQ	20410 MW	27530 TQ	USBLS	5/07

AE	Average entry wage	AW	Average wage paid	FQ	First quartile wage
AER	Average entry range	AWR	Average wage range	H	Hourly
AEX	Average experienced wage	AXR	Average experienced range	HI	Highest wage paid
ATC	Average total compensation	D	Daily	HR	High end range

LO	Lowest wage paid	MTC	Median total compensation	TCC	Total cash compensation
LR	Low end range	MW	Median wage paid	TQ	Third quartile wage
M	Monthly	MWR	Median wage range	W	Weekly
MCC	Median cash compensation	S	See annotated source	Y	Yearly

Occupation/Type/Industry	Location	Per	Low	Mid	High	Source	Date
Grader and Sorter							
Agricultural Products	Wisconsin	Y	21640 FQ	25060 MW	28730 TQ	USBLS	5/07
Agricultural Products	Puerto Rico	Y	12840 FQ	14750 MW	17660 TQ	USBLS	5/07
Agricultural Products	San Juan-Caguas-Guaynabo MSA, PR	Y	16780 FQ	18150 MW	19530 TQ	USBLS	5/07
Graduate Teaching Assistant	Arizona	Y	24440 FQ	30370 MW	36840 TQ	USBLS	5/07
	Little Rock-North Little Rock MSA, AR	Y	17930 FQ	19470 MW	21190 TQ	USBLS	5/07
	California	Y		30385 AW		CABLS	1/08-3/08
	Los Angeles-Long Beach-Glendale PMSA, CA	Y		32097 AW		CABLS	1/08-3/08
	Oakland-Fremont-Hayward MSA, CA	Y		30457 AW		CABLS	1/08-3/08
	Riverside-San Bernardino-Ontario MSA, CA	Y		33594 AW		CABLS	1/08-3/08
	San Diego-Carlsbad-San Marcos MSA, CA	Y		29718 AW		CABLS	1/08-3/08
	San Jose-Sunnyvale-Santa Clara MSA, CA	Y		24375 AW		CABLS	1/08-3/08
	Delaware	Y	16480 FQ	24880 MW	34620 TQ	USBLS	5/07
	Wilmington PMSA, DE-MD-NJ	Y	16590 FQ	24990 MW	34800 TQ	USBLS	5/07
	District of Columbia	Y	25090 FQ	31920 MW	38690 TQ	USBLS	5/07
	Washington-Arlington-Alexandria MSA, DC-VA-MD-WV	Y	21070 FQ	31690 MW	45750 TQ	USBLS	5/07
	Florida	Y	32120 FQ	35920 MW	42010 TQ	USBLS	5/07
	Miami-Fort Lauderdale-Miami Beach MSA, FL	Y	28520 FQ	34410 MW	42600 TQ	USBLS	5/07
	Georgia	Y	13250 FQ	15170 MW	23110 TQ	USBLS	5/07
	Illinois	Y	15950 FQ	22150 MW	32240 TQ	USBLS	5/07
	Chicago-Naperville-Joliet MSA, IL-IN-WI	Y	16520 FQ	22460 MW	34720 TQ	USBLS	5/07
	Indiana	Y	20860 FQ	27930 MW	33720 TQ	USBLS	5/07
	Louisiana	Y		25627 AW		LABLS	1/08-3/08
	Baton Rouge MSA, LA	Y	26660 FQ	32330 MW	45520 TQ	USBLS	5/07
	Maryland	Y		41275 MW		MDBLS	3/08
	Baltimore-Towson MSA, MD	Y	33880 FQ	42060 MW	50340 TQ	USBLS	5/07
	Bethesda-Gaithersburg-Frederick PMSA, MD	Y	16550 FQ	41030 MW	54670 TQ	USBLS	5/07
	Massachusetts	Y	35850 FQ	43620 MW	50990 TQ	USBLS	5/07
	Boston-Cambridge-Quincy NECTA, MA	Y	37940 FQ	45020 MW	51740 TQ	USBLS	5/07
	Worcester MSA, MA-CT	Y	32580 FQ	40660 MW	47560 TQ	USBLS	5/07
	Michigan	Y	34540 FQ	39110 MW	45030 TQ	USBLS	5/07
	Mississippi	Y	23920 FQ	29030 MW	38820 TQ	USBLS	5/07
	Missouri	Y	15000 FQ	20270 MW	24230 TQ	USBLS	5/07
	St. Louis MSA, MO-IL	Y	15400 FQ	22560 MW	28200 TQ	USBLS	5/07
	Nebraska	Y	14050 FQ	18520 MW	35720 TQ	USBLS	5/07
	New Jersey	Y	20700 FQ	28300 MW	39070 TQ	USBLS	5/07
	Newark-Union PMSA, NJ-PA	Y	22870 FQ	32210 MW	45320 TQ	USBLS	5/07
	New Mexico	Y	39050 FQ	42480 MW	45920 TQ	USBLS	5/07
	Albuquerque MSA, NM	Y	38960 FQ	42400 MW	45880 TQ	USBLS	5/07
	New York	Y	24090 FQ	27900 MW	36280 TQ	USBLS	5/07
	Albany-Schenectady-Troy MSA, NY	Y	28370 FQ	30460 MW	32530 TQ	USBLS	5/07
	Buffalo-Niagara Falls MSA, NY	Y	28290 FQ	30340 MW	32410 TQ	USBLS	5/07
	Nassau-Suffolk PMSA, NY	Y	26120 FQ	28140 MW	30170 TQ	USBLS	5/07
	New York-Northern New Jersey-Long Island MSA, NY-NJ-PA	Y	19210 FQ	28730 MW	41960 TQ	USBLS	5/07
	North Carolina	Y	22210 FQ	29550 MW	36970 TQ	USBLS	5/07
	North Dakota	Y	21230 FQ	36420 MW	55350 TQ	USBLS	5/07
	Ohio	Y	26810 FQ	39000 MW	47820 TQ	USBLS	5/07
	Oklahoma	Y	19870 FQ	21600 MW	23320 TQ	USBLS	5/07
	Oregon	Y	28367 FQ	34097 MW	40860 TQ	ORBLS	5/08
	Portland-Vancouver-Beaverton MSA, OR-WA	Y	21610 FQ	29400 MW	38670 TQ	USBLS	5/07
	Pennsylvania	Y	15390 FQ	24330 MW	31930 TQ	USBLS	5/07

Occupation/Type/Industry	Location	Per	Low	Mid	High	Source	Date

Graduate Teaching Assistant	Philadelphia-Camden-
	  Wilmington MSA, PA-NJ-DE-
	  MD
		Y	18920 FQ	26190 MW	33650 TQ	USBLS	5/07

	Pittsburgh MSA, PA	Y	15670 FQ	25840 MW	43590 TQ	USBLS	5/07
	South Carolina	Y	24760 FQ	29850 MW	37270 TQ	USBLS	5/07
	Tennessee	Y	14300 FQ	21070 MW	25930 TQ	USBLS	5/07
	Nashville-Davidson- Murfreesboro MSA, TN	Y	20980 FQ	22770 MW	25030 TQ	USBLS	5/07
	Texas	Y	20720 FQ	27640 MW	38520 TQ	USBLS	5/07
	Austin-Round Rock MSA, TX	Y	21120 FQ	27570 MW	32760 TQ	USBLS	5/07
	Dallas-Fort Worth-Arlington MSA, TX	Y	18280 FQ	25650 MW	37210 TQ	USBLS	5/07
	Houston-Sugar Land-Baytown MSA, TX	Y	22120 FQ	31820 MW	48970 TQ	USBLS	5/07
	Vermont	Y	25230 FQ	28440 MW	32980 TQ	USBLS	5/07
	Virginia Beach-Norfolk- Newport News MSA, VA-NC	Y	15440 FQ	18620 MW	21590 TQ	USBLS	5/07
	Washington	Y		34823 AW		WABLS	3/08
	Wisconsin	Y	23010 FQ	26060 MW	28940 TQ	USBLS	5/07
	Puerto Rico	Y	13600 FQ	15850 MW	41030 TQ	USBLS	5/07
	San Juan-Caguas-Guaynabo MSA, PR	Y	13370 FQ	15400 MW	38890 TQ	USBLS	5/07
Grain, Feed, and Seed Examiner							
State Government	Ohio	H	18.36 LO		23.87 HI	ODAS	2008
Grain Warehouse Financial Analyst							
State Government	Ohio	H	21.77 LO		31.86 HI	ODAS	2008
Graphic Artist							
Department of Transportation	Michigan	H	15.28 LO		27.47 HI	MDOT	10/1/07
Municipal Government	Carlsbad, CA	S	1730 LO		2103 HI	CCSS01	8/5/08
Graphic Design Supervisor							
Municipal Government	Cincinnati, OH	Y	53522 LO		71929 HI	COHSS	10/08
Graphic Designer	Alabama	Y	27550 FQ	35240 MW	48660 TQ	USBLS	5/07
	Birmingham-Hoover MSA, AL	Y	31070 FQ	41390 MW	58220 TQ	USBLS	5/07
	Alaska	Y	28830 FQ	33770 MW	45340 TQ	USBLS	5/07
	Anchorage MSA, AK	Y	28750 FQ	32960 MW	44520 TQ	USBLS	5/07
	Arizona	Y	31480 FQ	39040 MW	50510 TQ	USBLS	5/07
	Flagstaff MSA, AZ	Y	21670 FQ	35270 MW	45650 TQ	USBLS	5/07
	Phoenix-Mesa-Scottsdale MSA, AZ	Y	31900 FQ	39650 MW	51340 TQ	USBLS	5/07
	Tucson MSA, AZ	Y	33360 FQ	39460 MW	51190 TQ	USBLS	5/07
	Arkansas	Y	24920 FQ	31960 MW	40770 TQ	USBLS	5/07
	Little Rock-North Little Rock MSA, AR	Y	27740 FQ	35960 MW	43030 TQ	USBLS	5/07
	California	H	18.30 FQ	23.90 MW	31.54 TQ	CABLS	1/08-3/08
	Los Angeles-Long Beach- Glendale PMSA, CA	H	18.43 FQ	24.28 MW	33.79 TQ	CABLS	1/08-3/08
	Oakland-Fremont-Hayward MSA, CA	H	20.31 FQ	26.06 MW	30.96 TQ	CABLS	1/08-3/08
	Riverside-San Bernardino- Ontario MSA, CA	H	16.58 FQ	20.86 MW	24.96 TQ	CABLS	1/08-3/08
	Sacramento-Arden Arcade- Roseville MSA, CA	H	16.62 FQ	20.00 MW	26.75 TQ	CABLS	1/08-3/08
	San Diego-Carlsbad-San Marcos MSA, CA	H	16.82 FQ	21.81 MW	28.47 TQ	CABLS	1/08-3/08
	San Francisco-San Mateo- Redwood PMSA, CA	H	22.49 FQ	29.93 MW	38.07 TQ	CABLS	1/08-3/08
	San Jose-Sunnyvale-Santa Clara MSA, CA	H	21.98 FQ	30.44 MW	35.98 TQ	CABLS	1/08-3/08
	Santa Ana-Anaheim-Irvine PMSA, CA	Y	37140 FQ	46440 MW	57720 TQ	USBLS	5/07
	Colorado	Y	30490 FQ	39650 MW	52220 TQ	USBLS	5/07
	Denver-Aurora MSA, CO	Y	32540 FQ	41490 MW	54930 TQ	USBLS	5/07
	Pueblo MSA, CO	Y	26790 FQ	31400 MW	45010 TQ	USBLS	5/07
	Connecticut	H	16.18 AE	22.96 MW		CTBLS	1/08-3/08
	Bridgeport-Stamford-Norwalk MSA, CT	Y	37000 FQ	49040 MW	63330 TQ	USBLS	5/07

Occupation/Type/Industry	Location	Per	Low	Mid	High	Source	Date
Graphic Designer	Danbury MSA, CT	Y	35410 FQ	40120 MW	60300 TQ	USBLS	5/07
	Hartford-West Hartford-East Hartford MSA, CT	Y	33010 FQ	42860 MW	55290 TQ	USBLS	5/07
	New Haven MSA, CT	Y	38240 FQ	48240 MW	59770 TQ	USBLS	5/07
	Norwich-New London MSA, CT-RI	Y	37320 FQ	44780 MW	53530 TQ	USBLS	5/07
	Delaware	Y	31560 FQ	37410 MW	49880 TQ	USBLS	5/07
	Wilmington PMSA, DE-MD-NJ	Y	34160 FQ	40130 MW	54640 TQ	USBLS	5/07
	District of Columbia	Y	45770 FQ	59210 MW	80430 TQ	USBLS	5/07
	Washington-Arlington-Alexandria MSA, DC-VA-MD-WV	Y	41500 FQ	52290 MW	70350 TQ	USBLS	5/07
	Florida	Y	28800 FQ	36370 MW	46160 TQ	USBLS	5/07
	Fort Lauderdale-Pompano Beach-Deerfield Beach PMSA, FL	Y	31540 FQ	38500 MW	50660 TQ	USBLS	5/07
	Jacksonville MSA, FL	Y	29730 FQ	35550 MW	43610 TQ	USBLS	5/07
	Miami-Fort Lauderdale-Miami Beach MSA, FL	Y	32060 FQ	38900 MW	48740 TQ	USBLS	5/07
	Orlando-Kissimmee MSA, FL	Y	27490 FQ	38290 MW	47220 TQ	USBLS	5/07
	Tampa-St. Petersburg-Clearwater MSA, FL	Y	27550 FQ	33580 MW	42840 TQ	USBLS	5/07
	West Palm Beach-Boca Raton-Boynton Beach PMSA, FL	Y	32180 FQ	40820 MW	50950 TQ	USBLS	5/07
	Georgia	Y	32460 FQ	43620 MW	60070 TQ	USBLS	5/07
	Atlanta-Sandy Springs-Marietta MSA, GA	Y	36520 FQ	47820 MW	63540 TQ	USBLS	5/07
	Hawaii	Y	30640 FQ	39370 MW	60610 TQ	USBLS	5/07
	Honolulu MSA, HI	Y	31750 FQ	41810 MW	66730 TQ	USBLS	5/07
	Idaho	Y	25940 FQ	35810 MW	46330 TQ	USBLS	5/07
	Boise City-Nampa MSA, ID	Y	34640 FQ	44060 MW	51310 TQ	USBLS	5/07
	Illinois	Y	32540 FQ	42180 MW	54990 TQ	USBLS	5/07
	Chicago-Naperville-Joliet MSA, IL-IN-WI	Y	33900 FQ	43430 MW	57040 TQ	USBLS	5/07
	Indiana	Y	28160 FQ	35120 MW	45020 TQ	USBLS	5/07
	Evansville MSA, IN-KY	Y	24720 FQ	29830 MW	38050 TQ	USBLS	5/07
	Gary PMSA, IN	Y	28420 FQ	32240 MW	39800 TQ	USBLS	5/07
	Indianapolis-Carmel MSA, IN	Y	33010 FQ	39090 MW	50540 TQ	USBLS	5/07
	Iowa	Y	26060 FQ	32820 MW	42510 TQ	USBLS	5/07
	Des Moines-West Des Moines MSA, IA	Y	32460 FQ	39370 MW	48110 TQ	USBLS	5/07
	Dubuque MSA, IA	Y	27860 FQ	32470 MW	39530 TQ	USBLS	5/07
	Waterloo-Cedar Falls MSA, IA	Y	21710 FQ	28980 MW	42410 TQ	USBLS	5/07
	Kansas	Y	27400 FQ	35130 MW	45600 TQ	USBLS	5/07
	Wichita MSA, KS	Y	27790 FQ	37500 MW	48870 TQ	USBLS	5/07
	Kentucky	Y	27319 FQ	34629 MW	43115 TQ	KYBLS	2008
	Bowling Green MSA, KY	Y	22940 FQ	31390 MW	38080 TQ	USBLS	5/07
	Louisville-Jefferson County MSA, KY-IN	Y	27640 FQ	35420 MW	44250 TQ	USBLS	5/07
	Louisiana	H	12.28 FQ	15.43 MW	19.26 TQ	LABLS	1/08-3/08
	Baton Rouge MSA, LA	Y	27470 FQ	32300 MW	39730 TQ	USBLS	5/07
	New Orleans-Metairie-Kenner MSA, LA	Y	29460 FQ	35940 MW	43520 TQ	USBLS	5/07
	Maine	Y	25290 FQ	34090 MW	43710 TQ	USBLS	5/07
	Lewiston-Auburn MSA, ME	Y	24800 FQ	30880 MW	38280 TQ	USBLS	5/07
	Portland-South Portland-Biddeford MSA, ME	Y	27420 FQ	40160 MW	48010 TQ	USBLS	5/07
	Maryland	Y		45525 MW		MDBLS	3/08
	Baltimore-Towson MSA, MD	Y	34610 FQ	42660 MW	54630 TQ	USBLS	5/07
	Bethesda-Gaithersburg-Frederick PMSA, MD	Y	41510 FQ	50630 MW	68270 TQ	USBLS	5/07
	Massachusetts	Y	34850 FQ	46110 MW	59090 TQ	USBLS	5/07
	Boston-Cambridge-Quincy NECTA, MA	Y	34310 FQ	47220 MW	59920 TQ	USBLS	5/07
	New Bedford MSA, MA	Y	32540 FQ	39540 MW	53490 TQ	USBLS	5/07
	Worcester MSA, MA-CT	Y	34700 FQ	42340 MW	52190 TQ	USBLS	5/07
	Michigan	Y	32750 FQ	42970 MW	57620 TQ	USBLS	5/07
	Detroit-Warren-Livonia MSA, MI	Y	35300 FQ	48550 MW	63010 TQ	USBLS	5/07
	Grand Rapids-Wyoming MSA, MI	Y	33600 FQ	43270 MW	54610 TQ	USBLS	5/07

AE	Average entry wage	AW	Average wage paid	
AER	Average entry range	AWR	Average wage range	
AEX	Average experienced wage	AXR	Average experienced range	
ATC	Average total compensation	D	Daily	

FQ	First quartile wage
H	Hourly
HI	Highest wage paid
HR	High end range

LO	Lowest wage paid
LR	Low end range
M	Monthly
MCC	Median cash compensation

MTC	Median total compensation
MW	Median wage paid
MWR	Median wage range
S	See annotated source

TCC	Total cash compensation
TQ	Third quartile wage
W	Weekly
Y	Yearly

Occupation/Type/Industry	Location	Per	Low	Mid	High	Source	Date
Graphic Designer	Warren-Troy-Farmington Hills PMSA, MI	Y	34790 FQ	48770 MW	63280 TQ	USBLS	5/07
	Minnesota	Y	33406 FQ	42717 MW	55533 TQ	MNBLS	10/08-12/08
	Duluth-Superior MSA, MN-WI	Y	28143 FQ	34347 MW	47739 TQ	MNBLS	10/08-12/08
	Minneapolis-Saint Paul MSA, MN-WI	Y	36272 FQ	45196 MW	58640 TQ	MNBLS	10/08-12/08
	Rochester MSA, MN	Y	42147 FQ	52481 MW	66429 TQ	MNBLS	10/08-12/08
	Mississippi	Y	26650 FQ	32830 MW	43580 TQ	USBLS	5/07
	Gulfport-Biloxi MSA, MS	Y	31970 FQ	39570 MW	46830 TQ	USBLS	5/07
	Jackson MSA, MS	Y	30570 FQ	38000 MW	52630 TQ	USBLS	5/07
	Missouri	Y	26790 FQ	35190 MW	46330 TQ	USBLS	5/07
	Kansas City MSA, MO-KS	Y	30970 FQ	38340 MW	48130 TQ	USBLS	5/07
	St. Louis MSA, MO-IL	Y	31140 FQ	39940 MW	48960 TQ	USBLS	5/07
	Montana	Y	22360 FQ	29410 MW	37060 TQ	USBLS	5/07
	Billings MSA, MT	Y	28200 FQ	36550 MW	42930 TQ	USBLS	5/07
	Nebraska	Y	25740 FQ	34280 MW	45030 TQ	USBLS	5/07
	Omaha-Council Bluffs MSA, NE-IA	Y	28930 FQ	37280 MW	47440 TQ	USBLS	5/07
	Nevada	H	16.89 FQ	20.82 MW	28.45 TQ	NVBLS	5/08
	Las Vegas-Paradise MSA, NV	H	16.80 FQ	20.57 MW	28.59 TQ	NVBLS	5/08
	New Hampshire	H	14.44 AE	19.10 MW	22.51 AEX	NHBLS	6/08
	Manchester MSA, NH	Y	31780 FQ	36570 MW	53100 TQ	USBLS	5/07
	Nashua NECTA, NH-MA	Y	31380 FQ	38120 MW	44380 TQ	USBLS	5/07
	New Jersey	Y	35970 FQ	46250 MW	59890 TQ	USBLS	5/07
	Camden PMSA, NJ	Y	30140 FQ	40750 MW	52780 TQ	USBLS	5/07
	Edison PMSA, NJ	Y	31430 FQ	41750 MW	56190 TQ	USBLS	5/07
	Newark-Union PMSA, NJ-PA	Y	39590 FQ	47850 MW	61090 TQ	USBLS	5/07
	New Mexico	Y	21060 FQ	35020 MW	46350 TQ	USBLS	5/07
	Albuquerque MSA, NM	Y	18180 FQ	34350 MW	46090 TQ	USBLS	5/07
	New York	Y	39260 FQ	50520 MW	68540 TQ	USBLS	5/07
	Albany-Schenectady-Troy MSA, NY	Y	32210 FQ	39480 MW	50720 TQ	USBLS	5/07
	Binghamton MSA, NY	Y	27300 FQ	33630 MW	41410 TQ	USBLS	5/07
	Buffalo-Niagara Falls MSA, NY	Y	29900 FQ	37580 MW	47570 TQ	USBLS	5/07
	Nassau-Suffolk PMSA, NY	Y	37060 FQ	45990 MW	61160 TQ	USBLS	5/07
	New York-Northern New Jersey-Long Island MSA, NY-NJ-PA	Y	40970 FQ	51720 MW	68630 TQ	USBLS	5/07
	North Carolina	Y	29150 FQ	36990 MW	47650 TQ	USBLS	5/07
	Charlotte-Gastonia-Concord MSA, NC-SC	Y	32970 FQ	40050 MW	51020 TQ	USBLS	5/07
	Greensboro-High Point MSA, NC	Y	32030 FQ	38850 MW	49300 TQ	USBLS	5/07
	Raleigh-Cary MSA, NC	Y	32020 FQ	41170 MW	54410 TQ	USBLS	5/07
	North Dakota	Y	24050 FQ	29000 MW	33360 TQ	USBLS	5/07
	Fargo MSA, ND-MN	Y	24150 FQ	28980 MW	32660 TQ	USBLS	5/07
	Ohio	Y	29170 FQ	38790 MW	50170 TQ	USBLS	5/07
	Cincinnati-Middletown MSA, OH-KY-IN	Y	32030 FQ	42630 MW	54230 TQ	USBLS	5/07
	Cleveland-Elyria-Mentor MSA, OH	Y	27240 FQ	37070 MW	48800 TQ	USBLS	5/07
	Columbus MSA, OH	Y	35350 FQ	45210 MW	54980 TQ	USBLS	5/07
	Dayton MSA, OH	Y	29280 FQ	37300 MW	50080 TQ	USBLS	5/07
	Oklahoma	Y	28200 FQ	33770 MW	42530 TQ	USBLS	5/07
	Oklahoma City MSA, OK	Y	28250 FQ	34510 MW	44570 TQ	USBLS	5/07
	Tulsa MSA, OK	Y	29690 FQ	34960 MW	43940 TQ	USBLS	5/07
	Oregon	H	15.66 FQ	19.80 MW	25.18 TQ	ORBLS	5/08
	Portland-Vancouver-Beaverton MSA, OR-WA	Y	34150 FQ	43310 MW	52790 TQ	USBLS	5/07
	Pennsylvania	Y	28920 FQ	37050 MW	48510 TQ	USBLS	5/07
	Allentown-Bethlehem-Easton MSA, PA-NJ	Y	30530 FQ	37110 MW	48620 TQ	USBLS	5/07
	Philadelphia-Camden-Wilmington MSA, PA-NJ-DE-MD	Y	32830 FQ	41650 MW	55950 TQ	USBLS	5/07
	Pittsburgh MSA, PA	Y	26670 FQ	34020 MW	42930 TQ	USBLS	5/07
	Rhode Island	Y	35050 FQ	43390 MW	51730 TQ	USBLS	5/07
	Providence-Fall River-Warwick MSA, RI-MA	Y	34410 FQ	42940 MW	51540 TQ	USBLS	5/07
	South Carolina	Y	29320 FQ	35850 MW	45220 TQ	USBLS	5/07

AE	Average entry wage	AW	Average wage paid	FQ	First quartile wage
AER	Average entry range	AWR	Average wage range	H	Hourly
AEX	Average experienced wage	AXR	Average experienced range	HI	Highest wage paid
ATC	Average total compensation	D	Daily	HR	High end range

LO	Lowest wage paid	MTC	Median total compensation	TCC	Total cash compensation
LR	Low end range	MW	Median wage paid	TQ	Third quartile wage
M	Monthly	MWR	Median wage range	W	Weekly
MCC	Median cash compensation	S	See annotated source	Y	Yearly

Occupation/Type/Industry	Location	Per	Low	Mid	High	Source	Date
Graphic Designer	Charleston-North Charleston MSA, SC	Y	27730 FQ	34480 MW	41540 TQ	USBLS	5/07
	Columbia MSA, SC	Y	32560 FQ	37480 MW	45040 TQ	USBLS	5/07
	Myrtle Beach-Conway-North Myrtle Beach MSA, SC	Y	29310 FQ	33740 MW	37140 TQ	USBLS	5/07
	South Dakota	Y	27524 FQ	32664 MW	39548 TQ	SDBLS	7/08-9/08
	Sioux Falls MSA, SD	Y	29560 FQ	35176 MW	42319 TQ	SDBLS	7/08-9/08
	Tennessee	Y	26820 FQ	34540 MW	44840 TQ	USBLS	5/07
	Memphis MSA, TN-MS-AR	Y	29500 FQ	38790 MW	59250 TQ	USBLS	5/07
	Nashville-Davidson-Murfreesboro MSA, TN	Y	29030 FQ	35570 MW	44120 TQ	USBLS	5/07
	Texas	Y	29410 FQ	38660 MW	51970 TQ	USBLS	5/07
	Austin-Round Rock MSA, TX	Y	31710 FQ	40940 MW	52940 TQ	USBLS	5/07
	Brownsville-Harlingen MSA, TX	Y	26650 FQ	32840 MW	44400 TQ	USBLS	5/07
	Dallas-Fort Worth-Arlington MSA, TX	Y	32250 FQ	41370 MW	54780 TQ	USBLS	5/07
	El Paso MSA, TX	Y	24770 FQ	29240 MW	39490 TQ	USBLS	5/07
	Houston-Sugar Land-Baytown MSA, TX	Y	30230 FQ	39480 MW	54590 TQ	USBLS	5/07
	San Antonio MSA, TX	Y	31880 FQ	41020 MW	52880 TQ	USBLS	5/07
	Utah	Y	28450 FQ	37070 MW	45750 TQ	USBLS	5/07
	Salt Lake City MSA, UT	Y	32200 FQ	40630 MW	47830 TQ	USBLS	5/07
	Vermont	Y	28810 FQ	37230 MW	49110 TQ	USBLS	5/07
	Burlington-South Burlington MSA, VT	Y	33750 FQ	39320 MW	53050 TQ	USBLS	5/07
	Virginia	Y	34480 FQ	45260 MW	58330 TQ	USBLS	5/07
	Charlottesville MSA, VA	Y	33030 FQ	43720 MW	58390 TQ	USBLS	5/07
	Lynchburg MSA, VA	Y	29320 FQ	34560 MW	40460 TQ	USBLS	5/07
	Richmond MSA, VA	Y	35870 FQ	43500 MW	51450 TQ	USBLS	5/07
	Virginia Beach-Norfolk-Newport News MSA, VA-NC	Y	27490 FQ	36590 MW	48070 TQ	USBLS	5/07
	Washington	H	16.32 FQ	21.04 MW	26.64 TQ	WABLS	3/08
	Olympia MSA, WA	Y	36970 FQ	43560 MW	50580 TQ	USBLS	5/07
	Seattle-Tacoma-Bellevue MSA, WA	Y	37900 FQ	47370 MW	59480 TQ	USBLS	5/07
	West Virginia	Y	24220 FQ	30624 MW	41411 TQ	WVBLS	7/08-9/08
	Charleston MSA, WV	Y	32720 FQ	38470 MW	44020 TQ	USBLS	5/07
	Huntington-Ashland MSA, WV-KY-OH	Y	22770 FQ	27380 MW	31650 TQ	USBLS	5/07
	Wisconsin	Y	30790 FQ	38460 MW	47950 TQ	USBLS	5/07
	Appleton MSA, WI	Y	35410 FQ	45380 MW	58200 TQ	USBLS	5/07
	Milwaukee-Waukesha-West Allis MSA, WI	Y	33640 FQ	40700 MW	48710 TQ	USBLS	5/07
	Wyoming	Y	22608 FQ	28416 MW	38248 TQ	WYBLS	9/08
	Cheyenne MSA, WY	Y	24212 FQ	35592 MW	40757 TQ	WYBLS	9/08
	Puerto Rico	Y	17520 FQ	22450 MW	29370 TQ	USBLS	5/07
	San Juan-Caguas-Guaynabo MSA, PR	Y	18020 FQ	22870 MW	29620 TQ	USBLS	5/07
	Guam	Y	20370 FQ	25000 MW	29570 TQ	USBLS	5/07
Graphics Technician Municipal Government	Colorado Springs, CO	M	3249 LO			COSPRS	1/1/09
Grasscutter Public Schools	Baldwin County, AL	Y	19654 LO		31384 HI	BCPSSS	2008-2009
Grave Digger	Rhode Island	Y		33601 AW		RIM01	2009
Gravel Tax Appraiser Department of Revenue Administration	New Hampshire	Y			58308 HI	NHUL03	2008
Greenhouse Supervisor Municipal Government	Seattle, WA	H	23.28 LO		24.21 HI	CSSS	2007
Greenskeeper Municipal Government	Cincinnati, OH	Y	36517 LO		38340 HI	COHSS	10/08
Greenspace Manager Municipal Government	Cincinnati, OH	Y	38076 LO		51171 HI	COHSS	10/08
Greeting Card Writer	United States	S		35-200 AW		GCM	2008

AE	Average entry wage	AW	Average wage paid	FQ	First quartile wage	LO	Lowest wage paid	MTC	Median total compensation	TCC	Total cash compensation
AER	Average entry range	AWR	Average wage range	H	Hourly	LR	Low end range	MW	Median wage paid	TQ	Third quartile wage
AEX	Average experienced wage	AXR	Average experienced range	HI	Highest wage paid	M	Monthly	MWR	Median wage range	W	Weekly
ATC	Average total compensation	D	Daily	HR	High end range	MCC	Median cash compensation	S	See annotated source	Y	Yearly

728

Occupation/Type/Industry	Location	Per	Low	Mid	High	Source	Date
Greyhound Paddock Inspector							
Racing and Charitable Gaming Commission	New Hampshire	Y		27627 AW		NHUL03	2008
Grievance Officer							
Department of Corrections	Ohio	H	19.19 LO		30.13 HI	ODAS	2008
Grinding, Lapping, Polishing, and Buffing Machine Tool Setter, Operator, and Tender							
Metals and Plastics	Alabama	Y	21120 FQ	26190 MW	30820 TQ	USBLS	5/07
Metals and Plastics	Birmingham-Hoover MSA, AL	Y	21520 FQ	24720 MW	31690 TQ	USBLS	5/07
Metals and Plastics	Montgomery MSA, AL	Y	22280 FQ	27780 MW	34850 TQ	USBLS	5/07
Metals and Plastics	Arizona	Y	21430 FQ	27130 MW	32410 TQ	USBLS	5/07
Metals and Plastics	Phoenix-Mesa-Scottsdale MSA, AZ	Y	21900 FQ	27590 MW	32400 TQ	USBLS	5/07
Metals and Plastics	Tucson MSA, AZ	Y	21270 FQ	26220 MW	34830 TQ	USBLS	5/07
Metals and Plastics	Arkansas	Y	22400 FQ	26960 MW	31710 TQ	USBLS	5/07
Metals and Plastics	Fayetteville-Springdale-Rogers MSA, AR-MO	Y	22270 FQ	27750 MW	33720 TQ	USBLS	5/07
Metals and Plastics	Little Rock-North Little Rock MSA, AR	Y	26380 FQ	29550 MW	33120 TQ	USBLS	5/07
Metals and Plastics	California	H	9.79 FQ	12.25 MW	15.94 TQ	CABLS	1/08-3/08
Metals and Plastics	Los Angeles-Long Beach-Glendale PMSA, CA	H	10.03 FQ	13.37 MW	17.58 TQ	CABLS	1/08-3/08
Metals and Plastics	Modesto MSA, CA	H	10.65 FQ	13.18 MW	14.93 TQ	CABLS	1/08-3/08
Metals and Plastics	Oakland-Fremont-Hayward MSA, CA	H	11.52 FQ	14.07 MW	18.20 TQ	CABLS	1/08-3/08
Metals and Plastics	Riverside-San Bernardino-Ontario MSA, CA	H	8.76 FQ	10.65 MW	13.95 TQ	CABLS	1/08-3/08
Metals and Plastics	Sacramento-Arden Arcade-Roseville MSA, CA	H	10.39 FQ	11.74 MW	14.20 TQ	CABLS	1/08-3/08
Metals and Plastics	San Diego-Carlsbad-San Marcos MSA, CA	H	9.58 FQ	11.34 MW	13.87 TQ	CABLS	1/08-3/08
Metals and Plastics	San Francisco-San Mateo-Redwood PMSA, CA	H	12.19 FQ	14.32 MW	17.90 TQ	CABLS	1/08-3/08
Metals and Plastics	San Jose-Sunnyvale-Santa Clara MSA, CA	H	10.90 FQ	13.93 MW	18.15 TQ	CABLS	1/08-3/08
Metals and Plastics	Santa Ana-Anaheim-Irvine PMSA, CA	Y	19440 FQ	22630 MW	28520 TQ	USBLS	5/07
Metals and Plastics	Colorado	Y	22320 FQ	26250 MW	31360 TQ	USBLS	5/07
Metals and Plastics	Denver-Aurora MSA, CO	Y	22540 FQ	26220 MW	31160 TQ	USBLS	5/07
Metals and Plastics	Connecticut	H	10.95 AE	14.82 MW		CTBLS	1/08-3/08
Metals and Plastics	Bridgeport-Stamford-Norwalk MSA, CT	Y	23270 FQ	28580 MW	37030 TQ	USBLS	5/07
Metals and Plastics	Hartford-West Hartford-East Hartford MSA, CT	Y	26560 FQ	32620 MW	40560 TQ	USBLS	5/07
Metals and Plastics	Delaware	Y	26340 FQ	29980 MW	33840 TQ	USBLS	5/07
Metals and Plastics	Wilmington PMSA, DE-MD-NJ	Y	27460 FQ	30680 MW	34570 TQ	USBLS	5/07
Metals and Plastics	Washington-Arlington-Alexandria MSA, DC-VA-MD-WV	Y	20860 FQ	23620 MW	26690 TQ	USBLS	5/07
Metals and Plastics	Florida	Y	19830 FQ	24570 MW	30560 TQ	USBLS	5/07
Metals and Plastics	Fort Lauderdale-Pompano Beach-Deerfield Beach PMSA, FL	Y	20140 FQ	25080 MW	29090 TQ	USBLS	5/07
Metals and Plastics	Jacksonville MSA, FL	Y	17830 FQ	20000 MW	24670 TQ	USBLS	5/07
Metals and Plastics	Lakeland MSA, FL	Y	21230 FQ	24080 MW	27460 TQ	USBLS	5/07
Metals and Plastics	Miami-Fort Lauderdale-Miami Beach MSA, FL	Y	20530 FQ	26580 MW	31040 TQ	USBLS	5/07
Metals and Plastics	Orlando-Kissimmee MSA, FL	Y	19330 FQ	23120 MW	29490 TQ	USBLS	5/07
Metals and Plastics	Sarasota-Bradenton-Venice MSA, FL	Y	22460 FQ	27020 MW	31360 TQ	USBLS	5/07
Metals and Plastics	Tampa-St. Petersburg-Clearwater MSA, FL	Y	19070 FQ	23150 MW	29180 TQ	USBLS	5/07
Metals and Plastics	West Palm Beach-Boca Raton-Boynton Beach PMSA, FL	Y	25800 FQ	30540 MW	38680 TQ	USBLS	5/07
Metals and Plastics	Georgia	Y	21790 FQ	28350 MW	34570 TQ	USBLS	5/07
Metals and Plastics	Atlanta-Sandy Springs-Marietta MSA, GA	Y	22620 FQ	30470 MW	35750 TQ	USBLS	5/07

AE	Average entry wage	AW	Average wage paid	FQ	First quartile wage	LO	Lowest wage paid	MTC	Median total compensation	TCC	Total cash compensation
AER	Average entry range	AWR	Average wage range	H	Hourly	LR	Low end range	MW	Median wage paid	TQ	Third quartile wage
AEX	Average experienced wage	AXR	Average experienced range	HI	Highest wage paid	M	Monthly	MWR	Median wage range	W	Weekly
ATC	Average total compensation	D	Daily	HR	High end range	MCC	Median cash compensation	S	See annotated source	Y	Yearly

Occupation/Type/Industry	Location	Per	Low	Mid	High	Source	Date
Grinding, Lapping, Polishing, and Buffing Machine Tool Setter, Operator, and Tender							
Metals and Plastics	Idaho	Y	21480 FQ	25900 MW	42880 TQ	USBLS	5/07
Metals and Plastics	Boise City-Nampa MSA, ID	Y	22780 FQ	27020 MW	30240 TQ	USBLS	5/07
Metals and Plastics	Illinois	Y	23560 FQ	29480 MW	37010 TQ	USBLS	5/07
Metals and Plastics	Chicago-Naperville-Joliet MSA, IL-IN-WI	Y	23440 FQ	29220 MW	36080 TQ	USBLS	5/07
Metals and Plastics	Peoria MSA, IL	Y	23930 FQ	29580 MW	39880 TQ	USBLS	5/07
Metals and Plastics	Indiana	Y	25120 FQ	32830 MW	43390 TQ	USBLS	5/07
Metals and Plastics	Evansville MSA, IN-KY	Y	30050 FQ	33000 MW	35660 TQ	USBLS	5/07
Metals and Plastics	Gary PMSA, IN	Y	32340 FQ	36180 MW	39920 TQ	USBLS	5/07
Metals and Plastics	Indianapolis-Carmel MSA, IN	Y	22160 FQ	34240 MW	51700 TQ	USBLS	5/07
Metals and Plastics	Iowa	Y	24820 FQ	29210 MW	35570 TQ	USBLS	5/07
Metals and Plastics	Des Moines-West Des Moines MSA, IA	Y	24180 FQ	29950 MW	37740 TQ	USBLS	5/07
Metals and Plastics	Waterloo-Cedar Falls MSA, IA	Y	25810 FQ	28450 MW	31390 TQ	USBLS	5/07
Metals and Plastics	Kansas	Y	19850 FQ	27290 MW	35750 TQ	USBLS	5/07
Metals and Plastics	Wichita MSA, KS	Y	20760 FQ	29300 MW	42610 TQ	USBLS	5/07
Metals and Plastics	Kentucky	Y	22349 FQ	28468 MW	35211 TQ	KYBLS	2008
Metals and Plastics	Bowling Green MSA, KY	Y	17360 FQ	19370 MW	22910 TQ	USBLS	5/07
Metals and Plastics	Louisville-Jefferson County MSA, KY-IN	Y	20460 FQ	25780 MW	37170 TQ	USBLS	5/07
Metals and Plastics	Louisiana	H	8.99 FQ	11.93 MW	15.01 TQ	LABLS	1/08-3/08
Metals and Plastics	Baton Rouge MSA, LA	Y	19250 FQ	25060 MW	29010 TQ	USBLS	5/07
Metals and Plastics	Lafayette MSA, LA	Y	22090 FQ	26670 MW	30460 TQ	USBLS	5/07
Metals and Plastics	New Orleans-Metairie-Kenner MSA, LA	Y	17790 FQ	19560 MW	23260 TQ	USBLS	5/07
Metals and Plastics	Maine	Y	29830 FQ	37930 MW	44910 TQ	USBLS	5/07
Metals and Plastics	Portland-South Portland-Biddeford MSA, ME	Y	28470 FQ	35900 MW	42280 TQ	USBLS	5/07
Metals and Plastics	Maryland	Y		30900 MW		MDBLS	3/08
Metals and Plastics	Baltimore-Towson MSA, MD	Y	26020 FQ	30610 MW	37810 TQ	USBLS	5/07
Metals and Plastics	Cumberland MSA, MD-WV	Y	21650 FQ	25590 MW	28550 TQ	USBLS	5/07
Metals and Plastics	Hagerstown-Martinsburg MSA, MD-WV	Y	19310 FQ	32240 MW	41400 TQ	USBLS	5/07
Metals and Plastics	Massachusetts	Y	25780 FQ	31880 MW	38420 TQ	USBLS	5/07
Metals and Plastics	Boston-Cambridge-Quincy NECTA, MA	Y	25820 FQ	31380 MW	38970 TQ	USBLS	5/07
Metals and Plastics	Worcester MSA, MA-CT	Y	25820 FQ	32030 MW	38110 TQ	USBLS	5/07
Metals and Plastics	Michigan	Y	26530 FQ	33030 MW	45330 TQ	USBLS	5/07
Metals and Plastics	Detroit-Warren-Livonia MSA, MI	Y	28940 FQ	38790 MW	52520 TQ	USBLS	5/07
Metals and Plastics	Grand Rapids-Wyoming MSA, MI	Y	21840 FQ	28620 MW	41610 TQ	USBLS	5/07
Metals and Plastics	Muskegon-Norton Shores MSA, MI	Y	26190 FQ	29080 MW	35700 TQ	USBLS	5/07
Metals and Plastics	Warren-Troy-Farmington Hills PMSA, MI	Y	27910 FQ	35770 MW	47000 TQ	USBLS	5/07
Metals and Plastics	Minnesota	Y	28342 FQ	34251 MW	40700 TQ	MNBLS	10/08-12/08
Metals and Plastics	Duluth-Superior MSA, MN-WI	Y	18929 FQ	23885 MW	33806 TQ	MNBLS	10/08-12/08
Metals and Plastics	Minneapolis-Saint Paul MSA, MN-WI	Y	30965 FQ	36905 MW	43820 TQ	MNBLS	10/08-12/08
Metals and Plastics	Rochester MSA, MN	Y	34321 FQ	36981 MW	39641 TQ	MNBLS	10/08-12/08
Metals and Plastics	Mississippi	Y	21040 FQ	24160 MW	28760 TQ	USBLS	5/07
Metals and Plastics	Jackson MSA, MS	Y	20360 FQ	23250 MW	28030 TQ	USBLS	5/07
Metals and Plastics	Missouri	Y	22780 FQ	31750 MW	38490 TQ	USBLS	5/07
Metals and Plastics	Kansas City MSA, MO-KS	Y	20350 FQ	26620 MW	40700 TQ	USBLS	5/07
Metals and Plastics	St. Louis MSA, MO-IL	Y	27840 FQ	34520 MW	39520 TQ	USBLS	5/07
Metals and Plastics	Montana	Y	20100 FQ	22730 MW	27900 TQ	USBLS	5/07
Metals and Plastics	Nebraska	Y	25020 FQ	28750 MW	32930 TQ	USBLS	5/07
Metals and Plastics	Omaha-Council Bluffs MSA, NE-IA	Y	22460 FQ	26210 MW	32350 TQ	USBLS	5/07
Metals and Plastics	Nevada	H	11.69 FQ	13.52 MW	15.39 TQ	NVBLS	5/08
Metals and Plastics	Las Vegas-Paradise MSA, NV	H	11.63 FQ	13.17 MW	14.45 TQ	NVBLS	5/08
Metals and Plastics	New Hampshire	H	11.52 AE	15.04 MW	17.36 AEX	NHBLS	6/08
Metals and Plastics	Manchester MSA, NH	Y	25960 FQ	36320 MW	48740 TQ	USBLS	5/07
Metals and Plastics	Nashua NECTA, NH-MA	Y	27620 FQ	31650 MW	35070 TQ	USBLS	5/07
Metals and Plastics	New Jersey	Y	21490 FQ	27070 MW	34550 TQ	USBLS	5/07
Metals and Plastics	Camden PMSA, NJ	Y	27920 FQ	35610 MW	39730 TQ	USBLS	5/07
Metals and Plastics	Edison PMSA, NJ	Y	20270 FQ	26340 MW	30780 TQ	USBLS	5/07

AE	Average entry wage	AW	Average wage paid	FQ	First quartile wage	LO	Lowest wage paid	MTC	Median total compensation	TCC	Total cash compensation
AER	Average entry range	AWR	Average wage range	H	Hourly	LR	Low end range	MW	Median wage paid	TQ	Third quartile wage
AEX	Average experienced wage	AXR	Average experienced range	HI	Highest wage paid	M	Monthly	MWR	Median wage range	W	Weekly
ATC	Average total compensation	D	Daily	HR	High end range	MCC	Median cash compensation	S	See annotated source	Y	Yearly

Occupation/Type/Industry	Location	Per	Low	Mid	High	Source	Date
Grinding, Lapping, Polishing, and Buffing Machine Tool Setter, Operator, and Tender							
Metals and Plastics	Newark-Union PMSA, NJ-PA	Y	20810 FQ	26950 MW	35510 TQ	USBLS	5/07
Metals and Plastics	New Mexico	Y	20730 FQ	24250 MW	29150 TQ	USBLS	5/07
Metals and Plastics	Albuquerque MSA, NM	Y	19690 FQ	22840 MW	25410 TQ	USBLS	5/07
Metals and Plastics	New York	Y	22150 FQ	28620 MW	36620 TQ	USBLS	5/07
Metals and Plastics	Buffalo-Niagara Falls MSA, NY	Y	22280 FQ	31100 MW	44260 TQ	USBLS	5/07
Metals and Plastics	Nassau-Suffolk PMSA, NY	Y	22350 FQ	28750 MW	37270 TQ	USBLS	5/07
Metals and Plastics	New York-Northern New Jersey-Long Island MSA, NY-NJ-PA	Y	21260 FQ	27170 MW	35020 TQ	USBLS	5/07
Metals and Plastics	Syracuse MSA, NY	Y	22500 FQ	28040 MW	36230 TQ	USBLS	5/07
Metals and Plastics	Utica-Rome MSA, NY	Y	22100 FQ	24810 MW	31400 TQ	USBLS	5/07
Metals and Plastics	North Carolina	Y	24920 FQ	29300 MW	34600 TQ	USBLS	5/07
Metals and Plastics	Charlotte-Gastonia-Concord MSA, NC-SC	Y	27780 FQ	31730 MW	36650 TQ	USBLS	5/07
Metals and Plastics	Greensboro-High Point MSA, NC	Y	25740 FQ	30590 MW	42160 TQ	USBLS	5/07
Metals and Plastics	Raleigh-Cary MSA, NC	Y	18330 FQ	25810 MW	36060 TQ	USBLS	5/07
Metals and Plastics	North Dakota	Y	23170 FQ	26960 MW	30040 TQ	USBLS	5/07
Metals and Plastics	Ohio	Y	24050 FQ	30510 MW	37590 TQ	USBLS	5/07
Metals and Plastics	Cincinnati-Middletown MSA, OH-KY-IN	Y	29180 FQ	35850 MW	44250 TQ	USBLS	5/07
Metals and Plastics	Cleveland-Elyria-Mentor MSA, OH	Y	22580 FQ	27630 MW	34560 TQ	USBLS	5/07
Metals and Plastics	Columbus MSA, OH	Y	25610 FQ	31630 MW	36940 TQ	USBLS	5/07
Metals and Plastics	Dayton MSA, OH	Y	25400 FQ	34120 MW	40180 TQ	USBLS	5/07
Metals and Plastics	Oklahoma	Y	21520 FQ	26800 MW	34190 TQ	USBLS	5/07
Metals and Plastics	Oklahoma City MSA, OK	Y	20140 FQ	25080 MW	29410 TQ	USBLS	5/07
Metals and Plastics	Tulsa MSA, OK	Y	21940 FQ	28160 MW	38010 TQ	USBLS	5/07
Metals and Plastics	Oregon	H	12.27 FQ	14.56 MW	17.91 TQ	ORBLS	5/08
Metals and Plastics	Eugene-Springfield MSA, OR	Y	20650 FQ	22900 MW	25150 TQ	USBLS	5/07
Metals and Plastics	Portland-Vancouver-Beaverton MSA, OR-WA	Y	26670 FQ	31580 MW	39780 TQ	USBLS	5/07
Metals and Plastics	Pennsylvania	Y	24240 FQ	30820 MW	38320 TQ	USBLS	5/07
Metals and Plastics	Allentown-Bethlehem-Easton MSA, PA-NJ	Y	22580 FQ	25790 MW	35640 TQ	USBLS	5/07
Metals and Plastics	Philadelphia-Camden-Wilmington MSA, PA-NJ-DE-MD	Y	26000 FQ	31810 MW	38450 TQ	USBLS	5/07
Metals and Plastics	Pittsburgh MSA, PA	Y	24590 FQ	32270 MW	39700 TQ	USBLS	5/07
Metals and Plastics	Rhode Island	Y	22410 FQ	25460 MW	30470 TQ	USBLS	5/07
Metals and Plastics	Providence-Fall River-Warwick MSA, RI-MA	Y	22490 FQ	25720 MW	30930 TQ	USBLS	5/07
Metals and Plastics	South Carolina	Y	23970 FQ	31630 MW	40150 TQ	USBLS	5/07
Metals and Plastics	Charleston-North Charleston MSA, SC	Y	21710 FQ	26840 MW	35020 TQ	USBLS	5/07
Metals and Plastics	Columbia MSA, SC	Y	24970 FQ	30880 MW	36190 TQ	USBLS	5/07
Metals and Plastics	South Dakota	Y	21644 FQ	24885 MW	29250 TQ	SDBLS	7/08-9/08
Metals and Plastics	Sioux Falls MSA, SD	Y	22532 FQ	25587 MW	29393 TQ	SDBLS	7/08-9/08
Metals and Plastics	Tennessee	Y	24060 FQ	30430 MW	36720 TQ	USBLS	5/07
Metals and Plastics	Memphis MSA, TN-MS-AR	Y	22000 FQ	28900 MW	35680 TQ	USBLS	5/07
Metals and Plastics	Nashville-Davidson-Murfreesboro MSA, TN	Y	26530 FQ	31700 MW	42410 TQ	USBLS	5/07
Metals and Plastics	Texas	Y	18690 FQ	22910 MW	28660 TQ	USBLS	5/07
Metals and Plastics	Austin-Round Rock MSA, TX	Y	18550 FQ	21330 MW	24780 TQ	USBLS	5/07
Metals and Plastics	Brownsville-Harlingen MSA, TX	Y	13480 FQ	16880 MW	19750 TQ	USBLS	5/07
Metals and Plastics	Dallas-Fort Worth-Arlington MSA, TX	Y	20200 FQ	24550 MW	29020 TQ	USBLS	5/07
Metals and Plastics	El Paso MSA, TX	Y	17820 FQ	20620 MW	24120 TQ	USBLS	5/07
Metals and Plastics	Houston-Sugar Land-Baytown MSA, TX	Y	19050 FQ	23250 MW	30540 TQ	USBLS	5/07
Metals and Plastics	San Antonio MSA, TX	Y	16110 FQ	20540 MW	26760 TQ	USBLS	5/07
Metals and Plastics	Utah	Y	19980 FQ	24620 MW	31340 TQ	USBLS	5/07
Metals and Plastics	Salt Lake City MSA, UT	Y	19050 FQ	25960 MW	32690 TQ	USBLS	5/07
Metals and Plastics	Vermont	Y	22640 FQ	28970 MW	33870 TQ	USBLS	5/07
Metals and Plastics	Burlington-South Burlington MSA, VT	Y	22460 FQ	25780 MW	33390 TQ	USBLS	5/07

AE	Average entry wage	AW	Average wage paid	FQ	First quartile wage	LO	Lowest wage paid	MTC	Median total compensation	TCC	Total cash compensation
AER	Average entry range	AWR	Average wage range	H	Hourly	LR	Low end range	MW	Median wage paid	TQ	Third quartile wage
AEX	Average experienced wage	AXR	Average experienced range	HI	Highest wage paid	M	Monthly	MWR	Median wage range	W	Weekly
ATC	Average total compensation	D	Daily	HR	High end range	MCC	Median cash compensation	S	See annotated source	Y	Yearly

Occupation/Type/Industry	Location	Per	Low	Mid	High	Source	Date
Grinding, Lapping, Polishing, and Buffing Machine Tool Setter, Operator, and Tender							
Metals and Plastics	Virginia	Y	19230 FQ	25260 MW	32100 TQ	USBLS	5/07
Metals and Plastics	Richmond MSA, VA	Y	20750 FQ	22970 MW	25430 TQ	USBLS	5/07
Metals and Plastics	Virginia Beach-Norfolk-Newport News MSA, VA-NC	Y	23360 FQ	29620 MW	37650 TQ	USBLS	5/07
Metals and Plastics	Washington	H	11.93 FQ	14.28 MW	18.37 TQ	WABLS	3/08
Metals and Plastics	Seattle-Tacoma-Bellevue MSA, WA	Y	24640 FQ	29520 MW	37930 TQ	USBLS	5/07
Metals and Plastics	Wisconsin	Y	24410 FQ	30690 MW	37130 TQ	USBLS	5/07
Metals and Plastics	Milwaukee-Waukesha-West Allis MSA, WI	Y	23540 FQ	29430 MW	36100 TQ	USBLS	5/07
Metals and Plastics	Wyoming	Y	27427 FQ	32781 MW	41071 TQ	WYBLS	9/08
Metals and Plastics	Puerto Rico	Y	13770 FQ	17140 MW	22460 TQ	USBLS	5/07
Metals and Plastics	San Juan-Caguas-Guaynabo MSA, PR	Y	15160 FQ	19310 MW	24010 TQ	USBLS	5/07
Grinding and Polishing Worker							
Hand	Alabama	Y	17690 FQ	21320 MW	26250 TQ	USBLS	5/07
Hand	Birmingham-Hoover MSA, AL	Y	17740 FQ	22230 MW	27310 TQ	USBLS	5/07
Hand	Arizona	Y	18950 FQ	23270 MW	28870 TQ	USBLS	5/07
Hand	Phoenix-Mesa-Scottsdale MSA, AZ	Y	19000 FQ	23480 MW	29100 TQ	USBLS	5/07
Hand	Tucson MSA, AZ	Y	17830 FQ	20820 MW	24910 TQ	USBLS	5/07
Hand	Arkansas	Y	19030 FQ	23590 MW	28560 TQ	USBLS	5/07
Hand	Fort Smith MSA, AR-OK	Y	19700 FQ	22360 MW	27520 TQ	USBLS	5/07
Hand	California	H	9.08 FQ	11.12 MW	13.90 TQ	CABLS	1/08-3/08
Hand	Los Angeles-Long Beach-Glendale PMSA, CA	H	8.76 FQ	10.35 MW	12.47 TQ	CABLS	1/08-3/08
Hand	Modesto MSA, CA	H	9.14 FQ	11.00 MW	17.11 TQ	CABLS	1/08-3/08
Hand	Oakland-Fremont-Hayward MSA, CA	H	10.39 FQ	12.54 MW	14.35 TQ	CABLS	1/08-3/08
Hand	Riverside-San Bernardino-Ontario MSA, CA	H	9.38 FQ	11.87 MW	14.09 TQ	CABLS	1/08-3/08
Hand	Sacramento-Arden Arcade-Roseville MSA, CA	H	9.89 FQ	11.24 MW	13.54 TQ	CABLS	1/08-3/08
Hand	San Diego-Carlsbad-San Marcos MSA, CA	H	9.81 FQ	11.82 MW	15.01 TQ	CABLS	1/08-3/08
Hand	San Francisco-San Mateo-Redwood PMSA, CA	H	10.61 FQ	13.57 MW	18.79 TQ	CABLS	1/08-3/08
Hand	San Jose-Sunnyvale-Santa Clara MSA, CA	H	11.42 FQ	13.64 MW	15.26 TQ	CABLS	1/08-3/08
Hand	Santa Ana-Anaheim-Irvine PMSA, CA	Y	17380 FQ	20990 MW	26180 TQ	USBLS	5/07
Hand	Colorado	Y	21470 FQ	26940 MW	35540 TQ	USBLS	5/07
Hand	Denver-Aurora MSA, CO	Y	22560 FQ	28060 MW	37150 TQ	USBLS	5/07
Hand	Connecticut	H	10.78 AE	14.29 MW		CTBLS	1/08-3/08
Hand	Bridgeport-Stamford-Norwalk MSA, CT	Y	22730 FQ	26360 MW	29410 TQ	USBLS	5/07
Hand	Hartford-West Hartford-East Hartford MSA, CT	Y	25070 FQ	30350 MW	35200 TQ	USBLS	5/07
Hand	Washington-Arlington-Alexandria MSA, DC-VA-MD-WV	Y	21820 FQ	26850 MW	31750 TQ	USBLS	5/07
Hand	Florida	Y	20570 FQ	24850 MW	30380 TQ	USBLS	5/07
Hand	Fort Lauderdale-Pompano Beach-Deerfield Beach PMSA, FL	Y	19300 FQ	22610 MW	28010 TQ	USBLS	5/07
Hand	Jacksonville MSA, FL	Y	20380 FQ	23050 MW	27340 TQ	USBLS	5/07
Hand	Miami-Fort Lauderdale-Miami Beach MSA, FL	Y	19200 FQ	22990 MW	29000 TQ	USBLS	5/07
Hand	Orlando-Kissimmee MSA, FL	Y	20550 FQ	24530 MW	31630 TQ	USBLS	5/07
Hand	Tampa-St. Petersburg-Clearwater MSA, FL	Y	20750 FQ	24310 MW	28930 TQ	USBLS	5/07
Hand	West Palm Beach-Boca Raton-Boynton Beach PMSA, FL	Y	19720 FQ	23680 MW	29530 TQ	USBLS	5/07
Hand	Georgia	Y	21170 FQ	24440 MW	28560 TQ	USBLS	5/07
Hand	Atlanta-Sandy Springs-Marietta MSA, GA	Y	21100 FQ	23790 MW	28120 TQ	USBLS	5/07
Hand	Idaho	Y	18180 FQ	22820 MW	27670 TQ	USBLS	5/07

AE Average entry wage	**AW** Average wage paid	**FQ** First quartile wage	**LO** Lowest wage paid	**MTC** Median total compensation	**TCC** Total cash compensation
AER Average entry range	**AWR** Average wage range	**H** Hourly	**LR** Low end range	**MW** Median wage paid	**TQ** Third quartile wage
AEX Average experienced wage	**AXR** Average experienced range	**HI** Highest wage paid	**M** Monthly	**MWR** Median wage range	**W** Weekly
ATC Average total compensation	**D** Daily	**HR** High end range	**MCC** Median cash compensation	**S** See annotated source	**Y** Yearly

Grinding and Polishing Worker

Occupation/Type/Industry	Location	Per	Low	Mid	High	Source	Date
Hand	Boise City-Nampa MSA, ID	Y	18810 FQ	25390 MW	28700 TQ	USBLS	5/07
Hand	Illinois	Y	19690 FQ	23280 MW	29150 TQ	USBLS	5/07
Hand	Chicago-Naperville-Joliet MSA, IL-IN-WI	Y	19910 FQ	23780 MW	31390 TQ	USBLS	5/07
Hand	Indiana	Y	21430 FQ	26410 MW	32280 TQ	USBLS	5/07
Hand	Gary PMSA, IN	Y	20980 FQ	34390 MW	38460 TQ	USBLS	5/07
Hand	Indianapolis-Carmel MSA, IN	Y	25380 FQ	29110 MW	34100 TQ	USBLS	5/07
Hand	Iowa	Y	21420 FQ	24780 MW	30300 TQ	USBLS	5/07
Hand	Cedar Rapids MSA, IA	Y	22410 FQ	28660 MW	33280 TQ	USBLS	5/07
Hand	Kansas	Y	19340 FQ	23110 MW	29740 TQ	USBLS	5/07
Hand	Wichita MSA, KS	Y	18740 FQ	21770 MW	26880 TQ	USBLS	5/07
Hand	Kentucky	Y	20428 FQ	23328 MW	27300 TQ	KYBLS	2008
Hand	Louisville-Jefferson County MSA, KY-IN	Y	20710 FQ	22930 MW	25220 TQ	USBLS	5/07
Hand	Louisiana	H	10.90 FQ	12.62 MW	14.75 TQ	LABLS	1/08-3/08
Hand	Baton Rouge MSA, LA	Y	21510 FQ	23740 MW	28520 TQ	USBLS	5/07
Hand	New Orleans-Metairie-Kenner MSA, LA	Y	25690 FQ	27830 MW	30220 TQ	USBLS	5/07
Hand	Maine	Y	27510 FQ	31060 MW	38860 TQ	USBLS	5/07
Hand	Maryland	Y		27175 MW		MDBLS	3/08
Hand	Baltimore-Towson MSA, MD	Y	23370 FQ	26740 MW	30970 TQ	USBLS	5/07
Hand	Bethesda-Gaithersburg-Frederick PMSA, MD	Y	22270 FQ	27330 MW	31360 TQ	USBLS	5/07
Hand	Massachusetts	Y	22380 FQ	27180 MW	32080 TQ	USBLS	5/07
Hand	Boston-Cambridge-Quincy NECTA, MA	Y	23260 FQ	27380 MW	34020 TQ	USBLS	5/07
Hand	Worcester MSA, MA-CT	Y	22900 FQ	30180 MW	35890 TQ	USBLS	5/07
Hand	Michigan	Y	22620 FQ	27880 MW	34890 TQ	USBLS	5/07
Hand	Detroit-Warren-Livonia MSA, MI	Y	22190 FQ	27280 MW	34840 TQ	USBLS	5/07
Hand	Grand Rapids-Wyoming MSA, MI	Y	21860 FQ	26870 MW	38070 TQ	USBLS	5/07
Hand	Warren-Troy-Farmington Hills PMSA, MI	Y	22160 FQ	26770 MW	34720 TQ	USBLS	5/07
Hand	Minnesota	Y	25066 FQ	30613 MW	37465 TQ	MNBLS	10/08-12/08
Hand	Duluth-Superior MSA, MN-WI	Y	25948 FQ	28031 MW	30115 TQ	MNBLS	10/08-12/08
Hand	Minneapolis-Saint Paul MSA, MN-WI	Y	25015 FQ	31017 MW	37766 TQ	MNBLS	10/08-12/08
Hand	Mississippi	Y	18010 FQ	22560 MW	27420 TQ	USBLS	5/07
Hand	Missouri	Y	21370 FQ	26340 MW	30880 TQ	USBLS	5/07
Hand	Kansas City MSA, MO-KS	Y	24200 FQ	28240 MW	35110 TQ	USBLS	5/07
Hand	St. Louis MSA, MO-IL	Y	21850 FQ	26920 MW	34170 TQ	USBLS	5/07
Hand	Montana	Y	19910 FQ	22300 MW	29890 TQ	USBLS	5/07
Hand	Nebraska	Y	21830 FQ	24500 MW	41920 TQ	USBLS	5/07
Hand	Nevada	H	10.59 FQ	12.02 MW	16.06 TQ	NVBLS	5/08
Hand	New Hampshire	H	10.56 AE	13.37 MW	15.57 AEX	NHBLS	6/08
Hand	New Jersey	Y	21390 FQ	27210 MW	34550 TQ	USBLS	5/07
Hand	Camden PMSA, NJ	Y	24850 FQ	30310 MW	37870 TQ	USBLS	5/07
Hand	Edison PMSA, NJ	Y	19620 FQ	23710 MW	32730 TQ	USBLS	5/07
Hand	Newark-Union PMSA, NJ-PA	Y	19600 FQ	25470 MW	32120 TQ	USBLS	5/07
Hand	Vineland-Millville-Bridgeton MSA, NJ	Y	29270 FQ	38050 MW	44060 TQ	USBLS	5/07
Hand	New Mexico	Y	19710 FQ	21740 MW	23980 TQ	USBLS	5/07
Hand	Albuquerque MSA, NM	Y	19960 FQ	22280 MW	26090 TQ	USBLS	5/07
Hand	New York	Y	19570 FQ	23170 MW	29950 TQ	USBLS	5/07
Hand	Albany-Schenectady-Troy MSA, NY	Y	23090 FQ	27880 MW	30830 TQ	USBLS	5/07
Hand	Buffalo-Niagara Falls MSA, NY	Y	19040 FQ	21430 MW	24310 TQ	USBLS	5/07
Hand	Nassau-Suffolk PMSA, NY	Y	22610 FQ	29310 MW	34370 TQ	USBLS	5/07
Hand	New York-Northern New Jersey-Long Island MSA, NY-NJ-PA	Y	18870 FQ	23290 MW	29880 TQ	USBLS	5/07
Hand	North Carolina	Y	20540 FQ	24980 MW	29240 TQ	USBLS	5/07
Hand	Charlotte-Gastonia-Concord MSA, NC-SC	Y	19520 FQ	28880 MW	49680 TQ	USBLS	5/07
Hand	Raleigh-Cary MSA, NC	Y	16250 FQ	18050 MW	21560 TQ	USBLS	5/07
Hand	North Dakota	Y	21050 FQ	22800 MW	25370 TQ	USBLS	5/07
Hand	Ohio	Y	23070 FQ	27510 MW	31810 TQ	USBLS	5/07
Hand	Cincinnati-Middletown MSA, OH-KY-IN	Y	22160 FQ	26670 MW	31280 TQ	USBLS	5/07

AE	Average entry wage	AW	Average wage paid	FQ	First quartile wage	LO	Lowest wage paid	MTC	Median total compensation	TCC	Total cash compensation
AER	Average entry range	AWR	Average wage range	H	Hourly	LR	Low end range	MW	Median wage paid	TQ	Third quartile wage
AEX	Average experienced wage	AXR	Average experienced range	HI	Highest wage paid	M	Monthly	MWR	Median wage range	W	Weekly
ATC	Average total compensation	D	Daily	HR	High end range	MCC	Median cash compensation	S	See annotated source	Y	Yearly

Occupation/Type/Industry	Location	Per	Low	Mid	High	Source	Date
Grinding and Polishing Worker							
Hand	Cleveland-Elyria-Mentor MSA, OH	Y	26230 FQ	28930 MW	32000 TQ	USBLS	5/07
Hand	Columbus MSA, OH	Y	22420 FQ	29890 MW	44460 TQ	USBLS	5/07
Hand	Dayton MSA, OH	Y	23400 FQ	28080 MW	32460 TQ	USBLS	5/07
Hand	Oklahoma	Y	18370 FQ	22190 MW	27790 TQ	USBLS	5/07
Hand	Oklahoma City MSA, OK	Y	19040 FQ	24260 MW	29780 TQ	USBLS	5/07
Hand	Tulsa MSA, OK	Y	19670 FQ	22680 MW	26790 TQ	USBLS	5/07
Hand	Oregon	H	10.32 FQ	11.61 MW	13.58 TQ	ORBLS	5/08
Hand	Portland-Vancouver-Beaverton MSA, OR-WA	Y	20040 FQ	22920 MW	26560 TQ	USBLS	5/07
Hand	Pennsylvania	Y	22580 FQ	27170 MW	33800 TQ	USBLS	5/07
Hand	Allentown-Bethlehem-Easton MSA, PA-NJ	Y	23170 FQ	27180 MW	31840 TQ	USBLS	5/07
Hand	Philadelphia-Camden-Wilmington MSA, PA-NJ-DE-MD	Y	26030 FQ	32290 MW	40180 TQ	USBLS	5/07
Hand	Pittsburgh MSA, PA	Y	23130 FQ	28420 MW	34340 TQ	USBLS	5/07
Hand	Rhode Island	Y	21770 FQ	26200 MW	32320 TQ	USBLS	5/07
Hand	Providence-Fall River-Warwick MSA, RI-MA	Y	22360 FQ	27080 MW	31830 TQ	USBLS	5/07
Hand	South Carolina	Y	20600 FQ	24980 MW	30390 TQ	USBLS	5/07
Hand	Charleston-North Charleston MSA, SC	Y	23530 FQ	28030 MW	36470 TQ	USBLS	5/07
Hand	Columbia MSA, SC	Y	18290 FQ	24050 MW	29040 TQ	USBLS	5/07
Hand	South Dakota	Y	19336 FQ	22550 MW	25928 TQ	SDBLS	7/08-9/08
Hand	Sioux Falls MSA, SD	Y	21333 FQ	23752 MW	27026 TQ	SDBLS	7/08-9/08
Hand	Tennessee	Y	22150 FQ	26910 MW	31250 TQ	USBLS	5/07
Hand	Memphis MSA, TN-MS-AR	Y	23260 FQ	28000 MW	33000 TQ	USBLS	5/07
Hand	Nashville-Davidson-Murfreesboro MSA, TN	Y	21210 FQ	24300 MW	29660 TQ	USBLS	5/07
Hand	Texas	Y	17740 FQ	21690 MW	27190 TQ	USBLS	5/07
Hand	Austin-Round Rock MSA, TX	Y	17340 FQ	19540 MW	24310 TQ	USBLS	5/07
Hand	Dallas-Fort Worth-Arlington MSA, TX	Y	16430 FQ	19330 MW	25070 TQ	USBLS	5/07
Hand	Houston-Sugar Land-Baytown MSA, TX	Y	18040 FQ	22370 MW	27360 TQ	USBLS	5/07
Hand	San Antonio MSA, TX	Y	19040 FQ	23470 MW	28450 TQ	USBLS	5/07
Hand	Utah	Y	17700 FQ	21420 MW	25780 TQ	USBLS	5/07
Hand	Provo-Orem MSA, UT	Y	14800 FQ	17070 MW	19390 TQ	USBLS	5/07
Hand	Salt Lake City MSA, UT	Y	19230 FQ	21870 MW	25810 TQ	USBLS	5/07
Hand	Vermont	Y	24080 FQ	29070 MW	39400 TQ	USBLS	5/07
Hand	Virginia	Y	21930 FQ	27460 MW	33430 TQ	USBLS	5/07
Hand	Virginia Beach-Norfolk-Newport News MSA, VA-NC	Y	25960 FQ	37180 MW	46060 TQ	USBLS	5/07
Hand	Washington	H	11.05 FQ	13.46 MW	17.20 TQ	WABLS	3/08
Hand	Seattle-Tacoma-Bellevue MSA, WA	Y	22780 FQ	28170 MW	36080 TQ	USBLS	5/07
Hand	West Virginia	Y	18058 FQ	22482 MW	26283 TQ	WVBLS	7/08-9/08
Hand	Wisconsin	Y	23910 FQ	28000 MW	33400 TQ	USBLS	5/07
Hand	Milwaukee-Waukesha-West Allis MSA, WI	Y	23580 FQ	28030 MW	36550 TQ	USBLS	5/07
Hand	Wyoming	Y	18536 FQ	22238 MW	26194 TQ	WYBLS	9/08
Hand	Virgin Islands	Y	14490 FQ	15650 MW	17450 TQ	USBLS	5/07
Grocery Director	United States	Y		115000-145000 AWR		SMNEWS	2008
Groundskeeper	Liberty County, GA	Y	21882 LO		35838 HI	GACTY03	2008
Shea Stadium	New York, NY	H			21.00 HI	NYT04	2008
Growing Operations Supervisor	United States	Y	10000-19999 LO		60000-79999 HI	AMNUR	2007
Guidance Counselor							
Large Urban District	United States	Y		60876 AW		DADM	2007-2008
Medium Urban District	United States	Y		57684 AW		DADM	2007-2008
Rural District	United States	Y		49893 AW		DADM	2007-2008
Small Town District	United States	Y		55580 AW		DADM	2007-2008
Suburban District	United States	Y		63450 AW		DADM	2007-2008
Gunnery Sergeant							
U.S. Marines, Active Duty, Pay Grade E-7	United States	M	2516 LO		4521 HI	DOD1	2009

AE	Average entry wage	**AW**	Average wage paid	**FQ**	First quartile wage
AER	Average entry range	**AWR**	Average wage range	**H**	Hourly
AEX	Average experienced wage	**AXR**	Average experienced range	**HI**	Highest wage paid
ATC	Average total compensation	**D**	Daily	**HR**	High end range

LO	Lowest wage paid	**MTC**	Median total compensation	**TCC**	Total cash compensation
LR	Low end range	**MW**	Median wage paid	**TQ**	Third quartile wage
M	Monthly	**MWR**	Median wage range	**W**	Weekly
MCC	Median cash compensation	**S**	See annotated source	**Y**	Yearly

Occupation/Type/Industry	Location	Per	Low	Mid	High	Source	Date
Gymnastics Coach							
College Men	United States	Y		107400 AW		USATOD01	2006
College Women	United States	Y		91700 AW		USATOD01	2006
Gypsy Moth Program Manager							
State Government	Ohio	H	20.89 LO		26.11 HI	ODAS	2008
Hairdresser, Hairstylist, and Cosmetologist							
	Alabama	Y	15810 FQ	20590 MW	32640 TQ	USBLS	5/07
	Birmingham-Hoover MSA, AL	Y	21140 FQ	32550 MW	45800 TQ	USBLS	5/07
	Mobile MSA, AL	Y	15620 FQ	19360 MW	24420 TQ	USBLS	5/07
	Montgomery MSA, AL	Y	18480 FQ	24170 MW	34300 TQ	USBLS	5/07
	Alaska	Y	18550 FQ	23950 MW	35470 TQ	USBLS	5/07
	Anchorage MSA, AK	Y	18160 FQ	23900 MW	34800 TQ	USBLS	5/07
	Arizona	Y	15930 FQ	23360 MW	34840 TQ	USBLS	5/07
	Phoenix-Mesa-Scottsdale MSA, AZ	Y	15830 FQ	23700 MW	35980 TQ	USBLS	5/07
	Tucson MSA, AZ	Y	17890 FQ	23320 MW	32230 TQ	USBLS	5/07
	Arkansas	Y	15390 FQ	20030 MW	27100 TQ	USBLS	5/07
	Fayetteville-Springdale-Rogers MSA, AR-MO	Y	18810 FQ	23270 MW	32130 TQ	USBLS	5/07
	Little Rock-North Little Rock MSA, AR	Y	14500 FQ	15850 MW	25270 TQ	USBLS	5/07
	California	H	8.74 FQ	10.07 MW	13.91 TQ	CABLS	1/08-3/08
	Bakersfield MSA, CA	H	8.43 FQ	9.19 MW	11.06 TQ	CABLS	1/08-3/08
	Los Angeles-Long Beach-Glendale PMSA, CA	H	8.71 FQ	9.88 MW	14.78 TQ	CABLS	1/08-3/08
	Oakland-Fremont-Hayward MSA, CA	H	8.94 FQ	10.74 MW	14.17 TQ	CABLS	1/08-3/08
	Riverside-San Bernardino-Ontario MSA, CA	H	8.46 FQ	9.20 MW	11.09 TQ	CABLS	1/08-3/08
	Sacramento-Arden Arcade-Roseville MSA, CA	H	8.97 FQ	10.80 MW	14.93 TQ	CABLS	1/08-3/08
	San Diego-Carlsbad-San Marcos MSA, CA	H	8.88 FQ	10.84 MW	14.05 TQ	CABLS	1/08-3/08
	San Francisco-San Mateo-Redwood PMSA, CA	H	9.14 FQ	12.18 MW	21.83 TQ	CABLS	1/08-3/08
	San Jose-Sunnyvale-Santa Clara MSA, CA	H	8.67 FQ	9.65 MW	11.28 TQ	CABLS	1/08-3/08
	Santa Ana-Anaheim-Irvine PMSA, CA	Y	18100 FQ	21690 MW	27960 TQ	USBLS	5/07
	Colorado	Y	18520 FQ	22660 MW	28110 TQ	USBLS	5/07
	Boulder MSA, CO	Y	15520 FQ	20720 MW	30180 TQ	USBLS	5/07
	Denver-Aurora MSA, CO	Y	20620 FQ	23640 MW	29240 TQ	USBLS	5/07
	Connecticut	H	8.62 AE	12.70 MW		CTBLS	1/08-3/08
	Bridgeport-Stamford-Norwalk MSA, CT	Y	19860 FQ	28330 MW	38370 TQ	USBLS	5/07
	Hartford-West Hartford-East Hartford MSA, CT	Y	18440 FQ	26050 MW	35960 TQ	USBLS	5/07
	Delaware	Y	17890 FQ	23060 MW	32820 TQ	USBLS	5/07
	Wilmington PMSA, DE-MD-NJ	Y	16650 FQ	23140 MW	32310 TQ	USBLS	5/07
	Washington-Arlington-Alexandria MSA, DC-VA-MD-WV	Y	20250 FQ	29930 MW	42440 TQ	USBLS	5/07
	Florida	Y	17520 FQ	22610 MW	30320 TQ	USBLS	5/07
	Fort Lauderdale-Pompano Beach-Deerfield Beach PMSA, FL	Y	17810 FQ	22030 MW	25780 TQ	USBLS	5/07
	Jacksonville MSA, FL	Y	15660 FQ	20450 MW	36920 TQ	USBLS	5/07
	Lakeland MSA, FL	Y	22870 FQ	28090 MW	37560 TQ	USBLS	5/07
	Miami-Fort Lauderdale-Miami Beach MSA, FL	Y	18010 FQ	22460 MW	28610 TQ	USBLS	5/07
	Orlando-Kissimmee MSA, FL	Y	18650 FQ	24690 MW	36710 TQ	USBLS	5/07
	Tampa-St. Petersburg-Clearwater MSA, FL	Y	16310 FQ	20780 MW	27220 TQ	USBLS	5/07
	West Palm Beach-Boca Raton-Boynton Beach PMSA, FL	Y	19870 FQ	23500 MW	29520 TQ	USBLS	5/07
	Georgia	Y	18160 FQ	23150 MW	32170 TQ	USBLS	5/07
	Atlanta-Sandy Springs-Marietta MSA, GA	Y	20120 FQ	24260 MW	33730 TQ	USBLS	5/07
	Savannah MSA, GA	Y	14580 FQ	22490 MW	47240 TQ	USBLS	5/07

AE Average entry wage	**AW** Average wage paid	**FQ** First quartile wage	**LO** Lowest wage paid	**MTC** Median total compensation	**TCC** Total cash compensation
AER Average entry range	**AWR** Average wage range	**H** Hourly	**LR** Low end range	**MW** Median wage paid	**TQ** Third quartile wage
AEX Average experienced wage	**AXR** Average experienced range	**HI** Highest wage paid	**M** Monthly	**MWR** Median wage range	**W** Weekly
ATC Average total compensation	**D** Daily	**HR** High end range	**MCC** Median cash compensation	**S** See annotated source	**Y** Yearly

Occupation/Type/Industry	Location	Per	Low	Mid	High	Source	Date
Hairdresser, Hairstylist, and Cosmetologist	Hawaii	Y	22400 FQ	32020 MW	43910 TQ	USBLS	5/07
	Honolulu MSA, HI	Y	20590 FQ	29000 MW	44000 TQ	USBLS	5/07
	Idaho	Y	13660 FQ	16390 MW	20180 TQ	USBLS	5/07
	Boise City-Nampa MSA, ID	Y	13380 FQ	15710 MW	20730 TQ	USBLS	5/07
	Pocatello MSA, ID	Y	12510 FQ	13680 MW	14850 TQ	USBLS	5/07
	Illinois	Y	16930 FQ	22570 MW	28640 TQ	USBLS	5/07
	Chicago-Naperville-Joliet MSA, IL-IN-WI	Y	16900 FQ	22810 MW	28950 TQ	USBLS	5/07
	Rockford MSA, IL	Y	19280 FQ	25990 MW	31660 TQ	USBLS	5/07
	Indiana	Y	15230 FQ	20750 MW	27090 TQ	USBLS	5/07
	Gary PMSA, IN	Y	13460 FQ	17420 MW	28200 TQ	USBLS	5/07
	Indianapolis-Carmel MSA, IN	Y	18600 FQ	23830 MW	32210 TQ	USBLS	5/07
	Iowa	Y	16560 FQ	20630 MW	27300 TQ	USBLS	5/07
	Des Moines-West Des Moines MSA, IA	Y	17130 FQ	22150 MW	28290 TQ	USBLS	5/07
	Kansas	Y	15110 FQ	19280 MW	24550 TQ	USBLS	5/07
	Wichita MSA, KS	Y	15520 FQ	18130 MW	22620 TQ	USBLS	5/07
	Kentucky	Y	15210 FQ	19473 MW	24772 TQ	KYBLS	2008
	Lexington-Fayette MSA, KY	Y	20000 FQ	24830 MW	29270 TQ	USBLS	5/07
	Louisville-Jefferson County MSA, KY-IN	Y	17470 FQ	20380 MW	25200 TQ	USBLS	5/07
	Owensboro MSA, KY	Y	15760 FQ	18350 MW	21410 TQ	USBLS	5/07
	Louisiana	H	7.85 FQ	9.48 MW	12.79 TQ	LABLS	1/08-3/08
	Baton Rouge MSA, LA	Y	17390 FQ	20480 MW	26920 TQ	USBLS	5/07
	New Orleans-Metairie-Kenner MSA, LA	Y	15090 FQ	23840 MW	31360 TQ	USBLS	5/07
	Maine	Y	17900 FQ	23230 MW	29440 TQ	USBLS	5/07
	Portland-South Portland-Biddeford MSA, ME	Y	17490 FQ	22220 MW	29850 TQ	USBLS	5/07
	Maryland	Y		27225 MW		MDBLS	3/08
	Baltimore-Towson MSA, MD	Y	17260 FQ	25460 MW	40130 TQ	USBLS	5/07
	Bethesda-Gaithersburg-Frederick PMSA, MD	Y	21230 FQ	32210 MW	43260 TQ	USBLS	5/07
	Cumberland MSA, MD-WV	Y	14480 FQ	17760 MW	23240 TQ	USBLS	5/07
	Massachusetts	Y	22220 FQ	28420 MW	36110 TQ	USBLS	5/07
	Boston-Cambridge-Quincy NECTA, MA	Y	22920 FQ	28890 MW	35530 TQ	USBLS	5/07
	Worcester MSA, MA-CT	Y	19090 FQ	24960 MW	37640 TQ	USBLS	5/07
	Michigan	Y	15950 FQ	20600 MW	29670 TQ	USBLS	5/07
	Detroit-Warren-Livonia MSA, MI	Y	16570 FQ	21580 MW	30460 TQ	USBLS	5/07
	Grand Rapids-Wyoming MSA, MI	Y	14920 FQ	16220 MW	23250 TQ	USBLS	5/07
	Warren-Troy-Farmington Hills PMSA, MI	Y	16720 FQ	21500 MW	31310 TQ	USBLS	5/07
	Minnesota	Y	22344 FQ	27206 MW	35047 TQ	MNBLS	10/08-12/08
	Duluth-Superior MSA, MN-WI	Y	21382 FQ	23797 MW	26986 TQ	MNBLS	10/08-12/08
	Minneapolis-Saint Paul MSA, MN-WI	Y	23734 FQ	28764 MW	36877 TQ	MNBLS	10/08-12/08
	Rochester MSA, MN	Y	21806 FQ	25743 MW	35589 TQ	MNBLS	10/08-12/08
	Mississippi	Y	13930 FQ	18800 MW	24680 TQ	USBLS	5/07
	Jackson MSA, MS	Y	19510 FQ	22860 MW	25580 TQ	USBLS	5/07
	Missouri	Y	15740 FQ	20020 MW	27320 TQ	USBLS	5/07
	Jefferson City MSA, MO	Y	17790 FQ	25830 MW	33430 TQ	USBLS	5/07
	Kansas City MSA, MO-KS	Y	16010 FQ	19910 MW	25600 TQ	USBLS	5/07
	St. Joseph MSA, MO-KS	Y	16530 FQ	22350 MW	29230 TQ	USBLS	5/07
	St. Louis MSA, MO-IL	Y	17730 FQ	22920 MW	28710 TQ	USBLS	5/07
	Springfield MSA, MO	Y	15420 FQ	17220 MW	19010 TQ	USBLS	5/07
	Montana	Y	14700 FQ	17280 MW	20410 TQ	USBLS	5/07
	Billings MSA, MT	Y	17240 FQ	20060 MW	23530 TQ	USBLS	5/07
	Missoula MSA, MT	Y	14740 FQ	17120 MW	18980 TQ	USBLS	5/07
	Nebraska	Y	17040 FQ	20200 MW	27000 TQ	USBLS	5/07
	Omaha-Council Bluffs MSA, NE-IA	Y	17950 FQ	21740 MW	31930 TQ	USBLS	5/07
	Las Vegas-Paradise MSA, NV	H	7.62 FQ	9.80 MW	14.39 TQ	NVBLS	5/08
	New Hampshire	H	6.98 AE	10.24 MW	12.87 AEX	NHBLS	6/08
	Manchester MSA, NH	Y	14810 FQ	21130 MW	26140 TQ	USBLS	5/07
	Nashua NECTA, NH-MA	Y	21200 FQ	24580 MW	32920 TQ	USBLS	5/07
	New Jersey	Y	23700 FQ	28800 MW	35450 TQ	USBLS	5/07
	Camden PMSA, NJ	Y	25780 FQ	28790 MW	35780 TQ	USBLS	5/07
	Edison PMSA, NJ	Y	22380 FQ	28240 MW	34280 TQ	USBLS	5/07

AE	Average entry wage	AW	Average wage paid	FQ First quartile wage
AER	Average entry range	AWR	Average wage range	H Hourly
AEX	Average experienced wage	AXR	Average experienced range	HI Highest wage paid
ATC	Average total compensation	D	Daily	HR High end range

LO	Lowest wage paid	MTC Median total compensation	TCC Total cash compensation
LR	Low end range	MW Median wage paid	TQ Third quartile wage
M	Monthly	MWR Median wage range	W Weekly
MCC	Median cash compensation	S See annotated source	Y Yearly

Occupation/Type/Industry	Location	Per	Low	Mid	High	Source	Date
Hairdresser, Hairstylist, and Cosmetologist	Newark-Union PMSA, NJ-PA	Y	24420 FQ	29530 MW	36160 TQ	USBLS	5/07
	New Mexico	Y	13060 FQ	14950 MW	21650 TQ	USBLS	5/07
	Albuquerque MSA, NM	Y	13030 FQ	14890 MW	21080 TQ	USBLS	5/07
	Santa Fe MSA, NM	Y	13850 FQ	16370 MW	29780 TQ	USBLS	5/07
	New York	Y	17590 FQ	23410 MW	31560 TQ	USBLS	5/07
	Albany-Schenectady-Troy MSA, NY	Y	16210 FQ	22230 MW	26820 TQ	USBLS	5/07
	Buffalo-Niagara Falls MSA, NY	Y	18690 FQ	24390 MW	30510 TQ	USBLS	5/07
	Kingston MSA, NY	Y	15410 FQ	16760 MW	21710 TQ	USBLS	5/07
	Nassau-Suffolk PMSA, NY	Y	16430 FQ	22100 MW	29450 TQ	USBLS	5/07
	New York-Northern New Jersey-Long Island MSA, NY-NJ-PA	Y	20290 FQ	27170 MW	35010 TQ	USBLS	5/07
	Syracuse MSA, NY	Y	15700 FQ	16970 MW	19540 TQ	USBLS	5/07
	North Carolina	Y	15300 FQ	19960 MW	31350 TQ	USBLS	5/07
	Charlotte-Gastonia-Concord MSA, NC-SC	Y	15010 FQ	20740 MW	30270 TQ	USBLS	5/07
	Raleigh-Cary MSA, NC	Y	15740 FQ	22180 MW	59580 TQ	USBLS	5/07
	Winston-Salem MSA, NC	Y	15930 FQ	23670 MW	33210 TQ	USBLS	5/07
	North Dakota	Y	14910 FQ	20740 MW	27700 TQ	USBLS	5/07
	Fargo MSA, ND-MN	Y	14100 FQ	20790 MW	31820 TQ	USBLS	5/07
	Ohio	Y	15510 FQ	19750 MW	26920 TQ	USBLS	5/07
	Cincinnati-Middletown MSA, OH-KY-IN	Y	15350 FQ	21120 MW	27590 TQ	USBLS	5/07
	Cleveland-Elyria-Mentor MSA, OH	Y	16170 FQ	20700 MW	26460 TQ	USBLS	5/07
	Columbus MSA, OH	Y	15150 FQ	20000 MW	31980 TQ	USBLS	5/07
	Dayton MSA, OH	Y	16590 FQ	23670 MW	30030 TQ	USBLS	5/07
	Oklahoma	Y	14130 FQ	17220 MW	21720 TQ	USBLS	5/07
	Oklahoma City MSA, OK	Y	13620 FQ	15980 MW	20860 TQ	USBLS	5/07
	Tulsa MSA, OK	Y	15880 FQ	19530 MW	24060 TQ	USBLS	5/07
	Oregon	H	9.01 FQ	10.07 MW	12.70 TQ	ORBLS	5/08
	Portland-Vancouver-Beaverton MSA, OR-WA	Y	18190 FQ	20310 MW	25980 TQ	USBLS	5/07
	Pennsylvania	Y	15530 FQ	18920 MW	24530 TQ	USBLS	5/07
	Allentown-Bethlehem-Easton MSA, PA-NJ	Y	16890 FQ	21940 MW	27570 TQ	USBLS	5/07
	Erie MSA, PA	Y	17430 FQ	19540 MW	23380 TQ	USBLS	5/07
	Philadelphia-Camden-Wilmington MSA, PA-NJ-DE-MD	Y	18760 FQ	24260 MW	30440 TQ	USBLS	5/07
	Pittsburgh MSA, PA	Y	14890 FQ	17040 MW	21310 TQ	USBLS	5/07
	Rhode Island	Y	20340 FQ	25040 MW	29780 TQ	USBLS	5/07
	Providence-Fall River-Warwick MSA, RI-MA	Y	20500 FQ	25130 MW	30170 TQ	USBLS	5/07
	South Carolina	Y	16580 FQ	24240 MW	31080 TQ	USBLS	5/07
	Charleston-North Charleston MSA, SC	Y	22660 FQ	29130 MW	35800 TQ	USBLS	5/07
	Columbia MSA, SC	Y	15790 FQ	20150 MW	27760 TQ	USBLS	5/07
	South Dakota	Y	23297 FQ	25825 MW	29737 TQ	SDBLS	7/08-9/08
	Sioux Falls MSA, SD	Y	23237 FQ	25934 MW	30743 TQ	SDBLS	7/08-9/08
	Tennessee	Y	17790 FQ	23440 MW	34900 TQ	USBLS	5/07
	Memphis MSA, TN-MS-AR	Y	17490 FQ	22380 MW	32720 TQ	USBLS	5/07
	Nashville-Davidson-Murfreesboro MSA, TN	Y	19310 FQ	27500 MW	43850 TQ	USBLS	5/07
	Texas	Y	15850 FQ	20160 MW	25970 TQ	USBLS	5/07
	Austin-Round Rock MSA, TX	Y	19070 FQ	23020 MW	30180 TQ	USBLS	5/07
	Brownsville-Harlingen MSA, TX	Y	12340 FQ	13610 MW	14880 TQ	USBLS	5/07
	Dallas-Fort Worth-Arlington MSA, TX	Y	17000 FQ	20560 MW	25950 TQ	USBLS	5/07
	El Paso MSA, TX	Y	12870 FQ	14650 MW	18070 TQ	USBLS	5/07
	Houston-Sugar Land-Baytown MSA, TX	Y	15450 FQ	20570 MW	26220 TQ	USBLS	5/07
	San Antonio MSA, TX	Y	17510 FQ	20680 MW	26510 TQ	USBLS	5/07
	Utah	Y	15700 FQ	19290 MW	25330 TQ	USBLS	5/07
	Salt Lake City MSA, UT	Y	13790 FQ	16220 MW	22880 TQ	USBLS	5/07
	Vermont	Y	21070 FQ	26110 MW	34070 TQ	USBLS	5/07
	Burlington-South Burlington MSA, VT	Y	21620 FQ	29440 MW	47930 TQ	USBLS	5/07

AE	Average entry wage	AW	Average wage paid	FQ	First quartile wage	LO	Lowest wage paid	MTC	Median total compensation	TCC	Total cash compensation
AER	Average entry range	AWR	Average wage range	H	Hourly	LR	Low end range	MW	Median wage paid	TQ	Third quartile wage
AEX	Average experienced wage	AXR	Average experienced range	HI	Highest wage paid	M	Monthly	MWR	Median wage range	W	Weekly
ATC	Average total compensation	D	Daily	HR	High end range	MCC	Median cash compensation	S	See annotated source	Y	Yearly

Occupation/Type/Industry	Location	Per	Low	Mid	High	Source	Date
Hairdresser, Hairstylist, and Cosmetologist	Virginia	Y	17250 FQ	25350 MW	35070 TQ	USBLS	5/07
	Richmond MSA, VA	Y	23320 FQ	29700 MW	39500 TQ	USBLS	5/07
	Virginia Beach-Norfolk-Newport News MSA, VA-NC	Y	14540 FQ	21570 MW	28110 TQ	USBLS	5/07
	Washington	H	10.01 FQ	12.94 MW	16.92 TQ	WABLS	3/08
	Seattle-Tacoma-Bellevue MSA, WA	Y	21020 FQ	27090 MW	35960 TQ	USBLS	5/07
	West Virginia	Y	15197 FQ	19760 MW	26651 TQ	WVBLS	7/08-9/08
	Charleston MSA, WV	Y	16540 FQ	22950 MW	29290 TQ	USBLS	5/07
	Wisconsin	Y	17340 FQ	21210 MW	26710 TQ	USBLS	5/07
	Milwaukee-Waukesha-West Allis MSA, WI	Y	18280 FQ	21780 MW	27780 TQ	USBLS	5/07
	Wyoming	Y	20426 FQ	27456 MW	32635 TQ	WYBLS	9/08
	Casper MSA, WY	Y	14974 FQ	28319 MW	31586 TQ	WYBLS	9/08
	Cheyenne MSA, WY	Y	24307 FQ	29444 MW	33955 TQ	WYBLS	9/08
	Puerto Rico	Y	13370 FQ	15670 MW	21860 TQ	USBLS	5/07
	San Juan-Caguas-Guaynabo MSA, PR	Y	13390 FQ	15750 MW	22540 TQ	USBLS	5/07
	Guam	Y	15330 FQ	19780 MW	23890 TQ	USBLS	5/07
Handwriting Examiner							
Police Department	Long Beach, CA	W	4289 LO		5836 HI	CAC	2006-2007
Harbormaster							
Pease Development Authority	New Hampshire	Y		12182 AW		NHUL03	2008
Hardware Engineer	Southeast, MI	Y		67218 AW		MIOAKL03	2007
Hazardous Materials Removal Worker	Alabama	Y	24470 FQ	28290 MW	32240 TQ	USBLS	5/07
	Birmingham-Hoover MSA, AL	Y	24550 FQ	28790 MW	34190 TQ	USBLS	5/07
	Alaska	Y	45020 FQ	50200 MW	63450 TQ	USBLS	5/07
	Anchorage MSA, AK	Y	44460 FQ	49850 MW	60680 TQ	USBLS	5/07
	Arizona	Y	26280 FQ	28720 MW	31210 TQ	USBLS	5/07
	Phoenix-Mesa-Scottsdale MSA, AZ	Y	26500 FQ	28790 MW	31140 TQ	USBLS	5/07
	Arkansas	Y	32880 FQ	36010 MW	39710 TQ	USBLS	5/07
	Little Rock-North Little Rock MSA, AR	Y	30850 FQ	36990 MW	46000 TQ	USBLS	5/07
	California	H	15.98 FQ	18.27 MW	20.79 TQ	CABLS	1/08-3/08
	Los Angeles-Long Beach-Glendale PMSA, CA	H	15.82 FQ	18.31 MW	22.52 TQ	CABLS	1/08-3/08
	Oakland-Fremont-Hayward MSA, CA	H	15.05 FQ	17.47 MW	19.45 TQ	CABLS	1/08-3/08
	Oxnard-Thousand Oaks-Ventura MSA, CA	H	15.18 FQ	17.41 MW	19.61 TQ	CABLS	1/08-3/08
	Riverside-San Bernardino-Ontario MSA, CA	H	21.96 FQ	24.19 MW	28.07 TQ	CABLS	1/08-3/08
	Sacramento-Arden Arcade-Roseville MSA, CA	H	16.71 FQ	18.18 MW	20.47 TQ	CABLS	1/08-3/08
	San Diego-Carlsbad-San Marcos MSA, CA	H	15.99 FQ	18.23 MW	23.02 TQ	CABLS	1/08-3/08
	San Francisco-San Mateo-Redwood PMSA, CA	H	15.86 FQ	18.78 MW	24.82 TQ	CABLS	1/08-3/08
	San Jose-Sunnyvale-Santa Clara MSA, CA	H	18.05 FQ	20.94 MW	25.20 TQ	CABLS	1/08-3/08
	Santa Ana-Anaheim-Irvine PMSA, CA	Y	33090 FQ	36380 MW	39510 TQ	USBLS	5/07
	Colorado	Y	29400 FQ	35150 MW	39600 TQ	USBLS	5/07
	Denver-Aurora MSA, CO	Y	29480 FQ	35040 MW	39160 TQ	USBLS	5/07
	Connecticut	H	15.42 AE	19.98 MW		CTBLS	1/08-3/08
	Hartford-West Hartford-East Hartford MSA, CT	Y	32670 FQ	41700 MW	47730 TQ	USBLS	5/07
	Delaware	Y	31000 FQ	41770 MW	49140 TQ	USBLS	5/07
	Wilmington PMSA, DE-MD-NJ	Y	33690 FQ	43300 MW	49930 TQ	USBLS	5/07
	District of Columbia	Y	29990 FQ	36440 MW	45750 TQ	USBLS	5/07
	Washington-Arlington-Alexandria MSA, DC-VA-MD-WV	Y	27260 FQ	31420 MW	39190 TQ	USBLS	5/07
	Florida	Y	26750 FQ	31270 MW	38540 TQ	USBLS	5/07

AE Average entry wage	**AW** Average wage paid	**FQ** First quartile wage	**LO** Lowest wage paid	**MTC** Median total compensation	**TCC** Total cash compensation
AER Average entry range	**AWR** Average wage range	**H** Hourly	**LR** Low end range	**MW** Median wage paid	**TQ** Third quartile wage
AEX Average experienced wage	**AXR** Average experienced range	**HI** Highest wage paid	**M** Monthly	**MWR** Median wage range	**W** Weekly
ATC Average total compensation	**D** Daily	**HR** High end range	**MCC** Median cash compensation	**S** See annotated source	**Y** Yearly

Occupation/Type/Industry	Location	Per	Low	Mid	High	Source	Date
Hazardous Materials Removal Worker	Jacksonville MSA, FL	Y	26990 FQ	29820 MW	36240 TQ	USBLS	5/07
	Miami-Fort Lauderdale-Miami Beach MSA, FL	Y	23820 FQ	29070 MW	35490 TQ	USBLS	5/07
	Tampa-St. Petersburg-Clearwater MSA, FL	Y	26950 FQ	34310 MW	40420 TQ	USBLS	5/07
	Georgia	Y	15370 FQ	30200 MW	39810 TQ	USBLS	5/07
	Atlanta-Sandy Springs-Marietta MSA, GA	Y	14590 FQ	30000 MW	40000 TQ	USBLS	5/07
	Hawaii	Y	28470 FQ	33090 MW	47680 TQ	USBLS	5/07
	Honolulu MSA, HI	Y	28470 FQ	33090 MW	47680 TQ	USBLS	5/07
	Idaho	Y	28190 FQ	33810 MW	37100 TQ	USBLS	5/07
	Boise City-Nampa MSA, ID	Y	29670 FQ	34160 MW	37240 TQ	USBLS	5/07
	Illinois	Y	36560 FQ	49710 MW	71730 TQ	USBLS	5/07
	Chicago-Naperville-Joliet MSA, IL-IN-WI	Y	34270 FQ	49150 MW	73410 TQ	USBLS	5/07
	Indiana	Y	18620 FQ	30230 MW	37010 TQ	USBLS	5/07
	Gary PMSA, IN	Y	28830 FQ	33470 MW	41960 TQ	USBLS	5/07
	Indianapolis-Carmel MSA, IN	Y	17350 FQ	19110 MW	35310 TQ	USBLS	5/07
	Iowa	Y	24590 FQ	36330 MW	44770 TQ	USBLS	5/07
	Des Moines-West Des Moines MSA, IA	Y	25310 FQ	41980 MW	46250 TQ	USBLS	5/07
	Kansas	Y	30940 FQ	50330 MW	55900 TQ	USBLS	5/07
	Wichita MSA, KS	Y	27920 FQ	36190 MW	53030 TQ	USBLS	5/07
	Kentucky	Y	28832 FQ	33976 MW	41877 TQ	KYBLS	2008
	Louisville-Jefferson County MSA, KY-IN	Y	28810 FQ	32980 MW	39240 TQ	USBLS	5/07
	Louisiana	H	12.61 FQ	15.81 MW	20.21 TQ	LABLS	1/08-3/08
	Baton Rouge MSA, LA	Y	24560 FQ	33360 MW	44910 TQ	USBLS	5/07
	Houma-Bayou Cane-Thibodaux MSA, LA	Y	20090 FQ	24320 MW	31010 TQ	USBLS	5/07
	New Orleans-Metairie-Kenner MSA, LA	Y	28920 FQ	35240 MW	44190 TQ	USBLS	5/07
	Maine	Y	23920 FQ	29630 MW	36370 TQ	USBLS	5/07
	Portland-South Portland-Biddeford MSA, ME	Y	23440 FQ	29980 MW	37510 TQ	USBLS	5/07
	Maryland	Y		32050 MW		MDBLS	3/08
	Baltimore-Towson MSA, MD	Y	27280 FQ	31530 MW	36820 TQ	USBLS	5/07
	Bethesda-Gaithersburg-Frederick PMSA, MD	Y	26030 FQ	28530 MW	31020 TQ	USBLS	5/07
	Massachusetts	Y	28330 FQ	37110 MW	47190 TQ	USBLS	5/07
	Boston-Cambridge-Quincy NECTA, MA	Y	23670 FQ	35790 MW	46290 TQ	USBLS	5/07
	Worcester MSA, MA-CT	Y	32570 FQ	39160 MW	46070 TQ	USBLS	5/07
	Michigan	Y	31250 FQ	40840 MW	48480 TQ	USBLS	5/07
	Detroit-Warren-Livonia MSA, MI	Y	33640 FQ	41470 MW	49650 TQ	USBLS	5/07
	Grand Rapids-Wyoming MSA, MI	Y	30160 FQ	41580 MW	47510 TQ	USBLS	5/07
	Minnesota	Y	46170 FQ	58279 MW	63559 TQ	MNBLS	10/08-12/08
	Duluth-Superior MSA, MN-WI	Y	30815 FQ	38824 MW	58985 TQ	MNBLS	10/08-12/08
	Minneapolis-Saint Paul MSA, MN-WI	Y	54285 FQ	59744 MW	64381 TQ	MNBLS	10/08-12/08
	Rochester MSA, MN	Y	55394 FQ	60401 MW	65408 TQ	MNBLS	10/08-12/08
	Mississippi	Y	28280 FQ	33800 MW	38690 TQ	USBLS	5/07
	Jackson MSA, MS	Y	23530 FQ	27250 MW	30810 TQ	USBLS	5/07
	Missouri	Y	33810 FQ	51770 MW	59120 TQ	USBLS	5/07
	Kansas City MSA, MO-KS	Y	50640 FQ	56560 MW	61040 TQ	USBLS	5/07
	St. Louis MSA, MO-IL	Y	31710 FQ	42520 MW	56190 TQ	USBLS	5/07
	Nebraska	Y	19040 FQ	31920 MW	40090 TQ	USBLS	5/07
	Nevada	H	20.25 FQ	27.63 MW	31.33 TQ	NVBLS	5/08
	Las Vegas-Paradise MSA, NV	H	21.33 FQ	28.03 MW	31.53 TQ	NVBLS	5/08
	New Hampshire	H	13.43 AE	17.04 MW	18.44 AEX	NHBLS	6/08
	New Jersey	Y	42890 FQ	55000 MW	61850 TQ	USBLS	5/07
	Camden PMSA, NJ	Y	39350 FQ	48880 MW	54960 TQ	USBLS	5/07
	Edison PMSA, NJ	Y	47860 FQ	57390 MW	62590 TQ	USBLS	5/07
	Newark-Union PMSA, NJ-PA	Y	34450 FQ	54090 MW	60150 TQ	USBLS	5/07
	New Mexico	Y	28770 FQ	39340 MW	54040 TQ	USBLS	5/07
	Albuquerque MSA, NM	Y	26780 FQ	30430 MW	38780 TQ	USBLS	5/07
	New York	Y	37050 FQ	51620 MW	60000 TQ	USBLS	5/07
	Albany-Schenectady-Troy MSA, NY	Y	30240 FQ	36020 MW	40350 TQ	USBLS	5/07

AE	Average entry wage	AW	Average wage paid	FQ	First quartile wage
AER	Average entry range	AWR	Average wage range	H	Hourly
AEX	Average experienced wage	AXR	Average experienced range	HI	Highest wage paid
ATC	Average total compensation	D	Daily	HR	High end range

LO	Lowest wage paid	MTC	Median total compensation	TCC	Total cash compensation
LR	Low end range	MW	Median wage paid	TQ	Third quartile wage
M	Monthly	MWR	Median wage range	W	Weekly
MCC	Median cash compensation	S	See annotated source	Y	Yearly

Occupation/Type/Industry	Location	Per	Low	Mid	High	Source	Date
Hazardous Materials Removal Worker	Buffalo-Niagara Falls MSA, NY	Y	45270 FQ	55200 MW	61040 TQ	USBLS	5/07
	Nassau-Suffolk PMSA, NY	Y	49860 FQ	55030 MW	59860 TQ	USBLS	5/07
	New York-Northern New Jersey-Long Island MSA, NY-NJ-PA	Y	40820 FQ	54600 MW	61460 TQ	USBLS	5/07
	North Carolina	Y	19450 FQ	23340 MW	28620 TQ	USBLS	5/07
	Charlotte-Gastonia-Concord MSA, NC-SC	Y	21090 FQ	23460 MW	31890 TQ	USBLS	5/07
	Raleigh-Cary MSA, NC	Y	22040 FQ	24690 MW	30590 TQ	USBLS	5/07
	Ohio	Y	29170 FQ	35230 MW	43270 TQ	USBLS	5/07
	Cincinnati-Middletown MSA, OH-KY-IN	Y	28770 FQ	32990 MW	37240 TQ	USBLS	5/07
	Cleveland-Elyria-Mentor MSA, OH	Y	31120 FQ	37750 MW	42540 TQ	USBLS	5/07
	Columbus MSA, OH	Y	29360 FQ	33500 MW	43250 TQ	USBLS	5/07
	Oklahoma	Y	22330 FQ	24730 MW	31160 TQ	USBLS	5/07
	Oklahoma City MSA, OK	Y	28220 FQ	34300 MW	38910 TQ	USBLS	5/07
	Tulsa MSA, OK	Y	21900 FQ	24020 MW	27050 TQ	USBLS	5/07
	Oregon	H	14.07 FQ	17.15 MW	20.17 TQ	ORBLS	5/08
	Portland-Vancouver-Beaverton MSA, OR-WA	Y	31990 FQ	37390 MW	41750 TQ	USBLS	5/07
	Pennsylvania	Y	31370 FQ	39800 MW	47340 TQ	USBLS	5/07
	Philadelphia-Camden-Wilmington MSA, PA-NJ-DE-MD	Y	37380 FQ	44840 MW	52380 TQ	USBLS	5/07
	Rhode Island	Y	41460 FQ	49080 MW	57130 TQ	USBLS	5/07
	Providence-Fall River-Warwick MSA, RI-MA	Y	38720 FQ	48320 MW	56630 TQ	USBLS	5/07
	South Carolina	Y	29700 FQ	45720 MW	55360 TQ	USBLS	5/07
	Charleston-North Charleston MSA, SC	Y	27590 FQ	42010 MW	47080 TQ	USBLS	5/07
	Columbia MSA, SC	Y	22410 FQ	29520 MW	36700 TQ	USBLS	5/07
	Tennessee	Y	26510 FQ	30560 MW	38970 TQ	USBLS	5/07
	Memphis MSA, TN-MS-AR	Y	23790 FQ	28350 MW	33660 TQ	USBLS	5/07
	Nashville-Davidson-Murfreesboro MSA, TN	Y	27480 FQ	31130 MW	36520 TQ	USBLS	5/07
	Texas	Y	24250 FQ	28580 MW	32410 TQ	USBLS	5/07
	Austin-Round Rock MSA, TX	Y	21740 FQ	23770 MW	27550 TQ	USBLS	5/07
	Dallas-Fort Worth-Arlington MSA, TX	Y	24350 FQ	27900 MW	30690 TQ	USBLS	5/07
	El Paso MSA, TX	Y	16080 FQ	18550 MW	22550 TQ	USBLS	5/07
	Houston-Sugar Land-Baytown MSA, TX	Y	26070 FQ	30030 MW	36390 TQ	USBLS	5/07
	San Antonio MSA, TX	Y	26840 FQ	28880 MW	30920 TQ	USBLS	5/07
	Utah	Y	27640 FQ	36250 MW	45550 TQ	USBLS	5/07
	Salt Lake City MSA, UT	Y	27990 FQ	37570 MW	45970 TQ	USBLS	5/07
	Vermont	Y	33530 FQ	36170 MW	39080 TQ	USBLS	5/07
	Burlington-South Burlington MSA, VT	Y	33060 FQ	35960 MW	39360 TQ	USBLS	5/07
	Virginia	Y	27580 FQ	32050 MW	38220 TQ	USBLS	5/07
	Richmond MSA, VA	Y	27040 FQ	33250 MW	41480 TQ	USBLS	5/07
	Virginia Beach-Norfolk-Newport News MSA, VA-NC	Y	28660 FQ	32570 MW	37720 TQ	USBLS	5/07
	Washington	H	19.34 FQ	29.76 MW	33.78 TQ	WABLS	3/08
	Seattle-Tacoma-Bellevue MSA, WA	Y	36630 FQ	44800 MW	61490 TQ	USBLS	5/07
	West Virginia	Y	32543 FQ	41400 MW	47880 TQ	WVBLS	7/08-9/08
	Wisconsin	Y	32950 FQ	40450 MW	47890 TQ	USBLS	5/07
	Puerto Rico	Y	12740 FQ	14410 MW	16110 TQ	USBLS	5/07
	San Juan-Caguas-Guaynabo MSA, PR	Y	13040 FQ	15070 MW	18940 TQ	USBLS	5/07
Hazardous Materials Specialist							
Municipal Government	Colorado Springs, CO	M	4025 LO			COSPRS	1/1/09
State Government	Ohio	H	19.88 LO		26.28 HI	ODAS	2008
Hazardous Materials Training Coordinator							
State Highway Patrol	Missouri	S	1738 LO		2568 HI	MSHPSS	7/1/08

AE	Average entry wage	AW	Average wage paid	FQ	First quartile wage	LO	Lowest wage paid	MTC	Median total compensation	TCC	Total cash compensation
AER	Average entry range	AWR	Average wage range	H	Hourly	LR	Low end range	MW	Median wage paid	TQ	Third quartile wage
AEX	Average experienced wage	AXR	Average experienced range	HI	Highest wage paid	M	Monthly	MWR	Median wage range	W	Weekly
ATC	Average total compensation	D	Daily	HR	High end range	MCC	Median cash compensation	S	See annotated source	Y	Yearly

Occupation/Type/Industry	Location	Per	Low	Mid	High	Source	Date
Hazmat Diver	United States	Y		31183 AW		CBUILD	2008
Head Dispatcher							
Police Department	Montague, MA	H			16.62 HI	FRCOG	2009
Head Football Coach							
Big Ten Conference	United States	Y		1504176 AW		AAUP	2007-2008
Mid-American Conference	United States	Y		226475 AW		AAUP	2007-2008
Southeastern Conference	United States	Y		1941612 AW		AAUP	2007-2008
Western Athletic Conference	United States	Y		546508 AW		AAUP	2007-2008
Head of the Water Department	Detroit, MI	Y			240000 HI	WXYZ	2008
Health and Safety Engineer							
Except Mining Safety Engineers and Inspectors	Alabama	Y	52200 FQ	65450 MW	84230 TQ	USBLS	5/07
Except Mining Safety Engineers and Inspectors	Birmingham-Hoover MSA, AL	Y	49910 FQ	63210 MW	80650 TQ	USBLS	5/07
Except Mining Safety Engineers and Inspectors	Alaska	Y	62170 FQ	84570 MW	97270 TQ	USBLS	5/07
Except Mining Safety Engineers and Inspectors	Anchorage MSA, AK	Y	58060 FQ	74580 MW	90760 TQ	USBLS	5/07
Except Mining Safety Engineers and Inspectors	Arizona	Y	55650 FQ	72340 MW	87010 TQ	USBLS	5/07
Except Mining Safety Engineers and Inspectors	Phoenix-Mesa-Scottsdale MSA, AZ	Y	59200 FQ	75330 MW	89810 TQ	USBLS	5/07
Except Mining Safety Engineers and Inspectors	Tucson MSA, AZ	Y	54520 FQ	63760 MW	80070 TQ	USBLS	5/07
Except Mining Safety Engineers and Inspectors	Arkansas	Y	40840 FQ	56830 MW	72410 TQ	USBLS	5/07
Except Mining Safety Engineers and Inspectors	Little Rock-North Little Rock MSA, AR	Y	34020 FQ	41400 MW	60520 TQ	USBLS	5/07
Except Mining Safety Engineers and Inspectors	California	H	32.85 FQ	38.24 MW	45.72 TQ	CABLS	1/08-3/08
Except Mining Safety Engineers and Inspectors	Fresno MSA, CA	H	29.37 FQ	35.22 MW	43.75 TQ	CABLS	1/08-3/08
Except Mining Safety Engineers and Inspectors	Los Angeles-Long Beach-Glendale PMSA, CA	H	33.34 FQ	37.68 MW	44.47 TQ	CABLS	1/08-3/08
Except Mining Safety Engineers and Inspectors	Oakland-Fremont-Hayward MSA, CA	H	34.40 FQ	42.91 MW	48.71 TQ	CABLS	1/08-3/08
Except Mining Safety Engineers and Inspectors	Riverside-San Bernardino-Ontario MSA, CA	H	29.55 FQ	35.36 MW	40.11 TQ	CABLS	1/08-3/08
Except Mining Safety Engineers and Inspectors	Sacramento-Arden Arcade-Roseville MSA, CA	H	34.13 FQ	38.90 MW	45.33 TQ	CABLS	1/08-3/08
Except Mining Safety Engineers and Inspectors	San Diego-Carlsbad-San Marcos MSA, CA	H	33.92 FQ	38.77 MW	46.34 TQ	CABLS	1/08-3/08
Except Mining Safety Engineers and Inspectors	San Francisco-San Mateo-Redwood PMSA, CA	H	33.25 FQ	37.86 MW	44.79 TQ	CABLS	1/08-3/08
Except Mining Safety Engineers and Inspectors	San Jose-Sunnyvale-Santa Clara MSA, CA	H	37.32 FQ	44.25 MW	50.69 TQ	CABLS	1/08-3/08
Except Mining Safety Engineers and Inspectors	Santa Ana-Anaheim-Irvine PMSA, CA	Y	66110 FQ	79940 MW	94950 TQ	USBLS	5/07
Except Mining Safety Engineers and Inspectors	Santa Rosa-Petaluma MSA, CA	H	34.34 FQ	37.81 MW	42.28 TQ	CABLS	1/08-3/08
Except Mining Safety Engineers and Inspectors	Colorado	Y	55690 FQ	75670 MW	101140 TQ	USBLS	5/07
Except Mining Safety Engineers and Inspectors	Denver-Aurora MSA, CO	Y	52540 FQ	66730 MW	89570 TQ	USBLS	5/07
Except Mining Safety Engineers and Inspectors	Connecticut	H	25.98 AE	35.83 MW		CTBLS	1/08-3/08

AE Average entry wage	**AW** Average wage paid	**FQ** First quartile wage	**LO** Lowest wage paid	**MTC** Median total compensation	**TCC** Total cash compensation
AER Average entry range	**AWR** Average wage range	**H** Hourly	**LR** Low end range	**MW** Median wage paid	**TQ** Third quartile wage
AEX Average experienced wage	**AXR** Average experienced range	**HI** Highest wage paid	**M** Monthly	**MWR** Median wage range	**W** Weekly
ATC Average total compensation	**D** Daily	**HR** High end range	**MCC** Median cash compensation	**S** See annotated source	**Y** Yearly

Health and Safety Engineer

Occupation/Type/Industry	Location	Per	Low	Mid	High	Source	Date
Except Mining Safety Engineers and Inspectors	Bridgeport-Stamford-Norwalk MSA, CT	Y	61710 FQ	69320 MW	77820 TQ	USBLS	5/07
Except Mining Safety Engineers and Inspectors	Hartford-West Hartford-East Hartford MSA, CT	Y	63780 FQ	76820 MW	91110 TQ	USBLS	5/07
Except Mining Safety Engineers and Inspectors	Delaware	Y	68960 FQ	76660 MW	84450 TQ	USBLS	5/07
Except Mining Safety Engineers and Inspectors	Wilmington PMSA, DE-MD-NJ	Y	69160 FQ	77000 MW	84770 TQ	USBLS	5/07
Except Mining Safety Engineers and Inspectors	District of Columbia	Y	79780 FQ	89710 MW	100110 TQ	USBLS	5/07
Except Mining Safety Engineers and Inspectors	Washington-Arlington-Alexandria MSA, DC-VA-MD-WV	Y	62840 FQ	79630 MW	96620 TQ	USBLS	5/07
Except Mining Safety Engineers and Inspectors	Florida	Y	45860 FQ	59170 MW	79580 TQ	USBLS	5/07
Except Mining Safety Engineers and Inspectors	Fort Lauderdale-Pompano Beach-Deerfield Beach PMSA, FL	Y	41280 FQ	61980 MW	94570 TQ	USBLS	5/07
Except Mining Safety Engineers and Inspectors	Jacksonville MSA, FL	Y	54710 FQ	62370 MW	76910 TQ	USBLS	5/07
Except Mining Safety Engineers and Inspectors	Miami-Fort Lauderdale-Miami Beach MSA, FL	Y	40680 FQ	56790 MW	76860 TQ	USBLS	5/07
Except Mining Safety Engineers and Inspectors	Orlando-Kissimmee MSA, FL	Y	43630 FQ	52110 MW	78440 TQ	USBLS	5/07
Except Mining Safety Engineers and Inspectors	Tampa-St. Petersburg-Clearwater MSA, FL	Y	53710 FQ	63140 MW	81830 TQ	USBLS	5/07
Except Mining Safety Engineers and Inspectors	Georgia	Y	47320 FQ	59640 MW	78890 TQ	USBLS	5/07
Except Mining Safety Engineers and Inspectors	Atlanta-Sandy Springs-Marietta MSA, GA	Y	45920 FQ	59580 MW	83870 TQ	USBLS	5/07
Except Mining Safety Engineers and Inspectors	Hawaii	Y	59060 FQ	80130 MW	92730 TQ	USBLS	5/07
Except Mining Safety Engineers and Inspectors	Honolulu MSA, HI	Y	59530 FQ	80930 MW	93040 TQ	USBLS	5/07
Except Mining Safety Engineers and Inspectors	Idaho	Y	66120 FQ	79980 MW	93610 TQ	USBLS	5/07
Except Mining Safety Engineers and Inspectors	Illinois	Y	53940 FQ	68750 MW	84110 TQ	USBLS	5/07
Except Mining Safety Engineers and Inspectors	Chicago-Naperville-Joliet MSA, IL-IN-WI	Y	57680 FQ	71480 MW	86980 TQ	USBLS	5/07
Except Mining Safety Engineers and Inspectors	Indiana	Y	47510 FQ	56770 MW	63700 TQ	USBLS	5/07
Except Mining Safety Engineers and Inspectors	Gary PMSA, IN	Y	49020 FQ	58230 MW	65750 TQ	USBLS	5/07
Except Mining Safety Engineers and Inspectors	Indianapolis-Carmel MSA, IN	Y	51900 FQ	57410 MW	62810 TQ	USBLS	5/07
Except Mining Safety Engineers and Inspectors	Iowa	Y	57040 FQ	67200 MW	76600 TQ	USBLS	5/07
Except Mining Safety Engineers and Inspectors	Kansas	Y	45020 FQ	57580 MW	76030 TQ	USBLS	5/07
Except Mining Safety Engineers and Inspectors	Wichita MSA, KS	Y	48310 FQ	66320 MW	90820 TQ	USBLS	5/07
Except Mining Safety Engineers and Inspectors	Kentucky	Y	52167 FQ	64279 MW	80370 TQ	KYBLS	2008
Except Mining Safety Engineers and Inspectors	Louisville-Jefferson County MSA, KY-IN	Y	48160 FQ	63440 MW	88970 TQ	USBLS	5/07
Except Mining Safety Engineers and Inspectors	Louisiana	H	20.86 FQ	30.29 MW	39.78 TQ	LABLS	1/08-3/08
Except Mining Safety Engineers and Inspectors	Baton Rouge MSA, LA	Y	56340 FQ	75580 MW	90230 TQ	USBLS	5/07

AE	Average entry wage	AW	Average wage paid	FQ	First quartile wage
AER	Average entry range	AWR	Average wage range	H	Hourly
AEX	Average experienced wage	AXR	Average experienced range	HI	Highest wage paid
ATC	Average total compensation	D	Daily	HR	High end range

LO	Lowest wage paid	MTC	Median total compensation	TCC	Total cash compensation
LR	Low end range	MW	Median wage paid	TQ	Third quartile wage
M	Monthly	MWR	Median wage range	W	Weekly
MCC	Median cash compensation	S	See annotated source	Y	Yearly

Occupation/Type/Industry	Location	Per	Low	Mid	High	Source	Date
Health and Safety Engineer							
Except Mining Safety Engineers and Inspectors	Lafayette MSA, LA	Y	33150 FQ	35650 MW	38140 TQ	USBLS	5/07
Except Mining Safety Engineers and Inspectors	New Orleans-Metairie-Kenner MSA, LA	Y	56200 FQ	72830 MW	91250 TQ	USBLS	5/07
Except Mining Safety Engineers and Inspectors	Maine	Y	38050 FQ	49940 MW	61800 TQ	USBLS	5/07
Except Mining Safety Engineers and Inspectors	Maryland	Y		68300 MW		MDBLS	3/08
Except Mining Safety Engineers and Inspectors	Baltimore-Towson MSA, MD	Y	51700 FQ	62400 MW	79930 TQ	USBLS	5/07
Except Mining Safety Engineers and Inspectors	Bethesda-Gaithersburg-Frederick PMSA, MD	Y	69560 FQ	88070 MW	112960 TQ	USBLS	5/07
Except Mining Safety Engineers and Inspectors	Massachusetts	Y	68480 FQ	80810 MW	96250 TQ	USBLS	5/07
Except Mining Safety Engineers and Inspectors	Boston-Cambridge-Quincy NECTA, MA	Y	68590 FQ	79970 MW	95200 TQ	USBLS	5/07
Except Mining Safety Engineers and Inspectors	Michigan	Y	66170 FQ	76270 MW	89760 TQ	USBLS	5/07
Except Mining Safety Engineers and Inspectors	Detroit-Warren-Livonia MSA, MI	Y	68670 FQ	77880 MW	93560 TQ	USBLS	5/07
Except Mining Safety Engineers and Inspectors	Warren-Troy-Farmington Hills PMSA, MI	Y	67820 FQ	76970 MW	92400 TQ	USBLS	5/07
Except Mining Safety Engineers and Inspectors	Minnesota	Y	65849 FQ	75956 MW	88092 TQ	MNBLS	10/08-12/08
Except Mining Safety Engineers and Inspectors	Minneapolis-Saint Paul MSA, MN-WI	Y	67115 FQ	76625 MW	88374 TQ	MNBLS	10/08-12/08
Except Mining Safety Engineers and Inspectors	Rochester MSA, MN	Y	70398 FQ	79695 MW	91741 TQ	MNBLS	10/08-12/08
Except Mining Safety Engineers and Inspectors	Mississippi	Y	42880 FQ	55300 MW	72170 TQ	USBLS	5/07
Except Mining Safety Engineers and Inspectors	Missouri	Y	50000 FQ	67120 MW	82020 TQ	USBLS	5/07
Except Mining Safety Engineers and Inspectors	Kansas City MSA, MO-KS	Y	44330 FQ	57250 MW	76220 TQ	USBLS	5/07
Except Mining Safety Engineers and Inspectors	St. Louis MSA, MO-IL	Y	58340 FQ	71690 MW	87010 TQ	USBLS	5/07
Except Mining Safety Engineers and Inspectors	Montana	Y	54070 FQ	59660 MW	71820 TQ	USBLS	5/07
Except Mining Safety Engineers and Inspectors	Billings MSA, MT	Y	51950 FQ	55200 MW	58460 TQ	USBLS	5/07
Except Mining Safety Engineers and Inspectors	Nebraska	Y	48350 FQ	63960 MW	79480 TQ	USBLS	5/07
Except Mining Safety Engineers and Inspectors	Nevada	H	25.82 FQ	31.72 MW	40.87 TQ	NVBLS	5/08
Except Mining Safety Engineers and Inspectors	Las Vegas-Paradise MSA, NV	H	25.72 FQ	31.11 MW	39.03 TQ	NVBLS	5/08
Except Mining Safety Engineers and Inspectors	New Hampshire	H	21.38 AE	31.34 MW	40.35 AEX	NHBLS	6/08
Except Mining Safety Engineers and Inspectors	New Jersey	Y	68740 FQ	83950 MW	101910 TQ	USBLS	5/07
Except Mining Safety Engineers and Inspectors	Camden PMSA, NJ	Y	68230 FQ	84690 MW	106300 TQ	USBLS	5/07
Except Mining Safety Engineers and Inspectors	Edison PMSA, NJ	Y	74830 FQ	87150 MW	103610 TQ	USBLS	5/07
Except Mining Safety Engineers and Inspectors	Newark-Union PMSA, NJ-PA	Y	65650 FQ	80910 MW	96900 TQ	USBLS	5/07
Except Mining Safety Engineers and Inspectors	Trenton-Ewing MSA, NJ	Y	61430 FQ	83090 MW	107200 TQ	USBLS	5/07
Except Mining Safety Engineers and Inspectors	New Mexico	Y	50750 FQ	62470 MW	82330 TQ	USBLS	5/07
Except Mining Safety Engineers and Inspectors	Albuquerque MSA, NM	Y	54240 FQ	65160 MW	85300 TQ	USBLS	5/07
Except Mining Safety Engineers and Inspectors	New York	Y	54870 FQ	68260 MW	85820 TQ	USBLS	5/07

AE	Average entry wage	AW	Average wage paid	FQ	First quartile wage	LO	Lowest wage paid	MTC	Median total compensation	TCC	Total cash compensation
AER	Average entry range	AWR	Average wage range	H	Hourly	LR	Low end range	MW	Median wage paid	TQ	Third quartile wage
AEX	Average experienced wage	AXR	Average experienced range	HI	Highest wage paid	M	Monthly	MWR	Median wage range	W	Weekly
ATC	Average total compensation	D	Daily	HR	High end range	MCC	Median cash compensation	S	See annotated source	Y	Yearly

Occupation/Type/Industry	Location	Per	Low	Mid	High	Source	Date
Health and Safety Engineer							
Except Mining Safety Engineers and Inspectors	Albany-Schenectady-Troy MSA, NY	Y	49750 FQ	65630 MW	78980 TQ	USBLS	5/07
Except Mining Safety Engineers and Inspectors	Buffalo-Niagara Falls MSA, NY	Y	53470 FQ	62350 MW	76830 TQ	USBLS	5/07
Except Mining Safety Engineers and Inspectors	Nassau-Suffolk PMSA, NY	Y	52990 FQ	63670 MW	84820 TQ	USBLS	5/07
Except Mining Safety Engineers and Inspectors	New York-Northern New Jersey-Long Island MSA, NY-NJ-PA	Y	60700 FQ	76900 MW	93510 TQ	USBLS	5/07
Except Mining Safety Engineers and Inspectors	North Carolina	Y	52370 FQ	61960 MW	79350 TQ	USBLS	5/07
Except Mining Safety Engineers and Inspectors	Charlotte-Gastonia-Concord MSA, NC-SC	Y	52260 FQ	60990 MW	83220 TQ	USBLS	5/07
Except Mining Safety Engineers and Inspectors	Raleigh-Cary MSA, NC	Y	56080 FQ	66210 MW	78960 TQ	USBLS	5/07
Except Mining Safety Engineers and Inspectors	Ohio	Y	54970 FQ	69080 MW	86310 TQ	USBLS	5/07
Except Mining Safety Engineers and Inspectors	Cincinnati-Middletown MSA, OH-KY-IN	Y	58350 FQ	70040 MW	90740 TQ	USBLS	5/07
Except Mining Safety Engineers and Inspectors	Cleveland-Elyria-Mentor MSA, OH	Y	52180 FQ	69260 MW	85150 TQ	USBLS	5/07
Except Mining Safety Engineers and Inspectors	Columbus MSA, OH	Y	53810 FQ	62030 MW	75310 TQ	USBLS	5/07
Except Mining Safety Engineers and Inspectors	Dayton MSA, OH	Y	73750 FQ	89430 MW	99490 TQ	USBLS	5/07
Except Mining Safety Engineers and Inspectors	Oklahoma	Y	34020 FQ	47850 MW	67040 TQ	USBLS	5/07
Except Mining Safety Engineers and Inspectors	Oklahoma City MSA, OK	Y	33870 FQ	45720 MW	59970 TQ	USBLS	5/07
Except Mining Safety Engineers and Inspectors	Tulsa MSA, OK	Y	41980 FQ	58530 MW	83950 TQ	USBLS	5/07
Except Mining Safety Engineers and Inspectors	Oregon	H	29.06 FQ	35.30 MW	41.56 TQ	ORBLS	5/08
Except Mining Safety Engineers and Inspectors	Portland-Vancouver-Beaverton MSA, OR-WA	Y	60930 FQ	74140 MW	87120 TQ	USBLS	5/07
Except Mining Safety Engineers and Inspectors	Pennsylvania	Y	46030 FQ	62720 MW	78180 TQ	USBLS	5/07
Except Mining Safety Engineers and Inspectors	Allentown-Bethlehem-Easton MSA, PA-NJ	Y	41010 FQ	48350 MW	59120 TQ	USBLS	5/07
Except Mining Safety Engineers and Inspectors	Philadelphia-Camden-Wilmington MSA, PA-NJ-DE-MD	Y	52100 FQ	69620 MW	86780 TQ	USBLS	5/07
Except Mining Safety Engineers and Inspectors	Pittsburgh MSA, PA	Y	52030 FQ	67970 MW	81800 TQ	USBLS	5/07
Except Mining Safety Engineers and Inspectors	Rhode Island	Y	60900 FQ	71330 MW	82820 TQ	USBLS	5/07
Except Mining Safety Engineers and Inspectors	Providence-Fall River-Warwick MSA, RI-MA	Y	59710 FQ	72150 MW	84950 TQ	USBLS	5/07
Except Mining Safety Engineers and Inspectors	South Carolina	Y	57480 FQ	72290 MW	87180 TQ	USBLS	5/07
Except Mining Safety Engineers and Inspectors	Charleston-North Charleston MSA, SC	Y	30510 FQ	51020 MW	72470 TQ	USBLS	5/07
Except Mining Safety Engineers and Inspectors	Columbia MSA, SC	Y	43140 FQ	53480 MW	65290 TQ	USBLS	5/07
Except Mining Safety Engineers and Inspectors	South Dakota	Y	48217 FQ	62036 MW	81314 TQ	SDBLS	7/08-9/08
Except Mining Safety Engineers and Inspectors	Tennessee	Y	47860 FQ	65480 MW	90990 TQ	USBLS	5/07

AE	Average entry wage	AW	Average wage paid	FQ	First quartile wage	LO	Lowest wage paid	MTC	Median total compensation	TCC	Total cash compensation
AER	Average entry range	AWR	Average wage range	H	Hourly	LR	Low end range	MW	Median wage paid	TQ	Third quartile wage
AEX	Average experienced wage	AXR	Average experienced range	HI	Highest wage paid	M	Monthly	MWR	Median wage range	W	Weekly
ATC	Average total compensation	D	Daily	HR	High end range	MCC	Median cash compensation	S	See annotated source	Y	Yearly

744

Occupation/Type/Industry	Location	Per	Low	Mid	High	Source	Date
Health and Safety Engineer							
Except Mining Safety Engineers and Inspectors	Memphis MSA, TN-MS-AR	Y	41190 FQ	54840 MW	80610 TQ	USBLS	5/07
Except Mining Safety Engineers and Inspectors	Nashville-Davidson-Murfreesboro MSA, TN	Y	38690 FQ	50990 MW	60740 TQ	USBLS	5/07
Except Mining Safety Engineers and Inspectors	Texas	Y	55780 FQ	71710 MW	91080 TQ	USBLS	5/07
Except Mining Safety Engineers and Inspectors	Austin-Round Rock MSA, TX	Y	65890 FQ	78710 MW	93550 TQ	USBLS	5/07
Except Mining Safety Engineers and Inspectors	Corpus Christi MSA, TX	Y	50800 FQ	58670 MW	69640 TQ	USBLS	5/07
Except Mining Safety Engineers and Inspectors	Dallas-Fort Worth-Arlington MSA, TX	Y	49880 FQ	61570 MW	75630 TQ	USBLS	5/07
Except Mining Safety Engineers and Inspectors	Houston-Sugar Land-Baytown MSA, TX	Y	57630 FQ	76260 MW	98900 TQ	USBLS	5/07
Except Mining Safety Engineers and Inspectors	San Antonio MSA, TX	Y	51720 FQ	67530 MW	77080 TQ	USBLS	5/07
Except Mining Safety Engineers and Inspectors	Utah	Y	49030 FQ	61390 MW	74330 TQ	USBLS	5/07
Except Mining Safety Engineers and Inspectors	Salt Lake City MSA, UT	Y	49190 FQ	59850 MW	71300 TQ	USBLS	5/07
Except Mining Safety Engineers and Inspectors	Vermont	Y	51620 FQ	65990 MW	77340 TQ	USBLS	5/07
Except Mining Safety Engineers and Inspectors	Burlington-South Burlington MSA, VT	Y	50420 FQ	61090 MW	75950 TQ	USBLS	5/07
Except Mining Safety Engineers and Inspectors	Virginia	Y	54000 FQ	67350 MW	84310 TQ	USBLS	5/07
Except Mining Safety Engineers and Inspectors	Richmond MSA, VA	Y	56940 FQ	66890 MW	75880 TQ	USBLS	5/07
Except Mining Safety Engineers and Inspectors	Virginia Beach-Norfolk-Newport News MSA, VA-NC	Y	48990 FQ	63060 MW	77850 TQ	USBLS	5/07
Except Mining Safety Engineers and Inspectors	Washington	H	32.69 FQ	39.01 MW	45.84 TQ	WABLS	3/08
Except Mining Safety Engineers and Inspectors	Seattle-Tacoma-Bellevue MSA, WA	Y	62270 FQ	77430 MW	93180 TQ	USBLS	5/07
Except Mining Safety Engineers and Inspectors	West Virginia	Y	39528 FQ	53383 MW	75470 TQ	WVBLS	7/08-9/08
Except Mining Safety Engineers and Inspectors	Charleston MSA, WV	Y	37680 FQ	47060 MW	64190 TQ	USBLS	5/07
Except Mining Safety Engineers and Inspectors	Parkersburg-Marietta-Vienna MSA, WV-OH	Y	35280 FQ	38570 MW	69490 TQ	USBLS	5/07
Except Mining Safety Engineers and Inspectors	Wisconsin	Y	53600 FQ	68080 MW	84940 TQ	USBLS	5/07
Except Mining Safety Engineers and Inspectors	Milwaukee-Waukesha-West Allis MSA, WI	Y	49950 FQ	61960 MW	78880 TQ	USBLS	5/07
Except Mining Safety Engineers and Inspectors	Wyoming	Y	48249 FQ	64418 MW	76529 TQ	WYBLS	9/08
Except Mining Safety Engineers and Inspectors	Puerto Rico	Y	42630 FQ	69010 MW	81680 TQ	USBLS	5/07
Except Mining Safety Engineers and Inspectors	San Juan-Caguas-Guaynabo MSA, PR	Y	41710 FQ	66800 MW	79980 TQ	USBLS	5/07
Health Care Facilities Compliance Consultant							
State Government	Ohio	H	22.60 LO		31.62 HI	ODAS	2008
Health Caseworker							
Municipal Government	Cincinnati, OH	Y	36019 LO		48407 HI	COHSS	10/08
Health Counseling Supervisor							
Municipal Government	Cincinnati, OH	Y	46775 LO		64410 HI	COHSS	10/08

AE	Average entry wage	AW	Average wage paid	FQ	First quartile wage	LO	Lowest wage paid	MTC	Median total compensation	TCC	Total cash compensation
AER	Average entry range	AWR	Average wage range	H	Hourly	LR	Low end range	MW	Median wage paid	TQ	Third quartile wage
AEX	Average experienced wage	AXR	Average experienced range	HI	Highest wage paid	M	Monthly	MWR	Median wage range	W	Weekly
ATC	Average total compensation	D	Daily	HR	High end range	MCC	Median cash compensation	S	See annotated source	Y	Yearly

Occupation/Type/Industry	Location	Per	Low	Mid	High	Source	Date
Health Counselor							
Municipal Government	Cincinnati, OH	Y	40186 LO		54007 HI	COHSS	10/08
Health Director	Montague, MA	Y			58775 HI	FRCOG	2009
Health Educator	Alabama	Y	25250 FQ	37330 MW	52460 TQ	USBLS	5/07
	Birmingham-Hoover MSA, AL	Y	26780 FQ	35490 MW	54890 TQ	USBLS	5/07
	Tuscaloosa MSA, AL	Y	51490 FQ	56140 MW	60690 TQ	USBLS	5/07
	Alaska	Y	29160 FQ	35070 MW	47590 TQ	USBLS	5/07
	Anchorage MSA, AK	Y	28780 FQ	34500 MW	49650 TQ	USBLS	5/07
	Arizona	Y	27980 FQ	38010 MW	61340 TQ	USBLS	5/07
	Flagstaff MSA, AZ	Y	19910 FQ	21960 MW	24780 TQ	USBLS	5/07
	Phoenix-Mesa-Scottsdale MSA, AZ	Y	35280 FQ	46680 MW	68130 TQ	USBLS	5/07
	Tucson MSA, AZ	Y	26550 FQ	31920 MW	54490 TQ	USBLS	5/07
	Arkansas	Y	31520 FQ	46020 MW	58400 TQ	USBLS	5/07
	Little Rock-North Little Rock MSA, AR	Y	39730 FQ	50490 MW	60600 TQ	USBLS	5/07
	California	H	15.04 FQ	19.45 MW	29.51 TQ	CABLS	1/08-3/08
	Los Angeles-Long Beach-Glendale PMSA, CA	H	13.90 FQ	16.94 MW	23.10 TQ	CABLS	1/08-3/08
	Oakland-Fremont-Hayward MSA, CA	H	18.75 FQ	23.66 MW	36.21 TQ	CABLS	1/08-3/08
	Riverside-San Bernardino-Ontario MSA, CA	H	15.35 FQ	18.55 MW	26.07 TQ	CABLS	1/08-3/08
	Sacramento-Arden Arcade-Roseville MSA, CA	H	18.66 FQ	29.86 MW	36.53 TQ	CABLS	1/08-3/08
	San Diego-Carlsbad-San Marcos MSA, CA	H	13.63 FQ	17.06 MW	24.05 TQ	CABLS	1/08-3/08
	San Francisco-San Mateo-Redwood PMSA, CA	H	23.59 FQ	35.20 MW	44.97 TQ	CABLS	1/08-3/08
	San Jose-Sunnyvale-Santa Clara MSA, CA	H	20.76 FQ	23.61 MW	26.43 TQ	CABLS	1/08-3/08
	Santa Ana-Anaheim-Irvine PMSA, CA	Y	25590 FQ	42170 MW	60820 TQ	USBLS	5/07
	Colorado	Y	34730 FQ	44730 MW	61030 TQ	USBLS	5/07
	Colorado Springs MSA, CO	Y	26490 FQ	38940 MW	49040 TQ	USBLS	5/07
	Denver-Aurora MSA, CO	Y	37780 FQ	47690 MW	63580 TQ	USBLS	5/07
	Connecticut	H	17.76 AE	26.61 MW		CTBLS	1/08-3/08
	Bridgeport-Stamford-Norwalk MSA, CT	Y	35400 FQ	44030 MW	61760 TQ	USBLS	5/07
	Hartford-West Hartford-East Hartford MSA, CT	Y	41760 FQ	58510 MW	69450 TQ	USBLS	5/07
	Norwich-New London MSA, CT-RI	Y	36190 FQ	40130 MW	47020 TQ	USBLS	5/07
	Delaware	Y	35850 FQ	52590 MW	67980 TQ	USBLS	5/07
	Wilmington PMSA, DE-MD-NJ	Y	36750 FQ	55310 MW	68960 TQ	USBLS	5/07
	District of Columbia	Y	49700 FQ	65410 MW	83610 TQ	USBLS	5/07
	Washington-Arlington-Alexandria MSA, DC-VA-MD-WV	Y	52680 FQ	70780 MW	92210 TQ	USBLS	5/07
	Florida	Y	35120 FQ	46440 MW	59140 TQ	USBLS	5/07
	Fort Lauderdale-Pompano Beach-Deerfield Beach PMSA, FL	Y	36990 FQ	46340 MW	56670 TQ	USBLS	5/07
	Jacksonville MSA, FL	Y	34330 FQ	45960 MW	58810 TQ	USBLS	5/07
	Miami-Fort Lauderdale-Miami Beach MSA, FL	Y	38320 FQ	48980 MW	63110 TQ	USBLS	5/07
	Orlando-Kissimmee MSA, FL	Y	30930 FQ	38650 MW	54690 TQ	USBLS	5/07
	Tampa-St. Petersburg-Clearwater MSA, FL	Y	36590 FQ	49340 MW	60260 TQ	USBLS	5/07
	West Palm Beach-Boca Raton-Boynton Beach PMSA, FL	Y	38550 FQ	48700 MW	63100 TQ	USBLS	5/07
	Georgia	Y	39950 FQ	55900 MW	83010 TQ	USBLS	5/07
	Atlanta-Sandy Springs-Marietta MSA, GA	Y	48640 FQ	68900 MW	90930 TQ	USBLS	5/07
	Hawaii	Y	40050 FQ	48250 MW	71470 TQ	USBLS	5/07
	Honolulu MSA, HI	Y	41490 FQ	51730 MW	74430 TQ	USBLS	5/07
	Idaho	Y	38740 FQ	45010 MW	51000 TQ	USBLS	5/07
	Boise City-Nampa MSA, ID	Y	42160 FQ	46310 MW	51380 TQ	USBLS	5/07
	Illinois	Y	32200 FQ	44140 MW	60940 TQ	USBLS	5/07

AE	Average entry wage	AW	Average wage paid	FQ	First quartile wage	LO	Lowest wage paid	MTC	Median total compensation	TCC	Total cash compensation
AER	Average entry range	AWR	Average wage range	H	Hourly	LR	Low end range	MW	Median wage paid	TQ	Third quartile wage
AEX	Average experienced wage	AXR	Average experienced range	HI	Highest wage paid	M	Monthly	MWR	Median wage range	W	Weekly
ATC	Average total compensation	D	Daily	HR	High end range	MCC	Median cash compensation	S	See annotated source	Y	Yearly

Occupation/Type/Industry	Location	Per	Low	Mid	High	Source	Date
Health Educator	Chicago-Naperville-Joliet MSA, IL-IN-WI	Y	35810 FQ	46460 MW	63300 TQ	USBLS	5/07
	Indiana	Y	27620 FQ	37290 MW	53300 TQ	USBLS	5/07
	Gary PMSA, IN	Y	34830 FQ	49390 MW	67490 TQ	USBLS	5/07
	Indianapolis-Carmel MSA, IN	Y	35290 FQ	45910 MW	62930 TQ	USBLS	5/07
	Iowa	Y	31150 FQ	38040 MW	49790 TQ	USBLS	5/07
	Des Moines-West Des Moines MSA, IA	Y	34600 FQ	38030 MW	41490 TQ	USBLS	5/07
	Kansas	Y	29310 FQ	42020 MW	54370 TQ	USBLS	5/07
	Wichita MSA, KS	Y	37030 FQ	44860 MW	50690 TQ	USBLS	5/07
	Kentucky	Y	28856 FQ	38705 MW	51578 TQ	KYBLS	2008
	Lexington-Fayette MSA, KY	Y	21390 FQ	23500 MW	30570 TQ	USBLS	5/07
	Louisville-Jefferson County MSA, KY-IN	Y	29190 FQ	36670 MW	52940 TQ	USBLS	5/07
	Louisiana	H	11.43 FQ	18.49 MW	27.66 TQ	LABLS	1/08-3/08
	Baton Rouge MSA, LA	Y	42140 FQ	52300 MW	78110 TQ	USBLS	5/07
	New Orleans-Metairie-Kenner MSA, LA	Y	38100 FQ	53210 MW	63240 TQ	USBLS	5/07
	Maine	Y	31310 FQ	36560 MW	45380 TQ	USBLS	5/07
	Portland-South Portland-Biddeford MSA, ME	Y	29570 FQ	35690 MW	53690 TQ	USBLS	5/07
	Maryland	Y		76550 MW		MDBLS	3/08
	Baltimore-Towson MSA, MD	Y	42690 FQ	57610 MW	73430 TQ	USBLS	5/07
	Bethesda-Gaithersburg-Frederick PMSA, MD	Y	70310 FQ	87140 MW	103290 TQ	USBLS	5/07
	Massachusetts	Y	35830 FQ	46940 MW	64470 TQ	USBLS	5/07
	Boston-Cambridge-Quincy NECTA, MA	Y	37330 FQ	50200 MW	72250 TQ	USBLS	5/07
	New Bedford MSA, MA	Y	28440 FQ	33960 MW	43110 TQ	USBLS	5/07
	Springfield MSA, MA-CT	Y	37160 FQ	42420 MW	54990 TQ	USBLS	5/07
	Worcester MSA, MA-CT	Y	37080 FQ	42090 MW	50710 TQ	USBLS	5/07
	Michigan	Y	37790 FQ	50520 MW	63850 TQ	USBLS	5/07
	Detroit-Warren-Livonia MSA, MI	Y	37720 FQ	49200 MW	59970 TQ	USBLS	5/07
	Grand Rapids-Wyoming MSA, MI	Y	43570 FQ	64860 MW	78980 TQ	USBLS	5/07
	Warren-Troy-Farmington Hills PMSA, MI	Y	37640 FQ	49550 MW	58900 TQ	USBLS	5/07
	Minnesota	Y	36032 FQ	42748 MW	54278 TQ	MNBLS	10/08-12/08
	Duluth-Superior MSA, MN-WI	Y	30706 FQ	41660 MW	57699 TQ	MNBLS	10/08-12/08
	Minneapolis-Saint Paul MSA, MN-WI	Y	35760 FQ	41995 MW	53378 TQ	MNBLS	10/08-12/08
	Rochester MSA, MN	Y	51883 FQ	61012 MW	70086 TQ	MNBLS	10/08-12/08
	Mississippi	Y	28140 FQ	33650 MW	45910 TQ	USBLS	5/07
	Jackson MSA, MS	Y	29020 FQ	36410 MW	49770 TQ	USBLS	5/07
	Missouri	Y	28400 FQ	36600 MW	49250 TQ	USBLS	5/07
	Kansas City MSA, MO-KS	Y	31120 FQ	42020 MW	57320 TQ	USBLS	5/07
	St. Louis MSA, MO-IL	Y	23970 FQ	35290 MW	48780 TQ	USBLS	5/07
	Montana	Y	18410 FQ	31880 MW	42410 TQ	USBLS	5/07
	Billings MSA, MT	Y	17720 FQ	25510 MW	34970 TQ	USBLS	5/07
	Nebraska	Y	28890 FQ	40210 MW	52010 TQ	USBLS	5/07
	Omaha-Council Bluffs MSA, NE-IA	Y	32020 FQ	42530 MW	52010 TQ	USBLS	5/07
	Nevada	H	20.91 FQ	28.71 MW	36.55 TQ	NVBLS	5/08
	Las Vegas-Paradise MSA, NV	H	22.37 FQ	31.46 MW	37.49 TQ	NVBLS	5/08
	New Hampshire	H	15.38 AE	21.18 MW	24.50 AEX	NHBLS	6/08
	New Jersey	Y	39150 FQ	47450 MW	63230 TQ	USBLS	5/07
	Atlantic City MSA, NJ	Y	31890 FQ	38200 MW	66910 TQ	USBLS	5/07
	Camden PMSA, NJ	Y	35350 FQ	42190 MW	59010 TQ	USBLS	5/07
	Edison PMSA, NJ	Y	37340 FQ	44760 MW	53760 TQ	USBLS	5/07
	Newark-Union PMSA, NJ-PA	Y	41710 FQ	48040 MW	63040 TQ	USBLS	5/07
	New Mexico	Y	23560 FQ	28090 MW	38240 TQ	USBLS	5/07
	Albuquerque MSA, NM	Y	23430 FQ	27730 MW	37310 TQ	USBLS	5/07
	New York	Y	34770 FQ	41720 MW	53190 TQ	USBLS	5/07
	Albany-Schenectady-Troy MSA, NY	Y	33960 FQ	44770 MW	59130 TQ	USBLS	5/07
	Buffalo-Niagara Falls MSA, NY	Y	31140 FQ	41340 MW	49400 TQ	USBLS	5/07
	Nassau-Suffolk PMSA, NY	Y	43320 FQ	54610 MW	71870 TQ	USBLS	5/07
	New York-Northern New Jersey-Long Island MSA, NY-NJ-PA	Y	37590 FQ	45160 MW	57210 TQ	USBLS	5/07

Occupation/Type/Industry	Location	Per	Low	Mid	High	Source	Date
Health Educator	North Carolina	Y	35540 FQ	43500 MW	54950 TQ	USBLS	5/07
	Asheville MSA, NC	Y	37790 FQ	45460 MW	54070 TQ	USBLS	5/07
	Charlotte-Gastonia-Concord MSA, NC-SC	Y	38350 FQ	47760 MW	56230 TQ	USBLS	5/07
	Raleigh-Cary MSA, NC	Y	37810 FQ	44590 MW	52620 TQ	USBLS	5/07
	North Dakota	Y	19510 FQ	29580 MW	40920 TQ	USBLS	5/07
	Fargo MSA, ND-MN	Y	27750 FQ	30350 MW	36480 TQ	USBLS	5/07
	Ohio	Y	31370 FQ	41530 MW	53270 TQ	USBLS	5/07
	Cincinnati-Middletown MSA, OH-KY-IN	Y	28400 FQ	38880 MW	53230 TQ	USBLS	5/07
	Cleveland-Elyria-Mentor MSA, OH	Y	40510 FQ	52270 MW	61140 TQ	USBLS	5/07
	Columbus MSA, OH	Y	34430 FQ	39950 MW	49090 TQ	USBLS	5/07
	Dayton MSA, OH	Y	32680 FQ	37950 MW	48750 TQ	USBLS	5/07
	Oklahoma	Y	32530 FQ	43270 MW	55730 TQ	USBLS	5/07
	Oklahoma City MSA, OK	Y	35140 FQ	47050 MW	60330 TQ	USBLS	5/07
	Tulsa MSA, OK	Y	29680 FQ	39320 MW	48140 TQ	USBLS	5/07
	Oregon	H	18.27 FQ	24.77 MW	30.30 TQ	ORBLS	5/08
	Portland-Vancouver-Beaverton MSA, OR-WA	Y	44250 FQ	55560 MW	63550 TQ	USBLS	5/07
	Pennsylvania	Y	32230 FQ	44980 MW	58960 TQ	USBLS	5/07
	Allentown-Bethlehem-Easton MSA, PA-NJ	Y	33020 FQ	39890 MW	51520 TQ	USBLS	5/07
	Philadelphia-Camden-Wilmington MSA, PA-NJ-DE-MD	Y	33560 FQ	44150 MW	60500 TQ	USBLS	5/07
	Pittsburgh MSA, PA	Y	34540 FQ	51770 MW	66560 TQ	USBLS	5/07
	Rhode Island	Y	45150 FQ	59430 MW	72720 TQ	USBLS	5/07
	Providence-Fall River-Warwick MSA, RI-MA	Y	41490 FQ	54700 MW	70560 TQ	USBLS	5/07
	South Carolina	Y	32500 FQ	39370 MW	52010 TQ	USBLS	5/07
	Charleston-North Charleston MSA, SC	Y	25550 FQ	33110 MW	40970 TQ	USBLS	5/07
	Columbia MSA, SC	Y	32810 FQ	39950 MW	54340 TQ	USBLS	5/07
	South Dakota	Y	35865 FQ	40540 MW	47494 TQ	SDBLS	7/08-9/08
	Sioux Falls MSA, SD	Y	35939 FQ	39604 MW	47448 TQ	SDBLS	7/08-9/08
	Tennessee	Y	24810 FQ	34080 MW	50680 TQ	USBLS	5/07
	Kingsport-Bristol-Bristol MSA, TN-VA	Y	28450 FQ	32050 MW	37290 TQ	USBLS	5/07
	Memphis MSA, TN-MS-AR	Y	27850 FQ	32370 MW	47310 TQ	USBLS	5/07
	Nashville-Davidson-Murfreesboro MSA, TN	Y	23170 FQ	33270 MW	53440 TQ	USBLS	5/07
	Texas	Y	27640 FQ	35710 MW	52330 TQ	USBLS	5/07
	Austin-Round Rock MSA, TX	Y	29510 FQ	33470 MW	39680 TQ	USBLS	5/07
	Beaumont-Port Arthur MSA, TX	Y	22990 FQ	26800 MW	34210 TQ	USBLS	5/07
	Dallas-Fort Worth-Arlington MSA, TX	Y	30070 FQ	41500 MW	58830 TQ	USBLS	5/07
	El Paso MSA, TX	Y	24760 FQ	28740 MW	32600 TQ	USBLS	5/07
	Houston-Sugar Land-Baytown MSA, TX	Y	28490 FQ	36920 MW	55450 TQ	USBLS	5/07
	San Antonio MSA, TX	Y	27260 FQ	37770 MW	48880 TQ	USBLS	5/07
	Utah	Y	36790 FQ	44610 MW	51510 TQ	USBLS	5/07
	Salt Lake City MSA, UT	Y	41250 FQ	46770 MW	53640 TQ	USBLS	5/07
	Vermont	Y	32200 FQ	42990 MW	54890 TQ	USBLS	5/07
	Burlington-South Burlington MSA, VT	Y	33550 FQ	43660 MW	52920 TQ	USBLS	5/07
	Virginia	Y	32250 FQ	40630 MW	54250 TQ	USBLS	5/07
	Richmond MSA, VA	Y	37320 FQ	43990 MW	53130 TQ	USBLS	5/07
	Virginia Beach-Norfolk-Newport News MSA, VA-NC	Y	31230 FQ	37990 MW	45280 TQ	USBLS	5/07
	Washington	H	19.98 FQ	24.83 MW	30.17 TQ	WABLS	3/08
	Olympia MSA, WA	Y	48070 FQ	55930 MW	62420 TQ	USBLS	5/07
	Seattle-Tacoma-Bellevue MSA, WA	Y	41700 FQ	52450 MW	64590 TQ	USBLS	5/07
	West Virginia	Y	25963 FQ	30845 MW	39753 TQ	WVBLS	7/08-9/08
	Charleston MSA, WV	Y	18510 FQ	26890 MW	31660 TQ	USBLS	5/07
	Wisconsin	Y	34790 FQ	45640 MW	55660 TQ	USBLS	5/07
	Milwaukee-Waukesha-West Allis MSA, WI	Y	36940 FQ	45600 MW	53020 TQ	USBLS	5/07
	Wyoming	Y	36007 FQ	43838 MW	53653 TQ	WYBLS	9/08
	Cheyenne MSA, WY	Y	43379 FQ	50610 MW	62766 TQ	WYBLS	9/08

AE	Average entry wage	AW	Average wage paid	FQ	First quartile wage
AER	Average entry range	AWR	Average wage range	H	Hourly
AEX	Average experienced wage	AXR	Average experienced range	HI	Highest wage paid
ATC	Average total compensation	D	Daily	HR	High end range

LO Lowest wage paid   MTC Median total compensation TCC Total cash compensation
LR Low end range   MW Median wage paid   TQ Third quartile wage
M   Monthly   MWR Median wage range   W   Weekly
MCC Median cash compensation S See annotated source   Y   Yearly

Occupation/Type/Industry	Location	Per	Low	Mid	High	Source	Date
Health Educator	Puerto Rico	Y	19890 FQ	24990 MW	30620 TQ	USBLS	5/07
	San Juan-Caguas-Guaynabo MSA, PR	Y	20160 FQ	25690 MW	31120 TQ	USBLS	5/07
Health Officer							
County Government	Livingston County, MI	Y			106382 HI	LCPP	2009
Health Physicist							
Medical Facility	United States	Y		95357 AW		HPS	2007
Nuclear Power Utility	United States	Y		102202 AW		HPS	2007
University	United States	Y		73439 AW		HPS	2007
Health Physics Supervisor							
State Government	Ohio	H	27.93 LO		36.59 HI	ODAS	2008
Health Risk Assessor							
Department of Environmental Services	New Hampshire	Y		54886 AW		NHUL03	2008
Health Services Policy Analyst							
State Government	Ohio	H	24.90 LO		34.83 HI	ODAS	2008
Health Specialties Teacher							
Postsecondary	Alabama	Y	50350 FQ	80810 MW	109780 TQ	USBLS	5/07
Postsecondary	Montgomery MSA, AL	Y	25470 FQ	27830 MW	43900 TQ	USBLS	5/07
Postsecondary	Alaska	Y	56310 FQ	69530 MW	81970 TQ	USBLS	5/07
Postsecondary	Arizona	Y	67650 FQ	109570 MW		USBLS	5/07
Postsecondary	Phoenix-Mesa-Scottsdale MSA, AZ	Y	39440 FQ	83710 MW	120760 TQ	USBLS	5/07
Postsecondary	Arkansas	Y	35260 FQ	51370 MW	68390 TQ	USBLS	5/07
Postsecondary	Little Rock-North Little Rock MSA, AR	Y	33020 FQ	60850 MW	78260 TQ	USBLS	5/07
Postsecondary	California	Y		94108 AW		CABLS	1/08-3/08
Postsecondary	Los Angeles-Long Beach-Glendale PMSA, CA	Y		101952 AW		CABLS	1/08-3/08
Postsecondary	Oakland-Fremont-Hayward MSA, CA	Y		79556 AW		CABLS	1/08-3/08
Postsecondary	Riverside-San Bernardino-Ontario MSA, CA	Y		112002 AW		CABLS	1/08-3/08
Postsecondary	Sacramento-Arden Arcade-Roseville MSA, CA	Y		105316 AW		CABLS	1/08-3/08
Postsecondary	San Diego-Carlsbad-San Marcos MSA, CA	Y		103829 AW		CABLS	1/08-3/08
Postsecondary	San Francisco-San Mateo-Redwood PMSA, CA	Y		88939 AW		CABLS	1/08-3/08
Postsecondary	San Jose-Sunnyvale-Santa Clara MSA, CA	Y		71127 AW		CABLS	1/08-3/08
Postsecondary	Santa Ana-Anaheim-Irvine PMSA, CA	Y	50090 FQ	67700 MW	95490 TQ	USBLS	5/07
Postsecondary	Colorado	Y	49950 FQ	80500 MW	132860 TQ	USBLS	5/07
Postsecondary	Delaware	Y	39990 FQ	53080 MW	71540 TQ	USBLS	5/07
Postsecondary	Wilmington PMSA, DE-MD-NJ	Y	40300 FQ	53860 MW	75730 TQ	USBLS	5/07
Postsecondary	District of Columbia	Y	56580 FQ	83760 MW	106420 TQ	USBLS	5/07
Postsecondary	Washington-Arlington-Alexandria MSA, DC-VA-MD-WV	Y	56080 FQ	80600 MW	103760 TQ	USBLS	5/07
Postsecondary	Florida	Y	42400 FQ	71370 MW	137060 TQ	USBLS	5/07
Postsecondary	Fort Lauderdale-Pompano Beach-Deerfield Beach PMSA, FL	Y	27570 FQ	37690 MW	56900 TQ	USBLS	5/07
Postsecondary	Miami-Fort Lauderdale-Miami Beach MSA, FL	Y	34610 FQ	51230 MW	72410 TQ	USBLS	5/07
Postsecondary	Orlando-Kissimmee MSA, FL	Y	36160 FQ	55450 MW	69000 TQ	USBLS	5/07
Postsecondary	Tampa-St. Petersburg-Clearwater MSA, FL	Y	50700 FQ	75860 MW	127780 TQ	USBLS	5/07
Postsecondary	West Palm Beach-Boca Raton-Boynton Beach PMSA, FL	Y	44580 FQ	49480 MW	60830 TQ	USBLS	5/07
Postsecondary	Georgia	Y	54070 FQ	81920 MW	112430 TQ	USBLS	5/07
Postsecondary	Hawaii	Y	54400 FQ	69210 MW	96630 TQ	USBLS	5/07
Postsecondary	Honolulu MSA, HI	Y	54400 FQ	69210 MW	96630 TQ	USBLS	5/07
Postsecondary	Boise City-Nampa MSA, ID	Y	43730 FQ	52900 MW	60680 TQ	USBLS	5/07
Postsecondary	Illinois	Y	49260 FQ	71520 MW	108270 TQ	USBLS	5/07

AE   Average entry wage   AW   Average wage paid   FQ   First quartile wage   LO   Lowest wage paid   MTC   Median total compensation   TCC   Total cash compensation
AER   Average entry range   AWR   Average wage range   H   Hourly   LR   Low end range   MW   Median wage paid   TQ   Third quartile wage
AEX   Average experienced wage   AXR   Average experienced range   HI   Highest wage paid   M   Monthly   MWR   Median wage range   W   Weekly
ATC   Average total compensation   D   Daily   HR   High end range   MCC   Median cash compensation   S   See annotated source   Y   Yearly

749

Occupation/Type/Industry	Location	Per	Low	Mid	High	Source	Date
Health Specialties Teacher							
Postsecondary	Indiana	Y	47730 FQ	65880 MW	75990 TQ	USBLS	5/07
Postsecondary	Indianapolis-Carmel MSA, IN	Y	62060 FQ	69260 MW	76550 TQ	USBLS	5/07
Postsecondary	Iowa	Y	60660 FQ	99760 MW		USBLS	5/07
Postsecondary	Des Moines-West Des Moines MSA, IA	Y	41890 FQ	52400 MW	66340 TQ	USBLS	5/07
Postsecondary	Kansas	Y	33530 FQ	62220 MW	96830 TQ	USBLS	5/07
Postsecondary	Wichita MSA, KS	Y	34150 FQ	54910 MW	83020 TQ	USBLS	5/07
Postsecondary	Kentucky	Y	60486 FQ	95700 MW	147686 TQ	KYBLS	2008
Postsecondary	Louisiana	Y		63114 AW		LABLS	1/08-3/08
Postsecondary	Maine	Y	38570 FQ	55370 MW	69550 TQ	USBLS	5/07
Postsecondary	Portland-South Portland-Biddeford MSA, ME	Y	39900 FQ	56230 MW	69810 TQ	USBLS	5/07
Postsecondary	Maryland	Y		116625 MW		MDBLS	3/08
Postsecondary	Baltimore-Towson MSA, MD	Y	79240 FQ	119500 MW		USBLS	5/07
Postsecondary	Bethesda-Gaithersburg-Frederick PMSA, MD	Y	62620 FQ	74830 MW	88110 TQ	USBLS	5/07
Postsecondary	Massachusetts	Y	62930 FQ	98960 MW		USBLS	5/07
Postsecondary	Boston-Cambridge-Quincy NECTA, MA	Y	63780 FQ	103970 MW		USBLS	5/07
Postsecondary	Worcester MSA, MA-CT	Y	71300 FQ	89040 MW	111570 TQ	USBLS	5/07
Postsecondary	Michigan	Y	50690 FQ	72710 MW	103340 TQ	USBLS	5/07
Postsecondary	Detroit-Warren-Livonia MSA, MI	Y	49110 FQ	79170 MW	114400 TQ	USBLS	5/07
Postsecondary	Warren-Troy-Farmington Hills PMSA, MI	Y	30600 FQ	51300 MW	65750 TQ	USBLS	5/07
Postsecondary	Minnesota	Y	51767 FQ	71980 MW	121477 TQ	MNBLS	10/08-12/08
Postsecondary	Duluth-Superior MSA, MN-WI	Y	32788 FQ	49570 MW	59467 TQ	MNBLS	10/08-12/08
Postsecondary	Minneapolis-Saint Paul MSA, MN-WI	Y	51034 FQ	70431 MW	119217 TQ	MNBLS	10/08-12/08
Postsecondary	Missouri	Y	56380 FQ	85670 MW	132110 TQ	USBLS	5/07
Postsecondary	Kansas City MSA, MO-KS	Y	53690 FQ	78520 MW	137460 TQ	USBLS	5/07
Postsecondary	St. Louis MSA, MO-IL	Y	57590 FQ	87710 MW	130410 TQ	USBLS	5/07
Postsecondary	Montana	Y	40200 FQ	50660 MW	71810 TQ	USBLS	5/07
Postsecondary	Las Vegas-Paradise MSA, NV	Y	55433 FQ	85843 MW	118721 TQ	NVBLS	5/08
Postsecondary	New Jersey	Y	46970 FQ	64030 MW	86460 TQ	USBLS	5/07
Postsecondary	Camden PMSA, NJ	Y	36120 FQ	52720 MW	80300 TQ	USBLS	5/07
Postsecondary	Edison PMSA, NJ	Y	57040 FQ	75730 MW	93590 TQ	USBLS	5/07
Postsecondary	Newark-Union PMSA, NJ-PA	Y	48830 FQ	61860 MW	80920 TQ	USBLS	5/07
Postsecondary	New Mexico	Y	44380 FQ	54250 MW	80980 TQ	USBLS	5/07
Postsecondary	Albuquerque MSA, NM	Y	43380 FQ	55790 MW	84430 TQ	USBLS	5/07
Postsecondary	New York	Y	69920 FQ	114450 MW		USBLS	5/07
Postsecondary	Albany-Schenectady-Troy MSA, NY	Y	63760 FQ	107410 MW		USBLS	5/07
Postsecondary	Buffalo-Niagara Falls MSA, NY	Y	46170 FQ	60630 MW	94500 TQ	USBLS	5/07
Postsecondary	Nassau-Suffolk PMSA, NY	Y	49530 FQ	63400 MW	83840 TQ	USBLS	5/07
Postsecondary	New York-Northern New Jersey-Long Island MSA, NY-NJ-PA	Y	70060 FQ	110920 MW		USBLS	5/07
Postsecondary	North Carolina	Y	47930 FQ	81150 MW	128060 TQ	USBLS	5/07
Postsecondary	Charlotte-Gastonia-Concord MSA, NC-SC	Y	40570 FQ	55420 MW	71050 TQ	USBLS	5/07
Postsecondary	Greensboro-High Point MSA, NC	Y	49670 FQ	58480 MW	75880 TQ	USBLS	5/07
Postsecondary	Raleigh-Cary MSA, NC	Y	47340 FQ	60770 MW	89400 TQ	USBLS	5/07
Postsecondary	North Dakota	Y	39240 FQ	50830 MW	72240 TQ	USBLS	5/07
Postsecondary	Ohio	Y	51310 FQ	76890 MW	114060 TQ	USBLS	5/07
Postsecondary	Cincinnati-Middletown MSA, OH-KY-IN	Y	58400 FQ	89190 MW	140030 TQ	USBLS	5/07
Postsecondary	Cleveland-Elyria-Mentor MSA, OH	Y	42060 FQ	69980 MW	111350 TQ	USBLS	5/07
Postsecondary	Columbus MSA, OH	Y	49770 FQ	76700 MW	106900 TQ	USBLS	5/07
Postsecondary	Dayton MSA, OH	Y	51080 FQ	73700 MW	109580 TQ	USBLS	5/07
Postsecondary	Oklahoma	Y	62080 FQ	79240 MW	107420 TQ	USBLS	5/07
Postsecondary	Oklahoma City MSA, OK	Y	65630 FQ	83160 MW	112670 TQ	USBLS	5/07
Postsecondary	Tulsa MSA, OK	Y	31670 FQ	37160 MW	56720 TQ	USBLS	5/07
Postsecondary	Pennsylvania	Y	51930 FQ	65700 MW	93010 TQ	USBLS	5/07
Postsecondary	Erie MSA, PA	Y	56640 FQ	67560 MW	81300 TQ	USBLS	5/07
Postsecondary	Philadelphia-Camden-Wilmington MSA, PA-NJ-DE-MD	Y	47730 FQ	62300 MW	88840 TQ	USBLS	5/07

AE	Average entry wage	AW	Average wage paid	FQ	First quartile wage	LO	Lowest wage paid	MTC	Median total compensation	TCC	Total cash compensation
AER	Average entry range	AWR	Average wage range	H	Hourly	LR	Low end range	MW	Median wage paid	TQ	Third quartile wage
AEX	Average experienced wage	AXR	Average experienced range	HI	Highest wage paid	M	Monthly	MWR	Median wage range	W	Weekly
ATC	Average total compensation	D	Daily	HR	High end range	MCC	Median cash compensation	S	See annotated source	Y	Yearly

Occupation/Type/Industry	Location	Per	Low	Mid	High	Source	Date
Health Specialties Teacher							
Postsecondary	Pittsburgh MSA, PA	Y	56870 FQ	72330 MW	95430 TQ	USBLS	5/07
Postsecondary	Rhode Island	Y	61750 FQ	81440 MW	100080 TQ	USBLS	5/07
Postsecondary	Providence-Fall River-Warwick MSA, RI-MA	Y	61100 FQ	81940 MW	103600 TQ	USBLS	5/07
Postsecondary	South Carolina	Y	50710 FQ	60770 MW	83650 TQ	USBLS	5/07
Postsecondary	South Dakota	Y	47538 FQ	61825 MW	80251 TQ	SDBLS	7/08-9/08
Postsecondary	Rapid City MSA, SD	Y	46386 FQ	50559 MW	56400 TQ	SDBLS	7/08-9/08
Postsecondary	Sioux Falls MSA, SD	Y	42581 FQ	53609 MW	71808 TQ	SDBLS	7/08-9/08
Postsecondary	Tennessee	Y	43120 FQ	61770 MW	100370 TQ	USBLS	5/07
Postsecondary	Memphis MSA, TN-MS-AR	Y	42040 FQ	74040 MW	110790 TQ	USBLS	5/07
Postsecondary	Nashville-Davidson-Murfreesboro MSA, TN	Y	47630 FQ	66030 MW	113020 TQ	USBLS	5/07
Postsecondary	Texas	Y	56020 FQ	91400 MW		USBLS	5/07
Postsecondary	Austin-Round Rock MSA, TX	Y	34370 FQ	47430 MW	67470 TQ	USBLS	5/07
Postsecondary	Dallas-Fort Worth-Arlington MSA, TX	Y	57140 FQ	102710 MW		USBLS	5/07
Postsecondary	El Paso MSA, TX	Y	44480 FQ	59950 MW	76570 TQ	USBLS	5/07
Postsecondary	Houston-Sugar Land-Baytown MSA, TX	Y	66970 FQ	102730 MW		USBLS	5/07
Postsecondary	San Antonio MSA, TX	Y	30780 FQ	43810 MW	56250 TQ	USBLS	5/07
Postsecondary	Utah	Y	63850 FQ	112110 MW		USBLS	5/07
Postsecondary	Vermont	Y	54900 FQ	67290 MW	85250 TQ	USBLS	5/07
Postsecondary	Virginia	Y	52340 FQ	82470 MW	111850 TQ	USBLS	5/07
Postsecondary	Richmond MSA, VA	Y	59930 FQ	86560 MW	112310 TQ	USBLS	5/07
Postsecondary	Virginia Beach-Norfolk-Newport News MSA, VA-NC	Y	56770 FQ	83280 MW	109350 TQ	USBLS	5/07
Postsecondary	West Virginia	Y	38093 FQ	52243 MW	78225 TQ	WVBLS	7/08-9/08
Postsecondary	Charleston MSA, WV	Y	27860 FQ	41300 MW	56080 TQ	USBLS	5/07
Postsecondary	Wisconsin	Y	46670 FQ	62230 MW	86890 TQ	USBLS	5/07
Postsecondary	Milwaukee-Waukesha-West Allis MSA, WI	Y	46130 FQ	59240 MW	72450 TQ	USBLS	5/07
Postsecondary	Wyoming	Y	51008 FQ	66415 MW	93153 TQ	WYBLS	9/08
Postsecondary	Puerto Rico	Y	46660 FQ	59580 MW	75410 TQ	USBLS	5/07
Postsecondary	San Juan-Caguas-Guaynabo MSA, PR	Y	43840 FQ	62420 MW	77420 TQ	USBLS	5/07
Hearing Officer							
Parole Board	Ohio	H	23.87 LO		35.02 HI	ODAS	2008
Hearings Bailiff							
State Government	Ohio	H	14.36 LO		15.41 HI	ODAS	2008
Hearings Examiner							
Department of Safety	New Hampshire	Y		64911 AW		NHUL03	2008
Hearse Driver	Rhode Island	H		10.00-15.00 AWR		RIM01	2009
Heart Surgeon	Maryland	Y		200000 AW		WTGMD	2009
Heat Treating Equipment Setter, Operator, and Tender							
Metals and Plastics	Alabama	Y	25960 FQ	31210 MW	44560 TQ	USBLS	5/07
Metals and Plastics	Birmingham-Hoover MSA, AL	Y	22760 FQ	29160 MW	38760 TQ	USBLS	5/07
Metals and Plastics	Huntsville MSA, AL	Y	23170 FQ	27130 MW	35070 TQ	USBLS	5/07
Metals and Plastics	Arizona	Y	22410 FQ	27370 MW	31670 TQ	USBLS	5/07
Metals and Plastics	Phoenix-Mesa-Scottsdale MSA, AZ	Y	29850 FQ	32830 MW	36560 TQ	USBLS	5/07
Metals and Plastics	Arkansas	Y	26130 FQ	29450 MW	35720 TQ	USBLS	5/07
Metals and Plastics	Fayetteville-Springdale-Rogers MSA, AR-MO	Y	25820 FQ	28840 MW	32170 TQ	USBLS	5/07
Metals and Plastics	California	H	11.63 FQ	14.94 MW	19.11 TQ	CABLS	1/08-3/08
Metals and Plastics	Los Angeles-Long Beach-Glendale PMSA, CA	H	11.80 FQ	14.95 MW	18.94 TQ	CABLS	1/08-3/08
Metals and Plastics	Oakland-Fremont-Hayward MSA, CA	H	14.76 FQ	17.35 MW	20.23 TQ	CABLS	1/08-3/08
Metals and Plastics	Oxnard-Thousand Oaks-Ventura MSA, CA	H	10.96 FQ	14.13 MW	17.65 TQ	CABLS	1/08-3/08
Metals and Plastics	Riverside-San Bernardino-Ontario MSA, CA	H	13.43 FQ	17.38 MW	25.43 TQ	CABLS	1/08-3/08

AE	Average entry wage	AW	Average wage paid	FQ	First quartile wage	LO	Lowest wage paid	MTC Median total compensation TCC Total cash compensation
AER	Average entry range	AWR	Average wage range	H	Hourly	LR	Low end range	MW Median wage paid TQ Third quartile wage
AEX	Average experienced wage	AXR	Average experienced range	HI	Highest wage paid	M	Monthly	MWR Median wage range W Weekly
ATC	Average total compensation	D	Daily	HR	High end range	MCC	Median cash compensation	S See annotated source Y Yearly

Occupation/Type/Industry	Location	Per	Low	Mid	High	Source	Date
Heat Treating Equipment Setter, Operator, and Tender							
Metals and Plastics	San Diego-Carlsbad-San Marcos MSA, CA	H	13.94 FQ	16.08 MW	18.26 TQ	CABLS	1/08-3/08
Metals and Plastics	San Jose-Sunnyvale-Santa Clara MSA, CA	H	12.00 FQ	13.75 MW	18.00 TQ	CABLS	1/08-3/08
Metals and Plastics	Santa Ana-Anaheim-Irvine PMSA, CA	Y	19780 FQ	26250 MW	35490 TQ	USBLS	5/07
Metals and Plastics	Colorado	Y	25000 FQ	31880 MW	43280 TQ	USBLS	5/07
Metals and Plastics	Denver-Aurora MSA, CO	Y	21680 FQ	28800 MW	44100 TQ	USBLS	5/07
Metals and Plastics	Connecticut	H	12.87 AE	17.13 MW		CTBLS	1/08-3/08
Metals and Plastics	Bridgeport-Stamford-Norwalk MSA, CT	Y	31960 FQ	35380 MW	38330 TQ	USBLS	5/07
Metals and Plastics	Hartford-West Hartford-East Hartford MSA, CT	Y	27140 FQ	33770 MW	39840 TQ	USBLS	5/07
Metals and Plastics	Washington-Arlington-Alexandria MSA, DC-VA-MD-WV	Y	28750 FQ	32890 MW	36720 TQ	USBLS	5/07
Metals and Plastics	Florida	Y	21830 FQ	27240 MW	31810 TQ	USBLS	5/07
Metals and Plastics	Miami-Fort Lauderdale-Miami Beach MSA, FL	Y	15020 FQ	17130 MW	26020 TQ	USBLS	5/07
Metals and Plastics	Tampa-St. Petersburg-Clearwater MSA, FL	Y	22080 FQ	25550 MW	31240 TQ	USBLS	5/07
Metals and Plastics	Georgia	Y	26990 FQ	31230 MW	39120 TQ	USBLS	5/07
Metals and Plastics	Atlanta-Sandy Springs-Marietta MSA, GA	Y	28990 FQ	35210 MW	44220 TQ	USBLS	5/07
Metals and Plastics	Illinois	Y	24360 FQ	31290 MW	36390 TQ	USBLS	5/07
Metals and Plastics	Chicago-Naperville-Joliet MSA, IL-IN-WI	Y	25310 FQ	33230 MW	39030 TQ	USBLS	5/07
Metals and Plastics	Indiana	Y	26800 FQ	34540 MW	43720 TQ	USBLS	5/07
Metals and Plastics	Elkhart-Goshen MSA, IN	Y	21360 FQ	25140 MW	30130 TQ	USBLS	5/07
Metals and Plastics	Gary PMSA, IN	Y	35460 FQ	42910 MW	52490 TQ	USBLS	5/07
Metals and Plastics	Indianapolis-Carmel MSA, IN	Y	31150 FQ	37980 MW	51590 TQ	USBLS	5/07
Metals and Plastics	South Bend-Mishawaka MSA, IN-MI	Y	25310 FQ	32380 MW	36400 TQ	USBLS	5/07
Metals and Plastics	Iowa	Y	30130 FQ	36490 MW	43570 TQ	USBLS	5/07
Metals and Plastics	Kansas	Y	33660 FQ	42890 MW	48250 TQ	USBLS	5/07
Metals and Plastics	Wichita MSA, KS	Y	37540 FQ	44580 MW	49120 TQ	USBLS	5/07
Metals and Plastics	Kentucky	Y	28053 FQ	34185 MW	40078 TQ	KYBLS	2008
Metals and Plastics	Louisville-Jefferson County MSA, KY-IN	Y	26160 FQ	31480 MW	37220 TQ	USBLS	5/07
Metals and Plastics	Louisiana	H	11.42 FQ	13.63 MW	17.35 TQ	LABLS	1/08-3/08
Metals and Plastics	Maine	Y	27760 FQ	32470 MW	40960 TQ	USBLS	5/07
Metals and Plastics	Maryland	Y		42725 MW		MDBLS	3/08
Metals and Plastics	Massachusetts	Y	25000 FQ	31800 MW	37680 TQ	USBLS	5/07
Metals and Plastics	Boston-Cambridge-Quincy NECTA, MA	Y	25360 FQ	29830 MW	35670 TQ	USBLS	5/07
Metals and Plastics	Worcester MSA, MA-CT	Y	23420 FQ	29500 MW	36220 TQ	USBLS	5/07
Metals and Plastics	Michigan	Y	24520 FQ	31420 MW	37870 TQ	USBLS	5/07
Metals and Plastics	Detroit-Warren-Livonia MSA, MI	Y	24350 FQ	33170 MW	40140 TQ	USBLS	5/07
Metals and Plastics	Grand Rapids-Wyoming MSA, MI	Y	23020 FQ	27920 MW	32990 TQ	USBLS	5/07
Metals and Plastics	Warren-Troy-Farmington Hills PMSA, MI	Y	24510 FQ	33440 MW	39200 TQ	USBLS	5/07
Metals and Plastics	Minnesota	Y	28964 FQ	33505 MW	39134 TQ	MNBLS	10/08-12/08
Metals and Plastics	Minneapolis-Saint Paul MSA, MN-WI	Y	29597 FQ	35381 MW	41332 TQ	MNBLS	10/08-12/08
Metals and Plastics	Mississippi	Y	25830 FQ	29050 MW	31970 TQ	USBLS	5/07
Metals and Plastics	Missouri	Y	24280 FQ	27750 MW	33890 TQ	USBLS	5/07
Metals and Plastics	Kansas City MSA, MO-KS	Y	20300 FQ	24600 MW	30450 TQ	USBLS	5/07
Metals and Plastics	St. Louis MSA, MO-IL	Y	23910 FQ	30310 MW	36140 TQ	USBLS	5/07
Metals and Plastics	Nebraska	Y	23840 FQ	29780 MW	34210 TQ	USBLS	5/07
Metals and Plastics	Omaha-Council Bluffs MSA, NE-IA	Y	25690 FQ	27860 MW	30100 TQ	USBLS	5/07
Metals and Plastics	Nevada	H	11.80 FQ	14.10 MW	16.24 TQ	NVBLS	5/08
Metals and Plastics	New Hampshire	H	12.74 AE	17.83 MW	19.91 AEX	NHBLS	6/08
Metals and Plastics	New Jersey	Y	24590 FQ	29510 MW	37840 TQ	USBLS	5/07
Metals and Plastics	Camden PMSA, NJ	Y	26260 FQ	29860 MW	39960 TQ	USBLS	5/07
Metals and Plastics	Edison PMSA, NJ	Y	15420 FQ	25890 MW	35430 TQ	USBLS	5/07
Metals and Plastics	Newark-Union PMSA, NJ-PA	Y	28570 FQ	32390 MW	40730 TQ	USBLS	5/07
Metals and Plastics	New York	Y	26230 FQ	31410 MW	37120 TQ	USBLS	5/07

AE	Average entry wage	AW	Average wage paid	FQ	First quartile wage
AER	Average entry range	AWR	Average wage range	H	Hourly
AEX	Average experienced wage	AXR	Average experienced range	HI	Highest wage paid
ATC	Average total compensation	D	Daily	HR	High end range

LO Lowest wage paid
LR Low end range
M Monthly
MCC Median cash compensation

MTC Median total compensation
MW Median wage paid
MWR Median wage range
S See annotated source

TCC Total cash compensation
TQ Third quartile wage
W Weekly
Y Yearly

Occupation/Type/Industry	Location	Per	Low	Mid	High	Source	Date
Heat Treating Equipment Setter, Operator, and Tender							
Metals and Plastics	Binghamton MSA, NY	Y	21410 FQ	26060 MW	29720 TQ	USBLS	5/07
Metals and Plastics	Buffalo-Niagara Falls MSA, NY	Y	31130 FQ	34510 MW	37470 TQ	USBLS	5/07
Metals and Plastics	Nassau-Suffolk PMSA, NY	Y	25870 FQ	29990 MW	34760 TQ	USBLS	5/07
Metals and Plastics	New York-Northern New Jersey-Long Island MSA, NY-NJ-PA	Y	23880 FQ	29970 MW	36560 TQ	USBLS	5/07
Metals and Plastics	North Carolina	Y	26170 FQ	33050 MW	37630 TQ	USBLS	5/07
Metals and Plastics	Charlotte-Gastonia-Concord MSA, NC-SC	Y	22670 FQ	29410 MW	36840 TQ	USBLS	5/07
Metals and Plastics	Ohio	Y	23920 FQ	29530 MW	36260 TQ	USBLS	5/07
Metals and Plastics	Cincinnati-Middletown MSA, OH-KY-IN	Y	23390 FQ	31460 MW	40830 TQ	USBLS	5/07
Metals and Plastics	Cleveland-Elyria-Mentor MSA, OH	Y	21770 FQ	26660 MW	33330 TQ	USBLS	5/07
Metals and Plastics	Columbus MSA, OH	Y	27480 FQ	31820 MW	36410 TQ	USBLS	5/07
Metals and Plastics	Dayton MSA, OH	Y	28840 FQ	35090 MW	53230 TQ	USBLS	5/07
Metals and Plastics	Springfield MSA, OH	Y	24390 FQ	28260 MW	33750 TQ	USBLS	5/07
Metals and Plastics	Oklahoma	Y	26890 FQ	30840 MW	35790 TQ	USBLS	5/07
Metals and Plastics	Oklahoma City MSA, OK	Y	38110 FQ	43480 MW	48700 TQ	USBLS	5/07
Metals and Plastics	Tulsa MSA, OK	Y	26540 FQ	29390 MW	31730 TQ	USBLS	5/07
Metals and Plastics	Oregon	H	12.83 FQ	15.85 MW	19.00 TQ	ORBLS	5/08
Metals and Plastics	Portland-Vancouver-Beaverton MSA, OR-WA	Y	25480 FQ	32000 MW	37570 TQ	USBLS	5/07
Metals and Plastics	Pennsylvania	Y	29100 FQ	34720 MW	40530 TQ	USBLS	5/07
Metals and Plastics	Allentown-Bethlehem-Easton MSA, PA-NJ	Y	26110 FQ	30940 MW	45810 TQ	USBLS	5/07
Metals and Plastics	Philadelphia-Camden-Wilmington MSA, PA-NJ-DE-MD	Y	27440 FQ	33430 MW	42180 TQ	USBLS	5/07
Metals and Plastics	Pittsburgh MSA, PA	Y	29680 FQ	34380 MW	39140 TQ	USBLS	5/07
Metals and Plastics	Rhode Island	Y	22360 FQ	28710 MW	34470 TQ	USBLS	5/07
Metals and Plastics	Providence-Fall River-Warwick MSA, RI-MA	Y	22060 FQ	27830 MW	33560 TQ	USBLS	5/07
Metals and Plastics	South Carolina	Y	24550 FQ	32260 MW	37680 TQ	USBLS	5/07
Metals and Plastics	Charleston-North Charleston MSA, SC	Y	37850 FQ	41050 MW	44370 TQ	USBLS	5/07
Metals and Plastics	Columbia MSA, SC	Y	25310 FQ	27720 MW	30120 TQ	USBLS	5/07
Metals and Plastics	South Dakota	Y	21764 FQ	24008 MW	27770 TQ	SDBLS	7/08-9/08
Metals and Plastics	Tennessee	Y	27590 FQ	31200 MW	35380 TQ	USBLS	5/07
Metals and Plastics	Nashville-Davidson-Murfreesboro MSA, TN	Y	28910 FQ	32430 MW	36830 TQ	USBLS	5/07
Metals and Plastics	Texas	Y	21600 FQ	24470 MW	30080 TQ	USBLS	5/07
Metals and Plastics	Austin-Round Rock MSA, TX	Y	23030 FQ	28290 MW	34250 TQ	USBLS	5/07
Metals and Plastics	Dallas-Fort Worth-Arlington MSA, TX	Y	21360 FQ	23200 MW	25200 TQ	USBLS	5/07
Metals and Plastics	Houston-Sugar Land-Baytown MSA, TX	Y	21440 FQ	24380 MW	29800 TQ	USBLS	5/07
Metals and Plastics	Utah	Y	26310 FQ	32470 MW	39110 TQ	USBLS	5/07
Metals and Plastics	Salt Lake City MSA, UT	Y	24040 FQ	29700 MW	37000 TQ	USBLS	5/07
Metals and Plastics	Virginia	Y	26540 FQ	30790 MW	36400 TQ	USBLS	5/07
Metals and Plastics	Richmond MSA, VA	Y	31220 FQ	36050 MW	40640 TQ	USBLS	5/07
Metals and Plastics	Virginia Beach-Norfolk-Newport News MSA, VA-NC	Y	28450 FQ	33510 MW	37930 TQ	USBLS	5/07
Metals and Plastics	Washington	H	13.51 FQ	16.58 MW	18.93 TQ	WABLS	3/08
Metals and Plastics	Seattle-Tacoma-Bellevue MSA, WA	Y	28370 FQ	35330 MW	43110 TQ	USBLS	5/07
Metals and Plastics	Spokane MSA, WA	Y	29480 FQ	34980 MW	38260 TQ	USBLS	5/07
Metals and Plastics	West Virginia	Y	23506 FQ	31253 MW	36778 TQ	WVBLS	7/08-9/08
Metals and Plastics	Huntington-Ashland MSA, WV-KY-OH	Y	30680 FQ	33740 MW	36780 TQ	USBLS	5/07
Metals and Plastics	Wisconsin	Y	26260 FQ	32050 MW	37560 TQ	USBLS	5/07
Metals and Plastics	Milwaukee-Waukesha-West Allis MSA, WI	Y	27630 FQ	34140 MW	39110 TQ	USBLS	5/07
Metals and Plastics	Puerto Rico	Y	17720 FQ	20820 MW	25300 TQ	USBLS	5/07
Heating, Air Conditioning, and Refrigeration Mechanic and Installer	Alabama	Y	25710 FQ	30920 MW	38180 TQ	USBLS	5/07

AE	Average entry wage	AW	Average wage paid	FQ	First quartile wage
AER	Average entry range	AWR	Average wage range	H	Hourly
AEX	Average experienced wage	AXR	Average experienced range	HI	Highest wage paid
ATC	Average total compensation	D	Daily	HR	High end range

LO	Lowest wage paid	MTC	Median total compensation	TCC	Total cash compensation
LR	Low end range	MW	Median wage paid	TQ	Third quartile wage
M	Monthly	MWR	Median wage range	W	Weekly
MCC	Median cash compensation	S	See annotated source	Y	Yearly

Occupation/Type/Industry	Location	Per	Low	Mid	High	Source	Date
Heating, Air Conditioning, and Refrigeration Mechanic and Installer							
	Birmingham-Hoover MSA, AL	Y	25970 FQ	32530 MW	40180 TQ	USBLS	5/07
	Alaska	Y	45940 FQ	54620 MW	61340 TQ	USBLS	5/07
	Anchorage MSA, AK	Y	47820 FQ	55540 MW	61280 TQ	USBLS	5/07
	Arizona	Y	26140 FQ	34250 MW	43120 TQ	USBLS	5/07
	Phoenix-Mesa-Scottsdale MSA, AZ	Y	25440 FQ	33510 MW	43150 TQ	USBLS	5/07
	Tucson MSA, AZ	Y	33170 FQ	39490 MW	45360 TQ	USBLS	5/07
	Arkansas	Y	25900 FQ	32180 MW	39870 TQ	USBLS	5/07
	Fort Smith MSA, AR-OK	Y	25830 FQ	32880 MW	37950 TQ	USBLS	5/07
	Little Rock-North Little Rock MSA, AR	Y	29530 FQ	37930 MW	46950 TQ	USBLS	5/07
	California	H	16.74 FQ	22.38 MW	28.20 TQ	CABLS	1/08-3/08
	Bakersfield MSA, CA	H	13.18 FQ	16.49 MW	22.45 TQ	CABLS	1/08-3/08
	Los Angeles-Long Beach-Glendale PMSA, CA	H	15.00 FQ	22.09 MW	28.65 TQ	CABLS	1/08-3/08
	Oakland-Fremont-Hayward MSA, CA	H	21.34 FQ	26.61 MW	31.50 TQ	CABLS	1/08-3/08
	Riverside-San Bernardino-Ontario MSA, CA	H	14.83 FQ	20.17 MW	25.40 TQ	CABLS	1/08-3/08
	Sacramento-Arden Arcade-Roseville MSA, CA	H	17.40 FQ	21.27 MW	27.88 TQ	CABLS	1/08-3/08
	San Diego-Carlsbad-San Marcos MSA, CA	H	19.47 FQ	24.49 MW	28.30 TQ	CABLS	1/08-3/08
	San Francisco-San Mateo-Redwood PMSA, CA	H	23.78 FQ	27.11 MW	30.41 TQ	CABLS	1/08-3/08
	San Jose-Sunnyvale-Santa Clara MSA, CA	H	23.15 FQ	31.35 MW	37.13 TQ	CABLS	1/08-3/08
	Santa Ana-Anaheim-Irvine PMSA, CA	Y	41660 FQ	52530 MW	61680 TQ	USBLS	5/07
	Colorado	Y	32430 FQ	41360 MW	55630 TQ	USBLS	5/07
	Denver-Aurora MSA, CO	Y	35350 FQ	50310 MW	59000 TQ	USBLS	5/07
	Fort Collins-Loveland MSA, CO	Y	32280 FQ	36820 MW	47000 TQ	USBLS	5/07
	Pueblo MSA, CO	Y	27010 FQ	30300 MW	34900 TQ	USBLS	5/07
	Connecticut	H	16.47 AE	24.24 MW		CTBLS	1/08-3/08
	Bridgeport-Stamford-Norwalk MSA, CT	Y	45260 FQ	53800 MW	60740 TQ	USBLS	5/07
	Hartford-West Hartford-East Hartford MSA, CT	Y	39070 FQ	49170 MW	56880 TQ	USBLS	5/07
	Delaware	Y	31740 FQ	39180 MW	48000 TQ	USBLS	5/07
	Wilmington PMSA, DE-MD-NJ	Y	33310 FQ	42000 MW	50360 TQ	USBLS	5/07
	District of Columbia	Y	43500 FQ	52550 MW	59300 TQ	USBLS	5/07
	Washington-Arlington-Alexandria MSA, DC-VA-MD-WV	Y	35640 FQ	46160 MW	58810 TQ	USBLS	5/07
	Florida	Y	28650 FQ	35300 MW	43460 TQ	USBLS	5/07
	Fort Lauderdale-Pompano Beach-Deerfield Beach PMSA, FL	Y	28480 FQ	35280 MW	46660 TQ	USBLS	5/07
	Jacksonville MSA, FL	Y	31900 FQ	36700 MW	43440 TQ	USBLS	5/07
	Miami-Fort Lauderdale-Miami Beach MSA, FL	Y	29850 FQ	38210 MW	48490 TQ	USBLS	5/07
	Orlando-Kissimmee MSA, FL	Y	28280 FQ	35360 MW	41700 TQ	USBLS	5/07
	Sarasota-Bradenton-Venice MSA, FL	Y	28480 FQ	33930 MW	40780 TQ	USBLS	5/07
	Tampa-St. Petersburg-Clearwater MSA, FL	Y	30030 FQ	36110 MW	42660 TQ	USBLS	5/07
	West Palm Beach-Boca Raton-Boynton Beach PMSA, FL	Y	29260 FQ	35890 MW	43930 TQ	USBLS	5/07
	Georgia	Y	25370 FQ	33330 MW	44090 TQ	USBLS	5/07
	Atlanta-Sandy Springs-Marietta MSA, GA	Y	25500 FQ	36980 MW	47980 TQ	USBLS	5/07
	Hawaii	Y	31810 FQ	45250 MW	56310 TQ	USBLS	5/07
	Honolulu MSA, HI	Y	30550 FQ	44710 MW	57550 TQ	USBLS	5/07
	Idaho	Y	27900 FQ	35010 MW	42890 TQ	USBLS	5/07
	Boise City-Nampa MSA, ID	Y	27950 FQ	35230 MW	43480 TQ	USBLS	5/07
	Illinois	Y	33540 FQ	45310 MW	63690 TQ	USBLS	5/07

AE	Average entry wage	AW	Average wage paid	FQ	First quartile wage
AER	Average entry range	AWR	Average wage range	HI	Highest wage paid
AEX	Average experienced wage	AXR	Average experienced range	HR	High end range
ATC	Average total compensation	D	Daily		

LO	Lowest wage paid	MTC	Median total compensation
LR	Low end range	MW	Median wage paid
M	Monthly	MWR	Median wage range
MCC	Median cash compensation	S	See annotated source

TCC	Total cash compensation
TQ	Third quartile wage
W	Weekly
Y	Yearly

Occupation/Type/Industry	Location	Per	Low	Mid	High	Source	Date
Heating, Air Conditioning, and Refrigeration Mechanic and Installer							
	Chicago-Naperville-Joliet MSA, IL-IN-WI	Y	37210 FQ	48200 MW	67810 TQ	USBLS	5/07
	Peoria MSA, IL	Y	38920 FQ	45240 MW	60930 TQ	USBLS	5/07
	Indiana	Y	30570 FQ	37950 MW	48310 TQ	USBLS	5/07
	Gary PMSA, IN	Y	31550 FQ	42410 MW	51740 TQ	USBLS	5/07
	Indianapolis-Carmel MSA, IN	Y	33330 FQ	41580 MW	53980 TQ	USBLS	5/07
	Iowa	Y	24360 FQ	31900 MW	41100 TQ	USBLS	5/07
	Davenport-Moline-Rock Island MSA, IA-IL	Y	30430 FQ	39290 MW	47200 TQ	USBLS	5/07
	Des Moines-West Des Moines MSA, IA	Y	29360 FQ	37700 MW	48370 TQ	USBLS	5/07
	Kansas	Y	29560 FQ	37360 MW	49650 TQ	USBLS	5/07
	Wichita MSA, KS	Y	31710 FQ	40380 MW	47780 TQ	USBLS	5/07
	Kentucky	Y	26111 FQ	33287 MW	41250 TQ	KYBLS	2008
	Louisville-Jefferson County MSA, KY-IN	Y	27000 FQ	32920 MW	42560 TQ	USBLS	5/07
	Louisiana	H	11.96 FQ	14.57 MW	17.96 TQ	LABLS	1/08-3/08
	Baton Rouge MSA, LA	Y	25270 FQ	28730 MW	33740 TQ	USBLS	5/07
	New Orleans-Metairie-Kenner MSA, LA	Y	28080 FQ	34690 MW	39880 TQ	USBLS	5/07
	Maine	Y	31720 FQ	36950 MW	43200 TQ	USBLS	5/07
	Portland-South Portland-Biddeford MSA, ME	Y	36050 FQ	41260 MW	46850 TQ	USBLS	5/07
	Maryland	Y		45775 MW		MDBLS	3/08
	Baltimore-Towson MSA, MD	Y	33890 FQ	44180 MW	54360 TQ	USBLS	5/07
	Bethesda-Gaithersburg-Frederick PMSA, MD	Y	33810 FQ	48460 MW	61850 TQ	USBLS	5/07
	Massachusetts	Y	39950 FQ	49630 MW	60350 TQ	USBLS	5/07
	Boston-Cambridge-Quincy NECTA, MA	Y	42010 FQ	52290 MW	62180 TQ	USBLS	5/07
	Springfield MSA, MA-CT	Y	41200 FQ	50200 MW	57300 TQ	USBLS	5/07
	Worcester MSA, MA-CT	Y	36980 FQ	42100 MW	51360 TQ	USBLS	5/07
	Michigan	Y	34510 FQ	44240 MW	57170 TQ	USBLS	5/07
	Detroit-Warren-Livonia MSA, MI	Y	37900 FQ	46910 MW	60150 TQ	USBLS	5/07
	Grand Rapids-Wyoming MSA, MI	Y	30130 FQ	43370 MW	53350 TQ	USBLS	5/07
	Warren-Troy-Farmington Hills PMSA, MI	Y	33540 FQ	45460 MW	58220 TQ	USBLS	5/07
	Minnesota	Y	42125 FQ	50894 MW	61489 TQ	MNBLS	10/08-12/08
	Duluth-Superior MSA, MN-WI	Y	38171 FQ	48870 MW	57115 TQ	MNBLS	10/08-12/08
	Minneapolis-Saint Paul MSA, MN-WI	Y	44706 FQ	53559 MW	64478 TQ	MNBLS	10/08-12/08
	Rochester MSA, MN	Y	37130 FQ	44999 MW	54690 TQ	MNBLS	10/08-12/08
	Mississippi	Y	24730 FQ	29900 MW	36720 TQ	USBLS	5/07
	Jackson MSA, MS	Y	26800 FQ	33220 MW	43700 TQ	USBLS	5/07
	Missouri	Y	29850 FQ	38300 MW	50300 TQ	USBLS	5/07
	Joplin MSA, MO	Y	18210 FQ	22270 MW	35800 TQ	USBLS	5/07
	Kansas City MSA, MO-KS	Y	34840 FQ	43850 MW	57250 TQ	USBLS	5/07
	St. Louis MSA, MO-IL	Y	33650 FQ	41680 MW	53140 TQ	USBLS	5/07
	Montana	Y	28130 FQ	33820 MW	44600 TQ	USBLS	5/07
	Billings MSA, MT	Y	29860 FQ	33370 MW	36880 TQ	USBLS	5/07
	Nebraska	Y	28380 FQ	37240 MW	48120 TQ	USBLS	5/07
	Omaha-Council Bluffs MSA, NE-IA	Y	32100 FQ	41040 MW	54600 TQ	USBLS	5/07
	Nevada	H	16.97 FQ	21.25 MW	26.76 TQ	NVBLS	5/08
	Las Vegas-Paradise MSA, NV	H	17.01 FQ	21.06 MW	26.11 TQ	NVBLS	5/08
	New Hampshire	H	16.27 AE	19.52 MW	22.30 AEX	NHBLS	6/08
	Manchester MSA, NH	Y	39130 FQ	46570 MW	53650 TQ	USBLS	5/07
	Nashua NECTA, NH-MA	Y	36180 FQ	42430 MW	48880 TQ	USBLS	5/07
	New Jersey	Y	37130 FQ	47450 MW	60210 TQ	USBLS	5/07
	Atlantic City MSA, NJ	Y	38910 FQ	52960 MW	62740 TQ	USBLS	5/07
	Camden PMSA, NJ	Y	34360 FQ	42190 MW	56030 TQ	USBLS	5/07
	Edison PMSA, NJ	Y	38450 FQ	46680 MW	55860 TQ	USBLS	5/07
	Newark-Union PMSA, NJ-PA	Y	36630 FQ	49160 MW	64080 TQ	USBLS	5/07
	New Mexico	Y	26820 FQ	34970 MW	45050 TQ	USBLS	5/07
	Albuquerque MSA, NM	Y	25310 FQ	34200 MW	45390 TQ	USBLS	5/07
	Santa Fe MSA, NM	Y	38490 FQ	43150 MW	49080 TQ	USBLS	5/07
	New York	Y	32370 FQ	44060 MW	57880 TQ	USBLS	5/07

AE	Average entry wage	**AW**	Average wage paid	**FQ**	First quartile wage
AER	Average entry range	**AWR**	Average wage range	**H**	Hourly
AEX	Average experienced wage	**AXR**	Average experienced range	**HI**	Highest wage paid
ATC	Average total compensation	**D**	Daily	**HR**	High end range

LO	Lowest wage paid	**MTC**	Median total compensation	**TCC** Total cash compensation
LR	Low end range	**MW**	Median wage paid	**TQ** Third quartile wage
M	Monthly	**MWR**	Median wage range	**W** Weekly
MCC	Median cash compensation	**S**	See annotated source	**Y** Yearly

Occupation/Type/Industry	Location	Per	Low	Mid	High	Source	Date
Heating, Air Conditioning, and Refrigeration Mechanic and Installer	Albany-Schenectady-Troy MSA, NY	Y	27530 FQ	33990 MW	45720 TQ	USBLS	.5/07
	Buffalo-Niagara Falls MSA, NY	Y	33330 FQ	41320 MW	51970 TQ	USBLS	5/07
	Nassau-Suffolk PMSA, NY	Y	35370 FQ	49050 MW	58780 TQ	USBLS	5/07
	New York-Northern New Jersey-Long Island MSA, NY-NJ-PA	Y	37280 FQ	49770 MW	61230 TQ	USBLS	5/07
	North Carolina	Y	30210 FQ	36440 MW	44130 TQ	USBLS	5/07
	Charlotte-Gastonia-Concord MSA, NC-SC	Y	32960 FQ	39750 MW	47470 TQ	USBLS	5/07
	Greensboro-High Point MSA, NC	Y	31190 FQ	37120 MW	45900 TQ	USBLS	5/07
	Raleigh-Cary MSA, NC	Y	31440 FQ	38870 MW	48570 TQ	USBLS	5/07
	Winston-Salem MSA, NC	Y	30560 FQ	35680 MW	40970 TQ	USBLS	5/07
	North Dakota	Y	29740 FQ	35670 MW	49600 TQ	USBLS	5/07
	Bismarck MSA, ND	Y	33670 FQ	37100 MW	47910 TQ	USBLS	5/07
	Fargo MSA, ND-MN	Y	25500 FQ	32000 MW	46250 TQ	USBLS	5/07
	Ohio	Y	30020 FQ	37320 MW	47450 TQ	USBLS	5/07
	Cincinnati-Middletown MSA, OH-KY-IN	Y	33130 FQ	40800 MW	49920 TQ	USBLS	5/07
	Cleveland-Elyria-Mentor MSA, OH	Y	28830 FQ	38790 MW	49730 TQ	USBLS	5/07
	Columbus MSA, OH	Y	32630 FQ	40970 MW	51920 TQ	USBLS	5/07
	Dayton MSA, OH	Y	32590 FQ	36810 MW	43720 TQ	USBLS	5/07
	Oklahoma	Y	27660 FQ	34120 MW	45600 TQ	USBLS	5/07
	Oklahoma City MSA, OK	Y	28890 FQ	34280 MW	41710 TQ	USBLS	5/07
	Tulsa MSA, OK	Y	27900 FQ	35630 MW	51060 TQ	USBLS	5/07
	Oregon	H	14.70 FQ	18.99 MW	23.55 TQ	ORBLS	5/08
	Portland-Vancouver-Beaverton MSA, OR-WA	Y	32180 FQ	42160 MW	50460 TQ	USBLS	5/07
	Pennsylvania	Y	32060 FQ	40390 MW	49880 TQ	USBLS	5/07
	Allentown-Bethlehem-Easton MSA, PA-NJ	Y	33890 FQ	42180 MW	50020 TQ	USBLS	5/07
	Philadelphia-Camden-Wilmington MSA, PA-NJ-DE-MD	Y	36980 FQ	44980 MW	55110 TQ	USBLS	5/07
	Pittsburgh MSA, PA	Y	27870 FQ	35290 MW	45400 TQ	USBLS	5/07
	Rhode Island	Y	37070 FQ	44970 MW	55680 TQ	USBLS	5/07
	Providence-Fall River-Warwick MSA, RI-MA	Y	37830 FQ	46280 MW	57420 TQ	USBLS	5/07
	South Carolina	Y	28070 FQ	34630 MW	43140 TQ	USBLS	5/07
	Charleston-North Charleston MSA, SC	Y	31060 FQ	39420 MW	45670 TQ	USBLS	5/07
	Columbia MSA, SC	Y	26380 FQ	31480 MW	38440 TQ	USBLS	5/07
	South Dakota	Y	30225 FQ	36115 MW	43042 TQ	SDBLS	7/08-9/08
	Sioux Falls MSA, SD	Y	31854 FQ	39435 MW	48172 TQ	SDBLS	7/08-9/08
	Tennessee	Y	25860 FQ	30230 MW	38250 TQ	USBLS	5/07
	Knoxville MSA, TN	Y	25220 FQ	27720 MW	30510 TQ	USBLS	5/07
	Memphis MSA, TN-MS-AR	Y	29940 FQ	36900 MW	46460 TQ	USBLS	5/07
	Nashville-Davidson-Murfreesboro MSA, TN	Y	30920 FQ	35810 MW	40840 TQ	USBLS	5/07
	Texas	Y	27560 FQ	35060 MW	44150 TQ	USBLS	5/07
	Austin-Round Rock MSA, TX	Y	29660 FQ	36540 MW	42610 TQ	USBLS	5/07
	Dallas-Fort Worth-Arlington MSA, TX	Y	29710 FQ	38010 MW	46950 TQ	USBLS	5/07
	El Paso MSA, TX	Y	23840 FQ	30180 MW	36800 TQ	USBLS	5/07
	Houston-Sugar Land-Baytown MSA, TX	Y	29340 FQ	35720 MW	45780 TQ	USBLS	5/07
	San Antonio MSA, TX	Y	23110 FQ	30100 MW	40220 TQ	USBLS	5/07
	Utah	Y	28780 FQ	35360 MW	43550 TQ	USBLS	5/07
	Salt Lake City MSA, UT	Y	29380 FQ	37390 MW	48490 TQ	USBLS	5/07
	Vermont	Y	33040 FQ	38620 MW	48250 TQ	USBLS	5/07
	Burlington-South Burlington MSA, VT	Y	32520 FQ	42090 MW	49800 TQ	USBLS	5/07
	Virginia	Y	28540 FQ	36020 MW	45910 TQ	USBLS	5/07
	Lynchburg MSA, VA	Y	25690 FQ	31940 MW	39200 TQ	USBLS	5/07
	Richmond MSA, VA	Y	31150 FQ	38230 MW	47000 TQ	USBLS	5/07

AE Average entry wage	**AW** Average wage paid	**FQ** First quartile wage	**LO** Lowest wage paid	**MTC** Median total compensation **TCC** Total cash compensation
AER Average entry range	**AWR** Average wage range	**H** Hourly	**LR** Low end range	**MW** Median wage paid **TQ** Third quartile wage
AEX Average experienced wage	**AXR** Average experienced range	**HI** Highest wage paid	**M** Monthly	**MWR** Median wage range **W** Weekly
ATC Average total compensation	**D** Daily	**HR** High end range	**MCC** Median cash compensation	**S** See annotated source **Y** Yearly

Occupation/Type/Industry	Location	Per	Low	Mid	High	Source	Date
Heating, Air Conditioning, and Refrigeration Mechanic and Installer	Virginia Beach-Norfolk-Newport News MSA, VA-NC	Y	25910 FQ	32660 MW	42160 TQ	USBLS	5/07
	Washington	H	17.12 FQ	22.83 MW	29.01 TQ	WABLS	3/08
	Seattle-Tacoma-Bellevue MSA, WA	Y	40700 FQ	54620 MW	64640 TQ	USBLS	5/07
	West Virginia	Y	21955 FQ	28296 MW	38051 TQ	WVBLS	7/08-9/08
	Charleston MSA, WV	Y	22420 FQ	30860 MW	50690 TQ	USBLS	5/07
	Wisconsin	Y	33160 FQ	41310 MW	54010 TQ	USBLS	5/07
	Milwaukee-Waukesha-West Allis MSA, WI	Y	38540 FQ	49270 MW	65850 TQ	USBLS	5/07
	Wyoming	Y	28665 FQ	36047 MW	46181 TQ	WYBLS	9/08
	Cheyenne MSA, WY	Y	34181 FQ	43563 MW	51406 TQ	WYBLS	9/08
	Puerto Rico	Y	16570 FQ	19650 MW	26680 TQ	USBLS	5/07
	San Juan-Caguas-Guaynabo MSA, PR	Y	16840 FQ	19680 MW	26630 TQ	USBLS	5/07
	Virgin Islands	Y	26080 FQ	29220 MW	32530 TQ	USBLS	5/07
	Guam	Y	20540 FQ	26900 MW	33390 TQ	USBLS	5/07
Heavy Equipment Mechanic							
County Government	Chatham County, GA	Y	35186 LO		55587 HI	GACTY03	2008
County Government	Lumpkin County, GA	Y	28412 LO		43233 HI	GACTY03	2008
Department of Transportation	Michigan	H	17.61 LO		26.69 HI	MDOT	10/1/07
Heavy Equipment Operator							
County Government	Cherokee County, GA	Y	26806 LO		41549 HI	GACTG03	2008
County Government	Fulton County, GA	Y	30252 LO		50371 HI	AREGC	2007
Heavy Sign Maintenance Foreman							
Department of Transportation	New Hampshire	Y		47444 AW		NHUL03	2008
Helicopter Pilot							
Police/Fire Department	Baltimore County, MD	Y	44735 LO			BMAG	2009
Help Desk Specialist	San Francisco, CA	Y		53300 AW		BWEEK	2008
Help Desk/User Support Professional	United States	Y		55863 AW		MCP	2008
Helper							
Carpenter	Alabama	Y	18050 FQ	21750 MW	26110 TQ	USBLS	5/07
Carpenter	Birmingham-Hoover MSA, AL	Y	21150 FQ	24560 MW	28300 TQ	USBLS	5/07
Carpenter	Huntsville MSA, AL	Y	17760 FQ	22000 MW	28500 TQ	USBLS	5/07
Carpenter	Alaska	Y	30100 FQ	36560 MW	40710 TQ	USBLS	5/07
Carpenter	Arizona	Y	21040 FQ	26510 MW	30330 TQ	USBLS	5/07
Carpenter	Phoenix-Mesa-Scottsdale MSA, AZ	Y	21230 FQ	26750 MW	30520 TQ	USBLS	5/07
Carpenter	Tucson MSA, AZ	Y	20420 FQ	24520 MW	28740 TQ	USBLS	5/07
Carpenter	Arkansas	Y	19250 FQ	22270 MW	26240 TQ	USBLS	5/07
Carpenter	Fayetteville-Springdale-Rogers MSA, AR-MO	Y	19210 FQ	24070 MW	28340 TQ	USBLS	5/07
Carpenter	Little Rock-North Little Rock MSA, AR	Y	20260 FQ	23110 MW	26510 TQ	USBLS	5/07
Carpenter	California	H	10.96 FQ	13.04 MW	15.25 TQ	CABLS	1/08-3/08
Carpenter	Los Angeles-Long Beach-Glendale PMSA, CA	H	10.47 FQ	12.48 MW	14.62 TQ	CABLS	1/08-3/08
Carpenter	Oakland-Fremont-Hayward MSA, CA	H	12.29 FQ	13.60 MW	14.95 TQ	CABLS	1/08-3/08
Carpenter	Riverside-San Bernardino-Ontario MSA, CA	H	10.78 FQ	12.53 MW	14.62 TQ	CABLS	1/08-3/08
Carpenter	Sacramento-Arden Arcade-Roseville MSA, CA	H	10.73 FQ	12.29 MW	14.77 TQ	CABLS	1/08-3/08
Carpenter	San Diego-Carlsbad-San Marcos MSA, CA	H	10.83 FQ	13.20 MW	15.06 TQ	CABLS	1/08-3/08
Carpenter	San Francisco-San Mateo-Redwood PMSA, CA	H	13.87 FQ	15.36 MW	21.12 TQ	CABLS	1/08-3/08
Carpenter	San Jose-Sunnyvale-Santa Clara MSA, CA	H	12.75 FQ	15.28 MW	18.41 TQ	CABLS	1/08-3/08
Carpenter	Santa Ana-Anaheim-Irvine PMSA, CA	Y	22820 FQ	28170 MW	35830 TQ	USBLS	5/07
Carpenter	Colorado	Y	21590 FQ	26110 MW	31070 TQ	USBLS	5/07

AE	Average entry wage	AW	Average wage paid	FQ	First quartile wage	LO	Lowest wage paid	MTC	Median total compensation	TCC	Total cash compensation
AER	Average entry range	AWR	Average wage range	H	Hourly	LR	Low end range	MW	Median wage paid	TQ	Third quartile wage
AEX	Average experienced wage	AXR	Average experienced range	HI	Highest wage paid	M	Monthly	MWR	Median wage range	W	Weekly
ATC	Average total compensation	D	Daily	HR	High end range	MCC	Median cash compensation	S	See annotated source	Y	Yearly

Occupation/Type/Industry	Location	Per	Low	Mid	High	Source	Date
Helper							
Carpenter	Denver-Aurora MSA, CO	Y	21110 FQ	25190 MW	29990 TQ	USBLS	5/07
Carpenter	Connecticut	H	9.72 AE	13.13 MW		CTBLS	1/08-3/08
Carpenter	Bridgeport-Stamford-Norwalk MSA, CT	Y	23490 FQ	32730 MW	39670 TQ	USBLS	5/07
Carpenter	Hartford-West Hartford-East Hartford MSA, CT	Y	15920 FQ	25850 MW	30400 TQ	USBLS	5/07
Carpenter	Delaware	Y	20590 FQ	23420 MW	28150 TQ	USBLS	5/07
Carpenter	Dover MSA, DE	Y	20570 FQ	22090 MW	23610 TQ	USBLS	5/07
Carpenter	Wilmington PMSA, DE-MD-NJ	Y	20430 FQ	25320 MW	30600 TQ	USBLS	5/07
Carpenter	District of Columbia	Y	19430 FQ	30000 MW	35940 TQ	USBLS	5/07
Carpenter	Washington-Arlington-Alexandria MSA, DC-VA-MD-WV	Y	23230 FQ	27970 MW	31960 TQ	USBLS	5/07
Carpenter	Florida	Y	20050 FQ	23960 MW	28260 TQ	USBLS	5/07
Carpenter	Cape Coral-Fort Myers MSA, FL	Y	20070 FQ	25850 MW	29140 TQ	USBLS	5/07
Carpenter	Fort Lauderdale-Pompano Beach-Deerfield Beach PMSA, FL	Y	18060 FQ	22710 MW	28270 TQ	USBLS	5/07
Carpenter	Jacksonville MSA, FL	Y	21450 FQ	25870 MW	29440 TQ	USBLS	5/07
Carpenter	Miami-Fort Lauderdale-Miami Beach MSA, FL	Y	19090 FQ	23270 MW	27820 TQ	USBLS	5/07
Carpenter	Orlando-Kissimmee MSA, FL	Y	21120 FQ	23600 MW	27760 TQ	USBLS	5/07
Carpenter	Tampa-St. Petersburg-Clearwater MSA, FL	Y	17840 FQ	23890 MW	27690 TQ	USBLS	5/07
Carpenter	West Palm Beach-Boca Raton-Boynton Beach PMSA, FL	Y	23660 FQ	26870 MW	29610 TQ	USBLS	5/07
Carpenter	Georgia	Y	18950 FQ	23590 MW	28320 TQ	USBLS	5/07
Carpenter	Atlanta-Sandy Springs-Marietta MSA, GA	Y	22220 FQ	25850 MW	30170 TQ	USBLS	5/07
Carpenter	Augusta-Richmond County MSA, GA-SC	Y	16320 FQ	19850 MW	26170 TQ	USBLS	5/07
Carpenter	Savannah MSA, GA	Y	17710 FQ	25530 MW	29000 TQ	USBLS	5/07
Carpenter	Hawaii	Y	30120 FQ	36020 MW	43410 TQ	USBLS	5/07
Carpenter	Honolulu MSA, HI	Y	30060 FQ	35660 MW	41550 TQ	USBLS	5/07
Carpenter	Idaho	Y	23060 FQ	33850 MW	38180 TQ	USBLS	5/07
Carpenter	Illinois	Y	20910 FQ	26420 MW	34530 TQ	USBLS	5/07
Carpenter	Champaign-Urbana MSA, IL	Y	20740 FQ	22240 MW	23750 TQ	USBLS	5/07
Carpenter	Chicago-Naperville-Joliet MSA, IL-IN-WI	Y	22350 FQ	28280 MW	38190 TQ	USBLS	5/07
Carpenter	Indiana	Y	20170 FQ	24640 MW	29230 TQ	USBLS	5/07
Carpenter	Elkhart-Goshen MSA, IN	Y	22070 FQ	27500 MW	31840 TQ	USBLS	5/07
Carpenter	Gary PMSA, IN	Y	18450 FQ	22390 MW	28400 TQ	USBLS	5/07
Carpenter	Indianapolis-Carmel MSA, IN	Y	23570 FQ	27380 MW	30480 TQ	USBLS	5/07
Carpenter	Terre Haute MSA, IN	Y	14800 FQ	18000 MW	21100 TQ	USBLS	5/07
Carpenter	Iowa	Y	17870 FQ	22510 MW	26290 TQ	USBLS	5/07
Carpenter	Des Moines-West Des Moines MSA, IA	Y	21170 FQ	25990 MW	29020 TQ	USBLS	5/07
Carpenter	Kansas	Y	18970 FQ	23760 MW	29370 TQ	USBLS	5/07
Carpenter	Wichita MSA, KS	Y	21380 FQ	26460 MW	30070 TQ	USBLS	5/07
Carpenter	Kentucky	Y	17711 FQ	21423 MW	26384 TQ	KYBLS	2008
Carpenter	Louisville-Jefferson County MSA, KY-IN	Y	16650 FQ	20870 MW	28520 TQ	USBLS	5/07
Carpenter	Louisiana	H	7.79 FQ	9.96 MW	12.21 TQ	LABLS	1/08-3/08
Carpenter	Baton Rouge MSA, LA	Y	14560 FQ	17430 MW	22630 TQ	USBLS	5/07
Carpenter	New Orleans-Metairie-Kenner MSA, LA	Y	21650 FQ	25660 MW	30640 TQ	USBLS	5/07
Carpenter	Maine	Y	21670 FQ	25410 MW	28660 TQ	USBLS	5/07
Carpenter	Portland-South Portland-Biddeford MSA, ME	Y	20800 FQ	23290 MW	26850 TQ	USBLS	5/07
Carpenter	Maryland	Y		27500 MW		MDBLS	3/08
Carpenter	Baltimore-Towson MSA, MD	Y	22530 FQ	27460 MW	32050 TQ	USBLS	5/07
Carpenter	Bethesda-Gaithersburg-Frederick PMSA, MD	Y	19690 FQ	25630 MW	30890 TQ	USBLS	5/07
Carpenter	Massachusetts	Y	25670 FQ	31190 MW	39810 TQ	USBLS	5/07
Carpenter	Boston-Cambridge-Quincy NECTA, MA	Y	28100 FQ	36270 MW	41610 TQ	USBLS	5/07
Carpenter	Springfield MSA, MA-CT	Y	20270 FQ	23920 MW	28230 TQ	USBLS	5/07
Carpenter	Worcester MSA, MA-CT	Y	27230 FQ	29680 MW	32320 TQ	USBLS	5/07
Carpenter	Michigan	Y	18950 FQ	23070 MW	27610 TQ	USBLS	5/07

Helper

Occupation/Type/Industry	Location	Per	Low	Mid	High	Source	Date
Carpenter	Ann Arbor MSA, MI	Y	22700 FQ	25990 MW	29460 TQ	USBLS	5/07
Carpenter	Detroit-Warren-Livonia MSA, MI	Y	17220 FQ	23210 MW	27600 TQ	USBLS	5/07
Carpenter	Grand Rapids-Wyoming MSA, MI	Y	18060 FQ	25180 MW	29110 TQ	USBLS	5/07
Carpenter	Lansing-East Lansing MSA, MI	Y	18730 FQ	20870 MW	22950 TQ	USBLS	5/07
Carpenter	Warren-Troy-Farmington Hills PMSA, MI	Y	17340 FQ	23290 MW	27390 TQ	USBLS	5/07
Carpenter	Minnesota	Y	21888 FQ	25830 MW	31721 TQ	MNBLS	10/08-12/08
Carpenter	Duluth-Superior MSA, MN-WI	Y	24091 FQ	28760 MW	36558 TQ	MNBLS	10/08-12/08
Carpenter	Minneapolis-Saint Paul MSA, MN-WI	Y	24218 FQ	29181 MW	34229 TQ	MNBLS	10/08-12/08
Carpenter	Mississippi	Y	19090 FQ	21590 MW	24050 TQ	USBLS	5/07
Carpenter	Gulfport-Biloxi MSA, MS	Y	19650 FQ	23500 MW	28920 TQ	USBLS	5/07
Carpenter	Jackson MSA, MS	Y	20460 FQ	22290 MW	24150 TQ	USBLS	5/07
Carpenter	Missouri	Y	21840 FQ	28450 MW	35750 TQ	USBLS	5/07
Carpenter	Kansas City MSA, MO-KS	Y	23260 FQ	27670 MW	32220 TQ	USBLS	5/07
Carpenter	St. Louis MSA, MO-IL	Y	21410 FQ	28380 MW	35180 TQ	USBLS	5/07
Carpenter	Montana	Y	20080 FQ	23960 MW	28350 TQ	USBLS	5/07
Carpenter	Billings MSA, MT	Y	19790 FQ	22540 MW	26050 TQ	USBLS	5/07
Carpenter	Nebraska	Y	18470 FQ	23170 MW	27910 TQ	USBLS	5/07
Carpenter	Lincoln MSA, NE	Y	17950 FQ	20830 MW	26500 TQ	USBLS	5/07
Carpenter	Omaha-Council Bluffs MSA, NE-IA	Y	22760 FQ	26510 MW	29680 TQ	USBLS	5/07
Carpenter	Nevada	H	10.62 FQ	12.77 MW	15.40 TQ	NVBLS	5/08
Carpenter	Carson City MSA, NV	H	13.00 FQ	14.04 MW	15.05 TQ	NVBLS	5/08
Carpenter	Las Vegas-Paradise MSA, NV	H	10.55 FQ	12.50 MW	15.20 TQ	NVBLS	5/08
Carpenter	New Hampshire	H	8.86 AE	12.01 MW	14.73 AEX	NHBLS	6/08
Carpenter	Rochester-Dover MSA, NH-ME	Y	20430 FQ	22260 MW	24600 TQ	USBLS	5/07
Carpenter	New Jersey	Y	22180 FQ	27620 MW	32430 TQ	USBLS	5/07
Carpenter	Camden PMSA, NJ	Y	21370 FQ	25630 MW	29560 TQ	USBLS	5/07
Carpenter	Edison PMSA, NJ	Y	20340 FQ	27030 MW	31850 TQ	USBLS	5/07
Carpenter	Newark-Union PMSA, NJ-PA	Y	25830 FQ	29340 MW	37120 TQ	USBLS	5/07
Carpenter	New Mexico	Y	18290 FQ	23360 MW	28500 TQ	USBLS	5/07
Carpenter	Albuquerque MSA, NM	Y	20830 FQ	25170 MW	29250 TQ	USBLS	5/07
Carpenter	New York	Y	20060 FQ	23720 MW	29900 TQ	USBLS	5/07
Carpenter	Albany-Schenectady-Troy MSA, NY	Y	21760 FQ	27180 MW	34020 TQ	USBLS	5/07
Carpenter	Buffalo-Niagara Falls MSA, NY	Y	18300 FQ	21020 MW	23360 TQ	USBLS	5/07
Carpenter	Nassau-Suffolk PMSA, NY	Y	17350 FQ	26430 MW	31020 TQ	USBLS	5/07
Carpenter	New York-Northern New Jersey-Long Island MSA, NY-NJ-PA	Y	20740 FQ	24710 MW	30830 TQ	USBLS	5/07
Carpenter	North Carolina	Y	18980 FQ	22170 MW	25760 TQ	USBLS	5/07
Carpenter	Charlotte-Gastonia-Concord MSA, NC-SC	Y	21030 FQ	23620 MW	28230 TQ	USBLS	5/07
Carpenter	Raleigh-Cary MSA, NC	Y	17320 FQ	19320 MW	22510 TQ	USBLS	5/07
Carpenter	North Dakota	Y	20970 FQ	23400 MW	26570 TQ	USBLS	5/07
Carpenter	Fargo MSA, ND-MN	Y	19370 FQ	21680 MW	23660 TQ	USBLS	5/07
Carpenter	Ohio	Y	16790 FQ	23490 MW	28070 TQ	USBLS	5/07
Carpenter	Cincinnati-Middletown MSA, OH-KY-IN	Y	16920 FQ	22030 MW	30000 TQ	USBLS	5/07
Carpenter	Cleveland-Elyria-Mentor MSA, OH	Y	14980 FQ	15710 MW	16440 TQ	USBLS	5/07
Carpenter	Columbus MSA, OH	Y	23680 FQ	26500 MW	28960 TQ	USBLS	5/07
Carpenter	Oklahoma	Y	17690 FQ	20460 MW	23980 TQ	USBLS	5/07
Carpenter	Oklahoma City MSA, OK	Y	18880 FQ	21920 MW	26000 TQ	USBLS	5/07
Carpenter	Tulsa MSA, OK	Y	19960 FQ	23020 MW	26130 TQ	USBLS	5/07
Carpenter	Oregon	H	10.23 FQ	12.48 MW	14.52 TQ	ORBLS	5/08
Carpenter	Portland-Vancouver-Beaverton MSA, OR-WA	Y	20710 FQ	26340 MW	30030 TQ	USBLS	5/07
Carpenter	Pennsylvania	Y	21330 FQ	25160 MW	29620 TQ	USBLS	5/07
Carpenter	Allentown-Bethlehem-Easton MSA, PA-NJ	Y	21920 FQ	26990 MW	29600 TQ	USBLS	5/07
Carpenter	Philadelphia-Camden-Wilmington MSA, PA-NJ-DE-MD	Y	21780 FQ	26490 MW	33310 TQ	USBLS	5/07
Carpenter	Pittsburgh MSA, PA	Y	22520 FQ	25860 MW	29320 TQ	USBLS	5/07
Carpenter	Reading MSA, PA	Y	17170 FQ	19580 MW	23990 TQ	USBLS	5/07

AE	Average entry wage	AW	Average wage paid	FQ	First quartile wage	LO	Lowest wage paid
AER	Average entry range	AWR	Average wage range	H	Hourly	LR	Low end range
AEX	Average experienced wage	AXR	Average experienced range	HI	Highest wage paid	M	Monthly
ATC	Average total compensation	D	Daily	HR	High end range	MCC	Median cash compensation

MTC Median total compensation TCC Total cash compensation
MW Median wage paid TQ Third quartile wage
MWR Median wage range W Weekly
S See annotated source Y Yearly

Occupation/Type/Industry	Location	Per	Low	Mid	High	Source	Date
Helper							
Carpenter	Rhode Island	Y	25590 FQ	28600 MW	31790 TQ	USBLS	5/07
Carpenter	Providence-Fall River-Warwick MSA, RI-MA	Y	25930 FQ	29040 MW	33010 TQ	USBLS	5/07
Carpenter	South Carolina	Y	19880 FQ	22970 MW	26740 TQ	USBLS	5/07
Carpenter	Charleston-North Charleston MSA, SC	Y	21080 FQ	24120 MW	28720 TQ	USBLS	5/07
Carpenter	Columbia MSA, SC	Y	18460 FQ	22260 MW	26880 TQ	USBLS	5/07
Carpenter	Florence MSA, SC	Y	16820 FQ	21110 MW	23540 TQ	USBLS	5/07
Carpenter	South Dakota	Y	18202 FQ	19884 MW	22158 TQ	SDBLS	7/08-9/08
Carpenter	Sioux Falls MSA, SD	Y	18478 FQ	20220 MW	22764 TQ	SDBLS	7/08-9/08
Carpenter	Tennessee	Y	18800 FQ	22550 MW	26700 TQ	USBLS	5/07
Carpenter	Kingsport-Bristol-Bristol MSA, TN-VA	Y	17350 FQ	19300 MW	22480 TQ	USBLS	5/07
Carpenter	Memphis MSA, TN-MS-AR	Y	17920 FQ	21390 MW	24430 TQ	USBLS	5/07
Carpenter	Nashville-Davidson-Murfreesboro MSA, TN	Y	18380 FQ	24070 MW	29090 TQ	USBLS	5/07
Carpenter	Texas	Y	19530 FQ	22810 MW	26350 TQ	USBLS	5/07
Carpenter	Austin-Round Rock MSA, TX	Y	19940 FQ	22250 MW	25880 TQ	USBLS	5/07
Carpenter	Dallas-Fort Worth-Arlington MSA, TX	Y	20630 FQ	23630 MW	27690 TQ	USBLS	5/07
Carpenter	El Paso MSA, TX	Y	19230 FQ	22290 MW	26450 TQ	USBLS	5/07
Carpenter	Houston-Sugar Land-Baytown MSA, TX	Y	21280 FQ	24500 MW	27990 TQ	USBLS	5/07
Carpenter	San Antonio MSA, TX	Y	19010 FQ	22160 MW	25280 TQ	USBLS	5/07
Carpenter	Utah	Y	20870 FQ	23290 MW	26040 TQ	USBLS	5/07
Carpenter	Provo-Orem MSA, UT	Y	21300 FQ	22910 MW	24670 TQ	USBLS	5/07
Carpenter	Salt Lake City MSA, UT	Y	20040 FQ	23400 MW	27350 TQ	USBLS	5/07
Carpenter	Vermont	Y	23740 FQ	27180 MW	30760 TQ	USBLS	5/07
Carpenter	Burlington-South Burlington MSA, VT	Y	23880 FQ	29540 MW	34380 TQ	USBLS	5/07
Carpenter	Virginia	Y	21110 FQ	25590 MW	29940 TQ	USBLS	5/07
Carpenter	Lynchburg MSA, VA	Y	14350 FQ	19720 MW	22140 TQ	USBLS	5/07
Carpenter	Richmond MSA, VA	Y	19000 FQ	22540 MW	27540 TQ	USBLS	5/07
Carpenter	Virginia Beach-Norfolk-Newport News MSA, VA-NC	Y	22430 FQ	26170 MW	29980 TQ	USBLS	5/07
Carpenter	Washington	H	11.17 FQ	13.27 MW	15.37 TQ	WABLS	3/08
Carpenter	Bremerton-Silverdale MSA, WA	Y	19460 FQ	22030 MW	28560 TQ	USBLS	5/07
Carpenter	Seattle-Tacoma-Bellevue MSA, WA	Y	23170 FQ	27280 MW	31730 TQ	USBLS	5/07
Carpenter	West Virginia	Y	18614 FQ	22220 MW	26730 TQ	WVBLS	7/08-9/08
Carpenter	Charleston MSA, WV	Y	19170 FQ	27330 MW	32450 TQ	USBLS	5/07
Carpenter	Wisconsin	Y	20980 FQ	25730 MW	30500 TQ	USBLS	5/07
Carpenter	Milwaukee-Waukesha-West Allis MSA, WI	Y	25090 FQ	28320 MW	32360 TQ	USBLS	5/07
Carpenter	Wyoming	Y	23152 FQ	29127 MW	33247 TQ	WYBLS	9/08
Carpenter	Cheyenne MSA, WY	Y	18246 FQ	22892 MW	29381 TQ	WYBLS	9/08
Carpenter	Puerto Rico	Y	12550 FQ	13860 MW	15190 TQ	USBLS	5/07
Carpenter	San Juan-Caguas-Guaynabo MSA, PR	Y	12580 FQ	14000 MW	15460 TQ	USBLS	5/07
Carpenter	Virgin Islands	Y	24240 FQ	26440 MW	29270 TQ	USBLS	5/07
Carpenter	Guam	Y	14450 FQ	17850 MW	20680 TQ	USBLS	5/07
Electrician	Alabama	Y	18190 FQ	21380 MW	24680 TQ	USBLS	5/07
Electrician	Birmingham-Hoover MSA, AL	Y	19420 FQ	22320 MW	25450 TQ	USBLS	5/07
Electrician	Alaska	Y	24350 FQ	32180 MW	44790 TQ	USBLS	5/07
Electrician	Arizona	Y	17380 FQ	19730 MW	25750 TQ	USBLS	5/07
Electrician	Phoenix-Mesa-Scottsdale MSA, AZ	Y	17630 FQ	20160 MW	26060 TQ	USBLS	5/07
Electrician	Tucson MSA, AZ	Y	16730 FQ	18170 MW	22040 TQ	USBLS	5/07
Electrician	Arkansas	Y	20500 FQ	24150 MW	28580 TQ	USBLS	5/07
Electrician	Little Rock-North Little Rock MSA, AR	Y	20980 FQ	23590 MW	26590 TQ	USBLS	5/07
Electrician	California	H	11.24 FQ	14.07 MW	17.06 TQ	CABLS	1/08-3/08
Electrician	Los Angeles-Long Beach-Glendale PMSA, CA	H	10.40 FQ	13.07 MW	16.49 TQ	CABLS	1/08-3/08
Electrician	Oakland-Fremont-Hayward MSA, CA	H	13.19 FQ	16.42 MW	20.56 TQ	CABLS	1/08-3/08
Electrician	Riverside-San Bernardino-Ontario MSA, CA	H	10.30 FQ	13.41 MW	15.36 TQ	CABLS	1/08-3/08
Electrician	Sacramento-Arden Arcade-Roseville MSA, CA	H	11.17 FQ	13.22 MW	15.31 TQ	CABLS	1/08-3/08

AE	Average entry wage	AW	Average wage paid	FQ	First quartile wage	LO	Lowest wage paid	MTC	Median total compensation	TCC	Total cash compensation
AER	Average entry range	AWR	Average wage range	H	Hourly	LR	Low end range	MW	Median wage paid	TQ	Third quartile wage
AEX	Average experienced wage	AXR	Average experienced range	HI	Highest wage paid	M	Monthly	MWR	Median wage range	W	Weekly
ATC	Average total compensation	D	Daily	HR	High end range	MCC	Median cash compensation	S	See annotated source	Y	Yearly

Occupation/Type/Industry	Location	Per	Low	Mid	High	Source	Date
Helper							
Electrician	San Diego-Carlsbad-San Marcos MSA, CA	H	11.07 FQ	13.34 MW	15.80 TQ	CABLS	1/08-3/08
Electrician	San Francisco-San Mateo-Redwood PMSA, CA	H	18.22 FQ	23.53 MW	27.40 TQ	CABLS	1/08-3/08
Electrician	San Jose-Sunnyvale-Santa Clara MSA, CA	H	15.31 FQ	16.92 MW	18.63 TQ	CABLS	1/08-3/08
Electrician	Santa Ana-Anaheim-Irvine PMSA, CA	Y	25020 FQ	31050 MW	39200 TQ	USBLS	5/07
Electrician	Colorado	Y	24130 FQ	28440 MW	31950 TQ	USBLS	5/07
Electrician	Denver-Aurora MSA, CO	Y	25340 FQ	28570 MW	31710 TQ	USBLS	5/07
Electrician	Connecticut	H	10.54 AE	13.68 MW		CTBLS	1/08-3/08
Electrician	Bridgeport-Stamford-Norwalk MSA, CT	Y	21060 FQ	22920 MW	24780 TQ	USBLS	5/07
Electrician	Danbury MSA, CT	Y	26010 FQ	28480 MW	40100 TQ	USBLS	5/07
Electrician	Hartford-West Hartford-East Hartford MSA, CT	Y	22830 FQ	30700 MW	36810 TQ	USBLS	5/07
Electrician	Delaware	Y	22230 FQ	25580 MW	30560 TQ	USBLS	5/07
Electrician	Wilmington PMSA, DE-MD-NJ	Y	21800 FQ	26780 MW	32020 TQ	USBLS	5/07
Electrician	District of Columbia	Y	26050 FQ	33000 MW	45090 TQ	USBLS	5/07
Electrician	Washington-Arlington-Alexandria MSA, DC-VA-MD-WV	Y	25020 FQ	29350 MW	34530 TQ	USBLS	5/07
Electrician	Florida	Y	20920 FQ	24110 MW	28870 TQ	USBLS	5/07
Electrician	Fort Lauderdale-Pompano Beach-Deerfield Beach PMSA, FL	Y	22130 FQ	25120 MW	28940 TQ	USBLS	5/07
Electrician	Jacksonville MSA, FL	Y	20870 FQ	23740 MW	27890 TQ	USBLS	5/07
Electrician	Miami-Fort Lauderdale-Miami Beach MSA, FL	Y	21330 FQ	24140 MW	28650 TQ	USBLS	5/07
Electrician	Orlando-Kissimmee MSA, FL	Y	20350 FQ	22850 MW	26590 TQ	USBLS	5/07
Electrician	Tallahassee MSA, FL	Y	18580 FQ	22050 MW	26370 TQ	USBLS	5/07
Electrician	Tampa-St. Petersburg-Clearwater MSA, FL	Y	23100 FQ	27460 MW	30640 TQ	USBLS	5/07
Electrician	West Palm Beach-Boca Raton-Boynton Beach PMSA, FL	Y	22100 FQ	26670 MW	32030 TQ	USBLS	5/07
Electrician	Georgia	Y	20030 FQ	23670 MW	28330 TQ	USBLS	5/07
Electrician	Atlanta-Sandy Springs-Marietta MSA, GA	Y	21270 FQ	25410 MW	29830 TQ	USBLS	5/07
Electrician	Savannah MSA, GA	Y	20320 FQ	23250 MW	26330 TQ	USBLS	5/07
Electrician	Hawaii	Y	31440 FQ	36410 MW	43090 TQ	USBLS	5/07
Electrician	Honolulu MSA, HI	Y	34100 FQ	37960 MW	44650 TQ	USBLS	5/07
Electrician	Illinois	Y	22060 FQ	27120 MW	36290 TQ	USBLS	5/07
Electrician	Chicago-Naperville-Joliet MSA, IL-IN-WI	Y	24020 FQ	29590 MW	43820 TQ	USBLS	5/07
Electrician	Indiana	Y	20120 FQ	24530 MW	28740 TQ	USBLS	5/07
Electrician	Gary PMSA, IN	Y	21400 FQ	23900 MW	26800 TQ	USBLS	5/07
Electrician	Indianapolis-Carmel MSA, IN	Y	20100 FQ	23850 MW	28810 TQ	USBLS	5/07
Electrician	Iowa	Y	19760 FQ	23640 MW	28210 TQ	USBLS	5/07
Electrician	Sioux City MSA, IA-NE-SD	Y	18930 FQ	21830 MW	24460 TQ	USBLS	5/07
Electrician	Kansas	Y	21170 FQ	24320 MW	28050 TQ	USBLS	5/07
Electrician	Wichita MSA, KS	Y	21880 FQ	24110 MW	26640 TQ	USBLS	5/07
Electrician	Kentucky	Y	19940 FQ	23661 MW	28351 TQ	KYBLS	2008
Electrician	Bowling Green MSA, KY	Y	18510 FQ	21020 MW	23580 TQ	USBLS	5/07
Electrician	Louisville-Jefferson County MSA, KY-IN	Y	20870 FQ	24240 MW	30350 TQ	USBLS	5/07
Electrician	Louisiana	H	9.83 FQ	11.28 MW	13.50 TQ	LABLS	1/08-3/08
Electrician	Baton Rouge MSA, LA	Y	20800 FQ	23770 MW	27840 TQ	USBLS	5/07
Electrician	New Orleans-Metairie-Kenner MSA, LA	Y	22820 FQ	27210 MW	31590 TQ	USBLS	5/07
Electrician	Maine	Y	27490 FQ	31250 MW	35550 TQ	USBLS	5/07
Electrician	Portland-South Portland-Biddeford MSA, ME	Y	27450 FQ	32300 MW	37080 TQ	USBLS	5/07
Electrician	Maryland	Y		29375 MW		MDBLS	3/08
Electrician	Baltimore-Towson MSA, MD	Y	23280 FQ	27690 MW	31270 TQ	USBLS	5/07
Electrician	Bethesda-Gaithersburg-Frederick PMSA, MD	Y	26720 FQ	30190 MW	34150 TQ	USBLS	5/07
Electrician	Massachusetts	Y	25920 FQ	29690 MW	36440 TQ	USBLS	5/07
Electrician	Barnstable Town MSA, MA	Y	28860 FQ	32750 MW	45540 TQ	USBLS	5/07
Electrician	Boston-Cambridge-Quincy NECTA, MA	Y	25540 FQ	30270 MW	37170 TQ	USBLS	5/07

AE	Average entry wage	AW	Average wage paid	FQ First quartile wage
AER	Average entry range	AWR	Average wage range	H Hourly
AEX	Average experienced wage	AXR	Average experienced range	HI Highest wage paid
ATC	Average total compensation	D	Daily	HR High end range

LO Lowest wage paid	MTC Median total compensation	TCC Total cash compensation
LR Low end range	MW Median wage paid	TQ Third quartile wage
M Monthly	MWR Median wage range	W Weekly
MCC Median cash compensation	S See annotated source	Y Yearly

Helper

Occupation/Type/Industry	Location	Per	Low	Mid	High	Source	Date
Electrician	Worcester MSA, MA-CT	Y	25770 FQ	29220 MW	32630 TQ	USBLS	5/07
Electrician	Michigan	Y	21930 FQ	26200 MW	32070 TQ	USBLS	5/07
Electrician	Detroit-Warren-Livonia MSA, MI	Y	21250 FQ	25340 MW	30660 TQ	USBLS	5/07
Electrician	Grand Rapids-Wyoming MSA, MI	Y	23880 FQ	36210 MW	48730 TQ	USBLS	5/07
Electrician	Warren-Troy-Farmington Hills PMSA, MI	Y	20930 FQ	24580 MW	30290 TQ	USBLS	5/07
Electrician	Minnesota	Y	20192 FQ	26452 MW	32596 TQ	MNBLS	10/08-12/08
Electrician	Minneapolis-Saint Paul MSA, MN-WI	Y	22415 FQ	28264 MW	33207 TQ	MNBLS	10/08-12/08
Electrician	Mississippi	Y	20220 FQ	23590 MW	27830 TQ	USBLS	5/07
Electrician	Jackson MSA, MS	Y	21140 FQ	23320 MW	25820 TQ	USBLS	5/07
Electrician	Missouri	Y	19910 FQ	26720 MW	38750 TQ	USBLS	5/07
Electrician	Kansas City MSA, MO-KS	Y	22090 FQ	27520 MW	38500 TQ	USBLS	5/07
Electrician	St. Louis MSA, MO-IL	Y	26700 FQ	36210 MW	49690 TQ	USBLS	5/07
Electrician	Montana	Y	36140 FQ	43780 MW	47710 TQ	USBLS	5/07
Electrician	Nebraska	Y	20400 FQ	22900 MW	26470 TQ	USBLS	5/07
Electrician	Omaha-Council Bluffs MSA, NE-IA	Y	21130 FQ	23460 MW	27240 TQ	USBLS	5/07
Electrician	Nevada	H	10.61 FQ	13.11 MW	16.30 TQ	NVBLS	5/08
Electrician	Las Vegas-Paradise MSA, NV	H	10.36 FQ	13.31 MW	17.47 TQ	NVBLS	5/08
Electrician	New Hampshire	H	11.53 AE	15.42 MW	17.14 AEX	NHBLS	6/08
Electrician	New Jersey	Y	24860 FQ	30280 MW	37430 TQ	USBLS	5/07
Electrician	Camden PMSA, NJ	Y	23640 FQ	31180 MW	35730 TQ	USBLS	5/07
Electrician	Edison PMSA, NJ	Y	25260 FQ	29300 MW	37630 TQ	USBLS	5/07
Electrician	Newark-Union PMSA, NJ-PA	Y	24160 FQ	29750 MW	34800 TQ	USBLS	5/07
Electrician	New Mexico	Y	19030 FQ	23610 MW	31260 TQ	USBLS	5/07
Electrician	Albuquerque MSA, NM	Y	18980 FQ	26470 MW	35980 TQ	USBLS	5/07
Electrician	New York	Y	23970 FQ	29700 MW	36710 TQ	USBLS	5/07
Electrician	Albany-Schenectady-Troy MSA, NY	Y	22100 FQ	25830 MW	31780 TQ	USBLS	5/07
Electrician	Buffalo-Niagara Falls MSA, NY	Y	22010 FQ	27180 MW	33310 TQ	USBLS	5/07
Electrician	Nassau-Suffolk PMSA, NY	Y	19890 FQ	28290 MW	34210 TQ	USBLS	5/07
Electrician	New York-Northern New Jersey-Long Island MSA, NY-NJ-PA	Y	25270 FQ	31120 MW	38250 TQ	USBLS	5/07
Electrician	Syracuse MSA, NY	Y	25920 FQ	28210 MW	30500 TQ	USBLS	5/07
Electrician	North Carolina	Y	20850 FQ	24010 MW	28580 TQ	USBLS	5/07
Electrician	Charlotte-Gastonia-Concord MSA, NC-SC	Y	21590 FQ	24870 MW	28930 TQ	USBLS	5/07
Electrician	Raleigh-Cary MSA, NC	Y	21080 FQ	24430 MW	29660 TQ	USBLS	5/07
Electrician	North Dakota	Y	17530 FQ	21490 MW	27480 TQ	USBLS	5/07
Electrician	Fargo MSA, ND-MN	Y	20680 FQ	23460 MW	28850 TQ	USBLS	5/07
Electrician	Ohio	Y	19390 FQ	23200 MW	28930 TQ	USBLS	5/07
Electrician	Canton-Massillon MSA, OH	Y	21750 FQ	25760 MW	28960 TQ	USBLS	5/07
Electrician	Cincinnati-Middletown MSA, OH-KY-IN	Y	18800 FQ	23410 MW	28360 TQ	USBLS	5/07
Electrician	Cleveland-Elyria-Mentor MSA, OH	Y	21230 FQ	24310 MW	30690 TQ	USBLS	5/07
Electrician	Columbus MSA, OH	Y	19430 FQ	22520 MW	30030 TQ	USBLS	5/07
Electrician	Dayton MSA, OH	Y	16960 FQ	21280 MW	27520 TQ	USBLS	5/07
Electrician	Oklahoma	Y	21080 FQ	23640 MW	27980 TQ	USBLS	5/07
Electrician	Oklahoma City MSA, OK	Y	20610 FQ	23020 MW	26550 TQ	USBLS	5/07
Electrician	Tulsa MSA, OK	Y	21670 FQ	23790 MW	27680 TQ	USBLS	5/07
Electrician	Oregon	H	13.06 FQ	16.07 MW	19.54 TQ	ORBLS	5/08
Electrician	Portland-Vancouver-Beaverton MSA, OR-WA	Y	25390 FQ	30470 MW	36940 TQ	USBLS	5/07
Electrician	Pennsylvania	Y	21820 FQ	26730 MW	31150 TQ	USBLS	5/07
Electrician	Allentown-Bethlehem-Easton MSA, PA-NJ	Y	22950 FQ	27390 MW	30800 TQ	USBLS	5/07
Electrician	Philadelphia-Camden-Wilmington MSA, PA-NJ-DE-MD	Y	22590 FQ	27720 MW	32320 TQ	USBLS	5/07
Electrician	Pittsburgh MSA, PA	Y	18870 FQ	27360 MW	35680 TQ	USBLS	5/07
Electrician	Rhode Island	Y	24870 FQ	28050 MW	31210 TQ	USBLS	5/07
Electrician	Providence-Fall River-Warwick MSA, RI-MA	Y	25060 FQ	28120 MW	31260 TQ	USBLS	5/07
Electrician	South Carolina	Y	19640 FQ	22790 MW	26230 TQ	USBLS	5/07

AE	Average entry wage	AW	Average wage paid	FQ	First quartile wage
AER	Average entry range	AWR	Average wage range	H	Hourly
AEX	Average experienced wage	AXR	Average experienced range	HI	Highest wage paid
ATC	Average total compensation	D	Daily	HR	High end range

LO	Lowest wage paid	MTC	Median total compensation	TCC	Total cash compensation
LR	Low end range	MW	Median wage paid	TQ	Third quartile wage
M	Monthly	MWR	Median wage range	W	Weekly
MCC	Median cash compensation	S	See annotated source	Y	Yearly

Helper

Occupation/Type/Industry	Location	Per	Low	Mid	High	Source	Date
Electrician	Charleston-North Charleston MSA, SC	Y	19870 FQ	23230 MW	27070 TQ	USBLS	5/07
Electrician	Columbia MSA, SC	Y	19780 FQ	22640 MW	26460 TQ	USBLS	5/07
Electrician	Florence MSA, SC	Y	16790 FQ	19630 MW	24710 TQ	USBLS	5/07
Electrician	South Dakota	Y	19505 FQ	22532 MW	25253 TQ	SDBLS	7/08-9/08
Electrician	Sioux Falls MSA, SD	Y	21515 FQ	23363 MW	25925 TQ	SDBLS	7/08-9/08
Electrician	Tennessee	Y	20280 FQ	23620 MW	28290 TQ	USBLS	5/07
Electrician	Kingsport-Bristol-Bristol MSA, TN-VA	Y	19840 FQ	23430 MW	28550 TQ	USBLS	5/07
Electrician	Memphis MSA, TN-MS-AR	Y	20400 FQ	23660 MW	28410 TQ	USBLS	5/07
Electrician	Nashville-Davidson-Murfreesboro MSA, TN	Y	20780 FQ	23990 MW	28340 TQ	USBLS	5/07
Electrician	Texas	Y	20330 FQ	24500 MW	29430 TQ	USBLS	5/07
Electrician	Austin-Round Rock MSA, TX	Y	19410 FQ	22920 MW	27620 TQ	USBLS	5/07
Electrician	Beaumont-Port Arthur MSA, TX	Y	23780 FQ	28020 MW	32030 TQ	USBLS	5/07
Electrician	Dallas-Fort Worth-Arlington MSA, TX	Y	22650 FQ	26580 MW	30690 TQ	USBLS	5/07
Electrician	El Paso MSA, TX	Y	14850 FQ	18660 MW	23040 TQ	USBLS	5/07
Electrician	Houston-Sugar Land-Baytown MSA, TX	Y	21190 FQ	26090 MW	30550 TQ	USBLS	5/07
Electrician	San Antonio MSA, TX	Y	19210 FQ	22910 MW	27550 TQ	USBLS	5/07
Electrician	Utah	Y	19930 FQ	23200 MW	26950 TQ	USBLS	5/07
Electrician	Salt Lake City MSA, UT	Y	21080 FQ	24040 MW	27500 TQ	USBLS	5/07
Electrician	Vermont	Y	22090 FQ	26000 MW	28960 TQ	USBLS	5/07
Electrician	Burlington-South Burlington MSA, VT	Y	22950 FQ	25920 MW	28600 TQ	USBLS	5/07
Electrician	Virginia	Y	20780 FQ	24920 MW	29730 TQ	USBLS	5/07
Electrician	Richmond MSA, VA	Y	20270 FQ	23210 MW	27220 TQ	USBLS	5/07
Electrician	Virginia Beach-Norfolk-Newport News MSA, VA-NC	Y	18650 FQ	22990 MW	28300 TQ	USBLS	5/07
Electrician	Washington	H	10.54 FQ	12.58 MW	14.87 TQ	WABLS	3/08
Electrician	Seattle-Tacoma-Bellevue MSA, WA	Y	22470 FQ	26610 MW	30930 TQ	USBLS	5/07
Electrician	West Virginia	Y	21431 FQ	25655 MW	36104 TQ	WVBLS	7/08-9/08
Electrician	Charleston MSA, WV	Y	22470 FQ	33020 MW	36590 TQ	USBLS	5/07
Electrician	Wisconsin	Y	20560 FQ	24930 MW	29670 TQ	USBLS	5/07
Electrician	Milwaukee-Waukesha-West Allis MSA, WI	Y	20850 FQ	23650 MW	28320 TQ	USBLS	5/07
Electrician	Wyoming	Y	23136 FQ	28341 MW	35018 TQ	WYBLS	9/08
Electrician	Puerto Rico	Y	12990 FQ	14870 MW	17590 TQ	USBLS	5/07
Electrician	San Juan-Caguas-Guaynabo MSA, PR	Y	13140 FQ	15200 MW	18010 TQ	USBLS	5/07
Electrician	Virgin Islands	Y	21830 FQ	23820 MW	26210 TQ	USBLS	5/07
Electrician	Guam	Y	17510 FQ	20070 MW	23690 TQ	USBLS	5/07
Extraction Worker	Alabama	Y	23910 FQ	40680 MW	44350 TQ	USBLS	5/07
Extraction Worker	Alaska	Y	40430 FQ	61820 MW	72410 TQ	USBLS	5/07
Extraction Worker	Arizona	Y	20220 FQ	24950 MW	36220 TQ	USBLS	5/07
Extraction Worker	Tucson MSA, AZ	Y	20300 FQ	23950 MW	34210 TQ	USBLS	5/07
Extraction Worker	Arkansas	Y	23300 FQ	26860 MW	30900 TQ	USBLS	5/07
Extraction Worker	California	H	13.95 FQ	18.30 MW	22.78 TQ	CABLS	1/08-3/08
Extraction Worker	Bakersfield MSA, CA	H	15.41 FQ	21.02 MW	23.78 TQ	CABLS	1/08-3/08
Extraction Worker	Los Angeles-Long Beach-Glendale PMSA, CA	H	14.85 FQ	20.78 MW	23.90 TQ	CABLS	1/08-3/08
Extraction Worker	Riverside-San Bernardino-Ontario MSA, CA	H	10.60 FQ	13.05 MW	16.14 TQ	CABLS	1/08-3/08
Extraction Worker	Sacramento-Arden Arcade-Roseville MSA, CA	H	13.28 FQ	14.80 MW	16.90 TQ	CABLS	1/08-3/08
Extraction Worker	Santa Ana-Anaheim-Irvine PMSA, CA	Y	29320 FQ	41610 MW	54390 TQ	USBLS	5/07
Extraction Worker	Colorado	Y	27940 FQ	33020 MW	38590 TQ	USBLS	5/07
Extraction Worker	Denver-Aurora MSA, CO	Y	28410 FQ	31940 MW	39360 TQ	USBLS	5/07
Extraction Worker	Connecticut	H	11.12 AE	12.43 MW		CTBLS	1/08-3/08
Extraction Worker	Washington-Arlington-Alexandria MSA, DC-VA-MD-WV	Y	31020 FQ	36140 MW	40680 TQ	USBLS	5/07
Extraction Worker	Florida	Y	18670 FQ	22160 MW	25650 TQ	USBLS	5/07
Extraction Worker	Miami-Fort Lauderdale-Miami Beach MSA, FL	Y	17100 FQ	18600 MW	21480 TQ	USBLS	5/07
Extraction Worker	Georgia	Y	21260 FQ	28290 MW	36840 TQ	USBLS	5/07
Extraction Worker	Hawaii	Y	33550 FQ	36950 MW	40330 TQ	USBLS	5/07

AE Average entry wage	**AW** Average wage paid	**FQ** First quartile wage	**LO** Lowest wage paid	**MTC** Median total compensation	**TCC** Total cash compensation
AER Average entry range	**AWR** Average wage range	**H** Hourly	**LR** Low end range	**MW** Median wage paid	**TQ** Third quartile wage
AEX Average experienced wage	**AXR** Average experienced range	**HI** Highest wage paid	**M** Monthly	**MWR** Median wage range	**W** Weekly
ATC Average total compensation	**D** Daily	**HR** High end range	**MCC** Median cash compensation	**S** See annotated source	**Y** Yearly

Helper

Occupation/Type/Industry	Location	Per	Low	Mid	High	Source	Date
Extraction Worker	Honolulu MSA, HI	Y	33550 FQ	36950 MW	40330 TQ	USBLS	5/07
Extraction Worker	Idaho	Y	26990 FQ	29500 MW	32730 TQ	USBLS	5/07
Extraction Worker	Illinois	Y	23240 FQ	32330 MW	43000 TQ	USBLS	5/07
Extraction Worker	Chicago-Naperville-Joliet MSA, IL-IN-WI	Y	25950 FQ	34640 MW	61450 TQ	USBLS	5/07
Extraction Worker	Indiana	Y	17100 FQ	26560 MW	38610 TQ	USBLS	5/07
Extraction Worker	Indianapolis-Carmel MSA, IN	Y	32770 FQ	34830 MW	36890 TQ	USBLS	5/07
Extraction Worker	Kansas	Y	22920 FQ	25000 MW	27690 TQ	USBLS	5/07
Extraction Worker	Wichita MSA, KS	Y	22280 FQ	23940 MW	25590 TQ	USBLS	5/07
Extraction Worker	Kentucky	Y	26620 FQ	34243 MW	41103 TQ	KYBLS	2008
Extraction Worker	Louisville-Jefferson County MSA, KY-IN	Y	27470 FQ	31170 MW	36070 TQ	USBLS	5/07
Extraction Worker	Louisiana	H	11.96 FQ	15.20 MW	17.86 TQ	LABLS	1/08-3/08
Extraction Worker	New Orleans-Metairie-Kenner MSA, LA	Y	30850 FQ	33430 MW	36110 TQ	USBLS	5/07
Extraction Worker	Maryland	Y		30675 MW		MDBLS	3/08
Extraction Worker	Massachusetts	Y	21440 FQ	24490 MW	29900 TQ	USBLS	5/07
Extraction Worker	Michigan	Y	26170 FQ	32060 MW	43790 TQ	USBLS	5/07
Extraction Worker	Detroit-Warren-Livonia MSA, MI	Y	27660 FQ	30330 MW	32990 TQ	USBLS	5/07
Extraction Worker	Minnesota	Y	26620 FQ	34156 MW	41659 TQ	MNBLS	10/08-12/08
Extraction Worker	Mississippi	Y	21600 FQ	24600 MW	29700 TQ	USBLS	5/07
Extraction Worker	Missouri	Y	17960 FQ	20030 MW	32640 TQ	USBLS	5/07
Extraction Worker	St. Louis MSA, MO-IL	Y	31510 FQ	36540 MW	41140 TQ	USBLS	5/07
Extraction Worker	Montana	Y	25390 FQ	34890 MW	41300 TQ	USBLS	5/07
Extraction Worker	Nevada	H	13.81 FQ	16.71 MW	19.48 TQ	NVBLS	5/08
Extraction Worker	New Hampshire	H	11.75 AE	15.18 MW	18.01 AEX	NHBLS	6/08
Extraction Worker	New Jersey	Y	27790 FQ	30670 MW	34920 TQ	USBLS	5/07
Extraction Worker	New Mexico	Y	26200 FQ	30670 MW	37690 TQ	USBLS	5/07
Extraction Worker	New York	Y	24300 FQ	28940 MW	36070 TQ	USBLS	5/07
Extraction Worker	Albany-Schenectady-Troy MSA, NY	Y	24930 FQ	27270 MW	29600 TQ	USBLS	5/07
Extraction Worker	New York-Northern New Jersey-Long Island MSA, NY-NJ-PA	Y	23750 FQ	30100 MW	37840 TQ	USBLS	5/07
Extraction Worker	North Carolina	Y	20890 FQ	22770 MW	26130 TQ	USBLS	5/07
Extraction Worker	Charlotte-Gastonia-Concord MSA, NC-SC	Y	29160 FQ	32940 MW	36120 TQ	USBLS	5/07
Extraction Worker	North Dakota	Y	25260 FQ	28750 MW	34760 TQ	USBLS	5/07
Extraction Worker	Ohio	Y	25780 FQ	30440 MW	41050 TQ	USBLS	5/07
Extraction Worker	Columbus MSA, OH	Y	27090 FQ	29540 MW	31990 TQ	USBLS	5/07
Extraction Worker	Oklahoma	Y	25230 FQ	31460 MW	44330 TQ	USBLS	5/07
Extraction Worker	Oklahoma City MSA, OK	Y	27320 FQ	33060 MW	44070 TQ	USBLS	5/07
Extraction Worker	Tulsa MSA, OK	Y	23440 FQ	29210 MW	32640 TQ	USBLS	5/07
Extraction Worker	Portland-Vancouver-Beaverton MSA, OR-WA	Y	26530 FQ	28450 MW	30380 TQ	USBLS	5/07
Extraction Worker	Pennsylvania	Y	21370 FQ	28710 MW	35680 TQ	USBLS	5/07
Extraction Worker	Philadelphia-Camden-Wilmington MSA, PA-NJ-DE-MD	Y	23010 FQ	27140 MW	31320 TQ	USBLS	5/07
Extraction Worker	Pittsburgh MSA, PA	Y	19290 FQ	29380 MW	42090 TQ	USBLS	5/07
Extraction Worker	Rhode Island	Y	25520 FQ	27230 MW	28940 TQ	USBLS	5/07
Extraction Worker	Providence-Fall River-Warwick MSA, RI-MA	Y	25520 FQ	27230 MW	28940 TQ	USBLS	5/07
Extraction Worker	South Carolina	Y	19770 FQ	22500 MW	26580 TQ	USBLS	5/07
Extraction Worker	Columbia MSA, SC	Y	20580 FQ	22780 MW	28250 TQ	USBLS	5/07
Extraction Worker	Tennessee	Y	20880 FQ	24790 MW	29930 TQ	USBLS	5/07
Extraction Worker	Memphis MSA, TN-MS-AR	Y	21260 FQ	30290 MW	45800 TQ	USBLS	5/07
Extraction Worker	Texas	Y	21430 FQ	25530 MW	32450 TQ	USBLS	5/07
Extraction Worker	Dallas-Fort Worth-Arlington MSA, TX	Y	21170 FQ	23070 MW	25740 TQ	USBLS	5/07
Extraction Worker	Houston-Sugar Land-Baytown MSA, TX	Y	21840 FQ	26360 MW	33780 TQ	USBLS	5/07
Extraction Worker	San Antonio MSA, TX	Y	20930 FQ	24040 MW	29710 TQ	USBLS	5/07
Extraction Worker	Utah	Y	24340 FQ	28560 MW	36300 TQ	USBLS	5/07
Extraction Worker	Vermont	Y	34480 FQ	41050 MW	44500 TQ	USBLS	5/07
Extraction Worker	Virginia	Y	23690 FQ	27230 MW	30450 TQ	USBLS	5/07
Extraction Worker	Richmond MSA, VA	Y	26840 FQ	28630 MW	30420 TQ	USBLS	5/07
Extraction Worker	Washington	H	12.99 FQ	14.18 MW	15.48 TQ	WABLS	3/08
Extraction Worker	West Virginia	Y	30752 FQ	39519 MW	44174 TQ	WVBLS	7/08-9/08
Extraction Worker	Charleston MSA, WV	Y	35600 FQ	39780 MW	43670 TQ	USBLS	5/07

AE Average entry wage	**AW** Average wage paid	**FQ** First quartile wage	**LO** Lowest wage paid	**MTC** Median total compensation	**TCC** Total cash compensation
AER Average entry range	**AWR** Average wage range	**H** Hourly	**LR** Low end range	**MW** Median wage paid	**TQ** Third quartile wage
AEX Average experienced wage	**AXR** Average experienced range	**HI** Highest wage paid	**M** Monthly	**MWR** Median wage range	**W** Weekly
ATC Average total compensation	**D** Daily	**HR** High end range	**MCC** Median cash compensation	**S** See annotated source	**Y** Yearly

Occupation/Type/Industry	Location	Per	Low	Mid	High	Source	Date
Helper							
Extraction Worker	Wisconsin	Y	19030 FQ	21600 MW	30190 TQ	USBLS	5/07
Extraction Worker	Wyoming	Y	26026 FQ	38290 MW	48944 TQ	WYBLS	9/08
Extraction Worker	Puerto Rico	Y	12860 FQ	14430 MW	25050 TQ	USBLS	5/07
Extraction Worker	San Juan-Caguas-Guaynabo MSA, PR	Y	13040 FQ	14880 MW	25990 TQ	USBLS	5/07
Installation and Repair Worker	Alabama	Y	14890 FQ	18460 MW	23550 TQ	USBLS	5/07
Installation and Repair Worker	Birmingham-Hoover MSA, AL	Y	14640 FQ	18110 MW	23090 TQ	USBLS	5/07
Installation and Repair Worker	Mobile MSA, AL	Y	17900 FQ	21470 MW	24880 TQ	USBLS	5/07
Installation and Repair Worker	Montgomery MSA, AL	Y	17300 FQ	21170 MW	26090 TQ	USBLS	5/07
Installation and Repair Worker	Alaska	Y	24560 FQ	31140 MW	43910 TQ	USBLS	5/07
Installation and Repair Worker	Anchorage MSA, AK	Y	26290 FQ	35440 MW	48300 TQ	USBLS	5/07
Installation and Repair Worker	Arizona	Y	19980 FQ	24250 MW	30550 TQ	USBLS	5/07
Installation and Repair Worker	Flagstaff MSA, AZ	Y	15030 FQ	20080 MW	27360 TQ	USBLS	5/07
Installation and Repair Worker	Phoenix-Mesa-Scottsdale MSA, AZ	Y	20670 FQ	23980 MW	30210 TQ	USBLS	5/07
Installation and Repair Worker	Tucson MSA, AZ	Y	18020 FQ	22840 MW	28640 TQ	USBLS	5/07
Installation and Repair Worker	Arkansas	Y	17090 FQ	20630 MW	24810 TQ	USBLS	5/07
Installation and Repair Worker	Little Rock-North Little Rock MSA, AR	Y	17030 FQ	21400 MW	26580 TQ	USBLS	5/07
Installation and Repair Worker	California	H	9.22 FQ	11.51 MW	14.59 TQ	CABLS	1/08-3/08
Installation and Repair Worker	Fresno MSA, CA	H	8.00 FQ	8.72 MW	11.06 TQ	CABLS	1/08-3/08
Installation and Repair Worker	Los Angeles-Long Beach-Glendale PMSA, CA	H	9.21 FQ	11.37 MW	14.61 TQ	CABLS	1/08-3/08
Installation and Repair Worker	Modesto MSA, CA	H	9.47 FQ	11.83 MW	15.32 TQ	CABLS	1/08-3/08
Installation and Repair Worker	Oakland-Fremont-Hayward MSA, CA	H	9.48 FQ	13.46 MW	16.51 TQ	CABLS	1/08-3/08
Installation and Repair Worker	Riverside-San Bernardino-Ontario MSA, CA	H	8.67 FQ	10.42 MW	13.42 TQ	CABLS	1/08-3/08
Installation and Repair Worker	Sacramento-Arden Arcade-Roseville MSA, CA	H	9.56 FQ	11.44 MW	14.05 TQ	CABLS	1/08-3/08
Installation and Repair Worker	San Diego-Carlsbad-San Marcos MSA, CA	H	9.51 FQ	11.33 MW	13.84 TQ	CABLS	1/08-3/08
Installation and Repair Worker	San Francisco-San Mateo-Redwood PMSA, CA	H	10.68 FQ	13.30 MW	15.44 TQ	CABLS	1/08-3/08
Installation and Repair Worker	San Jose-Sunnyvale-Santa Clara MSA, CA	H	12.56 FQ	16.19 MW	22.27 TQ	CABLS	1/08-3/08
Installation and Repair Worker	Santa Ana-Anaheim-Irvine PMSA, CA	Y	18970 FQ	22920 MW	28330 TQ	USBLS	5/07
Installation and Repair Worker	Santa Rosa-Petaluma MSA, CA	H	9.95 FQ	12.99 MW	14.87 TQ	CABLS	1/08-3/08
Installation and Repair Worker	Colorado	Y	20090 FQ	25720 MW	35440 TQ	USBLS	5/07
Installation and Repair Worker	Denver-Aurora MSA, CO	Y	20460 FQ	26890 MW	36890 TQ	USBLS	5/07
Installation and Repair Worker	Connecticut	H	10.17 AE	14.13 MW		CTBLS	1/08-3/08
Installation and Repair Worker	Bridgeport-Stamford-Norwalk MSA, CT	Y	23060 FQ	30590 MW	40910 TQ	USBLS	5/07
Installation and Repair Worker	Hartford-West Hartford-East Hartford MSA, CT	Y	21840 FQ	28560 MW	35530 TQ	USBLS	5/07
Installation and Repair Worker	Delaware	Y	20290 FQ	25390 MW	30880 TQ	USBLS	5/07
Installation and Repair Worker	Wilmington PMSA, DE-MD-NJ	Y	21370 FQ	26740 MW	32440 TQ	USBLS	5/07
Installation and Repair Worker	District of Columbia	Y	31150 FQ	37990 MW	44270 TQ	USBLS	5/07
Installation and Repair Worker	Washington-Arlington-Alexandria MSA, DC-VA-MD-WV	Y	22910 FQ	29030 MW	35280 TQ	USBLS	5/07
Installation and Repair Worker	Florida	Y	17950 FQ	21680 MW	25620 TQ	USBLS	5/07
Installation and Repair Worker	Fort Lauderdale-Pompano Beach-Deerfield Beach PMSA, FL	Y	16720 FQ	20500 MW	27890 TQ	USBLS	5/07
Installation and Repair Worker	Jacksonville MSA, FL	Y	16740 FQ	20580 MW	23290 TQ	USBLS	5/07
Installation and Repair Worker	Lakeland MSA, FL	Y	16670 FQ	19390 MW	25820 TQ	USBLS	5/07
Installation and Repair Worker	Miami-Fort Lauderdale-Miami Beach MSA, FL	Y	16960 FQ	21490 MW	26390 TQ	USBLS	5/07
Installation and Repair Worker	Orlando-Kissimmee MSA, FL	Y	19190 FQ	23600 MW	28750 TQ	USBLS	5/07
Installation and Repair Worker	Tampa-St. Petersburg-Clearwater MSA, FL	Y	19840 FQ	22580 MW	25240 TQ	USBLS	5/07
Installation and Repair Worker	West Palm Beach-Boca Raton-Boynton Beach PMSA, FL	Y	19340 FQ	22410 MW	25310 TQ	USBLS	5/07
Installation and Repair Worker	Georgia	Y	17480 FQ	22040 MW	28030 TQ	USBLS	5/07
Installation and Repair Worker	Atlanta-Sandy Springs-Marietta MSA, GA	Y	18520 FQ	23880 MW	29920 TQ	USBLS	5/07
Installation and Repair Worker	Hawaii	Y	21350 FQ	27600 MW	35500 TQ	USBLS	5/07
Installation and Repair Worker	Honolulu MSA, HI	Y	20210 FQ	26240 MW	34160 TQ	USBLS	5/07

AE Average entry wage	**AW** Average wage paid	**FQ** First quartile wage	**LO** Lowest wage paid	**MTC** Median total compensation	**TCC** Total cash compensation
AER Average entry range	**AWR** Average wage range	**H** Hourly	**LR** Low end range	**MW** Median wage paid	**TQ** Third quartile wage
AEX Average experienced wage	**AXR** Average experienced range	**HI** Highest wage paid	**M** Monthly	**MWR** Median wage range	**W** Weekly
ATC Average total compensation	**D** Daily	**HR** High end range	**MCC** Median cash compensation	**S** See annotated source	**Y** Yearly

Occupation/Type/Industry	Location	Per	Low	Mid	High	Source	Date
Helper							
Installation and Repair Worker	Idaho	Y	16900 FQ	22900 MW	32240 TQ	USBLS	5/07
Installation and Repair Worker	Boise City-Nampa MSA, ID	Y	17660 FQ	21900 MW	28930 TQ	USBLS	5/07
Installation and Repair Worker	Idaho Falls MSA, ID	Y	18840 FQ	24630 MW	28070 TQ	USBLS	5/07
Installation and Repair Worker	Illinois	Y	20190 FQ	26650 MW	36250 TQ	USBLS	5/07
Installation and Repair Worker	Champaign-Urbana MSA, IL	Y	15640 FQ	19420 MW	27210 TQ	USBLS	5/07
Installation and Repair Worker	Chicago-Naperville-Joliet MSA, IL-IN-WI	Y	21420 FQ	27890 MW	37590 TQ	USBLS	5/07
Installation and Repair Worker	Peoria MSA, IL	Y	20360 FQ	26670 MW	30370 TQ	USBLS	5/07
Installation and Repair Worker	Indiana	Y	19100 FQ	23810 MW	30440 TQ	USBLS	5/07
Installation and Repair Worker	Evansville MSA, IN-KY	Y	19930 FQ	23240 MW	29430 TQ	USBLS	5/07
Installation and Repair Worker	Gary PMSA, IN	Y	18460 FQ	23360 MW	30120 TQ	USBLS	5/07
Installation and Repair Worker	Indianapolis-Carmel MSA, IN	Y	21050 FQ	25110 MW	30640 TQ	USBLS	5/07
Installation and Repair Worker	Iowa	Y	18150 FQ	22230 MW	26150 TQ	USBLS	5/07
Installation and Repair Worker	Davenport-Moline-Rock Island MSA, IA-IL	Y	20810 FQ	26170 MW	31730 TQ	USBLS	5/07
Installation and Repair Worker	Des Moines-West Des Moines MSA, IA	Y	18250 FQ	24040 MW	27400 TQ	USBLS	5/07
Installation and Repair Worker	Kansas	Y	16980 FQ	19820 MW	26310 TQ	USBLS	5/07
Installation and Repair Worker	Wichita MSA, KS	Y	16750 FQ	18710 MW	21800 TQ	USBLS	5/07
Installation and Repair Worker	Kentucky	Y	17923 FQ	22581 MW	27086 TQ	KYBLS	2008
Installation and Repair Worker	Louisville-Jefferson County MSA, KY-IN	Y	20920 FQ	25100 MW	32380 TQ	USBLS	5/07
Installation and Repair Worker	Louisiana	H	8.07 FQ	10.27 MW	12.97 TQ	LABLS	1/08-3/08
Installation and Repair Worker	Baton Rouge MSA, LA	Y	20340 FQ	24380 MW	29320 TQ	USBLS	5/07
Installation and Repair Worker	Lake Charles MSA, LA	Y	14460 FQ	20900 MW	27840 TQ	USBLS	5/07
Installation and Repair Worker	New Orleans-Metairie-Kenner MSA, LA	Y	16930 FQ	21880 MW	27720 TQ	USBLS	5/07
Installation and Repair Worker	Maine	Y	15980 FQ	20870 MW	26650 TQ	USBLS	5/07
Installation and Repair Worker	Portland-South Portland-Biddeford MSA, ME	Y	20590 FQ	23610 MW	28620 TQ	USBLS	5/07
Installation and Repair Worker	Maryland	Y		25750 MW		MDBLS	3/08
Installation and Repair Worker	Baltimore-Towson MSA, MD	Y	18500 FQ	23420 MW	30790 TQ	USBLS	5/07
Installation and Repair Worker	Bethesda-Gaithersburg-Frederick PMSA, MD	Y	21610 FQ	27620 MW	31740 TQ	USBLS	5/07
Installation and Repair Worker	Massachusetts	Y	21130 FQ	26050 MW	33390 TQ	USBLS	5/07
Installation and Repair Worker	Boston-Cambridge-Quincy NECTA, MA	Y	21180 FQ	27470 MW	34530 TQ	USBLS	5/07
Installation and Repair Worker	New Bedford MSA, MA	Y	23500 FQ	28030 MW	31760 TQ	USBLS	5/07
Installation and Repair Worker	Worcester MSA, MA-CT	Y	17990 FQ	22020 MW	28350 TQ	USBLS	5/07
Installation and Repair Worker	Michigan	Y	19140 FQ	24660 MW	33320 TQ	USBLS	5/07
Installation and Repair Worker	Detroit-Warren-Livonia MSA, MI	Y	20500 FQ	24810 MW	32850 TQ	USBLS	5/07
Installation and Repair Worker	Grand Rapids-Wyoming MSA, MI	Y	19480 FQ	26620 MW	34990 TQ	USBLS	5/07
Installation and Repair Worker	Lansing-East Lansing MSA, MI	Y	19860 FQ	24900 MW	33730 TQ	USBLS	5/07
Installation and Repair Worker	Warren-Troy-Farmington Hills PMSA, MI	Y	19740 FQ	24130 MW	30690 TQ	USBLS	5/07
Installation and Repair Worker	Minnesota	Y	19720 FQ	24608 MW	32475 TQ	MNBLS	10/08-12/08
Installation and Repair Worker	Duluth-Superior MSA, MN-WI	Y	19426 FQ	24073 MW	29202 TQ	MNBLS	10/08-12/08
Installation and Repair Worker	Minneapolis-Saint Paul MSA, MN-WI	Y	21692 FQ	26842 MW	36985 TQ	MNBLS	10/08-12/08
Installation and Repair Worker	Rochester MSA, MN	Y	22073 FQ	24350 MW	29347 TQ	MNBLS	10/08-12/08
Installation and Repair Worker	Mississippi	Y	17170 FQ	21530 MW	25720 TQ	USBLS	5/07
Installation and Repair Worker	Jackson MSA, MS	Y	19590 FQ	23030 MW	27580 TQ	USBLS	5/07
Installation and Repair Worker	Missouri	Y	18500 FQ	23530 MW	30250 TQ	USBLS	5/07
Installation and Repair Worker	Kansas City MSA, MO-KS	Y	21920 FQ	27240 MW	32770 TQ	USBLS	5/07
Installation and Repair Worker	St. Louis MSA, MO-IL	Y	20470 FQ	24860 MW	31250 TQ	USBLS	5/07
Installation and Repair Worker	Montana	Y	17940 FQ	21550 MW	26770 TQ	USBLS	5/07
Installation and Repair Worker	Billings MSA, MT	Y	17100 FQ	18980 MW	27660 TQ	USBLS	5/07
Installation and Repair Worker	Nebraska	Y	19150 FQ	21800 MW	25340 TQ	USBLS	5/07
Installation and Repair Worker	Omaha-Council Bluffs MSA, NE-IA	Y	20050 FQ	21920 MW	23830 TQ	USBLS	5/07
Installation and Repair Worker	Nevada	H	10.85 FQ	14.23 MW	18.32 TQ	NVBLS	5/08
Installation and Repair Worker	Carson City MSA, NV	H	8.89 FQ	10.59 MW	15.17 TQ	NVBLS	5/08
Installation and Repair Worker	Las Vegas-Paradise MSA, NV	H	11.88 FQ	14.56 MW	17.72 TQ	NVBLS	5/08
Installation and Repair Worker	New Hampshire	H	8.24 AE	11.69 MW	13.23 AEX	NHBLS	6/08
Installation and Repair Worker	Manchester MSA, NH	Y	25750 FQ	28620 MW	31340 TQ	USBLS	5/07
Installation and Repair Worker	Nashua NECTA, NH-MA	Y	13990 FQ	20240 MW	28900 TQ	USBLS	5/07
Installation and Repair Worker	New Jersey	Y	20060 FQ	25090 MW	32490 TQ	USBLS	5/07
Installation and Repair Worker	Atlantic City MSA, NJ	Y	19340 FQ	22750 MW	29870 TQ	USBLS	5/07
Installation and Repair Worker	Camden PMSA, NJ	Y	20110 FQ	24610 MW	30380 TQ	USBLS	5/07

AE Average entry wage	**AW** Average wage paid	**FQ** First quartile wage	**LO** Lowest wage paid	**MTC** Median total compensation	**TCC** Total cash compensation
AER Average entry range	**AWR** Average wage range	**H** Hourly	**LR** Low end range	**MW** Median wage paid	**TQ** Third quartile wage
AEX Average experienced wage	**AXR** Average experienced range	**HI** Highest wage paid	**M** Monthly	**MWR** Median wage range	**W** Weekly
ATC Average total compensation	**D** Daily	**HR** High end range	**MCC** Median cash compensation	**S** See annotated source	**Y** Yearly

Helper

Occupation/Type/Industry	Location	Per	Low	Mid	High	Source	Date
Installation and Repair Worker	Edison PMSA, NJ	Y	19550 FQ	24640 MW	32170 TQ	USBLS	5/07
Installation and Repair Worker	Newark-Union PMSA, NJ-PA	Y	20160 FQ	26630 MW	32770 TQ	USBLS	5/07
Installation and Repair Worker	Trenton-Ewing MSA, NJ	Y	21260 FQ	24000 MW	32550 TQ	USBLS	5/07
Installation and Repair Worker	New Mexico	Y	16790 FQ	20700 MW	24570 TQ	USBLS	5/07
Installation and Repair Worker	Albuquerque MSA, NM	Y	16560 FQ	21060 MW	25210 TQ	USBLS	5/07
Installation and Repair Worker	New York	Y	20790 FQ	28230 MW	37610 TQ	USBLS	5/07
Installation and Repair Worker	Albany-Schenectady-Troy MSA, NY	Y	17990 FQ	24020 MW	31220 TQ	USBLS	5/07
Installation and Repair Worker	Buffalo-Niagara Falls MSA, NY	Y	19400 FQ	24110 MW	32570 TQ	USBLS	5/07
Installation and Repair Worker	Nassau-Suffolk PMSA, NY	Y	20090 FQ	25210 MW	32960 TQ	USBLS	5/07
Installation and Repair Worker	New York-Northern New Jersey-Long Island MSA, NY-NJ-PA	Y	21380 FQ	29350 MW	39720 TQ	USBLS	5/07
Installation and Repair Worker	Utica-Rome MSA, NY	Y	18300 FQ	23950 MW	31190 TQ	USBLS	5/07
Installation and Repair Worker	North Carolina	Y	18330 FQ	22450 MW	27480 TQ	USBLS	5/07
Installation and Repair Worker	Charlotte-Gastonia-Concord MSA, NC-SC	Y	20350 FQ	24200 MW	28770 TQ	USBLS	5/07
Installation and Repair Worker	Raleigh-Cary MSA, NC	Y	16090 FQ	21530 MW	26890 TQ	USBLS	5/07
Installation and Repair Worker	North Dakota	Y	14580 FQ	19630 MW	25520 TQ	USBLS	5/07
Installation and Repair Worker	Fargo MSA, ND-MN	Y	15480 FQ	21710 MW	25860 TQ	USBLS	5/07
Installation and Repair Worker	Ohio	Y	17190 FQ	21690 MW	28210 TQ	USBLS	5/07
Installation and Repair Worker	Cincinnati-Middletown MSA, OH-KY-IN	Y	16200 FQ	20390 MW	26600 TQ	USBLS	5/07
Installation and Repair Worker	Cleveland-Elyria-Mentor MSA, OH	Y	18320 FQ	23220 MW	29030 TQ	USBLS	5/07
Installation and Repair Worker	Columbus MSA, OH	Y	20180 FQ	25180 MW	31550 TQ	USBLS	5/07
Installation and Repair Worker	Dayton MSA, OH	Y	20310 FQ	23570 MW	27380 TQ	USBLS	5/07
Installation and Repair Worker	Mansfield MSA, OH	Y	19820 FQ	23490 MW	32990 TQ	USBLS	5/07
Installation and Repair Worker	Oklahoma	Y	16920 FQ	20680 MW	25780 TQ	USBLS	5/07
Installation and Repair Worker	Oklahoma City MSA, OK	Y	17760 FQ	21870 MW	27150 TQ	USBLS	5/07
Installation and Repair Worker	Tulsa MSA, OK	Y	17560 FQ	20860 MW	25160 TQ	USBLS	5/07
Installation and Repair Worker	Oregon	H	9.95 FQ	12.30 MW	15.22 TQ	ORBLS	5/08
Installation and Repair Worker	Portland-Vancouver-Beaverton MSA, OR-WA	Y	20710 FQ	25980 MW	32020 TQ	USBLS	5/07
Installation and Repair Worker	Pennsylvania	Y	18880 FQ	23910 MW	30740 TQ	USBLS	5/07
Installation and Repair Worker	Allentown-Bethlehem-Easton MSA, PA-NJ	Y	18200 FQ	23410 MW	28430 TQ	USBLS	5/07
Installation and Repair Worker	Philadelphia-Camden-Wilmington MSA, PA-NJ-DE-MD	Y	20510 FQ	25010 MW	32710 TQ	USBLS	5/07
Installation and Repair Worker	Pittsburgh MSA, PA	Y	18500 FQ	24870 MW	31490 TQ	USBLS	5/07
Installation and Repair Worker	Rhode Island	Y	20860 FQ	24110 MW	28410 TQ	USBLS	5/07
Installation and Repair Worker	Providence-Fall River-Warwick MSA, RI-MA	Y	21010 FQ	24560 MW	29000 TQ	USBLS	5/07
Installation and Repair Worker	South Carolina	Y	16870 FQ	20140 MW	25860 TQ	USBLS	5/07
Installation and Repair Worker	Charleston-North Charleston MSA, SC	Y	16810 FQ	19860 MW	23020 TQ	USBLS	5/07
Installation and Repair Worker	Columbia MSA, SC	Y	16010 FQ	18590 MW	22780 TQ	USBLS	5/07
Installation and Repair Worker	South Dakota	Y	16658 FQ	17811 MW	18959 TQ	SDBLS	7/08-9/08
Installation and Repair Worker	Tennessee	Y	18840 FQ	23730 MW	30600 TQ	USBLS	5/07
Installation and Repair Worker	Memphis MSA, TN-MS-AR	Y	19730 FQ	24530 MW	31180 TQ	USBLS	5/07
Installation and Repair Worker	Nashville-Davidson-Murfreesboro MSA, TN	Y	19600 FQ	26210 MW	34100 TQ	USBLS	5/07
Installation and Repair Worker	Texas	Y	17230 FQ	21150 MW	26060 TQ	USBLS	5/07
Installation and Repair Worker	Austin-Round Rock MSA, TX	Y	20220 FQ	23610 MW	27450 TQ	USBLS	5/07
Installation and Repair Worker	Dallas-Fort Worth-Arlington MSA, TX	Y	17580 FQ	21400 MW	27980 TQ	USBLS	5/07
Installation and Repair Worker	El Paso MSA, TX	Y	16620 FQ	19210 MW	24550 TQ	USBLS	5/07
Installation and Repair Worker	Houston-Sugar Land-Baytown MSA, TX	Y	18680 FQ	23190 MW	28240 TQ	USBLS	5/07
Installation and Repair Worker	San Antonio MSA, TX	Y	17360 FQ	20630 MW	24110 TQ	USBLS	5/07
Installation and Repair Worker	Utah	Y	17910 FQ	21280 MW	26460 TQ	USBLS	5/07
Installation and Repair Worker	Salt Lake City MSA, UT	Y	19590 FQ	22890 MW	30470 TQ	USBLS	5/07
Installation and Repair Worker	Vermont	Y	19230 FQ	23790 MW	28550 TQ	USBLS	5/07
Installation and Repair Worker	Burlington-South Burlington MSA, VT	Y	20670 FQ	25520 MW	29080 TQ	USBLS	5/07
Installation and Repair Worker	Virginia	Y	19940 FQ	24810 MW	30310 TQ	USBLS	5/07
Installation and Repair Worker	Richmond MSA, VA	Y	20120 FQ	24000 MW	28310 TQ	USBLS	5/07
Installation and Repair Worker	Virginia Beach-Norfolk-Newport News MSA, VA-NC	Y	18420 FQ	22200 MW	27140 TQ	USBLS	5/07

AE	Average entry wage	**AW**	Average wage paid	**FQ**	First quartile wage
AER	Average entry range	**AWR**	Average wage range	**H**	Hourly
AEX	Average experienced wage	**AXR**	Average experienced range	**HI**	Highest wage paid
ATC	Average total compensation	**D**	Daily	**HR**	High end range

LO	Lowest wage paid	**MTC**	Median total compensation	**TCC**	Total cash compensation
LR	Low end range	**MW**	Median wage paid	**TQ**	Third quartile wage
M	Monthly	**MWR**	Median wage range	**W**	Weekly
MCC	Median cash compensation	**S**	See annotated source	**Y**	Yearly

Helper

Occupation/Type/Industry	Location	Per	Low	Mid	High	Source	Date
Helper							
Installation and Repair Worker	Washington	H	9.44 FQ	11.38 MW	14.36 TQ	WABLS	3/08
Installation and Repair Worker	Seattle-Tacoma-Bellevue MSA, WA	Y	21100 FQ	25720 MW	31020 TQ	USBLS	5/07
Installation and Repair Worker	West Virginia	Y	15142 FQ	18701 MW	26838 TQ	WVBLS	7/08-9/08
Installation and Repair Worker	Charleston MSA, WV	Y	14590 FQ	18060 MW	29040 TQ	USBLS	5/07
Installation and Repair Worker	Wisconsin	Y	17300 FQ	21360 MW	28010 TQ	USBLS	5/07
Installation and Repair Worker	Green Bay MSA, WI	Y	19390 FQ	23080 MW	27670 TQ	USBLS	5/07
Installation and Repair Worker	Milwaukee-Waukesha-West Allis MSA, WI	Y	18020 FQ	22070 MW	29580 TQ	USBLS	5/07
Installation and Repair Worker	Wyoming	Y	17954 FQ	21339 MW	31450 TQ	WYBLS	9/08
Installation and Repair Worker	Cheyenne MSA, WY	Y	15842 FQ	20570 MW	25604 TQ	WYBLS	9/08
Installation and Repair Worker	Puerto Rico	Y	13230 FQ	15580 MW	23160 TQ	USBLS	5/07
Installation and Repair Worker	San Juan-Caguas-Guaynabo MSA, PR	Y	13570 FQ	17100 MW	26390 TQ	USBLS	5/07
Installation and Repair Worker	Virgin Islands	Y	20160 FQ	25700 MW	36500 TQ	USBLS	5/07
Installation and Repair Worker	Guam	Y	14260 FQ	18250 MW	21820 TQ	USBLS	5/07
Mason, Tile and Marble Setter	Alabama	Y	17050 FQ	20150 MW	24420 TQ	USBLS	5/07
Mason, Tile and Marble Setter	Birmingham-Hoover MSA, AL	Y	17090 FQ	19820 MW	24270 TQ	USBLS	5/07
Mason, Tile and Marble Setter	Arizona	Y	19860 FQ	24230 MW	29210 TQ	USBLS	5/07
Mason, Tile and Marble Setter	Phoenix-Mesa-Scottsdale MSA, AZ	Y	19900 FQ	24990 MW	29520 TQ	USBLS	5/07
Mason, Tile and Marble Setter	Tucson MSA, AZ	Y	19120 FQ	25440 MW	29940 TQ	USBLS	5/07
Mason, Tile and Marble Setter	Arkansas	Y	19830 FQ	21980 MW	24120 TQ	USBLS	5/07
Mason, Tile and Marble Setter	Fayetteville-Springdale-Rogers MSA, AR-MO	Y	21270 FQ	23240 MW	25220 TQ	USBLS	5/07
Mason, Tile and Marble Setter	Little Rock-North Little Rock MSA, AR	Y	20760 FQ	22530 MW	24550 TQ	USBLS	5/07
Mason, Tile and Marble Setter	California	H	11.23 FQ	13.92 MW	17.71 TQ	CABLS	1/08-3/08
Mason, Tile and Marble Setter	Los Angeles-Long Beach-Glendale PMSA, CA	H	9.63 FQ	11.48 MW	14.84 TQ	CABLS	1/08-3/08
Mason, Tile and Marble Setter	Oakland-Fremont-Hayward MSA, CA	H	13.06 FQ	15.28 MW	18.35 TQ	CABLS	1/08-3/08
Mason, Tile and Marble Setter	Riverside-San Bernardino-Ontario MSA, CA	H	12.84 FQ	15.61 MW	19.40 TQ	CABLS	1/08-3/08
Mason, Tile and Marble Setter	Sacramento-Arden Arcade-Roseville MSA, CA	H	12.88 FQ	16.02 MW	21.83 TQ	CABLS	1/08-3/08
Mason, Tile and Marble Setter	San Diego-Carlsbad-San Marcos MSA, CA	H	11.10 FQ	13.79 MW	15.85 TQ	CABLS	1/08-3/08
Mason, Tile and Marble Setter	San Francisco-San Mateo-Redwood PMSA, CA	H	12.97 FQ	15.04 MW	20.49 TQ	CABLS	1/08-3/08
Mason, Tile and Marble Setter	San Jose-Sunnyvale-Santa Clara MSA, CA	H	12.95 FQ	15.33 MW	21.26 TQ	CABLS	1/08-3/08
Mason, Tile and Marble Setter	Santa Ana-Anaheim-Irvine PMSA, CA	Y	25760 FQ	31160 MW	44630 TQ	USBLS	5/07
Mason, Tile and Marble Setter	Colorado	Y	23750 FQ	27790 MW	32150 TQ	USBLS	5/07
Mason, Tile and Marble Setter	Denver-Aurora MSA, CO	Y	23540 FQ	28510 MW	32860 TQ	USBLS	5/07
Mason, Tile and Marble Setter	Connecticut	H	13.31 AE	17.91 MW		CTBLS	1/08-3/08
Mason, Tile and Marble Setter	Bridgeport-Stamford-Norwalk MSA, CT	Y	37300 FQ	42690 MW	47490 TQ	USBLS	5/07
Mason, Tile and Marble Setter	Hartford-West Hartford-East Hartford MSA, CT	Y	28560 FQ	35300 MW	46810 TQ	USBLS	5/07
Mason, Tile and Marble Setter	Delaware	Y	23690 FQ	28490 MW	35950 TQ	USBLS	5/07
Mason, Tile and Marble Setter	Wilmington PMSA, DE-MD-NJ	Y	24850 FQ	28890 MW	41800 TQ	USBLS	5/07
Mason, Tile and Marble Setter	District of Columbia	Y	20570 FQ	24860 MW	34320 TQ	USBLS	5/07
Mason, Tile and Marble Setter	Washington-Arlington-Alexandria MSA, DC-VA-MD-WV	Y	24890 FQ	28720 MW	33700 TQ	USBLS	5/07
Mason, Tile and Marble Setter	Florida	Y	21090 FQ	24780 MW	29080 TQ	USBLS	5/07
Mason, Tile and Marble Setter	Fort Lauderdale-Pompano Beach-Deerfield Beach PMSA, FL	Y	22650 FQ	27310 MW	30910 TQ	USBLS	5/07
Mason, Tile and Marble Setter	Jacksonville MSA, FL	Y	25110 FQ	27380 MW	29580 TQ	USBLS	5/07
Mason, Tile and Marble Setter	Miami-Fort Lauderdale-Miami Beach MSA, FL	Y	22920 FQ	26730 MW	30460 TQ	USBLS	5/07
Mason, Tile and Marble Setter	Orlando-Kissimmee MSA, FL	Y	20650 FQ	24500 MW	28740 TQ	USBLS	5/07
Mason, Tile and Marble Setter	Pensacola-Ferry Pass-Brent MSA, FL	Y	19660 FQ	21900 MW	24090 TQ	USBLS	5/07
Mason, Tile and Marble Setter	Tallahassee MSA, FL	Y	19540 FQ	23560 MW	28210 TQ	USBLS	5/07
Mason, Tile and Marble Setter	Tampa-St. Petersburg-Clearwater MSA, FL	Y	19660 FQ	22850 MW	26860 TQ	USBLS	5/07

AE	Average entry wage	**AW**	Average wage paid	**FQ**	First quartile wage	**LO**	Lowest wage paid
AER	Average entry range	**AWR**	Average wage range	**H**	Hourly	**LR**	Low end range
AEX	Average experienced wage	**AXR**	Average experienced range	**HI**	Highest wage paid	**M**	Monthly
ATC	Average total compensation	**D**	Daily	**HR**	High end range	**MCC**	Median cash compensation

MTC Median total compensation **TCC** Total cash compensation
MW Median wage paid **TQ** Third quartile wage
MWR Median wage range **W** Weekly
S See annotated source **Y** Yearly

Helper

Occupation/Type/Industry	Location	Per	Low	Mid	High	Source	Date
Mason, Tile and Marble Setter	West Palm Beach-Boca Raton-Boynton Beach PMSA, FL	Y	25850 FQ	28370 MW	32740 TQ	USBLS	5/07
Mason, Tile and Marble Setter	Georgia	Y	19670 FQ	22220 MW	25310 TQ	USBLS	5/07
Mason, Tile and Marble Setter	Atlanta-Sandy Springs-Marietta MSA, GA	Y	20780 FQ	23160 MW	27000 TQ	USBLS	5/07
Mason, Tile and Marble Setter	Hawaii	Y	27540 FQ	35040 MW	48550 TQ	USBLS	5/07
Mason, Tile and Marble Setter	Honolulu MSA, HI	Y	24220 FQ	47200 MW	52680 TQ	USBLS	5/07
Mason, Tile and Marble Setter	Idaho	Y	20540 FQ	26610 MW	33920 TQ	USBLS	5/07
Mason, Tile and Marble Setter	Boise City-Nampa MSA, ID	Y	21410 FQ	26570 MW	32750 TQ	USBLS	5/07
Mason, Tile and Marble Setter	Illinois	Y	29580 FQ	36910 MW	56680 TQ	USBLS	5/07
Mason, Tile and Marble Setter	Chicago-Naperville-Joliet MSA, IL-IN-WI	Y	29480 FQ	36730 MW	59170 TQ	USBLS	5/07
Mason, Tile and Marble Setter	Indiana	Y	24070 FQ	28700 MW	34040 TQ	USBLS	5/07
Mason, Tile and Marble Setter	Gary PMSA, IN	Y	26700 FQ	29440 MW	32180 TQ	USBLS	5/07
Mason, Tile and Marble Setter	Indianapolis-Carmel MSA, IN	Y	26600 FQ	29630 MW	33510 TQ	USBLS	5/07
Mason, Tile and Marble Setter	Iowa	Y	26290 FQ	30210 MW	35440 TQ	USBLS	5/07
Mason, Tile and Marble Setter	Kansas	Y	23290 FQ	28740 MW	34410 TQ	USBLS	5/07
Mason, Tile and Marble Setter	Wichita MSA, KS	Y	21140 FQ	23510 MW	27110 TQ	USBLS	5/07
Mason, Tile and Marble Setter	Kentucky	Y	21741 FQ	26803 MW	30849 TQ	KYBLS	2008
Mason, Tile and Marble Setter	Louisville-Jefferson County MSA, KY-IN	Y	21920 FQ	25410 MW	28550 TQ	USBLS	5/07
Mason, Tile and Marble Setter	Louisiana	H	9.76 FQ	10.94 MW	13.00 TQ	LABLS	1/08-3/08
Mason, Tile and Marble Setter	Baton Rouge MSA, LA	Y	20660 FQ	22960 MW	26560 TQ	USBLS	5/07
Mason, Tile and Marble Setter	New Orleans-Metairie-Kenner MSA, LA	Y	20170 FQ	28400 MW	36400 TQ	USBLS	5/07
Mason, Tile and Marble Setter	Maine	Y	22210 FQ	27220 MW	30200 TQ	USBLS	5/07
Mason, Tile and Marble Setter	Portland-South Portland-Biddeford MSA, ME	Y	15040 FQ	15760 MW	28730 TQ	USBLS	5/07
Mason, Tile and Marble Setter	Maryland	Y		28825 MW		MDBLS	3/08
Mason, Tile and Marble Setter	Baltimore-Towson MSA, MD	Y	26000 FQ	28900 MW	32050 TQ	USBLS	5/07
Mason, Tile and Marble Setter	Bethesda-Gaithersburg-Frederick PMSA, MD	Y	24790 FQ	27460 MW	29950 TQ	USBLS	5/07
Mason, Tile and Marble Setter	Massachusetts	Y	27930 FQ	31950 MW	51170 TQ	USBLS	5/07
Mason, Tile and Marble Setter	Boston-Cambridge-Quincy NECTA, MA	Y	27070 FQ	29780 MW	60470 TQ	USBLS	5/07
Mason, Tile and Marble Setter	Worcester MSA, MA-CT	Y	29220 FQ	33720 MW	37910 TQ	USBLS	5/07
Mason, Tile and Marble Setter	Michigan	Y	27870 FQ	31680 MW	40880 TQ	USBLS	5/07
Mason, Tile and Marble Setter	Detroit-Warren-Livonia MSA, MI	Y	28150 FQ	31730 MW	46310 TQ	USBLS	5/07
Mason, Tile and Marble Setter	Grand Rapids-Wyoming MSA, MI	Y	29130 FQ	32390 MW	36760 TQ	USBLS	5/07
Mason, Tile and Marble Setter	Warren-Troy-Farmington Hills PMSA, MI	Y	28000 FQ	31450 MW	44700 TQ	USBLS	5/07
Mason, Tile and Marble Setter	Minnesota	Y	25124 FQ	34061 MW	45369 TQ	MNBLS	10/08-12/08
Mason, Tile and Marble Setter	Minneapolis-Saint Paul MSA, MN-WI	Y	25777 FQ	37001 MW	48162 TQ	MNBLS	10/08-12/08
Mason, Tile and Marble Setter	Mississippi	Y	18020 FQ	20430 MW	23890 TQ	USBLS	5/07
Mason, Tile and Marble Setter	Missouri	Y	25520 FQ	32530 MW	44930 TQ	USBLS	5/07
Mason, Tile and Marble Setter	Kansas City MSA, MO-KS	Y	27910 FQ	34480 MW	40280 TQ	USBLS	5/07
Mason, Tile and Marble Setter	St. Louis MSA, MO-IL	Y	33380 FQ	42730 MW	53460 TQ	USBLS	5/07
Mason, Tile and Marble Setter	Montana	Y	18580 FQ	24460 MW	35560 TQ	USBLS	5/07
Mason, Tile and Marble Setter	Nebraska	Y	23040 FQ	27200 MW	31640 TQ	USBLS	5/07
Mason, Tile and Marble Setter	Omaha-Council Bluffs MSA, NE-IA	Y	25050 FQ	28970 MW	32900 TQ	USBLS	5/07
Mason, Tile and Marble Setter	Nevada	H	11.77 FQ	14.00 MW	17.31 TQ	NVBLS	5/08
Mason, Tile and Marble Setter	Las Vegas-Paradise MSA, NV	H	11.63 FQ	14.07 MW	18.03 TQ	NVBLS	5/08
Mason, Tile and Marble Setter	New Jersey	Y	24780 FQ	28550 MW	35290 TQ	USBLS	5/07
Mason, Tile and Marble Setter	Atlantic City MSA, NJ	Y	28830 FQ	32490 MW	35670 TQ	USBLS	5/07
Mason, Tile and Marble Setter	Camden PMSA, NJ	Y	26740 FQ	29720 MW	37510 TQ	USBLS	5/07
Mason, Tile and Marble Setter	Edison PMSA, NJ	Y	22520 FQ	25610 MW	30620 TQ	USBLS	5/07
Mason, Tile and Marble Setter	Newark-Union PMSA, NJ-PA	Y	23910 FQ	27220 MW	32670 TQ	USBLS	5/07
Mason, Tile and Marble Setter	New Mexico	Y	17600 FQ	19500 MW	23390 TQ	USBLS	5/07
Mason, Tile and Marble Setter	Albuquerque MSA, NM	Y	17840 FQ	19780 MW	23500 TQ	USBLS	5/07
Mason, Tile and Marble Setter	New York	Y	22860 FQ	27990 MW	47970 TQ	USBLS	5/07
Mason, Tile and Marble Setter	Albany-Schenectady-Troy MSA, NY	Y	27160 FQ	31510 MW	60420 TQ	USBLS	5/07
Mason, Tile and Marble Setter	Nassau-Suffolk PMSA, NY	Y	21410 FQ	24880 MW	29310 TQ	USBLS	5/07
Mason, Tile and Marble Setter	New York-Northern New Jersey-Long Island MSA, NY-NJ-PA	Y	23460 FQ	27740 MW	42280 TQ	USBLS	5/07
Mason, Tile and Marble Setter	North Carolina	Y	18970 FQ	21830 MW	24760 TQ	USBLS	5/07

AE	Average entry wage	AW	Average wage paid	FQ	First quartile wage	LO	Lowest wage paid	MTC	Median total compensation	TCC	Total cash compensation
AER	Average entry range	AWR	Average wage range	H	Hourly	LR	Low end range	MW	Median wage paid	TQ	Third quartile wage
AEX	Average experienced wage	AXR	Average experienced range	HI	Highest wage paid	M	Monthly	MWR	Median wage range	W	Weekly
ATC	Average total compensation	D	Daily	HR	High end range	MCC	Median cash compensation	S	See annotated source	Y	Yearly

Helper

Occupation/Type/Industry	Location	Per	Low	Mid	High	Source	Date
Mason, Tile and Marble Setter	Charlotte-Gastonia-Concord MSA, NC-SC	Y	20580 FQ	23130 MW	26330 TQ	USBLS	5/07
Mason, Tile and Marble Setter	Raleigh-Cary MSA, NC	Y	19570 FQ	22350 MW	25610 TQ	USBLS	5/07
Mason, Tile and Marble Setter	North Dakota	Y	21030 FQ	26520 MW	29340 TQ	USBLS	5/07
Mason, Tile and Marble Setter	Fargo MSA, ND-MN	Y	26100 FQ	28220 MW	30340 TQ	USBLS	5/07
Mason, Tile and Marble Setter	Ohio	Y	23080 FQ	28270 MW	34470 TQ	USBLS	5/07
Mason, Tile and Marble Setter	Cincinnati-Middletown MSA, OH-KY-IN	Y	22770 FQ	27920 MW	33250 TQ	USBLS	5/07
Mason, Tile and Marble Setter	Cleveland-Elyria-Mentor MSA, OH	Y	18170 FQ	21480 MW	24850 TQ	USBLS	5/07
Mason, Tile and Marble Setter	Columbus MSA, OH	Y	24660 FQ	28540 MW	31970 TQ	USBLS	5/07
Mason, Tile and Marble Setter	Dayton MSA, OH	Y	30900 FQ	35650 MW	38790 TQ	USBLS	5/07
Mason, Tile and Marble Setter	Oklahoma	Y	20110 FQ	23110 MW	27380 TQ	USBLS	5/07
Mason, Tile and Marble Setter	Oklahoma City MSA, OK	Y	21890 FQ	24750 MW	29110 TQ	USBLS	5/07
Mason, Tile and Marble Setter	Tulsa MSA, OK	Y	20980 FQ	22680 MW	24640 TQ	USBLS	5/07
Mason, Tile and Marble Setter	Oregon	H	13.22 FQ	15.24 MW	18.31 TQ	ORBLS	5/08
Mason, Tile and Marble Setter	Portland-Vancouver-Beaverton MSA, OR-WA	Y	27560 FQ	32330 MW	37980 TQ	USBLS	5/07
Mason, Tile and Marble Setter	Pennsylvania	Y	22780 FQ	28260 MW	34800 TQ	USBLS	5/07
Mason, Tile and Marble Setter	Allentown-Bethlehem-Easton MSA, PA-NJ	Y	22550 FQ	24880 MW	28510 TQ	USBLS	5/07
Mason, Tile and Marble Setter	Philadelphia-Camden-Wilmington MSA, PA-NJ-DE-MD	Y	26940 FQ	31410 MW	39470 TQ	USBLS	5/07
Mason, Tile and Marble Setter	Pittsburgh MSA, PA	Y	21620 FQ	24130 MW	29900 TQ	USBLS	5/07
Mason, Tile and Marble Setter	Rhode Island	Y	32330 FQ	36560 MW	40740 TQ	USBLS	5/07
Mason, Tile and Marble Setter	Providence-Fall River-Warwick MSA, RI-MA	Y	33520 FQ	37230 MW	41150 TQ	USBLS	5/07
Mason, Tile and Marble Setter	South Carolina	Y	18970 FQ	21710 MW	25030 TQ	USBLS	5/07
Mason, Tile and Marble Setter	Charleston-North Charleston MSA, SC	Y	19430 FQ	23200 MW	28160 TQ	USBLS	5/07
Mason, Tile and Marble Setter	Columbia MSA, SC	Y	19390 FQ	21350 MW	23560 TQ	USBLS	5/07
Mason, Tile and Marble Setter	Florence MSA, SC	Y	16870 FQ	20330 MW	24770 TQ	USBLS	5/07
Mason, Tile and Marble Setter	South Dakota	Y	21073 FQ	24364 MW	28947 TQ	SDBLS	7/08-9/08
Mason, Tile and Marble Setter	Sioux Falls MSA, SD	Y	19378 FQ	23158 MW	27574 TQ	SDBLS	7/08-9/08
Mason, Tile and Marble Setter	Tennessee	Y	20910 FQ	23630 MW	28600 TQ	USBLS	5/07
Mason, Tile and Marble Setter	Memphis MSA, TN-MS-AR	Y	18010 FQ	19740 MW	23910 TQ	USBLS	5/07
Mason, Tile and Marble Setter	Nashville-Davidson-Murfreesboro MSA, TN	Y	22210 FQ	24880 MW	34720 TQ	USBLS	5/07
Mason, Tile and Marble Setter	Texas	Y	19380 FQ	22270 MW	25260 TQ	USBLS	5/07
Mason, Tile and Marble Setter	Austin-Round Rock MSA, TX	Y	17660 FQ	19510 MW	23020 TQ	USBLS	5/07
Mason, Tile and Marble Setter	Dallas-Fort Worth-Arlington MSA, TX	Y	20110 FQ	22490 MW	25510 TQ	USBLS	5/07
Mason, Tile and Marble Setter	Houston-Sugar Land-Baytown MSA, TX	Y	20250 FQ	23580 MW	26720 TQ	USBLS	5/07
Mason, Tile and Marble Setter	San Antonio MSA, TX	Y	21430 FQ	23010 MW	24640 TQ	USBLS	5/07
Mason, Tile and Marble Setter	Utah	Y	18390 FQ	22440 MW	26360 TQ	USBLS	5/07
Mason, Tile and Marble Setter	Salt Lake City MSA, UT	Y	17190 FQ	19310 MW	23340 TQ	USBLS	5/07
Mason, Tile and Marble Setter	Vermont	Y	27420 FQ	29800 MW	31940 TQ	USBLS	5/07
Mason, Tile and Marble Setter	Virginia	Y	23340 FQ	26660 MW	30450 TQ	USBLS	5/07
Mason, Tile and Marble Setter	Richmond MSA, VA	Y	22840 FQ	25980 MW	28970 TQ	USBLS	5/07
Mason, Tile and Marble Setter	Roanoke MSA, VA	Y	20850 FQ	22790 MW	25910 TQ	USBLS	5/07
Mason, Tile and Marble Setter	Virginia Beach-Norfolk-Newport News MSA, VA-NC	Y	22550 FQ	25410 MW	27960 TQ	USBLS	5/07
Mason, Tile and Marble Setter	Washington	H	15.23 FQ	18.21 MW	22.31 TQ	WABLS	3/08
Mason, Tile and Marble Setter	Seattle-Tacoma-Bellevue MSA, WA	Y	32820 FQ	37150 MW	50180 TQ	USBLS	5/07
Mason, Tile and Marble Setter	West Virginia	Y	19484 FQ	22391 MW	32327 TQ	WVBLS	7/08-9/08
Mason, Tile and Marble Setter	Charleston MSA, WV	Y	23350 FQ	40360 MW	45480 TQ	USBLS	5/07
Mason, Tile and Marble Setter	Wisconsin	Y	26530 FQ	32450 MW	40610 TQ	USBLS	5/07
Mason, Tile and Marble Setter	Milwaukee-Waukesha-West Allis MSA, WI	Y	35230 FQ	42020 MW	55020 TQ	USBLS	5/07
Mason, Tile and Marble Setter	Wyoming	Y	24237 FQ	27916 MW	31593 TQ	WYBLS	9/08
Mason, Tile and Marble Setter	Puerto Rico	Y	12520 FQ	13710 MW	14900 TQ	USBLS	5/07
Mason, Tile and Marble Setter	San Juan-Caguas-Guaynabo MSA, PR	Y	12740 FQ	14160 MW	15770 TQ	USBLS	5/07
Painter, Paperhanger, Plasterer	Alabama	Y	14980 FQ	18170 MW	22840 TQ	USBLS	5/07
Painter, Paperhanger, Plasterer	Birmingham-Hoover MSA, AL	Y	17800 FQ	21880 MW	26990 TQ	USBLS	5/07
Painter, Paperhanger, Plasterer	Arizona	Y	18930 FQ	21860 MW	25260 TQ	USBLS	5/07
Painter, Paperhanger, Plasterer	Phoenix-Mesa-Scottsdale MSA, AZ	Y	18650 FQ	21300 MW	24440 TQ	USBLS	5/07

AE Average entry wage	**AW** Average wage paid	**FQ** First quartile wage	**LO** Lowest wage paid	**MTC** Median total compensation	**TCC** Total cash compensation
AER Average entry range	**AWR** Average wage range	**H** Hourly	**LR** Low end range	**MW** Median wage paid	**TQ** Third quartile wage
AEX Average experienced wage	**AXR** Average experienced range	**HI** Highest wage paid	**M** Monthly	**MWR** Median wage range	**W** Weekly
ATC Average total compensation	**D** Daily	**HR** High end range	**MCC** Median cash compensation	**S** See annotated source	**Y** Yearly

Helper

Occupation/Type/Industry	Location	Per	Low	Mid	High	Source	Date
Painter, Paperhanger, Plasterer	Tucson MSA, AZ	Y	21610 FQ	25210 MW	28830 TQ	USBLS	5/07
Painter, Paperhanger, Plasterer	Arkansas	Y	19850 FQ	21810 MW	23730 TQ	USBLS	5/07
Painter, Paperhanger, Plasterer	Little Rock-North Little Rock MSA, AR	Y	21160 FQ	22920 MW	25840 TQ	USBLS	5/07
Painter, Paperhanger, Plasterer	California	H	9.90 FQ	11.37 MW	13.13 TQ	CABLS	1/08-3/08
Painter, Paperhanger, Plasterer	Los Angeles-Long Beach-Glendale PMSA, CA	H	9.55 FQ	10.95 MW	12.44 TQ	CABLS	1/08-3/08
Painter, Paperhanger, Plasterer	Oakland-Fremont-Hayward MSA, CA	H	9.69 FQ	11.10 MW	12.82 TQ	CABLS	1/08-3/08
Painter, Paperhanger, Plasterer	Riverside-San Bernardino-Ontario MSA, CA	H	10.08 FQ	11.73 MW	13.61 TQ	CABLS	1/08-3/08
Painter, Paperhanger, Plasterer	Sacramento-Arden Arcade-Roseville MSA, CA	H	10.26 FQ	11.33 MW	13.11 TQ	CABLS	1/08-3/08
Painter, Paperhanger, Plasterer	San Diego-Carlsbad-San Marcos MSA, CA	H	9.84 FQ	11.13 MW	12.52 TQ	CABLS	1/08-3/08
Painter, Paperhanger, Plasterer	San Francisco-San Mateo-Redwood PMSA, CA	H	10.28 FQ	11.28 MW	12.25 TQ	CABLS	1/08-3/08
Painter, Paperhanger, Plasterer	San Jose-Sunnyvale-Santa Clara MSA, CA	H	10.18 FQ	11.24 MW	12.52 TQ	CABLS	1/08-3/08
Painter, Paperhanger, Plasterer	Santa Ana-Anaheim-Irvine PMSA, CA	Y	18670 FQ	23870 MW	27900 TQ	USBLS	5/07
Painter, Paperhanger, Plasterer	Colorado	Y	19620 FQ	24690 MW	28800 TQ	USBLS	5/07
Painter, Paperhanger, Plasterer	Denver-Aurora MSA, CO	Y	21750 FQ	24930 MW	28840 TQ	USBLS	5/07
Painter, Paperhanger, Plasterer	Connecticut	H	10.54 AE	14.70 MW		CTBLS	1/08-3/08
Painter, Paperhanger, Plasterer	Delaware	Y	26640 FQ	28870 MW	31180 TQ	USBLS	5/07
Painter, Paperhanger, Plasterer	Wilmington PMSA, DE-MD-NJ	Y	26640 FQ	28870 MW	31180 TQ	USBLS	5/07
Painter, Paperhanger, Plasterer	Washington-Arlington-Alexandria MSA, DC-VA-MD-WV	Y	17910 FQ	21180 MW	26690 TQ	USBLS	5/07
Painter, Paperhanger, Plasterer	Florida	Y	18290 FQ	21090 MW	24600 TQ	USBLS	5/07
Painter, Paperhanger, Plasterer	Fort Lauderdale-Pompano Beach-Deerfield Beach PMSA, FL	Y	19590 FQ	22710 MW	27000 TQ	USBLS	5/07
Painter, Paperhanger, Plasterer	Jacksonville MSA, FL	Y	19890 FQ	21590 MW	23290 TQ	USBLS	5/07
Painter, Paperhanger, Plasterer	Miami-Fort Lauderdale-Miami Beach MSA, FL	Y	17810 FQ	21070 MW	25030 TQ	USBLS	5/07
Painter, Paperhanger, Plasterer	Orlando-Kissimmee MSA, FL	Y	17800 FQ	20820 MW	23580 TQ	USBLS	5/07
Painter, Paperhanger, Plasterer	Tampa-St. Petersburg-Clearwater MSA, FL	Y	18140 FQ	20290 MW	23490 TQ	USBLS	5/07
Painter, Paperhanger, Plasterer	West Palm Beach-Boca Raton-Boynton Beach PMSA, FL	Y	19420 FQ	22770 MW	25350 TQ	USBLS	5/07
Painter, Paperhanger, Plasterer	Georgia	Y	18670 FQ	21360 MW	24680 TQ	USBLS	5/07
Painter, Paperhanger, Plasterer	Atlanta-Sandy Springs-Marietta MSA, GA	Y	21010 FQ	23350 MW	26750 TQ	USBLS	5/07
Painter, Paperhanger, Plasterer	Hawaii	Y	20380 FQ	33060 MW	36860 TQ	USBLS	5/07
Painter, Paperhanger, Plasterer	Idaho	Y	16900 FQ	18860 MW	23010 TQ	USBLS	5/07
Painter, Paperhanger, Plasterer	Illinois	Y	25030 FQ	29150 MW	36670 TQ	USBLS	5/07
Painter, Paperhanger, Plasterer	Chicago-Naperville-Joliet MSA, IL-IN-WI	Y	26660 FQ	30090 MW	36640 TQ	USBLS	5/07
Painter, Paperhanger, Plasterer	Indiana	Y	19140 FQ	22390 MW	27080 TQ	USBLS	5/07
Painter, Paperhanger, Plasterer	Indianapolis-Carmel MSA, IN	Y	18460 FQ	21410 MW	24270 TQ	USBLS	5/07
Painter, Paperhanger, Plasterer	Iowa	Y	18600 FQ	21850 MW	26110 TQ	USBLS	5/07
Painter, Paperhanger, Plasterer	Kansas	Y	19410 FQ	22210 MW	24490 TQ	USBLS	5/07
Painter, Paperhanger, Plasterer	Wichita MSA, KS	Y	20990 FQ	22910 MW	24970 TQ	USBLS	5/07
Painter, Paperhanger, Plasterer	Kentucky	Y	21201 FQ	23837 MW	27535 TQ	KYBLS	2008
Painter, Paperhanger, Plasterer	Louisiana	H	9.17 FQ	10.56 MW	11.97 TQ	LABLS	1/08-3/08
Painter, Paperhanger, Plasterer	Baton Rouge MSA, LA	Y	21200 FQ	24220 MW	29400 TQ	USBLS	5/07
Painter, Paperhanger, Plasterer	Lake Charles MSA, LA	Y	20090 FQ	21880 MW	23720 TQ	USBLS	5/07
Painter, Paperhanger, Plasterer	New Orleans-Metairie-Kenner MSA, LA	Y	19480 FQ	21480 MW	23320 TQ	USBLS	5/07
Painter, Paperhanger, Plasterer	Maryland	Y		25825 MW		MDBLS	3/08
Painter, Paperhanger, Plasterer	Baltimore-Towson MSA, MD	Y	20480 FQ	25450 MW	28890 TQ	USBLS	5/07
Painter, Paperhanger, Plasterer	Bethesda-Gaithersburg-Frederick PMSA, MD	Y	18350 FQ	25410 MW	28420 TQ	USBLS	5/07
Painter, Paperhanger, Plasterer	Massachusetts	Y	21860 FQ	26320 MW	29500 TQ	USBLS	5/07
Painter, Paperhanger, Plasterer	Boston-Cambridge-Quincy NECTA, MA	Y	26270 FQ	29390 MW	35160 TQ	USBLS	5/07
Painter, Paperhanger, Plasterer	Michigan	Y	23650 FQ	26730 MW	29400 TQ	USBLS	5/07
Painter, Paperhanger, Plasterer	Detroit-Warren-Livonia MSA, MI	Y	24800 FQ	26930 MW	29060 TQ	USBLS	5/07

AE	Average entry wage	AW	Average wage paid	FQ	First quartile wage
AER	Average entry range	AWR	Average wage range	H	Hourly
AEX	Average experienced wage	AXR	Average experienced range	HI	Highest wage paid
ATC	Average total compensation	D	Daily	HR	High end range

LO	Lowest wage paid	MTC	Median total compensation	TCC Total cash compensation
LR	Low end range	MW	Median wage paid	TQ Third quartile wage
M	Monthly	MWR	Median wage range	W Weekly
MCC	Median cash compensation	S	See annotated source	Y Yearly

Occupation/Type/Industry	Location	Per	Low	Mid	High	Source	Date
Helper							
Painter, Paperhanger, Plasterer	Minnesota	Y	23933 FQ	31205 MW	46391 TQ	MNBLS	10/08-12/08
Painter, Paperhanger, Plasterer	Minneapolis-Saint Paul MSA, MN-WI	Y	23111 FQ	33671 MW	53884 TQ	MNBLS	10/08-12/08
Painter, Paperhanger, Plasterer	Mississippi	Y	19080 FQ	21540 MW	23600 TQ	USBLS	5/07
Painter, Paperhanger, Plasterer	Jackson MSA, MS	Y	21270 FQ	22670 MW	24070 TQ	USBLS	5/07
Painter, Paperhanger, Plasterer	Missouri	Y	17900 FQ	19650 MW	22910 TQ	USBLS	5/07
Painter, Paperhanger, Plasterer	Montana	Y	21200 FQ	26190 MW	28990 TQ	USBLS	5/07
Painter, Paperhanger, Plasterer	Nevada	H	8.60 FQ	11.06 MW	14.43 TQ	NVBLS	5/08
Painter, Paperhanger, Plasterer	Las Vegas-Paradise MSA, NV	H	8.68 FQ	11.62 MW	14.54 TQ	NVBLS	5/08
Painter, Paperhanger, Plasterer	New Hampshire	H	9.90 AE	11.53 MW	12.61 AEX	NHBLS	6/08
Painter, Paperhanger, Plasterer	New Jersey	Y	19840 FQ	23150 MW	33690 TQ	USBLS	5/07
Painter, Paperhanger, Plasterer	Camden PMSA, NJ	Y	19400 FQ	22460 MW	32730 TQ	USBLS	5/07
Painter, Paperhanger, Plasterer	Newark-Union PMSA, NJ-PA	Y	22010 FQ	26600 MW	34850 TQ	USBLS	5/07
Painter, Paperhanger, Plasterer	New Mexico	Y	17000 FQ	19400 MW	23480 TQ	USBLS	5/07
Painter, Paperhanger, Plasterer	Albuquerque MSA, NM	Y	17540 FQ	20330 MW	23870 TQ	USBLS	5/07
Painter, Paperhanger, Plasterer	New York	Y	18340 FQ	20990 MW	29410 TQ	USBLS	5/07
Painter, Paperhanger, Plasterer	Buffalo-Niagara Falls MSA, NY	Y	17350 FQ	18520 MW	19690 TQ	USBLS	5/07
Painter, Paperhanger, Plasterer	Nassau-Suffolk PMSA, NY	Y	18140 FQ	20090 MW	29980 TQ	USBLS	5/07
Painter, Paperhanger, Plasterer	New York-Northern New Jersey-Long Island MSA, NY-NJ-PA	Y	19080 FQ	22600 MW	30880 TQ	USBLS	5/07
Painter, Paperhanger, Plasterer	North Carolina	Y	18480 FQ	20280 MW	22790 TQ	USBLS	5/07
Painter, Paperhanger, Plasterer	Charlotte-Gastonia-Concord MSA, NC-SC	Y	19740 FQ	21670 MW	23870 TQ	USBLS	5/07
Painter, Paperhanger, Plasterer	North Dakota	Y	21780 FQ	24040 MW	27640 TQ	USBLS	5/07
Painter, Paperhanger, Plasterer	Ohio	Y	18560 FQ	24760 MW	28770 TQ	USBLS	5/07
Painter, Paperhanger, Plasterer	Cincinnati-Middletown MSA, OH-KY-IN	Y	18190 FQ	20070 MW	26040 TQ	USBLS	5/07
Painter, Paperhanger, Plasterer	Oklahoma	Y	18760 FQ	22920 MW	26390 TQ	USBLS	5/07
Painter, Paperhanger, Plasterer	Oklahoma City MSA, OK	Y	23180 FQ	25620 MW	29570 TQ	USBLS	5/07
Painter, Paperhanger, Plasterer	Tulsa MSA, OK	Y	22900 FQ	25350 MW	28760 TQ	USBLS	5/07
Painter, Paperhanger, Plasterer	Oregon	H	10.27 FQ	12.31 MW	14.21 TQ	ORBLS	5/08
Painter, Paperhanger, Plasterer	Portland-Vancouver-Beaverton MSA, OR-WA	Y	21310 FQ	24830 MW	28870 TQ	USBLS	5/07
Painter, Paperhanger, Plasterer	Pennsylvania	Y	22110 FQ	26700 MW	30620 TQ	USBLS	5/07
Painter, Paperhanger, Plasterer	Philadelphia-Camden-Wilmington MSA, PA-NJ-DE-MD	Y	19840 FQ	24530 MW	31130 TQ	USBLS	5/07
Painter, Paperhanger, Plasterer	Pittsburgh MSA, PA	Y	23110 FQ	26770 MW	29410 TQ	USBLS	5/07
Painter, Paperhanger, Plasterer	Rhode Island	Y	20630 FQ	22290 MW	23930 TQ	USBLS	5/07
Painter, Paperhanger, Plasterer	Providence-Fall River-Warwick MSA, RI-MA	Y	20630 FQ	22290 MW	23930 TQ	USBLS	5/07
Painter, Paperhanger, Plasterer	South Carolina	Y	17720 FQ	20630 MW	23630 TQ	USBLS	5/07
Painter, Paperhanger, Plasterer	Myrtle Beach-Conway-North Myrtle Beach MSA, SC	Y	17310 FQ	19020 MW	20890 TQ	USBLS	5/07
Painter, Paperhanger, Plasterer	South Dakota	Y	17944 FQ	19895 MW	23460 TQ	SDBLS	7/08-9/08
Painter, Paperhanger, Plasterer	Sioux Falls MSA, SD	Y	18698 FQ	21297 MW	25419 TQ	SDBLS	7/08-9/08
Painter, Paperhanger, Plasterer	Tennessee	Y	21350 FQ	23800 MW	27780 TQ	USBLS	5/07
Painter, Paperhanger, Plasterer	Nashville-Davidson-Murfreesboro MSA, TN	Y	20160 FQ	22280 MW	24580 TQ	USBLS	5/07
Painter, Paperhanger, Plasterer	Texas	Y	17020 FQ	19440 MW	23340 TQ	USBLS	5/07
Painter, Paperhanger, Plasterer	Austin-Round Rock MSA, TX	Y	14370 FQ	16780 MW	18540 TQ	USBLS	5/07
Painter, Paperhanger, Plasterer	Dallas-Fort Worth-Arlington MSA, TX	Y	15720 FQ	19510 MW	23490 TQ	USBLS	5/07
Painter, Paperhanger, Plasterer	Houston-Sugar Land-Baytown MSA, TX	Y	17530 FQ	19730 MW	22820 TQ	USBLS	5/07
Painter, Paperhanger, Plasterer	San Antonio MSA, TX	Y	17000 FQ	18630 MW	20910 TQ	USBLS	5/07
Painter, Paperhanger, Plasterer	Utah	Y	18320 FQ	21520 MW	24020 TQ	USBLS	5/07
Painter, Paperhanger, Plasterer	Ogden-Clearfield MSA, UT	Y	17790 FQ	20830 MW	24240 TQ	USBLS	5/07
Painter, Paperhanger, Plasterer	Salt Lake City MSA, UT	Y	16820 FQ	21390 MW	23700 TQ	USBLS	5/07
Painter, Paperhanger, Plasterer	Virginia	Y	17590 FQ	20110 MW	22720 TQ	USBLS	5/07
Painter, Paperhanger, Plasterer	Richmond MSA, VA	Y	17200 FQ	18990 MW	20490 TQ	USBLS	5/07
Painter, Paperhanger, Plasterer	Virginia Beach-Norfolk-Newport News MSA, VA-NC	Y	16950 FQ	20230 MW	22710 TQ	USBLS	5/07
Painter, Paperhanger, Plasterer	Washington	H	10.90 FQ	12.89 MW	14.26 TQ	WABLS	3/08
Painter, Paperhanger, Plasterer	Seattle-Tacoma-Bellevue MSA, WA	Y	23490 FQ	26830 MW	29310 TQ	USBLS	5/07
Painter, Paperhanger, Plasterer	West Virginia	Y	19072 FQ	24268 MW	29919 TQ	WVBLS	7/08-9/08
Painter, Paperhanger, Plasterer	Wisconsin	Y	19670 FQ	23620 MW	28870 TQ	USBLS	5/07
Painter, Paperhanger, Plasterer	Wyoming	Y	21605 FQ	23324 MW	25041 TQ	WYBLS	9/08

AE Average entry wage	**AW** Average wage paid	**FQ** First quartile wage	**LO** Lowest wage paid	**MTC** Median total compensation	**TCC** Total cash compensation
AER Average entry range	**AWR** Average wage range	**H** Hourly	**LR** Low end range	**MW** Median wage paid	**TQ** Third quartile wage
AEX Average experienced wage	**AXR** Average experienced range	**HI** Highest wage paid	**M** Monthly	**MWR** Median wage range	**W** Weekly
ATC Average total compensation **D** Daily		**HR** High end range	**MCC** Median cash compensation	**S** See annotated source	**Y** Yearly

Occupation/Type/Industry	Location	Per	Low	Mid	High	Source	Date
Helper							
Painter, Paperhanger, Plasterer	Puerto Rico	Y	12560 FQ	13930 MW	15420 TQ	USBLS	5/07
Painter, Paperhanger, Plasterer	San Juan-Caguas-Guaynabo MSA, PR	Y	12480 FQ	13940 MW	15410 TQ	USBLS	5/07
Pipelayer, Plumber, Pipefitter, and Steamfitter	Alabama	Y	17180 FQ	20700 MW	26020 TQ	USBLS	5/07
Pipelayer, Plumber, Pipefitter, and Steamfitter	Birmingham-Hoover MSA, AL	Y	18700 FQ	24010 MW	29130 TQ	USBLS	5/07
Pipelayer, Plumber, Pipefitter, and Steamfitter	Alaska	Y	35330 FQ	47700 MW	57250 TQ	USBLS	5/07
Pipelayer, Plumber, Pipefitter, and Steamfitter	Arizona	Y	21180 FQ	23820 MW	28600 TQ	USBLS	5/07
Pipelayer, Plumber, Pipefitter, and Steamfitter	Flagstaff MSA, AZ	Y	20180 FQ	23620 MW	27240 TQ	USBLS	5/07
Pipelayer, Plumber, Pipefitter, and Steamfitter	Phoenix-Mesa-Scottsdale MSA, AZ	Y	21390 FQ	24070 MW	29160 TQ	USBLS	5/07
Pipelayer, Plumber, Pipefitter, and Steamfitter	Prescott MSA, AZ	Y	21040 FQ	24400 MW	27960 TQ	USBLS	5/07
Pipelayer, Plumber, Pipefitter, and Steamfitter	Tucson MSA, AZ	Y	20300 FQ	22740 MW	25920 TQ	USBLS	5/07
Pipelayer, Plumber, Pipefitter, and Steamfitter	Arkansas	Y	20410 FQ	23290 MW	27440 TQ	USBLS	5/07
Pipelayer, Plumber, Pipefitter, and Steamfitter	Little Rock-North Little Rock MSA, AR	Y	19670 FQ	23570 MW	29130 TQ	USBLS	5/07
Pipelayer, Plumber, Pipefitter, and Steamfitter	California	H	11.60 FQ	13.77 MW	16.00 TQ	CABLS	1/08-3/08
Pipelayer, Plumber, Pipefitter, and Steamfitter	Los Angeles-Long Beach-Glendale PMSA, CA	H	11.41 FQ	13.44 MW	15.05 TQ	CABLS	1/08-3/08
Pipelayer, Plumber, Pipefitter, and Steamfitter	Oakland-Fremont-Hayward MSA, CA	H	12.57 FQ	15.55 MW	19.18 TQ	CABLS	1/08-3/08
Pipelayer, Plumber, Pipefitter, and Steamfitter	Oxnard-Thousand Oaks-Ventura MSA, CA	H	10.10 FQ	11.68 MW	13.56 TQ	CABLS	1/08-3/08
Pipelayer, Plumber, Pipefitter, and Steamfitter	Riverside-San Bernardino-Ontario MSA, CA	H	11.75 FQ	13.54 MW	15.21 TQ	CABLS	1/08-3/08
Pipelayer, Plumber, Pipefitter, and Steamfitter	Sacramento-Arden Arcade-Roseville MSA, CA	H	10.82 FQ	12.21 MW	13.85 TQ	CABLS	1/08-3/08
Pipelayer, Plumber, Pipefitter, and Steamfitter	San Diego-Carlsbad-San Marcos MSA, CA	H	11.97 FQ	14.40 MW	18.29 TQ	CABLS	1/08-3/08
Pipelayer, Plumber, Pipefitter, and Steamfitter	San Francisco-San Mateo-Redwood PMSA, CA	H	20.03 FQ	22.07 MW	23.67 TQ	CABLS	1/08-3/08
Pipelayer, Plumber, Pipefitter, and Steamfitter	San Jose-Sunnyvale-Santa Clara MSA, CA	H	14.73 FQ	16.68 MW	19.71 TQ	CABLS	1/08-3/08
Pipelayer, Plumber, Pipefitter, and Steamfitter	Santa Ana-Anaheim-Irvine PMSA, CA	Y	23590 FQ	27540 MW	31230 TQ	USBLS	5/07
Pipelayer, Plumber, Pipefitter, and Steamfitter	Colorado	Y	23710 FQ	28410 MW	33920 TQ	USBLS	5/07
Pipelayer, Plumber, Pipefitter, and Steamfitter	Denver-Aurora MSA, CO	Y	26050 FQ	30030 MW	37900 TQ	USBLS	5/07
Pipelayer, Plumber, Pipefitter, and Steamfitter	Connecticut	H	11.39 AE	16.31 MW		CTBLS	1/08-3/08
Pipelayer, Plumber, Pipefitter, and Steamfitter	Bridgeport-Stamford-Norwalk MSA, CT	Y	20840 FQ	30450 MW	40560 TQ	USBLS	5/07
Pipelayer, Plumber, Pipefitter, and Steamfitter	Hartford-West Hartford-East Hartford MSA, CT	Y	26890 FQ	32440 MW	38730 TQ	USBLS	5/07
Pipelayer, Plumber, Pipefitter, and Steamfitter	Delaware	Y	21810 FQ	26340 MW	30350 TQ	USBLS	5/07

AE Average entry wage	**AW** Average wage paid	**FQ** First quartile wage	**LO** Lowest wage paid	**MTC** Median total compensation	**TCC** Total cash compensation
AER Average entry range	**AWR** Average wage range	**H** Hourly	**LR** Low end range	**MW** Median wage paid	**TQ** Third quartile wage
AEX Average experienced wage	**AXR** Average experienced range	**HI** Highest wage paid	**M** Monthly	**MWR** Median wage range	**W** Weekly
ATC Average total compensation	**D** Daily	**HR** High end range	**MCC** Median cash compensation	**S** See annotated source	**Y** Yearly

Occupation/Type/Industry	Location	Per	Low	Mid	High	Source	Date
Helper							
Pipelayer, Plumber, Pipefitter, and Steamfitter	Wilmington PMSA, DE-MD-NJ	Y	22800 FQ	27040 MW	30880 TQ	USBLS	5/07
Pipelayer, Plumber, Pipefitter, and Steamfitter	District of Columbia	Y	21890 FQ	26360 MW	29910 TQ	USBLS	5/07
Pipelayer, Plumber, Pipefitter, and Steamfitter	Washington-Arlington-Alexandria MSA, DC-VA-MD-WV	Y	25200 FQ	29320 MW	33840 TQ	USBLS	5/07
Pipelayer, Plumber, Pipefitter, and Steamfitter	Florida	Y	20340 FQ	23340 MW	27370 TQ	USBLS	5/07
Pipelayer, Plumber, Pipefitter, and Steamfitter	Fort Lauderdale-Pompano Beach-Deerfield Beach PMSA, FL	Y	19850 FQ	23710 MW	28720 TQ	USBLS	5/07
Pipelayer, Plumber, Pipefitter, and Steamfitter	Jacksonville MSA, FL	Y	21010 FQ	24060 MW	27640 TQ	USBLS	5/07
Pipelayer, Plumber, Pipefitter, and Steamfitter	Miami-Fort Lauderdale-Miami Beach MSA, FL	Y	20090 FQ	23930 MW	28570 TQ	USBLS	5/07
Pipelayer, Plumber, Pipefitter, and Steamfitter	Orlando-Kissimmee MSA, FL	Y	19930 FQ	22110 MW	24300 TQ	USBLS	5/07
Pipelayer, Plumber, Pipefitter, and Steamfitter	Tampa-St. Petersburg-Clearwater MSA, FL	Y	19880 FQ	22970 MW	27140 TQ	USBLS	5/07
Pipelayer, Plumber, Pipefitter, and Steamfitter	West Palm Beach-Boca Raton-Boynton Beach PMSA, FL	Y	20370 FQ	26790 MW	30440 TQ	USBLS	5/07
Pipelayer, Plumber, Pipefitter, and Steamfitter	Georgia	Y	21240 FQ	24900 MW	29800 TQ	USBLS	5/07
Pipelayer, Plumber, Pipefitter, and Steamfitter	Atlanta-Sandy Springs-Marietta MSA, GA	Y	22700 FQ	26830 MW	31290 TQ	USBLS	5/07
Pipelayer, Plumber, Pipefitter, and Steamfitter	Hawaii	Y	23450 FQ	27680 MW	32060 TQ	USBLS	5/07
Pipelayer, Plumber, Pipefitter, and Steamfitter	Honolulu MSA, HI	Y	23800 FQ	27740 MW	31480 TQ	USBLS	5/07
Pipelayer, Plumber, Pipefitter, and Steamfitter	Idaho	Y	24900 FQ	28130 MW	30920 TQ	USBLS	5/07
Pipelayer, Plumber, Pipefitter, and Steamfitter	Illinois	Y	26050 FQ	34210 MW	57080 TQ	USBLS	5/07
Pipelayer, Plumber, Pipefitter, and Steamfitter	Chicago-Naperville-Joliet MSA, IL-IN-WI	Y	27740 FQ	35750 MW	62060 TQ	USBLS	5/07
Pipelayer, Plumber, Pipefitter, and Steamfitter	Indiana	Y	23900 FQ	28170 MW	31900 TQ	USBLS	5/07
Pipelayer, Plumber, Pipefitter, and Steamfitter	Gary PMSA, IN	Y	25060 FQ	27780 MW	30740 TQ	USBLS	5/07
Pipelayer, Plumber, Pipefitter, and Steamfitter	Indianapolis-Carmel MSA, IN	Y	24970 FQ	28550 MW	32420 TQ	USBLS	5/07
Pipelayer, Plumber, Pipefitter, and Steamfitter	South Bend-Mishawaka MSA, IN-MI	Y	26090 FQ	28610 MW	35360 TQ	USBLS	5/07
Pipelayer, Plumber, Pipefitter, and Steamfitter	Iowa	Y	21380 FQ	27240 MW	30810 TQ	USBLS	5/07
Pipelayer, Plumber, Pipefitter, and Steamfitter	Cedar Rapids MSA, IA	Y	19520 FQ	24480 MW	27630 TQ	USBLS	5/07
Pipelayer, Plumber, Pipefitter, and Steamfitter	Des Moines-West Des Moines MSA, IA	Y	25050 FQ	28620 MW	32800 TQ	USBLS	5/07
Pipelayer, Plumber, Pipefitter, and Steamfitter	Kansas	Y	22550 FQ	27230 MW	31800 TQ	USBLS	5/07
Pipelayer, Plumber, Pipefitter, and Steamfitter	Wichita MSA, KS	Y	20260 FQ	23280 MW	28060 TQ	USBLS	5/07
Pipelayer, Plumber, Pipefitter, and Steamfitter	Kentucky	Y	20347 FQ	25108 MW	30004 TQ	KYBLS	2008
Pipelayer, Plumber, Pipefitter, and Steamfitter	Louisville-Jefferson County MSA, KY-IN	Y	19510 FQ	24800 MW	28800 TQ	USBLS	5/07

AE	Average entry wage	AW	Average wage paid	FQ	First quartile wage	LO	Lowest wage paid	MTC	Median total compensation	TCC	Total cash compensation
AER	Average entry range	AWR	Average wage range	H	Hourly	LR	Low end range	MW	Median wage paid	TQ	Third quartile wage
AEX	Average experienced wage	AXR	Average experienced range	HI	Highest wage paid	M	Monthly	MWR	Median wage range	W	Weekly
ATC	Average total compensation	D	Daily	HR	High end range	MCC	Median cash compensation	S	See annotated source	Y	Yearly

Helper

Occupation/Type/Industry	Location	Per	Low	Mid	High	Source	Date
Pipelayer, Plumber, Pipefitter, and Steamfitter	Louisiana	H	10.38 FQ	12.87 MW	15.96 TQ	LABLS	1/08-3/08
Pipelayer, Plumber, Pipefitter, and Steamfitter	Baton Rouge MSA, LA	Y	25980 FQ	32660 MW	38760 TQ	USBLS	5/07
Pipelayer, Plumber, Pipefitter, and Steamfitter	Houma-Bayou Cane-Thibodaux MSA, LA	Y	18190 FQ	21140 MW	25080 TQ	USBLS	5/07
Pipelayer, Plumber, Pipefitter, and Steamfitter	New Orleans-Metairie-Kenner MSA, LA	Y	20800 FQ	25850 MW	29730 TQ	USBLS	5/07
Pipelayer, Plumber, Pipefitter, and Steamfitter	Maine	Y	22000 FQ	25760 MW	31390 TQ	USBLS	5/07
Pipelayer, Plumber, Pipefitter, and Steamfitter	Portland-South Portland-Biddeford MSA, ME	Y	20290 FQ	25940 MW	38090 TQ	USBLS	5/07
Pipelayer, Plumber, Pipefitter, and Steamfitter	Maryland	Y		29650 MW		MDBLS	3/08
Pipelayer, Plumber, Pipefitter, and Steamfitter	Baltimore-Towson MSA, MD	Y	24710 FQ	28700 MW	32920 TQ	USBLS	5/07
Pipelayer, Plumber, Pipefitter, and Steamfitter	Bethesda-Gaithersburg-Frederick PMSA, MD	Y	26220 FQ	29840 MW	35030 TQ	USBLS	5/07
Pipelayer, Plumber, Pipefitter, and Steamfitter	Massachusetts	Y	24640 FQ	29450 MW	35800 TQ	USBLS	5/07
Pipelayer, Plumber, Pipefitter, and Steamfitter	Boston-Cambridge-Quincy NECTA, MA	Y	23050 FQ	29290 MW	35520 TQ	USBLS	5/07
Pipelayer, Plumber, Pipefitter, and Steamfitter	Springfield MSA, MA-CT	Y	25490 FQ	31510 MW	37120 TQ	USBLS	5/07
Pipelayer, Plumber, Pipefitter, and Steamfitter	Worcester MSA MA-CT	Y	25380 FQ	29940 MW	37130 TQ	USBLS	5/07
Pipelayer, Plumber, Pipefitter, and Steamfitter	Michigan	Y	21980 FQ	27560 MW	32080 TQ	USBLS	5/07
Pipelayer, Plumber, Pipefitter, and Steamfitter	Detroit-Warren-Livonia MSA, MI	Y	24000 FQ	28920 MW	33270 TQ	USBLS	5/07
Pipelayer, Plumber, Pipefitter, and Steamfitter	Grand Rapids-Wyoming MSA, MI	Y	21910 FQ	25360 MW	32860 TQ	USBLS	5/07
Pipelayer, Plumber, Pipefitter, and Steamfitter	Warren-Troy-Farmington Hills PMSA, MI	Y	24740 FQ	28000 MW	30780 TQ	USBLS	5/07
Pipelayer, Plumber, Pipefitter, and Steamfitter	Minnesota	Y	23417 FQ	30562 MW	39636 TQ	MNBLS	10/08-12/08
Pipelayer, Plumber, Pipefitter, and Steamfitter	Duluth-Superior MSA, MN-WI	Y	22415 FQ	25567 MW	28475 TQ	MNBLS	10/08-12/08
Pipelayer, Plumber, Pipefitter, and Steamfitter	Minneapolis-Saint Paul MSA, MN-WI	Y	27769 FQ	33492 MW	39931 TQ	MNBLS	10/08-12/08
Pipelayer, Plumber, Pipefitter, and Steamfitter	Mississippi	Y	19470 FQ	23090 MW	27560 TQ	USBLS	5/07
Pipelayer, Plumber, Pipefitter, and Steamfitter	Jackson MSA, MS	Y	19830 FQ	23220 MW	27370 TQ	USBLS	5/07
Pipelayer, Plumber, Pipefitter, and Steamfitter	Missouri	Y	20850 FQ	24290 MW	29120 TQ	USBLS	5/07
Pipelayer, Plumber, Pipefitter, and Steamfitter	Kansas City MSA, MO-KS	Y	23610 FQ	26940 MW	30870 TQ	USBLS	5/07
Pipelayer, Plumber, Pipefitter, and Steamfitter	St. Louis MSA, MO-IL	Y	25740 FQ	42070 MW	57890 TQ	USBLS	5/07
Pipelayer, Plumber, Pipefitter, and Steamfitter	Montana	Y	22040 FQ	24430 MW	30400 TQ	USBLS	5/07
Pipelayer, Plumber, Pipefitter, and Steamfitter	Billings MSA, MT	Y	24040 FQ	30030 MW	33570 TQ	USBLS	5/07
Pipelayer, Plumber, Pipefitter, and Steamfitter	Nebraska	Y	17560 FQ	23040 MW	28640 TQ	USBLS	5/07
Pipelayer, Plumber, Pipefitter, and Steamfitter	Omaha-Council Bluffs MSA, NE-IA	Y	24320 FQ	27810 MW	30750 TQ	USBLS	5/07
Pipelayer, Plumber, Pipefitter, and Steamfitter	Nevada	H	12.22 FQ	14.14 MW	16.49 TQ	NVBLS	5/08

AE	Average entry wage	AW	Average wage paid	FQ	First quartile wage	LO	Lowest wage paid	MTC	Median total compensation	TCC	Total cash compensation
AER	Average entry range	AWR	Average wage range	H	Hourly	LR	Low end range	MW	Median wage paid	TQ	Third quartile wage
AEX	Average experienced wage	AXR	Average experienced range	HI	Highest wage paid	M	Monthly	MWR	Median wage range	W	Weekly
ATC	Average total compensation	D	Daily	HR	High end range	MCC	Median cash compensation	S	See annotated source	Y	Yearly

Occupation/Type/Industry	Location	Per	Low	Mid	High	Source	Date
Helper							
Pipelayer, Plumber, Pipefitter, and Steamfitter	Las Vegas-Paradise MSA, NV	H	12.22 FQ	14.10 MW	16.33 TQ	NVBLS	5/08
Pipelayer, Plumber, Pipefitter, and Steamfitter	New Hampshire	H	11.13 AE	13.84 MW	15.41 AEX	NHBLS	6/08
Pipelayer, Plumber, Pipefitter, and Steamfitter	Manchester MSA, NH	Y	27300 FQ	29920 MW	33230 TQ	USBLS	5/07
Pipelayer, Plumber, Pipefitter, and Steamfitter	New Jersey	Y	24070 FQ	28810 MW	37300 TQ	USBLS	5/07
Pipelayer, Plumber, Pipefitter, and Steamfitter	Camden PMSA, NJ	Y	23010 FQ	26600 MW	31170 TQ	USBLS	5/07
Pipelayer, Plumber, Pipefitter, and Steamfitter	Edison PMSA, NJ	Y	23200 FQ	26390 MW	32130 TQ	USBLS	5/07
Pipelayer, Plumber, Pipefitter, and Steamfitter	Newark-Union PMSA, NJ-PA	Y	28350 FQ	38290 MW	44000 TQ	USBLS	5/07
Pipelayer, Plumber, Pipefitter, and Steamfitter	Ocean City MSA, NJ	Y	23260 FQ	26340 MW	29710 TQ	USBLS	5/07
Pipelayer, Plumber, Pipefitter, and Steamfitter	New Mexico	Y	20180 FQ	24980 MW	29510 TQ	USBLS	5/07
Pipelayer, Plumber, Pipefitter, and Steamfitter	Albuquerque MSA, NM	Y	20490 FQ	26040 MW	30670 TQ	USBLS	5/07
Pipelayer, Plumber, Pipefitter, and Steamfitter	New York	Y	22710 FQ	28270 MW	35430 TQ	USBLS	5/07
Pipelayer, Plumber, Pipefitter, and Steamfitter	Albany-Schenectady-Troy MSA, NY	Y	26700 FQ	30630 MW	33890 TQ	USBLS	5/07
Pipelayer, Plumber, Pipefitter, and Steamfitter	Buffalo-Niagara Falls MSA, NY	Y	26120 FQ	28490 MW	30890 TQ	USBLS	5/07
Pipelayer, Plumber, Pipefitter, and Steamfitter	Nassau-Suffolk PMSA, NY	Y	24060 FQ	28470 MW	34060 TQ	USBLS	5/07
Pipelayer, Plumber, Pipefitter, and Steamfitter	New York-Northern New Jersey-Long Island MSA, NY-NJ-PA	Y	22660 FQ	28130 MW	36890 TQ	USBLS	5/07
Pipelayer, Plumber, Pipefitter, and Steamfitter	North Carolina	Y	21060 FQ	24480 MW	29130 TQ	USBLS	5/07
Pipelayer, Plumber, Pipefitter, and Steamfitter	Charlotte-Gastonia-Concord MSA, NC-SC	Y	22320 FQ	26210 MW	29960 TQ	USBLS	5/07
Pipelayer, Plumber, Pipefitter, and Steamfitter	Raleigh-Cary MSA, NC	Y	21570 FQ	26180 MW	32000 TQ	USBLS	5/07
Pipelayer, Plumber, Pipefitter, and Steamfitter	North Dakota	Y	21470 FQ	25080 MW	28400 TQ	USBLS	5/07
Pipelayer, Plumber, Pipefitter, and Steamfitter	Fargo MSA, ND-MN	Y	22050 FQ	25370 MW	29850 TQ	USBLS	5/07
Pipelayer, Plumber, Pipefitter, and Steamfitter	Ohio	Y	20460 FQ	24810 MW	30540 TQ	USBLS	5/07
Pipelayer, Plumber, Pipefitter, and Steamfitter	Cincinnati-Middletown MSA, OH-KY-IN	Y	22180 FQ	26020 MW	31510 TQ	USBLS	5/07
Pipelayer, Plumber, Pipefitter, and Steamfitter	Cleveland-Elyria-Mentor MSA, OH	Y	15610 FQ	22050 MW	28450 TQ	USBLS	5/07
Pipelayer, Plumber, Pipefitter, and Steamfitter	Columbus MSA, OH	Y	20760 FQ	26070 MW	30220 TQ	USBLS	5/07
Pipelayer, Plumber, Pipefitter, and Steamfitter	Dayton MSA, OH	Y	20670 FQ	26180 MW	29610 TQ	USBLS	5/07
Pipelayer, Plumber, Pipefitter, and Steamfitter	Oklahoma	Y	19190 FQ	22860 MW	27440 TQ	USBLS	5/07
Pipelayer, Plumber, Pipefitter, and Steamfitter	Oklahoma City MSA, OK	Y	18530 FQ	22760 MW	27230 TQ	USBLS	5/07
Pipelayer, Plumber, Pipefitter, and Steamfitter	Tulsa MSA, OK	Y	21150 FQ	25630 MW	29070 TQ	USBLS	5/07
Pipelayer, Plumber, Pipefitter, and Steamfitter	Oregon	H	14.86 FQ	17.36 MW	19.25 TQ	ORBLS	5/08
Pipelayer, Plumber, Pipefitter, and Steamfitter	Portland-Vancouver-Beaverton MSA, OR-WA	Y	29450 FQ	34880 MW	38600 TQ	USBLS	5/07
Pipelayer, Plumber, Pipefitter, and Steamfitter	Pennsylvania	Y	21410 FQ	25940 MW	32390 TQ	USBLS	5/07

AE Average entry wage	**AW** Average wage paid	**FQ** First quartile wage	**LO** Lowest wage paid	**MTC** Median total compensation	**TCC** Total cash compensation
AER Average entry range	**AWR** Average wage range	**H** Hourly	**LR** Low end range	**MW** Median wage paid	**TQ** Third quartile wage
AEX Average experienced wage	**AXR** Average experienced range	**HI** Highest wage paid	**M** Monthly	**MWR** Median wage range	**W** Weekly
ATC Average total compensation	**D** Daily	**HR** High end range	**MCC** Median cash compensation	**S** See annotated source	**Y** Yearly

Helper

Occupation/Type/Industry	Location	Per	Low	Mid	High	Source	Date
Pipelayer, Plumber, Pipefitter, and Steamfitter	Allentown-Bethlehem-Easton MSA, PA-NJ	Y	18110 FQ	24550 MW	33010 TQ	USBLS	5/07
Pipelayer, Plumber, Pipefitter, and Steamfitter	Philadelphia-Camden-Wilmington MSA, PA-NJ-DE-MD	Y	20470 FQ	24590 MW	30030 TQ	USBLS	5/07
Pipelayer, Plumber, Pipefitter, and Steamfitter	Pittsburgh MSA, PA	Y	25070 FQ	32380 MW	37590 TQ	USBLS	5/07
Pipelayer, Plumber, Pipefitter, and Steamfitter	Providence-Fall River-Warwick MSA, RI-MA	Y	26430 FQ	28980 MW	31690 TQ	USBLS	5/07
Pipelayer, Plumber, Pipefitter, and Steamfitter	South Carolina	Y	19620 FQ	23550 MW	28050 TQ	USBLS	5/07
Pipelayer, Plumber, Pipefitter, and Steamfitter	Charleston-North Charleston MSA, SC	Y	19430 FQ	24970 MW	28850 TQ	USBLS	5/07
Pipelayer, Plumber, Pipefitter, and Steamfitter	Columbia MSA, SC	Y	18760 FQ	22810 MW	27220 TQ	USBLS	5/07
Pipelayer, Plumber, Pipefitter, and Steamfitter	South Dakota	Y	19757 FQ	22490 MW	25366 TQ	SDBLS	7/08-9/08
Pipelayer, Plumber, Pipefitter, and Steamfitter	Sioux Falls MSA, SD	Y	20318 FQ	23812 MW	27010 TQ	SDBLS	7/08-9/08
Pipelayer, Plumber, Pipefitter, and Steamfitter	Tennessee	Y	20370 FQ	23730 MW	28070 TQ	USBLS	5/07
Pipelayer, Plumber, Pipefitter, and Steamfitter	Memphis MSA, TN-MS-AR	Y	19950 FQ	22860 MW	26300 TQ	USBLS	5/07
Pipelayer, Plumber, Pipefitter, and Steamfitter	Nashville-Davidson-Murfreesboro MSA, TN	Y	21520 FQ	24980 MW	29160 TQ	USBLS	5/07
Pipelayer, Plumber, Pipefitter, and Steamfitter	Texas	Y	19940 FQ	23890 MW	28940 TQ	USBLS	5/07
Pipelayer, Plumber, Pipefitter, and Steamfitter	Austin-Round Rock MSA, TX	Y	21090 FQ	24470 MW	29420 TQ	USBLS	5/07
Pipelayer, Plumber, Pipefitter, and Steamfitter	Corpus Christi MSA, TX	Y	18690 FQ	21430 MW	26360 TQ	USBLS	5/07
Pipelayer, Plumber, Pipefitter, and Steamfitter	Dallas-Fort Worth-Arlington MSA, TX	Y	21350 FQ	25500 MW	30000 TQ	USBLS	5/07
Pipelayer, Plumber, Pipefitter, and Steamfitter	El Paso MSA, TX	Y	17590 FQ	19610 MW	22650 TQ	USBLS	5/07
Pipelayer, Plumber, Pipefitter, and Steamfitter	Houston-Sugar Land-Baytown MSA, TX	Y	21550 FQ	25740 MW	30490 TQ	USBLS	5/07
Pipelayer, Plumber, Pipefitter, and Steamfitter	San Antonio MSA, TX	Y	19770 FQ	22920 MW	26150 TQ	USBLS	5/07
Pipelayer, Plumber, Pipefitter, and Steamfitter	Utah	Y	19630 FQ	22890 MW	27360 TQ	USBLS	5/07
Pipelayer, Plumber, Pipefitter, and Steamfitter	Provo-Orem MSA, UT	Y	21250 FQ	23610 MW	29080 TQ	USBLS	5/07
Pipelayer, Plumber, Pipefitter, and Steamfitter	Salt Lake City MSA, UT	Y	21760 FQ	24270 MW	29340 TQ	USBLS	5/07
Pipelayer, Plumber, Pipefitter, and Steamfitter	Vermont	Y	24150 FQ	27250 MW	30510 TQ	USBLS	5/07
Pipelayer, Plumber, Pipefitter, and Steamfitter	Burlington-South Burlington MSA, VT	Y	25990 FQ	28900 MW	32660 TQ	USBLS	5/07
Pipelayer, Plumber, Pipefitter, and Steamfitter	Virginia	Y	20680 FQ	24050 MW	29600 TQ	USBLS	5/07
Pipelayer, Plumber, Pipefitter, and Steamfitter	Richmond MSA, VA	Y	20770 FQ	23670 MW	28980 TQ	USBLS	5/07
Pipelayer, Plumber, Pipefitter, and Steamfitter	Virginia Beach-Norfolk-Newport News MSA, VA-NC	Y	19000 FQ	21990 MW	25370 TQ	USBLS	5/07
Pipelayer, Plumber, Pipefitter, and Steamfitter	Washington	H	11.63 FQ	13.92 MW	17.66 TQ	WABLS	3/08
Pipelayer, Plumber, Pipefitter, and Steamfitter	Seattle-Tacoma-Bellevue MSA, WA	Y	25180 FQ	30170 MW	37600 TQ	USBLS	5/07

AE	Average entry wage	AW	Average wage paid	FQ	First quartile wage
AER	Average entry range	AWR	Average wage range	H	Hourly
AEX	Average experienced wage	AXR	Average experienced range	HI	Highest wage paid
ATC	Average total compensation	D	Daily	HR	High end range

LO	Lowest wage paid	MTC	Median total compensation	TCC	Total cash compensation
LR	Low end range	MW	Median wage paid	TQ	Third quartile wage
M	Monthly	MWR	Median wage range	W	Weekly
MCC	Median cash compensation	S	See annotated source	Y	Yearly

Helper

Occupation/Type/Industry	Location	Per	Low	Mid	High	Source	Date
Pipelayer, Plumber, Pipefitter, and Steamfitter	West Virginia	Y	17575 FQ	23049 MW	35774 TQ	WVBLS	7/08-9/08
Pipelayer, Plumber, Pipefitter, and Steamfitter	Charleston MSA, WV	Y	18080 FQ	38370 MW	64750 TQ	USBLS	5/07
Pipelayer, Plumber, Pipefitter, and Steamfitter	Wisconsin	Y	21230 FQ	24990 MW	29700 TQ	USBLS	5/07
Pipelayer, Plumber, Pipefitter, and Steamfitter	Milwaukee-Waukesha-West Allis MSA, WI	Y	25970 FQ	29370 MW	36350 TQ	USBLS	5/07
Pipelayer, Plumber, Pipefitter, and Steamfitter	Wyoming	Y	22666 FQ	25859 MW	29961 TQ	WYBLS	9/08
Pipelayer, Plumber, Pipefitter, and Steamfitter	Cheyenne MSA, WY	Y	21394 FQ	23627 MW	25821 TQ	WYBLS	9/08
Pipelayer, Plumber, Pipefitter, and Steamfitter	Puerto Rico	Y	13470 FQ	15960 MW	23500 TQ	USBLS	5/07
Pipelayer, Plumber, Pipefitter, and Steamfitter	San Juan-Caguas-Guaynabo MSA, PR	Y	13740 FQ	16730 MW	25170 TQ	USBLS	5/07
Pipelayer, Plumber, Pipefitter, and Steamfitter	Guam	Y	16490 FQ	17870 MW	20230 TQ	USBLS	5/07
Production Worker	Alabama	Y	16720 FQ	20840 MW	27910 TQ	USBLS	5/07
Production Worker	Birmingham-Hoover MSA, AL	Y	18630 FQ	24170 MW	34210 TQ	USBLS	5/07
Production Worker	Tuscaloosa MSA, AL	Y	16090 FQ	25540 MW	32210 TQ	USBLS	5/07
Production Worker	Alaska	Y	19200 FQ	23450 MW	29890 TQ	USBLS	5/07
Production Worker	Anchorage MSA, AK	Y	19790 FQ	22100 MW	25620 TQ	USBLS	5/07
Production Worker	Arizona	Y	15390 FQ	18930 MW	25190 TQ	USBLS	5/07
Production Worker	Phoenix-Mesa-Scottsdale MSA, AZ	Y	15360 FQ	19040 MW	25020 TQ	USBLS	5/07
Production Worker	Tucson MSA, AZ	Y	14770 FQ	16090 MW	19160 TQ	USBLS	5/07
Production Worker	Arkansas	Y	18020 FQ	21970 MW	26990 TQ	USBLS	5/07
Production Worker	Little Rock-North Little Rock MSA, AR	Y	16680 FQ	19720 MW	27270 TQ	USBLS	5/07
Production Worker	Pine Bluff MSA, AR	Y	20120 FQ	29170 MW	35480 TQ	USBLS	5/07
Production Worker	California	H	8.52 FQ	9.71 MW	11.84 TQ	CABLS	1/08-3/08
Production Worker	Los Angeles-Long Beach-Glendale PMSA, CA	H	8.39 FQ	9.40 MW	11.29 TQ	CABLS	1/08-3/08
Production Worker	Oakland-Fremont-Hayward MSA, CA	H	8.92 FQ	10.62 MW	13.03 TQ	CABLS	1/08-3/08
Production Worker	Riverside-San Bernardino-Ontario MSA, CA	H	8.42 FQ	9.56 MW	11.47 TQ	CABLS	1/08-3/08
Production Worker	Sacramento-Arden Arcade-Roseville MSA, CA	H	8.70 FQ	9.80 MW	11.82 TQ	CABLS	1/08-3/08
Production Worker	San Diego-Carlsbad-San Marcos MSA, CA	H	8.72 FQ	10.25 MW	12.16 TQ	CABLS	1/08-3/08
Production Worker	San Francisco-San Mateo-Redwood PMSA, CA	H	9.48 FQ	11.44 MW	13.83 TQ	CABLS	1/08-3/08
Production Worker	San Jose-Sunnyvale-Santa Clara MSA, CA	H	8.99 FQ	10.75 MW	13.35 TQ	CABLS	1/08-3/08
Production Worker	Santa Ana-Anaheim-Irvine PMSA, CA	Y	17170 FQ	19290 MW	23470 TQ	USBLS	5/07
Production Worker	Santa Rosa-Petaluma MSA, CA	H	9.54 FQ	11.05 MW	12.58 TQ	CABLS	1/08-3/08
Production Worker	Colorado	Y	18480 FQ	22570 MW	27660 TQ	USBLS	5/07
Production Worker	Denver-Aurora MSA, CO	Y	17930 FQ	21960 MW	27670 TQ	USBLS	5/07
Production Worker	Connecticut	H	8.70 AE	10.72 MW		CTBLS	1/08-3/08
Production Worker	Bridgeport-Stamford-Norwalk MSA, CT	Y	18150 FQ	20780 MW	24320 TQ	USBLS	5/07
Production Worker	Hartford-West Hartford-East Hartford MSA, CT	Y	22050 FQ	28410 MW	37920 TQ	USBLS	5/07
Production Worker	Delaware	Y	16040 FQ	18970 MW	22870 TQ	USBLS	5/07
Production Worker	Wilmington PMSA, DE-MD-NJ	Y	17610 FQ	21020 MW	25070 TQ	USBLS	5/07
Production Worker	District of Columbia	Y	24310 FQ	27310 MW	31560 TQ	USBLS	5/07
Production Worker	Washington-Arlington-Alexandria MSA, DC-VA-MD-WV	Y	19700 FQ	23640 MW	28600 TQ	USBLS	5/07
Production Worker	Florida	Y	16850 FQ	20670 MW	25870 TQ	USBLS	5/07
Production Worker	Fort Lauderdale-Pompano Beach-Deerfield Beach PMSA, FL	Y	15860 FQ	18450 MW	22240 TQ	USBLS	5/07
Production Worker	Jacksonville MSA, FL	Y	19790 FQ	22910 MW	27310 TQ	USBLS	5/07

Occupation/Type/Industry	Location	Per	Low	Mid	High	Source	Date
Helper							
Production Worker	Miami-Fort Lauderdale-Miami Beach MSA, FL	Y	15980 FQ	18770 MW	25400 TQ	USBLS	5/07
Production Worker	Orlando-Kissimmee MSA, FL	Y	16680 FQ	19160 MW	23460 TQ	USBLS	5/07
Production Worker	Tampa-St. Petersburg-Clearwater MSA, FL	Y	15260 FQ	19890 MW	25210 TQ	USBLS	5/07
Production Worker	Georgia	Y	17100 FQ	20510 MW	23910 TQ	USBLS	5/07
Production Worker	Atlanta-Sandy Springs-Marietta MSA, GA	Y	16780 FQ	20050 MW	24250 TQ	USBLS	5/07
Production Worker	Hawaii	Y	16190 FQ	18650 MW	23630 TQ	USBLS	5/07
Production Worker	Honolulu MSA, HI	Y	15880 FQ	17830 MW	22270 TQ	USBLS	5/07
Production Worker	Idaho	Y	17630 FQ	21880 MW	27680 TQ	USBLS	5/07
Production Worker	Boise City-Nampa MSA, ID	Y	16700 FQ	19120 MW	23030 TQ	USBLS	5/07
Production Worker	Coeur d'Alene MSA, ID	Y	19930 FQ	21970 MW	24040 TQ	USBLS	5/07
Production Worker	Illinois	Y	15890 FQ	19480 MW	27280 TQ	USBLS	5/07
Production Worker	Chicago-Naperville-Joliet MSA, IL-IN-WI	Y	15530 FQ	18650 MW	25480 TQ	USBLS	5/07
Production Worker	Indiana	Y	18110 FQ	21780 MW	26630 TQ	USBLS	5/07
Production Worker	Evansville MSA, IN-KY	Y	17330 FQ	19280 MW	22870 TQ	USBLS	5/07
Production Worker	Gary PMSA, IN	Y	18040 FQ	22180 MW	28560 TQ	USBLS	5/07
Production Worker	Indianapolis-Carmel MSA, IN	Y	17930 FQ	23170 MW	27500 TQ	USBLS	5/07
Production Worker	Terre Haute MSA, IN	Y	25160 FQ	28400 MW	31590 TQ	USBLS	5/07
Production Worker	Iowa	Y	19820 FQ	24190 MW	29130 TQ	USBLS	5/07
Production Worker	Cedar Rapids MSA, IA	Y	22720 FQ	28650 MW	36190 TQ	USBLS	5/07
Production Worker	Des Moines-West Des Moines MSA, IA	Y	21270 FQ	26790 MW	35750 TQ	USBLS	5/07
Production Worker	Kansas	Y	17180 FQ	20060 MW	25370 TQ	USBLS	5/07
Production Worker	Wichita MSA, KS	Y	16640 FQ	19860 MW	27550 TQ	USBLS	5/07
Production Worker	Kentucky	Y	18103 FQ	21571 MW	27456 TQ	KYBLS	2008
Production Worker	Louisville-Jefferson County MSA, KY-IN	Y	17670 FQ	21300 MW	27190 TQ	USBLS	5/07
Production Worker	Louisiana	H	8.37 FQ	10.43 MW	13.21 TQ	LABLS	1/08-3/08
Production Worker	Baton Rouge MSA, LA	Y	19180 FQ	23930 MW	30230 TQ	USBLS	5/07
Production Worker	Houma-Bayou Cane-Thibodaux MSA, LA	Y	19860 FQ	22990 MW	26660 TQ	USBLS	5/07
Production Worker	New Orleans-Metairie-Kenner MSA, LA	Y	19180 FQ	22390 MW	27280 TQ	USBLS	5/07
Production Worker	Maine	Y	19870 FQ	22260 MW	25210 TQ	USBLS	5/07
Production Worker	Portland-South Portland-Biddeford MSA, ME	Y	19660 FQ	22120 MW	25150 TQ	USBLS	5/07
Production Worker	Maryland	Y		23575 MW		MDBLS	3/08
Production Worker	Baltimore-Towson MSA, MD	Y	18240 FQ	22560 MW	27950 TQ	USBLS	5/07
Production Worker	Bethesda-Gaithersburg-Frederick PMSA, MD	Y	20800 FQ	24380 MW	28970 TQ	USBLS	5/07
Production Worker	Massachusetts	Y	18970 FQ	22940 MW	27840 TQ	USBLS	5/07
Production Worker	Barnstable Town MSA, MA	Y	18450 FQ	20870 MW	24490 TQ	USBLS	5/07
Production Worker	Boston-Cambridge-Quincy NECTA, MA	Y	19670 FQ	23790 MW	28550 TQ	USBLS	5/07
Production Worker	Springfield MSA, MA-CT	Y	17810 FQ	21180 MW	25560 TQ	USBLS	5/07
Production Worker	Worcester MSA, MA-CT	Y	17620 FQ	20280 MW	24520 TQ	USBLS	5/07
Production Worker	Michigan	Y	18780 FQ	23100 MW	29510 TQ	USBLS	5/07
Production Worker	Detroit-Warren-Livonia MSA, MI	Y	19370 FQ	24070 MW	30100 TQ	USBLS	5/07
Production Worker	Grand Rapids-Wyoming MSA, MI	Y	20780 FQ	23370 MW	28870 TQ	USBLS	5/07
Production Worker	Warren-Troy-Farmington Hills PMSA, MI	Y	18400 FQ	22260 MW	27920 TQ	USBLS	5/07
Production Worker	Minnesota	Y	19593 FQ	23791 MW	29773 TQ	MNBLS	10/08-12/08
Production Worker	Duluth-Supérior MSA, MN-WI	Y	19468 FQ	23739 MW	29866 TQ	MNBLS	10/08-12/08
Production Worker	Minneapolis-Saint Paul MSA, MN-WI	Y	19862 FQ	23833 MW	29804 TQ	MNBLS	10/08-12/08
Production Worker	Rochester MSA, MN	Y	22051 FQ	25673 MW	29769 TQ	MNBLS	10/08-12/08
Production Worker	Mississippi	Y	17360 FQ	21120 MW	24690 TQ	USBLS	5/07
Production Worker	Jackson MSA, MS	Y	15450 FQ	19790 MW	22660 TQ	USBLS	5/07
Production Worker	Missouri	Y	17440 FQ	20810 MW	24860 TQ	USBLS	5/07
Production Worker	Joplin MSA, MO	Y	16550 FQ	19330 MW	22210 TQ	USBLS	5/07
Production Worker	Kansas City MSA, MO-KS	Y	18710 FQ	22770 MW	29200 TQ	USBLS	5/07
Production Worker	St. Louis MSA, MO-IL	Y	18420 FQ	24090 MW	31980 TQ	USBLS	5/07
Production Worker	Montana	Y	18400 FQ	23020 MW	31240 TQ	USBLS	5/07
Production Worker	Billings MSA, MT	Y	15640 FQ	18400 MW	23310 TQ	USBLS	5/07
Production Worker	Nebraska	Y	19270 FQ	23010 MW	27660 TQ	USBLS	5/07

AE	Average entry wage	AW	Average wage paid	FQ	First quartile wage
AER	Average entry range	AWR	Average wage range	H	Hourly
AEX	Average experienced wage	AXR	Average experienced range	HI	Highest wage paid
ATC	Average total compensation	D	Daily	HR	High end range

LO	Lowest wage paid	MTC	Median total compensation	TCC	Total cash compensation
LR	Low end range	MW	Median wage paid	TQ	Third quartile wage
M	Monthly	MWR	Median wage range	W	Weekly
MCC	Median cash compensation	S	See annotated source	Y	Yearly

Occupation/Type/Industry	Location	Per	Low	Mid	High	Source	Date
Helper							
Production Worker	Omaha-Council Bluffs MSA, NE-IA	Y	19900 FQ	23180 MW	27490 TQ	USBLS	5/07
Production Worker	Nevada	H	8.49 FQ	10.15 MW	12.68 TQ	NVBLS	5/08
Production Worker	Las Vegas-Paradise MSA, NV	H	8.06 FQ	9.20 MW	11.50 TQ	NVBLS	5/08
Production Worker	New Hampshire	H	9.46 AE	11.25 MW	12.59 AEX	NHBLS	6/08
Production Worker	Manchester MSA, NH	Y	18700 FQ	21520 MW	24750 TQ	USBLS	5/07
Production Worker	Nashua NECTA, NH-MA	Y	21070 FQ	24120 MW	27320 TQ	USBLS	5/07
Production Worker	Portsmouth MSA, NH-ME	Y	21840 FQ	24030 MW	27550 TQ	USBLS	5/07
Production Worker	New Jersey	Y	16110 FQ	20030 MW	25790 TQ	USBLS	5/07
Production Worker	Camden PMSA, NJ	Y	15290 FQ	15950 MW	24180 TQ	USBLS	5/07
Production Worker	Edison PMSA, NJ	Y	19370 FQ	22730 MW	28000 TQ	USBLS	5/07
Production Worker	Newark-Union PMSA, NJ-PA	Y	16310 FQ	19320 MW	24600 TQ	USBLS	5/07
Production Worker	New Mexico	Y	16860 FQ	19900 MW	24640 TQ	USBLS	5/07
Production Worker	Albuquerque MSA, NM	Y	16850 FQ	19430 MW	23870 TQ	USBLS	5/07
Production Worker	New York	Y	16360 FQ	19960 MW	25720 TQ	USBLS	5/07
Production Worker	Albany-Schenectady-Troy MSA, NY	Y	18390 FQ	22870 MW	30740 TQ	USBLS	5/07
Production Worker	Buffalo-Niagara Falls MSA, NY	Y	16990 FQ	20870 MW	27620 TQ	USBLS	5/07
Production Worker	Nassau-Suffolk PMSA, NY	Y	16260 FQ	19240 MW	23710 TQ	USBLS	5/07
Production Worker	New York-Northern New Jersey-Long Island MSA, NY-NJ-PA	Y	16340 FQ	19850 MW	25140 TQ	USBLS	5/07
Production Worker	North Carolina	Y	17940 FQ	21470 MW	25270 TQ	USBLS	5/07
Production Worker	Charlotte-Gastonia-Concord MSA, NC-SC	Y	17000 FQ	19570 MW	23460 TQ	USBLS	5/07
Production Worker	Raleigh-Cary MSA, NC	Y	17920 FQ	20880 MW	25290 TQ	USBLS	5/07
Production Worker	Winston-Salem MSA, NC	Y	18920 FQ	24410 MW	33010 TQ	USBLS	5/07
Production Worker	North Dakota	Y	18590 FQ	21160 MW	23860 TQ	USBLS	5/07
Production Worker	Fargo MSA, ND-MN	Y	17580 FQ	19690 MW	22640 TQ	USBLS	5/07
Production Worker	Ohio	Y	18430 FQ	22710 MW	29070 TQ	USBLS	5/07
Production Worker	Cincinnati-Middletown MSA, OH-KY-IN	Y	18640 FQ	22860 MW	28700 TQ	USBLS	5/07
Production Worker	Cleveland-Elyria-Mentor MSA, OH	Y	17730 FQ	21790 MW	27760 TQ	USBLS	5/07
Production Worker	Columbus MSA, OH	Y	18220 FQ	21720 MW	26100 TQ	USBLS	5/07
Production Worker	Dayton MSA, OH	Y	17850 FQ	22210 MW	30420 TQ	USBLS	5/07
Production Worker	Oklahoma	Y	16880 FQ	19740 MW	25250 TQ	USBLS	5/07
Production Worker	Oklahoma City MSA, OK	Y	16920 FQ	19590 MW	26850 TQ	USBLS	5/07
Production Worker	Tulsa MSA, OK	Y	17850 FQ	21730 MW	26000 TQ	USBLS	5/07
Production Worker	Oregon	H	9.51 FQ	11.65 MW	14.68 TQ	ORBLS	5/08
Production Worker	Portland-Vancouver-Beaverton MSA, OR-WA	Y	19200 FQ	23700 MW	30320 TQ	USBLS	5/07
Production Worker	Pennsylvania	Y	18330 FQ	22870 MW	29180 TQ	USBLS	5/07
Production Worker	Allentown-Bethlehem-Easton MSA, PA-NJ	Y	17550 FQ	22690 MW	30310 TQ	USBLS	5/07
Production Worker	Philadelphia-Camden-Wilmington MSA, PA-NJ-DE-MD	Y	16590 FQ	21980 MW	28510 TQ	USBLS	5/07
Production Worker	Pittsburgh MSA, PA	Y	18660 FQ	23540 MW	30380 TQ	USBLS	5/07
Production Worker	Reading MSA, PA	Y	17500 FQ	23300 MW	28600 TQ	USBLS	5/07
Production Worker	Rhode Island	Y	17730 FQ	20620 MW	25830 TQ	USBLS	5/07
Production Worker	Providence-Fall River-Warwick MSA, RI-MA	Y	18210 FQ	21700 MW	26340 TQ	USBLS	5/07
Production Worker	South Carolina	Y	16900 FQ	19870 MW	24380 TQ	USBLS	5/07
Production Worker	Charleston-North Charleston MSA, SC	Y	16750 FQ	19650 MW	41980 TQ	USBLS	5/07
Production Worker	Columbia MSA, SC	Y	17030 FQ	20360 MW	24270 TQ	USBLS	5/07
Production Worker	South Dakota	Y	20278 FQ	22187 MW	24189 TQ	SDBLS	7/08-9/08
Production Worker	Tennessee	Y	17500 FQ	20560 MW	26290 TQ	USBLS	5/07
Production Worker	Memphis MSA, TN-MS-AR	Y	16900 FQ	19290 MW	26170 TQ	USBLS	5/07
Production Worker	Nashville-Davidson-Murfreesboro MSA, TN	Y	17360 FQ	19960 MW	24640 TQ	USBLS	5/07
Production Worker	Texas	Y	15000 FQ	18120 MW	21990 TQ	USBLS	5/07
Production Worker	Austin-Round Rock MSA, TX	Y	14990 FQ	18070 MW	21570 TQ	USBLS	5/07
Production Worker	Brownsville-Harlingen MSA, TX	Y	12920 FQ	14890 MW	17740 TQ	USBLS	5/07
Production Worker	Dallas-Fort Worth-Arlington MSA, TX	Y	15080 FQ	17880 MW	21250 TQ	USBLS	5/07
Production Worker	El Paso MSA, TX	Y	13110 FQ	15320 MW	19270 TQ	USBLS	5/07

AE Average entry wage	**AW** Average wage paid	**FQ** First quartile wage	**LO** Lowest wage paid	**MTC** Median total compensation	**TCC** Total cash compensation
AER Average entry range	**AWR** Average wage range	**H** Hourly	**LR** Low end range	**MW** Median wage paid	**TQ** Third quartile wage
AEX Average experienced wage	**AXR** Average experienced range	**HI** Highest wage paid	**M** Monthly	**MWR** Median wage range	**W** Weekly
ATC Average total compensation	**D** Daily	**HR** High end range	**MCC** Median cash compensation	**S** See annotated source	**Y** Yearly

Helper

Occupation/Type/Industry	Location	Per	Low	Mid	High	Source	Date
Production Worker	Houston-Sugar Land-Baytown MSA, TX	Y	15050 FQ	18460 MW	23100 TQ	USBLS	5/07
Production Worker	San Antonio MSA, TX	Y	14170 FQ	17450 MW	20170 TQ	USBLS	5/07
Production Worker	Utah	Y	17450 FQ	19960 MW	22970 TQ	USBLS	5/07
Production Worker	Provo-Orem MSA, UT	Y	17850 FQ	20290 MW	23290 TQ	USBLS	5/07
Production Worker	Salt Lake City MSA, UT	Y	17790 FQ	20320 MW	23150 TQ	USBLS	5/07
Production Worker	Vermont	Y	20900 FQ	23310 MW	27430 TQ	USBLS	5/07
Production Worker	Burlington-South Burlington MSA, VT	Y	22480 FQ	25220 MW	28440 TQ	USBLS	5/07
Production Worker	Virginia	Y	17910 FQ	20970 MW	24640 TQ	USBLS	5/07
Production Worker	Richmond MSA, VA	Y	18790 FQ	21860 MW	26770 TQ	USBLS	5/07
Production Worker	Virginia Beach-Norfolk-Newport News MSA, VA-NC	Y	17130 FQ	19570 MW	22730 TQ	USBLS	5/07
Production Worker	Washington	H	9.31 FQ	11.04 MW	14.01 TQ	WABLS	3/08
Production Worker	Bremerton-Silverdale MSA, WA	Y	18860 FQ	21030 MW	24750 TQ	USBLS	5/07
Production Worker	Olympia MSA, WA	Y	19370 FQ	21090 MW	22790 TQ	USBLS	5/07
Production Worker	Seattle-Tacoma-Bellevue MSA, WA	Y	20100 FQ	24520 MW	31280 TQ	USBLS	5/07
Production Worker	West Virginia	Y	18329 FQ	24065 MW	32273 TQ	WVBLS	7/08-9/08
Production Worker	Charleston MSA, WV	Y	17340 FQ	22300 MW	29070 TQ	USBLS	5/07
Production Worker	Wheeling MSA, WV-OH	Y	16230 FQ	24650 MW	28690 TQ	USBLS	5/07
Production Worker	Wisconsin	Y	19400 FQ	24050 MW	30300 TQ	USBLS	5/07
Production Worker	Milwaukee-Waukesha-West Allis MSA, WI	Y	15680 FQ	21320 MW	27560 TQ	USBLS	5/07
Production Worker	Wyoming	Y	20632 FQ	27861 MW	33677 TQ	WYBLS	9/08
Production Worker	Casper MSA, WY	Y	24120 FQ	28070 MW	31240 TQ	WYBLS	9/08
Production Worker	Cheyenne MSA, WY	Y	13583 FQ	16082 MW	21156 TQ	WYBLS	9/08
Production Worker	Puerto Rico	Y	12360 FQ	13550 MW	14750 TQ	USBLS	5/07
Production Worker	San Juan-Caguas-Guaynabo MSA, PR	Y	12370 FQ	13580 MW	14860 TQ	USBLS	5/07
Production Worker	Virgin Islands	Y	16220 FQ	18290 MW	21770 TQ	USBLS	5/07
Production Worker	Guam	Y	12460 FQ	13850 MW	15310 TQ	USBLS	5/07
Roofer	Alabama	Y	16150 FQ	20190 MW	22780 TQ	USBLS	5/07
Roofer	Birmingham-Hoover MSA, AL	Y	17850 FQ	19950 MW	22280 TQ	USBLS	5/07
Roofer	Arizona	Y	17170 FQ	20720 MW	24720 TQ	USBLS	5/07
Roofer	Phoenix-Mesa-Scottsdale MSA, AZ	Y	17620 FQ	21770 MW	25810 TQ	USBLS	5/07
Roofer	Tucson MSA, AZ	Y	17240 FQ	19330 MW	21880 TQ	USBLS	5/07
Roofer	Arkansas	Y	18420 FQ	21830 MW	25380 TQ	USBLS	5/07
Roofer	Fayetteville-Springdale-Rogers MSA, AR-MO	Y	23250 FQ	34080 MW	38450 TQ	USBLS	5/07
Roofer	Little Rock-North Little Rock MSA, AR	Y	20090 FQ	22450 MW	24890 TQ	USBLS	5/07
Roofer	California	H	9.89 FQ	11.71 MW	14.74 TQ	CABLS	1/08-3/08
Roofer	Los Angeles-Long Beach-Glendale PMSA, CA	H	9.09 FQ	10.71 MW	13.98 TQ	CABLS	1/08-3/08
Roofer	Oakland-Fremont-Hayward MSA, CA	H	10.33 FQ	12.38 MW	15.12 TQ	CABLS	1/08-3/08
Roofer	Riverside-San Bernardino-Ontario MSA, CA	H	10.64 FQ	12.40 MW	15.50 TQ	CABLS	1/08-3/08
Roofer	Sacramento-Arden Arcade-Roseville MSA, CA	H	9.68 FQ	12.26 MW	14.88 TQ	CABLS	1/08-3/08
Roofer	San Diego-Carlsbad-San Marcos MSA, CA	H	9.62 FQ	10.55 MW	11.79 TQ	CABLS	1/08-3/08
Roofer	San Francisco-San Mateo-Redwood PMSA, CA	H	12.54 FQ	14.81 MW	21.32 TQ	CABLS	1/08-3/08
Roofer	Santa Ana-Anaheim-Irvine PMSA, CA	Y	22330 FQ	25430 MW	28650 TQ	USBLS	5/07
Roofer	Colorado	Y	21000 FQ	23450 MW	26940 TQ	USBLS	5/07
Roofer	Boulder MSA, CO	Y	19330 FQ	22600 MW	26240 TQ	USBLS	5/07
Roofer	Denver-Aurora MSA, CO	Y	21330 FQ	23880 MW	26850 TQ	USBLS	5/07
Roofer	Connecticut	H	10.67 AE	11.87 MW		CTBLS	1/08-3/08
Roofer	Delaware	Y	24180 FQ	27050 MW	29790 TQ	USBLS	5/07
Roofer	Washington-Arlington-Alexandria MSA, DC-VA-MD-WV	Y	24340 FQ	28900 MW	33840 TQ	USBLS	5/07
Roofer	Florida	Y	20130 FQ	22340 MW	24560 TQ	USBLS	5/07
Roofer	Fort Lauderdale-Pompano Beach-Deerfield Beach PMSA, FL	Y	20480 FQ	24030 MW	27610 TQ	USBLS	5/07

AE	Average entry wage	AW	Average wage paid	FQ	First quartile wage	LO	Lowest wage paid	MTC	Median total compensation	TCC	Total cash compensation
AER	Average entry range	AWR	Average wage range	H	Hourly	LR	Low end range	MW	Median wage paid	TQ	Third quartile wage
AEX	Average experienced wage	AXR	Average experienced range	HI	Highest wage paid	M	Monthly	MWR	Median wage range	W	Weekly
ATC	Average total compensation	D	Daily	HR	High end range	MCC	Median cash compensation	S	See annotated source	Y	Yearly

Occupation/Type/Industry	Location	Per	Low	Mid	High	Source	Date
Helper							
Roofer	Jacksonville MSA, FL	Y	20870 FQ	22400 MW	23930 TQ	USBLS	5/07
Roofer	Miami-Fort Lauderdale-Miami Beach MSA, FL	Y	20900 FQ	22800 MW	24730 TQ	USBLS	5/07
Roofer	Orlando-Kissimmee MSA, FL	Y	17930 FQ	20830 MW	24590 TQ	USBLS	5/07
Roofer	Tampa-St. Petersburg-Clearwater MSA, FL	Y	20730 FQ	23070 MW	25800 TQ	USBLS	5/07
Roofer	West Palm Beach-Boca Raton-Boynton Beach PMSA, FL	Y	21150 FQ	22630 MW	24120 TQ	USBLS	5/07
Roofer	Georgia	Y	17720 FQ	20040 MW	23840 TQ	USBLS	5/07
Roofer	Atlanta-Sandy Springs-Marietta MSA, GA	Y	17890 FQ	20120 MW	24350 TQ	USBLS	5/07
Roofer	Savannah MSA, GA	Y	18110 FQ	20080 MW	22680 TQ	USBLS	5/07
Roofer	Idaho	Y	16950 FQ	21070 MW	24300 TQ	USBLS	5/07
Roofer	Illinois	Y	22110 FQ	25470 MW	30400 TQ	USBLS	5/07
Roofer	Chicago-Naperville-Joliet MSA, IL-IN-WI	Y	23420 FQ	26370 MW	30590 TQ	USBLS	5/07
Roofer	Indiana	Y	20940 FQ	24880 MW	28540 TQ	USBLS	5/07
Roofer	Indianapolis-Carmel MSA, IN	Y	22680 FQ	26410 MW	29490 TQ	USBLS	5/07
Roofer	Iowa	Y	20800 FQ	24560 MW	29980 TQ	USBLS	5/07
Roofer	Kansas	Y	17680 FQ	21250 MW	23900 TQ	USBLS	5/07
Roofer	Wichita MSA, KS	Y	20600 FQ	22210 MW	23810 TQ	USBLS	5/07
Roofer	Kentucky	Y	20889 FQ	25204 MW	30307 TQ	KYBLS	2008
Roofer	Louisville-Jefferson County MSA, KY-IN	Y	22100 FQ	25560 MW	29560 TQ	USBLS	5/07
Roofer	Louisiana	H	8.61 FQ	10.40 MW	11.98 TQ	LABLS	1/08-3/08
Roofer	New Orleans-Metairie-Kenner MSA, LA	Y	18350 FQ	22000 MW	25850 TQ	USBLS	5/07
Roofer	Maine	Y	21810 FQ	24750 MW	29160 TQ	USBLS	5/07
Roofer	Portland-South Portland-Biddeford MSA, ME	Y	21900 FQ	24730 MW	27660 TQ	USBLS	5/07
Roofer	Maryland	Y		28425 MW		MDBLS	3/08
Roofer	Baltimore-Towson MSA, MD	Y	23490 FQ	26890 MW	31170 TQ	USBLS	5/07
Roofer	Bethesda-Gaithersburg-Frederick PMSA, MD	Y	27980 FQ	33430 MW	37320 TQ	USBLS	5/07
Roofer	Massachusetts	Y	26690 FQ	29770 MW	33920 TQ	USBLS	5/07
Roofer	Boston-Cambridge-Quincy NECTA, MA	Y	27270 FQ	30360 MW	37590 TQ	USBLS	5/07
Roofer	Michigan	Y	19880 FQ	24770 MW	29570 TQ	USBLS	5/07
Roofer	Detroit-Warren-Livonia MSA, MI	Y	22310 FQ	27350 MW	44850 TQ	USBLS	5/07
Roofer	Grand Rapids-Wyoming MSA, MI	Y	20650 FQ	22160 MW	23680 TQ	USBLS	5/07
Roofer	Warren-Troy-Farmington Hills PMSA, MI	Y	23360 FQ	28900 MW	46700 TQ	USBLS	5/07
Roofer	Minnesota	Y	23511 FQ	28918 MW	34187 TQ	MNBLS	10/08-12/08
Roofer	Duluth-Superior MSA, MN-WI	Y	19844 FQ	23153 MW	28349 TQ	MNBLS	10/08-12/08
Roofer	Minneapolis-Saint Paul MSA, MN-WI	Y	28275 FQ	34461 MW	38434 TQ	MNBLS	10/08-12/08
Roofer	Mississippi	Y	15800 FQ	19870 MW	24410 TQ	USBLS	5/07
Roofer	Jackson MSA, MS	Y	21000 FQ	22850 MW	24710 TQ	USBLS	5/07
Roofer	Missouri	Y	19330 FQ	24600 MW	28200 TQ	USBLS	5/07
Roofer	St. Louis MSA, MO-IL	Y	24660 FQ	27260 MW	31080 TQ	USBLS	5/07
Roofer	Montana	Y	21050 FQ	24510 MW	31640 TQ	USBLS	5/07
Roofer	Nebraska	Y	16590 FQ	18650 MW	20800 TQ	USBLS	5/07
Roofer	Nevada	H	10.39 FQ	11.56 MW	13.22 TQ	NVBLS	5/08
Roofer	Las Vegas-Paradise MSA, NV	H	10.22 FQ	11.70 MW	14.07 TQ	NVBLS	5/08
Roofer	New Jersey	Y	21630 FQ	24360 MW	31300 TQ	USBLS	5/07
Roofer	Edison PMSA, NJ	Y	20710 FQ	22550 MW	24390 TQ	USBLS	5/07
Roofer	Newark-Union PMSA, NJ-PA	Y	29730 FQ	34220 MW	37990 TQ	USBLS	5/07
Roofer	New Mexico	Y	13460 FQ	16940 MW	22170 TQ	USBLS	5/07
Roofer	Albuquerque MSA, NM	Y	13090 FQ	15370 MW	21820 TQ	USBLS	5/07
Roofer	Las Cruces MSA, NM	Y	16180 FQ	17910 MW	19590 TQ	USBLS	5/07
Roofer	New York	Y	21210 FQ	23600 MW	28350 TQ	USBLS	5/07
Roofer	Buffalo-Niagara Falls MSA, NY	Y	20740 FQ	22190 MW	23650 TQ	USBLS	5/07
Roofer	Nassau-Suffolk PMSA, NY	Y	24460 FQ	27520 MW	29800 TQ	USBLS	5/07
Roofer	New York-Northern New Jersey-Long Island MSA, NY-NJ-PA	Y	21610 FQ	24740 MW	31380 TQ	USBLS	5/07
Roofer	North Carolina	Y	18660 FQ	21160 MW	23540 TQ	USBLS	5/07

AE	Average entry wage	AW	Average wage paid	FQ	First quartile wage
AER	Average entry range	AWR	Average wage range	H	Hourly
AEX	Average experienced wage	AXR	Average experienced range	HI	Highest wage paid
ATC	Average total compensation	D	Daily	HR	High end range

LO	Lowest wage paid	MTC	Median total compensation
LR	Low end range	MW	Median wage paid
M	Monthly	MWR	Median wage range
MCC	Median cash compensation	S	See annotated source

TCC	Total cash compensation		
TQ	Third quartile wage		
W	Weekly		
Y	Yearly		

Occupation/Type/Industry	Location	Per	Low	Mid	High	Source	Date
Helper							
Roofer	Charlotte-Gastonia-Concord MSA, NC-SC	Y	18950 FQ	21200 MW	23330 TQ	USBLS	5/07
Roofer	North Dakota	Y	21530 FQ	23320 MW	25160 TQ	USBLS	5/07
Roofer	Ohio	Y	21310 FQ	24520 MW	28270 TQ	USBLS	5/07
Roofer	Cincinnati-Middletown MSA, OH-KY-IN	Y	21200 FQ	24180 MW	28450 TQ	USBLS	5/07
Roofer	Cleveland-Elyria-Mentor MSA, OH	Y	25590 FQ	27500 MW	29400 TQ	USBLS	5/07
Roofer	Columbus MSA, OH	Y	21600 FQ	24870 MW	27660 TQ	USBLS	5/07
Roofer	Dayton MSA, OH	Y	23430 FQ	26170 MW	35150 TQ	USBLS	5/07
Roofer	Oklahoma	Y	17280 FQ	20640 MW	22850 TQ	USBLS	5/07
Roofer	Oklahoma City MSA, OK	Y	19330 FQ	21020 MW	22750 TQ	USBLS	5/07
Roofer	Tulsa MSA, OK	Y	13940 FQ	17880 MW	22240 TQ	USBLS	5/07
Roofer	Oregon	H	10.00 FQ	11.51 MW	16.16 TQ	ORBLS	5/08
Roofer	Portland-Vancouver-Beaverton MSA, OR-WA	Y	20950 FQ	25700 MW	35100 TQ	USBLS	5/07
Roofer	Pennsylvania	Y	19810 FQ	23700 MW	28240 TQ	USBLS	5/07
Roofer	Philadelphia-Camden-Wilmington MSA, PA-NJ-DE-MD	Y	20980 FQ	25480 MW	30380 TQ	USBLS	5/07
Roofer	Pittsburgh MSA, PA	Y	15090 FQ	23260 MW	28080 TQ	USBLS	5/07
Roofer	Rhode Island	Y	26630 FQ	28830 MW	31160 TQ	USBLS	5/07
Roofer	Providence-Fall River-Warwick MSA, RI-MA	Y	26860 FQ	28870 MW	30930 TQ	USBLS	5/07
Roofer	South Carolina	Y	17320 FQ	19210 MW	22180 TQ	USBLS	5/07
Roofer	Florence MSA, SC	Y	16270 FQ	17440 MW	18620 TQ	USBLS	5/07
Roofer	South Dakota	Y	22141 FQ	23892 MW	25750 TQ	SDBLS	7/08-9/08
Roofer	Tennessee	Y	20780 FQ	23110 MW	25890 TQ	USBLS	5/07
Roofer	Memphis MSA, TN-MS-AR	Y	21530 FQ	23580 MW	26470 TQ	USBLS	5/07
Roofer	Nashville-Davidson-Murfreesboro MSA, TN	Y	21270 FQ	23760 MW	27500 TQ	USBLS	5/07
Roofer	Texas	Y	17250 FQ	19630 MW	23210 TQ	USBLS	5/07
Roofer	Austin-Round Rock MSA, TX	Y	17250 FQ	18940 MW	21690 TQ	USBLS	5/07
Roofer	Dallas-Fort Worth-Arlington MSA, TX	Y	17160 FQ	19000 MW	21830 TQ	USBLS	5/07
Roofer	El Paso MSA, TX	Y	13320 FQ	15520 MW	17430 TQ	USBLS	5/07
Roofer	Houston-Sugar Land-Baytown MSA, TX	Y	19610 FQ	23480 MW	28180 TQ	USBLS	5/07
Roofer	San Antonio MSA, TX	Y	19180 FQ	22310 MW	27990 TQ	USBLS	5/07
Roofer	Utah	Y	20110 FQ	23640 MW	28790 TQ	USBLS	5/07
Roofer	Provo-Orem MSA, UT	Y	13790 FQ	16250 MW	20440 TQ	USBLS	5/07
Roofer	Salt Lake City MSA, UT	Y	21630 FQ	26100 MW	30230 TQ	USBLS	5/07
Roofer	Virginia	Y	21220 FQ	24910 MW	30130 TQ	USBLS	5/07
Roofer	Richmond MSA, VA	Y	20260 FQ	22840 MW	25100 TQ	USBLS	5/07
Roofer	Virginia Beach-Norfolk-Newport News MSA, VA-NC	Y	19470 FQ	23270 MW	27630 TQ	USBLS	5/07
Roofer	Washington	H	10.44 FQ	14.96 MW	18.18 TQ	WABLS	3/08
Roofer	Seattle-Tacoma-Bellevue MSA, WA	Y	21420 FQ	30780 MW	37280 TQ	USBLS	5/07
Roofer	West Virginia	Y	15997 FQ	18316 MW	20105 TQ	WVBLS	7/08-9/08
Roofer	Wisconsin	Y	23850 FQ	27730 MW	31590 TQ	USBLS	5/07
Roofer	Milwaukee-Waukesha-West Allis MSA, WI	Y	24920 FQ	28180 MW	31560 TQ	USBLS	5/07
Roofer	Wyoming	Y	20643 FQ	22797 MW	24886 TQ	WYBLS	9/08
Roofer	Puerto Rico	Y	12420 FQ	13950 MW	15520 TQ	USBLS	5/07
Roofer	San Juan-Caguas-Guaynabo MSA, PR	Y	12340 FQ	13790 MW	15260 TQ	USBLS	5/07
High Pressure Piping Inspector							
State Government	Ohio	H	18.36 LO		23.87 HI	ODAS	2008
Highway Engineer							
State Government	Indiana	Y	53586 LO		96512 HI	AFT02	3/1/08
State Government	West Virginia	Y	40932 LO		75720 HI	AFT02	3/1/08
Highway Garage Custodial Attendant							
Department of Transportation	New Hampshire	Y			28481 HI	NHUL03	2008
Highway Maintenance Worker	Alabama	Y	20930 FQ	23930 MW	28980 TQ	USBLS	5/07
	Birmingham-Hoover MSA, AL	Y	21750 FQ	24880 MW	29850 TQ	USBLS	5/07

AE Average entry wage	**AW** Average wage paid	**FQ** First quartile wage	**LO** Lowest wage paid	**MTC** Median total compensation **TCC** Total cash compensation
AER Average entry range	**AWR** Average wage range	**H** Hourly	**LR** Low end range	**MW** Median wage paid **TQ** Third quartile wage
AEX Average experienced wage	**AXR** Average experienced range	**HI** Highest wage paid	**M** Monthly	**MWR** Median wage range **W** Weekly
ATC Average total compensation **D** Daily		**HR** High end range	**MCC** Median cash compensation	**S** See annotated source **Y** Yearly

Occupation/Type/Industry	Location	Per	Low	Mid	High	Source	Date
Highway Maintenance Worker	Alaska	Y	48130 FQ	56130 MW	62890 TQ	USBLS	5/07
	Arizona	Y	26190 FQ	29360 MW	33810 TQ	USBLS	5/07
	Phoenix-Mesa-Scottsdale MSA, AZ	Y	25650 FQ	29990 MW	37210 TQ	USBLS	5/07
	Tucson MSA, AZ	Y	26480 FQ	29040 MW	32230 TQ	USBLS	5/07
	Arkansas	Y	20960 FQ	25160 MW	31090 TQ	USBLS	5/07
	Little Rock-North Little Rock MSA, AR	Y	20240 FQ	24530 MW	31350 TQ	USBLS	5/07
	California	H	19.68 FQ	23.18 MW	27.68 TQ	CABLS	1/08-3/08
	Los Angeles-Long Beach-Glendale PMSA, CA	H	21.70 FQ	25.70 MW	32.14 TQ	CABLS	1/08-3/08
	Oakland-Fremont-Hayward MSA, CA	H	20.62 FQ	23.64 MW	28.21 TQ	CABLS	1/08-3/08
	Riverside-San Bernardino-Ontario MSA, CA	H	19.01 FQ	22.41 MW	26.39 TQ	CABLS	1/08-3/08
	Sacramento-Arden Arcade-Roseville MSA, CA	H	20.56 FQ	23.05 MW	25.84 TQ	CABLS	1/08-3/08
	San Diego-Carlsbad-San Marcos MSA, CA	H	19.26 FQ	22.10 MW	24.80 TQ	CABLS	1/08-3/08
	San Francisco-San Mateo-Redwood PMSA, CA	H	23.57 FQ	28.21 MW	31.58 TQ	CABLS	1/08-3/08
	San Jose-Sunnyvale-Santa Clara MSA, CA	H	21.28 FQ	26.42 MW	30.32 TQ	CABLS	1/08-3/08
	Santa Ana-Anaheim-Irvine PMSA, CA	Y	43140 FQ	48190 MW	56630 TQ	USBLS	5/07
	Santa Rosa-Petaluma MSA, CA	H	22.17 FQ	25.15 MW	28.57 TQ	CABLS	1/08-3/08
	Colorado	Y	32820 FQ	37050 MW	42310 TQ	USBLS	5/07
	Colorado Springs MSA, CO	Y	31950 FQ	35850 MW	39620 TQ	USBLS	5/07
	Denver-Aurora MSA, CO	Y	33760 FQ	38080 MW	43850 TQ	USBLS	5/07
	Fort Collins-Loveland MSA, CO	Y	34320 FQ	37800 MW	42620 TQ	USBLS	5/07
	Connecticut	H	18.51 AE	22.48 MW		CTBLS	1/08-3/08
	Bridgeport-Stamford-Norwalk MSA, CT	Y	41540 FQ	46190 MW	50610 TQ	USBLS	5/07
	Hartford-West Hartford-East Hartford MSA, CT	Y	40760 FQ	45920 MW	51120 TQ	USBLS	5/07
	Delaware	Y	26160 FQ	28480 MW	30870 TQ	USBLS	5/07
	Wilmington PMSA, DE-MD-NJ	Y	26900 FQ	29250 MW	31730 TQ	USBLS	5/07
	Washington-Arlington-Alexandria MSA, DC-VA-MD-WV	Y	33650 FQ	41440 MW	49450 TQ	USBLS	5/07
	Florida	Y	23240 FQ	28090 MW	34590 TQ	USBLS	5/07
	Fort Lauderdale-Pompano Beach-Deerfield Beach PMSA, FL	Y	24580 FQ	28840 MW	34000 TQ	USBLS	5/07
	Jacksonville MSA, FL	Y	23450 FQ	27020 MW	32190 TQ	USBLS	5/07
	Miami-Fort Lauderdale-Miami Beach MSA, FL	Y	24310 FQ	29370 MW	36650 TQ	USBLS	5/07
	Orlando-Kissimmee MSA, FL	Y	23280 FQ	27660 MW	33400 TQ	USBLS	5/07
	Tallahassee MSA, FL	Y	21840 FQ	27630 MW	36000 TQ	USBLS	5/07
	Tampa-St. Petersburg-Clearwater MSA, FL	Y	24200 FQ	28070 MW	31820 TQ	USBLS	5/07
	West Palm Beach-Boca Raton-Boynton Beach PMSA, FL	Y	25630 FQ	30190 MW	36460 TQ	USBLS	5/07
	Georgia	Y	20490 FQ	23850 MW	28680 TQ	USBLS	5/07
	Atlanta-Sandy Springs-Marietta MSA, GA	Y	24440 FQ	28040 MW	32190 TQ	USBLS	5/07
	Idaho	Y	30420 FQ	34570 MW	39770 TQ	USBLS	5/07
	Boise City-Nampa MSA, ID	Y	30810 FQ	33830 MW	37010 TQ	USBLS	5/07
	Illinois	Y	33690 FQ	44630 MW	56470 TQ	USBLS	5/07
	Chicago-Naperville-Joliet MSA, IL-IN-WI	Y	36770 FQ	48280 MW	57790 TQ	USBLS	5/07
	Indiana	Y	24420 FQ	28310 MW	32010 TQ	USBLS	5/07
	Evansville MSA, IN-KY	Y	22990 FQ	26270 MW	31340 TQ	USBLS	5/07
	Gary PMSA, IN	Y	24380 FQ	29360 MW	33310 TQ	USBLS	5/07
	Indianapolis-Carmel MSA, IN	Y	24120 FQ	28740 MW	33180 TQ	USBLS	5/07
	Iowa	Y	31310 FQ	35950 MW	41260 TQ	USBLS	5/07
	Davenport-Moline-Rock Island MSA, IA-IL	Y	32800 FQ	37770 MW	46670 TQ	USBLS	5/07
	Des Moines-West Des Moines MSA, IA	Y	30660 FQ	36290 MW	43510 TQ	USBLS	5/07

AE	Average entry wage	AW	Average wage paid	FQ	First quartile wage	LO	Lowest wage paid	MTC	Median total compensation	TCC	Total cash compensation
AER	Average entry range	AWR	Average wage range	H	Hourly	LR	Low end range	MW	Median wage paid	TQ	Third quartile wage
AEX	Average experienced wage	AXR	Average experienced range	HI	Highest wage paid	M	Monthly	MWR	Median wage range	W	Weekly
ATC	Average total compensation	D	Daily	HR	High end range	MCC	Median cash compensation	S	See annotated source	Y	Yearly

Occupation/Type/Industry	Location	Per	Low	Mid	High	Source	Date
Highway Maintenance Worker	Kansas	Y	22950 FQ	26670 MW	31600 TQ	USBLS	5/07
	Wichita MSA, KS	Y	24550 FQ	28050 MW	32500 TQ	USBLS	5/07
	Kentucky	Y	23019 FQ	26399 MW	31215 TQ	KYBLS	2008
	Louisville-Jefferson County MSA, KY-IN	Y	23860 FQ	27370 MW	31520 TQ	USBLS	5/07
	Louisiana	H	9.51 FQ	12.14 MW	15.56 TQ	LABLS	1/08-3/08
	New Orleans-Metairie-Kenner MSA, LA	Y	20150 FQ	26310 MW	36330 TQ	USBLS	5/07
	Maine	Y	25290 FQ	28790 MW	32190 TQ	USBLS	5/07
	Portland-South Portland-Biddeford MSA, ME	Y	26930 FQ	30110 MW	34720 TQ	USBLS	5/07
	Maryland	Y		33725 MW		MDBLS	3/08
	Baltimore-Towson MSA, MD	Y	27330 FQ	33210 MW	38600 TQ	USBLS	5/07
	Massachusetts	Y	34510 FQ	39710 MW	46150 TQ	USBLS	5/07
	Boston-Cambridge-Quincy NECTA, MA	Y	36960 FQ	41350 MW	47140 TQ	USBLS	5/07
	Worcester MSA, MA-CT	Y	29180 FQ	38940 MW	46440 TQ	USBLS	5/07
	Michigan	Y	34050 FQ	37430 MW	41920 TQ	USBLS	5/07
	Detroit-Warren-Livonia MSA, MI	Y	35010 FQ	41360 MW	47520 TQ	USBLS	5/07
	Grand Rapids-Wyoming MSA, MI	Y	35830 FQ	42280 MW	47040 TQ	USBLS	5/07
	Warren-Troy-Farmington Hills PMSA, MI	Y	32080 FQ	43500 MW	49400 TQ	USBLS	5/07
	Minnesota	Y	36337 FQ	43029 MW	48720 TQ	MNBLS	10/08-12/08
	Duluth-Superior MSA, MN-WI	Y	36031 FQ	43914 MW	48920 TQ	MNBLS	10/08-12/08
	Minneapolis-Saint Paul MSA, MN-WI	Y	41944 FQ	46855 MW	51081 TQ	MNBLS	10/08-12/08
	Rochester MSA, MN	Y	31315 FQ	35377 MW	39073 TQ	MNBLS	10/08-12/08
	Mississippi	Y	19750 FQ	22730 MW	26030 TQ	USBLS	5/07
	Jackson MSA, MS	Y	21380 FQ	23790 MW	27000 TQ	USBLS	5/07
	Missouri	Y	24790 FQ	28570 MW	32200 TQ	USBLS	5/07
	Kansas City MSA, MO-KS	Y	27100 FQ	30350 MW	35610 TQ	USBLS	5/07
	St. Louis MSA, MO-IL	Y	29280 FQ	36400 MW	47310 TQ	USBLS	5/07
	Montana	Y	28300 FQ	32870 MW	37190 TQ	USBLS	5/07
	Billings MSA, MT	Y	32650 FQ	36900 MW	44220 TQ	USBLS	5/07
	Nebraska	Y	25510 FQ	28830 MW	32500 TQ	USBLS	5/07
	Omaha-Council Bluffs MSA, NE-IA	Y	31280 FQ	35240 MW	39250 TQ	USBLS	5/07
	Nevada	H	16.02 FQ	19.17 MW	22.91 TQ	NVBLS	5/08
	Las Vegas-Paradise MSA, NV	H	16.59 FQ	19.88 MW	23.88 TQ	NVBLS	5/08
	New Hampshire	H	10.99 AE	14.77 MW	16.66 AEX	NHBLS	6/08
	Nashua NECTA, NH-MA	Y	25420 FQ	31670 MW	37570 TQ	USBLS	5/07
	New Jersey	Y	33860 FQ	42130 MW	50880 TQ	USBLS	5/07
	Camden PMSA, NJ	Y	30400 FQ	36610 MW	41880 TQ	USBLS	5/07
	Edison PMSA, NJ	Y	38140 FQ	46340 MW	54640 TQ	USBLS	5/07
	Newark-Union PMSA, NJ-PA	Y	33330 FQ	40800 MW	48440 TQ	USBLS	5/07
	New Mexico	Y	22970 FQ	26790 MW	31580 TQ	USBLS	5/07
	New York	Y	28990 FQ	34520 MW	40110 TQ	USBLS	5/07
	Albany-Schenectady-Troy MSA, NY	Y	28130 FQ	34010 MW	39170 TQ	USBLS	5/07
	Buffalo-Niagara Falls MSA, NY	Y	30700 FQ	36180 MW	42060 TQ	USBLS	5/07
	Nassau-Suffolk PMSA, NY	Y	26810 FQ	35680 MW	44250 TQ	KYBLS	5/07
	New York-Northern New Jersey-Long Island MSA, NY-NJ-PA	Y	32600 FQ	41870 MW	52140 TQ	USBLS	5/07
	North Carolina	Y	21900 FQ	24800 MW	29170 TQ	USBLS	5/07
	Charlotte-Gastonia-Concord MSA, NC-SC	Y	22000 FQ	24580 MW	29410 TQ	USBLS	5/07
	Raleigh-Cary MSA, NC	Y	22450 FQ	25150 MW	29090 TQ	USBLS	5/07
	North Dakota	Y	26480 FQ	30500 MW	35660 TQ	USBLS	5/07
	Fargo MSA, ND-MN	Y	30410 FQ	37980 MW	43310 TQ	USBLS	5/07
	Ohio	Y	26180 FQ	32580 MW	39640 TQ	USBLS	5/07
	Cincinnati-Middletown MSA, OH-KY-IN	Y	24380 FQ	31560 MW	40620 TQ	USBLS	5/07
	Cleveland-Elyria-Mentor MSA, OH	Y	32990 FQ	38680 MW	45970 TQ	USBLS	5/07
	Columbus MSA, OH	Y	27700 FQ	34630 MW	39910 TQ	USBLS	5/07
	Dayton MSA, OH	Y	30970 FQ	36840 MW	43540 TQ	USBLS	5/07
	Oklahoma	Y	20530 FQ	23820 MW	27800 TQ	USBLS	5/07
	Oklahoma City MSA, OK	Y	22030 FQ	25820 MW	30710 TQ	USBLS	5/07

Occupation/Type/Industry	Location	Per	Low	Mid	High	Source	Date
Highway Maintenance Worker	Tulsa MSA, OK	Y	21330 FQ	25370 MW	30300 TQ	USBLS	5/07
	Oregon	H	15.86 FQ	18.18 MW	20.35 TQ	ORBLS	5/08
	Portland-Vancouver-Beaverton MSA, OR-WA	Y	34690 FQ	39590 MW	45130 TQ	USBLS	5/07
	Pennsylvania	Y	23890 FQ	30190 MW	37740 TQ	USBLS	5/07
	Allentown-Bethlehem-Easton MSA, PA-NJ	Y	28140 FQ	34480 MW	39190 TQ	USBLS	5/07
	Lancaster MSA, PA	Y	32440 FQ	35890 MW	39990 TQ	USBLS	5/07
	Philadelphia-Camden-Wilmington MSA, PA-NJ-DE-MD	Y	32890 FQ	39380 MW	46450 TQ	USBLS	5/07
	Pittsburgh MSA, PA	Y	24560 FQ	28800 MW	38770 TQ	USBLS	5/07
	Rhode Island	Y	32830 FQ	36410 MW	40310 TQ	USBLS	5/07
	Providence-Fall River-Warwick MSA, RI-MA	Y	31560 FQ	35850 MW	40200 TQ	USBLS	5/07
	South Carolina	Y	21170 FQ	24100 MW	28470 TQ	USBLS	5/07
	South Dakota	Y	23393 FQ	26814 MW	31090 TQ	SDBLS	7/08-9/08
	Sioux Falls MSA, SD	Y	27356 FQ	31176 MW	35913 TQ	SDBLS	7/08-9/08
	Tennessee	Y	19760 FQ	23140 MW	27420 TQ	USBLS	5/07
	Johnson City MSA, TN	Y	19980 FQ	23340 MW	27330 TQ	USBLS	5/07
	Memphis MSA, TN-MS-AR	Y	19880 FQ	23710 MW	28280 TQ	USBLS	5/07
	Nashville-Davidson-Murfreesboro MSA, TN	Y	20480 FQ	25000 MW	30160 TQ	USBLS	5/07
	Texas	Y	21760 FQ	26470 MW	31590 TQ	USBLS	5/07
	Austin-Round Rock MSA, TX	Y	21940 FQ	25420 MW	30470 TQ	USBLS	5/07
	Dallas-Fort Worth-Arlington MSA, TX	Y	24360 FQ	30090 MW	37330 TQ	USBLS	5/07
	Houston-Sugar Land-Baytown MSA, TX	Y	25210 FQ	29630 MW	35810 TQ	USBLS	5/07
	San Antonio MSA, TX	Y	21370 FQ	26920 MW	43290 TQ	USBLS	5/07
	Utah	Y	32770 FQ	39250 MW	43450 TQ	USBLS	5/07
	Ogden-Clearfield MSA, UT	Y	32060 FQ	37800 MW	43050 TQ	USBLS	5/07
	Salt Lake City MSA, UT	Y	38420 FQ	41480 MW	44930 TQ	USBLS	5/07
	Vermont	Y	27590 FQ	31190 MW	36130 TQ	USBLS	5/07
	Burlington-South Burlington MSA, VT	Y	28640 FQ	32010 MW	37150 TQ	USBLS	5/07
	Virginia	Y	29990 FQ	36170 MW	42370 TQ	USBLS	5/07
	Richmond MSA, VA	Y	30200 FQ	35650 MW	40160 TQ	USBLS	5/07
	Virginia Beach-Norfolk-Newport News MSA, VA-NC	Y	29270 FQ	34560 MW	39920 TQ	USBLS	5/07
	Washington	H	18.29 FQ	21.01 MW	23.82 TQ	WABLS	3/08
	Seattle-Tacoma-Bellevue MSA, WA	Y	41720 FQ	46710 MW	51690 TQ	USBLS	5/07
	West Virginia	Y	19605 FQ	25618 MW	31769 TQ	WVBLS	7/08-9/08
	Wheeling MSA, WV-OH	Y	22590 FQ	26430 MW	31190 TQ	USBLS	5/07
	Wisconsin	Y	27480 FQ	34970 MW	40200 TQ	USBLS	5/07
	Green Bay MSA, WI	Y	27330 FQ	36200 MW	43610 TQ	USBLS	5/07
	Milwaukee-Waukesha-West Allis MSA, WI	Y	39410 FQ	44150 MW	49430 TQ	USBLS	5/07
	Wyoming	Y	31383 FQ	36368 MW	43708 TQ	WYBLS	9/08
	Puerto Rico	Y	12560 FQ	14040 MW	15550 TQ	USBLS	5/07
	San Juan-Caguas-Guaynabo MSA, PR	Y	12770 FQ	14430 MW	16160 TQ	USBLS	5/07
	Virgin Islands	Y	17120 FQ	18410 MW	19710 TQ	USBLS	5/07
Highway Patrol Foreman							
Department of Transportation	New Hampshire	Y		53154 AW		NHUL03	2008
Historian	Alabama	Y	39710 FQ	54920 MW	80130 TQ	USBLS	5/07
	Arizona	Y	39750 FQ	50770 MW	61280 TQ	USBLS	5/07
	California	H	25.72 FQ	33.26 MW	42.91 TQ	CABLS	1/08-3/08
	Colorado	Y	52350 FQ	60740 MW	84230 TQ	USBLS	5/07
	Delaware	Y	40350 FQ	48090 MW	60180 TQ	USBLS	5/07
	District of Columbia	Y	69640 FQ	86160 MW	98750 TQ	USBLS	5/07
	Florida	Y	34650 FQ	54820 MW	74350 TQ	USBLS	5/07
	Georgia	Y	38090 FQ	49140 MW	65220 TQ	USBLS	5/07
	Illinois	Y	28060 FQ	38900 MW	70330 TQ	USBLS	5/07
	Indiana	Y	29620 FQ	37350 MW	56990 TQ	USBLS	5/07
	Kansas	Y	35090 FQ	40350 MW	67580 TQ	USBLS	5/07
	Kentucky	Y	33544 FQ	38158 MW	46145 TQ	KYBLS	2008
	Louisiana	H	17.05 FQ	19.34 MW	23.13 TQ	LABLS	1/08-3/08
	Maryland	Y		45225 MW		MDBLS	3/08

AE	Average entry wage	AW	Average wage paid	FQ First quartile wage	LO Lowest wage paid	MTC Median total compensation	TCC Total cash compensation
AER	Average entry range	AWR	Average wage range	H Hourly	LR Low end range	MW Median wage paid	TQ Third quartile wage
AEX	Average experienced wage	AXR	Average experienced range	HI Highest wage paid	M Monthly	MWR Median wage range	W Weekly
ATC	Average total compensation	D	Daily	HR High end range	MCC Median cash compensation	S See annotated source	Y Yearly

Occupation/Type/Industry	Location	Per	Low	Mid	High	Source	Date
Historian	Massachusetts	Y	31060 FQ	59650 MW	89120 TQ	USBLS	5/07
	Michigan	Y	42010 FQ	49580 MW	60710 TQ	USBLS	5/07
	Minnesota	Y	60409 FQ	83855 MW	94013 TQ	MNBLS	10/08-12/08
	Mississippi	Y	26190 FQ	30160 MW	48560 TQ	USBLS	5/07
	Missouri	Y	41750 FQ	47260 MW	55830 TQ	USBLS	5/07
	Nevada	H	21.44 FQ	27.47 MW	32.35 TQ	NVBLS	5/08
	New Jersey	Y	55580 FQ	69840 MW	76960 TQ	USBLS	5/07
	New York	Y	22710 FQ	26920 MW	32800 TQ	USBLS	5/07
	North Carolina	Y	33810 FQ	40420 MW	49000 TQ	USBLS	5/07
	Ohio	Y	51610 FQ	75110 MW	92980 TQ	USBLS	5/07
	Oklahoma	Y	23840 FQ	32580 MW	55610 TQ	USBLS	5/07
	Oregon	H	19.63 FQ	23.38 MW	28.07 TQ	ORBLS	5/08
	Pennsylvania	Y	28490 FQ	42440 MW	62940 TQ	USBLS	5/07
	Tennessee	Y	26990 FQ	38370 MW	48510 TQ	USBLS	5/07
	Texas	Y	36860 FQ	50850 MW	72750 TQ	USBLS	5/07
	Utah	Y	36250 FQ	46280 MW	64850 TQ	USBLS	5/07
	Virginia	Y	53860 FQ	74140 MW	94410 TQ	USBLS	5/07
	Washington	H	21.83 FQ	24.42 MW	30.95 TQ	WABLS	3/08
	West Virginia	Y	32776 FQ	37826 MW	42061 TQ	WVBLS	7/08-9/08
	Wisconsin	Y	17040 FQ	35790 MW	54890 TQ	USBLS	5/07
Department of Cultural Resources	New Hampshire	Y		48120 AW		NHUL03	2008
Private College or University	United States	Y		63281 AW		HISTORY	2007-2008
Public College or University	United States	Y		61062 AW		HISTORY	2007-2008
Historical Project Aide							
Municipal Government	Seaside, CA	S	800 LO		1120 HI	SSSS	8/08
History Teacher							
Postsecondary	Alabama	Y	42390 FQ	51540 MW	61520 TQ	USBLS	5/07
Postsecondary	Birmingham-Hoover MSA, AL	Y	44860 FQ	57620 MW	78450 TQ	USBLS	5/07
Postsecondary	Arizona	Y	41090 FQ	51820 MW	61470 TQ	USBLS	5/07
Postsecondary	Phoenix-Mesa-Scottsdale MSA, AZ	Y	36550 FQ	46950 MW	60890 TQ	USBLS	5/07
Postsecondary	Arkansas	Y	40680 FQ	48960 MW	61010 TQ	USBLS	5/07
Postsecondary	Little Rock-North Little Rock MSA, AR	Y	39120 FQ	48300 MW	63240 TQ	USBLS	5/07
Postsecondary	California	Y		82827 AW		CABLS	1/08-3/08
Postsecondary	Los Angeles-Long Beach-Glendale PMSA, CA	Y		80048 AW		CABLS	1/08-3/08
Postsecondary	Oakland-Fremont-Hayward MSA, CA	Y		85268 AW		CABLS	1/08-3/08
Postsecondary	Riverside-San Bernardino-Ontario MSA, CA	Y		81915 AW		CABLS	1/08-3/08
Postsecondary	Sacramento-Arden Arcade-Roseville MSA, CA	Y		81638 AW		CABLS	1/08-3/08
Postsecondary	San Diego-Carlsbad-San Marcos MSA, CA	Y		83596 AW		CABLS	1/08-3/08
Postsecondary	San Francisco-San Mateo-Redwood PMSA, CA	Y		81853 AW		CABLS	1/08-3/08
Postsecondary	Santa Ana-Anaheim-Irvine PMSA, CA	Y	65620 FQ	83550 MW	101620 TQ	USBLS	5/07
Postsecondary	Colorado	Y	32100 FQ	48870 MW	64620 TQ	USBLS	5/07
Postsecondary	Denver-Aurora MSA, CO	Y	30180 FQ	38520 MW	56820 TQ	USBLS	5/07
Postsecondary	Wilmington PMSA, DE-MD-NJ	Y	58830 FQ	76800 MW	102760 TQ	USBLS	5/07
Postsecondary	District of Columbia	Y	43650 FQ	53460 MW	71900 TQ	USBLS	5/07
Postsecondary	Washington-Arlington-Alexandria MSA, DC-VA-MD-WV	Y	46250 FQ	59500 MW	78040 TQ	USBLS	5/07
Postsecondary	Florida	Y	43600 FQ	56470 MW	72920 TQ	USBLS	5/07
Postsecondary	Jacksonville MSA, FL	Y	41380 FQ	51220 MW	76820 TQ	USBLS	5/07
Postsecondary	Miami-Fort Lauderdale-Miami Beach MSA, FL	Y	43290 FQ	57280 MW	74780 TQ	USBLS	5/07
Postsecondary	Orlando-Kissimmee MSA, FL	Y	32090 FQ	45630 MW	56770 TQ	USBLS	5/07
Postsecondary	Tampa-St. Petersburg-Clearwater MSA, FL	Y	47930 FQ	58770 MW	75630 TQ	USBLS	5/07
Postsecondary	West Palm Beach-Boca Raton-Boynton Beach PMSA, FL	Y	46250 FQ	53240 MW	60180 TQ	USBLS	5/07
Postsecondary	Georgia	Y	43170 FQ	54280 MW	69240 TQ	USBLS	5/07
Postsecondary	Atlanta-Sandy Springs-Marietta MSA, GA	Y	45530 FQ	55740 MW	72320 TQ	USBLS	5/07
Postsecondary	Hawaii	Y	45010 FQ	58010 MW	75350 TQ	USBLS	5/07

AE	Average entry wage	AW	Average wage paid	FQ	First quartile wage
AER	Average entry range	AWR	Average wage range	H	Hourly
AEX	Average experienced wage	AXR	Average experienced range	HI	Highest wage paid
ATC	Average total compensation	D	Daily	HR	High end range

LO	Lowest wage paid	MTC	Median total compensation
LR	Low end range	MW	Median wage paid
M	Monthly	MWR	Median wage range
MCC	Median cash compensation	S	See annotated source

TCC	Total cash compensation
TQ	Third quartile wage
W	Weekly
Y	Yearly

History Teacher

Occupation/Type/Industry	Location	Per	Low	Mid	High	Source	Date
Postsecondary	Honolulu MSA, HI	Y	45700 FQ	58640 MW	76780 TQ	USBLS	5/07
Postsecondary	Illinois	Y	39340 FQ	54890 MW	73030 TQ	USBLS	5/07
Postsecondary	Chicago-Naperville-Joliet MSA, IL-IN-WI	Y	40940 FQ	54790 MW	73210 TQ	USBLS	5/07
Postsecondary	Indiana	Y	48310 FQ	59800 MW	73150 TQ	USBLS	5/07
Postsecondary	Gary PMSA, IN	Y	42300 FQ	50260 MW	63540 TQ	USBLS	5/07
Postsecondary	Indianapolis-Carmel MSA, IN	Y	46010 FQ	59840 MW	72710 TQ	USBLS	5/07
Postsecondary	South Bend-Mishawaka MSA, IN-MI	Y	47400 FQ	59900 MW	76430 TQ	USBLS	5/07
Postsecondary	Iowa	Y	44670 FQ	58060 MW	75490 TQ	USBLS	5/07
Postsecondary	Des Moines-West Des Moines MSA, IA	Y	51450 FQ	69530 MW	85190 TQ	USBLS	5/07
Postsecondary	Kansas	Y	32910 FQ	45890 MW	65930 TQ	USBLS	5/07
Postsecondary	Kentucky	Y	37452 FQ	52971 MW	68785 TQ	KYBLS	2008
Postsecondary	Louisiana	Y		50948 AW		LABLS	1/08-3/08
Postsecondary	Baton Rouge MSA, LA	Y	38490 FQ	45390 MW	51940 TQ	USBLS	5/07
Postsecondary	Maine	Y	50000 FQ	60550 MW	77160 TQ	USBLS	5/07
Postsecondary	Portland-South Portland-Biddeford MSA, ME	Y	47550 FQ	56890 MW	72860 TQ	USBLS	5/07
Postsecondary	Maryland	Y		70775 MW		MDBLS	3/08
Postsecondary	Baltimore-Towson MSA, MD	Y	52860 FQ	71650 MW	101820 TQ	USBLS	5/07
Postsecondary	Bethesda-Gaithersburg-Frederick PMSA, MD	Y	61010 FQ	76540 MW	100810 TQ	USBLS	5/07
Postsecondary	Massachusetts	Y	57400 FQ	71490 MW	93740 TQ	USBLS	5/07
Postsecondary	Boston-Cambridge-Quincy NECTA, MA	Y	59080 FQ	71980 MW	93230 TQ	USBLS	5/07
Postsecondary	Springfield MSA, MA-CT	Y	55600 FQ	73780 MW	102760 TQ	USBLS	5/07
Postsecondary	Worcester MSA, MA-CT	Y	56620 FQ	73140 MW	95470 TQ	USBLS	5/07
Postsecondary	Michigan	Y	44150 FQ	57590 MW	74530 TQ	USBLS	5/07
Postsecondary	Detroit-Warren-Livonia MSA, MI	Y	36080 FQ	56980 MW	74070 TQ	USBLS	5/07
Postsecondary	Warren-Troy-Farmington Hills PMSA, MI	Y	27900 FQ	55710 MW	70940 TQ	USBLS	5/07
Postsecondary	Minnesota	Y	43815 FQ	55083 MW	70536 TQ	MNBLS	10/08-12/08
Postsecondary	Duluth-Superior MSA, MN-WI	Y	48387 FQ	54361 MW	63913 TQ	MNBLS	10/08-12/08
Postsecondary	Minneapolis-Saint Paul MSA, MN-WI	Y	46128 FQ	60137 MW	78540 TQ	MNBLS	10/08-12/08
Postsecondary	Mississippi	Y	44030 FQ	55060 MW	69360 TQ	USBLS	5/07
Postsecondary	Jackson MSA, MS	Y	42810 FQ	53720 MW	70650 TQ	USBLS	5/07
Postsecondary	Missouri	Y	41370 FQ	53770 MW	71840 TQ	USBLS	5/07
Postsecondary	Kansas City MSA, MO-KS	Y	36960 FQ	51050 MW	65780 TQ	USBLS	5/07
Postsecondary	St. Louis MSA, MO-IL	Y	33320 FQ	52580 MW	73400 TQ	USBLS	5/07
Postsecondary	Montana	Y	38220 FQ	49330 MW	60790 TQ	USBLS	5/07
Postsecondary	Nebraska	Y	46710 FQ	57550 MW	70500 TQ	USBLS	5/07
Postsecondary	Omaha-Council Bluffs MSA, NE-IA	Y	48110 FQ	59260 MW	74710 TQ	USBLS	5/07
Postsecondary	New Hampshire	Y	46199 AE	61435 MW	76481 AEX	NHBLS	6/08
Postsecondary	New Jersey	Y	50920 FQ	69800 MW	98990 TQ	USBLS	5/07
Postsecondary	Camden PMSA, NJ	Y	54350 FQ	67410 MW	99500 TQ	USBLS	5/07
Postsecondary	Edison PMSA, NJ	Y	60110 FQ	87250 MW	116130 TQ	USBLS	5/07
Postsecondary	Newark-Union PMSA, NJ-PA	Y	45740 FQ	64010 MW	91860 TQ	USBLS	5/07
Postsecondary	New Mexico	Y	47180 FQ	58210 MW	72940 TQ	USBLS	5/07
Postsecondary	New York	Y	49170 FQ	65250 MW	84180 TQ	USBLS	5/07
Postsecondary	Nassau-Suffolk PMSA, NY	Y	46520 FQ	59310 MW	77740 TQ	USBLS	5/07
Postsecondary	New York-Northern New Jersey-Long Island MSA, NY-NJ-PA	Y	54140 FQ	69620 MW	93020 TQ	USBLS	5/07
Postsecondary	North Carolina	Y	42620 FQ	51810 MW	66270 TQ	USBLS	5/07
Postsecondary	Charlotte-Gastonia-Concord MSA, NC-SC	Y	39750 FQ	51510 MW	65960 TQ	USBLS	5/07
Postsecondary	Raleigh-Cary MSA, NC	Y	36180 FQ	50330 MW	64660 TQ	USBLS	5/07
Postsecondary	North Dakota	Y	43990 FQ	55220 MW	67810 TQ	USBLS	5/07
Postsecondary	Fargo MSA, ND-MN	Y	36410 FQ	46160 MW	60020 TQ	USBLS	5/07
Postsecondary	Ohio	Y	45750 FQ	59760 MW	78110 TQ	USBLS	5/07
Postsecondary	Cincinnati-Middletown MSA, OH-KY-IN	Y	35300 FQ	53010 MW	68810 TQ	USBLS	5/07
Postsecondary	Cleveland-Elyria-Mentor MSA, OH	Y	44500 FQ	57540 MW	76340 TQ	USBLS	5/07
Postsecondary	Columbus MSA, OH	Y	60970 FQ	77360 MW	98340 TQ	USBLS	5/07
Postsecondary	Dayton MSA, OH	Y	34450 FQ	53090 MW	68160 TQ	USBLS	5/07
Postsecondary	Oklahoma	Y	31670 FQ	45780 MW	59630 TQ	USBLS	5/07

AE	Average entry wage	AW	Average wage paid	FQ	First quartile wage
AER	Average entry range	AWR	Average wage range	H	Hourly
AEX	Average experienced wage	AXR	Average experienced range	HI	Highest wage paid
ATC	Average total compensation	D	Daily	HR	High end range

LO	Lowest wage paid	MTC	Median total compensation	TCC	Total cash compensation
LR	Low end range	MW	Median wage paid	TQ	Third quartile wage
M	Monthly	MWR	Median wage range	W	Weekly
MCC	Median cash compensation	S	See annotated source	Y	Yearly

Occupation/Type/Industry	Location	Per	Low	Mid	High	Source	Date
History Teacher							
Postsecondary	Oklahoma City MSA, OK	Y	40460 FQ	52480 MW	68130 TQ	USBLS	5/07
Postsecondary	Tulsa MSA, OK	Y	31720 FQ	43390 MW	52920 TQ	USBLS	5/07
Postsecondary	Portland-Vancouver-Beaverton MSA, OR-WA	Y	49740 FQ	68120 MW	89430 TQ	USBLS	5/07
Postsecondary	Pennsylvania	Y	46900 FQ	63080 MW	82810 TQ	USBLS	5/07
Postsecondary	Allentown-Bethlehem-Easton MSA, PA-NJ	Y	51450 FQ	71090 MW	99030 TQ	USBLS	5/07
Postsecondary	Philadelphia-Camden-Wilmington MSA, PA-NJ-DE-MD	Y	49690 FQ	64750 MW	83770 TQ	USBLS	5/07
Postsecondary	Pittsburgh MSA, PA	Y	45600 FQ	70100 MW	90970 TQ	USBLS	5/07
Postsecondary	Rhode Island	Y	54300 FQ	69440 MW	91760 TQ	USBLS	5/07
Postsecondary	Providence-Fall River-Warwick MSA, RI-MA	Y	54070 FQ	68740 MW	90730 TQ	USBLS	5/07
Postsecondary	South Carolina	Y	47110 FQ	57820 MW	72340 TQ	USBLS	5/07
Postsecondary	Charleston-North Charleston MSA, SC	Y	47830 FQ	55360 MW	65720 TQ	USBLS	5/07
Postsecondary	Columbia MSA, SC	Y	57290 FQ	66800 MW	84090 TQ	USBLS	5/07
Postsecondary	South Dakota	Y	44678 FQ	52058 MW	67178 TQ	SDBLS	7/08-9/08
Postsecondary	Tennessee	Y	25300 FQ	48150 MW	63190 TQ	USBLS	5/07
Postsecondary	Memphis MSA, TN-MS-AR	Y	47790 FQ	56990 MW	73970 TQ	USBLS	5/07
Postsecondary	Nashville-Davidson-Murfreesboro MSA, TN	Y	44990 FQ	54950 MW	72940 TQ	USBLS	5/07
Postsecondary	Texas	Y	41210 FQ	56400 MW	75060 TQ	USBLS	5/07
Postsecondary	Austin-Round Rock MSA, TX	Y	14920 FQ	58200 MW	80260 TQ	USBLS	5/07
Postsecondary	Dallas-Fort Worth-Arlington MSA, TX	Y	35560 FQ	52930 MW	73970 TQ	USBLS	5/07
Postsecondary	El Paso MSA, TX	Y	48570 FQ	61710 MW	76830 TQ	USBLS	5/07
Postsecondary	San Antonio MSA, TX	Y	43230 FQ	53900 MW	63700 TQ	USBLS	5/07
Postsecondary	Utah	Y	43000 FQ	51720 MW	61600 TQ	USBLS	5/07
Postsecondary	Salt Lake City MSA, UT	Y	41350 FQ	53550 MW	63030 TQ	USBLS	5/07
Postsecondary	Vermont	Y	47930 FQ	56950 MW	69600 TQ	USBLS	5/07
Postsecondary	Burlington-South Burlington MSA, VT	Y	49120 FQ	58830 MW	71270 TQ	USBLS	5/07
Postsecondary	Virginia	Y	41620 FQ	55010 MW	71160 TQ	USBLS	5/07
Postsecondary	Richmond MSA, VA	Y	43020 FQ	55950 MW	75620 TQ	USBLS	5/07
Postsecondary	Virginia Beach-Norfolk-Newport News MSA, VA-NC	Y	37760 FQ	53100 MW	67730 TQ	USBLS	5/07
Postsecondary	Washington	Y		60849 AW		WABLS	3/08
Postsecondary	Seattle-Tacoma-Bellevue MSA, WA	Y	48480 FQ	59020 MW	76640 TQ	USBLS	5/07
Postsecondary	West Virginia	Y	44949 FQ	55148 MW	69387 TQ	WVBLS	7/08-9/08
Postsecondary	Wisconsin	Y	43450 FQ	55790 MW	74040 TQ	USBLS	5/07
Postsecondary	Milwaukee-Waukesha-West Allis MSA, WI	Y	42280 FQ	57390 MW	75990 TQ	USBLS	5/07
Postsecondary	Wyoming	Y	45271 FQ	56279 MW	64872 TQ	WYBLS	9/08
Postsecondary	Puerto Rico	Y	32020 FQ	40200 MW	60980 TQ	USBLS	5/07
Postsecondary	San Juan-Caguas-Guaynabo MSA, PR	Y	40890 FQ	52380 MW	75800 TQ	USBLS	5/07
Histotechnologist							
State Government	Ohio	H	19.88 LO		26.28 HI	ODAS	2008
Hockey Player							
National Hockey League	United States	Y		800000-2200000 MW		USATOD06	2007-2008
Hoist and Winch Operator	California	H	29.20 FQ	33.12 MW	35.86 TQ	CABLS	1/08-3/08
	Colorado	Y	32330 FQ	36000 MW	42600 TQ	USBLS	5/07
	Connecticut	H	13.54 AE	18.65 MW		CTBLS	1/08-3/08
	Florida	Y	22400 FQ	25970 MW	29400 TQ	USBLS	5/07
	Georgia	Y	34970 FQ	42270 MW	47970 TQ	USBLS	5/07
	Idaho	Y	41540 FQ	45530 MW	49520 TQ	USBLS	5/07
	Illinois	Y	31270 FQ	39460 MW	43680 TQ	USBLS	5/07
	Indiana	Y	27270 FQ	29530 MW	31810 TQ	USBLS	5/07
	Kansas	Y	20110 FQ	39980 MW	45020 TQ	USBLS	5/07
	Kentucky	Y	26333 FQ	28573 MW	30954 TQ	KYBLS	2008
	Louisiana	H	11.09 FQ	13.29 MW	20.48 TQ	LABLS	1/08-3/08
	Maryland	Y		40650 MW		MDBLS	3/08
	Massachusetts	Y	31550 FQ	33620 MW	35710 TQ	USBLS	5/07
	Michigan	Y	25850 FQ	28200 MW	33340 TQ	USBLS	5/07

Occupation/Type/Industry	Location	Per	Low	Mid	High	Source	Date
Hoist and Winch Operator	Mississippi	Y	21050 FQ	26820 MW	37170 TQ	USBLS	5/07
	New Jersey	Y	41250 FQ	48130 MW	52390 TQ	USBLS	5/07
	New Mexico	Y	49880 FQ	60670 MW	69910 TQ	USBLS	5/07
	Ohio	Y	30530 FQ	36950 MW	51210 TQ	USBLS	5/07
	Oregon	H	16.66 FQ	18.53 MW	20.44 TQ	ORBLS	5/08
	Pennsylvania	Y	28000 FQ	38350 MW	47030 TQ	USBLS	5/07
	Texas	Y	22830 FQ	26870 MW	35540 TQ	USBLS	5/07
	Virginia	Y	27620 FQ	30330 MW	36470 TQ	USBLS	5/07
	Washington	H	30.42 FQ	34.09 MW	36.77 TQ	WABLS	3/08
Home Appliance Repairer	Alabama	Y	21000 FQ	28120 MW	34980 TQ	USBLS	5/07
	Birmingham-Hoover MSA, AL	Y	27520 FQ	31540 MW	35080 TQ	USBLS	5/07
	Alaska	Y	31060 FQ	41750 MW	53270 TQ	USBLS	5/07
	Anchorage MSA, AK	Y	29500 FQ	38860 MW	50490 TQ	USBLS	5/07
	Arizona	Y	29430 FQ	36570 MW	47080 TQ	USBLS	5/07
	Phoenix-Mesa-Scottsdale MSA, AZ	Y	32340 FQ	36950 MW	45410 TQ	USBLS	5/07
	Tucson MSA, AZ	Y	20700 FQ	53830 MW	59960 TQ	USBLS	5/07
	Arkansas	Y	20100 FQ	26630 MW	41560 TQ	USBLS	5/07
	Little Rock-North Little Rock MSA, AR	Y	29710 FQ	41380 MW	46530 TQ	USBLS	5/07
	California	H	14.30 FQ	18.02 MW	23.38 TQ	CABLS	1/08-3/08
	Los Angeles-Long Beach-Glendale PMSA, CA	H	14.83 FQ	17.96 MW	22.93 TQ	CABLS	1/08-3/08
	Modesto MSA, CA	H	13.10 FQ	15.61 MW	17.65 TQ	CABLS	1/08-3/08
	Oakland-Fremont-Hayward MSA, CA	H	13.43 FQ	17.52 MW	23.11 TQ	CABLS	1/08-3/08
	Sacramento-Arden Arcade-Roseville MSA, CA	H	16.68 FQ	19.01 MW	31.29 TQ	CABLS	1/08-3/08
	San Diego-Carlsbad-San Marcos MSA, CA	H	12.56 FQ	16.00 MW	23.43 TQ	CABLS	1/08-3/08
	San Francisco-San Mateo-Redwood PMSA, CA	H	15.34 FQ	17.99 MW	22.42 TQ	CABLS	1/08-3/08
	San Jose-Sunnyvale-Santa Clara MSA, CA	H	19.28 FQ	21.00 MW	23.10 TQ	CABLS	1/08-3/08
	Santa Ana-Anaheim-Irvine PMSA, CA	Y	22710 FQ	29160 MW	38760 TQ	USBLS	5/07
	Colorado	Y	21270 FQ	35800 MW	45580 TQ	USBLS	5/07
	Denver-Aurora MSA, CO	Y	35010 FQ	44000 MW	50830 TQ	USBLS	5/07
	Connecticut	H	12.91 AE	17.54 MW		CTBLS	1/08-3/08
	Bridgeport-Stamford-Norwalk MSA, CT	Y	29540 FQ	38400 MW	48540 TQ	USBLS	5/07
	Norwich-New London MSA, CT-RI	Y	25720 FQ	27430 MW	29140 TQ	USBLS	5/07
	Delaware	Y	25900 FQ	29940 MW	39540 TQ	USBLS	5/07
	Wilmington PMSA, DE-MD-NJ	Y	26500 FQ	29810 MW	40610 TQ	USBLS	5/07
	Washington-Arlington-Alexandria MSA, DC-VA-MD-WV	Y	28070 FQ	39470 MW	48220 TQ	USBLS	5/07
	Florida	Y	28600 FQ	35470 MW	43770 TQ	USBLS	5/07
	Fort Lauderdale-Pompano Beach-Deerfield Beach PMSA, FL	Y	27300 FQ	34170 MW	39070 TQ	USBLS	5/07
	Jacksonville MSA, FL	Y	27200 FQ	35090 MW	43300 TQ	USBLS	5/07
	Miami-Fort Lauderdale-Miami Beach MSA, FL	Y	30040 FQ	37480 MW	47330 TQ	USBLS	5/07
	Orlando-Kissimmee MSA, FL	Y	31970 FQ	38860 MW	44660 TQ	USBLS	5/07
	Tampa-St. Petersburg-Clearwater MSA, FL	Y	27490 FQ	31500 MW	40540 TQ	USBLS	5/07
	West Palm Beach-Boca Raton-Boynton Beach PMSA, FL	Y	37460 FQ	42180 MW	50920 TQ	USBLS	5/07
	Georgia	Y	24600 FQ	29550 MW	36110 TQ	USBLS	5/07
	Atlanta-Sandy Springs-Marietta MSA, GA	Y	25140 FQ	31300 MW	41560 TQ	USBLS	5/07
	Augusta-Richmond County MSA, GA-SC	Y	25720 FQ	27940 MW	30150 TQ	USBLS	5/07
	Macon MSA, GA	Y	27320 FQ	31060 MW	35020 TQ	USBLS	5/07
	Hawaii	Y	26820 FQ	36250 MW	48530 TQ	USBLS	5/07
	Honolulu MSA, HI	Y	25270 FQ	35430 MW	47240 TQ	USBLS	5/07
	Idaho	Y	28520 FQ	34970 MW	41810 TQ	USBLS	5/07
	Boise City-Nampa MSA, ID	Y	29240 FQ	35430 MW	42370 TQ	USBLS	5/07

AE	Average entry wage	AW	Average wage paid	FQ	First quartile wage	LO	Lowest wage paid	MTC	Median total compensation	TCC	Total cash compensation
AER	Average entry range	AWR	Average wage range	H	Hourly	LR	Low end range	MW	Median wage paid	TQ	Third quartile wage
AEX	Average experienced wage	AXR	Average experienced range	HI	Highest wage paid	M	Monthly	MWR	Median wage range	W	Weekly
ATC	Average total compensation	D	Daily	HR	High end range	MCC	Median cash compensation	S	See annotated source	Y	Yearly

790

Occupation/Type/Industry	Location	Per	Low	Mid	High	Source	Date
Home Appliance Repairer	Illinois	Y	29220 FQ	36990 MW	50180 TQ	USBLS	5/07
	Chicago-Naperville-Joliet MSA, IL-IN-WI	Y	30880 FQ	43750 MW	54590 TQ	USBLS	5/07
	Indiana	Y	28000 FQ	35190 MW	43270 TQ	USBLS	5/07
	Fort Wayne MSA, IN	Y	33500 FQ	40960 MW	46870 TQ	USBLS	5/07
	Gary PMSA, IN	Y	23530 FQ	29990 MW	36480 TQ	USBLS	5/07
	Indianapolis-Carmel MSA, IN	Y	30720 FQ	35960 MW	43880 TQ	USBLS	5/07
	Iowa	Y	23600 FQ	30490 MW	38620 TQ	USBLS	5/07
	Des Moines-West Des Moines MSA, IA	Y	29840 FQ	38650 MW	51580 TQ	USBLS	5/07
	Iowa City MSA, IA	Y	22820 FQ	26600 MW	33240 TQ	USBLS	5/07
	Kansas	Y	24550 FQ	34500 MW	43170 TQ	USBLS	5/07
	Wichita MSA, KS	Y	14550 FQ	22590 MW	26590 TQ	USBLS	5/07
	Kentucky	Y	30439 FQ	37120 MW	44687 TQ	KYBLS	2008
	Louisville-Jefferson County MSA, KY-IN	Y	32280 FQ	38240 MW	45870 TQ	USBLS	5/07
	Louisiana	H	9.00 FQ	12.53 MW	15.85 TQ	LABLS	1/08-3/08
	Baton Rouge MSA, LA	Y	17190 FQ	26780 MW	36000 TQ	USBLS	5/07
	Maine	Y	24460 FQ	32520 MW	37810 TQ	USBLS	5/07
	Portland-South Portland-Biddeford MSA, ME	Y	26300 FQ	35770 MW	41270 TQ	USBLS	5/07
	Maryland	Y		38325 MW		MDBLS	3/08
	Baltimore-Towson MSA, MD	Y	31750 FQ	37790 MW	47880 TQ	USBLS	5/07
	Massachusetts	Y	29910 FQ	37170 MW	43830 TQ	USBLS	5/07
	Boston-Cambridge-Quincy NECTA, MA	Y	34280 FQ	41440 MW	45940 TQ	USBLS	5/07
	Michigan	Y	25300 FQ	34690 MW	43720 TQ	USBLS	5/07
	Detroit-Warren-Livonia MSA, MI	Y	32300 FQ	40030 MW	48360 TQ	USBLS	5/07
	Grand Rapids-Wyoming MSA, MI	Y	30480 FQ	33770 MW	36850 TQ	USBLS	5/07
	Warren-Troy-Farmington Hills PMSA, MI	Y	30510 FQ	36700 MW	45570 TQ	USBLS	5/07
	Minnesota	Y	35359 FQ	48744 MW	59496 TQ	MNBLS	10/08-12/08
	Duluth-Superior MSA, MN-WI	Y	44443 FQ	52457 MW	61268 TQ	MNBLS	10/08-12/08
	Minneapolis-Saint Paul MSA, MN-WI	Y	40247 FQ	51943 MW	60576 TQ	MNBLS	10/08-12/08
	Rochester MSA, MN	Y	55186 FQ	59598 MW	64011 TQ	MNBLS	10/08-12/08
	Mississippi	Y	21590 FQ	24680 MW	29940 TQ	USBLS	5/07
	Missouri	Y	27810 FQ	37580 MW	50990 TQ	USBLS	5/07
	Kansas City MSA, MO-KS	Y	32320 FQ	38510 MW	50230 TQ	USBLS	5/07
	St. Louis MSA, MO-IL	Y	32070 FQ	39660 MW	52090 TQ	USBLS	5/07
	Montana	Y	16960 FQ	21100 MW	28240 TQ	USBLS	5/07
	Billings MSA, MT	Y	16460 FQ	19360 MW	27690 TQ	USBLS	5/07
	Nebraska	Y	22420 FQ	28610 MW	35540 TQ	USBLS	5/07
	Omaha-Council Bluffs MSA, NE-IA	Y	21980 FQ	31040 MW	39780 TQ	USBLS	5/07
	Nevada	H	16.63 FQ	21.53 MW	26.10 TQ	NVBLS	5/08
	Las Vegas-Paradise MSA, NV	H	18.53 FQ	23.77 MW	26.98 TQ	NVBLS	5/08
	New Hampshire	H	15.23 AE	20.84 MW	23.72 AEX	NHBLS	6/08
	Nashua NECTA, NH-MA	Y	47840 FQ	51350 MW	56670 TQ	USBLS	5/07
	New Jersey	Y	33020 FQ	43300 MW	51710 TQ	USBLS	5/07
	Camden PMSA, NJ	Y	31490 FQ	42140 MW	50180 TQ	USBLS	5/07
	Edison PMSA, NJ	Y	40040 FQ	46410 MW	54150 TQ	USBLS	5/07
	Newark-Union PMSA, NJ-PA	Y	23980 FQ	41900 MW	50640 TQ	USBLS	5/07
	New Mexico	Y	20580 FQ	28310 MW	36030 TQ	USBLS	5/07
	Albuquerque MSA, NM	Y	19300 FQ	24980 MW	32490 TQ	USBLS	5/07
	New York	Y	24940 FQ	33110 MW	39570 TQ	USBLS	5/07
	Buffalo-Niagara Falls MSA, NY	Y	32320 FQ	36490 MW	52830 TQ	USBLS	5/07
	Nassau-Suffolk PMSA, NY	Y	30150 FQ	36340 MW	43020 TQ	USBLS	5/07
	New York-Northern New Jersey-Long Island MSA, NY-NJ-PA	Y	27940 FQ	37230 MW	46410 TQ	USBLS	5/07
	North Carolina	Y	25490 FQ	29210 MW	35110 TQ	USBLS	5/07
	Charlotte-Gastonia-Concord MSA, NC-SC	Y	26070 FQ	30480 MW	36180 TQ	USBLS	5/07
	Raleigh-Cary MSA, NC	Y	32080 FQ	35270 MW	41990 TQ	USBLS	5/07
	Winston-Salem MSA, NC	Y	24570 FQ	27580 MW	30920 TQ	USBLS	5/07
	North Dakota	Y	20150 FQ	24870 MW	31430 TQ	USBLS	5/07
	Fargo MSA, ND-MN	Y	20560 FQ	23720 MW	33080 TQ	USBLS	5/07
	Ohio	Y	27360 FQ	34860 MW	53660 TQ	USBLS	5/07

AE Average entry wage	**AW** Average wage paid	**FQ** First quartile wage	**LO** Lowest wage paid	**MTC** Median total compensation	**TCC** Total cash compensation
AER Average entry range	**AWR** Average wage range	**H** Hourly	**LR** Low end range	**MW** Median wage paid	**TQ** Third quartile wage
AEX Average experienced wage	**AXR** Average experienced range	**HI** Highest wage paid	**M** Monthly	**MWR** Median wage range	**W** Weekly
ATC Average total compensation	**D** Daily	**HR** High end range	**MCC** Median cash compensation	**S** See annotated source	**Y** Yearly

Home Appliance Repairer

Occupation/Type/Industry	Location	Per	Low	Mid	High	Source	Date
Home Appliance Repairer	Cincinnati-Middletown MSA, OH-KY-IN	Y	21680 FQ	28370 MW	37880 TQ	USBLS	5/07
	Cleveland-Elyria-Mentor MSA, OH	Y	47350 FQ	56680 MW	61390 TQ	USBLS	5/07
	Columbus MSA, OH	Y	30520 FQ	46860 MW	59690 TQ	USBLS	5/07
	Dayton MSA, OH	Y	26890 FQ	29440 MW	31820 TQ	USBLS	5/07
	Oklahoma	Y	25830 FQ	29480 MW	33480 TQ	USBLS	5/07
	Oklahoma City MSA, OK	Y	13570 FQ	18390 MW	29300 TQ	USBLS	5/07
	Tulsa MSA, OK	Y	28030 FQ	31300 MW	36870 TQ	USBLS	5/07
	Oregon	H	11.45 FQ	15.60 MW	21.13 TQ	ORBLS	5/08
	Medford MSA, OR	Y	25070 FQ	34560 MW	39640 TQ	USBLS	5/07
	Portland-Vancouver-Beaverton MSA, OR-WA	Y	23590 FQ	35850 MW	46210 TQ	USBLS	5/07
	Pennsylvania	Y	26180 FQ	30770 MW	37410 TQ	USBLS	5/07
	Allentown-Bethlehem-Easton MSA, PA-NJ	Y	27150 FQ	29740 MW	32510 TQ	USBLS	5/07
	Philadelphia-Camden-Wilmington MSA, PA-NJ-DE-MD	Y	28480 FQ	34460 MW	43060 TQ	USBLS	5/07
	Pittsburgh MSA, PA	Y	26870 FQ	31700 MW	37740 TQ	USBLS	5/07
	Rhode Island	Y	31950 FQ	40660 MW	48530 TQ	USBLS	5/07
	Providence-Fall River-Warwick MSA, RI-MA	Y	31520 FQ	39870 MW	46990 TQ	USBLS	5/07
	South Carolina	Y	18340 FQ	25700 MW	34280 TQ	USBLS	5/07
	Charleston-North Charleston MSA, SC	Y	17450 FQ	28190 MW	37360 TQ	USBLS	5/07
	Columbia MSA, SC	Y	29600 FQ	35380 MW	39200 TQ	USBLS	5/07
	South Dakota	Y	24458 FQ	34741 MW	42970 TQ	SDBLS	7/08-9/08
	Sioux Falls MSA, SD	Y	24164 FQ	30885 MW	44455 TQ	SDBLS	7/08-9/08
	Tennessee	Y	25490 FQ	28840 MW	32230 TQ	USBLS	5/07
	Memphis MSA, TN-MS-AR	Y	23180 FQ	27470 MW	32810 TQ	USBLS	5/07
	Nashville-Davidson-Murfreesboro MSA, TN	Y	27460 FQ	29460 MW	31550 TQ	USBLS	5/07
	Texas	Y	20340 FQ	26000 MW	32020 TQ	USBLS	5/07
	Dallas-Fort Worth-Arlington MSA, TX	Y	21820 FQ	25940 MW	30920 TQ	USBLS	5/07
	El Paso MSA, TX	Y	12770 FQ	14520 MW	19400 TQ	USBLS	5/07
	Houston-Sugar Land-Baytown MSA, TX	Y	18580 FQ	27060 MW	35240 TQ	USBLS	5/07
	San Antonio MSA, TX	Y	28190 FQ	33110 MW	54330 TQ	USBLS	5/07
	Utah	Y	25930 FQ	34890 MW	47660 TQ	USBLS	5/07
	Salt Lake City MSA, UT	Y	27670 FQ	38180 MW	49710 TQ	USBLS	5/07
	Vermont	Y	24770 FQ	30000 MW	36420 TQ	USBLS	5/07
	Burlington-South Burlington MSA, VT	Y	29360 FQ	32610 MW	36630 TQ	USBLS	5/07
	Virginia	Y	21360 FQ	31640 MW	42950 TQ	USBLS	5/07
	Richmond MSA, VA	Y	20800 FQ	34280 MW	44110 TQ	USBLS	5/07
	Virginia Beach-Norfolk-Newport News MSA, VA-NC	Y	23890 FQ	29700 MW	40020 TQ	USBLS	5/07
	Washington	H	15.76 FQ	17.68 MW	19.68 TQ	WABLS	3/08
	Seattle-Tacoma-Bellevue MSA, WA	Y	34010 FQ	37630 MW	43820 TQ	USBLS	5/07
	West Virginia	Y	16113 FQ	23654 MW	39778 TQ	WVBLS	7/08-9/08
	Wisconsin	Y	27260 FQ	32110 MW	38820 TQ	USBLS	5/07
	Milwaukee-Waukesha-West Allis MSA, WI	Y	27370 FQ	32680 MW	41890 TQ	USBLS	5/07
	Wyoming	Y	24264 FQ	29204 MW	42178 TQ	WYBLS	9/08
	Puerto Rico	Y	19530 FQ	24650 MW	28100 TQ	USBLS	5/07
Home Economics Teacher							
Postsecondary	Alabama	Y	45170 FQ	53130 MW	59090 TQ	USBLS	5/07
Postsecondary	Arizona	Y	28260 FQ	31090 MW	37300 TQ	USBLS	5/07
Postsecondary	Arkansas	Y	28090 FQ	32270 MW	48340 TQ	USBLS	5/07
Postsecondary	California	Y		97071 AW		CABLS	1/08-3/08
Postsecondary	Colorado	Y	40250 FQ	53950 MW	75730 TQ	USBLS	5/07
Postsecondary	Georgia	Y	47060 FQ	61630 MW	79550 TQ	USBLS	5/07
Postsecondary	Illinois	Y	41230 FQ	56260 MW	74590 TQ	USBLS	5/07
Postsecondary	Indiana	Y	39120 FQ	49150 MW	64460 TQ	USBLS	5/07
Postsecondary	Iowa	Y	71430 FQ	88340 MW	103570 TQ	USBLS	5/07
Postsecondary	Kansas	Y	30620 FQ	49490 MW	76080 TQ	USBLS	5/07
Postsecondary	Kentucky	Y	31571 FQ	44323 MW	63019 TQ	KYBLS	2008
Postsecondary	Michigan	Y	29320 FQ	55120 MW	78210 TQ	USBLS	5/07

AE	Average entry wage	AW	Average wage paid	FQ	First quartile wage	LO	Lowest wage paid
AER	Average entry range	AWR	Average wage range	H	Hourly	LR	Low end range
AEX	Average experienced wage	AXR	Average experienced range	HI	Highest wage paid	M	Monthly
ATC	Average total compensation	D	Daily	HR	High end range	MCC	Median cash compensation

MTC	Median total compensation	TCC	Total cash compensation
MW	Median wage paid	TQ	Third quartile wage
MWR	Median wage range	W	Weekly
S	See annotated source	Y	Yearly

Occupation/Type/Industry	Location	Per	Low	Mid	High	Source	Date
Home Economics Teacher							
Postsecondary	Minnesota	Y	41932 FQ	59404 MW	80308 TQ	MNBLS	10/08-12/08
Postsecondary	Mississippi	Y	43890 FQ	54790 MW	73160 TQ	USBLS	5/07
Postsecondary	Missouri	Y	41400 FQ	54760 MW	68050 TQ	USBLS	5/07
Postsecondary	New Jersey	Y	61430 FQ	75620 MW	97590 TQ	USBLS	5/07
Postsecondary	New Mexico	Y	38940 FQ	52300 MW	60920 TQ	USBLS	5/07
Postsecondary	North Carolina	Y	43220 FQ	50970 MW	62370 TQ	USBLS	5/07
Postsecondary	Ohio	Y	44870 FQ	59850 MW	80300 TQ	USBLS	5/07
Postsecondary	Oklahoma	Y	21510 FQ	23740 MW	36530 TQ	USBLS	5/07
Postsecondary	Pennsylvania	Y	40290 FQ	65800 MW	80000 TQ	USBLS	5/07
Postsecondary	Tennessee	Y	42970 FQ	50150 MW	61180 TQ	USBLS	5/07
Postsecondary	Texas	Y	40760 FQ	58870 MW	80720 TQ	USBLS	5/07
Postsecondary	Utah	Y	51650 FQ	56920 MW	62540 TQ	USBLS	5/07
Postsecondary	Virginia	Y	28410 FQ	38520 MW	70810 TQ	USBLS	5/07
Postsecondary	Washington	Y		60204 AW		WABLS	3/08
Postsecondary	Wisconsin	Y	40280 FQ	54310 MW	67920 TQ	USBLS	5/07
Postsecondary	Wyoming	Y	52382 FQ	64419 MW	74932 TQ	WYBLS	9/08
Home Health Aide	Alabama	Y	14070 FQ	16740 MW	19220 TQ	USBLS	5/07
	Birmingham-Hoover MSA, AL	Y	14800 FQ	17220 MW	19410 TQ	USBLS	5/07
	Huntsville MSA, AL	Y	13750 FQ	16420 MW	19680 TQ	USBLS	5/07
	Tuscaloosa MSA, AL	Y	14900 FQ	18810 MW	22310 TQ	USBLS	5/07
	Alaska	Y	24620 FQ	27770 MW	30490 TQ	USBLS	5/07
	Anchorage MSA, AK	Y	24100 FQ	27300 MW	29790 TQ	USBLS	5/07
	Arizona	Y	17940 FQ	20730 MW	23550 TQ	USBLS	5/07
	Phoenix-Mesa-Scottsdale MSA, AZ	Y	17790 FQ	20330 MW	23630 TQ	USBLS	5/07
	Prescott MSA, AZ	Y	17480 FQ	20030 MW	22890 TQ	USBLS	5/07
	Tucson MSA, AZ	Y	19820 FQ	21880 MW	23770 TQ	USBLS	5/07
	Arkansas	Y	15020 FQ	17210 MW	20340 TQ	USBLS	5/07
	Little Rock-North Little Rock MSA, AR	Y	15220 FQ	17880 MW	21370 TQ	USBLS	5/07
	California	H	8.68 FQ	9.80 MW	11.74 TQ	CABLS	1/08-3/08
	Bakersfield MSA, CA	H	8.35 FQ	9.09 MW	10.70 TQ	CABLS	1/08-3/08
	Los Angeles-Long Beach-Glendale PMSA, CA	H	8.57 FQ	9.52 MW	11.80 TQ	CABLS	1/08-3/08
	Oakland-Fremont-Hayward MSA, CA	H	8.95 FQ	10.51 MW	12.23 TQ	CABLS	1/08-3/08
	Riverside-San Bernardino-Ontario MSA, CA	H	8.50 FQ	9.33 MW	10.77 TQ	CABLS	1/08-3/08
	Sacramento-Arden Arcade-Roseville MSA, CA	H	8.85 FQ	10.00 MW	11.52 TQ	CABLS	1/08-3/08
	San Diego-Carlsbad-San Marcos MSA, CA	H	9.06 FQ	10.60 MW	13.40 TQ	CABLS	1/08-3/08
	San Francisco-San Mateo-Redwood PMSA, CA	H	9.24 FQ	10.77 MW	12.70 TQ	CABLS	1/08-3/08
	San Jose-Sunnyvale-Santa Clara MSA, CA	H	8.49 FQ	9.97 MW	12.47 TQ	CABLS	1/08-3/08
	Santa Ana-Anaheim-Irvine PMSA, CA	Y	18250 FQ	21230 MW	24590 TQ	USBLS	5/07
	Colorado	Y	18150 FQ	22210 MW	26950 TQ	USBLS	5/07
	Denver-Aurora MSA, CO	Y	19330 FQ	23780 MW	27950 TQ	USBLS	5/07
	Connecticut	H	10.81 AE	13.08 MW		CTBLS	1/08-3/08
	Bridgeport-Stamford-Norwalk MSA, CT	Y	22630 FQ	25280 MW	29460 TQ	USBLS	5/07
	Hartford-West Hartford-East Hartford MSA, CT	Y	23480 FQ	28650 MW	33590 TQ	USBLS	5/07
	New Haven MSA, CT	Y	22170 FQ	24540 MW	28270 TQ	USBLS	5/07
	Delaware	Y	21460 FQ	23930 MW	27190 TQ	USBLS	5/07
	Dover MSA, DE	Y	18320 FQ	25020 MW	28220 TQ	USBLS	5/07
	Wilmington PMSA, DE-MD-NJ	Y	21720 FQ	23890 MW	27280 TQ	USBLS	5/07
	District of Columbia	Y	19440 FQ	21690 MW	23740 TQ	USBLS	5/07
	Washington-Arlington-Alexandria MSA, DC-VA-MD-WV	Y	19230 FQ	21700 MW	24110 TQ	USBLS	5/07
	Florida	Y	17430 FQ	19850 MW	23210 TQ	USBLS	5/07
	Fort Lauderdale-Pompano Beach-Deerfield Beach PMSA, FL	Y	17410 FQ	19290 MW	22100 TQ	USBLS	5/07
	Jacksonville MSA, FL	Y	17530 FQ	19740 MW	22540 TQ	USBLS	5/07

AE	Average entry wage	AW	Average wage paid	FQ	First quartile wage
AER	Average entry range	AWR	Average wage range	H	Hourly
AEX	Average experienced wage	AXR	Average experienced range	HI	Highest wage paid
ATC	Average total compensation	D	Daily	HR	High end range

LO	Lowest wage paid	MTC	Median total compensation	TCC	Total cash compensation
LR	Low end range	MW	Median wage paid	TQ	Third quartile wage
M	Monthly	MWR	Median wage range	W	Weekly
MCC	Median cash compensation	S	See annotated source	Y	Yearly

Occupation/Type/Industry	Location	Per	Low	Mid	High	Source	Date
Home Health Aide	Miami-Fort Lauderdale-Miami Beach MSA, FL	Y	17000 FQ	19010 MW	21760 TQ	USBLS	5/07
	Orlando-Kissimmee MSA, FL	Y	18150 FQ	20640 MW	24070 TQ	USBLS	5/07
	Tampa-St. Petersburg-Clearwater MSA, FL	Y	20160 FQ	22720 MW	25250 TQ	USBLS	5/07
	West Palm Beach-Boca Raton-Boynton Beach PMSA, FL	Y	17780 FQ	19630 MW	22340 TQ	USBLS	5/07
	Georgia	Y	16080 FQ	17910 MW	19870 TQ	USBLS	5/07
	Atlanta-Sandy Springs-Marietta MSA, GA	Y	17180 FQ	18750 MW	20970 TQ	USBLS	5/07
	Hawaii	Y	21090 FQ	24520 MW	29200 TQ	USBLS	5/07
	Honolulu MSA, HI	Y	21250 FQ	24980 MW	29490 TQ	USBLS	5/07
	Idaho	Y	16610 FQ	18400 MW	20850 TQ	USBLS	5/07
	Boise City-Nampa MSA, ID	Y	16940 FQ	19030 MW	21880 TQ	USBLS	5/07
	Illinois	Y	18050 FQ	20500 MW	23460 TQ	USBLS	5/07
	Chicago-Naperville-Joliet MSA, IL-IN-WI	Y	18680 FQ	20950 MW	23640 TQ	USBLS	5/07
	Indiana	Y	17790 FQ	19940 MW	23060 TQ	USBLS	5/07
	Gary PMSA, IN	Y	18070 FQ	20630 MW	23260 TQ	USBLS	5/07
	Indianapolis-Carmel MSA, IN	Y	18410 FQ	20480 MW	23820 TQ	USBLS	5/07
	Terre Haute MSA, IN	Y	16780 FQ	18470 MW	21680 TQ	USBLS	5/07
	Iowa	Y	18240 FQ	21090 MW	24320 TQ	USBLS	5/07
	Davenport-Moline-Rock Island MSA, IA-IL	Y	17120 FQ	19710 MW	22740 TQ	USBLS	5/07
	Des Moines-West Des Moines MSA, IA	Y	21490 FQ	23210 MW	25020 TQ	USBLS	5/07
	Waterloo-Cedar Falls MSA, IA	Y	18540 FQ	20900 MW	23660 TQ	USBLS	5/07
	Kansas	Y	17110 FQ	18810 MW	21530 TQ	USBLS	5/07
	Wichita MSA, KS	Y	16980 FQ	18570 MW	20640 TQ	USBLS	5/07
	Kentucky	Y	19076 FQ	21696 MW	25278 TQ	KYBLS	2008
	Louisville-Jefferson County MSA, KY-IN	Y	18750 FQ	21350 MW	24990 TQ	USBLS	5/07
	Louisiana	H	6.47 FQ	7.60 MW	9.26 TQ	LABLS	1/08-3/08
	Baton Rouge MSA, LA	Y	13320 FQ	15430 MW	19020 TQ	USBLS	5/07
	Lake Charles MSA, LA	Y	12760 FQ	14350 MW	16660 TQ	USBLS	5/07
	New Orleans-Metairie-Kenner MSA, LA	Y	15090 FQ	17860 MW	21450 TQ	USBLS	5/07
	Maine	Y	19130 FQ	21880 MW	24710 TQ	USBLS	5/07
	Portland-South Portland-Biddeford MSA, ME	Y	18900 FQ	21570 MW	24820 TQ	USBLS	5/07
	Maryland	Y		22375 MW		MDBLS	3/08
	Baltimore-Towson MSA, MD	Y	19740 FQ	22230 MW	25640 TQ	USBLS	5/07
	Bethesda-Gaithersburg-Frederick PMSA, MD	Y	18300 FQ	21130 MW	24010 TQ	USBLS	5/07
	Massachusetts	Y	21850 FQ	24720 MW	28660 TQ	USBLS	5/07
	Barnstable Town MSA, MA	Y	23440 FQ	26920 MW	29630 TQ	USBLS	5/07
	Boston-Cambridge-Quincy NECTA, MA	Y	22220 FQ	25610 MW	29190 TQ	USBLS	5/07
	New Bedford MSA, MA	Y	21760 FQ	24750 MW	27980 TQ	USBLS	5/07
	Worcester MSA, MA-CT	Y	21900 FQ	24240 MW	28760 TQ	USBLS	5/07
	Michigan	Y	17210 FQ	19270 MW	22700 TQ	USBLS	5/07
	Detroit-Warren-Livonia MSA, MI	Y	17310 FQ	19290 MW	23020 TQ	USBLS	5/07
	Grand Rapids-Wyoming MSA, MI	Y	17810 FQ	20040 MW	23250 TQ	USBLS	5/07
	Warren-Troy-Farmington Hills PMSA, MI	Y	17650 FQ	20090 MW	24080 TQ	USBLS	5/07
	Minnesota	Y	20713 FQ	23368 MW	26160 TQ	MNBLS	10/08-12/08
	Duluth-Superior MSA, MN-WI	Y	19510 FQ	22333 MW	24884 TQ	MNBLS	10/08-12/08
	Minneapolis-Saint Paul MSA, MN-WI	Y	22103 FQ	24602 MW	28073 TQ	MNBLS	10/08-12/08
	Rochester MSA, MN	Y	21918 FQ	23714 MW	25807 TQ	MNBLS	10/08-12/08
	Mississippi	Y	15830 FQ	18310 MW	21500 TQ	USBLS	5/07
	Jackson MSA, MS	Y	15430 FQ	17770 MW	19960 TQ	USBLS	5/07
	Missouri	Y	16210 FQ	18220 MW	20870 TQ	USBLS	5/07
	Kansas City MSA, MO-KS	Y	18000 FQ	20850 MW	24890 TQ	USBLS	5/07
	St. Louis MSA, MO-IL	Y	16670 FQ	18860 MW	22390 TQ	USBLS	5/07
	Montana	Y	16860 FQ	19370 MW	22230 TQ	USBLS	5/07
	Billings MSA, MT	Y	18160 FQ	20800 MW	23130 TQ	USBLS	5/07
	Missoula MSA, MT	Y	17020 FQ	18860 MW	21860 TQ	USBLS	5/07
	Nebraska	Y	19530 FQ	22130 MW	24440 TQ	USBLS	5/07
	Lincoln MSA, NE	Y	22030 FQ	23850 MW	25860 TQ	USBLS	5/07

AE	Average entry wage	AW	Average wage paid	FQ	First quartile wage	LO	Lowest wage paid	MTC	Median total compensation	TCC	Total cash compensation
AER	Average entry range	AWR	Average wage range	H	Hourly	LR	Low end range	MW	Median wage paid	TQ	Third quartile wage
AEX	Average experienced wage	AXR	Average experienced range	HI	Highest wage paid	M	Monthly	MWR	Median wage range	W	Weekly
ATC	Average total compensation	D	Daily	HR	High end range	MCC	Median cash compensation	S	See annotated source	Y	Yearly

Occupation/Type/Industry	Location	Per	Low	Mid	High	Source	Date
Home Health Aide	Omaha-Council Bluffs MSA, NE-IA	Y	21120 FQ	23800 MW	33050 TQ	USBLS	5/07
	Nevada	H	9.52 FQ	10.80 MW	11.85 TQ	NVBLS	5/08
	Las Vegas-Paradise MSA, NV	H	9.66 FQ	10.75 MW	11.69 TQ	NVBLS	5/08
	New Hampshire	H	9.76 AE	11.33 MW	12.32 AEX	NHBLS	6/08
	Manchester MSA, NH	Y	19190 FQ	21410 MW	23430 TQ	USBLS	5/07
	Nashua NECTA, NH-MA	Y	23450 FQ	25630 MW	27840 TQ	USBLS	5/07
	Portsmouth MSA, NH-ME	Y	20580 FQ	22140 MW	23690 TQ	USBLS	5/07
	Rochester-Dover MSA, NH-ME	Y	20680 FQ	23770 MW	26660 TQ	USBLS	5/07
	New Jersey	Y	20590 FQ	22700 MW	24920 TQ	USBLS	5/07
	Atlantic City MSA, NJ	Y	25920 FQ	27870 MW	29820 TQ	USBLS	5/07
	Camden PMSA, NJ	Y	21340 FQ	23420 MW	26370 TQ	USBLS	5/07
	Edison PMSA, NJ	Y	20880 FQ	22740 MW	24820 TQ	USBLS	5/07
	Newark-Union PMSA, NJ-PA	Y	20430 FQ	22460 MW	24650 TQ	USBLS	5/07
	New Mexico	Y	17050 FQ	18770 MW	21620 TQ	USBLS	5/07
	Albuquerque MSA, NM	Y	17260 FQ	19040 MW	23990 TQ	USBLS	5/07
	New York	Y	17640 FQ	20870 MW	24600 TQ	USBLS	5/07
	Albany-Schenectady-Troy MSA, NY	Y	19130 FQ	22720 MW	28550 TQ	USBLS	5/07
	Buffalo-Niagara Falls MSA, NY	Y	18230 FQ	20960 MW	25170 TQ	USBLS	5/07
	Nassau-Suffolk PMSA, NY	Y	18280 FQ	21070 MW	24550 TQ	USBLS	5/07
	New York-Northern New Jersey-Long Island MSA, NY-NJ-PA	Y	17700 FQ	20900 MW	24010 TQ	USBLS	5/07
	North Carolina	Y	16930 FQ	19090 MW	22280 TQ	USBLS	5/07
	Asheville MSA, NC	Y	19100 FQ	21870 MW	24500 TQ	USBLS	5/07
	Charlotte-Gastonia-Concord MSA, NC-SC	Y	17710 FQ	20340 MW	23330 TQ	USBLS	5/07
	Raleigh-Cary MSA, NC	Y	17870 FQ	20260 MW	23340 TQ	USBLS	5/07
	Winston-Salem MSA, NC	Y	17380 FQ	19480 MW	22480 TQ	USBLS	5/07
	North Dakota	Y	17950 FQ	20260 MW	23050 TQ	USBLS	5/07
	Bismarck MSA, ND	Y	18950 FQ	21350 MW	23740 TQ	USBLS	5/07
	Fargo MSA, ND-MN	Y	18650 FQ	20930 MW	23300 TQ	USBLS	5/07
	Grand Forks MSA, ND-MN	Y	17410 FQ	18890 MW	20390 TQ	USBLS	5/07
	Ohio	Y	17440 FQ	19540 MW	22510 TQ	USBLS	5/07
	Cincinnati-Middletown MSA, OH-KY-IN	Y	19350 FQ	21800 MW	24020 TQ	USBLS	5/07
	Cleveland-Elyria-Mentor MSA, OH	Y	17670 FQ	19640 MW	22450 TQ	USBLS	5/07
	Columbus MSA, OH	Y	18170 FQ	20760 MW	23350 TQ	USBLS	5/07
	Dayton MSA, OH	Y	18010 FQ	20300 MW	23350 TQ	USBLS	5/07
	Oklahoma	Y	16000 FQ	18270 MW	21740 TQ	USBLS	5/07
	Oklahoma City MSA, OK	Y	16640 FQ	19390 MW	24660 TQ	USBLS	5/07
	Tulsa MSA, OK	Y	16210 FQ	18100 MW	20030 TQ	USBLS	5/07
	Oregon	H	8.88 FQ	9.76 MW	11.10 TQ	ORBLS	5/08
	Portland-Vancouver-Beaverton MSA, OR-WA	Y	18440 FQ	20520 MW	23040 TQ	USBLS	5/07
	Pennsylvania	Y	17130 FQ	19970 MW	23120 TQ	USBLS	5/07
	Allentown-Bethlehem-Easton MSA, PA-NJ	Y	17640 FQ	19800 MW	22910 TQ	USBLS	5/07
	Philadelphia-Camden-Wilmington MSA, PA-NJ-DE-MD	Y	19180 FQ	21930 MW	24520 TQ	USBLS	5/07
	Pittsburgh MSA, PA	Y	16890 FQ	19730 MW	22820 TQ	USBLS	5/07
	Rhode Island	Y	22030 FQ	24760 MW	30070 TQ	USBLS	5/07
	Providence-Fall River-Warwick MSA, RI-MA	Y	21960 FQ	24570 MW	29830 TQ	USBLS	5/07
	South Carolina	Y	16520 FQ	18260 MW	20270 TQ	USBLS	5/07
	Charleston-North Charleston MSA, SC	Y	16390 FQ	18270 MW	21010 TQ	USBLS	5/07
	Columbia MSA, SC	Y	17150 FQ	18810 MW	20930 TQ	USBLS	5/07
	South Dakota	Y	18997 FQ	21346 MW	24411 TQ	SDBLS	7/08-9/08
	Sioux Falls MSA, SD	Y	18428 FQ	20932 MW	24181 TQ	SDBLS	7/08-9/08
	Tennessee	Y	16780 FQ	18720 MW	21650 TQ	USBLS	5/07
	Memphis MSA, TN-MS-AR	Y	14480 FQ	19420 MW	26520 TQ	USBLS	5/07
	Nashville-Davidson-Murfreesboro MSA, TN	Y	17000 FQ	18820 MW	21370 TQ	USBLS	5/07
	Texas	Y	13570 FQ	16140 MW	19970 TQ	USBLS	5/07
	Austin-Round Rock MSA, TX	Y	16130 FQ	17800 MW	19950 TQ	USBLS	5/07

AE	Average entry wage	AW	Average wage paid	FQ	First quartile wage
AER	Average entry range	AWR	Average wage range	H	Hourly
AEX	Average experienced wage	AXR	Average experienced range	HI	Highest wage paid
ATC	Average total compensation	D	Daily	HR	High end range

LO	Lowest wage paid	MTC	Median total compensation	TCC	Total cash compensation
LR	Low end range	MW	Median wage paid	TQ	Third quartile wage
M	Monthly	MWR	Median wage range	W	Weekly
MCC	Median cash compensation	S	See annotated source	Y	Yearly

Occupation/Type/Industry	Location	Per	Low	Mid	High	Source	Date
Home Health Aide	Dallas-Fort Worth-Arlington						
	MSA, TX	Y	16360 FQ	19420 MW	23570 TQ	USBLS	5/07
	El Paso MSA, TX	Y	13190 FQ	15220 MW	18050 TQ	USBLS	5/07
	Houston-Sugar Land-Baytown						
	MSA, TX	Y	13380 FQ	15910 MW	20210 TQ	USBLS	5/07
	Midland MSA, TX	Y	13460 FQ	16380 MW	20200 TQ	USBLS	5/07
	San Antonio MSA, TX	Y	13480 FQ	15730 MW	18620 TQ	USBLS	5/07
	Utah	Y	17390 FQ	19340 MW	22130 TQ	USBLS	5/07
	Provo-Orem MSA, UT	Y	17020 FQ	19160 MW	22280 TQ	USBLS	5/07
	Salt Lake City MSA, UT	Y	17880 FQ	19840 MW	22510 TQ	USBLS	5/07
	Vermont	Y	18790 FQ	21670 MW	24650 TQ	USBLS	5/07
	Burlington-South Burlington						
	MSA, VT	Y	18310 FQ	20440 MW	23070 TQ	USBLS	5/07
	Virginia	Y	16820 FQ	18940 MW	22120 TQ	USBLS	5/07
	Richmond MSA, VA	Y	17020 FQ	18600 MW	20090 TQ	USBLS	5/07
	Virginia Beach-Norfolk-						
	Newport News MSA, VA-NC	Y	16170 FQ	18120 MW	20720 TQ	USBLS	5/07
	Washington	H	9.26 FQ	10.40 MW	11.67 TQ	WABLS	3/08
	Seattle-Tacoma-Bellevue						
	MSA, WA	Y	20920 FQ	23150 MW	25920 TQ	USBLS	5/07
	West Virginia	Y	14426 FQ	15930 MW	18203 TQ	WVBLS	7/08-9/08
	Charleston MSA, WV	Y	13910 FQ	15380 MW	17790 TQ	USBLS	5/07
	Wisconsin	Y	18300 FQ	20900 MW	23610 TQ	USBLS	5/07
	Milwaukee-Waukesha-West						
	Allis MSA, WI	Y	18140 FQ	20690 MW	23400 TQ	USBLS	5/07
	Racine MSA, WI	Y	16670 FQ	19270 MW	23700 TQ	USBLS	5/07
	Wyoming	Y	19259 FQ	22204 MW	25227 TQ	WYBLS	9/08
	Puerto Rico	Y	12480 FQ	13700 MW	14920 TQ	USBLS	5/07
	San Juan-Caguas-Guaynabo						
	MSA, PR	Y	12510 FQ	13770 MW	15060 TQ	USBLS	5/07
Homeland Security Chief	Louisiana	Y			165000 HI	DADV	2009
Horseracing Steward	Northern Virginia, VA	Y	53510-69907 LR		142764-172165 HR	VACG03	11/25/07
Hospital Aide	Ohio	H	14.36 LO		15.41 HI	ODAS	2008
Hospital Quality Assurance Coordinator	Virginia	Y	31352-40959 LR		64347-84062 HR	VACG04	11/25/07
Hospitalist	United States	Y	164000 AE			USNEWS01	2007
Host and Hostess							
Restaurant, Lounge, and Coffee Shop	Alabama	Y	13030 FQ	14870 MW	17640 TQ	USBLS	5/07
Restaurant, Lounge, and Coffee Shop	Birmingham-Hoover MSA, AL	Y	13680 FQ	16360 MW	19630 TQ	USBLS	5/07
Restaurant, Lounge, and Coffee Shop	Huntsville MSA, AL	Y	13020 FQ	14770 MW	17800 TQ	USBLS	5/07
Restaurant, Lounge, and Coffee Shop	Mobile MSA, AL	Y	12510 FQ	14060 MW	15640 TQ	USBLS	5/07
Restaurant, Lounge, and Coffee Shop	Alaska	Y	16610 FQ	18580 MW	20760 TQ	USBLS	5/07
Restaurant, Lounge, and Coffee Shop	Anchorage MSA, AK	Y	16550 FQ	18470 MW	20470 TQ	USBLS	5/07
Restaurant, Lounge, and Coffee Shop	Arizona	Y	14790 FQ	15840 MW	18470 TQ	USBLS	5/07
Restaurant, Lounge, and Coffee Shop	Phoenix-Mesa-Scottsdale						
	MSA, AZ	Y	14850 FQ	16000 MW	18730 TQ	USBLS	5/07
Restaurant, Lounge, and Coffee Shop	Tucson MSA, AZ	Y	14640 FQ	15380 MW	17560 TQ	USBLS	5/07
Restaurant, Lounge, and Coffee Shop	Arkansas	Y	14350 FQ	15520 MW	17720 TQ	USBLS	5/07
Restaurant, Lounge, and Coffee Shop	Fayetteville-Springdale-Rogers						
	MSA, AR-MO	Y	14700 FQ	16240 MW	18290 TQ	USBLS	5/07
Restaurant, Lounge, and Coffee Shop	Little Rock-North Little Rock						
	MSA, AR	Y	14240 FQ	15290 MW	17430 TQ	USBLS	5/07
Restaurant, Lounge, and Coffee Shop	California	H	8.05 FQ	8.81 MW	9.70 TQ	CABLS	1/08-3/08
Restaurant, Lounge, and Coffee Shop	Bakersfield MSA, CA	H	8.00 FQ	8.07 MW	8.90 TQ	CABLS	1/08-3/08
Restaurant, Lounge, and Coffee Shop	Los Angeles-Long Beach-						
	Glendale PMSA, CA	H	8.07 FQ	8.86 MW	9.83 TQ	CABLS	1/08-3/08
Restaurant, Lounge, and Coffee Shop	Oakland-Fremont-Hayward						
	MSA, CA	H	8.20 FQ	8.90 MW	9.77 TQ	CABLS	1/08-3/08
Restaurant, Lounge, and Coffee Shop	Riverside-San Bernardino-						
	Ontario MSA, CA	H	8.00 FQ	8.62 MW	9.36 TQ	CABLS	1/08-3/08
Restaurant, Lounge, and Coffee Shop	Sacramento-Arden Arcade-						
	Roseville MSA, CA	H	8.00 FQ	8.63 MW	9.30 TQ	CABLS	1/08-3/08
Restaurant, Lounge, and Coffee Shop	San Diego-Carlsbad-San						
	Marcos MSA, CA	H	8.17 FQ	8.91 MW	9.78 TQ	CABLS	1/08-3/08

AE	Average entry wage	AW	Average wage paid	FQ	First quartile wage	LO	Lowest wage paid	MTC	Median total compensation	TCC	Total cash compensation
AER	Average entry range	AWR	Average wage range	H	Hourly	LR	Low end range	MW	Median wage paid	TQ	Third quartile wage
AEX	Average experienced wage	AXR	Average experienced range	HI	Highest wage paid	M	Monthly	MWR	Median wage range	W	Weekly
ATC	Average total compensation	D	Daily	HR	High end range	MCC	Median cash compensation	S	See annotated source	Y	Yearly

796

Occupation/Type/Industry	Location	Per	Low	Mid	High	Source	Date
Host and Hostess							
Restaurant, Lounge, and Coffee Shop	San Francisco-San Mateo-Redwood PMSA, CA	H	9.02 FQ	10.51 MW	12.77 TQ	CABLS	1/08-3/08
Restaurant, Lounge, and Coffee Shop	San Jose-Sunnyvale-Santa Clara MSA, CA	H	8.34 FQ	9.03 MW	9.97 TQ	CABLS	1/08-3/08
Restaurant, Lounge, and Coffee Shop	Santa Ana-Anaheim-Irvine PMSA, CA	Y	16290 FQ	17750 MW	19440 TQ	USBLS	5/07
Restaurant, Lounge, and Coffee Shop	Colorado	Y	15260 FQ	17000 MW	19540 TQ	USBLS	5/07
Restaurant, Lounge, and Coffee Shop	Denver-Aurora MSA, CO	Y	15240 FQ	16980 MW	19670 TQ	USBLS	5/07
Restaurant, Lounge, and Coffee Shop	Connecticut	H	8.50 AE	9.68 MW		CTBLS	1/08-3/08
Restaurant, Lounge, and Coffee Shop	Bridgeport-Stamford-Norwalk MSA, CT	Y	17550 FQ	19290 MW	23230 TQ	USBLS	5/07
Restaurant, Lounge, and Coffee Shop	Hartford-West Hartford-East Hartford MSA, CT	Y	18100 FQ	20480 MW	25030 TQ	USBLS	5/07
Restaurant, Lounge, and Coffee Shop	Delaware	Y	14930 FQ	16740 MW	19240 TQ	USBLS	5/07
Restaurant, Lounge, and Coffee Shop	Wilmington PMSA, DE-MD-NJ	Y	15190 FQ	16950 MW	19060 TQ	USBLS	5/07
Restaurant, Lounge, and Coffee Shop	District of Columbia	Y	21190 FQ	24140 MW	27830 TQ	USBLS	5/07
Restaurant, Lounge, and Coffee Shop	Washington-Arlington-Alexandria MSA, DC-VA-MD-WV	Y	15760 FQ	18780 MW	22700 TQ	USBLS	5/07
Restaurant, Lounge, and Coffee Shop	Florida	Y	15060 FQ	16760 MW	19570 TQ	USBLS	5/07
Restaurant, Lounge, and Coffee Shop	Fort Lauderdale-Pompano Beach-Deerfield Beach PMSA, FL	Y	15130 FQ	17380 MW	20710 TQ	USBLS	5/07
Restaurant, Lounge, and Coffee Shop	Jacksonville MSA, FL	Y	14870 FQ	16120 MW	18180 TQ	USBLS	5/07
Restaurant, Lounge, and Coffee Shop	Miami-Fort Lauderdale-Miami Beach MSA, FL	Y	15180 FQ	17390 MW	21150 TQ	USBLS	5/07
Restaurant, Lounge, and Coffee Shop	Orlando-Kissimmee MSA, FL	Y	15360 FQ	17370 MW	19940 TQ	USBLS	5/07
Restaurant, Lounge, and Coffee Shop	Tampa-St. Petersburg-Clearwater MSA, FL	Y	15000 FQ	16280 MW	18760 TQ	USBLS	5/07
Restaurant, Lounge, and Coffee Shop	West Palm Beach-Boca Raton-Boynton Beach PMSA, FL	Y	15440 FQ	17580 MW	22610 TQ	USBLS	5/07
Restaurant, Lounge, and Coffee Shop	Georgia	Y	13240 FQ	15360 MW	18320 TQ	USBLS	5/07
Restaurant, Lounge, and Coffee Shop	Atlanta-Sandy Springs-Marietta MSA, GA	Y	13600 FQ	16090 MW	19130 TQ	USBLS	5/07
Restaurant, Lounge, and Coffee Shop	Hawaii	Y	16850 FQ	19540 MW	25950 TQ	USBLS	5/07
Restaurant, Lounge, and Coffee Shop	Honolulu MSA, HI	Y	16430 FQ	18740 MW	22750 TQ	USBLS	5/07
Restaurant, Lounge, and Coffee Shop	Idaho	Y	13130 FQ	15090 MW	17380 TQ	USBLS	5/07
Restaurant, Lounge, and Coffee Shop	Boise City-Nampa MSA, ID	Y	12940 FQ	14680 MW	16820 TQ	USBLS	5/07
Restaurant, Lounge, and Coffee Shop	Illinois	Y	15090 FQ	17000 MW	20090 TQ	USBLS	5/07
Restaurant, Lounge, and Coffee Shop	Chicago-Naperville-Joliet MSA, IL-IN-WI	Y	15320 FQ	17700 MW	21010 TQ	USBLS	5/07
Restaurant, Lounge, and Coffee Shop	Indiana	Y	13250 FQ	15350 MW	18070 TQ	USBLS	5/07
Restaurant, Lounge, and Coffee Shop	Gary PMSA, IN	Y	13070 FQ	14950 MW	17990 TQ	USBLS	5/07
Restaurant, Lounge, and Coffee Shop	Indianapolis-Carmel MSA, IN	Y	13650 FQ	16150 MW	18840 TQ	USBLS	5/07
Restaurant, Lounge, and Coffee Shop	Terre Haute MSA, IN	Y	13440 FQ	15720 MW	18160 TQ	USBLS	5/07
Restaurant, Lounge, and Coffee Shop	Iowa	Y	14230 FQ	15590 MW	18070 TQ	USBLS	5/07
Restaurant, Lounge, and Coffee Shop	Des Moines-West Des Moines MSA, IA	Y	14430 FQ	15950 MW	18440 TQ	USBLS	5/07
Restaurant, Lounge, and Coffee Shop	Kansas	Y	13010 FQ	14910 MW	17700 TQ	USBLS	5/07
Restaurant, Lounge, and Coffee Shop	Wichita MSA, KS	Y	12580 FQ	14070 MW	15730 TQ	USBLS	5/07
Restaurant, Lounge, and Coffee Shop	Kentucky	Y	13850 FQ	16160 MW	18669 TQ	KYBLS	2008
Restaurant, Lounge, and Coffee Shop	Elizabethtown MSA, KY	Y	12980 FQ	14820 MW	16400 TQ	USBLS	5/07
Restaurant, Lounge, and Coffee Shop	Louisville-Jefferson County MSA, KY-IN	Y	13670 FQ	15920 MW	18300 TQ	USBLS	5/07
Restaurant, Lounge, and Coffee Shop	Louisiana	H	6.26 FQ	7.16 MW	8.40 TQ	LABLS	1/08-3/08
Restaurant, Lounge, and Coffee Shop	Baton Rouge MSA, LA	Y	13260 FQ	15380 MW	17770 TQ	USBLS	5/07
Restaurant, Lounge, and Coffee Shop	Houma-Bayou Cane-Thibodaux MSA, LA	Y	12450 FQ	13700 MW	14980 TQ	USBLS	5/07
Restaurant, Lounge, and Coffee Shop	New Orleans-Metairie-Kenner MSA, LA	Y	13000 FQ	14870 MW	17760 TQ	USBLS	5/07
Restaurant, Lounge, and Coffee Shop	Maine	Y	16520 FQ	18840 MW	21930 TQ	USBLS	5/07
Restaurant, Lounge, and Coffee Shop	Portland-South Portland-Biddeford MSA, ME	Y	17640 FQ	20050 MW	23550 TQ	USBLS	5/07
Restaurant, Lounge, and Coffee Shop	Maryland	Y		17700 MW		MDBLS	3/08
Restaurant, Lounge, and Coffee Shop	Baltimore-Towson MSA, MD	Y	15340 FQ	17510 MW	20780 TQ	USBLS	5/07
Restaurant, Lounge, and Coffee Shop	Bethesda-Gaithersburg-Frederick PMSA, MD	Y	15720 FQ	18450 MW	21580 TQ	USBLS	5/07
Restaurant, Lounge, and Coffee Shop	Hagerstown-Martinsburg MSA, MD-WV	Y	14580 FQ	16000 MW	18430 TQ	USBLS	5/07
Restaurant, Lounge, and Coffee Shop	Massachusetts	Y	18290 FQ	20750 MW	23540 TQ	USBLS	5/07

AE	Average entry wage	AW	Average wage paid	FQ	First quartile wage	LO	Lowest wage paid	MTC	Median total compensation	TCC	Total cash compensation
AER	Average entry range	AWR	Average wage range	H	Hourly	LR	Low end range	MW	Median wage paid	TQ	Third quartile wage
AEX	Average experienced wage	AXR	Average experienced range	HI	Highest wage paid	M	Monthly	MWR	Median wage range	W	Weekly
ATC	Average total compensation	D	Daily	HR	High end range	MCC	Median cash compensation	S	See annotated source	Y	Yearly

797

Host and Hostess

Occupation/Type/Industry	Location	Per	Low	Mid	High	Source	Date
Host and Hostess							
Restaurant, Lounge, and Coffee Shop	Boston-Cambridge-Quincy NECTA, MA	Y	19150 FQ	21390 MW	23830 TQ	USBLS	5/07
Restaurant, Lounge, and Coffee Shop	Worcester MSA, MA-CT	Y	18660 FQ	21230 MW	23520 TQ	USBLS	5/07
Restaurant, Lounge, and Coffee Shop	Michigan	Y	15230 FQ	16110 MW	18620 TQ	USBLS	5/07
Restaurant, Lounge, and Coffee Shop	Detroit-Warren-Livonia MSA, MI	Y	15440 FQ	16440 MW	19190 TQ	USBLS	5/07
Restaurant, Lounge, and Coffee Shop	Grand Rapids-Wyoming MSA, MI	Y	15210 FQ	16040 MW	18440 TQ	USBLS	5/07
Restaurant, Lounge, and Coffee Shop	Warren-Troy-Farmington Hills PMSA, MI	Y	15370 FQ	16510 MW	19520 TQ	USBLS	5/07
Restaurant, Lounge, and Coffee Shop	Minnesota	Y	16028 FQ	18119 MW	20388 TQ	MNBLS	10/08-12/08
Restaurant, Lounge, and Coffee Shop	Duluth-Superior MSA, MN-WI	Y	15192 FQ	16635 MW	18966 TQ	MNBLS	10/08-12/08
Restaurant, Lounge, and Coffee Shop	Minneapolis-Saint Paul MSA, MN-WI	Y	16582 FQ	18611 MW	20807 TQ	MNBLS	10/08-12/08
Restaurant, Lounge, and Coffee Shop	Rochester MSA, MN	Y	15884 FQ	17934 MW	20153 TQ	MNBLS	10/08-12/08
Restaurant, Lounge, and Coffee Shop	Mississippi	Y	13350 FQ	15510 MW	18040 TQ	USBLS	5/07
Restaurant, Lounge, and Coffee Shop	Jackson MSA, MS	Y	14170 FQ	16210 MW	18040 TQ	USBLS	5/07
Restaurant, Lounge, and Coffee Shop	Pascagoula MSA, MS	Y	12410 FQ	13780 MW	15150 TQ	USBLS	5/07
Restaurant, Lounge, and Coffee Shop	Missouri	Y	14570 FQ	15780 MW	18580 TQ	USBLS	5/07
Restaurant, Lounge, and Coffee Shop	Kansas City MSA, MO-KS	Y	14280 FQ	15690 MW	18540 TQ	USBLS	5/07
Restaurant, Lounge, and Coffee Shop	St. Louis MSA, MO-IL	Y	14660 FQ	15900 MW	18750 TQ	USBLS	5/07
Restaurant, Lounge, and Coffee Shop	Montana	Y	13880 FQ	14960 MW	16470 TQ	USBLS	5/07
Restaurant, Lounge, and Coffee Shop	Billings MSA, MT	Y	14110 FQ	15390 MW	17430 TQ	USBLS	5/07
Restaurant, Lounge, and Coffee Shop	Nebraska	Y	13090 FQ	15100 MW	18130 TQ	USBLS	5/07
Restaurant, Lounge, and Coffee Shop	Omaha-Council Bluffs MSA, NE-IA	Y	13620 FQ	16060 MW	19140 TQ	USBLS	5/07
Restaurant, Lounge, and Coffee Shop	Nevada	H	8.08 FQ	9.57 MW	12.90 TQ	NVBLS	5/08
Restaurant, Lounge, and Coffee Shop	Las Vegas-Paradise MSA, NV	H	8.33 FQ	10.28 MW	13.58 TQ	NVBLS	5/08
Restaurant, Lounge, and Coffee Shop	New Hampshire	H	7.68 AE	9.50 MW	10.79 AEX	NHBLS	6/08
Restaurant, Lounge, and Coffee Shop	Manchester MSA, NH	Y	18150 FQ	21140 MW	24110 TQ	USBLS	5/07
Restaurant, Lounge, and Coffee Shop	Nashua NECTA, NH-MA	Y	16030 FQ	18020 MW	20270 TQ	USBLS	5/07
Restaurant, Lounge, and Coffee Shop	New Jersey	Y	16010 FQ	18100 MW	21310 TQ	USBLS	5/07
Restaurant, Lounge, and Coffee Shop	Camden PMSA, NJ	Y	15610 FQ	17300 MW	19870 TQ	USBLS	5/07
Restaurant, Lounge, and Coffee Shop	Edison PMSA, NJ	Y	16000 FQ	17810 MW	20220 TQ	USBLS	5/07
Restaurant, Lounge, and Coffee Shop	Newark-Union PMSA, NJ-PA	Y	16270 FQ	18770 MW	22490 TQ	USBLS	5/07
Restaurant, Lounge, and Coffee Shop	New Mexico	Y	13150 FQ	15160 MW	17970 TQ	USBLS	5/07
Restaurant, Lounge, and Coffee Shop	Albuquerque MSA, NM	Y	13350 FQ	15490 MW	17580 TQ	USBLS	5/07
Restaurant, Lounge, and Coffee Shop	New York	Y	15760 FQ	19000 MW	24750 TQ	USBLS	5/07
Restaurant, Lounge, and Coffee Shop	Albany-Schenectady-Troy MSA, NY	Y	15530 FQ	17840 MW	20500 TQ	USBLS	5/07
Restaurant, Lounge, and Coffee Shop	Buffalo-Niagara Falls MSA, NY	Y	15440 FQ	16500 MW	18620 TQ	USBLS	5/07
Restaurant, Lounge, and Coffee Shop	Nassau-Suffolk PMSA, NY	Y	16720 FQ	19150 MW	23300 TQ	USBLS	5/07
Restaurant, Lounge, and Coffee Shop	New York-Northern New Jersey-Long Island MSA, NY-NJ-PA	Y	16730 FQ	20520 MW	25690 TQ	USBLS	5/07
Restaurant, Lounge, and Coffee Shop	Syracuse MSA, NY	Y	15050 FQ	15600 MW	17330 TQ	USBLS	5/07
Restaurant, Lounge, and Coffee Shop	North Carolina	Y	14070 FQ	15390 MW	17890 TQ	USBLS	5/07
Restaurant, Lounge, and Coffee Shop	Charlotte-Gastonia-Concord MSA, NC-SC	Y	14050 FQ	15490 MW	18160 TQ	USBLS	5/07
Restaurant, Lounge, and Coffee Shop	Raleigh-Cary MSA, NC	Y	14450 FQ	16160 MW	18470 TQ	USBLS	5/07
Restaurant, Lounge, and Coffee Shop	Winston-Salem MSA, NC	Y	13960 FQ	15130 MW	16580 TQ	USBLS	5/07
Restaurant, Lounge, and Coffee Shop	North Dakota	Y	12850 FQ	14660 MW	16670 TQ	USBLS	5/07
Restaurant, Lounge, and Coffee Shop	Bismarck MSA, ND	Y	12960 FQ	14780 MW	16760 TQ	USBLS	5/07
Restaurant, Lounge, and Coffee Shop	Fargo MSA, ND-MN	Y	13140 FQ	15110 MW	17270 TQ	USBLS	5/07
Restaurant, Lounge, and Coffee Shop	Ohio	Y	14840 FQ	15720 MW	18070 TQ	USBLS	5/07
Restaurant, Lounge, and Coffee Shop	Cincinnati-Middletown MSA, OH-KY-IN	Y	14720 FQ	15660 MW	17980 TQ	USBLS	5/07
Restaurant, Lounge, and Coffee Shop	Cleveland-Elyria-Mentor MSA, OH	Y	15050 FQ	16060 MW	18570 TQ	USBLS	5/07
Restaurant, Lounge, and Coffee Shop	Columbus MSA, OH	Y	15030 FQ	16210 MW	18840 TQ	USBLS	5/07
Restaurant, Lounge, and Coffee Shop	Dayton MSA, OH	Y	14760 FQ	15530 MW	17600 TQ	USBLS	5/07
Restaurant, Lounge, and Coffee Shop	Mansfield MSA, OH	Y	14740 FQ	15310 MW	16460 TQ	USBLS	5/07
Restaurant, Lounge, and Coffee Shop	Oklahoma	Y	12840 FQ	14530 MW	17040 TQ	USBLS	5/07
Restaurant, Lounge, and Coffee Shop	Oklahoma City MSA, OK	Y	12860 FQ	14580 MW	17410 TQ	USBLS	5/07
Restaurant, Lounge, and Coffee Shop	Tulsa MSA, OK	Y	12980 FQ	14770 MW	17520 TQ	USBLS	5/07
Restaurant, Lounge, and Coffee Shop	Oregon	H	8.53 FQ	9.08 MW	9.83 TQ	ORBLS	5/08
Restaurant, Lounge, and Coffee Shop	Portland-Vancouver-Beaverton MSA, OR-WA	Y	17400 FQ	18540 MW	20340 TQ	USBLS	5/07
Restaurant, Lounge, and Coffee Shop	Pennsylvania	Y	14870 FQ	16980 MW	20680 TQ	USBLS	5/07

AE Average entry wage	**AW** Average wage paid	**FQ** First quartile wage	**LO** Lowest wage paid	**MTC** Median total compensation	**TCC** Total cash compensation
AER Average entry range	**AWR** Average wage range	**H** Hourly	**LR** Low end range	**MW** Median wage paid	**TQ** Third quartile wage
AEX Average experienced wage	**AXR** Average experienced range	**HI** Highest wage paid	**M** Monthly	**MWR** Median wage range	**W** Weekly
ATC Average total compensation	**D** Daily	**HR** High end range	**MCC** Median cash compensation	**S** See annotated source	**Y** Yearly

Occupation/Type/Industry	Location	Per	Low	Mid	High	Source	Date
Host and Hostess							
Restaurant, Lounge, and Coffee Shop	Allentown-Bethlehem-Easton MSA, PA-NJ	Y	15360 FQ	17420 MW	19950 TQ	USBLS	5/07
Restaurant, Lounge, and Coffee Shop	Erie MSA, PA	Y	14510 FQ	15630 MW	19190 TQ	USBLS	5/07
Restaurant, Lounge, and Coffee Shop	Philadelphia-Camden-Wilmington MSA, PA-NJ-DE-MD	Y	15460 FQ	18070 MW	22480 TQ	USBLS	5/07
Restaurant, Lounge, and Coffee Shop	Pittsburgh MSA, PA	Y	14920 FQ	16840 MW	20520 TQ	USBLS	5/07
Restaurant, Lounge, and Coffee Shop	York-Hanover MSA, PA	Y	14750 FQ	16860 MW	19760 TQ	USBLS	5/07
Restaurant, Lounge, and Coffee Shop	Rhode Island	Y	16260 FQ	17930 MW	20270 TQ	USBLS	5/07
Restaurant, Lounge, and Coffee Shop	Providence-Fall River-Warwick MSA, RI-MA	Y	16370 FQ	18040 MW	20340 TQ	USBLS	5/07
Restaurant, Lounge, and Coffee Shop	South Carolina	Y	13220 FQ	15340 MW	18020 TQ	USBLS	5/07
Restaurant, Lounge, and Coffee Shop	Charleston-North Charleston MSA, SC	Y	12870 FQ	14700 MW	17520 TQ	USBLS	5/07
Restaurant, Lounge, and Coffee Shop	Columbia MSA, SC	Y	13210 FQ	15220 MW	17290 TQ	USBLS	5/07
Restaurant, Lounge, and Coffee Shop	South Dakota	Y	15788 FQ	17912 MW	19667 TQ	SDBLS	7/08-9/08
Restaurant, Lounge, and Coffee Shop	Sioux Falls MSA, SD	Y	16485 FQ	18200 MW	19814 TQ	SDBLS	7/08-9/08
Restaurant, Lounge, and Coffee Shop	Tennessee	Y	13990 FQ	16330 MW	18440 TQ	USBLS	5/07
Restaurant, Lounge, and Coffee Shop	Memphis MSA, TN-MS-AR	Y	15240 FQ	17380 MW	19460 TQ	USBLS	5/07
Restaurant, Lounge, and Coffee Shop	Nashville-Davidson-Murfreesboro MSA, TN	Y	14520 FQ	16640 MW	18460 TQ	USBLS	5/07
Restaurant, Lounge, and Coffee Shop	Texas	Y	12910 FQ	14670 MW	17440 TQ	USBLS	5/07
Restaurant, Lounge, and Coffee Shop	Austin-Round Rock MSA, TX	Y	13380 FQ	15630 MW	18400 TQ	USBLS	5/07
Restaurant, Lounge, and Coffee Shop	Dallas-Fort Worth-Arlington MSA, TX	Y	13310 FQ	15530 MW	18740 TQ	USBLS	5/07
Restaurant, Lounge, and Coffee Shop	El Paso MSA, TX	Y	12320 FQ	13610 MW	14900 TQ	USBLS	5/07
Restaurant, Lounge, and Coffee Shop	Houston-Sugar Land-Baytown MSA, TX	Y	12850 FQ	14560 MW	17310 TQ	USBLS	5/07
Restaurant, Lounge, and Coffee Shop	San Antonio MSA, TX	Y	12760 FQ	14470 MW	16690 TQ	USBLS	5/07
Restaurant, Lounge, and Coffee Shop	Utah	Y	13670 FQ	16130 MW	18660 TQ	USBLS	5/07
Restaurant, Lounge, and Coffee Shop	Salt Lake City MSA, UT	Y	14110 FQ	16870 MW	19270 TQ	USBLS	5/07
Restaurant, Lounge, and Coffee Shop	Vermont	Y	16720 FQ	19190 MW	23710 TQ	USBLS	5/07
Restaurant, Lounge, and Coffee Shop	Burlington-South Burlington MSA, VT	Y	16360 FQ	18770 MW	23260 TQ	USBLS	5/07
Restaurant, Lounge, and Coffee Shop	Virginia	Y	13860 FQ	16510 MW	19530 TQ	USBLS	5/07
Restaurant, Lounge, and Coffee Shop	Richmond MSA, VA	Y	13460 FQ	15740 MW	18440 TQ	USBLS	5/07
Restaurant, Lounge, and Coffee Shop	Virginia Beach-Norfolk-Newport News MSA, VA-NC	Y	13430 FQ	15730 MW	18710 TQ	USBLS	5/07
Restaurant, Lounge, and Coffee Shop	Washington	H	8.53 FQ	9.11 MW	9.92 TQ	WABLS	3/08
Restaurant, Lounge, and Coffee Shop	Seattle-Tacoma-Bellevue MSA, WA	Y	17610 FQ	18860 MW	21070 TQ	USBLS	5/07
Restaurant, Lounge, and Coffee Shop	West Virginia	Y	14404 FQ	15935 MW	18411 TQ	WVBLS	7/08-9/08
Restaurant, Lounge, and Coffee Shop	Charleston MSA, WV	Y	13450 FQ	14570 MW	16290 TQ	USBLS	5/07
Restaurant, Lounge, and Coffee Shop	Huntington-Ashland MSA, WV-KY-OH	Y	14170 FQ	16180 MW	18340 TQ	USBLS	5/07
Restaurant, Lounge, and Coffee Shop	Wheeling MSA, WV-OH	Y	14440 FQ	14990 MW	16260 TQ	USBLS	5/07
Restaurant, Lounge, and Coffee Shop	Wisconsin	Y	15020 FQ	16750 MW	18960 TQ	USBLS	5/07
Restaurant, Lounge, and Coffee Shop	Appleton MSA, WI	Y	15580 FQ	17180 MW	18810 TQ	USBLS	5/07
Restaurant, Lounge, and Coffee Shop	Milwaukee-Waukesha-West Allis MSA, WI	Y	15610 FQ	17360 MW	19370 TQ	USBLS	5/07
Restaurant, Lounge, and Coffee Shop	Wyoming	Y	13114 FQ	14636 MW	16449 TQ	WYBLS	9/08
Restaurant, Lounge, and Coffee Shop	Cheyenne MSA, WY	Y	12901 FQ	14314 MW	15770 TQ	WYBLS	9/08
Restaurant, Lounge, and Coffee Shop	Puerto Rico	Y	12520 FQ	13880 MW	15280 TQ	USBLS	5/07
Restaurant, Lounge, and Coffee Shop	San Juan-Caguas-Guaynabo MSA, PR	Y	12530 FQ	13900 MW	15310 TQ	USBLS	5/07
Restaurant, Lounge, and Coffee Shop	Virgin Islands	Y	16900 FQ	18730 MW	22070 TQ	USBLS	5/07
Restaurant, Lounge, and Coffee Shop	Guam	Y	12660 FQ	14020 MW	15600 TQ	USBLS	5/07
Hostler							
Municipal Government	Cincinnati, OH	Y	20581 LO		31476 HI	COHSS	10/08
Hotel, Motel, and Resort Desk Clerk							
	Alabama	Y	13420 FQ	15690 MW	18280 TQ	USBLS	5/07
	Birmingham-Hoover MSA, AL	Y	13870 FQ	16460 MW	18970 TQ	USBLS	5/07
	Huntsville MSA, AL	Y	13880 FQ	16510 MW	19110 TQ	USBLS	5/07
	Montgomery MSA, AL	Y	14080 FQ	16510 MW	18390 TQ	USBLS	5/07
	Alaska	Y	17840 FQ	20640 MW	23680 TQ	USBLS	5/07
	Anchorage MSA, AK	Y	16950 FQ	20270 MW	23180 TQ	USBLS	5/07
	Arizona	Y	15580 FQ	18210 MW	21830 TQ	USBLS	5/07
	Phoenix-Mesa-Scottsdale MSA, AZ	Y	16910 FQ	20030 MW	23680 TQ	USBLS	5/07

Occupation/Type/Industry	Location	Per	Low	Mid	High	Source	Date
Hotel, Motel, and Resort Desk Clerk	Tucson MSA, AZ	Y	15120 FQ	17140 MW	19420 TQ	USBLS	5/07
	Arkansas	Y	14560 FQ	16030 MW	18200 TQ	USBLS	5/07
	Fort Smith MSA, AR-OK	Y	14120 FQ	15300 MW	17500 TQ	USBLS	5/07
	Little Rock-North Little Rock MSA, AR	Y	15290 FQ	17170 MW	18850 TQ	USBLS	5/07
	California	H	9.01 FQ	10.50 MW	12.32 TQ	CABLS	1/08-3/08
	Los Angeles-Long Beach-Glendale PMSA, CA	H	9.05 FQ	10.48 MW	12.07 TQ	CABLS	1/08-3/08
	Oakland-Fremont-Hayward MSA, CA	H	9.32 FQ	10.82 MW	12.34 TQ	CABLS	1/08-3/08
	Riverside-San Bernardino-Ontario MSA, CA	H	8.62 FQ	9.51 MW	10.98 TQ	CABLS	1/08-3/08
	Sacramento-Arden Arcade-Roseville MSA, CA	H	8.71 FQ	10.17 MW	12.39 TQ	CABLS	1/08-3/08
	San Diego-Carlsbad-San Marcos MSA, CA	H	8.83 FQ	10.12 MW	11.75 TQ	CABLS	1/08-3/08
	San Francisco-San Mateo-Redwood PMSA, CA	H	11.26 FQ	14.06 MW	17.25 TQ	CABLS	1/08-3/08
	San Jose-Sunnyvale-Santa Clara MSA, CA	H	10.23 FQ	11.61 MW	13.38 TQ	CABLS	1/08-3/08
	Santa Ana-Anaheim-Irvine PMSA, CA	Y	19590 FQ	22240 MW	25000 TQ	USBLS	5/07
	Colorado	Y	16880 FQ	19730 MW	24760 TQ	USBLS	5/07
	Denver-Aurora MSA, CO	Y	17270 FQ	19380 MW	23310 TQ	USBLS	5/07
	Connecticut	H	8.70 AE	10.67 MW		CTBLS	1/08-3/08
	Bridgeport-Stamford-Norwalk MSA, CT	Y	19720 FQ	22990 MW	26570 TQ	USBLS	5/07
	Hartford-West Hartford-East Hartford MSA, CT	Y	18070 FQ	21400 MW	25620 TQ	USBLS	5/07
	Norwich-New London MSA, CT-RI	Y	19070 FQ	21720 MW	24800 TQ	USBLS	5/07
	Delaware	Y	17770 FQ	20180 MW	23200 TQ	USBLS	5/07
	Dover MSA, DE	Y	16550 FQ	18150 MW	19880 TQ	USBLS	5/07
	Wilmington PMSA, DE-MD-NJ	Y	18690 FQ	21390 MW	24280 TQ	USBLS	5/07
	District of Columbia	Y	24880 FQ	28590 MW	32330 TQ	USBLS	5/07
	Washington-Arlington-Alexandria MSA, DC-VA-MD-WV	Y	19340 FQ	23300 MW	28410 TQ	USBLS	5/07
	Florida	Y	17560 FQ	20330 MW	24070 TQ	USBLS	5/07
	Fort Lauderdale-Pompano Beach-Deerfield Beach PMSA, FL	Y	17270 FQ	19050 MW	22630 TQ	USBLS	5/07
	Jacksonville MSA, FL	Y	16920 FQ	19130 MW	22070 TQ	USBLS	5/07
	Miami-Fort Lauderdale-Miami Beach MSA, FL	Y	17810 FQ	20700 MW	23860 TQ	USBLS	5/07
	Orlando-Kissimmee MSA, FL	Y	18240 FQ	22230 MW	33720 TQ	USBLS	5/07
	Sarasota-Bradenton-Venice MSA, FL	Y	18510 FQ	21210 MW	23580 TQ	USBLS	5/07
	Tampa-St. Petersburg-Clearwater MSA, FL	Y	17350 FQ	19640 MW	22910 TQ	USBLS	5/07
	West Palm Beach-Boca Raton-Boynton Beach PMSA, FL	Y	18640 FQ	21740 MW	24650 TQ	USBLS	5/07
	Georgia	Y	14660 FQ	17680 MW	20720 TQ	USBLS	5/07
	Athens-Clarke County MSA, GA	Y	14470 FQ	16870 MW	18780 TQ	USBLS	5/07
	Atlanta-Sandy Springs-Marietta MSA, GA	Y	15740 FQ	18830 MW	22390 TQ	USBLS	5/07
	Hawaii	Y	27710 FQ	32500 MW	36670 TQ	USBLS	5/07
	Honolulu MSA, HI	Y	28060 FQ	32750 MW	36590 TQ	USBLS	5/07
	Idaho	Y	13200 FQ	15290 MW	17960 TQ	USBLS	5/07
	Boise City-Nampa MSA, ID	Y	12930 FQ	14830 MW	17330 TQ	USBLS	5/07
	Lewiston MSA, ID-WA	Y	13200 FQ	15310 MW	18170 TQ	USBLS	5/07
	Illinois	Y	17230 FQ	19590 MW	23040 TQ	USBLS	5/07
	Champaign-Urbana MSA, IL	Y	14740 FQ	16930 MW	19310 TQ	USBLS	5/07
	Chicago-Naperville-Joliet MSA, IL-IN-WI	Y	17590 FQ	20180 MW	23710 TQ	USBLS	5/07
	Indiana	Y	15840 FQ	17680 MW	19600 TQ	USBLS	5/07
	Elkhart-Goshen MSA, IN	Y	14040 FQ	16200 MW	18320 TQ	USBLS	5/07
	Gary PMSA, IN	Y	15060 FQ	16760 MW	18290 TQ	USBLS	5/07
	Indianapolis-Carmel MSA, IN	Y	16800 FQ	18460 MW	20490 TQ	USBLS	5/07

AE Average entry wage	**AW** Average wage paid	**FQ** First quartile wage	**LO** Lowest wage paid	**MTC** Median total compensation	**TCC** Total cash compensation
AER Average entry range	**AWR** Average wage range	**H** Hourly	**LR** Low end range	**MW** Median wage paid	**TQ** Third quartile wage
AEX Average experienced wage	**AXR** Average experienced range	**HI** Highest wage paid	**M** Monthly	**MWR** Median wage range	**W** Weekly
ATC Average total compensation	**D** Daily	**HR** High end range	**MCC** Median cash compensation	**S** See annotated source	**Y** Yearly

Occupation/Type/Industry	Location	Per	Low	Mid	High	Source	Date
Hotel, Motel, and Resort Desk Clerk	South Bend-Mishawaka MSA, IN-MI	Y	16130 FQ	18040 MW	20560 TQ	USBLS	5/07
	Iowa	Y	15510 FQ	17530 MW	19650 TQ	USBLS	5/07
	Des Moines-West Des Moines MSA, IA	Y	17500 FQ	19610 MW	22670 TQ	USBLS	5/07
	Kansas	Y	13700 FQ	16340 MW	19550 TQ	USBLS	5/07
	Wichita MSA, KS	Y	14040 FQ	17000 MW	19690 TQ	USBLS	5/07
	Kentucky	Y	14525 FQ	17303 MW	19825 TQ	KYBLS	2008
	Louisville-Jefferson County MSA, KY-IN	Y	16460 FQ	18530 MW	21490 TQ	USBLS	5/07
	Louisiana	H	7.26 FQ	8.66 MW	10.59 TQ	LABLS	1/08-3/08
	Baton Rouge MSA, LA	Y	15840 FQ	17690 MW	19530 TQ	USBLS	5/07
	New Orleans-Metairie-Kenner MSA, LA	Y	16670 FQ	19920 MW	23490 TQ	USBLS	5/07
	Maine	Y	17960 FQ	21370 MW	24740 TQ	USBLS	5/07
	Portland-South Portland-Biddeford MSA, ME	Y	19980 FQ	22810 MW	27320 TQ	USBLS	5/07
	Maryland	Y		21350 MW		MDBLS	3/08
	Baltimore-Towson MSA, MD	Y	19000 FQ	21840 MW	24940 TQ	USBLS	5/07
	Bethesda-Gaithersburg-Frederick PMSA, MD	Y	17860 FQ	20610 MW	26080 TQ	USBLS	5/07
	Massachusetts	Y	20390 FQ	24050 MW	28220 TQ	USBLS	5/07
	Boston-Cambridge-Quincy NECTA, MA	Y	22000 FQ	25870 MW	29450 TQ	USBLS	5/07
	New Bedford MSA, MA	Y	19520 FQ	21640 MW	24300 TQ	USBLS	5/07
	Springfield MSA, MA-CT	Y	16950 FQ	19300 MW	23630 TQ	USBLS	5/07
	Worcester MSA, MA-CT	Y	19360 FQ	22220 MW	25410 TQ	USBLS	5/07
	Michigan	Y	16520 FQ	18500 MW	20960 TQ	USBLS	5/07
	Detroit-Warren-Livonia MSA, MI	Y	17760 FQ	20190 MW	22870 TQ	USBLS	5/07
	Grand Rapids-Wyoming MSA, MI	Y	16230 FQ	18120 MW	20610 TQ	USBLS	5/07
	Warren-Troy-Farmington Hills PMSA, MI	Y	18410 FQ	20690 MW	23110 TQ	USBLS	5/07
	Minnesota	Y	17370 FQ	19650 MW	22783 TQ	MNBLS	10/08-12/08
	Duluth-Superior MSA, MN-WI	Y	17266 FQ	19223 MW	21440 TQ	MNBLS	10/08-12/08
	Minneapolis-Saint Paul MSA, MN-WI	Y	19036 FQ	21471 MW	24635 TQ	MNBLS	10/08-12/08
	Rochester MSA, MN	Y	17820 FQ	19364 MW	21036 TQ	MNBLS	10/08-12/08
	Mississippi	Y	14460 FQ	16990 MW	19510 TQ	USBLS	5/07
	Jackson MSA, MS	Y	14220 FQ	16700 MW	18680 TQ	USBLS	5/07
	Pascagoula MSA, MS	Y	14650 FQ	17710 MW	21970 TQ	USBLS	5/07
	Missouri	Y	15860 FQ	17950 MW	20380 TQ	USBLS	5/07
	Joplin MSA, MO	Y	16110 FQ	17720 MW	19410 TQ	USBLS	5/07
	Kansas City MSA, MO-KS	Y	16910 FQ	19040 MW	21770 TQ	USBLS	5/07
	St. Louis MSA, MO-IL	Y	16860 FQ	19190 MW	22550 TQ	USBLS	5/07
	Montana	Y	14820 FQ	16750 MW	19200 TQ	USBLS	5/07
	Billings MSA, MT	Y	14080 FQ	15380 MW	18090 TQ	USBLS	5/07
	Nebraska	Y	14880 FQ	17180 MW	19240 TQ	USBLS	5/07
	Omaha-Council Bluffs MSA, NE-IA	Y	16570 FQ	18220 MW	20000 TQ	USBLS	5/07
	Nevada	H	9.90 FQ	12.87 MW	15.74 TQ	NVBLS	5/08
	Las Vegas-Paradise MSA, NV	H	11.11 FQ	14.04 MW	16.35 TQ	NVBLS	5/08
	New Hampshire	H	8.73 AE	10.53 MW	12.00 AEX	NHBLS	6/08
	Manchester MSA, NH	Y	21000 FQ	23280 MW	25820 TQ	USBLS	5/07
	Nashua NECTA, NH-MA	Y	17600 FQ	20610 MW	27280 TQ	USBLS	5/07
	New Jersey	Y	19410 FQ	22210 MW	25430 TQ	USBLS	5/07
	Camden PMSA, NJ	Y	18200 FQ	21150 MW	23810 TQ	USBLS	5/07
	Edison PMSA, NJ	Y	20240 FQ	23150 MW	27310 TQ	USBLS	5/07
	Newark-Union PMSA, NJ-PA	Y	19630 FQ	22400 MW	25800 TQ	USBLS	5/07
	Vineland-Millville-Bridgeton MSA, NJ	Y	18340 FQ	20870 MW	23620 TQ	USBLS	5/07
	New Mexico	Y	14820 FQ	17500 MW	20550 TQ	USBLS	5/07
	Albuquerque MSA, NM	Y	15100 FQ	17280 MW	19610 TQ	USBLS	5/07
	Santa Fe MSA, NM	Y	18950 FQ	21560 MW	23890 TQ	USBLS	5/07
	New York	Y	17870 FQ	22000 MW	29740 TQ	USBLS	5/07
	Albany-Schenectady-Troy MSA, NY	Y	17430 FQ	19970 MW	23170 TQ	USBLS	5/07
	Buffalo-Niagara Falls MSA, NY	Y	16480 FQ	18550 MW	22320 TQ	USBLS	5/07
	Nassau-Suffolk PMSA, NY	Y	21520 FQ	23910 MW	28700 TQ	USBLS	5/07

AE	Average entry wage	AW	Average wage paid	FQ	First quartile wage	LO	Lowest wage paid	MTC	Median total compensation	TCC	Total cash compensation
AER	Average entry range	AWR	Average wage range	H	Hourly	LR	Low end range	MW	Median wage paid	TQ	Third quartile wage
AEX	Average experienced wage	AXR	Average experienced range	HI	Highest wage paid	M	Monthly	MWR	Median wage range	W	Weekly
ATC	Average total compensation	D	Daily	HR	High end range	MCC	Median cash compensation	S	See annotated source	Y	Yearly

Occupation/Type/Industry	Location	Per	Low	Mid	High	Source	Date
Hotel, Motel, and Resort Desk Clerk	New York-Northern New Jersey-Long Island MSA, NY-NJ-PA	Y	21130 FQ	24680 MW	32370 TQ	USBLS	5/07
	North Carolina	Y	16650 FQ	18860 MW	21970 TQ	USBLS	5/07
	Charlotte-Gastonia-Concord MSA, NC-SC	Y	16740 FQ	19060 MW	21860 TQ	USBLS	5/07
	Raleigh-Cary MSA, NC	Y	17530 FQ	19400 MW	21690 TQ	USBLS	5/07
	North Dakota	Y	14200 FQ	16650 MW	18690 TQ	USBLS	5/07
	Fargo MSA, ND-MN	Y	16150 FQ	17670 MW	19190 TQ	USBLS	5/07
	Ohio	Y	15560 FQ	17420 MW	19610 TQ	USBLS	5/07
	Canton-Massillon MSA, OH	Y	14960 FQ	15660 MW	17700 TQ	USBLS	5/07
	Cincinnati-Middletown MSA, OH-KY-IN	Y	17110 FQ	19080 MW	21870 TQ	USBLS	5/07
	Cleveland-Elyria-Mentor MSA, OH	Y	16270 FQ	18520 MW	21060 TQ	USBLS	5/07
	Columbus MSA, OH	Y	15710 FQ	17580 MW	19550 TQ	USBLS	5/07
	Dayton MSA, OH	Y	15280 FQ	16440 MW	18480 TQ	USBLS	5/07
	Oklahoma	Y	14040 FQ	16740 MW	19230 TQ	USBLS	5/07
	Lawton MSA, OK	Y	13040 FQ	14690 MW	18260 TQ	USBLS	5/07
	Oklahoma City MSA, OK	Y	15450 FQ	17870 MW	20300 TQ	USBLS	5/07
	Tulsa MSA, OK	Y	14290 FQ	16830 MW	19420 TQ	USBLS	5/07
	Oregon	H	8.71 FQ	9.50 MW	10.95 TQ	ORBLS	5/08
	Portland-Vancouver-Beaverton MSA, OR-WA	Y	17870 FQ	19490 MW	21970 TQ	USBLS	5/07
	Pennsylvania	Y	16690 FQ	19390 MW	23360 TQ	USBLS	5/07
	Allentown-Bethlehem-Easton MSA, PA-NJ	Y	16830 FQ	19160 MW	22390 TQ	USBLS	5/07
	Philadelphia-Camden-Wilmington MSA, PA-NJ-DE-MD	Y	18480 FQ	21910 MW	25540 TQ	USBLS	5/07
	Pittsburgh MSA, PA	Y	16610 FQ	19120 MW	22620 TQ	USBLS	5/07
	Rhode Island	Y	20100 FQ	22360 MW	24650 TQ	USBLS	5/07
	Providence-Fall River-Warwick MSA, RI-MA	Y	19720 FQ	22130 MW	24340 TQ	USBLS	5/07
	South Carolina	Y	16150 FQ	18560 MW	21780 TQ	USBLS	5/07
	Charleston-North Charleston MSA, SC	Y	17640 FQ	20410 MW	23360 TQ	USBLS	5/07
	Columbia MSA, SC	Y	13380 FQ	16240 MW	19280 TQ	USBLS	5/07
	Myrtle Beach-Conway-North Myrtle Beach MSA, SC	Y	17510 FQ	19880 MW	23080 TQ	USBLS	5/07
	South Dakota	Y	15595 FQ	17955 MW	20413 TQ	SDBLS	7/08-9/08
	Sioux Falls MSA, SD	Y	16714 FQ	18557 MW	20729 TQ	SDBLS	7/08-9/08
	Tennessee	Y	15800 FQ	17780 MW	20000 TQ	USBLS	5/07
	Knoxville MSA, TN	Y	15490 FQ	17000 MW	18550 TQ	USBLS	5/07
	Memphis MSA, TN-MS-AR	Y	14770 FQ	16970 MW	19420 TQ	USBLS	5/07
	Nashville-Davidson-Murfreesboro MSA, TN	Y	16640 FQ	18310 MW	20270 TQ	USBLS	5/07
	Texas	Y	14280 FQ	16880 MW	19310 TQ	USBLS	5/07
	Austin-Round Rock MSA, TX	Y	16500 FQ	19170 MW	22080 TQ	USBLS	5/07
	Dallas-Fort Worth-Arlington MSA, TX	Y	15470 FQ	18300 MW	21430 TQ	USBLS	5/07
	El Paso MSA, TX	Y	13290 FQ	15240 MW	17710 TQ	USBLS	5/07
	Houston-Sugar Land-Baytown MSA, TX	Y	14660 FQ	17190 MW	19540 TQ	USBLS	5/07
	San Antonio MSA, TX	Y	15650 FQ	17530 MW	19390 TQ	USBLS	5/07
	Utah	Y	16510 FQ	18580 MW	21530 TQ	USBLS	5/07
	Provo-Orem MSA, UT	Y	15680 FQ	17210 MW	18670 TQ	USBLS	5/07
	Salt Lake City MSA, UT	Y	17390 FQ	19350 MW	22000 TQ	USBLS	5/07
	Vermont	Y	19650 FQ	22200 MW	24950 TQ	USBLS	5/07
	Burlington-South Burlington MSA, VT	Y	20110 FQ	22570 MW	25340 TQ	USBLS	5/07
	Virginia	Y	16280 FQ	18640 MW	22790 TQ	USBLS	5/07
	Richmond MSA, VA	Y	16680 FQ	18320 MW	20910 TQ	USBLS	5/07
	Virginia Beach-Norfolk-Newport News MSA, VA-NC	Y	16010 FQ	18180 MW	21020 TQ	USBLS	5/07
	Washington	H	8.76 FQ	9.61 MW	11.39 TQ	WABLS	3/08
	Seattle-Tacoma-Bellevue MSA, WA	Y	18440 FQ	20950 MW	24590 TQ	USBLS	5/07
	West Virginia	Y	14323 FQ	15887 MW	19084 TQ	WVBLS	7/08-9/08
	Charleston MSA, WV	Y	14060 FQ	16180 MW	19790 TQ	USBLS	5/07
	Wisconsin	Y	16670 FQ	18540 MW	21140 TQ	USBLS	5/07

AE	Average entry wage	AW	Average wage paid	FQ	First quartile wage
AER	Average entry range	AWR	Average wage range	H	Hourly
AEX	Average experienced wage	AXR	Average experienced range	HI	Highest wage paid
ATC	Average total compensation	D	Daily	HR	High end range

LO	Lowest wage paid	MTC	Median total compensation	TCC	Total cash compensation
LR	Low end range	MW	Median wage paid	TQ	Third quartile wage
M	Monthly	MWR	Median wage range	W	Weekly
MCC	Median cash compensation	S	See annotated source	Y	Yearly

Occupation/Type/Industry	Location	Per	Low	Mid	High	Source	Date
Hotel, Motel, and Resort Desk Clerk	Green Bay MSA, WI	Y	17680 FQ	19790 MW	23030 TQ	USBLS	5/07
	Milwaukee-Waukesha-West Allis MSA, WI	Y	17030 FQ	19190 MW	22560 TQ	USBLS	5/07
	Wyoming	Y	16844 FQ	18903 MW	21976 TQ	WYBLS	9/08
	Cheyenne MSA, WY	Y	17003 FQ	18627 MW	20421 TQ	WYBLS	9/08
	Puerto Rico	Y	12840 FQ	14390 MW	16570 TQ	USBLS	5/07
	San Juan-Caguas-Guaynabo MSA, PR	Y	12970 FQ	14550 MW	16900 TQ	USBLS	5/07
	Virgin Islands	Y	17780 FQ	20270 MW	23130 TQ	USBLS	5/07
	Guam	Y	12670 FQ	14220 MW	15890 TQ	USBLS	5/07
Hotel Executive Chef	United States	Y			86500 TQ	FORB02	2009
Housing Authority Director							
Municipal Government	Colorado Springs, CO	M	9115 LO			COSPRS	1/1/09
Housing Default Analyst							
State Government	Ohio	H	21.77 LO		31.86 HI	ODAS	2008
Housing Development Planner							
State Government	Ohio	H	23.87 LO		35.02 HI	ODAS	2008
Human Capital Management Analyst							
State Government	Ohio	H	19.19 LO		23.76 HI	ODAS	2008
Human Resources Assistant							
Except Payroll and Timekeeping	Alabama	Y	25320 FQ	30560 MW	37240 TQ	USBLS	5/07
Except Payroll and Timekeeping	Birmingham-Hoover MSA, AL	Y	27700 FQ	33160 MW	38660 TQ	USBLS	5/07
Except Payroll and Timekeeping	Alaska	Y	33260 FQ	37510 MW	43540 TQ	USBLS	5/07
Except Payroll and Timekeeping	Anchorage MSA, AK	Y	32720 FQ	37010 MW	42220 TQ	USBLS	5/07
Except Payroll and Timekeeping	Arizona	Y	29840 FQ	35790 MW	42140 TQ	USBLS	5/07
Except Payroll and Timekeeping	Phoenix-Mesa-Scottsdale MSA, AZ	Y	30350 FQ	36250 MW	43180 TQ	USBLS	5/07
Except Payroll and Timekeeping	Tucson MSA, AZ	Y	27560 FQ	33760 MW	38130 TQ	USBLS	5/07
Except Payroll and Timekeeping	Yuma MSA, AZ	Y	28190 FQ	33460 MW	40170 TQ	USBLS	5/07
Except Payroll and Timekeeping	Arkansas	Y	22330 FQ	28660 MW	35730 TQ	USBLS	5/07
Except Payroll and Timekeeping	Fort Smith MSA, AR-OK	Y	24830 FQ	32090 MW	38710 TQ	USBLS	5/07
Except Payroll and Timekeeping	Little Rock-North Little Rock MSA, AR	Y	15880 FQ	27930 MW	36030 TQ	USBLS	5/07
Except Payroll and Timekeeping	California	H	15.86 FQ	19.35 MW	23.53 TQ	CABLS	1/08-3/08
Except Payroll and Timekeeping	Los Angeles-Long Beach-Glendale PMSA, CA	H	15.08 FQ	18.44 MW	22.69 TQ	CABLS	1/08-3/08
Except Payroll and Timekeeping	Oakland-Fremont-Hayward MSA, CA	H	17.51 FQ	21.37 MW	25.15 TQ	CABLS	1/08-3/08
Except Payroll and Timekeeping	Riverside-San Bernardino-Ontario MSA, CA	H	14.49 FQ	17.87 MW	21.65 TQ	CABLS	1/08-3/08
Except Payroll and Timekeeping	Sacramento-Arden Arcade-Roseville MSA, CA	H	17.89 FQ	21.86 MW	25.84 TQ	CABLS	1/08-3/08
Except Payroll and Timekeeping	San Diego-Carlsbad-San Marcos MSA, CA	H	15.02 FQ	17.71 MW	20.96 TQ	CABLS	1/08-3/08
Except Payroll and Timekeeping	San Francisco-San Mateo-Redwood PMSA, CA	H	19.44 FQ	23.04 MW	26.89 TQ	CABLS	1/08-3/08
Except Payroll and Timekeeping	San Jose-Sunnyvale-Santa Clara MSA, CA	H	18.70 FQ	22.44 MW	27.09 TQ	CABLS	1/08-3/08
Except Payroll and Timekeeping	Santa Ana-Anaheim-Irvine PMSA, CA	Y	32030 FQ	38290 MW	46220 TQ	USBLS	5/07
Except Payroll and Timekeeping	Colorado	Y	30600 FQ	36420 MW	43240 TQ	USBLS	5/07
Except Payroll and Timekeeping	Boulder MSA, CO	Y	30850 FQ	36870 MW	47150 TQ	USBLS	5/07
Except Payroll and Timekeeping	Denver-Aurora MSA, CO	Y	32130 FQ	37490 MW	44320 TQ	USBLS	5/07
Except Payroll and Timekeeping	Connecticut	H	15.00 AE	19.93 MW		CTBLS	1/08-3/08
Except Payroll and Timekeeping	Bridgeport-Stamford-Norwalk MSA, CT	Y	33410 FQ	42950 MW	52820 TQ	USBLS	5/07
Except Payroll and Timekeeping	Hartford-West Hartford-East Hartford MSA, CT	Y	34510 FQ	40410 MW	47370 TQ	USBLS	5/07
Except Payroll and Timekeeping	Delaware	Y	29800 FQ	35120 MW	40500 TQ	USBLS	5/07
Except Payroll and Timekeeping	Wilmington PMSA, DE-MD-NJ	Y	31000 FQ	36250 MW	43320 TQ	USBLS	5/07
Except Payroll and Timekeeping	District of Columbia	Y	36080 FQ	43250 MW	50200 TQ	USBLS	5/07

AE	Average entry wage	AW	Average wage paid	FQ	First quartile wage
AER	Average entry range	AWR	Average wage range	H	Hourly
AEX	Average experienced wage	AXR	Average experienced range	HI	Highest wage paid
ATC	Average total compensation	D	Daily	HR	High end range

LO	Lowest wage paid	MTC	Median total compensation	TCC	Total cash compensation
LR	Low end range	MW	Median wage paid	TQ	Third quartile wage
M	Monthly	MWR	Median wage range	W	Weekly
MCC	Median cash compensation	S	See annotated source	Y	Yearly

Human Resources Assistant

Occupation/Type/Industry	Location	Per	Low	Mid	High	Source	Date
Except Payroll and Timekeeping	Washington-Arlington-Alexandria MSA, DC-VA-MD-WV	Y	35710 FQ	43040 MW	50520 TQ	USBLS	5/07
Except Payroll and Timekeeping	Florida	Y	27450 FQ	32720 MW	39850 TQ	USBLS	5/07
Except Payroll and Timekeeping	Fort Lauderdale-Pompano Beach-Deerfield Beach PMSA, FL	Y	29890 FQ	34910 MW	39320 TQ	USBLS	5/07
Except Payroll and Timekeeping	Jacksonville MSA, FL	Y	27630 FQ	32450 MW	37650 TQ	USBLS	5/07
Except Payroll and Timekeeping	Miami-Fort Lauderdale-Miami Beach MSA, FL	Y	28480 FQ	33530 MW	39210 TQ	USBLS	5/07
Except Payroll and Timekeeping	Orlando-Kissimmee MSA, FL	Y	25580 FQ	30170 MW	36290 TQ	USBLS	5/07
Except Payroll and Timekeeping	Sarasota-Bradenton-Venice MSA, FL	Y	27350 FQ	32080 MW	36940 TQ	USBLS	5/07
Except Payroll and Timekeeping	Tampa-St. Petersburg-Clearwater MSA, FL	Y	27350 FQ	33460 MW	39740 TQ	USBLS	5/07
Except Payroll and Timekeeping	West Palm Beach-Boca Raton-Boynton Beach PMSA, FL	Y	27630 FQ	31830 MW	37420 TQ	USBLS	5/07
Except Payroll and Timekeeping	Georgia	Y	27460 FQ	33020 MW	39170 TQ	USBLS	5/07
Except Payroll and Timekeeping	Atlanta-Sandy Springs-Marietta MSA, GA	Y	28710 FQ	34560 MW	41560 TQ	USBLS	5/07
Except Payroll and Timekeeping	Hawaii	Y	30070 FQ	35120 MW	40010 TQ	USBLS	5/07
Except Payroll and Timekeeping	Honolulu MSA, HI	Y	30070 FQ	35220 MW	40230 TQ	USBLS	5/07
Except Payroll and Timekeeping	Idaho	Y	29420 FQ	33690 MW	38480 TQ	USBLS	5/07
Except Payroll and Timekeeping	Boise City-Nampa MSA, ID	Y	30600 FQ	34050 MW	38200 TQ	USBLS	5/07
Except Payroll and Timekeeping	Lewiston MSA, ID-WA	Y	32980 FQ	41940 MW	48420 TQ	USBLS	5/07
Except Payroll and Timekeeping	Illinois	Y	29280 FQ	36200 MW	44290 TQ	USBLS	5/07
Except Payroll and Timekeeping	Chicago-Naperville-Joliet MSA, IL-IN-WI	Y	30440 FQ	37490 MW	46100 TQ	USBLS	5/07
Except Payroll and Timekeeping	Peoria MSA, IL	Y	24040 FQ	29080 MW	36270 TQ	USBLS	5/07
Except Payroll and Timekeeping	Indiana	Y	26700 FQ	31780 MW	37930 TQ	USBLS	5/07
Except Payroll and Timekeeping	Fort Wayne MSA, IN	Y	26440 FQ	31420 MW	39400 TQ	USBLS	5/07
Except Payroll and Timekeeping	Gary PMSA, IN	Y	25890 FQ	30250 MW	37740 TQ	USBLS	5/07
Except Payroll and Timekeeping	Indianapolis-Carmel MSA, IN	Y	28930 FQ	33950 MW	39090 TQ	USBLS	5/07
Except Payroll and Timekeeping	Iowa	Y	27230 FQ	32190 MW	38460 TQ	USBLS	5/07
Except Payroll and Timekeeping	Des Moines-West Des Moines MSA, IA	Y	28610 FQ	33580 MW	38700 TQ	USBLS	5/07
Except Payroll and Timekeeping	Kansas	Y	27420 FQ	33550 MW	38950 TQ	USBLS	5/07
Except Payroll and Timekeeping	Lawrence MSA, KS	Y	30670 FQ	34130 MW	36940 TQ	USBLS	5/07
Except Payroll and Timekeeping	Wichita MSA, KS	Y	27010 FQ	33000 MW	38080 TQ	USBLS	5/07
Except Payroll and Timekeeping	Kentucky	Y	28063 FQ	33747 MW	39327 TQ	KYBLS	2008
Except Payroll and Timekeeping	Louisville-Jefferson County MSA, KY-IN	Y	29180 FQ	34390 MW	39400 TQ	USBLS	5/07
Except Payroll and Timekeeping	Louisiana	H	12.03 FQ	14.59 MW	17.97 TQ	LABLS	1/08-3/08
Except Payroll and Timekeeping	Baton Rouge MSA, LA	Y	25620 FQ	31100 MW	37350 TQ	USBLS	5/07
Except Payroll and Timekeeping	New Orleans-Metairie-Kenner MSA, LA	Y	26240 FQ	31200 MW	40050 TQ	USBLS	5/07
Except Payroll and Timekeeping	Maine	Y	25760 FQ	30330 MW	35550 TQ	USBLS	5/07
Except Payroll and Timekeeping	Portland-South Portland-Biddeford MSA, ME	Y	27880 FQ	32200 MW	36780 TQ	USBLS	5/07
Except Payroll and Timekeeping	Maryland	Y		39375 MW		MDBLS	3/08
Except Payroll and Timekeeping	Baltimore-Towson MSA, MD	Y	31850 FQ	37270 MW	44500 TQ	USBLS	5/07
Except Payroll and Timekeeping	Bethesda-Gaithersburg-Frederick PMSA, MD	Y	36200 FQ	44130 MW	52120 TQ	USBLS	5/07
Except Payroll and Timekeeping	Hagerstown-Martinsburg MSA, MD-WV	Y	29620 FQ	34360 MW	39670 TQ	USBLS	5/07
Except Payroll and Timekeeping	Massachusetts	Y	32560 FQ	37950 MW	45380 TQ	USBLS	5/07
Except Payroll and Timekeeping	Boston-Cambridge-Quincy NECTA, MA	Y	33170 FQ	38570 MW	45680 TQ	USBLS	5/07
Except Payroll and Timekeeping	Worcester MSA, MA-CT	Y	32180 FQ	36880 MW	44180 TQ	USBLS	5/07
Except Payroll and Timekeeping	Michigan	Y	30010 FQ	36540 MW	44840 TQ	USBLS	5/07
Except Payroll and Timekeeping	Ann Arbor MSA, MI	Y	34300 FQ	41280 MW	46940 TQ	USBLS	5/07
Except Payroll and Timekeeping	Detroit-Warren-Livonia MSA, MI	Y	30460 FQ	36690 MW	45350 TQ	USBLS	5/07
Except Payroll and Timekeeping	Grand Rapids-Wyoming MSA, MI	Y	27930 FQ	34190 MW	42880 TQ	USBLS	5/07
Except Payroll and Timekeeping	Muskegon-Norton Shores MSA, MI	Y	35000 FQ	41220 MW	51130 TQ	USBLS	5/07
Except Payroll and Timekeeping	Warren-Troy-Farmington Hills PMSA, MI	Y	29250 FQ	35270 MW	44440 TQ	USBLS	5/07
Except Payroll and Timekeeping	Minnesota	Y	31400 FQ	37114 MW	42558 TQ	MNBLS	10/08-12/08
Except Payroll and Timekeeping	Duluth-Superior MSA, MN-WI	Y	29371 FQ	33544 MW	39862 TQ	MNBLS	10/08-12/08

AE	Average entry wage	AW	Average wage paid	FQ	First quartile wage
AER	Average entry range	AWR	Average wage range	H	Hourly
AEX	Average experienced wage	AXR	Average experienced range	HI	Highest wage paid
ATC	Average total compensation	D	Daily	HR	High end range

LO	Lowest wage paid	MTC	Median total compensation	TCC	Total cash compensation
LR	Low end range	MW	Median wage paid	TQ	Third quartile wage
M	Monthly	MWR	Median wage range	W	Weekly
MCC	Median cash compensation	S	See annotated source	Y	Yearly

Human Resources Assistant

Occupation/Type/Industry	Location	Per	Low	Mid	High	Source	Date
Except Payroll and Timekeeping	Minneapolis-Saint Paul MSA, MN-WI	Y	33721 FQ	38488 MW	43869 TQ	MNBLS	10/08-12/08
Except Payroll and Timekeeping	Rochester MSA, MN	Y	32984 FQ	37330 MW	41775 TQ	MNBLS	10/08-12/08
Except Payroll and Timekeeping	Mississippi	Y	26070 FQ	31220 MW	37320 TQ	USBLS	5/07
Except Payroll and Timekeeping	Jackson MSA, MS	Y	26260 FQ	32020 MW	38090 TQ	USBLS	5/07
Except Payroll and Timekeeping	Missouri	Y	28000 FQ	34180 MW	40190 TQ	USBLS	5/07
Except Payroll and Timekeeping	Kansas City MSA, MO-KS	Y	29880 FQ	35330 MW	41090 TQ	USBLS	5/07
Except Payroll and Timekeeping	St. Louis MSA, MO-IL	Y	30400 FQ	36120 MW	42450 TQ	USBLS	5/07
Except Payroll and Timekeeping	Montana	Y	25400 FQ	30740 MW	37230 TQ	USBLS	5/07
Except Payroll and Timekeeping	Billings MSA, MT	Y	25650 FQ	30630 MW	37440 TQ	USBLS	5/07
Except Payroll and Timekeeping	Nebraska	Y	26380 FQ	30770 MW	37380 TQ	USBLS	5/07
Except Payroll and Timekeeping	Omaha-Council Bluffs MSA, NE-IA	Y	27440 FQ	32220 MW	39620 TQ	USBLS	5/07
Except Payroll and Timekeeping	Nevada	H	12.94 FQ	15.11 MW	18.42 TQ	NVBLS	5/08
Except Payroll and Timekeeping	Carson City MSA, NV	H	16.26 FQ	18.39 MW	21.21 TQ	NVBLS	5/08
Except Payroll and Timekeeping	Las Vegas-Paradise MSA, NV	H	12.80 FQ	14.70 MW	17.67 TQ	NVBLS	5/08
Except Payroll and Timekeeping	New Hampshire	H	12.31 AE	16.19 MW	18.56 AEX	NHBLS	6/08
Except Payroll and Timekeeping	Manchester MSA, NH	Y	23700 FQ	30350 MW	39110 TQ	USBLS	5/07
Except Payroll and Timekeeping	Nashua NECTA, NH-MA	Y	32200 FQ	38120 MW	44420 TQ	USBLS	5/07
Except Payroll and Timekeeping	New Jersey	Y	31660 FQ	37860 MW	45170 TQ	USBLS	5/07
Except Payroll and Timekeeping	Camden PMSA, NJ	Y	31350 FQ	36800 MW	43290 TQ	USBLS	5/07
Except Payroll and Timekeeping	Edison PMSA, NJ	Y	29670 FQ	35530 MW	42830 TQ	USBLS	5/07
Except Payroll and Timekeeping	Newark-Union PMSA, NJ-PA	Y	34060 FQ	40690 MW	47820 TQ	USBLS	5/07
Except Payroll and Timekeeping	New Mexico	Y	26400 FQ	33740 MW	40930 TQ	USBLS	5/07
Except Payroll and Timekeeping	Albuquerque MSA, NM	Y	29100 FQ	35380 MW	40790 TQ	USBLS	5/07
Except Payroll and Timekeeping	New York	Y	30540 FQ	36670 MW	44510 TQ	USBLS	5/07
Except Payroll and Timekeeping	Albany-Schenectady-Troy MSA, NY	Y	28920 FQ	34130 MW	39290 TQ	USBLS	5/07
Except Payroll and Timekeeping	Buffalo-Niagara Falls MSA, NY	Y	26570 FQ	33570 MW	39700 TQ	USBLS	5/07
Except Payroll and Timekeeping	Nassau-Suffolk PMSA, NY	Y	33160 FQ	39890 MW	46920 TQ	USBLS	5/07
Except Payroll and Timekeeping	New York-Northern New Jersey-Long Island MSA, NY-NJ-PA	Y	32360 FQ	38650 MW	46390 TQ	USBLS	5/07
Except Payroll and Timekeeping	North Carolina	Y	26620 FQ	31580 MW	37650 TQ	USBLS	5/07
Except Payroll and Timekeeping	Charlotte-Gastonia-Concord MSA, NC-SC	Y	27240 FQ	32340 MW	38410 TQ	USBLS	5/07
Except Payroll and Timekeeping	Raleigh-Cary MSA, NC	Y	28220 FQ	33090 MW	38720 TQ	USBLS	5/07
Except Payroll and Timekeeping	North Dakota	Y	26160 FQ	30780 MW	36810 TQ	USBLS	5/07
Except Payroll and Timekeeping	Fargo MSA, ND-MN	Y	26370 FQ	31380 MW	37080 TQ	USBLS	5/07
Except Payroll and Timekeeping	Ohio	Y	27550 FQ	33510 MW	39990 TQ	USBLS	5/07
Except Payroll and Timekeeping	Cincinnati-Middletown MSA, OH-KY-IN	Y	29380 FQ	35620 MW	42320 TQ	USBLS	5/07
Except Payroll and Timekeeping	Cleveland-Elyria-Mentor MSA, OH	Y	26780 FQ	33720 MW	40720 TQ	USBLS	5/07
Except Payroll and Timekeeping	Columbus MSA, OH	Y	28930 FQ	34700 MW	40260 TQ	USBLS	5/07
Except Payroll and Timekeeping	Dayton MSA, OH	Y	29090 FQ	34680 MW	40480 TQ	USBLS	5/07
Except Payroll and Timekeeping	Oklahoma	Y	23800 FQ	28970 MW	36430 TQ	USBLS	5/07
Except Payroll and Timekeeping	Oklahoma City MSA, OK	Y	26880 FQ	32240 MW	38550 TQ	USBLS	5/07
Except Payroll and Timekeeping	Tulsa MSA, OK	Y	25820 FQ	29690 MW	35570 TQ	USBLS	5/07
Except Payroll and Timekeeping	Oregon	H	14.45 FQ	17.22 MW	20.13 TQ	ORBLS	5/08
Except Payroll and Timekeeping	Portland-Vancouver-Beaverton MSA, OR-WA	Y	31600 FQ	36840 MW	42900 TQ	USBLS	5/07
Except Payroll and Timekeeping	Pennsylvania	Y	27880 FQ	34540 MW	42950 TQ	USBLS	5/07
Except Payroll and Timekeeping	Allentown-Bethlehem-Easton MSA, PA-NJ	Y	28760 FQ	34440 MW	40950 TQ	USBLS	5/07
Except Payroll and Timekeeping	Philadelphia-Camden-Wilmington MSA, PA-NJ-DE-MD	Y	30010 FQ	36660 MW	44560 TQ	USBLS	5/07
Except Payroll and Timekeeping	Pittsburgh MSA, PA	Y	26410 FQ	33260 MW	42080 TQ	USBLS	5/07
Except Payroll and Timekeeping	Rhode Island	Y	27410 FQ	32630 MW	40090 TQ	USBLS	5/07
Except Payroll and Timekeeping	Providence-Fall River-Warwick MSA, RI-MA	Y	27390 FQ	32700 MW	39920 TQ	USBLS	5/07
Except Payroll and Timekeeping	South Carolina	Y	26760 FQ	32220 MW	38800 TQ	USBLS	5/07
Except Payroll and Timekeeping	Charleston-North Charleston MSA, SC	Y	27210 FQ	33380 MW	39580 TQ	USBLS	5/07
Except Payroll and Timekeeping	Columbia MSA, SC	Y	27050 FQ	32690 MW	39100 TQ	USBLS	5/07
Except Payroll and Timekeeping	Spartanburg MSA, SC	Y	28850 FQ	33780 MW	38140 TQ	USBLS	5/07
Except Payroll and Timekeeping	South Dakota	Y	24092 FQ	28117 MW	32289 TQ	SDBLS	7/08-9/08
Except Payroll and Timekeeping	Sioux Falls MSA, SD	Y	25620 FQ	28991 MW	32399 TQ	SDBLS	7/08-9/08
Except Payroll and Timekeeping	Tennessee	Y	27150 FQ	32680 MW	39160 TQ	USBLS	5/07

AE	Average entry wage	AW	Average wage paid	FQ	First quartile wage
AER	Average entry range	AWR	Average wage range	H	Hourly
AEX	Average experienced wage	AXR	Average experienced range	HI	Highest wage paid
ATC	Average total compensation	D	Daily	HR	High end range

LO	Lowest wage paid	MTC	Median total compensation	TCC	Total cash compensation
LR	Low end range	MW	Median wage paid	TQ	Third quartile wage
M	Monthly	MWR	Median wage range	W	Weekly
MCC	Median cash compensation	S	See annotated source	Y	Yearly

Occupation/Type/Industry	Location	Per	Low	Mid	High	Source	Date
Human Resources Assistant							
Except Payroll and Timekeeping	Memphis MSA, TN-MS-AR	Y	30560 FQ	35810 MW	41980 TQ	USBLS	5/07
Except Payroll and Timekeeping	Nashville-Davidson-Murfreesboro MSA, TN	Y	28200 FQ	34150 MW	40410 TQ	USBLS	5/07
Except Payroll and Timekeeping	Texas	Y	26660 FQ	32440 MW	39490 TQ	USBLS	5/07
Except Payroll and Timekeeping	Austin-Round Rock MSA, TX	Y	28340 FQ	34460 MW	41090 TQ	USBLS	5/07
Except Payroll and Timekeeping	Dallas-Fort Worth-Arlington MSA, TX	Y	28370 FQ	34280 MW	41160 TQ	USBLS	5/07
Except Payroll and Timekeeping	El Paso MSA, TX	Y	21560 FQ	27120 MW	31590 TQ	USBLS	5/07
Except Payroll and Timekeeping	Houston-Sugar Land-Baytown MSA, TX	Y	28180 FQ	34560 MW	41910 TQ	USBLS	5/07
Except Payroll and Timekeeping	San Antonio MSA, TX	Y	28120 FQ	34170 MW	39800 TQ	USBLS	5/07
Except Payroll and Timekeeping	Utah	Y	26080 FQ	31920 MW	39670 TQ	USBLS	5/07
Except Payroll and Timekeeping	Salt Lake City MSA, UT	Y	27530 FQ	32630 MW	40270 TQ	USBLS	5/07
Except Payroll and Timekeeping	Vermont	Y	28760 FQ	34060 MW	39180 TQ	USBLS	5/07
Except Payroll and Timekeeping	Burlington-South Burlington MSA, VT	Y	32400 FQ	35990 MW	39960 TQ	USBLS	5/07
Except Payroll and Timekeeping	Virginia	Y	30560 FQ	37230 MW	45880 TQ	USBLS	5/07
Except Payroll and Timekeeping	Richmond MSA, VA	Y	29900 FQ	36020 MW	42370 TQ	USBLS	5/07
Except Payroll and Timekeeping	Roanoke MSA, VA	Y	25770 FQ	29920 MW	37580 TQ	USBLS	5/07
Except Payroll and Timekeeping	Virginia Beach-Norfolk-Newport News MSA, VA-NC	Y	27520 FQ	31980 MW	37400 TQ	USBLS	5/07
Except Payroll and Timekeeping	Washington	H	15.45 FQ	17.72 MW	20.22 TQ	WABLS	3/08
Except Payroll and Timekeeping	Olympia MSA, WA	Y	33530 FQ	36660 MW	39810 TQ	USBLS	5/07
Except Payroll and Timekeeping	Seattle-Tacoma-Bellevue MSA, WA	Y	32910 FQ	37310 MW	42740 TQ	USBLS	5/07
Except Payroll and Timekeeping	West Virginia	Y	27065 FQ	33792 MW	41014 TQ	WVBLS	7/08-9/08
Except Payroll and Timekeeping	Charleston MSA, WV	Y	27870 FQ	33180 MW	38880 TQ	USBLS	5/07
Except Payroll and Timekeeping	Parkersburg-Marietta-Vienna MSA, WV-OH	Y	29700 FQ	34580 MW	39230 TQ	USBLS	5/07
Except Payroll and Timekeeping	Wisconsin	Y	29290 FQ	34710 MW	40300 TQ	USBLS	5/07
Except Payroll and Timekeeping	Green Bay MSA, WI	Y	27820 FQ	32690 MW	37540 TQ	USBLS	5/07
Except Payroll and Timekeeping	Milwaukee-Waukesha-West Allis MSA, WI	Y	30630 FQ	35550 MW	41080 TQ	USBLS	5/07
Except Payroll and Timekeeping	Wyoming	Y	30155 FQ	35385 MW	40236 TQ	WYBLS	9/08
Except Payroll and Timekeeping	Casper MSA, WY	Y	28250 FQ	32795 MW	37140 TQ	WYBLS	9/08
Except Payroll and Timekeeping	Cheyenne MSA, WY	Y	31777 FQ	36120 MW	39666 TQ	WYBLS	9/08
Except Payroll and Timekeeping	Puerto Rico	Y	15990 FQ	20540 MW	28940 TQ	USBLS	5/07
Except Payroll and Timekeeping	San Juan-Caguas-Guaynabo MSA, PR	Y	15930 FQ	20400 MW	28350 TQ	USBLS	5/07
Except Payroll and Timekeeping	Virgin Islands	Y	25860 FQ	28520 MW	31180 TQ	USBLS	5/07
Except Payroll and Timekeeping	Guam	Y	20560 FQ	28920 MW	37310 TQ	USBLS	5/07
Human Resources Director							
Compensation and Benefits	United States	Y		157600 MCC		HRFOC	2008
Recruiting	United States	Y		175500 MCC		HRFOC	2008
Training	United States	Y		154000 MCC		HRFOC	2008
Human Resources Generalist							
State Government	District of Columbia	Y	50510 LO		83550 HI	AFT02	3/1/08
Human Resources Manager							
Municipal Government	Colorado Springs, CO	M	6687 LO			COSPRS	1/1/09
Human Resources Specialist							
State Government	Illinois	Y	32088 LO		74832 HI	AFT02	3/1/08
Human Services Nurse							
State Government	South Dakota	Y	34818 LO		52228 HI	AFT02	3/1/08
HVAC Project Manager	New York, NY	Y		86200 AW		MEP01	2008
HVAC Service Technician	Georgia	Y		48360 AW		MEP01	2008
	New York, NY	Y		52000 AW		MEP01	2008
	Texas	Y		41600 AW		MEP01	2008
Hydrologic Technician	United States	Y		50337 AW		OOH01	2007
Hydrologist	Alaska	Y	59820 FQ	73600 MW	88980 TQ	USBLS	5/07
	Anchorage MSA, AK	Y	62120 FQ	80610 MW	95430 TQ	USBLS	5/07
	Arizona	Y	48500 FQ	57280 MW	73450 TQ	USBLS	5/07
	Phoenix-Mesa-Scottsdale MSA, AZ	Y	44820 FQ	52610 MW	60010 TQ	USBLS	5/07

AE	Average entry wage	AW	Average wage paid	FQ	First quartile wage
AER	Average entry range	AWR	Average wage range	H	Hourly
AEX	Average experienced wage	AXR	Average experienced range	HI	Highest wage paid
ATC	Average total compensation	D	Daily	HR	High end range

LO	Lowest wage paid	MTC	Median total compensation	TCC	Total cash compensation
LR	Low end range	MW	Median wage paid	TQ	Third quartile wage
M	Monthly	MWR	Median wage range	W	Weekly
MCC	Median cash compensation	S	See annotated source	Y	Yearly

Occupation/Type/Industry	Location	Per	Low	Mid	High	Source	Date
Hydrologist	Tucson MSA, AZ	Y	51470 FQ	64180 MW	84670 TQ	USBLS	5/07
	California	H	27.71 FQ	37.56 MW	46.49 TQ	CABLS	1/08-3/08
	Los Angeles-Long Beach- Glendale PMSA, CA	H	27.12 FQ	41.55 MW	48.09 TQ	CABLS	1/08-3/08
	Oakland-Fremont-Hayward MSA, CA	H	21.41 FQ	23.16 MW	24.92 TQ	CABLS	1/08-3/08
	Riverside-San Bernardino- Ontario MSA, CA	H	32.47 FQ	42.13 MW	56.42 TQ	CABLS	1/08-3/08
	Sacramento-Arden Arcade- Roseville MSA, CA	H	34.53 FQ	40.47 MW	45.58 TQ	CABLS	1/08-3/08
	San Diego-Carlsbad-San Marcos MSA, CA	H	27.38 FQ	32.90 MW	40.69 TQ	CABLS	1/08-3/08
	San Francisco-San Mateo- Redwood PMSA, CA	H	34.77 FQ	39.99 MW	54.90 TQ	CABLS	1/08-3/08
	Santa Ana-Anaheim-Irvine PMSA, CA	Y	61840 FQ	91180 MW	102910 TQ	USBLS	5/07
	Colorado	Y	61850 FQ	75030 MW	88980 TQ	USBLS	5/07
	Denver-Aurora MSA, CO	Y	65560 FQ	80050 MW	95600 TQ	USBLS	5/07
	Connecticut	H	18.68 AE	29.27 MW		CTBLS	1/08-3/08
	Hartford-West Hartford-East Hartford MSA, CT	Y	50370 FQ	71230 MW	82610 TQ	USBLS	5/07
	District of Columbia	Y	41570 FQ	59920 MW	88060 TQ	USBLS	5/07
	Washington-Arlington- Alexandria MSA, DC-VA- MD-WV	Y	53050 FQ	77460 MW	99000 TQ	USBLS	5/07
	Florida	Y	51910 FQ	73550 MW	91380 TQ	USBLS	5/07
	Fort Lauderdale-Pompano Beach-Deerfield Beach PMSA, FL	Y	64910 FQ	90000 MW	117400 TQ	USBLS	5/07
	Miami-Fort Lauderdale-Miami Beach MSA, FL	Y	55640 FQ	77000 MW	105480 TQ	USBLS	5/07
	Tampa-St. Petersburg- Clearwater MSA, FL	Y	45380 FQ	59080 MW	86200 TQ	USBLS	5/07
	Georgia	Y	71180 FQ	80970 MW	93930 TQ	USBLS	5/07
	Atlanta-Sandy Springs- Marietta MSA, GA	Y	72250 FQ	82170 MW	94900 TQ	USBLS	5/07
	Idaho	Y	54430 FQ	62400 MW	77160 TQ	USBLS	5/07
	Boise City-Nampa MSA, ID	Y	53550 FQ	63190 MW	81330 TQ	USBLS	5/07
	Illinois	Y	62260 FQ	76090 MW	90230 TQ	USBLS	5/07
	Indiana	Y	51530 FQ	65180 MW	80420 TQ	USBLS	5/07
	Kentucky	Y	64872 FQ	74116 MW	82898 TQ	KYBLS	2008
	Louisiana	H	31.38 FQ	36.82 MW	42.99 TQ	LABLS	1/08-3/08
	Maine	Y	57920 FQ	71270 MW	79940 TQ	USBLS	5/07
	Portland-South Portland- Biddeford MSA, ME	Y	55280 FQ	67180 MW	81900 TQ	USBLS	5/07
	Maryland	Y		67350 MW		MDBLS	3/08
	Baltimore-Towson MSA, MD	Y	46550 FQ	59970 MW	82430 TQ	USBLS	5/07
	Massachusetts	Y	72430 FQ	85370 MW	96450 TQ	USBLS	5/07
	Boston-Cambridge-Quincy NECTA, MA	Y	73510 FQ	88230 MW	102290 TQ	USBLS	5/07
	Michigan	Y	46230 FQ	53900 MW	71310 TQ	USBLS	5/07
	Minnesota	Y	58944 FQ	72064 MW	83248 TQ	MNBLS	10/08-12/08
	Minneapolis-Saint Paul MSA, MN-WI	Y	61455 FQ	75516 MW	85434 TQ	MNBLS	10/08-12/08
	Missouri	Y	63100 FQ	73350 MW	83900 TQ	USBLS	5/07
	Kansas City MSA, MO-KS	Y	66780 FQ	74490 MW	84800 TQ	USBLS	5/07
	Montana	Y	46400 FQ	57210 MW	74220 TQ	USBLS	5/07
	Nevada	H	30.54 FQ	38.31 MW	51.01 TQ	NVBLS	5/08
	Las Vegas-Paradise MSA, NV	H	32.97 FQ	41.47 MW	61.78 TQ	NVBLS	5/08
	Reno-Sparks MSA, NV	H	24.44 FQ	35.32 MW	47.07 TQ	NVBLS	5/08
	New Hampshire	H	28.01 AE	32.37 MW	38.77 AEX	NHBLS	6/08
	New Jersey	Y	61560 FQ	74990 MW	92390 TQ	USBLS	5/07
	Edison PMSA, NJ	Y	59030 FQ	64870 MW	78590 TQ	USBLS	5/07
	New Mexico	Y	50920 FQ	65360 MW	92830 TQ	USBLS	5/07
	Albuquerque MSA, NM	Y	49000 FQ	58500 MW	80350 TQ	USBLS	5/07
	New York	Y	40470 FQ	55950 MW	77260 TQ	USBLS	5/07
	Nassau-Suffolk PMSA, NY	Y	37660 FQ	46900 MW	61620 TQ	USBLS	5/07
	New York-Northern New Jersey-Long Island MSA, NY- NJ-PA	Y	40890 FQ	58000 MW	81970 TQ	USBLS	5/07
	North Carolina	Y	48530 FQ	55780 MW	62770 TQ	USBLS	5/07
	Raleigh-Cary MSA, NC	Y	48500 FQ	56590 MW	64940 TQ	USBLS	5/07

AE Average entry wage	**AW** Average wage paid	**FQ** First quartile wage	**LO** Lowest wage paid	**MTC** Median total compensation	**TCC** Total cash compensation
AER Average entry range	**AWR** Average wage range	**H** Hourly	**LR** Low end range	**MW** Median wage paid	**TQ** Third quartile wage
AEX Average experienced wage	**AXR** Average experienced range **HI**	Highest wage paid	**M** Monthly	**MWR** Median wage range	**W** Weekly
ATC Average total compensation **D**	Daily	**HR** High end range	**MCC** Median cash compensation **S**	See annotated source	**Y** Yearly

Occupation/Type/Industry	Location	Per	Low	Mid	High	Source	Date
Hydrologist	Ohio	Y	51780 FQ	70300 MW	86280 TQ	USBLS	5/07
	Cincinnati-Middletown MSA, OH-KY-IN	Y	64220 FQ	73510 MW	100190 TQ	USBLS	5/07
	Columbus MSA, OH	Y	47120 FQ	69840 MW	83150 TQ	USBLS	5/07
	Dayton MSA, OH	Y	50130 FQ	63520 MW	79770 TQ	USBLS	5/07
	Oklahoma	Y	66790 FQ	80630 MW	92390 TQ	USBLS	5/07
	Oklahoma City MSA, OK	Y	59360 FQ	81350 MW	93380 TQ	USBLS	5/07
	Oregon	H	28.59 FQ	35.36 MW	42.82 TQ	ORBLS	5/08
	Portland-Vancouver-Beaverton MSA, OR-WA	Y	62500 FQ	78450 MW	91650 TQ	USBLS	5/07
	Pennsylvania	Y	69220 FQ	84540 MW	96480 TQ	USBLS	5/07
	Philadelphia-Camden-Wilmington MSA, PA-NJ-DE-MD	Y	62780 FQ	83660 MW	97150 TQ	USBLS	5/07
	South Carolina	Y	45300 FQ	58650 MW	72930 TQ	USBLS	5/07
	Columbia MSA, SC	Y	42680 FQ	53070 MW	65450 TQ	USBLS	5/07
	South Dakota	Y	49464 FQ	57271 MW	74114 TQ	SDBLS	7/08-9/08
	Tennessee	Y	67590 FQ	77030 MW	92100 TQ	USBLS	5/07
	Texas	Y	52060 FQ	64820 MW	86370 TQ	USBLS	5/07
	Austin-Round Rock MSA, TX	Y	45750 FQ	58830 MW	75540 TQ	USBLS	5/07
	Dallas-Fort Worth-Arlington MSA, TX	Y	51090 FQ	75850 MW	112960 TQ	USBLS	5/07
	Houston-Sugar Land-Baytown MSA, TX	Y	58500 FQ	69760 MW	89950 TQ	USBLS	5/07
	San Antonio MSA, TX	Y	62580 FQ	80420 MW	90180 TQ	USBLS	5/07
	Utah	Y	54080 FQ	66560 MW	81710 TQ	USBLS	5/07
	Salt Lake City MSA, UT	Y	59580 FQ	72060 MW	87140 TQ	USBLS	5/07
	Virginia	Y	72380 FQ	87320 MW	101760 TQ	USBLS	5/07
	Washington	H	27.17 FQ	33.60 MW	41.57 TQ	WABLS	3/08
	Seattle-Tacoma-Bellevue MSA, WA	Y	53800 FQ	68780 MW	88200 TQ	USBLS	5/07
	Wisconsin	Y	50590 FQ	61190 MW	77670 TQ	USBLS	5/07
	Milwaukee-Waukesha-West Allis MSA, WI	Y	45700 FQ	51100 MW	64650 TQ	USBLS	5/07
	Wyoming	Y	45085 FQ	52648 MW	66344 TQ	WYBLS	9/08
Hydrometallurgist	United States	Y		64390 AW		SUSA03	2008
Ice Rink Specialist Municipal Government	Seattle, WA	H	21.00 LO		21.82 HI	CSSS	2007
Identification Technician Municipal Government	Seattle, WA	H	20.80 LO		24.21 HI	CSSS	2007
Image Consultant	United States	H	100.00 LO		300.00 HI	NYT01	2007
Imaging/Scanning Specialist	United States	Y	21000-25000 AER			IAAPHQ	2008
Immigration and Customs Inspector	United States	Y		59930 MW		RD01	2009
Import Coordinator Apparel Industry	United States	Y		53000 MW		247FASH	2009
Income Maintenance Caseworker	Caldwell County, NC	Y			30245 HI	NTOP	11/08
	Pennsylvania	Y	34875 LO		53008 HI	AFT02	3/1/08
Independent Medical Claims Consultant	United States	H	25.00 LO		125.00 HI	OMAG	2008
Industrial Engineer	Alabama	Y	53790 FQ	66410 MW	81890 TQ	USBLS	5/07
	Birmingham-Hoover MSA, AL	Y	52250 FQ	65410 MW	83070 TQ	USBLS	5/07
	Huntsville MSA, AL	Y	60470 FQ	76400 MW	94210 TQ	USBLS	5/07
	Tuscaloosa MSA, AL	Y	62070 FQ	70830 MW	80640 TQ	USBLS	5/07
	Alaska	Y	79350 FQ	94050 MW	108130 TQ	USBLS	5/07
	Arizona	Y	56740 FQ	69120 MW	84410 TQ	USBLS	5/07
	Phoenix-Mesa-Scottsdale MSA, AZ	Y	56570 FQ	67170 MW	82300 TQ	USBLS	5/07
	Tucson MSA, AZ	Y	61900 FQ	75970 MW	91820 TQ	USBLS	5/07
	Arkansas	Y	48190 FQ	59710 MW	73220 TQ	USBLS	5/07
	Little Rock-North Little Rock MSA, AR	Y	50820 FQ	61360 MW	73780 TQ	USBLS	5/07

AE Average entry wage	**AW** Average wage paid	**FQ** First quartile wage	**LO** Lowest wage paid	**MTC** Median total compensation	**TCC** Total cash compensation
AER Average entry range	**AWR** Average wage range	**H** Hourly	**LR** Low end range	**MW** Median wage paid	**TQ** Third quartile wage
AEX Average experienced wage	**AXR** Average experienced range	**HI** Highest wage paid	**M** Monthly	**MWR** Median wage range	**W** Weekly
ATC Average total compensation	**D** Daily	**HR** High end range	**MCC** Median cash compensation	**S** See annotated source	**Y** Yearly

Industrial Engineer

Occupation/Type/Industry	Location	Per	Low	Mid	High	Source	Date
Industrial Engineer	Pine Bluff MSA, AR	Y	58900 FQ	68930 MW	83010 TQ	USBLS	5/07
	California	H	31.97 FQ	39.57 MW	48.90 TQ	CABLS	1/08-3/08
	Los Angeles-Long Beach-Glendale PMSA, CA	H	30.71 FQ	37.37 MW	45.38 TQ	CABLS	1/08-3/08
	Oakland-Fremont-Hayward MSA, CA	H	35.00 FQ	43.24 MW	52.11 TQ	CABLS	1/08-3/08
	Riverside-San Bernardino-Ontario MSA, CA	H	25.36 FQ	32.59 MW	39.37 TQ	CABLS	1/08-3/08
	Sacramento-Arden Arcade-Roseville MSA, CA	H	30.31 FQ	36.18 MW	43.09 TQ	CABLS	1/08-3/08
	San Diego-Carlsbad-San Marcos MSA, CA	H	29.77 FQ	36.42 MW	44.83 TQ	CABLS	1/08-3/08
	San Francisco-San Mateo-Redwood PMSA, CA	H	36.23 FQ	43.22 MW	52.79 TQ	CABLS	1/08-3/08
	San Jose-Sunnyvale-Santa Clara MSA, CA	H	38.12 FQ	48.17 MW	58.50 TQ	CABLS	1/08-3/08
	Santa Ana-Anaheim-Irvine PMSA, CA	Y	62560 FQ	77060 MW	93210 TQ	USBLS	5/07
	Colorado	Y	63240 FQ	75920 MW	92030 TQ	USBLS	5/07
	Denver-Aurora MSA, CO	Y	63770 FQ	76210 MW	93150 TQ	USBLS	5/07
	Connecticut	H	28.23 AE	37.59 MW		CTBLS	1/08-3/08
	Bridgeport-Stamford-Norwalk MSA, CT	Y	63890 FQ	77400 MW	90700 TQ	USBLS	5/07
	Danbury MSA, CT	Y	59670 FQ	72570 MW	87690 TQ	USBLS	5/07
	Hartford-West Hartford-East Hartford MSA, CT	Y	65770 FQ	77870 MW	92620 TQ	USBLS	5/07
	Delaware	Y	59590 FQ	78410 MW	94960 TQ	USBLS	5/07
	Wilmington PMSA, DE-MD-NJ	Y	63910 FQ	80540 MW	95930 TQ	USBLS	5/07
	District of Columbia	Y	60980 FQ	78090 MW	95650 TQ	USBLS	5/07
	Washington-Arlington-Alexandria MSA, DC-VA-MD-WV	Y	62350 FQ	79770 MW	98630 TQ	USBLS	5/07
	Florida	Y	49360 FQ	64580 MW	82810 TQ	USBLS	5/07
	Fort Lauderdale-Pompano Beach-Deerfield Beach PMSA, FL	Y	50760 FQ	59020 MW	71060 TQ	USBLS	5/07
	Jacksonville MSA, FL	Y	48220 FQ	63830 MW	81320 TQ	USBLS	5/07
	Miami-Fort Lauderdale-Miami Beach MSA, FL	Y	46870 FQ	60330 MW	79400 TQ	USBLS	5/07
	Orlando-Kissimmee MSA, FL	Y	54190 FQ	71770 MW	91560 TQ	USBLS	5/07
	Tampa-St. Petersburg-Clearwater MSA, FL	Y	47870 FQ	62410 MW	77200 TQ	USBLS	5/07
	West Palm Beach-Boca Raton-Boynton Beach PMSA, FL	Y	57690 FQ	77000 MW	94740 TQ	USBLS	5/07
	Georgia	Y	55350 FQ	68420 MW	83480 TQ	USBLS	5/07
	Atlanta-Sandy Springs-Marietta MSA, GA	Y	55870 FQ	69680 MW	84660 TQ	USBLS	5/07
	Hawaii	Y	70480 FQ	78340 MW	87250 TQ	USBLS	5/07
	Honolulu MSA, HI	Y	70260 FQ	78050 MW	86160 TQ	USBLS	5/07
	Idaho	Y	62230 FQ	75390 MW	88220 TQ	USBLS	5/07
	Boise City-Nampa MSA, ID	Y	63680 FQ	74920 MW	86360 TQ	USBLS	5/07
	Illinois	Y	54920 FQ	67500 MW	84930 TQ	USBLS	5/07
	Chicago-Naperville-Joliet MSA, IL-IN-WI	Y	56840 FQ	70180 MW	87890 TQ	USBLS	5/07
	Indiana	Y	54110 FQ	65370 MW	78460 TQ	USBLS	5/07
	Fort Wayne MSA, IN	Y	53680 FQ	64590 MW	76770 TQ	USBLS	5/07
	Gary PMSA, IN	Y	58280 FQ	69510 MW	80030 TQ	USBLS	5/07
	Indianapolis-Carmel MSA, IN	Y	59520 FQ	71610 MW	85610 TQ	USBLS	5/07
	Iowa	Y	51920 FQ	61400 MW	74260 TQ	USBLS	5/07
	Des Moines-West Des Moines MSA, IA	Y	47280 FQ	57580 MW	71430 TQ	USBLS	5/07
	Sioux City MSA, IA-NE-SD	Y	62410 FQ	76240 MW	90160 TQ	USBLS	5/07
	Kansas	Y	54220 FQ	64790 MW	77660 TQ	USBLS	5/07
	Topeka MSA, KS	Y	47230 FQ	55810 MW	78380 TQ	USBLS	5/07
	Wichita MSA, KS	Y	54930 FQ	64870 MW	77100 TQ	USBLS	5/07
	Kentucky	Y	54336 FQ	64810 MW	77437 TQ	KYBLS	2008
	Elizabethtown MSA, KY	Y	52030 FQ	60340 MW	71690 TQ	USBLS	5/07
	Lexington-Fayette MSA, KY	Y	56700 FQ	69000 MW	84630 TQ	USBLS	5/07
	Louisville-Jefferson County MSA, KY-IN	Y	52740 FQ	62630 MW	75310 TQ	USBLS	5/07
	Louisiana	H	17.71 FQ	29.97 MW	38.90 TQ	LABLS	1/08-3/08

AE Average entry wage	**AW** Average wage paid	**FQ** First quartile wage	**LO** Lowest wage paid	**MTC** Median total compensation	**TCC** Total cash compensation
AER Average entry range	**AWR** Average wage range	**H** Hourly	**LR** Low end range	**MW** Median wage paid	**TQ** Third quartile wage
AEX Average experienced wage	**AXR** Average experienced range	**HI** Highest wage paid	**M** Monthly	**MWR** Median wage range	**W** Weekly
ATC Average total compensation	**D** Daily	**HR** High end range	**MCC** Median cash compensation	**S** See annotated source	**Y** Yearly

Occupation/Type/Industry	Location	Per	Low	Mid	High	Source	Date
Industrial Engineer	Baton Rouge MSA, LA	Y	33380 FQ	56600 MW	69800 TQ	USBLS	5/07
	New Orleans-Metairie-Kenner MSA, LA	Y	43170 FQ	66810 MW	81970 TQ	USBLS	5/07
	Maine	Y	55940 FQ	68350 MW	82530 TQ	USBLS	5/07
	Portland-South Portland-Biddeford MSA, ME	Y	55670 FQ	71290 MW	84400 TQ	USBLS	5/07
	Maryland	Y		76675 MW		MDBLS	3/08
	Baltimore-Towson MSA, MD	Y	63600 FQ	75640 MW	92420 TQ	USBLS	5/07
	Bethesda-Gaithersburg-Frederick PMSA, MD	Y	50690 FQ	66000 MW	85120 TQ	USBLS	5/07
	Massachusetts	Y	66790 FQ	79870 MW	95690 TQ	USBLS	5/07
	Boston-Cambridge-Quincy NECTA, MA	Y	68970 FQ	81610 MW	96500 TQ	USBLS	5/07
	Lynn-Peabody-Salem NECTA, MA	Y	72300 FQ	84970 MW	96910 TQ	USBLS	5/07
	Springfield MSA, MA-CT	Y	59340 FQ	70500 MW	81170 TQ	USBLS	5/07
	Worcester MSA, MA-CT	Y	59990 FQ	70320 MW	81490 TQ	USBLS	5/07
	Michigan	Y	62680 FQ	76520 MW	92260 TQ	USBLS	5/07
	Ann Arbor MSA, MI	Y	59990 FQ	75240 MW	91520 TQ	USBLS	5/07
	Detroit-Warren-Livonia MSA, MI	Y	68200 FQ	81720 MW	96340 TQ	USBLS	5/07
	Grand Rapids-Wyoming MSA, MI	Y	55310 FQ	66460 MW	77700 TQ	USBLS	5/07
	Warren-Troy-Farmington Hills PMSA, MI	Y	66340 FQ	79380 MW	94360 TQ	USBLS	5/07
	Minnesota	Y	62376 FQ	76280 MW	94223 TQ	MNBLS	10/08-12/08
	Duluth-Superior MSA, MN-WI	Y	60367 FQ	68841 MW	80538 TQ	MNBLS	10/08-12/08
	Minneapolis-Saint Paul MSA, MN-WI	Y	66278 FQ	79973 MW	97686 TQ	MNBLS	10/08-12/08
	Rochester MSA, MN	Y	63491 FQ	79358 MW	99351 TQ	MNBLS	10/08-12/08
	Mississippi	Y	53320 FQ	64080 MW	77550 TQ	USBLS	5/07
	Jackson MSA, MS	Y	56220 FQ	68600 MW	82690 TQ	USBLS	5/07
	Missouri	Y	58200 FQ	70320 MW	82950 TQ	USBLS	5/07
	Kansas City MSA, MO-KS	Y	62750 FQ	69610 MW	76590 TQ	USBLS	5/07
	St. Joseph MSA, MO-KS	Y	48160 FQ	58380 MW	68350 TQ	USBLS	5/07
	St. Louis MSA, MO-IL	Y	61210 FQ	75830 MW	90270 TQ	USBLS	5/07
	Springfield MSA, MO	Y	38480 FQ	48480 MW	70210 TQ	USBLS	5/07
	Montana	Y	50610 FQ	69810 MW	89740 TQ	USBLS	5/07
	Billings MSA, MT	Y	64170 FQ	82190 MW	100160 TQ	USBLS	5/07
	Nebraska	Y	52940 FQ	63260 MW	76480 TQ	USBLS	5/07
	Omaha-Council Bluffs MSA, NE-IA	Y	53630 FQ	67800 MW	83430 TQ	USBLS	5/07
	Nevada	H	23.99 FQ	28.80 MW	33.50 TQ	NVBLS	5/08
	Las Vegas-Paradise MSA, NV	H	23.29 FQ	28.65 MW	33.04 TQ	NVBLS	5/08
	New Hampshire	H	27.11 AE	36.09 MW	41.72 AEX	NHBLS	6/08
	Manchester MSA, NH	Y	61990 FQ	74060 MW	94870 TQ	USBLS	5/07
	Nashua NECTA, NH-MA	Y	64390 FQ	78580 MW	92200 TQ	USBLS	5/07
	New Jersey	Y	60180 FQ	75000 MW	91860 TQ	USBLS	5/07
	Camden PMSA, NJ	Y	61120 FQ	76740 MW	91850 TQ	USBLS	5/07
	Edison PMSA, NJ	Y	62870 FQ	79300 MW	99400 TQ	USBLS	5/07
	Newark-Union PMSA, NJ-PA	Y	55930 FQ	70110 MW	85450 TQ	USBLS	5/07
	New Mexico	Y	62310 FQ	78350 MW	98660 TQ	USBLS	5/07
	Albuquerque MSA, NM	Y	70380 FQ	83590 MW	104340 TQ	USBLS	5/07
	New York	Y	57230 FQ	71690 MW	90160 TQ	USBLS	5/07
	Albany-Schenectady-Troy MSA, NY	Y	62540 FQ	77650 MW	96660 TQ	USBLS	5/07
	Buffalo-Niagara Falls MSA, NY	Y	58190 FQ	70570 MW	84130 TQ	USBLS	5/07
	Ithaca MSA, NY	Y	64820 FQ	73170 MW	81360 TQ	USBLS	5/07
	Nassau-Suffolk PMSA, NY	Y	60860 FQ	75430 MW	94730 TQ	USBLS	5/07
	New York-Northern New Jersey-Long Island MSA, NY-NJ-PA	Y	62750 FQ	78630 MW	97310 TQ	USBLS	5/07
	North Carolina	Y	53980 FQ	66220 MW	80140 TQ	USBLS	5/07
	Charlotte-Gastonia-Concord MSA, NC-SC	Y	55440 FQ	66820 MW	79850 TQ	USBLS	5/07
	Raleigh-Cary MSA, NC	Y	59690 FQ	72840 MW	86330 TQ	USBLS	5/07
	North Dakota	Y	54590 FQ	66680 MW	81450 TQ	USBLS	5/07
	Fargo MSA, ND-MN	Y	55420 FQ	65950 MW	78210 TQ	USBLS	5/07
	Ohio	Y	55150 FQ	68680 MW	84460 TQ	USBLS	5/07
	Cincinnati-Middletown MSA, OH-KY-IN	Y	60460 FQ	73460 MW	90510 TQ	USBLS	5/07

AE	Average entry wage	AW	Average wage paid	FQ	First quartile wage	LO	Lowest wage paid	MTC	Median total compensation	TCC	Total cash compensation
AER	Average entry range	AWR	Average wage range	H	Hourly	LR	Low end range	MW	Median wage paid	TQ	Third quartile wage
AEX	Average experienced wage	AXR	Average experienced range	HI	Highest wage paid	M	Monthly	MWR	Median wage range	W	Weekly
ATC	Average total compensation	D	Daily	HR	High end range	MCC	Median cash compensation	S	See annotated source	Y	Yearly

Occupation/Type/Industry	Location	Per	Low	Mid	High	Source	Date
Industrial Engineer	Cleveland-Elyria-Mentor						
	MSA, OH	Y	56510 FQ	69820 MW	87090 TQ	USBLS	5/07
	Columbus MSA, OH	Y	55080 FQ	69470 MW	86970 TQ	USBLS	5/07
	Dayton MSA, OH	Y	63080 FQ	76100 MW	90670 TQ	USBLS	5/07
	Oklahoma	Y	51970 FQ	64810 MW	80180 TQ	USBLS	5/07
	Oklahoma City MSA, OK	Y	50010 FQ	64510 MW	82400 TQ	USBLS	5/07
	Tulsa MSA, OK	Y	51900 FQ	63490 MW	77440 TQ	USBLS	5/07
	Oregon	H	31.59 FQ	38.35 MW	45.51 TQ	ORBLS	5/08
	Eugene-Springfield MSA, OR	Y	60630 FQ	75760 MW	90480 TQ	USBLS	5/07
	Portland-Vancouver-Beaverton						
	MSA, OR-WA	Y	64760 FQ	77560 MW	92390 TQ	USBLS	5/07
	Pennsylvania	Y	53800 FQ	67550 MW	84420 TQ	USBLS	5/07
	Allentown-Bethlehem-Easton						
	MSA, PA-NJ	Y	54740 FQ	67490 MW	87090 TQ	USBLS	5/07
	Lancaster MSA, PA	Y	52450 FQ	65180 MW	79700 TQ	USBLS	5/07
	Philadelphia-Camden-						
	Wilmington MSA, PA-NJ-DE-						
	MD	Y	59580 FQ	75300 MW	93460 TQ	USBLS	5/07
	Pittsburgh MSA, PA	Y	57210 FQ	69820 MW	84710 TQ	USBLS	5/07
	Rhode Island	Y	59000 FQ	70410 MW	83320 TQ	USBLS	5/07
	Providence-Fall River-						
	Warwick MSA, RI-MA	Y	59910 FQ	71580 MW	84510 TQ	USBLS	5/07
	South Carolina	Y	54030 FQ	67230 MW	80940 TQ	USBLS	5/07
	Charleston-North Charleston						
	MSA, SC	Y	53620 FQ	67620 MW	81380 TQ	USBLS	5/07
	Columbia MSA, SC	Y	58650 FQ	70860 MW	81470 TQ	USBLS	5/07
	South Dakota	Y	55100 FQ	64047 MW	78739 TQ	SDBLS	7/08-9/08
	Sioux Falls MSA, SD	Y	54311 FQ	60986 MW	69304 TQ	SDBLS	7/08-9/08
	Tennessee	Y	52070 FQ	63950 MW	78210 TQ	USBLS	5/07
	Knoxville MSA, TN	Y	57500 FQ	71400 MW	87380 TQ	USBLS	5/07
	Memphis MSA, TN-MS-AR	Y	58030 FQ	73050 MW	91500 TQ	USBLS	5/07
	Nashville-Davidson-						
	Murfreesboro MSA, TN	Y	51690 FQ	61830 MW	75170 TQ	USBLS	5/07
	Texas	Y	60110 FQ	75490 MW	93910 TQ	USBLS	5/07
	Austin-Round Rock MSA, TX	Y	59880 FQ	78350 MW	100220 TQ	USBLS	5/07
	Dallas-Fort Worth-Arlington						
	MSA, TX	Y	62340 FQ	76290 MW	92230 TQ	USBLS	5/07
	El Paso MSA, TX	Y	46720 FQ	58850 MW	74740 TQ	USBLS	5/07
	Houston-Sugar Land-Baytown						
	MSA, TX	Y	61490 FQ	77490 MW	96350 TQ	USBLS	5/07
	San Antonio MSA, TX	Y	54260 FQ	62920 MW	76320 TQ	USBLS	5/07
	Utah	Y	57920 FQ	70980 MW	85900 TQ	USBLS	5/07
	Provo-Orem MSA, UT	Y	56660 FQ	68500 MW	80710 TQ	USBLS	5/07
	Salt Lake City MSA, UT	Y	60320 FQ	73330 MW	88790 TQ	USBLS	5/07
	Vermont	Y	60600 FQ	73020 MW	88890 TQ	USBLS	5/07
	Burlington-South Burlington						
	MSA, VT	Y	63000 FQ	76380 MW	96310 TQ	USBLS	5/07
	Virginia	Y	58000 FQ	73910 MW	93030 TQ	USBLS	5/07
	Charlottesville MSA, VA	Y	52940 FQ	60820 MW	74580 TQ	USBLS	5/07
	Richmond MSA, VA	Y	59680 FQ	71470 MW	85440 TQ	USBLS	5/07
	Virginia Beach-Norfolk-						
	Newport News MSA, VA-NC	Y	51430 FQ	64100 MW	79360 TQ	USBLS	5/07
	Washington	H	29.65 FQ	35.59 MW	42.86 TQ	WABLS	3/08
	Seattle-Tacoma-Bellevue						
	MSA, WA	Y	60600 FQ	73010 MW	88190 TQ	USBLS	5/07
	West Virginia	Y	54737 FQ	66599 MW	76429 TQ	WVBLS	7/08-9/08
	Charleston MSA, WV	Y	55220 FQ	67890 MW	76290 TQ	USBLS	5/07
	Wisconsin	Y	53960 FQ	64030 MW	77500 TQ	USBLS	5/07
	Milwaukee-Waukesha-West						
	Allis MSA, WI	Y	53490 FQ	64080 MW	78060 TQ	USBLS	5/07
	Wyoming	Y	50946 FQ	67973 MW	90831 TQ	WYBLS	9/08
	Puerto Rico	Y	47880 FQ	59820 MW	75880 TQ	USBLS	5/07
	San Juan-Caguas-Guaynabo						
	MSA, PR	Y	48690 FQ	62460 MW	78490 TQ	USBLS	5/07
Industrial Engineering Technician	Alabama	Y	36220 FQ	45910 MW	56590 TQ	USBLS	5/07
	Birmingham-Hoover MSA, AL	Y	43410 FQ	50770 MW	63740 TQ	USBLS	5/07
	Arizona	Y	29930 FQ	39640 MW	52520 TQ	USBLS	5/07
	Phoenix-Mesa-Scottsdale						
	MSA, AZ	Y	29200 FQ	38370 MW	52760 TQ	USBLS	5/07
	Tucson MSA, AZ	Y	36330 FQ	44720 MW	52880 TQ	USBLS	5/07
	Arkansas	Y	33870 FQ	39390 MW	50100 TQ	USBLS	5/07

AE	Average entry wage	AW	Average wage paid	FQ	First quartile wage	LO	Lowest wage paid	MTC	Median total compensation	TCC	Total cash compensation
AER	Average entry range	AWR	Average wage range	H	Hourly	LR	Low end range	MW	Median wage paid	TQ	Third quartile wage
AEX	Average experienced wage	AXR	Average experienced range	HI	Highest wage paid	M	Monthly	MWR	Median wage range	W	Weekly
ATC	Average total compensation	D	Daily	HR	High end range	MCC	Median cash compensation	S	See annotated source	Y	Yearly

Occupation/Type/Industry	Location	Per	Low	Mid	High	Source	Date
Industrial Engineering Technician	Little Rock-North Little Rock MSA, AR	Y	37070 FQ	43130 MW	52360 TQ	USBLS	5/07
	California	H	19.70 FQ	25.95 MW	34.25 TQ	CABLS	1/08-3/08
	Fresno MSA, CA	H	16.70 FQ	19.73 MW	24.34 TQ	CABLS	1/08-3/08
	Los Angeles-Long Beach-Glendale PMSA, CA	H	16.33 FQ	23.58 MW	31.41 TQ	CABLS	1/08-3/08
	Oakland-Fremont-Hayward MSA, CA	H	23.63 FQ	31.01 MW	43.25 TQ	CABLS	1/08-3/08
	Riverside-San Bernardino-Ontario MSA, CA	H	16.34 FQ	23.92 MW	30.75 TQ	CABLS	1/08-3/08
	Sacramento-Arden Arcade-Roseville MSA, CA	H	21.85 FQ	30.71 MW	45.30 TQ	CABLS	1/08-3/08
	San Diego-Carlsbad-San Marcos MSA, CA	H	19.46 FQ	24.70 MW	35.57 TQ	CABLS	1/08-3/08
	San Francisco-San Mateo-Redwood PMSA, CA	H	21.41 FQ	28.99 MW	39.77 TQ	CABLS	1/08-3/08
	San Jose-Sunnyvale-Santa Clara MSA, CA	H	22.46 FQ	28.88 MW	35.04 TQ	CABLS	1/08-3/08
	Santa Ana-Anaheim-Irvine PMSA, CA	Y	38630 FQ	48280 MW	59790 TQ	USBLS	5/07
	Colorado	Y	42560 FQ	52120 MW	66980 TQ	USBLS	5/07
	Denver-Aurora MSA, CO	Y	35900 FQ	48320 MW	62100 TQ	USBLS	5/07
	Connecticut	H	19.58 AE	27.10 MW		CTBLS	1/08-3/08
	Bridgeport-Stamford-Norwalk MSA, CT	Y	51440 FQ	59010 MW	68510 TQ	USBLS	5/07
	Hartford-West Hartford-East Hartford MSA, CT	Y	47840 FQ	57570 MW	66490 TQ	USBLS	5/07
	Delaware	Y	37960 FQ	49220 MW	59110 TQ	USBLS	5/07
	Wilmington PMSA, DE-MD-NJ	Y	39810 FQ	51430 MW	59470 TQ	USBLS	5/07
	District of Columbia	Y	36820 FQ	50750 MW	64870 TQ	USBLS	5/07
	Washington-Arlington-Alexandria MSA, DC-VA-MD-WV	Y	41550 FQ	54450 MW	74540 TQ	USBLS	5/07
	Florida	Y	33990 FQ	41460 MW	53320 TQ	USBLS	5/07
	Fort Lauderdale-Pompano Beach-Deerfield Beach PMSA, FL	Y	30090 FQ	37070 MW	46730 TQ	USBLS	5/07
	Jacksonville MSA, FL	Y	42100 FQ	53860 MW	64150 TQ	USBLS	5/07
	Miami-Fort Lauderdale-Miami Beach MSA, FL	Y	33790 FQ	43250 MW	53810 TQ	USBLS	5/07
	Orlando-Kissimmee MSA, FL	Y	35900 FQ	48380 MW	59990 TQ	USBLS	5/07
	Tampa-St. Petersburg-Clearwater MSA, FL	Y	32140 FQ	36710 MW	41620 TQ	USBLS	5/07
	West Palm Beach-Boca Raton-Boynton Beach PMSA, FL	Y	35730 FQ	46220 MW	59010 TQ	USBLS	5/07
	Georgia	Y	38180 FQ	48950 MW	62020 TQ	USBLS	5/07
	Atlanta-Sandy Springs-Marietta MSA, GA	Y	37800 FQ	47490 MW	69450 TQ	USBLS	5/07
	Idaho	Y	36260 FQ	49060 MW	72130 TQ	USBLS	5/07
	Boise City-Nampa MSA, ID	Y	38380 FQ	65870 MW	79900 TQ	USBLS	5/07
	Illinois	Y	36530 FQ	45480 MW	57270 TQ	USBLS	5/07
	Chicago-Naperville-Joliet MSA, IL-IN-WI	Y	37800 FQ	46880 MW	59710 TQ	USBLS	5/07
	Indiana	Y	36290 FQ	44060 MW	56210 TQ	USBLS	5/07
	Gary PMSA, IN	Y	41490 FQ	55100 MW	65150 TQ	USBLS	5/07
	Indianapolis-Carmel MSA, IN	Y	38170 FQ	47270 MW	62170 TQ	USBLS	5/07
	Iowa	Y	35290 FQ	42210 MW	54970 TQ	USBLS	5/07
	Des Moines-West Des Moines MSA, IA	Y	29940 FQ	38400 MW	45110 TQ	USBLS	5/07
	Kansas	Y	41310 FQ	53500 MW	61650 TQ	USBLS	5/07
	Wichita MSA, KS	Y	45500 FQ	57170 MW	63410 TQ	USBLS	5/07
	Kentucky	Y	36654 FQ	43314 MW	51066 TQ	KYBLS	2008
	Louisville-Jefferson County MSA, KY-IN	Y	25950 FQ	34970 MW	43170 TQ	USBLS	5/07
	Louisiana	H	17.89 FQ	23.47 MW	36.69 TQ	LABLS	1/08-3/08
	Baton Rouge MSA, LA	Y	35480 FQ	42580 MW	51110 TQ	USBLS	5/07
	New Orleans-Metairie-Kenner MSA, LA	Y	41210 FQ	63680 MW	88570 TQ	USBLS	5/07
	Maine	Y	37960 FQ	51700 MW	75190 TQ	USBLS	5/07
	Portland-South Portland-Biddeford MSA, ME	Y	36980 FQ	48050 MW	74540 TQ	USBLS	5/07

Occupation/Type/Industry	Location	Per	Low	Mid	High	Source	Date
Industrial Engineering Technician	Maryland	Y		49275 MW		MDBLS	3/08
	Baltimore-Towson MSA, MD	Y	35680 FQ	45820 MW	57140 TQ	USBLS	5/07
	Bethesda-Gaithersburg-Frederick PMSA, MD	Y	38480 FQ	48020 MW	62240 TQ	USBLS	5/07
	Massachusetts	Y	41580 FQ	50370 MW	61900 TQ	USBLS	5/07
	Boston-Cambridge-Quincy NECTA, MA	Y	43140 FQ	53680 MW	67660 TQ	USBLS	5/07
	Lynn-Peabody-Salem NECTA, MA	Y	43630 FQ	47840 MW	52660 TQ	USBLS	5/07
	New Bedford MSA, MA	Y	40070 FQ	45520 MW	52140 TQ	USBLS	5/07
	Worcester MSA, MA-CT	Y	40970 FQ	46380 MW	52880 TQ	USBLS	5/07
	Michigan	Y	36130 FQ	45210 MW	59540 TQ	USBLS	5/07
	Detroit-Warren-Livonia MSA, MI	Y	38860 FQ	47630 MW	62590 TQ	USBLS	5/07
	Grand Rapids-Wyoming MSA, MI	Y	33480 FQ	39740 MW	50470 TQ	USBLS	5/07
	Warren-Troy-Farmington Hills PMSA, MI	Y	40000 FQ	48480 MW	63690 TQ	USBLS	5/07
	Minnesota	Y	38720 FQ	45814 MW	54393 TQ	MNBLS	10/08-12/08
	Minneapolis-Saint Paul MSA, MN-WI	Y	41838 FQ	48429 MW	57573 TQ	MNBLS	10/08-12/08
	Rochester MSA, MN	Y	34445 FQ	38263 MW	41798 TQ	MNBLS	10/08-12/08
	Mississippi	Y	34620 FQ	41180 MW	54260 TQ	USBLS	5/07
	Jackson MSA, MS	Y	36920 FQ	45600 MW	70580 TQ	USBLS	5/07
	Missouri	Y	31500 FQ	40690 MW	55120 TQ	USBLS	5/07
	Kansas City MSA, MO-KS	Y	41850 FQ	54810 MW	67280 TQ	USBLS	5/07
	St. Louis MSA, MO-IL	Y	33140 FQ	43300 MW	59320 TQ	USBLS	5/07
	Montana	Y	33780 FQ	46450 MW	70220 TQ	USBLS	5/07
	Nebraska	Y	35970 FQ	46580 MW	55800 TQ	USBLS	5/07
	Omaha-Council Bluffs MSA, NE-IA	Y	34680 FQ	45460 MW	60190 TQ	USBLS	5/07
	Nevada	H	15.78 FQ	19.92 MW	24.38 TQ	NVBLS	5/08
	Las Vegas-Paradise MSA, NV	H	18.71 FQ	21.77 MW	24.87 TQ	NVBLS	5/08
	New Hampshire	H	17.90 AE	22.73 MW	26.23 AEX	NHBLS	6/08
	Nashua NECTA, NH-MA	Y	42400 FQ	48090 MW	58290 TQ	USBLS	5/07
	New Jersey	Y	35560 FQ	49470 MW	66760 TQ	USBLS	5/07
	Camden PMSA, NJ	Y	32080 FQ	49310 MW	66970 TQ	USBLS	5/07
	Edison PMSA, NJ	Y	34970 FQ	45610 MW	62590 TQ	USBLS	5/07
	Newark-Union PMSA, NJ-PA	Y	38740 FQ	49560 MW	61430 TQ	USBLS	5/07
	New Mexico	Y	44980 FQ	57470 MW	66740 TQ	USBLS	5/07
	Albuquerque MSA, NM	Y	42300 FQ	54410 MW	62710 TQ	USBLS	5/07
	New York	Y	37280 FQ	48950 MW	70680 TQ	USBLS	5/07
	Albany-Schenectady-Troy MSA, NY	Y	43370 FQ	53260 MW	70200 TQ	USBLS	5/07
	Buffalo-Niagara Falls MSA, NY	Y	34880 FQ	44670 MW	54830 TQ	USBLS	5/07
	Nassau-Suffolk PMSA, NY	Y	33380 FQ	44970 MW	57140 TQ	USBLS	5/07
	New York-Northern New Jersey-Long Island MSA, NY-NJ-PA	Y	36270 FQ	48710 MW	68860 TQ	USBLS	5/07
	North Carolina	Y	37770 FQ	48430 MW	61210 TQ	USBLS	5/07
	Charlotte-Gastonia-Concord MSA, NC-SC	Y	43010 FQ	50370 MW	75630 TQ	USBLS	5/07
	Raleigh-Cary MSA, NC	Y	45080 FQ	55500 MW	66350 TQ	USBLS	5/07
	Winston-Salem MSA, NC	Y	38460 FQ	47330 MW	68770 TQ	USBLS	5/07
	North Dakota	Y	34800 FQ	41210 MW	50100 TQ	USBLS	5/07
	Ohio	Y	39130 FQ	46430 MW	55090 TQ	USBLS	5/07
	Cincinnati-Middletown MSA, OH-KY-IN	Y	39800 FQ	49870 MW	62960 TQ	USBLS	5/07
	Cleveland-Elyria-Mentor MSA, OH	Y	41680 FQ	49100 MW	57190 TQ	USBLS	5/07
	Columbus MSA, OH	Y	38500 FQ	44440 MW	52110 TQ	USBLS	5/07
	Dayton MSA, OH	Y	38030 FQ	45570 MW	54410 TQ	USBLS	5/07
	Oklahoma	Y	48250 FQ	60450 MW	79450 TQ	USBLS	5/07
	Oklahoma City MSA, OK	Y	51740 FQ	57760 MW	63930 TQ	USBLS	5/07
	Tulsa MSA, OK	Y	49730 FQ	73630 MW	94100 TQ	USBLS	5/07
	Oregon	H	18.01 FQ	20.89 MW	24.40 TQ	ORBLS	5/08
	Portland-Vancouver-Beaverton MSA, OR-WA	Y	36460 FQ	42310 MW	49520 TQ	USBLS	5/07
	Pennsylvania	Y	37280 FQ	46780 MW	59900 TQ	USBLS	5/07
	Allentown-Bethlehem-Easton MSA, PA-NJ	Y	37880 FQ	51810 MW	69550 TQ	USBLS	5/07

AE	Average entry wage	AW	Average wage paid	FQ	First quartile wage	LO	Lowest wage paid	MTC	Median total compensation	TCC	Total cash compensation
AER	Average entry range	AWR	Average wage range	H	Hourly	LR	Low end range	MW	Median wage paid	TQ	Third quartile wage
AEX	Average experienced wage	AXR	Average experienced range	HI	Highest wage paid	M	Monthly	MWR	Median wage range	W	Weekly
ATC	Average total compensation	D	Daily	HR	High end range	MCC	Median cash compensation	S	See annotated source	Y	Yearly

Occupation/Type/Industry	Location	Per	Low	Mid	High	Source	Date
Industrial Engineering Technician	Erie MSA, PA	Y	25460 FQ	32230 MW	39940 TQ	USBLS	5/07
	Philadelphia-Camden-Wilmington MSA, PA-NJ-DE-MD	Y	41340 FQ	50110 MW	64160 TQ	USBLS	5/07
	Pittsburgh MSA, PA	Y	38510 FQ	50040 MW	66480 TQ	USBLS	5/07
	Rhode Island	Y	33400 FQ	39420 MW	47190 TQ	USBLS	5/07
	Providence-Fall River-Warwick MSA, RI-MA	Y	34130 FQ	40210 MW	48660 TQ	USBLS	5/07
	South Carolina	Y	36590 FQ	46860 MW	58930 TQ	USBLS	5/07
	Charleston-North Charleston MSA, SC	Y	41350 FQ	52470 MW	60050 TQ	USBLS	5/07
	Columbia MSA, SC	Y	38950 FQ	44260 MW	53020 TQ	USBLS	5/07
	South Dakota	Y	30889 FQ	37302 MW	43629 TQ	SDBLS	7/08-9/08
	Sioux Falls MSA, SD	Y	30309 FQ	35069 MW	40172 TQ	SDBLS	7/08-9/08
	Tennessee	Y	32890 FQ	41050 MW	53610 TQ	USBLS	5/07
	Memphis MSA, TN-MS-AR	Y	33330 FQ	42710 MW	51020 TQ	USBLS	5/07
	Nashville-Davidson-Murfreesboro MSA, TN	Y	39810 FQ	48720 MW	60140 TQ	USBLS	5/07
	Texas	Y	41560 FQ	57430 MW	79980 TQ	USBLS	5/07
	Austin-Round Rock MSA, TX	Y	34570 FQ	40550 MW	58050 TQ	USBLS	5/07
	Beaumont-Port Arthur MSA, TX	Y	38320 FQ	52720 MW	61370 TQ	USBLS	5/07
	Dallas-Fort Worth-Arlington MSA, TX	Y	50010 FQ	66360 MW	95320 TQ	USBLS	5/07
	El Paso MSA, TX	Y	36620 FQ	42590 MW	48040 TQ	USBLS	5/07
	Houston-Sugar Land-Baytown MSA, TX	Y	42740 FQ	59550 MW	74220 TQ	USBLS	5/07
	San Antonio MSA, TX	Y	38570 FQ	49450 MW	61790 TQ	USBLS	5/07
	Utah	Y	40270 FQ	52960 MW	60630 TQ	USBLS	5/07
	Salt Lake City MSA, UT	Y	34490 FQ	46340 MW	56210 TQ	USBLS	5/07
	Vermont	Y	33980 FQ	39130 MW	46140 TQ	USBLS	5/07
	Burlington-South Burlington MSA, VT	Y	37020 FQ	41730 MW	47750 TQ	USBLS	5/07
	Virginia	Y	35210 FQ	50030 MW	60650 TQ	USBLS	5/07
	Richmond MSA, VA	Y	49040 FQ	54020 MW	59180 TQ	USBLS	5/07
	Virginia Beach-Norfolk-Newport News MSA, VA-NC	Y	30740 FQ	39390 MW	53120 TQ	USBLS	5/07
	Washington	H	24.98 FQ	30.22 MW	35.34 TQ	WABLS	3/08
	Seattle-Tacoma-Bellevue MSA, WA	Y	53700 FQ	63700 MW	73260 TQ	USBLS	5/07
	West Virginia	Y	33994 FQ	42513 MW	53595 TQ	WVBLS	7/08-9/08
	Wisconsin	Y	36100 FQ	41000 MW	47870 TQ	USBLS	5/07
	Milwaukee-Waukesha-West Allis MSA, WI	Y	38270 FQ	44420 MW	51360 TQ	USBLS	5/07
	Puerto Rico	Y	34570 FQ	47760 MW	62210 TQ	USBLS	5/07
	San Juan-Caguas-Guaynabo MSA, PR	Y	34840 FQ	48000 MW	61370 TQ	USBLS	5/07
Industrial Hygienist	United States	Y		80000 MW		ISHN01	2007
Industrial Investigator							
Municipal Government	Cincinnati, OH	Y	42298 LO		56845 HI	COHSS	10/08
Industrial Machinery Mechanic	Alabama	Y	30890 FQ	38610 MW	49120 TQ	USBLS	5/07
	Birmingham-Hoover MSA, AL	Y	33650 FQ	40230 MW	46430 TQ	USBLS	5/07
	Huntsville MSA, AL	Y	39610 FQ	48900 MW	64280 TQ	USBLS	5/07
	Alaska	Y	38640 FQ	60620 MW	77490 TQ	USBLS	5/07
	Anchorage MSA, AK	Y	38130 FQ	55890 MW	65220 TQ	USBLS	5/07
	Fairbanks MSA, AK	Y	55120 FQ	61760 MW	70670 TQ	USBLS	5/07
	Arizona	Y	35420 FQ	43670 MW	56740 TQ	USBLS	5/07
	Phoenix-Mesa-Scottsdale MSA, AZ	Y	36860 FQ	49370 MW	63690 TQ	USBLS	5/07
	Tucson MSA, AZ	Y	31660 FQ	37700 MW	47880 TQ	USBLS	5/07
	Arkansas	Y	30880 FQ	37040 MW	46390 TQ	USBLS	5/07
	Little Rock-North Little Rock MSA, AR	Y	32100 FQ	39190 MW	44640 TQ	USBLS	5/07
	California	H	19.32 FQ	24.25 MW	29.49 TQ	CABLS	1/08-3/08
	Los Angeles-Long Beach-Glendale PMSA, CA	H	17.06 FQ	22.82 MW	28.39 TQ	CABLS	1/08-3/08
	Oakland-Fremont-Hayward MSA, CA	H	24.45 FQ	29.43 MW	35.66 TQ	CABLS	1/08-3/08

AE	Average entry wage	AW	Average wage paid	FQ	First quartile wage	LO	Lowest wage paid	MTC	Median total compensation	TCC	Total cash compensation
AER	Average entry range	AWR	Average wage range	H	Hourly	LR	Low end range	MW	Median wage paid	TQ	Third quartile wage
AEX	Average experienced wage	AXR	Average experienced range	HI	Highest wage paid	M	Monthly	MWR	Median wage range	W	Weekly
ATC	Average total compensation	D	Daily	HR	High end range	MCC	Median cash compensation	S	See annotated source	Y	Yearly

Industrial Machinery Mechanic

Occupation/Type/Industry	Location	Per	Low	Mid	High	Source	Date
Industrial Machinery Mechanic	Riverside-San Bernardino-Ontario MSA, CA	H	17.68 FQ	22.07 MW	26.98 TQ	CABLS	1/08-3/08
	Sacramento-Arden Arcade-Roseville MSA, CA	H	19.67 FQ	23.43 MW	29.85 TQ	CABLS	1/08-3/08
	San Diego-Carlsbad-San Marcos MSA, CA	H	18.77 FQ	22.75 MW	26.46 TQ	CABLS	1/08-3/08
	San Francisco-San Mateo-Redwood PMSA, CA	H	22.52 FQ	25.37 MW	32.68 TQ	CABLS	1/08-3/08
	San Jose-Sunnyvale-Santa Clara MSA, CA	H	18.30 FQ	24.79 MW	30.43 TQ	CABLS	1/08-3/08
	Santa Ana-Anaheim-Irvine PMSA, CA	Y	40620 FQ	50430 MW	61430 TQ	USBLS	5/07
	Colorado	Y	34070 FQ	42980 MW	51730 TQ	USBLS	5/07
	Boulder MSA, CO	Y	30550 FQ	37260 MW	48540 TQ	USBLS	5/07
	Denver-Aurora MSA, CO	Y	36340 FQ	44320 MW	51900 TQ	USBLS	5/07
	Pueblo MSA, CO	Y	41730 FQ	47930 MW	62490 TQ	USBLS	5/07
	Connecticut	H	16.56 AE	21.76 MW		CTBLS	1/08-3/08
	Bridgeport-Stamford-Norwalk MSA, CT	Y	37320 FQ	43850 MW	51330 TQ	USBLS	5/07
	Hartford-West Hartford-East Hartford MSA, CT	Y	37560 FQ	45850 MW	54640 TQ	USBLS	5/07
	Delaware	Y	37660 FQ	48900 MW	60290 TQ	USBLS	5/07
	Dover MSA, DE	Y	35970 FQ	48510 MW	55720 TQ	USBLS	5/07
	Wilmington PMSA, DE-MD-NJ	Y	42600 FQ	51000 MW	62670 TQ	USBLS	5/07
	District of Columbia	Y	50240 FQ	56500 MW	62240 TQ	USBLS	5/07
	Washington-Arlington-Alexandria MSA, DC-VA-MD-WV	Y	38160 FQ	47400 MW	57150 TQ	USBLS	5/07
	Florida	Y	32730 FQ	40330 MW	48950 TQ	USBLS	5/07
	Fort Lauderdale-Pompano Beach-Deerfield Beach PMSA, FL	Y	36660 FQ	45320 MW	55870 TQ	USBLS	5/07
	Jacksonville MSA, FL	Y	37150 FQ	43060 MW	50360 TQ	USBLS	5/07
	Miami-Fort Lauderdale-Miami Beach MSA, FL	Y	32590 FQ	41100 MW	51390 TQ	USBLS	5/07
	Orlando-Kissimmee MSA, FL	Y	34510 FQ	40980 MW	46610 TQ	USBLS	5/07
	Tampa-St. Petersburg-Clearwater MSA, FL	Y	33450 FQ	39870 MW	47490 TQ	USBLS	5/07
	West Palm Beach-Boca Raton-Boynton Beach PMSA, FL	Y	33450 FQ	40420 MW	49280 TQ	USBLS	5/07
	Georgia	Y	31600 FQ	38000 MW	46600 TQ	USBLS	5/07
	Atlanta-Sandy Springs-Marietta MSA, GA	Y	33700 FQ	39790 MW	46890 TQ	USBLS	5/07
	Hawaii	Y	40510 FQ	48370 MW	59470 TQ	USBLS	5/07
	Honolulu MSA, HI	Y	40690 FQ	52820 MW	62430 TQ	USBLS	5/07
	Idaho	Y	35620 FQ	42990 MW	50280 TQ	USBLS	5/07
	Boise City-Nampa MSA, ID	Y	39820 FQ	45200 MW	51510 TQ	USBLS	5/07
	Illinois	Y	36810 FQ	45720 MW	58260 TQ	USBLS	5/07
	Champaign-Urbana MSA, IL	Y	38470 FQ	45400 MW	54490 TQ	USBLS	5/07
	Chicago-Naperville-Joliet MSA, IL-IN-WI	Y	38960 FQ	49100 MW	58910 TQ	USBLS	5/07
	Indiana	Y	36880 FQ	46620 MW	56950 TQ	USBLS	5/07
	Evansville MSA, IN-KY	Y	37980 FQ	45590 MW	53630 TQ	USBLS	5/07
	Gary PMSA, IN	Y	48160 FQ	52680 MW	57270 TQ	USBLS	5/07
	Indianapolis-Carmel MSA, IN	Y	35880 FQ	43520 MW	56460 TQ	USBLS	5/07
	Iowa	Y	32230 FQ	37790 MW	45050 TQ	USBLS	5/07
	Cedar Rapids MSA, IA	Y	38760 FQ	45400 MW	51360 TQ	USBLS	5/07
	Des Moines-West Des Moines MSA, IA	Y	32930 FQ	37820 MW	45570 TQ	USBLS	5/07
	Kansas	Y	31060 FQ	37430 MW	48390 TQ	USBLS	5/07
	Wichita MSA, KS	Y	35820 FQ	49180 MW	55410 TQ	USBLS	5/07
	Kentucky	Y	35582 FQ	42458 MW	49830 TQ	KYBLS	2008
	Louisville-Jefferson County MSA, KY-IN	Y	37210 FQ	45730 MW	54500 TQ	USBLS	5/07
	Louisiana	H	15.55 FQ	19.61 MW	26.25 TQ	LABLS	1/08-3/08
	Baton Rouge MSA, LA	Y	33920 FQ	43800 MW	58930 TQ	USBLS	5/07
	Houma-Bayou Cane-Thibodaux MSA, LA	Y	36010 FQ	45800 MW	61440 TQ	USBLS	5/07
	New Orleans-Metairie-Kenner MSA, LA	Y	32210 FQ	40420 MW	53230 TQ	USBLS	5/07
	Maine	Y	33200 FQ	39370 MW	48040 TQ	USBLS	5/07

AE	Average entry wage	AW	Average wage paid	FQ	First quartile wage
AER	Average entry range	AWR	Average wage range	H	Hourly
AEX	Average experienced wage	AXR	Average experienced range	HI	Highest wage paid
ATC	Average total compensation	D	Daily	HR	High end range

LO	Lowest wage paid	MTC	Median total compensation
LR	Low end range	MW	Median wage paid
M	Monthly	MWR	Median wage range
MCC	Median cash compensation	S	See annotated source

TCC	Total cash compensation
TQ	Third quartile wage
W	Weekly
Y	Yearly

Industrial Machinery Mechanic

Occupation/Type/Industry	Location	Per	Low	Mid	High	Source	Date
Industrial Machinery Mechanic	Portland-South Portland-Biddeford MSA, ME	Y	34240 FQ	41500 MW	49420 TQ	USBLS	5/07
	Maryland	Y		47725 MW		MDBLS	3/08
	Baltimore-Towson MSA, MD	Y	40500 FQ	47290 MW	56620 TQ	USBLS	5/07
	Bethesda-Gaithersburg-Frederick PMSA, MD	Y	40880 FQ	49450 MW	58800 TQ	USBLS	5/07
	Salisbury MSA, MD	Y	34040 FQ	45250 MW	56930 TQ	USBLS	5/07
	Massachusetts	Y	39790 FQ	46790 MW	54690 TQ	USBLS	5/07
	Barnstable Town MSA, MA	Y	31460 FQ	48190 MW	56800 TQ	USBLS	5/07
	Boston-Cambridge-Quincy NECTA, MA	Y	40040 FQ	46440 MW	52520 TQ	USBLS	5/07
	Lynn-Peabody-Salem NECTA, MA	Y	52290 FQ	56020 MW	59770 TQ	USBLS	5/07
	Springfield MSA, MA-CT	Y	34980 FQ	42090 MW	52370 TQ	USBLS	5/07
	Worcester MSA, MA-CT	Y	40370 FQ	46650 MW	55580 TQ	USBLS	5/07
	Michigan	Y	38200 FQ	47860 MW	64560 TQ	USBLS	5/07
	Detroit-Warren-Livonia MSA, MI	Y	43300 FQ	57100 MW	68580 TQ	USBLS	5/07
	Grand Rapids-Wyoming MSA, MI	Y	36250 FQ	44100 MW	50950 TQ	USBLS	5/07
	Warren-Troy-Farmington Hills PMSA, MI	Y	42590 FQ	57090 MW	67630 TQ	USBLS	5/07
	Minnesota	Y	39377 FQ	46688 MW	54650 TQ	MNBLS	10/08-12/08
	Duluth-Superior MSA, MN-WI	Y	39052 FQ	48314 MW	58468 TQ	MNBLS	10/08-12/08
	Minneapolis-Saint Paul MSA, MN-WI	Y	42608 FQ	48891 MW	57429 TQ	MNBLS	10/08-12/08
	Rochester MSA, MN	Y	37935 FQ	42542 MW	48591 TQ	MNBLS	10/08-12/08
	Mississippi	Y	31900 FQ	39150 MW	57210 TQ	USBLS	5/07
	Jackson MSA, MS	Y	30270 FQ	37200 MW	48680 TQ	USBLS	5/07
	Missouri	Y	33270 FQ	41210 MW	53890 TQ	USBLS	5/07
	Kansas City MSA, MO-KS	Y	33520 FQ	41050 MW	50560 TQ	USBLS	5/07
	St. Louis MSA, MO-IL	Y	40590 FQ	49560 MW	59360 TQ	USBLS	5/07
	Springfield MSA, MO	Y	25970 FQ	32540 MW	37920 TQ	USBLS	5/07
	Montana	Y	41090 FQ	51240 MW	60070 TQ	USBLS	5/07
	Billings MSA, MT	Y	40240 FQ	44330 MW	53650 TQ	USBLS	5/07
	Nebraska	Y	31400 FQ	36580 MW	43970 TQ	USBLS	5/07
	Omaha-Council Bluffs MSA, NE-IA	Y	32480 FQ	37170 MW	43550 TQ	USBLS	5/07
	Nevada	H	20.61 FQ	24.90 MW	31.35 TQ	NVBLS	5/08
	Carson City MSA, NV	H	24.70 FQ	26.67 MW	28.64 TQ	NVBLS	5/08
	Las Vegas-Paradise MSA, NV	H	21.03 FQ	26.70 MW	37.30 TQ	NVBLS	5/08
	New Hampshire	H	16.35 AE	20.33 MW	24.27 AEX	NHBLS	6/08
	Manchester MSA, NH	Y	39780 FQ	46420 MW	52150 TQ	USBLS	5/07
	Nashua NECTA, NH-MA	Y	35410 FQ	40590 MW	56530 TQ	USBLS	5/07
	New Jersey	Y	38060 FQ	46080 MW	54870 TQ	USBLS	5/07
	Camden PMSA, NJ	Y	38490 FQ	47000 MW	55400 TQ	USBLS	5/07
	Edison PMSA, NJ	Y	41330 FQ	48460 MW	56940 TQ	USBLS	5/07
	Newark-Union PMSA, NJ-PA	Y	37900 FQ	45590 MW	52950 TQ	USBLS	5/07
	New Mexico	Y	31400 FQ	39090 MW	49670 TQ	USBLS	5/07
	Albuquerque MSA, NM	Y	33900 FQ	47090 MW	59900 TQ	USBLS	5/07
	Farmington MSA, NM	Y	28900 FQ	35470 MW	41250 TQ	USBLS	5/07
	New York	Y	34800 FQ	43380 MW	55750 TQ	USBLS	5/07
	Albany-Schenectady-Troy MSA, NY	Y	36520 FQ	44630 MW	55710 TQ	USBLS	5/07
	Buffalo-Niagara Falls MSA, NY	Y	36060 FQ	45620 MW	56970 TQ	USBLS	5/07
	Glens Falls MSA, NY	Y	33470 FQ	37580 MW	43660 TQ	USBLS	5/07
	Nassau-Suffolk PMSA, NY	Y	35980 FQ	46570 MW	59390 TQ	USBLS	5/07
	New York-Northern New Jersey-Long Island MSA, NY-NJ-PA	Y	38460 FQ	47270 MW	57480 TQ	USBLS	5/07
	North Carolina	Y	29290 FQ	35750 MW	43860 TQ	USBLS	5/07
	Charlotte-Gastonia-Concord MSA, NC-SC	Y	28810 FQ	36790 MW	46880 TQ	USBLS	5/07
	Greensboro-High Point MSA, NC	Y	29530 FQ	35990 MW	44780 TQ	USBLS	5/07
	Raleigh-Cary MSA, NC	Y	34370 FQ	40500 MW	52770 TQ	USBLS	5/07
	Winston-Salem MSA, NC	Y	25350 FQ	30800 MW	37550 TQ	USBLS	5/07
	North Dakota	Y	34830 FQ	42590 MW	53500 TQ	USBLS	5/07
	Fargo MSA, ND-MN	Y	30960 FQ	36200 MW	45020 TQ	USBLS	5/07
	Ohio	Y	37190 FQ	46820 MW	59260 TQ	USBLS	5/07

AE	Average entry wage	AW	Average wage paid	FQ	First quartile wage	LO	Lowest wage paid	MTC	Median total compensation	TCC	Total cash compensation
AER	Average entry range	AWR	Average wage range	H	Hourly	LR	Low end range	MW	Median wage paid	TQ	Third quartile wage
AEX	Average experienced wage	AXR	Average experienced range	HI	Highest wage paid	M	Monthly	MWR	Median wage range	W	Weekly
ATC	Average total compensation	D	Daily	HR	High end range	MCC	Median cash compensation	S	See annotated source	Y	Yearly

Occupation/Type/Industry	Location	Per	Low	Mid	High	Source	Date
Industrial Machinery Mechanic	Cincinnati-Middletown MSA, OH-KY-IN	Y	38840 FQ	47090 MW	57020 TQ	USBLS	5/07
	Cleveland-Elyria-Mentor MSA, OH	Y	37890 FQ	47180 MW	58230 TQ	USBLS	5/07
	Columbus MSA, OH	Y	35410 FQ	44420 MW	52920 TQ	USBLS	5/07
	Dayton MSA, OH	Y	43320 FQ	59020 MW	70870 TQ	USBLS	5/07
	Oklahoma	Y	30350 FQ	39830 MW	49140 TQ	USBLS	5/07
	Lawton MSA, OK	Y	18210 FQ	21960 MW	28740 TQ	USBLS	5/07
	Oklahoma City MSA, OK	Y	36880 FQ	44770 MW	51090 TQ	USBLS	5/07
	Tulsa MSA, OK	Y	28320 FQ	36220 MW	43270 TQ	USBLS	5/07
	Oregon	H	18.48 FQ	21.82 MW	25.98 TQ	ORBLS	5/08
	Portland-Vancouver-Beaverton MSA, OR-WA	Y	40520 FQ	48190 MW	57530 TQ	USBLS	5/07
	Pennsylvania	Y	33790 FQ	40390 MW	48470 TQ	USBLS	5/07
	Allentown-Bethlehem-Easton MSA, PA-NJ	Y	35660 FQ	42500 MW	48810 TQ	USBLS	5/07
	Philadelphia-Camden-Wilmington MSA, PA-NJ-DE-MD	Y	37330 FQ	45080 MW	52680 TQ	USBLS	5/07
	Pittsburgh MSA, PA	Y	34080 FQ	40650 MW	50760 TQ	USBLS	5/07
	Rhode Island	Y	33720 FQ	38580 MW	45740 TQ	USBLS	5/07
	Providence-Fall River-Warwick MSA, RI-MA	Y	34350 FQ	40080 MW	47880 TQ	USBLS	5/07
	South Carolina	Y	32700 FQ	39670 MW	49490 TQ	USBLS	5/07
	Charleston-North Charleston MSA, SC	Y	31790 FQ	39770 MW	46920 TQ	USBLS	5/07
	Columbia MSA, SC	Y	37390 FQ	43010 MW	51410 TQ	USBLS	5/07
	Florence MSA, SC	Y	33060 FQ	37350 MW	42840 TQ	USBLS	5/07
	South Dakota	Y	33096 FQ	37612 MW	42769 TQ	SDBLS	7/08-9/08
	Rapid City MSA, SD	Y	35971 FQ	41089 MW	45425 TQ	SDBLS	7/08-9/08
	Sioux Falls MSA, SD	Y	32654 FQ	37625 MW	43285 TQ	SDBLS	7/08-9/08
	Tennessee	Y	30060 FQ	37300 MW	44970 TQ	USBLS	5/07
	Memphis MSA, TN-MS-AR	Y	27850 FQ	40940 MW	46800 TQ	USBLS	5/07
	Nashville-Davidson-Murfreesboro MSA, TN	Y	34230 FQ	39840 MW	45680 TQ	USBLS	5/07
	Texas	Y	31420 FQ	39730 MW	49970 TQ	USBLS	5/07
	Austin-Round Rock MSA, TX	Y	33350 FQ	45740 MW	57140 TQ	USBLS	5/07
	Dallas-Fort Worth-Arlington MSA, TX	Y	33490 FQ	40400 MW	48790 TQ	USBLS	5/07
	El Paso MSA, TX	Y	25490 FQ	33180 MW	40210 TQ	USBLS	5/07
	Houston-Sugar Land-Baytown MSA, TX	Y	34250 FQ	42950 MW	54320 TQ	USBLS	5/07
	San Antonio MSA, TX	Y	28820 FQ	34160 MW	42260 TQ	USBLS	5/07
	Utah	Y	35750 FQ	43010 MW	49750 TQ	USBLS	5/07
	Salt Lake City MSA, UT	Y	38390 FQ	44650 MW	51080 TQ	USBLS	5/07
	Vermont	Y	32700 FQ	39210 MW	46740 TQ	USBLS	5/07
	Burlington-South Burlington MSA, VT	Y	37660 FQ	43910 MW	48990 TQ	USBLS	5/07
	Virginia	Y	34580 FQ	42380 MW	51110 TQ	USBLS	5/07
	Richmond MSA, VA	Y	39390 FQ	49050 MW	63750 TQ	USBLS	5/07
	Virginia Beach-Norfolk-Newport News MSA, VA-NC	Y	34500 FQ	41110 MW	47090 TQ	USBLS	5/07
	Washington	H	19.90 FQ	23.91 MW	30.62 TQ	WABLS	3/08
	Seattle-Tacoma-Bellevue MSA, WA	Y	41920 FQ	51040 MW	63210 TQ	USBLS	5/07
	West Virginia	Y	30352 FQ	41932 MW	50709 TQ	WVBLS	7/08-9/08
	Charleston MSA, WV	Y	28720 FQ	46940 MW	63010 TQ	USBLS	5/07
	Wisconsin	Y	37080 FQ	44580 MW	52850 TQ	USBLS	5/07
	Milwaukee-Waukesha-West Allis MSA, WI	Y	39690 FQ	46690 MW	55720 TQ	USBLS	5/07
	Wyoming	Y	39984 FQ	51649 MW	69071 TQ	WYBLS	9/08
	Cheyenne MSA, WY	Y	43227 FQ	53533 MW	61439 TQ	WYBLS	9/08
	Puerto Rico	Y	21910 FQ	29730 MW	37440 TQ	USBLS	5/07
	San Juan-Caguas-Guaynabo MSA, PR	Y	22500 FQ	29750 MW	37500 TQ	USBLS	5/07
	Virgin Islands	Y	41790 FQ	45800 MW	50000 TQ	USBLS	5/07
Industrial-Organizational Psychologist	California	H	23.62 FQ	30.07 MW	37.02 TQ	CABLS	1/08-3/08
	District of Columbia	Y	76030 FQ	93850 MW	135950 TQ	USBLS	5/07
	Massachusetts	Y	54830 FQ	69710 MW	85450 TQ	USBLS	5/07
	New York	Y	87080 FQ	105010 MW	127810 TQ	USBLS	5/07

AE Average entry wage	**AW** Average wage paid	**FQ** First quartile wage	**LO** Lowest wage paid	**MTC** Median total compensation	**TCC** Total cash compensation
AER Average entry range	**AWR** Average wage range	**H** Hourly	**LR** Low end range	**MW** Median wage paid	**TQ** Third quartile wage
AEX Average experienced wage	**AXR** Average experienced range	**HI** Highest wage paid	**M** Monthly	**MWR** Median wage range	**W** Weekly
ATC Average total compensation	**D** Daily	**HR** High end range	**MCC** Median cash compensation	**S** See annotated source	**Y** Yearly

Occupation/Type/Industry	Location	Per	Low	Mid	High	Source	Date
Industrial-Organizational Psychologist	Ohio	Y	44680 FQ	62160 MW	88390 TQ	USBLS	5/07
	Oregon	H	34.93 FQ	40.14 MW	46.21 TQ	ORBLS	5/08
	Pennsylvania	Y	68050 FQ	108820 MW	123420 TQ	USBLS	5/07
	Virginia	Y	74350 FQ	93600 MW	119190 TQ	USBLS	5/07
Industrial Production Manager	Alabama	Y	54580 FQ	71470 MW	91850 TQ	USBLS	5/07
	Birmingham-Hoover MSA, AL	Y	55690 FQ	73670 MW	95120 TQ	USBLS	5/07
	Mobile MSA, AL	Y	62160 FQ	81230 MW	103620 TQ	USBLS	5/07
	Alaska	Y	48640 FQ	58950 MW	70900 TQ	USBLS	5/07
	Anchorage MSA, AK	Y	51970 FQ	58080 MW	64960 TQ	USBLS	5/07
	Arizona	Y	56880 FQ	78270 MW	107460 TQ	USBLS	5/07
	Phoenix-Mesa-Scottsdale MSA, AZ	Y	57590 FQ	79280 MW	107910 TQ	USBLS	5/07
	Tucson MSA, AZ	Y	60550 FQ	83390 MW	124080 TQ	USBLS	5/07
	Arkansas	Y	56340 FQ	70840 MW	90310 TQ	USBLS	5/07
	Little Rock-North Little Rock MSA, AR	Y	62080 FQ	81610 MW	101270 TQ	USBLS	5/07
	California	H	32.40 FQ	42.44 MW	56.57 TQ	CABLS	1/08-3/08
	Los Angeles-Long Beach-Glendale PMSA, CA	H	31.57 FQ	41.31 MW	52.56 TQ	CABLS	1/08-3/08
	Oakland-Fremont-Hayward MSA, CA	H	37.08 FQ	47.67 MW	61.32 TQ	CABLS	1/08-3/08
	Riverside-San Bernardino-Ontario MSA, CA	H	27.34 FQ	35.28 MW	46.44 TQ	CABLS	1/08-3/08
	Sacramento-Arden Arcade-Roseville MSA, CA	H	30.41 FQ	38.78 MW	47.42 TQ	CABLS	1/08-3/08
	San Diego-Carlsbad-San Marcos MSA, CA	H	32.08 FQ	42.61 MW	59.56 TQ	CABLS	1/08-3/08
	San Francisco-San Mateo-Redwood PMSA, CA	H	39.23 FQ	53.22 MW		CABLS	1/08-3/08
	San Jose-Sunnyvale-Santa Clara MSA, CA	H	39.10 FQ	53.17 MW	66.76 TQ	CABLS	1/08-3/08
	Santa Ana-Anaheim-Irvine PMSA, CA	Y	63890 FQ	80310 MW	106860 TQ	USBLS	5/07
	Colorado	Y	55980 FQ	74290 MW	98520 TQ	USBLS	5/07
	Denver-Aurora MSA, CO	Y	54760 FQ	73080 MW	97490 TQ	USBLS	5/07
	Connecticut	H	30.53 AE	43.02 MW		CTBLS	1/08-3/08
	Bridgeport-Stamford-Norwalk MSA, CT	Y	81610 FQ	112140 MW	134430 TQ	USBLS	5/07
	Danbury MSA, CT	Y	71280 FQ	84540 MW	100130 TQ	USBLS	5/07
	Hartford-West Hartford-East Hartford MSA, CT	Y	70760 FQ	86670 MW	105800 TQ	USBLS	5/07
	Norwich-New London MSA, CT-RI	Y	72260 FQ	84100 MW	99500 TQ	USBLS	5/07
	Delaware	Y	76920 FQ	94570 MW	118670 TQ	USBLS	5/07
	Wilmington PMSA, DE-MD-NJ	Y	80930 FQ	97300 MW	118960 TQ	USBLS	5/07
	District of Columbia	Y	73260 FQ	92870 MW		USBLS	5/07
	Washington-Arlington-Alexandria MSA, DC-VA-MD-WV	Y	70630 FQ	92680 MW	119750 TQ	USBLS	5/07
	Florida	Y	62720 FQ	84040 MW	114170 TQ	USBLS	5/07
	Fort Lauderdale-Pompano Beach-Deerfield Beach PMSA, FL	Y	59210 FQ	76320 MW	101400 TQ	USBLS	5/07
	Jacksonville MSA, FL	Y	60200 FQ	81400 MW	121100 TQ	USBLS	5/07
	Miami-Fort Lauderdale-Miami Beach MSA, FL	Y	63150 FQ	79120 MW	106050 TQ	USBLS	5/07
	Orlando-Kissimmee MSA, FL	Y	59400 FQ	79470 MW	107160 TQ	USBLS	5/07
	Tampa-St. Petersburg-Clearwater MSA, FL	Y	66130 FQ	91110 MW	118140 TQ	USBLS	5/07
	West Palm Beach-Boca Raton-Boynton Beach PMSA, FL	Y	62180 FQ	86150 MW	127880 TQ	USBLS	5/07
	Georgia	Y	58630 FQ	75160 MW	94440 TQ	USBLS	5/07
	Athens-Clarke County MSA, GA	Y	62840 FQ	80950 MW	103260 TQ	USBLS	5/07
	Atlanta-Sandy Springs-Marietta MSA, GA	Y	63120 FQ	78240 MW	95910 TQ	USBLS	5/07
	Hawaii	Y	51570 FQ	64240 MW	95170 TQ	USBLS	5/07
	Honolulu MSA, HI	Y	49490 FQ	60100 MW	87480 TQ	USBLS	5/07
	Idaho	Y	50660 FQ	69200 MW	88950 TQ	USBLS	5/07

AE Average entry wage	**AW** Average wage paid	**FQ** First quartile wage	**LO** Lowest wage paid	**MTC** Median total compensation	**TCC** Total cash compensation
AER Average entry range	**AWR** Average wage range	**H** Hourly	**LR** Low end range	**MW** Median wage paid	**TQ** Third quartile wage
AEX Average experienced wage	**AXR** Average experienced range	**HI** Highest wage paid	**M** Monthly	**MWR** Median wage range	**W** Weekly
ATC Average total compensation	**D** Daily	**HR** High end range	**MCC** Median cash compensation	**S** See annotated source	**Y** Yearly

Industrial Production Manager

Occupation/Type/Industry	Location	Per	Low	Mid	High	Source	Date
Industrial Production Manager	Boise City-Nampa MSA, ID	Y	60690 FQ	77100 MW	97300 TQ	USBLS	5/07
	Idaho Falls MSA, ID	Y	48260 FQ	69940 MW	100010 TQ	USBLS	5/07
	Illinois	Y	62940 FQ	81080 MW	102460 TQ	USBLS	5/07
	Chicago-Naperville-Joliet MSA, IL-IN-WI	Y	65550 FQ	83810 MW	106860 TQ	USBLS	5/07
	Peoria MSA, IL	Y	49200 FQ	68580 MW	84710 TQ	USBLS	5/07
	Indiana	Y	57890 FQ	74550 MW	95320 TQ	USBLS	5/07
	Gary PMSA, IN	Y	60400 FQ	78760 MW	101450 TQ	USBLS	5/07
	Indianapolis-Carmel MSA, IN	Y	59870 FQ	77150 MW	98390 TQ	USBLS	5/07
	Iowa	Y	62500 FQ	83410 MW	105740 TQ	USBLS	5/07
	Des Moines-West Des Moines MSA, IA	Y	78370 FQ	87040 MW	95880 TQ	USBLS	5/07
	Kansas	Y	56020 FQ	72470 MW	95470 TQ	USBLS	5/07
	Wichita MSA, KS	Y	61190 FQ	84070 MW	110930 TQ	USBLS	5/07
	Kentucky	Y	60627 FQ	76603 MW	95491 TQ	KYBLS	2008
	Lexington-Fayette MSA, KY	Y	58770 FQ	72030 MW	88120 TQ	USBLS	5/07
	Louisville-Jefferson County MSA, KY-IN	Y	60190 FQ	75010 MW	95860 TQ	USBLS	5/07
	Louisiana	H	26.95 FQ	34.13 MW	43.65 TQ	LABLS	1/08-3/08
	Baton Rouge MSA, LA	Y	62030 FQ	76430 MW	94020 TQ	USBLS	5/07
	New Orleans-Metairie-Kenner MSA, LA	Y	54240 FQ	68030 MW	84630 TQ	USBLS	5/07
	Maine	Y	56010 FQ	72560 MW	93880 TQ	USBLS	5/07
	Portland-South Portland-Biddeford MSA, ME	Y	59210 FQ	71530 MW	96740 TQ	USBLS	5/07
	Maryland	Y		87025 MW		MDBLS	3/08
	Baltimore-Towson MSA, MD	Y	66750 FQ	88060 MW	114010 TQ	USBLS	5/07
	Bethesda-Gaithersburg-Frederick PMSA, MD	Y	71340 FQ	94970 MW	116190 TQ	USBLS	5/07
	Cumberland MSA, MD-WV	Y	71670 FQ	87410 MW	113660 TQ	USBLS	5/07
	Massachusetts	Y	71910 FQ	89550 MW	113630 TQ	USBLS	5/07
	Boston-Cambridge-Quincy NECTA, MA	Y	74810 FQ	92920 MW	119090 TQ	USBLS	5/07
	Worcester MSA, MA-CT	Y	68130 FQ	84240 MW	107080 TQ	USBLS	5/07
	Michigan	Y	66800 FQ	87940 MW	114020 TQ	USBLS	5/07
	Detroit-Warren-Livonia MSA, MI	Y	74670 FQ	95460 MW	119420 TQ	USBLS	5/07
	Grand Rapids-Wyoming MSA, MI	Y	58760 FQ	73420 MW	92680 TQ	USBLS	5/07
	Lansing-East Lansing MSA, MI	Y	71360 FQ	91090 MW	115540 TQ	USBLS	5/07
	Warren-Troy-Farmington Hills PMSA, MI	Y	71370 FQ	92610 MW	116990 TQ	USBLS	5/07
	Minnesota	Y	67887 FQ	85247 MW	109958 TQ	MNBLS	10/08-12/08
	Duluth-Superior MSA, MN-WI	Y	52549 FQ	74299 MW	102638 TQ	MNBLS	10/08-12/08
	Minneapolis-Saint Paul MSA, MN-WI	Y	73423 FQ	93150 MW	120562 TQ	MNBLS	10/08-12/08
	Rochester MSA, MN	Y	69602 FQ	81571 MW	95651 TQ	MNBLS	10/08-12/08
	Mississippi	Y	53390 FQ	69320 MW	88190 TQ	USBLS	5/07
	Hattiesburg MSA, MS	Y	67750 FQ	78690 MW	106100 TQ	USBLS	5/07
	Jackson MSA, MS	Y	57840 FQ	71930 MW	92100 TQ	USBLS	5/07
	Missouri	Y	60440 FQ	80190 MW	102290 TQ	USBLS	5/07
	Kansas City MSA, MO-KS	Y	61130 FQ	80270 MW	106120 TQ	USBLS	5/07
	St. Louis MSA, MO-IL	Y	66500 FQ	84670 MW	107330 TQ	USBLS	5/07
	Montana	Y	55610 FQ	69670 MW	81950 TQ	USBLS	5/07
	Nebraska	Y	56680 FQ	71880 MW	93250 TQ	USBLS	5/07
	Omaha-Council Bluffs MSA, NE-IA	Y	56800 FQ	72110 MW	94760 TQ	USBLS	5/07
	Nevada	H	23.81 FQ	31.90 MW	44.24 TQ	NVBLS	5/08
	Las Vegas-Paradise MSA, NV	H	23.57 FQ	32.96 MW	47.23 TQ	NVBLS	5/08
	Reno-Sparks MSA, NV	H	24.20 FQ	32.11 MW	40.25 TQ	NVBLS	5/08
	New Hampshire	H	29.45 AE	41.81 MW	50.88 AEX	NHBLS	6/08
	Manchester MSA, NH	Y	70310 FQ	85960 MW	110890 TQ	USBLS	5/07
	Nashua NECTA, NH-MA	Y	77910 FQ	93360 MW	113330 TQ	USBLS	5/07
	New Jersey	Y	72230 FQ	91640 MW	119110 TQ	USBLS	5/07
	Atlantic City MSA, NJ	Y	50960 FQ	75350 MW	90420 TQ	USBLS	5/07
	Camden PMSA, NJ	Y	71890 FQ	91960 MW	115800 TQ	USBLS	5/07
	Edison PMSA, NJ	Y	72640 FQ	92430 MW	115690 TQ	USBLS	5/07
	Newark-Union PMSA, NJ-PA	Y	71390 FQ	90290 MW	120200 TQ	USBLS	5/07
	Vineland-Millville-Bridgeton MSA, NJ	Y	62510 FQ	76590 MW	93630 TQ	USBLS	5/07
	New Mexico	Y	51960 FQ	68960 MW	91420 TQ	USBLS	5/07
	Albuquerque MSA, NM	Y	54460 FQ	72520 MW	95110 TQ	USBLS	5/07

AE Average entry wage	**AW** Average wage paid	**FQ** First quartile wage	**LO** Lowest wage paid	**MTC** Median total compensation	**TCC** Total cash compensation
AER Average entry range	**AWR** Average wage range	**H** Hourly	**LR** Low end range	**MW** Median wage paid	**TQ** Third quartile wage
AEX Average experienced wage	**AXR** Average experienced range	**HI** Highest wage paid	**M** Monthly	**MWR** Median wage range	**W** Weekly
ATC Average total compensation	**D** Daily	**HR** High end range	**MCC** Median cash compensation	**S** See annotated source	**Y** Yearly

Occupation/Type/Industry	Location	Per	Low	Mid	High	Source	Date
Industrial Production Manager	New York	Y	68460 FQ	88140 MW	112550 TQ	USBLS	5/07
	Albany-Schenectady-Troy MSA, NY	Y	70030 FQ	85830 MW	118940 TQ	USBLS	5/07
	Binghamton MSA, NY	Y	52460 FQ	69090 MW	87180 TQ	USBLS	5/07
	Buffalo-Niagara Falls MSA, NY	Y	66680 FQ	87530 MW	111860 TQ	USBLS	5/07
	Nassau-Suffolk PMSA, NY	Y	77210 FQ	94040 MW	114720 TQ	USBLS	5/07
	New York-Northern New Jersey-Long Island MSA, NY-NJ-PA	Y	75190 FQ	94640 MW	121240 TQ	USBLS	5/07
	North Carolina	Y	57510 FQ	74150 MW	94340 TQ	USBLS	5/07
	Charlotte-Gastonia-Concord MSA, NC-SC	Y	55300 FQ	69220 MW	88580 TQ	USBLS	5/07
	Raleigh-Cary MSA, NC	Y	67800 FQ	88040 MW	113000 TQ	USBLS	5/07
	North Dakota	Y	50720 FQ	71220 MW	90090 TQ	USBLS	5/07
	Fargo MSA, ND-MN	Y	48080 FQ	71620 MW	91170 TQ	USBLS	5/07
	Ohio	Y	60740 FQ	76840 MW	101890 TQ	USBLS	5/07
	Cincinnati-Middletown MSA, OH-KY-IN	Y	63530 FQ	81960 MW	103280 TQ	USBLS	5/07
	Cleveland-Elyria-Mentor MSA, OH	Y	64400 FQ	79890 MW	105350 TQ	USBLS	5/07
	Columbus MSA, OH	Y	61300 FQ	76500 MW	96110 TQ	USBLS	5/07
	Dayton MSA, OH	Y	61460 FQ	79260 MW	109490 TQ	USBLS	5/07
	Oklahoma	Y	48610 FQ	65250 MW	85650 TQ	USBLS	5/07
	Oklahoma City MSA, OK	Y	38130 FQ	56230 MW	82820 TQ	USBLS	5/07
	Tulsa MSA, OK	Y	56260 FQ	74750 MW	95520 TQ	USBLS	5/07
	Oregon	H	29.87 FQ	37.94 MW	48.44 TQ	ORBLS	5/08
	Portland-Vancouver-Beaverton MSA, OR-WA	Y	63730 FQ	79200 MW	104830 TQ	USBLS	5/07
	Pennsylvania	Y	58480 FQ	76880 MW	99960 TQ	USBLS	5/07
	Allentown-Bethlehem-Easton MSA, PA-NJ	Y	63390 FQ	85260 MW	106640 TQ	USBLS	5/07
	Philadelphia-Camden-Wilmington MSA, PA-NJ-DE-MD	Y	70010 FQ	88540 MW	112560 TQ	USBLS	5/07
	Pittsburgh MSA, PA	Y	53840 FQ	70610 MW	96150 TQ	USBLS	5/07
	Rhode Island	Y	69410 FQ	82650 MW	101120 TQ	USBLS	5/07
	Providence-Fall River-Warwick MSA, RI-MA	Y	68530 FQ	82060 MW	100840 TQ	USBLS	5/07
	South Carolina	Y	65560 FQ	82540 MW	102740 TQ	USBLS	5/07
	Charleston-North Charleston MSA, SC	Y	66520 FQ	84740 MW	107940 TQ	USBLS	5/07
	Columbia MSA, SC	Y	63370 FQ	81760 MW	100430 TQ	USBLS	5/07
	South Dakota	Y	63720 FQ	76396 MW	94576 TQ	SDBLS	7/08-9/08
	Rapid City MSA, SD	Y	67269 FQ	82731 MW	94290 TQ	SDBLS	7/08-9/08
	Sioux Falls MSA, SD	Y	66107 FQ	76585 MW	92217 TQ	SDBLS	7/08-9/08
	Tennessee	Y	46480 FQ	64690 MW	86560 TQ	USBLS	5/07
	Memphis MSA, TN-MS-AR	Y	52080 FQ	69620 MW	90810 TQ	USBLS	5/07
	Nashville-Davidson-Murfreesboro MSA, TN	Y	50260 FQ	71010 MW	91900 TQ	USBLS	5/07
	Texas	Y	70690 FQ	91640 MW	119580 TQ	USBLS	5/07
	Austin-Round Rock MSA, TX	Y	77450 FQ	111160 MW	144860 TQ	USBLS	5/07
	Beaumont-Port Arthur MSA, TX	Y	68410 FQ	83790 MW	113490 TQ	USBLS	5/07
	Dallas-Fort Worth-Arlington MSA, TX	Y	70950 FQ	92450 MW	118860 TQ	USBLS	5/07
	El Paso MSA, TX	Y	64820 FQ	78390 MW	108030 TQ	USBLS	5/07
	Houston-Sugar Land-Baytown MSA, TX	Y	77210 FQ	98350 MW	125040 TQ	USBLS	5/07
	San Antonio MSA, TX	Y	69430 FQ	86980 MW	104860 TQ	USBLS	5/07
	Utah	Y	61950 FQ	77990 MW	103410 TQ	USBLS	5/07
	Salt Lake City MSA, UT	Y	68430 FQ	87020 MW	112580 TQ	USBLS	5/07
	Vermont	Y	63590 FQ	81840 MW	109150 TQ	USBLS	5/07
	Burlington-South Burlington MSA, VT	Y	67240 FQ	83430 MW	112330 TQ	USBLS	5/07
	Virginia	Y	64520 FQ	81850 MW	110020 TQ	USBLS	5/07
	Richmond MSA, VA	Y	69290 FQ	85240 MW	119090 TQ	USBLS	5/07
	Virginia Beach-Norfolk-Newport News MSA, VA-NC	Y	69580 FQ	86900 MW	108920 TQ	USBLS	5/07
	Washington	H	34.32 FQ	44.88 MW	58.22 TQ	WABLS	3/08
	Seattle-Tacoma-Bellevue MSA, WA	Y	77960 FQ	97270 MW	123650 TQ	USBLS	5/07

AE	Average entry wage	AW	Average wage paid	FQ	First quartile wage
AER	Average entry range	AWR	Average wage range	H	Hourly
AEX	Average experienced wage	AXR	Average experienced range	HI	Highest wage paid
ATC	Average total compensation	D	Daily	HR	High end range

LO	Lowest wage paid	MTC	Median total compensation	TCC	Total cash compensation
LR	Low end range	MW	Median wage paid	TQ	Third quartile wage
M	Monthly	MWR	Median wage range	W	Weekly
MCC	Median cash compensation	S	See annotated source	Y	Yearly

Occupation/Type/Industry	Location	Per	Low	Mid	High	Source	Date
Industrial Production Manager	West Virginia	Y	53383 FQ	72346 MW	97507 TQ	WVBLS	7/08-9/08
	Charleston MSA, WV	Y	60930 FQ	79440 MW	102910 TQ	USBLS	5/07
	Wheeling MSA, WV-OH	Y	47710 FQ	61070 MW	88030 TQ	USBLS	5/07
	Wisconsin	Y	58610 FQ	74070 MW	94020 TQ	USBLS	5/07
	Milwaukee-Waukesha-West Allis MSA, WI	Y	64500 FQ	78140 MW	96910 TQ	USBLS	5/07
	Wyoming	Y	60648 FQ	90061 MW	115111 TQ	WYBLS	9/08
	Puerto Rico	Y	59260 FQ	82230 MW	104660 TQ	USBLS	5/07
	Aguadilla-Isabela-San Sebastian MSA, PR	Y	59480 FQ	79630 MW	100560 TQ	USBLS	5/07
	San Juan-Caguas-Guaynabo MSA, PR	Y	54500 FQ	81780 MW	105790 TQ	USBLS	5/07
Industrial Reemployment Specialist	Ohio	H	24.90 LO		34.83 HI	ODAS	2008
Industrial Rehabilitation Nurse	Ohio	H	22.60 LO		31.62 HI	ODAS	2008
Industrial Rehabilitation Work Simulator	Ohio	H	20.71 LO		26.11 HI	ODAS	2008
Industrial Safety Inspector	Ohio	H	17.22 LO		21.77 HI	ODAS	2008
Industrial Truck and Tractor Operator	Alabama	Y	21350 FQ	25590 MW	31250 TQ	USBLS	5/07
	Birmingham-Hoover MSA, AL	Y	23130 FQ	27970 MW	32840 TQ	USBLS	5/07
	Alaska	Y	24180 FQ	33390 MW	42730 TQ	USBLS	5/07
	Anchorage MSA, AK	Y	29050 FQ	36880 MW	45790 TQ	USBLS	5/07
	Arizona	Y	22540 FQ	27430 MW	33000 TQ	USBLS	5/07
	Phoenix-Mesa-Scottsdale MSA, AZ	Y	22710 FQ	27290 MW	32240 TQ	USBLS	5/07
	Prescott MSA, AZ	Y	30210 FQ	39200 MW	45500 TQ	USBLS	5/07
	Tucson MSA, AZ	Y	22800 FQ	27660 MW	33760 TQ	USBLS	5/07
	Arkansas	Y	21530 FQ	25400 MW	30150 TQ	USBLS	5/07
	Little Rock-North Little Rock MSA, AR	Y	21760 FQ	26390 MW	33150 TQ	USBLS	5/07
	California	H	11.78 FQ	14.94 MW	19.83 TQ	CABLS	1/08-3/08
	Los Angeles-Long Beach-Glendale PMSA, CA	H	11.69 FQ	15.16 MW	22.00 TQ	CABLS	1/08-3/08
	Oakland-Fremont-Hayward MSA, CA	H	13.74 FQ	17.95 MW	23.24 TQ	CABLS	1/08-3/08
	Riverside-San Bernardino-Ontario MSA, CA	H	11.54 FQ	13.94 MW	17.73 TQ	CABLS	1/08-3/08
	Sacramento-Arden Arcade-Roseville MSA, CA	H	12.35 FQ	14.72 MW	18.84 TQ	CABLS	1/08-3/08
	San Diego-Carlsbad-San Marcos MSA, CA	H	11.64 FQ	14.85 MW	20.43 TQ	CABLS	1/08-3/08
	San Francisco-San Mateo-Redwood PMSA, CA	H	13.37 FQ	17.27 MW	21.76 TQ	CABLS	1/08-3/08
	San Jose-Sunnyvale-Santa Clara MSA, CA	H	12.50 FQ	15.30 MW	19.39 TQ	CABLS	1/08-3/08
	Santa Ana-Anaheim-Irvine PMSA, CA	Y	24860 FQ	29960 MW	39300 TQ	USBLS	5/07
	Stockton MSA, CA	H	12.50 FQ	15.62 MW	18.89 TQ	CABLS	1/08-3/08
	Colorado	Y	23950 FQ	28910 MW	34930 TQ	USBLS	5/07
	Denver-Aurora MSA, CO	Y	25120 FQ	29860 MW	36000 TQ	USBLS	5/07
	Connecticut	H	11.33 AE	14.56 MW		CTBLS	1/08-3/08
	Bridgeport-Stamford-Norwalk MSA, CT	Y	25250 FQ	32000 MW	38080 TQ	USBLS	5/07
	Danbury MSA, CT	Y	25920 FQ	29960 MW	35680 TQ	USBLS	5/07
	Hartford-West Hartford-East Hartford MSA, CT	Y	25580 FQ	30580 MW	37360 TQ	USBLS	5/07
	Delaware	Y	23370 FQ	28030 MW	32830 TQ	USBLS	5/07
	Wilmington PMSA, DE-MD-NJ	Y	22970 FQ	26950 MW	31810 TQ	USBLS	5/07
	District of Columbia	Y	23310 FQ	32390 MW	38490 TQ	USBLS	5/07
	Washington-Arlington-Alexandria MSA, DC-VA-MD-WV	Y	24950 FQ	30560 MW	40220 TQ	USBLS	5/07
	Florida	Y	21450 FQ	25280 MW	31170 TQ	USBLS	5/07

AE Average entry wage	**AW** Average wage paid	**FQ** First quartile wage	**LO** Lowest wage paid	**MTC** Median total compensation	**TCC** Total cash compensation
AER Average entry range	**AWR** Average wage range	**H** Hourly	**LR** Low end range	**MW** Median wage paid	**TQ** Third quartile wage
AEX Average experienced wage	**AXR** Average experienced range	**HI** Highest wage paid	**M** Monthly	**MWR** Median wage range	**W** Weekly
ATC Average total compensation	**D** Daily	**HR** High end range	**MCC** Median cash compensation	**S** See annotated source	**Y** Yearly

Industrial Truck and Tractor Operator

Occupation/Type/Industry	Location	Per	Low	Mid	High	Source	Date
	Fort Lauderdale-Pompano Beach-Deerfield Beach PMSA, FL	Y	21600 FQ	24860 MW	31980 TQ	USBLS	5/07
	Jacksonville MSA, FL	Y	21960 FQ	25800 MW	32270 TQ	USBLS	5/07
	Miami-Fort Lauderdale-Miami Beach MSA, FL	Y	21680 FQ	25660 MW	33050 TQ	USBLS	5/07
	Orlando-Kissimmee MSA, FL	Y	22130 FQ	26160 MW	31810 TQ	USBLS	5/07
	Tampa-St. Petersburg-Clearwater MSA, FL	Y	20530 FQ	24550 MW	29990 TQ	USBLS	5/07
	West Palm Beach-Boca Raton-Boynton Beach PMSA, FL	Y	22660 FQ	26800 MW	31470 TQ	USBLS	5/07
	Georgia	Y	21680 FQ	25680 MW	30350 TQ	USBLS	5/07
	Atlanta-Sandy Springs-Marietta MSA, GA	Y	21740 FQ	25810 MW	30910 TQ	USBLS	5/07
	Hawaii	Y	25620 FQ	33250 MW	44800 TQ	USBLS	5/07
	Honolulu MSA, HI	Y	24310 FQ	31370 MW	44930 TQ	USBLS	5/07
	Idaho	Y	20420 FQ	25440 MW	30200 TQ	USBLS	5/07
	Boise City-Nampa MSA, ID	Y	21160 FQ	25200 MW	30060 TQ	USBLS	5/07
	Idaho Falls MSA, ID	Y	15220 FQ	20660 MW	25300 TQ	USBLS	5/07
	Lewiston MSA, ID-WA	Y	21620 FQ	26400 MW	30220 TQ	USBLS	5/07
	Illinois	Y	24140 FQ	29740 MW	37850 TQ	USBLS	5/07
	Champaign-Urbana MSA, IL	Y	25160 FQ	28150 MW	33130 TQ	USBLS	5/07
	Chicago-Naperville-Joliet MSA, IL-IN-WI	Y	24610 FQ	31170 MW	41430 TQ	USBLS	5/07
	Rockford MSA, IL	Y	22370 FQ	27230 MW	32580 TQ	USBLS	5/07
	Indiana	Y	24540 FQ	29410 MW	36400 TQ	USBLS	5/07
	Gary PMSA, IN	Y	31580 FQ	39420 MW	50480 TQ	USBLS	5/07
	Indianapolis-Carmel MSA, IN	Y	23660 FQ	27490 MW	32920 TQ	USBLS	5/07
	Iowa	Y	23350 FQ	27900 MW	33360 TQ	USBLS	5/07
	Des Moines-West Des Moines MSA, IA	Y	24750 FQ	29150 MW	34480 TQ	USBLS	5/07
	Kansas	Y	23270 FQ	27290 MW	32160 TQ	USBLS	5/07
	Wichita MSA, KS	Y	22050 FQ	26220 MW	31490 TQ	USBLS	5/07
	Kentucky	Y	22483 FQ	26394 MW	32527 TQ	KYBLS	2008
	Lexington-Fayette MSA, KY	Y	22240 FQ	26890 MW	35390 TQ	USBLS	5/07
	Louisville-Jefferson County MSA, KY-IN	Y	21750 FQ	24530 MW	30020 TQ	USBLS	5/07
	Louisiana	H	10.41 FQ	12.86 MW	15.36 TQ	LABLS	1/08-3/08
	Baton Rouge MSA, LA	Y	22020 FQ	26840 MW	30850 TQ	USBLS	5/07
	New Orleans-Metairie-Kenner MSA, LA	Y	21580 FQ	26760 MW	31730 TQ	USBLS	5/07
	Maine	Y	22650 FQ	26160 MW	32090 TQ	USBLS	5/07
	Lewiston-Auburn MSA, ME	Y	22480 FQ	25380 MW	31910 TQ	USBLS	5/07
	Portland-South Portland-Biddeford MSA, ME	Y	22630 FQ	25590 MW	33200 TQ	USBLS	5/07
	Maryland	Y		30350 MW		MDBLS	3/08
	Baltimore-Towson MSA, MD	Y	26050 FQ	30980 MW	37700 TQ	USBLS	5/07
	Bethesda-Gaithersburg-Frederick PMSA, MD	Y	23450 FQ	28340 MW	33230 TQ	USBLS	5/07
	Massachusetts	Y	25840 FQ	32270 MW	38110 TQ	USBLS	5/07
	Boston-Cambridge-Quincy NECTA, MA	Y	27010 FQ	33220 MW	38070 TQ	USBLS	5/07
	New Bedford MSA, MA	Y	22130 FQ	29100 MW	36220 TQ	USBLS	5/07
	Worcester MSA, MA-CT	Y	24980 FQ	29760 MW	36870 TQ	USBLS	5/07
	Michigan	Y	26380 FQ	33400 MW	49190 TQ	USBLS	5/07
	Detroit-Warren-Livonia MSA, MI	Y	28340 FQ	38090 MW	54160 TQ	USBLS	5/07
	Grand Rapids-Wyoming MSA, MI	Y	25680 FQ	30380 MW	38720 TQ	USBLS	5/07
	Warren-Troy-Farmington Hills PMSA, MI	Y	28580 FQ	40310 MW	56350 TQ	USBLS	5/07
	Minnesota	Y	27631 FQ	33915 MW	41291 TQ	MNBLS	10/08-12/08
	Duluth-Superior MSA, MN-WI	Y	29389 FQ	35642 MW	40885 TQ	MNBLS	10/08-12/08
	Minneapolis-Saint Paul MSA, MN-WI	Y	29608 FQ	36620 MW	43413 TQ	MNBLS	10/08-12/08
	Rochester MSA, MN	Y	23451 FQ	27331 MW	33871 TQ	MNBLS	10/08-12/08
	Mississippi	Y	21000 FQ	24440 MW	28530 TQ	USBLS	5/07
	Jackson MSA, MS	Y	21450 FQ	24630 MW	28720 TQ	USBLS	5/07
	Missouri	Y	22030 FQ	26960 MW	32710 TQ	USBLS	5/07
	Joplin MSA, MO	Y	19460 FQ	23690 MW	28980 TQ	USBLS	5/07
	Kansas City MSA, MO-KS	Y	24740 FQ	28680 MW	34320 TQ	USBLS	5/07

AE	Average entry wage	AW	Average wage paid	FQ	First quartile wage	LO	Lowest wage paid	MTC	Median total compensation	TCC	Total cash compensation
AER	Average entry range	AWR	Average wage range	H	Hourly	LR	Low end range	MW	Median wage paid	TQ	Third quartile wage
AEX	Average experienced wage	AXR	Average experienced range	HI	Highest wage paid	M	Monthly	MWR	Median wage range	W	Weekly
ATC	Average total compensation	D	Daily	HR	High end range	MCC	Median cash compensation	S	See annotated source	Y	Yearly

Industrial Truck and Tractor Operator

Occupation/Type/Industry	Location	Per	Low	Mid	High	Source	Date
	St. Louis MSA, MO-IL	Y	22960 FQ	28350 MW	34560 TQ	USBLS	5/07
	Montana	Y	24960 FQ	29780 MW	34750 TQ	USBLS	5/07
	Billings MSA, MT	Y	26010 FQ	29780 MW	34190 TQ	USBLS	5/07
	Nebraska	Y	23770 FQ	28300 MW	34170 TQ	USBLS	5/07
	Omaha-Council Bluffs MSA, NE-IA	Y	23440 FQ	28280 MW	34400 TQ	USBLS	5/07
	Nevada	H	12.11 FQ	14.52 MW	17.62 TQ	NVBLS	5/08
	Las Vegas-Paradise MSA, NV	H	12.25 FQ	14.61 MW	17.87 TQ	NVBLS	5/08
	Reno-Sparks MSA, NV	H	11.88 FQ	14.37 MW	17.12 TQ	NVBLS	5/08
	New Hampshire	H	11.57 AE	14.57 MW	16.27 AEX	NHBLS	6/08
	Manchester MSA, NH	Y	26620 FQ	30120 MW	34800 TQ	USBLS	5/07
	Nashua NECTA, NH-MA	Y	26700 FQ	30450 MW	34580 TQ	USBLS	5/07
	New Jersey	Y	24220 FQ	30280 MW	37260 TQ	USBLS	5/07
	Camden PMSA, NJ	Y	24580 FQ	30630 MW	36750 TQ	USBLS	5/07
	Edison PMSA, NJ	Y	25260 FQ	31350 MW	39130 TQ	USBLS	5/07
	Newark-Union PMSA, NJ-PA	Y	23900 FQ	30210 MW	38260 TQ	USBLS	5/07
	New Mexico	Y	20680 FQ	24820 MW	29340 TQ	USBLS	5/07
	Albuquerque MSA, NM	Y	22130 FQ	25830 MW	29590 TQ	USBLS	5/07
	New York	Y	24470 FQ	31040 MW	39070 TQ	USBLS	5/07
	Albany-Schenectady-Troy MSA, NY	Y	28310 FQ	34930 MW	42170 TQ	USBLS	5/07
	Buffalo-Niagara Falls MSA, NY	Y	25890 FQ	34270 MW	47470 TQ	USBLS	5/07
	Glens Falls MSA, NY	Y	31170 FQ	35220 MW	38640 TQ	USBLS	5/07
	Nassau-Suffolk PMSA, NY	Y	22570 FQ	28080 MW	37390 TQ	USBLS	5/07
	New York-Northern New Jersey-Long Island MSA, NY-NJ-PA	Y	24180 FQ	30830 MW	39230 TQ	USBLS	5/07
	Utica-Rome MSA, NY	Y	29870 FQ	33980 MW	36940 TQ	USBLS	5/07
	North Carolina	Y	21600 FQ	25800 MW	30840 TQ	USBLS	5/07
	Charlotte-Gastonia-Concord MSA, NC-SC	Y	22830 FQ	26980 MW	31720 TQ	USBLS	5/07
	Raleigh-Cary MSA, NC	Y	21660 FQ	25250 MW	30900 TQ	USBLS	5/07
	North Dakota	Y	24560 FQ	29060 MW	35240 TQ	USBLS	5/07
	Bismarck MSA, ND	Y	30570 FQ	35680 MW	44380 TQ	USBLS	5/07
	Fargo MSA, ND-MN	Y	23740 FQ	28730 MW	34000 TQ	USBLS	5/07
	Ohio	Y	23950 FQ	28550 MW	34420 TQ	USBLS	5/07
	Cincinnati-Middletown MSA, OH-KY-IN	Y	25430 FQ	29480 MW	34920 TQ	USBLS	5/07
	Cleveland-Elyria-Mentor MSA, OH	Y	25060 FQ	29460 MW	35050 TQ	USBLS	5/07
	Columbus MSA, OH	Y	22900 FQ	27100 MW	32060 TQ	USBLS	5/07
	Dayton MSA, OH	Y	24050 FQ	29070 MW	35450 TQ	USBLS	5/07
	Oklahoma	Y	21120 FQ	24470 MW	30360 TQ	USBLS	5/07
	Oklahoma City MSA, OK	Y	21700 FQ	24870 MW	30790 TQ	USBLS	5/07
	Tulsa MSA, OK	Y	21830 FQ	24700 MW	30770 TQ	USBLS	5/07
	Oregon	H	12.09 FQ	14.79 MW	18.14 TQ	ORBLS	5/08
	Portland-Vancouver-Beaverton MSA, OR-WA	Y	25290 FQ	31370 MW	39570 TQ	USBLS	5/07
	Pennsylvania	Y	24930 FQ	29720 MW	35920 TQ	USBLS	5/07
	Allentown-Bethlehem-Easton MSA, PA-NJ	Y	27630 FQ	32180 MW	36480 TQ	USBLS	5/07
	Philadelphia-Camden-Wilmington MSA, PA-NJ-DE-MD	Y	25090 FQ	30780 MW	37760 TQ	USBLS	5/07
	Pittsburgh MSA, PA	Y	23700 FQ	29950 MW	37000 TQ	USBLS	5/07
	Rhode Island	Y	24580 FQ	29660 MW	36480 TQ	USBLS	5/07
	Providence-Fall River-Warwick MSA, RI-MA	Y	24350 FQ	29400 MW	36860 TQ	USBLS	5/07
	South Carolina	Y	22250 FQ	26830 MW	31560 TQ	USBLS	5/07
	Charleston-North Charleston MSA, SC	Y	23570 FQ	29420 MW	42220 TQ	USBLS	5/07
	Columbia MSA, SC	Y	23000 FQ	27930 MW	33360 TQ	USBLS	5/07
	South Dakota	Y	23962 FQ	27192 MW	30606 TQ	SDBLS	7/08-9/08
	Sioux Falls MSA, SD	Y	24321 FQ	27349 MW	30426 TQ	SDBLS	7/08-9/08
	Tennessee	Y	22490 FQ	26940 MW	31910 TQ	USBLS	5/07
	Johnson City MSA, TN	Y	14160 FQ	20770 MW	27930 TQ	USBLS	5/07
	Memphis MSA, TN-MS-AR	Y	22440 FQ	26400 MW	30690 TQ	USBLS	5/07
	Nashville-Davidson-Murfreesboro MSA, TN	Y	23330 FQ	27620 MW	33160 TQ	USBLS	5/07
	Texas	Y	19890 FQ	23870 MW	29220 TQ	USBLS	5/07

AE	Average entry wage	AW	Average wage paid	FQ	First quartile wage
AER	Average entry range	AWR	Average wage range	H	Hourly
AEX	Average experienced wage	AXR	Average experienced range	HI	Highest wage paid
ATC	Average total compensation	D	Daily	HR	High end range

LO	Lowest wage paid	MTC	Median total compensation
LR	Low end range	MW	Median wage paid
M	Monthly	MWR	Median wage range
MCC	Median cash compensation	S	See annotated source

TCC	Total cash compensation		
TQ	Third quartile wage		
W	Weekly		
Y	Yearly		

Occupation/Type/Industry	Location	Per	Low	Mid	High	Source	Date
Industrial Truck and Tractor Operator	Austin-Round Rock MSA, TX	Y	20840 FQ	23870 MW	28650 TQ	USBLS	5/07
	Dallas-Fort Worth-Arlington MSA, TX	Y	21190 FQ	24820 MW	30140 TQ	USBLS	5/07
	El Paso MSA, TX	Y	14560 FQ	17930 MW	22300 TQ	USBLS	5/07
	Houston-Sugar Land-Baytown MSA, TX	Y	21180 FQ	24970 MW	30160 TQ	USBLS	5/07
	San Antonio MSA, TX	Y	19650 FQ	23000 MW	27730 TQ	USBLS	5/07
	Utah	Y	23080 FQ	27400 MW	32760 TQ	USBLS	5/07
	Provo-Orem MSA, UT	Y	22140 FQ	26770 MW	32140 TQ	USBLS	5/07
	St. George MSA, UT	Y	27280 FQ	30920 MW	36030 TQ	USBLS	5/07
	Salt Lake City MSA, UT	Y	23850 FQ	28350 MW	33810 TQ	USBLS	5/07
	Vermont	Y	22590 FQ	26960 MW	33110 TQ	USBLS	5/07
	Burlington-South Burlington MSA, VT	Y	23810 FQ	27610 MW	33980 TQ	USBLS	5/07
	Virginia	Y	22000 FQ	26420 MW	31380 TQ	USBLS	5/07
	Richmond MSA, VA	Y	22930 FQ	26950 MW	32550 TQ	USBLS	5/07
	Virginia Beach-Norfolk-Newport News MSA, VA-NC	Y	21500 FQ	25160 MW	29470 TQ	USBLS	5/07
	Washington	H	12.43 FQ	15.60 MW	19.77 TQ	WABLS	3/08
	Seattle-Tacoma-Bellevue MSA, WA	Y	27540 FQ	34820 MW	44490 TQ	USBLS	5/07
	West Virginia	Y	21386 FQ	27189 MW	36187 TQ	WVBLS	7/08-9/08
	Charleston MSA, WV	Y	23690 FQ	34310 MW	45680 TQ	USBLS	5/07
	Huntington-Ashland MSA, WV-KY-OH	Y	20470 FQ	26430 MW	34360 TQ	USBLS	5/07
	Wisconsin	Y	25560 FQ	30070 MW	35880 TQ	USBLS	5/07
	Milwaukee-Waukesha-West Allis MSA, WI	Y	25970 FQ	31530 MW	37650 TQ	USBLS	5/07
	Wyoming	Y	27053 FQ	31701 MW	37578 TQ	WYBLS	9/08
	Cheyenne MSA, WY	Y	24199 FQ	28473 MW	32856 TQ	WYBLS	9/08
	Puerto Rico	Y	13860 FQ	16740 MW	20630 TQ	USBLS	5/07
	San Juan-Caguas-Guaynabo MSA, PR	Y	13920 FQ	16870 MW	21030 TQ	USBLS	5/07
	Virgin Islands	Y	21400 FQ	25760 MW	31450 TQ	USBLS	5/07
	Guam	Y	17460 FQ	23120 MW	31070 TQ	USBLS	5/07
Industrial Waste Inspector	Cincinnati, OH	Y	44936 LO		50908 HI	COHSS	10/08
Infectious Disease Control Consultant	Ohio	H	24.90 LO		34.83 HI	ODAS	2008
Information Architect	Midwest	Y		89855 AW		IAI	6/07-10/07
	Northeast	Y		101996 AW		IAI	6/07-10/07
	South	Y		81406 AW		IAI	6/07-10/07
	West	Y		98310 AW		IAI	6/07-10/07
Information Security Architect Public Schools	Wake County, NC	Y		114717 MW		WCPS02	2008-2009
Information Security Manager	United States	Y		95807 AW		COWRLD1	5/20/08-7/25/08
Information Systems Auditor Local Government	United States	Y	55000-58237 LR		72849-85837 HR	GOVAUD	2008
Municipal Government	Colorado Springs, CO	M	5168 LO			COSPRS	1/1/09
Information Technology Engineer Computer Crimes, Sheriff's Department Crime Lab	San Diego County, CA	W	5451 LO		6642 HI	CAC	2006-2007
Information Technology Generalist	United States	Y		47800 MW		CNNM02	2007
Information Technology Infrastructure Support Manager Wayne County Airport Authority	Wayne County, MI	Y			102529 HI	FREEP06	2006
Information Technology Manager Municipal Government	Cincinnati, OH	Y	75782 LO		102305 HI	COHSS	10/08

AE	Average entry wage	AW	Average wage paid	FQ	First quartile wage	LO	Lowest wage paid	MTC	Median total compensation	TCC	Total cash compensation
AER	Average entry range	AWR	Average wage range	H	Hourly	LR	Low end range	MW	Median wage paid	TQ	Third quartile wage
AEX	Average experienced wage	AXR	Average experienced range	HI	Highest wage paid	M	Monthly	MWR	Median wage range	W	Weekly
ATC	Average total compensation	D	Daily	HR	High end range	MCC	Median cash compensation	S	See annotated source	Y	Yearly

Occupation/Type/Industry	Location	Per	Low	Mid	High	Source	Date
Information Technology Professional							
Cisco Certified Design Professional Certification	United States	Y		103800 AW		GLKNO1	10/20/08-11/11/08
Extranets	United States	Y		86286 AW		MCP	2008
Project Management Professional Certification	United States	Y		103100 AW		GLKNO1	10/20/08-11/11/08
Routers and Switches	United States	Y		75789 AW		MCP	2008
Web Services	United States	Y		83454 AW		MCP	2008
Wireless/Mobile Computing	United States	Y		76988 AW		MCP	2008
Information Technology Worker	Silicon Valley, CA	Y		97259 AW		WSJO01	2008
Information Writer							
State Government	Ohio	H	15.62 LO		21.77 HI	ODAS	2008
Inspector, Tester, Sorter, Sampler, and Weigher	Alabama	Y	19330 FQ	24670 MW	33950 TQ	USBLS	5/07
	Birmingham-Hoover MSA, AL	Y	19450 FQ	27790 MW	36850 TQ	USBLS	5/07
	Alaska	Y	30960 FQ	55330 MW	68740 TQ	USBLS	5/07
	Anchorage MSA, AK	Y	28840 FQ	41310 MW	60770 TQ	USBLS	5/07
	Arizona	Y	22240 FQ	29060 MW	37670 TQ	USBLS	5/07
	Phoenix-Mesa-Scottsdale MSA, AZ	Y	22190 FQ	28940 MW	37030 TQ	USBLS	5/07
	Tucson MSA, AZ	Y	24950 FQ	30970 MW	42520 TQ	USBLS	5/07
	Arkansas	Y	21950 FQ	27150 MW	34070 TQ	USBLS	5/07
	Fort Smith MSA, AR-OK	Y	21110 FQ	25320 MW	36140 TQ	USBLS	5/07
	Little Rock-North Little Rock MSA, AR	Y	21640 FQ	29760 MW	37510 TQ	USBLS	5/07
	Pine Bluff MSA, AR	Y	22710 FQ	27310 MW	31810 TQ	USBLS	5/07
	California	H	11.31 FQ	15.20 MW	20.54 TQ	CABLS	1/08-3/08
	Los Angeles-Long Beach-Glendale PMSA, CA	H	9.68 FQ	13.89 MW	19.74 TQ	CABLS	1/08-3/08
	Oakland-Fremont-Hayward MSA, CA	H	13.20 FQ	17.22 MW	23.00 TQ	CABLS	1/08-3/08
	Riverside-San Bernardino-Ontario MSA, CA	H	11.48 FQ	15.00 MW	18.98 TQ	CABLS	1/08-3/08
	Sacramento-Arden Arcade-Roseville MSA, CA	H	11.80 FQ	14.16 MW	20.63 TQ	CABLS	1/08-3/08
	San Diego-Carlsbad-San Marcos MSA, CA	H	12.51 FQ	15.95 MW	20.59 TQ	CABLS	1/08-3/08
	San Francisco-San Mateo-Redwood PMSA, CA	H	12.46 FQ	17.24 MW	23.14 TQ	CABLS	1/08-3/08
	San Jose-Sunnyvale-Santa Clara MSA, CA	H	14.16 FQ	17.68 MW	22.20 TQ	CABLS	1/08-3/08
	Santa Ana-Anaheim-Irvine PMSA, CA	Y	22730 FQ	29840 MW	39010 TQ	USBLS	5/07
	Colorado	Y	26600 FQ	33060 MW	41910 TQ	USBLS	5/07
	Denver-Aurora MSA, CO	Y	27350 FQ	33650 MW	42510 TQ	USBLS	5/07
	Connecticut	H	12.18 AE	17.78 MW		CTBLS	1/08-3/08
	Bridgeport-Stamford-Norwalk MSA, CT	Y	26920 FQ	36660 MW	43910 TQ	USBLS	5/07
	Hartford-West Hartford-East Hartford MSA, CT	Y	29410 FQ	37260 MW	46210 TQ	USBLS	5/07
	Delaware	Y	23300 FQ	30250 MW	39200 TQ	USBLS	5/07
	Dover MSA, DE	Y	31010 FQ	37090 MW	44980 TQ	USBLS	5/07
	Wilmington PMSA, DE-MD-NJ	Y	28230 FQ	35600 MW	45620 TQ	USBLS	5/07
	District of Columbia	Y	40460 FQ	44600 MW	48760 TQ	USBLS	5/07
	Washington-Arlington-Alexandria MSA, DC-VA-MD-WV	Y	29710 FQ	39850 MW	50720 TQ	USBLS	5/07
	Florida	Y	21360 FQ	27580 MW	36030 TQ	USBLS	5/07
	Fort Lauderdale-Pompano Beach-Deerfield Beach PMSA, FL	Y	21730 FQ	28100 MW	36700 TQ	USBLS	5/07
	Jacksonville MSA, FL	Y	25080 FQ	32880 MW	42500 TQ	USBLS	5/07
	Lakeland MSA, FL	Y	21270 FQ	26150 MW	32700 TQ	USBLS	5/07
	Miami-Fort Lauderdale-Miami Beach MSA, FL	Y	17330 FQ	25100 MW	33560 TQ	USBLS	5/07
	Orlando-Kissimmee MSA, FL	Y	22060 FQ	27290 MW	34970 TQ	USBLS	5/07

Occupation/Type/Industry	Location	Per	Low	Mid	High	Source	Date
Inspector, Tester, Sorter, Sampler, and Weigher							
	Sarasota-Bradenton-Venice MSA, FL	Y	24050 FQ	29030 MW	34480 TQ	USBLS	5/07
	Tampa-St. Petersburg-Clearwater MSA, FL	Y	21290 FQ	25960 MW	31450 TQ	USBLS	5/07
	West Palm Beach-Boca Raton-Boynton Beach PMSA, FL	Y	22390 FQ	27130 MW	36230 TQ	USBLS	5/07
	Georgia	Y	22260 FQ	27660 MW	34550 TQ	USBLS	5/07
	Atlanta-Sandy Springs-Marietta MSA, GA	Y	22050 FQ	27550 MW	34170 TQ	USBLS	5/07
	Augusta-Richmond County MSA, GA-SC	Y	21200 FQ	27700 MW	35000 TQ	USBLS	5/07
	Idaho	Y	19550 FQ	25120 MW	31700 TQ	USBLS	5/07
	Boise City-Nampa MSA, ID	Y	18540 FQ	24550 MW	30740 TQ	USBLS	5/07
	Coeur d'Alene MSA, ID	Y	16950 FQ	18880 MW	24760 TQ	USBLS	5/07
	Illinois	Y	22960 FQ	29900 MW	38810 TQ	USBLS	5/07
	Chicago-Naperville-Joliet MSA, IL-IN-WI	Y	23220 FQ	30650 MW	39000 TQ	USBLS	5/07
	Indiana	Y	23640 FQ	30540 MW	39220 TQ	USBLS	5/07
	Gary PMSA, IN	Y	33250 FQ	36840 MW	40330 TQ	USBLS	5/07
	Indianapolis-Carmel MSA, IN	Y	23300 FQ	32310 MW	47780 TQ	USBLS	5/07
	Iowa	Y	24860 FQ	31150 MW	38080 TQ	USBLS	5/07
	Des Moines-West Des Moines MSA, IA	Y	21230 FQ	29060 MW	39120 TQ	USBLS	5/07
	Kansas	Y	26220 FQ	33040 MW	45730 TQ	USBLS	5/07
	Wichita MSA, KS	Y	32340 FQ	45460 MW	53140 TQ	USBLS	5/07
	Kentucky	Y	22561 FQ	28477 MW	36246 TQ	KYBLS	2008
	Bowling Green MSA, KY	Y	20380 FQ	24810 MW	33800 TQ	USBLS	5/07
	Louisville-Jefferson County MSA, KY-IN	Y	21620 FQ	26810 MW	35750 TQ	USBLS	5/07
	Louisiana	H	11.64 FQ	16.29 MW	22.00 TQ	LABLS	1/08-3/08
	Baton Rouge MSA, LA	Y	29860 FQ	36690 MW	43780 TQ	USBLS	5/07
	New Orleans-Metairie-Kenner MSA, LA	Y	25010 FQ	36450 MW	48940 TQ	USBLS	5/07
	Maine	Y	22620 FQ	29700 MW	40300 TQ	USBLS	5/07
	Portland-South Portland-Biddeford MSA, ME	Y	22310 FQ	27310 MW	34110 TQ	USBLS	5/07
	Maryland	Y		36700 MW		MDBLS	3/08
	Baltimore-Towson MSA, MD	Y	20960 FQ	35520 MW	45800 TQ	USBLS	5/07
	Bethesda-Gaithersburg-Frederick PMSA, MD	Y	31490 FQ	37560 MW	46360 TQ	USBLS	5/07
	Cumberland MSA, MD-WV	Y	26430 FQ	32830 MW	41350 TQ	USBLS	5/07
	Hagerstown-Martinsburg MSA, MD-WV	Y	29080 FQ	32900 MW	37350 TQ	USBLS	5/07
	Massachusetts	Y	27760 FQ	35640 MW	46700 TQ	USBLS	5/07
	Boston-Cambridge-Quincy NECTA, MA	Y	31300 FQ	40260 MW	51240 TQ	USBLS	5/07
	Springfield MSA, MA-CT	Y	27810 FQ	33390 MW	41950 TQ	USBLS	5/07
	Worcester MSA, MA-CT	Y	28690 FQ	36840 MW	45760 TQ	USBLS	5/07
	Michigan	Y	24190 FQ	32990 MW	50880 TQ	USBLS	5/07
	Ann Arbor MSA, MI	Y	41160 FQ	55390 MW	61090 TQ	USBLS	5/07
	Detroit-Warren-Livonia MSA, MI	Y	24810 FQ	36060 MW	54720 TQ	USBLS	5/07
	Grand Rapids-Wyoming MSA, MI	Y	19890 FQ	25530 MW	33090 TQ	USBLS	5/07
	Warren-Troy-Farmington Hills PMSA, MI	Y	26830 FQ	38190 MW	55330 TQ	USBLS	5/07
	Minnesota	Y	27171 FQ	33609 MW	40285 TQ	MNBLS	10/08-12/08
	Duluth-Superior MSA, MN-WI	Y	22278 FQ	33484 MW	37289 TQ	MNBLS	10/08-12/08
	Minneapolis-Saint Paul MSA, MN-WI	Y	28923 FQ	35692 MW	42835 TQ	MNBLS	10/08-12/08
	Rochester MSA, MN	Y	20312 FQ	25050 MW	30667 TQ	MNBLS	10/08-12/08
	Mississippi	Y	20130 FQ	26020 MW	31600 TQ	USBLS	5/07
	Jackson MSA, MS	Y	20620 FQ	25980 MW	33610 TQ	USBLS	5/07
	Missouri	Y	24170 FQ	31080 MW	45020 TQ	USBLS	5/07
	Jefferson City MSA, MO	Y	29460 FQ	37070 MW	42870 TQ	USBLS	5/07
	Kansas City MSA, MO-KS	Y	26050 FQ	36080 MW	54790 TQ	USBLS	5/07
	St. Louis MSA, MO-IL	Y	27320 FQ	35720 MW	49080 TQ	USBLS	5/07
	Montana	Y	21990 FQ	29950 MW	36220 TQ	USBLS	5/07
	Billings MSA, MT	Y	14970 FQ	20550 MW	40900 TQ	USBLS	5/07
	Nebraska	Y	25300 FQ	29780 MW	36380 TQ	USBLS	5/07

Occupation/Type/Industry	Location	Per	Low	Mid	High	Source	Date
Inspector, Tester, Sorter, Sampler, and Weigher							
	Omaha-Council Bluffs MSA, NE-IA	Y	25030 FQ	29620 MW	36970 TQ	USBLS	5/07
	Nevada	H	10.56 FQ	13.56 MW	19.15 TQ	NVBLS	5/08
	Las Vegas-Paradise MSA, NV	H	10.01 FQ	11.60 MW	18.96 TQ	NVBLS	5/08
	New Hampshire	H	11.90 AE	15.92 MW	19.00 AEX	NHBLS	6/08
	Manchester MSA, NH	Y	30600 FQ	38180 MW	44970 TQ	USBLS	5/07
	Nashua NECTA, NH-MA	Y	27580 FQ	32930 MW	40880 TQ	USBLS	5/07
	New Jersey	Y	23690 FQ	31260 MW	40630 TQ	USBLS	5/07
	Camden PMSA, NJ	Y	22920 FQ	31070 MW	40550 TQ	USBLS	5/07
	Edison PMSA, NJ	Y	24780 FQ	31180 MW	40290 TQ	USBLS	5/07
	Newark-Union PMSA, NJ-PA	Y	26520 FQ	34290 MW	45420 TQ	USBLS	5/07
	New Mexico	Y	25190 FQ	32310 MW	42740 TQ	USBLS	5/07
	Albuquerque MSA, NM	Y	27130 FQ	34630 MW	44350 TQ	USBLS	5/07
	New York	Y	22580 FQ	30440 MW	40290 TQ	USBLS	5/07
	Albany-Schenectady-Troy MSA, NY	Y	24620 FQ	35080 MW	45720 TQ	USBLS	5/07
	Buffalo-Niagara Falls MSA, NY	Y	24370 FQ	33150 MW	48230 TQ	USBLS	5/07
	Kingston MSA, NY	Y	27940 FQ	33570 MW	42680 TQ	USBLS	5/07
	Nassau-Suffolk PMSA, NY	Y	25110 FQ	33660 MW	44490 TQ	USBLS	5/07
	New York-Northern New Jersey-Long Island MSA, NY-NJ-PA	Y	22370 FQ	30630 MW	42340 TQ	USBLS	5/07
	North Carolina	Y	21430 FQ	26690 MW	34800 TQ	USBLS	5/07
	Charlotte-Gastonia-Concord MSA, NC-SC	Y	21920 FQ	29640 MW	39020 TQ	USBLS	5/07
	Raleigh-Cary MSA, NC	Y	24220 FQ	29330 MW	36040 TQ	USBLS	5/07
	North Dakota	Y	24250 FQ	30310 MW	38620 TQ	USBLS	5/07
	Fargo MSA, ND-MN	Y	21720 FQ	27520 MW	36220 TQ	USBLS	5/07
	Ohio	Y	24660 FQ	31450 MW	40130 TQ	USBLS	5/07
	Cincinnati-Middletown MSA, OH-KY-IN	Y	26420 FQ	33550 MW	44230 TQ	USBLS	5/07
	Cleveland-Elyria-Mentor MSA, OH	Y	26440 FQ	32870 MW	41050 TQ	USBLS	5/07
	Columbus MSA, OH	Y	22520 FQ	29170 MW	37080 TQ	USBLS	5/07
	Dayton MSA, OH	Y	24720 FQ	31330 MW	43060 TQ	USBLS	5/07
	Oklahoma	Y	24450 FQ	32390 MW	43420 TQ	USBLS	5/07
	Oklahoma City MSA, OK	Y	24490 FQ	32940 MW	42870 TQ	USBLS	5/07
	Tulsa MSA, OK	Y	26830 FQ	34440 MW	44530 TQ	USBLS	5/07
	Oregon	H	11.92 FQ	15.47 MW	19.87 TQ	ORBLS	5/08
	Eugene-Springfield MSA, OR	Y	27060 FQ	33040 MW	39880 TQ	USBLS	5/07
	Portland-Vancouver-Beaverton MSA, OR-WA	Y	24650 FQ	32190 MW	41800 TQ	USBLS	5/07
	Pennsylvania	Y	24970 FQ	31780 MW	40220 TQ	USBLS	5/07
	Allentown-Bethlehem-Easton MSA, PA-NJ	Y	24520 FQ	31300 MW	39980 TQ	USBLS	5/07
	Philadelphia-Camden-Wilmington MSA, PA-NJ-DE-MD	Y	27290 FQ	35060 MW	44730 TQ	USBLS	5/07
	Pittsburgh MSA, PA	Y	26050 FQ	33090 MW	43790 TQ	USBLS	5/07
	Reading MSA, PA	Y	21360 FQ	26940 MW	36140 TQ	USBLS	5/07
	Rhode Island	Y	22250 FQ	29550 MW	37700 TQ	USBLS	5/07
	Providence-Fall River-Warwick MSA, RI-MA	Y	22010 FQ	28130 MW	35890 TQ	USBLS	5/07
	South Carolina	Y	23000 FQ	28180 MW	35240 TQ	USBLS	5/07
	Charleston-North Charleston MSA, SC	Y	25660 FQ	31050 MW	42320 TQ	USBLS	5/07
	Columbia MSA, SC	Y	26090 FQ	33410 MW	41070 TQ	USBLS	5/07
	Spartanburg MSA, SC	Y	23350 FQ	29450 MW	36000 TQ	USBLS	5/07
	South Dakota	Y	24630 FQ	27839 MW	31537 TQ	SDBLS	7/08-9/08
	Sioux Falls MSA, SD	Y	25442 FQ	27646 MW	29899 TQ	SDBLS	7/08-9/08
	Tennessee	Y	22320 FQ	27360 MW	34360 TQ	USBLS	5/07
	Johnson City MSA, TN	Y	19000 FQ	24560 MW	31620 TQ	USBLS	5/07
	Kingsport-Bristol-Bristol MSA, TN-VA	Y	21520 FQ	26670 MW	31490 TQ	USBLS	5/07
	Memphis MSA, TN-MS-AR	Y	22160 FQ	26000 MW	31200 TQ	USBLS	5/07
	Nashville-Davidson-Murfreesboro MSA, TN	Y	23180 FQ	29810 MW	43170 TQ	USBLS	5/07
	Texas	Y	21150 FQ	28690 MW	38060 TQ	USBLS	5/07
	Austin-Round Rock MSA, TX	Y	23240 FQ	30090 MW	42190 TQ	USBLS	5/07

Occupation/Type/Industry	Location	Per	Low	Mid	High	Source	Date
Inspector, Tester, Sorter, Sampler, and Weigher							
	Dallas-Fort Worth-Arlington MSA, TX	Y	22580 FQ	28630 MW	37210 TQ	USBLS	5/07
	El Paso MSA, TX	Y	14040 FQ	16660 MW	22850 TQ	USBLS	5/07
	Houston-Sugar Land-Baytown MSA, TX	Y	20670 FQ	29500 MW	38770 TQ	USBLS	5/07
	Midland MSA, TX	Y	15570 FQ	20530 MW	26210 TQ	USBLS	5/07
	San Antonio MSA, TX	Y	24820 FQ	31780 MW	38950 TQ	USBLS	5/07
	Utah	Y	23070 FQ	30290 MW	40540 TQ	USBLS	5/07
	Ogden-Clearfield MSA, UT	Y	24660 FQ	37020 MW	46330 TQ	USBLS	5/07
	Salt Lake City MSA, UT	Y	23190 FQ	29670 MW	38370 TQ	USBLS	5/07
	Vermont	Y	25530 FQ	29660 MW	35260 TQ	USBLS	5/07
	Burlington-South Burlington MSA, VT	Y	27840 FQ	32530 MW	38730 TQ	USBLS	5/07
	Virginia	Y	24020 FQ	31250 MW	43390 TQ	USBLS	5/07
	Charlottesville MSA, VA	Y	26880 FQ	33050 MW	37450 TQ	USBLS	5/07
	Richmond MSA, VA	Y	22590 FQ	28870 MW	42460 TQ	USBLS	5/07
	Virginia Beach-Norfolk-Newport News MSA, VA-NC	Y	28780 FQ	38910 MW	49080 TQ	USBLS	5/07
	Washington	H	13.04 FQ	18.48 MW	28.30 TQ	WABLS	3/08
	Seattle-Tacoma-Bellevue MSA, WA	Y	31540 FQ	45200 MW	63840 TQ	USBLS	5/07
	West Virginia	Y	24070 FQ	32938 MW	42357 TQ	WVBLS	7/08-9/08
	Charleston MSA, WV	Y	21070 FQ	32610 MW	42550 TQ	USBLS	5/07
	Parkersburg-Marietta-Vienna MSA, WV-OH	Y	19270 FQ	25450 MW	38130 TQ	USBLS	5/07
	Wisconsin	Y	24830 FQ	31340 MW	37760 TQ	USBLS	5/07
	Milwaukee-Waukesha-West Allis MSA, WI	Y	26280 FQ	32720 MW	39250 TQ	USBLS	5/07
	Wyoming	Y	30624 FQ	41868 MW	50276 TQ	WYBLS	9/08
	Cheyenne MSA, WY	Y	31351 FQ	37642 MW	44546 TQ	WYBLS	9/08
	Puerto Rico	Y	16860 FQ	24020 MW	35920 TQ	USBLS	5/07
	San Juan-Caguas-Guaynabo MSA, PR	Y	17110 FQ	24890 MW	36410 TQ	USBLS	5/07
	Virgin Islands	Y	27530 FQ	49590 MW	58190 TQ	USBLS	5/07
Inspector General							
United States House of Representatives	United States	Y			167800 HI	CRS01	1/08
Institutional Identification Officer							
State Government	Ohio	H	15.62 LO		18.36 HI	ODAS	2008
Instructional Coordinator							
	Alabama	Y	41480 FQ	60960 MW	73590 TQ	USBLS	5/07
	Birmingham-Hoover MSA, AL	Y	35700 FQ	55210 MW	68080 TQ	USBLS	5/07
	Alaska	Y	36430 FQ	50850 MW	70370 TQ	USBLS	5/07
	Anchorage MSA, AK	Y	20830 FQ	51340 MW	74830 TQ	USBLS	5/07
	Arizona	Y	34740 FQ	43100 MW	51570 TQ	USBLS	5/07
	Phoenix-Mesa-Scottsdale MSA, AZ	Y	35090 FQ	43380 MW	51250 TQ	USBLS	5/07
	Prescott MSA, AZ	Y	29680 FQ	38230 MW	47370 TQ	USBLS	5/07
	Tucson MSA, AZ	Y	34460 FQ	44280 MW	56280 TQ	USBLS	5/07
	Arkansas	Y	41620 FQ	52580 MW	62800 TQ	USBLS	5/07
	Little Rock-North Little Rock MSA, AR	Y	45970 FQ	56460 MW	64830 TQ	USBLS	5/07
	California	H	20.00 FQ	29.45 MW	39.65 TQ	CABLS	1/08-3/08
	Los Angeles-Long Beach-Glendale PMSA, CA	H	16.32 FQ	23.74 MW	35.16 TQ	CABLS	1/08-3/08
	Oakland-Fremont-Hayward MSA, CA	H	19.85 FQ	23.89 MW	34.57 TQ	CABLS	1/08-3/08
	Riverside-San Bernardino-Ontario MSA, CA	H	29.15 FQ	36.54 MW	43.29 TQ	CABLS	1/08-3/08
	Sacramento-Arden Arcade-Roseville MSA, CA	H	27.71 FQ	34.51 MW	39.18 TQ	CABLS	1/08-3/08
	San Diego-Carlsbad-San Marcos MSA, CA	H	17.71 FQ	25.07 MW	38.49 TQ	CABLS	1/08-3/08
	San Francisco-San Mateo-Redwood PMSA, CA	H	17.64 FQ	24.62 MW	39.02 TQ	CABLS	1/08-3/08
	San Jose-Sunnyvale-Santa Clara MSA, CA	H	21.72 FQ	28.90 MW	40.13 TQ	CABLS	1/08-3/08
	Santa Ana-Anaheim-Irvine PMSA, CA	Y	45220 FQ	63630 MW	86640 TQ	USBLS	5/07
	Colorado	Y	48380 FQ	61960 MW	75850 TQ	USBLS	5/07

AE Average entry wage	**AW** Average wage paid	**FQ** First quartile wage	**LO** Lowest wage paid	**MTC** Median total compensation	**TCC** Total cash compensation
AER Average entry range	**AWR** Average wage range	**H** Hourly	**LR** Low end range	**MW** Median wage paid	**TQ** Third quartile wage
AEX Average experienced wage	**AXR** Average experienced range	**HI** Highest wage paid	**M** Monthly	**MWR** Median wage range	**W** Weekly
ATC Average total compensation	**D** Daily	**HR** High end range	**MCC** Median cash compensation	**S** See annotated source	**Y** Yearly

Occupation/Type/Industry	Location	Per	Low	Mid	High	Source	Date
Instructional Coordinator	Colorado Springs MSA, CO	Y	53400 FQ	66900 MW	84130 TQ	USBLS	5/07
	Denver-Aurora MSA, CO	Y	51970 FQ	62050 MW	73850 TQ	USBLS	5/07
	Connecticut	H	21.92 AE	36.69 MW		CTBLS	1/08-3/08
	Bridgeport-Stamford-Norwalk MSA, CT	Y	43720 FQ	71820 MW	98700 TQ	USBLS	5/07
	Hartford-West Hartford-East Hartford MSA, CT	Y	61380 FQ	84810 MW	96400 TQ	USBLS	5/07
	Delaware	Y	41260 FQ	53920 MW	69710 TQ	USBLS	5/07
	Wilmington PMSA, DE-MD-NJ	Y	39650 FQ	53410 MW	68790 TQ	USBLS	5/07
	District of Columbia	Y	45390 FQ	66650 MW	91010 TQ	USBLS	5/07
	Washington-Arlington-Alexandria MSA, DC-VA-MD-WV	Y	43250 FQ	59940 MW	86160 TQ	USBLS	5/07
	Florida	Y	37590 FQ	49140 MW	67840 TQ	USBLS	5/07
	Fort Lauderdale-Pompano Beach-Deerfield Beach PMSA, FL	Y	36290 FQ	54050 MW	80600 TQ	USBLS	5/07
	Jacksonville MSA, FL	Y	37350 FQ	47100 MW	61820 TQ	USBLS	5/07
	Miami-Fort Lauderdale-Miami Beach MSA, FL	Y	34220 FQ	47030 MW	70360 TQ	USBLS	5/07
	Orlando-Kissimmee MSA, FL	Y	44070 FQ	57280 MW	71870 TQ	USBLS	5/07
	Tallahassee MSA, FL	Y	41840 FQ	47610 MW	55180 TQ	USBLS	5/07
	Tampa-St. Petersburg-Clearwater MSA, FL	Y	35790 FQ	52890 MW	71670 TQ	USBLS	5/07
	West Palm Beach-Boca Raton-Boynton Beach PMSA, FL	Y	29940 FQ	42130 MW	70560 TQ	USBLS	5/07
	Georgia	Y	34300 FQ	53640 MW	72150 TQ	USBLS	5/07
	Atlanta-Sandy Springs-Marietta MSA, GA	Y	37280 FQ	56690 MW	76020 TQ	USBLS	5/07
	Hawaii	Y	39400 FQ	45940 MW	55080 TQ	USBLS	5/07
	Honolulu MSA, HI	Y	39180 FQ	45610 MW	55660 TQ	USBLS	5/07
	Idaho	Y	27580 FQ	31440 MW	52620 TQ	USBLS	5/07
	Boise City-Nampa MSA, ID	Y	28510 FQ	31130 MW	49400 TQ	USBLS	5/07
	Illinois	Y	35240 FQ	51350 MW	73760 TQ	USBLS	5/07
	Chicago-Naperville-Joliet MSA, IL-IN-WI	Y	37700 FQ	54320 MW	81000 TQ	USBLS	5/07
	Indiana	Y	39670 FQ	50700 MW	68320 TQ	USBLS	5/07
	Gary PMSA, IN	Y	40490 FQ	55190 MW	79400 TQ	USBLS	5/07
	Indianapolis-Carmel MSA, IN	Y	41310 FQ	49020 MW	73470 TQ	USBLS	5/07
	Iowa	Y	41310 FQ	52760 MW	62330 TQ	USBLS	5/07
	Des Moines-West Des Moines MSA, IA	Y	50870 FQ	59900 MW	71200 TQ	USBLS	5/07
	Iowa City MSA, IA	Y	42410 FQ	48230 MW	57410 TQ	USBLS	5/07
	Kansas	Y	36210 FQ	48620 MW	60120 TQ	USBLS	5/07
	Kentucky	Y	42754 FQ	55880 MW	72218 TQ	KYBLS	2008
	Louisville-Jefferson County MSA, KY-IN	Y	35370 FQ	48590 MW	68750 TQ	USBLS	5/07
	Louisiana	H	17.21 FQ	21.18 MW	24.84 TQ	LABLS	1/08-3/08
	Baton Rouge MSA, LA	Y	30550 FQ	43200 MW	53260 TQ	USBLS	5/07
	New Orleans-Metairie-Kenner MSA, LA	Y	38980 FQ	44250 MW	49970 TQ	USBLS	5/07
	Maine	Y	35470 FQ	49120 MW	59390 TQ	USBLS	5/07
	Maryland	Y		53050 MW		MDBLS	3/08
	Baltimore-Towson MSA, MD	Y	38630 FQ	51730 MW	67060 TQ	USBLS	5/07
	Massachusetts	Y	48300 FQ	65230 MW	80060 TQ	USBLS	5/07
	Boston-Cambridge-Quincy NECTA, MA	Y	53320 FQ	68590 MW	81580 TQ	USBLS	5/07
	Springfield MSA, MA-CT	Y	37220 FQ	58940 MW	75100 TQ	USBLS	5/07
	Worcester MSA, MA-CT	Y	37590 FQ	53260 MW	66050 TQ	USBLS	5/07
	Michigan	Y	43500 FQ	61310 MW	79150 TQ	USBLS	5/07
	Detroit-Warren-Livonia MSA, MI	Y	41920 FQ	61530 MW	80110 TQ	USBLS	5/07
	Grand Rapids-Wyoming MSA, MI	Y	38320 FQ	55780 MW	95610 TQ	USBLS	5/07
	Warren-Troy-Farmington Hills PMSA, MI	Y	52220 FQ	73460 MW	91890 TQ	USBLS	5/07
	Minnesota	Y	48429 FQ	63589 MW	75715 TQ	MNBLS	10/08-12/08
	Duluth-Superior MSA, MN-WI	Y	55575 FQ	63589 MW	73560 TQ	MNBLS	10/08-12/08
	Minneapolis-Saint Paul MSA, MN-WI	Y	44893 FQ	65232 MW	76918 TQ	MNBLS	10/08-12/08
	Rochester MSA, MN	Y	52765 FQ	62326 MW	74181 TQ	MNBLS	10/08-12/08

AE	Average entry wage	AW	Average wage paid	FQ	First quartile wage
AER	Average entry range	AWR	Average wage range	H	Hourly
AEX	Average experienced wage	AXR	Average experienced range	HI	Highest wage paid
ATC	Average total compensation	D	Daily	HR	High end range

LO	Lowest wage paid	MTC	Median total compensation	TCC	Total cash compensation
LR	Low end range	MW	Median wage paid	TQ	Third quartile wage
M	Monthly	MWR	Median wage range	W	Weekly
MCC	Median cash compensation	S	See annotated source	Y	Yearly

Occupation/Type/Industry	Location	Per	Low	Mid	High	Source	Date
Instructional Coordinator	Mississippi	Y	39470 FQ	54900 MW	69770 TQ	USBLS	5/07
	Jackson MSA, MS	Y	33720 FQ	39980 MW	49000 TQ	USBLS	5/07
	Missouri	Y	38850 FQ	50630 MW	66220 TQ	USBLS	5/07
	Kansas City MSA, MO-KS	Y	41590 FQ	53430 MW	68420 TQ	USBLS	5/07
	St. Louis MSA, MO-IL	Y	42130 FQ	54820 MW	71180 TQ	USBLS	5/07
	Montana	Y	32830 FQ	41000 MW	50510 TQ	USBLS	5/07
	Nebraska	Y	38740 FQ	51960 MW	63370 TQ	USBLS	5/07
	Omaha-Council Bluffs MSA, NE-IA	Y	37660 FQ	52770 MW	66910 TQ	USBLS	5/07
	Nevada	H	23.57 FQ	31.86 MW	37.39 TQ	NVBLS	5/08
	Las Vegas-Paradise MSA, NV	H	24.11 FQ	33.33 MW	38.10 TQ	NVBLS	5/08
	New Hampshire	H	17.91 AE	26.66 MW	31.37 AEX	NHBLS	6/08
	Nashua NECTA, NH-MA	Y	50930 FQ	56980 MW	65930 TQ	USBLS	5/07
	New Jersey	Y	55040 FQ	74080 MW	88950 TQ	USBLS	5/07
	Camden PMSA, NJ	Y	54570 FQ	68370 MW	85270 TQ	USBLS	5/07
	Edison PMSA, NJ	Y	55270 FQ	72380 MW	87900 TQ	USBLS	5/07
	Newark-Union PMSA, NJ-PA	Y	40690 FQ	60770 MW	80390 TQ	USBLS	5/07
	New Mexico	Y	37730 FQ	52450 MW	67200 TQ	USBLS	5/07
	Albuquerque MSA, NM	Y	31230 FQ	51730 MW	68350 TQ	USBLS	5/07
	New York	Y	44410 FQ	60040 MW	80810 TQ	USBLS	5/07
	Albany-Schenectady-Troy MSA, NY	Y	39600 FQ	59920 MW	85860 TQ	USBLS	5/07
	Buffalo-Niagara Falls MSA, NY	Y	45720 FQ	61630 MW	77560 TQ	USBLS	5/07
	Nassau-Suffolk PMSA, NY	Y	44580 FQ	67820 MW	109080 TQ	USBLS	5/07
	New York-Northern New Jersey-Long Island MSA, NY-NJ-PA	Y	47580 FQ	64450 MW	84550 TQ	USBLS	5/07
	Syracuse MSA, NY	Y	41820 FQ	56290 MW	75170 TQ	USBLS	5/07
	North Carolina	Y	40740 FQ	50510 MW	62000 TQ	USBLS	5/07
	Charlotte-Gastonia-Concord MSA, NC-SC	Y	39510 FQ	49240 MW	61190 TQ	USBLS	5/07
	Raleigh-Cary MSA, NC	Y	44210 FQ	53670 MW	65600 TQ	USBLS	5/07
	Winston-Salem MSA, NC	Y	36230 FQ	48610 MW	59360 TQ	USBLS	5/07
	North Dakota	Y	37760 FQ	46970 MW	70470 TQ	USBLS	5/07
	Fargo MSA, ND-MN	Y	37190 FQ	45280 MW	88500 TQ	USBLS	5/07
	Ohio	Y	44210 FQ	59780 MW	77780 TQ	USBLS	5/07
	Cincinnati-Middletown MSA, OH-KY-IN	Y	37750 FQ	59640 MW	81350 TQ	USBLS	5/07
	Cleveland-Elyria-Mentor MSA, OH	Y	51630 FQ	63430 MW	77600 TQ	USBLS	5/07
	Columbus MSA, OH	Y	43770 FQ	61210 MW	80870 TQ	USBLS	5/07
	Dayton MSA, OH	Y	39600 FQ	56990 MW	72000 TQ	USBLS	5/07
	Mansfield MSA, OH	Y	57470 FQ	66710 MW	80410 TQ	USBLS	5/07
	Oklahoma	Y	32450 FQ	43500 MW	56610 TQ	USBLS	5/07
	Oklahoma City MSA, OK	Y	33270 FQ	41960 MW	51830 TQ	USBLS	5/07
	Tulsa MSA, OK	Y	36730 FQ	52790 MW	63320 TQ	USBLS	5/07
	Oregon	H	22.17 FQ	29.04 MW	36.95 TQ	ORBLS	5/08
	Portland-Vancouver-Beaverton MSA, OR-WA	Y	49840 FQ	62060 MW	76460 TQ	USBLS	5/07
	Pennsylvania	Y	38790 FQ	51720 MW	69280 TQ	USBLS	5/07
	Allentown-Bethlehem-Easton MSA, PA-NJ	Y	43380 FQ	49620 MW	62380 TQ	USBLS	5/07
	Philadelphia-Camden-Wilmington MSA, PA-NJ-DE-MD	Y	37470 FQ	53270 MW	74410 TQ	USBLS	5/07
	Pittsburgh MSA, PA	Y	43130 FQ	57690 MW	78200 TQ	USBLS	5/07
	Rhode Island	Y	40850 FQ	60180 MW	74970 TQ	USBLS	5/07
	Providence-Fall River-Warwick MSA, RI-MA	Y	41470 FQ	59320 MW	74500 TQ	USBLS	5/07
	South Carolina	Y	43820 FQ	56960 MW	69970 TQ	USBLS	5/07
	Charleston-North Charleston MSA, SC	Y	41750 FQ	57310 MW	76950 TQ	USBLS	5/07
	Columbia MSA, SC	Y	53630 FQ	63190 MW	73900 TQ	USBLS	5/07
	South Dakota	Y	38396 FQ	45698 MW	53552 TQ	SDBLS	7/08-9/08
	Sioux Falls MSA, SD	Y	32953 FQ	42323 MW	49078 TQ	SDBLS	7/08-9/08
	Tennessee	Y	36790 FQ	49480 MW	65320 TQ	USBLS	5/07
	Memphis MSA, TN-MS-AR	Y	37140 FQ	41530 MW	72870 TQ	USBLS	5/07
	Nashville-Davidson-Murfreesboro MSA, TN	Y	34450 FQ	46670 MW	68760 TQ	USBLS	5/07
	Texas	Y	43310 FQ	56590 MW	71360 TQ	USBLS	5/07
	Austin-Round Rock MSA, TX	Y	47990 FQ	59380 MW	73900 TQ	USBLS	5/07

AE Average entry wage	**AW** Average wage paid	**FQ** First quartile wage	**LO** Lowest wage paid	**MTC** Median total compensation	**TCC** Total cash compensation
AER Average entry range	**AWR** Average wage range	**H** Hourly	**LR** Low end range	**MW** Median wage paid	**TQ** Third quartile wage
AEX Average experienced wage	**AXR** Average experienced range	**HI** Highest wage paid	**M** Monthly	**MWR** Median wage range	**W** Weekly
ATC Average total compensation	**D** Daily	**HR** High end range	**MCC** Median cash compensation	**S** See annotated source	**Y** Yearly

Occupation/Type/Industry	Location	Per	Low	Mid	High	Source	Date
Instructional Coordinator	Dallas-Fort Worth-Arlington						
	MSA, TX	Y	46000 FQ	58230 MW	73910 TQ	USBLS	5/07
	El Paso MSA, TX	Y	57490 FQ	66780 MW	78520 TQ	USBLS	5/07
	Houston-Sugar Land-Baytown						
	MSA, TX	Y	44480 FQ	60100 MW	76650 TQ	USBLS	5/07
	San Antonio MSA, TX	Y	35570 FQ	49850 MW	68210 TQ	USBLS	5/07
	Utah	Y	30260 FQ	46420 MW	61950 TQ	USBLS	5/07
	Salt Lake City MSA, UT	Y	28460 FQ	44240 MW	63370 TQ	USBLS	5/07
	Vermont	Y	39460 FQ	52760 MW	61460 TQ	USBLS	5/07
	Burlington-South Burlington						
	MSA, VT	Y	29990 FQ	45990 MW	59460 TQ	USBLS	5/07
	Virginia	Y	46140 FQ	62530 MW	80650 TQ	USBLS	5/07
	Lynchburg MSA, VA	Y	33540 FQ	47600 MW	63150 TQ	USBLS	5/07
	Richmond MSA, VA	Y	49570 FQ	63370 MW	77140 TQ	USBLS	5/07
	Virginia Beach-Norfolk-						
	Newport News MSA, VA-NC	Y	43020 FQ	58900 MW	71750 TQ	USBLS	5/07
	Washington	H	23.46 FQ	30.50 MW	38.27 TQ	WABLS	3/08
	Olympia MSA, WA	Y	54460 FQ	62550 MW	74040 TQ	USBLS	5/07
	Seattle-Tacoma-Bellevue						
	MSA, WA	Y	50340 FQ	63340 MW	79730 TQ	USBLS	5/07
	West Virginia	Y	35329 FQ	47902 MW	60500 TQ	WVBLS	7/08-9/08
	Charleston MSA, WV	Y	31730 FQ	51850 MW	59110 TQ	USBLS	5/07
	Wheeling MSA, WV-OH	Y	31960 FQ	36190 MW	55630 TQ	USBLS	5/07
	Wisconsin	Y	41540 FQ	54570 MW	75100 TQ	USBLS	5/07
	Milwaukee-Waukesha-West						
	Allis MSA, WI	Y	39190 FQ	53340 MW	85840 TQ	USBLS	5/07
	Wyoming	Y	44999 FQ	54512 MW	65512 TQ	WYBLS	9/08
	Cheyenne MSA, WY	Y	45046 FQ	50995 MW	61803 TQ	WYBLS	9/08
	Puerto Rico	Y	27150 FQ	34440 MW	41380 TQ	USBLS	5/07
	San Juan-Caguas-Guaynabo						
	MSA, PR	Y	27880 FQ	35380 MW	41850 TQ	USBLS	5/07
	Virgin Islands	Y	62070 FQ	73290 MW	80990 TQ	USBLS	5/07
Instructional/Curriculum Director							
Large Urban District	United States	Y		115443 AW		DADM	2007-2008
Medium Urban District	United States	Y		105406 AW		DADM	2007-2008
Rural District	United States	Y		72128 AW		DADM	2007-2008
Small Town District	United States	Y		90545 AW		DADM	2007-2008
Suburban District	United States	Y		107768 AW		DADM	2007-2008
Instructional Designer	Central	Y		57312 AW		TRAIN	2008
	Great Lakes	Y		73313 AW		TRAIN	2008
	Mountain	Y		61537 AW		TRAIN	2008
	Northeast	Y		76174 AW		TRAIN	2008
	Pacific	Y		82681 AW		TRAIN	2008
	Southeast	Y		61390 AW		TRAIN	2008
Instructor							
Department of Corrections	Vermont	Y	36275 LO		56472 HI	AFT02	3/1/08
Finance/Banking/Real Estate/Insurance	United States	Y		69700 AW		AACSB	2007-2008
Quantitative Methods/Operations Research Statistics	United States	Y		55100 AW		AACSB	2007-2008
Instrumentation Engineer	United States	Y		97788 AW		AUTOM	2008
Insulation Worker							
Floor, Ceiling, and Wall	Alabama	Y	21000 FQ	26260 MW	34200 TQ	USBLS	5/07
Floor, Ceiling, and Wall	Birmingham-Hoover MSA, AL	Y	22090 FQ	27120 MW	32020 TQ	USBLS	5/07
Floor, Ceiling, and Wall	Montgomery MSA, AL	Y	18000 FQ	21870 MW	33190 TQ	USBLS	5/07
Floor, Ceiling, and Wall	Arizona	Y	18120 FQ	25790 MW	30200 TQ	USBLS	5/07
Floor, Ceiling, and Wall	Phoenix-Mesa-Scottsdale						
	MSA, AZ	Y	18190 FQ	25590 MW	28890 TQ	USBLS	5/07
Floor, Ceiling, and Wall	Tucson MSA, AZ	Y	21360 FQ	34540 MW	54850 TQ	USBLS	5/07
Floor, Ceiling, and Wall	Arkansas	Y	18700 FQ	24480 MW	30220 TQ	USBLS	5/07
Floor, Ceiling, and Wall	California	H	15.05 FQ	18.23 MW	21.88 TQ	CABLS	1/08-3/08
Floor, Ceiling, and Wall	Los Angeles-Long Beach-						
	Glendale PMSA, CA	H	13.09 FQ	16.15 MW	19.19 TQ	CABLS	1/08-3/08
Floor, Ceiling, and Wall	Oakland-Fremont-Hayward						
	MSA, CA	H	15.93 FQ	22.11 MW	29.76 TQ	CABLS	1/08-3/08
Floor, Ceiling, and Wall	Riverside-San Bernardino-						
	Ontario MSA, CA	H	11.97 FQ	16.39 MW	18.63 TQ	CABLS	1/08-3/08

AE Average entry wage	**AW** Average wage paid	**FQ** First quartile wage	**LO** Lowest wage paid	**MTC** Median total compensation	**TCC** Total cash compensation
AER Average entry range	**AWR** Average wage range	**H** Hourly	**LR** Low end range	**MW** Median wage paid	**TQ** Third quartile wage
AEX Average experienced wage	**AXR** Average experienced range	**HI** Highest wage paid	**M** Monthly	**MWR** Median wage range	**W** Weekly
ATC Average total compensation	**D** Daily	**HR** High end range	**MCC** Median cash compensation	**S** See annotated source	**Y** Yearly

Insulation Worker

Occupation/Type/Industry	Location	Per	Low	Mid	High	Source	Date
Floor, Ceiling, and Wall	Sacramento-Arden Arcade-Roseville MSA, CA	H	16.42 FQ	18.29 MW	20.78 TQ	CABLS	1/08-3/08
Floor, Ceiling, and Wall	San Diego-Carlsbad-San Marcos MSA, CA	H	11.44 FQ	15.72 MW	21.56 TQ	CABLS	1/08-3/08
Floor, Ceiling, and Wall	San Francisco-San Mateo-Redwood PMSA, CA	H	18.34 FQ	28.06 MW	37.60 TQ	CABLS	1/08-3/08
Floor, Ceiling, and Wall	Santa Ana-Anaheim-Irvine PMSA, CA	Y	37090 FQ	43280 MW	48140 TQ	USBLS	5/07
Floor, Ceiling, and Wall	Colorado	Y	24470 FQ	30230 MW	36950 TQ	USBLS	5/07
Floor, Ceiling, and Wall	Denver-Aurora MSA, CO	Y	24360 FQ	29680 MW	35410 TQ	USBLS	5/07
Floor, Ceiling, and Wall	Connecticut	H	13.57 AE	22.18 MW		CTBLS	1/08-3/08
Floor, Ceiling, and Wall	Delaware	Y	27560 FQ	34490 MW	42190 TQ	USBLS	5/07
Floor, Ceiling, and Wall	Dover MSA, DE	Y	23100 FQ	29920 MW	37680 TQ	USBLS	5/07
Floor, Ceiling, and Wall	Wilmington PMSA, DE-MD-NJ	Y	29970 FQ	37230 MW	47340 TQ	USBLS	5/07
Floor, Ceiling, and Wall	Washington-Arlington-Alexandria MSA, DC-VA-MD-WV	Y	26470 FQ	32990 MW	41050 TQ	USBLS	5/07
Floor, Ceiling, and Wall	Florida	Y	21270 FQ	29850 MW	48440 TQ	USBLS	5/07
Floor, Ceiling, and Wall	Fort Lauderdale-Pompano Beach-Deerfield Beach PMSA, FL	Y	31290 FQ	56030 MW	62540 TQ	USBLS	5/07
Floor, Ceiling, and Wall	Miami-Fort Lauderdale-Miami Beach MSA, FL	Y	48530 FQ	55620 MW	62960 TQ	USBLS	5/07
Floor, Ceiling, and Wall	Orlando-Kissimmee MSA, FL	Y	28670 FQ	44580 MW	60680 TQ	USBLS	5/07
Floor, Ceiling, and Wall	Tampa-St. Petersburg-Clearwater MSA, FL	Y	23170 FQ	29160 MW	35220 TQ	USBLS	5/07
Floor, Ceiling, and Wall	Georgia	Y	21250 FQ	25280 MW	32340 TQ	USBLS	5/07
Floor, Ceiling, and Wall	Atlanta-Sandy Springs-Marietta MSA, GA	Y	21020 FQ	25230 MW	36470 TQ	USBLS	5/07
Floor, Ceiling, and Wall	Idaho	Y	19460 FQ	25550 MW	35760 TQ	USBLS	5/07
Floor, Ceiling, and Wall	Illinois	Y	30520 FQ	38240 MW	66100 TQ	USBLS	5/07
Floor, Ceiling, and Wall	Chicago-Naperville-Joliet MSA, IL-IN-WI	Y	32000 FQ	38700 MW	68550 TQ	USBLS	5/07
Floor, Ceiling, and Wall	Indiana	Y	22490 FQ	29110 MW	39280 TQ	USBLS	5/07
Floor, Ceiling, and Wall	Gary PMSA, IN	Y	25760 FQ	33260 MW	42430 TQ	USBLS	5/07
Floor, Ceiling, and Wall	Iowa	Y	19980 FQ	25720 MW	38290 TQ	USBLS	5/07
Floor, Ceiling, and Wall	Kansas	Y	27540 FQ	34250 MW	44860 TQ	USBLS	5/07
Floor, Ceiling, and Wall	Wichita MSA, KS	Y	28680 FQ	35730 MW	45750 TQ	USBLS	5/07
Floor, Ceiling, and Wall	Kentucky	Y	32709 FQ	48914 MW	56172 TQ	KYBLS	2008
Floor, Ceiling, and Wall	Lexington-Fayette MSA, KY	Y	34230 FQ	45340 MW	50930 TQ	USBLS	5/07
Floor, Ceiling, and Wall	Louisville-Jefferson County MSA, KY-IN	Y	27110 FQ	44010 MW	53970 TQ	USBLS	5/07
Floor, Ceiling, and Wall	Louisiana	H	12.76 FQ	15.81 MW	17.93 TQ	LABLS	1/08-3/08
Floor, Ceiling, and Wall	Baton Rouge MSA, LA	Y	26340 FQ	30230 MW	34440 TQ	USBLS	5/07
Floor, Ceiling, and Wall	Lafayette MSA, LA	Y	25480 FQ	29190 MW	44590 TQ	USBLS	5/07
Floor, Ceiling, and Wall	Lake Charles MSA, LA	Y	31370 FQ	34990 MW	39740 TQ	USBLS	5/07
Floor, Ceiling, and Wall	Maine	Y	22370 FQ	27180 MW	33430 TQ	USBLS	5/07
Floor, Ceiling, and Wall	Maryland			39750 MW		MDBLS	3/08
Floor, Ceiling, and Wall	Baltimore-Towson MSA, MD	Y	32960 FQ	38580 MW	47920 TQ	USBLS	5/07
Floor, Ceiling, and Wall	Massachusetts	Y	26600 FQ	35110 MW	45720 TQ	USBLS	5/07
Floor, Ceiling, and Wall	Boston-Cambridge-Quincy NECTA, MA	Y	26360 FQ	36360 MW	46590 TQ	USBLS	5/07
Floor, Ceiling, and Wall	Worcester MSA, MA-CT	Y	25510 FQ	29860 MW	38200 TQ	USBLS	5/07
Floor, Ceiling, and Wall	Michigan	Y	26410 FQ	34000 MW	40020 TQ	USBLS	5/07
Floor, Ceiling, and Wall	Grand Rapids-Wyoming MSA, MI	Y	30710 FQ	37670 MW	46130 TQ	USBLS	5/07
Floor, Ceiling, and Wall	Minnesota	Y	31120 FQ	41248 MW	65076 TQ	MNBLS	10/08-12/08
Floor, Ceiling, and Wall	Minneapolis-Saint Paul MSA, MN-WI	Y	32427 FQ	45653 MW	66942 TQ	MNBLS	10/08-12/08
Floor, Ceiling, and Wall	Mississippi	Y	18570 FQ	27160 MW	30850 TQ	USBLS	5/07
Floor, Ceiling, and Wall	Missouri	Y	25720 FQ	31650 MW	41840 TQ	USBLS	5/07
Floor, Ceiling, and Wall	Kansas City MSA, MO-KS	Y	32080 FQ	40050 MW	46140 TQ	USBLS	5/07
Floor, Ceiling, and Wall	St. Louis MSA, MO-IL	Y	32950 FQ	44730 MW	60600 TQ	USBLS	5/07
Floor, Ceiling, and Wall	Nebraska	Y	30420 FQ	36300 MW	57750 TQ	USBLS	5/07
Floor, Ceiling, and Wall	Omaha-Council Bluffs MSA, NE-IA	Y	32550 FQ	43790 MW	66180 TQ	USBLS	5/07
Floor, Ceiling, and Wall	Nevada	H	14.22 FQ	15.73 MW	18.08 TQ	NVBLS	5/08
Floor, Ceiling, and Wall	Las Vegas-Paradise MSA, NV	H	14.23 FQ	15.53 MW	17.27 TQ	NVBLS	5/08
Floor, Ceiling, and Wall	New Hampshire	H	10.07 AE	14.42 MW	20.28 AEX	NHBLS	6/08
Floor, Ceiling, and Wall	New Jersey	Y	25960 FQ	34580 MW	56770 TQ	USBLS	5/07

AE	Average entry wage	AW	Average wage paid	FQ	First quartile wage	LO	Lowest wage paid	MTC	Median total compensation	TCC	Total cash compensation
AER	Average entry range	AWR	Average wage range	H	Hourly	LR	Low end range	MW	Median wage paid	TQ	Third quartile wage
AEX	Average experienced wage	AXR	Average experienced range	HI	Highest wage paid	M	Monthly	MWR	Median wage range	W	Weekly
ATC	Average total compensation	D	Daily	HR	High end range	MCC	Median cash compensation	S	See annotated source	Y	Yearly

Insulation Worker

Occupation/Type/Industry	Location	Per	Low	Mid	High	Source	Date
Insulation Worker							
Floor, Ceiling, and Wall	Camden PMSA, NJ	Y	70820 FQ	75910 MW	81010 TQ	USBLS	5/07
Floor, Ceiling, and Wall	Edison PMSA, NJ	Y	25890 FQ	43020 MW	58800 TQ	USBLS	5/07
Floor, Ceiling, and Wall	New Mexico	Y	21300 FQ	25800 MW	35040 TQ	USBLS	5/07
Floor, Ceiling, and Wall	Albuquerque MSA, NM	Y	23420 FQ	28540 MW	36050 TQ	USBLS	5/07
Floor, Ceiling, and Wall	New York	Y	27430 FQ	35460 MW	56170 TQ	USBLS	5/07
Floor, Ceiling, and Wall	Buffalo-Niagara Falls MSA, NY	Y	21790 FQ	27260 MW	36090 TQ	USBLS	5/07
Floor, Ceiling, and Wall	Nassau-Suffolk PMSA, NY	Y	32790 FQ	36340 MW	39890 TQ	USBLS	5/07
Floor, Ceiling, and Wall	New York-Northern New Jersey-Long Island MSA, NY-NJ-PA	Y	27910 FQ	36150 MW	58120 TQ	USBLS	5/07
Floor, Ceiling, and Wall	North Carolina	Y	21950 FQ	27850 MW	35260 TQ	USBLS	5/07
Floor, Ceiling, and Wall	Charlotte-Gastonia-Concord MSA, NC-SC	Y	23760 FQ	30270 MW	38700 TQ	USBLS	5/07
Floor, Ceiling, and Wall	Greensboro-High Point MSA, NC	Y	29990 FQ	35450 MW	45330 TQ	USBLS	5/07
Floor, Ceiling, and Wall	North Dakota	Y	24340 FQ	26430 MW	29140 TQ	USBLS	5/07
Floor, Ceiling, and Wall	Ohio	Y	23090 FQ	30190 MW	42960 TQ	USBLS	5/07
Floor, Ceiling, and Wall	Cincinnati-Middletown MSA, OH-KY-IN	Y	26480 FQ	33930 MW	51700 TQ	USBLS	5/07
Floor, Ceiling, and Wall	Cleveland-Elyria-Mentor MSA, OH	Y	32420 FQ	41190 MW	57960 TQ	USBLS	5/07
Floor, Ceiling, and Wall	Columbus MSA, OH	Y	16130 FQ	23800 MW	36370 TQ	USBLS	5/07
Floor, Ceiling, and Wall	Oklahoma	Y	30320 FQ	34480 MW	37960 TQ	USBLS	5/07
Floor, Ceiling, and Wall	Oklahoma City MSA, OK	Y	32950 FQ	35970 MW	43100 TQ	USBLS	5/07
Floor, Ceiling, and Wall	Oregon	H	12.51 FQ	15.54 MW	22.34 TQ	ORBLS	5/08
Floor, Ceiling, and Wall	Portland-Vancouver-Beaverton MSA, OR-WA	Y	28500 FQ	33440 MW	46250 TQ	USBLS	5/07
Floor, Ceiling, and Wall	Pennsylvania	Y	25210 FQ	32960 MW	49340 TQ	USBLS	5/07
Floor, Ceiling, and Wall	Lancaster MSA, PA	Y	21770 FQ	25140 MW	32910 TQ	USBLS	5/07
Floor, Ceiling, and Wall	Philadelphia-Camden-Wilmington MSA, PA-NJ-DE-MD	Y	29980 FQ	39190 MW	59680 TQ	USBLS	5/07
Floor, Ceiling, and Wall	Pittsburgh MSA, PA	Y	26170 FQ	48580 MW	57780 TQ	USBLS	5/07
Floor, Ceiling, and Wall	Providence-Fall River-Warwick MSA, RI-MA	Y	36990 FQ	44490 MW	48230 TQ	USBLS	5/07
Floor, Ceiling, and Wall	South Carolina	Y	23660 FQ	28990 MW	35760 TQ	USBLS	5/07
Floor, Ceiling, and Wall	Columbia MSA, SC	Y	22430 FQ	25060 MW	33760 TQ	USBLS	5/07
Floor, Ceiling, and Wall	Tennessee	Y	25050 FQ	31040 MW	37160 TQ	USBLS	5/07
Floor, Ceiling, and Wall	Memphis MSA, TN-MS-AR	Y	21660 FQ	26860 MW	32660 TQ	USBLS	5/07
Floor, Ceiling, and Wall	Nashville-Davidson-Murfreesboro MSA, TN	Y	24310 FQ	28750 MW	32300 TQ	USBLS	5/07
Floor, Ceiling, and Wall	Texas	Y	20950 FQ	25070 MW	31210 TQ	USBLS	5/07
Floor, Ceiling, and Wall	Dallas-Fort Worth-Arlington MSA, TX	Y	20470 FQ	25010 MW	32740 TQ	USBLS	5/07
Floor, Ceiling, and Wall	Houston-Sugar Land-Baytown MSA, TX	Y	21450 FQ	25820 MW	31280 TQ	USBLS	5/07
Floor, Ceiling, and Wall	San Antonio MSA, TX	Y	22080 FQ	25080 MW	31850 TQ	USBLS	5/07
Floor, Ceiling, and Wall	Utah	Y	22860 FQ	26860 MW	31130 TQ	USBLS	5/07
Floor, Ceiling, and Wall	Salt Lake City MSA, UT	Y	23320 FQ	26750 MW	30730 TQ	USBLS	5/07
Floor, Ceiling, and Wall	Vermont	Y	23610 FQ	26770 MW	30300 TQ	USBLS	5/07
Floor, Ceiling, and Wall	Virginia	Y	23410 FQ	30680 MW	39760 TQ	USBLS	5/07
Floor, Ceiling, and Wall	Virginia Beach-Norfolk-Newport News MSA, VA-NC	Y	24580 FQ	32920 MW	40230 TQ	USBLS	5/07
Floor, Ceiling, and Wall	Washington	H	11.53 FQ	14.68 MW	18.43 TQ	WABLS	3/08
Floor, Ceiling, and Wall	West Virginia	Y	29571 FQ	51916 MW	62984 TQ	WVBLS	7/08-9/08
Floor, Ceiling, and Wall	Wisconsin	Y	27090 FQ	32250 MW	38390 TQ	USBLS	5/07
Floor, Ceiling, and Wall	Wyoming	Y	22878 FQ	25623 MW	30141 TQ	WYBLS	9/08
Floor, Ceiling, and Wall	Puerto Rico	Y	14290 FQ	17750 MW	24500 TQ	USBLS	5/07
Floor, Ceiling, and Wall	San Juan-Caguas-Guaynabo MSA, PR	Y	14450 FQ	17970 MW	24350 TQ	USBLS	5/07
Mechanical	Alabama	Y	24340 FQ	29180 MW	34230 TQ	USBLS	5/07
Mechanical	Birmingham-Hoover MSA, AL	Y	25520 FQ	29970 MW	34010 TQ	USBLS	5/07
Mechanical	Alaska	Y	54970 FQ	62460 MW	71270 TQ	USBLS	5/07
Mechanical	Arizona	Y	26110 FQ	32350 MW	43330 TQ	USBLS	5/07
Mechanical	Phoenix-Mesa-Scottsdale MSA, AZ	Y	26460 FQ	33180 MW	43850 TQ	USBLS	5/07
Mechanical	Arkansas	Y	32260 FQ	35660 MW	38690 TQ	USBLS	5/07
Mechanical	California	H	16.53 FQ	21.69 MW	29.53 TQ	CABLS	1/08-3/08
Mechanical	Los Angeles-Long Beach-Glendale PMSA, CA	H	14.73 FQ	19.64 MW	25.38 TQ	CABLS	1/08-3/08

AE	Average entry wage	AW	Average wage paid	FQ	First quartile wage	LO	Lowest wage paid	MTC	Median total compensation	TCC	Total cash compensation
AER	Average entry range	AWR	Average wage range	H	Hourly	LR	Low end range	MW	Median wage paid	TQ	Third quartile wage
AEX	Average experienced wage	AXR	Average experienced range	HI	Highest wage paid	M	Monthly	MWR	Median wage range	W	Weekly
ATC	Average total compensation	D	Daily	HR	High end range	MCC	Median cash compensation	S	See annotated source	Y	Yearly

Occupation/Type/Industry	Location	Per	Low	Mid	High	Source	Date
Insulation Worker							
Mechanical	San Diego-Carlsbad-San Marcos MSA, CA	H	15.29 FQ	23.69 MW	37.02 TQ	CABLS	1/08-3/08
Mechanical	San Jose-Sunnyvale-Santa Clara MSA, CA	H	16.21 FQ	20.50 MW	25.45 TQ	CABLS	1/08-3/08
Mechanical	Santa Ana-Anaheim-Irvine PMSA, CA	Y	37500 FQ	47420 MW	69100 TQ	USBLS	5/07
Mechanical	Colorado	Y	26560 FQ	31800 MW	41440 TQ	USBLS	5/07
Mechanical	Denver-Aurora MSA, CO	Y	27810 FQ	32700 MW	42580 TQ	USBLS	5/07
Mechanical	Connecticut	H	13.92 AE	17.69 MW		CTBLS	1/08-3/08
Mechanical	Delaware	Y	34020 FQ	46650 MW	58220 TQ	USBLS	5/07
Mechanical	Wilmington PMSA, DE-MD-NJ	Y	36500 FQ	48990 MW	59100 TQ	USBLS	5/07
Mechanical	Washington-Arlington-Alexandria MSA, DC-VA-MD-WV	Y	29770 FQ	39740 MW	51650 TQ	USBLS	5/07
Mechanical	Florida	Y	25330 FQ	32770 MW	38460 TQ	USBLS	5/07
Mechanical	Fort Lauderdale-Pompano Beach-Deerfield Beach PMSA, FL	Y	33720 FQ	40320 MW	44120 TQ	USBLS	5/07
Mechanical	Jacksonville MSA, FL	Y	22540 FQ	24880 MW	33770 TQ	USBLS	5/07
Mechanical	Miami-Fort Lauderdale-Miami Beach MSA, FL	Y	29010 FQ	38760 MW	44830 TQ	USBLS	5/07
Mechanical	Orlando-Kissimmee MSA, FL	Y	29800 FQ	36950 MW	42230 TQ	USBLS	5/07
Mechanical	Tampa-St. Petersburg-Clearwater MSA, FL	Y	25180 FQ	32370 MW	36460 TQ	USBLS	5/07
Mechanical	Georgia	Y	24860 FQ	30430 MW	41290 TQ	USBLS	5/07
Mechanical	Atlanta-Sandy Springs-Marietta MSA, GA	Y	25030 FQ	30290 MW	42790 TQ	USBLS	5/07
Mechanical	Idaho	Y	28660 FQ	35450 MW	40760 TQ	USBLS	5/07
Mechanical	Illinois	Y	39080 FQ	50670 MW	79170 TQ	USBLS	5/07
Mechanical	Chicago-Naperville-Joliet MSA, IL-IN-WI	Y	39790 FQ	51150 MW	76160 TQ	USBLS	5/07
Mechanical	Indiana	Y	26500 FQ	38010 MW	64760 TQ	USBLS	5/07
Mechanical	Gary PMSA, IN	Y	29340 FQ	52750 MW	65450 TQ	USBLS	5/07
Mechanical	Iowa	Y	29150 FQ	34330 MW	41400 TQ	USBLS	5/07
Mechanical	Des Moines-West Des Moines MSA, IA	Y	28420 FQ	33130 MW	40170 TQ	USBLS	5/07
Mechanical	Kansas	Y	28670 FQ	35700 MW	57060 TQ	USBLS	5/07
Mechanical	Kentucky	Y	26063 FQ	40510 MW	53895 TQ	KYBLS	2008
Mechanical	Louisville-Jefferson County MSA, KY-IN	Y	31810 FQ	48270 MW	54370 TQ	USBLS	5/07
Mechanical	Louisiana	H	13.20 FQ	16.11 MW	18.99 TQ	LABLS	1/08-3/08
Mechanical	Baton Rouge MSA, LA	Y	27070 FQ	31570 MW	39270 TQ	USBLS	5/07
Mechanical	New Orleans-Metairie-Kenner MSA, LA	Y	34000 FQ	37120 MW	41080 TQ	USBLS	5/07
Mechanical	Maine	Y	29690 FQ	35060 MW	43200 TQ	USBLS	5/07
Mechanical	Maryland	Y		35125 MW		MDBLS	3/08
Mechanical	Baltimore-Towson MSA, MD	Y	26820 FQ	33410 MW	39940 TQ	USBLS	5/07
Mechanical	Bethesda-Gaithersburg-Frederick PMSA, MD	Y	26470 FQ	32000 MW	40800 TQ	USBLS	5/07
Mechanical	Massachusetts	Y	28280 FQ	36940 MW	63430 TQ	USBLS	5/07
Mechanical	Boston-Cambridge-Quincy NECTA, MA	Y	29130 FQ	38930 MW	66560 TQ	USBLS	5/07
Mechanical	Michigan	Y	29390 FQ	40390 MW	58890 TQ	USBLS	5/07
Mechanical	Detroit-Warren-Livonia MSA, MI	Y	37250 FQ	54620 MW	68710 TQ	USBLS	5/07
Mechanical	Warren-Troy-Farmington Hills PMSA, MI	Y	39470 FQ	60760 MW	70100 TQ	USBLS	5/07
Mechanical	Minnesota	Y	34377 FQ	64729 MW	89263 TQ	MNBLS	10/08-12/08
Mechanical	Minneapolis-Saint Paul MSA, MN-WI	Y	44283 FQ	70419 MW	94648 TQ	MNBLS	10/08-12/08
Mechanical	Mississippi	Y	20270 FQ	26630 MW	29820 TQ	USBLS	5/07
Mechanical	Jackson MSA, MS	Y	19370 FQ	24530 MW	28240 TQ	USBLS	5/07
Mechanical	Missouri	Y	30760 FQ	54790 MW	62800 TQ	USBLS	5/07
Mechanical	Kansas City MSA, MO-KS	Y	41780 FQ	55580 MW	61040 TQ	USBLS	5/07
Mechanical	St. Louis MSA, MO-IL	Y	34630 FQ	58190 MW	64720 TQ	USBLS	5/07
Mechanical	Nebraska	Y	26030 FQ	30370 MW	34910 TQ	USBLS	5/07
Mechanical	Nevada	H	26.54 FQ	29.32 MW	31.95 TQ	NVBLS	5/08
Mechanical	Las Vegas-Paradise MSA, NV	H	26.54 FQ	29.32 MW	31.95 TQ	NVBLS	5/08
Mechanical	New Jersey	Y	39230 FQ	68050 MW	81910 TQ	USBLS	5/07
Mechanical	Camden PMSA, NJ	Y	28400 FQ	36640 MW	46420 TQ	USBLS	5/07

AE	Average entry wage	AW	Average wage paid	FQ	First quartile wage
AER	Average entry range	AWR	Average wage range	H	Hourly
AEX	Average experienced wage	AXR	Average experienced range	HI	Highest wage paid
ATC	Average total compensation	D	Daily	HR	High end range

LO	Lowest wage paid	MTC	Median total compensation
LR	Low end range	MW	Median wage paid
M	Monthly	MWR	Median wage range
MCC	Median cash compensation	S	See annotated source

TCC	Total cash compensation
TQ	Third quartile wage
W	Weekly
Y	Yearly

Occupation/Type/Industry	Location	Per	Low	Mid	High	Source	Date
Insulation Worker							
Mechanical	Newark-Union PMSA, NJ-PA	Y	59240 FQ	76250 MW	90310 TQ	USBLS	5/07
Mechanical	New York	Y	54620 FQ	62410 MW	78840 TQ	USBLS	5/07
Mechanical	Buffalo-Niagara Falls MSA, NY	Y	57250 FQ	62190 MW	67570 TQ	USBLS	5/07
Mechanical	New York-Northern New Jersey-Long Island MSA, NY-NJ-PA	Y	54790 FQ	71270 MW	86730 TQ	USBLS	5/07
Mechanical	North Carolina	Y	22100 FQ	28540 MW	35880 TQ	USBLS	5/07
Mechanical	Charlotte-Gastonia-Concord MSA, NC-SC	Y	28310 FQ	36270 MW	42530 TQ	USBLS	5/07
Mechanical	Raleigh-Cary MSA, NC	Y	23320 FQ	29350 MW	34560 TQ	USBLS	5/07
Mechanical	North Dakota	Y	28120 FQ	32100 MW	36800 TQ	USBLS	5/07
Mechanical	Fargo MSA, ND-MN	Y	29320 FQ	32500 MW	36710 TQ	USBLS	5/07
Mechanical	Grand Forks MSA, ND-MN	Y	25500 FQ	32820 MW	41170 TQ	USBLS	5/07
Mechanical	Ohio	Y	26450 FQ	38210 MW	61220 TQ	USBLS	5/07
Mechanical	Cincinnati-Middletown MSA, OH-KY-IN	Y	22860 FQ	27540 MW	41830 TQ	USBLS	5/07
Mechanical	Oklahoma	Y	18580 FQ	33310 MW	43940 TQ	USBLS	5/07
Mechanical	Oklahoma City MSA, OK	Y	19300 FQ	22390 MW	25370 TQ	USBLS	5/07
Mechanical	Tulsa MSA, OK	Y	18320 FQ	34890 MW	46400 TQ	USBLS	5/07
Mechanical	Portland-Vancouver-Beaverton MSA, OR-WA	Y	26530 FQ	33430 MW	40760 TQ	USBLS	5/07
Mechanical	Pennsylvania	Y	44710 FQ	60830 MW	73220 TQ	USBLS	5/07
Mechanical	Philadelphia-Camden-Wilmington MSA, PA-NJ-DE-MD	Y	38010 FQ	54310 MW	68520 TQ	USBLS	5/07
Mechanical	Rhode Island	Y	33190 FQ	47310 MW	53660 TQ	USBLS	5/07
Mechanical	Providence-Fall River-Warwick MSA, RI-MA	Y	28720 FQ	43740 MW	53010 TQ	USBLS	5/07
Mechanical	South Carolina	Y	25760 FQ	32370 MW	36780 TQ	USBLS	5/07
Mechanical	Charleston-North Charleston MSA, SC	Y	30560 FQ	34460 MW	38100 TQ	USBLS	5/07
Mechanical	Columbia MSA, SC	Y	24940 FQ	33400 MW	36610 TQ	USBLS	5/07
Mechanical	Spartanburg MSA, SC	Y	25430 FQ	30310 MW	35270 TQ	USBLS	5/07
Mechanical	Tennessee	Y	28290 FQ	39410 MW	44530 TQ	USBLS	5/07
Mechanical	Memphis MSA, TN-MS-AR	Y	26500 FQ	31640 MW	41710 TQ	USBLS	5/07
Mechanical	Nashville-Davidson-Murfreesboro MSA, TN	Y	28190 FQ	41230 MW	46110 TQ	USBLS	5/07
Mechanical	Texas	Y	28520 FQ	34250 MW	39580 TQ	USBLS	5/07
Mechanical	Austin-Round Rock MSA, TX	Y	40500 FQ	45770 MW	55710 TQ	USBLS	5/07
Mechanical	Corpus Christi MSA, TX	Y	25200 FQ	30530 MW	36590 TQ	USBLS	5/07
Mechanical	Dallas-Fort Worth-Arlington MSA, TX	Y	26170 FQ	30670 MW	36500 TQ	USBLS	5/07
Mechanical	El Paso MSA, TX	Y	25220 FQ	29100 MW	32210 TQ	USBLS	5/07
Mechanical	Houston-Sugar Land-Baytown MSA, TX	Y	30930 FQ	35350 MW	39690 TQ	USBLS	5/07
Mechanical	San Antonio MSA, TX	Y	20410 FQ	40420 MW	44490 TQ	USBLS	5/07
Mechanical	Utah	Y	27100 FQ	29560 MW	37590 TQ	USBLS	5/07
Mechanical	Vermont	Y	30550 FQ	34870 MW	38560 TQ	USBLS	5/07
Mechanical	Burlington-South Burlington MSA, VT	Y	30550 FQ	34870 MW	38560 TQ	USBLS	5/07
Mechanical	Virginia	Y	27770 FQ	34680 MW	43710 TQ	USBLS	5/07
Mechanical	Richmond MSA, VA	Y	26070 FQ	29920 MW	34740 TQ	USBLS	5/07
Mechanical	Virginia Beach-Norfolk-Newport News MSA, VA-NC	Y	29000 FQ	37980 MW	45470 TQ	USBLS	5/07
Mechanical	Washington	H	15.05 FQ	19.53 MW	27.36 TQ	WABLS	3/08
Mechanical	Seattle-Tacoma-Bellevue MSA, WA	Y	32410 FQ	44550 MW	68000 TQ	USBLS	5/07
Mechanical	Wisconsin	Y	38680 FQ	55910 MW	63280 TQ	USBLS	5/07
Mechanical	Milwaukee-Waukesha-West Allis MSA, WI	Y	38320 FQ	59200 MW	66200 TQ	USBLS	5/07
Insurance Actuary Associate							
State Government	Ohio	H	29.14 LO		64.45 HI	ODAS	2008
Insurance Appraiser							
Auto Damage	Alabama	Y	40110 FQ	46480 MW	56940 TQ	USBLS	5/07
Auto Damage	Arizona	Y	41980 FQ	51200 MW	58980 TQ	USBLS	5/07
Auto Damage	Phoenix-Mesa-Scottsdale MSA, AZ	Y	41870 FQ	51380 MW	59250 TQ	USBLS	5/07
Auto Damage	Arkansas	Y	40310 FQ	49760 MW	59100 TQ	USBLS	5/07

AE Average entry wage	**AW** Average wage paid	**FQ** First quartile wage	**LO** Lowest wage paid	**MTC** Median total compensation	**TCC** Total cash compensation
AER Average entry range	**AWR** Average wage range	**H** Hourly	**LR** Low end range	**MW** Median wage paid	**TQ** Third quartile wage
AEX Average experienced wage	**AXR** Average experienced range	**HI** Highest wage paid	**M** Monthly	**MWR** Median wage range	**W** Weekly
ATC Average total compensation	**D** Daily	**HR** High end range	**MCC** Median cash compensation	**S** See annotated source	**Y** Yearly

Insurance Appraiser

Occupation/Type/Industry	Location	Per	Low	Mid	High	Source	Date
Auto Damage	Little Rock-North Little Rock MSA, AR	Y	41600 FQ	50870 MW	59410 TQ	USBLS	5/07
Auto Damage	California	H	20.89 FQ	26.73 MW	32.03 TQ	CABLS	1/08-3/08
Auto Damage	Los Angeles-Long Beach-Glendale PMSA, CA	H	22.71 FQ	27.26 MW	31.24 TQ	CABLS	1/08-3/08
Auto Damage	Oakland-Fremont-Hayward MSA, CA	H	25.53 FQ	30.62 MW	37.88 TQ	CABLS	1/08-3/08
Auto Damage	Riverside-San Bernardino-Ontario MSA, CA	H	19.90 FQ	26.53 MW	29.87 TQ	CABLS	1/08-3/08
Auto Damage	Sacramento-Arden Arcade-Roseville MSA, CA	H	21.78 FQ	26.78 MW	30.37 TQ	CABLS	1/08-3/08
Auto Damage	San Diego-Carlsbad-San Marcos MSA, CA	H	19.21 FQ	23.01 MW	29.38 TQ	CABLS	1/08-3/08
Auto Damage	San Jose-Sunnyvale-Santa Clara MSA, CA	H	27.15 FQ	33.01 MW	37.26 TQ	CABLS	1/08-3/08
Auto Damage	Santa Ana-Anaheim-Irvine PMSA, CA	Y	39910 FQ	50860 MW	62930 TQ	USBLS	5/07
Auto Damage	Colorado	Y	46590 FQ	53530 MW	60780 TQ	USBLS	5/07
Auto Damage	Denver-Aurora MSA, CO	Y	46620 FQ	53740 MW	61180 TQ	USBLS	5/07
Auto Damage	Connecticut	H	20.56 AE	26.66 MW		CTBLS	1/08-3/08
Auto Damage	Hartford-West Hartford-East Hartford MSA, CT	Y	45820 FQ	53650 MW	61940 TQ	USBLS	5/07
Auto Damage	Washington-Arlington-Alexandria MSA, DC-VA-MD-WV	Y	46380 FQ	52600 MW	59600 TQ	USBLS	5/07
Auto Damage	Florida	Y	39430 FQ	47600 MW	58390 TQ	USBLS	5/07
Auto Damage	Miami-Fort Lauderdale-Miami Beach MSA, FL	Y	39330 FQ	46550 MW	58680 TQ	USBLS	5/07
Auto Damage	Orlando-Kissimmee MSA, FL	Y	40740 FQ	51600 MW	62000 TQ	USBLS	5/07
Auto Damage	Tampa-St. Petersburg-Clearwater MSA, FL	Y	37950 FQ	44050 MW	54050 TQ	USBLS	5/07
Auto Damage	Georgia	Y	46210 FQ	53170 MW	60610 TQ	USBLS	5/07
Auto Damage	Atlanta-Sandy Springs-Marietta MSA, GA	Y	45530 FQ	51920 MW	61230 TQ	USBLS	5/07
Auto Damage	Hawaii	Y	44700 FQ	54220 MW	63530 TQ	USBLS	5/07
Auto Damage	Honolulu MSA, HI	Y	44700 FQ	54220 MW	63530 TQ	USBLS	5/07
Auto Damage	Idaho	Y	49180 FQ	52600 MW	56390 TQ	USBLS	5/07
Auto Damage	Boise City-Nampa MSA, ID	Y	50230 FQ	53500 MW	56770 TQ	USBLS	5/07
Auto Damage	Illinois	Y	39310 FQ	49740 MW	64980 TQ	USBLS	5/07
Auto Damage	Chicago-Naperville-Joliet MSA, IL-IN-WI	Y	44690 FQ	54660 MW	79550 TQ	USBLS	5/07
Auto Damage	Indiana	Y	45120 FQ	53260 MW	61820 TQ	USBLS	5/07
Auto Damage	Indianapolis-Carmel MSA, IN	Y	45600 FQ	53800 MW	62470 TQ	USBLS	5/07
Auto Damage	Iowa	Y	33670 FQ	39310 MW	45570 TQ	USBLS	5/07
Auto Damage	Des Moines-West Des Moines MSA, IA	Y	34950 FQ	40070 MW	46290 TQ	USBLS	5/07
Auto Damage	Kansas	Y	44760 FQ	51410 MW	59080 TQ	USBLS	5/07
Auto Damage	Wichita MSA, KS	Y	46120 FQ	53750 MW	60160 TQ	USBLS	5/07
Auto Damage	Kentucky	Y	45590 FQ	55848 MW	63478 TQ	KYBLS	2008
Auto Damage	Louisville-Jefferson County MSA, KY-IN	Y	43340 FQ	55140 MW	61960 TQ	USBLS	5/07
Auto Damage	Louisiana	H	17.39 FQ	25.53 MW	33.14 TQ	LABLS	1/08-3/08
Auto Damage	Maine	Y	43870 FQ	49950 MW	61620 TQ	USBLS	5/07
Auto Damage	Maryland	Y		52425 MW		MDBLS	3/08
Auto Damage	Baltimore-Towson MSA, MD	Y	38710 FQ	48650 MW	58850 TQ	USBLS	5/07
Auto Damage	Bethesda-Gaithersburg-Frederick PMSA, MD	Y	46150 FQ	53980 MW	60440 TQ	USBLS	5/07
Auto Damage	Massachusetts	Y	48180 FQ	56520 MW	63850 TQ	USBLS	5/07
Auto Damage	Boston-Cambridge-Quincy NECTA, MA	Y	50580 FQ	58420 MW	65320 TQ	USBLS	5/07
Auto Damage	Springfield MSA, MA-CT	Y	40800 FQ	43820 MW	46840 TQ	USBLS	5/07
Auto Damage	Worcester MSA, MA-CT	Y	51130 FQ	56410 MW	61860 TQ	USBLS	5/07
Auto Damage	Michigan	Y	41580 FQ	51580 MW	60840 TQ	USBLS	5/07
Auto Damage	Mississippi	Y	39370 FQ	44470 MW	49860 TQ	USBLS	5/07
Auto Damage	Jackson MSA, MS	Y	38230 FQ	43440 MW	48980 TQ	USBLS	5/07
Auto Damage	Missouri	Y	37790 FQ	47090 MW	56810 TQ	USBLS	5/07
Auto Damage	Kansas City MSA, MO-KS	Y	44240 FQ	49790 MW	57820 TQ	USBLS	5/07
Auto Damage	St. Louis MSA, MO-IL	Y	38090 FQ	47250 MW	57330 TQ	USBLS	5/07
Auto Damage	Montana	Y	43380 FQ	49620 MW	57510 TQ	USBLS	5/07
Auto Damage	Nevada	H	21.58 FQ	24.43 MW	27.21 TQ	NVBLS	5/08
Auto Damage	Las Vegas-Paradise MSA, NV	H	21.58 FQ	24.43 MW	27.21 TQ	NVBLS	5/08

AE	Average entry wage	AW	Average wage paid	FQ	First quartile wage	LO	Lowest wage paid	MTC	Median total compensation	TCC	Total cash compensation
AER	Average entry range	AWR	Average wage range	H	Hourly	LR	Low end range	MW	Median wage paid	TQ	Third quartile wage
AEX	Average experienced wage	AXR	Average experienced range	HI	Highest wage paid	M	Monthly	MWR	Median wage range	W	Weekly
ATC	Average total compensation	D	Daily	HR	High end range	MCC	Median cash compensation	S	See annotated source	Y	Yearly

Occupation/Type/Industry	Location	Per	Low	Mid	High	Source	Date
Insurance Appraiser							
Auto Damage	New Hampshire	H	19.96 AE	24.00 MW	26.04 AEX	NHBLS	6/08
Auto Damage	New Jersey	Y	46110 FQ	54820 MW	63130 TQ	USBLS	5/07
Auto Damage	Camden PMSA, NJ	Y	48870 FQ	56560 MW	63810 TQ	USBLS	5/07
Auto Damage	Edison PMSA, NJ	Y	55650 FQ	62630 MW	71570 TQ	USBLS	5/07
Auto Damage	Newark-Union PMSA, NJ-PA	Y	43460 FQ	51920 MW	60600 TQ	USBLS	5/07
Auto Damage	New York	Y	44460 FQ	50660 MW	58120 TQ	USBLS	5/07
Auto Damage	Albany-Schenectady-Troy MSA, NY	Y	48680 FQ	54410 MW	59870 TQ	USBLS	5/07
Auto Damage	Buffalo-Niagara Falls MSA, NY	Y	45210 FQ	48330 MW	51390 TQ	USBLS	5/07
Auto Damage	New York-Northern New Jersey-Long Island MSA, NY-NJ-PA	Y	45730 FQ	54420 MW	62610 TQ	USBLS	5/07
Auto Damage	North Carolina	Y	42890 FQ	49960 MW	59920 TQ	USBLS	5/07
Auto Damage	Charlotte-Gastonia-Concord MSA, NC-SC	Y	44540 FQ	52160 MW	62050 TQ	USBLS	5/07
Auto Damage	Raleigh-Cary MSA, NC	Y	42490 FQ	51480 MW	58290 TQ	USBLS	5/07
Auto Damage	Ohio	Y	43490 FQ	51980 MW	59710 TQ	USBLS	5/07
Auto Damage	Cincinnati-Middletown MSA, OH-KY-IN	Y	44130 FQ	52750 MW	61170 TQ	USBLS	5/07
Auto Damage	Cleveland-Elyria-Mentor MSA, OH	Y	48090 FQ	55230 MW	61450 TQ	USBLS	5/07
Auto Damage	Oklahoma	Y	38140 FQ	45620 MW	53260 TQ	USBLS	5/07
Auto Damage	Oklahoma City MSA, OK	Y	37970 FQ	44480 MW	51360 TQ	USBLS	5/07
Auto Damage	Tulsa MSA, OK	Y	35620 FQ	45070 MW	57160 TQ	USBLS	5/07
Auto Damage	Portland-Vancouver-Beaverton MSA, OR-WA	Y	43650 FQ	49900 MW	61690 TQ	USBLS	5/07
Auto Damage	Pennsylvania	Y	43090 FQ	51250 MW	59110 TQ	USBLS	5/07
Auto Damage	Philadelphia-Camden-Wilmington MSA, PA-NJ-DE-MD	Y	48070 FQ	55250 MW	61480 TQ	USBLS	5/07
Auto Damage	Pittsburgh MSA, PA	Y	34320 FQ	44540 MW	51860 TQ	USBLS	5/07
Auto Damage	South Carolina	Y	40340 FQ	49920 MW	59220 TQ	USBLS	5/07
Auto Damage	Columbia MSA, SC	Y	39220 FQ	49530 MW	58380 TQ	USBLS	5/07
Auto Damage	South Dakota	Y	33613 FQ	37042 MW	43591 TQ	SDBLS	7/08-9/08
Auto Damage	Tennessee	Y	35040 FQ	38700 MW	50650 TQ	USBLS	5/07
Auto Damage	Nashville-Davidson-Murfreesboro MSA, TN	Y	34960 FQ	38170 MW	48480 TQ	USBLS	5/07
Auto Damage	Texas	Y	42670 FQ	49530 MW	57900 TQ	USBLS	5/07
Auto Damage	Dallas-Fort Worth-Arlington MSA, TX	Y	43020 FQ	48480 MW	55150 TQ	USBLS	5/07
Auto Damage	Houston-Sugar Land-Baytown MSA, TX	Y	45400 FQ	54030 MW	60530 TQ	USBLS	5/07
Auto Damage	San Antonio MSA, TX	Y	39720 FQ	45430 MW	54930 TQ	USBLS	5/07
Auto Damage	Utah	Y	49350 FQ	53130 MW	57400 TQ	USBLS	5/07
Auto Damage	Virginia	Y	42320 FQ	50830 MW	62120 TQ	USBLS	5/07
Auto Damage	Richmond MSA, VA	Y	44040 FQ	52520 MW	64280 TQ	USBLS	5/07
Auto Damage	Washington	H	25.45 FQ	28.33 MW	31.35 TQ	WABLS	3/08
Auto Damage	Seattle-Tacoma-Bellevue MSA, WA	Y	50780 FQ	58010 MW	65610 TQ	USBLS	5/07
Auto Damage	West Virginia	Y	48106 FQ	57949 MW	83319 TQ	WVBLS	7/08-9/08
Auto Damage	Wisconsin	Y	40600 FQ	47990 MW	56890 TQ	USBLS	5/07
Auto Damage	Milwaukee-Waukesha-West Allis MSA, WI	Y	45720 FQ	53800 MW	59980 TQ	USBLS	5/07
Auto Damage	Puerto Rico	Y	26250 FQ	29180 MW	32130 TQ	USBLS	5/07
Auto Damage	San Juan-Caguas-Guaynabo MSA, PR	Y	26620 FQ	29580 MW	32550 TQ	USBLS	5/07
Insurance Claims and Policy Processing Clerk							
	Alabama	Y	23490 FQ	27470 MW	31540 TQ	USBLS	5/07
	Birmingham-Hoover MSA, AL	Y	24870 FQ	28330 MW	31800 TQ	USBLS	5/07
	Alaska	Y	27890 FQ	32620 MW	40680 TQ	USBLS	5/07
	Anchorage MSA, AK	Y	28300 FQ	34940 MW	43240 TQ	USBLS	5/07
	Arizona	Y	22900 FQ	28770 MW	36380 TQ	USBLS	5/07
	Phoenix-Mesa-Scottsdale MSA, AZ	Y	23200 FQ	29860 MW	37010 TQ	USBLS	5/07
	Tucson MSA, AZ	Y	23610 FQ	26150 MW	33800 TQ	USBLS	5/07
	Arkansas	Y	24150 FQ	29420 MW	38480 TQ	USBLS	5/07
	Little Rock-North Little Rock MSA, AR	Y	26040 FQ	31480 MW	41440 TQ	USBLS	5/07
	California	H	14.12 FQ	17.54 MW	22.13 TQ	CABLS	1/08-3/08

AE	Average entry wage	AW	Average wage paid	FQ	First quartile wage
AER	Average entry range	AWR	Average wage range	H	Hourly
AEX	Average experienced wage	AXR	Average experienced range	HI	Highest wage paid
ATC	Average total compensation	D	Daily	HR	High end range

LO	Lowest wage paid	MTC	Median total compensation	TCC	Total cash compensation
LR	Low end range	MW	Median wage paid	TQ	Third quartile wage
M	Monthly	MWR	Median wage range	W	Weekly
MCC	Median cash compensation	S	See annotated source	Y	Yearly

Occupation/Type/Industry	Location	Per	Low	Mid	High	Source	Date
Insurance Claims and Policy Processing Clerk							
	Los Angeles-Long Beach-Glendale PMSA, CA	H	13.43 FQ	17.02 MW	22.19 TQ	CABLS	1/08-3/08
	Oakland-Fremont-Hayward MSA, CA	H	15.85 FQ	20.82 MW	24.57 TQ	CABLS	1/08-3/08
	Oxnard-Thousand Oaks-Ventura MSA, CA	H	14.58 FQ	17.14 MW	22.07 TQ	CABLS	1/08-3/08
	Riverside-San Bernardino-Ontario MSA, CA	H	14.80 FQ	19.21 MW	24.84 TQ	CABLS	1/08-3/08
	Sacramento-Arden Arcade-Roseville MSA, CA	H	13.85 FQ	16.36 MW	20.21 TQ	CABLS	1/08-3/08
	San Diego-Carlsbad-San Marcos MSA, CA	H	14.44 FQ	17.12 MW	20.01 TQ	CABLS	1/08-3/08
	San Francisco-San Mateo-Redwood PMSA, CA	H	18.12 FQ	21.62 MW	25.73 TQ	CABLS	1/08-3/08
	San Jose-Sunnyvale-Santa Clara MSA, CA	H	14.50 FQ	19.53 MW	24.09 TQ	CABLS	1/08-3/08
	Santa Ana-Anaheim-Irvine PMSA, CA	Y	29200 FQ	35230 MW	41760 TQ	USBLS	5/07
	Santa Rosa-Petaluma MSA, CA	H	17.49 FQ	21.11 MW	24.45 TQ	CABLS	1/08-3/08
	Colorado	Y	29540 FQ	35890 MW	43490 TQ	USBLS	5/07
	Denver-Aurora MSA, CO	Y	30690 FQ	36510 MW	44000 TQ	USBLS	5/07
	Connecticut	H	14.71 AE	18.67 MW		CTBLS	1/08-3/08
	Bridgeport-Stamford-Norwalk MSA, CT	Y	34970 FQ	41180 MW	50170 TQ	USBLS	5/07
	Hartford-West Hartford-East Hartford MSA, CT	Y	32710 FQ	38160 MW	46200 TQ	USBLS	5/07
	Delaware	Y	30470 FQ	35500 MW	40290 TQ	USBLS	5/07
	Wilmington PMSA, DE-MD-NJ	Y	31150 FQ	35810 MW	40430 TQ	USBLS	5/07
	District of Columbia	Y	32600 FQ	37280 MW	49960 TQ	USBLS	5/07
	Washington-Arlington-Alexandria MSA, DC-VA-MD-WV	Y	27780 FQ	32980 MW	39270 TQ	USBLS	5/07
	Florida	Y	25450 FQ	30070 MW	37060 TQ	USBLS	5/07
	Fort Lauderdale-Pompano Beach-Deerfield Beach PMSA, FL	Y	26210 FQ	30640 MW	38320 TQ	USBLS	5/07
	Jacksonville MSA, FL	Y	22340 FQ	25540 MW	31710 TQ	USBLS	5/07
	Miami-Fort Lauderdale-Miami Beach MSA, FL	Y	27080 FQ	32300 MW	39440 TQ	USBLS	5/07
	Orlando-Kissimmee MSA, FL	Y	26080 FQ	29950 MW	36610 TQ	USBLS	5/07
	Tampa-St. Petersburg-Clearwater MSA, FL	Y	25680 FQ	31100 MW	38900 TQ	USBLS	5/07
	West Palm Beach-Boca Raton-Boynton Beach PMSA, FL	Y	28720 FQ	33960 MW	42790 TQ	USBLS	5/07
	Georgia	Y	24280 FQ	29630 MW	35520 TQ	USBLS	5/07
	Atlanta-Sandy Springs-Marietta MSA, GA	Y	24650 FQ	30670 MW	36810 TQ	USBLS	5/07
	Hawaii	Y	27760 FQ	33300 MW	38510 TQ	USBLS	5/07
	Honolulu MSA, HI	Y	27340 FQ	33130 MW	38540 TQ	USBLS	5/07
	Idaho	Y	25610 FQ	28220 MW	32660 TQ	USBLS	5/07
	Boise City-Nampa MSA, ID	Y	25510 FQ	27690 MW	29800 TQ	USBLS	5/07
	Coeur d'Alene MSA, ID	Y	28190 FQ	41600 MW	48050 TQ	USBLS	5/07
	Illinois	Y	27620 FQ	35210 MW	42190 TQ	USBLS	5/07
	Chicago-Naperville-Joliet MSA, IL-IN-WI	Y	28640 FQ	36240 MW	43440 TQ	USBLS	5/07
	Indiana	Y	24750 FQ	30290 MW	36480 TQ	USBLS	5/07
	Fort Wayne MSA, IN	Y	22550 FQ	27540 MW	34690 TQ	USBLS	5/07
	Gary PMSA, IN	Y	20560 FQ	26920 MW	33240 TQ	USBLS	5/07
	Indianapolis-Carmel MSA, IN	Y	27610 FQ	32450 MW	38690 TQ	USBLS	5/07
	Iowa	Y	23860 FQ	29250 MW	36120 TQ	USBLS	5/07
	Des Moines-West Des Moines MSA, IA	Y	25860 FQ	32350 MW	39370 TQ	USBLS	5/07
	Kansas	Y	25640 FQ	28800 MW	34370 TQ	USBLS	5/07
	Wichita MSA, KS	Y	22070 FQ	26310 MW	33230 TQ	USBLS	5/07
	Kentucky	Y	26752 FQ	31026 MW	37961 TQ	KYBLS	2008
	Louisville-Jefferson County MSA, KY-IN	Y	24010 FQ	28670 MW	34900 TQ	USBLS	5/07
	Louisiana	H	10.72 FQ	12.55 MW	14.98 TQ	LABLS	1/08-3/08
	Baton Rouge MSA, LA	Y	23190 FQ	26500 MW	30500 TQ	USBLS	5/07

AE	Average entry wage	AW	Average wage paid	FQ	First quartile wage
AER	Average entry range	AWR	Average wage range	H	Hourly
AEX	Average experienced wage	AXR	Average experienced range	HI	Highest wage paid
ATC	Average total compensation	D	Daily	HR	High end range

LO	Lowest wage paid	MTC	Median total compensation	TCC	Total cash compensation
LR	Low end range	MW	Median wage paid	TQ	Third quartile wage
M	Monthly	MWR	Median wage range	W	Weekly
MCC	Median cash compensation	S	See annotated source	Y	Yearly

Occupation/Type/Industry	Location	Per	Low	Mid	High	Source	Date
Insurance Claims and Policy Processing Clerk	New Orleans-Metairie-Kenner MSA, LA	Y	21530 FQ	25660 MW	31330 TQ	USBLS	5/07
	Maine	Y	27140 FQ	31380 MW	36980 TQ	USBLS	5/07
	Portland-South Portland-Biddeford MSA, ME	Y	27540 FQ	31780 MW	37000 TQ	USBLS	5/07
	Maryland	Y		36000 MW		MDBLS	3/08
	Baltimore-Towson MSA, MD	Y	30970 FQ	37570 MW	46070 TQ	USBLS	5/07
	Bethesda-Gaithersburg-Frederick PMSA, MD	Y	25920 FQ	30560 MW	37130 TQ	USBLS	5/07
	Massachusetts	Y	30100 FQ	35870 MW	42720 TQ	USBLS	5/07
	Boston-Cambridge-Quincy NECTA, MA	Y	32200 FQ	38010 MW	46060 TQ	USBLS	5/07
	New Bedford MSA, MA	Y	25880 FQ	31610 MW	35990 TQ	USBLS	5/07
	Springfield MSA, MA-CT	Y	30530 FQ	35010 MW	39430 TQ	USBLS	5/07
	Worcester MSA, MA-CT	Y	29030 FQ	33960 MW	40970 TQ	USBLS	5/07
	Michigan	Y	24570 FQ	31900 MW	40970 TQ	USBLS	5/07
	Ann Arbor MSA, MI	Y	28940 FQ	34590 MW	40660 TQ	USBLS	5/07
	Detroit-Warren-Livonia MSA, MI	Y	24800 FQ	33160 MW	42890 TQ	USBLS	5/07
	Flint MSA, MI	Y	22370 FQ	24750 MW	32340 TQ	USBLS	5/07
	Grand Rapids-Wyoming MSA, MI	Y	24830 FQ	30380 MW	37820 TQ	USBLS	5/07
	Warren-Troy-Farmington Hills PMSA, MI	Y	24950 FQ	35110 MW	45370 TQ	USBLS	5/07
	Minnesota	Y	30641 FQ	35990 MW	40965 TQ	MNBLS	10/08-12/08
	Duluth-Superior MSA, MN-WI	Y	26373 FQ	31681 MW	37895 TQ	MNBLS	10/08-12/08
	Minneapolis-Saint Paul MSA, MN-WI	Y	31151 FQ	36313 MW	41121 TQ	MNBLS	10/08-12/08
	Rochester MSA, MN	Y	23459 FQ	25646 MW	37062 TQ	MNBLS	10/08-12/08
	Mississippi	Y	24720 FQ	29280 MW	36720 TQ	USBLS	5/07
	Hattiesburg MSA, MS	Y	22930 FQ	25270 MW	29880 TQ	USBLS	5/07
	Jackson MSA, MS	Y	25920 FQ	30120 MW	37990 TQ	USBLS	5/07
	Missouri	Y	25030 FQ	30330 MW	39830 TQ	USBLS	5/07
	Kansas City MSA, MO-KS	Y	26710 FQ	29720 MW	38240 TQ	USBLS	5/07
	St. Louis MSA, MO-IL	Y	25220 FQ	31590 MW	44460 TQ	USBLS	5/07
	Montana	Y	23990 FQ	27950 MW	31530 TQ	USBLS	5/07
	Billings MSA, MT	Y	26120 FQ	31850 MW	37650 TQ	USBLS	5/07
	Great Falls MSA, MT	Y	23650 FQ	27760 MW	31590 TQ	USBLS	5/07
	Nebraska	Y	24940 FQ	29210 MW	35550 TQ	USBLS	5/07
	Omaha-Council Bluffs MSA, NE-IA	Y	26170 FQ	30710 MW	37500 TQ	USBLS	5/07
	Nevada	H	12.52 FQ	15.96 MW	18.34 TQ	NVBLS	5/08
	Las Vegas-Paradise MSA, NV	H	13.36 FQ	16.44 MW	18.57 TQ	NVBLS	5/08
	New Hampshire	H	11.74 AE	15.56 MW	18.61 AEX	NHBLS	6/08
	Manchester MSA, NH	Y	27990 FQ	32720 MW	40060 TQ	USBLS	5/07
	Nashua NECTA, NH-MA	Y	24190 FQ	30740 MW	39170 TQ	USBLS	5/07
	New Jersey	Y	29310 FQ	35090 MW	41060 TQ	USBLS	5/07
	Camden PMSA, NJ	Y	29020 FQ	34590 MW	40610 TQ	USBLS	5/07
	Edison PMSA, NJ	Y	28730 FQ	34690 MW	41380 TQ	USBLS	5/07
	Newark-Union PMSA, NJ-PA	Y	30360 FQ	35640 MW	40800 TQ	USBLS	5/07
	New Mexico	Y	21620 FQ	25640 MW	31530 TQ	USBLS	5/07
	Albuquerque MSA, NM	Y	21910 FQ	26430 MW	31840 TQ	USBLS	5/07
	New York	Y	27430 FQ	33430 MW	40500 TQ	USBLS	5/07
	Albany-Schenectady-Troy MSA, NY	Y	27000 FQ	31490 MW	37420 TQ	USBLS	5/07
	Binghamton MSA, NY	Y	27320 FQ	33840 MW	39230 TQ	USBLS	5/07
	Buffalo-Niagara Falls MSA, NY	Y	26610 FQ	30410 MW	35430 TQ	USBLS	5/07
	Nassau-Suffolk PMSA, NY	Y	32380 FQ	38360 MW	47470 TQ	USBLS	5/07
	New York-Northern New Jersey-Long Island MSA, NY-NJ-PA	Y	29900 FQ	35940 MW	42990 TQ	USBLS	5/07
	North Carolina	Y	26470 FQ	31620 MW	38320 TQ	USBLS	5/07
	Charlotte-Gastonia-Concord MSA, NC-SC	Y	27570 FQ	33650 MW	41660 TQ	USBLS	5/07
	Raleigh-Cary MSA, NC	Y	26460 FQ	33850 MW	38630 TQ	USBLS	5/07
	North Dakota	Y	23420 FQ	27080 MW	31320 TQ	USBLS	5/07
	Fargo MSA, ND-MN	Y	22740 FQ	26240 MW	28800 TQ	USBLS	5/07
	Ohio	Y	27300 FQ	32410 MW	39470 TQ	USBLS	5/07
	Cincinnati-Middletown MSA, OH-KY-IN	Y	28130 FQ	32790 MW	41630 TQ	USBLS	5/07

AE Average entry wage	**AW** Average wage paid	**FQ** First quartile wage	**LO** Lowest wage paid	**MTC** Median total compensation	**TCC** Total cash compensation
AER Average entry range	**AWR** Average wage range	**H** Hourly	**LR** Low end range	**MW** Median wage paid	**TQ** Third quartile wage
AEX Average experienced wage	**AXR** Average experienced range	**HI** Highest wage paid	**M** Monthly	**MWR** Median wage range	**W** Weekly
ATC Average total compensation	**D** Daily	**HR** High end range	**MCC** Median cash compensation	**S** See annotated source	**Y** Yearly

Insurance Claims and Policy Processing Clerk

Occupation/Type/Industry	Location	Per	Low	Mid	High	Source	Date
Insurance Claims and Policy Processing Clerk	Cleveland-Elyria-Mentor MSA, OH	Y	27660 FQ	32600 MW	38480 TQ	USBLS	5/07
	Columbus MSA, OH	Y	27120 FQ	33250 MW	39530 TQ	USBLS	5/07
	Dayton MSA, OH	Y	28230 FQ	34650 MW	42500 TQ	USBLS	5/07
	Oklahoma	Y	22450 FQ	28580 MW	33430 TQ	USBLS	5/07
	Lawton MSA, OK	Y	17880 FQ	22530 MW	33670 TQ	USBLS	5/07
	Oklahoma City MSA, OK	Y	25490 FQ	30270 MW	36760 TQ	USBLS	5/07
	Tulsa MSA, OK	Y	25880 FQ	29060 MW	32270 TQ	USBLS	5/07
	Oregon	H	13.38 FQ	16.28 MW	18.92 TQ	ORBLS	5/08
	Portland-Vancouver-Beaverton MSA, OR-WA	Y	30560 FQ	35100 MW	40680 TQ	USBLS	5/07
	Pennsylvania	Y	26110 FQ	31100 MW	38190 TQ	USBLS	5/07
	Allentown-Bethlehem-Easton MSA, PA-NJ	Y	29100 FQ	33880 MW	38630 TQ	USBLS	5/07
	Philadelphia-Camden-Wilmington MSA, PA-NJ-DE-MD	Y	26970 FQ	32960 MW	40260 TQ	USBLS	5/07
	Pittsburgh MSA, PA	Y	24720 FQ	28910 MW	35410 TQ	USBLS	5/07
	Rhode Island	Y	29160 FQ	34030 MW	38940 TQ	USBLS	5/07
	Providence-Fall River-Warwick MSA, RI-MA	Y	28950 FQ	33760 MW	38520 TQ	USBLS	5/07
	South Carolina	Y	24790 FQ	28920 MW	33760 TQ	USBLS	5/07
	Charleston-North Charleston MSA, SC	Y	26310 FQ	29030 MW	31910 TQ	USBLS	5/07
	Columbia MSA, SC	Y	25650 FQ	28990 MW	32400 TQ	USBLS	5/07
	Florence MSA, SC	Y	23810 FQ	27220 MW	30320 TQ	USBLS	5/07
	South Dakota	Y	21500 FQ	24997 MW	29720 TQ	SDBLS	7/08-9/08
	Sioux Falls MSA, SD	Y	22096 FQ	26417 MW	30510 TQ	SDBLS	7/08-9/08
	Tennessee	Y	27890 FQ	32750 MW	42160 TQ	USBLS	5/07
	Memphis MSA, TN-MS-AR	Y	29130 FQ	35170 MW	44440 TQ	USBLS	5/07
	Nashville-Davidson-Murfreesboro MSA, TN	Y	29810 FQ	36890 MW	44700 TQ	USBLS	5/07
	Texas	Y	23290 FQ	29250 MW	35500 TQ	USBLS	5/07
	Austin-Round Rock MSA, TX	Y	26350 FQ	32120 MW	38640 TQ	USBLS	5/07
	Beaumont-Port Arthur MSA, TX	Y	21380 FQ	23890 MW	28400 TQ	USBLS	5/07
	Dallas-Fort Worth-Arlington MSA, TX	Y	25920 FQ	30690 MW	36500 TQ	USBLS	5/07
	El Paso MSA, TX	Y	22970 FQ	28670 MW	32150 TQ	USBLS	5/07
	Houston-Sugar Land-Baytown MSA, TX	Y	23120 FQ	29710 MW	36740 TQ	USBLS	5/07
	San Antonio MSA, TX	Y	25820 FQ	30180 MW	34660 TQ	USBLS	5/07
	Utah	Y	22830 FQ	28000 MW	34310 TQ	USBLS	5/07
	Salt Lake City MSA, UT	Y	24630 FQ	29990 MW	35780 TQ	USBLS	5/07
	Vermont	Y	26900 FQ	31470 MW	37380 TQ	USBLS	5/07
	Burlington-South Burlington MSA, VT	Y	29490 FQ	35660 MW	43670 TQ	USBLS	5/07
	Virginia	Y	26420 FQ	31200 MW	37020 TQ	USBLS	5/07
	Richmond MSA, VA	Y	27380 FQ	32950 MW	39560 TQ	USBLS	5/07
	Virginia Beach-Norfolk-Newport News MSA, VA-NC	Y	25120 FQ	29960 MW	34950 TQ	USBLS	5/07
	Washington	H	13.86 FQ	16.42 MW	19.47 TQ	WABLS	3/08
	Seattle-Tacoma-Bellevue MSA, WA	Y	30240 FQ	35820 MW	42610 TQ	USBLS	5/07
	West Virginia	Y	22485 FQ	25410 MW	30809 TQ	WVBLS	7/08-9/08
	Charleston MSA, WV	Y	22930 FQ	26500 MW	31180 TQ	USBLS	5/07
	Wisconsin	Y	25620 FQ	29870 MW	36260 TQ	USBLS	5/07
	Milwaukee-Waukesha-West Allis MSA, WI	Y	27320 FQ	32290 MW	39310 TQ	USBLS	5/07
	Wyoming	Y	22804 FQ	26469 MW	30880 TQ	WYBLS	9/08
	Cheyenne MSA, WY	Y	23369 FQ	26765 MW	31921 TQ	WYBLS	9/08
	Puerto Rico	Y	18190 FQ	22090 MW	26960 TQ	USBLS	5/07
	San Juan-Caguas-Guaynabo MSA, PR	Y	18260 FQ	22110 MW	26930 TQ	USBLS	5/07
	Virgin Islands	Y	21940 FQ	25040 MW	29840 TQ	USBLS	5/07
	Guam	Y	18090 FQ	21710 MW	28620 TQ	USBLS	5/07
Insurance Clerk State Highway Patrol	Missouri	S	1081 LO		1498 HI	MSHPSS	7/1/08

AE	Average entry wage	AW	Average wage paid	FQ	First quartile wage
AER	Average entry range	AWR	Average wage range	H	Hourly
AEX	Average experienced wage	AXR	Average experienced range	HI	Highest wage paid
ATC	Average total compensation	D	Daily	HR	High end range

LO	Lowest wage paid	MTC	Median total compensation	TCC	Total cash compensation
LR	Low end range	MW	Median wage paid	TQ	Third quartile wage
M	Monthly	MWR	Median wage range	W	Weekly
MCC	Median cash compensation	S	See annotated source	Y	Yearly

Occupation/Type/Industry	Location	Per	Low	Mid	High	Source	Date
Insurance Examination Data Specialist							
State Government	Ohio	H	23.87 LO		35.02 HI	ODAS	2008
Insurance Examiner							
State Government	Ohio	H	19.88 LO		26.28 HI	ODAS	2008
Insurance Sales Agent	Alabama	Y	29740 FQ	39610 MW	64900 TQ	USBLS	5/07
	Birmingham-Hoover MSA, AL	Y	30450 FQ	47310 MW	85500 TQ	USBLS	5/07
	Montgomery MSA, AL	Y	31490 FQ	44190 MW	74740 TQ	USBLS	5/07
	Alaska	Y	30430 FQ	37750 MW	47330 TQ	USBLS	5/07
	Arizona	Y	32430 FQ	43320 MW	59090 TQ	USBLS	5/07
	Flagstaff MSA, AZ	Y	33370 FQ	41030 MW	69490 TQ	USBLS	5/07
	Phoenix-Mesa-Scottsdale MSA, AZ	Y	34160 FQ	44740 MW	62090 TQ	USBLS	5/07
	Tucson MSA, AZ	Y	23850 FQ	33210 MW	47130 TQ	USBLS	5/07
	Arkansas	Y	23790 FQ	30210 MW	51110 TQ	USBLS	5/07
	Little Rock-North Little Rock MSA, AR	Y	24930 FQ	38660 MW	60190 TQ	USBLS	5/07
	California	H	18.61 FQ	25.88 MW	40.50 TQ	CABLS	1/08-3/08
	Bakersfield MSA, CA	H	12.87 FQ	24.17 MW	34.48 TQ	CABLS	1/08-3/08
	Los Angeles-Long Beach-Glendale PMSA, CA	H	19.00 FQ	24.39 MW	39.26 TQ	CABLS	1/08-3/08
	Oakland-Fremont-Hayward MSA, CA	H	21.97 FQ	27.29 MW	34.55 TQ	CABLS	1/08-3/08
	Riverside-San Bernardino-Ontario MSA, CA	H	16.28 FQ	23.23 MW	31.72 TQ	CABLS	1/08-3/08
	Sacramento-Arden Arcade-Roseville MSA, CA	H	18.07 FQ	24.52 MW	50.68 TQ	CABLS	1/08-3/08
	San Diego-Carlsbad-San Marcos MSA, CA	H	20.30 FQ	28.11 MW	39.24 TQ	CABLS	1/08-3/08
	San Francisco-San Mateo-Redwood PMSA, CA	H	25.80 FQ	38.40 MW	60.73 TQ	CABLS	1/08-3/08
	San Jose-Sunnyvale-Santa Clara MSA, CA	H	20.28 FQ	26.89 MW	46.16 TQ	CABLS	1/08-3/08
	Santa Ana-Anaheim-Irvine PMSA, CA	Y	35000 FQ	53420 MW	86830 TQ	USBLS	5/07
	Colorado	Y	32310 FQ	42600 MW	68840 TQ	USBLS	5/07
	Denver-Aurora MSA, CO	Y	33950 FQ	45030 MW	75460 TQ	USBLS	5/07
	Fort Collins-Loveland MSA, CO	Y	29950 FQ	36700 MW	45120 TQ	USBLS	5/07
	Connecticut	H	18.28 AE	27.51 MW		CTBLS	1/08-3/08
	Bridgeport-Stamford-Norwalk MSA, CT	Y	44460 FQ	61250 MW	113580 TQ	USBLS	5/07
	Hartford-West Hartford-East Hartford MSA, CT	Y	45690 FQ	59760 MW	87750 TQ	USBLS	5/07
	New Haven MSA, CT	Y	36780 FQ	44620 MW	65570 TQ	USBLS	5/07
	Delaware	Y	36210 FQ	47540 MW	69340 TQ	USBLS	5/07
	Wilmington PMSA, DE-MD-NJ	Y	35020 FQ	47340 MW	67100 TQ	USBLS	5/07
	District of Columbia	Y	44500 FQ	51350 MW	62390 TQ	USBLS	5/07
	Washington-Arlington-Alexandria MSA, DC-VA-MD-WV	Y	36780 FQ	46280 MW	67520 TQ	USBLS	5/07
	Florida	Y	31980 FQ	42200 MW	61360 TQ	USBLS	5/07
	Fort Lauderdale-Pompano Beach-Deerfield Beach PMSA, FL	Y	34700 FQ	44810 MW	59800 TQ	USBLS	5/07
	Jacksonville MSA, FL	Y	32810 FQ	49460 MW	66300 TQ	USBLS	5/07
	Miami-Fort Lauderdale-Miami Beach MSA, FL	Y	31790 FQ	42430 MW	59180 TQ	USBLS	5/07
	Orlando-Kissimmee MSA, FL	Y	32760 FQ	44960 MW	71210 TQ	USBLS	5/07
	Tallahassee MSA, FL	Y	31750 FQ	42150 MW	56660 TQ	USBLS	5/07
	Tampa-St. Petersburg-Clearwater MSA, FL	Y	31140 FQ	40290 MW	62610 TQ	USBLS	5/07
	West Palm Beach-Boca Raton-Boynton Beach PMSA, FL	Y	35290 FQ	46440 MW	63460 TQ	USBLS	5/07
	Georgia	Y	29370 FQ	39940 MW	62050 TQ	USBLS	5/07
	Athens-Clarke County MSA, GA	Y	31790 FQ	37210 MW	53040 TQ	USBLS	5/07
	Atlanta-Sandy Springs-Marietta MSA, GA	Y	32730 FQ	43850 MW	67190 TQ	USBLS	5/07

AE	Average entry wage	AW	Average wage paid	FQ	First quartile wage
AER	Average entry range	AWR	Average wage range	H	Hourly
AEX	Average experienced wage	AXR	Average experienced range	HI	Highest wage paid
ATC	Average total compensation	D	Daily	HR	High end range

LO	Lowest wage paid	MTC	Median total compensation
LR	Low end range	MW	Median wage paid
M	Monthly	MWR	Median wage range
MCC	Median cash compensation	S	See annotated source

TCC	Total cash compensation		
TQ	Third quartile wage		
W	Weekly		
Y	Yearly		

Occupation/Type/Industry	Location	Per	Low	Mid	High	Source	Date
Insurance Sales Agent	Savannah MSA, GA	Y	35670 FQ	50040 MW	68090 TQ	USBLS	5/07
	Hawaii	Y	26230 FQ	40360 MW	54550 TQ	USBLS	5/07
	Honolulu MSA, HI	Y	23900 FQ	39110 MW	50370 TQ	USBLS	5/07
	Idaho	Y	23960 FQ	34740 MW	42380 TQ	USBLS	5/07
	Boise City-Nampa MSA, ID	Y	32590 FQ	36220 MW	42330 TQ	USBLS	5/07
	Illinois	Y	33600 FQ	45450 MW	75680 TQ	USBLS	5/07
	Chicago-Naperville-Joliet MSA, IL-IN-WI	Y	35680 FQ	50090 MW	85980 TQ	USBLS	5/07
	Indiana	Y	29790 FQ	42240 MW	63850 TQ	USBLS	5/07
	Gary PMSA, IN	Y	22880 FQ	30910 MW	67750 TQ	USBLS	5/07
	Indianapolis-Carmel MSA, IN	Y	34910 FQ	46930 MW	65960 TQ	USBLS	5/07
	Iowa	Y	30870 FQ	41440 MW	62410 TQ	USBLS	5/07
	Des Moines-West Des Moines MSA, IA	Y	35190 FQ	61990 MW	77180 TQ	USBLS	5/07
	Kansas	Y	29690 FQ	41390 MW	67240 TQ	USBLS	5/07
	Wichita MSA, KS	Y	29880 FQ	45590 MW	62420 TQ	USBLS	5/07
	Kentucky	Y	27706 FQ	37592 MW	63682 TQ	KYBLS	2008
	Louisville-Jefferson County MSA, KY-IN	Y	31250 FQ	45280 MW	71580 TQ	USBLS	5/07
	Owensboro MSA, KY	Y	27930 FQ	31170 MW	53240 TQ	USBLS	5/07
	Louisiana	H	14.44 FQ	18.96 MW	27.61 TQ	LABLS	1/08-3/08
	Baton Rouge MSA, LA	Y	33180 FQ	39850 MW	55820 TQ	USBLS	5/07
	New Orleans-Metairie-Kenner MSA, LA	Y	36280 FQ	47940 MW	61150 TQ	USBLS	5/07
	Maine	Y	33860 FQ	43290 MW	68990 TQ	USBLS	5/07
	Lewiston-Auburn MSA, ME	Y	35080 FQ	40690 MW	50100 TQ	USBLS	5/07
	Portland-South Portland-Biddeford MSA, ME	Y	35450 FQ	49840 MW	83240 TQ	USBLS	5/07
	Maryland	Y		46500 MW		MDBLS	3/08
	Baltimore-Towson MSA, MD	Y	34410 FQ	46100 MW	79490 TQ	USBLS	5/07
	Bethesda-Gaithersburg-Frederick PMSA, MD	Y	36910 FQ	47920 MW	83700 TQ	USBLS	5/07
	Massachusetts	Y	40340 FQ	59720 MW	88640 TQ	USBLS	5/07
	Boston-Cambridge-Quincy NECTA, MA	Y	40360 FQ	62280 MW	93750 TQ	USBLS	5/07
	New Bedford MSA, MA	Y	25620 FQ	39930 MW	59980 TQ	USBLS	5/07
	Worcester MSA, MA-CT	Y	44580 FQ	59920 MW	78660 TQ	USBLS	5/07
	Michigan	Y	33680 FQ	47530 MW	83860 TQ	USBLS	5/07
	Detroit-Warren-Livonia MSA, MI	Y	37480 FQ	61750 MW	96110 TQ	USBLS	5/07
	Grand Rapids-Wyoming MSA, MI	Y	33480 FQ	44080 MW	72880 TQ	USBLS	5/07
	Warren-Troy-Farmington Hills PMSA, MI	Y	42670 FQ	72060 MW	99670 TQ	USBLS	5/07
	Minnesota	Y	39393 FQ	49861 MW	72231 TQ	MNBLS	10/08-12/08
	Duluth-Superior MSA, MN-WI	Y	34149 FQ	44881 MW	71154 TQ	MNBLS	10/08-12/08
	Minneapolis-Saint Paul MSA, MN-WI	Y	43215 FQ	57454 MW	77211 TQ	MNBLS	10/08-12/08
	Rochester MSA, MN	Y	35832 FQ	41452 MW	69420 TQ	MNBLS	10/08-12/08
	Mississippi	Y	24850 FQ	35570 MW	47790 TQ	USBLS	5/07
	Jackson MSA, MS	Y	33470 FQ	42990 MW	51770 TQ	USBLS	5/07
	Pascagoula MSA, MS	Y	27050 FQ	35800 MW	49970 TQ	USBLS	5/07
	Missouri	Y	28870 FQ	37110 MW	67600 TQ	USBLS	5/07
	Kansas City MSA, MO-KS	Y	30330 FQ	40370 MW	74580 TQ	USBLS	5/07
	St. Louis MSA, MO-IL	Y	25660 FQ	35840 MW	67030 TQ	USBLS	5/07
	Montana	Y	28570 FQ	36510 MW	56120 TQ	USBLS	5/07
	Billings MSA, MT	Y	87170 FQ	96520 MW	105760 TQ	USBLS	5/07
	Nebraska	Y	24870 FQ	36830 MW	51270 TQ	USBLS	5/07
	Omaha-Council Bluffs MSA, NE-IA	Y	25810 FQ	40370 MW	57360 TQ	USBLS	5/07
	Nevada	H	16.78 FQ	22.22 MW	29.84 TQ	NVBLS	5/08
	Las Vegas-Paradise MSA, NV	H	16.97 FQ	21.83 MW	30.78 TQ	NVBLS	5/08
	New Hampshire	H	18.37 AE	25.52 MW	44.60 AEX	NHBLS	6/08
	Manchester MSA, NH	Y	39360 FQ	45490 MW	63290 TQ	USBLS	5/07
	Nashua NECTA, NH-MA	Y	40480 FQ	47200 MW	58440 TQ	USBLS	5/07
	New Jersey	Y	43880 FQ	61560 MW	94790 TQ	USBLS	5/07
	Camden PMSA, NJ	Y	39870 FQ	54750 MW	78180 TQ	USBLS	5/07
	Edison PMSA, NJ	Y	42500 FQ	51570 MW	100010 TQ	USBLS	5/07
	Newark-Union PMSA, NJ-PA	Y	49280 FQ	75810 MW	99290 TQ	USBLS	5/07
	New Mexico	Y	26230 FQ	34280 MW	45970 TQ	USBLS	5/07
	Albuquerque MSA, NM	Y	24600 FQ	36490 MW	52310 TQ	USBLS	5/07
	New York	Y	37700 FQ	49100 MW	78630 TQ	USBLS	5/07

AE Average entry wage	**AW** Average wage paid	**FQ** First quartile wage	**LO** Lowest wage paid	**MTC** Median total compensation	**TCC** Total cash compensation
AER Average entry range	**AWR** Average wage range	**H** Hourly	**LR** Low end range	**MW** Median wage paid	**TQ** Third quartile wage
AEX Average experienced wage	**AXR** Average experienced range	**HI** Highest wage paid	**M** Monthly	**MWR** Median wage range	**W** Weekly
ATC Average total compensation	**D** Daily	**HR** High end range	**MCC** Median cash compensation	**S** See annotated source	**Y** Yearly

Occupation/Type/Industry	Location	Per	Low	Mid	High	Source	Date
Insurance Sales Agent	Albany-Schenectady-Troy MSA, NY	Y	40630 FQ	48430 MW	69090 TQ	USBLS	5/07
	Buffalo-Niagara Falls MSA, NY	Y	37500 FQ	48780 MW	70640 TQ	USBLS	5/07
	Nassau-Suffolk PMSA, NY	Y	35870 FQ	44740 MW	70520 TQ	USBLS	5/07
	New York-Northern New Jersey-Long Island MSA, NY-NJ-PA	Y	40210 FQ	53080 MW	92000 TQ	USBLS	5/07
	North Carolina	Y	27220 FQ	36430 MW	53920 TQ	USBLS	5/07
	Asheville MSA, NC	Y	27780 FQ	35800 MW	48740 TQ	USBLS	5/07
	Charlotte-Gastonia-Concord MSA, NC-SC	Y	33570 FQ	45550 MW	68690 TQ	USBLS	5/07
	Raleigh-Cary MSA, NC	Y	30260 FQ	38010 MW	76870 TQ	USBLS	5/07
	North Dakota	Y	30180 FQ	39620 MW	60810 TQ	USBLS	5/07
	Bismarck MSA, ND	Y	30860 FQ	56940 MW	107990 TQ	USBLS	5/07
	Fargo MSA, ND-MN	Y	29490 FQ	39310 MW	74660 TQ	USBLS	5/07
	Ohio	Y	29120 FQ	40190 MW	61920 TQ	USBLS	5/07
	Cincinnati-Middletown MSA, OH-KY-IN	Y	32360 FQ	47580 MW	71010 TQ	USBLS	5/07
	Cleveland-Elyria-Mentor MSA, OH	Y	27840 FQ	34940 MW	60630 TQ	USBLS	5/07
	Columbus MSA, OH	Y	33910 FQ	44600 MW	67120 TQ	USBLS	5/07
	Dayton MSA, OH	Y	29070 FQ	38230 MW	47770 TQ	USBLS	5/07
	Oklahoma	Y	27060 FQ	38980 MW	56710 TQ	USBLS	5/07
	Oklahoma City MSA, OK	Y	26900 FQ	36180 MW	50680 TQ	USBLS	5/07
	Tulsa MSA, OK	Y	30070 FQ	44130 MW	67360 TQ	USBLS	5/07
	Oregon	H	14.04 FQ	19.45 MW	30.77 TQ	ORBLS	5/08
	Portland-Vancouver-Beaverton MSA, OR-WA	Y	31610 FQ	45690 MW	65890 TQ	USBLS	5/07
	Pennsylvania	Y	33380 FQ	46970 MW	68930 TQ	USBLS	5/07
	Allentown-Bethlehem-Easton MSA, PA-NJ	Y	30810 FQ	37490 MW	62770 TQ	USBLS	5/07
	Philadelphia-Camden-Wilmington MSA, PA-NJ-DE-MD	Y	39140 FQ	51310 MW	75070 TQ	USBLS	5/07
	Pittsburgh MSA, PA	Y	32080 FQ	47600 MW	72650 TQ	USBLS	5/07
	Rhode Island	Y	43450 FQ	58490 MW	76930 TQ	USBLS	5/07
	Providence-Fall River-Warwick MSA, RI-MA	Y	38190 FQ	54470 MW	76770 TQ	USBLS	5/07
	South Carolina	Y	28340 FQ	36040 MW	54960 TQ	USBLS	5/07
	Charleston-North Charleston MSA, SC	Y	28320 FQ	35230 MW	46580 TQ	USBLS	5/07
	Columbia MSA, SC	Y	33910 FQ	44920 MW	60550 TQ	USBLS	5/07
	South Dakota	Y	32374 FQ	39279 MW	54292 TQ	SDBLS	7/08-9/08
	Sioux Falls MSA, SD	Y	35320 FQ	44398 MW	92097 TQ	SDBLS	7/08-9/08
	Tennessee	Y	29080 FQ	38790 MW	62100 TQ	USBLS	5/07
	Memphis MSA, TN-MS-AR	Y	29930 FQ	41250 MW	66420 TQ	USBLS	5/07
	Nashville-Davidson-Murfreesboro MSA, TN	Y	29430 FQ	39780 MW	63430 TQ	USBLS	5/07
	Texas	Y	30520 FQ	39330 MW	53800 TQ	USBLS	5/07
	Austin-Round Rock MSA, TX	Y	30920 FQ	38930 MW	52800 TQ	USBLS	5/07
	Dallas-Fort Worth-Arlington MSA, TX	Y	34360 FQ	43690 MW	68930 TQ	USBLS	5/07
	El Paso MSA, TX	Y	29030 FQ	38460 MW	48270 TQ	USBLS	5/07
	Houston-Sugar Land-Baytown MSA, TX	Y	30030 FQ	39360 MW	51490 TQ	USBLS	5/07
	San Antonio MSA, TX	Y	28710 FQ	35330 MW	47740 TQ	USBLS	5/07
	Utah	Y	27490 FQ	40400 MW	58650 TQ	USBLS	5/07
	Salt Lake City MSA, UT	Y	29760 FQ	47260 MW	62980 TQ	USBLS	5/07
	Vermont	Y	34360 FQ	46590 MW	71600 TQ	USBLS	5/07
	Burlington-South Burlington MSA, VT	Y	25270 FQ	43300 MW	77360 TQ	USBLS	5/07
	Virginia	Y	32490 FQ	42400 MW	59640 TQ	USBLS	5/07
	Lynchburg MSA, VA	Y	32200 FQ	41030 MW	51060 TQ	USBLS	5/07
	Richmond MSA, VA	Y	36470 FQ	48280 MW	63530 TQ	USBLS	5/07
	Virginia Beach-Norfolk-Newport News MSA, VA-NC	Y	30690 FQ	39130 MW	58580 TQ	USBLS	5/07
	Washington	H	18.43 FQ	23.75 MW	32.47 TQ	WABLS	3/08
	Seattle-Tacoma-Bellevue MSA, WA	Y	40950 FQ	52700 MW	75110 TQ	USBLS	5/07
	West Virginia	Y	22374 FQ	30572 MW	42357 TQ	WVBLS	7/08-9/08
	Charleston MSA, WV	Y	23710 FQ	38190 MW	62810 TQ	USBLS	5/07

AE Average entry wage	**AW** Average wage paid	**FQ** First quartile wage	**LO** Lowest wage paid	**MTC** Median total compensation	**TCC** Total cash compensation
AER Average entry range	**AWR** Average wage range	**H** Hourly	**LR** Low end range	**MW** Median wage paid	**TQ** Third quartile wage
AEX Average experienced wage	**AXR** Average experienced range	**HI** Highest wage paid	**M** Monthly	**MWR** Median wage range	**W** Weekly
ATC Average total compensation	**D** Daily	**HR** High end range	**MCC** Median cash compensation	**S** See annotated source	**Y** Yearly

Occupation/Type/Industry	Location	Per	Low	Mid	High	Source	Date
Insurance Sales Agent	Wisconsin	Y	35600 FQ	49540 MW	83030 TQ	USBLS	5/07
	Green Bay MSA, WI	Y	40010 FQ	57040 MW	71390 TQ	USBLS	5/07
	Milwaukee-Waukesha-West Allis MSA, WI	Y	47170 FQ	73720 MW	128970 TQ	USBLS	5/07
	Wyoming	Y	27929 FQ	34073 MW	52564 TQ	WYBLS	9/08
	Cheyenne MSA, WY	Y	15243 FQ	19135 MW	29385 TQ	WYBLS	9/08
	Puerto Rico	Y	14630 FQ	24430 MW	37490 TQ	USBLS	5/07
	San Juan-Caguas-Guaynabo MSA, PR	Y	14620 FQ	25110 MW	39110 TQ	USBLS	5/07
	Virgin Islands	Y	32870 FQ	37980 MW	49130 TQ	USBLS	5/07
	Guam	Y	19570 FQ	24680 MW	39130 TQ	USBLS	5/07
Insurance Underwriter	Alabama	Y	38730 FQ	44360 MW	53920 TQ	USBLS	5/07
	Birmingham-Hoover MSA, AL	Y	40380 FQ	44810 MW	52170 TQ	USBLS	5/07
	Alaska	Y	58630 FQ	69090 MW	79980 TQ	USBLS	5/07
	Anchorage MSA, AK	Y	58990 FQ	70330 MW	80780 TQ	USBLS	5/07
	Arizona	Y	37590 FQ	45810 MW	58060 TQ	USBLS	5/07
	Phoenix-Mesa-Scottsdale MSA, AZ	Y	37190 FQ	45120 MW	56200 TQ	USBLS	5/07
	Arkansas	Y	34150 FQ	43480 MW	62300 TQ	USBLS	5/07
	Little Rock-North Little Rock MSA, AR	Y	34100 FQ	43430 MW	63140 TQ	USBLS	5/07
	California	H	22.29 FQ	29.51 MW	39.35 TQ	CABLS	1/08-3/08
	Los Angeles-Long Beach-Glendale PMSA, CA	H	21.71 FQ	29.40 MW	40.46 TQ	CABLS	1/08-3/08
	Oakland-Fremont-Hayward MSA, CA	H	22.19 FQ	28.78 MW	37.49 TQ	CABLS	1/08-3/08
	Riverside-San Bernardino-Ontario MSA, CA	H	20.71 FQ	25.86 MW	34.82 TQ	CABLS	1/08-3/08
	Sacramento-Arden Arcade-Roseville MSA, CA	H	22.07 FQ	29.96 MW	40.40 TQ	CABLS	1/08-3/08
	San Diego-Carlsbad-San Marcos MSA, CA	H	20.09 FQ	24.08 MW	32.20 TQ	CABLS	1/08-3/08
	San Francisco-San Mateo-Redwood PMSA, CA	H	26.16 FQ	35.31 MW	52.20 TQ	CABLS	1/08-3/08
	San Jose-Sunnyvale-Santa Clara MSA, CA	H	22.65 FQ	27.51 MW	35.83 TQ	CABLS	1/08-3/08
	Santa Ana-Anaheim-Irvine PMSA, CA	Y	49090 FQ	63370 MW	80830 TQ	USBLS	5/07
	Colorado	Y	41540 FQ	56530 MW	73250 TQ	USBLS	5/07
	Denver-Aurora MSA, CO	Y	42960 FQ	57740 MW	73770 TQ	USBLS	5/07
	Connecticut	H	20.96 AE	29.74 MW		CTBLS	1/08-3/08
	Bridgeport-Stamford-Norwalk MSA, CT	Y	50930 FQ	65830 MW	92740 TQ	USBLS	5/07
	Hartford-West Hartford-East Hartford MSA, CT	Y	47220 FQ	62710 MW	87860 TQ	USBLS	5/07
	Delaware	Y	44540 FQ	58170 MW	76810 TQ	USBLS	5/07
	Wilmington PMSA, DE-MD-NJ	Y	43830 FQ	57180 MW	75960 TQ	USBLS	5/07
	District of Columbia	Y	42810 FQ	58310 MW	75900 TQ	USBLS	5/07
	Washington-Arlington-Alexandria MSA, DC-VA-MD-WV	Y	41510 FQ	52010 MW	70860 TQ	USBLS	5/07
	Florida	Y	38160 FQ	47410 MW	61970 TQ	USBLS	5/07
	Fort Lauderdale-Pompano Beach-Deerfield Beach PMSA, FL	Y	41590 FQ	51210 MW	62680 TQ	USBLS	5/07
	Jacksonville MSA, FL	Y	40570 FQ	47050 MW	58880 TQ	USBLS	5/07
	Miami-Fort Lauderdale-Miami Beach MSA, FL	Y	34040 FQ	45530 MW	60210 TQ	USBLS	5/07
	Orlando-Kissimmee MSA, FL	Y	38530 FQ	48420 MW	76300 TQ	USBLS	5/07
	Tampa-St. Petersburg-Clearwater MSA, FL	Y	42860 FQ	52100 MW	64190 TQ	USBLS	5/07
	West Palm Beach-Boca Raton-Boynton Beach PMSA, FL	Y	38610 FQ	50000 MW	68520 TQ	USBLS	5/07
	Georgia	Y	39760 FQ	51240 MW	69390 TQ	USBLS	5/07
	Atlanta-Sandy Springs-Marietta MSA, GA	Y	40980 FQ	53340 MW	72060 TQ	USBLS	5/07
	Hawaii	Y	37870 FQ	50500 MW	63190 TQ	USBLS	5/07
	Honolulu MSA, HI	Y	40760 FQ	52580 MW	64580 TQ	USBLS	5/07
	Idaho	Y	39560 FQ	49800 MW	64600 TQ	USBLS	5/07
	Boise City-Nampa MSA, ID	Y	46380 FQ	59810 MW	73060 TQ	USBLS	5/07

AE Average entry wage	**AW** Average wage paid	**FQ** First quartile wage	**LO** Lowest wage paid	**MTC** Median total compensation	**TCC** Total cash compensation
AER Average entry range	**AWR** Average wage range	**H** Hourly	**LR** Low end range	**MW** Median wage paid	**TQ** Third quartile wage
AEX Average experienced wage	**AXR** Average experienced range	**HI** Highest wage paid	**M** Monthly	**MWR** Median wage range	**W** Weekly
ATC Average total compensation	**D** Daily	**HR** High end range	**MCC** Median cash compensation	**S** See annotated source	**Y** Yearly

Occupation/Type/Industry	Location	Per	Low	Mid	High	Source	Date
Insurance Underwriter	Illinois	Y	43980 FQ	59340 MW	80780 TQ	USBLS	5/07
	Chicago-Naperville-Joliet MSA, IL-IN-WI	Y	44400 FQ	59420 MW	80450 TQ	USBLS	5/07
	Indiana	Y	43880 FQ	55480 MW	72760 TQ	USBLS	5/07
	Fort Wayne MSA, IN	Y	41250 FQ	51820 MW	73910 TQ	USBLS	5/07
	Indianapolis-Carmel MSA, IN	Y	44600 FQ	54920 MW	72000 TQ	USBLS	5/07
	Iowa	Y	36940 FQ	49630 MW	66060 TQ	USBLS	5/07
	Des Moines-West Des Moines MSA, IA	Y	39760 FQ	52550 MW	67000 TQ	USBLS	5/07
	Kansas	Y	37110 FQ	51550 MW	67500 TQ	USBLS	5/07
	Wichita MSA, KS	Y	30710 FQ	48150 MW	64800 TQ	USBLS	5/07
	Kentucky	Y	34764 FQ	45251 MW	59251 TQ	KYBLS	2008
	Louisville-Jefferson County MSA, KY-IN	Y	35050 FQ	47740 MW	60240 TQ	USBLS	5/07
	Louisiana	H	16.16 FQ	19.71 MW	25.42 TQ	LABLS	1/08-3/08
	Baton Rouge MSA, LA	Y	36720 FQ	45060 MW	55310 TQ	USBLS	5/07
	New Orleans-Metairie-Kenner MSA, LA	Y	34390 FQ	40180 MW	59510 TQ	USBLS	5/07
	Maine	Y	41280 FQ	56090 MW	70670 TQ	USBLS	5/07
	Portland-South Portland-Biddeford MSA, ME	Y	41870 FQ	57350 MW	72040 TQ	USBLS	5/07
	Maryland	Y		56850 MW		MDBLS	3/08
	Baltimore-Towson MSA, MD	Y	40500 FQ	58590 MW	72960 TQ	USBLS	5/07
	Bethesda-Gaithersburg-Frederick PMSA, MD	Y	43040 FQ	54010 MW	68210 TQ	USBLS	5/07
	Massachusetts	Y	49360 FQ	63950 MW	84300 TQ	USBLS	5/07
	Boston-Cambridge-Quincy NECTA, MA	Y	52450 FQ	66250 MW	88670 TQ	USBLS	5/07
	Springfield MSA, MA-CT	Y	41630 FQ	49470 MW	66420 TQ	USBLS	5/07
	Worcester MSA, MA-CT	Y	42270 FQ	53210 MW	67720 TQ	USBLS	5/07
	Michigan	Y	43470 FQ	55200 MW	70380 TQ	USBLS	5/07
	Detroit-Warren-Livonia MSA, MI	Y	45000 FQ	56200 MW	69980 TQ	USBLS	5/07
	Grand Rapids-Wyoming MSA, MI	Y	37950 FQ	46630 MW	57630 TQ	USBLS	5/07
	Warren-Troy-Farmington Hills PMSA, MI	Y	46170 FQ	58260 MW	72940 TQ	USBLS	5/07
	Minnesota	Y	43655 FQ	56032 MW	71818 TQ	MNBLS	10/08-12/08
	Minneapolis-Saint Paul MSA, MN-WI	Y	44510 FQ	58315 MW	74184 TQ	MNBLS	10/08-12/08
	Mississippi	Y	33840 FQ	45820 MW	62170 TQ	USBLS	5/07
	Jackson MSA, MS	Y	37250 FQ	47810 MW	63370 TQ	USBLS	5/07
	Missouri	Y	38250 FQ	50410 MW	68650 TQ	USBLS	5/07
	Kansas City MSA, MO-KS	Y	39810 FQ	53910 MW	70690 TQ	USBLS	Weekly
	St. Louis MSA, MO-IL	Y	40020 FQ	51640 MW	71610 TQ	USBLS	5/07
	Montana	Y	28300 FQ	36870 MW	46820 TQ	USBLS	5/07
	Nebraska	Y	37660 FQ	49960 MW	66920 TQ	USBLS	5/07
	Lincoln MSA, NE	Y	35060 FQ	42730 MW	60590 TQ	USBLS	5/07
	Omaha-Council Bluffs MSA, NE-IA	Y	40780 FQ	53600 MW	69290 TQ	USBLS	5/07
	Nevada	H	19.94 FQ	27.47 MW	40.94 TQ	NVBLS	5/08
	Las Vegas-Paradise MSA, NV	H	19.63 FQ	26.53 MW	39.41 TQ	NVBLS	5/08
	New Hampshire	H	21.42 AE	30.47 MW	37.25 AEX	NHBLS	6/08
	Manchester MSA, NH	Y	49100 FQ	59290 MW	79710 TQ	USBLS	5/07
	New Jersey	Y	52380 FQ	68930 MW	88430 TQ	USBLS	5/07
	Camden PMSA, NJ	Y	47800 FQ	65010 MW	86690 TQ	USBLS	5/07
	Edison PMSA, NJ	Y	49070 FQ	67200 MW	82160 TQ	USBLS	5/07
	Newark-Union PMSA, NJ-PA	Y	54890 FQ	71370 MW	92120 TQ	USBLS	5/07
	New Mexico	Y	39540 FQ	50640 MW	59890 TQ	USBLS	5/07
	Albuquerque MSA, NM	Y	39030 FQ	50010 MW	60020 TQ	USBLS	5/07
	New York	Y	48160 FQ	65290 MW	97600 TQ	USBLS	5/07
	Albany-Schenectady-Troy MSA, NY	Y	44190 FQ	55960 MW	85110 TQ	USBLS	5/07
	Buffalo-Niagara Falls MSA, NY	Y	39570 FQ	53930 MW	77950 TQ	USBLS	5/07
	Nassau-Suffolk PMSA, NY	Y	43910 FQ	55890 MW	80450 TQ	USBLS	5/07
	New York-Northern New Jersey-Long Island MSA, NY-NJ-PA	Y	53170 FQ	70640 MW	99180 TQ	USBLS	5/07
	Utica-Rome MSA, NY	Y	37480 FQ	48910 MW	69740 TQ	USBLS	5/07
	North Carolina	Y	39170 FQ	50350 MW	68180 TQ	USBLS	5/07

AE	Average entry wage	AW	Average wage paid	FQ	First quartile wage	LO	Lowest wage paid	MTC	Median total compensation
AER	Average entry range	AWR	Average wage range	H	Hourly	LR	Low end range	MW	Median wage paid
AEX	Average experienced wage	AXR	Average experienced range	HI	Highest wage paid	M	Monthly	MWR	Median wage range
ATC	Average total compensation	D	Daily	HR	High end range	MCC	Median cash compensation	S	See annotated source

TCC	Total cash compensation
TQ	Third quartile wage
W	Weekly
Y	Yearly

Occupation/Type/Industry	Location	Per	Low	Mid	High	Source	Date
Insurance Underwriter	Charlotte-Gastonia-Concord MSA, NC-SC	Y	42100 FQ	51600 MW	74090 TQ	USBLS	5/07
	Raleigh-Cary MSA, NC	Y	36750 FQ	47000 MW	64640 TQ	USBLS	5/07
	North Dakota	Y	30770 FQ	40870 MW	54570 TQ	USBLS	5/07
	Fargo MSA, ND-MN	Y	29320 FQ	36720 MW	56730 TQ	USBLS	5/07
	Ohio	Y	43650 FQ	55330 MW	69220 TQ	USBLS	5/07
	Cincinnati-Middletown MSA, OH-KY-IN	Y	45540 FQ	56370 MW	70390 TQ	USBLS	5/07
	Cleveland-Elyria-Mentor MSA, OH	Y	44330 FQ	56000 MW	70680 TQ	USBLS	5/07
	Columbus MSA, OH	Y	44750 FQ	56690 MW	70120 TQ	USBLS	5/07
	Dayton MSA, OH	Y	36200 FQ	46310 MW	60650 TQ	USBLS	5/07
	Oklahoma	Y	35850 FQ	40570 MW	48540 TQ	USBLS	5/07
	Oklahoma City MSA, OK	Y	35150 FQ	41960 MW	47920 TQ	USBLS	5/07
	Tulsa MSA, OK	Y	35980 FQ	40000 MW	48700 TQ	USBLS	5/07
	Portland-Vancouver-Beaverton MSA, OR-WA	Y	45510 FQ	57130 MW	73050 TQ	USBLS	5/07
	Pennsylvania	Y	43450 FQ	56950 MW	77010 TQ	USBLS	5/07
	Allentown-Bethlehem-Easton MSA, PA-NJ	Y	46950 FQ	58820 MW	77030 TQ	USBLS	5/07
	Philadelphia-Camden-Wilmington MSA, PA-NJ-DE-MD	Y	46430 FQ	62220 MW	82940 TQ	USBLS	5/07
	Pittsburgh MSA, PA	Y	39370 FQ	47540 MW	64990 TQ	USBLS	5/07
	Providence-Fall River-Warwick MSA, RI-MA	Y	44150 FQ	53260 MW	71710 TQ	USBLS	5/07
	South Carolina	Y	30340 FQ	36920 MW	50040 TQ	USBLS	5/07
	Charleston-North Charleston MSA, SC	Y	32710 FQ	44560 MW	54530 TQ	USBLS	5/07
	Columbia MSA, SC	Y	36210 FQ	41090 MW	48370 TQ	USBLS	5/07
	South Dakota	Y	45427 FQ	53862 MW	62879 TQ	SDBLS	7/08-9/08
	Sioux Falls MSA, SD	Y	46416 FQ	54163 MW	62247 TQ	SDBLS	7/08-9/08
	Tennessee	Y	44710 FQ	56800 MW	72280 TQ	USBLS	5/07
	Memphis MSA, TN-MS-AR	Y	44000 FQ	56850 MW	68850 TQ	USBLS	5/07
	Nashville-Davidson-Murfreesboro MSA, TN	Y	49650 FQ	62660 MW	76200 TQ	USBLS	5/07
	Texas	Y	41610 FQ	53400 MW	71270 TQ	USBLS	5/07
	Austin-Round Rock MSA, TX	Y	41340 FQ	53860 MW	69080 TQ	USBLS	5/07
	Dallas-Fort Worth-Arlington MSA, TX	Y	43970 FQ	58940 MW	74590 TQ	USBLS	5/07
	El Paso MSA, TX	Y	35540 FQ	47670 MW	71860 TQ	USBLS	5/07
	Houston-Sugar Land-Baytown MSA, TX	Y	43490 FQ	53810 MW	72640 TQ	USBLS	5/07
	San Antonio MSA, TX	Y	38000 FQ	49690 MW	63510 TQ	USBLS	5/07
	Utah	Y	41850 FQ	54970 MW	70590 TQ	USBLS	5/07
	Salt Lake City MSA, UT	Y	40180 FQ	50910 MW	62830 TQ	USBLS	5/07
	Vermont	Y	34810 FQ	41160 MW	51760 TQ	USBLS	5/07
	Burlington-South Burlington MSA, VT	Y	44000 FQ	48550 MW	57190 TQ	USBLS	5/07
	Virginia	Y	36150 FQ	48480 MW	60900 TQ	USBLS	5/07
	Charlottesville MSA, VA	Y	32940 FQ	35840 MW	45130 TQ	USBLS	5/07
	Richmond MSA, VA	Y	43600 FQ	54150 MW	64870 TQ	USBLS	5/07
	Virginia Beach-Norfolk-Newport News MSA, VA-NC	Y	31620 FQ	44310 MW	54340 TQ	USBLS	5/07
	Washington	H	21.83 FQ	27.34 MW	35.88 TQ	WABLS	3/08
	Seattle-Tacoma-Bellevue MSA, WA	Y	46320 FQ	58760 MW	75050 TQ	USBLS	5/07
	West Virginia	Y	26772 FQ	41079 MW	60281 TQ	WVBLS	7/08-9/08
	Wisconsin	Y	37310 FQ	45770 MW	59030 TQ	USBLS	5/07
	Milwaukee-Waukesha-West Allis MSA, WI	Y	39210 FQ	50570 MW	64480 TQ	USBLS	5/07
	Racine MSA, WI	Y	24500 FQ	61410 MW	88760 TQ	USBLS	5/07
	Wyoming	Y	34765 FQ	47406 MW	68402 TQ	WYBLS	9/08
	Puerto Rico	Y	24720 FQ	29250 MW	36740 TQ	USBLS	5/07
	San Juan-Caguas-Guaynabo MSA, PR	Y	24910 FQ	29340 MW	36890 TQ	USBLS	5/07
	Guam	Y	18440 FQ	24560 MW	30660 TQ	USBLS	5/07
Intensivist	United States	Y		296034 AW		CEJ01	2008
Interior Designer	Alabama	Y	34580 FQ	40780 MW	55120 TQ	USBLS	5/07
	Birmingham-Hoover MSA, AL	Y	35080 FQ	40750 MW	61850 TQ	USBLS	5/07

AE	Average entry wage	**AW**	Average wage paid	**FQ**	First quartile wage	**LO**	Lowest wage paid	**MTC** Median total compensation **TCC** Total cash compensation
AER	Average entry range	**AWR**	Average wage range	**H**	Hourly	**LR**	Low end range	**MW** Median wage paid **TQ** Third quartile wage
AEX	Average experienced wage	**AXR**	Average experienced range	**HI**	Highest wage paid	**M**	Monthly	**MWR** Median wage range **W** Weekly
ATC	Average total compensation	**D**	Daily	**HR**	High end range	**MCC**	Median cash compensation	**S** See annotated source **Y** Yearly

Occupation/Type/Industry	Location	Per	Low	Mid	High	Source	Date
Interior Designer	Alaska	Y	39690 FQ	65240 MW	76310 TQ	USBLS	5/07
	Anchorage MSA, AK	Y	56770 FQ	68760 MW	77800 TQ	USBLS	5/07
	Arizona	Y	31070 FQ	40780 MW	49100 TQ	USBLS	5/07
	Phoenix-Mesa-Scottsdale MSA, AZ	Y	31610 FQ	41170 MW	50570 TQ	USBLS	5/07
	Tucson MSA, AZ	Y	38370 FQ	42560 MW	46870 TQ	USBLS	5/07
	Arkansas	Y	26880 FQ	32590 MW	44730 TQ	USBLS	5/07
	Little Rock-North Little Rock MSA, AR	Y	29820 FQ	37760 MW	50650 TQ	USBLS	5/07
	California	H	19.96 FQ	25.40 MW	34.67 TQ	CABLS	1/08-3/08
	Los Angeles-Long Beach-Glendale PMSA, CA	H	20.05 FQ	26.91 MW	37.05 TQ	CABLS	1/08-3/08
	Oakland-Fremont-Hayward MSA, CA	H	23.59 FQ	27.99 MW	31.75 TQ	CABLS	1/08-3/08
	Riverside-San Bernardino-Ontario MSA, CA	H	18.35 FQ	26.87 MW	43.77 TQ	CABLS	1/08-3/08
	Sacramento-Arden Arcade-Roseville MSA, CA	H	19.50 FQ	22.59 MW	25.61 TQ	CABLS	1/08-3/08
	San Diego-Carlsbad-San Marcos MSA, CA	H	20.46 FQ	24.95 MW	30.51 TQ	CABLS	1/08-3/08
	San Francisco-San Mateo-Redwood PMSA, CA	H	20.99 FQ	28.43 MW	38.23 TQ	CABLS	1/08-3/08
	San Jose-Sunnyvale-Santa Clara MSA, CA	H	21.84 FQ	27.03 MW	36.83 TQ	CABLS	1/08-3/08
	Santa Ana-Anaheim-Irvine PMSA, CA	Y	36700 FQ	49720 MW	72060 TQ	USBLS	5/07
	Colorado	Y	29540 FQ	39050 MW	52490 TQ	USBLS	5/07
	Denver-Aurora MSA, CO	Y	32400 FQ	42260 MW	55960 TQ	USBLS	5/07
	Fort Collins-Loveland MSA, CO	Y	29650 FQ	36390 MW	42610 TQ	USBLS	5/07
	Connecticut	H	15.47 AE	26.01 MW		CTBLS	1/08-3/08
	Bridgeport-Stamford-Norwalk MSA, CT	Y	40140 FQ	65540 MW	86610 TQ	USBLS	5/07
	Hartford-West Hartford-East Hartford MSA, CT	Y	33860 FQ	48870 MW	66160 TQ	USBLS	5/07
	Delaware	Y	18860 FQ	37010 MW	47730 TQ	USBLS	5/07
	Wilmington PMSA, DE-MD-NJ	Y	18490 FQ	36730 MW	47290 TQ	USBLS	5/07
	District of Columbia	Y	43800 FQ	56730 MW	76380 TQ	USBLS	5/07
	Washington-Arlington-Alexandria MSA, DC-VA-MD-WV	Y	37730 FQ	56620 MW	81820 TQ	USBLS	5/07
	Florida	Y	31220 FQ	40640 MW	53900 TQ	USBLS	5/07
	Fort Lauderdale-Pompano Beach-Deerfield Beach PMSA, FL	Y	35420 FQ	43180 MW	53030 TQ	USBLS	5/07
	Jacksonville MSA, FL	Y	19160 FQ	41570 MW	48400 TQ	USBLS	5/07
	Miami-Fort Lauderdale-Miami Beach MSA, FL	Y	34510 FQ	44490 MW	60410 TQ	USBLS	5/07
	Orlando-Kissimmee MSA, FL	Y	33140 FQ	38890 MW	48640 TQ	USBLS	5/07
	Tampa-St. Petersburg-Clearwater MSA, FL	Y	27940 FQ	38430 MW	53510 TQ	USBLS	5/07
	West Palm Beach-Boca Raton-Boynton Beach PMSA, FL	Y	38650 FQ	50590 MW	68850 TQ	USBLS	5/07
	Georgia	Y	35530 FQ	46400 MW	66330 TQ	USBLS	5/07
	Atlanta-Sandy Springs-Marietta MSA, GA	Y	36470 FQ	49630 MW	68100 TQ	USBLS	5/07
	Hawaii	Y	47000 FQ	59180 MW	68640 TQ	USBLS	5/07
	Honolulu MSA, HI	Y	50680 FQ	61530 MW	70960 TQ	USBLS	5/07
	Idaho	Y	35640 FQ	44810 MW	51520 TQ	USBLS	5/07
	Boise City-Nampa MSA, ID	Y	43450 FQ	46560 MW	49670 TQ	USBLS	5/07
	Illinois	Y	38090 FQ	48760 MW	61180 TQ	USBLS	5/07
	Chicago-Naperville-Joliet MSA, IL-IN-WI	Y	39150 FQ	49210 MW	61260 TQ	USBLS	5/07
	Indiana	Y	29190 FQ	36460 MW	52450 TQ	USBLS	5/07
	Gary PMSA, IN	Y	24880 FQ	34340 MW	50110 TQ	USBLS	5/07
	Indianapolis-Carmel MSA, IN	Y	34250 FQ	40950 MW	60610 TQ	USBLS	5/07
	Iowa	Y	29080 FQ	34930 MW	43060 TQ	USBLS	5/07
	Des Moines-West Des Moines MSA, IA	Y	30540 FQ	35240 MW	41120 TQ	USBLS	5/07
	Kansas	Y	30400 FQ	35210 MW	44120 TQ	USBLS	5/07
	Wichita MSA, KS	Y	29800 FQ	34580 MW	49160 TQ	USBLS	5/07

AE Average entry wage	**AW** Average wage paid	**FQ** First quartile wage	**LO** Lowest wage paid	**MTC** Median total compensation **TCC** Total cash compensation
AER Average entry range	**AWR** Average wage range	**H** Hourly	**LR** Low end range	**MW** Median wage paid **TQ** Third quartile wage
AEX Average experienced wage	**AXR** Average experienced range	**HI** Highest wage paid	**M** Monthly	**MWR** Median wage range **W** Weekly
ATC Average total compensation	**D** Daily	**HR** High end range	**MCC** Median cash compensation	**S** See annotated source **Y** Yearly

Occupation/Type/Industry	Location	Per	Low	Mid	High	Source	Date
Interior Designer	Kentucky	Y	27752 FQ	34844 MW	41527 TQ	KYBLS	2008
	Louisville-Jefferson County MSA, KY-IN	Y	31300 FQ	38200 MW	57190 TQ	USBLS	5/07
	Louisiana	H	15.80 FQ	17.47 MW	19.36 TQ	LABLS	1/08-3/08
	Baton Rouge MSA, LA	Y	30210 FQ	34040 MW	37770 TQ	USBLS	5/07
	New Orleans-Metairie-Kenner MSA, LA	Y	35390 FQ	40050 MW	91510 TQ	USBLS	5/07
	Maine	Y	32610 FQ	38080 MW	47130 TQ	USBLS	5/07
	Portland-South Portland-Biddeford MSA, ME	Y	32290 FQ	37310 MW	42510 TQ	USBLS	5/07
	Maryland	Y		53700 MW		MDBLS	3/08
	Baltimore-Towson MSA, MD	Y	39410 FQ	49220 MW	67930 TQ	USBLS	5/07
	Bethesda-Gaithersburg-Frederick PMSA, MD	Y	52720 FQ	58780 MW	64840 TQ	USBLS	5/07
	Massachusetts	Y	39470 FQ	55650 MW	71790 TQ	USBLS	5/07
	Barnstable Town MSA, MA	Y	31110 FQ	38990 MW	53160 TQ	USBLS	5/07
	Boston-Cambridge-Quincy NECTA, MA	Y	41190 FQ	57020 MW	72970 TQ	USBLS	5/07
	Lynn-Peabody-Salem NECTA, MA	Y	40030 FQ	58930 MW	69830 TQ	USBLS	5/07
	Michigan	Y	38320 FQ	48150 MW	65430 TQ	USBLS	5/07
	Detroit-Warren-Livonia MSA, MI	Y	42390 FQ	48590 MW	59630 TQ	USBLS	5/07
	Grand Rapids-Wyoming MSA, MI	Y	36550 FQ	124650 MW		USBLS	5/07
	Warren-Troy-Farmington Hills PMSA, MI	Y	41910 FQ	48180 MW	59390 TQ	USBLS	5/07
	Minnesota	Y	38522 FQ	47425 MW	61235 TQ	MNBLS	10/08-12/08
	Duluth-Superior MSA, MN-WI	Y	32767 FQ	38731 MW	46452 TQ	MNBLS	10/08-12/08
	Minneapolis-Saint Paul MSA, MN-WI	Y	40698 FQ	49204 MW	63641 TQ	MNBLS	10/08-12/08
	Rochester MSA, MN	Y	37560 FQ	47702 MW	71008 TQ	MNBLS	10/08-12/08
	Mississippi	Y	22070 FQ	26230 MW	32780 TQ	USBLS	5/07
	Jackson MSA, MS	Y	21620 FQ	24510 MW	31380 TQ	USBLS	5/07
	Missouri	Y	31200 FQ	40270 MW	53620 TQ	USBLS	5/07
	Kansas City MSA, MO-KS	Y	33220 FQ	37840 MW	47900 TQ	USBLS	5/07
	St. Louis MSA, MO-IL	Y	32090 FQ	43350 MW	57670 TQ	USBLS	5/07
	Montana	Y	27420 FQ	36630 MW	48700 TQ	USBLS	5/07
	Billings MSA, MT	Y	14670 FQ	19060 MW	31970 TQ	USBLS	5/07
	Nebraska	Y	35320 FQ	39480 MW	47940 TQ	USBLS	5/07
	Omaha-Council Bluffs MSA, NE-IA	Y	35110 FQ	39090 MW	46730 TQ	USBLS	5/07
	Nevada	H	18.27 FQ	22.92 MW	40.31 TQ	NVBLS	5/08
	Las Vegas-Paradise MSA, NV	H	17.96 FQ	24.35 MW	44.65 TQ	NVBLS	5/08
	New Hampshire	H	16.87 AE	22.54 MW	30.24 AEX	NHBLS	6/08
	Manchester MSA, NH	Y	48930 FQ	67710 MW	74060 TQ	USBLS	5/07
	New Jersey	Y	35860 FQ	54190 MW	75900 TQ	USBLS	5/07
	Camden PMSA, NJ	Y	38290 FQ	48000 MW	60590 TQ	USBLS	5/07
	Edison PMSA, NJ	Y	44350 FQ	57400 MW	104490 TQ	USBLS	5/07
	Newark-Union PMSA, NJ-PA	Y	36900 FQ	69470 MW	77810 TQ	USBLS	5/07
	New Mexico	Y	27490 FQ	42510 MW	51350 TQ	USBLS	5/07
	Albuquerque MSA, NM	Y	27360 FQ	42470 MW	53820 TQ	KYBLS	5/07
	New York	Y	42350 FQ	52570 MW	75690 TQ	USBLS	5/07
	Buffalo-Niagara Falls MSA, NY	Y	32770 FQ	38230 MW	47190 TQ	USBLS	5/07
	Nassau-Suffolk PMSA, NY	Y	44020 FQ	50300 MW	60290 TQ	USBLS	5/07
	New York-Northern New Jersey-Long Island MSA, NY-NJ-PA	Y	42450 FQ	56050 MW	78560 TQ	USBLS	5/07
	Syracuse MSA, NY	Y	34660 FQ	47330 MW	70360 TQ	USBLS	5/07
	North Carolina	Y	30830 FQ	39580 MW	51900 TQ	USBLS	5/07
	Charlotte-Gastonia-Concord MSA, NC-SC	Y	32580 FQ	38980 MW	49680 TQ	USBLS	5/07
	Raleigh-Cary MSA, NC	Y	30760 FQ	40200 MW	47290 TQ	USBLS	5/07
	North Dakota	Y	21930 FQ	33370 MW	39490 TQ	USBLS	5/07
	Fargo MSA, ND-MN	Y	18550 FQ	26930 MW	37490 TQ	USBLS	5/07
	Ohio	Y	29420 FQ	38010 MW	47160 TQ	USBLS	5/07
	Cincinnati-Middletown MSA, OH-KY-IN	Y	32140 FQ	38070 MW	48700 TQ	USBLS	5/07
	Cleveland-Elyria-Mentor MSA, OH	Y	23060 FQ	27140 MW	40290 TQ	USBLS	5/07
	Columbus MSA, OH	Y	36310 FQ	41540 MW	54810 TQ	USBLS	5/07

AE	Average entry wage	AW	Average wage paid	FQ	First quartile wage	LO	Lowest wage paid	MTC Median total compensation TCC Total cash compensation
AER	Average entry range	AWR	Average wage range	H	Hourly	LR	Low end range	MW Median wage paid TQ Third quartile wage
AEX	Average experienced wage	AXR	Average experienced range	HI	Highest wage paid	M	Monthly	MWR Median wage range W Weekly
ATC	Average total compensation	D	Daily	HR	High end range	MCC	Median cash compensation	S See annotated source Y Yearly

Occupation/Type/Industry	Location	Per	Low	Mid	High	Source	Date
Interior Designer	Dayton MSA, OH	Y	30110 FQ	39660 MW	50900 TQ	USBLS	5/07
	Oklahoma	Y	27490 FQ	37750 MW	53810 TQ	USBLS	5/07
	Oklahoma City MSA, OK	Y	25080 FQ	37140 MW	53280 TQ	USBLS	5/07
	Tulsa MSA, OK	Y	33530 FQ	39190 MW	54900 TQ	USBLS	5/07
	Oregon	H	16.73 FQ	21.75 MW	26.36 TQ	ORBLS	5/08
	Portland-Vancouver-Beaverton MSA, OR-WA	Y	35720 FQ	45440 MW	56660 TQ	USBLS	5/07
	Pennsylvania	Y	34980 FQ	43230 MW	60490 TQ	USBLS	5/07
	Allentown-Bethlehem-Easton MSA, PA-NJ	Y	27430 FQ	30960 MW	38210 TQ	USBLS	5/07
	Philadelphia-Camden-Wilmington MSA, PA-NJ-DE-MD	Y	35280 FQ	44060 MW	58140 TQ	USBLS	5/07
	Pittsburgh MSA, PA	Y	37060 FQ	61120 MW	105160 TQ	USBLS	5/07
	Rhode Island	Y	32230 FQ	39560 MW	52720 TQ	USBLS	5/07
	Providence-Fall River-Warwick MSA, RI-MA	Y	32440 FQ	38970 MW	51350 TQ	USBLS	5/07
	South Carolina	Y	28890 FQ	38810 MW	54790 TQ	USBLS	5/07
	Charleston-North Charleston MSA, SC	Y	26050 FQ	33770 MW	43780 TQ	USBLS	5/07
	Columbia MSA, SC	Y	35390 FQ	53640 MW	67230 TQ	USBLS	5/07
	South Dakota	Y	29318 FQ	37846 MW	48924 TQ	SDBLS	7/08-9/08
	Sioux Falls MSA, SD	Y	31395 FQ	43337 MW	53893 TQ	SDBLS	7/08-9/08
	Tennessee	Y	34990 FQ	41970 MW	51430 TQ	USBLS	5/07
	Memphis MSA, TN-MS-AR	Y	29300 FQ	40240 MW	47100 TQ	USBLS	5/07
	Nashville-Davidson-Murfreesboro MSA, TN	Y	37900 FQ	43900 MW	51700 TQ	USBLS	5/07
	Texas	Y	29070 FQ	38180 MW	49250 TQ	USBLS	5/07
	Austin-Round Rock MSA, TX	Y	32850 FQ	38250 MW	48230 TQ	USBLS	5/07
	Dallas-Fort Worth-Arlington MSA, TX	Y	33410 FQ	39840 MW	48840 TQ	USBLS	5/07
	El Paso MSA, TX	Y	32140 FQ	39020 MW	68090 TQ	USBLS	5/07
	Houston-Sugar Land-Baytown MSA, TX	Y	25510 FQ	37170 MW	54900 TQ	USBLS	5/07
	San Antonio MSA, TX	Y	20790 FQ	28570 MW	38440 TQ	USBLS	5/07
	Utah	Y	28070 FQ	32640 MW	56890 TQ	USBLS	5/07
	Provo-Orem MSA, UT	Y	26000 FQ	28330 MW	32070 TQ	USBLS	5/07
	Salt Lake City MSA, UT	Y	28550 FQ	33580 MW	58650 TQ	USBLS	5/07
	Vermont	Y	35580 FQ	45070 MW	52710 TQ	USBLS	5/07
	Burlington-South Burlington MSA, VT	Y	44290 FQ	48060 MW	51820 TQ	USBLS	5/07
	Virginia	Y	32420 FQ	44310 MW	75790 TQ	USBLS	5/07
	Richmond MSA, VA	Y	40260 FQ	56920 MW	73040 TQ	USBLS	5/07
	Roanoke MSA, VA	Y	32650 FQ	44640 MW	74450 TQ	USBLS	5/07
	Virginia Beach-Norfolk-Newport News MSA, VA-NC	Y	21520 FQ	32070 MW	46610 TQ	USBLS	5/07
	Washington	H	16.57 FQ	20.13 MW	27.77 TQ	WABLS	3/08
	Bremerton-Silverdale MSA, WA	Y	33770 FQ	39100 MW	45850 TQ	USBLS	5/07
	Seattle-Tacoma-Bellevue MSA, WA	Y	34440 FQ	42290 MW	58460 TQ	USBLS	5/07
	West Virginia	Y	22384 FQ	25807 MW	39092 TQ	WVBLS	7/08-9/08
	Charleston MSA, WV	Y	30060 FQ	39360 MW	44010 TQ	USBLS	5/07
	Wisconsin	Y	29470 FQ	40930 MW	53570 TQ	USBLS	5/07
	Milwaukee-Waukesha-West Allis MSA, WI	Y	31000 FQ	43660 MW	56610 TQ	USBLS	5/07
	Wyoming	Y	37227 FQ	43953 MW	49898 TQ	WYBLS	9/08
	Puerto Rico	Y	18540 FQ	21380 MW	25030 TQ	USBLS	5/07
	San Juan-Caguas-Guaynabo MSA, PR	Y	18590 FQ	21310 MW	24930 TQ	USBLS	5/07
Commercial Real Estate	United States	Y	35000-55000 AER			WSJ03	2007
Intermediate Interior Designer	Sacramento, CA	Y		41200 MW		SBJ	2008
Intern Coordinator White House Staff	United States	Y			57500 HI	WPOST02	2008
Internal Auditor Municipal Government	Cincinnati, OH	Y	44033 LO		60634 HI	COHSS	10/08

AE Average entry wage	**AW** Average wage paid	**FQ** First quartile wage	**LO** Lowest wage paid	**MTC** Median total compensation	**TCC** Total cash compensation
AER Average entry range	**AWR** Average wage range	**H** Hourly	**LR** Low end range	**MW** Median wage paid	**TQ** Third quartile wage
AEX Average experienced wage	**AXR** Average experienced range	**HI** Highest wage paid	**M** Monthly	**MWR** Median wage range	**W** Weekly
ATC Average total compensation	**D** Daily	**HR** High end range	**MCC** Median cash compensation	**S** See annotated source	**Y** Yearly

Occupation/Type/Industry	Location	Per	Low	Mid	High	Source	Date
International Management Analyst	United States	Y		71150 MW		RD01	2009
Internet Technology Architect/ Strategist	United States	Y		121044 AW		COWRLD2	5/20/08-7/25/08
Internist	Alabama	Y	143670 FQ			USBLS	5/07
	Alaska	Y	119590 FQ			USBLS	5/07
	Arizona	Y	139880 FQ			USBLS	5/07
	Tucson MSA, AZ	Y	120670 FQ	143720 MW		USBLS	5/07
	California	H	57.54 FQ			CABLS	1/08-3/08
	Los Angeles-Long Beach-Glendale PMSA, CA	H	64.01 FQ			CABLS	1/08-3/08
	Oakland-Fremont-Hayward MSA, CA	H	66.95 FQ			CABLS	1/08-3/08
	Riverside-San Bernardino-Ontario MSA, CA	H	62.02 FQ			CABLS	1/08-3/08
	Sacramento-Arden Arcade-Roseville MSA, CA	H	62.24 FQ			CABLS	1/08-3/08
	San Diego-Carlsbad-San Marcos MSA, CA	H	34.14 FQ	68.92 MW		CABLS	1/08-3/08
	San Francisco-San Mateo-Redwood PMSA, CA	H	59.32 FQ			CABLS	1/08-3/08
	San Jose-Sunnyvale-Santa Clara MSA, CA	H	61.36 FQ			CABLS	1/08-3/08
	Connecticut	H	40.20 AE	77.99 AW		CTBLS	1/08-3/08
	Bridgeport-Stamford-Norwalk MSA, CT	Y	126450 FQ			USBLS	5/07
	Hartford-West Hartford-East Hartford MSA, CT	Y	45020 FQ	129090 MW		USBLS	5/07
	District of Columbia	Y	116030 FQ			USBLS	5/07
	Washington-Arlington-Alexandria MSA, DC-VA-MD-WV	Y	124690 FQ			USBLS	5/07
	Florida	Y	141430 FQ			USBLS	5/07
	Fort Lauderdale-Pompano Beach-Deerfield Beach PMSA, FL	Y	145420 FQ			USBLS	5/07
	Miami-Fort Lauderdale-Miami Beach MSA, FL	Y	145050 FQ			USBLS	5/07
	Orlando-Kissimmee MSA, FL	Y	108000 FQ	143390 MW		USBLS	5/07
	Georgia	Y	130940 FQ			USBLS	5/07
	Atlanta-Sandy Springs-Marietta MSA, GA	Y	124830 FQ			USBLS	5/07
	Hawaii	Y	132690 FQ			USBLS	5/07
	Honolulu MSA, HI	Y	140130 FQ			USBLS	5/07
	Illinois	Y	99980 FQ			USBLS	5/07
	Chicago-Naperville-Joliet MSA, IL-IN-WI	Y	94690 FQ			USBLS	5/07
	Indiana	Y	142730 FQ			USBLS	5/07
	Indianapolis-Carmel MSA, IN	Y	125990 FQ			USBLS	5/07
	Kansas	Y	135140 FQ			USBLS	5/07
	Wichita MSA, KS	Y	143310 FQ			USBLS	5/07
	Kentucky	Y	136708 FQ			KYBLS	2008
	Louisville-Jefferson County MSA, KY-IN	Y	145340 FQ			USBLS	5/07
	Louisiana	Y		184938 AW		LABLS	1/08-3/08
	Baton Rouge MSA, LA	Y	133320 FQ			USBLS	5/07
	Maine	Y	122260 FQ	144760 MW		USBLS	5/07
	Portland-South Portland-Biddeford MSA, ME	Y	122640 FQ			USBLS	5/07
	Maryland	Y		170175 AW		MDBLS	3/08
	Baltimore-Towson MSA, MD	Y	136600 FQ			USBLS	5/07
	Bethesda-Gaithersburg-Frederick PMSA, MD	Y	102110 FQ			USBLS	5/07
	Massachusetts	Y	128950 FQ			USBLS	5/07
	Worcester MSA, MA-CT	Y	95590 FQ	136240 MW		USBLS	5/07
	Michigan	Y	130950 FQ			USBLS	5/07
	Detroit-Warren-Livonia MSA, MI	Y	133930 FQ			USBLS	5/07
	Grand Rapids-Wyoming MSA, MI	Y	118030 FQ			USBLS	5/07

AE	Average entry wage	AW	Average wage paid	FQ	First quartile wage	LO	Lowest wage paid	MTC	Median total compensation	TCC	Total cash compensation
AER	Average entry range	AWR	Average wage range	H	Hourly	LR	Low end range	MW	Median wage paid	TQ	Third quartile wage
AEX	Average experienced wage	AXR	Average experienced range	HI	Highest wage paid	M	Monthly	MWR	Median wage range	W	Weekly
ATC	Average total compensation	D	Daily	HR	High end range	MCC	Median cash compensation	S	See annotated source	Y	Yearly

Occupation/Type/Industry	Location	Per	Low	Mid	High	Source	Date
Internist	Warren-Troy-Farmington Hills PMSA, MI	Y	133850 FQ			USBLS	5/07
	Minnesota	Y	151336 FQ	188822 AW		MNBLS	10/08-12/08
	Minneapolis-Saint Paul MSA, MN-WI	Y	150531 FQ	189230 AW		MNBLS	10/08-12/08
	Missouri	Y	130940 FQ			USBLS	5/07
	Kansas City MSA, MO-KS	Y	129470 FQ			USBLS	5/07
	St. Louis MSA, MO-IL	Y	119490 FQ			USBLS	5/07
	Montana	Y	125310 FQ	139490 MW		USBLS	5/07
	Nebraska	Y	130230 FQ			USBLS	5/07
	Omaha-Council Bluffs MSA, NE-IA	Y	122700 FQ			USBLS	5/07
	New Hampshire	H		97.53 AW		NHBLS	6/08
	New Jersey	Y	130400 FQ			USBLS	5/07
	Camden PMSA, NJ	Y	144710 FQ			USBLS	5/07
	Newark-Union PMSA, NJ-PA	Y	129100 FQ			USBLS	5/07
	New York	Y	131110 FQ			USBLS	5/07
	Albany-Schenectady-Troy MSA, NY	Y	125680 FQ			USBLS	5/07
	Buffalo-Niagara Falls MSA, NY	Y	142070 FQ			USBLS	5/07
	Nassau-Suffolk PMSA, NY	Y	137550 FQ			USBLS	5/07
	New York-Northern New Jersey-Long Island MSA, NY-NJ-PA	Y	130280 FQ			USBLS	5/07
	Raleigh-Cary MSA, NC	Y	141910 FQ			USBLS	5/07
	North Dakota	Y	128390 FQ			USBLS	5/07
	Ohio	Y	121310 FQ			USBLS	5/07
	Cincinnati-Middletown MSA, OH-KY-IN	Y	73250 FQ			USBLS	5/07
	Cleveland-Elyria-Mentor MSA, OH	Y	112090 FQ	141060 MW		USBLS	5/07
	Columbus MSA, OH	Y	144570 FQ			USBLS	5/07
	Dayton MSA, OH	Y	133270 FQ			USBLS	5/07
	Oklahoma	Y	137990 FQ			USBLS	5/07
	Portland-Vancouver-Beaverton MSA, OR-WA	Y	145490 FQ			USBLS	5/07
	Pennsylvania	Y	76220 FQ			USBLS	5/07
	Philadelphia-Camden-Wilmington MSA, PA-NJ-DE-MD	Y	53200 FQ			USBLS	5/07
	Rhode Island	Y	129830 FQ			USBLS	5/07
	Providence-Fall River-Warwick MSA, RI-MA	Y	130010 FQ			USBLS	5/07
	Tennessee	Y	139700 FQ			USBLS	5/07
	Memphis MSA, TN-MS-AR	Y	134830 FQ			USBLS	5/07
	Nashville-Davidson-Murfreesboro MSA, TN	Y	125950 FQ			USBLS	5/07
	Texas	Y	122310 FQ			USBLS	5/07
	Austin-Round Rock MSA, TX	Y	97370 FQ	131040 MW		USBLS	5/07
	Dallas-Fort Worth-Arlington MSA, TX	Y	135200 FQ			USBLS	5/07
	Houston-Sugar Land-Baytown MSA, TX	Y	48520 FQ			USBLS	5/07
	Vermont	Y	47550 FQ	96330 MW	144540 TQ	USBLS	5/07
	Virginia	Y	117790 FQ	144470 MW		USBLS	5/07
	Richmond MSA, VA	Y	129910 FQ			USBLS	5/07
	Virginia Beach-Norfolk-Newport News MSA, VA-NC	Y	114210 FQ			USBLS	5/07
	Washington	Y		177077 AW		WABLS	3/08
	Seattle-Tacoma-Bellevue MSA, WA	Y	136810 FQ			USBLS	5/07
	West Virginia	Y	116951 FQ	163687 AW		WVBLS	7/08-9/08
	Wyoming	Y	120238 FQ	136218 MW		WYBLS	9/08
	Puerto Rico	Y	51620 FQ	60840 MW	85530 TQ	USBLS	5/07
	San Juan-Caguas-Guaynabo MSA, PR	Y	49660 FQ	64760 MW	92090 TQ	USBLS	5/07
	Virgin Islands	Y	75110 FQ	85330 MW	94420 TQ	USBLS	5/07
Interpreter and Translator	Alabama	Y	24970 FQ	30540 MW	37790 TQ	USBLS	5/07
	Birmingham-Hoover MSA, AL	Y	26010 FQ	28700 MW	31480 TQ	USBLS	5/07
	Alaska	Y	25610 FQ	38530 MW	48960 TQ	USBLS	5/07

AE	Average entry wage	AW	Average wage paid	FQ	First quartile wage	LO	Lowest wage paid	MTC	Median total compensation	TCC	Total cash compensation
AER	Average entry range	AWR	Average wage range	H	Hourly	LR	Low end range	MW	Median wage paid	TQ	Third quartile wage
AEX	Average experienced wage	AXR	Average experienced range	HI	Highest wage paid	M	Monthly	MWR	Median wage range	W	Weekly
ATC	Average total compensation	D	Daily	HR	High end range	MCC	Median cash compensation	S	See annotated source	Y	Yearly

Occupation/Type/Industry	Location	Per	Low	Mid	High	Source	Date
Interpreter and Translator	Arizona	Y	25210 FQ	32980 MW	40320 TQ	USBLS	5/07
	Flagstaff MSA, AZ	Y	34980 FQ	38180 MW	41160 TQ	USBLS	5/07
	Phoenix-Mesa-Scottsdale MSA, AZ	Y	25290 FQ	32360 MW	40100 TQ	USBLS	5/07
	Tucson MSA, AZ	Y	28550 FQ	36210 MW	45490 TQ	USBLS	5/07
	California	H	15.08 FQ	19.66 MW	25.57 TQ	CABLS	1/08-3/08
	Fresno MSA, CA	H	13.98 FQ	17.77 MW	21.77 TQ	CABLS	1/08-3/08
	Los Angeles-Long Beach-Glendale PMSA, CA	H	13.93 FQ	18.98 MW	26.12 TQ	CABLS	1/08-3/08
	Oakland-Fremont-Hayward MSA, CA	H	16.52 FQ	24.16 MW	31.14 TQ	CABLS	1/08-3/08
	Riverside-San Bernardino-Ontario MSA, CA	H	14.91 FQ	18.61 MW	24.75 TQ	CABLS	1/08-3/08
	Sacramento-Arden Arcade-Roseville MSA, CA	H	14.85 FQ	18.16 MW	23.08 TQ	CABLS	1/08-3/08
	San Diego-Carlsbad-San Marcos MSA, CA	H	17.43 FQ	21.36 MW	24.73 TQ	CABLS	1/08-3/08
	San Francisco-San Mateo-Redwood PMSA, CA	H	19.59 FQ	26.57 MW	30.68 TQ	CABLS	1/08-3/08
	San Jose-Sunnyvale-Santa Clara MSA, CA	H	14.25 FQ	21.44 MW	28.07 TQ	CABLS	1/08-3/08
	Santa Ana-Anaheim-Irvine PMSA, CA	Y	31460 FQ	41210 MW	48760 TQ	USBLS	5/07
	Colorado	Y	32020 FQ	40870 MW	50890 TQ	USBLS	5/07
	Boulder MSA, CO	Y	41990 FQ	49040 MW	64610 TQ	USBLS	5/07
	Denver-Aurora MSA, CO	Y	37810 FQ	44670 MW	53740 TQ	USBLS	5/07
	Connecticut	H	13.84 AE	22.73 MW		CTBLS	1/08-3/08
	Hartford-West Hartford-East Hartford MSA, CT	Y	44910 FQ	57480 MW	67920 TQ	USBLS	5/07
	District of Columbia	Y	44910 FQ	63520 MW	80140 TQ	USBLS	5/07
	Washington-Arlington-Alexandria MSA, DC-VA-MD-WV	Y	37050 FQ	58020 MW	101560 TQ	USBLS	5/07
	Florida	Y	23410 FQ	34370 MW	47570 TQ	USBLS	5/07
	Fort Lauderdale-Pompano Beach-Deerfield Beach PMSA, FL	Y	33380 FQ	37910 MW	46600 TQ	USBLS	5/07
	Miami-Fort Lauderdale-Miami Beach MSA, FL	Y	15480 FQ	24150 MW	38870 TQ	USBLS	5/07
	Orlando-Kissimmee MSA, FL	Y	30350 FQ	44010 MW	58640 TQ	USBLS	5/07
	Tampa-St. Petersburg-Clearwater MSA, FL	Y	37140 FQ	49420 MW	71420 TQ	USBLS	5/07
	Georgia	Y	22460 FQ	30090 MW	40170 TQ	USBLS	5/07
	Atlanta-Sandy Springs-Marietta MSA, GA	Y	25540 FQ	31300 MW	40000 TQ	USBLS	5/07
	Hawaii	Y	25200 FQ	35060 MW	38950 TQ	USBLS	5/07
	Honolulu MSA, HI	Y	30690 FQ	35530 MW	38840 TQ	USBLS	5/07
	Idaho	Y	23700 FQ	30190 MW	36870 TQ	USBLS	5/07
	Boise City-Nampa MSA, ID	Y	18920 FQ	27340 MW	31580 TQ	USBLS	5/07
	Illinois	Y	23060 FQ	32340 MW	42930 TQ	USBLS	5/07
	Chicago-Naperville-Joliet MSA, IL-IN-WI	Y	24030 FQ	33710 MW	44180 TQ	USBLS	5/07
	Indiana	Y	24610 FQ	29460 MW	36940 TQ	USBLS	5/07
	Gary PMSA, IN	Y	27680 FQ	30450 MW	32920 TQ	USBLS	5/07
	Indianapolis-Carmel MSA, IN	Y	28180 FQ	31950 MW	38240 TQ	USBLS	5/07
	Iowa	Y	25420 FQ	29370 MW	35470 TQ	USBLS	5/07
	Des Moines-West Des Moines MSA, IA	Y	25980 FQ	30000 MW	36410 TQ	USBLS	5/07
	Sioux City MSA, IA-NE-SD	Y	22210 FQ	27020 MW	32060 TQ	USBLS	5/07
	Kansas	Y	21080 FQ	28660 MW	43830 TQ	USBLS	5/07
	Wichita MSA, KS	Y	40590 FQ	44530 MW	48330 TQ	USBLS	5/07
	Kentucky	Y	28422 FQ	37696 MW	46550 TQ	KYBLS	2008
	Lexington-Fayette MSA, KY	Y	31320 FQ	42260 MW	49680 TQ	USBLS	5/07
	Louisville-Jefferson County MSA, KY-IN	Y	24610 FQ	30840 MW	38100 TQ	USBLS	5/07
	Maine	Y	24700 FQ	29060 MW	32490 TQ	USBLS	5/07
	Maryland	Y		47825 MW		MDBLS	3/08
	Baltimore-Towson MSA, MD	Y	36320 FQ	44900 MW	64720 TQ	USBLS	5/07
	Bethesda-Gaithersburg-Frederick PMSA, MD	Y	40300 FQ	47820 MW	62140 TQ	USBLS	5/07
	Massachusetts	Y	31990 FQ	38790 MW	52200 TQ	USBLS	5/07

AE	Average entry wage	AW	Average wage paid	FQ	First quartile wage
AER	Average entry range	AWR	Average wage range	H	Hourly
AEX	Average experienced wage	AXR	Average experienced range	HI	Highest wage paid
ATC	Average total compensation	D	Daily	HR	High end range

LO	Lowest wage paid	MTC	Median total compensation	TCC	Total cash compensation
LR	Low end range	MW	Median wage paid	TQ	Third quartile wage
M	Monthly	MWR	Median wage range	W	Weekly
MCC	Median cash compensation	S	See annotated source	Y	Yearly

Occupation/Type/Industry	Location	Per	Low	Mid	High	Source	Date
Interpreter and Translator	Boston-Cambridge-Quincy NECTA, MA	Y	34620 FQ	44960 MW	57080 TQ	USBLS	5/07
	Lynn-Peabody-Salem NECTA, MA	Y	28430 FQ	31240 MW	35980 TQ	USBLS	5/07
	Worcester MSA, MA-CT	Y	32440 FQ	35980 MW	39410 TQ	USBLS	5/07
	Michigan	Y	33420 FQ	41240 MW	51440 TQ	USBLS	5/07
	Flint MSA, MI	Y	34760 FQ	42180 MW	51140 TQ	USBLS	5/07
	Grand Rapids-Wyoming MSA, MI	Y	37350 FQ	42690 MW	48950 TQ	USBLS	5/07
	Minnesota	Y	33217 FQ	43188 MW	54477 TQ	MNBLS	10/08-12/08
	Duluth-Superior MSA, MN-WI	Y	34117 FQ	39850 MW	55470 TQ	MNBLS	10/08-12/08
	Minneapolis-Saint Paul MSA, MN-WI	Y	32108 FQ	43366 MW	54811 TQ	MNBLS	10/08-12/08
	Rochester MSA, MN	Y	35921 FQ	40363 MW	46474 TQ	MNBLS	10/08-12/08
	Mississippi	Y	20780 FQ	28710 MW	37080 TQ	USBLS	5/07
	Missouri	Y	27630 FQ	35060 MW	53010 TQ	USBLS	5/07
	Kansas City MSA, MO-KS	Y	26720 FQ	34520 MW	51460 TQ	USBLS	5/07
	St. Louis MSA, MO-IL	Y	26810 FQ	36980 MW	53890 TQ	USBLS	5/07
	Nebraska	Y	25260 FQ	33230 MW	44680 TQ	USBLS	5/07
	Omaha-Council Bluffs MSA, NE-IA	Y	29250 FQ	33280 MW	37210 TQ	USBLS	5/07
	Nevada	H	14.90 FQ	17.78 MW	31.57 TQ	NVBLS	5/08
	Las Vegas-Paradise MSA, NV	H	14.90 FQ	17.95 MW	33.59 TQ	NVBLS	5/08
	New Hampshire	H	16.16 AE	21.55 MW	23.87 AEX	NHBLS	6/08
	Manchester MSA, NH	Y	33350 FQ	38390 MW	46560 TQ	USBLS	5/07
	New Jersey	Y	34670 FQ	46100 MW	58050 TQ	USBLS	5/07
	Camden PMSA, NJ	Y	33640 FQ	38470 MW	48070 TQ	USBLS	5/07
	Edison PMSA, NJ	Y	40170 FQ	48000 MW	57060 TQ	USBLS	5/07
	Newark-Union PMSA, NJ-PA	Y	24990 FQ	40580 MW	55720 TQ	USBLS	5/07
	New Mexico	Y	27600 FQ	30660 MW	37150 TQ	USBLS	5/07
	Albuquerque MSA, NM	Y	27600 FQ	30410 MW	35520 TQ	USBLS	5/07
	New York	Y	35530 FQ	48470 MW	62390 TQ	USBLS	5/07
	Buffalo-Niagara Falls MSA, NY	Y	31170 FQ	40250 MW	51530 TQ	USBLS	5/07
	Nassau-Suffolk PMSA, NY	Y	31390 FQ	37370 MW	52380 TQ	USBLS	5/07
	New York-Northern New Jersey-Long Island MSA, NY-NJ-PA	Y	38630 FQ	51960 MW	64070 TQ	USBLS	5/07
	North Carolina	Y	24380 FQ	29050 MW	35810 TQ	USBLS	5/07
	Charlotte-Gastonia-Concord MSA, NC-SC	Y	27800 FQ	32680 MW	39000 TQ	USBLS	5/07
	Raleigh-Cary MSA, NC	Y	27810 FQ	31630 MW	42880 TQ	USBLS	5/07
	Ohio	Y	34630 FQ	41290 MW	50200 TQ	USBLS	5/07
	Cincinnati-Middletown MSA, OH-KY-IN	Y	32900 FQ	41130 MW	50040 TQ	USBLS	5/07
	Cleveland-Elyria-Mentor MSA, OH	Y	36490 FQ	42100 MW	50020 TQ	USBLS	5/07
	Columbus MSA, OH	Y	34320 FQ	41480 MW	52900 TQ	USBLS	5/07
	Dayton MSA, OH	Y	32940 FQ	37530 MW	46010 TQ	USBLS	5/07
	Oklahoma	Y	18270 FQ	22590 MW	26770 TQ	USBLS	5/07
	Oklahoma City MSA, OK	Y	21950 FQ	24820 MW	29560 TQ	USBLS	5/07
	Tulsa MSA, OK	Y	22720 FQ	26300 MW	32290 TQ	USBLS	5/07
	Oregon	H	17.01 FQ	21.50 MW	25.32 TQ	ORBLS	5/08
	Portland-Vancouver-Beaverton MSA, OR-WA	Y	39400 FQ	47400 MW	57580 TQ	USBLS	5/07
	Salem MSA, OR	Y	34080 FQ	40330 MW	49810 TQ	USBLS	5/07
	Pittsburgh MSA, PA	Y	23540 FQ	28010 MW	31530 TQ	USBLS	5/07
	Rhode Island	Y	31100 FQ	35280 MW	41400 TQ	USBLS	5/07
	Providence-Fall River-Warwick MSA, RI-MA	Y	29380 FQ	33970 MW	40250 TQ	USBLS	5/07
	South Carolina	Y	26270 FQ	31480 MW	36840 TQ	USBLS	5/07
	Charleston-North Charleston MSA, SC	Y	25020 FQ	27870 MW	30470 TQ	USBLS	5/07
	Columbia MSA, SC	Y	23350 FQ	30860 MW	44900 TQ	USBLS	5/07
	South Dakota	Y	33626 FQ	41593 MW	46806 TQ	SDBLS	7/08-9/08
	Sioux Falls MSA, SD	Y	35273 FQ	42497 MW	47383 TQ	SDBLS	7/08-9/08
	Tennessee	Y	22810 FQ	29320 MW	36260 TQ	USBLS	5/07
	Knoxville MSA, TN	Y	13480 FQ	20070 MW	31620 TQ	USBLS	5/07
	Memphis MSA, TN-MS-AR	Y	34080 FQ	37320 MW	41810 TQ	USBLS	5/07
	Nashville-Davidson-Murfreesboro MSA, TN	Y	24180 FQ	28630 MW	34770 TQ	USBLS	5/07
	Texas	Y	27810 FQ	38670 MW	56330 TQ	USBLS	5/07

AE	Average entry wage	AW	Average wage paid	FQ	First quartile wage	LO	Lowest wage paid	MTC	Median total compensation	TCC	Total cash compensation
AER	Average entry range	AWR	Average wage range	H	Hourly	LR	Low end range	MW	Median wage paid	TQ	Third quartile wage
AEX	Average experienced wage	AXR	Average experienced range	HI	Highest wage paid	M	Monthly	MWR	Median wage range	W	Weekly
ATC	Average total compensation	D	Daily	HR	High end range	MCC	Median cash compensation	S	See annotated source	Y	Yearly

Occupation/Type/Industry	Location	Per	Low	Mid	High	Source	Date
Interpreter and Translator	Austin-Round Rock MSA, TX	Y	50030 FQ	64340 MW	78020 TQ	USBLS	5/07
	Dallas-Fort Worth-Arlington						
	MSA, TX	Y	26670 FQ	36280 MW	47010 TQ	USBLS	5/07
	El Paso MSA, TX	Y	31720 FQ	37610 MW	49030 TQ	USBLS	5/07
	Houston-Sugar Land-Baytown						
	MSA, TX	Y	30680 FQ	42330 MW	64310 TQ	USBLS	5/07
	San Antonio MSA, TX	Y	33700 FQ	38240 MW	42310 TQ	USBLS	5/07
	Utah	Y	23960 FQ	30840 MW	40500 TQ	USBLS	5/07
	Salt Lake City MSA, UT	Y	24510 FQ	32960 MW	42550 TQ	USBLS	5/07
	Vermont	Y	29850 FQ	34600 MW	38650 TQ	USBLS	5/07
	Burlington-South Burlington						
	MSA, VT	Y	31910 FQ	35920 MW	39330 TQ	USBLS	5/07
	Virginia	Y	29020 FQ	51690 MW	101440 TQ	USBLS	5/07
	Richmond MSA, VA	Y	27680 FQ	38700 MW	56170 TQ	USBLS	5/07
	Virginia Beach-Norfolk-						
	Newport News MSA, VA-NC	Y	34850 FQ	39400 MW	60850 TQ	USBLS	5/07
	Washington	H	17.17 FQ	19.76 MW	25.69 TQ	WABLS	3/08
	Seattle-Tacoma-Bellevue						
	MSA, WA	Y	34910 FQ	38720 MW	46450 TQ	USBLS	5/07
	West Virginia	Y	19391 FQ	22543 MW	25212 TQ	WVBLS	7/08-9/08
	Charleston MSA, WV	Y	20480 FQ	22270 MW	23990 TQ	USBLS	5/07
	Wisconsin	Y	30070 FQ	38010 MW	47260 TQ	USBLS	5/07
	Milwaukee-Waukesha-West						
	Allis MSA, WI	Y	30210 FQ	38320 MW	45510 TQ	USBLS	5/07
	Wyoming	Y	23078 FQ	32493 MW	43414 TQ	WYBLS	9/08
	Puerto Rico	Y	28610 FQ	34590 MW	47440 TQ	USBLS	5/07
	San Juan-Caguas-Guaynabo						
	MSA, PR	Y	27930 FQ	32220 MW	42780 TQ	USBLS	5/07
Interpreter/Tutor							
Montana State School for the Deaf and							
Blind	Montana	Y	21326 LO			MTSDB	10/08-6/09
Interviewer							
Except Eligibility and Loan	Alabama	Y	19790 FQ	24580 MW	31480 TQ	USBLS	5/07
Except Eligibility and Loan	Birmingham-Hoover MSA, AL	Y	20920 FQ	25500 MW	30630 TQ	USBLS	5/07
Except Eligibility and Loan	Huntsville MSA, AL	Y	20650 FQ	24720 MW	29680 TQ	USBLS	5/07
Except Eligibility and Loan	Alaska	Y	25960 FQ	30370 MW	35140 TQ	USBLS	5/07
Except Eligibility and Loan	Anchorage MSA, AK	Y	23270 FQ	29230 MW	32550 TQ	USBLS	5/07
Except Eligibility and Loan	Arizona	Y	22210 FQ	26120 MW	30050 TQ	USBLS	5/07
Except Eligibility and Loan	Phoenix-Mesa-Scottsdale						
	MSA, AZ	Y	22280 FQ	26670 MW	30270 TQ	USBLS	5/07
Except Eligibility and Loan	Tucson MSA, AZ	Y	22170 FQ	24650 MW	29410 TQ	USBLS	5/07
Except Eligibility and Loan	Arkansas	Y	17830 FQ	21740 MW	27110 TQ	USBLS	5/07
Except Eligibility and Loan	Little Rock-North Little Rock						
	MSA, AR	Y	17670 FQ	22100 MW	28040 TQ	USBLS	5/07
Except Eligibility and Loan	California	H	12.20 FQ	15.65 MW	20.38 TQ	CABLS	1/08-3/08
Except Eligibility and Loan	Bakersfield MSA, CA	H	11.25 FQ	14.11 MW	18.60 TQ	CABLS	1/08-3/08
Except Eligibility and Loan	Fresno MSA, CA	H	13.01 FQ	16.19 MW	21.52 TQ	CABLS	1/08-3/08
Except Eligibility and Loan	Los Angeles-Long Beach-						
	Glendale PMSA, CA	H	9.88 FQ	13.82 MW	17.72 TQ	CABLS	1/08-3/08
Except Eligibility and Loan	Oakland-Fremont-Hayward						
	MSA, CA	H	15.78 FQ	20.13 MW	23.19 TQ	CABLS	1/08-3/08
Except Eligibility and Loan	Riverside-San Bernardino-						
	Ontario MSA, CA	H	13.94 FQ	18.22 MW	22.73 TQ	CABLS	1/08-3/08
Except Eligibility and Loan	Sacramento-Arden Arcade-						
	Roseville MSA, CA	H	15.21 FQ	17.31 MW	19.54 TQ	CABLS	1/08-3/08
Except Eligibility and Loan	San Diego-Carlsbad-San						
	Marcos MSA, CA	H	11.32 FQ	14.72 MW	19.08 TQ	CABLS	1/08-3/08
Except Eligibility and Loan	San Francisco-San Mateo-						
	Redwood PMSA, CA	H	14.84 FQ	19.16 MW	22.88 TQ	CABLS	1/08-3/08
Except Eligibility and Loan	San Jose-Sunnyvale-Santa						
	Clara MSA, CA	H	16.95 FQ	21.33 MW	23.61 TQ	CABLS	1/08-3/08
Except Eligibility and Loan	Santa Ana-Anaheim-Irvine						
	PMSA, CA	Y	27920 FQ	34320 MW	43990 TQ	USBLS	5/07
Except Eligibility and Loan	Colorado	Y	22760 FQ	28380 MW	35200 TQ	USBLS	5/07
Except Eligibility and Loan	Boulder MSA, CO	Y	17080 FQ	19560 MW	28490 TQ	USBLS	5/07
Except Eligibility and Loan	Denver-Aurora MSA, CO	Y	25010 FQ	30010 MW	36810 TQ	USBLS	5/07
Except Eligibility and Loan	Connecticut	H	12.86 AE	16.19 MW		CTBLS	1/08-3/08
Except Eligibility and Loan	Bridgeport-Stamford-Norwalk						
	MSA, CT	Y	25860 FQ	30630 MW	38500 TQ	USBLS	5/07

AE	Average entry wage	**AW**	Average wage paid	**FQ**	First quartile wage	**LO** Lowest wage paid
AER	Average entry range	**AWR**	Average wage range	**H**	Hourly	**LR** Low end range
AEX	Average experienced wage	**AXR**	Average experienced range	**HI**	Highest wage paid	**M** Monthly
ATC	Average total compensation	**D**	Daily	**HR**	High end range	**MCC** Median cash compensation

MTC Median total compensation	**TCC** Total cash compensation
MW Median wage paid	**TQ** Third quartile wage
MWR Median wage range	**W** Weekly
S See annotated source	**Y** Yearly

Interviewer

Occupation/Type/Industry	Location	Per	Low	Mid	High	Source	Date
Except Eligibility and Loan	Hartford-West Hartford-East Hartford MSA, CT	Y	29540 FQ	34990 MW	40500 TQ	USBLS	5/07
Except Eligibility and Loan	Delaware	Y	24670 FQ	29210 MW	34360 TQ	USBLS	5/07
Except Eligibility and Loan	Dover MSA, DE	Y	25350 FQ	28630 MW	31860 TQ	USBLS	5/07
Except Eligibility and Loan	Wilmington PMSA, DE-MD-NJ	Y	26240 FQ	30100 MW	34960 TQ	USBLS	5/07
Except Eligibility and Loan	District of Columbia	Y	25430 FQ	33470 MW	38860 TQ	USBLS	5/07
Except Eligibility and Loan	Washington-Arlington-Alexandria MSA, DC-VA-MD-WV	Y	26110 FQ	30990 MW	37760 TQ	USBLS	5/07
Except Eligibility and Loan	Florida	Y	22170 FQ	27010 MW	31590 TQ	USBLS	5/07
Except Eligibility and Loan	Fort Lauderdale-Pompano Beach-Deerfield Beach PMSA, FL	Y	26680 FQ	30100 MW	35280 TQ	USBLS	5/07
Except Eligibility and Loan	Jacksonville MSA, FL	Y	24450 FQ	28320 MW	32890 TQ	USBLS	5/07
Except Eligibility and Loan	Lakeland MSA, FL	Y	18140 FQ	21300 MW	24960 TQ	USBLS	5/07
Except Eligibility and Loan	Miami-Fort Lauderdale-Miami Beach MSA, FL	Y	22740 FQ	27740 MW	32150 TQ	USBLS	5/07
Except Eligibility and Loan	Orlando-Kissimmee MSA, FL	Y	21710 FQ	25800 MW	30230 TQ	USBLS	5/07
Except Eligibility and Loan	Sarasota-Bradenton-Venice MSA, FL	Y	18570 FQ	22270 MW	26250 TQ	USBLS	5/07
Except Eligibility and Loan	West Palm Beach-Boca Raton-Boynton Beach PMSA, FL	Y	22010 FQ	25760 MW	29770 TQ	USBLS	5/07
Except Eligibility and Loan	Georgia	Y	20490 FQ	25240 MW	29820 TQ	USBLS	5/07
Except Eligibility and Loan	Atlanta-Sandy Springs-Marietta MSA, GA	Y	21280 FQ	26660 MW	30630 TQ	USBLS	5/07
Except Eligibility and Loan	Hawaii	Y	18410 FQ	25580 MW	29960 TQ	USBLS	5/07
Except Eligibility and Loan	Honolulu MSA, HI	Y	17820 FQ	22280 MW	29620 TQ	USBLS.	5/07
Except Eligibility and Loan	Idaho	Y	13500 FQ	16800 MW	24400 TQ	USBLS	5/07
Except Eligibility and Loan	Boise City-Nampa MSA, ID	Y	18790 FQ	22600 MW	28520 TQ	USBLS	5/07
Except Eligibility and Loan	Illinois	Y	19870 FQ	24030 MW	31380 TQ	USBLS	5/07
Except Eligibility and Loan	Chicago-Naperville-Joliet MSA, IL-IN-WI	Y	19800 FQ	23990 MW	31210 TQ	USBLS	5/07
Except Eligibility and Loan	Indiana	Y	21620 FQ	25180 MW	30280 TQ	USBLS	5/07
Except Eligibility and Loan	Gary PMSA, IN	Y	20630 FQ	24170 MW	28700 TQ	USBLS	5/07
Except Eligibility and Loan	Indianapolis-Carmel MSA, IN	Y	22780 FQ	27850 MW	35760 TQ	USBLS	5/07
Except Eligibility and Loan	Iowa	Y	20500 FQ	23670 MW	29740 TQ	USBLS	5/07
Except Eligibility and Loan	Des Moines-West Des Moines MSA, IA	Y	26210 FQ	33200 MW	41670 TQ	USBLS	5/07
Except Eligibility and Loan	Kansas	Y	20300 FQ	23690 MW	28930 TQ	USBLS	5/07
Except Eligibility and Loan	Wichita MSA, KS	Y	21870 FQ	25340 MW	28760 TQ	USBLS	5/07
Except Eligibility and Loan	Kentucky	Y	20734 FQ	25246 MW	29848 TQ	KYBLS	2008
Except Eligibility and Loan	Louisville-Jefferson County MSA, KY-IN	Y	21400 FQ	24520 MW	28700 TQ	USBLS	5/07
Except Eligibility and Loan	Louisiana	H	9.10 FQ	10.82 MW	12.90 TQ	LABLS	1/08-3/08
Except Eligibility and Loan	Baton Rouge MSA, LA	Y	18140 FQ	22970 MW	28930 TQ	USBLS	5/07
Except Eligibility and Loan	Houma-Bayou Cane-Thibodaux MSA, LA	Y	20960 FQ	23010 MW	25080 TQ	USBLS	5/07
Except Eligibility and Loan	New Orleans-Metairie-Kenner MSA, LA	Y	21810 FQ	25170 MW	29580 TQ	USBLS	5/07
Except Eligibility and Loan	Maine	Y	20900 FQ	24060 MW	29040 TQ	USBLS	5/07
Except Eligibility and Loan	Portland-South Portland-Biddeford MSA, ME	Y	20320 FQ	24930 MW	30350 TQ	USBLS	5/07
Except Eligibility and Loan	Maryland	Y		29450 MW		MDBLS	3/08
Except Eligibility and Loan	Baltimore-Towson MSA, MD	Y	26500 FQ	29260 MW	32350 TQ	USBLS	5/07
Except Eligibility and Loan	Bethesda-Gaithersburg-Frederick PMSA, MD	Y	24100 FQ	27820 MW	33530 TQ	USBLS	5/07
Except Eligibility and Loan	Massachusetts	Y	27780 FQ	32130 MW	37240 TQ	USBLS	5/07
Except Eligibility and Loan	Boston-Cambridge-Quincy NECTA, MA	Y	28400 FQ	32550 MW	37350 TQ	USBLS	5/07
Except Eligibility and Loan	Worcester MSA, MA-CT	Y	27800 FQ	32340 MW	37330 TQ	USBLS	5/07
Except Eligibility and Loan	Michigan	Y	24790 FQ	28610 MW	33030 TQ	USBLS	5/07
Except Eligibility and Loan	Detroit-Warren-Livonia MSA, MI	Y	26000 FQ	29370 MW	33290 TQ	USBLS	5/07
Except Eligibility and Loan	Grand Rapids-Wyoming MSA, MI	Y	26230 FQ	29360 MW	32940 TQ	USBLS	5/07
Except Eligibility and Loan	Warren-Troy-Farmington Hills PMSA, MI	Y	25340 FQ	29340 MW	33450 TQ	USBLS	5/07
Except Eligibility and Loan	Minnesota	Y	24188 FQ	29964 MW	36615 TQ	MNBLS	10/08-12/08
Except Eligibility and Loan	Duluth-Superior MSA, MN-WI	Y	24854 FQ	28726 MW	33440 TQ	MNBLS	10/08-12/08

AE	Average entry wage	AW	Average wage paid	FQ	First quartile wage	LO	Lowest wage paid
AER	Average entry range	AWR	Average wage range	H	Hourly	LR	Low end range
AEX	Average experienced wage	AXR	Average experienced range	HI	Highest wage paid	M	Monthly
ATC	Average total compensation	D	Daily	HR	High end range	MCC	Median cash compensation

MTC	Median total compensation	TCC	Total cash compensation
MW	Median wage paid	TQ	Third quartile wage
MWR	Median wage range	W	Weekly
S	See annotated source	Y	Yearly

Occupation/Type/Industry	Location	Per	Low	Mid	High	Source	Date
Interviewer							
Except Eligibility and Loan	Minneapolis-Saint Paul MSA, MN-WI	Y	23917 FQ	30734 MW	37937 TQ	MNBLS	10/08-12/08
Except Eligibility and Loan	Rochester MSA, MN	Y	30885 FQ	33695 MW	36854 TQ	MNBLS	10/08-12/08
Except Eligibility and Loan	Mississippi	Y	20310 FQ	23700 MW	28200 TQ	USBLS	5/07
Except Eligibility and Loan	Jackson MSA, MS	Y	19190 FQ	23410 MW	28740 TQ	USBLS	5/07
Except Eligibility and Loan	Missouri	Y	20210 FQ	24760 MW	30740 TQ	USBLS	5/07
Except Eligibility and Loan	Kansas City MSA, MO-KS	Y	23350 FQ	27770 MW	32240 TQ	USBLS	5/07
Except Eligibility and Loan	St. Louis MSA, MO-IL	Y	20920 FQ	25540 MW	32110 TQ	USBLS	5/07
Except Eligibility and Loan	Montana	Y	20990 FQ	23410 MW	27660 TQ	USBLS	5/07
Except Eligibility and Loan	Nebraska	Y	17760 FQ	23180 MW	29360 TQ	USBLS	5/07
Except Eligibility and Loan	Omaha-Council Bluffs MSA, NE-IA	Y	17860 FQ	23590 MW	29860 TQ	USBLS	5/07
Except Eligibility and Loan	Nevada	H	12.06 FQ	14.12 MW	16.51 TQ	NVBLS	5/08
Except Eligibility and Loan	Las Vegas-Paradise MSA, NV	H	12.34 FQ	14.51 MW	17.32 TQ	NVBLS	5/08
Except Eligibility and Loan	New Hampshire	H	11.01 AE	14.10 MW	15.51 AEX	NHBLS	6/08
Except Eligibility and Loan	Manchester MSA, NH	Y	24820 FQ	28260 MW	31370 TQ	USBLS	5/07
Except Eligibility and Loan	Nashua NECTA, NH-MA	Y	23430 FQ	27420 MW	31710 TQ	USBLS	5/07
Except Eligibility and Loan	New Jersey	Y	24080 FQ	28800 MW	33280 TQ	USBLS	5/07
Except Eligibility and Loan	Camden PMSA, NJ	Y	21990 FQ	27750 MW	31290 TQ	USBLS	5/07
Except Eligibility and Loan	Edison PMSA, NJ	Y	23460 FQ	28940 MW	34480 TQ	USBLS	5/07
Except Eligibility and Loan	Newark-Union PMSA, NJ-PA	Y	26550 FQ	29450 MW	32890 TQ	USBLS	5/07
Except Eligibility and Loan	New Mexico	Y	21690 FQ	25210 MW	29810 TQ	USBLS	5/07
Except Eligibility and Loan	Albuquerque MSA, NM	Y	23660 FQ	26700 MW	30720 TQ	USBLS	5/07
Except Eligibility and Loan	New York	Y	23410 FQ	31100 MW	37280 TQ	USBLS	5/07
Except Eligibility and Loan	Albany-Schenectady-Troy MSA, NY	Y	22030 FQ	26990 MW	33820 TQ	USBLS	5/07
Except Eligibility and Loan	Buffalo-Niagara Falls MSA, NY	Y	23530 FQ	28610 MW	33010 TQ	USBLS	5/07
Except Eligibility and Loan	Ithaca MSA, NY	Y	22710 FQ	27320 MW	33390 TQ	USBLS	5/07
Except Eligibility and Loan	Nassau-Suffolk PMSA, NY	Y	21920 FQ	31590 MW	37970 TQ	USBLS	5/07
Except Eligibility and Loan	New York-Northern New Jersey-Long Island MSA, NY-NJ-PA	Y	25080 FQ	31140 MW	37000 TQ	USBLS	5/07
Except Eligibility and Loan	North Carolina	Y	21500 FQ	25450 MW	30330 TQ	USBLS	5/07
Except Eligibility and Loan	Charlotte-Gastonia-Concord MSA, NC-SC	Y	23420 FQ	27600 MW	32930 TQ	USBLS	5/07
Except Eligibility and Loan	Raleigh-Cary MSA, NC	Y	22350 FQ	27980 MW	32270 TQ	USBLS	5/07
Except Eligibility and Loan	North Dakota	Y	20710 FQ	22590 MW	24860 TQ	USBLS	5/07
Except Eligibility and Loan	Bismarck MSA, ND	Y	21860 FQ	23660 MW	25900 TQ	USBLS	5/07
Except Eligibility and Loan	Fargo MSA, ND-MN	Y	20480 FQ	22130 MW	23780 TQ	USBLS	5/07
Except Eligibility and Loan	Ohio	Y	23450 FQ	27340 MW	31030 TQ	USBLS	5/07
Except Eligibility and Loan	Cincinnati-Middletown MSA, OH-KY-IN	Y	20890 FQ	25670 MW	30200 TQ	USBLS	5/07
Except Eligibility and Loan	Cleveland-Elyria-Mentor MSA, OH	Y	26750 FQ	29530 MW	32490 TQ	USBLS	5/07
Except Eligibility and Loan	Columbus MSA, OH	Y	22890 FQ	26690 MW	30730 TQ	USBLS	5/07
Except Eligibility and Loan	Dayton MSA, OH	Y	24550 FQ	27930 MW	31360 TQ	USBLS	5/07
Except Eligibility and Loan	Oklahoma	Y	18690 FQ	21960 MW	25330 TQ	USBLS	5/07
Except Eligibility and Loan	Oklahoma City MSA, OK	Y	20810 FQ	23220 MW	26210 TQ	USBLS	5/07
Except Eligibility and Loan	Tulsa MSA, OK	Y	18510 FQ	21810 MW	26680 TQ	USBLS	5/07
Except Eligibility and Loan	Oregon	H	10.84 FQ	13.85 MW	16.48 TQ	ORBLS	5/08
Except Eligibility and Loan	Portland-Vancouver-Beaverton MSA, OR-WA	Y	25900 FQ	31260 MW	35740 TQ	USBLS	5/07
Except Eligibility and Loan	Pennsylvania	Y	23960 FQ	28190 MW	33360 TQ	USBLS	5/07
Except Eligibility and Loan	Allentown-Bethlehem-Easton MSA, PA-NJ	Y	25710 FQ	30030 MW	34250 TQ	USBLS	5/07
Except Eligibility and Loan	Philadelphia-Camden-Wilmington MSA, PA-NJ-DE-MD	Y	24910 FQ	28950 MW	33890 TQ	USBLS	5/07
Except Eligibility and Loan	Pittsburgh MSA, PA	Y	24250 FQ	28150 MW	33060 TQ	USBLS	5/07
Except Eligibility and Loan	Rhode Island	Y	23620 FQ	29710 MW	35690 TQ	USBLS	5/07
Except Eligibility and Loan	Providence-Fall River-Warwick MSA, RI-MA	Y	24240 FQ	30040 MW	36080 TQ	USBLS	5/07
Except Eligibility and Loan	South Carolina	Y	21390 FQ	24230 MW	28700 TQ	USBLS	5/07
Except Eligibility and Loan	Charleston-North Charleston MSA, SC	Y	22150 FQ	25040 MW	28930 TQ	USBLS	5/07
Except Eligibility and Loan	Columbia MSA, SC	Y	22030 FQ	24970 MW	30240 TQ	USBLS	5/07
Except Eligibility and Loan	Myrtle Beach-Conway-North Myrtle Beach MSA, SC	Y	25900 FQ	28620 MW	31350 TQ	USBLS	5/07
Except Eligibility and Loan	Spartanburg MSA, SC	Y	23050 FQ	26440 MW	31000 TQ	USBLS	5/07
Except Eligibility and Loan	South Dakota	Y	20985 FQ	22945 MW	25122 TQ	SDBLS	7/08-9/08

AE	Average entry wage	AW	Average wage paid	FQ	First quartile wage	LO	Lowest wage paid	MTC	Median total compensation	TCC	Total cash compensation
AER	Average entry range	AWR	Average wage range	H	Hourly	LR	Low end range	MW	Median wage paid	TQ	Third quartile wage
AEX	Average experienced wage	AXR	Average experienced range	HI	Highest wage paid	M	Monthly	MWR	Median wage range	W	Weekly
ATC	Average total compensation	D	Daily	HR	High end range	MCC	Median cash compensation	S	See annotated source	Y	Yearly

Occupation/Type/Industry	Location	Per	Low	Mid	High	Source	Date
Interviewer							
Except Eligibility and Loan	Sioux Falls MSA, SD	Y	22671 FQ	24760 MW	28074 TQ	SDBLS	7/08-9/08
Except Eligibility and Loan	Tennessee	Y	21010 FQ	25990 MW	31560 TQ	USBLS	5/07
Except Eligibility and Loan	Knoxville MSA, TN	Y	20880 FQ	23050 MW	26610 TQ	USBLS	5/07
Except Eligibility and Loan	Memphis MSA, TN-MS-AR	Y	20770 FQ	25000 MW	29590 TQ	USBLS	5/07
Except Eligibility and Loan	Nashville-Davidson-Murfreesboro MSA, TN	Y	24660 FQ	29040 MW	34730 TQ	USBLS	5/07
Except Eligibility and Loan	Texas	Y	21930 FQ	26680 MW	31160 TQ	USBLS	5/07
Except Eligibility and Loan	Austin-Round Rock MSA, TX	Y	21260 FQ	25320 MW	30180 TQ	USBLS	5/07
Except Eligibility and Loan	Beaumont-Port Arthur MSA, TX	Y	22800 FQ	26230 MW	30060 TQ	USBLS	5/07
Except Eligibility and Loan	Dallas-Fort Worth-Arlington MSA, TX	Y	22900 FQ	27450 MW	31620 TQ	USBLS	5/07
Except Eligibility and Loan	El Paso MSA, TX	Y	13300 FQ	15660 MW	26460 TQ	USBLS	5/07
Except Eligibility and Loan	Houston-Sugar Land-Baytown MSA, TX	Y	25200 FQ	29070 MW	34010 TQ	USBLS	5/07
Except Eligibility and Loan	San Antonio MSA, TX	Y	20730 FQ	24430 MW	29450 TQ	USBLS	5/07
Except Eligibility and Loan	Utah	Y	16810 FQ	20730 MW	26690 TQ	USBLS	5/07
Except Eligibility and Loan	Salt Lake City MSA, UT	Y	20330 FQ	25270 MW	29470 TQ	USBLS	5/07
Except Eligibility and Loan	Vermont	Y	20160 FQ	25690 MW	30650 TQ	USBLS	5/07
Except Eligibility and Loan	Burlington-South Burlington MSA, VT	Y	18710 FQ	22750 MW	29410 TQ	USBLS	5/07
Except Eligibility and Loan	Virginia	Y	24020 FQ	28420 MW	34070 TQ	USBLS	5/07
Except Eligibility and Loan	Richmond MSA, VA	Y	24610 FQ	27930 MW	31770 TQ	USBLS	5/07
Except Eligibility and Loan	Virginia Beach-Norfolk-Newport News MSA, VA-NC	Y	21450 FQ	26000 MW	29930 TQ	USBLS	5/07
Except Eligibility and Loan	Washington	H	10.35 FQ	14.42 MW	17.50 TQ	WABLS	3/08
Except Eligibility and Loan	Olympia MSA, WA	Y	25350 FQ	29120 MW	33260 TQ	USBLS	5/07
Except Eligibility and Loan	Seattle-Tacoma-Bellevue MSA, WA	Y	23220 FQ	31430 MW	37220 TQ	USBLS	5/07
Except Eligibility and Loan	West Virginia	Y	19303 FQ	22594 MW	25670 TQ	WVBLS	7/08-9/08
Except Eligibility and Loan	Charleston MSA, WV	Y	18460 FQ	21400 MW	24270 TQ	USBLS	5/07
Except Eligibility and Loan	Huntington-Ashland MSA, WV-KY-OH	Y	16500 FQ	21550 MW	26210 TQ	USBLS	5/07
Except Eligibility and Loan	Parkersburg-Marietta-Vienna MSA, WV-OH	Y	17810 FQ	20370 MW	23450 TQ	USBLS	5/07
Except Eligibility and Loan	Wisconsin	Y	23170 FQ	27060 MW	31230 TQ	USBLS	5/07
Except Eligibility and Loan	Milwaukee-Waukesha-West Allis MSA, WI	Y	23330 FQ	28610 MW	35450 TQ	USBLS	5/07
Except Eligibility and Loan	Racine MSA, WI	Y	24370 FQ	27380 MW	31040 TQ	USBLS	5/07
Except Eligibility and Loan	Wyoming	Y	17431 FQ	19925 MW	23332 TQ	WYBLS	9/08
Except Eligibility and Loan	Cheyenne MSA, WY	Y	17880 FQ	19043 MW	20206 TQ	WYBLS	9/08
Except Eligibility and Loan	Puerto Rico	Y	13460 FQ	15860 MW	22860 TQ	USBLS	5/07
Except Eligibility and Loan	San Juan-Caguas-Guaynabo MSA, PR	Y	13640 FQ	16550 MW	24180 TQ	USBLS	5/07
Inventory Bookkeeper							
Public Schools	Baldwin County, AL	Y	30964 LO		38886 HI	BCPSSS	2008-2009
Inventory Clerk	United States	Y		33042 MTC		IOMA03	2008
Investment Banker	United States	Y		258000 MW		USNEWS02	2008
Investments Officer							
State Government	Ohio	H	33.83 LO		44.38 HI	ODAS	2008
IRA Specialist	United States	Y		38700 MW		CNNM04	2007
Iron Worker							
Reinforcing	United States	H		46.93 AW		ENR02	9/08
Structural	United States	H		48.13 AW		ENR02	9/08
Irrigation Specialist							
Municipal Government	Seaside, CA	S	2006 LO		2366 HI	SSSS	8/08
Municipal Government	Cincinnati, OH	Y	37647 LO		40748 HI	COHSS	10/08
Jail Inspector							
State Government	Ohio	H	21.77 LO		31.86 HI	ODAS	2008
Jailer	Oklahoma County, OK	Y	25000 LO			DOKL	2009
Janitor and Cleaner							
Except Maids and Housekeeping Cleaners	Alabama	Y	14010 FQ	17150 MW	21200 TQ	USBLS	5/07

AE	Average entry wage	AW	Average wage paid	FQ	First quartile wage	LO	Lowest wage paid	MTC	Median total compensation	TCC	Total cash compensation
AER	Average entry range	AWR	Average wage range	H	Hourly	LR	Low end range	MW	Median wage paid	TQ	Third quartile wage
AEX	Average experienced wage	AXR	Average experienced range	HI	Highest wage paid	M	Monthly	MWR	Median wage range	W	Weekly
ATC	Average total compensation	D	Daily	HR	High end range	MCC	Median cash compensation	S	See annotated source	Y	Yearly

Janitor and Cleaner

Occupation/Type/Industry	Location	Per	Low	Mid	High	Source	Date
Janitor and Cleaner							
Except Maids and Housekeeping Cleaners	Birmingham-Hoover MSA, AL	Y	13630 FQ	16520 MW	20930 TQ	USBLS	5/07
Except Maids and Housekeeping Cleaners	Alaska	Y	22640 FQ	28050 MW	35780 TQ	USBLS	5/07
Except Maids and Housekeeping Cleaners	Anchorage MSA, AK	Y	21580 FQ	26200 MW	36360 TQ	USBLS	5/07
Except Maids and Housekeeping Cleaners	Arizona	Y	15700 FQ	18500 MW	22870 TQ	USBLS	5/07
Except Maids and Housekeeping Cleaners	Phoenix-Mesa-Scottsdale MSA, AZ	Y	15590 FQ	18270 MW	22580 TQ	USBLS	
Except Maids and Housekeeping Cleaners	Tucson MSA, AZ	Y	15690 FQ	18650 MW	23020 TQ	USBLS	5/07
Except Maids and Housekeeping Cleaners	Arkansas	Y	15270 FQ	18040 MW	22300 TQ	USBLS	5/07
Except Maids and Housekeeping Cleaners	Fayetteville-Springdale-Rogers MSA, AR-MO	Y	17160 FQ	20470 MW	24500 TQ	USBLS	
Except Maids and Housekeeping Cleaners	Little Rock-North Little Rock MSA, AR	Y	15220 FQ	18070 MW	22780 TQ	USBLS	5/07
Except Maids and Housekeeping Cleaners	Pine Bluff MSA, AR	Y	14670 FQ	16800 MW	19770 TQ	USBLS	5/07
Except Maids and Housekeeping Cleaners	California	H	8.95 FQ	10.81 MW	14.25 TQ	CABLS	1/08-3/08
Except Maids and Housekeeping Cleaners	Los Angeles-Long Beach-Glendale PMSA, CA	H	8.78 FQ	10.31 MW	13.18 TQ	CABLS	1/08-3/08
Except Maids and Housekeeping Cleaners	Oakland-Fremont-Hayward MSA, CA	H	9.68 FQ	11.90 MW	16.67 TQ	CABLS	1/08-3/08
Except Maids and Housekeeping Cleaners	Riverside-San Bernardino-Ontario MSA, CA	H	9.25 FQ	11.79 MW	15.94 TQ	CABLS	1/08-3/08
Except Maids and Housekeeping Cleaners	Sacramento-Arden Arcade-Roseville MSA, CA	H	9.02 FQ	10.80 MW	14.38 TQ	CABLS	1/08-3/08
Except Maids and Housekeeping Cleaners	San Diego-Carlsbad-San Marcos MSA, CA	H	8.77 FQ	10.16 MW	13.48 TQ	CABLS	1/08-3/08
Except Maids and Housekeeping Cleaners	San Francisco-San Mateo-Redwood PMSA, CA	H	9.14 FQ	11.51 MW	15.84 TQ	CABLS	1/08-3/08
Except Maids and Housekeeping Cleaners	San Jose-Sunnyvale-Santa Clara MSA, CA	H	9.41 FQ	11.16 MW	14.20 TQ	CABLS	1/08-3/08
Except Maids and Housekeeping Cleaners	Santa Ana-Anaheim-Irvine PMSA, CA	Y	17700 FQ	20710 MW	25400 TQ	USBLS	5/07
Except Maids and Housekeeping Cleaners	Colorado	Y	17530 FQ	21690 MW	27460 TQ	USBLS	5/07
Except Maids and Housekeeping Cleaners	Denver-Aurora MSA, CO	Y	17060 FQ	20420 MW	26480 TQ	USBLS	5/07
Except Maids and Housekeeping Cleaners	Connecticut	H	9.11 AE	12.12 MW		CTBLS	1/08-3/08
Except Maids and Housekeeping Cleaners	Bridgeport-Stamford-Norwalk MSA, CT	Y	18420 FQ	24660 MW	38170 TQ	USBLS	5/07
Except Maids and Housekeeping Cleaners	Hartford-West Hartford-East Hartford MSA, CT	Y	19720 FQ	23750 MW	31330 TQ	USBLS	5/07
Except Maids and Housekeeping Cleaners	Delaware	Y	16580 FQ	19720 MW	25670 TQ	USBLS	5/07
Except Maids and Housekeeping Cleaners	Wilmington PMSA, DE-MD-NJ	Y	16510 FQ	19840 MW	26550 TQ	USBLS	5/07
Except Maids and Housekeeping Cleaners	District of Columbia	Y	20580 FQ	23810 MW	28120 TQ	USBLS	5/07
Except Maids and Housekeeping Cleaners	Washington-Arlington-Alexandria MSA, DC-VA-MD-WV	Y	17310 FQ	21450 MW	26170 TQ	USBLS	5/07
Except Maids and Housekeeping Cleaners	Florida	Y	16300 FQ	19250 MW	23390 TQ	USBLS	5/07
Except Maids and Housekeeping Cleaners	Fort Lauderdale-Pompano Beach-Deerfield Beach PMSA, FL	Y	16320 FQ	18980 MW	23520 TQ	USBLS	5/07
Except Maids and Housekeeping Cleaners	Jacksonville MSA, FL	Y	16840 FQ	20300 MW	25140 TQ	USBLS	5/07
Except Maids and Housekeeping Cleaners	Miami-Fort Lauderdale-Miami Beach MSA, FL	Y	16220 FQ	19030 MW	23190 TQ	USBLS	5/07
Except Maids and Housekeeping Cleaners	Orlando-Kissimmee MSA, FL	Y	16360 FQ	19220 MW	22890 TQ	USBLS	5/07
Except Maids and Housekeeping Cleaners	Tallahassee MSA, FL	Y	15440 FQ	17950 MW	21820 TQ	USBLS	5/07
Except Maids and Housekeeping Cleaners	Tampa-St. Petersburg-Clearwater MSA, FL	Y	16350 FQ	18970 MW	22850 TQ	USBLS	5/07
Except Maids and Housekeeping Cleaners	West Palm Beach-Boca Raton-Boynton Beach PMSA, FL	Y	16730 FQ	19470 MW	23430 TQ	USBLS	5/07
Except Maids and Housekeeping Cleaners	Georgia	Y	15120 FQ	18520 MW	23250 TQ	USBLS	5/07
Except Maids and Housekeeping Cleaners	Atlanta-Sandy Springs-Marietta MSA, GA	Y	16000 FQ	19650 MW	24820 TQ	USBLS	5/07
Except Maids and Housekeeping Cleaners	Hawaii	Y	16790 FQ	23220 MW	29360 TQ	USBLS	5/07
Except Maids and Housekeeping Cleaners	Honolulu MSA, HI	Y	16250 FQ	21370 MW	28060 TQ	USBLS	5/07
Except Maids and Housekeeping Cleaners	Idaho	Y	16860 FQ	21240 MW	25490 TQ	USBLS	5/07
Except Maids and Housekeeping Cleaners	Boise City-Nampa MSA, ID	Y	16590 FQ	21080 MW	25370 TQ	USBLS	5/07
Except Maids and Housekeeping Cleaners	Illinois	Y	17770 FQ	22300 MW	29050 TQ	USBLS	5/07
Except Maids and Housekeeping Cleaners	Chicago-Naperville-Joliet MSA, IL-IN-WI	Y	18090 FQ	22720 MW	29260 TQ	USBLS	5/07
Except Maids and Housekeeping Cleaners	Indiana	Y	16920 FQ	20550 MW	26050 TQ	USBLS	5/07
Except Maids and Housekeeping Cleaners	Gary PMSA, IN	Y	16610 FQ	21050 MW	27060 TQ	USBLS	5/07
Except Maids and Housekeeping Cleaners	Indianapolis-Carmel MSA, IN	Y	16520 FQ	19460 MW	24020 TQ	USBLS	5/07

AE	Average entry wage	AW	Average wage paid	FQ	First quartile wage	LO	Lowest wage paid	MTC	Median total compensation	TCC	Total cash compensation
AER	Average entry range	AWR	Average wage range	H	Hourly	LR	Low end range	MW	Median wage paid	TQ	Third quartile wage
AEX	Average experienced wage	AXR	Average experienced range	HI	Highest wage paid	M	Monthly	MWR	Median wage range	W	Weekly
ATC	Average total compensation	D	Daily	HR	High end range	MCC	Median cash compensation	S	See annotated source	Y	Yearly

Janitor and Cleaner

Occupation/Type/Industry	Location	Per	Low	Mid	High	Source	Date
Janitor and Cleaner							
Except Maids and Housekeeping Cleaners	South Bend-Mishawaka MSA, IN-MI	Y	15110 FQ	20910 MW	28710 TQ	USBLS	5/07
Except Maids and Housekeeping Cleaners	Iowa	Y	17010 FQ	20680 MW	26150 TQ	USBLS	5/07
Except Maids and Housekeeping Cleaners	Des Moines-West Des Moines MSA, IA	Y	16940 FQ	20050 MW	25480 TQ	USBLS	5/07
Except Maids and Housekeeping Cleaners	Kansas	Y	16310 FQ	19800 MW	24310 TQ	USBLS	5/07
Except Maids and Housekeeping Cleaners	Wichita MSA, KS	Y	15540 FQ	18790 MW	23640 TQ	USBLS	5/07
Except Maids and Housekeeping Cleaners	Kentucky	Y	16894 FQ	19938 MW	24315 TQ	KYBLS	2008
Except Maids and Housekeeping Cleaners	Bowling Green MSA, KY	Y	15930 FQ	19200 MW	24140 TQ	USBLS	5/07
Except Maids and Housekeeping Cleaners	Louisville-Jefferson County MSA, KY-IN	Y	16880 FQ	20520 MW	24960 TQ	USBLS	5/07
Except Maids and Housekeeping Cleaners	Louisiana	H	6.72 FQ	8.17 MW	9.87 TQ	LABLS	1/08-3/08
Except Maids and Housekeeping Cleaners	Baton Rouge MSA, LA	Y	13490 FQ	16080 MW	20250 TQ	USBLS	5/07
Except Maids and Housekeeping Cleaners	Houma-Bayou Cane-Thibodaux MSA, LA	Y	16170 FQ	19070 MW	23750 TQ	USBLS	5/07
Except Maids and Housekeeping Cleaners	New Orleans-Metairie-Kenner MSA, LA	Y	14670 FQ	17670 MW	21170 TQ	USBLS	5/07
Except Maids and Housekeeping Cleaners	Maine	Y	19750 FQ	23520 MW	28440 TQ	USBLS	5/07
Except Maids and Housekeeping Cleaners	Portland-South Portland-Biddeford MSA, ME	Y	20820 FQ	24570 MW	29970 TQ	USBLS	5/07
Except Maids and Housekeeping Cleaners	Maryland	Y		20425 MW		MDBLS	3/08
Except Maids and Housekeeping Cleaners	Baltimore-Towson MSA, MD	Y	17010 FQ	19700 MW	24120 TQ	USBLS	5/07
Except Maids and Housekeeping Cleaners	Bethesda-Gaithersburg-Frederick PMSA, MD	Y	15750 FQ	18930 MW	24330 TQ	USBLS	5/07
Except Maids and Housekeeping Cleaners	Salisbury MSA, MD	Y	18330 FQ	21800 MW	25080 TQ	USBLS	5/07
Except Maids and Housekeeping Cleaners	Massachusetts	Y	21300 FQ	25880 MW	31550 TQ	USBLS	5/07
Except Maids and Housekeeping Cleaners	Boston-Cambridge-Quincy NECTA, MA	Y	21990 FQ	26190 MW	31180 TQ	USBLS	5/07
Except Maids and Housekeeping Cleaners	Worcester MSA, MA-CT	Y	19560 FQ	24000 MW	31760 TQ	USBLS	5/07
Except Maids and Housekeeping Cleaners	Michigan	Y	18150 FQ	23060 MW	30650 TQ	USBLS	5/07
Except Maids and Housekeeping Cleaners	Ann Arbor MSA, MI	Y	21370 FQ	27830 MW	33360 TQ	USBLS	5/07
Except Maids and Housekeeping Cleaners	Detroit-Warren-Livonia MSA, MI	Y	18600 FQ	23220 MW	31330 TQ	USBLS	5/07
Except Maids and Housekeeping Cleaners	Grand Rapids-Wyoming MSA, MI	Y	18130 FQ	22360 MW	30090 TQ	USBLS	5/07
Except Maids and Housekeeping Cleaners	Lansing-East Lansing MSA, MI	Y	17220 FQ	21510 MW	30970 TQ	USBLS	5/07
Except Maids and Housekeeping Cleaners	Warren-Troy-Farmington Hills PMSA, MI	Y	18540 FQ	23380 MW	32270 TQ	USBLS	5/07
Except Maids and Housekeeping Cleaners	Minnesota	Y	20002 FQ	24320 MW	30227 TQ	MNBLS	10/08-12/08
Except Maids and Housekeeping Cleaners	Duluth-Superior MSA, MN-WI	Y	17304 FQ	21267 MW	29391 TQ	MNBLS	10/08-12/08
Except Maids and Housekeeping Cleaners	Minneapolis-Saint Paul MSA, MN-WI	Y	21214 FQ	24947 MW	30687 TQ	MNBLS	10/08-12/08
Except Maids and Housekeeping Cleaners	Rochester MSA, MN	Y	23353 FQ	30677 MW	35547 TQ	MNBLS	10/08-12/08
Except Maids and Housekeeping Cleaners	Mississippi	Y	14580 FQ	17640 MW	20760 TQ	USBLS	5/07
Except Maids and Housekeeping Cleaners	Jackson MSA, MS	Y	14920 FQ	18010 MW	21460 TQ	USBLS	5/07
Except Maids and Housekeeping Cleaners	Missouri	Y	16580 FQ	19850 MW	24550 TQ	USBLS	5/07
Except Maids and Housekeeping Cleaners	Kansas City MSA, MO-KS	Y	17100 FQ	20900 MW	25600 TQ	USBLS	5/07
Except Maids and Housekeeping Cleaners	St. Louis MSA, MO-IL	Y	17200 FQ	20590 MW	25820 TQ	USBLS	5/07
Except Maids and Housekeeping Cleaners	Montana	Y	16410 FQ	20180 MW	25010 TQ	USBLS	5/07
Except Maids and Housekeeping Cleaners	Billings MSA, MT	Y	16110 FQ	19060 MW	24160 TQ	USBLS	5/07
Except Maids and Housekeeping Cleaners	Great Falls MSA, MT	Y	17010 FQ	21280 MW	27150 TQ	USBLS	5/07
Except Maids and Housekeeping Cleaners	Missoula MSA, MT	Y	16230 FQ	18900 MW	22850 TQ	USBLS	5/07
Except Maids and Housekeeping Cleaners	Nebraska	Y	16800 FQ	19860 MW	23960 TQ	USBLS	5/07
Except Maids and Housekeeping Cleaners	Omaha-Council Bluffs MSA, NE-IA	Y	17360 FQ	20350 MW	24720 TQ	USBLS	5/07
Except Maids and Housekeeping Cleaners	Nevada	H	9.27 FQ	12.04 MW	14.22 TQ	NVBLS	5/08
Except Maids and Housekeeping Cleaners	Las Vegas-Paradise MSA, NV	H	9.79 FQ	12.59 MW	14.38 TQ	NVBLS	5/08
Except Maids and Housekeeping Cleaners	Reno-Sparks MSA, NV	H	7.94 FQ	9.80 MW	12.20 TQ	NVBLS	5/08
Except Maids and Housekeeping Cleaners	New Hampshire	H	8.92 AE	11.60 MW	13.71 AEX	NHBLS	6/08
Except Maids and Housekeeping Cleaners	Manchester MSA, NH	Y	19900 FQ	22990 MW	27980 TQ	USBLS	5/07
Except Maids and Housekeeping Cleaners	Nashua NECTA, NH-MA	Y	19370 FQ	23880 MW	28990 TQ	USBLS	5/07
Except Maids and Housekeeping Cleaners	New Jersey	Y	17770 FQ	23040 MW	31010 TQ	USBLS	5/07
Except Maids and Housekeeping Cleaners	Camden PMSA, NJ	Y	18810 FQ	23610 MW	30380 TQ	USBLS	5/07
Except Maids and Housekeeping Cleaners	Edison PMSA, NJ	Y	18100 FQ	23320 MW	29830 TQ	USBLS	5/07
Except Maids and Housekeeping Cleaners	Newark-Union PMSA, NJ-PA	Y	17920 FQ	23120 MW	32070 TQ	USBLS	5/07
Except Maids and Housekeeping Cleaners	New Mexico	Y	15590 FQ	18630 MW	22820 TQ	USBLS	5/07
Except Maids and Housekeeping Cleaners	Albuquerque MSA, NM	Y	15530 FQ	18320 MW	22480 TQ	USBLS	5/07
Except Maids and Housekeeping Cleaners	Las Cruces MSA, NM	Y	14150 FQ	16960 MW	20080 TQ	USBLS	5/07
Except Maids and Housekeeping Cleaners	New York	Y	18520 FQ	24360 MW	32850 TQ	USBLS	5/07
Except Maids and Housekeeping Cleaners	Albany-Schenectady-Troy MSA, NY	Y	19570 FQ	23280 MW	28950 TQ	USBLS	5/07

Occupation/Type/Industry	Location	Per	Low	Mid	High	Source	Date
Janitor and Cleaner							
Except Maids and Housekeeping Cleaners	Binghamton MSA, NY	Y	16350 FQ	18490 MW	22800 TQ	USBLS	5/07
Except Maids and Housekeeping Cleaners	Buffalo-Niagara Falls MSA, NY	Y	17750 FQ	21480 MW	26730 TQ	USBLS	5/07
Except Maids and Housekeeping Cleaners	Glens Falls MSA, NY	Y	17700 FQ	21340 MW	26250 TQ	USBLS	5/07
Except Maids and Housekeeping Cleaners	Ithaca MSA, NY	Y	20270 FQ	23760 MW	28980 TQ	USBLS	5/07
Except Maids and Housekeeping Cleaners	Nassau-Suffolk PMSA, NY	Y	18890 FQ	25020 MW	36500 TQ	USBLS	5/07
Except Maids and Housekeeping Cleaners	New York-Northern New Jersey-Long Island MSA, NY-NJ-PA	Y	18610 FQ	25160 MW	34330 TQ	USBLS	5/07
Except Maids and Housekeeping Cleaners	North Carolina	Y	16060 FQ	19130 MW	22890 TQ	USBLS	5/07
Except Maids and Housekeeping Cleaners	Charlotte-Gastonia-Concord MSA, NC-SC	Y	16970 FQ	19920 MW	23490 TQ	USBLS	5/07
Except Maids and Housekeeping Cleaners	Raleigh-Cary MSA, NC	Y	17080 FQ	19530 MW	23120 TQ	USBLS	5/07
Except Maids and Housekeeping Cleaners	North Dakota	Y	17010 FQ	20500 MW	25260 TQ	USBLS	5/07
Except Maids and Housekeeping Cleaners	Bismarck MSA, ND	Y	18380 FQ	22150 MW	28300 TQ	USBLS	5/07
Except Maids and Housekeeping Cleaners	Fargo MSA, ND-MN	Y	17760 FQ	20510 MW	25530 TQ	USBLS	5/07
Except Maids and Housekeeping Cleaners	Ohio	Y	17210 FQ	21280 MW	29090 TQ	USBLS	5/07
Except Maids and Housekeeping Cleaners	Cincinnati-Middletown MSA, OH-KY-IN	Y	17770 FQ	21920 MW	28860 TQ	USBLS	5/07
Except Maids and Housekeeping Cleaners	Cleveland-Elyria-Mentor MSA, OH	Y	17180 FQ	21290 MW	29100 TQ	USBLS	5/07
Except Maids and Housekeeping Cleaners	Columbus MSA, OH	Y	17340 FQ	19940 MW	27960 TQ	USBLS	5/07
Except Maids and Housekeeping Cleaners	Dayton MSA, OH	Y	18080 FQ	22680 MW	31680 TQ	USBLS	5/07
Except Maids and Housekeeping Cleaners	Oklahoma	Y	14920 FQ	17870 MW	21620 TQ	USBLS	5/07
Except Maids and Housekeeping Cleaners	Oklahoma City MSA, OK	Y	15190 FQ	18160 MW	22180 TQ	USBLS	5/07
Except Maids and Housekeeping Cleaners	Tulsa MSA, OK	Y	15060 FQ	18030 MW	21800 TQ	USBLS	5/07
Except Maids and Housekeeping Cleaners	Oregon	H	9.32 FQ	10.90 MW	13.11 TQ	ORBLS	5/08
Except Maids and Housekeeping Cleaners	Medford MSA, OR	Y	18490 FQ	22000 MW	26200 TQ	USBLS	5/07
Except Maids and Housekeeping Cleaners	Portland-Vancouver-Beaverton MSA, OR-WA	Y	19180 FQ	22240 MW	26200 TQ	USBLS	5/07
Except Maids and Housekeeping Cleaners	Pennsylvania	Y	17580 FQ	21850 MW	27570 TQ	USBLS	5/07
Except Maids and Housekeeping Cleaners	Allentown-Bethlehem-Easton MSA, PA-NJ	Y	17790 FQ	21510 MW	28640 TQ	USBLS	5/07
Except Maids and Housekeeping Cleaners	Philadelphia-Camden-Wilmington MSA, PA-NJ-DE-MD	Y	18390 FQ	22830 MW	28670 TQ	USBLS	5/07
Except Maids and Housekeeping Cleaners	Pittsburgh MSA, PA	Y	16840 FQ	21180 MW	27130 TQ	USBLS	5/07
Except Maids and Housekeeping Cleaners	Reading MSA, PA	Y	19410 FQ	23710 MW	30880 TQ	USBLS	5/07
Except Maids and Housekeeping Cleaners	Rhode Island	Y	19470 FQ	24650 MW	32500 TQ	USBLS	5/07
Except Maids and Housekeeping Cleaners	Providence-Fall River-Warwick MSA, RI-MA	Y	19330 FQ	24450 MW	31930 TQ	USBLS	5/07
Except Maids and Housekeeping Cleaners	South Carolina	Y	14590 FQ	17710 MW	21690 TQ	USBLS	5/07
Except Maids and Housekeeping Cleaners	Charleston-North Charleston MSA, SC	Y	13610 FQ	15870 MW	18820 TQ	USBLS	5/07
Except Maids and Housekeeping Cleaners	Columbia MSA, SC	Y	14590 FQ	18180 MW	22510 TQ	USBLS	5/07
Except Maids and Housekeeping Cleaners	Spartanburg MSA, SC	Y	15300 FQ	18200 MW	22000 TQ	USBLS	5/07
Except Maids and Housekeeping Cleaners	South Dakota	Y	17558 FQ	20400 MW	24073 TQ	SDBLS	7/08-9/08
Except Maids and Housekeeping Cleaners	Sioux Falls MSA, SD	Y	18221 FQ	21582 MW	24896 TQ	SDBLS	7/08-9/08
Except Maids and Housekeeping Cleaners	Tennessee	Y	15770 FQ	18800 MW	23350 TQ	USBLS	5/07
Except Maids and Housekeeping Cleaners	Johnson City MSA, TN	Y	13530 FQ	16200 MW	20490 TQ	USBLS	5/07
Except Maids and Housekeeping Cleaners	Kingsport-Bristol-Bristol MSA, TN-VA	Y	14650 FQ	18100 MW	21190 TQ	USBLS	5/07
Except Maids and Housekeeping Cleaners	Memphis MSA, TN-MS-AR	Y	15240 FQ	20240 MW	24610 TQ	USBLS	5/07
Except Maids and Housekeeping Cleaners	Nashville-Davidson-Murfreesboro MSA, TN	Y	17160 FQ	20240 MW	24950 TQ	USBLS	5/07
Except Maids and Housekeeping Cleaners	Texas	Y	14140 FQ	17270 MW	21440 TQ	USBLS	5/07
Except Maids and Housekeeping Cleaners	Austin-Round Rock MSA, TX	Y	14730 FQ	18780 MW	23250 TQ	USBLS	5/07
Except Maids and Housekeeping Cleaners	Brownsville-Harlingen MSA, TX	Y	13830 FQ	16840 MW	20880 TQ	USBLS	5/07
Except Maids and Housekeeping Cleaners	Dallas-Fort Worth-Arlington MSA, TX	Y	14250 FQ	17480 MW	22090 TQ	USBLS	5/07
Except Maids and Housekeeping Cleaners	El Paso MSA, TX	Y	13770 FQ	16860 MW	21100 TQ	USBLS	5/07
Except Maids and Housekeeping Cleaners	Houston-Sugar Land-Baytown MSA, TX	Y	13710 FQ	16420 MW	20650 TQ	USBLS	5/07
Except Maids and Housekeeping Cleaners	San Antonio MSA, TX	Y	16040 FQ	18690 MW	22940 TQ	USBLS	5/07
Except Maids and Housekeeping Cleaners	Utah	Y	15560 FQ	18820 MW	23720 TQ	USBLS	5/07
Except Maids and Housekeeping Cleaners	St. George MSA, UT	Y	16970 FQ	20970 MW	27240 TQ	USBLS	5/07
Except Maids and Housekeeping Cleaners	Salt Lake City MSA, UT	Y	16490 FQ	19250 MW	24150 TQ	USBLS	5/07
Except Maids and Housekeeping Cleaners	Vermont	Y	19990 FQ	22820 MW.	26460 TQ	USBLS	5/07
Except Maids and Housekeeping Cleaners	Burlington-South Burlington MSA, VT	Y	20340 FQ	22910 MW	26530 TQ	USBLS	5/07

AE	Average entry wage	AW	Average wage paid	FQ	First quartile wage
AER	Average entry range	AWR	Average wage range	H	Hourly
AEX	Average experienced wage	AXR	Average experienced range	HI	Highest wage paid
ATC	Average total compensation	D	Daily	HR	High end range

LO	Lowest wage paid	MTC	Median total compensation	TCC	Total cash compensation
LR	Low end range	MW	Median wage paid	TQ	Third quartile wage
M	Monthly	MWR	Median wage range	W	Weekly
MCC	Median cash compensation	S	See annotated source	Y	Yearly

Occupation/Type/Industry	Location	Per	Low	Mid	High	Source	Date
Janitor and Cleaner							
Except Maids and Housekeeping Cleaners	Virginia	Y	15890 FQ	19190 MW	23670 TQ	USBLS	5/07
Except Maids and Housekeeping Cleaners	Richmond MSA, VA	Y	15950 FQ	19210 MW	23800 TQ	USBLS	5/07
Except Maids and Housekeeping Cleaners	Virginia Beach-Norfolk-Newport News MSA, VA-NC	Y	15210 FQ	18700 MW	23080 TQ	USBLS	5/07
Except Maids and Housekeeping Cleaners	Washington	H	9.94 FQ	12.03 MW	15.02 TQ	WABLS	3/08
Except Maids and Housekeeping Cleaners	Bremerton-Silverdale MSA, WA	Y	20140 FQ	23940 MW	30410 TQ	USBLS	5/07
Except Maids and Housekeeping Cleaners	Seattle-Tacoma-Bellevue MSA, WA	Y	21320 FQ	25460 MW	31940 TQ	USBLS	5/07
Except Maids and Housekeeping Cleaners	West Virginia	Y	15280 FQ	18894 MW	24480 TQ	WVBLS	7/08-9/08
Except Maids and Housekeeping Cleaners	Charleston MSA, WV	Y	13960 FQ	15860 MW	20870 TQ	USBLS	5/07
Except Maids and Housekeeping Cleaners	Wisconsin	Y	17810 FQ	21600 MW	27300 TQ	USBLS	5/07
Except Maids and Housekeeping Cleaners	Appleton MSA, WI	Y	18410 FQ	21850 MW	26190 TQ	USBLS	5/07
Except Maids and Housekeeping Cleaners	Milwaukee-Waukesha-West Allis MSA, WI	Y	17500 FQ	20590 MW	26830 TQ	USBLS	5/07
Except Maids and Housekeeping Cleaners	Racine MSA, WI	Y	16340 FQ	19290 MW	24720 TQ	USBLS	5/07
Except Maids and Housekeeping Cleaners	Wyoming	Y	18595 FQ	22747 MW	28526 TQ	WYBLS	9/08
Except Maids and Housekeeping Cleaners	Cheyenne MSA, WY	Y	19737 FQ	22896 MW	27751 TQ	WYBLS	9/08
Except Maids and Housekeeping Cleaners	Puerto Rico	Y	12850 FQ	14490 MW	17130 TQ	USBLS	5/07
Except Maids and Housekeeping Cleaners	Aguadilla-Isabela-San Sebastian MSA, PR	Y	12360 FQ	13520 MW	14690 TQ	USBLS	5/07
Except Maids and Housekeeping Cleaners	San Juan-Caguas-Guaynabo MSA, PR	Y	12930 FQ	14650 MW	17470 TQ	USBLS	5/07
Except Maids and Housekeeping Cleaners	Virgin Islands	Y	16230 FQ	18380 MW	21330 TQ	USBLS	5/07
Except Maids and Housekeeping Cleaners	Guam	Y	12790 FQ	14530 MW	17520 TQ	USBLS	5/07
Jeweler and Precious Stone and Metal Worker	Alabama	Y	26570 FQ	34200 MW	42010 TQ	USBLS	5/07
	Birmingham-Hoover MSA, AL	Y	35580 FQ	39670 MW	44070 TQ	USBLS	5/07
	Alaska	Y	22890 FQ	29620 MW	35370 TQ	USBLS	5/07
	Arizona	Y	28550 FQ	35700 MW	43120 TQ	USBLS	5/07
	Phoenix-Mesa-Scottsdale MSA, AZ	Y	31030 FQ	36130 MW	42930 TQ	USBLS	5/07
	Tucson MSA, AZ	Y	24550 FQ	41510 MW	49400 TQ	USBLS	5/07
	Arkansas	Y	26690 FQ	32020 MW	36690 TQ	USBLS	5/07
	California	H	8.99 FQ	12.67 MW	17.21 TQ	CABLS	1/08-3/08
	Los Angeles-Long Beach-Glendale PMSA, CA	H	8.60 FQ	10.35 MW	15.39 TQ	CABLS	1/08-3/08
	Oakland-Fremont-Hayward MSA, CA	H	10.89 FQ	13.53 MW	15.69 TQ	CABLS	1/08-3/08
	Riverside-San Bernardino-Ontario MSA, CA	H	9.98 FQ	12.24 MW	15.43 TQ	CABLS	1/08-3/08
	Sacramento-Arden Arcade-Roseville MSA, CA	H	10.99 FQ	13.70 MW	23.74 TQ	CABLS	1/08-3/08
	San Diego-Carlsbad-San Marcos MSA, CA	H	11.86 FQ	15.62 MW	17.68 TQ	CABLS	1/08-3/08
	San Jose-Sunnyvale-Santa Clara MSA, CA	H	17.59 FQ	27.33 MW	31.72 TQ	CABLS	1/08-3/08
	Santa Ana-Anaheim-Irvine PMSA, CA	Y	22480 FQ	28390 MW	31910 TQ	USBLS	5/07
	Colorado	Y	17130 FQ	26970 MW	41290 TQ	USBLS	5/07
	Denver-Aurora MSA, CO	Y	24160 FQ	28500 MW	46030 TQ	USBLS	5/07
	Connecticut	H	16.90 AE	23.06 MW		CTBLS	1/08-3/08
	Bridgeport-Stamford-Norwalk MSA, CT	Y	36510 FQ	48750 MW	59540 TQ	USBLS	5/07
	Hartford-West Hartford-East Hartford MSA, CT	Y	43620 FQ	47730 MW	98910 TQ	USBLS	5/07
	Delaware	Y	24820 FQ	31550 MW	45120 TQ	USBLS	5/07
	Wilmington PMSA, DE-MD-NJ	Y	22080 FQ	31090 MW	48320 TQ	USBLS	5/07
	Washington-Arlington-Alexandria MSA, DC-VA-MD-WV	Y	13840 FQ	17880 MW	42120 TQ	USBLS	5/07
	Florida	Y	26130 FQ	30510 MW	35990 TQ	USBLS	5/07
	Fort Lauderdale-Pompano Beach-Deerfield Beach PMSA, FL	Y	28350 FQ	31190 MW	37830 TQ	USBLS	5/07
	Jacksonville MSA, FL	Y	17580 FQ	19560 MW	24210 TQ	USBLS	5/07
	Miami-Fort Lauderdale-Miami Beach MSA, FL	Y	26290 FQ	30420 MW	34920 TQ	USBLS	5/07
	Orlando-Kissimmee MSA, FL	Y	28790 FQ	32250 MW	35330 TQ	USBLS	5/07

Occupation/Type/Industry	Location	Per	Low	Mid	High	Source	Date
Jeweler and Precious Stone and Metal Worker							
	Tampa-St. Petersburg-Clearwater MSA, FL	Y	26490 FQ	33310 MW	54820 TQ	USBLS	5/07
	West Palm Beach-Boca Raton-Boynton Beach PMSA, FL	Y	32940 FQ	35920 MW	38950 TQ	USBLS	5/07
	Georgia	Y	29680 FQ	35170 MW	40120 TQ	USBLS	5/07
	Atlanta-Sandy Springs-Marietta MSA, GA	Y	34440 FQ	37570 MW	42700 TQ	USBLS	5/07
	Hawaii	Y	20680 FQ	24540 MW	40430 TQ	USBLS	5/07
	Honolulu MSA, HI	Y	20070 FQ	23370 MW	30770 TQ	USBLS	5/07
	Idaho	Y	24430 FQ	30360 MW	36160 TQ	USBLS	5/07
	Illinois	Y	22910 FQ	30780 MW	39460 TQ	USBLS	5/07
	Chicago-Naperville-Joliet MSA, IL-IN-WI	Y	22980 FQ	30230 MW	40530 TQ	USBLS	5/07
	Indiana	Y	25570 FQ	33710 MW	47260 TQ	USBLS	5/07
	Indianapolis-Carmel MSA, IN	Y	29740 FQ	42680 MW	48290 TQ	USBLS	5/07
	Iowa	Y	30140 FQ	34270 MW	37610 TQ	USBLS	5/07
	Kansas	Y	20060 FQ	33550 MW	43500 TQ	USBLS	5/07
	Kentucky	Y	19757 FQ	30667 MW	48125 TQ	KYBLS	2008
	Louisville-Jefferson County MSA, KY-IN	Y	23650 FQ	36010 MW	57980 TQ	USBLS	5/07
	Louisiana	H	9.25 FQ	10.75 MW	15.08 TQ	LABLS	1/08-3/08
	New Orleans-Metairie-Kenner MSA, LA	Y	34440 FQ	40560 MW	48260 TQ	USBLS	5/07
	Maine	Y	28950 FQ	32520 MW	38710 TQ	USBLS	5/07
	Portland-South Portland-Biddeford MSA, ME	Y	31360 FQ	35840 MW	42760 TQ	USBLS	5/07
	Maryland	Y		33075 MW		MDBLS	3/08
	Baltimore-Towson MSA, MD	Y	26010 FQ	32550 MW	39290 TQ	USBLS	5/07
	Massachusetts	Y	24110 FQ	32750 MW	41160 TQ	USBLS	5/07
	Boston-Cambridge-Quincy NECTA, MA	Y	29250 FQ	36160 MW	40610 TQ	USBLS	5/07
	Michigan	Y	26330 FQ	33740 MW	44350 TQ	USBLS	5/07
	Detroit-Warren-Livonia MSA, MI	Y	30330 FQ	37720 MW	45940 TQ	USBLS	5/07
	Warren-Troy-Farmington Hills PMSA, MI	Y	29550 FQ	37990 MW	46720 TQ	USBLS	5/07
	Minnesota	Y	29794 FQ	36180 MW	47925 TQ	MNBLS	10/08-12/08
	Minneapolis-Saint Paul MSA, MN-WI	Y	28881 FQ	36729 MW	49584 TQ	MNBLS	10/08-12/08
	Mississippi	Y	20100 FQ	30890 MW	35580 TQ	USBLS	5/07
	Missouri	Y	30870 FQ	38110 MW	47370 TQ	USBLS	5/07
	Kansas City MSA, MO-KS	Y	21780 FQ	33280 MW	42980 TQ	USBLS	5/07
	St. Louis MSA, MO-IL	Y	32850 FQ	39100 MW	50060 TQ	USBLS	5/07
	Montana	Y	21870 FQ	25930 MW	33770 TQ	USBLS	5/07
	Nebraska	Y	20030 FQ	28130 MW	32320 TQ	USBLS	5/07
	Lincoln MSA, NE	Y	20550 FQ	28160 MW	31140 TQ	USBLS	5/07
	Nevada	H	14.81 FQ	16.81 MW	18.82 TQ	NVBLS	5/08
	Las Vegas-Paradise MSA, NV	H	15.85 FQ	17.40 MW	19.69 TQ	NVBLS	5/08
	New Hampshire	H	14.78 AE	20.04 MW	24.68 AEX	NHBLS	6/08
	New Jersey	Y	28800 FQ	36860 MW	45320 TQ	USBLS	5/07
	Camden PMSA, NJ	Y	29430 FQ	34740 MW	40220 TQ	USBLS	5/07
	Edison PMSA, NJ	Y	41460 FQ	54500 MW	59350 TQ	USBLS	5/07
	Newark-Union PMSA, NJ-PA	Y	32170 FQ	36450 MW	41590 TQ	USBLS	5/07
	New Mexico	Y	17920 FQ	22840 MW	28890 TQ	USBLS	5/07
	Albuquerque MSA, NM	Y	19300 FQ	23380 MW	30330 TQ	USBLS	5/07
	New York	Y	24480 FQ	34220 MW	51240 TQ	USBLS	5/07
	Buffalo-Niagara Falls MSA, NY	Y	34350 FQ	42320 MW	57050 TQ	USBLS	5/07
	Nassau-Suffolk PMSA, NY	Y	26070 FQ	36590 MW	48500 TQ	USBLS	5/07
	New York-Northern New Jersey-Long Island MSA, NY-NJ-PA	Y	24740 FQ	35150 MW	49450 TQ	USBLS	5/07
	North Carolina	Y	24930 FQ	32660 MW	46390 TQ	USBLS	5/07
	Charlotte-Gastonia-Concord MSA, NC-SC	Y	32080 FQ	34680 MW	37120 TQ	USBLS	5/07
	North Dakota	Y	28240 FQ	36270 MW	50500 TQ	USBLS	5/07
	Ohio	Y	22370 FQ	28840 MW	39620 TQ	USBLS	5/07
	Cincinnati-Middletown MSA, OH-KY-IN	Y	24580 FQ	34070 MW	42120 TQ	USBLS	5/07
	Cleveland-Elyria-Mentor MSA, OH	Y	21130 FQ	23840 MW	34150 TQ	USBLS	5/07

AE	Average entry wage	AW	Average wage paid	FQ	First quartile wage
AER	Average entry range	AWR	Average wage range	H	Hourly
AEX	Average experienced wage	AXR	Average experienced range	HI	Highest wage paid
ATC	Average total compensation	D	Daily	HR	High end range

LO	Lowest wage paid	MTC	Median total compensation	TCC	Total cash compensation
LR	Low end range	MW	Median wage paid	TQ	Third quartile wage
M	Monthly	MWR	Median wage range	W	Weekly
MCC	Median cash compensation	S	See annotated source	Y	Yearly

Occupation/Type/Industry	Location	Per	Low	Mid	High	Source	Date
Jeweler and Precious Stone and Metal Worker	Columbus MSA, OH	Y	23440 FQ	27550 MW	31720 TQ	USBLS	5/07
	Dayton MSA, OH	Y	24770 FQ	31740 MW	45070 TQ	USBLS	5/07
	Oklahoma	Y	30000 FQ	32440 MW	34980 TQ	USBLS	5/07
	Oklahoma City MSA, OK	Y	30190 FQ	32500 MW	34800 TQ	USBLS	5/07
	Oregon	H	9.58 FQ	13.58 MW	20.08 TQ	ORBLS	5/08
	Portland-Vancouver-Beaverton MSA, OR-WA	Y	23610 FQ	34060 MW	45230 TQ	USBLS	5/07
	Pennsylvania	Y	31370 FQ	43200 MW	51420 TQ	USBLS	5/07
	Allentown-Bethlehem-Easton MSA, PA-NJ	Y	40420 FQ	44070 MW	47800 TQ	USBLS	5/07
	Philadelphia-Camden-Wilmington MSA, PA-NJ-DE-MD	Y	30820 FQ	43840 MW	51220 TQ	USBLS	5/07
	Pittsburgh MSA, PA	Y	21980 FQ	37740 MW	54100 TQ	USBLS	5/07
	Rhode Island	Y	23140 FQ	26980 MW	31370 TQ	USBLS	5/07
	Providence-Fall River-Warwick MSA, RI-MA	Y	22470 FQ	26740 MW	31290 TQ	USBLS	5/07
	South Carolina	Y	29170 FQ	34760 MW	38870 TQ	USBLS	5/07
	Charleston-North Charleston MSA, SC	Y	32290 FQ	37360 MW	42360 TQ	USBLS	5/07
	Columbia MSA, SC	Y	29890 FQ	34250 MW	37070 TQ	USBLS	5/07
	South Dakota	Y	20871 FQ	25525 MW	31563 TQ	SDBLS	7/08-9/08
	Sioux Falls MSA, SD	Y	24221 FQ	43045 MW	48138 TQ	SDBLS	7/08-9/08
	Tennessee	Y	30840 FQ	33960 MW	36980 TQ	USBLS	5/07
	Nashville-Davidson-Murfreesboro MSA, TN	Y	31260 FQ	33730 MW	36250 TQ	USBLS	5/07
	Texas	Y	23310 FQ	28590 MW	37220 TQ	USBLS	5/07
	Austin-Round Rock MSA, TX	Y	25360 FQ	30820 MW	40680 TQ	USBLS	5/07
	Dallas-Fort Worth-Arlington MSA, TX	Y	27240 FQ	31660 MW	39360 TQ	USBLS	5/07
	Houston-Sugar Land-Baytown MSA, TX	Y	21210 FQ	23550 MW	26660 TQ	USBLS	5/07
	San Antonio MSA, TX	Y	19320 FQ	31950 MW	60640 TQ	USBLS	5/07
	Utah	Y	20180 FQ	26900 MW	35460 TQ	USBLS	5/07
	Salt Lake City MSA, UT	Y	24160 FQ	29200 MW	34740 TQ	USBLS	5/07
	Vermont	Y	27950 FQ	33800 MW	38920 TQ	USBLS	5/07
	Virginia	Y	23720 FQ	30260 MW	36020 TQ	USBLS	5/07
	Washington	H	14.13 FQ	17.45 MW	21.51 TQ	WABLS	3/08
	Seattle-Tacoma-Bellevue MSA, WA	Y	32320 FQ	40020 MW	49850 TQ	USBLS	5/07
	West Virginia	Y	24039 FQ	26223 MW	34143 TQ	WVBLS	7/08-9/08
	Wisconsin	Y	27650 FQ	35330 MW	44000 TQ	USBLS	5/07
	Milwaukee-Waukesha-West Allis MSA, WI	Y	32250 FQ	38830 MW	48460 TQ	USBLS	5/07
	Wyoming	Y	29351 FQ	49666 MW	54838 TQ	WYBLS	9/08
	Puerto Rico	Y	16890 FQ	18620 MW	20830 TQ	USBLS	5/07
	San Juan-Caguas-Guaynabo MSA, PR	Y	17120 FQ	18730 MW	20840 TQ	USBLS	5/07
	Virgin Islands	Y	25810 FQ	29280 MW	34940 TQ	USBLS	5/07
Job Analyst	United States	Y		45100 AW		SUSA06	2009
Job Printer	Alabama	Y	20900 FQ	26830 MW	32870 TQ	USBLS	5/07
	Birmingham-Hoover MSA, AL	Y	22720 FQ	28170 MW	32310 TQ	USBLS	5/07
	Arizona	Y	25230 FQ	31380 MW	40310 TQ	USBLS	5/07
	Phoenix-Mesa-Scottsdale MSA, AZ	Y	26190 FQ	33230 MW	43930 TQ	USBLS	5/07
	Tucson MSA, AZ	Y	24940 FQ	30860 MW	34990 TQ	USBLS	5/07
	Arkansas	Y	18970 FQ	26060 MW	33880 TQ	USBLS	5/07
	Little Rock-North Little Rock MSA, AR	Y	18280 FQ	22600 MW	35850 TQ	USBLS	5/07
	California	H	13.95 FQ	18.95 MW	24.56 TQ	CABLS	1/08-3/08
	Los Angeles-Long Beach-Glendale PMSA, CA	H	11.97 FQ	15.56 MW	23.71 TQ	CABLS	1/08-3/08
	Oakland-Fremont-Hayward MSA, CA	H	19.23 FQ	24.47 MW	28.33 TQ	CABLS	1/08-3/08
	Riverside-San Bernardino-Ontario MSA, CA	H	14.18 FQ	18.14 MW	22.10 TQ	CABLS	1/08-3/08
	Sacramento-Arden Arcade-Roseville MSA, CA	H	14.76 FQ	18.00 MW	24.23 TQ	CABLS	1/08-3/08

AE	Average entry wage	**AW**	Average wage paid	**FQ**	First quartile wage	**LO**	Lowest wage paid	**MTC**	Median total compensation
AER	Average entry range	**AWR**	Average wage range	**H**	Hourly	**LR**	Low end range	**MW**	Median wage paid
AEX	Average experienced wage	**AXR**	Average experienced range	**HI**	Highest wage paid	**M**	Monthly	**MWR**	Median wage range
ATC	Average total compensation	**D**	Daily	**HR**	High end range	**MCC**	Median cash compensation	**S**	See annotated source

TCC Total cash compensation
TQ Third quartile wage
W Weekly
Y Yearly

Occupation/Type/Industry	Location	Per	Low	Mid	High	Source	Date
Job Printer	San Diego-Carlsbad-San Marcos MSA, CA	H	18.01 FQ	20.36 MW	22.68 TQ	CABLS	1/08-3/08
	San Francisco-San Mateo-Redwood PMSA, CA	H	13.50 FQ	21.64 MW	33.63 TQ	CABLS	1/08-3/08
	San Jose-Sunnyvale-Santa Clara MSA, CA	H	17.10 FQ	20.66 MW	25.82 TQ	CABLS	1/08-3/08
	Santa Ana-Anaheim-Irvine PMSA, CA	Y	33690 FQ	39920 MW	47530 TQ	USBLS	5/07
	Stockton MSA, CA	H	11.60 FQ	15.90 MW	20.64 TQ	CABLS	1/08-3/08
	Colorado	Y	22300 FQ	30500 MW	38330 TQ	USBLS	5/07
	Denver-Aurora MSA, CO	Y	27140 FQ	34870 MW	41740 TQ	USBLS	5/07
	Connecticut	H	12.46 AE	16.30 MW		CTBLS	1/08-3/08
	Bridgeport-Stamford-Norwalk MSA, CT	Y	29510 FQ	33760 MW	50620 TQ	USBLS	5/07
	Hartford-West Hartford-East Hartford MSA, CT	Y	27210 FQ	35300 MW	44620 TQ	USBLS	5/07
	Delaware	Y	28810 FQ	32170 MW	45820 TQ	USBLS	5/07
	Wilmington PMSA, DE-MD-NJ	Y	28710 FQ	32040 MW	46180 TQ	USBLS	5/07
	District of Columbia	Y	23760 FQ	28840 MW	34270 TQ	USBLS	5/07
	Washington-Arlington-Alexandria MSA, DC-VA-MD-WV	Y	26760 FQ	33590 MW	44500 TQ	USBLS	5/07
	Florida	Y	22110 FQ	27600 MW	33230 TQ	USBLS	5/07
	Fort Lauderdale-Pompano Beach-Deerfield Beach PMSA, FL	Y	22070 FQ	25090 MW	31550 TQ	USBLS	5/07
	Jacksonville MSA, FL	Y	22980 FQ	25760 MW	29530 TQ	USBLS	5/07
	Lakeland MSA, FL	Y	25940 FQ	28200 MW	30470 TQ	USBLS	5/07
	Miami-Fort Lauderdale-Miami Beach MSA, FL	Y	22210 FQ	26690 MW	33830 TQ	USBLS	5/07
	Orlando-Kissimmee MSA, FL	Y	21960 FQ	27820 MW	32720 TQ	USBLS	5/07
	Sarasota-Bradenton-Venice MSA, FL	Y	15070 FQ	26530 MW	36200 TQ	USBLS	5/07
	Tampa-St. Petersburg-Clearwater MSA, FL	Y	25850 FQ	29760 MW	33400 TQ	USBLS	5/07
	West Palm Beach-Boca Raton-Boynton Beach PMSA, FL	Y	28620 FQ	36360 MW	47980 TQ	USBLS	5/07
	Georgia	Y	22790 FQ	31250 MW	40430 TQ	USBLS	5/07
	Atlanta-Sandy Springs-Marietta MSA, GA	Y	25030 FQ	34020 MW	41630 TQ	USBLS	5/07
	Hawaii	Y	19970 FQ	28330 MW	37770 TQ	USBLS	5/07
	Honolulu MSA, HI	Y	19650 FQ	28450 MW	37630 TQ	USBLS	5/07
	Idaho	Y	24180 FQ	27990 MW	32530 TQ	USBLS	5/07
	Illinois	Y	30550 FQ	36260 MW	44110 TQ	USBLS	5/07
	Chicago-Naperville-Joliet MSA, IL-IN-WI	Y	30580 FQ	36940 MW	46100 TQ	USBLS	5/07
	Indiana	Y	23580 FQ	30890 MW	37070 TQ	USBLS	5/07
	Indianapolis-Carmel MSA, IN	Y	18000 FQ	29250 MW	34830 TQ	USBLS	5/07
	Terre Haute MSA, IN	Y	23750 FQ	32540 MW	39670 TQ	USBLS	5/07
	Iowa	Y	25660 FQ	35010 MW	42420 TQ	USBLS	5/07
	Cedar Rapids MSA, IA	Y	27860 FQ	36570 MW	42320 TQ	USBLS	5/07
	Kansas	Y	26970 FQ	32850 MW	41320 TQ	USBLS	5/07
	Wichita MSA, KS	Y	24010 FQ	34990 MW	43860 TQ	USBLS	5/07
	Kentucky	Y	19317 FQ	27665 MW	34974 TQ	KYBLS	2008
	Louisville-Jefferson County MSA, KY-IN	Y	23600 FQ	30740 MW	36560 TQ	USBLS	5/07
	Louisiana	H	9.82 FQ	11.70 MW	14.26 TQ	LABLS	1/08-3/08
	Baton Rouge MSA, LA	Y	20890 FQ	23540 MW	29860 TQ	USBLS	5/07
	New Orleans-Metairie-Kenner MSA, LA	Y	18760 FQ	22120 MW	25150 TQ	USBLS	5/07
	Maine	Y	23010 FQ	31890 MW	39960 TQ	USBLS	5/07
	Portland-South Portland-Biddeford MSA, ME	Y	21600 FQ	23440 MW	28560 TQ	USBLS	5/07
	Maryland	Y		37150 MW		MDBLS	3/08
	Baltimore-Towson MSA, MD	Y	33270 FQ	40870 MW	50310 TQ	USBLS	5/07
	Bethesda-Gaithersburg-Frederick PMSA, MD	Y	30320 FQ	36730 MW	48070 TQ	USBLS	5/07
	Massachusetts	Y	27770 FQ	35510 MW	47760 TQ	USBLS	5/07
	Boston-Cambridge-Quincy NECTA, MA	Y	27030 FQ	34350 MW	47670 TQ	USBLS	5/07
	Worcester MSA, MA-CT	Y	29360 FQ	35040 MW	39840 TQ	USBLS	5/07

AE	Average entry wage	AW	Average wage paid	FQ	First quartile wage
AER	Average entry range	AWR	Average wage range	H	Hourly
AEX	Average experienced wage	AXR	Average experienced range	HI	Highest wage paid
ATC	Average total compensation	D	Daily	HR	High end range

LO	Lowest wage paid	MTC	Median total compensation	TCC	Total cash compensation
LR	Low end range	MW	Median wage paid	TQ	Third quartile wage
M	Monthly	MWR	Median wage range	W	Weekly
MCC	Median cash compensation	S	See annotated source	Y	Yearly

Occupation/Type/Industry	Location	Per	Low	Mid	High	Source	Date
Job Printer	Michigan	Y	27150 FQ	34340 MW	41880 TQ	USBLS	5/07
	Detroit-Warren-Livonia MSA, MI	Y	31040 FQ	37350 MW	45570 TQ	USBLS	5/07
	Grand Rapids-Wyoming MSA, MI	Y	30540 FQ	35660 MW	41710 TQ	USBLS	5/07
	Warren-Troy-Farmington Hills PMSA, MI	Y	32230 FQ	38040 MW	45850 TQ	USBLS	5/07
	Minnesota	Y	33484 FQ	42514 MW	50786 TQ	MNBLS	10/08-12/08
	Minneapolis-Saint Paul MSA, MN-WI	Y	38916 FQ	45416 MW	54415 TQ	MNBLS	10/08-12/08
	Rochester MSA, MN	Y	31141 FQ	38734 MW	45148 TQ	MNBLS	10/08-12/08
	Mississippi	Y	27520 FQ	31730 MW	36130 TQ	USBLS	5/07
	Jackson MSA, MS	Y	21470 FQ	27200 MW	31870 TQ	USBLS	5/07
	Missouri	Y	28290 FQ	34310 MW	43580 TQ	USBLS	5/07
	Kansas City MSA, MO-KS	Y	28360 FQ	33760 MW	44260 TQ	USBLS	5/07
	St. Louis MSA, MO-IL	Y	32200 FQ	40070 MW	54360 TQ	USBLS	5/07
	Montana	Y	25380 FQ	32710 MW	38710 TQ	USBLS	5/07
	Nebraska	Y	26410 FQ	31720 MW	41450 TQ	USBLS	5/07
	Omaha-Council Bluffs MSA, NE-IA	Y	27770 FQ	32340 MW	39080 TQ	USBLS	5/07
	Nevada	H	14.03 FQ	17.18 MW	20.82 TQ	NVBLS	5/08
	Las Vegas-Paradise MSA, NV	H	14.40 FQ	17.60 MW	21.16 TQ	NVBLS	5/08
	New Hampshire	H	14.93 AE	19.27 MW	20.91 AEX	NHBLS	6/08
	Nashua NECTA, NH-MA	Y	31850 FQ	35320 MW	42340 TQ	USBLS	5/07
	New Jersey	Y	23780 FQ	38920 MW	50690 TQ	USBLS	5/07
	Camden PMSA, NJ	Y	22410 FQ	30390 MW	41950 TQ	USBLS	5/07
	Edison PMSA, NJ	Y	35930 FQ	43460 MW	49420 TQ	USBLS	5/07
	Newark-Union PMSA, NJ-PA	Y	21830 FQ	47310 MW	56740 TQ	USBLS	5/07
	New Mexico	Y	28570 FQ	34700 MW	39010 TQ	USBLS	5/07
	Albuquerque MSA, NM	Y	34680 FQ	37620 MW	41660 TQ	USBLS	5/07
	New York	Y	26900 FQ	34360 MW	44890 TQ	USBLS	5/07
	Albany-Schenectady-Troy MSA, NY	Y	32290 FQ	39150 MW	49780 TQ	USBLS	5/07
	Buffalo-Niagara Falls MSA, NY	Y	20780 FQ	29300 MW	38800 TQ	USBLS	5/07
	Nassau-Suffolk PMSA, NY	Y	27540 FQ	35990 MW	50270 TQ	USBLS	5/07
	New York-Northern New Jersey-Long Island MSA, NY-NJ-PA	Y	26400 FQ	35300 MW	48260 TQ	USBLS	5/07
	North Carolina	Y	25750 FQ	31650 MW	40480 TQ	USBLS	5/07
	Charlotte-Gastonia-Concord MSA, NC-SC	Y	24150 FQ	29490 MW	42480 TQ	USBLS	5/07
	Raleigh-Cary MSA, NC	Y	26720 FQ	31390 MW	37630 TQ	USBLS	5/07
	North Dakota	Y	22180 FQ	28650 MW	37690 TQ	USBLS	5/07
	Ohio	Y	24450 FQ	33200 MW	40330 TQ	USBLS	5/07
	Canton-Massillon MSA, OH	Y	26710 FQ	31200 MW	36790 TQ	USBLS	5/07
	Cincinnati-Middletown MSA, OH-KY-IN	Y	30380 FQ	35790 MW	43540 TQ	USBLS	5/07
	Cleveland-Elyria-Mentor MSA, OH	Y	20830 FQ	36050 MW	46300 TQ	USBLS	5/07
	Columbus MSA, OH	Y	20990 FQ	33350 MW	39160 TQ	USBLS	5/07
	Dayton MSA, OH	Y	22580 FQ	29040 MW	36240 TQ	USBLS	5/07
	Oklahoma	Y	21250 FQ	29060 MW	35680 TQ	USBLS	5/07
	Oklahoma City MSA, OK	Y	26320 FQ	31820 MW	36670 TQ	USBLS	5/07
	Tulsa MSA, OK	Y	22540 FQ	28360 MW	35750 TQ	USBLS	5/07
	Oregon	H	13.37 FQ	16.76 MW	20.84 TQ	ORBLS	5/08
	Portland-Vancouver-Beaverton MSA, OR-WA	Y	28170 FQ	35200 MW	41600 TQ	USBLS	5/07
	Pennsylvania	Y	25870 FQ	32060 MW	39630 TQ	USBLS	5/07
	Allentown-Bethlehem-Easton MSA, PA-NJ	Y	25540 FQ	35300 MW	41380 TQ	USBLS	5/07
	Erie MSA, PA	Y	28360 FQ	34570 MW	38380 TQ	USBLS	5/07
	Philadelphia-Camden-Wilmington MSA, PA-NJ-DE-MD	Y	25850 FQ	31310 MW	38850 TQ	USBLS	5/07
	Pittsburgh MSA, PA	Y	27800 FQ	32650 MW	40060 TQ	USBLS	5/07
	Rhode Island	Y	28980 FQ	36500 MW	46700 TQ	USBLS	5/07
	Providence-Fall River-Warwick MSA, RI-MA	Y	29140 FQ	36560 MW	46410 TQ	USBLS	5/07
	South Carolina	Y	25090 FQ	28920 MW	36230 TQ	USBLS	5/07
	Charleston-North Charleston MSA, SC	Y	24200 FQ	29210 MW	36830 TQ	USBLS	5/07

AE	Average entry wage	AW	Average wage paid	FQ	First quartile wage
AER	Average entry range	AWR	Average wage range	H	Hourly
AEX	Average experienced wage	AXR	Average experienced range	HI	Highest wage paid
ATC	Average total compensation	D	Daily	HR	High end range

LO	Lowest wage paid	MTC	Median total compensation
LR	Low end range	MW	Median wage paid
M	Monthly	MWR	Median wage range
MCC	Median cash compensation	S	See annotated source

TCC	Total cash compensation
TQ	Third quartile wage
W	Weekly
Y	Yearly

Occupation/Type/Industry	Location	Per	Low	Mid	High	Source	Date
Job Printer	Columbia MSA, SC	Y	22890 FQ	29210 MW	36110 TQ	USBLS	5/07
	South Dakota	Y	22334 FQ	24529 MW	32782 TQ	SDBLS	7/08-9/08
	Tennessee	Y	27550 FQ	34090 MW	39170 TQ	USBLS	5/07
	Memphis MSA, TN-MS-AR	Y	31160 FQ	35380 MW	39810 TQ	USBLS	5/07
	Nashville-Davidson-Murfreesboro MSA, TN	Y	31530 FQ	36160 MW	41490 TQ	USBLS	5/07
	Texas	Y	21950 FQ	28870 MW	36210 TQ	USBLS	5/07
	Austin-Round Rock MSA, TX	Y	24790 FQ	32330 MW	38540 TQ	USBLS	5/07
	Dallas-Fort Worth-Arlington MSA, TX	Y	22300 FQ	29460 MW	36720 TQ	USBLS	5/07
	Houston-Sugar Land-Baytown MSA, TX	Y	25850 FQ	32290 MW	38390 TQ	USBLS	5/07
	San Antonio MSA, TX	Y	21430 FQ	29850 MW	37670 TQ	USBLS	5/07
	Utah	Y	23670 FQ	28910 MW	37690 TQ	USBLS	5/07
	Salt Lake City MSA, UT	Y	22070 FQ	28320 MW	37370 TQ	USBLS	5/07
	Vermont	Y	32950 FQ	38440 MW	43950 TQ	USBLS	5/07
	Burlington-South Burlington MSA, VT	Y	32960 FQ	36470 MW	40630 TQ	USBLS	5/07
	Virginia	Y	23950 FQ	32510 MW	43880 TQ	USBLS	5/07
	Richmond MSA, VA	Y	22930 FQ	25780 MW	41730 TQ	USBLS	5/07
	Virginia Beach-Norfolk-Newport News MSA, VA-NC	Y	27440 FQ	33140 MW	40120 TQ	USBLS	5/07
	Washington	H	13.77 FQ	17.22 MW	21.72 TQ	WABLS	3/08
	Seattle-Tacoma-Bellevue MSA, WA	Y	30980 FQ	39100 MW	47450 TQ	USBLS	5/07
	West Virginia	Y	25008 FQ	28888 MW	33067 TQ	WVBLS	7/08-9/08
	Wisconsin	Y	27040 FQ	31760 MW	38410 TQ	USBLS	5/07
	Milwaukee-Waukesha-West Allis MSA, WI	Y	28680 FQ	36110 MW	43660 TQ	USBLS	5/07
	Wyoming	Y	21885 FQ	32799 MW	37105 TQ	WYBLS	9/08
	Puerto Rico	Y	17120 FQ	21670 MW	25310 TQ	USBLS	5/07
	San Juan-Caguas-Guaynabo MSA, PR	Y	18450 FQ	22410 MW	26020 TQ	USBLS	5/07
	Virgin Islands	Y	21820 FQ	24000 MW	28430 TQ	USBLS	5/07
Journeyman Heavy Equipment Operator	Michigan	H	25.00 LO		32.00 HI	FREEP09	2009
Journeyman Plumber	Chicago, IL	Y			250000 HI	TME01	2008
Judge							
District Court	Michigan	Y			138272 HI	FREEP04	2008
Probate Court	Bibb County, GA	Y			143085 HI	GACTY02	2008
Probate Court	Douglas County, GA	Y			76762 HI	GACTY02	2008
Probate Court	Michigan	Y			139919 HI	FREEP04	2008
State Court	Gwinnett County, GA	Y			160040 HI	GACTY02	2008
State Court	Stephens County, GA	Y			31193 HI	GACTY02	2008
State Court of Appeals	Michigan	Y			151441 HI	FREEP01	2007
State Court of Appeals	Mississippi	Y			105050 HI	HATAM	7/08
State Court of Appeals	North Carolina	Y		128011 AW		NCLW	2008
State Supreme Court	Nebraska	Y			131285 HI	NEST	2008
Superior Court	DeKalb County, GA	Y			155716 HI	GACTY02	2008
Superior Court	Peach County, GA	Y			4100 HI	GACTY02	2008
Tax Court of the United States	United States	Y			169300 HI	CRS02	1/08
U.S. Court of Appeals for the Armed Services	United States	Y			179500 HI	CRS02	1/08
U.S. Court of Appeals for Veterans Claims	United States	Y			169300 HI	CRS02	1/08
U.S. Court of Federal Claims	United States	Y			169300 HI	CRS02	1/08
U.S. Court of International Trade	United States	Y			169300 HI	CRS02	1/08
U.S. Courts of Appeal	United States	Y			179500 HI	CRS02	1/08
U.S. District Courts	United States	Y			169300 HI	CRS02	1/08
Judge, Magistrate Judge, and Magistrate	Alabama	Y	31910 FQ	45120 MW	100320 TQ	USBLS	5/07
	Birmingham-Hoover MSA, AL	Y	25490 FQ	41880 MW	51420 TQ	USBLS	5/07
	Arizona	Y	66670 FQ	76990 MW	107850 TQ	USBLS	5/07
	Phoenix-Mesa-Scottsdale MSA, AZ	Y	71000 FQ	80020 MW	121910 TQ	USBLS	5/07
	Arkansas	Y	23920 FQ	32180 MW	49890 TQ	USBLS	5/07
	Little Rock-North Little Rock MSA, AR	Y	23770 FQ	47640 MW	84000 TQ	USBLS	5/07

AE	Average entry wage	AW	Average wage paid	FQ	First quartile wage	LO	Lowest wage paid	MTC	Median total compensation	TCC	Total cash compensation
AER	Average entry range	AWR	Average wage range	H	Hourly	LR	Low end range	MW	Median wage paid	TQ	Third quartile wage
AEX	Average experienced wage	AXR	Average experienced range	HI	Highest wage paid	M	Monthly	MWR	Median wage range	W	Weekly
ATC	Average total compensation	D	Daily	HR	High end range	MCC	Median cash compensation	S	See annotated source	Y	Yearly

Judge, Magistrate Judge, and Magistrate

Occupation/Type/Industry	Location	Per	Low	Mid	High	Source	Date
Judge, Magistrate Judge, and Magistrate	Sacramento-Arden Arcade-Roseville MSA, CA	H	69.72 FQ			CABLS	1/08-3/08
	Colorado	Y	101940 FQ	114330 MW	125440 TQ	USBLS	5/07
	Denver-Aurora MSA, CO	Y	102790 FQ	114430 MW	124970 TQ	USBLS	5/07
	Connecticut	H	63.75 AE	71.79 MW		CTBLS	1/08-3/08
	Wilmington PMSA, DE-MD-NJ	Y	75510 FQ			USBLS	5/07
	Florida	Y	139320 FQ			USBLS	5/07
	Jacksonville MSA, FL	Y	138830 FQ			USBLS	5/07
	Miami-Fort Lauderdale-Miami Beach MSA, FL	Y	138960 FQ			USBLS	5/07
	Orlando-Kissimmee MSA, FL	Y	140110 FQ			USBLS	5/07
	Tampa-St. Petersburg-Clearwater MSA, FL	Y	138120 FQ			USBLS	5/07
	Georgia	Y	45520 FQ	78260 MW	120680 TQ	USBLS	5/07
	Atlanta-Sandy Springs-Marietta MSA, GA	Y	56680 FQ	110540 MW	131330 TQ	USBLS	5/07
	Idaho	Y	114790 FQ	133660 MW		USBLS	5/07
	Illinois	Y	140600 FQ			USBLS	5/07
	Chicago-Naperville-Joliet MSA, IL-IN-WI	Y	134660 FQ			USBLS	5/07
	Indiana	Y	50630 FQ	108250 MW	121200 TQ	USBLS	5/07
	Gary PMSA, IN	Y	48980 FQ	98880 MW	119070 TQ	USBLS	5/07
	Indianapolis-Carmel MSA, IN	Y	34950 FQ	53790 MW	115330 TQ	USBLS	5/07
	Iowa	Y	36790 FQ	106350 MW	121430 TQ	USBLS	5/07
	Kansas	Y	76750 FQ	114690 MW	133010 TQ	USBLS	5/07
	Wichita MSA, KS	Y	110940 FQ	119800 MW	128870 TQ	USBLS	5/07
	Louisiana	H	6.87 FQ	20.51 MW	37.11 TQ	LABLS	1/08-3/08
	New Orleans-Metairie-Kenner MSA, LA	Y	43190 FQ	50700 MW	78510 TQ	USBLS	5/07
	Maine	Y	80710 FQ	115160 MW	125280 TQ	USBLS	5/07
	Maryland	Y		55650 MW		MDBLS	3/08
	Baltimore-Towson MSA, MD	Y	50900 FQ	54630 MW	58350 TQ	USBLS	5/07
	Massachusetts	Y	96860 FQ	128900 MW		USBLS	5/07
	Michigan	Y	53170 FQ	99060 MW		USBLS	5/07
	Detroit-Warren-Livonia MSA, MI	Y	86950 FQ	106810 MW		USBLS	5/07
	Grand Rapids-Wyoming MSA, MI	Y	46990 FQ	67640 MW	144270 TQ	USBLS	5/07
	Warren-Troy-Farmington Hills PMSA, MI	Y	50250 FQ	107910 MW	140550 TQ	USBLS	5/07
	Minnesota	Y	113055 FQ	122492 MW	131929 TQ	MNBLS	10/08-12/08
	Minneapolis-Saint Paul MSA, MN-WI	Y	107478 FQ	119897 MW	130757 TQ	MNBLS	10/08-12/08
	Mississippi	Y	26200 FQ	31960 MW	40060 TQ	USBLS	5/07
	Jackson MSA, MS	Y	23430 FQ	30370 MW	73800 TQ	USBLS	5/07
	Missouri	Y	90850 FQ	102760 MW	123920 TQ	USBLS	5/07
	Kansas City MSA, MO-KS	Y	88080 FQ	112380 MW	132330 TQ	USBLS	5/07
	St. Louis MSA, MO-IL	Y	101640 FQ	123800 MW		USBLS	5/07
	Nevada	H	42.34 FQ	64.80 MW		NVBLS	5/08
	Las Vegas-Paradise MSA, NV	H	56.59 FQ	68.85 MW		NVBLS	5/08
	New Jersey	Y	118950 FQ	144020 MW		USBLS	5/07
	Camden PMSA, NJ	Y	119120 FQ	142970 MW		USBLS	5/07
	Edison PMSA, NJ	Y	117550 FQ	143790 MW		USBLS	5/07
	Newark-Union PMSA, NJ-PA	Y	134270 FQ			USBLS	5/07
	New Mexico	Y	15910 FQ	35510 MW	52330 TQ	USBLS	5/07
	New York	Y	108090 FQ	122700 MW	141600 TQ	USBLS	5/07
	Albany-Schenectady-Troy MSA, NY	Y	102550 FQ	117560 MW	130840 TQ	USBLS	5/07
	Buffalo-Niagara Falls MSA, NY	Y	107810 FQ	117730 MW	128130 TQ	USBLS	5/07
	Nassau-Suffolk PMSA, NY	Y	111070 FQ	125470 MW	144230 TQ	USBLS	5/07
	New York-Northern New Jersey-Long Island MSA, NY-NJ-PA	Y	115590 FQ	136850 MW		USBLS	5/07
	Syracuse MSA, NY	Y	109600 FQ	122530 MW	139440 TQ	USBLS	5/07
	Utica-Rome MSA, NY	Y	103200 FQ	117240 MW	130810 TQ	USBLS	5/07
	North Dakota	Y	106180 FQ	115960 MW	125630 TQ	USBLS	5/07
	Ohio	Y	37490 FQ	50640 MW	71630 TQ	USBLS	5/07
	Cincinnati-Middletown MSA, OH-KY-IN	Y	39120 FQ	61240 MW	108910 TQ	USBLS	5/07

AE	Average entry wage	AW	Average wage paid	FQ First quartile wage
AER	Average entry range	AWR	Average wage range	H Hourly
AEX	Average experienced wage	AXR	Average experienced range	HI Highest wage paid
ATC	Average total compensation	D	Daily	HR High end range

LO Lowest wage paid	MTC Median total compensation	TCC Total cash compensation
LR Low end range	MW Median wage paid	TQ Third quartile wage
M Monthly	MWR Median wage range	W Weekly
MCC Median cash compensation	S See annotated source	Y Yearly

Occupation/Type/Industry	Location	Per	Low	Mid	High	Source	Date
Judge, Magistrate Judge, and Magistrate							
	Cleveland-Elyria-Mentor MSA, OH	Y	36340 FQ	45470 MW	64460 TQ	USBLS	5/07
	Columbus MSA, OH	Y	36400 FQ	40200 MW	72290 TQ	USBLS	5/07
	Dayton MSA, OH	Y	42610 FQ	64730 MW	73450 TQ	USBLS	5/07
	Oklahoma	Y	74570 FQ	89700 MW	98920 TQ	USBLS	5/07
	Oklahoma City MSA, OK	Y	85890 FQ	93320 MW	100770 TQ	USBLS	5/07
	Tulsa MSA, OK	Y	74870 FQ	87620 MW	97660 TQ	USBLS	5/07
	Oregon	H	42.73 FQ	46.25 MW	49.77 TQ	ORBLS	5/08
	Portland-Vancouver-Beaverton MSA, OR-WA	Y	86220 FQ	93910 MW	101600 TQ	USBLS	5/07
	Pennsylvania	Y	53680 FQ	63750 MW	77860 TQ	USBLS	5/07
	Philadelphia-Camden-Wilmington MSA, PA-NJ-DE-MD	Y	82670 FQ	143180 MW		USBLS	5/07
	Providence-Fall River-Warwick MSA, RI-MA	Y	138550 FQ			USBLS	5/07
	South Carolina	Y	26530 FQ	45880 MW	73990 TQ	USBLS	5/07
	Charleston-North Charleston MSA, SC	Y	21890 FQ	41310 MW	79950 TQ	USBLS	5/07
	Columbia MSA, SC	Y	28650 FQ	48380 MW	115740 TQ	USBLS	5/07
	South Dakota	Y	75414 FQ	87753 MW	98711 TQ	SDBLS	7/08-9/08
	Tennessee	Y	31880 FQ	74850 MW	138080 TQ	USBLS	5/07
	Memphis MSA, TN-MS-AR	Y	29800 FQ	50210 MW	144180 TQ	USBLS	5/07
	Nashville-Davidson-Murfreesboro MSA, TN	Y	36820 FQ	93260 MW	139400 TQ	USBLS	5/07
	Texas	Y	16040 FQ	43070 MW	83800 TQ	USBLS	5/07
	Austin-Round Rock MSA, TX	Y	24740 FQ	54850 MW	68790 TQ	USBLS	5/07
	Corpus Christi MSA, TX	Y	15100 FQ	57550 MW	83090 TQ	USBLS	5/07
	Dallas-Fort Worth-Arlington MSA, TX	Y	33300 FQ	76950 MW	123880 TQ	USBLS	5/07
	Houston-Sugar Land-Baytown MSA, TX	Y	15920 FQ	52910 MW	95520 TQ	USBLS	5/07
	San Antonio MSA, TX	Y	16190 FQ	72280 MW	83030 TQ	USBLS	5/07
	Utah	Y	37700 FQ	51730 MW	93600 TQ	USBLS	5/07
	Salt Lake City MSA, UT	Y	77910 FQ	95840 MW	108890 TQ	USBLS	5/07
	Vermont	Y	23860 FQ	107820 MW	120820 TQ	USBLS	5/07
	Washington	H	36.56 FQ	47.96 MW	60.52 TQ	WABLS	3/08
	Seattle-Tacoma-Bellevue MSA, WA	Y	77140 FQ	101900 MW	123300 TQ	USBLS	5/07
	West Virginia	Y	33622 FQ	49451 MW	90367 TQ	WVBLS	7/08-9/08
	Wisconsin	Y	14670 FQ	15790 MW	73350 TQ	USBLS	5/07
	Wyoming	Y	42845 FQ	48453 MW	58740 TQ	WYBLS	9/08
Junior Civil Engineer							
Municipal Government	Walnut Creek, CA	Y	73971 LO		89243 HI	WCSWP	7/11/08
Junior Planner							
Municipal Government	Carlsbad, CA	S	1818 LO		2210 HI	CCSS01	8/5/08
Junior ROTC Instructor							
Master's Degree, Public Schools	Baldwin County, AL	Y	26189 LO		33318 HI	BCPSSS	2008-2009
Nondegreed, Public Schools	Baldwin County, AL	Y	21455 LO		28122 HI	BCPSSS	2008-2009
Juvenile Correctional Officer							
State Government	Ohio	H	16.35 LO		19.88 HI	ODAS	2008
Juvenile Justice Program Coordinator							
Municipal Government	Carlsbad, CA	S	1969 LO		2393 HI	CCSS01	8/5/08
Juvenile Parole Officer							
State Government	Ohio	H	18.99 LO		23.76 HI	ODAS	2008
K-12 Curriculum Designer	United States	H		30.87 MW		YAHHJ	2007
Kindergarten Teacher							
Except Special Education	Alabama	Y	35060 FQ	40520 MW	46520 TQ	USBLS	5/07
Except Special Education	Birmingham-Hoover MSA, AL	Y	35780 FQ	41350 MW	46800 TQ	USBLS	5/07
Except Special Education	Alaska	Y	43950 FQ	54050 MW	69020 TQ	USBLS	5/07
Except Special Education	Arizona	Y	31030 FQ	36810 MW	43740 TQ	USBLS	5/07

AE	Average entry wage	AW	Average wage paid	FQ	First quartile wage	LO	Lowest wage paid	MTC	Median total compensation	TCC	Total cash compensation
AER	Average entry range	AWR	Average wage range	H	Hourly	LR	Low end range	MW	Median wage paid	TQ	Third quartile wage
AEX	Average experienced wage	AXR	Average experienced range	HI	Highest wage paid	M	Monthly	MWR	Median wage range	W	Weekly
ATC	Average total compensation	D	Daily	HR	High end range	MCC	Median cash compensation	S	See annotated source	Y	Yearly

Occupation/Type/Industry	Location	Per	Low	Mid	High	Source	Date
Kindergarten Teacher							
Except Special Education	Phoenix-Mesa-Scottsdale MSA, AZ	Y	34100 FQ	39030 MW	46810 TQ	USBLS	5/07
Except Special Education	Tucson MSA, AZ	Y	27820 FQ	32530 MW	37620 TQ	USBLS	5/07
Except Special Education	Yuma MSA, AZ	Y	26950 FQ	29800 MW	38640 TQ	USBLS	5/07
Except Special Education	Arkansas	Y	34860 FQ	40030 MW	46190 TQ	USBLS	5/07
Except Special Education	Fort Smith MSA, AR-OK	Y	33880 FQ	37840 MW	43960 TQ	USBLS	5/07
Except Special Education	Little Rock-North Little Rock MSA, AR	Y	34360 FQ	40970 MW	49870 TQ	USBLS	5/07
Except Special Education	California	Y		55140 AW		CABLS	1/08-3/08
Except Special Education	Los Angeles-Long Beach-Glendale PMSA, CA	Y		53489 AW		CABLS	1/08-3/08
Except Special Education	Oakland-Fremont-Hayward MSA, CA	Y		52176 AW		CABLS	1/08-3/08
Except Special Education	Riverside-San Bernardino-Ontario MSA, CA	Y		56678 AW		CABLS	1/08-3/08
Except Special Education	Sacramento-Arden Arcade-Roseville MSA, CA	Y		53663 MW		CABLS	1/08-3/08
Except Special Education	San Diego-Carlsbad-San Marcos MSA, CA	Y		46854 AW		CABLS	1/08-3/08
Except Special Education	San Francisco-San Mateo-Redwood PMSA, CA	Y		53222 AW		CABLS	1/08-3/08
Except Special Education	San Jose-Sunnyvale-Santa Clara MSA, CA	Y		54770 AW		CABLS	1/08-3/08
Except Special Education	Santa Ana-Anaheim-Irvine PMSA, CA	Y	33480 FQ	50700 MW	70450 TQ	USBLS	5/07
Except Special Education	Colorado	Y	34900 FQ	41520 MW	52380 TQ	USBLS	5/07
Except Special Education	Denver-Aurora MSA, CO	Y	35710 FQ	44110 MW	56600 TQ	USBLS	5/07
Except Special Education	Bridgeport-Stamford-Norwalk MSA, CT	Y	48430 FQ	61580 MW	75610 TQ	USBLS	5/07
Except Special Education	Hartford-West Hartford-East Hartford MSA, CT	Y	45750 FQ	64240 MW	72890 TQ	USBLS	5/07
Except Special Education	Delaware	Y	35370 FQ	44460 MW	59960 TQ	USBLS	5/07
Except Special Education	Wilmington PMSA, DE-MD-NJ	Y	35690 FQ	46250 MW	59750 TQ	USBLS	5/07
Except Special Education	District of Columbia	Y	26490 FQ	35910 MW	44650 TQ	USBLS	5/07
Except Special Education	Washington-Arlington-Alexandria MSA, DC-VA-MD-WV	Y	40390 FQ	52190 MW	73770 TQ	USBLS	5/07
Except Special Education	Florida	Y	38060 FQ	47070 MW	59830 TQ	USBLS	5/07
Except Special Education	Jacksonville MSA, FL	Y	35880 FQ	40700 MW	55550 TQ	USBLS	5/07
Except Special Education	Miami-Fort Lauderdale-Miami Beach MSA, FL	Y	37390 FQ	47590 MW	63990 TQ	USBLS	5/07
Except Special Education	Orlando-Kissimmee MSA, FL	Y	37120 FQ	42910 MW	51570 TQ	USBLS	5/07
Except Special Education	Tampa-St. Petersburg-Clearwater MSA, FL	Y	42280 FQ	49980 MW	61270 TQ	USBLS	5/07
Except Special Education	West Palm Beach-Boca Raton-Boynton Beach PMSA, FL	Y	34100 FQ	38580 MW	49780 TQ	USBLS	5/07
Except Special Education	Georgia	Y	35430 FQ	44520 MW	54470 TQ	USBLS	5/07
Except Special Education	Atlanta-Sandy Springs-Marietta MSA, GA	Y	34290 FQ	43650 MW	53690 TQ	USBLS	5/07
Except Special Education	Hawaii	Y	32180 FQ	36500 MW	41630 TQ	USBLS	5/07
Except Special Education	Honolulu MSA, HI	Y	33150 FQ	37160 MW	42410 TQ	USBLS	5/07
Except Special Education	Idaho	Y	23030 FQ	27200 MW	32130 TQ	USBLS	5/07
Except Special Education	Boise City-Nampa MSA, ID	Y	23240 FQ	26850 MW	30220 TQ	USBLS	5/07
Except Special Education	Illinois	Y	31770 FQ	39320 MW	50450 TQ	USBLS	5/07
Except Special Education	Chicago-Naperville-Joliet MSA, IL-IN-WI	Y	33730 FQ	40050 MW	52630 TQ	USBLS	5/07
Except Special Education	Indiana	Y	35180 FQ	44340 MW	56700 TQ	USBLS	5/07
Except Special Education	Gary PMSA, IN	Y	34460 FQ	41850 MW	52890 TQ	USBLS	5/07
Except Special Education	Indianapolis-Carmel MSA, IN	Y	36520 FQ	48850 MW	60310 TQ	USBLS	5/07
Except Special Education	Iowa	Y	31120 FQ	37400 MW	44750 TQ	USBLS	5/07
Except Special Education	Des Moines-West Des Moines MSA, IA	Y	32980 FQ	40200 MW	48380 TQ	USBLS	5/07
Except Special Education	Iowa City MSA, IA	Y	31920 FQ	37120 MW	47740 TQ	USBLS	5/07
Except Special Education	Waterloo-Cedar Falls MSA, IA	Y	28030 FQ	35000 MW	42540 TQ	USBLS	5/07
Except Special Education	Kansas	Y	34120 FQ	39470 MW	45790 TQ	USBLS	5/07
Except Special Education	Lawrence MSA, KS	Y	31590 FQ	37010 MW	43360 TQ	USBLS	5/07
Except Special Education	Wichita MSA, KS	Y	36950 FQ	42560 MW	48170 TQ	USBLS	5/07
Except Special Education	Kentucky	Y	36166 FQ	44886 MW	53632 TQ	KYBLS	2008
Except Special Education	Louisville-Jefferson County MSA, KY-IN	Y	34470 FQ	45090 MW	57330 TQ	USBLS	5/07

AE	Average entry wage	AW	Average wage paid	FQ	First quartile wage	LO	Lowest wage paid
AER	Average entry range	AWR	Average wage range	H	Hourly	LR	Low end range
AEX	Average experienced wage	AXR	Average experienced range	HI	Highest wage paid	M	Monthly
ATC	Average total compensation	D	Daily	HR	High end range	MCC	Median cash compensation

MTC Median total compensation   TCC Total cash compensation
MW Median wage paid   TQ Third quartile wage
MWR Median wage range   W Weekly
S See annotated source   Y Yearly

Kindergarten Teacher

Occupation/Type/Industry	Location	Per	Low	Mid	High	Source	Date
Kindergarten Teacher							
Except Special Education	Louisiana	Y		39845 AW		LABLS	1/08-3/08
Except Special Education	Baton Rouge MSA, LA	Y	36450 FQ	41900 MW	47320 TQ	USBLS	5/07
Except Special Education	New Orleans-Metairie-Kenner MSA, LA	Y	37530 FQ	43120 MW	48100 TQ	USBLS	5/07
Except Special Education	Shreveport-Bossier City MSA, LA	Y	31740 FQ	38050 MW	47460 TQ	USBLS	5/07
Except Special Education	Maine	Y	35060 FQ	43740 MW	52040 TQ	USBLS	5/07
Except Special Education	Portland-South Portland-Biddeford MSA, ME	Y	36520 FQ	45490 MW	54780 TQ	USBLS	5/07
Except Special Education	Maryland	Y		49900 MW		MDBLS	3/08
Except Special Education	Baltimore-Towson MSA, MD	Y	40640 FQ	48900 MW	60830 TQ	USBLS	5/07
Except Special Education	Bethesda-Gaithersburg-Frederick PMSA, MD	Y	39130 FQ	49900 MW	67280 TQ	USBLS	5/07
Except Special Education	Massachusetts	Y	39090 FQ	50540 MW	61810 TQ	USBLS	5/07
Except Special Education	Boston-Cambridge-Quincy NECTA, MA	Y	35820 FQ	47560 MW	61620 TQ	USBLS	5/07
Except Special Education	New Bedford MSA, MA	Y	43960 FQ	52570 MW	61980 TQ	USBLS	5/07
Except Special Education	Worcester MSA, MA-CT	Y	42420 FQ	52420 MW	62240 TQ	USBLS	5/07
Except Special Education	Michigan	Y	41420 FQ	53310 MW	66570 TQ	USBLS	5/07
Except Special Education	Detroit-Warren-Livonia MSA, MI	Y	44150 FQ	57280 MW	68870 TQ	USBLS	5/07
Except Special Education	Grand Rapids-Wyoming MSA, MI	Y	34880 FQ	41260 MW	48140 TQ	USBLS	5/07
Except Special Education	Warren-Troy-Farmington Hills PMSA, MI	Y	44700 FQ	57750 MW	68850 TQ	USBLS	5/07
Except Special Education	Minnesota	Y	37957 FQ	47383 MW	61172 TQ	MNBLS	10/08-12/08
Except Special Education	Duluth-Superior MSA, MN-WI	Y	44443 FQ	55251 MW	62009 TQ	MNBLS	10/08-12/08
Except Special Education	Minneapolis-Saint Paul MSA, MN-WI	Y	38072 FQ	48147 MW	63443 TQ	MNBLS	10/08-12/08
Except Special Education	Rochester MSA, MN	Y	40742 FQ	47052 MW	52468 TQ	MNBLS	10/08-12/08
Except Special Education	Mississippi	Y	30040 FQ	37340 MW	44680 TQ	USBLS	5/07
Except Special Education	Jackson MSA, MS	Y	24540 FQ	33810 MW	42430 TQ	USBLS	5/07
Except Special Education	Missouri	Y	32800 FQ	38680 MW	47710 TQ	USBLS	5/07
Except Special Education	Jefferson City MSA, MO	Y	32440 FQ	37700 MW	45490 TQ	USBLS	5/07
Except Special Education	Kansas City MSA, MO-KS	Y	35440 FQ	40730 MW	49100 TQ	USBLS	5/07
Except Special Education	St. Louis MSA, MO-IL	Y	32750 FQ	41850 MW	53540 TQ	USBLS	5/07
Except Special Education	Montana	Y	26000 FQ	34630 MW	45240 TQ	USBLS	5/07
Except Special Education	Billings MSA, MT	Y	27880 FQ	36830 MW	48570 TQ	USBLS	5/07
Except Special Education	Missoula MSA, MT	Y	22770 FQ	29050 MW	36260 TQ	USBLS	5/07
Except Special Education	Nebraska	Y	35510 FQ	41490 MW	49020 TQ	USBLS	5/07
Except Special Education	Omaha-Council Bluffs MSA, NE-IA	Y	34210 FQ	38770 MW	46220 TQ	USBLS	5/07
Except Special Education	Nevada	Y	31182 FQ	39050 MW	48735 TQ	NVBLS	5/08
Except Special Education	Las Vegas-Paradise MSA, NV	Y	28241 FQ	37506 MW	46803 TQ	NVBLS	5/08
Except Special Education	New Hampshire	Y	25109 AE	38612 MW	46619 AEX	NHBLS	6/08
Except Special Education	Manchester MSA, NH	Y	33140 FQ	38400 MW	54400 TQ	USBLS	5/07
Except Special Education	Nashua NECTA, NH-MA	Y	34060 FQ	43570 MW	50840 TQ	USBLS	5/07
Except Special Education	Rochester-Dover MSA, NH-ME	Y	33890 FQ	39980 MW	50650 TQ	USBLS	5/07
Except Special Education	New Jersey	Y	44390 FQ	52380 MW	70330 TQ	USBLS	5/07
Except Special Education	Camden PMSA, NJ	Y	47790 FQ	62220 MW	72610 TQ	USBLS	5/07
Except Special Education	Edison PMSA, NJ	Y	44160 FQ	51700 MW	69790 TQ	USBLS	5/07
Except Special Education	Newark-Union PMSA, NJ-PA	Y	43440 FQ	50300 MW	66340 TQ	USBLS	5/07
Except Special Education	Trenton-Ewing MSA, NJ	Y	43380 FQ	52430 MW	71970 TQ	USBLS	5/07
Except Special Education	New Mexico	Y	35820 FQ	42400 MW	51580 TQ	USBLS	5/07
Except Special Education	Albuquerque MSA, NM	Y	35620 FQ	42610 MW	52320 TQ	USBLS	5/07
Except Special Education	Farmington MSA, NM	Y	35770 FQ	43940 MW	49570 TQ	USBLS	5/07
Except Special Education	New York	Y	45850 FQ	60430 MW	78060 TQ	USBLS	5/07
Except Special Education	Albany-Schenectady-Troy MSA, NY	Y	40940 FQ	57460 MW	72930 TQ	USBLS	5/07
Except Special Education	Buffalo-Niagara Falls MSA, NY	Y	43270 FQ	57470 MW	74790 TQ	USBLS	5/07
Except Special Education	Nassau-Suffolk PMSA, NY	Y	58420 FQ	77040 MW	99210 TQ	USBLS	5/07
Except Special Education	New York-Northern New Jersey-Long Island MSA, NY-NJ-PA	Y	46330 FQ	60540 MW	79080 TQ	USBLS	5/07
Except Special Education	North Carolina	Y	30410 FQ	37170 MW	45470 TQ	USBLS	5/07
Except Special Education	Charlotte-Gastonia-Concord MSA, NC-SC	Y	30140 FQ	36000 MW	45110 TQ	USBLS	5/07
Except Special Education	Raleigh-Cary MSA, NC	Y	30690 FQ	36770 MW	44860 TQ	USBLS	5/07
Except Special Education	North Dakota	Y	29410 FQ	36790 MW	46120 TQ	USBLS	5/07

AE	Average entry wage	AW	Average wage paid	FQ	First quartile wage	LO	Lowest wage paid	MTC	Median total compensation	TCC	Total cash compensation
AER	Average entry range	AWR	Average wage range	H	Hourly	LR	Low end range	MW	Median wage paid	TQ	Third quartile wage
AEX	Average experienced wage	AXR	Average experienced range	HI	Highest wage paid	M	Monthly	MWR	Median wage range	W	Weekly
ATC	Average total compensation	D	Daily	HR	High end range	MCC	Median cash compensation	S	See annotated source	Y	Yearly

Occupation/Type/Industry	Location	Per	Low	Mid	High	Source	Date
Kindergarten Teacher							
Except Special Education	Fargo MSA, ND-MN	Y	31680 FQ	40490 MW	55610 TQ	USBLS	5/07
Except Special Education	Ohio	Y	37190 FQ	48850 MW	60700 TQ	USBLS	5/07
Except Special Education	Canton-Massillon MSA, OH	Y	40040 FQ	51350 MW	60470 TQ	USBLS	5/07
Except Special Education	Cincinnati-Middletown MSA, OH-KY-IN	Y	38000 FQ	50020 MW	62870 TQ	USBLS	5/07
Except Special Education	Cleveland-Elyria-Mentor MSA, OH	Y	41290 FQ	58480 MW	72410 TQ	USBLS	5/07
Except Special Education	Columbus MSA, OH	Y	37760 FQ	50930 MW	63450 TQ	USBLS	5/07
Except Special Education	Dayton MSA, OH	Y	36760 FQ	48110 MW	57740 TQ	USBLS	5/07
Except Special Education	Mansfield MSA, OH	Y	23250 FQ	37520 MW	48540 TQ	USBLS	5/07
Except Special Education	Oklahoma	Y	31290 FQ	35610 MW	40390 TQ	USBLS	5/07
Except Special Education	Oklahoma City MSA, OK	Y	29520 FQ	33910 MW	38010 TQ	USBLS	5/07
Except Special Education	Tulsa MSA, OK	Y	33400 FQ	39960 MW	47600 TQ	USBLS	5/07
Except Special Education	Oregon	Y	29297 FQ	40967 MW	52458 TQ	ORBLS	5/08
Except Special Education	Medford MSA, OR	Y	37080 FQ	43020 MW	53060 TQ	USBLS	5/07
Except Special Education	Portland-Vancouver-Beaverton MSA, OR-WA	Y	31030 FQ	41260 MW	53320 TQ	USBLS	5/07
Except Special Education	Pennsylvania	Y	35910 FQ	47250 MW	62430 TQ	USBLS	5/07
Except Special Education	Allentown-Bethlehem-Easton MSA, PA-NJ	Y	32850 FQ	47650 MW	62670 TQ	USBLS	5/07
Except Special Education	Lancaster MSA, PA	Y	38540 FQ	46250 MW	58510 TQ	USBLS	5/07
Except Special Education	Philadelphia-Camden-Wilmington MSA, PA-NJ-DE-MD	Y	36950 FQ	49000 MW	66910 TQ	USBLS	5/07
Except Special Education	Pittsburgh MSA, PA	Y	40610 FQ	53620 MW	69630 TQ	USBLS	5/07
Except Special Education	Rhode Island	Y	50670 FQ	64310 MW	74090 TQ	USBLS	5/07
Except Special Education	Providence-Fall River-Warwick MSA, RI-MA	Y	47290 FQ	62090 MW	72930 TQ	USBLS	5/07
Except Special Education	South Carolina	Y	34020 FQ	42630 MW	51770 TQ	USBLS	5/07
Except Special Education	Charleston-North Charleston MSA, SC	Y	33970 FQ	47620 MW	61390 TQ	USBLS	5/07
Except Special Education	Columbia MSA, SC	Y	33630 FQ	42870 MW	53280 TQ	USBLS	5/07
Except Special Education	South Dakota	Y	30540 FQ	34935 MW	40064 TQ	SDBLS	7/08-9/08
Except Special Education	Sioux Falls MSA, SD	Y	30507 FQ	34773 MW	39538 TQ	SDBLS	7/08-9/08
Except Special Education	Tennessee	Y	34580 FQ	39800 MW	45970 TQ	USBLS	5/07
Except Special Education	Memphis MSA, TN-MS-AR	Y	34420 FQ	39660 MW	45110 TQ	USBLS	5/07
Except Special Education	Nashville-Davidson-Murfreesboro MSA, TN	Y	33780 FQ	39200 MW	47340 TQ	USBLS	5/07
Except Special Education	Texas	Y	37280 FQ	43250 MW	49110 TQ	USBLS	5/07
Except Special Education	Austin-Round Rock MSA, TX	Y	36140 FQ	40140 MW	47170 TQ	USBLS	5/07
Except Special Education	Dallas-Fort Worth-Arlington MSA, TX	Y	40380 FQ	45520 MW	50600 TQ	USBLS	5/07
Except Special Education	El Paso MSA, TX	Y	38810 FQ	44340 MW	50790 TQ	USBLS	5/07
Except Special Education	Houston-Sugar Land-Baytown MSA, TX	Y	38970 FQ	44030 MW	49520 TQ	USBLS	5/07
Except Special Education	San Antonio MSA, TX	Y	37420 FQ	44220 MW	50560 TQ	USBLS	5/07
Except Special Education	Utah	Y	24730 FQ	32160 MW	44710 TQ	USBLS	5/07
Except Special Education	Provo-Orem MSA, UT	Y	27780 FQ	30900 MW	43170 TQ	USBLS	5/07
Except Special Education	Salt Lake City MSA, UT	Y	23110 FQ	32290 MW	47970 TQ	USBLS	5/07
Except Special Education	Vermont	Y	33610 FQ	43440 MW	55830 TQ	USBLS	5/07
Except Special Education	Burlington-South Burlington MSA, VT	Y	37670 FQ	50830 MW	60980 TQ	USBLS	5/07
Except Special Education	Virginia	Y	37700 FQ	48970 MW	65090 TQ	USBLS	5/07
Except Special Education	Richmond MSA, VA	Y	41660 FQ	50690 MW	59350 TQ	USBLS	5/07
Except Special Education	Virginia Beach-Norfolk-Newport News MSA, VA-NC	Y	30950 FQ	37120 MW	47310 TQ	USBLS	5/07
Except Special Education	Washington	Y		48344 AW		WABLS	3/08
Except Special Education	Seattle-Tacoma-Bellevue MSA, WA	Y	39510 FQ	48690 MW	59130 TQ	USBLS	5/07
Except Special Education	West Virginia	Y	39034 FQ	44548 MW	49302 TQ	WVBLS	7/08-9/08
Except Special Education	Charleston MSA, WV	Y	36920 FQ	41940 MW	46890 TQ	USBLS	5/07
Except Special Education	Wisconsin	Y	36540 FQ	43800 MW	51870 TQ	USBLS	5/07
Except Special Education	Milwaukee-Waukesha-West Allis MSA, WI	Y	33910 FQ	43480 MW	58830 TQ	USBLS	5/07
Except Special Education	Wyoming	Y	40476 FQ	46935 MW	54022 TQ	WYBLS	9/08
Except Special Education	Puerto Rico	Y	13480 FQ	15780 MW	19170 TQ	USBLS	5/07
Except Special Education	San Juan-Caguas-Guaynabo MSA, PR	Y	13530 FQ	15840 MW	19020 TQ	USBLS	5/07
Except Special Education	Virgin Islands	Y	20490 FQ	30250 MW	37160 TQ	USBLS	5/07

AE Average entry wage	**AW** Average wage paid	**FQ** First quartile wage	**LO** Lowest wage paid	**MTC** Median total compensation	**TCC** Total cash compensation
AER Average entry range	**AWR** Average wage range	**H** Hourly	**LR** Low end range	**MW** Median wage paid	**TQ** Third quartile wage
AEX Average experienced wage	**AXR** Average experienced range	**HI** Highest wage paid	**M** Monthly	**MWR** Median wage range	**W** Weekly
ATC Average total compensation	**D** Daily	**HR** High end range	**MCC** Median cash compensation	**S** See annotated source	**Y** Yearly

Occupation/Type/Industry	Location	Per	Low	Mid	High	Source	Date
Kitchen Aide							
Municipal Government	Carlsbad, CA	H	8.00 LO		12.00 HI	CCSS	1/1/08
Lab Director							
Sheriff's Department Forensic Laboratory	San Bernardino, CA	W	7767 LO		9938 HI	CAC	2006-2007
Lab Machinist							
State Government	Ohio	H	20.81 LO		26.28 HI	ODAS	2008
Labor Relations Coordinator							
Municipal Government	Seattle, WA	H	32.80 LO		38.22 HI	CSSS	2008
Labor Relations Manager	United States	Y		100700 MW		CNNM03	2007
Labor Relations Mediator							
State Government	Ohio	H	30.68 LO		40.22 HI	ODAS	2008
Laborer							
County Government	Liberty County, GA	Y	21882 LO		37648 HI	GACTY03	2008
Department of Transportation	Michigan	H	14.41 LO		19.09 HI	MDOT	10/1/07
Municipal Government	Biloxi, MS	Y			22836 HI	MML	2008
Municipal Government	Eupora, MS	Y			18700 HI	MML	2008
Municipal Government	Harwood, ND	M			1440 HI	NDLC02	2008
Municipal Government	McVille, ND	M			1500 HI	NDLC02	2008
Laborer and Freight, Stock, and Material Mover							
Hand	Alabama	Y	16250 FQ	19540 MW	24070 TQ	USBLS	5/07
Hand	Birmingham-Hoover MSA, AL	Y	16930 FQ	19840 MW	23990 TQ	USBLS	5/07
Hand	Alaska	Y	23430 FQ	30060 MW	39360 TQ	USBLS	5/07
Hand	Anchorage MSA, AK	Y	22200 FQ	29050 MW	39840 TQ	USBLS	5/07
Hand	Fairbanks MSA, AK	Y	24360 FQ	28130 MW	32000 TQ	USBLS	5/07
Hand	Arizona	Y	17260 FQ	21350 MW	26900 TQ	USBLS	5/07
Hand	Flagstaff MSA, AZ	Y	15510 FQ	22350 MW	33040 TQ	USBLS	5/07
Hand	Phoenix-Mesa-Scottsdale MSA, AZ	Y	17610 FQ	21800 MW	27330 TQ	USBLS	5/07
Hand	Tucson MSA, AZ	Y	16360 FQ	19380 MW	24850 TQ	USBLS	5/07
Hand	Arkansas	Y	16200 FQ	19070 MW	23900 TQ	USBLS	5/07
Hand	Little Rock-North Little Rock MSA, AR	Y	16270 FQ	19050 MW	24090 TQ	USBLS	5/07
Hand	Pine Bluff MSA, AR	Y	16740 FQ	19330 MW	23690 TQ	USBLS	5/07
Hand	California	H	8.80 FQ	10.72 MW	14.00 TQ	CABLS	1/08-3/08
Hand	Los Angeles-Long Beach-Glendale PMSA, CA	H	8.54 FQ	10.12 MW	13.41 TQ	CABLS	1/08-3/08
Hand	Oakland-Fremont-Hayward MSA, CA	H	9.74 FQ	12.27 MW	15.39 TQ	CABLS	1/08-3/08
Hand	Riverside-San Bernardino-Ontario MSA, CA	H	8.74 FQ	10.19 MW	13.97 TQ	CABLS	1/08-3/08
Hand	Sacramento-Arden Arcade-Roseville MSA, CA	H	9.60 FQ	11.53 MW	14.47 TQ	CABLS	1/08-3/08
Hand	San Diego-Carlsbad-San Marcos MSA, CA	H	9.28 FQ	11.17 MW	13.83 TQ	CABLS	1/08-3/08
Hand	San Francisco-San Mateo-Redwood PMSA, CA	H	10.89 FQ	13.80 MW	17.30 TQ	CABLS	1/08-3/08
Hand	San Jose-Sunnyvale-Santa Clara MSA, CA	H	9.91 FQ	12.49 MW	15.35 TQ	CABLS	1/08-3/08
Hand	Santa Ana-Anaheim-Irvine PMSA, CA	Y	17420 FQ	21100 MW	26450 TQ	USBLS	5/07
Hand	Colorado	Y	18880 FQ	23320 MW	29930 TQ	USBLS	5/07
Hand	Boulder MSA, CO	Y	19660 FQ	23250 MW	27680 TQ	USBLS	5/07
Hand	Denver-Aurora MSA, CO	Y	19600 FQ	24060 MW	30830 TQ	USBLS	5/07
Hand	Fort Collins-Loveland MSA, CO	Y	16500 FQ	20390 MW	28860 TQ	USBLS	5/07
Hand	Pueblo MSA, CO	Y	17770 FQ	26300 MW	34900 TQ	USBLS	5/07
Hand	Connecticut	H	9.59 AE	12.43 MW		CTBLS	1/08-3/08
Hand	Bridgeport-Stamford-Norwalk MSA, CT	Y	19760 FQ	24580 MW	32100 TQ	USBLS	5/07
Hand	Hartford-West Hartford-East Hartford MSA, CT	Y	21230 FQ	25910 MW	31480 TQ	USBLS	5/07
Hand	Delaware	Y	19770 FQ	25410 MW	33890 TQ	USBLS	5/07
Hand	Wilmington PMSA, DE-MD-NJ	Y	21750 FQ	27710 MW	35610 TQ	USBLS	5/07

Occupation/Type/Industry	Location	Per	Low	Mid	High	Source	Date
Laborer and Freight, Stock, and Material Mover							
Hand	District of Columbia	Y	21920 FQ	26370 MW	30950 TQ	USBLS	5/07
Hand	Washington-Arlington-Alexandria MSA, DC-VA-MD-WV	Y	19790 FQ	24050 MW	30030 TQ	USBLS	5/07
Hand	Florida	Y	16970 FQ	20490 MW	25570 TQ	USBLS	5/07
Hand	Fort Lauderdale-Pompano Beach-Deerfield Beach PMSA, FL	Y	16880 FQ	20710 MW	26950 TQ	USBLS	5/07
Hand	Jacksonville MSA, FL	Y	18410 FQ	22830 MW	29980 TQ	USBLS	5/07
Hand	Miami-Fort Lauderdale-Miami Beach MSA, FL	Y	17080 FQ	20570 MW	26170 TQ	USBLS	5/07
Hand	Orlando-Kissimmee MSA, FL	Y	16900 FQ	20100 MW	24910 TQ	USBLS	5/07
Hand	Tampa-St. Petersburg-Clearwater MSA, FL	Y	17280 FQ	21090 MW	25930 TQ	USBLS	5/07
Hand	West Palm Beach-Boca Raton-Boynton Beach PMSA, FL	Y	16340 FQ	18420 MW	23000 TQ	USBLS	5/07
Hand	Georgia	Y	17250 FQ	20930 MW	26420 TQ	USBLS	5/07
Hand	Atlanta-Sandy Springs-Marietta MSA, GA	Y	18030 FQ	21820 MW	27270 TQ	USBLS	5/07
Hand	Savannah MSA, GA	Y	17520 FQ	24450 MW	40190 TQ	USBLS	5/07
Hand	Hawaii	Y	19410 FQ	24900 MW	32060 TQ	USBLS	5/07
Hand	Honolulu MSA, HI	Y	19390 FQ	25260 MW	33400 TQ	USBLS	5/07
Hand	Idaho	Y	16380 FQ	19980 MW	25860 TQ	USBLS	5/07
Hand	Boise City-Nampa MSA, ID	Y	16400 FQ	19020 MW	23050 TQ	USBLS	5/07
Hand	Lewiston MSA, ID-WA	Y	18100 FQ	22260 MW	29250 TQ	USBLS	5/07
Hand	Illinois	Y	17680 FQ	22550 MW	29350 TQ	USBLS	5/07
Hand	Chicago-Naperville-Joliet MSA, IL-IN-WI	Y	17400 FQ	22310 MW	29430 TQ	USBLS	5/07
Hand	Peoria MSA, IL	Y	17750 FQ	21030 MW	24660 TQ	USBLS	5/07
Hand	Rockford MSA, IL	Y	19840 FQ	26790 MW	32870 TQ	USBLS	5/07
Hand	Indiana	Y	18450 FQ	22600 MW	28340 TQ	USBLS	5/07
Hand	Gary PMSA, IN	Y	18740 FQ	24790 MW	34380 TQ	USBLS	5/07
Hand	Indianapolis-Carmel MSA, IN	Y	18880 FQ	22580 MW	27840 TQ	USBLS	5/07
Hand	Iowa	Y	17480 FQ	21790 MW	27660 TQ	USBLS	5/07
Hand	Des Moines-West Des Moines MSA, IA	Y	17920 FQ	21090 MW	27590 TQ	USBLS	5/07
Hand	Iowa City MSA, IA	Y	18060 FQ	21310 MW	26610 TQ	USBLS	5/07
Hand	Waterloo-Cedar Falls MSA, IA	Y	17660 FQ	23320 MW	27970 TQ	USBLS	5/07
Hand	Kansas	Y	17520 FQ	21690 MW	27350 TQ	USBLS	5/07
Hand	Lawrence MSA, KS	Y	21270 FQ	26970 MW	38780 TQ	USBLS	5/07
Hand	Topeka MSA, KS	Y	16640 FQ	19260 MW	23490 TQ	USBLS	5/07
Hand	Wichita MSA, KS	Y	15940 FQ	19720 MW	24850 TQ	USBLS	5/07
Hand	Kentucky	Y	17905 FQ	21611 MW	26644 TQ	KYBLS	2008
Hand	Louisville-Jefferson County MSA, KY-IN	Y	18720 FQ	21930 MW	26630 TQ	USBLS	5/07
Hand	Louisiana	H	7.69 FQ	9.47 MW	11.73 TQ	LABLS	1/08-3/08
Hand	Baton Rouge MSA, LA	Y	16670 FQ	19730 MW	23880 TQ	USBLS	5/07
Hand	Houma-Bayou Cane-Thibodaux MSA, LA	Y	15450 FQ	19180 MW	23420 TQ	USBLS	5/07
Hand	New Orleans-Metairie-Kenner MSA, LA	Y	16230 FQ	20260 MW	25760 TQ	USBLS	5/07
Hand	Maine	Y	18430 FQ	22130 MW	26170 TQ	USBLS	5/07
Hand	Portland-South Portland-Biddeford MSA, ME	Y	19530 FQ	22520 MW	25730 TQ	USBLS	5/07
Hand	Maryland	Y		23700 MW		MDBLS	3/08
Hand	Baltimore-Towson MSA, MD	Y	18070 FQ	23240 MW	30690 TQ	USBLS	5/07
Hand	Bethesda-Gaithersburg-Frederick PMSA, MD	Y	18990 FQ	23590 MW	28990 TQ	USBLS	5/07
Hand	Massachusetts	Y	20770 FQ	26110 MW	32760 TQ	USBLS	5/07
Hand	Boston-Cambridge-Quincy NECTA, MA	Y	22070 FQ	27120 MW	33600 TQ	USBLS	5/07
Hand	Lynn-Peabody-Salem NECTA, MA	Y	20370 FQ	24100 MW	31020 TQ	USBLS	5/07
Hand	Worcester MSA, MA-CT	Y	21520 FQ	27260 MW	33450 TQ	USBLS	5/07
Hand	Michigan	Y	18800 FQ	23940 MW	32090 TQ	USBLS	5/07
Hand	Detroit-Warren-Livonia MSA, MI	Y	18660 FQ	24080 MW	33610 TQ	USBLS	5/07
Hand	Grand Rapids-Wyoming MSA, MI	Y	20570 FQ	25060 MW	35180 TQ	USBLS	5/07

AE Average entry wage	**AW** Average wage paid	**FQ** First quartile wage	**LO** Lowest wage paid	**MTC** Median total compensation	**TCC** Total cash compensation
AER Average entry range	**AWR** Average wage range	**H** Hourly	**LR** Low end range	**MW** Median wage paid	**TQ** Third quartile wage
AEX Average experienced wage	**AXR** Average experienced range	**HI** Highest wage paid	**M** Monthly	**MWR** Median wage range	**W** Weekly
ATC Average total compensation	**D** Daily	**HR** High end range	**MCC** Median cash compensation	**S** See annotated source	**Y** Yearly

Occupation/Type/Industry	Location	Per	Low	Mid	High	Source	Date
Laborer and Freight, Stock, and Material Mover							
Hand	Warren-Troy-Farmington Hills PMSA, MI	Y	17710 FQ	22950 MW	33990 TQ	USBLS	5/07
Hand	Minnesota	Y	20838 FQ	25592 MW	33291 TQ	MNBLS	10/08-12/08
Hand	Duluth-Superior MSA, MN-WI	Y	19017 FQ	23449 MW	31002 TQ	MNBLS	10/08-12/08
Hand	Minneapolis-Saint Paul MSA, MN-WI	Y	21233 FQ	26247 MW	35007 TQ	MNBLS	10/08-12/08
Hand	Rochester MSA, MN	Y	19477 FQ	23252 MW	29423 TQ	MNBLS	10/08-12/08
Hand	Mississippi	Y	16170 FQ	19690 MW	24560 TQ	USBLS	5/07
Hand	Jackson MSA, MS	Y	17630 FQ	21640 MW	27630 TQ	USBLS	5/07
Hand	Pascagoula MSA, MS	Y	17460 FQ	20750 MW	23760 TQ	USBLS	5/07
Hand	Missouri	Y	17850 FQ	22250 MW	29270 TQ	USBLS	5/07
Hand	Kansas City MSA, MO-KS	Y	19360 FQ	23600 MW	30320 TQ	USBLS	5/07
Hand	St. Joseph MSA, MO-KS	Y	19520 FQ	26610 MW	30390 TQ	USBLS	5/07
Hand	St. Louis MSA, MO-IL	Y	18480 FQ	23620 MW	31210 TQ	USBLS	5/07
Hand	Montana	Y	17370 FQ	21420 MW	27430 TQ	USBLS	5/07
Hand	Billings MSA, MT	Y	17560 FQ	21040 MW	26660 TQ	USBLS	5/07
Hand	Missoula MSA, MT	Y	16520 FQ	20320 MW	25080 TQ	USBLS	5/07
Hand	Nebraska	Y	18770 FQ	22750 MW	28030 TQ	USBLS	5/07
Hand	Omaha-Council Bluffs MSA, NE-IA	Y	19460 FQ	23180 MW	28220 TQ	USBLS	5/07
Hand	Nevada	H	9.35 FQ	11.42 MW	14.27 TQ	NVBLS	5/08
Hand	Las Vegas-Paradise MSA, NV	H	9.57 FQ	11.64 MW	14.66 TQ	NVBLS	5/08
Hand	New Hampshire	H	9.10 AE	11.92 MW	14.98 AEX	NHBLS	6/08
Hand	Manchester MSA, NH	Y	19870 FQ	22140 MW	25310 TQ	USBLS	5/07
Hand	Nashua NECTA, NH-MA	Y	21030 FQ	28010 MW	37760 TQ	USBLS	5/07
Hand	New Jersey	Y	18280 FQ	23270 MW	29950 TQ	USBLS	5/07
Hand	Camden PMSA, NJ	Y	19890 FQ	25500 MW	32420 TQ	USBLS	5/07
Hand	Edison PMSA, NJ	Y	19080 FQ	23450 MW	29240 TQ	USBLS	5/07
Hand	Newark-Union PMSA, NJ-PA	Y	18500 FQ	24600 MW	31700 TQ	USBLS	5/07
Hand	Ocean City MSA, NJ	Y	19140 FQ	23110 MW	30620 TQ	USBLS	5/07
Hand	New Mexico	Y	15180 FQ	18660 MW	23930 TQ	USBLS	5/07
Hand	Albuquerque MSA, NM	Y	15760 FQ	19110 MW	24460 TQ	USBLS	5/07
Hand	Santa Fe MSA, NM	Y	20250 FQ	23490 MW	27980 TQ	USBLS	5/07
Hand	New York	Y	18610 FQ	23160 MW	30170 TQ	USBLS	5/07
Hand	Albany-Schenectady-Troy MSA, NY	Y	19400 FQ	23380 MW	29220 TQ	USBLS	5/07
Hand	Binghamton MSA, NY	Y	16750 FQ	19290 MW	23890 TQ	USBLS	5/07
Hand	Buffalo-Niagara Falls MSA, NY	Y	17980 FQ	22810 MW	30100 TQ	USBLS	5/07
Hand	Nassau-Suffolk PMSA, NY	Y	19290 FQ	24170 MW	31870 TQ	USBLS	5/07
Hand	New York-Northern New Jersey-Long Island MSA, NY-NJ-PA	Y	18330 FQ	23230 MW	30280 TQ	USBLS	5/07
Hand	Syracuse MSA, NY	Y	18890 FQ	22690 MW	28650 TQ	USBLS	5/07
Hand	North Carolina	Y	17300 FQ	20880 MW	25730 TQ	USBLS	5/07
Hand	Charlotte-Gastonia-Concord MSA, NC-SC	Y	17890 FQ	21470 MW	26600 TQ	USBLS	5/07
Hand	Durham MSA, NC	Y	16730 FQ	21100 MW	25650 TQ	USBLS	5/07
Hand	Raleigh-Cary MSA, NC	Y	17210 FQ	20780 MW	25010 TQ	USBLS	5/07
Hand	North Dakota	Y	17540 FQ	21680 MW	26390 TQ	USBLS	5/07
Hand	Bismarck MSA, ND	Y	15880 FQ	18810 MW	23540 TQ	USBLS	5/07
Hand	Fargo MSA, ND-MN	Y	18950 FQ	23080 MW	28440 TQ	USBLS	5/07
Hand	Ohio	Y	17790 FQ	22340 MW	28830 TQ	USBLS	5/07
Hand	Cincinnati-Middletown MSA, OH-KY-IN	Y	18440 FQ	22450 MW	28280 TQ	USBLS	5/07
Hand	Cleveland-Elyria-Mentor MSA, OH	Y	16630 FQ	22100 MW	29300 TQ	USBLS	5/07
Hand	Columbus MSA, OH	Y	18310 FQ	22450 MW	28270 TQ	USBLS	5/07
Hand	Dayton MSA, OH	Y	19300 FQ	23400 MW	28800 TQ	USBLS	5/07
Hand	Springfield MSA, OH	Y	17390 FQ	20790 MW	29080 TQ	USBLS	5/07
Hand	Oklahoma	Y	16720 FQ	19950 MW	25110 TQ	USBLS	5/07
Hand	Oklahoma City MSA, OK	Y	17030 FQ	20200 MW	25830 TQ	USBLS	5/07
Hand	Tulsa MSA, OK	Y	17390 FQ	20860 MW	25870 TQ	USBLS	5/07
Hand	Oregon	H	9.55 FQ	11.57 MW	14.53 TQ	ORBLS	5/08
Hand	Portland-Vancouver-Beaverton MSA, OR-WA	Y	19910 FQ	23840 MW	29280 TQ	USBLS	5/07
Hand	Pennsylvania	Y	18730 FQ	23420 MW	30600 TQ	USBLS	5/07
Hand	Allentown-Bethlehem-Easton MSA, PA-NJ	Y	19750 FQ	24060 MW	29770 TQ	USBLS	5/07

AE Average entry wage	**AW** Average wage paid	**FQ** First quartile wage	**LO** Lowest wage paid	**MTC** Median total compensation	**TCC** Total cash compensation
AER Average entry range	**AWR** Average wage range	**H** Hourly	**LR** Low end range	**MW** Median wage paid	**TQ** Third quartile wage
AEX Average experienced wage	**AXR** Average experienced range	**HI** Highest wage paid	**M** Monthly	**MWR** Median wage range	**W** Weekly
ATC Average total compensation	**D** Daily	**HR** High end range	**MCC** Median cash compensation	**S** See annotated source	**Y** Yearly

Occupation/Type/Industry	Location	Per	Low	Mid	High	Source	Date
Laborer and Freight, Stock, and Material Mover							
Hand	Philadelphia-Camden-Wilmington MSA, PA-NJ-DE-MD	Y	19880 FQ	24560 MW	31980 TQ	USBLS	5/07
Hand	Pittsburgh MSA, PA	Y	17890 FQ	22540 MW	30260 TQ	USBLS	5/07
Hand	Rhode Island	Y	20450 FQ	25430 MW	31700 TQ	USBLS	5/07
Hand	Providence-Fall River-Warwick MSA, RI-MA	Y	20270 FQ	25320 MW	31380 TQ	USBLS	5/07
Hand	South Carolina	Y	17220 FQ	20790 MW	26670 TQ	USBLS	5/07
Hand	Charleston-North Charleston MSA, SC	Y	17080 FQ	19860 MW	27020 TQ	USBLS	5/07
Hand	Columbia MSA, SC	Y	17220 FQ	19930 MW	24790 TQ.	USBLS	5/07
Hand	South Dakota	Y	18145 FQ	20852 MW	24402 TQ	SDBLS	7/08-9/08
Hand	Sioux Falls MSA, SD	Y	19635 FQ	22741 MW	25739 TQ	SDBLS	7/08-9/08
Hand	Tennessee	Y	17210 FQ	20330 MW	25440 TQ	USBLS	5/07
Hand	Kingsport-Bristol-Bristol MSA, TN-VA	Y	14920 FQ	18800 MW	22480 TQ	USBLS	5/07
Hand	Memphis MSA, TN-MS-AR	Y	17320 FQ	19820 MW	25140 TQ	USBLS	5/07
Hand	Nashville-Davidson-Murfreesboro MSA, TN	Y	16960 FQ	20140 MW	25070 TQ	USBLS	5/07
Hand	Texas	Y	16080 FQ	19780 MW	24750 TQ	USBLS	5/07
Hand	Austin-Round Rock MSA, TX	Y	18120 FQ	21820 MW	26080 TQ	USBLS	5/07
Hand	Brownsville-Harlingen MSA, TX	Y	12900 FQ	14780 MW	18060 TQ	USBLS	5/07
Hand	Dallas-Fort Worth-Arlington MSA, TX	Y	17630 FQ	21340 MW	26090 TQ	USBLS	5/07
Hand	El Paso MSA, TX	Y	14000 FQ	16960 MW	20590 TQ	USBLS	5/07
Hand	Houston-Sugar Land-Baytown MSA, TX	Y	15980 FQ	20010 MW	24910 TQ	USBLS	5/07
Hand	San Antonio MSA, TX	Y	16520 FQ	19330 MW	24220 TQ	USBLS	5/07
Hand	Utah	Y	18140 FQ	21330 MW	25260 TQ	USBLS	5/07
Hand	St. George MSA, UT	Y	19370 FQ	25110 MW	30650 TQ	USBLS	5/07
Hand	Salt Lake City MSA, UT	Y	18480 FQ	21890 MW	25930 TQ	USBLS	5/07
Hand	Vermont	Y	19500 FQ	22900 MW	27960 TQ	USBLS	5/07
Hand	Burlington-South Burlington MSA, VT	Y	18860 FQ	22080 MW	26460 TQ	USBLS	5/07
Hand	Virginia	Y	17990 FQ	22000 MW	27220 TQ	USBLS	5/07
Hand	Richmond MSA, VA	Y	19270 FQ	22950 MW	28570 TQ	USBLS	5/07
Hand	Virginia Beach-Norfolk-Newport News MSA, VA-NC	Y	16920 FQ	20250 MW	24980 TQ	USBLS	5/07
Hand	Washington	H	9.55 FQ	11.63 MW	14.92 TQ	WABLS	3/08
Hand	Seattle-Tacoma-Bellevue MSA, WA	Y	19900 FQ	24510 MW	31760 TQ	USBLS	5/07
Hand	West Virginia	Y	15444 FQ	19225 MW	25564 TQ	WVBLS	7/08-9/08
Hand	Charleston MSA, WV	Y	15740 FQ	19740 MW	28910 TQ	USBLS	5/07
Hand	Huntington-Ashland MSA, WV-KY-OH	Y	14710 FQ	18170 MW	25120 TQ	USBLS	5/07
Hand	Wisconsin	Y	18910 FQ	23690 MW	29780 TQ	USBLS	5/07
Hand	Milwaukee-Waukesha-West Allis MSA, WI	Y	19070 FQ	23610 MW	29540 TQ	USBLS	5/07
Hand	Wyoming	Y	19161 FQ	24082 MW	29191 TQ	WYBLS	9/08
Hand	Cheyenne MSA, WY	Y	20126 FQ	23461 MW	28034 TQ	WYBLS	9/08
Hand	Puerto Rico	Y	12930 FQ	14690 MW	18370 TQ	USBLS	5/07
Hand	San German-Cabo Rojo MSA, PR	Y	12670 FQ	14100 MW	17950 TQ	USBLS	5/07
Hand	San Juan-Caguas-Guaynabo MSA, PR	Y	13030 FQ	14970 MW	18660 TQ	USBLS	5/07
Hand	Virgin Islands	Y	16170 FQ	18990 MW	25690 TQ	USBLS	5/07
Hand	Guam	Y	13740 FQ	17030 MW	23770 TQ	USBLS	5/07
Lake Lands Administrator							
State Government	Ohio	H	19.70 LO		45.31 HI	ODAS	2008
Lance Corporal							
U.S. Marines, Active Duty, Pay Grade E-3	United States	M	1650 LO		1860 HI	DOD1	2009
Land Development Review Manager							
Municipal Government	Colorado Springs, CO	M	6687 LO			COSPRS	1/1/09

AE Average entry wage	**AW** Average wage paid	**FQ** First quartile wage	**LO** Lowest wage paid	**MTC** Median total compensation	**TCC** Total cash compensation
AER Average entry range	**AWR** Average wage range	**H** Hourly	**LR** Low end range	**MW** Median wage paid	**TQ** Third quartile wage
AEX Average experienced wage	**AXR** Average experienced range	**HI** Highest wage paid	**M** Monthly	**MWR** Median wage range	**W** Weekly
ATC Average total compensation	**D** Daily	**HR** High end range	**MCC** Median cash compensation	**S** See annotated source	**Y** Yearly

Occupation/Type/Industry	Location	Per	Low	Mid	High	Source	Date
Land Surveyor							
Department of Transportation	Michigan	H	16.87 LO		30.90 HI	MDOT	10/1/07
Small Organization	United States	Y	44829 FQ	49407 MW	53895 TQ	ALA06	2008
Land Surveyor Mapper							
Department of Resources and Economic Development	New Hampshire	Y			62127 HI	NHUL03	2008
Land Use Inspector							
Municipal Government	Colorado Springs, CO	M	3488 LO			COSPRS	1/1/09
Landfill Inmate Supervisor	Bartow County, GA	Y			39374 HI	GACTY03	2008
	Paulding County, GA	Y	32510 LO		50398 HI	GACTY03	2008
Landfill Manager							
Certified	Coweta County, GA	Y	30758 LO		46138 HI	GACTY03	2008
Certified	Newton County, GA	Y	41538 LO		62379 HI	GACTY03	2008
Landfill Operator	Deerfield, MA	H			16.00 HI	FRCOG	2009
Landscape Architect	Alabama	Y	56570 FQ	71910 MW	83740 TQ	USBLS	5/07
	Alaska	Y	63790 FQ	75040 MW	86630 TQ	USBLS	5/07
	Anchorage MSA, AK	Y	62010 FQ	73860 MW	85010 TQ	USBLS	5/07
	Arizona	Y	56320 FQ	65680 MW	84870 TQ	USBLS	5/07
	Phoenix-Mesa-Scottsdale MSA, AZ	Y	57400 FQ	66330 MW	87590 TQ	USBLS	5/07
	Tucson MSA, AZ	Y	44980 FQ	59410 MW	74250 TQ	USBLS	5/07
	Arkansas	Y	35680 FQ	38540 MW	41730 TQ	USBLS	5/07
	California	H	23.20 FQ	31.95 MW	38.82 TQ	CABLS	1/08-3/08
	Los Angeles-Long Beach-Glendale PMSA, CA	H	21.92 FQ	24.18 MW	34.00 TQ	CABLS	1/08-3/08
	Oakland-Fremont-Hayward MSA, CA	H	20.54 FQ	32.07 MW	39.63 TQ	CABLS	1/08-3/08
	Riverside-San Bernardino-Ontario MSA, CA	H	20.64 FQ	22.25 MW	23.86 TQ	CABLS	1/08-3/08
	Sacramento-Arden Arcade-Roseville MSA, CA	H	27.78 FQ	36.40 MW	45.86 TQ	CABLS	1/08-3/08
	San Diego-Carlsbad-San Marcos MSA, CA	H	33.02 FQ	36.44 MW	39.93 TQ	CABLS	1/08-3/08
	San Francisco-San Mateo-Redwood PMSA, CA	H	23.81 FQ	28.85 MW	36.09 TQ	CABLS	1/08-3/08
	San Jose-Sunnyvale-Santa Clara MSA, CA	H	26.61 FQ	29.64 MW	43.51 TQ	CABLS	1/08-3/08
	Santa Ana-Anaheim-Irvine PMSA, CA	Y	66920 FQ	76010 MW	84880 TQ	USBLS	5/07
	Colorado	Y	44490 FQ	54080 MW	73590 TQ	USBLS	5/07
	Denver-Aurora MSA, CO	Y	44650 FQ	52480 MW	69670 TQ	USBLS	5/07
	Fort Collins-Loveland MSA, CO	Y	48470 FQ	59340 MW	74100 TQ	USBLS	5/07
	Connecticut	H	20.75 AE	34.22 MW		CTBLS	1/08-3/08
	Bridgeport-Stamford-Norwalk MSA, CT	Y	44190 FQ	56020 MW	90300 TQ	USBLS	5/07
	Hartford-West Hartford-East Hartford MSA, CT	Y	48060 FQ	74480 MW	91490 TQ	USBLS	5/07
	Delaware	Y	49310 FQ	54990 MW	60550 TQ	USBLS	5/07
	Wilmington PMSA, DE-MD-NJ	Y	49720 FQ	55470 MW	63730 TQ	USBLS	5/07
	District of Columbia	Y	64240 FQ	83860 MW	107200 TQ	USBLS	5/07
	Washington-Arlington-Alexandria MSA, DC-VA-MD-WV	Y	48690 FQ	59840 MW	77910 TQ	USBLS	5/07
	Florida	Y	37620 FQ	51000 MW	72120 TQ	USBLS	5/07
	Fort Lauderdale-Pompano Beach-Deerfield Beach PMSA, FL	Y	48560 FQ	54800 MW	66160 TQ	USBLS	5/07
	Miami-Fort Lauderdale-Miami Beach MSA, FL	Y	43230 FQ	50720 MW	66730 TQ	USBLS	5/07
	Orlando-Kissimmee MSA, FL	Y	45280 FQ	57430 MW	82480 TQ	USBLS	5/07
	Tampa-St. Petersburg-Clearwater MSA, FL	Y	39010 FQ	59880 MW	80210 TQ	USBLS	5/07
	West Palm Beach-Boca Raton-Boynton Beach PMSA, FL	Y	46690 FQ	57040 MW	76880 TQ	USBLS	5/07
	Georgia	Y	37720 FQ	47440 MW	61750 TQ	USBLS	5/07

AE	Average entry wage	AW	Average wage paid	FQ	First quartile wage	LO	Lowest wage paid	MTC	Median total compensation	TCC	Total cash compensation
AER	Average entry range	AWR	Average wage range	H	Hourly	LR	Low end range	MW	Median wage paid	TQ	Third quartile wage
AEX	Average experienced wage	AXR	Average experienced range	HI	Highest wage paid	M	Monthly	MWR	Median wage range	W	Weekly
ATC	Average total compensation	D	Daily	HR	High end range	MCC	Median cash compensation	S	See annotated source	Y	Yearly

Occupation/Type/Industry	Location	Per	Low	Mid	High	Source	Date
Landscape Architect	Atlanta-Sandy Springs-						
	Marietta MSA, GA	Y	39180 FQ	48460 MW	61460 TQ	USBLS	5/07
	Hawaii	Y	41680 FQ	58850 MW	73160 TQ	USBLS	5/07
	Honolulu MSA, HI	Y	41450 FQ	58120 MW	72800 TQ	USBLS	5/07
	Idaho	Y	45110 FQ	56720 MW	69870 TQ	USBLS	5/07
	Illinois	Y	51230 FQ	59170 MW	72410 TQ	USBLS	5/07
	Chicago-Naperville-Joliet						
	MSA, IL-IN-WI	Y	52380 FQ	59370 MW	71740 TQ	USBLS	5/07
	Peoria MSA, IL	Y	36280 FQ	47710 MW	63360 TQ	USBLS	5/07
	Indiana	Y	39320 FQ	47320 MW	60360 TQ	USBLS	5/07
	Indianapolis-Carmel MSA, IN	Y	44160 FQ	55970 MW	66560 TQ	USBLS	5/07
	Iowa	Y	34250 FQ	53240 MW	72760 TQ	USBLS	5/07
	Des Moines-West Des Moines						
	MSA, IA	Y	52110 FQ	65830 MW	81320 TQ	USBLS	5/07
	Kansas	Y	42420 FQ	50660 MW	63600 TQ	USBLS	5/07
	Wichita MSA, KS	Y	41140 FQ	55140 MW	66300 TQ	USBLS	5/07
	Kentucky	Y	42195 FQ	51557 MW	66337 TQ	KYBLS	2008
	Louisville-Jefferson County						
	MSA, KY-IN	Y	45980 FQ	53140 MW	69790 TQ	USBLS	5/07
	Louisiana	H	17.85 FQ	22.43 MW	27.67 TQ	LABLS	1/08-3/08
	New Orleans-Metairie-Kenner						
	MSA, LA	Y	42790 FQ	48440 MW	58670 TQ	USBLS	5/07
	Maine	Y	48100 FQ	58710 MW	69480 TQ	USBLS	5/07
	Portland-South Portland-						
	Biddeford MSA, ME	Y	52470 FQ	63110 MW	73300 TQ	USBLS	5/07
	Maryland	Y		59400 MW		MDBLS	3/08
	Baltimore-Towson MSA, MD	Y	47990 FQ	59510 MW	76940 TQ	USBLS	5/07
	Bethesda-Gaithersburg-						
	Frederick PMSA, MD	Y	49070 FQ	54630 MW	59900 TQ	USBLS	5/07
	Massachusetts	Y	53650 FQ	70680 MW	83660 TQ	USBLS	5/07
	Boston-Cambridge-Quincy						
	NECTA, MA	Y	55150 FQ	73600 MW	84240 TQ	USBLS	5/07
	Michigan	Y	42580 FQ	56140 MW	71570 TQ	USBLS	5/07
	Detroit-Warren-Livonia MSA,						
	MI	Y	46150 FQ	65950 MW	76800 TQ	USBLS	5/07
	Grand Rapids-Wyoming MSA,						
	MI	Y	40400 FQ	44000 MW	47560 TQ	USBLS	5/07
	Warren-Troy-Farmington Hills						
	PMSA, MI	Y	49910 FQ	67810 MW	77990 TQ	USBLS	5/07
	Minnesota	Y	45908 FQ	57919 MW	74365 TQ	MNBLS	10/08-12/08
	Minneapolis-Saint Paul MSA,						
	MN-WI	Y	47917 FQ	59708 MW	76458 TQ	MNBLS	10/08-12/08
	Rochester MSA, MN	Y	36525 FQ	39211 MW	41897 TQ	MNBLS	10/08-12/08
	Mississippi	Y	44670 FQ	57670 MW	64700 TQ	USBLS	5/07
	Kansas City MSA, MO-KS	Y	40860 FQ	47120 MW	63830 TQ	USBLS	5/07
	Montana	Y	33380 FQ	39380 MW	55030 TQ	USBLS	5/07
	Nebraska	Y	40870 FQ	51570 MW	82140 TQ	USBLS	5/07
	Omaha-Council Bluffs MSA,						
	NE-IA	Y	38340 FQ	51620 MW	96260 TQ	USBLS	5/07
	Nevada	H	22.65 FQ	31.13 MW	38.74 TQ	NVBLS	5/08
	Las Vegas-Paradise MSA, NV	H	24.11 FQ	33.29 MW	37.96 TQ	NVBLS	5/08
	New Hampshire	H	28.25 AE	33.78 MW	40.19 AEX	NHBLS	6/08
	New Jersey	Y	51770 FQ	66130 MW	84460 TQ	USBLS	5/07
	Camden PMSA, NJ	Y	48480 FQ	54720 MW	60490 TQ	USBLS	5/07
	Edison PMSA, NJ	Y	61440 FQ	75640 MW	98300 TQ	USBLS	5/07
	Newark-Union PMSA, NJ-PA	Y	40020 FQ	62770 MW	75150 TQ	USBLS	5/07
	New Mexico	Y	38520 FQ	57300 MW	88170 TQ	USBLS	5/07
	Albuquerque MSA, NM	Y	44960 FQ	65980 MW	99180 TQ	USBLS	5/07
	New York	Y	55970 FQ	65890 MW	80520 TQ	USBLS	5/07
	Albany-Schenectady-Troy						
	MSA, NY	Y	61820 FQ	70160 MW	82120 TQ	USBLS	5/07
	Buffalo-Niagara Falls MSA,						
	NY	Y	64780 FQ	71060 MW	78670 TQ	USBLS	5/07
	Nassau-Suffolk PMSA, NY	Y	57560 FQ	63160 MW	83810 TQ	USBLS	5/07
	New York-Northern New						
	Jersey-Long Island MSA, NY-						
	NJ-PA	Y	53830 FQ	65510 MW	85250 TQ	USBLS	5/07
	North Carolina	Y	47480 FQ	57840 MW	78080 TQ	USBLS	5/07
	Charlotte-Gastonia-Concord						
	MSA, NC-SC	Y	48490 FQ	57530 MW	72520 TQ	USBLS	5/07
	Raleigh-Cary MSA, NC	Y	48210 FQ	67110 MW	80200 TQ	USBLS	5/07
	Ohio	Y	43460 FQ	48430 MW	55560 TQ	USBLS	5/07

AE	Average entry wage	AW	Average wage paid	FQ	First quartile wage
AER	Average entry range	AWR	Average wage range	H	Hourly
AEX	Average experienced wage	AXR	Average experienced range	HI	Highest wage paid
ATC	Average total compensation	D	Daily	HR	High end range

LO	Lowest wage paid	MTC	Median total compensation
LR	Low end range	MW	Median wage paid
M	Monthly	MWR	Median wage range
MCC	Median cash compensation	S	See annotated source

TCC	Total cash compensation
TQ	Third quartile wage
W	Weekly
Y	Yearly

Landscape Architect

Occupation/Type/Industry	Location	Per	Low	Mid	High	Source	Date
Landscape Architect	Cincinnati-Middletown MSA, OH-KY-IN	Y	40290 FQ	48620 MW	57500 TQ	USBLS	5/07
	Cleveland-Elyria-Mentor MSA, OH	Y	44410 FQ	47480 MW	50610 TQ	USBLS	5/07
	Columbus MSA, OH	Y	41650 FQ	51080 MW	69310 TQ	USBLS	5/07
	Oklahoma	Y	30470 FQ	43400 MW	51910 TQ	USBLS	5/07
	Tulsa MSA, OK	Y	29000 FQ	43180 MW	51770 TQ	USBLS	5/07
	Oregon	H	19.75 FQ	30.45 MW	36.30 TQ	ORBLS	5/08
	Portland-Vancouver-Beaverton MSA, OR-WA	Y	45710 FQ	62540 MW	79570 TQ	USBLS	5/07
	Pennsylvania	Y	39360 FQ	52240 MW	65850 TQ	USBLS	5/07
	Allentown-Bethlehem-Easton MSA, PA-NJ	Y	25030 FQ	48650 MW	65230 TQ	USBLS	5/07
	Philadelphia-Camden-Wilmington MSA, PA-NJ-DE-MD	Y	44320 FQ	54760 MW	64640 TQ	USBLS	5/07
	Pittsburgh MSA, PA	Y	44370 FQ	55110 MW	67080 TQ	USBLS	5/07
	Providence-Fall River-Warwick MSA, RI-MA	Y	48750 FQ	56930 MW	69720 TQ	USBLS	5/07
	South Carolina	Y	36990 FQ	49850 MW	71230 TQ	USBLS	5/07
	Charleston-North Charleston MSA, SC	Y	37610 FQ	50920 MW	62030 TQ	USBLS	5/07
	South Dakota	Y	39579 FQ	50569 MW	61675 TQ	SDBLS	7/08-9/08
	Sioux Falls MSA, SD	Y	44307 FQ	54459 MW	64064 TQ	SDBLS	7/08-9/08
	Tennessee	Y	38960 FQ	51580 MW	72880 TQ	USBLS	5/07
	Memphis MSA, TN-MS-AR	Y	41950 FQ	54530 MW	70970 TQ	USBLS	5/07
	Nashville-Davidson-Murfreesboro MSA, TN	Y	46290 FQ	60870 MW	77300 TQ	USBLS	5/07
	Texas	Y	42990 FQ	57140 MW	74080 TQ	USBLS	5/07
	Austin-Round Rock MSA, TX	Y	43430 FQ	53330 MW	67590 TQ	USBLS	5/07
	Dallas-Fort Worth-Arlington MSA, TX	Y	52230 FQ	65540 MW	92520 TQ	USBLS	5/07
	Houston-Sugar Land-Baytown MSA, TX	Y	40110 FQ	54150 MW	65620 TQ	USBLS	5/07
	Utah	Y	44470 FQ	55890 MW	74830 TQ	USBLS	5/07
	Salt Lake City MSA, UT	Y	42300 FQ	49160 MW	69260 TQ	USBLS	5/07
	Vermont	Y	32360 FQ	37560 MW	49840 TQ	USBLS	5/07
	Burlington-South Burlington MSA, VT	Y	35220 FQ	39330 MW	53590 TQ	USBLS	5/07
	Virginia	Y	42090 FQ	50910 MW	68650 TQ	USBLS	5/07
	Richmond MSA, VA	Y	44380 FQ	50300 MW	64950 TQ	USBLS	5/07
	Virginia Beach-Norfolk-Newport News MSA, VA-NC	Y	43360 FQ	51260 MW	71970 TQ	USBLS	5/07
	Washington	H	24.82 FQ	28.27 MW	33.89 TQ	WABLS	3/08
	Seattle-Tacoma-Bellevue MSA, WA	Y	50950 FQ	57750 MW	68480 TQ	USBLS	5/07
	West Virginia	Y	25383 FQ	58352 MW	70727 TQ	WVBLS	7/08-9/08
	Wisconsin	Y	44710 FQ	51310 MW	66330 TQ	USBLS	5/07
	Milwaukee-Waukesha-West Allis MSA, WI	Y	51610 FQ	60760 MW	73400 TQ	USBLS	5/07
	Wyoming	Y	56269 FQ	62612 MW	71569 TQ	WYBLS	9/08
	Virgin Islands	Y	32210 FQ	34490 MW	36780 TQ	USBLS	5/07
Landscape Designer	United States	Y	10000-19999 LO		80000-99999 HI	AMNUR	2007
Municipal Government	Seattle, WA	H	24.38 LO		26.36 HI	CSSS	2007
Landscaping and Groundskeeping Worker	Alabama	Y	16810 FQ	19590 MW	24280 TQ	USBLS	5/07
	Birmingham-Hoover MSA, AL	Y	17450 FQ	20090 MW	25000 TQ	USBLS	5/07
	Huntsville MSA, AL	Y	16590 FQ	20020 MW	23300 TQ	USBLS	5/07
	Alaska	Y	21660 FQ	27090 MW	32020 TQ	USBLS	5/07
	Anchorage MSA, AK	Y	20570 FQ	26400 MW	30650 TQ	USBLS	5/07
	Arizona	Y	17230 FQ	20170 MW	24560 TQ	USBLS	5/07
	Phoenix-Mesa-Scottsdale MSA, AZ	Y	17120 FQ	20000 MW	24380 TQ	USBLS	5/07
	Prescott MSA, AZ	Y	20170 FQ	23310 MW	26190 TQ	USBLS	5/07
	Tucson MSA, AZ	Y	17260 FQ	20100 MW	24010 TQ	USBLS	5/07
	Arkansas	Y	16430 FQ	19410 MW	23980 TQ	USBLS	5/07
	Little Rock-North Little Rock MSA, AR	Y	16860 FQ	19800 MW	24730 TQ	USBLS	5/07
	California	H	9.41 FQ	11.38 MW	14.55 TQ	CABLS	1/08-3/08

AE Average entry wage	**AW** Average wage paid	**FQ** First quartile wage	**LO** Lowest wage paid	**MTC** Median total compensation	**TCC** Total cash compensation
AER Average entry range	**AWR** Average wage range	**H** Hourly	**LR** Low end range	**MW** Median wage paid	**TQ** Third quartile wage
AEX Average experienced wage	**AXR** Average experienced range	**HI** Highest wage paid	**M** Monthly	**MWR** Median wage range	**W** Weekly
ATC Average total compensation	**D** Daily	**HR** High end range	**MCC** Median cash compensation	**S** See annotated source	**Y** Yearly

Occupation/Type/Industry	Location	Per	Low	Mid	High	Source	Date
Landscaping and Groundskeeping Worker							
	Los Angeles-Long Beach-Glendale PMSA, CA	H	9.72 FQ	11.96 MW	15.92 TQ	CABLS	1/08-3/08
	Oakland-Fremont-Hayward MSA, CA	H	10.51 FQ	12.99 MW	16.98 TQ	CABLS	1/08-3/08
	Riverside-San Bernardino-Ontario MSA, CA	H	8.86 FQ	10.22 MW	12.36 TQ	CABLS	1/08-3/08
	Sacramento-Arden Arcade-Roseville MSA, CA	H	9.24 FQ	10.98 MW	13.15 TQ	CABLS	1/08-3/08
	San Diego-Carlsbad-San Marcos MSA, CA	H	9.88 FQ	11.40 MW	13.69 TQ	CABLS	1/08-3/08
	San Francisco-San Mateo-Redwood PMSA, CA	H	11.67 FQ	14.34 MW	19.45 TQ	CABLS	1/08-3/08
	San Jose-Sunnyvale-Santa Clara MSA, CA	H	10.15 FQ	12.31 MW	15.18 TQ	CABLS	1/08-3/08
	Santa Ana-Anaheim-Irvine PMSA, CA	Y	17530 FQ	19870 MW	24070 TQ	USBLS	5/07
	Stockton MSA, CA	H	9.47 FQ	11.25 MW	14.88 TQ	CABLS	1/08-3/08
	Colorado	Y	19720 FQ	23750 MW	29840 TQ	USBLS	5/07
	Denver-Aurora MSA, CO	Y	19900 FQ	23630 MW	29760 TQ	USBLS	5/07
	Connecticut	H	9.97 AE	13.48 MW		CTBLS	1/08-3/08
	Bridgeport-Stamford-Norwalk MSA, CT	Y	22260 FQ	27930 MW	33180 TQ	USBLS	5/07
	Hartford-West Hartford-East Hartford MSA, CT	Y	22780 FQ	27860 MW	35350 TQ	USBLS	5/07
	Delaware	Y	20110 FQ	23620 MW	29320 TQ	USBLS	5/07
	Dover MSA, DE	Y	19610 FQ	22360 MW	25120 TQ	USBLS	5/07
	Wilmington PMSA, DE-MD-NJ	Y	20450 FQ	24320 MW	30040 TQ	USBLS	5/07
	District of Columbia	Y	25730 FQ	28810 MW	36020 TQ	USBLS	5/07
	Washington-Arlington-Alexandria MSA, DC-VA-MD-WV	Y	19280 FQ	23170 MW	28550 TQ	USBLS	5/07
	Florida	Y	17680 FQ	20720 MW	25110 TQ	USBLS	5/07
	Fort Lauderdale-Pompano Beach-Deerfield Beach PMSA, FL	Y	18090 FQ	21650 MW	28100 TQ	USBLS	5/07
	Jacksonville MSA, FL	Y	17510 FQ	20260 MW	23970 TQ	USBLS	5/07
	Miami-Fort Lauderdale-Miami Beach MSA, FL	Y	17130 FQ	19990 MW	25180 TQ	USBLS	5/07
	Orlando-Kissimmee MSA, FL	Y	19530 FQ	22410 MW	25980 TQ	USBLS	5/07
	Tampa-St. Petersburg-Clearwater MSA, FL	Y	17720 FQ	21010 MW	25660 TQ	USBLS	5/07
	West Palm Beach-Boca Raton-Boynton Beach PMSA, FL	Y	16920 FQ	19470 MW	23940 TQ	USBLS	5/07
	Georgia	Y	18150 FQ	21300 MW	25000 TQ	USBLS	5/07
	Atlanta-Sandy Springs-Marietta MSA, GA	Y	18860 FQ	21940 MW	25490 TQ	USBLS	5/07
	Hawaii	Y	23080 FQ	27780 MW	32260 TQ	USBLS	5/07
	Honolulu MSA, HI	Y	21810 FQ	26910 MW	32070 TQ	USBLS	5/07
	Idaho	Y	18590 FQ	22550 MW	26680 TQ	USBLS	5/07
	Boise City-Nampa MSA, ID	Y	20180 FQ	23070 MW	26280 TQ	USBLS	5/07
	Illinois	Y	18500 FQ	22700 MW	28840 TQ	USBLS	5/07
	Chicago-Naperville-Joliet MSA, IL-IN-WI	Y	18690 FQ	23010 MW	29060 TQ	USBLS	5/07
	Indiana	Y	17590 FQ	21290 MW	26150 TQ	USBLS	5/07
	Gary PMSA, IN	Y	17670 FQ	22520 MW	27580 TQ	USBLS	5/07
	Indianapolis-Carmel MSA, IN	Y	17770 FQ	21040 MW	26200 TQ	USBLS	5/07
	Terre Haute MSA, IN	Y	15470 FQ	18470 MW	23620 TQ	USBLS	5/07
	Iowa	Y	17280 FQ	21200 MW	27620 TQ	USBLS	5/07
	Des Moines-West Des Moines MSA, IA	Y	19130 FQ	23400 MW	30030 TQ	USBLS	5/07
	Kansas	Y	17420 FQ	20770 MW	25480 TQ	USBLS	5/07
	Lawrence MSA, KS	Y	17860 FQ	20250 MW	25780 TQ	USBLS	5/07
	Wichita MSA, KS	Y	17020 FQ	19600 MW	22800 TQ	USBLS	5/07
	Kentucky	Y	18077 FQ	21440 MW	25894 TQ	KYBLS	2008
	Lexington-Fayette MSA, KY	Y	18130 FQ	21020 MW	26120 TQ	USBLS	5/07
	Louisville-Jefferson County MSA, KY-IN	Y	19350 FQ	22890 MW	26980 TQ	USBLS	5/07
	Owensboro MSA, KY	Y	13430 FQ	16000 MW	18870 TQ	USBLS	5/07
	Louisiana	H	7.51 FQ	9.39 MW	11.57 TQ	LABLS	1/08-3/08
	Baton Rouge MSA, LA	Y	15920 FQ	19630 MW	23810 TQ	USBLS	5/07

Occupation/Type/Industry	Location	Per	Low	Mid	High	Source	Date
Landscaping and Groundskeeping Worker							
	New Orleans-Metairie-Kenner MSA, LA	Y	18550 FQ	21970 MW	25790 TQ	USBLS	5/07
	Maine	Y	19440 FQ	24450 MW	29940 TQ	USBLS	5/07
	Portland-South Portland-Biddeford MSA, ME	Y	22250 FQ	27260 MW	32270 TQ	USBLS	5/07
	Maryland	Y		23925 MW		MDBLS	3/08
	Baltimore-Towson MSA, MD	Y	20030 FQ	23800 MW	30020 TQ	USBLS	5/07
	Bethesda-Gaithersburg-Frederick PMSA, MD	Y	19430 FQ	23170 MW	28560 TQ	USBLS	5/07
	Massachusetts	Y	23420 FQ	28690 MW	35200 TQ	USBLS	5/07
	Boston-Cambridge-Quincy NECTA, MA	Y	23860 FQ	29870 MW	37110 TQ	USBLS	5/07
	Worcester MSA, MA-CT	Y	21920 FQ	27050 MW	31560 TQ	USBLS	5/07
	Michigan	Y	18390 FQ	22510 MW	28640 TQ	USBLS	5/07
	Detroit-Warren-Livonia MSA, MI	Y	19560 FQ	23300 MW	29630 TQ	USBLS	5/07
	Grand Rapids-Wyoming MSA, MI	Y	18840 FQ	22840 MW	27040 TQ	USBLS	5/07
	Warren-Troy-Farmington Hills PMSA, MI	Y	19770 FQ	23470 MW	29790 TQ	USBLS	5/07
	Minnesota	Y	20545 FQ	25010 MW	32507 TQ	MNBLS	10/08-12/08
	Duluth-Superior MSA, MN-WI	Y	17137 FQ	20932 MW	30646 TQ	MNBLS	10/08-12/08
	Minneapolis-Saint Paul MSA, MN-WI	Y	22197 FQ	26829 MW	34127 TQ	MNBLS	10/08-12/08
	Rochester MSA, MN	Y	22681 FQ	26944 MW	37431 TQ	MNBLS	10/08-12/08
	Mississippi	Y	16430 FQ	19360 MW	23000 TQ	USBLS	5/07
	Gulfport-Biloxi MSA, MS	Y	17110 FQ	20430 MW	24090 TQ	USBLS	5/07
	Jackson MSA, MS	Y	17440 FQ	20320 MW	23590 TQ	USBLS	5/07
	Missouri	Y	18340 FQ	22680 MW	30090 TQ	USBLS	5/07
	Kansas City MSA, MO-KS	Y	19230 FQ	23140 MW	29410 TQ	USBLS	5/07
	St. Louis MSA, MO-IL	Y	19500 FQ	23670 MW	31920 TQ	USBLS	5/07
	Montana	Y	17120 FQ	21080 MW	27200 TQ	USBLS	5/07
	Billings MSA, MT	Y	17240 FQ	20150 MW	25730 TQ	USBLS	5/07
	Missoula MSA, MT	Y	17540 FQ	20160 MW	26870 TQ	USBLS	5/07
	Nebraska	Y	17890 FQ	21760 MW	26330 TQ	USBLS	5/07
	Omaha-Council Bluffs MSA, NE-IA	Y	19710 FQ	22810 MW	26820 TQ	USBLS	5/07
	Nevada	H	9.18 FQ	11.14 MW	13.95 TQ	NVBLS	5/08
	Las Vegas-Paradise MSA, NV	H	9.02 FQ	10.84 MW	13.56 TQ	NVBLS	5/08
	New Hampshire	H	9.63 AE	12.43 MW	14.53 AEX	NHBLS	6/08
	Manchester MSA, NH	Y	20700 FQ	24660 MW	32460 TQ	USBLS	5/07
	Nashua NECTA, NH-MA	Y	24000 FQ	27240 MW	31120 TQ	USBLS	5/07
	New Jersey	Y	20420 FQ	24660 MW	30990 TQ	USBLS	5/07
	Camden PMSA, NJ	Y	19510 FQ	24110 MW	29850 TQ	USBLS	5/07
	Edison PMSA, NJ	Y	19610 FQ	24280 MW	30680 TQ	USBLS	5/07
	Newark-Union PMSA, NJ-PA	Y	21300 FQ	25740 MW	32230 TQ	USBLS	5/07
	New Mexico	Y	16040 FQ	19600 MW	23920 TQ	USBLS	5/07
	Albuquerque MSA, NM	Y	15520 FQ	19380 MW	23450 TQ	USBLS	5/07
	New York	Y	19200 FQ	24160 MW	31940 TQ	USBLS	5/07
	Albany-Schenectady-Troy MSA, NY	Y	19920 FQ	23040 MW	28800 TQ	USBLS	5/07
	Buffalo-Niagara Falls MSA, NY	Y	18530 FQ	22590 MW	30280 TQ	USBLS	5/07
	Glens Falls MSA, NY	Y	19980 FQ	22760 MW	26960 TQ	USBLS	5/07
	Nassau-Suffolk PMSA, NY	Y	18870 FQ	23660 MW	30990 TQ	USBLS	5/07
	New York-Northern New Jersey-Long Island MSA, NY-NJ-PA	Y	20350 FQ	24980 MW	32590 TQ	USBLS	5/07
	Syracuse MSA, NY	Y	17570 FQ	22470 MW	28820 TQ	USBLS	5/07
	North Carolina	Y	17600 FQ	20750 MW	24560 TQ	USBLS	5/07
	Charlotte-Gastonia-Concord MSA, NC-SC	Y	17770 FQ	20650 MW	24850 TQ	USBLS	5/07
	Raleigh-Cary MSA, NC	Y	17500 FQ	20520 MW	24490 TQ	USBLS	5/07
	North Dakota	Y	17010 FQ	21010 MW	25660 TQ	USBLS	5/07
	Fargo MSA, ND-MN	Y	19360 FQ	22830 MW	27960 TQ	USBLS	5/07
	Ohio	Y	17680 FQ	21490 MW	26850 TQ	USBLS	5/07
	Cincinnati-Middletown MSA, OH-KY-IN	Y	18470 FQ	21870 MW	27440 TQ	USBLS	5/07
	Cleveland-Elyria-Mentor MSA, OH	Y	18050 FQ	22310 MW	28480 TQ	USBLS	5/07
	Columbus MSA, OH	Y	19210 FQ	22650 MW	27090 TQ	USBLS	5/07

AE	Average entry wage	AW	Average wage paid	FQ	First quartile wage	LO	Lowest wage paid	MTC	Median total compensation	TCC	Total cash compensation
AER	Average entry range	AWR	Average wage range	H	Hourly	LR	Low end range	MW	Median wage paid	TQ	Third quartile wage
AEX	Average experienced wage	AXR	Average experienced range	HI	Highest wage paid	M	Monthly	MWR	Median wage range	W	Weekly
ATC	Average total compensation	D	Daily	HR	High end range	MCC	Median cash compensation	S	See annotated source	Y	Yearly

880

Landscaping and Groundskeeping Worker

Occupation/Type/Industry	Location	Per	Low	Mid	High	Source	Date
Landscaping and Groundskeeping Worker	Dayton MSA, OH	Y	19050 FQ	23020 MW	28710 TQ	USBLS	5/07
	Oklahoma	Y	16380 FQ	19320 MW	23580 TQ	USBLS	5/07
	Oklahoma City MSA, OK	Y	16540 FQ	19120 MW	23290 TQ	USBLS	5/07
	Tulsa MSA, OK	Y	17140 FQ	20340 MW	24750 TQ	USBLS	5/07
	Oregon	H	9.31 FQ	11.06 MW	13.70 TQ	ORBLS	5/08
	Medford MSA, OR	Y	18810 FQ	24440 MW	32500 TQ	USBLS	5/07
	Portland-Vancouver-Beaverton MSA, OR-WA	Y	19110 FQ	22590 MW	27780 TQ	USBLS	5/07
	Pennsylvania	Y	19060 FQ	23570 MW	30170 TQ	USBLS	5/07
	Allentown-Bethlehem-Easton MSA, PA-NJ	Y	19460 FQ	23270 MW	28330 TQ	USBLS	5/07
	Erie MSA, PA	Y	15190 FQ	18470 MW	25190 TQ	USBLS	5/07
	Philadelphia-Camden-Wilmington MSA, PA-NJ-DE-MD	Y	20820 FQ	25370 MW	31830 TQ	USBLS	5/07
	Pittsburgh MSA, PA	Y	18260 FQ	22410 MW	28970 TQ	USBLS	5/07
	Rhode Island	Y	21550 FQ	25660 MW	31320 TQ	USBLS	5/07
	Providence-Fall River-Warwick MSA, RI-MA	Y	21640 FQ	25390 MW	31180 TQ	USBLS	5/07
	South Carolina	Y	17550 FQ	20670 MW	24960 TQ	USBLS	5/07
	Charleston-North Charleston MSA, SC	Y	17700 FQ	20710 MW	23770 TQ	USBLS	5/07
	Columbia MSA, SC	Y	18170 FQ	21090 MW	24590 TQ	USBLS	5/07
	Myrtle Beach-Conway-North Myrtle Beach MSA, SC	Y	17210 FQ	19360 MW	22900 TQ	USBLS	5/07
	South Dakota	Y	18302 FQ	21616 MW	25100 TQ	SDBLS	7/08-9/08
	Sioux Falls MSA, SD	Y	19835 FQ	23243 MW	27050 TQ	SDBLS	7/08-9/08
	Tennessee	Y	17670 FQ	21060 MW	25230 TQ	USBLS	5/07
	Johnson City MSA, TN	Y	16740 FQ	19720 MW	23660 TQ	USBLS	5/07
	Memphis MSA, TN-MS-AR	Y	18040 FQ	21440 MW	26260 TQ	USBLS	5/07
	Nashville-Davidson-Murfreesboro MSA, TN	Y	19740 FQ	22580 MW	26290 TQ	USBLS	5/07
	Texas	Y	16060 FQ	18800 MW	23240 TQ	USBLS	5/07
	Austin-Round Rock MSA, TX	Y	16550 FQ	19080 MW	23120 TQ	USBLS	5/07
	Beaumont-Port Arthur MSA, TX	Y	13230 FQ	15090 MW	20160 TQ	USBLS	5/07
	Dallas-Fort Worth-Arlington MSA, TX	Y	17110 FQ	19920 MW	25080 TQ	USBLS	5/07
	El Paso MSA, TX	Y	14110 FQ	17170 MW	21210 TQ	USBLS	5/07
	Houston-Sugar Land-Baytown MSA, TX	Y	15300 FQ	18150 MW	22570 TQ	USBLS	5/07
	San Antonio MSA, TX	Y	16610 FQ	19210 MW	22910 TQ	USBLS	5/07
	Utah	Y	17060 FQ	20330 MW	24740 TQ	USBLS	5/07
	Salt Lake City MSA, UT	Y	18290 FQ	21710 MW	25790 TQ	USBLS	5/07
	Vermont	Y	21410 FQ	24660 MW	30190 TQ	USBLS	5/07
	Burlington-South Burlington MSA, VT	Y	21140 FQ	23940 MW	28310 TQ	USBLS	5/07
	Virginia	Y	18450 FQ	22180 MW	26880 TQ	USBLS	5/07
	Richmond MSA, VA	Y	18290 FQ	21790 MW	25870 TQ	USBLS	5/07
	Roanoke MSA, VA	Y	17880 FQ	20900 MW	26590 TQ	USBLS	5/07
	Virginia Beach-Norfolk-Newport News MSA, VA-NC	Y	18320 FQ	21720 MW	25510 TQ	USBLS	5/07
	Washington	H	10.59 FQ	12.70 MW	16.02 TQ	WABLS	3/08
	Olympia MSA, WA	Y	20450 FQ	22780 MW	26840 TQ	USBLS	5/07
	Seattle-Tacoma-Bellevue MSA, WA	Y	22410 FQ	27210 MW	34240 TQ	USBLS	5/07
	West Virginia	Y	15198 FQ	18159 MW	22660 TQ	WVBLS	7/08-9/08
	Charleston MSA, WV	Y	14120 FQ	16570 MW	19680 TQ	USBLS	5/07
	Huntington-Ashland MSA, WV-KY-OH	Y	16110 FQ	18320 MW	21230 TQ	USBLS	5/07
	Parkersburg-Marietta-Vienna MSA, WV-OH	Y	14850 FQ	17220 MW	21070 TQ	USBLS	5/07
	Wheeling MSA, WV-OH	Y	14630 FQ	17580 MW	22680 TQ	USBLS	5/07
	Wisconsin	Y	19280 FQ	23940 MW	30080 TQ	USBLS	5/07
	Milwaukee-Waukesha-West Allis MSA, WI	Y	19950 FQ	24350 MW	30760 TQ	USBLS	5/07
	Wyoming	Y	19527 FQ	24144 MW	31013 TQ	WYBLS	9/08
	Cheyenne MSA, WY	Y	20660 FQ	23857 MW	27634 TQ	WYBLS	9/08
	Puerto Rico	Y	12790 FQ	14400 MW	16920 TQ	USBLS	5/07
	San Juan-Caguas-Guaynabo MSA, PR	Y	12830 FQ	14480 MW	17280 TQ	USBLS	5/07

AE Average entry wage	**AW** Average wage paid	**FQ** First quartile wage	**LO** Lowest wage paid	**MTC** Median total compensation	**TCC** Total cash compensation
AER Average entry range	**AWR** Average wage range	**H** Hourly	**LR** Low end range	**MW** Median wage paid	**TQ** Third quartile wage
AEX Average experienced wage	**AXR** Average experienced range	**HI** Highest wage paid	**M** Monthly	**MWR** Median wage range	**W** Weekly
ATC Average total compensation	**D** Daily	**HR** High end range	**MCC** Median cash compensation	**S** See annotated source	**Y** Yearly

Occupation/Type/Industry	Location	Per	Low	Mid	High	Source	Date
Landscaping and Groundskeeping Worker	Virgin Islands	Y	17360 FQ	19560 MW	23170 TQ	USBLS	5/07
	Guam	Y	13350 FQ	15730 MW	18710 TQ	USBLS	5/07
Language Specialist							
Federal Government	United States	Y		76287 AW		OOH02	2007
Latent Print Examiner							
Municipal Government	Seattle, WA	H	27.63 LO		32.19 HI	CSSS	2008
Police Department	Mesa, AZ	W	3548 LO		4782 HI	CAC	2006-2007
Police Department Crime Lab	Oregon	W	3432 LO		4987 HI	CAC	2006-2007
Lathe and Turning Machine Tool Setter, Operator, and Tender							
Metals and Plastics	Alabama	Y	26690 FQ	30330 MW	35100 TQ	USBLS	5/07
Metals and Plastics	Birmingham-Hoover MSA, AL	Y	28400 FQ	31440 MW	37010 TQ	USBLS	5/07
Metals and Plastics	Huntsville MSA, AL	Y	27200 FQ	29020 MW	31070 TQ	USBLS	5/07
Metals and Plastics	Arizona	Y	27960 FQ	32480 MW	39970 TQ	USBLS	5/07
Metals and Plastics	Phoenix-Mesa-Scottsdale MSA, AZ	Y	28150 FQ	33790 MW	40780 TQ	USBLS	5/07
Metals and Plastics	Tucson MSA, AZ	Y	27650 FQ	30750 MW	36640 TQ	USBLS	5/07
Metals and Plastics	Arkansas	Y	24360 FQ	29030 MW	34080 TQ	USBLS	5/07
Metals and Plastics	Little Rock-North Little Rock MSA, AR	Y	24510 FQ	27620 MW	32970 TQ	USBLS	5/07
Metals and Plastics	California	H	11.22 FQ	15.23 MW	20.45 TQ	CABLS	1/08-3/08
Metals and Plastics	Los Angeles-Long Beach-Glendale PMSA, CA	H	10.07 FQ	14.02 MW	18.41 TQ	CABLS	1/08-3/08
Metals and Plastics	Oakland-Fremont-Hayward MSA, CA	H	11.43 FQ	19.39 MW	24.00 TQ	CABLS	1/08-3/08
Metals and Plastics	Riverside-San Bernardino-Ontario MSA, CA	H	12.38 FQ	15.71 MW	20.70 TQ	CABLS	1/08-3/08
Metals and Plastics	Sacramento-Arden Arcade-Roseville MSA, CA	H	12.97 FQ	14.07 MW	15.11 TQ	CABLS	1/08-3/08
Metals and Plastics	San Diego-Carlsbad-San Marcos MSA, CA	H	12.80 FQ	17.18 MW	21.93 TQ	CABLS	1/08-3/08
Metals and Plastics	San Francisco-San Mateo-Redwood PMSA, CA	H	12.35 FQ	14.23 MW	17.19 TQ	CABLS	1/08-3/08
Metals and Plastics	San Jose-Sunnyvale-Santa Clara MSA, CA	H	18.51 FQ	21.82 MW	27.12 TQ	CABLS	1/08-3/08
Metals and Plastics	Santa Ana-Anaheim-Irvine PMSA, CA	Y	24020 FQ	33070 MW	41390 TQ	USBLS	5/07
Metals and Plastics	Colorado	Y	31910 FQ	38070 MW	43760 TQ	USBLS	5/07
Metals and Plastics	Denver-Aurora MSA, CO	Y	37920 FQ	41590 MW	46550 TQ	USBLS	5/07
Metals and Plastics	Connecticut	H	13.26 AE	17.99 MW		CTBLS	1/08-3/08
Metals and Plastics	Bridgeport-Stamford-Norwalk MSA, CT	Y	34370 FQ	41730 MW	51080 TQ	USBLS	5/07
Metals and Plastics	Hartford-West Hartford-East Hartford MSA, CT	Y	32880 FQ	39080 MW	46120 TQ	USBLS	5/07
Metals and Plastics	Washington-Arlington-Alexandria MSA, DC-VA-MD-WV	Y	40200 FQ	44050 MW	47530 TQ	USBLS	5/07
Metals and Plastics	Florida	Y	23110 FQ	28350 MW	34940 TQ	USBLS	5/07
Metals and Plastics	Fort Lauderdale-Pompano Beach-Deerfield Beach PMSA, FL	Y	23600 FQ	32500 MW	37330 TQ	USBLS	5/07
Metals and Plastics	Jacksonville MSA, FL	Y	20090 FQ	21390 MW	22680 TQ	USBLS	5/07
Metals and Plastics	Orlando-Kissimmee MSA, FL	Y	17570 FQ	19320 MW	30650 TQ	USBLS	5/07
Metals and Plastics	Tampa-St. Petersburg-Clearwater MSA, FL	Y	25820 FQ	28870 MW	34420 TQ	USBLS	5/07
Metals and Plastics	Georgia	Y	26110 FQ	33520 MW	40410 TQ	USBLS	5/07
Metals and Plastics	Atlanta-Sandy Springs-Marietta MSA, GA	Y	24280 FQ	31990 MW	43990 TQ	USBLS	5/07
Metals and Plastics	Idaho	Y	22260 FQ	26440 MW	30390 TQ	USBLS	5/07
Metals and Plastics	Illinois	Y	26180 FQ	34350 MW	44170 TQ	USBLS	5/07
Metals and Plastics	Chicago-Naperville-Joliet MSA, IL-IN-WI	Y	26700 FQ	35140 MW	45450 TQ	USBLS	5/07
Metals and Plastics	Indiana	Y	25540 FQ	31270 MW	39660 TQ	USBLS	5/07
Metals and Plastics	Gary PMSA, IN	Y	28090 FQ	35510 MW	46300 TQ	USBLS	5/07
Metals and Plastics	Indianapolis-Carmel MSA, IN	Y	29930 FQ	38700 MW	53700 TQ	USBLS	5/07
Metals and Plastics	Iowa	Y	28030 FQ	33810 MW	39000 TQ	USBLS	5/07
Metals and Plastics	Kansas	Y	25340 FQ	30110 MW	36800 TQ	USBLS	5/07
Metals and Plastics	Wichita MSA, KS	Y	24530 FQ	31110 MW	44260 TQ	USBLS	5/07

Lathe and Turning Machine Tool Setter, Operator, and Tender

Occupation/Type/Industry	Location	Per	Low	Mid	High	Source	Date
Lathe and Turning Machine Tool Setter, Operator, and Tender							
Metals and Plastics	Kentucky	Y	27634 FQ	32574 MW	37334 TQ	KYBLS	2008
Metals and Plastics	Louisville-Jefferson County MSA, KY-IN	Y	25030 FQ	33080 MW	38110 TQ	USBLS	5/07
Metals and Plastics	Louisiana	H	12.84 FQ	16.17 MW	19.12 TQ	LABLS	1/08-3/08
Metals and Plastics	New Orleans-Metairie-Kenner MSA, LA	Y	31290 FQ	36370 MW	42230 TQ	USBLS	5/07
Metals and Plastics	Maine	Y	30300 FQ	34350 MW	38660 TQ	USBLS	5/07
Metals and Plastics	Portland-South Portland-Biddeford MSA, ME	Y	31520 FQ	35110 MW	39160 TQ	USBLS	5/07
Metals and Plastics	Maryland	Y		41525 MW		MDBLS	3/08
Metals and Plastics	Baltimore-Towson MSA, MD	Y	33640 FQ	37980 MW	44330 TQ	USBLS	5/07
Metals and Plastics	Massachusetts	Y	29160 FQ	37220 MW	45500 TQ	USBLS	5/07
Metals and Plastics	Boston-Cambridge-Quincy NECTA, MA	Y	30600 FQ	36530 MW	45940 TQ	USBLS	5/07
Metals and Plastics	Worcester MSA, MA-CT	Y	36880 FQ	40890 MW	44530 TQ	USBLS	5/07
Metals and Plastics	Michigan	Y	30240 FQ	38430 MW	49990 TQ	USBLS	5/07
Metals and Plastics	Detroit-Warren-Livonia MSA, MI	Y	33980 FQ	42300 MW	53480 TQ	USBLS	5/07
Metals and Plastics	Grand Rapids-Wyoming MSA, MI	Y	27260 FQ	38640 MW	48750 TQ	USBLS	5/07
Metals and Plastics	Muskegon-Norton Shores MSA, MI	Y	32160 FQ	34940 MW	38140 TQ	USBLS	5/07
Metals and Plastics	Warren-Troy-Farmington Hills PMSA, MI	Y	36230 FQ	44010 MW	53590 TQ	USBLS	5/07
Metals and Plastics	Minnesota	Y	31338 FQ	36926 MW	45168 TQ	MNBLS	10/08-12/08
Metals and Plastics	Minneapolis-Saint Paul MSA, MN-WI	Y	32821 FQ	38502 MW	45562 TQ	MNBLS	10/08-12/08
Metals and Plastics	Mississippi	Y	22860 FQ	26260 MW	28990 TQ	USBLS	5/07
Metals and Plastics	Missouri	Y	24690 FQ	29000 MW	34670 TQ	USBLS	5/07
Metals and Plastics	Kansas City MSA, MO-KS	Y	27370 FQ	30530 MW	35280 TQ	USBLS	5/07
Metals and Plastics	St. Louis MSA, MO-IL	Y	23660 FQ	29550 MW	40410 TQ	USBLS	5/07
Metals and Plastics	Montana	Y	23880 FQ	27120 MW	30830 TQ	USBLS	5/07
Metals and Plastics	Nebraska	Y	29480 FQ	32630 MW	35530 TQ	USBLS	5/07
Metals and Plastics	Omaha-Council Bluffs MSA, NE-IA	Y	23400 FQ	28820 MW	34640 TQ	USBLS	5/07
Metals and Plastics	Nevada	H	13.11 FQ	16.50 MW	20.55 TQ	NVBLS	5/08
Metals and Plastics	Las Vegas-Paradise MSA, NV	H	16.42 FQ	17.83 MW	19.42 TQ	NVBLS	5/08
Metals and Plastics	New Hampshire	H	13.52 AE	16.83 MW	18.98 AEX	NHBLS	6/08
Metals and Plastics	Nashua NECTA, NH-MA	Y	30350 FQ	35900 MW	42670 TQ	USBLS	5/07
Metals and Plastics	New Jersey	Y	25170 FQ	30180 MW	40830 TQ	USBLS	5/07
Metals and Plastics	Camden PMSA, NJ	Y	37100 FQ	49680 MW	57290 TQ	USBLS	5/07
Metals and Plastics	Edison PMSA, NJ	Y	26380 FQ	28500 MW	30750 TQ	USBLS	5/07
Metals and Plastics	Newark-Union PMSA, NJ-PA	Y	23390 FQ	32040 MW	43590 TQ	USBLS	5/07
Metals and Plastics	New Mexico	Y	24950 FQ	26880 MW	28840 TQ	USBLS	5/07
Metals and Plastics	New York	Y	26690 FQ	33100 MW	40360 TQ	USBLS	5/07
Metals and Plastics	Albany-Schenectady-Troy MSA, NY	Y	23260 FQ	28000 MW	34960 TQ	USBLS	5/07
Metals and Plastics	Buffalo-Niagara Falls MSA, NY	Y	30120 FQ	36080 MW	45070 TQ	USBLS	5/07
Metals and Plastics	Nassau-Suffolk PMSA, NY	Y	26420 FQ	37720 MW	52340 TQ	USBLS	5/07
Metals and Plastics	New York-Northern New Jersey-Long Island MSA, NY-NJ-PA	Y	25060 FQ	31460 MW	43670 TQ	USBLS	5/07
Metals and Plastics	North Carolina	Y	28750 FQ	33670 MW	37370 TQ	USBLS	5/07
Metals and Plastics	Charlotte-Gastonia-Concord MSA, NC-SC	Y	27940 FQ	37570 MW	42680 TQ	USBLS	5/07
Metals and Plastics	Raleigh-Cary MSA, NC	Y	21700 FQ	29600 MW	34600 TQ	USBLS	5/07
Metals and Plastics	Winston-Salem MSA, NC	Y	27720 FQ	32050 MW	36310 TQ	USBLS	5/07
Metals and Plastics	Fargo MSA, ND-MN	Y	26630 FQ	34570 MW	37920 TQ	USBLS	5/07
Metals and Plastics	Ohio	Y	24760 FQ	32120 MW	38770 TQ	USBLS	5/07
Metals and Plastics	Cincinnati-Middletown MSA, OH-KY-IN	Y	22280 FQ	31520 MW	37110 TQ	USBLS	5/07
Metals and Plastics	Cleveland-Elyria-Mentor MSA, OH	Y	24910 FQ	33020 MW	38230 TQ	USBLS	5/07
Metals and Plastics	Columbus MSA, OH	Y	28000 FQ	34020 MW	39010 TQ	USBLS	5/07
Metals and Plastics	Dayton MSA, OH	Y	29450 FQ	36300 MW	44780 TQ	USBLS	5/07
Metals and Plastics	Oklahoma	Y	23220 FQ	29810 MW	36120 TQ	USBLS	5/07
Metals and Plastics	Oklahoma City MSA, OK	Y	21010 FQ	23730 MW	29190 TQ	USBLS	5/07
Metals and Plastics	Tulsa MSA, OK	Y	27230 FQ	32920 MW	38250 TQ	USBLS	5/07
Metals and Plastics	Oregon	H	15.91 FQ	20.03 MW	24.19 TQ	ORBLS	5/08

AE Average entry wage	**AW** Average wage paid	**FQ** First quartile wage	**LO** Lowest wage paid	**MTC** Median total compensation	**TCC** Total cash compensation
AER Average entry range	**AWR** Average wage range	**H** Hourly	**LR** Low end range	**MW** Median wage paid	**TQ** Third quartile wage
AEX Average experienced wage	**AXR** Average experienced range	**HI** Highest wage paid	**M** Monthly	**MWR** Median wage range	**W** Weekly
ATC Average total compensation	**D** Daily	**HR** High end range	**MCC** Median cash compensation	**S** See annotated source	**Y** Yearly

Occupation/Type/Industry	Location	Per	Low	Mid	High	Source	Date
Lathe and Turning Machine Tool Setter, Operator, and Tender							
Metals and Plastics	Portland-Vancouver-Beaverton MSA, OR-WA	Y	32370 FQ	41400 MW	50730 TQ	USBLS	5/07
Metals and Plastics	Pennsylvania	Y	28280 FQ	33680 MW	40370 TQ	USBLS	5/07
Metals and Plastics	Allentown-Bethlehem-Easton MSA, PA-NJ	Y	29450 FQ	35190 MW	42830 TQ	USBLS	5/07
Metals and Plastics	Erie MSA, PA	Y	25070 FQ	29890 MW	34130 TQ	USBLS	5/07
Metals and Plastics	Lancaster MSA, PA	Y	29660 FQ	35190 MW	39910 TQ	USBLS	5/07
Metals and Plastics	Philadelphia-Camden-Wilmington MSA, PA-NJ-DE-MD	Y	32040 FQ	38300 MW	46640 TQ	USBLS	5/07
Metals and Plastics	Pittsburgh MSA, PA	Y	27660 FQ	34130 MW	42580 TQ	USBLS	5/07
Metals and Plastics	Rhode Island	Y	27060 FQ	32530 MW	37950 TQ	USBLS	5/07
Metals and Plastics	Providence-Fall River-Warwick MSA, RI-MA	Y	25430 FQ	31930 MW	37970 TQ	USBLS	5/07
Metals and Plastics	South Carolina	Y	28030 FQ	34730 MW	43420 TQ	USBLS	5/07
Metals and Plastics	Columbia MSA, SC	Y	24720 FQ	29410 MW	34970 TQ	USBLS	5/07
Metals and Plastics	South Dakota	Y	25175 FQ	29120 MW	33974 TQ	SDBLS	7/08-9/08
Metals and Plastics	Tennessee	Y	25500 FQ	30760 MW	36210 TQ	USBLS	5/07
Metals and Plastics	Memphis MSA, TN-MS-AR	Y	23780 FQ	26480 MW	29580 TQ	USBLS	5/07
Metals and Plastics	Nashville-Davidson-Murfreesboro MSA, TN	Y	28260 FQ	32860 MW	39530 TQ	USBLS	5/07
Metals and Plastics	Texas	Y	22010 FQ	27660 MW	35320 TQ	USBLS	5/07
Metals and Plastics	Austin-Round Rock MSA, TX	Y	20230 FQ	23440 MW	29620 TQ	USBLS	5/07
Metals and Plastics	Dallas-Fort Worth-Arlington MSA, TX	Y	22200 FQ	28010 MW	34610 TQ	USBLS	5/07
Metals and Plastics	El Paso MSA, TX	Y	13430 FQ	16360 MW	31280 TQ	USBLS	5/07
Metals and Plastics	Houston-Sugar Land-Baytown MSA, TX	Y	23060 FQ	29300 MW	38610 TQ	USBLS	5/07
Metals and Plastics	San Antonio MSA, TX	Y	22140 FQ	24900 MW	32730 TQ	USBLS	5/07
Metals and Plastics	Utah	Y	22900 FQ	28140 MW	32590 TQ	USBLS	5/07
Metals and Plastics	Salt Lake City MSA, UT	Y	22660 FQ	28190 MW	32750 TQ	USBLS	5/07
Metals and Plastics	Vermont	Y	23830 FQ	28780 MW	34400 TQ	USBLS	5/07
Metals and Plastics	Virginia	Y	24060 FQ	30180 MW	36250 TQ	USBLS	5/07
Metals and Plastics	Virginia Beach-Norfolk-Newport News MSA, VA-NC	Y	23330 FQ	27730 MW	37800 TQ	USBLS	5/07
Metals and Plastics	Washington	H	15.34 FQ	17.93 MW	20.80 TQ	WABLS	3/08
Metals and Plastics	Seattle-Tacoma-Bellevue MSA, WA	Y	32060 FQ	37140 MW	43100 TQ	USBLS	5/07
Metals and Plastics	West Virginia	Y	28592 FQ	33089 MW	39837 TQ	WVBLS	7/08-9/08
Metals and Plastics	Wisconsin	Y	27120 FQ	32580 MW	37840 TQ	USBLS	5/07
Metals and Plastics	Milwaukee-Waukesha-West Allis MSA, WI	Y	27520 FQ	33650 MW	38930 TQ	USBLS	5/07
Metals and Plastics	Wyoming	Y	30505 FQ	37390 MW	46720 TQ	WYBLS	9/08
Metals and Plastics	Puerto Rico	Y	14140 FQ	17150 MW	20830 TQ	USBLS	5/07
Metals and Plastics	San Juan-Caguas-Guaynabo MSA, PR	Y	14140 FQ	17130 MW	20860 TQ	USBLS	5/07
Laundry and Dry-Cleaning Worker							
	Alabama	Y	14050 FQ	16940 MW	19870 TQ	USBLS	5/07
	Birmingham-Hoover MSA, AL	Y	13950 FQ	17080 MW	19750 TQ	USBLS	5/07
	Alaska	Y	19740 FQ	22890 MW	28430 TQ	USBLS	5/07
	Anchorage MSA, AK	Y	20330 FQ	22890 MW	28030 TQ	USBLS	5/07
	Arizona	Y	15910 FQ	18410 MW	22900 TQ	USBLS	5/07
	Phoenix-Mesa-Scottsdale MSA, AZ	Y	16010 FQ	18580 MW	23030 TQ	USBLS	5/07
	Tucson MSA, AZ	Y	15990 FQ	18550 MW	25980 TQ	USBLS	5/07
	Arkansas	Y	14280 FQ	15680 MW	18610 TQ	USBLS	5/07
	Little Rock-North Little Rock MSA, AR	Y	15030 FQ	17150 MW	19970 TQ	USBLS	5/07
	California	H	8.28 FQ	9.36 MW	11.01 TQ	CABLS	1/08-3/08
	Los Angeles-Long Beach-Glendale PMSA, CA	H	8.00 FQ	8.76 MW	9.93 TQ	CABLS	1/08-3/08
	Oakland-Fremont-Hayward MSA, CA	H	9.59 FQ	10.75 MW	11.99 TQ	CABLS	1/08-3/08
	Riverside-San Bernardino-Ontario MSA, CA	H	8.08 FQ	8.79 MW	9.66 TQ	CABLS	1/08-3/08
	Sacramento-Arden Arcade-Roseville MSA, CA	H	8.85 FQ	9.92 MW	11.15 TQ	CABLS	1/08-3/08

AE	Average entry wage	AW	Average wage paid	FQ	First quartile wage
AER	Average entry range	AWR	Average wage range	H	Hourly
AEX	Average experienced wage	AXR	Average experienced range	HI	Highest wage paid
ATC	Average total compensation	D	Daily	HR	High end range

LO	Lowest wage paid	MTC	Median total compensation	TCC	Total cash compensation
LR	Low end range	MW	Median wage paid	TQ	Third quartile wage
M	Monthly	MWR	Median wage range	W	Weekly
MCC	Median cash compensation	S	See annotated source	Y	Yearly

Occupation/Type/Industry	Location	Per	Low	Mid	High	Source	Date
Laundry and Dry-Cleaning Worker	San Diego-Carlsbad-San Marcos MSA, CA	H	8.44 FQ	9.23 MW	10.51 TQ	CABLS	1/08-3/08
	San Francisco-San Mateo-Redwood PMSA, CA	H	9.26 FQ	10.84 MW	13.50 TQ	CABLS	1/08-3/08
	San Jose-Sunnyvale-Santa Clara MSA, CA	H	8.65 FQ	9.88 MW	11.44 TQ	CABLS	1/08-3/08
	Santa Ana-Anaheim-Irvine PMSA, CA	Y	17630 FQ	20100 MW	23000 TQ	USBLS	5/07
	Colorado	Y	17040 FQ	19680 MW	23920 TQ	USBLS	5/07
	Denver-Aurora MSA, CO	Y	17420 FQ	20150 MW	23720 TQ	USBLS	5/07
	Connecticut	H	8.87 AE	11.17 MW		CTBLS	1/08-3/08
	Bridgeport-Stamford-Norwalk MSA, CT	Y	17690 FQ	20780 MW	26970 TQ	USBLS	5/07
	Hartford-West Hartford-East Hartford MSA, CT	Y	19630 FQ	23130 MW	28140 TQ	USBLS	5/07
	Delaware	Y	15300 FQ	18820 MW	25080 TQ	USBLS	5/07
	Wilmington PMSA, DE-MD-NJ	Y	15140 FQ	17960 MW	23500 TQ	USBLS	5/07
	District of Columbia	Y	17240 FQ	22360 MW	29300 TQ	USBLS	5/07
	Washington-Arlington-Alexandria MSA, DC-VA-MD-WV	Y	15360 FQ	18980 MW	24260 TQ	USBLS	5/07
	Florida	Y	15720 FQ	17940 MW	20880 TQ	USBLS	5/07
	Fort Lauderdale-Pompano Beach-Deerfield Beach PMSA, FL	Y	15140 FQ	17190 MW	19740 TQ	USBLS	5/07
	Jacksonville MSA, FL	Y	16220 FQ	18000 MW	20890 TQ	USBLS	5/07
	Miami-Fort Lauderdale-Miami Beach MSA, FL	Y	15290 FQ	17770 MW	21390 TQ	USBLS	5/07
	Orlando-Kissimmee MSA, FL	Y	15490 FQ	17720 MW	20780 TQ	USBLS	5/07
	Pensacola-Ferry Pass-Brent MSA, FL	Y	15440 FQ	16820 MW	18570 TQ	USBLS	5/07
	Tampa-St. Petersburg-Clearwater MSA, FL	Y	15940 FQ	17750 MW	19620 TQ	USBLS	5/07
	West Palm Beach-Boca Raton-Boynton Beach PMSA, FL	Y	15130 FQ	17180 MW	20950 TQ	USBLS	5/07
	Georgia	Y	14630 FQ	17010 MW	19320 TQ	USBLS	5/07
	Atlanta-Sandy Springs-Marietta MSA, GA	Y	15530 FQ	17520 MW	19710 TQ	USBLS	5/07
	Savannah MSA, GA	Y	15460 FQ	17340 MW	19370 TQ	USBLS	5/07
	Hawaii	Y	21510 FQ	26960 MW	30750 TQ	USBLS	5/07
	Honolulu MSA, HI	Y	19820 FQ	25200 MW	29650 TQ	USBLS	5/07
	Idaho	Y	14710 FQ	18110 MW	21490 TQ	USBLS	5/07
	Boise City-Nampa MSA, ID	Y	13610 FQ	16210 MW	19900 TQ	USBLS	5/07
	Illinois	Y	15630 FQ	17750 MW	20280 TQ	USBLS	5/07
	Chicago-Naperville-Joliet MSA, IL-IN-WI	Y	15790 FQ	17850 MW	20580 TQ	USBLS	5/07
	Indiana	Y	16330 FQ	18600 MW	21930 TQ	USBLS	5/07
	Evansville MSA, IN-KY	Y	16280 FQ	18680 MW	22190 TQ	USBLS	5/07
	Gary PMSA, IN	Y	15800 FQ	18000 MW	21100 TQ	USBLS	5/07
	Indianapolis-Carmel MSA, IN	Y	17120 FQ	19210 MW	22460 TQ	USBLS	5/07
	Iowa	Y	16250 FQ	19170 MW	22630 TQ	USBLS	5/07
	Davenport-Moline-Rock Island MSA, IA-IL	Y	15980 FQ	18340 MW	20970 TQ	USBLS	5/07
	Des Moines-West Des Moines MSA, IA	Y	18480 FQ	21020 MW	24220 TQ	USBLS	5/07
	Kansas	Y	15300 FQ	17700 MW	20290 TQ	USBLS	5/07
	Wichita MSA, KS	Y	15220 FQ	17320 MW	19310 TQ	USBLS	5/07
	Kentucky	Y	14848 FQ	17549 MW	19951 TQ	KYBLS	2008
	Elizabethtown MSA, KY	Y	12940 FQ	14980 MW	18950 TQ	USBLS	5/07
	Louisville-Jefferson County MSA, KY-IN	Y	16000 FQ	18340 MW	21020 TQ	USBLS	5/07
	Louisiana	H	6.34 FQ	7.41 MW	9.01 TQ	LABLS	1/08-3/08
	Baton Rouge MSA, LA	Y	13940 FQ	16970 MW	21260 TQ	USBLS	5/07
	New Orleans-Metairie-Kenner MSA, LA	Y	13890 FQ	17090 MW	20670 TQ	USBLS	5/07
	Maine	Y	17470 FQ	19490 MW	22410 TQ	USBLS	5/07
	Portland-South Portland-Biddeford MSA, ME	Y	17950 FQ	20060 MW	23130 TQ	USBLS	5/07
	Maryland	Y		19125 MW		MDBLS	3/08
	Baltimore-Towson MSA, MD	Y	16690 FQ	19310 MW	22750 TQ	USBLS	5/07

AE Average entry wage	**AW** Average wage paid	**FQ** First quartile wage	**LO** Lowest wage paid	**MTC** Median total compensation	**TCC** Total cash compensation
AER Average entry range	**AWR** Average wage range	**H** Hourly	**LR** Low end range	**MW** Median wage paid	**TQ** Third quartile wage
AEX Average experienced wage	**AXR** Average experienced range	**HI** Highest wage paid	**M** Monthly	**MWR** Median wage range	**W** Weekly
ATC Average total compensation	**D** Daily	**HR** High end range	**MCC** Median cash compensation	**S** See annotated source	**Y** Yearly

Occupation/Type/Industry	Location	Per	Low	Mid	High	Source	Date
Laundry and Dry-Cleaning Worker	Bethesda-Gaithersburg-Frederick PMSA, MD	Y	14430 FQ	17560 MW	21660 TQ	USBLS	5/07
	Hagerstown-Martinsburg MSA, MD-WV	Y	20300 FQ	24050 MW	28510 TQ	USBLS	5/07
	Massachusetts	Y	17570 FQ	20200 MW	24310 TQ	USBLS	5/07
	Boston-Cambridge-Quincy NECTA, MA	Y	17560 FQ	20160 MW	25230 TQ	USBLS	5/07
	Worcester MSA, MA-CT	Y	17490 FQ	20540 MW	23880 TQ	USBLS	5/07
	Michigan	Y	17300 FQ	21120 MW	24450 TQ	USBLS	5/07
	Detroit-Warren-Livonia MSA, MI	Y	19080 FQ	21930 MW	24660 TQ	USBLS	5/07
	Flint MSA, MI	Y	17700 FQ	21010 MW	24620 TQ	USBLS	5/07
	Grand Rapids-Wyoming MSA, MI	Y	16580 FQ	21420 MW	25690 TQ	USBLS	5/07
	Lansing-East Lansing MSA, MI	Y	14940 FQ	17520 MW	22250 TQ	USBLS	5/07
	Warren-Troy-Farmington Hills PMSA, MI	Y	18560 FQ	22470 MW	26160 TQ	USBLS	5/07
	Minnesota	Y	21034 FQ	25326 MW	29856 TQ	MNBLS	10/08-12/08
	Duluth-Superior MSA, MN-WI	Y	19924 FQ	23708 MW	29960 TQ	MNBLS	10/08-12/08
	Minneapolis-Saint Paul MSA, MN-WI	Y	23159 FQ	27067 MW	30685 TQ	MNBLS	10/08-12/08
	Rochester MSA, MN	Y	23181 FQ	31282 MW	34801 TQ	MNBLS	10/08-12/08
	Mississippi	Y	13700 FQ	16310 MW	18940 TQ	USBLS	5/07
	Jackson MSA, MS	Y	13780 FQ	16590 MW	19330 TQ	USBLS	5/07
	Missouri	Y	15240 FQ	17630 MW	21080 TQ	USBLS	5/07
	Kansas City MSA, MO-KS	Y	15520 FQ	18430 MW	22160 TQ	USBLS	5/07
	St. Louis MSA, MO-IL	Y	15400 FQ	18180 MW	21710 TQ	USBLS	5/07
	Springfield MSA, MO	Y	14800 FQ	16060 MW	18830 TQ	USBLS	5/07
	Montana	Y	16190 FQ	19240 MW	24250 TQ	USBLS	5/07
	Billings MSA, MT	Y	20140 FQ	23890 MW	28010 TQ	USBLS	5/07
	Nebraska	Y	15300 FQ	17990 MW	21760 TQ	USBLS	5/07
	Omaha-Council Bluffs MSA, NE-IA	Y	16150 FQ	19580 MW	23140 TQ	USBLS	5/07
	Nevada	H	9.80 FQ	10.85 MW	11.96 TQ	NVBLS	5/08
	Las Vegas-Paradise MSA, NV	H	10.19 FQ	11.09 MW	12.10 TQ	NVBLS	5/08
	New Hampshire	H	7.95 AE	10.02 MW	12.37 AEX	NHBLS	6/08
	Manchester MSA, NH	Y	17800 FQ	25010 MW	39970 TQ	USBLS	5/07
	Nashua NECTA, NH-MA	Y	19020 FQ	21120 MW	23370 TQ	USBLS	5/07
	New Jersey	Y	16140 FQ	18850 MW	23470 TQ	USBLS	5/07
	Camden PMSA, NJ	Y	16860 FQ	19640 MW	22750 TQ	USBLS	5/07
	Edison PMSA, NJ	Y	15580 FQ	17990 MW	22660 TQ	USBLS	5/07
	Newark-Union PMSA, NJ-PA	Y	17080 FQ	19440 MW	24650 TQ	USBLS	5/07
	Ocean City MSA, NJ	Y	19750 FQ	21770 MW	25520 TQ	USBLS	5/07
	New Mexico	Y	13750 FQ	16270 MW	18650 TQ	USBLS	5/07
	Albuquerque MSA, NM	Y	13570 FQ	16090 MW	18580 TQ	USBLS	5/07
	New York	Y	16500 FQ	19560 MW	24980 TQ	USBLS	5/07
	Albany-Schenectady-Troy MSA, NY	Y	18170 FQ	21430 MW	25660 TQ	USBLS	5/07
	Binghamton MSA, NY	Y	17890 FQ	20350 MW	24440 TQ	USBLS	5/07
	Buffalo-Niagara Falls MSA, NY	Y	15430 FQ	17560 MW	21990 TQ	USBLS	5/07
	Nassau-Suffolk PMSA, NY	Y	16700 FQ	19170 MW	23400 TQ	USBLS	5/07
	New York-Northern New Jersey-Long Island MSA, NY-NJ-PA	Y	16470 FQ	19490 MW	25330 TQ	USBLS	5/07
	Utica-Rome MSA, NY	Y	15010 FQ	16390 MW	18870 TQ	USBLS	5/07
	North Carolina	Y	14960 FQ	17240 MW	19800 TQ	USBLS	5/07
	Charlotte-Gastonia-Concord MSA, NC-SC	Y	15480 FQ	18050 MW	22150 TQ	USBLS	5/07
	Raleigh-Cary MSA, NC	Y	16440 FQ	19180 MW	21610 TQ	USBLS	5/07
	North Dakota	Y	16710 FQ	18710 MW	21560 TQ	USBLS	5/07
	Fargo MSA, ND-MN	Y	16950 FQ	19140 MW	21840 TQ	USBLS	5/07
	Grand Forks MSA, ND-MN	Y	17490 FQ	19440 MW	22710 TQ	USBLS	5/07
	Ohio	Y	16030 FQ	18670 MW	22230 TQ	USBLS	5/07
	Cincinnati-Middletown MSA, OH-KY-IN	Y	17290 FQ	19740 MW	23290 TQ	USBLS	5/07
	Cleveland-Elyria-Mentor MSA, OH	Y	16720 FQ	19990 MW	23670 TQ	USBLS	5/07
	Columbus MSA, OH	Y	16860 FQ	19550 MW	22570 TQ	USBLS	5/07
	Dayton MSA, OH	Y	16590 FQ	18750 MW	21570 TQ	USBLS	5/07
	Oklahoma	Y	14040 FQ	16660 MW	19330 TQ	USBLS	5/07

AE	Average entry wage	AW	Average wage paid	FQ	First quartile wage
AER	Average entry range	AWR	Average wage range	H	Hourly
AEX	Average experienced wage	AXR	Average experienced range	HI	Highest wage paid
ATC	Average total compensation	D	Daily	HR	High end range

LO	Lowest wage paid	MTC	Median total compensation
LR	Low end range	MW	Median wage paid
M	Monthly	MWR	Median wage range
MCC	Median cash compensation	S	See annotated source

TCC	Total cash compensation		
TQ	Third quartile wage		
W	Weekly		
Y	Yearly		

Occupation/Type/Industry	Location	Per	Low	Mid	High	Source	Date
Laundry and Dry-Cleaning Worker							
	Oklahoma City MSA, OK	Y	15600 FQ	17780 MW	20550 TQ	USBLS	5/07
	Tulsa MSA, OK	Y	14090 FQ	16680 MW	19510 TQ	USBLS	5/07
	Oregon	H	8.68 FQ	9.47 MW	10.97 TQ	ORBLS	5/08
	Portland-Vancouver-Beaverton MSA, OR-WA	Y	18040 FQ	20080 MW	23310 TQ	USBLS	5/07
	Salem MSA, OR	Y	17630 FQ	19040 MW	21620 TQ	USBLS	5/07
	Pennsylvania	Y	16720 FQ	19830 MW	23830 TQ	USBLS	5/07
	Allentown-Bethlehem-Easton MSA, PA-NJ	Y	16880 FQ	20400 MW	23670 TQ	USBLS	5/07
	Philadelphia-Camden-Wilmington MSA, PA-NJ-DE-MD	Y	16280 FQ	19970 MW	24300 TQ	USBLS	5/07
	Pittsburgh MSA, PA	Y	17120 FQ	19510 MW	23120 TQ	USBLS	5/07
	Reading MSA, PA	Y	16260 FQ	20510 MW	23400 TQ	USBLS	5/07
	Rhode Island	Y	17140 FQ	19760 MW	24940 TQ	USBLS	5/07
	Providence-Fall River-Warwick MSA, RI-MA	Y	17150 FQ	19570 MW	24510 TQ	USBLS	5/07
	South Carolina	Y	14860 FQ	17300 MW	19320 TQ	USBLS	5/07
	Charleston-North Charleston MSA, SC	Y	16090 FQ	18400 MW	20780 TQ	USBLS	5/07
	Columbia MSA, SC	Y	15450 FQ	17550 MW	19670 TQ	USBLS	5/07
	Spartanburg MSA, SC	Y	17030 FQ	18160 MW	19280 TQ	USBLS	5/07
	South Dakota	Y	17042 FQ	19148 MW	22115 TQ	SDBLS	7/08-9/08
	Sioux Falls MSA, SD	Y	18116 FQ	21165 MW	24338 TQ	SDBLS	7/08-9/08
	Tennessee	Y	15360 FQ	17750 MW	20360 TQ	USBLS	5/07
	Memphis MSA, TN-MS-AR	Y	15360 FQ	17650 MW	20700 TQ	USBLS	5/07
	Nashville-Davidson-Murfreesboro MSA, TN	Y	15130 FQ	17650 MW	20040 TQ	USBLS	5/07
	Texas	Y	13330 FQ	15630 MW	18550 TQ	USBLS	5/07
	Austin-Round Rock MSA, TX	Y	14750 FQ	16830 MW	18830 TQ	USBLS	5/07
	Brownsville-Harlingen MSA, TX	Y	12770 FQ	14360 MW	17060 TQ	USBLS	5/07
	Dallas-Fort Worth-Arlington MSA, TX	Y	13870 FQ	16430 MW	19640 TQ	USBLS	5/07
	El Paso MSA, TX	Y	12240 FQ	13470 MW	14710 TQ	USBLS	5/07
	Houston-Sugar Land-Baytown MSA, TX	Y	13330 FQ	15700 MW	18560 TQ	USBLS	5/07
	San Antonio MSA, TX	Y	13400 FQ	15960 MW	18910 TQ	USBLS	5/07
	Utah	Y	15900 FQ	17780 MW	19680 TQ	USBLS	5/07
	Ogden-Clearfield MSA, UT	Y	12670 FQ	14380 MW	16710 TQ	USBLS	5/07
	Salt Lake City MSA, UT	Y	16560 FQ	18120 MW	19720 TQ	USBLS	5/07
	Vermont	Y	16660 FQ	18860 MW	22160 TQ	USBLS	5/07
	Burlington-South Burlington MSA, VT	Y	16800 FQ	20110 MW	25210 TQ	USBLS	5/07
	Virginia	Y	15790 FQ	18480 MW	22100 TQ	USBLS	5/07
	Charlottesville MSA, VA	Y	17160 FQ	19220 MW	21990 TQ	USBLS	5/07
	Richmond MSA, VA	Y	16370 FQ	18440 MW	21580 TQ	USBLS	5/07
	Roanoke MSA, VA	Y	16080 FQ	18520 MW	22430 TQ	USBLS	5/07
	Virginia Beach-Norfolk-Newport News MSA, VA-NC	Y	15550 FQ	18400 MW	22070 TQ	USBLS	5/07
	Washington	H	8.90 FQ	10.20 MW	12.22 TQ	WABLS	3/08
	Seattle-Tacoma-Bellevue MSA, WA	Y	18780 FQ	21750 MW	25600 TQ	USBLS	5/07
	West Virginia	Y	15086 FQ	17855 MW	21756 TQ	WVBLS	7/08-9/08
	Charleston MSA, WV	Y	14530 FQ	16730 MW	19120 TQ	USBLS	5/07
	Wisconsin	Y	17030 FQ	20010 MW	23700 TQ	USBLS	5/07
	Appleton MSA, WI	Y	17320 FQ	19470 MW	23900 TQ	USBLS	5/07
	Milwaukee-Waukesha-West Allis MSA, WI	Y	16320 FQ	19600 MW	24090 TQ	USBLS	5/07
	Wyoming	Y	16937 FQ	19058 MW	22005 TQ	WYBLS	9/08
	Cheyenne MSA, WY	Y	16210 FQ	18765 MW	22201 TQ	WYBLS	9/08
	Puerto Rico	Y	12560 FQ	14140 MW	16550 TQ	USBLS	5/07
	San Juan-Caguas-Guaynabo MSA, PR	Y	12610 FQ	14280 MW	17120 TQ	USBLS	5/07
	Virgin Islands	Y	14740 FQ	16780 MW	19140 TQ	USBLS	5/07
	Guam	Y	12220 FQ	13490 MW	14780 TQ	USBLS	5/07
Laundry Foreman Department of Health and Human Services, Juvenile Justice Services	New Hampshire	Y			35448 HI	NHUL03	2008

AE Average entry wage	**AW** Average wage paid	**FQ** First quartile wage	**LO** Lowest wage paid	**MTC** Median total compensation	**TCC** Total cash compensation
AER Average entry range	**AWR** Average wage range	**H** Hourly	**LR** Low end range	**MW** Median wage paid	**TQ** Third quartile wage
AEX Average experienced wage	**AXR** Average experienced range	**HI** Highest wage paid	**M** Monthly	**MWR** Median wage range	**W** Weekly
ATC Average total compensation	**D** Daily	**HR** High end range	**MCC** Median cash compensation	**S** See annotated source	**Y** Yearly

Occupation/Type/Industry	Location	Per	Low	Mid	High	Source	Date
Law Clerk	Alabama	Y	27160 FQ	31430 MW	44090 TQ	USBLS	5/07
	Birmingham-Hoover MSA, AL	Y	29180 FQ	32350 MW	45720 TQ	USBLS	5/07
	Arizona	Y	31330 FQ	38710 MW	49840 TQ	USBLS	5/07
	Phoenix-Mesa-Scottsdale MSA, AZ	Y	32110 FQ	41070 MW	52650 TQ	USBLS	5/07
	Tucson MSA, AZ	Y	29910 FQ	35460 MW	42070 TQ	USBLS	5/07
	Arkansas	Y	20620 FQ	25230 MW	35550 TQ	USBLS	5/07
	Little Rock-North Little Rock MSA, AR	Y	22670 FQ	35540 MW	45080 TQ	USBLS	5/07
	California	H	16.00 FQ	18.71 MW	25.63 TQ	CABLS	1/08-3/08
	Los Angeles-Long Beach-Glendale PMSA, CA	H	16.75 FQ	21.82 MW	30.93 TQ	CABLS	1/08-3/08
	Oakland-Fremont-Hayward MSA, CA	H	24.60 FQ	27.28 MW	29.83 TQ	CABLS	1/08-3/08
	Sacramento-Arden Arcade-Roseville MSA, CA	H	15.01 FQ	18.36 MW	23.83 TQ	CABLS	1/08-3/08
	San Diego-Carlsbad-San Marcos MSA, CA	H	14.00 FQ	16.40 MW	18.54 TQ	CABLS	1/08-3/08
	San Francisco-San Mateo-Redwood PMSA, CA	H	22.37 FQ	27.71 MW	31.92 TQ	CABLS	1/08-3/08
	San Jose-Sunnyvale-Santa Clara MSA, CA	H	18.59 FQ	23.28 MW	29.27 TQ	CABLS	1/08-3/08
	Santa Ana-Anaheim-Irvine PMSA, CA	Y	35000 FQ	38400 MW	42220 TQ	USBLS	5/07
	Colorado	Y	30520 FQ	39180 MW	45390 TQ	USBLS	5/07
	Denver-Aurora MSA, CO	Y	29990 FQ	39530 MW	45810 TQ	USBLS	5/07
	Connecticut	H	16.15 AE	23.62 MW		CTBLS	1/08-3/08
	Bridgeport-Stamford-Norwalk MSA, CT	Y	26200 FQ	29810 MW	45080 TQ	USBLS	5/07
	Hartford-West Hartford-East Hartford MSA, CT	Y	45000 FQ	57290 MW	66470 TQ	USBLS	5/07
	Delaware	Y	34200 FQ	38560 MW	49930 TQ	USBLS	5/07
	Wilmington PMSA, DE-MD-NJ	Y	34640 FQ	39830 MW	51440 TQ	USBLS	5/07
	District of Columbia	Y	46310 FQ	59110 MW	74910 TQ	USBLS	5/07
	Washington-Arlington-Alexandria MSA, DC-VA-MD-WV	Y	32990 FQ	44950 MW	61400 TQ	USBLS	5/07
	Florida	Y	28450 FQ	36600 MW	46730 TQ	USBLS	5/07
	Fort Lauderdale-Pompano Beach-Deerfield Beach PMSA, FL	Y	26640 FQ	37870 MW	47120 TQ	USBLS	5/07
	Jacksonville MSA, FL	Y	27260 FQ	30320 MW	33480 TQ	USBLS	5/07
	Miami-Fort Lauderdale-Miami Beach MSA, FL	Y	30200 FQ	37350 MW	48940 TQ	USBLS	5/07
	Orlando-Kissimmee MSA, FL	Y	28290 FQ	31420 MW	37030 TQ	USBLS	5/07
	Tallahassee MSA, FL	Y	28090 FQ	34820 MW	39290 TQ	USBLS	5/07
	Tampa-St. Petersburg-Clearwater MSA, FL	Y	29330 FQ	41780 MW	48110 TQ	USBLS	5/07
	West Palm Beach-Boca Raton-Boynton Beach PMSA, FL	Y	32220 FQ	42900 MW	48540 TQ	USBLS	5/07
	Georgia	Y	21610 FQ	39460 MW	51150 TQ	USBLS	5/07
	Athens-Clarke County MSA, GA	Y	17440 FQ	19410 MW	24470 TQ	USBLS	5/07
	Atlanta-Sandy Springs-Marietta MSA, GA	Y	23170 FQ	44680 MW	55180 TQ	USBLS	5/07
	Hawaii	Y	42980 FQ	47970 MW	54290 TQ	USBLS	5/07
	Idaho	Y	30800 FQ	37050 MW	47060 TQ	USBLS	5/07
	Illinois	Y	29870 FQ	40590 MW	49810 TQ	USBLS	5/07
	Chicago-Naperville-Joliet MSA, IL-IN-WI	Y	30940 FQ	41270 MW	49590 TQ	USBLS	5/07
	Indiana	Y	26920 FQ	32070 MW	52000 TQ	USBLS	5/07
	Gary PMSA, IN	Y	28550 FQ	32780 MW	37770 TQ	USBLS	5/07
	Indianapolis-Carmel MSA, IN	Y	27670 FQ	37240 MW	58950 TQ	USBLS	5/07
	Iowa	Y	24740 FQ	28320 MW	35790 TQ	USBLS	5/07
	Des Moines-West Des Moines MSA, IA	Y	24360 FQ	27060 MW	37530 TQ	USBLS	5/07
	Kansas	Y	21670 FQ	27140 MW	35110 TQ	USBLS	5/07
	Kentucky	Y	25362 FQ	30305 MW	38351 TQ	KYBLS	2008
	Louisville-Jefferson County MSA, KY-IN	Y	28200 FQ	33610 MW	52710 TQ	USBLS	5/07
	Louisiana	H	9.78 FQ	15.52 MW	20.67 TQ	LABLS	1/08-3/08

AE	Average entry wage	AW	Average wage paid	FQ	First quartile wage	LO	Lowest wage paid	MTC	Median total compensation	TCC	Total cash compensation
AER	Average entry range	AWR	Average wage range	H	Hourly	LR	Low end range	MW	Median wage paid	TQ	Third quartile wage
AEX	Average experienced wage	AXR	Average experienced range	HI	Highest wage paid	M	Monthly	MWR	Median wage range	W	Weekly
ATC	Average total compensation	D	Daily	HR	High end range	MCC	Median cash compensation	S	See annotated source	Y	Yearly

Law Clerk

Occupation/Type/Industry	Location	Per	Low	Mid	High	Source	Date
Law Clerk	Baton Rouge MSA, LA	Y	18730 FQ	29670 MW	35590 TQ	USBLS	5/07
	New Orleans-Metairie-Kenner MSA, LA	Y	24970 FQ	38820 MW	46640 TQ	USBLS	5/07
	Maine	Y	36650 FQ	43930 MW	49260 TQ	USBLS	5/07
	Maryland	Y		47850 MW		MDBLS	3/08
	Baltimore-Towson MSA, MD	Y	36500 FQ	47150 MW	60640 TQ	USBLS	5/07
	Bethesda-Gaithersburg-Frederick PMSA, MD	Y	27750 FQ	34030 MW	47530 TQ	USBLS	5/07
	Massachusetts	Y	43060 FQ	47650 MW	52610 TQ	USBLS	5/07
	Boston-Cambridge-Quincy NECTA, MA	Y	43850 FQ	48290 MW	52830 TQ	USBLS	5/07
	Michigan	Y	31310 FQ	39630 MW	48480 TQ	USBLS	5/07
	Detroit-Warren-Livonia MSA, MI	Y	31220 FQ	38270 MW	48020 TQ	USBLS	5/07
	Warren-Troy-Farmington Hills PMSA, MI	Y	29490 FQ	32890 MW	37510 TQ	USBLS	5/07
	Minnesota	Y	36806 FQ	45908 MW	51254 TQ	MNBLS	10/08-12/08
	Minneapolis-Saint Paul MSA, MN-WI	Y	34535 FQ	44652 MW	51129 TQ	MNBLS	10/08-12/08
	Mississippi	Y	20540 FQ	25700 MW	32800 TQ	USBLS	5/07
	Jackson MSA, MS	Y	28950 FQ	36260 MW	68870 TQ	USBLS	5/07
	Missouri	Y	20230 FQ	24480 MW	33970 TQ	USBLS	5/07
	Kansas City MSA, MO-KS	Y	21580 FQ	29280 MW	41200 TQ	USBLS	5/07
	St. Louis MSA, MO-IL	Y	29680 FQ	37960 MW	48890 TQ	USBLS	5/07
	Montana	Y	34010 FQ	39060 MW	47420 TQ	USBLS	5/07
	Nebraska	Y	26300 FQ	34990 MW	46940 TQ	USBLS	5/07
	Omaha-Council Bluffs MSA, NE-IA	Y	25470 FQ	34640 MW	45360 TQ	USBLS	5/07
	Nevada	H	20.22 FQ	24.12 MW	28.98 TQ	NVBLS	5/08
	Las Vegas-Paradise MSA, NV	H	20.16 FQ	23.53 MW	28.23 TQ	NVBLS	5/08
	New Jersey	Y	33450 FQ	38220 MW	46290 TQ	USBLS	5/07
	Camden PMSA, NJ	Y	32760 FQ	37000 MW	42040 TQ	USBLS	5/07
	Edison PMSA, NJ	Y	35040 FQ	38690 MW	45500 TQ	USBLS	5/07
	Newark-Union PMSA, NJ-PA	Y	34270 FQ	39730 MW	50450 TQ	USBLS	5/07
	New Mexico	Y	28950 FQ	36390 MW	53740 TQ	USBLS	5/07
	Albuquerque MSA, NM	Y	27660 FQ	30620 MW	47770 TQ	USBLS	5/07
	New York	Y	30990 FQ	37830 MW	49810 TQ	USBLS	5/07
	Albany-Schenectady-Troy MSA, NY	Y	25620 FQ	31080 MW	44920 TQ	USBLS	5/07
	Buffalo-Niagara Falls MSA, NY	Y	30250 FQ	35930 MW	42320 TQ	USBLS	5/07
	Nassau-Suffolk PMSA, NY	Y	22570 FQ	31730 MW	36210 TQ	USBLS	5/07
	New York-Northern New Jersey-Long Island MSA, NY-NJ-PA	Y	33190 FQ	39070 MW	50750 TQ	USBLS	5/07
	North Carolina	Y	23410 FQ	40150 MW	49000 TQ	USBLS	5/07
	Charlotte-Gastonia-Concord MSA, NC-SC	Y	41090 FQ	47130 MW	66940 TQ	USBLS	5/07
	Raleigh-Cary MSA, NC	Y	23490 FQ	35590 MW	48030 TQ	USBLS	5/07
	North Dakota	Y	32700 FQ	38320 MW	45690 TQ	USBLS	5/07
	Ohio	Y	26140 FQ	31050 MW	38990 TQ	USBLS	5/07
	Cincinnati-Middletown MSA, OH-KY-IN	Y	26270 FQ	30220 MW	37110 TQ	USBLS	5/07
	Cleveland-Elyria-Mentor MSA, OH	Y	27740 FQ	33530 MW	43740 TQ	USBLS	5/07
	Columbus MSA, OH	Y	26300 FQ	31460 MW	37390 TQ	USBLS	5/07
	Dayton MSA, OH	Y	27890 FQ	30520 MW	35100 TQ	USBLS	5/07
	Oklahoma	Y	27170 FQ	33950 MW	45130 TQ	USBLS	5/07
	Oklahoma City MSA, OK	Y	25070 FQ	37510 MW	56530 TQ	USBLS	5/07
	Tulsa MSA, OK	Y	29790 FQ	33760 MW	37620 TQ	USBLS	5/07
	Oregon	H	15.69 FQ	20.55 MW	26.13 TQ	ORBLS	5/08
	Portland-Vancouver-Beaverton MSA, OR-WA	Y	31440 FQ	36980 MW	56350 TQ	USBLS	5/07
	Pennsylvania	Y	29500 FQ	37970 MW	48250 TQ	USBLS	5/07
	Allentown-Bethlehem-Easton MSA, PA-NJ	Y	30910 FQ	36770 MW	41720 TQ	USBLS	5/07
	Philadelphia-Camden-Wilmington MSA, PA-NJ-DE-MD	Y	35450 FQ	44500 MW	53590 TQ	USBLS	5/07
	Pittsburgh MSA, PA	Y	25620 FQ	31000 MW	41930 TQ	USBLS	5/07
	Rhode Island	Y	51080 FQ	59460 MW	70310 TQ	USBLS	5/07

AE Average entry wage	**AW** Average wage paid	**FQ** First quartile wage	**LO** Lowest wage paid	**MTC** Median total compensation	**TCC** Total cash compensation
AER Average entry range	**AWR** Average wage range	**H** Hourly	**LR** Low end range	**MW** Median wage paid	**TQ** Third quartile wage
AEX Average experienced wage	**AXR** Average experienced range	**HI** Highest wage paid	**M** Monthly	**MWR** Median wage range	**W** Weekly
ATC Average total compensation	**D** Daily	**HR** High end range	**MCC** Median cash compensation	**S** See annotated source	**Y** Yearly

Occupation/Type/Industry	Location	Per	Low	Mid	High	Source	Date
Law Clerk	Providence-Fall River-Warwick MSA, RI-MA	Y	49260 FQ	58710 MW	68960 TQ	USBLS	5/07
	South Carolina	Y	26530 FQ	31040 MW	45670 TQ	USBLS	5/07
	Charleston-North Charleston MSA, SC	Y	29860 FQ	46790 MW	60560 TQ	USBLS	5/07
	Columbia MSA, SC	Y	27200 FQ	32610 MW	46170 TQ	USBLS	5/07
	Tennessee	Y	14890 FQ	21940 MW	28670 TQ	USBLS	5/07
	Memphis MSA, TN-MS-AR	Y	13460 FQ	18000 MW	23560 TQ	USBLS	5/07
	Texas	Y	26770 FQ	34220 MW	45680 TQ	USBLS	5/07
	Austin-Round Rock MSA, TX	Y	28400 FQ	39830 MW	47440 TQ	USBLS	5/07
	Dallas-Fort Worth-Arlington MSA, TX	Y	28300 FQ	33360 MW	43190 TQ	USBLS	5/07
	Houston-Sugar Land-Baytown MSA, TX	Y	28340 FQ	38900 MW	51640 TQ	USBLS	5/07
	San Antonio MSA, TX	Y	30890 FQ	35460 MW	55300 TQ	USBLS	5/07
	Utah	Y	26540 FQ	36370 MW	44800 TQ	USBLS	5/07
	Salt Lake City MSA, UT	Y	31160 FQ	42310 MW	49190 TQ	USBLS	5/07
	Virginia	Y	28940 FQ	34530 MW	44740 TQ	USBLS	5/07
	Richmond MSA, VA	Y	26830 FQ	29720 MW	33860 TQ	USBLS	5/07
	Virginia Beach-Norfolk-Newport News MSA, VA-NC	Y	31760 FQ	39230 MW	46990 TQ	USBLS	5/07
	Washington	H	16.49 FQ	21.92 MW	26.05 TQ	WABLS	3/08
	Seattle-Tacoma-Bellevue MSA, WA	Y	42230 FQ	48380 MW	60800 TQ	USBLS	5/07
	Spokane MSA, WA	Y	27100 FQ	29730 MW	38500 TQ	USBLS	5/07
	West Virginia	Y	28172 FQ	32004 MW	45684 TQ	WVBLS	7/08-9/08
	Wisconsin	Y	31790 FQ	37600 MW	53000 TQ	USBLS	5/07
	Milwaukee-Waukesha-West Allis MSA, WI	Y	32160 FQ	42500 MW	58490 TQ	USBLS	5/07
	Racine MSA, WI	Y	28970 FQ	33430 MW	36700 TQ	USBLS	5/07
	Wyoming	Y	20803 FQ	30378 MW	39496 TQ	WYBLS	9/08
	Puerto Rico	Y	26000 FQ	30990 MW	40820 TQ	USBLS	5/07
	San Juan-Caguas-Guaynabo MSA, PR	Y	24470 FQ	29820 MW	35310 TQ	USBLS	5/07
Law Enforcement Instructor	Cincinnati, OH	Y	44936 LO		48365 HI	COHSS	10/08
Law Enforcement Training Specialist							
Police Standards and Training Council	New Hampshire	Y		64788 AW		NHUL03	2008
Law Firm Recruitment Coordinator	Bay Area, CA	Y		57800-72818 AW		BALRA	10/07
Law Revision Counsel							
United States House of Representatives	United States	Y			167800 HI	CRS01	1/08
Law School Dean	United States	Y		430000 AW		NYT06	2006
Law Teacher							
Postsecondary	Alabama	Y	59930 FQ	92480 MW	123430 TQ	USBLS	5/07
Postsecondary	California	Y		92610 AW		CABLS	1/08-3/08
Postsecondary	Los Angeles-Long Beach-Glendale PMSA, CA	Y		100158 AW		CABLS	1/08-3/08
Postsecondary	San Diego-Carlsbad-San Marcos MSA, CA	Y		105736 AW		CABLS	1/08-3/08
Postsecondary	Santa Ana-Anaheim-Irvine PMSA, CA	Y	74610 FQ	94080 MW	112720 TQ	USBLS	5/07
Postsecondary	Colorado	Y	73070 FQ	103760 MW	131560 TQ	USBLS	5/07
Postsecondary	Hartford-West Hartford-East Hartford MSA, CT	Y	68200 FQ	123710 MW		USBLS	5/07
Postsecondary	District of Columbia	Y	68750 FQ	94930 MW	127200 TQ	USBLS	5/07
Postsecondary	Washington-Arlington-Alexandria MSA, DC-VA-MD-WV	Y	66160 FQ	93330 MW	126950 TQ	USBLS	5/07
Postsecondary	Florida	Y	70850 FQ	97660 MW	134080 TQ	USBLS	5/07
Postsecondary	Jacksonville MSA, FL	Y	65210 FQ	88040 MW	98610 TQ	USBLS	5/07
Postsecondary	Miami-Fort Lauderdale-Miami Beach MSA, FL	Y	63500 FQ	78700 MW	101140 TQ	USBLS	5/07
Postsecondary	Tampa-St. Petersburg-Clearwater MSA, FL	Y	95560 FQ	137010 MW		USBLS	5/07

AE Average entry wage	**AW** Average wage paid	**FQ** First quartile wage	**LO** Lowest wage paid	**MTC** Median total compensation	**TCC** Total cash compensation
AER Average entry range	**AWR** Average wage range	**H** Hourly	**LR** Low end range	**MW** Median wage paid	**TQ** Third quartile wage
AEX Average experienced wage	**AXR** Average experienced range	**HI** Highest wage paid	**M** Monthly	**MWR** Median wage range	**W** Weekly
ATC Average total compensation **D** Daily		**HR** High end range	**MCC** Median cash compensation	**S** See annotated source	**Y** Yearly

Occupation/Type/Industry	Location	Per	Low	Mid	High	Source	Date
Law Teacher							
Postsecondary	Georgia	Y	64420 FQ	102720 MW		USBLS	5/07
Postsecondary	Atlanta-Sandy Springs-Marietta MSA, GA	Y	63370 FQ	99040 MW		USBLS	5/07
Postsecondary	Illinois	Y	59400 FQ	100660 MW	136190 TQ	USBLS	5/07
Postsecondary	Chicago-Naperville-Joliet MSA, IL-IN-WI	Y	68880 FQ	105680 MW	136980 TQ	USBLS	5/07
Postsecondary	Indiana	Y	62340 FQ	92190 MW	125300 TQ	USBLS	5/07
Postsecondary	Kansas	Y	30440 FQ	84310 MW	121680 TQ	USBLS	5/07
Postsecondary	Kentucky	Y	49837 FQ	93625 MW	129576 TQ	KYBLS	2008
Postsecondary	Louisiana	Y		119955 AW		LABLS	1/08-3/08
Postsecondary	Maryland	Y		115850 MW		MDBLS	3/08
Postsecondary	Baltimore-Towson MSA, MD	Y	81010 FQ	117890 MW		USBLS	5/07
Postsecondary	Massachusetts	Y	45860 FQ	79190 MW	134140 TQ	USBLS	5/07
Postsecondary	Boston-Cambridge-Quincy NECTA, MA	Y	44340 FQ	88650 MW	140450 TQ	USBLS	5/07
Postsecondary	Michigan	Y	31780 FQ	88170 MW	113480 TQ	USBLS	5/07
Postsecondary	Detroit-Warren-Livonia MSA, MI	Y	31360 FQ	92610 MW	121440 TQ	USBLS	5/07
Postsecondary	Minnesota	Y	74386 FQ	103356 MW	131039 TQ	MNBLS	10/08-12/08
Postsecondary	Minneapolis-Saint Paul MSA, MN-WI	Y	79178 FQ	104392 MW	128874 TQ	MNBLS	10/08-12/08
Postsecondary	Mississippi	Y	57330 FQ	84190 MW	114010 TQ	USBLS	5/07
Postsecondary	Missouri	Y	69200 FQ	86360 MW	112630 TQ	USBLS	5/07
Postsecondary	St. Louis MSA, MO-IL	Y	68430 FQ	81740 MW	101980 TQ	USBLS	5/07
Postsecondary	New Jersey	Y	66540 FQ	103290 MW	140880 TQ	USBLS	5/07
Postsecondary	Newark-Union PMSA, NJ-PA	Y	73090 FQ	109280 MW		USBLS	5/07
Postsecondary	New York	Y	48870 FQ	83030 MW	119210 TQ	USBLS	5/07
Postsecondary	New York-Northern New Jersey-Long Island MSA, NY-NJ-PA	Y	54410 FQ	86830 MW	127090 TQ	USBLS	5/07
Postsecondary	North Carolina	Y	50910 FQ	85270 MW	141740 TQ	USBLS	5/07
Postsecondary	North Dakota	Y	90940 FQ	116930 MW		USBLS	5/07
Postsecondary	Ohio	Y	51900 FQ	88100 MW	130230 TQ	USBLS	5/07
Postsecondary	Cincinnati-Middletown MSA, OH-KY-IN	Y	45890 FQ	86500 MW	127170 TQ	USBLS	5/07
Postsecondary	Cleveland-Elyria-Mentor MSA, OH	Y	48070 FQ	83770 MW	123230 TQ	USBLS	5/07
Postsecondary	Dayton MSA, OH	Y	31200 FQ	72810 MW	122380 TQ	USBLS	5/07
Postsecondary	Oklahoma	Y	27600 FQ	76080 MW	111700 TQ	USBLS	5/07
Postsecondary	Portland-Vancouver-Beaverton MSA, OR-WA	Y	77480 FQ	95590 MW	118680 TQ	USBLS	5/07
Postsecondary	Pennsylvania	Y	52420 FQ	67230 MW	82720 TQ	USBLS	5/07
Postsecondary	Philadelphia-Camden-Wilmington MSA, PA-NJ-DE-MD	Y	63120 FQ	84890 MW	123520 TQ	USBLS	5/07
Postsecondary	South Carolina	Y	43170 FQ	47770 MW	89070 TQ	USBLS	5/07
Postsecondary	Charleston-North Charleston MSA, SC	Y	42130 FQ	45710 MW	77620 TQ	USBLS	5/07
Postsecondary	Tennessee	Y	49390 FQ	85050 MW	114080 TQ	USBLS	5/07
Postsecondary	Nashville-Davidson-Murfreesboro MSA, TN	Y	48310 FQ	76760 MW	92490 TQ	USBLS	5/07
Postsecondary	Texas	Y	56620 FQ	95330 MW	129120 TQ	USBLS	5/07
Postsecondary	Houston-Sugar Land-Baytown MSA, TX	Y	30420 FQ	68240 MW	116360 TQ	USBLS	5/07
Postsecondary	Virginia	Y	43560 FQ	67110 MW	118050 TQ	USBLS	5/07
Postsecondary	Washington	Y		97566 AW		WABLS	3/08
Postsecondary	Wisconsin	Y	58770 FQ	87140 MW	119170 TQ	USBLS	5/07
Postsecondary	Puerto Rico	Y	55770 FQ	64630 MW	75410 TQ	USBLS	5/07
Postsecondary	San Juan-Caguas-Guaynabo MSA, PR	Y	58700 FQ	69750 MW	81350 TQ	USBLS	5/07
Lawyer	Alabama	Y	68340 FQ	92840 MW	133100 TQ	USBLS	5/07
	Birmingham-Hoover MSA, AL	Y	70380 FQ	95140 MW	144170 TQ	USBLS	5/07
	Mobile MSA, AL	Y	69760 FQ	91720 MW	140860 TQ	USBLS	5/07
	Alaska	Y	73570 FQ	91630 MW	111910 TQ	USBLS	5/07
	Anchorage MSA, AK	Y	72710 FQ	90590 MW	110710 TQ	USBLS	5/07
	Arizona	Y	74860 FQ	101070 MW	142210 TQ	USBLS	5/07
	Phoenix-Mesa-Scottsdale MSA, AZ	Y	82100 FQ	107330 MW		USBLS	5/07
	Prescott MSA, AZ	Y	48780 FQ	68860 MW	90730 TQ	USBLS	5/07
	Tucson MSA, AZ	Y	67020 FQ	92470 MW	132140 TQ	USBLS	5/07

AE	Average entry wage	AW	Average wage paid	FQ	First quartile wage
AER	Average entry range	AWR	Average wage range	H	Hourly
AEX	Average experienced wage	AXR	Average experienced range	HI	Highest wage paid
ATC	Average total compensation	D	Daily	HR	High end range

LO Lowest wage paid   MTC Median total compensation   TCC Total cash compensation
LR Low end range   MW Median wage paid   TQ Third quartile wage
M Monthly   MWR Median wage range   W Weekly
MCC Median cash compensation   S See annotated source   Y Yearly

Occupation/Type/Industry	Location	Per	Low	Mid	High	Source	Date
Lawyer	Yuma MSA, AZ	Y	47260 FQ	64180 MW	91340 TQ	USBLS	5/07
	Arkansas	Y	48100 FQ	63610 MW	104490 TQ	USBLS	5/07
	Little Rock-North Little Rock MSA, AR	Y	53730 FQ	74410 MW	120910 TQ	USBLS	5/07
	California	H	46.14 FQ	63.19 MW		CABLS	1/08-3/08
	Los Angeles-Long Beach-Glendale PMSA, CA	H	46.85 FQ	64.75 MW		CABLS	1/08-3/08
	Oakland-Fremont-Hayward MSA, CA	H	42.01 FQ	57.98 MW		CABLS	1/08-3/08
	Oxnard-Thousand Oaks-Ventura MSA, CA	H	48.30 FQ	62.06 MW		CABLS	1/08-3/08
	Riverside-San Bernardino-Ontario MSA, CA	H	41.35 FQ	54.73 MW	66.93 TQ	CABLS	1/08-3/08
	Sacramento-Arden Arcade-Roseville MSA, CA	H	39.93 FQ	51.20 MW	62.25 TQ	CABLS	1/08-3/08
	San Diego-Carlsbad-San Marcos MSA, CA	H	40.54 FQ	61.76 MW		CABLS	1/08-3/08
	San Francisco-San Mateo-Redwood PMSA, CA	H	54.28 FQ			CABLS	1/08-3/08
	San Jose-Sunnyvale-Santa Clara MSA, CA	H	64.44 FQ			CABLS	1/08-3/08
	Santa Ana-Anaheim-Irvine PMSA, CA	Y	101000 FQ	131430 MW		USBLS	5/07
	Colorado	Y	67450 FQ	98060 MW	140220 TQ	USBLS	5/07
	Denver-Aurora MSA, CO	Y	72630 FQ	104160 MW		USBLS	5/07
	Fort Collins-Loveland MSA, CO	Y	62590 FQ	84390 MW	113120 TQ	USBLS	5/07
	Pueblo MSA, CO	Y	55740 FQ	74990 MW	104640 TQ	USBLS	5/07
	Connecticut	H	31.95 AE	53.06 MW		CTBLS	1/08-3/08
	Bridgeport-Stamford-Norwalk MSA, CT	Y	66870 FQ	100030 MW		USBLS	5/07
	Hartford-West Hartford-East Hartford MSA, CT	Y	88020 FQ	114780 MW		USBLS	5/07
	Delaware	Y	86240 FQ	128720 MW		USBLS	5/07
	Wilmington PMSA, DE-MD-NJ	Y	91020 FQ	133550 MW		USBLS	5/07
	District of Columbia	Y	107460 FQ	140240 MW		USBLS	5/07
	Washington-Arlington-Alexandria MSA, DC-VA-MD-WV	Y	96950 FQ	134560 MW		USBLS	5/07
	Florida	Y	58710 FQ	89680 MW	144330 TQ	USBLS	5/07
	Fort Lauderdale-Pompano Beach-Deerfield Beach PMSA, FL	Y	54600 FQ	87250 MW		USBLS	5/07
	Jacksonville MSA, FL	Y	62220 FQ	85200 MW	128260 TQ	USBLS	5/07
	Miami-Fort Lauderdale-Miami Beach MSA, FL	Y	56010 FQ	90350 MW		USBLS	5/07
	Orlando-Kissimmee MSA, FL	Y	73250 FQ	104200 MW		USBLS	5/07
	Tampa-St. Petersburg-Clearwater MSA, FL	Y	66250 FQ	95800 MW		USBLS	5/07
	West Palm Beach-Boca Raton-Boynton Beach PMSA, FL	Y	29700 FQ	81630 MW		USBLS	5/07
	Georgia	Y	77040 FQ	117200 MW		USBLS	5/07
	Atlanta-Sandy Springs-Marietta MSA, GA	Y	85140 FQ	128170 MW		USBLS	5/07
	Hawaii	Y	68230 FQ	85010 MW	106990 TQ	USBLS	5/07
	Honolulu MSA, HI	Y	69060 FQ	87120 MW	110380 TQ	USBLS	5/07
	Idaho	Y	52180 FQ	79360 MW	116820 TQ	USBLS	5/07
	Boise City-Nampa MSA, ID	Y	69930 FQ	98120 MW	139570 TQ	USBLS	5/07
	Illinois	Y	75230 FQ	116120 MW		USBLS	5/07
	Chicago-Naperville-Joliet MSA, IL-IN-WI	Y	76930 FQ	118290 MW		USBLS	5/07
	Indiana	Y	51140 FQ	74180 MW	108960 TQ	USBLS	5/07
	Gary PMSA, IN	Y	48380 FQ	76820 MW		USBLS	5/07
	Indianapolis-Carmel MSA, IN	Y	57800 FQ	80150 MW	116870 TQ	USBLS	5/07
	Iowa	Y	57750 FQ	81320 MW	122740 TQ	USBLS	5/07
	Des Moines-West Des Moines MSA, IA	Y	70860 FQ	95760 MW	135620 TQ	USBLS	5/07
	Waterloo-Cedar Falls MSA, IA	Y	53730 FQ	68220 MW	88720 TQ	USBLS	5/07
	Kansas	Y	53150 FQ	73600 MW	104280 TQ	USBLS	5/07
	Lawrence MSA, KS	Y	54690 FQ	64040 MW	76110 TQ	USBLS	5/07
	Wichita MSA, KS	Y	54310 FQ	81440 MW	115580 TQ	USBLS	5/07

AE Average entry wage	**AW** Average wage paid	**FQ** First quartile wage	**LO** Lowest wage paid	**MTC** Median total compensation	**TCC** Total cash compensation
AER Average entry range	**AWR** Average wage range	**H** Hourly	**LR** Low end range	**MW** Median wage paid	**TQ** Third quartile wage
AEX Average experienced wage	**AXR** Average experienced range	**HI** Highest wage paid	**M** Monthly	**MWR** Median wage range	**W** Weekly
ATC Average total compensation	**D** Daily	**HR** High end range	**MCC** Median cash compensation	**S** See annotated source	**Y** Yearly

Occupation/Type/Industry	Location	Per	Low	Mid	High	Source	Date
Lawyer	Kentucky	Y	51646 FQ	75191 MW	112129 TQ	KYBLS	2008
	Louisville-Jefferson County MSA, KY-IN	Y	46890 FQ	82400 MW	122190 TQ	USBLS	5/07
	Louisiana	H	28.69 FQ	42.52 MW	61.47 TQ	LABLS	1/08-3/08
	Baton Rouge MSA, LA	Y	57970 FQ	79910 MW	111010 TQ	USBLS	5/07
	Lake Charles MSA, LA	Y	73180 FQ	133540 MW		USBLS	5/07
	New Orleans-Metairie-Kenner MSA, LA	Y	71030 FQ	96120 MW	127300 TQ	USBLS	5/07
	Maine	Y	62980 FQ	80120 MW	107150 TQ	USBLS	5/07
	Portland-South Portland-Biddeford MSA, ME	Y	66950 FQ	87080 MW	137240 TQ	USBLS	5/07
	Maryland	Y		103350 MW		MDBLS	3/08
	Baltimore-Towson MSA, MD	Y	78650 FQ	103480 MW	144140 TQ	USBLS	5/07
	Bethesda-Gaithersburg-Frederick PMSA, MD	Y	65220 FQ	102280 MW	139070 TQ	USBLS	5/07
	Cumberland MSA, MD-WV	Y	54670 FQ	72960 MW	131130 TQ	USBLS	5/07
	Massachusetts	Y	75710 FQ	114190 MW		USBLS	5/07
	Boston-Cambridge-Quincy NECTA, MA	Y	81880 FQ	121750 MW		USBLS	5/07
	Worcester MSA, MA-CT	Y	75330 FQ	102680 MW	143340 TQ	USBLS	5/07
	Michigan	Y	68080 FQ	96460 MW		USBLS	5/07
	Detroit-Warren-Livonia MSA, MI	Y	69820 FQ	100330 MW		USBLS	5/07
	Flint MSA, MI	Y	56580 FQ	92790 MW		USBLS	5/07
	Grand Rapids-Wyoming MSA, MI	Y	55120 FQ	94610 MW	133910 TQ	USBLS	5/07
	Warren-Troy-Farmington Hills PMSA, MI	Y	67590 FQ	93180 MW		USBLS	5/07
	Minnesota	Y	76050 FQ	103450 MW	145425 TQ	MNBLS	10/08-12/08
	Duluth-Superior MSA, MN-WI	Y	60806 FQ	87255 MW	119311 TQ	MNBLS	10/08-12/08
	Minneapolis-Saint Paul MSA, MN-WI	Y	81365 FQ	111036 MW		MNBLS	10/08-12/08
	Rochester MSA, MN	Y	70954 FQ	83524 MW	133167 TQ	MNBLS	10/08-12/08
	Mississippi	Y	38830 FQ	63280 MW	98800 TQ	USBLS	5/07
	Gulfport-Biloxi MSA, MS	Y	70040 FQ	103150 MW	136380 TQ	USBLS	5/07
	Jackson MSA, MS	Y	62770 FQ	85560 MW	115690 TQ	USBLS	5/07
	Missouri	Y	63910 FQ	91340 MW	133170 TQ	USBLS	5/07
	Joplin MSA, MO	Y	55470 FQ	70150 MW	101000 TQ	USBLS	5/07
	Kansas City MSA, MO-KS	Y	66990 FQ	90420 MW	123750 TQ	USBLS	5/07
	St. Louis MSA, MO-IL	Y	66230 FQ	99320 MW		USBLS	5/07
	Montana	Y	41860 FQ	56900 MW	77260 TQ	USBLS	5/07
	Billings MSA, MT	Y	55260 FQ	75730 MW	117660 TQ	USBLS	5/07
	Nebraska	Y	50580 FQ	76080 MW	122840 TQ	USBLS	5/07
	Omaha-Council Bluffs MSA, NE-IA	Y	54450 FQ	86970 MW	140660 TQ	USBLS	5/07
	Nevada	H	40.64 FQ	53.12 MW		NVBLS	5/08
	Las Vegas-Paradise MSA, NV	H	40.16 FQ	52.50 MW		NVBLS	5/08
	New Hampshire	H	26.19 AE	39.50 MW	57.01 AEX	NHBLS	6/08
	Manchester MSA, NH	Y	59500 FQ	87110 MW	137880 TQ	USBLS	5/07
	Nashua NECTA, NH-MA	Y	64930 FQ	81860 MW	96920 TQ	USBLS	5/07
	New Jersey	Y	78150 FQ	109290 MW		USBLS	5/07
	Camden PMSA, NJ	Y	74620 FQ	104660 MW		USBLS	5/07
	Edison PMSA, NJ	Y	72430 FQ	107270 MW		USBLS	5/07
	Newark-Union PMSA, NJ-PA	Y	85510 FQ	115080 MW		USBLS	5/07
	New Mexico	Y	62310 FQ	81210 MW	104260 TQ	USBLS	5/07
	Albuquerque MSA, NM	Y	64370 FQ	82640 MW	104480 TQ	USBLS	5/07
	New York	Y	89580 FQ	127070 MW		USBLS	5/07
	Albany-Schenectady-Troy MSA, NY	Y	69320 FQ	90190 MW	118360 TQ	USBLS	5/07
	Buffalo-Niagara Falls MSA, NY	Y	64840 FQ	87340 MW	118240 TQ	USBLS	5/07
	Glens Falls MSA, NY	Y	62420 FQ	76820 MW	101180 TQ	USBLS	5/07
	Nassau-Suffolk PMSA, NY	Y	83220 FQ	105710 MW		USBLS	5/07
	New York-Northern New Jersey-Long Island MSA, NY-NJ-PA	Y	93000 FQ	131020 MW		USBLS	5/07
	Utica-Rome MSA, NY	Y	74640 FQ	88300 MW	102130 TQ	USBLS	5/07
	North Carolina	Y	59440 FQ	88300 MW	134840 TQ	USBLS	5/07
	Charlotte-Gastonia-Concord MSA, NC-SC	Y	61730 FQ	97190 MW		USBLS	5/07
	Raleigh-Cary MSA, NC	Y	65890 FQ	95890 MW	140040 TQ	USBLS	5/07
	Winston-Salem MSA, NC	Y	71920 FQ	98950 MW	126720 TQ	USBLS	5/07

AE	Average entry wage	AW	Average wage paid	FQ	First quartile wage	LO	Lowest wage paid	MTC	Median total compensation	TCC	Total cash compensation
AER	Average entry range	AWR	Average wage range	H	Hourly	LR	Low end range	MW	Median wage paid	TQ	Third quartile wage
AEX	Average experienced wage	AXR	Average experienced range	HI	Highest wage paid	M	Monthly	MWR	Median wage range	W	Weekly
ATC	Average total compensation	D	Daily	HR	High end range	MCC	Median cash compensation	S	See annotated source	Y	Yearly

Occupation/Type/Industry	Location	Per	Low	Mid	High	Source	Date
Lawyer	North Dakota	Y	55470 FQ	74210 MW	121870 TQ	USBLS	5/07
	Fargo MSA, ND-MN	Y	62410 FQ	103800 MW		USBLS	5/07
	Ohio	Y	64240 FQ	91770 MW	127380 TQ	USBLS	5/07
	Cincinnati-Middletown MSA, OH-KY-IN	Y	69590 FQ	102730 MW	133220 TQ	USBLS	5/07
	Cleveland-Elyria-Mentor MSA, OH	Y	64340 FQ	95270 MW	130850 TQ	USBLS	5/07
	Columbus MSA, OH	Y	62850 FQ	83200 MW	112830 TQ	USBLS	5/07
	Dayton MSA, OH	Y	76190 FQ	104670 MW	139310 TQ	USBLS	5/07
	Oklahoma	Y	54090 FQ	78500 MW	139410 TQ	USBLS	5/07
	Oklahoma City MSA, OK	Y	52100 FQ	76820 MW	142380 TQ	USBLS	5/07
	Tulsa MSA, OK	Y	63020 FQ	90790 MW		USBLS	5/07
	Oregon	H	29.65 FQ	43.00 MW	56.41 TQ	ORBLS	5/08
	Portland-Vancouver-Beaverton MSA, OR-WA	Y	66150 FQ	96210 MW	123470 TQ	USBLS	5/07
	Salem MSA, OR	Y	61640 FQ	82320 MW	99730 TQ	USBLS	5/07
	Pennsylvania	Y	66770 FQ	97590 MW	139110 TQ	USBLS	5/07
	Allentown-Bethlehem-Easton MSA, PA-NJ	Y	50060 FQ	83660 MW	133120 TQ	USBLS	5/07
	Philadelphia-Camden-Wilmington MSA, PA-NJ-DE-MD	Y	75110 FQ	108340 MW		USBLS	5/07
	Pittsburgh MSA, PA	Y	62210 FQ	91640 MW	129450 TQ	USBLS	5/07
	Reading MSA, PA	Y	62120 FQ	113990 MW		USBLS	5/07
	Rhode Island	Y	57250 FQ	85410 MW	127030 TQ	USBLS	5/07
	Providence-Fall River-Warwick MSA, RI-MA	Y	57780 FQ	85970 MW	130420 TQ	USBLS	5/07
	South Carolina	Y	61210 FQ	86590 MW	131580 TQ	USBLS	5/07
	Charleston-North Charleston MSA, SC	Y	59620 FQ	81040 MW	135640 TQ	USBLS	5/07
	Columbia MSA, SC	Y	63900 FQ	92160 MW	128350 TQ	USBLS	5/07
	South Dakota	Y	59356 FQ	73674 MW	97313 TQ	SDBLS	7/08-9/08
	Sioux Falls MSA, SD	Y	62525 FQ	77139 MW	114623 TQ	SDBLS	7/08-9/08
	Tennessee	Y	66030 FQ	93430 MW	136000 TQ	USBLS	5/07
	Memphis MSA, TN-MS-AR	Y	70150 FQ	96230 MW		USBLS	5/07
	Nashville-Davidson-Murfreesboro MSA, TN	Y	69310 FQ	95320 MW	123060 TQ	USBLS	5/07
	Texas	Y	71150 FQ	109070 MW		USBLS	5/07
	Austin-Round Rock MSA, TX	Y	61210 FQ	88520 MW	131190 TQ	USBLS	5/07
	Dallas-Fort Worth-Arlington MSA, TX	Y	80710 FQ	126970 MW		USBLS	5/07
	El Paso MSA, TX	Y	73670 FQ	94460 MW	139160 TQ	USBLS	5/07
	Houston-Sugar Land-Baytown MSA, TX	Y	80350 FQ	122680 MW		USBLS	5/07
	Midland MSA, TX	Y	87630 FQ	134640 MW		USBLS	5/07
	San Antonio MSA, TX	Y	62160 FQ	87460 MW	133780 TQ	USBLS	5/07
	Utah	Y	70780 FQ	93330 MW		USBLS	5/07
	Salt Lake City MSA, UT	Y	73350 FQ	101240 MW		USBLS	5/07
	Vermont	Y	61540 FQ	86410 MW	120860 TQ	USBLS	5/07
	Burlington-South Burlington MSA, VT	Y	72270 FQ	94260 MW	136230 TQ	USBLS	5/07
	Virginia	Y	78720 FQ	111670 MW		USBLS	5/07
	Lynchburg MSA, VA	Y	58770 FQ	112700 MW	129290 TQ	USBLS	5/07
	Richmond MSA, VA	Y	75540 FQ	105360 MW		USBLS	5/07
	Roanoke MSA, VA	Y	60350 FQ	78900 MW	130090 TQ	USBLS	5/07
	Virginia Beach-Norfolk-Newport News MSA, VA-NC	Y	74510 FQ	102730 MW		USBLS	5/07
	Washington	H	24.63 FQ	40.15 MW	57.85 TQ	WABLS	3/08
	West Virginia	Y	59399 FQ	75391 MW	101675 TQ	WVBLS	7/08-9/08
	Charleston MSA, WV	Y	59130 FQ	72540 MW	100900 TQ	USBLS	5/07
	Wisconsin	Y	62000 FQ	94440 MW	130940 TQ	USBLS	5/07
	Milwaukee-Waukesha-West Allis MSA, WI	Y	57970 FQ	104820 MW	137490 TQ	USBLS	5/07
	Wyoming	Y	48269 FQ	67844 MW	94192 TQ	WYBLS	9/08
	Cheyenne MSA, WY	Y	57692 FQ	73687 MW	89735 TQ	WYBLS	9/08
	Puerto Rico	Y	39470 FQ	52560 MW	74390 TQ	USBLS	5/07
	San Juan-Caguas-Guaynabo MSA, PR	Y	39550 FQ	52180 MW	72440 TQ	USBLS	5/07
	Virgin Islands	Y	74090 FQ	89530 MW	106180 TQ	USBLS	5/07
	Guam	Y	66870 FQ	83540 MW	108540 TQ	USBLS	5/07
First-Year Associate, Large Law Firm	United States	Y		99000-129000 AWR		ABAJ	2008

AE	Average entry wage	**AW**	Average wage paid	**FQ**	First quartile wage
AER	Average entry range	**AWR**	Average wage range	**H**	Hourly
AEX	Average experienced wage	**AXR**	Average experienced range	**HI**	Highest wage paid
ATC	Average total compensation	**D**	Daily	**HR**	High end range

LO	Lowest wage paid	**MTC**	Median total compensation	**TCC**	Total cash compensation
LR	Low end range	**MW**	Median wage paid	**TQ**	Third quartile wage
M	Monthly	**MWR**	Median wage range	**W**	Weekly
MCC	Median cash compensation	**S**	See annotated source	**Y**	Yearly

Occupation/Type/Industry	Location	Per	Low	Mid	High	Source	Date
Lawyer							
First-Year Associate, Small/Medium Law Firm	United States	Y		53750-78750 AWR		ABAJ	2008
Lay-Out Worker							
Metals and Plastics	Alabama	Y	26410 FQ	29910 MW	35470 TQ	USBLS	5/07
Metals and Plastics	Mobile MSA, AL	Y	27440 FQ	31020 MW	36050 TQ	USBLS	5/07
Metals and Plastics	Arkansas	Y	27320 FQ	29860 MW	33390 TQ	USBLS	5/07
Metals and Plastics	California	H	9.91 FQ	14.23 MW	18.20 TQ	CABLS	1/08-3/08
Metals and Plastics	Los Angeles-Long Beach-Glendale PMSA, CA	H	9.72 FQ	13.84 MW	16.72 TQ	CABLS	1/08-3/08
Metals and Plastics	Riverside-San Bernardino-Ontario MSA, CA	H	10.21 FQ	12.31 MW	16.13 TQ	CABLS	1/08-3/08
Metals and Plastics	Sacramento-Arden Arcade-Roseville MSA, CA	H	14.79 FQ	17.11 MW	20.07 TQ	CABLS	1/08-3/08
Metals and Plastics	San Diego-Carlsbad-San Marcos MSA, CA	H	10.11 FQ	14.69 MW	18.30 TQ	CABLS	1/08-3/08
Metals and Plastics	San Jose-Sunnyvale-Santa Clara MSA, CA	H	9.83 FQ	15.35 MW	23.73 TQ	CABLS	1/08-3/08
Metals and Plastics	Santa Ana-Anaheim-Irvine PMSA, CA	Y	17830 FQ	21950 MW	39970 TQ	USBLS	5/07
Metals and Plastics	Colorado	Y	33110 FQ	45590 MW	52990 TQ	USBLS	5/07
Metals and Plastics	Denver-Aurora MSA, CO	Y	36520 FQ	48150 MW	53900 TQ	USBLS	5/07
Metals and Plastics	Connecticut	H	15.86 AE	21.03 MW		CTBLS	1/08-3/08
Metals and Plastics	Florida	Y	24910 FQ	28810 MW	33420 TQ	USBLS	5/07
Metals and Plastics	Jacksonville MSA, FL	Y	29450 FQ	33900 MW	37980 TQ	USBLS	5/07
Metals and Plastics	Miami-Fort Lauderdale-Miami Beach MSA, FL	Y	22510 FQ	27030 MW	30150 TQ	USBLS	5/07
Metals and Plastics	Orlando-Kissimmee MSA, FL	Y	19640 FQ	29470 MW	42770 TQ	USBLS	5/07
Metals and Plastics	Tampa-St. Petersburg-Clearwater MSA, FL	Y	22750 FQ	24800 MW	27560 TQ	USBLS	5/07
Metals and Plastics	Georgia	Y	18560 FQ	27950 MW	39710 TQ	USBLS	5/07
Metals and Plastics	Illinois	Y	27290 FQ	37390 MW	50050 TQ	USBLS	5/07
Metals and Plastics	Chicago-Naperville-Joliet MSA, IL-IN-WI	Y	22940 FQ	36450 MW	48160 TQ	USBLS	5/07
Metals and Plastics	Rockford MSA, IL	Y	39470 FQ	46320 MW	72970 TQ	USBLS	5/07
Metals and Plastics	Indiana	Y	23940 FQ	34470 MW	40490 TQ	USBLS	5/07
Metals and Plastics	Gary PMSA, IN	Y	37920 FQ	41510 MW	46560 TQ	USBLS	5/07
Metals and Plastics	Indianapolis-Carmel MSA, IN	Y	35380 FQ	37930 MW	40470 TQ	USBLS	5/07
Metals and Plastics	Iowa	Y	27670 FQ	32120 MW	36780 TQ	USBLS	5/07
Metals and Plastics	Kansas	Y	27010 FQ	30420 MW	34940 TQ	USBLS	5/07
Metals and Plastics	Kentucky	Y	26388 FQ	32098 MW	37747 TQ	KYBLS	2008
Metals and Plastics	Louisiana	H	13.39 FQ	16.98 MW	20.14 TQ	LABLS	1/08-3/08
Metals and Plastics	Baton Rouge MSA, LA	Y	22600 FQ	33280 MW	39390 TQ	USBLS	5/07
Metals and Plastics	Maine	Y	39550 FQ	43870 MW	48140 TQ	USBLS	5/07
Metals and Plastics	Maryland	Y		46300 MW		MDBLS	3/08
Metals and Plastics	Baltimore-Towson MSA, MD	Y	31760 FQ	48520 MW	57320 TQ	USBLS	5/07
Metals and Plastics	Massachusetts	Y	20980 FQ	26440 MW	32400 TQ	USBLS	5/07
Metals and Plastics	Michigan	Y	33680 FQ	48460 MW	60810 TQ	USBLS	5/07
Metals and Plastics	Detroit-Warren-Livonia MSA, MI	Y	35470 FQ	56320 MW	66730 TQ	USBLS	5/07
Metals and Plastics	Grand Rapids-Wyoming MSA, MI	Y	34870 FQ	39660 MW	47180 TQ	USBLS	5/07
Metals and Plastics	Warren-Troy-Farmington Hills PMSA, MI	Y	35700 FQ	58090 MW	66500 TQ	USBLS	5/07
Metals and Plastics	Minnesota	Y	31421 FQ	39383 MW	51688 TQ	MNBLS	10/08-12/08
Metals and Plastics	Minneapolis-Saint Paul MSA, MN-WI	Y	31867 FQ	41487 MW	54518 TQ	MNBLS	10/08-12/08
Metals and Plastics	Mississippi	Y	31020 FQ	33470 MW	36010 TQ	USBLS	5/07
Metals and Plastics	Missouri	Y	23980 FQ	30000 MW	35180 TQ	USBLS	5/07
Metals and Plastics	St. Louis MSA, MO-IL	Y	25630 FQ	30870 MW	37600 TQ	USBLS	5/07
Metals and Plastics	Nevada	H	13.94 FQ	16.64 MW	22.63 TQ	NVBLS	5/08
Metals and Plastics	Las Vegas-Paradise MSA, NV	H	13.85 FQ	16.23 MW	22.81 TQ	NVBLS	5/08
Metals and Plastics	New Hampshire	H	11.53 AE	19.54 MW	23.74 AEX	NHBLS	6/08
Metals and Plastics	New Jersey	Y	35410 FQ	46620 MW	56230 TQ	USBLS	5/07
Metals and Plastics	Newark-Union PMSA, NJ-PA	Y	26570 FQ	29880 MW	38540 TQ	USBLS	5/07
Metals and Plastics	New York	Y	32280 FQ	35910 MW	39730 TQ	USBLS	5/07
Metals and Plastics	Buffalo-Niagara Falls MSA, NY	Y	33780 FQ	36270 MW	39420 TQ	USBLS	5/07

AE	Average entry wage	AW	Average wage paid	FQ	First quartile wage	LO	Lowest wage paid	MTC	Median total compensation	TCC	Total cash compensation
AER	Average entry range	AWR	Average wage range	H	Hourly	LR	Low end range	MW	Median wage paid	TQ	Third quartile wage
AEX	Average experienced wage	AXR	Average experienced range	HI	Highest wage paid	M	Monthly	MWR	Median wage range	W	Weekly
ATC	Average total compensation	D	Daily	HR	High end range	MCC	Median cash compensation	S	See annotated source	Y	Yearly

895

Occupation/Type/Industry	Location	Per	Low	Mid	High	Source	Date
Lay-Out Worker							
Metals and Plastics	New York-Northern New Jersey-Long Island MSA, NY-NJ-PA	Y	31270 FQ	45220 MW	55970 TQ	USBLS	5/07
Metals and Plastics	North Carolina	Y	27880 FQ	31620 MW	36630 TQ	USBLS	5/07
Metals and Plastics	Ohio	Y	27610 FQ	35120 MW.	44780 TQ	USBLS	5/07
Metals and Plastics	Cincinnati-Middletown MSA, OH-KY-IN	Y	28180 FQ	36550 MW	45010 TQ	USBLS	5/07
Metals and Plastics	Columbus MSA, OH	Y	32210 FQ	40920 MW	44770 TQ	USBLS	5/07
Metals and Plastics	Oklahoma	Y	21650 FQ	24220 MW	28760 TQ	USBLS	5/07
Metals and Plastics	Tulsa MSA, OK	Y	21770 FQ	23930 MW	27600 TQ	USBLS	5/07
Metals and Plastics	Oregon	H	19.33 FQ	21.15 MW	23.13 TQ	ORBLS	5/08
Metals and Plastics	Portland-Vancouver-Beaverton MSA, OR-WA	Y	39470 FQ	43100 MW	46760 TQ	USBLS	5/07
Metals and Plastics	Pennsylvania	Y	29160 FQ	34480 MW	39840 TQ	USBLS	5/07
Metals and Plastics	Philadelphia-Camden-Wilmington MSA, PA-NJ-DE-MD	Y	29680 FQ	36350 MW	46180 TQ	USBLS	5/07
Metals and Plastics	Pittsburgh MSA, PA	Y	29180 FQ	33800 MW	37320 TQ	USBLS	5/07
Metals and Plastics	Providence-Fall River-Warwick MSA, RI-MA	Y	16840 FQ	18210 MW	23810 TQ	USBLS	5/07.
Metals and Plastics	South Carolina	Y	26740 FQ	32960 MW	39410 TQ	USBLS	5/07
Metals and Plastics	South Dakota	Y	22888 FQ	26413 MW	37249 TQ	SDBLS	7/08-9/08
Metals and Plastics	Tennessee	Y	30110 FQ	33720 MW	38940 TQ	USBLS	5/07
Metals and Plastics	Nashville-Davidson-Murfreesboro MSA, TN	Y	29170 FQ	34190 MW	43960 TQ	USBLS	5/07
Metals and Plastics	Texas	Y	23920 FQ	30350 MW	39670 TQ	USBLS	5/07
Metals and Plastics	Austin-Round Rock MSA, TX	Y	18440 FQ	21270 MW	24840 TQ	USBLS	5/07
Metals and Plastics	Dallas-Fort Worth-Arlington MSA, TX	Y	23870 FQ	29380 MW	42800 TQ	USBLS	5/07
Metals and Plastics	Houston-Sugar Land-Baytown MSA, TX	Y	25810 FQ	31230 MW	39020 TQ	USBLS	5/07
Metals and Plastics	San Antonio MSA, TX	Y	22080 FQ	24570 MW	29860 TQ	USBLS	5/07
Metals and Plastics	Utah	Y	22030 FQ	28610 MW	36590 TQ	USBLS	5/07
Metals and Plastics	Salt Lake City MSA, UT	Y	27870 FQ	34430 MW	41550 TQ	USBLS	5/07
Metals and Plastics	Virginia	Y	35230 FQ	42010 MW	46930 TQ	USBLS	5/07
Metals and Plastics	Virginia Beach-Norfolk-Newport News MSA, VA-NC	Y	37080 FQ	42770 MW	47350 TQ	USBLS	5/07
Metals and Plastics	Washington	H	19.63 FQ	23.59 MW	28.48 TQ	WABLS	3/08
Metals and Plastics	Seattle-Tacoma-Bellevue MSA, WA	Y	28700 FQ	42760 MW	51920 TQ	USBLS	5/07
Metals and Plastics	West Virginia	Y	26902 FQ	30267 MW	34927 TQ	WVBLS	7/08-9/08
Metals and Plastics	Wisconsin	Y	33740 FQ	37910 MW	41890 TQ	USBLS	5/07
Metals and Plastics	Milwaukee-Waukesha-West Allis MSA, WI	Y	38400 FQ	43240 MW	47790 TQ	USBLS	5/07
Layout Design Artist							
State Government	Ohio	H	17.22 LO		21.77 HI	ODAS	2008
Lead Computer Operator							
Municipal Government	Cincinnati, OH	Y	43264 LO		48214 HI	COHSS	10/08
Lead Fingerprint Examiner							
Coroner Crime Lab	Contra Costa County, CA	W	5266 LO		6401 HI	CAC	2006-2007
Lead Information Technology Security Professional	United States	Y		108000 AW		SCMAG	2008
Lead Programmer/Analyst							
State Government	Mississippi	Y	55274 LO		96730 HI	AFT02	3/1/08
Lead Transit Dispatcher							
Municipal Government	Colorado Springs, CO	M	3427 LO			COSPRS	1/1/09
Lean/Continuous Improvement Manager							
Manufacturing	United States	Y		85171 AW		IWEEK	2008
Legal Assistant							
Municipal Government	Walnut Creek, CA	Y	57096 LO		68695 HI	WCSWP	7/11/08

AE	Average entry wage	AW	Average wage paid	FQ	First quartile wage
AER	Average entry range	AWR	Average wage range	H	Hourly
AEX	Average experienced wage	AXR	Average experienced range	HI	Highest wage paid
ATC	Average total compensation	D	Daily	HR	High end range

LO	Lowest wage paid	MTC	Median total compensation
LR	Low end range	MW	Median wage paid
M	Monthly	MWR	Median wage range
MCC	Median cash compensation	S	See annotated source

TCC	Total cash compensation
TQ	Third quartile wage
W	Weekly
Y	Yearly

Occupation/Type/Industry	Location	Per	Low	Mid	High	Source	Date
Legal Intern							
Municipal Government	Carlsbad, CA	H	15.00 LO		25.00 HI	CCSS	1/1/08
Legal Secretary	Alabama	Y	25030 FQ	31840 MW	39700 TQ	USBLS	5/07
	Birmingham-Hoover MSA, AL	Y	26270 FQ	36560 MW	44620 TQ	USBLS	5/07
	Mobile MSA, AL	Y	28280 FQ	34300 MW	39130 TQ	USBLS	5/07
	Alaska	Y	34390 FQ	41810 MW	50880 TQ	USBLS	5/07
	Anchorage MSA, AK	Y	35900 FQ	43360 MW	52040 TQ	USBLS	5/07
	Arizona	Y	33270 FQ	40020 MW	47980 TQ	USBLS	5/07
	Phoenix-Mesa-Scottsdale MSA, AZ	Y	35560 FQ	42010 MW	49050 TQ	USBLS	5/07
	Tucson MSA, AZ	Y	29240 FQ	33110 MW	42370 TQ	USBLS	5/07
	Arkansas	Y	23380 FQ	27900 MW	32570 TQ	USBLS	5/07
	Jonesboro MSA, AR	Y	22870 FQ	25150 MW	29690 TQ	USBLS	5/07
	Little Rock-North Little Rock MSA, AR	Y	26030 FQ	31880 MW	39440 TQ	USBLS	5/07
	California	H	18.04 FQ	24.17 MW	30.41 TQ	CABLS	1/08-3/08
	Los Angeles-Long Beach-Glendale PMSA, CA	H	20.53 FQ	25.63 MW	31.26 TQ	CABLS	1/08-3/08
	Oakland-Fremont-Hayward MSA, CA	H	17.37 FQ	25.42 MW	30.59 TQ	CABLS	1/08-3/08
	Riverside-San Bernardino-Ontario MSA, CA	H	14.85 FQ	18.08 MW	21.32 TQ	CABLS	1/08-3/08
	Sacramento-Arden Arcade-Roseville MSA, CA	H	16.68 FQ	21.78 MW	25.79 TQ	CABLS	1/08-3/08
	San Diego-Carlsbad-San Marcos MSA, CA	H	17.25 FQ	24.34 MW	29.95 TQ	CABLS	1/08-3/08
	San Francisco-San Mateo-Redwood PMSA, CA	H	20.50 FQ	28.56 MW	34.41 TQ	CABLS	1/08-3/08
	San Jose-Sunnyvale-Santa Clara MSA, CA	H	26.95 FQ	32.33 MW	37.78 TQ	CABLS	1/08-3/08
	Santa Ana-Anaheim-Irvine PMSA, CA	Y	34480 FQ	44390 MW	57240 TQ	USBLS	5/07
	Santa Rosa-Petaluma MSA, CA	H	15.61 FQ	23.50 MW	27.09 TQ	CABLS	1/08-3/08
	Colorado	Y	33320 FQ	44080 MW	52710 TQ	USBLS	5/07
	Denver-Aurora MSA, CO	Y	36830 FQ	47010 MW	54660 TQ	USBLS	5/07
	Connecticut	H	16.03 AE	21.58 MW		CTBLS	1/08-3/08
	Bridgeport-Stamford-Norwalk MSA, CT	Y	42740 FQ	47600 MW	55270 TQ	USBLS	5/07
	Hartford-West Hartford-East Hartford MSA, CT	Y	38720 FQ	44980 MW	51660 TQ	USBLS	5/07
	Delaware	Y	34020 FQ	42470 MW	51150 TQ	USBLS	5/07
	Wilmington PMSA, DE-MD-NJ	Y	36360 FQ	44490 MW	52850 TQ	USBLS	5/07
	District of Columbia	Y	52020 FQ	60830 MW	70770 TQ	USBLS	5/07
	Washington-Arlington-Alexandria MSA, DC-VA-MD-WV	Y	46960 FQ	58060 MW	68690 TQ	USBLS	5/07
	Florida	Y	29070 FQ	36560 MW	45070 TQ	USBLS	5/07
	Fort Lauderdale-Pompano Beach-Deerfield Beach PMSA, FL	Y	30250 FQ	39370 MW	46180 TQ	USBLS	5/07
	Jacksonville MSA, FL	Y	25990 FQ	35630 MW	41090 TQ	USBLS	5/07
	Miami-Fort Lauderdale-Miami Beach MSA, FL	Y	30110 FQ	38960 MW	47570 TQ	USBLS	5/07
	Orlando-Kissimmee MSA, FL	Y	33980 FQ	40720 MW	46690 TQ	USBLS	5/07
	Tampa-St. Petersburg-Clearwater MSA, FL	Y	27630 FQ	33380 MW	43540 TQ	USBLS	5/07
	West Palm Beach-Boca Raton-Boynton Beach PMSA, FL	Y	31610 FQ	38240 MW	45950 TQ	USBLS	5/07
	Georgia	Y	26040 FQ	31900 MW	50780 TQ	USBLS	5/07
	Atlanta-Sandy Springs-Marietta MSA, GA	Y	27830 FQ	41630 MW	56820 TQ	USBLS	5/07
	Savannah MSA, GA	Y	24600 FQ	29550 MW	36480 TQ	USBLS	5/07
	Hawaii	Y	37190 FQ	43110 MW	48680 TQ	USBLS	5/07
	Honolulu MSA, HI	Y	38300 FQ	44120 MW	49430 TQ	USBLS	5/07
	Idaho	Y	23870 FQ	29650 MW	36740 TQ	USBLS	5/07
	Boise City-Nampa MSA, ID	Y	27430 FQ	32220 MW	41840 TQ	USBLS	5/07
	Idaho Falls MSA, ID	Y	19700 FQ	28380 MW	34250 TQ	USBLS	5/07
	Pocatello MSA, ID	Y	20420 FQ	22950 MW	26300 TQ	USBLS	5/07
	Illinois	Y	29870 FQ	39550 MW	50830 TQ	USBLS	5/07

AE	Average entry wage	**AW**	Average wage paid	**FQ**	First quartile wage
AER	Average entry range	**AWR**	Average wage range	**H**	Hourly
AEX	Average experienced wage	**AXR**	Average experienced range	**HI**	Highest wage paid
ATC	Average total compensation	**D**	Daily	**HR**	High end range

LO	Lowest wage paid	**MTC**	Median total compensation	**TCC**	Total cash compensation
LR	Low end range	**MW**	Median wage paid	**TQ**	Third quartile wage
M	Monthly	**MWR**	Median wage range	**W**	Weekly
MCC	Median cash compensation	**S**	See annotated source	**Y**	Yearly

Occupation/Type/Industry	Location	Per	Low	Mid	High	Source	Date
Legal Secretary	Chicago-Naperville-Joliet MSA, IL-IN-WI	Y	30570 FQ	41160 MW	52980 TQ	USBLS	5/07
	Indiana	Y	25710 FQ	31730 MW	40480 TQ	USBLS	5/07
	Gary PMSA, IN	Y	23240 FQ	27830 MW	33440 TQ	USBLS	5/07
	Indianapolis-Carmel MSA, IN	Y	29120 FQ	38490 MW	47580 TQ	USBLS	5/07
	Iowa	Y	25600 FQ	29860 MW	35880 TQ	USBLS	5/07
	Des Moines-West Des Moines MSA, IA	Y	28940 FQ	36290 MW	43960 TQ	USBLS	5/07
	Kansas	Y	23270 FQ	28100 MW	32420 TQ	USBLS	5/07
	Lawrence MSA, KS	Y	27890 FQ	29660 MW	31430 TQ	USBLS	5/07
	Wichita MSA, KS	Y	24060 FQ	29240 MW	33480 TQ	USBLS	5/07
	Kentucky	Y	27662 FQ	33297 MW	41180 TQ	KYBLS	2008
	Louisville-Jefferson County MSA, KY-IN	Y	31670 FQ	37790 MW	44630 TQ	USBLS	5/07
	Louisiana	H	13.06 FQ	16.98 MW	20.68 TQ	LABLS	1/08-3/08
	Baton Rouge MSA, LA	Y	27350 FQ	34690 MW	42480 TQ	USBLS	5/07
	New Orleans-Metairie-Kenner MSA, LA	Y	34630 FQ	41360 MW	46250 TQ	USBLS	5/07
	Maine	Y	28520 FQ	33360 MW	38640 TQ	USBLS	5/07
	Portland-South Portland-Biddeford MSA, ME	Y	29300 FQ	38700 MW	44570 TQ	USBLS	5/07
	Maryland	Y		40325 MW		MDBLS	3/08
	Baltimore-Towson MSA, MD	Y	33320 FQ	39760 MW	48720 TQ	USBLS	5/07
	Bethesda-Gaithersburg-Frederick PMSA, MD	Y	33430 FQ	38720 MW	49840 TQ	USBLS	5/07
	Massachusetts	Y	35470 FQ	46300 MW	56600 TQ	USBLS	5/07
	Boston-Cambridge-Quincy NECTA, MA	Y	42170 FQ	50260 MW	60650 TQ	USBLS	5/07
	Worcester MSA, MA-CT	Y	38650 FQ	45720 MW	51690 TQ	USBLS	5/07
	Michigan	Y	32950 FQ	39220 MW	46670 TQ	USBLS	5/07
	Detroit-Warren-Livonia MSA, MI	Y	34570 FQ	40960 MW	47930 TQ	USBLS	5/07
	Grand Rapids-Wyoming MSA, MI	Y	33970 FQ	40690 MW	46310 TQ	USBLS	5/07
	Warren-Troy-Farmington Hills PMSA, MI	Y	34090 FQ	40410 MW	47680 TQ	USBLS	5/07
	Minnesota	Y	38322 FQ	47543 MW	55734 TQ	MNBLS	10/08-12/08
	Duluth-Superior MSA, MN-WI	Y	31140 FQ	37229 MW	42495 TQ	MNBLS	10/08-12/08
	Minneapolis-Saint Paul MSA, MN-WI	Y	41912 FQ	49979 MW	57566 TQ	MNBLS	10/08-12/08
	Rochester MSA, MN	Y	35342 FQ	38596 MW	41750 TQ	MNBLS	10/08-12/08
	Mississippi	Y	28210 FQ	36020 MW	42510 TQ	USBLS	5/07
	Jackson MSA, MS	Y	36770 FQ	41670 MW	45760 TQ	USBLS	5/07
	Missouri	Y	28120 FQ	35630 MW	42890 TQ	USBLS	5/07
	Kansas City MSA, MO-KS	Y	31990 FQ	37510 MW	44050 TQ	USBLS	5/07
	St. Louis MSA, MO-IL	Y	32570 FQ	38200 MW	44950 TQ	USBLS	5/07
	Springfield MSA, MO	Y	24590 FQ	28630 MW	33400 TQ	USBLS	5/07
	Montana	Y	22400 FQ	26450 MW	31470 TQ	USBLS	5/07
	Billings MSA, MT	Y	26710 FQ	30440 MW	35960 TQ	USBLS	5/07
	Nebraska	Y	25590 FQ	32090 MW	39890 TQ	USBLS	5/07
	Omaha-Council Bluffs MSA, NE-IA	Y	28460 FQ	35370 MW	41250 TQ	USBLS	5/07
	Nevada	H	17.69 FQ	21.29 MW	25.24 TQ	NVBLS	5/08
	Las Vegas-Paradise MSA, NV	H	17.79 FQ	21.53 MW	26.19 TQ	NVBLS	5/08
	New Hampshire	H	13.96 AE	16.56 MW	18.38 AEX	NHBLS	6/08
	Manchester MSA, NH	Y	32950 FQ	36900 MW	45590 TQ	USBLS	5/07
	Portsmouth MSA, NH-ME	Y	32160 FQ	34640 MW	37110 TQ	USBLS	5/07
	New Jersey	Y	35530 FQ	43320 MW	50960 TQ	USBLS	5/07
	Camden PMSA, NJ	Y	32730 FQ	39240 MW	46600 TQ	USBLS	5/07
	Edison PMSA, NJ	Y	36710 FQ	43010 MW	50240 TQ	USBLS	5/07
	Newark-Union PMSA, NJ-PA	Y	38530 FQ	46410 MW	54290 TQ	USBLS	5/07
	New Mexico	Y	27090 FQ	31150 MW	37070 TQ	USBLS	5/07
	Albuquerque MSA, NM	Y	27110 FQ	30360 MW	35930 TQ	USBLS	5/07
	New York	Y	32270 FQ	40620 MW	52780 TQ	USBLS	5/07
	Albany-Schenectady-Troy MSA, NY	Y	29380 FQ	33190 MW	41060 TQ	USBLS	5/07
	Buffalo-Niagara Falls MSA, NY	Y	27340 FQ	32460 MW	39820 TQ	USBLS	5/07
	Nassau-Suffolk PMSA, NY	Y	32760 FQ	40260 MW	48120 TQ	USBLS	5/07
	New York-Northern New Jersey-Long Island MSA, NY-NJ-PA	Y	35080 FQ	44070 MW	54540 TQ	USBLS	5/07

AE	Average entry wage	AW	Average wage paid	FQ	First quartile wage
AER	Average entry range	AWR	Average wage range	H	Hourly
AEX	Average experienced wage	AXR	Average experienced range	HI	Highest wage paid
ATC	Average total compensation	D	Daily	HR	High end range

LO	Lowest wage paid	MTC	Median total compensation
LR	Low end range	MW	Median wage paid
M	Monthly	MWR	Median wage range
MCC	Median cash compensation	S	See annotated source

TCC	Total cash compensation
TQ	Third quartile wage
W	Weekly
Y	Yearly

Occupation/Type/Industry	Location	Per	Low	Mid	High	Source	Date
Legal Secretary	North Carolina	Y	26370 FQ	32350 MW	42290 TQ	USBLS	5/07
	Charlotte-Gastonia-Concord MSA, NC-SC	Y	29790 FQ	39130 MW	51610 TQ	USBLS	5/07
	Raleigh-Cary MSA, NC	Y	35040 FQ	42060 MW	50370 TQ	USBLS	5/07
	North Dakota	Y	21030 FQ	26290 MW	31530 TQ	USBLS	5/07
	Fargo MSA, ND-MN	Y	23940 FQ	27990 MW	32950 TQ	USBLS	5/07
	Ohio	Y	28180 FQ	34660 MW	43690 TQ	USBLS	5/07
	Cincinnati-Middletown MSA, OH-KY-IN	Y	30740 FQ	38210 MW	47220 TQ	USBLS	5/07
	Cleveland-Elyria-Mentor MSA, OH	Y	29690 FQ	38060 MW	45550 TQ	USBLS	5/07
	Columbus MSA, OH	Y	33640 FQ	40930 MW	47550 TQ	USBLS	5/07
	Dayton MSA, OH	Y	29170 FQ	33270 MW	40740 TQ	USBLS	5/07
	Oklahoma	Y	22730 FQ	28710 MW	35490 TQ	USBLS	5/07
	Oklahoma City MSA, OK	Y	25470 FQ	32730 MW	38150 TQ	USBLS	5/07
	Tulsa MSA, OK	Y	24160 FQ	29680 MW	34820 TQ	USBLS	5/07
	Oregon	H	15.17 FQ	18.94 MW	23.92 TQ	ORBLS	5/08
	Portland-Vancouver-Beaverton MSA, OR-WA	Y	36070 FQ	44530 MW	52540 TQ	USBLS	5/07
	Pennsylvania	Y	26550 FQ	34250 MW	43700 TQ	USBLS	5/07
	Allentown-Bethlehem-Easton MSA, PA-NJ	Y	22990 FQ	28900 MW	35990 TQ	USBLS	5/07
	Philadelphia-Camden-Wilmington MSA, PA-NJ-DE-MD	Y	32370 FQ	41080 MW	50600 TQ	USBLS	5/07
	Pittsburgh MSA, PA	Y	27100 FQ	33220 MW	37930 TQ	USBLS	5/07
	Rhode Island	Y	31500 FQ	36780 MW	44700 TQ	USBLS	5/07
	Providence-Fall River-Warwick MSA, RI-MA	Y	29500 FQ	35910 MW	43890 TQ	USBLS	5/07
	South Carolina	Y	25900 FQ	30880 MW	38110 TQ	USBLS	5/07
	Charleston-North Charleston MSA, SC	Y	26950 FQ	29910 MW	34860 TQ	USBLS	5/07
	Columbia MSA, SC	Y	27830 FQ	31810 MW	39570 TQ	USBLS	5/07
	South Dakota	Y	26346 FQ	31169 MW	37740 TQ	SDBLS	7/08-9/08
	Sioux Falls MSA, SD	Y	33382 FQ	37113 MW	40611 TQ	SDBLS	7/08-9/08
	Tennessee	Y	26080 FQ	32410 MW	39270 TQ	USBLS	5/07
	Memphis MSA, TN-MS-AR	Y	30130 FQ	36040 MW	41770 TQ	USBLS	5/07
	Nashville-Davidson-Murfreesboro MSA, TN	Y	27660 FQ	33230 MW	40400 TQ	USBLS	5/07
	Texas	Y	27600 FQ	37410 MW	51500 TQ	USBLS	5/07
	Austin-Round Rock MSA, TX	Y	24650 FQ	33750 MW	44240 TQ	USBLS	5/07
	Dallas-Fort Worth-Arlington MSA, TX	Y	33350 FQ	46220 MW	56050 TQ	USBLS	5/07
	El Paso MSA, TX	Y	28030 FQ	31340 MW	35630 TQ	USBLS	5/07
	Houston-Sugar Land-Baytown MSA, TX	Y	31670 FQ	45030 MW	57420 TQ	USBLS	5/07
	San Antonio MSA, TX	Y	26260 FQ	37380 MW	45720 TQ	USBLS	5/07
	Utah	Y	30170 FQ	36020 MW	44140 TQ	USBLS	5/07
	Provo-Orem MSA, UT	Y	25820 FQ	29660 MW	33630 TQ	USBLS	5/07
	Salt Lake City MSA, UT	Y	33210 FQ	38890 MW	46610 TQ	USBLS	5/07
	Vermont	Y	30640 FQ	37100 MW	45020 TQ	USBLS	5/07
	Burlington-South Burlington MSA, VT	Y	37070 FQ	41960 MW	46610 TQ	USBLS	5/07
	Virginia	Y	32200 FQ	41100 MW	51500 TQ	USBLS	5/07
	Richmond MSA, VA	Y	36920 FQ	42860 MW	48010 TQ	USBLS	5/07
	Virginia Beach-Norfolk-Newport News MSA, VA-NC	Y	32540 FQ	35940 MW	39340 TQ	USBLS	5/07
	Washington	H	16.07 FQ	19.76 MW	24.51 TQ	WABLS	3/08
	Seattle-Tacoma-Bellevue MSA, WA	Y	36920 FQ	46370 MW	55650 TQ	USBLS	5/07
	West Virginia	Y	26093 FQ	30824 MW	36052 TQ	WVBLS	7/08-9/08
	Charleston MSA, WV	Y	28480 FQ	33340 MW	36960 TQ	USBLS	5/07
	Wisconsin	Y	27300 FQ	33590 MW	41420 TQ	USBLS	5/07
	Milwaukee-Waukesha-West Allis MSA, WI	Y	28350 FQ	35390 MW	44280 TQ	USBLS	5/07
	Racine MSA, WI	Y	27170 FQ	34260 MW	38940 TQ	USBLS	5/07
	Cheyenne MSA, WY	Y	29723 FQ	35513 MW	40177 TQ	WYBLS	9/08
	Puerto Rico	Y	18690 FQ	22890 MW	27750 TQ	USBLS	5/07
	San Juan-Caguas-Guaynabo MSA, PR	Y	19390 FQ	23420 MW	28210 TQ	USBLS	5/07
	Virgin Islands	Y	30680 FQ	35690 MW	40130 TQ	USBLS	5/07
	Guam	Y	20890 FQ	29350 MW	38140 TQ	USBLS	5/07

AE	Average entry wage	**AW**	Average wage paid	**FQ**	First quartile wage	**LO**	Lowest wage paid	**MTC** Median total compensation **TCC** Total cash compensation
AER	Average entry range	**AWR**	Average wage range	**H**	Hourly	**LR**	Low end range	**MW** Median wage paid **TQ** Third quartile wage
AEX	Average experienced wage	**AXR**	Average experienced range	**HI**	Highest wage paid	**M**	Monthly	**MWR** Median wage range **W** Weekly
ATC	Average total compensation	**D**	Daily	**HR**	High end range	**MCC**	Median cash compensation	**S** See annotated source **Y** Yearly

Occupation/Type/Industry	Location	Per	Low	Mid	High	Source	Date
Legislative Budget Assistant	New Hampshire	Y			107132 HI	NHUL02	2008
Legislative Counsel							
United States House of Representatives	United States	Y			167800 HI	CRS01	1/08
United States Senate	United States	Y			163700 HI	CRS01	2007
Legislative Proofreader	Rhode Island	Y		35713 AW		RIM01	2009
Legislator	Alabama	Y	12500 FQ	13770 MW	15090 TQ	USBLS	5/07
	Birmingham-Hoover MSA, AL	Y	12400 FQ	13440 MW	14480 TQ	USBLS	5/07
	Arizona	Y	21140 FQ	33620 MW	39760 TQ	USBLS	5/07
	Phoenix-Mesa-Scottsdale MSA, AZ	Y	19150 FQ	25460 MW	48200 TQ	USBLS	5/07
	Tucson MSA, AZ	Y	15220 FQ	23370 MW	43700 TQ	USBLS	5/07
	Arkansas	Y	14410 FQ	15910 MW	47090 TQ	USBLS	5/07
	Little Rock-North Little Rock MSA, AR	Y	14300 FQ	15530 MW	49960 TQ	USBLS	5/07
	California	Y		49475 AW		CABLS	1/08-3/08
	Los Angeles-Long Beach-Glendale PMSA, CA	Y		48644 AW		CABLS	1/08-3/08
	Oakland-Fremont-Hayward MSA, CA	Y		49300 AW		CABLS	1/08-3/08
	Riverside-San Bernardino-Ontario MSA, CA	Y		48285 AW		CABLS	1/08-3/08
	Sacramento-Arden Arcade-Roseville MSA, CA	Y		65382 AW		CABLS	1/08-3/08
	San Diego-Carlsbad-San Marcos MSA, CA	Y		51474 AW		CABLS	1/08-3/08
	San Francisco-San Mateo-Redwood PMSA, CA	Y		52233 AW		CABLS	1/08-3/08
	San Jose-Sunnyvale-Santa Clara MSA, CA	Y		57382 AW		CABLS	1/08-3/08
	Santa Ana-Anaheim-Irvine PMSA, CA	Y	35630 FQ	51780 MW	112300 TQ	USBLS	5/07
	Colorado	Y	14940 FQ	15910 MW	52360 TQ	USBLS	5/07
	Denver-Aurora MSA, CO	Y	15130 FQ	48110 MW	60670 TQ	USBLS	5/07
	Bridgeport-Stamford-Norwalk MSA, CT	Y	15980 FQ	16090 MW	61300 TQ	USBLS	5/07
	Hartford-West Hartford-East Hartford MSA, CT	Y	28940 FQ	34140 MW	40130 TQ	USBLS	5/07
	New Haven MSA, CT	Y	15960 FQ	16080 MW	46320 TQ	USBLS	5/07
	Delaware	Y	14420 FQ	15170 MW	29370 TQ	USBLS	5/07
	Wilmington PMSA, DE-MD-NJ	Y	14560 FQ	15330 MW	33420 TQ	USBLS	5/07
	Washington-Arlington-Alexandria MSA, DC-VA-MD-WV	Y	14670 FQ	28910 MW	56260 TQ	USBLS	5/07
	Florida	Y	25910 FQ	30210 MW	38690 TQ	USBLS	5/07
	Fort Lauderdale-Pompano Beach-Deerfield Beach PMSA, FL	Y	25290 FQ	28030 MW	30940 TQ	USBLS	5/07
	Jacksonville MSA, FL	Y	27920 FQ	32160 MW	56920 TQ	USBLS	5/07
	Miami-Fort Lauderdale-Miami Beach MSA, FL	Y	26270 FQ	29160 MW	33030 TQ	USBLS	5/07
	Orlando-Kissimmee MSA, FL	Y	26620 FQ	31820 MW	57270 TQ	USBLS	5/07
	Tampa-St. Petersburg-Clearwater MSA, FL	Y	22360 FQ	29890 MW	44280 TQ	USBLS	5/07
	West Palm Beach-Boca Raton-Boynton Beach PMSA, FL	Y	27970 FQ	30930 MW	45030 TQ	USBLS	5/07
	Georgia	Y	12810 FQ	14450 MW	17890 TQ	USBLS	5/07
	Atlanta-Sandy Springs-Marietta MSA, GA	Y	13780 FQ	16990 MW	20710 TQ	USBLS	5/07
	Hawaii	Y	35750 FQ	39040 MW	46770 TQ	USBLS	5/07
	Idaho	Y	12760 FQ	14510 MW	18720 TQ	USBLS	5/07
	Illinois	Y	14590 FQ	15120 MW	31330 TQ	USBLS	5/07
	Chicago-Naperville-Joliet MSA, IL-IN-WI	Y	14660 FQ	15720 MW	34630 TQ	USBLS	5/07
	Indiana	Y	14060 FQ	28070 MW	63950 TQ	USBLS	5/07
	Gary PMSA, IN	Y	20460 FQ	23670 MW	73160 TQ	USBLS	5/07
	Indianapolis-Carmel MSA, IN	Y	12750 FQ	14110 MW	42160 TQ	USBLS	5/07
	South Bend-Mishawaka MSA, IN-MI	Y	13730 FQ	15960 MW	41590 TQ	USBLS	5/07

Legislator

Occupation/Type/Industry	Location	Per	Low	Mid	High	Source	Date
Legislator	Iowa	Y	14090 FQ	15350 MW	27240 TQ	USBLS	5/07
	Kansas	Y	21740 FQ	29410 MW	54720 TQ	USBLS	5/07
	Wichita MSA, KS	Y	15250 FQ	27320 MW	38600 TQ	USBLS	5/07
	Louisiana	Y		16626 AW		LABLS	1/08-3/08
	Baton Rouge MSA, LA	Y	12370 FQ	13660 MW	14980 TQ	USBLS	5/07
	New Orleans-Metairie-Kenner MSA, LA	Y	13300 FQ	17020 MW	29880 TQ	USBLS	5/07
	Maine	Y	14920 FQ	16320 MW	32520 TQ	USBLS	5/07
	Portland-South Portland-Biddeford MSA, ME	Y	15030 FQ	20380 MW	29990 TQ	USBLS	5/07
	Maryland	Y		15700 MW		MDBLS	3/08
	Baltimore-Towson MSA, MD	Y	14310 FQ	15770 MW	67800 TQ	USBLS	5/07
	Worcester MSA, MA-CT	Y	16070 FQ	22570 MW	36170 TQ	USBLS	5/07
	Michigan	Y	15670 FQ	37180 MW	52730 TQ	USBLS	5/07
	Detroit-Warren-Livonia MSA, MI	Y	16450 FQ	40040 MW	49720 TQ	USBLS	5/07
	Grand Rapids-Wyoming MSA, MI	Y	20290 FQ	42010 MW	63930 TQ	USBLS	5/07
	Warren-Troy-Farmington Hills PMSA, MI	Y	15620 FQ	42360 MW	51210 TQ	USBLS	5/07
	Minnesota	Y	14597 FQ	15306 MW	16317 TQ	MNBLS	10/08-12/08
	Duluth-Superior MSA, MN-WI	Y	14545 FQ	15306 MW	16213 TQ	MNBLS	10/08-12/08
	Minneapolis-Saint Paul MSA, MN-WI	Y	14711 FQ	15295 MW	16275 TQ	MNBLS	10/08-12/08
	Rochester MSA, MN	Y	15992 FQ	18644 MW	28140 TQ	MNBLS	10/08-12/08
	Mississippi	Y	19390 FQ	23380 MW	31440 TQ	USBLS	5/07
	Jackson MSA, MS	Y	14620 FQ	20140 MW	27590 TQ	USBLS	5/07
	Missouri	Y	26120 FQ	29140 MW	32160 TQ	USBLS	5/07
	Kansas City MSA, MO-KS	Y	19360 FQ	36180 MW	60870 TQ	USBLS	5/07
	St. Louis MSA, MO-IL	Y	14480 FQ	14900 MW	15780 TQ	USBLS	5/07
	Montana	Y	13750 FQ	14700 MW	29810 TQ	USBLS	5/07
	Nebraska	Y	12570 FQ	14090 MW	15960 TQ	USBLS	5/07
	Omaha-Council Bluffs MSA, NE-IA	Y	13130 FQ	14710 MW	18770 TQ	USBLS	5/07
	Nevada	H	12.26 FQ	17.08 MW	20.08 TQ	NVBLS	5/08
	Las Vegas-Paradise MSA, NV	H	7.38 FQ	20.13 MW	33.32 TQ	NVBLS	5/08
	New Hampshire	Y	13538 AE	13852 MW	14440 AEX	NHBLS	6/08
	Nashua NECTA, NH-MA	Y	12550 FQ	14200 MW	15860 TQ	USBLS	5/07
	New Jersey	Y	15350 FQ	16260 MW	45230 TQ	USBLS	5/07
	Camden PMSA, NJ	Y	15340 FQ	16220 MW	40190 TQ	USBLS	5/07
	Edison PMSA, NJ	Y	15380 FQ	16100 MW	44630 TQ	USBLS	5/07
	Newark-Union PMSA, NJ-PA	Y	15320 FQ	16070 MW	48140 TQ	USBLS	5/07
	New Mexico	Y	12920 FQ	14640 MW	22320 TQ	USBLS	5/07
	Albuquerque MSA, NM	Y	12840 FQ	14550 MW	19840 TQ	USBLS	5/07
	New York	Y	66450 FQ	74650 MW	83040 TQ	USBLS	5/07
	Albany-Schenectady-Troy MSA, NY	Y	69230 FQ	75400 MW	81550 TQ	USBLS	5/07
	Buffalo-Niagara Falls MSA, NY	Y	64200 FQ	78140 MW	91790 TQ	USBLS	5/07
	Kingston MSA, NY	Y	71100 FQ	76750 MW	82090 TQ	USBLS	5/07
	Nassau-Suffolk PMSA, NY	Y	60190 FQ	71730 MW	80750 TQ	USBLS	5/07
	New York-Northern New Jersey-Long Island MSA, NY-NJ-PA	Y	15720 FQ	46790 MW	74990 TQ	USBLS	5/07
	Ohio	Y	14800 FQ	15410 MW	21150 TQ	USBLS	5/07
	Oklahoma	Y	13420 FQ	15950 MW	37720 TQ	USBLS	5/07
	Oklahoma City MSA, OK	Y	15910 FQ	35240 MW	39540 TQ	USBLS	5/07
	Tulsa MSA, OK	Y	13420 FQ	16810 MW	36280 TQ	USBLS	5/07
	Portland-Vancouver-Beaverton MSA, OR-WA	Y	29680 FQ	47510 MW	58810 TQ	USBLS	5/07
	Pennsylvania	Y	14190 FQ	14860 MW	16290 TQ	USBLS	5/07
	Allentown-Bethlehem-Easton MSA, PA-NJ	Y	14140 FQ	14760 MW	15500 TQ	USBLS	5/07
	Philadelphia-Camden-Wilmington MSA, PA-NJ-DE-MD	Y	14680 FQ	15590 MW	44680 TQ	USBLS	5/07
	Pittsburgh MSA, PA	Y	14290 FQ	15150 MW	17500 TQ	USBLS	5/07
	Rhode Island	Y	15520 FQ	15720 MW	15920 TQ	USBLS	5/07
	Providence-Fall River-Warwick MSA, RI-MA	Y	15560 FQ	15750 MW	15930 TQ	USBLS	5/07
	South Carolina	Y	12600 FQ	14050 MW	15760 TQ	USBLS	5/07

Occupation/Type/Industry	Location	Per	Low	Mid	High	Source	Date
Legislator	Charleston-North Charleston						
	MSA, SC	Y	12450 FQ	13770 MW	15120 TQ	USBLS	5/07
	Columbia MSA, SC	Y	12530 FQ	14040 MW	15630 TQ	USBLS	5/07
	Florence MSA, SC	Y	12300 FQ	13330 MW	14350 TQ	USBLS	5/07
	South Dakota	Y	28910 FQ	33126 MW	38605 TQ	SDBLS	7/08-9/08
	Sioux Falls MSA, SD	Y	27321 FQ	29437 MW	33138 TQ	SDBLS	7/08-9/08
	Tennessee	Y	12360 FQ	13610 MW	14860 TQ	USBLS	5/07
	Johnson City MSA, TN	Y	12320 FQ	13240 MW	14160 TQ	USBLS	5/07
	Memphis MSA, TN-MS-AR	Y	13350 FQ	14940 MW	29370 TQ	USBLS	5/07
	Nashville-Davidson-						
	Murfreesboro MSA, TN	Y	12290 FQ	13460 MW	14640 TQ	USBLS	5/07
	Texas	Y	12770 FQ	14330 MW	20860 TQ	USBLS	5/07
	Dallas-Fort Worth-Arlington						
	MSA, TX	Y	12710 FQ	14260 MW	16100 TQ	USBLS	5/07
	Houston-Sugar Land-Baytown						
	MSA, TX	Y	12720 FQ	14180 MW	16010 TQ	USBLS	5/07
	San Antonio MSA, TX	Y	12490 FQ	13900 MW	15300 TQ	USBLS	5/07
	Utah	Y	13770 FQ	19530 MW	32430 TQ	USBLS	5/07
	Ogden-Clearfield MSA, UT	Y	13520 FQ	15870 MW	19020 TQ	USBLS	5/07
	Salt Lake City MSA, UT	Y	22000 FQ	27670 MW	30860 TQ	USBLS	5/07
	Virginia	Y	12570 FQ	13980 MW	15640 TQ	USBLS	5/07
	Richmond MSA, VA	Y	12640 FQ	14010 MW	16370 TQ	USBLS	5/07
	Virginia Beach-Norfolk-						
	Newport News MSA, VA-NC	Y	12840 FQ	14780 MW	21920 TQ	USBLS	5/07
	Washington	H	17.27 FQ	22.39 MW	37.98 TQ	WABLS	3/08
	Seattle-Tacoma-Bellevue						
	MSA, WA	Y	38990 FQ	80640 MW	109270 TQ	USBLS	5/07
	West Virginia	Y	14121 FQ	15317 MW	34189 TQ	WVBLS	7/08-9/08
	Charleston MSA, WV	Y	14430 FQ	22190 MW	36860 TQ	USBLS	5/07
	Wheeling MSA, WV-OH	Y	14770 FQ	25160 MW	46440 TQ	USBLS	5/07
	Wisconsin	Y	14340 FQ	14910 MW	16020 TQ	USBLS	5/07
	Milwaukee-Waukesha-West						
	Allis MSA, WI	Y	14350 FQ	14980 MW	26600 TQ	USBLS	5/07
	San Juan-Caguas-Guaynabo						
	MSA, PR	Y	25720 FQ	72800 MW	80330 TQ	USBLS	5/07
State Government	Alaska	Y			24000 HI	ANCDN	2008
State Government	California	Y			116000 HI	BGLOBE	2009
State Government	Hawaii	Y			35900 HI	STARB	2008
State Government	Louisiana	Y			16800 HI	STLEG1	2008
State Government	Massachusetts	Y			61400 HI	BGLOBE	2009
State Government	Michigan	Y			79650 HI	TCRE	2009
State Government	Washington	Y			42106 HI	WCC	9/1/08
State Government	Wisconsin	Y			49943 HI	LTEL	2009
Librarian	Alabama	Y	37440 FQ	44720 MW	50530 TQ	USBLS	5/07
	Birmingham-Hoover MSA, AL	Y	37950 FQ	45630 MW	52300 TQ	USBLS	5/07
	Alaska	Y	42040 FQ	55900 MW	66830 TQ	USBLS	5/07
	Arizona	Y	34180 FQ	42320 MW	52820 TQ	USBLS	5/07
	Flagstaff MSA, AZ	Y	24910 FQ	35920 MW	46150 TQ	USBLS	5/07
	Phoenix-Mesa-Scottsdale						
	MSA, AZ	Y	36320 FQ	43950 MW	53530 TQ	USBLS	5/07
	Tucson MSA, AZ	Y	31450 FQ	43960 MW	56700 TQ	USBLS	5/07
	Arkansas	Y	40290 FQ	46590 MW	53530 TQ	USBLS	5/07
	Fayetteville-Springdale-Rogers						
	MSA, AR-MO	Y	43190 FQ	50620 MW	60850 TQ	USBLS	5/07
	Little Rock-North Little Rock						
	MSA, AR	Y	41430 FQ	50780 MW	59930 TQ	USBLS	5/07
	California	H	22.87 FQ	29.75 MW	36.92 TQ	CABLS	1/08-3/08
	Los Angeles-Long Beach-						
	Glendale PMSA, CA	H	22.69 FQ	29.46 MW	36.41 TQ	CABLS	1/08-3/08
	Oakland-Fremont-Hayward						
	MSA, CA	H	23.69 FQ	29.63 MW	35.83 TQ	CABLS	1/08-3/08
	Oxnard-Thousand Oaks-						
	Ventura MSA, CA	H	18.58 FQ	26.30 MW	34.34 TQ	CABLS	1/08-3/08
	Riverside-San Bernardino-						
	Ontario MSA, CA	H	21.48 FQ	28.17 MW	35.38 TQ	CABLS	1/08-3/08
	Sacramento-Arden Arcade-						
	Roseville MSA, CA	H	23.26 FQ	28.94 MW	35.28 TQ	CABLS	1/08-3/08
	San Diego-Carlsbad-San						
	Marcos MSA, CA	H	23.93 FQ	28.46 MW	33.11 TQ	CABLS	1/08-3/08
	San Francisco-San Mateo-						
	Redwood PMSA, CA	H	25.54 FQ	34.16 MW	40.23 TQ	CABLS	1/08-3/08

AE Average entry wage	**AW** Average wage paid	**FQ** First quartile wage	**LO** Lowest wage paid	**MTC** Median total compensation	**TCC** Total cash compensation
AER Average entry range	**AWR** Average wage range	**H** Hourly	**LR** Low end range	**MW** Median wage paid	**TQ** Third quartile wage
AEX Average experienced wage	**AXR** Average experienced range	**HI** Highest wage paid	**M** Monthly	**MWR** Median wage range	**W** Weekly
ATC Average total compensation	**D** Daily	**HR** High end range	**MCC** Median cash compensation	**S** See annotated source	**Y** Yearly

Occupation/Type/Industry	Location	Per	Low	Mid	High	Source	Date
Librarian	San Jose-Sunnyvale-Santa Clara MSA, CA	H	27.34 FQ	35.50 MW	41.73 TQ	CABLS	1/08-3/08
	Santa Ana-Anaheim-Irvine PMSA, CA	Y	51070 FQ	65240 MW	78630 TQ	USBLS	5/07
	Colorado	Y	41760 FQ	53690 MW	70410 TQ	USBLS	5/07
	Colorado Springs MSA, CO	Y	52200 FQ	66780 MW	80970 TQ	USBLS	5/07
	Denver-Aurora MSA, CO	Y	42060 FQ	53400 MW	69240 TQ	USBLS	5/07
	Connecticut	H	19.27 AE	28.83 MW		CTBLS	1/08-3/08
	Bridgeport-Stamford-Norwalk MSA, CT	Y	47790 FQ	58290 MW	74460 TQ	USBLS	5/07
	Danbury MSA, CT	Y	51510 FQ	58970 MW	67100 TQ	USBLS	5/07
	Hartford-West Hartford-East Hartford MSA, CT	Y	44270 FQ	57720 MW	71840 TQ	USBLS	5/07
	Waterbury MSA, CT	Y	40870 FQ	57580 MW	76040 TQ	USBLS	5/07
	Delaware	Y	40740 FQ	58260 MW	72850 TQ	USBLS	5/07
	Wilmington PMSA, DE-MD-NJ	Y	44530 FQ	63060 MW	74680 TQ	USBLS	5/07
	District of Columbia	Y	52810 FQ	64290 MW	76850 TQ	USBLS	5/07
	Washington-Arlington-Alexandria MSA, DC-VA-MD-WV	Y	52040 FQ	65590 MW	80340 TQ	USBLS	5/07
	Florida	Y	41400 FQ	51810 MW	65340 TQ	USBLS	5/07
	Fort Lauderdale-Pompano Beach-Deerfield Beach PMSA, FL	Y	39140 FQ	55480 MW	79290 TQ	USBLS	5/07
	Jacksonville MSA, FL	Y	39210 FQ	47900 MW	58600 TQ	USBLS	5/07
	Miami-Fort Lauderdale-Miami Beach MSA, FL	Y	41130 FQ	53290 MW	70410 TQ	USBLS	5/07
	Orlando-Kissimmee MSA, FL	Y	42590 FQ	53180 MW	66070 TQ	USBLS	5/07
	Tampa-St. Petersburg-Clearwater MSA, FL	Y	43510 FQ	53940 MW	66520 TQ	USBLS	5/07
	West Palm Beach-Boca Raton-Boynton Beach PMSA, FL	Y	42780 FQ	50600 MW	62440 TQ	USBLS	5/07
	Georgia	Y	46920 FQ	56610 MW	65470 TQ	USBLS	5/07
	Atlanta-Sandy Springs-Marietta MSA, GA	Y	47700 FQ	58540 MW	68740 TQ	USBLS	5/07
	Savannah MSA, GA	Y	45040 FQ	53390 MW	61930 TQ	USBLS	5/07
	Hawaii	Y	44320 FQ	55180 MW	64880 TQ	USBLS	5/07
	Honolulu MSA, HI	Y	41970 FQ	52850 MW	64260 TQ	USBLS	5/07
	Idaho	Y	37290 FQ	44700 MW	55800 TQ	USBLS	5/07
	Boise City-Nampa MSA, ID	Y	38790 FQ	45080 MW	56650 TQ	USBLS	5/07
	Illinois	Y	40720 FQ	54690 MW	71160 TQ	USBLS	5/07
	Chicago-Naperville-Joliet MSA, IL-IN-WI	Y	45180 FQ	58650 MW	75160 TQ	USBLS	5/07
	Indiana	Y	35070 FQ	45890 MW	57910 TQ	USBLS	5/07
	Gary PMSA, IN	Y	35540 FQ	47170 MW	58290 TQ	USBLS	5/07
	Indianapolis-Carmel MSA, IN	Y	37930 FQ	46580 MW	59530 TQ	USBLS	5/07
	South Bend-Mishawaka MSA, IN-MI	Y	38730 FQ	46660 MW	56140 TQ	USBLS	5/07
	Iowa	Y	35100 FQ	45490 MW	55530 TQ	USBLS	5/07
	Des Moines-West Des Moines MSA, IA	Y	40300 FQ	51690 MW	59020 TQ	USBLS	5/07
	Kansas	Y	35550 FQ	43770 MW	51130 TQ	USBLS	5/07
	Wichita MSA, KS	Y	37390 FQ	45850 MW	53620 TQ	USBLS	5/07
	Kentucky	Y	41554 FQ	51030 MW	60055 TQ	KYBLS	2008
	Louisville-Jefferson County MSA, KY-IN	Y	38730 FQ	51550 MW	63140 TQ	USBLS	5/07
	Louisiana	H	18.30 FQ	21.29 MW	24.08 TQ	LABLS	1/08-3/08
	Baton Rouge MSA, LA	Y	37550 FQ	44160 MW	50240 TQ	USBLS	5/07
	Lafayette MSA, LA	Y	40040 FQ	45740 MW	51190 TQ	USBLS	5/07
	New Orleans-Metairie-Kenner MSA, LA	Y	41520 FQ	47340 MW	54020 TQ	USBLS	5/07
	Shreveport-Bossier City MSA, LA	Y	40690 FQ	48650 MW	54630 TQ	USBLS	5/07
	Maine	Y	33370 FQ	42880 MW	53640 TQ	USBLS	5/07
	Lewiston-Auburn MSA, ME	Y	36970 FQ	46490 MW	59150 TQ	USBLS	5/07
	Portland-South Portland-Biddeford MSA, ME	Y	36870 FQ	45270 MW	55290 TQ	USBLS	5/07
	Maryland	Y		59400 MW		MDBLS	3/08
	Baltimore-Towson MSA, MD	Y	41100 FQ	52260 MW	68040 TQ	USBLS	5/07
	Bethesda-Gaithersburg-Frederick PMSA, MD	Y	57700 FQ	72450 MW	85900 TQ	USBLS	5/07

AE	Average entry wage	AW	Average wage paid	FQ	First quartile wage
AER	Average entry range	AWR	Average wage range	H	Hourly
AEX	Average experienced wage	AXR	Average experienced range	HI	Highest wage paid
ATC	Average total compensation	D	Daily	HR	High end range

LO	Lowest wage paid	MTC	Median total compensation	TCC	Total cash compensation
LR	Low end range	MW	Median wage paid	TQ	Third quartile wage
M	Monthly	MWR	Median wage range	W	Weekly
MCC	Median cash compensation	S	See annotated source	Y	Yearly

Librarian

Occupation/Type/Industry	Location	Per	Low	Mid	High	Source	Date
Librarian	Massachusetts	Y	45330 FQ	57040 MW	69740 TQ	USBLS	5/07
	Boston-Cambridge-Quincy NECTA, MA	Y	48600 FQ	59910 MW	73930 TQ	USBLS	5/07
	Worcester MSA, MA-CT	Y	41300 FQ	53850 MW	65560 TQ	USBLS	5/07
	Michigan	Y	40510 FQ	51610 MW	65900 TQ	USBLS	5/07
	Detroit-Warren-Livonia MSA, MI	Y	42880 FQ	51710 MW	69700 TQ	USBLS	5/07
	Grand Rapids-Wyoming MSA, MI	Y	37780 FQ	50080 MW	62550 TQ	USBLS	5/07
	Warren-Troy-Farmington Hills PMSA, MI	Y	43470 FQ	54040 MW	74120 TQ	USBLS	5/07
	Minnesota	Y	45741 FQ	54299 MW	63819 TQ	MNBLS	10/08-12/08
	Duluth-Superior MSA, MN-WI	Y	42403 FQ	50333 MW	60325 TQ	MNBLS	10/08-12/08
	Minneapolis-Saint Paul MSA, MN-WI	Y	47038 FQ	56496 MW	65703 TQ	MNBLS	10/08-12/08
	Rochester MSA, MN	Y	45026 FQ	52380 MW	62193 TQ	MNBLS	10/08-12/08
	Mississippi	Y	32150 FQ	41140 MW	49620 TQ	USBLS	5/07
	Jackson MSA, MS	Y	25450 FQ	38560 MW	48210 TQ	USBLS	5/07
	Missouri	Y	37700 FQ	47560 MW	59400 TQ	USBLS	5/07
	Jefferson City MSA, MO	Y	35760 FQ	40980 MW	48170 TQ	USBLS	5/07
	Joplin MSA, MO	Y	30760 FQ	39200 MW	47080 TQ	USBLS	5/07
	Kansas City MSA, MO-KS	Y	40170 FQ	49260 MW	59160 TQ	USBLS	5/07
	St. Louis MSA, MO-IL	Y	40680 FQ	53110 MW	64040 TQ	USBLS	5/07
	Montana	Y	26620 FQ	37270 MW	47090 TQ	USBLS	5/07
	Billings MSA, MT	Y	26010 FQ	43180 MW	55400 TQ	USBLS	5/07
	Nebraska	Y	36630 FQ	44480 MW	51850 TQ	USBLS	5/07
	Omaha-Council Bluffs MSA, NE-IA	Y	41350 FQ	46560 MW	52410 TQ	USBLS	5/07
	Nevada	H	24.13 FQ	28.56 MW	33.76 TQ	NVBLS	5/08
	Las Vegas-Paradise MSA, NV	H	24.65 FQ	28.85 MW	34.09 TQ	NVBLS	5/08
	New Hampshire	H	15.01 AE	21.17 MW	25.52 AEX	NHBLS	6/08
	Manchester MSA, NH	Y	42570 FQ	50950 MW	58260 TQ	USBLS	5/07
	Nashua NECTA, NH-MA	Y	39220 FQ	49970 MW	59660 TQ	USBLS	5/07
	Portsmouth MSA, NH-ME	Y	35780 FQ	47140 MW	55470 TQ	USBLS	5/07
	New Jersey	Y	47240 FQ	58100 MW	73450 TQ	USBLS	5/07
	Camden PMSA, NJ	Y	45680 FQ	59490 MW	73520 TQ	USBLS	5/07
	Edison PMSA, NJ	Y	47610 FQ	56270 MW	68290 TQ	USBLS	5/07
	Newark-Union PMSA, NJ-PA	Y	47190 FQ	59020 MW	74940 TQ	USBLS	5/07
	New Mexico	Y	34180 FQ	42980 MW	54020 TQ	USBLS	5/07
	Albuquerque MSA, NM	Y	34960 FQ	41690 MW	49990 TQ	USBLS	5/07
	New York	Y	45080 FQ	55590 MW	68570 TQ	USBLS	5/07
	Albany-Schenectady-Troy MSA, NY	Y	42040 FQ	49690 MW	62280 TQ	USBLS	5/07
	Binghamton MSA, NY	Y	42500 FQ	49360 MW	61340 TQ	USBLS	5/07
	Buffalo-Niagara Falls MSA, NY	Y	39940 FQ	52410 MW	67310 TQ	USBLS	5/07
	Nassau-Suffolk PMSA, NY	Y	49380 FQ	60580 MW	77200 TQ	USBLS	5/07
	New York-Northern New Jersey-Long Island MSA, NY-NJ-PA	Y	47980 FQ	58400 MW	73500 TQ	USBLS	5/07
	North Carolina	Y	38990 FQ	46160 MW	54660 TQ	USBLS	5/07
	Charlotte-Gastonia-Concord MSA, NC-SC	Y	39700 FQ	48590 MW	57860 TQ	USBLS	5/07
	Raleigh-Cary MSA, NC	Y	41990 FQ	49040 MW	58290 TQ	USBLS	5/07
	North Dakota	Y	29940 FQ	39290 MW	48060 TQ	USBLS	5/07
	Fargo MSA, ND-MN	Y	39240 FQ	45300 MW	55390 TQ	USBLS	5/07
	Ohio	Y	40760 FQ	53210 MW	65380 TQ	USBLS	5/07
	Canton-Massillon MSA, OH	Y	32340 FQ	44740 MW	58250 TQ	USBLS	5/07
	Cincinnati-Middletown MSA, OH-KY-IN	Y	42600 FQ	53320 MW	67490 TQ	USBLS	5/07
	Cleveland-Elyria-Mentor MSA, OH	Y	39250 FQ	50250 MW	65210 TQ	USBLS	5/07
	Columbus MSA, OH	Y	44820 FQ	55530 MW	67420 TQ	USBLS	5/07
	Dayton MSA, OH	Y	53890 FQ	64650 MW	83230 TQ	USBLS	5/07
	Mansfield MSA, OH	Y	39830 FQ	49520 MW	60500 TQ	USBLS	5/07
	Oklahoma	Y	31990 FQ	38290 MW	45880 TQ	USBLS	5/07
	Oklahoma City MSA, OK	Y	33200 FQ	40080 MW	47400 TQ	USBLS	5/07
	Tulsa MSA, OK	Y	33780 FQ	40600 MW	49100 TQ	USBLS	5/07
	Oregon	H	21.48 FQ	26.72 MW	31.15 TQ	ORBLS	5/08
	Portland-Vancouver-Beaverton MSA, OR-WA	Y	46380 FQ	56940 MW	66670 TQ	USBLS	5/07
	Pennsylvania	Y	34780 FQ	49950 MW	61510 TQ	USBLS	5/07

AE	Average entry wage	AW	Average wage paid	FQ	First quartile wage	LO	Lowest wage paid	MTC	Median total compensation	TCC	Total cash compensation
AER	Average entry range	AWR	Average wage range	H	Hourly	LR	Low end range	MW	Median wage paid	TQ	Third quartile wage
AEX	Average experienced wage	AXR	Average experienced range	HI	Highest wage paid	M	Monthly	MWR	Median wage range	W	Weekly
ATC	Average total compensation	D	Daily	HR	High end range	MCC	Median cash compensation	S	See annotated source	Y	Yearly

Occupation/Type/Industry	Location	Per	Low	Mid	High	Source	Date
Librarian	Allentown-Bethlehem-Easton MSA, PA-NJ	Y	43140 FQ	55220 MW	66320 TQ	USBLS	5/07
	Philadelphia-Camden-Wilmington MSA, PA-NJ-DE-MD	Y	37660 FQ	52540 MW	65320 TQ	USBLS	5/07
	Pittsburgh MSA, PA	Y	32870 FQ	46920 MW	58690 TQ	USBLS	5/07
	Rhode Island	Y	48230 FQ	57950 MW	68910 TQ	USBLS	5/07
	Providence-Fall River-Warwick MSA, RI-MA	Y	46940 FQ	57120 MW	68010 TQ	USBLS	5/07
	South Carolina	Y	38440 FQ	48200 MW	57680 TQ	USBLS	5/07
	Charleston-North Charleston MSA, SC	Y	36750 FQ	44940 MW	57220 TQ	USBLS	5/07
	Columbia MSA, SC	Y	37420 FQ	46260 MW	57210 TQ	USBLS	5/07
	Spartanburg MSA, SC	Y	40680 FQ	51450 MW	58560 TQ	USBLS	5/07
	South Dakota	Y	27516 FQ	34029 MW	41307 TQ	SDBLS	7/08-9/08
	Sioux Falls MSA, SD	Y	31547 FQ	37269 MW	49534 TQ	SDBLS	7/08-9/08
	Tennessee	Y	34950 FQ	42880 MW	49300 TQ	USBLS	5/07
	Memphis MSA, TN-MS-AR	Y	37490 FQ	44090 MW	49660 TQ	USBLS	5/07
	Nashville-Davidson-Murfreesboro MSA, TN	Y	37110 FQ	44930 MW	52310 TQ	USBLS	5/07
	Texas	Y	42400 FQ	48850 MW	56940 TQ	USBLS	5/07
	Austin-Round Rock MSA, TX	Y	42260 FQ	49150 MW	57630 TQ	USBLS	5/07
	Brownsville-Harlingen MSA, TX	Y	37210 FQ	47290 MW	56640 TQ	USBLS	5/07
	Corpus Christi MSA, TX	Y	42050 FQ	48190 MW	55210 TQ	USBLS	5/07
	Dallas-Fort Worth-Arlington MSA, TX	Y	43780 FQ	49940 MW	58600 TQ	USBLS	5/07
	El Paso MSA, TX	Y	42930 FQ	49220 MW	56240 TQ	USBLS	5/07
	Houston-Sugar Land-Baytown MSA, TX	Y	43720 FQ	50110 MW	58480 TQ	USBLS	5/07
	San Antonio MSA, TX	Y	43390 FQ	50960 MW	59380 TQ	USBLS	5/07
	Utah	Y	33650 FQ	44670 MW	55610 TQ	USBLS	5/07
	Ogden-Clearfield MSA, UT	Y	34100 FQ	44430 MW	54020 TQ	USBLS	5/07
	Salt Lake City MSA, UT	Y	40100 FQ	48170 MW	58550 TQ	USBLS	5/07
	Vermont	Y	30740 FQ	35940 MW	48670 TQ	USBLS	5/07
	Burlington-South Burlington MSA, VT	Y	31750 FQ	36380 MW	50350 TQ	USBLS	5/07
	Virginia	Y	44200 FQ	55390 MW	71140 TQ	USBLS	5/07
	Richmond MSA, VA	Y	44500 FQ	53790 MW	66080 TQ	USBLS	5/07
	Virginia Beach-Norfolk-Newport News MSA, VA-NC	Y	43480 FQ	51940 MW	62430 TQ	USBLS	5/07
	Washington	H	24.67 FQ	29.10 MW	33.67 TQ	WABLS	3/08
	Seattle-Tacoma-Bellevue MSA, WA	Y	53910 FQ	62590 MW	72280 TQ	USBLS	5/07
	West Virginia	Y	34820 FQ	43797 MW	51473 TQ	WVBLS	7/08-9/08
	Charleston MSA, WV	Y	35740 FQ	42560 MW	49780 TQ	USBLS	5/07
	Wisconsin	Y	39820 FQ	48760 MW	59570 TQ	USBLS	5/07
	Milwaukee-Waukesha-West Allis MSA, WI	Y	41800 FQ	51950 MW	68560 TQ	USBLS	5/07
	Wyoming	Y	33364 FQ	45426 MW	55139 TQ	WYBLS	9/08
	Cheyenne MSA, WY	Y	43265 FQ	52852 MW	72474 TQ	WYBLS	9/08
	Puerto Rico	Y	26420 FQ	30460 MW	36020 TQ	USBLS	5/07
	San Juan-Caguas-Guaynabo MSA, PR	Y	25610 FQ	30070 MW	35530 TQ	USBLS	5/07
	Virgin Islands	Y	30380 FQ	42980 MW	56810 TQ	USBLS	5/07
	Guam	Y	34700 FQ	41660 MW	55380 TQ	USBLS	5/07
Adult Services	United States	Y		35993 AW		LIBJ	2007
ALA-Accredited Master's Degree	United States	Y		53251 MW		ALA01	2008
Department of Environmental Quality	Oregon	M	3386 LO		4951 HI	ODEQSS	11/1/08
Electronic or Digital Services	United States	Y		44657 AW		LIBJ	2007
Interlibrary Loans/Document Delivery	United States	Y		33779 AW		LIBJ	2007
Substitute	Warwick, MA	Y			400 HI	FRCOG	2009
Youth Services	United States	Y		35929 AW		LIBJ	2007
Librarian of Congress							
Federal Government	United States	Y			172200 HI	CRS02	1/08
Library Aide							
Montana State School for the Deaf and Blind	Montana	H	9.00 LO			MTSDB	10/08-6/09
Summer	Bernardston, MA	H			8.40 HI	FRCOG	2009

AE Average entry wage	**AW** Average wage paid	**FQ** First quartile wage	**LO** Lowest wage paid	**MTC** Median total compensation	**TCC** Total cash compensation
AER Average entry range	**AWR** Average wage range	**H** Hourly	**LR** Low end range	**MW** Median wage paid	**TQ** Third quartile wage
AEX Average experienced wage	**AXR** Average experienced range	**HI** Highest wage paid	**M** Monthly	**MWR** Median wage range	**W** Weekly
ATC Average total compensation	**D** Daily	**HR** High end range	**MCC** Median cash compensation	**S** See annotated source	**Y** Yearly

Library Assistant

Occupation/Type/Industry	Location	Per	Low	Mid	High	Source	Date
Clerical	Alabama	Y	14130 FQ	17180 MW	20820 TQ	USBLS	5/07
Clerical	Birmingham-Hoover MSA, AL	Y	14620 FQ	18960 MW	24140 TQ	USBLS	5/07
Clerical	Mobile MSA, AL	Y	17130 FQ	18800 MW	20640 TQ	USBLS	5/07
Clerical	Alaska	Y	28730 FQ	34270 MW	39500 TQ	USBLS	5/07
Clerical	Anchorage MSA, AK	Y	27890 FQ	32910 MW	37230 TQ	USBLS	5/07
Clerical	Arizona	Y	19690 FQ	24750 MW	30550 TQ	USBLS	5/07
Clerical	Phoenix-Mesa-Scottsdale MSA, AZ	Y	21870 FQ	27170 MW	32120 TQ	USBLS	5/07
Clerical	Tucson MSA, AZ	Y	18980 FQ	22210 MW	31480 TQ	USBLS	5/07
Clerical	Arkansas	Y	14370 FQ	15610 MW	18850 TQ	USBLS	5/07
Clerical	Little Rock-North Little Rock MSA, AR	Y	14030 FQ	14990 MW	17050 TQ	USBLS	5/07
Clerical	California	H	10.94 FQ	14.41 MW	18.04 TQ	CABLS	1/08-3/08
Clerical	Bakersfield MSA, CA	H	12.93 FQ	14.34 MW	15.86 TQ	CABLS	1/08-3/08
Clerical	Fresno MSA, CA	H	8.44 FQ	9.27 MW	13.43 TQ	CABLS	1/08-3/08
Clerical	Los Angeles-Long Beach-Glendale PMSA, CA	H	10.46 FQ	12.20 MW	16.80 TQ	CABLS	1/08-3/08
Clerical	Oakland-Fremont-Hayward MSA, CA	H	13.44 FQ	16.51 MW	19.14 TQ	CABLS	1/08-3/08
Clerical	Oxnard-Thousand Oaks-Ventura MSA, CA	H	10.97 FQ	14.24 MW	18.00 TQ	CABLS	1/08-3/08
Clerical	Riverside-San Bernardino-Ontario MSA, CA	H	10.74 FQ	15.58 MW	18.10 TQ	CABLS	1/08-3/08
Clerical	Sacramento-Arden Arcade-Roseville MSA, CA	H	12.31 FQ	14.97 MW	17.38 TQ	CABLS	1/08-3/08
Clerical	San Diego-Carlsbad-San Marcos MSA, CA	H	9.68 FQ	12.43 MW	17.01 TQ	CABLS	1/08-3/08
Clerical	San Francisco-San Mateo-Redwood PMSA, CA	H	11.12 FQ	14.24 MW	19.41 TQ	CABLS	1/08-3/08
Clerical	San Jose-Sunnyvale-Santa Clara MSA, CA	H	11.81 FQ	16.87 MW	20.64 TQ	CABLS	1/08-3/08
Clerical	Santa Ana-Anaheim-Irvine PMSA, CA	Y	26510 FQ	33370 MW	39970 TQ	USBLS	5/07
Clerical	Colorado	Y	17810 FQ	20310 MW	24800 TQ	USBLS	5/07
Clerical	Denver-Aurora MSA, CO	Y	18320 FQ	20170 MW	23460 TQ	USBLS	5/07
Clerical	Connecticut	H	8.63 AE	11.57 MW		CTBLS	1/08-3/08
Clerical	Bridgeport-Stamford-Norwalk MSA, CT	Y	18030 FQ	22300 MW	29490 TQ	USBLS	5/07
Clerical	Hartford-West Hartford-East Hartford MSA, CT	Y	17900 FQ	23850 MW	32840 TQ	USBLS	5/07
Clerical	Delaware	Y	17270 FQ	25900 MW	30840 TQ	USBLS	5/07
Clerical	Wilmington PMSA, DE-MD-NJ	Y	19680 FQ	26910 MW	31460 TQ	USBLS	5/07
Clerical	District of Columbia	Y	18870 FQ	27470 MW	36900 TQ	USBLS	5/07
Clerical	Washington-Arlington-Alexandria MSA, DC-VA-MD-WV	Y	19290 FQ	25980 MW	32880 TQ	USBLS	5/07
Clerical	Florida	Y	18750 FQ	22760 MW	27560 TQ	USBLS	5/07
Clerical	Fort Lauderdale-Pompano Beach-Deerfield Beach PMSA, FL	Y	17790 FQ	27660 MW	33070 TQ	USBLS	5/07
Clerical	Jacksonville MSA, FL	Y	19480 FQ	23130 MW	27760 TQ	USBLS	5/07
Clerical	Miami-Fort Lauderdale-Miami Beach MSA, FL	Y	18590 FQ	23640 MW	29470 TQ	USBLS	5/07
Clerical	Orlando-Kissimmee MSA, FL	Y	19520 FQ	22520 MW	25190 TQ	USBLS	5/07
Clerical	Tampa-St. Petersburg-Clearwater MSA, FL	Y	16980 FQ	21320 MW	25530 TQ	USBLS	5/07
Clerical	West Palm Beach-Boca Raton-Boynton Beach PMSA, FL	Y	16550 FQ	22740 MW	28540 TQ	USBLS	5/07
Clerical	Georgia	Y	16260 FQ	20060 MW	24840 TQ	USBLS	5/07
Clerical	Atlanta-Sandy Springs-Marietta MSA, GA	Y	16800 FQ	20360 MW	24800 TQ	USBLS	5/07
Clerical	Hawaii	Y	23870 FQ	27090 MW	30150 TQ	USBLS	5/07
Clerical	Honolulu MSA, HI	Y	23940 FQ	27120 MW	30180 TQ	USBLS	5/07
Clerical	Idaho	Y	22480 FQ	29010 MW	36370 TQ	USBLS	5/07
Clerical	Boise City-Nampa MSA, ID	Y	26260 FQ	32290 MW	38350 TQ	USBLS	5/07
Clerical	Illinois	Y	16970 FQ	21950 MW	29880 TQ	USBLS	5/07
Clerical	Chicago-Naperville-Joliet MSA, IL-IN-WI	Y	17230 FQ	22800 MW	31020 TQ	USBLS	5/07
Clerical	Indiana	Y	14590 FQ	19000 MW	23920 TQ	USBLS	5/07
Clerical	Fort Wayne MSA, IN	Y	13220 FQ	14870 MW	20710 TQ	USBLS	5/07

AE   Average entry wage   AW   Average wage paid   FQ   First quartile wage   LO   Lowest wage paid   MTC   Median total compensation   TCC   Total cash compensation
AER Average entry range   AWR Average wage range   H   Hourly   LR   Low end range   MW   Median wage paid   TQ   Third quartile wage
AEX Average experienced wage   AXR Average experienced range HI   Highest wage paid   M   Monthly   MWR   Median wage range   W   Weekly
ATC Average total compensation D   Daily   HR   High end range   MCC Median cash compensation   S   See annotated source   Y   Yearly

906

Library Assistant

Occupation/Type/Industry	Location	Per	Low	Mid	High	Source	Date
Clerical	Gary PMSA, IN	Y	13880 FQ	17680 MW	22970 TQ	USBLS	5/07
Clerical	Indianapolis-Carmel MSA, IN	Y	14510 FQ	18680 MW	24480 TQ	USBLS	5/07
Clerical	Iowa	Y	15390 FQ	18540 MW	25760 TQ	USBLS	5/07
Clerical	Des Moines-West Des Moines MSA, IA	Y	16520 FQ	18830 MW	28960 TQ	USBLS	5/07
Clerical	Sioux City MSA, IA-NE-SD	Y	17190 FQ	20300 MW	27020 TQ	USBLS	5/07
Clerical	Kansas	Y	15180 FQ	18530 MW	22950 TQ	USBLS	5/07
Clerical	Topeka MSA, KS	Y	18230 FQ	22450 MW	26010 TQ	USBLS	5/07
Clerical	Wichita MSA, KS	Y	14590 FQ	19440 MW	27120 TQ	USBLS	5/07
Clerical	Kentucky	Y	16023 FQ	20626 MW	26030 TQ	KYBLS	2008
Clerical	Louisville-Jefferson County MSA, KY-IN	Y	21020 FQ	25700 MW	28750 TQ	USBLS	5/07
Clerical	Louisiana	H	7.51 FQ	9.11 MW	11.54 TQ	LABLS	1/08-3/08
Clerical	Baton Rouge MSA, LA	Y	17630 FQ	19380 MW	22410 TQ	USBLS	5/07
Clerical	New Orleans-Metairie-Kenner MSA, LA	Y	15920 FQ	20580 MW	29200 TQ	USBLS	5/07
Clerical	Maine	Y	16090 FQ	20700 MW	26690 TQ	USBLS	5/07
Clerical	Bangor MSA, ME	Y	20360 FQ	24850 MW	27370 TQ	USBLS	5/07
Clerical	Portland-South Portland-Biddeford MSA, ME	Y	15980 FQ	22090 MW	28460 TQ	USBLS	5/07
Clerical	Maryland	Y		22125 MW		MDBLS	3/08
Clerical	Baltimore-Towson MSA, MD	Y	15780 FQ	19580 MW	29650 TQ	USBLS	5/07
Clerical	Bethesda-Gaithersburg-Frederick PMSA, MD	Y	18070 FQ	24580 MW	30730 TQ	USBLS	5/07
Clerical	Massachusetts	Y	20760 FQ	27940 MW	35630 TQ	USBLS	5/07
Clerical	Boston-Cambridge-Quincy NECTA, MA	Y	21930 FQ	30250 MW	37070 TQ	USBLS	5/07
Clerical	Worcester MSA, MA-CT	Y	16660 FQ	26600 MW	30740 TQ	USBLS	5/07
Clerical	Michigan	Y	16870 FQ	20210 MW	27110 TQ	USBLS	5/07
Clerical	Detroit-Warren-Livonia MSA, MI	Y	16750 FQ	19510 MW	26240 TQ	USBLS	5/07
Clerical	Grand Rapids-Wyoming MSA, MI	Y	20880 FQ	25870 MW	29040 TQ	USBLS	5/07
Clerical	Warren-Troy-Farmington Hills PMSA, MI	Y	16740 FQ	20640 MW	26520 TQ	USBLS	5/07
Clerical	Minnesota	Y	19691 FQ	25947 MW	31556 TQ	MNBLS	10/08-12/08
Clerical	Duluth-Superior MSA, MN-WI	Y	15070 FQ	17412 MW	27518 TQ	MNBLS	10/08-12/08
Clerical	Minneapolis-Saint Paul MSA, MN-WI	Y	22762 FQ	28507 MW	32878 TQ	MNBLS	10/08-12/08
Clerical	Mississippi	Y	14240 FQ	17460 MW	20970 TQ	USBLS	5/07
Clerical	Jackson MSA, MS	Y	13390 FQ	16670 MW	20900 TQ	USBLS	5/07
Clerical	Missouri	Y	15010 FQ	18040 MW	22540 TQ	USBLS	5/07
Clerical	Joplin MSA, MO	Y	14380 FQ	15330 MW	19140 TQ	USBLS	5/07
Clerical	Kansas City MSA, MO-KS	Y	14860 FQ	18640 MW	23290 TQ	USBLS	5/07
Clerical	St. Louis MSA, MO-IL	Y	16450 FQ	19250 MW	25110 TQ	USBLS	5/07
Clerical	Montana	Y	16660 FQ	19480 MW	23930 TQ	USBLS	5/07
Clerical	Billings MSA, MT	Y	19360 FQ	22050 MW	25870 TQ	USBLS	5/07
Clerical	Nebraska	Y	13890 FQ	16830 MW	21630 TQ	USBLS	5/07
Clerical	Lincoln MSA, NE	Y	20770 FQ	22960 MW	25070 TQ	USBLS	5/07
Clerical	Omaha-Council Bluffs MSA, NE-IA	Y	14080 FQ	16710 MW	21330 TQ	USBLS	5/07
Clerical	Nevada	H	12.79 FQ	14.71 MW	18.55 TQ	NVBLS	5/08
Clerical	Las Vegas-Paradise MSA, NV	H	12.26 FQ	14.01 MW	16.59 TQ	NVBLS	5/08
Clerical	New Hampshire	H	8.25 AE	11.10 MW	12.61 AEX	NHBLS	6/08
Clerical	Manchester MSA, NH	Y	18040 FQ	21570 MW	26350 TQ	USBLS	5/07
Clerical	Nashua NECTA, NH-MA	Y	16980 FQ	20360 MW	26280 TQ	USBLS	5/07
Clerical	New Jersey	Y	18040 FQ	23690 MW	29270 TQ	USBLS	5/07
Clerical	Camden PMSA, NJ	Y	15940 FQ	18530 MW	22940 TQ	USBLS	5/07
Clerical	Edison PMSA, NJ	Y	23150 FQ	26920 MW	32790 TQ	USBLS	5/07
Clerical	Newark-Union PMSA, NJ-PA	Y	17690 FQ	22340 MW	28450 TQ	USBLS	5/07
Clerical	New Mexico	Y	14430 FQ	17960 MW	23390 TQ	USBLS	5/07
Clerical	Albuquerque MSA, NM	Y	13630 FQ	16100 MW	24460 TQ	USBLS	5/07
Clerical	New York	Y	17230 FQ	23270 MW	30890 TQ	USBLS	5/07
Clerical	Albany-Schenectady-Troy MSA, NY	Y	17780 FQ	22450 MW	29060 TQ	USBLS	5/07
Clerical	Buffalo-Niagara Falls MSA, NY	Y	15820 FQ	18140 MW	25410 TQ	USBLS	5/07
Clerical	Glens Falls MSA, NY	Y	16920 FQ	18800 MW	27150 TQ	USBLS	5/07
Clerical	Nassau-Suffolk PMSA, NY	Y	23800 FQ	29070 MW	34720 TQ	USBLS	5/07

AE	Average entry wage	AW	Average wage paid	FQ	First quartile wage
AER	Average entry range	AWR	Average wage range	H	Hourly
AEX	Average experienced wage	AXR	Average experienced range	HI	Highest wage paid
ATC	Average total compensation	D	Daily	HR	High end range

LO	Lowest wage paid	MTC	Median total compensation
LR	Low end range	MW	Median wage paid
M	Monthly	MWR	Median wage range
MCC	Median cash compensation	S	See annotated source

TCC	Total cash compensation
TQ	Third quartile wage
W	Weekly
Y	Yearly

Occupation/Type/Industry	Location	Per	Low	Mid	High	Source	Date
Library Assistant							
Clerical	New York-Northern New Jersey-Long Island MSA, NY-NJ-PA	Y	18020 FQ	25480 MW	32540 TQ	USBLS	5/07
Clerical	North Carolina	Y	16550 FQ	20740 MW	25030 TQ	USBLS	5/07
Clerical	Charlotte-Gastonia-Concord MSA, NC-SC	Y	19500 FQ	21910 MW	24750 TQ	USBLS	5/07
Clerical	Raleigh-Cary MSA, NC	Y	14400 FQ	17430 MW	20190 TQ	USBLS	5/07
Clerical	North Dakota	Y	13720 FQ	16610 MW	22880 TQ	USBLS	5/07
Clerical	Fargo MSA, ND-MN	Y	14920 FQ	17460 MW	20160 TQ	USBLS	5/07
Clerical	Ohio	Y	17300 FQ	23360 MW	29740 TQ	USBLS	5/07
Clerical	Canton-Massillon MSA, OH	Y	16790 FQ	19970 MW	23530 TQ	USBLS	5/07
Clerical	Cincinnati-Middletown MSA, OH-KY-IN	Y	16860 FQ	22390 MW	28650 TQ	USBLS	5/07
Clerical	Cleveland-Elyria-Mentor MSA, OH	Y	16100 FQ	22140 MW	29800 TQ	USBLS	5/07
Clerical	Columbus MSA, OH	Y	17180 FQ	21150 MW	27790 TQ	USBLS	5/07
Clerical	Mansfield MSA, OH	Y	21230 FQ	23990 MW	35150 TQ	USBLS	5/07
Clerical	Oklahoma	Y	13810 FQ	16520 MW	20820 TQ	USBLS	5/07
Clerical	Oklahoma City MSA, OK	Y	14070 FQ	16590 MW	20890 TQ	USBLS	5/07
Clerical	Tulsa MSA, OK	Y	13370 FQ	15930 MW	19160 TQ	USBLS	5/07
Clerical	Oregon	H	10.37 FQ	13.17 MW	15.58 TQ	ORBLS	5/08
Clerical	Eugene-Springfield MSA, OR	Y	19960 FQ	26490 MW	29210 TQ	USBLS	5/07
Clerical	Medford MSA, OR	Y	20030 FQ	26720 MW	29770 TQ	USBLS	5/07
Clerical	Portland-Vancouver-Beaverton MSA, OR-WA	Y	24420 FQ	28770 MW	33700 TQ	USBLS	5/07
Clerical	Pennsylvania	Y	15830 FQ	20520 MW	25620 TQ	USBLS	5/07
Clerical	Allentown-Bethlehem-Easton MSA, PA-NJ	Y	17250 FQ	22220 MW	26030 TQ	USBLS	5/07
Clerical	Lancaster MSA, PA	Y	18850 FQ	21660 MW	24390 TQ	USBLS	5/07
Clerical	Philadelphia-Camden-Wilmington MSA, PA-NJ-DE-MD	Y	16260 FQ	20830 MW	26770 TQ	USBLS	5/07
Clerical	Pittsburgh MSA, PA	Y	14930 FQ	19280 MW	24140 TQ	USBLS	5/07
Clerical	Rhode Island	Y	19370 FQ	23750 MW	29190 TQ	USBLS	5/07
Clerical	Providence-Fall River-Warwick MSA, RI-MA	Y	19480 FQ	23880 MW	29320 TQ	USBLS	5/07
Clerical	South Carolina	Y	18080 FQ	21850 MW	24640 TQ	USBLS	5/07
Clerical	Charleston-North Charleston MSA, SC	Y	16030 FQ	19430 MW	22880 TQ	USBLS	5/07
Clerical	Columbia MSA, SC	Y	21820 FQ	23550 MW	25330 TQ	USBLS	5/07
Clerical	South Dakota	Y	17091 FQ	19160 MW	23335 TQ	SDBLS	7/08-9/08
Clerical	Tennessee	Y	16600 FQ	21560 MW	25810 TQ	USBLS	5/07
Clerical	Memphis MSA, TN-MS-AR	Y	14620 FQ	19630 MW	24920 TQ	USBLS	5/07
Clerical	Nashville-Davidson-Murfreesboro MSA, TN	Y	20620 FQ	23370 MW	27730 TQ	USBLS	5/07
Clerical	Texas	Y	16770 FQ	20580 MW	25030 TQ	USBLS	5/07
Clerical	Austin-Round Rock MSA, TX	Y	19740 FQ	24190 MW	31260 TQ	USBLS	5/07
Clerical	Beaumont-Port Arthur MSA, TX	Y	15940 FQ	21230 MW	24810 TQ	USBLS	5/07
Clerical	Brownsville-Harlingen MSA, TX	Y	17110 FQ	19780 MW	23510 TQ	USBLS	5/07
Clerical	Dallas-Fort Worth-Arlington MSA, TX	Y	16870 FQ	21770 MW	26130 TQ	USBLS	5/07
Clerical	El Paso MSA, TX	Y	17990 FQ	22510 MW	28110 TQ	USBLS	5/07
Clerical	Houston-Sugar Land-Baytown MSA, TX	Y	17110 FQ	20370 MW	24730 TQ	USBLS	5/07
Clerical	San Antonio MSA, TX	Y	17180 FQ	19930 MW	23980 TQ	USBLS	5/07
Clerical	Utah	Y	17230 FQ	20000 MW	24450 TQ	USBLS	5/07
Clerical	Provo-Orem MSA, UT	Y	15570 FQ	18970 MW	24300 TQ	USBLS	5/07
Clerical	Salt Lake City MSA, UT	Y	17430 FQ	19660 MW	24420 TQ	USBLS	5/07
Clerical	Vermont	Y	21320 FQ	25470 MW	28270 TQ	USBLS	5/07
Clerical	Burlington-South Burlington MSA, VT	Y	24710 FQ	26700 MW	28680 TQ	USBLS	5/07
Clerical	Virginia	Y	18860 FQ	23490 MW	29460 TQ	USBLS	5/07
Clerical	Lynchburg MSA, VA	Y	14300 FQ	19310 MW	24320 TQ	USBLS	5/07
Clerical	Richmond MSA, VA	Y	18710 FQ	23330 MW	28290 TQ	USBLS	5/07
Clerical	Roanoke MSA, VA	Y	16570 FQ	21050 MW	27140 TQ	USBLS	5/07
Clerical	Virginia Beach-Norfolk-Newport News MSA, VA-NC	Y	17380 FQ	20910 MW	25330 TQ	USBLS	5/07
Clerical	Washington	H	10.40 FQ	12.13 MW	14.45 TQ	WABLS	3/08

AE	Average entry wage	AW	Average wage paid	FQ	First quartile wage
AER	Average entry range	AWR	Average wage range	H	Hourly
AEX	Average experienced wage	AXR	Average experienced range	HI	Highest wage paid
ATC	Average total compensation	D	Daily	HR	High end range

LO Lowest wage paid MTC Median total compensation TCC Total cash compensation
LR Low end range MW Median wage paid TQ Third quartile wage
M Monthly MWR Median wage range W Weekly
MCC Median cash compensation S See annotated source Y Yearly

Occupation/Type/Industry	Location	Per	Low	Mid	High	Source	Date
Library Assistant							
Clerical	Seattle-Tacoma-Bellevue MSA, WA	Y	21770 FQ	24450 MW	30080 TQ	USBLS	5/07
Clerical	West Virginia	Y	14445 FQ	16059 MW	19474 TQ	WVBLS	7/08-9/08
Clerical	Charleston MSA, WV	Y	14220 FQ	16540 MW	20250 TQ	USBLS	5/07
Clerical	Wisconsin	Y	16430 FQ	21780 MW	26750 TQ	USBLS	5/07
Clerical	Appleton MSA, WI	Y	24560 FQ	28810 MW	33590 TQ	USBLS	5/07
Clerical	Milwaukee-Waukesha-West Allis MSA, WI	Y	16560 FQ	21990 MW	27150 TQ	USBLS	5/07
Clerical	Wyoming	Y	16859 FQ	21651 MW	25491 TQ	WYBLS	9/08
Clerical	Puerto Rico	Y	13810 FQ	16560 MW	23050 TQ	USBLS	5/07
Clerical	San Juan-Caguas-Guaynabo MSA, PR	Y	14270 FQ	18330 MW	27570 TQ	USBLS	5/07
Clerical	Virgin Islands	Y	17270 FQ	20190 MW	23470 TQ	USBLS	5/07
Library Associate	Ohio	H	15.62 LO		18.36 HI	ODAS	2008
Library Consultant	Ohio	H	22.60 LO		30.13 HI	ODAS	2008
Library Delivery Driver							
Department of Cultural Resources	New Hampshire	Y		27158 AW		NHUL03	2008
Library Director	Orange, MA	Y			50542 HI	FRCOG	2009
Library Page	Carlsbad, CA	H	9.00 LO		12.50 HI	CCSS	1/1/08
Library Science Teacher							
Postsecondary	Alabama	Y	41200 FQ	51660 MW	63840 TQ	USBLS	5/07
Postsecondary	California	Y		87586 AW		CABLS	1/08-3/08
Postsecondary	Colorado	Y	48950 FQ	56470 MW	65830 TQ	USBLS	5/07
Postsecondary	District of Columbia	Y	57760 FQ	65380 MW	72480 TQ	USBLS	5/07
Postsecondary	Florida	Y	51850 FQ	63210 MW	77170 TQ	USBLS	5/07
Postsecondary	Georgia	Y	40880 FQ	48540 MW	59420 TQ	USBLS	5/07
Postsecondary	Illinois	Y	36070 FQ	52210 MW	64760 TQ	USBLS	5/07
Postsecondary	Indiana	Y	41730 FQ	57030 MW	71200 TQ	USBLS	5/07
Postsecondary	Iowa	Y	47060 FQ	53550 MW	64100 TQ	USBLS	5/07
Postsecondary	Kentucky	Y	49215 FQ	59609 MW	77447 TQ	KYBLS	2008
Postsecondary	Louisiana	Y		53752 AW		LABLS	1/08-3/08
Postsecondary	Maryland	Y		55750 MW		MDBLS	3/08
Postsecondary	Massachusetts	Y	35620 FQ	39580 MW	56180 TQ	USBLS	5/07
Postsecondary	Michigan	Y	41880 FQ	54180 MW	74390 TQ	USBLS	5/07
Postsecondary	Minnesota	Y	49130 FQ	62846 MW	80496 TQ	MNBLS	10/08-12/08
Postsecondary	Mississippi	Y	44910 FQ	56090 MW	71860 TQ	USBLS	5/07
Postsecondary	Missouri	Y	45090 FQ	54740 MW	65780 TQ	USBLS	5/07
Postsecondary	New Jersey	Y	55940 FQ	72720 MW	95930 TQ	USBLS	5/07
Postsecondary	New York	Y	50950 FQ	64780 MW	76810 TQ	USBLS	5/07
Postsecondary	North Carolina	Y	50000 FQ	60400 MW	77270 TQ	USBLS	5/07
Postsecondary	Ohio	Y	49540 FQ	59620 MW	71290 TQ	USBLS	5/07
Postsecondary	Oklahoma	Y	35590 FQ	41930 MW	53640 TQ	USBLS	5/07
Postsecondary	Pennsylvania	Y	46520 FQ	57910 MW	74690 TQ	USBLS	5/07
Postsecondary	South Carolina	Y	39810 FQ	51320 MW	64250 TQ	USBLS	5/07
Postsecondary	Tennessee	Y	45010 FQ	52960 MW	64270 TQ	USBLS	5/07
Postsecondary	Texas	Y	40430 FQ	51050 MW	70560 TQ	USBLS	5/07
Postsecondary	Washington	Y		74604 AW		WABLS	3/08
Postsecondary	Wisconsin	Y	50000 FQ	56290 MW	62250 TQ	USBLS	5/07
Library Specialist	South Carolina	Y	24635 LO		45578 HI	AFT02	3/1/08
Library Technician	Alabama	Y	17500 FQ	22540 MW	28260 TQ	USBLS	5/07
	Birmingham-Hoover MSA, AL	Y	18490 FQ	23740 MW	31330 TQ	USBLS	5/07
	Tuscaloosa MSA, AL	Y	19580 FQ	23570 MW	28640 TQ	USBLS	5/07
	Alaska	Y	29090 FQ	34410 MW	40260 TQ	USBLS	5/07
	Anchorage MSA, AK	Y	31350 FQ	37040 MW	41620 TQ	USBLS	5/07
	Arizona	Y	20450 FQ	25760 MW	32370 TQ	USBLS	5/07
	Phoenix-Mesa-Scottsdale MSA, AZ	Y	21160 FQ	26100 MW	31420 TQ	USBLS	5/07
	Tucson MSA, AZ	Y	22870 FQ	29110 MW	37430 TQ	USBLS	5/07
	Arkansas	Y	17580 FQ	22130 MW	27420 TQ	USBLS	5/07
	Fayetteville-Springdale-Rogers MSA, AR-MO	Y	18520 FQ	23070 MW	29350 TQ	USBLS	5/07
	Little Rock-North Little Rock MSA, AR	Y	20080 FQ	23530 MW	28620 TQ	USBLS	5/07
	California	H	13.44 FQ	16.69 MW	20.21 TQ	CABLS	1/08-3/08

AE	Average entry wage	**AW**	Average wage paid	**FQ** First quartile wage	**LO** Lowest wage paid	**MTC** Median total compensation	**TCC** Total cash compensation
AER	Average entry range	**AWR**	Average wage range	**H** Hourly	**LR** Low end range	**MW** Median wage paid	**TQ** Third quartile wage
AEX	Average experienced wage	**AXR**	Average experienced range	**HI** Highest wage paid	**M** Monthly	**MWR** Median wage range	**W** Weekly
ATC	Average total compensation	**D**	Daily	**HR** High end range	**MCC** Median cash compensation	**S** See annotated source	**Y** Yearly

Occupation/Type/Industry	Location	Per	Low	Mid	High	Source	Date
Library Technician	Bakersfield MSA, CA	H	12.24 FQ	15.38 MW	18.45 TQ	CABLS	1/08-3/08
	Los Angeles-Long Beach-Glendale PMSA, CA	H	11.24 FQ	16.25 MW	20.96 TQ	CABLS	1/08-3/08
	Oakland-Fremont-Hayward MSA, CA	H	13.56 FQ	19.11 MW	23.91 TQ	CABLS	1/08-3/08
	Riverside-San Bernardino-Ontario MSA, CA	H	14.40 FQ	16.89 MW	19.11 TQ	CABLS	1/08-3/08
	Sacramento-Arden Arcade-Roseville MSA, CA	H	12.75 FQ	16.91 MW	19.59 TQ	CABLS	1/08-3/08
	San Diego-Carlsbad-San Marcos MSA, CA	H	14.92 FQ	17.44 MW	20.27 TQ	CABLS	1/08-3/08
	San Francisco-San Mateo-Redwood PMSA, CA	H	14.58 FQ	17.61 MW	25.88 TQ	CABLS	1/08-3/08
	San Jose-Sunnyvale-Santa Clara MSA, CA	H	14.10 FQ	16.77 MW	21.12 TQ	CABLS	1/08-3/08
	Santa Ana-Anaheim-Irvine PMSA, CA	Y	30690 FQ	36960 MW	43560 TQ	USBLS	5/07
	Stockton MSA, CA	H	14.33 FQ	16.40 MW	18.89 TQ	CABLS	1/08-3/08
	Colorado	Y	23710 FQ	28840 MW	34300 TQ	USBLS	5/07
	Colorado Springs MSA, CO	Y	21150 FQ	26390 MW	31940 TQ	USBLS	5/07
	Denver-Aurora MSA, CO	Y	25010 FQ	29870 MW	35540 TQ	USBLS	5/07
	Fort Collins-Loveland MSA, CO	Y	26790 FQ	29810 MW	32830 TQ	USBLS	5/07
	Connecticut	H	10.97 AE	16.01 MW		CTBLS	1/08-3/08
	Bridgeport-Stamford-Norwalk MSA, CT	Y	25060 FQ	31080 MW	42890 TQ	USBLS	5/07
	Hartford-West Hartford-East Hartford MSA, CT	Y	27140 FQ	33400 MW	41590 TQ	USBLS	5/07
	Delaware	Y	22510 FQ	30130 MW	40710 TQ	USBLS	5/07
	Wilmington PMSA, DE-MD-NJ	Y	26520 FQ	31460 MW	41210 TQ	USBLS	5/07
	District of Columbia	Y	34850 FQ	44960 MW	56160 TQ	USBLS	5/07
	Washington-Arlington-Alexandria MSA, DC-VA-MD-WV	Y	31240 FQ	41840 MW	50880 TQ	USBLS	5/07
	Florida	Y	23460 FQ	28580 MW	35220 TQ	USBLS	5/07
	Fort Lauderdale-Pompano Beach-Deerfield Beach PMSA, FL	Y	27090 FQ	32740 MW	38600 TQ	USBLS	5/07
	Jacksonville MSA, FL	Y	21970 FQ	24310 MW	32480 TQ	USBLS	5/07
	Miami-Fort Lauderdale-Miami Beach MSA, FL	Y	28220 FQ	34140 MW	40290 TQ	USBLS	5/07
	Orlando-Kissimmee MSA, FL	Y	23260 FQ	28040 MW	33560 TQ	USBLS	5/07
	Tampa-St. Petersburg-Clearwater MSA, FL	Y	22690 FQ	26690 MW	31360 TQ	USBLS	5/07
	West Palm Beach-Boca Raton-Boynton Beach PMSA, FL	Y	31550 FQ	36790 MW	42530 TQ	USBLS	5/07
	Georgia	Y	19870 FQ	26070 MW	32990 TQ	USBLS	5/07
	Atlanta-Sandy Springs-Marietta MSA, GA	Y	22340 FQ	28240 MW	34950 TQ	USBLS	5/07
	Augusta-Richmond County MSA, GA-SC	Y	14500 FQ	18020 MW	23880 TQ	USBLS	5/07
	Hawaii	Y	26020 FQ	32300 MW	37730 TQ	USBLS	5/07
	Honolulu MSA, HI	Y	25380 FQ	32030 MW	37480 TQ	USBLS	5/07
	Idaho	Y	19320 FQ	23490 MW	29660 TQ	USBLS	5/07
	Boise City-Nampa MSA, ID	Y	17040 FQ	20510 MW	24080 TQ	USBLS	5/07
	Illinois	Y	19220 FQ	25490 MW	32840 TQ	USBLS	5/07
	Chicago-Naperville-Joliet MSA, IL-IN-WI	Y	21000 FQ	27440 MW	34390 TQ	USBLS	5/07
	Indiana	Y	19600 FQ	23550 MW	28800 TQ	USBLS	5/07
	Gary PMSA, IN	Y	17550 FQ	22570 MW	28170 TQ	USBLS	5/07
	Indianapolis-Carmel MSA, IN	Y	19690 FQ	22870 MW	26330 TQ	USBLS	5/07
	South Bend-Mishawaka MSA, IN-MI	Y	18640 FQ	23200 MW	29100 TQ	USBLS	5/07
	Iowa	Y	17080 FQ	20690 MW	25960 TQ	USBLS	5/07
	Des Moines-West Des Moines MSA, IA	Y	18810 FQ	23010 MW	29280 TQ	USBLS	5/07
	Kansas	Y	17710 FQ	22090 MW	28000 TQ	USBLS	5/07
	Wichita MSA, KS	Y	14590 FQ	17450 MW	20540 TQ	USBLS	5/07
	Kentucky	Y	20562 FQ	25881 MW	31721 TQ	KYBLS	2008
	Louisville-Jefferson County MSA, KY-IN	Y	24790 FQ	29160 MW	33910 TQ	USBLS	5/07

AE	Average entry wage	AW	Average wage paid	FQ	First quartile wage
AER	Average entry range	AWR	Average wage range	H	Hourly
AEX	Average experienced wage	AXR	Average experienced range	HI	Highest wage paid
ATC	Average total compensation	D	Daily	HR	High end range

AE Average entry wage AW Average wage paid FQ First quartile wage LO Lowest wage paid MTC Median total compensation TCC Total cash compensation
AER Average entry range AWR Average wage range H Hourly LR Low end range MW Median wage paid TQ Third quartile wage
AEX Average experienced wage AXR Average experienced range HI Highest wage paid M Monthly MWR Median wage range W Weekly
ATC Average total compensation D Daily HR High end range MCC Median cash compensation S See annotated source Y Yearly

Occupation/Type/Industry	Location	Per	Low	Mid	High	Source	Date
Library Technician	Louisiana	H	9.30 FQ	11.95 MW	14.66 TQ	LABLS	1/08-3/08
	Baton Rouge MSA, LA	Y	14540 FQ	23560 MW	29470 TQ	USBLS	5/07
	New Orleans-Metairie-Kenner MSA, LA	Y	22670 FQ	27090 MW	33230 TQ	USBLS	5/07
	Maine	Y	22620 FQ	27930 MW	33190 TQ	USBLS	5/07
	Portland-South Portland-Biddeford MSA, ME	Y	25300 FQ	29150 MW	33340 TQ	USBLS	5/07
	Maryland	Y		33225 MW		MDBLS	3/08
	Baltimore-Towson MSA, MD	Y	25690 FQ	32030 MW	39990 TQ	USBLS	5/07
	Bethesda-Gaithersburg-Frederick PMSA, MD	Y	24590 FQ	37680 MW	48310 TQ	USBLS	5/07
	Massachusetts	Y	27430 FQ	34770 MW	43810 TQ	USBLS	5/07
	Boston-Cambridge-Quincy NECTA, MA	Y	29510 FQ	39010 MW	47970 TQ	USBLS	5/07
	Worcester MSA, MA-CT	Y	23150 FQ	32020 MW	38810 TQ	USBLS	5/07
	Montague, MA	Y			31908 HI	FRCOG	2009
	Michigan	Y	18450 FQ	25620 MW	33640 TQ	USBLS	5/07
	Detroit-Warren-Livonia MSA, MI	Y	21050 FQ	28780 MW	37300 TQ	USBLS	5/07
	Grand Rapids-Wyoming MSA, MI	Y	22210 FQ	27350 MW	32370 TQ	USBLS	5/07
	Warren-Troy-Farmington Hills PMSA, MI	Y	19640 FQ	27700 MW	36510 TQ	USBLS	5/07
	Minnesota	Y	28206 FQ	34745 MW	42142 TQ	MNBLS	10/08-12/08
	Duluth-Superior MSA, MN-WI	Y	26553 FQ	33625 MW	39013 TQ	MNBLS	10/08-12/08
	Minneapolis-Saint Paul MSA, MN-WI	Y	31732 FQ	37245 MW	44684 TQ	MNBLS	10/08-12/08
	Rochester MSA, MN	Y	26859 FQ	37277 MW	44988 TQ	MNBLS	10/08-12/08
	Mississippi	Y	16060 FQ	21000 MW	26810 TQ	USBLS	5/07
	Jackson MSA, MS	Y	17240 FQ	21060 MW	24740 TQ	USBLS	5/07
	Missouri	Y	23210 FQ	28540 MW	34450 TQ	USBLS	5/07
	Kansas City MSA, MO-KS	Y	21680 FQ	26990 MW	34230 TQ	USBLS	5/07
	St. Louis MSA, MO-IL	Y	23430 FQ	28540 MW	34000 TQ	USBLS	5/07
	Montana	Y	17240 FQ	21080 MW	26370 TQ	USBLS	5/07
	Nebraska	Y	17240 FQ	21370 MW	27650 TQ	USBLS	5/07
	Omaha-Council Bluffs MSA, NE-IA	Y	18510 FQ	24950 MW	32670 TQ	USBLS	5/07
	Nevada	H	9.57 FQ	16.41 MW	20.03 TQ	NVBLS	5/08
	New Hampshire	H	10.23 AE	13.59 MW	15.68 AEX	NHBLS	6/08
	Manchester MSA, NH	Y	24030 FQ	29770 MW	35270 TQ	USBLS	5/07
	Nashua NECTA, NH-MA	Y	22340 FQ	28330 MW	34780 TQ	USBLS	5/07
	New Jersey	Y	22460 FQ	28810 MW	37320 TQ	USBLS	5/07
	Atlantic City MSA, NJ	Y	22140 FQ	28220 MW	35770 TQ	USBLS	5/07
	Camden PMSA, NJ	Y	21500 FQ	26310 MW	33830 TQ	USBLS	5/07
	Edison PMSA, NJ	Y	23560 FQ	29550 MW	37170 TQ	USBLS	5/07
	Newark-Union PMSA, NJ-PA	Y	22310 FQ	29180 MW	37860 TQ	USBLS	5/07
	New Mexico	Y	17470 FQ	23060 MW	29440 TQ	USBLS	5/07
	Albuquerque MSA, NM	Y	16360 FQ	27090 MW	32830 TQ	USBLS	5/07
	New York	Y	19270 FQ	27460 MW	37840 TQ	USBLS	5/07
	Albany-Schenectady-Troy MSA, NY	Y	23270 FQ	28620 MW	40260 TQ	USBLS	5/07
	Buffalo-Niagara Falls MSA, NY	Y	19580 FQ	28130 MW	37220 TQ	USBLS	5/07
	Nassau-Suffolk PMSA, NY	Y	17360 FQ	21970 MW	30240 TQ	USBLS	5/07
	New York-Northern New Jersey-Long Island MSA, NY-NJ-PA	Y	21120 FQ	29710 MW	39300 TQ	USBLS	5/07
	North Carolina	Y	23690 FQ	27920 MW	33070 TQ	USBLS	5/07
	Charlotte-Gastonia-Concord MSA, NC-SC	Y	23610 FQ	27570 MW	32260 TQ	USBLS	5/07
	Greensboro-High Point MSA, NC	Y	23390 FQ	27900 MW	33320 TQ	USBLS	5/07
	Raleigh-Cary MSA, NC	Y	25380 FQ	28250 MW	32450 TQ	USBLS	5/07
	North Dakota	Y	14620 FQ	18630 MW	24190 TQ	USBLS	5/07
	Fargo MSA, ND-MN	Y	21580 FQ	28810 MW	36650 TQ	USBLS	5/07
	Ohio	Y	22140 FQ	28450 MW	35940 TQ	USBLS	5/07
	Cincinnati-Middletown MSA, OH-KY-IN	Y	23230 FQ	28410 MW	34380 TQ	USBLS	5/07
	Cleveland-Elyria-Mentor MSA, OH	Y	23260 FQ	33540 MW	40250 TQ	USBLS	5/07
	Columbus MSA, OH	Y	25050 FQ	31570 MW	37410 TQ	USBLS	5/07
	Dayton MSA, OH	Y	27430 FQ	34240 MW	40330 TQ	USBLS	5/07

AE	Average entry wage	AW	Average wage paid	FQ	First quartile wage
AER	Average entry range	AWR	Average wage range	H	Hourly
AEX	Average experienced wage	AXR	Average experienced range	HI	Highest wage paid
ATC	Average total compensation	D	Daily	HR	High end range

LO	Lowest wage paid	MTC	Median total compensation	TCC	Total cash compensation
LR	Low end range	MW	Median wage paid	TQ	Third quartile wage
M	Monthly	MWR	Median wage range	W	Weekly
MCC	Median cash compensation	S	See annotated source	Y	Yearly

Occupation/Type/Industry	Location	Per	Low	Mid	High	Source	Date
Library Technician	Oklahoma	Y	14040 FQ	17820 MW	24030 TQ	USBLS	5/07
	Oklahoma City MSA, OK	Y	15230 FQ	21080 MW	28140 TQ	USBLS	5/07
	Tulsa MSA, OK	Y	16450 FQ	21520 MW	30820 TQ	USBLS	5/07
	Oregon	H	12.85 FQ	15.23 MW	18.34 TQ	ORBLS	5/08
	Portland-Vancouver-Beaverton MSA, OR-WA	Y	30450 FQ	35790 MW	42660 TQ	USBLS	5/07
	Pennsylvania	Y	19450 FQ	24950 MW	30410 TQ	USBLS	5/07
	Allentown-Bethlehem-Easton MSA, PA-NJ	Y	20390 FQ	24760 MW	29930 TQ	USBLS	5/07
	Philadelphia-Camden-Wilmington MSA, PA-NJ-DE-MD	Y	22470 FQ	27440 MW	32590 TQ	USBLS	5/07
	Pittsburgh MSA, PA	Y	16860 FQ	22130 MW	28500 TQ	USBLS	5/07
	Rhode Island	Y	21100 FQ	31050 MW	38330 TQ	USBLS	5/07
	Providence-Fall River-Warwick MSA, RI-MA	Y	21370 FQ	31240 MW	38660 TQ	USBLS	5/07
	South Carolina	Y	17330 FQ	21680 MW	28280 TQ	USBLS	5/07
	Charleston-North Charleston MSA, SC	Y	17880 FQ	20860 MW	28050 TQ	USBLS	5/07
	Columbia MSA, SC	Y	19720 FQ	25900 MW	31510 TQ	USBLS	5/07
	Myrtle Beach-Conway-North Myrtle Beach MSA, SC	Y	15100 FQ	18430 MW	23380 TQ	USBLS	5/07
	South Dakota	Y	20718 FQ	23508 MW	26456 TQ	SDBLS	7/08-9/08
	Sioux Falls MSA, SD	Y	22266 FQ	25276 MW	30425 TQ	SDBLS	7/08-9/08
	Tennessee	Y	17220 FQ	23090 MW	31020 TQ	USBLS	5/07
	Johnson City MSA, TN	Y	18840 FQ	22230 MW	26390 TQ	USBLS	5/07
	Kingsport-Bristol-Bristol MSA, TN-VA	Y	15040 FQ	21680 MW	26260 TQ	USBLS	5/07
	Memphis MSA, TN-MS-AR	Y	16970 FQ	22240 MW	25960 TQ	USBLS	5/07
	Nashville-Davidson-Murfreesboro MSA, TN	Y	18940 FQ	29110 MW	48280 TQ	USBLS	5/07
	Texas	Y	18220 FQ	24230 MW	30060 TQ	USBLS	5/07
	Austin-Round Rock MSA, TX	Y	21050 FQ	25110 MW	29850 TQ	USBLS	5/07
	Brownsville-Harlingen MSA, TX	Y	23130 FQ	28680 MW	38650 TQ	USBLS	5/07
	Dallas-Fort Worth-Arlington MSA, TX	Y	20920 FQ	27410 MW	33450 TQ	USBLS	5/07
	Houston-Sugar Land-Baytown MSA, TX	Y	20060 FQ	26710 MW	30950 TQ	USBLS	5/07
	San Antonio MSA, TX	Y	22000 FQ	26430 MW	32430 TQ	USBLS	5/07
	Utah	Y	18320 FQ	23130 MW	29430 TQ	USBLS	5/07
	Ogden-Clearfield MSA, UT	Y	21760 FQ	27490 MW	33450 TQ	USBLS	5/07
	Salt Lake City MSA, UT	Y	21550 FQ	24420 MW	31420 TQ	USBLS	5/07
	Vermont	Y	22770 FQ	26490 MW	30040 TQ	USBLS	5/07
	Burlington-South Burlington MSA, VT	Y	24560 FQ	27010 MW	29680 TQ	USBLS	5/07
	Virginia	Y	24480 FQ	31900 MW	41620 TQ	USBLS	5/07
	Richmond MSA, VA	Y	25790 FQ	33070 MW	38860 TQ	USBLS	5/07
	Virginia Beach-Norfolk-Newport News MSA, VA-NC	Y	27010 FQ	30770 MW	36380 TQ	USBLS	5/07
	Washington	H	14.35 FQ	16.96 MW	19.60 TQ	WABLS	3/08
	Seattle-Tacoma-Bellevue MSA, WA	Y	31830 FQ	36350 MW	41440 TQ	USBLS	5/07
	West Virginia	Y	16181 FQ	23658 MW	30808 TQ	WVBLS	7/08-9/08
	Charleston MSA, WV	Y	15540 FQ	22000 MW	28260 TQ	USBLS	5/07
	Wisconsin	Y	21070 FQ	26060 MW	33720 TQ	USBLS	5/07
	Milwaukee-Waukesha-West Allis MSA, WI	Y	22110 FQ	27460 MW	40220 TQ	USBLS	5/07
	Wyoming	Y	18111 FQ	21458 MW	27468 TQ	WYBLS	9/08
	Puerto Rico	Y	15390 FQ	17910 MW	21650 TQ	USBLS	5/07
	San Juan-Caguas-Guaynabo MSA, PR	Y	15630 FQ	17860 MW	20620 TQ	USBLS	5/07
	Virgin Islands	Y	17820 FQ	20010 MW	22480 TQ	USBLS	5/07
Licensed Practical and Licensed Vocational Nurse	Alabama	Y	27270 FQ	31440 MW	36030 TQ	USBLS	5/07
	Birmingham-Hoover MSA, AL	Y	28480 FQ	32480 MW	37080 TQ	USBLS	5/07
	Alaska	Y	40280 FQ	46130 MW	53500 TQ	USBLS	5/07
	Anchorage MSA, AK	Y	40910 FQ	45830 MW	52070 TQ	USBLS	5/07
	Arizona	Y	35100 FQ	42100 MW	47510 TQ	USBLS	5/07
	Phoenix-Mesa-Scottsdale MSA, AZ	Y	35070 FQ	42740 MW	47930 TQ	USBLS	5/07

AE	Average entry wage	AW	Average wage paid	FQ	First quartile wage
AER	Average entry range	AWR	Average wage range	H	Hourly
AEX	Average experienced wage	AXR	Average experienced range	HI	Highest wage paid
ATC	Average total compensation	D	Daily	HR	High end range

LO   Lowest wage paid
LR   Low end range
M   Monthly
MCC Median cash compensation

MTC Median total compensation
MW   Median wage paid
MWR Median wage range
S   See annotated source

TCC Total cash compensation
TQ   Third quartile wage
W   Weekly
Y   Yearly

Licensed Practical and Licensed Vocational Nurse

Occupation/Type/Industry	Location	Per	Low	Mid	High	Source	Date
Licensed Practical and Licensed Vocational Nurse							
	Tucson MSA, AZ	Y	35870 FQ	41720 MW	46820 TQ	USBLS	5/07
	Arkansas	Y	27500 FQ	31580 MW	36880 TQ	USBLS	5/07
	Fayetteville-Springdale-Rogers MSA, AR-MO	Y	29730 FQ	34600 MW	39660 TQ	USBLS	5/07
	Fort Smith MSA, AR-OK	Y	26960 FQ	30300 MW	34870 TQ	USBLS	5/07
	Jonesboro MSA, AR	Y	26250 FQ	29190 MW	32270 TQ	USBLS	5/07
	Little Rock-North Little Rock MSA, AR	Y	31460 FQ	35890 MW	40040 TQ	USBLS	5/07
	California	H	19.39 FQ	22.59 MW	26.35 TQ	CABLS	1/08-3/08
	Los Angeles-Long Beach-Glendale PMSA, CA	H	19.37 FQ	22.29 MW	25.41 TQ	CABLS	1/08-3/08
	Oakland-Fremont-Hayward MSA, CA	H	24.04 FQ	27.55 MW	30.76 TQ	CABLS	1/08-3/08
	Riverside-San Bernardino-Ontario MSA, CA	H	17.77 FQ	20.01 MW	23.14 TQ	CABLS	1/08-3/08
	Sacramento-Arden Arcade-Roseville MSA, CA	H	20.12 FQ	23.99 MW	27.90 TQ	CABLS	1/08-3/08
	San Diego-Carlsbad-San Marcos MSA, CA	H	18.29 FQ	21.02 MW	23.48 TQ	CABLS	1/08-3/08
	San Francisco-San Mateo-Redwood PMSA, CA	H	24.09 FQ	28.15 MW	31.28 TQ	CABLS	1/08-3/08
	San Jose-Sunnyvale-Santa Clara MSA, CA	H	24.15 FQ	27.83 MW	30.86 TQ	CABLS	1/08-3/08
	Santa Ana-Anaheim-Irvine PMSA, CA	Y	41510 FQ	47380 MW	53720 TQ	USBLS	5/07
	Colorado	Y	33870 FQ	39780 MW	46320 TQ	USBLS	5/07
	Denver-Aurora MSA, CO	Y	37870 FQ	43310 MW	48390 TQ	USBLS	5/07
	Connecticut	H	20.32 AE	25.21 MW		CTBLS	1/08-3/08
	Bridgeport-Stamford-Norwalk MSA, CT	Y	48580 FQ	55400 MW	61250 TQ	USBLS	5/07
	Hartford-West Hartford-East Hartford MSA, CT	Y	44710 FQ	51360 MW	59310 TQ	USBLS	5/07
	Delaware	Y	38660 FQ	45140 MW	51220 TQ	USBLS	5/07
	Wilmington PMSA, DE-MD-NJ	Y	40950 FQ	46280 MW	51890 TQ	USBLS	5/07
	District of Columbia	Y	41350 FQ	47390 MW	57130 TQ	USBLS	5/07
	Washington-Arlington-Alexandria MSA, DC-VA-MD-WV	Y	39230 FQ	45290 MW	52060 TQ	USBLS	5/07
	Florida	Y	33680 FQ	38240 MW	43940 TQ	USBLS	5/07
	Fort Lauderdale-Pompano Beach-Deerfield Beach PMSA, FL	Y	35820 FQ	39730 MW	45360 TQ	USBLS	5/07
	Jacksonville MSA, FL	Y	33840 FQ	38000 MW	42670 TQ	USBLS	5/07
	Miami-Fort Lauderdale-Miami Beach MSA, FL	Y	35560 FQ	40090 MW	46040 TQ	USBLS	5/07
	Orlando-Kissimmee MSA, FL	Y	33110 FQ	37440 MW	42270 TQ	USBLS	5/07
	Tampa-St. Petersburg-Clearwater MSA, FL	Y	34310 FQ	38940 MW	44570 TQ	USBLS	5/07
	West Palm Beach-Boca Raton-Boynton Beach PMSA, FL	Y	36300 FQ	41490 MW	47340 TQ	USBLS	5/07
	Georgia	Y	29030 FQ	34450 MW	39750 TQ	USBLS	5/07
	Atlanta-Sandy Springs-Marietta MSA, GA	Y	31380 FQ	36950 MW	42950 TQ	USBLS	5/07
	Hawaii	Y	35380 FQ	39650 MW	44900 TQ	USBLS	5/07
	Honolulu MSA, HI	Y	36630 FQ	40670 MW	45850 TQ	USBLS	5/07
	Idaho	Y	31710 FQ	35960 MW	41100 TQ	USBLS	5/07
	Boise City-Nampa MSA, ID	Y	34320 FQ	38500 MW	44820 TQ	USBLS	5/07
	Illinois	Y	33080 FQ	39010 MW	46380 TQ	USBLS	5/07
	Chicago-Naperville-Joliet MSA, IL-IN-WI	Y	36350 FQ	42670 MW	48660 TQ	USBLS	5/07
	Indiana	Y	32660 FQ	36890 MW	41690 TQ	USBLS	5/07
	Elkhart-Goshen MSA, IN	Y	31870 FQ	35940 MW	41070 TQ	USBLS	5/07
	Gary PMSA, IN	Y	32370 FQ	38480 MW	45100 TQ	USBLS	5/07
	Indianapolis-Carmel MSA, IN	Y	34700 FQ	39770 MW	46080 TQ	USBLS	5/07
	Iowa	Y	30050 FQ	34250 MW	38530 TQ	USBLS	5/07
	Des Moines-West Des Moines MSA, IA	Y	33220 FQ	37100 MW	41230 TQ	USBLS	5/07
	Dubuque MSA, IA	Y	31420 FQ	36040 MW	40500 TQ	USBLS	5/07
	Kansas	Y	30660 FQ	34970 MW	39110 TQ	USBLS	5/07
	Wichita MSA, KS	Y	31590 FQ	35350 MW	39140 TQ	USBLS	5/07

AE Average entry wage	**AW** Average wage paid	**FQ** First quartile wage	**LO** Lowest wage paid	**MTC** Median total compensation **TCC** Total cash compensation
AER Average entry range	**AWR** Average wage range	**H** Hourly	**LR** Low end range	**MW** Median wage paid **TQ** Third quartile wage
AEX Average experienced wage	**AXR** Average experienced range	**HI** Highest wage paid	**M** Monthly	**MWR** Median wage range **W** Weekly
ATC Average total compensation **D** Daily		**HR** High end range	**MCC** Median cash compensation	**S** See annotated source **Y** Yearly

Occupation/Type/Industry	Location	Per	Low	Mid	High	Source	Date
Licensed Practical and Licensed Vocational Nurse	Kentucky	Y	31172 FQ	36060 MW	40931 TQ	KYBLS	2008
	Louisville-Jefferson County MSA, KY-IN	Y	33420 FQ	37510 MW	41980 TQ	USBLS	5/07
	Louisiana	H	13.63 FQ	15.92 MW	18.37 TQ	LABLS	1/08-3/08
	Baton Rouge MSA, LA	Y	29940 FQ	35120 MW	40850 TQ	USBLS	5/07
	New Orleans-Metairie-Kenner MSA, LA	Y	29970 FQ	34870 MW	39010 TQ	USBLS	5/07
	Maine	Y	33340 FQ	37240 MW	42200 TQ	USBLS	5/07
	Portland-South Portland-Biddeford MSA, ME	Y	38250 FQ	42940 MW	47760 TQ	USBLS	5/07
	Maryland	Y		47875 MW		MDBLS	3/08
	Baltimore-Towson MSA, MD	Y	41860 FQ	47540 MW	55650 TQ	USBLS	5/07
	Bethesda-Gaithersburg-Frederick PMSA, MD	Y	39810 FQ	46940 MW	55030 TQ	USBLS	5/07
	Cumberland MSA, MD-WV	Y	31870 FQ	35700 MW	39550 TQ	USBLS	5/07
	Massachusetts	Y	42700 FQ	48500 MW	55790 TQ	USBLS	5/07
	Boston-Cambridge-Quincy NECTA, MA	Y	43740 FQ	49840 MW	57110 TQ	USBLS	5/07
	Worcester MSA, MA-CT	Y	43670 FQ	50320 MW	57290 TQ	USBLS	5/07
	Michigan	Y	34220 FQ	39900 MW	46620 TQ	USBLS	5/07
	Detroit-Warren-Livonia MSA, MI	Y	39560 FQ	45320 MW	51260 TQ	USBLS	5/07
	Grand Rapids-Wyoming MSA, MI	Y	30880 FQ	36070 MW	41910 TQ	USBLS	5/07
	Lansing-East Lansing MSA, MI	Y	34730 FQ	40020 MW	45550 TQ	USBLS	5/07
	Warren-Troy-Farmington Hills PMSA, MI	Y	38610 FQ	45400 MW	52520 TQ	USBLS	5/07
	Minnesota	Y	34755 FQ	39348 MW	45081 TQ	MNBLS	10/08-12/08
	Duluth-Superior MSA, MN-WI	Y	34305 FQ	38155 MW	42445 TQ	MNBLS	10/08-12/08
	Minneapolis-Saint Paul MSA, MN-WI	Y	38187 FQ	42801 MW	48325 TQ	MNBLS	10/08-12/08
	Rochester MSA, MN	Y	37821 FQ	43396 MW	49097 TQ	MNBLS	10/08-12/08
	Mississippi	Y	26620 FQ	30740 MW	36030 TQ	USBLS	5/07
	Jackson MSA, MS	Y	26880 FQ	32330 MW	37340 TQ	USBLS	5/07
	Missouri	Y	28130 FQ	32950 MW	38070 TQ	USBLS	5/07
	Kansas City MSA, MO-KS	Y	31890 FQ	36290 MW	40450 TQ	USBLS	5/07
	St. Joseph MSA, MO-KS	Y	28540 FQ	32620 MW	36380 TQ	USBLS	5/07
	St. Louis MSA, MO-IL	Y	32750 FQ	36820 MW	41240 TQ	USBLS	5/07
	Montana	Y	28130 FQ	32180 MW	36920 TQ	USBLS	5/07
	Billings MSA, MT	Y	30150 FQ	33990 MW	37960 TQ	USBLS	5/07
	Nebraska	Y	29740 FQ	34330 MW	39010 TQ	USBLS	5/07
	Omaha-Council Bluffs MSA, NE-IA	Y	33100 FQ	37440 MW	42110 TQ	USBLS	5/07
	Nevada	H	19.26 FQ	21.90 MW	24.18 TQ	NVBLS	5/08
	Carson City MSA, NV	H	20.16 FQ	22.22 MW	24.39 TQ	NVBLS	5/08
	Las Vegas-Paradise MSA, NV	H	18.81 FQ	21.65 MW	23.98 TQ	NVBLS	5/08
	New Hampshire	H	17.04 AE	20.87 MW	22.93 AEX	NHBLS	6/08
	Manchester MSA, NH	Y	40970 FQ	47180 MW	52420 TQ	USBLS	5/07
	Nashua NECTA, NH-MA	Y	34550 FQ	38880 MW	44870 TQ	USBLS	5/07
	New Jersey	Y	42850 FQ	48460 MW	55350 TQ	USBLS	5/07
	Camden PMSA, NJ	Y	41020 FQ	46410 MW	52730 TQ	USBLS	5/07
	Edison PMSA, NJ	Y	43000 FQ	48920 MW	55710 TQ	USBLS	5/07
	Newark-Union PMSA, NJ-PA	Y	43570 FQ	48770 MW	55640 TQ	USBLS	5/07
	New Mexico	Y	36870 FQ	43450 MW	51050 TQ	USBLS	5/07
	Albuquerque MSA, NM	Y	42440 FQ	47880 MW	59970 TQ	USBLS	5/07
	New York	Y	33160 FQ	39270 MW	47110 TQ	USBLS	5/07
	Albany-Schenectady-Troy MSA, NY	Y	32890 FQ	37380 MW	43550 TQ	USBLS	5/07
	Buffalo-Niagara Falls MSA, NY	Y	31700 FQ	36020 MW	40310 TQ	USBLS	5/07
	Kingston MSA, NY	Y	34070 FQ	38230 MW	44170 TQ	USBLS	5/07
	Nassau-Suffolk PMSA, NY	Y	40320 FQ	45750 MW	51210 TQ	USBLS	5/07
	New York-Northern New Jersey-Long Island MSA, NY-NJ-PA	Y	41180 FQ	47090 MW	53460 TQ	USBLS	5/07
	North Carolina	Y	33290 FQ	37780 MW	43100 TQ	USBLS	5/07
	Charlotte-Gastonia-Concord MSA, NC-SC	Y	34800 FQ	39190 MW	44700 TQ	USBLS	5/07
	Greensboro-High Point MSA, NC	Y	34400 FQ	39390 MW	44910 TQ	USBLS	5/07
	Raleigh-Cary MSA, NC	Y	31850 FQ	37290 MW	43740 TQ	USBLS	5/07

AE Average entry wage · AER Average entry range · AEX Average experienced wage · ATC Average total compensation · AW Average wage paid · AWR Average wage range · AXR Average experienced range · D Daily · FQ First quartile wage · H Hourly · HI Highest wage paid · HR High end range · LO Lowest wage paid · LR Low end range · M Monthly · MCC Median cash compensation · MTC Median total compensation · MW Median wage paid · MWR Median wage range · S See annotated source · TCC Total cash compensation · TQ Third quartile wage · W Weekly · Y Yearly

Occupation/Type/Industry	Location	Per	Low	Mid	High	Source	Date
Licensed Practical and Licensed Vocational Nurse	North Dakota	Y	29000 FQ	33290 MW	37580 TQ	USBLS	5/07
	Fargo MSA, ND-MN	Y	28820 FQ	32780 MW	37300 TQ	USBLS	5/07
	Ohio	Y	33920 FQ	38310 MW	43950 TQ	USBLS	5/07
	Cincinnati-Middletown MSA, OH-KY-IN	Y	35730 FQ	41160 MW	46580 TQ	USBLS	5/07
	Cleveland-Elyria-Mentor MSA, OH	Y	36550 FQ	41440 MW	46830 TQ	USBLS	5/07
	Columbus MSA, OH	Y	35450 FQ	40060 MW	46210 TQ	USBLS	5/07
	Dayton MSA, OH	Y	35330 FQ	39650 MW	45090 TQ	USBLS	5/07
	Oklahoma	Y	27020 FQ	31040 MW	36030 TQ	USBLS	5/07
	Oklahoma City MSA, OK	Y	28040 FQ	32420 MW	37170 TQ	USBLS	5/07
	Tulsa MSA, OK	Y	26960 FQ	31800 MW	36920 TQ	USBLS	5/07
	Oregon	H	18.07 FQ	21.04 MW	23.53 TQ	ORBLS	5/08
	Eugene-Springfield MSA, OR	Y	33690 FQ	38400 MW	43670 TQ	USBLS	5/07
	Portland-Vancouver-Beaverton MSA, OR-WA	Y	41860 FQ	45980 MW	50390 TQ	USBLS	5/07
	Pennsylvania	Y	32330 FQ	38430 MW	46360 TQ	USBLS	5/07
	Allentown-Bethlehem-Easton MSA, PA-NJ	Y	30950 FQ	37890 MW	44410 TQ	USBLS	5/07
	Philadelphia-Camden-Wilmington MSA, PA-NJ-DE-MD	Y	40370 FQ	46770 MW	53950 TQ	USBLS	5/07
	Pittsburgh MSA, PA	Y	31810 FQ	36510 MW	41180 TQ	USBLS	5/07
	Rhode Island	Y	41750 FQ	47290 MW	53550 TQ	USBLS	5/07
	Providence-Fall River-Warwick MSA, RI-MA	Y	41620 FQ	47180 MW	53100 TQ	USBLS	5/07
	South Carolina	Y	31220 FQ	35770 MW	40250 TQ	USBLS	5/07
	Charleston-North Charleston MSA, SC	Y	33180 FQ	38120 MW	43360 TQ	USBLS	5/07
	Columbia MSA, SC	Y	33040 FQ	37150 MW	41580 TQ	USBLS	5/07
	Myrtle Beach-Conway-North Myrtle Beach MSA, SC	Y	30440 FQ	34060 MW	37310 TQ	USBLS	5/07
	Spartanburg MSA, SC	Y	28980 FQ	33810 MW	37870 TQ	USBLS	5/07
	South Dakota	Y	28652 FQ	32118 MW	36852 TQ	SDBLS	7/08-9/08
	Rapid City MSA, SD	Y	29997 FQ	34003 MW	38617 TQ	SDBLS	7/08-9/08
	Sioux Falls MSA, SD	Y	29485 FQ	32989 MW	37978 TQ	SDBLS	7/08-9/08
	Tennessee	Y	29020 FQ	34020 MW	38990 TQ	USBLS	5/07
	Clarksville MSA, TN-KY	Y	29860 FQ	33970 MW	37530 TQ	USBLS	5/07
	Memphis MSA, TN-MS-AR	Y	32500 FQ	38060 MW	45180 TQ	USBLS	5/07
	Nashville-Davidson-Murfreesboro MSA, TN	Y	32790 FQ	36840 MW	41460 TQ	USBLS	5/07
	Texas	Y	31850 FQ	36800 MW	42290 TQ	USBLS	5/07
	Austin-Round Rock MSA, TX	Y	35080 FQ	39430 MW	44810 TQ	USBLS	5/07
	Dallas-Fort Worth-Arlington MSA, TX	Y	34440 FQ	39700 MW	46260 TQ	USBLS	5/07
	El Paso MSA, TX	Y	33190 FQ	38440 MW	48230 TQ	USBLS	5/07
	Houston-Sugar Land-Baytown MSA, TX	Y	34500 FQ	39140 MW	44910 TQ	USBLS	5/07
	San Antonio MSA, TX	Y	32700 FQ	36120 MW	39990 TQ	USBLS	5/07
	Utah	Y	29630 FQ	35700 MW	41830 TQ	USBLS	5/07
	Salt Lake City MSA, UT	Y	33720 FQ	39120 MW	44330 TQ	USBLS	5/07
	Vermont	Y	33960 FQ	38260 MW	43710 TQ	USBLS	5/07
	Burlington-South Burlington MSA, VT	Y	35660 FQ	40850 MW	46500 TQ	USBLS	5/07
	Virginia	Y	31040 FQ	36060 MW	41550 TQ	USBLS	5/07
	Richmond MSA, VA	Y	33480 FQ	37960 MW	44190 TQ	USBLS	5/07
	Virginia Beach-Norfolk-Newport News MSA, VA-NC	Y	30620 FQ	34410 MW	37900 TQ	USBLS	5/07
	Washington	H	17.90 FQ	20.45 MW	23.24 TQ	WABLS	3/08
	Olympia MSA, WA	Y	34550 FQ	39670 MW	45550 TQ	USBLS	5/07
	Seattle-Tacoma-Bellevue MSA, WA	Y	38990 FQ	44200 MW	49580 TQ	USBLS	5/07
	West Virginia	Y	27623 FQ	31338 MW	36464 TQ	WVBLS	7/08-9/08
	Charleston MSA, WV	Y	27420 FQ	30480 MW	35350 TQ	USBLS	5/07
	Parkersburg-Marietta-Vienna MSA, WV-OH	Y	26050 FQ	28810 MW	32410 TQ	USBLS	5/07
	Wisconsin	Y	34130 FQ	38550 MW	44780 TQ	USBLS	5/07
	Appleton MSA, WI	Y	33970 FQ	37600 MW	42030 TQ	USBLS	5/07
	Green Bay MSA, WI	Y	33230 FQ	37260 MW	42000 TQ	USBLS	5/07
	Milwaukee-Waukesha-West Allis MSA, WI	Y	38140 FQ	44070 MW	49990 TQ	USBLS	5/07

AE Average entry wage	**AW** Average wage paid	**FQ** First quartile wage	**LO** Lowest wage paid	**MTC** Median total compensation	**TCC** Total cash compensation
AER Average entry range	**AWR** Average wage range	**H** Hourly	**LR** Low end range	**MW** Median wage paid	**TQ** Third quartile wage
AEX Average experienced wage	**AXR** Average experienced range	**HI** Highest wage paid	**M** Monthly	**MWR** Median wage range	**W** Weekly
ATC Average total compensation	**D** Daily	**HR** High end range	**MCC** Median cash compensation	**S** See annotated source	**Y** Yearly

Occupation/Type/Industry	Location	Per	Low	Mid	High	Source	Date
Licensed Practical and Licensed Vocational Nurse	Wyoming	Y	32582 FQ	37721 MW	43837 TQ	WYBLS	9/08
	Cheyenne MSA, WY	Y	33151 FQ	40445 MW	47832 TQ	WYBLS	9/08
	Puerto Rico	Y	13780 FQ	16410 MW	19770 TQ	USBLS	5/07
	Aguadilla-Isabela-San Sebastian MSA, PR	Y	12890 FQ	14200 MW	16130 TQ	USBLS	5/07
	San Juan-Caguas-Guaynabo MSA, PR	Y	14000 FQ	16830 MW	20100 TQ	USBLS	5/07
	Virgin Islands	Y	27140 FQ	31100 MW	37950 TQ	USBLS	5/07
	Guam	Y	26370 FQ	34000 MW	37840 TQ	USBLS	5/07
Licensed Practical Nurse							
State Hospital	Vermont	Y	40909 LO		58710 HI	AFT02	3/1/08
Lieutenant							
Department of Corrections	Connecticut	Y	53196 LO		70283 HI	AFT02	3/1/08
Department of Corrections	New Hampshire	Y		69826 AW		NHUL03	2008
Fire Department	Marietta, GA	Y	46505 LO		62259 HI	GACTY01	2008
Police Department	Roswell, GA	Y	52348 LO		83757 HI	GACTY01	2008
Lieutenant Governor	Florida	Y			127399 HI	SFSUNS	2009
	Nebraska	Y			75000 HI	NEST	2008
Lifeguard, Ski Patrol, and Other Recreational Protective Service Worker	Alabama	Y	13180 FQ	15190 MW	18230 TQ	USBLS	5/07
	Birmingham-Hoover MSA, AL	Y	12770 FQ	14290 MW	16200 TQ	USBLS	5/07
	Alaska	Y	21050 FQ	26030 MW	30880 TQ	USBLS	5/07
	Anchorage MSA, AK	Y	22640 FQ	26450 MW	29660 TQ	USBLS	5/07
	Arizona	Y	15400 FQ	18020 MW	22100 TQ	USBLS	5/07
	Phoenix-Mesa-Scottsdale MSA, AZ	Y	16800 FQ	19950 MW	22880 TQ	USBLS	5/07
	Arkansas	Y	13960 FQ	14620 MW	15700 TQ	USBLS	5/07
	Little Rock-North Little Rock MSA, AR	Y	13890 FQ	14470 MW	15330 TQ	USBLS	5/07
	California	H	9.28 FQ	11.21 MW	14.27 TQ	CABLS	1/08-3/08
	Los Angeles-Long Beach-Glendale PMSA, CA	H	9.14 FQ	11.47 MW	15.36 TQ	CABLS	1/08-3/08
	Oakland-Fremont-Hayward MSA, CA	H	9.68 FQ	11.54 MW	14.54 TQ	CABLS	1/08-3/08
	Riverside-San Bernardino-Ontario MSA, CA	H	8.77 FQ	10.12 MW	12.32 TQ	CABLS	1/08-3/08
	Sacramento-Arden Arcade-Roseville MSA, CA	H	8.40 FQ	9.49 MW	11.62 TQ	CABLS	1/08-3/08
	San Diego-Carlsbad-San Marcos MSA, CA	H	10.95 FQ	12.83 MW	15.47 TQ	CABLS	1/08-3/08
	San Francisco-San Mateo-Redwood PMSA, CA	H	10.62 FQ	12.49 MW	16.78 TQ	CABLS	1/08-3/08
	San Jose-Sunnyvale-Santa Clara MSA, CA	H	9.96 FQ	11.16 MW	12.28 TQ	CABLS	1/08-3/08
	Santa Ana-Anaheim-Irvine PMSA, CA	Y	20520 FQ	24480 MW	33620 TQ	USBLS	5/07
	Colorado	Y	16680 FQ	19080 MW	22310 TQ	USBLS	5/07
	Colorado Springs MSA, CO	Y	15690 FQ	17410 MW	19370 TQ	USBLS	5/07
	Denver-Aurora MSA, CO	Y	17130 FQ	19310 MW	22010 TQ	USBLS	5/07
	Connecticut	H	8.64 AE	9.72 MW		CTBLS	1/08-3/08
	Bridgeport-Stamford-Norwalk MSA, CT	Y	17710 FQ	20430 MW	24520 TQ	USBLS	5/07
	Hartford-West Hartford-East Hartford MSA, CT	Y	17730 FQ	19390 MW	22120 TQ	USBLS	5/07
	Delaware	Y	17090 FQ	19850 MW	23150 TQ	USBLS	5/07
	Wilmington PMSA, DE-MD-NJ	Y	15950 FQ	18250 MW	21840 TQ	USBLS	5/07
	District of Columbia	Y	21490 FQ	23080 MW	24720 TQ	USBLS	5/07
	Washington-Arlington-Alexandria MSA, DC-VA-MD-WV	Y	16490 FQ	18380 MW	21180 TQ	USBLS	5/07
	Florida	Y	17240 FQ	20150 MW	26360 TQ	USBLS	5/07
	Fort Lauderdale-Pompano Beach-Deerfield Beach PMSA, FL	Y	19580 FQ	25950 MW	30400 TQ	USBLS	5/07

AE	Average entry wage	AW	Average wage paid	FQ	First quartile wage	LO	Lowest wage paid	MTC	Median total compensation	TCC	Total cash compensation
AER	Average entry range	AWR	Average wage range	H	Hourly	LR	Low end range	MW	Median wage paid	TQ	Third quartile wage
AEX	Average experienced wage	AXR	Average experienced range	HI	Highest wage paid	M	Monthly	MWR	Median wage range	W	Weekly
ATC	Average total compensation	D	Daily	HR	High end range	MCC	Median cash compensation	S	See annotated source	Y	Yearly

916

Occupation/Type/Industry	Location	Per	Low	Mid	High	Source	Date
Lifeguard, Ski Patrol, and Other Recreational Protective Service Worker	Jacksonville MSA, FL	Y	19960 FQ	22950 MW	26200 TQ	USBLS	5/07
	Miami-Fort Lauderdale-Miami Beach MSA, FL	Y	21760 FQ	26870 MW	31890 TQ	USBLS	5/07
	Orlando-Kissimmee MSA, FL	Y	16330 FQ	17820 MW	19370 TQ	USBLS	5/07
	Tampa-St. Petersburg-Clearwater MSA, FL	Y	16440 FQ	18420 MW	21520 TQ	USBLS	5/07
	West Palm Beach-Boca Raton-Boynton Beach PMSA, FL	Y	23130 FQ	27600 MW	32180 TQ	USBLS	5/07
	Georgia	Y	14330 FQ	17420 MW	20140 TQ	USBLS	5/07
	Atlanta-Sandy Springs-Marietta MSA, GA	Y	14750 FQ	17750 MW	20290 TQ	USBLS	5/07
	Hawaii	Y	23400 FQ	31980 MW	40120 TQ	USBLS	5/07
	Honolulu MSA, HI	Y	20890 FQ	31130 MW	39950 TQ	USBLS	5/07
	Idaho	Y	14190 FQ	16620 MW	18680 TQ	USBLS	5/07
	Boise City-Nampa MSA, ID	Y	15660 FQ	17340 MW	18980 TQ	USBLS	5/07
	Illinois	Y	15320 FQ	17180 MW	19570 TQ	USBLS	5/07
	Chicago-Naperville-Joliet MSA, IL-IN-WI	Y	15540 FQ	17600 MW	20130 TQ	USBLS	5/07
	Peoria MSA, IL	Y	14740 FQ	15670 MW	18680 TQ	USBLS	5/07
	Indiana	Y	13250 FQ	15400 MW	18270 TQ	USBLS	5/07
	Gary PMSA, IN	Y	12790 FQ	14740 MW	17790 TQ	USBLS	5/07
	Indianapolis-Carmel MSA, IN	Y	14660 FQ	17380 MW	19730 TQ	USBLS	5/07
	Iowa	Y	13970 FQ	15050 MW	17220 TQ	USBLS	5/07
	Cedar Rapids MSA, IA	Y	13800 FQ	14700 MW	18930 TQ	USBLS	5/07
	Des Moines-West Des Moines MSA, IA	Y	15860 FQ	17680 MW	19790 TQ	USBLS	5/07
	Kansas	Y	13300 FQ	15530 MW	18000 TQ	USBLS	5/07
	Wichita MSA, KS	Y	13010 FQ	15040 MW	17680 TQ	USBLS	5/07
	Kentucky	Y	13678 FQ	15780 MW	17994 TQ	KYBLS	2008
	Louisville-Jefferson County MSA, KY-IN	Y	14110 FQ	16450 MW	18410 TQ	USBLS	5/07
	Louisiana	H	6.15 FQ	6.96 MW	8.41 TQ	LABLS	1/08-3/08
	Baton Rouge MSA, LA	Y	13120 FQ	15390 MW	17580 TQ	USBLS	5/07
	New Orleans-Metairie-Kenner MSA, LA	Y	12700 FQ	14230 MW	17040 TQ	USBLS	5/07
	Maine	Y	14900 FQ	16010 MW	19590 TQ	USBLS	5/07
	Portland-South Portland-Biddeford MSA, ME	Y	14800 FQ	17110 MW	23990 TQ	USBLS	5/07
	Maryland	Y		18900 MW		MDBLS	3/08
	Baltimore-Towson MSA, MD	Y	15400 FQ	18520 MW	22650 TQ	USBLS	5/07
	Bethesda-Gaithersburg-Frederick PMSA, MD	Y	16140 FQ	18540 MW	21870 TQ	USBLS	5/07
	Massachusetts	Y	18400 FQ	21700 MW	26580 TQ	USBLS	5/07
	Barnstable Town MSA, MA	Y	21360 FQ	24280 MW	28530 TQ	USBLS	5/07
	Boston-Cambridge-Quincy NECTA, MA	Y	19670 FQ	23170 MW	27920 TQ	USBLS	5/07
	Lynn-Peabody-Salem NECTA, MA	Y	17690 FQ	19520 MW	23250 TQ	USBLS	5/07
	Springfield MSA, MA-CT	Y	17170 FQ	19040 MW	23500 TQ	USBLS	5/07
	Worcester MSA, MA-CT	Y	17190 FQ	19150 MW	27390 TQ	USBLS	5/07
	Michigan	Y	16300 FQ	18330 MW	21770 TQ	USBLS	5/07
	Detroit-Warren-Livonia MSA, MI	Y	16750 FQ	19150 MW	23720 TQ	USBLS	5/07
	Grand Rapids-Wyoming MSA, MI	Y	16990 FQ	18830 MW	20750 TQ	USBLS	5/07
	Warren-Troy-Farmington Hills PMSA, MI	Y	16430 FQ	18480 MW	23380 TQ	USBLS	5/07
	Minnesota	Y	17597 FQ	20190 MW	23818 TQ	MNBLS	10/08-12/08
	Duluth-Superior MSA, MN-WI	Y	18266 FQ	19970 MW	21999 TQ	MNBLS	10/08-12/08
	Minneapolis-Saint Paul MSA, MN-WI	Y	18140 FQ	20639 MW	24090 TQ	MNBLS	10/08-12/08
	Mississippi	Y	13520 FQ	15640 MW	18170 TQ	USBLS	5/07
	Jackson MSA, MS	Y	13260 FQ	15490 MW	18600 TQ	USBLS	5/07
	Missouri	Y	14810 FQ	16580 MW	18930 TQ	USBLS	5/07
	Kansas City MSA, MO-KS	Y	16070 FQ	17680 MW	19260 TQ	USBLS	5/07
	St. Louis MSA, MO-IL	Y	14990 FQ	16860 MW	19020 TQ	USBLS	5/07
	Montana	Y	13840 FQ	14890 MW	17190 TQ	USBLS	5/07
	Billings MSA, MT	Y	14440 FQ	15980 MW	18660 TQ	USBLS	5/07
	Nebraska	Y	13410 FQ	15670 MW	17960 TQ	USBLS	5/07

AE Average entry wage	**AW** Average wage paid	**FQ** First quartile wage	**LO** Lowest wage paid	**MTC** Median total compensation	**TCC** Total cash compensation
AER Average entry range	**AWR** Average wage range	**H** Hourly	**LR** Low end range	**MW** Median wage paid	**TQ** Third quartile wage
AEX Average experienced wage	**AXR** Average experienced range	**HI** Highest wage paid	**M** Monthly	**MWR** Median wage range	**W** Weekly
ATC Average total compensation	**D** Daily	**HR** High end range	**MCC** Median cash compensation	**S** See annotated source	**Y** Yearly

Occupation/Type/Industry	Location	Per	Low	Mid	High	Source	Date
Lifeguard, Ski Patrol, and Other Recreational Protective Service Worker							
	Omaha-Council Bluffs MSA, NE-IA	Y	16200 FQ	17700 MW	19240 TQ	USBLS	5/07
	Nevada	H	8.53 FQ	9.37 MW	10.37 TQ	NVBLS	5/08
	Las Vegas-Paradise MSA, NV	H	8.60 FQ	9.36 MW	10.30 TQ	NVBLS	5/08
	New Hampshire	H	8.71 AE	10.70 MW	11.71 AEX	NHBLS	6/08
	Nashua NECTA, NH-MA	Y	19040 FQ	21350 MW	23430 TQ	USBLS	5/07
	New Jersey	Y	16610 FQ	18600 MW	21930 TQ	USBLS	5/07
	Camden PMSA, NJ	Y	16770 FQ	18380 MW	21250 TQ	USBLS	5/07
	Edison PMSA, NJ	Y	16660 FQ	18350 MW	21230 TQ	USBLS	5/07
	Newark-Union PMSA, NJ-PA	Y	17200 FQ	19360 MW	23440 TQ	USBLS	5/07
	New Mexico	Y	13390 FQ	15700 MW	19300 TQ	USBLS	5/07
	Albuquerque MSA, NM	Y	13040 FQ	14990 MW	17430 TQ	USBLS	5/07
	New York	Y	16740 FQ	20130 MW	24350 TQ	USBLS	5/07
	Albany-Schenectady-Troy MSA, NY	Y	16690 FQ	18540 MW	21100 TQ	USBLS	5/07
	Buffalo-Niagara Falls MSA, NY	Y	15760 FQ	16800 MW	18650 TQ	USBLS	5/07
	Kingston MSA, NY	Y	16100 FQ	19960 MW	23190 TQ	USBLS	5/07
	Nassau-Suffolk PMSA, NY	Y	19740 FQ	22800 MW	26220 TQ	USBLS	5/07
	New York-Northern New Jersey-Long Island MSA, NY-NJ-PA	Y	17550 FQ	20620 MW	24780 TQ	USBLS	5/07
	North Carolina	Y	14910 FQ	16850 MW	19000 TQ	USBLS	5/07
	Charlotte-Gastonia-Concord MSA, NC-SC	Y	16780 FQ	18840 MW	21430 TQ	USBLS	5/07
	Greensboro-High Point MSA, NC	Y	16020 FQ	17750 MW	19710 TQ	USBLS	5/07
	Raleigh-Cary MSA, NC	Y	15510 FQ	16940 MW	18340 TQ	USBLS	5/07
	North Dakota	Y	13850 FQ	16600 MW	18750 TQ	USBLS	5/07
	Fargo MSA, ND-MN	Y	16450 FQ	17910 MW	19370 TQ	USBLS	5/07
	Grand Forks MSA, ND-MN	Y	13670 FQ	14980 MW	18110 TQ	USBLS	5/07
	Ohio	Y	14940 FQ	15790 MW	18430 TQ	USBLS	5/07
	Cincinnati-Middletown MSA, OH-KY-IN	Y	14770 FQ	15350 MW	16490 TQ	USBLS	5/07
	Cleveland-Elyria-Mentor MSA, OH	Y	15280 FQ	16260 MW	18700 TQ	USBLS	5/07
	Columbus MSA, OH	Y	16640 FQ	19050 MW	22140 TQ	USBLS	5/07
	Dayton MSA, OH	Y	14930 FQ	15630 MW	19050 TQ	USBLS	5/07
	Oklahoma	Y	13420 FQ	15530 MW	18270 TQ	USBLS	5/07
	Oklahoma City MSA, OK	Y	13260 FQ	15170 MW	17340 TQ	USBLS	5/07
	Tulsa MSA, OK	Y	13880 FQ	15870 MW	18190 TQ	USBLS	5/07
	Oregon	H	8.56 FQ	9.11 MW	9.97 TQ	ORBLS	5/08
	Portland-Vancouver-Beaverton MSA, OR-WA	Y	17440 FQ	18630 MW	20870 TQ	USBLS	5/07
	Pennsylvania	Y	14470 FQ	15650 MW	18660 TQ	USBLS	5/07
	Allentown-Bethlehem-Easton MSA, PA-NJ	Y	14330 FQ	15590 MW	19210 TQ	USBLS	5/07
	Philadelphia-Camden-Wilmington MSA, PA-NJ-DE-MD	Y	15320 FQ	17450 MW	21080 TQ	USBLS	5/07
	Pittsburgh MSA, PA	Y	14260 FQ	15040 MW	17250 TQ	USBLS	5/07
	Rhode Island	Y	17170 FQ	18850 MW	21010 TQ	USBLS	5/07
	Providence-Fall River-Warwick MSA, RI-MA	Y	16890 FQ	18490 MW	20260 TQ	USBLS	5/07
	South Carolina	Y	14860 FQ	17060 MW	19050 TQ	USBLS	5/07
	Charleston-North Charleston MSA, SC	Y	15150 FQ	16880 MW	18460 TQ	USBLS	5/07
	Columbia MSA, SC	Y	15790 FQ	17120 MW	18520 TQ	USBLS	5/07
	South Dakota	Y	15506 FQ	17566 MW	19528 TQ	SDBLS	7/08-9/08
	Sioux Falls MSA, SD	Y	18150 FQ	22233 MW	24672 TQ	SDBLS	7/08-9/08
	Tennessee	Y	13510 FQ	15900 MW	18460 TQ	USBLS	5/07
	Memphis MSA, TN-MS-AR	Y	12990 FQ	14860 MW	17920 TQ	USBLS	5/07
	Nashville-Davidson-Murfreesboro MSA, TN	Y	15830 FQ	17680 MW	19710 TQ	USBLS	5/07
	Texas	Y	13610 FQ	16050 MW	18800 TQ	USBLS	5/07
	Austin-Round Rock MSA, TX	Y	16040 FQ	18790 MW	22320 TQ	USBLS	5/07
	Dallas-Fort Worth-Arlington MSA, TX	Y	14220 FQ	16750 MW	18920 TQ	USBLS	5/07
	El Paso MSA, TX	Y	12470 FQ	13850 MW	15350 TQ	USBLS	5/07

AE Average entry wage	**AW** Average wage paid	**FQ** First quartile wage	**LO** Lowest wage paid	**MTC** Median total compensation	**TCC** Total cash compensation
AER Average entry range	**AWR** Average wage range	**H** Hourly	**LR** Low end range	**MW** Median wage paid	**TQ** Third quartile wage
AEX Average experienced wage	**AXR** Average experienced range	**HI** Highest wage paid	**M** Monthly	**MWR** Median wage range	**W** Weekly
ATC Average total compensation	**D** Daily	**HR** High end range	**MCC** Median cash compensation	**S** See annotated source	**Y** Yearly

Occupation/Type/Industry	Location	Per	Low	Mid	High	Source	Date
Lifeguard, Ski Patrol, and Other Recreational Protective Service Worker							
	Houston-Sugar Land-Baytown MSA, TX	Y	14430 FQ	17150 MW	19820 TQ	USBLS	5/07
	San Antonio MSA, TX	Y	13040 FQ	15050 MW	17610 TQ	USBLS	5/07
	Utah	Y	13430 FQ	15640 MW	18410 TQ	USBLS	5/07
	Salt Lake City MSA, UT	Y	13730 FQ	16010 MW	18720 TQ	USBLS	5/07
	Vermont	Y	17130 FQ	18620 MW	20460 TQ	USBLS	5/07
	Burlington-South Burlington MSA, VT	Y	16300 FQ	17700 MW	19140 TQ	USBLS	5/07
	Virginia	Y	15390 FQ	17790 MW	20170 TQ	USBLS	5/07
	Richmond MSA, VA	Y	15260 FQ	18360 MW	23790 TQ	USBLS	5/07
	Virginia Beach-Norfolk-Newport News MSA, VA-NC	Y	15030 FQ	17500 MW	19720 TQ	USBLS	5/07
	Washington	H	8.70 FQ	9.43 MW	11.09 TQ	WABLS	3/08
	Seattle-Tacoma-Bellevue MSA, WA	Y	18000 FQ	19740 MW	23060 TQ	USBLS	5/07
	West Virginia	Y	13962 FQ	15032 MW	16494 TQ	WVBLS	7/08-9/08
	Charleston MSA, WV	Y	13150 FQ	13910 MW	14670 TQ	USBLS	5/07
	Wisconsin	Y	15790 FQ	17620 MW	19580 TQ	USBLS	5/07
	Milwaukee-Waukesha-West Allis MSA, WI	Y	16640 FQ	18100 MW	19670 TQ	USBLS	5/07
	Racine MSA, WI	Y	15860 FQ	17520 MW	19360 TQ	USBLS	5/07
	Wyoming	Y	13729 FQ	15654 MW	18937 TQ	WYBLS	9/08
	Cheyenne MSA, WY	Y	16749 FQ	18177 MW	19617 TQ	WYBLS	9/08
	Puerto Rico	Y	13460 FQ	15790 MW	19680 TQ	USBLS	5/07
	San Juan-Caguas-Guaynabo MSA, PR	Y	13670 FQ	16310 MW	20530 TQ	USBLS	5/07
	Virgin Islands	Y	18710 FQ	21910 MW	25500 TQ	USBLS	5/07
	Guam	Y	13960 FQ	16910 MW	20200 TQ	USBLS	5/07
Light Equipment Operator	Fayette County, GA	Y	30458 LO		46346 HI	GACTY03	2008
	Rockdale County, GA	Y	20742 LO		33114 HI	GACTY03	2008
Linen Control Supervisor							
New Hampshire Hospital	New Hampshire	Y		27433 AW		NHUL03	2008
Linguist, Translator or Interpreter							
With Security Clearance	United States	Y		70952 AW		CLJOBS	3/20/07-2/20/08
Without Security Clearance	United States	Y		62789 AW		CLJOBS	3/20/07-2/20/08
Liquor Control Chemist							
State Government	Ohio	H	19.88 LO		26.28 HI	ODAS	2008
Litter Control Officer							
Municipal Government	Cincinnati, OH	Y	39113 LO		41597 HI	COHSS	10/08
Livestock Inspector							
State Government	Indiana	Y	29614 LO		51168 HI	AFT02	3/1/08
State Government	Ohio	H	17.22 LO		21.77 HI	ODAS	2008
Loading Machine Operator							
Underground Mining	Alabama	Y	33070 FQ	40100 MW	45160 TQ	USBLS	5/07
Underground Mining	California	H	14.84 FQ	16.76 MW	19.05 TQ	CABLS	1/08-3/08
Underground Mining	Georgia	Y	22740 FQ	27310 MW	35640 TQ	USBLS	5/07
Underground Mining	Illinois	Y	27980 FQ	33680 MW	40580 TQ	USBLS	5/07
Underground Mining	Kentucky	Y	35895 FQ	39800 MW	44371 TQ	KYBLS	2008
Underground Mining	Missouri	Y	27070 FQ	29560 MW	32370 TQ	USBLS	5/07
Underground Mining	New York	Y	31130 FQ	34970 MW	38800 TQ	USBLS	5/07
Underground Mining	Ohio	Y	30340 FQ	43860 MW	48100 TQ	USBLS	5/07
Underground Mining	Pennsylvania	Y	30690 FQ	34730 MW	40710 TQ	USBLS	5/07
Underground Mining	Utah	Y	43660 FQ	86050 MW	96250 TQ	USBLS	5/07
Loan Counselor							
	Alabama	Y	29790 FQ	35040 MW	41140 TQ	USBLS	5/07
	Birmingham-Hoover MSA, AL	Y	30090 FQ	33350 MW	38690 TQ	USBLS	5/07
	Alaska	Y	34860 FQ	37670 MW	40500 TQ	USBLS	5/07
	Arizona	Y	31240 FQ	37640 MW	61580 TQ	USBLS	5/07
	Phoenix-Mesa-Scottsdale MSA, AZ	Y	31480 FQ	38180 MW	62500 TQ	USBLS	5/07
	Tucson MSA, AZ	Y	28550 FQ	36880 MW	70920 TQ	USBLS	5/07
	Arkansas	Y	30260 FQ	39110 MW	46990 TQ	USBLS	5/07

AE	Average entry wage	AW	Average wage paid	FQ	First quartile wage	LO	Lowest wage paid	MTC	Median total compensation	TCC	Total cash compensation
AER	Average entry range	AWR	Average wage range	H	Hourly	LR	Low end range	MW	Median wage paid	TQ	Third quartile wage
AEX	Average experienced wage	AXR	Average experienced range	HI	Highest wage paid	M	Monthly	MWR	Median wage range	W	Weekly
ATC	Average total compensation	D	Daily	HR	High end range	MCC	Median cash compensation	S	See annotated source	Y	Yearly

Loan Counselor

Occupation/Type/Industry	Location	Per	Low	Mid	High	Source	Date
Loan Counselor	Little Rock-North Little Rock MSA, AR	Y	29220 FQ	36440 MW	50940 TQ	USBLS	5/07
	California	H	15.80 FQ	19.27 MW	25.26 TQ	CABLS	1/08-3/08
	Los Angeles-Long Beach-Glendale PMSA, CA	H	15.39 FQ	18.59 MW	24.43 TQ	CABLS	1/08-3/08
	Oakland-Fremont-Hayward MSA, CA	H	17.91 FQ	22.96 MW	29.49 TQ	CABLS	1/08-3/08
	Riverside-San Bernardino-Ontario MSA, CA	H	15.66 FQ	19.02 MW	23.17 TQ	CABLS	1/08-3/08
	Sacramento-Arden Arcade-Roseville MSA, CA	H	17.24 FQ	19.02 MW	23.01 TQ	CABLS	1/08-3/08
	San Diego-Carlsbad-San Marcos MSA, CA	H	13.99 FQ	19.41 MW	27.06 TQ	CABLS	1/08-3/08
	San Francisco-San Mateo-Redwood PMSA, CA	H	19.61 FQ	24.21 MW	29.00 TQ	CABLS	1/08-3/08
	San Jose-Sunnyvale-Santa Clara MSA, CA	H	16.05 FQ	17.97 MW	22.44 TQ	CABLS	1/08-3/08
	Santa Ana-Anaheim-Irvine PMSA, CA	Y	34680 FQ	43770 MW	57320 TQ	USBLS	5/07
	Colorado	Y	33280 FQ	41120 MW	55700 TQ	USBLS	5/07
	Denver-Aurora MSA, CO	Y	34780 FQ	42770 MW	56750 TQ	USBLS	5/07
	Connecticut	H	16.11 AE	20.79 MW		CTBLS	1/08-3/08
	Bridgeport-Stamford-Norwalk MSA, CT	Y	38250 FQ	43250 MW	51050 TQ	USBLS	5/07
	Hartford-West Hartford-East Hartford MSA, CT	Y	34460 FQ	37710 MW	46520 TQ	USBLS	5/07
	Delaware	Y	30060 FQ	38470 MW	50440 TQ	USBLS	5/07
	Wilmington PMSA, DE-MD-NJ	Y	35940 FQ	45240 MW	58660 TQ	USBLS	5/07
	District of Columbia	Y	43130 FQ	61850 MW	80860 TQ	USBLS	5/07
	Washington-Arlington-Alexandria MSA, DC-VA-MD-WV	Y	32260 FQ	43020 MW	63070 TQ	USBLS	5/07
	Florida	Y	28840 FQ	34600 MW	44990 TQ	USBLS	5/07
	Fort Lauderdale-Pompano Beach-Deerfield Beach PMSA, FL	Y	27350 FQ	30960 MW	36060 TQ	USBLS	5/07
	Jacksonville MSA, FL	Y	29530 FQ	37400 MW	57010 TQ	USBLS	5/07
	Miami-Fort Lauderdale-Miami Beach MSA, FL	Y	27750 FQ	32240 MW	38810 TQ	USBLS	5/07
	Orlando-Kissimmee MSA, FL	Y	32840 FQ	39440 MW	45850 TQ	USBLS	5/07
	Tampa-St. Petersburg-Clearwater MSA, FL	Y	29620 FQ	37580 MW	58300 TQ	USBLS	5/07
	West Palm Beach-Boca Raton-Boynton Beach PMSA, FL	Y	26480 FQ	31150 MW	44200 TQ	USBLS	5/07
	Georgia	Y	28650 FQ	38240 MW	49580 TQ	USBLS	5/07
	Atlanta-Sandy Springs-Marietta MSA, GA	Y	30880 FQ	41130 MW	52970 TQ	USBLS	5/07
	Hawaii	Y	29910 FQ	32910 MW	43350 TQ	USBLS	5/07
	Honolulu MSA, HI	Y	29600 FQ	32740 MW	44420 TQ	USBLS	5/07
	Boise City-Nampa MSA, ID	Y	29080 FQ	35230 MW	38580 TQ	USBLS	5/07
	Illinois	Y	34980 FQ	42470 MW	59300 TQ	USBLS	5/07
	Chicago-Naperville-Joliet MSA, IL-IN-WI	Y	34870 FQ	42220 MW	60030 TQ	USBLS	5/07
	Indiana	Y	29270 FQ	33640 MW	40730 TQ	USBLS	5/07
	Evansville MSA, IN-KY	Y	28040 FQ	35210 MW	45200 TQ	USBLS	5/07
	Gary PMSA, IN	Y	32240 FQ	35360 MW	38940 TQ	USBLS	5/07
	Indianapolis-Carmel MSA, IN	Y	28750 FQ	32780 MW	37810 TQ	USBLS	5/07
	Iowa	Y	28440 FQ	32080 MW	37460 TQ	USBLS	5/07
	Des Moines-West Des Moines MSA, IA	Y	30010 FQ	34170 MW	38050 TQ	USBLS	5/07
	Sioux City MSA, IA-NE-SD	Y	28180 FQ	30360 MW	32470 TQ	USBLS	5/07
	Kansas	Y	29190 FQ	34540 MW	41860 TQ	USBLS	5/07
	Wichita MSA, KS	Y	28530 FQ	32150 MW	39760 TQ	USBLS	5/07
	Kentucky	Y	30695 FQ	36793 MW	48276 TQ	KYBLS	2008
	Louisville-Jefferson County MSA, KY-IN	Y	32050 FQ	42160 MW	56000 TQ	USBLS	5/07
	Louisiana	H	16.52 FQ	21.72 MW	27.97 TQ	LABLS	1/08-3/08
	Baton Rouge MSA, LA	Y	33590 FQ	45190 MW	60610 TQ	USBLS	5/07
	New Orleans-Metairie-Kenner MSA, LA	Y	36830 FQ	47850 MW	61750 TQ	USBLS	5/07
	Maine	Y	30480 FQ	35110 MW	40700 TQ	USBLS	5/07

AE Average entry wage	**AW** Average wage paid	**FQ** First quartile wage	**LO** Lowest wage paid	**MTC** Median total compensation	**TCC** Total cash compensation
AER Average entry range	**AWR** Average wage range	**H** Hourly	**LR** Low end range	**MW** Median wage paid	**TQ** Third quartile wage
AEX Average experienced wage	**AXR** Average experienced range	**HI** Highest wage paid	**M** Monthly	**MWR** Median wage range	**W** Weekly
ATC Average total compensation	**D** Daily	**HR** High end range	**MCC** Median cash compensation	**S** See annotated source	**Y** Yearly

Occupation/Type/Industry	Location	Per	Low	Mid	High	Source	Date
Loan Counselor	Maryland	Y		39225 ᴍᴡ		MDBLS	3/08
	Baltimore-Towson MSA, MD	Y	34960 ꜰǫ	40610 ᴍᴡ	50840 ᴛǫ	USBLS	5/07
	Bethesda-Gaithersburg-Frederick PMSA, MD	Y	27150 ꜰǫ	35650 ᴍᴡ	47870 ᴛǫ	USBLS	5/07
	Massachusetts	Y	37760 ꜰǫ	46630 ᴍᴡ	61880 ᴛǫ	USBLS	5/07
	Boston-Cambridge-Quincy NECTA, MA	Y	39270 ꜰǫ	49000 ᴍᴡ	68850 ᴛǫ	USBLS	5/07
	Worcester MSA, MA-CT	Y	36340 ꜰǫ	42470 ᴍᴡ	56440 ᴛǫ	USBLS	5/07
	Michigan	Y	32170 ꜰǫ	41770 ᴍᴡ	53770 ᴛǫ	USBLS	5/07
	Detroit-Warren-Livonia MSA, MI	Y	32860 ꜰǫ	42970 ᴍᴡ	54840 ᴛǫ	USBLS	5/07
	Grand Rapids-Wyoming MSA, MI	Y	30410 ꜰǫ	37630 ᴍᴡ	47070 ᴛǫ	USBLS	5/07
	Warren-Troy-Farmington Hills PMSA, MI	Y	40470 ꜰǫ	48660 ᴍᴡ	58700 ᴛǫ	USBLS	5/07
	Minnesota	Y	34981 ꜰǫ	40892 ᴍᴡ	48744 ᴛǫ	MNBLS	10/08-12/08
	Duluth-Superior MSA, MN-WI	Y	29653 ꜰǫ	33490 ᴍᴡ	37681 ᴛǫ	MNBLS	10/08-12/08
	Minneapolis-Saint Paul MSA, MN-WI	Y	34480 ꜰǫ	39964 ᴍᴡ	48149 ᴛǫ	MNBLS	10/08-12/08
	Rochester MSA, MN	Y	28684 ꜰǫ	30738 ᴍᴡ	32793 ᴛǫ	MNBLS	10/08-12/08
	Mississippi	Y	38820 ꜰǫ	46840 ᴍᴡ	54660 ᴛǫ	USBLS	5/07
	Jackson MSA, MS	Y	37950 ꜰǫ	45290 ᴍᴡ	51160 ᴛǫ	USBLS	5/07
	Missouri	Y	27770 ꜰǫ	34710 ᴍᴡ	44650 ᴛǫ	USBLS	5/07
	Kansas City MSA, MO-KS	Y	30440 ꜰǫ	37830 ᴍᴡ	44730 ᴛǫ	USBLS	5/07
	St. Louis MSA, MO-IL	Y	28280 ꜰǫ	33310 ᴍᴡ	44990 ᴛǫ	USBLS	5/07
	Montana	Y	27810 ꜰǫ	33570 ᴍᴡ	40750 ᴛǫ	USBLS	5/07
	Nebraska	Y	28730 ꜰǫ	33570 ᴍᴡ	42930 ᴛǫ	USBLS	5/07
	Omaha-Council Bluffs MSA, NE-IA	Y	27620 ꜰǫ	30900 ᴍᴡ	37470 ᴛǫ	USBLS	5/07
	Nevada	H	14.64 ꜰǫ	20.00 ᴍᴡ	27.68 ᴛǫ	NVBLS	5/08
	Las Vegas-Paradise MSA, NV	H	14.97 ꜰǫ	20.62 ᴍᴡ	28.99 ᴛǫ	NVBLS	5/08
	New Hampshire	H	14.71 ᴀᴇ	19.08 ᴍᴡ	24.63 ᴀᴇˣ	NHBLS	6/08
	Manchester MSA, NH	Y	44570 ꜰǫ	49230 ᴍᴡ	55260 ᴛǫ	USBLS	5/07
	New Jersey	Y	32690 ꜰǫ	40290 ᴍᴡ	49330 ᴛǫ	USBLS	5/07
	Camden PMSA, NJ	Y	33060 ꜰǫ	37530 ᴍᴡ	46880 ᴛǫ	USBLS	5/07
	Edison PMSA, NJ	Y	33890 ꜰǫ	40740 ᴍᴡ	48290 ᴛǫ	USBLS	5/07
	Newark-Union PMSA, NJ-PA	Y	30990 ꜰǫ	40850 ᴍᴡ	51480 ᴛǫ	USBLS	5/07
	New Mexico	Y	27500 ꜰǫ	31670 ᴍᴡ	37100 ᴛǫ	USBLS	5/07
	Albuquerque MSA, NM	Y	27500 ꜰǫ	31980 ᴍᴡ	37060 ᴛǫ	USBLS	5/07
	New York	Y	31930 ꜰǫ	38650 ᴍᴡ	50080 ᴛǫ	USBLS	5/07
	Albany-Schenectady-Troy MSA, NY	Y	37980 ꜰǫ	44200 ᴍᴡ	50990 ᴛǫ	USBLS	5/07
	Buffalo-Niagara Falls MSA, NY	Y	32730 ꜰǫ	37910 ᴍᴡ	50820 ᴛǫ	USBLS	5/07
	Nassau-Suffolk PMSA, NY	Y	36090 ꜰǫ	43720 ᴍᴡ	59760 ᴛǫ	USBLS	5/07
	New York-Northern New Jersey-Long Island MSA, NY-NJ-PA	Y	31960 ꜰǫ	39310 ᴍᴡ	50940 ᴛǫ	USBLS	5/07
	North Carolina	Y	27670 ꜰǫ	31110 ᴍᴡ	36880 ᴛǫ	USBLS	5/07
	Charlotte-Gastonia-Concord MSA, NC-SC	Y	30950 ꜰǫ	35270 ᴍᴡ	48720 ᴛǫ	USBLS	5/07
	Durham MSA, NC	Y	27410 ꜰǫ	30410 ᴍᴡ	34540 ᴛǫ	USBLS	3/08
	Raleigh-Cary MSA, NC	Y	34890 ꜰǫ	42470 ᴍᴡ	48800 ᴛǫ	USBLS	5/07
	North Dakota	Y	26450 ꜰǫ	29650 ᴍᴡ	33460 ᴛǫ	USBLS	5/07
	Ohio	Y	30160 ꜰǫ	36680 ᴍᴡ	45470 ᴛǫ	USBLS	5/07
	Cincinnati-Middletown MSA, OH-KY-IN	Y	29550 ꜰǫ	35010 ᴍᴡ	42790 ᴛǫ	USBLS	5/07
	Cleveland-Elyria-Mentor MSA, OH	Y	30010 ꜰǫ	37530 ᴍᴡ	46400 ᴛǫ	USBLS	5/07
	Columbus MSA, OH	Y	31300 ꜰǫ	38490 ᴍᴡ	46800 ᴛǫ	USBLS	5/07
	Dayton MSA, OH	Y	30350 ꜰǫ	35940 ᴍᴡ	42600 ᴛǫ	USBLS	5/07
	Oklahoma	Y	27090 ꜰǫ	32270 ᴍᴡ	43050 ᴛǫ	USBLS	5/07
	Oklahoma City MSA, OK	Y	28480 ꜰǫ	33910 ᴍᴡ	40920 ᴛǫ	USBLS	5/07
	Tulsa MSA, OK	Y	28030 ꜰǫ	32340 ᴍᴡ	43120 ᴛǫ	USBLS	5/07
	Oregon	H	15.77 ꜰǫ	18.40 ᴍᴡ	22.00 ᴛǫ	ORBLS	5/08
	Portland-Vancouver-Beaverton MSA, OR-WA	Y	33580 ꜰǫ	38730 ᴍᴡ	45370 ᴛǫ	USBLS	5/07
	Pennsylvania	Y	30520 ꜰǫ	37060 ᴍᴡ	47750 ᴛǫ	USBLS	5/07
	Philadelphia-Camden-Wilmington MSA, PA-NJ-DE-MD	Y	32370 ꜰǫ	38440 ᴍᴡ	47630 ᴛǫ	USBLS	5/07
	Pittsburgh MSA, PA	Y	30900 ꜰǫ	37170 ᴍᴡ	49000 ᴛǫ	USBLS	5/07

AE Average entry wage	**AW** Average wage paid	**FQ** First quartile wage	**LO** Lowest wage paid	**MTC** Median total compensation	**TCC** Total cash compensation
AER Average entry range	**AWR** Average wage range	**H** Hourly	**LR** Low end range	**MW** Median wage paid	**TQ** Third quartile wage
AEX Average experienced wage	**AXR** Average experienced range	**HI** Highest wage paid	**M** Monthly	**MWR** Median wage range	**W** Weekly
ATC Average total compensation	**D** Daily	**HR** High end range	**MCC** Median cash compensation	**S** See annotated source	**Y** Yearly

Occupation/Type/Industry	Location	Per	Low	Mid	High	Source	Date
Loan Counselor	Rhode Island	Y	33500 FQ	41110 MW	46600 TQ	USBLS	5/07
	Providence-Fall River-Warwick MSA, RI-MA	Y	32970 FQ	39510 MW	45680 TQ	USBLS	5/07
	South Carolina	Y	28430 FQ	33130 MW	41660 TQ	USBLS	5/07
	Charleston-North Charleston MSA, SC	Y	33150 FQ	42410 MW	57300 TQ	USBLS	5/07
	Columbia MSA, SC	Y	29230 FQ	32350 MW	37490 TQ	USBLS	5/07
	South Dakota	Y	31004 FQ	35453 MW	41347 TQ	SDBLS	7/08-9/08
	Tennessee	Y	28420 FQ	32960 MW	38490 TQ	USBLS	5/07
	Memphis MSA, TN-MS-AR	Y	32250 FQ	36340 MW	41140 TQ	USBLS	5/07
	Nashville-Davidson-Murfreesboro MSA, TN	Y	28300 FQ	31950 MW	36640 TQ	USBLS	5/07
	Texas	Y	26520 FQ	31620 MW	37590 TQ	USBLS	5/07
	Austin-Round Rock MSA, TX	Y	29540 FQ	33690 MW	38830 TQ	USBLS	5/07
	Dallas-Fort Worth-Arlington MSA, TX	Y	25490 FQ	31540 MW	37360 TQ	USBLS	5/07
	El Paso MSA, TX	Y	27830 FQ	31760 MW	37320 TQ	USBLS	5/07
	Houston-Sugar Land-Baytown MSA, TX	Y	28250 FQ	34010 MW	40770 TQ	USBLS	5/07
	San Antonio MSA, TX	Y	26070 FQ	30510 MW	35750 TQ	USBLS	5/07
	Utah	Y	28680 FQ	33820 MW	43070 TQ	USBLS	5/07
	Salt Lake City MSA, UT	Y	28270 FQ	32010 MW	37980 TQ	USBLS	5/07
	Vermont	Y	29430 FQ	35860 MW	50430 TQ	USBLS	5/07
	Burlington-South Burlington MSA, VT	Y	29730 FQ	35260 MW	45750 TQ	USBLS	5/07
	Virginia	Y	32900 FQ	41100 MW	58310 TQ	USBLS	5/07
	Richmond MSA, VA	Y	32710 FQ	39450 MW	49800 TQ	USBLS	5/07
	Virginia Beach-Norfolk-Newport News MSA, VA-NC	Y	27970 FQ	35860 MW	51640 TQ	USBLS	5/07
	Washington	H	16.97 FQ	19.06 MW	22.58 TQ	WABLS	3/08
	Seattle-Tacoma-Bellevue MSA, WA	Y	36120 FQ	39900 MW	46120 TQ	USBLS	5/07
	West Virginia	Y	25775 FQ	34037 MW	44123 TQ	WVBLS	7/08-9/08
	Wisconsin	Y	29450 FQ	35580 MW	49840 TQ	USBLS	5/07
	Milwaukee-Waukesha-West Allis MSA, WI	Y	32820 FQ	44220 MW	54010 TQ	USBLS	5/07
	Wyoming	Y	37817 FQ	62108 MW	78528 TQ	WYBLS	9/08
	Puerto Rico	Y	28360 FQ	35110 MW	44260 TQ	USBLS	5/07
	San Juan-Caguas-Guaynabo MSA, PR	Y	29320 FQ	37220 MW	45520 TQ	USBLS	5/07
Loan Interviewer and Clerk	Alabama	Y	22200 FQ	26750 MW	32790 TQ	USBLS	5/07
	Birmingham-Hoover MSA, AL	Y	23000 FQ	28590 MW	34870 TQ	USBLS	5/07
	Alaska	Y	30830 FQ	36630 MW	44200 TQ	USBLS	5/07
	Anchorage MSA, AK	Y	30800 FQ	37120 MW	45530 TQ	USBLS	5/07
	Arizona	Y	27600 FQ	32730 MW	39170 TQ	USBLS	5/07
	Flagstaff MSA, AZ	Y	28380 FQ	33280 MW	38670 TQ	USBLS	5/07
	Phoenix-Mesa-Scottsdale MSA, AZ	Y	27860 FQ	33000 MW	39850 TQ	USBLS	5/07
	Tucson MSA, AZ	Y	25620 FQ	32240 MW	36190 TQ	USBLS	5/07
	Arkansas	Y	22360 FQ	27330 MW	32010 TQ	USBLS	5/07
	Fort Smith MSA, AR-OK	Y	18600 FQ	22300 MW	30030 TQ	USBLS	5/07
	Little Rock-North Little Rock MSA, AR	Y	24650 FQ	29450 MW	34230 TQ	USBLS	5/07
	California	H	14.63 FQ	18.16 MW	22.57 TQ	CABLS	1/08-3/08
	Los Angeles-Long Beach-Glendale PMSA, CA	H	14.10 FQ	17.85 MW	22.35 TQ	CABLS	1/08-3/08
	Oakland-Fremont-Hayward MSA, CA	H	15.78 FQ	19.01 MW	23.00 TQ	CABLS	1/08-3/08
	Riverside-San Bernardino-Ontario MSA, CA	H	13.61 FQ	16.38 MW	21.09 TQ	CABLS	1/08-3/08
	Sacramento-Arden Arcade-Roseville MSA, CA	H	16.63 FQ	20.00 MW	24.88 TQ	CABLS	1/08-3/08
	San Diego-Carlsbad-San Marcos MSA, CA	H	14.68 FQ	18.19 MW	23.10 TQ	CABLS	1/08-3/08
	San Francisco-San Mateo-Redwood PMSA, CA	H	16.86 FQ	19.97 MW	23.76 TQ	CABLS	1/08-3/08
	San Jose-Sunnyvale-Santa Clara MSA, CA	H	15.46 FQ	19.52 MW	23.49 TQ	CABLS	1/08-3/08
	Santa Ana-Anaheim-Irvine PMSA, CA	Y	29950 FQ	37550 MW	46510 TQ	USBLS	5/07
	Colorado	Y	28460 FQ	35190 MW	42990 TQ	USBLS	5/07

AE	Average entry wage	AW	Average wage paid	FQ	First quartile wage	LO	Lowest wage paid	MTC	Median total compensation	TCC	Total cash compensation
AER	Average entry range	AWR	Average wage range	H	Hourly	LR	Low end range	MW	Median wage paid	TQ	Third quartile wage
AEX	Average experienced wage	AXR	Average experienced range	HI	Highest wage paid	M	Monthly	MWR	Median wage range	W	Weekly
ATC	Average total compensation	D	Daily	HR	High end range	MCC	Median cash compensation	S	See annotated source	Y	Yearly

Occupation/Type/Industry	Location	Per	Low	Mid	High	Source	Date
Loan Interviewer and Clerk	Denver-Aurora MSA, CO	Y	31740 FQ	37550 MW	45500 MW	USBLS	5/07
	Connecticut	H	12.94 AE	17.82 MW		CTBLS	1/08-3/08
	Bridgeport-Stamford-Norwalk MSA, CT	Y	29520 FQ	36930 MW	44730 TQ	USBLS	5/07
	Hartford-West Hartford-East Hartford MSA, CT	Y	30830 FQ	37600 MW	44070 TQ	USBLS	5/07
	Delaware	Y	27550 FQ	31210 MW	37790 TQ	USBLS	5/07
	Wilmington PMSA, DE-MD-NJ	Y	27950 FQ	31860 MW	38670 TQ	USBLS	5/07
	District of Columbia	Y	28400 FQ	35480 MW	44050 TQ	USBLS	5/07
	Washington-Arlington-Alexandria MSA, DC-VA-MD-WV	Y	31190 FQ	36750 MW	44180 TQ	USBLS	5/07
	Florida	Y	25460 FQ	31200 MW	38640 TQ	USBLS	5/07
	Fort Lauderdale-Pompano Beach-Deerfield Beach PMSA, FL	Y	26340 FQ	32850 MW	39730 TQ	USBLS	5/07
	Jacksonville MSA, FL	Y	27770 FQ	32410 MW	39040 TQ	USBLS	5/07
	Miami-Fort Lauderdale-Miami Beach MSA, FL	Y	25670 FQ	32730 MW	40350 TQ	USBLS	5/07
	Orlando-Kissimmee MSA, FL	Y	25430 FQ	31390 MW	41160 TQ	USBLS	5/07
	Pensacola-Ferry Pass-Brent MSA, FL	Y	23260 FQ	27830 MW	31860 TQ	USBLS	5/07
	Tallahassee MSA, FL	Y	20260 FQ	24650 MW	29790 TQ	USBLS	5/07
	Tampa-St. Petersburg-Clearwater MSA, FL	Y	25620 FQ	31180 MW	38030 TQ	USBLS	5/07
	West Palm Beach-Boca Raton-Boynton Beach PMSA, FL	Y	27000 FQ	34850 MW	42870 TQ	USBLS	5/07
	Georgia	Y	19880 FQ	27280 MW	34210 TQ	USBLS	5/07
	Atlanta-Sandy Springs-Marietta MSA, GA	Y	16740 FQ	27840 MW	35670 TQ	USBLS	5/07
	Augusta-Richmond County MSA, GA-SC	Y	23190 FQ	28420 MW	35780 TQ	USBLS	5/07
	Hawaii	Y	22580 FQ	26540 MW	35850 TQ	USBLS	5/07
	Idaho	Y	24200 FQ	28090 MW	33620 TQ	USBLS	5/07
	Boise City-Nampa MSA, ID	Y	25170 FQ	29290 MW	35810 TQ	USBLS	5/07
	Idaho Falls MSA, ID	Y	21320 FQ	24210 MW	28570 TQ	USBLS	5/07
	Illinois	Y	27170 FQ	34300 MW	43100 TQ	USBLS	5/07
	Chicago-Naperville-Joliet MSA, IL-IN-WI	Y	27780 FQ	35630 MW	44230 TQ	USBLS	5/07
	Rockford MSA, IL	Y	24480 FQ	29680 MW	39270 TQ	USBLS	5/07
	Indiana	Y	22870 FQ	27470 MW	34730 TQ	USBLS	5/07
	Gary PMSA, IN	Y	23210 FQ	27790 MW	35040 TQ	USBLS	5/07
	Indianapolis-Carmel MSA, IN	Y	23190 FQ	29510 MW	39090 TQ	USBLS	5/07
	Terre Haute MSA, IN	Y	21340 FQ	23310 MW	27030 TQ	USBLS	5/07
	Iowa	Y	25430 FQ	29050 MW	33770 TQ	USBLS	5/07
	Davenport-Moline-Rock Island MSA, IA-IL	Y	24200 FQ	29330 MW	36120 TQ	USBLS	5/07
	Des Moines-West Des Moines MSA, IA	Y	26950 FQ	30270 MW	35420 TQ	USBLS	5/07
	Kansas	Y	23380 FQ	29270 MW	35920 TQ	USBLS	5/07
	Wichita MSA, KS	Y	27220 FQ	32740 MW	37440 TQ	USBLS	5/07
	Kentucky	Y	22768 FQ	28407 MW	34157 TQ	KYBLS	2008
	Louisville-Jefferson County MSA, KY-IN	Y	24760 FQ	29540 MW	35160 TQ	USBLS	5/07
	Louisiana	H	10.14 FQ	12.01 MW	14.39 TQ	LABLS	1/08-3/08
	Baton Rouge MSA, LA	Y	22460 FQ	27170 MW	34300 TQ	USBLS	5/07
	Houma-Bayou Cane-Thibodaux MSA, LA	Y	21560 FQ	26500 MW	31510 TQ	USBLS	5/07
	Lafayette MSA, LA	Y	21750 FQ	25050 MW	28860 TQ	USBLS	5/07
	New Orleans-Metairie-Kenner MSA, LA	Y	20140 FQ	23760 MW	29150 TQ	USBLS	5/07
	Maine	Y	23620 FQ	28060 MW	34050 TQ	USBLS	5/07
	Portland-South Portland-Biddeford MSA, ME	Y	23980 FQ	29550 MW	36230 TQ	USBLS	5/07
	Maryland	Y		35725 MW		MDBLS	3/08
	Baltimore-Towson MSA, MD	Y	26310 FQ	34400 MW	43540 TQ	USBLS	5/07
	Bethesda-Gaithersburg-Frederick PMSA, MD	Y	30470 FQ	35460 MW	41580 TQ	USBLS	5/07
	Massachusetts	Y	27830 FQ	34520 MW	43120 TQ	USBLS	5/07
	Barnstable Town MSA, MA	Y	29590 FQ	33580 MW	45310 TQ	USBLS	5/07

AE	Average entry wage	AW	Average wage paid	FQ	First quartile wage
AER	Average entry range	AWR	Average wage range	H	Hourly
AEX	Average experienced wage	AXR	Average experienced range	HI	Highest wage paid
ATC	Average total compensation	D	Daily	HR	High end range

LO	Lowest wage paid	MTC	Median total compensation	TCC	Total cash compensation
LR	Low end range	MW	Median wage paid	TQ	Third quartile wage
M	Monthly	MWR	Median wage range	W	Weekly
MCC	Median cash compensation	S	See annotated source	Y	Yearly

Occupation/Type/Industry	Location	Per	Low	Mid	High	Source	Date
Loan Interviewer and Clerk	Boston-Cambridge-Quincy NECTA, MA	Y	27860 FQ	35290 MW	45470 TQ	USBLS	5/07
	Worcester MSA, MA-CT	Y	30280 FQ	35220 MW	41300 TQ	USBLS	5/07
	Michigan	Y	26420 FQ	32010 MW	37970 TQ	USBLS	5/07
	Detroit-Warren-Livonia MSA, MI	Y	28190 FQ	33480 MW	39450 TQ	USBLS	5/07
	Grand Rapids-Wyoming MSA, MI	Y	29170 FQ	34410 MW	38430 TQ	USBLS	5/07
	Warren-Troy-Farmington Hills PMSA, MI	Y	29240 FQ	34440 MW	40350 TQ	USBLS	5/07
	Minnesota	Y	29360 FQ	34887 MW	41621 TQ	MNBLS	10/08-12/08
	Duluth-Superior MSA, MN-WI	Y	27529 FQ	31473 MW	37583 TQ	MNBLS	10/08-12/08
	Minneapolis-Saint Paul MSA, MN-WI	Y	30349 FQ	36094 MW	43036 TQ	MNBLS	10/08-12/08
	Rochester MSA, MN	Y	27159 FQ	32003 MW	38413 TQ	MNBLS	10/08-12/08
	Mississippi	Y	22800 FQ	27890 MW	32680 TQ	USBLS	5/07
	Jackson MSA, MS	Y	24280 FQ	28660 MW	35000 TQ	USBLS	5/07
	Missouri	Y	23920 FQ	28840 MW	35260 TQ	USBLS	5/07
	Joplin MSA, MO	Y	22730 FQ	27090 MW	34740 TQ	USBLS	5/07
	Kansas City MSA, MO-KS	Y	25830 FQ	30330 MW	36820 TQ	USBLS	5/07
	St. Louis MSA, MO-IL	Y	25440 FQ	30230 MW	36810 TQ	USBLS	5/07
	Montana	Y	22470 FQ	26040 MW	30440 TQ	USBLS	5/07
	Billings MSA, MT	Y	22660 FQ	25350 MW	29530 TQ	USBLS	5/07
	Great Falls MSA, MT	Y	21330 FQ	24220 MW	27400 TQ	USBLS	5/07
	Nebraska	Y	24440 FQ	28420 MW	33250 TQ	USBLS	5/07
	Omaha-Council Bluffs MSA, NE-IA	Y	26830 FQ	30350 MW	36000 TQ	USBLS	5/07
	Nevada	H	13.22 FQ	16.52 MW	21.66 TQ	NVBLS	5/08
	Las Vegas-Paradise MSA, NV	H	13.02 FQ	16.11 MW	21.22 TQ	NVBLS	5/08
	New Hampshire	H	12.61 AE	15.37 MW	18.33 AEX	NHBLS	6/08
	Manchester MSA, NH	Y	28040 FQ	33740 MW	41770 TQ	USBLS	5/07
	Nashua NECTA, NH-MA	Y	26600 FQ	32380 MW	41960 TQ	USBLS	5/07
	New Jersey	Y	28530 FQ	35230 MW	42920 TQ	USBLS	5/07
	Camden PMSA, NJ	Y	28590 FQ	34940 MW	41450 TQ	USBLS	5/07
	Edison PMSA, NJ	Y	29270 FQ	36610 MW	44380 TQ	USBLS	5/07
	Newark-Union PMSA, NJ-PA	Y	31060 FQ	37540 MW	46540 TQ	USBLS	5/07
	New Mexico	Y	19750 FQ	24320 MW	30400 TQ	USBLS	5/07
	Albuquerque MSA, NM	Y	20110 FQ	24570 MW	32100 TQ	USBLS	5/07
	Las Cruces MSA, NM	Y	21220 FQ	25810 MW	29960 TQ	USBLS	5/07
	New York	Y	28290 FQ	35410 MW	43720 TQ	USBLS	5/07
	Albany-Schenectady-Troy MSA, NY	Y	26850 FQ	30860 MW	36270 TQ	USBLS	5/07
	Buffalo-Niagara Falls MSA, NY	Y	26910 FQ	31350 MW	39320 TQ	USBLS	5/07
	Nassau-Suffolk PMSA, NY	Y	29570 FQ	37310 MW	44660 TQ	USBLS	5/07
	New York-Northern New Jersey-Long Island MSA, NY-NJ-PA	Y	29840 FQ	37180 MW	45580 TQ	USBLS	5/07
	North Carolina	Y	26020 FQ	30020 MW	35360 TQ	USBLS	5/07
	Charlotte-Gastonia-Concord MSA, NC-SC	Y	27540 FQ	31180 MW	35710 TQ	USBLS	5/07
	Raleigh-Cary MSA, NC	Y	26490 FQ	31480 MW	38470 TQ	USBLS	5/07
	North Dakota	Y	23900 FQ	27860 MW	32490 TQ	USBLS	5/07
	Fargo MSA, ND-MN	Y	27330 FQ	30910 MW	35660 TQ	USBLS	5/07
	Ohio	Y	24020 FQ	29570 MW	36500 TQ	USBLS	5/07
	Cincinnati-Middletown MSA, OH-KY-IN	Y	22800 FQ	28500 MW	36280 TQ	USBLS	5/07
	Cleveland-Elyria-Mentor MSA, OH	Y	26560 FQ	31470 MW	38340 TQ	USBLS	5/07
	Columbus MSA, OH	Y	22560 FQ	30750 MW	37920 TQ	USBLS	5/07
	Oklahoma	Y	22480 FQ	27470 MW	34390 TQ	USBLS	5/07
	Oklahoma City MSA, OK	Y	23350 FQ	28330 MW	36630 TQ	USBLS	5/07
	Tulsa MSA, OK	Y	26480 FQ	31540 MW	40100 TQ	USBLS	5/07
	Oregon	H	13.21 FQ	16.09 MW	20.33 TQ	ORBLS	5/08
	Portland-Vancouver-Beaverton MSA, OR-WA	Y	28450 FQ	34720 MW	43190 TQ	USBLS	5/07
	Pennsylvania	Y	22550 FQ	27650 MW	33860 TQ	USBLS	5/07
	Allentown-Bethlehem-Easton MSA, PA-NJ	Y	20790 FQ	26060 MW	32740 TQ	USBLS	5/07
	Philadelphia-Camden-Wilmington MSA, PA-NJ-DE-MD	Y	24980 FQ	30410 MW	38010 TQ	USBLS	5/07

AE	Average entry wage	AW	Average wage paid	FQ	First quartile wage	LO	Lowest wage paid	MTC	Median total compensation
AER	Average entry range	AWR	Average wage range	H	Hourly	LR	Low end range	MW	Median wage paid
AEX	Average experienced wage	AXR	Average experienced range	HI	Highest wage paid	M	Monthly	MWR	Median wage range
ATC	Average total compensation	D	Daily	HR	High end range	MCC	Median cash compensation	S	See annotated source

TCC	Total cash compensation	
TQ	Third quartile wage	
W	Weekly	
Y	Yearly	

Occupation/Type/Industry	Location	Per	Low	Mid	High	Source	Date
Loan Interviewer and Clerk	Pittsburgh MSA, PA	Y	22940 FQ	27990 MW	34280 TQ	USBLS	5/07
	Rhode Island	Y	26280 FQ	31070 MW	37670 TQ	USBLS	5/07
	Providence-Fall River- Warwick MSA, RI-MA	Y	25650 FQ	30710 MW	37210 TQ	USBLS	5/07
	South Carolina	Y	25700 FQ	29470 MW	33510 TQ	USBLS	5/07
	Charleston-North Charleston MSA, SC	Y	24650 FQ	30590 MW	38630 TQ	USBLS	5/07
	Columbia MSA, SC	Y	25120 FQ	32470 MW	38660 TQ	USBLS	5/07
	South Dakota	Y	24039 FQ	27694 MW	31291 TQ	SDBLS	7/08-9/08
	Sioux Falls MSA, SD	Y	23948 FQ	27577 MW	30973 TQ	SDBLS	7/08-9/08
	Tennessee	Y	23280 FQ	28830 MW	35600 TQ	USBLS	5/07
	Memphis MSA, TN-MS-AR	Y	22770 FQ	28630 MW	35850 TQ	USBLS	5/07
	Nashville-Davidson- Murfreesboro MSA, TN	Y	26350 FQ	30730 MW	37130 TQ	USBLS	5/07
	Texas	Y	27960 FQ	33780 MW	40470 TQ	USBLS	5/07
	Austin-Round Rock MSA, TX	Y	27070 FQ	31150 MW	36830 TQ	USBLS	5/07
	Dallas-Fort Worth-Arlington MSA, TX	Y	30550 FQ	36050 MW	42580 TQ	USBLS	5/07
	El Paso MSA, TX	Y	24770 FQ	29230 MW	35390 TQ	USBLS	5/07
	Houston-Sugar Land-Baytown MSA, TX	Y	31750 FQ	37890 MW	44440 TQ	USBLS	5/07
	San Antonio MSA, TX	Y	27030 FQ	32210 MW	39250 TQ	USBLS	5/07
	Utah	Y	20570 FQ	23190 MW	29520 TQ	USBLS	5/07
	Salt Lake City MSA, UT	Y	20450 FQ	22860 MW	29380 TQ	USBLS	5/07
	Vermont	Y	26630 FQ	29820 MW	34900 TQ	USBLS	5/07
	Burlington-South Burlington MSA, VT	Y	26890 FQ	30660 MW	37800 TQ	USBLS	5/07
	Virginia	Y	29430 FQ	35600 MW	42430 TQ	USBLS	5/07
	Lynchburg MSA, VA	Y	27880 FQ	30590 MW	33870 TQ	USBLS	5/07
	Richmond MSA, VA	Y	28920 FQ	35010 MW	40520 TQ	USBLS	5/07
	Roanoke MSA, VA	Y	27450 FQ	33100 MW	38260 TQ	USBLS	5/07
	Virginia Beach-Norfolk- Newport News MSA, VA-NC	Y	28750 FQ	34500 MW	40510 TQ	USBLS	5/07
	Washington	H	14.42 FQ	17.71 MW	21.40 TQ	WABLS	3/08
	Seattle-Tacoma-Bellevue MSA, WA	Y	31000 FQ	37950 MW	45410 TQ	USBLS	5/07
	West Virginia	Y	21836 FQ	26027 MW	31439 TQ	WVBLS	7/08-9/08
	Charleston MSA, WV	Y	21950 FQ	25420 MW	29830 TQ	USBLS	5/07
	Wisconsin	Y	25170 FQ	30520 MW	37320 TQ	USBLS	5/07
	Milwaukee-Waukesha-West Allis MSA, WI	Y	28080 FQ	33960 MW	40520 TQ	USBLS	5/07
	Wyoming	Y	22088 FQ	25968 MW	29955 TQ	WYBLS	9/08
	Cheyenne MSA, WY	Y	17735 FQ	20898 MW	31031 TQ	WYBLS	9/08
	Puerto Rico	Y	14590 FQ	17390 MW	20810 TQ	USBLS	5/07
	San Juan-Caguas-Guaynabo MSA, PR	Y	14740 FQ	17490 MW	20920 TQ	USBLS	5/07
	Virgin Islands	Y	23190 FQ	27980 MW	34000 TQ	USBLS	5/07
	Guam	Y	19520 FQ	22630 MW	26110 TQ	USBLS	5/07
Loan Officer	Alabama	Y	39300 FQ	57300 MW	79870 TQ	USBLS	5/07
	Birmingham-Hoover MSA, AL	Y	43790 FQ	62400 MW	86580 TQ	USBLS	5/07
	Huntsville MSA, AL	Y	39540 FQ	58820 MW	79470 TQ	USBLS	5/07
	Montgomery MSA, AL	Y	37630 FQ	51020 MW	78540 TQ	USBLS	5/07
	Alaska	Y	51920 FQ	69030 MW	102900 TQ	USBLS	5/07
	Anchorage MSA, AK	Y	58120 FQ	86620 MW	106540 TQ	USBLS	5/07
	Arizona	Y	39250 FQ	53910 MW	75950 TQ	USBLS	5/07
	Phoenix-Mesa-Scottsdale MSA, AZ	Y	39940 FQ	56090 MW	78940 TQ	USBLS	5/07
	Tucson MSA, AZ	Y	38020 FQ	43500 MW	53870 TQ	USBLS	5/07
	Arkansas	Y	40850 FQ	54080 MW	71010 TQ	USBLS	5/07
	Little Rock-North Little Rock MSA, AR	Y	43320 FQ	54300 MW	76220 TQ	USBLS	5/07
	Pine Bluff MSA, AR	Y	42550 FQ	61040 MW	81980 TQ	USBLS	5/07
	California	H	22.73 FQ	31.19 MW	44.22 TQ	CABLS	1/08-3/08
	Los Angeles-Long Beach- Glendale PMSA, CA	H	23.37 FQ	31.14 MW	44.24 TQ	CABLS	1/08-3/08
	Oakland-Fremont-Hayward MSA, CA	H	23.26 FQ	31.64 MW	43.16 TQ	CABLS	1/08-3/08
	Riverside-San Bernardino- Ontario MSA, CA	H	22.31 FQ	31.32 MW	40.11 TQ	CABLS	1/08-3/08
	Sacramento-Arden Arcade- Roseville MSA, CA	H	23.45 FQ	32.49 MW	47.26 TQ	CABLS	1/08-3/08

AE Average entry wage	**AW** Average wage paid	**FQ** First quartile wage	**LO** Lowest wage paid	**MTC** Median total compensation	**TCC** Total cash compensation
AER Average entry range	**AWR** Average wage range	**H** Hourly	**LR** Low end range	**MW** Median wage paid	**TQ** Third quartile wage
AEX Average experienced wage	**AXR** Average experienced range	**HI** Highest wage paid	**M** Monthly	**MWR** Median wage range	**W** Weekly
ATC Average total compensation	**D** Daily	**HR** High end range	**MCC** Median cash compensation	**S** See annotated source	**Y** Yearly

Occupation/Type/Industry	Location	Per	Low	Mid	High	Source	Date
Loan Officer	San Diego-Carlsbad-San Marcos MSA, CA	H	22.70 FQ	30.05 MW	40.72 TQ	CABLS	1/08-3/08
	San Francisco-San Mateo-Redwood PMSA, CA	H	25.98 FQ	39.48 MW	57.70 TQ	CABLS	1/08-3/08
	San Jose-Sunnyvale-Santa Clara MSA, CA	H	21.01 FQ	29.93 MW	50.82 TQ	CABLS	1/08-3/08
	Santa Ana-Anaheim-Irvine PMSA, CA	Y	47010 FQ	63640 MW	89880 TQ	USBLS	5/07
	Colorado	Y	39360 FQ	51880 MW	75400 TQ	USBLS	5/07
	Denver-Aurora MSA, CO	Y	39570 FQ .	51750 MW	76160 TQ	USBLS	5/07
	Connecticut	H	19.73 AE	31.70 MW		CTBLS	1/08-3/08
	Bridgeport-Stamford-Norwalk MSA, CT	Y	56810 FQ	71620 MW	97190 TQ	USBLS	5/07
	Hartford-West Hartford-East Hartford MSA, CT	Y	42240 FQ	54150 MW	77000 TQ	USBLS	5/07
	New Haven MSA, CT	Y	48120 FQ	61500 MW	80940 TQ	USBLS	5/07
	Delaware	Y	38080 FQ	48460 MW	74120 TQ	USBLS	5/07
	Wilmington PMSA, DE-MD-NJ	Y	37660 FQ	46860 MW	70060 TQ	USBLS	5/07
	District of Columbia	Y	41490 FQ	54190 MW	64590 TQ	USBLS	5/07
	Washington-Arlington-Alexandria MSA, DC-VA-MD-WV	Y	39390 FQ	51680 MW	68440 TQ	USBLS	5/07
	Florida	Y	36830 FQ	48840 MW	67290 TQ	USBLS	5/07
	Cape Coral-Fort Myers MSA, FL	Y	37940 FQ	46790 MW	60760 TQ	USBLS	5/07
	Fort Lauderdale-Pompano Beach-Deerfield Beach PMSA, FL	Y	33990 FQ	44170 MW	61710 TQ	USBLS	5/07
	Jacksonville MSA, FL	Y	37190 FQ	49160 MW	69900 TQ	USBLS	5/07
	Lakeland MSA, FL	Y	39420 FQ	57350 MW	69870 TQ	USBLS	5/07
	Miami-Fort Lauderdale-Miami Beach MSA, FL	Y	40070 FQ	51800 MW	71330 TQ	USBLS	5/07
	Orlando-Kissimmee MSA, FL	Y	30790 FQ	41500 MW	61910 TQ	USBLS	5/07
	Sarasota-Bradenton-Venice MSA, FL	Y	37400 FQ	50230 MW	64510 TQ	USBLS	5/07
	Tampa-St. Petersburg-Clearwater MSA, FL	Y	36480 FQ	49470 MW	69680 TQ	USBLS	5/07
	West Palm Beach-Boca Raton-Boynton Beach PMSA, FL	Y	44510 FQ	57310 MW	83340 TQ	USBLS	5/07
	Georgia	Y	40780 FQ	54610 MW	80170 TQ	USBLS	5/07
	Atlanta-Sandy Springs-Marietta MSA, GA	Y	40080 FQ	54460 MW	82970 TQ	USBLS	5/07
	Hawaii	Y	37640 FQ	55690 MW	88710 TQ	USBLS	5/07
	Honolulu MSA, HI	Y	37930 FQ	56130 MW	84890 TQ	USBLS	5/07
	Idaho	Y	32490 FQ	45900 MW	62820 TQ	USBLS	5/07
	Boise City-Nampa MSA, ID	Y	38780 FQ	50080 MW	65500 TQ	USBLS	5/07
	Illinois	Y	39780 FQ	56330 MW	78270 TQ	USBLS	5/07
	Chicago-Naperville-Joliet MSA, IL-IN-WI	Y	41870 FQ	57540 MW	80530 TQ	USBLS	5/07
	Indiana	Y	34840 FQ	47160 MW	73210 TQ	USBLS	5/07
	Elkhart-Goshen MSA, IN	Y	36940 FQ	48030 MW	66500 TQ	USBLS	5/07
	Evansville MSA, IN-KY	Y	34330 FQ	44940 MW	60440 TQ	USBLS	5/07
	Gary PMSA, IN	Y	33010 FQ	45000 MW	64710 TQ	USBLS	5/07
	Indianapolis-Carmel MSA, IN	Y	35320 FQ	55410 MW	91270 TQ	USBLS	5/07
	Iowa	Y	37690 FQ	47970 MW	63590 TQ	USBLS	5/07
	Davenport-Moline-Rock Island MSA, IA-IL	Y	34340 FQ	48450 MW	69840 TQ	USBLS	5/07
	Des Moines-West Des Moines MSA, IA	Y	37350 FQ	47490 MW	63840 TQ	USBLS	5/07
	Kansas	Y	34680 FQ	45830 MW	65620 TQ	USBLS	5/07
	Wichita MSA, KS	Y	32580 FQ	43980 MW	68740 TQ	USBLS	5/07
	Kentucky	Y	33241 FQ	45678 MW	62115 TQ	KYBLS	2008
	Louisville-Jefferson County MSA, KY-IN	Y	30380 FQ	43110 MW	58750 TQ	USBLS	5/07
	Louisiana	H	14.61 FQ	18.38 MW	26.01 TQ	LABLS	1/08-3/08
	Baton Rouge MSA, LA	Y	27970 FQ	34500 MW	45670 TQ	USBLS	5/07
	Lake Charles MSA, LA	Y	27520 FQ	32240 MW	44930 TQ	USBLS	5/07
	New Orleans-Metairie-Kenner MSA, LA	Y	33410 FQ	43870 MW	62010 TQ	USBLS	5/07
	Shreveport-Bossier City MSA, LA	Y	32220 FQ	38490 MW	52430 TQ	USBLS	5/07

AE	Average entry wage	AW	Average wage paid	FQ	First quartile wage	LO	Lowest wage paid	MTC	Median total compensation	TCC	Total cash compensation
AER	Average entry range	AWR	Average wage range	H	Hourly	LR	Low end range	MW	Median wage paid	TQ	Third quartile wage
AEX	Average experienced wage	AXR	Average experienced range	HI	Highest wage paid	M	Monthly	MWR	Median wage range	W	Weekly
ATC	Average total compensation	D	Daily	HR	High end range	MCC	Median cash compensation	S	See annotated source	Y	Yearly

Occupation/Type/Industry	Location	Per	Low	Mid	High	Source	Date
Loan Officer	Maine	Y	37480 FQ	49380 MW	65110 TQ	USBLS	5/07
	Lewiston-Auburn MSA, ME	Y	35790 FQ	46570 MW	56690 TQ	USBLS	5/07
	Portland-South Portland-Biddeford MSA, ME	Y	38190 FQ	49380 MW	69450 TQ	USBLS	5/07
	Maryland	Y		55175 MW		MDBLS	3/08
	Baltimore-Towson MSA, MD	Y	43480 FQ	56200 MW	82360 TQ	USBLS	5/07
	Bethesda-Gaithersburg-Frederick PMSA, MD	Y	43240 FQ	56690 MW	84790 TQ	USBLS	5/07
	Massachusetts	Y	49700 FQ	72760 MW	99830 TQ	USBLS	5/07
	Boston-Cambridge-Quincy NECTA, MA	Y	52110 FQ	77350 MW	104160 TQ	USBLS	5/07
	Worcester MSA, MA-CT	Y	45680 FQ	63920 MW	90710 TQ	USBLS	5/07
	Michigan	Y	38410 FQ	51180 MW	64470 TQ	USBLS	5/07
	Detroit-Warren-Livonia MSA, MI	Y	40790 FQ	53310 MW	63600 TQ	USBLS	5/07
	Grand Rapids-Wyoming MSA, MI	Y	36520 FQ	48630 MW	74950 TQ	USBLS	5/07
	Warren-Troy-Farmington Hills PMSA, MI	Y	40380 FQ	47610 MW	61940 TQ	USBLS	5/07
	Minnesota	Y	43812 FQ	59347 MW	85163 TQ	MNBLS	10/08-12/08
	Duluth-Superior MSA, MN-WI	Y	30737 FQ	44802 MW	74091 TQ	MNBLS	10/08-12/08
	Minneapolis-Saint Paul MSA, MN-WI	Y	45355 FQ	64196 MW	92754 TQ	MNBLS	10/08-12/08
	Rochester MSA, MN	Y	42326 FQ	49436 MW	60935 TQ	MNBLS	10/08-12/08
	Mississippi	Y	36870 FQ	49240 MW	69950 TQ	USBLS	5/07
	Jackson MSA, MS	Y	45690 FQ	66010 MW	77010 TQ	USBLS	5/07
	Missouri	Y	37490 FQ	51000 MW	72610 TQ	USBLS	5/07
	Kansas City MSA, MO-KS	Y	35880 FQ	48240 MW	72470 TQ	USBLS	5/07
	St. Louis MSA, MO-IL	Y	36680 FQ	50870 MW	73250 TQ	USBLS	5/07
	Springfield MSA, MO	Y	45240 FQ	59990 MW	80730 TQ	USBLS	5/07
	Montana	Y	33460 FQ	47390 MW	65410 TQ	USBLS	5/07
	Billings MSA, MT	Y	35480 FQ	47060 MW	70280 TQ	USBLS	5/07
	Great Falls MSA, MT	Y	27020 FQ	31900 MW	49020 TQ	USBLS	5/07
	Nebraska	Y	39500 FQ	53010 MW	68370 TQ	USBLS	5/07
	Lincoln MSA, NE	Y	36160 FQ	53510 MW	76930 TQ	USBLS	5/07
	Omaha-Council Bluffs MSA, NE-IA	Y	37660 FQ	47100 MW	66140 TQ	USBLS	5/07
	Nevada	H	17.33 FQ	24.46 MW	32.51 TQ	NVBLS	5/08
	Las Vegas-Paradise MSA, NV	H	17.37 FQ	23.83 MW	31.88 TQ	NVBLS	5/08
	New Hampshire	H	17.24 AE	25.28 MW	42.36 AEX	NHBLS	6/08
	Manchester MSA, NH	Y	40930 FQ	50360 MW	70200 TQ	USBLS	5/07
	Nashua NECTA, NH-MA	Y	34380 FQ	52820 MW	136040 TQ	USBLS	5/07
	New Jersey	Y	41150 FQ	56570 MW	75110 TQ	USBLS	5/07
	Camden PMSA, NJ	Y	43370 FQ	58540 MW	78630 TQ	USBLS	5/07
	Edison PMSA, NJ	Y	41180 FQ	59630 MW	79000 TQ	USBLS	5/07
	Newark-Union PMSA, NJ-PA	Y	37570 FQ	54100 MW	73350 TQ	USBLS	5/07
	Ocean City MSA, NJ	Y	44730 FQ	60830 MW	92340 TQ	USBLS	5/07
	New Mexico	Y	36100 FQ	47980 MW	68990 TQ	USBLS	5/07
	Albuquerque MSA, NM	Y	37440 FQ	48930 MW	85440 TQ	USBLS	5/07
	New York	Y	43480 FQ	62420 MW	88330 TQ	USBLS	5/07
	Albany-Schenectady-Troy MSA, NY	Y	48390 FQ	72310 MW	96780 TQ	USBLS	5/07
	Buffalo-Niagara Falls MSA, NY	Y	39250 FQ	45880 MW	55540 TQ	USBLS	5/07
	Nassau-Suffolk PMSA, NY	Y	42050 FQ	63990 MW	81440 TQ	USBLS	5/07
	New York-Northern New Jersey-Long Island MSA, NY-NJ-PA	Y	43900 FQ	61320 MW	84430 TQ	USBLS	5/07
	North Carolina	Y	36820 FQ	45850 MW	59280 TQ	USBLS	5/07
	Charlotte-Gastonia-Concord MSA, NC-SC	Y	38680 FQ	49860 MW	66380 TQ	USBLS	5/07
	Raleigh-Cary MSA, NC	Y	40480 FQ	48930 MW	59430 TQ	USBLS	5/07
	North Dakota	Y	39960 FQ	52960 MW	68080 TQ	USBLS	5/07
	Fargo MSA, ND-MN	Y	36050 FQ	51220 MW	70230 TQ	USBLS	5/07
	Ohio	Y	34440 FQ	45520 MW	63250 TQ	USBLS	5/07
	Canton-Massillon MSA, OH	Y	30290 FQ	39830 MW	63480 TQ	USBLS	5/07
	Cincinnati-Middletown MSA, OH-KY-IN	Y	36490 FQ	45920 MW	63490 TQ	USBLS	5/07
	Cleveland-Elyria-Mentor MSA, OH	Y	35650 FQ	44720 MW	59990 TQ	USBLS	5/07
	Columbus MSA, OH	Y	33350 FQ	45720 MW	64280 TQ	USBLS	5/07
	Dayton MSA, OH	Y	36000 FQ	45820 MW	59700 TQ	USBLS	5/07

AE Average entry wage	**AW** Average wage paid	**FQ** First quartile wage	**LO** Lowest wage paid	**MTC** Median total compensation	**TCC** Total cash compensation
AER Average entry range	**AWR** Average wage range	**H** Hourly	**LR** Low end range	**MW** Median wage paid	**TQ** Third quartile wage
AEX Average experienced wage	**AXR** Average experienced range	**HI** Highest wage paid	**M** Monthly	**MWR** Median wage range	**W** Weekly
ATC Average total compensation	**D** Daily	**HR** High end range	**MCC** Median cash compensation	**S** See annotated source	**Y** Yearly

Occupation/Type/Industry	Location	Per	Low	Mid	High	Source	Date
Loan Officer	Oklahoma	Y	31200 FQ	43890 MW	65340 TQ	USBLS	5/07
	Oklahoma City MSA, OK	Y	29970 FQ	47070 MW	75530 TQ	USBLS	5/07
	Tulsa MSA, OK	Y	33000 FQ	40710 MW	57620 TQ	USBLS	5/07
	Oregon	H	18.44 FQ	25.83 MW	38.76 TQ	ORBLS	5/08
	Portland-Vancouver-Beaverton MSA, OR-WA	Y	38170 FQ	53300 MW	80820 TQ	USBLS	5/07
	Pennsylvania	Y	36490 FQ	45050 MW	58000 TQ	USBLS	5/07
	Allentown-Bethlehem-Easton MSA, PA-NJ	Y	35100 FQ	44520 MW	58170 TQ	USBLS	5/07
	Philadelphia-Camden-Wilmington MSA, PA-NJ-DE-MD	Y	37470 FQ	47550 MW	68150 TQ	USBLS	5/07
	Pittsburgh MSA, PA	Y	38330 FQ	47280 MW	58400 TQ	USBLS	5/07
	Rhode Island	Y	52830 FQ	65800 MW	91150 TQ	USBLS	5/07
	Providence-Fall River-Warwick MSA, RI-MA	Y	52460 FQ	66130 MW	90850 TQ	USBLS	5/07
	South Carolina	Y	35480 FQ	48710 MW	66330 TQ	USBLS	5/07
	Charleston-North Charleston MSA, SC	Y	36280 FQ	47790 MW	62020 TQ	USBLS	5/07
	Columbia MSA, SC	Y	40690 FQ	55820 MW	79640 TQ	USBLS	5/07
	South Dakota	Y	39117 FQ	47959 MW	61000 TQ	SDBLS	7/08-9/08
	Sioux Falls MSA, SD	Y	35935 FQ	42736 MW	58972 TQ	SDBLS	7/08-9/08
	Tennessee	Y	31510 FQ	43130 MW	64660 TQ	USBLS	5/07
	Memphis MSA, TN-MS-AR	Y	30370 FQ	43840 MW	72280 TQ	USBLS	5/07
	Nashville-Davidson-Murfreesboro MSA, TN	Y	34470 FQ	45140 MW	64040 TQ	USBLS	5/07
	Texas	Y	42280 FQ	57340 MW	79590 TQ	USBLS	5/07
	Austin-Round Rock MSA, TX	Y	49250 FQ	61330 MW	75060 TQ	USBLS	5/07
	Beaumont-Port Arthur MSA, TX	Y	36060 FQ	50490 MW	61640 TQ	USBLS	5/07
	Dallas-Fort Worth-Arlington MSA, TX	Y	46400 FQ	61360 MW	87480 TQ	USBLS	5/07
	El Paso MSA, TX	Y	33930 FQ	46460 MW	59820 TQ	USBLS	5/07
	Houston-Sugar Land-Baytown MSA, TX	Y	42750 FQ	57410 MW	81370 TQ	USBLS	5/07
	San Antonio MSA, TX	Y	40710 FQ	55500 MW	86610 TQ	USBLS	5/07
	Utah	Y	37080 FQ	45990 MW	66820 TQ	USBLS	5/07
	Logan MSA, UT-ID	Y	33970 FQ	49880 MW	59130 TQ	USBLS	5/07
	St. George MSA, UT	Y	36310 FQ	49690 MW	63130 TQ	USBLS	5/07
	Salt Lake City MSA, UT	Y	38170 FQ	46270 MW	65610 TQ	USBLS	5/07
	Vermont	Y	34540 FQ	48040 MW	69360 TQ	USBLS	5/07
	Burlington-South Burlington MSA, VT	Y	36450 FQ	45460 MW	65240 TQ	USBLS	5/07
	Virginia	Y	38180 FQ	50690 MW	68160 TQ	USBLS	5/07
	Lynchburg MSA, VA	Y	29420 FQ	38270 MW	47400 TQ	USBLS	5/07
	Richmond MSA, VA	Y	39400 FQ	58300 MW	89760 TQ	USBLS	5/07
	Virginia Beach-Norfolk-Newport News MSA, VA-NC	Y	36120 FQ	51480 MW	67390 TQ	USBLS	5/07
	Washington	H	19.75 FQ	28.16 MW	40.24 TQ	WABLS	3/08
	Seattle-Tacoma-Bellevue MSA, WA	Y	41500 FQ	60670 MW	90000 TQ	USBLS	5/07
	West Virginia	Y	36298 FQ	48604 MW	64411 TQ	WVBLS	7/08-9/08
	Charleston MSA, WV	Y	33390 FQ	41720 MW	58500 TQ	USBLS	5/07
	Wheeling MSA, WV-OH	Y	34160 FQ	41040 MW	67270 TQ	USBLS	5/07
	Wisconsin	Y	39560 FQ	51650 MW	73670 TQ	USBLS	5/07
	Milwaukee-Waukesha-West Allis MSA, WI	Y	40720 FQ	54950 MW	87070 TQ	USBLS	5/07
	Wyoming	Y	32802 FQ	47040 MW	66009 TQ	WYBLS	9/08
	Cheyenne MSA, WY	Y	27317 FQ	31927 MW	51466 TQ	WYBLS	9/08
	Puerto Rico	Y	23620 FQ	28140 MW	33450 TQ	USBLS	5/07
	San Juan-Caguas-Guaynabo MSA, PR	Y	23690 FQ	27920 MW	32330 TQ	USBLS	5/07
	Virgin Islands	Y	32690 FQ	39980 MW	58350 TQ	USBLS	5/07
	Guam	Y	32370 FQ	40600 MW	56850 TQ	USBLS	5/07
Lobbyist	United States	Y		93100 MW		CNNM04	2007
Auburn University	Auburn, AL	Y			180000 HI	AMIW01	2008
Local Area Network Engineer							
Public Schools	North Carolina	M	3556 LO		6343 HI	NCSS	2008-2009

AE Average entry wage	**AW** Average wage paid	**FQ** First quartile wage	**LO** Lowest wage paid	**MTC** Median total compensation	**TCC** Total cash compensation
AER Average entry range	**AWR** Average wage range	**H** Hourly	**LR** Low end range	**MW** Median wage paid	**TQ** Third quartile wage
AEX Average experienced wage	**AXR** Average experienced range	**HI** Highest wage paid	**M** Monthly	**MWR** Median wage range	**W** Weekly
ATC Average total compensation	**D** Daily	**HR** High end range	**MCC** Median cash compensation	**S** See annotated source	**Y** Yearly

Occupation/Type/Industry	Location	Per	Low	Mid	High	Source	Date
Locker Room, Coatroom, and Dressing Room Attendant	Alabama	Y	14190 FQ	17000 MW	19970 TQ	USBLS	5/07
	Birmingham-Hoover MSA, AL	Y	14300 FQ	17070 MW	19860 TQ	USBLS	5/07
	Arizona	Y	16010 FQ	19630 MW	25360 TQ	USBLS	5/07
	Phoenix-Mesa-Scottsdale MSA, AZ	Y	16010 FQ	19810 MW	26430 TQ	USBLS	5/07
	Tucson MSA, AZ	Y	15860 FQ	18570 MW	22280 TQ	USBLS	5/07
	Arkansas	Y	14540 FQ	16080 MW	22400 TQ	USBLS	5/07
	California	H	8.84 FQ	10.47 MW	12.94 TQ	CABLS	1/08-3/08
	Los Angeles-Long Beach-Glendale PMSA, CA	H	8.66 FQ	10.31 MW	13.28 TQ	CABLS	1/08-3/08
	Oakland-Fremont-Hayward MSA, CA	H	8.00 FQ	9.14 MW	11.73 TQ	CABLS	1/08-3/08
	Riverside-San Bernardino-Ontario MSA, CA	H	8.74 FQ	9.91 MW	12.31 TQ	CABLS	1/08-3/08
	Sacramento-Arden Arcade-Roseville MSA, CA	H	8.81 FQ	10.43 MW	11.76 TQ	CABLS	1/08-3/08
	San Diego-Carlsbad-San Marcos MSA, CA	H	8.74 FQ	10.39 MW	13.99 TQ	CABLS	1/08-3/08
	San Francisco-San Mateo-Redwood PMSA, CA	H	9.86 FQ	12.56 MW	16.17 TQ	CABLS	1/08-3/08
	San Jose-Sunnyvale-Santa Clara MSA, CA	H	9.30 FQ	15.26 MW	17.87 TQ	CABLS	1/08-3/08
	Santa Ana-Anaheim-Irvine PMSA, CA	Y	19810 FQ	22010 MW	24740 TQ	USBLS	5/07
	Colorado	Y	16580 FQ	18500 MW	22650 TQ	USBLS	5/07
	Denver-Aurora MSA, CO	Y	16580 FQ	18250 MW	21620 TQ	USBLS	5/07
	Connecticut	H	8.45 AE	10.05 MW		CTBLS	1/08-3/08
	Bridgeport-Stamford-Norwalk MSA, CT	Y	21330 FQ	25830 MW	33310 TQ	USBLS	5/07
	Hartford-West Hartford-East Hartford MSA, CT	Y	16790 FQ	19440 MW	21800 TQ	USBLS	5/07
	District of Columbia	Y	16810 FQ	20200 MW	29200 TQ	USBLS	5/07
	Washington-Arlington-Alexandria MSA, DC-VA-MD-WV	Y	16330 FQ	19170 MW	24330 TQ	USBLS	5/07
	Florida	Y	16590 FQ	19610 MW	23850 TQ	USBLS	5/07
	Fort Lauderdale-Pompano Beach-Deerfield Beach PMSA, FL	Y	15740 FQ	18070 MW	25960 TQ	USBLS	5/07
	Jacksonville MSA, FL	Y	17270 FQ	20930 MW	24000 TQ	USBLS	5/07
	Miami-Fort Lauderdale-Miami Beach MSA, FL	Y	16430 FQ	19380 MW	23820 TQ	USBLS	5/07
	Orlando-Kissimmee MSA, FL	Y	15530 FQ	17340 MW	19750 TQ	USBLS	5/07
	Tampa-St. Petersburg-Clearwater MSA, FL	Y	15680 FQ	18600 MW	21840 TQ	USBLS	5/07
	West Palm Beach-Boca Raton-Boynton Beach PMSA, FL	Y	16320 FQ	21350 MW	25540 TQ	USBLS	5/07
	Georgia	Y	17900 FQ	20270 MW	23830 TQ	USBLS	5/07
	Atlanta-Sandy Springs-Marietta MSA, GA	Y	18010 FQ	20260 MW	23900 TQ	USBLS	5/07
	Hawaii	Y	18430 FQ	22740 MW	28020 TQ	USBLS	5/07
	Honolulu MSA, HI	Y	16580 FQ	20620 MW	23740 TQ	USBLS	5/07
	Illinois	Y	16400 FQ	20450 MW	23790 TQ	USBLS	5/07
	Chicago-Naperville-Joliet MSA, IL-IN-WI	Y	16250 FQ	20460 MW	23780 TQ	USBLS	5/07
	Indiana	Y	13620 FQ	16480 MW	19620 TQ	USBLS	5/07
	Indianapolis-Carmel MSA, IN	Y	14890 FQ	17480 MW	20470 TQ	USBLS	5/07
	Iowa	Y	13830 FQ	14760 MW	17100 TQ	USBLS	5/07
	Kansas	Y	13500 FQ	15900 MW	18520 TQ	USBLS	5/07
	Kentucky	Y	16427 FQ	18422 MW	21037 TQ	KYBLS	2008
	Louisiana	H	7.26 FQ	8.73 MW	10.74 TQ	LABLS	1/08-3/08
	New Orleans-Metairie-Kenner MSA, LA	Y	15750 FQ	18550 MW	22170 TQ	USBLS	5/07
	Maryland	Y		18275 MW		MDBLS	3/08
	Baltimore-Towson MSA, MD	Y	14120 FQ	15140 MW	18230 TQ	USBLS	5/07
	Bethesda-Gaithersburg-Frederick PMSA, MD	Y	17110 FQ	18740 MW	20610 TQ	USBLS	5/07
	Massachusetts	Y	17180 FQ	19130 MW	23170 TQ	USBLS	5/07
	Boston-Cambridge-Quincy NECTA, MA	Y	17950 FQ	21060 MW	24330 TQ	USBLS	5/07
	Worcester MSA, MA-CT	Y	16500 FQ	17390 MW	18280 TQ	USBLS	5/07

AE	Average entry wage	**AW**	Average wage paid	**FQ**	First quartile wage
AER	Average entry range	**AWR**	Average wage range	**H**	Hourly
AEX	Average experienced wage	**AXR**	Average experienced range	**HI**	Highest wage paid
ATC	Average total compensation	**D**	Daily	**HR**	High end range

LO	Lowest wage paid	**MTC**	Median total compensation	**TCC**	Total cash compensation
LR	Low end range	**MW**	Median wage paid	**TQ**	Third quartile wage
M	Monthly	**MWR**	Median wage range	**W**	Weekly
MCC	Median cash compensation	**S**	See annotated source	**Y**	Yearly

Occupation/Type/Industry	Location	Per	Low	Mid	High	Source	Date
Locker Room, Coatroom, and Dressing Room Attendant	Michigan	Y	15050 FQ	16870 MW	19210 TQ	USBLS	5/07
	Detroit-Warren-Livonia MSA, MI	Y	14900 FQ	16080 MW	19180 TQ	USBLS	5/07
	Grand Rapids-Wyoming MSA, MI	Y	17080 FQ	18680 MW	21140 TQ	USBLS	5/07
	Lansing-East Lansing MSA, MI	Y	15710 FQ	16940 MW	18630 TQ	USBLS	5/07
	Warren-Troy-Farmington Hills PMSA, MI	Y	15060 FQ	17370 MW	22750 TQ	USBLS	5/07
	Minnesota	Y	16896 FQ	19573 MW	23452 TQ	MNBLS	10/08-12/08
	Minneapolis-Saint Paul MSA, MN-WI	Y	16875 FQ	19667 MW	23881 TQ	MNBLS	10/08-12/08
	Rochester MSA, MN	Y	18031 FQ	19587 MW	21286 TQ	MNBLS	10/08-12/08
	Mississippi	Y	12620 FQ	14280 MW	15900 TQ	USBLS	5/07
	Missouri	Y	14760 FQ	16930 MW	21390 TQ	USBLS	5/07
	Kansas City MSA, MO-KS	Y	13860 FQ	16270 MW	18820 TQ	USBLS	5/07
	St. Louis MSA, MO-IL	Y	16430 FQ	20480 MW	24920 TQ	USBLS	5/07
	Montana	Y	14140 FQ	15480 MW	19920 TQ	USBLS	5/07
	Nebraska	Y	14760 FQ	17970 MW	22090 TQ	USBLS	5/07
	Omaha-Council Bluffs MSA, NE-IA	Y	14270 FQ	16200 MW	18670 TQ	USBLS	5/07
	Las Vegas-Paradise MSA, NV	H	6.84 FQ	10.00 MW	12.86 TQ	NVBLS	5/08
	New Jersey	Y	17110 FQ	20130 MW	24050 TQ	USBLS	5/07
	Camden PMSA, NJ	Y	15770 FQ	17770 MW	21980 TQ	USBLS	5/07
	Edison PMSA, NJ	Y	17320 FQ	20230 MW	23560 TQ	USBLS	5/07
	Newark-Union PMSA, NJ-PA	Y	17410 FQ	19380 MW	22560 TQ	USBLS	5/07
	New York	Y	17220 FQ	21420 MW	27230 TQ	USBLS	5/07
	Albany-Schenectady-Troy MSA, NY	Y	17910 FQ	25340 MW	28460 TQ	USBLS	5/07
	Buffalo-Niagara Falls MSA, NY	Y	15930 FQ	18190 MW	21190 TQ	USBLS	5/07
	Nassau-Suffolk PMSA, NY	Y	17750 FQ	22000 MW	27950 TQ	USBLS	5/07
	New York-Northern New Jersey-Long Island MSA, NY-NJ-PA	Y	16770 FQ	20730 MW	27550 TQ	USBLS	5/07
	North Carolina	Y	18300 FQ	21770 MW	25910 TQ	USBLS	5/07
	Ohio	Y	15560 FQ	17590 MW	20170 TQ	USBLS	5/07
	Cincinnati-Middletown MSA, OH-KY-IN	Y	16520 FQ	19040 MW	23100 TQ	USBLS	5/07
	Cleveland-Elyria-Mentor MSA, OH	Y	15820 FQ	18430 MW	23000 TQ	USBLS	5/07
	Columbus MSA, OH	Y	15710 FQ	17360 MW	19130 TQ	USBLS	5/07
	Dayton MSA, OH	Y	16330 FQ	17900 MW	19710 TQ	USBLS	5/07
	Oklahoma	Y	13490 FQ	16160 MW	19270 TQ	USBLS	5/07
	Oregon	H	8.64 FQ	9.23 MW	10.74 TQ	ORBLS	5/08
	Portland-Vancouver-Beaverton MSA, OR-WA	Y	17540 FQ	18840 MW	23150 TQ	USBLS	5/07
	Pennsylvania	Y	16010 FQ	19600 MW	24000 TQ	USBLS	5/07
	Allentown-Bethlehem-Easton MSA, PA-NJ	Y	15650 FQ	19090 MW	24000 TQ	USBLS	5/07
	Philadelphia-Camden-Wilmington MSA, PA-NJ-DE-MD	Y	16680 FQ	21190 MW	25230 TQ	USBLS	5/07
	Pittsburgh MSA, PA	Y	15360 FQ	18430 MW	22820 TQ	USBLS	5/07
	Rhode Island	Y	17130 FQ	18910 MW	22280 TQ	USBLS	5/07
	Providence-Fall River-Warwick MSA, RI-MA	Y	17320 FQ	19310 MW	22680 TQ	USBLS	5/07
	South Carolina	Y	14480 FQ	17570 MW	22670 TQ	USBLS	5/07
	South Dakota	Y	16327 FQ	19428 MW	23586 TQ	SDBLS	7/08-9/08
	Sioux Falls MSA, SD	Y	20245 FQ	23375 MW	25374 TQ	SDBLS	7/08-9/08
	Tennessee	Y	15670 FQ	18380 MW	23070 TQ	USBLS	5/07
	Memphis MSA, TN-MS-AR	Y	16140 FQ	19300 MW	25350 TQ	USBLS	5/07
	Texas	Y	15100 FQ	17980 MW	21100 TQ	USBLS	5/07
	Austin-Round Rock MSA, TX	Y	17360 FQ	20050 MW	24290 TQ	USBLS	5/07
	Dallas-Fort Worth-Arlington MSA, TX	Y	14230 FQ	17300 MW	21390 TQ	USBLS	5/07
	Houston-Sugar Land-Baytown MSA, TX	Y	16490 FQ	18530 MW	20900 TQ	USBLS	5/07
	San Antonio MSA, TX	Y	14360 FQ	17940 MW	21330 TQ	USBLS	5/07
	Utah	Y	14860 FQ	17360 MW	19200 TQ	USBLS	5/07
	Salt Lake City MSA, UT	Y	14090 FQ	16870 MW	18720 TQ	USBLS	5/07
	Virginia	Y	14600 FQ	19020 MW	24460 TQ	USBLS	5/07

AE Average entry wage	**AW** Average wage paid	**FQ** First quartile wage	**LO** Lowest wage paid	**MTC** Median total compensation	**TCC** Total cash compensation
AER Average entry range	**AWR** Average wage range	**H** Hourly	**LR** Low end range	**MW** Median wage paid	**TQ** Third quartile wage
AEX Average experienced wage	**AXR** Average experienced range	**HI** Highest wage paid	**M** Monthly	**MWR** Median wage range	**W** Weekly
ATC Average total compensation	**D** Daily	**HR** High end range	**MCC** Median cash compensation	**S** See annotated source	**Y** Yearly

Occupation/Type/Industry	Location	Per	Low	Mid	High	Source	Date
Locker Room, Coatroom, and Dressing Room Attendant	Richmond MSA, VA	Y	13780 FQ	16520 MW	19870 TQ	USBLS	5/07
	Virginia Beach-Norfolk-Newport News MSA, VA-NC	Y	13180 FQ	15510 MW	21640 TQ	USBLS	5/07
	Washington	H	8.96 FQ	10.26 MW	12.33 TQ	WABLS	3/08
	Seattle-Tacoma-Bellevue MSA, WA	Y	18580 FQ	21490 MW	25810 TQ	USBLS	5/07
	West Virginia	Y	15463 FQ	18507 MW	23818 TQ	WVBLS	7/08-9/08
	Wisconsin	Y	16120 FQ	19260 MW	23220 TQ	USBLS	5/07
	Milwaukee-Waukesha-West Allis MSA, WI	Y	16540 FQ	19230 MW	23640 TQ	USBLS	5/07
	Puerto Rico	Y	13160 FQ	15250 MW	19630 TQ	USBLS	5/07
	San Juan-Caguas-Guaynabo MSA, PR	Y	14120 FQ	17350 MW	21380 TQ	USBLS	5/07
Locksmith							
Public Schools	North Carolina	M	2276 LO		2811 HI	NCSS	2008-2009
Locksmith and Safe Repairer	Alabama	Y	17190 FQ	19150 MW	22770 TQ	USBLS	5/07
	Birmingham-Hoover MSA, AL	Y	17490 FQ	18850 MW	20210 TQ	USBLS	5/07
	Arizona	Y	27170 FQ	36430 MW	41620 TQ	USBLS	5/07
	Phoenix-Mesa-Scottsdale MSA, AZ	Y	34960 FQ	38730 MW	43690 TQ	USBLS	5/07
	Tucson MSA, AZ	Y	18380 FQ	22070 MW	35530 TQ	USBLS	5/07
	Arkansas	Y	20130 FQ	24040 MW	28890 TQ	USBLS	5/07
	Little Rock-North Little Rock MSA, AR	Y	20300 FQ	22440 MW	26980 TQ	USBLS	5/07
	California	H	15.16 FQ	18.45 MW	23.06 TQ	CABLS	1/08-3/08
	Los Angeles-Long Beach-Glendale PMSA, CA	H	14.14 FQ	17.45 MW	23.58 TQ	CABLS	1/08-3/08
	Modesto MSA, CA	H	10.85 FQ	14.72 MW	17.47 TQ	CABLS	1/08-3/08
	Oakland-Fremont-Hayward MSA, CA	H	18.66 FQ	23.26 MW	28.82 TQ	CABLS	1/08-3/08
	Riverside-San Bernardino-Ontario MSA, CA	H	16.03 FQ	19.32 MW	22.41 TQ	CABLS	1/08-3/08
	Sacramento-Arden Arcade-Roseville MSA, CA	H	12.35 FQ	15.27 MW	24.58 TQ	CABLS	1/08-3/08
	San Diego-Carlsbad-San Marcos MSA, CA	H	16.81 FQ	18.17 MW	19.57 TQ	CABLS	1/08-3/08
	San Francisco-San Mateo-Redwood PMSA, CA	H	17.07 FQ	19.37 MW	23.56 TQ	CABLS	1/08-3/08
	San Jose-Sunnyvale-Santa Clara MSA, CA	H	17.66 FQ	26.07 MW	30.02 TQ	CABLS	1/08-3/08
	Santa Ana-Anaheim-Irvine PMSA, CA	Y	24750 FQ	30350 MW	53140 TQ	USBLS	5/07
	Colorado	Y	23550 FQ	31960 MW	45190 TQ	USBLS	5/07
	Denver-Aurora MSA, CO	Y	24350 FQ	39280 MW	49520 TQ	USBLS	5/07
	Connecticut	H	19.46 AE	24.73 MW		CTBLS	1/08-3/08
	Bridgeport-Stamford-Norwalk MSA, CT	Y	45080 FQ	54820 MW	60250 TQ	USBLS	5/07
	District of Columbia	Y	38990 FQ	45340 MW	51800 TQ	USBLS	5/07
	Washington-Arlington-Alexandria MSA, DC-VA-MD-WV	Y	37720 FQ	44730 MW	50490 TQ	USBLS	5/07
	Florida	Y	19750 FQ	24980 MW	33790 TQ	USBLS	5/07
	Fort Lauderdale-Pompano Beach-Deerfield Beach PMSA, FL	Y	14950 FQ	20640 MW	28700 TQ	USBLS	5/07
	Jacksonville MSA, FL	Y	28840 FQ	34060 MW	39230 TQ	USBLS	5/07
	Miami-Fort Lauderdale-Miami Beach MSA, FL	Y	15000 FQ	25610 MW	39640 TQ	USBLS	5/07
	Orlando-Kissimmee MSA, FL	Y	22360 FQ	24160 MW	25870 TQ	USBLS	5/07
	Tampa-St. Petersburg-Clearwater MSA, FL	Y	19880 FQ	22350 MW	26810 TQ	USBLS	5/07
	Georgia	Y	14430 FQ	24580 MW	40080 TQ	USBLS	5/07
	Atlanta-Sandy Springs-Marietta MSA, GA	Y	13560 FQ	23990 MW	42640 TQ	USBLS	5/07
	Hawaii	Y	35370 FQ	41110 MW	45920 TQ	USBLS	5/07
	Honolulu MSA, HI	Y	33730 FQ	37730 MW	43700 TQ	USBLS	5/07
	Idaho	Y	19770 FQ	25310 MW	29230 TQ	USBLS	5/07
	Boise City-Nampa MSA, ID	Y	20750 FQ	25890 MW	29690 TQ	USBLS	5/07
	Illinois	Y	23010 FQ	35650 MW	47350 TQ	USBLS	5/07

AE Average entry wage	**AW** Average wage paid	**FQ** First quartile wage	**LO** Lowest wage paid	**MTC** Median total compensation	**TCC** Total cash compensation
AER Average entry range	**AWR** Average wage range	**H** Hourly	**LR** Low end range	**MW** Median wage paid	**TQ** Third quartile wage
AEX Average experienced wage	**AXR** Average experienced range	**HI** Highest wage paid	**M** Monthly	**MWR** Median wage range	**W** Weekly
ATC Average total compensation	**D** Daily	**HR** High end range	**MCC** Median cash compensation	**S** See annotated source	**Y** Yearly

Occupation/Type/Industry	Location	Per	Low	Mid	High	Source	Date
Locksmith and Safe Repairer	Chicago-Naperville-Joliet MSA, IL-IN-WI	Y	22590 FQ	27600 MW	45770 TQ	USBLS	5/07
	Indiana	Y	25270 FQ	29520 MW	36400 TQ	USBLS	5/07
	Iowa	Y	26590 FQ	29630 MW	34020 TQ	USBLS	5/07
	Des Moines-West Des Moines MSA, IA	Y	27310 FQ	29930 MW	33270 TQ	USBLS	5/07
	Kansas	Y	24310 FQ	30500 MW	37170 TQ	USBLS	5/07
	Kentucky	Y	21823 FQ	26466 MW	38595 TQ	KYBLS	2008
	Louisville-Jefferson County MSA, KY-IN	Y	34170 FQ	37810 MW	44120 TQ	USBLS	5/07
	Louisiana	H	10.96 FQ	15.96 MW	20.66 TQ	LABLS	1/08-3/08
	New Orleans-Metairie-Kenner MSA, LA	Y	31720 FQ	45430 MW	54160 TQ	USBLS	5/07
	Maine	Y	24060 FQ	30700 MW	49080 TQ	USBLS	5/07
	Maryland	Y		42775 MW		MDBLS	3/08
	Baltimore-Towson MSA, MD	Y	29280 FQ	40700 MW	48280 TQ	USBLS	5/07
	Massachusetts	Y	32500 FQ	37510 MW	44940 TQ	USBLS	5/07
	Boston-Cambridge-Quincy NECTA, MA	Y	33580 FQ	38050 MW	47120 TQ	USBLS	5/07
	Worcester MSA, MA-CT	Y	29400 FQ	36560 MW	45270 TQ	USBLS	5/07
	Michigan	Y	22450 FQ	31110 MW	48780 TQ	USBLS	5/07
	Detroit-Warren-Livonia MSA, MI	Y	22440 FQ	42160 MW	62580 TQ	USBLS	5/07
	Minnesota	Y	26989 FQ	35055 MW	44328 TQ	MNBLS	10/08-12/08
	Minneapolis-Saint Paul MSA, MN-WI	Y	19027 FQ	25615 MW	33083 TQ	MNBLS	10/08-12/08
	Mississippi	Y	25950 FQ	28870 MW	34330 TQ	USBLS	5/07
	Jackson MSA, MS	Y	24030 FQ	26840 MW	29240 TQ	USBLS	5/07
	Missouri	Y	27410 FQ	32000 MW	39640 TQ	USBLS	5/07
	Kansas City MSA, MO-KS	Y	35210 FQ	49170 MW	54930 TQ	USBLS	5/07
	St. Louis MSA, MO-IL	Y	27010 FQ	30490 MW	35230 TQ	USBLS	5/07
	Montana	Y	19920 FQ	30920 MW	38880 TQ	USBLS	5/07
	Nebraska	Y	13450 FQ	18770 MW	27550 TQ	USBLS	5/07
	Omaha-Council Bluffs MSA, NE-IA	Y	12680 FQ	14100 MW	24590 TQ	USBLS	5/07
	Nevada	H	12.36 FQ	15.85 MW	21.66 TQ	NVBLS	5/08
	Las Vegas-Paradise MSA, NV	H	11.93 FQ	14.90 MW	21.87 TQ	NVBLS	5/08
	Reno-Sparks MSA, NV	H	16.40 FQ	17.68 MW	19.81 TQ	NVBLS	5/08
	New Hampshire	H	13.50 AE	15.88 MW	19.44 AEX	NHBLS	6/08
	New Jersey	Y	34150 FQ	42000 MW	48450 TQ	USBLS	5/07
	Camden PMSA, NJ	Y	39940 FQ	47120 MW	54830 TQ	USBLS	5/07
	Edison PMSA, NJ	Y	37230 FQ	41460 MW	48130 TQ	USBLS	5/07
	Newark-Union PMSA, NJ-PA	Y	38910 FQ	46010 MW	52900 TQ	USBLS	5/07
	New Mexico	Y	29010 FQ	34290 MW	44690 TQ	USBLS	5/07
	New York	Y	29270 FQ	37060 MW	48060 TQ	USBLS	5/07
	Albany-Schenectady-Troy MSA, NY	Y	30980 FQ	36120 MW	41370 TQ	USBLS	5/07
	Buffalo-Niagara Falls MSA, NY	Y	27930 FQ	32760 MW	36960 TQ	USBLS	5/07
	New York-Northern New Jersey-Long Island MSA, NY-NJ-PA	Y	30860 FQ	42040 MW	49930 TQ	USBLS	5/07
	North Carolina	Y	21480 FQ	28540 MW	36900 TQ	USBLS	5/07
	Asheville MSA, NC	Y	21640 FQ	24800 MW	27960 TQ	USBLS	5/07
	Charlotte-Gastonia-Concord MSA, NC-SC	Y	34050 FQ	37040 MW	40300 TQ	USBLS	5/07
	Raleigh-Cary MSA, NC	Y	27190 FQ	33230 MW	41230 TQ	USBLS	5/07
	Ohio	Y	24280 FQ	31850 MW	38950 TQ	USBLS	5/07
	Cincinnati-Middletown MSA, OH-KY-IN	Y	34630 FQ	39170 MW	47820 TQ	USBLS	5/07
	Columbus MSA, OH	Y	28320 FQ	34390 MW	39660 TQ	USBLS	5/07
	Oklahoma	Y	24280 FQ	28930 MW	34630 TQ	USBLS	5/07
	Oklahoma City MSA, OK	Y	19700 FQ	24820 MW	34750 TQ	USBLS	5/07
	Tulsa MSA, OK	Y	25780 FQ	28850 MW	32250 TQ	USBLS	5/07
	Oregon	H	14.07 FQ	16.25 MW	17.93 TQ	ORBLS	5/08
	Portland-Vancouver-Beaverton MSA, OR-WA	Y	32570 FQ	35140 MW	37880 TQ	USBLS	5/07
	Pennsylvania	Y	30720 FQ	39110 MW	47470 TQ	USBLS	5/07
	Philadelphia-Camden-Wilmington MSA, PA-NJ-DE-MD	Y	37910 FQ	44460 MW	50260 TQ	USBLS	5/07
	Pittsburgh MSA, PA	Y	27700 FQ	30310 MW	36770 TQ	USBLS	5/07

AE Average entry wage	**AW** Average wage paid	**FQ** First quartile wage	**LO** Lowest wage paid	**MTC** Median total compensation	**TCC** Total cash compensation
AER Average entry range	**AWR** Average wage range	**H** Hourly	**LR** Low end range	**MW** Median wage paid	**TQ** Third quartile wage
AEX Average experienced wage	**AXR** Average experienced range	**HI** Highest wage paid	**M** Monthly	**MWR** Median wage range	**W** Weekly
ATC Average total compensation	**D** Daily	**HR** High end range	**MCC** Median cash compensation	**S** See annotated source	**Y** Yearly

Occupation/Type/Industry	Location	Per	Low	Mid	High	Source	Date
Locksmith and Safe Repairer	Rhode Island	Y	40530 FQ	43610 MW	46740 TQ	USBLS	5/07
	Providence-Fall River-Warwick MSA, RI-MA	Y	37900 FQ	41570 MW	45690 TQ	USBLS	5/07
	South Carolina	Y	26520 FQ	29150 MW	31760 TQ	USBLS	5/07
	Charleston-North Charleston MSA, SC	Y	15000 FQ	27180 MW	29900 TQ	USBLS	5/07
	Columbia MSA, SC	Y	28530 FQ	31050 MW	34770 TQ	USBLS	5/07
	Tennessee	Y	25600 FQ	31460 MW	35950 TQ	USBLS	5/07
	Memphis MSA, TN-MS-AR	Y	29910 FQ	32440 MW	35050 TQ	USBLS	5/07
	Nashville-Davidson-Murfreesboro MSA, TN	Y	31920 FQ	35630 MW	38920 TQ	USBLS	5/07
	Texas	Y	24640 FQ	32190 MW	40190 TQ	USBLS	5/07
	Austin-Round Rock MSA, TX	Y	29200 FQ	34700 MW	39520 TQ	USBLS	5/07
	Dallas-Fort Worth-Arlington MSA, TX	Y	28710 FQ	40020 MW	53750 TQ	USBLS	5/07
	El Paso MSA, TX	Y	13570 FQ	20530 MW	28120 TQ	USBLS	5/07
	Houston-Sugar Land-Baytown MSA, TX	Y	28630 FQ	34440 MW	39130 TQ	USBLS	5/07
	San Antonio MSA, TX	Y	17310 FQ	27940 MW	37240 TQ	USBLS	5/07
	Utah	Y	22600 FQ	33820 MW	45020 TQ	USBLS	5/07
	Salt Lake City MSA, UT	Y	32820 FQ	43740 MW	48670 TQ	USBLS	5/07
	Virginia	Y	35940 FQ	42320 MW	49430 TQ	USBLS	5/07
	Richmond MSA, VA	Y	36400 FQ	40760 MW	53840 TQ	USBLS	5/07
	Virginia Beach-Norfolk-Newport News MSA, VA-NC	Y	37520 FQ	42050 MW	45580 TQ	USBLS	5/07
	Washington	H	14.77 FQ	19.54 MW	24.11 TQ	WABLS	3/08
	Seattle-Tacoma-Bellevue MSA, WA	Y	41870 FQ	48040 MW	54940 TQ	USBLS	5/07
	West Virginia	Y	19049 FQ	27771 MW	34471 TQ	WVBLS	7/08-9/08
	Wisconsin	Y	31140 FQ	35310 MW	39110 TQ	USBLS	5/07
	Milwaukee-Waukesha-West Allis MSA, WI	Y	33190 FQ	36080 MW	38950 TQ	USBLS	5/07
	Wyoming	Y	21354 FQ	23154 MW	24963 TQ	WYBLS	9/08
	Puerto Rico	Y	20180 FQ	25610 MW	27720 TQ	USBLS	5/07
Locksmith/Security System Technician	United States	Y		43600 MW		USNEWS07	2008
Locomotive Engineer	Alabama	Y	36470 FQ	43580 MW	48500 TQ	USBLS	5/07
	Arizona	Y	45090 FQ	55980 MW	97900 TQ	USBLS	5/07
	Arkansas	Y	52380 FQ	65480 MW	75890 TQ	USBLS	5/07
	California	H	24.13 FQ	28.98 MW	41.61 TQ	CABLS	1/08-3/08
	Colorado	Y	46620 FQ	60280 MW	84530 TQ	USBLS	5/07
	Florida	Y	42160 FQ	46420 MW	50690 TQ	USBLS	5/07
	Georgia	Y	39110 FQ	44340 MW	48250 TQ	USBLS	5/07
	Illinois	Y	51690 FQ	68530 MW	87960 TQ	USBLS	5/07
	Indiana	Y	40650 FQ	45450 MW	51070 TQ	USBLS	5/07
	Iowa	Y	43480 FQ	56680 MW	72200 TQ	USBLS	5/07
	Kansas	Y	58150 FQ	80470 MW	97440 TQ	USBLS	5/07
	Kentucky	Y	41101 FQ	44435 MW	47706 TQ	KYBLS	2008
	Louisiana	H	24.48 FQ	31.23 MW	41.60 TQ	LABLS	1/08-3/08
	Maine	Y	49260 FQ	59580 MW	78810 TQ	USBLS	5/07
	Maryland	Y		72300 MW		MDBLS	3/08
	Massachusetts	Y	45390 FQ	57970 MW	69930 TQ	USBLS	5/07
	Michigan	Y	46080 FQ	53500 MW	83140 TQ	USBLS	5/07
	Minnesota	Y	50352 FQ	56698 MW	81885 TQ	MNBLS	10/08-12/08
	Mississippi	Y	49630 FQ	74380 MW	87900 TQ	USBLS	5/07
	Missouri	Y	62410 FQ	76810 MW	91280 TQ	USBLS	5/07
	Nebraska	Y	65160 FQ	77340 MW	91840 TQ	USBLS	5/07
	Nevada	H	36.96 FQ	49.33 MW	63.58 TQ	NVBLS	5/08
	New Jersey	Y	41320 FQ	53360 MW	64540 TQ	USBLS	5/07
	New York	Y	32470 FQ	47860 MW	55750 TQ	USBLS	5/07
	North Carolina	Y	32330 FQ	39760 MW	45650 TQ	USBLS	5/07
	Ohio	Y	40210 FQ	44440 MW	48930 TQ	USBLS	5/07
	Oklahoma	Y	37200 FQ	63430 MW	80340 TQ	USBLS	5/07
	Oregon	H	25.42 FQ	32.09 MW	40.35 TQ	ORBLS	5/08
	Pennsylvania	Y	46900 FQ	57420 MW	77000 TQ	USBLS	5/07
	South Carolina	Y	42350 FQ	45760 MW	49300 TQ	USBLS	5/07
	Tennessee	Y	62500 FQ	79980 MW	94140 TQ	USBLS	5/07
	Texas	Y	70360 FQ	86060 MW	100930 TQ	USBLS	5/07
	Vermont	Y	31470 FQ	43730 MW	79130 TQ	USBLS	5/07
	Virginia	Y	60710 FQ	80090 MW	94230 TQ	USBLS	5/07

AE	Average entry wage	**AW**	Average wage paid	**FQ**	First quartile wage	**LO** Lowest wage paid	**MTC** Median total compensation	**TCC** Total cash compensation
AER	Average entry range	**AWR**	Average wage range	**H**	Hourly	**LR** Low end range	**MW** Median wage paid	**TQ** Third quartile wage
AEX	Average experienced wage	**AXR**	Average experienced range	**HI**	Highest wage paid	**M** Monthly	**MWR** Median wage range	**W** Weekly
ATC	Average total compensation	**D**	Daily	**HR**	High end range	**MCC** Median cash compensation	**S** See annotated source	**Y** Yearly

Occupation/Type/Industry	Location	Per	Low	Mid	High	Source	Date
Locomotive Engineer	West Virginia	Y	60524 FQ	81628 MW	97053 TQ	WVBLS	7/08-9/08
	Wisconsin	Y	53760 FQ	62580 MW	79910 TQ	USBLS	5/07
	Wyoming	Y	69496 FQ	84399 MW	96742 TQ	WYBLS	9/08
Locomotive Firer	California	H	17.29 FQ	20.24 MW	23.06 TQ	CABLS	1/08-3/08
	Pennsylvania	Y	34600 FQ	40640 MW	46310 TQ	USBLS	5/07
Lodging Manager	Alabama	Y	27430 FQ	36740 MW	47310 TQ	USBLS	5/07
	Birmingham-Hoover MSA, AL	Y	28890 FQ	38740 MW	53050 TQ	USBLS	5/07
	Alaska	Y	30040 FQ	43170 MW	56430 TQ	USBLS	5/07
	Anchorage MSA, AK	Y	28670 FQ	40780 MW	52550 TQ	USBLS	5/07
	Arizona	Y	27950 FQ	36590 MW	52200 TQ	USBLS	5/07
	Phoenix-Mesa-Scottsdale MSA, AZ	Y	33010 FQ	42930 MW	60520 TQ	USBLS	5/07
	Tucson MSA, AZ	Y	25480 FQ	30950 MW	51550 TQ	USBLS	5/07
	Arkansas	Y	28870 FQ	32590 MW	40810 TQ	USBLS	5/07
	Little Rock-North Little Rock MSA, AR	Y	33140 FQ	36750 MW	47060 TQ	USBLS	5/07
	California	H	17.33 FQ	22.71 MW	30.81 TQ	CABLS	1/08-3/08
	Los Angeles-Long Beach-Glendale PMSA, CA	H	19.62 FQ	24.06 MW	33.65 TQ	CABLS	1/08-3/08
	Oakland-Fremont-Hayward MSA, CA	H	14.91 FQ	20.59 MW	29.44 TQ	CABLS	1/08-3/08
	Riverside-San Bernardino-Ontario MSA, CA	H	16.76 FQ	19.68 MW	26.78 TQ	CABLS	1/08-3/08
	Sacramento-Arden Arcade-Roseville MSA, CA	H	19.21 FQ	23.42 MW	29.83 TQ	CABLS	1/08-3/08
	San Diego-Carlsbad-San Marcos MSA, CA	H	19.33 FQ	25.91 MW	34.33 TQ	CABLS	1/08-3/08
	San Francisco-San Mateo-Redwood PMSA, CA	H	14.30 FQ	18.93 MW	28.12 TQ	CABLS	1/08-3/08
	San Jose-Sunnyvale-Santa Clara MSA, CA	H	20.95 FQ	28.03 MW	35.92 TQ	CABLS	1/08-3/08
	Santa Ana-Anaheim-Irvine PMSA, CA	Y	42080 FQ	49940 MW	64460 TQ	USBLS	5/07
	Colorado	Y	34860 FQ	44860 MW	61600 TQ	USBLS	5/07
	Denver-Aurora MSA, CO	Y	41250 FQ	47520 MW	62630 TQ	USBLS	5/07
	Connecticut	H	16.51 AE	25.62 MW		CTBLS	1/08-3/08
	Bridgeport-Stamford-Norwalk MSA, CT	Y	44380 FQ	53320 MW	64710 TQ	USBLS	5/07
	Hartford-West Hartford-East Hartford MSA, CT	Y	32890 FQ	45040 MW	65280 TQ	USBLS	5/07
	Delaware	Y	45070 FQ	56130 MW	69060 TQ	USBLS	5/07
	Wilmington PMSA, DE-MD-NJ	Y	41730 FQ	56970 MW	73020 TQ	USBLS	5/07
	District of Columbia	Y	45840 FQ	65400 MW	88780 TQ	USBLS	5/07
	Washington-Arlington-Alexandria MSA, DC-VA-MD-WV	Y	48950 FQ	64220 MW	83250 TQ	USBLS	5/07
	Florida	Y	38750 FQ	49200 MW	68270 TQ	USBLS	5/07
	Fort Lauderdale-Pompano Beach-Deerfield Beach PMSA, FL	Y	41500 FQ	51380 MW	85550 TQ	USBLS	5/07
	Jacksonville MSA, FL	Y	41070 FQ	52230 MW	66080 TQ	USBLS	5/07
	Miami-Fort Lauderdale-Miami Beach MSA, FL	Y	40710 FQ	54270 MW	79350 TQ	USBLS	5/07
	Orlando-Kissimmee MSA, FL	Y	42150 FQ	49470 MW	65560 TQ	USBLS	5/07
	Tampa-St. Petersburg-Clearwater MSA, FL	Y	37300 FQ	47180 MW	59860 TQ	USBLS	5/07
	West Palm Beach-Boca Raton-Boynton Beach PMSA, FL	Y	35370 FQ	45310 MW	66380 TQ	USBLS	5/07
	Georgia	Y	34290 FQ	45110 MW	62520 TQ	USBLS	5/07
	Atlanta-Sandy Springs-Marietta MSA, GA	Y	34190 FQ	50670 MW	69700 TQ	USBLS	5/07
	Savannah MSA, GA	Y	38790 FQ	45860 MW	50710 TQ	USBLS	5/07
	Hawaii	Y	37820 FQ	48490 MW	70440 TQ	USBLS	5/07
	Honolulu MSA, HI	Y	40150 FQ	49210 MW	73800 TQ	USBLS	5/07
	Idaho	Y	25020 FQ	31640 MW	46170 TQ	USBLS	5/07
	Boise City-Nampa MSA, ID	Y	25420 FQ	27920 MW	43640 TQ	USBLS	5/07
	Illinois	Y	38590 FQ	50780 MW	64340 TQ	USBLS	5/07
	Chicago-Naperville-Joliet MSA, IL-IN-WI	Y	39280 FQ	51810 MW	65880 TQ	USBLS	5/07

AE	Average entry wage	AW	Average wage paid	FQ	First quartile wage
AER	Average entry range	AWR	Average wage range	H	Hourly
AEX	Average experienced wage	AXR	Average experienced range	HI	Highest wage paid
ATC	Average total compensation	D	Daily	HR	High end range

LO	Lowest wage paid	MTC	Median total compensation	TCC	Total cash compensation
LR	Low end range	MW	Median wage paid	TQ	Third quartile wage
M	Monthly	MWR	Median wage range	W	Weekly
MCC	Median cash compensation	S	See annotated source	Y	Yearly

Lodging Manager

Occupation/Type/Industry	Location	Per	Low	Mid	High	Source	Date
Lodging Manager	Indiana	Y	29770 FQ	39690 MW	46960 TQ	USBLS	5/07
	Indianapolis-Carmel MSA, IN	Y	35690 FQ	42910 MW	48920 TQ	USBLS	5/07
	Iowa	Y	31110 FQ	36530 MW	43810 TQ	USBLS	5/07
	Des Moines-West Des Moines MSA, IA	Y	32240 FQ	37970 MW	47150 TQ	USBLS	5/07
	Kansas	Y	33500 FQ	42720 MW	50370 TQ	USBLS	5/07
	Wichita MSA, KS	Y	32620 FQ	38480 MW	43660 TQ	USBLS	5/07
	Kentucky	Y	30826 FQ	41326 MW	55162 TQ	KYBLS	2008
	Louisville-Jefferson County MSA, KY-IN	Y	31530 FQ	45100 MW	57700 TQ	USBLS	5/07
	Louisiana	H	13.62 FQ	16.63 MW	26.51 TQ	LABLS	1/08-3/08
	Baton Rouge MSA, LA	Y	36120 FQ	40590 MW	53310 TQ	USBLS	5/07
	New Orleans-Metairie-Kenner MSA, LA	Y	28110 FQ	32820 MW	53180 TQ	USBLS	5/07
	Maine	Y	34880 FQ	43350 MW	59780 TQ	USBLS	5/07
	Portland-South Portland-Biddeford MSA, ME	Y	33870 FQ	40750 MW	50900 TQ	USBLS	5/07
	Maryland	Y		57025 MW		MDBLS	3/08
	Baltimore-Towson MSA, MD	Y	41930 FQ	50930 MW	75880 TQ	USBLS	5/07
	Bethesda-Gaithersburg-Frederick PMSA, MD	Y	55260 FQ	70240 MW	132520 TQ	USBLS	5/07
	Massachusetts	Y	39750 FQ	49060 MW	65820 TQ	USBLS	5/07
	Boston-Cambridge-Quincy NECTA, MA	Y	44070 FQ	56950 MW	77900 TQ	USBLS	5/07
	Springfield MSA, MA-CT	Y	43850 FQ	55610 MW	72140 TQ	USBLS	5/07
	Worcester MSA, MA-CT	Y	36790 FQ	52220 MW	66670 TQ	USBLS	5/07
	Michigan	Y	37480 FQ	47800 MW	62410 TQ	USBLS	5/07
	Detroit-Warren-Livonia MSA, MI	Y	42540 FQ	49880 MW	66350 TQ	USBLS	5/07
	Grand Rapids-Wyoming MSA, MI	Y	35770 FQ	44730 MW	49250 TQ	USBLS	5/07
	Warren-Troy-Farmington Hills PMSA, MI	Y	42150 FQ	47610 MW	61700 TQ	USBLS	5/07
	Minnesota	Y	34876 FQ	42018 MW	52195 TQ	MNBLS	10/08-12/08
	Duluth-Superior MSA, MN-WI	Y	31477 FQ	39433 MW	50735 TQ	MNBLS	10/08-12/08
	Minneapolis-Saint Paul MSA, MN-WI	Y	36774 FQ	44448 MW	56991 TQ	MNBLS	10/08-12/08
	Rochester MSA, MN	Y	37558 FQ	40858 MW	55116 TQ	MNBLS	10/08-12/08
	Mississippi	Y	28010 FQ	34520 MW	45230 TQ	USBLS	5/07
	Jackson MSA, MS	Y	28800 FQ	32910 MW	45300 TQ	USBLS	5/07
	Missouri	Y	37760 FQ	51630 MW	61450 TQ	USBLS	5/07
	Kansas City MSA, MO-KS	Y	40900 FQ	52200 MW	60390 TQ	USBLS	5/07
	St. Louis MSA, MO-IL	Y	35440 FQ	48070 MW	62690 TQ	USBLS	5/07
	Montana	Y	24670 FQ	33050 MW	40880 TQ	USBLS	5/07
	Billings MSA, MT	Y	25110 FQ	38830 MW	45500 TQ	USBLS	5/07
	Nebraska	Y	28410 FQ	34670 MW	44100 TQ	USBLS	5/07
	Omaha-Council Bluffs MSA, NE-IA	Y	34530 FQ	37920 MW	41600 TQ	USBLS	5/07
	Nevada	H	20.36 FQ	26.95 MW	40.12 TQ	NVBLS	5/08
	Las Vegas-Paradise MSA, NV	H	22.36 FQ	28.37 MW	44.34 TQ	NVBLS	5/08
	New Hampshire	H	16.27 AE	22.81 MW	28.45 AEX	NHBLS	6/08
	Nashua NECTA, NH-MA	Y	26890 FQ	37780 MW	46350 TQ	USBLS	5/07
	New Jersey	Y	39000 FQ	55980 MW	82830 TQ	USBLS	5/07
	Camden PMSA, NJ	Y	36720 FQ	42880 MW	79690 TQ	USBLS	5/07
	Edison PMSA, NJ	Y	54800 FQ	64950 MW	93390 TQ	USBLS	5/07
	Newark-Union PMSA, NJ-PA	Y	37490 FQ	58140 MW	81520 TQ	USBLS	5/07
	New Mexico	Y	24850 FQ	36470 MW	46640 TQ	USBLS	5/07
	Albuquerque MSA, NM	Y	32890 FQ	38300 MW	47290 TQ	USBLS	5/07
	New York	Y	45240 FQ	59970 MW	79680 TQ	USBLS	5/07
	Albany-Schenectady-Troy MSA, NY	Y	49260 FQ	63630 MW	77780 TQ	USBLS	5/07
	Buffalo-Niagara Falls MSA, NY	Y	39580 FQ	55420 MW	62620 TQ	USBLS	5/07
	Nassau-Suffolk PMSA, NY	Y	48570 FQ	56260 MW	65640 TQ	USBLS	5/07
	New York-Northern New Jersey-Long Island MSA, NY-NJ-PA	Y	51900 FQ	68920 MW	89990 TQ	USBLS	5/07
	North Carolina	Y	31780 FQ	39040 MW	49420 TQ	USBLS	5/07
	Charlotte-Gastonia-Concord MSA, NC-SC	Y	32950 FQ	40940 MW	50640 TQ	USBLS	5/07
	Greensboro-High Point MSA, NC	Y	31570 FQ	37480 MW	43230 TQ	USBLS	5/07

AE	Average entry wage	AW	Average wage paid	FQ First quartile wage
AER	Average entry range	AWR	Average wage range	H Hourly
AEX	Average experienced wage	AXR	Average experienced range	HI Highest wage paid
ATC	Average total compensation	D	Daily	HR High end range

LO	Lowest wage paid
LR	Low end range
M	Monthly
MCC	Median cash compensation

MTC	Median total compensation
MW	Median wage paid
MWR	Median wage range
S	See annotated source

TCC	Total cash compensation
TQ	Third quartile wage
W	Weekly
Y	Yearly

Occupation/Type/Industry	Location	Per	Low	Mid	High	Source	Date
Lodging Manager	Winston-Salem MSA, NC	Y	31990 FQ	35520 MW	40310 TQ	USBLS	5/07
	North Dakota	Y	29970 FQ	39350 MW	48130 TQ	USBLS	5/07
	Fargo MSA, ND-MN	Y	33490 FQ	41610 MW	50300 TQ	USBLS	5/07
	Ohio	Y	31000 FQ	40290 MW	57300 TQ	USBLS	5/07
	Cincinnati-Middletown MSA, OH-KY-IN	Y	32170 FQ	47480 MW	66570 TQ	USBLS	5/07
	Cleveland-Elyria-Mentor MSA, OH	Y	31720 FQ	50080 MW	71340 TQ	USBLS	5/07
	Columbus MSA, OH	Y	38060 FQ	50110 MW	70260 TQ	USBLS	5/07
	Dayton MSA, OH	Y	27460 FQ	37770 MW	48250 TQ	USBLS	5/07
	Oklahoma	Y	14130 FQ	20140 MW	29780 TQ	USBLS	5/07
	Oklahoma City MSA, OK	Y	19190 FQ	26910 MW	31640 TQ	USBLS	5/07
	Tulsa MSA, OK	Y	22870 FQ	34310 MW	43590 TQ	USBLS	5/07
	Oregon	H	15.80 FQ	20.33 MW	27.39 TQ	ORBLS	5/08
	Portland-Vancouver-Beaverton MSA, OR-WA	Y	39350 FQ	49850 MW	63760 TQ	USBLS	5/07
	Pennsylvania	Y	33360 FQ	43070 MW	57350 TQ	USBLS	5/07
	Allentown-Bethlehem-Easton MSA, PA-NJ	Y	30170 FQ	42150 MW	54280 TQ	USBLS	5/07
	Philadelphia-Camden-Wilmington MSA, PA-NJ-DE-MD	Y	39310 FQ	51440 MW	75720 TQ	USBLS	5/07
	Pittsburgh MSA, PA	Y	29580 FQ	38820 MW	50020 TQ	USBLS	5/07
	Rhode Island	Y	48790 FQ	55760 MW	65020 TQ	USBLS	5/07
	Providence-Fall River-Warwick MSA, RI-MA	Y	43470 FQ	53940 MW	66720 TQ	USBLS	5/07
	South Carolina	Y	34230 FQ	43890 MW	62290 TQ	USBLS	5/07
	Charleston-North Charleston MSA, SC	Y	32110 FQ	48490 MW	69400 TQ	USBLS	5/07
	Columbia MSA, SC	Y	33840 FQ	37890 MW	48210 TQ	USBLS	5/07
	South Dakota	Y	37804 FQ	42891 MW	49859 TQ	SDBLS	7/08-9/08
	Sioux Falls MSA, SD	Y	36259 FQ	41223 MW	58669 TQ	SDBLS	7/08-9/08
	Tennessee	Y	29500 FQ	35920 MW	43300 TQ	USBLS	5/07
	Memphis MSA, TN-MS-AR	Y	34550 FQ	42540 MW	50540 TQ	USBLS	5/07
	Nashville-Davidson-Murfreesboro MSA, TN	Y	28610 FQ	34730 MW	38950 TQ	USBLS	5/07
	Texas	Y	39030 FQ	49290 MW	63660 TQ	USBLS	5/07
	Austin-Round Rock MSA, TX	Y	43850 FQ	58270 MW	86550 TQ	USBLS	5/07
	Brownsville-Harlingen MSA, TX	Y	35400 FQ	39840 MW	45480 TQ	USBLS	5/07
	Dallas-Fort Worth-Arlington MSA, TX	Y	43690 FQ	54620 MW	76820 TQ	USBLS	5/07
	El Paso MSA, TX	Y	51620 FQ	144020 MW		USBLS	5/07
	Houston-Sugar Land-Baytown MSA, TX	Y	42990 FQ	50750 MW	61480 TQ	USBLS	5/07
	San Antonio MSA, TX	Y	37870 FQ	50100 MW	65870 TQ	USBLS	5/07
	Utah	Y	37550 FQ	54020 MW	79760 TQ	USBLS	5/07
	Salt Lake City MSA, UT	Y	37490 FQ	61090 MW	92530 TQ	USBLS	5/07
	Vermont	Y	33440 FQ	47570 MW	68170 TQ	USBLS	5/07
	Virginia	Y	40020 FQ	53620 MW	71320 TQ	USBLS	5/07
	Richmond MSA, VA	Y	45070 FQ	56350 MW	74210 TQ	USBLS	5/07
	Virginia Beach-Norfolk-Newport News MSA, VA-NC	Y	41960 FQ	54870 MW	71810 TQ	USBLS	5/07
	Washington	H	27.84 FQ	34.89 MW	43.10 TQ	WABLS	3/08
	Seattle-Tacoma-Bellevue MSA, WA	Y	57120 FQ	72010 MW	86810 TQ	USBLS	5/07
	Spokane MSA, WA	Y	64380 FQ	87170 MW	120690 TQ	USBLS	5/07
	West Virginia	Y	30280 FQ	36464 MW	45011 TQ	WVBLS	7/08-9/08
	Wisconsin	Y	34880 FQ	43400 MW	55000 TQ	USBLS	5/07
	Milwaukee-Waukesha-West Allis MSA, WI	Y	40750 FQ	48020 MW	68170 TQ	USBLS	5/07
	Wyoming	Y	30364 FQ	37948 MW	47672 TQ	WYBLS	9/08
	Cheyenne MSA, WY	Y	22524 FQ	31501 MW	39919 TQ	WYBLS	9/08
	Puerto Rico	Y	27150 FQ	36600 MW	80050 TQ	USBLS	5/07
	San Juan-Caguas-Guaynabo MSA, PR	Y	30300 FQ	40690 MW	88210 TQ	USBLS	5/07
	Virgin Islands	Y	36980 FQ	45040 MW	57490 TQ	USBLS	5/07
	Guam	Y	25600 FQ	30360 MW	36500 TQ	USBLS	5/07
Log Grader and Scaler	Alabama	Y	23840 FQ	28340 MW	32770 TQ	USBLS	5/07
	Arkansas	Y	24730 FQ	29090 MW	36360 TQ	USBLS	5/07
	California	H	15.00 FQ	19.24 MW	22.75 TQ	CABLS	1/08-3/08

AE	Average entry wage	AW	Average wage paid	FQ	First quartile wage
AER	Average entry range	AWR	Average wage range	H	Hourly
AEX	Average experienced wage	AXR	Average experienced range	HI	Highest wage paid
ATC	Average total compensation	D	Daily	HR	High end range

LO	Lowest wage paid	MTC	Median total compensation
LR	Low end range	MW	Median wage paid
M	Monthly	MWR	Median wage range
MCC	Median cash compensation	S	See annotated source

TCC	Total cash compensation
TQ	Third quartile wage
W	Weekly
Y	Yearly

936

Occupation/Type/Industry	Location	Per	Low	Mid	High	Source	Date
Log Grader and Scaler	Georgia	Y	21090 FQ	32210 MW	37810 TQ	USBLS	5/07
	Idaho	Y	32500 FQ	36010 MW	39390 TQ	USBLS	5/07
	Indiana	Y	28000 FQ	32150 MW	39790 TQ	USBLS	5/07
	Kentucky	Y	24216 FQ	29695 MW	37297 TQ	KYBLS	2008
	Louisiana	H	10.99 FQ	14.85 MW	17.48 TQ	LABLS	1/08-3/08
	Maine	Y	28030 FQ	32040 MW	37090 TQ	USBLS	5/07
	Michigan	Y	28160 FQ	32430 MW	37990 TQ	USBLS	5/07
	Minnesota	Y	30615 FQ	41638 MW	50723 TQ	MNBLS	10/08-12/08
	Mississippi	Y	22930 FQ	31650 MW	41640 TQ	USBLS	5/07
	Missouri	Y	20240 FQ	22100 MW	23990 TQ	USBLS	5/07
	Montana	Y	31560 FQ	35580 MW	40710 TQ	USBLS	5/07
	New Hampshire	H	15.26 AE	18.03 MW	19.41 AEX	NHBLS	6/08
	New York	Y	27540 FQ	32900 MW	43470 TQ	USBLS	5/07
	North Carolina	Y	25020 FQ	28610 MW	33080 TQ	USBLS	5/07
	Ohio	Y	27440 FQ	31210 MW	35480 TQ	USBLS	5/07
	Oregon	H	18.10 FQ	21.45 MW	29.34 TQ	ORBLS	5/08
	Pennsylvania	Y	21320 FQ	26740 MW	34040 TQ	USBLS	5/07
	South Carolina	Y	22770 FQ	32200 MW	39660 TQ	USBLS	5/07
	South Dakota	Y	24209 FQ	28081 MW	32600 TQ	SDBLS	7/08-9/08
	Tennessee	Y	19470 FQ	27980 MW	35440 TQ	USBLS	5/07
	Virginia	Y	27110 FQ	32070 MW	42000 TQ	USBLS	5/07
	Washington	H	15.81 FQ	18.30 MW	22.13 TQ	WABLS	3/08
	West Virginia	Y	23932 FQ	28950 MW	32973 TQ	WVBLS	7/08-9/08
	Wisconsin	Y	25800 FQ	29760 MW	35210 TQ	USBLS	5/07
	Wyoming	Y	23517 FQ	25570 MW	28571 TQ	WYBLS	9/08
Logging Equipment Operator	Alabama	Y	22770 FQ	26590 MW	33110 TQ	USBLS	5/07
	Alaska	Y	33160 FQ	38840 MW	45270 TQ	USBLS	5/07
	Arkansas	Y	23720 FQ	30750 MW	37770 TQ	USBLS	5/07
	California	H	16.11 FQ	18.37 MW	21.94 TQ	CABLS	1/08-3/08
	Colorado	Y	27440 FQ	32980 MW	37580 TQ	USBLS	5/07
	Florida	Y	23830 FQ	27750 MW	33880 TQ	USBLS	5/07
	Georgia	Y	23410 FQ	28810 MW	34860 TQ	USBLS	5/07
	Idaho	Y	33950 FQ	40220 MW	46600 TQ	USBLS	5/07
	Illinois	Y	22000 FQ	24660 MW	32240 TQ	USBLS	5/07
	Indiana	Y	21590 FQ	25060 MW	31520 TQ	USBLS	5/07
	Kentucky	Y	20135 FQ	23115 MW	27835 TQ	KYBLS	2008
	Louisiana	H	13.02 FQ	14.87 MW	18.59 TQ	LABLS	1/08-3/08
	Maine	Y	24900 FQ	29280 MW	33720 TQ	USBLS	5/07
	Maryland	Y		29925 MW		MDBLS	3/08
	Massachusetts	Y	23410 FQ	30540 MW	36490 TQ	USBLS	5/07
	Michigan	Y	23050 FQ	27240 MW	31530 TQ	USBLS	5/07
	Minnesota	Y	28760 FQ	38224 MW	44494 TQ	MNBLS	10/08-12/08
	Mississippi	Y	24090 FQ	28280 MW	32690 TQ	USBLS	5/07
	Missouri	Y	16900 FQ	18430 MW	26560 TQ	USBLS	5/07
	Montana	Y	30640 FQ	35950 MW	40900 TQ	USBLS	5/07
	New Hampshire	H	13.77 AE	17.78 MW	19.52 AEX	NHBLS	6/08
	New York	Y	23920 FQ	29210 MW	36340 TQ	USBLS	5/07
	North Carolina	Y	22780 FQ	28050 MW	33470 TQ	USBLS	5/07
	Ohio	Y	22110 FQ	27140 MW	33030 TQ	USBLS	5/07
	Oklahoma	Y	22540 FQ	28470 MW	36370 TQ	USBLS	5/07
	Oregon	H	16.64 FQ	18.72 MW	21.56 TQ	ORBLS	5/08
	Pennsylvania	Y	20170 FQ	24100 MW	29190 TQ	USBLS	5/07
	South Carolina	Y	25000 FQ	29920 MW	37640 TQ	USBLS	5/07
	South Dakota	Y	29407 FQ	35409 MW	40334 TQ	SDBLS	7/08-9/08
	Tennessee	Y	22640 FQ	27560 MW	38290 TQ	USBLS	5/07
	Texas	Y	27920 FQ	33260 MW	37050 TQ	USBLS	5/07
	Vermont	Y	23240 FQ	27680 MW	31180 TQ	USBLS	5/07
	Virginia	Y	22890 FQ	28360 MW	33900 TQ	USBLS	5/07
	Washington	H	17.45 FQ	20.35 MW	23.21 TQ	WABLS	3/08
	West Virginia	Y	19195 FQ	23849 MW	29984 TQ	WVBLS	7/08-9/08
	Wisconsin	Y	23160 FQ	26690 MW	30120 TQ	USBLS	5/07
	Wyoming	Y	29610 FQ	36267 MW	42000 TQ	WYBLS	9/08
Logistician	Alabama	Y	57470 FQ	73110 MW	89070 TQ	USBLS	5/07
	Birmingham-Hoover MSA, AL	Y	56800 FQ	70260 MW	81070 TQ	USBLS	5/07
	Montgomery MSA, AL	Y	50790 FQ	61760 MW	70440 TQ	USBLS	5/07
	Alaska	Y	54610 FQ	63480 MW	83600 TQ	USBLS	5/07
	Anchorage MSA, AK	Y	53870 FQ	62980 MW	83090 TQ	USBLS	5/07
	Arizona	Y	47880 FQ	59850 MW	75820 TQ	USBLS	5/07
	Phoenix-Mesa-Scottsdale MSA, AZ	Y	46550 FQ	58210 MW	75190 TQ	USBLS	5/07

AE	Average entry wage	**AW**	Average wage paid	**FQ**	First quartile wage	**LO** Lowest wage paid	**MTC** Median total compensation	**TCC** Total cash compensation
AER	Average entry range	**AWR**	Average wage range	**H**	Hourly	**LR** Low end range	**MW** Median wage paid	**TQ** Third quartile wage
AEX	Average experienced wage	**AXR**	Average experienced range	**HI**	Highest wage paid	**M** Monthly	**MWR** Median wage range	**W** Weekly
ATC	Average total compensation	**D**	Daily	**HR**	High end range	**MCC** Median cash compensation	**S** See annotated source	**Y** Yearly

Occupation/Type/Industry	Location	Per	Low	Mid	High	Source	Date
Logistician	Tucson MSA, AZ	Y	53560 FQ	62740 MW	75600 TQ	USBLS	5/07
	Arkansas	Y	48100 FQ	61590 MW	72050 TQ	USBLS	5/07
	Fayetteville-Springdale-Rogers MSA, AR-MO	Y	49280 FQ	63630 MW	72870 TQ	USBLS	5/07
	Little Rock-North Little Rock MSA, AR	Y	44800 FQ	57180 MW	70880 TQ	USBLS	5/07
	California	H	27.65 FQ	34.47 MW	42.50 TQ	CABLS	1/08-3/08
	Los Angeles-Long Beach-Glendale PMSA, CA	H	27.98 FQ	34.40 MW	42.56 TQ	CABLS	1/08-3/08
	Modesto MSA, CA	H	27.53 FQ	29.89 MW	32.41 TQ	CABLS	1/08-3/08
	Oakland-Fremont-Hayward MSA, CA	H	30.53 FQ	38.25 MW	47.11 TQ	CABLS	1/08-3/08
	Oxnard-Thousand Oaks-Ventura MSA, CA	H	31.38 FQ	39.02 MW	47.88 TQ	CABLS	1/08-3/08
	Riverside-San Bernardino-Ontario MSA, CA	H	26.06 FQ	31.47 MW	37.80 TQ	CABLS	1/08-3/08
	Sacramento-Arden Arcade-Roseville MSA, CA	H	24.66 FQ	32.99 MW	40.02 TQ	CABLS	1/08-3/08
	San Diego-Carlsbad-San Marcos MSA, CA	H	27.41 FQ	34.02 MW	40.94 TQ	CABLS	1/08-3/08
	San Francisco-San Mateo-Redwood PMSA, CA	H	26.12 FQ	33.38 MW	43.18 TQ	CABLS	1/08-3/08
	San Jose-Sunnyvale-Santa Clara MSA, CA	H	31.13 FQ	37.32 MW	44.66 TQ	CABLS	1/08-3/08
	Santa Ana-Anaheim-Irvine PMSA, CA	Y	52470 FQ	64550 MW	80870 TQ	USBLS	5/07
	Colorado	Y	52310 FQ	67870 MW	84330 TQ	USBLS	5/07
	Denver-Aurora MSA, CO	Y	52820 FQ	67890 MW	84350 TQ	USBLS	5/07
	Connecticut	H	21.76 AE	30.75 MW		CTBLS	1/08-3/08
	Bridgeport-Stamford-Norwalk MSA, CT	Y	45260 FQ	59010 MW	70860 TQ	USBLS	5/07
	Hartford-West Hartford-East Hartford MSA, CT	Y	51780 FQ	67300 MW	83580 TQ	USBLS	5/07
	Norwich-New London MSA, CT-RI	Y	45610 FQ	56940 MW	77480 TQ	USBLS	5/07
	Delaware	Y	55420 FQ	68110 MW	91100 TQ	USBLS	5/07
	Wilmington PMSA, DE-MD-NJ	Y	56860 FQ	71770 MW	94570 TQ	USBLS	5/07
	District of Columbia	Y	66310 FQ	80770 MW	98290 TQ	USBLS	5/07
	Washington-Arlington-Alexandria MSA, DC-VA-MD-WV	Y	59750 FQ	77560 MW	96530 TQ	USBLS	5/07
	Florida	Y	47340 FQ	59270 MW	75790 TQ	USBLS	5/07
	Cape Coral-Fort Myers MSA, FL	Y	48220 FQ	57000 MW	65750 TQ	USBLS	5/07
	Fort Lauderdale-Pompano Beach-Deerfield Beach PMSA, FL	Y	51870 FQ	63260 MW	79960 TQ	USBLS	5/07
	Jacksonville MSA, FL	Y	49290 FQ	65160 MW	78230 TQ	USBLS	5/07
	Miami-Fort Lauderdale-Miami Beach MSA, FL	Y	44730 FQ	55520 MW	75180 TQ	USBLS	5/07
	Orlando-Kissimmee MSA, FL	Y	52150 FQ	66860 MW	83670 TQ	USBLS	5/07
	Tampa-St. Petersburg-Clearwater MSA, FL	Y	48200 FQ	63010 MW	79330 TQ	USBLS	5/07
	West Palm Beach-Boca Raton-Boynton Beach PMSA, FL	Y	53290 FQ	63790 MW	84700 TQ	USBLS	5/07
	Georgia	Y	50160 FQ	61360 MW	75300 TQ	USBLS	5/07
	Atlanta-Sandy Springs-Marietta MSA, GA	Y	47290 FQ	59010 MW	75220 TQ	USBLS	5/07
	Hawaii	Y	57810 FQ	71810 MW	86830 TQ	USBLS	5/07
	Honolulu MSA, HI	Y	59130 FQ	72600 MW	87430 TQ	USBLS	5/07
	Idaho	Y	40120 FQ	50750 MW	61850 TQ	USBLS	5/07
	Boise City-Nampa MSA, ID	Y	38950 FQ	49100 MW	59910 TQ	USBLS	5/07
	Illinois	Y	48700 FQ	62300 MW	79350 TQ	USBLS	5/07
	Chicago-Naperville-Joliet MSA, IL-IN-WI	Y	43690 FQ	57920 MW	75360 TQ	USBLS	5/07
	Indiana	Y	44210 FQ	60820 MW	78080 TQ	USBLS	5/07
	Fort Wayne MSA, IN	Y	46620 FQ	58480 MW	84190 TQ	USBLS	5/07
	Gary PMSA, IN	Y	29960 FQ	37400 MW	71500 TQ	USBLS	5/07
	Indianapolis-Carmel MSA, IN	Y	52110 FQ	66470 MW	83630 TQ	USBLS	5/07
	Iowa	Y	43980 FQ	60650 MW	78140 TQ	USBLS	5/07

Occupation/Type/Industry	Location	Per	Low	Mid	High	Source	Date
Logistician	Des Moines-West Des Moines MSA, IA	Y	40060 FQ	51000 MW	67100 TQ	USBLS	5/07
	Kansas	Y	53380 FQ	65990 MW	79160 TQ	USBLS	5/07
	Wichita MSA, KS	Y	55510 FQ	64990 MW	75380 TQ	USBLS	5/07
	Kentucky	Y	47786 FQ	59183 MW	73010 TQ	KYBLS	2008
	Elizabethtown MSA, KY	Y	52070 FQ	61580 MW	75960 TQ	USBLS	5/07
	Louisville-Jefferson County MSA, KY-IN	Y	45990 FQ	58990 MW	74610 TQ	USBLS	5/07
	Louisiana	H	21.36 FQ	27.04 MW	35.80 TQ	LABLS	1/08-3/08
	Baton Rouge MSA, LA	Y	42390 FQ	49220 MW	61770 TQ	USBLS	5/07
	New Orleans-Metairie-Kenner MSA, LA	Y	47720 FQ	63150 MW	79810 TQ	USBLS	5/07
	Maine	Y	49360 FQ	59120 MW	70310 TQ	USBLS	5/07
	Portland-South Portland-Biddeford MSA, ME	Y	36660 FQ	44940 MW	67350 TQ	USBLS	5/07
	Maryland	Y		76225 MW		MDBLS	3/08
	Baltimore-Towson MSA, MD	Y	52650 FQ	68150 MW	82660 TQ	USBLS	5/07
	Bethesda-Gaithersburg-Frederick PMSA, MD	Y	65090 FQ	79760 MW	98960 TQ	USBLS	5/07
	Massachusetts	Y	53260 FQ	69830 MW	88430 TQ	USBLS	5/07
	Boston-Cambridge-Quincy NECTA, MA	Y	51810 FQ	69420 MW	88260 TQ	USBLS	5/07
	Lynn-Peabody-Salem NECTA, MA	Y	66990 FQ	77340 MW	95660 TQ	USBLS	5/07
	Worcester MSA, MA-CT	Y	55930 FQ	66490 MW	77480 TQ	USBLS	5/07
	Michigan	Y	53050 FQ	69890 MW	86600 TQ	USBLS	5/07
	Detroit-Warren-Livonia MSA, MI	Y	57720 FQ	74950 MW	92500 TQ	USBLS	5/07
	Grand Rapids-Wyoming MSA, MI	Y	40570 FQ	51990 MW	68980 TQ	USBLS	5/07
	Warren-Troy-Farmington Hills PMSA, MI	Y	60730 FQ	75230 MW	91710 TQ	USBLS	5/07
	Minnesota	Y	53456 FQ	67126 MW	85612 TQ	MNBLS	10/08-12/08
	Duluth-Superior MSA, MN-WI	Y	42936 FQ	59327 MW	80774 TQ	MNBLS	10/08-12/08
	Minneapolis-Saint Paul MSA, MN-WI	Y	54739 FQ	69576 MW	87603 TQ	MNBLS	10/08-12/08
	Mississippi	Y	40990 FQ	51100 MW	63810 TQ	USBLS	5/07
	Jackson MSA, MS	Y	46330 FQ	57250 MW	68010 TQ	USBLS	5/07
	Missouri	Y	49690 FQ	62410 MW	77160 TQ	USBLS	5/07
	Kansas City MSA, MO-KS	Y	46640 FQ	64760 MW	81330 TQ	USBLS	5/07
	St. Louis MSA, MO-IL	Y	53890 FQ	65560 MW	78350 TQ	USBLS	5/07
	Montana	Y	39040 FQ	55150 MW	72870 TQ	USBLS	5/07
	Nebraska	Y	42860 FQ	56460 MW	78750 TQ	USBLS	5/07
	Omaha-Council Bluffs MSA, NE-IA	Y	40270 FQ	51510 MW	72250 TQ	USBLS	5/07
	Las Vegas-Paradise MSA, NV	H	23.69 FQ	28.35 MW	34.97 TQ	NVBLS	5/08
	New Hampshire	H	23.27 AE	29.14 MW	34.59 AEX	NHBLS	6/08
	Nashua NECTA, NH-MA	Y	53550 FQ	59920 MW	73450 TQ	USBLS	5/07
	New Jersey	Y	62010 FQ	77280 MW	94060 TQ	USBLS	5/07
	Camden PMSA, NJ	Y	49600 FQ	61570 MW	77490 TQ	USBLS	5/07
	Edison PMSA, NJ	Y	69360 FQ	85510 MW	100090 TQ	USBLS	5/07
	Newark-Union PMSA, NJ-PA	Y	61500 FQ	76780 MW	93480 TQ	USBLS	5/07
	New Mexico	Y	53960 FQ	65690 MW	90890 TQ	USBLS	5/07
	Albuquerque MSA, NM	Y	57970 FQ	74270 MW	97720 TQ	USBLS	5/07
	New York	Y	50160 FQ	67510 MW	81810 TQ	USBLS	5/07
	Albany-Schenectady-Troy MSA, NY	Y	43830 FQ	52800 MW	65410 TQ	USBLS	5/07
	Binghamton MSA, NY	Y	54710 FQ	67440 MW	81160 TQ	USBLS	5/07
	Buffalo-Niagara Falls MSA, NY	Y	46310 FQ	56170 MW	67780 TQ	USBLS	5/07
	Nassau-Suffolk PMSA, NY	Y	45690 FQ	54180 MW	73060 TQ	USBLS	5/07
	New York-Northern New Jersey-Long Island MSA, NY-NJ-PA	Y	59510 FQ	75250 MW	92300 TQ	USBLS	5/07
	Syracuse MSA, NY	Y	47640 FQ	54050 MW	71030 TQ	USBLS	5/07
	Utica-Rome MSA, NY	Y	41570 FQ	44790 MW	48290 TQ	USBLS	5/07
	North Carolina	Y	46150 FQ	56770 MW	73100 TQ	USBLS	5/07
	Charlotte-Gastonia-Concord MSA, NC-SC	Y	44920 FQ	52780 MW	66880 TQ	USBLS	5/07
	Raleigh-Cary MSA, NC	Y	51900 FQ	67540 MW	82130 TQ	USBLS	5/07
	North Dakota	Y	52450 FQ	58650 MW	64910 TQ	USBLS	5/07
	Ohio	Y	50720 FQ	66590 MW	82050 TQ	USBLS	5/07

AE	Average entry wage	AW	Average wage paid	FQ	First quartile wage	LO Lowest wage paid	MTC Median total compensation	TCC Total cash compensation
AER	Average entry range	AWR	Average wage range	H	Hourly	LR Low end range	MW Median wage paid	TQ Third quartile wage
AEX	Average experienced wage	AXR	Average experienced range	HI	Highest wage paid	M Monthly	MWR Median wage range	W Weekly
ATC	Average total compensation	D	Daily	HR	High end range	MCC Median cash compensation	S See annotated source	Y Yearly

Occupation/Type/Industry	Location	Per	Low	Mid	High	Source	Date
Logistician	Cincinnati-Middletown MSA, OH-KY-IN	Y	46290 FQ	59890 MW	75140 TQ	USBLS	5/07
	Cleveland-Elyria-Mentor MSA, OH	Y	52670 FQ	67840 MW	86210 TQ	USBLS	5/07
	Columbus MSA, OH	Y	49950 FQ	64530 MW	79860 TQ	USBLS	5/07
	Dayton MSA, OH	Y	65420 FQ	78410 MW	92910 TQ	USBLS	5/07
	Oklahoma	Y	51800 FQ	62080 MW	75070 TQ	USBLS	5/07
	Oklahoma City MSA, OK	Y	53430 FQ	62680 MW	75150 TQ	USBLS	5/07
	Tulsa MSA, OK	Y	44720 FQ	58340 MW	72660 TQ	USBLS	5/07
	Oregon	H	24.32 FQ	28.97 MW	35.50 TQ	ORBLS	5/08
	Portland-Vancouver-Beaverton MSA, OR-WA	Y	50850 FQ	60200 MW	73760 TQ	USBLS	5/07
	Pennsylvania	Y	49880 FQ	64280 MW	77770 TQ	USBLS	5/07
	Allentown-Bethlehem-Easton MSA, PA-NJ	Y	44800 FQ	53820 MW	74190 TQ	USBLS	5/07
	Philadelphia-Camden-Wilmington MSA, PA-NJ-DE-MD	Y	53110 FQ	66660 MW	80310 TQ	USBLS	5/07
	Pittsburgh MSA, PA	Y	44820 FQ	57940 MW	72160 TQ	USBLS	5/07
	Rhode Island	Y	51860 FQ	63770 MW	86670 TQ	USBLS	5/07
	Providence-Fall River-Warwick MSA, RI-MA	Y	51290 FQ	63290 MW	86270 TQ	USBLS	5/07
	South Carolina	Y	48150 FQ	60700 MW	75160 TQ	USBLS	5/07
	Charleston-North Charleston MSA, SC	Y	51570 FQ	66110 MW	81020 TQ	USBLS	5/07
	Columbia MSA, SC	Y	44700 FQ	55260 MW	67610 TQ	USBLS	5/07
	South Dakota	Y	52521 FQ	61084 MW	72681 TQ	SDBLS	7/08-9/08
	Tennessee	Y	39930 FQ	53500 MW	68260 TQ	USBLS	5/07
	Memphis MSA, TN-MS-AR	Y	46760 FQ	58080 MW	69730 TQ	USBLS	5/07
	Nashville-Davidson-Murfreesboro MSA, TN	Y	42760 FQ	53630 MW	66720 TQ	USBLS	5/07
	Texas	Y	33240 FQ	52350 MW	73520 TQ	USBLS	5/07
	Austin-Round Rock MSA, TX	Y	29970 FQ	51850 MW	75430 TQ	USBLS	5/07
	Dallas-Fort Worth-Arlington MSA, TX	Y	44280 FQ	57600 MW	76610 TQ	USBLS	5/07
	El Paso MSA, TX	Y	42620 FQ	52300 MW	71400 TQ	USBLS	5/07
	Houston-Sugar Land-Baytown MSA, TX	Y	43290 FQ	58600 MW	79350 TQ	USBLS	5/07
	San Antonio MSA, TX	Y	27300 FQ	29760 MW	44700 TQ	USBLS	5/07
	Utah	Y	51730 FQ	62990 MW	75030 TQ	USBLS	5/07
	Salt Lake City MSA, UT	Y	48510 FQ	59610 MW	70980 TQ	USBLS	5/07
	Virginia	Y	53550 FQ	69910 MW	90030 TQ	USBLS	5/07
	Charlottesville MSA, VA	Y	42670 FQ	55450 MW	82410 TQ	USBLS	5/07
	Richmond MSA, VA	Y	54810 FQ	67950 MW	84420 TQ	USBLS	5/07
	Virginia Beach-Norfolk-Newport News MSA, VA-NC	Y	46470 FQ	59530 MW	76260 TQ	USBLS	5/07
	Washington	H	26.78 FQ	31.48 MW	37.05 TQ	WABLS	3/08
	Seattle-Tacoma-Bellevue MSA, WA	Y	55340 FQ	64610 MW	75200 TQ	USBLS	5/07
	Spokane MSA, WA	Y	47760 FQ	55630 MW	64030 TQ	USBLS	5/07
	West Virginia	Y	43270 FQ	58711 MW	68541 TQ	WVBLS	7/08-9/08
	Wisconsin	Y	48920 FQ	60020 MW	72690 TQ	USBLS	5/07
	Appleton MSA, WI	Y	49660 FQ	57600 MW	69260 TQ	USBLS	5/07
	Milwaukee-Waukesha-West Allis MSA, WI	Y	49070 FQ	61500 MW	73290 TQ	USBLS	5/07
	Wyoming	Y	54423 FQ	63126 MW	79042 TQ	WYBLS	9/08
	Puerto Rico	Y	41980 FQ	51920 MW	70370 TQ	USBLS	5/07
	San Juan-Caguas-Guaynabo MSA, PR	Y	40540 FQ	54940 MW	75790 TQ	USBLS	5/07
Lottery Game Security Specialist	Ohio	H	15.09 LO		17.03 HI	ODAS	2008
Lumberjack	United States	Y		32124 AW		WSJ09	2009
Machine Feeder and Offbearer	Alabama	Y	17730 FQ	22450 MW	28590 TQ	USBLS	5/07
	Birmingham-Hoover MSA, AL	Y	17590 FQ	22440 MW	32210 TQ	USBLS	5/07
	Alaska	Y	18160 FQ	20260 MW	24710 TQ	USBLS	5/07
	Arizona	Y	18700 FQ	23790 MW	28810 TQ	USBLS	5/07
	Phoenix-Mesa-Scottsdale MSA, AZ	Y	18730 FQ	24690 MW	29210 TQ	USBLS	5/07
	Tucson MSA, AZ	Y	20720 FQ	22610 MW	24540 TQ	USBLS	5/07
	Arkansas	Y	20040 FQ	23730 MW	28330 TQ	USBLS	5/07

AE	Average entry wage	**AW**	Average wage paid	**FQ**	First quartile wage	**LO**	Lowest wage paid	**MTC**	Median total compensation	**TCC**	Total cash compensation
AER	Average entry range	**AWR**	Average wage range	**H**	Hourly	**LR**	Low end range	**MW**	Median wage paid	**TQ**	Third quartile wage
AEX	Average experienced wage	**AXR**	Average experienced range	**HI**	Highest wage paid			**MWR**	Median wage range	**W**	Weekly
ATC	Average total compensation	**D**	Daily	**HR**	High end range	**M**	Monthly	**S**	See annotated source	**Y**	Yearly
						MCC	Median cash compensation				

Occupation/Type/Industry	Location	Per	Low	Mid	High	Source	Date
Machine Feeder and Offbearer	Little Rock-North Little Rock MSA, AR	Y	20870 FQ	24530 MW	27690 TQ	USBLS	5/07
	California	H	9.00 FQ	10.92 MW	14.51 TQ	CABLS	1/08-3/08
	Los Angeles-Long Beach-Glendale PMSA, CA	H	8.79 FQ	10.25 MW	12.89 TQ	CABLS	1/08-3/08
	Oakland-Fremont-Hayward MSA, CA	H	9.62 FQ	11.34 MW	13.70 TQ	CABLS	1/08-3/08
	Riverside-San Bernardino-Ontario MSA, CA	H	9.26 FQ	11.09 MW	14.01 TQ	CABLS	1/08-3/08
	Sacramento-Arden Arcade-Roseville MSA, CA	H	8.67 FQ	9.64 MW	11.09 TQ	CABLS	1/08-3/08
	San Diego-Carlsbad-San Marcos MSA, CA	H	8.92 FQ	10.83 MW	13.70 TQ	CABLS	1/08-3/08
	San Francisco-San Mateo-Redwood PMSA, CA	H	9.14 FQ	10.84 MW	12.87 TQ	CABLS	1/08-3/08
	San Jose-Sunnyvale-Santa Clara MSA, CA	H	10.58 FQ	14.81 MW	20.68 TQ	CABLS	1/08-3/08
	Santa Ana-Anaheim-Irvine PMSA, CA	Y	18240 FQ	21360 MW	25940 TQ	USBLS	5/07
	Colorado	Y	17440 FQ	22820 MW	32580 TQ	USBLS	5/07
	Denver-Aurora MSA, CO	Y	16360 FQ	20960 MW	26210 TQ	USBLS	5/07
	Connecticut	H	9.38 AE	11.64 MW		CTBLS	1/08-3/08
	Bridgeport-Stamford-Norwalk MSA, CT	Y	21020 FQ	25410 MW	29880 TQ	USBLS	5/07
	Hartford-West Hartford-East Hartford MSA, CT	Y	21070 FQ	23970 MW	30950 TQ	USBLS	5/07
	New Haven MSA, CT	Y	19070 FQ	22130 MW	27130 TQ	USBLS	5/07
	Washington-Arlington-Alexandria MSA, DC-VA-MD-WV	Y	18010 FQ	21780 MW	32110 TQ	USBLS	5/07
	Florida	Y	18310 FQ	22300 MW	28480 TQ	USBLS	5/07
	Fort Lauderdale-Pompano Beach-Deerfield Beach PMSA, FL	Y	16770 FQ	18380 MW	22020 TQ	USBLS	5/07
	Jacksonville MSA, FL	Y	21960 FQ	25530 MW	32230 TQ	USBLS	5/07
	Miami-Fort Lauderdale-Miami Beach MSA, FL	Y	17200 FQ	19380 MW	23820 TQ	USBLS	5/07
	Orlando-Kissimmee MSA, FL	Y	17430 FQ	22150 MW	30320 TQ	USBLS	5/07
	Tampa-St. Petersburg-Clearwater MSA, FL	Y	17390 FQ	19920 MW	24500 TQ	USBLS	5/07
	West Palm Beach-Boca Raton-Boynton Beach PMSA, FL	Y	17380 FQ	19090 MW	22140 TQ	USBLS	5/07
	Georgia	Y	17960 FQ	22070 MW	27470 TQ	USBLS	5/07
	Atlanta-Sandy Springs-Marietta MSA, GA	Y	19320 FQ	23790 MW	28920 TQ	USBLS	5/07
	Hawaii	Y	18570 FQ	24330 MW	27880 TQ	USBLS	5/07
	Honolulu MSA, HI	Y	18330 FQ	24430 MW	28070 TQ	USBLS	5/07
	Idaho	Y	19260 FQ	24390 MW	30110 TQ	USBLS	5/07
	Boise City-Nampa MSA, ID	Y	13670 FQ	20380 MW	29670 TQ	USBLS	5/07
	Illinois	Y	18730 FQ	24960 MW	32490 TQ	USBLS	5/07
	Chicago-Naperville-Joliet MSA, IL-IN-WI	Y	18500 FQ	24200 MW	32300 TQ	USBLS	5/07
	Indiana	Y	18850 FQ	22890 MW	28990 TQ	USBLS	5/07
	Evansville MSA, IN-KY	Y	21040 FQ	23430 MW	29920 TQ	USBLS	5/07
	Gary PMSA, IN	Y	19580 FQ	24160 MW	31240 TQ	USBLS	5/07
	Indianapolis-Carmel MSA, IN	Y	22290 FQ	30620 MW	37260 TQ	USBLS	5/07
	Iowa	Y	17770 FQ	24090 MW	28630 TQ	USBLS	5/07
	Cedar Rapids MSA, IA	Y	31010 FQ	36500 MW	42100 TQ	USBLS	5/07
	Des Moines-West Des Moines MSA, IA	Y	14190 FQ	15470 MW	26170 TQ	USBLS	5/07
	Kansas	Y	20240 FQ	26090 MW	32840 TQ	USBLS	5/07
	Wichita MSA, KS	Y	19210 FQ	22650 MW	27800 TQ	USBLS	5/07
	Kentucky	Y	20250 FQ	23881 MW	29834 TQ	KYBLS	2008
	Louisville-Jefferson County MSA, KY-IN	Y	20090 FQ	24000 MW	29370 TQ	USBLS	5/07
	Owensboro MSA, KY	Y	32130 FQ	35960 MW	40610 TQ	USBLS	5/07
	Louisiana	H	7.98 FQ	11.24 MW	14.00 TQ	LABLS	1/08-3/08
	Lafayette MSA, LA	Y	12490 FQ	13930 MW	15420 TQ	USBLS	5/07
	New Orleans-Metairie-Kenner MSA, LA	Y	21330 FQ	26740 MW	29660 TQ	USBLS	5/07
	Maine	Y	23430 FQ	26820 MW	29840 TQ	USBLS	5/07

AE Average entry wage	**AW** Average wage paid	**FQ** First quartile wage	**LO** Lowest wage paid	**MTC** Median total compensation	**TCC** Total cash compensation
AER Average entry range	**AWR** Average wage range	**H** Hourly	**LR** Low end range	**MW** Median wage paid	**TQ** Third quartile wage
AEX Average experienced wage	**AXR** Average experienced range	**HI** Highest wage paid	**M** Monthly	**MWR** Median wage range	**W** Weekly
ATC Average total compensation	**D** Daily	**HR** High end range	**MCC** Median cash compensation	**S** See annotated source	**Y** Yearly

Occupation/Type/Industry	Location	Per	Low	Mid	High	Source	Date
Machine Feeder and Offbearer	Portland-South Portland- Biddeford MSA, ME	Y	24990 FQ	27200 MW	29350 TQ	USBLS	5/07
	Maryland	Y		27500 MW		MDBLS	3/08
	Baltimore-Towson MSA, MD	Y	22130 FQ	26580 MW	30370 TQ	USBLS	5/07
	Bethesda-Gaithersburg- Frederick PMSA, MD	Y	25560 FQ	30270 MW	35820 TQ	USBLS	5/07
	Massachusetts	Y	20690 FQ	25940 MW	32810 TQ	USBLS	5/07
	Boston-Cambridge-Quincy NECTA, MA	Y	20590 FQ	27220 MW	33000 TQ	USBLS	5/07
	Lynn-Peabody-Salem NECTA, MA	Y	19840 FQ	22670 MW	31230 TQ	USBLS	5/07
	Worcester MSA, MA-CT	Y	18760 FQ	23950 MW	31960 TQ	USBLS	5/07
	Michigan	Y	21100 FQ	26230 MW	31440 TQ	USBLS	5/07
	Detroit-Warren-Livonia MSA, MI	Y	22210 FQ	26720 MW	31140 TQ	USBLS	5/07
	Grand Rapids-Wyoming MSA, MI	Y	17780 FQ	20180 MW	25090 TQ	USBLS	5/07
	Warren-Troy-Farmington Hills PMSA, MI	Y	21150 FQ	25150 MW	29890 TQ	USBLS	5/07
	Minnesota	Y	26757 FQ	32021 MW	39085 TQ	MNBLS	10/08-12/08
	Duluth-Superior MSA, MN-WI	Y	22866 FQ	42945 MW	51830 TQ	MNBLS	10/08-12/08
	Minneapolis-Saint Paul MSA, MN-WI	Y	27943 FQ	34008 MW	40823 TQ	MNBLS	10/08-12/08
	Rochester MSA, MN	Y	23107 FQ	27224 MW	30586 TQ	MNBLS	10/08-12/08
	Mississippi	Y	19550 FQ	23650 MW	28430 TQ	USBLS	5/07
	Hattiesburg MSA, MS	Y	17010 FQ	18160 MW	19310 TQ	USBLS	5/07
	Jackson MSA, MS	Y	13400 FQ	17330 MW	24750 TQ	USBLS	5/07
	Missouri	Y	20900 FQ	27570 MW	34630 TQ	USBLS	5/07
	Kansas City MSA, MO-KS	Y	24680 FQ	30540 MW	37250 TQ	USBLS	5/07
	St. Louis MSA, MO-IL	Y	19720 FQ	24620 MW	32780 TQ	USBLS	5/07
	Montana	Y	22020 FQ	32950 MW	36350 TQ	USBLS	5/07
	Nebraska	Y	20380 FQ	24750 MW	29410 TQ	USBLS	5/07
	Omaha-Council Bluffs MSA, NE-IA	Y	19000 FQ	21730 MW	24730 TQ	USBLS	5/07
	Nevada	H	9.71 FQ	13.39 MW	16.94 TQ	NVBLS	5/08
	Las Vegas-Paradise MSA, NV	H	10.70 FQ	14.52 MW	19.88 TQ	NVBLS	5/08
	New Hampshire	H	10.33 AE	13.56 MW	15.29 AEX	NHBLS	6/08
	New Jersey	Y	16910 FQ	20660 MW	24630 TQ	USBLS	5/07
	Camden PMSA, NJ	Y	19210 FQ	21620 MW	24400 TQ	USBLS	5/07
	Edison PMSA, NJ	Y	15740 FQ	18410 MW	22350 TQ	USBLS	5/07
	Newark-Union PMSA, NJ-PA	Y	15960 FQ	20380 MW	24970 TQ	USBLS	5/07
	New Mexico	Y	15980 FQ	26280 MW	29130 TQ	USBLS	5/07
	Albuquerque MSA, NM	Y	16650 FQ	27060 MW	29740 TQ	USBLS	5/07
	New York	Y	18060 FQ	23400 MW	32300 TQ	USBLS	5/07
	Albany-Schenectady-Troy MSA, NY	Y	26590 FQ	34120 MW	37760 TQ	USBLS	5/07
	Buffalo-Niagara Falls MSA, NY	Y	20090 FQ	25210 MW	50460 TQ	USBLS	5/07
	Nassau-Suffolk PMSA, NY	Y	21290 FQ	28880 MW	38760 TQ	USBLS	5/07
	New York-Northern New Jersey-Long Island MSA, NY- NJ-PA	Y	16000 FQ	20390 MW	26180 TQ	USBLS	5/07
	North Carolina	Y	19050 FQ	23240 MW	28570 TQ	USBLS	5/07
	Asheville MSA, NC	Y	18960 FQ	21080 MW	23160 TQ	USBLS	5/07
	Charlotte-Gastonia-Concord MSA, NC-SC	Y	18130 FQ	21840 MW	27430 TQ	USBLS	5/07
	Raleigh-Cary MSA, NC	Y	16060 FQ	19380 MW	26500 TQ	USBLS	5/07
	North Dakota	Y	21600 FQ	25520 MW	28950 TQ	USBLS	5/07
	Ohio	Y	20560 FQ	24610 MW	33040 TQ	USBLS	5/07
	Cincinnati-Middletown MSA, OH-KY-IN	Y	21610 FQ	24200 MW	29230 TQ	USBLS	5/07
	Cleveland-Elyria-Mentor MSA, OH	Y	20770 FQ	26220 MW	48400 TQ	USBLS	5/07
	Columbus MSA, OH	Y	23170 FQ	35660 MW	45020 TQ	USBLS	5/07
	Dayton MSA, OH	Y	21020 FQ	23970 MW	28640 TQ	USBLS	5/07
	Oklahoma	Y	19590 FQ	23350 MW	28330 TQ	USBLS	5/07
	Oklahoma City MSA, OK	Y	18560 FQ	21970 MW	25810 TQ	USBLS	5/07
	Tulsa MSA, OK	Y	17920 FQ	21140 MW	26930 TQ	USBLS	5/07
	Oregon	H	10.16 FQ	12.47 MW	15.94 TQ	ORBLS	5/08
	Portland-Vancouver-Beaverton MSA, OR-WA	Y	19130 FQ	22480 MW	28310 TQ	USBLS	5/07
	Pennsylvania	Y	20040 FQ	25380 MW	31160 TQ	USBLS	5/07

AE	Average entry wage	AW	Average wage paid	FQ	First quartile wage
AER	Average entry range	AWR	Average wage range	H	Hourly
AEX	Average experienced wage	AXR	Average experienced range	HI	Highest wage paid
ATC	Average total compensation	D	Daily	HR	High end range

LO	Lowest wage paid	MTC	Median total compensation	TCC	Total cash compensation
LR	Low end range	MW	Median wage paid	TQ	Third quartile wage
M	Monthly	MWR	Median wage range	W	Weekly
MCC	Median cash compensation	S	See annotated source	Y	Yearly

Occupation/Type/Industry	Location	Per	Low	Mid	High	Source	Date
Machine Feeder and Offbearer	Allentown-Bethlehem-Easton MSA, PA-NJ	Y	21110 FQ	24570 MW	30880 TQ	USBLS	5/07
	Philadelphia-Camden-Wilmington MSA, PA-NJ-DE-MD	Y	18860 FQ	22430 MW	27940 TQ	USBLS	5/07
	Pittsburgh MSA, PA	Y	20170 FQ	24090 MW	31510 TQ	USBLS	5/07
	Rhode Island	Y	18560 FQ	24760 MW	32990 TQ	USBLS	5/07
	Providence-Fall River-Warwick MSA, RI-MA	Y	18380 FQ	23180 MW	32110 TQ	USBLS	5/07
	South Carolina	Y	19950 FQ	24860 MW	29480 TQ	USBLS	5/07
	Charleston-North Charleston MSA, SC	Y	24210 FQ	27870 MW	32020 TQ	USBLS	5/07
	Columbia MSA, SC	Y	19290 FQ	24320 MW	28540 TQ	USBLS	5/07
	Spartanburg MSA, SC	Y	20220 FQ	22620 MW	24870 TQ	USBLS	5/07
	South Dakota	Y	18662 FQ	21376 MW	24846 TQ	SDBLS	7/08-9/08
	Sioux Falls MSA, SD	Y	19540 FQ	22845 MW	26246 TQ	SDBLS	7/08-9/08
	Tennessee	Y	17460 FQ	22050 MW	26860 TQ	USBLS	5/07
	Kingsport-Bristol-Bristol MSA, TN-VA	Y	12570 FQ	13870 MW	19400 TQ	USBLS	5/07
	Memphis MSA, TN-MS-AR	Y	14340 FQ	18310 MW	26490 TQ	USBLS	5/07
	Nashville-Davidson-Murfreesboro MSA, TN	Y	19470 FQ	23880 MW	27740 TQ	USBLS	5/07
	Texas	Y	18990 FQ	25120 MW	30810 TQ	USBLS	5/07
	Austin-Round Rock MSA, TX	Y	24010 FQ	27900 MW	32430 TQ	USBLS	5/07
	Dallas-Fort Worth-Arlington MSA, TX	Y	20570 FQ	25490 MW	31860 TQ	USBLS	5/07
	El Paso MSA, TX	Y	14630 FQ	19960 MW	26540 TQ	USBLS	5/07
	Houston-Sugar Land-Baytown MSA, TX	Y	17610 FQ	22390 MW	28710 TQ	USBLS	5/07
	San Antonio MSA, TX	Y	23320 FQ	29640 MW	35250 TQ	USBLS	5/07
	Utah	Y	20840 FQ	25100 MW	29830 TQ	USBLS	5/07
	Salt Lake City MSA, UT	Y	19890 FQ	23080 MW	27560 TQ	USBLS	5/07
	Vermont	Y	19380 FQ	21490 MW	24660 TQ	USBLS	5/07
	Burlington-South Burlington MSA, VT	Y	17800 FQ	19530 MW	23780 TQ	USBLS	5/07
	Virginia	Y	17890 FQ	21140 MW	25840 TQ	USBLS	5/07
	Richmond MSA, VA	Y	18560 FQ	22160 MW	27970 TQ	USBLS	5/07
	Virginia Beach-Norfolk-Newport News MSA, VA-NC	Y	18060 FQ	21480 MW	26430 TQ	USBLS	5/07
	Washington	H	9.94 FQ	12.48 MW	15.82 TQ	WABLS	3/08
	Seattle-Tacoma-Bellevue MSA, WA	Y	22210 FQ	27700 MW	34140 TQ	USBLS	5/07
	West Virginia	Y	14372 FQ	16443 MW	20908 TQ	WVBLS	7/08-9/08
	Wisconsin	Y	22230 FQ	26900 MW	32600 TQ	USBLS	5/07
	Appleton MSA, WI	Y	22860 FQ	26980 MW	31430 TQ	USBLS	5/07
	Milwaukee-Waukesha-West Allis MSA, WI	Y	22750 FQ	27680 MW	34350 TQ	USBLS	5/07
	Wyoming	Y	26015 FQ	54454 MW	61840 TQ	WYBLS	9/08
	Puerto Rico	Y	13460 FQ	16490 MW	19200 TQ	USBLS	5/07
	San Juan-Caguas-Guaynabo MSA, PR	Y	13240 FQ	15780 MW	18820 TQ	USBLS	5/07
Machinist	Alabama	Y	27420 FQ	34670 MW	40940 TQ	USBLS	5/07
	Birmingham-Hoover MSA, AL	Y	30660 FQ	36510 MW	45700 TQ	USBLS	5/07
	Huntsville MSA, AL	Y	29710 FQ	36090 MW	43190 TQ	USBLS	5/07
	Alaska	Y	41400 FQ	50680 MW	67450 TQ	USBLS	5/07
	Arizona	Y	27280 FQ	35320 MW	43450 TQ	USBLS	5/07
	Flagstaff MSA, AZ	Y	27980 FQ	37690 MW	50010 TQ	USBLS	5/07
	Phoenix-Mesa-Scottsdale MSA, AZ	Y	26960 FQ	35130 MW	43410 TQ	USBLS	5/07
	Tucson MSA, AZ	Y	30480 FQ	36540 MW	43430 TQ	USBLS	5/07
	Arkansas	Y	26350 FQ	32400 MW	38820 TQ	USBLS	5/07
	Little Rock-North Little Rock MSA, AR	Y	27570 FQ	33120 MW	44990 TQ	USBLS	5/07
	California	H	13.58 FQ	17.96 MW	23.31 TQ	CABLS	1/08-3/08
	Los Angeles-Long Beach-Glendale PMSA, CA	H	12.43 FQ	16.59 MW	21.93 TQ	CABLS	1/08-3/08
	Oakland-Fremont-Hayward MSA, CA	H	16.69 FQ	21.45 MW	27.78 TQ	CABLS	1/08-3/08
	Riverside-San Bernardino-Ontario MSA, CA	H	11.74 FQ	15.87 MW	20.23 TQ	CABLS	1/08-3/08

AE Average entry wage	**AW** Average wage paid	**FQ** First quartile wage	**LO** Lowest wage paid	**MTC** Median total compensation	**TCC** Total cash compensation
AER Average entry range	**AWR** Average wage range	**H** Hourly	**LR** Low end range	**MW** Median wage paid	**TQ** Third quartile wage
AEX Average experienced wage	**AXR** Average experienced range	**HI** Highest wage paid	**M** Monthly	**MWR** Median wage range	**W** Weekly
ATC Average total compensation	**D** Daily	**HR** High end range	**MCC** Median cash compensation	**S** See annotated source	**Y** Yearly

Occupation/Type/Industry	Location	Per	Low	Mid	High	Source	Date
Machinist	Sacramento-Arden Arcade-Roseville MSA, CA	H	13.51 FQ	18.11 MW	23.40 TQ	CABLS	1/08-3/08
	San Diego-Carlsbad-San Marcos MSA, CA	H	15.00 FQ	19.15 MW	23.90 TQ	CABLS	1/08-3/08
	San Francisco-San Mateo-Redwood PMSA, CA	H	17.34 FQ	22.27 MW	27.67 TQ	CABLS	1/08-3/08
	San Jose-Sunnyvale-Santa Clara MSA, CA	H	15.77 FQ	20.63 MW	26.61 TQ	CABLS	1/08-3/08
	Santa Ana-Anaheim-Irvine PMSA, CA	Y	26150 FQ	35690 MW	46410 TQ	USBLS	5/07
	Santa Rosa-Petaluma MSA, CA	H	16.48 FQ	22.15 MW	26.69 TQ	CABLS	1/08-3/08
	Colorado	Y	29670 FQ	37130 MW	45770 TQ	USBLS	5/07
	Denver-Aurora MSA, CO	Y	28710 FQ	37200 MW	45770 TQ	USBLS	5/07
	Pueblo MSA, CO	Y	29410 FQ	33870 MW	37240 TQ	USBLS	5/07
	Connecticut	H	12.46 AE	18.42 MW		CTBLS	1/08-3/08
	Bridgeport-Stamford-Norwalk MSA, CT	Y	28640 FQ	38390 MW	49540 TQ	USBLS	5/07
	Hartford-West Hartford-East Hartford MSA, CT	Y	33590 FQ	40420 MW	47070 TQ	USBLS	5/07
	Delaware	Y	38580 FQ	45790 MW	56540 TQ	USBLS	5/07
	Dover MSA, DE	Y	24150 FQ	29910 MW	39820 TQ	USBLS	5/07
	Wilmington PMSA, DE-MD-NJ	Y	41160 FQ	47260 MW	56720 TQ	USBLS	5/07
	District of Columbia	Y	55300 FQ	65770 MW	74110 TQ	USBLS	5/07
	Washington-Arlington-Alexandria MSA, DC-VA-MD-WV	Y	33810 FQ	44970 MW	56830 TQ	USBLS	5/07
	Florida	Y	25250 FQ	33390 MW	40580 TQ	USBLS	5/07
	Fort Lauderdale-Pompano Beach-Deerfield Beach PMSA, FL	Y	26620 FQ	33280 MW	41820 TQ	USBLS	5/07
	Jacksonville MSA, FL	Y	31000 FQ	39460 MW	45920 TQ	USBLS	5/07
	Miami-Fort Lauderdale-Miami Beach MSA, FL	Y	23430 FQ	31540 MW	40270 TQ	USBLS	5/07
	Orlando-Kissimmee MSA, FL	Y	29100 FQ	34890 MW	40610 TQ	USBLS	5/07
	Tallahassee MSA, FL	Y	20570 FQ	23460 MW	30460 TQ	USBLS	5/07
	Tampa-St. Petersburg-Clearwater MSA, FL	Y	24820 FQ	33180 MW	38160 TQ	USBLS	5/07
	West Palm Beach-Boca Raton-Boynton Beach PMSA, FL	Y	19740 FQ	33030 MW	40530 TQ	USBLS	5/07
	Georgia	Y	21020 FQ	29840 MW	38570 TQ	USBLS	5/07
	Athens-Clarke County MSA, GA	Y	26110 FQ	32580 MW	39600 TQ	USBLS	5/07
	Atlanta-Sandy Springs-Marietta MSA, GA	Y	22910 FQ	32510 MW	40650 TQ	USBLS	5/07
	Hawaii	Y	33920 FQ	49270 MW	60520 TQ	USBLS	5/07
	Honolulu MSA, HI	Y	34420 FQ	51330 MW	61300 TQ	USBLS	5/07
	Idaho	Y	24160 FQ	33040 MW	40270 TQ	USBLS	5/07
	Boise City-Nampa MSA, ID	Y	20490 FQ	31000 MW	37660 TQ	USBLS	5/07
	Illinois	Y	27210 FQ	35540 MW	45370 TQ	USBLS	5/07
	Chicago-Naperville-Joliet MSA, IL-IN-WI	Y	26670 FQ	35060 MW	45130 TQ	USBLS	5/07
	Indiana	Y	27990 FQ	35470 MW	46350 TQ	USBLS	5/07
	Fort Wayne MSA, IN	Y	29670 FQ	33750 MW	38240 TQ	USBLS	5/07
	Gary PMSA, IN	Y	34640 FQ	39840 MW	47920 TQ	USBLS	5/07
	Indianapolis-Carmel MSA, IN	Y	27110 FQ	36950 MW	54060 TQ	USBLS	5/07
	Iowa	Y	26970 FQ	33690 MW	39410 TQ	USBLS	5/07
	Des Moines-West Des Moines MSA, IA	Y	33340 FQ	37500 MW	44140 TQ	USBLS	5/07
	Dubuque MSA, IA	Y	30540 FQ	34310 MW	37620 TQ	USBLS	5/07
	Kansas	Y	25720 FQ	31120 MW	37200 TQ	USBLS	5/07
	Wichita MSA, KS	Y	25100 FQ	30960 MW	38910 TQ	USBLS	5/07
	Kentucky	Y	25000 FQ	33667 MW	43606 TQ	KYBLS	2008
	Louisville-Jefferson County MSA, KY-IN	Y	31520 FQ	40370 MW	46270 TQ	USBLS	5/07
	Owensboro MSA, KY	Y	19210 FQ	24630 MW	35470 TQ	USBLS	5/07
	Louisiana	H	14.72 FQ	18.05 MW	21.66 TQ	LABLS	1/08-3/08
	Baton Rouge MSA, LA	Y	36290 FQ	41270 MW	46720 TQ	USBLS	5/07
	New Orleans-Metairie-Kenner MSA, LA	Y	33690 FQ	41780 MW	51050 TQ	USBLS	5/07
	Maine	Y	33360 FQ	41560 MW	48290 TQ	USBLS	5/07

AE	Average entry wage	AW	Average wage paid	FQ	First quartile wage	LO	Lowest wage paid	MTC	Median total compensation	TCC	Total cash compensation
AER	Average entry range	AWR	Average wage range	H	Hourly	LR	Low end range	MW	Median wage paid	TQ	Third quartile wage
AEX	Average experienced wage	AXR	Average experienced range	HI	Highest wage paid	M	Monthly	MWR	Median wage range	W	Weekly
ATC	Average total compensation	D	Daily	HR	High end range	MCC	Median cash compensation	S	See annotated source	Y	Yearly

Occupation/Type/Industry	Location	Per	Low	Mid	High	Source	Date
Machinist	Portland-South Portland-Biddeford MSA, ME	Y	32890 FQ	38970 MW	47820 TQ	USBLS	5/07
	Maryland	Y		43200 MW		MDBLS	3/08
	Baltimore-Towson MSA, MD	Y	30680 FQ	42910 MW	51630 TQ	USBLS	5/07
	Bethesda-Gaithersburg-Frederick PMSA, MD	Y	31340 FQ	42590 MW	55120 TQ	USBLS	5/07
	Cumberland MSA, MD-WV	Y	30290 FQ	36050 MW	42010 TQ	USBLS	5/07
	Massachusetts	Y	32780 FQ	40360 MW	48580 TQ	USBLS	5/07
	Boston-Cambridge-Quincy NECTA, MA	Y	31820 FQ	40480 MW	50090 TQ	USBLS	5/07
	Worcester MSA, MA-CT	Y	34060 FQ	40550 MW	47910 TQ	USBLS	5/07
	Michigan	Y	29470 FQ	37320 MW	47380 TQ	USBLS	5/07
	Detroit-Warren-Livonia MSA, MI	Y	32450 FQ	40060 MW	49480 TQ	USBLS	5/07
	Grand Rapids-Wyoming MSA, MI	Y	26880 FQ	33810 MW	43830 TQ	USBLS	5/07
	Warren-Troy-Farmington Hills PMSA, MI	Y	31800 FQ	39300 MW	47410 TQ	USBLS	5/07
	Minnesota	Y	32199 FQ	40513 MW	49242 TQ	MNBLS	10/08-12/08
	Duluth-Superior MSA, MN-WI	Y	32676 FQ	39570 MW	46795 TQ	MNBLS	10/08-12/08
	Minneapolis-Saint Paul MSA, MN-WI	Y	33132 FQ	42223 MW	50838 TQ	MNBLS	10/08-12/08
	Rochester MSA, MN	Y	29056 FQ	34840 MW	43962 TQ	MNBLS	10/08-12/08
	Mississippi	Y	31930 FQ	35410 MW	38810 TQ	USBLS	5/07
	Jackson MSA, MS	Y	34320 FQ	36780 MW	39230 TQ	USBLS	5/07
	Missouri	Y	25300 FQ	31080 MW	41170 TQ	USBLS	5/07
	Kansas City MSA, MO-KS	Y	27280 FQ	34640 MW	43690 TQ	USBLS	5/07
	St. Louis MSA, MO-IL	Y	31790 FQ	38710 MW	48930 TQ	USBLS	5/07
	Montana	Y	27940 FQ	33600 MW	38210 TQ	USBLS	5/07
	Billings MSA, MT	Y	28620 FQ	33660 MW	38080 TQ	USBLS	5/07
	Nebraska	Y	26370 FQ	31920 MW	38760 TQ	USBLS	5/07
	Omaha-Council Bluffs MSA, NE-IA	Y	26290 FQ	31510 MW	36770 TQ	USBLS	5/07
	Nevada	H	15.81 FQ	19.22 MW	23.49 TQ	NVBLS	5/08
	Las Vegas-Paradise MSA, NV	H	15.31 FQ	18.67 MW	22.78 TQ	NVBLS	5/08
	New Hampshire	H	13.47 AE	18.29 MW	21.69 AEX	NHBLS	6/08
	Manchester MSA, NH	Y	35560 FQ	47640 MW	55390 TQ	USBLS	5/07
	Nashua NECTA, NH-MA	Y	30460 FQ	36300 MW	46260 TQ	USBLS	5/07
	New Jersey	Y	32390 FQ	39740 MW	48490 TQ	USBLS	5/07
	Camden PMSA, NJ	Y	38180 FQ	44600 MW	54590 TQ	USBLS	5/07
	Edison PMSA, NJ	Y	32760 FQ	40880 MW	51240 TQ	USBLS	5/07
	Newark-Union PMSA, NJ-PA	Y	30730 FQ	37910 MW	45910 TQ	USBLS	5/07
	New Mexico	Y	29420 FQ	41460 MW	54050 TQ	USBLS	5/07
	Albuquerque MSA, NM	Y	31500 FQ	48750 MW	54780 TQ	USBLS	5/07
	New York	Y	27330 FQ	35960 MW	45600 TQ	USBLS	5/07
	Albany-Schenectady-Troy MSA, NY	Y	35970 FQ	44310 MW	58180 TQ	USBLS	5/07
	Binghamton MSA, NY	Y	19260 FQ	23990 MW	31820 TQ	USBLS	5/07
	Buffalo-Niagara Falls MSA, NY	Y	28880 FQ	38520 MW	48400 TQ	USBLS	5/07
	Nassau-Suffolk PMSA, NY	Y	29040 FQ	38310 MW	49110 TQ	USBLS	5/07
	New York-Northern New Jersey-Long Island MSA, NY-NJ-PA	Y	29480 FQ	38150 MW	47860 TQ	USBLS	5/07
	North Carolina	Y	25680 FQ	33110 MW	39890 TQ	USBLS	5/07
	Charlotte-Gastonia-Concord MSA, NC-SC	Y	24770 FQ	31860 MW	39470 TQ	USBLS	5/07
	Raleigh-Cary MSA, NC	Y	25380 FQ	30380 MW	37940 TQ	USBLS	5/07
	North Dakota	Y	25690 FQ	32970 MW	43970 TQ	USBLS	5/07
	Fargo MSA, ND-MN	Y	31400 FQ	39270 MW	47960 TQ	USBLS	5/07
	Ohio	Y	27620 FQ	34100 MW	40410 TQ	USBLS	5/07
	Cincinnati-Middletown MSA, OH-KY-IN	Y	27870 FQ	34280 MW	40430 TQ	USBLS	5/07
	Cleveland-Elyria-Mentor MSA, OH	Y	26780 FQ	33740 MW	41080 TQ	USBLS	5/07
	Columbus MSA, OH	Y	28750 FQ	34970 MW	39930 TQ	USBLS	5/07
	Dayton MSA, OH	Y	28560 FQ	35780 MW	44150 TQ	USBLS	5/07
	Springfield MSA, OH	Y	26450 FQ	33280 MW	39580 TQ	USBLS	5/07
	Oklahoma	Y	24980 FQ	32160 MW	39480 TQ	USBLS	5/07
	Oklahoma City MSA, OK	Y	27270 FQ	35310 MW	43720 TQ	USBLS	5/07
	Tulsa MSA, OK	Y	27380 FQ	33600 MW	38740 TQ	USBLS	5/07
	Oregon	H	16.31 FQ	19.78 MW	23.46 TQ	ORBLS	5/08

AE	Average entry wage	AW	Average wage paid	FQ First quartile wage
AER	Average entry range	AWR	Average wage range	H Hourly
AEX	Average experienced wage	AXR	Average experienced range	HI Highest wage paid
ATC	Average total compensation	D	Daily	HR High end range

LO	Lowest wage paid	MTC	Median total compensation	TCC	Total cash compensation
LR	Low end range	MW	Median wage paid	TQ	Third quartile wage
M	Monthly	MWR	Median wage range	W	Weekly
MCC	Median cash compensation	S	See annotated source	Y	Yearly

Occupation/Type/Industry	Location	Per	Low	Mid	High	Source	Date
Machinist	Portland-Vancouver-Beaverton MSA, OR-WA	Y	34350 FQ	41320 MW	49190 TQ	USBLS	5/07
	Pennsylvania	Y	29150 FQ	35680 MW	43570 TQ	USBLS	5/07
	Allentown-Bethlehem-Easton MSA, PA-NJ	Y	31710 FQ	37450 MW	45410 TQ	USBLS	5/07
	Lancaster MSA, PA	Y	27080 FQ	33830 MW	41330 TQ	USBLS	5/07
	Philadelphia-Camden-Wilmington MSA, PA-NJ-DE-MD	Y	33880 FQ	41420 MW	50530 TQ	USBLS	5/07
	Pittsburgh MSA, PA	Y	27580 FQ	34040 MW	41680 TQ	USBLS	5/07
	Rhode Island	Y	32370 FQ	38880 MW	45450 TQ	USBLS	5/07
	Providence-Fall River-Warwick MSA, RI-MA	Y	30370 FQ	37730 MW	44490 TQ	USBLS	5/07
	South Carolina	Y	24240 FQ	31710 MW	38730 TQ	USBLS	5/07
	Charleston-North Charleston MSA, SC	Y	25700 FQ	31470 MW	41020 TQ	USBLS	5/07
	Columbia MSA, SC	Y	25240 FQ	30730 MW	37550 TQ	USBLS	5/07
	Myrtle Beach-Conway-North Myrtle Beach MSA, SC	Y	27570 FQ	34980 MW	44280 TQ	USBLS	5/07
	Spartanburg MSA, SC	Y	27920 FQ	34870 MW	40600 TQ	USBLS	5/07
	South Dakota	Y	27604 FQ	31244 MW	35841 TQ	SDBLS	7/08-9/08
	Rapid City MSA, SD	Y	29983 FQ	35667 MW	40405 TQ	SDBLS	7/08-9/08
	Sioux Falls MSA, SD	Y	29557 FQ	32988 MW	37304 TQ	SDBLS	7/08-9/08
	Tennessee	Y	27960 FQ	35600 MW	45260 TQ	USBLS	5/07
	Kingsport-Bristol-Bristol MSA, TN-VA	Y	29020 FQ	34170 MW	39280 TQ	USBLS	5/07
	Memphis MSA, TN-MS-AR	Y	30650 FQ	38610 MW	45650 TQ	USBLS	5/07
	Nashville-Davidson-Murfreesboro MSA, TN	Y	27650 FQ	34340 MW	41930 TQ	USBLS	5/07
	Texas	Y	25020 FQ	31120 MW	39380 TQ	USBLS	5/07
	Austin-Round Rock MSA, TX	Y	28250 FQ	33770 MW	40610 TQ	USBLS	5/07
	Beaumont-Port Arthur MSA, TX	Y	30280 FQ	35290 MW	42250 TQ	USBLS	5/07
	Brownsville-Harlingen MSA, TX	Y	14720 FQ	22170 MW	27960 TQ	USBLS	5/07
	Corpus Christi MSA, TX	Y	27770 FQ	35900 MW	52390 TQ	USBLS	5/07
	Dallas-Fort Worth-Arlington MSA, TX	Y	24280 FQ	30540 MW	38650 TQ	USBLS	5/07
	El Paso MSA, TX	Y	24870 FQ	29450 MW	36200 TQ	USBLS	5/07
	Houston-Sugar Land-Baytown MSA, TX	Y	25210 FQ	31830 MW	40490 TQ	USBLS	5/07
	San Antonio MSA, TX	Y	20930 FQ	29950 MW	37660 TQ	USBLS	5/07
	Utah	Y	29890 FQ	37630 MW	48010 TQ	USBLS	5/07
	Salt Lake City MSA, UT	Y	28810 FQ	36300 MW	46810 TQ	USBLS	5/07
	Vermont	Y	27300 FQ	36040 MW	46150 TQ	USBLS	5/07
	Burlington-South Burlington MSA, VT	Y	26080 FQ	32300 MW	37530 TQ	USBLS	5/07
	Virginia	Y	29560 FQ	36430 MW	43880 TQ	USBLS	5/07
	Richmond MSA, VA	Y	29510 FQ	37080 MW	44920 TQ	USBLS	5/07
	Virginia Beach-Norfolk-Newport News MSA, VA-NC	Y	33350 FQ	39600 MW	46240 TQ	USBLS	5/07
	Washington	H	17.16 FQ	21.05 MW	25.66 TQ	WABLS	3/08
	Seattle-Tacoma-Bellevue MSA, WA	Y	36560 FQ	44990 MW	56200 TQ	USBLS	5/07
	Spokane MSA, WA	Y	27650 FQ	37320 MW	44440 TQ	USBLS	5/07
	West Virginia	Y	29267 FQ	36962 MW	43970 TQ	WVBLS	7/08-9/08
	Charleston MSA, WV	Y	32720 FQ	43170 MW	49020 TQ	USBLS	5/07
	Wisconsin	Y	28980 FQ	36140 MW	44500 TQ	USBLS	5/07
	Appleton MSA, WI	Y	32180 FQ	37160 MW	44370 TQ	USBLS	5/07
	Green Bay MSA, WI	Y	31800 FQ	36360 MW	40660 TQ	USBLS	5/07
	Milwaukee-Waukesha-West Allis MSA, WI	Y	28940 FQ	36690 MW	46900 TQ	USBLS	5/07
	Wyoming	Y	33018 FQ	39349 MW	47344 TQ	WYBLS	9/08
	Puerto Rico	Y	17810 FQ	22200 MW	31940 TQ	USBLS	5/07
	San Juan-Caguas-Guaynabo MSA, PR	Y	17250 FQ	21810 MW	33240 TQ	USBLS	5/07
Wind Power Component Manufacturing	New York	H		17.00 AW		GCJR	2008
Magazine Staff Science Writer	United States	Y	30000 LO			CASW	2008
Maid and Housekeeping Cleaner	Alabama	Y	13350 FQ	15610 MW	18500 TQ	USBLS	5/07
	Birmingham-Hoover MSA, AL	Y	14100 FQ	16950 MW	19430 TQ	USBLS	5/07

AE	Average entry wage	AW	Average wage paid	FQ	First quartile wage
AER	Average entry range	AWR	Average wage range	H	Hourly
AEX	Average experienced wage	AXR	Average experienced range	HI	Highest wage paid
ATC	Average total compensation	D	Daily	HR	High end range

LO	Lowest wage paid	MTC	Median total compensation
LR	Low end range	MW	Median wage paid
M	Monthly	MWR	Median wage range
MCC	Median cash compensation	S	See annotated source

TCC	Total cash compensation
TQ	Third quartile wage
W	Weekly
Y	Yearly

Occupation/Type/Industry	Location	Per	Low	Mid	High	Source	Date
Maid and Housekeeping Cleaner	Alaska	Y	18930 FQ	22020 MW	25400 TQ	USBLS	5/07
	Anchorage MSA, AK	Y	19000 FQ	21510 MW	24140 TQ	USBLS	5/07
	Arizona	Y	15300 FQ	17610 MW	20630 TQ	USBLS	5/07
	Phoenix-Mesa-Scottsdale MSA, AZ	Y	15640 FQ	18320 MW	21770 TQ	USBLS	5/07
	Tucson MSA, AZ	Y	15310 FQ	17320 MW	19800 TQ	USBLS	5/07
	Arkansas	Y	14280 FQ	15400 MW	17660 TQ	USBLS	5/07
	Fayetteville-Springdale-Rogers MSA, AR-MO	Y	14480 FQ	16080 MW	18500 TQ	USBLS	5/07
	Fort Smith MSA, AR-OK	Y	14120 FQ	15360 MW	17630 TQ	USBLS	5/07
	Jonesboro MSA, AR	Y	14240 FQ	15330 MW	17550 TQ	USBLS	5/07
	Little Rock-North Little Rock MSA, AR	Y	14500 FQ	15920 MW	18130 TQ	USBLS	5/07
	California	H	8.52 FQ	9.58 MW	11.64 TQ	CABLS	1/08-3/08
	Los Angeles-Long Beach-Glendale PMSA, CA	H	8.62 FQ	9.74 MW	11.79 TQ	CABLS	1/08-3/08
	Oakland-Fremont-Hayward MSA, CA	H	9.10 FQ	10.76 MW	14.03 TQ	CABLS	1/08-3/08
	Riverside-San Bernardino-Ontario MSA, CA	H	8.21 FQ	9.01 MW	10.11 TQ	CABLS	1/08-3/08
	Sacramento-Arden Arcade-Roseville MSA, CA	H	8.54 FQ	9.54 MW	11.80 TQ	CABLS	1/08-3/08
	San Diego-Carlsbad-San Marcos MSA, CA	H	8.46 FQ	9.38 MW	10.84 TQ	CABLS	1/08-3/08
	San Francisco-San Mateo-Redwood PMSA, CA	H	10.16 FQ	12.95 MW	16.07 TQ	CABLS	1/08-3/08
	San Jose-Sunnyvale-Santa Clara MSA, CA	H	8.91 FQ	10.15 MW	12.46 TQ	CABLS	1/08-3/08
	Santa Ana-Anaheim-Irvine PMSA, CA	Y	16860 FQ	18800 MW	22170 TQ	USBLS	5/07
	Colorado	Y	16340 FQ	18930 MW	23010 TQ	USBLS	5/07
	Denver-Aurora MSA, CO	Y	16340 FQ	18790 MW	22410 TQ	USBLS	5/07
	Connecticut	H	9.05 AE	11.29 MW		CTBLS	1/08-3/08
	Bridgeport-Stamford-Norwalk MSA, CT	Y	18780 FQ	22220 MW	26160 TQ	USBLS	5/07
	Danbury MSA, CT	Y	18410 FQ	20710 MW	23500 TQ	USBLS	5/07
	Hartford-West Hartford-East Hartford MSA, CT	Y	20610 FQ	23890 MW	28160 TQ	USBLS	5/07
	Delaware	Y	16800 FQ	18770 MW	21880 TQ	USBLS	5/07
	Wilmington PMSA, DE-MD-NJ	Y	17260 FQ	19680 MW	23180 TQ	USBLS	5/07
	District of Columbia	Y	24900 FQ	28100 MW	31040 TQ	USBLS	5/07
	Washington-Arlington-Alexandria MSA, DC-VA-MD-WV	Y	18680 FQ	22140 MW	27020 TQ	USBLS	5/07
	Florida	Y	15470 FQ	17550 MW	20070 TQ	USBLS	5/07
	Fort Lauderdale-Pompano Beach-Deerfield Beach PMSA, FL	Y	15260 FQ	17400 MW	20210 TQ	USBLS	5/07
	Jacksonville MSA, FL	Y	15570 FQ	17340 MW	19550 TQ	USBLS	5/07
	Miami-Fort Lauderdale-Miami Beach MSA, FL	Y	15400 FQ	17640 MW	20380 TQ	USBLS	5/07
	Orlando-Kissimmee MSA, FL	Y	15700 FQ	17790 MW	20310 TQ	USBLS	5/07
	Tallahassee MSA, FL	Y	14700 FQ	15790 MW	18030 TQ	USBLS	5/07
	Tampa-St. Petersburg-Clearwater MSA, FL	Y	15440 FQ	17530 MW	20000 TQ	USBLS	5/07
	West Palm Beach-Boca Raton-Boynton Beach PMSA, FL	Y	16000 FQ	18180 MW	20950 TQ	USBLS	5/07
	Georgia	Y	13950 FQ	16610 MW	19120 TQ	USBLS	5/07
	Atlanta-Sandy Springs-Marietta MSA, GA	Y	15300 FQ	17580 MW	19880 TQ	USBLS	5/07
	Augusta-Richmond County MSA, GA-SC	Y	12880 FQ	14550 MW	16820 TQ	USBLS	5/07
	Hawaii	Y	24810 FQ	27780 MW	30480 TQ	USBLS	5/07
	Honolulu MSA, HI	Y	23300 FQ	27010 MW	29710 TQ	USBLS	5/07
	Idaho	Y	13330 FQ	15560 MW	19530 TQ	USBLS	5/07
	Boise City-Nampa MSA, ID	Y	13580 FQ	16030 MW	21440 TQ	USBLS	5/07
	Pocatello MSA, ID	Y	12940 FQ	14700 MW	17050 TQ	USBLS	5/07
	Illinois	Y	16030 FQ	18610 MW	22730 TQ	USBLS	5/07
	Champaign-Urbana MSA, IL	Y	15620 FQ	17950 MW	21810 TQ	USBLS	5/07
	Chicago-Naperville-Joliet MSA, IL-IN-WI	Y	16560 FQ	19310 MW	23580 TQ	USBLS	5/07

AE Average entry wage	**AW** Average wage paid	**FQ** First quartile wage	**LO** Lowest wage paid	**MTC** Median total compensation	**TCC** Total cash compensation
AER Average entry range	**AWR** Average wage range	**H** Hourly	**LR** Low end range	**MW** Median wage paid	**TQ** Third quartile wage
AEX Average experienced wage	**AXR** Average experienced range	**HI** Highest wage paid	**M** Monthly	**MWR** Median wage range	**W** Weekly
ATC Average total compensation	**D** Daily	**HR** High end range	**MCC** Median cash compensation	**S** See annotated source	**Y** Yearly

Maid and Housekeeping Cleaner

Occupation/Type/Industry	Location	Per	Low	Mid	High	Source	Date
Maid and Housekeeping Cleaner	Indiana	Y	15020 FQ	17450 MW	20040 TQ	USBLS	5/07
	Fort Wayne MSA, IN	Y	15400 FQ	17720 MW	20130 TQ	USBLS	5/07
	Gary PMSA, IN	Y	15760 FQ	18440 MW	22690 TQ	USBLS	5/07
	Indianapolis-Carmel MSA, IN	Y	15160 FQ	17480 MW	19820 TQ	USBLS	5/07
	Iowa	Y	15880 FQ	18270 MW	21260 TQ	USBLS	5/07
	Davenport-Moline-Rock Island MSA, IA-IL	Y	14910 FQ	16680 MW	19340 TQ	USBLS	5/07
	Des Moines-West Des Moines MSA, IA	Y	16280 FQ	18560 MW	21820 TQ	USBLS	5/07
	Kansas	Y	14260 FQ	16940 MW	19370 TQ	USBLS	5/07
	Lawrence MSA, KS	Y	15790 FQ	18250 MW	21730 TQ	USBLS	5/07
	Wichita MSA, KS	Y	14700 FQ	17350 MW	19930 TQ	USBLS	5/07
	Kentucky	Y	15050 FQ	17854 MW	20498 TQ	KYBLS	2008
	Bowling Green MSA, KY	Y	13160 FQ	15270 MW	18340 TQ	USBLS	5/07
	Louisville-Jefferson County MSA, KY-IN	Y	16790 FQ	18870 MW	21660 TQ	USBLS	5/07
	Louisiana	H	6.24 FQ	7.08 MW	8.47 TQ	LABLS	1/08-3/08
	Baton Rouge MSA, LA	Y	13060 FQ	14960 MW	18040 TQ	USBLS	5/07
	New Orleans-Metairie-Kenner MSA, LA	Y	14590 FQ	17190 MW	19950 TQ	USBLS	5/07
	Maine	Y	16870 FQ	19320 MW	22700 TQ	USBLS	5/07
	Portland-South Portland-Biddeford MSA, ME	Y	17350 FQ	19730 MW	23270 TQ	USBLS	5/07
	Maryland	Y		20050 MW		MDBLS	3/08
	Baltimore-Towson MSA, MD	Y	17000 FQ	20120 MW	23620 TQ	USBLS	5/07
	Bethesda-Gaithersburg-Frederick PMSA, MD	Y	18180 FQ	20890 MW	24370 TQ	USBLS	5/07
	Massachusetts	Y	19050 FQ	22330 MW	26260 TQ	USBLS	5/07
	Boston-Cambridge-Quincy NECTA, MA	Y	20290 FQ	24030 MW	28090 TQ	USBLS	5/07
	Worcester MSA, MA-CT	Y	19100 FQ	21440 MW	23940 TQ	USBLS	5/07
	Michigan	Y	16580 FQ	19760 MW	23700 TQ	USBLS	5/07
	Detroit-Warren-Livonia MSA, MI	Y	18060 FQ	21450 MW	24880 TQ	USBLS	5/07
	Grand Rapids-Wyoming MSA, MI	Y	17190 FQ	19690 MW	23180 TQ	USBLS	5/07
	Warren-Troy-Farmington Hills PMSA, MI	Y	17280 FQ	20320 MW	23720 TQ	USBLS	5/07
	Minnesota	Y	17649 FQ	20943 MW	25773 TQ	MNBLS	10/08-12/08
	Duluth-Superior MSA, MN-WI	Y	16990 FQ	19803 MW	24445 TQ	MNBLS	10/08-12/08
	Minneapolis-Saint Paul MSA, MN-WI	Y	18705 FQ	22469 MW	27896 TQ	MNBLS	10/08-12/08
	Rochester MSA, MN	Y	17853 FQ	20717 MW	28184 TQ	MNBLS	10/08-12/08
	Mississippi	Y	13310 FQ	15440 MW	17970 TQ	USBLS	5/07
	Jackson MSA, MS	Y	13200 FQ	15260 MW	17700 TQ	USBLS	5/07
	Missouri	Y	15660 FQ	17990 MW	20870 TQ	USBLS	5/07
	Jefferson City MSA, MO	Y	16170 FQ	18050 MW	20170 TQ	USBLS	5/07
	Kansas City MSA, MO-KS	Y	16610 FQ	18820 MW	21830 TQ	USBLS	5/07
	St. Louis MSA, MO-IL	Y	16680 FQ	18890 MW	22520 TQ	USBLS	5/07
	Springfield MSA, MO	Y	15430 FQ	17340 MW	19290 TQ	USBLS	5/07
	Montana	Y	14420 FQ	16190 MW	18690 TQ	USBLS	5/07
	Billings MSA, MT	Y	14120 FQ	15580 MW	18700 TQ	USBLS	5/07
	Nebraska	Y	14520 FQ	17210 MW	19500 TQ	USBLS	5/07
	Omaha-Council Bluffs MSA, NE-IA	Y	16190 FQ	18360 MW	20780 TQ	USBLS	5/07
	Nevada	H	9.57 FQ	12.60 MW	14.21 TQ	NVBLS	5/08
	Las Vegas-Paradise MSA, NV	H	10.69 FQ	13.14 MW	14.45 TQ	NVBLS	5/08
	New Hampshire	H	8.39 AE	10.35 MW	11.62 AEX	NHBLS	6/08
	Manchester MSA, NH	Y	17860 FQ	20330 MW	22840 TQ	USBLS	5/07
	Nashua NECTA, NH-MA	Y	18720 FQ	21670 MW	24850 TQ	USBLS	5/07
	New Jersey	Y	17350 FQ	20060 MW	23880 TQ	USBLS	5/07
	Camden PMSA, NJ	Y	16630 FQ	18600 MW	22450 TQ	USBLS	5/07
	Edison PMSA, NJ	Y	17120 FQ	19460 MW	22760 TQ	USBLS	5/07
	Newark-Union PMSA, NJ-PA	Y	17920 FQ	21630 MW	26830 TQ	USBLS	5/07
	Vineland-Millville-Bridgeton MSA, NJ	Y	20200 FQ	25880 MW	30420 TQ	USBLS	5/07
	New Mexico	Y	13560 FQ	15980 MW	18800 TQ	USBLS	5/07
	Albuquerque MSA, NM	Y	13730 FQ	16240 MW	18740 TQ	USBLS	5/07
	Las Cruces MSA, NM	Y	12630 FQ	14110 MW	15770 TQ	USBLS	5/07
	New York	Y	19010 FQ	25180 MW	34280 TQ	USBLS	5/07
	Albany-Schenectady-Troy MSA, NY	Y	16870 FQ	19400 MW	22770 TQ	USBLS	5/07

AE Average entry wage	**AW** Average wage paid	**FQ** First quartile wage	**LO** Lowest wage paid	**MTC** Median total compensation	**TCC** Total cash compensation
AER Average entry range	**AWR** Average wage range	**H** Hourly	**LR** Low end range	**MW** Median wage paid	**TQ** Third quartile wage
AEX Average experienced wage	**AXR** Average experienced range	**HI** Highest wage paid	**M** Monthly	**MWR** Median wage range	**W** Weekly
ATC Average total compensation	**D** Daily	**HR** High end range	**MCC** Median cash compensation	**S** See annotated source	**Y** Yearly

Occupation/Type/Industry	Location	Per	Low	Mid	High	Source	Date
Maid and Housekeeping Cleaner	Buffalo-Niagara Falls MSA, NY	Y	16000 FQ	18690 MW	22740 TQ	USBLS	5/07
	Nassau-Suffolk PMSA, NY	Y	20010 FQ	27060 MW	33870 TQ	USBLS	5/07
	New York-Northern New Jersey-Long Island MSA, NY-NJ-PA	Y	20530 FQ	27060 MW	34980 TQ	USBLS	5/07
	Utica-Rome MSA, NY	Y	15960 FQ	18150 MW	20930 TQ	USBLS	5/07
	North Carolina	Y	14760 FQ	16920 MW	19600 TQ	USBLS	5/07
	Charlotte-Gastonia-Concord MSA, NC-SC	Y	15260 FQ	17410 MW	19850 TQ	USBLS	5/07
	Raleigh-Cary MSA, NC	Y	15420 FQ	17530 MW	20060 TQ	USBLS	5/07
	North Dakota	Y	14430 FQ	17100 MW	19730 TQ	USBLS	5/07
	Bismarck MSA, ND	Y	15780 FQ	18080 MW	20900 TQ	USBLS	5/07
	Fargo MSA, ND-MN	Y	15200 FQ	17290 MW	19540 TQ	USBLS	5/07
	Ohio	Y	16010 FQ	18450 MW	21740 TQ	USBLS	5/07
	Canton-Massillon MSA, OH	Y	15360 FQ	17860 MW	21630 TQ	USBLS	5/07
	Cincinnati-Middletown MSA, OH-KY-IN	Y	17240 FQ	19820 MW	23010 TQ	USBLS	5/07
	Cleveland-Elyria-Mentor MSA, OH	Y	16650 FQ	19090 MW	22830 TQ	USBLS	5/07
	Columbus MSA, OH	Y	16130 FQ	18510 MW	21280 TQ	USBLS	5/07
	Dayton MSA, OH	Y	15810 FQ	17960 MW	20430 TQ	USBLS	5/07
	Oklahoma	Y	13540 FQ	15810 MW	18280 TQ	USBLS	5/07
	Oklahoma City MSA, OK	Y	13580 FQ	15860 MW	18350 TQ	USBLS	5/07
	Tulsa MSA, OK	Y	14440 FQ	16670 MW	19000 TQ	USBLS	5/07
	Oregon	H	8.61 FQ	9.21 MW	10.31 TQ	ORBLS	5/08
	Portland-Vancouver-Beaverton MSA, OR-WA	Y	17640 FQ	19070 MW	22270 TQ	USBLS	5/07
	Pennsylvania	Y	16120 FQ	18680 MW	22300 TQ	USBLS	5/07
	Allentown-Bethlehem-Easton MSA, PA-NJ	Y	15920 FQ	17930 MW	21220 TQ	USBLS	5/07
	Philadelphia-Camden-Wilmington MSA, PA-NJ-DE-MD	Y	17330 FQ	20170 MW	23890 TQ	USBLS	5/07
	Pittsburgh MSA, PA	Y	15860 FQ	18470 MW	21900 TQ	USBLS	5/07
	Rhode Island	Y	18450 FQ	22090 MW	26660 TQ	USBLS	5/07
	Providence-Fall River-Warwick MSA, RI-MA	Y	18410 FQ	21800 MW	26040 TQ	USBLS	5/07
	South Carolina	Y	14130 FQ	16760 MW	19220 TQ	USBLS	5/07
	Charleston-North Charleston MSA, SC	Y	14400 FQ	17090 MW	20000 TQ	USBLS	5/07
	Columbia MSA, SC	Y	13520 FQ	15910 MW	18660 TQ	USBLS	5/07
	South Dakota	Y	14533 FQ	17286 MW	20067 TQ	SDBLS	7/08-9/08
	Sioux Falls MSA, SD	Y	15512 FQ	18782 MW	22801 TQ	SDBLS	7/08-9/08
	Tennessee	Y	14160 FQ	16870 MW	19440 TQ	USBLS	5/07
	Memphis MSA, TN-MS-AR	Y	14320 FQ	16430 MW	18530 TQ	USBLS	5/07
	Nashville-Davidson-Murfreesboro MSA, TN	Y	15400 FQ	17970 MW	20470 TQ	USBLS	5/07
	Texas	Y	13330 FQ	15540 MW	18400 TQ	USBLS	5/07
	Austin-Round Rock MSA, TX	Y	14120 FQ	16650 MW	19200 TQ	USBLS	5/07
	Dallas-Fort Worth-Arlington MSA, TX	Y	14100 FQ	16670 MW	19070 TQ	USBLS	5/07
	El Paso MSA, TX	Y	12910 FQ	14580 MW	17010 TQ	USBLS	5/07
	Houston-Sugar Land-Baytown MSA, TX	Y	13360 FQ	15660 MW	18540 TQ	USBLS	5/07
	San Antonio MSA, TX	Y	13470 FQ	16050 MW	19060 TQ	USBLS	5/07
	Utah	Y	14550 FQ	17230 MW	19760 TQ	USBLS	5/07
	St. George MSA, UT	Y	16740 FQ	18530 MW	20330 TQ	USBLS	5/07
	Salt Lake City MSA, UT	Y	15530 FQ	17770 MW	20180 TQ	USBLS	5/07
	Vermont	Y	17780 FQ	20510 MW	23840 TQ	USBLS	5/07
	Burlington-South Burlington MSA, VT	Y	17780 FQ	20200 MW	23250 TQ	USBLS	5/07
	Virginia	Y	15420 FQ	18060 MW	21310 TQ	USBLS	5/07
	Richmond MSA, VA	Y	15740 FQ	17890 MW	20180 TQ	USBLS	5/07
	Virginia Beach-Norfolk-Newport News MSA, VA-NC	Y	14460 FQ	17090 MW	19730 TQ	USBLS	5/07
	Washington	H	8.85 FQ	9.83 MW	11.68 TQ	WABLS	3/08
	Seattle-Tacoma-Bellevue MSA, WA	Y	18760 FQ	21850 MW	25600 TQ	USBLS	5/07
	West Virginia	Y	14658 FQ	16534 MW	19479 TQ	WVBLS	7/08-9/08
	Charleston MSA, WV	Y	14430 FQ	16530 MW	18920 TQ	USBLS	5/07
	Wisconsin	Y	16230 FQ	18510 MW	21740 TQ	USBLS	5/07

AE	Average entry wage	AW	Average wage paid	FQ	First quartile wage	LO	Lowest wage paid	MTC	Median total compensation	TCC	Total cash compensation
AER	Average entry range	AWR	Average wage range	H	Hourly	LR	Low end range	MW	Median wage paid	TQ	Third quartile wage
AEX	Average experienced wage	AXR	Average experienced range	HI	Highest wage paid	M	Monthly	MWR	Median wage range	W	Weekly
ATC	Average total compensation	D	Daily	HR	High end range	MCC	Median cash compensation	S	See annotated source	Y	Yearly

Occupation/Type/Industry	Location	Per	Low	Mid	High	Source	Date
Maid and Housekeeping Cleaner	Milwaukee-Waukesha-West Allis MSA, WI	Y	16590 FQ	18890 MW	22790 TQ	USBLS	5/07
	Wyoming	Y	15585 FQ	18131 MW	20590 TQ	WYBLS	9/08
	Cheyenne MSA, WY	Y	14677 FQ	17441 MW	19767 TQ	WYBLS	9/08
	Puerto Rico	Y	12410 FQ	13780 MW	15190 TQ	USBLS	5/07
	Aguadilla-Isabela-San Sebastian MSA, PR	Y	12240 FQ	13400 MW	14560 TQ	USBLS	5/07
	San Juan-Caguas-Guaynabo MSA, PR	Y	12660 FQ	14130 MW	16230 TQ	USBLS	5/07
	Virgin Islands	Y	16200 FQ	18090 MW	20650 TQ	USBLS	5/07
	Guam	Y	12550 FQ	13970 MW	15490 TQ	USBLS	5/07
Mail Clerk and Mail Machine Operator							
Except Postal Service	Alabama	Y	17630 FQ	22200 MW	27490 TQ	USBLS	5/07
Except Postal Service	Birmingham-Hoover MSA, AL	Y	21060 FQ	24500 MW	29630 TQ	USBLS	5/07
Except Postal Service	Mobile MSA, AL	Y	15360 FQ	17970 MW	24490 TQ	USBLS	5/07
Except Postal Service	Alaska	Y	21770 FQ	27000 MW	33800 TQ	USBLS	5/07
Except Postal Service	Anchorage MSA, AK	Y	20840 FQ	23350 MW	30330 TQ	USBLS	5/07
Except Postal Service	Arizona	Y	17300 FQ	20820 MW	26280 TQ	USBLS	5/07
Except Postal Service	Flagstaff MSA, AZ	Y	14990 FQ	16730 MW	24300 TQ	USBLS	5/07
Except Postal Service	Phoenix-Mesa-Scottsdale MSA, AZ	Y	16980 FQ	20020 MW	25730 TQ	USBLS	5/07
Except Postal Service	Tucson MSA, AZ	Y	21060 FQ	23500 MW	28170 TQ	USBLS	5/07
Except Postal Service	Arkansas	Y	17530 FQ	22650 MW	29240 TQ	USBLS	5/07
Except Postal Service	Fort Smith MSA, AR-OK	Y	15350 FQ	17890 MW	22780 TQ	USBLS	5/07
Except Postal Service	Little Rock-North Little Rock MSA, AR	Y	20820 FQ	25790 MW	38610 TQ	USBLS	5/07
Except Postal Service	California	H	9.95 FQ	12.28 MW	15.62 TQ	CABLS	1/08-3/08
Except Postal Service	Fresno MSA, CA	H	10.41 FQ	11.39 MW	12.60 TQ	CABLS	1/08-3/08
Except Postal Service	Los Angeles-Long Beach-Glendale PMSA, CA	H	9.84 FQ	11.74 MW	15.05 TQ	CABLS	1/08-3/08
Except Postal Service	Oakland-Fremont-Hayward MSA, CA	H	10.04 FQ	12.44 MW	16.87 TQ	CABLS	1/08-3/08
Except Postal Service	Riverside-San Bernardino-Ontario MSA, CA	H	10.29 FQ	12.24 MW	15.14 TQ	CABLS	1/08-3/08
Except Postal Service	Sacramento-Arden Arcade-Roseville MSA, CA	H	10.08 FQ	13.74 MW	17.47 TQ	CABLS	1/08-3/08
Except Postal Service	San Diego-Carlsbad-San Marcos MSA, CA	H	9.44 FQ	12.58 MW	15.46 TQ	CABLS	1/08-3/08
Except Postal Service	San Francisco-San Mateo-Redwood PMSA, CA	H	12.69 FQ	15.55 MW	18.38 TQ	CABLS	1/08-3/08
Except Postal Service	San Jose-Sunnyvale-Santa Clara MSA, CA	H	15.06 FQ	17.02 MW	19.49 TQ	CABLS	1/08-3/08
Except Postal Service	Santa Ana-Anaheim-Irvine PMSA, CA	Y	20440 FQ	24870 MW	29910 TQ	USBLS	5/07
Except Postal Service	Colorado	Y	21770 FQ	26390 MW	32230 TQ	USBLS	5/07
Except Postal Service	Denver-Aurora MSA, CO	Y	23340 FQ	28050 MW	34010 TQ	USBLS	5/07
Except Postal Service	Connecticut	H	8.97 AE	12.78 MW		CTBLS	1/08-3/08
Except Postal Service	Bridgeport-Stamford-Norwalk MSA, CT	Y	22880 FQ	27810 MW	33100 TQ	USBLS	5/07
Except Postal Service	Hartford-West Hartford-East Hartford MSA, CT	Y	17880 FQ	22180 MW	31040 TQ	USBLS	5/07
Except Postal Service	Norwich-New London MSA, CT-RI	Y	28060 FQ	31130 MW	35840 TQ	USBLS	5/07
Except Postal Service	Delaware	Y	17920 FQ	23290 MW	28810 TQ	USBLS	5/07
Except Postal Service	Wilmington PMSA, DE-MD-NJ	Y	22160 FQ	26470 MW	30630 TQ	USBLS	5/07
Except Postal Service	District of Columbia	Y	27270 FQ	32720 MW	38220 TQ	USBLS	5/07
Except Postal Service	Washington-Arlington-Alexandria MSA, DC-VA-MD-WV	Y	22090 FQ	29060 MW	36350 TQ	USBLS	5/07
Except Postal Service	Florida	Y	17490 FQ	22330 MW	27870 TQ	USBLS	5/07
Except Postal Service	Fort Lauderdale-Pompano Beach-Deerfield Beach PMSA, FL	Y	20030 FQ	23250 MW	27340 TQ	USBLS	5/07
Except Postal Service	Jacksonville MSA, FL	Y	18830 FQ	22400 MW	25950 TQ	USBLS	5/07
Except Postal Service	Miami-Fort Lauderdale-Miami Beach MSA, FL	Y	19420 FQ	25470 MW	31540 TQ	USBLS	5/07
Except Postal Service	Orlando-Kissimmee MSA, FL	Y	22150 FQ	25850 MW	29460 TQ	USBLS	5/07
Except Postal Service	Tampa-St. Petersburg-Clearwater MSA, FL	Y	18630 FQ	22840 MW	29870 TQ	USBLS	5/07

AE Average entry wage	**AW** Average wage paid	**FQ** First quartile wage	**LO** Lowest wage paid	**MTC** Median total compensation	**TCC** Total cash compensation
AER Average entry range	**AWR** Average wage range	**H** Hourly	**LR** Low end range	**MW** Median wage paid	**TQ** Third quartile wage
AEX Average experienced wage	**AXR** Average experienced range	**HI** Highest wage paid	**M** Monthly	**MWR** Median wage range	**W** Weekly
ATC Average total compensation	**D** Daily	**HR** High end range	**MCC** Median cash compensation	**S** See annotated source	**Y** Yearly

Occupation/Type/Industry	Location	Per	Low	Mid	High	Source	Date
Mail Clerk and Mail Machine Operator							
Except Postal Service	West Palm Beach-Boca Raton-Boynton Beach PMSA, FL	Y	26570 FQ	32170 MW	43580 TQ	USBLS	5/07
Except Postal Service	Georgia	Y	19990 FQ	23740 MW	28750 TQ	USBLS	5/07
Except Postal Service	Atlanta-Sandy Springs-Marietta MSA, GA	Y	20550 FQ	24310 MW	29220 TQ	USBLS	5/07
Except Postal Service	Augusta-Richmond County MSA, GA-SC	Y	18420 FQ	24840 MW	29870 TQ	USBLS	5/07
Except Postal Service	Hawaii	Y	20020 FQ	24790 MW	31580 TQ	USBLS	5/07
Except Postal Service	Honolulu MSA, HI	Y	20160 FQ	25780 MW	32680 TQ	USBLS	5/07
Except Postal Service	Idaho	Y	21840 FQ	26680 MW	30640 TQ	USBLS	5/07
Except Postal Service	Boise City-Nampa MSA, ID	Y	24510 FQ	28820 MW	32950 TQ	USBLS	5/07
Except Postal Service	Illinois	Y	17770 FQ	23290 MW	30160 TQ	USBLS	5/07
Except Postal Service	Champaign-Urbana MSA, IL	Y	18910 FQ	23140 MW	27200 TQ	USBLS	5/07
Except Postal Service	Chicago-Naperville-Joliet MSA, IL-IN-WI	Y	17270 FQ	23160 MW	30220 TQ	USBLS	5/07
Except Postal Service	Indiana	Y	19880 FQ	24090 MW	29380 TQ	USBLS	5/07
Except Postal Service	Gary PMSA, IN	Y	18110 FQ	22130 MW	28340 TQ	USBLS	5/07
Except Postal Service	Indianapolis-Carmel MSA, IN	Y	20540 FQ	24270 MW	30070 TQ	USBLS	5/07
Except Postal Service	Terre Haute MSA, IN	Y	13940 FQ	17620 MW	25700 TQ	USBLS	5/07
Except Postal Service	Iowa	Y	20520 FQ	23450 MW	28100 TQ	USBLS	5/07
Except Postal Service	Des Moines-West Des Moines MSA, IA	Y	21890 FQ	25030 MW	30480 TQ	USBLS	5/07
Except Postal Service	Kansas	Y	18980 FQ	23440 MW	28930 TQ	USBLS	5/07
Except Postal Service	Wichita MSA, KS	Y	18540 FQ	22530 MW	28360 TQ	USBLS	5/07
Except Postal Service	Kentucky	Y	19742 FQ	23995 MW	29370 TQ	KYBLS	2008
Except Postal Service	Louisville-Jefferson County MSA, KY-IN	Y	18490 FQ	22910 MW	29270 TQ	USBLS	5/07
Except Postal Service	Louisiana	H	8.21 FQ	9.93 MW	12.48 TQ	LABLS	1/08-3/08
Except Postal Service	Baton Rouge MSA, LA	Y	17110 FQ	19760 MW	23850 TQ	USBLS	5/07
Except Postal Service	New Orleans-Metairie-Kenner MSA, LA	Y	20380 FQ	23840 MW	29800 TQ	USBLS	5/07
Except Postal Service	Maine	Y	18400 FQ	23250 MW	28470 TQ	USBLS	5/07
Except Postal Service	Portland-South Portland-Biddeford MSA, ME	Y	20210 FQ	24470 MW	29230 TQ	USBLS	5/07
Except Postal Service	Maryland	Y		25500 MW		MDBLS	3/08
Except Postal Service	Baltimore-Towson MSA, MD	Y	20250 FQ	24710 MW	30750 TQ	USBLS	5/07
Except Postal Service	Bethesda-Gaithersburg-Frederick PMSA, MD	Y	24740 FQ	29020 MW	36070 TQ	USBLS	5/07
Except Postal Service	Massachusetts	Y	22910 FQ	27700 MW	32860 TQ	USBLS	5/07
Except Postal Service	Boston-Cambridge-Quincy NECTA, MA	Y	23380 FQ	28320 MW	34030 TQ	USBLS	5/07
Except Postal Service	Worcester MSA, MA-CT	Y	21160 FQ	23270 MW	26330 TQ	USBLS	5/07
Except Postal Service	Michigan	Y	20180 FQ	24890 MW	30430 TQ	USBLS	5/07
Except Postal Service	Detroit-Warren-Livonia MSA, MI	Y	20020 FQ	24790 MW	30420 TQ	USBLS	5/07
Except Postal Service	Grand Rapids-Wyoming MSA, MI	Y	23580 FQ	26970 MW	30430 TQ	USBLS	5/07
Except Postal Service	Warren-Troy-Farmington Hills PMSA, MI	Y	19030 FQ	25020 MW	31770 TQ	USBLS	5/07
Except Postal Service	Minnesota	Y	20305 FQ	24531 MW	30578 TQ	MNBLS	10/08-12/08
Except Postal Service	Duluth-Superior MSA, MN-WI	Y	15320 FQ	20659 MW	25145 TQ	MNBLS	10/08-12/08
Except Postal Service	Minneapolis-Saint Paul MSA, MN-WI	Y	20888 FQ	25572 MW	31796 TQ	MNBLS	10/08-12/08
Except Postal Service	Rochester MSA, MN	Y	24595 FQ	28587 MW	34192 TQ	MNBLS	10/08-12/08
Except Postal Service	Mississippi	Y	17270 FQ	20850 MW	25110 TQ	USBLS	5/07
Except Postal Service	Jackson MSA, MS	Y	17130 FQ	20490 MW	25140 TQ	USBLS	5/07
Except Postal Service	Missouri	Y	19780 FQ	24210 MW	29380 TQ	USBLS	5/07
Except Postal Service	Kansas City MSA, MO-KS	Y	21720 FQ	25740 MW	31550 TQ	USBLS	5/07
Except Postal Service	St. Louis MSA, MO-IL	Y	21110 FQ	25080 MW	29400 TQ	USBLS	5/07
Except Postal Service	Montana	Y	17590 FQ	20520 MW	25370 TQ	USBLS	5/07
Except Postal Service	Billings MSA, MT	Y	16380 FQ	18350 MW	22030 TQ	USBLS	5/07
Except Postal Service	Nebraska	Y	21050 FQ	24240 MW	28700 TQ	USBLS	5/07
Except Postal Service	Omaha-Council Bluffs MSA, NE-IA	Y	22000 FQ	25180 MW	29140 TQ	USBLS	5/07
Except Postal Service	Nevada	H	9.01 FQ	10.74 MW	13.94 TQ	NVBLS	5/08
Except Postal Service	Las Vegas-Paradise MSA, NV	H	8.81 FQ	9.98 MW	12.22 TQ	NVBLS	5/08
Except Postal Service	New Hampshire	H	9.79 AE	12.02 MW	14.63 AEX	NHBLS	6/08
Except Postal Service	Manchester MSA, NH	Y	21650 FQ	25860 MW	33990 TQ	USBLS	5/07
Except Postal Service	Nashua NECTA, NH-MA	Y	25720 FQ	29390 MW	33480 TQ	USBLS	5/07
Except Postal Service	New Jersey	Y	21340 FQ	26420 MW	32630 TQ	USBLS	5/07

AE	Average entry wage	AW	Average wage paid	FQ	First quartile wage
AER	Average entry range	AWR	Average wage range	H	Hourly
AEX	Average experienced wage	AXR	Average experienced range	HI	Highest wage paid
ATC	Average total compensation	D	Daily	HR	High end range

LO	Lowest wage paid	MTC	Median total compensation	TCC	Total cash compensation
LR	Low end range	MW	Median wage paid	TQ	Third quartile wage
M	Monthly	MWR	Median wage range	W	Weekly
MCC	Median cash compensation	S	See annotated source	Y	Yearly

Occupation/Type/Industry	Location	Per	Low	Mid	High	Source	Date
Mail Clerk and Mail Machine Operator							
Except Postal Service	Camden PMSA, NJ	Y	18740 FQ	22370 MW	27460 TQ	USBLS	5/07
Except Postal Service	Edison PMSA, NJ	Y	20440 FQ	24120 MW	31050 TQ	USBLS	5/07
Except Postal Service	Newark-Union PMSA, NJ-PA	Y	23860 FQ	28100 MW	32620 TQ	USBLS	5/07
Except Postal Service	Trenton-Ewing MSA, NJ	Y	25270 FQ	31830 MW	39390 TQ	USBLS	5/07
Except Postal Service	New Mexico	Y	18930 FQ	22600 MW	26820 TQ	USBLS	5/07
Except Postal Service	Albuquerque MSA, NM	Y	18950 FQ	22710 MW	26460 TQ	USBLS	5/07
Except Postal Service	New York	Y	22250 FQ	27370 MW	33570 TQ	USBLS	5/07
Except Postal Service	Albany-Schenectady-Troy MSA, NY	Y	23080 FQ	27240 MW	31550 TQ	USBLS	5/07
Except Postal Service	Buffalo-Niagara Falls MSA, NY	Y	21920 FQ	27350 MW	32680 TQ	USBLS	5/07
Except Postal Service	Nassau-Suffolk PMSA, NY	Y	19960 FQ	24210 MW	29710 TQ	USBLS	5/07
Except Postal Service	New York-Northern New Jersey-Long Island MSA, NY-NJ-PA	Y	22060 FQ	27200 MW	33520 TQ	USBLS	5/07
Except Postal Service	Syracuse MSA, NY	Y	25310 FQ	28490 MW	31610 TQ	USBLS	5/07
Except Postal Service	North Carolina	Y	18710 FQ	22880 MW	27330 TQ	USBLS	5/07
Except Postal Service	Charlotte-Gastonia-Concord MSA, NC-SC	Y	20930 FQ	24100 MW	28330 TQ	USBLS	5/07
Except Postal Service	Durham MSA, NC	Y	21240 FQ	24460 MW	28320 TQ	USBLS	5/07
Except Postal Service	Raleigh-Cary MSA, NC	Y	21990 FQ	24490 MW	28010 TQ	USBLS	5/07
Except Postal Service	North Dakota	Y	19510 FQ	21490 MW	23470 TQ	USBLS	5/07
Except Postal Service	Fargo MSA, ND-MN	Y	19930 FQ	21620 MW	23320 TQ	USBLS	5/07
Except Postal Service	Ohio	Y	20090 FQ	24190 MW	29400 TQ	USBLS	5/07
Except Postal Service	Cincinnati-Middletown MSA, OH-KY-IN	Y	21380 FQ	25160 MW	30280 TQ	USBLS	5/07
Except Postal Service	Cleveland-Elyria-Mentor MSA, OH	Y	20760 FQ	24410 MW	29690 TQ	USBLS	5/07
Except Postal Service	Columbus MSA, OH	Y	21120 FQ	25400 MW	29590 TQ	USBLS	5/07
Except Postal Service	Dayton MSA, OH	Y	17610 FQ	20130 MW	26530 TQ	USBLS	5/07
Except Postal Service	Oklahoma	Y	16780 FQ	20650 MW	26340 TQ	USBLS	5/07
Except Postal Service	Oklahoma City MSA, OK	Y	16580 FQ	21170 MW	27390 TQ	USBLS	5/07
Except Postal Service	Tulsa MSA, OK	Y	17200 FQ	20430 MW	24130 TQ	USBLS	5/07
Except Postal Service	Oregon	H	10.40 FQ	12.93 MW	15.31 TQ	ORBLS	5/08
Except Postal Service	Portland-Vancouver-Beaverton MSA, OR-WA	Y	22080 FQ	27110 MW	32290 TQ	USBLS	5/07
Except Postal Service	Pennsylvania	Y	19180 FQ	23870 MW	29620 TQ	USBLS	5/07
Except Postal Service	Allentown-Bethlehem-Easton MSA, PA-NJ	Y	21060 FQ	23840 MW	27120 TQ	USBLS	5/07
Except Postal Service	Philadelphia-Camden-Wilmington MSA, PA-NJ-DE-MD	Y	21150 FQ	25670 MW	31440 TQ	USBLS	5/07
Except Postal Service	Pittsburgh MSA, PA	Y	19050 FQ	23830 MW	29040 TQ	USBLS	5/07
Except Postal Service	Rhode Island	Y	21890 FQ	26730 MW	32730 TQ	USBLS	5/07
Except Postal Service	Providence-Fall River-Warwick MSA, RI-MA	Y	21920 FQ	26820 MW	32740 TQ	USBLS	5/07
Except Postal Service	South Carolina	Y	20240 FQ	23170 MW	27170 TQ	USBLS	5/07
Except Postal Service	Charleston-North Charleston MSA, SC	Y	17520 FQ	21580 MW	27890 TQ	USBLS	5/07
Except Postal Service	Columbia MSA, SC	Y	20560 FQ	23350 MW	27550 TQ	USBLS	5/07
Except Postal Service	Florence MSA, SC	Y	17160 FQ	20780 MW	23520 TQ	USBLS	5/07
Except Postal Service	South Dakota	Y	18935 FQ	22448 MW	26266 TQ	SDBLS	7/08-9/08
Except Postal Service	Sioux Falls MSA, SD	Y	18615 FQ	22369 MW	26507 TQ	SDBLS	7/08-9/08
Except Postal Service	Tennessee	Y	17870 FQ	22440 MW	28670 TQ	USBLS	5/07
Except Postal Service	Memphis MSA, TN-MS-AR	Y	17260 FQ	20880 MW	28880 TQ	USBLS	5/07
Except Postal Service	Nashville-Davidson-Murfreesboro MSA, TN	Y	18730 FQ	22030 MW	27730 TQ	USBLS	5/07
Except Postal Service	Texas	Y	20840 FQ	24830 MW	29730 TQ	USBLS	5/07
Except Postal Service	Austin-Round Rock MSA, TX	Y	22420 FQ	26330 MW	30520 TQ	USBLS	5/07
Except Postal Service	Dallas-Fort Worth-Arlington MSA, TX	Y	21770 FQ	25420 MW	29920 TQ	USBLS	5/07
Except Postal Service	El Paso MSA, TX	Y	18830 FQ	23810 MW	28880 TQ	USBLS	5/07
Except Postal Service	Houston-Sugar Land-Baytown MSA, TX	Y	20280 FQ	24610 MW	30260 TQ	USBLS	5/07
Except Postal Service	San Antonio MSA, TX	Y	19980 FQ	23660 MW	28740 TQ	USBLS	5/07
Except Postal Service	Utah	Y	17770 FQ	21690 MW	25140 TQ	USBLS	5/07
Except Postal Service	Provo-Orem MSA, UT	Y	17440 FQ	20020 MW	25110 TQ	USBLS	5/07
Except Postal Service	Salt Lake City MSA, UT	Y	17500 FQ	21660 MW	25460 TQ	USBLS	5/07
Except Postal Service	Vermont	Y	25150 FQ	27720 MW	30280 TQ	USBLS	5/07

AE	Average entry wage	AW	Average wage paid	FQ	First quartile wage
AER	Average entry range	AWR	Average wage range	H	Hourly
AEX	Average experienced wage	AXR	Average experienced range	HI	Highest wage paid
ATC	Average total compensation	D	Daily	HR	High end range

LO	Lowest wage paid	MTC	Median total compensation	TCC	Total cash compensation
LR	Low end range	MW	Median wage paid	TQ	Third quartile wage
M	Monthly	MWR	Median wage range	W	Weekly
MCC	Median cash compensation	S	See annotated source	Y	Yearly

Occupation/Type/Industry	Location	Per	Low	Mid	High	Source	Date
Mail Clerk and Mail Machine Operator							
Except Postal Service	Burlington-South Burlington MSA, VT	Y	21100 FQ	26880 MW	29850 TQ	USBLS	5/07
Except Postal Service	Virginia	Y	18500 FQ	25420 MW	32490 TQ	USBLS	5/07
Except Postal Service	Richmond MSA, VA	Y	21960 FQ	26020 MW	30420 TQ	USBLS	5/07
Except Postal Service	Virginia Beach-Norfolk-Newport News MSA, VA-NC	Y	18420 FQ	22460 MW	29720 TQ	USBLS	5/07
Except Postal Service	Washington	H	11.06 FQ	14.57 MW	18.07 TQ	WABLS	3/08
Except Postal Service	Seattle-Tacoma-Bellevue MSA, WA	Y	23170 FQ	30650 MW	37710 TQ	USBLS	5/07
Except Postal Service	West Virginia	Y	17333 FQ	21921 MW	28728 TQ	WVBLS	7/08-9/08
Except Postal Service	Charleston MSA, WV	Y	16400 FQ	19170 MW	24750 TQ	USBLS	5/07
Except Postal Service	Wisconsin	Y	20920 FQ	24280 MW	29350 TQ	USBLS	5/07
Except Postal Service	Milwaukee-Waukesha-West Allis MSA, WI	Y	21130 FQ	24640 MW	30630 TQ	USBLS	5/07
Except Postal Service	Puerto Rico	Y	13380 FQ	15700 MW	21610 TQ	USBLS	5/07
Except Postal Service	San Juan-Caguas-Guaynabo MSA, PR	Y	13150 FQ	15130 MW	18710 TQ	USBLS	5/07
Mail Clerk/Messenger							
Municipal Government	Carlsbad, CA	S	1117 LO		1357 HI	CCSS01	8/5/08
Mail Clerk/Screener							
State Government	Ohio	H	14.85 LO		16.35 HI	ODAS	2008
Mail/Copy Technician							
State Supreme Court	Michigan	Y		38127 AW		LSJ02	7/11/07
Mail Courier							
Municipal Government	Seattle, WA	H	12.76 LO		13.77 HI	CSSS	2007
Mail Docketing Clerk							
State Court of Appeals	Michigan	Y		35939 AW		LSJ02	7/11/07
Main Street Manager							
Municipal Government	East Point, GA	Y	41390 LO		64554 HI	AREGC	2007
Maintenance and Repair Worker							
General	Alabama	Y	23920 FQ	31440 MW	39190 TQ	USBLS	5/07
General	Birmingham-Hoover MSA, AL	Y	26640 FQ	33240 MW	38950 TQ	USBLS	5/07
General	Montgomery MSA, AL	Y	23220 FQ	32600 MW	44800 TQ	USBLS	5/07
General	Alaska	Y	31130 FQ	41670 MW	54900 TQ	USBLS	5/07
General	Anchorage MSA, AK	Y	30240 FQ	41750 MW	54060 TQ	USBLS	5/07
General	Arizona	Y	23390 FQ	30120 MW	39030 TQ	USBLS	5/07
General	Phoenix-Mesa-Scottsdale MSA, AZ	Y	24150 FQ	30810 MW	39750 TQ	USBLS	5/07
General	Tucson MSA, AZ	Y	21580 FQ	27990 MW	35750 TQ	USBLS	5/07
General	Arkansas	Y	21580 FQ	28150 MW	35840 TQ	USBLS	5/07
General	Little Rock-North Little Rock MSA, AR	Y	24280 FQ	30030 MW	37290 TQ	USBLS	5/07
General	California	H	13.14 FQ	17.60 MW	23.22 TQ	CABLS	1/08-3/08
General	Los Angeles-Long Beach-Glendale PMSA, CA	H	12.57 FQ	16.81 MW	22.91 TQ	CABLS	1/08-3/08
General	Oakland-Fremont-Hayward MSA, CA	H	15.53 FQ	20.70 MW	26.14 TQ	CABLS	1/08-3/08
General	Riverside-San Bernardino-Ontario MSA, CA	H	12.84 FQ	17.34 MW	22.64 TQ	CABLS	1/08-3/08
General	Sacramento-Arden Arcade-Roseville MSA, CA	H	13.51 FQ	17.54 MW	22.35 TQ	CABLS	1/08-3/08
General	San Diego-Carlsbad-San Marcos MSA, CA	H	12.98 FQ	16.46 MW	21.47 TQ	CABLS	1/08-3/08
General	San Francisco-San Mateo-Redwood PMSA, CA	H	15.45 FQ	20.62 MW	27.30 TQ	CABLS	1/08-3/08
General	San Jose-Sunnyvale-Santa Clara MSA, CA	H	16.30 FQ	21.31 MW	28.15 TQ	CABLS	1/08-3/08
General	Santa Ana-Anaheim-Irvine PMSA, CA	Y	25990 FQ	34140 MW	45770 TQ	USBLS	5/07
General	Colorado	Y	25780 FQ	32760 MW	41950 TQ	USBLS	5/07
General	Denver-Aurora MSA, CO	Y	27110 FQ	34440 MW	44310 TQ	USBLS	5/07
General	Fort Collins-Loveland MSA, CO	Y	24030 FQ	32370 MW	40810 TQ	USBLS	5/07

AE	Average entry wage	AW	Average wage paid	FQ	First quartile wage
AER	Average entry range	AWR	Average wage range	H	Hourly
AEX	Average experienced wage	AXR	Average experienced range	HI	Highest wage paid
ATC	Average total compensation	D	Daily	HR	High end range

LO	Lowest wage paid	MTC	Median total compensation
LR	Low end range	MW	Median wage paid
M	Monthly	MWR	Median wage range
MCC	Median cash compensation	S	See annotated source

TCC	Total cash compensation
TQ	Third quartile wage
W	Weekly
Y	Yearly

Maintenance and Repair Worker

Occupation/Type/Industry	Location	Per	Low	Mid	High	Source	Date
General	Connecticut	H	13.75 AE	19.70 MW		CTBLS	1/08-3/08
General	Bridgeport-Stamford-Norwalk MSA, CT	Y	29920 FQ	38720 MW	47600 TQ	USBLS	5/07
General	Hartford-West Hartford-East Hartford MSA, CT	Y	32740 FQ	40780 MW	48640 TQ	USBLS	5/07
General	Delaware	Y	26660 FQ	34420 MW	44260 TQ	USBLS	5/07
General	Wilmington PMSA, DE-MD-NJ	Y	28500 FQ	36970 MW	46960 TQ	USBLS	5/07
General	District of Columbia	Y	31420 FQ	39540 MW	47670 TQ	USBLS	5/07
General	Washington-Arlington-Alexandria MSA, DC-VA-MD-WV	Y	29620 FQ	38250 MW	51040 TQ	USBLS	5/07
General	Florida	Y	22520 FQ	28310 MW	35680 TQ	USBLS	5/07
General	Fort Lauderdale-Pompano Beach-Deerfield Beach PMSA, FL	Y	23490 FQ	29310 MW	36690 TQ	USBLS	5/07
General	Jacksonville MSA, FL	Y	22600 FQ	29900 MW	38100 TQ	USBLS	5/07
General	Miami-Fort Lauderdale-Miami Beach MSA, FL	Y	22960 FQ	28600 MW	35690 TQ	USBLS	5/07
General	Orlando-Kissimmee MSA, FL	Y	22140 FQ	27160 MW	33600 TQ	USBLS	5/07
General	Pensacola-Ferry Pass-Brent MSA, FL	Y	22160 FQ	30010 MW	41360 TQ	USBLS	5/07
General	Tampa-St. Petersburg-Clearwater MSA, FL	Y	21170 FQ	27070 MW	34120 TQ	USBLS	5/07
General	West Palm Beach-Boca Raton-Boynton Beach PMSA, FL	Y	24940 FQ	29960 MW	36750 TQ	USBLS	5/07
General	Georgia	Y	24870 FQ	31800 MW	39700 TQ	USBLS	5/07
General	Atlanta-Sandy Springs-Marietta MSA, GA	Y	26320 FQ	33300 MW	40980 TQ	USBLS	5/07
General	Hawaii	Y	26710 FQ	34130 MW	45220 TQ	USBLS	5/07
General	Honolulu MSA, HI	Y	26050 FQ	33040 MW	44940 TQ	USBLS	5/07
General	Idaho	Y	22410 FQ	28510 MW	38160 TQ	USBLS	5/07
General	Boise City-Nampa MSA, ID	Y	22840 FQ	28080 MW	35490 TQ	USBLS	5/07
General	Lewiston MSA, ID-WA	Y	21430 FQ	31960 MW	42030 TQ	USBLS	5/07
General	Illinois	Y	27730 FQ	37490 MW	49230 TQ	USBLS	5/07
General	Champaign-Urbana MSA, IL	Y	23880 FQ	30060 MW	39090 TQ	USBLS	5/07
General	Chicago-Naperville-Joliet MSA, IL-IN-WI	Y	29940 FQ	40470 MW	51400 TQ	USBLS	5/07
General	Indiana	Y	26070 FQ	34140 MW	43640 TQ	USBLS	5/07
General	Evansville MSA, IN-KY	Y	26030 FQ	35660 MW	47380 TQ	USBLS	5/07
General	Gary PMSA, IN	Y	35000 FQ	44300 MW	50760 TQ	USBLS	5/07
General	Indianapolis-Carmel MSA, IN	Y	25730 FQ	32720 MW	40940 TQ	USBLS	5/07
General	Iowa	Y	24860 FQ	32100 MW	40050 TQ	USBLS	5/07
General	Des Moines-West Des Moines MSA, IA	Y	24780 FQ	31410 MW	40730 TQ	USBLS	5/07
General	Kansas	Y	23340 FQ	30110 MW	38910 TQ	USBLS	5/07
General	Wichita MSA, KS	Y	22940 FQ	29310 MW	37240 TQ	USBLS	5/07
General	Kentucky	Y	23266 FQ	30936 MW	40167 TQ	KYBLS	2008
General	Louisville-Jefferson County MSA, KY-IN	Y	23640 FQ	31390 MW	40870 TQ	USBLS	5/07
General	Louisiana	H	10.65 FQ	13.92 MW	18.06 TQ	LABLS	1/08-3/08
General	Baton Rouge MSA, LA	Y	23730 FQ	31120 MW	41420 TQ	USBLS	5/07
General	Lake Charles MSA, LA	Y	22290 FQ	28240 MW	36190 TQ	USBLS	5/07
General	New Orleans-Metairie-Kenner MSA, LA	Y	23330 FQ	30250 MW	38930 TQ	USBLS	5/07
General	Maine	Y	25250 FQ	31020 MW	38440 TQ	USBLS	5/07
General	Portland-South Portland-Biddeford MSA, ME	Y	24650 FQ	29820 MW	36510 TQ	USBLS	5/07
General	Maryland	Y		34775 MW		MDBLS	3/08
General	Baltimore-Towson MSA, MD	Y	26590 FQ	33440 MW	42230 TQ	USBLS	5/07
General	Bethesda-Gaithersburg-Frederick PMSA, MD	Y	28170 FQ	35390 MW	44730 TQ	USBLS	5/07
General	Cumberland MSA, MD-WV	Y	19770 FQ	26020 MW	33390 TQ	USBLS	5/07
General	Massachusetts	Y	31640 FQ	38860 MW	46990 TQ	USBLS	5/07
General	Boston-Cambridge-Quincy NECTA, MA	Y	33420 FQ	40460 MW	48250 TQ	USBLS	5/07
General	Worcester MSA, MA-CT	Y	29060 FQ	35460 MW	42370 TQ	USBLS	5/07
General	Michigan	Y	27760 FQ	36940 MW	46190 TQ	USBLS	5/07
General	Detroit-Warren-Livonia MSA, MI	Y	29540 FQ	39430 MW	48830 TQ	USBLS	5/07
General	Flint MSA, MI	Y	26970 FQ	35770 MW	44750 TQ	USBLS	5/07

AE	Average entry wage	AW	Average wage paid	FQ	First quartile wage	LO	Lowest wage paid	MTC	Median total compensation	TCC	Total cash compensation
AER	Average entry range	AWR	Average wage range	H	Hourly	LR	Low end range	MW	Median wage paid	TQ	Third quartile wage
AEX	Average experienced wage	AXR	Average experienced range	HI	Highest wage paid	M	Monthly	MWR	Median wage range	W	Weekly
ATC	Average total compensation	D	Daily	HR	High end range	MCC	Median cash compensation	S	See annotated source	Y	Yearly

Occupation/Type/Industry	Location	Per	Low	Mid	High	Source	Date
Maintenance and Repair Worker							
General	Grand Rapids-Wyoming MSA, MI	Y	27920 FQ	36910 MW	44980 TQ	USBLS	5/07
General	Warren-Troy-Farmington Hills PMSA, MI	Y	28800 FQ	38240 MW	47320 TQ	USBLS	5/07
General	Minnesota	Y	31101 FQ	38653 MW	47045 TQ	MNBLS	10/08-12/08
General	Duluth-Superior MSA, MN-WI	Y	27503 FQ	37352 MW	46667 TQ	MNBLS	10/08-12/08
General	Minneapolis-Saint Paul MSA, MN-WI	Y	34541 FQ	41422 MW	49153 TQ	MNBLS	10/08-12/08
General	Rochester MSA, MN	Y	28341 FQ	35377 MW	45105 TQ	MNBLS	10/08-12/08
General	Mississippi	Y	21350 FQ	26490 MW	33240 TQ	USBLS	5/07
General	Jackson MSA, MS	Y	21500 FQ	26570 MW	34030 TQ	USBLS	5/07
General	Missouri	Y	23700 FQ	31310 MW	40450 TQ	USBLS	5/07
General	Kansas City MSA, MO-KS	Y	24990 FQ	32420 MW	41840 TQ	USBLS	5/07
General	St. Louis MSA, MO-IL	Y	27110 FQ	35520 MW	46060 TQ	USBLS	5/07
General	Montana	Y	22750 FQ	31630 MW	38260 TQ	USBLS	5/07
General	Billings MSA, MT	Y	21640 FQ	27750 MW	35640 TQ	USBLS	5/07
General	Missoula MSA, MT	Y	20750 FQ	27600 MW	36220 TQ	USBLS	5/07
General	Nebraska	Y	23350 FQ	30170 MW	37850 TQ	USBLS	5/07
General	Omaha-Council Bluffs MSA, NE-IA	Y	25740 FQ	32380 MW	39610 TQ	USBLS	5/07
General	Nevada	H	13.39 FQ	18.30 MW	24.19 TQ	NVBLS	5/08
General	Las Vegas-Paradise MSA, NV	H	13.96 FQ	19.42 MW	25.25 TQ	NVBLS	5/08
General	New Hampshire	H	12.31 AE	16.94 MW	19.70 AEX	NHBLS	6/08
General	Manchester MSA, NH	Y	29580 FQ	36680 MW	43530 TQ	USBLS	5/07
General	Nashua NECTA, NH-MA	Y	28550 FQ	36320 MW	43050 TQ	USBLS	5/07
General	New Jersey	Y	28310 FQ	37000 MW	46290 TQ	USBLS	5/07
General	Camden PMSA, NJ	Y	29320 FQ	37380 MW	45250 TQ	USBLS	5/07
General	Edison PMSA, NJ	Y	27820 FQ	37420 MW	47230 TQ	USBLS	5/07
General	Newark-Union PMSA, NJ-PA	Y	28390 FQ	37130 MW	47620 TQ	USBLS	5/07
General	New Mexico	Y	20880 FQ	26600 MW	35070 TQ	USBLS	5/07
General	Albuquerque MSA, NM	Y	21340 FQ	27310 MW	34740 TQ	USBLS	5/07
General	New York	Y	26700 FQ	35020 MW	44580 TQ	USBLS	5/07
General	Albany-Schenectady-Troy MSA, NY	Y	25390 FQ	32960 MW	42650 TQ	USBLS	5/07
General	Buffalo-Niagara Falls MSA, NY	Y	25260 FQ	34260 MW	44480 TQ	USBLS	5/07
General	Glens Falls MSA, NY	Y	26980 FQ	33530 MW	41610 TQ	USBLS	5/07
General	Nassau-Suffolk PMSA, NY	Y	28900 FQ	37870 MW	48430 TQ	USBLS	5/07
General	New York-Northern New Jersey-Long Island MSA, NY-NJ-PA	Y	27890 FQ	36950 MW	46310 TQ	USBLS	5/07
General	North Carolina	Y	26050 FQ	32800 MW	40110 TQ	USBLS	5/07
General	Charlotte-Gastonia-Concord MSA, NC-SC	Y	28000 FQ	35210 MW	44040 TQ	USBLS	5/07
General	Raleigh-Cary MSA, NC	Y	26330 FQ	33720 MW	41850 TQ	USBLS	5/07
General	North Dakota	Y	25320 FQ	31550 MW	43000 TQ	USBLS	5/07
General	Fargo MSA, ND-MN	Y	25160 FQ	30090 MW	36810 TQ	USBLS	5/07
General	Ohio	Y	26110 FQ	34280 MW	42840 TQ	USBLS	5/07
General	Cincinnati-Middletown MSA, OH-KY-IN	Y	27380 FQ	36330 MW	45150 TQ	USBLS	5/07
General	Cleveland-Elyria-Mentor MSA, OH	Y	26820 FQ	35970 MW	45400 TQ	USBLS	5/07
General	Columbus MSA, OH	Y	26520 FQ	34270 MW	42160 TQ	USBLS	5/07
General	Dayton MSA, OH	Y	24110 FQ	31520 MW	38930 TQ	USBLS	5/07
General	Springfield MSA, OH	Y	22130 FQ	29250 MW	36280 TQ	USBLS	5/07
General	Oklahoma	Y	22350 FQ	29150 MW	37770 TQ	USBLS	5/07
General	Oklahoma City MSA, OK	Y	23730 FQ	30190 MW	37710 TQ	USBLS	5/07
General	Tulsa MSA, OK	Y	24160 FQ	30860 MW	39660 TQ	USBLS	5/07
General	Oregon	H	12.15 FQ	16.08 MW	20.44 TQ	ORBLS	5/08
General	Portland-Vancouver-Beaverton MSA, OR-WA	Y	26980 FQ	35190 MW	44290 TQ	USBLS	5/07
General	Pennsylvania	Y	25510 FQ	33120 MW	41380 TQ	USBLS	5/07
General	Allentown-Bethlehem-Easton MSA, PA-NJ	Y	26650 FQ	34000 MW	41620 TQ	USBLS	5/07
General	Philadelphia-Camden-Wilmington MSA, PA-NJ-DE-MD	Y	27950 FQ	35960 MW	45100 TQ	USBLS	5/07
General	Pittsburgh MSA, PA	Y	24210 FQ	33080 MW	41250 TQ	USBLS	5/07
General	Rhode Island	Y	27670 FQ	35550 MW	43280 TQ	USBLS	5/07
General	Providence-Fall River-Warwick MSA, RI-MA	Y	27500 FQ	35300 MW	43080 TQ	USBLS	5/07

AE	Average entry wage	AW	Average wage paid	FQ	First quartile wage	LO	Lowest wage paid	MTC	Median total compensation	TCC	Total cash compensation
AER	Average entry range	AWR	Average wage range	H	Hourly	LR	Low end range	MW	Median wage paid	TQ	Third quartile wage
AEX	Average experienced wage	AXR	Average experienced range	HI	Highest wage paid	M	Monthly	MWR	Median wage range	W	Weekly
ATC	Average total compensation	D	Daily	HR	High end range	MCC	Median cash compensation	S	See annotated source	Y	Yearly

Occupation/Type/Industry	Location	Per	Low	Mid	High	Source	Date
Maintenance and Repair Worker							
General	South Carolina	Y	23850 FQ	31180 MW	39890 TQ	USBLS	5/07
General	Charleston-North Charleston MSA, SC	Y	21870 FQ	30150 MW	39870 TQ	USBLS	5/07
General	Columbia MSA, SC	Y	25690 FQ	32940 MW	41350 TQ	USBLS	5/07
General	South Dakota	Y	23963 FQ	27928 MW	32107 TQ	SDBLS	7/08-9/08
General	Sioux Falls MSA, SD	Y	24974 FQ	28306 MW	31688 TQ	SDBLS	7/08-9/08
General	Tennessee	Y	23790 FQ	31140 MW	40300 TQ	USBLS	5/07
General	Memphis MSA, TN-MS-AR	Y	24180 FQ	31430 MW	43110 TQ	USBLS	5/07
General	Nashville-Davidson-Murfreesboro MSA, TN	Y	24340 FQ	32630 MW	42450 TQ	USBLS	5/07
General	Texas	Y	20220 FQ	26210 MW	34520 TQ	USBLS	5/07
General	Austin-Round Rock MSA, TX	Y	23420 FQ	28300 MW	35100 TQ	USBLS	5/07
General	Dallas-Fort Worth-Arlington MSA, TX	Y	22750 FQ	29550 MW	37770 TQ	USBLS	5/07
General	El Paso MSA, TX	Y	15820 FQ	19910 MW	28030 TQ	USBLS	5/07
General	Houston-Sugar Land-Baytown MSA, TX	Y	21230 FQ	27340 MW	36400 TQ	USBLS	5/07
General	San Antonio MSA, TX	Y	20170 FQ	25760 MW	32560 TQ	USBLS	5/07
General	Utah	Y	23580 FQ	30880 MW	40990 TQ	USBLS	5/07
General	Ogden-Clearfield MSA, UT	Y	25750 FQ	32890 MW	41200 TQ	USBLS	5/07
General	Salt Lake City MSA, UT	Y	25470 FQ	32970 MW	43340 TQ	USBLS	5/07
General	Vermont	Y	25670 FQ	31250 MW	38110 TQ	USBLS	5/07
General	Burlington-South Burlington MSA, VT	Y	26440 FQ	31870 MW	38640 TQ	USBLS	5/07
General	Virginia	Y	26700 FQ	34090 MW	45140 TQ	USBLS	5/07
General	Richmond MSA, VA	Y	27700 FQ	35040 MW	45710 TQ	USBLS	5/07
General	Virginia Beach-Norfolk-Newport News MSA, VA-NC	Y	24650 FQ	30600 MW	37780 TQ	USBLS	5/07
General	Washington	H	14.06 FQ	18.14 MW	22.68 TQ	WABLS	3/08
General	Bremerton-Silverdale MSA, WA	Y	29340 FQ	38670 MW	47010 TQ	USBLS	5/07
General	Seattle-Tacoma-Bellevue MSA, WA	Y	30090 FQ	38740 MW	48610 TQ	USBLS	5/07
General	West Virginia	Y	19004 FQ	26092 MW	36706 TQ	WVBLS	7/08-9/08
General	Charleston MSA, WV	Y	18610 FQ	26920 MW	41110 TQ	USBLS	5/07
General	Wisconsin	Y	28490 FQ	35890 MW	43590 TQ	USBLS	5/07
General	Milwaukee-Waukesha-West Allis MSA, WI	Y	29380 FQ	37090 MW	44790 TQ	USBLS	5/07
General	Wyoming	Y	25235 FQ	34814 MW	50236 TQ	WYBLS	9/08
General	Cheyenne MSA, WY	Y	22151 FQ	30194 MW	41898 TQ	WYBLS	9/08
General	Puerto Rico	Y	14450 FQ	18300 MW	25840 TQ	USBLS	5/07
General	San Juan-Caguas-Guaynabo MSA, PR	Y	14630 FQ	18720 MW	26880 TQ	USBLS	5/07
General	Virgin Islands	Y	20030 FQ	23870 MW	29280 TQ	USBLS	5/07
General	Guam	Y	16750 FQ	21900 MW	27740 TQ	USBLS	5/07
Maintenance Assistant							
Municipal Government	Carlsbad, CA	H	9.00 LO		17.00 HI	CCSS	1/1/08
Maintenance Machinist							
Municipal Government	Cincinnati, OH	Y	44100 LO		47537 HI	COHSS	10/08
Maintenance Superintendent							
Public Works	Forsyth County, GA	Y	67299 LO		100948 HI	GACTY03	2008
Public Works	Rabun County, GA	Y	31069 LO		47275 HI	GACTY03	2008
Maintenance Worker							
Machinery	Alabama	Y	24210 FQ	30320 MW	37680 TQ	USBLS	5/07
Machinery	Birmingham-Hoover MSA, AL	Y	26780 FQ	32140 MW	38710 TQ	USBLS	5/07
Machinery	Alaska	Y	18970 FQ	33220 MW	49390 TQ	USBLS	5/07
Machinery	Arizona	Y	29060 FQ	38980 MW	48330 TQ	USBLS	5/07
Machinery	Phoenix-Mesa-Scottsdale MSA, AZ	Y	30030 FQ	42050 MW	50960 TQ	USBLS	5/07
Machinery	Tucson MSA, AZ	Y	33350 FQ	39090 MW	45280 TQ	USBLS	5/07
Machinery	Arkansas	Y	24790 FQ	28880 MW	34610 TQ	USBLS	5/07
Machinery	Little Rock-North Little Rock MSA, AR	Y	24480 FQ	27800 MW	31900 TQ	USBLS	5/07
Machinery	California	H	13.26 FQ	19.48 MW	24.16 TQ	CABLS	1/08-3/08
Machinery	Los Angeles-Long Beach-Glendale PMSA, CA	H	11.83 FQ	15.02 MW	20.42 TQ	CABLS	1/08-3/08

AE   Average entry wage   AW   Average wage paid   FQ   First quartile wage   LO   Lowest wage paid   MTC   Median total compensation   TCC   Total cash compensation
AER   Average entry range   AWR   Average wage range   H   Hourly   LR   Low end range   MW   Median wage paid   TQ   Third quartile wage
AEX   Average experienced wage   AXR   Average experienced range   HI   Highest wage paid   M   Monthly   MWR   Median wage range   W   Weekly
ATC   Average total compensation   D   Daily   HR   High end range   MCC   Median cash compensation   S   See annotated source   Y   Yearly

Maintenance Worker

Occupation/Type/Industry	Location	Per	Low	Mid	High	Source	Date
Machinery	Oakland-Fremont-Hayward MSA, CA	H	17.39 FQ	20.76 MW	28.60 TQ	CABLS	1/08-3/08
Machinery	Riverside-San Bernardino-Ontario MSA, CA	H	11.61 FQ	18.40 MW	23.74 TQ	CABLS	1/08-3/08
Machinery	Sacramento-Arden Arcade-Roseville MSA, CA	H	15.58 FQ	21.45 MW	23.78 TQ	CABLS	1/08-3/08
Machinery	San Diego-Carlsbad-San Marcos MSA, CA	H	21.53 FQ	26.17 MW	29.65 TQ	CABLS	1/08-3/08
Machinery	San Francisco-San Mateo-Redwood PMSA, CA	H	18.55 FQ	22.63 MW	29.11 TQ	CABLS	1/08-3/08
Machinery	San Jose-Sunnyvale-Santa Clara MSA, CA	H	12.55 FQ	18.38 MW	25.05 TQ	CABLS	1/08-3/08
Machinery	Santa Ana-Anaheim-Irvine PMSA, CA	Y	22550 FQ	30790 MW	41010 TQ	USBLS	5/07
Machinery	Colorado	Y	27490 FQ	43760 MW	51520 TQ	USBLS	5/07
Machinery	Boulder MSA, CO	Y	35070 FQ	42440 MW	51990 TQ	USBLS	5/07
Machinery	Denver-Aurora MSA, CO	Y	25920 FQ	41850 MW	49190 TQ	USBLS	5/07
Machinery	Connecticut	H	13.38 AE	20.60 MW		CTBLS	1/08-3/08
Machinery	Bridgeport-Stamford-Norwalk MSA, CT	Y	34220 FQ	45510 MW	51360 TQ	USBLS	5/07
Machinery	Hartford-West Hartford-East Hartford MSA, CT	Y	29530 FQ	35880 MW	44570 TQ	USBLS	5/07
Machinery	Delaware	Y	30710 FQ	40250 MW	49670 TQ	USBLS	5/07
Machinery	Wilmington PMSA, DE-MD-NJ	Y	25820 FQ	36390 MW	48640 TQ	USBLS	5/07
Machinery	District of Columbia	Y	36440 FQ	51930 MW	58240 TQ	USBLS	5/07
Machinery	Washington-Arlington-Alexandria MSA, DC-VA-MD-WV	Y	27380 FQ	33170 MW	42550 TQ	USBLS	5/07
Machinery	Florida	Y	27820 FQ	34390 MW	43830 TQ	USBLS	5/07
Machinery	Fort Lauderdale-Pompano Beach-Deerfield Beach PMSA, FL	Y	29130 FQ	37190 MW	46350 TQ	USBLS	5/07
Machinery	Jacksonville MSA, FL	Y	27870 FQ	35350 MW	44240 TQ	USBLS	5/07
Machinery	Miami-Fort Lauderdale-Miami Beach MSA, FL	Y	28410 FQ	35230 MW	45750 TQ	USBLS	5/07
Machinery	Orlando-Kissimmee MSA, FL	Y	32440 FQ	40980 MW	46950 TQ	USBLS	5/07
Machinery	Tampa-St. Petersburg-Clearwater MSA, FL	Y	25980 FQ	30250 MW	36860 TQ	USBLS	5/07
Machinery	West Palm Beach-Boca Raton-Boynton Beach PMSA, FL	Y	27570 FQ	33490 MW	41630 TQ	USBLS	5/07
Machinery	Georgia	Y	23960 FQ	28550 MW	35480 TQ	USBLS	5/07
Machinery	Atlanta-Sandy Springs-Marietta MSA, GA	Y	23470 FQ	27730 MW	34490 TQ	USBLS	5/07
Machinery	Augusta-Richmond County MSA, GA-SC	Y	27480 FQ	31400 MW	36810 TQ	USBLS	5/07
Machinery	Hawaii	Y	32210 FQ	41210 MW	47620 TQ	USBLS	5/07
Machinery	Honolulu MSA, HI	Y	32010 FQ	40020 MW	46260 TQ	USBLS	5/07
Machinery	Idaho	Y	27900 FQ	30940 MW	38120 TQ	USBLS	5/07
Machinery	Boise City-Nampa MSA, ID	Y	27840 FQ	30470 MW	36770 TQ	USBLS	5/07
Machinery	Illinois	Y	32970 FQ	45390 MW	55210 TQ	USBLS	5/07
Machinery	Chicago-Naperville-Joliet MSA, IL-IN-WI	Y	33030 FQ	48310 MW	56350 TQ	USBLS	5/07
Machinery	Indiana	Y	32050 FQ	38880 MW	50380 TQ	USBLS	5/07
Machinery	Elkhart-Goshen MSA, IN	Y	26990 FQ	33840 MW	41890 TQ	USBLS	5/07
Machinery	Fort Wayne MSA, IN	Y	35890 FQ	42400 MW	49450 TQ	USBLS	5/07
Machinery	Gary PMSA, IN	Y	31830 FQ	38650 MW	54620 TQ	USBLS	5/07
Machinery	Indianapolis-Carmel MSA, IN	Y	34190 FQ	38840 MW	47590 TQ	USBLS	5/07
Machinery	Iowa	Y	29720 FQ	34730 MW	38860 TQ	USBLS	5/07
Machinery	Des Moines-West Des Moines MSA, IA	Y	28910 FQ	34760 MW	43630 TQ	USBLS	5/07
Machinery	Kansas	Y	24150 FQ	29150 MW	38160 TQ	USBLS	5/07
Machinery	Wichita MSA, KS	Y	25360 FQ	30090 MW	38010 TQ	USBLS	5/07
Machinery	Kentucky	Y	31841 FQ	38166 MW	47473 TQ	KYBLS	2008
Machinery	Louisville-Jefferson County MSA, KY-IN	Y	32830 FQ	37730 MW	49600 TQ	USBLS	5/07
Machinery	Louisiana	H	12.47 FQ	15.73 MW	21.88 TQ	LABLS	1/08-3/08
Machinery	Baton Rouge MSA, LA	Y	31070 FQ	43240 MW	50130 TQ	USBLS	5/07
Machinery	New Orleans-Metairie-Kenner MSA, LA	Y	27820 FQ	33620 MW	45210 TQ	USBLS	5/07
Machinery	Maine	Y	26800 FQ	34100 MW	38610 TQ	USBLS	5/07

AE	Average entry wage	AW	Average wage paid	FQ	First quartile wage	LO	Lowest wage paid	MTC	Median total compensation	TCC	Total cash compensation
AER	Average entry range	AWR	Average wage range	H	Hourly	LR	Low end range	MW	Median wage paid	TQ	Third quartile wage
AEX	Average experienced wage	AXR	Average experienced range	HI	Highest wage paid	M	Monthly	MWR	Median wage range	W	Weekly
ATC	Average total compensation	D	Daily	HR	High end range	MCC	Median cash compensation	S	See annotated source	Y	Yearly

Maintenance Worker

Occupation/Type/Industry	Location	Per	Low	Mid	High	Source	Date
Machinery	Lewiston-Auburn MSA, ME	Y	19530 FQ	28400 MW	36310 TQ	USBLS	5/07
Machinery	Portland-South Portland-Biddeford MSA, ME	Y	29410 FQ	34060 MW	38340 TQ	USBLS	5/07
Machinery	Maryland	Y		34175 MW		MDBLS	3/08
Machinery	Baltimore-Towson MSA, MD	Y	24900 FQ	33220 MW	38810 TQ	USBLS	5/07
Machinery	Bethesda-Gaithersburg-Frederick PMSA, MD	Y	29380 FQ	36060 MW	41300 TQ	USBLS	5/07
Machinery	Massachusetts	Y	32780 FQ	38850 MW	46870 TQ	USBLS	5/07
Machinery	Boston-Cambridge-Quincy NECTA, MA	Y	34910 FQ	41080 MW	48770 TQ	USBLS	5/07
Machinery	Lynn-Peabody-Salem NECTA, MA	Y	42000 FQ	49130 MW	56050 TQ	USBLS	5/07
Machinery	Worcester MSA, MA-CT	Y	31290 FQ	36330 MW	43580 TQ	USBLS	5/07
Machinery	Michigan	Y	34220 FQ	42810 MW	49580 TQ	USBLS	5/07
Machinery	Detroit-Warren-Livonia MSA, MI	Y	37030 FQ	44020 MW	49490 TQ	USBLS	5/07
Machinery	Flint MSA, MI	Y	44040 FQ	52390 MW	58090 TQ	USBLS	5/07
Machinery	Grand Rapids-Wyoming MSA, MI	Y	30360 FQ	37750 MW	51670 TQ	USBLS	5/07
Machinery	Warren-Troy-Farmington Hills PMSA, MI	Y	34640 FQ	41960 MW	50510 TQ	USBLS	5/07
Machinery	Minnesota	Y	28457 FQ	35013 MW	43185 TQ	MNBLS	10/08-12/08
Machinery	Duluth-Superior MSA, MN-WI	Y	32989 FQ	37331 MW	41685 TQ	MNBLS	10/08-12/08
Machinery	Minneapolis-Saint Paul MSA, MN-WI	Y	32894 FQ	39975 MW	47737 TQ	MNBLS	10/08-12/08
Machinery	Rochester MSA, MN	Y	28478 FQ	30457 MW	32359 TQ	MNBLS	10/08-12/08
Machinery	Mississippi	Y	27730 FQ	33720 MW	40740 TQ	USBLS	5/07
Machinery	Jackson MSA, MS	Y	26520 FQ	34150 MW	45640 TQ	USBLS	5/07
Machinery	Missouri	Y	29990 FQ	35730 MW	42380 TQ	USBLS	5/07
Machinery	Kansas City MSA, MO-KS	Y	25480 FQ	32460 MW	40890 TQ	USBLS	5/07
Machinery	St. Louis MSA, MO-IL	Y	33300 FQ	39950 MW	47330 TQ	USBLS	5/07
Machinery	Montana	Y	28050 FQ	33720 MW	38930 TQ	USBLS	5/07
Machinery	Nebraska	Y	28350 FQ	36130 MW	43160 TQ	USBLS	5/07
Machinery	Omaha-Council Bluffs MSA, NE-IA	Y	27550 FQ	35680 MW	41580 TQ	USBLS	5/07
Machinery	Nevada	H	13.73 FQ	18.02 MW	22.17 TQ	NVBLS	5/08
Machinery	Las Vegas-Paradise MSA, NV	H	12.19 FQ	17.80 MW	22.00 TQ	NVBLS	5/08
Machinery	New Hampshire	H	13.04 AE	24.33 MW	25.55 AEX	NHBLS	6/08
Machinery	Nashua NECTA, NH-MA	Y	48130 FQ	51950 MW	55780 TQ	USBLS	5/07
Machinery	New Jersey	Y	32230 FQ	39690 MW	50220 TQ	USBLS	5/07
Machinery	Camden PMSA, NJ	Y	30960 FQ	39710 MW	46650 TQ	USBLS	5/07
Machinery	Edison PMSA, NJ	Y	35050 FQ	44820 MW	57870 TQ	USBLS	5/07
Machinery	Newark-Union PMSA, NJ-PA	Y	32620 FQ	38070 MW	46350 TQ	USBLS	5/07
Machinery	Trenton-Ewing MSA, NJ	Y	29010 FQ	35770 MW	45020 TQ	USBLS	5/07
Machinery	New Mexico	Y	23520 FQ	33900 MW	40350 TQ	USBLS	5/07
Machinery	Albuquerque MSA, NM	Y	27120 FQ	33280 MW	37990 TQ	USBLS	5/07
Machinery	New York	Y	30740 FQ	41610 MW	53250 TQ	USBLS	5/07
Machinery	Albany-Schenectady-Troy MSA, NY	Y	34100 FQ	39700 MW	46060 TQ	USBLS	5/07
Machinery	Buffalo-Niagara Falls MSA, NY	Y	31010 FQ	39890 MW	47280 TQ	USBLS	5/07
Machinery	Nassau-Suffolk PMSA, NY	Y	36090 FQ	43280 MW	53940 TQ	USBLS	5/07
Machinery	New York-Northern New Jersey-Long Island MSA, NY-NJ-PA	Y	32300 FQ	41430 MW	55090 TQ	USBLS	5/07
Machinery	North Carolina	Y	26650 FQ	32580 MW	41700 TQ	USBLS	5/07
Machinery	Charlotte-Gastonia-Concord MSA, NC-SC	Y	26330 FQ	30650 MW	35610 TQ	USBLS	5/07
Machinery	Greensboro-High Point MSA, NC	Y	28580 FQ	34480 MW	41480 TQ	USBLS	5/07
Machinery	Raleigh-Cary MSA, NC	Y	25960 FQ	33120 MW	40110 TQ	USBLS	5/07
Machinery	North Dakota	Y	27470 FQ	35110 MW	54270 TQ	USBLS	5/07
Machinery	Ohio	Y	30170 FQ	37520 MW	46860 TQ	USBLS	5/07
Machinery	Cincinnati-Middletown MSA, OH-KY-IN	Y	31770 FQ	40820 MW	57010 TQ	USBLS	5/07
Machinery	Cleveland-Elyria-Mentor MSA, OH	Y	29540 FQ	37280 MW	48620 TQ	USBLS	5/07
Machinery	Columbus MSA, OH	Y	31390 FQ	40840 MW	47630 TQ	USBLS	5/07
Machinery	Dayton MSA, OH	Y	32190 FQ	39820 MW	47320 TQ	USBLS	5/07
Machinery	Springfield MSA, OH	Y	36270 FQ	46940 MW	58090 TQ	USBLS	5/07
Machinery	Oklahoma	Y	22580 FQ	28620 MW	36630 TQ	USBLS	5/07

AE	Average entry wage	AW	Average wage paid	FQ	First quartile wage	LO	Lowest wage paid	MTC	Median total compensation	TCC	Total cash compensation
AER	Average entry range	AWR	Average wage range	H	Hourly	LR	Low end range	MW	Median wage paid	TQ	Third quartile wage
AEX	Average experienced wage	AXR	Average experienced range	HI	Highest wage paid	M	Monthly	MWR	Median wage range	W	Weekly
ATC	Average total compensation	D	Daily	HR	High end range	MCC	Median cash compensation	S	See annotated source	Y	Yearly

Occupation/Type/Industry	Location	Per	Low	Mid	High	Source	Date
Maintenance Worker							
Machinery	Oklahoma City MSA, OK	Y	26480 FQ	34460 MW	49910 TQ	USBLS	5/07
Machinery	Tulsa MSA, OK	Y	21550 FQ	27180 MW	32550 TQ	USBLS	5/07
Machinery	Oregon	H	11.73 FQ	14.96 MW	18.64 TQ	ORBLS	5/08
Machinery	Portland-Vancouver-Beaverton MSA, OR-WA	Y	21310 FQ	29470 MW	37210 TQ	USBLS	5/07
Machinery	Pennsylvania	Y	28170 FQ	36210 MW	46480 TQ	USBLS	5/07
Machinery	Allentown-Bethlehem-Easton MSA, PA-NJ	Y	28300 FQ	32470 MW	39570 TQ	USBLS	5/07
Machinery	Philadelphia-Camden-Wilmington MSA, PA-NJ-DE-MD	Y	32030 FQ	40190 MW	51680 TQ	USBLS	5/07
Machinery	Pittsburgh MSA, PA	Y	27610 FQ	40060 MW	52840 TQ	USBLS	5/07
Machinery	York-Hanover MSA, PA	Y	28990 FQ	34860 MW	42130 TQ	USBLS	5/07
Machinery	Rhode Island	Y	28860 FQ	36930 MW	44090 TQ	USBLS	5/07
Machinery	Providence-Fall River-Warwick MSA, RI-MA	Y	30040 FQ	37440 MW	44610 TQ	USBLS	5/07
Machinery	South Carolina	Y	27010 FQ	32240 MW	39120 TQ	USBLS	5/07
Machinery	Charleston-North Charleston MSA, SC	Y	30890 FQ	40220 MW	47280 TQ	USBLS	5/07
Machinery	Columbia MSA, SC	Y	21480 FQ	31020 MW	48170 TQ	USBLS	5/07
Machinery	South Dakota	Y	21415 FQ	23600 MW	25838 TQ	SDBLS	7/08-9/08
Machinery	Sioux Falls MSA, SD	Y	20852 FQ	22822 MW	24563 TQ	SDBLS	7/08-9/08
Machinery	Tennessee	Y	26830 FQ	31920 MW	38330 TQ	USBLS	5/07
Machinery	Knoxville MSA, TN	Y	31450 FQ	36680 MW	40970 TQ	USBLS	5/07
Machinery	Memphis MSA, TN-MS-AR	Y	32390 FQ	36390 MW	40710 TQ	USBLS	5/07
Machinery	Nashville-Davidson-Murfreesboro MSA, TN	Y	25460 FQ	34200 MW	41040 TQ	USBLS	5/07
Machinery	Texas	Y	22460 FQ	29100 MW	38030 TQ	USBLS	5/07
Machinery	Austin-Round Rock MSA, TX	Y	26430 FQ	30840 MW	36800 TQ	USBLS	5/07
Machinery	Dallas-Fort Worth-Arlington MSA, TX	Y	22690 FQ	31470 MW	46400 TQ	USBLS	5/07
Machinery	El Paso MSA, TX	Y	19240 FQ	26010 MW	34530 TQ	USBLS	5/07
Machinery	Houston-Sugar Land-Baytown MSA, TX	Y	24670 FQ	29640 MW	38030 TQ	USBLS	5/07
Machinery	San Antonio MSA, TX	Y	22370 FQ	31510 MW	37600 TQ	USBLS	5/07
Machinery	Utah	Y	27100 FQ	34280 MW	43070 TQ	USBLS	5/07
Machinery	Salt Lake City MSA, UT	Y	27440 FQ	36410 MW	44050 TQ	USBLS	5/07
Machinery	Vermont	Y	27050 FQ	32050 MW	36650 TQ	USBLS	5/07
Machinery	Burlington-South Burlington MSA, VT	Y	26270 FQ	33370 MW	39550 TQ	USBLS	5/07
Machinery	Virginia	Y	28970 FQ	36700 MW	48690 TQ	USBLS	5/07
Machinery	Richmond MSA, VA	Y	43910 FQ	55340 MW	68240 TQ	USBLS	5/07
Machinery	Virginia Beach-Norfolk-Newport News MSA, VA-NC	Y	26850 FQ	34290 MW	46540 TQ	USBLS	5/07
Machinery	Washington	H	14.36 FQ	17.41 MW	21.79 TQ	WABLS	3/08
Machinery	Seattle-Tacoma-Bellevue MSA, WA	Y	28330 FQ	34430 MW	42710 TQ	USBLS	5/07
Machinery	West Virginia	Y	24693 FQ	35025 MW	42712 TQ	WVBLS	7/08-9/08
Machinery	Charleston MSA, WV	Y	25890 FQ	40910 MW	47770 TQ	USBLS	5/07
Machinery	Wheeling MSA, WV-OH	Y	34340 FQ	41100 MW	47050 TQ	USBLS	5/07
Machinery	Wisconsin	Y	28250 FQ	36090 MW	43410 TQ	USBLS	5/07
Machinery	Appleton MSA, WI	Y	18390 FQ	36210 MW	45920 TQ	USBLS	5/07
Machinery	Milwaukee-Waukesha-West Allis MSA, WI	Y	27720 FQ	33940 MW	42750 TQ	USBLS	5/07
Machinery	Wyoming	Y	53364 FQ	65686 MW	71932 TQ	WYBLS	9/08
Machinery	Puerto Rico	Y	16680 FQ	21090 MW	29770 TQ	USBLS	5/07
Machinery	San Juan-Caguas-Guaynabo MSA, PR	Y	16110 FQ	19050 MW	22560 TQ	USBLS	5/07
Machinery	Virgin Islands	Y	24950 FQ	36420 MW	45930 TQ	USBLS	5/07
Machinery	Guam	Y	20170 FQ	24750 MW	34720 TQ	USBLS	5/07
Public Works	Floyd County, GA	Y	21757 LO		35485 HI	GACTY03	2008
Major							
Police Department	Griffin, GA	Y	46675 LO		70863 HI	GACTY01	2008
Police Department	Roswell, GA	Y	63629 LO		101807 HI	GACTY01	2008
Majority Leader							
State Senate	Washington	Y			50106 HI	WCC	9/1/08
United States House of Representatives	United States	Y			188100 HI	CRS02	1/08
United States Senate	United States	Y			188100 HI	CRS02	1/08

AE	Average entry wage	AW	Average wage paid	FQ	First quartile wage
AER	Average entry range	AWR	Average wage range	H	Hourly
AEX	Average experienced wage	AXR	Average experienced range	HI	Highest wage paid
ATC	Average total compensation	D	Daily	HR	High end range

LO	Lowest wage paid	MTC	Median total compensation
LR	Low end range	MW	Median wage paid
M	Monthly	MWR	Median wage range
MCC	Median cash compensation	S	See annotated source

TCC	Total cash compensation
TQ	Third quartile wage
W	Weekly
Y	Yearly

Occupation/Type/Industry	Location	Per	Low	Mid	High	Source	Date
Makeup Artist							
Theatrical and Performance	California	H	13.06 FQ	23.83 MW	34.05 TQ	CABLS	1/08-3/08
Theatrical and Performance	Florida	Y	37650 FQ	62450 MW	70860 TQ	USBLS	5/07
Theatrical and Performance	Georgia	Y	22370 FQ	34740 MW	38680 TQ	USBLS	5/07
Theatrical and Performance	Illinois	Y	16200 FQ	26120 MW	32560 TQ	USBLS	5/07
Theatrical and Performance	Maryland	Y		18075 MW		MDBLS	3/08
Theatrical and Performance	New York	Y	37980 FQ	58750 MW	71060 TQ	USBLS	5/07
Theatrical and Performance	Texas	Y	19810 FQ	24040 MW	40970 TQ	USBLS	5/07
Theatrical and Performance	Virginia	Y	19450 FQ	21930 MW	24360 TQ	USBLS	5/07
Mammography Technologist							
Suburban	United States	H	18.00 LO		25.50 HI	RTODAY	2007
Urban	United States	H	20.79 LO		42.10 HI	RTODAY	2007
Management Accountant							
Cost Accounting	United States	Y		96627 ATC		STFIN	2007
Internal Auditing	United States	Y		112954 ATC		STFIN	2007
Public Accounting	United States	Y		135659 ATC		STFIN	2007
Management Analyst	Alabama	Y	51760 FQ	68320 MW	92850 TQ	USBLS	5/07
	Birmingham-Hoover MSA, AL	Y	49140 FQ	69910 MW	108110 TQ	USBLS	5/07
	Alaska	Y	55390 FQ	67470 MW	85720 TQ	USBLS	5/07
	Anchorage MSA, AK	Y	57870 FQ	70890 MW	89280 TQ	USBLS	5/07
	Arizona	Y	44500 FQ	59670 MW	80080 TQ	USBLS	5/07
	Phoenix-Mesa-Scottsdale MSA, AZ	Y	45960 FQ	62120 MW	82040 TQ	USBLS	5/07
	Tucson MSA, AZ	Y	38860 FQ	52060 MW	69250 TQ	USBLS	5/07
	Arkansas	Y	37550 FQ	50760 MW	64640 TQ	USBLS	5/07
	Little Rock-North Little Rock MSA, AR	Y	37650 FQ	47490 MW	63410 TQ	USBLS	5/07
	California	H	27.88 FQ	36.49 MW	49.41 TQ	CABLS	1/08-3/08
	Bakersfield MSA, CA	H	30.79 FQ	38.03 MW	46.51 TQ	CABLS	1/08-3/08
	Los Angeles-Long Beach-Glendale PMSA, CA	H	28.37 FQ	36.47 MW	48.06 TQ	CABLS	1/08-3/08
	Oakland-Fremont-Hayward MSA, CA	H	30.94 FQ	39.53 MW	49.96 TQ	CABLS	1/08-3/08
	Riverside-San Bernardino-Ontario MSA, CA	H	25.90 FQ	31.10 MW	40.69 TQ	CABLS	1/08-3/08
	Sacramento-Arden Arcade-Roseville MSA, CA	H	25.22 FQ	30.41 MW	39.73 TQ	CABLS	1/08-3/08
	San Diego-Carlsbad-San Marcos MSA, CA	H	28.02 FQ	36.54 MW	48.51 TQ	CABLS	1/08-3/08
	San Francisco-San Mateo-Redwood PMSA, CA	H	32.96 FQ	43.68 MW	62.85 TQ	CABLS	1/08-3/08
	San Jose-Sunnyvale-Santa Clara MSA, CA	H	32.64 FQ	42.60 MW	58.89 TQ	CABLS	1/08-3/08
	Santa Ana-Anaheim-Irvine PMSA, CA	Y	47170 FQ	65830 MW	92950 TQ	USBLS	5/07
	Colorado	Y	61120 FQ	78960 MW	102210 TQ	USBLS	5/07
	Denver-Aurora MSA, CO	Y	63120 FQ	79150 MW	100010 TQ	USBLS	5/07
	Connecticut	H	25.29 AE	36.96 MW		CTBLS	1/08-3/08
	Bridgeport-Stamford-Norwalk MSA, CT	Y	69020 FQ	91830 MW	142210 TQ	USBLS	5/07
	Hartford-West Hartford-East Hartford MSA, CT	Y	55260 FQ	69610 MW	83910 TQ	USBLS	5/07
	Delaware	Y	56840 FQ	81920 MW	109610 TQ	USBLS	5/07
	Wilmington PMSA, DE-MD-NJ	Y	58610 FQ	85010 MW	111150 TQ	USBLS	5/07
	District of Columbia	Y	60260 FQ	78230 MW	93790 TQ	USBLS	5/07
	Washington-Arlington-Alexandria MSA, DC-VA-MD-WV	Y	63880 FQ	83530 MW	102120 TQ	USBLS	5/07
	Florida	Y	44960 FQ	61790 MW	94160 TQ	USBLS	5/07
	Cape Coral-Fort Myers MSA, FL	Y	55650 FQ	72540 MW	118420 TQ	USBLS	5/07
	Fort Lauderdale-Pompano Beach-Deerfield Beach PMSA, FL	Y	54540 FQ	88160 MW	140050 TQ	USBLS	5/07
	Jacksonville MSA, FL	Y	48800 FQ	60980 MW	79870 TQ	USBLS	5/07
	Miami-Fort Lauderdale-Miami Beach MSA, FL	Y	49300 FQ	75250 MW	108350 TQ	USBLS	5/07
	Orlando-Kissimmee MSA, FL	Y	50100 FQ	64810 MW	95330 TQ	USBLS	5/07

Occupation/Type/Industry	Location	Per	Low	Mid	High	Source	Date
Management Analyst	Pensacola-Ferry Pass-Brent MSA, FL	Y	43580 FQ	58970 MW	84450 TQ	USBLS	5/07
	Tallahassee MSA, FL	Y	39090 FQ	47370 MW	59200 TQ	USBLS	5/07
	Tampa-St. Petersburg-Clearwater MSA, FL	Y	41790 FQ	60530 MW	96170 TQ	USBLS	5/07
	West Palm Beach-Boca Raton-Boynton Beach PMSA, FL	Y	53910 FQ	83910 MW	104970 TQ	USBLS	5/07
	Georgia	Y	52700 FQ	72550 MW	103190 TQ	USBLS	5/07
	Atlanta-Sandy Springs-Marietta MSA, GA	Y	54410 FQ	75020 MW	107280 TQ	USBLS	5/07
	Macon MSA, GA	Y	48650 FQ	67890 MW	87870 TQ	USBLS	5/07
	Hawaii	Y	54080 FQ	67820 MW	81760 TQ	USBLS	5/07
	Honolulu MSA, HI	Y	54300 FQ	68210 MW	83260 TQ	USBLS	5/07
	Idaho	Y	39410 FQ	59670 MW	96600 TQ	USBLS	5/07
	Boise City-Nampa MSA, ID	Y	41280 FQ	67300 MW	94470 TQ	USBLS	5/07
	Lewiston MSA, ID-WA	Y	36310 FQ	49380 MW	116060 TQ	USBLS	5/07
	Illinois	Y	53740 FQ	72950 MW	101370 TQ	USBLS	5/07
	Chicago-Naperville-Joliet MSA, IL-IN-WI	Y	53880 FQ	73550 MW	102740 TQ	USBLS	5/07
	Indiana	Y	46270 FQ	60390 MW	80580 TQ	USBLS	5/07
	Gary PMSA, IN	Y	43980 FQ	64290 MW	103570 TQ	USBLS	5/07
	Indianapolis-Carmel MSA, IN	Y	46760 FQ	61270 MW	80450 TQ	USBLS	5/07
	Terre Haute MSA, IN	Y	39700 FQ	49140 MW	58560 TQ	USBLS	5/07
	Iowa	Y	48660 FQ	59360 MW	75130 TQ	USBLS	5/07
	Des Moines-West Des Moines MSA, IA	Y	49430 FQ	59010 MW	72390 TQ	USBLS	5/07
	Kansas	Y	52480 FQ	64770 MW	84680 TQ	USBLS	5/07
	Topeka MSA, KS	Y	46980 FQ	55050 MW	62860 TQ	USBLS	5/07
	Wichita MSA, KS	Y	52960 FQ	64870 MW	80410 TQ	USBLS	5/07
	Kentucky	Y	50888 FQ	65983 MW	84405 TQ	KYBLS	2008
	Louisville-Jefferson County MSA, KY-IN	Y	49610 FQ	62210 MW	74280 TQ	USBLS	5/07
	Louisiana	H	21.18 FQ	27.44 MW	36.60 TQ	LABLS	1/08-3/08
	Baton Rouge MSA, LA	Y	43740 FQ	50040 MW	64250 TQ	USBLS	5/07
	New Orleans-Metairie-Kenner MSA, LA	Y	53980 FQ	69020 MW	88210 TQ	USBLS	5/07
	Maine	Y	48830 FQ	61830 MW	77920 TQ	USBLS	5/07
	Portland-South Portland-Biddeford MSA, ME	Y	49730 FQ	61970 MW	82860 TQ	USBLS	5/07
	Maryland	Y		78925 MW		MDBLS	3/08
	Baltimore-Towson MSA, MD	Y	53380 FQ	76070 MW	96530 TQ	USBLS	5/07
	Bethesda-Gaithersburg-Frederick PMSA, MD	Y	64270 FQ	83210 MW	102240 TQ	USBLS	5/07
	Massachusetts	Y	63040 FQ	84150 MW	114720 TQ	USBLS	5/07
	Boston-Cambridge-Quincy NECTA, MA	Y	64910 FQ	86820 MW	116130 TQ	USBLS	5/07
	Worcester MSA, MA-CT	Y	59890 FQ	80040 MW		USBLS	5/07
	Michigan	Y	55470 FQ	75170 MW	110250 TQ	USBLS	5/07
	Detroit-Warren-Livonia MSA, MI	Y	59500 FQ	85200 MW	124210 TQ	USBLS	5/07
	Grand Rapids-Wyoming MSA, MI	Y	48130 FQ	62070 MW	84200 TQ	USBLS	5/07
	Warren-Troy-Farmington Hills PMSA, MI	Y	58980 FQ	84800 MW	128520 TQ	USBLS	5/07
	Minnesota	Y	62934 FQ	79575 MW	106465 TQ	MNBLS	10/08-12/08
	Duluth-Superior MSA, MN-WI	Y	45751 FQ	61745 MW	78939 TQ	MNBLS	10/08-12/08
	Minneapolis-Saint Paul MSA, MN-WI	Y	63914 FQ	80607 MW	108602 TQ	MNBLS	10/08-12/08
	Rochester MSA, MN	Y	55357 FQ	64084 MW	80591 TQ	MNBLS	10/08-12/08
	Mississippi	Y	43980 FQ	56890 MW	72350 TQ	USBLS	5/07
	Jackson MSA, MS	Y	38550 FQ	51300 MW	64420 TQ	USBLS	5/07
	Pascagoula MSA, MS	Y	57020 FQ	66370 MW	87950 TQ	USBLS	5/07
	Missouri	Y	50540 FQ	64070 MW	82170 TQ	USBLS	5/07
	Joplin MSA, MO	Y	29110 FQ	36700 MW	68410 TQ	USBLS	5/07
	Kansas City MSA, MO-KS	Y	53900 FQ	69050 MW	90070 TQ	USBLS	5/07
	St. Louis MSA, MO-IL	Y	53940 FQ	66150 MW	86440 TQ	USBLS	5/07
	Montana	Y	47790 FQ	57460 MW	70710 TQ	USBLS	5/07
	Billings MSA, MT	Y	53050 FQ	64360 MW	76810 TQ	USBLS	5/07
	Nebraska	Y	47120 FQ	58940 MW	75780 TQ	USBLS	5/07
	Omaha-Council Bluffs MSA, NE-IA	Y	47660 FQ	59890 MW	76890 TQ	USBLS	5/07
	Nevada	H	26.73 FQ	33.88 MW	45.42 TQ	NVBLS	5/08

AE Average entry wage	**AW** Average wage paid	**FQ** First quartile wage	**LO** Lowest wage paid	**MTC** Median total compensation	**TCC** Total cash compensation
AER Average entry range	**AWR** Average wage range	**H** Hourly	**LR** Low end range	**MW** Median wage paid	**TQ** Third quartile wage
AEX Average experienced wage	**AXR** Average experienced range	**HI** Highest wage paid	**M** Monthly	**MWR** Median wage range	**W** Weekly
ATC Average total compensation	**D** Daily	**HR** High end range	**MCC** Median cash compensation	**S** See annotated source	**Y** Yearly

Occupation/Type/Industry	Location	Per	Low	Mid	High	Source	Date
Management Analyst	Las Vegas-Paradise MSA, NV	H	26.08 FQ	33.81 MW	43.96 TQ	NVBLS	5/08
	New Hampshire	H	26.29 AE	39.51 MW	57.66 AEX	NHBLS	6/08
	Manchester MSA, NH	Y	68540 FQ	79850 MW	91000 TQ	USBLS	5/07
	Nashua NECTA, NH-MA	Y	54600 FQ	67340 MW	80730 TQ	USBLS	5/07
	New Jersey	Y	64310 FQ	83830 MW	107280 TQ	USBLS	5/07
	Atlantic City MSA, NJ	Y	62320 FQ	81850 MW	100150 TQ	USBLS	5/07
	Camden PMSA, NJ	Y	56930 FQ	76370 MW	117750 TQ	USBLS	5/07
	Edison PMSA, NJ	Y	65570 FQ	90200 MW	116910 TQ	USBLS	5/07
	Newark-Union PMSA, NJ-PA	Y	64740 FQ	83200 MW	106910 TQ	USBLS	5/07
	New Mexico	Y	47390 FQ	63610 MW	91600 TQ	USBLS	5/07
	Albuquerque MSA, NM	Y	50470 FQ	66760 MW	93940 TQ	USBLS	5/07
	New York	Y	55400 FQ	75300 MW	103450 TQ	USBLS	5/07
	Albany-Schenectady-Troy MSA, NY	Y	46890 FQ	57860 MW	73430 TQ	USBLS	5/07
	Buffalo-Niagara Falls MSA, NY	Y	50260 FQ	63120 MW	78990 TQ	USBLS	5/07
	Ithaca MSA, NY	Y	45620 FQ	63900 MW	101650 TQ	USBLS	5/07
	Nassau-Suffolk PMSA, NY	Y	56690 FQ	75410 MW	97300 TQ	USBLS	5/07
	New York-Northern New Jersey-Long Island MSA, NY-NJ-PA	Y	61010 FQ	82250 MW	111740 TQ	USBLS	5/07
	North Carolina	Y	53740 FQ	70550 MW	95890 TQ	USBLS	5/07
	Charlotte-Gastonia-Concord MSA, NC-SC	Y	57810 FQ	80680 MW	106070 TQ	USBLS	5/07
	Raleigh-Cary MSA, NC	Y	52690 FQ	64420 MW	83310 TQ	USBLS	5/07
	North Dakota	Y	46560 FQ	58570 MW	72850 TQ	USBLS	5/07
	Fargo MSA, ND-MN	Y	48200 FQ	59140 MW	72000 TQ	USBLS	5/07
	Ohio	Y	53550 FQ	69520 MW	91340 TQ	USBLS	5/07
	Cincinnati-Middletown MSA, OH-KY-IN	Y	53910 FQ	73520 MW	94630 TQ	USBLS	5/07
	Cleveland-Elyria-Mentor MSA, OH	Y	54790 FQ	72670 MW	96500 TQ	USBLS	5/07
	Columbus MSA, OH	Y	54380 FQ	66040 MW	81270 TQ	USBLS	5/07
	Dayton MSA, OH	Y	52010 FQ	69970 MW	90590 TQ	USBLS	5/07
	Oklahoma	Y	40860 FQ	52980 MW	69370 TQ	USBLS	5/07
	Oklahoma City MSA, OK	Y	44830 FQ	58170 MW	72150 TQ	USBLS	5/07
	Tulsa MSA, OK	Y	39900 FQ	49510 MW	68170 TQ	USBLS	5/07
	Oregon	H	24.09 FQ	29.14 MW	36.37 TQ	ORBLS	5/08
	Portland-Vancouver-Beaverton MSA, OR-WA	Y	53550 FQ	65890 MW	82740 TQ	USBLS	5/07
	Pennsylvania	Y	54120 FQ	73440 MW	100090 TQ	USBLS	5/07
	Allentown-Bethlehem-Easton MSA, PA-NJ	Y	41580 FQ	61170 MW	89020 TQ	USBLS	5/07
	Philadelphia-Camden-Wilmington MSA, PA-NJ-DE-MD	Y	58380 FQ	79890 MW	104680 TQ	USBLS	5/07
	Pittsburgh MSA, PA	Y	56590 FQ	74600 MW	125160 TQ	USBLS	5/07
	Rhode Island	Y	50960 FQ	66730 MW	84870 TQ	USBLS	5/07
	Providence-Fall River-Warwick MSA, RI-MA	Y	51620 FQ	66260 MW	85260 TQ	USBLS	5/07
	South Carolina	Y	46900 FQ	61850 MW	79110 TQ	USBLS	5/07
	Charleston-North Charleston MSA, SC	Y	45850 FQ	60010 MW	76330 TQ	USBLS	5/07
	Columbia MSA, SC	Y	52520 FQ	62730 MW	75850 TQ	USBLS	5/07
	Florence MSA, SC	Y	36810 FQ	49000 MW	69140 TQ	USBLS	5/07
	South Dakota	Y	50232 FQ	60794 MW	77218 TQ	SDBLS	7/08-9/08
	Sioux Falls MSA, SD	Y	53200 FQ	62712 MW	80173 TQ	SDBLS	7/08-9/08
	Tennessee	Y	44710 FQ	59270 MW	79230 TQ	USBLS	5/07
	Memphis MSA, TN-MS-AR	Y	46080 FQ	59850 MW	76870 TQ	USBLS	5/07
	Nashville-Davidson-Murfreesboro MSA, TN	Y	48950 FQ	60800 MW	79160 TQ	USBLS	5/07
	Texas	Y	43480 FQ	60770 MW	84520 TQ	USBLS	5/07
	Austin-Round Rock MSA, TX	Y	40690 FQ	56640 MW	64730 TQ	USBLS	5/07
	Dallas-Fort Worth-Arlington MSA, TX	Y	49490 FQ	69030 MW	96690 TQ	USBLS	5/07
	El Paso MSA, TX	Y	40330 FQ	54350 MW	65650 TQ	USBLS	5/07
	Houston-Sugar Land-Baytown MSA, TX	Y	45740 FQ	66460 MW	94020 TQ	USBLS	5/07
	San Antonio MSA, TX	Y	43380 FQ	58170 MW	73400 TQ	USBLS	5/07
	Utah	Y	47450 FQ	62690 MW	84390 TQ	USBLS	5/07
	Salt Lake City MSA, UT	Y	45710 FQ	63720 MW	102970 TQ	USBLS	5/07
	Vermont	Y	54130 FQ	72750 MW	103820 TQ	USBLS	5/07

Occupation/Type/Industry	Location	Per	Low	Mid	High	Source	Date
Management Analyst	Burlington-South Burlington						
	MSA, VT	Y	59510 FQ	78990 MW	106850 TQ	USBLS	5/07
	Virginia	Y	61220 FQ	81640 MW	104970 TQ	USBLS	5/07
	Charlottesville MSA, VA	Y	49920 FQ	61440 MW	78410 TQ	USBLS	5/07
	Lynchburg MSA, VA	Y	31340 FQ	49470 MW	86250 TQ	USBLS	5/07
	Richmond MSA, VA	Y	52190 FQ	67410 MW	87330 TQ	USBLS	5/07
	Virginia Beach-Norfolk-						
	Newport News MSA, VA-NC	Y	55070 FQ	69770 MW	87600 TQ	USBLS	5/07
	Washington	H	28.94 FQ	35.95 MW	45.20 TQ	WABLS	3/08
	Seattle-Tacoma-Bellevue						
	MSA, WA	Y	61810 FQ	75820 MW	94840 TQ	USBLS	5/07
	West Virginia	Y	57282 FQ	72970 MW	84260 TQ	WVBLS	7/08-9/08
	Charleston MSA, WV	Y	44250 FQ	63260 MW	83150 TQ	USBLS	5/07
	Wisconsin	Y	45680 FQ	59140 MW	76530 TQ	USBLS	5/07
	Milwaukee-Waukesha-West						
	Allis MSA, WI	Y	41670 FQ	56900 MW	77770 TQ	USBLS	5/07
	Wyoming	Y	48847 FQ	63132 MW	77475 TQ	WYBLS	9/08
	Cheyenne MSA, WY	Y	46754 FQ	53824 MW	66462 TQ	WYBLS	9/08
	Puerto Rico	Y	38640 FQ	53510 MW	67660 TQ	USBLS	5/07
	San Juan-Caguas-Guaynabo						
	MSA, PR	Y	37150 FQ	51560 MW	66310 TQ	USBLS	5/07
	Virgin Islands	Y	42800 FQ	48100 MW	53560 TQ	USBLS	5/07
	Guam	Y	36200 FQ	46540 MW	59740 TQ	USBLS	5/07
Manicurist and Pedicurist	Alabama	Y	15190 FQ	17200 MW	18830 TQ	USBLS	5/07
	Birmingham-Hoover MSA, AL	Y	12610 FQ	13880 MW	15360 TQ	USBLS	5/07
	Arizona	Y	15030 FQ	16940 MW	20640 TQ	USBLS	5/07
	Phoenix-Mesa-Scottsdale						
	MSA, AZ	Y	15250 FQ	16920 MW	19390 TQ	USBLS	5/07
	Tucson MSA, AZ	Y	14740 FQ	17330 MW	25530 TQ	USBLS	5/07
	Arkansas	Y	15370 FQ	20670 MW	24340 TQ	USBLS	5/07
	California	H	8.00 FQ	8.69 MW	9.63 TQ	CABLS	1/08-3/08
	Los Angeles-Long Beach-						
	Glendale PMSA, CA	H	8.00 FQ	8.53 MW	9.27 TQ	CABLS	1/08-3/08
	Oakland-Fremont-Hayward						
	MSA, CA	H	8.53 FQ	10.79 MW	12.11 TQ	CABLS	1/08-3/08
	Riverside-San Bernardino-						
	Ontario MSA, CA	H	8.00 FQ	8.00 MW	8.62 TQ	CABLS	1/08-3/08
	Sacramento-Arden Arcade-						
	Roseville MSA, CA	H	8.00 FQ	8.49 MW	9.11 TQ	CABLS	1/08-3/08
	San Diego-Carlsbad-San						
	Marcos MSA, CA	H	8.00 FQ	8.74 MW	9.56 TQ	CABLS	1/08-3/08
	San Francisco-San Mateo-						
	Redwood PMSA, CA	H	8.43 FQ	9.36 MW	10.38 TQ	CABLS	1/08-3/08
	San Jose-Sunnyvale-Santa						
	Clara MSA, CA	H	8.93 FQ	13.34 MW	19.11 TQ	CABLS	1/08-3/08
	Santa Ana-Anaheim-Irvine						
	PMSA, CA	Y	16640 FQ	17810 MW	19050 TQ	USBLS	5/07
	Colorado	Y	15500 FQ	25190 MW	30930 TQ	USBLS	5/07
	Denver-Aurora MSA, CO	Y	15330 FQ	22660 MW	29030 TQ	USBLS	5/07
	Connecticut	H	8.30 AE	9.98 MW		CTBLS	1/08-3/08
	Bridgeport-Stamford-Norwalk						
	MSA, CT	Y	17090 FQ	19990 MW	26080 TQ	USBLS	5/07
	Hartford-West Hartford-East						
	Hartford MSA, CT	Y	16910 FQ	18460 MW	24690 TQ	USBLS	5/07
	Delaware	Y	14770 FQ	18140 MW	20650 TQ	USBLS	5/07
	Wilmington PMSA, DE-MD-						
	NJ	Y	14430 FQ	17770 MW	30770 TQ	USBLS	5/07
	District of Columbia	Y	27800 FQ	30040 MW	32490 TQ	USBLS	5/07
	Washington-Arlington-						
	Alexandria MSA, DC-VA-						
	MD-WV	Y	15620 FQ	22670 MW	31940 TQ	USBLS	5/07
	Florida	Y	16850 FQ	22760 MW	31830 TQ	USBLS	5/07
	Fort Lauderdale-Pompano						
	Beach-Deerfield Beach						
	PMSA, FL	Y	17820 FQ	20040 MW	27410 TQ	USBLS	5/07
	Jacksonville MSA, FL	Y	30220 FQ	32910 MW	35590 TQ	USBLS	5/07
	Miami-Fort Lauderdale-Miami						
	Beach MSA, FL	Y	16970 FQ	21730 MW	30900 TQ	USBLS	5/07
	Orlando-Kissimmee MSA, FL	Y	18770 FQ	23440 MW	31040 TQ	USBLS	5/07
	Sarasota-Bradenton-Venice						
	MSA, FL	Y	18020 FQ	27350 MW	31270 TQ	USBLS	5/07

AE	Average entry wage	**AW**	Average wage paid	**FQ**	First quartile wage
AER	Average entry range	**AWR**	Average wage range	**H**	Hourly
AEX	Average experienced wage	**AXR**	Average experienced range	**HI**	Highest wage paid
ATC	Average total compensation	**D**	Daily	**HR**	High end range

LO	Lowest wage paid	**MTC**	Median total compensation
LR	Low end range	**MW**	Median wage paid
		MWR	Median wage range
		MCC	Median cash compensation

S	See annotated source
TCC	Total cash compensation
TQ	Third quartile wage
W	Weekly
Y	Yearly

Manicurist and Pedicurist

Occupation/Type/Industry	Location	Per	Low	Mid	High	Source	Date
Manicurist and Pedicurist	Tampa-St. Petersburg-Clearwater MSA, FL	Y	14800 FQ	16210 MW	22370 TQ	USBLS	5/07
	West Palm Beach-Boca Raton-Boynton Beach PMSA, FL	Y	15260 FQ	17650 MW	21710 TQ	USBLS	5/07
	Georgia	Y	15630 FQ	18460 MW	24330 TQ	USBLS	5/07
	Atlanta-Sandy Springs-Marietta MSA, GA	Y	16860 FQ	19000 MW	24770 TQ	USBLS	5/07
	Hawaii	Y	18730 FQ	24080 MW	30980 TQ	USBLS	5/07
	Honolulu MSA, HI	Y	17790 FQ	22590 MW	29410 TQ	USBLS	5/07
	Idaho	Y	17630 FQ	23950 MW	28980 TQ	USBLS	5/07
	Coeur d'Alene MSA, ID	Y	20260 FQ	25240 MW	27650 TQ	USBLS	5/07
	Illinois	Y	22510 FQ	25930 MW	28420 TQ	USBLS	5/07
	Chicago-Naperville-Joliet MSA, IL-IN-WI	Y	23250 FQ	26050 MW	28430 TQ	USBLS	5/07
	Indiana	Y	17000 FQ	19470 MW	23680 TQ	USBLS	5/07
	Gary PMSA, IN	Y	15070 FQ	19600 MW	31140 TQ	USBLS	5/07
	Indianapolis-Carmel MSA, IN	Y	15780 FQ	23180 MW	27960 TQ	USBLS	5/07
	Iowa	Y	15270 FQ	22670 MW	31810 TQ	USBLS	5/07
	Des Moines-West Des Moines MSA, IA	Y	18180 FQ	30310 MW	34920 TQ	USBLS	5/07
	Kansas	Y	14100 FQ	19280 MW	33460 TQ	USBLS	5/07
	Wichita MSA, KS	Y	22270 FQ	33470 MW	36840 TQ	USBLS	5/07
	Kentucky	Y	15709 FQ	18519 MW	21267 TQ	KYBLS	2008
	Louisville-Jefferson County MSA, KY-IN	Y	17160 FQ	18750 MW	22010 TQ	USBLS	5/07
	Louisiana	H	6.37 FQ	7.60 MW	10.61 TQ	LABLS	1/08-3/08
	Baton Rouge MSA, LA	Y	12480 FQ	14150 MW	16630 TQ	USBLS	5/07
	New Orleans-Metairie-Kenner MSA, LA	Y	22320 FQ	25970 MW	28920 TQ	USBLS	5/07
	Maine	Y	15110 FQ	15900 MW	19600 TQ	USBLS	5/07
	Lewiston-Auburn MSA, ME	Y	14940 FQ	15510 MW	21910 TQ	USBLS	5/07
	Maryland	Y		27850 MW		MDBLS	3/08
	Baltimore-Towson MSA, MD	Y	18670 FQ	29600 MW	36060 TQ	USBLS	5/07
	Bethesda-Gaithersburg-Frederick PMSA, MD	Y	19660 FQ	27740 MW	35880 TQ	USBLS	5/07
	Hagerstown-Martinsburg MSA, MD-WV	Y	17280 FQ	25750 MW	37790 TQ	USBLS	5/07
	Massachusetts	Y	18110 FQ	22250 MW	27640 TQ	USBLS	5/07
	Boston-Cambridge-Quincy NECTA, MA	Y	18010 FQ	22090 MW	28000 TQ	USBLS	5/07
	Michigan	Y	15440 FQ	17740 MW	25910 TQ	USBLS	5/07
	Detroit-Warren-Livonia MSA, MI	Y	15440 FQ	17030 MW	20560 TQ	USBLS	5/07
	Warren-Troy-Farmington Hills PMSA, MI	Y	15300 FQ	16710 MW	19920 TQ	USBLS	5/07
	Minnesota	Y	20890 FQ	22908 MW	24958 TQ	MNBLS	10/08-12/08
	Duluth-Superior MSA, MN-WI	Y	21884 FQ	28199 MW	42931 TQ	MNBLS	10/08-12/08
	Minneapolis-Saint Paul MSA, MN-WI	Y	20974 FQ	22877 MW	24780 TQ	MNBLS	10/08-12/08
	Rochester MSA, MN	Y	17997 FQ	19951 MW	28146 TQ	MNBLS	10/08-12/08
	Mississippi	Y	16420 FQ	18130 MW	21730 TQ	USBLS	5/07
	Missouri	Y	14530 FQ	15630 MW	20800 TQ	USBLS	5/07
	Kansas City MSA, MO-KS	Y	14140 FQ	15260 MW	16430 TQ	USBLS	5/07
	St. Louis MSA, MO-IL	Y	14580 FQ	15740 MW	21220 TQ	USBLS	5/07
	Montana	Y	13540 FQ	14290 MW	15040 TQ	USBLS	5/07
	Nebraska	Y	14540 FQ	29430 MW	38030 TQ	USBLS	5/07
	Las Vegas-Paradise MSA, NV	H	6.68 FQ	8.95 MW	13.71 TQ	NVBLS	5/08
	Nashua NECTA, NH-MA	Y	21550 FQ	31230 MW	34480 TQ	USBLS	5/07
	New Jersey	Y	20340 FQ	24790 MW	29560 TQ	USBLS	5/07
	Camden PMSA, NJ	Y	18550 FQ	27640 MW	33170 TQ	USBLS	5/07
	Edison PMSA, NJ	Y	26350 FQ	28860 MW	31470 TQ	USBLS	5/07
	Newark-Union PMSA, NJ-PA	Y	21590 FQ	24630 MW	29550 TQ	USBLS	5/07
	New York	Y	16080 FQ	18840 MW	22670 TQ	USBLS	5/07
	Albany-Schenectady-Troy MSA, NY	Y	15370 FQ	16840 MW	25870 TQ	USBLS	5/07
	Buffalo-Niagara Falls MSA, NY	Y	16320 FQ	17980 MW	19640 TQ	USBLS	5/07
	Nassau-Suffolk PMSA, NY	Y	16620 FQ	18770 MW	22890 TQ	USBLS	5/07
	New York-Northern New Jersey-Long Island MSA, NY-NJ-PA	Y	16470 FQ	20480 MW	24580 TQ	USBLS	5/07
	North Carolina	Y	17860 FQ	24820 MW	30910 TQ	USBLS	5/07

AE	Average entry wage	AW	Average wage paid	FQ	First quartile wage	LO	Lowest wage paid	MTC	Median total compensation	TCC	Total cash compensation
AER	Average entry range	AWR	Average wage range	H	Hourly	LR	Low end range	MW	Median wage paid	TQ	Third quartile wage
AEX	Average experienced wage	AXR	Average experienced range	HI	Highest wage paid	M	Monthly	MWR	Median wage range	W	Weekly
ATC	Average total compensation	D	Daily	HR	High end range	MCC	Median cash compensation	S	See annotated source	Y	Yearly

Occupation/Type/Industry	Location	Per	Low	Mid	High	Source	Date
Manicurist and Pedicurist	Charlotte-Gastonia-Concord MSA, NC-SC	Y	18390 FQ	27370 MW	30200 TQ	USBLS	5/07
	Durham MSA, NC	Y	18950 FQ	35070 MW	39200 TQ	USBLS	5/07
	Raleigh-Cary MSA, NC	Y	23080 FQ	26840 MW	35870 TQ	USBLS	5/07
	North Dakota	Y	18970 FQ	27910 MW	31510 TQ	USBLS	5/07
	Ohio	Y	15830 FQ	21270 MW	29150 TQ	USBLS	5/07
	Cincinnati-Middletown MSA, OH-KY-IN	Y	20040 FQ	25670 MW	36290 TQ	USBLS	5/07
	Cleveland-Elyria-Mentor MSA, OH	Y	15760 FQ	21140 MW	28040 TQ	USBLS	5/07
	Columbus MSA, OH	Y	15320 FQ	18050 MW	25810 TQ	USBLS	5/07
	Dayton MSA, OH	Y	16020 FQ	19760 MW	33100 TQ	USBLS	5/07
	Oklahoma	Y	12550 FQ	14060 MW	15580 TQ	USBLS	5/07
	Oregon	H	9.09 FQ	11.32 MW	15.97 TQ	ORBLS	5/08
	Portland-Vancouver-Beaverton MSA, OR-WA	Y	18100 FQ	23230 MW	34490 TQ	USBLS	5/07
	Pennsylvania	Y	15410 FQ	18760 MW	22400 TQ	USBLS	5/07
	Allentown-Bethlehem-Easton MSA, PA-NJ	Y	21820 FQ	24740 MW	28380 TQ	USBLS	5/07
	Lancaster MSA, PA	Y	14600 FQ	15810 MW	19080 TQ	USBLS	5/07
	Philadelphia-Camden-Wilmington MSA, PA-NJ-DE-MD	Y	15520 FQ	19460 MW	25190 TQ	USBLS	5/07
	Pittsburgh MSA, PA	Y	17980 FQ	20980 MW	23390 TQ	USBLS	5/07
	Rhode Island	Y	17760 FQ	21460 MW	24200 TQ	USBLS	5/07
	Providence-Fall River-Warwick MSA, RI-MA	Y	18060 FQ	21270 MW	24000 TQ	USBLS	5/07
	South Carolina	Y	17900 FQ	21200 MW	23710 TQ	USBLS	5/07
	Charleston-North Charleston MSA, SC	Y	19330 FQ	21710 MW	23970 TQ	USBLS	5/07
	Columbia MSA, SC	Y	21420 FQ	23410 MW	25400 TQ	USBLS	5/07
	South Dakota	Y	21136 FQ	23263 MW	25196 TQ	SDBLS	7/08-9/08
	Sioux Falls MSA, SD	Y	22746 FQ	24151 MW	25694 TQ	SDBLS	7/08-9/08
	Tennessee	Y	15610 FQ	18330 MW	27470 TQ	USBLS	5/07
	Memphis MSA, TN-MS-AR	Y	16210 FQ	17820 MW	20930 TQ	USBLS	5/07
	Nashville-Davidson-Murfreesboro MSA, TN	Y	14380 FQ	17650 MW	32890 TQ	USBLS	5/07
	Texas	Y	14210 FQ	18180 MW	23320 TQ	USBLS	5/07
	Austin-Round Rock MSA, TX	Y	18660 FQ	25050 MW	37180 TQ	USBLS	5/07
	Corpus Christi MSA, TX	Y	13060 FQ	14960 MW	21010 TQ	USBLS	5/07
	Dallas-Fort Worth-Arlington MSA, TX	Y	17030 FQ	21050 MW	26860 TQ	USBLS	5/07
	Houston-Sugar Land-Baytown MSA, TX	Y	14120 FQ	18710 MW	25470 TQ	USBLS	5/07
	San Antonio MSA, TX	Y	13470 FQ	16380 MW	18670 TQ	USBLS	5/07
	Utah	Y	15020 FQ	17970 MW	20920 TQ	USBLS	5/07
	Vermont	Y	22430 FQ	29290 MW	33970 TQ	USBLS	5/07
	Virginia	Y	16930 FQ	21970 MW	24550 TQ	USBLS	5/07
	Richmond MSA, VA	Y	16450 FQ	21130 MW	24370 TQ	USBLS	5/07
	Virginia Beach-Norfolk-Newport News MSA, VA-NC	Y	21260 FQ	22940 MW	24630 TQ	USBLS	5/07
	Seattle-Tacoma-Bellevue MSA, WA	Y	16500 FQ	16750 MW	18890 TQ	USBLS	5/07
	West Virginia	Y	14210 FQ	15686 MW	18247 TQ	WVBLS	7/08-9/08
	Wisconsin	Y	15330 FQ	17250 MW	21720 TQ	USBLS	5/07
	Milwaukee-Waukesha-West Allis MSA, WI	Y	16950 FQ	19500 MW	24200 TQ	USBLS	5/07
	Puerto Rico	Y	12590 FQ	14220 MW	17130 TQ	USBLS	5/07
	San Juan-Caguas-Guaynabo MSA, PR	Y	12590 FQ	14300 MW	18590 TQ	USBLS	5/07
Manufactured Building and Mobile Home Installer	Alabama	Y	20790 FQ	23000 MW	25200 TQ	USBLS	5/07
	Arizona	Y	22440 FQ	25720 MW	29820 TQ	USBLS	5/07
	Arkansas	Y	19420 FQ	21330 MW	24330 TQ	USBLS	5/07
	California	H	10.61 FQ	13.34 MW	16.08 TQ	CABLS	1/08-3/08
	Colorado	Y	21970 FQ	26820 MW	31370 TQ	USBLS	5/07
	Delaware	Y	25500 FQ	29150 MW	36040 TQ	USBLS	5/07
	Florida	Y	22050 FQ	27850 MW	34270 TQ	USBLS	5/07
	Georgia	Y	22540 FQ	30310 MW	36700 TQ	USBLS	5/07
	Illinois	Y	26320 FQ	28160 MW	30530 TQ	USBLS	5/07
	Indiana	Y	23890 FQ	28500 MW	35070 TQ	USBLS	5/07

AE Average entry wage	**AW** Average wage paid	**FQ** First quartile wage	**LO** Lowest wage paid	**MTC** Median total compensation	**TCC** Total cash compensation
AER Average entry range	**AWR** Average wage range	**H** Hourly	**LR** Low end range	**MW** Median wage paid	**TQ** Third quartile wage
AEX Average experienced wage	**AXR** Average experienced range	**HI** Highest wage paid	**M** Monthly	**MWR** Median wage range	**W** Weekly
ATC Average total compensation	**D** Daily	**HR** High end range	**MCC** Median cash compensation	**S** See annotated source	**Y** Yearly

Occupation/Type/Industry	Location	Per	Low	Mid	High	Source	Date
Manufactured Building and Mobile Home Installer	Iowa	Y	21930 FQ	26100 MW	29840 TQ	USBLS	5/07
	Kansas	Y	23970 FQ	29040 MW	38740 TQ	USBLS	5/07
	Kentucky	Y	19023 FQ	23073 TQ	29081 TQ	KYBLS	2008
	Louisiana	H	12.53 FQ	14.48 MW	17.94 TQ	LABLS	1/08-3/08
	Maine	Y	21850 FQ	26960 MW	30280 TQ	USBLS	5/07
	Maryland	Y		27150 MW		MDBLS	3/08
	Michigan	Y	26000 FQ	38510 MW	49830 TQ	USBLS	5/07
	Minnesota	Y	27891 FQ	31866 MW	37688 TQ	MNBLS	10/08-12/08
	Mississippi	Y	20950 FQ	23690 MW	27220 TQ	USBLS	5/07
	Missouri	Y	23340 FQ	27580 MW	30490 TQ	USBLS	5/07
	Montana	Y	21950 FQ	28200 MW	31460 TQ	USBLS	5/07
	Nebraska	Y	22440 FQ	26920 MW	31380 TQ	USBLS	5/07
	New Hampshire	H	11.26 AE	14.17 MW	15.41 AEX	NHBLS	6/08
	New Mexico	Y	17520 FQ	20090 MW	22280 TQ	USBLS	5/07
	New York	Y	18210 FQ	22770 MW	33860 TQ	USBLS	5/07
	North Carolina	Y	22070 FQ	25830 MW	31140 TQ	USBLS	5/07
	North Dakota	Y	24350 FQ	27810 MW	32390 TQ	USBLS	5/07
	Ohio	Y	20440 FQ	24600 MW	29600 TQ	USBLS	5/07
	Oklahoma	Y	19030 FQ	24560 MW	30890 TQ	USBLS	5/07
	Oregon	H	14.47 FQ	17.56 MW	22.79 TQ	ORBLS	5/08
	Pennsylvania	Y	23590 FQ	26590 MW	30710 TQ	USBLS	5/07
	South Carolina	Y	23720 FQ	28500 MW	35250 TQ	USBLS	5/07
	South Dakota	Y	23910 FQ	27334 MW	32145 TQ	SDBLS	7/08-9/08
	Tennessee	Y	22600 FQ	27700 MW	31770 TQ	USBLS	5/07
	Texas	Y	19800 FQ	22660 MW	27930 TQ	USBLS	5/07
	Vermont	Y	27740 FQ	32170 MW	36210 TQ	USBLS	5/07
	Virginia	Y	20660 FQ	22810 MW	27900 TQ	USBLS	5/07
	Washington	H	11.10 FQ	12.86 MW	16.09 TQ	WABLS	3/08
	West Virginia	Y	14461 FQ	16138 MW	23547 TQ	WVBLS	7/08-9/08
	Wisconsin	Y	27680 FQ	33280 MW	36840 TQ	USBLS	5/07
	Wyoming	Y	28394 FQ	33468 MW	37420 TQ	WYBLS	9/08
Manufacturing Manager							
Aerospace/Defense	United States	Y		92044 AW		IWEEK01	2009
Apparel/Textiles	United States	Y		84512 AW		IWEEK01	2009
Consulting/Education	United States	Y		113418 AW		IWEEK01	2009
Medical Devices/Lab Equipment	United States	Y		102617 AW		IWEEK01	2009
Pharmaceuticals/Healthcare	United States	Y		110830 AW		IWEEK01	2009
Manufacturing Worker							
Renewable Energy Manufacturing Facilities	United States	H	11.00 LO		22.00 HI	CHTW	2008
Marine Engineer and Naval Architect	Alabama	Y	68460 FQ	74250 MW	80430 TQ	USBLS	5/07
	Arizona	Y	37380 FQ	46630 MW	60460 TQ	USBLS	5/07
	California	H	26.50 FQ	29.52 MW	44.14 TQ	CABLS	1/08-3/08
	Connecticut	H	29.72 AE	40.13 MW		CTBLS	1/08-3/08
	District of Columbia	Y	89570 FQ	111750 MW	128290 TQ	USBLS	5/07
	Washington-Arlington-Alexandria MSA, DC-VA-MD-WV	Y	63990 FQ	94420 MW	118780 TQ	USBLS	5/07
	Florida	Y	64360 FQ	74560 MW	92210 TQ	USBLS	5/07
	Fort Lauderdale-Pompano Beach-Deerfield Beach PMSA, FL	Y	57000 FQ	61790 MW	66560 TQ	USBLS	5/07
	Miami-Fort Lauderdale-Miami Beach MSA, FL	Y	61790 FQ	70490 MW	87540 TQ	USBLS	5/07
	Tampa-St. Petersburg-Clearwater MSA, FL	Y	69380 FQ	76540 MW	91830 TQ	USBLS	5/07
	Hawaii	Y	62170 FQ	78580 MW	112530 TQ	USBLS	5/07
	Honolulu MSA, HI	Y	62060 FQ	78890 MW	114170 TQ	USBLS	5/07
	Louisiana	H	22.59 FQ	29.31 MW	38.95 TQ	LABLS	1/08-3/08
	Baton Rouge MSA, LA	Y	53140 FQ	60220 MW	66300 TQ	USBLS	5/07
	New Orleans-Metairie-Kenner MSA, LA	Y	51120 FQ	68650 MW	86450 TQ	USBLS	5/07
	Maine	Y	58810 FQ	75520 MW	90850 TQ	USBLS	5/07
	Maryland	Y		84125 MW		MDBLS	3/08
	Baltimore-Towson MSA, MD	Y	54800 FQ	62670 MW	73450 TQ	USBLS	5/07
	Massachusetts	Y	70290 FQ	81220 MW	91680 TQ	USBLS	5/07
	Boston-Cambridge-Quincy NECTA, MA	Y	70080 FQ	79720 MW	90160 TQ	USBLS	5/07

AE	Average entry wage	AW	Average wage paid	FQ First quartile wage
AER	Average entry range	AWR	Average wage range	H Hourly
AEX	Average experienced wage	AXR	Average experienced range	HI Highest wage paid
ATC	Average total compensation	D	Daily	HR High end range

LO   Lowest wage paid   MTC Median total compensation   TCC Total cash compensation
LR   Low end range   MW   Median wage paid   TQ   Third quartile wage
M   Monthly   MWR Median wage range   W   Weekly
MCC Median cash compensation   S See annotated source   Y   Yearly

Occupation/Type/Industry	Location	Per	Low	Mid	High	Source	Date
Marine Engineer and Naval Architect							
	Michigan	Y	49830 FQ	61320 MW	82290 TQ	USBLS	5/07
	Mississippi	Y	71150 FQ	77430 MW	83770 TQ	USBLS	5/07
	Missouri	Y	91940 FQ	139540 MW		USBLS	5/07
	New Jersey	Y	65260 FQ	83180 MW	94270 TQ	USBLS	5/07
	New York	Y	51760 FQ	60570 MW	72980 TQ	USBLS	5/07
	New York-Northern New Jersey-Long Island MSA, NY-NJ-PA	Y	54180 FQ	65500 MW	88590 TQ	USBLS	5/07
	Pennsylvania	Y	67440 FQ	86970 MW	98260 TQ	USBLS	5/07
	Philadelphia-Camden-Wilmington MSA, PA-NJ-DE-MD	Y	64660 FQ	82120 MW	95340 TQ	USBLS	5/07
	Texas	Y	68220 FQ	90180 MW	113700 TQ	USBLS	5/07
	Houston-Sugar Land-Baytown MSA, TX	Y	66880 FQ	89830 MW	123940 TQ	USBLS	5/07
	Virginia	Y	56050 FQ	69600 MW	88920 TQ	USBLS	5/07
	Virginia Beach-Norfolk-Newport News MSA, VA-NC	Y	58100 FQ	69060 MW	83890 TQ	USBLS	5/07
	Washington	H	32.15 FQ	39.44 MW	44.84 TQ	WABLS	3/08
	Seattle-Tacoma-Bellevue MSA, WA	Y	62630 FQ	78020 MW	91270 TQ	USBLS	5/07
	Wisconsin	Y	46650 FQ	57090 MW	68200 TQ	USBLS	5/07
Marine Equipment Servicer							
Municipal Government	Seattle, WA	H	29.34 LO		30.43 HI	CSSS	2008
Marine Patrol Captain							
Department of Safety	New Hampshire	Y			75968 HI	NHUL03	2008
Market Reporter							
State Government	Ohio	H	15.62 LO		18.36 HI	ODAS	2008
Market Research Analyst							
	Alabama	Y	35820 FQ	49540 MW	68200 TQ	USBLS	5/07
	Birmingham-Hoover MSA, AL	Y	44580 FQ	60170 MW	73440 TQ	USBLS	5/07
	Alaska	Y	41810 FQ	50280 MW	63840 TQ	USBLS	5/07
	Anchorage MSA, AK	Y	43570 FQ	49420 MW	62680 TQ	USBLS	5/07
	Arizona	Y	35710 FQ	49150 MW	72930 TQ	USBLS	5/07
	Phoenix-Mesa-Scottsdale MSA, AZ	Y	38490 FQ	52140 MW	76240 TQ	USBLS	5/07
	Tucson MSA, AZ	Y	32010 FQ	38530 MW	59260 TQ	USBLS	5/07
	Arkansas	Y	37120 FQ	58600 MW	79280 TQ	USBLS	5/07
	Little Rock-North Little Rock MSA, AR	Y	36090 FQ	41750 MW	61790 TQ	USBLS	5/07
	California	H	22.61 FQ	31.28 MW	44.93 TQ	CABLS	1/08-3/08
	Los Angeles-Long Beach-Glendale PMSA, CA	H	21.13 FQ	28.05 MW	38.94 TQ	CABLS	1/08-3/08
	Oakland-Fremont-Hayward MSA, CA	H	28.15 FQ	35.91 MW	48.00 TQ	CABLS	1/08-3/08
	Riverside-San Bernardino-Ontario MSA, CA	H	19.38 FQ	23.88 MW	30.67 TQ	CABLS	1/08-3/08
	Sacramento-Arden Arcade-Roseville MSA, CA	H	18.04 FQ	23.86 MW	35.14 TQ	CABLS	1/08-3/08
	San Diego-Carlsbad-San Marcos MSA, CA	H	21.69 FQ	28.74 MW	41.62 TQ	CABLS	1/08-3/08
	San Francisco-San Mateo-Redwood PMSA, CA	H	29.66 FQ	40.21 MW	51.19 TQ	CABLS	1/08-3/08
	San Jose-Sunnyvale-Santa Clara MSA, CA	H	32.60 FQ	46.66 MW	64.57 TQ	CABLS	1/08-3/08
	Santa Ana-Anaheim-Irvine PMSA, CA	Y	42550 FQ	57460 MW	74650 TQ	USBLS	5/07
	Colorado	Y	45680 FQ	66940 MW	88210 TQ	USBLS	5/07
	Denver-Aurora MSA, CO	Y	47590 FQ	68240 MW	86470 TQ	USBLS	5/07
	Connecticut	H	20.38 AE	30.30 MW		CTBLS	1/08-3/08
	Bridgeport-Stamford-Norwalk MSA, CT	Y	48630 FQ	68150 MW	95020 TQ	USBLS	5/07
	Hartford-West Hartford-East Hartford MSA, CT	Y	47870 FQ	62330 MW	80970 TQ	USBLS	5/07
	Delaware	Y	56890 FQ	74330 MW	95720 TQ	USBLS	5/07
	Wilmington PMSA, DE-MD-NJ	Y	57830 FQ	75230 MW	95990 TQ	USBLS	5/07
	District of Columbia	Y	45420 FQ	59720 MW	80000 TQ	USBLS	5/07

AE	Average entry wage	AW	Average wage paid	FQ	First quartile wage	LO Lowest wage paid
AER	Average entry range	AWR	Average wage range	H	Hourly	LR Low end range
AEX	Average experienced wage	AXR	Average experienced range	HI	Highest wage paid	M Monthly
ATC	Average total compensation	D	Daily	HR	High end range	MCC Median cash compensation

MTC Median total compensation	TCC Total cash compensation
MW Median wage paid	TQ Third quartile wage
MWR Median wage range	W Weekly
S See annotated source	Y Yearly

Occupation/Type/Industry	Location	Per	Low	Mid	High	Source	Date
Market Research Analyst	Washington-Arlington-Alexandria MSA, DC-VA-MD-WV	Y	48850 FQ	68230 MW	95340 TQ	USBLS	5/07
	Florida	Y	37830 FQ	51290 MW	72540 TQ	USBLS	5/07
	Fort Lauderdale-Pompano Beach-Deerfield Beach PMSA, FL	Y	36050 FQ	44640 MW	57800 TQ	USBLS	5/07
	Jacksonville MSA, FL	Y	44900 FQ	54240 MW	67710 TQ	USBLS	5/07
	Miami-Fort Lauderdale-Miami Beach MSA, FL	Y	38180 FQ	50760 MW	72370 TQ	USBLS	5/07
	Orlando-Kissimmee MSA, FL	Y	42660 FQ	54660 MW	70990 TQ	USBLS	5/07
	Tampa-St. Petersburg-Clearwater MSA, FL	Y	34320 FQ	50290 MW	76120 TQ	USBLS	5/07
	West Palm Beach-Boca Raton-Boynton Beach PMSA, FL	Y	41100 FQ	55650 MW	82810 TQ	USBLS	5/07
	Georgia	Y	42420 FQ	56540 MW	76220 TQ	USBLS	5/07
	Atlanta-Sandy Springs-Marietta MSA, GA	Y	45030 FQ	58740 MW	78690 TQ	USBLS	5/07
	Hawaii	Y	42290 FQ	55370 MW	71520 TQ	USBLS	5/07
	Honolulu MSA, HI	Y	41790 FQ	56540 MW	72950 TQ	USBLS	5/07
	Idaho	Y	41470 FQ	47060 MW	53740 TQ	USBLS	5/07
	Boise City-Nampa MSA, ID	Y	42500 FQ	49860 MW	70120 TQ	USBLS	5/07
	Illinois	Y	38060 FQ	54890 MW	77760 TQ	USBLS	5/07
	Chicago-Naperville-Joliet MSA, IL-IN-WI	Y	39200 FQ	56250 MW	78880 TQ	USBLS	5/07
	Indiana	Y	36980 FQ	47830 MW	65250 TQ	USBLS	5/07
	Gary PMSA, IN	Y	41490 FQ	50710 MW	59910 TQ	USBLS	5/07
	Indianapolis-Carmel MSA, IN	Y	37550 FQ	49110 MW	70700 TQ	USBLS	5/07
	South Bend-Mishawaka MSA, IN-MI	Y	43460 FQ	51370 MW	67380 TQ	USBLS	5/07
	Iowa	Y	37060 FQ	48750 MW	67250 TQ	USBLS	5/07
	Des Moines-West Des Moines MSA, IA	Y	40620 FQ	50840 MW	65610 TQ	USBLS	5/07
	Sioux City MSA, IA-NE-SD	Y	42390 FQ	49450 MW	72470 TQ	USBLS	5/07
	Kansas	Y	38080 FQ	50410 MW	66460 TQ	USBLS	5/07
	Topeka MSA, KS	Y	46010 FQ	54040 MW	63650 TQ	USBLS	5/07
	Wichita MSA, KS	Y	36110 FQ	45060 MW	60440 TQ	USBLS	5/07
	Kentucky	Y	40372 FQ	60110 MW	87941 TQ	KYBLS	2008
	Louisville-Jefferson County MSA, KY-IN	Y	45480 FQ	66220 MW	96070 TQ	USBLS	5/07
	Louisiana	H	15.49 FQ	18.81 MW	23.74 TQ	LABLS	1/08-3/08
	Baton Rouge MSA, LA	Y	34850 FQ	42820 MW	53700 TQ	USBLS	5/07
	New Orleans-Metairie-Kenner MSA, LA	Y	34030 FQ	39030 MW	48000 TQ	USBLS	5/07
	Maine	Y	37450 FQ	49960 MW	70990 TQ	USBLS	5/07
	Portland-South Portland-Biddeford MSA, ME	Y	43100 FQ	61050 MW	76590 TQ	USBLS	5/07
	Maryland	Y		64950 MW		MDBLS	3/08
	Baltimore-Towson MSA, MD	Y	44950 FQ	62770 MW	82790 TQ	USBLS	5/07
	Bethesda-Gaithersburg-Frederick PMSA, MD	Y	49190 FQ	66450 MW	99780 TQ	USBLS	5/07
	Massachusetts	Y	49710 FQ	67910 MW	93270 TQ	USBLS	5/07
	Boston-Cambridge-Quincy NECTA, MA	Y	50430 FQ	68630 MW	91790 TQ	USBLS	5/07
	Worcester MSA, MA-CT	Y	54050 FQ	67590 MW	89180 TQ	USBLS	5/07
	Michigan	Y	49240 FQ	65360 MW	92340 TQ	USBLS	5/07
	Detroit-Warren-Livonia MSA, MI	Y	52050 FQ	68930 MW	94670 TQ	USBLS	5/07
	Flint MSA, MI	Y	52980 FQ	59320 MW	70570 TQ	USBLS	5/07
	Grand Rapids-Wyoming MSA, MI	Y	44200 FQ	59670 MW	88090 TQ	USBLS	5/07
	Muskegon-Norton Shores MSA, MI	Y	24910 FQ	44700 MW	85430 TQ	USBLS	5/07
	Warren-Troy-Farmington Hills PMSA, MI	Y	47410 FQ	63390 MW	89160 TQ	USBLS	5/07
	Minnesota	Y	53388 FQ	69239 MW	90038 TQ	MNBLS	10/08-12/08
	Duluth-Superior MSA, MN-WI	Y	38145 FQ	51254 MW	64813 TQ	MNBLS	10/08-12/08
	Minneapolis-Saint Paul MSA, MN-WI	Y	54864 FQ	70724 MW	91701 TQ	MNBLS	10/08-12/08
	Rochester MSA, MN	Y	52316 FQ	80885 MW	115161 TQ	MNBLS	10/08-12/08
	Mississippi	Y	32550 FQ	42040 MW	51270 TQ	USBLS	5/07
	Jackson MSA, MS	Y	32600 FQ	40780 MW	57020 TQ	USBLS	5/07

Occupation/Type/Industry	Location	Per	Low	Mid	High	Source	Date
Market Research Analyst	Missouri	Y	38610 FQ	52670 MW	73960 TQ	USBLS	5/07
	Kansas City MSA, MO-KS	Y	42330 FQ	55570 MW	74130 TQ	USBLS	5/07
	St. Louis MSA, MO-IL	Y	41380 FQ	54940 MW	76320 TQ	USBLS	5/07
	Montana	Y	33360 FQ	41670 MW	57330 TQ	USBLS	5/07
	Billings MSA, MT	Y	35370 FQ	43260 MW	71650 TQ	USBLS	5/07
	Nebraska	Y	39960 FQ	54050 MW	71340 TQ	USBLS	5/07
	Omaha-Council Bluffs MSA, NE-IA	Y	41870 FQ	56150 MW	75310 TQ	USBLS	5/07
	Nevada	H	16.72 FQ	24.32 MW	35.21 TQ	NVBLS	5/08
	Las Vegas-Paradise MSA, NV	H	16.12 FQ	22.23 MW	32.92 TQ	NVBLS	5/08
	New Hampshire	H	23.02 AE	30.36 MW	40.10 AEX	NHBLS	6/08
	Manchester MSA, NH	Y	53050 FQ	60300 MW	77220 TQ	USBLS	5/07
	Nashua NECTA, NH-MA	Y	50230 FQ	69060 MW	110980 TQ	USBLS	5/07
	New Jersey	Y	49720 FQ	66650 MW	92240 TQ	USBLS	5/07
	Camden PMSA, NJ	Y	48730 FQ	64780 MW	88900 TQ	USBLS	5/07
	Edison PMSA, NJ	Y	48130 FQ	66380 MW	93220 TQ	USBLS	5/07
	Newark-Union PMSA, NJ-PA	Y	53850 FQ	77710 MW	101060 TQ	USBLS	5/07
	New Mexico	Y	42110 FQ	52390 MW	73250 TQ	USBLS	5/07
	Albuquerque MSA, NM	Y	42930 FQ	53810 MW	74500 TQ	USBLS	5/07
	Las Cruces MSA, NM	Y	45530 FQ	65480 MW	75550 TQ	USBLS	5/07
	New York	Y	46250 FQ	63940 MW	91510 TQ	USBLS	5/07
	Albany-Schenectady-Troy MSA, NY	Y	44050 FQ	58550 MW	73450 TQ	USBLS	5/07
	Buffalo-Niagara Falls MSA, NY	Y	41280 FQ	54960 MW	72870 TQ	USBLS	5/07
	Nassau-Suffolk PMSA, NY	Y	47240 FQ	63490 MW	91160 TQ	USBLS	5/07
	New York-Northern New Jersey-Long Island MSA, NY-NJ-PA	Y	48490 FQ	67320 MW	94920 TQ	USBLS	5/07
	North Carolina	Y	45720 FQ	61060 MW	84910 TQ	USBLS	5/07
	Charlotte-Gastonia-Concord MSA, NC-SC	Y	47370 FQ	62720 MW	80580 TQ	USBLS	5/07
	Greensboro-High Point MSA, NC	Y	33560 FQ	46830 MW	67780 TQ	USBLS	5/07
	Raleigh-Cary MSA, NC	Y	47880 FQ	66170 MW	90130 TQ	USBLS	5/07
	North Dakota	Y	44160 FQ	49170 MW	57800 TQ	USBLS	5/07
	Fargo MSA, ND-MN	Y	45700 FQ	50580 MW	71170 TQ	USBLS	5/07
	Ohio	Y	44220 FQ	57960 MW	79260 TQ	USBLS	5/07
	Cincinnati-Middletown MSA, OH-KY-IN	Y	41880 FQ	56910 MW	77570 TQ	USBLS	5/07
	Cleveland-Elyria-Mentor MSA, OH	Y	45440 FQ	57880 MW	81420 TQ	USBLS	5/07
	Columbus MSA, OH	Y	50340 FQ	68840 MW	97870 TQ	USBLS	5/07
	Dayton MSA, OH	Y	38810 FQ	51150 MW	69820 TQ	USBLS	5/07
	Oklahoma	Y	33100 FQ	45940 MW	63530 TQ	USBLS	5/07
	Oklahoma City MSA, OK	Y	26000 FQ	36890 MW	51700 TQ	USBLS	5/07
	Tulsa MSA, OK	Y	41560 FQ	56210 MW	83360 TQ	USBLS	5/07
	Oregon	H	24.11 FQ	34.39 MW	46.16 TQ	ORBLS	5/08
	Portland-Vancouver-Beaverton MSA, OR-WA	Y	49750 FQ	70820 MW	95060 TQ	USBLS	5/07
	Pennsylvania	Y	35390 FQ	47680 MW	71230 TQ	USBLS	5/07
	Allentown-Bethlehem-Easton MSA, PA-NJ	Y	38390 FQ	48580 MW	77400 TQ	USBLS	5/07
	Philadelphia-Camden-Wilmington MSA, PA-NJ-DE-MD	Y	42630 FQ	60640 MW	86710 TQ	USBLS	5/07
	Pittsburgh MSA, PA	Y	30270 FQ	41090 MW	57250 TQ	USBLS	5/07
	Rhode Island	Y	39340 FQ	50600 MW	72220 TQ	USBLS	5/07
	Providence-Fall River-Warwick MSA, RI-MA	Y	36160 FQ	49360 MW	70850 TQ	USBLS	5/07
	South Carolina	Y	36340 FQ	49350 MW	64970 TQ	USBLS	5/07
	Charleston-North Charleston MSA, SC	Y	46300 FQ	54880 MW	68790 TQ	USBLS	5/07
	Columbia MSA, SC	Y	41170 FQ	47250 MW	53030 TQ	USBLS	5/07
	South Dakota	Y	36062 FQ	46035 MW	61656 TQ	SDBLS	7/08-9/08
	Sioux Falls MSA, SD	Y	36159 FQ	45340 MW	60456 TQ	SDBLS	7/08-9/08
	Tennessee	Y	35060 FQ	48470 MW	68010 TQ	USBLS	5/07
	Knoxville MSA, TN	Y	30800 FQ	38570 MW	63400 TQ	USBLS	5/07
	Memphis MSA, TN-MS-AR	Y	34230 FQ	58310 MW	109480 TQ	USBLS	5/07
	Nashville-Davidson-Murfreesboro MSA, TN	Y	40320 FQ	49250 MW	60840 TQ	USBLS	5/07
	Texas	Y	43850 FQ	63940 MW	92430 TQ	USBLS	5/07

AE	Average entry wage	AW	Average wage paid	FQ	First quartile wage	LO Lowest wage paid	MTC Median total compensation	TCC Total cash compensation
AER	Average entry range	AWR	Average wage range	H	Hourly	LR Low end range	MW Median wage paid	TQ Third quartile wage
AEX	Average experienced wage	AXR	Average experienced range	HI	Highest wage paid	M Monthly	MWR Median wage range	W Weekly
ATC	Average total compensation	D	Daily	HR	High end range	MCC Median cash compensation	S See annotated source	Y Yearly

Occupation/Type/Industry	Location	Per	Low	Mid	High	Source	Date
Market Research Analyst	Austin-Round Rock MSA, TX	Y	56330 FQ	85860 MW	108030 TQ	USBLS	5/07
	Beaumont-Port Arthur MSA, TX	Y	36380 FQ	54050 MW	84070 TQ	USBLS	5/07
	Dallas-Fort Worth-Arlington MSA, TX	Y	46960 FQ	64780 MW	91280 TQ	USBLS	5/07
	El Paso MSA, TX	Y	33140 FQ	37400 MW	42650 TQ	USBLS	5/07
	Houston-Sugar Land-Baytown MSA, TX	Y	45070 FQ	69580 MW	96380 TQ	USBLS	5/07
	San Antonio MSA, TX	Y	42410 FQ	56000 MW	77510 TQ	USBLS	5/07
	Utah	Y	37180 FQ	54980 MW	77160 TQ	USBLS	5/07
	Salt Lake City MSA, UT	Y	36420 FQ	55230 MW	77000 TQ	USBLS	5/07
	Vermont	Y	32820 FQ	46120 MW	63940 TQ	USBLS	5/07
	Burlington-South Burlington MSA, VT	Y	28960 FQ	40420 MW	59910 TQ	USBLS	5/07
	Virginia	Y	45660 FQ	66340 MW	94080 TQ	USBLS	5/07
	Richmond MSA, VA	Y	38240 FQ	57130 MW	78120 TQ	USBLS	5/07
	Virginia Beach-Norfolk-Newport News MSA, VA-NC	Y	35530 FQ	48780 MW	68840 TQ	USBLS	5/07
	Washington	H	27.52 FQ	41.35 MW	53.01 TQ	WABLS	3/08
	Seattle-Tacoma-Bellevue MSA, WA	Y	60280 FQ	88700 MW	111280 TQ	USBLS	5/07
	West Virginia	Y	31533 FQ	40356 MW	64590 TQ	WVBLS	7/08-9/08
	Charleston MSA, WV	Y	33090 FQ	50550 MW	87780 TQ	USBLS	5/07
	Wisconsin	Y	42940 FQ	56220 MW	76650 TQ	USBLS	5/07
	Milwaukee-Waukesha-West Allis MSA, WI	Y	44580 FQ	60000 MW	96830 TQ	USBLS	5/07
	Wyoming	Y	37778 FQ	45731 MW	54553 TQ	WYBLS	9/08
	Casper MSA, WY	Y	36563 FQ	44801 MW	53777 TQ	WYBLS	9/08
	Cheyenne MSA, WY	Y	37914 FQ	43326 MW	49477 TQ	WYBLS	9/08
	Puerto Rico	Y	27590 FQ	40280 MW	59890 TQ	USBLS	5/07
	San Juan-Caguas-Guaynabo MSA, PR	Y	27950 FQ	40860 MW	60360 TQ	USBLS	5/07
Marketing Executive	United States	Y		186000 AW		USATOD03	2008
Marketing Manager	Alabama	Y	63360 FQ	86910 MW	113960 TQ	USBLS	5/07
	Birmingham-Hoover MSA, AL	Y	63060 FQ	84660 MW	111530 TQ	USBLS	5/07
	Alaska	Y	48400 FQ	71270 MW	92850 TQ	USBLS	5/07
	Anchorage MSA, AK	Y	48390 FQ	71120 MW	92570 TQ	USBLS	5/07
	Arizona	Y	47180 FQ	66900 MW	97700 TQ	USBLS	5/07
	Phoenix-Mesa-Scottsdale MSA, AZ	Y	49780 FQ	70600 MW	104690 TQ	USBLS	5/07
	Prescott MSA, AZ	Y	37210 FQ	46890 MW	57840 TQ	USBLS	5/07
	Tucson MSA, AZ	Y	42850 FQ	58950 MW	79800 TQ	USBLS	5/07
	Arkansas	Y	63320 FQ	71850 MW	90730 TQ	USBLS	5/07
	Little Rock-North Little Rock MSA, AR	Y	58240 FQ	80710 MW	127530 TQ	USBLS	5/07
	California	H	43.40 FQ	60.41 MW		CABLS	1/08-3/08
	Los Angeles-Long Beach-Glendale PMSA, CA	H	39.51 FQ	56.09 MW		CABLS	1/08-3/08
	Oakland-Fremont-Hayward MSA, CA	H	45.80 FQ	60.82 MW		CABLS	1/08-3/08
	Riverside-San Bernardino-Ontario MSA, CA	H	36.77 FQ	47.23 MW	66.41 TQ	CABLS	1/08-3/08
	Sacramento-Arden Arcade-Roseville MSA, CA	H	33.45 FQ	46.04 MW	62.47 TQ	CABLS	1/08-3/08
	San Diego-Carlsbad-San Marcos MSA, CA	H	39.24 FQ	55.32 MW		CABLS	1/08-3/08
	San Francisco-San Mateo-Redwood PMSA, CA	H	54.88 FQ			CABLS	1/08-3/08
	San Jose-Sunnyvale-Santa Clara MSA, CA	H	57.45 FQ			CABLS	1/08-3/08
	Santa Ana-Anaheim-Irvine PMSA, CA	Y	84040 FQ	112290 MW		USBLS	5/07
	Colorado	Y	66200 FQ	92400 MW	129950 TQ	USBLS	5/07
	Denver-Aurora MSA, CO	Y	70700 FQ	94930 MW	131930 TQ	USBLS	5/07
	Connecticut	H	30.36 AE	50.85 MW		CTBLS	1/08-3/08
	Bridgeport-Stamford-Norwalk MSA, CT	Y	85100 FQ	122020 MW		USBLS	5/07
	Danbury MSA, CT	Y	90230 FQ	105850 MW	136030 TQ	USBLS	5/07
	Hartford-West Hartford-East Hartford MSA, CT	Y	74470 FQ	100760 MW	129350 TQ	USBLS	5/07

AE	Average entry wage	AW	Average wage paid	FQ	First quartile wage	LO	Lowest wage paid	MTC	Median total compensation	TCC	Total cash compensation
AER	Average entry range	AWR	Average wage range	H	Hourly	LR	Low end range	MW	Median wage paid	TQ	Third quartile wage
AEX	Average experienced wage	AXR	Average experienced range	HI	Highest wage paid	M	Monthly	MWR	Median wage range	W	Weekly
ATC	Average total compensation	D	Daily	HR	High end range	MCC	Median cash compensation	S	See annotated source	Y	Yearly

Occupation/Type/Industry	Location	Per	Low	Mid	High	Source	Date
Marketing Manager	Norwich-New London MSA, CT-RI	Y	51100 FQ	63250 MW	101040 TQ	USBLS	5/07
	Delaware	Y	96230 FQ	129310 MW		USBLS	5/07
	Wilmington PMSA, DE-MD-NJ	Y	97920 FQ	130740 MW		USBLS	5/07
	District of Columbia	Y	74140 FQ	95770 MW	119960 TQ	USBLS	5/07
	Washington-Arlington-Alexandria MSA, DC-VA-MD-WV	Y	80270 FQ	109930 MW		USBLS	5/07
	Florida	Y	69600 FQ	99680 MW	134990 TQ	USBLS	5/07
	Fort Lauderdale-Pompano Beach-Deerfield Beach PMSA, FL	Y	78740 FQ	103540 MW	145040 TQ	USBLS	5/07
	Jacksonville MSA, FL	Y	68290 FQ	100090 MW	138400 TQ	USBLS	5/07
	Miami-Fort Lauderdale-Miami Beach MSA, FL	Y	73820 FQ	102350 MW	145400 TQ	USBLS	5/07
	Orlando-Kissimmee MSA, FL	Y	51970 FQ	91040 MW	120550 TQ	USBLS	5/07
	Tampa-St. Petersburg-Clearwater MSA, FL	Y	72260 FQ	103330 MW	129020 TQ	USBLS	5/07
	West Palm Beach-Boca Raton-Boynton Beach PMSA, FL	Y	66210 FQ	90720 MW		USBLS	5/07
	Georgia	Y	70090 FQ	96500 MW	129180 TQ	USBLS	5/07
	Atlanta-Sandy Springs-Marietta MSA, GA	Y	72800 FQ	99650 MW	132480 TQ	USBLS	5/07
	Augusta-Richmond County MSA, GA-SC	Y	53290 FQ	80160 MW	102150 TQ	USBLS	5/07
	Hawaii	Y	52150 FQ	74160 MW	98160 TQ	USBLS	5/07
	Honolulu MSA, HI	Y	50890 FQ	71780 MW	95060 TQ	USBLS	5/07
	Idaho	Y	48980 FQ	69390 MW	91090 TQ	USBLS	5/07
	Boise City-Nampa MSA, ID	Y	56160 FQ	78090 MW	97290 TQ	USBLS	5/07
	Illinois	Y	70190 FQ	97720 MW	131730 TQ	USBLS	5/07
	Chicago-Naperville-Joliet MSA, IL-IN-WI	Y	72380 FQ	100430 MW	134070 TQ	USBLS	5/07
	Indiana	Y	58680 FQ	81790 MW	114600 TQ	USBLS	5/07
	Gary PMSA, IN	Y	60360 FQ	84730 MW	112590 TQ	USBLS	5/07
	Indianapolis-Carmel MSA, IN	Y	64840 FQ	90020 MW	125680 TQ	USBLS	5/07
	Iowa	Y	55920 FQ	77710 MW	106500 TQ	USBLS	5/07
	Cedar Rapids MSA, IA	Y	69670 FQ	92190 MW	121200 TQ	USBLS	5/07
	Des Moines-West Des Moines MSA, IA	Y	69520 FQ	90030 MW	115200 TQ	USBLS	5/07
	Kansas	Y	60580 FQ	83390 MW	126750 TQ	USBLS	5/07
	Wichita MSA, KS	Y	47890 FQ	80790 MW	113700 TQ	USBLS	5/07
	Kentucky	Y	58639 FQ	81761 MW	115673 TQ	KYBLS	2008
	Lexington-Fayette MSA, KY	Y	62300 FQ	84400 MW	124960 TQ	USBLS	5/07
	Louisville-Jefferson County MSA, KY-IN	Y	57320 FQ	76720 MW	117040 TQ	USBLS	5/07
	Louisiana	H	24.82 FQ	30.55 MW	46.00 TQ	LABLS	1/08-3/08
	Baton Rouge MSA, LA	Y	49980 FQ	58470 MW	109230 TQ	USBLS	5/07
	New Orleans-Metairie-Kenner MSA, LA	Y	58380 FQ	74680 MW	102000 TQ	USBLS	5/07
	Shreveport-Bossier City MSA, LA	Y	51440 FQ	62140 MW	75610 TQ	USBLS	5/07
	Maine	Y	57180 FQ	74560 MW	100100 TQ	USBLS	5/07
	Portland-South Portland-Biddeford MSA, ME	Y	67450 FQ	85310 MW	111670 TQ	USBLS	5/07
	Maryland	Y		97850 MW		MDBLS	3/08
	Baltimore-Towson MSA, MD	Y	73440 FQ	101650 MW	137990 TQ	USBLS	5/07
	Bethesda-Gaithersburg-Frederick PMSA, MD	Y	70780 FQ	94470 MW	136320 TQ	USBLS	5/07
	Hagerstown-Martinsburg MSA, MD-WV	Y	43610 FQ	59400 MW	93310 TQ	USBLS	5/07
	Massachusetts	Y	87730 FQ	115430 MW		USBLS	5/07
	Boston-Cambridge-Quincy NECTA, MA	Y	91000 FQ	117470 MW		USBLS	5/07
	Worcester MSA, MA-CT	Y	62370 FQ	102410 MW	141790 TQ	USBLS	5/07
	Michigan	Y	64930 FQ	90070 MW	117400 TQ	USBLS	5/07
	Ann Arbor MSA, MI	Y	64910 FQ	92200 MW	119210 TQ	USBLS	5/07
	Detroit-Warren-Livonia MSA, MI	Y	67390 FQ	94690 MW	124400 TQ	USBLS	5/07
	Grand Rapids-Wyoming MSA, MI	Y	63000 FQ	81840 MW	99950 TQ	USBLS	5/07

AE	Average entry wage	AW	Average wage paid	FQ	First quartile wage
AER	Average entry range	AWR	Average wage range	H	Hourly
AEX	Average experienced wage	AXR	Average experienced range	HI	Highest wage paid
ATC	Average total compensation	D	Daily	HR	High end range

LO	Lowest wage paid	MTC	Median total compensation
LR	Low end range	MW	Median wage paid
M	Monthly	MWR	Median wage range
MCC	Median cash compensation	S	See annotated source

TCC	Total cash compensation	
TQ	Third quartile wage	
W	Weekly	
Y	Yearly	

Occupation/Type/Industry	Location	Per	Low	Mid	High	Source	Date
Marketing Manager	Warren-Troy-Farmington Hills PMSA, MI	Y	77820 FQ	100500 MW	129410 TQ	USBLS	5/07
	Minnesota	Y	90356 FQ	115546 MW	146628 TQ	MNBLS	10/08-12/08
	Duluth-Superior MSA, MN-WI	Y	56730 FQ	77750 MW	97686 TQ	MNBLS	10/08-12/08
	Minneapolis-Saint Paul MSA, MN-WI	Y	92347 FQ	117527 MW	148359 TQ	MNBLS	10/08-12/08
	Rochester MSA, MN	Y	80081 FQ	110410 MW	127947 TQ	MNBLS	10/08-12/08
	Mississippi	Y	47570 FQ	62800 MW	90050 TQ	USBLS	5/07
	Jackson MSA, MS	Y	50780 FQ	68430 MW	110670 TQ	USBLS	5/07
	Missouri	Y	72240 FQ	96150 MW	129720 TQ	USBLS	5/07
	Kansas City MSA, MO-KS	Y	69550 FQ	90330 MW	126090 TQ	USBLS	5/07
	St. Louis MSA, MO-IL	Y	76620 FQ	102550 MW	135550 TQ	USBLS	5/07
	Montana	Y	49110 FQ	62260 MW	80730 TQ	USBLS	5/07
	Billings MSA, MT	Y	53380 FQ	70290 MW	77860 TQ	USBLS	5/07
	Nebraska	Y	68600 FQ	89690 MW	117230 TQ	USBLS	5/07
	Omaha-Council Bluffs MSA, NE-IA	Y	75680 FQ	92230 MW	123110 TQ	USBLS	5/07
	Nevada	H	30.55 FQ	38.99 MW	51.75 TQ	NVBLS	5/08
	Las Vegas-Paradise MSA, NV	H	32.15 FQ	40.20 MW	54.59 TQ	NVBLS	5/08
	New Hampshire	H	28.06 AE	41.87 MW	56.02 AEX	NHBLS	6/08
	Manchester MSA, NH	Y	72510 FQ	90470 MW	108190 TQ	USBLS	5/07
	Nashua NECTA, NH-MA	Y	76830 FQ	103210 MW	135110 TQ	USBLS	5/07
	New Jersey	Y	95480 FQ	121490 MW		USBLS	5/07
	Camden PMSA, NJ	Y	87540 FQ	119280 MW		USBLS	5/07
	Edison PMSA, NJ	Y	100400 FQ	129020 MW		USBLS	5/07
	Newark-Union PMSA, NJ-PA	Y	97210 FQ	121080 MW		USBLS	5/07
	New Mexico	Y	39780 FQ	65010 MW	95710 TQ	USBLS	5/07
	Albuquerque MSA, NM	Y	51140 FQ	83930 MW	130010 TQ	USBLS	5/07
	New York	Y	99120 FQ	135490 MW		USBLS	5/07
	Albany-Schenectady-Troy MSA, NY	Y	74430 FQ	105470 MW	140800 TQ	USBLS	5/07
	Buffalo-Niagara Falls MSA, NY	Y	75770 FQ	96610 MW	125660 TQ	USBLS	5/07
	Nassau-Suffolk PMSA, NY	Y	109990 FQ			USBLS	5/07
	New York-Northern New Jersey-Long Island MSA, NY-NJ-PA	Y	101200 FQ	134140 MW		USBLS	5/07
	North Carolina	Y	75950 FQ	100070 MW	132710 TQ	USBLS	5/07
	Charlotte-Gastonia-Concord MSA, NC-SC	Y	79520 FQ	98740 MW	131520 TQ	USBLS	5/07
	Raleigh-Cary MSA, NC	Y	82120 FQ	105720 MW	135310 TQ	USBLS	5/07
	Winston-Salem MSA, NC	Y	81340 FQ	101910 MW	131610 TQ	USBLS	5/07
	North Dakota	Y	56200 FQ	68040 MW	79900 TQ	USBLS	5/07
	Fargo MSA, ND-MN	Y	58090 FQ	68390 MW	79960 TQ	USBLS	5/07
	Ohio	Y	74510 FQ	96030 MW	125290 TQ	USBLS	5/07
	Cincinnati-Middletown MSA, OH-KY-IN	Y	71480 FQ	96440 MW	131600 TQ	USBLS	5/07
	Cleveland-Elyria-Mentor MSA, OH	Y	78290 FQ	98850 MW	131260 TQ	USBLS	5/07
	Columbus MSA, OH	Y	74050 FQ	93640 MW	122270 TQ	USBLS	5/07
	Dayton MSA, OH	Y	76370 FQ	95620 MW	121450 TQ	USBLS	5/07
	Oklahoma	Y	48040 FQ	73520 MW	103850 TQ	USBLS	5/07
	Oklahoma City MSA, OK	Y	42090 FQ	64730 MW	84940 TQ	USBLS	5/07
	Tulsa MSA, OK	Y	58490 FQ	87010 MW	111190 TQ	USBLS	5/07
	Oregon	H	33.03 FQ	44.96 MW	59.64 TQ	ORBLS	5/08
	Portland-Vancouver-Beaverton MSA, OR-WA	Y	73210 FQ	100100 MW	128200 TQ	USBLS	5/07
	Pennsylvania	Y	66290 FQ	93030 MW	130840 TQ	USBLS	5/07
	Allentown-Bethlehem-Easton MSA, PA-NJ	Y	69690 FQ	95350 MW	144140 TQ	USBLS	5/07
	Philadelphia-Camden-Wilmington MSA, PA-NJ-DE-MD	Y	79340 FQ	111690 MW		USBLS	5/07
	Pittsburgh MSA, PA	Y	66690 FQ	89080 MW	117230 TQ	USBLS	5/07
	Rhode Island	Y	58290 FQ	83250 MW	119430 TQ	USBLS	5/07
	Providence-Fall River-Warwick MSA, RI-MA	Y	59050 FQ	84080 MW	119290 TQ	USBLS	5/07
	South Carolina	Y	57050 FQ	77830 MW	106170 TQ	USBLS	5/07
	Charleston-North Charleston MSA, SC	Y	56610 FQ	76020 MW	103530 TQ	USBLS	5/07
	Columbia MSA, SC	Y	53150 FQ	65920 MW	93310 TQ	USBLS	5/07
	South Dakota	Y	79743 FQ	96897 MW	115125 TQ	SDBLS	7/08-9/08

AE — Average entry wage
AER — Average entry range
AEX — Average experienced wage
ATC — Average total compensation
AW — Average wage paid
AWR — Average wage range
AXR — Average experienced range
D — Daily
FQ — First quartile wage
H — Hourly
HI — Highest wage paid
HR — High end range
LO — Lowest wage paid
LR — Low end range
M — Monthly
MCC — Median cash compensation
MTC — Median total compensation
MW — Median wage paid
MWR — Median wage range
S — See annotated source
TCC — Total cash compensation
TQ — Third quartile wage
W — Weekly
Y — Yearly

Occupation/Type/Industry	Location	Per	Low	Mid	High	Source	Date
Marketing Manager	Sioux Falls MSA, SD	Y	82616 FQ	97781 MW	116569 TQ	SDBLS	7/08-9/08
	Tennessee	Y	48110 FQ	72640 MW	107910 TQ	USBLS	5/07
	Memphis MSA, TN-MS-AR	Y	54620 FQ	86410 MW	126290 TQ	USBLS	5/07
	Nashville-Davidson-Murfreesboro MSA, TN	Y	49960 FQ	72170 MW	100950 TQ	USBLS	5/07
	Texas	Y	79970 FQ	110070 MW		USBLS	5/07
	Austin-Round Rock MSA, TX	Y	90730 FQ	116710 MW		USBLS	5/07
	Dallas-Fort Worth-Arlington MSA, TX	Y	85540 FQ	114550 MW		USBLS	5/07
	El Paso MSA, TX	Y	60010 FQ	76280 MW	117400 TQ	USBLS	5/07
	Houston-Sugar Land-Baytown MSA, TX	Y	78000 FQ	109120 MW		USBLS	5/07
	San Antonio MSA, TX	Y	70820 FQ	96940 MW	123510 TQ	USBLS	5/07
	Utah	Y	57960 FQ	80150 MW	105880 TQ	USBLS	5/07
	Salt Lake City MSA, UT	Y	60170 FQ	79670 MW	105520 TQ	USBLS	5/07
	Vermont	Y	56530 FQ	77950 MW	127610 TQ	USBLS	5/07
	Burlington-South Burlington MSA, VT	Y	59190 FQ	89610 MW	144920 TQ	USBLS	5/07
	Virginia	Y	93470 FQ	124850 MW		USBLS	5/07
	Charlottesville MSA, VA	Y	59040 FQ	85530 MW	101400 TQ	USBLS	5/07
	Richmond MSA, VA	Y	80520 FQ	126500 MW		USBLS	5/07
	Virginia Beach-Norfolk-Newport News MSA, VA-NC	Y	70170 FQ	91730 MW	121430 TQ	USBLS	5/07
	Washington	H	42.64 FQ	55.55 MW		WABLS	3/08
	Seattle-Tacoma-Bellevue MSA, WA	Y	91080 FQ	120150 MW		USBLS	5/07
	West Virginia	Y	48400 FQ	72008 MW	108383 TQ	WVBLS	7/08-9/08
	Charleston MSA, WV	Y	43640 FQ	50940 MW	72460 TQ	USBLS	5/07
	Wisconsin	Y	66070 FQ	91410 MW	124580 TQ	USBLS	5/07
	Milwaukee-Waukesha-West Allis MSA, WI	Y	70640 FQ	101820 MW	141110 TQ	USBLS	5/07
	Wyoming	Y	45464 FQ	70553 MW	93771 TQ	WYBLS	9/08
	Cheyenne MSA, WY	Y	37657 FQ	41563 MW	80314 TQ	WYBLS	9/08
	Puerto Rico	Y	51990 FQ	76970 MW	108220 TQ	USBLS	5/07
	San Juan-Caguas-Guaynabo MSA, PR	Y	52320 FQ	76720 MW	106140 TQ	USBLS	5/07
	Virgin Islands	Y	49640 FQ	61510 MW	80630 TQ	USBLS	5/07
	Guam	Y	35430 FQ	51230 MW	62980 TQ	USBLS	5/07
Marriage and Family Therapist	Alabama	Y	30070 FQ	35560 MW	46280 TQ	USBLS	5/07
	Birmingham-Hoover MSA, AL	Y	28620 FQ	31340 MW	36180 TQ	USBLS	5/07
	Arizona	Y	41580 FQ	47200 MW	53070 TQ	USBLS	5/07
	Phoenix-Mesa-Scottsdale MSA, AZ	Y	45110 FQ	49430 MW	54000 TQ	USBLS	5/07
	Tucson MSA, AZ	Y	30410 FQ	37050 MW	51410 TQ	USBLS	5/07
	California	H	14.31 FQ	20.15 MW	26.14 TQ	CABLS	1/08-3/08
	Bakersfield MSA, CA	H	22.97 FQ	25.95 MW	31.62 TQ	CABLS	1/08-3/08
	Los Angeles-Long Beach-Glendale PMSA, CA	H	18.95 FQ	22.97 MW	27.04 TQ	CABLS	1/08-3/08
	Oakland-Fremont-Hayward MSA, CA	H	18.35 FQ	20.86 MW	29.56 TQ	CABLS	1/08-3/08
	Riverside-San Bernardino-Ontario MSA, CA	H	17.77 FQ	20.26 MW	22.86 TQ	CABLS	1/08-3/08
	Sacramento-Arden Arcade-Roseville MSA, CA	H	20.34 FQ	24.68 MW	29.22 TQ	CABLS	1/08-3/08
	San Diego-Carlsbad-San Marcos MSA, CA	H	17.77 FQ	21.39 MW	26.03 TQ	CABLS	1/08-3/08
	San Francisco-San Mateo-Redwood PMSA, CA	H	8.43 FQ	9.18 MW	19.34 TQ	CABLS	1/08-3/08
	San Jose-Sunnyvale-Santa Clara MSA, CA	H	11.84 FQ	16.99 MW	26.65 TQ	CABLS	1/08-3/08
	Santa Ana-Anaheim-Irvine PMSA, CA	Y	26640 FQ	33030 MW	50310 TQ	USBLS	5/07
	Colorado	Y	27650 FQ	46970 MW	56740 TQ	USBLS	5/07
	Denver-Aurora MSA, CO	Y	30150 FQ	36390 MW	46900 TQ	USBLS	5/07
	Connecticut	H	19.11 AE	25.54 MW		CTBLS	1/08-3/08
	Bridgeport-Stamford-Norwalk MSA, CT	Y	52830 FQ	62800 MW	74330 TQ	USBLS	5/07
	Danbury MSA, CT	Y	35120 FQ	44950 MW	56080 TQ	USBLS	5/07
	Hartford-West Hartford-East Hartford MSA, CT	Y	44370 FQ	51350 MW	59680 TQ	USBLS	5/07

AE	Average entry wage	AW	Average wage paid	FQ	First quartile wage	LO	Lowest wage paid	MTC	Median total compensation	TCC	Total cash compensation
AER	Average entry range	AWR	Average wage range	H	Hourly	LR	Low end range	MW	Median wage paid	TQ	Third quartile wage
AEX	Average experienced wage	AXR	Average experienced range	HI	Highest wage paid	M	Monthly	MWR	Median wage range	W	Weekly
ATC	Average total compensation	D	Daily	HR	High end range	MCC	Median cash compensation	S	See annotated source	Y	Yearly

Occupation/Type/Industry	Location	Per	Low	Mid	High	Source	Date
Marriage and Family Therapist	Washington-Arlington-Alexandria MSA, DC-VA-MD-WV	Y	41680 FQ	51420 MW	61060 TQ	USBLS	5/07
	Florida	Y	33450 FQ	41490 MW	54510 TQ	USBLS	5/07
	Fort Lauderdale-Pompano Beach-Deerfield Beach PMSA, FL	Y	38430 FQ	56930 MW	69640 TQ	USBLS	5/07
	Jacksonville MSA, FL	Y	36870 FQ	43710 MW	52470 TQ	USBLS	5/07
	Miami-Fort Lauderdale-Miami Beach MSA, FL	Y	35780 FQ	46000 MW	62260 TQ	USBLS	5/07
	Orlando-Kissimmee MSA, FL	Y	28020 FQ	31200 MW	36670 TQ	USBLS	5/07
	Tampa-St. Petersburg-Clearwater MSA, FL	Y	30660 FQ	40080 MW	57470 TQ	USBLS	5/07
	West Palm Beach-Boca Raton-Boynton Beach PMSA, FL	Y	35860 FQ	44270 MW	49730 TQ	USBLS	5/07
	Georgia	Y	30780 FQ	42480 MW	61260 TQ	USBLS	5/07
	Idaho	Y	34400 FQ	43790 MW	49840 TQ	USBLS	5/07
	Illinois	Y	26310 FQ	35520 MW	46860 TQ	USBLS	5/07
	Chicago-Naperville-Joliet MSA, IL-IN-WI	Y	35340 FQ	40980 MW	57850 TQ	USBLS	5/07
	Indiana	Y	31810 FQ	37710 MW	46460 TQ	USBLS	5/07
	Indianapolis-Carmel MSA, IN	Y	34390 FQ	37810 MW	53470 TQ	USBLS	5/07
	Iowa	Y	26900 FQ	32640 MW	43080 TQ	USBLS	5/07
	Des Moines-West Des Moines MSA, IA	Y	27380 FQ	33640 MW	46540 TQ	USBLS	5/07
	Kansas	Y	14730 FQ	36130 MW	51640 TQ	USBLS	5/07
	Kentucky	Y	24492 FQ	29693 MW	43017 TQ	KYBLS	2008
	Louisville-Jefferson County MSA, KY-IN	Y	22660 FQ	25400 MW	31780 TQ	USBLS	5/07
	Maine	Y	30910 FQ	35290 MW	46770 TQ	USBLS	5/07
	Maryland	Y		44850 MW		MDBLS	3/08
	Baltimore-Towson MSA, MD	Y	38330 FQ	43590 MW	47880 TQ	USBLS	5/07
	Bethesda-Gaithersburg-Frederick PMSA, MD	Y	38320 FQ	43760 MW	50560 TQ	USBLS	5/07
	Massachusetts	Y	30620 FQ	42710 MW	60550 TQ	USBLS	5/07
	Boston-Cambridge-Quincy NECTA, MA	Y	40540 FQ	48840 MW	63060 TQ	USBLS	5/07
	Michigan	Y	26270 FQ	37870 MW	53020 TQ	USBLS	5/07
	Detroit-Warren-Livonia MSA, MI	Y	23630 FQ	31720 MW	40380 TQ	USBLS	5/07
	Warren-Troy-Farmington Hills PMSA, MI	Y	23020 FQ	28490 MW	36660 TQ	USBLS	5/07
	Minnesota	Y	46714 FQ	52531 MW	60294 TQ	MNBLS	10/08-12/08
	Minneapolis-Saint Paul MSA, MN-WI	Y	46734 FQ	52279 MW	59645 TQ	MNBLS	10/08-12/08
	Missouri	Y	33150 FQ	41100 MW	52330 TQ	USBLS	5/07
	Nebraska	Y	32930 FQ	36640 MW	44500 TQ	USBLS	5/07
	Omaha-Council Bluffs MSA, NE-IA	Y	32070 FQ	37330 MW	47080 TQ	USBLS	5/07
	Nevada	H	19.40 FQ	26.90 MW	34.68 TQ	NVBLS	5/08
	Las Vegas-Paradise MSA, NV	H	16.82 FQ	19.89 MW	26.94 TQ	NVBLS	5/08
	New Hampshire	H	15.37 AE	19.04 MW	23.18 AEX	NHBLS	6/08
	New Jersey	Y	45010 FQ	51520 MW	65150 TQ	USBLS	5/07
	Camden PMSA, NJ	Y	44270 FQ	51700 MW	66530 TQ	USBLS	5/07
	Edison PMSA, NJ	Y	42840 FQ	48950 MW	60120 TQ	USBLS	5/07
	Newark-Union PMSA, NJ-PA	Y	45910 FQ	51360 MW	65150 TQ	USBLS	5/07
	New Mexico	Y	33070 FQ	36620 MW	40440 TQ	USBLS	5/07
	New York	Y	31630 FQ	37010 MW	45990 TQ	USBLS	5/07
	Albany-Schenectady-Troy MSA, NY	Y	37180 FQ	41550 MW	46140 TQ	USBLS	5/07
	New York-Northern New Jersey-Long Island MSA, NY-NJ-PA	Y	43460 FQ	49760 MW	62150 TQ	USBLS	5/07
	North Carolina	Y	41890 FQ	48690 MW	65640 TQ	USBLS	5/07
	Ohio	Y	35960 FQ	40460 MW	49570 TQ	USBLS	5/07
	Cincinnati-Middletown MSA, OH-KY-IN	Y	32770 FQ	41790 MW	51090 TQ	USBLS	5/07
	Cleveland-Elyria-Mentor MSA, OH	Y	35660 FQ	38990 MW	45280 TQ	USBLS	5/07
	Oklahoma	Y	33220 FQ	38170 MW	44530 TQ	USBLS	5/07
	Oklahoma City MSA, OK	Y	34210 FQ	38820 MW	44480 TQ	USBLS	5/07
	Oregon	H	16.54 FQ	19.60 MW	24.32 TQ	ORBLS	5/08

AE	Average entry wage	AW	Average wage paid	FQ	First quartile wage
AER	Average entry range	AWR	Average wage range	H	Hourly
AEX	Average experienced wage	AXR	Average experienced range	HI	Highest wage paid
ATC	Average total compensation	D	Daily	HR	High end range

LO	Lowest wage paid	MTC	Median total compensation
LR	Low end range	MW	Median wage paid
M	Monthly	MWR	Median wage range
MCC	Median cash compensation	S	See annotated source

TCC	Total cash compensation	
TQ	Third quartile wage	
W	Weekly	
Y	Yearly	

Occupation/Type/Industry	Location	Per	Low	Mid	High	Source	Date
Marriage and Family Therapist	Portland-Vancouver-Beaverton MSA, OR-WA	Y	31910 FQ	38510 MW	51140 TQ	USBLS	5/07
	Pennsylvania	Y	35180 FQ	45090 MW	55270 TQ	USBLS	5/07
	Allentown-Bethlehem-Easton MSA, PA-NJ	Y	43090 FQ	49280 MW	59110 TQ	USBLS	5/07
	Philadelphia-Camden-Wilmington MSA, PA-NJ-DE-MD	Y	43670 FQ	51250 MW	63200 TQ	USBLS	5/07
	Pittsburgh MSA, PA	Y	30420 FQ	37550 MW	51610 TQ	USBLS	5/07
	Providence-Fall River-Warwick MSA, RI-MA	Y	42660 FQ	46250 MW	50090 TQ	USBLS	5/07
	South Carolina	Y	32120 FQ	34580 MW	37010 TQ	USBLS	5/07
	South Dakota	Y	35604 FQ	39872 MW	46063 TQ	SDBLS	7/08-9/08
	Tennessee	Y	27160 FQ	30490 MW	38600 TQ	USBLS	5/07
	Memphis MSA, TN-MS-AR	Y	34240 FQ	37210 MW	40570 TQ	USBLS	5/07
	Nashville-Davidson-Murfreesboro MSA, TN	Y	24950 FQ	28150 MW	30710 TQ	USBLS	5/07
	Texas	Y	27090 FQ	33240 MW	45400 TQ	USBLS	5/07
	Austin-Round Rock MSA, TX	Y	26920 FQ	29020 MW	31110 TQ	USBLS	5/07
	El Paso MSA, TX	Y	32800 FQ	35800 MW	38800 TQ	USBLS	5/07
	Houston-Sugar Land-Baytown MSA, TX	Y	23410 FQ	26050 MW	42120 TQ	USBLS	5/07
	Utah	Y	41240 FQ	45130 MW	49500 TQ	USBLS	5/07
	Salt Lake City MSA, UT	Y	40030 FQ	44050 MW	48080 TQ	USBLS	5/07
	Vermont	Y	38650 FQ	44630 MW	52360 TQ	USBLS	5/07
	Virginia	Y	31590 FQ	42940 MW	55740 TQ	USBLS	5/07
	Virginia Beach-Norfolk-Newport News MSA, VA-NC	Y	28500 FQ	31020 MW	36300 TQ	USBLS	5/07
	Washington	H	17.32 FQ	21.58 MW	25.06 TQ	WABLS	3/08
	Seattle-Tacoma-Bellevue MSA, WA	Y	40210 FQ	46840 MW	54610 TQ	USBLS	5/07
	West Virginia	Y	26360 FQ	36516 MW	49243 TQ	WVBLS	7/08-9/08
	Wisconsin	Y	33320 FQ	39700 MW	54490 TQ	USBLS	5/07
	Milwaukee-Waukesha-West Allis MSA, WI	Y	39570 FQ	54320 MW	73170 TQ	USBLS	5/07
	Wyoming	Y	36701 FQ	42688 MW	50760 TQ	WYBLS	9/08
Mascot							
PawSox	Rhode Island	H			9.00 HI	RIM01	2009
Mason							
New Hampshire Hospital	New Hampshire	Y			19740 HI	NHUL03	2008
Massage Therapist	Alabama	Y	14640 FQ	20630 MW	44920 TQ	USBLS	5/07
	Arizona	Y	21770 FQ	33110 MW	38650 TQ	USBLS	5/07
	Phoenix-Mesa-Scottsdale MSA, AZ	Y	18420 FQ	33580 MW	41980 TQ	USBLS	5/07
	Tucson MSA, AZ	Y	28530 FQ	33330 MW	36430 TQ	USBLS	5/07
	Arkansas	Y	22770 FQ	38760 MW	48230 TQ	USBLS	5/07
	Little Rock-North Little Rock MSA, AR	Y	23430 FQ	29340 MW	43690 TQ	USBLS	5/07
	California	H	12.52 FQ	20.41 MW	28.53 TQ	CABLS	1/08-3/08
	Los Angeles-Long Beach-Glendale PMSA, CA	H	13.44 FQ	17.81 MW	26.40 TQ	CABLS	1/08-3/08
	Oakland-Fremont-Hayward MSA, CA	H	15.60 FQ	20.46 MW	23.66 TQ	CABLS	1/08-3/08
	Riverside-San Bernardino-Ontario MSA, CA	H	11.28 FQ	23.23 MW	35.51 TQ	CABLS	1/08-3/08
	Sacramento-Arden Arcade-Roseville MSA, CA	H	17.58 FQ	24.62 MW	33.09 TQ	CABLS	1/08-3/08
	San Diego-Carlsbad-San Marcos MSA, CA	H	16.42 FQ	23.01 MW	25.96 TQ	CABLS	1/08-3/08
	San Francisco-San Mateo-Redwood PMSA, CA	H	18.26 FQ	27.45 MW	33.74 TQ	CABLS	1/08-3/08
	San Jose-Sunnyvale-Santa Clara MSA, CA	H	13.78 FQ	22.90 MW	34.60 TQ	CABLS	1/08-3/08
	Santa Ana-Anaheim-Irvine PMSA, CA	Y	18360 FQ	23980 MW	35210 TQ	USBLS	5/07
	Colorado	Y	25170 FQ	38660 MW	51120 TQ	USBLS	5/07
	Denver-Aurora MSA, CO	Y	30730 FQ	38710 MW	48230 TQ	USBLS	5/07
	Connecticut	H	13.63 AE	22.36 MW		CTBLS	1/08-3/08

AE	Average entry wage	AW	Average wage paid	FQ	First quartile wage	LO	Lowest wage paid	MTC Median total compensation	TCC Total cash compensation
AER	Average entry range	AWR	Average wage range	H	Hourly	LR	Low end range	MW Median wage paid	TQ Third quartile wage
AEX	Average experienced wage	AXR	Average experienced range	HI	Highest wage paid	M	Monthly	MWR Median wage range	W Weekly
ATC	Average total compensation	D	Daily	HR	High end range	MCC Median cash compensation	S See annotated source	Y Yearly

Massage Therapist

Occupation/Type/Industry	Location	Per	Low	Mid	High	Source	Date
Massage Therapist	Bridgeport-Stamford-Norwalk MSA, CT	Y	42130 FQ	62930 MW	79940 TQ	USBLS	5/07
	Hartford-West Hartford-East Hartford MSA, CT	Y	31260 FQ	36510 MW	72010 TQ	USBLS	5/07
	Delaware	Y	15130 FQ	27380 MW	53010 TQ	USBLS	5/07
	Wilmington PMSA, DE-MD-NJ	Y	20970 FQ	29080 MW	59320 TQ	USBLS	5/07
	District of Columbia	Y	37360 FQ	47920 MW	68050 TQ	USBLS	5/07
	Washington-Arlington-Alexandria MSA, DC-VA-MD-WV	Y	24820 FQ	36220 MW	50380 TQ	USBLS	5/07
	Florida	Y	22290 FQ	32220 MW	46330 TQ	USBLS	5/07
	Fort Lauderdale-Pompano Beach-Deerfield Beach PMSA, FL	Y	17230 FQ	29010 MW	40650 TQ	USBLS	5/07
	Jacksonville MSA, FL	Y	22370 FQ	28320 MW	43130 TQ	USBLS	5/07
	Miami-Fort Lauderdale-Miami Beach MSA, FL	Y	22930 FQ	32950 MW	56040 TQ	USBLS	5/07
	Orlando-Kissimmee MSA, FL	Y	21340 FQ	33760 MW	40550 TQ	USBLS	5/07
	Tampa-St. Petersburg-Clearwater MSA, FL	Y	24400 FQ	30130 MW	40990 TQ	USBLS	5/07
	West Palm Beach-Boca Raton-Boynton Beach PMSA, FL	Y	28060 FQ	36280 MW	57410 TQ	USBLS	5/07
	Georgia	Y	21470 FQ	33600 MW	44330 TQ	USBLS	5/07
	Atlanta-Sandy Springs-Marietta MSA, GA	Y	28590 FQ	37470 MW	47370 TQ	USBLS	5/07
	Savannah MSA, GA	Y	19100 FQ	21730 MW	24960 TQ	USBLS	5/07
	Hawaii	Y	35190 FQ	41710 MW	53960 TQ	USBLS	5/07
	Honolulu MSA, HI	Y	36570 FQ	43600 MW	55070 TQ	USBLS	5/07
	Idaho	Y	25940 FQ	30890 MW	48380 TQ	USBLS	5/07
	Boise City-Nampa MSA, ID	Y	28740 FQ	31750 MW	41350 TQ	USBLS	5/07
	Coeur d'Alene MSA, ID	Y	18090 FQ	28880 MW	32820 TQ	USBLS	5/07
	Illinois	Y	26900 FQ	39120 MW	64500 TQ	USBLS	5/07
	Chicago-Naperville-Joliet MSA, IL-IN-WI	Y	28230 FQ	41550 MW	66800 TQ	USBLS	5/07
	Indiana	Y	21460 FQ	29190 MW	51010 TQ	USBLS	5/07
	Gary PMSA, IN	Y	24670 FQ	29080 MW	33780 TQ	USBLS	5/07
	Indianapolis-Carmel MSA, IN	Y	22700 FQ	41980 MW	60010 TQ	USBLS	5/07
	Iowa	Y	21870 FQ	28820 MW	38230 TQ	USBLS	5/07
	Kansas	Y	20170 FQ	33510 MW	52500 TQ	USBLS	5/07
	Wichita MSA, KS	Y	20580 FQ	25260 MW	38460 TQ	USBLS	5/07
	Kentucky	Y	22843 FQ	29438 MW	38722 TQ	KYBLS	2008
	Louisville-Jefferson County MSA, KY-IN	Y	17630 FQ	27700 MW	39280 TQ	USBLS	5/07
	Louisiana	H	7.22 FQ	11.79 MW	15.63 TQ	LABLS	1/08-3/08
	New Orleans-Metairie-Kenner MSA, LA	Y	14040 FQ	25110 MW	30320 TQ	USBLS	5/07
	Portland-South Portland-Biddeford MSA, ME	Y	16180 FQ	37260 MW	48920 TQ	USBLS	5/07
	Maryland	Y		34225 MW		MDBLS	3/08
	Baltimore-Towson MSA, MD	Y	25650 FQ	34080 MW	38610 TQ	USBLS	5/07
	Bethesda-Gaithersburg-Frederick PMSA, MD	Y	32730 FQ	36920 MW	47710 TQ	USBLS	5/07
	Massachusetts	Y	24570 FQ	33850 MW	50110 TQ	USBLS	5/07
	Boston-Cambridge-Quincy NECTA, MA	Y	24970 FQ	36230 MW	58410 TQ	USBLS	5/07
	Grand Rapids-Wyoming MSA, MI	Y	20280 FQ	24150 MW	38510 TQ	USBLS	5/07
	Minnesota	Y	28272 FQ	33416 MW	45796 TQ	MNBLS	10/08-12/08
	Minneapolis-Saint Paul MSA, MN-WI	Y	27990 FQ	34776 MW	47145 TQ	MNBLS	10/08-12/08
	Rochester MSA, MN	Y	33967 FQ	42756 MW	49409 TQ	MNBLS	10/08-12/08
	Mississippi	Y	18430 FQ	23580 MW	27460 TQ	USBLS	5/07
	Missouri	Y	17000 FQ	25460 MW	38690 TQ	USBLS	5/07
	Kansas City MSA, MO-KS	Y	18830 FQ	30410 MW	40440 TQ	USBLS	5/07
	St. Louis MSA, MO-IL	Y	15940 FQ	29910 MW	46870 TQ	USBLS	5/07
	Montana	Y	18790 FQ	26880 MW	48210 TQ	USBLS	5/07
	Billings MSA, MT	Y	26790 FQ	33640 MW	53740 TQ	USBLS	5/07
	Nebraska	Y	17500 FQ	22360 MW	36990 TQ	USBLS	5/07
	Omaha-Council Bluffs MSA, NE-IA	Y	24770 FQ	35070 MW	52050 TQ	USBLS	5/07
	Nevada	H	6.61 FQ	7.89 MW	13.10 TQ	NVBLS	5/08

AE	Average entry wage	AW	Average wage paid	FQ	First quartile wage
AER	Average entry range	AWR	Average wage range	H	Hourly
AEX	Average experienced wage	AXR	Average experienced range	HI	Highest wage paid
ATC	Average total compensation	D	Daily	HR	High end range

LO Lowest wage paid · LR Low end range · M Monthly · MCC Median cash compensation · MTC Median total compensation · MW Median wage paid · MWR Median wage range · S See annotated source · TCC Total cash compensation · TQ Third quartile wage · W Weekly · Y Yearly

Massage Therapist

Occupation/Type/Industry	Location	Per	Low	Mid	High	Source	Date
Massage Therapist	Las Vegas-Paradise MSA, NV	H	6.62 FQ	7.94 MW	13.38 TQ	NVBLS	5/08
	New Hampshire	H	16.45 AE	30.59 MW	32.00 AEX	NHBLS	6/08
	Nashua NECTA, NH-MA	Y	38140 FQ	41780 MW	45380 TQ	USBLS	5/07
	New Jersey	Y	35070 FQ	42870 MW	58390 TQ	USBLS	5/07
	Camden PMSA, NJ	Y	38620 FQ	60520 MW	93490 TQ	USBLS	5/07
	Edison PMSA, NJ	Y	34280 FQ	42590 MW	62020 TQ	USBLS	5/07
	Newark-Union PMSA, NJ-PA	Y	32010 FQ	36270 MW	60480 TQ	USBLS	5/07
	New Mexico	Y	23200 FQ	28060 MW	48290 TQ	USBLS	5/07
	Albuquerque MSA, NM	Y	25880 FQ	32360 MW	44540 TQ	USBLS	5/07
	New York	Y	31920 FQ	45550 MW	64100 TQ	USBLS	5/07
	Albany-Schenectady-Troy MSA, NY	Y	28360 FQ	32710 MW	47060 TQ	USBLS	5/07
	Buffalo-Niagara Falls MSA, NY	Y	15430 FQ	16150 MW	29460 TQ	USBLS	5/07
	Nassau-Suffolk PMSA, NY	Y	31190 FQ	42120 MW	55190 TQ	USBLS	5/07
	New York-Northern New Jersey-Long Island MSA, NY-NJ-PA	Y	34500 FQ	46170 MW	63820 TQ	USBLS	5/07
	North Carolina	Y	23740 FQ	41820 MW	53900 TQ	USBLS	5/07
	Charlotte-Gastonia-Concord MSA, NC-SC	Y	15450 FQ	25350 MW	40810 TQ	USBLS	5/07
	Raleigh-Cary MSA, NC	Y	45290 FQ	51480 MW	57730 TQ	USBLS	5/07
	North Dakota	Y	21040 FQ	23240 MW	25290 TQ	USBLS	5/07
	Ohio	Y	22180 FQ	29620 MW	39870 TQ	USBLS	5/07
	Cincinnati-Middletown MSA, OH-KY-IN	Y	16110 FQ	26290 MW	32590 TQ	USBLS	5/07
	Cleveland-Elyria-Mentor MSA, OH	Y	22370 FQ	29310 MW	41890 TQ	USBLS	5/07
	Columbus MSA, OH	Y	22090 FQ	32740 MW	40750 TQ	USBLS	5/07
	Dayton MSA, OH	Y	26170 FQ	32960 MW	36690 TQ	USBLS	5/07
	Oklahoma City MSA, OK	Y	16580 FQ	18030 MW	19470 TQ	USBLS	5/07
	Tulsa MSA, OK	Y	21990 FQ	32220 MW	39330 TQ	USBLS	5/07
	Oregon	H	19.42 FQ	25.02 MW	30.72 MW	ORBLS	5/08
	Portland-Vancouver-Beaverton MSA, OR-WA	Y	43810 FQ	54070 MW	61850 TQ	USBLS	5/07
	Pennsylvania	Y	18530 FQ	29140 MW	45600 TQ	USBLS	5/07
	Philadelphia-Camden-Wilmington MSA, PA-NJ-DE-MD	Y	28720 FQ	42010 MW	57010 TQ	USBLS	5/07
	Pittsburgh MSA, PA	Y	15630 FQ	26040 MW	32500 TQ	USBLS	5/07
	Rhode Island	Y	31010 FQ	41710 MW	46730 TQ	USBLS	5/07
	Providence-Fall River-Warwick MSA, RI-MA	Y	25750 FQ	36890 MW	46140 TQ	USBLS	5/07
	South Carolina	Y	21840 FQ	32360 MW	68210 TQ	USBLS	5/07
	Charleston-North Charleston MSA, SC	Y	19150 FQ	66460 MW	89970 TQ	USBLS	5/07
	South Dakota	Y	26307 FQ	35248 MW	39742 TQ	SDBLS	7/08-9/08
	Sioux Falls MSA, SD	Y	30047 FQ	36952 MW	40513 TQ	SDBLS	7/08-9/08
	Tennessee	Y	22340 FQ	31270 MW	40980 TQ	USBLS	5/07
	Clarksville MSA, TN-KY	Y	18800 FQ	27060 MW	31830 TQ	USBLS	5/07
	Knoxville MSA, TN	Y	20810 FQ	28790 MW	36070 TQ	USBLS	5/07
	Memphis MSA, TN-MS-AR	Y	21400 FQ	30990 MW	36260 TQ	USBLS	5/07
	Nashville-Davidson-Murfreesboro MSA, TN	Y	26370 FQ	37580 MW	54840 TQ	USBLS	5/07
	Texas	Y	22950 FQ	29390 MW	43420 TQ	USBLS	5/07
	Austin-Round Rock MSA, TX	Y	16110 FQ	22660 MW	28890 TQ	USBLS	5/07
	Corpus Christi MSA, TX	Y	34060 FQ	40410 MW	47370 TQ	USBLS	5/07
	Dallas-Fort Worth-Arlington MSA, TX	Y	24980 FQ	31390 MW	44390 TQ	USBLS	5/07
	El Paso MSA, TX	Y	19530 FQ	28050 MW	36200 TQ	USBLS	5/07
	Houston-Sugar Land-Baytown MSA, TX	Y	24560 FQ	28230 MW	41410 TQ	USBLS	5/07
	San Antonio MSA, TX	Y	25510 FQ	42920 MW	47660 TQ	USBLS	5/07
	Utah	Y	17030 FQ	23790 MW	39900 TQ	USBLS	5/07
	Salt Lake City MSA, UT	Y	17170 FQ	23300 MW	31900 TQ	USBLS	5/07
	Vermont	Y	27590 FQ	42530 MW	70840 TQ	USBLS	5/07
	Virginia	Y	22240 FQ	36340 MW	52310 TQ	USBLS	5/07
	Richmond MSA, VA	Y	35640 FQ	44890 MW	57200 TQ	USBLS	5/07
	Virginia Beach-Norfolk-Newport News MSA, VA-NC	Y	16170 FQ	21760 MW	32030 TQ	USBLS	5/07
	Washington	H	19.78 FQ	28.90 MW	34.78 TQ	WABLS	3/08

AE Average entry wage; AER Average entry range; AEX Average experienced wage; ATC Average total compensation; AW Average wage paid; AWR Average wage range; AXR Average experienced range; D Daily; FQ First quartile wage; H Hourly; HI Highest wage paid; HR High end range; LO Lowest wage paid; LR Low end range; M Monthly; MCC Median cash compensation; MTC Median total compensation; MW Median wage paid; MWR Median wage range; S See annotated source; TCC Total cash compensation; TQ Third quartile wage; W Weekly; Y Yearly

Occupation/Type/Industry	Location	Per	Low	Mid	High	Source	Date
Massage Therapist	Seattle-Tacoma-Bellevue						
	MSA, WA	Y	45840 FQ	61540 MW	72750 TQ	USBLS	5/07
	West Virginia	Y	20239 FQ	31192 MW	50899 TQ	WVBLS	7/08-9/08
	Wisconsin	Y	19940 FQ	31990 MW	38730 TQ	USBLS	5/07
	Milwaukee-Waukesha-West						
	Allis MSA, WI	Y	16130 FQ	24520 MW	37150 TQ	USBLS	5/07
	Wyoming	Y	19911 FQ	26108 MW	40563 TQ	WYBLS	9/08
	Puerto Rico	Y	16620 FQ	18680 MW	23850 TQ	USBLS	5/07
	San Juan-Caguas-Guaynabo						
	MSA, PR	Y	16710 FQ	18540 MW	22210 TQ	USBLS	5/07
	Guam	Y	12690 FQ	14430 MW	16610 TQ	USBLS	5/07
Cruise Ship	United States	M	2600 LO		3600 HI	CRU04	2008
Master Bridge Maintenance Worker							
State Government	Maine	Y	25022 LO		32677 HI	AFT02	3/1/08
Master Chief Petty Officer							
U.S. Navy, Active Duty, Pay Grade E-9	United States	M	4421 LO		6863 HI	DOD1	2009
Master Gunnery Sergeant							
U.S. Marines, Active Duty, Pay Grade E-9	United States	M	4421 LO		6863 HI	DOD1	2009
Master Sergeant							
U.S. Air Force, Active Duty, Pay Grade E-7	United States	M	2516 LO		4521 HI	DOD1	2009
U.S. Army, Active Duty, Pay Grade E-8	United States	M	3619 LO		5161 HI	DOD1	2009
U.S. Marines, Active Duty, Pay Grade E-8	United States	M	3619 LO		5161 HI	DOD1	2009
Materials Engineer	United States	Y	76949 AE		99933 AEX	AVWK	2007
	Alabama	Y	60950 FQ	76220 MW	97710 TQ	USBLS	5/07
	Birmingham-Hoover MSA, AL	Y	57060 FQ	66570 MW	76310 TQ	USBLS	5/07
	Arizona	Y	53960 FQ	70510 MW	85360 TQ	USBLS	5/07
	Phoenix-Mesa-Scottsdale						
	MSA, AZ	Y	55250 FQ	71310 MW	85780 TQ	USBLS	5/07
	Tucson MSA, AZ	Y	48800 FQ	66050 MW	80190 TQ	USBLS	5/07
	Arkansas	Y	61960 FQ	71970 MW	80360 TQ	USBLS	5/07
	California	H	33.53 FQ	40.78 MW	48.60 TQ	CABLS	1/08-3/08
	Los Angeles-Long Beach-						
	Glendale PMSA, CA	H	33.78 FQ	42.51 MW	50.37 TQ	CABLS	1/08-3/08
	Oakland-Fremont-Hayward						
	MSA, CA	H	33.44 FQ	37.54 MW	41.83 TQ	CABLS	1/08-3/08
	Riverside-San Bernardino-						
	Ontario MSA, CA	H	32.10 FQ	36.67 MW	40.74 TQ	CABLS	1/08-3/08
	Sacramento-Arden Arcade-						
	Roseville MSA, CA	H	34.04 FQ	39.29 MW	44.97 TQ	CABLS	1/08-3/08
	San Diego-Carlsbad-San						
	Marcos MSA, CA	H	35.39 FQ	41.93 MW	48.29 TQ	CABLS	1/08-3/08
	San Francisco-San Mateo-						
	Redwood PMSA, CA	H	30.35 FQ	37.56 MW	46.93 TQ	CABLS	1/08-3/08
	San Jose-Sunnyvale-Santa						
	Clara MSA, CA	H	37.54 FQ	45.28 MW	51.99 TQ	CABLS	1/08-3/08
	Santa Ana-Anaheim-Irvine						
	PMSA, CA	Y	58760 FQ	72120 MW	88910 TQ	USBLS	5/07
	Colorado	Y	75410 FQ	95880 MW	114870 TQ	USBLS	5/07
	Denver-Aurora MSA, CO	Y	70750 FQ	91680 MW	119960 TQ	USBLS	5/07
	Connecticut	H	32.40 AE	41.08 MW		CTBLS	1/08-3/08
	Bridgeport-Stamford-Norwalk						
	MSA, CT	Y	67180 FQ	75360 MW	86800 TQ	USBLS	5/07
	Hartford-West Hartford-East						
	Hartford MSA, CT	Y	72200 FQ	84740 MW	98730 TQ	USBLS	5/07
	Washington-Arlington-						
	Alexandria MSA, DC-VA-						
	MD-WV	Y	76420 FQ	97680 MW	126250 TQ	USBLS	5/07
	Florida	Y	49520 FQ	67430 MW	89650 TQ	USBLS	5/07
	Jacksonville MSA, FL	Y	78970 FQ	92620 MW	134110 TQ	USBLS	5/07
	Miami-Fort Lauderdale-Miami						
	Beach MSA, FL	Y	39720 FQ	61330 MW	86100 TQ	USBLS	5/07
	Orlando-Kissimmee MSA, FL	Y	52820 FQ	61450 MW	77240 TQ	USBLS	5/07
	Georgia	Y	54790 FQ	67370 MW	80680 TQ	USBLS	5/07
	Atlanta-Sandy Springs-						
	Marietta MSA, GA	Y	58560 FQ	69320 MW	80560 TQ	USBLS	5/07
	Idaho	Y	52990 FQ	66460 MW	78860 TQ	USBLS	5/07

AE	Average entry wage	AW	Average wage paid	FQ	First quartile wage
AER	Average entry range	AWR	Average wage range	H	Hourly
AEX	Average experienced wage	AXR	Average experienced range	HI	Highest wage paid
ATC	Average total compensation	D	Daily	HR	High end range

LO	Lowest wage paid	MTC	Median total compensation
LR	Low end range	MW	Median wage paid
M	Monthly	MWR	Median wage range
MCC	Median cash compensation	S	See annotated source

TCC	Total cash compensation	
TQ	Third quartile wage	
W	Weekly	
Y	Yearly	

Occupation/Type/Industry	Location	Per	Low	Mid	High	Source	Date
Materials Engineer	Boise City-Nampa MSA, ID	Y	56800 FQ	66050 MW	76330 TQ	USBLS	5/07
	Illinois	Y	60910 FQ	74110 MW	89700 TQ	USBLS	5/07
	Chicago-Naperville-Joliet MSA, IL-IN-WI	Y	64180 FQ	76960 MW	95560 TQ	USBLS	5/07
	Indiana	Y	58370 FQ	71080 MW	87520 TQ	USBLS	5/07
	Gary PMSA, IN	Y	67870 FQ	79210 MW	104050 TQ	USBLS	5/07
	Indianapolis-Carmel MSA, IN	Y	61330 FQ	80010 MW	103590 TQ	USBLS	5/07
	Iowa	Y	55600 FQ	68310 MW	82920 TQ	USBLS	5/07
	Kansas	Y	58550 FQ	83100 MW	94890 TQ	USBLS	5/07
	Wichita MSA, KS	Y	74400 FQ	84310 MW	95190 TQ	USBLS	5/07
	Kentucky	Y	60338 FQ	77007 MW	93116 TQ	KYBLS	2008
	Louisville-Jefferson County MSA, KY-IN	Y	77010 FQ	88310 MW	96290 TQ	USBLS	5/07
	Louisiana	H	27.93 FQ	35.95 MW	44.84 TQ	LABLS	1/08-3/08
	Maine	Y	55910 FQ	70250 MW	85320 TQ	USBLS	5/07
	Maryland	Y		96725 MW		MDBLS	3/08
	Baltimore-Towson MSA, MD	Y	85150 FQ	95110 MW	114680 TQ	USBLS	5/07
	Bethesda-Gaithersburg-Frederick PMSA, MD	Y	80020 FQ	98310 MW	123040 TQ	USBLS	5/07
	Massachusetts	Y	66970 FQ	86180 MW	103280 TQ	USBLS	5/07
	Boston-Cambridge-Quincy NECTA, MA	Y	72930 FQ	90400 MW	106150 TQ	USBLS	5/07
	Worcester MSA, MA-CT	Y	70200 FQ	83060 MW	96780 TQ	USBLS	5/07
	Michigan	Y	64270 FQ	77110 MW	95900 TQ	USBLS	5/07
	Detroit-Warren-Livonia MSA, MI	Y	66990 FQ	80340 MW	105530 TQ	USBLS	5/07
	Grand Rapids-Wyoming MSA, MI	Y	62380 FQ	72560 MW	81510 TQ	USBLS	5/07
	Warren-Troy-Farmington Hills PMSA, MI	Y	65830 FQ	81720 MW	111280 TQ	USBLS	5/07
	Minnesota	Y	59687 FQ	79136 MW	102498 TQ	MNBLS	10/08-12/08
	Minneapolis-Saint Paul MSA, MN-WI	Y	62763 FQ	81229 MW	101578 TQ	MNBLS	10/08-12/08
	Mississippi	Y	49050 FQ	68650 MW	81340 TQ	USBLS	5/07
	Missouri	Y	48390 FQ	67830 MW	92430 TQ	USBLS	5/07
	Kansas City MSA, MO-KS	Y	41800 FQ	60370 MW	89680 TQ	USBLS	5/07
	St. Louis MSA, MO-IL	Y	67860 FQ	88260 MW	101160 TQ	USBLS	5/07
	Montana	Y	45160 FQ	49400 MW	59050 TQ	USBLS	5/07
	Nebraska	Y	51280 FQ	64410 MW	88600 TQ	USBLS	5/07
	Omaha-Council Bluffs MSA, NE-IA	Y	52870 FQ	88260 MW	101020 TQ	USBLS	5/07
	Nevada	H	26.82 FQ	31.45 MW	37.13 TQ	NVBLS	5/08
	Las Vegas-Paradise MSA, NV	H	28.36 FQ	31.80 MW	37.04 TQ	NVBLS	5/08
	New Hampshire	H	23.75 AE	34.50 MW	43.35 AEX	NHBLS	6/08
	New Jersey	Y	65510 FQ	80530 MW	93810 TQ	USBLS	5/07
	Camden PMSA, NJ	Y	60740 FQ	79750 MW	96070 TQ	USBLS	5/07
	Edison PMSA, NJ	Y	61590 FQ	81150 MW	95400 TQ	USBLS	5/07
	Newark-Union PMSA, NJ-PA	Y	66540 FQ	77740 MW	99550 TQ	USBLS	5/07
	New Mexico	Y	56830 FQ	75390 MW	99580 TQ	USBLS	5/07
	Albuquerque MSA, NM	Y	58640 FQ	80380 MW	103790 TQ	USBLS	5/07
	New York	Y	52150 FQ	71310 MW	91100 TQ	USBLS	5/07
	Albany-Schenectady-Troy MSA, NY	Y	65990 FQ	78980 MW	99360 TQ	USBLS	5/07
	Buffalo-Niagara Falls MSA, NY	Y	54850 FQ	64000 MW	72990 TQ	USBLS	5/07
	Nassau-Suffolk PMSA, NY	Y	44670 FQ	55850 MW	80710 TQ	USBLS	5/07
	New York-Northern New Jersey-Long Island MSA, NY-NJ-PA	Y	49820 FQ	73010 MW	90850 TQ	USBLS	5/07
	North Carolina	Y	59530 FQ	70140 MW	81880 TQ	USBLS	5/07
	Charlotte-Gastonia-Concord MSA, NC-SC	Y	31720 FQ	56880 MW	72330 TQ	USBLS	5/07
	Ohio	Y	59080 FQ	81370 MW	100740 TQ	USBLS	5/07
	Cincinnati-Middletown MSA, OH-KY-IN	Y	54770 FQ	72830 MW	95440 TQ	USBLS	5/07
	Cleveland-Elyria-Mentor MSA, OH	Y	66790 FQ	84280 MW	107730 TQ	USBLS	5/07
	Columbus MSA, OH	Y	52970 FQ	73630 MW	93010 TQ	USBLS	5/07
	Dayton MSA, OH	Y	68380 FQ	94030 MW	116360 TQ	USBLS	5/07
	Oklahoma	Y	45020 FQ	57660 MW	75230 TQ	USBLS	5/07
	Oklahoma City MSA, OK	Y	57840 FQ	75510 MW	91000 TQ	USBLS	5/07
	Tulsa MSA, OK	Y	41130 FQ	53670 MW	66690 TQ	USBLS	5/07

AE Average entry wage	**AW** Average wage paid	**FQ** First quartile wage	**LO** Lowest wage paid	**MTC** Median total compensation	**TCC** Total cash compensation
AER Average entry range	**AWR** Average wage range	**H** Hourly	**LR** Low end range	**MW** Median wage paid	**TQ** Third quartile wage
AEX Average experienced wage	**AXR** Average experienced range	**HI** Highest wage paid	**M** Monthly	**MWR** Median wage range	**W** Weekly
ATC Average total compensation	**D** Daily	**HR** High end range	**MCC** Median cash compensation	**S** See annotated source	**Y** Yearly

Occupation/Type/Industry	Location	Per	Low	Mid	High	Source	Date
Materials Engineer	Oregon	H	31.05 FQ	39.20 MW	46.32 TQ	ORBLS	5/08
	Portland-Vancouver-Beaverton MSA, OR-WA	Y	65520 FQ	81210 MW	94980 TQ	USBLS	5/07
	Pennsylvania	Y	58680 FQ	72880 MW	91050 TQ	USBLS	5/07
	Allentown-Bethlehem-Easton MSA, PA-NJ	Y	57220 FQ	73630 MW	94420 TQ	USBLS	5/07
	Philadelphia-Camden-Wilmington MSA, PA-NJ-DE-MD	Y	60540 FQ	81670 MW	99330 TQ	USBLS	5/07
	Pittsburgh MSA, PA	Y	60670 FQ	74200 MW	90230 TQ	USBLS	5/07
	Rhode Island	Y	62010 FQ	71560 MW	84510 TQ	USBLS	5/07
	Providence-Fall River-Warwick MSA, RI-MA	Y	55630 FQ	67380 MW	79520 TQ	USBLS	5/07
	South Carolina	Y	45670 FQ	63690 MW	77360 TQ	USBLS	5/07
	Columbia MSA, SC	Y	56990 FQ	66480 MW	77420 TQ	USBLS	5/07
	Tennessee	Y	58210 FQ	89850 MW	116410 TQ	USBLS	5/07
	Knoxville MSA, TN	Y	63600 FQ	83890 MW	98740 TQ	USBLS	5/07
	Nashville-Davidson-Murfreesboro MSA, TN	Y	41190 FQ	56340 MW	70840 TQ	USBLS	5/07
	Texas	Y	60600 FQ	81950 MW	99790 TQ	USBLS	5/07
	Austin-Round Rock MSA, TX	Y	59010 FQ	74850 MW	93890 TQ	USBLS	5/07
	Dallas-Fort Worth-Arlington MSA, TX	Y	68510 FQ	82600 MW	101550 TQ	USBLS	5/07
	El Paso MSA, TX	Y	39210 FQ	52590 MW	70470 TQ	USBLS	5/07
	Houston-Sugar Land-Baytown MSA, TX	Y	69020 FQ	88610 MW	103530 TQ	USBLS	5/07
	San Antonio MSA, TX	Y	68560 FQ	85910 MW	108950 TQ	USBLS	5/07
	Utah	Y	57180 FQ	70450 MW	79650 TQ	USBLS	5/07
	Ogden-Clearfield MSA, UT	Y	48580 FQ	58470 MW	72680 TQ	USBLS	5/07
	Salt Lake City MSA, UT	Y	67930 FQ	74650 MW	81420 TQ	USBLS	5/07
	Virginia	Y	62970 FQ	85260 MW	125210 TQ	USBLS	5/07
	Richmond MSA, VA	Y	57530 FQ	87930 MW	112890 TQ	USBLS	5/07
	Virginia Beach-Norfolk-Newport News MSA, VA-NC	Y	67910 FQ	85830 MW	106190 TQ	USBLS	5/07
	Washington	H	31.80 FQ	39.35 MW	46.72 TQ	WABLS	3/08
	Seattle-Tacoma-Bellevue MSA, WA	Y	68660 FQ	83260 MW	97860 TQ	USBLS	5/07
	West Virginia	Y	46228 FQ	65398 MW	76058 TQ	WVBLS	7/08-9/08
	Wisconsin	Y	52350 FQ	67890 MW	83760 TQ	USBLS	5/07
	Milwaukee-Waukesha-West Allis MSA, WI	Y	52060 FQ	69600 MW	90740 TQ	USBLS	5/07
Materials Handling Professional	United States	Y		73000 MW		MMH	2008
Materials Management Professional	Central	Y		62232 AW		HPURCH01	2008
	Mountain	Y		56722 AW		HPURCH01	2008
	Northeast	Y		62437 AW		HPURCH01	2008
	Pacific	Y		69133 AW		HPURCH01	2008
	Southeast	Y		56973 AW		HPURCH01	2008
Materials Scientist	Arizona	Y	38850 FQ	63830 MW	91400 TQ	USBLS	5/07
	Phoenix-Mesa-Scottsdale MSA, AZ	Y	36520 FQ	52380 MW	89420 TQ	USBLS	5/07
	Arkansas	Y	80390 FQ	86730 MW	93470 TQ	USBLS	5/07
	California	H	34.46 FQ	43.63 MW	53.25 TQ	CABLS	1/08-3/08
	Los Angeles-Long Beach-Glendale PMSA, CA	H	32.97 FQ	44.01 MW	52.48 TQ	CABLS	1/08-3/08
	Oakland-Fremont-Hayward MSA, CA	H	42.12 FQ	51.07 MW	59.70 TQ	CABLS	1/08-3/08
	Riverside-San Bernardino-Ontario MSA, CA	H	30.63 FQ	35.85 MW	40.82 TQ	CABLS	1/08-3/08
	San Diego-Carlsbad-San Marcos MSA, CA	H	30.51 FQ	36.25 MW	43.81 TQ	CABLS	1/08-3/08
	San Francisco-San Mateo-Redwood PMSA, CA	H	47.10 FQ	53.57 MW	59.68 TQ	CABLS	1/08-3/08
	San Jose-Sunnyvale-Santa Clara MSA, CA	H	42.72 FQ	50.67 MW	59.81 TQ	CABLS	1/08-3/08
	Santa Ana-Anaheim-Irvine PMSA, CA	Y	70680 FQ	90100 MW	106370 TQ	USBLS	5/07
	Colorado	Y	61010 FQ	75020 MW	92000 TQ	USBLS	5/07
	Boulder MSA, CO	Y	60400 FQ	71620 MW	84020 TQ	USBLS	5/07

AE	Average entry wage	AW	Average wage paid	FQ	First quartile wage	LO	Lowest wage paid	MTC Median total compensation	TCC	Total cash compensation
AER	Average entry range	AWR	Average wage range	H	Hourly	LR	Low end range	MW Median wage paid	TQ	Third quartile wage
AEX	Average experienced wage	AXR	Average experienced range	HI	Highest wage paid	M	Monthly	MWR Median wage range	W	Weekly
ATC	Average total compensation	D	Daily	HR	High end range	MCC	Median cash compensation	S See annotated source	Y	Yearly

Occupation/Type/Industry	Location	Per	Low	Mid	High	Source	Date
Materials Scientist	Denver-Aurora MSA, CO	Y	60940 FQ	74460 MW	91790 TQ	USBLS	5/07
	Connecticut	H	31.30 AE	37.35 MW		CTBLS	1/08-3/08
	Delaware	Y	44110 FQ	62590 MW	94880 TQ	USBLS	5/07
	Wilmington PMSA, DE-MD-NJ	Y	44110 FQ	62590 MW	94880 TQ	USBLS	5/07
	District of Columbia	Y	74230 FQ	85940 MW	114530 TQ	USBLS	5/07
	Washington-Arlington-Alexandria MSA, DC-VA-MD-WV	Y	84270 FQ	96080 MW	111860 TQ	USBLS	5/07
	Florida	Y	53400 FQ	70380 MW	86240 TQ	USBLS	5/07
	Georgia	Y	69650 FQ	81980 MW	92700 TQ	USBLS	5/07
	Atlanta-Sandy Springs-Marietta MSA, GA	Y	69590 FQ	81980 MW	92680 TQ	USBLS	5/07
	Illinois	Y	44120 FQ	73570 MW	100600 TQ	USBLS	5/07
	Chicago-Naperville-Joliet MSA, IL-IN-WI	Y	67370 FQ	88770 MW	106760 TQ	USBLS	5/07
	Indiana	Y	51310 FQ	65110 MW	79980 TQ	USBLS	5/07
	Iowa	Y	74820 FQ	92060 MW	106140 TQ	USBLS	5/07
	Kansas	Y	57360 FQ	68290 MW	94950 TQ	USBLS	5/07
	Kentucky	Y	54411 FQ	72744 MW	100913 TQ	KYBLS	2008
	Louisville-Jefferson County MSA, KY-IN	Y	69790 FQ	84240 MW	104930 TQ	USBLS	5/07
	Maine	Y	47590 FQ	63040 MW	80440 TQ	USBLS	5/07
	Maryland	Y		100925 MW		MDBLS	3/08
	Baltimore-Towson MSA, MD	Y	62920 FQ	85170 MW	129010 TQ	USBLS	5/07
	Massachusetts	Y	76350 FQ	92160 MW	109040 TQ	USBLS	5/07
	Boston-Cambridge-Quincy NECTA, MA	Y	79010 FQ	93790 MW	111670 TQ	USBLS	5/07
	Michigan	Y	48750 FQ	69660 MW	87720 TQ	USBLS	5/07
	Detroit-Warren-Livonia MSA, MI	Y	50000 FQ	62790 MW	83080 TQ	USBLS	5/07
	Warren-Troy-Farmington Hills PMSA, MI	Y	47820 FQ	58790 MW	79030 TQ	USBLS	5/07
	Minnesota	Y	73539 FQ	87841 MW	101693 TQ	MNBLS	10/08-12/08
	Minneapolis-Saint Paul MSA, MN-WI	Y	76468 FQ	89734 MW	102739 TQ	MNBLS	10/08-12/08
	Missouri	Y	49240 FQ	60600 MW	87250 TQ	USBLS	5/07
	Kansas City MSA, MO-KS	Y	56340 FQ	64400 MW	95310 TQ	USBLS	5/07
	St. Louis MSA, MO-IL	Y	50330 FQ	61190 MW	88490 TQ	USBLS	5/07
	New Hampshire	H	25.73 AE	40.55 MW	46.51 AEX	NHBLS	6/08
	Nashua NECTA, NH-MA	Y	65100 FQ	84850 MW	102520 TQ	USBLS	5/07
	New Jersey	Y	75870 FQ	96140 MW	116230 TQ	USBLS	5/07
	Edison PMSA, NJ	Y	69580 FQ	83050 MW	104420 TQ	USBLS	5/07
	Newark-Union PMSA, NJ-PA	Y	81860 FQ	98830 MW	118390 TQ	USBLS	5/07
	Albuquerque MSA, NM	Y	53300 FQ	61920 MW	88670 TQ	USBLS	5/07
	New York	Y	55490 FQ	68280 MW	82720 TQ	USBLS	5/07
	Nassau-Suffolk PMSA, NY	Y	52910 FQ	60630 MW	76420 TQ	USBLS	5/07
	New York-Northern New Jersey-Long Island MSA, NY-NJ-PA	Y	57750 FQ	72370 MW	94080 TQ	USBLS	5/07
	North Carolina	Y	70690 FQ	83890 MW	111530 TQ	USBLS	5/07
	Charlotte-Gastonia-Concord MSA, NC-SC	Y	40180 FQ	76570 MW	94720 TQ	USBLS	5/07
	Raleigh-Cary MSA, NC	Y	77890 FQ	86280 MW	131450 TQ	USBLS	5/07
	Ohio	Y	55460 FQ	74730 MW	96860 TQ	USBLS	5/07
	Cincinnati-Middletown MSA, OH-KY-IN	Y	49950 FQ	64800 MW	84140 TQ	USBLS	5/07
	Cleveland-Elyria-Mentor MSA, OH	Y	65240 FQ	84380 MW	105100 TQ	USBLS	5/07
	Columbus MSA, OH	Y	62350 FQ	77980 MW	96700 TQ	USBLS	5/07
	Dayton MSA, OH	Y	54840 FQ	86550 MW	98630 TQ	USBLS	5/07
	Oregon	H	25.83 FQ	28.20 MW	33.52 TQ	ORBLS	5/08
	Portland-Vancouver-Beaverton MSA, OR-WA	Y	51840 FQ	55870 MW	59860 TQ	USBLS	5/07
	Pennsylvania	Y	57440 FQ	76050 MW	98110 TQ	USBLS	5/07
	Philadelphia-Camden-Wilmington MSA, PA-NJ-DE-MD	Y	53710 FQ	73640 MW	97960 TQ	USBLS	5/07
	Pittsburgh MSA, PA	Y	61690 FQ	80600 MW	99660 TQ	USBLS	5/07
	South Carolina	Y	58950 FQ	73080 MW	95150 TQ	USBLS	5/07
	Tennessee	Y	53980 FQ	67450 MW	77850 TQ	USBLS	5/07
	Memphis MSA, TN-MS-AR	Y	73040 FQ	100170 MW	112940 TQ	USBLS	5/07

AE	Average entry wage	AW	Average wage paid	FQ	First quartile wage	LO	Lowest wage paid	MTC	Median total compensation	TCC	Total cash compensation
AER	Average entry range	AWR	Average wage range	H	Hourly	LR	Low end range	MW	Median wage paid	TQ	Third quartile wage
AEX	Average experienced wage	AXR	Average experienced range	HI	Highest wage paid	M	Monthly	MWR	Median wage range	W	Weekly
ATC	Average total compensation	D	Daily	HR	High end range	MCC	Median cash compensation	S	See annotated source	Y	Yearly

Occupation/Type/Industry	Location	Per	Low	Mid	High	Source	Date
Materials Scientist	Texas	Y	59310 FQ	73690 MW	90100 TQ	USBLS	5/07
	Austin-Round Rock MSA, TX	Y	42180 FQ	69580 MW	86830 TQ	USBLS	5/07
	Dallas-Fort Worth-Arlington MSA, TX	Y	64310 FQ	75860 MW	90530 TQ	USBLS	5/07
	Houston-Sugar Land-Baytown MSA, TX	Y	53800 FQ	63770 MW	87690 TQ	USBLS	5/07
	San Antonio MSA, TX	Y	42320 FQ	69210 MW	83440 TQ	USBLS	5/07
	Utah	Y	37750 FQ	57300 MW	76690 TQ	USBLS	5/07
	Virginia	Y	60540 FQ	89640 MW	110120 TQ	USBLS	5/07
	Washington	H	24.85 FQ	38.58 MW	48.42 TQ	WABLS	3/08
	Seattle-Tacoma-Bellevue MSA, WA	Y	41860 FQ	49770 MW	80180 TQ	USBLS	5/07
	Wisconsin	Y	58490 FQ	78170 MW	98230 TQ	USBLS	5/07
	Milwaukee-Waukesha-West Allis MSA, WI	Y	53480 FQ	77630 MW	102010 TQ	USBLS	5/07
Mathematical Science Teacher							
Postsecondary	Alabama	Y	39210 FQ	53440 MW	69370 TQ	USBLS	5/07
Postsecondary	Birmingham-Hoover MSA, AL	Y	43030 FQ	58000 MW	86280 TQ	USBLS	5/07
Postsecondary	Alaska	Y	50780 FQ	63520 MW	78070 TQ	USBLS	5/07
Postsecondary	Anchorage MSA, AK	Y	70140 FQ	82330 MW	98810 TQ	USBLS	5/07
Postsecondary	Arizona	Y	35320 FQ	47170 MW	58280 TQ	USBLS	5/07
Postsecondary	Phoenix-Mesa-Scottsdale MSA, AZ	Y	31460 FQ	45240 MW	56510 TQ	USBLS	5/07
Postsecondary	Tucson MSA, AZ	Y	41910 FQ	50910 MW	78040 TQ	USBLS	5/07
Postsecondary	Arkansas	Y	36690 FQ	47110 MW	60150 TQ	USBLS	5/07
Postsecondary	Little Rock-North Little Rock MSA, AR	Y	36410 FQ	45210 MW	63520 TQ	USBLS	5/07
Postsecondary	California	Y		95584 AW		CABLS	1/08-3/08
Postsecondary	Fresno MSA, CA	Y		66030 AW		CABLS	1/08-3/08
Postsecondary	Los Angeles-Long Beach-Glendale PMSA, CA	Y		93533 AW		CABLS	1/08-3/08
Postsecondary	Oakland-Fremont-Hayward MSA, CA	Y		100691 AW		CABLS	1/08-3/08
Postsecondary	Riverside-San Bernardino-Ontario MSA, CA	Y		78069 AW		CABLS	1/08-3/08
Postsecondary	Sacramento-Arden Arcade-Roseville MSA, CA	Y		100076 AW		CABLS	1/08-3/08
Postsecondary	San Diego-Carlsbad-San Marcos MSA, CA	Y		105900 AW		CABLS	1/08-3/08
Postsecondary	San Francisco-San Mateo-Redwood PMSA, CA	Y		112463 AW		CABLS	1/08-3/08
Postsecondary	San Jose-Sunnyvale-Santa Clara MSA, CA	Y		99245 AW		CABLS	1/08-3/08
Postsecondary	Santa Ana-Anaheim-Irvine PMSA, CA	Y	69290 FQ	82780 MW	101890 TQ	USBLS	5/07
Postsecondary	Colorado	Y	39340 FQ	52370 MW	75700 TQ	USBLS	5/07
Postsecondary	Denver-Aurora MSA, CO	Y	38630 FQ	49340 MW	67470 TQ	USBLS	5/07
Postsecondary	Fort Collins-Loveland MSA, CO	Y	50580 FQ	74790 MW	103540 TQ	USBLS	5/07
Postsecondary	Hartford-West Hartford-East Hartford MSA, CT	Y	46240 FQ	64540 MW	84230 TQ	USBLS	5/07
Postsecondary	Delaware	Y	54530 FQ	63740 MW	78030 TQ	USBLS	5/07
Postsecondary	Wilmington PMSA, DE-MD-NJ	Y	52300 FQ	61180 MW	83810 TQ	USBLS	5/07
Postsecondary	District of Columbia	Y	51800 FQ	63780 MW	81120 TQ	USBLS	5/07
Postsecondary	Washington-Arlington-Alexandria MSA, DC-VA-MD-WV	Y	48610 FQ	61920 MW	81560 TQ	USBLS	5/07
Postsecondary	Florida	Y	41330 FQ	58130 MW	75250 TQ	USBLS	5/07
Postsecondary	Jacksonville MSA, FL	Y	35780 FQ	49860 MW	62040 TQ	USBLS	5/07
Postsecondary	Orlando-Kissimmee MSA, FL	Y	33760 FQ	48820 MW	70130 TQ	USBLS	5/07
Postsecondary	Tampa-St. Petersburg-Clearwater MSA, FL	Y	42280 FQ	57230 MW	79500 TQ	USBLS	5/07
Postsecondary	West Palm Beach-Boca Raton-Boynton Beach PMSA, FL	Y	45990 FQ	56690 MW	73380 TQ	USBLS	5/07
Postsecondary	Georgia	Y	41710 FQ	53770 MW	70270 TQ	USBLS	5/07
Postsecondary	Atlanta-Sandy Springs-Marietta MSA, GA	Y	46590 FQ	59610 MW	76420 TQ	USBLS	5/07
Postsecondary	Augusta-Richmond County MSA, GA-SC	Y	41070 FQ	50440 MW	59480 TQ	USBLS	5/07
Postsecondary	Hawaii	Y	47260 FQ	61140 MW	79320 TQ	USBLS	5/07

AE	Average entry wage	AW	Average wage paid	FQ	First quartile wage	LO	Lowest wage paid	MTC	Median total compensation	TCC	Total cash compensation
AER	Average entry range	AWR	Average wage range	H	Hourly	LR	Low end range	MW	Median wage paid	TQ	Third quartile wage
AEX	Average experienced wage	AXR	Average experienced range	HI	Highest wage paid	M	Monthly	MWR	Median wage range	W	Weekly
ATC	Average total compensation	D	Daily	HR	High end range	MCC	Median cash compensation	S	See annotated source	Y	Yearly

Occupation/Type/Industry	Location	Per	Low	Mid	High	Source	Date
Mathematical Science Teacher							
Postsecondary	Honolulu MSA, HI	Y	51270 FQ	66560 MW	84550 TQ	USBLS	5/07
Postsecondary	Illinois	Y	37710 FQ	55010 MW	73690 TQ	USBLS	5/07
Postsecondary	Chicago-Naperville-Joliet MSA, IL-IN-WI	Y	40170 FQ	56560 MW	76060 TQ	USBLS	5/07
Postsecondary	Indiana	Y	43760 FQ	56880 MW	73670 TQ	USBLS	5/07
Postsecondary	Gary PMSA, IN	Y	49570 FQ	58520 MW	68540 TQ	USBLS	5/07
Postsecondary	Indianapolis-Carmel MSA, IN	Y	38280 FQ	57570 MW	78570 TQ	USBLS	5/07
Postsecondary	Iowa	Y	44480 FQ	64930 MW	92020 TQ	USBLS	5/07
Postsecondary	Des Moines-West Des Moines MSA, IA	Y	39440 FQ	61080 MW	87110 TQ	USBLS	5/07
Postsecondary	Kansas	Y	32990 FQ	47230 MW	76200 TQ	USBLS	5/07
Postsecondary	Wichita MSA, KS	Y	45850 FQ	69780 MW	94450 TQ	USBLS	5/07
Postsecondary	Kentucky	Y	39728 FQ	51367 MW	65073 TQ	KYBLS	2008
Postsecondary	Louisville-Jefferson County MSA, KY-IN	Y	42810 FQ	51880 MW	67060 TQ	USBLS	5/07
Postsecondary	Louisiana	Y		60492 AW		LABLS	1/08-3/08
Postsecondary	Baton Rouge MSA, LA	Y	53670 FQ	65180 MW	81940 TQ	USBLS	5/07
Postsecondary	New Orleans-Metairie-Kenner MSA, LA	Y	34860 FQ	47750 MW	68140 TQ	USBLS.	5/07
Postsecondary	Maine	Y	44780 FQ	53890 MW	63710 TQ	USBLS	5/07
Postsecondary	Bangor MSA, ME	Y	47760 FQ	56050 MW	71490 TQ	USBLS	5/07
Postsecondary	Portland-South Portland-Biddeford MSA, ME	Y	46850 FQ	53730 MW	61560 TQ	USBLS	5/07
Postsecondary	Maryland	Y		65875 MW		MDBLS	3/08
Postsecondary	Baltimore-Towson MSA, MD	Y	54060 FQ	65100 MW	92440 TQ	USBLS	5/07
Postsecondary	Bethesda-Gaithersburg-Frederick PMSA, MD	Y	55770 FQ	68760 MW	91820 TQ	USBLS	5/07
Postsecondary	Massachusetts	Y	54660 FQ	70850 MW	96940 TQ	USBLS	5/07
Postsecondary	Boston-Cambridge-Quincy NECTA, MA	Y	52900 FQ	68530 MW	94980 TQ	USBLS	5/07
Postsecondary	Worcester MSA, MA-CT	Y	57260 FQ	69540 MW	93580 TQ	USBLS	5/07
Postsecondary	Michigan	Y	38970 FQ	60860 MW	79060 TQ	USBLS	5/07
Postsecondary	Detroit-Warren-Livonia MSA, MI	Y	28390 FQ	41950 MW	79150 TQ	USBLS	5/07
Postsecondary	Warren-Troy-Farmington Hills PMSA, MI	Y	28710 FQ	62820 MW	84040 TQ	USBLS	5/07
Postsecondary	Minnesota	Y	43460 FQ	55826 MW	68140 TQ	MNBLS	10/08-12/08
Postsecondary	Duluth-Superior MSA, MN-WI	Y	45469 FQ	59101 MW	76866 TQ	MNBLS	10/08-12/08
Postsecondary	Minneapolis-Saint Paul MSA, MN-WI	Y	43209 FQ	55763 MW	69228 TQ	MNBLS	10/08-12/08
Postsecondary	Mississippi	Y	40890 FQ	51440 MW	65770 TQ	USBLS	5/07
Postsecondary	Jackson MSA, MS	Y	39620 FQ	47350 MW	59080 TQ	USBLS	5/07
Postsecondary	Missouri	Y	39670 FQ	55750 MW	76890 TQ	USBLS	5/07
Postsecondary	Kansas City MSA, MO-KS	Y	36290 FQ	49800 MW	66470 TQ	USBLS	5/07
Postsecondary	St. Louis MSA, MO-IL	Y	32570 FQ	53630 MW	75610 TQ	USBLS	5/07
Postsecondary	Montana	Y	37560 FQ	47150 MW	57790 TQ	USBLS	5/07
Postsecondary	Nebraska	Y	41180 FQ	53650 MW	70850 TQ	USBLS	5/07
Postsecondary	Omaha-Council Bluffs MSA, NE-IA	Y	34540 FQ	51990 MW	62590 TQ	USBLS	5/07
Postsecondary	New Hampshire	Y	37295 AE	58914 MW	77470 AEX	NHBLS	6/08
Postsecondary	New Jersey	Y	48430 FQ	67610 MW	98060 TQ	USBLS	5/07
Postsecondary	Camden PMSA, NJ	Y	47660 FQ	71920 MW	101030 TQ	USBLS	5/07
Postsecondary	Edison PMSA, NJ	Y	54920 FQ	73430 MW	117410 TQ	USBLS	5/07
Postsecondary	Newark-Union PMSA, NJ-PA	Y	44550 FQ	61730 MW	86240 TQ	USBLS	5/07
Postsecondary	New Mexico	Y	47070 FQ	59540 MW	74320 TQ	USBLS	5/07
Postsecondary	Albuquerque MSA, NM	Y	44240 FQ	51620 MW	69210 TQ	USBLS	5/07
Postsecondary	New York	Y	46850 FQ	61990 MW	96250 TQ	USBLS	5/07
Postsecondary	Albany-Schenectady-Troy MSA, NY	Y	46580 FQ	77510 MW	110420 TQ	USBLS	5/07
Postsecondary	Buffalo-Niagara Falls MSA, NY	Y	39280 FQ	47550 MW	62570 TQ	USBLS	5/07
Postsecondary	Nassau-Suffolk PMSA, NY	Y	47090 FQ	58760 MW	74870 TQ	USBLS	5/07
Postsecondary	New York-Northern New Jersey-Long Island MSA, NY-NJ-PA	Y	51130 FQ	68800 MW	106060 TQ	USBLS	5/07
Postsecondary	North Carolina	Y	42760 FQ	51950 MW	65500 TQ	USBLS	5/07
Postsecondary	Charlotte-Gastonia-Concord MSA, NC-SC	Y	38220 FQ	50270 MW	66710 TQ	USBLS	5/07
Postsecondary	Raleigh-Cary MSA, NC	Y	52890 FQ	70870 MW	92750 TQ	USBLS	5/07
Postsecondary	North Dakota	Y	35550 FQ	46740 MW	59320 TQ	USBLS	5/07
Postsecondary	Fargo MSA, ND-MN	Y	43210 FQ	51850 MW	58640 TQ	USBLS	5/07

AE	Average entry wage	AW	Average wage paid	FQ	First quartile wage	LO	Lowest wage paid	MTC	Median total compensation	TCC	Total cash compensation
AER	Average entry range	AWR	Average wage range	H	Hourly	LR	Low end range	MW	Median wage paid	TQ	Third quartile wage
AEX	Average experienced wage	AXR	Average experienced range	HI	Highest wage paid	M	Monthly	MWR	Median wage range	W	Weekly
ATC	Average total compensation	D	Daily	HR	High end range	MCC	Median cash compensation	S	See annotated source	Y	Yearly

Occupation/Type/Industry	Location	Per	Low	Mid	High	Source	Date
Mathematical Science Teacher							
Postsecondary	Ohio	Y	41500 FQ	59260 MW	81370 TQ	USBLS	5/07
Postsecondary	Cincinnati-Middletown MSA, OH-KY-IN	Y	37620 FQ	52360 MW	73930 TQ	USBLS	5/07
Postsecondary	Cleveland-Elyria-Mentor MSA, OH	Y	37710 FQ	55620 MW	73900 TQ	USBLS	5/07
Postsecondary	Columbus MSA, OH	Y	64960 FQ	86590 MW	100230 TQ	USBLS	5/07
Postsecondary	Dayton MSA, OH	Y	30600 FQ	44910 MW	64380 TQ	USBLS	5/07
Postsecondary	Oklahoma	Y	28340 FQ	37270 MW	47750 TQ	USBLS	5/07
Postsecondary	Oklahoma City MSA, OK	Y	29020 FQ	37720 MW	54860 TQ	USBLS	5/07
Postsecondary	Tulsa MSA, OK	Y	23940 FQ	33650 MW	44420 TQ	USBLS	5/07
Postsecondary	Portland-Vancouver-Beaverton MSA, OR-WA	Y	43970 FQ	75070 MW	107130 TQ	USBLS	5/07
Postsecondary	Pennsylvania	Y	47770 FQ	64130 MW	85070 TQ	USBLS	5/07
Postsecondary	Allentown-Bethlehem-Easton MSA, PA-NJ	Y	58320 FQ	75530 MW	106380 TQ	USBLS	5/07
Postsecondary	Erie MSA, PA	Y	45850 FQ	56390 MW	67750 TQ	USBLS	5/07
Postsecondary	Lancaster MSA, PA	Y	46290 FQ	60060 MW	76670 TQ	USBLS	5/07
Postsecondary	Philadelphia-Camden-Wilmington MSA, PA-NJ-DE-MD	Y	49020 FQ	64380 MW	88030 TQ	USBLS	5/07
Postsecondary	Pittsburgh MSA, PA	Y	44370 FQ	62210 MW	80630 TQ	USBLS	5/07
Postsecondary	Rhode Island	Y	55290 FQ	76650 MW	97610 TQ	USBLS	5/07
Postsecondary	Providence-Fall River-Warwick MSA, RI-MA	Y	55090 FQ	75860 MW	97100 TQ	USBLS	5/07
Postsecondary	South Carolina	Y	46620 FQ	55390 MW	69060 TQ	USBLS	5/07
Postsecondary	Charleston-North Charleston MSA, SC	Y	46750 FQ	52940 MW	65840 TQ	USBLS	5/07
Postsecondary	Columbia MSA, SC	Y	54120 FQ	65720 MW	86240 TQ	USBLS	5/07
Postsecondary	South Dakota	Y	42570 FQ	52311 MW	66612 TQ	SDBLS	7/08-9/08
Postsecondary	Sioux Falls MSA, SD	Y	43227 FQ	52152 MW	61546 TQ	SDBLS	7/08-9/08
Postsecondary	Tennessee	Y	41910 FQ	49910 MW	63320 TQ	USBLS	5/07
Postsecondary	Memphis MSA, TN-MS-AR	Y	45870 FQ	59000 MW	86910 TQ	USBLS	5/07
Postsecondary	Nashville-Davidson-Murfreesboro MSA, TN	Y	43780 FQ	53670 MW	68070 TQ	USBLS	5/07
Postsecondary	Texas	Y	36090 FQ	51970 MW	75820 TQ	USBLS	5/07
Postsecondary	Austin-Round Rock MSA, TX	Y	14090 FQ	39030 MW	79890 TQ	USBLS	5/07
Postsecondary	Dallas-Fort Worth-Arlington MSA, TX	Y	25740 FQ	46430 MW	70120 TQ	USBLS	5/07
Postsecondary	El Paso MSA, TX	Y	44190 FQ	55730 MW	72360 TQ	USBLS	5/07
Postsecondary	San Antonio MSA, TX	Y	43120 FQ	55350 MW	65250 TQ	USBLS	5/07
Postsecondary	Utah	Y	44540 FQ	55980 MW	75840 TQ	USBLS	5/07
Postsecondary	Salt Lake City MSA, UT	Y	39280 FQ	48910 MW	84340 TQ	USBLS	5/07
Postsecondary	Vermont	Y	44130 FQ	53210 MW	63190 TQ	USBLS	5/07
Postsecondary	Burlington-South Burlington MSA, VT	Y	42930 FQ	52650 MW	66190 TQ	USBLS	5/07
Postsecondary	Virginia	Y	38760 FQ	51110 MW	68490 TQ	USBLS	5/07
Postsecondary	Lynchburg MSA, VA	Y	33360 FQ	46630 MW	57490 TQ	USBLS	5/07
Postsecondary	Richmond MSA, VA	Y	41940 FQ	54030 MW	70150 TQ	USBLS	5/07
Postsecondary	Virginia Beach-Norfolk-Newport News MSA, VA-NC	Y	35600 FQ	46160 MW	64620 TQ	USBLS	5/07
Postsecondary	Washington	Y		67278 AW		WABLS	3/08
Postsecondary	Seattle-Tacoma-Bellevue MSA, WA	Y	47500 FQ	61750 MW	89190 TQ	USBLS	5/07
Postsecondary	West Virginia	Y	41315 FQ	53015 MW	68471 TQ	WVBLS	7/08-9/08
Postsecondary	Wisconsin	Y	42710 FQ	55610 MW	76100 TQ	USBLS	5/07
Postsecondary	Milwaukee-Waukesha-West Allis MSA, WI	Y	40760 FQ	54800 MW	78920 TQ	USBLS	5/07
Postsecondary	Wyoming	Y	43695 FQ	51760 MW	63748 TQ	WYBLS	9/08
Postsecondary	Puerto Rico	Y	35280 FQ	45580 MW	71620 TQ	USBLS	5/07
Postsecondary	San Juan-Caguas-Guaynabo MSA, PR	Y	35760 FQ	49100 MW	73720 TQ	USBLS	5/07
Mathematical Technician	California	H	12.91 FQ	16.90 MW	22.23 TQ	CABLS	1/08-3/08
	Florida	Y	28760 FQ	32220 MW	37060 TQ	USBLS	5/07
	Minnesota	Y	37256 FQ	45186 MW	56224 TQ	MNBLS	10/08-12/08
	New Jersey	Y	45230 FQ	127320 MW		USBLS	5/07
	New York	Y	34430 FQ	47640 MW	69660 TQ	USBLS	5/07
	Ohio	Y	30490 FQ	38670 MW	46820 TQ	USBLS	5/07
	Oregon	H	18.12 FQ	21.60 MW	25.08 TQ	ORBLS	5/08
	Virginia	Y	33230 FQ	50480 MW	68360 TQ	USBLS	5/07

AE	Average entry wage	AW	Average wage paid	FQ	First quartile wage	LO	Lowest wage paid	MTC	Median total compensation	TCC	Total cash compensation
AER	Average entry range	AWR	Average wage range	H	Hourly	LR	Low end range	MW	Median wage paid	TQ	Third quartile wage
AEX	Average experienced wage	AXR	Average experienced range	HI	Highest wage paid	M	Monthly	MWR	Median wage range	W	Weekly
ATC	Average total compensation	D	Daily	HR	High end range	MCC	Median cash compensation	S	See annotated source	Y	Yearly

Occupation/Type/Industry	Location	Per	Low	Mid	High	Source	Date
Mathematician	Alabama	Y	86620 FQ	95480 MW	104440 TQ	USBLS	5/07
	California	H	41.21 FQ	52.85 MW	64.31 TQ	CABLS	1/08-3/08
	Colorado	Y	85490 FQ	107120 MW	123570 TQ	USBLS	5/07
	Connecticut	H	28.93 AE	43.99 MW		CTBLS	1/08-3/08
	District of Columbia	Y	88800 FQ	107380 MW	131500 TQ	USBLS	5/07
	Florida	Y	57510 FQ	76530 MW	92460 TQ	USBLS	5/07
	Illinois	Y	62110 FQ	74480 MW	105350 TQ	USBLS	5/07
	Maryland	Y		98500 MW		MDBLS	3/08
	Massachusetts	Y	59720 FQ	79130 MW	98910 TQ	USBLS	5/07
	Mississippi	Y	50200 FQ	77490 MW	94700 TQ	USBLS	5/07
	New Jersey	Y	85910 FQ	98860 MW	115710 TQ	USBLS	5/07
	New Mexico	Y	49230 FQ	59810 MW	83570 TQ	USBLS	5/07
	New York	Y	69670 FQ	84820 MW	108580 TQ	USBLS	5/07
	North Carolina	Y	46810 FQ	54290 MW	97140 TQ	USBLS	5/07
	Ohio	Y	72830 FQ	90190 MW	102230 TQ	USBLS	5/07
	Tennessee	Y	83530 FQ	94510 MW	104850 TQ	USBLS	5/07
	Texas	Y	39780 FQ	65270 MW	105690 TQ	USBLS	5/07
	Utah	Y	58880 FQ	71210 MW	79380 TQ	USBLS	5/07
	Virginia	Y	80810 FQ	97750 MW	119000 TQ	USBLS	5/07
	Wisconsin	Y	53010 FQ	61560 MW	75340 TQ	USBLS	5/07
Mayor	Atlanta, GA	Y			147500 HI	GACTY04	2008
	Chicago, IL	Y			210000 HI	ILLOOP	2009
	Baltimore, MD	Y			151700 HI	BMAG	2009
	Newton, MA	Y			97500 HI	BGLOBE2	2008
	Ferndale, MI	Y			8142 HI	FREEP05	2007
	Lincoln Park, MI	Y			14500 HI	NHERLD5	2009
	Oak Park, MI	Y			6010 HI	FREEP05	2007
	Rochester Hills, MI	Y			99279 HI	FREEP05	2007
	Wixom, MI	Y			1800 HI	FREEP05	2007
	Minneapolis, MN	Y			94000 HI	MMTHLY	2008
	Biloxi, MS	Y			110379 HI	MML	2008
	Hattiesburg, MS	Y			81890 HI	MML	2008
	Monticello, MS	Y			36000 HI	MML	2008
	Tupelo, MS	Y			89554 HI	MML	2008
	Morristown, NJ	Y			26000 HI	MGREEN	2008
	Arthur, ND	M			25 HI	NDLC02	2008
	Bismarck, ND	M			1500 HI	NDLC01	2008
	Cooperstown, ND	M			100 HI	NDLC01	2008
	Willston, ND	M			900 HI	NDLC01	2008
	Cincinnati, OH	Y			131904 HI	COHSS	10/08
	Toledo, OH	Y			136000 HI	TBLADE	2009
	Bethlehem, PA	Y			80000 HI	MORNC	2009
	Lebanon, PA	Y			37000 HI	PLIVE	2008
	Sioux Falls, SD	Y			105601 HI	SFMS	2008
MCDST Professional	United States	Y		63910 AW		CERT03	2008
MCSE Professional	United States	Y		89440 AW		CERT03	2008
Meat, Poultry, and Fish Cutter and Trimmer	Alabama	Y	17080 FQ	20110 MW	22600 TQ	USBLS	5/07
	Birmingham-Hoover MSA, AL	Y	17210 FQ	20220 MW	24200 TQ	USBLS	5/07
	Alaska	Y	18280 FQ	20600 MW	23670 TQ	USBLS	5/07
	Arizona	Y	16310 FQ	24130 MW	34860 TQ	USBLS	5/07
	Phoenix-Mesa-Scottsdale MSA, AZ	Y	15850 FQ	22540 MW	34000 TQ	USBLS	5/07
	Tucson MSA, AZ	Y	26230 FQ	33540 MW	37360 TQ	USBLS	5/07
	Arkansas	Y	17150 FQ	19550 MW	22370 TQ	USBLS	5/07
	Little Rock-North Little Rock MSA, AR	Y	17330 FQ	20390 MW	22390 TQ	USBLS	5/07
	California	H	8.49 FQ	9.80 MW	12.07 TQ	CABLS	1/08-3/08
	Bakersfield MSA, CA	H	8.70 FQ	10.26 MW	13.86 TQ	CABLS	1/08-3/08
	Fresno MSA, CA	H	8.09 FQ	8.93 MW	9.80 TQ	CABLS	1/08-3/08
	Los Angeles-Long Beach-Glendale PMSA, CA	H	8.25 FQ	9.13 MW	11.37 TQ	CABLS	1/08-3/08
	Modesto MSA, CA	H	10.00 FQ	10.88 MW	11.76 TQ	CABLS	1/08-3/08
	Oakland-Fremont-Hayward MSA, CA	H	9.27 FQ	11.99 MW	15.99 TQ	CABLS	1/08-3/08
	Riverside-San Bernardino-Ontario MSA, CA	H	8.19 FQ	9.28 MW	12.43 TQ	CABLS	1/08-3/08

AE	Average entry wage	AW	Average wage paid	FQ	First quartile wage	LO	Lowest wage paid	MTC Median total compensation
AER	Average entry range	AWR	Average wage range	H	Hourly	LR	Low end range	MW Median wage paid
AEX	Average experienced wage	AXR	Average experienced range	HI	Highest wage paid	M	Monthly	MWR Median wage range
ATC	Average total compensation	D	Daily	HR	High end range	MCC	Median cash compensation	S See annotated source

TCC	Total cash compensation
TQ	Third quartile wage
W	Weekly
Y	Yearly

Occupation/Type/Industry	Location	Per	Low	Mid	High	Source	Date
Meat, Poultry, and Fish Cutter and Trimmer	Sacramento-Arden Arcade-Roseville MSA, CA	H	9.86 FQ	11.69 MW	15.14 TQ	CABLS	1/08-3/08
	San Diego-Carlsbad-San Marcos MSA, CA	H	8.45 FQ	9.72 MW	13.08 TQ	CABLS	1/08-3/08
	San Francisco-San Mateo-Redwood PMSA, CA	H	9.82 FQ	12.21 MW	16.98 TQ	CABLS	1/08-3/08
	San Jose-Sunnyvale-Santa Clara MSA, CA	H	8.59 FQ	10.60 MW	15.03 TQ	CABLS	1/08-3/08
	Santa Ana-Anaheim-Irvine PMSA, CA	Y	16900 FQ	18480 MW	22090 TQ	USBLS	5/07
	Colorado	Y	21940 FQ	24540 MW	28210 TQ	USBLS	5/07
	Denver-Aurora MSA, CO	Y	20340 FQ	22960 MW	25490 TQ	USBLS	5/07
	Connecticut	H	9.20 AE	11.32 MW		CTBLS	1/08-3/08
	Bridgeport-Stamford-Norwalk MSA, CT	Y	20730 FQ	27120 MW	32910 TQ	USBLS	5/07
	New Haven MSA, CT	Y	18870 FQ	21920 MW	29550 TQ	USBLS	5/07
	Delaware	Y	16910 FQ	19260 MW	22340 TQ	USBLS	5/07
	Wilmington PMSA, DE-MD-NJ	Y	16000 FQ	19740 MW	24510 TQ	USBLS	5/07
	District of Columbia	Y	23650 FQ	33850 MW	41510 TQ	USBLS	5/07
	Washington-Arlington-Alexandria MSA, DC-VA-MD-WV	Y	20850 FQ	25110 MW	33850 TQ	USBLS	5/07
	Florida	Y	16830 FQ	20470 MW	25530 TQ	USBLS	5/07
	Fort Lauderdale-Pompano Beach-Deerfield Beach PMSA, FL	Y	17670 FQ	21550 MW	26270 TQ	USBLS	5/07
	Jacksonville MSA, FL	Y	19580 FQ	21830 MW	24830 TQ	USBLS	5/07
	Lakeland MSA, FL	Y	17550 FQ	21810 MW	26750 TQ	USBLS	5/07
	Miami-Fort Lauderdale-Miami Beach MSA, FL	Y	16770 FQ	21090 MW	26050 TQ	USBLS	5/07
	Orlando-Kissimmee MSA, FL	Y	19380 FQ	26270 MW	36010 TQ	USBLS	5/07
	Tampa-St. Petersburg-Clearwater MSA, FL	Y	14640 FQ	17870 MW	22640 TQ	USBLS	5/07
	West Palm Beach-Boca Raton-Boynton Beach PMSA, FL	Y	21320 FQ	25760 MW	29440 TQ	USBLS	5/07
	Georgia	Y	16940 FQ	19370 MW	22030 TQ	USBLS	5/07
	Atlanta-Sandy Springs-Marietta MSA, GA	Y	15740 FQ	18240 MW	21630 TQ	USBLS	5/07
	Hawaii	Y	18490 FQ	23880 MW	30280 TQ	USBLS	5/07
	Honolulu MSA, HI	Y	18160 FQ	23700 MW	30340 TQ	USBLS	5/07
	Idaho	Y	17710 FQ	20260 MW	23370 TQ	USBLS	5/07
	Boise City-Nampa MSA, ID	Y	17680 FQ	20340 MW	23440 TQ	USBLS	5/07
	Illinois	Y	21100 FQ	23710 MW	27760 TQ	USBLS	5/07
	Chicago-Naperville-Joliet MSA, IL-IN-WI	Y	19690 FQ	22850 MW	28900 TQ	USBLS	5/07
	Indiana	Y	20480 FQ	22390 MW	24300 TQ	USBLS	5/07
	Gary PMSA, IN	Y	15890 FQ	19130 MW	23570 TQ	USBLS	5/07
	Indianapolis-Carmel MSA, IN	Y	18410 FQ	21550 MW	25570 TQ	USBLS	5/07
	Iowa	Y	22030 FQ	25790 MW	28790 TQ	USBLS	5/07
	Kansas	Y	22630 FQ	25910 MW	28500 TQ	USBLS	5/07
	Wichita MSA, KS	Y	26460 FQ	28890 MW	31340 TQ	USBLS	5/07
	Kentucky	Y	18885 FQ	21502 MW	23939 TQ	KYBLS	2008
	Louisville-Jefferson County MSA, KY-IN	Y	16850 FQ	18210 MW	19550 TQ	USBLS	5/07
	Louisiana	H	7.34 FQ	8.90 MW	10.77 TQ	LABLS	1/08-3/08
	Baton Rouge MSA, LA	Y	15810 FQ	22840 MW	29220 TQ	USBLS	5/07
	New Orleans-Metairie-Kenner MSA, LA	Y	15730 FQ	17650 MW	20170 TQ	USBLS	5/07
	Shreveport-Bossier City MSA, LA	Y	13470 FQ	16160 MW	20290 TQ	USBLS	5/07
	Maine	Y	16840 FQ	19630 MW	23910 TQ	USBLS	5/07
	Portland-South Portland-Biddeford MSA, ME	Y	18780 FQ	21660 MW	24730 TQ	USBLS	5/07
	Maryland	Y		23300 MW		MDBLS	3/08
	Baltimore-Towson MSA, MD	Y	19120 FQ	27760 MW	39430 TQ	USBLS	5/07
	Bethesda-Gaithersburg-Frederick PMSA, MD	Y	17870 FQ	27870 MW	41480 TQ	USBLS	5/07
	Massachusetts	Y	21530 FQ	27250 MW	35230 TQ	USBLS	5/07
	Boston-Cambridge-Quincy NECTA, MA	Y	22030 FQ	27660 MW	36600 TQ	USBLS	5/07

AE	Average entry wage	AW	Average wage paid	FQ	First quartile wage
AER	Average entry range	AWR	Average wage range	H	Hourly
AEX	Average experienced wage	AXR	Average experienced range	HI	Highest wage paid
ATC	Average total compensation	D	Daily	HR	High end range

LO	Lowest wage paid	MTC	Median total compensation	TCC	Total cash compensation
LR	Low end range	MW	Median wage paid	TQ	Third quartile wage
M	Monthly	MWR	Median wage range	W	Weekly
MCC	Median cash compensation	S	See annotated source	Y	Yearly

Occupation/Type/Industry	Location	Per	Low	Mid	High	Source	Date
Meat, Poultry, and Fish Cutter and Trimmer	New Bedford MSA, MA	Y	19160 FQ	24210 MW	29510 TQ	USBLS	5/07
	Worcester MSA, MA-CT	Y	20040 FQ	32620 MW	40030 TQ	USBLS	5/07
	Michigan	Y	19400 FQ	22610 MW	26860 TQ	USBLS	5/07
	Detroit-Warren-Livonia MSA, MI	Y	15540 FQ	21240 MW	27050 TQ	USBLS	5/07
	Grand Rapids-Wyoming MSA, MI	Y	20150 FQ	22660 MW	26680 TQ	USBLS	5/07
	Warren-Troy-Farmington Hills PMSA, MI	Y	15120 FQ	19250 MW	26210 TQ	USBLS	5/07
	Minnesota	Y	21573 FQ	23729 MW	25885 TQ	MNBLS	10/08-12/08
	Minneapolis-Saint Paul MSA, MN-WI	Y	21324 FQ	25523 MW	30633 TQ	MNBLS	10/08-12/08
	Mississippi	Y	16940 FQ	19730 MW	22500 TQ	USBLS	5/07
	Jackson MSA, MS	Y	17180 FQ	19030 MW	22570 TQ	USBLS	5/07
	Missouri	Y	19170 FQ	21410 MW	24110 TQ	USBLS	5/07
	Kansas City MSA, MO-KS	Y	19500 FQ	22760 MW	25540 TQ	USBLS	5/07
	St. Louis MSA, MO-IL	Y	16760 FQ	19030 MW	24610 TQ	USBLS	5/07
	Montana	Y	20200 FQ	22880 MW	26960 TQ	USBLS	5/07
	Nebraska	Y	20360 FQ	24490 MW	28220 TQ	USBLS	5/07
	Omaha-Council Bluffs MSA, NE-IA	Y	19500 FQ	22000 MW	25440 TQ	USBLS	5/07
	Nevada	H	9.52 FQ	11.98 MW	15.72 TQ	NVBLS	5/08
	Las Vegas-Paradise MSA, NV	H	9.26 FQ	11.75 MW	15.21 TQ	NVBLS	5/08
	New Hampshire	H	8.81 AE	11.69 MW	13.39 AEX	NHBLS	6/08
	New Jersey	Y	17400 FQ	21680 MW	31950 TQ	USBLS	5/07
	Camden PMSA, NJ	Y	17810 FQ	21650 MW	26950 TQ	USBLS	5/07
	Edison PMSA, NJ	Y	18660 FQ	24460 MW	31170 TQ	USBLS	5/07
	Newark-Union PMSA, NJ-PA	Y	16650 FQ	18290 MW	30700 TQ	USBLS	5/07
	New Mexico	Y	18770 FQ	21610 MW	24990 TQ	USBLS	5/07
	Albuquerque MSA, NM	Y	24360 FQ	26200 MW	28060 TQ	USBLS	5/07
	Las Cruces MSA, NM	Y	14500 FQ	19140 MW	23030 TQ	USBLS	5/07
	New York	Y	16850 FQ	19940 MW	24840 TQ	USBLS	5/07
	Buffalo-Niagara Falls MSA, NY	Y	15600 FQ	17250 MW	19810 TQ	USBLS	5/07
	Nassau-Suffolk PMSA, NY	Y	17900 FQ	22160 MW	30130 TQ	USBLS	5/07
	New York-Northern New Jersey-Long Island MSA, NY-NJ-PA	Y	17540 FQ	21830 MW	30840 TQ	USBLS	5/07
	North Carolina	Y	17450 FQ	19660 MW	22330 TQ	USBLS	5/07
	Charlotte-Gastonia-Concord MSA, NC-SC	Y	20040 FQ	21590 MW	23140 TQ	USBLS	5/07
	Greensboro-High Point MSA, NC	Y	15560 FQ	19000 MW	26530 TQ	USBLS	5/07
	North Dakota	Y	20310 FQ	21990 MW	23670 TQ	USBLS	5/07
	Fargo MSA, ND-MN	Y	20380 FQ	21920 MW	23460 TQ	USBLS	5/07
	Ohio	Y	16230 FQ	19910 MW	25290 TQ	USBLS	5/07
	Cincinnati-Middletown MSA, OH-KY-IN	Y	16260 FQ	18530 MW	26770 TQ	USBLS	5/07
	Cleveland-Elyria-Mentor MSA, OH	Y	16560 FQ	20670 MW	25550 TQ	USBLS	5/07
	Columbus MSA, OH	Y	18650 FQ	22020 MW	25150 TQ	USBLS	5/07
	Dayton MSA, OH	Y	15720 FQ	16940 MW	18210 TQ	USBLS	5/07
	Oklahoma	Y	17280 FQ	19310 MW	21940 TQ	USBLS	5/07
	Oklahoma City MSA, OK	Y	17040 FQ	19440 MW	23040 TQ	USBLS	5/07
	Tulsa MSA, OK	Y	17140 FQ	22200 MW	32130 TQ	USBLS	5/07
	Oregon	H	8.67 FQ	9.49 MW	11.84 TQ	ORBLS	5/08
	Portland-Vancouver-Beaverton MSA, OR-WA	Y	18720 FQ	22620 MW	29920 TQ	USBLS	5/07
	Pennsylvania	Y	21130 FQ	23850 MW	28060 TQ	USBLS	5/07
	Allentown-Bethlehem-Easton MSA, PA-NJ	Y	21840 FQ	24640 MW	29080 TQ	USBLS	5/07
	Philadelphia-Camden-Wilmington MSA, PA-NJ-DE-MD	Y	20800 FQ	23620 MW	27860 TQ	USBLS	5/07
	Pittsburgh MSA, PA	Y	17830 FQ	20850 MW	23750 TQ	USBLS	5/07
	Rhode Island	Y	17270 FQ	21350 MW	28060 TQ	USBLS	5/07
	Providence-Fall River-Warwick MSA, RI-MA	Y	17440 FQ	21890 MW	29430 TQ	USBLS	5/07
	South Carolina	Y	16300 FQ	17640 MW	18970 TQ	USBLS	5/07
	Charleston-North Charleston MSA, SC	Y	22850 FQ	26530 MW	30960 TQ	USBLS	5/07

AE	Average entry wage	AW	Average wage paid	FQ	First quartile wage	LO	Lowest wage paid	MTC	Median total compensation	TCC	Total cash compensation
AER	Average entry range	AWR	Average wage range	H	Hourly	LR	Low end range	MW	Median wage paid	TQ	Third quartile wage
AEX	Average experienced wage	AXR	Average experienced range	HI	Highest wage paid	M	Monthly	MWR	Median wage range	W	Weekly
ATC	Average total compensation	D	Daily	HR	High end range	MCC	Median cash compensation	S	See annotated source	Y	Yearly

Occupation/Type/Industry	Location	Per	Low	Mid	High	Source	Date
Meat, Poultry, and Fish Cutter and Trimmer	Tennessee	Y	16950 FQ	18940 MW	20890 TQ	USBLS	5/07
	Nashville-Davidson-Murfreesboro MSA, TN	Y	16120 FQ	18040 MW	19930 TQ	USBLS	5/07
	Texas	Y	16200 FQ	19070 MW	23770 TQ	USBLS	5/07
	Austin-Round Rock MSA, TX	Y	15260 FQ	17760 MW	23830 TQ	USBLS	5/07
	Dallas-Fort Worth-Arlington MSA, TX	Y	16250 FQ	17810 MW	19380 TQ	USBLS	5/07
	Houston-Sugar Land-Baytown MSA, TX	Y	14200 FQ.	19300 MW	23080 TQ	USBLS	5/07
	San Antonio MSA, TX	Y	17270 FQ	20310 MW	24190 TQ	USBLS	5/07
	Utah	Y	18940 FQ	22940 MW	27240 TQ	USBLS	5/07
	Salt Lake City MSA, UT	Y	20940 FQ	25480 MW	28380 TQ	USBLS	5/07
	Vermont	Y	17880 FQ	20510 MW	25350 TQ	USBLS	5/07
	Burlington-South Burlington MSA, VT	Y	17450 FQ	19250 MW	24160 TQ	USBLS	5/07
	Virginia	Y	18290 FQ	21510 MW	23720 TQ	USBLS	5/07
	Richmond MSA, VA	Y	25960 FQ	28540 MW	39940 TQ	USBLS	5/07
	Virginia Beach-Norfolk-Newport News MSA, VA-NC	Y	13500 FQ	19020 MW	21890 TQ	USBLS	5/07
	Washington	H	8.93 FQ	10.41 MW	12.52 TQ	WABLS	3/08
	Olympia MSA, WA	Y	20290 FQ	21820 MW	23330 TQ	USBLS	5/07
	Seattle-Tacoma-Bellevue MSA, WA	Y	19110 FQ	22550 MW	27850 TQ	USBLS	5/07
	Wisconsin	Y	20780 FQ	22770 MW	24800 TQ	USBLS	5/07
	Milwaukee-Waukesha-West Allis MSA, WI	Y	21530 FQ	23280 MW	24980 TQ	USBLS	5/07
	Wyoming	Y	18093 FQ	21043 MW	24987 TQ	WYBLS	9/08
	Puerto Rico	Y	12390 FQ	13720 MW	15180 TQ	USBLS	5/07
	San Juan-Caguas-Guaynabo MSA, PR	Y	12430 FQ	13860 MW	15350 TQ	USBLS	5/07
	Guam	Y	12590 FQ	14130 MW	15610 TQ	USBLS	5/07
Meat Inspection Administrator State Government	Ohio	H	33.83 LO		44.38 HI	ODAS	2008
Meat Inspector State Government	Ohio	H	18.36 LO		23.87 HI	ODAS	2008
Mechanic Highway Department	Deerfield, MA	Y			45247 HI	FRCOG	2009
Mechanical Door Repairer	Alabama	Y	18580 FQ	23770 MW	29220 TQ	USBLS	5/07
	Alaska	Y	55670 FQ	61920 MW	69790 TQ	USBLS	5/07
	Arizona	Y	23620 FQ	28460 MW	35210 TQ	USBLS	5/07
	Arkansas	Y	21500 FQ	25470 MW	30350 TQ	USBLS	5/07
	California	H	14.88 FQ	18.03 MW	23.59 TQ	CABLS	1/08-3/08
	Colorado	Y	25710 FQ	32620 MW	38680 TQ	USBLS	5/07
	Connecticut	H	13.96 AE	19.11 MW		CTBLS	1/08-3/08
	Florida	Y	24370 FQ	29380 MW	37150 TQ	USBLS	5/07
	Georgia	Y	26700 FQ	34220 MW	42560 TQ	USBLS	5/07
	Idaho	Y	25350 FQ	27920 MW	32550 TQ	USBLS	5/07
	Illinois	Y	25930 FQ	28520 MW	41490 TQ	USBLS	5/07
	Indiana	Y	27810 FQ	33910 MW	41320 TQ	USBLS	5/07
	Iowa	Y	26890 FQ	31210 MW	39310 TQ	USBLS	5/07
	Kansas	Y	22980 FQ	28910 MW	33830 TQ	USBLS	5/07
	Kentucky	Y	26037 FQ	31126 MW	35788 TQ	KYBLS	2008
	Louisiana	H	13.26 FQ	16.37 MW	19.54 TQ	LABLS	1/08-3/08
	Maine	Y	25890 FQ	29970 MW	35930 TQ	USBLS	5/07
	Maryland	Y		34050 MW		MDBLS	3/08
	Massachusetts	Y	32790 FQ	43000 MW	49130 TQ	USBLS	5/07
	Michigan	Y	31410 FQ	37070 MW	44360 TQ	USBLS	5/07
	Minnesota	Y	31667 FQ	36985 MW	42303 TQ	MNBLS	10/08-12/08
	Mississippi	Y	22560 FQ	27150 MW	30780 TQ	USBLS	5/07
	Missouri	Y	25500 FQ	29290 MW	37000 TQ	USBLS	5/07
	Montana	Y	27940 FQ	32050 MW	38860 TQ	USBLS	5/07
	Nebraska	Y	22680 FQ	26420 MW	33160 TQ	USBLS	5/07
	Nevada	H	11.90 FQ	16.92 MW	23.11 TQ	NVBLS	5/08
	New Hampshire	H	13.60 AE	17.90 MW	20.50 AEX	NHBLS	6/08
	New Jersey	Y	28240 FQ	34220 MW	39520 TQ	USBLS	5/07
	New York	Y	25230 FQ	29450 MW	36120 TQ	USBLS	5/07
	North Carolina	Y	26880 FQ	32860 MW	38100 TQ	USBLS	5/07

AE	Average entry wage	AW	Average wage paid	FQ	First quartile wage	LO	Lowest wage paid	MTC	Median total compensation	TCC	Total cash compensation
AER	Average entry range	AWR	Average wage range	H	Hourly	LR	Low end range	MW	Median wage paid	TQ	Third quartile wage
AEX	Average experienced wage	AXR	Average experienced range	HI	Highest wage paid	M	Monthly	MWR	Median wage range	W	Weekly
ATC	Average total compensation	D	Daily	HR	High end range	MCC	Median cash compensation	S	See annotated source	Y	Yearly

Occupation/Type/Industry	Location	Per	Low	Mid	High	Source	Date
Mechanical Door Repairer	North Dakota	Y	24140 FQ	28110 MW	34460 TQ	USBLS	5/07
	Ohio	Y	26200 FQ	31450 MW	38940 TQ	USBLS	5/07
	Oklahoma	Y	20820 FQ	24590 MW	29480 TQ	USBLS	5/07
	Oregon	H	14.23 FQ	17.48 MW	22.54 TQ	ORBLS	5/08
	Pennsylvania	Y	28440 FQ	38490 MW	53490 TQ	USBLS	5/07
	Rhode Island	Y	31050 FQ	36790 MW	43150 TQ	USBLS	5/07
	South Carolina	Y	27440 FQ	32420 MW	37030 TQ	USBLS	5/07
	South Dakota	Y	28826 FQ	32505 MW	39894 TQ	SDBLS	7/08-9/08
	Tennessee	Y	23620 FQ	33150 MW	38510 TQ	USBLS	5/07
	Texas	Y	22100 FQ	28860 MW	36000 TQ	USBLS	5/07
	Utah	Y	30130 FQ	37530 MW	47730 TQ	USBLS	5/07
	Virginia	Y	27720 FQ	32600 MW	37570 TQ	USBLS	5/07
	Washington	H	12.94 FQ	15.14 MW	19.33 TQ	WABLS	3/08
	West Virginia	Y	25906 FQ	31969 MW	40056 TQ	WVBLS	7/08-9/08
	Wisconsin	Y	32490 FQ	40570 MW	47580 TQ	USBLS	5/07
	Wyoming	Y	28124 FQ	31988 MW	37642 TQ	WYBLS	9/08
	Puerto Rico	Y	13400 FQ	15910 MW	20770 TQ	USBLS	5/07
Mechanical Drafter	Alabama	Y	31620 FQ	40880 MW	54200 TQ	USBLS	5/07
	Birmingham-Hoover MSA, AL	Y	36940 FQ	45390 MW	53100 TQ	USBLS	5/07
	Huntsville MSA, AL	Y	31910 FQ	45940 MW	66100 TQ	USBLS	5/07
	Alaska	Y	43430 FQ	80400 MW	97640 TQ	USBLS	5/07
	Anchorage MSA, AK	Y	43240 FQ	80600 MW	97960 TQ	USBLS	5/07
	Arizona	Y	33880 FQ	40770 MW	51140 TQ	USBLS	5/07
	Phoenix-Mesa-Scottsdale MSA, AZ	Y	33680 FQ	40370 MW	50630 TQ	USBLS	5/07
	Tucson MSA, AZ	Y	35910 FQ	45480 MW	59640 TQ	USBLS	5/07
	Arkansas	Y	31390 FQ	36220 MW	42340 TQ	USBLS	5/07
	Little Rock-North Little Rock MSA, AR	Y	30820 FQ	36790 MW	46530 TQ	USBLS	5/07
	California	H	18.92 FQ	24.71 MW	30.29 TQ	CABLS	1/08-3/08
	Los Angeles-Long Beach-Glendale PMSA, CA	H	18.70 FQ	23.60 MW	28.76 TQ	CABLS	1/08-3/08
	Oakland-Fremont-Hayward MSA, CA	H	21.56 FQ	26.80 MW	32.59 TQ	CABLS	1/08-3/08
	Riverside-San Bernardino-Ontario MSA, CA	H	18.45 FQ	22.39 MW	28.17 TQ	CABLS	1/08-3/08
	Sacramento-Arden Arcade-Roseville MSA, CA	H	17.12 FQ	19.99 MW	28.47 TQ	CABLS	1/08-3/08
	San Diego-Carlsbad-San Marcos MSA, CA	H	16.11 FQ	22.01 MW	29.96 TQ	CABLS	1/08-3/08
	San Francisco-San Mateo-Redwood PMSA, CA	H	24.12 FQ	29.69 MW	36.05 TQ	CABLS	1/08-3/08
	San Jose-Sunnyvale-Santa Clara MSA, CA	H	24.61 FQ	29.66 MW	38.35 TQ	CABLS	1/08-3/08
	Santa Ana-Anaheim-Irvine PMSA, CA	Y	37570 FQ	50180 MW	62510 TQ	USBLS	5/07
	Colorado	Y	36900 FQ	47400 MW	59280 TQ	USBLS	5/07
	Denver-Aurora MSA, CO	Y	42640 FQ	52140 MW	64980 TQ	USBLS	5/07
	Connecticut	H	19.62 AE	24.42 MW		CTBLS	1/08-3/08
	Bridgeport-Stamford-Norwalk MSA, CT	Y	38240 FQ	50120 MW	59950 TQ	USBLS	5/07
	Hartford-West Hartford-East Hartford MSA, CT	Y	44800 FQ	52550 MW	61450 TQ	USBLS	5/07
	Delaware	Y	38100 FQ	51540 MW	69850 TQ	USBLS	5/07
	Wilmington PMSA, DE-MD-NJ	Y	39650 FQ	53510 MW	74710 TQ	USBLS	5/07
	Washington-Arlington-Alexandria MSA, DC-VA-MD-WV	Y	34560 FQ	46350 MW	61380 TQ	USBLS	5/07
	Florida	Y	35050 FQ	41380 MW	51640 TQ	USBLS	5/07
	Fort Lauderdale-Pompano Beach-Deerfield Beach PMSA, FL	Y	35560 FQ	40310 MW	46520 TQ	USBLS	5/07
	Jacksonville MSA, FL	Y	34200 FQ	38450 MW	46240 TQ	USBLS	5/07
	Miami-Fort Lauderdale-Miami Beach MSA, FL	Y	34710 FQ	40420 MW	48690 TQ	USBLS	5/07
	Orlando-Kissimmee MSA, FL	Y	34210 FQ	43680 MW	55160 TQ	USBLS	5/07
	Tampa-St. Petersburg-Clearwater MSA, FL	Y	35000 FQ	40750 MW	50630 TQ	USBLS	5/07
	West Palm Beach-Boca Raton-Boynton Beach PMSA, FL	Y	36560 FQ	48390 MW	63990 TQ	USBLS	5/07

AE	Average entry wage	AW	Average wage paid	FQ	First quartile wage
AER	Average entry range	AWR	Average wage range	H	Hourly
AEX	Average experienced wage	AXR	Average experienced range	HI	Highest wage paid
ATC	Average total compensation	D	Daily	HR	High end range

LO	Lowest wage paid	MTC	Median total compensation
LR	Low end range	MW	Median wage paid
M	Monthly	MWR	Median wage range
MCC	Median cash compensation	S	See annotated source

TCC	Total cash compensation
TQ	Third quartile wage
W	Weekly
Y	Yearly

989

Occupation/Type/Industry	Location	Per	Low	Mid	High	Source	Date
Mechanical Drafter	Georgia	Y	33460 FQ	43310 MW	55410 TQ	USBLS	5/07
	Atlanta-Sandy Springs-Marietta MSA, GA	Y	36270 FQ	45090 MW	56650 TQ	USBLS	5/07
	Augusta-Richmond County MSA, GA-SC	Y	38380 FQ	47670 MW	56690 TQ	USBLS	5/07
	Hawaii	Y	24300 FQ	53290 MW	58790 TQ	USBLS	5/07
	Honolulu MSA, HI	Y	24300 FQ	53290 MW	58790 TQ	USBLS	5/07
	Idaho	Y	33450 FQ	38720 MW	51080 TQ	USBLS	5/07
	Boise City-Nampa MSA, ID	Y	35170 FQ	43660 MW	56740 TQ	USBLS	5/07
	Illinois	Y	36070 FQ	44950 MW	56570 TQ	USBLS	5/07
	Chicago-Naperville-Joliet MSA, IL-IN-WI	Y	36540 FQ	45900 MW	58690 TQ	USBLS	5/07
	Indiana	Y	34080 FQ	43170 MW	52280 TQ	USBLS	5/07
	Evansville MSA, IN-KY	Y	30800 FQ	38830 MW	53340 TQ	USBLS	5/07
	Gary PMSA, IN	Y	36740 FQ	51200 MW	62660 TQ	USBLS	5/07
	Indianapolis-Carmel MSA, IN	Y	38940 FQ	45880 MW	55100 TQ	USBLS	5/07
	South Bend-Mishawaka MSA, IN-MI	Y	34700 FQ	40810 MW	47270 TQ	USBLS	5/07
	Iowa	Y	31570 FQ	40550 MW	50700 TQ	USBLS	5/07
	Des Moines-West Des Moines MSA, IA	Y	30450 FQ	39920 MW	49860 TQ	USBLS	5/07
	Iowa City MSA, IA	Y	25690 FQ	27390 MW	29090 TQ	USBLS	5/07
	Kansas	Y	32140 FQ	38730 MW	47610 TQ	USBLS	5/07
	Wichita MSA, KS	Y	35310 FQ	41680 MW	57590 TQ	USBLS	5/07
	Kentucky	Y	33827 FQ	40979 MW	49961 TQ	KYBLS	2008
	Louisville-Jefferson County MSA, KY-IN	Y	30470 FQ	36020 MW	43000 TQ	USBLS	5/07
	Louisiana	H	13.49 FQ	17.77 MW	22.53 TQ	LABLS	1/08-3/08
	Baton Rouge MSA, LA	Y	31560 FQ	37790 MW	44760 TQ	USBLS	5/07
	New Orleans-Metairie-Kenner MSA, LA	Y	25510 FQ	33000 MW	45650 TQ	USBLS	5/07
	Maine	Y	43030 FQ	46630 MW	50240 TQ	USBLS	5/07
	Portland-South Portland-Biddeford MSA, ME	Y	38010 FQ	44790 MW	51890 TQ	USBLS	5/07
	Maryland	Y		45275 MW		MDBLS	3/08
	Baltimore-Towson MSA, MD	Y	33310 FQ	39440 MW	52470 TQ	USBLS	5/07
	Bethesda-Gaithersburg-Frederick PMSA, MD	Y	42630 FQ	49060 MW	57670 TQ	USBLS	5/07
	Massachusetts	Y	44880 FQ	57880 MW	72920 TQ	USBLS	5/07
	Boston-Cambridge-Quincy NECTA, MA	Y	53450 FQ	64380 MW	83730 TQ	USBLS	5/07
	Worcester MSA, MA-CT	Y	40280 FQ	49720 MW	64050 TQ	USBLS	5/07
	Michigan	Y	40290 FQ	50130 MW	60470 TQ	USBLS	5/07
	Detroit-Warren-Livonia MSA, MI	Y	42910 FQ	54160 MW	65020 TQ	USBLS	5/07
	Grand Rapids-Wyoming MSA, MI	Y	43770 FQ	51460 MW	58470 TQ	USBLS	5/07
	Warren-Troy-Farmington Hills PMSA, MI	Y	43730 FQ	54430 MW	64520 TQ	USBLS	5/07
	Minnesota	Y	41577 FQ	49810 MW	59289 TQ	MNBLS	10/08-12/08
	Duluth-Superior MSA, MN-WI	Y	44119 FQ	49496 MW	55742 TQ	MNBLS	10/08-12/08
	Minneapolis-Saint Paul MSA, MN-WI	Y	45625 FQ	53127 MW	62334 TQ	MNBLS	10/08-12/08
	Rochester MSA, MN	Y	38683 FQ	47243 MW	57514 TQ	MNBLS	10/08-12/08
	Mississippi	Y	28420 FQ	31070 MW	35410 TQ	USBLS	5/07
	Jackson MSA, MS	Y	34170 FQ	37480 MW	41280 TQ	USBLS	5/07
	Pascagoula MSA, MS	Y	28220 FQ	30460 MW	32690 TQ	USBLS	5/07
	Missouri	Y	35300 FQ	44540 MW	54370 TQ	USBLS	5/07
	Kansas City MSA, MO-KS	Y	38430 FQ	44830 MW	50620 TQ	USBLS	5/07
	St. Louis MSA, MO-IL	Y	39120 FQ	47620 MW	59360 TQ	USBLS	5/07
	Montana	Y	34170 FQ	44160 MW	55670 TQ	USBLS	5/07
	Nebraska	Y	29190 FQ	34270 MW	40030 TQ	USBLS	5/07
	Omaha-Council Bluffs MSA, NE-IA	Y	30580 FQ	35170 MW	41720 TQ	USBLS	5/07
	Nevada	H	19.26 FQ	23.48 MW	28.93 TQ	NVBLS	5/08
	Las Vegas-Paradise MSA, NV	H	20.80 FQ	26.78 MW	30.01 TQ	NVBLS	5/08
	Reno-Sparks MSA, NV	H	18.97 FQ	21.23 MW	25.50 TQ	NVBLS	5/08
	New Hampshire	H	15.29 AE	21.94 MW	25.84 AEX	NHBLS	6/08
	New Jersey	Y	40150 FQ	49310 MW	61690 TQ	USBLS	5/07
	Camden PMSA, NJ	Y	41080 FQ	50880 MW	61760 TQ	USBLS	5/07
	Edison PMSA, NJ	Y	42850 FQ	50910 MW	61980 TQ	USBLS	5/07
	Newark-Union PMSA, NJ-PA	Y	39770 FQ	49600 MW	62860 TQ	USBLS	5/07

AE	Average entry wage	AW	Average wage paid	FQ	First quartile wage	LO	Lowest wage paid	MTC	Median total compensation	TCC	Total cash compensation
AER	Average entry range	AWR	Average wage range	H	Hourly	LR	Low end range	MW	Median wage paid	TQ	Third quartile wage
AEX	Average experienced wage	AXR	Average experienced range	HI	Highest wage paid	M	Monthly	MWR	Median wage range	W	Weekly
ATC	Average total compensation	D	Daily	HR	High end range	MCC	Median cash compensation	S	See annotated source	Y	Yearly

990

Occupation/Type/Industry	Location	Per	Low	Mid	High	Source	Date
Mechanical Drafter	New Mexico	Y	37740 FQ	49190 MW	65690 TQ	USBLS	5/07
	Albuquerque MSA, NM	Y	37580 FQ	47500 MW	59930 TQ	USBLS	5/07
	New York	Y	39960 FQ	47920 MW	59130 TQ	USBLS	5/07
	Albany-Schenectady-Troy MSA, NY	Y	35200 FQ	43790 MW	58460 TQ	USBLS	5/07
	Buffalo-Niagara Falls MSA, NY	Y	39400 FQ	46770 MW	56140 TQ	USBLS	5/07
	Nassau-Suffolk PMSA, NY	Y	48070 FQ	58820 MW	70400 TQ	USBLS	5/07
	New York-Northern New Jersey-Long Island MSA, NY-NJ-PA	Y	42950 FQ	52060 MW	64790 TQ	USBLS	5/07
	North Carolina	Y	37630 FQ	47750 MW	60750 TQ	USBLS	5/07
	Charlotte-Gastonia-Concord MSA, NC-SC	Y	40380 FQ	51600 MW	61800 TQ	USBLS	5/07
	Raleigh-Cary MSA, NC	Y	39640 FQ	49350 MW	58550 TQ	USBLS	5/07
	North Dakota	Y	25430 FQ	32630 MW	38580 TQ	USBLS	5/07
	Fargo MSA, ND-MN	Y	24720 FQ	32600 MW	37690 TQ	USBLS	5/07
	Ohio	Y	32360 FQ	39630 MW	48180 TQ	USBLS	5/07
	Cincinnati-Middletown MSA, OH-KY-IN	Y	34790 FQ	42870 MW	50820 TQ	USBLS	5/07
	Cleveland-Elyria-Mentor MSA, OH	Y	33930 FQ	40890 MW	50010 TQ	USBLS	5/07
	Columbus MSA, OH	Y	34100 FQ	41310 MW	48690 TQ	USBLS	5/07
	Dayton MSA, OH	Y	33880 FQ	39090 MW	48790 TQ	USBLS	5/07
	Oklahoma	Y	29730 FQ	40590 MW	50790 TQ	USBLS	5/07
	Oklahoma City MSA, OK	Y	29190 FQ	37980 MW	44800 TQ	USBLS	5/07
	Tulsa MSA, OK	Y	34690 FQ	45000 MW	56950 TQ	USBLS	5/07
	Oregon	H	17.87 FQ	22.49 MW	27.46 TQ	ORBLS	5/08
	Portland-Vancouver-Beaverton MSA, OR-WA	Y	40830 FQ	49070 MW	58250 TQ	USBLS	5/07
	Pennsylvania	Y	35310 FQ	43820 MW	53990 TQ	USBLS	5/07
	Allentown-Bethlehem-Easton MSA, PA-NJ	Y	37520 FQ	44590 MW	54120 TQ	USBLS	5/07
	Erie MSA, PA	Y	36460 FQ	50910 MW	64990 TQ	USBLS	5/07
	Philadelphia-Camden-Wilmington MSA, PA-NJ-DE-MD	Y	38850 FQ	48260 MW	59510 TQ	USBLS	5/07
	Pittsburgh MSA, PA	Y	35630 FQ	44070 MW	52750 TQ	USBLS	5/07
	Rhode Island	Y	41890 FQ	47750 MW	53310 TQ	USBLS	5/07
	Providence-Fall River-Warwick MSA, RI-MA	Y	41610 FQ	47540 MW	53750 TQ	USBLS	5/07
	South Carolina	Y	40740 FQ	50750 MW	65860 TQ	USBLS	5/07
	Charleston-North Charleston MSA, SC	Y	42170 FQ	50970 MW	57860 TQ	USBLS	5/07
	Columbia MSA, SC	Y	36060 FQ	44220 MW	54670 TQ	USBLS	5/07
	South Dakota	Y	29008 FQ	32813 MW	38382 TQ	SDBLS	7/08-9/08
	Sioux Falls MSA, SD	Y	29417 FQ	33577 MW	38175 TQ	SDBLS	7/08-9/08
	Tennessee	Y	34640 FQ	43920 MW	56250 TQ	USBLS	5/07
	Kingsport-Bristol-Bristol MSA, TN-VA	Y	29760 FQ	39110 MW	47540 TQ	USBLS	5/07
	Memphis MSA, TN-MS-AR	Y	38110 FQ	53380 MW	59900 TQ	USBLS	5/07
	Nashville-Davidson-Murfreesboro MSA, TN	Y	35000 FQ	48470 MW	58520 TQ	USBLS	5/07
	Texas	Y	36140 FQ	46370 MW	59480 TQ	USBLS	5/07
	Austin-Round Rock MSA, TX	Y	41310 FQ	50590 MW	60390 TQ	USBLS	5/07
	Dallas-Fort Worth-Arlington MSA, TX	Y	36240 FQ	45230 MW	56490 TQ	USBLS	5/07
	El Paso MSA, TX	Y	19710 FQ	31390 MW	46030 TQ	USBLS	5/07
	Houston-Sugar Land-Baytown MSA, TX	Y	38700 FQ	50950 MW	65630 TQ	USBLS	5/07
	San Antonio MSA, TX	Y	33920 FQ	39770 MW	52150 TQ	USBLS	5/07
	Utah	Y	34120 FQ	42920 MW	51280 TQ	USBLS	5/07
	Provo-Orem MSA, UT	Y	36880 FQ	48300 MW	73200 TQ	USBLS	5/07
	Salt Lake City MSA, UT	Y	33010 FQ	41910 MW	50890 TQ	USBLS	5/07
	Vermont	Y	40600 FQ	47520 MW	55090 TQ	USBLS	5/07
	Burlington-South Burlington MSA, VT	Y	42390 FQ	47290 MW	51990 TQ	USBLS	5/07
	Virginia	Y	33510 FQ	42140 MW	54110 TQ	USBLS	5/07
	Richmond MSA, VA	Y	36130 FQ	41250 MW	49900 TQ	USBLS	5/07
	Roanoke MSA, VA	Y	28360 FQ	38400 MW	46780 TQ	USBLS	5/07
	Washington	H	20.09 FQ	26.31 MW	33.65 TQ	WABLS	3/08

AE Average entry wage	**AW** Average wage paid	**FQ** First quartile wage	**LO** Lowest wage paid	**MTC** Median total compensation	**TCC** Total cash compensation
AER Average entry range	**AWR** Average wage range	**H** Hourly	**LR** Low end range	**MW** Median wage paid	**TQ** Third quartile wage
AEX Average experienced wage	**AXR** Average experienced range	**HI** Highest wage paid	**M** Monthly	**MWR** Median wage range	**W** Weekly
ATC Average total compensation	**D** Daily	**HR** High end range	**MCC** Median cash compensation	**S** See annotated source	**Y** Yearly

Mechanical Drafter

Occupation/Type/Industry	Location	Per	Low	Mid	High	Source	Date
Mechanical Drafter	Seattle-Tacoma-Bellevue MSA, WA	Y	47240 FQ	61190 MW	73740 TQ	USBLS	5/07
	West Virginia	Y	28499 FQ	37628 MW	46881 TQ	WVBLS	7/08-9/08
	Charleston MSA, WV	Y	31490 FQ	36360 MW	44630 TQ	USBLS	5/07
	Wisconsin	Y	37480 FQ	45760 MW	54750 TQ	USBLS	5/07
	Milwaukee-Waukesha-West Allis MSA, WI	Y	38630 FQ	47420 MW	56340 TQ	USBLS	5/07
	Wyoming	Y	35602 FQ	42830 MW	51632 TQ	WYBLS	9/08
	Cheyenne MSA, WY	Y	36795 FQ	47139 MW	58004 TQ	WYBLS	9/08
	Puerto Rico	Y	27090 FQ	32310 MW	40950 TQ	USBLS	5/07
	San Juan-Caguas-Guaynabo MSA, PR	Y	27290 FQ	32370 MW	40590 TQ	USBLS	5/07
Mechanical Engineer	Alabama	Y	58220 FQ	73450 MW	94450 TQ	USBLS	5/07
	Birmingham-Hoover MSA, AL	Y	49490 FQ	65880 MW	81330 TQ	USBLS	5/07
	Mobile MSA, AL	Y	66550 FQ	79880 MW	97410 TQ	USBLS	5/07
	Alaska	Y	71790 FQ	87820 MW	101140 TQ	USBLS	5/07
	Anchorage MSA, AK	Y	73590 FQ	88730 MW	101920 TQ	USBLS	5/07
	Arizona	Y	54250 FQ	66830 MW	82960 TQ	USBLS	5/07
	Phoenix-Mesa-Scottsdale MSA, AZ	Y	55790 FQ	66890 MW	82560 TQ	USBLS	5/07
	Tucson MSA, AZ	Y	52750 FQ	69550 MW	87720 TQ	USBLS	5/07
	Arkansas	Y	50570 FQ	62050 MW	77280 TQ	USBLS	5/07
	Fayetteville-Springdale-Rogers MSA, AR-MO	Y	45640 FQ	54700 MW	64310 TQ	USBLS	5/07
	Little Rock-North Little Rock MSA, AR	Y	54300 FQ	66410 MW	86490 TQ	USBLS	5/07
	California	H	31.77 FQ	40.36 MW	50.02 TQ	CABLS	1/08-3/08
	Los Angeles-Long Beach-Glendale PMSA, CA	H	31.93 FQ	39.87 MW	48.98 TQ	CABLS	1/08-3/08
	Oakland-Fremont-Hayward MSA, CA	H	35.60 FQ	44.57 MW	53.78 TQ	CABLS	1/08-3/08
	Riverside-San Bernardino-Ontario MSA, CA	H	26.55 FQ	37.27 MW	45.23 TQ	CABLS	1/08-3/08
	Sacramento-Arden Arcade-Roseville MSA, CA	H	31.83 FQ	38.77 MW	47.62 TQ	CABLS	1/08-3/08
	San Diego-Carlsbad-San Marcos MSA, CA	H	29.76 FQ	38.53 MW	48.09 TQ	CABLS	1/08-3/08
	San Francisco-San Mateo-Redwood PMSA, CA	H	32.30 FQ	37.81 MW	45.87 TQ	CABLS	1/08-3/08
	San Jose-Sunnyvale-Santa Clara MSA, CA	H	37.20 FQ	47.93 MW	59.72 TQ	CABLS	1/08-3/08
	Santa Ana-Anaheim-Irvine PMSA, CA	Y	60530 FQ	79540 MW	97490 TQ	USBLS	5/07
	Colorado	Y	61340 FQ	77760 MW	97630 TQ	USBLS	5/07
	Denver-Aurora MSA, CO	Y	61530 FQ	77390 MW	99350 TQ	USBLS	5/07
	Connecticut	H	27.07 AE	34.89 MW		CTBLS	1/08-3/08
	Bridgeport-Stamford-Norwalk MSA, CT	Y	59510 FQ	77040 MW	94090 TQ	USBLS	5/07
	Hartford-West Hartford-East Hartford MSA, CT	Y	61480 FQ	72120 MW	84690 TQ	USBLS	5/07
	Delaware	Y	65330 FQ	79490 MW	94960 TQ	USBLS	5/07
	Wilmington PMSA, DE-MD-NJ	Y	64740 FQ	77470 MW	93440 TQ	USBLS	5/07
	District of Columbia	Y	74670 FQ	91230 MW	104440 TQ	USBLS	5/07
	Washington-Arlington-Alexandria MSA, DC-VA-MD-WV	Y	66320 FQ	84580 MW	101070 TQ	USBLS	5/07
	Florida	Y	54890 FQ	69690 MW	89150 TQ	USBLS	5/07
	Fort Lauderdale-Pompano Beach-Deerfield Beach PMSA, FL	Y	55040 FQ	65490 MW	76010 TQ	USBLS	5/07
	Jacksonville MSA, FL	Y	52530 FQ	67550 MW	82880 TQ	USBLS	5/07
	Miami-Fort Lauderdale-Miami Beach MSA, FL	Y	51410 FQ	66550 MW	85450 TQ	USBLS	5/07
	Orlando-Kissimmee MSA, FL	Y	53960 FQ	69120 MW	89130 TQ	USBLS	5/07
	Sarasota-Bradenton-Venice MSA, FL	Y	52180 FQ	62670 MW	74170 TQ	USBLS	5/07
	Tallahassee MSA, FL	Y	49300 FQ	70880 MW	79820 TQ	USBLS	5/07
	Tampa-St. Petersburg-Clearwater MSA, FL	Y	52560 FQ	61040 MW	77040 TQ	USBLS	5/07

AE	Average entry wage	AW	Average wage paid	FQ	First quartile wage	LO	Lowest wage paid	MTC	Median total compensation	TCC	Total cash compensation
AER	Average entry range	AWR	Average wage range	H	Hourly	LR	Low end range	MW	Median wage paid	TQ	Third quartile wage
AEX	Average experienced wage	AXR	Average experienced range	HI	Highest wage paid	M	Monthly	MWR	Median wage range	W	Weekly
ATC	Average total compensation	D	Daily	HR	High end range	MCC	Median cash compensation	S	See annotated source	Y	Yearly

992

Occupation/Type/Industry	Location	Per	Low	Mid	High	Source	Date
Mechanical Engineer	West Palm Beach-Boca Raton-Boynton Beach PMSA, FL	Y	64690 FQ	82290 MW	98550 TQ	USBLS	5/07
	Georgia	Y	58750 FQ	72060 MW	84560 TQ	USBLS	5/07
	Atlanta-Sandy Springs-Marietta MSA, GA	Y	61370 FQ	73180 MW	85050 TQ	USBLS	5/07
	Hawaii	Y	65030 FQ	80900 MW	97280 TQ	USBLS	5/07
	Honolulu MSA, HI	Y	64980 FQ	80840 MW	97420 TQ	USBLS	5/07
	Idaho	Y	55690 FQ	86010 MW	120620 TQ	USBLS	5/07
	Boise City-Nampa MSA, ID	Y	70330 FQ	93830 MW	127170 TQ	USBLS	5/07
	Illinois	Y	53860 FQ	67150 MW	82550 TQ	USBLS	5/07
	Chicago-Naperville-Joliet MSA, IL-IN-WI	Y	55350 FQ	70020 MW	87100 TQ	USBLS	5/07
	Indiana	Y	54800 FQ	67010 MW	80660 TQ	USBLS	5/07
	Evansville MSA, IN-KY	Y	56530 FQ	68450 MW	77920 TQ	USBLS	5/07
	Gary PMSA, IN	Y	64270 FQ	74110 MW	88010 TQ	USBLS	5/07
	Indianapolis-Carmel MSA, IN	Y	58010 FQ	70660 MW	84250 TQ	USBLS	5/07
	Iowa	Y	51180 FQ	62190 MW	77840 TQ	USBLS	5/07
	Des Moines-West Des Moines MSA, IA	Y	45860 FQ	57390 MW	78690 TQ	USBLS	5/07
	Sioux City MSA, IA-NE-SD	Y	49970 FQ	64710 MW	84330 TQ	USBLS	5/07
	Kansas	Y	51920 FQ	64830 MW	81110 TQ	USBLS	5/07
	Wichita MSA, KS	Y	54380 FQ	64650 MW	77870 TQ	USBLS	5/07
	Kentucky	Y	54541 FQ	65299 MW	78617 TQ	KYBLS	2008
	Louisville-Jefferson County MSA, KY-IN	Y	48780 FQ	63700 MW	79540 TQ	USBLS	5/07
	Louisiana	H	26.57 FQ	33.40 MW	43.56 TQ	LABLS	1/08-3/08
	Baton Rouge MSA, LA	Y	63050 FQ	82020 MW	97970 TQ	USBLS	5/07
	Houma-Bayou Cane-Thibodaux MSA, LA	Y	53940 FQ	60990 MW	70150 TQ	USBLS	5/07
	New Orleans-Metairie-Kenner MSA, LA	Y	50900 FQ	64300 MW	87270 TQ	USBLS	5/07
	Maine	Y	53570 FQ	67210 MW	83850 TQ	USBLS	5/07
	Bangor MSA, ME	Y	50890 FQ	58070 MW	70400 TQ	USBLS	5/07
	Portland-South Portland-Biddeford MSA, ME	Y	51870 FQ	63560 MW	79330 TQ	USBLS	5/07
	Maryland	Y		85625 MW		MDBLS	3/08
	Baltimore-Towson MSA, MD	Y	63420 FQ	80070 MW	98560 TQ	USBLS	5/07
	Bethesda-Gaithersburg-Frederick PMSA, MD	Y	65530 FQ	87150 MW	99940 TQ	USBLS	5/07
	Massachusetts	Y	65800 FQ	80610 MW	98870 TQ	USBLS	5/07
	Boston-Cambridge-Quincy NECTA, MA	Y	66960 FQ	82760 MW	101420 TQ	USBLS	5/07
	New Bedford MSA, MA	Y	71920 FQ	86000 MW	95460 TQ	USBLS	5/07
	Worcester MSA, MA-CT	Y	61760 FQ	72770 MW	84080 TQ	USBLS	5/07
	Michigan	Y	60600 FQ	76190 MW	93540 TQ	USBLS	5/07
	Detroit-Warren-Livonia MSA, MI	Y	66650 FQ	81100 MW	96990 TQ	USBLS	5/07
	Grand Rapids-Wyoming MSA, MI	Y	52870 FQ	63830 MW	79280 TQ	USBLS	5/07
	Warren-Troy-Farmington Hills PMSA, MI	Y	63760 FQ	77670 MW	93840 TQ	USBLS	5/07
	Minnesota	Y	58222 FQ	70400 MW	84754 TQ	MNBLS	10/08-12/08
	Duluth-Superior MSA, MN-WI	Y	51495 FQ	63244 MW	80925 TQ	MNBLS	10/08-12/08
	Minneapolis-Saint Paul MSA, MN-WI	Y	59174 FQ	71907 MW	85884 TQ	MNBLS	10/08-12/08
	Rochester MSA, MN	Y	59203 FQ	72623 MW	83198 TQ	MNBLS	10/08-12/08
	Mississippi	Y	50470 FQ	62910 MW	76450 TQ	USBLS	5/07
	Jackson MSA, MS	Y	56770 FQ	65040 MW	82670 TQ	USBLS	5/07
	Missouri	Y	55220 FQ	67780 MW	81560 TQ	USBLS	5/07
	Kansas City MSA, MO-KS	Y	53820 FQ	68160 MW	87530 TQ	USBLS	5/07
	St. Louis MSA, MO-IL	Y	58310 FQ	70300 MW	82730 TQ	USBLS	5/07
	Montana	Y	45500 FQ	52980 MW	70000 TQ	USBLS	5/07
	Billings MSA, MT	Y	44870 FQ	53570 MW	76010 TQ	USBLS	5/07
	Missoula MSA, MT	Y	43030 FQ	46340 MW	49660 TQ	USBLS	5/07
	Nebraska	Y	49690 FQ	62870 MW	79970 TQ	USBLS	5/07
	Omaha-Council Bluffs MSA, NE-IA	Y	47460 FQ	64600 MW	87580 TQ	USBLS	5/07
	Nevada	H	30.14 FQ	37.17 MW	46.46 TQ	NVBLS	5/08
	Las Vegas-Paradise MSA, NV	H	32.52 FQ	41.90 MW	48.66 TQ	NVBLS	5/08
	Reno-Sparks MSA, NV	H	28.94 FQ	36.11 MW	48.28 TQ	NVBLS	5/08
	New Hampshire	H	24.64 AE	33.51 MW	41.54 AEX	NHBLS	6/08
	Manchester MSA, NH	Y	55640 FQ	63690 MW	75020 TQ	USBLS	5/07

AE	Average entry wage	**AW**	Average wage paid	**FQ**	First quartile wage	**LO**	Lowest wage paid	**MTC**	Median total compensation	**TCC**	Total cash compensation
AER	Average entry range	**AWR**	Average wage range	**H**	Hourly	**LR**	Low end range	**MW**	Median wage paid	**TQ**	Third quartile wage
AEX	Average experienced wage	**AXR**	Average experienced range	**HI**	Highest wage paid	**M**	Monthly	**MWR**	Median wage range	**W**	Weekly
ATC	Average total compensation	**D**	Daily	**HR**	High end range	**MCC**	Median cash compensation	**S**	See annotated source	**Y**	Yearly

Occupation/Type/Industry	Location	Per	Low	Mid	High	Source	Date
Mechanical Engineer	Nashua NECTA, NH-MA	Y	66950 FQ	79740 MW	100220 TQ	USBLS	5/07
	New Jersey	Y	62110 FQ	79120 MW	102830 TQ	USBLS	5/07
	Camden PMSA, NJ	Y	57570 FQ	74940 MW	99780 TQ	USBLS	5/07
	Edison PMSA, NJ	Y	64500 FQ	81200 MW	102340 TQ	USBLS	5/07
	Newark-Union PMSA, NJ-PA	Y	61670 FQ	77500 MW	102770 TQ	USBLS	5/07
	New Mexico	Y	69960 FQ	88390 MW	105400 TQ	USBLS	5/07
	Albuquerque MSA, NM	Y	71500 FQ	90630 MW	108150 TQ	USBLS	5/07
	New York	Y	57140 FQ	70720 MW	87920 TQ	USBLS	5/07
	Albany-Schenectady-Troy MSA, NY	Y	64040 FQ	80180 MW	99760 TQ	USBLS	5/07
	Buffalo-Niagara Falls MSA, NY	Y	54690 FQ	66750 MW	80150 TQ	USBLS	5/07
	Nassau-Suffolk PMSA, NY	Y	62550 FQ	80880 MW	101030 TQ	USBLS	5/07
	New York-Northern New Jersey-Long Island MSA, NY-NJ-PA	Y	62210 FQ	78450 MW	100100 TQ	USBLS	5/07
	North Carolina	Y	54490 FQ	65450 MW	78290 TQ	USBLS	5/07
	Charlotte-Gastonia-Concord MSA, NC-SC	Y	54260 FQ	63990 MW	78770 TQ	USBLS	5/07
	Greensboro-High Point MSA, NC	Y	57740 FQ	70350 MW	85310 TQ	USBLS	5/07
	Raleigh-Cary MSA, NC	Y	52720 FQ	65880 MW	80220 TQ	USBLS	5/07
	North Dakota	Y	54630 FQ	65470 MW	79920 TQ	USBLS	5/07
	Fargo MSA, ND-MN	Y	50630 FQ	63150 MW	84380 TQ	USBLS	5/07
	Ohio	Y	52170 FQ	63580 MW	78670 TQ	USBLS	5/07
	Cincinnati-Middletown MSA, OH-KY-IN	Y	54860 FQ	69030 MW	83650 TQ	USBLS	5/07
	Cleveland-Elyria-Mentor MSA, OH	Y	52840 FQ	65310 MW	78590 TQ	USBLS	5/07
	Columbus MSA, OH	Y	53750 FQ	65350 MW	79660 TQ	USBLS	5/07
	Dayton MSA, OH	Y	55380 FQ	64070 MW	78240 TQ	USBLS	5/07
	Oklahoma	Y	55280 FQ	68180 MW	82620 TQ	USBLS	5/07
	Oklahoma City MSA, OK	Y	57980 FQ	71020 MW	84610 TQ	USBLS	5/07
	Tulsa MSA, OK	Y	55550 FQ	66690 MW	81890 TQ	USBLS	5/07
	Oregon	H	27.39 FQ	35.12 MW	43.46 TQ	ORBLS	5/08
	Portland-Vancouver-Beaverton MSA, OR-WA	Y	58320 FQ	73460 MW	90180 TQ	USBLS	5/07
	Pennsylvania	Y	55530 FQ	70030 MW	88610 TQ	USBLS	5/07
	Allentown-Bethlehem-Easton MSA, PA-NJ	Y	58760 FQ	72170 MW	87190 TQ	USBLS	5/07
	Philadelphia-Camden-Wilmington MSA, PA-NJ-DE-MD	Y	62200 FQ	78930 MW	97620 TQ	USBLS	5/07
	Pittsburgh MSA, PA	Y	56540 FQ	70340 MW	88200 TQ	USBLS	5/07
	York-Hanover MSA, PA	Y	51880 FQ	65100 MW	80100 TQ	USBLS	5/07
	Rhode Island	Y	64410 FQ	78890 MW	96830 TQ	USBLS	5/07
	Providence-Fall River-Warwick MSA, RI-MA	Y	63680 FQ	77400 MW	95500 TQ	USBLS	5/07
	South Carolina	Y	58490 FQ	71210 MW	84100 TQ	USBLS	5/07
	Charleston-North Charleston MSA, SC	Y	59300 FQ	71120 MW	83730 TQ	USBLS	5/07
	Columbia MSA, SC	Y	57590 FQ	70120 MW	80250 TQ	USBLS	5/07
	South Dakota	Y	52818 FQ	63085 MW	76269 TQ	SDBLS	7/08-9/08
	Sioux Falls MSA, SD	Y	51490 FQ	61228 MW	72856 TQ	SDBLS	7/08-9/08
	Tennessee	Y	53470 FQ	65060 MW	81840 TQ	USBLS	5/07
	Kingsport-Bristol-Bristol MSA, TN-VA	Y	54290 FQ	59680 MW	65330 TQ	USBLS	5/07
	Memphis MSA, TN-MS-AR	Y	53120 FQ	67130 MW	82700 TQ	USBLS	5/07
	Nashville-Davidson-Murfreesboro MSA, TN	Y	53670 FQ	67390 MW	81010 TQ	USBLS	5/07
	Texas	Y	62310 FQ	79390 MW	100110 TQ	USBLS	5/07
	Austin-Round Rock MSA, TX	Y	56500 FQ	71100 MW	93080 TQ	USBLS	5/07
	Dallas-Fort Worth-Arlington MSA, TX	Y	65340 FQ	83750 MW	101110 TQ	USBLS	5/07
	El Paso MSA, TX	Y	46730 FQ	56410 MW	68670 TQ	USBLS	5/07
	Houston-Sugar Land-Baytown MSA, TX	Y	66880 FQ	82880 MW	105490 TQ	USBLS	5/07
	San Antonio MSA, TX	Y	48100 FQ	62960 MW	83710 TQ	USBLS	5/07
	Utah	Y	61350 FQ	73240 MW	88950 TQ	USBLS	5/07
	Ogden-Clearfield MSA, UT	Y	63890 FQ	75590 MW	89660 TQ	USBLS	5/07
	Salt Lake City MSA, UT	Y	61080 FQ	72310 MW	89480 TQ	USBLS	5/07
	Vermont	Y	49640 FQ	59580 MW	71970 TQ	USBLS	5/07

Occupation/Type/Industry	Location	Per	Low	Mid	High	Source	Date
Mechanical Engineer	Burlington-South Burlington MSA, VT	Y	49800 FQ	57890 MW	71070 TQ	USBLS	5/07
	Virginia	Y	57840 FQ	73910 MW	92470 TQ	USBLS	5/07
	Richmond MSA, VA	Y	61740 FQ	75950 MW	93670 TQ	USBLS	5/07
	Virginia Beach-Norfolk-Newport News MSA, VA-NC	Y	59710 FQ	74630 MW	90180 TQ	USBLS	5/07
	Washington	H	31.31 FQ	38.72 MW	46.13 TQ	WABLS	3/08
	Seattle-Tacoma-Bellevue MSA, WA	Y	64830 FQ	79890 MW	95320 TQ	USBLS	5/07
	West Virginia	Y	54129 FQ	66247 MW	86108 TQ	WVBLS	7/08-9/08
	Charleston MSA, WV	Y	53910 FQ	62850 MW	77020 TQ	USBLS	5/07
	Wisconsin	Y	52410 FQ	63600 MW	77000 TQ	USBLS	5/07
	Milwaukee-Waukesha-West Allis MSA, WI	Y	52310 FQ	62830 MW	75910 TQ	USBLS	5/07
	Wyoming	Y	54305 FQ	72071 MW	89928 TQ	WYBLS	9/08
	Cheyenne MSA, WY	Y	52414 FQ	79227 MW	98541 TQ	WYBLS	9/08
	Puerto Rico	Y	42510 FQ	58560 MW	72490 TQ	USBLS	5/07
	San Juan-Caguas-Guaynabo MSA, PR	Y	41650 FQ	57610 MW	71500 TQ	USBLS	5/07
	Virgin Islands	Y	68240 FQ	75480 MW	83180 TQ	USBLS	5/07
Green or Sustainability Skills	West Coast	Y	75000 LO		100000 HI	MDES	2008
Mechanical Engineering Technician	Alabama	Y	31560 FQ	41100 MW	55110 TQ	USBLS	5/07
	Birmingham-Hoover MSA, AL	Y	52100 FQ	58330 MW	66670 TQ	USBLS	5/07
	Huntsville MSA, AL	Y	33010 FQ	41250 MW	53520 TQ	USBLS	5/07
	Alaska	Y	36980 FQ	49930 MW	60040 TQ	USBLS	5/07
	Arizona	Y	34730 FQ	46340 MW	58060 TQ	USBLS	5/07
	Phoenix-Mesa-Scottsdale MSA, AZ	Y	32530 FQ	46070 MW	59410 TQ	USBLS	5/07
	Tucson MSA, AZ	Y	42410 FQ	46640 MW	50950 TQ	USBLS	5/07
	Arkansas	Y	34940 FQ	39660 MW	46890 TQ	USBLS	5/07
	Little Rock-North Little Rock MSA, AR	Y	35710 FQ	39870 MW	45950 TQ	USBLS	5/07
	California	H	19.50 FQ	24.90 MW	32.25 TQ	CABLS	1/08-3/08
	Los Angeles-Long Beach-Glendale PMSA, CA	H	19.77 FQ	24.53 MW	32.98 TQ	CABLS	1/08-3/08
	Oakland-Fremont-Hayward MSA, CA	H	25.42 FQ	31.92 MW	36.57 TQ	CABLS	1/08-3/08
	Riverside-San Bernardino-Ontario MSA, CA	H	17.80 FQ	24.16 MW	29.01 TQ	CABLS	1/08-3/08
	Sacramento-Arden Arcade-Roseville MSA, CA	H	19.01 FQ	22.50 MW	27.92 TQ	CABLS	1/08-3/08
	San Diego-Carlsbad-San Marcos MSA, CA	H	17.27 FQ	21.45 MW	28.41 TQ	CABLS	1/08-3/08
	San Francisco-San Mateo-Redwood PMSA, CA	H	19.06 FQ	26.81 MW	34.60 TQ	CABLS	1/08-3/08
	San Jose-Sunnyvale-Santa Clara MSA, CA	H	24.19 FQ	29.51 MW	35.39 TQ	CABLS	1/08-3/08
	Santa Ana-Anaheim-Irvine PMSA, CA	Y	38760 FQ	48070 MW	62470 TQ	USBLS	5/07
	Colorado	Y	41240 FQ	51910 MW	62500 TQ	USBLS	5/07
	Denver-Aurora MSA, CO	Y	44110 FQ	52910 MW	63610 TQ	USBLS	5/07
	Connecticut	H	17.95 AE	23.74 MW		CTBLS	1/08-3/08
	Bridgeport-Stamford-Norwalk MSA, CT	Y	41670 FQ	52410 MW	62110 TQ	USBLS	5/07
	Hartford-West Hartford-East Hartford MSA, CT	Y	46810 FQ	57010 MW	64220 TQ	USBLS	5/07
	Delaware	Y	45680 FQ	53740 MW	62770 TQ	USBLS	5/07
	Wilmington PMSA, DE-MD-NJ	Y	45730 FQ	53800 MW	62800 TQ	USBLS	5/07
	Washington-Arlington-Alexandria MSA, DC-VA-MD-WV	Y	37340 FQ	48500 MW	63920 TQ	USBLS	5/07
	Florida	Y	35370 FQ	43400 MW	51860 TQ	USBLS	5/07
	Fort Lauderdale-Pompano Beach-Deerfield Beach PMSA, FL	Y	23740 FQ	35130 MW	48980 TQ	USBLS	5/07
	Miami-Fort Lauderdale-Miami Beach MSA, FL	Y	34820 FQ	41310 MW	50470 TQ	USBLS	5/07
	Orlando-Kissimmee MSA, FL	Y	34060 FQ	40480 MW	45860 TQ	USBLS	5/07

AE	Average entry wage	AW	Average wage paid	FQ	First quartile wage	LO	Lowest wage paid	MTC	Median total compensation	TCC	Total cash compensation
AER	Average entry range	AWR	Average wage range	H	Hourly	LR	Low end range	MW	Median wage paid	TQ	Third quartile wage
AEX	Average experienced wage	AXR	Average experienced range	HI	Highest wage paid	M	Monthly	MWR	Median wage range	W	Weekly
ATC	Average total compensation	D	Daily	HR	High end range	MCC	Median cash compensation	S	See annotated source	Y	Yearly

Mechanical Engineering Technician

Occupation/Type/Industry	Location	Per	Low	Mid	High	Source	Date
Mechanical Engineering Technician	Tampa-St. Petersburg-Clearwater MSA, FL	Y	38050 FQ	45130 MW	51260 TQ	USBLS	5/07
	West Palm Beach-Boca Raton-Boynton Beach PMSA, FL	Y	36550 FQ	42180 MW	50250 TQ	USBLS	5/07
	Georgia	Y	41360 FQ	46380 MW	51740 TQ	USBLS	5/07
	Atlanta-Sandy Springs-Marietta MSA, GA	Y	42800 FQ	47060 MW	51610 TQ	USBLS	5/07
	Idaho	Y	28230 FQ	31090 MW	35550 TQ	USBLS	5/07
	Boise City-Nampa MSA, ID	Y	28050 FQ	30510 MW	32940 TQ	USBLS	5/07
	Illinois	Y	37900 FQ	46880 MW	61730 TQ	USBLS	5/07
	Chicago-Naperville-Joliet MSA, IL-IN-WI	Y	40880 FQ	51860 MW	64660 TQ	USBLS	5/07
	Indiana	Y	32210 FQ	43590 MW	52160 TQ	USBLS	5/07
	Gary PMSA, IN	Y	44610 FQ	52320 MW	59130 TQ	USBLS	5/07
	Indianapolis-Carmel MSA, IN	Y	24180 FQ	35230 MW	52400 TQ	USBLS	5/07
	Iowa	Y	35660 FQ	40700 MW	48640 TQ	USBLS	5/07
	Davenport-Moline-Rock Island MSA, IA-IL	Y	43400 FQ	51970 MW	60310 TQ	USBLS	5/07
	Kansas	Y	36930 FQ	46130 MW	59150 TQ	USBLS	5/07
	Wichita MSA, KS	Y	35940 FQ	41930 MW	48900 TQ	USBLS	5/07
	Kentucky	Y	35584 FQ	45041 MW	57257 TQ	KYBLS	2008
	Louisville-Jefferson County MSA, KY-IN	Y	33370 FQ	41110 MW	51790 TQ	USBLS	5/07
	Louisiana	H	17.66 FQ	19.72 MW	23.24 TQ	LABLS	1/08-3/08
	New Orleans-Metairie-Kenner MSA, LA	Y	36090 FQ	39970 MW	45980 TQ	USBLS	5/07
	Maine	Y	37300 FQ	44890 MW	51860 TQ	USBLS	5/07
	Portland-South Portland-Biddeford MSA, ME	Y	35870 FQ	43470 MW	52540 TQ	USBLS	5/07
	Maryland	Y		53975 MW		MDBLS	3/08
	Baltimore-Towson MSA, MD	Y	38390 FQ	50630 MW	64730 TQ	USBLS	5/07
	Bethesda-Gaithersburg-Frederick PMSA, MD	Y	46240 FQ	54680 MW	66590 TQ	USBLS	5/07
	Massachusetts	Y	42490 FQ	49110 MW	58760 TQ	USBLS	5/07
	Boston-Cambridge-Quincy NECTA, MA	Y	43730 FQ	51250 MW	60750 TQ	USBLS	5/07
	Lynn-Peabody-Salem NECTA, MA	Y	43780 FQ	50620 MW	60030 TQ	USBLS	5/07
	Worcester MSA, MA-CT	Y	38140 FQ	42970 MW	47240 TQ	USBLS	5/07
	Michigan	Y	37230 FQ	47410 MW	60330 TQ	USBLS	5/07
	Detroit-Warren-Livonia MSA, MI	Y	37300 FQ	47340 MW	60200 TQ	USBLS	5/07
	Grand Rapids-Wyoming MSA, MI	Y	36230 FQ	47550 MW	58530 TQ	USBLS	5/07
	Warren-Troy-Farmington Hills PMSA, MI	Y	40020 FQ	50290 MW	61670 TQ	USBLS	5/07
	Minnesota	Y	41472 FQ	50637 MW	61559 TQ	MNBLS	10/08-12/08
	Duluth-Superior MSA, MN-WI	Y	54236 FQ	60022 MW	65462 TQ	MNBLS	10/08-12/08
	Minneapolis-Saint Paul MSA, MN-WI	Y	44098 FQ	53221 MW	63955 TQ	MNBLS	10/08-12/08
	Rochester MSA, MN	Y	41245 FQ	51181 MW	62161 TQ	MNBLS	10/08-12/08
	Mississippi	Y	37890 FQ	44160 MW	48510 TQ	USBLS	5/07
	Jackson MSA, MS	Y	31700 FQ	41870 MW	46950 TQ	USBLS	5/07
	Missouri	Y	37660 FQ	46690 MW	58500 TQ	USBLS	5/07
	Kansas City MSA, MO-KS	Y	46260 FQ	58690 MW	68660 TQ	USBLS	5/07
	St. Louis MSA, MO-IL	Y	39230 FQ	47950 MW	59310 TQ	USBLS	5/07
	Montana	Y	35170 FQ	40640 MW	50890 TQ	USBLS	5/07
	Nebraska	Y	35920 FQ	44770 MW	58640 TQ	USBLS	5/07
	Omaha-Council Bluffs MSA, NE-IA	Y	32410 FQ	39400 MW	55960 TQ	USBLS	5/07
	Nevada	H	19.09 FQ	23.67 MW	28.35 TQ	NVBLS	5/08
	Las Vegas-Paradise MSA, NV	H	21.23 FQ	24.71 MW	30.45 TQ	NVBLS	5/08
	New Hampshire	H	17.10 AE	22.10 MW	25.22 AEX	NHBLS	6/08
	Nashua NECTA, NH-MA	Y	39420 FQ	44670 MW	52400 TQ	USBLS	5/07
	New Jersey	Y	36930 FQ	45650 MW	55840 TQ	USBLS	5/07
	Camden PMSA, NJ	Y	35320 FQ	42640 MW	50190 TQ	USBLS	5/07
	Edison PMSA, NJ	Y	38890 FQ	46900 MW	61070 TQ	USBLS	5/07
	Newark-Union PMSA, NJ-PA	Y	34970 FQ	43760 MW	53880 TQ	USBLS	5/07
	Trenton-Ewing MSA, NJ	Y	44310 FQ	52400 MW	60270 TQ	USBLS	5/07
	New Mexico	Y	44740 FQ	53490 MW	64160 TQ	USBLS	5/07
	Albuquerque MSA, NM	Y	44790 FQ	52010 MW	60530 TQ	USBLS	5/07

AE	Average entry wage	AW	Average wage paid	FQ	First quartile wage	LO	Lowest wage paid	MTC	Median total compensation	TCC	Total cash compensation
AER	Average entry range	AWR	Average wage range	H	Hourly	LR	Low end range	MW	Median wage paid	TQ	Third quartile wage
AEX	Average experienced wage	AXR	Average experienced range	HI	Highest wage paid	M	Monthly	MWR	Median wage range	W	Weekly
ATC	Average total compensation	D	Daily	HR	High end range	MCC	Median cash compensation	S	See annotated source	Y	Yearly

Occupation/Type/Industry	Location	Per	Low	Mid	High	Source	Date
Mechanical Engineering Technician	New York	Y	38490 FQ	47360 MW	60240 TQ	USBLS	5/07
	Albany-Schenectady-Troy MSA, NY	Y	43640 FQ	57770 MW	73860 TQ	USBLS	5/07
	Buffalo-Niagara Falls MSA, NY	Y	36170 FQ	45830 MW	59090 TQ	USBLS	5/07
	Nassau-Suffolk PMSA, NY	Y	44100 FQ	57850 MW	71380 TQ	USBLS	5/07
	New York-Northern New Jersey-Long Island MSA, NY-NJ-PA	Y	39110 FQ	48200 MW	61860 TQ	USBLS	5/07
	North Carolina	Y	37830 FQ	46700 MW	60780 TQ	USBLS	5/07
	Charlotte-Gastonia-Concord MSA, NC-SC	Y	45150 FQ	52360 MW	68630 TQ	USBLS	5/07
	North Dakota	Y	37520 FQ	44130 MW	50440 TQ	USBLS	5/07
	Fargo MSA, ND-MN	Y	38910 FQ	44850 MW	50300 TQ	USBLS	5/07
	Ohio	Y	35950 FQ	45360 MW	56100 TQ	USBLS	5/07
	Cincinnati-Middletown MSA, OH-KY-IN	Y	32620 FQ	43250 MW	56800 TQ	USBLS	5/07
	Cleveland-Elyria-Mentor MSA, OH	Y	41300 FQ	48200 MW	59570 TQ	USBLS	5/07
	Columbus MSA, OH	Y	40340 FQ	47770 MW	58100 TQ	USBLS	5/07
	Dayton MSA, OH	Y	34560 FQ	44960 MW	56130 TQ	USBLS	5/07
	Oklahoma	Y	37310 FQ	45700 MW	58140 TQ	USBLS	5/07
	Oklahoma City MSA, OK	Y	36940 FQ	42810 MW	47140 TQ	USBLS	5/07
	Tulsa MSA, OK	Y	35870 FQ	45500 MW	59390 TQ	USBLS	5/07
	Oregon	H	23.92 FQ	28.49 MW	33.35 TQ	ORBLS	5/08
	Portland-Vancouver-Beaverton MSA, OR-WA	Y	50150 FQ	58580 MW	69080 TQ	USBLS	5/07
	Pennsylvania	Y	34140 FQ	43200 MW	52040 TQ	USBLS	5/07
	Allentown-Bethlehem-Easton MSA, PA-NJ	Y	36450 FQ	43600 MW	49230 TQ	USBLS	5/07
	Lancaster MSA, PA	Y	42260 FQ	47540 MW	55300 TQ	USBLS	5/07
	Philadelphia-Camden-Wilmington MSA, PA-NJ-DE-MD	Y	36430 FQ	45440 MW	53890 TQ	USBLS	5/07
	Pittsburgh MSA, PA	Y	32720 FQ	41620 MW	50900 TQ	USBLS	5/07
	Rhode Island	Y	34520 FQ	42220 MW	51640 TQ	USBLS	5/07
	Providence-Fall River-Warwick MSA, RI-MA	Y	35860 FQ	45530 MW	53850 TQ	USBLS	5/07
	South Carolina	Y	39820 FQ	48620 MW	59000 TQ	USBLS	5/07
	Charleston-North Charleston MSA, SC	Y	40710 FQ	50490 MW	58230 TQ	USBLS	5/07
	Columbia MSA, SC	Y	36370 FQ	42630 MW	48720 TQ	USBLS	5/07
	Spartanburg MSA, SC	Y	48800 FQ	58030 MW	68960 TQ	USBLS	5/07
	South Dakota	Y	31817 FQ	38232 MW	44706 TQ	SDBLS	7/08-9/08
	Sioux Falls MSA, SD	Y	29809 FQ	35319 MW	40707 TQ	SDBLS	7/08-9/08
	Tennessee	Y	35460 FQ	43570 MW	55630 TQ	USBLS	5/07
	Memphis MSA, TN-MS-AR	Y	33690 FQ	38890 MW	48380 TQ	USBLS	5/07
	Nashville-Davidson-Murfreesboro MSA, TN	Y	36930 FQ	43350 MW	51980 TQ	USBLS	5/07
	Texas	Y	40610 FQ	52460 MW	65130 TQ	USBLS	5/07
	Austin-Round Rock MSA, TX	Y	43400 FQ	52280 MW	60400 TQ	USBLS	5/07
	Dallas-Fort Worth-Arlington MSA, TX	Y	45090 FQ	59390 MW	72090 TQ	USBLS	5/07
	Houston-Sugar Land-Baytown MSA, TX	Y	41220 FQ	52600 MW	63960 TQ	USBLS	5/07
	San Antonio MSA, TX	Y	33000 FQ	43470 MW	55380 TQ	USBLS	5/07
	Utah	Y	30800 FQ	42450 MW	50600 TQ	USBLS	5/07
	Salt Lake City MSA, UT	Y	29200 FQ	43860 MW	51450 TQ	USBLS	5/07
	Vermont	Y	35030 FQ	43240 MW	54870 TQ	USBLS	5/07
	Virginia	Y	35550 FQ	43950 MW	55340 TQ	USBLS	5/07
	Richmond MSA, VA	Y	42630 FQ	48210 MW	60230 TQ	USBLS	5/07
	Virginia Beach-Norfolk-Newport News MSA, VA-NC	Y	30550 FQ	36600 MW	48140 TQ	USBLS	5/07
	Washington	H	22.67 FQ	27.18 MW	31.59 TQ	WABLS	3/08
	Seattle-Tacoma-Bellevue MSA, WA	Y	47850 FQ	56200 MW	64630 TQ	USBLS	5/07
	West Virginia	Y	32350 FQ	40001 MW	48629 TQ	WVBLS	7/08-9/08
	Wisconsin	Y	35910 FQ	45150 MW	55250 TQ	USBLS	5/07
	Milwaukee-Waukesha-West Allis MSA, WI	Y	39370 FQ	49560 MW	59560 TQ	USBLS	5/07
	Puerto Rico	Y	32540 FQ	39180 MW	50840 TQ	USBLS	5/07

AE Average entry wage	**AW** Average wage paid	**FQ** First quartile wage	**LO** Lowest wage paid	**MTC** Median total compensation	**TCC** Total cash compensation
AER Average entry range	**AWR** Average wage range	**H** Hourly	**LR** Low end range	**MW** Median wage paid	**TQ** Third quartile wage
AEX Average experienced wage	**AXR** Average experienced range	**HI** Highest wage paid	**M** Monthly	**MWR** Median wage range	**W** Weekly
ATC Average total compensation	**D** Daily	**HR** High end range	**MCC** Median cash compensation	**S** See annotated source	**Y** Yearly

Occupation/Type/Industry	Location	Per	Low	Mid	High	Source	Date
Mechanical Engineering Technician	San Juan-Caguas-Guaynabo MSA, PR	Y	35090 FQ	40000 MW	50490 TQ	USBLS	5/07
Media Coordinator							
White House Staff	United States	Y			47000 HI	WPOST02	2008
Mediation Services Specialist							
Municipal Government	Cincinnati, OH	Y	14616 LO		27144 HI	COHSS	10/08
Mediation Specialist							
Municipal Government	Gresham, OR	Y	49764 LO		64692 HI	GOSS01	7/1/08
Mediator	United States	Y		66800 MW		USNEWS02	2008
Medic	St. Petersburg, FL	Y			59984 HI	FIREH	2006
	Elgin, IL	Y			66648 HI	FIREH	2006
	Hammond, IN	Y			47452 HI	FIREH	2006
	Hebron, KY	Y			43913 HI	FIREH	2006
	Brockton, MA	Y			45101 HI	FIREH	2006
	Elizabeth, NJ	Y			72356 HI	FIREH	2006
	South Euclid, OH	Y			77822 HI	FIREH	2006
	Pawtucket, RI	Y			51498 HI	FIREH	2006
	Spokane, WA	Y			74710 HI	FIREH	2006
	Kenosha, WI	Y			58601 HI	FIREH	2006
Medicaid Health Systems Analyst							
State Government	Ohio	H	20.71 LO		26.11 HI	ODAS	2008
Medical and Clinical Laboratory Technician	Alabama	Y	23380 FQ	28430 MW	35240 TQ	USBLS	5/07
	Birmingham-Hoover MSA, AL	Y	24370 FQ	29500 MW	35730 TQ	USBLS	5/07
	Alaska	Y	34950 FQ	43810 MW	54460 TQ	USBLS	5/07
	Anchorage MSA, AK	Y	35080 FQ	43080 MW	50850 TQ	USBLS	5/07
	Arizona	Y	29880 FQ	39160 MW	49150 TQ	USBLS	5/07
	Phoenix-Mesa-Scottsdale MSA, AZ	Y	33440 FQ	38840 MW	47510 TQ	USBLS	5/07
	Tucson MSA, AZ	Y	27130 FQ	43740 MW	51470 TQ	USBLS	5/07
	Arkansas	Y	25160 FQ	30910 MW	37920 TQ	USBLS	5/07
	Little Rock-North Little Rock MSA, AR	Y	27910 FQ	32380 MW	39610 TQ	USBLS	5/07
	California	H	14.34 FQ	17.81 MW	22.62 TQ	CABLS	1/08-3/08
	Los Angeles-Long Beach-Glendale PMSA, CA	H	13.77 FQ	17.06 MW	20.64 TQ	CABLS	1/08-3/08
	Oakland-Fremont-Hayward MSA, CA	H	14.32 FQ	19.13 MW	24.77 TQ	CABLS	1/08-3/08
	Riverside-San Bernardino-Ontario MSA, CA	H	14.65 FQ	18.07 MW	23.92 TQ	CABLS	1/08-3/08
	Sacramento-Arden Arcade-Roseville MSA, CA	H	13.61 FQ	17.18 MW	19.75 TQ	CABLS	1/08-3/08
	San Diego-Carlsbad-San Marcos MSA, CA	H	14.01 FQ	17.64 MW	23.53 TQ	CABLS	1/08-3/08
	San Francisco-San Mateo-Redwood PMSA, CA	H	16.45 FQ	20.34 MW	29.95 TQ	CABLS	1/08-3/08
	San Jose-Sunnyvale-Santa Clara MSA, CA	H	19.90 FQ	23.43 MW	35.36 TQ	CABLS	1/08-3/08
	Santa Ana-Anaheim-Irvine PMSA, CA	Y	29270 FQ	35500 MW	43190 TQ	USBLS	5/07
	Colorado	Y	26340 FQ	31450 MW	37620 TQ	USBLS	5/07
	Denver-Aurora MSA, CO	Y	27240 FQ	32360 MW	37400 TQ	USBLS	5/07
	Connecticut	H	15.69 AE	20.72 MW		CTBLS	1/08-3/08
	Bridgeport-Stamford-Norwalk MSA, CT	Y	35120 FQ	40200 MW	50900 TQ	USBLS	5/07
	Hartford-West Hartford-East Hartford MSA, CT	Y	32810 FQ	39110 MW	46670 TQ	USBLS	5/07
	New Haven MSA, CT	Y	37980 FQ	49350 MW	61670 TQ	USBLS	5/07
	Delaware	Y	25090 FQ	31690 MW	43970 TQ	USBLS	5/07
	Wilmington PMSA, DE-MD-NJ	Y	28930 FQ	38880 MW	49980 TQ	USBLS	5/07
	District of Columbia	Y	34850 FQ	41610 MW	49270 TQ	USBLS	5/07

AE	Average entry wage	**AW**	Average wage paid	**FQ**	First quartile wage
AER	Average entry range	**AWR**	Average wage range	**H**	Hourly
AEX	Average experienced wage	**AXR**	Average experienced range	**HI**	Highest wage paid
ATC	Average total compensation	**D**	Daily	**HR**	High end range

LO	Lowest wage paid	**MTC**	Median total compensation	**TCC**	Total cash compensation
LR	Low end range	**MW**	Median wage paid	**TQ**	Third quartile wage
		MWR	Median wage range	**W**	Weekly
M	Monthly	**S**	See annotated source	**Y**	Yearly
MCC	Median cash compensation				

Occupation/Type/Industry	Location	Per	Low	Mid	High	Source	Date
Medical and Clinical Laboratory Technician	Washington-Arlington-Alexandria MSA, DC-VA-MD-WV	Y	31410 FQ	39540 MW	48530 TQ	USBLS	5/07
	Florida	Y	27030 FQ	34460 MW	43420 TQ	USBLS	5/07
	Fort Lauderdale-Pompano Beach-Deerfield Beach PMSA, FL	Y	26150 FQ	32690 MW	44950 TQ	USBLS	5/07
	Jacksonville MSA, FL	Y	28800 FQ	32840 MW	41040 TQ	USBLS	5/07
	Miami-Fort Lauderdale-Miami Beach MSA, FL	Y	25930 FQ	34390 MW	46440 TQ	USBLS	5/07
	Orlando-Kissimmee MSA, FL	Y	32900 FQ	37930 MW	44620 TQ	USBLS	5/07
	Tampa-St. Petersburg-Clearwater MSA, FL	Y	25360 FQ	30780 MW	38410 TQ	USBLS	5/07
	West Palm Beach-Boca Raton-Boynton Beach PMSA, FL	Y	27760 FQ	37870 MW	49800 TQ	USBLS	5/07
	Georgia	Y	25590 FQ	30320 MW	38210 TQ	USBLS	5/07
	Atlanta-Sandy Springs-Marietta MSA, GA	Y	27030 FQ	31310 MW	39360 TQ	USBLS	5/07
	Hawaii	Y	32180 FQ	39300 MW	49390 TQ	USBLS	5/07
	Honolulu MSA, HI	Y	35160 FQ	43630 MW	51880 TQ	USBLS	5/07
	Idaho	Y	27100 FQ	32930 MW	45690 TQ	USBLS	5/07
	Boise City-Nampa MSA, ID	Y	27620 FQ	34230 MW	45620 TQ	USBLS	5/07
	Illinois	Y	28650 FQ	36840 MW	47910 TQ	USBLS	5/07
	Chicago-Naperville-Joliet MSA, IL-IN-WI	Y	28960 FQ	36560 MW	46220 TQ	USBLS	5/07
	Rockford MSA, IL	Y	29230 FQ	43440 MW	56320 TQ	USBLS	5/07
	Indiana	Y	27740 FQ	35210 MW	45670 TQ	USBLS	5/07
	Gary PMSA, IN	Y	35320 FQ	43180 MW	49360 TQ	USBLS	5/07
	Indianapolis-Carmel MSA, IN	Y	27870 FQ	37530 MW	49470 TQ	USBLS	5/07
	Iowa	Y	29320 FQ	35600 MW	41920 TQ	USBLS	5/07
	Davenport-Moline-Rock Island MSA, IA-IL	Y	26280 FQ	31120 MW	37590 TQ	USBLS	5/07
	Des Moines-West Des Moines MSA, IA	Y	33300 FQ	39210 MW	44760 TQ	USBLS	5/07
	Kansas	Y	22690 FQ	28560 MW	35480 TQ	USBLS	5/07
	Wichita MSA, KS	Y	22790 FQ	29230 MW	34690 TQ	USBLS	5/07
	Kentucky	Y	27418 FQ	33156 MW	41403 TQ	KYBLS	2008
	Lexington-Fayette MSA, KY	Y	27170 FQ	34480 MW	45200 TQ	USBLS	5/07
	Louisville-Jefferson County MSA, KY-IN	Y	26390 FQ	31290 MW	39930 TQ	USBLS	5/07
	Louisiana	H	10.71 FQ	13.37 MW	17.54 TQ	LABLS	1/08-3/08
	Baton Rouge MSA, LA	Y	22700 FQ	28870 MW	37630 TQ	USBLS	5/07
	New Orleans-Metairie-Kenner MSA, LA	Y	22120 FQ	26700 MW	35250 TQ	USBLS	5/07
	Maine	Y	28380 FQ	33630 MW	41450 TQ	USBLS	5/07
	Portland-South Portland-Biddeford MSA, ME	Y	29460 FQ	33720 MW	41790 TQ	USBLS	5/07
	Maryland	Y		41425 MW		MDBLS	3/08
	Baltimore-Towson MSA, MD	Y	28390 FQ	35860 MW	48890 TQ	USBLS	5/07
	Bethesda-Gaithersburg-Frederick PMSA, MD	Y	40800 FQ	47610 MW	56860 TQ	USBLS	5/07
	Massachusetts	Y	29410 FQ	35610 MW	43150 TQ	USBLS	5/07
	Boston-Cambridge-Quincy NECTA, MA	Y	29570 FQ	35550 MW	42160 TQ	USBLS	5/07
	Springfield MSA, MA-CT	Y	28030 FQ	33050 MW	41590 TQ	USBLS	5/07
	Worcester MSA, MA-CT	Y	32130 FQ	37530 MW	44530 TQ	USBLS	5/07
	Michigan	Y	25770 FQ	30760 MW	39350 TQ	USBLS	5/07
	Detroit-Warren-Livonia MSA, MI	Y	26650 FQ	31410 MW	39810 TQ	USBLS	5/07
	Grand Rapids-Wyoming MSA, MI	Y	26230 FQ	30000 MW	34790 TQ	USBLS	5/07
	Warren-Troy-Farmington Hills PMSA, MI	Y	27000 FQ	32810 MW	40830 TQ	USBLS	5/07
	Minnesota	Y	36063 FQ	41671 MW	48335 TQ	MNBLS	10/08-12/08
	Duluth-Superior MSA, MN-WI	Y	35571 FQ	40206 MW	46703 TQ	MNBLS	10/08-12/08
	Minneapolis-Saint Paul MSA, MN-WI	Y	35655 FQ	41660 MW	48063 TQ	MNBLS	10/08-12/08
	Rochester MSA, MN	Y	40846 FQ	47411 MW	54870 TQ	MNBLS	10/08-12/08
	Mississippi	Y	22920 FQ	28750 MW	35310 TQ	USBLS	5/07
	Jackson MSA, MS	Y	22190 FQ	28100 MW	35670 TQ	USBLS	5/07
	Pascagoula MSA, MS	Y	23450 FQ	28220 MW	35470 TQ	USBLS	5/07

AE	Average entry wage	AW	Average wage paid	FQ	First quartile wage	LO	Lowest wage paid	MTC	Median total compensation	TCC	Total cash compensation
AER	Average entry range	AWR	Average wage range	H	Hourly	LR	Low end range	MW	Median wage paid	TQ	Third quartile wage
AEX	Average experienced wage	AXR	Average experienced range	HI	Highest wage paid	M	Monthly	MWR	Median wage range	W	Weekly
ATC	Average total compensation	D	Daily	HR	High end range	MCC	Median cash compensation	S	See annotated source	Y	Yearly

Occupation/Type/Industry	Location	Per	Low	Mid	High	Source	Date
Medical and Clinical Laboratory Technician	Missouri	Y	23900 FQ	29980 MW	39090 TQ	USBLS	5/07
	Kansas City MSA, MO-KS	Y	23810 FQ	29690 MW	37090 TQ	USBLS	5/07
	St. Louis MSA, MO-IL	Y	25910 FQ	32520 MW	43010 TQ	USBLS	5/07
	Montana	Y	26330 FQ	33320 MW	44950 TQ	USBLS	5/07
	Nebraska	Y	24330 FQ	29620 MW	35900 TQ	USBLS	5/07
	Omaha-Council Bluffs MSA, NE-IA	Y	24920 FQ	29820 MW	35940 TQ	USBLS	5/07
	Nevada	H	12.91 FQ	16.02 MW	19.77 TQ	NVBLS	5/08
	Las Vegas-Paradise MSA, NV	H	12.89 FQ	15.82 MW	19.75 TQ	NVBLS	5/08
	Reno-Sparks MSA, NV	H	12.77 FQ	15.87 MW	18.91 TQ	NVBLS	5/08
	New Hampshire	H	13.25 AE	18.25 MW	20.99 AEX	NHBLS	6/08
	Nashua NECTA, NH-MA	Y	41660 FQ	46030 MW	50600 TQ	USBLS	5/07
	New Jersey	Y	31890 FQ	41030 MW	49840 TQ	USBLS	5/07
	Camden PMSA, NJ	Y	31560 FQ	42240 MW	49990 TQ	USBLS	5/07
	Edison PMSA, NJ	Y	30740 FQ	38140 MW	46510 TQ	USBLS	5/07
	Newark-Union PMSA, NJ-PA	Y	38410 FQ	45520 MW	54500 TQ	USBLS	5/07
	New Mexico	Y	27810 FQ	34990 MW	46730 TQ	USBLS	5/07
	Albuquerque MSA, NM	Y	29120 FQ	35000 MW	47720 TQ	USBLS	5/07
	Las Cruces MSA, NM	Y	22640 FQ	27240 MW	31560 TQ	USBLS	5/07
	New York	Y	33000 FQ	40770 MW	51040 TQ	USBLS	5/07
	Albany-Schenectady-Troy MSA, NY	Y	29100 FQ	33750 MW	38750 TQ	USBLS	5/07
	Buffalo-Niagara Falls MSA, NY	Y	32060 FQ	38970 MW	45020 TQ	USBLS	5/07
	Kingston MSA, NY	Y	28370 FQ	34250 MW	39960 TQ	USBLS	5/07
	Nassau-Suffolk PMSA, NY	Y	33910 FQ	43930 MW	53330 TQ	USBLS	5/07
	New York-Northern New Jersey-Long Island MSA, NY-NJ-PA	Y	34440 FQ	42990 MW	52510 TQ	USBLS	5/07
	Syracuse MSA, NY	Y	31470 FQ	40250 MW	52110 TQ	USBLS	5/07
	North Carolina	Y	28630 FQ	34590 MW	41320 TQ	USBLS	5/07
	Charlotte-Gastonia-Concord MSA, NC-SC	Y	30280 FQ	36870 MW	44200 TQ	USBLS	5/07
	Raleigh-Cary MSA, NC	Y	29940 FQ	35860 MW	42520 TQ	USBLS	5/07
	North Dakota	Y	26500 FQ	30350 MW	35680 TQ	USBLS	5/07
	Fargo MSA, ND-MN	Y	25180 FQ	28610 MW	32460 TQ	USBLS	5/07
	Ohio	Y	29630 FQ	34990 MW	40710 TQ	USBLS	5/07
	Canton-Massillon MSA, OH	Y	31230 FQ	36570 MW	43360 TQ	USBLS	5/07
	Cincinnati-Middletown MSA, OH-KY-IN	Y	27940 FQ	32590 MW	39260 TQ	USBLS	5/07
	Cleveland-Elyria-Mentor MSA, OH	Y	29530 FQ	34340 MW	39380 TQ	USBLS	5/07
	Columbus MSA, OH	Y	30530 FQ	35450 MW	41300 TQ	USBLS	5/07
	Dayton MSA, OH	Y	29820 FQ	36060 MW	43540 TQ	USBLS	5/07
	Oklahoma	Y	23460 FQ	29320 MW	37650 TQ	USBLS	5/07
	Oklahoma City MSA, OK	Y	24250 FQ	31930 MW	41480 TQ	USBLS	5/07
	Tulsa MSA, OK	Y	22940 FQ	26620 MW	30530 TQ	USBLS	5/07
	Oregon	H	13.92 FQ	16.87 MW	21.32 TQ	ORBLS	5/08
	Portland-Vancouver-Beaverton MSA, OR-WA	Y	28480 FQ	34510 MW	42630 TQ	USBLS	5/07
	Pennsylvania	Y	28350 FQ	35800 MW	45080 TQ	USBLS	5/07
	Allentown-Bethlehem-Easton MSA, PA-NJ	Y	29270 FQ	35880 MW	42440 TQ	USBLS	5/07
	Philadelphia-Camden-Wilmington MSA, PA-NJ-DE-MD	Y	31830 FQ	40140 MW	48930 TQ	USBLS	5/07
	Pittsburgh MSA, PA	Y	27240 FQ	32820 MW	41940 TQ	USBLS	5/07
	Reading MSA, PA	Y	25500 FQ	35940 MW	49930 TQ	USBLS	5/07
	Rhode Island	Y	43750 FQ	52190 MW	60620 TQ	USBLS	5/07
	Providence-Fall River-Warwick MSA, RI-MA	Y	34710 FQ	47040 MW	57230 TQ	USBLS	5/07
	South Carolina	Y	25640 FQ	31140 MW	37730 TQ	USBLS	5/07
	Charleston-North Charleston MSA, SC	Y	28520 FQ	33710 MW	38330 TQ	USBLS	5/07
	Columbia MSA, SC	Y	23860 FQ	29330 MW	37130 TQ	USBLS	5/07
	South Dakota	Y	26773 FQ	31395 MW	37465 TQ	SDBLS	7/08-9/08
	Sioux Falls MSA, SD	Y	26447 FQ	31096 MW	36865 TQ	SDBLS	7/08-9/08
	Tennessee	Y	24840 FQ	30810 MW	38370 TQ	USBLS	5/07
	Memphis MSA, TN-MS-AR	Y	25550 FQ	30830 MW	38150 TQ	USBLS	5/07
	Nashville-Davidson-Murfreesboro MSA, TN	Y	25710 FQ	30840 MW	37470 TQ	USBLS	5/07

AE	Average entry wage	AW	Average wage paid	FQ	First quartile wage	LO	Lowest wage paid	MTC	Median total compensation	TCC Total cash compensation
AER	Average entry range	AWR	Average wage range	H	Hourly	LR	Low end range	MW	Median wage paid	TQ Third quartile wage
AEX	Average experienced wage	AXR	Average experienced range	HI	Highest wage paid	M	Monthly	MWR	Median wage range	W Weekly
ATC	Average total compensation	D	Daily	HR	High end range	MCC	Median cash compensation	S	See annotated source	Y Yearly

Occupation/Type/Industry	Location	Per	Low	Mid	High	Source	Date
Medical and Clinical Laboratory Technician	Texas	Y	25850 FQ	30850 MW	37970 TQ	USBLS	5/07
	Austin-Round Rock MSA, TX	Y	26370 FQ	32230 MW	40090 TQ	USBLS	5/07
	Beaumont-Port Arthur MSA, TX	Y	23320 FQ	28530 MW	33910 TQ	USBLS	5/07
	Dallas-Fort Worth-Arlington MSA, TX	Y	26960 FQ	31280 MW	37400 TQ	USBLS	5/07
	El Paso MSA, TX	Y	21820 FQ	27900 MW	34680 TQ	USBLS	5/07
	Houston-Sugar Land-Baytown MSA, TX	Y	27060 FQ	32600 MW	42520 TQ	USBLS	5/07
	San Antonio MSA, TX	Y	25400 FQ	31110 MW	37920 TQ	USBLS	5/07
	Utah	Y	22890 FQ	27470 MW	33400 TQ	USBLS	5/07
	St. George MSA, UT	Y	21950 FQ	24260 MW	29040 TQ	USBLS	5/07
	Salt Lake City MSA, UT	Y	23070 FQ	27770 MW	33570 TQ	USBLS	5/07
	Vermont	Y	21410 FQ	25320 MW	37430 TQ	USBLS	5/07
	Burlington-South Burlington MSA, VT	Y	20320 FQ	22630 MW	26300 TQ	USBLS	5/07
	Virginia	Y	26710 FQ	32790 MW	39980 TQ	USBLS	5/07
	Charlottesville MSA, VA	Y	26570 FQ	32690 MW	41600 TQ	USBLS	5/07
	Richmond MSA, VA	Y	27290 FQ	32820 MW	39730 TQ	USBLS	5/07
	Virginia Beach-Norfolk-Newport News MSA, VA-NC	Y	26340 FQ	32260 MW	38610 TQ	USBLS	5/07
	Washington	H	14.55 FQ	17.28 MW	20.24 TQ	WABLS	3/08
	Seattle-Tacoma-Bellevue MSA, WA	Y	30510 FQ	35670 MW	41280 TQ	USBLS	5/07
	West Virginia	Y	24440 FQ	31994 MW	39920 TQ	WVBLS	7/08-9/08
	Charleston MSA, WV	Y	23950 FQ	31960 MW	39820 TQ	USBLS	5/07
	Wisconsin	Y	32980 FQ	38080 MW	44680 TQ	USBLS	5/07
	Appleton MSA, WI	Y	31880 FQ	39000 MW	45290 TQ	USBLS	5/07
	Milwaukee-Waukesha-West Allis MSA, WI	Y	33740 FQ	37710 MW	43470 TQ	USBLS	5/07
	Wyoming	Y	23990 FQ	30050 MW	39067 TQ	WYBLS	9/08
	Cheyenne MSA, WY	Y	26281 FQ	31177 MW	42158 TQ	WYBLS	9/08
	Puerto Rico	Y	13810 FQ	16850 MW	21660 TQ	USBLS	5/07
	San Juan-Caguas-Guaynabo MSA, PR	Y	13500 FQ	15870 MW	20190 TQ	USBLS	5/07
	Virgin Islands	Y	25220 FQ	29200 MW	33820 TQ	USBLS	5/07
Medical and Clinical Laboratory Technologist	Alabama	Y	40040 FQ	46850 MW	54190 TQ	USBLS	5/07
	Birmingham-Hoover MSA, AL	Y	42060 FQ	48900 MW	57180 TQ	USBLS	5/07
	Mobile MSA, AL	Y	40080 FQ	45450 MW	51430 TQ	USBLS	5/07
	Alaska	Y	56910 FQ	64990 MW	74360 TQ	USBLS	5/07
	Anchorage MSA, AK	Y	57130 FQ	65600 MW	74640 TQ	USBLS	5/07
	Arizona	Y	39960 FQ	49220 MW	57410 TQ	USBLS	5/07
	Phoenix-Mesa-Scottsdale MSA, AZ	Y	37820 FQ	48060 MW	56490 TQ	USBLS	5/07
	Prescott MSA, AZ	Y	48230 FQ	55320 MW	61170 TQ	USBLS	5/07
	Tucson MSA, AZ	Y	45200 FQ	51760 MW	58610 TQ	USBLS	5/07
	Arkansas	Y	38720 FQ	46270 MW	54620 TQ	USBLS	5/07
	Jonesboro MSA, AR	Y	35760 FQ	42220 MW	52790 TQ	USBLS	5/07
	Little Rock-North Little Rock MSA, AR	Y	41780 FQ	49710 MW	58340 TQ	USBLS	5/07
	California	H	29.49 FQ	34.57 MW	38.67 TQ	CABLS	1/08-3/08
	Los Angeles-Long Beach-Glendale PMSA, CA	H	30.50 FQ	34.98 MW	38.46 TQ	CABLS	1/08-3/08
	Modesto MSA, CA	H	27.49 FQ	33.48 MW	38.27 TQ	CABLS	1/08-3/08
	Oakland-Fremont-Hayward MSA, CA	H	26.82 FQ	33.69 MW	40.89 TQ	CABLS	1/08-3/08
	Riverside-San Bernardino-Ontario MSA, CA	H	29.37 FQ	33.72 MW	37.45 TQ	CABLS	1/08-3/08
	Sacramento-Arden Arcade-Roseville MSA, CA	H	27.94 FQ	34.62 MW	39.77 TQ	CABLS	1/08-3/08
	San Diego-Carlsbad-San Marcos MSA, CA	H	27.34 FQ	32.00 MW	36.54 TQ	CABLS	1/08-3/08
	San Francisco-San Mateo-Redwood PMSA, CA	H	29.65 FQ	34.94 MW	39.72 TQ	CABLS	1/08-3/08
	San Jose-Sunnyvale-Santa Clara MSA, CA	H	35.18 FQ	39.58 MW	45.87 TQ	CABLS	1/08-3/08
	Santa Ana-Anaheim-Irvine PMSA, CA	Y	53680 FQ	63790 MW	75090 TQ	USBLS	5/07

AE	Average entry wage	AW	Average wage paid	FQ	First quartile wage
AER	Average entry range	AWR	Average wage range	H	Hourly
AEX	Average experienced wage	AXR	Average experienced range	HI	Highest wage paid
ATC	Average total compensation	D	Daily	HR	High end range
LO	Lowest wage paid	MTC	Median total compensation	TCC	Total cash compensation
LR	Low end range	MW	Median wage paid	TQ	Third quartile wage
M	Monthly	MWR	Median wage range	W	Weekly
MCC	Median cash compensation	S	See annotated source	Y	Yearly

Occupation/Type/Industry	Location	Per	Low	Mid	High	Source	Date
Medical and Clinical Laboratory Technologist	Colorado	Y	42140 FQ	52890 MW	61100 TQ	USBLS	5/07
	Denver-Aurora MSA, CO	Y	40450 FQ	52220 MW	61130 TQ	USBLS	5/07
	Fort Collins-Loveland MSA, CO	Y	44340 FQ	53650 MW	61960 TQ	USBLS	5/07
	Connecticut	H	23.50 AE	29.46 MW		CTBLS	1/08-3/08
	Bridgeport-Stamford-Norwalk MSA, CT	Y	53140 FQ	62080 MW	71450 TQ	USBLS	5/07
	Hartford-West Hartford-East Hartford MSA, CT	Y	52510 FQ	58770 MW	64780 TQ	USBLS	5/07
	Delaware	Y	45790 FQ	54470 MW	61630 TQ	USBLS	5/07
	Wilmington PMSA, DE-MD-NJ	Y	47460 FQ	55070 MW	61480 TQ	USBLS	5/07
	District of Columbia	Y	45540 FQ	55400 MW	63320 TQ	USBLS	5/07
	Washington-Arlington-Alexandria MSA, DC-VA-MD-WV	Y	46420 FQ	55450 MW	64270 TQ	USBLS	5/07
	Florida	Y	42850 FQ	49700 MW	58620 TQ	USBLS	5/07
	Fort Lauderdale-Pompano Beach-Deerfield Beach PMSA, FL	Y	46250 FQ	53920 MW	61760 TQ	USBLS	5/07
	Jacksonville MSA, FL	Y	39410 FQ	49120 MW	59180 TQ	USBLS	5/07
	Lakeland MSA, FL	Y	43440 FQ	48640 MW	56220 TQ	USBLS	5/07
	Miami-Fort Lauderdale-Miami Beach MSA, FL	Y	44720 FQ	53270 MW	61120 TQ	USBLS	5/07
	Orlando-Kissimmee MSA, FL	Y	40150 FQ	46240 MW	52690 TQ	USBLS	5/07
	Tampa-St. Petersburg-Clearwater MSA, FL	Y	42640 FQ	48900 MW	57300 TQ	USBLS	5/07
	West Palm Beach-Boca Raton-Boynton Beach PMSA, FL	Y	40500 FQ	51640 MW	60150 TQ	USBLS	5/07
	Georgia	Y	42970 FQ	50660 MW	58840 TQ	USBLS	5/07
	Atlanta-Sandy Springs-Marietta MSA, GA	Y	43870 FQ	52080 MW	59980 TQ	USBLS	5/07
	Hawaii	Y	34200 FQ	50190 MW	60220 TQ	USBLS	5/07
	Honolulu MSA, HI	Y	33430 FQ	47610 MW	60330 TQ	USBLS	5/07
	Idaho	Y	30600 FQ	44330 MW	53410 TQ	USBLS	5/07
	Boise City-Nampa MSA, ID	Y	43550 FQ	50440 MW	58660 TQ	USBLS	5/07
	Illinois	Y	42100 FQ	49100 MW	58200 TQ	USBLS	5/07
	Chicago-Naperville-Joliet MSA, IL-IN-WI	Y	42960 FQ	50020 MW	58940 TQ	USBLS	5/07
	Indiana	Y	39780 FQ	47810 MW	56590 TQ	USBLS	5/07
	Gary PMSA, IN	Y	41880 FQ	48320 MW	55900 TQ	USBLS	5/07
	Indianapolis-Carmel MSA, IN	Y	35880 FQ	47700 MW	57150 TQ	USBLS	5/07
	Iowa	Y	40770 FQ	47520 MW	55410 TQ	USBLS	5/07
	Des Moines-West Des Moines MSA, IA	Y	43260 FQ	51460 MW	59220 TQ	USBLS	5/07
	Iowa City MSA, IA	Y	44030 FQ	50990 MW	57470 TQ	USBLS	5/07
	Sioux City MSA, IA-NE-SD	Y	35390 FQ	43060 MW	51830 TQ	USBLS	5/07
	Waterloo-Cedar Falls MSA, IA	Y	41160 FQ	48830 MW	56010 TQ	USBLS	5/07
	Kansas	Y	41570 FQ	50030 MW	59740 TQ	USBLS	5/07
	Wichita MSA, KS	Y	41180 FQ	50770 MW	58720 TQ	USBLS	5/07
	Kentucky	Y	42944 FQ	50526 MW	58563 TQ	KYBLS	2008
	Elizabethtown MSA, KY	Y	42850 FQ	46410 MW	49970 TQ	USBLS	5/07
	Louisville-Jefferson County MSA, KY-IN	Y	42880 FQ	51330 MW	58510 TQ	USBLS	5/07
	Louisiana	H	16.92 FQ	21.30 MW	25.11 TQ	LABLS	1/08-3/08
	Baton Rouge MSA, LA	Y	25070 FQ	42390 MW	51600 TQ	USBLS	5/07
	New Orleans-Metairie-Kenner MSA, LA	Y	34990 FQ	44080 MW	52300 TQ	USBLS	5/07
	Shreveport-Bossier City MSA, LA	Y	35780 FQ	44870 MW	53760 TQ	USBLS	5/07
	Maine	Y	41300 FQ	47580 MW	55220 TQ	USBLS	5/07
	Portland-South Portland-Biddeford MSA, ME	Y	40300 FQ	46810 MW	52830 TQ	USBLS	5/07
	Maryland	Y		60275 MW		MDBLS	3/08
	Baltimore-Towson MSA, MD	Y	48410 FQ	57840 MW	65950 TQ	USBLS	5/07
	Bethesda-Gaithersburg-Frederick PMSA, MD	Y	56000 FQ	65130 MW	74870 TQ	USBLS	5/07
	Massachusetts	Y	41350 FQ	54020 MW	63430 TQ	USBLS	5/07
	Boston-Cambridge-Quincy NECTA, MA	Y	40050 FQ	53250 MW	63600 TQ	USBLS	5/07
	Worcester MSA, MA-CT	Y	45860 FQ	56810 MW	65880 TQ	USBLS	5/07

AE	Average entry wage	AW	Average wage paid	FQ	First quartile wage	LO	Lowest wage paid	MTC	Median total compensation	TCC	Total cash compensation
AER	Average entry range	AWR	Average wage range	H	Hourly	LR	Low end range	MW	Median wage paid	TQ	Third quartile wage
AEX	Average experienced wage	AXR	Average experienced range	HI	Highest wage paid	M	Monthly	MWR	Median wage range	W	Weekly
ATC	Average total compensation	D	Daily	HR	High end range	MCC	Median cash compensation	S	See annotated source	Y	Yearly

1002

Occupation/Type/Industry	Location	Per	Low	Mid	High	Source	Date
Medical and Clinical Laboratory Technologist							
	Michigan	Y	45810 FQ	52730 MW	59850 TQ	USBLS	5/07
	Detroit-Warren-Livonia MSA, MI	Y	46440 FQ	53220 MW	60480 TQ	USBLS	5/07
	Grand Rapids-Wyoming MSA, MI	Y	46310 FQ	53060 MW	59930 TQ	USBLS	5/07
	Warren-Troy-Farmington Hills PMSA, MI	Y	44950 FQ	52190 MW	61000 TQ	USBLS	5/07
	Minnesota	Y	48398 FQ	56077 MW	64949 TQ	MNBLS	10/08-12/08
	Duluth-Superior MSA, MN-WI	Y	50480 FQ	58400 MW	65179 TQ	MNBLS	10/08-12/08
	Minneapolis-Saint Paul MSA, MN-WI	Y	48251 FQ	57898 MW	65462 TQ	MNBLS	10/08-12/08
	Rochester MSA, MN	Y	48837 FQ	54077 MW	64855 TQ	MNBLS	10/08-12/08
	Mississippi	Y	38700 FQ	46050 MW	53520 TQ	USBLS	5/07
	Hattiesburg MSA, MS	Y	33720 FQ	41040 MW	47400 TQ	USBLS	5/07
	Jackson MSA, MS	Y	39790 FQ	47240 MW	57420 TQ	USBLS	5/07
	Missouri	Y	42760 FQ	50200 MW	58000 TQ	USBLS	5/07
	Joplin MSA, MO	Y	37930 FQ	46370 MW	54890 TQ	USBLS	5/07
	Kansas City MSA, MO-KS	Y	44210 FQ	53760 MW	61640 TQ	USBLS	5/07
	St. Louis MSA, MO-IL	Y	43810 FQ	50680 MW	58180 TQ	USBLS	5/07
	Montana	Y	39510 FQ	47180 MW	56430 TQ	USBLS	5/07
	Billings MSA, MT	Y	45000 FQ	52380 MW	58720 TQ	USBLS	5/07
	Nebraska	Y	36870 FQ	46500 MW	55250 TQ	USBLS	5/07
	Omaha-Council Bluffs MSA, NE-IA	Y	33810 FQ	45380 MW	54560 TQ	USBLS	5/07
	Nevada	H	26.82 FQ	30.75 MW	36.28 TQ	NVBLS	5/08
	Las Vegas-Paradise MSA, NV	H	26.36 FQ	30.59 MW	36.17 TQ	NVBLS	5/08
	New Hampshire	H	21.30 AE	25.05 MW	26.97 AEX	NHBLS	6/08
	Manchester MSA, NH	Y	47670 FQ	54640 MW	60650 TQ	USBLS	5/07
	Nashua NECTA, NH-MA	Y	47060 FQ	53820 MW	60030 TQ	USBLS	5/07
	New Jersey	Y	52170 FQ	58810 MW	66560 TQ	USBLS	5/07
	Camden PMSA, NJ	Y	52370 FQ	57610 MW	63280 TQ	USBLS	5/07
	Edison PMSA, NJ	Y	51420 FQ	58960 MW	67970 TQ	USBLS	5/07
	Newark-Union PMSA, NJ-PA	Y	52680 FQ	59350 MW	68080 TQ	USBLS	5/07
	New Mexico	Y	33030 FQ	45210 MW	54740 TQ	USBLS	5/07
	Albuquerque MSA, NM	Y	28900 FQ	42880 MW	52450 TQ	USBLS	5/07
	New York	Y	47190 FQ	55650 MW	64140 TQ	USBLS	5/07
	Albany-Schenectady-Troy MSA, NY	Y	43590 FQ	49840 MW	57810 TQ	USBLS	5/07
	Buffalo-Niagara Falls MSA, NY	Y	41360 FQ	49170 MW	56710 TQ	USBLS	5/07
	Nassau-Suffolk PMSA, NY	Y	54550 FQ	61990 MW	70860 TQ	USBLS	5/07
	New York-Northern New Jersey-Long Island MSA, NY-NJ-PA	Y	51530 FQ	58860 MW	66950 TQ	USBLS	5/07
	North Carolina	Y	39080 FQ	47050 MW	55670 TQ	USBLS	5/07
	Charlotte-Gastonia-Concord MSA, NC-SC	Y	45390 FQ	53670 MW	60410 TQ	USBLS	5/07
	Raleigh-Cary MSA, NC	Y	39490 FQ	45690 MW	52470 TQ	USBLS	5/07
	North Dakota	Y	39480 FQ	46720 MW	55540 TQ	USBLS	5/07
	Fargo MSA, ND-MN	Y	38770 FQ	45730 MW	54630 TQ	USBLS	5/07
	Ohio	Y	43340 FQ	49270 MW	56040 TQ	USBLS	5/07
	Cincinnati-Middletown MSA, OH-KY-IN	Y	42500 FQ	50380 MW	57980 TQ	USBLS	5/07
	Cleveland-Elyria-Mentor MSA, OH	Y	44500 FQ	49700 MW	55160 TQ	USBLS	5/07
	Columbus MSA, OH	Y	41630 FQ	47490 MW	54650 TQ	USBLS	5/07
	Dayton MSA, OH	Y	42820 FQ	48110 MW	56450 TQ	USBLS	5/07
	Oklahoma	Y	36920 FQ	45330 MW	54720 TQ	USBLS	5/07
	Lawton MSA, OK	Y	41960 FQ	50090 MW	57540 TQ	USBLS	5/07
	Oklahoma City MSA, OK	Y	36070 FQ	46600 MW	58480 TQ	USBLS	5/07
	Tulsa MSA, OK	Y	38290 FQ	45390 MW	53710 TQ	USBLS	5/07
	Oregon	H	24.22 FQ	27.89 MW	31.48 TQ	ORBLS	5/08
	Portland-Vancouver-Beaverton MSA, OR-WA	Y	48820 FQ	56520 MW	64240 TQ	USBLS	5/07
	Pennsylvania	Y	41580 FQ	47750 MW	56700 TQ	USBLS	5/07
	Allentown-Bethlehem-Easton MSA, PA-NJ	Y	41130 FQ	46280 MW	54920 TQ	USBLS	5/07
	Philadelphia-Camden-Wilmington MSA, PA-NJ-DE-MD	Y	45920 FQ	54380 MW	62680 TQ	USBLS	5/07
	Pittsburgh MSA, PA	Y	41590 FQ	46860 MW	52360 TQ	USBLS	5/07

Occupation/Type/Industry	Location	Per	Low	Mid	High	Source	Date
Medical and Clinical Laboratory Technologist	Rhode Island	Y	52130 FQ	58630 MW	65460 TQ	USBLS	5/07
	Providence-Fall River- Warwick MSA, RI-MA	Y	50650 FQ	57640 MW	64650 TQ	USBLS	5/07
	South Carolina	Y	37460 FQ	45270 MW	53680 TQ	USBLS	5/07
	Charleston-North Charleston MSA, SC	Y	37710 FQ	44820 MW	53660 TQ	USBLS	5/07
	Columbia MSA, SC	Y	39600 FQ	47590 MW	56090 TQ	USBLS	5/07
	South Dakota	Y	38286 FQ	46170 MW	55785 TQ	SDBLS	7/08-9/08
	Sioux Falls MSA, SD	Y	39383 FQ	48018 MW	57509 TQ	SDBLS	7/08-9/08
	Tennessee	Y	43930 FQ	51260 MW	58910 TQ	USBLS	5/07
	Clarksville MSA, TN-KY	Y	37410 FQ	43770 MW	51570 TQ	USBLS	5/07
	Memphis MSA, TN-MS-AR	Y	45390 FQ	52380 MW	59360 TQ	USBLS	5/07
	Nashville-Davidson- Murfreesboro MSA, TN	Y	47480 FQ	54210 MW	59840 TQ	USBLS	5/07
	Texas	Y	41380 FQ	48130 MW	56440 TQ	USBLS	5/07
	Austin-Round Rock MSA, TX	Y	41050 FQ	46510 MW	52720 TQ	USBLS	5/07
	Dallas-Fort Worth-Arlington MSA, TX	Y	42730 FQ	49170 MW	57040 TQ	USBLS	5/07
	El Paso MSA, TX	Y	41320 FQ	49280 MW	58260 TQ	USBLS	5/07
	Houston-Sugar Land-Baytown MSA, TX	Y	43290 FQ	50430 MW	58890 TQ	USBLS	5/07
	San Antonio MSA, TX	Y	42550 FQ	49350 MW	57120 TQ	USBLS	5/07
	Utah	Y	41800 FQ	49880 MW	58670 TQ	USBLS	5/07
	Salt Lake City MSA, UT	Y	40840 FQ	48510 MW	57690 TQ	USBLS	5/07
	Vermont	Y	45200 FQ	52440 MW	59190 TQ	USBLS	5/07
	Virginia	Y	40840 FQ	48680 MW	57490 TQ	USBLS	5/07
	Richmond MSA, VA	Y	38770 FQ	47250 MW	56550 TQ	USBLS	5/07
	Virginia Beach-Norfolk- Newport News MSA, VA-NC	Y	40290 FQ	47400 MW	55250 TQ	USBLS	5/07
	Washington	H	24.33 FQ	28.43 MW	32.80 TQ	WABLS	3/08
	Seattle-Tacoma-Bellevue MSA, WA	Y	49780 FQ	58480 MW	67300 TQ	USBLS	5/07
	West Virginia	Y	40636 FQ	47505 MW	54302 TQ	WVBLS	7/08-9/08
	Charleston MSA, WV	Y	40970 FQ	45480 MW	50330 TQ	USBLS	5/07
	Huntington-Ashland MSA, WV-KY-OH	Y	44090 FQ	50140 MW	57880 TQ	USBLS	5/07
	Wisconsin	Y	44820 FQ	52010 MW	59190 TQ	USBLS	5/07
	Green Bay MSA, WI	Y	43330 FQ	52390 MW	60310 TQ	USBLS	5/07
	Milwaukee-Waukesha-West Allis MSA, WI	Y	46410 FQ	53490 MW	60250 TQ	USBLS	5/07
	Racine MSA, WI	Y	47310 FQ	53580 MW	59180 TQ	USBLS	5/07
	Wyoming	Y	46172 FQ	53172 MW	60343 TQ	WYBLS	9/08
	Cheyenne MSA, WY	Y	46543 FQ	52128 MW	60162 TQ	WYBLS	9/08
	Puerto Rico	Y	23670 FQ	26980 MW	30070 TQ	USBLS	5/07
	San Juan-Caguas-Guaynabo MSA, PR	Y	24830 FQ	27410 MW	30050 TQ	USBLS	5/07
	Guam	Y	18770 FQ	27630 MW	43280 TQ	USBLS	5/07
Medical and Health Services Manager	Alabama	Y	56940 FQ	72030 MW	96620 TQ	USBLS	5/07
	Birmingham-Hoover MSA, AL	Y	53710 FQ	71180 MW	96760 TQ	USBLS	5/07
	Huntsville MSA, AL	Y	55290 FQ	65580 MW	84320 TQ	USBLS	5/07
	Alaska	Y	57760 FQ	77490 MW	100910 TQ	USBLS	5/07
	Anchorage MSA, AK	Y	58600 FQ	78870 MW	108470 TQ	USBLS	5/07
	Arizona	Y	46500 FQ	65970 MW	85400 TQ	USBLS	5/07
	Phoenix-Mesa-Scottsdale MSA, AZ	Y	45250 FQ	63650 MW	82960 TQ	USBLS	5/07
	Tucson MSA, AZ	Y	51020 FQ	71380 MW	94530 TQ	USBLS	5/07
	Arkansas	Y	50370 FQ	65540 MW	81520 TQ	USBLS	5/07
	Fayetteville-Springdale-Rogers MSA, AR-MO	Y	59130 FQ	75050 MW	92840 TQ	USBLS	5/07
	Little Rock-North Little Rock MSA, AR	Y	52210 FQ	69130 MW	85370 TQ	USBLS	5/07
	California	H	33.97 FQ	44.98 MW	58.77 TQ	CABLS	1/08-3/08
	Los Angeles-Long Beach- Glendale PMSA, CA	H	36.11 FQ	46.58 MW	60.91 TQ	CABLS	1/08-3/08
	Oakland-Fremont-Hayward MSA, CA	H	35.83 FQ	49.98 MW	63.80 TQ	CABLS	1/08-3/08
	Riverside-San Bernardino- Ontario MSA, CA	H	31.26 FQ	42.12 MW	54.68 TQ	CABLS	1/08-3/08

AE	Average entry wage	AW	Average wage paid	FQ	First quartile wage	LO	Lowest wage paid	MTC	Median total compensation	TCC	Total cash compensation
AER	Average entry range	AWR	Average wage range	H	Hourly	LR	Low end range	MW	Median wage paid	TQ	Third quartile wage
AEX	Average experienced wage	AXR	Average experienced range	HI	Highest wage paid	M	Monthly	MWR	Median wage range	W	Weekly
ATC	Average total compensation	D	Daily	HR	High end range	MCC	Median cash compensation	S	See annotated source	Y	Yearly

1004

Occupation/Type/Industry	Location	Per	Low	Mid	High	Source	Date
Medical and Health Services Manager	Sacramento-Arden Arcade-Roseville MSA, CA	H	37.59 FQ	48.04 MW	61.25 TQ	CABLS	1/08-3/08
	San Diego-Carlsbad-San Marcos MSA, CA	H	35.69 FQ	45.80 MW	57.60 TQ	CABLS	1/08-3/08
	San Francisco-San Mateo-Redwood PMSA, CA	H	35.58 FQ	46.72 MW	62.18 TQ	CABLS	1/08-3/08
	San Jose-Sunnyvale-Santa Clara MSA, CA	H	37.54 FQ	53.29 MW	66.42 TQ	CABLS	1/08-3/08
	Santa Ana-Anaheim-Irvine PMSA, CA	Y	67830 FQ	85890 MW	112330 TQ	USBLS	5/07
	Colorado	Y	60230 FQ	80540 MW	102110 TQ	USBLS	5/07
	Denver-Aurora MSA, CO	Y	66120 FQ	86220 MW	108470 TQ	USBLS	5/07
	Connecticut	H	30.31 AE	42.29 MW		CTBLS	1/08-3/08
	Bridgeport-Stamford-Norwalk MSA, CT	Y	61660 FQ	77120 MW	95830 TQ	USBLS	5/07
	Hartford-West Hartford-East Hartford MSA, CT	Y	72770 FQ	88260 MW	109370 TQ	USBLS	5/07
	Norwich-New London MSA, CT-RI	Y	68490 FQ	83670 MW	101480 TQ	USBLS	5/07
	Waterbury MSA, CT	Y	67840 FQ	85670 MW	110870 TQ	USBLS	5/07
	Delaware	Y	61410 FQ	76070 MW	93410 TQ	USBLS	5/07
	Wilmington PMSA, DE-MD-NJ	Y	62730 FQ	77940 MW	95700 TQ	USBLS	5/07
	District of Columbia	Y	67990 FQ	79660 MW	96640 TQ	USBLS	5/07
	Washington-Arlington-Alexandria MSA, DC-VA-MD-WV	Y	72730 FQ	88010 MW	104000 TQ	USBLS	5/07
	Florida	Y	65320 FQ	83940 MW	112400 TQ	USBLS	5/07
	Fort Lauderdale-Pompano Beach-Deerfield Beach PMSA, FL	Y	67480 FQ	86690 MW	115740 TQ	USBLS	5/07
	Jacksonville MSA, FL	Y	62860 FQ	77160 MW	94610 TQ	USBLS	5/07
	Lakeland MSA, FL	Y	63660 FQ	79360 MW	100890 TQ	USBLS	5/07
	Miami-Fort Lauderdale-Miami Beach MSA, FL	Y	69080 FQ	88130 MW	115610 TQ	USBLS	5/07
	Orlando-Kissimmee MSA, FL	Y	64900 FQ	86030 MW	123390 TQ	USBLS	5/07
	Tampa-St. Petersburg-Clearwater MSA, FL	Y	62520 FQ	83350 MW	117640 TQ	USBLS	5/07
	West Palm Beach-Boca Raton-Boynton Beach PMSA, FL	Y	67550 FQ	82510 MW	103700 TQ	USBLS	5/07
	Georgia	Y	54790 FQ	71450 MW	93760 TQ	USBLS	5/07
	Atlanta-Sandy Springs-Marietta MSA, GA	Y	54920 FQ	73390 MW	97720 TQ	USBLS	5/07
	Hawaii	Y	70520 FQ	85870 MW	104900 TQ	USBLS	5/07
	Honolulu MSA, HI	Y	73030 FQ	87670 MW	106950 TQ	USBLS	5/07
	Idaho	Y	51810 FQ	65060 MW	75780 TQ	USBLS	5/07
	Boise City-Nampa MSA, ID	Y	58310 FQ	68060 MW	76770 TQ	USBLS	5/07
	Illinois	Y	57450 FQ	72740 MW	93260 TQ	USBLS	5/07
	Chicago-Naperville-Joliet MSA, IL-IN-WI	Y	60290 FQ	75840 MW	96440 TQ	USBLS	5/07
	Peoria MSA, IL	Y	62270 FQ	73940 MW		USBLS	5/07
	Indiana	Y	54680 FQ	68780 MW	87040 TQ	USBLS	5/07
	Gary PMSA, IN	Y	56560 FQ	74110 MW	91840 TQ	USBLS	5/07
	Indianapolis-Carmel MSA, IN	Y	58600 FQ	73700 MW	94020 TQ	USBLS	5/07
	Iowa	Y	52200 FQ	64090 MW	81110 TQ	USBLS	5/07
	Cedar Rapids MSA, IA	Y	53090 FQ	67370 MW	80580 TQ	USBLS	5/07
	Des Moines-West Des Moines MSA, IA	Y	55490 FQ	70650 MW	106300 TQ	USBLS	5/07
	Kansas	Y	52230 FQ	65990 MW	81980 TQ	USBLS	5/07
	Topeka MSA, KS	Y	54380 FQ	66110 MW	82270 TQ	USBLS	5/07
	Wichita MSA, KS	Y	53860 FQ	66680 MW	80050 TQ	USBLS	5/07
	Kentucky	Y	60348 FQ	74550 MW	95175 TQ	KYBLS	2008
	Bowling Green MSA, KY	Y	58330 FQ	66060 MW	84810 TQ	USBLS	5/07
	Louisville-Jefferson County MSA, KY-IN	Y	59740 FQ	73250 MW	93830 TQ	USBLS	5/07
	Louisiana	H	24.44 FQ	29.54 MW	36.45 TQ	LABLS	1/08-3/08
	Baton Rouge MSA, LA	Y	53370 FQ	64120 MW	77590 TQ	USBLS	5/07
	New Orleans-Metairie-Kenner MSA, LA	Y	51520 FQ	61820 MW	80210 TQ	USBLS	5/07
	Maine	Y	56110 FQ	70250 MW	91910 TQ	USBLS	5/07
	Lewiston-Auburn MSA, ME	Y	52710 FQ	63920 MW	84550 TQ	USBLS	5/07

AE Average entry wage	**AW** Average wage paid	**FQ** First quartile wage	**LO** Lowest wage paid	**MTC** Median total compensation	**TCC** Total cash compensation
AER Average entry range	**AWR** Average wage range	**H** Hourly	**LR** Low end range	**MW** Median wage paid	**TQ** Third quartile wage
AEX Average experienced wage	**AXR** Average experienced range	**HI** Highest wage paid	**M** Monthly	**MWR** Median wage range	**W** Weekly
ATC Average total compensation	**D** Daily	**HR** High end range	**MCC** Median cash compensation	**S** See annotated source	**Y** Yearly

Medical and Health Services Manager

Occupation/Type/Industry	Location	Per	Low	Mid	High	Source	Date
Medical and Health Services Manager	Portland-South Portland-Biddeford MSA, ME	Y	63930 FQ	85360 MW	119420 TQ	USBLS	5/07
	Maryland	Y		87100 MW		MDBLS	3/08
	Baltimore-Towson MSA, MD	Y	66350 FQ	81400 MW	101410 TQ	USBLS	5/07
	Bethesda-Gaithersburg-Frederick PMSA, MD	Y	76370 FQ	91040 MW	105330 TQ	USBLS	5/07
	Massachusetts	Y	69590 FQ	88840 MW	116580 TQ	USBLS	5/07
	Boston-Cambridge-Quincy NECTA, MA	Y	76830 FQ	97420 MW	125990 TQ	USBLS	5/07
	Worcester MSA, MA-CT	Y	63590 FQ	77900 MW	95900 TQ	USBLS	5/07
	Michigan	Y	60270 FQ	74570 MW	94610 TQ	USBLS	5/07
	Detroit-Warren-Livonia MSA, MI	Y	61300 FQ	76240 MW	99330 TQ	USBLS	5/07
	Grand Rapids-Wyoming MSA, MI	Y	59830 FQ	73050 MW	91220 TQ	USBLS	5/07
	Muskegon-Norton Shores MSA, MI	Y	64280 FQ	74620 MW	84010 TQ	USBLS	5/07
	Warren-Troy-Farmington Hills PMSA, MI	Y	59400 FQ	72540 MW	93060 TQ	USBLS	5/07
	Minnesota	Y	68460 FQ	85132 MW	105912 TQ	MNBLS	10/08-12/08
	Duluth-Superior MSA, MN-WI	Y	59233 FQ	72652 MW	88521 TQ	MNBLS	10/08-12/08
	Minneapolis-Saint Paul MSA, MN-WI	Y	72985 FQ	90564 MW	109687 TQ	MNBLS	10/08-12/08
	Rochester MSA, MN	Y	80633 FQ	98912 MW	122476 TQ	MNBLS	10/08-12/08
	Mississippi	Y	52260 FQ	66360 MW	82090 TQ	USBLS	5/07
	Jackson MSA, MS	Y	52710 FQ	67940 MW	85980 TQ	USBLS	5/07
	Pascagoula MSA, MS	Y	57260 FQ	72350 MW	95130 TQ	USBLS	5/07
	Missouri	Y	53070 FQ	69160 MW	91900 TQ	USBLS	5/07
	Kansas City MSA, MO-KS	Y	54580 FQ	70300 MW	91380 TQ	USBLS	5/07
	St. Joseph MSA, MO-KS	Y	47470 FQ	61170 MW	142300 TQ	USBLS	5/07
	St. Louis MSA, MO-IL	Y	59890 FQ	74310 MW	94870 TQ	USBLS	5/07
	Montana	Y	50530 FQ	66560 MW	82640 TQ	USBLS	5/07
	Billings MSA, MT	Y	49180 FQ	64030 MW	81550 TQ	USBLS	5/07
	Nebraska	Y	53550 FQ	66940 MW	86430 TQ	USBLS	5/07
	Omaha-Council Bluffs MSA, NE-IA	Y	56740 FQ	71360 MW	91960 TQ	USBLS	5/07
	Nevada	H	32.03 FQ	40.31 MW	48.25 TQ	NVBLS	5/08
	Las Vegas-Paradise MSA, NV	H	31.15 FQ	39.44 MW	47.75 TQ	NVBLS	5/08
	New Hampshire	H	27.74 AE	37.97 MW	49.70 AEX	NHBLS	6/08
	Manchester MSA, NH	Y	67390 FQ	87190 MW	102580 TQ	USBLS	5/07
	Nashua NECTA, NH-MA	Y	56120 FQ	69170 MW	81200 TQ	USBLS	5/07
	New Jersey	Y	78390 FQ	92990 MW	113230 TQ	USBLS	5/07
	Camden PMSA, NJ	Y	76260 FQ	90380 MW	107340 TQ	USBLS	5/07
	Edison PMSA, NJ	Y	76300 FQ	90980 MW	110960 TQ	USBLS`	5/07
	Newark-Union PMSA, NJ-PA	Y	80970 FQ	95310 MW	116330 TQ	USBLS	5/07
	New Mexico	Y	54850 FQ	72820 MW	95200 TQ	USBLS	5/07
	Albuquerque MSA, NM	Y	61090 FQ	78260 MW	104430 TQ	USBLS	5/07
	Las Cruces MSA, NM	Y	49240 FQ	69740 MW	91620 TQ	USBLS	5/07
	New York	Y	71670 FQ	90940 MW	115700 TQ	USBLS	5/07
	Albany-Schenectady-Troy MSA, NY	Y	66470 FQ	78710 MW	97080 TQ	USBLS	5/07
	Buffalo-Niagara Falls MSA, NY	Y	65390 FQ	79580 MW	101670 TQ	USBLS	5/07
	Nassau-Suffolk PMSA, NY	Y	81390 FQ	95820 MW	118380 TQ	USBLS	5/07
	New York-Northern New Jersey-Long Island MSA, NY-NJ-PA	Y	79500 FQ	96160 MW	121060 TQ	USBLS	5/07
	North Carolina	Y	60910 FQ	74260 MW	94190 TQ	USBLS	5/07
	Charlotte-Gastonia-Concord MSA, NC-SC	Y	60090 FQ	76990 MW	109140 TQ	USBLS	5/07
	Raleigh-Cary MSA, NC	Y	60610 FQ	75560 MW	96750 TQ	USBLS	5/07
	North Dakota	Y	49850 FQ	62300 MW	84890 TQ	USBLS	5/07
	Fargo MSA, ND-MN	Y	48390 FQ	60810 MW	83260 TQ	USBLS	5/07
	Grand Forks MSA, ND-MN	Y	61090 FQ	77090 MW	98200 TQ	USBLS	5/07
	Ohio	Y	60690 FQ	72770 MW	88540 TQ	USBLS	5/07
	Canton-Massillon MSA, OH	Y	64910 FQ	78250 MW	93220 TQ	USBLS	5/07
	Cincinnati-Middletown MSA, OH-KY-IN	Y	60520 FQ	73350 MW	92670 TQ	USBLS	5/07
	Cleveland-Elyria-Mentor MSA, OH	Y	64090 FQ	75620 MW	92000 TQ	USBLS	5/07
	Columbus MSA, OH	Y	59650 FQ	70650 MW	82510 TQ	USBLS	5/07

AE	Average entry wage	AW	Average wage paid	FQ	First quartile wage	LO	Lowest wage paid	MTC	Median total compensation	TCC	Total cash compensation
AER	Average entry range	AWR	Average wage range	H	Hourly	LR	Low end range	MW	Median wage paid	TQ	Third quartile wage
AEX	Average experienced wage	AXR	Average experienced range	HI	Highest wage paid	M	Monthly	MWR	Median wage range	W	Weekly
ATC	Average total compensation	D	Daily	HR	High end range	MCC	Median cash compensation	S	See annotated source	Y	Yearly

Occupation/Type/Industry	Location	Per	Low	Mid	High	Source	Date
Medical and Health Services Manager							
	Dayton MSA, OH	Y	61770 FQ	75940 MW	94700 TQ	USBLS	5/07
	Mansfield MSA, OH	Y	55640 FQ	70510 MW	80420 TQ	USBLS	5/07
	Oklahoma	Y	47240 FQ	60990 MW	75850 TQ	USBLS	5/07
	Oklahoma City MSA, OK	Y	54100 FQ	65820 MW	81370 TQ	USBLS	5/07
	Tulsa MSA, OK	Y	40100 FQ	55410 MW	72470 TQ	USBLS	5/07
	Oregon	H	29.32 FQ	40.50 MW	51.48 TQ	ORBLS	5/08
	Portland-Vancouver-Beaverton MSA, OR-WA	Y	66870 FQ	88290 MW	112460 TQ	USBLS	5/07
	Pennsylvania	Y	55270 FQ	71100 MW	91040 TQ	USBLS	5/07
	Allentown-Bethlehem-Easton MSA, PA-NJ	Y	53860 FQ	70860 MW	90040 TQ	USBLS	5/07
	Philadelphia-Camden-Wilmington MSA, PA-NJ-DE-MD	Y	63760 FQ	78370 MW	98010 TQ	USBLS	5/07
	Pittsburgh MSA, PA	Y	56950 FQ	71460 MW	90130 TQ	USBLS	5/07
	Rhode Island	Y	71260 FQ	88440 MW	109270 TQ	USBLS	5/07
	Providence-Fall River-Warwick MSA, RI-MA	Y	66790 FQ	83290 MW	105430 TQ	USBLS	5/07
	South Carolina	Y	52810 FQ	68590 MW	86140 TQ	USBLS	5/07
	Charleston-North Charleston MSA, SC	Y	46140 FQ	67830 MW	83890 TQ	USBLS	5/07
	Columbia MSA, SC	Y	55450 FQ	69870 MW	86310 TQ	USBLS	5/07
	South Dakota	Y	60667 FQ	73675 MW	94498 TQ	SDBLS	7/08-9/08
	Sioux Falls MSA, SD	Y	62987 FQ	78280 MW	104791 TQ	SDBLS	7/08-9/08
	Tennessee	Y	53980 FQ	68930 MW	89280 TQ	USBLS	5/07
	Johnson City MSA, TN	Y	47240 FQ	66590 MW	95980 TQ	USBLS	5/07
	Knoxville MSA, TN	Y	49030 FQ	59450 MW	76520 TQ	USBLS	5/07
	Memphis MSA, TN-MS-AR	Y	59260 FQ	73730 MW	93800 TQ	USBLS	5/07
	Nashville-Davidson-Murfreesboro MSA, TN	Y	60200 FQ	77050 MW	97140 TQ	USBLS	5/07
	Texas	Y	54560 FQ	69670 MW	86420 TQ	USBLS	5/07
	Austin-Round Rock MSA, TX	Y	58400 FQ	68370 MW	80440 TQ	USBLS	5/07
	Dallas-Fort Worth-Arlington MSA, TX	Y	54600 FQ	68720 MW	86660 TQ	USBLS	5/07
	El Paso MSA, TX	Y	52680 FQ	66730 MW	83900 TQ	USBLS	5/07
	Houston-Sugar Land-Baytown MSA, TX	Y	60730 FQ	77740 MW	96630 TQ	USBLS	5/07
	San Antonio MSA, TX	Y	59000 FQ	71890 MW	85910 TQ	USBLS	5/07
	Utah	Y	61110 FQ	73750 MW	91120 TQ	USBLS	5/07
	Salt Lake City MSA, UT	Y	61780 FQ	74260 MW	93220 TQ	USBLS	5/07
	Vermont	Y	65490 FQ	83700 MW	117570 TQ	USBLS	5/07
	Burlington-South Burlington MSA, VT	Y	65520 FQ	90190 MW	130450 TQ	USBLS	5/07
	Virginia	Y	62500 FQ	79280 MW	99260 TQ	USBLS	5/07
	Richmond MSA, VA	Y	62760 FQ	79200 MW	98850 TQ	USBLS	5/07
	Virginia Beach-Norfolk-Newport News MSA, VA-NC	Y	54450 FQ	73790 MW	95100 TQ	USBLS	5/07
	Washington	H	42.35 FQ	49.30 MW	61.68 TQ	WABLS	3/08
	Bremerton-Silverdale MSA, WA	Y	86800 FQ	99290 MW	121330 TQ	USBLS	5/07
	Seattle-Tacoma-Bellevue MSA, WA	Y	88670 FQ	103600 MW	129620 TQ	USBLS	5/07
	West Virginia	Y	49205 FQ	62863 MW	83996 TQ	WVBLS	7/08-9/08
	Charleston MSA, WV	Y	45550 FQ	56350 MW	74580 TQ	USBLS	5/07
	Wisconsin	Y	60380 FQ	74840 MW	91970 TQ	USBLS	5/07
	Milwaukee-Waukesha-West Allis MSA, WI	Y	60200 FQ	74490 MW	90160 TQ	USBLS	5/07
	Wyoming	Y	55810 FQ	71546 MW	87653 TQ	WYBLS	9/08
	Cheyenne MSA, WY	Y	60301 FQ	76487 MW	89104 TQ	WYBLS	9/08
	Puerto Rico	Y	32720 FQ	47290 MW	70740 TQ	USBLS	5/07
	San Juan-Caguas-Guaynabo MSA, PR	Y	34230 FQ	49100 MW	69290 TQ	USBLS	5/07
Medical and Public Health Social Worker							
	Alabama	Y	32150 FQ	38200 MW	46050 TQ	USBLS	5/07
	Birmingham-Hoover MSA, AL	Y	34950 FQ	42300 MW	50610 TQ	USBLS	5/07
	Huntsville MSA, AL	Y	34980 FQ	41000 MW	48230 TQ	USBLS	5/07
	Alaska	Y	40490 FQ	52210 MW	61400 TQ	USBLS	5/07
	Anchorage MSA, AK	Y	42020 FQ	51690 MW	61490 TQ	USBLS	5/07
	Arizona	Y	32940 FQ	42720 MW	54190 TQ	USBLS	5/07

AE Average entry wage	**AW** Average wage paid	**FQ** First quartile wage	**LO** Lowest wage paid	**MTC** Median total compensation	**TCC** Total cash compensation
AER Average entry range	**AWR** Average wage range	**H** Hourly	**LR** Low end range	**MW** Median wage paid	**TQ** Third quartile wage
AEX Average experienced wage	**AXR** Average experienced range	**HI** Highest wage paid	**M** Monthly	**MWR** Median wage range	**W** Weekly
ATC Average total compensation	**D** Daily	**HR** High end range	**MCC** Median cash compensation	**S** See annotated source	**Y** Yearly

Occupation/Type/Industry	Location	Per	Low	Mid	High	Source	Date
Medical and Public Health Social Worker							
	Phoenix-Mesa-Scottsdale MSA, AZ	Y	31780 FQ	41880 MW	55090 TQ	USBLS	5/07
	Tucson MSA, AZ	Y	38550 FQ	44560 MW	51500 TQ	USBLS	5/07
	Yuma MSA, AZ	Y	36130 FQ	46020 MW	59480 TQ	USBLS	5/07
	Arkansas	Y	32220 FQ	42100 MW	51380 TQ	USBLS	5/07
	Little Rock-North Little Rock MSA, AR	Y	37770 FQ	46670 MW	55150 TQ	USBLS	5/07
	California	H	21.34 FQ	27.78 MW	34.67 TQ	CABLS	1/08-3/08
	Bakersfield MSA, CA	H	16.85 FQ	19.32 MW	26.67 TQ	CABLS	1/08-3/08
	Los Angeles-Long Beach-Glendale PMSA, CA	H	18.69 FQ	25.84 MW	34.03 TQ	CABLS	1/08-3/08
	Oakland-Fremont-Hayward MSA, CA	H	22.83 FQ	27.86 MW	35.48 TQ	CABLS	1/08-3/08
	Riverside-San Bernardino-Ontario MSA, CA	H	22.16 FQ	27.13 MW	31.59 TQ	CABLS	1/08-3/08
	Sacramento-Arden Arcade-Roseville MSA, CA	H	21.15 FQ	27.89 MW	35.92 TQ	CABLS	1/08-3/08
	San Diego-Carlsbad-San Marcos MSA, CA	H	24.81 FQ	29.37 MW	33.53 TQ	CABLS	1/08-3/08
	San Francisco-San Mateo-Redwood PMSA, CA	H	24.45 FQ	30.54 MW	36.82 TQ	CABLS	1/08-3/08
	San Jose-Sunnyvale-Santa Clara MSA, CA	H	23.22 FQ	28.32 MW	36.57 TQ	CABLS	1/08-3/08
	Santa Ana-Anaheim-Irvine PMSA, CA	Y	45410 FQ	58990 MW	71110 TQ	USBLS	
	Colorado	Y	36140 FQ	43010 MW	51350 TQ	USBLS	
	Denver-Aurora MSA, CO	Y	39320 FQ	45140 MW	52450 TQ	USBLS	
	Connecticut	H	20.13 AE	26.15 MW		CTBLS	1/08-3/08
	Bridgeport-Stamford-Norwalk MSA, CT	Y	44910 FQ	55520 MW	69160 TQ	USBLS	5/07
	Hartford-West Hartford-East Hartford MSA, CT	Y	44710 FQ	51950 MW	62030 TQ	USBLS	5/07
	Delaware	Y	42010 FQ	48130 MW	55670 TQ	USBLS	5/07
	Wilmington PMSA, DE-MD-NJ	Y	43320 FQ	49580 MW	57530 TQ	USBLS	5/07
	District of Columbia	Y	51990 FQ	60850 MW	71570 TQ	USBLS	5/07
	Washington-Arlington-Alexandria MSA, DC-VA-MD-WV	Y	46060 FQ	56880 MW	67000 TQ	USBLS	5/07
	Florida	Y	34090 FQ	42030 MW	50900 TQ	USBLS	5/07
	Fort Lauderdale-Pompano Beach-Deerfield Beach PMSA, FL	Y	38560 FQ	45280 MW	52120 TQ	USBLS	5/07
	Jacksonville MSA, FL	Y	31820 FQ	39330 MW	49890 TQ	USBLS	5/07
	Miami-Fort Lauderdale-Miami Beach MSA, FL	Y	37840 FQ	45650 MW	54700 TQ	USBLS	5/07
	Orlando-Kissimmee MSA, FL	Y	31760 FQ	38050 MW	45810 TQ	USBLS	5/07
	Pensacola-Ferry Pass-Brent MSA, FL	Y	15770 FQ	38610 MW	47500 TQ	USBLS	5/07
	Sarasota-Bradenton-Venice MSA, FL	Y	36650 FQ	45030 MW	57000 TQ	USBLS	5/07
	Tallahassee MSA, FL	Y	19240 FQ	24380 MW	34900 TQ	USBLS	5/07
	Tampa-St. Petersburg-Clearwater MSA, FL	Y	34100 FQ	40620 MW	48290 TQ	USBLS	5/07
	West Palm Beach-Boca Raton-Boynton Beach PMSA, FL	Y	38150 FQ	44810 MW	53100 TQ	USBLS	5/07
	Georgia	Y	33230 FQ	40700 MW	51810 TQ	USBLS	5/07
	Atlanta-Sandy Springs-Marietta MSA, GA	Y	35400 FQ	44540 MW	55700 TQ	USBLS	5/07
	Macon MSA, GA	Y	28690 FQ	32330 MW	47190 TQ	USBLS	5/07
	Hawaii	Y	42880 FQ	53720 MW	65790 TQ	USBLS	5/07
	Honolulu MSA, HI	Y	43730 FQ	53850 MW	65640 TQ	USBLS	5/07
	Idaho	Y	34740 FQ	39630 MW	47910 TQ	USBLS	5/07
	Boise City-Nampa MSA, ID	Y	36610 FQ	41300 MW	53680 TQ	USBLS	5/07
	Illinois	Y	34600 FQ	45470 MW	56620 TQ	USBLS	5/07
	Chicago-Naperville-Joliet MSA, IL-IN-WI	Y	38700 FQ	47740 MW	58430 TQ	USBLS	5/07
	Indiana	Y	33840 FQ	41880 MW	51330 TQ	USBLS	5/07
	Evansville MSA, IN-KY	Y	31180 FQ	36170 MW	45160 TQ	USBLS	5/07
	Fort Wayne MSA, IN	Y	29230 FQ	38210 MW	52890 TQ	USBLS	5/07
	Gary PMSA, IN	Y	41980 FQ	50050 MW	57380 TQ	USBLS	5/07

AE	Average entry wage	AW	Average wage paid	FQ	First quartile wage	LO	Lowest wage paid	MTC	Median total compensation	TCC	Total cash compensation
AER	Average entry range	AWR	Average wage range	H	Hourly	LR	Low end range	MW	Median wage paid	TQ	Third quartile wage
AEX	Average experienced wage	AXR	Average experienced range	HI	Highest wage paid	M	Monthly	MWR	Median wage range	W	Weekly
ATC	Average total compensation	D	Daily	HR	High end range	MCC	Median cash compensation	S	See annotated source	Y	Yearly

1008

Occupation/Type/Industry	Location	Per	Low	Mid	High	Source	Date
Medical and Public Health Social Worker	Indianapolis-Carmel MSA, IN	Y	36970 FQ	44090 MW	52560 TQ	USBLS	5/07
	South Bend-Mishawaka MSA, IN-MI	Y	31610 FQ	43130 MW	53100 TQ	USBLS	5/07
	Iowa	Y	31700 FQ	37830 MW	45960 TQ	USBLS	5/07
	Des Moines-West Des Moines MSA, IA	Y	34390 FQ	42260 MW	51780 TQ	USBLS	5/07
	Iowa City MSA, IA	Y	35790 FQ	42340 MW	48230 TQ	USBLS	5/07
	Kansas	Y	34180 FQ	42240 MW	49000 TQ	USBLS	5/07
	Wichita MSA, KS	Y	39150 FQ	45490 MW	53130 TQ	USBLS	5/07
	Kentucky	Y	32835 FQ	39303 MW	46724 TQ	KYBLS	2008
	Louisville-Jefferson County MSA, KY-IN	Y	32320 FQ	39550 MW	46170 TQ	USBLS	5/07
	Louisiana	H	15.64 FQ	19.42 MW	23.85 TQ	LABLS	1/08-3/08
	Baton Rouge MSA, LA	Y	33260 FQ	39120 MW	46520 TQ	USBLS	5/07
	New Orleans-Metairie-Kenner MSA, LA	Y	33690 FQ	43120 MW	51440 TQ	USBLS	5/07
	Maine	Y	29610 FQ	36760 MW	46180 TQ	USBLS	5/07
	Portland-South Portland-Biddeford MSA, ME	Y	30100 FQ	39630 MW	48390 TQ	USBLS	5/07
	Maryland	Y		53575 MW		MDBLS	3/08
	Baltimore-Towson MSA, MD	Y	42600 FQ	52990 MW	61500 TQ	USBLS	5/07
	Bethesda-Gaithersburg-Frederick PMSA, MD	Y	46090 FQ	56080 MW	65990 TQ	USBLS	5/07
	Massachusetts	Y	36190 FQ	49160 MW	60820 TQ	USBLS	5/07
	Boston-Cambridge-Quincy NECTA, MA	Y	39410 FQ	51700 MW	61500 TQ	USBLS	5/07
	Worcester MSA, MA-CT	Y	27900 FQ	40650 MW	57150 TQ	USBLS	5/07
	Michigan	Y	38890 FQ	46040 MW	54560 TQ	USBLS	5/07
	Detroit-Warren-Livonia MSA, MI	Y	39490 FQ	46460 MW	55450 TQ	USBLS	5/07
	Grand Rapids-Wyoming MSA, MI	Y	40980 FQ	46330 MW	52580 TQ	USBLS	5/07
	Warren-Troy-Farmington Hills PMSA, MI	Y	41780 FQ	47290 MW	56540 TQ	USBLS	5/07
	Minnesota	Y	41660 FQ	49109 MW	57416 TQ	MNBLS	10/08-12/08
	Duluth-Superior MSA, MN-WI	Y	41001 FQ	46797 MW	53137 TQ	MNBLS	10/08-12/08
	Minneapolis-Saint Paul MSA, MN-WI	Y	44077 FQ	51076 MW	59394 TQ	MNBLS	10/08-12/08
	Rochester MSA, MN	Y	48286 FQ	56346 MW	63777 TQ	MNBLS	10/08-12/08
	Mississippi	Y	26680 FQ	33630 MW	41080 TQ	USBLS	5/07
	Jackson MSA, MS	Y	23310 FQ	28910 MW	38680 TQ	USBLS	5/07
	Missouri	Y	30810 FQ	38540 MW	47700 TQ	USBLS	5/07
	Kansas City MSA, MO-KS	Y	33740 FQ	41780 MW	50130 TQ	USBLS	5/07
	St. Louis MSA, MO-IL	Y	34610 FQ	41350 MW	49510 TQ	USBLS	5/07
	Montana	Y	26530 FQ	35340 MW	42420 TQ	USBLS	5/07
	Billings MSA, MT	Y	36420 FQ	39930 MW	51860 TQ	USBLS	5/07
	Nebraska	Y	30160 FQ	36600 MW	44690 TQ	USBLS	5/07
	Omaha-Council Bluffs MSA, NE-IA	Y	32510 FQ	39150 MW	48120 TQ	USBLS	5/07
	Nevada	H	22.46 FQ	26.31 MW	30.72 TQ	NVBLS	5/08
	Las Vegas-Paradise MSA, NV	H	22.41 FQ	26.48 MW	31.49 TQ	NVBLS	5/08
	New Hampshire	H	17.57 AE	23.33 MW	27.96 AEX	NHBLS	6/08
	Nashua NECTA, NH-MA	Y	46170 FQ	57840 MW	73790 TQ	USBLS	5/07
	New Jersey	Y	43520 FQ	51610 MW	59930 TQ	USBLS	5/07
	Camden PMSA, NJ	Y	39070 FQ	47070 MW	57440 TQ	USBLS	5/07
	Edison PMSA, NJ	Y	43110 FQ	49350 MW	57030 TQ	USBLS	5/07
	Newark-Union PMSA, NJ-PA	Y	47080 FQ	55330 MW	62130 TQ	USBLS	5/07
	New Mexico	Y	25070 FQ	40110 MW	51690 TQ	USBLS	5/07
	Albuquerque MSA, NM	Y	18520 FQ	38070 MW	55280 TQ	USBLS	5/07
	New York	Y	38150 FQ	47910 MW	61180 TQ	USBLS	5/07
	Albany-Schenectady-Troy MSA, NY	Y	33540 FQ	40920 MW	52080 TQ	USBLS	5/07
	Buffalo-Niagara Falls MSA, NY	Y	31280 FQ	39150 MW	52820 TQ	USBLS	5/07
	Glens Falls MSA, NY	Y	34800 FQ	37850 MW	40760 TQ	USBLS	5/07
	Nassau-Suffolk PMSA, NY	Y	45180 FQ	55720 MW	65530 TQ	USBLS	5/07
	New York-Northern New Jersey-Long Island MSA, NY-NJ-PA	Y	42680 FQ	52120 MW	63470 TQ	USBLS	5/07
	Utica-Rome MSA, NY	Y	25540 FQ	36870 MW	46400 TQ	USBLS	5/07
	North Carolina	Y	34670 FQ	40530 MW	47980 TQ	USBLS	5/07

AE Average entry wage	**AW** Average wage paid	**FQ** First quartile wage	**LO** Lowest wage paid
AER Average entry range	**AWR** Average wage range	**H** Hourly	**LR** Low end range
AEX Average experienced wage	**AXR** Average experienced range	**HI** Highest wage paid	**M** Monthly
ATC Average total compensation	**D** Daily	**HR** High end range	**MCC** Median cash compensation

MTC Median total compensation	**TCC** Total cash compensation	
MW Median wage paid	**TQ** Third quartile wage	
MWR Median wage range	**W** Weekly	
S See annotated source	**Y** Yearly	

Occupation/Type/Industry	Location	Per	Low	Mid	High	Source	Date
Medical and Public Health Social Worker							
	Charlotte-Gastonia-Concord MSA, NC-SC	Y	36460 FQ	41400 MW	47240 TQ	USBLS	5/07
	Raleigh-Cary MSA, NC	Y	33010 FQ	40090 MW	47960 TQ	USBLS	5/07
	North Dakota	Y	31590 FQ	36410 MW	42070 TQ	USBLS	5/07
	Fargo MSA, ND-MN	Y	34440 FQ	38110 MW	44030 TQ	USBLS	5/07
	Ohio	Y	35540 FQ	42460 MW	49810 TQ	USBLS	5/07
	Cincinnati-Middletown MSA, OH-KY-IN	Y	33580 FQ	42280 MW	49700 TQ	USBLS	5/07
	Cleveland-Elyria-Mentor MSA, OH	Y	37840 FQ	44650 MW	51940 TQ	USBLS	5/07
	Columbus MSA, OH	Y	36190 FQ	41970 MW	49930 TQ	USBLS	5/07
	Dayton MSA, OH	Y	36560 FQ	43300 MW	51640 TQ	USBLS	5/07
	Springfield MSA, OH	Y	37220 FQ	42150 MW	47220 TQ	USBLS	5/07
	Oklahoma	Y	27170 FQ	35860 MW	47760 TQ	USBLS	5/07
	Oklahoma City MSA, OK	Y	27970 FQ	35620 MW	46990 TQ	USBLS	5/07
	Tulsa MSA, OK	Y	31620 FQ	40730 MW	51210 TQ	USBLS	5/07
	Oregon	H	18.30 FQ	24.43 MW	29.89 TQ	ORBLS	5/08
	Portland-Vancouver-Beaverton MSA, OR-WA	Y	39730 FQ	52480 MW	63260 TQ	USBLS	5/07
	Pennsylvania	Y	31840 FQ	40500 MW	50770 TQ	USBLS	5/07
	Allentown-Bethlehem-Easton MSA, PA-NJ	Y	34650 FQ	40260 MW	50350 TQ	USBLS	5/07
	Philadelphia-Camden-Wilmington MSA, PA-NJ-DE-MD	Y	35260 FQ	45050 MW	55240 TQ	USBLS	5/07
	Pittsburgh MSA, PA	Y	33700 FQ	41330 MW	50330 TQ	USBLS	5/07
	Rhode Island	Y	42080 FQ	48750 MW	57500 TQ	USBLS	5/07
	Providence-Fall River-Warwick MSA, RI-MA	Y	34710 FQ	45610 MW	56310 TQ	USBLS	5/07
	South Carolina	Y	29600 FQ	36020 MW	45880 TQ	USBLS	5/07
	Charleston-North Charleston MSA, SC	Y	30140 FQ	40150 MW	51320 TQ	USBLS	5/07
	Columbia MSA, SC	Y	34180 FQ	39610 MW	47660 TQ	USBLS	5/07
	Florence MSA, SC	Y	26740 FQ	30680 MW	36610 TQ	USBLS	5/07
	Spartanburg MSA, SC	Y	34140 FQ	45820 MW	63590 TQ	USBLS	5/07
	South Dakota	Y	29640 FQ	37104 MW	48305 TQ	SDBLS	7/08-9/08
	Sioux Falls MSA, SD	Y	35176 FQ	44053 MW	54856 TQ	SDBLS	7/08-9/08
	Tennessee	Y	33850 FQ	44840 MW	54900 TQ	USBLS	5/07
	Kingsport-Bristol-Bristol MSA, TN-VA	Y	31900 FQ	41250 MW	47660 TQ	USBLS	5/07
	Memphis MSA, TN-MS-AR	Y	41990 FQ	50040 MW	59040 TQ	USBLS	5/07
	Nashville-Davidson-Murfreesboro MSA, TN	Y	35690 FQ	46740 MW	55730 TQ	USBLS	5/07
	Texas	Y	34430 FQ	43790 MW	54210 TQ	USBLS	5/07
	Austin-Round Rock MSA, TX	Y	33290 FQ	41990 MW	49970 TQ	USBLS	5/07
	Dallas-Fort Worth-Arlington MSA, TX	Y	36590 FQ	45620 MW	56690 TQ	USBLS	5/07
	El Paso MSA, TX	Y	34820 FQ	43270 MW	56510 TQ	USBLS	5/07
	Houston-Sugar Land-Baytown MSA, TX	Y	37030 FQ	47820 MW	59160 TQ	USBLS	5/07
	Midland MSA, TX	Y	29870 FQ	43260 MW	57920 TQ	USBLS	5/07
	San Antonio MSA, TX	Y	32480 FQ	41620 MW	51200 TQ	USBLS	5/07
	Utah	Y	35290 FQ	44850 MW	55140 TQ	USBLS	5/07
	Salt Lake City MSA, UT	Y	38500 FQ	47750 MW	56100 TQ	USBLS	5/07
	Vermont	Y	32680 FQ	41920 MW	50700 TQ	USBLS	5/07
	Burlington-South Burlington MSA, VT	Y	39010 FQ	46710 MW	54170 TQ	USBLS	5/07
	Virginia	Y	35530 FQ	45420 MW	56390 TQ	USBLS	5/07
	Richmond MSA, VA	Y	38100 FQ	46150 MW	56520 TQ	USBLS	5/07
	Virginia Beach-Norfolk-Newport News MSA, VA-NC	Y	33610 FQ	38770 MW	49590 TQ	USBLS	5/07
	Washington	H	21.09 FQ	24.50 MW	28.92 TQ	WABLS	3/08
	Seattle-Tacoma-Bellevue MSA, WA	Y	44080 FQ	52110 MW	61110 TQ	USBLS	5/07
	West Virginia	Y	27679 FQ	36105 MW	46097 TQ	WVBLS	7/08-9/08
	Charleston MSA, WV	Y	17860 FQ	28060 MW	43400 TQ	USBLS	5/07
	Wisconsin	Y	36980 FQ	43730 MW	51590 TQ	USBLS	5/07
	Milwaukee-Waukesha-West Allis MSA, WI	Y	37690 FQ	44400 MW	52360 TQ	USBLS	5/07
	Wyoming	Y	30665 FQ	34996 MW	44155 TQ	WYBLS	9/08
	Cheyenne MSA, WY	Y	29743 FQ	32198 MW	34815 TQ	WYBLS	9/08

AE	Average entry wage	AW	Average wage paid	FQ	First quartile wage
AER	Average entry range	AWR	Average wage range	H	Hourly
AEX	Average experienced wage	AXR	Average experienced range	HI	Highest wage paid
ATC	Average total compensation	D	Daily	HR	High end range

LO	Lowest wage paid	MTC	Median total compensation
LR	Low end range	MW	Median wage paid
M	Monthly	MWR	Median wage range
MCC	Median cash compensation	S	See annotated source

TCC	Total cash compensation
TQ	Third quartile wage
W	Weekly
Y	Yearly

Occupation/Type/Industry	Location	Per	Low	Mid	High	Source	Date
Medical and Public Health Social Worker	Puerto Rico	Y	17490 FQ	22040 MW	26990 TQ	USBLS	5/07
	San Juan-Caguas-Guaynabo MSA, PR	Y	17690 FQ	22520 MW	27670 TQ	USBLS	5/07
	Virgin Islands	Y	29800 FQ	33560 MW	38260 TQ	USBLS	5/07
Medical Appliance Technician	Alabama	Y	24100 FQ	33240 MW	39800 TQ	USBLS	5/07
	Arizona	Y	22640 FQ	27480 MW	43970 TQ	USBLS	5/07
	Phoenix-Mesa-Scottsdale MSA, AZ	Y	25110 FQ	32150 MW	52560 TQ	USBLS	5/07
	Tucson MSA, AZ	Y	21400 FQ	24400 MW	38070 TQ	USBLS	5/07
	Arkansas	Y	21830 FQ	23920 MW	26930 TQ	USBLS	5/07
	Little Rock-North Little Rock MSA, AR	Y	21960 FQ	23470 MW	24980 TQ	USBLS	5/07
	California	H	12.58 FQ	16.36 MW	21.32 TQ	CABLS	1/08-3/08
	Los Angeles-Long Beach-Glendale PMSA, CA	H	16.35 FQ	20.36 MW	27.57 TQ	CABLS	1/08-3/08
	Oakland-Fremont-Hayward MSA, CA	H	16.56 FQ	20.58 MW	25.68 TQ	CABLS	1/08-3/08
	Riverside-San Bernardino-Ontario MSA, CA	H	11.92 FQ	15.10 MW	19.76 TQ	CABLS	1/08-3/08
	San Diego-Carlsbad-San Marcos MSA, CA	H	11.69 FQ	15.06 MW	21.63 TQ	CABLS	1/08-3/08
	San Francisco-San Mateo-Redwood PMSA, CA	H	17.27 FQ	19.94 MW	27.55 TQ	CABLS	1/08-3/08
	San Jose-Sunnyvale-Santa Clara MSA, CA	H	16.40 FQ	20.56 MW	24.17 TQ	CABLS	1/08-3/08
	Santa Ana-Anaheim-Irvine PMSA, CA	Y	24330 FQ	30050 MW	38200 TQ	USBLS	5/07
	Colorado	Y	23010 FQ	34540 MW	49930 TQ	USBLS	5/07
	Denver-Aurora MSA, CO	Y	22570 FQ	41310 MW	53190 TQ	USBLS	5/07
	Connecticut	H	13.14 AE	17.42 MW		CTBLS	1/08-3/08
	Bridgeport-Stamford-Norwalk MSA, CT	Y	29890 FQ	37170 MW	43950 TQ	USBLS	5/07
	Hartford-West Hartford-East Hartford MSA, CT	Y	27520 FQ	33210 MW	37270 TQ	USBLS	5/07
	Wilmington PMSA, DE-MD-NJ	Y	22350 FQ	28790 MW	39270 TQ	USBLS	5/07
	Florida	Y	22450 FQ	28850 MW	42210 TQ	USBLS	5/07
	Jacksonville MSA, FL	Y	27880 FQ	30760 MW	46110 TQ	USBLS	5/07
	Miami-Fort Lauderdale-Miami Beach MSA, FL	Y	22940 FQ	32920 MW	51260 TQ	USBLS	5/07
	Tampa-St. Petersburg-Clearwater MSA, FL	Y	19710 FQ	27080 MW	31240 TQ	USBLS	5/07
	West Palm Beach-Boca Raton-Boynton Beach PMSA, FL	Y	23200 FQ	34780 MW	55100 TQ	USBLS	5/07
	Georgia	Y	22860 FQ	29760 MW	38490 TQ	USBLS	5/07
	Atlanta-Sandy Springs-Marietta MSA, GA	Y	19070 FQ	23770 MW	35170 TQ	USBLS	5/07
	Illinois	Y	25180 FQ	32460 MW	43880 TQ	USBLS	5/07
	Chicago-Naperville-Joliet MSA, IL-IN-WI	Y	30170 FQ	36920 MW	52590 TQ	USBLS	5/07
	Indiana	Y	25980 FQ	31690 MW	44560 TQ	USBLS	5/07
	Indianapolis-Carmel MSA, IN	Y	28070 FQ	35840 MW	42770 TQ	USBLS	5/07
	Iowa	Y	22980 FQ	33700 MW	37870 TQ	USBLS	5/07
	Des Moines-West Des Moines MSA, IA	Y	33910 FQ	36270 MW	38630 TQ	USBLS	5/07
	Kansas	Y	26850 FQ	28750 MW	30660 TQ	USBLS	5/07
	Kentucky	Y	23535 FQ	30051 MW	37187 TQ	KYBLS	2008
	Louisville-Jefferson County MSA, KY-IN	Y	25340 FQ	31670 MW	37080 TQ	USBLS	5/07
	Louisiana	H	11.13 FQ	15.27 MW	20.31 TQ	LABLS	1/08-3/08
	New Orleans-Metairie-Kenner MSA, LA	Y	21220 FQ	29070 MW	43010 TQ	USBLS	5/07
	Maryland	Y		38550 MW		MDBLS	3/08
	Baltimore-Towson MSA, MD	Y	29100 FQ	38690 MW	48270 TQ	USBLS	5/07
	Massachusetts	Y	31210 FQ	38820 MW	53830 TQ	USBLS	5/07
	Boston-Cambridge-Quincy NECTA, MA	Y	33320 FQ	43410 MW	62770 TQ	USBLS	5/07
	Worcester MSA, MA-CT	Y	32630 FQ	37230 MW	44900 TQ	USBLS	5/07
	Michigan	Y	30610 FQ	40500 MW	54080 TQ	USBLS	5/07

AE	Average entry wage	**AW**	Average wage paid	**FQ**	First quartile wage	**LO**	Lowest wage paid
AER	Average entry range	**AWR**	Average wage range	**H**	Hourly	**LR**	Low end range
AEX	Average experienced wage	**AXR**	Average experienced range	**HI**	Highest wage paid	**M**	Monthly
ATC	Average total compensation	**D**	Daily	**HR**	High end range	**MCC**	Median cash compensation

MTC Median total compensation	**TCC** Total cash compensation
MW Median wage paid	**TQ** Third quartile wage
MWR Median wage range	**W** Weekly
S See annotated source	**Y** Yearly

Occupation/Type/Industry	Location	Per	Low	Mid	High	Source	Date
Medical Appliance Technician	Detroit-Warren-Livonia MSA, MI	Y	40180 FQ	50680 MW	58220 TQ	USBLS	5/07
	Lansing-East Lansing MSA, MI	Y	30300 FQ	39930 MW	52060 TQ	USBLS	5/07
	Warren-Troy-Farmington Hills PMSA, MI	Y	41510 FQ	51650 MW	58650 TQ	USBLS	5/07
	Minnesota	Y	34272 FQ	45873 MW	56436 TQ	MNBLS	10/08-12/08
	Minneapolis-Saint Paul MSA, MN-WI	Y	31079 FQ	36864 MW	45261 TQ	MNBLS	10/08-12/08
	Mississippi	Y	20290 FQ	27260 MW	41670 TQ	USBLS	5/07
	Jackson MSA, MS	Y	19890 FQ	25850 MW	33820 TQ	USBLS	5/07
	Missouri	Y	29240 FQ	45490 MW	53190 TQ	USBLS	5/07
	St. Louis MSA, MO-IL	Y	37990 FQ	50570 MW	55500 TQ	USBLS	5/07
	Nebraska	Y	28840 FQ	39260 MW	54420 TQ	USBLS	5/07
	Omaha-Council Bluffs MSA, NE-IA	Y	35260 FQ	45510 MW	56700 TQ	USBLS	5/07
	Nevada	H	14.31 FQ	19.42 MW	23.19 TQ	NVBLS	5/08
	Las Vegas-Paradise MSA, NV	H	19.06 FQ	22.98 MW	37.06 TQ	NVBLS	5/08
	New Hampshire	H	12.48 AE	23.32 MW	26.55 AEX	NHBLS	6/08
	New Jersey	Y	27080 FQ	42080 MW	57300 TQ	USBLS	5/07
	Edison PMSA, NJ	Y	32020 FQ	41820 MW	54400 TQ	USBLS	5/07
	New Mexico	Y	30880 FQ	36230 MW	43250 TQ	USBLS	5/07
	New York	Y	20660 FQ	27430 MW	33800 TQ	USBLS	5/07
	Buffalo-Niagara Falls MSA, NY	Y	16600 FQ	18070 MW	22420 TQ	USBLS	5/07
	Nassau-Suffolk PMSA, NY	Y	23830 FQ	35190 MW	48450 TQ	USBLS	5/07
	New York-Northern New Jersey-Long Island MSA, NY-NJ-PA	Y	29340 FQ	36180 MW	53750 TQ	USBLS	5/07
	North Carolina	Y	30310 FQ	36870 MW	44360 TQ	USBLS	5/07
	Ohio	Y	24940 FQ	32330 MW	36240 TQ	USBLS	5/07
	Cincinnati-Middletown MSA, OH-KY-IN	Y	22830 FQ	26450 MW	35380 TQ	USBLS	5/07
	Cleveland-Elyria-Mentor MSA, OH	Y	30820 FQ	34710 MW	39390 TQ	USBLS	5/07
	Columbus MSA, OH	Y	28710 FQ	32960 MW	36420 TQ	USBLS	5/07
	Oklahoma	Y	20210 FQ	22620 MW	33930 TQ	USBLS	5/07
	Oregon	H	12.97 FQ	16.82 MW	19.21 TQ	ORBLS	5/08
	Portland-Vancouver-Beaverton MSA, OR-WA	Y	21890 FQ	31810 MW	38100 TQ	USBLS	5/07
	Pennsylvania	Y	26460 FQ	34910 MW	46510 TQ	USBLS	5/07
	Allentown-Bethlehem-Easton MSA, PA-NJ	Y	25730 FQ	50930 MW	66640 TQ	USBLS	5/07
	Philadelphia-Camden-Wilmington MSA, PA-NJ-DE-MD	Y	30250 FQ	41920 MW	64900 TQ	USBLS	5/07
	Pittsburgh MSA, PA	Y	22050 FQ	28240 MW	39960 TQ	USBLS	5/07
	Rhode Island	Y	16240 FQ	17090 MW	17940 TQ	USBLS	5/07
	Providence-Fall River-Warwick MSA, RI-MA	Y	16240 FQ	17090 MW	17940 TQ	USBLS	5/07
	South Carolina	Y	21080 FQ	25710 MW	34010 TQ	USBLS	5/07
	South Dakota	Y	31482 FQ	33477 MW	36178 TQ	SDBLS	7/08-9/08
	Tennessee	Y	23440 FQ	28610 MW	38490 TQ	USBLS	5/07
	Texas	Y	24100 FQ	31990 MW	39830 TQ	USBLS	5/07
	Austin-Round Rock MSA, TX	Y	25070 FQ	32380 MW	40370 TQ	USBLS	5/07
	Dallas-Fort Worth-Arlington MSA, TX	Y	19620 FQ	24210 MW	37350 TQ	USBLS	5/07
	Houston-Sugar Land-Baytown MSA, TX	Y	33410 FQ	37200 MW	40910 TQ	USBLS	5/07
	San Antonio MSA, TX	Y	20450 FQ	30330 MW	37530 TQ	USBLS	5/07
	Utah	Y	23630 FQ	29870 MW	35920 TQ	USBLS	5/07
	Salt Lake City MSA, UT	Y	26400 FQ	30940 MW	37430 TQ	USBLS	5/07
	Virginia	Y	29130 FQ	39310 MW	75650 TQ	USBLS	5/07
	Richmond MSA, VA	Y	26280 FQ	32980 MW	45330 TQ	USBLS	5/07
	Virginia Beach-Norfolk-Newport News MSA, VA-NC	Y	31450 FQ	35230 MW	54320 TQ	USBLS	5/07
	Washington	H	13.19 FQ	17.40 MW	22.34 TQ	WABLS	3/08
	Seattle-Tacoma-Bellevue MSA, WA	Y	35060 FQ	44740 MW	51000 TQ	USBLS	5/07
	West Virginia	Y	26313 FQ	34078 MW	38961 TQ	WVBLS	7/08-9/08
	Wisconsin	Y	23460 FQ	27860 MW	36620 TQ	USBLS	5/07
	Milwaukee-Waukesha-West Allis MSA, WI	Y	26930 FQ	30790 MW	46780 TQ	USBLS	5/07

AE	Average entry wage	AW	Average wage paid	FQ	First quartile wage	LO	Lowest wage paid	MTC	Median total compensation	TCC	Total cash compensation
AER	Average entry range	AWR	Average wage range	H	Hourly	LR	Low end range	MW	Median wage paid	TQ	Third quartile wage
AEX	Average experienced wage	AXR	Average experienced range	HI	Highest wage paid	M	Monthly	MWR	Median wage range	W	Weekly
ATC	Average total compensation	D	Daily	HR	High end range	MCC	Median cash compensation	S	See annotated source	Y	Yearly

Occupation/Type/Industry	Location	Per	Low	Mid	High	Source	Date
Medical Appliance Technician	Puerto Rico	Y	16910 FQ	22340 MW	33580 TQ	USBLS	5/07
Medical Assistant	United States	Y		27200 AW		AAHS	2009
	Alabama	Y	19600 FQ	23210 MW	27640 TQ	USBLS	5/07
	Birmingham-Hoover MSA, AL	Y	21500 FQ	25300 MW	30410 TQ	USBLS	5/07
	Montgomery MSA, AL	Y	20620 FQ	25570 MW	30010 TQ	USBLS	5/07
	Alaska	Y	28670 FQ	32550 MW	38240 TQ	USBLS	5/07
	Anchorage MSA, AK	Y	29060 FQ	33130 MW	38930 TQ	USBLS	5/07
	Arizona	Y	24110 FQ	28050 MW	32120 TQ	USBLS	5/07
	Phoenix-Mesa-Scottsdale MSA, AZ	Y	24950 FQ	28850 MW	33120 TQ	USBLS	5/07
	Prescott MSA, AZ	Y	23940 FQ	27570 MW	30250 TQ	USBLS	5/07
	Tucson MSA, AZ	Y	22730 FQ	26010 MW	29710 TQ	USBLS	5/07
	Arkansas	Y	20720 FQ	23450 MW	27410 TQ	USBLS	5/07
	Jonesboro MSA, AR	Y	18330 FQ	20860 MW	24110 TQ	USBLS	5/07
	Little Rock-North Little Rock MSA, AR	Y	21560 FQ	23850 MW	27950 TQ	USBLS	5/07
	California	H	11.79 FQ	14.34 MW	17.87 TQ	CABLS	1/08-3/08
	Los Angeles-Long Beach-Glendale PMSA, CA	H	12.10 FQ	14.88 MW	18.37 TQ	CABLS	1/08-3/08
	Oakland-Fremont-Hayward MSA, CA	H	13.72 FQ	16.48 MW	21.29 TQ	CABLS	1/08-3/08
	Riverside-San Bernardino-Ontario MSA, CA	H	10.65 FQ	12.38 MW	14.96 TQ	CABLS	1/08-3/08
	Sacramento-Arden Arcade-Roseville MSA, CA	H	11.40 FQ	14.14 MW	17.87 TQ	CABLS	1/08-3/08
	San Diego-Carlsbad-San Marcos MSA, CA	H	11.28 FQ	13.32 MW	15.63 TQ	CABLS	1/08-3/08
	San Francisco-San Mateo-Redwood PMSA, CA	H	14.80 FQ	18.29 MW	22.63 TQ	CABLS	1/08-3/08
	San Jose-Sunnyvale-Santa Clara MSA, CA	H	14.44 FQ	17.77 MW	20.77 TQ	CABLS	1/08-3/08
	Santa Ana-Anaheim-Irvine PMSA, CA	Y	25070 FQ	29160 MW	35610 TQ	USBLS	5/07
	Stockton MSA, CA	H	10.80 FQ	12.61 MW	14.68 TQ	CABLS	1/08-3/08
	Colorado	Y	26060 FQ	29970 MW	35280 TQ	USBLS	5/07
	Colorado Springs MSA, CO	Y	24020 FQ	27650 MW	31210 TQ	USBLS	5/07
	Denver-Aurora MSA, CO	Y	27170 FQ	31230 MW	36440 TQ	USBLS	5/07
	Connecticut	H	13.08 AE	15.50 MW		CTBLS	1/08-3/08
	Bridgeport-Stamford-Norwalk MSA, CT	Y	28030 FQ	32710 MW	37670 TQ	USBLS	5/07
	Hartford-West Hartford-East Hartford MSA, CT	Y	27570 FQ	31080 MW	36570 TQ	USBLS	5/07
	Delaware	Y	26150 FQ	29850 MW	35460 TQ	USBLS	5/07
	Wilmington PMSA, DE-MD-NJ	Y	26030 FQ	29430 MW	34380 TQ	USBLS	5/07
	District of Columbia	Y	29850 FQ	35020 MW	41810 TQ	USBLS	5/07
	Washington-Arlington-Alexandria MSA, DC-VA-MD-WV	Y	26980 FQ	31140 MW	36750 TQ	USBLS	5/07
	Florida	Y	22460 FQ	26290 MW	30680 TQ	USBLS	5/07
	Fort Lauderdale-Pompano Beach-Deerfield Beach PMSA, FL	Y	23790 FQ	27620 MW	31290 TQ	USBLS	5/07
	Jacksonville MSA, FL	Y	22840 FQ	26650 MW	31150 TQ	USBLS	5/07
	Miami-Fort Lauderdale-Miami Beach MSA, FL	Y	23130 FQ	27750 MW	32270 TQ	USBLS	5/07
	Orlando-Kissimmee MSA, FL	Y	22730 FQ	25870 MW	29740 TQ	USBLS	5/07
	Pensacola-Ferry Pass-Brent MSA, FL	Y	20370 FQ	23390 MW	27060 TQ	USBLS	5/07
	Tampa-St. Petersburg-Clearwater MSA, FL	Y	22200 FQ	25270 MW	29750 TQ	USBLS	5/07
	West Palm Beach-Boca Raton-Boynton Beach PMSA, FL	Y	25920 FQ	29120 MW	32960 TQ	USBLS	5/07
	Georgia	Y	22930 FQ	27610 MW	31870 TQ	USBLS	5/07
	Atlanta-Sandy Springs-Marietta MSA, GA	Y	25670 FQ	29470 MW	33060 TQ	USBLS	5/07
	Hawaii	Y	25520 FQ	29600 MW	34740 TQ	USBLS	5/07
	Honolulu MSA, HI	Y	25400 FQ	29560 MW	34650 TQ	USBLS	5/07
	Idaho	Y	22390 FQ	27620 MW	35930 TQ	USBLS	5/07
	Boise City-Nampa MSA, ID	Y	23920 FQ	29950 MW	40450 TQ	USBLS	5/07
	Lewiston MSA, ID-WA	Y	24530 FQ	27430 MW	30440 TQ	USBLS	5/07

AE	Average entry wage	AW	Average wage paid	FQ	First quartile wage
AER	Average entry range	AWR	Average wage range	H	Hourly
AEX	Average experienced wage	AXR	Average experienced range	HI	Highest wage paid
ATC	Average total compensation	D	Daily	HR	High end range

LO	Lowest wage paid	MTC	Median total compensation	TCC Total cash compensation
LR	Low end range	MW	Median wage paid	TQ Third quartile wage
M	Monthly	MWR	Median wage range	W Weekly
MCC	Median cash compensation	S	See annotated source	Y Yearly

Occupation/Type/Industry	Location	Per	Low	Mid	High	Source	Date
Medical Assistant	Pocatello MSA, ID	Y	25640 FQ	27800 MW	29850 TQ	USBLS	5/07
	Illinois	Y	23710 FQ	28070 MW	32870 TQ	USBLS	5/07
	Chicago-Naperville-Joliet MSA, IL-IN-WI	Y	24230 FQ	28580 MW	33550 TQ	USBLS	5/07
	Indiana	Y	22700 FQ	26220 MW	30310 TQ	USBLS	5/07
	Gary PMSA, IN	Y	21170 FQ	24150 MW	29180 TQ	USBLS	5/07
	Indianapolis-Carmel MSA, IN	Y	25200 FQ	28640 MW	33080 TQ	USBLS	5/07
	Iowa	Y	22940 FQ	27190 MW	31520 TQ	USBLS	5/07
	Des Moines-West Des Moines MSA, IA	Y	26490 FQ	30370 MW	34660 TQ	USBLS	5/07
	Kansas	Y	21470 FQ	25010 MW	29420 TQ	USBLS	5/07
	Wichita MSA, KS	Y	21420 FQ	24150 MW	27780 TQ	USBLS	5/07
	Kentucky	Y	21642 FQ	25088 MW	29918 TQ	KYBLS	2008
	Louisville-Jefferson County MSA, KY-IN	Y	23310 FQ	27190 MW	30770 TQ	USBLS	5/07
	Louisiana	H	8.68 FQ	10.54 MW	12.74 TQ	LABLS	1/08-3/08
	Baton Rouge MSA, LA	Y	18780 FQ	22050 MW	26170 TQ	USBLS	5/07
	New Orleans-Metairie-Kenner MSA, LA	Y	17720 FQ	22340 MW	27750 TQ	USBLS	5/07
	Shreveport-Bossier City MSA, LA	Y	20050 FQ	23540 MW	28150 TQ	USBLS	5/07
	Maine	Y	23330 FQ	27610 MW	32090 TQ	USBLS	5/07
	Lewiston-Auburn MSA, ME	Y	22460 FQ	24890 MW	28830 TQ	USBLS	5/07
	Portland-South Portland-Biddeford MSA, ME	Y	27260 FQ	30950 MW	35770 TQ	USBLS	5/07
	Maryland	Y		29625 MW		MDBLS	3/08
	Baltimore-Towson MSA, MD	Y	24130 FQ	28500 MW	33080 TQ	USBLS	5/07
	Bethesda-Gaithersburg-Frederick PMSA, MD	Y	27910 FQ	31260 MW	36210 TQ	USBLS	5/07
	Hagerstown-Martinsburg MSA, MD-WV	Y	24060 FQ	27930 MW	31840 TQ	USBLS	5/07
	Massachusetts	Y	27340 FQ	31770 MW	37830 TQ	USBLS	5/07
	Barnstable Town MSA, MA	Y	30950 FQ	36020 MW	40800 TQ	USBLS	5/07
	Boston-Cambridge-Quincy NECTA, MA	Y	28620 FQ	33640 MW	39460 TQ	USBLS	5/07
	New Bedford MSA, MA	Y	25380 FQ	29040 MW	37670 TQ	USBLS	5/07
	Worcester MSA, MA-CT	Y	26860 FQ	31240 MW	38210 TQ	USBLS	5/07
	Michigan	Y	23600 FQ	27420 MW	31540 TQ	USBLS	5/07
	Detroit-Warren-Livonia MSA, MI	Y	24180 FQ	27880 MW	31890 TQ	USBLS	5/07
	Grand Rapids-Wyoming MSA, MI	Y	22670 FQ	26540 MW	31600 TQ	USBLS	5/07
	Warren-Troy-Farmington Hills PMSA, MI	Y	24610 FQ	28630 MW	32730 TQ	USBLS	5/07
	Minnesota	Y	27519 FQ	31953 MW	37829 TQ	MNBLS	10/08-12/08
	Duluth-Superior MSA, MN-WI	Y	23410 FQ	27247 MW	31127 TQ	MNBLS	10/08-12/08
	Minneapolis-Saint Paul MSA, MN-WI	Y	29056 FQ	33510 MW	38822 TQ	MNBLS	10/08-12/08
	Rochester MSA, MN	Y	32526 FQ	39264 MW	47150 TQ	MNBLS	10/08-12/08
	Mississippi	Y	19160 FQ	23390 MW	27970 TQ	USBLS	5/07
	Hattiesburg MSA, MS	Y	18430 FQ	23740 MW	27450 TQ	USBLS	5/07
	Jackson MSA, MS	Y	20980 FQ	24900 MW	29210 TQ	USBLS	5/07
	Missouri	Y	21290 FQ	24730 MW	29680 TQ	USBLS	5/07
	Kansas City MSA, MO-KS	Y	24840 FQ	28400 MW	31640 TQ	USBLS	5/07
	St. Louis MSA, MO-IL	Y	21840 FQ	25140 MW	30140 TQ	USBLS	5/07
	Montana	Y	21920 FQ	26090 MW	29800 TQ	USBLS	5/07
	Billings MSA, MT	Y	22770 FQ	26070 MW	29160 TQ	USBLS	5/07
	Missoula MSA, MT	Y	22750 FQ	25180 MW	29250 TQ	USBLS	5/07
	Nebraska	Y	22580 FQ	25840 MW	29900 TQ	USBLS	5/07
	Omaha-Council Bluffs MSA, NE-IA	Y	24660 FQ	27650 MW	31200 TQ	USBLS	5/07
	Nevada	H	12.49 FQ	14.30 MW	16.71 TQ	NVBLS	5/08
	Las Vegas-Paradise MSA, NV	H	12.41 FQ	14.10 MW	16.28 TQ	NVBLS	5/08
	New Hampshire	H	12.98 AE	14.85 MW	16.14 AEX	NHBLS	6/08
	Manchester MSA, NH	Y	27660 FQ	30760 MW	34630 TQ	USBLS	5/07
	Nashua NECTA, NH-MA	Y	26570 FQ	30290 MW	35090 TQ	USBLS	5/07
	Rochester-Dover MSA, NH-ME	Y	25620 FQ	28680 MW	32380 TQ	USBLS	5/07
	New Jersey	Y	26380 FQ	30910 MW	36880 TQ	USBLS	5/07
	Camden PMSA, NJ	Y	24880 FQ	29020 MW	32670 TQ	USBLS	5/07
	Edison PMSA, NJ	Y	26520 FQ	30110 MW	35220 TQ	USBLS	5/07
	Newark-Union PMSA, NJ-PA	Y	27740 FQ	33380 MW	38350 TQ	USBLS	5/07

AE	Average entry wage	AW	Average wage paid	FQ	First quartile wage
AER	Average entry range	AWR	Average wage range	H	Hourly
AEX	Average experienced wage	AXR	Average experienced range	HI	Highest wage paid
ATC	Average total compensation	D	Daily	HR	High end range

LO	Lowest wage paid	MTC	Median total compensation	TCC	Total cash compensation
LR	Low end range	MW	Median wage paid	TQ	Third quartile wage
M	Monthly	MWR	Median wage range	W	Weekly
MCC	Median cash compensation	S	See annotated source	Y	Yearly

Medical Assistant

Occupation/Type/Industry	Location	Per	Low	Mid	High	Source	Date
Medical Assistant	New Mexico	Y	21650 FQ	25650 MW	30230 TQ	USBLS	5/07
	Albuquerque MSA, NM	Y	22510 FQ	26540 MW	30490 TQ	USBLS	5/07
	New York	Y	25270 FQ	29270 MW	35060 TQ	USBLS	5/07
	Albany-Schenectady-Troy MSA, NY	Y	25450 FQ	28270 MW	32230 TQ	USBLS	5/07
	Binghamton MSA, NY	Y	19950 FQ	22620 MW	25340 TQ	USBLS	5/07
	Buffalo-Niagara Falls MSA, NY	Y	23460 FQ	26730 MW	30590 TQ	USBLS	5/07
	Nassau-Suffolk PMSA, NY	Y	25840 FQ	29720 MW	35160 TQ	USBLS	5/07
	New York-Northern New Jersey-Long Island MSA, NY-NJ-PA	Y	26530 FQ	30890 MW	37020 TQ	USBLS	5/07
	North Carolina	Y	22730 FQ	26680 MW	30640 TQ	USBLS	5/07
	Charlotte-Gastonia-Concord MSA, NC-SC	Y	23490 FQ	27120 MW	30970 TQ	USBLS	5/07
	Raleigh-Cary MSA, NC	Y	25570 FQ	28780 MW	32880 TQ	USBLS	5/07
	North Dakota	Y	22440 FQ	27050 MW	31420 TQ	USBLS	5/07
	Bismarck MSA, ND	Y	22460 FQ	25600 MW	29130 TQ	USBLS	5/07
	Fargo MSA, ND-MN	Y	20320 FQ	26180 MW	31810 TQ	USBLS	5/07
	Ohio	Y	21930 FQ	25410 MW	29720 TQ	USBLS	5/07
	Canton-Massillon MSA, OH	Y	21340 FQ	24030 MW	28440 TQ	USBLS	5/07
	Cincinnati-Middletown MSA, OH-KY-IN	Y	23480 FQ	27140 MW	31220 TQ	USBLS	5/07
	Cleveland-Elyria-Mentor MSA, OH	Y	22170 FQ	25280 MW	29600 TQ	USBLS	5/07
	Columbus MSA, OH	Y	22320 FQ	26240 MW	30620 TQ	USBLS	5/07
	Dayton MSA, OH	Y	22700 FQ	26090 MW	29860 TQ	USBLS	5/07
	Oklahoma	Y	20590 FQ	24210 MW	28470 TQ	USBLS	5/07
	Oklahoma City MSA, OK	Y	21010 FQ	24850 MW	28870 TQ	USBLS	5/07
	Tulsa MSA, OK	Y	22060 FQ	25510 MW	29290 TQ	USBLS	5/07
	Oregon	H	13.22 FQ	14.98 MW	17.20 TQ	ORBLS	5/08
	Medford MSA, OR	Y	26170 FQ	28780 MW	31970 TQ	USBLS	5/07
	Portland-Vancouver-Beaverton MSA, OR-WA	Y	27800 FQ	31570 MW	36150 TQ	USBLS	5/07
	Pennsylvania	Y	22250 FQ	26020 MW	30470 TQ	USBLS	5/07
	Allentown-Bethlehem-Easton MSA, PA-NJ	Y	22590 FQ	26720 MW	31310 TQ	USBLS	5/07
	Philadelphia-Camden-Wilmington MSA, PA-NJ-DE-MD	Y	25000 FQ	28730 MW	32890 TQ	USBLS	5/07
	Pittsburgh MSA, PA	Y	21580 FQ	24720 MW	28820 TQ	USBLS	5/07
	Rhode Island	Y	25200 FQ	28960 MW	33790 TQ	USBLS	5/07
	Providence-Fall River-Warwick MSA, RI-MA	Y	25260 FQ	29000 MW	33540 TQ	USBLS	5/07
	South Carolina	Y	22270 FQ	25860 MW	30390 TQ	USBLS	5/07
	Charleston-North Charleston MSA, SC	Y	21890 FQ	25200 MW	29780 TQ	USBLS	5/07
	Columbia MSA, SC	Y	23920 FQ	27900 MW	31610 TQ	USBLS	5/07
	South Dakota	Y	22179 FQ	25189 MW	29019 TQ	SDBLS	7/08-9/08
	Sioux Falls MSA, SD	Y	23003 FQ	26175 MW	29693 TQ	SDBLS	7/08-9/08
	Tennessee	Y	22150 FQ	25680 MW	29690 TQ	USBLS	5/07
	Memphis MSA, TN-MS-AR	Y	22800 FQ	26450 MW	29700 TQ	USBLS	5/07
	Nashville-Davidson-Murfreesboro MSA, TN	Y	23920 FQ	27460 MW	31440 TQ	USBLS	5/07
	Texas	Y	20330 FQ	24660 MW	29680 TQ	USBLS	5/07
	Austin-Round Rock MSA, TX	Y	21710 FQ	26810 MW	30790 TQ	USBLS	5/07
	Corpus Christi MSA, TX	Y	17690 FQ	20030 MW	24300 TQ	USBLS	5/07
	Dallas-Fort Worth-Arlington MSA, TX	Y	23570 FQ	27600 MW	32200 TQ	USBLS	5/07
	El Paso MSA, TX	Y	16250 FQ	19070 MW	23100 TQ	USBLS	5/07
	Houston-Sugar Land-Baytown MSA, TX	Y	21230 FQ	25870 MW	30100 TQ	USBLS	5/07
	San Antonio MSA, TX	Y	19170 FQ	22310 MW	26100 TQ	USBLS	5/07
	Utah	Y	21400 FQ	24480 MW	28660 TQ	USBLS	5/07
	St. George MSA, UT	Y	22030 FQ	24650 MW	28550 TQ	USBLS	5/07
	Salt Lake City MSA, UT	Y	22150 FQ	25160 MW	28980 TQ	USBLS	5/07
	Vermont	Y	26140 FQ	29400 MW	33910 TQ	USBLS	5/07
	Burlington-South Burlington MSA, VT	Y	26020 FQ	29120 MW	33410 TQ	USBLS	5/07
	Virginia	Y	22770 FQ	26990 MW	32100 TQ	USBLS	5/07
	Richmond MSA, VA	Y	23630 FQ	27030 MW	31110 TQ	USBLS	5/07

AE	Average entry wage	AW	Average wage paid	FQ	First quartile wage
AER	Average entry range	AWR	Average wage range	H	Hourly
AEX	Average experienced wage	AXR	Average experienced range	HI	Highest wage paid
ATC	Average total compensation	D	Daily	HR	High end range

LO	Lowest wage paid	MTC	Median total compensation	TCC	Total cash compensation
LR	Low end range	MW	Median wage paid	TQ	Third quartile wage
M	Monthly	MWR	Median wage range	W	Weekly
MCC	Median cash compensation	S	See annotated source	Y	Yearly

Occupation/Type/Industry	Location	Per	Low	Mid	High	Source	Date
Medical Assistant	Virginia Beach-Norfolk-						
	Newport News MSA, VA-NC	Y	21530 FQ	24810 MW	29650 TQ	USBLS	5/07
	Washington	H	13.42 FQ	15.39 MW	17.78 TQ	WABLS	3/08
	Olympia MSA, WA	Y	27640 FQ	31140 MW	35850 TQ	USBLS	5/07
	Seattle-Tacoma-Bellevue						
	MSA, WA	Y	29400 FQ	33510 MW	37850 TQ	USBLS	5/07
	West Virginia	Y	18674 FQ	21889 MW	25323 TQ	WVBLS	7/08-9/08
	Charleston MSA, WV	Y	19190 FQ	21950 MW	24930 TQ	USBLS	5/07
	Huntington-Ashland MSA,						
	WV-KY-OH	Y	19490 FQ	22600 MW	26520 TQ	USBLS	5/07
	Wisconsin	Y	25230 FQ	28700 MW	32280 TQ	USBLS	5/07
	Milwaukee-Waukesha-West						
	Allis MSA, WI	Y	24120 FQ	28540 MW	32850 TQ	USBLS	5/07
	Wyoming	Y	20318 FQ	23356 MW	26634 TQ	WYBLS	9/08
	Cheyenne MSA, WY	Y	23100 FQ	26104 MW	30546 TQ	WYBLS	9/08
	Puerto Rico	Y	17240 FQ	21260 MW	25280 TQ	USBLS	5/07
	San Juan-Caguas-Guaynabo						
	MSA, PR	Y	16680 FQ	19140 MW	23040 TQ	USBLS	5/07
	Virgin Islands	Y	25430 FQ	27690 MW	29920 TQ	USBLS	5/07
	Guam	Y *	19030 FQ	23050 MW	27470 TQ	USBLS	5/07
Medical Billing/Coding Specialist	United States	Y		38700 AW		AAHS	2009
Medical Coder							
Credentialed	United States	Y		43100 AW		AAPC	2008
Not Credentialed	United States	Y		36500 AW		AAPC	2008
Medical Coding Clerk							
New Hampshire Hospital	New Hampshire	Y		34008 AW		NHUL03	2008
Medical Equipment Preparer	Alabama	Y	18680 FQ	21640 MW	24570 TQ	USBLS	5/07
	Birmingham-Hoover MSA, AL	Y	19760 FQ	22430 MW	25230 TQ	USBLS	5/07
	Arizona	Y	22430 FQ	26150 MW	30430 TQ	USBLS	5/07
	Phoenix-Mesa-Scottsdale						
	MSA, AZ	Y	24170 FQ	27830 MW	32050 TQ	USBLS	5/07
	Tucson MSA, AZ	Y	20770 FQ	23600 MW	27110 TQ	USBLS	5/07
	Arkansas	Y	18580 FQ	22380 MW	26550 TQ	USBLS	5/07
	Little Rock-North Little Rock						
	MSA, AR	Y	21040 FQ	23520 MW	26630 TQ	USBLS	5/07
	California	H	10.95 FQ	13.83 MW	17.06 TQ	CABLS	1/08-3/08
	Los Angeles-Long Beach-						
	Glendale PMSA, CA	H	10.21 FQ	13.38 MW	16.31 TQ	CABLS	1/08-3/08
	Modesto MSA, CA	H	9.71 FQ	12.99 MW	14.59 TQ	CABLS	1/08-3/08
	Oakland-Fremont-Hayward						
	MSA, CA	H	12.07 FQ	17.05 MW	23.75 TQ	CABLS	1/08-3/08
	Riverside-San Bernardino-						
	Ontario MSA, CA	H	10.59 FQ	13.21 MW	15.35 TQ	CABLS	1/08-3/08
	Sacramento-Arden Arcade-						
	Roseville MSA, CA	H	12.48 FQ	14.70 MW	20.04 TQ	CABLS	1/08-3/08
	San Diego-Carlsbad-San						
	Marcos MSA, CA	H	13.06 FQ	15.01 MW	16.79 TQ	CABLS	1/08-3/08
	San Francisco-San Mateo-						
	Redwood PMSA, CA	H	11.04 FQ	15.43 MW	22.22 TQ	CABLS	1/08-3/08
	San Jose-Sunnyvale-Santa						
	Clara MSA, CA	H	9.87 FQ	14.42 MW	19.75 TQ	CABLS	1/08-3/08
	Santa Ana-Anaheim-Irvine						
	PMSA, CA	Y	19110 FQ	27830 MW	33890 TQ	USBLS	5/07
	Stockton MSA, CA	H	13.32 FQ	15.40 MW	21.18 TQ	CABLS	1/08-3/08
	Colorado	Y	24440 FQ	28290 MW	32160 TQ	USBLS	5/07
	Denver-Aurora MSA, CO	Y	25380 FQ	28920 MW	32400 TQ	USBLS	5/07
	Connecticut	H	12.78 AE	15.18 MW		CTBLS	1/08-3/08
	Bridgeport-Stamford-Norwalk						
	MSA, CT	Y	25210 FQ	29830 MW	36610 TQ	USBLS	5/07
	Hartford-West Hartford-East						
	Hartford MSA, CT	Y	27710 FQ	31090 MW	35890 TQ	USBLS	5/07
	New Haven MSA, CT	Y	27030 FQ	30030 MW	34410 TQ	USBLS	5/07
	Delaware	Y	25740 FQ	29790 MW	35290 TQ	USBLS	5/07
	Wilmington PMSA, DE-MD-						
	NJ	Y	26680 FQ	31050 MW	35770 TQ	USBLS	5/07
	District of Columbia	Y	27970 FQ	32260 MW	36100 TQ	USBLS	5/07

AE	Average entry wage	AW	Average wage paid	FQ	First quartile wage	LO	Lowest wage paid	MTC	Median total compensation	TCC	Total cash compensation
AER	Average entry range	AWR	Average wage range	H	Hourly	LR	Low end range	MW	Median wage paid	TQ	Third quartile wage
AEX	Average experienced wage	AXR	Average experienced range	HI	Highest wage paid	M	Monthly	MWR	Median wage range	W	Weekly
ATC	Average total compensation	D	Daily	HR	High end range	MCC	Median cash compensation	S	See annotated source	Y	Yearly

1016

Medical Equipment Preparer

Occupation/Type/Industry	Location	Per	Low	Mid	High	Source	Date
Medical Equipment Preparer	Washington-Arlington-Alexandria MSA, DC-VA-MD-WV	Y	27570 FQ	31820 MW	35490 TQ	USBLS	5/07
	Florida	Y	20790 FQ	23410 MW	26980 TQ	USBLS	5/07
	Jacksonville MSA, FL	Y	20130 FQ	23070 MW	26840 TQ	USBLS	5/07
	Orlando-Kissimmee MSA, FL	Y	20750 FQ	22810 MW	25160 TQ	USBLS	5/07
	Pensacola-Ferry Pass-Brent MSA, FL	Y	19990 FQ	22480 MW	25350 TQ	USBLS	5/07
	Tampa-St. Petersburg-Clearwater MSA, FL	Y	19980 FQ	22780 MW	25620 TQ	USBLS	5/07
	West Palm Beach-Boca Raton-Boynton Beach PMSA, FL	Y	21220 FQ	23510 MW	26610 TQ	USBLS	5/07
	Georgia	Y	21170 FQ	25260 MW	30160 TQ	USBLS	5/07
	Atlanta-Sandy Springs-Marietta MSA, GA	Y	23650 FQ	27770 MW	32040 TQ	USBLS	5/07
	Hawaii	Y	27190 FQ	30020 MW	34270 TQ	USBLS	5/07
	Honolulu MSA, HI	Y	28130 FQ	31060 MW	35730 TQ	USBLS	5/07
	Idaho	Y	19630 FQ	24130 MW	28820 TQ	USBLS	5/07
	Illinois	Y	22840 FQ	26870 MW	32030 TQ	USBLS	5/07
	Chicago-Naperville-Joliet MSA, IL-IN-WI	Y	23550 FQ	27460 MW	32630 TQ	USBLS	5/07
	Indiana	Y	23200 FQ	27200 MW	31420 TQ	USBLS	5/07
	Gary PMSA, IN	Y	21470 FQ	25150 MW	28840 TQ	USBLS	5/07
	Indianapolis-Carmel MSA, IN	Y	25330 FQ	28970 MW	34650 TQ	USBLS	5/07
	Iowa	Y	23240 FQ	26310 MW	29690 TQ	USBLS	5/07
	Kansas	Y	22100 FQ	26770 MW	32080 TQ	USBLS	5/07
	Wichita MSA, KS	Y	22300 FQ	25080 MW	28880 TQ	USBLS	5/07
	Kentucky	Y	22073 FQ	26390 MW	30403 TQ	KYBLS	2008
	Lexington-Fayette MSA, KY	Y	22510 FQ	25970 MW	29830 TQ	USBLS	5/07
	Louisville-Jefferson County MSA, KY-IN	Y	23120 FQ	27090 MW	30230 TQ	USBLS	5/07
	Louisiana	H	8.69 FQ	10.00 MW	11.79 TQ	LABLS	1/08-3/08
	Baton Rouge MSA, LA	Y	17780 FQ	20940 MW	24980 TQ	USBLS	5/07
	New Orleans-Metairie-Kenner MSA, LA	Y	18680 FQ	22000 MW	27210 TQ	USBLS	5/07
	Maine	Y	23890 FQ	28760 MW	32830 TQ	USBLS	5/07
	Portland-South Portland-Biddeford MSA, ME	Y	24620 FQ	28680 MW	32690 TQ	USBLS	5/07
	Maryland	Y		28475 MW		MDBLS	3/08
	Baltimore-Towson MSA, MD	Y	22920 FQ	26400 MW	30650 TQ	USBLS	5/07
	Bethesda-Gaithersburg-Frederick PMSA, MD	Y	31900 FQ	34280 MW	36700 TQ	USBLS	5/07
	Massachusetts	Y	26800 FQ	31120 MW	36890 TQ	USBLS	5/07
	Boston-Cambridge-Quincy NECTA, MA	Y	27070 FQ	31520 MW	37480 TQ	USBLS	5/07
	Springfield MSA, MA-CT	Y	27360 FQ	30520 MW	35110 TQ	USBLS	5/07
	Worcester MSA, MA-CT	Y	26650 FQ	31150 MW	36880 TQ	USBLS	5/07
	Michigan	Y	26510 FQ	29610 MW	33200 TQ	USBLS	5/07
	Detroit-Warren-Livonia MSA, MI	Y	27070 FQ	29670 MW	32400 TQ	USBLS	5/07
	Lansing-East Lansing MSA, MI	Y	28210 FQ	30900 MW	34180 TQ	USBLS	5/07
	Warren-Troy-Farmington Hills PMSA, MI	Y	25050 FQ	27900 MW	30740 TQ	USBLS	5/07
	Minnesota	Y	29297 FQ	33835 MW	38738 TQ	MNBLS	10/08-12/08
	Duluth-Superior MSA, MN-WI	Y	27467 FQ	30949 MW	35340 TQ	MNBLS	10/08-12/08
	Minneapolis-Saint Paul MSA, MN-WI	Y	30938 FQ	36083 MW	40380 TQ	MNBLS	10/08-12/08
	Rochester MSA, MN	Y	29663 FQ	33195 MW	37731 TQ	MNBLS	10/08-12/08
	Mississippi	Y	18150 FQ	20580 MW	23240 TQ	USBLS	5/07
	Missouri	Y	21030 FQ	25620 MW	31120 TQ	USBLS	5/07
	Kansas City MSA, MO-KS	Y	24810 FQ	29290 MW	34620 TQ	USBLS	5/07
	St. Louis MSA, MO-IL	Y	21730 FQ	26270 MW	32140 TQ	USBLS	5/07
	Springfield MSA, MO	Y	19460 FQ	26250 MW	32420 TQ	USBLS	5/07
	Montana	Y	22060 FQ	24670 MW	28740 TQ	USBLS	5/07
	Nebraska	Y	23860 FQ	27230 MW	31060 TQ	USBLS	5/07
	Omaha-Council Bluffs MSA, NE-IA	Y	24490 FQ	27560 MW	31860 TQ	USBLS	5/07
	Nevada	H	13.71 FQ	16.55 MW	18.72 TQ	NVBLS	5/08
	Las Vegas-Paradise MSA, NV	H	15.62 FQ	17.55 MW	19.50 TQ	NVBLS	5/08
	New Hampshire	H	9.90 AE	13.43 MW	15.13 AEX	NHBLS	6/08
	Manchester MSA, NH	Y	14230 FQ	25180 MW	28820 TQ	USBLS	5/07
	New Jersey	Y	26670 FQ	30370 MW	35730 TQ	USBLS	5/07

AE Average entry wage	**AW** Average wage paid	**FQ** First quartile wage	**LO** Lowest wage paid	**MTC** Median total compensation	**TCC** Total cash compensation
AER Average entry range	**AWR** Average wage range	**H** Hourly	**LR** Low end range	**MW** Median wage paid	**TQ** Third quartile wage
AEX Average experienced wage	**AXR** Average experienced range	**HI** Highest wage paid	**M** Monthly	**MWR** Median wage range	**W** Weekly
ATC Average total compensation	**D** Daily	**HR** High end range	**MCC** Median cash compensation	**S** See annotated source	**Y** Yearly

Occupation/Type/Industry	Location	Per	Low	Mid	High	Source	Date
Medical Equipment Preparer	Camden PMSA, NJ	Y	26340 FQ	30170 MW	35060 TQ	USBLS	5/07
	Edison PMSA, NJ	Y	25970 FQ	29320 MW	34470 TQ	USBLS	5/07
	Newark-Union PMSA, NJ-PA	Y	27130 FQ	30810 MW	35690 TQ	USBLS	5/07
	New Mexico	Y	21650 FQ	24440 MW	34080 TQ	USBLS	5/07
	New York	Y	27440 FQ	34110 MW	38600 TQ	USBLS	5/07
	Albany-Schenectady-Troy MSA, NY	Y	23510 FQ	26950 MW	30990 TQ	USBLS	5/07
	Buffalo-Niagara Falls MSA, NY	Y	26940 FQ	30330 MW	35390 TQ	USBLS	5/07
	Nassau-Suffolk PMSA, NY	Y	32880 FQ	36870 MW	40840 TQ	USBLS	5/07
	New York-Northern New Jersey-Long Island MSA, NY-NJ-PA	Y	28680 FQ	34100 MW	38540 TQ	USBLS	5/07
	North Carolina	Y	22540 FQ	26020 MW	30470 TQ	USBLS	5/07
	Charlotte-Gastonia-Concord MSA, NC-SC	Y	24250 FQ	28060 MW	33270 TQ	USBLS	5/07
	Raleigh-Cary MSA, NC	Y	22320 FQ	27020 MW	30450 TQ	USBLS	5/07
	North Dakota	Y	21410 FQ	23820 MW	28100 TQ	USBLS	5/07
	Fargo MSA, ND-MN	Y	20870 FQ	22690 MW	25000 TQ	USBLS	5/07
	Ohio	Y	22790 FQ	26660 MW	30720 TQ	USBLS	5/07
	Cincinnati-Middletown MSA, OH-KY-IN	Y	22370 FQ	26310 MW	30550 TQ	USBLS	5/07
	Cleveland-Elyria-Mentor MSA, OH	Y	24220 FQ	28430 MW	32900 TQ	USBLS	5/07
	Columbus MSA, OH	Y	22920 FQ	27070 MW	31260 TQ	USBLS	5/07
	Dayton MSA, OH	Y	23490 FQ	26990 MW	31150 TQ	USBLS	5/07
	Oklahoma	Y	19930 FQ	23370 MW	29040 TQ	USBLS	5/07
	Oklahoma City MSA, OK	Y	21360 FQ	24660 MW	29810 TQ	USBLS	5/07
	Tulsa MSA, OK	Y	20550 FQ	23620 MW	28490 TQ	USBLS	5/07
	Oregon	H	12.03 FQ	14.05 MW	16.40 TQ	ORBLS	5/08
	Portland-Vancouver-Beaverton MSA, OR-WA	Y	26050 FQ	30420 MW	35570 TQ	USBLS	5/07
	Pennsylvania	Y	23480 FQ	27430 MW	31600 TQ	USBLS	5/07
	Allentown-Bethlehem-Easton MSA, PA-NJ	Y	25060 FQ	27920 MW	31100 TQ	USBLS	5/07
	Philadelphia-Camden-Wilmington MSA, PA-NJ-DE-MD	Y	26750 FQ	30670 MW	35930 TQ	USBLS	5/07
	Pittsburgh MSA, PA	Y	22290 FQ	25170 MW	29130 TQ	USBLS	5/07
	Rhode Island	Y	27100 FQ	30340 MW	35900 TQ	USBLS	5/07
	Providence-Fall River-Warwick MSA, RI-MA	Y	27120 FQ	30550 MW	36070 TQ	USBLS	5/07
	South Carolina	Y	22590 FQ	26250 MW	30740 TQ	USBLS	5/07
	Charleston-North Charleston MSA, SC	Y	22070 FQ	24570 MW	27370 TQ	USBLS	5/07
	Columbia MSA, SC	Y	23180 FQ	28450 MW	34800 TQ	USBLS	5/07
	South Dakota	Y	22688 FQ	25802 MW	30165 TQ	SDBLS	7/08-9/08
	Sioux Falls MSA, SD	Y	21980 FQ	24571 MW	28434 TQ	SDBLS	7/08-9/08
	Tennessee	Y	21680 FQ	25910 MW	30780 TQ	USBLS	5/07
	Nashville-Davidson-Murfreesboro MSA, TN	Y	25160 FQ	29100 MW	34050 TQ	USBLS	5/07
	Texas	Y	21290 FQ	24810 MW	29240 TQ	USBLS	5/07
	Austin-Round Rock MSA, TX	Y	22120 FQ	25490 MW	29180 TQ	USBLS	5/07
	Dallas-Fort Worth-Arlington MSA, TX	Y	21990 FQ	25760 MW	30040 TQ	USBLS	5/07
	El Paso MSA, TX	Y	21480 FQ	25390 MW	28850 TQ	USBLS	5/07
	Houston-Sugar Land-Baytown MSA, TX	Y	23130 FQ	26750 MW	30240 TQ	USBLS	5/07
	San Antonio MSA, TX	Y	20240 FQ	23080 MW	27750 TQ	USBLS	5/07
	Ogden-Clearfield MSA, UT	Y	22240 FQ	24650 MW	28730 TQ	USBLS	5/07
	Vermont	Y	23620 FQ	27700 MW	31810 TQ	USBLS	5/07
	Virginia	Y	21800 FQ	26370 MW	31390 TQ	USBLS	5/07
	Richmond MSA, VA	Y	20500 FQ	24330 MW	28980 TQ	USBLS	5/07
	Virginia Beach-Norfolk-Newport News MSA, VA-NC	Y	20060 FQ	23250 MW	27270 TQ	USBLS	5/07
	Washington	H	12.19 FQ	14.68 MW	17.50 TQ	WABLS	3/08
	Seattle-Tacoma-Bellevue MSA, WA	Y	25430 FQ	31600 MW	37170 TQ	USBLS	5/07
	Spokane MSA, WA	Y	22530 FQ	27950 MW	33520 TQ	USBLS	5/07
	West Virginia	Y	21636 FQ	26081 MW	30839 TQ	WVBLS	7/08-9/08
	Wisconsin	Y	24930 FQ	28250 MW	31650 TQ	USBLS	5/07
	Green Bay MSA, WI	Y	25790 FQ	29440 MW	32650 TQ	USBLS	5/07

Occupation/Type/Industry	Location	Per	Low	Mid	High	Source	Date
Medical Equipment Preparer	Milwaukee-Waukesha-West Allis MSA, WI	Y	25270 FQ	28070 MW	31150 TQ	USBLS	5/07
	Wyoming	Y	22380 FQ	25424 MW	31002 TQ	WYBLS	9/08
	Puerto Rico	Y	12990 FQ	14820 MW	17810 TQ	USBLS	5/07
	San Juan-Caguas-Guaynabo MSA, PR	Y	12720 FQ	14290 MW	16130 TQ	USBLS	5/07
Medical Equipment Repairer	Alabama	Y	29530 FQ	38590 MW	48260 TQ	USBLS	5/07
	Birmingham-Hoover MSA, AL	Y	32570 FQ	44770 MW	53540 TQ	USBLS	5/07
	Mobile MSA, AL	Y	30030 FQ	37090 MW	44540 TQ	USBLS	5/07
	Montgomery MSA, AL	Y	34970 FQ	40500 MW	49910 TQ	USBLS	5/07
	Arizona	Y	26980 FQ	33080 MW	44460 TQ	USBLS	5/07
	Phoenix-Mesa-Scottsdale MSA, AZ	Y	28900 FQ	34920 MW	45550 TQ	USBLS	5/07
	Tucson MSA, AZ	Y	21620 FQ	25790 MW	35310 TQ	USBLS	5/07
	Arkansas	Y	27010 FQ	36310 MW	48050 TQ	USBLS	5/07
	Little Rock-North Little Rock MSA, AR	Y	28000 FQ	39480 MW	50760 TQ	USBLS	5/07
	California	H	17.02 FQ	23.59 MW	32.70 TQ	CABLS	1/08-3/08
	Fresno MSA, CA	H	10.51 FQ	11.27 MW	12.04 TQ	CABLS	1/08-3/08
	Los Angeles-Long Beach-Glendale PMSA, CA	H	16.51 FQ	21.47 MW	28.94 TQ	CABLS	1/08-3/08
	Oakland-Fremont-Hayward MSA, CA	H	16.65 FQ	19.13 MW	29.20 TQ	CABLS	1/08-3/08
	Riverside-San Bernardino-Ontario MSA, CA	H	15.25 FQ	17.44 MW	19.59 TQ	CABLS	1/08-3/08
	Sacramento-Arden Arcade-Roseville MSA, CA	H	14.54 FQ	17.67 MW	24.32 TQ	CABLS	1/08-3/08
	San Diego-Carlsbad-San Marcos MSA, CA	H	17.93 FQ	34.29 MW	42.60 TQ	CABLS	1/08-3/08
	San Francisco-San Mateo-Redwood PMSA, CA	H	18.97 FQ	27.17 MW	33.50 TQ	CABLS	1/08-3/08
	San Jose-Sunnyvale-Santa Clara MSA, CA	H	17.23 FQ	21.80 MW	28.79 TQ	CABLS	1/08-3/08
	Santa Ana-Anaheim-Irvine PMSA, CA	Y	48590 FQ	71970 MW	92990 TQ	USBLS	5/07
	Colorado	Y	30310 FQ	46190 MW	58380 TQ	USBLS	5/07
	Denver-Aurora MSA, CO	Y	34570 FQ	51580 MW	62700 TQ	USBLS	5/07
	Connecticut	H	15.78 AE	23.20 MW		CTBLS	1/08-3/08
	Hartford-West Hartford-East Hartford MSA, CT	Y	41760 FQ	52470 MW	58080 TQ	USBLS	5/07
	Delaware	Y	27710 FQ	30410 MW	40660 TQ	USBLS	5/07
	Wilmington PMSA, DE-MD-NJ	Y	28250 FQ	30900 MW	47420 TQ	USBLS	5/07
	District of Columbia	Y	28580 FQ	32580 MW	42290 TQ	USBLS	5/07
	Washington-Arlington-Alexandria MSA, DC-VA-MD-WV	Y	29110 FQ	36280 MW	47030 TQ	USBLS	5/07
	Florida	Y	29190 FQ	37900 MW	47470 TQ	USBLS	5/07
	Fort Lauderdale-Pompano Beach-Deerfield Beach PMSA, FL	Y	32770 FQ	40400 MW	45900 TQ	USBLS	5/07
	Jacksonville MSA, FL	Y	35960 FQ	42660 MW	51550 TQ	USBLS	5/07
	Miami-Fort Lauderdale-Miami Beach MSA, FL	Y	24090 FQ	36440 MW	46040 TQ	USBLS	5/07
	Orlando-Kissimmee MSA, FL	Y	24160 FQ	31610 MW	48280 TQ	USBLS	5/07
	Tampa-St. Petersburg-Clearwater MSA, FL	Y	33300 FQ	38890 MW	48010 TQ	USBLS	5/07
	West Palm Beach-Boca Raton-Boynton Beach PMSA, FL	Y	33720 FQ	42800 MW	55100 TQ	USBLS	5/07
	Georgia	Y	30560 FQ	38800 MW	49370 TQ	USBLS	5/07
	Atlanta-Sandy Springs-Marietta MSA, GA	Y	29730 FQ	37790 MW	49840 TQ	USBLS	5/07
	Idaho	Y	38230 FQ	44730 MW	53810 TQ	USBLS	5/07
	Illinois	Y	28610 FQ	35690 MW	47480 TQ	USBLS	5/07
	Chicago-Naperville-Joliet MSA, IL-IN-WI	Y	28500 FQ	35410 MW	47090 TQ	USBLS	5/07
	Indiana	Y	30390 FQ	36910 MW	47890 TQ	USBLS	5/07
	Fort Wayne MSA, IN	Y	30490 FQ	42820 MW	48890 TQ	USBLS	5/07
	Gary PMSA, IN	Y	23850 FQ	27990 MW	38920 TQ	USBLS	5/07
	Indianapolis-Carmel MSA, IN	Y	31410 FQ	36100 MW	45350 TQ	USBLS	5/07
	Iowa	Y	33390 FQ	43980 MW	51390 TQ	USBLS	5/07

AE	Average entry wage	**AW**	Average wage paid	**FQ**	First quartile wage	**LO**	Lowest wage paid	**MTC**	Median total compensation	**TCC**	Total cash compensation
AER	Average entry range	**AWR**	Average wage range	**H**	Hourly	**LR**	Low end range	**MW**	Median wage paid	**TQ**	Third quartile wage
AEX	Average experienced wage	**AXR**	Average experienced range	**HI**	Highest wage paid	**M**	Monthly	**MWR**	Median wage range	**W**	Weekly
ATC	Average total compensation	**D**	Daily	**HR**	High end range	**MCC**	Median cash compensation	**S**	See annotated source	**Y**	Yearly

Occupation/Type/Industry	Location	Per	Low	Mid	High	Source	Date
Medical Equipment Repairer	Des Moines-West Des Moines MSA, IA	Y	42370 FQ	46400 MW	50430 TQ	USBLS	5/07
	Kansas	Y	24430 FQ	38310 MW	50730 TQ	USBLS	5/07
	Wichita MSA, KS	Y	44160 FQ	53780 MW	88000 TQ	USBLS	5/07
	Kentucky	Y	23785 FQ	30999 MW	46580 TQ	KYBLS	2008
	Louisville-Jefferson County MSA, KY-IN	Y	29070 FQ	40500 MW	51240 TQ	USBLS	5/07
	Louisiana	H	14.69 FQ	21.63 MW	29.18 TQ	LABLS	1/08-3/08
	Baton Rouge MSA, LA	Y	46300 FQ	54300 MW	62970 TQ	USBLS	5/07
	New Orleans-Metairie-Kenner MSA, LA	Y	32340 FQ	47820 MW	68240 TQ	USBLS	5/07
	Maine	Y	39480 FQ	46700 MW	54650 TQ	USBLS	5/07
	Portland-South Portland-Biddeford MSA, ME	Y	39190 FQ	45930 MW	52980 TQ	USBLS	5/07
	Maryland	Y		40075 MW		MDBLS	3/08
	Baltimore-Towson MSA, MD	Y	32980 FQ	41600 MW	49410 TQ	USBLS	5/07
	Bethesda-Gaithersburg-Frederick PMSA, MD	Y	24040 FQ	26570 MW	29410 TQ	USBLS	5/07
	Massachusetts	Y	28600 FQ	32900 MW	45870 TQ	USBLS	5/07
	Boston-Cambridge-Quincy NECTA, MA	Y	27800 FQ	31430 MW	44750 TQ	USBLS	5/07
	Worcester MSA, MA-CT	Y	29060 FQ	32650 MW	38360 TQ	USBLS	5/07
	Michigan	Y	33380 FQ	40160 MW	55360 TQ	USBLS	5/07
	Detroit-Warren-Livonia MSA, MI	Y	36570 FQ	45790 MW	63470 TQ	USBLS	5/07
	Grand Rapids-Wyoming MSA, MI	Y	31460 FQ	35910 MW	44500 TQ	USBLS	5/07
	Warren-Troy-Farmington Hills PMSA, MI	Y	35860 FQ	39700 MW	48830 TQ	USBLS	5/07
	Minnesota	Y	38894 FQ	53758 MW	65695 TQ	MNBLS	10/08-12/08
	Duluth-Superior MSA, MN-WI	Y	46352 FQ	53978 MW	61625 TQ	MNBLS	10/08-12/08
	Minneapolis-Saint Paul MSA, MN-WI	Y	38401 FQ	54094 MW	66786 TQ	MNBLS	10/08-12/08
	Rochester MSA, MN	Y	49347 FQ	59588 MW	68781 TQ	MNBLS	10/08-12/08
	Mississippi	Y	29320 FQ	37150 MW	51110 TQ	USBLS	5/07
	Jackson MSA, MS	Y	42000 FQ	51160 MW	59600 TQ	USBLS	5/07
	Missouri	Y	32590 FQ	39800 MW	50970 TQ	USBLS	5/07
	Kansas City MSA, MO-KS	Y	30870 FQ	43420 MW	56770 TQ	USBLS	5/07
	St. Louis MSA, MO-IL	Y	32400 FQ	38780 MW	46960 TQ	USBLS	5/07
	Montana	Y	34320 FQ	46960 MW	55640 TQ	USBLS	5/07
	Nebraska	Y	36020 FQ	47040 MW	58640 TQ	USBLS	5/07
	Omaha-Council Bluffs MSA, NE-IA	Y	32110 FQ	39500 MW	57690 TQ	USBLS	5/07
	Nevada	H	15.89 FQ	20.78 MW	30.25 TQ	NVBLS	5/08
	New Hampshire	H	13.14 AE	15.22 MW	21.71 AEX	NHBLS	6/08
	Nashua NECTA, NH-MA	Y	28170 FQ	32560 MW	45350 TQ	USBLS	5/07
	New Jersey	Y	35760 FQ	45300 MW	56900 TQ	USBLS	5/07
	Camden PMSA, NJ	Y	33250 FQ	38420 MW	47610 TQ	USBLS	5/07
	Edison PMSA, NJ	Y	32620 FQ	44460 MW	58820 TQ	USBLS	5/07
	Newark-Union PMSA, NJ-PA	Y	39680 FQ	46040 MW	55130 TQ	USBLS	5/07
	New Mexico	Y	21080 FQ	23410 MW	39630 TQ	USBLS	5/07
	Albuquerque MSA, NM	Y	21070 FQ	23220 MW	53080 TQ	USBLS	5/07
	New York	Y	33620 FQ	42720 MW	54770 TQ	USBLS	5/07
	Albany-Schenectady-Troy MSA, NY	Y	37050 FQ	46350 MW	56490 TQ	USBLS	5/07
	Buffalo-Niagara Falls MSA, NY	Y	32390 FQ	41410 MW	51090 TQ	USBLS	5/07
	Nassau-Suffolk PMSA, NY	Y	26020 FQ	43100 MW	59040 TQ	USBLS	5/07
	New York-Northern New Jersey-Long Island MSA, NY-NJ-PA	Y	37000 FQ	45820 MW	58380 TQ	USBLS	5/07
	North Carolina	Y	35580 FQ	44920 MW	53160 TQ	USBLS	5/07
	Charlotte-Gastonia-Concord MSA, NC-SC	Y	37660 FQ	44960 MW	53690 TQ	USBLS	5/07
	Raleigh-Cary MSA, NC	Y	39800 FQ	46380 MW	52080 TQ	USBLS	5/07
	North Dakota	Y	33010 FQ	39830 MW	47240 TQ	USBLS	5/07
	Ohio	Y	31640 FQ	43330 MW	55780 TQ	USBLS	5/07
	Cincinnati-Middletown MSA, OH-KY-IN	Y	29530 FQ	39830 MW	63240 TQ	USBLS	5/07
	Cleveland-Elyria-Mentor MSA, OH	Y	37820 FQ	44870 MW	52860 TQ	USBLS	5/07
	Columbus MSA, OH	Y	34810 FQ	46850 MW	55560 TQ	USBLS	5/07

AE	Average entry wage	AW	Average wage paid	FQ	First quartile wage
AER	Average entry range	AWR	Average wage range	H	Hourly
AEX	Average experienced wage	AXR	Average experienced range	HI	Highest wage paid
ATC	Average total compensation	D	Daily	HR	High end range

LO	Lowest wage paid	MTC	Median total compensation
LR	Low end range	MW	Median wage paid
M	Monthly	MWR	Median wage range
MCC	Median cash compensation	S	See annotated source

TCC	Total cash compensation
TQ	Third quartile wage
W	Weekly
Y	Yearly

Occupation/Type/Industry	Location	Per	Low	Mid	High	Source	Date
Medical Equipment Repairer	Dayton MSA, OH	Y	26630 FQ	30140 MW	43950 TQ	USBLS	5/07
	Oklahoma	Y	27910 FQ	34640 MW	45970 TQ	USBLS	5/07
	Oklahoma City MSA, OK	Y	30370 FQ	36880 MW	46840 TQ	USBLS	5/07
	Tulsa MSA, OK	Y	31480 FQ	35940 MW	48470 TQ	USBLS	5/07
	Oregon	H	19.23 FQ	25.79 MW	31.24 TQ	ORBLS	5/08
	Eugene-Springfield MSA, OR	Y	32040 FQ	39060 MW	48520 TQ	USBLS	5/07
	Portland-Vancouver-Beaverton MSA, OR-WA	Y	46820 FQ	56690 MW	66520 TQ	USBLS	5/07
	Pennsylvania	Y	32070 FQ	41950 MW	50510 TQ	USBLS	5/07
	Allentown-Bethlehem-Easton MSA, PA-NJ	Y	33470 FQ	42690 MW	55340 TQ	USBLS	5/07
	Lancaster MSA, PA	Y	36570 FQ	43790 MW	50070 TQ	USBLS	5/07
	Philadelphia-Camden-Wilmington MSA, PA-NJ-DE-MD	Y	34750 FQ	44490 MW	52890 TQ	USBLS	5/07
	Pittsburgh MSA, PA	Y	30190 FQ	37350 MW	46310 TQ	USBLS	5/07
	Rhode Island	Y	30590 FQ	41100 MW	53940 TQ	USBLS	5/07
	Providence-Fall River-Warwick MSA, RI-MA	Y	32810 FQ	42640 MW	54510 TQ	USBLS	5/07
	South Carolina	Y	26760 FQ	31040 MW	42330 TQ	USBLS	5/07
	Charleston-North Charleston MSA, SC	Y	27820 FQ	30470 MW	35450 TQ	USBLS	5/07
	Columbia MSA, SC	Y	20290 FQ	27290 MW	31700 TQ	USBLS	5/07
	South Dakota	Y	36587 FQ	44928 MW	53478 TQ	SDBLS	7/08-9/08
	Sioux Falls MSA, SD	Y	38198 FQ	49668 MW	60865 TQ	SDBLS	7/08-9/08
	Tennessee	Y	30220 FQ	41300 MW	51230 TQ	USBLS	5/07
	Memphis MSA, TN-MS-AR	Y	27130 FQ	34480 MW	44880 TQ	USBLS	5/07
	Nashville-Davidson-Murfreesboro MSA, TN	Y	31600 FQ	42350 MW	49380 TQ	USBLS	5/07
	Texas	Y	26880 FQ	35670 MW	48170 TQ	USBLS	5/07
	Austin-Round Rock MSA, TX	Y	24760 FQ	35120 MW	50660 TQ	USBLS	5/07
	Dallas-Fort Worth-Arlington MSA, TX	Y	33760 FQ	45940 MW	58390 TQ	USBLS	5/07
	El Paso MSA, TX	Y	32730 FQ	35370 MW	38030 TQ	USBLS	5/07
	Houston-Sugar Land-Baytown MSA, TX	Y	28710 FQ	38250 MW	48790 TQ	USBLS	5/07
	San Antonio MSA, TX	Y	25190 FQ	29130 MW	34320 TQ	USBLS	5/07
	Utah	Y	47060 FQ	59280 MW	70700 TQ	USBLS	5/07
	Provo-Orem MSA, UT	Y	31060 FQ	48460 MW	58750 TQ	USBLS	5/07
	Salt Lake City MSA, UT	Y	47920 FQ	61250 MW	72080 TQ	USBLS	5/07
	Vermont	Y	35040 FQ	39310 MW	46790 TQ	USBLS	5/07
	Virginia	Y	29350 FQ	37460 MW	47890 TQ	USBLS	5/07
	Richmond MSA, VA	Y	34680 FQ	44110 MW	51120 TQ	USBLS	5/07
	Virginia Beach-Norfolk-Newport News MSA, VA-NC	Y	27460 FQ	29870 MW	34600 TQ	USBLS	5/07
	Washington	H	15.47 FQ	20.72 MW	28.99 TQ	WABLS	3/08
	Seattle-Tacoma-Bellevue MSA, WA	Y	31940 FQ	43180 MW	60930 TQ	USBLS	5/07
	West Virginia	Y	24285 FQ	29665 MW	42171 TQ	WVBLS	7/08-9/08
	Charleston MSA, WV	Y	21950 FQ	27550 MW	37560 TQ	USBLS	5/07
	Wisconsin	Y	36580 FQ	48010 MW	57340 TQ	USBLS	5/07
	Milwaukee-Waukesha-West Allis MSA, WI	Y	36370 FQ	50900 MW	59770 TQ	USBLS	5/07
	Wyoming	Y	25052 FQ	30284 MW	45581 TQ	WYBLS	9/08
	Puerto Rico	Y	19910 FQ	28050 MW	37370 TQ	USBLS	5/07
	San Juan-Caguas-Guaynabo MSA, PR	Y	20730 FQ	28760 MW	38080 TQ	USBLS	5/07
Medical Librarian	United States	Y		58000 AW		EXHC	5/08
Medical Office Administrator	United States	Y	36750-51750 AER			IAAPHQ	2008
Medical Office Specialist Municipal Government	Colorado Springs, CO	M	2935 LO			COSPRS	1/1/09
Medical Product Manager	United States	Y		106200 AW		MMM	2008
Medical Records and Health Information Technician	Alabama	Y	19540 FQ	23140 MW	30670 TQ	USBLS	5/07
	Birmingham-Hoover MSA, AL	Y	20460 FQ	24010 MW	33580 TQ	USBLS	5/07
	Montgomery MSA, AL	Y	18310 FQ	21820 MW	28320 TQ	USBLS	5/07

AE Average entry wage	**AW** Average wage paid	**FQ** First quartile wage	**LO** Lowest wage paid	**MTC** Median total compensation	**TCC** Total cash compensation
AER Average entry range	**AWR** Average wage range	**H** Hourly	**LR** Low end range	**MW** Median wage paid	**TQ** Third quartile wage
AEX Average experienced wage	**AXR** Average experienced range	**HI** Highest wage paid	**M** Monthly	**MWR** Median wage range	**W** Weekly
ATC Average total compensation	**D** Daily	**HR** High end range	**MCC** Median cash compensation	**S** See annotated source	**Y** Yearly

Occupation/Type/Industry	Location	Per	Low	Mid	High	Source	Date
Medical Records and Health Information Technician							
	Alaska	Y	29330 FQ	34640 MW	39490 TQ	USBLS	5/07
	Anchorage MSA, AK	Y	28450 FQ	33550 MW	37940 TQ	USBLS	5/07
	Arizona	Y	23680 FQ	27840 MW	32110 TQ	USBLS	5/07
	Flagstaff MSA, AZ	Y	26130 FQ	28530 MW	30980 TQ	USBLS	5/07
	Phoenix-Mesa-Scottsdale MSA, AZ	Y	24820 FQ	28260 MW	32160 TQ	USBLS	5/07
	Prescott MSA, AZ	Y	21450 FQ	23980 MW	29230 TQ	USBLS	5/07
	Tucson MSA, AZ	Y	21050 FQ	24110 MW	31260 TQ	USBLS	5/07
	Arkansas	Y	20350 FQ	25520 MW	35940 TQ	USBLS	5/07
	Fayetteville-Springdale-Rogers MSA, AR-MO	Y	24950 FQ	35100 MW	41840 TQ	USBLS	5/07
	Little Rock-North Little Rock MSA, AR	Y	22350 FQ	31090 MW	40110 TQ	USBLS	5/07
	California	H	12.76 FQ	15.98 MW	20.86 TQ	CABLS	1/08-3/08
	Los Angeles-Long Beach-Glendale PMSA, CA	H	12.40 FQ	15.24 MW	20.75 TQ	CABLS	1/08-3/08
	Oakland-Fremont-Hayward MSA, CA	H	15.66 FQ	18.87 MW	23.23 TQ	CABLS	1/08-3/08
	Riverside-San Bernardino-Ontario MSA, CA	H	11.54 FQ	14.97 MW	19.44 TQ	CABLS	1/08-3/08
	Sacramento-Arden Arcade-Roseville MSA, CA	H	13.55 FQ	16.60 MW	21.39 TQ	CABLS	1/08-3/08
	San Diego-Carlsbad-San Marcos MSA, CA	H	12.30 FQ	14.77 MW	18.39 TQ	CABLS	1/08-3/08
	San Francisco-San Mateo-Redwood PMSA, CA	H	15.54 FQ	19.13 MW	26.49 TQ	CABLS	1/08-3/08
	San Jose-Sunnyvale-Santa Clara MSA, CA	H	17.12 FQ	20.68 MW	25.15 TQ	CABLS	1/08-3/08
	Santa Ana-Anaheim-Irvine PMSA, CA	Y	26950 FQ	34490 MW	45460 TQ	USBLS	5/07
	Colorado	Y	26320 FQ	32650 MW	41290 TQ	USBLS	5/07
	Denver-Aurora MSA, CO	Y	27740 FQ	33880 MW	42220 TQ	USBLS	5/07
	Fort Collins-Loveland MSA, CO	Y	26080 FQ	30720 MW	41840 TQ	USBLS	5/07
	Connecticut	H	13.13 AE	16.42 MW		CTBLS	1/08-3/08
	Bridgeport-Stamford-Norwalk MSA, CT	Y	27410 FQ	31220 MW	39900 TQ	USBLS	5/07
	Hartford-West Hartford-East Hartford MSA, CT	Y	28180 FQ	33650 MW	43170 TQ	USBLS	5/07
	New Haven MSA, CT	Y	28220 FQ	32330 MW	39540 TQ	USBLS	5/07
	Norwich-New London MSA, CT-RI	Y	30750 FQ	35690 MW	42760 TQ	USBLS	5/07
	Delaware	Y	25350 FQ	29050 MW	34610 TQ	USBLS	5/07
	Wilmington PMSA, DE-MD-NJ	Y	26440 FQ	29740 MW	35670 TQ	USBLS	5/07
	District of Columbia	Y	31440 FQ	36130 MW	40490 TQ	USBLS	5/07
	Washington-Arlington-Alexandria MSA, DC-VA-MD-WV	Y	29520 FQ	36390 MW	44800 TQ	USBLS	5/07
	Florida	Y	22870 FQ	28410 MW	36540 TQ	USBLS	5/07
	Fort Lauderdale-Pompano Beach-Deerfield Beach PMSA, FL	Y	24580 FQ	29730 MW	38280 TQ	USBLS	5/07
	Jacksonville MSA, FL	Y	23610 FQ	28600 MW	34260 TQ	USBLS	5/07
	Miami-Fort Lauderdale-Miami Beach MSA, FL	Y	23280 FQ	29090 MW	37780 TQ	USBLS	5/07
	Orlando-Kissimmee MSA, FL	Y	22110 FQ	27520 MW	35790 TQ	USBLS	5/07
	Sarasota-Bradenton-Venice MSA, FL	Y	24610 FQ	28010 MW	31660 TQ	USBLS	5/07
	Tallahassee MSA, FL	Y	22780 FQ	27850 MW	31730 TQ	USBLS	5/07
	Tampa-St. Petersburg-Clearwater MSA, FL	Y	21960 FQ	27770 MW	38350 TQ	USBLS	5/07
	West Palm Beach-Boca Raton-Boynton Beach PMSA, FL	Y	24340 FQ	29420 MW	38380 TQ	USBLS	5/07
	Georgia	Y	22130 FQ	27080 MW	32870 TQ	USBLS	5/07
	Atlanta-Sandy Springs-Marietta MSA, GA	Y	23930 FQ	28580 MW	34750 TQ	USBLS	5/07
	Macon MSA, GA	Y	22440 FQ	26220 MW	30470 TQ	USBLS	5/07
	Hawaii	Y	28150 FQ	33850 MW	43880 TQ	USBLS	5/07
	Honolulu MSA, HI	Y	29710 FQ	36080 MW	45900 TQ	USBLS	5/07
	Idaho	Y	23510 FQ	28310 MW	35390 TQ	USBLS	5/07

AE	Average entry wage	AW	Average wage paid	FQ	First quartile wage	LO	Lowest wage paid	MTC	Median total compensation	TCC	Total cash compensation
AER	Average entry range	AWR	Average wage range	H	Hourly	LR	Low end range	MW	Median wage paid	TQ	Third quartile wage
AEX	Average experienced wage	AXR	Average experienced range	HI	Highest wage paid	M	Monthly	MWR	Median wage range	W	Weekly
ATC	Average total compensation	D	Daily	HR	High end range	MCC	Median cash compensation	S	See annotated source	Y	Yearly

Occupation/Type/Industry	Location	Per	Low	Mid	High	Source	Date
Medical Records and Health Information Technician	Boise City-Nampa MSA, ID	Y	23610 FQ	29140 MW	36470 TQ	USBLS	5/07
	Illinois	Y	22630 FQ	28480 MW	35500 TQ	USBLS	5/07
	Chicago-Naperville-Joliet MSA, IL-IN-WI	Y	24040 FQ	29390 MW	36330 TQ	USBLS	5/07
	Indiana	Y	22460 FQ	27300 MW	34400 TQ	USBLS	5/07
	Evansville MSA, IN-KY	Y	20700 FQ	25530 MW	32150 TQ	USBLS	5/07
	Fort Wayne MSA, IN	Y	22720 FQ	26840 MW	33120 TQ	USBLS	5/07
	Gary PMSA, IN	Y	20990 FQ	26350 MW	32010 TQ	USBLS	5/07
	Indianapolis-Carmel MSA, IN	Y	24200 FQ	28870 MW	38520 TQ	USBLS	5/07
	South Bend-Mishawaka MSA, IN-MI	Y	20860 FQ	25360 MW	32820 TQ	USBLS	5/07
	Iowa	Y	21740 FQ	26620 MW	33440 TQ	USBLS	5/07
	Des Moines-West Des Moines MSA, IA	Y	23870 FQ	29600 MW	37290 TQ	USBLS	5/07
	Sioux City MSA, IA-NE-SD	Y	21590 FQ	23840 MW	28660 TQ	USBLS	5/07
	Waterloo-Cedar Falls MSA, IA	Y	23760 FQ	28880 MW	34420 TQ	USBLS	5/07
	Kansas	Y	21340 FQ	25840 MW	32790 TQ	USBLS	5/07
	Wichita MSA, KS	Y	20770 FQ	23700 MW	30480 TQ	USBLS	5/07
	Kentucky	Y	23051 FQ	29160 MW	37526 TQ	KYBLS	2008
	Louisville-Jefferson County MSA, KY-IN	Y	24630 FQ	29440 MW	37650 TQ	USBLS	5/07
	Owensboro MSA, KY	Y	20290 FQ	26430 MW	33160 TQ	USBLS	5/07
	Louisiana	H	8.51 FQ	10.62 MW	14.50 TQ	LABLS	1/08-3/08
	Baton Rouge MSA, LA	Y	18630 FQ	23040 MW	30080 TQ	USBLS	5/07
	New Orleans-Metairie-Kenner MSA, LA	Y	19930 FQ	23800 MW	30250 TQ	USBLS	5/07
	Maine	Y	24020 FQ	29180 MW	35860 TQ	USBLS	5/07
	Portland-South Portland-Biddeford MSA, ME	Y	24530 FQ	29420 MW	35430 TQ	USBLS	5/07
	Maryland	Y		35175 MW		MDBLS	3/08
	Baltimore-Towson MSA, MD	Y	26210 FQ	35460 MW	49640 TQ	USBLS	5/07
	Bethesda-Gaithersburg-Frederick PMSA, MD	Y	29610 FQ	36210 MW	47050 TQ	USBLS	5/07
	Massachusetts	Y	25570 FQ	30900 MW	39470 TQ	USBLS	5/07
	Boston-Cambridge-Quincy NECTA, MA	Y	26290 FQ	32510 MW	42430 TQ	USBLS	5/07
	Lynn-Peabody-Salem NECTA, MA	Y	26330 FQ	31100 MW	38680 TQ	USBLS	5/07
	Worcester MSA, MA-CT	Y	27170 FQ	30570 MW	36650 TQ	USBLS	5/07
	Michigan	Y	24120 FQ	30020 MW	39630 TQ	USBLS	5/07
	Detroit-Warren-Livonia MSA, MI	Y	26020 FQ	31320 MW	41970 TQ	USBLS	5/07
	Grand Rapids-Wyoming MSA, MI	Y	25250 FQ	30460 MW	39710 TQ	USBLS	5/07
	Lansing-East Lansing MSA, MI	Y	22460 FQ	28460 MW	36160 TQ	USBLS	5/07
	Warren-Troy-Farmington Hills PMSA, MI	Y	25420 FQ	31120 MW	40570 TQ	USBLS	5/07
	Minnesota	Y	29534 FQ	35529 MW	42246 TQ	MNBLS	10/08-12/08
	Duluth-Superior MSA, MN-WI	Y	30779 FQ	36220 MW	41880 TQ	MNBLS	10/08-12/08
	Minneapolis-Saint Paul MSA, MN-WI	Y	30623 FQ	36523 MW	43292 TQ	MNBLS	10/08-12/08
	Rochester MSA, MN	Y	35563 FQ	40483 MW	49077 TQ	MNBLS	10/08-12/08
	Mississippi	Y	19540 FQ	23630 MW	30360 TQ	USBLS	5/07
	Jackson MSA, MS	Y	20730 FQ	25980 MW	33580 TQ	USBLS	5/07
	Missouri	Y	22060 FQ	26930 MW	34100 TQ	USBLS	5/07
	Kansas City MSA, MO-KS	Y	24770 FQ	29610 MW	36710 TQ	USBLS	5/07
	St. Louis MSA, MO-IL	Y	22340 FQ	26670 MW	34040 TQ	USBLS	5/07
	Montana	Y	21800 FQ	27540 MW	34470 TQ	USBLS	5/07
	Billings MSA, MT	Y	23710 FQ	29100 MW	35100 TQ	USBLS	5/07
	Missoula MSA, MT	Y	21660 FQ	25230 MW	37850 TQ	USBLS	5/07
	Nebraska	Y	22770 FQ	27990 MW	35590 TQ	USBLS	5/07
	Omaha-Council Bluffs MSA, NE-IA	Y	23580 FQ	28970 MW	36920 TQ	USBLS	5/07
	Nevada	H	12.67 FQ	15.57 MW	19.78 TQ	NVBLS	5/08
	Las Vegas-Paradise MSA, NV	H	13.04 FQ	15.78 MW	19.99 TQ	NVBLS	5/08
	New Hampshire	H	11.31 AE	14.30 MW	17.43 AEX	NHBLS	6/08
	Manchester MSA, NH	Y	23690 FQ	27290 MW	32160 TQ	USBLS	5/07
	Nashua NECTA, NH-MA	Y	23610 FQ	27970 MW	33440 TQ	USBLS	5/07
	Rochester-Dover MSA, NH-ME	Y	24790 FQ	31000 MW	37300 TQ	USBLS	5/07
	New Jersey	Y	32010 FQ	39770 MW	52740 TQ	USBLS	5/07

AE	Average entry wage	AW	Average wage paid	FQ	First quartile wage	
AER	Average entry range	AWR	Average wage range	H	Hourly	
AEX	Average experienced wage	AXR	Average experienced range	HI	Highest wage paid	
ATC	Average total compensation	D	Daily	HR	High end range	

LO	Lowest wage paid	MTC	Median total compensation	TCC	Total cash compensation
LR	Low end range	MW	Median wage paid	TQ	Third quartile wage
M	Monthly	MWR	Median wage range	W	Weekly
MCC	Median cash compensation	S	See annotated source	Y	Yearly

Occupation/Type/Industry	Location	Per	Low	Mid	High	Source	Date
Medical Records and Health Information Technician	Atlantic City MSA, NJ	Y	32850 FQ	39230 MW	49700 TQ	USBLS	5/07
	Camden PMSA, NJ	Y	31570 FQ	36840 MW	51330 TQ	USBLS	5/07
	Edison PMSA, NJ	Y	31960 FQ	39620 MW	51470 TQ	USBLS	5/07
	Newark-Union PMSA, NJ-PA	Y	31810 FQ	41690 MW	54310 TQ	USBLS	5/07
	New Mexico	Y	21820 FQ	28110 MW	35180 TQ	USBLS	5/07
	Albuquerque MSA, NM	Y	25120 FQ	30280 MW	37150 TQ	USBLS	5/07
	New York	Y	27450 FQ	34970 MW	42380 TQ	USBLS	5/07
	Albany-Schenectady-Troy MSA, NY	Y	22940 FQ	27270 MW	36160 TQ	USBLS	5/07
	Buffalo-Niagara Falls MSA, NY	Y	30460 FQ	36560 MW	44750 TQ	USBLS	5/07
	Nassau-Suffolk PMSA, NY	Y	30340 FQ	37520 MW	44970 TQ	USBLS	5/07
	New York-Northern New Jersey-Long Island MSA, NY-NJ-PA	Y	32630 FQ	38400 MW	46570 TQ	USBLS	5/07
	North Carolina	Y	22210 FQ	26460 MW	32790 TQ	USBLS	5/07
	Charlotte-Gastonia-Concord MSA, NC-SC	Y	24750 FQ	28820 MW	34130 TQ	USBLS	5/07
	Raleigh-Cary MSA, NC	Y	21000 FQ	25370 MW	33490 TQ	USBLS	5/07
	North Dakota	Y	22790 FQ	27250 MW	34900 TQ	USBLS	5/07
	Fargo MSA, ND-MN	Y	21860 FQ	23880 MW	30150 TQ	USBLS	5/07
	Grand Forks MSA, ND-MN	Y	29010 FQ	33600 MW	38730 TQ	USBLS	5/07
	Ohio	Y	24320 FQ	29470 MW	37110 TQ	USBLS	5/07
	Cincinnati-Middletown MSA, OH-KY-IN	Y	25360 FQ	31030 MW	39570 TQ	USBLS	5/07
	Cleveland-Elyria-Mentor MSA, OH	Y	27450 FQ	34080 MW	42520 TQ	USBLS	5/07
	Columbus MSA, OH	Y	23610 FQ	27850 MW	34610 TQ	USBLS	5/07
	Dayton MSA, OH	Y	24520 FQ	28650 MW	34090 TQ	USBLS	5/07
	Oklahoma	Y	21010 FQ	25610 MW	33310 TQ	USBLS	5/07
	Lawton MSA, OK	Y	21820 FQ	27760 MW	34460 TQ	USBLS	5/07
	Oklahoma City MSA, OK	Y	22690 FQ	27500 MW	35700 TQ	USBLS	5/07
	Tulsa MSA, OK	Y	21720 FQ	25410 MW	31820 TQ	USBLS	5/07
	Oregon	H	11.91 FQ	14.85 MW	19.05 TQ	ORBLS	5/08
	Medford MSA, OR	Y	22020 FQ	26040 MW	33020 TQ	USBLS	5/07
	Portland-Vancouver-Beaverton MSA, OR-WA	Y	27890 FQ	35020 MW	43020 TQ	USBLS	5/07
	Pennsylvania	Y	23840 FQ	29020 MW	36380 TQ	USBLS	5/07
	Allentown-Bethlehem-Easton MSA, PA-NJ	Y	24860 FQ	28610 MW	34160 TQ	USBLS	5/07
	Philadelphia-Camden-Wilmington MSA, PA-NJ-DE-MD	Y	25410 FQ	30440 MW	37890 TQ	USBLS	5/07
	Pittsburgh MSA, PA	Y	24140 FQ	29760 MW	37250 TQ	USBLS	5/07
	Rhode Island	Y	28750 FQ	34150 MW	40650 TQ	USBLS	5/07
	Providence-Fall River-Warwick MSA, RI-MA	Y	27800 FQ	32850 MW	39650 TQ	USBLS	5/07
	South Carolina	Y	21010 FQ	25280 MW	31140 TQ	USBLS	5/07
	Charleston-North Charleston MSA, SC	Y	21310 FQ	25170 MW	29160 TQ	USBLS	5/07
	Columbia MSA, SC	Y	22560 FQ	27880 MW	35440 TQ	USBLS	5/07
	South Dakota	Y	23585 FQ	28050 MW	35507 TQ	SDBLS	7/08-9/08
	Sioux Falls MSA, SD	Y	24018 FQ	28104 MW	33733 TQ	SDBLS	7/08-9/08
	Tennessee	Y	21180 FQ	25330 MW	33050 TQ	USBLS	5/07
	Clarksville MSA, TN-KY	Y	20860 FQ	25050 MW	34420 TQ	USBLS	5/07
	Kingsport-Bristol-Bristol MSA, TN-VA	Y	20800 FQ	24950 MW	39190 TQ	USBLS	5/07
	Memphis MSA, TN-MS-AR	Y	21370 FQ	24900 MW	32350 TQ	USBLS	5/07
	Nashville-Davidson-Murfreesboro MSA, TN	Y	23550 FQ	29190 MW	37840 TQ	USBLS	5/07
	Texas	Y	22030 FQ	27730 MW	36810 TQ	USBLS	5/07
	Austin-Round Rock MSA, TX	Y	21640 FQ	26630 MW	31660 TQ	USBLS	5/07
	Dallas-Fort Worth-Arlington MSA, TX	Y	24210 FQ	29050 MW	37700 TQ	USBLS	5/07
	El Paso MSA, TX	Y	21990 FQ	28080 MW	37800 TQ	USBLS	5/07
	Houston-Sugar Land-Baytown MSA, TX	Y	25520 FQ	31810 MW	42910 TQ	USBLS	5/07
	San Antonio MSA, TX	Y	21790 FQ	27920 MW	38860 TQ	USBLS	5/07
	Utah	Y	22540 FQ	27450 MW	34290 TQ	USBLS	5/07
	Salt Lake City MSA, UT	Y	24240 FQ	29580 MW	35840 TQ	USBLS	5/07
	Vermont	Y	24250 FQ	29350 MW	36460 TQ	USBLS	5/07

AE	Average entry wage	AW	Average wage paid	FQ	First quartile wage
AER	Average entry range	AWR	Average wage range	H	Hourly
AEX	Average experienced wage	AXR	Average experienced range	HI	Highest wage paid
ATC	Average total compensation	D	Daily	HR	High end range

LO Lowest wage paid   MTC Median total compensation TCC Total cash compensation
LR Low end range   MW Median wage paid TQ Third quartile wage
M Monthly   MWR Median wage range W Weekly
MCC Median cash compensation   S See annotated source Y Yearly

Occupation/Type/Industry	Location	Per	Low	Mid	High	Source	Date
Medical Records and Health Information Technician	Burlington-South Burlington MSA, VT	Y	23910 FQ	30210 MW	37290 TQ	USBLS	5/07
	Virginia	Y	23690 FQ	30550 MW	40410 TQ	USBLS	5/07
	Richmond MSA, VA	Y	21460 FQ	27830 MW	38940 TQ	USBLS	5/07
	Virginia Beach-Norfolk-Newport News MSA, VA-NC	Y	22380 FQ	28050 MW	36790 TQ	USBLS	5/07
	Washington	H	13.20 FQ	15.67 MW	19.39 TQ	WABLS	3/08
	Olympia MSA, WA	Y	26240 FQ	35370 MW	45370 TQ	USBLS	5/07
	Seattle-Tacoma-Bellevue MSA, WA	Y	28600 FQ	33950 MW	41380 TQ	USBLS	5/07
	West Virginia	Y	19255 FQ	24530 MW	32750 TQ	WVBLS	7/08-9/08
	Charleston MSA, WV	Y	19130 FQ	23800 MW	28560 TQ	USBLS	5/07
	Appleton MSA, WI	Y	21950 FQ	24710 MW	30390 TQ	USBLS	5/07
	Milwaukee-Waukesha-West Allis MSA, WI	Y	28410 FQ	35550 MW	45460 TQ	USBLS	5/07
	Wyoming	Y	26062 FQ	30571 MW	35650 TQ	WYBLS	9/08
	Cheyenne MSA, WY	Y	29340 FQ	33214 MW	38798 TQ	WYBLS	9/08
	Puerto Rico	Y	13860 FQ	16600 MW	21820 TQ	USBLS	5/07
	San Juan-Caguas-Guaynabo MSA, PR	Y	14060 FQ	16880 MW	21170 TQ	USBLS	5/07
	Guam	Y	16640 FQ	22100 MW	32250 TQ	USBLS	5/07
Medical Resident							
UNC Hospitals	North Carolina	Y			44720-53560 HR	UNCHC	1/1/08
Medical Review Nurse							
State Government	Ohio	H	24.90 LO		34.83 HI	ODAS	2008
Medical Scientist							
Except Epidemiologist	Arizona	Y	45580 FQ	60830 MW	73440 TQ	USBLS	5/07
Except Epidemiologist	Phoenix-Mesa-Scottsdale MSA, AZ	Y	41540 FQ	59330 MW	72580 TQ	USBLS	5/07
Except Epidemiologist	Arkansas	Y	43330 FQ	54570 MW	69680 TQ	USBLS	5/07
Except Epidemiologist	Little Rock-North Little Rock MSA, AR	Y	41670 FQ	51040 MW	62610 TQ	USBLS	5/07
Except Epidemiologist	California	H	28.42 FQ	37.80 MW	49.09 TQ	CABLS	1/08-3/08
Except Epidemiologist	Bakersfield MSA, CA	H	32.84 FQ	36.37 MW	39.89 TQ	CABLS	1/08-3/08
Except Epidemiologist	Los Angeles-Long Beach-Glendale PMSA, CA	H	23.23 FQ	31.35 MW	39.18 TQ	CABLS	1/08-3/08
Except Epidemiologist	Modesto MSA, CA	H	24.78 FQ	42.30 MW	47.80 TQ	CABLS	1/08-3/08
Except Epidemiologist	Oakland-Fremont-Hayward MSA, CA	H	27.64 FQ	38.03 MW	49.21 TQ	CABLS	1/08-3/08
Except Epidemiologist	Riverside-San Bernardino-Ontario MSA, CA	H	26.82 FQ	40.16 MW	53.22 TQ	CABLS	1/08-3/08
Except Epidemiologist	Sacramento-Arden Arcade-Roseville MSA, CA	H	34.26 FQ	41.26 MW	49.30 TQ	CABLS	1/08-3/08
Except Epidemiologist	San Diego-Carlsbad-San Marcos MSA, CA	H	22.72 FQ	30.97 MW	40.57 TQ	CABLS	1/08-3/08
Except Epidemiologist	San Francisco-San Mateo-Redwood PMSA, CA	H	33.03 FQ	41.29 MW	52.19 TQ	CABLS	1/08-3/08
Except Epidemiologist	San Jose-Sunnyvale-Santa Clara MSA, CA	H	35.41 FQ	46.35 MW	60.89 TQ	CABLS	1/08-3/08
Except Epidemiologist	Santa Ana-Anaheim-Irvine PMSA, CA	Y	59210 FQ	79040 MW	98120 TQ	USBLS	5/07
Except Epidemiologist	Colorado	Y	54700 FQ	70440 MW	93580 TQ	USBLS	5/07
Except Epidemiologist	Denver-Aurora MSA, CO	Y	53620 FQ	70500 MW	96550 TQ	USBLS	5/07
Except Epidemiologist	Connecticut	H	25.95 AE	38.59 MW		CTBLS	1/08-3/08
Except Epidemiologist	Hartford-West Hartford-East Hartford MSA, CT	Y	58540 FQ	70430 MW	82280 TQ	USBLS	5/07
Except Epidemiologist	Delaware	Y	72190 FQ	94350 MW	115840 TQ	USBLS	5/07
Except Epidemiologist	Wilmington PMSA, DE-MD-NJ	Y	74800 FQ	95490 MW	116940 TQ	USBLS	5/07
Except Epidemiologist	District of Columbia	Y	43750 FQ	72480 MW	105100 TQ	USBLS	5/07
Except Epidemiologist	Washington-Arlington-Alexandria MSA, DC-VA-MD-WV	Y	67310 FQ	91730 MW	114780 TQ	USBLS	5/07
Except Epidemiologist	Florida	Y	44020 FQ	62360 MW	84710 TQ	USBLS	5/07
Except Epidemiologist	Fort Lauderdale-Pompano Beach-Deerfield Beach PMSA, FL	Y	42090 FQ	47010 MW	63550 TQ	USBLS	5/07

AE	Average entry wage	AW	Average wage paid	FQ	First quartile wage
AER	Average entry range	AWR	Average wage range	H	Hourly
AEX	Average experienced wage	AXR	Average experienced range	HI	Highest wage paid
ATC	Average total compensation	D	Daily	HR	High end range

LO Lowest wage paid · LR Low end range · M Monthly · MCC Median cash compensation · MTC Median total compensation · MW Median wage paid · MWR Median wage range · S See annotated source · TCC Total cash compensation · TQ Third quartile wage · W Weekly · Y Yearly

Occupation/Type/Industry	Location	Per	Low	Mid	High	Source	Date
Medical Scientist							
Except Epidemiologist	Jacksonville MSA, FL	Y	35180 FQ	49640 MW	67950 TQ	USBLS	5/07
Except Epidemiologist	Miami-Fort Lauderdale-Miami Beach MSA, FL	Y	42460 FQ	50720 MW	76620 TQ	USBLS	5/07
Except Epidemiologist	Orlando-Kissimmee MSA, FL	Y	71810 FQ	84530 MW	94600 TQ	USBLS	5/07
Except Epidemiologist	Tampa-St. Petersburg-Clearwater MSA, FL	Y	37820 FQ	48700 MW	68770 TQ	USBLS	5/07
Except Epidemiologist	West Palm Beach-Boca Raton-Boynton Beach PMSA, FL	Y	38170 FQ	55560 MW	99690 TQ	USBLS	5/07
Except Epidemiologist	Georgia	Y	67010 FQ	130650 MW		USBLS	5/07
Except Epidemiologist	Atlanta-Sandy Springs-Marietta MSA, GA	Y	47700 FQ	67270 MW	109830 TQ	USBLS	5/07
Except Epidemiologist	Hawaii	Y	44070 FQ	58090 MW	76250 TQ	USBLS	5/07
Except Epidemiologist	Honolulu MSA, HI	Y	43930 FQ	58650 MW	77330 TQ	USBLS	5/07
Except Epidemiologist	Idaho	Y	28910 FQ	36690 MW	47240 TQ	USBLS	5/07
Except Epidemiologist	Boise City-Nampa MSA, ID	Y	26430 FQ	33380 MW	42030 TQ	USBLS	5/07
Except Epidemiologist	Illinois	Y	51400 FQ	60740 MW	89920 TQ	USBLS	5/07
Except Epidemiologist	Chicago-Naperville-Joliet MSA, IL-IN-WI	Y	52130 FQ	61190 MW	96460 TQ	USBLS	5/07
Except Epidemiologist	Indiana	Y	39190 FQ	52880 MW	60560 TQ	USBLS	5/07
Except Epidemiologist	Indianapolis-Carmel MSA, IN	Y	38970 FQ	52630 MW	60100 TQ	USBLS	5/07
Except Epidemiologist	Iowa	Y	42990 FQ	53200 MW	67860 TQ	USBLS	5/07
Except Epidemiologist	Kansas	Y	46400 FQ	51340 MW	70250 TQ	USBLS	5/07
Except Epidemiologist	Wichita MSA, KS	Y	46820 FQ	52940 MW	66380 TQ	USBLS	5/07
Except Epidemiologist	Kentucky	Y	36627 FQ	43955 MW	53098 TQ	KYBLS	2008
Except Epidemiologist	Louisville-Jefferson County MSA, KY-IN	Y	35730 FQ	43920 MW	55320 TQ	USBLS	5/07
Except Epidemiologist	Louisiana	H	18.73 FQ	27.18 MW	33.62 TQ	LABLS	1/08-3/08
Except Epidemiologist	Maine	Y	41880 FQ	61250 MW	97380 TQ	USBLS	5/07
Except Epidemiologist	Portland-South Portland-Biddeford MSA, ME	Y	43100 FQ	63920 MW	100620 TQ	USBLS	5/07
Except Epidemiologist	Maryland	Y		77325 MW		MDBLS	3/08
Except Epidemiologist	Baltimore-Towson MSA, MD	Y	40250 FQ	47920 MW	69510 TQ	USBLS	5/07
Except Epidemiologist	Bethesda-Gaithersburg-Frederick PMSA, MD	Y	77750 FQ	95880 MW	117080 TQ	USBLS	5/07
Except Epidemiologist	Massachusetts	Y	59140 FQ	83340 MW	110560 TQ	USBLS	5/07
Except Epidemiologist	Boston-Cambridge-Quincy NECTA, MA	Y	57160 FQ	82350 MW	110820 TQ	USBLS	5/07
Except Epidemiologist	Worcester MSA, MA-CT	Y	67430 FQ	80940 MW	98990 TQ	USBLS	5/07
Except Epidemiologist	Michigan	Y	43440 FQ	52990 MW	72140 TQ	USBLS	5/07
Except Epidemiologist	Detroit-Warren-Livonia MSA, MI	Y	46300 FQ	63360 MW	74080 TQ	USBLS	5/07
Except Epidemiologist	Warren-Troy-Farmington Hills PMSA, MI	Y	72850 FQ			USBLS	5/07
Except Epidemiologist	Minnesota	Y	50145 FQ	63746 MW	86899 TQ	MNBLS	10/08-12/08
Except Epidemiologist	Duluth-Superior MSA, MN-WI	Y	60607 FQ	85759 MW	105365 TQ	MNBLS	10/08-12/08
Except Epidemiologist	Minneapolis-Saint Paul MSA, MN-WI	Y	49863 FQ	63516 MW	86606 TQ	MNBLS	10/08-12/08
Except Epidemiologist	Mississippi	Y	34450 FQ	41830 MW	55230 TQ	USBLS	5/07
Except Epidemiologist	Missouri	Y	50040 FQ	61300 MW	78250 TQ	USBLS	5/07
Except Epidemiologist	Kansas City MSA, MO-KS	Y	46200 FQ	51280 MW	73280 TQ	USBLS	5/07
Except Epidemiologist	St. Louis MSA, MO-IL	Y	51740 FQ	62630 MW	78850 TQ	USBLS	5/07
Except Epidemiologist	Montana	Y	44420 FQ	50750 MW	63140 TQ	USBLS	5/07
Except Epidemiologist	Nebraska	Y	35360 FQ	44740 MW	64440 TQ	USBLS	5/07
Except Epidemiologist	Omaha-Council Bluffs MSA, NE-IA	Y	34040 FQ	39790 MW	51920 TQ	USBLS	5/07
Except Epidemiologist	Nevada	H	22.76 FQ	35.10 MW	48.02 TQ	NVBLS	5/08
Except Epidemiologist	Las Vegas-Paradise MSA, NV	H	21.99 FQ	30.47 MW	46.94 TQ	NVBLS	5/08
Except Epidemiologist	New Jersey	Y	64110 FQ	80730 MW	107690 TQ	USBLS	5/07
Except Epidemiologist	Camden PMSA, NJ	Y	63230 FQ	76750 MW	94920 TQ	USBLS	5/07
Except Epidemiologist	Edison PMSA, NJ	Y	61490 FQ	79390 MW	106420 TQ	USBLS	5/07
Except Epidemiologist	Newark-Union PMSA, NJ-PA	Y	65220 FQ	80550 MW	107630 TQ	USBLS	5/07
Except Epidemiologist	Trenton-Ewing MSA, NJ	Y	67810 FQ	83960 MW	101580 TQ	USBLS	5/07
Except Epidemiologist	New York	Y	49290 FQ	68170 MW	96010 TQ	USBLS	5/07
Except Epidemiologist	Albany-Schenectady-Troy MSA, NY	Y	40600 FQ	51010 MW	71710 TQ	USBLS	5/07
Except Epidemiologist	Buffalo-Niagara Falls MSA, NY	Y	51030 FQ	59950 MW	85430 TQ	USBLS	5/07
Except Epidemiologist	Nassau-Suffolk PMSA, NY	Y	46680 FQ	61300 MW	99050 TQ	USBLS	5/07
Except Epidemiologist	New York-Northern New Jersey-Long Island MSA, NY-NJ-PA	Y	61450 FQ	79160 MW	107800 TQ	USBLS	5/07

AE	Average entry wage	AW	Average wage paid	FQ	First quartile wage
AER	Average entry range	AWR	Average wage range	H	Hourly
AEX	Average experienced wage	AXR	Average experienced range	HI	Highest wage paid
ATC	Average total compensation	D	Daily	HR	High end range

LO	Lowest wage paid	MTC	Median total compensation	TCC	Total cash compensation
LR	Low end range	MW	Median wage paid	TQ	Third quartile wage
M	Monthly	MWR	Median wage range	W	Weekly
MCC	Median cash compensation	S	See annotated source	Y	Yearly

Occupation/Type/Industry	Location	Per	Low	Mid	High	Source	Date
Medical Scientist							
Except Epidemiologist	North Carolina	Y	55090 FQ	72930 MW	99290 TQ	USBLS	5/07
Except Epidemiologist	Raleigh-Cary MSA, NC	Y	48420 FQ	63250 MW	84180 TQ	USBLS	5/07
Except Epidemiologist	North Dakota	Y	38180 FQ	68050 MW	84140 TQ	USBLS	5/07
Except Epidemiologist	Ohio	Y	41680 FQ	55380 MW	69450 TQ	USBLS	5/07
Except Epidemiologist	Cincinnati-Middletown MSA, OH-KY-IN	Y	48600 FQ	57730 MW	70400 TQ	USBLS	5/07
Except Epidemiologist	Cleveland-Elyria-Mentor MSA, OH	Y	50840 FQ	60420 MW	75790 TQ	USBLS	5/07
Except Epidemiologist	Columbus MSA, OH	Y	33840 FQ	44610 MW	59530 TQ	USBLS	5/07
Except Epidemiologist	Dayton MSA, OH	Y	59770 FQ	67470 MW	97080 TQ	USBLS	5/07
Except Epidemiologist	Oklahoma	Y	40150 FQ	44440 MW	48700 TQ	USBLS	5/07
Except Epidemiologist	Oklahoma City MSA, OK	Y	40040 FQ	44280 MW	48510 TQ	USBLS	5/07
Except Epidemiologist	Tulsa MSA, OK	Y	45330 FQ	53000 MW	138500 TQ	USBLS	5/07
Except Epidemiologist	Oregon	H	21.33 FQ	27.20 MW	44.97 TQ	ORBLS	5/08
Except Epidemiologist	Portland-Vancouver-Beaverton MSA, OR-WA	Y	45780 FQ	65200 MW	95010 TQ	USBLS	5/07
Except Epidemiologist	Pennsylvania	Y	51730 FQ	77060 MW	103720 TQ	USBLS	5/07
Except Epidemiologist	Philadelphia-Camden-Wilmington MSA, PA-NJ-DE-MD	Y	66890 FQ	89520 MW	109740 TQ	USBLS	5/07
Except Epidemiologist	Pittsburgh MSA, PA	Y	27270 FQ	35290 MW	52020 TQ	USBLS	5/07
Except Epidemiologist	Rhode Island	Y	43280 FQ	58440 MW	79860 TQ	USBLS	5/07
Except Epidemiologist	Providence-Fall River-Warwick MSA, RI-MA	Y	45330 FQ	60640 MW	89390 TQ	USBLS	5/07
Except Epidemiologist	South Carolina	Y	39310 FQ	51390 MW	103250 TQ	USBLS	5/07
Except Epidemiologist	Tennessee	Y	32930 FQ	41450 MW	60160 TQ	USBLS	5/07
Except Epidemiologist	Nashville-Davidson-Murfreesboro MSA, TN	Y	32250 FQ	55450 MW	66310 TQ	USBLS	5/07
Except Epidemiologist	Texas	Y	37440 FQ	46430 MW	58520 TQ	USBLS	5/07
Except Epidemiologist	Austin-Round Rock MSA, TX	Y	43470 FQ	57430 MW	74260 TQ	USBLS	5/07
Except Epidemiologist	Dallas-Fort Worth-Arlington MSA, TX	Y	38890 FQ	47360 MW	59460 TQ	USBLS	5/07
Except Epidemiologist	Houston-Sugar Land-Baytown MSA, TX	Y	36250 FQ	45450 MW	56340 TQ	USBLS	5/07
Except Epidemiologist	San Antonio MSA, TX	Y	49670 FQ	83340 MW	107300 TQ	USBLS	5/07
Except Epidemiologist	Utah	Y	37580 FQ	49040 MW	66170 TQ	USBLS	5/07
Except Epidemiologist	Salt Lake City MSA, UT	Y	37170 FQ	47900 MW	64410 TQ	USBLS	5/07
Except Epidemiologist	Vermont	Y	63380 FQ	96990 MW	144150 TQ	USBLS	5/07
Except Epidemiologist	Burlington-South Burlington MSA, VT	Y	64950 FQ	97760 MW	145200 TQ	USBLS	5/07
Except Epidemiologist	Virginia	Y	50900 FQ	63570 MW	91220 TQ	USBLS	5/07
Except Epidemiologist	Richmond MSA, VA	Y	56890 FQ	70710 MW	93460 TQ	USBLS	5/07
Except Epidemiologist	Virginia Beach-Norfolk-Newport News MSA, VA-NC	Y	40470 FQ	69680 MW	88720 TQ	USBLS	5/07
Except Epidemiologist	Washington	H	22.71 FQ	30.72 MW	40.90 TQ	WABLS	3/08
Except Epidemiologist	Seattle-Tacoma-Bellevue MSA, WA	Y	45150 FQ	59110 MW	80450 TQ	USBLS	5/07
Except Epidemiologist	West Virginia	Y	50865 FQ	81203 MW	117122 TQ	WVBLS	7/08-9/08
Except Epidemiologist	Charleston MSA, WV	Y	48860 FQ	63770 MW	106010 TQ	USBLS	5/07
Except Epidemiologist	Milwaukee-Waukesha-West Allis MSA, WI	Y	44130 FQ	57610 MW	78620 TQ	USBLS	5/07
Except Epidemiologist	Wyoming	Y	45131 FQ	52643 MW	76304 TQ	WYBLS	9/08
Except Epidemiologist	San Juan-Caguas-Guaynabo MSA, PR	Y	41390 FQ	52970 MW	64130 TQ	USBLS	5/07
Medical Secretary	Alabama	Y	20130 FQ	23210 MW	28300 TQ	USBLS	5/07
	Birmingham-Hoover MSA, AL	Y	21090 FQ	25740 MW	30720 TQ	USBLS	5/07
	Alaska	Y	28740 FQ	32170 MW	36840 TQ	USBLS	5/07
	Anchorage MSA, AK	Y	29410 FQ	32730 MW	37100 TQ	USBLS	5/07
	Arizona	Y	25190 FQ	29450 MW	34410 TQ	USBLS	5/07
	Phoenix-Mesa-Scottsdale MSA, AZ	Y	26290 FQ	30310 MW	35320 TQ	USBLS	5/07
	Prescott MSA, AZ	Y	24060 FQ	27600 MW	30580 TQ	USBLS	5/07
	Tucson MSA, AZ	Y	22570 FQ	28150 MW	33190 TQ	USBLS	5/07
	Fayetteville-Springdale-Rogers MSA, AR-MO	Y	19330 FQ	22420 MW	25760 TQ	USBLS	5/07
	California	H	11.38 FQ	14.38 MW	18.10 TQ	CABLS	1/08-3/08
	Los Angeles-Long Beach-Glendale PMSA, CA	H	11.23 FQ	14.19 MW	17.77 TQ	CABLS	1/08-3/08
	Oakland-Fremont-Hayward MSA, CA	H	12.04 FQ	16.69 MW	21.96 TQ	CABLS	1/08-3/08

AE	Average entry wage	AW	Average wage paid	FQ	First quartile wage
AER	Average entry range	AWR	Average wage range	H	Hourly
AEX	Average experienced wage	AXR	Average experienced range	HI	Highest wage paid
ATC	Average total compensation	D	Daily	HR	High end range

LO	Lowest wage paid	MTC	Median total compensation	TCC	Total cash compensation
LR	Low end range	MW	Median wage paid	TQ	Third quartile wage
M	Monthly	MWR	Median wage range	W	Weekly
MCC	Median cash compensation	S	See annotated source	Y	Yearly

Medical Secretary

Occupation/Type/Industry	Location	Per	Low	Mid	High	Source	Date
Medical Secretary	Riverside-San Bernardino-Ontario MSA, CA	H	10.81 FQ	12.80 MW	15.56 TQ	CABLS	1/08-3/08
	Sacramento-Arden Arcade-Roseville MSA, CA	H	12.12 FQ	15.25 MW	18.80 TQ	CABLS	1/08-3/08
	San Diego-Carlsbad-San Marcos MSA, CA	H	11.33 FQ	13.74 MW	16.27 TQ	CABLS	1/08-3/08
	San Francisco-San Mateo-Redwood PMSA, CA	H	13.91 FQ	18.11 MW	23.17 TQ	CABLS	1/08-3/08
	San Jose-Sunnyvale-Santa Clara MSA, CA	H	12.62 FQ	17.69 MW	21.43 TQ	CABLS	1/08-3/08
	Santa Ana-Anaheim-Irvine PMSA, CA	Y	22440 FQ	28850 MW	35780 TQ	USBLS	5/07
	Colorado	Y	26070 FQ	32370 MW	39430 TQ	USBLS	5/07
	Boulder MSA, CO	Y	24540 FQ	29710 MW	37200 TQ	USBLS	5/07
	Denver-Aurora MSA, CO	Y	29590 FQ	35180 MW	41290 TQ	USBLS	5/07
	Connecticut	H	13.49 AE	16.87 MW		CTBLS	1/08-3/08
	Bridgeport-Stamford-Norwalk MSA, CT	Y	29930 FQ	36100 MW	41360 TQ	USBLS	5/07
	Hartford-West Hartford-East Hartford MSA, CT	Y	29110 FQ	33650 MW	39260 TQ	USBLS	5/07
	Delaware	Y	25310 FQ	30730 MW	36340 TQ	USBLS	5/07
	Dover MSA, DE	Y	22760 FQ	25720 MW	32110 TQ	USBLS	5/07
	Wilmington PMSA, DE-MD-NJ	Y	27290 FQ	32540 MW	37390 TQ	USBLS	5/07
	District of Columbia	Y	30690 FQ	34730 MW	39110 TQ	USBLS	5/07
	Washington-Arlington-Alexandria MSA, DC-VA-MD-WV	Y	28180 FQ	33570 MW	39210 TQ	USBLS	5/07
	Florida	Y	22260 FQ	26460 MW	31320 TQ	USBLS	5/07
	Fort Lauderdale-Pompano Beach-Deerfield Beach PMSA, FL	Y	24240 FQ	27860 MW	31390 TQ	USBLS	5/07
	Jacksonville MSA, FL	Y	23490 FQ	27960 MW	32590 TQ	USBLS	5/07
	Miami-Fort Lauderdale-Miami Beach MSA, FL	Y	23150 FQ	27680 MW	32000 TQ	USBLS	5/07
	Orlando-Kissimmee MSA, FL	Y	21510 FQ	24500 MW	29640 TQ	USBLS	5/07
	Tampa-St. Petersburg-Clearwater MSA, FL	Y	22480 FQ	26480 MW	31210 TQ	USBLS	5/07
	West Palm Beach-Boca Raton-Boynton Beach PMSA, FL	Y	23930 FQ	28900 MW	34400 TQ	USBLS	5/07
	Georgia	Y	22370 FQ	26970 MW	31280 TQ	USBLS	5/07
	Athens-Clarke County MSA, GA	Y	23080 FQ	28430 MW	32850 TQ	USBLS	5/07
	Atlanta-Sandy Springs-Marietta MSA, GA	Y	25060 FQ	28820 MW	32370 TQ	USBLS	5/07
	Hawaii	Y	27980 FQ	32480 MW	37610 TQ	USBLS	5/07
	Honolulu MSA, HI	Y	28160 FQ	32470 MW	36900 TQ	USBLS	5/07
	Idaho	Y	21580 FQ	25990 MW	30780 TQ	USBLS	5/07
	Boise City-Nampa MSA, ID	Y	23480 FQ	28350 MW	32780 TQ	USBLS	5/07
	Illinois	Y	25730 FQ	31190 MW	38820 TQ	USBLS	5/07
	Chicago-Naperville-Joliet MSA, IL-IN-WI	Y	26860 FQ	32040 MW	40090 TQ	USBLS	5/07
	Indiana	Y	23420 FQ	27620 MW	32150 TQ	USBLS	5/07
	Gary PMSA, IN	Y	22770 FQ	26980 MW	31160 TQ	USBLS	5/07
	Indianapolis-Carmel MSA, IN	Y	24940 FQ	28810 MW	33650 TQ	USBLS	5/07
	Iowa	Y	22460 FQ	27230 MW	32250 TQ	USBLS	5/07
	Cedar Rapids MSA, IA	Y	24660 FQ	27460 MW	30590 TQ	USBLS	5/07
	Davenport-Moline-Rock Island MSA, IA-IL	Y	24820 FQ	28730 MW	34440 TQ	USBLS	5/07
	Des Moines-West Des Moines MSA, IA	Y	25750 FQ	30490 MW	35840 TQ	USBLS	5/07
	Kansas	Y	22050 FQ	25630 MW	30830 TQ	USBLS	5/07
	Topeka MSA, KS	Y	22850 FQ	26160 MW	31240 TQ	USBLS	5/07
	Wichita MSA, KS	Y	21190 FQ	23310 MW	27830 TQ	USBLS	5/07
	Kentucky	Y	21380 FQ	25255 MW	29726 TQ	KYBLS	2008
	Louisville-Jefferson County MSA, KY-IN	Y	23090 FQ	27030 MW	31110 TQ	USBLS	5/07
	Louisiana	H	9.22 FQ	11.01 MW	13.37 TQ	LABLS	1/08-3/08
	Baton Rouge MSA, LA	Y	23440 FQ	27320 MW	31980 TQ	USBLS	5/07
	Houma-Bayou Cane-Thibodaux MSA, LA	Y	18360 FQ	20830 MW	23120 TQ	USBLS	5/07

AE	Average entry wage	AW	Average wage paid	FQ	First quartile wage
AER	Average entry range	AWR	Average wage range	H	Hourly
AEX	Average experienced wage	AXR	Average experienced range	HI	Highest wage paid
ATC	Average total compensation	D	Daily	HR	High end range

LO	Lowest wage paid	MTC	Median total compensation	TCC	Total cash compensation
LR	Low end range	MW	Median wage paid	TQ	Third quartile wage
M	Monthly	MWR	Median wage range	W	Weekly
MCC	Median cash compensation	S	See annotated source	Y	Yearly

Occupation/Type/Industry	Location	Per	Low	Mid	High	Source	Date
Medical Secretary	New Orleans-Metairie-Kenner MSA, LA	Y	21090 FQ	24630 MW	30140 TQ	USBLS	5/07
	Maine	Y	23410 FQ	27450 MW	31590 TQ	USBLS	5/07
	Portland-South Portland-Biddeford MSA, ME	Y	27070 FQ	30840 MW	35720 TQ	USBLS	5/07
	Maryland	Y		32125 MW		MDBLS	3/08
	Baltimore-Towson MSA, MD	Y	27290 FQ	32300 MW	37860 TQ	USBLS	5/07
	Bethesda-Gaithersburg-Frederick PMSA, MD	Y	27210 FQ	32580 MW	37870 TQ	USBLS	5/07
	Hagerstown-Martinsburg MSA, MD-WV	Y	22710 FQ	26960 MW	30910 TQ	USBLS	5/07
	Massachusetts	Y	28610 FQ	33820 MW	39680 TQ	USBLS	5/07
	Boston-Cambridge-Quincy NECTA, MA	Y	29420 FQ	34710 MW	40540 TQ	USBLS	5/07
	Springfield MSA, MA-CT	Y	26350 FQ	31160 MW	37330 TQ	USBLS	5/07
	Worcester MSA, MA-CT	Y	29070 FQ	34190 MW	40540 TQ	USBLS	5/07
	Michigan	Y	26120 FQ	29890 MW	35090 TQ	USBLS	5/07
	Detroit-Warren-Livonia MSA, MI	Y	27120 FQ	30950 MW	36470 TQ	USBLS	5/07
	Grand Rapids-Wyoming MSA, MI	Y	25580 FQ	29260 MW	33590 TQ	USBLS	5/07
	Warren-Troy-Farmington Hills PMSA, MI	Y	26980 FQ	31090 MW	38340 TQ	USBLS	5/07
	Minnesota	Y	29610 FQ	34304 MW	39238 TQ	MNBLS	10/08-12/08
	Duluth-Superior MSA, MN-WI	Y	28195 FQ	32108 MW	36979 TQ	MNBLS	10/08-12/08
	Minneapolis-Saint Paul MSA, MN-WI	Y	30443 FQ	34752 MW	39342 TQ	MNBLS	10/08-12/08
	Rochester MSA, MN	Y	33580 FQ	37862 MW	42653 TQ	MNBLS	10/08-12/08
	Mississippi	Y	21530 FQ	25570 MW	31950 TQ	USBLS	5/07
	Jackson MSA, MS	Y	22610 FQ	26110 MW	30640 TQ	USBLS	5/07
	Missouri	Y	22160 FQ	26740 MW	31620 TQ	USBLS	5/07
	Kansas City MSA, MO-KS	Y	25790 FQ	29650 MW	33890 TQ	USBLS	5/07
	St. Louis MSA, MO-IL	Y	23320 FQ	27940 MW	32410 TQ	USBLS	5/07
	Springfield MSA, MO	Y	19540 FQ	23870 MW	30460 TQ	USBLS	5/07
	Montana	Y	21850 FQ	26940 MW	31370 TQ	USBLS	5/07
	Billings MSA, MT	Y	23860 FQ	29100 MW	35380 TQ	USBLS	5/07
	Nebraska	Y	23910 FQ	28120 MW	32530 TQ	USBLS	5/07
	Omaha-Council Bluffs MSA, NE-IA	Y	25720 FQ	29220 MW	33770 TQ	USBLS	5/07
	Nevada	H	13.74 FQ	16.19 MW	19.04 TQ	NVBLS	5/08
	Las Vegas-Paradise MSA, NV	H	13.43 FQ	15.78 MW	19.02 TQ	NVBLS	5/08
	New Hampshire	H	12.83 AE	15.87 MW	18.04 AEX	NHBLS	6/08
	Manchester MSA, NH	Y	27200 FQ	31330 MW	35270 TQ	USBLS	5/07
	Nashua NECTA, NH-MA	Y	31430 FQ	36590 MW	43140 TQ	USBLS	5/07
	New Jersey	Y	27670 FQ	32720 MW	39390 TQ	USBLS	5/07
	Camden PMSA, NJ	Y	29350 FQ	33670 MW	39550 TQ	USBLS	5/07
	Edison PMSA, NJ	Y	27500 FQ	32330 MW	39360 TQ	USBLS	5/07
	Newark-Union PMSA, NJ-PA	Y	28550 FQ	33430 MW	39960 TQ	USBLS	5/07
	Trenton-Ewing MSA, NJ	Y	26540 FQ	30730 MW	35270 TQ	USBLS	5/07
	New Mexico	Y	20620 FQ	24910 MW	31230 TQ	USBLS	5/07
	Albuquerque MSA, NM	Y	23920 FQ	29970 MW	36790 TQ	USBLS	5/07
	Santa Fe MSA, NM	Y	23690 FQ	30530 MW	34370 TQ	USBLS	5/07
	New York	Y	25720 FQ	30610 MW	37570 TQ	USBLS	5/07
	Albany-Schenectady-Troy MSA, NY	Y	25530 FQ	28800 MW	32490 TQ	USBLS	5/07
	Buffalo-Niagara Falls MSA, NY	Y	24510 FQ	28020 MW	32130 TQ	USBLS	5/07
	Nassau-Suffolk PMSA, NY	Y	29430 FQ	34820 MW	40580 TQ	USBLS	5/07
	New York-Northern New Jersey-Long Island MSA, NY-NJ-PA	Y	27910 FQ	33330 MW	40350 TQ	USBLS	5/07
	North Carolina	Y	22940 FQ	26670 MW	30540 TQ	USBLS	5/07
	Charlotte-Gastonia-Concord MSA, NC-SC	Y	24900 FQ	28330 MW	32030 TQ	USBLS	5/07
	Raleigh-Cary MSA, NC	Y	24730 FQ	27820 MW	30920 TQ	USBLS	5/07
	North Dakota	Y	21770 FQ	25170 MW	29330 TQ	USBLS	5/07
	Fargo MSA, ND-MN	Y	21470 FQ	25070 MW	29510 TQ	USBLS	5/07
	Grand Forks MSA, ND-MN	Y	23670 FQ	26990 MW	30470 TQ	USBLS	5/07
	Ohio	Y	23000 FQ	27400 MW	32070 TQ	USBLS	5/07
	Cincinnati-Middletown MSA, OH-KY-IN	Y	23670 FQ	27560 MW	32110 TQ	USBLS	5/07

AE	Average entry wage	AW	Average wage paid	FQ	First quartile wage
AER	Average entry range	AWR	Average wage range	H	Hourly
AEX	Average experienced wage	AXR	Average experienced range	HI	Highest wage paid
ATC	Average total compensation	D	Daily	HR	High end range

LO	Lowest wage paid	MTC	Median total compensation	TCC	Total cash compensation
LR	Low end range	MW	Median wage paid	TQ	Third quartile wage
M	Monthly	MWR	Median wage range	W	Weekly
MCC	Median cash compensation	S	See annotated source	Y	Yearly

Occupation/Type/Industry	Location	Per	Low	Mid	High	Source	Date
Medical Secretary	Cleveland-Elyria-Mentor MSA, OH	Y	24210 FQ	28580 MW	33940 TQ	USBLS	5/07
	Columbus MSA, OH	Y	25210 FQ	29360 MW	34360 TQ	USBLS	5/07
	Dayton MSA, OH	Y	23530 FQ	27300 MW	31080 TQ	USBLS	5/07
	Oklahoma	Y	20360 FQ	23330 MW	27860 TQ	USBLS	5/07
	Oklahoma City MSA, OK	Y	20580 FQ	23400 MW	27660 TQ	USBLS	5/07
	Tulsa MSA, OK	Y	22010 FQ	25180 MW	29410 TQ	USBLS	5/07
	Oregon	H	13.12 FQ	15.48 MW	18.40 TQ	ORBLS	5/08
	Eugene-Springfield MSA, OR	Y	27190 FQ	31820 MW	37100 TQ	USBLS	5/07
	Portland-Vancouver-Beaverton MSA, OR-WA	Y	28600 FQ	33740 MW	39910 TQ	USBLS	5/07
	Pennsylvania	Y	22660 FQ	27040 MW	31760 TQ	USBLS	5/07
	Allentown-Bethlehem-Easton MSA, PA-NJ	Y	23870 FQ	27440 MW	32270 TQ	USBLS	5/07
	Philadelphia-Camden-Wilmington MSA, PA-NJ-DE-MD	Y	27170 FQ	31830 MW	37710 TQ	USBLS	5/07
	Pittsburgh MSA, PA	Y	21660 FQ	25240 MW	29560 TQ	USBLS	5/07
	Reading MSA, PA	Y	22690 FQ	25910 MW	29450 TQ	USBLS	5/07
	Rhode Island	Y	27980 FQ	31920 MW	36880 TQ	USBLS	5/07
	Providence-Fall River-Warwick MSA, RI-MA	Y	27860 FQ	31750 MW	36740 TQ	USBLS	5/07
	South Carolina	Y	22200 FQ	25900 MW	30070 TQ	USBLS	5/07
	Charleston-North Charleston MSA, SC	Y	23680 FQ	27200 MW	31600 TQ	USBLS	5/07
	Columbia MSA, SC	Y	22830 FQ	26190 MW	30160 TQ	USBLS	5/07
	Florence MSA, SC	Y	18840 FQ	23550 MW	27660 TQ	USBLS	5/07
	South Dakota	Y	26324 FQ	29741 MW	34496 TQ	SDBLS	7/08-9/08
	Sioux Falls MSA, SD	Y	27375 FQ	31776 MW	37995 TQ	SDBLS	7/08-9/08
	Tennessee	Y	21990 FQ	25890 MW	30950 TQ	USBLS	5/07
	Memphis MSA, TN-MS-AR	Y	23120 FQ	27230 MW	31990 TQ	USBLS	5/07
	Nashville-Davidson-Murfreesboro MSA, TN	Y	23280 FQ	27620 MW	32880 TQ	USBLS	5/07
	Texas	Y	21870 FQ	26720 MW	31560 TQ	USBLS	5/07
	Austin-Round Rock MSA, TX	Y	23930 FQ	27150 MW	30700 TQ	USBLS	5/07
	Dallas-Fort Worth-Arlington MSA, TX	Y	23460 FQ	27860 MW	32340 TQ	USBLS	5/07
	El Paso MSA, TX	Y	18100 FQ	22690 MW	27440 TQ	USBLS	5/07
	Houston-Sugar Land-Baytown MSA, TX	Y	25780 FQ	29750 MW	35140 TQ	USBLS	5/07
	San Antonio MSA, TX	Y	20130 FQ	23800 MW	28710 TQ	USBLS	5/07
	Utah	Y	21430 FQ	24860 MW	29840 TQ	USBLS	5/07
	St. George MSA, UT	Y	22840 FQ	26840 MW	31170 TQ	USBLS	5/07
	Salt Lake City MSA, UT	Y	21770 FQ	25280 MW	30230 TQ	USBLS	5/07
	Vermont	Y	26550 FQ	30690 MW	40330 TQ	USBLS	5/07
	Burlington-South Burlington MSA, VT	Y	28160 FQ	34860 MW	44890 TQ	USBLS	5/07
	Virginia	Y	23860 FQ	28740 MW	35050 TQ	USBLS	5/07
	Richmond MSA, VA	Y	24350 FQ	28580 MW	33710 TQ	USBLS	5/07
	Virginia Beach-Norfolk-Newport News MSA, VA-NC	Y	22330 FQ	26180 MW	31380 TQ	USBLS	5/07
	Washington	H	13.86 FQ	16.33 MW	19.58 TQ	WABLS	3/08
	Seattle-Tacoma-Bellevue MSA, WA	Y	30560 FQ	35940 MW	42840 TQ	USBLS	5/07
	West Virginia	Y	20139 FQ	24440 MW	29220 TQ	WVBLS	7/08-9/08
	Charleston MSA, WV	Y	21660 FQ	24580 MW	28590 TQ	USBLS	5/07
	Huntington-Ashland MSA, WV-KY-OH	Y	20980 FQ	24070 MW	28160 TQ	USBLS	5/07
	Wisconsin	Y	24300 FQ	28910 MW	34510 TQ	USBLS	5/07
	Milwaukee-Waukesha-West Allis MSA, WI	Y	23540 FQ	29160 MW	36850 TQ	USBLS	5/07
	Wyoming	Y	23166 FQ	28006 MW	32683 TQ	WYBLS	9/08
	Cheyenne MSA, WY	Y	22931 FQ	26539 MW	31724 TQ	WYBLS	9/08
	Puerto Rico	Y	13090 FQ	15110 MW	19060 TQ	USBLS	5/07
	San Juan-Caguas-Guaynabo MSA, PR	Y	13650 FQ	16480 MW	22040 TQ	USBLS	5/07
	Virgin Islands	Y	25340 FQ	29960 MW	35200 TQ	USBLS	5/07
Medical/Surgical Registered Nurse							
Florida Health Care System	Florida	Y		54851 AW		FHA	2007

AE Average entry wage	AW Average wage paid	FQ First quartile wage	LO Lowest wage paid
AER Average entry range	AWR Average wage range	H Hourly	LR Low end range
AEX Average experienced wage	AXR Average experienced range	HI Highest wage paid	M Monthly
ATC Average total compensation	D Daily	HR High end range	MCC Median cash compensation

MTC Median total compensation	TCC Total cash compensation	
MW Median wage paid	TQ Third quartile wage	
MWR Median wage range	W Weekly	
S See annotated source	Y Yearly	

Occupation/Type/Industry	Location	Per	Low	Mid	High	Source	Date
Medical Transcriptionist	Alabama	Y	23000 FQ	26900 MW	30830 TQ	USBLS	5/07
	Birmingham-Hoover MSA, AL	Y	24140 FQ	28710 MW	33860 TQ	USBLS	5/07
	Tuscaloosa MSA, AL	Y	24070 FQ	26830 MW	29260 TQ	USBLS	5/07
	Alaska	Y	34910 FQ	39160 MW	45440 TQ	USBLS	5/07
	Anchorage MSA, AK	Y	36040 FQ	40750 MW	47210 TQ	USBLS	5/07
	Arizona	Y	30150 FQ	34010 MW	37280 TQ	USBLS	5/07
	Phoenix-Mesa-Scottsdale MSA, AZ	Y	31210 FQ	34580 MW	37610 TQ	USBLS	5/07
	Tucson MSA, AZ	Y	28070 FQ	32140 MW	35580 TQ	USBLS	5/07
	Arkansas	Y	22580 FQ	26520 MW	30290 TQ	USBLS	5/07
	Little Rock-North Little Rock MSA, AR	Y	23180 FQ	28180 MW	32380 TQ	USBLS	5/07
	California	H	16.52 FQ	19.44 MW	23.04 TQ	CABLS	1/08-3/08
	Los Angeles-Long Beach-Glendale PMSA, CA	H	17.43 FQ	21.23 MW	24.54 TQ	CABLS	1/08-3/08
	Oakland-Fremont-Hayward MSA, CA	H	17.35 FQ	20.93 MW	25.32 TQ	CABLS	1/08-3/08
	Riverside-San Bernardino-Ontario MSA, CA	H	15.39 FQ	18.81 MW	21.06 TQ	CABLS	1/08-3/08
	Sacramento-Arden Arcade-Roseville MSA, CA	H	16.40 FQ	18.94 MW	22.26 TQ	CABLS	1/08-3/08
	San Diego-Carlsbad-San Marcos MSA, CA	H	15.22 FQ	18.17 MW	21.18 TQ	CABLS	1/08-3/08
	San Francisco-San Mateo-Redwood PMSA, CA	H	17.09 FQ	20.69 MW	24.16 TQ	CABLS	1/08-3/08
	San Jose-Sunnyvale-Santa Clara MSA, CA	H	19.58 FQ	22.75 MW	25.66 TQ	CABLS	1/08-3/08
	Santa Ana-Anaheim-Irvine PMSA, CA	Y	35970 FQ	43460 MW	49280 TQ	USBLS	5/07
	Santa Rosa-Petaluma MSA, CA	H	17.31 FQ	20.09 MW	22.87 TQ	CABLS	1/08-3/08
	Colorado	Y	28850 FQ	34590 MW	40540 TQ	USBLS	5/07
	Boulder MSA, CO	Y	32810 FQ	36540 MW	41800 TQ	USBLS	5/07
	Denver-Aurora MSA, CO	Y	30940 FQ	36240 MW	43380 TQ	USBLS	5/07
	Pueblo MSA, CO	Y	26860 FQ	31320 MW	37430 TQ	USBLS	5/07
	Connecticut	H	13.43 AE	18.55 MW		CTBLS	1/08-3/08
	Bridgeport-Stamford-Norwalk MSA, CT	Y	26100 FQ	35960 MW	41890 TQ	USBLS	5/07
	Hartford-West Hartford-East Hartford MSA, CT	Y	29360 FQ	36170 MW	41940 TQ	USBLS	5/07
	Delaware	Y	28360 FQ	32660 MW	37850 TQ	USBLS	5/07
	Wilmington PMSA, DE-MD-NJ	Y	30050 FQ	34310 MW	39300 TQ	USBLS	5/07
	District of Columbia	Y	28520 FQ	34020 MW	40100 TQ	USBLS	5/07
	Washington-Arlington-Alexandria MSA, DC-VA-MD-WV	Y	33070 FQ	39220 MW	45220 TQ	USBLS	5/07
	Florida	Y	26290 FQ	29730 MW	34180 TQ	USBLS	5/07
	Fort Lauderdale-Pompano Beach-Deerfield Beach PMSA, FL	Y	28520 FQ	33270 MW	38620 TQ	USBLS	5/07
	Jacksonville MSA, FL	Y	26290 FQ	29310 MW	33350 TQ	USBLS	5/07
	Miami-Fort Lauderdale-Miami Beach MSA, FL	Y	28140 FQ	32410 MW	37690 TQ	USBLS	5/07
	Orlando-Kissimmee MSA, FL	Y	27180 FQ	30110 MW	33270 TQ	USBLS	5/07
	Sarasota-Bradenton-Venice MSA, FL	Y	28890 FQ	34130 MW	37630 TQ	USBLS	5/07
	Tallahassee MSA, FL	Y	25610 FQ	31190 MW	38880 TQ	USBLS	5/07
	Tampa-St. Petersburg-Clearwater MSA, FL	Y	25400 FQ	29370 MW	33890 TQ	USBLS	5/07
	West Palm Beach-Boca Raton-Boynton Beach PMSA, FL	Y	27770 FQ	32400 MW	37570 TQ	USBLS	5/07
	Georgia	Y	25510 FQ	30360 MW	36160 TQ	USBLS	5/07
	Atlanta-Sandy Springs-Marietta MSA, GA	Y	27670 FQ	32910 MW	39440 TQ	USBLS	5/07
	Hawaii	Y	28140 FQ	35240 MW	42780 TQ	USBLS	5/07
	Honolulu MSA, HI	Y	32760 FQ	38190 MW	46590 TQ	USBLS	5/07
	Idaho	Y	25670 FQ	29330 MW	33250 TQ	USBLS	5/07
	Boise City-Nampa MSA, ID	Y	25850 FQ	29190 MW	33440 TQ	USBLS	5/07
	Coeur d'Alene MSA, ID	Y	25340 FQ	29120 MW	32860 TQ	USBLS	5/07
	Illinois	Y	26290 FQ	31830 MW	39100 TQ	USBLS	5/07
	Chicago-Naperville-Joliet MSA, IL-IN-WI	Y	27710 FQ	33960 MW	40490 TQ	USBLS	5/07

AE Average entry wage	**AW** Average wage paid	**FQ** First quartile wage	**LO** Lowest wage paid	**MTC** Median total compensation	**TCC** Total cash compensation
AER Average entry range	**AWR** Average wage range	**H** Hourly	**LR** Low end range	**MW** Median wage paid	**TQ** Third quartile wage
AEX Average experienced wage	**AXR** Average experienced range	**HI** Highest wage paid	**M** Monthly	**MWR** Median wage range	**W** Weekly
ATC Average total compensation	**D** Daily	**HR** High end range	**MCC** Median cash compensation	**S** See annotated source	**Y** Yearly

Occupation/Type/Industry	Location	Per	Low	Mid	High	Source	Date
Medical Transcriptionist	Indiana	Y	26070 FQ	29510 MW	33860 TQ	USBLS	5/07
	Evansville MSA, IN-KY	Y	20130 FQ	26390 MW	33190 TQ	USBLS	5/07
	Fort Wayne MSA, IN	Y	25330 FQ	28680 MW	32900 TQ	USBLS	5/07
	Gary PMSA, IN	Y	26370 FQ	30040 MW	34840 TQ	USBLS	5/07
	Indianapolis-Carmel MSA, IN	Y	26500 FQ	30530 MW	35400 TQ	USBLS	5/07
	Iowa	Y	24790 FQ	28250 MW	32130 TQ	USBLS	5/07
	Des Moines-West Des Moines MSA, IA	Y	24900 FQ	29200 MW	33270 TQ	USBLS	5/07
	Sioux City MSA, IA-NE-SD	Y	23720 FQ	28460 MW	32860 TQ	USBLS	5/07
	Kansas	Y	23740 FQ	27910 MW	32370 TQ	USBLS	5/07
	Wichita MSA, KS	Y	25740 FQ	28690 MW	31770 TQ	USBLS	5/07
	Kentucky	Y	24614 FQ	29117 MW	33580 TQ	KYBLS	2008
	Louisville-Jefferson County MSA, KY-IN	Y	26860 FQ	30310 MW	34910 TQ	USBLS	5/07
	Louisiana	H	10.90 FQ	13.24 MW	15.32 TQ	LABLS	1/08-3/08
	Baton Rouge MSA, LA	Y	25300 FQ	28960 MW	33140 TQ	USBLS	5/07
	Lafayette MSA, LA	Y	20560 FQ	25800 MW	29970 TQ	USBLS	5/07
	New Orleans-Metairie-Kenner MSA, LA	Y	24710 FQ	29010 MW	32600 TQ	USBLS	5/07
	Maine	Y	25270 FQ	29490 MW	34360 TQ	USBLS	5/07
	Portland-South Portland-Biddeford MSA, ME	Y	27270 FQ	31660 MW	37550 TQ	USBLS	5/07
	Maryland	Y		36500 MW		MDBLS	3/08
	Baltimore-Towson MSA, MD	Y	27940 FQ	35240 MW	41400 TQ	USBLS	5/07
	Bethesda-Gaithersburg-Frederick PMSA, MD	Y	34870 FQ	41720 MW	46740 TQ	USBLS	5/07
	Massachusetts	Y	32140 FQ	36980 MW	43450 TQ	USBLS	5/07
	Boston-Cambridge-Quincy NECTA, MA	Y	32450 FQ	36860 MW	41580 TQ	USBLS	5/07
	Worcester MSA, MA-CT	Y	31580 FQ	35720 MW	39160 TQ	USBLS	5/07
	Michigan	Y	26840 FQ	31190 MW	36840 TQ	USBLS	5/07
	Detroit-Warren-Livonia MSA, MI	Y	29910 FQ	34960 MW	39490 TQ	USBLS	5/07
	Grand Rapids-Wyoming MSA, MI	Y	27830 FQ	31620 MW	36870 TQ	USBLS	5/07
	Warren-Troy-Farmington Hills PMSA, MI	Y	29610 FQ	34780 MW	39480 TQ	USBLS	5/07
	Minnesota	Y	31085 FQ	36407 MW	41635 TQ	MNBLS	10/08-12/08
	Duluth-Superior MSA, MN-WI	Y	29684 FQ	33761 MW	38299 TQ	MNBLS	10/08-12/08
	Minneapolis-Saint Paul MSA, MN-WI	Y	33615 FQ	38216 MW	43820 TQ	MNBLS	10/08-12/08
	Mississippi	Y	22690 FQ	26210 MW	29800 TQ	USBLS	5/07
	Jackson MSA, MS	Y	24510 FQ	28370 MW	33340 TQ	USBLS	5/07
	Missouri	Y	26090 FQ	30650 MW	36060 TQ	USBLS	5/07
	Kansas City MSA, MO-KS	Y	26720 FQ	31510 MW	36420 TQ	USBLS	5/07
	St. Louis MSA, MO-IL	Y	28200 FQ	32490 MW	37230 TQ	USBLS	5/07
	Montana	Y	23750 FQ	28120 MW	31760 TQ	USBLS	5/07
	Billings MSA, MT	Y	25620 FQ	30950 MW	35060 TQ	USBLS	5/07
	Nebraska	Y	24140 FQ	28310 MW	32560 TQ	USBLS	5/07
	Omaha-Council Bluffs MSA, NE-IA	Y	27100 FQ	30500 MW	34130 TQ	USBLS	5/07
	Nevada	H	15.08 FQ	17.55 MW	20.09 TQ	NVBLS	5/08
	Las Vegas-Paradise MSA, NV	H	15.41 FQ	18.02 MW	20.41 TQ	NVBLS	5/08
	New Hampshire	H	13.27 AE	15.69 MW	17.29 AEX	NHBLS	6/08
	Manchester MSA, NH	Y	31770 FQ	35140 MW	38500 TQ	USBLS	5/07
	New Jersey	Y	31630 FQ	36660 MW	43800 TQ	USBLS	5/07
	Camden PMSA, NJ	Y	30990 FQ	35890 MW	41230 TQ	USBLS	5/07
	Edison PMSA, NJ	Y	30710 FQ	35120 MW	42050 TQ	USBLS	5/07
	Newark-Union PMSA, NJ-PA	Y	33520 FQ	38780 MW	45470 TQ	USBLS	5/07
	New Mexico	Y	24580 FQ	27250 MW	30010 TQ	USBLS	5/07
	Albuquerque MSA, NM	Y	25270 FQ	27170 MW	29040 TQ	USBLS	5/07
	New York	Y	27320 FQ	32700 MW	39970 TQ	USBLS	5/07
	Albany-Schenectady-Troy MSA, NY	Y	28070 FQ	31260 MW	35940 TQ	USBLS	5/07
	Buffalo-Niagara Falls MSA, NY	Y	24170 FQ	27950 MW	31880 TQ	USBLS	5/07
	Nassau-Suffolk PMSA, NY	Y	33840 FQ	39520 MW	45080 TQ	USBLS	5/07
	New York-Northern New Jersey-Long Island MSA, NY-NJ-PA	Y	32470 FQ	38500 MW	45230 TQ	USBLS	5/07
	Syracuse MSA, NY	Y	25860 FQ	30920 MW	37080 TQ	USBLS	5/07
	Utica-Rome MSA, NY	Y	25070 FQ	28350 MW	31710 TQ	USBLS	5/07

AE Average entry wage	**AW** Average wage paid	**FQ** First quartile wage	**LO** Lowest wage paid	**MTC** Median total compensation	**TCC** Total cash compensation
AER Average entry range	**AWR** Average wage range	**H** Hourly	**LR** Low end range	**MW** Median wage paid	**TQ** Third quartile wage
AEX Average experienced wage	**AXR** Average experienced range	**HI** Highest wage paid	**M** Monthly	**MWR** Median wage range	**W** Weekly
ATC Average total compensation	**D** Daily	**HR** High end range	**MCC** Median cash compensation	**S** See annotated source	**Y** Yearly

Occupation/Type/Industry	Location	Per	Low	Mid	High	Source	Date
Medical Transcriptionist	North Carolina	Y	27270 FQ	31480 MW	36900 TQ	USBLS	5/07
	Charlotte-Gastonia-Concord MSA, NC-SC	Y	28530 FQ	32370 MW	36310 TQ	USBLS	5/07
	Durham MSA, NC	Y	29060 FQ	33080 MW	37260 TQ	USBLS	5/07
	Raleigh-Cary MSA, NC	Y	28100 FQ	34910 MW	40710 TQ	USBLS	5/07
	North Dakota	Y	22460 FQ	26370 MW	31540 TQ	USBLS	5/07
	Fargo MSA, ND-MN	Y	22550 FQ	25780 MW	29970 TQ	USBLS	5/07
	Ohio	Y	26310 FQ	30220 MW	35260 TQ	USBLS	5/07
	Cincinnati-Middletown MSA, OH-KY-IN	Y	28690 FQ	33210 MW	37990 TQ	USBLS	5/07
	Cleveland-Elyria-Mentor MSA, OH	Y	27620 FQ	31280 MW	36140 TQ	USBLS	5/07
	Columbus MSA, OH	Y	27580 FQ	31010 MW	35880 TQ	USBLS	5/07
	Dayton MSA, OH	Y	27020 FQ	30040 MW	33510 TQ	USBLS	5/07
	Oklahoma	Y	22360 FQ	26660 MW	30910 TQ	USBLS	5/07
	Oklahoma City MSA, OK	Y	20090 FQ	25100 MW	29530 TQ	USBLS	5/07
	Tulsa MSA, OK	Y	26310 FQ	29990 MW	34870 TQ	USBLS	5/07
	Oregon	H	14.23 FQ	17.11 MW	19.66 TQ	ORBLS	5/08
	Eugene-Springfield MSA, OR	Y	30610 FQ	34290 MW	37330 TQ	USBLS	5/07
	Medford MSA, OR	Y	27900 FQ	31320 MW	35050 TQ	USBLS	5/07
	Portland-Vancouver-Beaverton MSA, OR-WA	Y	33160 FQ	38130 MW	43630 TQ	USBLS	5/07
	Pennsylvania	Y	25420 FQ	29220 MW	34110 TQ	USBLS	5/07
	Allentown-Bethlehem-Easton MSA, PA-NJ	Y	25420 FQ	30100 MW	35020 TQ	USBLS	5/07
	Philadelphia-Camden-Wilmington MSA, PA-NJ-DE-MD	Y	27810 FQ	33330 MW	38080 TQ	USBLS	5/07
	Pittsburgh MSA, PA	Y	26230 FQ	28990 MW	32540 TQ	USBLS	5/07
	Rhode Island	Y	27890 FQ	32550 MW	38730 TQ	USBLS	5/07
	Providence-Fall River-Warwick MSA, RI-MA	Y	27300 FQ	31870 MW	38380 TQ	USBLS	5/07
	South Carolina	Y	25340 FQ	29350 MW	33870 TQ	USBLS	5/07
	Charleston-North Charleston MSA, SC	Y	25270 FQ	28630 MW	32230 TQ	USBLS	5/07
	Columbia MSA, SC	Y	27250 FQ	31070 MW	37300 TQ	USBLS	5/07
	Spartanburg MSA, SC	Y	17860 FQ	26560 MW	31750 TQ	USBLS	5/07
	South Dakota	Y	24297 FQ	28277 MW	32680 TQ	SDBLS	7/08-9/08
	Sioux Falls MSA, SD	Y	26822 FQ	30184 MW	34093 TQ	SDBLS	7/08-9/08
	Tennessee	Y	25540 FQ	29320 MW	33940 TQ	USBLS	5/07
	Memphis MSA, TN-MS-AR	Y	27320 FQ	31480 MW	39240 TQ	USBLS	5/07
	Nashville-Davidson-Murfreesboro MSA, TN	Y	29050 FQ	32870 MW	37470 TQ	USBLS	5/07
	Texas	Y	25730 FQ	31170 MW	37470 TQ	USBLS	5/07
	Austin-Round Rock MSA, TX	Y	26650 FQ	29130 MW	32730 TQ	USBLS	5/07
	Dallas-Fort Worth-Arlington MSA, TX	Y	31540 FQ	36230 MW	40870 TQ	USBLS	5/07
	El Paso MSA, TX	Y	19720 FQ	24710 MW	31240 TQ	USBLS	5/07
	Houston-Sugar Land-Baytown MSA, TX	Y	29010 FQ	35520 MW	40610 TQ	USBLS	5/07
	San Antonio MSA, TX	Y	23800 FQ	28560 MW	33740 TQ	USBLS	5/07
	Utah	Y	24020 FQ	28880 MW	33080 TQ	USBLS	5/07
	Salt Lake City MSA, UT	Y	28490 FQ	31920 MW	36600 TQ	USBLS	5/07
	Vermont	Y	25810 FQ	30060 MW	34490 TQ	USBLS	5/07
	Burlington-South Burlington MSA, VT	Y	26210 FQ	30600 MW	35430 TQ	USBLS	5/07
	Virginia	Y	24780 FQ	29480 MW	35510 TQ	USBLS	5/07
	Richmond MSA, VA	Y	24000 FQ	28130 MW	33560 TQ	USBLS	5/07
	Virginia Beach-Norfolk-Newport News MSA, VA-NC	Y	25210 FQ	29570 MW	33570 TQ	USBLS	5/07
	Washington	H	15.32 FQ	17.59 MW	20.42 TQ	WABLS	3/08
	Seattle-Tacoma-Bellevue MSA, WA	Y	33990 FQ	38850 MW	46580 TQ	USBLS	5/07
	West Virginia	Y	20303 FQ	24225 MW	29461 TQ	WVBLS	7/08-9/08
	Charleston MSA, WV	Y	21220 FQ	23820 MW	29360 TQ	USBLS	5/07
	Wisconsin	Y	27710 FQ	31510 MW	36150 TQ	USBLS	5/07
	Appleton MSA, WI	Y	27400 FQ	30390 MW	35170 TQ	USBLS	5/07
	Milwaukee-Waukesha-West Allis MSA, WI	Y	29020 FQ	32710 MW	37550 TQ	USBLS	5/07
	Wyoming	Y	23279 FQ	27733 MW	31788 TQ	WYBLS	9/08
	Cheyenne MSA, WY	Y	26850 FQ	29758 MW	32672 TQ	WYBLS	9/08
	Puerto Rico	Y	16620 FQ	20000 MW	24370 TQ	USBLS	5/07

Occupation/Type/Industry	Location	Per	Low	Mid	High	Source	Date
Medical Transcriptionist	San Juan-Caguas-Guaynabo MSA, PR	Y	17600 FQ	21330 MW	25940 TQ	USBLS	5/07
Meeting and Convention Planner	Alabama	Y	28160 FQ	36920 MW	47080 TQ	USBLS	5/07
	Birmingham-Hoover MSA, AL	Y	35260 FQ	44910 MW	52380 TQ	USBLS	5/07
	Alaska	Y	33940 FQ	37850 MW	42210 TQ	USBLS	5/07
	Arizona	Y	25000 FQ	40330 MW	55120 TQ	USBLS	5/07
	Phoenix-Mesa-Scottsdale MSA, AZ	Y	22430 FQ	42430 MW	58110 TQ	USBLS	5/07
	Tucson MSA, AZ	Y	34930 FQ	40840 MW	46680 TQ	USBLS	5/07
	Arkansas	Y	26160 FQ	29430 MW	42000 TQ	USBLS	5/07
	Little Rock-North Little Rock MSA, AR	Y	27790 FQ	38120 MW	45220 TQ	USBLS	5/07
	California	H	18.11 FQ	22.73 MW	29.30 TQ	CABLS	1/08-3/08
	Los Angeles-Long Beach-Glendale PMSA, CA	H	19.61 FQ	25.08 MW	32.23 TQ	CABLS	1/08-3/08
	Oakland-Fremont-Hayward MSA, CA	H	20.49 FQ	24.92 MW	34.06 TQ	CABLS	1/08-3/08
	Riverside-San Bernardino-Ontario MSA, CA	H	15.54 FQ	19.80 MW	25.02 TQ	CABLS	1/08-3/08
	Sacramento-Arden Arcade-Roseville MSA, CA	H	19.04 FQ	23.32 MW	28.92 TQ	CABLS	1/08-3/08
	San Diego-Carlsbad-San Marcos MSA, CA	H	17.18 FQ	19.98 MW	25.06 TQ	CABLS	1/08-3/08
	San Francisco-San Mateo-Redwood PMSA, CA	H	20.07 FQ	24.68 MW	31.35 TQ	CABLS	1/08-3/08
	San Jose-Sunnyvale-Santa Clara MSA, CA	H	18.40 FQ	24.12 MW	32.62 TQ	CABLS	1/08-3/08
	Santa Ana-Anaheim-Irvine PMSA, CA	Y	37950 FQ	43700 MW	56240 TQ	USBLS	5/07
	Colorado	Y	33170 FQ	40370 MW	51390 TQ	USBLS	5/07
	Denver-Aurora MSA, CO	Y	35500 FQ	42920 MW	53790 TQ	USBLS	5/07
	Connecticut	H	17.99 AE	25.62 MW		CTBLS	1/08-3/08
	Bridgeport-Stamford-Norwalk MSA, CT	Y	47570 FQ	59070 MW	68310 TQ	USBLS	5/07
	Hartford-West Hartford-East Hartford MSA, CT	Y	35200 FQ	40810 MW	50750 TQ	USBLS	5/07
	Delaware	Y	35240 FQ	44560 MW	60070 TQ	USBLS	5/07
	Wilmington PMSA, DE-MD-NJ	Y	35050 FQ	42650 MW	59530 TQ	USBLS	5/07
	District of Columbia	Y	41260 FQ	50250 MW	62260 TQ	USBLS	5/07
	Washington-Arlington-Alexandria MSA, DC-VA-MD-WV	Y	39530 FQ	49450 MW	63620 TQ	USBLS	5/07
	Florida	Y	31970 FQ	38810 MW	51230 TQ	USBLS	5/07
	Fort Lauderdale-Pompano Beach-Deerfield Beach PMSA, FL	Y	46840 FQ	57480 MW	63300 TQ	USBLS	5/07
	Jacksonville MSA, FL	Y	42200 FQ	46230 MW	50150 TQ	USBLS	5/07
	Miami-Fort Lauderdale-Miami Beach MSA, FL	Y	36080 FQ	50160 MW	61080 TQ	USBLS	5/07
	Orlando-Kissimmee MSA, FL	Y	28360 FQ	32410 MW	48460 TQ	USBLS	5/07
	Tampa-St. Petersburg-Clearwater MSA, FL	Y	32670 FQ	35830 MW	39420 TQ	USBLS	5/07
	West Palm Beach-Boca Raton-Boynton Beach PMSA, FL	Y	35200 FQ	38860 MW	51850 TQ	USBLS	5/07
	Georgia	Y	34760 FQ	45040 MW	75430 TQ	USBLS	5/07
	Atlanta-Sandy Springs-Marietta MSA, GA	Y	35980 FQ	47790 MW	82880 TQ	USBLS	5/07
	Augusta-Richmond County MSA, GA-SC	Y	28630 FQ	32540 MW	44280 TQ	USBLS	5/07
	Hawaii	Y	35080 FQ	44280 MW	56120 TQ	USBLS	5/07
	Honolulu MSA, HI	Y	34440 FQ	39480 MW	49640 TQ	USBLS	5/07
	Idaho	Y	33430 FQ	41790 MW	52390 TQ	USBLS	5/07
	Boise City-Nampa MSA, ID	Y	35490 FQ	43410 MW	52410 TQ	USBLS	5/07
	Illinois	Y	36320 FQ	47520 MW	64700 TQ	USBLS	5/07
	Chicago-Naperville-Joliet MSA, IL-IN-WI	Y	36130 FQ	47350 MW	64480 TQ	USBLS	5/07
	Indiana	Y	29890 FQ	36480 MW	45250 TQ	USBLS	5/07
	Gary PMSA, IN	Y	27790 FQ	31420 MW	35390 TQ	USBLS	5/07
	Indianapolis-Carmel MSA, IN	Y	33370 FQ	38410 MW	47270 TQ	USBLS	5/07
	Iowa	Y	31530 FQ	39700 MW	50510 TQ	USBLS	5/07

AE	Average entry wage	AW	Average wage paid	FQ First quartile wage
AER	Average entry range	AWR	Average wage range	H Hourly
AEX	Average experienced wage	AXR	Average experienced range	HI Highest wage paid
ATC	Average total compensation	D	Daily	HR High end range

LO Lowest wage paid — MTC Median total compensation — TCC Total cash compensation
LR Low end range — MW Median wage paid — TQ Third quartile wage
M Monthly — MWR Median wage range — W Weekly
MCC Median cash compensation — S See annotated source — Y Yearly

Occupation/Type/Industry	Location	Per	Low	Mid	High	Source	Date
Meeting and Convention Planner	Des Moines-West Des Moines MSA, IA	Y	36180 FQ	44410 MW	53440 TQ	USBLS	5/07
	Kansas	Y	27460 FQ	36560 MW	46170 TQ	USBLS	5/07
	Wichita MSA, KS	Y	27560 FQ	39900 MW	48190 TQ	USBLS	5/07
	Kentucky	Y	30166 FQ	37440 MW	47004 TQ	KYBLS	2008
	Lexington-Fayette MSA, KY	Y	31140 FQ	38100 MW	44560 TQ	USBLS	5/07
	Louisville-Jefferson County MSA, KY-IN	Y	29120 FQ	38070 MW	48560 TQ	USBLS	5/07
	Louisiana	H	13.72 FQ	18.17 MW	22.32 TQ	LABLS	1/08-3/08
	Baton Rouge MSA, LA	Y	34840 FQ	38410 MW	42510 TQ	USBLS	5/07
	New Orleans-Metairie-Kenner MSA, LA	Y	34290 FQ	42940 MW	51660 TQ	USBLS	5/07
	Maine	Y	29580 FQ	35640 MW	44460 TQ	USBLS	5/07
	Portland-South Portland-Biddeford MSA, ME	Y	29200 FQ	33810 MW	41870 TQ	USBLS	5/07
	Maryland	Y		47225 MW		MDBLS	3/08
	Baltimore-Towson MSA, MD	Y	37120 FQ	47240 MW	64750 TQ	USBLS	5/07
	Bethesda-Gaithersburg-Frederick PMSA, MD	Y	33370 FQ	42700 MW	61480 TQ	USBLS	5/07
	Massachusetts	Y	41450 FQ	49210 MW	61370 TQ	USBLS	5/07
	Barnstable Town MSA, MA	Y	23890 FQ	46340 MW	56920 TQ	USBLS	5/07
	Boston-Cambridge-Quincy NECTA, MA	Y	42720 FQ	49710 MW	61090 TQ	USBLS	5/07
	Worcester MSA, MA-CT	Y	40710 FQ	54850 MW	74280 TQ	USBLS	5/07
	Michigan	Y	30200 FQ	39610 MW	50030 TQ	USBLS	5/07
	Detroit-Warren-Livonia MSA, MI	Y	36190 FQ	43440 MW	54070 TQ	USBLS	5/07
	Grand Rapids-Wyoming MSA, MI	Y	29510 FQ	44940 MW	51990 TQ	USBLS	5/07
	Warren-Troy-Farmington Hills PMSA, MI	Y	33080 FQ	40860 MW	54230 TQ	USBLS	5/07
	Minnesota	Y	36409 FQ	45793 MW	56928 TQ	MNBLS	10/08-12/08
	Duluth-Superior MSA, MN-WI	Y	33218 FQ	42029 MW	48566 TQ	MNBLS	10/08-12/08
	Minneapolis-Saint Paul MSA, MN-WI	Y	37076 FQ	47117 MW	59410 TQ	MNBLS	10/08-12/08
	Rochester MSA, MN	Y	40178 FQ	45913 MW	53534 TQ	MNBLS	10/08-12/08
	Mississippi	Y	21620 FQ	32910 MW	46350 TQ	USBLS	5/07
	Jackson MSA, MS	Y	30510 FQ	45670 MW	59980 TQ	USBLS	5/07
	Missouri	Y	31270 FQ	39080 MW	51080 TQ	USBLS	5/07
	Kansas City MSA, MO-KS	Y	34150 FQ	40350 MW	50250 TQ	USBLS	5/07
	St. Louis MSA, MO-IL	Y	31030 FQ	40070 MW	54640 TQ	USBLS	5/07
	Montana	Y	24470 FQ	31000 MW	41000 TQ	USBLS	5/07
	Billings MSA, MT	Y	28700 FQ	34390 MW	38770 TQ	USBLS	5/07
	Nebraska	Y	30830 FQ	35900 MW	43660 TQ	USBLS	5/07
	Omaha-Council Bluffs MSA, NE-IA	Y	30740 FQ	34890 MW	40080 TQ	USBLS	5/07
	Nevada	H	17.59 FQ	23.21 MW	27.17 TQ	NVBLS	5/08
	Las Vegas-Paradise MSA, NV	H	16.92 FQ	20.22 MW	26.18 TQ	NVBLS	5/08
	Reno-Sparks MSA, NV	H	23.63 FQ	25.46 MW	27.53 TQ	NVBLS	5/08
	New Hampshire	H	14.94 AE	19.57 MW	25.54 AEX	NHBLS	6/08
	New Jersey	Y	36750 FQ	45070 MW	57870 TQ	USBLS	5/07
	Camden PMSA, NJ	Y	38120 FQ	47450 MW	71960 TQ	USBLS	5/07
	Edison PMSA, NJ	Y	34140 FQ	43620 MW	54330 TQ	USBLS	5/07
	Newark-Union PMSA, NJ-PA	Y	37970 FQ	44680 MW	57960 TQ	USBLS	5/07
	New Mexico	Y	27680 FQ	35770 MW	42440 TQ	USBLS	5/07
	Albuquerque MSA, NM	Y	27720 FQ	36390 MW	42880 TQ	USBLS	5/07
	New York	Y	41100 FQ	53550 MW	71340 TQ	USBLS	5/07
	Albany-Schenectady-Troy MSA, NY	Y	35030 FQ	43730 MW	61690 TQ	USBLS	5/07
	Buffalo-Niagara Falls MSA, NY	Y	33930 FQ	41600 MW	47730 TQ	USBLS	5/07
	Nassau-Suffolk PMSA, NY	Y	30630 FQ	50680 MW	68870 TQ	USBLS	5/07
	New York-Northern New Jersey-Long Island MSA, NY-NJ-PA	Y	41430 FQ	53440 MW	70430 TQ	USBLS	5/07
	North Carolina	Y	31240 FQ	38520 MW	48900 TQ	USBLS	5/07
	Charlotte-Gastonia-Concord MSA, NC-SC	Y	33720 FQ	42700 MW	52970 TQ	USBLS	5/07
	Greensboro-High Point MSA, NC	Y	28760 FQ	36230 MW	50210 TQ	USBLS	5/07
	Raleigh-Cary MSA, NC	Y	32700 FQ	40980 MW	50360 TQ	USBLS	5/07
	Winston-Salem MSA, NC	Y	35750 FQ	43880 MW	51090 TQ	USBLS	5/07

Occupation/Type/Industry	Location	Per	Low	Mid	High	Source	Date
Meeting and Convention Planner	North Dakota	Y	24300 FQ	29820 MW	36400 TQ	USBLS	5/07
	Ohio	Y	30500 FQ	38090 MW	47640 TQ	USBLS	5/07
	Cincinnati-Middletown MSA, OH-KY-IN	Y	31490 FQ	37350 MW	53910 TQ	USBLS	5/07
	Cleveland-Elyria-Mentor MSA, OH	Y	33380 FQ	41650 MW	49830 TQ	USBLS	5/07
	Columbus MSA, OH	Y	29870 FQ	37300 MW	51460 TQ	USBLS	5/07
	Dayton MSA, OH	Y	21780 FQ	36050 MW	48130 TQ	USBLS	5/07
	Oklahoma	Y	22500 FQ	31490 MW	39810 TQ	USBLS	5/07
	Oklahoma City MSA, OK	Y	22150 FQ	32850 MW	40400 TQ	USBLS	5/07
	Tulsa MSA, OK	Y	24390 FQ	30800 MW	39030 TQ	USBLS	5/07
	Oregon	H	14.27 FQ	18.12 MW	21.99 TQ	ORBLS	5/08
	Portland-Vancouver-Beaverton MSA, OR-WA	Y	29730 FQ	38880 MW	45690 TQ	USBLS	5/07
	Pennsylvania	Y	29810 FQ	39780 MW	50530 TQ	USBLS	5/07
	Allentown-Bethlehem-Easton MSA, PA-NJ	Y	28550 FQ	34480 MW	44090 TQ	USBLS	5/07
	Lancaster MSA, PA	Y	25860 FQ	32570 MW	36860 TQ	USBLS	5/07
	Philadelphia-Camden-Wilmington MSA, PA-NJ-DE-MD	Y	34980 FQ	45260 MW	57330 TQ	USBLS	5/07
	Pittsburgh MSA, PA	Y	26010 FQ	34740 MW	43760 TQ	USBLS	5/07
	Rhode Island	Y	38990 FQ	44420 MW	54130 TQ	USBLS	5/07
	Providence-Fall River-Warwick MSA, RI-MA	Y	38450 FQ	43990 MW	53230 TQ	USBLS	5/07
	South Carolina	Y	28390 FQ	34030 MW	45170 TQ	USBLS	5/07
	Charleston-North Charleston MSA, SC	Y	28330 FQ	31860 MW	37920 TQ	USBLS	5/07
	Columbia MSA, SC	Y	29320 FQ	35540 MW	56400 TQ	USBLS	5/07
	South Dakota	Y	26242 FQ	30132 MW	35463 TQ	SDBLS	7/08-9/08
	Sioux Falls MSA, SD	Y	27688 FQ	34492 MW	40067 TQ	SDBLS	7/08-9/08
	Tennessee	Y	30570 FQ	40230 MW	50970 TQ	USBLS	5/07
	Memphis MSA, TN-MS-AR	Y	33780 FQ	44440 MW	55700 TQ	USBLS	5/07
	Nashville-Davidson-Murfreesboro MSA, TN	Y	29800 FQ	39050 MW	50530 TQ	USBLS	5/07
	Texas	Y	33380 FQ	43510 MW	60060 TQ	USBLS	5/07
	Austin-Round Rock MSA, TX	Y	35710 FQ	45550 MW	58400 TQ	USBLS	5/07
	Corpus Christi MSA, TX	Y	23410 FQ	26910 MW	36280 TQ	USBLS	5/07
	Dallas-Fort Worth-Arlington MSA, TX	Y	36790 FQ	47260 MW	65970 TQ	USBLS	5/07
	El Paso MSA, TX	Y	34690 FQ	42550 MW	50040 TQ	USBLS	5/07
	Houston-Sugar Land-Baytown MSA, TX	Y	36340 FQ	46110 MW	65910 TQ	USBLS	5/07
	San Antonio MSA, TX	Y	30780 FQ	37210 MW	52060 TQ	USBLS	5/07
	Utah	Y	30140 FQ	39110 MW	55720 TQ	USBLS	5/07
	Salt Lake City MSA, UT	Y	33310 FQ	45580 MW	72960 TQ	USBLS	5/07
	Vermont	Y	27610 FQ	35670 MW	45610 TQ	USBLS	5/07
	Virginia	Y	36710 FQ	45740 MW	60510 TQ	USBLS	5/07
	Richmond MSA, VA	Y	40900 FQ	46370 MW	52760 TQ	USBLS	5/07
	Virginia Beach-Norfolk-Newport News MSA, VA-NC	Y	32900 FQ	39560 MW	50410 TQ	USBLS	5/07
	Washington	H	17.77 FQ	21.35 MW	26.25 TQ	WABLS	3/08
	Seattle-Tacoma-Bellevue MSA, WA	Y	36900 FQ	44230 MW	54330 TQ	USBLS	5/07
	West Virginia	Y	25105 FQ	38385 MW	52496 TQ	WVBLS	7/08-9/08
	Charleston MSA, WV	Y	51040 FQ	73810 MW	80770 TQ	USBLS	5/07
	Wisconsin	Y	29250 FQ	35820 MW	42950 TQ	USBLS	5/07
	Milwaukee-Waukesha-West Allis MSA, WI	Y	30740 FQ	36430 MW	42600 TQ	USBLS	5/07
	Wyoming	Y	23160 FQ	30109 MW	37386 TQ	WYBLS	9/08
	Puerto Rico	Y	18490 FQ	23660 MW	30190 TQ	USBLS	5/07
	San Juan-Caguas-Guaynabo MSA, PR	Y	18810 FQ	23600 MW	31370 TQ	USBLS	5/07
Member of the House of Representatives Federal Government	United States	Y			174000 HI	TSEAT	2009
Men's Hockey Coach University of New Hampshire	Durham, NH	Y			196660 HI	NHUL01	2008

Occupation/Type/Industry	Location	Per	Low	Mid	High	Source	Date
Mental Health and Substance Abuse Social Worker	Alabama	Y	23960 FQ	31280 MW	40610 TQ	USBLS	5/07
	Birmingham-Hoover MSA, AL	Y	24700 FQ	30940 MW	40820 TQ	USBLS	5/07
	Alaska	Y	30000 FQ	35740 MW	41790 TQ	USBLS	5/07
	Anchorage MSA, AK	Y	28290 FQ	34010 MW	39170 TQ	USBLS	5/07
	Arizona	Y	27560 FQ	35500 MW	43540 TQ	USBLS	5/07
	Phoenix-Mesa-Scottsdale MSA, AZ	Y	29760 FQ	37150 MW	48430 TQ	USBLS	5/07
	Tucson MSA, AZ	Y	24320 FQ	34780 MW	40500 TQ	USBLS	5/07
	Arkansas	Y	26200 FQ	34620 MW	45780 TQ	USBLS	5/07
	Little Rock-North Little Rock MSA, AR	Y	35620 FQ	45360 MW	55720 TQ	USBLS	5/07
	California	H	14.37 FQ	17.79 MW	23.84 TQ	CABLS	1/08-3/08
	Bakersfield MSA, CA	H	13.43 FQ	16.82 MW	20.69 TQ	CABLS	1/08-3/08
	Los Angeles-Long Beach-Glendale PMSA, CA	H	14.13 FQ	16.96 MW	23.61 TQ	CABLS	1/08-3/08
	Oakland-Fremont-Hayward MSA, CA	H	16.39 FQ	20.20 MW	24.34 TQ	CABLS	1/08-3/08
	Riverside-San Bernardino-Ontario MSA, CA	H	13.83 FQ	17.61 MW	22.00 TQ	CABLS	1/08-3/08
	Sacramento-Arden Arcade-Roseville MSA, CA	H	15.87 FQ	19.39 MW	25.00 TQ	CABLS	1/08-3/08
	San Diego-Carlsbad-San Marcos MSA, CA	H	13.31 FQ	17.57 MW	24.68 TQ	CABLS	1/08-3/08
	San Francisco-San Mateo-Redwood PMSA, CA	H	16.06 FQ	19.20 MW	23.46 TQ	CABLS	1/08-3/08
	San Jose-Sunnyvale-Santa Clara MSA, CA	H	17.82 FQ	20.84 MW	26.88 TQ	CABLS	1/08-3/08
	Santa Ana-Anaheim-Irvine PMSA, CA	Y	28700 FQ	34470 MW	46190 TQ	USBLS	5/07
	Colorado	Y	25970 FQ	30210 MW	37840 TQ	USBLS	5/07
	Denver-Aurora MSA, CO	Y	27180 FQ	31300 MW	38440 TQ	USBLS	5/07
	Connecticut	H	16.18 AE	22.82 MW		CTBLS	1/08-3/08
	Bridgeport-Stamford-Norwalk MSA, CT	Y	40500 FQ	49590 MW	58080 TQ	USBLS	5/07
	Hartford-West Hartford-East Hartford MSA, CT	Y	39110 FQ	50940 MW	60990 TQ	USBLS	5/07
	Waterbury MSA, CT	Y	30640 FQ	39490 MW	57350 TQ	USBLS	5/07
	Delaware	Y	31650 FQ	39590 MW	50000 TQ	USBLS	5/07
	Wilmington PMSA, DE-MD-NJ	Y	33960 FQ	41880 MW	50410 TQ	USBLS	5/07
	District of Columbia	Y	36580 FQ	44440 MW	50560 TQ	USBLS	5/07
	Washington-Arlington-Alexandria MSA, DC-VA-MD-WV	Y	42120 FQ	50320 MW	61370 TQ	USBLS	5/07
	Florida	Y	27550 FQ	33180 MW	39750 TQ	USBLS	5/07
	Fort Lauderdale-Pompano Beach-Deerfield Beach PMSA, FL	Y	29070 FQ	34410 MW	40440 TQ	USBLS	5/07
	Jacksonville MSA, FL	Y	27710 FQ	32470 MW	37600 TQ	USBLS	5/07
	Miami-Fort Lauderdale-Miami Beach MSA, FL	Y	29220 FQ	36090 MW	44550 TQ	USBLS	5/07
	Orlando-Kissimmee MSA, FL	Y	27260 FQ	30340 MW	35270 TQ	USBLS	5/07
	Tampa-St. Petersburg-Clearwater MSA, FL	Y	24820 FQ	29180 MW	35600 TQ	USBLS	5/07
	West Palm Beach-Boca Raton-Boynton Beach PMSA, FL	Y	23610 FQ	29090 MW	36290 TQ	USBLS	5/07
	Georgia	Y	24230 FQ	33720 MW	39920 TQ	USBLS	5/07
	Atlanta-Sandy Springs-Marietta MSA, GA	Y	24850 FQ	34320 MW	40180 TQ	USBLS	5/07
	Hawaii	Y	35030 FQ	47110 MW	66120 TQ	USBLS	5/07
	Honolulu MSA, HI	Y	34620 FQ	48250 MW	70610 TQ	USBLS	5/07
	Idaho	Y	19120 FQ	26980 MW	39640 TQ	USBLS	5/07
	Boise City-Nampa MSA, ID	Y	18220 FQ	22550 MW	33850 TQ	USBLS	5/07
	Illinois	Y	27680 FQ	32700 MW	40700 TQ	USBLS	5/07
	Chicago-Naperville-Joliet MSA, IL-IN-WI	Y	28890 FQ	34010 MW	44420 TQ	USBLS	5/07
	Indiana	Y	28790 FQ	35280 MW	46130 TQ	USBLS	5/07
	Gary PMSA, IN	Y	28170 FQ	31790 MW	37690 TQ	USBLS	5/07
	Indianapolis-Carmel MSA, IN	Y	29910 FQ	36520 MW	45760 TQ	USBLS	5/07
	Iowa	Y	28510 FQ	35110 MW	45610 TQ	USBLS	5/07

AE	Average entry wage	AW	Average wage paid	FQ	First quartile wage	LO	Lowest wage paid	MTC	Median total compensation	TCC	Total cash compensation
AER	Average entry range	AWR	Average wage range	H	Hourly	LR	Low end range	MW	Median wage paid	TQ	Third quartile wage
AEX	Average experienced wage	AXR	Average experienced range	HI	Highest wage paid	M	Monthly	MWR	Median wage range	W	Weekly
ATC	Average total compensation	D	Daily	HR	High end range	MCC	Median cash compensation	S	See annotated source	Y	Yearly

Occupation/Type/Industry	Location	Per	Low	Mid	High	Source	Date
Mental Health and Substance Abuse Social Worker	Des Moines-West Des Moines MSA, IA	Y	33590 FQ	46420 MW	56500 TQ	USBLS	5/07
	Kansas	Y	29300 FQ	35490 MW	42870 TQ	USBLS	5/07
	Wichita MSA, KS	Y	29590 FQ	36980 MW	45350 TQ	USBLS	5/07
	Kentucky	Y	31611 FQ	38399 MW	47340 TQ	KYBLS	2008
	Lexington-Fayette MSA, KY	Y	32440 FQ	37560 MW	50720 TQ	USBLS	5/07
	Louisville-Jefferson County MSA, KY-IN	Y	31420 FQ	39040 MW	46310 TQ	USBLS	5/07
	Louisiana	H	14.76 FQ	18.91 MW	23.62 TQ	LABLS	1/08-3/08
	Baton Rouge MSA, LA	Y	30080 FQ	36680 MW	52670 TQ	USBLS	5/07
	New Orleans-Metairie-Kenner MSA, LA	Y	35210 FQ	44430 MW	52250 TQ	USBLS	5/07
	Maine	Y	30410 FQ	40640 MW	50950 TQ	USBLS	5/07
	Portland-South Portland-Biddeford MSA, ME	Y	24600 FQ	32860 MW	44460 TQ	USBLS	5/07
	Maryland	Y		46400 MW		MDBLS	3/08
	Baltimore-Towson MSA, MD	Y	39970 FQ	46420 MW	52890 TQ	USBLS	5/07
	Bethesda-Gaithersburg-Frederick PMSA, MD	Y	36040 FQ	41980 MW	55620 TQ	USBLS	5/07
	Massachusetts	Y	30080 FQ	37880 MW	48320 TQ	USBLS	5/07
	Barnstable Town MSA, MA	Y	32110 FQ	37580 MW	55310 TQ	USBLS	5/07
	Boston-Cambridge-Quincy NECTA, MA	Y	31040 FQ	38550 MW	48180 TQ	USBLS	5/07
	Lynn-Peabody-Salem NECTA, MA	Y	36030 FQ	45220 MW	54370 TQ	USBLS	5/07
	Worcester MSA, MA-CT	Y	25880 FQ	31650 MW	39130 TQ	USBLS	5/07
	Michigan	Y	32010 FQ	39110 MW	48500 TQ	USBLS	5/07
	Detroit-Warren-Livonia MSA, MI	Y	30450 FQ	37390 MW	45450 TQ	USBLS	5/07
	Grand Rapids-Wyoming MSA, MI	Y	32960 FQ	39950 MW	49400 TQ	USBLS	5/07
	Muskegon-Norton Shores MSA, MI	Y	33890 FQ	39480 MW	47150 TQ	USBLS	5/07
	Warren-Troy-Farmington Hills PMSA, MI	Y	35580 FQ	40490 MW	47510 TQ	USBLS	5/07
	Minnesota	Y	39599 FQ	49821 MW	59551 TQ	MNBLS	10/08-12/08
	Duluth-Superior MSA, MN-WI	Y	39651 FQ	52478 MW	62532 TQ	MNBLS	10/08-12/08
	Minneapolis-Saint Paul MSA, MN-WI	Y	41053 FQ	50114 MW	59300 TQ	MNBLS	10/08-12/08
	Mississippi	Y	25920 FQ	32610 MW	40130 TQ	USBLS	5/07
	Jackson MSA, MS	Y	26190 FQ	31270 MW	36920 TQ	USBLS	5/07
	Missouri	Y	25650 FQ	30960 MW	39270 TQ	USBLS	5/07
	Kansas City MSA, MO-KS	Y	28980 FQ	34950 MW	41530 TQ	USBLS	5/07
	St. Louis MSA, MO-IL	Y	26740 FQ	32340 MW	40580 TQ	USBLS	5/07
	Montana	Y	28830 FQ	34490 MW	39940 TQ	USBLS	5/07
	Billings MSA, MT	Y	32860 FQ	37100 MW	42450 TQ	USBLS	5/07
	Nebraska	Y	25950 FQ	30680 MW	37380 TQ	USBLS	5/07
	Omaha-Council Bluffs MSA, NE-IA	Y	25510 FQ	30820 MW	41370 TQ	USBLS	5/07
	Nevada	H	20.54 FQ	23.44 MW	27.84 TQ	NVBLS	5/08
	Las Vegas-Paradise MSA, NV	H	20.18 FQ	23.12 MW	27.59 TQ	NVBLS	5/08
	New Hampshire	H	13.40 AE	16.83 MW	21.03 AEX	NHBLS	6/08
	Manchester MSA, NH	Y	36870 FQ	41820 MW	49310 TQ	USBLS	5/07
	New Jersey	Y	42290 FQ	52500 MW	67050 TQ	USBLS	5/07
	Camden PMSA, NJ	Y	47500 FQ	55710 MW	64540 TQ	USBLS	5/07
	Edison PMSA, NJ	Y	45860 FQ	66170 MW	82210 TQ	USBLS	5/07
	Newark-Union PMSA, NJ-PA	Y	43340 FQ	51440 MW	59930 TQ	USBLS	5/07
	Vineland-Millville-Bridgeton MSA, NJ	Y	32180 FQ	35380 MW	38510 TQ	USBLS	5/07
	New Mexico	Y	27910 FQ	40590 MW	49670 TQ	USBLS	5/07
	Albuquerque MSA, NM	Y	25220 FQ	37910 MW	49080 TQ	USBLS	5/07
	New York	Y	34900 FQ	41360 MW	51980 TQ	USBLS	5/07
	Albany-Schenectady-Troy MSA, NY	Y	33830 FQ	39090 MW	47670 TQ	USBLS	5/07
	Buffalo-Niagara Falls MSA, NY	Y	30220 FQ	35260 MW	40260 TQ	USBLS	5/07
	Nassau-Suffolk PMSA, NY	Y	35800 FQ	40430 MW	49580 TQ	USBLS	5/07
	New York-Northern New Jersey-Long Island MSA, NY-NJ-PA	Y	36930 FQ	44430 MW	55630 TQ	USBLS	5/07
	North Carolina	Y	32930 FQ	38400 MW	46650 TQ	USBLS	5/07

AE	Average entry wage	AW	Average wage paid	FQ	First quartile wage	LO	Lowest wage paid	MTC	Median total compensation	TCC	Total cash compensation
AER	Average entry range	AWR	Average wage range	H	Hourly	LR	Low end range	MW	Median wage paid	TQ	Third quartile wage
AEX	Average experienced wage	AXR	Average experienced range	HI	Highest wage paid	M	Monthly	MWR	Median wage range	W	Weekly
ATC	Average total compensation	D	Daily	HR	High end range	MCC	Median cash compensation	S	See annotated source	Y	Yearly

Occupation/Type/Industry	Location	Per	Low	Mid	High	Source	Date
Mental Health and Substance Abuse Social Worker	Charlotte-Gastonia-Concord MSA, NC-SC	Y	34430 FQ	37740 MW	42210 TQ	USBLS	5/07
	Greensboro-High Point MSA, NC	Y	29590 FQ	37020 MW	50890 TQ	USBLS	5/07
	Raleigh-Cary MSA, NC	Y	32420 FQ	39280 MW	45860 TQ	USBLS	5/07
	North Dakota	Y	34160 FQ	37990 MW	44720 TQ	USBLS	5/07
	Fargo MSA, ND-MN	Y	33760 FQ	37090 MW	41240 TQ	USBLS	5/07
	Ohio	Y	28580 FQ	33570 MW	40750 TQ	USBLS	5/07
	Canton-Massillon MSA, OH	Y	28780 FQ	33500 MW	44660 TQ	USBLS	5/07
	Cincinnati-Middletown MSA, OH-KY-IN	Y	28200 FQ	32240 MW	38890 TQ	USBLS	5/07
	Cleveland-Elyria-Mentor MSA, OH	Y	29690 FQ	36170 MW	46030 TQ	USBLS	5/07
	Columbus MSA, OH	Y	30170 FQ	34530 MW	40520 TQ	USBLS	5/07
	Dayton MSA, OH	Y	28340 FQ	32510 MW	40980 TQ	USBLS	5/07
	Oklahoma	Y	26170 FQ	32500 MW	40510 TQ	USBLS	5/07
	Oklahoma City MSA, OK	Y	25770 FQ	33120 MW	41210 TQ	USBLS	5/07
	Tulsa MSA, OK	Y	29200 FQ	35350 MW	43100 TQ	USBLS	5/07
	Oregon	H	12.95 FQ	16.69 MW	22.69 TQ	ORBLS	5/08
	Portland-Vancouver-Beaverton MSA, OR-WA	Y	24030 FQ	30340 MW	39810 TQ	USBLS	5/07
	Pennsylvania	Y	26910 FQ	33730 MW	42660 TQ	USBLS	5/07
	Allentown-Bethlehem-Easton MSA, PA-NJ	Y	26150 FQ	30320 MW	41040 TQ	USBLS	5/07
	Philadelphia-Camden-Wilmington MSA, PA-NJ-DE-MD	Y	26630 FQ	34240 MW	44830 TQ	USBLS	5/07
	Pittsburgh MSA, PA	Y	31870 FQ	37150 MW	45170 TQ	USBLS	5/07
	Reading MSA, PA	Y	26210 FQ	30050 MW	40480 TQ	USBLS	5/07
	Rhode Island	Y	33170 FQ	41560 MW	57590 TQ	USBLS	5/07
	Providence-Fall River-Warwick MSA, RI-MA	Y	33660 FQ	42680 MW	57260 TQ	USBLS	5/07
	South Carolina	Y	18850 FQ	25210 MW	33400 TQ	USBLS	5/07
	Columbia MSA, SC	Y	29010 FQ	34280 MW	41600 TQ	USBLS	5/07
	South Dakota	Y	28577 FQ	32855 MW	38540 TQ	SDBLS	7/08-9/08
	Sioux Falls MSA, SD	Y	26995 FQ	30023 MW	34878 TQ	SDBLS	7/08-9/08
	Tennessee	Y	22410 FQ	28910 MW	37180 TQ	USBLS	5/07
	Memphis MSA, TN-MS-AR	Y	27550 FQ	35380 MW	44380 TQ	USBLS	5/07
	Nashville-Davidson-Murfreesboro MSA, TN	Y	19340 FQ	26920 MW	35200 TQ	USBLS	5/07
	Texas	Y	26340 FQ	31020 MW	38370 TQ	USBLS	5/07
	Austin-Round Rock MSA, TX	Y	25490 FQ	28840 MW	37480 TQ	USBLS	5/07
	Dallas-Fort Worth-Arlington MSA, TX	Y	25640 FQ	29970 MW	34520 TQ	USBLS	5/07
	El Paso MSA, TX	Y	19650 FQ	25410 MW	31380 TQ	USBLS	5/07
	Houston-Sugar Land-Baytown MSA, TX	Y	26500 FQ	31790 MW	39350 TQ	USBLS	5/07
	San Antonio MSA, TX	Y	29410 FQ	36220 MW	46140 TQ	USBLS	5/07
	Utah	Y	31010 FQ	38120 MW	46240 TQ	USBLS	5/07
	Provo-Orem MSA, UT	Y	33190 FQ	39410 MW	47220 TQ	USBLS	5/07
	Salt Lake City MSA, UT	Y	30410 FQ	36660 MW	44190 TQ	USBLS	5/07
	Vermont	Y	30410 FQ	36020 MW	44270 TQ	USBLS	5/07
	Burlington-South Burlington MSA, VT	Y	40670 FQ	47460 MW	59300 TQ	USBLS	5/07
	Virginia	Y	35520 FQ	46680 MW	59900 TQ	USBLS	5/07
	Richmond MSA, VA	Y	35860 FQ	44010 MW	56160 TQ	USBLS	5/07
	Virginia Beach-Norfolk-Newport News MSA, VA-NC	Y	30830 FQ	39210 MW	53190 TQ	USBLS	5/07
	Washington	H	14.53 FQ	17.26 MW	22.32 TQ	WABLS	3/08
	Seattle-Tacoma-Bellevue MSA, WA	Y	30400 FQ	35740 MW	46970 TQ	USBLS	5/07
	West Virginia	Y	18938 FQ	23265 MW	29328 TQ	WVBLS	7/08-9/08
	Charleston MSA, WV	Y	21990 FQ	27000 MW	37370 TQ	USBLS	5/07
	Huntington-Ashland MSA, WV-KY-OH	Y	21150 FQ	26170 MW	33710 TQ	USBLS	5/07
	Wisconsin	Y	24240 FQ	37480 MW	50010 TQ	USBLS	5/07
	Milwaukee-Waukesha-West Allis MSA, WI	Y	34690 FQ	39340 MW	48490 TQ	USBLS	5/07
	Wyoming	Y	24440 FQ	30327 MW	38957 TQ	WYBLS	9/08
	Cheyenne MSA, WY	Y	24240 FQ	29139 MW	41427 TQ	WYBLS	9/08
	Puerto Rico	Y	16490 FQ	19270 MW	24440 TQ	USBLS	5/07

AE	Average entry wage	AW	Average wage paid	FQ	First quartile wage	LO	Lowest wage paid	MTC	Median total compensation	TCC	Total cash compensation
AER	Average entry range	AWR	Average wage range	H	Hourly	LR	Low end range	MW	Median wage paid	TQ	Third quartile wage
AEX	Average experienced wage	AXR	Average experienced range	HI	Highest wage paid	M	Monthly	MWR	Median wage range	W	Weekly
ATC	Average total compensation	D	Daily	HR	High end range	MCC	Median cash compensation	S	See annotated source	Y	Yearly

Occupation/Type/Industry	Location	Per	Low	Mid	High	Source	Date
Mental Health and Substance Abuse Social Worker	San Juan-Caguas-Guaynabo MSA, PR	Y	16580 FQ	19370 MW	25280 TQ	USBLS	5/07
Mental Health Counselor	Alabama	Y	26970 FQ	35060 MW	40200 TQ	USBLS	5/07
	Birmingham-Hoover MSA, AL	Y	26130 FQ	35350 MW	39930 TQ	USBLS	5/07
	Montgomery MSA, AL	Y	34450 FQ	40370 MW	60110 TQ	USBLS	5/07
	Anchorage MSA, AK	Y	42010 FQ	55310 MW	65500 TQ	USBLS	5/07
	Arizona	Y	21670 FQ	33040 MW	52520 TQ	USBLS	5/07
	Phoenix-Mesa-Scottsdale MSA, AZ	Y	21620 FQ	30200 MW	60620 TQ	USBLS	5/07
	Tucson MSA, AZ	Y	18200 FQ	37260 MW	47400 TQ	USBLS	5/07
	Arkansas	Y	26360 FQ	32100 MW	47370 TQ	USBLS	5/07
	Little Rock-North Little Rock MSA, AR	Y	28540 FQ	31880 MW	45530 TQ	USBLS	5/07
	California	H	14.62 FQ	20.07 MW	29.96 TQ	CABLS	1/08-3/08
	Los Angeles-Long Beach-Glendale PMSA, CA	H	14.20 FQ	18.17 MW	27.73 TQ	CABLS	1/08-3/08
	Oakland-Fremont-Hayward MSA, CA	H	14.41 FQ	19.59 MW	31.03 TQ	CABLS	1/08-3/08
	Oxnard-Thousand Oaks-Ventura MSA, CA	H	14.26 FQ	18.39 MW	25.12 TQ	CABLS	1/08-3/08
	Riverside-San Bernardino-Ontario MSA, CA	H	21.22 FQ	34.95 MW	38.79 TQ	CABLS	1/08-3/08
	Sacramento-Arden Arcade-Roseville MSA, CA	H	17.58 FQ	24.12 MW	30.34 TQ	CABLS	1/08-3/08
	San Diego-Carlsbad-San Marcos MSA, CA	H	13.45 FQ	16.78 MW	30.42 TQ	CABLS	1/08-3/08
	San Francisco-San Mateo-Redwood PMSA, CA	H	18.82 FQ	23.08 MW	27.88 TQ	CABLS	1/08-3/08
	San Jose-Sunnyvale-Santa Clara MSA, CA	H	17.58 FQ	22.00 MW	34.37 TQ	CABLS	1/08-3/08
	Santa Ana-Anaheim-Irvine PMSA, CA	Y	23280 FQ	27540 MW	44560 TQ	USBLS	5/07
	Colorado	Y	27440 FQ	32390 MW	42230 TQ	USBLS	5/07
	Denver-Aurora MSA, CO	Y	27430 FQ	31330 MW	41040 TQ	USBLS	5/07
	Connecticut	H	13.41 AE	17.30 MW		CTBLS	1/08-3/08
	Bridgeport-Stamford-Norwalk MSA, CT	Y	30910 FQ	39130 MW	53070 TQ	USBLS	5/07
	Hartford-West Hartford-East Hartford MSA, CT	Y	27250 FQ	31660 MW	41020 TQ	USBLS	5/07
	Delaware	Y	29200 FQ	37830 MW	49830 TQ	USBLS	5/07
	Wilmington PMSA, DE-MD-NJ	Y	27990 FQ	34820 MW	44570 TQ	USBLS	5/07
	District of Columbia	Y	33170 FQ	39950 MW	48270 TQ	USBLS	5/07
	Washington-Arlington-Alexandria MSA, DC-VA-MD-WV	Y	35500 FQ	43650 MW	56680 TQ	USBLS	5/07
	Florida	Y	29230 FQ	35870 MW	46670 TQ	USBLS	5/07
	Cape Coral-Fort Myers MSA, FL	Y	27200 FQ	29950 MW	38950 TQ	USBLS	5/07
	Fort Lauderdale-Pompano Beach-Deerfield Beach PMSA, FL	Y	29380 FQ	37270 MW	49530 TQ	USBLS	5/07
	Jacksonville MSA, FL	Y	26770 FQ	32770 MW	38820 TQ	USBLS	5/07
	Miami-Fort Lauderdale-Miami Beach MSA, FL	Y	32260 FQ	41590 MW	55150 TQ	USBLS	5/07
	Orlando-Kissimmee MSA, FL	Y	35530 FQ	45810 MW	58700 TQ	USBLS	5/07
	Tampa-St. Petersburg-Clearwater MSA, FL	Y	28680 FQ	33290 MW	38880 TQ	USBLS	5/07
	West Palm Beach-Boca Raton-Boynton Beach PMSA, FL	Y	33720 FQ	39150 MW	47430 TQ	USBLS	5/07
	Georgia	Y	28220 FQ	37320 MW	48580 TQ	USBLS	5/07
	Atlanta-Sandy Springs-Marietta MSA, GA	Y	27150 FQ	37510 MW	50040 TQ	USBLS	5/07
	Savannah MSA, GA	Y	23780 FQ	28520 MW	36700 TQ	USBLS	5/07
	Hawaii	Y	29820 FQ	35040 MW	43430 TQ	USBLS	5/07
	Honolulu MSA, HI	Y	29670 FQ	34500 MW	42020 TQ	USBLS	5/07
	Idaho	Y	25310 FQ	34300 MW	48920 TQ	USBLS	5/07
	Idaho Falls MSA, ID	Y	47190 FQ	62580 MW	70130 TQ	USBLS	5/07
	Lewiston MSA, ID-WA	Y	21590 FQ	29010 MW	39250 TQ	USBLS	5/07
	Illinois	Y	28820 FQ	36980 MW	47020 TQ	USBLS	5/07

Occupation/Type/Industry	Location	Per	Low	Mid	High	Source	Date
Mental Health Counselor	Chicago-Naperville-Joliet MSA, IL-IN-WI	Y	30240 FQ	40050 MW	48500 TQ	USBLS	5/07
	Indiana	Y	27760 FQ	34130 MW	45330 TQ	USBLS	5/07
	Gary PMSA, IN	Y	23100 FQ	35680 MW	45720 TQ	USBLS	5/07
	Indianapolis-Carmel MSA, IN	Y	30770 FQ	38630 MW	49960 TQ	USBLS	5/07
	Terre Haute MSA, IN	Y	32450 FQ	36020 MW	39560 TQ	USBLS	5/07
	Iowa	Y	22560 FQ	28880 MW	42660 TQ	USBLS	5/07
	Des Moines-West Des Moines MSA, IA	Y	27890 FQ	42560 MW	48510 TQ	USBLS	5/07
	Kansas	Y	28080 FQ	33060 MW	40710 TQ	USBLS	5/07
	Wichita MSA, KS	Y	36130 FQ	43540 MW	51130 TQ	USBLS	5/07
	Kentucky	Y	28434 FQ	35036 MW	41735 TQ	KYBLS	2008
	Louisville-Jefferson County MSA, KY-IN	Y	24280 FQ	29370 MW	38780 TQ	USBLS	5/07
	Louisiana	H	10.94 FQ	13.23 MW	15.99 TQ	LABLS	1/08-3/08
	Baton Rouge MSA, LA	Y	26050 FQ	31100 MW	35550 TQ	USBLS	5/07
	Lake Charles MSA, LA	Y	18920 FQ	35950 MW	45520 TQ	USBLS	5/07
	New Orleans-Metairie-Kenner MSA, LA	Y	23170 FQ	27450 MW	31910 TQ	USBLS	5/07
	Shreveport-Bossier City MSA, LA	Y	18660 FQ	21500 MW	23700 TQ	USBLS	5/07
	Maine	Y	31950 FQ	40130 MW	49390 TQ	USBLS	5/07
	Portland-South Portland-Biddeford MSA, ME	Y	34680 FQ	41440 MW	52020 TQ	USBLS	5/07
	Maryland	Y		37600 MW		MDBLS	3/08
	Baltimore-Towson MSA, MD	Y	29960 FQ	37780 MW	47470 TQ	USBLS	5/07
	Bethesda-Gaithersburg-Frederick PMSA, MD	Y	33050 FQ	41160 MW	50500 TQ	USBLS	5/07
	Hagerstown-Martinsburg MSA, MD-WV	Y	34680 FQ	39160 MW	45990 TQ	USBLS	5/07
	Massachusetts	Y	28780 FQ	35060 MW	43380 TQ	USBLS	5/07
	Boston-Cambridge-Quincy NECTA, MA	Y	29860 FQ	35370 MW	43070 TQ	USBLS	5/07
	New Bedford MSA, MA	Y	41850 FQ	52940 MW	62600 TQ	USBLS	5/07
	Worcester MSA, MA-CT	Y	28400 FQ	34490 MW	42750 TQ	USBLS	5/07
	Michigan	Y	30870 FQ	41920 MW	54420 TQ	USBLS	5/07
	Detroit-Warren-Livonia MSA, MI	Y	31320 FQ	40770 MW	50200 TQ	USBLS	5/07
	Grand Rapids-Wyoming MSA, MI	Y	21410 FQ	23840 MW	45230 TQ	USBLS	5/07
	Warren-Troy-Farmington Hills PMSA, MI	Y	31180 FQ	40840 MW	51440 TQ	USBLS	5/07
	Minnesota	Y	35090 FQ	42989 MW	51777 TQ	MNBLS	10/08-12/08
	Duluth-Superior MSA, MN-WI	Y	32485 FQ	38375 MW	46787 TQ	MNBLS	10/08-12/08
	Minneapolis-Saint Paul MSA, MN-WI	Y	36335 FQ	44506 MW	53127 TQ	MNBLS	10/08-12/08
	Mississippi	Y	29670 FQ	36900 MW	45380 TQ	USBLS	5/07
	Jackson MSA, MS	Y	33190 FQ	41840 MW	47470 TQ	USBLS	5/07
	Missouri	Y	29660 FQ	39530 MW	49940 TQ	USBLS	5/07
	Jefferson City MSA, MO	Y	33040 FQ	39660 MW	47290 TQ	USBLS	5/07
	Kansas City MSA, MO-KS	Y	31070 FQ	40220 MW	51620 TQ	USBLS	5/07
	St. Louis MSA, MO-IL	Y	33810 FQ	40100 MW	48950 TQ	USBLS	5/07
	Montana	Y	26330 FQ	33470 MW	58460 TQ	USBLS	5/07
	Billings MSA, MT	Y	23390 FQ	141180 MW		USBLS	5/07
	Nebraska	Y	24160 FQ	34790 MW	45360 TQ	USBLS	5/07
	Omaha-Council Bluffs MSA, NE-IA	Y	34840 FQ	40290 MW	59100 TQ	USBLS	5/07
	Nevada	H	20.79 FQ	23.96 MW	28.29 TQ	NVBLS	5/08
	Las Vegas-Paradise MSA, NV	H	20.40 FQ	23.30 MW	26.75 TQ	NVBLS	5/08
	New Hampshire	H	14.59 AE	19.04 MW	23.28 AEX	NHBLS	6/08
	Manchester MSA, NH	Y	29180 FQ	34710 MW	40270 TQ	USBLS	5/07
	New Jersey	Y	29720 FQ	36100 MW	46880 TQ	USBLS	5/07
	Camden PMSA, NJ	Y	35780 FQ	41470 MW	52310 TQ	USBLS	5/07
	Edison PMSA, NJ	Y	28290 FQ	34590 MW	43920 TQ	USBLS	5/07
	Newark-Union PMSA, NJ-PA	Y	30360 FQ	35430 MW	48160 TQ	USBLS	5/07
	Trenton-Ewing MSA, NJ	Y	35020 FQ	40770 MW	46100 TQ	USBLS	5/07
	New Mexico	Y	31270 FQ	43860 MW	56420 TQ	USBLS	5/07
	Albuquerque MSA, NM	Y	34010 FQ	50580 MW	59030 TQ	USBLS	5/07
	New York	Y	24630 FQ	30770 MW	44350 TQ	USBLS	5/07
	Albany-Schenectady-Troy MSA, NY	Y	23450 FQ	39800 MW	61680 TQ	USBLS	5/07

AE	Average entry wage	AW	Average wage paid	FQ First quartile wage
AER	Average entry range	AWR	Average wage range	H Hourly
AEX	Average experienced wage	AXR	Average experienced range	HI Highest wage paid
ATC	Average total compensation	D	Daily	HR High end range

LO	Lowest wage paid	MTC	Median total compensation	TCC	Total cash compensation
LR	Low end range	MW	Median wage paid	TQ	Third quartile wage
M	Monthly	MWR	Median wage range	W	Weekly
MCC	Median cash compensation	S	See annotated source	Y	Yearly

Occupation/Type/Industry	Location	Per	Low	Mid	High	Source	Date
Mental Health Counselor	Buffalo-Niagara Falls MSA, NY	Y	23900 FQ	27650 MW	31690 TQ	USBLS	5/07
	Nassau-Suffolk PMSA, NY	Y	27460 FQ	30330 MW	37570 TQ	USBLS	5/07
	New York-Northern New Jersey-Long Island MSA, NY-NJ-PA	Y	26440 FQ	32210 MW	45670 TQ	USBLS	5/07
	North Carolina	Y	29940 FQ	37360 MW	47230 TQ	USBLS	5/07
	Charlotte-Gastonia-Concord MSA, NC-SC	Y	28800 FQ	32460 MW	40090 TQ	USBLS	5/07
	Raleigh-Cary MSA, NC	Y	37410 FQ	55660 MW	62640 TQ	USBLS	5/07
	Fargo MSA, ND-MN	Y	32830 FQ	35250 MW	37690 TQ	USBLS	5/07
	Ohio	Y	33620 FQ	39550 MW	47690 TQ	USBLS	5/07
	Cincinnati-Middletown MSA, OH-KY-IN	Y	32430 FQ	37690 MW	44820 TQ	USBLS	5/07
	Cleveland-Elyria-Mentor MSA, OH	Y	32170 FQ	37860 MW	45070 TQ	USBLS	5/07
	Columbus MSA, OH	Y	33490 FQ	40930 MW	48760 TQ	USBLS	5/07
	Dayton MSA, OH	Y	36410 FQ	42120 MW	49550 TQ	USBLS	5/07
	Oklahoma	Y	30470 FQ	36750 MW	45780 TQ	USBLS	5/07
	Oklahoma City MSA, OK	Y	31490 FQ	38160 MW	47660 TQ	USBLS	5/07
	Tulsa MSA, OK	Y	33080 FQ	38930 MW	46820 TQ	USBLS	5/07
	Oregon	H	15.97 FQ	21.42 MW	28.04 TQ	ORBLS	5/08
	Eugene-Springfield MSA, OR	Y	25230 FQ	37090 MW	50160 TQ	USBLS	5/07
	Portland-Vancouver-Beaverton MSA, OR-WA	Y	33590 FQ	45950 MW	60380 TQ	USBLS	5/07
	Pennsylvania	Y	25860 FQ	31520 MW	39970 TQ	USBLS	5/07
	Allentown-Bethlehem-Easton MSA, PA-NJ	Y	29470 FQ	36670 MW	49120 TQ	USBLS	5/07
	Philadelphia-Camden-Wilmington MSA, PA-NJ-DE-MD	Y	28400 FQ	36720 MW	47390 TQ	USBLS	5/07
	Pittsburgh MSA, PA	Y	24450 FQ	28220 MW	33170 TQ	USBLS	5/07
	York-Hanover MSA, PA	Y	26470 FQ	29500 MW	33960 TQ	USBLS	5/07
	Rhode Island	Y	29950 FQ	35720 MW	43880 TQ	USBLS	5/07
	Providence-Fall River-Warwick MSA, RI-MA	Y	28680 FQ	34480 MW	42920 TQ	USBLS	5/07
	South Carolina	Y	27280 FQ	36340 MW	49250 TQ	USBLS	5/07
	Columbia MSA, SC	Y	27880 FQ	39560 MW	55620 TQ	USBLS	5/07
	South Dakota	Y	32085 FQ	37156 MW	43347 TQ	SDBLS	7/08-9/08
	Sioux Falls MSA, SD	Y	33930 FQ	39117 MW	46071 TQ	SDBLS	7/08-9/08
	Tennessee	Y	23040 FQ	25990 MW	35780 TQ	USBLS	5/07
	Memphis MSA, TN-MS-AR	Y	23260 FQ	25630 MW	38400 TQ	USBLS	5/07
	Nashville-Davidson-Murfreesboro MSA, TN	Y	23670 FQ	28420 MW	38020 TQ	USBLS	5/07
	Texas	Y	29480 FQ	35950 MW	42810 TQ	USBLS	5/07
	Austin-Round Rock MSA, TX	Y	31300 FQ	37410 MW	43330 TQ	USBLS	5/07
	Dallas-Fort Worth-Arlington MSA, TX	Y	33400 FQ	37070 MW	41540 TQ	USBLS	5/07
	El Paso MSA, TX	Y	21020 FQ	28960 MW	43080 TQ	USBLS	5/07
	Houston-Sugar Land-Baytown MSA, TX	Y	33370 FQ	37550 MW	43140 TQ	USBLS	5/07
	San Antonio MSA, TX	Y	32540 FQ	37670 MW	46760 TQ	USBLS	5/07
	Utah	Y	38990 FQ	45450 MW	53830 TQ	USBLS	5/07
	Ogden-Clearfield MSA, UT	Y	35930 FQ	43360 MW	49230 TQ	USBLS	5/07
	Salt Lake City MSA, UT	Y	40970 FQ	46040 MW	52510 TQ	USBLS	5/07
	Vermont	Y	39110 FQ	46240 MW	57520 TQ	USBLS	5/07
	Burlington-South Burlington MSA, VT	Y	42420 FQ	48500 MW	58830 TQ	USBLS	5/07
	Virginia	Y	33220 FQ	41790 MW	54960 TQ	USBLS	5/07
	Richmond MSA, VA	Y	35130 FQ	49260 MW	59960 TQ	USBLS	5/07
	Virginia Beach-Norfolk-Newport News MSA, VA-NC	Y	33520 FQ	42420 MW	50430 TQ	USBLS	5/07
	Washington	H	16.73 FQ	20.16 MW	24.99 TQ	WABLS	3/08
	Seattle-Tacoma-Bellevue MSA, WA	Y	33930 FQ	40500 MW	50560 TQ	USBLS	5/07
	West Virginia	Y	29142 FQ	36756 MW	44534 TQ	WVBLS	7/08-9/08
	Charleston MSA, WV	Y	30130 FQ	36530 MW	42060 TQ	USBLS	5/07
	Huntington-Ashland MSA, WV-KY-OH	Y	29300 FQ	37090 MW	45730 TQ	USBLS	5/07
	Wisconsin	Y	27760 FQ	42450 MW	52900 TQ	USBLS	5/07
	Milwaukee-Waukesha-West Allis MSA, WI	Y	27000 FQ	38870 MW	48400 TQ	USBLS	5/07

AE	Average entry wage	AW	Average wage paid	FQ	First quartile wage	LO	Lowest wage paid	MTC	Median total compensation	TCC	Total cash compensation
AER	Average entry range	AWR	Average wage range	H	Hourly	LR	Low end range	MW	Median wage paid	TQ	Third quartile wage
AEX	Average experienced wage	AXR	Average experienced range	HI	Highest wage paid	M	Monthly	MWR	Median wage range	W	Weekly
ATC	Average total compensation	D	Daily	HR	High end range	MCC	Median cash compensation	S	See annotated source	Y	Yearly

1042

Occupation/Type/Industry	Location	Per	Low	Mid	High	Source	Date
Mental Health Counselor	Wyoming	Y	35121 FQ	40313 MW	48418 TQ	WYBLS	9/08
	Cheyenne MSA, WY	Y	35354 FQ	41615 MW	47803 TQ	WYBLS	9/08
	Puerto Rico	Y	24280 FQ	29100 MW	34870 TQ	USBLS	5/07
	San Juan-Caguas-Guaynabo MSA, PR	Y	22150 FQ	28890 MW	35180 TQ	USBLS	5/07
Mental Health Specialist							
State Government	Oregon	Y	39100 LO		54800 HI	AFT02	3/1/08
Mental Health Worker Trainee							
New Hampshire Hospital	New Hampshire	Y		12031 AW		NHUL03	2008
Merchandise Displayer and Window Trimmer	Alabama	Y	17680 FQ	21130 MW	27420 TQ	USBLS	5/07
	Birmingham-Hoover MSA, AL	Y	19860 FQ	24810 MW	29440 TQ	USBLS	5/07
	Alaska	Y	21010 FQ	26720 MW	31170 TQ	USBLS	5/07
	Anchorage MSA, AK	Y	20570 FQ	26390 MW	30720 TQ	USBLS	5/07
	Arizona	Y	18670 FQ	23430 MW	28940 TQ	USBLS	5/07
	Phoenix-Mesa-Scottsdale MSA, AZ	Y	19670 FQ	24630 MW	29680 TQ	USBLS	5/07
	Tucson MSA, AZ	Y	16400 FQ	21500 MW	27490 TQ	USBLS	5/07
	Arkansas	Y	16470 FQ	22300 MW	28480 TQ	USBLS	5/07
	Little Rock-North Little Rock MSA, AR	Y	21720 FQ	25240 MW	29980 TQ	USBLS	5/07
	California	H	10.39 FQ	12.82 MW	16.42 TQ	CABLS	1/08-3/08
	Los Angeles-Long Beach-Glendale PMSA, CA	H	11.03 FQ	13.83 MW	19.39 TQ	CABLS	1/08-3/08
	Oakland-Fremont-Hayward MSA, CA	H	11.09 FQ	14.84 MW	19.45 TQ	CABLS	1/08-3/08
	Riverside-San Bernardino-Ontario MSA, CA	H	10.24 FQ	12.32 MW	14.49 TQ	CABLS	1/08-3/08
	Sacramento-Arden Arcade-Roseville MSA, CA	H	9.63 FQ	12.60 MW	16.61 TQ	CABLS	1/08-3/08
	San Diego-Carlsbad-San Marcos MSA, CA	H	9.31 FQ	11.34 MW	15.21 TQ	CABLS	1/08-3/08
	San Francisco-San Mateo-Redwood PMSA, CA	H	10.48 FQ	13.72 MW	18.31 TQ	CABLS	1/08-3/08
	San Jose-Sunnyvale-Santa Clara MSA, CA	H	10.97 FQ	14.72 MW	18.81 TQ	CABLS	1/08-3/08
	Santa Ana-Anaheim-Irvine PMSA, CA	Y	20140 FQ	26230 MW	32190 TQ	USBLS	5/07
	Colorado	Y	18010 FQ	22790 MW	28560 TQ	USBLS	5/07
	Boulder MSA, CO	Y	22110 FQ	27560 MW	31380 TQ	USBLS	5/07
	Denver-Aurora MSA, CO	Y	19470 FQ	23390 MW	28620 TQ	USBLS	5/07
	Connecticut	H	9.26 AE	12.50 MW		CTBLS	1/08-3/08
	Bridgeport-Stamford-Norwalk MSA, CT	Y	18050 FQ	20170 MW	32470 TQ	USBLS	5/07
	Hartford-West Hartford-East Hartford MSA, CT	Y	20000 FQ	29150 MW	38010 TQ	USBLS	5/07
	Delaware	Y	24970 FQ	30160 MW	36990 TQ	USBLS	5/07
	Wilmington PMSA, DE-MD-NJ	Y	24520 FQ	29140 MW	36070 TQ	USBLS	5/07
	District of Columbia	Y	16950 FQ	27230 MW	35760 TQ	USBLS	5/07
	Washington-Arlington-Alexandria MSA, DC-VA-MD-WV	Y	18920 FQ	24790 MW	40710 TQ	USBLS	5/07
	Florida	Y	19820 FQ	23910 MW	29450 TQ	USBLS	5/07
	Fort Lauderdale-Pompano Beach-Deerfield Beach PMSA, FL	Y	20530 FQ	26080 MW	35090 TQ	USBLS	5/07
	Jacksonville MSA, FL	Y	22250 FQ	26760 MW	30140 TQ	USBLS	5/07
	Miami-Fort Lauderdale-Miami Beach MSA, FL	Y	19230 FQ	24290 MW	31080 TQ	USBLS	5/07
	Orlando-Kissimmee MSA, FL	Y	21090 FQ	25750 MW	30120 TQ	USBLS	5/07
	Tampa-St. Petersburg-Clearwater MSA, FL	Y	18650 FQ	22430 MW	25370 TQ	USBLS	5/07
	West Palm Beach-Boca Raton-Boynton Beach PMSA, FL	Y	20270 FQ	23220 MW	27520 TQ	USBLS	5/07
	Georgia	Y	18270 FQ	22890 MW	29740 TQ	USBLS	5/07
	Atlanta-Sandy Springs-Marietta MSA, GA	Y	17890 FQ	21520 MW	29570 TQ	USBLS	5/07
	Savannah MSA, GA	Y	19360 FQ	28540 MW	35460 TQ	USBLS	5/07

AE	Average entry wage	**AW**	Average wage paid	**FQ**	First quartile wage
AER	Average entry range	**AWR**	Average wage range	**H**	Hourly
AEX	Average experienced wage	**AXR**	Average experienced range	**HI**	Highest wage paid
ATC	Average total compensation	**D**	Daily	**HR**	High end range

LO	Lowest wage paid	**MTC**	Median total compensation
LR	Low end range	**MW**	Median wage paid
M	Monthly	**MWR**	Median wage range
MCC	Median cash compensation	**S**	See annotated source

TCC	Total cash compensation
TQ	Third quartile wage
W	Weekly
Y	Yearly

Occupation/Type/Industry	Location	Per	Low	Mid	High	Source	Date
Merchandise Displayer and Window Trimmer							
	Hawaii	Y	26530 FQ	31270 MW	40240 TQ	USBLS	5/07
	Honolulu MSA, HI	Y	26640 FQ	32460 MW	41010 TQ	USBLS	5/07
	Idaho	Y	18690 FQ	24800 MW	29050 TQ	USBLS	5/07
	Boise City-Nampa MSA, ID	Y	22670 FQ	26530 MW	29590 TQ	USBLS	5/07
	Illinois	Y	20800 FQ	24520 MW	31750 TQ	USBLS	5/07
	Chicago-Naperville-Joliet MSA, IL-IN-WI	Y	21220 FQ	24650 MW	32250 TQ	USBLS	5/07
	Indiana	Y	16710 FQ	22720 MW	30690 TQ	USBLS	5/07
	Gary PMSA, IN	Y	19880 FQ	22300 MW	25240 TQ	USBLS	5/07
	Indianapolis-Carmel MSA, IN	Y	18900 FQ	25820 MW	30460 TQ	USBLS	5/07
	Iowa	Y	19560 FQ	22530 MW	25400 TQ	USBLS	5/07
	Des Moines-West Des Moines MSA, IA	Y	18670 FQ	21460 MW	24220 TQ	USBLS	5/07
	Kansas	Y	15150 FQ	20960 MW	28660 TQ	USBLS	5/07
	Wichita MSA, KS	Y	22390 FQ	27730 MW	38930 TQ	USBLS	5/07
	Kentucky	Y	18896 FQ	22478 MW	26834 TQ	KYBLS	2008
	Louisville-Jefferson County MSA, KY-IN	Y	19350 FQ	22840 MW	28350 TQ	USBLS	5/07
	Louisiana	H	6.84 FQ	9.45 MW	13.50 TQ	LABLS	1/08-3/08
	Baton Rouge MSA, LA	Y	15810 FQ	18730 MW	23690 TQ	USBLS	5/07
	New Orleans-Metairie-Kenner MSA, LA	Y	13750 FQ	17620 MW	29250 TQ	USBLS	5/07
	Maine	Y	23500 FQ	28120 MW	34500 TQ	USBLS	5/07
	Portland-South Portland-Biddeford MSA, ME	Y	25640 FQ	29750 MW	38370 TQ	USBLS	5/07
	Maryland	Y		28225 MW		MDBLS	3/08
	Baltimore-Towson MSA, MD	Y	18740 FQ	25000 MW	34980 TQ	USBLS	5/07
	Bethesda-Gaithersburg-Frederick PMSA, MD	Y	18330 FQ	22840 MW	35580 TQ	USBLS	5/07
	Massachusetts	Y	25180 FQ	31620 MW	39410 TQ	USBLS	5/07
	Barnstable Town MSA, MA	Y	20280 FQ	22700 MW	25960 TQ	USBLS	5/07
	Boston-Cambridge-Quincy NECTA, MA	Y	25550 FQ	32520 MW	41550 TQ	USBLS	5/07
	Worcester MSA, MA-CT	Y	24340 FQ	32380 MW	39800 TQ	USBLS	5/07
	Michigan	Y	20820 FQ	26010 MW	32930 TQ	USBLS	5/07
	Detroit-Warren-Livonia MSA, MI	Y	20900 FQ	25370 MW	31140 TQ	USBLS	5/07
	Grand Rapids-Wyoming MSA, MI	Y	24120 FQ	35910 MW	53050 TQ	USBLS	5/07
	Warren-Troy-Farmington Hills PMSA, MI	Y	21720 FQ	25830 MW	31730 TQ	USBLS	5/07
	Minnesota	Y	22807 FQ	29221 MW	39024 TQ	MNBLS	10/08-12/08
	Duluth-Superior MSA, MN-WI	Y	20746 FQ	23226 MW	25967 TQ	MNBLS	10/08-12/08
	Minneapolis-Saint Paul MSA, MN-WI	Y	24314 FQ	31324 MW	41618 TQ	MNBLS	10/08-12/08
	Rochester MSA, MN	Y	23388 FQ	27410 MW	31000 TQ	MNBLS	10/08-12/08
	Mississippi	Y	13290 FQ	14920 MW	22630 TQ	USBLS	5/07
	Jackson MSA, MS	Y	12950 FQ	14240 MW	21970 TQ	USBLS	5/07
	Missouri	Y	20790 FQ	24410 MW	30340 TQ	USBLS	5/07
	Kansas City MSA, MO-KS	Y	17490 FQ	25830 MW	31350 TQ	USBLS	5/07
	St. Joseph MSA, MO-KS	Y	15550 FQ	26430 MW	30080 TQ	USBLS	5/07
	St. Louis MSA, MO-IL	Y	20930 FQ	23930 MW	29770 TQ	USBLS	5/07
	Montana	Y	16840 FQ	18560 MW	22480 TQ	USBLS	5/07
	Billings MSA, MT	Y	16570 FQ	17870 MW	19160 TQ	USBLS	5/07
	Nebraska	Y	17490 FQ	20030 MW	26120 TQ	USBLS	5/07
	Omaha-Council Bluffs MSA, NE-IA	Y	16820 FQ	23610 MW	29370 TQ	USBLS	5/07
	Nevada	H	10.19 FQ	11.64 MW	14.50 TQ	NVBLS	5/08
	Las Vegas-Paradise MSA, NV	H	10.32 FQ	11.73 MW	14.73 TQ	NVBLS	5/08
	New Hampshire	H	10.13 AE	13.05 MW	15.64 AEX	NHBLS	6/08
	Manchester MSA, NH	Y	25610 FQ	28820 MW	32100 TQ	USBLS	5/07
	New Jersey	Y	25190 FQ	29300 MW	36690 TQ	USBLS	5/07
	Atlantic City MSA, NJ	Y	21950 FQ	26110 MW	29380 TQ	USBLS	5/07
	Camden PMSA, NJ	Y	27390 FQ	32670 MW	39270 TQ	USBLS	5/07
	Edison PMSA, NJ	Y	20720 FQ	28640 MW	38780 TQ	USBLS	5/07
	Newark-Union PMSA, NJ-PA	Y	22940 FQ	29460 MW	36340 TQ	USBLS	5/07
	New Mexico	Y	24950 FQ	28760 MW	33480 TQ	USBLS	5/07
	Albuquerque MSA, NM	Y	25570 FQ	29380 MW	34700 TQ	USBLS	5/07
	New York	Y	24010 FQ	31650 MW	40340 TQ	USBLS	5/07
	Albany-Schenectady-Troy MSA, NY	Y	27810 FQ	32450 MW	48760 TQ	USBLS	5/07

AE	Average entry wage	AW	Average wage paid	FQ	First quartile wage	LO	Lowest wage paid	MTC	Median total compensation	TCC	Total cash compensation
AER	Average entry range	AWR	Average wage range	H	Hourly	LR	Low end range	MW	Median wage paid	TQ	Third quartile wage
AEX	Average experienced wage	AXR	Average experienced range	HI	Highest wage paid	M	Monthly	MWR	Median wage range	W	Weekly
ATC	Average total compensation	D	Daily	HR	High end range	MCC	Median cash compensation	S	See annotated source	Y	Yearly

1044

Occupation/Type/Industry	Location	Per	Low	Mid	High	Source	Date
Merchandise Displayer and Window Trimmer	Binghamton MSA, NY	Y	25180 FQ	31160 MW	47050 TQ	USBLS	5/07
	Buffalo-Niagara Falls MSA, NY	Y	19210 FQ	23680 MW	31580 TQ	USBLS	5/07
	Nassau-Suffolk PMSA, NY	Y	22350 FQ	27630 MW	37000 TQ	USBLS	5/07
	New York-Northern New Jersey-Long Island MSA, NY-NJ-PA	Y	25280 FQ	31570 MW	40250 TQ	USBLS	5/07
	North Carolina	Y	17750 FQ	23440 MW	32150 TQ	USBLS	5/07
	Charlotte-Gastonia-Concord MSA, NC-SC	Y	17910 FQ	23650 MW	34060 TQ	USBLS	5/07
	Raleigh-Cary MSA, NC	Y	17750 FQ	21550 MW	28440 TQ	USBLS	5/07
	North Dakota	Y	20250 FQ	24850 MW	29400 TQ	USBLS	5/07
	Fargo MSA, ND-MN	Y	22490 FQ	27310 MW	30130 TQ	USBLS	5/07
	Ohio	Y	18570 FQ	22720 MW	28270 TQ	USBLS	5/07
	Canton-Massillon MSA, OH	Y	16820 FQ	19430 MW	24320 TQ	USBLS	5/07
	Cincinnati-Middletown MSA, OH-KY-IN	Y	17620 FQ	20200 MW	25010 TQ	USBLS	5/07
	Cleveland-Elyria-Mentor MSA, OH	Y	19820 FQ	24260 MW	30220 TQ	USBLS	5/07
	Columbus MSA, OH	Y	17050 FQ	22150 MW	29460 TQ	USBLS	5/07
	Dayton MSA, OH	Y	20170 FQ	24540 MW	28700 TQ	USBLS	5/07
	Oklahoma	Y	14660 FQ	21410 MW	25900 TQ	USBLS	5/07
	Oklahoma City MSA, OK	Y	15550 FQ	21580 MW	29250 TQ	USBLS	5/07
	Tulsa MSA, OK	Y	19770 FQ	23260 MW	25670 TQ	USBLS	5/07
	Oregon	H	11.54 FQ	13.44 MW	15.45 TQ	ORBLS	5/08
	Portland-Vancouver-Beaverton MSA, OR-WA	Y	23990 FQ	27480 MW	31840 TQ	USBLS	5/07
	Pennsylvania	Y	17850 FQ	21760 MW	28260 TQ	USBLS	5/07
	Allentown-Bethlehem-Easton MSA, PA-NJ	Y	17670 FQ	20350 MW	24300 TQ	USBLS	5/07
	Philadelphia-Camden-Wilmington MSA, PA-NJ-DE-MD	Y	23780 FQ	28960 MW	36710 TQ	USBLS	5/07
	Pittsburgh MSA, PA	Y	21580 FQ	30630 MW	49090 TQ	USBLS	5/07
	Rhode Island	Y	25800 FQ	31120 MW	36190 TQ	USBLS	5/07
	Providence-Fall River-Warwick MSA, RI-MA	Y	25230 FQ	30640 MW	35870 TQ	USBLS	5/07
	South Carolina	Y	14700 FQ	19400 MW	26280 TQ	USBLS	5/07
	Charleston-North Charleston MSA, SC	Y	20030 FQ	23540 MW	26930 TQ	USBLS	5/07
	Columbia MSA, SC	Y	13710 FQ	16260 MW	21810 TQ	USBLS	5/07
	South Dakota	Y	19123 FQ	21969 MW	24893 TQ	SDBLS	7/08-9/08
	Sioux Falls MSA, SD	Y	19750 FQ	23166 MW	26236 TQ	SDBLS	7/08-9/08
	Tennessee	Y	17620 FQ	24610 MW	30270 TQ	USBLS	5/07
	Memphis MSA, TN-MS-AR	Y	14710 FQ	24100 MW	30260 TQ	USBLS	5/07
	Nashville-Davidson-Murfreesboro MSA, TN	Y	19150 FQ	27030 MW	31030 TQ	USBLS	5/07
	Texas	Y	18430 FQ	23120 MW	30160 TQ	USBLS	5/07
	Austin-Round Rock MSA, TX	Y	19830 FQ	22350 MW	26020 TQ	USBLS	5/07
	Brownsville-Harlingen MSA, TX	Y	13300 FQ	15180 MW	24140 TQ	USBLS	5/07
	Dallas-Fort Worth-Arlington MSA, TX	Y	19840 FQ	25010 MW	35480 TQ	USBLS	5/07
	El Paso MSA, TX	Y	17430 FQ	20860 MW	24200 TQ	USBLS	5/07
	Houston-Sugar Land-Baytown MSA, TX	Y	17130 FQ	21290 MW	26460 TQ	USBLS	5/07
	San Antonio MSA, TX	Y	18650 FQ	23470 MW	30740 TQ	USBLS	5/07
	Utah	Y	20580 FQ	25950 MW	31910 TQ	USBLS	5/07
	Salt Lake City MSA, UT	Y	24240 FQ	28550 MW	34220 TQ	USBLS	5/07
	Vermont	Y	21210 FQ	26800 MW	31780 TQ	USBLS	5/07
	Burlington-South Burlington MSA, VT	Y	21070 FQ	25620 MW	29760 TQ	USBLS	5/07
	Virginia	Y	18900 FQ	23170 MW	29350 TQ	USBLS	5/07
	Richmond MSA, VA	Y	20380 FQ	23740 MW	28920 TQ	USBLS	5/07
	Virginia Beach-Norfolk-Newport News MSA, VA-NC	Y	18630 FQ	24000 MW	29140 TQ	USBLS	5/07
	Washington	H	11.24 FQ	13.90 MW	17.17 TQ	WABLS	3/08
	Seattle-Tacoma-Bellevue MSA, WA	Y	24340 FQ	29890 MW	36050 TQ	USBLS	5/07
	Spokane MSA, WA	Y	18720 FQ	27130 MW	35390 TQ	USBLS	5/07
	West Virginia	Y	15395 FQ	19682 MW	25725 TQ	WVBLS	7/08-9/08

AE Average entry wage	**AW** Average wage paid	**FQ** First quartile wage	**LO** Lowest wage paid	**MTC** Median total compensation	**TCC** Total cash compensation
AER Average entry range	**AWR** Average wage range	**H** Hourly	**LR** Low end range	**MW** Median wage paid	**TQ** Third quartile wage
AEX Average experienced wage	**AXR** Average experienced range	**HI** Highest wage paid	**M** Monthly	**MWR** Median wage range	**W** Weekly
ATC Average total compensation	**D** Daily	**HR** High end range	**MCC** Median cash compensation	**S** See annotated source	**Y** Yearly

Occupation/Type/Industry	Location	Per	Low	Mid	High	Source	Date
Merchandise Displayer and Window Trimmer	Wisconsin	Y	21190 FQ	26150 MW	32030 TQ	USBLS	5/07
	Milwaukee-Waukesha-West Allis MSA, WI	Y	24350 FQ	30480 MW	38450 TQ	USBLS	5/07
	Wyoming	Y	16951 FQ	19813 MW	24546 TQ	WYBLS	9/08
	Puerto Rico	Y	14880 FQ	21370 MW	32060 TQ	USBLS	5/07
	San Juan-Caguas-Guaynabo MSA, PR	Y	15310 FQ	22200 MW	32140 TQ	USBLS	5/07
Merchandiser							
Apparel Industry	United States	Y		73000 MW		247FASH	2009
Messaging Administrator	United States	Y	87250 LO		120000 HI	FREEP08	2009
Messaging/E-mail/Groupware Specialist	United States	Y		72204 AW		COWRLD	5/20/08-7/25/08
Metal-Refining Furnace Operator and Tender	Alabama	Y	26040 FQ	33140 MW	38850 TQ	USBLS	5/07
	Birmingham-Hoover MSA, AL	Y	30440 FQ	35230 MW	39450 TQ	USBLS	5/07
	Arizona	Y	31580 FQ	36210 MW	50400 TQ	USBLS	5/07
	Phoenix-Mesa-Scottsdale MSA, AZ	Y	28590 FQ	32200 MW	34990 TQ	USBLS	5/07
	Arkansas	Y	33360 FQ	43570 MW	55750 TQ	USBLS	5/07
	California	H	11.21 FQ	13.57 MW	15.67 TQ	CABLS	1/08-3/08
	Los Angeles-Long Beach-Glendale PMSA, CA	H	10.74 FQ	13.34 MW	15.83 TQ	CABLS	1/08-3/08
	Oakland-Fremont-Hayward MSA, CA	H	12.61 FQ	14.54 MW	16.14 TQ	CABLS	1/08-3/08
	Riverside-San Bernardino-Ontario MSA, CA	H	11.41 FQ	12.96 MW	15.18 TQ	CABLS	1/08-3/08
	Santa Ana-Anaheim-Irvine PMSA, CA	Y	21830 FQ	27180 MW	31790 TQ	USBLS	5/07
	Connecticut	H	14.73 AE	18.98 MW		CTBLS	1/08-3/08
	Florida	Y	26990 FQ	29550 MW	31920 TQ	USBLS	5/07
	Jacksonville MSA, FL	Y	27590 FQ	29690 MW	31720 TQ	USBLS	5/07
	Georgia	Y	24060 FQ	28890 MW	34940 TQ	USBLS	5/07
	Atlanta-Sandy Springs-Marietta MSA, GA	Y	26850 FQ	30310 MW	41590 TQ	USBLS	5/07
	Illinois	Y	26280 FQ	29190 MW	40970 TQ	USBLS	5/07
	Chicago-Naperville-Joliet MSA, IL-IN-WI	Y	27300 FQ	38130 MW	45920 TQ	USBLS	5/07
	Indiana	Y	33150 FQ	40380 MW	45860 TQ	USBLS	5/07
	Indianapolis-Carmel MSA, IN	Y	37020 FQ	40730 MW	44210 TQ	USBLS	5/07
	Iowa	Y	28700 FQ	35080 MW	40970 TQ	USBLS	5/07
	Davenport-Moline-Rock Island MSA, IA-IL	Y	35550 FQ	40340 MW	45880 TQ	USBLS	5/07
	Kansas	Y	22100 FQ	26550 MW	31920 TQ	USBLS	5/07
	Wichita MSA, KS	Y	21190 FQ	22780 MW	24830 TQ	USBLS	5/07
	Kentucky	Y	30826 FQ	37169 MW	43540 TQ	KYBLS	2008
	Louisville-Jefferson County MSA, KY-IN	Y	19750 FQ	32170 MW	36720 TQ	USBLS	5/07
	Maryland	Y		42800 MW		MDBLS	3/08
	Massachusetts	Y	34170 FQ	37690 MW	44350 TQ	USBLS	5/07
	Michigan	Y	28750 FQ	35540 MW	47230 TQ	USBLS	5/07
	Detroit-Warren-Livonia MSA, MI	Y	29990 FQ	34990 MW	39420 TQ	USBLS	5/07
	Grand Rapids-Wyoming MSA, MI	Y	30960 FQ	34440 MW	37400 TQ	USBLS	5/07
	Warren-Troy-Farmington Hills PMSA, MI	Y	27130 FQ	29980 MW	33810 TQ	USBLS	5/07
	Minnesota	Y	32074 FQ	35755 MW	39041 TQ	MNBLS	10/08-12/08
	Minneapolis-Saint Paul MSA, MN-WI	Y	34210 FQ	37133 MW	40057 TQ	MNBLS	10/08-12/08
	Mississippi	Y	27070 FQ	29080 MW	31150 TQ	USBLS	5/07
	Missouri	Y	30190 FQ	33800 MW	36860 TQ	USBLS	5/07
	St. Louis MSA, MO-IL	Y	32110 FQ	45890 MW	58080 TQ	USBLS	5/07
	Nebraska	Y	55870 FQ	68750 MW	75760 TQ	USBLS	5/07
	Nevada	H	20.40 FQ	24.83 MW	28.24 TQ	NVBLS	5/08
	New Hampshire	H	13.21 AE	17.26 MW	19.43 AEX	NHBLS	6/08
	New Jersey	Y	27230 FQ	31570 MW	42890 TQ	USBLS	5/07
	Camden PMSA, NJ	Y	26570 FQ	29810 MW	37320 TQ	USBLS	5/07

AE Average entry wage	**AW** Average wage paid	**FQ** First quartile wage	**LO** Lowest wage paid	**MTC** Median total compensation	**TCC** Total cash compensation
AER Average entry range	**AWR** Average wage range	**H** Hourly	**LR** Low end range	**MW** Median wage paid	**TQ** Third quartile wage
AEX Average experienced wage	**AXR** Average experienced range	**HI** Highest wage paid	**M** Monthly	**MWR** Median wage range	**W** Weekly
ATC Average total compensation	**D** Daily	**HR** High end range	**MCC** Median cash compensation	**S** See annotated source	**Y** Yearly

Occupation/Type/Industry	Location	Per	Low	Mid	High	Source	Date
Metal-Refining Furnace Operator and Tender	Edison PMSA, NJ	Y	43740 FQ	46670 MW	49710 TQ	USBLS	5/07
	Newark-Union PMSA, NJ-PA	Y	29080 FQ	32850 MW	43280 TQ	USBLS	5/07
	New Mexico	Y	27990 FQ	30940 MW	35410 TQ	USBLS	5/07
	New York	Y	34390 FQ	39130 MW	50470 TQ	USBLS	5/07
	Buffalo-Niagara Falls MSA, NY	Y	36300 FQ	52460 MW	58010 TQ	USBLS	5/07
	New York-Northern New Jersey-Long Island MSA, NY-NJ-PA	Y	28390 FQ	34970 MW	45820 TQ	USBLS	5/07
	North Carolina	Y	26310 FQ	36620 MW	43620 TQ	USBLS	5/07
	Charlotte-Gastonia-Concord MSA, NC-SC	Y	33160 FQ	39320 MW	44010 TQ	USBLS	5/07
	Ohio	Y	30900 FQ	36580 MW	45670 TQ	USBLS	5/07
	Canton-Massillon MSA, OH	Y	23120 FQ	28680 MW	33230 TQ	USBLS	5/07
	Cincinnati-Middletown MSA, OH-KY-IN	Y	27280 FQ	35670 MW	54280 TQ	USBLS	5/07
	Cleveland-Elyria-Mentor MSA, OH	Y	34080 FQ	39090 MW	45830 TQ	USBLS	5/07
	Oklahoma	Y	27250 FQ	29830 MW	33330 TQ	USBLS	5/07
	Tulsa MSA, OK	Y	27420 FQ	29970 MW	33000 TQ	USBLS	5/07
	Oregon	H	12.98 FQ	15.55 MW	20.71 TQ	ORBLS	5/08
	Portland-Vancouver-Beaverton MSA, OR-WA	Y	27940 FQ	32780 MW	39630 TQ	USBLS	5/07
	Pennsylvania	Y	27190 FQ	33910 MW	40060 TQ	USBLS	5/07
	Allentown-Bethlehem-Easton MSA, PA-NJ	Y	20930 FQ	22980 MW	32870 TQ	USBLS	5/07
	Philadelphia-Camden-Wilmington MSA, PA-NJ-DE-MD	Y	29460 FQ	37890 MW	46280 TQ	USBLS	5/07
	Pittsburgh MSA, PA	Y	29000 FQ	36200 MW	41410 TQ	USBLS	5/07
	Rhode Island	Y	24150 FQ	32340 MW	36530 TQ	USBLS	5/07
	Providence-Fall River-Warwick MSA, RI-MA	Y	27290 FQ	33910 MW	37970 TQ	USBLS	5/07
	South Carolina	Y	32100 FQ	42130 MW	46490 TQ	USBLS	5/07
	Charleston-North Charleston MSA, SC	Y	42300 FQ	45090 MW	48070 TQ	USBLS	5/07
	Columbia MSA, SC	Y	26350 FQ	30840 MW	35800 TQ	USBLS	5/07
	South Dakota	Y	26392 FQ	30430 MW	34082 TQ	SDBLS	7/08-9/08
	Tennessee	Y	29560 FQ	35190 MW	40740 TQ	USBLS	5/07
	Texas	Y	18900 FQ	26240 MW	32480 TQ	USBLS	5/07
	Dallas-Fort Worth-Arlington MSA, TX	Y	23450 FQ	27500 MW	31450 TQ	USBLS	5/07
	Houston-Sugar Land-Baytown MSA, TX	Y	20700 FQ	25130 MW	29710 TQ	USBLS	5/07
	Utah	Y	22430 FQ	28720 MW	39240 TQ	USBLS	5/07
	Salt Lake City MSA, UT	Y	25740 FQ	29050 MW	37240 TQ	USBLS	5/07
	Virginia	Y	26100 FQ	31720 MW	37390 TQ	USBLS	5/07
	Roanoke MSA, VA	Y	22800 FQ	25550 MW	32760 TQ	USBLS	5/07
	Virginia Beach-Norfolk-Newport News MSA, VA-NC	Y	30110 FQ	35260 MW	39230 TQ	USBLS	5/07
	Washington	H	15.85 FQ	18.31 MW	21.21 TQ	WABLS	3/08
	Seattle-Tacoma-Bellevue MSA, WA	Y	28900 FQ	32150 MW	36370 TQ	USBLS	5/07
	West Virginia	Y	35699 FQ	38674 MW	41195 TQ	WVBLS	7/08-9/08
	Wisconsin	Y	29790 FQ	35110 MW	41720 TQ	USBLS	5/07
	Milwaukee-Waukesha-West Allis MSA, WI	Y	28890 FQ	35150 MW	42980 TQ	USBLS	5/07
Metal Technician	East North Central	Y		46356 AW		BSB	2007
	East South Central	Y		47833 AW		BSB	2007
	Pacific	Y		54506 AW		BSB	2007
	South Atlantic	Y		52831 AW		BSB	2007
	West North Central	Y		41714 AW		BSB	2007
	West South Central	Y		48515 AW		BSB	2007
Metallurgical Engineer	Southeast, MI	Y		82183 AW		MIOAKL03	2007
Meteorological Technician	United States	Y		63396 AW		OOH01	2007
Meter Reader Utilities	Alabama	Y	23080 FQ	28560 MW	36540 TQ	USBLS	5/07

AE	Average entry wage	AW	Average wage paid	FQ	First quartile wage	LO	Lowest wage paid	MTC	Median total compensation	TCC	Total cash compensation
AER	Average entry range	AWR	Average wage range	H	Hourly	LR	Low end range	MW	Median wage paid	TQ	Third quartile wage
AEX	Average experienced wage	AXR	Average experienced range	HI	Highest wage paid	M	Monthly	MWR	Median wage range	W	Weekly
ATC	Average total compensation	D	Daily	HR	High end range	MCC	Median cash compensation	S	See annotated source	Y	Yearly

Meter Reader

Occupation/Type/Industry	Location	Per	Low	Mid	High	Source	Date
Meter Reader							
Utilities	Birmingham-Hoover MSA, AL	Y	26420 FQ	32520 MW	40100 TQ	USBLS	5/07
Utilities	Alaska	Y	24640 FQ	37370 MW	54250 TQ	USBLS	5/07
Utilities	Arizona	Y	29310 FQ	36260 MW	51840 TQ	USBLS	5/07
Utilities	Phoenix-Mesa-Scottsdale MSA, AZ	Y	31500 FQ	39080 MW	55200 TQ	USBLS	5/07
Utilities	Tucson MSA, AZ	Y	25880 FQ	31600 MW	44150 TQ	USBLS	5/07
Utilities	Arkansas	Y	17430 FQ	21730 MW	26790 TQ	USBLS	5/07
Utilities	Little Rock-North Little Rock MSA, AR	Y	19780 FQ	23130 MW	27550 TQ	USBLS	5/07
Utilities	California	H	16.31 FQ	19.11 MW	25.69 TQ	CABLS	1/08-3/08
Utilities	Los Angeles-Long Beach-Glendale PMSA, CA	H	14.78 FQ	17.15 MW	20.07 TQ	CABLS	1/08-3/08
Utilities	Modesto MSA, CA	H	20.58 FQ	25.83 MW	29.45 TQ	CABLS	1/08-3/08
Utilities	Oakland-Fremont-Hayward MSA, CA	H	24.38 FQ	27.79 MW	30.52 TQ	CABLS	1/08-3/08
Utilities	Riverside-San Bernardino-Ontario MSA, CA	H	15.48 FQ	17.83 MW	21.69 TQ	CABLS	1/08-3/08
Utilities	Sacramento-Arden Arcade-Roseville MSA, CA	H	16.13 FQ	17.53 MW	21.42 TQ	CABLS	1/08-3/08
Utilities	San Diego-Carlsbad-San Marcos MSA, CA	H	17.10 FQ	19.03 MW	21.66 TQ	CABLS	1/08-3/08
Utilities	San Francisco-San Mateo-Redwood PMSA, CA	H	18.74 FQ	23.70 MW	28.43 TQ	CABLS	1/08-3/08
Utilities	San Jose-Sunnyvale-Santa Clara MSA, CA	H	19.91 FQ	26.76 MW	29.41 TQ	CABLS	1/08-3/08
Utilities	Santa Ana-Anaheim-Irvine PMSA, CA	Y	32790 FQ	36450 MW	44470 TQ	USBLS	5/07
Utilities	Colorado	Y	32990 FQ	38570 MW	46720 TQ	USBLS	5/07
Utilities	Denver-Aurora MSA, CO	Y	32260 FQ	40810 MW	49590 TQ	USBLS	5/07
Utilities	Connecticut	H	15.74 AE	21.62 MW		CTBLS	1/08-3/08
Utilities	Hartford-West Hartford-East Hartford MSA, CT	Y	35860 FQ	39560 MW	48180 TQ	USBLS	5/07
Utilities	Delaware	Y	36820 FQ	43720 MW	49010 TQ	USBLS	5/07
Utilities	Wilmington PMSA, DE-MD-NJ	Y	40330 FQ	45480 MW	50730 TQ	USBLS	5/07
Utilities	Washington-Arlington-Alexandria MSA, DC-VA-MD-WV	Y	32810 FQ	42190 MW	49740 TQ	USBLS	5/07
Utilities	Florida	Y	25460 FQ	29330 MW	33590 TQ	USBLS	5/07
Utilities	Fort Lauderdale-Pompano Beach-Deerfield Beach PMSA, FL	Y	27480 FQ	30440 MW	34500 TQ	USBLS	5/07
Utilities	Jacksonville MSA, FL	Y	22510 FQ	25390 MW	33250 TQ	USBLS	5/07
Utilities	Miami-Fort Lauderdale-Miami Beach MSA, FL	Y	27200 FQ	30470 MW	35090 TQ	USBLS	5/07
Utilities	Orlando-Kissimmee MSA, FL	Y	24650 FQ	29750 MW	35370 TQ	USBLS	5/07
Utilities	Tampa-St. Petersburg-Clearwater MSA, FL	Y	25060 FQ	27970 MW	31050 TQ	USBLS	5/07
Utilities	West Palm Beach-Boca Raton-Boynton Beach PMSA, FL	Y	27070 FQ	30240 MW	34630 TQ	USBLS	5/07
Utilities	Georgia	Y	23440 FQ	26960 MW	32480 TQ	USBLS	5/07
Utilities	Atlanta-Sandy Springs-Marietta MSA, GA	Y	24330 FQ	27460 MW	33220 TQ	USBLS	5/07
Utilities	Hawaii	Y	38850 FQ	45610 MW	50080 TQ	USBLS	5/07
Utilities	Idaho	Y	26720 FQ	33310 MW	45320 TQ	USBLS	5/07
Utilities	Boise City-Nampa MSA, ID	Y	31360 FQ	37550 MW	43440 TQ	USBLS	5/07
Utilities	Illinois	Y	21110 FQ	32380 MW	38350 TQ	USBLS	5/07
Utilities	Chicago-Naperville-Joliet MSA, IL-IN-WI	Y	17580 FQ	32570 MW	49770 TQ	USBLS	5/07
Utilities	Peoria MSA, IL	Y	21450 FQ	23810 MW	31620 TQ	USBLS	5/07
Utilities	Rockford MSA, IL	Y	29780 FQ	37990 MW	52890 TQ	USBLS	5/07
Utilities	Indiana	Y	26390 FQ	33010 MW	41520 TQ	USBLS	5/07
Utilities	Indianapolis-Carmel MSA, IN	Y	30600 FQ	35240 MW	40920 TQ	USBLS	5/07
Utilities	Iowa	Y	20330 FQ	33120 MW	39020 TQ	USBLS	5/07
Utilities	Des Moines-West Des Moines MSA, IA	Y	27660 FQ	33890 MW	38270 TQ	USBLS	5/07
Utilities	Kansas	Y	18430 FQ	27810 MW	35470 TQ	USBLS	5/07
Utilities	Wichita MSA, KS	Y	22420 FQ	25250 MW	32770 TQ	USBLS	5/07
Utilities	Kentucky	Y	20911 FQ	26922 MW	33274 TQ	KYBLS	2008
Utilities	Louisville-Jefferson County MSA, KY-IN	Y	22200 FQ	26430 MW	29500 TQ	USBLS	5/07

AE	Average entry wage	AW	Average wage paid	FQ	First quartile wage	LO	Lowest wage paid	MTC	Median total compensation	TCC	Total cash compensation
AER	Average entry range	AWR	Average wage range	H	Hourly	LR	Low end range	MW	Median wage paid	TQ	Third quartile wage
AEX	Average experienced wage	AXR	Average experienced range	HI	Highest wage paid	M	Monthly	MWR	Median wage range	W	Weekly
ATC	Average total compensation	D	Daily	HR	High end range	MCC	Median cash compensation	S	See annotated source	Y	Yearly

1048

Meter Reader

Occupation/Type/Industry	Location	Per	Low	Mid	High	Source	Date
Meter Reader							
Utilities	Louisiana	H	8.90 FQ	11.33 MW	14.56 TQ	LABLS	1/08-3/08
Utilities	Baton Rouge MSA, LA	Y	23880 FQ	30050 MW	36580 TQ	USBLS	5/07
Utilities	New Orleans-Metairie-Kenner MSA, LA	Y	19320 FQ	24470 MW	30960 TQ	USBLS	5/07
Utilities	Maine	Y	25890 FQ	31240 MW	38340 TQ	USBLS	5/07
Utilities	Maryland	Y		43975 MW		MDBLS	3/08
Utilities	Baltimore-Towson MSA, MD	Y	32800 FQ	42350 MW	47110 TQ	USBLS	5/07
Utilities	Bethesda-Gaithersburg-Frederick PMSA, MD	Y	36090 FQ	44590 MW	49270 TQ	USBLS	5/07
Utilities	Massachusetts	Y	33580 FQ	39810 MW	47800 TQ	USBLS	5/07
Utilities	Boston-Cambridge-Quincy NECTA, MA	Y	27540 FQ	37880 MW	45180 TQ	USBLS	5/07
Utilities	Michigan	Y	32100 FQ	35860 MW	41090 TQ	USBLS	5/07
Utilities	Detroit-Warren-Livonia MSA, MI	Y	32160 FQ	36360 MW	43450 TQ	USBLS	5/07
Utilities	Grand Rapids-Wyoming MSA, MI	Y	33740 FQ	36810 MW	41500 TQ	USBLS	5/07
Utilities	Warren-Troy-Farmington Hills PMSA, MI	Y	32180 FQ	36000 MW	42610 TQ	USBLS	5/07
Utilities	Minnesota	Y	34929 FQ	42839 MW	54797 TQ	MNBLS	10/08-12/08
Utilities	Duluth-Superior MSA, MN-WI	Y	35324 FQ	38852 MW	42610 TQ	MNBLS	10/08-12/08
Utilities	Minneapolis-Saint Paul MSA, MN-WI	Y	31921 FQ	41527 MW	55006 TQ	MNBLS	10/08-12/08
Utilities	Rochester MSA, MN	Y	36295 FQ	39552 MW	43667 TQ	MNBLS	10/08-12/08
Utilities	Mississippi	Y	19670 FQ	23690 MW	28430 TQ	USBLS	5/07
Utilities	Hattiesburg MSA, MS	Y	16910 FQ	20570 MW	29740 TQ	USBLS	5/07
Utilities	Missouri	Y	21570 FQ	27460 MW	35920 TQ	USBLS	5/07
Utilities	Kansas City MSA, MO-KS	Y	24170 FQ	32480 MW	40580 TQ	USBLS	5/07
Utilities	St. Louis MSA, MO-IL	Y	30740 FQ	34160 MW	37210 TQ	USBLS	5/07
Utilities	Montana	Y	21940 FQ	30700 MW	41530 TQ	USBLS	5/07
Utilities	Nebraska	Y	30120 FQ	38620 MW	44510 TQ	USBLS	5/07
Utilities	Omaha-Council Bluffs MSA, NE-IA	Y	14580 FQ	36650 MW	43970 TQ	USBLS	5/07
Utilities	Nevada	H	17.19 FQ	21.59 MW	26.48 TQ	NVBLS	5/08
Utilities	Las Vegas-Paradise MSA, NV	H	17.41 FQ	21.20 MW	24.80 TQ	NVBLS	5/08
Utilities	New Hampshire	H	12.25 AE	18.07 MW	20.95 AEX	NHBLS	6/08
Utilities	Nashua NECTA, NH-MA	Y	35920 FQ	42510 MW	47540 TQ	USBLS	5/07
Utilities	New Jersey	Y	34510 FQ	44470 MW	53020 TQ	USBLS	5/07
Utilities	Camden PMSA, NJ	Y	33730 FQ	42690 MW	47480 TQ	USBLS	5/07
Utilities	Edison PMSA, NJ	Y	39320 FQ	43760 MW	47800 TQ	USBLS	5/07
Utilities	Newark-Union PMSA, NJ-PA	Y	41880 FQ	50350 MW	57110 TQ	USBLS	5/07
Utilities	New Mexico	Y	19660 FQ	25660 MW	33660 TQ	USBLS	5/07
Utilities	Albuquerque MSA, NM	Y	21150 FQ	25970 MW	33630 TQ	USBLS	5/07
Utilities	New York	Y	29160 FQ	39630 MW	54100 TQ	USBLS	5/07
Utilities	Buffalo-Niagara Falls MSA, NY	Y	22790 FQ	25380 MW	38220 TQ	USBLS	5/07
Utilities	Nassau-Suffolk PMSA, NY	Y	32340 FQ	53690 MW	60370 TQ	USBLS	5/07
Utilities	New York-Northern New Jersey-Long Island MSA, NY-NJ-PA	Y	35200 FQ	45370 MW	55380 TQ	USBLS	5/07
Utilities	North Carolina	Y	22480 FQ	26860 MW	31360 TQ	USBLS	5/07
Utilities	Charlotte-Gastonia-Concord MSA, NC-SC	Y	26420 FQ	30250 MW	35490 TQ	USBLS	5/07
Utilities	Raleigh-Cary MSA, NC	Y	24360 FQ	27750 MW	31070 TQ	USBLS	5/07
Utilities	Ohio	Y	23950 FQ	32500 MW	39700 TQ	USBLS	5/07
Utilities	Cincinnati-Middletown MSA, OH-KY-IN	Y	22830 FQ	28440 MW	42990 TQ	USBLS	5/07
Utilities	Cleveland-Elyria-Mentor MSA, OH	Y	28600 FQ	37050 MW	42150 TQ	USBLS	5/07
Utilities	Columbus MSA, OH	Y	26440 FQ	33850 MW	39670 TQ	USBLS	5/07
Utilities	Dayton MSA, OH	Y	25810 FQ	31100 MW	36930 TQ	USBLS	5/07
Utilities	Oklahoma	Y	21270 FQ	25100 MW	30700 TQ	USBLS	5/07
Utilities	Oklahoma City MSA, OK	Y	24970 FQ	29220 MW	36080 TQ	USBLS	5/07
Utilities	Tulsa MSA, OK	Y	22030 FQ	24510 MW	28520 TQ	USBLS	5/07
Utilities	Oregon	H	15.85 FQ	18.05 MW	20.66 TQ	ORBLS	5/08
Utilities	Portland-Vancouver-Beaverton MSA, OR-WA	Y	36310 FQ	40480 MW	45550 TQ	USBLS	5/07
Utilities	Pennsylvania	Y	28750 FQ	37850 MW	45600 TQ	USBLS	5/07
Utilities	Allentown-Bethlehem-Easton MSA, PA-NJ	Y	30630 FQ	36710 MW	44240 TQ	USBLS	5/07

AE	Average entry wage	AW	Average wage paid	FQ	First quartile wage	LO	Lowest wage paid	MTC	Median total compensation	TCC	Total cash compensation
AER	Average entry range	AWR	Average wage range	H	Hourly	LR	Low end range	MW	Median wage paid	TQ	Third quartile wage
AEX	Average experienced wage	AXR	Average experienced range	HI	Highest wage paid	M	Monthly	MWR	Median wage range	W	Weekly
ATC	Average total compensation	D	Daily	HR	High end range	MCC	Median cash compensation	S	See annotated source	Y	Yearly

Occupation/Type/Industry	Location	Per	Low	Mid	High	Source	Date
Meter Reader							
Utilities	Philadelphia-Camden-Wilmington MSA, PA-NJ-DE-MD	Y	37200 FQ	42870 MW	50470 TQ	USBLS	5/07
Utilities	Pittsburgh MSA, PA	Y	23200 FQ	32320 MW	45090 TQ	USBLS	5/07
Utilities	Rhode Island	Y	39980 FQ	43320 MW	46870 TQ	USBLS	5/07
Utilities	Providence-Fall River-Warwick MSA, RI-MA	Y	39800 FQ	44090 MW	49480 TQ	USBLS	5/07
Utilities	South Carolina	Y	24770 FQ	28340 MW	33500 TQ	USBLS	5/07
Utilities	Charleston-North Charleston MSA, SC	Y	26640 FQ	30300 MW	34330 TQ	USBLS	5/07
Utilities	Columbia MSA, SC	Y	23570 FQ	28370 MW	33890 TQ	USBLS	5/07
Utilities	South Dakota	Y	23068 FQ	26808 MW	34600 TQ	SDBLS	7/08-9/08
Utilities	Tennessee	Y	25260 FQ	31190 MW	39500 TQ	USBLS	5/07
Utilities	Memphis MSA, TN-MS-AR	Y	26040 FQ	29290 MW	32720 TQ	USBLS	5/07
Utilities	Nashville-Davidson-Murfreesboro MSA, TN	Y	28660 FQ	34810 MW	42170 TQ	USBLS	5/07
Utilities	Texas	Y	22510 FQ	27340 MW	31740 TQ	USBLS	5/07
Utilities	Austin-Round Rock MSA, TX	Y	25770 FQ	29070 MW	32880 TQ	USBLS	5/07
Utilities	Brownsville-Harlingen MSA, TX	Y	19120 FQ	23290 MW	27290 TQ	USBLS	5/07
Utilities	Dallas-Fort Worth-Arlington MSA, TX	Y	26290 FQ	29320 MW	32600 TQ	USBLS	5/07
Utilities	El Paso MSA, TX	Y	20640 FQ	22710 MW	24850 TQ	USBLS	5/07
Utilities	Houston-Sugar Land-Baytown MSA, TX	Y	23910 FQ	27760 MW	31610 TQ	USBLS	5/07
Utilities	San Antonio MSA, TX	Y	20570 FQ	24980 MW	30290 TQ	USBLS	5/07
Utilities	Utah	Y	23500 FQ	32170 MW	38640 TQ	USBLS	5/07
Utilities	Salt Lake City MSA, UT	Y	24070 FQ	33220 MW	38060 TQ	USBLS	5/07
Utilities	Vermont	Y	32930 FQ	37800 MW	44610 TQ	USBLS	5/07
Utilities	Virginia	Y	22510 FQ	29660 MW	38740 TQ	USBLS	5/07
Utilities	Richmond MSA, VA	Y	30030 FQ	40120 MW	46110 TQ	USBLS	5/07
Utilities	Virginia Beach-Norfolk-Newport News MSA, VA-NC	Y	20650 FQ	27620 MW	35240 TQ	USBLS	5/07
Utilities	Washington	H	17.70 FQ	20.88 MW	25.08 TQ	WABLS	3/08
Utilities	Seattle-Tacoma-Bellevue MSA, WA	Y	36110 FQ	40320 MW	46610 TQ	USBLS	5/07
Utilities	West Virginia	Y	20422 FQ	27653 MW	38415 TQ	WVBLS	7/08-9/08
Utilities	Charleston MSA, WV	Y	22190 FQ	37720 MW	50560 TQ	USBLS	5/07
Utilities	Parkersburg-Marietta-Vienna MSA, WV-OH	Y	26660 FQ	29300 MW	37640 TQ	USBLS	5/07
Utilities	Wisconsin	Y	27980 FQ	35040 MW	44530 TQ	USBLS	5/07
Utilities	Milwaukee-Waukesha-West Allis MSA, WI	Y	28520 FQ	33750 MW	44960 TQ	USBLS	5/07
Utilities	Wyoming	Y	28188 FQ	34381 MW	41218 TQ	WYBLS	9/08
Utilities	Puerto Rico	Y	26800 FQ	28850 MW	30890 TQ	USBLS	5/07
Water Department	Erving, MA	Y			600 HI	FRCOG	2009
Microbiologist							
	Alabama	Y	38590 FQ	53140 MW	65190 TQ	USBLS	5/07
	Alaska	Y	45450 FQ	51140 MW	61050 TQ	USBLS	5/07
	Arizona	Y	48000 FQ	67140 MW	88190 TQ	USBLS	5/07
	Arkansas	Y	42960 FQ	54170 MW	65670 TQ	USBLS	5/07
	California	H	27.33 FQ	33.87 MW	42.14 TQ	CABLS	1/08-3/08
	Los Angeles-Long Beach-Glendale PMSA, CA	H	19.58 FQ	29.28 MW	38.22 TQ	CABLS	1/08-3/08
	Oakland-Fremont-Hayward MSA, CA	H	29.44 FQ	35.79 MW	45.28 TQ	CABLS	1/08-3/08
	Riverside-San Bernardino-Ontario MSA, CA	H	32.54 FQ	42.14 MW	47.14 TQ	CABLS	1/08-3/08
	Sacramento-Arden Arcade-Roseville MSA, CA	H	23.96 FQ	28.84 MW	33.77 TQ	CABLS	1/08-3/08
	San Diego-Carlsbad-San Marcos MSA, CA	H	27.97 FQ	36.50 MW	45.00 TQ	CABLS	1/08-3/08
	San Francisco-San Mateo-Redwood PMSA, CA	H	28.74 FQ	34.78 MW	43.38 TQ	CABLS	1/08-3/08
	San Jose-Sunnyvale-Santa Clara MSA, CA	H	30.65 FQ	38.20 MW	50.28 TQ	CABLS	1/08-3/08
	Santa Ana-Anaheim-Irvine PMSA, CA	Y	57900 FQ	65900 MW	82270 TQ	USBLS	5/07
	Colorado	Y	44780 FQ	60530 MW	82690 TQ	USBLS	5/07
	Denver-Aurora MSA, CO	Y	46100 FQ	71370 MW	86330 TQ	USBLS	5/07
	Connecticut	H	22.61 AE	33.85 MW		CTBLS	1/08-3/08

AE	Average entry wage	AW	Average wage paid	FQ	First quartile wage	LO Lowest wage paid	MTC Median total compensation	TCC Total cash compensation
AER	Average entry range	AWR	Average wage range	H	Hourly	LR Low end range	MW Median wage paid	TQ Third quartile wage
AEX	Average experienced wage	AXR	Average experienced range	HI	Highest wage paid	M Monthly	MWR Median wage range	W Weekly
ATC	Average total compensation	D	Daily	HR	High end range	MCC Median cash compensation	S See annotated source	Y Yearly

Occupation/Type/Industry	Location	Per	Low	Mid	High	Source	Date
Microbiologist	Delaware	Y	48900 FQ	59530 MW	74670 TQ	USBLS	5/07
	Wilmington PMSA, DE-MD-NJ	Y	56770 FQ	66610 MW	81670 TQ	USBLS	5/07
	District of Columbia	Y	48100 FQ	81890 MW	108570 TQ	USBLS	5/07
	Washington-Arlington-Alexandria MSA, DC-VA-MD-WV	Y	64600 FQ	88730 MW	114300 TQ	USBLS	5/07
	Florida	Y	36870 FQ	49110 MW	72770 TQ	USBLS	5/07
	Miami-Fort Lauderdale-Miami Beach MSA, FL	Y	34030 FQ	40080 MW	55260 TQ	USBLS	5/07
	Orlando-Kissimmee MSA, FL	Y	35430 FQ	50530 MW	71710 TQ	USBLS	5/07
	Georgia	Y	67150 FQ	81220 MW	100730 TQ	USBLS	5/07
	Atlanta-Sandy Springs-Marietta MSA, GA	Y	68280 FQ	82330 MW	101720 TQ	USBLS	5/07
	Hawaii	Y	38900 FQ	50260 MW	60510 TQ	USBLS	5/07
	Idaho	Y	36560 FQ	42450 MW	49450 TQ	USBLS	5/07
	Illinois	Y	50120 FQ	62240 MW	77310 TQ	USBLS	5/07
	Chicago-Naperville-Joliet MSA, IL-IN-WI	Y	50000 FQ	62550 MW	76980 TQ	USBLS	5/07
	Indianapolis-Carmel MSA, IN	Y	34340 FQ	38280 MW	46790 TQ	USBLS	5/07
	Iowa	Y	48040 FQ	59280 MW	73570 TQ	USBLS	5/07
	Des Moines-West Des Moines MSA, IA	Y	54240 FQ	59240 MW	64250 TQ	USBLS	5/07
	Kansas	Y	35940 FQ	42680 MW	48600 TQ	USBLS	5/07
	Kentucky	Y	40368 FQ	46115 MW	51813 TQ	KYBLS	2008
	Louisiana	H	23.82 FQ	33.94 MW	49.82 TQ	LABLS	1/08-3/08
	New Orleans-Metairie-Kenner MSA, LA	Y	48170 FQ	53600 MW	98470 TQ	USBLS	5/07
	Maine	Y	44560 FQ	54430 MW	91930 TQ	USBLS	5/07
	Maryland	Y		94450 MW		MDBLS	3/08
	Baltimore-Towson MSA, MD	Y	55540 FQ	88590 MW	109290 TQ	USBLS	5/07
	Bethesda-Gaithersburg-Frederick PMSA, MD	Y	73190 FQ	93570 MW	118730 TQ	USBLS	5/07
	Massachusetts	Y	44360 FQ	52680 MW	69890 TQ	USBLS	5/07
	Boston-Cambridge-Quincy NECTA, MA	Y	43580 FQ	51360 MW	66240 TQ	USBLS	5/07
	Worcester MSA, MA-CT	Y	54930 FQ	67850 MW	77240 TQ	USBLS	5/07
	Michigan	Y	42920 FQ	53050 MW	61950 TQ	USBLS	5/07
	Detroit-Warren-Livonia MSA, MI	Y	47190 FQ	55080 MW	64110 TQ	USBLS	5/07
	Minnesota	Y	46211 FQ	55606 MW	68402 TQ	MNBLS	10/08-12/08
	Minneapolis-Saint Paul MSA, MN-WI	Y	45521 FQ	54749 MW	65493 TQ	MNBLS	10/08-12/08
	Mississippi	Y	40770 FQ	50310 MW	69020 TQ	USBLS	5/07
	Missouri	Y	44860 FQ	56060 MW	73230 TQ	USBLS	5/07
	Kansas City MSA, MO-KS	Y	39650 FQ	49570 MW	71030 TQ	USBLS	5/07
	St. Louis MSA, MO-IL	Y	47130 FQ	56020 MW	67340 TQ	USBLS	5/07
	Montana	Y	39840 FQ	55690 MW	74130 TQ	USBLS	5/07
	Nebraska	Y	44690 FQ	56020 MW	74230 TQ	USBLS	5/07
	Nevada	H	22.25 FQ	27.19 MW	31.82 TQ	NVBLS	5/08
	Las Vegas-Paradise MSA, NV	H	29.33 FQ	32.89 MW	38.10 TQ	NVBLS	5/08
	New Jersey	Y	53760 FQ	74360 MW	92900 TQ	USBLS	5/07
	Edison PMSA, NJ	Y	66910 FQ	86360 MW	100670 TQ	USBLS	5/07
	Newark-Union PMSA, NJ-PA	Y	46300 FQ	61150 MW	80970 TQ	USBLS	5/07
	Trenton-Ewing MSA, NJ	Y	52640 FQ	66570 MW	82950 TQ	USBLS	5/07
	New York	Y	47100 FQ	62500 MW	81560 TQ	USBLS	5/07
	Albany-Schenectady-Troy MSA, NY	Y	42740 FQ	50170 MW	67240 TQ	USBLS	5/07
	Nassau-Suffolk PMSA, NY	Y	45830 FQ	57640 MW	80040 TQ	USBLS	5/07
	New York-Northern New Jersey-Long Island MSA, NY-NJ-PA	Y	51550 FQ	71250 MW	90750 TQ	USBLS	5/07
	North Carolina	Y	40810 FQ	51110 MW	69220 TQ	USBLS	5/07
	Durham MSA, NC	Y	46990 FQ	56850 MW	69290 TQ	USBLS	5/07
	Raleigh-Cary MSA, NC	Y	37030 FQ	43400 MW	66620 TQ	USBLS	5/07
	Ohio	Y	43340 FQ	60640 MW	81800 TQ	USBLS	5/07
	Cincinnati-Middletown MSA, OH-KY-IN	Y	55870 FQ	75810 MW	95560 TQ	USBLS	5/07
	Cleveland-Elyria-Mentor MSA, OH	Y	35530 FQ	39770 MW	51240 TQ	USBLS	5/07
	Columbus MSA, OH	Y	46480 FQ	62480 MW	83080 TQ	USBLS	5/07
	Oklahoma	Y	36440 FQ	43970 MW	52180 TQ	USBLS	5/07

AE Average entry wage	**AW** Average wage paid	**FQ** First quartile wage	**LO** Lowest wage paid	**MTC** Median total compensation	**TCC** Total cash compensation
AER Average entry range	**AWR** Average wage range	**H** Hourly	**LR** Low end range	**MW** Median wage paid	**TQ** Third quartile wage
AEX Average experienced wage	**AXR** Average experienced range	**HI** Highest wage paid	**M** Monthly	**MWR** Median wage range	**W** Weekly
ATC Average total compensation	**D** Daily	**HR** High end range	**MCC** Median cash compensation	**S** See annotated source	**Y** Yearly

Occupation/Type/Industry	Location	Per	Low	Mid	High	Source	Date
Microbiologist	Oregon	H	20.06 FQ	23.88 MW	29.96 TQ	ORBLS	5/08
	Portland-Vancouver-Beaverton MSA, OR-WA	Y	41270 FQ	48140 MW	58590 TQ	USBLS	5/07
	Pennsylvania	Y	50840 FQ	63300 MW	81090 TQ	USBLS	5/07
	Philadelphia-Camden-Wilmington MSA, PA-NJ-DE-MD	Y	53280 FQ	66030 MW	84290 TQ	USBLS	5/07
	South Carolina	Y	41840 FQ	51830 MW	65130 TQ	USBLS	5/07
	South Dakota	Y	35269 FQ	42996 MW	49803 TQ	SDBLS	7/08-9/08
	Tennessee	Y	42390 FQ	47790 MW	54660 TQ	USBLS	5/07
	Nashville-Davidson-Murfreesboro MSA, TN	Y	41400 FQ	46300 MW	51160 TQ	USBLS	5/07
	Texas	Y	36260 FQ	45160 MW	53600 TQ	USBLS	5/07
	Austin-Round Rock MSA, TX	Y	33890 FQ	43730 MW	50160 TQ	USBLS	5/07
	Dallas-Fort Worth-Arlington MSA, TX	Y	37120 FQ	43120 MW	50790 TQ	USBLS	5/07
	Houston-Sugar Land-Baytown MSA, TX	Y	35210 FQ	44030 MW	58750 TQ	USBLS	5/07
	San Antonio MSA, TX	Y	45970 FQ	61070 MW	75920 TQ	USBLS	5/07
	Utah	Y	39200 FQ	47110 MW	61170 TQ	USBLS	5/07
	Ogden-Clearfield MSA, UT	Y	37570 FQ	42970 MW	52280 TQ	USBLS	5/07
	Salt Lake City MSA, UT	Y	41000 FQ	48670 MW	62970 TQ	USBLS	5/07
	Virginia	Y	42910 FQ	51160 MW	63500 TQ	USBLS	5/07
	Washington	H	21.50 FQ	27.31 MW	35.48 TQ	WABLS	3/08
	Seattle-Tacoma-Bellevue MSA, WA	Y	44210 FQ	56690 MW	73770 TQ	USBLS	5/07
	West Virginia	Y	31367 FQ	37631 MW	52389 TQ	WVBLS	7/08-9/08
	Charleston MSA, WV	Y	30360 FQ	35370 MW	40150 TQ	USBLS	5/07
	Wisconsin	Y	43000 FQ	55270 MW	75460 TQ	USBLS	5/07
	Milwaukee-Waukesha-West Allis MSA, WI	Y	38540 FQ	52210 MW	72060 TQ	USBLS	5/07
	Puerto Rico	Y	35270 FQ	43430 MW	53300 TQ	USBLS	5/07
	San Juan-Caguas-Guaynabo MSA, PR	Y	35430 FQ	43260 MW	52020 TQ	USBLS	5/07
Department of Environmental Quality	Oregon	M	2696 LO		4716 HI	ODEQSS	11/1/08
Small Organization	United States	Y	61961 FQ	70293 MW	78625 TQ	ALA03	2008
Microphone Boom Operator							
Journeyman, Major Motion Picture	West Coast	H			36.34-40.53 HR	MPEG01	8/3/08-7/31/09
Microsoft Internet Security/ Acceleration Server Expert	United States	Y		76634 AW		REDMAG	2008
Microsoft Project Server Expert	United States	Y		92532 AW		REDMAG	2008
Middle School Teacher							
Except Special and Vocational Education	Alabama	Y	37440 FQ	43370 MW	48770 TQ	USBLS	5/07
Except Special and Vocational Education	Birmingham-Hoover MSA, AL	Y	39930 FQ	45060 MW	50320 TQ	USBLS	5/07
Except Special and Vocational Education	Huntsville MSA, AL	Y	40640 FQ	45660 MW	50580 TQ	USBLS	5/07
Except Special and Vocational Education	Montgomery MSA, AL	Y	33710 FQ	37990 MW	43700 TQ	USBLS	5/07
Except Special and Vocational Education	Alaska	Y	47780 FQ	57310 MW	66430 TQ	USBLS	5/07
Except Special and Vocational Education	Arizona	Y	31760 FQ	37790 MW	46270 TQ	USBLS	5/07
Except Special and Vocational Education	Phoenix-Mesa-Scottsdale MSA, AZ	Y	32840 FQ	38790 MW	47000 TQ	USBLS	5/07
Except Special and Vocational Education	Prescott MSA, AZ	Y	30320 FQ	36430 MW	42580 TQ	USBLS	5/07
Except Special and Vocational Education	Tucson MSA, AZ	Y	30740 FQ	37290 MW	48880 TQ	USBLS	5/07
Except Special and Vocational Education	Arkansas	Y	35000 FQ	41000 MW	47930 TQ	USBLS	5/07
Except Special and Vocational Education	Fayetteville-Springdale-Rogers MSA, AR-MO	Y	35930 FQ	41160 MW	47380 TQ	USBLS	5/07
Except Special and Vocational Education	Little Rock-North Little Rock MSA, AR	Y	35050 FQ	43500 MW	52190 TQ	USBLS	5/07
Except Special and Vocational Education	California	Y		62369 AW		CABLS	1/08-3/08
Except Special and Vocational Education	Fresno MSA, CA	Y		65230 AW		CABLS	1/08-3/08
Except Special and Vocational Education	Los Angeles-Long Beach-Glendale PMSA, CA	Y		59682 AW		CABLS	1/08-3/08
Except Special and Vocational Education	Oakland-Fremont-Hayward MSA, CA	Y		66071 AW		CABLS	1/08-3/08
Except Special and Vocational Education	Riverside-San Bernardino-Ontario MSA, CA	Y		59344 AW		CABLS	1/08-3/08
Except Special and Vocational Education	Sacramento-Arden Arcade-Roseville MSA, CA	Y		57662 MW		CABLS	1/08-3/08

Occupation/Type/Industry	Location	Per	Low	Mid	High	Source	Date
Middle School Teacher							
Except Special and Vocational Education	San Diego-Carlsbad-San Marcos MSA, CA	Y		67630 AW		CABLS	1/08-3/08
Except Special and Vocational Education	San Francisco-San Mateo-Redwood PMSA, CA	Y		64256 AW		CABLS	1/08-3/08
Except Special and Vocational Education	San Jose-Sunnyvale-Santa Clara MSA, CA	Y		65405 AW		CABLS	1/08-3/08
Except Special and Vocational Education	Santa Ana-Anaheim-Irvine PMSA, CA	Y	52710 FQ	65450 MW	79260 TQ	USBLS	5/07
Except Special and Vocational Education	Stockton MSA, CA	Y		67609 AW		CABLS	1/08-3/08
Except Special and Vocational Education	Colorado	Y	36580 FQ	44370 MW	55690 TQ	USBLS	5/07
Except Special and Vocational Education	Denver-Aurora MSA, CO	Y	38500 FQ	48380 MW	60240 TQ	USBLS	5/07
Except Special and Vocational Education	Bridgeport-Stamford-Norwalk MSA, CT	Y	53400 FQ	63400 MW	78690 TQ	USBLS	5/07
Except Special and Vocational Education	Hartford-West Hartford-East Hartford MSA, CT	Y	50070 FQ	66100 MW	77310 TQ	USBLS	5/07
Except Special and Vocational Education	Norwich-New London MSA, CT-RI	Y	48160 FQ	62000 MW	72740 TQ	USBLS	5/07
Except Special and Vocational Education	Delaware	Y	40800 FQ	50310 MW	65470 TQ	USBLS	5/07
Except Special and Vocational Education	Wilmington PMSA, DE-MD-NJ	Y	42090 FQ	52380 MW	66550 TQ	USBLS	5/07
Except Special and Vocational Education	District of Columbia	Y	41180 FQ	49570 MW	65260 TQ	USBLS	5/07
Except Special and Vocational Education	Washington-Arlington-Alexandria MSA, DC-VA-MD-WV	Y	45360 FQ	58470 MW	76310 TQ	USBLS	5/07
Except Special and Vocational Education	Florida	Y	39180 FQ	47930 MW	60280 TQ	USBLS	5/07
Except Special and Vocational Education	Jacksonville MSA, FL	Y	35710 FQ	40090 MW	51250 TQ	USBLS	5/07
Except Special and Vocational Education	Miami-Fort Lauderdale-Miami Beach MSA, FL	Y	41560 FQ	50680 MW	64600 TQ	USBLS	5/07
Except Special and Vocational Education	Orlando-Kissimmee MSA, FL	Y	37700 FQ	43790 MW	53410 TQ	USBLS	5/07
Except Special and Vocational Education	Sarasota-Bradenton-Venice MSA, FL	Y	40480 FQ	49310 MW	61240 TQ	USBLS	5/07
Except Special and Vocational Education	Tampa-St. Petersburg-Clearwater MSA, FL	Y	44180 FQ	51420 MW	62540 TQ	USBLS	5/07
Except Special and Vocational Education	West Palm Beach-Boca Raton-Boynton Beach PMSA, FL	Y	36610 FQ	43060 MW	53270 TQ	USBLS	5/07
Except Special and Vocational Education	Georgia	Y	39640 FQ	48240 MW	57940 TQ	USBLS	5/07
Except Special and Vocational Education	Atlanta-Sandy Springs-Marietta MSA, GA	Y	41400 FQ	49330 MW	59370 TQ	USBLS	5/07
Except Special and Vocational Education	Hawaii	Y	35180 FQ	45080 MW	60820 TQ	USBLS	5/07
Except Special and Vocational Education	Honolulu MSA, HI	Y	36020 FQ	46950 MW	63770 TQ	USBLS	5/07
Except Special and Vocational Education	Idaho	Y	31520 FQ	39780 MW	48630 TQ	USBLS	5/07
Except Special and Vocational Education	Illinois	Y	38060 FQ	48720 MW	63810 TQ	USBLS	5/07
Except Special and Vocational Education	Chicago-Naperville-Joliet MSA, IL-IN-WI	Y	40610 FQ	51770 MW	67180 TQ	USBLS	5/07
Except Special and Vocational Education	Indiana	Y	37390 FQ	48960 MW	60060 TQ	USBLS	5/07
Except Special and Vocational Education	Gary PMSA, IN	Y	38500 FQ	49000 MW	58750 TQ	USBLS	5/07
Except Special and Vocational Education	Indianapolis-Carmel MSA, IN	Y	38480 FQ	49360 MW	64410 TQ	USBLS	5/07
Except Special and Vocational Education	Iowa	Y	29740 FQ	38650 MW	49450 TQ	USBLS	5/07
Except Special and Vocational Education	Des Moines-West Des Moines MSA, IA	Y	33310 FQ	43410 MW	53850 TQ	USBLS	5/07
Except Special and Vocational Education	Kansas	Y	32070 FQ	38500 MW	45650 TQ	USBLS	5/07
Except Special and Vocational Education	Wichita MSA, KS	Y	34630 FQ	41420 MW	47360 TQ	USBLS	5/07
Except Special and Vocational Education	Kentucky	Y	38431 FQ	45703 MW	53177 TQ	KYBLS	2008
Except Special and Vocational Education	Louisville-Jefferson County MSA, KY-IN	Y	39200 FQ	49210 MW	59340 TQ	USBLS	5/07
Except Special and Vocational Education	Louisiana	Y		40581 AW		LABLS	1/08-3/08
Except Special and Vocational Education	Baton Rouge MSA, LA	Y	28840 FQ	34400 MW	45200 TQ	USBLS	5/07
Except Special and Vocational Education	New Orleans-Metairie-Kenner MSA, LA	Y	32620 FQ	40730 MW	50460 TQ	USBLS	5/07
Except Special and Vocational Education	Maine	Y	35950 FQ	44340 MW	52320 TQ	USBLS	5/07
Except Special and Vocational Education	Portland-South Portland-Biddeford MSA, ME	Y	37850 FQ	46010 MW	54070 TQ	USBLS	5/07
Except Special and Vocational Education	Maryland	Y		52275 MW		MDBLS	3/08
Except Special and Vocational Education	Baltimore-Towson MSA, MD	Y	39450 FQ	48110 MW	61200 TQ	USBLS	5/07
Except Special and Vocational Education	Bethesda-Gaithersburg-Frederick PMSA, MD	Y	47660 FQ	63680 MW	82320 TQ	USBLS	5/07
Except Special and Vocational Education	Massachusetts	Y	44410 FQ	55960 MW	66370 TQ	USBLS	5/07
Except Special and Vocational Education	Boston-Cambridge-Quincy NECTA, MA	Y	46530 FQ	58390 MW	70690 TQ	USBLS	5/07
Except Special and Vocational Education	Worcester MSA, MA-CT	Y	45040 FQ	54450 MW	63430 TQ	USBLS	5/07
Except Special and Vocational Education	Michigan	Y	42660 FQ	55940 MW	66810 TQ	USBLS	5/07

AE	Average entry wage	AW	Average wage paid	FQ	First quartile wage	LO	Lowest wage paid	MTC Median total compensation TCC Total cash compensation
AER	Average entry range	AWR	Average wage range	H	Hourly	LR	Low end range	MW Median wage paid TQ Third quartile wage
AEX	Average experienced wage	AXR	Average experienced range	HI	Highest wage paid	M	Monthly	MWR Median wage range W Weekly
ATC	Average total compensation	D	Daily	HR	High end range	MCC	Median cash compensation	S See annotated source Y Yearly

Middle School Teacher

Occupation/Type/Industry	Location	Per	Low	Mid	High	Source	Date
Middle School Teacher							
Except Special and Vocational Education	Detroit-Warren-Livonia MSA, MI	Y	45860 FQ	59610 MW	70590 TQ	USBLS	5/07
Except Special and Vocational Education	Flint MSA, MI	Y	37270 FQ	52610 MW	65490 TQ	USBLS	5/07
Except Special and Vocational Education	Grand Rapids-Wyoming MSA, MI	Y	36670 FQ	49180 MW	62650 TQ	USBLS	5/07
Except Special and Vocational Education	Warren-Troy-Farmington Hills PMSA, MI	Y	50380 FQ	61700 MW	70810 TQ	USBLS	5/07
Except Special and Vocational Education	Minnesota	Y	38040 FQ	46578 MW	58170 TQ	MNBLS	10/08-12/08
Except Special and Vocational Education	Duluth-Superior MSA, MN-WI	Y	39055 FQ	48618 MW	58128 TQ	MNBLS	10/08-12/08
Except Special and Vocational Education	Minneapolis-Saint Paul MSA, MN-WI	Y	38396 FQ	47310 MW	60482 TQ	MNBLS	10/08-12/08
Except Special and Vocational Education	Rochester MSA, MN	Y	38501 FQ	46195 MW	54921 TQ	MNBLS	10/08-12/08
Except Special and Vocational Education	Mississippi	Y	34290 FQ	39120 MW	46790 TQ	USBLS	5/07
Except Special and Vocational Education	Jackson MSA, MS	Y	34530 FQ	38480 MW	45270 TQ	USBLS	5/07
Except Special and Vocational Education	Missouri	Y	34690 FQ	41120 MW	51010 TQ	USBLS	5/07
Except Special and Vocational Education	Joplin MSA, MO	Y	29880 FQ	34540 MW	39900 TQ	USBLS	5/07
Except Special and Vocational Education	Kansas City MSA, MO-KS	Y	34570 FQ	41110 MW	50490 TQ	USBLS	5/07
Except Special and Vocational Education	St. Louis MSA, MO-IL	Y	37020 FQ	45020 MW	55870 TQ	USBLS	5/07
Except Special and Vocational Education	Montana	Y	23650 FQ	33800 MW	46080 TQ	USBLS	5/07
Except Special and Vocational Education	Billings MSA, MT	Y	23550 FQ	30990 MW	43520 TQ	USBLS	5/07
Except Special and Vocational Education	Nebraska	Y	35620 FQ	42440 MW	51160 TQ	USBLS	5/07
Except Special and Vocational Education	Omaha-Council Bluffs MSA, NE-IA	Y	35070 FQ	40950 MW	49070 TQ	USBLS	5/07
Except Special and Vocational Education	Nevada	Y	36973 FQ	44810 MW	53224 TQ	NVBLS	5/08
Except Special and Vocational Education	Las Vegas-Paradise MSA, NV	Y	36117 FQ	43417 MW	51717 TQ	NVBLS	5/08
Except Special and Vocational Education	New Hampshire	Y	35969 AE	48499 MW	56408 AEX	NHBLS	6/08
Except Special and Vocational Education	Manchester MSA, NH	Y	36830 FQ	46470 MW	56420 TQ	USBLS	5/07
Except Special and Vocational Education	Nashua NECTA, NH-MA	Y	40480 FQ	48870 MW	59150 TQ	USBLS	5/07
Except Special and Vocational Education	New Jersey	Y	45550 FQ	54920 MW	73140 TQ	USBLS	5/07
Except Special and Vocational Education	Camden PMSA, NJ	Y	46800 FQ	56290 MW	71680 TQ	USBLS	5/07
Except Special and Vocational Education	Edison PMSA, NJ	Y	45300 FQ	54150 MW	74510 TQ	USBLS	5/07
Except Special and Vocational Education	Newark-Union PMSA, NJ-PA	Y	46210 FQ	55980 MW	73170 TQ	USBLS	5/07
Except Special and Vocational Education	New Mexico	Y	37020 FQ	44840 MW	54220 TQ	USBLS	5/07
Except Special and Vocational Education	Albuquerque MSA, NM	Y	37570 FQ	44260 MW	52100 TQ	USBLS	5/07
Except Special and Vocational Education	Las Cruces MSA, NM	Y	32550 FQ	52710 MW	71490 TQ	USBLS	5/07
Except Special and Vocational Education	New York	Y	47670 FQ	61000 MW	78160 TQ	USBLS	5/07
Except Special and Vocational Education	Albany-Schenectady-Troy MSA, NY	Y	43790 FQ	52520 MW	70230 TQ	USBLS	5/07
Except Special and Vocational Education	Buffalo-Niagara Falls MSA, NY	Y	42270 FQ	50700 MW	67230 TQ	USBLS	5/07
Except Special and Vocational Education	Glens Falls MSA, NY	Y	43680 FQ	52670 MW	66690 TQ	USBLS	5/07
Except Special and Vocational Education	Nassau-Suffolk PMSA, NY	Y	60500 FQ	76420 MW	95920 TQ	USBLS	5/07
Except Special and Vocational Education	New York-Northern New Jersey-Long Island MSA, NY-NJ-PA	Y	48870 FQ	62670 MW	80810 TQ	USBLS	5/07
Except Special and Vocational Education	North Carolina	Y	31200 FQ	38090 MW	46620 TQ	USBLS	5/07
Except Special and Vocational Education	Asheville MSA, NC	Y	32160 FQ	39150 MW	47620 TQ	USBLS	5/07
Except Special and Vocational Education	Charlotte-Gastonia-Concord MSA, NC-SC	Y	34210 FQ	39840 MW	48010 TQ	USBLS	5/07
Except Special and Vocational Education	Raleigh-Cary MSA, NC	Y	36980 FQ	45570 MW	56150 TQ	USBLS	5/07
Except Special and Vocational Education	Grand Forks MSA, ND-MN	Y	35240 FQ	44070 MW	52970 TQ	USBLS	5/07
Except Special and Vocational Education	Ohio	Y	41740 FQ	52910 MW	64140 TQ	USBLS	5/07
Except Special and Vocational Education	Cincinnati-Middletown MSA, OH-KY-IN	Y	40700 FQ	51530 MW	64170 TQ	USBLS	5/07
Except Special and Vocational Education	Cleveland-Elyria-Mentor MSA, OH	Y	46130 FQ	59090 MW	72420 TQ	USBLS	5/07
Except Special and Vocational Education	Columbus MSA, OH	Y	44810 FQ	55970 MW	69340 TQ	USBLS	5/07
Except Special and Vocational Education	Dayton MSA, OH	Y	37460 FQ	48840 MW	60290 TQ	USBLS	5/07
Except Special and Vocational Education	Springfield MSA, OH	Y	30500 FQ	40080 MW	55810 TQ	USBLS	5/07
Except Special and Vocational Education	Oklahoma	Y	32210 FQ	36600 MW	41760 TQ	USBLS	5/07
Except Special and Vocational Education	Oklahoma City MSA, OK	Y	31880 FQ	36170 MW	41100 TQ	USBLS	5/07
Except Special and Vocational Education	Tulsa MSA, OK	Y	33980 FQ	39250 MW	46900 TQ	USBLS	5/07
Except Special and Vocational Education	Oregon	Y	41385 FQ	49774 MW	59773 TQ	ORBLS	5/08
Except Special and Vocational Education	Portland-Vancouver-Beaverton MSA, OR-WA	Y	42090 FQ	50150 MW	60610 TQ	USBLS	5/07
Except Special and Vocational Education	Pennsylvania	Y	39780 FQ	50480 MW	64830 TQ	USBLS	5/07
Except Special and Vocational Education	Allentown-Bethlehem-Easton MSA, PA-NJ	Y	41440 FQ	49390 MW	64360 TQ	USBLS	5/07
Except Special and Vocational Education	Philadelphia-Camden-Wilmington MSA, PA-NJ-DE-MD	Y	43080 FQ	52840 MW	68770 TQ	USBLS	5/07

AE	Average entry wage	AW	Average wage paid	FQ	First quartile wage	LO	Lowest wage paid	MTC	Median total compensation	TCC	Total cash compensation
AER	Average entry range	AWR	Average wage range	H	Hourly	LR	Low end range	MW	Median wage paid	TQ	Third quartile wage
AEX	Average experienced wage	AXR	Average experienced range	HI	Highest wage paid	M	Monthly	MWR	Median wage range	W	Weekly
ATC	Average total compensation	D	Daily	HR	High end range	MCC	Median cash compensation	S	See annotated source	Y	Yearly

Occupation/Type/Industry	Location	Per	Low	Mid	High	Source	Date
Middle School Teacher							
Except Special and Vocational Education	Pittsburgh MSA, PA	Y	39490 FQ	49750 MW	64750 TQ	USBLS	5/07
Except Special and Vocational Education	Rhode Island	Y	47770 FQ	61360 MW	72050 TQ	USBLS	5/07
Except Special and Vocational Education	Providence-Fall River-Warwick MSA, RI-MA	Y	41670 FQ	57490 MW	70010 TQ	USBLS	5/07
Except Special and Vocational Education	South Carolina	Y	34730 FQ	41930 MW	51220 TQ	USBLS	5/07
Except Special and Vocational Education	Charleston-North Charleston MSA, SC	Y	34830 FQ	40980 MW	50420 TQ	USBLS	5/07
Except Special and Vocational Education	Columbia MSA, SC	Y	33250 FQ	40220 MW	51030 TQ	USBLS	5/07
Except Special and Vocational Education	South Dakota	Y	31458 FQ	37481 MW	45416 TQ	SDBLS	7/08-9/08
Except Special and Vocational Education	Sioux Falls MSA, SD	Y	31387 FQ	37332 MW	44970 TQ	SDBLS	7/08-9/08
Except Special and Vocational Education	Tennessee	Y	35720 FQ	41460 MW	48600 TQ	USBLS	5/07
Except Special and Vocational Education	Kingsport-Bristol-Bristol MSA, TN-VA	Y	36100 FQ	41580 MW	49300 TQ	USBLS	5/07
Except Special and Vocational Education	Memphis MSA, TN-MS-AR	Y	34450 FQ	40810 MW	50370 TQ	USBLS	5/07
Except Special and Vocational Education	Nashville-Davidson-Murfreesboro MSA, TN	Y	35760 FQ	41420 MW	48910 TQ	USBLS	5/07
Except Special and Vocational Education	Texas	Y	38960 FQ	44880 MW	50860 TQ	USBLS	5/07
Except Special and Vocational Education	Austin-Round Rock MSA, TX	Y	37450 FQ	42320 MW	49460 TQ	USBLS	5/07
Except Special and Vocational Education	Dallas-Fort Worth-Arlington MSA, TX	Y	42170 FQ	46830 MW	51780 TQ	USBLS	5/07
Except Special and Vocational Education	El Paso MSA, TX	Y	39980 FQ	45040 MW	50790 TQ	USBLS	5/07
Except Special and Vocational Education	Houston-Sugar Land-Baytown MSA, TX	Y	40450 FQ	45980 MW	52190 TQ	USBLS	5/07
Except Special and Vocational Education	San Antonio MSA, TX	Y	41360 FQ	46740 MW	52640 TQ	USBLS	5/07
Except Special and Vocational Education	Utah	Y	35040 FQ	45100 MW	55970 TQ	USBLS	5/07
Except Special and Vocational Education	Salt Lake City MSA, UT	Y	32700 FQ	45330 MW	58250 TQ	USBLS	5/07
Except Special and Vocational Education	Vermont	Y	37290 FQ	46410 MW	58030 TQ	USBLS	5/07
Except Special and Vocational Education	Burlington-South Burlington MSA, VT	Y	40220 FQ	50150 MW	61640 TQ	USBLS	5/07
Except Special and Vocational Education	Virginia	Y	39920 FQ	49280 MW	62720 TQ	USBLS	5/07
Except Special and Vocational Education	Charlottesville MSA, VA	Y	43910 FQ	59210 MW	72960 TQ	USBLS	5/07
Except Special and Vocational Education	Richmond MSA, VA	Y	41690 FQ	51820 MW	60940 TQ	USBLS	5/07
Except Special and Vocational Education	Virginia Beach-Norfolk-Newport News MSA, VA-NC	Y	39470 FQ	46940 MW	58070 TQ	USBLS	5/07
Except Special and Vocational Education	Washington	Y		53022 AW		WABLS	3/08
Except Special and Vocational Education	Seattle-Tacoma-Bellevue MSA, WA	Y	44460 FQ	53020 MW	63650 TQ	USBLS	5/07
Except Special and Vocational Education	West Virginia	Y	35382 FQ	41994 MW	48251 TQ	WVBLS	7/08-9/08
Except Special and Vocational Education	Charleston MSA, WV	Y	35860 FQ	42030 MW	48090 TQ	USBLS	5/07
Except Special and Vocational Education	Wisconsin	Y	37580 FQ	47290 MW	58610 TQ	USBLS	5/07
Except Special and Vocational Education	Appleton MSA, WI	Y	36970 FQ	45390 MW	55280 TQ	USBLS	5/07
Except Special and Vocational Education	Milwaukee-Waukesha-West Allis MSA, WI	Y	41690 FQ	54490 MW	67800 TQ	USBLS	5/07
Except Special and Vocational Education	Wyoming	Y	43884 FQ	51326 MW	59350 TQ	WYBLS	9/08
Except Special and Vocational Education	Puerto Rico	Y	25570 FQ	28270 MW	31220 TQ	USBLS	5/07
Except Special and Vocational Education	San German-Cabo Rojo MSA, PR	Y	26170 FQ	28290 MW	30330 TQ	USBLS	5/07
Except Special and Vocational Education	San Juan-Caguas-Guaynabo MSA, PR	Y	25250 FQ	27890 MW	30300 TQ	USBLS	5/07
Except Special and Vocational Education	Virgin Islands	Y	34760 FQ	45210 MW	59810 TQ	USBLS	5/07
Military Analyst							
U.S. Central Intelligence Agency	District of Columbia	Y	46460 LO		90698 HI	CIA02	2008
Milker	California	H		10.49 AW		FELS	2008
Milling and Planing Machine Setter, Operator, and Tender							
Metals and Plastics	Alabama	Y	26770 FQ	31550 MW	37360 TQ	USBLS	5/07
Metals and Plastics	Birmingham-Hoover MSA, AL	Y	27530 FQ	30290 MW	35680 TQ	USBLS	5/07
Metals and Plastics	Arizona	Y	24400 FQ	31850 MW	39870 TQ	USBLS	5/07
Metals and Plastics	Phoenix-Mesa-Scottsdale MSA, AZ	Y	24500 FQ	31920 MW	38140 TQ	USBLS	5/07
Metals and Plastics	Tucson MSA, AZ	Y	24420 FQ	31330 MW	42310 TQ	USBLS	5/07
Metals and Plastics	Arkansas	Y	26770 FQ	33160 MW	37710 TQ	USBLS	5/07
Metals and Plastics	Little Rock-North Little Rock MSA, AR	Y	22630 FQ	26090 MW	29250 TQ	USBLS	5/07
Metals and Plastics	California	H	12.18 FQ	15.95 MW	20.39 TQ	CABLS	1/08-3/08
Metals and Plastics	Los Angeles-Long Beach-Glendale PMSA, CA	H	11.31 FQ	14.62 MW	18.86 TQ	CABLS	1/08-3/08

Occupation/Type/Industry	Location	Per	Low	Mid	High	Source	Date
Milling and Planing Machine Setter, Operator, and Tender							
Metals and Plastics	Oakland-Fremont-Hayward MSA, CA	H	15.68 FQ	20.63 MW	26.63 TQ	CABLS	1/08-3/08
Metals and Plastics	Riverside-San Bernardino-Ontario MSA, CA	H	12.46 FQ	17.76 MW	21.71 TQ	CABLS	1/08-3/08
Metals and Plastics	Sacramento-Arden Arcade-Roseville MSA, CA	H	11.02 FQ	12.15 MW	16.91 TQ	CABLS	1/08-3/08
Metals and Plastics	San Diego-Carlsbad-San Marcos MSA, CA	H	9.65 FQ	12.62 MW	15.90 TQ	CABLS	1/08-3/08
Metals and Plastics	San Francisco-San Mateo-Redwood PMSA, CA	H	12.85 FQ	15.88 MW	19.20 TQ	CABLS	1/08-3/08
Metals and Plastics	San Jose-Sunnyvale-Santa Clara MSA, CA	H	18.51 FQ	25.00 MW	31.09 TQ	CABLS	1/08-3/08
Metals and Plastics	Santa Ana-Anaheim-Irvine PMSA, CA	Y	28280 FQ	34310 MW	40310 TQ	USBLS	5/07
Metals and Plastics	Colorado	Y	24860 FQ	29610 MW	36190 TQ	USBLS	5/07
Metals and Plastics	Denver-Aurora MSA, CO	Y	29040 FQ	34590 MW	43000 TQ	USBLS	5/07
Metals and Plastics	Connecticut	H	11.67 AE	16.49 MW		CTBLS	1/08-3/08
Metals and Plastics	Bridgeport-Stamford-Norwalk MSA, CT	Y	25500 FQ	28940 MW	34510 TQ	USBLS	5/07
Metals and Plastics	Danbury MSA, CT	Y	32370 FQ	36160 MW	42140 TQ	USBLS	5/07
Metals and Plastics	Hartford-West Hartford-East Hartford MSA, CT	Y	33920 FQ	40480 MW	47090 TQ	USBLS	5/07
Metals and Plastics	Florida	Y	21120 FQ	27940 MW	35620 TQ	USBLS	5/07
Metals and Plastics	Fort Lauderdale-Pompano Beach-Deerfield Beach PMSA, FL	Y	29760 FQ	35010 MW	39960 TQ	USBLS	5/07
Metals and Plastics	Miami-Fort Lauderdale-Miami Beach MSA, FL	Y	26520 FQ	33930 MW	39100 TQ	USBLS	5/07
Metals and Plastics	Tampa-St. Petersburg-Clearwater MSA, FL	Y	23300 FQ	26330 MW	29460 TQ	USBLS	5/07
Metals and Plastics	Georgia	Y	22070 FQ	24730 MW	32680 TQ	USBLS	5/07
Metals and Plastics	Atlanta-Sandy Springs-Marietta MSA, GA	Y	22360 FQ	33010 MW	38290 TQ	USBLS	5/07
Metals and Plastics	Idaho	Y	17470 FQ	19200 MW	27180 TQ	USBLS	5/07
Metals and Plastics	Illinois	Y	28860 FQ	36950 MW	46430 TQ	USBLS	5/07
Metals and Plastics	Chicago-Naperville-Joliet MSA, IL-IN-WI	Y	27600 FQ	35640 MW	47180 TQ	USBLS	5/07
Metals and Plastics	Indiana	Y	25040 FQ	34030 MW	48570 TQ	USBLS	5/07
Metals and Plastics	Gary PMSA, IN	Y	30610 FQ	36850 MW	48360 TQ	USBLS	5/07
Metals and Plastics	Indianapolis-Carmel MSA, IN	Y	17910 FQ	28830 MW	49210 TQ	USBLS	5/07
Metals and Plastics	Iowa	Y	27660 FQ	31780 MW	37410 TQ	USBLS	5/07
Metals and Plastics	Kansas	Y	26810 FQ	32900 MW	42600 TQ	USBLS	5/07
Metals and Plastics	Wichita MSA, KS	Y	26200 FQ	33910 MW	45370 TQ	USBLS	5/07
Metals and Plastics	Kentucky	Y	23032 FQ	29019 MW	38582 TQ	KYBLS	2008
Metals and Plastics	Louisville-Jefferson County MSA, KY-IN	Y	22220 FQ	39610 MW	45870 TQ	USBLS	5/07
Metals and Plastics	Louisiana	H	12.73 FQ	14.92 MW	18.60 TQ	LABLS	1/08-3/08
Metals and Plastics	Portland-South Portland-Biddeford MSA, ME	Y	27490 FQ	31280 MW	35580 TQ	USBLS	5/07
Metals and Plastics	Maryland	Y		41875 MW		MDBLS	3/08
Metals and Plastics	Baltimore-Towson MSA, MD	Y	26470 FQ	32220 MW	41170 TQ	USBLS	5/07
Metals and Plastics	Massachusetts	Y	29910 FQ	37370 MW	48590 TQ	USBLS	5/07
Metals and Plastics	Boston-Cambridge-Quincy NECTA, MA	Y	30040 FQ	35420 MW	42700 TQ	USBLS	5/07
Metals and Plastics	Worcester MSA, MA-CT	Y	32770 FQ	39550 MW	48850 TQ	USBLS	5/07
Metals and Plastics	Michigan	Y	27810 FQ	34480 MW	40310 TQ	USBLS	5/07
Metals and Plastics	Detroit-Warren-Livonia MSA, MI	Y	30590 FQ	35930 MW	41050 TQ	USBLS	5/07
Metals and Plastics	Grand Rapids-Wyoming MSA, MI	Y	29380 FQ	36480 MW	43800 TQ	USBLS	5/07
Metals and Plastics	Muskegon-Norton Shores MSA, MI	Y	34050 FQ	37930 MW	43800 TQ	USBLS	5/07
Metals and Plastics	Warren-Troy-Farmington Hills PMSA, MI	Y	32310 FQ	36900 MW	42670 TQ	USBLS	5/07
Metals and Plastics	Minnesota	Y	30747 FQ	36345 MW	42503 TQ	MNBLS	10/08-12/08
Metals and Plastics	Minneapolis-Saint Paul MSA, MN-WI	Y	32178 FQ	38471 MW	45624 TQ	MNBLS	10/08-12/08
Metals and Plastics	Mississippi	Y	22410 FQ	26570 MW	29840 TQ	USBLS	5/07
Metals and Plastics	Missouri	Y	25120 FQ	31700 MW	38040 TQ	USBLS	5/07
Metals and Plastics	Kansas City MSA, MO-KS	Y	28010 FQ	32230 MW	41670 TQ	USBLS	5/07

AE   Average entry wage   AW   Average wage paid   FQ   First quartile wage   LO   Lowest wage paid   MTC Median total compensation   TCC Total cash compensation
AER Average entry range   AWR Average wage range   H   Hourly   LR   Low end range   MW   Median wage paid   TQ   Third quartile wage
AEX Average experienced wage   AXR Average experienced range HI   Highest wage paid   M   Monthly   MWR Median wage range   W   Weekly
ATC Average total compensation D   Daily   HR   High end range   MCC Median cash compensation S See annotated source   Y   Yearly

1056

Occupation/Type/Industry	Location	Per	Low	Mid	High	Source	Date
Milling and Planing Machine Setter, Operator, and Tender							
Metals and Plastics	St. Louis MSA, MO-IL	Y	24490 FQ	29690 MW	36310 TQ	USBLS	5/07
Metals and Plastics	Montana	Y	26060 FQ	30700 MW	35600 TQ	USBLS	5/07
Metals and Plastics	Nebraska	Y	26430 FQ	29460 MW	32760 TQ	USBLS	5/07
Metals and Plastics	Nevada	H	16.18 FQ	19.16 MW	22.65 TQ	NVBLS	5/08
Metals and Plastics	Reno-Sparks MSA, NV	H	16.69 FQ	19.30 MW	24.08 TQ	NVBLS	5/08
Metals and Plastics	New Hampshire	H	12.47 AE	17.84 MW	19.58 AEX	NHBLS	6/08
Metals and Plastics	Nashua NECTA, NH-MA	Y	26420 FQ	31200 MW	41390 TQ	USBLS	5/07
Metals and Plastics	New Jersey	Y	26600 FQ	32510 MW	36540 TQ	USBLS	5/07
Metals and Plastics	Camden PMSA, NJ	Y	30000 FQ	32280 MW	35030 TQ	USBLS	5/07
Metals and Plastics	Edison PMSA, NJ	Y	20910 FQ	30970 MW	34750 TQ	USBLS	5/07
Metals and Plastics	Newark-Union PMSA, NJ-PA	Y	27730 FQ	38520 MW	46740 TQ	USBLS	5/07
Metals and Plastics	New Mexico	Y	22140 FQ	25180 MW	27700 TQ	USBLS	5/07
Metals and Plastics	Albuquerque MSA, NM	Y	21950 FQ	24860 MW	27400 TQ	USBLS	5/07
Metals and Plastics	New York	Y	24540 FQ	30640 MW	37490 TQ	USBLS	5/07
Metals and Plastics	Buffalo-Niagara Falls MSA, NY	Y	30550 FQ	36000 MW	45180 TQ	USBLS	5/07
Metals and Plastics	Nassau-Suffolk PMSA, NY	Y	25940 FQ	34620 MW	51720 TQ	USBLS	5/07
Metals and Plastics	New York-Northern New Jersey-Long Island MSA, NY-NJ-PA	Y	23000 FQ	31360 MW	44010 TQ	USBLS	5/07
Metals and Plastics	North Carolina	Y	24300 FQ	29280 MW	35710 TQ	USBLS	5/07
Metals and Plastics	Asheville MSA, NC	Y	28800 FQ	32630 MW	36590 TQ	USBLS	5/07
Metals and Plastics	Charlotte-Gastonia-Concord MSA, NC-SC	Y	20810 FQ	26860 MW	35130 TQ	USBLS	5/07
Metals and Plastics	Raleigh-Cary MSA, NC	Y	30930 FQ	36430 MW	42950 TQ	USBLS	5/07
Metals and Plastics	Ohio	Y	24800 FQ	30260 MW	35610 TQ	USBLS	5/07
Metals and Plastics	Canton-Massillon MSA, OH	Y	26940 FQ	32010 MW	35750 TQ	USBLS	5/07
Metals and Plastics	Cincinnati-Middletown MSA, OH-KY-IN	Y	28830 FQ	34730 MW	39580 TQ	USBLS	5/07
Metals and Plastics	Cleveland-Elyria-Mentor MSA, OH	Y	26490 FQ	30490 MW	34500 TQ	USBLS	5/07
Metals and Plastics	Columbus MSA, OH	Y	23250 FQ	29760 MW	36250 TQ	USBLS	5/07
Metals and Plastics	Dayton MSA, OH	Y	26610 FQ	29730 MW	34230 TQ	USBLS	5/07
Metals and Plastics	Oklahoma	Y	22010 FQ	27700 MW	35810 TQ	USBLS	5/07
Metals and Plastics	Oklahoma City MSA, OK	Y	20760 FQ	24390 MW	31670 TQ	USBLS	5/07
Metals and Plastics	Tulsa MSA, OK	Y	21550 FQ	25220 MW	35910 TQ	USBLS	5/07
Metals and Plastics	Oregon	H	14.53 AE	18.67 MW	22.30 TQ	ORBLS	5/08
Metals and Plastics	Portland-Vancouver-Beaverton MSA, OR-WA	Y	30090 FQ	38580 MW	46940 TQ	USBLS	5/07
Metals and Plastics	Pennsylvania	Y	27620 FQ	34060 MW	40800 TQ	USBLS	5/07
Metals and Plastics	Lancaster MSA, PA	Y	33820 FQ	41500 MW	47390 TQ	USBLS	5/07
Metals and Plastics	Philadelphia-Camden-Wilmington MSA, PA-NJ-DE-MD	Y	28370 FQ	32830 MW	37350 TQ	USBLS	5/07
Metals and Plastics	Pittsburgh MSA, PA	Y	26480 FQ	34950 MW	43850 TQ	USBLS	5/07
Metals and Plastics	Rhode Island	Y	34840 FQ	40770 MW	46550 TQ	USBLS	5/07
Metals and Plastics	Providence-Fall River-Warwick MSA, RI-MA	Y	31250 FQ	38880 MW	45420 TQ	USBLS	5/07
Metals and Plastics	South Carolina	Y	26210 FQ	31800 MW	36350 TQ	USBLS	5/07
Metals and Plastics	Charleston-North Charleston MSA, SC	Y	26730 FQ	28700 MW	30660 TQ	USBLS	5/07
Metals and Plastics	Columbia MSA, SC	Y	18700 FQ	29230 MW	33670 TQ	USBLS	5/07
Metals and Plastics	South Dakota	Y	27754 FQ	33405 MW	37414 TQ	SDBLS	7/08-9/08
Metals and Plastics	Tennessee	Y	23590 FQ	30570 MW	35410 TQ	USBLS	5/07
Metals and Plastics	Memphis MSA, TN-MS-AR	Y	30480 FQ	32680 MW	35140 TQ	USBLS	5/07
Metals and Plastics	Nashville-Davidson-Murfreesboro MSA, TN	Y	21690 FQ	31150 MW	37670 TQ	USBLS	5/07
Metals and Plastics	Texas	Y	22260 FQ	28740 MW	37560 TQ	USBLS	5/07
Metals and Plastics	Dallas-Fort Worth-Arlington MSA, TX	Y	23840 FQ	29040 MW	36590 TQ	USBLS	5/07
Metals and Plastics	Houston-Sugar Land-Baytown MSA, TX	Y	23980 FQ	31560 MW	43420 TQ	USBLS	5/07
Metals and Plastics	San Antonio MSA, TX	Y	20450 FQ	25640 MW	28720 TQ	USBLS	5/07
Metals and Plastics	Utah	Y	30110 FQ	33510 MW	38910 TQ	USBLS	5/07
Metals and Plastics	Vermont	Y	30080 FQ	34140 MW	37720 TQ	USBLS	5/07
Metals and Plastics	Virginia	Y	25510 FQ	29310 MW	39120 TQ	USBLS	5/07
Metals and Plastics	Virginia Beach-Norfolk-Newport News MSA, VA-NC	Y	26440 FQ	28200 MW	30070 TQ	USBLS	5/07
Metals and Plastics	Washington	H	14.62 FQ	19.13 MW	24.09 TQ	WABLS	3/08

AE Average entry wage	**AW** Average wage paid	**FQ** First quartile wage	**LO** Lowest wage paid	**MTC** Median total compensation	**TCC** Total cash compensation
AER Average entry range	**AWR** Average wage range	**H** Hourly	**LR** Low end range	**MW** Median wage paid	**TQ** Third quartile wage
AEX Average experienced wage	**AXR** Average experienced range	**HI** Highest wage paid	**M** Monthly	**MWR** Median wage range	**W** Weekly
ATC Average total compensation	**D** Daily	**HR** High end range	**MCC** Median cash compensation	**S** See annotated source	**Y** Yearly

Occupation/Type/Industry	Location	Per	Low	Mid	High	Source	Date
Milling and Planing Machine Setter, Operator, and Tender							
Metals and Plastics	Seattle-Tacoma-Bellevue MSA, WA	Y	30110 FQ	38950 MW	49000 TQ	USBLS	5/07
Metals and Plastics	West Virginia	Y	29090 FQ	33812 MW	38180 TQ	WVBLS	7/08-9/08
Metals and Plastics	Wisconsin	Y	24920 FQ	28930 MW	35400 TQ	USBLS	5/07
Metals and Plastics	Milwaukee-Waukesha-West Allis MSA, WI	Y	26670 FQ	29230 MW	35270 TQ	USBLS	5/07
Millwright	Alabama	Y	31450 FQ	38380 MW	44730 TQ	USBLS	5/07
	Birmingham-Hoover MSA, AL	Y	32310 FQ	38670 MW	44450 TQ	USBLS	5/07
	Arizona	Y	34040 FQ	38020 MW	48010 TQ	USBLS	5/07
	Phoenix-Mesa-Scottsdale MSA, AZ	Y	33750 FQ	37220 MW	41160 TQ	USBLS	5/07
	Arkansas	Y	32570 FQ	37340 MW	42580 TQ	USBLS	5/07
	Little Rock-North Little Rock MSA, AR	Y	26770 FQ	29850 MW	34120 TQ	USBLS	5/07
	California	H	19.83 FQ	25.45 MW	33.24 TQ	CABLS	1/08-3/08
	Los Angeles-Long Beach-Glendale PMSA, CA	H	22.89 FQ	26.80 MW	30.23 TQ	CABLS	1/08-3/08
	Oakland-Fremont-Hayward MSA, CA	H	32.83 FQ	35.44 MW	38.37 TQ	CABLS	1/08-3/08
	Riverside-San Bernardino-Ontario MSA, CA	H	17.18 FQ	19.55 MW	21.72 TQ	CABLS	1/08-3/08
	Sacramento-Arden Arcade-Roseville MSA, CA	H	21.88 FQ	25.14 MW	28.44 TQ	CABLS	1/08-3/08
	San Diego-Carlsbad-San Marcos MSA, CA	H	14.26 FQ	16.66 MW	33.51 TQ	CABLS	1/08-3/08
	San Francisco-San Mateo-Redwood PMSA, CA	H	18.46 FQ	27.27 MW	33.11 TQ	CABLS	1/08-3/08
	Santa Ana-Anaheim-Irvine PMSA, CA	Y	33490 FQ	43340 MW	50510 TQ	USBLS	5/07
	Colorado	Y	30280 FQ	36040 MW	49450 TQ	USBLS	5/07
	Denver-Aurora MSA, CO	Y	28650 FQ	35330 MW	51000 TQ	USBLS	5/07
	Connecticut	H	16.19 AE	21.24 MW		CTBLS	1/08-3/08
	Bridgeport-Stamford-Norwalk MSA, CT	Y	37040 FQ	42440 MW	47380 TQ	USBLS	5/07
	Hartford-West Hartford-East Hartford MSA, CT	Y	34820 FQ	41870 MW	53240 TQ	USBLS	5/07
	New Haven MSA, CT	Y	34910 FQ	39290 MW	50720 TQ	USBLS	5/07
	Delaware	Y	42460 FQ	61580 MW	70420 TQ	USBLS	5/07
	Wilmington PMSA, DE-MD-NJ	Y	48740 FQ	64460 MW	71540 TQ	USBLS	5/07
	Washington-Arlington-Alexandria MSA, DC-VA-MD-WV	Y	48940 FQ	60310 MW	71130 TQ	USBLS	5/07
	Florida	Y	31230 FQ	37060 MW	46360 TQ	USBLS	5/07
	Fort Lauderdale-Pompano Beach-Deerfield Beach PMSA, FL	Y	41310 FQ	44770 MW	48240 TQ	USBLS	5/07
	Jacksonville MSA, FL	Y	32830 FQ	36820 MW	54400 TQ	USBLS	5/07
	Miami-Fort Lauderdale-Miami Beach MSA, FL	Y	35150 FQ	42640 MW	47000 TQ	USBLS	5/07
	Orlando-Kissimmee MSA, FL	Y	24710 FQ	42080 MW	47840 TQ	USBLS	5/07
	Tampa-St. Petersburg-Clearwater MSA, FL	Y	28600 FQ	33600 MW	41610 TQ	USBLS	5/07
	Georgia	Y	30160 FQ	36490 MW	44880 TQ	USBLS	5/07
	Atlanta-Sandy Springs-Marietta MSA, GA	Y	32750 FQ	38820 MW	46750 TQ	USBLS	5/07
	Idaho	Y	33430 FQ	43020 MW	51180 TQ	USBLS	5/07
	Boise City-Nampa MSA, ID	Y	34560 FQ	43610 MW	48800 TQ	USBLS	5/07
	Illinois	Y	38530 FQ	66150 MW	75040 TQ	USBLS	5/07
	Chicago-Naperville-Joliet MSA, IL-IN-WI	Y	45370 FQ	62110 MW	73500 TQ	USBLS	5/07
	Rockford MSA, IL	Y	36570 FQ	69870 MW	76770 TQ	USBLS	5/07
	Indiana	Y	43270 FQ	53460 MW	67310 TQ	USBLS	5/07
	Elkhart-Goshen MSA, IN	Y	37080 FQ	48070 MW	56940 TQ	USBLS	5/07
	Gary PMSA, IN	Y	41640 FQ	51880 MW	58380 TQ	USBLS	5/07
	Indianapolis-Carmel MSA, IN	Y	44210 FQ	55680 MW	68160 TQ	USBLS	5/07
	Iowa	Y	30140 FQ	38810 MW	53610 TQ	USBLS	5/07
	Kansas	Y	29760 FQ	44060 MW	69190 TQ	USBLS	5/07
	Kentucky	Y	41483 FQ	47931 MW	56988 TQ	KYBLS	2008

AE Average entry wage	**AW** Average wage paid	**FQ** First quartile wage	**LO** Lowest wage paid	**MTC** Median total compensation	**TCC** Total cash compensation
AER Average entry range	**AWR** Average wage range	**H** Hourly	**LR** Low end range	**MW** Median wage paid	**TQ** Third quartile wage
AEX Average experienced wage	**AXR** Average experienced range	**HI** Highest wage paid	**M** Monthly	**MWR** Median wage range	**W** Weekly
ATC Average total compensation	**D** Daily	**HR** High end range	**MCC** Median cash compensation	**S** See annotated source	**Y** Yearly

Millwright

Occupation/Type/Industry	Location	Per	Low	Mid	High	Source	Date
Millwright	Louisville-Jefferson County MSA, KY-IN	Y	42540 FQ	48940 MW	63890 TQ	USBLS	5/07
	Owensboro MSA, KY	Y	41790 FQ	44880 MW	48010 TQ	USBLS	5/07
	Louisiana	H	16.50 FQ	19.06 MW	22.27 TQ	LABLS	1/08-3/08
	Baton Rouge MSA, LA	Y	36120 FQ	41250 MW	45580 TQ	USBLS	5/07
	New Orleans-Metairie-Kenner MSA, LA	Y	38720 FQ	45420 MW	59700 TQ	USBLS	5/07
	Maine	Y	34610 FQ	41280 MW	49110 TQ	USBLS	5/07
	Portland-South Portland-Biddeford MSA, ME	Y	38550 FQ	44780 MW	50250 TQ	USBLS	5/07
	Maryland	Y		56000 MW		MDBLS	3/08
	Baltimore-Towson MSA, MD	Y	45190 FQ	50960 MW	58430 TQ	USBLS	5/07
	Bethesda-Gaithersburg-Frederick PMSA, MD	Y	58510 FQ	68980 MW	76770 TQ	USBLS	5/07
	Massachusetts	Y	37560 FQ	43790 MW	50260 TQ	USBLS	5/07
	Boston-Cambridge-Quincy NECTA, MA	Y	37440 FQ	41750 MW	47820 TQ	USBLS	5/07
	Worcester MSA, MA-CT	Y	33190 FQ	41770 MW	48660 TQ	USBLS	5/07
	Michigan	Y	57480 FQ	67720 MW	74460 TQ	USBLS	5/07
	Detroit-Warren-Livonia MSA, MI	Y	61580 FQ	69340 MW	75310 TQ	USBLS	5/07
	Grand Rapids-Wyoming MSA, MI	Y	61850 FQ	72280 MW	78320 TQ	USBLS	5/07
	Warren-Troy-Farmington Hills PMSA, MI	Y	64130 FQ	70360 MW	75820 TQ	USBLS	5/07
	Minnesota	Y	47097 FQ	58394 MW	67342 TQ	MNBLS	10/08-12/08
	Duluth-Superior MSA, MN-WI	Y	44779 FQ	51712 MW	61468 TQ	MNBLS	10/08-12/08
	Minneapolis-Saint Paul MSA, MN-WI	Y	49321 FQ	61342 MW	72377 TQ	MNBLS	10/08-12/08
	Mississippi	Y	28350 FQ	34400 MW	41350 TQ	USBLS	5/07
	Missouri	Y	36210 FQ	47410 MW	64400 TQ	USBLS	5/07
	Kansas City MSA, MO-KS	Y	35260 FQ	56290 MW	71890 TQ	USBLS	5/07
	St. Louis MSA, MO-IL	Y	46160 FQ	59730 MW	66310 TQ	USBLS	5/07
	Montana	Y	33850 FQ	39260 MW	44750 TQ	USBLS	5/07
	Nebraska	Y	28040 FQ	31650 MW	36700 TQ	USBLS	5/07
	Omaha-Council Bluffs MSA, NE-IA	Y	29520 FQ	33820 MW	37510 TQ	USBLS	5/07
	Nevada	H	23.54 FQ	32.06 MW	36.75 TQ	NVBLS	5/08
	New Hampshire	H	20.89 AE	27.89 MW	31.63 AEX	NHBLS	6/08
	New Jersey	Y	47670 FQ	66530 MW	75160 TQ	USBLS	5/07
	Camden PMSA, NJ	Y	38790 FQ	45310 MW	54530 TQ	USBLS	5/07
	Edison PMSA, NJ	Y	53290 FQ	66230 MW	73330 TQ	USBLS	5/07
	Newark-Union PMSA, NJ-PA	Y	43650 FQ	67210 MW	82850 TQ	USBLS	5/07
	New Mexico	Y	34100 FQ	36460 MW	38810 TQ	USBLS	5/07
	New York	Y	40240 FQ	50800 MW	68190 TQ	USBLS	5/07
	Albany-Schenectady-Troy MSA, NY	Y	47900 FQ	55030 MW	59670 TQ	USBLS	5/07
	Buffalo-Niagara Falls MSA, NY	Y	60910 FQ	70890 MW	77640 TQ	USBLS	5/07
	New York-Northern New Jersey-Long Island MSA, NY-NJ-PA	Y	53370 FQ	68780 MW	77810 TQ	USBLS	5/07
	North Carolina	Y	31620 FQ	37670 MW	44710 TQ	USBLS	5/07
	Charlotte-Gastonia-Concord MSA, NC-SC	Y	22350 FQ	34310 MW	41640 TQ	USBLS	5/07
	Raleigh-Cary MSA, NC	Y	32290 FQ	36910 MW	42440 TQ	USBLS	5/07
	North Dakota	Y	35320 FQ	42010 MW	50050 TQ	USBLS	5/07
	Ohio	Y	41320 FQ	60510 MW	72450 TQ	USBLS	5/07
	Cincinnati-Middletown MSA, OH-KY-IN	Y	39960 FQ	57250 MW	71900 TQ	USBLS	5/07
	Cleveland-Elyria-Mentor MSA, OH	Y	42960 FQ	58510 MW	73800 TQ	USBLS	5/07
	Columbus MSA, OH	Y	56380 FQ	63370 MW	69380 TQ	USBLS	5/07
	Dayton MSA, OH	Y	49360 FQ	61830 MW	72030 TQ	USBLS	5/07
	Oklahoma	Y	28610 FQ	38710 MW	53780 TQ	USBLS	5/07
	Oklahoma City MSA, OK	Y	22920 FQ	31630 MW	45880 TQ	USBLS	5/07
	Tulsa MSA, OK	Y	37670 FQ	60140 MW	73260 TQ	USBLS	5/07
	Oregon	H	17.15 FQ	20.39 MW	25.64 TQ	ORBLS	5/08
	Eugene-Springfield MSA, OR	Y	33100 FQ	35950 MW	39630 TQ	USBLS	5/07
	Portland-Vancouver-Beaverton MSA, OR-WA	Y	39690 FQ	50990 MW	66500 TQ	USBLS	5/07
	Pennsylvania	Y	33450 FQ	39790 MW	47180 TQ	USBLS	5/07

AE	Average entry wage	AW	Average wage paid	FQ	First quartile wage
AER	Average entry range	AWR	Average wage range	H	Hourly
AEX	Average experienced wage	AXR	Average experienced range	HI	Highest wage paid
ATC	Average total compensation	D	Daily	HR	High end range

LO	Lowest wage paid	MTC	Median total compensation
LR	Low end range	MW	Median wage paid
M	Monthly	MWR	Median wage range
MCC	Median cash compensation	S	See annotated source

TCC	Total cash compensation
TQ	Third quartile wage
W	Weekly
Y	Yearly

Occupation/Type/Industry	Location	Per	Low	Mid	High	Source	Date
Millwright	Allentown-Bethlehem-Easton MSA, PA-NJ	Y	15600 FQ	42140 MW	49250 TQ	USBLS	5/07
	Philadelphia-Camden-Wilmington MSA, PA-NJ-DE-MD	Y	37810 FQ	45050 MW	58850 TQ	USBLS	5/07
	Pittsburgh MSA, PA	Y	40390 FQ	46920 MW	55980 TQ	USBLS	5/07
	Rhode Island	Y	61390 FQ	65990 MW	70720 TQ	USBLS	5/07
	Providence-Fall River-Warwick MSA, RI-MA	Y	49780 FQ	64080 MW	69750 TQ	USBLS	5/07
	South Carolina	Y	33960 FQ	39070 MW	45710 TQ	USBLS	5/07
	Charleston-North Charleston MSA, SC	Y	42920 FQ	88650 MW	98240 TQ	USBLS	5/07
	Columbia MSA, SC	Y	32980 FQ	39950 MW	45980 TQ	USBLS	5/07
	South Dakota	Y	32153 FQ	37737 MW	44588 TQ	SDBLS	7/08-9/08
	Tennessee	Y	33240 FQ	42640 MW	52200 TQ	USBLS	5/07
	Knoxville MSA, TN	Y	31540 FQ	41300 MW	46070 TQ	USBLS	5/07
	Memphis MSA, TN-MS-AR	Y	31100 FQ	37110 MW	43580 TQ	USBLS	5/07
	Nashville-Davidson-Murfreesboro MSA, TN	Y	33710 FQ	41040 MW	48860 TQ	USBLS	5/07
	Texas	Y	31280 FQ	42990 MW	50610 TQ	USBLS	5/07
	Austin-Round Rock MSA, TX	Y	24580 FQ	34460 MW	44960 TQ	USBLS	5/07
	Dallas-Fort Worth-Arlington MSA, TX	Y	40280 FQ	46470 MW	57500 TQ	USBLS	5/07
	Houston-Sugar Land-Baytown MSA, TX	Y	37970 FQ	46720 MW	52780 TQ	USBLS	5/07
	Utah	Y	42290 FQ	45700 MW	49050 TQ	USBLS	5/07
	Salt Lake City MSA, UT	Y	43530 FQ	46340 MW	49210 TQ	USBLS	5/07
	Vermont	Y	34040 FQ	38160 MW	43990 TQ	USBLS	5/07
	Virginia	Y	34230 FQ	40120 MW	53620 TQ	USBLS	5/07
	Richmond MSA, VA	Y	32490 FQ	37240 MW	50220 TQ	USBLS	5/07
	Virginia Beach-Norfolk-Newport News MSA, VA-NC	Y	43390 FQ	53850 MW	63040 TQ	USBLS	5/07
	Washington	H	19.93 FQ	24.75 MW	31.90 TQ	WABLS	3/08
	Seattle-Tacoma-Bellevue MSA, WA	Y	42290 FQ	54380 MW	67170 TQ	USBLS	5/07
	West Virginia	Y	32317 FQ	38078 MW	43260 TQ	WVBLS	7/08-9/08
	Wisconsin	Y	43790 FQ	51890 MW	61060 TQ	USBLS	5/07
	Milwaukee-Waukesha-West Allis MSA, WI	Y	50440 FQ	58590 MW	65860 TQ	USBLS	5/07
	Wyoming	Y	35615 FQ	48335 MW	61213 TQ	WYBLS	9/08
	Puerto Rico	Y	27460 FQ	32470 MW	44190 TQ	USBLS	5/07
Mine Cutting and Channeling Machine Operator	Alabama	Y	31980 FQ	37990 MW	43200 TQ	USBLS	5/07
	Arizona	Y	21730 FQ	23880 MW	40330 TQ	USBLS	5/07
	Arkansas	Y	21250 FQ	28050 MW	42570 TQ	USBLS	5/07
	California	H	13.89 FQ	16.34 MW	19.51 TQ	CABLS	1/08-3/08
	Colorado	Y	40610 FQ	45440 MW	50290 TQ	USBLS	5/07
	Georgia	Y	28890 FQ	36850 MW	43610 TQ	USBLS	5/07
	Illinois	Y	34260 FQ	40670 MW	45730 TQ	USBLS	5/07
	Indiana	Y	36580 FQ	41680 MW	46080 TQ	USBLS	5/07
	Kentucky	Y	32445 FQ	44708 MW	53430 TQ	KYBLS	2008
	Maryland	Y		31150 MW		MDBLS	3/08
	Michigan	Y	26240 FQ	29310 MW	43390 TQ	USBLS	5/07
	Minnesota	Y	28233 FQ	38150 MW	47245 TQ	MNBLS	10/08-12/08
	Missouri	Y	22670 FQ	25360 MW	31250 TQ	USBLS	5/07
	Nevada	H	21.99 FQ	23.97 MW	26.01 TQ	NVBLS	5/08
	New York	Y	29090 FQ	34300 MW	39180 TQ	USBLS	5/07
	Ohio	Y	25870 FQ	33890 MW	41250 TQ	USBLS	5/07
	Pennsylvania	Y	29140 FQ	39250 MW	46630 TQ	USBLS	5/07
	Tennessee	Y	25160 FQ	30220 MW	38460 TQ	USBLS	5/07
	Texas	Y	22140 FQ	26190 MW	30040 TQ	USBLS	5/07
	Utah	Y	34890 FQ	38840 MW	44330 TQ	USBLS	5/07
	Vermont	Y	39580 FQ	42400 MW	45220 TQ	USBLS	5/07
	Virginia	Y	29720 FQ	34680 MW	41820 TQ	USBLS	5/07
	West Virginia	Y	37386 FQ	42322 MW	47974 TQ	WVBLS	7/08-9/08
	Wyoming	Y	37146 FQ	46021 MW	57009 TQ	WYBLS	9/08
Mine Rescue Operations Coordinator State Government	Ohio	H	19.88 LO		26.28 HI	ODAS	2008

AE	Average entry wage	**AW**	Average wage paid	**FQ**	First quartile wage	**LO**	Lowest wage paid	**MTC**	Median total compensation	**TCC**	Total cash compensation
AER	Average entry range	**AWR**	Average wage range	**H**	Hourly	**LR**	Low end range	**MW**	Median wage paid	**TQ**	Third quartile wage
AEX	Average experienced wage	**AXR**	Average experienced range	**HI**	Highest wage paid	**M**	Monthly	**MWR**	Median wage range	**W**	Weekly
ATC	Average total compensation	**D**	Daily	**HR**	High end range	**MCC**	Median cash compensation	**S**	See annotated source	**Y**	Yearly

Occupation/Type/Industry	Location	Per	Low	Mid	High	Source	Date
Mine Ventilation Engineer	United States	Y		61770 AW		SUSA03	2008
Minicomputer Systems Programmer							
State Government	Ohio	H	23.87 LO		35.02 HI	ODAS	2008
Mining and Geological Engineer							
Including Mining Safety Engineers	Alabama	Y	60410 FQ	81920 MW	96950 TQ	USBLS	5/07
Including Mining Safety Engineers	Arizona	Y	48620 FQ	62720 MW	79410 TQ	USBLS	5/07
Including Mining Safety Engineers	California	H	35.73 FQ	43.81 MW	49.18 TQ	CABLS	1/08-3/08
Including Mining Safety Engineers	Colorado	Y	74290 FQ	93720 MW	119650 TQ	USBLS	5/07
Including Mining Safety Engineers	Florida	Y	53030 FQ	63580 MW	90330 TQ	USBLS	5/07
Including Mining Safety Engineers	Georgia	Y	60830 FQ	77180 MW	91770 TQ	USBLS	5/07
Including Mining Safety Engineers	Idaho	Y	53000 FQ	60310 MW	75200 TQ	USBLS	5/07
Including Mining Safety Engineers	Illinois	Y	51130 FQ	71690 MW	100820 TQ	USBLS	5/07
Including Mining Safety Engineers	Indiana	Y	63860 FQ	73860 MW	80630 TQ	USBLS	5/07
Including Mining Safety Engineers	Kentucky	Y	63008 FQ	76147 MW	88379 TQ	KYBLS	2008
Including Mining Safety Engineers	Louisiana	H	28.85 FQ	35.30 MW	44.13 TQ	LABLS	1/08-3/08
Including Mining Safety Engineers	Michigan	Y	57540 FQ	69430 MW	82410 TQ	USBLS	5/07
Including Mining Safety Engineers	Minnesota	Y	63244 FQ	77378 MW	94265 TQ	MNBLS	10/08-12/08
Including Mining Safety Engineers	Missouri	Y	46920 FQ	71000 MW	89450 TQ	USBLS	5/07
Including Mining Safety Engineers	Montana	Y	55750 FQ	66240 MW	78690 TQ	USBLS	5/07
Including Mining Safety Engineers	Nevada	H	29.21 FQ	35.78 MW	42.18 TQ	NVBLS	5/08
Including Mining Safety Engineers	New Mexico	Y	59480 FQ	68740 MW	91700 TQ	USBLS	5/07
Including Mining Safety Engineers	Ohio	Y	46960 FQ	58570 MW	76380 TQ	USBLS	5/07
Including Mining Safety Engineers	Oklahoma	Y	66290 FQ	111010 MW		USBLS	5/07
Including Mining Safety Engineers	Pennsylvania	Y	46960 FQ	58970 MW	74040 TQ	USBLS	5/07
Including Mining Safety Engineers	South Carolina	Y	47190 FQ	59050 MW	70570 TQ	USBLS	5/07
Including Mining Safety Engineers	South Dakota	Y	59313 FQ	68168 MW	74987 TQ	SDBLS	7/08-9/08
Including Mining Safety Engineers	Tennessee	Y	38270 FQ	42570 MW	48380 TQ	USBLS	5/07
Including Mining Safety Engineers	Texas	Y	68360 FQ	84880 MW	128810 TQ	USBLS	5/07
Including Mining Safety Engineers	Utah	Y	67820 FQ	78560 MW	95930 TQ	USBLS	5/07
Including Mining Safety Engineers	Virginia	Y	71020 FQ	111990 MW	125290 TQ	USBLS	5/07
Including Mining Safety Engineers	Washington	H	26.76 FQ	32.77 MW	41.24 TQ	WABLS	3/08
Including Mining Safety Engineers	West Virginia	Y	53724 FQ	73638 MW	91587 TQ	WVBLS	7/08-9/08
Including Mining Safety Engineers	Wyoming	Y	70382 FQ	83042 MW	100557 TQ	WYBLS	9/08
Mining Worker	Beulah-Hazen, ND	Y		76679 AW		BTRIB	2007
Minister							
Presbyterian Church	United States	Y		55652 AW		BOPP01	5/1/08
Minor League Baseball Player							
Rookie, PawSox	Rhode Island	Y		30000 AW		RIM01	2009
Minority Business Coordinator							
State Government	Ohio	H	16.35 LO		19.88 HI	ODAS	2008
Minority Leader							
State House of Representatives	Washington	Y			46106 HI	WCC	9/1/08
State Senate	Washington	Y			46106 HI	WCC	9/1/08
Minute Clerk							
Municipal Government	Seattle, WA	H	21.59 LO		25.13 HI	CSSS	2008
Missionary							
Single Person, Evangelical Lutheran Church in America	United States	Y		40000 ATC		ELCA	2008
Mixing and Blending Machine Setter, Operator, and Tender	Alabama	Y	24370 FQ	30680 MW	38860 TQ	USBLS	5/07
	Birmingham-Hoover MSA, AL	Y	25720 FQ	29770 MW	34850 TQ	USBLS	5/07
	Alaska	Y	30630 FQ	43660 MW	62640 TQ	USBLS	5/07
	Arizona	Y	21320 FQ	27630 MW	35520 TQ	USBLS	5/07
	Phoenix-Mesa-Scottsdale MSA, AZ	Y	21040 FQ	28840 MW	36120 TQ	USBLS	5/07
	Tucson MSA, AZ	Y	20040 FQ	23010 MW	27940 TQ	USBLS	5/07
	Arkansas	Y	23370 FQ	28210 MW	34870 TQ	USBLS	5/07
	Little Rock-North Little Rock MSA, AR	Y	27610 FQ	31800 MW	37480 TQ	USBLS	5/07
	California	H	10.37 FQ	13.79 MW	17.43 TQ	CABLS	1/08-3/08
	Fresno MSA, CA	H	9.42 FQ	11.40 MW	14.66 TQ	CABLS	1/08-3/08

AE Average entry wage	**AW** Average wage paid	**FQ** First quartile wage	**LO** Lowest wage paid	**MTC** Median total compensation	**TCC** Total cash compensation
AER Average entry range	**AWR** Average wage range	**H** Hourly	**LR** Low end range	**MW** Median wage paid	**TQ** Third quartile wage
AEX Average experienced wage	**AXR** Average experienced range	**HI** Highest wage paid	**M** Monthly	**MWR** Median wage range	**W** Weekly
ATC Average total compensation	**D** Daily	**HR** High end range	**MCC** Median cash compensation	**S** See annotated source	**Y** Yearly

Occupation/Type/Industry	Location	Per	Low	Mid	High	Source	Date
Mixing and Blending Machine Setter, Operator, and Tender							
	Los Angeles-Long Beach-Glendale PMSA, CA	H	9.06 FQ	13.19 MW	16.89 TQ	CABLS	1/08-3/08
	Oakland-Fremont-Hayward MSA, CA	H	12.95 FQ	16.03 MW	18.69 TQ	CABLS	1/08-3/08
	Oxnard-Thousand Oaks-Ventura MSA, CA	H	14.06 FQ	17.15 MW	19.84 TQ	CABLS	1/08-3/08
	Riverside-San Bernardino-Ontario MSA, CA	H	11.00 FQ	13.43 MW	15.99 TQ	CABLS	1/08-3/08
	Sacramento-Arden Arcade-Roseville MSA, CA	H	13.56 FQ	16.52 MW	19.30 TQ	CABLS	1/08-3/08
	San Diego-Carlsbad-San Marcos MSA, CA	H	11.09 FQ	13.30 MW	17.63 TQ	CABLS	1/08-3/08
	San Francisco-San Mateo-Redwood PMSA, CA	H	12.14 FQ	14.08 MW	17.46 TQ	CABLS	1/08-3/08
	San Jose-Sunnyvale-Santa Clara MSA, CA	H	13.56 FQ	16.51 MW	19.26 TQ	CABLS	1/08-3/08
	Santa Ana-Anaheim-Irvine PMSA, CA	Y	18680 FQ	25210 MW	31830 TQ	USBLS	5/07
	Colorado	Y	22880 FQ	31240 MW	37200 TQ	USBLS	5/07
	Denver-Aurora MSA, CO	Y	24560 FQ	31510 MW	37650 TQ	USBLS	5/07
	Fort Collins-Loveland MSA, CO	Y	25060 FQ	28180 MW	31210 TQ	USBLS	5/07
	Connecticut	H	12.49 AE	16.57 MW		CTBLS	1/08-3/08
	Bridgeport-Stamford-Norwalk MSA, CT	Y	27410 FQ	31750 MW	41200 TQ	USBLS	5/07
	Hartford-West Hartford-East Hartford MSA, CT	Y	28360 FQ	34280 MW	40920 TQ	USBLS	5/07
	Delaware	Y	30010 FQ	36240 MW	43440 TQ	USBLS	5/07
	Wilmington PMSA, DE-MD-NJ	Y	31000 FQ	38040 MW	45220 TQ	USBLS	5/07
	Washington-Arlington-Alexandria MSA, DC-VA-MD-WV	Y	28750 FQ	34100 MW	44970 TQ	USBLS	5/07
	Florida	Y	21150 FQ	26660 MW	32560 TQ	USBLS	5/07
	Fort Lauderdale-Pompano Beach-Deerfield Beach PMSA, FL	Y	15800 FQ	22390 MW	29310 TQ	USBLS	5/07
	Jacksonville MSA, FL	Y	20890 FQ	23380 MW	30710 TQ	USBLS	5/07
	Lakeland MSA, FL	Y	26560 FQ	34480 MW	39410 TQ	USBLS	5/07
	Miami-Fort Lauderdale-Miami Beach MSA, FL	Y	18600 FQ	23680 MW	29270 TQ	USBLS	5/07
	Orlando-Kissimmee MSA, FL	Y	22280 FQ	27210 MW	33630 TQ	USBLS	5/07
	Tampa-St. Petersburg-Clearwater MSA, FL	Y	20080 FQ	26970 MW	31550 TQ	USBLS	5/07
	West Palm Beach-Boca Raton-Boynton Beach PMSA, FL	Y	19410 FQ	23780 MW	29330 TQ	USBLS	5/07
	Georgia	Y	23840 FQ	29580 MW	36360 TQ	USBLS	5/07
	Atlanta-Sandy Springs-Marietta MSA, GA	Y	25360 FQ	30960 MW	37240 TQ	USBLS	5/07
	Augusta-Richmond County MSA, GA-SC	Y	33560 FQ	48940 MW	56680 TQ	USBLS	5/07
	Hawaii	Y	21600 FQ	30120 MW	35400 TQ	USBLS	5/07
	Honolulu MSA, HI	Y	20590 FQ	23530 MW	33650 TQ	USBLS	5/07
	Idaho	Y	25990 FQ	30020 MW	44850 TQ	USBLS	5/07
	Boise City-Nampa MSA, ID	Y	23370 FQ	25940 MW	28590 TQ	USBLS	5/07
	Illinois	Y	24590 FQ	30770 MW	39140 TQ	USBLS	5/07
	Chicago-Naperville-Joliet MSA, IL-IN-WI	Y	24110 FQ	29520 MW	38410 TQ	USBLS	5/07
	Indiana	Y	24600 FQ	32190 MW	41120 TQ	USBLS	5/07
	Gary PMSA, IN	Y	23890 FQ	33100 MW	42980 TQ	USBLS	5/07
	Indianapolis-Carmel MSA, IN	Y	22400 FQ	27580 MW	42660 TQ	USBLS	5/07
	Iowa	Y	24240 FQ	28630 MW	33750 TQ	USBLS	5/07
	Des Moines-West Des Moines MSA, IA	Y	26950 FQ	32270 MW	36250 TQ	USBLS	5/07
	Kansas	Y	24030 FQ	30830 MW	41370 TQ	USBLS	5/07
	Wichita MSA, KS	Y	23960 FQ	30100 MW	42600 TQ	USBLS	5/07
	Kentucky	Y	23945 FQ	29547 MW	36134 TQ	KYBLS	2008
	Louisville-Jefferson County MSA, KY-IN	Y	25190 FQ	30500 MW	41660 TQ	USBLS	5/07
	Louisiana	H	11.33 FQ	15.27 MW	21.14 TQ	LABLS	1/08-3/08
	Baton Rouge MSA, LA	Y	27920 FQ	43270 MW	59740 TQ	USBLS	5/07

AE Average entry wage	**AW** Average wage paid	**FQ** First quartile wage	**LO** Lowest wage paid	**MTC** Median total compensation	**TCC** Total cash compensation
AER Average entry range	**AWR** Average wage range	**H** Hourly	**LR** Low end range	**MW** Median wage paid	**TQ** Third quartile wage
AEX Average experienced wage	**AXR** Average experienced range	**HI** Highest wage paid	**M** Monthly	**MWR** Median wage range	**W** Weekly
ATC Average total compensation	**D** Daily	**HR** High end range	**MCC** Median cash compensation	**S** See annotated source	**Y** Yearly

Occupation/Type/Industry	Location	Per	Low	Mid	High	Source	Date
Mixing and Blending Machine Setter, Operator, and Tender	New Orleans-Metairie-Kenner MSA, LA	Y	36070 FQ	41930 MW	46180 TQ	USBLS	5/07
	Maine	Y	30370 FQ	36040 MW	46520 TQ	USBLS	5/07
	Portland-South Portland-Biddeford MSA, ME	Y	34400 FQ	42160 MW	51170 TQ	USBLS	5/07
	Maryland	Y		38925 MW		MDBLS	3/08
	Baltimore-Towson MSA, MD	Y	33200 FQ	39190 MW	44510 TQ	USBLS	5/07
	Massachusetts	Y	28660 FQ	33620 MW	38470 TQ	USBLS	5/07
	Boston-Cambridge-Quincy NECTA, MA	Y	30000 FQ	34360 MW	38880 TQ	USBLS	5/07
	Worcester MSA, MA-CT	Y	28280 FQ	31980 MW	35930 TQ	USBLS	5/07
	Michigan	Y	24590 FQ	31770 MW	39060 TQ	USBLS	5/07
	Ann Arbor MSA, MI	Y	25470 FQ	30530 MW	36810 TQ	USBLS	5/07
	Detroit-Warren-Livonia MSA, MI	Y	24910 FQ	31930 MW	38560 TQ	USBLS	5/07
	Grand Rapids-Wyoming MSA, MI	Y	22600 FQ	31230 MW	43270 TQ	USBLS	5/07
	Lansing-East Lansing MSA, MI	Y	26680 FQ	29580 MW	32530 TQ	USBLS	5/07
	Warren-Troy-Farmington Hills PMSA, MI	Y	26670 FQ	33460 MW	38760 TQ	USBLS	5/07
	Minnesota	Y	28363 FQ	34096 MW	40876 TQ	MNBLS	10/08-12/08
	Duluth-Superior MSA, MN-WI	Y	18442 FQ	25678 MW	31100 TQ	MNBLS	10/08-12/08
	Minneapolis-Saint Paul MSA, MN-WI	Y	29566 FQ	35962 MW	43125 TQ	MNBLS	10/08-12/08
	Rochester MSA, MN	Y	25725 FQ	30502 MW	42364 TQ	MNBLS	10/08-12/08
	Mississippi	Y	22300 FQ	28610 MW	35220 TQ	USBLS	5/07
	Jackson MSA, MS	Y	19910 FQ	22150 MW	26800 TQ	USBLS	5/07
	Missouri	Y	24820 FQ	32400 MW	38970 TQ	USBLS	5/07
	Kansas City MSA, MO-KS	Y	28120 FQ	35320 MW	45720 TQ	USBLS	5/07
	St. Louis MSA, MO-IL	Y	29260 FQ	35280 MW	40720 TQ	USBLS	5/07
	Montana	Y	21990 FQ	30670 MW	59190 TQ	USBLS	5/07
	Billings MSA, MT	Y	23930 FQ	31200 MW	54720 TQ	USBLS	5/07
	Nebraska	Y	22920 FQ	28970 MW	39910 TQ	USBLS	5/07
	Omaha-Council Bluffs MSA, NE-IA	Y	23240 FQ	33070 MW	42950 TQ	USBLS	5/07
	Nevada	H	12.85 FQ	16.35 MW	19.40 TQ	NVBLS	5/08
	Las Vegas-Paradise MSA, NV	H	11.77 FQ	16.69 MW	19.60 TQ	NVBLS	5/08
	New Hampshire	H	14.10 AE	16.87 MW	18.13 AEX	NHBLS	6/08
	Manchester MSA, NH	Y	33960 FQ	37490 MW	43620 TQ	USBLS	5/07
	Nashua NECTA, NH-MA	Y	29440 FQ	33600 MW	37230 TQ	USBLS	5/07
	New Jersey	Y	22850 FQ	30920 MW	40120 TQ	USBLS	5/07
	Camden PMSA, NJ	Y	25310 FQ	32570 MW	38820 TQ	USBLS	5/07
	Edison PMSA, NJ	Y	23660 FQ	30880 MW	40240 TQ	USBLS	5/07
	Newark-Union PMSA, NJ-PA	Y	21700 FQ	28970 MW	37450 TQ	USBLS	5/07
	New Mexico	Y	22100 FQ	26990 MW	38330 TQ	USBLS	5/07
	Albuquerque MSA, NM	Y	22140 FQ	27820 MW	49830 TQ	USBLS	5/07
	New York	Y	26750 FQ	34940 MW	43950 TQ	USBLS	5/07
	Albany-Schenectady-Troy MSA, NY	Y	23390 FQ	33940 MW	50990 TQ	USBLS	5/07
	Binghamton MSA, NY	Y	18510 FQ	24830 MW	32050 TQ	USBLS	5/07
	Buffalo-Niagara Falls MSA, NY	Y	24680 FQ	30180 MW	43830 TQ	USBLS	5/07
	Glens Falls MSA, NY	Y	32660 FQ	38750 MW	43150 TQ	USBLS	5/07
	Nassau-Suffolk PMSA, NY	Y	23980 FQ	31010 MW	44010 TQ	USBLS	5/07
	New York-Northern New Jersey-Long Island MSA, NY-NJ-PA	Y	24080 FQ	32300 MW	42480 TQ	USBLS	5/07
	North Carolina	Y	23320 FQ	28520 MW	36640 TQ	USBLS	5/07
	Charlotte-Gastonia-Concord MSA, NC-SC	Y	24930 FQ	30340 MW	37990 TQ	USBLS	5/07
	Raleigh-Cary MSA, NC	Y	24290 FQ	28540 MW	31810 TQ	USBLS	5/07
	North Dakota	Y	19230 FQ	22950 MW	27550 TQ	USBLS	5/07
	Fargo MSA, ND-MN	Y	22140 FQ	25810 MW	29230 TQ	USBLS	5/07
	Ohio	Y	26840 FQ	33760 MW	41260 TQ	USBLS	5/07
	Cincinnati-Middletown MSA, OH-KY-IN	Y	32160 FQ	37660 MW	44440 TQ	USBLS	5/07
	Cleveland-Elyria-Mentor MSA, OH	Y	26970 FQ	34300 MW	43260 TQ	USBLS	5/07
	Columbus MSA, OH	Y	28200 FQ	34320 MW	43320 TQ	USBLS	5/07
	Dayton MSA, OH	Y	26010 FQ	33500 MW	40770 TQ	USBLS	5/07
	Oklahoma	Y	21350 FQ	29090 MW	33830 TQ	USBLS	5/07

AE	Average entry wage	AW	Average wage paid	FQ	First quartile wage	LO	Lowest wage paid	MTC	Median total compensation	TCC	Total cash compensation
AER	Average entry range	AWR	Average wage range	H	Hourly	LR	Low end range	MW	Median wage paid	TQ	Third quartile wage
AEX	Average experienced wage	AXR	Average experienced range	HI	Highest wage paid	M	Monthly	MWR	Median wage range	W	Weekly
ATC	Average total compensation	D	Daily	HR	High end range	MCC	Median cash compensation	S	See annotated source	Y	Yearly

Occupation/Type/Industry	Location	Per	Low	Mid	High	Source	Date
Mixing and Blending Machine Setter, Operator, and Tender	Oklahoma City MSA, OK	Y	16530 FQ	20770 MW	32940 TQ	USBLS	5/07
	Tulsa MSA, OK	Y	25040 FQ	31220 MW	34320 TQ	USBLS	5/07
	Oregon	H	11.32 FQ	14.46 MW	18.30 TQ	ORBLS	5/08
	Portland-Vancouver-Beaverton MSA, OR-WA	Y	26020 FQ	32930 MW	41120 TQ	USBLS	5/07
	Pennsylvania	Y	26710 FQ	33510 MW	40620 TQ	USBLS	5/07
	Allentown-Bethlehem-Easton MSA, PA-NJ	Y	29680 FQ	35110 MW	41020 TQ	USBLS	5/07
	Philadelphia-Camden-Wilmington MSA, PA-NJ-DE-MD	Y	29300 FQ	35760 MW	42860 TQ	USBLS	5/07
	Pittsburgh MSA, PA	Y	27100 FQ	33210 MW	39940 TQ	USBLS	5/07
	Rhode Island	Y	22300 FQ	26380 MW	32770 TQ	USBLS	5/07
	Providence-Fall River-Warwick MSA, RI-MA	Y	22470 FQ	26620 MW	32430 TQ	USBLS	5/07
	South Carolina	Y	25960 FQ	30970 MW	36750 TQ	USBLS	5/07
	Charleston-North Charleston MSA, SC	Y	24290 FQ	30500 MW	35910 TQ	USBLS	5/07
	Columbia MSA, SC	Y	23130 FQ	29150 MW	35260 TQ	USBLS	5/07
	Florence MSA, SC	Y	24330 FQ	35530 MW	40870 TQ	USBLS	5/07
	South Dakota	Y	24227 FQ	28586 MW	32580 TQ	SDBLS	7/08-9/08
	Sioux Falls MSA, SD	Y	25332 FQ	28142 MW	30809 TQ	SDBLS	7/08-9/08
	Tennessee	Y	23600 FQ	28650 MW	36250 TQ	USBLS	5/07
	Kingsport-Bristol-Bristol MSA, TN-VA	Y	26080 FQ	39540 MW	46240 TQ	USBLS	5/07
	Memphis MSA, TN-MS-AR	Y	21820 FQ	28660 MW	36280 TQ	USBLS	5/07
	Nashville-Davidson-Murfreesboro MSA, TN	Y	24800 FQ	28820 MW	35620 TQ	USBLS	5/07
	Texas	Y	20190 FQ	25200 MW	32080 TQ	USBLS	5/07
	Austin-Round Rock MSA, TX	Y	21010 FQ	25430 MW	52360 TQ	USBLS	5/07
	Dallas-Fort Worth-Arlington MSA, TX	Y	20650 FQ	24970 MW	32210 TQ	USBLS	5/07
	El Paso MSA, TX	Y	14410 FQ	17650 MW	21280 TQ	USBLS	5/07
	Houston-Sugar Land-Baytown MSA, TX	Y	21470 FQ	27670 MW	36130 TQ	USBLS	5/07
	San Antonio MSA, TX	Y	20410 FQ	22810 MW	26380 TQ	USBLS	5/07
	Utah	Y	21560 FQ	25220 MW	31150 TQ	USBLS	5/07
	Provo-Orem MSA, UT	Y	20590 FQ	23230 MW	27230 TQ	USBLS	5/07
	Salt Lake City MSA, UT	Y	26450 FQ	29710 MW	34330 TQ	USBLS	5/07
	Vermont	Y	26170 FQ	30210 MW	35160 TQ	USBLS	5/07
	Burlington-South Burlington MSA, VT	Y	24750 FQ	28910 MW	35030 TQ	USBLS	5/07
	Virginia	Y	23250 FQ	31330 MW	39440 TQ	USBLS	5/07
	Richmond MSA, VA	Y	24440 FQ	34870 MW	44470 TQ	USBLS	5/07
	Virginia Beach-Norfolk-Newport News MSA, VA-NC	Y	21310 FQ	26090 MW	37150 TQ	USBLS	5/07
	Washington	H	12.81 FQ	15.85 MW	19.55 TQ	WABLS	3/08
	Seattle-Tacoma-Bellevue MSA, WA	Y	27000 FQ	33100 MW	43130 TQ	USBLS	5/07
	West Virginia	Y	21696 FQ	29518 MW	37347 TQ	WVBLS	7/08-9/08
	Charleston MSA, WV	Y	22970 FQ	25560 MW	29590 TQ	USBLS	5/07
	Wisconsin	Y	27030 FQ	32750 MW	40300 TQ	USBLS	5/07
	Green Bay MSA, WI	Y	25400 FQ	29280 MW	34960 TQ	USBLS	5/07
	Milwaukee-Waukesha-West Allis MSA, WI	Y	27710 FQ	34710 MW	46190 TQ	USBLS	5/07
	Wyoming	Y	27920 FQ	32112 MW	37547 TQ	WYBLS	9/08
	Cheyenne MSA, WY	Y	25070 FQ	35213 MW	39424 TQ	WYBLS	9/08
	Puerto Rico	Y	17620 FQ	24120 MW	32720 TQ	USBLS	5/07
	San Juan-Caguas-Guaynabo MSA, PR	Y	17780 FQ	24120 MW	33000 TQ	USBLS	5/07
Mobile Heavy Equipment Mechanic							
Except Engines	Alabama	Y	31650 FQ	40090 MW	46880 TQ	USBLS	5/07
Except Engines	Birmingham-Hoover MSA, AL	Y	29600 FQ	40620 MW	50260 TQ	USBLS	5/07
Except Engines	Alaska	Y	52690 FQ	61930 MW	72710 TQ	USBLS	5/07
Except Engines	Anchorage MSA, AK	Y	49780 FQ	61450 MW	72030 TQ	USBLS	5/07
Except Engines	Arizona	Y	37760 FQ	44180 MW	49760 TQ	USBLS	5/07
Except Engines	Phoenix-Mesa-Scottsdale MSA, AZ	Y	36370 FQ	43790 MW	50860 TQ	USBLS	5/07

AE	Average entry wage	**AW**	Average wage paid	**FQ**	First quartile wage	**LO**	Lowest wage paid	**MTC**	Median total compensation	**TCC**	Total cash compensation
AER	Average entry range	**AWR**	Average wage range	**H**	Hourly	**LR**	Low end range	**MW**	Median wage paid	**TQ**	Third quartile wage
AEX	Average experienced wage	**AXR**	Average experienced range	**HI**	Highest wage paid	**M**	Monthly	**MWR**	Median wage range	**W**	Weekly
ATC	Average total compensation	**D**	Daily	**HR**	High end range	**MCC**	Median cash compensation	**S**	See annotated source	**Y**	Yearly

Mobile Heavy Equipment Mechanic

Occupation/Type/Industry	Location	Per	Low	Mid	High	Source	Date
Except Engines	Tucson MSA, AZ	Y	41510 FQ	45400 MW	49410 TQ	USBLS	5/07
Except Engines	Arkansas	Y	29890 FQ	35070 MW	40340 TQ	USBLS	5/07
Except Engines	Little Rock-North Little Rock MSA, AR	Y	30180 FQ	36580 MW	45790 TQ	USBLS	5/07
Except Engines	California	H	19.35 FQ	24.53 MW	31.58 TQ	CABLS	1/08-3/08
Except Engines	Los Angeles-Long Beach-Glendale PMSA, CA	H	19.63 FQ	27.88 MW	35.28 TQ	CABLS	1/08-3/08
Except Engines	Oakland-Fremont-Hayward MSA, CA	H	25.63 FQ	31.51 MW	36.86 TQ	CABLS	1/08-3/08
Except Engines	Riverside-San Bernardino-Ontario MSA, CA	H	18.48 FQ	22.96 MW	27.75 TQ	CABLS	1/08-3/08
Except Engines	Sacramento-Arden Arcade-Roseville MSA, CA	H	17.60 FQ	21.76 MW	25.80 TQ	CABLS	1/08-3/08
Except Engines	San Diego-Carlsbad-San Marcos MSA, CA	H	22.35 FQ	29.12 MW	36.02 TQ	CABLS	1/08-3/08
Except Engines	San Francisco-San Mateo-Redwood PMSA, CA	H	23.82 FQ	28.90 MW	33.06 TQ	CABLS	1/08-3/08
Except Engines	San Jose-Sunnyvale-Santa Clara MSA, CA	H	18.29 FQ	27.47 MW	34.48 TQ	CABLS	1/08-3/08
Except Engines	Santa Ana-Anaheim-Irvine PMSA, CA	Y	33920 FQ	45370 MW	55680 TQ	USBLS	5/07
Except Engines	Santa Rosa-Petaluma MSA, CA	H	23.72 FQ	27.24 MW	30.77 TQ	CABLS	1/08-3/08
Except Engines	Colorado	Y	36140 FQ	43500 MW	51110 TQ	USBLS	5/07
Except Engines	Denver-Aurora MSA, CO	Y	36800 FQ	43940 MW	51150 TQ	USBLS	5/07
Except Engines	Connecticut	H	18.13 AE	23.35 MW		CTBLS	1/08-3/08
Except Engines	Bridgeport-Stamford-Norwalk MSA, CT	Y	47650 FQ	56790 MW	64430 TQ	USBLS	5/07
Except Engines	Hartford-West Hartford-East Hartford MSA, CT	Y	40700 FQ	47520 MW	53370 TQ	USBLS	5/07
Except Engines	Delaware	Y	35670 FQ	43170 MW	51540 TQ	USBLS	5/07
Except Engines	Wilmington PMSA, DE-MD-NJ	Y.	39880 FQ	48440 MW	55230 TQ	USBLS	5/07
Except Engines	District of Columbia	Y	41780 FQ	49770 MW	57550 TQ	USBLS	5/07
Except Engines	Washington-Arlington-Alexandria MSA, DC-VA-MD-WV	Y	36030 FQ	43530 MW	52010 TQ	USBLS	5/07
Except Engines	Florida	Y	30110 FQ	36970 MW	44950 TQ	USBLS	5/07
Except Engines	Fort Lauderdale-Pompano Beach-Deerfield Beach PMSA, FL	Y	28110 FQ	33940 MW	42110 TQ	USBLS	5/07
Except Engines	Jacksonville MSA, FL	Y	32360 FQ	36600 MW	40740 TQ	USBLS	5/07
Except Engines	Miami-Fort Lauderdale-Miami Beach MSA, FL	Y	32840 FQ	40680 MW	52600 TQ	USBLS	5/07
Except Engines	Orlando-Kissimmee MSA, FL	Y	30810 FQ	36320 MW	42210 TQ	USBLS	5/07
Except Engines	Tampa-St. Petersburg-Clearwater MSA, FL	Y	30610 FQ	38350 MW	45630 TQ	USBLS	5/07
Except Engines	West Palm Beach-Boca Raton-Boynton Beach PMSA, FL	Y	34830 FQ	40480 MW	50100 TQ	USBLS	5/07
Except Engines	Georgia	Y	32260 FQ	38280 MW	46500 TQ	USBLS	5/07
Except Engines	Atlanta-Sandy Springs-Marietta MSA, GA	Y	34430 FQ	41050 MW	49140 TQ	USBLS	5/07
Except Engines	Hawaii	Y	44720 FQ	54250 MW	64830 TQ	USBLS	5/07
Except Engines	Honolulu MSA, HI	Y	49610 FQ	58240 MW	67310 TQ	USBLS	5/07
Except Engines	Idaho	Y	31380 FQ	37650 MW	45390 TQ	USBLS	5/07
Except Engines	Boise City-Nampa MSA, ID	Y	30260 FQ	36720 MW	45920 TQ	USBLS	5/07
Except Engines	Illinois	Y	38680 FQ	49190 MW	65270 TQ	USBLS	5/07
Except Engines	Chicago-Naperville-Joliet MSA, IL-IN-WI	Y	43960 FQ	55310 MW	70150 TQ	USBLS	5/07
Except Engines	Indiana	Y	32690 FQ	40100 MW	48860 TQ	USBLS	5/07
Except Engines	Gary PMSA, IN	Y	45750 FQ	52980 MW	58640 TQ	USBLS	5/07
Except Engines	Indianapolis-Carmel MSA, IN	Y	36140 FQ	42430 MW	48680 TQ	USBLS	5/07
Except Engines	Iowa	Y	32630 FQ	39710 MW	47670 TQ	USBLS	5/07
Except Engines	Des Moines-West Des Moines MSA, IA	Y	37600 FQ	44210 MW	50310 TQ	USBLS	5/07
Except Engines	Kansas	Y	31970 FQ	40710 MW	48170 TQ	USBLS	5/07
Except Engines	Wichita MSA, KS	Y	32300 FQ	40200 MW	50460 TQ	USBLS	5/07
Except Engines	Kentucky	Y	33290 FQ	38584 MW	46563 TQ	KYBLS	2008
Except Engines	Louisville-Jefferson County MSA, KY-IN	Y	33500 FQ	38760 MW	47450 TQ	USBLS	5/07
Except Engines	Louisiana	H	14.73 FQ	18.03 MW	21.62 TQ	LABLS	1/08-3/08

AE	Average entry wage	AW	Average wage paid	FQ	First quartile wage
AER	Average entry range	AWR	Average wage range	H	Hourly
AEX	Average experienced wage	AXR	Average experienced range	HI	Highest wage paid
ATC	Average total compensation	D	Daily	HR	High end range

LO	Lowest wage paid	MTC	Median total compensation	TCC	Total cash compensation
LR	Low end range	MW	Median wage paid	TQ	Third quartile wage
M	Monthly	MWR	Median wage range	W	Weekly
MCC	Median cash compensation	S	See annotated source	Y	Yearly

Occupation/Type/Industry	Location	Per	Low	Mid	High	Source	Date
Mobile Heavy Equipment Mechanic							
Except Engines	Baton Rouge MSA, LA	Y	35100 FQ	41300 MW	48320 TQ	USBLS	5/07
Except Engines	New Orleans-Metairie-Kenner MSA, LA	Y	31040 FQ	37220 MW	43650 TQ	USBLS	5/07
Except Engines	Maine	Y	31090 FQ	37010 MW	44370 TQ	USBLS	5/07
Except Engines	Bangor MSA, ME	Y	32130 FQ	38830 MW	45240 TQ	USBLS	5/07
Except Engines	Portland-South Portland-Biddeford MSA, ME	Y	36370 FQ	42660 MW	50670 TQ	USBLS	5/07
Except Engines	Maryland	Y		43900 MW		MDBLS	3/08
Except Engines	Baltimore-Towson MSA, MD	Y	35170 FQ	42720 MW	49920 TQ	USBLS	5/07
Except Engines	Bethesda-Gaithersburg-Frederick PMSA, MD	Y	35450 FQ	40080 MW	47530 TQ	USBLS	5/07
Except Engines	Massachusetts	Y	40450 FQ	46230 MW	53400 TQ	USBLS	5/07
Except Engines	Boston-Cambridge-Quincy NECTA, MA	Y	41910 FQ	47720 MW	56440 TQ	USBLS	5/07
Except Engines	Worcester MSA, MA-CT	Y	41910 FQ	46660 MW	53200 TQ	USBLS	5/07
Except Engines	Michigan	Y	34000 FQ	44110 MW	57610 TQ	USBLS	5/07
Except Engines	Detroit-Warren-Livonia MSA, MI	Y	45240 FQ	56290 MW	69510 TQ	USBLS	5/07
Except Engines	Grand Rapids-Wyoming MSA, MI	Y	37940 FQ	44400 MW	53040 TQ	USBLS	5/07
Except Engines	Warren-Troy-Farmington Hills PMSA, MI	Y	49610 FQ	60010 MW	69240 TQ	USBLS	5/07
Except Engines	Minnesota	Y	43468 FQ	49772 MW	57503 TQ	MNBLS	10/08-12/08
Except Engines	Duluth-Superior MSA, MN-WI	Y	45146 FQ	52688 MW	60272 TQ	MNBLS	10/08-12/08
Except Engines	Minneapolis-Saint Paul MSA, MN-WI	Y	45817 FQ	51964 MW	59632 TQ	MNBLS	10/08-12/08
Except Engines	Rochester MSA, MN	Y	42772 FQ	50499 MW	57996 TQ	MNBLS	10/08-12/08
Except Engines	Mississippi	Y	28730 FQ	34060 MW	40220 TQ	USBLS	5/07
Except Engines	Jackson MSA, MS	Y	29790 FQ	34290 MW	39300 TQ	USBLS	5/07
Except Engines	Missouri	Y	32740 FQ	39940 MW	48860 TQ	USBLS	5/07
Except Engines	Kansas City MSA, MO-KS	Y	35140 FQ	43070 MW	50600 TQ	USBLS	5/07
Except Engines	St. Louis MSA, MO-IL	Y	35070 FQ	43730 MW	50850 TQ	USBLS	5/07
Except Engines	Montana	Y	31970 FQ	39690 MW	47630 TQ	USBLS	5/07
Except Engines	Billings MSA, MT	Y	29080 FQ	34780 MW	41850 TQ	USBLS	5/07
Except Engines	Great Falls MSA, MT	Y	34130 FQ	43930 MW	51280 TQ	USBLS	5/07
Except Engines	Missoula MSA, MT	Y	29350 FQ	39550 MW	46380 TQ	USBLS	5/07
Except Engines	Nebraska	Y	31000 FQ	37410 MW	44450 TQ	USBLS	5/07
Except Engines	Omaha-Council Bluffs MSA, NE-IA	Y	32510 FQ	37900 MW	44500 TQ	USBLS	5/07
Except Engines	Nevada	H	21.12 FQ	24.74 MW	28.69 TQ	NVBLS	5/08
Except Engines	Las Vegas-Paradise MSA, NV	H	19.50 FQ	23.35 MW	27.88 TQ	NVBLS	5/08
Except Engines	New Hampshire	H	16.78 AE	20.39 MW	23.22 AEX	NHBLS	6/08
Except Engines	Manchester MSA, NH	Y	36920 FQ	41550 MW	48600 TQ	USBLS	5/07
Except Engines	Nashua NECTA, NH-MA	Y	39980 FQ	44620 MW	50400 TQ	USBLS	5/07
Except Engines	New Jersey	Y	40390 FQ	50140 MW	59690 TQ	USBLS	5/07
Except Engines	Camden PMSA, NJ	Y	39700 FQ	46660 MW	55260 TQ	USBLS	5/07
Except Engines	Edison PMSA, NJ	Y	35730 FQ	47720 MW	56340 TQ	USBLS	5/07
Except Engines	Newark-Union PMSA, NJ-PA	Y	46480 FQ	56110 MW	61830 TQ	USBLS	5/07
Except Engines	New Mexico	Y	32550 FQ	40570 MW	47790 TQ	USBLS	5/07
Except Engines	Albuquerque MSA, NM	Y	32130 FQ	39090 MW	48310 TQ	USBLS	5/07
Except Engines	New York	Y	34720 FQ	43720 MW	52980 TQ	USBLS	5/07
Except Engines	Albany-Schenectady-Troy MSA, NY	Y	35630 FQ	41240 MW	48860 TQ	USBLS	5/07
Except Engines	Buffalo-Niagara Falls MSA, NY	Y	39010 FQ	46770 MW	53350 TQ	USBLS	5/07
Except Engines	Nassau-Suffolk PMSA, NY	Y	37160 FQ	51160 MW	65580 TQ	USBLS	5/07
Except Engines	New York-Northern New Jersey-Long Island MSA, NY-NJ-PA	Y	41950 FQ	51970 MW	62530 TQ	USBLS	5/07
Except Engines	North Carolina	Y	32150 FQ	38010 MW	45970 TQ	USBLS	5/07
Except Engines	Asheville MSA, NC	Y	29190 FQ	35360 MW	42260 TQ	USBLS	5/07
Except Engines	Charlotte-Gastonia-Concord MSA, NC-SC	Y	33920 FQ	39230 MW	45590 TQ	USBLS	5/07
Except Engines	Raleigh-Cary MSA, NC	Y	30820 FQ	36720 MW	44560 TQ	USBLS	5/07
Except Engines	North Dakota	Y	33150 FQ	39860 MW	54100 TQ	USBLS	5/07
Except Engines	Bismarck MSA, ND	Y	35040 FQ	40290 MW	54870 TQ	USBLS	5/07
Except Engines	Fargo MSA, ND-MN	Y	30400 FQ	37370 MW	45420 TQ	USBLS	5/07
Except Engines	Ohio	Y	32910 FQ	40750 MW	51220 TQ	USBLS	5/07

AE	Average entry wage	AW	Average wage paid	FQ	First quartile wage
AER	Average entry range	AWR	Average wage range	H	Hourly
AEX	Average experienced wage	AXR	Average experienced range	HI	Highest wage paid
ATC	Average total compensation	D	Daily	HR	High end range

LO	Lowest wage paid	MTC	Median total compensation
LR	Low end range	MW	Median wage paid
M	Monthly	MWR	Median wage range
MCC	Median cash compensation	S	See annotated source

TCC	Total cash compensation		
TQ	Third quartile wage		
W	Weekly		
Y	Yearly		

Mobile Heavy Equipment Mechanic

Occupation/Type/Industry	Location	Per	Low	Mid	High	Source	Date
Except Engines	Cincinnati-Middletown MSA, OH-KY-IN	Y	35240 FQ	42140 MW	50210 TQ	USBLS	5/07
Except Engines	Cleveland-Elyria-Mentor MSA, OH	Y	38070 FQ	44700 MW	62200 TQ	USBLS	5/07
Except Engines	Columbus MSA, OH	Y	35820 FQ	45360 MW	55940 TQ	USBLS	5/07
Except Engines	Dayton MSA, OH	Y	30120 FQ	38180 MW	52960 TQ	USBLS	5/07
Except Engines	Oklahoma	Y	28080 FQ	35050 MW	43190 TQ	USBLS	5/07
Except Engines	Oklahoma City MSA, OK	Y	27330 FQ	32690 MW	40970 TQ	USBLS	5/07
Except Engines	Tulsa MSA, OK	Y	33910 FQ	39380 MW	46820 TQ	USBLS	5/07
Except Engines	Oregon	H	17.27 FQ	21.36 MW	25.07 TQ	ORBLS	5/08
Except Engines	Medford MSA, OR	Y	33480 FQ	40840 MW	47170 TQ	USBLS	5/07
Except Engines	Portland-Vancouver-Beaverton MSA, OR-WA	Y	38440 FQ	46290 MW	55350 TQ	USBLS	5/07
Except Engines	Pennsylvania	Y	36060 FQ	42850 MW	48930 TQ	USBLS	5/07
Except Engines	Allentown-Bethlehem-Easton MSA, PA-NJ	Y	36870 FQ	43650 MW	50700 TQ	USBLS	5/07
Except Engines	Philadelphia-Camden-Wilmington MSA, PA-NJ-DE-MD	Y	39510 FQ	45060 MW	52870 TQ	USBLS	5/07
Except Engines	Pittsburgh MSA, PA	Y	36580 FQ	43170 MW	48780 TQ	USBLS	5/07
Except Engines	Reading MSA, PA	Y	32620 FQ	37780 MW	44260 TQ	USBLS	5/07
Except Engines	Rhode Island	Y	37280 FQ	41910 MW	47080 TQ	USBLS	5/07
Except Engines	Providence-Fall River-Warwick MSA, RI-MA	Y	35540 FQ	39820 MW	46240 TQ	USBLS	5/07
Except Engines	South Carolina	Y	31920 FQ	38240 MW	46660 TQ	USBLS	5/07
Except Engines	Charleston-North Charleston MSA, SC	Y	32310 FQ	39450 MW	47420 TQ	USBLS	5/07
Except Engines	Columbia MSA, SC	Y	34530 FQ	41650 MW	49080 TQ	USBLS	5/07
Except Engines	Spartanburg MSA, SC	Y	33340 FQ	39010 MW	51700 TQ	USBLS	5/07
Except Engines	South Dakota	Y	33226 FQ	39601 MW	46198 TQ	SDBLS	7/08-9/08
Except Engines	Sioux Falls MSA, SD	Y	32933 FQ	39024 MW	45068 TQ	SDBLS	7/08-9/08
Except Engines	Tennessee	Y	29850 FQ	35220 MW	41150 TQ	USBLS	5/07
Except Engines	Kingsport-Bristol-Bristol MSA, TN-VA	Y	28430 FQ	39710 MW	44710 TQ	USBLS	5/07
Except Engines	Memphis MSA, TN-MS-AR	Y	29770 FQ	36670 MW	44520 TQ	USBLS	5/07
Except Engines	Nashville-Davidson-Murfreesboro MSA, TN	Y	32040 FQ	36000 MW	41290 TQ	USBLS	5/07
Except Engines	Texas	Y	28950 FQ	35920 MW	43850 TQ	USBLS	5/07
Except Engines	Austin-Round Rock MSA, TX	Y	31210 FQ	35520 MW	41660 TQ	USBLS	5/07
Except Engines	Beaumont-Port Arthur MSA, TX	Y	28710 FQ	36600 MW	45030 TQ	USBLS	5/07
Except Engines	Dallas-Fort Worth-Arlington MSA, TX	Y	30960 FQ	37620 MW	45420 TQ	USBLS	5/07
Except Engines	El Paso MSA, TX	Y	23830 FQ	33710 MW	42420 TQ	USBLS	5/07
Except Engines	Houston-Sugar Land-Baytown MSA, TX	Y	27900 FQ	36050 MW	44950 TQ	USBLS	5/07
Except Engines	San Antonio MSA, TX	Y	30090 FQ	36020 MW	42110 TQ	USBLS	5/07
Except Engines	Utah	Y	36050 FQ	43820 MW	50820 TQ	USBLS	5/07
Except Engines	Salt Lake City MSA, UT	Y	37010 FQ	44270 MW	50520 TQ	USBLS	5/07
Except Engines	Vermont	Y	33630 FQ	39680 MW	45830 TQ	USBLS	5/07
Except Engines	Burlington-South Burlington MSA, VT	Y	35350 FQ	41180 MW	45830 TQ	USBLS	5/07
Except Engines	Virginia	Y	32830 FQ	38960 MW	46180 TQ	USBLS	5/07
Except Engines	Richmond MSA, VA	Y	34520 FQ	39750 MW	46340 TQ	USBLS	5/07
Except Engines	Roanoke MSA, VA	Y	30820 FQ	34950 MW	39160 TQ	USBLS	5/07
Except Engines	Virginia Beach-Norfolk-Newport News MSA, VA-NC	Y	31750 FQ	39730 MW	46780 TQ	USBLS	5/07
Except Engines	Washington	H	19.97 FQ	23.78 MW	29.68 TQ	WABLS	3/08
Except Engines	Seattle-Tacoma-Bellevue MSA, WA	Y	44010 FQ	53360 MW	66330 TQ	USBLS	5/07
Except Engines	West Virginia	Y	29937 FQ	38561 MW	47880 TQ	WVBLS	7/08-9/08
Except Engines	Charleston MSA, WV	Y	31590 FQ	41290 MW	47110 TQ	USBLS	5/07
Except Engines	Parkersburg-Marietta-Vienna MSA, WV-OH	Y	26650 FQ	34440 MW	42700 TQ	USBLS	5/07
Except Engines	Wisconsin	Y	36060 FQ	42450 MW	50260 TQ	USBLS	5/07
Except Engines	Milwaukee-Waukesha-West Allis MSA, WI	Y	40610 FQ	47680 MW	56820 TQ	USBLS	5/07
Except Engines	Wyoming	Y	39643 FQ	46070 MW	52146 TQ	WYBLS	9/08
Except Engines	Cheyenne MSA, WY	Y	37211 FQ	46677 MW	53060 TQ	WYBLS	9/08
Except Engines	Puerto Rico	Y	17210 FQ	19930 MW	24190 TQ	USBLS	5/07

AE	Average entry wage	AW	Average wage paid	FQ	First quartile wage
AER	Average entry range	AWR	Average wage range	H	Hourly
AEX	Average experienced wage	AXR	Average experienced range	HI	Highest wage paid
ATC	Average total compensation	D	Daily	HR	High end range

LO	Lowest wage paid	MTC	Median total compensation	TCC	Total cash compensation
LR	Low end range	MW	Median wage paid	TQ	Third quartile wage
M	Monthly	MWR	Median wage range	W	Weekly
MCC	Median cash compensation	S	See annotated source	Y	Yearly

Occupation/Type/Industry	Location	Per	Low	Mid	High	Source	Date
Mobile Heavy Equipment Mechanic							
Except Engines	San Juan-Caguas-Guaynabo MSA, PR	Y	17040 FQ	19600 MW	22910 TQ	USBLS	5/07
Except Engines	Virgin Islands	Y	33440 FQ	39740 MW	45020 TQ	USBLS	5/07
Except Engines	Guam	Y	27320 FQ	30870 MW	35480 TQ	USBLS	5/07
Model	Kentucky	Y	18479 FQ	23839 MW	27390 TQ	KYBLS	2008
	Maryland	Y		23825 MW		MDBLS	3/08
	Missouri	Y	20150 FQ	22330 MW	24300 TQ	USBLS	5/07
	New York	Y	22400 FQ	30080 MW	36220 TQ	USBLS	5/07
	North Carolina	Y	14140 FQ	22460 MW	30220 TQ	USBLS	5/07
	Oregon	H	9.72 FQ	10.80 MW	11.88 TQ	ORBLS	5/08
	Texas	Y	19830 FQ	24150 MW	28410 TQ	USBLS	5/07
	Virginia	Y	21060 FQ	23460 MW	29320 TQ	USBLS	5/07
	Washington	H	11.66 FQ	14.96 MW	17.59 TQ	WABLS	3/08
Model Maker							
Metals and Plastics	Arizona	Y	23900 FQ	29310 MW	38470 TQ	USBLS	5/07
Metals and Plastics	Phoenix-Mesa-Scottsdale MSA, AZ	Y	23120 FQ	27430 MW	34800 TQ	USBLS	5/07
Metals and Plastics	Arkansas	Y	30290 FQ	35030 MW	43590 TQ	USBLS	5/07
Metals and Plastics	California	H	12.27 FQ	17.53 MW	26.41 TQ	CABLS	1/08-3/08
Metals and Plastics	Los Angeles-Long Beach-Glendale PMSA, CA	H	11.59 FQ	19.26 MW	26.86 TQ	CABLS	1/08-3/08
Metals and Plastics	Oakland-Fremont-Hayward MSA, CA	H	11.01 FQ	13.27 MW	17.32 TQ	CABLS	1/08-3/08
Metals and Plastics	Riverside-San Bernardino-Ontario MSA, CA	H	13.72 FQ	15.21 MW	24.47 TQ	CABLS	1/08-3/08
Metals and Plastics	San Diego-Carlsbad-San Marcos MSA, CA	H	18.38 FQ	33.29 MW	48.04 TQ	CABLS	1/08-3/08
Metals and Plastics	San Francisco-San Mateo-Redwood PMSA, CA	H	24.09 FQ	32.89 MW	39.09 TQ	CABLS	1/08-3/08
Metals and Plastics	San Jose-Sunnyvale-Santa Clara MSA, CA	H	14.93 FQ	20.39 MW	28.97 TQ	CABLS	1/08-3/08
Metals and Plastics	Santa Ana-Anaheim-Irvine PMSA, CA	Y	28460 FQ	32680 MW	40440 TQ	USBLS	5/07
Metals and Plastics	Colorado	Y	26390 FQ	35660 MW	47470 TQ	USBLS	5/07
Metals and Plastics	Denver-Aurora MSA, CO	Y	27490 FQ	33850 MW	45420 TQ	USBLS	5/07
Metals and Plastics	Connecticut	H	15.32 AE	23.72 MW		CTBLS	1/08-3/08
Metals and Plastics	Washington-Arlington-Alexandria MSA, DC-VA-MD-WV	Y	28050 FQ	32910 MW	41700 TQ	USBLS	5/07
Metals and Plastics	Florida	Y	24220 FQ	31710 MW	37660 TQ	USBLS	5/07
Metals and Plastics	Miami-Fort Lauderdale-Miami Beach MSA, FL	Y	22320 FQ	26210 MW	31400 TQ	USBLS	5/07
Metals and Plastics	Illinois	Y	32640 FQ	44760 MW	59220 TQ	USBLS	5/07
Metals and Plastics	Chicago-Naperville-Joliet MSA, IL-IN-WI	Y	35340 FQ	48510 MW	61750 TQ	USBLS	5/07
Metals and Plastics	Indiana	Y	29740 FQ	36320 MW	47590 TQ	USBLS	5/07
Metals and Plastics	Indianapolis-Carmel MSA, IN	Y	27800 FQ	30560 MW	38640 TQ	USBLS	5/07
Metals and Plastics	South Bend-Mishawaka MSA, IN-MI	Y	26660 FQ	29860 MW	42250 TQ	USBLS	5/07
Metals and Plastics	Iowa	Y	30820 FQ	42450 MW	50780 TQ	USBLS	5/07
Metals and Plastics	Kansas	Y	29200 FQ	50560 MW	56230 TQ	USBLS	5/07
Metals and Plastics	Wichita MSA, KS	Y	50240 FQ	53970 MW	57700 TQ	USBLS	5/07
Metals and Plastics	Kentucky	Y	34531 FQ	38150 MW	48258 TQ	KYBLS	2008
Metals and Plastics	Louisiana	H	9.39 FQ	11.63 MW	18.30 TQ	LABLS	1/08-3/08
Metals and Plastics	Maryland	Y		37275 MW		MDBLS	3/08
Metals and Plastics	Baltimore-Towson MSA, MD	Y	31320 FQ	36880 MW	44410 TQ	USBLS	5/07
Metals and Plastics	Massachusetts	Y	38500 FQ	45260 MW	52580 TQ	USBLS	5/07
Metals and Plastics	Boston-Cambridge-Quincy NECTA, MA	Y	42450 FQ	48680 MW	56980 TQ	USBLS	5/07
Metals and Plastics	Grand Rapids-Wyoming MSA, MI	Y	40200 FQ	44750 MW	49520 TQ	USBLS	5/07
Metals and Plastics	Minnesota	Y	37610 FQ	48516 MW	58479 TQ	MNBLS	10/08-12/08
Metals and Plastics	Minneapolis-Saint Paul MSA, MN-WI	Y	43094 FQ	54705 MW	61381 TQ	MNBLS	10/08-12/08
Metals and Plastics	Missouri	Y	34360 FQ	61490 MW	73060 TQ	USBLS	5/07
Metals and Plastics	New Jersey	Y	30770 FQ	37330 MW	50720 TQ	USBLS	5/07
Metals and Plastics	Camden PMSA, NJ	Y	25020 FQ	34450 MW	47290 TQ	USBLS	5/07
Metals and Plastics	Edison PMSA, NJ	Y	31480 FQ	35830 MW	47040 TQ	USBLS	5/07

AE	Average entry wage	AW	Average wage paid	FQ	First quartile wage	LO	Lowest wage paid	MTC	Median total compensation
AER	Average entry range	AWR	Average wage range	H	Hourly	LR	Low end range	MW	Median wage paid
AEX	Average experienced wage	AXR	Average experienced range	HI	Highest wage paid	M	Monthly	MWR	Median wage range
ATC	Average total compensation	D	Daily	HR	High end range	MCC	Median cash compensation	S	See annotated source

TCC	Total cash compensation
TQ	Third quartile wage
W	Weekly
Y	Yearly

Model Maker

Occupation/Type/Industry	Location	Per	Low	Mid	High	Source	Date
Model Maker							
Metals and Plastics	Newark-Union PMSA, NJ-PA	Y	28350 FQ	31790 MW	37110 TQ	USBLS	5/07
Metals and Plastics	New York	Y	38820 FQ	46610 MW	55340 TQ	USBLS	5/07
Metals and Plastics	Buffalo-Niagara Falls MSA, NY	Y	49230 FQ	53040 MW	56950 TQ	USBLS	5/07
Metals and Plastics	Nassau-Suffolk PMSA, NY	Y	36810 FQ	46970 MW	61150 TQ	USBLS	5/07
Metals and Plastics	New York-Northern New Jersey-Long Island MSA, NY-NJ-PA	Y	33670 FQ	43370 MW	56470 TQ	USBLS	5/07
Metals and Plastics	North Carolina	Y	31490 FQ	35220 MW	39660 TQ	USBLS	5/07
Metals and Plastics	Charlotte-Gastonia-Concord MSA, NC-SC	Y	29310 FQ	33050 MW	37510 TQ	USBLS	5/07
Metals and Plastics	Ohio	Y	27430 FQ	35920 MW	57970 TQ	USBLS	5/07
Metals and Plastics	Cincinnati-Middletown MSA, OH-KY-IN	Y	29440 FQ	37340 MW	53350 TQ	USBLS	5/07
Metals and Plastics	Cleveland-Elyria-Mentor MSA, OH	Y	26900 FQ	30930 MW	40270 TQ	USBLS	5/07
Metals and Plastics	Oklahoma	Y	18870 FQ	22820 MW	28110 TQ	USBLS	5/07
Metals and Plastics	Tulsa MSA, OK	Y	18280 FQ	21860 MW	29020 TQ	USBLS	5/07
Metals and Plastics	Oregon	H	23.77 FQ	28.70 MW	34.76 TQ	ORBLS	5/08
Metals and Plastics	Portland-Vancouver-Beaverton MSA, OR-WA	Y	50240 FQ	58900 MW	70010 TQ	USBLS	5/07
Metals and Plastics	Pennsylvania	Y	26360 FQ	32970 MW	38880 TQ	USBLS	5/07
Metals and Plastics	Philadelphia-Camden-Wilmington MSA, PA-NJ-DE-MD	Y	35740 FQ	45580 MW	64150 TQ	USBLS	5/07
Metals and Plastics	Pittsburgh MSA, PA	Y	22330 FQ	29220 MW	38180 TQ	USBLS	5/07
Metals and Plastics	Rhode Island	Y	18630 FQ	29660 MW	42980 TQ	USBLS	5/07
Metals and Plastics	Providence-Fall River-Warwick MSA, RI-MA	Y	19620 FQ	36540 MW	45070 TQ	USBLS	5/07
Metals and Plastics	South Carolina	Y	32960 FQ	36510 MW	40840 TQ	USBLS	5/07
Metals and Plastics	Tennessee	Y	28430 FQ	34620 MW	38720 TQ	USBLS	5/07
Metals and Plastics	Nashville-Davidson-Murfreesboro MSA, TN	Y	23780 FQ	27690 MW	32730 TQ	USBLS	5/07
Metals and Plastics	Texas	Y	22920 FQ	29420 MW	39790 TQ	USBLS	5/07
Metals and Plastics	Houston-Sugar Land-Baytown MSA, TX	Y	27110 FQ	33540 MW	43390 TQ	USBLS	5/07
Metals and Plastics	Utah	Y	38490 FQ	44240 MW	51420 TQ	USBLS	5/07
Metals and Plastics	Vermont	Y	33260 FQ	39010 MW	43180 TQ	USBLS	5/07
Metals and Plastics	Virginia	Y	20080 FQ	30710 MW	42880 TQ	USBLS	5/07
Metals and Plastics	Washington	H	30.04 FQ	32.27 MW	34.67 TQ	WABLS	3/08
Metals and Plastics	Seattle-Tacoma-Bellevue MSA, WA	Y	62430 FQ	67000 MW	71710 TQ	USBLS	5/07
Metals and Plastics	Wisconsin	Y	38450 FQ	45710 MW	55120 TQ	USBLS	5/07
Metals and Plastics	Appleton MSA, WI	Y	28980 FQ	43010 MW	52720 TQ	USBLS	5/07
Metals and Plastics	Milwaukee-Waukesha-West Allis MSA, WI	Y	44070 FQ	52190 MW	61590 TQ	USBLS	5/07
Wood	Arkansas	Y	22230 FQ	26100 MW	30580 TQ	USBLS	5/07
Wood	California	H	10.22 FQ	11.36 MW	16.75 TQ	CABLS	1/08-3/08
Wood	Santa Ana-Anaheim-Irvine PMSA, CA	Y	19980 FQ	21430 MW	22890 TQ	USBLS	5/07
Wood	Georgia	Y	26260 FQ	28440 MW	30620 TQ	USBLS	5/07
Wood	Illinois	Y	27140 FQ	34530 MW	54480 TQ	USBLS	5/07
Wood	Chicago-Naperville-Joliet MSA, IL-IN-WI	Y	31180 FQ	40000 MW	58900 TQ	USBLS	5/07
Wood	Indiana	Y	24890 FQ	27350 MW	30250 TQ	USBLS	5/07
Wood	Maryland	Y		30175 MW		MDBLS	3/08
Wood	Michigan	Y	69680 FQ	74300 MW	79270 TQ	USBLS	5/07
Wood	Detroit-Warren-Livonia MSA, MI	Y	70730 FQ	75280 MW	79880 TQ	USBLS	5/07
Wood	Warren-Troy-Farmington Hills PMSA, MI	Y	70730 FQ	75280 MW	79880 TQ	USBLS	5/07
Wood	Minnesota	Y	28923 FQ	33785 MW	37071 TQ	MNBLS	10/08-12/08
Wood	Minneapolis-Saint Paul MSA, MN-WI	Y	29752 FQ	34739 MW	38170 TQ	MNBLS	10/08-12/08
Wood	Mississippi	Y	19070 FQ	23080 MW	32620 TQ	USBLS	5/07
Wood	Missouri	Y	23670 FQ	27590 MW	31520 TQ	USBLS	5/07
Wood	New Jersey	Y	31700 FQ	36540 MW	42930 TQ	USBLS	5/07
Wood	New York	Y	24130 FQ	28050 MW	34500 TQ	USBLS	5/07
Wood	New York-Northern New Jersey-Long Island MSA, NY-NJ-PA	Y	30890 FQ	36490 MW	42860 TQ	USBLS	5/07

AE	Average entry wage	**AW**	Average wage paid	**FQ**	First quartile wage	**LO** Lowest wage paid **MTC** Median total compensation **TCC** Total cash compensation
AER	Average entry range	**AWR**	Average wage range	**H**	Hourly	**LR** Low end range **MW** Median wage paid **TQ** Third quartile wage
AEX	Average experienced wage	**AXR**	Average experienced range	**HI**	Highest wage paid	**M** Monthly **MWR** Median wage range **W** Weekly
ATC	Average total compensation	**D**	Daily	**HR**	High end range	**MCC** Median cash compensation **S** See annotated source **Y** Yearly

Occupation/Type/Industry	Location	Per	Low	Mid	High	Source	Date
Model Maker							
Wood	North Carolina	Y	24330 FQ	29030 MW	35340 TQ	USBLS	5/07
Wood	Pennsylvania	Y	27620 FQ	36760 MW	52530 TQ	USBLS	5/07
Wood	Texas	Y	22870 FQ	27940 MW	35130 TQ	USBLS	5/07
Wood	Dallas-Fort Worth-Arlington MSA, TX	Y	23660 FQ	27860 MW	36280 TQ	USBLS	5/07
Wood	Virginia	Y	24370 FQ	28510 MW	35150 TQ	USBLS	5/07
Mold Technician	United States	Y	46250 LO	48750 AW	51250 HI	SOPE	4/08-5/08
Molder, Shaper, and Caster							
Except Metals and Plastics	Alabama	Y	17550 FQ	22650 MW	28920 TQ	USBLS	5/07
Except Metals and Plastics	Birmingham-Hoover MSA, AL	Y	21320 FQ	26260 MW	30400 TQ	USBLS	5/07
Except Metals and Plastics	Arizona	Y	19450 FQ	23670 MW	31700 TQ	USBLS	5/07
Except Metals and Plastics	Phoenix-Mesa-Scottsdale MSA, AZ	Y	20510 FQ	24200 MW	30540 TQ	USBLS	5/07
Except Metals and Plastics	Tucson MSA, AZ	Y	16970 FQ	18720 MW	30190 TQ	USBLS	5/07
Except Metals and Plastics	Arkansas	Y	17430 FQ	21350 MW	26770 TQ	USBLS	5/07
Except Metals and Plastics	Little Rock-North Little Rock MSA, AR	Y	17740 FQ	24130 MW	28360 TQ	USBLS	5/07
Except Metals and Plastics	California	H	9.87 FQ	11.96 MW	14.94 TQ	CABLS	1/08-3/08
Except Metals and Plastics	Los Angeles-Long Beach-Glendale PMSA, CA	H	9.02 FQ	10.71 MW	13.60 TQ	CABLS	1/08-3/08
Except Metals and Plastics	Oakland-Fremont-Hayward MSA, CA	H	9.16 FQ	10.81 MW	15.53 TQ	CABLS	1/08-3/08
Except Metals and Plastics	Riverside-San Bernardino-Ontario MSA, CA	H	9.00 FQ	11.31 MW	13.82 TQ	CABLS	1/08-3/08
Except Metals and Plastics	Sacramento-Arden Arcade-Roseville MSA, CA	H	11.72 FQ	13.68 MW	15.38 TQ	CABLS	1/08-3/08
Except Metals and Plastics	San Diego-Carlsbad-San Marcos MSA, CA	H	10.15 FQ	12.08 MW	14.36 TQ	CABLS	1/08-3/08
Except Metals and Plastics	San Francisco-San Mateo-Redwood PMSA, CA	H	10.24 FQ	13.31 MW	17.70 TQ	CABLS	1/08-3/08
Except Metals and Plastics	San Jose-Sunnyvale-Santa Clara MSA, CA	H	10.66 FQ	12.14 MW	15.00 TQ	CABLS	1/08-3/08
Except Metals and Plastics	Santa Ana-Anaheim-Irvine PMSA, CA	Y	21510 FQ	26940 MW	33790 TQ	USBLS	5/07
Except Metals and Plastics	Colorado	Y	22110 FQ	27980 MW	35870 TQ	USBLS	5/07
Except Metals and Plastics	Denver-Aurora MSA, CO	Y	25800 FQ	33460 MW	39690 TQ	USBLS	5/07
Except Metals and Plastics	Connecticut	H	13.77 AE	17.62 MW		CTBLS	1/08-3/08
Except Metals and Plastics	Bridgeport-Stamford-Norwalk MSA, CT	Y	37340 FQ	42470 MW	46750 TQ	USBLS	5/07
Except Metals and Plastics	Delaware	Y	20400 FQ	22780 MW	27630 TQ	USBLS	5/07
Except Metals and Plastics	Wilmington PMSA, DE-MD-NJ	Y	19190 FQ	21000 MW	22820 TQ	USBLS	5/07
Except Metals and Plastics	Washington-Arlington-Alexandria MSA, DC-VA-MD-WV	Y	24220 FQ	28740 MW	36470 TQ	USBLS	5/07
Except Metals and Plastics	Florida	Y	21350 FQ	27730 MW	34700 TQ	USBLS	5/07
Except Metals and Plastics	Cape Coral-Fort Myers MSA, FL	Y	21090 FQ	26930 MW	34050 TQ	USBLS	5/07
Except Metals and Plastics	Fort Lauderdale-Pompano Beach-Deerfield Beach PMSA, FL	Y	30880 FQ	40330 MW	43900 TQ	USBLS	5/07
Except Metals and Plastics	Miami-Fort Lauderdale-Miami Beach MSA, FL	Y	19830 FQ	25250 MW	35600 TQ	USBLS	5/07
Except Metals and Plastics	Orlando-Kissimmee MSA, FL	Y	21450 FQ	27860 MW	36910 TQ	USBLS	5/07
Except Metals and Plastics	Tampa-St. Petersburg-Clearwater MSA, FL	Y	22940 FQ	27430 MW	31940 TQ	USBLS	5/07
Except Metals and Plastics	West Palm Beach-Boca Raton-Boynton Beach PMSA, FL	Y	21730 FQ	28080 MW	35640 TQ	USBLS	5/07
Except Metals and Plastics	Georgia	Y	24250 FQ	29990 MW	42340 TQ	USBLS	5/07
Except Metals and Plastics	Atlanta-Sandy Springs-Marietta MSA, GA	Y	26290 FQ	31780 MW	43630 TQ	USBLS	5/07
Except Metals and Plastics	Hawaii	Y	24230 FQ	32070 MW	43090 TQ	USBLS	5/07
Except Metals and Plastics	Honolulu MSA, HI	Y	22350 FQ	25000 MW	31950 TQ	USBLS	5/07
Except Metals and Plastics	Idaho	Y	14770 FQ	23130 MW	27980 TQ	USBLS	5/07
Except Metals and Plastics	Boise City-Nampa MSA, ID	Y	23680 FQ	27140 MW	31140 TQ	USBLS	5/07
Except Metals and Plastics	Illinois	Y	19610 FQ	27760 MW	35760 TQ	USBLS	5/07
Except Metals and Plastics	Chicago-Naperville-Joliet MSA, IL-IN-WI	Y	20480 FQ	28590 MW	37200 TQ	USBLS	5/07
Except Metals and Plastics	Indiana	Y	20060 FQ	27150 MW	32470 TQ	USBLS	5/07

AE Average entry wage	**AW** Average wage paid	**FQ** First quartile wage	**LO** Lowest wage paid	**MTC** Median total compensation **TCC** Total cash compensation
AER Average entry range	**AWR** Average wage range	**H** Hourly	**LR** Low end range	**MW** Median wage paid **TQ** Third quartile wage
AEX Average experienced wage	**AXR** Average experienced range **HI** Highest wage paid		**M** Monthly	**MWR** Median wage range **W** Weekly
ATC Average total compensation **D** Daily		**HR** High end range	**MCC** Median cash compensation **S** See annotated source	**Y** Yearly

Occupation/Type/Industry	Location	Per	Low	Mid	High	Source	Date
Molder, Shaper, and Caster							
Except Metals and Plastics	Gary PMSA, IN	Y	27950 FQ	31470 MW	35750 TQ	USBLS	5/07
Except Metals and Plastics	Indianapolis-Carmel MSA, IN	Y	21720 FQ	32600 MW	38380 TQ	USBLS	5/07
Except Metals and Plastics	Iowa	Y	22550 FQ	28100 MW	33510 TQ	USBLS	5/07
Except Metals and Plastics	Des Moines-West Des Moines MSA, IA	Y	20110 FQ	25290 MW	30830 TQ	USBLS	5/07
	Kansas	Y	21290 FQ	24000 MW	34340 TQ	USBLS	5/07
Except Metals and Plastics	Wichita MSA, KS	Y	18960 FQ	25050 MW	37580 TQ	USBLS	5/07
Except Metals and Plastics	Kentucky	Y	18854 FQ	24092 MW	31406 TQ	KYBLS	2008
Except Metals and Plastics	Louisville-Jefferson County MSA, KY-IN	Y	21810 FQ	27050 MW	34060 TQ	USBLS	5/07
Except Metals and Plastics	Louisiana	H	9.37 FQ	12.50 MW	15.90 TQ	LABLS	1/08-3/08
Except Metals and Plastics	Baton Rouge MSA, LA	Y	22060 FQ	26850 MW	33200 TQ	USBLS	5/07
Except Metals and Plastics	Lafayette MSA, LA	Y	17910 FQ	23180 MW	28300 TQ	USBLS	5/07
Except Metals and Plastics	Maine	Y	23800 FQ	26980 MW	30070 TQ	USBLS	5/07
Except Metals and Plastics	Portland-South Portland-Biddeford MSA, ME	Y	25210 FQ	27590 MW	29840 TQ	USBLS	5/07
	Maryland	Y		25525 MW		MDBLS	3/08
Except Metals and Plastics	Baltimore-Towson MSA, MD	Y	22390 FQ	24880 MW	29970 TQ	USBLS	5/07
Except Metals and Plastics	Bethesda-Gaithersburg-Frederick PMSA, MD	Y	22440 FQ	24490 MW	30290 TQ	USBLS	5/07
Except Metals and Plastics	Massachusetts	Y	25830 FQ	30860 MW	38760 TQ	USBLS	5/07
Except Metals and Plastics	Boston-Cambridge-Quincy NECTA, MA	Y	25990 FQ	32140 MW	47470 TQ	USBLS	5/07
Except Metals and Plastics	Worcester MSA, MA-CT	Y	27240 FQ	31010 MW	36520 TQ	USBLS	5/07
Except Metals and Plastics	Michigan	Y	24610 FQ	28880 MW	37560 TQ	USBLS	5/07
Except Metals and Plastics	Detroit-Warren-Livonia MSA, MI	Y	23780 FQ	29300 MW	46750 TQ	USBLS	5/07
Except Metals and Plastics	Grand Rapids-Wyoming MSA, MI	Y	26440 FQ	29330 MW	32250 TQ	USBLS	5/07
Except Metals and Plastics	Warren-Troy-Farmington Hills PMSA, MI	Y	24030 FQ	29950 MW	49110 TQ	USBLS	5/07
Except Metals and Plastics	Minnesota	Y	27119 FQ	33567 MW	39062 TQ	MNBLS	10/08-12/08
Except Metals and Plastics	Minneapolis-Saint Paul MSA, MN-WI	Y	22599 FQ	30208 MW	39601 TQ	MNBLS	10/08-12/08
Except Metals and Plastics	Mississippi	Y	18030 FQ	22510 MW	27380 TQ	USBLS	5/07
Except Metals and Plastics	Missouri	Y	21150 FQ	25100 MW	38000 TQ	USBLS	5/07
Except Metals and Plastics	Kansas City MSA, MO-KS	Y	21980 FQ	24690 MW	32800 TQ	USBLS	5/07
Except Metals and Plastics	St. Louis MSA, MO-IL	Y	20370 FQ	29390 MW	43360 TQ	USBLS	5/07
Except Metals and Plastics	Nebraska	Y	24280 FQ	27830 MW	30920 TQ	USBLS	5/07
Except Metals and Plastics	Omaha-Council Bluffs MSA, NE-IA	Y	26190 FQ	28330 MW	30640 TQ	USBLS	5/07
Except Metals and Plastics	Nevada	H	11.80 FQ	14.44 MW	17.08 TQ	NVBLS	5/08
Except Metals and Plastics	Las Vegas-Paradise MSA, NV	H	11.42 FQ	14.02 MW	16.41 TQ	NVBLS	5/08
Except Metals and Plastics	New Hampshire	H	11.57 AE	15.25 MW	18.50 AEX	NHBLS	6/08
Except Metals and Plastics	Nashua NECTA, NH-MA	Y	23430 FQ	29320 MW	38520 TQ	USBLS	5/07
Except Metals and Plastics	New Jersey	Y	23820 FQ	31640 MW	36810 TQ	USBLS	5/07
Except Metals and Plastics	Camden PMSA, NJ	Y	23020 FQ	28070 MW	36650 TQ	USBLS	5/07
Except Metals and Plastics	Edison PMSA, NJ	Y	22370 FQ	27110 MW	33370 TQ	USBLS	5/07
Except Metals and Plastics	Newark-Union PMSA, NJ-PA	Y	17360 FQ	26160 MW	33560 TQ	USBLS	5/07
Except Metals and Plastics	New Mexico	Y	16740 FQ	20030 MW	24820 TQ	USBLS	5/07
Except Metals and Plastics	Albuquerque MSA, NM	Y	17660 FQ	21150 MW	25360 TQ	USBLS	5/07
Except Metals and Plastics	New York	Y	22230 FQ	27510 MW	34290 TQ	USBLS	5/07
Except Metals and Plastics	Albany-Schenectady-Troy MSA, NY	Y	28230 FQ	30980 MW	33420 TQ	USBLS	5/07
Except Metals and Plastics	Buffalo-Niagara Falls MSA, NY	Y	21380 FQ	23550 MW	29590 TQ	USBLS	5/07
Except Metals and Plastics	Nassau-Suffolk PMSA, NY	Y	23970 FQ	31700 MW	39070 TQ	USBLS	5/07
Except Metals and Plastics	New York-Northern New Jersey-Long Island MSA, NY-NJ-PA	Y	21780 FQ	28150 MW	35700 TQ	USBLS	5/07
Except Metals and Plastics	North Carolina	Y	18940 FQ	24120 MW	33220 TQ	USBLS	5/07
Except Metals and Plastics	Charlotte-Gastonia-Concord MSA, NC-SC	Y	22820 FQ	27310 MW	30840 TQ	USBLS	5/07
Except Metals and Plastics	Greensboro-High Point MSA, NC	Y	24330 FQ	27210 MW	29720 TQ	USBLS	5/07
Except Metals and Plastics	Raleigh-Cary MSA, NC	Y	17840 FQ	19510 MW	23390 TQ	USBLS	5/07
Except Metals and Plastics	North Dakota	Y	19170 FQ	23490 MW	30770 TQ	USBLS	5/07
Except Metals and Plastics	Ohio	Y	20930 FQ	25970 MW	31490 TQ	USBLS	5/07
Except Metals and Plastics	Cincinnati-Middletown MSA, OH-KY-IN	Y	18940 FQ	21680 MW	25290 TQ	USBLS	5/07

AE Average entry wage	**AW** Average wage paid	**FQ** First quartile wage	**LO** Lowest wage paid	**MTC** Median total compensation	**TCC** Total cash compensation
AER Average entry range	**AWR** Average wage range	**H** Hourly	**LR** Low end range	**MW** Median wage paid	**TQ** Third quartile wage
AEX Average experienced wage	**AXR** Average experienced range	**HI** Highest wage paid	**M** Monthly	**MWR** Median wage range	**W** Weekly
ATC Average total compensation	**D** Daily	**HR** High end range	**MCC** Median cash compensation	**S** See annotated source	**Y** Yearly

Occupation/Type/Industry	Location	Per	Low	Mid	High	Source	Date
Molder, Shaper, and Caster							
Except Metals and Plastics	Cleveland-Elyria-Mentor MSA, OH	Y	21910 FQ	24910 MW	28340 TQ	USBLS	5/07
Except Metals and Plastics	Columbus MSA, OH	Y	19260 FQ	24290 MW	29930 TQ	USBLS	5/07
Except Metals and Plastics	Dayton MSA, OH	Y	20450 FQ	28870 MW	33500 TQ	USBLS	5/07
Except Metals and Plastics	Oklahoma	Y	20730 FQ	24340 MW	31110 TQ	USBLS	5/07
Except Metals and Plastics	Oklahoma City MSA, OK	Y	20470 FQ	25240 MW	30930 TQ	USBLS	5/07
Except Metals and Plastics	Tulsa MSA, OK	Y	21290 FQ	24440 MW	31670 TQ	USBLS	5/07
Except Metals and Plastics	Oregon	H	10.16 FQ	13.02 MW	17.84 TQ	ORBLS	5/08
Except Metals and Plastics	Portland-Vancouver-Beaverton MSA, OR-WA	Y	19580 FQ	25090 MW	35430 TQ	USBLS	5/07
Except Metals and Plastics	Pennsylvania	Y	22070 FQ	28290 MW	35390 TQ	USBLS	5/07
Except Metals and Plastics	Allentown-Bethlehem-Easton MSA, PA-NJ	Y	31050 FQ	34660 MW	37660 TQ	USBLS	5/07
Except Metals and Plastics	Philadelphia-Camden-Wilmington MSA, PA-NJ-DE-MD	Y	21740 FQ	30660 MW	37530 TQ	USBLS	5/07
Except Metals and Plastics	Pittsburgh MSA, PA	Y	23160 FQ	27690 MW	34440 TQ	USBLS	5/07
Except Metals and Plastics	Reading MSA, PA	Y	19330 FQ	24710 MW	29530 TQ	USBLS	5/07
Except Metals and Plastics	Rhode Island	Y	21380 FQ	27990 MW	34230 TQ	USBLS	5/07
Except Metals and Plastics	Providence-Fall River-Warwick MSA, RI-MA	Y	22730 FQ	27930 MW	33220 TQ	USBLS	5/07
Except Metals and Plastics	South Carolina	Y	22570 FQ	27930 MW	34270 TQ	USBLS	5/07
Except Metals and Plastics	Columbia MSA, SC	Y	18620 FQ	21210 MW	23530 TQ	USBLS	5/07
Except Metals and Plastics	South Dakota	Y	20558 FQ	22741 MW	25545 TQ	SDBLS	7/08-9/08
Except Metals and Plastics	Tennessee	Y	21710 FQ	26130 MW	29860 TQ	USBLS	5/07
Except Metals and Plastics	Memphis MSA, TN-MS-AR	Y	21250 FQ	24750 MW	29320 TQ	USBLS	5/07
Except Metals and Plastics	Nashville-Davidson-Murfreesboro MSA, TN	Y	24400 FQ	27280 MW	29750 TQ	USBLS	5/07
Except Metals and Plastics	Texas	Y	18710 FQ	22310 MW	28400 TQ	USBLS	5/07
Except Metals and Plastics	Austin-Round Rock MSA, TX	Y	20670 FQ	24260 MW	31620 TQ	USBLS	5/07
Except Metals and Plastics	Dallas-Fort Worth-Arlington MSA, TX	Y	18870 FQ	21910 MW	26820 TQ	USBLS	5/07
Except Metals and Plastics	Houston-Sugar Land-Baytown MSA, TX	Y	17520 FQ	19650 MW	23180 TQ	USBLS	5/07
Except Metals and Plastics	San Antonio MSA, TX	Y	21840 FQ	26390 MW	29530 TQ	USBLS	5/07
Except Metals and Plastics	Utah	Y	20970 FQ	29060 MW	37440 TQ	USBLS	5/07
Except Metals and Plastics	Salt Lake City MSA, UT	Y	19760 FQ	31980 MW	37150 TQ	USBLS	5/07
Except Metals and Plastics	Vermont	Y	24530 FQ	27440 MW	31490 TQ	USBLS	5/07
Except Metals and Plastics	Virginia	Y	23650 FQ	28650 MW	35250 TQ	USBLS	5/07
Except Metals and Plastics	Richmond MSA, VA	Y	20270 FQ	23190 MW	30090 TQ	USBLS	5/07
Except Metals and Plastics	Virginia Beach-Norfolk-Newport News MSA, VA-NC	Y	20370 FQ	25370 MW	28910 TQ	USBLS	5/07
Except Metals and Plastics	Washington	H	10.59 FQ	14.23 MW	17.66 TQ	WABLS	3/08
Except Metals and Plastics	Seattle-Tacoma-Bellevue MSA, WA	Y	24560 FQ	32740 MW	37330 TQ	USBLS	5/07
Except Metals and Plastics	West Virginia	Y	15536 FQ	21210 MW	25153 TQ	WVBLS	7/08-9/08
Except Metals and Plastics	Huntington-Ashland MSA, WV-KY-OH	Y	19570 FQ	23580 MW	27820 TQ	USBLS	5/07
Except Metals and Plastics	Wisconsin	Y	25930 FQ	30520 MW	36100 TQ	USBLS	5/07
Except Metals and Plastics	Green Bay MSA, WI	Y	24030 FQ	29940 MW	34550 TQ	USBLS	5/07
Except Metals and Plastics	Milwaukee-Waukesha-West Allis MSA, WI	Y	26830 FQ	30590 MW	35940 TQ	USBLS	5/07
Except Metals and Plastics	Puerto Rico	Y	14560 FQ	17250 MW	19510 TQ	USBLS	5/07
Except Metals and Plastics	San Juan-Caguas-Guaynabo MSA, PR	Y	14870 FQ	17410 MW	19510 TQ	USBLS	5/07
Molding, Coremaking, and Casting Machine Setter, Operator, and Tender							
Metals and Plastics	Alabama	Y	20510 FQ	24900 MW	30530 TQ	USBLS	5/07
Metals and Plastics	Birmingham-Hoover MSA, AL	Y	19860 FQ	23960 MW	28790 TQ	USBLS	5/07
Metals and Plastics	Arizona	Y	19350 FQ	25820 MW	37040 TQ	USBLS	5/07
Metals and Plastics	Phoenix-Mesa-Scottsdale MSA, AZ	Y	19400 FQ	26480 MW	37490 TQ	USBLS	5/07
Metals and Plastics	Arkansas	Y	22030 FQ	25710 MW	30310 TQ	USBLS	5/07
Metals and Plastics	Fort Smith MSA, AR-OK	Y	22390 FQ	24950 MW	32980 TQ	USBLS	5/07
Metals and Plastics	Little Rock-North Little Rock MSA, AR	Y	23880 FQ	27580 MW	34190 TQ	USBLS	5/07
Metals and Plastics	California	H	8.75 FQ	10.75 MW	14.18 TQ	CABLS	1/08-3/08

AE	Average entry wage	AW	Average wage paid	FQ	First quartile wage	LO	Lowest wage paid	MTC	Median total compensation	TCC	Total cash compensation
AER	Average entry range	AWR	Average wage range	H	Hourly	LR	Low end range	MW	Median wage paid	TQ	Third quartile wage
AEX	Average experienced wage	AXR	Average experienced range	HI	Highest wage paid	M	Monthly	MWR	Median wage range	W	Weekly
ATC	Average total compensation	D	Daily	HR	High end range	MCC	Median cash compensation	S	See annotated source	Y	Yearly

1072

Occupation/Type/Industry	Location	Per	Low	Mid	High	Source	Date
Molding, Coremaking, and Casting Machine Setter, Operator, and Tender							
Metals and Plastics	Los Angeles-Long Beach-Glendale PMSA, CA	H	8.55 FQ	10.41 MW	13.69 TQ	CABLS	1/08-3/08
Metals and Plastics	Oakland-Fremont-Hayward MSA, CA	H	9.06 FQ	11.90 MW	17.71 TQ	CABLS	1/08-3/08
Metals and Plastics	Riverside-San Bernardino-Ontario MSA, CA	H	8.50 FQ	9.45 MW	14.36 TQ	CABLS	1/08-3/08
Metals and Plastics	Sacramento-Arden Arcade-Roseville MSA, CA	H	8.73 FQ	11.01 MW	14.31 TQ	CABLS	1/08-3/08
Metals and Plastics	San Diego-Carlsbad-San Marcos MSA, CA	H	8.98 FQ	10.73 MW	13.81 TQ	CABLS	1/08-3/08
Metals and Plastics	San Francisco-San Mateo-Redwood PMSA, CA	H	10.32 FQ	13.11 MW	17.49 TQ	CABLS	1/08-3/08
Metals and Plastics	San Jose-Sunnyvale-Santa Clara MSA, CA	H	9.37 FQ	11.47 MW	14.50 TQ	CABLS	1/08-3/08
Metals and Plastics	Santa Ana-Anaheim-Irvine PMSA, CA	Y	17290 FQ	20930 MW	26700 TQ	USBLS	5/07
Metals and Plastics	Colorado	Y	20070 FQ	25720 MW	32610 TQ	USBLS	5/07
Metals and Plastics	Denver-Aurora MSA, CO	Y	19700 FQ	24620 MW	29260 TQ	USBLS	5/07
Metals and Plastics	Fort Collins-Loveland MSA, CO	Y	21970 FQ	29980 MW	42900 TQ	USBLS	5/07
Metals and Plastics	Connecticut	H	10.05 AE	13.81 MW		CTBLS	1/08-3/08
Metals and Plastics	Bridgeport-Stamford-Norwalk MSA, CT	Y	21600 FQ	26710 MW	40580 TQ	USBLS	5/07
Metals and Plastics	Danbury MSA, CT	Y	20880 FQ	28290 MW	40840 TQ	USBLS	5/07
Metals and Plastics	Hartford-West Hartford-East Hartford MSA, CT	Y	24220 FQ	28890 MW	37560 TQ	USBLS	5/07
Metals and Plastics	Wilmington PMSA, DE-MD-NJ	Y	22390 FQ	24990 MW	31340 TQ	USBLS	5/07
Metals and Plastics	Washington-Arlington-Alexandria MSA, DC-VA-MD-WV	Y	22420 FQ	25250 MW	30450 TQ	USBLS	5/07
Metals and Plastics	Florida	Y	20120 FQ	25270 MW	31430 TQ	USBLS	5/07
Metals and Plastics	Fort Lauderdale-Pompano Beach-Deerfield Beach PMSA, FL	Y	19360 FQ	24060 MW	30040 TQ	USBLS	5/07
Metals and Plastics	Jacksonville MSA, FL	Y	27380 FQ	32540 MW	36320 TQ	USBLS	5/07
Metals and Plastics	Miami-Fort Lauderdale-Miami Beach MSA, FL	Y	17550 FQ	21620 MW	26740 TQ	USBLS	5/07
Metals and Plastics	Orlando-Kissimmee MSA, FL	Y	21410 FQ	26370 MW	31350 TQ	USBLS	5/07
Metals and Plastics	Tampa-St. Petersburg-Clearwater MSA, FL	Y	19580 FQ	24830 MW	32250 TQ	USBLS	5/07
Metals and Plastics	West Palm Beach-Boca Raton-Boynton Beach PMSA, FL	Y	20430 FQ	24530 MW	27080 TQ	USBLS	5/07
Metals and Plastics	Georgia	Y	22260 FQ	27150 MW	34840 TQ	USBLS	5/07
Metals and Plastics	Atlanta-Sandy Springs-Marietta MSA, GA	Y	25130 FQ	30960 MW	36420 TQ	USBLS	5/07
Metals and Plastics	Augusta-Richmond County MSA, GA-SC	Y	23240 FQ	26670 MW	29510 TQ	USBLS	5/07
Metals and Plastics	Hawaii	Y	36820 FQ	54550 MW	60900 TQ	USBLS	5/07
Metals and Plastics	Honolulu MSA, HI	Y	36820 FQ	54550 MW	60900 TQ	USBLS	5/07
Metals and Plastics	Idaho	Y	20990 FQ	26950 MW	34360 TQ	USBLS	5/07
Metals and Plastics	Illinois	Y	20630 FQ	26260 MW	33570 TQ	USBLS	5/07
Metals and Plastics	Champaign-Urbana MSA, IL	Y	22680 FQ	27800 MW	35670 TQ	USBLS	5/07
Metals and Plastics	Chicago-Naperville-Joliet MSA, IL-IN-WI	Y	19800 FQ	25940 MW	33980 TQ	USBLS	5/07
Metals and Plastics	Indiana	Y	22800 FQ	28330 MW	34670 TQ	USBLS	5/07
Metals and Plastics	Fort Wayne MSA, IN	Y	26130 FQ	29470 MW	32250 TQ	USBLS	5/07
Metals and Plastics	Gary PMSA, IN	Y	17950 FQ	23580 MW	38020 TQ	USBLS	5/07
Metals and Plastics	Indianapolis-Carmel MSA, IN	Y	26500 FQ	32810 MW	37700 TQ	USBLS	5/07
Metals and Plastics	Iowa	Y	21170 FQ	25210 MW	30130 TQ	USBLS	5/07
Metals and Plastics	Des Moines-West Des Moines MSA, IA	Y	25110 FQ	28440 MW	31680 TQ	USBLS	5/07
Metals and Plastics	Kansas	Y	20830 FQ	24440 MW	30320 TQ	USBLS	5/07
Metals and Plastics	Wichita MSA, KS	Y	18600 FQ	23500 MW	36650 TQ	USBLS	5/07
Metals and Plastics	Kentucky	Y	21332 FQ	27168 MW	32265 TQ	KYBLS	2008
Metals and Plastics	Bowling Green MSA, KY	Y	18750 FQ	26850 MW	30120 TQ	USBLS	5/07
Metals and Plastics	Louisville-Jefferson County MSA, KY-IN	Y	20940 FQ	25480 MW	31490 TQ	USBLS	5/07

AE	Average entry wage	**AW**	Average wage paid	**FQ**	First quartile wage
AER	Average entry range	**AWR**	Average wage range	**H**	Hourly
AEX	Average experienced wage	**AXR**	Average experienced range	**HI**	Highest wage paid
ATC	Average total compensation	**D**	Daily	**HR**	High end range

LO	Lowest wage paid	**MTC**	Median total compensation
LR	Low end range	**MW**	Median wage paid
M	Monthly	**MWR**	Median wage range
MCC	Median cash compensation	**S**	See annotated source

TCC	Total cash compensation
TQ	Third quartile wage
W	Weekly
Y	Yearly

Molding, Coremaking, and Casting Machine Setter, Operator, and Tender

Occupation/Type/Industry	Location	Per	Low	Mid	High	Source	Date
Metals and Plastics	Louisiana	H	8.42 FQ	10.29 MW	12.74 TQ	LABLS	1/08-3/08
Metals and Plastics	New Orleans-Metairie-Kenner MSA, LA	Y	16790 FQ	18900 MW	24580 TQ	USBLS	5/07
Metals and Plastics	Maine	Y	22970 FQ	33770 MW	43160 TQ	USBLS	5/07
Metals and Plastics	Maryland	Y		30575 MW		MDBLS	3/08
Metals and Plastics	Baltimore-Towson MSA, MD	Y	25490 FQ	32540 MW	42680 TQ	USBLS	5/07
Metals and Plastics	Massachusetts	Y	23680 FQ	30070 MW	37210 TQ	USBLS	5/07
Metals and Plastics	Boston-Cambridge-Quincy NECTA, MA	Y	28360 FQ	34580 MW	39610 TQ	USBLS	5/07
Metals and Plastics	Worcester MSA, MA-CT	Y	23930 FQ	29270 MW	35970 TQ	USBLS	5/07
Metals and Plastics	Michigan	Y	21880 FQ	28010 MW	38450 TQ	USBLS	5/07
Metals and Plastics	Detroit-Warren-Livonia MSA, MI	Y	23250 FQ	34460 MW	49640 TQ	USBLS	5/07
Metals and Plastics	Grand Rapids-Wyoming MSA, MI	Y	21020 FQ	25590 MW	30280 TQ	USBLS	5/07
Metals and Plastics	Lansing-East Lansing MSA, MI	Y	21350 FQ	26220 MW	35770 TQ	USBLS	5/07
Metals and Plastics	Warren-Troy-Farmington Hills PMSA, MI	Y	23120 FQ	35350 MW	49710 TQ	USBLS	5/07
Metals and Plastics	Minnesota	Y	25927 FQ	30913 MW	37714 TQ	MNBLS	10/08-12/08
Metals and Plastics	Duluth-Superior MSA, MN-WI	Y	33733 FQ	36532 MW	41425 TQ	MNBLS	10/08-12/08
Metals and Plastics	Minneapolis-Saint Paul MSA, MN-WI	Y	25491 FQ	30447 MW	37869 TQ	MNBLS	10/08-12/08
Metals and Plastics	Mississippi	Y	16900 FQ	21420 MW	26710 TQ	USBLS	5/07
Metals and Plastics	Missouri	Y	20490 FQ	24840 MW	32790 TQ	USBLS	5/07
Metals and Plastics	Kansas City MSA, MO-KS	Y	19890 FQ	23420 MW	29180 TQ	USBLS	5/07
Metals and Plastics	St. Louis MSA, MO-IL	Y	21230 FQ	26770 MW	37480 TQ	USBLS	5/07
Metals and Plastics	Montana	Y	17530 FQ	23560 MW	27270 TQ	USBLS	5/07
Metals and Plastics	Nebraska	Y	21480 FQ	27730 MW	35130 TQ	USBLS	5/07
Metals and Plastics	Lincoln MSA, NE	Y	21800 FQ	25960 MW	33510 TQ	USBLS	5/07
Metals and Plastics	Omaha-Council Bluffs MSA, NE-IA	Y	18430 FQ	21290 MW	27140 TQ	USBLS	5/07
Metals and Plastics	Nevada	H	7.61 FQ	12.64 MW	17.01 TQ	NVBLS	5/08
Metals and Plastics	Las Vegas-Paradise MSA, NV	H	9.88 FQ	14.02 MW	18.26 TQ	NVBLS	5/08
Metals and Plastics	New Hampshire	H	10.44 AE	14.40 MW	16.86 AEX	NHBLS	6/08
Metals and Plastics	Nashua NECTA, NH-MA	Y	22230 FQ	27950 MW	35200 TQ	USBLS	5/07
Metals and Plastics	New Jersey	Y	17990 FQ	22990 MW	32890 TQ	USBLS	5/07
Metals and Plastics	Camden PMSA, NJ	Y	20420 FQ	25610 MW	34730 TQ	USBLS	5/07
Metals and Plastics	Edison PMSA, NJ	Y	17320 FQ	22270 MW	33610 TQ	USBLS	5/07
Metals and Plastics	Newark-Union PMSA, NJ-PA	Y	20280 FQ	23020 MW	27990 TQ	USBLS	5/07
Metals and Plastics	New Mexico	Y	17640 FQ	20620 MW	23440 TQ	USBLS	5/07
Metals and Plastics	Albuquerque MSA, NM	Y	17690 FQ	19510 MW	22760 TQ	USBLS	5/07
Metals and Plastics	New York	Y	20240 FQ	26750 MW	35170 TQ	USBLS	5/07
Metals and Plastics	Buffalo-Niagara Falls MSA, NY	Y	24670 FQ	27930 MW	35330 TQ	USBLS	5/07
Metals and Plastics	Nassau-Suffolk PMSA, NY	Y	19550 FQ	31390 MW	43580 TQ	USBLS	5/07
Metals and Plastics	New York-Northern New Jersey-Long Island MSA, NY-NJ-PA	Y	18360 FQ	23620 MW	34240 TQ	USBLS	5/07
Metals and Plastics	North Carolina	Y	21320 FQ	26100 MW	34110 TQ	USBLS	5/07
Metals and Plastics	Charlotte-Gastonia-Concord MSA, NC-SC	Y	22910 FQ	29000 MW	36200 TQ	USBLS	5/07
Metals and Plastics	Raleigh-Cary MSA, NC	Y	28410 FQ	36530 MW	44340 TQ	USBLS	5/07
Metals and Plastics	North Dakota	Y	21000 FQ	27010 MW	31110 TQ	USBLS	5/07
Metals and Plastics	Ohio	Y	20510 FQ	26270 MW	32660 TQ	USBLS	5/07
Metals and Plastics	Cincinnati-Middletown MSA, OH-KY-IN	Y	21540 FQ	26850 MW	35920 TQ	USBLS	5/07
Metals and Plastics	Cleveland-Elyria-Mentor MSA, OH	Y	22200 FQ	29640 MW	55900 TQ	USBLS	5/07
Metals and Plastics	Columbus MSA, OH	Y	24220 FQ	29980 MW	36340 TQ	USBLS	5/07
Metals and Plastics	Dayton MSA, OH	Y	25060 FQ	30260 MW	37160 TQ	USBLS	5/07
Metals and Plastics	Oklahoma	Y	18060 FQ	22760 MW	30070 TQ	USBLS	5/07
Metals and Plastics	Tulsa MSA, OK	Y	17970 FQ	22620 MW	29500 TQ	USBLS	5/07
Metals and Plastics	Oregon	H	9.07 FQ	12.10 MW	16.56 TQ	ORBLS	5/08
Metals and Plastics	Portland-Vancouver-Beaverton MSA, OR-WA	Y	19130 FQ	26240 MW	35370 TQ	USBLS	5/07
Metals and Plastics	Pennsylvania	Y	22060 FQ	27720 MW	34890 TQ	USBLS	5/07
Metals and Plastics	Allentown-Bethlehem-Easton MSA, PA-NJ	Y	23170 FQ	27690 MW	36750 TQ	USBLS	5/07

AE	Average entry wage	AW	Average wage paid	FQ	First quartile wage
AER	Average entry range	AWR	Average wage range	H	Hourly
AEX	Average experienced wage	AXR	Average experienced range	HI	Highest wage paid
ATC	Average total compensation	D	Daily	HR	High end range

LO	Lowest wage paid	MTC	Median total compensation
LR	Low end range	MW	Median wage paid
M	Monthly	MWR	Median wage range
MCC	Median cash compensation	S	See annotated source

TCC	Total cash compensation
TQ	Third quartile wage
W	Weekly
Y	Yearly

Occupation/Type/Industry	Location	Per	Low	Mid	High	Source	Date
Molding, Coremaking, and Casting Machine Setter, Operator, and Tender							
Metals and Plastics	Lancaster MSA, PA	Y	24360 FQ	27690 MW	32720 TQ	USBLS	5/07
Metals and Plastics	Philadelphia-Camden-Wilmington MSA, PA-NJ-DE-MD	Y	21160 FQ	27780 MW	34860 TQ	USBLS	5/07
Metals and Plastics	Pittsburgh MSA, PA	Y	24500 FQ	31030 MW	36280 TQ	USBLS	5/07
Metals and Plastics	Rhode Island	Y	21210 FQ	24790 MW	32050 TQ	USBLS	5/07
Metals and Plastics	Providence-Fall River-Warwick MSA, RI-MA	Y	21490 FQ	25130 MW	32060 TQ	USBLS	5/07
Metals and Plastics	South Carolina	Y	23690 FQ	27790 MW	32730 TQ	USBLS	5/07
Metals and Plastics	Columbia MSA, SC	Y	24830 FQ	28590 MW	32300 TQ	USBLS	5/07
Metals and Plastics	South Dakota	Y	22283 FQ	25504 MW	29864 TQ	SDBLS	7/08-9/08
Metals and Plastics	Sioux Falls MSA, SD	Y	23433 FQ	27413 MW	31111 TQ	SDBLS	7/08-9/08
Metals and Plastics	Tennessee	Y	20310 FQ	25590 MW	33430 TQ	USBLS	5/07
Metals and Plastics	Johnson City MSA, TN	Y	31930 FQ	34670 MW	37380 TQ	USBLS	5/07
Metals and Plastics	Memphis MSA, TN-MS-AR	Y	20610 FQ	25360 MW	31280 TQ	USBLS	5/07
Metals and Plastics	Nashville-Davidson-Murfreesboro MSA, TN	Y	21060 FQ	25980 MW	32030 TQ	USBLS	5/07
Metals and Plastics	Texas	Y	18460 FQ	22490 MW	28070 TQ	USBLS	5/07
Metals and Plastics	Austin-Round Rock MSA, TX	Y	20630 FQ	23170 MW	26510 TQ	USBLS	5/07
Metals and Plastics	Brownsville-Harlingen MSA, TX	Y	14720 FQ	18130 MW	29930 TQ	USBLS	5/07
Metals and Plastics	Corpus Christi MSA, TX	Y	22100 FQ	44870 MW	55020 TQ	USBLS	5/07
Metals and Plastics	Dallas-Fort Worth-Arlington MSA, TX	Y	18190 FQ	22470 MW	28740 TQ	USBLS	5/07
Metals and Plastics	El Paso MSA, TX	Y	19290 FQ	21570 MW	26560 TQ	USBLS	5/07
Metals and Plastics	Houston-Sugar Land-Baytown MSA, TX	Y	19450 FQ	23180 MW	28200 TQ	USBLS	5/07
Metals and Plastics	San Antonio MSA, TX	Y	17690 FQ	21080 MW	26810 TQ	USBLS	5/07
Metals and Plastics	Utah	Y	19930 FQ	23660 MW	36450 TQ	USBLS	5/07
Metals and Plastics	Provo-Orem MSA, UT	Y	19780 FQ	23170 MW	28010 TQ	USBLS	5/07
Metals and Plastics	Salt Lake City MSA, UT	Y	19530 FQ	23740 MW	35000 TQ	USBLS	5/07
Metals and Plastics	Vermont	Y	22330 FQ	25920 MW	31930 TQ	USBLS	5/07
Metals and Plastics	Burlington-South Burlington MSA, VT	Y	22930 FQ	27460 MW	31570 TQ	USBLS	5/07
Metals and Plastics	Virginia	Y	22080 FQ	27870 MW	32330 TQ	USBLS	5/07
Metals and Plastics	Richmond MSA, VA	Y	20910 FQ	27140 MW	35360 TQ	USBLS	5/07
Metals and Plastics	Virginia Beach-Norfolk-Newport News MSA, VA-NC	Y	21940 FQ	26790 MW	30660 TQ	USBLS	5/07
Metals and Plastics	Washington	H	11.54 FQ	14.46 MW	17.70 TQ	WABLS	3/08
Metals and Plastics	Seattle-Tacoma-Bellevue MSA, WA	Y	24410 FQ	29800 MW	35670 TQ	USBLS	5/07
Metals and Plastics	Wisconsin	Y	23260 FQ	28580 MW	35220 TQ	USBLS	5/07
Metals and Plastics	Green Bay MSA, WI	Y	22340 FQ	25120 MW	31170 TQ	USBLS	5/07
Metals and Plastics	Milwaukee-Waukesha-West Allis MSA, WI	Y	23170 FQ	30440 MW	37240 TQ	USBLS	5/07
Metals and Plastics	Puerto Rico	Y	14500 FQ	17640 MW	20660 TQ	USBLS	5/07
Metals and Plastics	Aguadilla-Isabela-San Sebastian MSA, PR	Y	13010 FQ	14680 MW	17560 TQ	USBLS	5/07
Metals and Plastics	San Juan-Caguas-Guaynabo MSA, PR	Y	15040 FQ	17910 MW	20640 TQ	USBLS	5/07
Moldmaker/Designer	United States	Y		66000 AW		IMM	1/14/08-2/20/08
Molecular Biologist							
Department of Health and Human Services	New Hampshire	Y			80527 HI	NHUL03	2008
Tenured	United States	Y		101000 AW		SCI01	2008
Molecular Microbiologist							
State Government	Ohio	H	33.83 LO		44.38 HI	ODAS	2008
Mortgage/Escrow Assistant	United States	Y	26250-33500 AER			IAAPHQ	2008
Motion Picture Projectionist	Alabama	Y	12550 FQ	13660 MW	14760 TQ	USBLS	5/07
	Birmingham-Hoover MSA, AL	Y	13900 FQ	16240 MW	18300 TQ	USBLS	5/07
	Alaska	Y	16900 FQ	18120 MW	20850 TQ	USBLS	5/07
	Arizona	Y	14690 FQ	16000 MW	20580 TQ	USBLS	5/07
	Phoenix-Mesa-Scottsdale MSA, AZ	Y	14620 FQ	15950 MW	22150 TQ	USBLS	5/07

AE Average entry wage	**AW** Average wage paid	**FQ** First quartile wage	**LO** Lowest wage paid	**MTC** Median total compensation	**TCC** Total cash compensation
AER Average entry range	**AWR** Average wage range	**H** Hourly	**LR** Low end range	**MW** Median wage paid	**TQ** Third quartile wage
AEX Average experienced wage	**AXR** Average experienced range	**HI** Highest wage paid	**M** Monthly	**MWR** Median wage range	**W** Weekly
ATC Average total compensation	**D** Daily	**HR** High end range	**MCC** Median cash compensation	**S** See annotated source	**Y** Yearly

Motion Picture Projectionist

Occupation/Type/Industry	Location	Per	Low	Mid	High	Source	Date
Motion Picture Projectionist	Arkansas	Y	14270 FQ	15390 MW	19000 TQ	USBLS	5/07
	Little Rock-North Little Rock MSA, AR	Y	14090 FQ	14880 MW	15990 TQ	USBLS	5/07
	California	H	9.14 FQ	10.68 MW	12.80 TQ	CABLS	1/08-3/08
	Los Angeles-Long Beach-Glendale PMSA, CA	H	9.71 FQ	11.26 MW	21.52 TQ	CABLS	1/08-3/08
	Oakland-Fremont-Hayward MSA, CA	H	8.49 FQ	9.21 MW	10.93 TQ	CABLS	1/08-3/08
	Riverside-San Bernardino-Ontario MSA, CA	H	9.05 FQ	10.12 MW	11.78 TQ	CABLS	1/08-3/08
	Sacramento-Arden Arcade-Roseville MSA, CA	H	8.79 FQ	9.93 MW	12.60 TQ	CABLS	1/08-3/08
	San Diego-Carlsbad-San Marcos MSA, CA	H	9.50 FQ	10.96 MW	12.41 TQ	CABLS	1/08-3/08
	San Francisco-San Mateo-Redwood PMSA, CA	H	10.08 FQ	11.24 MW	15.75 TQ	CABLS	1/08-3/08
	San Jose-Sunnyvale-Santa Clara MSA, CA	H	9.71 FQ	11.22 MW	14.72 TQ	CABLS	1/08-3/08
	Santa Ana-Anaheim-Irvine PMSA, CA	Y	19800 FQ	22490 MW	24960 TQ	USBLS	5/07
	Colorado	Y	17390 FQ	20820 MW	23360 TQ	USBLS	5/07
	Denver-Aurora MSA, CO	Y	19650 FQ	21320 MW	23020 TQ	USBLS	5/07
	Connecticut	H	9.95 AE	12.65 MW		CTBLS	1/08-3/08
	Washington-Arlington-Alexandria MSA, DC-VA-MD-WV	Y	14380 FQ	17060 MW	19570 TQ	USBLS	5/07
	Florida	Y	15730 FQ	17890 MW	21540 TQ	USBLS	5/07
	Fort Lauderdale-Pompano Beach-Deerfield Beach PMSA, FL	Y	15250 FQ	18130 MW	21150 TQ	USBLS	5/07
	Jacksonville MSA, FL	Y	14860 FQ	16170 MW	19540 TQ	USBLS	5/07
	Miami-Fort Lauderdale-Miami Beach MSA, FL	Y	15900 FQ	17980 MW	21350 TQ	USBLS	5/07
	Orlando-Kissimmee MSA, FL	Y	16110 FQ	18590 MW	23650 TQ	USBLS	5/07
	Tampa-St. Petersburg-Clearwater MSA, FL	Y	15640 FQ	17380 MW	19080 TQ	USBLS	5/07
	West Palm Beach-Boca Raton-Boynton Beach PMSA, FL	Y	16520 FQ	18440 MW	21840 TQ	USBLS	5/07
	Georgia	Y	13930 FQ	16220 MW	18930 TQ	USBLS	5/07
	Atlanta-Sandy Springs-Marietta MSA, GA	Y	15110 FQ	17130 MW	19870 TQ	USBLS	5/07
	Boise City-Nampa MSA, ID	Y	19690 FQ	25390 MW	29310 TQ	USBLS	5/07
	Illinois	Y	15690 FQ	18630 MW	28050 TQ	USBLS	5/07
	Chicago-Naperville-Joliet MSA, IL-IN-WI	Y	16430 FQ	20530 MW	43810 TQ	USBLS	5/07
	Indiana	Y	15540 FQ	19030 MW	22940 TQ	USBLS	5/07
	Indianapolis-Carmel MSA, IN	Y	14860 FQ	17380 MW	19650 TQ	USBLS	5/07
	Iowa	Y	13730 FQ	14560 MW	16400 TQ	USBLS	5/07
	Des Moines-West Des Moines MSA, IA	Y	14490 FQ	16340 MW	21610 TQ	USBLS	5/07
	Kansas	Y	13650 FQ	18900 MW	23030 TQ	USBLS	5/07
	Wichita MSA, KS	Y	13430 FQ	15800 MW	21810 TQ	USBLS	5/07
	Kentucky	Y	14258 FQ	16804 MW	21430 TQ	KYBLS	2008
	Louisville-Jefferson County MSA, KY-IN	Y	14250 FQ	17880 MW	25140 TQ	USBLS	5/07
	Louisiana	H	6.76 FQ	8.33 MW	10.21 TQ	LABLS	1/08-3/08
	New Orleans-Metairie-Kenner MSA, LA	Y	13520 FQ	15740 MW	18120 TQ	USBLS	5/07
	Maine	Y	16950 FQ	18770 MW	22030 TQ	USBLS	5/07
	Portland-South Portland-Biddeford MSA, ME	Y	16600 FQ	18070 MW	19690 TQ	USBLS	5/07
	Baltimore-Towson MSA, MD	Y	17270 FQ	19380 MW	22950 TQ	USBLS	5/07
	Massachusetts	Y	18670 FQ	22440 MW	29460 TQ	USBLS	5/07
	Boston-Cambridge-Quincy NECTA, MA	Y	19030 FQ	24630 MW	30800 TQ	USBLS	5/07
	Michigan	Y	15680 FQ	18410 MW	21910 TQ	USBLS	5/07
	Detroit-Warren-Livonia MSA, MI	Y	15930 FQ	19410 MW	22950 TQ	USBLS	5/07
	Warren-Troy-Farmington Hills PMSA, MI	Y	16120 FQ	19880 MW	23030 TQ	USBLS	5/07
	Minnesota	Y	15244 FQ	17356 MW	21058 TQ	MNBLS	10/08-12/08

AE Average entry wage	AW Average wage paid	FQ First quartile wage	LO Lowest wage paid	MTC Median total compensation	TCC Total cash compensation
AER Average entry range	AWR Average wage range	H Hourly	LR Low end range	MW Median wage paid	TQ Third quartile wage
AEX Average experienced wage	AXR Average experienced range	HI Highest wage paid	M Monthly	MWR Median wage range	W Weekly
ATC Average total compensation	D Daily	HR High end range	MCC Median cash compensation	S See annotated source	Y Yearly

Occupation/Type/Industry	Location	Per	Low	Mid	High	Source	Date
Motion Picture Projectionist	Minneapolis-Saint Paul MSA, MN-WI	Y	15349 FQ	18642 MW	22668 TQ	MNBLS	10/08-12/08
	Mississippi	Y	13110 FQ	14820 MW	21020 TQ	USBLS	5/07
	Missouri	Y	14350 FQ	15240 MW	18750 TQ	USBLS	5/07
	Kansas City MSA, MO-KS	Y	14870 FQ	18140 MW	23820 TQ	USBLS	5/07
	St. Louis MSA, MO-IL	Y	14410 FQ	15070 MW	18750 TQ	USBLS	5/07
	Montana	Y	13770 FQ	14740 MW	16400 TQ	USBLS	5/07
	Nebraska	Y	14080 FQ	17080 MW	23870 TQ	USBLS	5/07
	Omaha-Council Bluffs MSA, NE-IA	Y	15050 FQ	17820 MW	25910 TQ	USBLS	5/07
	Las Vegas-Paradise MSA, NV	H	7.82 FQ	9.56 MW	11.52 TQ	NVBLS	5/08
	New Hampshire	H	7.02 AE	8.79 MW	10.63 AEX	NHBLS	6/08
	New Jersey	Y	18300 FQ	22370 MW	26920 TQ	USBLS	5/07
	Edison PMSA, NJ	Y	17670 FQ	21600 MW	24350 TQ	USBLS	5/07
	Newark-Union PMSA, NJ-PA	Y	15930 FQ	22810 MW	28630 TQ	USBLS	5/07
	New York	Y	20770 FQ	26400 MW	32320 TQ	USBLS	5/07
	Buffalo-Niagara Falls MSA, NY	Y	15820 FQ	17790 MW	23120 TQ	USBLS	5/07
	Nassau-Suffolk PMSA, NY	Y	18530 FQ	26590 MW	32340 TQ	USBLS	5/07
	New York-Northern New Jersey-Long Island MSA, NY-NJ-PA	Y	20560 FQ	25180 MW	32200 TQ	USBLS	5/07
	North Carolina	Y	15090 FQ	17190 MW	19090 TQ	USBLS	5/07
	Charlotte-Gastonia-Concord MSA, NC-SC	Y	16110 FQ	17340 MW	18570 TQ	USBLS	5/07
	Raleigh-Cary MSA, NC	Y	14400 FQ	16450 MW	19240 TQ	USBLS	5/07
	North Dakota	Y	13740 FQ	16200 MW	18450 TQ	USBLS	5/07
	Ohio	Y	16210 FQ	21710 MW	27360 TQ	USBLS	5/07
	Cleveland-Elyria-Mentor MSA, OH	Y	15080 FQ	18730 MW	36420 TQ	USBLS	5/07
	Oklahoma	Y	13300 FQ	15290 MW	17720 TQ	USBLS	5/07
	Oregon	H	8.82 FQ	10.32 MW	12.97 TQ	ORBLS	5/08
	Portland-Vancouver-Beaverton MSA, OR-WA	Y	20610 FQ	24370 MW	29090 TQ	USBLS	5/07
	Pennsylvania	Y	14650 FQ	16940 MW	25810 TQ	USBLS	5/07
	Philadelphia-Camden-Wilmington MSA, PA-NJ-DE-MD	Y	15610 FQ	18070 MW	36590 TQ	USBLS	5/07
	Pittsburgh MSA, PA	Y	14100 FQ	14690 MW	16730 TQ	USBLS	5/07
	Rhode Island	Y	16790 FQ	21610 MW	24620 TQ	USBLS	5/07
	Providence-Fall River-Warwick MSA, RI-MA	Y	16790 FQ	21610 MW	24620 TQ	USBLS	5/07
	South Carolina	Y	16420 FQ	19280 MW	23070 TQ	USBLS	5/07
	Charleston-North Charleston MSA, SC	Y	16130 FQ	19580 MW	23620 TQ	USBLS	5/07
	Columbia MSA, SC	Y	15630 FQ	18300 MW	21590 TQ	USBLS	5/07
	South Dakota	Y	16031 FQ	18467 MW	21145 TQ	SDBLS	7/08-9/08
	Sioux Falls MSA, SD	Y	18523 FQ	20293 MW	23223 TQ	SDBLS	7/08-9/08
	Tennessee	Y	15210 FQ	18240 MW	23090 TQ	USBLS	5/07
	Memphis MSA, TN-MS-AR	Y	16100 FQ	18730 MW	26570 TQ	USBLS	5/07
	Texas	Y	13470 FQ	15800 MW	21110 TQ	USBLS	5/07
	Austin-Round Rock MSA, TX	Y	14300 FQ	16740 MW	19300 TQ	USBLS	5/07
	Dallas-Fort Worth-Arlington MSA, TX	Y	13910 FQ	16690 MW	20970 TQ	USBLS	5/07
	Houston-Sugar Land-Baytown MSA, TX	Y	12810 FQ	14440 MW	26180 TQ	USBLS	5/07
	Utah	Y	13260 FQ	15380 MW	18550 TQ	USBLS	5/07
	Salt Lake City MSA, UT	Y	14360 FQ	19320 MW	22980 TQ	USBLS	5/07
	Vermont	Y	16960 FQ	21780 MW	24390 TQ	USBLS	5/07
	Virginia	Y	13810 FQ	16640 MW	20230 TQ	USBLS	5/07
	Virginia Beach-Norfolk-Newport News MSA, VA-NC	Y	16380 FQ	18810 MW	26990 TQ	USBLS	5/07
	Washington	H	8.86 FQ	10.77 MW	14.46 TQ	WABLS	3/08
	Seattle-Tacoma-Bellevue MSA, WA	Y	17520 FQ	23080 MW	32420 TQ	USBLS	5/07
	West Virginia	Y	13922 FQ	14871 MW	17270 TQ	WVBLS	7/08-9/08
	Wisconsin	Y	15730 FQ	17320 MW	18950 TQ	USBLS	5/07
	Milwaukee-Waukesha-West Allis MSA, WI	Y	16760 FQ	18110 MW	19670 TQ	USBLS	5/07
	Wyoming	Y	17155 FQ	19163 MW	21308 TQ	WYBLS	9/08
	Puerto Rico	Y	12510 FQ	13910 MW	15390 TQ	USBLS	5/07

Occupation/Type/Industry	Location	Per	Low	Mid	High	Source	Date
Motion Picture Projectionist	San Juan-Caguas-Guaynabo MSA, PR	Y	12450 FQ	13830 MW	15250 TQ	USBLS	5/07
Motor Carrier Enforcement Inspector							
State Government	Ohio	H	17.22 LO		21.77 HI	ODAS	2008
Motorboat Mechanic	Alabama	Y	25310 FQ	31650 MW	38280 TQ	USBLS	5/07
	Alaska	Y	33000 FQ	41140 MW	47140 TQ	USBLS	5/07
	Arizona	Y	28290 FQ	36710 MW	43790 TQ	USBLS	5/07
	Phoenix-Mesa-Scottsdale MSA, AZ	Y	25050 FQ	38620 MW	45080 TQ	USBLS	5/07
	Arkansas	Y	22930 FQ	30180 MW	36520 TQ	USBLS	5/07
	California	H	14.76 FQ	18.42 MW	25.87 TQ	CABLS	1/08-3/08
	Los Angeles-Long Beach-Glendale PMSA, CA	H	16.75 FQ	25.57 MW	28.30 TQ	CABLS	1/08-3/08
	Oakland-Fremont-Hayward MSA, CA	H	17.57 FQ	27.21 MW	32.30 TQ	CABLS	1/08-3/08
	Riverside-San Bernardino-Ontario MSA, CA	H	11.83 FQ	18.13 MW	23.38 TQ	CABLS	1/08-3/08
	Sacramento-Arden Arcade-Roseville MSA, CA	H	16.87 FQ	18.90 MW	24.46 TQ	CABLS	1/08-3/08
	San Diego-Carlsbad-San Marcos MSA, CA	H	12.62 FQ	14.70 MW	17.17 TQ	CABLS	1/08-3/08
	San Francisco-San Mateo-Redwood PMSA, CA	H	16.34 FQ	23.70 MW	29.49 TQ	CABLS	1/08-3/08
	Santa Ana-Anaheim-Irvine PMSA, CA	Y	33880 FQ	37580 MW	41300 TQ	USBLS	5/07
	Colorado	Y	27890 FQ	33910 MW	41950 TQ	USBLS	5/07
	Denver-Aurora MSA, CO	Y	28270 FQ	38670 MW	44420 TQ	USBLS	5/07
	Connecticut	H	16.87 AE	21.45 MW		CTBLS	1/08-3/08
	Bridgeport-Stamford-Norwalk MSA, CT	Y	43600 FQ	48330 MW	54980 TQ	USBLS	5/07
	Hartford-West Hartford-East Hartford MSA, CT	Y	35190 FQ	38940 MW	45280 TQ	USBLS	5/07
	Delaware	Y	24170 FQ	29170 MW	35570 TQ	USBLS	5/07
	Wilmington PMSA, DE-MD-NJ	Y	29570 FQ	36080 MW	43300 TQ	USBLS	5/07
	Washington-Arlington-Alexandria MSA, DC-VA-MD-WV	Y	29410 FQ	46900 MW	57100 TQ	USBLS	5/07
	Florida	Y	27900 FQ	35930 MW	46220 TQ	USBLS	5/07
	Fort Lauderdale-Pompano Beach-Deerfield Beach PMSA, FL	Y	20660 FQ	33030 MW	46570 TQ	USBLS	5/07
	Jacksonville MSA, FL	Y	27630 FQ	33360 MW	41690 TQ	USBLS	5/07
	Miami-Fort Lauderdale-Miami Beach MSA, FL	Y	23610 FQ	35730 MW	48660 TQ	USBLS	5/07
	Orlando-Kissimmee MSA, FL	Y	24450 FQ	35710 MW	47620 TQ	USBLS	5/07
	Tallahassee MSA, FL	Y	33380 FQ	36600 MW	39420 TQ	USBLS	5/07
	Tampa-St. Petersburg-Clearwater MSA, FL	Y	35650 FQ	47040 MW	53500 TQ	USBLS	5/07
	West Palm Beach-Boca Raton-Boynton Beach PMSA, FL	Y	27710 FQ	34100 MW	41090 TQ	USBLS	5/07
	Georgia	Y	27200 FQ	31860 MW	41140 TQ	USBLS	5/07
	Atlanta-Sandy Springs-Marietta MSA, GA	Y	28420 FQ	32900 MW	49830 TQ	USBLS	5/07
	Hawaii	Y	26910 FQ	34210 MW	39850 TQ	USBLS	5/07
	Idaho	Y	27760 FQ	31870 MW	42610 TQ	USBLS	5/07
	Illinois	Y	29760 FQ	34640 MW	38760 TQ	USBLS	5/07
	Chicago-Naperville-Joliet MSA, IL-IN-WI	Y	30120 FQ	34970 MW	39880 TQ	USBLS	5/07
	Indiana	Y	25670 FQ	30940 MW	36750 TQ	USBLS	5/07
	Gary PMSA, IN	Y	26640 FQ	28820 MW	30980 TQ	USBLS	5/07
	Indianapolis-Carmel MSA, IN	Y	28630 FQ	32660 MW	40940 TQ	USBLS	5/07
	Iowa	Y	24370 FQ	28370 MW	32200 TQ	USBLS	5/07
	Kansas	Y	26850 FQ	28900 MW	31160 TQ	USBLS	5/07
	Kentucky	Y	19812 FQ	23677 MW	32583 TQ	KYBLS	2008
	Louisville-Jefferson County MSA, KY-IN	Y	22470 FQ	31090 MW	37620 TQ	USBLS	5/07
	Louisiana	H	13.86 FQ	17.97 MW	21.59 TQ	LABLS	1/08-3/08
	Maine	Y	28140 FQ	34980 MW	42120 TQ	USBLS	5/07

AE	Average entry wage	**AW**	Average wage paid	**FQ**	First quartile wage	**LO** Lowest wage paid	**MTC** Median total compensation	**TCC** Total cash compensation
AER	Average entry range	**AWR**	Average wage range	**H**	Hourly	**LR** Low end range	**MW** Median wage paid	**TQ** Third quartile wage
AEX	Average experienced wage	**AXR**	Average experienced range	**HI**	Highest wage paid	**M** Monthly	**MWR** Median wage range	**W** Weekly
ATC	Average total compensation	**D**	Daily	**HR**	High end range	**MCC** Median cash compensation	**S** See annotated source	**Y** Yearly

Motorboat Mechanic

Occupation/Type/Industry	Location	Per	Low	Mid	High	Source	Date
Motorboat Mechanic	Portland-South Portland-Biddeford MSA, ME	Y	29200 FQ	33930 MW	38180 TQ	USBLS	5/07
	Maryland	Y		42750 MW		MDBLS	3/08
	Baltimore-Towson MSA, MD	Y	33140 FQ	45440 MW	55210 TQ	USBLS	5/07
	Massachusetts	Y	34750 FQ	42400 MW	49110 TQ	USBLS	5/07
	Boston-Cambridge-Quincy NECTA, MA	Y	36930 FQ	43840 MW	51180 TQ	USBLS	5/07
	New Bedford MSA, MA	Y	35820 FQ	43130 MW	48260 TQ	USBLS	5/07
	Worcester MSA, MA-CT	Y	30360 FQ	34980 MW	40410 TQ	USBLS	5/07
	Michigan	Y	27830 FQ	33170 MW	37280 TQ	USBLS	5/07
	Detroit-Warren-Livonia MSA, MI	Y	30780 FQ	36220 MW	42640 TQ	USBLS	5/07
	Warren-Troy-Farmington Hills PMSA, MI	Y	31950 FQ	37470 MW	43130 TQ	USBLS	5/07
	Minnesota	Y	29422 FQ	35475 MW	40080 TQ	MNBLS	10/08-12/08
	Duluth-Superior MSA, MN-WI	Y	27660 FQ	32003 MW	35517 TQ	MNBLS	10/08-12/08
	Minneapolis-Saint Paul MSA, MN-WI	Y	28793 FQ	33241 MW	38653 TQ	MNBLS	10/08-12/08
	Mississippi	Y	22130 FQ	26710 MW	32680 TQ	USBLS	5/07
	Missouri	Y	25110 FQ	30840 MW	39380 TQ	USBLS	5/07
	St. Louis MSA, MO-IL	Y	29970 FQ	36010 MW	41750 TQ	USBLS	5/07
	Montana	Y	14850 FQ	18910 MW	30870 TQ	USBLS	5/07
	Nebraska	Y	30500 FQ	36110 MW	41120 TQ	USBLS	5/07
	Nevada	H	16.54 FQ	22.99 MW	27.60 TQ	NVBLS	5/08
	Las Vegas-Paradise MSA, NV	H	15.93 FQ	21.31 MW	26.75 TQ	NVBLS	5/08
	New Hampshire	H	15.75 AE	21.41 MW	23.47 AEX	NHBLS	6/08
	New Jersey	Y	31270 FQ	39080 MW	49000 TQ	USBLS	5/07
	Camden PMSA, NJ	Y	34190 FQ	39050 MW	46570 TQ	USBLS	5/07
	Edison PMSA, NJ	Y	31520 FQ	40670 MW	50790 TQ	USBLS	5/07
	Newark-Union PMSA, NJ-PA	Y	29670 FQ	41270 MW	51230 TQ	USBLS	5/07
	New York	Y	26440 FQ	32940 MW	43610 TQ	USBLS	5/07
	Albany-Schenectady-Troy MSA, NY	Y	22780 FQ	25880 MW	31070 TQ	USBLS	5/07
	Buffalo-Niagara Falls MSA, NY	Y	21110 FQ	28270 MW	35450 TQ	USBLS	5/07
	Nassau-Suffolk PMSA, NY	Y	40590 FQ	47810 MW	54660 TQ	USBLS	5/07
	New York-Northern New Jersey-Long Island MSA, NY-NJ-PA	Y	36380 FQ	45260 MW	53350 TQ	USBLS	5/07
	North Carolina	Y	25850 FQ	32040 MW	38990 TQ	USBLS	5/07
	Ohio	Y	22550 FQ	27480 MW	33690 TQ	USBLS	5/07
	Cincinnati-Middletown MSA, OH-KY-IN	Y	21030 FQ	25370 MW	34020 TQ	USBLS	5/07
	Columbus MSA, OH	Y	29230 FQ	34460 MW	39160 TQ	USBLS	5/07
	Oklahoma	Y	20490 FQ	26210 MW	34090 TQ	USBLS	5/07
	Tulsa MSA, OK	Y	18070 FQ	23740 MW	33510 TQ	USBLS	5/07
	Oregon	H	13.60 FQ	17.45 MW	22.13 TQ	ORBLS	5/08
	Portland-Vancouver-Beaverton MSA, OR-WA	Y	33860 FQ	39190 MW	46590 TQ	USBLS	5/07
	Pennsylvania	Y	23850 FQ	29800 MW	35650 TQ	USBLS	5/07
	Philadelphia-Camden-Wilmington MSA, PA-NJ-DE-MD	Y	32630 FQ	37620 MW	44500 TQ	USBLS	5/07
	Pittsburgh MSA, PA	Y	22920 FQ	29550 MW	35210 TQ	USBLS	5/07
	Rhode Island	Y	30450 FQ	37610 MW	45250 TQ	USBLS	5/07
	Providence-Fall River-Warwick MSA, RI-MA	Y	31750 FQ	38900 MW	45090 TQ	USBLS	5/07
	South Carolina	Y	26890 FQ	31550 MW	36990 TQ	USBLS	5/07
	Charleston-North Charleston MSA, SC	Y	27280 FQ	32450 MW	41470 TQ	USBLS	5/07
	Columbia MSA, SC	Y	30820 FQ	35640 MW	40110 TQ	USBLS	5/07
	South Dakota	Y	23705 FQ	27752 MW	31132 TQ	SDBLS	7/08-9/08
	Tennessee	Y	25390 FQ	29130 MW	36370 TQ	USBLS	5/07
	Nashville-Davidson-Murfreesboro MSA, TN	Y	23950 FQ	30740 MW	45860 TQ	USBLS	5/07
	Texas	Y	21560 FQ	29100 MW	38260 TQ	USBLS	5/07
	Austin-Round Rock MSA, TX	Y	27180 FQ	34020 MW	47950 TQ	USBLS	5/07
	Dallas-Fort Worth-Arlington MSA, TX	Y	25930 FQ	29900 MW	35700 TQ	USBLS	5/07
	Houston-Sugar Land-Baytown MSA, TX	Y	15390 FQ	24810 MW	37530 TQ	USBLS	5/07
	San Antonio MSA, TX	Y	13570 FQ	20920 MW	26690 TQ	USBLS	5/07

AE	Average entry wage	AW	Average wage paid	FQ	First quartile wage
AER	Average entry range	AWR	Average wage range	H	Hourly
AEX	Average experienced wage	AXR	Average experienced range	HI	Highest wage paid
ATC	Average total compensation	D	Daily	HR	High end range

LO	Lowest wage paid	MTC	Median total compensation	TCC	Total cash compensation
LR	Low end range	MW	Median wage paid	TQ	Third quartile wage
M	Monthly	MWR	Median wage range	W	Weekly
MCC	Median cash compensation	S	See annotated source	Y	Yearly

Occupation/Type/Industry	Location	Per	Low	Mid	High	Source	Date
Motorboat Mechanic	Utah	Y	22240 FQ	32370 MW	38860 TQ	USBLS	5/07
	Vermont	Y	27580 FQ	32760 MW	36430 TQ	USBLS	5/07
	Burlington-South Burlington MSA, VT	Y	24880 FQ	31310 MW	36590 TQ	USBLS	5/07
	Virginia	Y	30320 FQ	37180 MW	49410 TQ	USBLS	5/07
	Richmond MSA, VA	Y	31080 FQ	46240 MW	54670 TQ	USBLS	5/07
	Virginia Beach-Norfolk-Newport News MSA, VA-NC	Y	32890 FQ	36880 MW	41610 TQ	USBLS	5/07
	Washington	H	15.22 FQ	18.85 MW	22.63 TQ	WABLS	3/08
	Seattle-Tacoma-Bellevue MSA, WA	Y	34290 FQ	42340 MW	48480 TQ	USBLS	5/07
	West Virginia	Y	27032 FQ	33262 MW	47015 TQ	WVBLS	7/08-9/08
	Wisconsin	Y	23620 FQ	29520 MW	36130 TQ	USBLS	5/07
	Virgin Islands	Y	28580 FQ	32490 MW	38030 TQ	USBLS	5/07
Motorboat Operator	California	H	11.81 FQ	21.59 MW	24.55 TQ	CABLS	1/08-3/08
	Connecticut	H	12.33 AE	18.13 MW		CTBLS	1/08-3/08
	Florida	Y	21150 FQ	27990 MW	37020 TQ	USBLS	5/07
	Hawaii	Y	21320 FQ	26710 MW	36000 TQ	USBLS	5/07
	Illinois	Y	24510 FQ	30870 MW	44670 TQ	USBLS	5/07
	Louisiana	H	14.53 FQ	20.96 MW	24.34 TQ	LABLS	1/08-3/08
	Maine	Y	33130 FQ	40600 MW	46880 TQ	USBLS	5/07
	Maryland	Y		53975 MW		MDBLS	3/08
	Michigan	Y	15640 FQ	32430 MW	39550 TQ	USBLS	5/07
	New Jersey	Y	26820 FQ	32260 MW	54740 TQ	USBLS	5/07
	New York	Y	26660 FQ	29750 MW	32780 TQ	USBLS	5/07
	Ohio	Y	36890 FQ	41770 MW	46340 TQ	USBLS	5/07
	Oregon	H	17.64 FQ	19.44 MW	22.32 TQ	ORBLS	5/08
	Rhode Island	Y	25400 FQ	29770 MW	40030 TQ	USBLS	5/07
	Texas	Y	14720 FQ	19700 MW	36590 TQ	USBLS	5/07
	Washington	H	20.65 FQ	26.16 MW	29.50 TQ	WABLS	3/08
	Wisconsin	Y	24410 FQ	28490 MW	33880 TQ	USBLS	5/07
Motorcycle Mechanic	Alabama	Y	21930 FQ	27430 MW	34150 TQ	USBLS	5/07
	Birmingham-Hoover MSA, AL	Y	23360 FQ	27110 MW	32930 TQ	USBLS	5/07
	Arizona	Y	22640 FQ	28830 MW	36880 TQ	USBLS	5/07
	Phoenix-Mesa-Scottsdale MSA, AZ	Y	22510 FQ	28600 MW	34720 TQ	USBLS	5/07
	Tucson MSA, AZ	Y	23110 FQ	30550 MW	41200 TQ	USBLS	5/07
	Arkansas	Y	22540 FQ	26790 MW	31030 TQ	USBLS	5/07
	California	H	14.35 FQ	19.29 MW	24.53 TQ	CABLS	1/08-3/08
	Los Angeles-Long Beach-Glendale PMSA, CA	H	12.28 FQ	15.57 MW	21.37 TQ	CABLS	1/08-3/08
	Oakland-Fremont-Hayward MSA, CA	H	16.20 FQ	19.78 MW	25.85 TQ	CABLS	1/08-3/08
	Riverside-San Bernardino-Ontario MSA, CA	H	15.95 FQ	24.25 MW	29.66 TQ	CABLS	1/08-3/08
	Sacramento-Arden Arcade-Roseville MSA, CA	H	16.62 FQ	19.91 MW	23.20 TQ	CABLS	1/08-3/08
	San Diego-Carlsbad-San Marcos MSA, CA	H	19.42 FQ	22.84 MW	27.19 TQ	CABLS	1/08-3/08
	San Jose-Sunnyvale-Santa Clara MSA, CA	H	14.34 FQ	21.32 MW	26.65 TQ	CABLS	1/08-3/08
	Santa Ana-Anaheim-Irvine PMSA, CA	Y	30190 FQ	39650 MW	50030 TQ	USBLS	5/07
	Colorado	Y	27780 FQ	34750 MW	43070 TQ	USBLS	5/07
	Denver-Aurora MSA, CO	Y	32570 FQ	37330 MW	44510 TQ	USBLS	5/07
	Connecticut	H	12.45 AE	16.29 MW		CTBLS	1/08-3/08
	Bridgeport-Stamford-Norwalk MSA, CT	Y	33180 FQ	37370 MW	54330 TQ	USBLS	5/07
	Hartford-West Hartford-East Hartford MSA, CT	Y	24350 FQ	29340 MW	35180 TQ	USBLS	5/07
	Delaware	Y	24850 FQ	31240 MW	38790 TQ	USBLS	5/07
	Washington-Arlington-Alexandria MSA, DC-VA-MD-WV	Y	28580 FQ	35690 MW	45590 TQ	USBLS	5/07
	Florida	Y	27030 FQ	33540 MW	39420 TQ	USBLS	5/07
	Fort Lauderdale-Pompano Beach-Deerfield Beach PMSA, FL	Y	34420 FQ	42380 MW	46940 TQ	USBLS	5/07
	Jacksonville MSA, FL	Y	26580 FQ	34610 MW	39170 TQ	USBLS	5/07
	Lakeland MSA, FL	Y	24040 FQ	28410 MW	35420 TQ	USBLS	5/07

AE	Average entry wage	AW	Average wage paid	FQ First quartile wage
AER	Average entry range	AWR	Average wage range	H Hourly
AEX	Average experienced wage	AXR	Average experienced range	HI Highest wage paid
ATC	Average total compensation	D	Daily	HR High end range

LO Lowest wage paid — MTC Median total compensation — TCC Total cash compensation
LR Low end range — MW Median wage paid — TQ Third quartile wage
M Monthly — MWR Median wage range — W Weekly
MCC Median cash compensation — S See annotated source — Y Yearly

Motorcycle Mechanic

Occupation/Type/Industry	Location	Per	Low	Mid	High	Source	Date
Motorcycle Mechanic	Miami-Fort Lauderdale-Miami Beach MSA, FL	Y	30450 FQ	36550 MW	44520 TQ	USBLS	5/07
	Orlando-Kissimmee MSA, FL	Y	32750 FQ	35600 MW	38640 TQ	USBLS	5/07
	Tampa-St. Petersburg-Clearwater MSA, FL	Y	26040 FQ	31120 MW	52580 TQ	USBLS	5/07
	Georgia	Y	25110 FQ	30870 MW	41090 TQ	USBLS	5/07
	Atlanta-Sandy Springs-Marietta MSA, GA	Y	26380 FQ	33480 MW	46160 TQ	USBLS	5/07
	Hawaii	Y	27580 FQ	32370 MW	41650 TQ	USBLS	5/07
	Idaho	Y	21730 FQ	24300 MW	30020 TQ	USBLS	5/07
	Illinois	Y	25170 FQ	29980 MW	37780 TQ	USBLS	5/07
	Chicago-Naperville-Joliet MSA, IL-IN-WI	Y	23150 FQ	31230 MW	41090 TQ	USBLS	5/07
	Indiana	Y	23640 FQ	27680 MW	32200 TQ	USBLS	5/07
	Iowa	Y	21320 FQ	27160 MW	32930 TQ	USBLS	5/07
	Des Moines-West Des Moines MSA, IA	Y	24640 FQ	29100 MW	35280 TQ	USBLS	5/07
	Kansas	Y	26810 FQ	29960 MW	34760 TQ	USBLS	5/07
	Kentucky	Y	22446 FQ	28119 MW	35173 TQ	KYBLS	2008
	Louisville-Jefferson County MSA, KY-IN	Y	21440 FQ	26720 MW	34180 TQ	USBLS	5/07
		H	11.00 FQ	13.48 MW	16.52 TQ	LABLS	1/08-3/08
	Louisiana	Y	22350 FQ	24190 MW	26270 TQ	USBLS	5/07
	Baton Rouge MSA, LA	Y					
	New Orleans-Metairie-Kenner MSA, LA	Y	24150 FQ	29300 MW	36010 TQ	USBLS	5/07
	Maine	Y	25080 FQ	29340 MW	35850 TQ	USBLS	5/07
	Maryland	Y		34625 MW		MDBLS	3/08
	Bethesda-Gaithersburg-Frederick PMSA, MD	Y	25570 FQ	32080 MW	40410 TQ	USBLS	5/07
	Massachusetts	Y	25250 FQ	32080 MW	41770 TQ	USBLS	5/07
	Boston-Cambridge-Quincy NECTA, MA	Y	23320 FQ	27420 MW	32510 TQ	USBLS	5/07
	Springfield MSA, MA-CT	Y	24630 FQ	29180 MW	33950 TQ	USBLS	5/07
	Michigan	Y	24140 FQ	34620 MW	43670 TQ	USBLS	5/07
	Detroit-Warren-Livonia MSA, MI	Y	32270 FQ	41270 MW	47750 TQ	USBLS	5/07
	Warren-Troy-Farmington Hills PMSA, MI	Y	27670 FQ	40430 MW	47820 TQ	USBLS	5/07
	Minnesota	Y	20622 FQ	30440 MW	38810 TQ	MNBLS	10/08-12/08
	Duluth-Superior MSA, MN-WI	Y	33482 FQ	37741 MW	45125 TQ	MNBLS	10/08-12/08
	Minneapolis-Saint Paul MSA, MN-WI	Y	30283 FQ	36576 MW	49216 TQ	MNBLS	10/08-12/08
	Mississippi	Y	20920 FQ	26670 MW	30420 TQ	USBLS	5/07
	Missouri	Y	23140 FQ	30850 MW	38410 TQ	USBLS	5/07
	Kansas City MSA, MO-KS	Y	26830 FQ	32800 MW	38710 TQ	USBLS	5/07
	St. Louis MSA, MO-IL	Y	28020 FQ	33870 MW	41910 TQ	USBLS	5/07
	Montana	Y	20730 FQ	26010 MW	31750 TQ	USBLS	5/07
	Nebraska	Y	17910 FQ	20180 MW	25390 TQ	USBLS	5/07
	Omaha-Council Bluffs MSA, NE-IA	Y	17630 FQ	19580 MW	27620 TQ	USBLS	5/07
	Nevada	H	13.48 FQ	16.92 MW	22.94 TQ	NVBLS	5/08
	Las Vegas-Paradise MSA, NV	H	13.27 FQ	15.50 MW	22.72 TQ	NVBLS	5/08
	New Hampshire	H	13.23 AE	16.95 MW	19.55 AEX	NHBLS	6/08
	New Jersey	Y	24000 FQ	31610 MW	37540 TQ	USBLS	5/07
	Edison PMSA, NJ	Y	22710 FQ	31460 MW	37010 TQ	USBLS	5/07
	New Mexico	Y	23130 FQ	30290 MW	36070 TQ	USBLS	5/07
	New York	Y	22620 FQ	26970 MW	33510 TQ	USBLS	5/07
	Albany-Schenectady-Troy MSA, NY	Y	30480 FQ	33680 MW	36600 TQ	USBLS	5/07
	New York-Northern New Jersey-Long Island MSA, NY-NJ-PA	Y	23200 FQ	28710 MW	36500 TQ	USBLS	5/07
	North Carolina	Y	22940 FQ	29000 MW	37560 TQ	USBLS	5/07
	Charlotte-Gastonia-Concord MSA, NC-SC	Y	20980 FQ	28710 MW	37840 TQ	USBLS	5/07
	Raleigh-Cary MSA, NC	Y	28620 FQ	33370 MW	41720 TQ	USBLS	5/07
	North Dakota	Y	20410 FQ	26080 MW	34230 TQ	USBLS	5/07
	Ohio	Y	21540 FQ	26900 MW	31280 TQ	USBLS	5/07
	Cincinnati-Middletown MSA, OH-KY-IN	Y	26030 FQ	30640 MW	37460 TQ	USBLS	5/07
	Cleveland-Elyria-Mentor MSA, OH	Y	23470 FQ	27990 MW	32810 TQ	USBLS	5/07

AE	Average entry wage	**AW**	Average wage paid	**FQ**	First quartile wage
AER	Average entry range	**AWR**	Average wage range	**H**	Hourly
AEX	Average experienced wage	**AXR**	Average experienced range	**HI**	Highest wage paid
ATC	Average total compensation	**D**	Daily	**HR**	High end range

LO	Lowest wage paid	**MTC**	Median total compensation
LR	Low end range	**MW**	Median wage paid
M	Monthly	**MWR**	Median wage range
MCC	Median cash compensation	**S**	See annotated source

TCC	Total cash compensation
TQ	Third quartile wage
W	Weekly
Y	Yearly

Occupation/Type/Industry	Location	Per	Low	Mid	High	Source	Date
Motorcycle Mechanic	Columbus MSA, OH	Y	21540 FQ	27530 MW	32280 TQ	USBLS	5/07
	Oklahoma	Y	23330 FQ	31290 MW	45390 TQ	USBLS	5/07
	Oklahoma City MSA, OK	Y	28520 FQ	36390 MW	47380 TQ	USBLS	5/07
	Oregon	H	11.61 FQ	14.18 MW	17.18 TQ	ORBLS	5/08
	Portland-Vancouver-Beaverton MSA, OR-WA	Y	27090 FQ	31670 MW	44150 TQ	USBLS	5/07
	Pennsylvania	Y	20590 FQ	29920 MW	40890 TQ	USBLS	5/07
	Philadelphia-Camden-Wilmington MSA, PA-NJ-DE-MD	Y	33260 FQ	40260 MW	46550 TQ	USBLS	5/07
	Pittsburgh MSA, PA	Y	19710 FQ	27450 MW	36110 TQ	USBLS	5/07
	Rhode Island	Y	24300 FQ	27950 MW	33510 TQ	USBLS	5/07
	Providence-Fall River-Warwick MSA, RI-MA	Y	24770 FQ	28670 MW	35180 TQ	USBLS	5/07
	South Carolina	Y	22830 FQ	27630 MW	32990 TQ	USBLS	5/07
	Columbia MSA, SC	Y	26780 FQ	31030 MW	40240 TQ	USBLS	5/07
	South Dakota	Y	23965 FQ	28934 MW	35055 TQ	SDBLS	7/08-9/08
	Sioux Falls MSA, SD	Y	24077 FQ	27664 MW	30920 TQ	SDBLS	7/08-9/08
	Tennessee	Y	22810 FQ	30150 MW	36370 TQ	USBLS	5/07
	Memphis MSA, TN-MS-AR	Y	22510 FQ	30940 MW	36630 TQ	USBLS	5/07
	Nashville-Davidson-Murfreesboro MSA, TN	Y	27780 FQ	33960 MW	41500 TQ	USBLS	5/07
	Texas	Y	23000 FQ	30370 MW	37880 TQ	USBLS	5/07
	Austin-Round Rock MSA, TX	Y	26150 FQ	31040 MW	36580 TQ	USBLS	5/07
	Dallas-Fort Worth-Arlington MSA, TX	Y	26990 FQ	35330 MW	43730 TQ	USBLS	5/07
	Houston-Sugar Land-Baytown MSA, TX	Y	22310 FQ	26700 MW	36030 TQ	USBLS	5/07
	San Antonio MSA, TX	Y	28920 FQ	36870 MW	61440 TQ	USBLS	5/07
	Utah	Y	26140 FQ	29770 MW	35180 TQ	USBLS	5/07
	Vermont	Y	27590 FQ	32790 MW	37070 TQ	USBLS	5/07
	Virginia	Y	24820 FQ	31520 MW	38350 TQ	USBLS	5/07
	Richmond MSA, VA	Y	23950 FQ	33820 MW	43130 TQ	USBLS	5/07
	Virginia Beach-Norfolk-Newport News MSA, VA-NC	Y	23540 FQ	26650 MW	30610 TQ	USBLS	5/07
	Washington	H	14.56 FQ	17.56 MW	21.23 TQ	WABLS	3/08
	Seattle-Tacoma-Bellevue MSA, WA	Y	28820 FQ	34690 MW	40120 TQ	USBLS	5/07
	West Virginia	Y	17874 FQ	21968 MW	27515 TQ	WVBLS	7/08-9/08
	Charleston MSA, WV	Y	17060 FQ	19040 MW	32340 TQ	USBLS	5/07
	Wisconsin	Y	24390 FQ	29540 MW	38550 TQ	USBLS	5/07
	Milwaukee-Waukesha-West Allis MSA, WI	Y	24520 FQ	29830 MW	38770 TQ	USBLS	5/07
	Wyoming	Y	21985 FQ	28251 MW	36025 TQ	WYBLS	9/08
	Cheyenne MSA, WY	Y	17043 FQ	21986 MW	42111 TQ	WYBLS	9/08
Movie and Television Script Writer	Maryland	Y		60000 AW		WTGMD	2009
Mower Operator	United States	H	8.00 AE		10.40 AEX	LANDL	2007
Multi-Media Artist and Animator	Alabama	Y	38550 FQ	45080 MW	50400 TQ	USBLS	5/07
	Birmingham-Hoover MSA, AL	Y	42540 FQ	46470 MW	50730 TQ	USBLS	5/07
	Arizona	Y	30880 FQ	41670 MW	52520 TQ	USBLS	5/07
	Phoenix-Mesa-Scottsdale MSA, AZ	Y	33770 FQ	44640 MW	55500 TQ	USBLS	5/07
	Arkansas	Y	28900 FQ	47860 MW	64570 TQ	USBLS	5/07
	California	H	26.34 FQ	35.05 MW	47.20 TQ	CABLS	1/08-3/08
	Los Angeles-Long Beach-Glendale PMSA, CA	H	26.93 FQ	35.56 MW	48.24 TQ	CABLS	1/08-3/08
	Oakland-Fremont-Hayward MSA, CA	H	26.13 FQ	32.36 MW	41.65 TQ	CABLS	1/08-3/08
	Riverside-San Bernardino-Ontario MSA, CA	H	22.84 FQ	28.82 MW	33.77 TQ	CABLS	1/08-3/08
	Sacramento-Arden Arcade-Roseville MSA, CA	H	27.08 FQ	33.99 MW	45.95 TQ	CABLS	1/08-3/08
	San Diego-Carlsbad-San Marcos MSA, CA	H	14.81 FQ	23.30 MW	37.40 TQ	CABLS	1/08-3/08
	San Francisco-San Mateo-Redwood PMSA, CA	H	29.86 FQ	40.74 MW	49.87 TQ	CABLS	1/08-3/08
	San Jose-Sunnyvale-Santa Clara MSA, CA	H	33.23 FQ	44.55 MW	54.22 TQ	CABLS	1/08-3/08

AE Average entry wage	**AW** Average wage paid	**FQ** First quartile wage	**LO** Lowest wage paid	**MTC** Median total compensation	**TCC** Total cash compensation
AER Average entry range	**AWR** Average wage range	**H** Hourly	**LR** Low end range	**MW** Median wage paid	**TQ** Third quartile wage
AEX Average experienced wage	**AXR** Average experienced range	**HI** Highest wage paid	**M** Monthly	**MWR** Median wage range	**W** Weekly
ATC Average total compensation	**D** Daily	**HR** High end range	**MCC** Median cash compensation	**S** See annotated source	**Y** Yearly

Occupation/Type/Industry	Location	Per	Low	Mid	High	Source	Date
Multi-Media Artist and Animator	Santa Ana-Anaheim-Irvine PMSA, CA	Y	45800 FQ	61140 MW	77740 TQ	USBLS	5/07
	Colorado	Y	40160 FQ	46700 MW	57720 TQ	USBLS	5/07
	Denver-Aurora MSA, CO	Y	41840 FQ	47590 MW	59820 TQ	USBLS	5/07
	Connecticut	H	14.86 AE	22.66 MW		CTBLS	1/08-3/08
	Bridgeport-Stamford-Norwalk MSA, CT	Y	44870 FQ	60430 MW	72260 TQ	USBLS	5/07
	Delaware	Y	33530 FQ	38610 MW	45880 TQ	USBLS	5/07
	Wilmington PMSA, DE-MD-NJ	Y	33390 FQ	38220 MW	45550 TQ	USBLS	5/07
	District of Columbia	Y	54410 FQ	61580 MW	79440 TQ	USBLS	5/07
	Washington-Arlington-Alexandria MSA, DC-VA-MD-WV	Y	45410 FQ	57740 MW	71280 TQ	USBLS	5/07
	Florida	Y	36580 FQ	43320 MW	55960 TQ	USBLS	5/07
	Fort Lauderdale-Pompano Beach-Deerfield Beach PMSA, FL	Y	35590 FQ	39690 MW	46290 TQ	USBLS	5/07
	Miami-Fort Lauderdale-Miami Beach MSA, FL	Y	36160 FQ	41580 MW	52710 TQ	USBLS	5/07
	Orlando-Kissimmee MSA, FL	Y	37290 FQ	44220 MW	52710 TQ	USBLS	5/07
	Tampa-St. Petersburg-Clearwater MSA, FL	Y	37640 FQ	49710 MW	73420 TQ	USBLS	5/07
	West Palm Beach-Boca Raton-Boynton Beach PMSA, FL	Y	36050 FQ	42190 MW	52440 TQ	USBLS	5/07
	Georgia	Y	24400 FQ	42960 MW	62680 TQ	USBLS	5/07
	Atlanta-Sandy Springs-Marietta MSA, GA	Y	23950 FQ	45940 MW	63430 TQ	USBLS	5/07
	Illinois	Y	36670 FQ	44880 MW	61670 TQ	USBLS	5/07
	Chicago-Naperville-Joliet MSA, IL-IN-WI	Y	37430 FQ	46720 MW	64050 TQ	USBLS	5/07
	Indiana	Y	43480 FQ	53110 MW	58990 TQ	USBLS	5/07
	Indianapolis-Carmel MSA, IN	Y	50610 FQ	55780 MW	60200 TQ	USBLS	5/07
	Iowa	Y	23880 FQ	31440 MW	51220 TQ	USBLS	5/07
	Kansas	Y	27660 FQ	31090 MW	41140 TQ	USBLS	5/07
	Kentucky	Y	39996 FQ	48753 MW	59371 TQ	KYBLS	2008
	Louisville-Jefferson County MSA, KY-IN	Y	43280 FQ	47890 MW	53180 TQ	USBLS	5/07
	Louisiana	H	12.90 FQ	14.59 MW	17.72 TQ	LABLS	1/08-3/08
	Baton Rouge MSA, LA	Y	26220 FQ	29360 MW	35090 TQ	USBLS	5/07
	Maine	Y	37160 FQ	44630 MW	51060 TQ	USBLS	5/07
	Portland-South Portland-Biddeford MSA, ME	Y	35630 FQ	43740 MW	49740 TQ	USBLS	5/07
	Maryland	Y		51100 MW		MDBLS	3/08
	Baltimore-Towson MSA, MD	Y	36330 FQ	40740 MW	54370 TQ	USBLS	5/07
	Bethesda-Gaithersburg-Frederick PMSA, MD	Y	46310 FQ	69110 MW	84980 TQ	USBLS	5/07
	Massachusetts	Y	40600 FQ	49210 MW	62630 TQ	USBLS	5/07
	Boston-Cambridge-Quincy NECTA, MA	Y	42290 FQ	50930 MW	64490 TQ	USBLS	5/07
	Worcester MSA, MA-CT	Y	36090 FQ	47690 MW	60610 TQ	USBLS	5/07
	Michigan	Y	33530 FQ	39860 MW	53900 TQ	USBLS	5/07
	Detroit-Warren-Livonia MSA, MI	Y	33370 FQ	38680 MW	50570 TQ	USBLS	5/07
	Warren-Troy-Farmington Hills PMSA, MI	Y	32910 FQ	37680 MW	46350 TQ	USBLS	5/07
	Minnesota	Y	36460 FQ	46462 MW	60471 TQ	MNBLS	10/08-12/08
	Duluth-Superior MSA, MN-WI	Y	27557 FQ	35561 MW	40865 TQ	MNBLS	10/08-12/08
	Minneapolis-Saint Paul MSA, MN-WI	Y	37224 FQ	48304 MW	63704 TQ	MNBLS	10/08-12/08
	Rochester MSA, MN	Y	39301 FQ	44973 MW	50987 TQ	MNBLS	10/08-12/08
	Mississippi	Y	28340 FQ	41590 MW	49990 TQ	USBLS	5/07
	Missouri	Y	37520 FQ	47660 MW	64570 TQ	USBLS	5/07
	Kansas City MSA, MO-KS	Y	36840 FQ	47420 MW	64450 TQ	USBLS	5/07
	St. Louis MSA, MO-IL	Y	40180 FQ	47180 MW	65440 TQ	USBLS	5/07
	Montana	Y	28690 FQ	34980 MW	44630 TQ	USBLS	5/07
	Nebraska	Y	34040 FQ	38790 MW	45430 TQ	USBLS	5/07
	Omaha-Council Bluffs MSA, NE-IA	Y	33790 FQ	38750 MW	44760 TQ	USBLS	5/07
	Nevada	H	20.51 FQ	24.80 MW	29.77 TQ	NVBLS	5/08
	Las Vegas-Paradise MSA, NV	H	20.02 FQ	24.59 MW	29.11 TQ	NVBLS	5/08
	New Jersey	Y	35140 FQ	50260 MW	64130 TQ	USBLS	5/07

AE	Average entry wage	**AW**	Average wage paid	**FQ**	First quartile wage	**LO**	Lowest wage paid	**MTC** Median total compensation	**TCC** Total cash compensation
AER	Average entry range	**AWR**	Average wage range	**H**	Hourly	**LR**	Low end range	**MW** Median wage paid	**TQ** Third quartile wage
AEX	Average experienced wage	**AXR**	Average experienced range	**HI**	Highest wage paid	**M**	Monthly	**MWR** Median wage range	**W** Weekly
ATC	Average total compensation	**D**	Daily	**HR**	High end range	**MCC**	Median cash compensation	**S** See annotated source	**Y** Yearly

Occupation/Type/Industry	Location	Per	Low	Mid	High	Source	Date
Multi-Media Artist and Animator	Edison PMSA, NJ	Y	33870 FQ	43440 MW	57650 TQ	USBLS	5/07
	Newark-Union PMSA, NJ-PA	Y	38020 FQ	54170 MW	63550 TQ	USBLS	5/07
	New Mexico	Y	43620 FQ	49280 MW	56990 TQ	USBLS	5/07
	Albuquerque MSA, NM	Y	43730 FQ	49130 MW	56380 TQ	USBLS	5/07
	New York	Y	43850 FQ	57070 MW	72840 TQ	USBLS	5/07
	Albany-Schenectady-Troy MSA, NY	Y	39570 FQ	49030 MW	60560 TQ	USBLS	5/07
	Buffalo-Niagara Falls MSA, NY	Y	41380 FQ	47530 MW	56270 TQ	USBLS	5/07
	Nassau-Suffolk PMSA, NY	Y	40350 FQ	57320 MW	82490 TQ	USBLS	5/07
	New York-Northern New Jersey-Long Island MSA, NY-NJ-PA	Y	44400 FQ	57980 MW	73790 TQ	USBLS	5/07
	North Carolina	Y	36050 FQ	46310 MW	65760 TQ	USBLS	5/07
	Charlotte-Gastonia-Concord MSA, NC-SC	Y	35340 FQ	44530 MW	51340 TQ	USBLS	5/07
	Raleigh-Cary MSA, NC	Y	35150 FQ	47840 MW	74540 TQ	USBLS	5/07
	Ohio	Y	36540 FQ	44930 MW	51750 TQ	USBLS	5/07
	Cincinnati-Middletown MSA, OH-KY-IN	Y	39040 FQ	46380 MW	56820 TQ	USBLS	5/07
	Cleveland-Elyria-Mentor MSA, OH	Y	43400 FQ	48750 MW	53590 TQ	USBLS	5/07
	Columbus MSA, OH	Y	31810 FQ	40280 MW	52300 TQ	USBLS	5/07
	Dayton MSA, OH	Y	35080 FQ	39940 MW	45710 TQ	USBLS	5/07
	Oklahoma	Y	28860 FQ	38260 MW	50120 TQ	USBLS	5/07
	Oregon	H	19.54 FQ	25.25 MW	34.08 TQ	ORBLS	5/08
	Portland-Vancouver-Beaverton MSA, OR-WA	Y	42550 FQ	53130 MW	72180 TQ	USBLS	5/07
	Pennsylvania	Y	36880 FQ	50800 MW	62600 TQ	USBLS	5/07
	Philadelphia-Camden-Wilmington MSA, PA-NJ-DE-MD	Y	36330 FQ	48520 MW	61110 TQ	USBLS	5/07
	Pittsburgh MSA, PA	Y	30640 FQ	43970 MW	60890 TQ	USBLS	5/07
	Rhode Island	Y	39070 FQ	44020 MW	49250 TQ	USBLS	5/07
	Providence-Fall River-Warwick MSA, RI-MA	Y	39270 FQ	43990 MW	48620 TQ	USBLS	5/07
	South Carolina	Y	31090 FQ	43430 MW	56150 TQ	USBLS	5/07
	Columbia MSA, SC	Y	23480 FQ	27270 MW	45250 TQ	USBLS	5/07
	South Dakota	Y	28952 FQ	32778 MW	41063 TQ	SDBLS	7/08-9/08
	Sioux Falls MSA, SD	Y	31015 FQ	37251 MW	49910 TQ	SDBLS	7/08-9/08
	Tennessee	Y	33900 FQ	43760 MW	58810 TQ	USBLS	5/07
	Memphis MSA, TN-MS-AR	Y	33150 FQ	54160 MW	64120 TQ	USBLS	5/07
	Nashville-Davidson-Murfreesboro MSA, TN	Y	35930 FQ	43030 MW	53680 TQ	USBLS	5/07
	Texas	Y	31190 FQ	47680 MW	69410 TQ	USBLS	5/07
	Austin-Round Rock MSA, TX	Y	53290 FQ	74100 MW	90790 TQ	USBLS	5/07
	Dallas-Fort Worth-Arlington MSA, TX	Y	26160 FQ	41550 MW	63280 TQ	USBLS	5/07
	Houston-Sugar Land-Baytown MSA, TX	Y	42720 FQ	51340 MW	64270 TQ	USBLS	5/07
	San Antonio MSA, TX	Y	29730 FQ	42720 MW	52770 TQ	USBLS	5/07
	Utah	Y	32870 FQ	52290 MW	65330 TQ	USBLS	5/07
	Salt Lake City MSA, UT	Y	44480 FQ	56850 MW	69870 TQ	USBLS	5/07
	Vermont	Y	40500 FQ	48410 MW	60100 TQ	USBLS	5/07
	Virginia	Y	40990 FQ	53990 MW	64140 TQ	USBLS	5/07
	Richmond MSA, VA	Y	25700 FQ	29920 MW	46200 TQ	USBLS	5/07
	Virginia Beach-Norfolk-Newport News MSA, VA-NC	Y	37670 FQ	50410 MW	59240 TQ	USBLS	5/07
	Washington	H	20.30 FQ	26.39 MW	36.02 TQ	WABLS	3/08
	Seattle-Tacoma-Bellevue MSA, WA	Y	43110 FQ	55460 MW	75530 TQ	USBLS	5/07
	West Virginia	Y	33320 FQ	44434 MW	55059 TQ	WVBLS	7/08-9/08
	Wisconsin	Y	39710 FQ	46320 MW	51920 TQ	USBLS	5/07
	Green Bay MSA, WI	Y	40570 FQ	46660 MW	54900 TQ	USBLS	5/07
	Milwaukee-Waukesha-West Allis MSA, WI	Y	43470 FQ	47600 MW	51810 TQ	USBLS	5/07
Multimedia Specialist State Supreme Court	Michigan	Y			55144 HI	LSJ02	7/11/07

AE Average entry wage	**AW** Average wage paid	**FQ** First quartile wage	**LO** Lowest wage paid	**MTC** Median total compensation	**TCC** Total cash compensation
AER Average entry range	**AWR** Average wage range	**H** Hourly	**LR** Low end range	**MW** Median wage paid	**TQ** Third quartile wage
AEX Average experienced wage	**AXR** Average experienced range	**HI** Highest wage paid	**M** Monthly	**MWR** Median wage range	**W** Weekly
ATC Average total compensation	**D** Daily	**HR** High end range	**MCC** Median cash compensation	**S** See annotated source	**Y** Yearly

Multiple Machine Tool Setter, Operator, and Tender

Occupation/Type/Industry	Location	Per	Low	Mid	High	Source	Date
Multiple Machine Tool Setter, Operator, and Tender							
Metals and Plastics	Alabama	Y	21070 FQ	26850 MW	31820 TQ	USBLS	5/07
Metals and Plastics	Birmingham-Hoover MSA, AL	Y	23640 FQ	28550 MW	33140 TQ	USBLS	5/07
Metals and Plastics	Arizona	Y	21160 FQ	24370 MW	28530 TQ	USBLS	5/07
Metals and Plastics	Phoenix-Mesa-Scottsdale MSA, AZ	Y	21000 FQ	23920 MW	27920 TQ	USBLS	5/07
	Tucson MSA, AZ	Y	21820 FQ	25860 MW	30580 TQ	USBLS	5/07
Metals and Plastics	Arkansas	Y	25240 FQ	32390 MW	36770 TQ	USBLS	5/07
Metals and Plastics	California	H	11.10 FQ	13.86 MW	17.25 TQ	CABLS	1/08-3/08
Metals and Plastics	Fresno MSA, CA	H	11.50 FQ	16.13 MW	21.31 TQ	CABLS	1/08-3/08
Metals and Plastics	Los Angeles-Long Beach-Glendale PMSA, CA	H	11.23 FQ	13.70 MW	17.47 TQ	CABLS	1/08-3/08
Metals and Plastics	Oakland-Fremont-Hayward MSA, CA	H	13.56 FQ	18.52 MW	32.79 TQ	CABLS	1/08-3/08
Metals and Plastics	Riverside-San Bernardino-Ontario MSA, CA	H	10.22 FQ	12.76 MW	15.69 TQ	CABLS	1/08-3/08
Metals and Plastics	Sacramento-Arden Arcade-Roseville MSA, CA	H	11.13 FQ	15.03 MW	18.14 TQ	CABLS	1/08-3/08
Metals and Plastics	San Diego-Carlsbad-San Marcos MSA, CA	H	9.49 FQ	12.46 MW	15.94 TQ	CABLS	1/08-3/08
Metals and Plastics	San Francisco-San Mateo-Redwood PMSA, CA	H	11.02 FQ	13.10 MW	16.16 TQ	CABLS	1/08-3/08
Metals and Plastics	San Jose-Sunnyvale-Santa Clara MSA, CA	H	12.50 FQ	14.48 MW	17.11 TQ	CABLS	1/08-3/08
Metals and Plastics	Santa Ana-Anaheim-Irvine PMSA, CA	Y	22450 FQ	28410 MW	35850 TQ	USBLS	5/07
Metals and Plastics	Colorado	Y	22210 FQ	28540 MW	46360 TQ	USBLS	5/07
Metals and Plastics	Denver-Aurora MSA, CO	Y	25000 FQ	41710 MW	52620 TQ	USBLS	5/07
Metals and Plastics	Connecticut	H	13.65 AE	18.34 MW		CTBLS	1/08-3/08
Metals and Plastics	Bridgeport-Stamford-Norwalk MSA, CT	Y	29190 FQ	36160 MW	44890 TQ	USBLS	5/07
Metals and Plastics	Hartford-West Hartford-East Hartford MSA, CT	Y	34610 FQ	38980 MW	43930 TQ	USBLS	5/07
Metals and Plastics	Delaware	Y	19450 FQ	21980 MW	25750 TQ	USBLS	5/07
Metals and Plastics	Washington-Arlington-Alexandria MSA, DC-VA-MD-WV	Y	20810 FQ	24730 MW	34900 TQ	USBLS	5/07
Metals and Plastics	Florida	Y	20160 FQ	24750 MW	30580 TQ	USBLS	5/07
Metals and Plastics	Fort Lauderdale-Pompano Beach-Deerfield Beach PMSA, FL	Y	17900 FQ	23060 MW	32410 TQ	USBLS	5/07
Metals and Plastics	Jacksonville MSA, FL	Y	21640 FQ	29060 MW	36750 TQ	USBLS	5/07
Metals and Plastics	Miami-Fort Lauderdale-Miami Beach MSA, FL	Y	17710 FQ	22840 MW	31390 TQ	USBLS	5/07
Metals and Plastics	Orlando-Kissimmee MSA, FL	Y	18840 FQ	21520 MW	24910 TQ	USBLS	5/07
Metals and Plastics	Tampa-St. Petersburg-Clearwater MSA, FL	Y	21040 FQ	25370 MW	29860 TQ	USBLS	5/07
Metals and Plastics	Georgia	Y	23370 FQ	28340 MW	32480 TQ	USBLS	5/07
Metals and Plastics	Atlanta-Sandy Springs-Marietta MSA, GA	Y	22770 FQ	27530 MW	31690 TQ	USBLS	5/07
Metals and Plastics	Idaho	Y	26160 FQ	32860 MW	44850 TQ	USBLS	5/07
Metals and Plastics	Illinois	Y	23530 FQ	29340 MW	38130 TQ	USBLS	5/07
Metals and Plastics	Chicago-Naperville-Joliet MSA, IL-IN-WI	Y	23130 FQ	29700 MW	39560 TQ	USBLS	5/07
Metals and Plastics	Indiana	Y	25690 FQ	33150 MW	41190 TQ	USBLS	5/07
Metals and Plastics	Elkhart-Goshen MSA, IN	Y	25760 FQ	31570 MW	36310 TQ	USBLS	5/07
Metals and Plastics	Gary PMSA, IN	Y	21060 FQ	26280 MW	30360 TQ	USBLS	5/07
Metals and Plastics	Indianapolis-Carmel MSA, IN	Y	33690 FQ	37670 MW	44080 TQ	USBLS	5/07
Metals and Plastics	Iowa	Y	24570 FQ	29270 MW	35080 TQ	USBLS	5/07
Metals and Plastics	Des Moines-West Des Moines MSA, IA	Y	24940 FQ	29440 MW	35040 TQ	USBLS	5/07
Metals and Plastics	Kansas	Y	22620 FQ	27130 MW	32030 TQ	USBLS	5/07
Metals and Plastics	Wichita MSA, KS	Y	25640 FQ	29390 MW	36600 TQ	USBLS	5/07
Metals and Plastics	Kentucky	Y	21448 FQ	26344 MW	34276 TQ	KYBLS	2008
Metals and Plastics	Louisville-Jefferson County MSA, KY-IN	Y	21280 FQ	26260 MW	32240 TQ	USBLS	5/07
Metals and Plastics	Louisiana	H	11.36 FQ	14.15 MW	18.13 TQ	LABLS	1/08-3/08
Metals and Plastics	New Orleans-Metairie-Kenner MSA, LA	Y	27130 FQ	30960 MW	40390 TQ	USBLS	5/07
Metals and Plastics	Maine	Y	22960 FQ	28300 MW	34720 TQ	USBLS	5/07
Metals and Plastics	Maryland	Y		29550 MW		MDBLS	3/08

AE	Average entry wage	AW	Average wage paid	FQ	First quartile wage	LO	Lowest wage paid	MTC	Median total compensation	TCC	Total cash compensation
AER	Average entry range	AWR	Average wage range	H	Hourly	LR	Low end range	MW	Median wage paid	TQ	Third quartile wage
AEX	Average experienced wage	AXR	Average experienced range	HI	Highest wage paid	M	Monthly	MWR	Median wage range	W	Weekly
ATC	Average total compensation	D	Daily	HR	High end range	MCC	Median cash compensation	S	See annotated source	Y	Yearly

Multiple Machine Tool Setter, Operator, and Tender

Occupation/Type/Industry	Location	Per	Low	Mid	High	Source	Date
Metals and Plastics	Baltimore-Towson MSA, MD	Y	26980 FQ	29250 MW	31390 TQ	USBLS	5/07
Metals and Plastics	Massachusetts	Y	26580 FQ	32030 MW	37750 TQ	USBLS	5/07
Metals and Plastics	Boston-Cambridge-Quincy NECTA, MA	Y	27670 FQ	33360 MW	40880 TQ	USBLS	5/07
Metals and Plastics	Worcester MSA, MA-CT	Y	32410 FQ	37000 MW	46410 TQ	USBLS	5/07
Metals and Plastics	Michigan	Y	25000 FQ	33210 MW	53440 TQ	USBLS	5/07
Metals and Plastics	Detroit-Warren-Livonia MSA, MI	Y	25560 FQ	37040 MW	57140 TQ	USBLS	5/07
Metals and Plastics	Grand Rapids-Wyoming MSA, MI	Y	25980 FQ	29660 MW	38230 TQ	USBLS	5/07
Metals and Plastics	Warren-Troy-Farmington Hills PMSA, MI	Y	29000 FQ	52400 MW	59260 TQ	USBLS	5/07
Metals and Plastics	Minnesota	Y	29255 FQ	37921 MW	44784 TQ	MNBLS	10/08-12/08
Metals and Plastics	Duluth-Superior MSA, MN-WI	Y	23211 FQ	25647 MW	38564 TQ	MNBLS	10/08-12/08
Metals and Plastics	Minneapolis-Saint Paul MSA, MN-WI	Y	34521 FQ	41187 MW	46101 TQ	MNBLS	10/08-12/08
Metals and Plastics	Mississippi	Y	21930 FQ	27510 MW	34920 TQ	USBLS	5/07
Metals and Plastics	Missouri	Y	23710 FQ	28350 MW	33680 TQ	USBLS	5/07
Metals and Plastics	Kansas City MSA, MO-KS	Y	19930 FQ	25360 MW	31080 TQ	USBLS	5/07
Metals and Plastics	St. Louis MSA, MO-IL	Y	26350 FQ	31130 MW	37140 TQ	USBLS	5/07
Metals and Plastics	Montana	Y	27550 FQ	32220 MW	38980 TQ	USBLS	5/07
Metals and Plastics	Nebraska	Y	25210 FQ	28860 MW	34540 TQ	USBLS	5/07
Metals and Plastics	Nevada	H	13.56 FQ	16.31 MW	19.07 TQ	NVBLS	5/08
Metals and Plastics	New Hampshire	H	14.08 AE	19.35 MW	21.42 AEX	NHBLS	6/08
Metals and Plastics	Manchester MSA, NH	Y	38420 FQ	41640 MW	44890 TQ	USBLS	5/07
Metals and Plastics	Nashua NECTA, NH-MA	Y	37600 FQ	53730 MW	60230 TQ	USBLS	5/07
Metals and Plastics	New Jersey	Y	21680 FQ	29530 MW	36640 TQ	USBLS	5/07
Metals and Plastics	Camden PMSA, NJ	Y	33710 FQ	36730 MW	40150 TQ	USBLS	5/07
Metals and Plastics	Edison PMSA, NJ	Y	23380 FQ	29730 MW	36160 TQ	USBLS	5/07
Metals and Plastics	Newark-Union PMSA, NJ-PA	Y	17750 FQ	21700 MW	29590 TQ	USBLS	5/07
Metals and Plastics	New Mexico	Y	50280 FQ	53590 MW	56910 TQ	USBLS	5/07
Metals and Plastics	New York	Y	21800 FQ	30090 MW	41350 TQ	USBLS	5/07
Metals and Plastics	Albany-Schenectady-Troy MSA, NY	Y	22910 FQ	26800 MW	31080 TQ	USBLS	5/07
Metals and Plastics	Binghamton MSA, NY	Y	15920 FQ	19180 MW	28120 TQ	USBLS	5/07
Metals and Plastics	Buffalo-Niagara Falls MSA, NY	Y	21980 FQ	37350 MW	46410 TQ	USBLS	5/07
Metals and Plastics	Nassau-Suffolk PMSA, NY	Y	20100 FQ	27780 MW	37260 TQ	USBLS	5/07
Metals and Plastics	New York-Northern New Jersey-Long Island MSA, NY-NJ-PA	Y	21920 FQ	30460 MW	40190 TQ	USBLS	5/07
Metals and Plastics	North Carolina	Y	26210 FQ	33250 MW	48130 TQ	USBLS	5/07
Metals and Plastics	Asheville MSA, NC	Y	31700 FQ	35330 MW	38900 TQ	USBLS	5/07
Metals and Plastics	Charlotte-Gastonia-Concord MSA, NC-SC	Y	25750 FQ	31370 MW	40520 TQ	USBLS	5/07
Metals and Plastics	Raleigh-Cary MSA, NC	Y	32930 FQ	36860 MW	41820 TQ	USBLS	5/07
Metals and Plastics	North Dakota	Y	21140 FQ	25530 MW	40600 TQ	USBLS	5/07
Metals and Plastics	Ohio	Y	26250 FQ	33870 MW	42260 TQ	USBLS	5/07
Metals and Plastics	Cincinnati-Middletown MSA, OH-KY-IN	Y	27110 FQ	40260 MW	56760 TQ	USBLS	5/07
Metals and Plastics	Cleveland-Elyria-Mentor MSA, OH	Y	23960 FQ	30870 MW	38930 TQ	USBLS	5/07
Metals and Plastics	Columbus MSA, OH	Y	26550 FQ	33280 MW	40000 TQ	USBLS	5/07
Metals and Plastics	Dayton MSA, OH	Y	22590 FQ	31920 MW	39790 TQ	USBLS	5/07
Metals and Plastics	Oklahoma	Y	24070 FQ	33740 MW	43880 TQ	USBLS	5/07
Metals and Plastics	Oklahoma City MSA, OK	Y	22200 FQ	31240 MW	36120 TQ	USBLS	5/07
Metals and Plastics	Tulsa MSA, OK	Y	27540 FQ	39290 MW	46790 TQ	USBLS	5/07
Metals and Plastics	Oregon	H	12.43 FQ	15.24 MW	19.50 TQ	ORBLS	5/08
Metals and Plastics	Portland-Vancouver-Beaverton MSA, OR-WA	Y	25620 FQ	32260 MW	40310 TQ	USBLS	5/07
Metals and Plastics	Pennsylvania	Y	25780 FQ	31040 MW	37580 TQ	USBLS	5/07
Metals and Plastics	Allentown-Bethlehem-Easton MSA, PA-NJ	Y	25790 FQ	29940 MW	36000 TQ	USBLS	5/07
Metals and Plastics	Lancaster MSA, PA	Y	28240 FQ	33840 MW	37820 TQ	USBLS	5/07
Metals and Plastics	Philadelphia-Camden-Wilmington MSA, PA-NJ-DE-MD	Y	26620 FQ	32590 MW	38530 TQ	USBLS	5/07
Metals and Plastics	Pittsburgh MSA, PA	Y	24220 FQ	30730 MW	36700 TQ	USBLS	5/07
Metals and Plastics	Rhode Island	Y	22550 FQ	28490 MW	34840 TQ	USBLS	5/07

AE	Average entry wage	AW	Average wage paid	FQ	First quartile wage
AER	Average entry range	AWR	Average wage range	H	Hourly
AEX	Average experienced wage	AXR	Average experienced range	HI	Highest wage paid
ATC	Average total compensation	D	Daily	HR	High end range

LO	Lowest wage paid	MTC	Median total compensation	TCC	Total cash compensation
LR	Low end range	MW	Median wage paid	TQ	Third quartile wage
M	Monthly	MWR	Median wage range	W	Weekly
MCC	Median cash compensation	S	See annotated source	Y	Yearly

Occupation/Type/Industry	Location	Per	Low	Mid	High	Source	Date
Multiple Machine Tool Setter, Operator, and Tender							
Metals and Plastics	Providence-Fall River-Warwick MSA, RI-MA	Y	22820 FQ	28380 MW	34410 TQ	USBLS	5/07
Metals and Plastics	South Carolina	Y	23010 FQ	29540 MW	35750 TQ	USBLS	5/07
Metals and Plastics	Charleston-North Charleston MSA, SC	Y	24220 FQ	28320 MW	31600 TQ	USBLS	5/07
Metals and Plastics	Columbia MSA, SC	Y	21360 FQ	29070 MW	37050 TQ	USBLS	5/07
Metals and Plastics	South Dakota	Y	22933 FQ	25499 MW	29539 TQ	SDBLS	7/08-9/08
Metals and Plastics	Sioux Falls MSA, SD	Y	24300 FQ	28314 MW	33234 TQ	SDBLS	7/08-9/08
Metals and Plastics	Tennessee	Y	23690 FQ	28390 MW	34820 TQ	USBLS	5/07
Metals and Plastics	Kingsport-Bristol-Bristol MSA, TN-VA	Y	22910 FQ	28060 MW	33360 TQ	USBLS	5/07
Metals and Plastics	Memphis MSA, TN-MS-AR	Y	20390 FQ	25410 MW	29840 TQ	USBLS	5/07
Metals and Plastics	Nashville-Davidson-Murfreesboro MSA, TN	Y	22950 FQ	26110 MW	31160 TQ	USBLS	5/07
Metals and Plastics	Texas	Y	20740 FQ	26200 MW	30820 TQ	USBLS	5/07
Metals and Plastics	Austin-Round Rock MSA, TX	Y	18140 FQ	23520 MW	30440 TQ	USBLS	5/07
Metals and Plastics	Dallas-Fort Worth-Arlington MSA, TX	Y	25170 FQ	28300 MW	35290 TQ	USBLS	5/07
Metals and Plastics	El Paso MSA, TX	Y	12900 FQ	14780 MW	19710 TQ	USBLS	5/07
Metals and Plastics	Houston-Sugar Land-Baytown MSA, TX	Y	21160 FQ	24870 MW	29100 TQ	USBLS	5/07
Metals and Plastics	San Antonio MSA, TX	Y	20820 FQ	23250 MW	29550 TQ	USBLS	5/07
Metals and Plastics	Utah	Y	19100 FQ	24160 MW	30880 TQ	USBLS	5/07
Metals and Plastics	Salt Lake City MSA, UT	Y	21550 FQ	25510 MW	31680 TQ	USBLS	5/07
Metals and Plastics	Burlington-South Burlington MSA, VT	Y	27910 FQ	31390 MW	38400 TQ	USBLS	5/07
Metals and Plastics	Virginia	Y	26740 FQ	32760 MW	36280 TQ	USBLS	5/07
Metals and Plastics	Virginia Beach-Norfolk-Newport News MSA, VA-NC	Y	27060 FQ	30750 MW	34400 TQ	USBLS	5/07
Metals and Plastics	Washington	H	13.04 FQ	17.21 MW	21.04 TQ	WABLS	3/08
Metals and Plastics	Seattle-Tacoma-Bellevue MSA, WA	Y	28080 FQ	37000 MW	44950 TQ	USBLS	5/07
Metals and Plastics	Spokane MSA, WA	Y	27220 FQ	34360 MW	40500 TQ	USBLS	5/07
Metals and Plastics	West Virginia	Y	21854 FQ	27915 MW	32052 TQ	WVBLS	7/08-9/08
Metals and Plastics	Wisconsin	Y	27480 FQ	34170 MW	39660 TQ	USBLS	5/07
Metals and Plastics	Milwaukee-Waukesha-West Allis MSA, WI	Y	25790 FQ	34580 MW	46200 TQ	USBLS	5/07
Metals and Plastics	Puerto Rico	Y	14070 FQ	17260 MW	20650 TQ	USBLS	5/07
Metals and Plastics	San Juan-Caguas-Guaynabo MSA, PR	Y	14810 FQ	19000 MW	21710 TQ	USBLS	5/07
Municipal Accounts Auditor							
Department of Revenue Administration	New Hampshire	Y		45841 AW		NHUL03	2008
Municipal Court Administrator	Colorado Springs, CO	M	7388 LO			COSPRS	1/1/09
Municipal Judge	Ashley, ND	M			180 HI	NDLC02	2008
	Bismarck, ND	M			5503 HI	NDLC01	2008
	Lincoln, ND	M			250 HI	NDLC01	2008
	Zap, ND	M			75 HI	NDLC02	2008
Municipal Secretary	Whately, MA	H			15.15 HI	FRCOG	2009
Museum Archivist	Colorado Springs, CO	M	4006 LO			COSPRS	1/1/09
Museum Cataloguer	United States	Y		66050 AW		SUSA02	2008
Museum Director							
Baltimore Museum of Art	Baltimore, MD	Y			238968 HI	BMAG	2009
Museum Exhibit Designer	Colorado Springs, CO	M	4006 LO			COSPRS	1/1/09
Museum Guard	Colorado Springs, CO	M	2243 LO			COSPRS	1/1/09
Museum Guard Supervisor	Colorado Springs, CO	M	2646 LO			COSPRS	1/1/09
Museum Store Associate							
State Government	Ohio	H	13.03 LO		14.36 HI	ODAS	2008
Museum Technician and Conservator	Alabama	Y	23270 FQ	30320 MW	38990 TQ	USBLS	5/07

AE	Average entry wage	**AW**	Average wage paid	**FQ**	First quartile wage	**LO** Lowest wage paid **MTC** Median total compensation **TCC** Total cash compensation
AER	Average entry range	**AWR**	Average wage range	**H**	Hourly	**LR** Low end range **MW** Median wage paid **TQ** Third quartile wage
AEX	Average experienced wage	**AXR**	Average experienced range	**HI**	Highest wage paid	**M** Monthly **MWR** Median wage range **W** Weekly
ATC	Average total compensation	**D**	Daily	**HR**	High end range	**MCC** Median cash compensation **S** See annotated source **Y** Yearly

Occupation/Type/Industry	Location	Per	Low	Mid	High	Source	Date
Museum Technician and Conservator							
	Arizona	Y	24190 FQ	32370 MW	38770 TQ	USBLS	5/07
	Phoenix-Mesa-Scottsdale MSA, AZ	Y	23470 FQ	30770 MW	38680 TQ	USBLS	5/07
	Tucson MSA, AZ	Y	24690 FQ	34160 MW	39420 TQ	USBLS	5/07
	Arkansas	Y	21150 FQ	25280 MW	32600 TQ	USBLS	5/07
	California	H	16.70 FQ	20.45 MW	25.82 TQ	CABLS	1/08-3/08
	Los Angeles-Long Beach-Glendale PMSA, CA	H	17.10 FQ	21.62 MW	26.60 TQ	CABLS	1/08-3/08
	Oakland-Fremont-Hayward MSA, CA	H	18.42 FQ	22.29 MW	28.27 TQ	CABLS	1/08-3/08
	Riverside-San Bernardino-Ontario MSA, CA	H	16.40 FQ	20.36 MW	23.35 TQ	CABLS	1/08-3/08
	San Diego-Carlsbad-San Marcos MSA, CA	H	13.72 FQ	16.45 MW	19.56 TQ	CABLS	1/08-3/08
	San Francisco-San Mateo-Redwood PMSA, CA	H	17.56 FQ	21.30 MW	26.52 TQ	CABLS	1/08-3/08
	San Jose-Sunnyvale-Santa Clara MSA, CA	H	15.73 FQ	17.66 MW	19.55 TQ	CABLS	1/08-3/08
	Santa Ana-Anaheim-Irvine PMSA, CA	Y	34260 FQ	40160 MW	49260 TQ	USBLS	5/07
	Colorado	Y	30740 FQ	37860 MW	48870 TQ	USBLS	5/07
	Connecticut	H	12.72 AE	20.42 MW		CTBLS	1/08-3/08
	Hartford-West Hartford-East Hartford MSA, CT	Y	25700 FQ	31430 MW	37580 TQ	USBLS	5/07
	Delaware	Y	26320 FQ	32710 MW	39430 TQ	USBLS	5/07
	Wilmington PMSA, DE-MD-NJ	Y	26320 FQ	32710 MW	39430 TQ	USBLS	5/07
	District of Columbia	Y	44200 FQ	56460 MW	70830 TQ	USBLS	5/07
	Washington-Arlington-Alexandria MSA, DC-VA-MD-WV	Y	38320 FQ	52160 MW	68910 TQ	USBLS	5/07
	Florida	Y	26380 FQ	33890 MW	43010 TQ	USBLS	5/07
	Fort Lauderdale-Pompano Beach-Deerfield Beach PMSA, FL	Y	14300 FQ	14730 MW	25400 TQ	USBLS	5/07
	Jacksonville MSA, FL	Y	39230 FQ	47510 MW	55690 TQ	USBLS	5/07
	Miami-Fort Lauderdale-Miami Beach MSA, FL	Y	26120 FQ	33450 MW	42030 TQ	USBLS	5/07
	Tampa-St. Petersburg-Clearwater MSA, FL	Y	19520 FQ	27970 MW	31730 TQ	USBLS	5/07
	West Palm Beach-Boca Raton-Boynton Beach PMSA, FL	Y	33590 FQ	39030 MW	51600 TQ	USBLS	5/07
	Georgia	Y	25810 FQ	32620 MW	43760 TQ	USBLS	5/07
	Atlanta-Sandy Springs-Marietta MSA, GA	Y	29120 FQ	35560 MW	46880 TQ	USBLS	5/07
	Illinois	Y	29210 FQ	37410 MW	47420 TQ	USBLS	5/07
	Chicago-Naperville-Joliet MSA, IL-IN-WI	Y	29460 FQ	37460 MW	47330 TQ	USBLS	5/07
	Indiana	Y	27470 FQ	33360 MW	38380 TQ	USBLS	5/07
	Indianapolis-Carmel MSA, IN	Y	26320 FQ	33120 MW	38310 TQ	USBLS	5/07
	Iowa	Y	28440 FQ	41920 MW	52750 TQ	USBLS	5/07
	Kansas	Y	25360 FQ	29480 MW	36290 TQ	USBLS	5/07
	Kentucky	Y	25350 FQ	30881 MW	40388 TQ	KYBLS	2008
	Louisiana	H	10.07 FQ	10.99 MW	11.92 TQ	LABLS	1/08-3/08
	New Orleans-Metairie-Kenner MSA, LA	Y	21020 FQ	22750 MW	24490 TQ	USBLS	5/07
	Maine	Y	26820 FQ	32070 MW	37040 TQ	USBLS	5/07
	Maryland	Y		45550 MW		MDBLS	3/08
	Baltimore-Towson MSA, MD	Y	30220 FQ	42820 MW	51790 TQ	USBLS	5/07
	Massachusetts	Y	33070 FQ	40670 MW	51090 TQ	USBLS	5/07
	Boston-Cambridge-Quincy NECTA, MA	Y	36660 FQ	43560 MW	53600 TQ	USBLS	5/07
	Worcester MSA, MA-CT	Y	27070 FQ	29990 MW	44060 TQ	USBLS	5/07
	Michigan	Y	22690 FQ	28410 MW	36880 TQ	USBLS	5/07
	Detroit-Warren-Livonia MSA, MI	Y	26150 FQ	31060 MW	40730 TQ	USBLS	5/07
	Minnesota	Y	27819 FQ	36157 MW	41022 TQ	MNBLS	10/08-12/08
	Minneapolis-Saint Paul MSA, MN-WI	Y	32066 FQ	37601 MW	41807 TQ	MNBLS	10/08-12/08
	Missouri	Y	25350 FQ	31170 MW	38490 TQ	USBLS	5/07
	Kansas City MSA, MO-KS	Y	27270 FQ	31150 MW	40790 TQ	USBLS	5/07

AE	Average entry wage	AW	Average wage paid	FQ	First quartile wage	LO	Lowest wage paid	MTC	Median total compensation	TCC	Total cash compensation
AER	Average entry range	AWR	Average wage range	H	Hourly	LR	Low end range	MW	Median wage paid	TQ	Third quartile wage
AEX	Average experienced wage	AXR	Average experienced range	HI	Highest wage paid	M	Monthly	MWR	Median wage range	W	Weekly
ATC	Average total compensation	D	Daily	HR	High end range	MCC	Median cash compensation	S	See annotated source	Y	Yearly

1088

Occupation/Type/Industry	Location	Per	Low	Mid	High	Source	Date
Museum Technician and Conservator	St. Louis MSA, MO-IL	Y	24920 FQ	30880 MW	37950 TQ	USBLS	5/07
	Montana	Y	14840 FQ	17700 MW	34130 TQ	USBLS	5/07
	Nebraska	Y	19820 FQ	24830 MW	36150 TQ	USBLS	5/07
	Omaha-Council Bluffs MSA, NE-IA	Y	19260 FQ	23010 MW	36000 TQ	USBLS	5/07
	Nevada	H	19.26 FQ	22.12 MW	24.33 TQ	NVBLS	5/08
	New Jersey	Y	18970 FQ	32740 MW	49750 TQ	USBLS	5/07
	Newark-Union PMSA, NJ-PA	Y	32950 FQ	41750 MW	56690 TQ	USBLS	5/07
	New Mexico	Y	26880 FQ	32100 MW	36760 TQ	USBLS	5/07
	Albuquerque MSA, NM	Y	29460 FQ	34700 MW	38050 TQ	USBLS	5/07
	New York	Y	33190 FQ	41530 MW	55800 TQ	USBLS	5/07
	Albany-Schenectady-Troy MSA, NY	Y	43210 FQ	48510 MW	61300 TQ	USBLS	5/07
	North Carolina	Y	29350 FQ	35120 MW	40580 TQ	USBLS	5/07
	Charlotte-Gastonia-Concord MSA, NC-SC	Y	28190 FQ	35100 MW	44730 TQ	USBLS	5/07
	Raleigh-Cary MSA, NC	Y	31740 FQ	37380 MW	45200 TQ	USBLS	5/07
	Ohio	Y	24700 FQ	30290 MW	36960 TQ	USBLS	5/07
	Cleveland-Elyria-Mentor MSA, OH	Y	28480 FQ	33820 MW	37740 TQ	USBLS	5/07
	Dayton MSA, OH	Y	23370 FQ	27460 MW	32410 TQ	USBLS	5/07
	Oklahoma	Y	25400 FQ	29100 MW	37440 TQ	USBLS	5/07
	Oregon	H	12.04 FQ	14.27 MW	17.43 TQ	ORBLS	5/08
	Portland-Vancouver-Beaverton MSA, OR-WA	Y	25310 FQ	29540 MW	36860 TQ	USBLS	5/07
	Pennsylvania	Y	28650 FQ	35460 MW	45920 TQ	USBLS	5/07
	Philadelphia-Camden-Wilmington MSA, PA-NJ-DE-MD	Y	28470 FQ	33820 MW	42650 TQ	USBLS	5/07
	Pittsburgh MSA, PA	Y	29090 FQ	39370 MW	52190 TQ	USBLS	5/07
	Rhode Island	Y	24800 FQ	33870 MW	43640 TQ	USBLS	5/07
	Providence-Fall River-Warwick MSA, RI-MA	Y	24800 FQ	33870 MW	43640 TQ	USBLS	5/07
	South Carolina	Y	25860 FQ	31340 MW	38940 TQ	USBLS	5/07
	South Dakota	Y	22272 FQ	25346 MW	31683 TQ	SDBLS	7/08-9/08
	Tennessee	Y	23470 FQ	27350 MW	34530 TQ	USBLS	5/07
	Texas	Y	24690 FQ	32490 MW	41140 TQ	USBLS	5/07
	Austin-Round Rock MSA, TX	Y	22690 FQ	24950 MW	36250 TQ	USBLS	5/07
	Dallas-Fort Worth-Arlington MSA, TX	Y	29680 FQ	35660 MW	39920 TQ	USBLS	5/07
	Houston-Sugar Land-Baytown MSA, TX	Y	24690 FQ	34100 MW	60440 TQ	USBLS	5/07
	San Antonio MSA, TX	Y	22150 FQ	28110 MW	35100 TQ	USBLS	5/07
	Utah	Y	23710 FQ	28510 MW	37070 TQ	USBLS	5/07
	Salt Lake City MSA, UT	Y	23580 FQ	27180 MW	32090 TQ	USBLS	5/07
	Vermont	Y	27270 FQ	32670 MW	49910 TQ	USBLS	5/07
	Virginia	Y	23740 FQ	30580 MW	42410 TQ	USBLS	5/07
	Richmond MSA, VA	Y	26870 FQ	29470 MW	32590 TQ	USBLS	5/07
	Virginia Beach-Norfolk-Newport News MSA, VA-NC	Y	27860 FQ	32470 MW	43610 TQ	USBLS	5/07
	Washington	H	13.83 FQ	17.54 MW	21.50 TQ	WABLS	3/08
	Seattle-Tacoma-Bellevue MSA, WA	Y	30020 FQ	37290 MW	45010 TQ	USBLS	5/07
	West Virginia	Y	16195 FQ	27418 MW	34298 TQ	WVBLS	7/08-9/08
	Wisconsin	Y	26210 FQ	33960 MW	47100 TQ	USBLS	5/07
	Milwaukee-Waukesha-West Allis MSA, WI	Y	25220 FQ	31940 MW	43000 TQ	USBLS	5/07
	Puerto Rico	Y	22790 FQ	25990 MW	30400 TQ	USBLS	5/07
Music Director and Composer	Arizona	Y	18010 FQ	22160 MW	41340 TQ	USBLS	5/07
	California	H	16.17 FQ	27.61 MW	58.94 TQ	CABLS	1/08-3/08
	Los Angeles-Long Beach-Glendale PMSA, CA	H	20.08 FQ	58.76 MW		CABLS	1/08-3/08
	Oakland-Fremont-Hayward MSA, CA	H	17.34 FQ	21.55 MW	26.99 TQ	CABLS	1/08-3/08
	Oxnard-Thousand Oaks-Ventura MSA, CA	H	51.87 FQ	55.62 MW	59.37 TQ	CABLS	1/08-3/08
	Riverside-San Bernardino-Ontario MSA, CA	H	11.77 FQ	19.56 MW	29.31 TQ	CABLS	1/08-3/08
	San Diego-Carlsbad-San Marcos MSA, CA	H	16.20 FQ	31.04 MW	54.52 TQ	CABLS	1/08-3/08

AE	Average entry wage	**AW**	Average wage paid	**FQ**	First quartile wage	**LO**	Lowest wage paid	**MTC**	Median total compensation
AER	Average entry range	**AWR**	Average wage range	**H**	Hourly	**LR**	Low end range	**MW**	Median wage paid
AEX	Average experienced wage	**AXR**	Average experienced range	**HI**	Highest wage paid	**M**	Monthly	**MWR**	Median wage range
ATC	Average total compensation	**D**	Daily	**HR**	High end range	**MCC**	Median cash compensation	**S**	See annotated source

TCC Total cash compensation
TQ Third quartile wage
W Weekly
Y Yearly

Occupation/Type/Industry	Location	Per	Low	Mid	High	Source	Date
Music Director and Composer	San Francisco-San Mateo-Redwood PMSA, CA	H	24.37 FQ	30.01 MW	44.75 TQ	CABLS	1/08-3/08
	San Jose-Sunnyvale-Santa Clara MSA, CA	H	16.49 FQ	27.61 MW	35.12 TQ	CABLS	1/08-3/08
	Santa Ana-Anaheim-Irvine PMSA, CA	Y	16410 FQ	31670 MW	44820 TQ	USBLS	5/07
	Colorado	Y	15130 FQ	25750 MW	41430 TQ	USBLS	5/07
	Colorado Springs MSA, CO	Y	14630 FQ	15010 MW	38170 TQ	USBLS	5/07
	Denver-Aurora MSA, CO	Y	15600 FQ	29510 MW	39610 TQ	USBLS	5/07
	Connecticut	H	20.02 AE	24.24 MW		CTBLS	1/08-3/08
	District of Columbia	Y	44370 FQ	79130 MW	94910 TQ	USBLS	5/07
	Washington-Arlington-Alexandria MSA, DC-VA-MD-WV	Y	38230 FQ	53910 MW	81040 TQ	USBLS	5/07
	Florida	Y	32590 FQ	40880 MW	47850 TQ	USBLS	5/07
	Fort Lauderdale-Pompano Beach-Deerfield Beach PMSA, FL	Y	35510 FQ	41300 MW	49050 TQ	USBLS	5/07
	Jacksonville MSA, FL	Y	24830 FQ	32690 MW	38630 TQ	USBLS	5/07
	Miami-Fort Lauderdale-Miami Beach MSA, FL	Y	36040 FQ	41530 MW	46780 TQ	USBLS	5/07
	Orlando-Kissimmee MSA, FL	Y	36120 FQ	53130 MW	60420 TQ	USBLS	5/07
	Tampa-St. Petersburg-Clearwater MSA, FL	Y	41350 FQ	45480 MW	49590 TQ	USBLS	5/07
	Hawaii	Y	27040 FQ	31580 MW	38530 TQ	USBLS	5/07
	Honolulu MSA, HI	Y	29840 FQ	35810 MW	41130 TQ	USBLS	5/07
	Illinois	Y	26270 FQ	38800 MW	51620 TQ	USBLS	5/07
	Chicago-Naperville-Joliet MSA, IL-IN-WI	Y	30870 FQ	39760 MW	52570 TQ	USBLS	5/07
	Indiana	Y	16700 FQ	27690 MW	42230 TQ	USBLS	5/07
	Indianapolis-Carmel MSA, IN	Y	17710 FQ	25950 MW	29580 TQ	USBLS	5/07
	Iowa	Y	15340 FQ	26900 MW	33230 TQ	USBLS	5/07
	Kentucky	Y	30941 FQ	38426 MW	51090 TQ	KYBLS	2008
	Louisiana	H	13.55 FQ	17.44 MW	24.95 TQ	LABLS	1/08-3/08
	Maryland	Y		50800 MW		MDBLS	3/08
	Baltimore-Towson MSA, MD	Y	43820 FQ	70470 MW	80150 TQ	USBLS	5/07
	Massachusetts	Y	40110 FQ	53030 MW	95830 TQ	USBLS	5/07
	Boston-Cambridge-Quincy NECTA, MA	Y	41510 FQ	60600 MW	103010 TQ	USBLS	5/07
	Michigan	Y	30630 FQ	34460 MW	39210 TQ	USBLS	5/07
	Detroit-Warren-Livonia MSA, MI	Y	29620 FQ	36710 MW	46430 TQ	USBLS	5/07
	Warren-Troy-Farmington Hills PMSA, MI	Y	30180 FQ	37700 MW	50990 TQ	USBLS	5/07
	Minnesota	Y	46065 FQ	58557 MW	66278 TQ	MNBLS	10/08-12/08
	Minneapolis-Saint Paul MSA, MN-WI	Y	51474 FQ	60398 MW	67345 TQ	MNBLS	10/08-12/08
	Missouri	Y	37420 FQ	68530 MW	79190 TQ	USBLS	5/07
	St. Louis MSA, MO-IL	Y	43110 FQ	68520 MW	78510 TQ	USBLS	5/07
	Montana	Y	14740 FQ	17890 MW	27900 TQ	USBLS	5/07
	Billings MSA, MT	Y	13840 FQ	14890 MW	17560 TQ	USBLS	5/07
	Nevada	Y	90431 FQ	104866 MW	125588 TQ	NVBLS	5/08
	Las Vegas-Paradise MSA, NV	Y	92559 FQ	106040 MW	126814 TQ	NVBLS	5/08
	New Jersey	Y	24090 FQ	41400 MW	50890 TQ	USBLS	5/07
	Edison PMSA, NJ	Y	24370 FQ	40780 MW	45340 TQ	USBLS	5/07
	New York	Y	19760 FQ	37670 MW	56750 TQ	USBLS	5/07
	Albany-Schenectady-Troy MSA, NY	Y	30810 FQ	36810 MW	56850 TQ	USBLS	5/07
	New York-Northern New Jersey-Long Island MSA, NY-NJ-PA	Y	23340 FQ	39090 MW	56450 TQ	USBLS	5/07
	North Carolina	Y	41800 FQ	70940 MW	104600 TQ	USBLS	5/07
	Ohio	Y	32450 FQ	43710 MW	90100 TQ	USBLS	5/07
	Columbus MSA, OH	Y	27850 FQ	32870 MW	45820 TQ	USBLS	5/07
	Oregon	Y	32072 FQ	40431 MW	52069 TQ	ORBLS	5/08
	Portland-Vancouver-Beaverton MSA, OR-WA	Y	28880 FQ	36340 MW	46430 TQ	USBLS	5/07
	Salem MSA, OR	Y	39980 FQ	47150 MW	66520 TQ	USBLS	5/07
	Pennsylvania	Y	16390 FQ	30150 MW	42380 TQ	USBLS	5/07
	Philadelphia-Camden-Wilmington MSA, PA-NJ-DE-MD	Y	17810 FQ	33260 MW	44120 TQ	USBLS	5/07

AE	Average entry wage	AW	Average wage paid	FQ	First quartile wage
AER	Average entry range	AWR	Average wage range	H	Hourly
AEX	Average experienced wage	AXR	Average experienced range	HI	Highest wage paid
ATC	Average total compensation	D	Daily	HR	High end range

LO	Lowest wage paid	MTC	Median total compensation
LR	Low end range	MW	Median wage paid
M	Monthly	MWR	Median wage range
MCC	Median cash compensation	S	See annotated source

TCC	Total cash compensation
TQ	Third quartile wage
W	Weekly
Y	Yearly

Occupation/Type/Industry	Location	Per	Low	Mid	High	Source	Date
Music Director and Composer	Pittsburgh MSA, PA	Y	18520 FQ	30390 MW	40060 TQ	USBLS	5/07
	Rhode Island	Y	25890 FQ	45280 MW	53320 TQ	USBLS	5/07
	Providence-Fall River- Warwick MSA, RI-MA	Y	27000 FQ	45900 MW	53560 TQ	USBLS	5/07
	Texas	Y	23360 FQ	42370 MW	50920 TQ	USBLS	5/07
	Dallas-Fort Worth-Arlington MSA, TX	Y	23240 FQ	43020 MW	50760 TQ	USBLS	5/07
	Virginia	Y	25800 FQ	31040 MW	55610 TQ	USBLS	5/07
	Richmond MSA, VA	Y	25330 FQ	27260 MW	29180 TQ	USBLS	5/07
	Washington	H	20.17 FQ	28.19 MW	35.44 TQ	WABLS	3/08
	Seattle-Tacoma-Bellevue MSA, WA	Y	39480 FQ	54570 MW	70650 TQ	USBLS	5/07
	Spokane MSA, WA	Y	37790 FQ	56360 MW	75500 TQ	USBLS	5/07
	Wisconsin	Y	30910 FQ	47110 MW	58660 TQ	USBLS	5/07
Music Producer	United States	Y		45000 MW		FLOOP	2007
Music/Re-Recording Mixer Journeyman, Major Motion Picture	West Coast	H			50.41- 59.43 HR	MPEG01	8/3/08-7/31/09
Musical Instrument Repairer and Tuner	Alabama	Y	18830 FQ	24840 MW	34710 TQ	USBLS	5/07
	Arizona	Y	30190 FQ	35760 MW	39230 TQ	USBLS	5/07
	California	H	13.62 FQ	16.99 MW	23.53 TQ	CABLS	1/08-3/08
	Los Angeles-Long Beach- Glendale PMSA, CA	H	13.02 FQ	15.78 MW	17.67 TQ	CABLS	1/08-3/08
	Sacramento-Arden Arcade- Roseville MSA, CA	H	16.47 FQ	25.68 MW	29.17 TQ	CABLS	1/08-3/08
	Colorado	Y	32730 FQ	36650 MW	41090 TQ	USBLS	5/07
	Connecticut	H	9.11 AE	15.08 MW		CTBLS	1/08-3/08
	Wilmington PMSA, DE-MD- NJ	Y	18590 FQ	25590 MW	32790 TQ	USBLS	5/07

	Washington-Arlington-
	  Alexandria MSA, DC-VA-
	  MD-WV
		Y	32450 FQ	43020 MW	49550 TQ	USBLS	5/07

	Florida	Y	23020 FQ	29270 MW	42820 TQ	USBLS	5/07

	Fort Lauderdale-Pompano
	  Beach-Deerfield Beach
	  PMSA, FL
		Y	22210 FQ	33210 MW	37310 TQ	USBLS	5/07

	Miami-Fort Lauderdale-Miami Beach MSA, FL	Y	23570 FQ	29970 MW	39940 TQ	USBLS	5/07
	Georgia	Y	21080 FQ	26960 MW	32150 TQ	USBLS	5/07
	Atlanta-Sandy Springs- Marietta MSA, GA	Y	20130 FQ	26470 MW	31390 TQ	USBLS	5/07
	Illinois	Y	31440 FQ	42360 MW	59470 TQ	USBLS	5/07
	Indiana	Y	21580 FQ	31430 MW	39950 TQ	USBLS	5/07
	Iowa	Y	29780 FQ	37010 MW	48190 TQ	USBLS	5/07
	Kansas	Y	24860 FQ	30330 MW	38040 TQ	USBLS	5/07
	Kentucky	Y	25879 FQ	31051 MW	45043 TQ	KYBLS	2008
	Louisville-Jefferson County MSA, KY-IN	Y	24890 FQ	30780 MW	43260 TQ	USBLS	5/07
	Louisiana	H	16.31 FQ	17.76 MW	19.22 TQ	LABLS	1/08-3/08
	Maryland	Y		40225 MW		MDBLS	3/08
	Bethesda-Gaithersburg- Frederick PMSA, MD	Y	28960 FQ	41060 MW	46490 TQ	USBLS	5/07
	Massachusetts	Y	34780 FQ	40110 MW	45700 TQ	USBLS	5/07
	Boston-Cambridge-Quincy NECTA, MA	Y	28360 FQ	33270 MW	42860 TQ	USBLS	5/07
	Michigan	Y	31820 FQ	44180 MW	53920 TQ	USBLS	5/07
	Minnesota	Y	34237 FQ	38024 MW	41810 TQ	MNBLS	10/08-12/08
	Minneapolis-Saint Paul MSA, MN-WI	Y	34950 FQ	38475 MW	42010 TQ	MNBLS	10/08-12/08
	Missouri	Y	26110 FQ	32280 MW	38490 TQ	USBLS	5/07
	St. Louis MSA, MO-IL	Y	28180 FQ	33490 MW	39920 TQ	USBLS	5/07
	Nebraska	Y	14840 FQ	25560 MW	30020 TQ	USBLS	5/07
	Nevada	H	9.02 FQ	12.78 MW	14.59 TQ	NVBLS	5/08
	Las Vegas-Paradise MSA, NV	H	8.98 FQ	12.71 MW	14.46 TQ	NVBLS	5/08
	New Hampshire	H	12.99 AE	14.41 MW	18.33 AEX	NHBLS	6/08
	New Jersey	Y	29640 FQ	36070 MW	44650 TQ	USBLS	5/07
	Edison PMSA, NJ	Y	29080 FQ	35230 MW	46540 TQ	USBLS	5/07
	Newark-Union PMSA, NJ-PA	Y	32300 FQ	37100 MW	44290 TQ	USBLS	5/07

AE Average entry wage	**AW** Average wage paid	**FQ** First quartile wage	**LO** Lowest wage paid	**MTC** Median total compensation	**TCC** Total cash compensation
AER Average entry range	**AWR** Average wage range	**H** Hourly	**LR** Low end range	**MW** Median wage paid	**TQ** Third quartile wage
AEX Average experienced wage	**AXR** Average experienced range	**HI** Highest wage paid	**M** Monthly	**MWR** Median wage range	**W** Weekly
ATC Average total compensation	**D** Daily	**HR** High end range	**MCC** Median cash compensation	**S** See annotated source	**Y** Yearly

Occupation/Type/Industry	Location	Per	Low	Mid	High	Source	Date
Musical Instrument Repairer and Tuner	New York	Y	17720 FQ	26600 MW	34360 TQ	USBLS	5/07
	Buffalo-Niagara Falls MSA, NY	Y	25100 FQ	30310 MW	36880 TQ	USBLS	5/07
	New York-Northern New Jersey-Long Island MSA, NY-NJ-PA	Y	24050 FQ	32870 MW	40620 TQ	USBLS	5/07
	North Carolina	Y	30450 FQ	35100 MW	39840 TQ	USBLS	5/07
	Ohio	Y	20890 FQ	30590 MW	37840 TQ	USBLS	5/07
	Cleveland-Elyria-Mentor MSA, OH	Y	17370 FQ	30800 MW	36250 TQ	USBLS	5/07
	Oklahoma	Y	28000 FQ	34710 MW	40970 TQ	USBLS	5/07
	Portland-Vancouver-Beaverton MSA, OR-WA	Y	18560 FQ	25330 MW	35520 TQ	USBLS	5/07
	Pennsylvania	Y	19040 FQ	23920 MW	38810 TQ	USBLS	5/07
	Allentown-Bethlehem-Easton MSA, PA-NJ	Y	20610 FQ	25850 MW	37920 TQ	USBLS	5/07
	Philadelphia-Camden-Wilmington MSA, PA-NJ-DE-MD	Y	20850 FQ	26470 MW	36640 TQ	USBLS	5/07
	Pittsburgh MSA, PA	Y	18560 FQ	22990 MW	43470 TQ	USBLS	5/07
	South Carolina	Y	21040 FQ	23960 MW	29990 TQ	USBLS	5/07
	South Dakota	Y	19679 FQ	22421 MW	28921 TQ	SDBLS	7/08-9/08
	Tennessee	Y	14930 FQ	28840 MW	36170 TQ	USBLS	5/07
	Texas	Y	22080 FQ	30040 MW	37250 TQ	USBLS	5/07
	Houston-Sugar Land-Baytown MSA, TX	Y	28300 FQ	34130 MW	43680 TQ	USBLS	5/07
	Vermont	Y	24840 FQ	27530 MW	32420 TQ	USBLS	5/07
	Virginia	Y	28790 FQ	35830 MW	58320 TQ	USBLS	5/07
	Washington	H	11.70 FQ	13.67 MW	23.50 TQ	WABLS	3/08
	West Virginia	Y	14397 FQ	16282 MW	33005 TQ	WVBLS	7/08-9/08
	Wisconsin	Y	21170 FQ	26850 MW	36430 TQ	USBLS	5/07
	Milwaukee-Waukesha-West Allis MSA, WI	Y	19870 FQ	22370 MW	32660 TQ	USBLS	5/07
Musician							
Symphony Orchestra	Baltimore, MD	W		1475 AW		BSO	2007-2008
Symphony Orchestra	Boston, MA	W		2360 AW		BSO	2007-2008
Symphony Orchestra	New York, NY	W		2155 AW		BSO	2007-2008
Symphony Orchestra	Philadelphia, PA	W		2200 AW		BSO	2007-2008
Touring Production	Detroit, MI	S			151 HI	CRDB01	2009
Musician and Singer	Alabama	H	6.89 FQ	15.09 MW	20.98 TQ	USBLS	5/07
	Arizona	H	8.59 FQ	9.65 MW	17.21 TQ	USBLS	5/07
	Arkansas	H	11.60 FQ	21.29 MW	34.64 TQ	USBLS	5/07
	California	H	21.04 FQ	32.05 MW	56.96 TQ	CABLS	1/08-3/08
	Colorado	H	7.80 FQ	21.89 MW	38.43 TQ	USBLS	5/07
	Connecticut	H	8.22 AE	11.95 MW		CTBLS	1/08-3/08
	District of Columbia	H	11.80 FQ	22.40 MW	32.35 TQ	USBLS	5/07
	Florida	H	10.87 FQ	20.12 MW	24.04 TQ	USBLS	5/07
	Georgia	H	11.06 FQ	18.20 MW	43.28 TQ	USBLS	5/07
	Hawaii	H	16.40 FQ	22.25 MW	49.63 TQ	USBLS	5/07
	Idaho	H	6.45 FQ	7.53 MW	14.01 TQ	USBLS	5/07
	Illinois	H	7.79 FQ	16.36 MW	31.42 TQ	USBLS	5/07
	Indiana	H	9.14 FQ	21.34 MW	43.43 TQ	USBLS	5/07
	Iowa	H	7.29 FQ	14.04 MW	21.08 TQ	USBLS	5/07
	Kansas	H	6.69 FQ	11.15 MW	28.17 TQ	USBLS	5/07
	Louisiana	H	11.78 FQ	13.11 MW	14.46 TQ	LABLS	1/08-3/08
	Maryland	H		35.50 MW		MDBLS	3/08
	Massachusetts	H	11.65 FQ	14.55 MW	27.00 TQ	USBLS	5/07
	Michigan	H	7.54 FQ	13.59 MW	23.70 TQ	USBLS	5/07
	Minnesota	H	20.35 FQ	24.50 MW	59.02 TQ	MNBLS	10/08-12/08
	Missouri	H	11.08 FQ	17.76 MW	25.13 TQ	USBLS	5/07
	Montana	H	6.72 FQ	7.38 MW	13.60 TQ	USBLS	5/07
	Nebraska	H	12.80 FQ	40.79 MW	48.73 TQ	USBLS	5/07
	Nevada	H	19.77 FQ	23.11 MW	28.19 TQ	NVBLS	5/08
	New Jersey	H	10.47 FQ	15.72 MW	20.43 TQ	USBLS	5/07
	New Mexico	H	6.26 FQ	7.36 MW	15.89 TQ	USBLS	5/07
	New York	H	8.24 FQ	15.81 MW	46.01 TQ	USBLS	5/07
	Ohio	H	11.62 FQ	27.90 MW	46.24 TQ	USBLS	5/07
	Oklahoma	H	6.59 FQ	10.45 MW	22.82 TQ	USBLS	5/07
	Pennsylvania	H	7.62 FQ	12.44 MW	34.70 TQ	USBLS	5/07

AE	Average entry wage	**AW**	Average wage paid	**FQ**	First quartile wage
AER	Average entry range	**AWR**	Average wage range	**H**	Hourly
AEX	Average experienced wage	**AXR**	Average experienced range	**HI**	Highest wage paid
ATC	Average total compensation	**D**	Daily	**HR**	High end range

LO	Lowest wage paid	**MTC**	Median total compensation	**TCC**	Total cash compensation
LR	Low end range	**MW**	Median wage paid	**TQ**	Third quartile wage
M	Monthly	**MWR**	Median wage range	**W**	Weekly
MCC	Median cash compensation	**S**	See annotated source	**Y**	Yearly

Occupation/Type/Industry	Location	Per	Low	Mid	High	Source	Date
Musician and Singer	Rhode Island	H	10.48 FQ	19.64 MW	23.32 TQ	USBLS	5/07
	South Carolina	H	6.53 FQ	11.77 MW	26.21 TQ	USBLS	5/07
	South Dakota	H	10.37 FQ	11.25 MW	12.76 TQ	SDBLS	7/08-9/08
	Tennessee	H	14.01 FQ	17.59 MW	34.39 TQ	USBLS	5/07
	Texas	H	7.09 FQ	13.85 MW	18.87 TQ	USBLS	5/07
	Utah	H	14.06 FQ	31.68 MW	35.63 TQ	USBLS	5/07
	Virginia	H	8.89 FQ	19.79 MW	26.38 TQ	USBLS	5/07
	Washington	H	20.33 FQ	23.01 MW	36.92 TQ	WABLS	3/08
	West Virginia	H	16.29 FQ	17.90 MW	33.26 TQ	WVBLS	7/08-9/08
	Wisconsin	H	7.41 FQ	19.97 MW	33.44 TQ	USBLS	5/07
Nanny							
Full-Time, Live In	District of Columbia	H		14.64 AW		4NTAX01	9/07-2/08
Full-Time, Live In	New York, NY	H		15.95 AW		4NTAX	9/07-2/08
Full-Time, Live Out	District of Columbia	H		16.12 AW		4NTAX01	9/07-2/08
Full-Time, Live Out	New York, NY	H		16.79 AW		4NTAX	9/07-2/08
National Guard Member	Rhode Island	Y		38000 AW		RIM01	2009
Natural Resources Specialist							
State Government	Illinois	Y	43740 LO		65244 HI	AFT02	3/1/08
Natural Sciences Manager	Alabama	Y	78680 FQ	94690 MW	119320 TQ	USBLS	5/07
	Birmingham-Hoover MSA, AL	Y	81060 FQ	97600 MW	123120 TQ	USBLS	5/07
	Alaska	Y	74350 FQ	89260 MW	102800 TQ	USBLS	5/07
	Anchorage MSA, AK	Y	76150 FQ	91230 MW	105210 TQ	USBLS	5/07
	Arizona	Y	64480 FQ	85380 MW	102390 TQ	USBLS	5/07
	Phoenix-Mesa-Scottsdale MSA, AZ	Y	66130 FQ	87330 MW	103350 TQ	USBLS	5/07
	Tucson MSA, AZ	Y	80790 FQ	98810 MW	122230 TQ	USBLS	5/07
	Arkansas	Y	75850 FQ	91290 MW	109160 TQ	USBLS	5/07
	Little Rock-North Little Rock MSA, AR	Y	79900 FQ	91650 MW*	103280 TQ	USBLS	5/07
	California	H	45.65 FQ	61.37 MW		CABLS	1/08-3/08
	Bakersfield MSA, CA	H	31.85 FQ	45.54 MW	53.56 TQ	CABLS	1/08-3/08
	Los Angeles-Long Beach-Glendale PMSA, CA	H	39.81 FQ	54.09 MW		CABLS	1/08-3/08
	Oakland-Fremont-Hayward MSA, CA	H	47.28 FQ	62.11 MW		CABLS	1/08-3/08
	Riverside-San Bernardino-Ontario MSA, CA	H	41.30 FQ	55.47 MW		CABLS	1/08-3/08
	Sacramento-Arden Arcade-Roseville MSA, CA	H	40.21 FQ	47.75 MW	58.16 TQ	CABLS	1/08-3/08
	San Diego-Carlsbad-San Marcos MSA, CA	H	50.70 FQ	65.19 MW		CABLS	1/08-3/08
	San Francisco-San Mateo-Redwood PMSA, CA	H	59.66 FQ			CABLS	1/08-3/08
	San Jose-Sunnyvale-Santa Clara MSA, CA	H	60.98 FQ			CABLS	1/08-3/08
	Santa Ana-Anaheim-Irvine PMSA, CA	Y	76040 FQ	103080 MW	128920 TQ	USBLS	5/07
	Colorado	Y	91170 FQ	111170 MW	131550 TQ	USBLS	5/07
	Denver-Aurora MSA, CO	Y	92110 FQ	110460 MW	130460 TQ	USBLS	5/07
	Connecticut	H	30.88 AE	51.60 MW		CTBLS	1/08-3/08
	Bridgeport-Stamford-Norwalk MSA, CT	Y	100660 FQ	117340 MW		USBLS	5/07
	Hartford-West Hartford-East Hartford MSA, CT	Y	86220 FQ	102390 MW	117250 TQ	USBLS	5/07
	Delaware	Y	116800 FQ	144450 MW		USBLS	5/07
	Wilmington PMSA, DE-MD-NJ	Y	122700 FQ			USBLS	5/07
	District of Columbia	Y	94280 FQ	114450 MW	134460 TQ	USBLS	5/07
	Washington-Arlington-Alexandria MSA, DC-VA-MD-WV	Y	94450 FQ	114460 MW	139080 TQ	USBLS	5/07
	Florida	Y	77860 FQ	94670 MW	120090 TQ	USBLS	5/07
	Fort Lauderdale-Pompano Beach-Deerfield Beach PMSA, FL	Y	87280 FQ	101540 MW		USBLS	5/07
	Miami-Fort Lauderdale-Miami Beach MSA, FL	Y	91680 FQ	112420 MW		USBLS	5/07
	Orlando-Kissimmee MSA, FL	Y	85530 FQ	111540 MW	131090 TQ	USBLS	5/07

AE	Average entry wage	AW	Average wage paid	FQ	First quartile wage
AER	Average entry range	AWR	Average wage range	H	Hourly
AEX	Average experienced wage	AXR	Average experienced range	HI	Highest wage paid
ATC	Average total compensation	D	Daily	HR	High end range

LO	Lowest wage paid	MTC	Median total compensation	TCC	Total cash compensation
LR	Low end range	MW	Median wage paid	TQ	Third quartile wage
M	Monthly	MWR	Median wage range	W	Weekly
MCC	Median cash compensation	S	See annotated source	Y	Yearly

Occupation/Type/Industry	Location	Per	Low	Mid	High	Source	Date
Natural Sciences Manager	Tampa-St. Petersburg-Clearwater MSA, FL	Y	55790 FQ	88220 MW	108630 TQ	USBLS	5/07
	Georgia	Y	70120 FQ	89180 MW	110750 TQ	USBLS	5/07
	Atlanta-Sandy Springs-Marietta MSA, GA	Y	72330 FQ	91080 MW	112070 TQ	USBLS	5/07
	Hawaii	Y	85410 FQ	101490 MW	127380 TQ	USBLS	5/07
	Honolulu MSA, HI	Y	87460 FQ	102990 MW	131240 TQ	USBLS	5/07
	Idaho	Y	71980 FQ	84710 MW	99330 TQ	USBLS	5/07
	Boise City-Nampa MSA, ID	Y	77380 FQ	90310 MW	103090 TQ	USBLS	5/07
	Illinois	Y	75890 FQ	94790 MW	117410 TQ	USBLS	5/07
	Chicago-Naperville-Joliet MSA, IL-IN-WI	Y	72560 FQ	93440 MW	117000 TQ	USBLS	5/07
	Indiana	Y	43630 FQ	51230 MW	64450 TQ	USBLS	5/07
	Gary PMSA, IN	Y	44410 FQ	48140 MW	51860 TQ	USBLS	5/07
	Indianapolis-Carmel MSA, IN	Y	42130 FQ	48800 MW	58780 TQ	USBLS	5/07
	Iowa	Y	80730 FQ	93460 MW	120360 TQ	USBLS	5/07
	Des Moines-West Des Moines MSA, IA	Y	87690 FQ	105500 MW	143600 TQ	USBLS	5/07
	Kansas	Y	82720 FQ	94700 MW	113460 TQ	USBLS	5/07
	Kentucky	Y	70469 FQ	84842 MW	103833 TQ	KYBLS	2008
	Louisville-Jefferson County MSA, KY-IN	Y	81940 FQ	93990 MW	109700 TQ	USBLS	5/07
	Louisiana	H	30.26 FQ	40.93 MW	49.20 TQ	LABLS	1/08-3/08
	Baton Rouge MSA, LA	Y	56790 FQ	77120 MW	97360 TQ	USBLS	5/07
	New Orleans-Metairie-Kenner MSA, LA	Y	67930 FQ	96250 MW	116220 TQ	USBLS	5/07
	Maine	Y	67800 FQ	79810 MW	98620 TQ	USBLS	5/07
	Portland-South Portland-Biddeford MSA, ME	Y	84800 FQ	98490 MW	144890 TQ	USBLS	5/07
	Maryland	Y		108500 MW		MDBLS	3/08
	Baltimore-Towson MSA, MD	Y	55070 FQ	87280 MW	109890 TQ	USBLS	5/07
	Bethesda-Gaithersburg-Frederick PMSA, MD	Y	93410 FQ	112180 MW	140770 TQ	USBLS	5/07
	Massachusetts	Y	93910 FQ	125990 MW		USBLS	5/07
	Boston-Cambridge-Quincy NECTA, MA	Y	90710 FQ	128730 MW		USBLS	5/07
	Springfield MSA, MA-CT	Y	82370 FQ	92030 MW	102210 TQ	USBLS	5/07
	Worcester MSA, MA-CT	Y	48750 FQ	110410 MW	130680 TQ	USBLS	5/07
	Michigan	Y	70180 FQ	87070 MW	112640 TQ	USBLS	5/07
	Ann Arbor MSA, MI	Y	101540 FQ	121790 MW	137890 TQ	USBLS	5/07
	Detroit-Warren-Livonia MSA, MI	Y	67030 FQ	77430 MW	94860 TQ	USBLS	5/07
	Warren-Troy-Farmington Hills PMSA, MI	Y	66300 FQ	74380 MW	82450 TQ	USBLS	5/07
	Minnesota	Y	88844 FQ	112398 MW	148400 TQ	MNBLS	10/08-12/08
	Duluth-Superior MSA, MN-WI	Y	81879 FQ	93140 MW	105224 TQ	MNBLS	10/08-12/08
	Minneapolis-Saint Paul MSA, MN-WI	Y	92472 FQ	118091 MW		MNBLS	10/08-12/08
	Rochester MSA, MN	Y	108235 FQ	120212 MW	130116 TQ	MNBLS	10/08-12/08
	Mississippi	Y	66490 FQ	86560 MW	105460 TQ	USBLS	5/07
	Jackson MSA, MS	Y	69390 FQ	82950 MW	98260 TQ	USBLS	5/07
	Missouri	Y	70990 FQ	93900 MW	119280 TQ	USBLS	5/07
	Kansas City MSA, MO-KS	Y	83810 FQ	98410 MW	118470 TQ	USBLS	5/07
	St. Louis MSA, MO-IL	Y	77580 FQ	103480 MW	129940 TQ	USBLS	5/07
	Montana	Y	67280 FQ	77930 MW	91570 TQ	USBLS	5/07
	Billings MSA, MT	Y	70590 FQ	80710 MW	93190 TQ	USBLS	5/07
	Nebraska	Y	69300 FQ	87840 MW	104520 TQ	USBLS	5/07
	Omaha-Council Bluffs MSA, NE-IA	Y	53330 FQ	86440 MW	113260 TQ	USBLS	5/07
	Nevada	H	30.14 FQ	38.59 MW	49.27 TQ	NVBLS	5/08
	Las Vegas-Paradise MSA, NV	H	32.18 FQ	38.73 MW	50.68 TQ	NVBLS	5/08
	New Hampshire	H	23.38 AE	42.70 MW	50.32 AEX	NHBLS	6/08
	New Jersey	Y	105330 FQ	133270 MW		USBLS	5/07
	Camden PMSA, NJ	Y	94730 FQ	113270 MW	131590 TQ	USBLS	5/07
	Edison PMSA, NJ	Y	114330 FQ	145160 MW		USBLS	5/07
	Newark-Union PMSA, NJ-PA	Y	104370 FQ	135370 MW		USBLS	5/07
	New Mexico	Y	72270 FQ	86000 MW	110250 TQ	USBLS	5/07
	Albuquerque MSA, NM	Y	78430 FQ	94310 MW	124740 TQ	USBLS	5/07
	New York	Y	87390 FQ	109370 MW		USBLS	5/07
	Albany-Schenectady-Troy MSA, NY	Y	85940 FQ	103480 MW	124500 TQ	USBLS	5/07

AE	Average entry wage	AW	Average wage paid	FQ	First quartile wage	LO	Lowest wage paid	MTC Median total compensation	TCC Total cash compensation
AER	Average entry range	AWR	Average wage range	H	Hourly	LR	Low end range	MW Median wage paid	TQ Third quartile wage
AEX	Average experienced wage	AXR	Average experienced range	HI	Highest wage paid	M	Monthly	MWR Median wage range	W Weekly
ATC	Average total compensation	D	Daily	HR	High end range	MCC	Median cash compensation	S See annotated source	Y Yearly

Occupation/Type/Industry	Location	Per	Low	Mid	High	Source	Date
Natural Sciences Manager	Buffalo-Niagara Falls MSA, NY	Y	85980 FQ	113520 MW		USBLS	5/07
	Nassau-Suffolk PMSA, NY	Y	90800 FQ	107930 MW	144100 TQ	USBLS	5/07
	New York-Northern New Jersey-Long Island MSA, NY-NJ-PA	Y	104010 FQ	135180 MW		USBLS	5/07
	North Carolina	Y	83390 FQ	103280 MW	132860 TQ	USBLS	5/07
	Charlotte-Gastonia-Concord MSA, NC-SC	Y	88710 FQ	98830 MW	118240 TQ	USBLS	5/07
	Durham MSA, NC	Y	82090 FQ	106640 MW	138680 TQ	USBLS	5/07
	Raleigh-Cary MSA, NC	Y	88270 FQ	107480 MW	142830 TQ	USBLS	5/07
	Ohio	Y	72790 FQ	92180 MW	114320 TQ	USBLS	5/07
	Cincinnati-Middletown MSA, OH-KY-IN	Y	83920 FQ	98270 MW	118070 TQ	USBLS	5/07
	Cleveland-Elyria-Mentor MSA, OH	Y	66600 FQ	92190 MW	118120 TQ	USBLS	5/07
	Columbus MSA, OH	Y	73970 FQ	93210 MW	115400 TQ	USBLS	5/07
	Dayton MSA, OH	Y	80900 FQ	100310 MW	124570 TQ	USBLS	5/07
	Oklahoma	Y	72950 FQ	89480 MW	112150 TQ	USBLS	5/07
	Oklahoma City MSA, OK	Y	78330 FQ	103070 MW	128020 TQ	USBLS	5/07
	Tulsa MSA, OK	Y	67490 FQ	82180 MW	97520 TQ	USBLS	5/07
	Oregon	H	37.29 FQ	45.46 MW	55.78 TQ	ORBLS	5/08
	Portland-Vancouver-Beaverton MSA, OR-WA	Y	81750 FQ	96520 MW	118510 TQ	USBLS	5/07
	Pennsylvania	Y	92630 FQ	133250 MW		USBLS	5/07
	Philadelphia-Camden-Wilmington MSA, PA-NJ-DE-MD	Y	102990 FQ	143910 MW		USBLS	5/07
	Pittsburgh MSA, PA	Y	63780 FQ	101560 MW	129180 TQ	USBLS	5/07
	South Carolina	Y	69130 FQ	88170 MW	109670 TQ	USBLS	5/07
	Charleston-North Charleston MSA, SC	Y	53210 FQ	84210 MW	118500 TQ	USBLS	5/07
	Columbia MSA, SC	Y	76980 FQ	87420 MW	100610 TQ	USBLS	5/07
	South Dakota	Y	76740 FQ	88196 MW	103188 TQ	SDBLS	7/08-9/08
	Tennessee	Y	67830 FQ	88170 MW	109070 TQ	USBLS	5/07
	Memphis MSA, TN-MS-AR	Y	83170 FQ	99660 MW	122760 TQ	USBLS	5/07
	Nashville-Davidson-Murfreesboro MSA, TN	Y	67400 FQ	79780 MW	96380 TQ	USBLS	5/07
	Texas	Y	83520 FQ	102330 MW	130650 TQ	USBLS	5/07
	Austin-Round Rock MSA, TX	Y	79110 FQ	96430 MW	120680 TQ	USBLS	5/07
	Dallas-Fort Worth-Arlington MSA, TX	Y	87260 FQ	104470 MW	128710 TQ	USBLS	5/07
	Houston-Sugar Land-Baytown MSA, TX	Y	88130 FQ	104210 MW	133670 TQ	USBLS	5/07
	San Antonio MSA, TX	Y	73980 FQ	89420 MW	124600 TQ	USBLS	5/07
	Utah	Y	71120 FQ	83190 MW	98940 TQ	USBLS	5/07
	Salt Lake City MSA, UT	Y	73070 FQ	83950 MW	99880 TQ	USBLS	5/07
	Vermont	Y	75380 FQ	87640 MW	99210 TQ	USBLS	5/07
	Virginia	Y	92620 FQ	113060 MW	139480 TQ	USBLS	5/07
	Richmond MSA, VA	Y	81500 FQ	102350 MW	130500 TQ	USBLS	5/07
	Virginia Beach-Norfolk-Newport News MSA, VA-NC	Y	82190 FQ	91760 MW	101970 TQ	USBLS	5/07
	Washington	H	44.36 FQ	54.34 MW	67.55 TQ	WABLS	3/08
	Seattle-Tacoma-Bellevue MSA, WA	Y	97660 FQ	119150 MW		USBLS	5/07
	West Virginia	Y	71583 FQ	87362 MW	109229 TQ	WVBLS	7/08-9/08
	Charleston MSA, WV	Y	60060 FQ	72990 MW	97550 TQ	USBLS	5/07
	Wisconsin	Y	78770 FQ	94920 MW	117490 TQ	USBLS	5/07
	Milwaukee-Waukesha-West Allis MSA, WI	Y	79120 FQ	98180 MW	127590 TQ	USBLS	5/07
	Wyoming	Y	67894 FQ	76379 MW	84703 TQ	WYBLS	9/08
	Casper MSA, WY	Y	66261 FQ	80193 MW	93002 TQ	WYBLS	9/08
	Puerto Rico	Y	53100 FQ	90140 MW	101710 TQ	USBLS	5/07
	San Juan-Caguas-Guaynabo MSA, PR	Y	40000 FQ	88790 MW	101460 TQ	USBLS	5/07
Naturalist Municipal Government	Seattle, WA	H	21.18 LO		24.63 HI	CSSS	2008
Naturalist Aide State Government	Ohio	H	15.09 LO		17.03 HI	ODAS	2008

AE	Average entry wage	**AW**	Average wage paid	**FQ**	First quartile wage	**LO**	Lowest wage paid	**MTC** Median total compensation **TCC** Total cash compensation
AER	Average entry range	**AWR**	Average wage range	**H**	Hourly	**LR**	Low end range	**MW** Median wage paid **TQ** Third quartile wage
AEX	Average experienced wage	**AXR**	Average experienced range	**HI**	Highest wage paid	**M**	Monthly	**MWR** Median wage range **W** Weekly
ATC	Average total compensation	**D**	Daily	**HR**	High end range	**MCC**	Median cash compensation	**S** See annotated source **Y** Yearly

Occupation/Type/Industry	Location	Per	Low	Mid	High	Source	Date
Neighborhood Canvasser							
United States Census Bureau	Michigan	H			16.00 HI	FREEP10	2009
Neonatologist	United States	Y		265400 AW		CEJ01	2008
Net Construction Specialist							
State Government	Ohio	H	16.09 LO		18.36 HI	ODAS	2008
Network and Computer Systems Administrator							
	Alabama	Y	45600 FQ	58210 MW	74730 TQ	USBLS	5/07
	Birmingham-Hoover MSA, AL	Y	49330 FQ	63000 MW	78980 TQ	USBLS	5/07
	Montgomery MSA, AL	Y	48300 FQ	64860 MW	94760 TQ	USBLS	5/07
	Alaska	Y	49870 FQ	60310 MW	75960 TQ	USBLS	5/07
	Anchorage MSA, AK	Y	52560 FQ	61570 MW	77580 TQ	USBLS	5/07
	Arizona	Y	45990 FQ	58850 MW	75860 TQ	USBLS	5/07
	Phoenix-Mesa-Scottsdale MSA, AZ	Y	47980 FQ	60320 MW	78330 TQ	USBLS	5/07
	Tucson MSA, AZ	Y	41700 FQ	52780 MW	66910 TQ	USBLS	5/07
	Arkansas	Y	39670 FQ	50830 MW	64120 TQ	USBLS	5/07
	Little Rock-North Little Rock MSA, AR	Y	45230 FQ	58730 MW	72200 TQ	USBLS	5/07
	California	H	28.16 FQ	36.31 MW	46.04 TQ	CABLS	1/08-3/08
	Fresno MSA, CA	H	22.30 FQ	29.35 MW	37.51 TQ	CABLS	1/08-3/08
	Los Angeles-Long Beach-Glendale PMSA, CA	H	27.12 FQ	34.44 MW	43.20 TQ	CABLS	1/08-3/08
	Oakland-Fremont-Hayward MSA, CA	H	31.43 FQ	39.50 MW	47.41 TQ	CABLS	1/08-3/08
	Riverside-San Bernardino-Ontario MSA, CA	H	25.25 FQ	33.18 MW	39.45 TQ	CABLS	1/08-3/08
	Sacramento-Arden Arcade-Roseville MSA, CA	H	26.51 FQ	34.20 MW	42.53 TQ	CABLS	1/08-3/08
	San Diego-Carlsbad-San Marcos MSA, CA	H	26.83 FQ	33.66 MW	40.83 TQ	CABLS	1/08-3/08
	San Francisco-San Mateo-Redwood PMSA, CA	H	34.27 FQ	43.58 MW	53.94 TQ	CABLS	1/08-3/08
	San Jose-Sunnyvale-Santa Clara MSA, CA	H	35.10 FQ	45.86 MW	57.47 TQ	CABLS	1/08-3/08
	Santa Ana-Anaheim-Irvine PMSA, CA	Y	53820 FQ	68070 MW	84470 TQ	USBLS	5/07
	Stockton MSA, CA	H	24.47 FQ	32.80 MW	41.01 TQ	CABLS	1/08-3/08
	Colorado	Y	53970 FQ	69620 MW	86030 TQ	USBLS	5/07
	Boulder MSA, CO	Y	56700 FQ	71280 MW	86230 TQ	USBLS	5/07
	Denver-Aurora MSA, CO	Y	57770 FQ	73510 MW	90750 TQ	USBLS	5/07
	Pueblo MSA, CO	Y	40360 FQ	53660 MW	68480 TQ	USBLS	5/07
	Connecticut	H	24.16 AE	35.40 MW		CTBLS	1/08-3/08
	Bridgeport-Stamford-Norwalk MSA, CT	Y	64270 FQ	80630 MW	98860 TQ	USBLS	5/07
	Hartford-West Hartford-East Hartford MSA, CT	Y	51430 FQ	63780 MW	77750 TQ	USBLS	5/07
	Delaware	Y	49020 FQ	65390 MW	92670 TQ	USBLS	5/07
	Wilmington PMSA, DE-MD-NJ	Y	52360 FQ	71520 MW	97050 TQ	USBLS	5/07
	District of Columbia	Y	55700 FQ	68270 MW	86750 TQ	USBLS	5/07
	Washington-Arlington-Alexandria MSA, DC-VA-MD-WV	Y	57460 FQ	74860 MW	95160 TQ	USBLS	5/07
	Florida	Y	49590 FQ	63120 MW	80720 TQ	USBLS	5/07
	Fort Lauderdale-Pompano Beach-Deerfield Beach PMSA, FL	Y	51700 FQ	64270 MW	85150 TQ	USBLS	5/07
	Jacksonville MSA, FL	Y	51310 FQ	62210 MW	78420 TQ	USBLS	5/07
	Miami-Fort Lauderdale-Miami Beach MSA, FL	Y	52130 FQ	67400 MW	88410 TQ	USBLS	5/07
	Orlando-Kissimmee MSA, FL	Y	50240 FQ	64670 MW	82250 TQ	USBLS	5/07
	Tampa-St. Petersburg-Clearwater MSA, FL	Y	48360 FQ	61850 MW	79670 TQ	USBLS	5/07
	West Palm Beach-Boca Raton-Boynton Beach PMSA, FL	Y	53640 FQ	66910 MW	85200 TQ	USBLS	5/07
	Georgia	Y	50100 FQ	64710 MW	81300 TQ	USBLS	5/07
	Atlanta-Sandy Springs-Marietta MSA, GA	Y	53490 FQ	68450 MW	84030 TQ	USBLS	5/07
	Macon MSA, GA	Y	49120 FQ	62560 MW	77690 TQ	USBLS	5/07

AE	Average entry wage	AW	Average wage paid	FQ	First quartile wage	LO	Lowest wage paid	MTC	Median total compensation	TCC	Total cash compensation
AER	Average entry range	AWR	Average wage range	H	Hourly	LR	Low end range	MW	Median wage paid	TQ	Third quartile wage
AEX	Average experienced wage	AXR	Average experienced range	HI	Highest wage paid	M	Monthly	MWR	Median wage range	W	Weekly
ATC	Average total compensation	D	Daily	HR	High end range	MCC	Median cash compensation	S	See annotated source	Y	Yearly

1096

Occupation/Type/Industry	Location	Per	Low	Mid	High	Source	Date
Network and Computer Systems Administrator	Hawaii	Y	44820 FQ	55550 MW	68750 TQ	USBLS	5/07
	Honolulu MSA, HI	Y	44210 FQ	54300 MW	67550 TQ	USBLS	5/07
	Idaho	Y	35840 FQ	46180 MW	67720 TQ	USBLS	5/07
	Boise City-Nampa MSA, ID	Y	37230 FQ	44560 MW	60780 TQ	USBLS	5/07
	Illinois	Y	52000 FQ	65680 MW	81910 TQ	USBLS	5/07
	Chicago-Naperville-Joliet MSA, IL-IN-WI	Y	54150 FQ	67870 MW	83620 TQ	USBLS	5/07
	Indiana	Y	41860 FQ	54810 MW	67580 TQ	USBLS	5/07
	Elkhart-Goshen MSA, IN	Y	43270 FQ	55120 MW	64780 TQ	USBLS	5/07
	Gary PMSA, IN	Y	39430 FQ	49780 MW	63610 TQ	USBLS	5/07
	Indianapolis-Carmel MSA, IN	Y	45940 FQ	59280 MW	73330 TQ	USBLS	5/07
	Iowa	Y	45600 FQ	57270 MW	73130 TQ	USBLS	5/07
	Davenport-Moline-Rock Island MSA, IA-IL	Y	38970 FQ	52400 MW	62780 TQ	USBLS	5/07
	Des Moines-West Des Moines MSA, IA	Y	50180 FQ	63970 MW	80880 TQ	USBLS	5/07
	Kansas	Y	43380 FQ	56590 MW	71380 TQ	USBLS	5/07
	Wichita MSA, KS	Y	44290 FQ	52620 MW	65200 TQ	USBLS	5/07
	Kentucky	Y	38661 FQ	49865 MW	64453 TQ	KYBLS	2008
	Lexington-Fayette MSA, KY	Y	40900 FQ	51250 MW	67680 TQ	USBLS	5/07
	Louisville-Jefferson County MSA, KY-IN	Y	42750 FQ	54290 MW	66480 TQ	USBLS	5/07
	Owensboro MSA, KY	Y	43290 FQ	51560 MW	60790 TQ	USBLS	5/07
	Louisiana	H	20.08 FQ	25.14 MW	30.86 TQ	LABLS	1/08-3/08
	Baton Rouge MSA, LA	Y	40510 FQ	49220 MW	59050 TQ	USBLS	5/07
	Lake Charles MSA, LA	Y	41390 FQ	50940 MW	63200 TQ	USBLS	5/07
	New Orleans-Metairie-Kenner MSA, LA	Y	45930 FQ	57510 MW	70730 TQ	USBLS	5/07
	Maine	Y	47260 FQ	57690 MW	68360 TQ	USBLS	5/07
	Portland-South Portland-Biddeford MSA, ME	Y	50940 FQ	61700 MW	72830 TQ	USBLS	5/07
	Maryland	Y		74725 MW		MDBLS	3/08
	Baltimore-Towson MSA, MD	Y	57000 FQ	72460 MW	90820 TQ	USBLS	5/07
	Bethesda-Gaithersburg-Frederick PMSA, MD	Y	60520 FQ	77330 MW	98390 TQ	USBLS	5/07
	Massachusetts	Y	57970 FQ	74120 MW	91190 TQ	USBLS	5/07
	Boston-Cambridge-Quincy NECTA, MA	Y	60520 FQ	76350 MW	93930 TQ	USBLS	5/07
	Worcester MSA, MA-CT	Y	55220 FQ	66530 MW	87090 TQ	USBLS	5/07
	Michigan	Y	47470 FQ	58870 MW	73370 TQ	USBLS	5/07
	Detroit-Warren-Livonia MSA, MI	Y	50260 FQ	62040 MW	76090 TQ	USBLS	5/07
	Grand Rapids-Wyoming MSA, MI	Y	41900 FQ	49860 MW	63430 TQ	USBLS	5/07
	Muskegon-Norton Shores MSA, MI	Y	42950 FQ	54240 MW	66230 TQ	USBLS	5/07
	Warren-Troy-Farmington Hills PMSA, MI	Y	50490 FQ	62230 MW	76380 TQ	USBLS	5/07
	Minnesota	Y	55533 FQ	68287 MW	85570 TQ	MNBLS	10/08-12/08
	Duluth-Superior MSA, MN-WI	Y	51034 FQ	62281 MW	74062 TQ	MNBLS	10/08-12/08
	Minneapolis-Saint Paul MSA, MN-WI	Y	58368 FQ	72168 MW	89065 TQ	MNBLS	10/08-12/08
	Rochester MSA, MN	Y	47433 FQ	55465 MW	69561 TQ	MNBLS	10/08-12/08
	Mississippi	Y	40030 FQ	49430 MW	61270 TQ	USBLS	5/07
	Gulfport-Biloxi MSA, MS	Y	45670 FQ	56080 MW	64340 TQ	USBLS	5/07
	Jackson MSA, MS	Y	37560 FQ	47490 MW	58890 TQ	USBLS	5/07
	Missouri	Y	47140 FQ	60430 MW	74940 TQ	USBLS	5/07
	Kansas City MSA, MO-KS	Y	47890 FQ	62260 MW	76550 TQ	USBLS	5/07
	St. Joseph MSA, MO-KS	Y	38530 FQ	47030 MW	68270 TQ	USBLS	5/07
	St. Louis MSA, MO-IL	Y	52680 FQ	64110 MW	77440 TQ	USBLS	5/07
	Montana	Y	38740 FQ	48540 MW	59860 TQ	USBLS	5/07
	Billings MSA, MT	Y	41160 FQ	49390 MW	57050 TQ	USBLS	5/07
	Nebraska	Y	48560 FQ	58830 MW	71730 TQ	USBLS	5/07
	Omaha-Council Bluffs MSA, NE-IA	Y	50290 FQ	60170 MW	74010 TQ	USBLS	5/07
	Nevada	H	23.22 FQ	28.54 MW	39.22 TQ	NVBLS	5/08
	Las Vegas-Paradise MSA, NV	H	23.13 FQ	28.43 MW	39.55 TQ	NVBLS	5/08
	New Hampshire	H	22.44 AE	30.13 MW	35.52 AEX	NHBLS	6/08
	Manchester MSA, NH	Y	54870 FQ	69600 MW	80640 TQ	USBLS	5/07
	Nashua NECTA, NH-MA	Y	46450 FQ	61060 MW	74670 TQ	USBLS	5/07
	Portsmouth MSA, NH-ME	Y	51050 FQ	58370 MW	73470 TQ	USBLS	5/07

AE Average entry wage	**AW** Average wage paid	**FQ** First quartile wage	**LO** Lowest wage paid	**MTC** Median total compensation	**TCC** Total cash compensation
AER Average entry range	**AWR** Average wage range	**H** Hourly	**LR** Low end range	**MW** Median wage paid	**TQ** Third quartile wage
AEX Average experienced wage	**AXR** Average experienced range	**HI** Highest wage paid	**M** Monthly	**MWR** Median wage range	**W** Weekly
ATC Average total compensation	**D** Daily	**HR** High end range	**MCC** Median cash compensation	**S** See annotated source	**Y** Yearly

Network and Computer Systems Administrator

Occupation/Type/Industry	Location	Per	Low	Mid	High	Source	Date
Network and Computer Systems Administrator	New Jersey	Y	59990 FQ	74910 MW	91910 TQ	USBLS	5/07
	Camden PMSA, NJ	Y	56140 FQ	69790 MW	80800 TQ	USBLS	5/07
	Edison PMSA, NJ	Y	62360 FQ	79560 MW	97330 TQ	USBLS	5/07
	Newark-Union PMSA, NJ-PA	Y	56820 FQ	72190 MW	87620 TQ	USBLS	5/07
	New Mexico	Y	37420 FQ	52130 MW	66250 TQ	USBLS	5/07
	Albuquerque MSA, NM	Y	47480 FQ	60060 MW	78360 TQ	USBLS	5/07
	Farmington MSA, NM	Y	53910 FQ	63040 MW	75020 TQ	USBLS	5/07
	New York	Y	57680 FQ	74520 MW	94870 TQ	USBLS	5/07
	Albany-Schenectady-Troy MSA, NY	Y	44380 FQ	55980 MW	70340 TQ	USBLS	5/07
	Buffalo-Niagara Falls MSA, NY	Y	47540 FQ	58390 MW	72480 TQ	USBLS	5/07
	Nassau-Suffolk PMSA, NY	Y	59890 FQ	74880 MW	93630 TQ	USBLS	5/07
	New York-Northern New Jersey-Long Island MSA, NY-NJ-PA	Y	63170 FQ	79410 MW	97830 TQ	USBLS	5/07
	North Carolina	Y	48320 FQ	61140 MW	77680 TQ	USBLS	5/07
	Charlotte-Gastonia-Concord MSA, NC-SC	Y	53080 FQ	65870 MW	83810 TQ	USBLS	5/07
	Raleigh-Cary MSA, NC	Y	45680 FQ	58880 MW	75850 TQ	USBLS	5/07
	North Dakota	Y	39290 FQ	45790 MW	54900 TQ	USBLS	5/07
	Fargo MSA, ND-MN	Y	40320 FQ	46850 MW	57190 TQ	USBLS	5/07
	Ohio	Y	48280 FQ	60880 MW	75600 TQ	USBLS	5/07
	Canton-Massillon MSA, OH	Y	47110 FQ	56440 MW	66090 TQ	USBLS	5/07
	Cincinnati-Middletown MSA, OH-KY-IN	Y	51210 FQ	63880 MW	76960 TQ	USBLS	5/07
	Cleveland-Elyria-Mentor MSA, OH	Y	49390 FQ	61750 MW	77110 TQ	USBLS	5/07
	Columbus MSA, OH	Y	48770 FQ	62610 MW	78170 TQ	USBLS	5/07
	Dayton MSA, OH	Y	46940 FQ	56380 MW	67310 TQ	USBLS	5/07
	Oklahoma	Y	41770 FQ	51520 MW	64190 TQ	USBLS	5/07
	Oklahoma City MSA, OK	Y	42590 FQ	51850 MW	65010 TQ	USBLS	5/07
	Tulsa MSA, OK	Y	45110 FQ	56060 MW	67320 TQ	USBLS	5/07
	Oregon	H	23.79 FQ	29.97 MW	37.46 TQ	ORBLS	5/08
	Portland-Vancouver-Beaverton MSA, OR-WA	Y	50400 FQ	63840 MW	78390 TQ	USBLS	5/07
	Pennsylvania	Y	47730 FQ	61220 MW	79730 TQ	USBLS	5/07
	Allentown-Bethlehem-Easton MSA, PA-NJ	Y	43740 FQ	57370 MW	76950 TQ	USBLS	5/07
	Erie MSA, PA	Y	41340 FQ	54890 MW	73850 TQ	USBLS	5/07
	Philadelphia-Camden-Wilmington MSA, PA-NJ-DE-MD	Y	52370 FQ	68180 MW	88190 TQ	USBLS	5/07
	Pittsburgh MSA, PA	Y	46540 FQ	61680 MW	77730 TQ	USBLS	5/07
	Rhode Island	Y	55490 FQ	65180 MW	81030 TQ	USBLS	5/07
	Providence-Fall River-Warwick MSA, RI-MA	Y	54810 FQ	64880 MW	80570 TQ	USBLS	5/07
	South Carolina	Y	44260 FQ	53580 MW	68660 TQ	USBLS	5/07
	Charleston-North Charleston MSA, SC	Y	43070 FQ	48520 MW	57370 TQ	USBLS	5/07
	Columbia MSA, SC	Y	41650 FQ	51380 MW	64710 TQ	USBLS	5/07
	South Dakota	Y	41248 FQ	49530 MW	59778 TQ	SDBLS	7/08-9/08
	Sioux Falls MSA, SD	Y	42662 FQ	50859 MW	61715 TQ	SDBLS	7/08-9/08
	Tennessee	Y	48840 FQ	62430 MW	77460 TQ	USBLS	5/07
	Memphis MSA, TN-MS-AR	Y	54940 FQ	70610 MW	85060 TQ	USBLS	5/07
	Nashville-Davidson-Murfreesboro MSA, TN	Y	52080 FQ	65160 MW	77680 TQ	USBLS	5/07
	Texas	Y	48170 FQ	61090 MW	77050 TQ	USBLS	5/07
	Austin-Round Rock MSA, TX	Y	44730 FQ	53590 MW	67450 TQ	USBLS	5/07
	Dallas-Fort Worth-Arlington MSA, TX	Y	53210 FQ	66030 MW	83180 TQ	USBLS	5/07
	El Paso MSA, TX	Y	40380 FQ	49180 MW	59910 TQ	USBLS	5/07
	Houston-Sugar Land-Baytown MSA, TX	Y	52590 FQ	64310 MW	78720 TQ	USBLS	5/07
	San Antonio MSA, TX	Y	43660 FQ	56390 MW	70600 TQ	USBLS	5/07
	Utah	Y	45670 FQ	56990 MW	72360 TQ	USBLS	5/07
	Salt Lake City MSA, UT	Y	45610 FQ	57450 MW	74220 TQ	USBLS	5/07
	Vermont	Y	45300 FQ	56050 MW	69120 TQ	USBLS	5/07
	Burlington-South Burlington MSA, VT	Y	47440 FQ	59470 MW	73100 TQ	USBLS	5/07
	Virginia	Y	53970 FQ	71920 MW	92710 TQ	USBLS	5/07

AE	Average entry wage	AW	Average wage paid	FQ	First quartile wage	LO	Lowest wage paid	MTC	Median total compensation	TCC	Total cash compensation
AER	Average entry range	AWR	Average wage range	H	Hourly	LR	Low end range	MW	Median wage paid	TQ	Third quartile wage
AEX	Average experienced wage	AXR	Average experienced range	HI	Highest wage paid	M	Monthly	MWR	Median wage range	W	Weekly
ATC	Average total compensation	D	Daily	HR	High end range	MCC	Median cash compensation	S	See annotated source	Y	Yearly

Occupation/Type/Industry	Location	Per	Low	Mid	High	Source	Date
Network and Computer Systems Administrator	Lynchburg MSA, VA	Y	42880 FQ	55690 MW	75860 TQ	USBLS	5/07
	Richmond MSA, VA	Y	53630 FQ	65380 MW	82320 TQ	USBLS	5/07
	Virginia Beach-Norfolk-Newport News MSA, VA-NC	Y	46840 FQ	58800 MW	74130 TQ	USBLS	5/07
	Washington	H	28.64 FQ	35.09 MW	41.89 TQ	WABLS	3/08
	Seattle-Tacoma-Bellevue MSA, WA	Y	62960 FQ	74910 MW	89610 TQ	USBLS	5/07
	West Virginia	Y	38720 FQ	52404 MW	70695 TQ	WVBLS	7/08-9/08
	Charleston MSA, WV	Y	37290 FQ	49600 MW	70590 TQ	USBLS	5/07
	Huntington-Ashland MSA, WV-KY-OH	Y	34010 FQ	46680 MW	56870 TQ	USBLS	5/07
	Wisconsin	Y	47230 FQ	58370 MW	71590 TQ	USBLS	5/07
	Milwaukee-Waukesha-West Allis MSA, WI	Y	49870 FQ	61720 MW	75560 TQ	USBLS	5/07
	Wyoming	Y	40517 FQ	49961 MW	60267 TQ	WYBLS	9/08
	Cheyenne MSA, WY	Y	45587 FQ	53889 MW	64025 TQ	WYBLS	9/08
	Puerto Rico	Y	33190 FQ	42270 MW	52780 TQ	USBLS	5/07
	San Juan-Caguas-Guaynabo MSA, PR	Y	33730 FQ	42370 MW	53190 TQ	USBLS	5/07
	Virgin Islands	Y	52550 FQ	61130 MW	73940 TQ	USBLS	5/07
	Guam	Y	32210 FQ	39580 MW	51640 TQ	USBLS	5/07
Network Engineer							
Municipal Government	Colorado Springs, CO	M	4699 LO			COSPRS	1/1/09
Network Security Administrator	United States	Y		77500-106250 AWR		ESECP	2009
Network Systems and Data Communications Analyst	United States	Y		65000 MW		MSN04	2008
	Alabama	Y	46340 FQ	64100 MW	79990 TQ	USBLS	5/07
	Birmingham-Hoover MSA, AL	Y	47040 FQ	65270 MW	77160 TQ	USBLS	5/07
	Mobile MSA, AL	Y	39880 FQ	49080 MW	74250 TQ	USBLS	5/07
	Alaska	Y	46910 FQ	59900 MW	75850 TQ	USBLS	5/07
	Anchorage MSA, AK	Y	45750 FQ	60070 MW	76410 TQ	USBLS	5/07
	Arizona	Y	44980 FQ	59320 MW	77540 TQ	USBLS	5/07
	Phoenix-Mesa-Scottsdale MSA, AZ	Y	44390 FQ	58890 MW	78430 TQ	USBLS	5/07
	Tucson MSA, AZ	Y	50220 FQ	62400 MW	74380 TQ	USBLS	5/07
	Arkansas	Y	42920 FQ	55720 MW	72570 TQ	USBLS	5/07
	Little Rock-North Little Rock MSA, AR	Y	40890 FQ	53050 MW	61810 TQ	USBLS	5/07
	California	H	27.36 FQ	35.99 MW	46.38 TQ	CABLS	1/08-3/08
	Los Angeles-Long Beach-Glendale PMSA, CA	H	24.95 FQ	33.49 MW	42.28 TQ	CABLS	1/08-3/08
	Oakland-Fremont-Hayward MSA, CA	H	29.78 FQ	36.87 MW	45.96 TQ	CABLS	1/08-3/08
	Riverside-San Bernardino-Ontario MSA, CA	H	21.33 FQ	28.64 MW	36.29 TQ	CABLS	1/08-3/08
	Sacramento-Arden Arcade-Roseville MSA, CA	H	24.83 FQ	32.78 MW	42.81 TQ	CABLS	1/08-3/08
	San Diego-Carlsbad-San Marcos MSA, CA	H	28.54 FQ	35.65 MW	43.71 TQ	CABLS	1/08-3/08
	San Francisco-San Mateo-Redwood PMSA, CA	H	31.40 FQ	42.43 MW	52.28 TQ	CABLS	1/08-3/08
	San Jose-Sunnyvale-Santa Clara MSA, CA	H	33.33 FQ	44.28 MW	55.37 TQ	CABLS	1/08-3/08
	Santa Ana-Anaheim-Irvine PMSA, CA	Y	55870 FQ	72230 MW	90770 TQ	USBLS	5/07
	Colorado	Y	52080 FQ	69580 MW	88790 TQ	USBLS	5/07
	Denver-Aurora MSA, CO	Y	58490 FQ	75960 MW	93310 TQ	USBLS	5/07
	Connecticut	H	25.60 AE	36.05 MW		CTBLS	1/08-3/08
	Bridgeport-Stamford-Norwalk MSA, CT	Y	61270 FQ	73730 MW	92310 TQ	USBLS	5/07
	Hartford-West Hartford-East Hartford MSA, CT	Y	58130 FQ	71600 MW	83820 TQ	USBLS	5/07
	Delaware	Y	45590 FQ	61450 MW	85930 TQ	USBLS	5/07
	Wilmington PMSA, DE-MD-NJ	Y	46260 FQ	62450 MW	88110 TQ	USBLS	5/07
	District of Columbia	Y	57200 FQ	70620 MW	88000 TQ	USBLS	5/07

AE	Average entry wage	AW	Average wage paid	FQ	First quartile wage
AER	Average entry range	AWR	Average wage range	H	Hourly
AEX	Average experienced wage	AXR	Average experienced range	HI	Highest wage paid
ATC	Average total compensation	D	Daily	HR	High end range

LO	Lowest wage paid	MTC	Median total compensation	TCC	Total cash compensation
LR	Low end range	MW	Median wage paid	TQ	Third quartile wage
		MWR	Median wage range	W	Weekly
M	Monthly				
MCC	Median cash compensation	S	See annotated source	Y	Yearly

Occupation/Type/Industry	Location	Per	Low	Mid	High	Source	Date
Network Systems and Data Communications Analyst	Washington-Arlington-Alexandria MSA, DC-VA-MD-WV	Y	65070 FQ	80690 MW	100750 TQ	USBLS	5/07
	Florida	Y	44330 FQ	57390 MW	75900 TQ	USBLS	5/07
	Fort Lauderdale-Pompano Beach-Deerfield Beach PMSA, FL	Y	40460 FQ	51720 MW	72920 TQ	USBLS	5/07
	Jacksonville MSA, FL	Y	48790 FQ	63240 MW	79310 TQ	USBLS	5/07
	Miami-Fort Lauderdale-Miami Beach MSA, FL	Y	44400 FQ	58800 MW	79370 TQ	USBLS	5/07
	Orlando-Kissimmee MSA, FL	Y	44800 FQ	57640 MW	74630 TQ	USBLS	5/07
	Tampa-St. Petersburg-Clearwater MSA, FL	Y	50760 FQ	66450 MW	86350 TQ	USBLS	5/07
	West Palm Beach-Boca Raton-Boynton Beach PMSA, FL	Y	48310 FQ	63410 MW	85750 TQ	USBLS	5/07
	Georgia	Y	51220 FQ	66820 MW	84050 TQ	USBLS	5/07
	Atlanta-Sandy Springs-Marietta MSA, GA	Y	54980 FQ	70020 MW	87380 TQ	USBLS	5/07
	Augusta-Richmond County MSA, GA-SC	Y	46800 FQ	69220 MW	78820 TQ	USBLS	5/07
	Macon MSA, GA	Y	36680 FQ	40240 MW	47620 TQ	USBLS	5/07
	Savannah MSA, GA	Y	43580 FQ	55280 MW	79080 TQ	USBLS	5/07
	Hawaii	Y	52050 FQ	65730 MW	79040 TQ	USBLS	5/07
	Honolulu MSA, HI	Y	52180 FQ	66080 MW	79020 TQ	USBLS	5/07
	Idaho	Y	40260 FQ	54720 MW	74580 TQ	USBLS	5/07
	Boise City-Nampa MSA, ID	Y	47540 FQ	61510 MW	78110 TQ	USBLS	5/07
	Illinois	Y	54930 FQ	69090 MW	86470 TQ	USBLS	5/07
	Chicago-Naperville-Joliet MSA, IL-IN-WI	Y	56470 FQ	70760 MW	89060 TQ	USBLS	5/07
	Indiana	Y	49560 FQ	63830 MW	82160 TQ	USBLS	5/07
	Gary PMSA, IN	Y	37550 FQ	50610 MW	63460 TQ	USBLS	5/07
	Indianapolis-Carmel MSA, IN	Y	56430 FQ	70810 MW	87130 TQ	USBLS	5/07
	Iowa	Y	45870 FQ	59830 MW	78340 TQ	USBLS	5/07
	Des Moines-West Des Moines MSA, IA	Y	49520 FQ	62580 MW	85100 TQ	USBLS	5/07
	Kansas	Y	45440 FQ	58860 MW	75440 TQ	USBLS	5/07
	Wichita MSA, KS	Y	51690 FQ	67270 MW	85440 TQ	USBLS	5/07
	Kentucky	Y	43531 FQ	56381 MW	71630 TQ	KYBLS	2008
	Bowling Green MSA, KY	Y	29990 FQ	41740 MW	54550 TQ	USBLS	5/07
	Louisville-Jefferson County MSA, KY-IN	Y	43490 FQ	56970 MW	76640 TQ	USBLS	5/07
	Owensboro MSA, KY	Y	54400 FQ	64800 MW	75850 TQ	USBLS	5/07
	Louisiana	H	18.72 FQ	23.21 MW	29.49 TQ	LABLS	1/08-3/08
	Baton Rouge MSA, LA	Y	38950 FQ	47470 MW	60240 TQ	USBLS	5/07
	New Orleans-Metairie-Kenner MSA, LA	Y	37540 FQ	53430 MW	64370 TQ	USBLS	5/07
	Maine	Y	44780 FQ	59790 MW	77400 TQ	USBLS	5/07
	Portland-South Portland-Biddeford MSA, ME	Y	50760 FQ	62690 MW	81720 TQ	USBLS	5/07
	Maryland	Y		78125 MW		MDBLS	3/08
	Baltimore-Towson MSA, MD	Y	54640 FQ	71740 MW	91790 TQ	USBLS	5/07
	Bethesda-Gaithersburg-Frederick PMSA, MD	Y	70280 FQ	88180 MW	106790 TQ	USBLS	5/07
	Cumberland MSA, MD-WV	Y	64210 FQ	75120 MW	88570 TQ	USBLS	5/07
	Hagerstown-Martinsburg MSA, MD-WV	Y	27950 FQ	36080 MW	56400 TQ	USBLS	5/07
	Massachusetts	Y	63050 FQ	80660 MW	98090 TQ	USBLS	5/07
	Boston-Cambridge-Quincy NECTA, MA	Y	65500 FQ	82890 MW	102050 TQ	USBLS	5/07
	Worcester MSA, MA-CT	Y	51820 FQ	67790 MW	96630 TQ	USBLS	5/07
	Michigan	Y	53400 FQ	64170 MW	80180 TQ	USBLS	5/07
	Detroit-Warren-Livonia MSA, MI	Y	55120 FQ	65550 MW	80480 TQ	USBLS	5/07
	Grand Rapids-Wyoming MSA, MI	Y	54390 FQ	71370 MW	96070 TQ	USBLS	5/07
	Lansing-East Lansing MSA, MI	Y	44190 FQ	55680 MW	71440 TQ	USBLS	5/07
	Muskegon-Norton Shores MSA, MI	Y	49720 FQ	60290 MW	71690 TQ	USBLS	5/07
	Warren-Troy-Farmington Hills PMSA, MI	Y	56310 FQ	66350 MW	80710 TQ	USBLS	5/07
	Minnesota	Y	65912 FQ	80768 MW	97979 TQ	MNBLS	10/08-12/08

AE	Average entry wage	AW	Average wage paid	FQ	First quartile wage	LO	Lowest wage paid	MTC Median total compensation TCC Total cash compensation
AER	Average entry range	AWR	Average wage range	H	Hourly	LR	Low end range	MW Median wage paid TQ Third quartile wage
AEX	Average experienced wage	AXR	Average experienced range	HI	Highest wage paid	M	Monthly	MWR Median wage range W Weekly
ATC	Average total compensation	D	Daily	HR	High end range	MCC	Median cash compensation	S See annotated source Y Yearly

1100

Occupation/Type/Industry	Location	Per	Low	Mid	High	Source	Date
Network Systems and Data Communications Analyst	Duluth-Superior MSA, MN-WI	Y	56004 FQ	71279 MW	85141 TQ	MNBLS	10/08-12/08
	Minneapolis-Saint Paul MSA, MN-WI	Y	67220 FQ	81657 MW	98585 TQ	MNBLS	10/08-12/08
	Rochester MSA, MN	Y	89274 FQ	100893 MW	113060 TQ	MNBLS	10/08-12/08
	Mississippi	Y	40310 FQ	50300 MW	69020 TQ	USBLS	5/07
	Jackson MSA, MS	Y	33890 FQ	48670 MW	72980 TQ	USBLS	5/07
	Missouri	Y	47950 FQ	64670 MW	80580 TQ	USBLS	5/07
	Kansas City MSA, MO-KS	Y	45230 FQ	59390 MW	76010 TQ	USBLS	5/07
	St. Louis MSA, MO-IL	Y	57500 FQ	69990 MW	83030 TQ	USBLS	5/07
	Montana	Y	38530 FQ	47120 MW	60230 TQ	USBLS	5/07
	Billings MSA, MT	Y	18370 FQ	41310 MW	62540 TQ	USBLS	5/07
	Nebraska	Y	47190 FQ	60110 MW	77020 TQ	USBLS	5/07
	Omaha-Council Bluffs MSA, NE-IA	Y	51070 FQ	64510 MW	80670 TQ	USBLS	5/07
	Nevada	H	27.10 FQ	33.33 MW	39.67 TQ	NVBLS	5/08
	Las Vegas-Paradise MSA, NV	H	27.56 FQ	33.31 MW	39.64 TQ	NVBLS	5/08
	New Hampshire	H	20.76 AE	30.24 MW	37.21 AEX	NHBLS	6/08
	Manchester MSA, NH	Y	59430 FQ	68910 MW	82510 TQ	USBLS	5/07
	Nashua NECTA, NH-MA	Y	56130 FQ	73060 MW	98060 TQ	USBLS	5/07
	New Jersey	Y	67110 FQ	81550 MW	99620 TQ	USBLS	5/07
	Camden PMSA, NJ	Y	59630 FQ	74660 MW	95220 TQ	USBLS	5/07
	Edison PMSA, NJ	Y	65990 FQ	80780 MW	98140 TQ	USBLS	5/07
	Newark-Union PMSA, NJ-PA	Y	71660 FQ	84120 MW	100400 TQ	USBLS	5/07
	New Mexico	Y	48250 FQ	63640 MW	77520 TQ	USBLS	5/07
	Albuquerque MSA, NM	Y	51750 FQ	63900 MW	79810 TQ	USBLS	5/07
	New York	Y	59010 FQ	74590 MW	94250 TQ	USBLS	5/07
	Albany-Schenectady-Troy MSA, NY	Y	56360 FQ	66640 MW	79370 TQ	USBLS	5/07
	Buffalo-Niagara Falls MSA, NY	Y	51240 FQ	64400 MW	80800 TQ	USBLS	5/07
	Nassau-Suffolk PMSA, NY	Y	55760 FQ	68150 MW	89770 TQ	USBLS	5/07
	New York-Northern New Jersey-Long Island MSA, NY-NJ-PA	Y	63050 FQ	78900 MW	98250 TQ	USBLS	5/07
	North Carolina	Y	49800 FQ	64220 MW	81620 TQ	USBLS	5/07
	Charlotte-Gastonia-Concord MSA, NC-SC	Y	54810 FQ	72040 MW	89380 TQ	USBLS	5/07
	Raleigh-Cary MSA, NC	Y	54090 FQ	65090 MW	80240 TQ	USBLS	5/07
	North Dakota	Y	39260 FQ	47300 MW	58740 TQ	USBLS	5/07
	Bismarck MSA, ND	Y	45470 FQ	54130 MW	62590 TQ	USBLS	5/07
	Fargo MSA, ND-MN	Y	36610 FQ	43210 MW	53190 TQ	USBLS	5/07
	Ohio	Y	56560 FQ	69250 MW	84740 TQ	USBLS	5/07
	Cincinnati-Middletown MSA, OH-KY-IN	Y	57460 FQ	72440 MW	90530 TQ	USBLS	5/07
	Cleveland-Elyria-Mentor MSA, OH	Y	58530 FQ	72250 MW	87560 TQ	USBLS	5/07
	Columbus MSA, OH	Y	56260 FQ	67760 MW	83870 TQ	USBLS	5/07
	Dayton MSA, OH	Y	54180 FQ	66760 MW	80830 TQ	USBLS	5/07
	Oklahoma	Y	40050 FQ	52800 MW	69340 TQ	USBLS	5/07
	Oklahoma City MSA, OK	Y	41100 FQ	53710 MW	68010 TQ	USBLS	5/07
	Tulsa MSA, OK	Y	44000 FQ	54780 MW	70860 TQ	USBLS	5/07
	Oregon	H	24.67 FQ	30.97 MW	38.07 TQ	ORBLS	5/08
	Portland-Vancouver-Beaverton MSA, OR-WA	Y	52560 FQ	65250 MW	79470 TQ	USBLS	5/07
	Pennsylvania	Y	51520 FQ	67590 MW	83390 TQ	USBLS	5/07
	Allentown-Bethlehem-Easton MSA, PA-NJ	Y	52620 FQ	66440 MW	91710 TQ	USBLS	5/07
	Philadelphia-Camden-Wilmington MSA, PA-NJ-DE-MD	Y	53000 FQ	70450 MW	90050 TQ	USBLS	5/07
	Pittsburgh MSA, PA	Y	49110 FQ	62130 MW	77080 TQ	USBLS	5/07
	Rhode Island	Y	58450 FQ	73290 MW	86170 TQ	USBLS	5/07
	Providence-Fall River-Warwick MSA, RI-MA	Y	58770 FQ	73560 MW	87610 TQ	USBLS	5/07
	South Carolina	Y	44950 FQ	59160 MW	78800 TQ	USBLS	5/07
	Charleston-North Charleston MSA, SC	Y	48290 FQ	62680 MW	78340 TQ	USBLS	5/07
	Columbia MSA, SC	Y	45400 FQ	58540 MW	77200 TQ	USBLS	5/07
	South Dakota	Y	41792 FQ	48949 MW	60202 TQ	SDBLS	7/08-9/08
	Sioux Falls MSA, SD	Y	40355 FQ	49243 MW	62817 TQ	SDBLS	7/08-9/08
	Tennessee	Y	46070 FQ	62600 MW	80620 TQ	USBLS	5/07

AE	Average entry wage	**AW**	Average wage paid	**FQ**	First quartile wage	**LO** Lowest wage paid
AER	Average entry range	**AWR**	Average wage range	**H**	Hourly	**LR** Low end range
AEX	Average experienced wage	**AXR**	Average experienced range	**HI**	Highest wage paid	**M** Monthly
ATC	Average total compensation	**D**	Daily	**HR**	High end range	**MCC** Median cash compensation

MTC Median total compensation **TCC** Total cash compensation
MW Median wage paid **TQ** Third quartile wage
MWR Median wage range **W** Weekly
S See annotated source **Y** Yearly

Occupation/Type/Industry	Location	Per	Low	Mid	High	Source	Date
Network Systems and Data Communications Analyst	Memphis MSA, TN-MS-AR	Y	48310 FQ	61960 MW	75690 TQ	USBLS	5/07
	Nashville-Davidson-Murfreesboro MSA, TN	Y	47360 FQ	62680 MW	80990 TQ	USBLS	5/07
	Texas	Y	49290 FQ	64110 MW	83850 TQ	USBLS	5/07
	Austin-Round Rock MSA, TX	Y	43340 FQ	58210 MW	76180 TQ	USBLS	5/07
	Dallas-Fort Worth-Arlington MSA, TX	Y	54940 FQ	71700 MW	91190 TQ	USBLS	5/07
	El Paso MSA, TX	Y	40910 FQ	57640 MW	76920 TQ	USBLS	5/07
	Houston-Sugar Land-Baytown MSA, TX	Y	49340 FQ	63210 MW	81540 TQ	USBLS	5/07
	San Antonio MSA, TX	Y	41600 FQ	56110 MW	69860 TQ	USBLS	5/07
	Utah	Y	43170 FQ	57870 MW	80210 TQ	USBLS	5/07
	Provo-Orem MSA, UT	Y	41160 FQ	57700 MW	83740 TQ	USBLS	5/07
	St. George MSA, UT	Y	99280 FQ	107710 MW	115960 TQ	USBLS	5/07
	Salt Lake City MSA, UT	Y	43160 FQ	57130 MW	75870 TQ	USBLS	5/07
	Vermont	Y	51720 FQ	64200 MW	77620 TQ	USBLS	5/07
	Burlington-South Burlington MSA, VT	Y	56970 FQ	71240 MW	82280 TQ	USBLS	5/07
	Virginia	Y	59780 FQ	76640 MW	97100 TQ	USBLS	5/07
	Richmond MSA, VA	Y	54760 FQ	68900 MW	83790 TQ	USBLS	5/07
	Virginia Beach-Norfolk-Newport News MSA, VA-NC	Y	46580 FQ	58640 MW	74380 TQ	USBLS	5/07
	Washington	H	29.12 FQ	37.58 MW	47.02 TQ	WABLS	3/08
	Bremerton-Silverdale MSA, WA	Y	40740 FQ	58010 MW	73180 TQ	USBLS	5/07
	Seattle-Tacoma-Bellevue MSA, WA	Y	63890 FQ	81830 MW	99260 TQ	USBLS	5/07
	West Virginia	Y	34009 FQ	42027 MW	62619 TQ	WVBLS	7/08-9/08
	Charleston MSA, WV	Y	32340 FQ	39120 MW	51760 TQ	USBLS	5/07
	Wisconsin	Y	48000 FQ	59370 MW	73410 TQ	USBLS	5/07
	Milwaukee-Waukesha-West Allis MSA, WI	Y	51120 FQ	62340 MW	76880 TQ	USBLS	5/07
	Wyoming	Y	37375 FQ	49641 MW	63742 TQ	WYBLS	9/08
	Cheyenne MSA, WY	Y	42734 FQ	51249 MW	62782 TQ	WYBLS	9/08
	Puerto Rico	Y	27410 FQ	34870 MW	45870 TQ	USBLS	5/07
	San Juan-Caguas-Guaynabo MSA, PR	Y	27280 FQ	34890 MW	46000 TQ	USBLS	5/07
	Guam	Y	38710 FQ	55090 MW	60670 TQ	USBLS	5/07
Neuropsychologist							
Institution	United States	Y		81000 MW		TCN	2/05-5/31/05
Private Practice	United States	Y		100000 MW		TCN	2/05-5/31/05
New Accounts Clerk	Alabama	Y	21470 FQ	24510 MW	28770 TQ	USBLS	5/07
	Birmingham-Hoover MSA, AL	Y	21510 FQ	24280 MW	29450 TQ	USBLS	5/07
	Alaska	Y	27480 FQ	29830 MW	32370 TQ	USBLS	5/07
	Arizona	Y	26310 FQ	29780 MW	34620 TQ	USBLS	5/07
	Tucson MSA, AZ	Y	27520 FQ	30770 MW	35090 TQ	USBLS	5/07
	Arkansas	Y	22010 FQ	25210 MW	29440 TQ	USBLS	5/07
	Little Rock-North Little Rock MSA, AR	Y	24630 FQ	27170 MW	31160 TQ	USBLS	5/07
	California	H	13.42 FQ	15.79 MW	18.54 TQ	CABLS	1/08-3/08
	Los Angeles-Long Beach-Glendale PMSA, CA	H	13.00 FQ	15.08 MW	18.55 TQ	CABLS	1/08-3/08
	Oakland-Fremont-Hayward MSA, CA	H	13.34 FQ	14.98 MW	18.41 TQ	CABLS	1/08-3/08
	Riverside-San Bernardino-Ontario MSA, CA	H	13.34 FQ	15.60 MW	18.11 TQ	CABLS	1/08-3/08
	Sacramento-Arden Arcade-Roseville MSA, CA	H	14.15 FQ	16.08 MW	18.18 TQ	CABLS	1/08-3/08
	San Diego-Carlsbad-San Marcos MSA, CA	H	12.56 FQ	16.49 MW	18.55 TQ	CABLS	1/08-3/08
	San Francisco-San Mateo-Redwood PMSA, CA	H	14.22 FQ	16.94 MW	19.23 TQ	CABLS	1/08-3/08
	San Jose-Sunnyvale-Santa Clara MSA, CA	H	14.46 FQ	17.13 MW	21.48 TQ	CABLS	1/08-3/08
	Santa Ana-Anaheim-Irvine PMSA, CA	Y	30190 FQ	34510 MW	39220 TQ	USBLS	5/07
	Colorado	Y	26820 FQ	30240 MW	34480 TQ	USBLS	5/07
	Denver-Aurora MSA, CO	Y	28430 FQ	31590 MW	35570 TQ	USBLS	5/07
	Connecticut	H	12.22 AE	15.45 MW		CTBLS	1/08-3/08

AE	Average entry wage	**AW**	Average wage paid	**FQ**	First quartile wage	**LO** Lowest wage paid **MTC** Median total compensation **TCC** Total cash compensation
AER	Average entry range	**AWR**	Average wage range	**H**	Hourly	**LR** Low end range **MW** Median wage paid **TQ** Third quartile wage
AEX	Average experienced wage	**AXR**	Average experienced range	**HI**	Highest wage paid	**M** Monthly **MWR** Median wage range **W** Weekly
ATC	Average total compensation	**D**	Daily	**HR**	High end range	**MCC** Median cash compensation **S** See annotated source **Y** Yearly

New Accounts Clerk

Occupation/Type/Industry	Location	Per	Low	Mid	High	Source	Date
New Accounts Clerk	Bridgeport-Stamford-Norwalk MSA, CT	Y	29040 FQ	35310 MW	41810 TQ	USBLS	5/07
	Hartford-West Hartford-East Hartford MSA, CT	Y	24590 FQ	28670 MW	33630 TQ	USBLS	5/07
	Delaware	Y	28110 FQ	31940 MW	36370 TQ	USBLS	5/07
	Wilmington PMSA, DE-MD-NJ	Y	28180 FQ	32020 MW	36590 TQ	USBLS	5/07
	District of Columbia	Y	31690 FQ	35700 MW	39820 TQ	USBLS	5/07
	Washington-Arlington-Alexandria MSA, DC-VA-MD-WV	Y	29850 FQ	34270 MW	38790 TQ	USBLS	5/07
	Florida	Y	23580 FQ	28270 MW	33850 TQ	USBLS	5/07
	Fort Lauderdale-Pompano Beach-Deerfield Beach PMSA, FL	Y	24370 FQ	29380 MW	33900 TQ	USBLS	5/07
	Jacksonville MSA, FL	Y	25350 FQ	30380 MW	34930 TQ	USBLS	5/07
	Miami-Fort Lauderdale-Miami Beach MSA, FL	Y	24940 FQ	30560 MW	35950 TQ	USBLS	5/07
	Orlando-Kissimmee MSA, FL	Y	25120 FQ	29460 MW	35610 TQ	USBLS	5/07
	Tampa-St. Petersburg-Clearwater MSA, FL	Y	21620 FQ	25400 MW	31370 TQ	USBLS	5/07
	West Palm Beach-Boca Raton-Boynton Beach PMSA, FL	Y	25360 FQ	32260 MW	37330 TQ	USBLS	5/07
	Georgia	Y	25000 FQ	29700 MW	35050 TQ	USBLS	5/07
	Atlanta-Sandy Springs-Marietta MSA, GA	Y	25450 FQ	30280 MW	35590 TQ	USBLS	5/07
	Hawaii	Y	25370 FQ	28250 MW	31600 TQ	USBLS	5/07
	Honolulu MSA, HI	Y	24980 FQ	28240 MW	32730 TQ	USBLS	5/07
	Idaho	Y	22020 FQ	24440 MW	29780 TQ	USBLS	5/07
	Boise City-Nampa MSA, ID	Y	22920 FQ	27190 MW	31830 TQ	USBLS	5/07
	Illinois	Y	26660 FQ	31810 MW	37560 TQ	USBLS	5/07
	Champaign-Urbana MSA, IL	Y	25090 FQ	30260 MW	35670 TQ	USBLS	5/07
	Chicago-Naperville-Joliet MSA, IL-IN-WI	Y	27760 FQ	32810 MW	38000 TQ	USBLS	5/07
	Rockford MSA, IL	Y	24420 FQ	29770 MW	35510 TQ	USBLS	5/07
	Indiana	Y	25370 FQ	29240 MW	34150 TQ	USBLS	5/07
	Gary PMSA, IN	Y	24750 FQ	28340 MW	32940 TQ	USBLS	5/07
	Indianapolis-Carmel MSA, IN	Y	27580 FQ	32310 MW	36100 TQ	USBLS	5/07
	Iowa	Y	25240 FQ	28920 MW	34470 TQ	USBLS	5/07
	Des Moines-West Des Moines MSA, IA	Y	29200 FQ	34190 MW	42160 TQ	USBLS	5/07
	Kansas	Y	23690 FQ	27100 MW	30820 TQ	USBLS	5/07
	Wichita MSA, KS	Y	24120 FQ	26850 MW	29630 TQ	USBLS	5/07
	Kentucky	Y	23676 FQ	27987 MW	32103 TQ	KYBLS	2008
	Louisville-Jefferson County MSA, KY-IN	Y	24720 FQ	28210 MW	31640 TQ	USBLS	5/07
	Louisiana	H	9.94 FQ	12.15 MW	14.29 TQ	LABLS	1/08-3/08
	Baton Rouge MSA, LA	Y	19970 FQ	24020 MW	28070 TQ	USBLS	5/07
	New Orleans-Metairie-Kenner MSA, LA	Y	23180 FQ	27340 MW	31850 TQ	USBLS	5/07
	Maine	Y	25530 FQ	28080 MW	31200 TQ	USBLS	5/07
	Portland-South Portland-Biddeford MSA, ME	Y	27760 FQ	31200 MW	37890 TQ	USBLS	5/07
	Maryland	Y		34025 MW		MDBLS	3/08
	Baltimore-Towson MSA, MD	Y	28950 FQ	33340 MW	37040 TQ	USBLS	5/07
	Bethesda-Gaithersburg-Frederick PMSA, MD	Y	30610 FQ	34280 MW	38710 TQ	USBLS	5/07
	Massachusetts	Y	28780 FQ	34340 MW	40410 TQ	USBLS	5/07
	Boston-Cambridge-Quincy NECTA, MA	Y	29070 FQ	35070 MW	40750 TQ	USBLS	5/07
	New Bedford MSA, MA	Y	23140 FQ	29520 MW	34760 TQ	USBLS	5/07
	Worcester MSA, MA-CT	Y	27420 FQ	29870 MW	34680 TQ	USBLS	5/07
	Michigan	Y	25680 FQ	29410 MW	35120 TQ	USBLS	5/07
	Detroit-Warren-Livonia MSA, MI	Y	26580 FQ	30280 MW	36110 TQ	USBLS	5/07
	Flint MSA, MI	Y	22970 FQ	27310 MW	34780 TQ	USBLS	5/07
	Grand Rapids-Wyoming MSA, MI	Y	24390 FQ	30590 MW	36910 TQ	USBLS	5/07
	Warren-Troy-Farmington Hills PMSA, MI	Y	26540 FQ	29880 MW	35730 TQ	USBLS	5/07
	Minnesota	Y	25728 FQ	31223 MW	36833 TQ	MNBLS	10/08-12/08
	Duluth-Superior MSA, MN-WI	Y	26613 FQ	29652 MW	33003 TQ	MNBLS	10/08-12/08

AE	Average entry wage	AW	Average wage paid	FQ	First quartile wage	LO	Lowest wage paid	MTC	Median total compensation	TCC	Total cash compensation
AER	Average entry range	AWR	Average wage range	H	Hourly	LR	Low end range	MW	Median wage paid	TQ	Third quartile wage
AEX	Average experienced wage	AXR	Average experienced range	HI	Highest wage paid	M	Monthly	MWR	Median wage range	W	Weekly
ATC	Average total compensation	D	Daily	HR	High end range	MCC	Median cash compensation	S	See annotated source	Y	Yearly

Occupation/Type/Industry	Location	Per	Low	Mid	High	Source	Date
New Accounts Clerk	Minneapolis-Saint Paul MSA, MN-WI	Y	26321 FQ	32347 MW	37406 TQ	MNBLS	10/08-12/08
	Rochester MSA, MN	Y	23597 FQ	28770 MW	36573 TQ	MNBLS	10/08-12/08
	Mississippi	Y	22920 FQ	25990 MW	30310 TQ	USBLS	5/07
	Jackson MSA, MS	Y	22720 FQ	26140 MW	29850 TQ	USBLS	5/07
	Missouri	Y	23400 FQ	27890 MW	32320 TQ	USBLS	5/07
	Joplin MSA, MO	Y	20800 FQ	24310 MW	31910 TQ	USBLS	5/07
	Kansas City MSA, MO-KS	Y	24780 FQ	28790 MW	34010 TQ	USBLS	5/07
	St. Louis MSA, MO-IL	Y	24950 FQ	29100 MW	35430 TQ	USBLS	5/07
	Montana	Y	24340 FQ	27490 MW	30290 TQ	USBLS	5/07
	Billings MSA, MT	Y	24410 FQ	28180 MW	31940 TQ	USBLS	5/07
	Nebraska	Y	22770 FQ	28090 MW	32590 TQ	USBLS	5/07
	Omaha-Council Bluffs MSA, NE-IA	Y	25250 FQ	29430 MW	33660 TQ	USBLS	5/07
	Nevada	H	13.85 FQ	15.76 MW	18.02 TQ	NVBLS	5/08
	Las Vegas-Paradise MSA, NV	H	13.92 FQ	15.63 MW	17.71 TQ	NVBLS	5/08
	New Hampshire	H	11.26 AE	13.72 MW	14.99 AEX	NHBLS	6/08
	Manchester MSA, NH	Y	25820 FQ	28820 MW	32620 TQ	USBLS	5/07
	Nashua NECTA, NH-MA	Y	23410 FQ	28060 MW	30840 TQ	USBLS	5/07
	Rochester-Dover MSA, NH-ME	Y	24390 FQ	27340 MW	30070 TQ	USBLS	5/07
	New Jersey	Y	27350 FQ	33080 MW	38850 TQ	USBLS	5/07
	Camden PMSA, NJ	Y	25290 FQ	31300 MW	37050 TQ	USBLS	5/07
	Edison PMSA, NJ	Y	27950 FQ	33590 MW	39900 TQ	USBLS	5/07
	Newark-Union PMSA, NJ-PA	Y	26220 FQ	33180 MW	40630 TQ	USBLS	5/07
	New Mexico	Y	23930 FQ	28160 MW	32480 TQ	USBLS	5/07
	Albuquerque MSA, NM	Y	26210 FQ	29370 MW	33950 TQ	USBLS	5/07
	New York	Y	26460 FQ	30830 MW	37140 TQ	USBLS	5/07
	Albany-Schenectady-Troy MSA, NY	Y	25010 FQ	27350 MW	29890 TQ	USBLS	5/07
	Buffalo-Niagara Falls MSA, NY	Y	28160 FQ	32460 MW	37880 TQ	USBLS	5/07
	Nassau-Suffolk PMSA, NY	Y	26820 FQ	31200 MW	37290 TQ	USBLS	5/07
	New York-Northern New Jersey-Long Island MSA, NY-NJ-PA	Y	26840 FQ	32350 MW	38830 TQ	USBLS	5/07
	North Carolina	Y	23670 FQ	28920 MW	35740 TQ	USBLS	5/07
	Charlotte-Gastonia-Concord MSA, NC-SC	Y	24450 FQ	30950 MW	36900 TQ	USBLS	5/07
	Raleigh-Cary MSA, NC	Y	26320 FQ	32620 MW	43460 TQ	USBLS	5/07
	North Dakota	Y	22090 FQ	26180 MW	29410 TQ	USBLS	5/07
	Fargo MSA, ND-MN	Y	22970 FQ	28770 MW	35630 TQ	USBLS	5/07
	Ohio	Y	23700 FQ	27920 MW	32800 TQ	USBLS	5/07
	Cincinnati-Middletown MSA, OH-KY-IN	Y	23610 FQ	28240 MW	33910 TQ	USBLS	5/07
	Cleveland-Elyria-Mentor MSA, OH	Y	26820 FQ	31070 MW	36580 TQ	USBLS	5/07
	Columbus MSA, OH	Y	22680 FQ	26120 MW	32210 TQ	USBLS	5/07
	Dayton MSA, OH	Y	25980 FQ	28520 MW	31190 TQ	USBLS	5/07
	Oklahoma	Y	21850 FQ	25110 MW	30340 TQ	USBLS	5/07
	Oklahoma City MSA, OK	Y	22440 FQ	25100 MW	30960 TQ	USBLS	5/07
	Tulsa MSA, OK	Y	23140 FQ	27580 MW	33520 TQ	USBLS	5/07
	Oregon	H	12.35 FQ	14.73 MW	17.01 TQ	ORBLS	5/08
	Medford MSA, OR	Y	30720 FQ	34240 MW	37960 TQ	USBLS	5/07
	Portland-Vancouver-Beaverton MSA, OR-WA	Y	27130 FQ	31130 MW	35830 TQ	USBLS	5/07
	Pennsylvania	Y	22930 FQ	26730 MW	30340 TQ	USBLS	5/07
	Allentown-Bethlehem-Easton MSA, PA-NJ	Y	22340 FQ	24870 MW	28360 TQ	USBLS	5/07
	Philadelphia-Camden-Wilmington MSA, PA-NJ-DE-MD	Y	24360 FQ	28510 MW	33790 TQ	USBLS	5/07
	Pittsburgh MSA, PA	Y	23270 FQ	26880 MW	30310 TQ	USBLS	5/07
	Reading MSA, PA	Y	21810 FQ	26530 MW	31170 TQ	USBLS	5/07
	Rhode Island	Y	24560 FQ	28370 MW	32850 TQ	USBLS	5/07
	Providence-Fall River-Warwick MSA, RI-MA	Y	24810 FQ	28720 MW	33060 TQ	USBLS	5/07
	South Carolina	Y	26120 FQ	29390 MW	33310 TQ	USBLS	5/07
	Charleston-North Charleston MSA, SC	Y	26090 FQ	28820 MW	31760 TQ	USBLS	5/07
	Columbia MSA, SC	Y	26150 FQ	28990 MW	32260 TQ	USBLS	5/07
	South Dakota	Y	23789 FQ	26390 MW	29432 TQ	SDBLS	7/08-9/08

AE	Average entry wage	AW	Average wage paid	FQ	First quartile wage
AER	Average entry range	AWR	Average wage range	H	Hourly
AEX	Average experienced wage	AXR	Average experienced range	HI	Highest wage paid
ATC	Average total compensation	D	Daily	HR	High end range

LO	Lowest wage paid	MTC	Median total compensation	TCC	Total cash compensation
LR	Low end range	MW	Median wage paid	TQ	Third quartile wage
M	Monthly	MWR	Median wage range	W	Weekly
MCC	Median cash compensation	S	See annotated source	Y	Yearly

Occupation/Type/Industry	Location	Per	Low	Mid	High	Source	Date
New Accounts Clerk	Sioux Falls MSA, SD	Y	24637 FQ	26608 MW	29784 TQ	SDBLS	7/08-9/08
	Tennessee	Y	23990 FQ	28600 MW	33190 TQ	USBLS	5/07
	Memphis MSA, TN-MS-AR	Y	27200 FQ	29830 MW	33120 TQ	USBLS	5/07
	Nashville-Davidson- Murfreesboro MSA, TN	Y	23180 FQ	28260 MW	34050 TQ	USBLS	5/07
	Texas	Y	24980 FQ	29950 MW	35490 TQ	USBLS	5/07
	Austin-Round Rock MSA, TX	Y	27420 FQ	31840 MW	35740 TQ	USBLS	5/07
	Dallas-Fort Worth-Arlington MSA, TX	Y	27770 FQ	32540 MW	37020 TQ	USBLS	5/07
	El Paso MSA, TX	Y	24660 FQ	30970 MW	35700 TQ	USBLS	5/07
	Houston-Sugar Land-Baytown MSA, TX	Y	27350 FQ	31420 MW	36570 TQ	USBLS	5/07
	San Antonio MSA, TX	Y	25450 FQ	30190 MW	37110 TQ	USBLS	5/07
	Utah	Y	23710 FQ	27650 MW	31920 TQ	USBLS	5/07
	Ogden-Clearfield MSA, UT	Y	19750 FQ	23680 MW	30610 TQ	USBLS	5/07
	Salt Lake City MSA, UT	Y	25230 FQ	28500 MW	32320 TQ	USBLS	5/07
	Vermont	Y	26980 FQ	29640 MW	32450 TQ	USBLS	5/07
	Virginia	Y	26430 FQ	29820 MW	35210 TQ	USBLS	5/07
	Richmond MSA, VA	Y	26830 FQ	29850 MW	35600 TQ	USBLS	5/07
	Virginia Beach-Norfolk- Newport News MSA, VA-NC	Y	26280 FQ	28590 MW	31140 TQ	USBLS	5/07
	Washington	H	13.21 FQ	15.19 MW	18.12 TQ	WABLS	3/08
	Seattle-Tacoma-Bellevue MSA, WA	Y	29140 FQ	34360 MW	40000 TQ	USBLS	5/07
	West Virginia	Y	24142 FQ	27405 MW	30529 TQ	WVBLS	7/08-9/08
	Charleston MSA, WV	Y	22360 FQ	26100 MW	29870 TQ	USBLS	5/07
	Wisconsin	Y	25830 FQ	29110 MW	33470 TQ	USBLS	5/07
	Milwaukee-Waukesha-West Allis MSA, WI	Y	26950 FQ	30810 MW	35110 TQ	USBLS	5/07
	Wyoming	Y	22684 FQ	25518 MW	30157 TQ	WYBLS	9/08
	Cheyenne MSA, WY	Y	24567 FQ	28445 MW	32758 TQ	WYBLS	9/08
	Puerto Rico	Y	15650 FQ	19010 MW	23090 TQ	USBLS	5/07
	San Juan-Caguas-Guaynabo MSA, PR	Y	15160 FQ	18910 MW	22730 TQ	USBLS	5/07
Newsperson Experienced, Associated Press	United States	W	1193.40 LO			EDPUB	3/09
Night Avionics Technician	United States	H		24.00 AW		AVJOB06	2009
Night Mechanic Airline	United States	H		19.00 AW		AVJOB07	2009
Night Nanny	Delaware	H	13.00 LO			ADA	2008
Noise Compatibility Manager Dallas/Fort Worth International Airport	Dallas-Fort Worth, TX	Y			106942 HI	CBSTV	2008
Noise Control Program Specialist Municipal Government	Seattle, WA	H	30.43 LO		35.44 HI	CSSS	2008
Nonfarm Animal Caretaker	Alabama	Y	15390 FQ	18920 MW	23130 TQ	USBLS	5/07
	Birmingham-Hoover MSA, AL	Y	18410 FQ	21350 MW	27480 TQ	USBLS	5/07
	Alaska	Y	17700 FQ	19640 MW	27730 TQ	USBLS	5/07
	Anchorage MSA, AK	Y	17410 FQ	19010 MW	23730 TQ	USBLS	5/07
	Arizona	Y	15400 FQ	17730 MW	22620 TQ	USBLS	5/07
	Phoenix-Mesa-Scottsdale MSA, AZ	Y	15350 FQ	17510 MW	21930 TQ	USBLS	5/07
	Tucson MSA, AZ	Y	15840 FQ	19190 MW	25870 TQ	USBLS	5/07
	Arkansas	Y	14590 FQ	16460 MW	19750 TQ	USBLS	5/07
	Little Rock-North Little Rock MSA, AR	Y	15830 FQ	18170 MW	21670 TQ	USBLS	5/07
	California	H	8.55 FQ	9.59 MW	12.47 TQ	CABLS	1/08-3/08
	Los Angeles-Long Beach- Glendale PMSA, CA	H	8.48 FQ	9.31 MW	11.17 TQ	CABLS	1/08-3/08
	Oakland-Fremont-Hayward MSA, CA	H	9.51 FQ	11.55 MW	15.90 TQ	CABLS	1/08-3/08
	Oxnard-Thousand Oaks- Ventura MSA, CA	H	8.60 FQ	9.40 MW	10.56 TQ	CABLS	1/08-3/08
	Riverside-San Bernardino- Ontario MSA, CA	H	8.38 FQ	9.31 MW	11.29 TQ	CABLS	1/08-3/08
	Sacramento-Arden Arcade- Roseville MSA, CA	H	8.27 FQ	9.19 MW	11.33 TQ	CABLS	1/08-3/08

AE	Average entry wage	**AW**	Average wage paid	**FQ**	First quartile wage
AER	Average entry range	**AWR**	Average wage range	**H**	Hourly
AEX	Average experienced wage	**AXR**	Average experienced range	**HI**	Highest wage paid
ATC	Average total compensation	**D**	Daily	**HR**	High end range

LO	Lowest wage paid	**MTC**	Median total compensation	**TCC**	Total cash compensation
LR	Low end range	**MW**	Median wage paid	**TQ**	Third quartile wage
M	Monthly	**MWR**	Median wage range	**W**	Weekly
MCC	Median cash compensation	**S**	See annotated source	**Y**	Yearly

Occupation/Type/Industry	Location	Per	Low	Mid	High	Source	Date
Nonfarm Animal Caretaker	San Diego-Carlsbad-San Marcos MSA, CA	H	8.61 FQ	10.11 MW	14.90 TQ	CABLS	1/08-3/08
	San Francisco-San Mateo-Redwood PMSA, CA	H	11.57 FQ	13.76 MW	16.05 TQ	CABLS	1/08-3/08
	San Jose-Sunnyvale-Santa Clara MSA, CA	H	9.61 FQ	17.65 MW	21.36 TQ	CABLS	1/08-3/08
	Santa Ana-Anaheim-Irvine PMSA, CA	Y	16870 FQ	18370 MW	20510 TQ	USBLS	5/07
	Colorado	Y	17360 FQ	20140 MW	27300 TQ	USBLS	5/07
	Boulder MSA, CO	Y	17760 FQ	20120 MW	28160 TQ	USBLS	5/07
	Denver-Aurora MSA, CO	Y	18220 FQ	21590 MW	33940 TQ	USBLS	5/07
	Connecticut	H	8.68 AE	10.28 MW		CTBLS	1/08-3/08
	Bridgeport-Stamford-Norwalk MSA, CT	Y	19110 FQ	22830 MW	27790 TQ	USBLS	5/07
	Danbury MSA, CT	Y	17380 FQ	18710 MW	20420 TQ	USBLS	5/07
	Hartford-West Hartford-East Hartford MSA, CT	Y	17110 FQ	18570 MW	21310 TQ	USBLS	5/07
	Waterbury MSA, CT	Y	19810 FQ	22360 MW	25350 TQ	USBLS	5/07
	Delaware	Y	16530 FQ	18600 MW	21550 TQ	USBLS	5/07
	Wilmington PMSA, DE-MD-NJ	Y	16390 FQ	19270 MW	23300 TQ	USBLS	5/07
	District of Columbia	Y	21120 FQ	22980 MW	24770 TQ	USBLS	5/07
	Washington-Arlington-Alexandria MSA, DC-VA-MD-WV	Y	17560 FQ	21590 MW	25780 TQ	USBLS	5/07
	Florida	Y	16680 FQ	19930 MW	25300 TQ	USBLS	5/07
	Fort Lauderdale-Pompano Beach-Deerfield Beach PMSA, FL	Y	16510 FQ	20090 MW	23620 TQ	USBLS	5/07
	Jacksonville MSA, FL	Y	17120 FQ	20800 MW	23830 TQ	USBLS	5/07
	Miami-Fort Lauderdale-Miami Beach MSA, FL	Y	17420 FQ	20290 MW	28320 TQ	USBLS	5/07
	Orlando-Kissimmee MSA, FL	Y	18580 FQ	25080 MW	33760 TQ	USBLS	5/07
	Tampa-St. Petersburg-Clearwater MSA, FL	Y	16200 FQ	20090 MW	24570 TQ	USBLS	5/07
	West Palm Beach-Boca Raton-Boynton Beach PMSA, FL	Y	18090 FQ	20320 MW	30270 TQ	USBLS	5/07
	Georgia	Y	15720 FQ	18130 MW	22900 TQ	USBLS	5/07
	Atlanta-Sandy Springs-Marietta MSA, GA	Y	16390 FQ	18650 MW	24680 TQ	USBLS	5/07
	Hawaii	Y	19010 FQ	27550 MW	35400 TQ	USBLS	5/07
	Honolulu MSA, HI	Y	20560 FQ	30770 MW	36120 TQ	USBLS	5/07
	Idaho	Y	14960 FQ	21270 MW	40660 TQ	USBLS	5/07
	Boise City-Nampa MSA, ID	Y	18810 FQ	39300 MW	43670 TQ	USBLS	5/07
	Illinois	Y	16020 FQ	18090 MW	21650 TQ	USBLS	5/07
	Chicago-Naperville-Joliet MSA, IL-IN-WI	Y	16190 FQ	18260 MW	22130 TQ	USBLS	5/07
	Indiana	Y	14770 FQ	17790 MW	22620 TQ	USBLS	5/07
	Gary PMSA, IN	Y	13450 FQ	16410 MW	20140 TQ	USBLS	5/07
	Indianapolis-Carmel MSA, IN	Y	16350 FQ	19000 MW	26210 TQ	USBLS	5/07
	South Bend-Mishawaka MSA, IN-MI	Y	14720 FQ	16860 MW	19130 TQ	USBLS	5/07
	Terre Haute MSA, IN	Y	13290 FQ	16320 MW	22830 TQ	USBLS	5/07
	Iowa	Y	14740 FQ	17230 MW	23470 TQ	USBLS	5/07
	Des Moines-West Des Moines MSA, IA	Y	14790 FQ	16310 MW	21060 TQ	USBLS	5/07
	Kansas	Y	15450 FQ	18520 MW	23310 TQ	USBLS	5/07
	Wichita MSA, KS	Y	17060 FQ	20740 MW	25000 TQ	USBLS	5/07
	Kentucky	Y	15854 FQ	19299 MW	24117 TQ	KYBLS	2008
	Louisville-Jefferson County MSA, KY-IN	Y	15800 FQ	19880 MW	26820 TQ	USBLS	5/07
	Louisiana	H	7.61 FQ	9.10 MW	11.67 TQ	LABLS	1/08-3/08
	Baton Rouge MSA, LA	Y	15980 FQ	21000 MW	25450 TQ	USBLS	5/07
	Lake Charles MSA, LA	Y	13140 FQ	14980 MW	17800 TQ	USBLS	5/07
	New Orleans-Metairie-Kenner MSA, LA	Y	17930 FQ	20490 MW	27960 TQ	USBLS	5/07
	Shreveport-Bossier City MSA, LA	Y	14970 FQ	18480 MW	24320 TQ	USBLS	5/07
	Maine	Y	17570 FQ	19870 MW	23320 TQ	USBLS	5/07
	Bangor MSA, ME	Y	16750 FQ	18850 MW	27050 TQ	USBLS	5/07
	Portland-South Portland-Biddeford MSA, ME	Y	18500 FQ	21010 MW	24760 TQ	USBLS	5/07

AE	Average entry wage	AW	Average wage paid	FQ	First quartile wage	LO	Lowest wage paid
AER	Average entry range	AWR	Average wage range	H	Hourly	LR	Low end range
AEX	Average experienced wage	AXR	Average experienced range	HI	Highest wage paid	M	Monthly
ATC	Average total compensation	D	Daily	HR	High end range	MCC	Median cash compensation

MTC	Median total compensation	TCC	Total cash compensation
MW	Median wage paid	TQ	Third quartile wage
MWR	Median wage range	W	Weekly
S	See annotated source	Y	Yearly

Occupation/Type/Industry	Location	Per	Low	Mid	High	Source	Date
Nonfarm Animal Caretaker	Maryland	Y		21725 MW		MDBLS	3/08
	Baltimore-Towson MSA, MD	Y	16050 FQ	21730 MW	26330 TQ	USBLS	5/07
	Bethesda-Gaithersburg-Frederick PMSA, MD	Y	19220 FQ	23940 MW	29190 TQ	USBLS	5/07
	Massachusetts	Y	18200 FQ	21580 MW	27380 TQ	USBLS	5/07
	Boston-Cambridge-Quincy NECTA, MA	Y	19290 FQ	26290 MW	34430 TQ	USBLS	5/07
	Worcester MSA, MA-CT	Y	16940 FQ	19070 MW	23440 TQ	USBLS	5/07
	Michigan	Y	16150 FQ	19270 MW	23400 TQ	USBLS	5/07
	Detroit-Warren-Livonia MSA, MI	Y	16830 FQ	20720 MW	23520 TQ	USBLS	5/07
	Grand Rapids-Wyoming MSA, MI	Y	17260 FQ	21000 MW	25500 TQ	USBLS	5/07
	Warren-Troy-Farmington Hills PMSA, MI	Y	16120 FQ	19090 MW	22740 TQ	USBLS	5/07
	Minnesota	Y	15840 FQ	18444 MW	23295 TQ	MNBLS	10/08-12/08
	Duluth-Superior MSA, MN-WI	Y	15213 FQ	17304 MW	22961 TQ	MNBLS	10/08-12/08
	Minneapolis-Saint Paul MSA, MN-WI	Y	16206 FQ	18862 MW	24288 TQ	MNBLS	10/08-12/08
	Rochester MSA, MN	Y	16847 FQ	22718 MW	29317 TQ	MNBLS	10/08-12/08
	Mississippi	Y	15410 FQ	17910 MW	22300 TQ	USBLS	5/07
	Jackson MSA, MS	Y	16660 FQ	19400 MW	24760 TQ	USBLS	5/07
	Missouri	Y	15130 FQ	17820 MW	22320 TQ	USBLS	5/07
	Kansas City MSA, MO-KS	Y	16380 FQ	18770 MW	22420 TQ	USBLS	5/07
	St. Louis MSA, MO-IL	Y	15380 FQ	17920 MW	23220 TQ	USBLS	5/07
	Montana	Y	14840 FQ	16940 MW	19430 TQ	USBLS	5/07
	Billings MSA, MT	Y	16360 FQ	19620 MW	22620 TQ	USBLS	5/07
	Nebraska	Y	15280 FQ	18240 MW	22270 TQ	USBLS	5/07
	Omaha-Council Bluffs MSA, NE-IA	Y	15570 FQ	18390 MW	22840 TQ	USBLS	5/07
	Las Vegas-Paradise MSA, NV	H	8.14 FQ	9.32 MW	13.39 TQ	NVBLS	5/08
	New Hampshire	H	7.87 AE	9.28 MW	11.02 AEX	NHBLS	6/08
	Manchester MSA, NH	Y	17270 FQ	18840 MW	21770 TQ	USBLS	5/07
	Nashua NECTA, NH-MA	Y	16200 FQ	17650 MW	20040 TQ	USBLS	5/07
	New Jersey	Y	17020 FQ	19650 MW	26140 TQ	USBLS	5/07
	Camden PMSA, NJ	Y	17200 FQ	20260 MW	25040 TQ	USBLS	5/07
	Edison PMSA, NJ	Y	16690 FQ	19040 MW	23570 TQ	USBLS	5/07
	Newark-Union PMSA, NJ-PA	Y	16170 FQ	19210 MW	29280 TQ	USBLS	5/07
	New Mexico	Y	16580 FQ	21310 MW	26780 TQ	USBLS	5/07
	Albuquerque MSA, NM	Y	18890 FQ	25600 MW	30510 TQ	USBLS	5/07
	New York	Y	16830 FQ	20420 MW	25820 TQ	USBLS	5/07
	Albany-Schenectady-Troy MSA, NY	Y	15500 FQ	20780 MW	28400 TQ	USBLS	5/07
	Buffalo-Niagara Falls MSA, NY	Y	15410 FQ	16280 MW	18930 TQ	USBLS	5/07
	Nassau-Suffolk PMSA, NY	Y	18210 FQ	21440 MW	26150 TQ	USBLS	5/07
	New York-Northern New Jersey-Long Island MSA, NY-NJ-PA	Y	17000 FQ	20420 MW	26240 TQ	USBLS	5/07
	North Carolina	Y	15600 FQ	18180 MW	21930 TQ	USBLS	5/07
	Charlotte-Gastonia-Concord MSA, NC-SC	Y	15890 FQ	18600 MW	22510 TQ	USBLS	5/07
	Raleigh-Cary MSA, NC	Y	17120 FQ	19190 MW	22620 TQ	USBLS	5/07
	North Dakota	Y	14020 FQ	16520 MW	18770 TQ	USBLS	5/07
	Fargo MSA, ND-MN	Y	17400 FQ	19180 MW	21620 TQ	USBLS	5/07
	Ohio	Y	15470 FQ	17850 MW	22290 TQ	USBLS	5/07
	Cincinnati-Middletown MSA, OH-KY-IN	Y	14880 FQ	18060 MW	27320 TQ	USBLS	5/07
	Cleveland-Elyria-Mentor MSA, OH	Y	15580 FQ	18070 MW	21530 TQ	USBLS	5/07
	Columbus MSA, OH	Y	16390 FQ	18510 MW	22450 TQ	USBLS	5/07
	Dayton MSA, OH	Y	14870 FQ	17050 MW	21640 TQ	USBLS	5/07
	Oklahoma	Y	14720 FQ	17420 MW	22780 TQ	USBLS	5/07
	Oklahoma City MSA, OK	Y	14580 FQ	17190 MW	21870 TQ	USBLS	5/07
	Tulsa MSA, OK	Y	16190 FQ	20000 MW	29550 TQ	USBLS	5/07
	Oregon	H	8.74 FQ	9.61 MW	12.16 TQ	ORBLS	5/08
	Portland-Vancouver-Beaverton MSA, OR-WA	Y	17600 FQ	19300 MW	24950 TQ	USBLS	5/07
	Pennsylvania	Y	15080 FQ	17220 MW	20770 TQ	USBLS	5/07
	Allentown-Bethlehem-Easton MSA, PA-NJ	Y	17230 FQ	19920 MW	23980 TQ	USBLS	5/07

Occupation/Type/Industry	Location	Per	Low	Mid	High	Source	Date
Nonfarm Animal Caretaker	Philadelphia-Camden-Wilmington MSA, PA-NJ-DE-MD	Y	15390 FQ	18030 MW	23090 TQ	USBLS	5/07
	Pittsburgh MSA, PA	Y	14990 FQ	17080 MW	20010 TQ	USBLS	5/07
	Rhode Island	Y	19460 FQ	24820 MW	32550 TQ	USBLS	5/07
	Providence-Fall River-Warwick MSA, RI-MA	Y	19310 FQ	23520 MW	30240 TQ	USBLS	5/07
	South Carolina	Y	15330 FQ	18300 MW	22460 TQ	USBLS	5/07
	Charleston-North Charleston MSA, SC	Y	15380 FQ	18900 MW	22990 TQ	USBLS	5/07
	Columbia MSA, SC	Y	14320 FQ	17370 MW	21300 TQ	USBLS	5/07
	South Dakota	Y	16290 FQ	18851 MW	22198 TQ	SDBLS	7/08-9/08
	Sioux Falls MSA, SD	Y	15818 FQ	18715 MW	21521 TQ	SDBLS	7/08-9/08
	Tennessee	Y	15960 FQ	18770 MW	23220 TQ	USBLS	5/07
	Clarksville MSA, TN-KY	Y	13000 FQ	14960 MW	17890 TQ	USBLS	5/07
	Johnson City MSA, TN	Y	16840 FQ	18810 MW	21320 TQ	USBLS	5/07
	Memphis MSA, TN-MS-AR	Y	17090 FQ	21220 MW	24200 TQ	USBLS	5/07
	Nashville-Davidson-Murfreesboro MSA, TN	Y	17080 FQ	19410 MW	24160 TQ	USBLS	5/07
	Texas	Y	15340 FQ	18050 MW	21600 TQ	USBLS	5/07
	Austin-Round Rock MSA, TX	Y	15820 FQ	18040 MW	20620 TQ	USBLS	5/07
	Brownsville-Harlingen MSA, TX	Y	15120 FQ	19610 MW	22750 TQ	USBLS	5/07
	Dallas-Fort Worth-Arlington MSA, TX	Y	15730 FQ	18650 MW	23330 TQ	USBLS	5/07
	El Paso MSA, TX	Y	13070 FQ	15440 MW	23540 TQ	USBLS	5/07
	Houston-Sugar Land-Baytown MSA, TX	Y	15420 FQ	17760 MW	20950 TQ	USBLS	5/07
	San Antonio MSA, TX	Y	16950 FQ	19600 MW	22150 TQ	USBLS	5/07
	Utah	Y	14350 FQ	17560 MW	20680 TQ	USBLS	5/07
	Provo-Orem MSA, UT	Y	15150 FQ	21120 MW	23380 TQ	USBLS	5/07
	Salt Lake City MSA, UT	Y	14860 FQ	17620 MW	20120 TQ	USBLS	5/07
	Vermont	Y	17120 FQ	18920 MW	23490 TQ	USBLS	5/07
	Burlington-South Burlington MSA, VT	Y	17540 FQ	20340 MW	24790 TQ	USBLS	5/07
	Virginia	Y	16050 FQ	19330 MW	24480 TQ	USBLS	5/07
	Lynchburg MSA, VA	Y	13490 FQ	16570 MW	20700 TQ	USBLS	5/07
	Richmond MSA, VA	Y	14590 FQ	18670 MW	37780 TQ	USBLS	5/07
	Virginia Beach-Norfolk-Newport News MSA, VA-NC	Y	15540 FQ	18000 MW	22530 TQ	USBLS	5/07
	Washington	H	8.84 FQ	9.87 MW	12.38 TQ	WABLS	3/08
	Olympia MSA, WA	Y	17990 FQ	19740 MW	23930 TQ	USBLS	5/07
	Seattle-Tacoma-Bellevue MSA, WA	Y	18250 FQ	20660 MW	26680 TQ	USBLS	5/07
	West Virginia	Y	14289 FQ	15686 MW	20520 TQ	WVBLS	7/08-9/08
	Charleston MSA, WV	Y	14790 FQ	19130 MW	24160 TQ	USBLS	5/07
	Wisconsin	Y	15400 FQ	18420 MW	23720 TQ	USBLS	5/07
	Milwaukee-Waukesha-West Allis MSA, WI	Y	16420 FQ	20380 MW	27600 TQ	USBLS	5/07
	Wyoming	Y	18084 FQ	21012 MW	27805 TQ	WYBLS	9/08
	Casper MSA, WY	Y	16528 FQ	18499 MW	27786 TQ	WYBLS	9/08
	Cheyenne MSA, WY	Y	17965 FQ	19519 MW	23180 TQ	WYBLS	9/08
	Puerto Rico	Y	12680 FQ	13950 MW	15600 TQ	USBLS	5/07
	San Juan-Caguas-Guaynabo MSA, PR	Y	12710 FQ	13980 MW	15820 TQ	USBLS	5/07
	Virgin Islands	Y	16660 FQ	21160 MW	27840 TQ	USBLS	5/07
Nosologist State Government	Ohio	H	15.62 LO		18.36 HI	ODAS	2008
Nuclear Boiler Inspector State Government	Ohio	H	21.77 LO		31.86 HI	ODAS	2008
Nuclear Engineer	Arizona	Y	85290 FQ	93160 MW	101030 TQ	USBLS	5/07
	California	H	39.19 FQ	47.78 MW	57.46 TQ	CABLS	1/08-3/08
	Colorado	Y	109490 FQ	119400 MW	129310 TQ	USBLS	5/07
	Florida	Y	79230 FQ	91310 MW	101800 TQ	USBLS	5/07
	Georgia	Y	85420 FQ	102220 MW	123390 TQ	USBLS	5/07
	Illinois	Y	96290 FQ	110320 MW	124000 TQ	USBLS	5/07
	Maryland	Y		119600 MW		MDBLS	3/08
	Mississippi	Y	94720 FQ	105460 MW	127560 TQ	USBLS	5/07
	Nevada	H	53.52 FQ	62.12 MW		NVBLS	5/08

AE Average entry wage	**AW** Average wage paid	**FQ** First quartile wage	**LO** Lowest wage paid	**MTC** Median total compensation	**TCC** Total cash compensation
AER Average entry range	**AWR** Average wage range	**H** Hourly	**LR** Low end range	**MW** Median wage paid	**TQ** Third quartile wage
AEX Average experienced wage	**AXR** Average experienced range	**HI** Highest wage paid	**M** Monthly	**MWR** Median wage range	**W** Weekly
ATC Average total compensation	**D** Daily	**HR** High end range	**MCC** Median cash compensation	**S** See annotated source	**Y** Yearly

Occupation/Type/Industry	Location	Per	Low	Mid	High	Source	Date
Nuclear Engineer	New Jersey	Y	83560 FQ	96980 MW	111840 TQ	USBLS	5/07
	New Mexico	Y	99290 FQ	114940 MW	129260 TQ	USBLS	5/07
	New York	Y	82710 FQ	96310 MW	116470 TQ	USBLS	5/07
	North Carolina	Y	73030 FQ	89250 MW	101930 TQ	USBLS	5/07
	Ohio	Y	72310 FQ	86430 MW	100220 TQ	USBLS	5/07
	Pennsylvania	Y	80870 FQ	99210 MW	124190 TQ	USBLS	5/07
	South Carolina	Y	83820 FQ	94330 MW	104560 TQ	USBLS	5/07
	Tennessee	Y	100680 FQ	116060 MW	134360 TQ	USBLS	5/07
	Texas	Y	64540 FQ	93340 MW	129440 TQ	USBLS	5/07
	Virginia	Y	75580 FQ	90820 MW	108190 TQ	USBLS	5/07
	Washington	H	33.68 FQ	39.75 MW	45.98 TQ	WABLS	3/08
Consulting Firm	United States	Y	53667 AE			NAYGN	2007
Government or Regulatory	United States	Y	52800 AE			NAYGN	2007
Research	United States	Y	80200 AE			NAYGN	2007
Utility	United States	Y	56613 AE			NAYGN	2007
Vendor	United States	Y	58175 AE			NAYGN	2007
Nuclear Medicine Technologist	Alabama	Y	46570 FQ	56370 MW	66480 TQ	USBLS	5/07
	Birmingham-Hoover MSA, AL	Y	46420 FQ	56160 MW	67490 TQ	USBLS	5/07
	Mobile MSA, AL	Y	49050 FQ	56770 MW	63440 TQ	USBLS	5/07
	Arizona	Y	60330 FQ	70550 MW	77590 TQ	USBLS	5/07
	Phoenix-Mesa-Scottsdale MSA, AZ	Y	61360 FQ	70860 MW	77580 TQ	USBLS	5/07
	Tucson MSA, AZ	Y	52150 FQ	65190 MW	78290 TQ	USBLS	5/07
	Arkansas	Y	55030 FQ	61000 MW	68540 TQ	USBLS	5/07
	Little Rock-North Little Rock MSA, AR	Y	56830 FQ	63220 MW	71990 TQ	USBLS	5/07
	California	H	31.26 FQ	37.06 MW	45.06 TQ	CABLS	1/08-3/08
	Los Angeles-Long Beach-Glendale PMSA, CA	H	29.15 FQ	32.43 MW	39.44 TQ	CABLS	1/08-3/08
	Oakland-Fremont-Hayward MSA, CA	H	39.57 FQ	50.55 MW	60.18 TQ	CABLS	1/08-3/08
	Riverside-San Bernardino-Ontario MSA, CA	H	34.65 FQ	38.53 MW	45.89 TQ	CABLS	1/08-3/08
	Sacramento-Arden Arcade-Roseville MSA, CA	H	35.54 FQ	43.22 MW	49.30 TQ	CABLS	1/08-3/08
	San Diego-Carlsbad-San Marcos MSA, CA	H	28.86 FQ	33.61 MW	41.50 TQ	CABLS	1/08-3/08
	San Francisco-San Mateo-Redwood PMSA, CA	H	33.38 FQ	40.38 MW	51.64 TQ	CABLS	1/08-3/08
	San Jose-Sunnyvale-Santa Clara MSA, CA	H	34.68 FQ	41.50 MW	48.75 TQ	CABLS	1/08-3/08
	Santa Ana-Anaheim-Irvine PMSA, CA	Y	74120 FQ	86300 MW	95410 TQ	USBLS	5/07
	Santa Rosa-Petaluma MSA, CA	H	36.36 FQ	43.33 MW	48.87 TQ	CABLS	1/08-3/08
	Colorado	Y	58380 FQ	66960 MW	74550 TQ	USBLS	5/07
	Denver-Aurora MSA, CO	Y	61920 FQ	68710 MW	75070 TQ	USBLS	5/07
	Connecticut	H	30.23 AE	35.95 MW		CTBLS	1/08-3/08
	Bridgeport-Stamford-Norwalk MSA, CT	Y	63540 FQ	72330 MW	80580 TQ	USBLS	5/07
	Hartford-West Hartford-East Hartford MSA, CT	Y	67390 FQ	73440 MW	79450 TQ	USBLS	5/07
	Delaware	Y	58210 FQ	65570 MW	74260 TQ	USBLS	5/07
	Wilmington PMSA, DE-MD-NJ	Y	59110 FQ	66330 MW	74810 TQ	USBLS	5/07
	District of Columbia	Y	49330 FQ	59830 MW	73620 TQ	USBLS	5/07
	Washington-Arlington-Alexandria MSA, DC-VA-MD-WV	Y	59600 FQ	71280 MW	85220 TQ	USBLS	5/07
	Florida	Y	55130 FQ	63270 MW	73370 TQ	USBLS	5/07
	Fort Lauderdale-Pompano Beach-Deerfield Beach PMSA, FL	Y	54130 FQ	65780 MW	78050 TQ	USBLS	5/07
	Jacksonville MSA, FL	Y	61660 FQ	70700 MW	77670 TQ	USBLS	5/07
	Miami-Fort Lauderdale-Miami Beach MSA, FL	Y	55410 FQ	64500 MW	75600 TQ	USBLS	5/07
	Orlando-Kissimmee MSA, FL	Y	53990 FQ	61660 MW	71490 TQ	USBLS	5/07
	Tampa-St. Petersburg-Clearwater MSA, FL	Y	55440 FQ	63840 MW	73170 TQ	USBLS	5/07
	West Palm Beach-Boca Raton-Boynton Beach PMSA, FL	Y	45110 FQ	62050 MW	73220 TQ	USBLS	5/07
	Georgia	Y	54920 FQ	62460 MW	72210 TQ	USBLS	5/07

AE	Average entry wage	**AW**	Average wage paid	**FQ**	First quartile wage
AER	Average entry range	**AWR**	Average wage range	**H**	Hourly
AEX	Average experienced wage	**AXR**	Average experienced range	**HI**	Highest wage paid
ATC	Average total compensation	**D**	Daily	**HR**	High end range

LO	Lowest wage paid	**MTC**	Median total compensation	**TCC** Total cash compensation
LR	Low end range	**MW**	Median wage paid	**TQ** Third quartile wage
M	Monthly	**MWR**	Median wage range	**W** Weekly
MCC	Median cash compensation	**S**	See annotated source	**Y** Yearly

Occupation/Type/Industry	Location	Per	Low	Mid	High	Source	Date
Nuclear Medicine Technologist	Atlanta-Sandy Springs-Marietta MSA, GA	Y	57290 FQ	65350 MW	74510 TQ	USBLS	5/07
	Hawaii	Y	54760 FQ	69440 MW	76960 TQ	USBLS	5/07
	Idaho	Y	54520 FQ	60780 MW	69570 TQ	USBLS	5/07
	Boise City-Nampa MSA, ID	Y	54540 FQ	60870 MW	70720 TQ	USBLS	5/07
	Illinois	Y	56740 FQ	64480 MW	76220 TQ	USBLS	5/07
	Chicago-Naperville-Joliet MSA, IL-IN-WI	Y	57310 FQ	65840 MW	77020 TQ	USBLS	5/07
	Indiana	Y	53390 FQ	61270 MW	72300 TQ	USBLS	5/07
	Gary PMSA, IN	Y	64910 FQ	72170 MW	79050 TQ	USBLS	5/07
	Indianapolis-Carmel MSA, IN	Y	59010 FQ	69760 MW	79880 TQ	USBLS	5/07
	Iowa	Y	52350 FQ	60140 MW	67660 TQ	USBLS	5/07
	Des Moines-West Des Moines MSA, IA	Y	51430 FQ	61910 MW	71880 TQ	USBLS	5/07
	Kansas	Y	52240 FQ	61640 MW	72990 TQ	USBLS	5/07
	Kentucky	Y	52034 FQ	58791 MW	65238 TQ	KYBLS	2008
	Louisville-Jefferson County MSA, KY-IN	Y	50860 FQ	57510 MW	63330 TQ	USBLS	5/07
	Louisiana	H	25.70 FQ	29.04 MW	33.82 TQ	LABLS	1/08-3/08
	Baton Rouge MSA, LA	Y	53970 FQ	58800 MW	67140 TQ	USBLS	5/07
	New Orleans-Metairie-Kenner MSA, LA	Y	55100 FQ	61990 MW	70080 TQ	USBLS	5/07
	Maine	Y	55860 FQ	65730 MW	73960 TQ	USBLS	5/07
	Maryland	Y		78225 MW		MDBLS	3/08
	Baltimore-Towson MSA, MD	Y	63940 FQ	74950 MW	83420 TQ	USBLS	5/07
	Bethesda-Gaithersburg-Frederick PMSA, MD	Y	81710 FQ	91340 MW	98800 TQ	USBLS	5/07
	Massachusetts	Y	60620 FQ	70140 MW	79430 TQ	USBLS	5/07
	Boston-Cambridge-Quincy NECTA, MA	Y	63090 FQ	72270 MW	81040 TQ	USBLS	5/07
	Worcester MSA, MA-CT	Y	53250 FQ	58830 MW	64400 TQ	USBLS	5/07
	Michigan	Y	54140 FQ	63440 MW	71500 TQ	USBLS	5/07
	Ann Arbor MSA, MI	Y	67250 FQ	72170 MW	77100 TQ	USBLS	5/07
	Detroit-Warren-Livonia MSA, MI	Y	61870 FQ	67300 MW	73210 TQ	USBLS	5/07
	Grand Rapids-Wyoming MSA, MI	Y	48800 FQ	57330 MW	64310 TQ	USBLS	5/07
	Warren-Troy-Farmington Hills PMSA, MI	Y	63600 FQ	68370 MW	73620 TQ	USBLS	5/07
	Minnesota	Y	64562 FQ	73267 MW	80758 TQ	MNBLS	10/08-12/08
	Minneapolis-Saint Paul MSA, MN-WI	Y	64656 FQ	72890 MW	80245 TQ	MNBLS	10/08-12/08
	Mississippi	Y	53110 FQ	58880 MW	64920 TQ	USBLS	5/07
	Jackson MSA, MS	Y	52440 FQ	59230 MW	65880 TQ	USBLS	5/07
	Missouri	Y	55510 FQ	63180 MW	72800 TQ	USBLS	5/07
	Kansas City MSA, MO-KS	Y	58290 FQ	67030 MW	75270 TQ	USBLS	5/07
	St. Louis MSA, MO-IL	Y	54940 FQ	61400 MW	72300 TQ	USBLS	5/07
	Montana	Y	54390 FQ	60540 MW	67980 TQ	USBLS	5/07
	Nebraska	Y	54140 FQ	63010 MW	74440 TQ	USBLS	5/07
	Omaha-Council Bluffs MSA, NE-IA	Y	51440 FQ	60900 MW	69640 TQ	USBLS	5/07
	Nevada	H	30.19 FQ	35.86 MW	43.66 TQ	NVBLS	5/08
	Las Vegas-Paradise MSA, NV	H	31.17 FQ	38.98 MW	46.31 TQ	NVBLS	5/08
	New Hampshire	H	26.94 AE	34.05 MW	36.19 AEX	NHBLS	6/08
	New Jersey	Y	68450 FQ	77410 MW	87740 TQ	USBLS	5/07
	Camden PMSA, NJ	Y	65690 FQ	73400 MW	80470 TQ	USBLS	5/07
	Edison PMSA, NJ	Y	70210 FQ	80080 MW	90800 TQ	USBLS	5/07
	Newark-Union PMSA, NJ-PA	Y	69840 FQ	79120 MW	89320 TQ	USBLS	5/07
	New Mexico	Y	33100 FQ	47100 MW	65550 TQ	USBLS	5/07
	Albuquerque MSA, NM	Y	31350 FQ	36960 MW	56060 TQ	USBLS	5/07
	New York	Y	57700 FQ	67770 MW	76870 TQ	USBLS	5/07
	Albany-Schenectady-Troy MSA, NY	Y	62860 FQ	72030 MW	79310 TQ	USBLS	5/07
	Buffalo-Niagara Falls MSA, NY	Y	57780 FQ	66560 MW	74870 TQ	USBLS	5/07
	Nassau-Suffolk PMSA, NY	Y	63380 FQ	71200 MW	80600 TQ	USBLS	5/07
	New York-Northern New Jersey-Long Island MSA, NY-NJ-PA	Y	65790 FQ	74240 MW	83830 TQ	USBLS	5/07
	North Carolina	Y	52930 FQ	59430 MW	66930 TQ	USBLS	5/07
	Charlotte-Gastonia-Concord MSA, NC-SC	Y	56110 FQ	63830 MW	71510 TQ	USBLS	5/07

AE Average entry wage	**AW** Average wage paid	**FQ** First quartile wage	**LO** Lowest wage paid	**MTC** Median total compensation **TCC** Total cash compensation
AER Average entry range	**AWR** Average wage range	**H** Hourly	**LR** Low end range	**MW** Median wage paid **TQ** Third quartile wage
AEX Average experienced wage	**AXR** Average experienced range	**HI** Highest wage paid	**M** Monthly	**MWR** Median wage range **W** Weekly
ATC Average total compensation	**D** Daily	**HR** High end range	**MCC** Median cash compensation	**S** See annotated source **Y** Yearly

Occupation/Type/Industry	Location	Per	Low	Mid	High	Source	Date
Nuclear Medicine Technologist	Raleigh-Cary MSA, NC	Y	51720 FQ	58470 MW	64610 TQ	USBLS	5/07
	Ohio	Y	55670 FQ	62250 MW	69670 TQ	USBLS	5/07
	Cincinnati-Middletown MSA, OH-KY-IN	Y	56260 FQ	63340 MW	70940 TQ	USBLS	5/07
	Cleveland-Elyria-Mentor MSA, OH	Y	59540 FQ	66000 MW	73840 TQ	USBLS	5/07
	Columbus MSA, OH	Y	56330 FQ	64010 MW	72600 TQ	USBLS	5/07
	Dayton MSA, OH	Y	57500 FQ	63950 MW	71330 TQ	USBLS	5/07
	Oklahoma	Y	48970 FQ	58320 MW	70600 TQ	USBLS	5/07
	Oklahoma City MSA, OK	Y	52930 FQ	63770 MW	83520 TQ	USBLS	5/07
	Tulsa MSA, OK	Y	46870 FQ	56980 MW	70420 TQ	USBLS	5/07
	Oregon	H	31.98 FQ	35.43 MW	38.68 TQ	ORBLS	5/08
	Portland-Vancouver-Beaverton MSA, OR-WA	Y	67050 FQ	72760 MW	78860 TQ	USBLS	5/07
	Pennsylvania	Y	49330 FQ	57750 MW	68760 TQ	USBLS	5/07
	Allentown-Bethlehem-Easton MSA, PA-NJ	Y	55950 FQ	61370 MW	68260 TQ	USBLS	5/07
	Philadelphia-Camden-Wilmington MSA, PA-NJ-DE-MD	Y	58050 FQ	68830 MW	78540 TQ	USBLS	5/07
	Pittsburgh MSA, PA	Y	45690 FQ	51900 MW	58180 TQ	USBLS	5/07
	Rhode Island	Y	69780 FQ	75140 MW	80510 TQ	USBLS	5/07
	Providence-Fall River-Warwick MSA, RI-MA	Y	69240 FQ	74690 MW	80380 TQ	USBLS	5/07
	South Carolina	Y	51590 FQ	59620 MW	72030 TQ	USBLS	5/07
	Charleston-North Charleston MSA, SC	Y	49900 FQ	55610 MW	61710 TQ	USBLS	5/07
	Columbia MSA, SC	Y	49450 FQ	56640 MW	64580 TQ	USBLS	5/07
	South Dakota	Y	48846 FQ	56471 MW	64997 TQ	SDBLS	7/08-9/08
	Sioux Falls MSA, SD	Y	47006 FQ	53639 MW	64590 TQ	SDBLS	7/08-9/08
	Tennessee	Y	54190 FQ	60560 MW	69140 TQ	USBLS	5/07
	Memphis MSA, TN-MS-AR	Y	55030 FQ	60410 MW	67850 TQ	USBLS	5/07
	Nashville-Davidson-Murfreesboro MSA, TN	Y	56780 FQ	65330 MW	73660 TQ	USBLS	5/07
	Texas	Y	56190 FQ	63770 MW	75750 TQ	USBLS	5/07
	Austin-Round Rock MSA, TX	Y	54460 FQ	60070 MW	66680 TQ	USBLS	5/07
	Dallas-Fort Worth-Arlington MSA, TX	Y	57830 FQ	64200 MW	73590 TQ	USBLS	5/07
	El Paso MSA, TX	Y	52460 FQ	71540 MW	84490 TQ	USBLS	5/07
	Houston-Sugar Land-Baytown MSA, TX	Y	60140 FQ	71760 MW	83020 TQ	USBLS	5/07
	San Antonio MSA, TX	Y	54880 FQ	60430 MW	66130 TQ	USBLS	5/07
	Utah	Y	49960 FQ	57600 MW	65280 TQ	USBLS	5/07
	Salt Lake City MSA, UT	Y	49140 FQ	57520 MW	64990 TQ	USBLS	5/07
	Vermont	Y	54180 FQ	60330 MW	67970 TQ	USBLS	5/07
	Virginia	Y	51510 FQ	59820 MW	68590 TQ	USBLS	5/07
	Richmond MSA, VA	Y	51140 FQ	58730 MW	68120 TQ	USBLS	5/07
	Virginia Beach-Norfolk-Newport News MSA, VA-NC	Y	54570 FQ	60610 MW	66610 TQ	USBLS	5/07
	Washington	H	33.17 FQ	36.72 MW	40.74 TQ	WABLS	3/08
	Seattle-Tacoma-Bellevue MSA, WA	Y	69660 FQ	76820 MW	85730 TQ	USBLS	5/07
	West Virginia	Y	45196 FQ	53467 MW	65797 TQ	WVBLS	7/08-9/08
	Charleston MSA, WV	Y	43780 FQ	49680 MW	57050 TQ	USBLS	5/07
	Wisconsin	Y	59300 FQ	66980 MW	74830 TQ	USBLS	5/07
	Milwaukee-Waukesha-West Allis MSA, WI	Y	62670 FQ	69840 MW	76390 TQ	USBLS	5/07
	Wyoming	Y	49198 FQ	58269 MW	66165 TQ	WYBLS	9/08
	Puerto Rico	Y	28960 FQ	33290 MW	38930 TQ	USBLS	5/07
	San Juan-Caguas-Guaynabo MSA, PR	Y	28930 FQ	32750 MW	39010 TQ	USBLS	5/07
Nuclear Power Reactor Operator	Florida	Y	69010 FQ	76200 MW	83540 TQ	USBLS	5/07
	Illinois	Y	69100 FQ	80750 MW	112010 TQ	USBLS	5/07
	Maryland	Y		76975 MW		MDBLS	3/08
	Michigan	Y	58360 FQ	65330 MW	74980 TQ	USBLS	5/07
	New York-Northern New Jersey-Long Island MSA, NY-NJ-PA	Y	64850 FQ	73980 MW	84160 TQ	USBLS	5/07
	North Carolina	Y	56360 FQ	61210 MW	66080 TQ	USBLS	5/07
	Ohio	Y	56050 FQ	61130 MW	69990 TQ	USBLS	5/07
	Pennsylvania	Y	55500 FQ	62850 MW	72710 TQ	USBLS	5/07

AE	Average entry wage	**AW**	Average wage paid	**FQ**	First quartile wage	**LO**	Lowest wage paid	**MTC**	Median total compensation	**TCC**	Total cash compensation
AER	Average entry range	**AWR**	Average wage range	**H**	Hourly	**LR**	Low end range	**MW**	Median wage paid	**TQ**	Third quartile wage
AEX	Average experienced wage	**AXR**	Average experienced range	**HI**	Highest wage paid	**M**	Monthly	**MWR**	Median wage range	**W**	Weekly
ATC	Average total compensation	**D**	Daily	**HR**	High end range	**MCC**	Median cash compensation	**S**	See annotated source	**Y**	Yearly

Occupation/Type/Industry	Location	Per	Low	Mid	High	Source	Date
Nuclear Power Reactor Operator	Pittsburgh MSA, PA	Y	54140 FQ	60360 MW	67300 TQ	USBLS	5/07
	South Carolina	Y	56860 FQ	61940 MW	68780 TQ	USBLS	5/07
Nuclear Technician	California	H	24.34 FQ	30.17 MW	37.81 TQ	CABLS	1/08-3/08
	Connecticut	H	31.83 AE	36.24 MW		CTBLS	1/08-3/08
	Florida	Y	55540 FQ	63000 MW	68520 TQ	USBLS	5/07
	Georgia	Y	42190 FQ	61480 MW	76100 TQ	USBLS	5/07
	Illinois	Y	51660 FQ	66480 MW	79330 TQ	USBLS	5/07
	Louisiana	H	20.12 FQ	23.57 MW	30.27 TQ	LABLS	1/08-3/08
	Maryland	Y		65100 MW		MDBLS	3/08
	Massachusetts	Y	41930 FQ	50010 MW	78900 TQ	USBLS	5/07
	Michigan	Y	67160 FQ	74400 MW	81720 TQ	USBLS	5/07
	Mississippi	Y	56510 FQ	68200 MW	80670 TQ	USBLS	5/07
	Missouri	Y	51100 FQ	63570 MW	78510 TQ	USBLS	5/07
	New Jersey	Y	49560 FQ	70270 MW	80480 TQ	USBLS	5/07
	New York	Y	50930 FQ	71280 MW	80940 TQ	USBLS	5/07
	Ohio	Y	42640 FQ	52970 MW	69220 TQ	USBLS	5/07
	South Carolina	Y	43950 FQ	57340 MW	63470 TQ	USBLS	5/07
	Texas	Y	45650 FQ	59300 MW	91070 TQ	USBLS	5/07
	Virginia	Y	56750 FQ	67710 MW	79100 TQ	USBLS	5/07
Numerical Tool and Process Control Programmer	Alabama	Y	26230 FQ	32980 MW	41840 TQ	USBLS	5/07
	Arizona	Y	34900 FQ	42120 MW	53230 TQ	USBLS	5/07
	Phoenix-Mesa-Scottsdale MSA, AZ	Y	36050 FQ	44460 MW	55810 TQ	USBLS	5/07
	Arkansas	Y	32110 FQ	36890 MW	48270 TQ	USBLS	5/07
	California	H	19.56 FQ	24.76 MW	33.14 TQ	CABLS	1/08-3/08
	Los Angeles-Long Beach-Glendale PMSA, CA	H	21.55 FQ	28.09 MW	37.49 TQ	CABLS	1/08-3/08
	Oakland-Fremont-Hayward MSA, CA	H	26.24 FQ	30.78 MW	36.04 TQ	CABLS	1/08-3/08
	Oxnard-Thousand Oaks-Ventura MSA, CA	H	18.88 FQ	20.74 MW	23.20 TQ	CABLS	1/08-3/08
	Riverside-San Bernardino-Ontario MSA, CA	H	19.68 FQ	23.19 MW	33.74 TQ	CABLS	1/08-3/08
	Sacramento-Arden Arcade-Roseville MSA, CA	H	18.73 FQ	21.87 MW	24.72 TQ	CABLS	1/08-3/08
	San Diego-Carlsbad-San Marcos MSA, CA	H	17.55 FQ	21.69 MW	26.49 TQ	CABLS	1/08-3/08
	San Francisco-San Mateo-Redwood PMSA, CA	H	23.38 FQ	28.32 MW	33.14 TQ	CABLS	1/08-3/08
	San Jose-Sunnyvale-Santa Clara MSA, CA	H	22.69 FQ	26.52 MW	32.38 TQ	CABLS	1/08-3/08
	Santa Ana-Anaheim-Irvine PMSA, CA	Y	33160 FQ	40180 MW	60590 TQ	USBLS	5/07
	Santa Rosa-Petaluma MSA, CA	H	16.65 FQ	18.89 MW	24.29 TQ	CABLS	1/08-3/08
	Colorado	Y	40120 FQ	46050 MW	55610 TQ	USBLS	5/07
	Denver-Aurora MSA, CO	Y	42510 FQ	47800 MW	57550 TQ	USBLS	5/07
	Connecticut	H	19.01 AE	23.85 MW		CTBLS	1/08-3/08
	Bridgeport-Stamford-Norwalk MSA, CT	Y	43860 FQ	50170 MW	55940 TQ	USBLS	5/07
	Hartford-West Hartford-East Hartford MSA, CT	Y	43030 FQ	50240 MW	57060 TQ	USBLS	5/07
	Washington-Arlington-Alexandria MSA, DC-VA-MD-WV	Y	42130 FQ	46920 MW	51900 TQ	USBLS	5/07
	Florida	Y	29720 FQ	38180 MW	46370 TQ	USBLS	5/07
	Miami-Fort Lauderdale-Miami Beach MSA, FL	Y	30430 FQ	36220 MW	45130 TQ	USBLS	5/07
	Tampa-St. Petersburg-Clearwater MSA, FL	Y	41070 FQ	44590 MW	50010 TQ	USBLS	5/07
	Georgia	Y	28480 FQ	34170 MW	44580 TQ	USBLS	5/07
	Atlanta-Sandy Springs-Marietta MSA, GA	Y	29720 FQ	34780 MW	39920 TQ	USBLS	5/07
	Idaho	Y	32160 FQ	36850 MW	41820 TQ	USBLS	5/07
	Illinois	Y	39570 FQ	47070 MW	57910 TQ	USBLS	5/07
	Chicago-Naperville-Joliet MSA, IL-IN-WI	Y	39770 FQ	46330 MW	55780 TQ	USBLS	5/07
	Indiana	Y	26440 FQ	32900 MW	40000 TQ	USBLS	5/07
	Indianapolis-Carmel MSA, IN	Y	32390 FQ	38780 MW	49300 TQ	USBLS	5/07
	Iowa	Y	35920 FQ	43370 MW	54600 TQ	USBLS	5/07

AE	Average entry wage	AW	Average wage paid	FQ	First quartile wage	LO	Lowest wage paid	MTC	Median total compensation	TCC	Total cash compensation
AER	Average entry range	AWR	Average wage range	H	Hourly	LR	Low end range	MW	Median wage paid	TQ	Third quartile wage
AEX	Average experienced wage	AXR	Average experienced range	HI	Highest wage paid	M	Monthly	MWR	Median wage range	W	Weekly
ATC	Average total compensation	D	Daily	HR	High end range	MCC	Median cash compensation	S	See annotated source	Y	Yearly

Numerical Tool and Process Control Programmer

Occupation/Type/Industry	Location	Per	Low	Mid	High	Source	Date
Numerical Tool and Process Control Programmer	Kansas	Y	37590 FQ	46210 MW	53600 TQ	USBLS	5/07
	Wichita MSA, KS	Y	48170 FQ	54300 MW	59410 TQ	USBLS	5/07
	Kentucky	Y	35129 FQ	39610 MW	46763 TQ	KYBLS	2008
	Louisville-Jefferson County MSA, KY-IN	Y	33510 FQ	38410 MW	46500 TQ	USBLS	5/07
	Louisiana	H	16.29 FQ	19.39 MW	24.62 TQ	LABLS	1/08-3/08
	Maine	Y	38850 FQ	43530 MW	49620 TQ	USBLS	5/07
	Maryland	Y		48800 MW		MDBLS	3/08
	Baltimore-Towson MSA, MD	Y	43230 FQ	50610 MW	57770 TQ	USBLS	
	Massachusetts	Y	42120 FQ	49380 MW	58280 TQ	USBLS	5/07
	Boston-Cambridge-Quincy NECTA, MA	Y	42110 FQ	48870 MW	56010 TQ	USBLS	5/07
	Worcester MSA, MA-CT	Y	38720 FQ	46170 MW	54080 TQ	USBLS	5/07
	Michigan	Y	35870 FQ	43530 MW	52890 TQ	USBLS	5/07
	Detroit-Warren-Livonia MSA, MI	Y	37960 FQ	46800 MW	57940 TQ	USBLS	5/07
	Grand Rapids-Wyoming MSA, MI	Y	39800 FQ	46610 MW	52410 TQ	USBLS	5/07
	Warren-Troy-Farmington Hills PMSA, MI	Y	39320 FQ	47680 MW	57750 TQ	USBLS	5/07
	Minnesota	Y	40409 FQ	48060 MW	57058 TQ	MNBLS	10/08-12/08
	Minneapolis-Saint Paul MSA, MN-WI	Y	44204 FQ	51885 MW	61288 TQ	MNBLS	10/08-12/08
	Mississippi	Y	29600 FQ	38220 MW	45480 TQ	USBLS	5/07
	Missouri	Y	31230 FQ	42040 MW	53410 TQ	USBLS	5/07
	Kansas City MSA, MO-KS	Y	40650 FQ	45800 MW	51940 TQ	USBLS	5/07
	St. Louis MSA, MO-IL	Y	36610 FQ	46330 MW	63090 TQ	USBLS	5/07
	Nebraska	Y	33720 FQ	36940 MW	40440 TQ	USBLS	5/07
	Nevada	H	20.17 FQ	22.54 MW	24.83 TQ	NVBLS	5/08
	Las Vegas-Paradise MSA, NV	H	20.44 FQ	22.47 MW	24.43 TQ	NVBLS	5/08
	New Hampshire	H	16.14 AE	19.69 MW	22.94 AEX	NHBLS	6/08
	Nashua NECTA, NH-MA	Y	32580 FQ	35740 MW	47270 TQ	USBLS	5/07
	New Jersey	Y	35980 FQ	43480 MW	57560 TQ	USBLS	5/07
	Camden PMSA, NJ	Y	35320 FQ	39260 MW	51790 TQ	USBLS	5/07
	Edison PMSA, NJ	Y	27610 FQ	45900 MW	63540 TQ	USBLS	5/07
	Newark-Union PMSA, NJ-PA	Y	39150 FQ	52650 MW	65530 TQ	USBLS	5/07
	New York	Y	28910 FQ	36910 MW	45620 TQ	USBLS	5/07
	Buffalo-Niagara Falls MSA, NY	Y	19360 FQ	34940 MW	44130 TQ	USBLS	5/07
	Nassau-Suffolk PMSA, NY	Y	31450 FQ	40920 MW	49410 TQ	USBLS	5/07
	New York-Northern New Jersey-Long Island MSA, NY-NJ-PA	Y	31280 FQ	41200 MW	52020 TQ	USBLS	5/07
	North Carolina	Y	34570 FQ	39810 MW	49680 TQ	USBLS	5/07
	Asheville MSA, NC	Y	34370 FQ	36830 MW	39340 TQ	USBLS	5/07
	Charlotte-Gastonia-Concord MSA, NC-SC	Y	39510 FQ	47380 MW	63480 TQ	USBLS	5/07
	Ohio	Y	34960 FQ	43300 MW	51690 TQ	USBLS	5/07
	Cincinnati-Middletown MSA, OH-KY-IN	Y	37230 FQ	45650 MW	54260 TQ	USBLS	5/07
	Cleveland-Elyria-Mentor MSA, OH	Y	38420 FQ	48120 MW	54640 TQ	USBLS	5/07
	Columbus MSA, OH	Y	21970 FQ	26920 MW	38330 TQ	USBLS	5/07
	Dayton MSA, OH	Y	35950 FQ	43330 MW	50070 TQ	USBLS	5/07
	Oklahoma	Y	34520 FQ	42910 MW	53390 TQ	USBLS	5/07
	Tulsa MSA, OK	Y	33370 FQ	39630 MW	48040 TQ	USBLS	5/07
	Oregon	H	20.42 FQ	25.03 MW	30.74 TQ	ORBLS	5/08
	Portland-Vancouver-Beaverton MSA, OR-WA	Y	43440 FQ	53640 MW	66340 TQ	USBLS	5/07
	Pennsylvania	Y	35710 FQ	43650 MW	49980 TQ	USBLS	5/07
	Allentown-Bethlehem-Easton MSA, PA-NJ	Y	45990 FQ	57770 MW	68050 TQ	USBLS	5/07
	Philadelphia-Camden-Wilmington MSA, PA-NJ-DE-MD	Y	37480 FQ	45100 MW	57770 TQ	USBLS	5/07
	Pittsburgh MSA, PA	Y	38660 FQ	45260 MW	51280 TQ	USBLS	5/07
	Rhode Island	Y	35440 FQ	40600 MW	48460 TQ	USBLS	5/07
	Providence-Fall River-Warwick MSA, RI-MA	Y	35100 FQ	40360 MW	48370 TQ	USBLS	5/07
	South Carolina	Y	29460 FQ	33880 MW	39650 TQ	USBLS	5/07
	Columbia MSA, SC	Y	28740 FQ	33920 MW	45120 TQ	USBLS	5/07

AE	Average entry wage	AW	Average wage paid	FQ First quartile wage
AER	Average entry range	AWR	Average wage range	H Hourly
AEX	Average experienced wage	AXR	Average experienced range	HI Highest wage paid
ATC	Average total compensation	D	Daily	HR High end range

LO	Lowest wage paid	MTC Median total compensation
LR	Low end range	MW Median wage paid
M	Monthly	MWR Median wage range
		MCC Median cash compensation S See annotated source

TCC	Total cash compensation
TQ	Third quartile wage
W	Weekly
Y	Yearly

Occupation/Type/Industry	Location	Per	Low	Mid	High	Source	Date
Numerical Tool and Process Control Programmer	South Dakota	Y	24031 FQ	29934 MW	37128 TQ	SDBLS	7/08-9/08
	Sioux Falls MSA, SD	Y	23327 FQ	27153 MW	33013 TQ	SDBLS	7/08-9/08
	Tennessee	Y	30750 FQ	34430 MW	38830 TQ	USBLS	5/07
	Memphis MSA, TN-MS-AR	Y	29770 FQ	54110 MW	60560 TQ	USBLS	5/07
	Nashville-Davidson-Murfreesboro MSA, TN	Y	43740 FQ	50750 MW	57550 TQ	USBLS	5/07
	Texas	Y	29420 FQ	39370 MW	51490 TQ	USBLS	5/07
	Austin-Round Rock MSA, TX	Y	21510 FQ	39280 MW	48860 TQ	USBLS	5/07
	Dallas-Fort Worth-Arlington MSA, TX	Y	28110 FQ	33220 MW	48630 TQ	USBLS	5/07
	Houston-Sugar Land-Baytown MSA, TX	Y	30090 FQ	40930 MW	52460 TQ	USBLS	5/07
	Utah	Y	38650 FQ	45080 MW	49840 TQ	USBLS	5/07
	Salt Lake City MSA, UT	Y	41890 FQ	45750 MW	49370 TQ	USBLS	5/07
	Vermont	Y	36500 FQ	44050 MW	52850 TQ	USBLS	5/07
	Burlington-South Burlington MSA, VT	Y	35030 FQ	40130 MW	46100 TQ	USBLS	5/07
	Virginia	Y	37610 FQ	44250 MW	52140 TQ	USBLS	5/07
	Richmond MSA, VA	Y	46020 FQ	57460 MW	68250 TQ	USBLS	5/07
	Virginia Beach-Norfolk-Newport News MSA, VA-NC	Y	34690 FQ	39220 MW	47640 TQ	USBLS	5/07
	Washington	H	23.06 FQ	29.40 MW	36.00 TQ	WABLS	3/08
	Seattle-Tacoma-Bellevue MSA, WA	Y	50060 FQ	63120 MW	75860 TQ	USBLS	5/07
	Wisconsin	Y	36850 FQ	43110 MW	50550 TQ	USBLS	5/07
	Milwaukee-Waukesha-West Allis MSA, WI	Y	41240 FQ	48080 MW	56180 TQ	USBLS	5/07
Nurse	United States	Y		56785 AW		ADVN	2008
Nurse Aide							
Certified, Home Health Agency	United States	H		11.00 MW		IOMA01	2006-2007
Certified, Hospital	United States	H		11.49 MW		IOMA01	2006-2007
Certified, Nursing Home	United States	H		10.33 MW		IOMA01	2006-2007
Nurse Manager	United States	Y		70000 AW		EZART	2009
Nurse Midwife							
Certified	Midwest	Y		79700 MW		WFMGMT	9/1/06
Certified	Northeast	Y		81400 MW		WFMGMT	9/1/06
Certified	South	Y		81700 MW		WFMGMT	9/1/06
Certified	West	Y		85100 MW		WFMGMT	9/1/06
Nurse Practitioner	United States	Y		81397 AW		AFNP	2007
	Los Angeles, CA	Y		102599 AW		AFNP	2007
	Oakland, CA	Y		88143 AW		AFNP	2007
	Chicago, IL	Y		86552 AW		AFNP	2007
	Rockford, IL	Y		78700 AW		AFNP	2007
	Buffalo, NY	Y		75762 AW		AFNP	2007
	New York, NY	Y		96955 AW		AFNP	2007
Department of Corrections	New Hampshire	Y		59540 AW		NHUL03	2008
Nurse Specialist							
New Hampshire Hospital	New Hampshire	Y		75065 AW		NHUL03	2008
Nursery Propagator	California	H		9.25 AW		FELS	2008
Nursery Technician							
State Government	Ohio	H	15.62 LO		18.36 HI	ODAS	2008
Nursing Aide, Orderly, and Attendant	Alabama	Y	17180 FQ	19390 MW	22630 TQ	USBLS	5/07
	Birmingham-Hoover MSA, AL	Y	18390 FQ	21460 MW	23890 TQ	USBLS	5/07
	Huntsville MSA, AL	Y	17060 FQ	18730 MW	21250 TQ	USBLS	5/07
	Montgomery MSA, AL	Y	17310 FQ	19210 MW	22200 TQ	USBLS	5/07
	Tuscaloosa MSA, AL	Y	16750 FQ	18850 MW	22710 TQ	USBLS	5/07
	Alaska	Y	27990 FQ	31060 MW	35880 TQ	USBLS	5/07
	Arizona	Y	19740 FQ	22870 MW	26860 TQ	USBLS	5/07
	Phoenix-Mesa-Scottsdale MSA, AZ	Y	19810 FQ	23360 MW	27710 TQ	USBLS	5/07
	Tucson MSA, AZ	Y	19910 FQ	22200 MW	24730 TQ	USBLS	5/07

AE	Average entry wage	**AW**	Average wage paid	**FQ**	First quartile wage	**LO**	Lowest wage paid	**MTC** Median total compensation **TCC** Total cash compensation
AER	Average entry range	**AWR**	Average wage range	**H**	Hourly	**LR**	Low end range	**MW** Median wage paid **TQ** Third quartile wage
AEX	Average experienced wage	**AXR**	Average experienced range	**HI**	Highest wage paid	**M**	Monthly	**MWR** Median wage range **W** Weekly
ATC	Average total compensation	**D**	Daily	**HR**	High end range	**MCC**	Median cash compensation	**S** See annotated source **Y** Yearly

Occupation/Type/Industry	Location	Per	Low	Mid	High	Source	Date
Nursing Aide, Orderly, and Attendant	Arkansas	Y	16850 FQ	18780 MW	21350 TQ	USBLS	5/07
	Little Rock-North Little Rock MSA, AR	Y	17900 FQ	19990 MW	23060 TQ	USBLS	5/07
	California	H	10.53 FQ	12.27 MW	14.78 TQ	CABLS	1/08-3/08
	Los Angeles-Long Beach-Glendale PMSA, CA	H	10.08 FQ	11.49 MW	13.92 TQ	CABLS	1/08-3/08
	Oakland-Fremont-Hayward MSA, CA	H	12.33 FQ	13.91 MW	15.89 TQ	CABLS	1/08-3/08
	Oxnard-Thousand Oaks-Ventura MSA, CA	H	11.33 FQ	13.12 MW	14.93 TQ	CABLS	1/08-3/08
	Riverside-San Bernardino-Ontario MSA, CA	H	10.31 FQ	11.65 MW	13.68 TQ	CABLS	1/08-3/08
	Sacramento-Arden Arcade-Roseville MSA, CA	H	11.37 FQ	13.19 MW	15.13 TQ	CABLS	1/08-3/08
	San Diego-Carlsbad-San Marcos MSA, CA	H	10.43 FQ	11.73 MW	13.72 TQ	CABLS	1/08-3/08
	San Francisco-San Mateo-Redwood PMSA, CA	H	13.55 FQ	17.24 MW	23.41 TQ	CABLS	1/08-3/08
	San Jose-Sunnyvale-Santa Clara MSA, CA	H	13.37 FQ	15.51 MW	18.94 TQ	CABLS	1/08-3/08
	Santa Ana-Anaheim-Irvine PMSA, CA	Y	21470 FQ	23690 MW	27240 TQ	USBLS	5/07
	Colorado	Y	21840 FQ	25380 MW	29540 TQ	USBLS	5/07
	Colorado Springs MSA, CO	Y	21420 FQ	24500 MW	28160 TQ	USBLS	5/07
	Denver-Aurora MSA, CO	Y	23600 FQ	27050 MW	30830 TQ	USBLS	5/07
	Connecticut	H	11.87 AE	14.41 MW		CTBLS	1/08-3/08
	Bridgeport-Stamford-Norwalk MSA, CT	Y	26380 FQ	29560 MW	33250 TQ	USBLS	5/07
	Hartford-West Hartford-East Hartford MSA, CT	Y	26600 FQ	29850 MW	33820 TQ	USBLS	5/07
	Delaware	Y	22890 FQ	26910 MW	30440 TQ	USBLS	5/07
	Wilmington PMSA, DE-MD-NJ	Y	23420 FQ	27080 MW	30520 TQ	USBLS	5/07
	District of Columbia	Y	22450 FQ	26280 MW	31040 TQ	USBLS	5/07
	Washington-Arlington-Alexandria MSA, DC-VA-MD-WV	Y	22220 FQ	26220 MW	31590 TQ	USBLS	5/07
	Florida	Y	19860 FQ	22600 MW	25520 TQ	USBLS	5/07
	Fort Lauderdale-Pompano Beach-Deerfield Beach PMSA, FL	Y	19200 FQ	22090 MW	25480 TQ	USBLS	5/07
	Jacksonville MSA, FL	Y	20630 FQ	22970 MW	25630 TQ	USBLS	5/07
	Miami-Fort Lauderdale-Miami Beach MSA, FL	Y	18870 FQ	21950 MW	25310 TQ	USBLS	5/07
	Orlando-Kissimmee MSA, FL	Y	20070 FQ	22580 MW	25330 TQ	USBLS	5/07
	Pensacola-Ferry Pass-Brent MSA, FL	Y	20540 FQ	22420 MW	24400 TQ	USBLS	5/07
	Tampa-St. Petersburg-Clearwater MSA, FL	Y	20290 FQ	22750 MW	25400 TQ	USBLS	5/07
	West Palm Beach-Boca Raton-Boynton Beach PMSA, FL	Y	19410 FQ	22040 MW	24610 TQ	USBLS	5/07
	Georgia	Y	16580 FQ	19250 MW	23260 TQ	USBLS	5/07
	Atlanta-Sandy Springs-Marietta MSA, GA	Y	18190 FQ	21240 MW	25430 TQ	USBLS	5/07
	Hawaii	Y	23750 FQ	26950 MW	30010 TQ	USBLS	5/07
	Honolulu MSA, HI	Y	22960 FQ	26330 MW	29960 TQ	USBLS	5/07
	Idaho	Y	18110 FQ	20910 MW	24100 TQ	USBLS	5/07
	Boise City-Nampa MSA, ID	Y	20690 FQ	22820 MW	25410 TQ	USBLS	5/07
	Pocatello MSA, ID	Y	16470 FQ	18720 MW	21330 TQ	USBLS	5/07
	Illinois	Y	19200 FQ	22390 MW	25790 TQ	USBLS	5/07
	Chicago-Naperville-Joliet MSA, IL-IN-WI	Y	20250 FQ	23260 MW	27140 TQ	USBLS	5/07
	Peoria MSA, IL	Y	20310 FQ	22860 MW	26260 TQ	USBLS	5/07
	Indiana	Y	19720 FQ	22560 MW	25680 TQ	USBLS	5/07
	Evansville MSA, IN-KY	Y	20110 FQ	22850 MW	25860 TQ	USBLS	5/07
	Gary PMSA, IN	Y	18930 FQ	22000 MW	25440 TQ	USBLS	5/07
	Indianapolis-Carmel MSA, IN	Y	21200 FQ	24030 MW	28220 TQ	USBLS	5/07
	Iowa	Y	20010 FQ	22560 MW	25350 TQ	USBLS	5/07
	Des Moines-West Des Moines MSA, IA	Y	21700 FQ	24390 MW	28300 TQ	USBLS	5/07
	Kansas	Y	18660 FQ	21360 MW	24320 TQ	USBLS	5/07

AE Average entry wage	**AW** Average wage paid	**FQ** First quartile wage	**LO** Lowest wage paid	**MTC** Median total compensation	**TCC** Total cash compensation
AER Average entry range	**AWR** Average wage range	**H** Hourly	**LR** Low end range	**MW** Median wage paid	**TQ** Third quartile wage
AEX Average experienced wage	**AXR** Average experienced range	**HI** Highest wage paid	**M** Monthly	**MWR** Median wage range	**W** Weekly
ATC Average total compensation	**D** Daily	**HR** High end range	**MCC** Median cash compensation	**S** See annotated source	**Y** Yearly

Occupation/Type/Industry	Location	Per	Low	Mid	High	Source	Date
Nursing Aide, Orderly, and Attendant	Lawrence MSA, KS	Y	20650 FQ	22810 MW	25140 TQ	USBLS	5/07
	Wichita MSA, KS	Y	19350 FQ	21780 MW	24400 TQ	USBLS	5/07
	Kentucky	Y	18534 FQ	21970 MW	25522 TQ	KYBLS	2008
	Louisville-Jefferson County MSA, KY-IN	Y	20650 FQ	23320 MW	26510 TQ	USBLS	5/07
	Louisiana	H	6.77 FQ	8.14 MW	9.65 TQ	LABLS	1/08-3/08
	Baton Rouge MSA, LA	Y	15060 FQ	17950 MW	20860 TQ	USBLS	5/07
	Houma-Bayou Cane-Thibodaux MSA, LA	Y	16940 FQ	19170 MW	26810 TQ	USBLS	5/07
	Lafayette MSA, LA	Y	13000 FQ	14690 MW	18300 TQ	USBLS	5/07
	Lake Charles MSA, LA	Y	13500 FQ	15960 MW	18730 TQ	USBLS	5/07
	New Orleans-Metairie-Kenner MSA, LA	Y	16610 FQ	19160 MW	23120 TQ	USBLS	5/07
	Maine	Y	19870 FQ	22430 MW	25370 TQ	USBLS	5/07
	Lewiston-Auburn MSA, ME	Y	20800 FQ	23330 MW	26940 TQ	USBLS	5/07
	Portland-South Portland-Biddeford MSA, ME	Y	22310 FQ	25190 MW	29080 TQ	USBLS	5/07
	Maryland	Y		27725 MW		MDBLS	3/08
	Baltimore-Towson MSA, MD	Y.	23110 FQ	27250 MW	32150 TQ	USBLS	5/07
	Bethesda-Gaithersburg-Frederick PMSA, MD	Y	23670 FQ	28910 MW	35860 TQ	USBLS	5/07
	Massachusetts	Y	23960 FQ	27570 MW	31300 TQ	USBLS	5/07
	Barnstable Town MSA, MA	Y	24640 FQ	27620 MW	31140 TQ	USBLS	5/07
	Boston-Cambridge-Quincy NECTA, MA	Y	25010 FQ	28370 MW	32000 TQ	USBLS	5/07
	Worcester MSA, MA-CT	Y	24120 FQ	27830 MW	31820 TQ	USBLS	5/07
	Michigan	Y	21810 FQ	24910 MW	28620 TQ	USBLS	5/07
	Detroit-Warren-Livonia MSA, MI	Y	22500 FQ	25820 MW	29310 TQ	USBLS	5/07
	Grand Rapids-Wyoming MSA, MI	Y	20920 FQ	23650 MW	27370 TQ	USBLS	5/07
	Warren-Troy-Farmington Hills PMSA, MI	Y	22970 FQ	25930 MW	29150 TQ	USBLS	5/07
	Minnesota	Y	23337 FQ	26798 MW	31472 TQ	MNBLS	10/08-12/08
	Duluth-Superior MSA, MN-WI	Y	22229 FQ	25637 MW	30426 TQ	MNBLS	10/08-12/08
	Minneapolis-Saint Paul MSA, MN-WI	Y	26223 FQ	29924 MW	33730 TQ	MNBLS	10/08-12/08
	Rochester MSA, MN	Y	24320 FQ	28716 MW	33494 TQ	MNBLS	10/08-12/08
	Mississippi	Y	16030 FQ	18030 MW	20390 TQ	USBLS	5/07
	Gulfport-Biloxi MSA, MS	Y	18180 FQ	22180 MW	28450 TQ	USBLS	5/07
	Jackson MSA, MS	Y	16620 FQ	18270 MW	20180 TQ	USBLS	5/07
	Missouri	Y	17410 FQ	20320 MW	23650 TQ	USBLS	5/07
	Joplin MSA, MO	Y	17380 FQ	19490 MW	22050 TQ	USBLS	5/07
	Kansas City MSA, MO-KS	Y	20140 FQ	23180 MW	26760 TQ	USBLS	5/07
	St. Louis MSA, MO-IL	Y	18890 FQ	21780 MW	24470 TQ	USBLS	5/07
	Montana	Y	18050 FQ	20590 MW	23360 TQ	USBLS	5/07
	Billings MSA, MT	Y	18990 FQ	20950 MW	23220 TQ	USBLS	5/07
	Nebraska	Y	19510 FQ	22280 MW	25180 TQ	USBLS	5/07
	Lincoln MSA, NE	Y	20960 FQ	23560 MW	27400 TQ	USBLS	5/07
	Omaha-Council Bluffs MSA, NE-IA	Y	21270 FQ	23870 MW	27280 TQ	USBLS	5/07
	Nevada	H	11.20 FQ	13.23 MW	15.24 TQ	NVBLS	5/08
	Las Vegas-Paradise MSA, NV	H	11.27 FQ	13.34 MW	15.54 TQ	NVBLS	5/08
	New Hampshire	H	11.09 AE	13.46 MW	14.84 AEX	NHBLS	6/08
	Manchester MSA, NH	Y	24000 FQ	28260 MW	32750 TQ	USBLS	5/07
	Nashua NECTA, NH-MA	Y	22570 FQ	24910 MW	28800 TQ	USBLS	5/07
	New Jersey	Y	22170 FQ	25480 MW	29490 TQ	USBLS	5/07
	Atlantic City MSA, NJ	Y	21290 FQ	25240 MW	30950 TQ	USBLS	5/07
	Camden PMSA, NJ	Y	21980 FQ	25450 MW	29330 TQ	USBLS	5/07
	Edison PMSA, NJ	Y	22570 FQ	25720 MW	29510 TQ	USBLS	5/07
	Newark-Union PMSA, NJ-PA	Y	22010 FQ	25090 MW	29050 TQ	USBLS	5/07
	New Mexico	Y	18190 FQ	21260 MW	24710 TQ	USBLS	5/07
	Albuquerque MSA, NM	Y	19730 FQ	22640 MW	26000 TQ	USBLS	5/07
	Farmington MSA, NM	Y	17760 FQ	21160 MW	25290 TQ	USBLS	5/07
	Santa Fe MSA, NM	Y	21380 FQ	24170 MW	28490 TQ	USBLS	5/07
	New York	Y	24120 FQ	29850 MW	34970 TQ	USBLS	5/07
	Albany-Schenectady-Troy MSA, NY	Y	21320 FQ	23910 MW	27500 TQ	USBLS	5/07
	Binghamton MSA, NY	Y	21240 FQ	23960 MW	28510 TQ	USBLS	5/07
	Buffalo-Niagara Falls MSA, NY	Y	21630 FQ	24860 MW	28290 TQ	USBLS	5/07

AE	Average entry wage	AW	Average wage paid	FQ	First quartile wage
AER	Average entry range	AWR	Average wage range	H	Hourly
AEX	Average experienced wage	AXR	Average experienced range	HI	Highest wage paid
ATC	Average total compensation	D	Daily	HR	High end range

LO	Lowest wage paid	MTC	Median total compensation
LR	Low end range	MW	Median wage paid
M	Monthly	MWR	Median wage range
MCC	Median cash compensation	S	See annotated source

TCC	Total cash compensation
TQ	Third quartile wage
W	Weekly
Y	Yearly

Occupation/Type/Industry	Location	Per	Low	Mid	High	Source	Date
Nursing Aide, Orderly, and Attendant	Glens Falls MSA, NY	Y	21780 FQ	25700 MW	33870 TQ	USBLS	5/07
	Nassau-Suffolk PMSA, NY	Y	30240 FQ	33930 MW	37250 TQ	USBLS	5/07
	New York-Northern New Jersey-Long Island MSA, NY-NJ-PA	Y	25880 FQ	30830 MW	35590 TQ	USBLS	5/07
	North Carolina	Y	19640 FQ	22590 MW	25820 TQ	USBLS	5/07
	Charlotte-Gastonia-Concord MSA, NC-SC	Y	19840 FQ	22360 MW	25300 TQ	USBLS	5/07
	Raleigh-Cary MSA, NC	Y	21630 FQ	24370 MW	27810 TQ	USBLS	5/07
	Winston-Salem MSA, NC	Y	20850 FQ	23570 MW	26510 TQ	USBLS	5/07
	North Dakota	Y	19810 FQ	22430 MW	25030 TQ	USBLS	5/07
	Fargo MSA, ND-MN	Y	21080 FQ	23010 MW	25290 TQ	USBLS	5/07
	Grand Forks MSA, ND-MN	Y	21210 FQ	23430 MW	26450 TQ	USBLS	5/07
	Ohio	Y	20100 FQ	22930 MW	26200 TQ	USBLS	5/07
	Cincinnati-Middletown MSA, OH-KY-IN	Y	21340 FQ	23870 MW	27430 TQ	USBLS	5/07
	Cleveland-Elyria-Mentor MSA, OH	Y	21020 FQ	23820 MW	27140 TQ	USBLS	5/07
	Columbus MSA, OH	Y	21090 FQ	24180 MW	27740 TQ	USBLS	5/07
	Dayton MSA, OH	Y	20840 FQ	23240 MW	26430 TQ	USBLS	5/07
	Oklahoma	Y	16830 FQ	18920 MW	21640 TQ	USBLS	5/07
	Oklahoma City MSA, OK	Y	17640 FQ	19780 MW	22600 TQ	USBLS	5/07
	Tulsa MSA, OK	Y	17940 FQ	20220 MW	22810 TQ	USBLS	5/07
	Oregon	H	10.38 FQ	11.98 MW	14.25 TQ	ORBLS	5/08
	Portland-Vancouver-Beaverton MSA, OR-WA	Y	21910 FQ	25660 MW	30240 TQ	USBLS	5/07
	Pennsylvania	Y	21040 FQ	24300 MW	28300 TQ	USBLS	5/07
	Allentown-Bethlehem-Easton MSA, PA-NJ	Y	20410 FQ	23230 MW	27300 TQ	USBLS	5/07
	Erie MSA, PA	Y	19390 FQ	22600 MW	26040 TQ	USBLS	5/07
	Lancaster MSA, PA	Y	21990 FQ	25090 MW	29090 TQ	USBLS	5/07
	Philadelphia-Camden-Wilmington MSA, PA-NJ-DE-MD	Y	22480 FQ	25910 MW	29590 TQ	USBLS	5/07
	Pittsburgh MSA, PA	Y	20270 FQ	23610 MW	27100 TQ	USBLS	5/07
	Rhode Island	Y	23170 FQ	26750 MW	30870 TQ	USBLS	5/07
	Providence-Fall River-Warwick MSA, RI-MA	Y	23170 FQ	26720 MW	30740 TQ	USBLS	5/07
	South Carolina	Y	16930 FQ	19310 MW	22670 TQ	USBLS	5/07
	Charleston-North Charleston MSA, SC	Y	16930 FQ	19200 MW	23260 TQ	USBLS	5/07
	Columbia MSA, SC	Y	15250 FQ	18510 MW	22100 TQ	USBLS	5/07
	Spartanburg MSA, SC	Y	19110 FQ	22050 MW	24460 TQ	USBLS	5/07
	South Dakota	Y	19069 FQ	21953 MW	25125 TQ	SDBLS	7/08-9/08
	Sioux Falls MSA, SD	Y	21682 FQ	24003 MW	26509 TQ	SDBLS	7/08-9/08
	Tennessee	Y	18470 FQ	21260 MW	24010 TQ	USBLS	5/07
	Johnson City MSA, TN	Y	17490 FQ	20390 MW	23700 TQ	USBLS	5/07
	Memphis MSA, TN-MS-AR	Y	18630 FQ	21480 MW	24390 TQ	USBLS	5/07
	Nashville-Davidson-Murfreesboro MSA, TN	Y	19900 FQ	22450 MW	25570 TQ	USBLS	5/07
	Texas	Y	17150 FQ	20140 MW	23780 TQ	USBLS	5/07
	Austin-Round Rock MSA, TX	Y	20000 FQ	22420 MW	25100 TQ	USBLS	5/07
	Dallas-Fort Worth-Arlington MSA, TX	Y	18960 FQ	21880 MW	25330 TQ	USBLS	5/07
	El Paso MSA, TX	Y	14010 FQ	17390 MW	22700 TQ	USBLS	5/07
	Houston-Sugar Land-Baytown MSA, TX	Y	18780 FQ	22280 MW	25970 TQ	USBLS	5/07
	Midland MSA, TX	Y	16350 FQ	18160 MW	20720 TQ	USBLS	5/07
	San Antonio MSA, TX	Y	17050 FQ	20070 MW	23120 TQ	USBLS	5/07
	Utah	Y	18010 FQ	20260 MW	23270 TQ	USBLS	5/07
	Logan MSA, UT-ID	Y	18240 FQ	20650 MW	23230 TQ	USBLS	5/07
	Provo-Orem MSA, UT	Y	17550 FQ	19680 MW	22520 TQ	USBLS	5/07
	Salt Lake City MSA, UT	Y	18600 FQ	20890 MW	24140 TQ	USBLS	5/07
	Vermont	Y	20810 FQ	23630 MW	27710 TQ	USBLS	5/07
	Burlington-South Burlington MSA, VT	Y	21930 FQ	25590 MW	29460 TQ	USBLS	5/07
	Virginia	Y	18870 FQ	21890 MW	25200 TQ	USBLS	5/07
	Richmond MSA, VA	Y	19230 FQ	22760 MW	26420 TQ	USBLS	5/07
	Virginia Beach-Norfolk-Newport News MSA, VA-NC	Y	18580 FQ	21000 MW	23430 TQ	USBLS	5/07
	Washington	H	10.48 FQ	12.12 MW	14.33 TQ	WABLS	3/08

AE	Average entry wage	AW	Average wage paid	FQ	First quartile wage
AER	Average entry range	AWR	Average wage range	H	Hourly
AEX	Average experienced wage	AXR	Average experienced range	HI	Highest wage paid
ATC	Average total compensation	D	Daily	HR	High end range

LO Lowest wage paid
LR Low end range
M Monthly
MCC Median cash compensation

MTC Median total compensation
MW Median wage paid
MWR Median wage range
S See annotated source

TCC Total cash compensation
TQ Third quartile wage
W Weekly
Y Yearly

Occupation/Type/Industry	Location	Per	Low	Mid	High	Source	Date
Nursing Aide, Orderly, and Attendant	Seattle-Tacoma-Bellevue MSA, WA	Y	23420 FQ	27030 MW	31010 TQ	USBLS	5/07
	West Virginia	Y	17351 FQ	19854 MW	23267 TQ	WVBLS	7/08-9/08
	Charleston MSA, WV	Y	16980 FQ	18890 MW	22030 TQ	USBLS	5/07
	Wisconsin	Y	21790 FQ	24670 MW	28590 TQ	USBLS	5/07
	Milwaukee-Waukesha-West Allis MSA, WI	Y	21470 FQ	24590 MW	28980 TQ	USBLS	5/07
	Wyoming	Y	21222 FQ	23794 MW	27317 TQ	WYBLS	9/08
	Cheyenne MSA, WY	Y	23431 FQ	27105 MW	30777 TQ	WYBLS	9/08
	Puerto Rico	Y	12800 FQ	14430 MW	17470 TQ	USBLS	5/07
	San Juan-Caguas-Guaynabo MSA, PR	Y	12770 FQ	14390 MW	17230 TQ	USBLS	5/07
	Virgin Islands	Y	14710 FQ	16720 MW	18650 TQ	USBLS	5/07
Nursing Coordinator Department of Corrections	New Hampshire	Y		76741 AW		NHUL03	2008
Nursing Director Municipal Government	Cincinnati, OH	Y	75782 LO		102305 HI	COHSS	10/08
Nursing Home Administrator	United States	Y		85464 MW		MLTCN01	2008
Nursing Instructor and Teacher							
Postsecondary	Alabama	Y	42710 FQ	52820 MW	65450 TQ	USBLS	5/07
Postsecondary	Birmingham-Hoover MSA, AL	Y	50020 FQ	67090 MW	80220 TQ	USBLS	5/07
Postsecondary	Alaska	Y	62230 FQ	72120 MW	80670 TQ	USBLS	5/07
Postsecondary	Arizona	Y	41000 FQ	52060 MW	59400 TQ	USBLS	5/07
Postsecondary	Phoenix-Mesa-Scottsdale MSA, AZ	Y	30850 FQ	39980 MW	54160 TQ	USBLS	5/07
Postsecondary	Arkansas	Y	38820 FQ	46510 MW	56590 TQ	USBLS	5/07
Postsecondary	Little Rock-North Little Rock MSA, AR	Y	42930 FQ	52540 MW	62410 TQ	USBLS	5/07
Postsecondary	California	Y		77926 AW		CABLS	1/08-3/08
Postsecondary	Los Angeles-Long Beach-Glendale PMSA, CA	Y		77474 AW		CABLS	1/08-3/08
Postsecondary	Oakland-Fremont-Hayward MSA, CA	Y		68799 AW		CABLS	1/08-3/08
Postsecondary	Riverside-San Bernardino-Ontario MSA, CA	Y		81351 AW		CABLS	1/08-3/08
Postsecondary	Sacramento-Arden Arcade-Roseville MSA, CA	Y		97707 AW		CABLS	1/08-3/08
Postsecondary	San Diego-Carlsbad-San Marcos MSA, CA	Y		78069 AW		CABLS	1/08-3/08
Postsecondary	San Francisco-San Mateo-Redwood PMSA, CA	Y		90559 AW		CABLS	1/08-3/08
Postsecondary	San Jose-Sunnyvale-Santa Clara MSA, CA	Y		62687 AW		CABLS	1/08-3/08
Postsecondary	Santa Ana-Anaheim-Irvine PMSA, CA	Y	52070 FQ	69410 MW	80400 TQ	USBLS	
Postsecondary	Colorado	Y	44100 FQ	60630 MW	73870 TQ	USBLS	5/07
Postsecondary	Denver-Aurora MSA, CO	Y	52430 FQ	65560 MW	76230 TQ	USBLS	5/07
Postsecondary	Bridgeport-Stamford-Norwalk MSA, CT	Y	45930 FQ	63690 MW	76670 TQ	USBLS	5/07
Postsecondary	Hartford-West Hartford-East Hartford MSA, CT	Y	57660 FQ	70190 MW	92290 TQ	USBLS	5/07
Postsecondary	Delaware	Y	50270 FQ	63170 MW	74420 TQ	USBLS	5/07
Postsecondary	District of Columbia	Y	66890 FQ	76840 MW	110460 TQ	USBLS	5/07
Postsecondary	Washington-Arlington-Alexandria MSA, DC-VA-MD-WV	Y	61300 FQ	73210 MW	84560 TQ	USBLS	5/07
Postsecondary	Florida	Y	49340 FQ	61150 MW	75070 TQ	USBLS	5/07
Postsecondary	Fort Lauderdale-Pompano Beach-Deerfield Beach PMSA, FL	Y	57480 FQ	69250 MW	77880 TQ	USBLS	5/07
Postsecondary	Jacksonville MSA, FL	Y	46390 FQ	51570 MW	65040 TQ	USBLS	5/07
Postsecondary	Miami-Fort Lauderdale-Miami Beach MSA, FL	Y	59110 FQ	71340 MW	79380 TQ	USBLS	5/07
Postsecondary	Orlando-Kissimmee MSA, FL	Y	54750 FQ	62180 MW	70070 TQ	USBLS	5/07
Postsecondary	Tampa-St. Petersburg-Clearwater MSA, FL	Y	48980 FQ	59540 MW	72450 TQ	USBLS	5/07

Occupation/Type/Industry	Location	Per	Low	Mid	High	Source	Date
Nursing Instructor and Teacher							
Postsecondary	West Palm Beach-Boca Raton-Boynton Beach PMSA, FL	Y	57250 FQ	67750 MW	86720 TQ	USBLS	5/07
Postsecondary	Georgia	Y	46230 FQ	55800 MW	66470 TQ	USBLS	5/07
Postsecondary	Atlanta-Sandy Springs-Marietta MSA, GA	Y	51710 FQ	59310 MW	70910 TQ	USBLS	5/07
Postsecondary	Illinois	Y	41540 FQ	55720 MW	68810 TQ	USBLS	5/07
Postsecondary	Chicago-Naperville-Joliet MSA, IL-IN-WI	Y	42670 FQ	56750 MW	69710 TQ	USBLS	5/07
Postsecondary	Indiana	Y	44360 FQ	53160 MW	66780 TQ	USBLS	5/07
Postsecondary	Gary PMSA, IN	Y	44610 FQ	52890 MW	62280 TQ	USBLS	5/07
Postsecondary	Indianapolis-Carmel MSA, IN	Y	54410 FQ	80800 MW	96890 TQ	USBLS	5/07
Postsecondary	Iowa	Y	40660 FQ	49120 MW	61220 TQ	USBLS	5/07
Postsecondary	Des Moines-West Des Moines MSA, IA	Y	47810 FQ	54770 MW	61900 TQ	USBLS	5/07
Postsecondary	Kansas	Y	38940 FQ	50920 MW	64920 TQ	USBLS	5/07
Postsecondary	Kentucky	Y	44786 FQ	54665 MW	67727 TQ	KYBLS	2008
Postsecondary	Louisville-Jefferson County MSA, KY-IN	Y	48880 FQ	56770 MW	66900 TQ	USBLS	5/07
Postsecondary	Louisiana	Y		60759 AW		LABLS	1/08-3/08
Postsecondary	Baton Rouge MSA, LA	Y	52110 FQ	57840 MW	63500 TQ	USBLS	5/07
Postsecondary	New Orleans-Metairie-Kenner MSA, LA	Y	58570 FQ	90520 MW	111540 TQ	USBLS	5/07
Postsecondary	Maine	Y	44370 FQ	54160 MW	65880 TQ	USBLS	5/07
Postsecondary	Portland-South Portland-Biddeford MSA, ME	Y	44720 FQ	53860 MW	68090 TQ	USBLS	5/07
Postsecondary	Maryland	Y		71525 MW		MDBLS	3/08
Postsecondary	Baltimore-Towson MSA, MD	Y	55090 FQ	70980 MW	92400 TQ	USBLS	5/07
Postsecondary	Bethesda-Gaithersburg-Frederick PMSA, MD	Y	68540 FQ	75230 MW	82090 TQ	USBLS	5/07
Postsecondary	Massachusetts	Y	50040 FQ	64730 MW	84550 TQ	USBLS	5/07
Postsecondary	Boston-Cambridge-Quincy NECTA, MA	Y	49020 FQ	63140 MW	83360 TQ	USBLS	5/07
Postsecondary	Worcester MSA, MA-CT	Y	76840 FQ	89690 MW	100070 TQ	USBLS	5/07
Postsecondary	Michigan	Y	45940 FQ	60390 MW	73150 TQ	USBLS	5/07
Postsecondary	Detroit-Warren-Livonia MSA, MI	Y	39560 FQ	52360 MW	71620 TQ	USBLS	5/07
Postsecondary	Warren-Troy-Farmington Hills PMSA, MI	Y	38740 FQ	46980 MW	70430 TQ	USBLS	5/07
Postsecondary	Minnesota	Y	50302 FQ	62825 MW	77860 TQ	MNBLS	10/08-12/08
Postsecondary	Duluth-Superior MSA, MN-WI	Y	42822 FQ	50386 MW	66686 TQ	MNBLS	10/08-12/08
Postsecondary	Minneapolis-Saint Paul MSA, MN-WI	Y	54048 FQ	64165 MW	77734 TQ	MNBLS	10/08-12/08
Postsecondary	Rochester MSA, MN	Y	78601 FQ	88261 MW	97165 TQ	MNBLS	10/08-12/08
Postsecondary	Mississippi	Y	42950 FQ	53120 MW	62210 TQ	USBLS	5/07
Postsecondary	Jackson MSA, MS	Y	30480 FQ	44170 MW	57620 TQ	USBLS	5/07
Postsecondary	Missouri	Y	43960 FQ	54870 MW	66430 TQ	USBLS	5/07
Postsecondary	Kansas City MSA, MO-KS	Y	44810 FQ	55510 MW	68630 TQ	USBLS	5/07
Postsecondary	St. Louis MSA, MO-IL	Y	40630 FQ	55110 MW	65140 TQ	USBLS	5/07
Postsecondary	Montana	Y	34140 FQ	40580 MW	49900 TQ	USBLS	5/07
Postsecondary	Nebraska	Y	41390 FQ	50070 MW	60720 TQ	USBLS	5/07
Postsecondary	Omaha-Council Bluffs MSA, NE-IA	Y	43190 FQ	54210 MW	62490 TQ	USBLS	5/07
Postsecondary	New Hampshire	Y	36760 AE	55763 MW	64647 AEX	NHBLS	6/08
Postsecondary	Manchester MSA, NH	Y	43780 FQ	56780 MW	68080 TQ	USBLS	5/07
Postsecondary	Nashua NECTA, NH-MA	Y	43890 FQ	58590 MW	66850 TQ	USBLS	5/07
Postsecondary	New Jersey	Y	58300 FQ	72880 MW	86450 TQ	USBLS	5/07
Postsecondary	Camden PMSA, NJ	Y	58400 FQ	71220 MW	83380 TQ	USBLS	5/07
Postsecondary	Edison PMSA, NJ	Y	66140 FQ	79700 MW	91780 TQ	USBLS	5/07
Postsecondary	Newark-Union PMSA, NJ-PA	Y	54890 FQ	73550 MW	89450 TQ	USBLS	5/07
Postsecondary	New Mexico	Y	46030 FQ	57450 MW	73490 TQ	USBLS	5/07
Postsecondary	Albuquerque MSA, NM	Y	48010 FQ	59900 MW	80210 TQ	USBLS	5/07
Postsecondary	New York	Y	47880 FQ	59140 MW	80310 TQ	USBLS	5/07
Postsecondary	Albany-Schenectady-Troy MSA, NY	Y	58870 FQ	70170 MW	77110 TQ	USBLS	5/07
Postsecondary	Buffalo-Niagara Falls MSA, NY	Y	43680 FQ	60030 MW	70130 TQ	USBLS	5/07
Postsecondary	Nassau-Suffolk PMSA, NY	Y	45730 FQ	59450 MW	88860 TQ	USBLS	5/07
Postsecondary	New York-Northern New Jersey-Long Island MSA, NY-NJ-PA	Y	50610 FQ	65630 MW	88720 TQ	USBLS	5/07
Postsecondary	Syracuse MSA, NY	Y	46220 FQ	58430 MW	71520 TQ	USBLS	5/07

AE Average entry wage	**AW** Average wage paid	**FQ** First quartile wage	**LO** Lowest wage paid	**MTC** Median total compensation	**TCC** Total cash compensation
AER Average entry range	**AWR** Average wage range	**H** Hourly	**LR** Low end range	**MW** Median wage paid	**TQ** Third quartile wage
AEX Average experienced wage	**AXR** Average experienced range	**HI** Highest wage paid	**M** Monthly	**MWR** Median wage range	**W** Weekly
ATC Average total compensation	**D** Daily	**HR** High end range	**MCC** Median cash compensation	**S** See annotated source	**Y** Yearly

Occupation/Type/Industry	Location	Per	Low	Mid	High	Source	Date
Nursing Instructor and Teacher							
Postsecondary	North Carolina	Y	46230 FQ	54400 MW	62920 TQ	USBLS	5/07
Postsecondary	Charlotte-Gastonia-Concord MSA, NC-SC	Y	45020 FQ	52350 MW	62600 TQ	USBLS	5/07
Postsecondary	Greensboro-High Point MSA, NC	Y	49160 FQ	59220 MW	72890 TQ	USBLS	5/07
Postsecondary	North Dakota	Y	42400 FQ	48170 MW	58130 TQ	USBLS	5/07
Postsecondary	Fargo MSA, ND-MN	Y	39500 FQ	45750 MW	53210 TQ	USBLS	5/07
Postsecondary	Ohio	Y	46640 FQ	58400 MW	73820 TQ	USBLS	5/07
Postsecondary	Cincinnati-Middletown MSA, OH-KY-IN	Y	43550 FQ	54250 MW	66080 TQ	USBLS	5/07
Postsecondary	Cleveland-Elyria-Mentor MSA, OH	Y	48880 FQ	60540 MW	77650 TQ	USBLS	5/07
Postsecondary	Columbus MSA, OH	Y	54440 FQ	68370 MW	90970 TQ	USBLS	5/07
Postsecondary	Dayton MSA, OH	Y	44050 FQ	55870 MW	65730 TQ	USBLS	5/07
Postsecondary	Oklahoma	Y	38320 FQ	45930 MW	55870 TQ	USBLS	5/07
Postsecondary	Oklahoma City MSA, OK	Y	40910 FQ	48470 MW	59350 TQ	USBLS	5/07
Postsecondary	Tulsa MSA, OK	Y	30440 FQ	42770 MW	48970 TQ	USBLS	5/07
Postsecondary	Portland-Vancouver-Beaverton MSA, OR-WA	Y	51730 FQ	65560 MW	83300 TQ	USBLS	5/07
Postsecondary	Pennsylvania	Y	45180 FQ	57940 MW	71050 TQ	USBLS	5/07
Postsecondary	Allentown-Bethlehem-Easton MSA, PA-NJ	Y	48270 FQ	59470 MW	77390 TQ	USBLS	5/07
Postsecondary	Philadelphia-Camden-Wilmington MSA, PA-NJ-DE-MD	Y	43200 FQ	60660 MW	75610 TQ	USBLS	5/07
Postsecondary	Pittsburgh MSA, PA	Y	47520 FQ	56630 MW	64390 TQ	USBLS	5/07
Postsecondary	Rhode Island	Y	48940 FQ	58690 MW	71830 TQ	USBLS	5/07
Postsecondary	Providence-Fall River-Warwick MSA, RI-MA	Y	48040 FQ	56970 MW	70840 TQ	USBLS	5/07
Postsecondary	South Carolina	Y	51740 FQ	59650 MW	68230 TQ	USBLS	5/07
Postsecondary	South Dakota	Y	42307 FQ	52301 MW	66742 TQ	SDBLS	7/08-9/08
Postsecondary	Sioux Falls MSA, SD	Y	42949 FQ	48813 MW	56600 TQ	SDBLS	7/08-9/08
Postsecondary	Tennessee	Y	43170 FQ	51890 MW	70090 TQ	USBLS	5/07
Postsecondary	Memphis MSA, TN-MS-AR	Y	48330 FQ	62660 MW	78660 TQ	USBLS	5/07
Postsecondary	Nashville-Davidson-Murfreesboro MSA, TN	Y	43940 FQ	57680 MW	75750 TQ	USBLS	5/07
Postsecondary	Texas	Y	43530 FQ	53470 MW	68000 TQ	USBLS	5/07
Postsecondary	Austin-Round Rock MSA, TX	Y	41620 FQ	54100 MW	76960 TQ	USBLS	5/07
Postsecondary	Dallas-Fort Worth-Arlington MSA, TX	Y	34730 FQ	51760 MW	65550 TQ	USBLS	5/07
Postsecondary	El Paso MSA, TX	Y	43520 FQ	52870 MW	64940 TQ	USBLS	5/07
Postsecondary	Houston-Sugar Land-Baytown MSA, TX	Y	47450 FQ	61650 MW	83800 TQ	USBLS	5/07
Postsecondary	San Antonio MSA, TX	Y	43540 FQ	51280 MW	63070 TQ	USBLS	5/07
Postsecondary	Utah	Y	44540 FQ	51830 MW	63340 TQ	USBLS	5/07
Postsecondary	Salt Lake City MSA, UT	Y	44990 FQ	56400 MW	73650 TQ	USBLS	5/07
Postsecondary	Vermont	Y	55210 FQ	65360 MW	81410 TQ	USBLS	5/07
Postsecondary	Virginia	Y	45120 FQ	57160 MW	70090 TQ	USBLS	5/07
Postsecondary	Richmond MSA, VA	Y	36770 FQ	47760 MW	59750 TQ	USBLS	5/07
Postsecondary	Virginia Beach-Norfolk-Newport News MSA, VA-NC	Y	43650 FQ	55460 MW	67360 TQ	USBLS	5/07
Postsecondary	Washington	Y		60981 AW		WABLS	3/08
Postsecondary	Seattle-Tacoma-Bellevue MSA, WA	Y	47290 FQ	61940 MW	80230 TQ	USBLS	5/07
Postsecondary	West Virginia	Y	41546 FQ	50939 MW	62676 TQ	WVBLS	7/08-9/08
Postsecondary	Charleston MSA, WV	Y	39430 FQ	46270 MW	54750 TQ	USBLS	5/07
Postsecondary	Wisconsin	Y	49670 FQ	58940 MW	72510 TQ	USBLS	5/07
Postsecondary	Green Bay MSA, WI	Y	48110 FQ	57520 MW	68910 TQ	USBLS	5/07
Postsecondary	Milwaukee-Waukesha-West Allis MSA, WI	Y	49130 FQ	57500 MW	70900 TQ	USBLS	5/07
Postsecondary	Wyoming	Y	45825 FQ	51778 MW	60107 TQ	WYBLS	9/08
Nursing Professor							
Alamo Community College District	San Antonio, TX	Y			43000 HI	SAEN	2009
Nutrition Consultant							
Department of Health and Human Services, Office of Health Management	New Hampshire	Y		50838 AW		NHUL03	2008
Nutritionist							
Public Health	Ohio	H	22.60 LO		31.62 HI	ODAS	2008

AE	Average entry wage	AW	Average wage paid	FQ	First quartile wage	LO	Lowest wage paid	MTC	Median total compensation	TCC	Total cash compensation
AER	Average entry range	AWR	Average wage range	H	Hourly	LR	Low end range	MW	Median wage paid	TQ	Third quartile wage
AEX	Average experienced wage	AXR	Average experienced range	HI	Highest wage paid	M	Monthly	MWR	Median wage range	W	Weekly
ATC	Average total compensation	D	Daily	HR	High end range	MCC	Median cash compensation	S	See annotated source	Y	Yearly

Occupation/Type/Industry	Location	Per	Low	Mid	High	Source	Date
Obstetrician and Gynecologist	United States	Y		237500 ATC		MEDEC01	2007
	Arizona	Y	142030 FQ			USBLS	5/07
	Phoenix-Mesa-Scottsdale MSA, AZ	Y	93030 FQ			USBLS	5/07
	California	H	68.91 FQ			CABLS	1/08-3/08
	Los Angeles-Long Beach-Glendale PMSA, CA	H	40.93 FQ			CABLS	1/08-3/08
	Connecticut	H	52.03 AE	87.81 AW		CTBLS	1/08-3/08
	Hartford-West Hartford-East Hartford MSA, CT	Y	137730 FQ			USBLS	5/07
	Delaware	Y	108200 FQ			USBLS	5/07
	Wilmington PMSA, DE-MD-NJ	Y	109400 FQ			USBLS	5/07
	District of Columbia	Y	76610 FQ	105650 MW		USBLS	5/07
	Washington-Arlington-Alexandria MSA, DC-VA-MD-WV	Y	106800 FQ	132080 MW		USBLS	5/07
	Tampa-St. Petersburg-Clearwater MSA, FL	Y	133370 FQ			USBLS	5/07
	Hawaii	Y	134520 FQ			USBLS	5/07
	Honolulu MSA, HI	Y	133730 FQ	144260 MW		USBLS	5/07
	Illinois	Y	100040 FQ			USBLS	5/07
	Chicago-Naperville-Joliet MSA, IL-IN-WI	Y	93270 FQ			USBLS	5/07
	Gary PMSA, IN	Y	76040 FQ			USBLS	5/07
	Indianapolis-Carmel MSA, IN	Y	118950 FQ			USBLS	5/07
	Louisiana	Y		187329 AW		LABLS	1/08-3/08
	Baton Rouge MSA, LA	Y	107200 FQ			USBLS	5/07
	Boston-Cambridge-Quincy NECTA, MA	Y	131740 FQ			USBLS	5/07
	Michigan	Y	116530 FQ			USBLS	5/07
	Detroit-Warren-Livonia MSA, MI	Y	83100 FQ			USBLS	5/07
	Grand Rapids-Wyoming MSA, MI	Y	142130 FQ			USBLS	5/07
	Warren-Troy-Farmington Hills PMSA, MI	Y	118410 FQ			USBLS	5/07
	Minnesota	Y		188885 AW		MNBLS	10/08-12/08
	Duluth-Superior MSA, MN-WI	Y	97414 FQ	105888 MW		MNBLS	10/08-12/08
	Minneapolis-Saint Paul MSA, MN-WI	Y	143856 FQ	181321 AW		MNBLS	10/08-12/08
	St. Louis MSA, MO-IL	Y	119210 FQ			USBLS	5/07
	Montana	Y	73180 FQ	108200 MW		USBLS	5/07
	Nevada	H	62.57 FQ	91.90 AW		NVBLS	5/08
	Las Vegas-Paradise MSA, NV	H	61.89 FQ	91.22 AW		NVBLS	5/08
	New Jersey	Y	145510 FQ			USBLS	5/07
	Edison PMSA, NJ	Y	129240 FQ			USBLS	5/07
	Newark-Union PMSA, NJ-PA	Y	118820 FQ			USBLS	5/07
	New Mexico	Y	135720 FQ			USBLS	5/07
	Albuquerque MSA, NM	Y	134330 FQ			USBLS	5/07
	Cincinnati-Middletown MSA, OH-KY-IN	Y	133810 FQ			USBLS	5/07
	Oklahoma	Y	142120 FQ			USBLS	5/07
	Oklahoma City MSA, OK	Y	128040 FQ			USBLS	5/07
	South Carolina	Y	142240 FQ			USBLS	5/07
	Charleston-North Charleston MSA, SC	Y	135690 FQ			USBLS	5/07
	Columbia MSA, SC	Y	131730 FQ			USBLS	5/07
	Tennessee	Y	141930 FQ			USBLS	5/07
	Memphis MSA, TN-MS-AR	Y	86390 FQ	134110 MW		USBLS	5/07
	Houston-Sugar Land-Baytown MSA, TX	Y	48570 FQ			USBLS	5/07
	Vermont	Y	85050 FQ			USBLS	5/07
	Burlington-South Burlington MSA, VT	Y	52490 FQ	111480 MW		USBLS	5/07
	Virginia	Y	118080 FQ			USBLS	5/07
	Richmond MSA, VA	Y	121120 FQ			USBLS	5/07
	Washington	Y		187836 AW		WABLS	3/08
	Seattle-Tacoma-Bellevue MSA, WA	Y	122880 FQ			USBLS	5/07
	West Virginia	Y	138376 FQ	189363 AW		WVBLS	7/08-9/08
	Puerto Rico	Y	72630 FQ	94510 MW		USBLS	5/07

AE	Average entry wage	AW	Average wage paid	FQ	First quartile wage
AER	Average entry range	AWR	Average wage range	H	Hourly
AEX	Average experienced wage	AXR	Average experienced range	HI	Highest wage paid
ATC	Average total compensation	D	Daily	HR	High end range

LO	Lowest wage paid	MTC	Median total compensation	TCC	Total cash compensation
LR	Low end range	MW	Median wage paid	TQ	Third quartile wage
M	Monthly	MWR	Median wage range	W	Weekly
MCC	Median cash compensation	S	See annotated source	Y	Yearly

Occupation/Type/Industry	Location	Per	Low	Mid	High	Source	Date
Obstetrician and Gynecologist	San Juan-Caguas-Guaynabo MSA, PR	Y	64490 FQ	100970 MW		USBLS	5/07
Occupational Health and Safety Specialist							
	Alabama	Y	46420 FQ	62370 MW	79600 TQ	USBLS	5/07
	Birmingham-Hoover MSA, AL	Y	48670 FQ	68250 MW	87520 TQ	USBLS	5/07
	Mobile MSA, AL	Y	37110 FQ	50730 MW	71210 TQ	USBLS	5/07
	Alaska	Y	66480 FQ	79100 MW	100490 TQ	USBLS	5/07
	Anchorage MSA, AK	Y	67610 FQ	77200 MW	95750 TQ	USBLS	5/07
	Arizona	Y	44460 FQ	56360 MW	70030 TQ	USBLS	5/07
	Phoenix-Mesa-Scottsdale MSA, AZ	Y	48230 FQ	59190 MW	75430 TQ	USBLS	5/07
	Tucson MSA, AZ	Y	38910 FQ	46640 MW	60280 TQ	USBLS	5/07
	Arkansas	Y	39340 FQ	53970 MW	65750 TQ	USBLS	5/07
	Little Rock-North Little Rock MSA, AR	Y	39360 FQ	53150 MW	69470 TQ	USBLS	5/07
	California	H	26.73 FQ	34.03 MW	40.88 TQ	CABLS	1/08-3/08
	Bakersfield MSA, CA	H	24.47 FQ	34.00 MW	40.27 TQ	CABLS	1/08-3/08
	Los Angeles-Long Beach-Glendale PMSA, CA	H	25.61 FQ	32.39 MW	39.47 TQ	CABLS	1/08-3/08
	Oakland-Fremont-Hayward MSA, CA	H	28.74 FQ	35.95 MW	43.15 TQ	CABLS	1/08-3/08
	Riverside-San Bernardino-Ontario MSA, CA	H	24.63 FQ	31.70 MW	38.02 TQ	CABLS	1/08-3/08
	Sacramento-Arden Arcade-Roseville MSA, CA	H	27.67 FQ	32.92 MW	37.99 TQ	CABLS	1/08-3/08
	San Diego-Carlsbad-San Marcos MSA, CA	H	28.04 FQ	34.13 MW	39.46 TQ	CABLS	1/08-3/08
	San Francisco-San Mateo-Redwood PMSA, CA	H	35.46 FQ	42.74 MW	48.45 TQ	CABLS	1/08-3/08
	San Jose-Sunnyvale-Santa Clara MSA, CA	H	27.85 FQ	38.10 MW	46.08 TQ	CABLS	1/08-3/08
	Santa Ana-Anaheim-Irvine PMSA, CA	Y	52720 FQ	68770 MW	83230 TQ	USBLS	5/07
	Colorado	Y	54030 FQ	66830 MW	81770 TQ	USBLS	5/07
	Denver-Aurora MSA, CO	Y	58780 FQ	71550 MW	85880 TQ	USBLS	5/07
	Connecticut	H	23.19 AE	30.14 MW		CTBLS	1/08-3/08
	Bridgeport-Stamford-Norwalk MSA, CT	Y	51830 FQ	64390 MW	78640 TQ	USBLS	5/07
	Hartford-West Hartford-East Hartford MSA, CT	Y	52400 FQ	60060 MW	70120 TQ	USBLS	5/07
	Delaware	Y	47390 FQ	59820 MW	74870 TQ	USBLS	5/07
	Wilmington PMSA, DE-MD-NJ	Y	47670 FQ	60720 MW	74640 TQ	USBLS	5/07
	District of Columbia	Y	62260 FQ	79060 MW	95900 TQ	USBLS	5/07
	Washington-Arlington-Alexandria MSA, DC-VA-MD-WV	Y	58260 FQ	73920 MW	89290 TQ	USBLS	5/07
	Florida	Y	45140 FQ	57380 MW	71560 TQ	USBLS	5/07
	Fort Lauderdale-Pompano Beach-Deerfield Beach PMSA, FL	Y	45870 FQ	67460 MW	78440 TQ	USBLS	5/07
	Jacksonville MSA, FL	Y	44600 FQ	57050 MW	66610 TQ	USBLS	5/07
	Miami-Fort Lauderdale-Miami Beach MSA, FL	Y	45580 FQ	61050 MW	75260 TQ	USBLS	5/07
	Orlando-Kissimmee MSA, FL	Y	47890 FQ	60000 MW	75180 TQ	USBLS	5/07
	Tampa-St. Petersburg-Clearwater MSA, FL	Y	45120 FQ	56190 MW	69980 TQ	USBLS	5/07
	West Palm Beach-Boca Raton-Boynton Beach PMSA, FL	Y	42970 FQ	51430 MW	73720 TQ	USBLS	5/07
	Georgia	Y	39290 FQ	58070 MW	74460 TQ	USBLS	5/07
	Atlanta-Sandy Springs-Marietta MSA, GA	Y	25970 FQ	56580 MW	76650 TQ	USBLS	5/07
	Hawaii	Y	52810 FQ	64450 MW	77950 TQ	USBLS	5/07
	Honolulu MSA, HI	Y	52810 FQ	64750 MW	78580 TQ	USBLS	5/07
	Idaho	Y	32500 FQ	57200 MW	71640 TQ	USBLS	5/07
	Boise City-Nampa MSA, ID	Y	48530 FQ	62860 MW	72760 TQ	USBLS	5/07
	Illinois	Y	45830 FQ	62840 MW	78790 TQ	USBLS	5/07
	Chicago-Naperville-Joliet MSA, IL-IN-WI	Y	43790 FQ	60230 MW	77800 TQ	USBLS	5/07
	Indiana	Y	40380 FQ	51500 MW	68190 TQ	USBLS	5/07
	Gary PMSA, IN	Y	33210 FQ	49090 MW	74370 TQ	USBLS	5/07

AE	Average entry wage	AW	Average wage paid	FQ	First quartile wage	LO	Lowest wage paid	MTC	Median total compensation	TCC	Total cash compensation
AER	Average entry range	AWR	Average wage range	H	Hourly	LR	Low end range	MW	Median wage paid	TQ	Third quartile wage
AEX	Average experienced wage	AXR	Average experienced range	HI	Highest wage paid	M	Monthly	MWR	Median wage range	W	Weekly
ATC	Average total compensation	D	Daily	HR	High end range	MCC	Median cash compensation	S	See annotated source	Y	Yearly

Occupation/Type/Industry	Location	Per	Low	Mid	High	Source	Date
Occupational Health and Safety Specialist	Indianapolis-Carmel MSA, IN	Y	41600 FQ	51780 MW	65550 TQ	USBLS	5/07
	Iowa	Y	45060 FQ	56990 MW	66150 TQ	USBLS	5/07
	Des Moines-West Des Moines MSA, IA	Y	49180 FQ	58670 MW	69650 TQ	USBLS	5/07
	Kansas	Y	44250 FQ	52700 MW	65030 TQ	USBLS	5/07
	Wichita MSA, KS	Y	46590 FQ	57500 MW	69370 TQ	USBLS	5/07
	Kentucky	Y	45916 FQ	56415 MW	69678 TQ	KYBLS	2008
	Louisville-Jefferson County MSA, KY-IN	Y	40310 FQ	54420 MW	66910 TQ	USBLS	5/07
	Louisiana	H	21.25 FQ	27.33 MW	22.40 TQ	LABLS	1/08-3/08
	Baton Rouge MSA, LA	Y	38960 FQ	47810 MW	68630 TQ	USBLS	5/07
	Lake Charles MSA, LA	Y	52170 FQ	66660 MW	75640 TQ	USBLS	5/07
	New Orleans-Metairie-Kenner MSA, LA	Y	54310 FQ	62370 MW	72570 TQ	USBLS	5/07
	Maine	Y	53400 FQ	62720 MW	74170 TQ	USBLS	5/07
	Portland-South Portland-Biddeford MSA, ME	Y	55110 FQ	61740 MW	70260 TQ	USBLS	5/07
	Maryland	Y		72875 MW		MDBLS	3/08
	Baltimore-Towson MSA, MD	Y	52430 FQ	68640 MW	80980 TQ	USBLS	5/07
	Bethesda-Gaithersburg-Frederick PMSA, MD	Y	64790 FQ	75820 MW	88180 TQ	USBLS	5/07
	Massachusetts	Y	53580 FQ	65980 MW	78810 TQ	USBLS	5/07
	Boston-Cambridge-Quincy NECTA, MA	Y	56860 FQ	68070 MW	79690 TQ	USBLS	5/07
	Worcester MSA, MA-CT	Y	46940 FQ	53260 MW	65270 TQ	USBLS	5/07
	Michigan	Y	49460 FQ	60670 MW	75150 TQ	USBLS	5/07
	Detroit-Warren-Livonia MSA, MI	Y	51080 FQ	60700 MW	75670 TQ	USBLS	5/07
	Grand Rapids-Wyoming MSA, MI	Y	51720 FQ	61040 MW	73660 TQ	USBLS	5/07
	Warren-Troy-Farmington Hills PMSA, MI	Y	51650 FQ	59840 MW	71270 TQ	USBLS	5/07
	Minnesota	Y	54299 FQ	65870 MW	78017 TQ	MNBLS	10/08-12/08
	Duluth-Superior MSA, MN-WI	Y	56799 FQ	65389 MW	76123 TQ	MNBLS	10/08-12/08
	Minneapolis-Saint Paul MSA, MN-WI	Y	58316 FQ	69563 MW	80475 TQ	MNBLS	10/08-12/08
	Rochester MSA, MN	Y	52730 FQ	63520 MW	77176 TQ	MNBLS	10/08-12/08
	Mississippi	Y	43300 FQ	56740 MW	69220 TQ	USBLS	5/07
	Jackson MSA, MS	Y	47540 FQ	59670 MW	72040 TQ	USBLS	5/07
	Missouri	Y	41060 FQ	52760 MW	68530 TQ	USBLS	5/07
	Kansas City MSA, MO-KS	Y	45730 FQ	60260 MW	73810 TQ	USBLS	5/07
	St. Louis MSA, MO-IL	Y	50930 FQ	63350 MW	77210 TQ	USBLS	5/07
	Montana	Y	42460 FQ	52190 MW	64910 TQ	USBLS	5/07
	Billings MSA, MT	Y	42290 FQ	58260 MW	72770 TQ	USBLS	5/07
	Nebraska	Y	38190 FQ	49250 MW	63720 TQ	USBLS	5/07
	Omaha-Council Bluffs MSA, NE-IA	Y	40810 FQ	54150 MW	69870 TQ	USBLS	5/07
	Nevada	H	24.49 FQ	30.02 MW	37.41 TQ	NVBLS	5/08
	Las Vegas-Paradise MSA, NV	H	24.72 FQ	30.08 MW	38.24 TQ	NVBLS	5/08
	New Hampshire	H	22.35 AE	30.04 MW	35.70 AEX	NHBLS	6/08
	Manchester MSA, NH	Y	61060 FQ	75510 MW	84660 TQ	USBLS	5/07
	Nashua NECTA, NH-MA	Y	53510 FQ	59940 MW	85250 TQ	USBLS	5/07
	New Jersey	Y	57880 FQ	70270 MW	80770 TQ	USBLS	5/07
	Camden PMSA, NJ	Y	54650 FQ	68330 MW	79230 TQ	USBLS	5/07
	Edison PMSA, NJ	Y	57160 FQ	69930 MW	83590 TQ	USBLS	5/07
	Newark-Union PMSA, NJ-PA	Y	60180 FQ	71590 MW	82300 TQ	USBLS	5/07
	New Mexico	Y	51530 FQ	60730 MW	73260 TQ	USBLS	5/07
	Albuquerque MSA, NM	Y	52440 FQ	69040 MW	82850 TQ	USBLS	5/07
	New York	Y	49720 FQ	60680 MW	75220 TQ	USBLS	5/07
	Albany-Schenectady-Troy MSA, NY	Y	50120 FQ	61090 MW	74570 TQ	USBLS	5/07
	Buffalo-Niagara Falls MSA, NY	Y	46440 FQ	53490 MW	67060 TQ	USBLS	5/07
	Nassau-Suffolk PMSA, NY	Y	56210 FQ	62960 MW	73700 TQ	USBLS	5/07
	New York-Northern New Jersey-Long Island MSA, NY-NJ-PA	Y	54560 FQ	66410 MW	81720 TQ	USBLS	5/07
	North Carolina	Y	44810 FQ	56580 MW	67490 TQ	USBLS	5/07
	Charlotte-Gastonia-Concord MSA, NC-SC	Y	42140 FQ	56750 MW	65340 TQ	USBLS	5/07

AE	Average entry wage	AW	Average wage paid	FQ	First quartile wage	LO	Lowest wage paid	MTC Median total compensation TCC Total cash compensation
AER	Average entry range	AWR	Average wage range	H	Hourly	LR	Low end range	MW Median wage paid TQ Third quartile wage
AEX	Average experienced wage	AXR	Average experienced range	HI	Highest wage paid	M	Monthly	MWR Median wage range W Weekly
ATC	Average total compensation	D	Daily	HR	High end range	MCC	Median cash compensation	S See annotated source Y Yearly

Occupation/Type/Industry	Location	Per	Low	Mid	High	Source	Date
Occupational Health and Safety Specialist	Greensboro-High Point MSA, NC	Y	43720 FQ	52340 MW	62430 TQ	USBLS	5/07
	Raleigh-Cary MSA, NC	Y	50640 FQ	65340 MW	72270 TQ	USBLS	5/07
	North Dakota	Y	48970 FQ	58780 MW	70990 TQ	USBLS	5/07
	Ohio	Y	47710 FQ	62300 MW	78590 TQ	USBLS	5/07
	Cincinnati-Middletown MSA, OH-KY-IN	Y	57740 FQ	73970 MW	104650 TQ	USBLS	5/07
	Cleveland-Elyria-Mentor MSA, OH	Y	47230 FQ	60630 MW	75290 TQ	USBLS	5/07
	Columbus MSA, OH	Y	50220 FQ	69320 MW	82460 TQ	USBLS	5/07
	Dayton MSA, OH	Y	53820 FQ	65410 MW	76670 TQ	USBLS	5/07
	Oklahoma	Y	28740 FQ	49370 MW	65690 TQ	USBLS	5/07
	Oklahoma City MSA, OK	Y	25250 FQ	44800 MW	65320 TQ	USBLS	5/07
	Tulsa MSA, OK	Y	45510 FQ	57730 MW	69690 TQ	USBLS	5/07
	Oregon	H	19.14 FQ	26.53 MW	32.12 TQ	ORBLS	5/08
	Portland-Vancouver-Beaverton MSA, OR-WA	Y	51590 FQ	59390 MW	69150 TQ	USBLS	5/07
	Pennsylvania	Y	42450 FQ	56180 MW	69740 TQ	USBLS	5/07
	Allentown-Bethlehem-Easton MSA, PA-NJ	Y	45000 FQ	58310 MW	70300 TQ	USBLS	5/07
	Lancaster MSA, PA	Y	40570 FQ	53530 MW	67650 TQ	USBLS	5/07
	Philadelphia-Camden-Wilmington MSA, PA-NJ-DE-MD	Y	48040 FQ	62680 MW	77700 TQ	USBLS	5/07
	Pittsburgh MSA, PA	Y	43710 FQ	57840 MW	72660 TQ	USBLS	5/07
	York-Hanover MSA, PA	Y	39390 FQ	49680 MW	63700 TQ	USBLS	5/07
	Rhode Island	Y	57940 FQ	72210 MW	85940 TQ	USBLS	5/07
	Providence-Fall River-Warwick MSA, RI-MA	Y	57930 FQ	71210 MW	84590 TQ	USBLS	5/07
	South Carolina	Y	33990 FQ	43600 MW	60990 TQ	USBLS	5/07
	Charleston-North Charleston MSA, SC	Y	35090 FQ	45480 MW	63980 TQ	USBLS	5/07
	Columbia MSA, SC	Y	32580 FQ	39080 MW	48840 TQ	USBLS	5/07
	South Dakota	Y	46364 FQ	52849 MW	68564 TQ	SDBLS	7/08-9/08
	Sioux Falls MSA, SD	Y	47862 FQ	56123 MW	71600 TQ	SDBLS	7/08-9/08
	Tennessee	Y	50020 FQ	65090 MW	81300 TQ	USBLS	5/07
	Memphis MSA, TN-MS-AR	Y	40040 FQ	55330 MW	70130 TQ	USBLS	5/07
	Nashville-Davidson-Murfreesboro MSA, TN	Y	50460 FQ	60850 MW	74290 TQ	USBLS	5/07
	Texas	Y	41950 FQ	56740 MW	72490 TQ	USBLS	5/07
	Austin-Round Rock MSA, TX	Y	37090 FQ	51990 MW	74520 TQ	USBLS	5/07
	Dallas-Fort Worth-Arlington MSA, TX	Y	43770 FQ	57590 MW	74380 TQ	USBLS	5/07
	El Paso MSA, TX	Y	32730 FQ	51590 MW	69160 TQ	USBLS	5/07
	Houston-Sugar Land-Baytown MSA, TX	Y	51630 FQ	61270 MW	75740 TQ	USBLS	5/07
	San Antonio MSA, TX	Y	37510 FQ	58810 MW	73040 TQ	USBLS	5/07
	Utah	Y	45710 FQ	58430 MW	72060 TQ	USBLS	5/07
	Salt Lake City MSA, UT	Y	45530 FQ	58580 MW	72700 TQ	USBLS	5/07
	Vermont	Y	39720 FQ	49480 MW	61330 TQ	USBLS	5/07
	Burlington-South Burlington MSA, VT	Y	37390 FQ	50580 MW	64690 TQ	USBLS	5/07
	Virginia	Y	46210 FQ	59420 MW	74570 TQ	USBLS	5/07
	Richmond MSA, VA	Y	47080 FQ	59820 MW	72910 TQ	USBLS	5/07
	Roanoke MSA, VA	Y	44530 FQ	53520 MW	62600 TQ	USBLS	5/07
	Virginia Beach-Norfolk-Newport News MSA, VA-NC	Y	46930 FQ	59850 MW	73730 TQ	USBLS	5/07
	Washington	H	25.05 FQ	29.74 MW	36.86 TQ	WABLS	3/08
	Seattle-Tacoma-Bellevue MSA, WA	Y	51240 FQ	63340 MW	80370 TQ	USBLS	5/07
	West Virginia	Y	47189 FQ	61724 MW	78423 TQ	WVBLS	7/08-9/08
	Charleston MSA, WV	Y	44760 FQ	54110 MW	71750 TQ	USBLS	5/07
	Wheeling MSA, WV-OH	Y	52250 FQ	71880 MW	84680 TQ	USBLS	5/07
	Wisconsin	Y	47670 FQ	58910 MW	70880 TQ	USBLS	5/07
	Milwaukee-Waukesha-West Allis MSA, WI	Y	54270 FQ	67710 MW	76700 TQ	USBLS	5/07
	Wyoming	Y	53927 FQ	64992 MW	80462 TQ	WYBLS	9/08
	Cheyenne MSA, WY	Y	33137 FQ	56679 MW	65049 TQ	WYBLS	9/08
	Puerto Rico	Y	32240 FQ	39730 MW	52880 TQ	USBLS	5/07
	San Juan-Caguas-Guaynabo MSA, PR	Y	31870 FQ	38950 MW	50870 TQ	USBLS	5/07

AE Average entry wage	**AW** Average wage paid	**FQ** First quartile wage	**LO** Lowest wage paid	**MTC** Median total compensation	**TCC** Total cash compensation
AER Average entry range	**AWR** Average wage range	**H** Hourly	**LR** Low end range	**MW** Median wage paid	**TQ** Third quartile wage
AEX Average experienced wage	**AXR** Average experienced range	**HI** Highest wage paid	**M** Monthly	**MWR** Median wage range	**W** Weekly
ATC Average total compensation	**D** Daily	**HR** High end range	**MCC** Median cash compensation	**S** See annotated source	**Y** Yearly

Occupation/Type/Industry	Location	Per	Low	Mid	High	Source	Date
Occupational Health and Safety Technician	Alabama	Y	36250 FQ	41320 MW	74430 TQ	USBLS	5/07
	Birmingham-Hoover MSA, AL	Y	36800 FQ	41660 MW	94330 TQ	USBLS	5/07
	Alaska	Y	51430 FQ	58270 MW	70890 TQ	USBLS	5/07
	Arizona	Y	46520 FQ	65720 MW	87990 TQ	USBLS	5/07
	Phoenix-Mesa-Scottsdale MSA, AZ	Y	58060 FQ	75100 MW	94780 TQ	USBLS	5/07
	Arkansas	Y	26080 FQ	30220 MW	37960 TQ	USBLS	5/07
	Little Rock-North Little Rock MSA, AR	Y	25100 FQ	30040 MW	37150 TQ	USBLS	5/07
	California	H	18.26 FQ	22.27 MW	26.06 TQ	CABLS	1/08-3/08
	Los Angeles-Long Beach-Glendale PMSA, CA	H	20.01 FQ	24.47 MW	29.68 TQ	CABLS	1/08-3/08
	Oakland-Fremont-Hayward MSA, CA	H	17.98 FQ	21.86 MW	25.39 TQ	CABLS	1/08-3/08
	Riverside-San Bernardino-Ontario MSA, CA	H	16.95 FQ	20.45 MW	23.42 TQ	CABLS	1/08-3/08
	Sacramento-Arden Arcade-Roseville MSA, CA	H	21.47 FQ	23.44 MW	25.26 TQ	CABLS	1/08-3/08
	San Diego-Carlsbad-San Marcos MSA, CA	H	20.39 FQ	22.92 MW	25.68 TQ	CABLS	1/08-3/08
	San Francisco-San Mateo-Redwood PMSA, CA	H	21.17 FQ	23.29 MW	25.63 TQ	CABLS	1/08-3/08
	San Jose-Sunnyvale-Santa Clara MSA, CA	H	17.87 FQ	22.15 MW	27.21 TQ	CABLS	1/08-3/08
	Colorado	Y	35890 FQ	48980 MW	68040 TQ	USBLS	5/07
	Denver-Aurora MSA, CO	Y	42220 FQ	57620 MW	68140 TQ	USBLS	5/07
	Connecticut	H	19.82 AE	24.96 MW		CTBLS	1/08-3/08
	Hartford-West Hartford-East Hartford MSA, CT	Y	42730 FQ	50080 MW	59900 TQ	USBLS	5/07
	Washington-Arlington-Alexandria MSA, DC-VA-MD-WV	Y	27310 FQ	48220 MW	73360 TQ	USBLS	5/07
	Florida	Y	34820 FQ	41220 MW	49570 TQ	USBLS	5/07
	Miami-Fort Lauderdale-Miami Beach MSA, FL	Y	43200 FQ	75640 MW	95020 TQ	USBLS	5/07
	Orlando-Kissimmee MSA, FL	Y	34160 FQ	41130 MW	48410 TQ	USBLS	5/07
	Georgia	Y	29050 FQ	41360 MW	59110 TQ	USBLS	5/07
	Atlanta-Sandy Springs-Marietta MSA, GA	Y	37670 FQ	52760 MW	74440 TQ	USBLS	5/07
	Boise City-Nampa MSA, ID	Y	17160 FQ	18410 MW	19650 TQ	USBLS	5/07
	Illinois	Y	34490 FQ	45750 MW	59640 TQ	USBLS	5/07
	Chicago-Naperville-Joliet MSA, IL-IN-WI	Y	33000 FQ	40730 MW	56230 TQ	USBLS	5/07
	Indiana	Y	30410 FQ	37180 MW	49250 TQ	USBLS	5/07
	Gary PMSA, IN	Y	30380 FQ	35040 MW	39020 TQ	USBLS	5/07
	Indianapolis-Carmel MSA, IN	Y	30460 FQ	37030 MW	56800 TQ	USBLS	5/07
	Iowa	Y	33230 FQ	38360 MW	48090 TQ	USBLS	5/07
	Kansas	Y	33980 FQ	41040 MW	49400 TQ	USBLS	5/07
	Kentucky	Y	30940 FQ	43446 MW	57078 TQ	KYBLS	2008
	Louisville-Jefferson County MSA, KY-IN	Y	30870 FQ	42510 MW	65070 TQ	USBLS	5/07
	Louisiana	H	15.86 FQ	21.42 MW	27.97 TQ	LABLS	1/08-3/08
	Baton Rouge MSA, LA	Y	32610 FQ	38340 MW	50010 TQ	USBLS	5/07
	New Orleans-Metairie-Kenner MSA, LA	Y	40330 FQ	47600 MW	54950 TQ	USBLS	5/07
	Maine	Y	31460 FQ	39170 MW	48450 TQ	USBLS	5/07
	Maryland	Y		47450 MW		MDBLS	3/08
	Baltimore-Towson MSA, MD	Y	37890 FQ	47180 MW	72860 TQ	USBLS	5/07
	Massachusetts	Y	39160 FQ	46300 MW	55610 TQ	USBLS	5/07
	Boston-Cambridge-Quincy NECTA, MA	Y	42590 FQ	47810 MW	61140 TQ	USBLS	5/07
	Michigan	Y	23740 FQ	32970 MW	44400 TQ	USBLS	5/07
	Detroit-Warren-Livonia MSA, MI	Y	30910 FQ	37310 MW	48910 TQ	USBLS	5/07
	Warren-Troy-Farmington Hills PMSA, MI	Y	36370 FQ	43310 MW	47960 TQ	USBLS	5/07
	Minnesota	Y	44391 FQ	49946 MW	56736 TQ	MNBLS	10/08-12/08
	Minneapolis-Saint Paul MSA, MN-WI	Y	46190 FQ	52405 MW	62072 TQ	MNBLS	10/08-12/08
	Mississippi	Y	25450 FQ	29370 MW	42830 TQ	USBLS	5/07
	Missouri	Y	37490 FQ	45850 MW	54820 TQ	USBLS	5/07

AE Average entry wage	**AW** Average wage paid	**FQ** First quartile wage	**LO** Lowest wage paid	**MTC** Median total compensation	**TCC** Total cash compensation
AER Average entry range	**AWR** Average wage range	**H** Hourly	**LR** Low end range	**MW** Median wage paid	**TQ** Third quartile wage
AEX Average experienced wage	**AXR** Average experienced range	**HI** Highest wage paid	**M** Monthly	**MWR** Median wage range	**W** Weekly
ATC Average total compensation	**D** Daily	**HR** High end range	**MCC** Median cash compensation	**S** See annotated source	**Y** Yearly

Occupation/Type/Industry	Location	Per	Low	Mid	High	Source	Date
Occupational Health and Safety Technician	Kansas City MSA, MO-KS	Y	35700 FQ	42420 MW	48180 TQ	USBLS	5/07
	St. Louis MSA, MO-IL	Y	40820 FQ	47380 MW	59830 TQ	USBLS	5/07
	Nebraska	Y	29280 FQ	38320 MW	53730 TQ	USBLS	5/07
	Omaha-Council Bluffs MSA, NE-IA	Y	25930 FQ	37070 MW	50830 TQ	USBLS	5/07
	Nevada	H	17.12 FQ	22.20 MW	26.19 TQ	NVBLS	5/08
	Las Vegas-Paradise MSA, NV	H	19.35 FQ	22.62 MW	25.86 TQ	NVBLS	5/08
	New Hampshire	H	14.91 AE	18.55 MW	26.06 AEX	NHBLS	6/08
	New Jersey	Y	35780 FQ	51310 MW	58340 TQ	USBLS	5/07
	Edison PMSA, NJ	Y	49200 FQ	55290 MW	60010 TQ	USBLS	5/07
	Newark-Union PMSA, NJ-PA	Y	29840 FQ	44760 MW	53390 TQ	USBLS	5/07
	New Mexico	Y	45360 FQ	53050 MW	66570 TQ	USBLS	5/07
	Albuquerque MSA, NM	Y	48720 FQ	58880 MW	70090 TQ	USBLS	5/07
	New York	Y	37770 FQ	44350 MW	50480 TQ	USBLS	5/07
	New York-Northern New Jersey-Long Island MSA, NY-NJ-PA	Y	37890 FQ	45900 MW	52700 TQ	USBLS	5/07
	North Carolina	Y	35160 FQ	44160 MW	55890 TQ	USBLS	5/07
	Charlotte-Gastonia-Concord MSA, NC-SC	Y	33230 FQ	41360 MW	53860 TQ	USBLS	5/07
	Durham MSA, NC	Y	44900 FQ	54420 MW	67560 TQ	USBLS	5/07
	North Dakota	Y	33590 FQ	48660 MW	59460 TQ	USBLS	5/07
	Ohio	Y	39060 FQ	47040 MW	55260 TQ	USBLS	5/07
	Cincinnati-Middletown MSA, OH-KY-IN	Y	44440 FQ	50150 MW	56800 TQ	USBLS	5/07
	Cleveland-Elyria-Mentor MSA, OH	Y	37440 FQ	45500 MW	55140 TQ	USBLS	5/07
	Columbus MSA, OH	Y	37890 FQ	45530 MW	56010 TQ	USBLS	5/07
	Oklahoma	Y	33780 FQ	47390 MW	65740 TQ	USBLS	5/07
	Oregon	H	21.11 FQ	26.58 MW	29.81 TQ	ORBLS	5/08
	Portland-Vancouver-Beaverton MSA, OR-WA	Y	37990 FQ	49890 MW	59520 TQ	USBLS	5/07
	Pennsylvania	Y	29050 FQ	36470 MW	49030 TQ	USBLS	5/07
	Philadelphia-Camden-Wilmington MSA, PA-NJ-DE-MD	Y	30050 FQ	39260 MW	47840 TQ	USBLS	5/07
	Pittsburgh MSA, PA	Y	31410 FQ	39290 MW	53580 TQ	USBLS	5/07
	South Carolina	Y	28610 FQ	38240 MW	51890 TQ	USBLS	5/07
	Tennessee	Y	39320 FQ	49040 MW	61080 TQ	USBLS	5/07
	Texas	Y	26050 FQ	42420 MW	57510 TQ	USBLS	5/07
	Dallas-Fort Worth-Arlington MSA, TX	Y	23060 FQ	26510 MW	49340 TQ	USBLS	5/07
	Houston-Sugar Land-Baytown MSA, TX	Y	33210 FQ	48240 MW	68490 TQ	USBLS	5/07
	San Antonio MSA, TX	Y	34500 FQ	46520 MW	72360 TQ	USBLS	5/07
	Utah	Y	27130 FQ	40920 MW	57890 TQ	USBLS	5/07
	Salt Lake City MSA, UT	Y	29240 FQ	46240 MW	60010 TQ	USBLS	5/07
	Virginia	Y	30940 FQ	43010 MW	62770 TQ	USBLS	5/07
	Virginia Beach-Norfolk-Newport News MSA, VA-NC	Y	30400 FQ	37660 MW	47710 TQ	USBLS	5/07
	Washington	H	18.85 FQ	23.33 MW	28.67 TQ	WABLS	3/08
	Seattle-Tacoma-Bellevue MSA, WA	Y	41170 FQ	53220 MW	61510 TQ	USBLS	5/07
	West Virginia	Y	26194 FQ	38889 MW	62891 TQ	WVBLS	7/08-9/08
	Wisconsin	Y	35510 FQ	43900 MW	52950 TQ	USBLS	5/07
	Milwaukee-Waukesha-West Allis MSA, WI	Y	41850 FQ	48280 MW	58250 TQ	USBLS	5/07
	Wyoming	Y	29511 FQ	46598 MW	63034 TQ	WYBLS	9/08
	Puerto Rico	Y	28210 FQ	33540 MW	38600 TQ	USBLS	5/07
	San Juan-Caguas-Guaynabo MSA, PR	Y	30290 FQ	34520 MW	39010 TQ	USBLS	5/07
Occupational Therapist	Alabama	Y	53360 FQ	62370 MW	75210 TQ	USBLS	5/07
	Birmingham-Hoover MSA, AL	Y	55030 FQ	65000 MW	76400 TQ	USBLS	5/07
	Alaska	Y	56020 FQ	68200 MW	79170 TQ	USBLS	5/07
	Arizona	Y	34060 FQ	50140 MW	71780 TQ	USBLS	5/07
	Phoenix-Mesa-Scottsdale MSA, AZ	Y	28790 FQ	44370 MW	63210 TQ	USBLS	5/07
	Tucson MSA, AZ	Y	53680 FQ	71070 MW	89690 TQ	USBLS	5/07
	Arkansas	Y	55830 FQ	67480 MW	79540 TQ	USBLS	5/07

AE	Average entry wage	**AW**	Average wage paid	**FQ**	First quartile wage	**LO** Lowest wage paid **MTC** Median total compensation **TCC** Total cash compensation
AER	Average entry range	**AWR**	Average wage range	**H**	Hourly	**LR** Low end range **MW** Median wage paid **TQ** Third quartile wage
AEX	Average experienced wage	**AXR**	Average experienced range	**HI**	Highest wage paid	**M** Monthly **MWR** Median wage range **W** Weekly
ATC	Average total compensation	**D**	Daily	**HR**	High end range	**MCC** Median cash compensation **S** See annotated source **Y** Yearly

Occupation/Type/Industry	Location	Per	Low	Mid	High	Source	Date
Occupational Therapist	Little Rock-North Little Rock MSA, AR	Y	54260 FQ	66780 MW	80270 TQ	USBLS	5/07
	California	H	32.07 FQ	37.97 MW	44.51 TQ	CABLS	1/08-3/08
	Los Angeles-Long Beach-Glendale PMSA, CA	H	29.63 FQ	37.57 MW	45.51 TQ	CABLS	1/08-3/08
	Oakland-Fremont-Hayward MSA, CA	H	32.70 FQ	38.71 MW	44.64 TQ	CABLS	1/08-3/08
	Riverside-San Bernardino-Ontario MSA, CA	H	33.78 FQ	38.08 MW	42.19 TQ	CABLS	1/08-3/08
	Sacramento-Arden Arcade-Roseville MSA, CA	H	31.97 FQ	39.92 MW	45.95 TQ	CABLS	1/08-3/08
	San Diego-Carlsbad-San Marcos MSA, CA	H	32.07 FQ	37.43 MW	42.57 TQ	CABLS	1/08-3/08
	San Francisco-San Mateo-Redwood PMSA, CA	H	36.45 FQ	42.56 MW	. 48.53 TQ	CABLS	1/08-3/08
	San Jose-Sunnyvale-Santa Clara MSA, CA	H	32.33 FQ	37.42 MW	44.20 TQ	CABLS	1/08-3/08
	Santa Ana-Anaheim-Irvine PMSA, CA	Y	67810 FQ	76230 MW	86620 TQ	USBLS	5/07
	Colorado	Y	52270 FQ	59920 MW	69620 TQ	USBLS	5/07
	Denver-Aurora MSA, CO	Y	53200 FQ	60460 MW	69800 TQ	USBLS	5/07
	Connecticut	H	24.54 AE	33.10 MW		CTBLS	1/08-3/08
	Bridgeport-Stamford-Norwalk MSA, CT	Y	55600 FQ	67030 MW	89130 TQ	USBLS	5/07
	Hartford-West Hartford-East Hartford MSA, CT	Y	57320 FQ	70050 MW	85310 TQ	USBLS	5/07
	Delaware	Y	38650 FQ	54540 MW	73900 TQ	USBLS	5/07
	Wilmington PMSA, DE-MD-NJ	Y	41990 FQ	62200 MW	76530 TQ	USBLS	5/07
	District of Columbia	Y	45620 FQ	61760 MW	73090 TQ	USBLS	5/07
	Washington-Arlington-Alexandria MSA, DC-VA-MD-WV	Y	56950 FQ	70280 MW	86130 TQ	USBLS	5/07
	Florida	Y	58250 FQ	69830 MW	81180 TQ	USBLS	5/07
	Fort Lauderdale-Pompano Beach-Deerfield Beach PMSA, FL	Y	64430 FQ	73570 MW	84180 TQ	USBLS	5/07
	Jacksonville MSA, FL	Y	48100 FQ	62650 MW	77190 TQ	USBLS	5/07
	Miami-Fort Lauderdale-Miami Beach MSA, FL	Y	61800 FQ	72090 MW	82390 TQ	USBLS	5/07
	Orlando-Kissimmee MSA, FL	Y	58950 FQ	66940 MW	75950 TQ	USBLS	5/07
	Tampa-St. Petersburg-Clearwater MSA, FL	Y	66290 FQ	76150 MW	88320 TQ	USBLS	5/07
	West Palm Beach-Boca Raton-Boynton Beach PMSA, FL	Y	61940 FQ	71520 MW	80370 TQ	USBLS	5/07
	Georgia	Y	55590 FQ	68540 MW	82200 TQ	USBLS	5/07
	Atlanta-Sandy Springs-Marietta MSA, GA	Y	58030 FQ	72190 MW	84320 TQ	USBLS	5/07
	Hawaii	Y	48260 FQ	59980 MW	70770 TQ	USBLS	5/07
	Honolulu MSA, HI	Y	52000 FQ	62090 MW	72220 TQ	USBLS	5/07
	Idaho	Y	18960 FQ	48860 MW	60650 TQ	USBLS	5/07
	Boise City-Nampa MSA, ID	Y	54390 FQ	58360 MW	62750 TQ	USBLS	5/07
	Illinois	Y	59070 FQ	69670 MW	83230 TQ	USBLS	5/07
	Chicago-Naperville-Joliet MSA, IL-IN-WI	Y	58360 FQ	69330 MW	83150 TQ	USBLS	5/07
	Rockford MSA, IL	Y	62800 FQ	72920 MW	83600 TQ	USBLS	5/07
	Indiana	Y	51830 FQ	61620 MW	76080 TQ	USBLS	5/07
	Gary PMSA, IN	Y	19820 FQ	55920 MW	80040 TQ	USBLS	5/07
	Indianapolis-Carmel MSA, IN	Y	54860 FQ	62960 MW	78590 TQ	USBLS	5/07
	Iowa	Y	50720 FQ	57980 MW	65560 TQ	USBLS	5/07
	Des Moines-West Des Moines MSA, IA	Y	48270 FQ	55840 MW	63580 TQ	USBLS	5/07
	Sioux City MSA, IA-NE-SD	Y	52530 FQ	63210 MW	89210 TQ	USBLS	5/07
	Kansas	Y	52790 FQ	61220 MW	72000 TQ	USBLS	5/07
	Wichita MSA, KS	Y	51380 FQ	58780 MW	66920 TQ	USBLS	5/07
	Kentucky	Y	59371 FQ	71580 MW	83645 TQ	KYBLS	2008
	Louisville-Jefferson County MSA, KY-IN	Y	57080 FQ	67240 MW	78710 TQ	USBLS	5/07
	Louisiana	H	26.58 FQ	32.26 MW	37.54 TQ	LABLS	1/08-3/08
	Baton Rouge MSA, LA	Y	51400 FQ	61680 MW	73680 TQ	USBLS	5/07
	New Orleans-Metairie-Kenner MSA, LA	Y	58330 FQ	71400 MW	81800 TQ	USBLS	5/07

AE Average entry wage	**AW** Average wage paid	**FQ** First quartile wage	**LO** Lowest wage paid	**MTC** Median total compensation	**TCC** Total cash compensation
AER Average entry range	**AWR** Average wage range	**H** Hourly	**LR** Low end range	**MW** Median wage paid	**TQ** Third quartile wage
AEX Average experienced wage	**AXR** Average experienced range	**HI** Highest wage paid	**M** Monthly	**MWR** Median wage range	**W** Weekly
ATC Average total compensation	**D** Daily	**HR** High end range	**MCC** Median cash compensation	**S** See annotated source	**Y** Yearly

1127

Occupational Therapist

Occupation/Type/Industry	Location	Per	Low	Mid	High	Source	Date
Occupational Therapist	Maine	Y	40030 FQ	50330 MW	59370 TQ	USBLS	5/07
	Portland-South Portland-Biddeford MSA, ME	Y	41090 FQ	48850 MW	59670 TQ	USBLS	5/07
	Maryland	Y		75650 MW		MDBLS	3/08
	Baltimore-Towson MSA, MD	Y	61620 FQ	73710 MW	84350 TQ	USBLS	5/07
	Bethesda-Gaithersburg-Frederick PMSA, MD	Y	63650 FQ	75480 MW	87070 TQ	USBLS	5/07
	Massachusetts	Y	52160 FQ	64210 MW	76490 TQ	USBLS	5/07
	Boston-Cambridge-Quincy NECTA, MA	Y	55060 FQ	66210 MW	78260 TQ	USBLS	5/07
	Worcester MSA, MA-CT	Y	53950 FQ	66370 MW	78030 TQ	USBLS	5/07
	Michigan	Y	50240 FQ	58780 MW	70180 TQ	USBLS	5/07
	Detroit-Warren-Livonia MSA, MI	Y	52150 FQ	60940 MW	73480 TQ	USBLS	5/07
	Grand Rapids-Wyoming MSA, MI	Y	47890 FQ	57240 MW	66410 TQ	USBLS	5/07
	Warren-Troy-Farmington Hills PMSA, MI	Y	53520 FQ	62130 MW	76170 TQ	USBLS	5/07
	Minnesota	Y	54759 FQ	61005 MW	67921 TQ	MNBLS	10/08-12/08
	Duluth-Superior MSA, MN-WI	Y	52123 FQ	58358 MW	64311 TQ	MNBLS	10/08-12/08
	Minneapolis-Saint Paul MSA, MN-WI	Y	55544 FQ	61298 MW	67847 TQ	MNBLS	10/08-12/08
	Rochester MSA, MN	Y	59257 FQ	66988 MW	78534 TQ	MNBLS	10/08-12/08
	Mississippi	Y	55500 FQ	66220 MW	77850 TQ	USBLS	5/07
	Jackson MSA, MS	Y	55010 FQ	64170 MW	72580 TQ	USBLS	5/07
	Missouri	Y	48500 FQ	57660 MW	68270 TQ	USBLS	5/07
	Joplin MSA, MO	Y	44550 FQ	50110 MW	59920 TQ	USBLS	5/07
	Kansas City MSA, MO-KS	Y	50970 FQ	58820 MW	68220 TQ	USBLS	5/07
	St. Louis MSA, MO-IL	Y	49100 FQ	58580 MW	68430 TQ	USBLS	5/07
	Montana	Y	49450 FQ	56410 MW	62760 TQ	USBLS	5/07
	Billings MSA, MT	Y	48380 FQ	54540 MW	60170 TQ	USBLS	5/07
	Missoula MSA, MT	Y	53730 FQ	58360 MW	62990 TQ	USBLS	5/07
	Nebraska	Y	46240 FQ	56690 MW	67700 TQ	USBLS	5/07
	Omaha-Council Bluffs MSA, NE-IA	Y	45060 FQ	54260 MW	62880 TQ	USBLS	5/07
	Nevada	H	24.86 FQ	34.28 MW	42.91 TQ	NVBLS	5/08
	Las Vegas-Paradise MSA, NV	H	25.34 FQ	34.70 MW	46.98 TQ	NVBLS	5/08
	New Hampshire	H	20.37 AE	27.57 MW	31.54 AEX	NHBLS	6/08
	Manchester MSA, NH	Y	49110 FQ	57780 MW	66290 TQ	USBLS	5/07
	Nashua NECTA, NH-MA	Y	42400 FQ	51980 MW	60280 TQ	USBLS	5/07
	New Jersey	Y	59060 FQ	72920 MW	91870 TQ	USBLS	5/07
	Camden PMSA, NJ	Y	56130 FQ	67670 MW	79720 TQ	USBLS	5/07
	Edison PMSA, NJ	Y	58900 FQ	74720 MW	96600 TQ	USBLS	5/07
	Newark-Union PMSA, NJ-PA	Y	60370 FQ	78320 MW	96700 TQ	USBLS	5/07
	New Mexico	Y	42940 FQ	53500 MW	64780 TQ	USBLS	5/07
	Albuquerque MSA, NM	Y	42460 FQ	53340 MW	65960 TQ	USBLS	5/07
	New York	Y	51450 FQ	60290 MW	74200 TQ	USBLS	5/07
	Albany-Schenectady-Troy MSA, NY	Y	47370 FQ	56430 MW	66830 TQ	USBLS	5/07
	Buffalo-Niagara Falls MSA, NY	Y	34640 FQ	46040 MW	58410 TQ	USBLS	5/07
	Glens Falls MSA, NY	Y	40260 FQ	47640 MW	60370 TQ	USBLS	5/07
	Kingston MSA, NY	Y	53950 FQ	63090 MW	75480 TQ	USBLS	5/07
	Nassau-Suffolk PMSA, NY	Y	54090 FQ	61950 MW	74950 TQ	USBLS	5/07
	New York-Northern New Jersey-Long Island MSA, NY-NJ-PA	Y	56490 FQ	65570 MW	84800 TQ	USBLS	5/07
	North Carolina	Y	53470 FQ	63140 MW	75400 TQ	USBLS	5/07
	Charlotte-Gastonia-Concord MSA, NC-SC	Y	51830 FQ	62180 MW	73250 TQ	USBLS	5/07
	Raleigh-Cary MSA, NC	Y	50430 FQ	64880 MW	74710 TQ	USBLS	5/07
	North Dakota	Y	44540 FQ	50060 MW	61010 TQ	USBLS	5/07
	Fargo MSA, ND-MN	Y	44640 FQ	50180 MW	61800 TQ	USBLS	5/07
	Ohio	Y	59020 FQ	69670 MW	81270 TQ	USBLS	5/07
	Cincinnati-Middletown MSA, OH-KY-IN	Y	56690 FQ	67220 MW	79140 TQ	USBLS	5/07
	Cleveland-Elyria-Mentor MSA, OH	Y	64700 FQ	72860 MW	81610 TQ	USBLS	5/07
	Columbus MSA, OH	Y	56780 FQ	69060 MW	85210 TQ	USBLS	5/07
	Dayton MSA, OH	Y	58410 FQ	67710 MW	81730 TQ	USBLS	5/07
	Oklahoma City MSA, OK	Y	42800 FQ	56970 MW	73780 TQ	USBLS	5/07
	Tulsa MSA, OK	Y	39400 FQ	48380 MW	61170 TQ	USBLS	5/07

Occupation/Type/Industry	Location	Per	Low	Mid	High	Source	Date
Occupational Therapist	Oregon	H	26.64 FQ	31.57 MW	36.02 TQ	ORBLS	5/08
	Portland-Vancouver-Beaverton MSA, OR-WA	Y	50880 FQ	61950 MW	71740 TQ	USBLS	5/07
	Pennsylvania	Y	49650 FQ	59770 MW	72900 TQ	USBLS	5/07
	Allentown-Bethlehem-Easton MSA, PA-NJ	Y	50610 FQ	62050 MW	83990 TQ	USBLS	5/07
	Philadelphia-Camden-Wilmington MSA, PA-NJ-DE-MD	Y	53130 FQ	64860 MW	77560 TQ	USBLS	5/07
	Pittsburgh MSA, PA	Y	46810 FQ	56290 MW	63830 TQ	USBLS	5/07
	Rhode Island	Y	53020 FQ	61610 MW	74140 TQ	USBLS	5/07
	Providence-Fall River-Warwick MSA, RI-MA	Y	52620 FQ	61630 MW	74830 TQ	USBLS	5/07
	South Carolina	Y	47480 FQ	60740 MW	76660 TQ	USBLS	5/07
	Charleston-North Charleston MSA, SC	Y	53770 FQ	60630 MW	69840 TQ	USBLS	5/07
	Columbia MSA, SC	Y	59380 FQ	70940 MW	84800 TQ	USBLS	5/07
	South Dakota	Y	49231 FQ	56865 MW	64628 TQ	SDBLS	7/08-9/08
	Rapid City MSA, SD	Y	47179 FQ	55770 MW	63787 TQ	SDBLS	7/08-9/08
	Sioux Falls MSA, SD	Y	49610 FQ	57344 MW	65190 TQ	SDBLS	7/08-9/08
	Tennessee	Y	54080 FQ	62880 MW	78230 TQ	USBLS	5/07
	Memphis MSA, TN-MS-AR	Y	56790 FQ	71930 MW	91080 TQ	USBLS	5/07
	Nashville-Davidson-Murfreesboro MSA, TN	Y	53290 FQ	59750 MW	68180 TQ	USBLS	5/07
	Texas	Y	55130 FQ	67670 MW	83140 TQ	USBLS	5/07
	Austin-Round Rock MSA, TX	Y	45200 FQ	56940 MW	70790 TQ	USBLS	5/07
	Dallas-Fort Worth-Arlington MSA, TX	Y	56410 FQ	69550 MW	84870 TQ	USBLS	5/07
	El Paso MSA, TX	Y	64950 FQ	80900 MW	106820 TQ	USBLS	5/07
	Houston-Sugar Land-Baytown MSA, TX	Y	56450 FQ	67810 MW	81950 TQ	USBLS	5/07
	San Antonio MSA, TX	Y	55170 FQ	68330 MW	91460 TQ	USBLS	5/07
	Utah	Y	53480 FQ	61110 MW	71600 TQ	USBLS	5/07
	Provo-Orem MSA, UT	Y	51750 FQ	57640 MW	67140 TQ	USBLS	5/07
	Salt Lake City MSA, UT	Y	57690 FQ	65610 MW	75330 TQ	USBLS	5/07
	Vermont	Y	52620 FQ	59860 MW	71940 TQ	USBLS	5/07
	Burlington-South Burlington MSA, VT	Y	50120 FQ	56600 MW	62800 TQ	USBLS	5/07
	Virginia	Y	54150 FQ	66580 MW	82470 TQ	USBLS	5/07
	Richmond MSA, VA	Y	52570 FQ	62880 MW	76560 TQ	USBLS	5/07
	Virginia Beach-Norfolk-Newport News MSA, VA-NC	Y	52080 FQ	70110 MW	84340 TQ	USBLS	5/07
	Washington	H	26.54 FQ	31.47 MW	36.08 TQ	WABLS	3/08
	Seattle-Tacoma-Bellevue MSA, WA	Y	55540 FQ	65390 MW	74360 TQ	USBLS	5/07
	West Virginia	Y	53040 FQ	60043 MW	73756 TQ	WVBLS	7/08-9/08
	Charleston MSA, WV	Y	53990 FQ	66900 MW	82210 TQ	USBLS	5/07
	Parkersburg-Marietta-Vienna MSA, WV-OH	Y	48000 FQ	58790 MW	72920 TQ	USBLS	5/07
	Wisconsin	Y	49390 FQ	57150 MW	64660 TQ	USBLS	5/07
	Milwaukee-Waukesha-West Allis MSA, WI	Y	49820 FQ	56880 MW	63780 TQ	USBLS	5/07
	Wyoming	Y	46549 FQ	56078 MW	65970 TQ	WYBLS	9/08
	Cheyenne MSA, WY	Y	55661 FQ	61846 MW	68200 TQ	WYBLS	9/08
	Puerto Rico	Y	24800 FQ	30190 MW	46920 TQ	USBLS	5/07
	San Juan-Caguas-Guaynabo MSA, PR	Y	24530 FQ	29770 MW	41830 TQ	USBLS	5/07
Occupational Therapist Aide	Arizona	Y	24270 FQ	28350 MW	34190 TQ	USBLS	5/07
	Phoenix-Mesa-Scottsdale MSA, AZ	Y	26100 FQ	28880 MW	31660 TQ	USBLS	5/07
	Arkansas	Y	25220 FQ	29580 MW	35770 TQ	USBLS	5/07
	California	H	10.90 FQ	13.53 MW	17.09 TQ	CABLS	1/08-3/08
	Los Angeles-Long Beach-Glendale PMSA, CA	H	9.81 FQ	11.27 MW	14.57 TQ	CABLS	1/08-3/08
	Oakland-Fremont-Hayward MSA, CA	H	10.25 FQ	12.55 MW	14.64 TQ	CABLS	1/08-3/08
	Riverside-San Bernardino-Ontario MSA, CA	H	10.02 FQ	12.50 MW	16.26 TQ	CABLS	1/08-3/08
	Sacramento-Arden Arcade-Roseville MSA, CA	H	10.99 FQ	12.06 MW	18.43 TQ	CABLS	1/08-3/08

AE	Average entry wage	AW	Average wage paid	FQ	First quartile wage
AER	Average entry range	AWR	Average wage range	H	Hourly
AEX	Average experienced wage	AXR	Average experienced range	HI	Highest wage paid
ATC	Average total compensation	D	Daily	HR	High end range

LO	Lowest wage paid	MTC	Median total compensation	TCC	Total cash compensation
LR	Low end range	MW	Median wage paid	TQ	Third quartile wage
M	Monthly	MWR	Median wage range	W	Weekly
MCC	Median cash compensation	S	See annotated source	Y	Yearly

Occupation/Type/Industry	Location	Per	Low	Mid	High	Source	Date
Occupational Therapist Aide	San Diego-Carlsbad-San Marcos MSA, CA	H	10.81 FQ	14.15 MW	22.28 TQ	CABLS	1/08-3/08
	San Francisco-San Mateo-Redwood PMSA, CA	H	11.78 FQ	13.85 MW	15.46 TQ	CABLS	1/08-3/08
	San Jose-Sunnyvale-Santa Clara MSA, CA	H	10.97 FQ	12.21 MW	17.05 TQ	CABLS	1/08-3/08
	Santa Ana-Anaheim-Irvine PMSA, CA	Y	27820 FQ	30690 MW	35330 TQ	USBLS	5/07
	Colorado	Y	29220 FQ	34710 MW	39950 TQ	USBLS	5/07
	Connecticut	H	10.50 AE	14.76 MW		CTBLS	1/08-3/08
	Bridgeport-Stamford-Norwalk MSA, CT	Y	22780 FQ	28070 MW	37720 TQ	USBLS	5/07
	District of Columbia	Y	21390 FQ	23310 MW	25260 TQ	USBLS	5/07
	Washington-Arlington-Alexandria MSA, DC-VA-MD-WV	Y	21910 FQ	24410 MW	27900 TQ	USBLS	5/07
	Florida	Y	20750 FQ	23000 MW	25700 TQ	USBLS	5/07
	Miami-Fort Lauderdale-Miami Beach MSA, FL	Y	19830 FQ	21940 MW	24010 TQ	USBLS	5/07
	Georgia	Y	19830 FQ	25240 MW	29630 TQ	USBLS	5/07
	Hawaii	Y	25690 FQ	27550 MW	29400 TQ	USBLS	5/07
	Honolulu MSA, HI	Y	25690 FQ	27550 MW	29400 TQ	USBLS	5/07
	Illinois	Y	24210 FQ	29270 MW	41900 TQ	USBLS	5/07
	Chicago-Naperville-Joliet MSA, IL-IN-WI	Y	23330 FQ	28550 MW	39830 TQ	USBLS	5/07
	Indiana	Y	19560 FQ	23740 MW	28940 TQ	USBLS	5/07
	Gary PMSA, IN	Y	17040 FQ	18680 MW	28870 TQ	USBLS	5/07
	Iowa	Y	19810 FQ	23130 MW	30660 TQ	USBLS	5/07
	Kansas	Y	22090 FQ	24890 MW	35200 TQ	USBLS	5/07
	Kentucky	Y	20961 FQ	24016 MW	30127 TQ	KYBLS	2008
	Louisville-Jefferson County MSA, KY-IN	Y	21790 FQ	24680 MW	48200 TQ	USBLS	5/07
	Louisiana	H	9.16 FQ	10.79 MW	13.81 TQ	LABLS	1/08-3/08
	Maine	Y	24280 FQ	27680 MW	30690 TQ	USBLS	5/07
	Baltimore-Towson MSA, MD	Y	35180 FQ	51400 MW	58680 TQ	USBLS	5/07
	Massachusetts	Y	27370 FQ	31840 MW	36900 TQ	USBLS	5/07
	Boston-Cambridge-Quincy NECTA, MA	Y	26570 FQ	30550 MW	34360 TQ	USBLS	5/07
	Michigan	Y	21850 FQ	24840 MW	29090 TQ	USBLS	5/07
	Detroit-Warren-Livonia MSA, MI	Y	21960 FQ	25170 MW	29130 TQ	USBLS	5/07
	Minnesota	Y	26076 FQ	30959 MW	38163 TQ	MNBLS	10/08-12/08
	Minneapolis-Saint Paul MSA, MN-WI	Y	29046 FQ	34640 MW	40694 TQ	MNBLS	10/08-12/08
	Mississippi	Y	22410 FQ	25270 MW	32470 TQ	USBLS	5/07
	Missouri	Y	20710 FQ	23960 MW	34390 TQ	USBLS	5/07
	Kansas City MSA, MO-KS	Y	21060 FQ	22900 MW	26040 TQ	USBLS	5/07
	St. Louis MSA, MO-IL	Y	21280 FQ	26010 MW	38800 TQ	USBLS	5/07
	Nebraska	Y	20370 FQ	24300 MW	35540 TQ	USBLS	5/07
	Nevada	H	11.88 FQ	13.59 MW	15.49 TQ	NVBLS	5/08
	Reno-Sparks MSA, NV	H	12.43 FQ	13.65 MW	14.82 TQ	NVBLS	5/08
	New Hampshire	H	12.15 AE	13.26 MW	14.20 AEX	NHBLS	6/08
	New Jersey	Y	23930 FQ	28760 MW	36190 TQ	USBLS	5/07
	Newark-Union PMSA, NJ-PA	Y	23070 FQ	27780 MW	35570 TQ	USBLS	5/07
	New Mexico	Y	20840 FQ	22610 MW	25540 TQ	USBLS	5/07
	New York	Y	26410 FQ	30110 MW	35100 TQ	USBLS	5/07
	Albany-Schenectady-Troy MSA, NY	Y	21790 FQ	25650 MW	29580 TQ	USBLS	5/07
	Buffalo-Niagara Falls MSA, NY	Y	25550 FQ	31430 MW	35900 TQ	USBLS	5/07
	Nassau-Suffolk PMSA, NY	Y	29410 FQ	33610 MW	39730 TQ	USBLS	5/07
	New York-Northern New Jersey-Long Island MSA, NY-NJ-PA	Y	27060 FQ	30520 MW	35760 TQ	USBLS	5/07
	North Carolina	Y	21390 FQ	26220 MW	41240 TQ	USBLS	5/07
	Charlotte-Gastonia-Concord MSA, NC-SC	Y	22640 FQ	36380 MW	52890 TQ	USBLS	5/07
	Ohio	Y	22220 FQ	25030 MW	28790 TQ	USBLS	5/07
	Cleveland-Elyria-Mentor MSA, OH	Y	21950 FQ	24200 MW	27460 TQ	USBLS	5/07
	Oklahoma	Y	17540 FQ	19810 MW	24560 TQ	USBLS	5/07
	Oklahoma City MSA, OK	Y	17770 FQ	19920 MW	24720 TQ	USBLS	5/07

AE	Average entry wage	AW	Average wage paid	FQ	First quartile wage	LO	Lowest wage paid	MTC	Median total compensation	TCC	Total cash compensation
AER	Average entry range	AWR	Average wage range	H	Hourly	LR	Low end range	MW	Median wage paid	TQ	Third quartile wage
AEX	Average experienced wage	AXR	Average experienced range	HI	Highest wage paid	M	Monthly	MWR	Median wage range	W	Weekly
ATC	Average total compensation	D	Daily	HR	High end range	MCC	Median cash compensation	S	See annotated source	Y	Yearly

1130

Occupation/Type/Industry	Location	Per	Low	Mid	High	Source	Date
Occupational Therapist Aide	Oregon	H	13.96 FQ	21.02 MW	24.95 TQ	ORBLS	5/08
	Pennsylvania	Y	21440 FQ	25690 MW	31490 TQ	USBLS	5/07
	Allentown-Bethlehem-Easton MSA, PA-NJ	Y	21900 FQ	23340 MW	24780 TQ	USBLS	5/07
	Philadelphia-Camden-Wilmington MSA, PA-NJ-DE-MD	Y	24190 FQ	27860 MW	32400 TQ	USBLS	5/07
	Pittsburgh MSA, PA	Y	25870 FQ	29210 MW	35150 TQ	USBLS	5/07
	South Carolina	Y	16100 FQ	18530 MW	22690 TQ	USBLS	5/07
	Columbia MSA, SC	Y	16980 FQ	18330 MW	20120 TQ	USBLS	5/07
	Tennessee	Y	20430 FQ	24060 MW	32600 TQ	USBLS	5/07
	Knoxville MSA, TN	Y	19820 FQ	21720 MW	23600 TQ	USBLS	5/07
	Texas	Y	18210 FQ	21840 MW	29690 TQ	USBLS	5/07
	Dallas-Fort Worth-Arlington MSA, TX	Y	19440 FQ	23090 MW	34950 TQ	USBLS	5/07
	Houston-Sugar Land-Baytown MSA, TX	Y	17150 FQ	19340 MW	25160 TQ	USBLS	5/07
	San Antonio MSA, TX	Y	20420 FQ	22060 MW	23770 TQ	USBLS	5/07
	Utah	Y	17780 FQ	21220 MW	37300 TQ	USBLS	5/07
	Virginia	Y	23950 FQ	28340 MW	36930 TQ	USBLS	5/07
	Richmond MSA, VA	Y	23970 FQ	26370 MW	33860 TQ	USBLS	5/07
	Washington	H	10.70 FQ	12.41 MW	14.99 TQ	WABLS	3/08
	Seattle-Tacoma-Bellevue MSA, WA	Y	22270 FQ	27080 MW	35580 TQ	USBLS	5/07
	West Virginia	Y	21806 FQ	24259 MW	29463 TQ	WVBLS	7/08-9/08
	Wisconsin	Y	19110 FQ	22240 MW	27420 TQ	USBLS	5/07
	Wyoming	Y	22872 FQ	26431 MW	29528 TQ	WYBLS	9/08
	Puerto Rico	Y	19500 FQ	21900 MW	23900 TQ	USBLS	5/07
	San Juan-Caguas-Guaynabo MSA, PR	Y	19500 FQ	21900 MW	23900 TQ	USBLS	5/07
Occupational Therapist Assistant	Alabama	Y	39540 FQ	45900 MW	52720 TQ	USBLS	5/07
	Birmingham-Hoover MSA, AL	Y	41590 FQ	47030 MW	54600 TQ	USBLS	5/07
	Arizona	Y	40820 FQ	47920 MW	56820 TQ	USBLS	5/07
	Phoenix-Mesa-Scottsdale MSA, AZ	Y	42850 FQ	50560 MW	57930 TQ	USBLS	5/07
	Tucson MSA, AZ	Y	40230 FQ	45780 MW	51590 TQ	USBLS	5/07
	Arkansas	Y	43430 FQ	52470 MW	58680 TQ	USBLS	5/07
	Little Rock-North Little Rock MSA, AR	Y	52380 FQ	56600 MW	60950 TQ	USBLS	5/07
	California	H	22.02 FQ	26.30 MW	30.24 TQ	CABLS	1/08-3/08
	Los Angeles-Long Beach-Glendale PMSA, CA	H	23.49 FQ	27.37 MW	30.53 TQ	CABLS	1/08-3/08
	Oakland-Fremont-Hayward MSA, CA	H	19.05 FQ	24.76 MW	27.74 TQ	CABLS	1/08-3/08
	Riverside-San Bernardino-Ontario MSA, CA	H	22.79 FQ	25.80 MW	30.63 TQ	CABLS	1/08-3/08
	Sacramento-Arden Arcade-Roseville MSA, CA	H	22.50 FQ	25.82 MW	29.85 TQ	CABLS	1/08-3/08
	San Diego-Carlsbad-San Marcos MSA, CA	H	21.18 FQ	25.13 MW	28.42 TQ	CABLS	1/08-3/08
	San Francisco-San Mateo-Redwood PMSA, CA	H	22.21 FQ	24.47 MW	27.72 TQ	CABLS	1/08-3/08
	Santa Ana-Anaheim-Irvine PMSA, CA	Y	48760 FQ	56160 MW	64180 TQ	USBLS	5/07
	Colorado	Y	34190 FQ	40230 MW	46480 TQ	USBLS	5/07
	Denver-Aurora MSA, CO	Y	34660 FQ	39930 MW	46330 TQ	USBLS	5/07
	Connecticut	H	18.87 AE	24.29 MW		CTBLS	1/08-3/08
	Bridgeport-Stamford-Norwalk MSA, CT	Y	44330 FQ	49410 MW	56210 TQ	USBLS	5/07
	Hartford-West Hartford-East Hartford MSA, CT	Y	42610 FQ	50280 MW	57030 TQ	USBLS	5/07
	Delaware	Y	43110 FQ	51910 MW	58690 TQ	USBLS	5/07
	Wilmington PMSA, DE-MD-NJ	Y	43490 FQ	52330 MW	58940 TQ	USBLS	5/07
	District of Columbia	Y	32510 FQ	42210 MW	47970 TQ	USBLS	5/07
	Washington-Arlington-Alexandria MSA, DC-VA-MD-WV	Y	27840 FQ	41780 MW	52770 TQ	USBLS	5/07
	Florida	Y	47200 FQ	54170 MW	60100 TQ	USBLS	5/07

AE	Average entry wage	AW	Average wage paid	FQ	First quartile wage	LO	Lowest wage paid	MTC	Median total compensation	TCC	Total cash compensation
AER	Average entry range	AWR	Average wage range	H	Hourly	LR	Low end range	MW	Median wage paid	TQ	Third quartile wage
AEX	Average experienced wage	AXR	Average experienced range	HI	Highest wage paid	M	Monthly	MWR	Median wage range	W	Weekly
ATC	Average total compensation	D	Daily	HR	High end range	MCC	Median cash compensation	S	See annotated source	Y	Yearly

1131

Occupation/Type/Industry	Location	Per	Low	Mid	High	Source	Date
Occupational Therapist Assistant	Fort Lauderdale-Pompano Beach-Deerfield Beach PMSA, FL	Y	51430 FQ	55850 MW	60190 TQ	USBLS	5/07
	Jacksonville MSA, FL	Y	43550 FQ	49830 MW	58070 TQ	USBLS	5/07
	Miami-Fort Lauderdale-Miami Beach MSA, FL	Y	50050 FQ	55400 MW	60160 TQ	USBLS	5/07
	Orlando-Kissimmee MSA, FL	Y	42550 FQ	47250 MW	55990 TQ	USBLS	5/07
	Tampa-St. Petersburg-Clearwater MSA, FL	Y	47130 FQ	55310 MW	62000 TQ	USBLS	5/07
	West Palm Beach-Boca Raton-Boynton Beach PMSA, FL	Y	48820 FQ	55420 MW	60260 TQ	USBLS	5/07
	Georgia	Y	36100 FQ	49850 MW	59870 TQ	USBLS	5/07
	Atlanta-Sandy Springs-Marietta MSA, GA	Y	37100 FQ	52500 MW	60670 TQ	USBLS	5/07
	Hawaii	Y	30460 FQ	38190 MW	45160 TQ	USBLS	5/07
	Idaho	Y	22560 FQ	49040 MW	86240 TQ	USBLS	5/07
	Illinois	Y	30010 FQ	46400 MW	58670 TQ	USBLS	5/07
	Chicago-Naperville-Joliet MSA, IL-IN-WI	Y	34780 FQ	50840 MW	60140 TQ	USBLS	5/07
	Indiana	Y	34350 FQ	45130 MW	56070 TQ	USBLS	5/07
	Gary PMSA, IN	Y	40630 FQ	48050 MW	54890 TQ	USBLS	5/07
	Indianapolis-Carmel MSA, IN	Y	28170 FQ	45950 MW	57600 TQ	USBLS	5/07
	Iowa	Y	34330 FQ	40090 MW	46610 TQ	USBLS	5/07
	Des Moines-West Des Moines MSA, IA	Y	36610 FQ	40830 MW	45700 TQ	USBLS	5/07
	Kansas	Y	38400 FQ	44550 MW	51800 TQ	USBLS	5/07
	Wichita MSA, KS	Y	36760 FQ	43660 MW	51540 TQ	USBLS	5/07
	Kentucky	Y	42812 FQ	48442 MW	55760 TQ	KYBLS	2008
	Louisville-Jefferson County MSA, KY-IN	Y	45410 FQ	52440 MW	58840 TQ	USBLS	5/07
	Louisiana	H	18.26 FQ	21.82 MW	25.15 TQ	LABLS	1/08-3/08
	Baton Rouge MSA, LA	Y	41800 FQ	46950 MW	54260 TQ	USBLS	5/07
	New Orleans-Metairie-Kenner MSA, LA	Y	45020 FQ	50420 MW	66960 TQ	USBLS	5/07
	Maryland	Y		42050 MW		MDBLS	3/08
	Baltimore-Towson MSA, MD	Y	42890 FQ	54040 MW	63460 TQ	USBLS	5/07
	Massachusetts	Y	36150 FQ	43820 MW	50620 TQ	USBLS	5/07
	Boston-Cambridge-Quincy NECTA, MA	Y	39870 FQ	45920 MW	52010 TQ	USBLS	5/07
	Worcester MSA, MA-CT	Y	33380 FQ	37000 MW	41510 TQ	USBLS	5/07
	Michigan	Y	33630 FQ	40450 MW	45900 TQ	USBLS	5/07
	Detroit-Warren-Livonia MSA, MI	Y	33440 FQ	41540 MW	48820 TQ	USBLS	5/07
	Flint MSA, MI	Y	38880 FQ	42230 MW	45510 TQ	USBLS	5/07
	Grand Rapids-Wyoming MSA, MI	Y	32390 FQ	36130 MW	40070 TQ	USBLS	5/07
	Warren-Troy-Farmington Hills PMSA, MI	Y	30270 FQ	37430 MW	45270 TQ	USBLS	5/07
	Minnesota	Y	34629 FQ	40035 MW	45859 TQ	MNBLS	10/08-12/08
	Duluth-Superior MSA, MN-WI	Y	35581 FQ	38644 MW	42868 TQ	MNBLS	10/08-12/08
	Minneapolis-Saint Paul MSA, MN-WI	Y	35309 FQ	41373 MW	47197 TQ	MNBLS	10/08-12/08
	Rochester MSA, MN	Y	37390 FQ	41269 MW	47020 TQ	MNBLS	10/08-12/08
	Mississippi	Y	32910 FQ	43280 MW	49670 TQ	USBLS	5/07
	Jackson MSA, MS	Y	32190 FQ	41180 MW	46410 TQ	USBLS	5/07
	Missouri	Y	35000 FQ	42500 MW	49440 TQ	USBLS	5/07
	Kansas City MSA, MO-KS	Y	29940 FQ	42390 MW	49830 TQ	USBLS	5/07
	St. Louis MSA, MO-IL	Y	37650 FQ	43200 MW	49390 TQ	USBLS	5/07
	Montana	Y	26440 FQ	31920 MW	38610 TQ	USBLS	5/07
	Nebraska	Y	33560 FQ	43550 MW	52000 TQ	USBLS	5/07
	Omaha-Council Bluffs MSA, NE-IA	Y	39320 FQ	48170 MW	56730 TQ	USBLS	5/07
	Nevada	H	12.48 FQ	14.70 MW	26.38 TQ	NVBLS	5/08
	Las Vegas-Paradise MSA, NV	H	12.42 FQ	14.61 MW	26.48 TQ	NVBLS	5/08
	New Hampshire	H	16.41 AE	20.88 MW	23.09 AEX	NHBLS	6/08
	New Jersey	Y	39990 FQ	48390 MW	58790 TQ	USBLS	5/07
	Camden PMSA, NJ	Y	32610 FQ	44620 MW	52240 TQ	USBLS	5/07
	Edison PMSA, NJ	Y	45440 FQ	51530 MW	72370 TQ	USBLS	5/07
	Newark-Union PMSA, NJ-PA	Y	36950 FQ	45960 MW	54950 TQ	USBLS	5/07
	New Mexico	Y	31260 FQ	38810 MW	50710 TQ	USBLS	5/07
	Albuquerque MSA, NM	Y	47050 FQ	56230 MW	63550 TQ	USBLS	5/07
	New York	Y	34580 FQ	42490 MW	51350 TQ	USBLS	5/07

AE	Average entry wage	AW	Average wage paid	FQ	First quartile wage
AER	Average entry range	AWR	Average wage range	H	Hourly
AEX	Average experienced wage	AXR	Average experienced range	HI	Highest wage paid
ATC	Average total compensation	D	Daily	HR	High end range

LO	Lowest wage paid	MTC	Median total compensation
LR	Low end range	MW	Median wage paid
M	Monthly	MWR	Median wage range
MCC	Median cash compensation	S	See annotated source

TCC	Total cash compensation
TQ	Third quartile wage
W	Weekly
Y	Yearly

Occupation/Type/Industry	Location	Per	Low	Mid	High	Source	Date
Occupational Therapist Assistant	Albany-Schenectady-Troy MSA, NY	Y	32090 FQ	36120 MW	40490 TQ	USBLS	5/07
	Buffalo-Niagara Falls MSA, NY	Y	29470 FQ	34510 MW	39200 TQ	USBLS	5/07
	Nassau-Suffolk PMSA, NY	Y	42580 FQ	49900 MW	57780 TQ	USBLS	5/07
	New York-Northern New Jersey-Long Island MSA, NY-NJ-PA	Y	41620 FQ	48850 MW	56880 TQ	USBLS	5/07
	North Carolina	Y	33870 FQ	44840 MW	53710 TQ	USBLS	5/07
	Charlotte-Gastonia-Concord MSA, NC-SC	Y	37650 FQ	44260 MW	52460 TQ	USBLS	5/07
	Raleigh-Cary MSA, NC	Y	39890 FQ	45780 MW	52350 TQ	USBLS	5/07
	North Dakota	Y	29380 FQ	34050 MW	38560 TQ	USBLS	5/07
	Ohio	Y	41820 FQ	47370 MW	54170 TQ	USBLS	5/07
	Cincinnati-Middletown MSA, OH-KY-IN	Y	40940 FQ	45840 MW	50400 TQ	USBLS	5/07
	Cleveland-Elyria-Mentor MSA, OH	Y	44160 FQ	51020 MW	57620 TQ	USBLS	5/07
	Columbus MSA, OH	Y	41070 FQ	46360 MW	53690 TQ	USBLS	5/07
	Dayton MSA, OH	Y	38430 FQ	44420 MW	50600 TQ	USBLS	5/07
	Oklahoma	Y	35390 FQ	44890 MW	52930 TQ	USBLS	5/07
	Oklahoma City MSA, OK	Y	42170 FQ	48040 MW	61700 TQ	USBLS	5/07
	Tulsa MSA, OK	Y	31330 FQ	42440 MW	51090 TQ	USBLS	5/07
	Oregon	H	20.08 FQ	22.19 MW	24.14 TQ	ORBLS	5/08
	Portland-Vancouver-Beaverton MSA, OR-WA	Y	41930 FQ	45600 MW	49440 TQ	USBLS	5/07
	Pennsylvania	Y	33680 FQ	40170 MW	47450 TQ	USBLS	5/07
	Allentown-Bethlehem-Easton MSA, PA-NJ	Y	34160 FQ	38530 MW	43490 TQ	USBLS	5/07
	Philadelphia-Camden-Wilmington MSA, PA-NJ-DE-MD	Y	38410 FQ	45870 MW	54240 TQ	USBLS	5/07
	Pittsburgh MSA, PA	Y	35210 FQ	40440 MW	47500 TQ	USBLS	5/07
	Rhode Island	Y	30920 FQ	42960 MW	51930 TQ	USBLS	5/07
	Providence-Fall River-Warwick MSA, RI-MA	Y	31750 FQ	43160 MW	50140 TQ	USBLS	5/07
	South Carolina	Y	33350 FQ	42210 MW	51080 TQ	USBLS	5/07
	Columbia MSA, SC	Y	41930 FQ	48430 MW	54560 TQ	USBLS	5/07
	South Dakota	Y	29288 FQ	33350 MW	37475 TQ	SDBLS	7/08-9/08
	Sioux Falls MSA, SD	Y	31968 FQ	34998 MW	38185 TQ	SDBLS	7/08-9/08
	Tennessee	Y	38480 FQ	45900 MW	53760 TQ	USBLS	5/07
	Memphis MSA, TN-MS-AR	Y	28030 FQ	30660 MW	38060 TQ	USBLS	5/07
	Nashville-Davidson-Murfreesboro MSA, TN	Y	42230 FQ	49300 MW	57020 TQ	USBLS	5/07
	Texas	Y	40040 FQ	50680 MW	59850 TQ	USBLS	5/07
	Austin-Round Rock MSA, TX	Y	36990 FQ	46600 MW	53830 TQ	USBLS	5/07
	Dallas-Fort Worth-Arlington MSA, TX	Y	41730 FQ	50810 MW	60150 TQ	USBLS	5/07
	El Paso MSA, TX	Y	44560 FQ	55460 MW	61090 TQ	USBLS	5/07
	Houston-Sugar Land-Baytown MSA, TX	Y	33320 FQ	45930 MW	57600 TQ	USBLS	5/07
	San Antonio MSA, TX	Y	50610 FQ	56310 MW	63300 TQ	USBLS	5/07
	Utah	Y	38210 FQ	43610 MW	49260 TQ	USBLS	5/07
	Salt Lake City MSA, UT	Y	39490 FQ	45270 MW	50780 TQ	USBLS	5/07
	Vermont	Y	35090 FQ	39610 MW	52950 TQ	USBLS	5/07
	Virginia	Y	39900 FQ	47790 MW	56240 TQ	USBLS	5/07
	Charlottesville MSA, VA	Y	31470 FQ	37750 MW	44530 TQ	USBLS	5/07
	Richmond MSA, VA	Y	39250 FQ	47760 MW	55280 TQ	USBLS	5/07
	Virginia Beach-Norfolk-Newport News MSA, VA-NC	Y	40410 FQ	50320 MW	58740 TQ	USBLS	5/07
	Washington	H	20.78 FQ	22.74 MW	25.24 TQ	WABLS	3/08
	Seattle-Tacoma-Bellevue MSA, WA	Y	43400 FQ	47770 MW	53990 TQ	USBLS	5/07
	West Virginia	Y	37844 FQ	44153 MW	51760 TQ	WVBLS	7/08-9/08
	Milwaukee-Waukesha-West Allis MSA, WI	Y	35270 FQ	40560 MW	46660 TQ	USBLS	5/07
	Wyoming	Y	33207 FQ	39990 MW	47320 TQ	WYBLS	9/08
	Puerto Rico	Y	17960 FQ	20950 MW	25220 TQ	USBLS	5/07
Oceanographer	United States	Y		77890 AW		COSOC	11/06

Occupation/Type/Industry	Location	Per	Low	Mid	High	Source	Date
Offensive Coordinator							
Texas A&M University	Texas	Y			330000 HI	AASTATE	2008
University of Texas	Texas	Y			425000 HI	AASTATE	2008
Office Aide							
Municipal Government	Carlsbad, CA	H	8.00 LO		14.00 HI	CCSS	1/1/08
Office Assistant							
State Government	Kansas	Y	18741 LO		25064 HI	AFT02	3/1/08
Office Clerk							
General	Alabama	Y	15270 FQ	19970 MW	25060 TQ	USBLS	5/07
General	Birmingham-Hoover MSA, AL	Y	15750 FQ	20860 MW	26110 TQ	USBLS	5/07
General	Montgomery MSA, AL	Y	16620 FQ	21310 MW	25930 TQ	USBLS	5/07
General	Alaska	Y	24710 FQ	29650 MW	36240 TQ	USBLS	5/07
General	Anchorage MSA, AK	Y	24890 FQ	29900 MW	36600 TQ	USBLS	5/07
General	Fairbanks MSA, AK	Y	26230 FQ	30850 MW	37010 TQ	USBLS	5/07
General	Arizona	Y	19110 FQ	24600 MW	31650 TQ	USBLS	5/07
General	Phoenix-Mesa-Scottsdale MSA, AZ	Y	19570 FQ	25390 MW	32830 TQ	USBLS	5/07
General	Tucson MSA, AZ	Y	19750 FQ	24300 MW	29760 TQ	USBLS	5/07
General	Arkansas	Y	15640 FQ	19350 MW	23800 TQ	USBLS	5/07
General	Little Rock-North Little Rock MSA, AR	Y	16000 FQ	20160 MW	25560 TQ	USBLS	5/07
General	California	H	10.17 FQ	13.17 MW	16.86 TQ	CABLS	1/08-3/08
General	Los Angeles-Long Beach-Glendale PMSA, CA	H	9.63 FQ	12.38 MW	16.28 TQ	CABLS	1/08-3/08
General	Oakland-Fremont-Hayward MSA, CA	H	12.54 FQ	15.77 MW	20.64 TQ	CABLS	1/08-3/08
General	Riverside-San Bernardino-Ontario MSA, CA	H	10.02 FQ	12.24 MW	15.39 TQ	CABLS	1/08-3/08
General	Sacramento-Arden Arcade-Roseville MSA, CA	H	10.70 FQ	14.16 MW	17.49 TQ	CABLS	1/08-3/08
General	San Diego-Carlsbad-San Marcos MSA, CA	H	10.50 FQ	13.36 MW	16.26 TQ	CABLS	1/08-3/08
General	San Francisco-San Mateo-Redwood PMSA, CA	H	10.95 FQ	15.26 MW	19.68 TQ	CABLS	1/08-3/08
General	San Jose-Sunnyvale-Santa Clara MSA, CA	H	11.74 FQ	15.31 MW	20.11 TQ	CABLS	1/08-3/08
General	Santa Ana-Anaheim-Irvine PMSA, CA	Y	21040 FQ	27280 MW	34100 TQ	USBLS	5/07
General	Colorado	Y	21080 FQ	26710 MW	32730 TQ	USBLS	5/07
General	Denver-Aurora MSA, CO	Y	22690 FQ	28210 MW	34680 TQ	USBLS	5/07
General	Connecticut	H	10.09 AE	14.39 MW		CTBLS	1/08-3/08
General	Bridgeport-Stamford-Norwalk MSA, CT	Y	22340 FQ	29070 MW	36770 TQ	USBLS	5/07
General	Hartford-West Hartford-East Hartford MSA, CT	Y	24060 FQ	29820 MW	37650 TQ	USBLS	5/07
General	Waterbury MSA, CT	Y	22460 FQ	28050 MW	35250 TQ	USBLS	5/07
General	Delaware	Y	17300 FQ	25080 MW	32040 TQ	USBLS	5/07
General	Wilmington PMSA, DE-MD-NJ	Y	16420 FQ	24970 MW	32310 TQ	USBLS	5/07
General	District of Columbia	Y	25690 FQ	31020 MW	37980 TQ	USBLS	5/07
General	Washington-Arlington-Alexandria MSA, DC-VA-MD-WV	Y	24360 FQ	30980 MW	38760 TQ	USBLS	5/07
General	Florida	Y	17680 FQ	22820 MW	28780 TQ	USBLS	5/07
General	Cape Coral-Fort Myers MSA, FL	Y	16600 FQ	22410 MW	28020 TQ	USBLS	5/07
General	Fort Lauderdale-Pompano Beach-Deerfield Beach PMSA, FL	Y	17150 FQ	22730 MW	28920 TQ	USBLS	5/07
General	Jacksonville MSA, FL	Y	19140 FQ	23240 MW	28650 TQ	USBLS	5/07
General	Miami-Fort Lauderdale-Miami Beach MSA, FL	Y	17660 FQ	22770 MW	28930 TQ	USBLS	5/07
General	Orlando-Kissimmee MSA, FL	Y	17640 FQ	22710 MW	28290 TQ	USBLS	5/07
General	Tampa-St. Petersburg-Clearwater MSA, FL	Y	18090 FQ	23640 MW	29750 TQ	USBLS	5/07
General	West Palm Beach-Boca Raton-Boynton Beach PMSA, FL	Y	17980 FQ	23090 MW	29380 TQ	USBLS	5/07
General	Georgia	Y	17520 FQ	22960 MW	29030 TQ	USBLS	5/07

AE Average entry wage	**AW** Average wage paid	**FQ** First quartile wage	**LO** Lowest wage paid	**MTC** Median total compensation	**TCC** Total cash compensation
AER Average entry range	**AWR** Average wage range	**H** Hourly	**LR** Low end range	**MW** Median wage paid	**TQ** Third quartile wage
AEX Average experienced wage	**AXR** Average experienced range	**HI** Highest wage paid	**M** Monthly	**MWR** Median wage range	**W** Weekly
ATC Average total compensation	**D** Daily	**HR** High end range	**MCC** Median cash compensation	**S** See annotated source	**Y** Yearly

Office Clerk

Occupation/Type/Industry	Location	Per	Low	Mid	High	Source	Date
Office Clerk							
General	Atlanta-Sandy Springs-Marietta MSA, GA	Y	18910 FQ	24370 MW	30330 TQ	USBLS	5/07
General	Hawaii	Y	19330 FQ	25000 MW	31320 TQ	USBLS	5/07
General	Honolulu MSA, HI	Y	18760 FQ	24470 MW	31540 TQ	USBLS	5/07
General	Idaho	Y	18110 FQ	22980 MW	28900 TQ	USBLS	5/07
General	Boise City-Nampa MSA, ID	Y	18970 FQ	24280 MW	29780 TQ	USBLS	5/07
General	Illinois	Y	19010 FQ	24750 MW	31830 TQ	USBLS	5/07
General	Champaign-Urbana MSA, IL	Y	15750 FQ	22290 MW	28220 TQ	USBLS	5/07
General	Chicago-Naperville-Joliet MSA, IL-IN-WI	Y	19700 FQ	25640 MW	32800 TQ	USBLS	5/07
General	Indiana	Y	17530 FQ	22320 MW	27990 TQ	USBLS	5/07
General	Gary PMSA, IN	Y	16800 FQ	21050 MW	28140 TQ	USBLS	5/07
General	Indianapolis-Carmel MSA, IN	Y	20040 FQ	24630 MW	30240 TQ	USBLS	5/07
General	Iowa	Y	19380 FQ	23920 MW	29570 TQ	USBLS	5/07
General	Des Moines-West Des Moines MSA, IA	Y	21230 FQ	26080 MW	31350 TQ	USBLS	5/07
General	Kansas	Y	17820 FQ	22510 MW	27680 TQ	USBLS	5/07
General	Lawrence MSA, KS	Y	13800 FQ	17450 MW	25720 TQ	USBLS	5/07
General	Topeka MSA, KS	Y	19410 FQ	22740 MW	27410 TQ	USBLS	5/07
General	Wichita MSA, KS	Y	19190 FQ	23170 MW	28370 TQ	USBLS	5/07
General	Kentucky	Y	18127 FQ	23545 MW	29707 TQ	KYBLS	2008
General	Bowling Green MSA, KY	Y	16910 FQ	22410 MW	27630 TQ	USBLS	5/07
General	Louisville-Jefferson County MSA, KY-IN	Y	19650 FQ	24490 MW	30280 TQ	USBLS	5/07
General	Louisiana	H	7.00 FQ	8.91 MW	11.42 TQ	LABLS	1/08-3/08
General	Baton Rouge MSA, LA	Y	15300 FQ	19100 MW	24140 TQ	USBLS	5/07
General	Lake Charles MSA, LA	Y	13690 FQ	16810 MW	22760 TQ	USBLS	5/07
General	New Orleans-Metairie-Kenner MSA, LA	Y	16010 FQ	20230 MW	25590 TQ	USBLS	5/07
General	Maine	Y	18640 FQ	24040 MW	29520 TQ	USBLS	5/07
General	Portland-South Portland-Biddeford MSA, ME	Y	20910 FQ	26470 MW	31130 TQ	USBLS	5/07
General	Maryland	Y		28650 MW		MDBLS	3/08
General	Baltimore-Towson MSA, MD	Y	22440 FQ	28130 MW	35120 TQ	USBLS	5/07
General	Bethesda-Gaithersburg-Frederick PMSA, MD	Y	22730 FQ	29700 MW	38930 TQ	USBLS	5/07
General	Cumberland MSA, MD-WV	Y	14720 FQ	18910 MW	24840 TQ	USBLS	5/07
General	Massachusetts	Y	22870 FQ	28710 MW	35840 TQ	USBLS	5/07
General	Boston-Cambridge-Quincy NECTA, MA	Y	23260 FQ	29410 MW	36900 TQ	USBLS	5/07
General	Worcester MSA, MA-CT	Y	22500 FQ	27570 MW	33210 TQ	USBLS	5/07
General	Michigan	Y	19500 FQ	24750 MW	31220 TQ	USBLS	5/07
General	Detroit-Warren-Livonia MSA, MI	Y	19570 FQ	25010 MW	31250 TQ	USBLS	5/07
General	Grand Rapids-Wyoming MSA, MI	Y	21380 FQ	26080 MW	32540 TQ	USBLS	5/07
General	Warren-Troy-Farmington Hills PMSA, MI	Y	18840 FQ	24240 MW	30770 TQ	USBLS	5/07
General	Minnesota	Y	22835 FQ	28216 MW	34034 TQ	MNBLS	10/08-12/08
General	Duluth-Superior MSA, MN-WI	Y	21253 FQ	25822 MW	31400 TQ	MNBLS	10/08-12/08
General	Minneapolis-Saint Paul MSA, MN-WI	Y	24281 FQ	29850 MW	35897 TQ	MNBLS	10/08-12/08
General	Rochester MSA, MN	Y	23743 FQ	28954 MW	33946 TQ	MNBLS	10/08-12/08
General	Mississippi	Y	15440 FQ	19610 MW	24010 TQ	USBLS	5/07
General	Jackson MSA, MS	Y	16270 FQ	20850 MW	24880 TQ	USBLS	5/07
General	Missouri	Y	19370 FQ	24250 MW	30980 TQ	USBLS	5/07
General	Joplin MSA, MO	Y	17680 FQ	21810 MW	27070 TQ	USBLS	5/07
General	Kansas City MSA, MO-KS	Y	20990 FQ	26290 MW	32560 TQ	USBLS	5/07
General	St. Louis MSA, MO-IL	Y	20710 FQ	26310 MW	32990 TQ	USBLS	5/07
General	Montana	Y	17180 FQ	21740 MW	26620 TQ	USBLS	5/07
General	Billings MSA, MT	Y	16830 FQ	20050 MW	24850 TQ	USBLS	5/07
General	Nebraska	Y	16500 FQ	21310 MW	26510 TQ	USBLS	5/07
General	Omaha-Council Bluffs MSA, NE-IA	Y	19880 FQ	24270 MW	29980 TQ	USBLS	5/07
General	Nevada	H	9.93 FQ	12.44 MW	15.53 TQ	NVBLS	5/08
General	Las Vegas-Paradise MSA, NV	H	10.13 FQ	12.65 MW	15.61 TQ	NVBLS	5/08
General	New Hampshire	H	10.12 AE	13.91 MW	16.43 AEX	NHBLS	6/08
General	Manchester MSA, NH	Y	23910 FQ	28090 MW	33310 TQ	USBLS	5/07
General	Nashua NECTA, NH-MA	Y	23920 FQ	28990 MW	34850 TQ	USBLS	5/07
General	New Jersey	Y	20050 FQ	25800 MW	33030 TQ	USBLS	5/07
General	Camden PMSA, NJ	Y	20380 FQ	25470 MW	32380 TQ	USBLS	5/07

AE	Average entry wage	AW	Average wage paid	FQ	First quartile wage
AER	Average entry range	AWR	Average wage range	H	Hourly
AEX	Average experienced wage	AXR	Average experienced range	HI	Highest wage paid
ATC	Average total compensation	D	Daily	HR	High end range

LO	Lowest wage paid	MTC	Median total compensation	TCC	Total cash compensation
LR	Low end range	MW	Median wage paid	TQ	Third quartile wage
M	Monthly	MWR	Median wage range	W	Weekly
MCC	Median cash compensation	S	See annotated source	Y	Yearly

Occupation/Type/Industry	Location	Per	Low	Mid	High	Source	Date
Office Clerk							
General	Edison PMSA, NJ	Y	19930 FQ	25550 MW	32220 TQ	USBLS	5/07
General	Newark-Union PMSA, NJ-PA	Y	20520 FQ	26310 MW	34040 TQ	USBLS	5/07
General	New Mexico	Y	15890 FQ	20490 MW	27070 TQ	USBLS	5/07
General	Albuquerque MSA, NM	Y	16880 FQ	21370 MW	27290 TQ	USBLS	5/07
General	New York	Y	19340 FQ	25530 MW	32190 TQ	USBLS	5/07
General	Albany-Schenectady-Troy MSA, NY	Y	21190 FQ	26150 MW	31430 TQ	USBLS	5/07
General	Buffalo-Niagara Falls MSA, NY	Y	18230 FQ	22970 MW	28350 TQ	USBLS	5/07
General	Ithaca MSA, NY	Y	20990 FQ	24740 MW	28230 TQ	USBLS	5/07
General	Nassau-Suffolk PMSA, NY	Y	20070 FQ	26060 MW	33710 TQ	USBLS	5/07
General	New York-Northern New Jersey-Long Island MSA, NY-NJ-PA	Y	19950 FQ	26610 MW	33580 TQ	USBLS	5/07
General	North Carolina	Y	18420 FQ	23170 MW	28910 TQ	USBLS	5/07
General	Charlotte-Gastonia-Concord MSA, NC-SC	Y	19460 FQ	24420 MW	30070 TQ	USBLS	5/07
General	Durham MSA, NC	Y	22850 FQ	28650 MW	34440 TQ	USBLS	5/07
General	Raleigh-Cary MSA, NC	Y	19790 FQ	24650 MW	29820 TQ	USBLS	5/07
General	North Dakota	Y	16610 FQ	20870 MW	25160 TQ	USBLS	5/07
General	Fargo MSA, ND-MN	Y	19290 FQ	23620 MW	28600 TQ	USBLS	5/07
General	Ohio	Y	18220 FQ	23430 MW	29720 TQ	USBLS	5/07
General	Cincinnati-Middletown MSA, OH-KY-IN	Y	19470 FQ	25090 MW	31330 TQ	USBLS	5/07
General	Cleveland-Elyria-Mentor MSA, OH	Y	18400 FQ	23890 MW	30650 TQ	USBLS	5/07
General	Columbus MSA, OH	Y	20290 FQ	25510 MW	31490 TQ	USBLS	5/07
General	Dayton MSA, OH	Y	19430 FQ	24060 MW	30520 TQ	USBLS	5/07
General	Springfield MSA, OH	Y	16340 FQ	22330 MW	27960 TQ	USBLS	5/07
General	Oklahoma	Y	16550 FQ	21090 MW	26600 TQ	USBLS	5/07
General	Oklahoma City MSA, OK	Y	16730 FQ	21530 MW	27010 TQ	USBLS	5/07
General	Tulsa MSA, OK	Y	18890 FQ	23140 MW	29770 TQ	USBLS	5/07
General	Oregon	H	10.66 FQ	13.11 MW	16.11 TQ	ORBLS	5/08
General	Portland-Vancouver-Beaverton MSA, OR-WA	Y	22510 FQ	27780 MW	34260 TQ	USBLS	5/07
General	Pennsylvania	Y	19110 FQ	24670 MW	31720 TQ	USBLS	5/07
General	Allentown-Bethlehem-Easton MSA, PA-NJ	Y	19670 FQ	25140 MW	32200 TQ	USBLS	5/07
General	Erie MSA, PA	Y	19320 FQ	23880 MW	29930 TQ	USBLS	5/07
General	Philadelphia-Camden-Wilmington MSA, PA-NJ-DE-MD	Y	20300 FQ	26920 MW	34660 TQ	USBLS	5/07
General	Pittsburgh MSA, PA	Y	18500 FQ	23380 MW	29710 TQ	USBLS	5/07
General	Rhode Island	Y	20360 FQ	24840 MW	30400 TQ	USBLS	5/07
General	Providence-Fall River-Warwick MSA, RI-MA	Y	20440 FQ	25060 MW	30750 TQ	USBLS	5/07
General	South Carolina	Y	18150 FQ	22780 MW	28120 TQ	USBLS	5/07
General	Charleston-North Charleston MSA, SC	Y	18200 FQ	22610 MW	27280 TQ	USBLS	5/07
General	Columbia MSA, SC	Y	20580 FQ	24590 MW	29690 TQ	USBLS	5/07
General	Myrtle Beach-Conway-North Myrtle Beach MSA, SC	Y	17640 FQ	21860 MW	26690 TQ	USBLS	5/07
General	South Dakota	Y	16816 FQ	19759 MW	23854 TQ	SDBLS	7/08-9/08
General	Sioux Falls MSA, SD	Y	18052 FQ	21499 MW	24731 TQ	SDBLS	7/08-9/08
General	Tennessee	Y	19790 FQ	24580 MW	30770 TQ	USBLS	5/07
General	Clarksville MSA, TN-KY	Y	17920 FQ	22080 MW	27490 TQ	USBLS	5/07
General	Memphis MSA, TN-MS-AR	Y	20540 FQ	25070 MW	31300 TQ	USBLS	5/07
General	Nashville-Davidson-Murfreesboro MSA, TN	Y	21520 FQ	26850 MW	33200 TQ	USBLS	5/07
General	Texas	Y	16560 FQ	21170 MW	26620 TQ	USBLS	5/07
General	Austin-Round Rock MSA, TX	Y	17640 FQ	21700 MW	26350 TQ	USBLS	5/07
General	Dallas-Fort Worth-Arlington MSA, TX	Y	17850 FQ	22790 MW	28970 TQ	USBLS	5/07
General	El Paso MSA, TX	Y	14610 FQ	18230 MW	23170 TQ	USBLS	5/07
General	Houston-Sugar Land-Baytown MSA, TX	Y	17730 FQ	22580 MW	28550 TQ	USBLS	5/07
General	San Antonio MSA, TX	Y	16710 FQ	21560 MW	26400 TQ	USBLS	5/07
General	Utah	Y	18160 FQ	22440 MW	27370 TQ	USBLS	5/07
General	Salt Lake City MSA, UT	Y	19260 FQ	23580 MW	28720 TQ	USBLS	5/07
General	Vermont	Y	20270 FQ	24210 MW	28940 TQ	USBLS	5/07

AE	Average entry wage	AW	Average wage paid	FQ	First quartile wage	LO	Lowest wage paid	MTC	Median total compensation	TCC	Total cash compensation
AER	Average entry range	AWR	Average wage range	H	Hourly	LR	Low end range	MW	Median wage paid	TQ	Third quartile wage
AEX	Average experienced wage	AXR	Average experienced range	HI	Highest wage paid	M	Monthly	MWR	Median wage range	W	Weekly
ATC	Average total compensation	D	Daily	HR	High end range	MCC	Median cash compensation	S	See annotated source	Y	Yearly

Office Clerk

Occupation/Type/Industry	Location	Per	Low	Mid	High	Source	Date
General	Burlington-South Burlington MSA, VT	Y	20810 FQ	25180 MW	29750 TQ	USBLS	5/07
General	Virginia	Y	20810 FQ	26930 MW	34120 TQ	USBLS	5/07
General	Richmond MSA, VA	Y	21630 FQ	27200 MW	34190 TQ	USBLS	5/07
General	Virginia Beach-Norfolk-Newport News MSA, VA-NC	Y	20110 FQ	24930 MW	30640 TQ	USBLS	5/07
General	Washington	H	10.98 FQ	13.48 MW	16.10	WABLS	3/08
General	Seattle-Tacoma-Bellevue MSA, WA	Y	23910 FQ	29240 MW	35210 TQ	USBLS	5/07
General	West Virginia	Y	16592 FQ	21662 MW	27481 TQ	WVBLS	7/08-9/08
General	Charleston MSA, WV	Y	17540 FQ	21940 MW	27700 TQ	USBLS	5/07
General	Wisconsin	Y	20450 FQ	24860 MW	30180 TQ	USBLS	5/07
General	Milwaukee-Waukesha-West Allis MSA, WI	Y	20820 FQ	25530 MW	31310 TQ	USBLS	5/07
General	Wyoming	Y	19951 FQ	23622 MW	28861 TQ	WYBLS	9/08
General	Cheyenne MSA, WY	Y	21511 FQ	24406 MW	28368 TQ	WYBLS	9/08
General	Puerto Rico	Y	13670 FQ	16450 MW	20300 TQ	USBLS	5/07
General	San Juan-Caguas-Guaynabo MSA, PR	Y	14020 FQ	17150 MW	21030 TQ	USBLS	5/07
General	Virgin Islands	Y	17530 FQ	19980 MW	23240 TQ	USBLS	5/07
General	Guam	Y	13490 FQ	16070 MW	21990 TQ	USBLS	5/07

Office Machine Operator

Occupation/Type/Industry	Location	Per	Low	Mid	High	Source	Date
Except Computer	Alabama	Y	18020 FQ	20910 MW	23900 TQ	USBLS	5/07
Except Computer	Birmingham-Hoover MSA, AL	Y	19850 FQ	22200 MW	24660 TQ	USBLS	5/07
Except Computer	Alaska	Y	20180 FQ	24640 MW	33110 TQ	USBLS	5/07
Except Computer	Anchorage MSA, AK	Y	19350 FQ	23630 MW	31390 TQ	USBLS	5/07
Except Computer	Arizona	Y	20020 FQ	25790 MW	31610 TQ	USBLS	5/07
Except Computer	Phoenix-Mesa-Scottsdale MSA, AZ	Y	21420 FQ	26700 MW	32740 TQ	USBLS	5/07
Except Computer	Tucson MSA, AZ	Y	15150 FQ	21370 MW	28790 TQ	USBLS	5/07
Except Computer	Arkansas	Y	17810 FQ	19810 MW	25410 TQ	USBLS	5/07
Except Computer	Little Rock-North Little Rock MSA, AR	Y	18040 FQ	19970 MW	26280 TQ	USBLS	5/07
Except Computer	California	H	10.59 FQ	13.55 MW	17.06 TQ	CABLS	1/08-3/08
Except Computer	Los Angeles-Long Beach-Glendale PMSA, CA	H	10.60 FQ	13.38 MW	16.23 TQ	CABLS	1/08-3/08
Except Computer	Oakland-Fremont-Hayward MSA, CA	H	10.58 FQ	13.59 MW	18.16 TQ	CABLS	1/08-3/08
Except Computer	Riverside-San Bernardino-Ontario MSA, CA	H	9.36 FQ	12.28 MW	16.31 TQ	CABLS	1/08-3/08
Except Computer	Sacramento-Arden Arcade-Roseville MSA, CA	H	12.67 FQ	14.49 MW	17.17 TQ	CABLS	1/08-3/08
Except Computer	San Diego-Carlsbad-San Marcos MSA, CA	H	11.50 FQ	14.12 MW	16.72 TQ	CABLS	1/08-3/08
Except Computer	San Francisco-San Mateo-Redwood PMSA, CA	H	10.50 FQ	15.49 MW	18.62 TQ	CABLS	1/08-3/08
Except Computer	San Jose-Sunnyvale-Santa Clara MSA, CA	H	9.46 FQ	14.39 MW	19.25 TQ	CABLS	1/08-3/08
Except Computer	Santa Ana-Anaheim-Irvine PMSA, CA	Y	22080 FQ	27750 MW	35220 TQ	USBLS	5/07
Except Computer	Stockton MSA, CA	H	10.73 FQ	13.98 MW	17.01 TQ	CABLS	1/08-3/08
Except Computer	Colorado	Y	21990 FQ	26550 MW	32670 TQ	USBLS	5/07
Except Computer	Denver-Aurora MSA, CO	Y	22440 FQ	26720 MW	32610 TQ	USBLS	5/07
Except Computer	Connecticut	H	9.39 AE	13.67 MW		CTBLS	1/08-3/08
Except Computer	Bridgeport-Stamford-Norwalk MSA, CT	Y	24470 FQ	33700 MW	41450 TQ	USBLS	5/07
Except Computer	Hartford-West Hartford-East Hartford MSA, CT	Y	19360 FQ	24680 MW	34590 TQ	USBLS	5/07
Except Computer	Delaware	Y	24280 FQ	28110 MW	31620 TQ	USBLS	5/07
Except Computer	Wilmington PMSA, DE-MD-NJ	Y	24690 FQ	28400 MW	31870 TQ	USBLS	5/07
Except Computer	District of Columbia	Y	25580 FQ	29060 MW	35890 TQ	USBLS	5/07
Except Computer	Washington-Arlington-Alexandria MSA, DC-VA-MD-WV	Y	23220 FQ	27850 MW	33790 TQ	USBLS	5/07
Except Computer	Florida	Y	19710 FQ	23510 MW	29030 TQ	USBLS	5/07
Except Computer	Cape Coral-Fort Myers MSA, FL	Y	24410 FQ	28510 MW	32630 TQ	USBLS	5/07

AE	Average entry wage	AW	Average wage paid	FQ	First quartile wage	LO	Lowest wage paid	MTC	Median total compensation	TCC	Total cash compensation
AER	Average entry range	AWR	Average wage range	H	Hourly	LR	Low end range	MW	Median wage paid	TQ	Third quartile wage
AEX	Average experienced wage	AXR	Average experienced range	HI	Highest wage paid	M	Monthly	MWR	Median wage range	W	Weekly
ATC	Average total compensation	D	Daily	HR	High end range	MCC	Median cash compensation	S	See annotated source	Y	Yearly

Office Machine Operator

Occupation/Type/Industry	Location	Per	Low	Mid	High	Source	Date
Except Computer	Fort Lauderdale-Pompano Beach-Deerfield Beach PMSA, FL	Y	22470 FQ	27290 MW	38870 TQ	USBLS	5/07
Except Computer	Jacksonville MSA, FL	Y	17600 FQ	19720 MW	25710 TQ	USBLS	5/07
Except Computer	Miami-Fort Lauderdale-Miami Beach MSA, FL	Y	20070 FQ	24420 MW	32700 TQ	USBLS	5/07
Except Computer	Orlando-Kissimmee MSA, FL	Y	20990 FQ	23860 MW	27570 TQ	USBLS	5/07
Except Computer	Tampa-St. Petersburg-Clearwater MSA, FL	Y	20530 FQ	23550 MW	28120 TQ	USBLS	5/07
Except Computer	West Palm Beach-Boca Raton-Boynton Beach PMSA, FL	Y	20460 FQ	27190 MW	37240 TQ	USBLS	5/07
Except Computer	Georgia	Y	20160 FQ	23540 MW	29610 TQ	USBLS	5/07
Except Computer	Atlanta-Sandy Springs-Marietta MSA, GA	Y	20640 FQ	24090 MW	30210 TQ	USBLS	5/07
Except Computer	Hawaii	Y	18260 FQ	21100 MW	24490 TQ	USBLS	5/07
Except Computer	Honolulu MSA, HI	Y	18200 FQ	21030 MW	24420 TQ	USBLS	5/07
Except Computer	Idaho	Y	25940 FQ	34610 MW	41360 TQ	USBLS	5/07
Except Computer	Boise City-Nampa MSA, ID	Y	24680 FQ	32040 MW	40650 TQ	USBLS	5/07
Except Computer	Illinois	Y	21570 FQ	25320 MW	31920 TQ	USBLS	5/07
Except Computer	Chicago-Naperville-Joliet MSA, IL-IN-WI	Y	21660 FQ	25210 MW	31540 TQ	USBLS	5/07
Except Computer	Indiana	Y	19070 FQ	24350 MW	30330 TQ	USBLS	5/07
Except Computer	Gary PMSA, IN	Y	18090 FQ	20720 MW	24080 TQ	USBLS	5/07
Except Computer	Indianapolis-Carmel MSA, IN	Y	21140 FQ	25660 MW	31500 TQ	USBLS	5/07
Except Computer	Terre Haute MSA, IN	Y	17210 FQ	20270 MW	34430 TQ	USBLS	5/07
Except Computer	Iowa	Y	17280 FQ	21090 MW	28460 TQ	USBLS	5/07
Except Computer	Davenport-Moline-Rock Island MSA, IA-IL	Y	18450 FQ	21360 MW	25600 TQ	USBLS	5/07
Except Computer	Kansas	Y	21780 FQ	25340 MW	31990 TQ	USBLS	5/07
Except Computer	Wichita MSA, KS	Y	23900 FQ	32700 MW	37610 TQ	USBLS	5/07
Except Computer	Kentucky	Y	17519 FQ	23063 MW	28651 TQ	KYBLS	2008
Except Computer	Louisville-Jefferson County MSA, KY-IN	Y	21890 FQ	26430 MW	31040 TQ	USBLS	5/07
Except Computer	Owensboro MSA, KY	Y	17620 FQ	20390 MW	25200 TQ	USBLS	5/07
Except Computer	Louisiana	H	9.41 FQ	11.30 MW	15.06 TQ	LABLS	1/08-3/08
Except Computer	Baton Rouge MSA, LA	Y	19400 FQ	25120 MW	32800 TQ	USBLS	5/07
Except Computer	New Orleans-Metairie-Kenner MSA, LA	Y	19120 FQ	24890 MW	32410 TQ	USBLS	5/07
Except Computer	Maine	Y	18690 FQ	26260 MW	32830 TQ	USBLS	5/07
Except Computer	Portland-South Portland-Biddeford MSA, ME	Y	14850 FQ	26060 MW	33140 TQ	USBLS	5/07
Except Computer	Maryland	Y		26925 MW		MDBLS	3/08
Except Computer	Baltimore-Towson MSA, MD	Y	24160 FQ	28150 MW	32700 TQ	USBLS	5/07
Except Computer	Bethesda-Gaithersburg-Frederick PMSA, MD	Y	22340 FQ	27720 MW	33470 TQ	USBLS	5/07
Except Computer	Massachusetts	Y	20070 FQ	26830 MW	32680 TQ	USBLS	5/07
Except Computer	Boston-Cambridge-Quincy NECTA, MA	Y	19720 FQ	26610 MW	32620 TQ	USBLS	5/07
Except Computer	Worcester MSA, MA-CT	Y	24520 FQ	28760 MW	33470 TQ	USBLS	5/07
Except Computer	Michigan	Y	21990 FQ	26270 MW	32650 TQ	USBLS	5/07
Except Computer	Detroit-Warren-Livonia MSA, MI	Y	22550 FQ	26690 MW	33110 TQ	USBLS	5/07
Except Computer	Grand Rapids-Wyoming MSA, MI	Y	22980 FQ	27900 MW	31200 TQ	USBLS	5/07
Except Computer	Warren-Troy-Farmington Hills PMSA, MI	Y	22810 FQ	26710 MW	33160 TQ	USBLS	5/07
Except Computer	Minnesota	Y	23355 FQ	27383 MW	32223 TQ	MNBLS	10/08-12/08
Except Computer	Duluth-Superior MSA, MN-WI	Y	25187 FQ	33732 MW	39550 TQ	MNBLS	10/08-12/08
Except Computer	Minneapolis-Saint Paul MSA, MN-WI	Y	23574 FQ	27737 MW	32462 TQ	MNBLS	10/08-12/08
Except Computer	Rochester MSA, MN	Y	27994 FQ	30136 MW	32442 TQ	MNBLS	10/08-12/08
Except Computer	Mississippi	Y	19150 FQ	22260 MW	25800 TQ	USBLS	5/07
Except Computer	Jackson MSA, MS	Y	19580 FQ	23020 MW	26840 TQ	USBLS	5/07
Except Computer	Missouri	Y	20820 FQ	24590 MW	29940 TQ	USBLS	5/07
Except Computer	Jefferson City MSA, MO	Y	18230 FQ	24970 MW	32400 TQ	USBLS	5/07
Except Computer	Kansas City MSA, MO-KS	Y	22350 FQ	28730 MW	35390 TQ	USBLS	5/07
Except Computer	St. Louis MSA, MO-IL	Y	20260 FQ	23160 MW	27080 TQ	USBLS	5/07
Except Computer	Montana	Y	20410 FQ	24790 MW	30870 TQ	USBLS	5/07
Except Computer	Billings MSA, MT	Y	21100 FQ	22710 MW	24340 TQ	USBLS	5/07
Except Computer	Nebraska	Y	20680 FQ	23570 MW	28700 TQ	USBLS	5/07

AE Average entry wage	**AW** Average wage paid	**FQ** First quartile wage	**LO** Lowest wage paid	**MTC** Median total compensation	**TCC** Total cash compensation
AER Average entry range	**AWR** Average wage range	**H** Hourly	**LR** Low end range	**MW** Median wage paid	**TQ** Third quartile wage
AEX Average experienced wage	**AXR** Average experienced range	**HI** Highest wage paid	**M** Monthly	**MWR** Median wage range	**W** Weekly
ATC Average total compensation	**D** Daily	**HR** High end range	**MCC** Median cash compensation	**S** See annotated source	**Y** Yearly

Occupation/Type/Industry	Location	Per	Low	Mid	High	Source	Date
Office Machine Operator							
Except Computer	Omaha-Council Bluffs MSA, NE-IA	Y	21270 FQ	24340 MW	29910 TQ	USBLS	5/07
Except Computer	Nevada	H	9.85 FQ	11.97 MW	14.50 TQ	NVBLS	5/08
Except Computer	Las Vegas-Paradise MSA, NV	H	9.83 FQ	11.92 MW	14.30 TQ	NVBLS	5/08
Except Computer	New Hampshire	H	10.89 AE	15.18 MW	17.47 AEX	NHBLS	6/08
Except Computer	Manchester MSA, NH	Y	19650 FQ	22720 MW	25270 TQ	USBLS	5/07
Except Computer	New Jersey	Y	21000 FQ	27240 MW	34820 TQ	USBLS	5/07
Except Computer	Camden PMSA, NJ	Y	22220 FQ	25280 MW	31650 TQ	USBLS	5/07
Except Computer	Edison PMSA, NJ	Y	22890 FQ	28630 MW	34390 TQ	USBLS	5/07
Except Computer	Newark-Union PMSA, NJ-PA	Y	19990 FQ	26680 MW	35110 TQ	USBLS	5/07
Except Computer	Albuquerque MSA, NM	Y	26150 FQ	28830 MW	39350 TQ	USBLS	5/07
Except Computer	New York	Y	21740 FQ	25870 MW	30960 TQ	USBLS	5/07
Except Computer	Albany-Schenectady-Troy MSA, NY	Y	18520 FQ	21380 MW	26140 TQ	USBLS	5/07
Except Computer	Buffalo-Niagara Falls MSA, NY	Y	17570 FQ	20060 MW	24920 TQ	USBLS	5/07
Except Computer	Nassau-Suffolk PMSA, NY	Y	23930 FQ	31240 MW	39740 TQ	USBLS	5/07
Except Computer	New York-Northern New Jersey-Long Island MSA, NY-NJ-PA	Y	22410 FQ	26700 MW	32270 TQ	USBLS	5/07
Except Computer	North Carolina	Y	19490 FQ	23190 MW	29990 TQ	USBLS	5/07
Except Computer	Charlotte-Gastonia-Concord MSA, NC-SC	Y	18020 FQ	21710 MW	30100 TQ	USBLS	5/07
Except Computer	Durham MSA, NC	Y	22980 FQ	25060 MW	28780 TQ	USBLS	5/07
Except Computer	Raleigh-Cary MSA, NC	Y	20970 FQ	23140 MW	29410 TQ	USBLS	5/07
Except Computer	North Dakota	Y	20610 FQ	24760 MW	28270 TQ	USBLS	5/07
Except Computer	Fargo MSA, ND-MN	Y	21430 FQ	26190 MW	28990 TQ	USBLS	5/07
Except Computer	Ohio	Y	21290 FQ	25590 MW	32260 TQ	USBLS	5/07
Except Computer	Cincinnati-Middletown MSA, OH-KY-IN	Y	23630 FQ	28620 MW	34960 TQ	USBLS	5/07
Except Computer	Cleveland-Elyria-Mentor MSA, OH	Y	21740 FQ	25920 MW	35090 TQ	USBLS	5/07
Except Computer	Columbus MSA, OH	Y	21070 FQ	24940 MW	31580 TQ	USBLS	5/07
Except Computer	Dayton MSA, OH	Y	21450 FQ	24760 MW	30640 TQ	USBLS	5/07
Except Computer	Oklahoma	Y	17900 FQ	22880 MW	30040 TQ	USBLS	5/07
Except Computer	Oklahoma City MSA, OK	Y	22560 FQ	30290 MW	40900 TQ	USBLS	5/07
Except Computer	Tulsa MSA, OK	Y	16810 FQ	20460 MW	25610 TQ	USBLS	5/07
Except Computer	Oregon	H	9.50 FQ	11.89 MW	15.40 TQ	ORBLS	5/08
Except Computer	Medford MSA, OR	Y	20830 FQ	26080 MW	31020 TQ	USBLS	5/07
Except Computer	Portland-Vancouver-Beaverton MSA, OR-WA	Y	19050 FQ	24040 MW	31210 TQ	USBLS	5/07
Except Computer	Pennsylvania	Y	20480 FQ	24600 MW	31110 TQ	USBLS	5/07
Except Computer	Allentown-Bethlehem-Easton MSA, PA-NJ	Y	19000 FQ	22020 MW	26270 TQ	USBLS	5/07
Except Computer	Philadelphia-Camden-Wilmington MSA, PA-NJ-DE-MD	Y	22130 FQ	27690 MW	33410 TQ	USBLS	5/07
Except Computer	Pittsburgh MSA, PA	Y	20180 FQ	23240 MW	27820 TQ	USBLS	5/07
Except Computer	Rhode Island	Y	23610 FQ	27850 MW	31040 TQ	USBLS	5/07
Except Computer	Providence-Fall River-Warwick MSA, RI-MA	Y	22210 FQ	27410 MW	30890 TQ	USBLS	5/07
Except Computer	South Carolina	Y	18130 FQ	22390 MW	27770 TQ	USBLS	5/07
Except Computer	Columbia MSA, SC	Y	17060 FQ	21180 MW	26200 TQ	USBLS	5/07
Except Computer	South Dakota	Y	19070 FQ	21405 MW	25347 TQ	SDBLS	7/08-9/08
Except Computer	Sioux Falls MSA, SD	Y	19361 FQ	22005 MW	25715 TQ	SDBLS	7/08-9/08
Except Computer	Tennessee	Y	21050 FQ	25710 MW	29700 TQ	USBLS	5/07
Except Computer	Memphis MSA, TN-MS-AR	Y	21580 FQ	26000 MW	29660 TQ	USBLS	5/07
Except Computer	Nashville-Davidson-Murfreesboro MSA, TN	Y	19300 FQ	24960 MW	30030 TQ	USBLS	5/07
Except Computer	Texas	Y	20140 FQ	24270 MW	29420 TQ	USBLS	5/07
Except Computer	Austin-Round Rock MSA, TX	Y	20480 FQ	25160 MW	29960 TQ	USBLS	5/07
Except Computer	Corpus Christi MSA, TX	Y	20800 FQ	23180 MW	27030 TQ	USBLS	5/07
Except Computer	Dallas-Fort Worth-Arlington MSA, TX	Y	22350 FQ	26460 MW	30840 TQ	USBLS	5/07
Except Computer	El Paso MSA, TX	Y	19370 FQ	22850 MW	27060 TQ	USBLS	5/07
Except Computer	Houston-Sugar Land-Baytown MSA, TX	Y	18900 FQ	23000 MW	28230 TQ	USBLS	5/07
Except Computer	San Antonio MSA, TX	Y	18280 FQ	21540 MW	26690 TQ	USBLS	5/07
Except Computer	Utah	Y	22070 FQ	26930 MW	36190 TQ	USBLS	5/07
Except Computer	Salt Lake City MSA, UT	Y	22600 FQ	27170 MW	35010 TQ	USBLS	5/07
Except Computer	Vermont	Y	22540 FQ	26690 MW	32020 TQ	USBLS	5/07

AE	Average entry wage	AW	Average wage paid	FQ	First quartile wage	LO Lowest wage paid	MTC Median total compensation	TCC Total cash compensation
AER	Average entry range	AWR	Average wage range	H	Hourly	LR Low end range	MW Median wage paid	TQ Third quartile wage
AEX	Average experienced wage	AXR	Average experienced range	HI	Highest wage paid	M Monthly	MWR Median wage range	W Weekly
ATC	Average total compensation	D	Daily	HR	High end range	MCC Median cash compensation	S See annotated source	Y Yearly

Occupation/Type/Industry	Location	Per	Low	Mid	High	Source	Date
Office Machine Operator							
Except Computer	Burlington-South Burlington MSA, VT	Y	24040 FQ	28520 MW	36490 TQ	USBLS	5/07
Except Computer	Virginia	Y	22150 FQ	26660 MW	32010 TQ	USBLS	5/07
Except Computer	Richmond MSA, VA	Y	21330 FQ	25500 MW	31130 TQ	USBLS	5/07
Except Computer	Virginia Beach-Norfolk-Newport News MSA, VA-NC	Y	19630 FQ	23470 MW	28940 TQ	USBLS	5/07
Except Computer	Washington	H	9.78 FQ	11.97 MW	15.87 TQ	WABLS	3/08
Except Computer	Seattle-Tacoma-Bellevue MSA, WA	Y	20760 FQ	25240 MW	34820 TQ	USBLS	5/07
Except Computer	West Virginia	Y	17768 FQ	20063 MW	25563 TQ	WVBLS	7/08-9/08
Except Computer	Charleston MSA, WV	Y	17230 FQ	18870 MW	23950 TQ	USBLS	5/07
Except Computer	Wisconsin	Y	20950 FQ	23740 MW	28670 TQ	USBLS	5/07
Except Computer	Milwaukee-Waukesha-West Allis MSA, WI	Y	21150 FQ	24070 MW	30320 TQ	USBLS	5/07
Except Computer	Wyoming	Y	13627 FQ	15438 MW	20196 TQ	WYBLS	9/08
Except Computer	Cheyenne MSA, WY	Y	21076 FQ	22871 MW	24650 TQ	WYBLS	9/08
Except Computer	Puerto Rico	Y	16700 FQ	19820 MW	25430 TQ	USBLS	5/07
Except Computer	San Juan-Caguas-Guaynabo MSA, PR	Y	16860 FQ	19710 MW	24560 TQ	USBLS	5/07
Office Worker							
United States Census Bureau	United States	H	8.25 LO		19.00 HI	DNEWS02	2008-2009
Oil and Gas Well Inspector							
State Government	Ohio	H	16.35 LO		19.88 HI	ODAS	2008
Oiler-Rigger							
Municipal Government	Seattle, WA	H	19.91 LO		20.67 HI	CSSS	7/5/06
Ombudsman							
Department of Health and Human Services	New Hampshire	Y		58805 AW		NHUL03	2008
On-Camera Host							
Infomercial	United States	S	1134 LO			AFTRA2	10/30/06-10/29/08
Open Space Ranger							
Municipal Government	Walnut Creek, CA	Y	53885 LO		65514 HI	WCSWP	6/27/08
Operating Engineer and Other Construction Equipment Operator	Alabama	Y	26070 FQ	30570 MW	37060 TQ	USBLS	5/07
	Birmingham-Hoover MSA, AL	Y	28030 FQ	32730 MW	39560 TQ	USBLS	5/07
	Alaska	Y	48640 FQ	58800 MW	68380 TQ	USBLS	5/07
	Anchorage MSA, AK	Y	47140 FQ	58740 MW	70060 TQ	USBLS	5/07
	Arizona	Y	34460 FQ	40700 MW	47270 TQ	USBLS	5/07
	Flagstaff MSA, AZ	Y	31770 FQ	37290 MW	47600 TQ	USBLS	5/07
	Phoenix-Mesa-Scottsdale MSA, AZ	Y	35130 FQ	41820 MW	47960 TQ	USBLS	5/07
	Tucson MSA, AZ	Y	31860 FQ	38910 MW	45490 TQ	USBLS	5/07
	Arkansas	Y	24170 FQ	28150 MW	32640 TQ	USBLS	5/07
	Little Rock-North Little Rock MSA, AR	Y	23700 FQ	30060 MW	37050 TQ	USBLS	5/07
	California	H	22.91 FQ	29.94 MW	36.14 TQ	CABLS	1/08-3/08
	Los Angeles-Long Beach-Glendale PMSA, CA	H	24.92 FQ	33.32 MW	38.13 TQ	CABLS	1/08-3/08
	Oakland-Fremont-Hayward MSA, CA	H	26.87 FQ	32.41 MW	37.57 TQ	CABLS	1/08-3/08
	Riverside-San Bernardino-Ontario MSA, CA	H	22.53 FQ	28.60 MW	33.68 TQ	CABLS	1/08-3/08
	Sacramento-Arden Arcade-Roseville MSA, CA	H	23.10 FQ	29.42 MW	35.48 TQ	CABLS	1/08-3/08
	San Diego-Carlsbad-San Marcos MSA, CA	H	23.90 FQ	30.33 MW	36.00 TQ	CABLS	1/08-3/08
	San Francisco-San Mateo-Redwood PMSA, CA	H	30.16 FQ	34.86 MW	39.26 TQ	CABLS	1/08-3/08
	San Jose-Sunnyvale-Santa Clara MSA, CA	H	24.27 FQ	31.29 MW	36.04 TQ	CABLS	1/08-3/08
	Santa Ana-Anaheim-Irvine PMSA, CA	Y	52360 FQ	66680 MW	77780 TQ	USBLS	5/07
	Colorado	Y	34620 FQ	41320 MW	47970 TQ	USBLS	5/07
	Denver-Aurora MSA, CO	Y	36800 FQ	42810 MW	48770 TQ	USBLS	5/07

Occupation/Type/Industry	Location	Per	Low	Mid	High	Source	Date
Operating Engineer and Other Construction Equipment Operator							
	Connecticut	H	19.64 AE	25.58 MW		CTBLS	1/08-3/08
	Bridgeport-Stamford-Norwalk MSA, CT	Y	55150 FQ	63360 MW	78540 TQ	USBLS	5/07
	Hartford-West Hartford-East Hartford MSA, CT	Y	41440 FQ	49400 MW	59200 TQ	USBLS	5/07
	Delaware	Y	33880 FQ	40300 MW	50000 TQ	USBLS	5/07
	Wilmington PMSA, DE-MD-NJ	Y	37400 FQ	45870 MW	54840 TQ	USBLS	5/07
	District of Columbia	Y	43810 FQ	49340 MW	56910 TQ	USBLS	5/07
	Washington-Arlington-Alexandria MSA, DC-VA-MD-WV	Y	35570 FQ	42820 MW	50260 TQ	USBLS	5/07
	Florida	Y	26780 FQ	31700 MW	38340 TQ	USBLS	5/07
	Fort Lauderdale-Pompano Beach-Deerfield Beach PMSA, FL	Y	28870 FQ	34700 MW	40730 TQ	USBLS	5/07
	Jacksonville MSA, FL	Y	26760 FQ	30680 MW	36530 TQ	USBLS	5/07
	Miami-Fort Lauderdale-Miami Beach MSA, FL	Y	29570 FQ	35860 MW	43430 TQ	USBLS	5/07
	Orlando-Kissimmee MSA, FL	Y	27680 FQ	32890 MW	39530 TQ	USBLS	5/07
	Tampa-St. Petersburg-Clearwater MSA, FL	Y	25460 FQ	29330 MW	34570 TQ	USBLS	5/07
	West Palm Beach-Boca Raton-Boynton Beach PMSA, FL	Y	27560 FQ	32590 MW	39270 TQ	USBLS	5/07
	Georgia	Y	25100 FQ	29640 MW	35600 TQ	USBLS	5/07
	Atlanta-Sandy Springs-Marietta MSA, GA	Y	27490 FQ	32020 MW	38180 TQ	USBLS	5/07
	Savannah MSA, GA	Y	22550 FQ	26180 MW	32630 TQ	USBLS	5/07
	Hawaii	Y	51150 FQ	67350 MW	75690 TQ	USBLS	5/07
	Honolulu MSA, HI	Y	55130 FQ	67850 MW	76740 TQ	USBLS	5/07
	Idaho	Y	30180 FQ	35660 MW	41260 TQ	USBLS	5/07
	Boise City-Nampa MSA, ID	Y	27090 FQ	33540 MW	37770 TQ	USBLS	5/07
	Idaho Falls MSA, ID	Y	33120 FQ	39020 MW	50290 TQ	USBLS	5/07
	Illinois	Y	52330 FQ	69690 MW	83990 TQ	USBLS	5/07
	Chicago-Naperville-Joliet MSA, IL-IN-WI	Y	60620 FQ	75620 MW	86780 TQ	USBLS	5/07
	Indiana	Y	32900 FQ	42130 MW	56990 TQ	USBLS	5/07
	Gary PMSA, IN	Y	45090 FQ	60450 MW	72650 TQ	USBLS	5/07
	Indianapolis-Carmel MSA, IN	Y	35640 FQ	47980 MW	58470 TQ	USBLS	5/07
	Iowa	Y	32790 FQ	39320 MW	47070 TQ	USBLS	5/07
	Des Moines-West Des Moines MSA, IA	Y	38480 FQ	44300 MW	50900 TQ	USBLS	5/07
	Kansas	Y	26810 FQ	31590 MW	40580 TQ	USBLS	5/07
	Wichita MSA, KS	Y	26410 FQ	30090 MW	35390 TQ	USBLS	5/07
	Kentucky	Y	31290 FQ	36503 MW	42705 TQ	KYBLS	2008
	Elizabethtown MSA, KY	Y	28260 FQ	35150 MW	49600 TQ	USBLS	5/07
	Louisville-Jefferson County MSA, KY-IN	Y	32930 FQ	39020 MW	48040 TQ	USBLS	5/07
	Louisiana	H	12.71 FQ	15.55 MW	19.53 TQ	LABLS	1/08-3/08
	Baton Rouge MSA, LA	Y	26140 FQ	32220 MW	43290 TQ	USBLS	5/07
	Lake Charles MSA, LA	Y	26350 FQ	34700 MW	42190 TQ	USBLS	5/07
	New Orleans-Metairie-Kenner MSA, LA	Y	29290 FQ	35350 MW	42830 TQ	USBLS	5/07
	Maine	Y	27500 FQ	31990 MW	37670 TQ	USBLS	5/07
	Portland-South Portland-Biddeford MSA, ME	Y	28740 FQ	31990 MW	36890 TQ	USBLS	5/07
	Maryland	Y		41650 MW		MDBLS	3/08
	Baltimore-Towson MSA, MD	Y	34910 FQ	39800 MW	46580 TQ	USBLS	5/07
	Bethesda-Gaithersburg-Frederick PMSA, MD	Y	35820 FQ	42730 MW	52680 TQ	USBLS	5/07
	Massachusetts	Y	44500 FQ	55070 MW	68000 TQ	USBLS	5/07
	Boston-Cambridge-Quincy NECTA, MA	Y	50830 FQ	62700 MW	73130 TQ	USBLS	5/07
	New Bedford MSA, MA	Y	41420 FQ	49270 MW	56440 TQ	USBLS	5/07
	Worcester MSA, MA-CT	Y	41860 FQ	48340 MW	63740 TQ	USBLS	5/07
	Michigan	Y	36940 FQ	44050 MW	51930 TQ	USBLS	5/07
	Detroit-Warren-Livonia MSA, MI	Y	42170 FQ	48600 MW	56070 TQ	USBLS	5/07
	Flint MSA, MI	Y	44320 FQ	50980 MW	60730 TQ	USBLS	5/07

AE Average entry wage	**AW** Average wage paid	**FQ** First quartile wage	**LO** Lowest wage paid	**MTC** Median total compensation **TCC** Total cash compensation
AER Average entry range	**AWR** Average wage range	**H** Hourly	**LR** Low end range	**MW** Median wage paid **TQ** Third quartile wage
AEX Average experienced wage	**AXR** Average experienced range **HI** Highest wage paid		**M** Monthly	**MWR** Median wage range **W** Weekly
ATC Average total compensation **D** Daily		**HR** High end range	**MCC** Median cash compensation **S** See annotated source	**Y** Yearly

Occupation/Type/Industry	Location	Per	Low	Mid	High	Source	Date
Operating Engineer and Other Construction Equipment Operator							
	Grand Rapids-Wyoming MSA, MI	Y	31350 FQ	39380 MW	45720 TQ	USBLS	5/07
	Muskegon-Norton Shores MSA, MI	Y	33910 FQ	37510 MW	42760 TQ	USBLS	5/07
	Warren-Troy-Farmington Hills PMSA, MI	Y	42250 FQ	49410 MW	57270 TQ	USBLS	5/07
	Minnesota	Y	41322 FQ	51945 MW	62810 TQ	MNBLS	10/08-12/08
	Duluth-Superior MSA, MN-WI	Y	44167 FQ	49142 MW	53958 TQ	MNBLS	10/08-12/08
	Minneapolis-Saint Paul MSA, MN-WI	Y	51376 FQ	60397 MW	69566 TQ	MNBLS	10/08-12/08
	Rochester MSA, MN	Y	40006 FQ	49706 MW	58719 TQ	MNBLS	10/08-12/08
	Mississippi	Y	23160 FQ	27390 MW	31380 TQ	USBLS	5/07
	Jackson MSA, MS	Y	23260 FQ	27520 MW	30550 TQ	USBLS	5/07
	Pascagoula MSA, MS	Y	22970 FQ	26460 MW	30590 TQ	USBLS	5/07
	Missouri	Y	32590 FQ	43640 MW	56620 TQ	USBLS	5/07
	Kansas City MSA, MO-KS	Y	34300 FQ	46960 MW	58060 TQ	USBLS	5/07
	St. Louis MSA, MO-IL	Y	42490 FQ	53100 MW	59450 TQ	USBLS	5/07
	Montana	Y	33800 FQ	40110 MW	46810 TQ	USBLS	5/07
	Billings MSA, MT	Y	35470 FQ	42400 MW	46820 TQ	USBLS	5/07
	Nebraska	Y	27600 FQ	33550 MW	41010 TQ	USBLS	5/07
	Omaha-Council Bluffs MSA, NE-IA	Y	30230 FQ	38520 MW	45730 TQ	USBLS	5/07
	Nevada	H	19.52 FQ	23.72 MW	30.13 TQ	NVBLS	5/08
	Las Vegas-Paradise MSA, NV	H	19.65 FQ	25.75 MW	32.59 TQ	NVBLS	5/08
	New Hampshire	H	16.40 AE	20.07 MW	22.16 AEX	NHBLS	6/08
	Manchester MSA, NH	Y	35780 FQ	39530 MW	43040 TQ	USBLS	5/07
	Nashua NECTA, NH-MA	Y	35440 FQ	41640 MW	48720 TQ	USBLS	5/07
	New Jersey	Y	42910 FQ	56340 MW	72810 TQ	USBLS	5/07
	Camden PMSA, NJ	Y	40180 FQ	52440 MW	70630 TQ	USBLS	5/07
	Edison PMSA, NJ	Y	42080 FQ	53050 MW	72140 TQ	USBLS	5/07
	Newark-Union PMSA, NJ-PA	Y	43690 FQ	56410 MW	71770 TQ	USBLS	5/07
	Vineland-Millville-Bridgeton MSA, NJ	Y	34740 FQ	44750 MW	59410 TQ	USBLS	5/07
	New Mexico	Y	28720 FQ	33770 MW	40380 TQ	USBLS	5/07
	Albuquerque MSA, NM	Y	29830 FQ	33930 MW	39660 TQ	USBLS	5/07
	New York	Y	39950 FQ	54800 MW	77150 TQ	USBLS	5/07
	Albany-Schenectady-Troy MSA, NY	Y	37750 FQ	46350 MW	59520 TQ	USBLS	5/07
	Buffalo-Niagara Falls MSA, NY	Y	29890 FQ	43040 MW	55270 TQ	USBLS	5/07
	Nassau-Suffolk PMSA, NY	Y	49000 FQ	63990 MW	82470 TQ	USBLS	5/07
	New York-Northern New Jersey-Long Island MSA, NY-NJ-PA	Y	49940 FQ	67990 MW	84480 TQ	USBLS	5/07
	North Carolina	Y	26580 FQ	30700 MW	36430 TQ	USBLS	5/07
	Charlotte-Gastonia-Concord MSA, NC-SC	Y	27330 FQ	31150 MW	36670 TQ	USBLS	5/07
	Raleigh-Cary MSA, NC	Y	27290 FQ	30990 MW	36810 TQ	USBLS	5/07
	Winston-Salem MSA, NC	Y	24930 FQ	29600 MW	35100 TQ	USBLS	5/07
	North Dakota	Y	30540 FQ	37050 MW	46130 TQ	USBLS	5/07
	Fargo MSA, ND-MN	Y	32580 FQ	37610 MW	42790 TQ	USBLS	5/07
	Ohio	Y	36110 FQ	46780 MW	57460 TQ	USBLS	5/07
	Canton-Massillon MSA, OH	Y	34940 FQ	39540 MW	49660 TQ	USBLS	5/07
	Cincinnati-Middletown MSA, OH-KY-IN	Y	33420 FQ	42360 MW	51450 TQ	USBLS	5/07
	Cleveland-Elyria-Mentor MSA, OH	Y	44650 FQ	54020 MW	64220 TQ	USBLS	5/07
	Columbus MSA, OH	Y	36000 FQ	41890 MW	53670 TQ	USBLS	5/07
	Dayton MSA, OH	Y	36060 FQ	46160 MW	59020 TQ	USBLS	5/07
	Springfield MSA, OH	Y	36320 FQ	40300 MW	56090 TQ	USBLS	5/07
	Oklahoma	Y	25330 FQ	29330 MW	34860 TQ	USBLS	5/07
	Oklahoma City MSA, OK	Y	25730 FQ	29310 MW	34390 TQ	USBLS	5/07
	Tulsa MSA, OK	Y	26560 FQ	29930 MW	34510 TQ	USBLS	5/07
	Oregon	H	17.97 FQ	21.64 MW	26.65 TQ	ORBLS	5/08
	Portland-Vancouver-Beaverton MSA, OR-WA	Y	41990 FQ	49950 MW	59650 TQ	USBLS	5/07
	Salem MSA, OR	Y	35840 FQ	40010 MW	48640 TQ	USBLS	5/07
	Pennsylvania	Y	33420 FQ	41260 MW	52330 TQ	USBLS	5/07

AE	Average entry wage	AW	Average wage paid	FQ	First quartile wage	LO	Lowest wage paid	MTC	Median total compensation	TCC	Total cash compensation
AER	Average entry range	AWR	Average wage range	H	Hourly	LR	Low end range	MW	Median wage paid	TQ	Third quartile wage
AEX	Average experienced wage	AXR	Average experienced range	HI	Highest wage paid	M	Monthly	MWR	Median wage range	W	Weekly
ATC	Average total compensation	D	Daily	HR	High end range	MCC	Median cash compensation	S	See annotated source	Y	Yearly

Occupation/Type/Industry	Location	Per	Low	Mid	High	Source	Date
Operating Engineer and Other Construction Equipment Operator	Allentown-Bethlehem-Easton MSA, PA-NJ	Y	33530 FQ	39410 MW	48320 TQ	USBLS	5/07
	Philadelphia-Camden-Wilmington MSA, PA-NJ-DE-MD	Y	39130 FQ	47900 MW	62700 TQ	USBLS	5/07
	Pittsburgh MSA, PA	Y	35200 FQ	44180 MW	53320 TQ	USBLS	5/07
	Rhode Island	Y	49200 FQ	56920 MW	64410 TQ	USBLS	5/07
	Providence-Fall River-Warwick MSA, RI-MA	Y	49420 FQ	56970 MW	64740 TQ	USBLS	5/07
	South Carolina	Y	25020 FQ	30070 MW	35350 TQ	USBLS	5/07
	Charleston-North Charleston MSA, SC	Y	27360 FQ	31700 MW	35910 TQ	USBLS	5/07
	Columbia MSA, SC	Y	24460 FQ	29840 MW	35900 TQ	USBLS	5/07
	Spartanburg MSA, SC	Y	26000 FQ	30540 MW	35170 TQ	USBLS	5/07
	South Dakota	Y	29065 FQ	33023 MW	38981 TQ	SDBLS	7/08-9/08
	Sioux Falls MSA, SD	Y	31221 FQ	36312 MW	40558 TQ	SDBLS	7/08-9/08
	Tennessee	Y	26430 FQ	30640 MW	36280 TQ	USBLS	5/07
	Johnson City MSA, TN	Y	22140 FQ	25310 MW	29170 TQ	USBLS	5/07
	Memphis MSA, TN-MS-AR	Y	25250 FQ	31500 MW	38050 TQ	USBLS	5/07
	Nashville-Davidson-Murfreesboro MSA, TN	Y	27290 FQ	31320 MW	36470 TQ	USBLS	5/07
	Texas	Y	25120 FQ	29230 MW	34600 TQ	USBLS	5/07
	Austin-Round Rock MSA, TX	Y	25910 FQ	29390 MW	34290 TQ	USBLS	5/07
	Dallas-Fort Worth-Arlington MSA, TX	Y	25540 FQ	29990 MW	36250 TQ	USBLS	5/07
	El Paso MSA, TX	Y	21980 FQ	25930 MW	30880 TQ	USBLS	5/07
	Houston-Sugar Land-Baytown MSA, TX	Y	26550 FQ	30260 MW	35920 TQ	USBLS	5/07
	San Antonio MSA, TX	Y	24200 FQ	28030 MW	32380 TQ	USBLS	5/07
	Utah	Y	29660 FQ	35070 MW	40190 TQ	USBLS	5/07
	Salt Lake City MSA, UT	Y	26150 FQ	34000 MW	39120 TQ	USBLS	5/07
	Vermont	Y	29800 FQ	33900 MW	39000 TQ	USBLS	5/07
	Burlington-South Burlington MSA, VT	Y	31330 FQ	34380 MW	37400 TQ	USBLS	5/07
	Virginia	Y	28330 FQ	34230 MW	41560 TQ	USBLS	5/07
	Richmond MSA, VA	Y	29020 FQ	34020 MW	40030 TQ	USBLS	5/07
	Virginia Beach-Norfolk-Newport News MSA, VA-NC	Y	27840 FQ	33150 MW	40080 TQ	USBLS	5/07
	Washington	H	19.52 FQ	25.08 MW	30.68 TQ	WABLS	3/08
	Seattle-Tacoma-Bellevue MSA, WA	Y	45090 FQ	56030 MW	65500 TQ	USBLS	5/07
	West Virginia	Y	26682 FQ	33285 MW	44496 TQ	WVBLS	7/08-9/08
	Charleston MSA, WV	Y	26940 FQ	37110 MW	47150 TQ	USBLS	5/07
	Huntington-Ashland MSA, WV-KY-OH	Y	31040 FQ	38450 MW	49060 TQ	USBLS	5/07
	Wisconsin	Y	39230 FQ	49100 MW	58490 TQ	USBLS	5/07
	Appleton MSA, WI	Y	41390 FQ	55810 MW	68860 TQ	USBLS	5/07
	Milwaukee-Waukesha-West Allis MSA, WI	Y	46460 FQ	55300 MW	61880 TQ	USBLS	5/07
	Wyoming	Y	35357 FQ	41279 MW	53295 TQ	WYBLS	9/08
	Cheyenne MSA, WY	Y	32294 FQ	38388 MW	46105 TQ	WYBLS	9/08
	Puerto Rico	Y	16300 FQ	19060 MW	22740 TQ	USBLS	5/07
	San Juan-Caguas-Guaynabo MSA, PR	Y	16900 FQ	19740 MW	23430 TQ	USBLS	5/07
	Virgin Islands	Y	30120 FQ	35180 MW	39250 TQ	USBLS	5/07
	Guam	Y	22150 FQ	25820 MW	30110 TQ	USBLS	5/07
Operational Zoologist and Wildlife Biologist State Government	New Mexico	Y	27664 LO		49171 HI	AFT02	3/1/08
Operations Research Analyst	Alabama	Y	51430 FQ	77450 MW	96520 TQ	USBLS	5/07
	Birmingham-Hoover MSA, AL	Y	53090 FQ	74950 MW	91620 TQ	USBLS	5/07
	Montgomery MSA, AL	Y	39560 FQ	45840 MW	51350 TQ	USBLS	5/07
	Arizona	Y	41780 FQ	52900 MW	70770 TQ	USBLS	5/07
	Phoenix-Mesa-Scottsdale MSA, AZ	Y	42110 FQ	53710 MW	71660 TQ	USBLS	5/07
	Tucson MSA, AZ	Y	37320 FQ	43270 MW	48270 TQ	USBLS	5/07
	Arkansas	Y	39230 FQ	50940 MW	62760 TQ	USBLS	5/07

AE	Average entry wage	**AW**	Average wage paid	**FQ**	First quartile wage	**LO**	Lowest wage paid	**MTC**	Median total compensation	**TCC**	Total cash compensation
AER	Average entry range	**AWR**	Average wage range	**H**	Hourly	**LR**	Low end range	**MW**	Median wage paid	**TQ**	Third quartile wage
AEX	Average experienced wage	**AXR**	Average experienced range	**HI**	Highest wage paid	**M**	Monthly	**MWR**	Median wage range	**W**	Weekly
ATC	Average total compensation	**D**	Daily	**HR**	High end range	**MCC**	Median cash compensation	**S**	See annotated source	**Y**	Yearly

Operations Research Analyst

Occupation/Type/Industry	Location	Per	Low	Mid	High	Source	Date
Operations Research Analyst	California	H	27.36 FQ	34.31 MW	44.02 TQ	CABLS	1/08-3/08
	Los Angeles-Long Beach- Glendale PMSA, CA	H	25.47 FQ	33.19 MW	44.18 TQ	CABLS	1/08-3/08
	Oakland-Fremont-Hayward MSA, CA	H	27.55 FQ	34.68 MW	42.09 TQ	CABLS	1/08-3/08
	Riverside-San Bernardino- Ontario MSA, CA	H	25.82 FQ	34.67 MW	45.42 TQ	CABLS	1/08-3/08
	Sacramento-Arden Arcade- Roseville MSA, CA	H	27.69 FQ	31.53 MW	36.70 TQ	CABLS	1/08-3/08
	San Diego-Carlsbad-San Marcos MSA, CA	H	28.94 FQ	38.07 MW	50.00 TQ	CABLS	1/08-3/08
	San Francisco-San Mateo- Redwood PMSA, CA	H	26.79 FQ	33.78 MW	45.78 TQ	CABLS	1/08-3/08
	San Jose-Sunnyvale-Santa Clara MSA, CA	H	27.02 FQ	38.96 MW	51.57 TQ	CABLS	1/08-3/08
	Santa Ana-Anaheim-Irvine PMSA, CA	Y	55880 FQ	69110 MW	82070 TQ	USBLS	5/07
	Colorado	Y	51860 FQ	65720 MW	85140 TQ	USBLS	5/07
	Denver-Aurora MSA, CO	Y	50430 FQ	60970 MW	75040 TQ	USBLS	5/07
	Connecticut	H	23.05 AE	35.18 MW		CTBLS	1/08-3/08
	Bridgeport-Stamford-Norwalk MSA, CT	Y	59510 FQ	74200 MW	90330 TQ	USBLS	5/07
	Hartford-West Hartford-East Hartford MSA, CT	Y	52700 FQ	73470 MW	90840 TQ	USBLS	5/07
	Delaware	Y	52600 FQ	71310 MW	101030 TQ	USBLS	5/07
	Wilmington PMSA, DE-MD- NJ	Y	52610 FQ	71220 MW	102000 TQ	USBLS	5/07
	District of Columbia	Y	58260 FQ	82740 MW	99430 TQ	USBLS	5/07
	Washington-Arlington- Alexandria MSA, DC-VA- MD-WV	Y	64370 FQ	88910 MW	113310 TQ	USBLS	5/07
	Florida	Y	42470 FQ	54530 MW	70190 TQ	USBLS	5/07
	Fort Lauderdale-Pompano Beach-Deerfield Beach PMSA, FL	Y	41460 FQ	53370 MW	67540 TQ	USBLS	5/07
	Jacksonville MSA, FL	Y	42450 FQ	52600 MW	64660 TQ	USBLS	5/07
	Miami-Fort Lauderdale-Miami Beach MSA, FL	Y	44180 FQ	55440 MW	68810 TQ	USBLS	5/07
	Orlando-Kissimmee MSA, FL	Y	39250 FQ	52880 MW	73060 TQ	USBLS	5/07
	Pensacola-Ferry Pass-Brent MSA, FL	Y	38540 FQ	53270 MW	79750 TQ	USBLS	5/07
	Tampa-St. Petersburg- Clearwater MSA, FL	Y	42140 FQ	53310 MW	64640 TQ	USBLS	5/07
	West Palm Beach-Boca Raton- Boynton Beach PMSA, FL	Y	47990 FQ	59100 MW	74850 TQ	USBLS	5/07
	Georgia	Y	42000 FQ	53290 MW	69930 TQ	USBLS	5/07
	Atlanta-Sandy Springs- Marietta MSA, GA	Y	43250 FQ	54820 MW	72780 TQ	USBLS	5/07
	Hawaii	Y	61840 FQ	71060 MW	85640 TQ	USBLS	5/07
	Honolulu MSA, HI	Y	60300 FQ	71010 MW	86330 TQ	USBLS	5/07
	Idaho	Y	52800 FQ	61290 MW	73500 TQ	USBLS	5/07
	Boise City-Nampa MSA, ID	Y	52590 FQ	62640 MW	74960 TQ	USBLS	5/07
	Illinois	Y	55890 FQ	69350 MW	83620 TQ	USBLS	5/07
	Chicago-Naperville-Joliet MSA, IL-IN-WI	Y	55650 FQ	68500 MW	82270 TQ	USBLS	5/07
	Indiana	Y	51410 FQ	63730 MW	87590 TQ	USBLS	5/07
	Gary PMSA, IN	Y	44370 FQ	53850 MW	63050 TQ	USBLS	5/07
	Indianapolis-Carmel MSA, IN	Y	50850 FQ	64540 MW	90820 TQ	USBLS	5/07
	Iowa	Y	40900 FQ	51330 MW	60200 TQ	USBLS	5/07
	Des Moines-West Des Moines MSA, IA	Y	39890 FQ	49760 MW	59040 TQ	USBLS	5/07
	Kansas	Y	57380 FQ	74330 MW	93000 TQ	USBLS	5/07
	Wichita MSA, KS	Y	31110 FQ	54500 MW	66510 TQ	USBLS	5/07
	Kentucky	Y	43530 FQ	56076 MW	74867 TQ	KYBLS	2008
	Louisville-Jefferson County MSA, KY-IN	Y	41510 FQ	50490 MW	64670 TQ	USBLS	5/07
	Louisiana	H	15.92 FQ	21.14 MW	27.70 TQ	LABLS	1/08-3/08
	Baton Rouge MSA, LA	Y	32930 FQ	43020 MW	55210 TQ	USBLS	5/07
	New Orleans-Metairie-Kenner MSA, LA	Y	35240 FQ	49040 MW	64920 TQ	USBLS	5/07
	Maine	Y	50400 FQ	64140 MW	75720 TQ	USBLS	5/07

AE Average entry wage	**AW** Average wage paid	**FQ** First quartile wage	**LO** Lowest wage paid	**MTC** Median total compensation **TCC** Total cash compensation
AER Average entry range	**AWR** Average wage range	**H** Hourly	**LR** Low end range	**MW** Median wage paid **TQ** Third quartile wage
AEX Average experienced wage	**AXR** Average experienced range	**HI** Highest wage paid	**M** Monthly	**MWR** Median wage range **W** Weekly
ATC Average total compensation **D** Daily		**HR** High end range	**MCC** Median cash compensation **S** See annotated source	**Y** Yearly

Operations Research Analyst

Occupation/Type/Industry	Location	Per	Low	Mid	High	Source	Date
Operations Research Analyst	Portland-South Portland-Biddeford MSA, ME	Y	52470 FQ	64620 MW	75600 TQ	USBLS	5/07
	Maryland	Y		85475 MW		MDBLS	3/08
	Baltimore-Towson MSA, MD	Y	64820 FQ	88760 MW	111670 TQ	USBLS	5/07
	Bethesda-Gaithersburg-Frederick PMSA, MD	Y	50680 FQ	69790 MW	99720 TQ	USBLS	5/07
	Massachusetts	Y	55710 FQ	76730 MW	97890 TQ	USBLS	5/07
	Boston-Cambridge-Quincy NECTA, MA	Y	56620 FQ	78580 MW	98670 TQ	USBLS	5/07
	Worcester MSA, MA-CT	Y	36470 FQ	40330 MW	81220 TQ	USBLS	5/07
	Michigan	Y	58400 FQ	76940 MW	105330 TQ	USBLS	5/07
	Ann Arbor MSA, MI	Y	74680 FQ	109430 MW	127150 TQ	USBLS	5/07
	Detroit-Warren-Livonia MSA, MI	Y	59100 FQ	77290 MW	104660 TQ	USBLS	5/07
	Grand Rapids-Wyoming MSA, MI	Y	55180 FQ	71190 MW	92720 TQ	USBLS	5/07
	Warren-Troy-Farmington Hills PMSA, MI	Y	58700 FQ	77790 MW	110040 TQ	USBLS	5/07
	Minnesota	Y	48492 FQ	62585 MW	94850 TQ	MNBLS	10/08-12/08
	Minneapolis-Saint Paul MSA, MN-WI	Y	48105 FQ	61371 MW	95007 TQ	MNBLS	10/08-12/08
	Mississippi	Y	45040 FQ	58140 MW	72530 TQ	USBLS	5/07
	Missouri	Y	50980 FQ	64580 MW	82630 TQ	USBLS	5/07
	Kansas City MSA, MO-KS	Y	57030 FQ	70820 MW	88990 TQ	USBLS	5/07
	St. Louis MSA, MO-IL	Y	53340 FQ	70130 MW	90150 TQ	USBLS	5/07
	Montana	Y	35080 FQ	39640 MW	49310 TQ	USBLS	5/07
	Nebraska	Y	51990 FQ	69940 MW	85060 TQ	USBLS	5/07
	Lincoln MSA, NE	Y	37670 FQ	45230 MW	59590 TQ	USBLS	5/07
	Omaha-Council Bluffs MSA, NE-IA	Y	54150 FQ	70660 MW	84580 TQ	USBLS	5/07
	Nevada	H	26.78 FQ	33.01 MW	45.59 TQ	NVBLS	5/08
	Las Vegas-Paradise MSA, NV	H	26.68 FQ	34.70 MW	47.32 TQ	NVBLS	5/08
	New Hampshire	H	21.92 AE	29.58 MW	33.82 AEX	NHBLS	6/08
	Manchester MSA, NH	Y	53740 FQ	60660 MW	70310 TQ	USBLS	5/07
	New Jersey	Y	67410 FQ	88160 MW	114250 TQ	USBLS	5/07
	Camden PMSA, NJ	Y	68150 FQ	84470 MW	106850 TQ	USBLS	5/07
	Edison PMSA, NJ	Y	74730 FQ	93630 MW	115990 TQ	USBLS	5/07
	Newark-Union PMSA, NJ-PA	Y	64700 FQ	97120 MW	125780 TQ	USBLS	5/07
	New Mexico	Y	62070 FQ	83260 MW	101240 TQ	USBLS	5/07
	Albuquerque MSA, NM	Y	56350 FQ	86240 MW	107750 TQ	USBLS	5/07
	New York	Y	54650 FQ	72120 MW	100450 TQ	USBLS	5/07
	Albany-Schenectady-Troy MSA, NY	Y	44190 FQ	56010 MW	79890 TQ	USBLS	5/07
	Buffalo-Niagara Falls MSA, NY	Y	46220 FQ	63730 MW	81450 TQ	USBLS	5/07
	Nassau-Suffolk PMSA, NY	Y	58300 FQ	74580 MW	97410 TQ	USBLS	5/07
	New York-Northern New Jersey-Long Island MSA, NY-NJ-PA	Y	60980 FQ	83290 MW	112590 TQ	USBLS	5/07
	North Carolina	Y	51410 FQ	62380 MW	76380 TQ	USBLS	5/07
	Charlotte-Gastonia-Concord MSA, NC-SC	Y	41300 FQ	56180 MW	78240 TQ	USBLS	5/07
	Raleigh-Cary MSA, NC	Y	53630 FQ	64360 MW	76240 TQ	USBLS	5/07
	North Dakota	Y	43510 FQ	53270 MW	68620 TQ	MDBLS	3/07
	Ohio	Y	58960 FQ	73820 MW	90290 TQ	USBLS	5/07
	Cincinnati-Middletown MSA, OH-KY-IN	Y	55740 FQ	74110 MW	85380 TQ	USBLS	5/07
	Cleveland-Elyria-Mentor MSA, OH	Y	57460 FQ	67560 MW	81870 TQ	USBLS	5/07
	Columbus MSA, OH	Y	60890 FQ	74710 MW	92370 TQ	USBLS	5/07
	Dayton MSA, OH	Y	56470 FQ	75730 MW	97070 TQ	USBLS	5/07
	Oklahoma	Y	48320 FQ	65790 MW	89550 TQ	USBLS	5/07
	Oklahoma City MSA, OK	Y	43280 FQ	55700 MW	72970 TQ	USBLS	5/07
	Oregon	H	23.85 FQ	32.29 MW	41.36 TQ	ORBLS	5/08
	Portland-Vancouver-Beaverton MSA, OR-WA	Y	49100 FQ	64300 MW	82290 TQ	USBLS	5/07
	Pennsylvania	Y	51550 FQ	64920 MW	85590 TQ	USBLS	5/07
	Allentown-Bethlehem-Easton MSA, PA-NJ	Y	65880 FQ	78450 MW	117270 TQ	USBLS	5/07
	Philadelphia-Camden-Wilmington MSA, PA-NJ-DE-MD	Y	57180 FQ	73490 MW	100350 TQ	USBLS	5/07

AE	Average entry wage	AW	Average wage paid	FQ	First quartile wage
AER	Average entry range	AWR	Average wage range	H	Hourly
AEX	Average experienced wage	AXR	Average experienced range	HI	Highest wage paid
ATC	Average total compensation	D	Daily	HR	High end range

LO	Lowest wage paid	MTC	Median total compensation	TCC	Total cash compensation
LR	Low end range	MW	Median wage paid	TQ	Third quartile wage
M	Monthly	MWR	Median wage range	W	Weekly
MCC	Median cash compensation	S	See annotated source	Y	Yearly

Occupation/Type/Industry	Location	Per	Low	Mid	High	Source	Date
Operations Research Analyst	Pittsburgh MSA, PA	Y	42410 FQ	51670 MW	68130 TQ	USBLS	5/07
	Rhode Island	Y	52890 FQ	76380 MW	98020 TQ	USBLS	5/07
	Providence-Fall River- Warwick MSA, RI-MA	Y	54920 FQ	76450 MW	98260 TQ	USBLS	5/07
	South Carolina	Y	45020 FQ	60740 MW	79480 TQ	USBLS	5/07
	Charleston-North Charleston MSA, SC	Y	51870 FQ	63090 MW	74510 TQ	USBLS	5/07
	Columbia MSA, SC	Y	43930 FQ	57380 MW	71420 TQ	USBLS	5/07
	South Dakota	Y	38418 FQ	43838 MW	50666 TQ	SDBLS	7/08-9/08
	Sioux Falls MSA, SD	Y	38926 FQ	43993 MW	50678 TQ	SDBLS	7/08-9/08
	Tennessee	Y	47690 FQ	60860 MW	77650 TQ	USBLS	5/07
	Knoxville MSA, TN	Y	34610 FQ	46440 MW	57990 TQ	USBLS	5/07
	Memphis MSA, TN-MS-AR	Y	70920 FQ	86140 MW	98830 TQ	USBLS	5/07
	Nashville-Davidson- Murfreesboro MSA, TN	Y	52240 FQ	66600 MW	76950 TQ	USBLS	5/07
	Texas	Y	49680 FQ	69750 MW	89360 TQ	USBLS	5/07
	Austin-Round Rock MSA, TX	Y	52670 FQ	71130 MW	87970 TQ	USBLS	5/07
	Dallas-Fort Worth-Arlington MSA, TX	Y	42510 FQ	65030 MW	88370 TQ	USBLS	5/07
	El Paso MSA, TX	Y	66660 FQ	78830 MW	92040 TQ	USBLS	5/07
	Houston-Sugar Land-Baytown MSA, TX	Y	55180 FQ	70450 MW	90280 TQ	USBLS	5/07
	San Antonio MSA, TX	Y	57890 FQ	78730 MW	92220 TQ	USBLS	5/07
	Utah	Y	43480 FQ	52980 MW	65460 TQ	USBLS	5/07
	Salt Lake City MSA, UT	Y	42660 FQ	50530 MW	62360 TQ	USBLS	5/07
	Vermont	Y	88020 FQ	95700 MW	103390 TQ	USBLS	5/07
	Burlington-South Burlington MSA, VT	Y	89760 FQ	96680 MW	103600 TQ	USBLS	5/07
	Virginia	Y	65600 FQ	88270 MW	111090 TQ	USBLS	5/07
	Richmond MSA, VA	Y	46490 FQ	66060 MW	88240 TQ	USBLS	5/07
	Virginia Beach-Norfolk- Newport News MSA, VA-NC	Y	61850 FQ	80960 MW	95600 TQ	USBLS	5/07
	Washington	H	30.21 FQ	38.48 MW	47.26 TQ	WABLS	3/08
	Seattle-Tacoma-Bellevue MSA, WA	Y	65250 FQ	82130 MW	99150 TQ	USBLS	5/07
	West Virginia	Y	43825 FQ	53773 MW	63332 TQ	WVBLS	7/08-9/08
	Wisconsin	Y	44380 FQ	56780 MW	72550 TQ	USBLS	5/07
	Milwaukee-Waukesha-West Allis MSA, WI	Y	48210 FQ	60710 MW	74590 TQ	USBLS	5/07
	Wyoming	Y	54330 FQ	69407 MW	85720 TQ	WYBLS	9/08
Ophthalmic Laboratory Technician	Alabama	Y	21710 FQ	26670 MW	34100 TQ	USBLS	5/07
	Birmingham-Hoover MSA, AL	Y	22180 FQ	27270 MW	35070 TQ	USBLS	5/07
	Arizona	Y	18700 FQ	24500 MW	35220 TQ	USBLS	5/07
	Phoenix-Mesa-Scottsdale MSA, AZ	Y	18410 FQ	23320 MW	33240 TQ	USBLS	5/07
	Tucson MSA, AZ	Y	19270 FQ	25480 MW	35160 TQ	USBLS	5/07
	Arkansas	Y	21010 FQ	24280 MW	28560 TQ	USBLS	5/07
	Little Rock-North Little Rock MSA, AR	Y	17100 FQ	21800 MW	38190 TQ	USBLS	5/07
	California	H	10.51 FQ	14.77 MW	20.03 TQ	CABLS	1/08-3/08
	Los Angeles-Long Beach- Glendale PMSA, CA	H	8.96 FQ	11.31 MW	17.60 TQ	CABLS	1/08-3/08
	Oakland-Fremont-Hayward MSA, CA	H	13.44 FQ	18.53 MW	22.40 TQ	CABLS	1/08-3/08
	Riverside-San Bernardino- Ontario MSA, CA	H	11.16 FQ	14.47 MW	18.52 TQ	CABLS	1/08-3/08
	Sacramento-Arden Arcade- Roseville MSA, CA	H	11.55 FQ	14.51 MW	16.92 TQ	CABLS	1/08-3/08
	San Diego-Carlsbad-San Marcos MSA, CA	H	9.43 FQ	13.87 MW	20.30 TQ	CABLS	1/08-3/08
	San Francisco-San Mateo- Redwood PMSA, CA	H	14.59 FQ	17.92 MW	21.52 TQ	CABLS	1/08-3/08
	San Jose-Sunnyvale-Santa Clara MSA, CA	H	13.77 FQ	18.84 MW	23.33 TQ	CABLS	1/08-3/08
	Santa Ana-Anaheim-Irvine PMSA, CA	Y	17620 FQ	19380 MW	26740 TQ	USBLS	5/07
	Colorado	Y	25610 FQ	30500 MW	37810 TQ	USBLS	5/07
	Denver-Aurora MSA, CO	Y	29400 FQ	34670 MW	39640 TQ	USBLS	5/07
	Connecticut	H	9.83 AE	15.33 MW		CTBLS	1/08-3/08

AE	Average entry wage	**AW**	Average wage paid	**FQ**	First quartile wage	**LO** Lowest wage paid	**MTC** Median total compensation	**TCC** Total cash compensation
AER	Average entry range	**AWR**	Average wage range	**H**	Hourly	**LR** Low end range	**MW** Median wage paid	**TQ** Third quartile wage
AEX	Average experienced wage	**AXR**	Average experienced range	**HI**	Highest wage paid	**M** Monthly	**MWR** Median wage range	**W** Weekly
ATC	Average total compensation	**D**	Daily	**HR**	High end range	**MCC** Median cash compensation	**S** See annotated source	**Y** Yearly

Occupation/Type/Industry	Location	Per	Low	Mid	High	Source	Date
Ophthalmic Laboratory Technician	Bridgeport-Stamford-Norwalk MSA, CT	Y	23970 FQ	37090 MW	45400 TQ	USBLS	5/07
	Hartford-West Hartford-East Hartford MSA, CT	Y	24160 FQ	31970 MW	40780 TQ	USBLS	5/07
	Delaware	Y	19790 FQ	23550 MW	28860 TQ	USBLS	5/07
	Dover MSA, DE	Y	18920 FQ	23170 MW	28970 TQ	USBLS	5/07
	Wilmington PMSA, DE-MD-NJ	Y	21060 FQ	23960 MW	28730 TQ	USBLS	5/07
	Washington-Arlington-Alexandria MSA, DC-VA-MD-WV	Y	23220 FQ	26730 MW	31500 TQ	USBLS	5/07
	Florida	Y	20680 FQ	26550 MW	33160 TQ	USBLS	5/07
	Fort Lauderdale-Pompano Beach-Deerfield Beach PMSA, FL	Y	22780 FQ	27690 MW	31710 TQ	USBLS	5/07
	Jacksonville MSA, FL	Y	23560 FQ	33530 MW	39710 TQ	USBLS	5/07
	Miami-Fort Lauderdale-Miami Beach MSA, FL	Y	21500 FQ	27180 MW	31780 TQ	USBLS	5/07
	Orlando-Kissimmee MSA, FL	Y	25680 FQ	33560 MW	39500 TQ	USBLS	5/07
	Tampa-St. Petersburg-Clearwater MSA, FL	Y	22220 FQ	26670 MW	32990 TQ	USBLS	5/07
	West Palm Beach-Boca Raton-Boynton Beach PMSA, FL	Y	25800 FQ	28450 MW	31310 TQ	USBLS	5/07
	Georgia	Y	21490 FQ	25900 MW	30010 TQ	USBLS	5/07
	Atlanta-Sandy Springs-Marietta MSA, GA	Y	21700 FQ	26020 MW	29740 TQ	USBLS	5/07
	Hawaii	Y	19380 FQ	32830 MW	37840 TQ	USBLS	5/07
	Honolulu MSA, HI	Y	18920 FQ	31880 MW	36960 TQ	USBLS	5/07
	Idaho	Y	17790 FQ	20190 MW	24430 TQ	USBLS	5/07
	Boise City-Nampa MSA, ID	Y	17630 FQ	19660 MW	23540 TQ	USBLS	5/07
	Illinois	Y	25770 FQ	33530 MW	43480 TQ	USBLS	5/07
	Chicago-Naperville-Joliet MSA, IL-IN-WI	Y	26580 FQ	35370 MW	44080 TQ	USBLS	5/07
	Indiana	Y	22280 FQ	26550 MW	30170 TQ	USBLS	5/07
	Gary PMSA, IN	Y	21240 FQ	23610 MW	27230 TQ	USBLS	5/07
	Indianapolis-Carmel MSA, IN	Y	29280 FQ	32810 MW	36550 TQ	USBLS	5/07
	Iowa	Y	20270 FQ	24340 MW	30970 TQ	USBLS	5/07
	Davenport-Moline-Rock Island MSA, IA-IL	Y	22090 FQ	27930 MW	32540 TQ	USBLS	5/07
	Des Moines-West Des Moines MSA, IA	Y	20070 FQ	26090 MW	35950 TQ	USBLS	5/07
	Iowa City MSA, IA	Y	21440 FQ	25650 MW	29250 TQ	USBLS	5/07
	Kansas	Y	21350 FQ	25410 MW	32320 TQ	USBLS	5/07
	Wichita MSA, KS	Y	21580 FQ	24060 MW	30710 TQ	USBLS	5/07
	Kentucky	Y	19934 FQ	26283 MW	38520 TQ	KYBLS	2008
	Louisville-Jefferson County MSA, KY-IN	Y	22190 FQ	26490 MW	31320 TQ	USBLS	5/07
	Louisiana	H	8.73 FQ	11.11 MW	13.60 TQ	LABLS	1/08-3/08
	New Orleans-Metairie-Kenner MSA, LA	Y	16770 FQ	20670 MW	24460 TQ	USBLS	5/07
	Shreveport-Bossier City MSA, LA	Y	24730 FQ	28640 MW	33760 TQ	USBLS	5/07
	Maine	Y	24790 FQ	26810 MW	28860 TQ	USBLS	5/07
	Portland-South Portland-Biddeford MSA, ME	Y	25310 FQ	26960 MW	28610 TQ	USBLS	5/07
	Maryland	Y		25425 MW		MDBLS	3/08
	Baltimore-Towson MSA, MD	Y	22640 FQ	25080 MW	28640 TQ	USBLS	5/07
	Bethesda-Gaithersburg-Frederick PMSA, MD	Y	22550 FQ	25990 MW	29790 TQ	USBLS	5/07
	Massachusetts	Y	24300 FQ	28220 MW	33780 TQ	USBLS	5/07
	Boston-Cambridge-Quincy NECTA, MA	Y	23590 FQ	27060 MW	30620 TQ	USBLS	5/07
	Michigan	Y	27640 FQ	33910 MW	39050 TQ	USBLS	5/07
	Detroit-Warren-Livonia MSA, MI	Y	27560 FQ	33200 MW	37160 TQ	USBLS	5/07
	Warren-Troy-Farmington Hills PMSA, MI	Y	29590 FQ	33900 MW	37340 TQ	USBLS	5/07
	Minnesota	Y	23833 FQ	28819 MW	35941 TQ	MNBLS	10/08-12/08
	Duluth-Superior MSA, MN-WI	Y	17499 FQ	18857 MW	20215 TQ	MNBLS	10/08-12/08
	Minneapolis-Saint Paul MSA, MN-WI	Y	25699 FQ	30934 MW	37019 TQ	MNBLS	10/08-12/08

Occupation/Type/Industry	Location	Per	Low	Mid	High	Source	Date
Ophthalmic Laboratory Technician	Mississippi	Y	20090 FQ	27560 MW	33260 TQ	USBLS	5/07
	Jackson MSA, MS	Y	30030 FQ	32630 MW	35170 TQ	USBLS	5/07
	Missouri	Y	23340 FQ	29860 MW	36920 TQ	USBLS	5/07
	Kansas City MSA, MO-KS	Y	23170 FQ	30340 MW	36630 TQ	USBLS	5/07
	St. Louis MSA, MO-IL	Y	22960 FQ	30480 MW	37870 TQ	USBLS	5/07
	Montana	Y	20870 FQ	24980 MW	30770 TQ	USBLS	5/07
	Nebraska	Y	20760 FQ	24410 MW	30160 TQ	USBLS	5/07
	Omaha-Council Bluffs MSA, NE-IA	Y	20080 FQ	24080 MW	28300 TQ	USBLS	5/07
	Nevada	H	10.69 FQ	13.47 MW	15.39 TQ	NVBLS	5/08
	Las Vegas-Paradise MSA, NV	H	8.99 FQ	11.72 MW	14.35 TQ	NVBLS	5/08
	New Hampshire	H	8.12 AE	9.55 MW	11.83 AEX	NHBLS	6/08
	Nashua NECTA, NH-MA	Y	15750 FQ	16790 MW	17820 TQ	USBLS	5/07
	New Jersey	Y	22150 FQ	28830 MW	40900 TQ	USBLS	5/07
	Camden PMSA, NJ	Y	23570 FQ	29150 MW	35260 TQ	USBLS	5/07
	Edison PMSA, NJ	Y	22100 FQ	31480 MW	43960 TQ	USBLS	5/07
	New Mexico	Y	22890 FQ	27510 MW	35540 TQ	USBLS	5/07
	Albuquerque MSA, NM	Y	23320 FQ	27440 MW	34930 TQ	USBLS	5/07
	New York	Y	22050 FQ	28430 MW	36420 TQ	USBLS	5/07
	Albany-Schenectady-Troy MSA, NY	Y	35020 FQ	37580 MW	40290 TQ	USBLS	5/07
	Buffalo-Niagara Falls MSA, NY	Y	26150 FQ	29680 MW	34040 TQ	USBLS	5/07
	Nassau-Suffolk PMSA, NY	Y	27160 FQ	31620 MW	36610 TQ	USBLS	5/07
	New York-Northern New Jersey-Long Island MSA, NY-NJ-PA	Y	22690 FQ	29470 MW	39630 TQ	USBLS	5/07
	North Carolina	Y	22810 FQ	27950 MW	33020 TQ	USBLS	5/07
	Charlotte-Gastonia-Concord MSA, NC-SC	Y	27750 FQ	31260 MW	35080 TQ	USBLS	5/07
	North Dakota	Y	21580 FQ	26890 MW	33820 TQ	USBLS	5/07
	Ohio	Y	18060 FQ	23080 MW	32140 TQ	USBLS	5/07
	Cincinnati-Middletown MSA, OH-KY-IN	Y	21870 FQ	31740 MW	40670 TQ	USBLS	5/07
	Cleveland-Elyria-Mentor MSA, OH	Y	17370 FQ	26370 MW	34500 TQ	USBLS	5/07
	Dayton MSA, OH	Y	31460 FQ	34050 MW	36380 TQ	USBLS	5/07
	Oklahoma	Y	18620 FQ	23970 MW	30110 TQ	USBLS	5/07
	Lawton MSA, OK	Y	13730 FQ	18040 MW	24190 TQ	USBLS	5/07
	Oklahoma City MSA, OK	Y	17440 FQ	19630 MW	25690 TQ	USBLS	5/07
	Tulsa MSA, OK	Y	21460 FQ	26730 MW	31760 TQ	USBLS	5/07
	Oregon	H	11.98 FQ	15.07 MW	17.79 TQ	ORBLS	5/08
	Portland-Vancouver-Beaverton MSA, OR-WA	Y	25330 FQ	32420 MW	37020 TQ	USBLS	5/07
	Pennsylvania	Y	20430 FQ	24890 MW	32020 TQ	USBLS	5/07
	Allentown-Bethlehem-Easton MSA, PA-NJ	Y	23260 FQ	32650 MW	37260 TQ	USBLS	5/07
	Philadelphia-Camden-Wilmington MSA, PA-NJ-DE-MD	Y	21540 FQ	25930 MW	32090 TQ	USBLS	5/07
	Pittsburgh MSA, PA	Y	16790 FQ	19670 MW	26020 TQ	USBLS	5/07
	Rhode Island	Y	20520 FQ	23120 MW	26290 TQ	USBLS	5/07
	Providence-Fall River-Warwick MSA, RI-MA	Y	20520 FQ	23120 MW	26290 TQ	USBLS	5/07
	South Carolina	Y	21570 FQ	25490 MW	34530 TQ	USBLS	5/07
	Columbia MSA, SC	Y	20610 FQ	22280 MW	25250 TQ	USBLS	5/07
	South Dakota	Y	22640 FQ	24855 MW	27831 TQ	SDBLS	7/08-9/08
	Sioux Falls MSA, SD	Y	22918 FQ	25393 MW	28703 TQ	SDBLS	7/08-9/08
	Tennessee	Y	19960 FQ	24200 MW	29280 TQ	USBLS	5/07
	Memphis MSA, TN-MS-AR	Y	21500 FQ	26930 MW	31300 TQ	USBLS	5/07
	Nashville-Davidson-Murfreesboro MSA, TN	Y	23050 FQ	26580 MW	33000 TQ	USBLS	5/07
	Texas	Y	18220 FQ	21860 MW	28580 TQ	USBLS	5/07
	Austin-Round Rock MSA, TX	Y	21230 FQ	23590 MW	26740 TQ	USBLS	5/07
	Dallas-Fort Worth-Arlington MSA, TX	Y	18160 FQ	20810 MW	25720 TQ	USBLS	5/07
	El Paso MSA, TX	Y	16250 FQ	17970 MW	19610 TQ	USBLS	5/07
	Houston-Sugar Land-Baytown MSA, TX	Y	17570 FQ	21230 MW	25620 TQ	USBLS	5/07
	San Antonio MSA, TX	Y	20490 FQ	38940 MW	67000 TQ	USBLS	5/07
	Utah	Y	17660 FQ	20400 MW	25110 TQ	USBLS	5/07

Occupation/Type/Industry	Location	Per	Low	Mid	High	Source	Date
Ophthalmic Laboratory Technician	Virginia	Y	17560 FQ	23050 MW	30140 TQ	USBLS	5/07
	Richmond MSA, VA	Y	25440 FQ	29730 MW	33300 TQ	USBLS	5/07
	Virginia Beach-Norfolk-Newport News MSA, VA-NC	Y	15670 FQ	18940 MW	25010 TQ	USBLS	5/07
	Washington	H	12.53 FQ	15.59 MW	21.71 TQ	WABLS	3/08
	Seattle-Tacoma-Bellevue MSA, WA	Y	26300 FQ	32860 MW	45250 TQ	USBLS	5/07
	West Virginia	Y	18224 FQ	21720 MW	25582 TQ	WVBLS	7/08-9/08
	Wisconsin	Y	22390 FQ	27850 MW	35200 TQ	USBLS	5/07
	Green Bay MSA, WI	Y	23190 FQ	28730 MW	36220 TQ	USBLS	5/07
	Milwaukee-Waukesha-West Allis MSA, WI	Y	20850 FQ	25120 MW	30830 TQ	USBLS	5/07
	Puerto Rico	Y	13920 FQ	17030 MW	21830 TQ	USBLS	5/07
	San Juan-Caguas-Guaynabo MSA, PR	Y	14530 FQ	18130 MW	22300 TQ	USBLS	5/07
Opinion Clerk State Court of Appeals	Michigan	Y			51072 HI	LSJ02	7/11/07
Optician, Dispensing	Alabama	Y	21310 FQ	24110 MW	29490 TQ	USBLS	5/07
	Birmingham-Hoover MSA, AL	Y	21010 FQ	23290 MW	25880 TQ	USBLS	5/07
	Alaska	Y	30600 FQ	39870 MW	48850 TQ	USBLS	5/07
	Anchorage MSA, AK	Y	32270 FQ	42890 MW	49170 TQ	USBLS	5/07
	Arizona	Y	25910 FQ	30170 MW	37490 TQ	USBLS	5/07
	Flagstaff MSA, AZ	Y	25540 FQ	28680 MW	32920 TQ	USBLS	5/07
	Phoenix-Mesa-Scottsdale MSA, AZ	Y	26550 FQ	30060 MW	36650 TQ	USBLS	5/07
	Tucson MSA, AZ	Y	26210 FQ	34020 MW	38660 TQ	USBLS	5/07
	Arkansas	Y	21510 FQ	25970 MW	34950 TQ	USBLS	5/07
	Little Rock-North Little Rock MSA, AR	Y	23520 FQ	32310 MW	36370 TQ	USBLS	5/07
	California	H	13.78 FQ	17.46 MW	21.17 TQ	CABLS	1/08-3/08
	Los Angeles-Long Beach-Glendale PMSA, CA	H	11.12 FQ	16.77 MW	20.49 TQ	CABLS	1/08-3/08
	Oakland-Fremont-Hayward MSA, CA	H	17.14 FQ	19.78 MW	23.44 TQ	CABLS	1/08-3/08
	Riverside-San Bernardino-Ontario MSA, CA	H	12.39 FQ	15.32 MW	18.40 TQ	CABLS	1/08-3/08
	Sacramento-Arden Arcade-Roseville MSA, CA	H	13.98 FQ	16.11 MW	20.08 TQ	CABLS	1/08-3/08
	San Diego-Carlsbad-San Marcos MSA, CA	H	18.16 FQ	21.92 MW	33.78 TQ	CABLS	1/08-3/08
	San Francisco-San Mateo-Redwood PMSA, CA	H	17.84 FQ	20.02 MW	25.41 TQ	CABLS	1/08-3/08
	San Jose-Sunnyvale-Santa Clara MSA, CA	H	16.96 FQ	19.72 MW	22.46 TQ	CABLS	1/08-3/08
	Santa Ana-Anaheim-Irvine PMSA, CA	Y	30230 FQ	35990 MW	43920 TQ	USBLS	5/07
	Stockton MSA, CA	H	12.50 FQ	14.48 MW	17.26 TQ	CABLS	1/08-3/08
	Colorado	Y	27360 FQ	33700 MW	39520 TQ	USBLS	5/07
	Colorado Springs MSA, CO	Y	21040 FQ	25180 MW	34370 TQ	USBLS	5/07
	Denver-Aurora MSA, CO	Y	33100 FQ	37090 MW	42720 TQ	USBLS	5/07
	Pueblo MSA, CO	Y	22170 FQ	27140 MW	32510 TQ	USBLS	5/07
	Connecticut	H	16.57 AE	24.15 MW		CTBLS	1/08-3/08
	Bridgeport-Stamford-Norwalk MSA, CT	Y	43330 FQ	54480 MW	61180 TQ	USBLS	5/07
	Hartford-West Hartford-East Hartford MSA, CT	Y	48680 FQ	53740 MW	59210 TQ	USBLS	5/07
	Delaware	Y	17830 FQ	27310 MW	33170 TQ	USBLS	5/07
	Wilmington PMSA, DE-MD-NJ	Y	18000 FQ	22580 MW	35380 TQ	USBLS	5/07
	District of Columbia	Y	28970 FQ	32990 MW	37120 TQ	USBLS	5/07
	Washington-Arlington-Alexandria MSA, DC-VA-MD-WV	Y	32640 FQ	42990 MW	51240 TQ	USBLS	5/07
	Florida	Y	29920 FQ	37330 MW	45300 TQ	USBLS	5/07
	Cape Coral-Fort Myers MSA, FL	Y	35280 FQ	43080 MW	47850 TQ	USBLS	5/07
	Fort Lauderdale-Pompano Beach-Deerfield Beach PMSA, FL	Y	30980 FQ	35470 MW	39710 TQ	USBLS	5/07

AE	Average entry wage	**AW**	Average wage paid	**FQ**	First quartile wage	**LO**	Lowest wage paid
AER	Average entry range	**AWR**	Average wage range	**H**	Hourly	**LR**	Low end range
AEX	Average experienced wage	**AXR**	Average experienced range	**HI**	Highest wage paid	**M**	Monthly
ATC	Average total compensation	**D**	Daily	**HR**	High end range	**MCC**	Median cash compensation

MTC	Median total compensation	**TCC**	Total cash compensation
MW	Median wage paid	**TQ**	Third quartile wage
MWR	Median wage range	**W**	Weekly
S	See annotated source	**Y**	Yearly

Occupation/Type/Industry	Location	Per	Low	Mid	High	Source	Date
Optician, Dispensing	Jacksonville MSA, FL	Y	27490 FQ	38570 MW	46810 TQ	USBLS	5/07
	Miami-Fort Lauderdale-Miami Beach MSA, FL	Y	29850 FQ	35880 MW	41670 TQ	USBLS	5/07
	Orlando-Kissimmee MSA, FL	Y	30820 FQ	36790 MW	45490 TQ	USBLS	5/07
	Tallahassee MSA, FL	Y	33680 FQ	40320 MW	45990 TQ	USBLS	5/07
	Tampa-St. Petersburg-Clearwater MSA, FL	Y	32420 FQ	37820 MW	47010 TQ	USBLS	5/07
	West Palm Beach-Boca Raton-Boynton Beach PMSA, FL	Y	30590 FQ	36210 MW	47400 TQ	USBLS	5/07
	Georgia	Y	26540 FQ	34170 MW	41430 TQ	USBLS	5/07
	Atlanta-Sandy Springs-Marietta MSA, GA	Y	30540 FQ	35670 MW	41360 TQ	USBLS	5/07
	Macon MSA, GA	Y	40940 FQ	44650 MW	48290 TQ	USBLS	5/07
	Hawaii	Y	32310 FQ	41070 MW	49150 TQ	USBLS	5/07
	Honolulu MSA, HI	Y	33800 FQ	42270 MW	50230 TQ	USBLS	5/07
	Idaho	Y	20400 FQ	24750 MW	33550 TQ	USBLS	5/07
	Boise City-Nampa MSA, ID	Y	19020 FQ	21900 MW	26220 TQ	USBLS	5/07
	Illinois	Y	23170 FQ	27760 MW	34620 TQ	USBLS	5/07
	Chicago-Naperville-Joliet MSA, IL-IN-WI	Y	23960 FQ	28420 MW	35070 TQ	USBLS	5/07
	Indiana	Y	21470 FQ	25440 MW	30620 TQ	USBLS	5/07
	Elkhart-Goshen MSA, IN	Y	22210 FQ	26570 MW	31530 TQ	USBLS	5/07
	Fort Wayne MSA, IN	Y	15440 FQ	22760 MW	28960 TQ	USBLS	5/07
	Gary PMSA, IN	Y	21520 FQ	24210 MW	28430 TQ	USBLS	5/07
	Indianapolis-Carmel MSA, IN	Y	22940 FQ	27550 MW	32250 TQ	USBLS	5/07
	Iowa	Y	21210 FQ	25280 MW	30650 TQ	USBLS	5/07
	Des Moines-West Des Moines MSA, IA	Y	25600 FQ	28790 MW	31960 TQ	USBLS	5/07
	Kansas	Y	21380 FQ	26010 MW	30480 TQ	USBLS	5/07
	Topeka MSA, KS	Y	18480 FQ	25150 MW	28650 TQ	USBLS	5/07
	Wichita MSA, KS	Y	17910 FQ	22140 MW	26160 TQ	USBLS	5/07
	Kentucky	Y	29020 FQ	35939 MW	41722 TQ	KYBLS	2008
	Louisville-Jefferson County MSA, KY-IN	Y	26660 FQ	35400 MW	41720 TQ	USBLS	5/07
	Louisiana	H	10.05 FQ	12.52 MW	15.31 TQ	LABLS	1/08-3/08
	Baton Rouge MSA, LA	Y	18040 FQ	22040 MW	25900 TQ	USBLS	5/07
	New Orleans-Metairie-Kenner MSA, LA	Y	25480 FQ	29400 MW	35650 TQ	USBLS	5/07
	Maine	Y	26040 FQ	30670 MW	36830 TQ	USBLS	5/07
	Portland-South Portland-Biddeford MSA, ME	Y	31790 FQ	36230 MW	43320 TQ	USBLS	5/07
	Maryland	Y		33825 MW		MDBLS	3/08
	Baltimore-Towson MSA, MD	Y	23300 FQ	33440 MW	39030 TQ	USBLS	5/07
	Bethesda-Gaithersburg-Frederick PMSA, MD	Y	26280 FQ	34090 MW	43380 TQ	USBLS	5/07
	Salisbury MSA, MD	Y	23970 FQ	28790 MW	35060 TQ	USBLS	5/07
	Massachusetts	Y	35620 FQ	44200 MW	52130 TQ	USBLS	5/07
	Boston-Cambridge-Quincy NECTA, MA	Y	37610 FQ	48840 MW	63860 TQ	USBLS	5/07
	New Bedford MSA, MA	Y	26780 FQ	36530 MW	45530 TQ	USBLS	5/07
	Worcester MSA, MA-CT	Y	38670 FQ	41770 MW	45730 TQ	USBLS	5/07
	Michigan	Y	26320 FQ	30080 MW	35500 TQ	USBLS	5/07
	Detroit-Warren-Livonia MSA, MI	Y	27450 FQ	31220 MW	37350 TQ	USBLS	5/07
	Grand Rapids-Wyoming MSA, MI	Y	27830 FQ	31480 MW	36280 TQ	USBLS	5/07
	Warren-Troy-Farmington Hills PMSA, MI	Y	27050 FQ	30740 MW	37120 TQ	USBLS	5/07
	Minnesota	Y	27704 FQ	35059 MW	41179 TQ	MNBLS	10/08-12/08
	Duluth-Superior MSA, MN-WI	Y	21311 FQ	26134 MW	33981 TQ	MNBLS	10/08-12/08
	Minneapolis-Saint Paul MSA, MN-WI	Y	30926 FQ	36680 MW	42602 TQ	MNBLS	10/08-12/08
	Rochester MSA, MN	Y	27300 FQ	33388 MW	41154 TQ	MNBLS	10/08-12/08
	Mississippi	Y	21990 FQ	27720 MW	35170 TQ	USBLS	5/07
	Jackson MSA, MS	Y	24430 FQ	31910 MW	43420 TQ	USBLS	5/07
	Missouri	Y	20450 FQ	25380 MW	31240 TQ	USBLS	5/07
	Kansas City MSA, MO-KS	Y	25250 FQ	29270 MW	33510 TQ	USBLS	5/07
	St. Louis MSA, MO-IL	Y	22300 FQ	27520 MW	32080 TQ	USBLS	5/07
	Montana	Y	19710 FQ	23710 MW	28150 TQ	USBLS	5/07
	Billings MSA, MT	Y	21700 FQ	26320 MW	29810 TQ	USBLS	5/07
	Nebraska	Y	21560 FQ	24940 MW	30780 TQ	USBLS	5/07

Occupation/Type/Industry	Location	Per	Low	Mid	High	Source	Date
Optician, Dispensing	Omaha-Council Bluffs MSA, NE-IA	Y	23660 FQ	28380 MW	33850 TQ	USBLS	5/07
	Nevada	H	15.33 FQ	24.06 MW	29.93 TQ	NVBLS	5/08
	Las Vegas-Paradise MSA, NV	H	14.20 FQ	24.70 MW	30.26 TQ	NVBLS	5/08
	Reno-Sparks MSA, NV	H	17.72 FQ	23.99 MW	30.34 TQ	NVBLS	5/08
	New Hampshire	H	13.29 AE	17.84 MW	20.14 AEX	NHBLS	6/08
	Nashua NECTA, NH-MA	Y	29790 FQ	38130 MW	44610 TQ	USBLS	5/07
	New Jersey	Y	42630 FQ	48050 MW	55250 TQ	USBLS	5/07
	Camden PMSA, NJ	Y	41850 FQ	49420 MW	58050 TQ	USBLS	5/07
	Edison PMSA, NJ	Y	44070 FQ	49260 MW	57350 TQ	USBLS	5/07
	Newark-Union PMSA, NJ-PA	Y	43130 FQ	48380 MW	54900 TQ	USBLS	5/07
	New Mexico	Y	20820 FQ	28090 MW	34640 TQ	USBLS	5/07
	Albuquerque MSA, NM	Y	23430 FQ	28160 MW	33690 TQ	USBLS	5/07
	New York	Y	38480 FQ	45360 MW	52050 TQ	USBLS	5/07
	Albany-Schenectady-Troy MSA, NY	Y	30470 FQ	43800 MW	48300 TQ	USBLS	5/07
	Buffalo-Niagara Falls MSA, NY	Y	35660 FQ	41680 MW	46730 TQ	USBLS	5/07
	Nassau-Suffolk PMSA, NY	Y	37990 FQ	45430 MW	60170 TQ	USBLS	5/07
	New York-Northern New Jersey-Long Island MSA, NY-NJ-PA	Y	42150 FQ	48020 MW	55500 TQ	USBLS	5/07
	Syracuse MSA, NY	Y	38980 FQ	45170 MW	50890 TQ	USBLS	5/07
	North Carolina	Y	26960 FQ	33590 MW	43050 TQ	USBLS	5/07
	Charlotte-Gastonia-Concord MSA, NC-SC	Y	27100 FQ	32650 MW	43200 TQ	USBLS	5/07
	Durham MSA, NC	Y	27780 FQ	41420 MW	51270 TQ	USBLS	5/07
	Raleigh-Cary MSA, NC	Y	36580 FQ	43700 MW	48880 TQ	USBLS	5/07
	North Dakota	Y	20470 FQ	24840 MW	29300 TQ	USBLS	5/07
	Fargo MSA, ND-MN	Y	21020 FQ	24730 MW	28590 TQ	USBLS	5/07
	Ohio	Y	27780 FQ	32790 MW	37610 TQ	USBLS	5/07
	Cincinnati-Middletown MSA, OH-KY-IN	Y	27270 FQ	32890 MW	37320 TQ	USBLS	5/07
	Cleveland-Elyria-Mentor MSA, OH	Y	30860 FQ	35700 MW	40360 TQ	USBLS	5/07
	Columbus MSA, OH	Y	28880 FQ	32820 MW	37000 TQ	USBLS	5/07
	Dayton MSA, OH	Y	29120 FQ	32850 MW	36940 TQ	USBLS	5/07
	Oklahoma	Y	19510 FQ	23500 MW	29540 TQ	USBLS	5/07
	Oklahoma City MSA, OK	Y	19620 FQ	22520 MW	28030 TQ	USBLS	5/07
	Tulsa MSA, OK	Y	19190 FQ	26720 MW	31650 TQ	USBLS	5/07
	Oregon	H	13.21 FQ	14.89 MW	19.63 TQ	ORBLS	5/08
	Portland-Vancouver-Beaverton MSA, OR-WA	Y	27670 FQ	31220 MW	44150 TQ	USBLS	5/07
	Pennsylvania	Y	23770 FQ	30650 MW	38180 TQ	USBLS	5/07
	Allentown-Bethlehem-Easton MSA, PA-NJ	Y	23930 FQ	33800 MW	45800 TQ	USBLS	5/07
	Erie MSA, PA	Y	21980 FQ	25730 MW	31470 TQ	USBLS	5/07
	Lancaster MSA, PA	Y	27510 FQ	31280 MW	36590 TQ	USBLS	5/07
	Philadelphia-Camden-Wilmington MSA, PA-NJ-DE-MD	Y	32230 FQ	39070 MW	47280 TQ	USBLS	5/07
	Pittsburgh MSA, PA	Y	21860 FQ	28930 MW	36630 TQ	USBLS	5/07
	Rhode Island	Y	35900 FQ	43980 MW	49590 TQ	USBLS	5/07
	Providence-Fall River-Warwick MSA, RI-MA	Y	34480 FQ	43390 MW	49420 TQ	USBLS	5/07
	South Carolina	Y	23850 FQ	28770 MW	35650 TQ	USBLS	5/07
	Charleston-North Charleston MSA, SC	Y	24950 FQ	28740 MW	32100 TQ	USBLS	5/07
	Columbia MSA, SC	Y	23320 FQ	29300 MW	36030 TQ	USBLS	5/07
	South Dakota	Y	23183 FQ	26889 MW	31917 TQ	SDBLS	7/08-9/08
	Sioux Falls MSA, SD	Y	24403 FQ	29330 MW	36392 TQ	SDBLS	7/08-9/08
	Tennessee	Y	26390 FQ	31570 MW	39060 TQ	USBLS	5/07
	Memphis MSA, TN-MS-AR	Y	26440 FQ	29590 MW	34910 TQ	USBLS	5/07
	Nashville-Davidson-Murfreesboro MSA, TN	Y	31770 FQ	39420 MW	44570 TQ	USBLS	5/07
	Texas	Y	21560 FQ	26960 MW	32790 TQ	USBLS	5/07
	Austin-Round Rock MSA, TX	Y	24780 FQ	28480 MW	32780 TQ	USBLS	5/07
	Dallas-Fort Worth-Arlington MSA, TX	Y	25340 FQ	29310 MW	38460 TQ	USBLS	5/07
	El Paso MSA, TX	Y	18190 FQ	20800 MW	24780 TQ	USBLS	5/07
	Houston-Sugar Land-Baytown MSA, TX	Y	21380 FQ	26730 MW	32780 TQ	USBLS	5/07

AE	Average entry wage	AW	Average wage paid	FQ	First quartile wage	LO	Lowest wage paid	MTC	Median total compensation	TCC	Total cash compensation
AER	Average entry range	AWR	Average wage range	H	Hourly	LR	Low end range	MW	Median wage paid	TQ	Third quartile wage
AEX	Average experienced wage	AXR	Average experienced range	HI	Highest wage paid	M	Monthly	MWR	Median wage range	W	Weekly
ATC	Average total compensation	D	Daily	HR	High end range	MCC	Median cash compensation	S	See annotated source	Y	Yearly

Occupation/Type/Industry	Location	Per	Low	Mid	High	Source	Date
Optician, Dispensing	San Antonio MSA, TX	Y	21480 FQ	26470 MW	29620 TQ	USBLS	5/07
	Utah	Y	21750 FQ	27200 MW	32630 TQ	USBLS	5/07
	Salt Lake City MSA, UT	Y	27250 FQ	30760 MW	43020 TQ	USBLS	5/07
	Vermont	Y	26500 FQ	31720 MW	36960 TQ	USBLS	5/07
	Burlington-South Burlington MSA, VT	Y	31050 FQ	38900 MW	43810 TQ	USBLS	5/07
	Virginia	Y	33850 FQ	41970 MW	50490 TQ	USBLS	5/07
	Lynchburg MSA, VA	Y	25890 FQ	37010 MW	42410 TQ	USBLS	5/07
	Richmond MSA, VA	Y	35320 FQ	39020 MW	44120 TQ	USBLS	5/07
	Virginia Beach-Norfolk-Newport News MSA, VA-NC	Y	30330 FQ	36310 MW	42790 TQ	USBLS	5/07
	Washington	H	13.54 FQ	16.04 MW	21.73 TQ	WABLS	3/08
	Seattle-Tacoma-Bellevue MSA, WA	Y	27610 FQ	31650 MW	44960 TQ	USBLS	5/07
	West Virginia	Y	18889 FQ	24188 MW	32830 TQ	WVBLS	7/08-9/08
	Wisconsin	Y	23030 FQ	28460 MW	34940 TQ	USBLS	5/07
	Milwaukee-Waukesha-West Allis MSA, WI	Y	27270 FQ	33580 MW	39910 TQ	USBLS	5/07
	Wyoming	Y	21548 FQ	27170 MW	38109 TQ	WYBLS	9/08
	Cheyenne MSA, WY	Y	18193 FQ	20370 MW	26745 TQ	WYBLS	9/08
	Puerto Rico	Y	16020 FQ	20670 MW	24030 TQ	USBLS	5/07
	San Juan-Caguas-Guaynabo MSA, PR	Y	18110 FQ	21560 MW	24540 TQ	USBLS	5/07
Optometrist	Alabama	Y	63320 FQ	78050 MW	102390 TQ	USBLS	5/07
	Birmingham-Hoover MSA, AL	Y	67620 FQ	78080 MW	105790 TQ	USBLS	5/07
	Alaska	Y	83670 FQ	125760 MW		USBLS	5/07
	Anchorage MSA, AK	Y	80540 FQ	128010 MW		USBLS	5/07
	Arizona	Y	85720 FQ	98460 MW	136680 TQ	USBLS	5/07
	Phoenix-Mesa-Scottsdale MSA, AZ	Y	87270 FQ	99520 MW		USBLS	5/07
	Tucson MSA, AZ	Y	83790 FQ	93570 MW	104500 TQ	USBLS	5/07
	Arkansas	Y	58760 FQ	89930 MW		USBLS	5/07
	Little Rock-North Little Rock MSA, AR	Y	70900 FQ			USBLS	5/07
	California	H	32.83 FQ	44.40 MW	53.58 TQ	CABLS	1/08-3/08
	Los Angeles-Long Beach-Glendale PMSA, CA	H	29.15 FQ	35.86 MW	51.31 TQ	CABLS	1/08-3/08
	Oakland-Fremont-Hayward MSA, CA	H	39.03 FQ	53.52 MW	64.87 TQ	CABLS	1/08-3/08
	Riverside-San Bernardino-Ontario MSA, CA	H	47.62 FQ	68.32 MW		CABLS	1/08-3/08
	Sacramento-Arden Arcade-Roseville MSA, CA	H	34.53 FQ	50.89 MW	60.48 TQ	CABLS	1/08-3/08
	San Diego-Carlsbad-San Marcos MSA, CA	H	39.06 FQ	43.75 MW	47.25 TQ	CABLS	1/08-3/08
	San Francisco-San Mateo-Redwood PMSA, CA	H	41.24 FQ	45.85 MW	51.36 TQ	CABLS	1/08-3/08
	San Jose-Sunnyvale-Santa Clara MSA, CA	H	24.50 FQ	42.10 MW	48.58 TQ	CABLS	1/08-3/08
	Santa Ana-Anaheim-Irvine PMSA, CA	Y	55450 FQ	76700 MW	100490 TQ	USBLS	5/07
	Colorado	Y	44910 FQ	64510 MW	99600 TQ	USBLS	5/07
	Denver-Aurora MSA, CO	Y	38470 FQ	58090 MW	104980 TQ	USBLS	5/07
	Connecticut	H	34.73 AE	48.94 MW		CTBLS	1/08-3/08
	Bridgeport-Stamford-Norwalk MSA, CT	Y	93670 FQ	115220 MW		USBLS	5/07
	Hartford-West Hartford-East Hartford MSA, CT	Y	80680 FQ	102400 MW	120390 TQ	USBLS	5/07
	Delaware	Y	72900 FQ	81140 MW	104270 TQ	USBLS	5/07
	Wilmington PMSA, DE-MD-NJ	Y	71810 FQ	80010 MW	94050 TQ	USBLS	5/07
	District of Columbia	Y	65740 FQ	76780 MW	91150 TQ	USBLS	5/07
	Washington-Arlington-Alexandria MSA, DC-VA-MD-WV	Y	85800 FQ	98090 MW	115140 TQ	USBLS	5/07
	Florida	Y	51570 FQ	91570 MW	130380 TQ	USBLS	5/07
	Fort Lauderdale-Pompano Beach-Deerfield Beach PMSA, FL	Y	34320 FQ	98420 MW	114020 TQ	USBLS	5/07
	Jacksonville MSA, FL	Y	93550 FQ	111670 MW	125550 TQ	USBLS	5/07

Occupation/Type/Industry	Location	Per	Low	Mid	High	Source	Date
Optometrist	Miami-Fort Lauderdale-Miami Beach MSA, FL	Y	36710 FQ	77650 MW	104520 TQ	USBLS	5/07
	Orlando-Kissimmee MSA, FL	Y	83870 FQ	141200 MW		USBLS	5/07
	Tampa-St. Petersburg-Clearwater MSA, FL	Y	37700 FQ	48700 MW	105570 TQ	USBLS	5/07
	West Palm Beach-Boca Raton-Boynton Beach PMSA, FL	Y	34260 FQ	57170 MW	65380 TQ	USBLS	5/07
	Georgia	Y	71860 FQ	98020 MW		USBLS	5/07
	Atlanta-Sandy Springs-Marietta MSA, GA	Y	88790 FQ	109550 MW		USBLS	5/07
	Hawaii	Y	64420 FQ	89860 MW	120880 TQ	USBLS	5/07
	Honolulu MSA, HI	Y	62680 FQ	80170 MW	109370 TQ	USBLS	5/07
	Idaho	Y	32100 FQ	48910 MW	59430 TQ	USBLS	5/07
	Boise City-Nampa MSA, ID	Y	53440 FQ	58090 MW	81130 TQ	USBLS	5/07
	Illinois	Y	71830 FQ	98490 MW	121310 TQ	USBLS	5/07
	Chicago-Naperville-Joliet MSA, IL-IN-WI	Y	73290 FQ	99980 MW	120820 TQ	USBLS	5/07
	Indiana	Y	69500 FQ	88370 MW	123510 TQ	USBLS	5/07
	Gary PMSA, IN	Y	83140 FQ	94840 MW	105480 TQ	USBLS	5/07
	Indianapolis-Carmel MSA, IN	Y	74630 FQ	86520 MW		USBLS	5/07
	Iowa	Y	65800 FQ	85030 MW	110220 TQ	USBLS	5/07
	Des Moines-West Des Moines MSA, IA	Y	83260 FQ	102430 MW		USBLS	5/07
	Kansas	Y	69390 FQ	89340 MW	127800 TQ	USBLS	5/07
	Wichita MSA, KS	Y	85700 FQ	113520 MW	135840 TQ	USBLS	5/07
	Kentucky	Y	80332 FQ	101942 MW	137004 TQ	KYBLS	2008
	Louisville-Jefferson County MSA, KY-IN	Y	66940 FQ	106010 MW	131160 TQ	USBLS	5/07
	Louisiana	H	40.62 FQ	61.04 MW		LABLS	1/08-3/08
	New Orleans-Metairie-Kenner MSA, LA	Y	109750 FQ			USBLS	5/07
	Maine	Y	70300 FQ	107740 MW	128220 TQ	USBLS	5/07
	Maryland	Y		102000 MW		MDBLS	3/08
	Baltimore-Towson MSA, MD	Y	61820 FQ	99450 MW	116740 TQ	USBLS	5/07
	Bethesda-Gaithersburg-Frederick PMSA, MD	Y	88860 FQ	97530 MW	109480 TQ	USBLS	5/07
	Massachusetts	Y	54450 FQ	87520 MW	109660 TQ	USBLS	5/07
	Boston-Cambridge-Quincy NECTA, MA	Y	51080 FQ	83390 MW	100490 TQ	USBLS	5/07
	Michigan	Y	78470 FQ	100170 MW	121030 TQ	USBLS	5/07
	Detroit-Warren-Livonia MSA, MI	Y	85670 FQ	105100 MW	119090 TQ	USBLS	5/07
	Grand Rapids-Wyoming MSA, MI	Y	71640 FQ	89650 MW		USBLS	5/07
	Warren-Troy-Farmington Hills PMSA, MI	Y	87650 FQ	107200 MW	122040 TQ	USBLS	5/07
	Minnesota	Y	86627 FQ	106369 MW		MNBLS	10/08-12/08
	Duluth-Superior MSA, MN-WI	Y	76437 FQ	86585 MW	122084 TQ	MNBLS	10/08-12/08
	Minneapolis-Saint Paul MSA, MN-WI	Y	92381 FQ	109257 MW		MNBLS	10/08-12/08
	Mississippi	Y	47520 FQ	63490 MW	93760 TQ	USBLS	5/07
	Jackson MSA, MS	Y	53110 FQ	69570 MW	94130 TQ	USBLS	5/07
	Missouri	Y	65110 FQ	83710 MW	106290 TQ	USBLS	5/07
	Kansas City MSA, MO-KS	Y	73350 FQ	83040 MW	121820 TQ	USBLS	5/07
	St. Louis MSA, MO-IL	Y	55430 FQ	92840 MW	107020 TQ	USBLS	5/07
	Montana	Y	31580 FQ	52860 MW	82030 TQ	USBLS	5/07
	Nebraska	Y	65120 FQ	85430 MW	125100 TQ	USBLS	5/07
	Omaha-Council Bluffs MSA, NE-IA	Y	52960 FQ	79950 MW	101240 TQ	USBLS	5/07
	Nevada	H	25.92 FQ	32.97 MW		NVBLS	5/08
	New Hampshire	H	36.39 AE	54.73 MW	63.46 AEX	NHBLS	6/08
	New Jersey	Y	81670 FQ	92540 MW	103480 TQ	USBLS	5/07
	Camden PMSA, NJ	Y	84820 FQ	94460 MW	102970 TQ	USBLS	5/07
	Edison PMSA, NJ	Y	86730 FQ	94930 MW	103590 TQ	USBLS	5/07
	Newark-Union PMSA, NJ-PA	Y	82880 FQ	93840 MW	128140 TQ	USBLS	5/07
	New Mexico	Y	67280 FQ	102900 MW	134530 TQ	USBLS	5/07
	Albuquerque MSA, NM	Y	76010 FQ	106770 MW	127860 TQ	USBLS	5/07
	New York	Y	93120 FQ	106060 MW	124460 TQ	USBLS	5/07
	Albany-Schenectady-Troy MSA, NY	Y	88660 FQ	94280 MW	99910 TQ	USBLS	5/07
	Buffalo-Niagara Falls MSA, NY	Y	87050 FQ	94800 MW	105390 TQ	USBLS	5/07

AE Average entry wage	**AW** Average wage paid	**FQ** First quartile wage	**LO** Lowest wage paid	**MTC** Median total compensation	**TCC** Total cash compensation
AER Average entry range	**AWR** Average wage range	**H** Hourly	**LR** Low end range	**MW** Median wage paid	**TQ** Third quartile wage
AEX Average experienced wage	**AXR** Average experienced range	**HI** Highest wage paid	**M** Monthly	**MWR** Median wage range	**W** Weekly
ATC Average total compensation	**D** Daily	**HR** High end range	**MCC** Median cash compensation	**S** See annotated source	**Y** Yearly

|

Occupation/Type/Industry	Location	Per	Low	Mid	High	Source	Date
Optometrist	Nassau-Suffolk PMSA, NY	Y	101730 FQ	114720 MW	129190 TQ	USBLS	5/07
	New York-Northern New Jersey-Long Island MSA, NY-NJ-PA	Y	90290 FQ	104780 MW	123230 TQ	USBLS	5/07
	Syracuse MSA, NY	Y	95790 FQ	108740 MW	122240 TQ	USBLS	5/07
	North Carolina	Y	83030 FQ	114770 MW		USBLS	5/07
	Charlotte-Gastonia-Concord MSA, NC-SC	Y	65770 FQ	103010 MW		USBLS	5/07
	Raleigh-Cary MSA, NC	Y	85960 FQ	111880 MW		USBLS	5/07
	North Dakota	Y	62190 FQ	87120 MW	126750 TQ	USBLS	5/07
	Fargo MSA, ND-MN	Y	57060 FQ	62980 MW	89680 TQ	USBLS	5/07
	Ohio	Y	79480 FQ	98960 MW	127820 TQ	USBLS	5/07
	Cincinnati-Middletown MSA, OH-KY-IN	Y	90460 FQ	107340 MW		USBLS	5/07
	Cleveland-Elyria-Mentor MSA, OH	Y	59320 FQ	79870 MW	99080 TQ	USBLS	5/07
	Columbus MSA, OH	Y	73320 FQ	89030 MW	100550 TQ	USBLS	5/07
	Dayton MSA, OH	Y	106800 FQ	120860 MW	138850 TQ	USBLS	5/07
	Oklahoma	Y	42210 FQ	68980 MW	111800 TQ	USBLS	5/07
	Oklahoma City MSA, OK	Y	39800 FQ	58560 MW	94600 TQ	USBLS	5/07
	Tulsa MSA, OK	Y	71280 FQ	80730 MW		USBLS	5/07
	Oregon	H	28.68 FQ	39.92 MW	48.98 TQ	ORBLS	5/08
	Portland-Vancouver-Beaverton MSA, OR-WA	Y	57900 FQ	86890 MW	99750 TQ	USBLS	5/07
	Pennsylvania	Y	67790 FQ	84600 MW	110640 TQ	USBLS	5/07
	Allentown-Bethlehem-Easton MSA, PA-NJ	Y	78660 FQ	92100 MW	105460 TQ	USBLS	5/07
	Philadelphia-Camden-Wilmington MSA, PA-NJ-DE-MD	Y	68830 FQ	84130 MW	100530 TQ	USBLS	5/07
	Pittsburgh MSA, PA	Y	66750 FQ	92130 MW	127300 TQ	USBLS	5/07
	Rhode Island	Y	88760 FQ	118950 MW		USBLS	5/07
	Providence-Fall River-Warwick MSA, RI-MA	Y	86070 FQ	110050 MW		USBLS	5/07
	South Carolina	Y	54360 FQ	68660 MW	108570 TQ	USBLS	5/07
	South Dakota	Y	78299 FQ	95915 MW	151376 TQ	SDBLS	7/08-9/08
	Sioux Falls MSA, SD	Y	73864 FQ	82077 MW	94181 TQ	SDBLS	7/08-9/08
	Tennessee	Y	65390 FQ	80290 MW	113120 TQ	USBLS	5/07
	Memphis MSA, TN-MS-AR	Y	90990 FQ	112620 MW		USBLS	5/07
	Texas	Y	66440 FQ	96130 MW	144490 TQ	USBLS	5/07
	Austin-Round Rock MSA, TX	Y	59950 FQ	66060 MW	83270 TQ	USBLS	5/07
	Dallas-Fort Worth-Arlington MSA, TX	Y	66750 FQ	98130 MW		USBLS	5/07
	Houston-Sugar Land-Baytown MSA, TX	Y	56210 FQ	88280 MW	119310 TQ	USBLS	5/07
	San Antonio MSA, TX	Y	101200 FQ	109840 MW	119650 TQ	USBLS	5/07
	Utah	Y	78600 FQ	92580 MW	123020 TQ	USBLS	5/07
	Salt Lake City MSA, UT	Y	83610 FQ	96040 MW	123840 TQ	USBLS	5/07
	Vermont	Y	107150 FQ			USBLS	5/07
	Virginia	Y	81420 FQ	98150 MW	118310 TQ	USBLS	5/07
	Richmond MSA, VA	Y	86180 FQ	102450 MW	121560 TQ	USBLS	5/07
	Virginia Beach-Norfolk-Newport News MSA, VA-NC	Y	76870 FQ	88710 MW	103400 TQ	USBLS	5/07
	Washington	H	41.73 FQ	51.13 MW		WABLS	3/08
	Seattle-Tacoma-Bellevue MSA, WA	Y	92740 FQ	117630 MW		USBLS	5/07
	West Virginia	Y	30138 FQ	89327 MW		WVBLS	7/08-9/08
	Wisconsin	Y	65910 FQ	90910 MW	103360 TQ	USBLS	5/07
	Milwaukee-Waukesha-West Allis MSA, WI	Y	59760 FQ	89690 MW	102280 TQ	USBLS	5/07
	Wyoming	Y	53025 FQ	66588 MW	104079 TQ	WYBLS	9/08
	Puerto Rico	Y	40950 FQ	54710 MW	66490 TQ	USBLS	5/07
	San Juan-Caguas-Guaynabo MSA, PR	Y	43490 FQ	56770 MW	66850 TQ	USBLS	5/07
Oral and Maxillofacial Surgeon	Arkansas	Y	93380 FQ			USBLS	5/07
	California	H	32.07 FQ			CABLS	1/08-3/08
	San Jose-Sunnyvale-Santa Clara MSA, CA	H	37.28 FQ			CABLS	1/08-3/08
	Kansas	H		98.66 AW		JWRLD	4/07-6/07
	Boston-Cambridge-Quincy NECTA, MA	Y	97700 FQ			USBLS	5/07

AE	Average entry wage	AW	Average wage paid	FQ	First quartile wage
AER	Average entry range	AWR	Average wage range	H	Hourly
AEX	Average experienced wage	AXR	Average experienced range	HI	Highest wage paid
ATC	Average total compensation	D	Daily	HR	High end range

LO	Lowest wage paid	MTC	Median total compensation	TCC	Total cash compensation
LR	Low end range	MW	Median wage paid	TQ	Third quartile wage
M	Monthly	MWR	Median wage range	W	Weekly
MCC	Median cash compensation	S	See annotated source	Y	Yearly

Occupation/Type/Industry	Location	Per	Low	Mid	High	Source	Date
Oral and Maxillofacial Surgeon	Minnesota	Y		213325 AW		MNBLS	10/08-12/08
	Minneapolis-Saint Paul MSA, MN-WI	Y		206818 AW		MNBLS	10/08-12/08
	Missouri	Y	97170 FQ			USBLS	5/07
	New Jersey	Y	91510 FQ			USBLS	5/07
	Camden PMSA, NJ	Y	48170 FQ	56700 MW	144260 TQ	USBLS	5/07
	Edison PMSA, NJ	Y	98540 FQ			USBLS	5/07
	Newark-Union PMSA, NJ-PA	Y	90180 FQ	138810 MW		USBLS	5/07
	New York	Y	124460 FQ			USBLS	5/07
	New York-Northern New Jersey-Long Island MSA, NY-NJ-PA	Y	104350 FQ			USBLS	5/07
	North Carolina	Y	144440 FQ			USBLS	5/07
	Raleigh-Cary MSA, NC	Y	104570 FQ			USBLS	5/07
	Philadelphia-Camden-Wilmington MSA, PA-NJ-DE-MD	Y	44530 FQ	57980 MW		USBLS	5/07
	South Carolina	Y	145110 FQ			USBLS	5/07
	Texas	Y	57900 FQ			USBLS	5/07
	Virginia Beach-Norfolk-Newport News MSA, VA-NC	Y	118040 FQ			USBLS	5/07
	Wyoming	Y		193488 AW		WYBLS	9/08
Oral Health Specialist							
State Government	Ohio	H	24.90 LO		34.83 HI	ODAS	2008
Order Clerk	Alabama	Y	18570 FQ	22940 MW	29530 TQ	USBLS	5/07
	Birmingham-Hoover MSA, AL	Y	18940 FQ	24110 MW	32080 TQ	USBLS	5/07
	Montgomery MSA, AL	Y	19740 FQ	23570 MW	30810 TQ	USBLS	5/07
	Alaska	Y	25070 FQ	30890 MW	41950 TQ	USBLS	5/07
	Anchorage MSA, AK	Y	25920 FQ	31300 MW	42300 TQ	USBLS	5/07
	Arizona	Y	21410 FQ	26510 MW	31770 TQ	USBLS	5/07
	Phoenix-Mesa-Scottsdale MSA, AZ	Y	21550 FQ	26580 MW	32420 TQ	USBLS	5/07
	Tucson MSA, AZ	Y	21650 FQ	26120 MW	31050 TQ	USBLS	5/07
	Arkansas	Y	18160 FQ	21750 MW	28260 TQ	USBLS	5/07
	Little Rock-North Little Rock MSA, AR	Y	18550 FQ	22160 MW	29210 TQ	USBLS	5/07
	California	H	11.25 FQ	14.08 MW	17.50 TQ	CABLS	1/08-3/08
	Los Angeles-Long Beach-Glendale PMSA, CA	H	10.59 FQ	13.21 MW	16.56 TQ	CABLS	1/08-3/08
	Oakland-Fremont-Hayward MSA, CA	H	13.00 FQ	15.64 MW	18.85 TQ	CABLS	1/08-3/08
	Riverside-San Bernardino-Ontario MSA, CA	H	11.36 FQ	13.87 MW	17.00 TQ	CABLS	1/08-3/08
	Sacramento-Arden Arcade-Roseville MSA, CA	H	12.70 FQ	14.74 MW	18.11 TQ	CABLS	1/08-3/08
	San Diego-Carlsbad-San Marcos MSA, CA	H	11.43 FQ	13.87 MW	16.67 TQ	CABLS	1/08-3/08
	San Francisco-San Mateo-Redwood PMSA, CA	H	13.07 FQ	16.22 MW	19.41 TQ	CABLS	1/08-3/08
	San Jose-Sunnyvale-Santa Clara MSA, CA	H	13.96 FQ	17.70 MW	22.37 TQ	CABLS	1/08-3/08
	Santa Ana-Anaheim-Irvine PMSA, CA	Y	25310 FQ	30180 MW	36290 TQ	USBLS	5/07
	Santa Rosa-Petaluma MSA, CA	H	11.74 FQ	15.56 MW	18.95 TQ	CABLS	1/08-3/08
	Colorado	Y	23040 FQ	28800 MW	36230 TQ	USBLS	5/07
	Boulder MSA, CO	Y	28970 FQ	34780 MW	40270 TQ	USBLS	5/07
	Colorado Springs MSA, CO	Y	22650 FQ	31190 MW	35620 TQ	USBLS	5/07
	Denver-Aurora MSA, CO	Y	24870 FQ	29210 MW	37380 TQ	USBLS	5/07
	Pueblo MSA, CO	Y	17130 FQ	19440 MW	22940 TQ	USBLS	5/07
	Connecticut	H	10.78 AE	15.08 MW		CTBLS	1/08-3/08
	Bridgeport-Stamford-Norwalk MSA, CT	Y	24170 FQ	29940 MW	36820 TQ	USBLS	5/07
	Hartford-West Hartford-East Hartford MSA, CT	Y	25610 FQ	32120 MW	37440 TQ	USBLS	5/07
	Delaware	Y	24520 FQ	34700 MW	42580 TQ	USBLS	5/07
	Wilmington PMSA, DE-MD-NJ	Y	27980 FQ	36800 MW	44560 TQ	USBLS	5/07
	District of Columbia	Y	29280 FQ	37040 MW	48290 TQ	USBLS	5/07

AE	Average entry wage	AW	Average wage paid	FQ	First quartile wage	LO	Lowest wage paid	MTC	Median total compensation	TCC	Total cash compensation
AER	Average entry range	AWR	Average wage range	H	Hourly	LR	Low end range	MW	Median wage paid	TQ	Third quartile wage
AEX	Average experienced wage	AXR	Average experienced range	HI	Highest wage paid	M	Monthly	MWR	Median wage range	W	Weekly
ATC	Average total compensation	D	Daily	HR	High end range	MCC	Median cash compensation	S	See annotated source	Y	Yearly

Order Clerk

Occupation/Type/Industry	Location	Per	Low	Mid	High	Source	Date
Order Clerk	Washington-Arlington- Alexandria MSA, DC-VA- MD-WV	Y	24230 FQ	31910 MW	40980 TQ	USBLS	5/07
	Florida	Y	19340 FQ	24160 MW	30100 TQ	USBLS	5/07
	Fort Lauderdale-Pompano Beach-Deerfield Beach PMSA, FL	Y	22370 FQ	26900 MW	33340 TQ	USBLS	5/07
	Jacksonville MSA, FL	Y	21080 FQ	25490 MW	31720 TQ	USBLS	5/07
	Lakeland MSA, FL	Y	18230 FQ	23620 MW	29980 TQ	USBLS	5/07
	Miami-Fort Lauderdale-Miami Beach MSA, FL	Y	16470 FQ	22970 MW	29520 TQ	USBLS	5/07
	Orlando-Kissimmee MSA, FL	Y	21070 FQ	24480 MW	29810 TQ	USBLS	5/07
	Tampa-St. Petersburg- Clearwater MSA, FL	Y	22550 FQ	27380 MW	32350 TQ	USBLS	5/07
	West Palm Beach-Boca Raton- Boynton Beach PMSA, FL	Y	20110 FQ	27110 MW	31350 TQ	USBLS	5/07
	Georgia	Y	21100 FQ	26140 MW	32350 TQ	USBLS	5/07
	Atlanta-Sandy Springs- Marietta MSA, GA	Y	22910 FQ	28720 MW	35580 TQ	USBLS	5/07
	Hawaii	Y	20950 FQ	25610 MW	31830 TQ	USBLS	5/07
	Honolulu MSA, HI	Y	20700 FQ	25400 MW	31960 TQ	USBLS	5/07
	Idaho	Y	19070 FQ	29860 MW	42790 TQ	USBLS	5/07
	Boise City-Nampa MSA, ID	Y	19130 FQ	41540 MW	46240 TQ	USBLS	5/07
	Illinois	Y	20320 FQ	27370 MW	35240 TQ	USBLS	5/07
	Chicago-Naperville-Joliet MSA, IL-IN-WI	Y	20990 FQ	28460 MW	36300 TQ	USBLS	5/07
	Peoria MSA, IL	Y	20610 FQ	24300 MW	31720 TQ	USBLS	5/07
	Indiana	Y	21340 FQ	26880 MW	32930 TQ	USBLS	5/07
	Elkhart-Goshen MSA, IN	Y	20930 FQ	27220 MW	30600 TQ	USBLS	5/07
	Gary PMSA, IN	Y	21340 FQ	28640 MW	35410 TQ	USBLS	5/07
	Indianapolis-Carmel MSA, IN	Y	23820 FQ	30170 MW	36320 TQ	USBLS	5/07
	Iowa	Y	22830 FQ	28330 MW	34990 TQ	USBLS	5/07
	Des Moines-West Des Moines MSA, IA	Y	27270 FQ	38340 MW	52350 TQ	USBLS	5/07
	Kansas	Y	18460 FQ	23010 MW	29590 TQ	USBLS	5/07
	Wichita MSA, KS	Y	17450 FQ	22780 MW	30710 TQ	USBLS	5/07
	Kentucky	Y	21019 FQ	25599 MW	30750 TQ	KYBLS	2008
	Louisville-Jefferson County MSA, KY-IN	Y	20110 FQ	26040 MW	30490 TQ	USBLS	5/07
	Louisiana	H	8.81 FQ	10.95 MW	13.91 TQ	LABLS	1/08-3/08
	Baton Rouge MSA, LA	Y	18280 FQ	21800 MW	27030 TQ	USBLS	5/07
	New Orleans-Metairie-Kenner MSA, LA	Y	19570 FQ	23740 MW	29780 TQ	USBLS	5/07
	Portland-South Portland- Biddeford MSA, ME	Y	20960 FQ	23520 MW	29130 TQ	USBLS	5/07
	Maryland	Y		30825 MW		MDBLS	3/08
	Baltimore-Towson MSA, MD	Y	25030 FQ	31560 MW	41110 TQ	USBLS	5/07
	Bethesda-Gaithersburg- Frederick PMSA, MD	Y	24330 FQ	29810 MW	39680 TQ	USBLS	5/07
	Massachusetts	Y	25820 FQ	31620 MW	40570 TQ	USBLS	5/07
	Boston-Cambridge-Quincy NECTA, MA	Y	26830 FQ	33350 MW	44980 TQ	USBLS	5/07
	Worcester MSA, MA-CT	Y	24200 FQ	30030 MW	35840 TQ	USBLS	5/07
	Michigan	Y	23830 FQ	31010 MW	39340 TQ	USBLS	5/07
	Detroit-Warren-Livonia MSA, MI	Y	26810 FQ	34740 MW	43250 TQ	USBLS	5/07
	Grand Rapids-Wyoming MSA, MI	Y	24870 FQ	30710 MW	37670 TQ	USBLS	5/07
	Warren-Troy-Farmington Hills PMSA, MI	Y	27070 FQ	34090 MW	41330 TQ	USBLS	5/07
	Minnesota	Y	25051 FQ	32535 MW	41090 TQ	MNBLS	10/08-12/08
	Duluth-Superior MSA, MN-WI	Y	20930 FQ	24021 MW	29371 TQ	MNBLS	10/08-12/08
	Minneapolis-Saint Paul MSA, MN-WI	Y	27706 FQ	34897 MW	43994 TQ	MNBLS	10/08-12/08
	Rochester MSA, MN	Y	21706 FQ	24979 MW	33170 TQ	MNBLS	10/08-12/08
	Mississippi	Y	19460 FQ	23630 MW	29080 TQ	USBLS	5/07
	Jackson MSA, MS	Y	21450 FQ	27160 MW	33730 TQ	USBLS	5/07
	Missouri	Y	18010 FQ	22350 MW	30030 TQ	USBLS	5/07
	Kansas City MSA, MO-KS	Y	19350 FQ	24120 MW	32450 TQ	USBLS	5/07
	St. Louis MSA, MO-IL	Y	22390 FQ	29050 MW	35360 TQ	USBLS	5/07
	Montana	Y	19250 FQ	24350 MW	30840 TQ	USBLS	5/07
	Billings MSA, MT	Y	21830 FQ	25680 MW	31400 TQ	USBLS	5/07

AE	Average entry wage	**AW**	Average wage paid	**FQ**	First quartile wage
AER	Average entry range	**AWR**	Average wage range	**H**	Hourly
AEX	Average experienced wage	**AXR**	Average experienced range	**HI**	Highest wage paid
ATC	Average total compensation **D**	Daily		**HR**	High end range

LO	Lowest wage paid	**MTC**	Median total compensation	**TCC** Total cash compensation
LR	Low end range	**MW**	Median wage paid	**TQ** Third quartile wage
M	Monthly	**MWR**	Median wage range	**W** Weekly
MCC	Median cash compensation	**S**	See annotated source	**Y** Yearly

Order Clerk

Occupation/Type/Industry	Location	Per	Low	Mid	High	Source	Date
Order Clerk	Missoula MSA, MT	Y	17400 FQ	20900 MW	23960 TQ	USBLS	5/07
	Nebraska	Y	18920 FQ	22180 MW	26520 TQ	USBLS	5/07
	Omaha-Council Bluffs MSA, NE-IA	Y	21080 FQ	23920 MW	29150 TQ	USBLS	5/07
	Nevada	H	10.31 FQ	11.93 MW	14.61 TQ	NVBLS	5/08
	Las Vegas-Paradise MSA, NV	H	9.87 FQ	11.79 MW	14.52 TQ	NVBLS	5/08
	New Hampshire	H	9.63 AE	13.16 MW	16.16 AEX	NHBLS	6/08
	Manchester MSA, NH	Y	23530 FQ	32570 MW	41020 TQ	USBLS	5/07
	Nashua NECTA, NH-MA	Y	26010 FQ	31240 MW	37220 TQ	USBLS	5/07
	New Jersey	Y	25970 FQ	33100 MW	42850 TQ	USBLS	5/07
	Camden PMSA, NJ	Y	26210 FQ	31690 MW	39720 TQ	USBLS	5/07
	Edison PMSA, NJ	Y	24420 FQ	36030 MW	46970 TQ	USBLS	5/07
	Newark-Union PMSA, NJ-PA	Y	26330 FQ	32940 MW	43520 TQ	USBLS	5/07
	New Mexico	Y	17670 FQ	21830 MW	27950 TQ	USBLS	5/07
	Albuquerque MSA, NM	Y	19850 FQ	22750 MW	26930 TQ	USBLS	5/07
	Farmington MSA, NM	Y	17080 FQ	19390 MW	27180 TQ	USBLS	5/07
	New York	Y	22200 FQ	28990 MW	37030 TQ	USBLS	5/07
	Albany-Schenectady-Troy MSA, NY	Y	20650 FQ	26320 MW	34370 TQ	USBLS	5/07
	Buffalo-Niagara Falls MSA, NY	Y	21910 FQ	26260 MW	33760 TQ	USBLS	5/07
	Nassau-Suffolk PMSA, NY	Y	25110 FQ	30660 MW	38390 TQ	USBLS	5/07
	New York-Northern New Jersey-Long Island MSA, NY-NJ-PA	Y	25440 FQ	32700 MW	41580 TQ	USBLS	5/07
	Utica-Rome MSA, NY	Y	18410 FQ	22290 MW	27760 TQ	USBLS	5/07
	North Carolina	Y	21740 FQ	27010 MW	33000 TQ	USBLS	5/07
	Charlotte-Gastonia-Concord MSA, NC-SC	Y	22360 FQ	27560 MW	34160 TQ	USBLS	5/07
	Raleigh-Cary MSA, NC	Y	23430 FQ	28090 MW	35420 TQ	USBLS	5/07
	North Dakota	Y	20660 FQ	25470 MW	31290 TQ	USBLS	5/07
	Fargo MSA, ND-MN	Y	24170 FQ	29240 MW	34880 TQ	USBLS	5/07
	Ohio	Y	21490 FQ	26940 MW	31780 TQ	USBLS	5/07
	Canton-Massillon MSA, OH	Y	17750 FQ	22860 MW	28570 TQ	USBLS	5/07
	Cincinnati-Middletown MSA, OH-KY-IN	Y	22200 FQ	27260 MW	33000 TQ	USBLS	5/07
	Cleveland-Elyria-Mentor MSA, OH	Y	20470 FQ	25820 MW	30870 TQ	USBLS	5/07
	Columbus MSA, OH	Y	22030 FQ	26800 MW	30130 TQ	USBLS	5/07
	Dayton MSA, OH	Y	24850 FQ	29890 MW	37620 TQ	USBLS	5/07
	Oklahoma	Y	18850 FQ	23870 MW	30680 TQ	USBLS	5/07
	Oklahoma City MSA, OK	Y	19100 FQ	22750 MW	27790 TQ	USBLS	5/07
	Tulsa MSA, OK	Y	18710 FQ	26270 MW	31690 TQ	USBLS	5/07
	Oregon	H	10.96 FQ	13.99 MW	17.58 TQ	ORBLS	5/08
	Medford MSA, OR	Y	19740 FQ	24250 MW	27900 TQ	USBLS	5/07
	Portland-Vancouver-Beaverton MSA, OR-WA	Y	25570 FQ	31490 MW	38250 TQ	USBLS	5/07
	Pennsylvania	Y	20630 FQ	26040 MW	34850 TQ	USBLS	5/07
	Allentown-Bethlehem-Easton MSA, PA-NJ	Y	25380 FQ	32240 MW	38840 TQ	USBLS	5/07
	Philadelphia-Camden-Wilmington MSA, PA-NJ-DE-MD	Y	22580 FQ	30100 MW	41460 TQ	USBLS	5/07
	Pittsburgh MSA, PA	Y	20600 FQ	25910 MW	33550 TQ	USBLS	5/07
	Rhode Island	Y	23150 FQ	28940 MW	35040 TQ	USBLS	5/07
	Providence-Fall River-Warwick MSA, RI-MA	Y	23190 FQ	29660 MW	36210 TQ	USBLS	5/07
	South Carolina	Y	20190 FQ	24810 MW	31530 TQ	USBLS	5/07
	Charleston-North Charleston MSA, SC	Y	16980 FQ	21850 MW	28270 TQ	USBLS	5/07
	Columbia MSA, SC	Y	20780 FQ	24950 MW	30080 TQ	USBLS	5/07
	Florence MSA, SC	Y	20180 FQ	24860 MW	30320 TQ	USBLS	5/07
	Myrtle Beach-Conway-North Myrtle Beach MSA, SC	Y	20030 FQ	23190 MW	28250 TQ	USBLS	5/07
	South Dakota	Y	21134 FQ	24215 MW	28651 TQ	SDBLS	7/08-9/08
	Sioux Falls MSA, SD	Y	22746 FQ	25839 MW	30257 TQ	SDBLS	7/08-9/08
	Tennessee	Y	18170 FQ	21940 MW	28780 TQ	USBLS	5/07
	Memphis MSA, TN-MS-AR	Y	21040 FQ	24540 MW	29560 TQ	USBLS	5/07
	Nashville-Davidson-Murfreesboro MSA, TN	Y	19590 FQ	23410 MW	30090 TQ	USBLS	5/07
	Texas	Y	19660 FQ	24900 MW	31560 TQ	USBLS	5/07
	Austin-Round Rock MSA, TX	Y	20500 FQ	24540 MW	32140 TQ	USBLS	5/07

AE Average entry wage	AW Average wage paid	FQ First quartile wage	LO Lowest wage paid	MTC Median total compensation TCC Total cash compensation
AER Average entry range	AWR Average wage range	H Hourly	LR Low end range	MW Median wage paid TQ Third quartile wage
AEX Average experienced wage	AXR Average experienced range	HI Highest wage paid	M Monthly	MWR Median wage range W Weekly
ATC Average total compensation	D Daily	HR High end range	MCC Median cash compensation	S See annotated source Y Yearly

Occupation/Type/Industry	Location	Per	Low	Mid	High	Source	Date
Order Clerk	Dallas-Fort Worth-Arlington						
	MSA, TX	Y	20900 FQ	26210 MW	35360 TQ	USBLS	5/07
	El Paso MSA, TX	Y	16600 FQ	18800 MW	23200 TQ	USBLS	5/07
	Houston-Sugar Land-Baytown						
	MSA, TX	Y	20590 FQ	26260 MW	31370 TQ	USBLS	5/07
	San Antonio MSA, TX	Y	19570 FQ	25570 MW	31020 TQ	USBLS	5/07
	Utah	Y	19340 FQ	23400 MW	30510 TQ	USBLS	5/07
	Logan MSA, UT-ID	Y	20680 FQ	23470 MW	27900 TQ	USBLS	5/07
	Salt Lake City MSA, UT	Y	19610 FQ	24690 MW	34600 TQ	USBLS	5/07
	Vermont	Y	23720 FQ	27940 MW	32830 TQ	USBLS	5/07
	Burlington-South Burlington						
	MSA, VT	Y	25980 FQ	29080 MW	34490 TQ	USBLS	5/07
	Virginia	Y	20270 FQ	27210 MW	37940 TQ	USBLS	5/07
	Richmond MSA, VA	Y	25940 FQ	35200 MW	51590 TQ	USBLS	5/07
	Virginia Beach-Norfolk-						
	Newport News MSA, VA-NC	Y	18290 FQ	22590 MW	31460 TQ	USBLS	5/07
	Washington	H	11.85 FQ	14.78 MW	18.85 TQ	WABLS	3/08
	Seattle-Tacoma-Bellevue						
	MSA, WA	Y	25820 FQ	32020 MW	41340 TQ	USBLS	5/07
	Wisconsin	Y	24560 FQ	28390 MW	31830 TQ	USBLS	5/07
	Green Bay MSA, WI	Y	26500 FQ	31920 MW	38640 TQ	USBLS	5/07
	Milwaukee-Waukesha-West						
	Allis MSA, WI	Y	24480 FQ	30110 MW	37950 TQ	USBLS	5/07
	Wyoming	Y	19197 FQ	22609 MW	28685 TQ	WYBLS	9/08
	Cheyenne MSA, WY	Y	18717 FQ	20739 MW	23577 TQ	WYBLS	9/08
	Puerto Rico	Y	14620 FQ	18240 MW	22850 TQ	USBLS	5/07
	San Juan-Caguas-Guaynabo						
	MSA, PR	Y	14220 FQ	17760 MW	22630 TQ	USBLS	5/07
Order Filler/Picker	United States	H		12.00 AW		MMH01	2008
Organist							
Bachelor's Degree in Organ or Sacred Music or CAGO Certificate	United States	Y		63131-83123 ATC		AGO	2009
Doctorate in Organ or Sacred Music or FAGO Certificate	United States	Y		80915-107967 ATC		AGO	2009
Orthodontist	Colorado	Y	110240 FQ			USBLS	5/07
	Louisiana	Y		166784 AW		LABLS	1/08-3/08
	Maryland	Y		189250 AW		MDBLS	3/08
	Montana	Y	85040 FQ	91820 MW	98600 TQ	USBLS	5/07
	Nevada	H	41.96 FQ	90.52 AW		NVBLS	5/08
	New Jersey	Y	117450 FQ			USBLS	5/07
	New York	Y	116820 FQ			USBLS	5/07
	Oklahoma	Y	132220 FQ			USBLS	5/07
	Utah	Y	58800 FQ	63580 MW	68260 TQ	USBLS	5/07
	West Virginia	Y		193453 AW		WVBLS	7/08-9/08
Orthopaedic Technologist	United States	Y		44458 AW		NAOT	2008
Orthopedic Surgeon	United States	Y			400000 HI	LLIFE	2008
Spine	United States	Y		611670 AW		CEJ01	2008
Orthoptist	United States	Y	50000 AE			WIHC	2007
Orthotist and Prosthetist	Alabama	Y	47350 FQ	58510 MW	73920 TQ	USBLS	5/07
	Birmingham-Hoover MSA, AL	Y	55520 FQ	69540 MW	81040 TQ	USBLS	5/07
	Arizona	Y	34000 FQ	37370 MW	70390 TQ	USBLS	5/07
	Phoenix-Mesa-Scottsdale						
	MSA, AZ	Y	33890 FQ	37150 MW	70560 TQ	USBLS	5/07
	Arkansas	Y	48160 FQ	54530 MW	60610 TQ	USBLS	5/07
	California	H	18.45 FQ	22.40 MW	26.85 TQ	CABLS	1/08-3/08
	Los Angeles-Long Beach-						
	Glendale PMSA, CA	H	17.89 FQ	22.20 MW	27.40 TQ	CABLS	1/08-3/08
	Oakland-Fremont-Hayward						
	MSA, CA	H	20.08 FQ	21.45 MW	22.82 TQ	CABLS	1/08-3/08
	Riverside-San Bernardino-						
	Ontario MSA, CA	H	11.79 FQ	20.93 MW	24.02 TQ	CABLS	1/08-3/08
	San Diego-Carlsbad-San						
	Marcos MSA, CA	H	19.67 FQ	22.57 MW	28.69 TQ	CABLS	1/08-3/08

AE	Average entry wage	**AW**	Average wage paid	**FQ**	First quartile wage	**LO**	Lowest wage paid	**MTC** Median total compensation	**TCC** Total cash compensation
AER	Average entry range	**AWR**	Average wage range	**H**	Hourly	**LR**	Low end range	**MW** Median wage paid	**TQ** Third quartile wage
AEX	Average experienced wage	**AXR**	Average experienced range	**HI**	Highest wage paid	**M**	Monthly	**MWR** Median wage range	**W** Weekly
ATC	Average total compensation	**D**	Daily	**HR**	High end range	**MCC**	Median cash compensation	**S** See annotated source	**Y** Yearly

Orthotist and Prosthetist

Occupation/Type/Industry	Location	Per	Low	Mid	High	Source	Date
Orthotist and Prosthetist	San Francisco-San Mateo-Redwood PMSA, CA	H	20.85 FQ	25.87 MW	29.83 TQ	CABLS	1/08-3/08
	Colorado	Y	30250 FQ	36220 MW	58150 TQ	USBLS	5/07
	Washington-Arlington-Alexandria MSA, DC-VA-MD-WV	Y	40010 FQ	62320 MW	108780 TQ	USBLS	5/07
	Florida	Y	53370 FQ	76660 MW	107130 TQ	USBLS	5/07
	Jacksonville MSA, FL	Y	58530 FQ	103990 MW	117410 TQ	USBLS	5/07
	Miami-Fort Lauderdale-Miami Beach MSA, FL	Y	65600 FQ	78190 MW	105790 TQ	USBLS	5/07
	Tampa-St. Petersburg-Clearwater MSA, FL	Y	44310 FQ	60910 MW	85760 TQ	USBLS	5/07
	West Palm Beach-Boca Raton-Boynton Beach PMSA, FL	Y	68970 FQ	78830 MW	101960 TQ	USBLS	5/07
	Georgia	Y	22980 FQ	30880 MW	45330 TQ	USBLS	5/07
	Atlanta-Sandy Springs-Marietta MSA, GA	Y	22150 FQ	27650 MW	38220 TQ	USBLS	5/07
	Illinois	Y	54600 FQ	65460 MW	91220 TQ	USBLS	5/07
	Chicago-Naperville-Joliet MSA, IL-IN-WI	Y	58940 FQ	73340 MW	94270 TQ	USBLS	5/07
	Indiana	Y	61750 FQ	100600 MW	132520 TQ	USBLS	5/07
	Iowa	Y	82550 FQ	92770 MW	100930 TQ	USBLS	5/07
	Kentucky	Y	41194 FQ	58718 MW	74551 TQ	KYBLS	2008
	Louisiana	H	18.85 FQ	21.81 MW	25.31 TQ	LABLS	1/08-3/08
	Maryland	Y		52225 MW		MDBLS	3/08
	Massachusetts	Y	39810 FQ	48550 MW	59920 TQ	USBLS	5/07
	Boston-Cambridge-Quincy NECTA, MA	Y	35960 FQ	44910 MW	52620 TQ	USBLS	5/07
	Michigan	Y	38160 FQ	64530 MW	83200 TQ	USBLS	5/07
	Detroit-Warren-Livonia MSA, MI	Y	46780 FQ	74730 MW	91330 TQ	USBLS	5/07
	Minnesota	Y	63129 FQ	75119 MW	83750 TQ	MNBLS	10/08-12/08
	Minneapolis-Saint Paul MSA, MN-WI	Y	65713 FQ	76604 MW	84671 TQ	MNBLS	10/08-12/08
	Mississippi	Y	35370 FQ	46570 MW	89220 TQ	USBLS	5/07
	Jackson MSA, MS	Y	29620 FQ	49320 MW	88560 TQ	USBLS	5/07
	Missouri	Y	52570 FQ	70580 MW	82290 TQ	USBLS	5/07
	Kansas City MSA, MO-KS	Y	74340 FQ	81650 MW	92410 TQ	USBLS	5/07
	Nevada	H	17.97 FQ	21.18 MW	29.51 TQ	NVBLS	5/08
	New Hampshire	H	25.57 AE	37.17 MW	62.95 AEX	NHBLS	6/08
	New Jersey	Y	41420 FQ	50750 MW	65650 TQ	USBLS	5/07
	Camden PMSA, NJ	Y	42690 FQ	49610 MW	55680 TQ	USBLS	5/07
	Newark-Union PMSA, NJ-PA	Y	42410 FQ	62690 MW	83760 TQ	USBLS	5/07
	New York	Y	58700 FQ	69330 MW	78460 TQ	USBLS	5/07
	Nassau-Suffolk PMSA, NY	Y	60510 FQ	101190 MW	128350 TQ	USBLS	5/07
	New York-Northern New Jersey-Long Island MSA, NY-NJ-PA	Y	59160 FQ	70120 MW	79180 TQ	USBLS	5/07
	North Carolina	Y	28460 FQ	33210 MW	51240 TQ	USBLS	5/07
	Raleigh-Cary MSA, NC	Y	27990 FQ	31910 MW	40760 TQ	USBLS	5/07
	Ohio	Y	43330 FQ	61820 MW	77260 TQ	USBLS	5/07
	Cincinnati-Middletown MSA, OH-KY-IN	Y	64410 FQ	70710 MW	77300 TQ	USBLS	5/07
	Cleveland-Elyria-Mentor MSA, OH	Y	42730 FQ	53720 MW	71750 TQ	USBLS	5/07
	Columbus MSA, OH	Y	51550 FQ	74910 MW	84240 TQ	USBLS	5/07
	Oklahoma	Y	39460 FQ	50740 MW	61140 TQ	USBLS	5/07
	Oklahoma City MSA, OK	Y	40860 FQ	52200 MW	62190 TQ	USBLS	5/07
	Oregon	H	33.63 FQ	36.46 MW	39.48 TQ	ORBLS	5/08
	Portland-Vancouver-Beaverton MSA, OR-WA	Y	68880 FQ	74880 MW	80870 TQ	USBLS	5/07
	Pennsylvania	Y	46510 FQ	75080 MW	93930 TQ	USBLS	5/07
	Philadelphia-Camden-Wilmington MSA, PA-NJ-DE-MD	Y	40650 FQ	50740 MW	65640 TQ	USBLS	5/07
	Pittsburgh MSA, PA	Y	43800 FQ	52770 MW	74520 TQ	USBLS	5/07
	Rhode Island	Y	46330 FQ	51240 MW	75000 TQ	USBLS	5/07
	Providence-Fall River-Warwick MSA, RI-MA	Y	46840 FQ	52450 MW	74090 TQ	USBLS	5/07
	South Carolina	Y	56140 FQ	74200 MW	83070 TQ	USBLS	5/07
	Charleston-North Charleston MSA, SC	Y	66850 FQ	72360 MW	77860 TQ	USBLS	5/07

AE	Average entry wage	AW	Average wage paid	FQ	First quartile wage
AER	Average entry range	AWR	Average wage range	H	Hourly
AEX	Average experienced wage	AXR	Average experienced range	HI	Highest wage paid
ATC	Average total compensation	D	Daily	HR	High end range

LO	Lowest wage paid	MTC	Median total compensation	TCC	Total cash compensation
LR	Low end range	MW	Median wage paid	TQ	Third quartile wage
M	Monthly	MWR	Median wage range	W	Weekly
MCC	Median cash compensation	S	See annotated source	Y	Yearly

Occupation/Type/Industry	Location	Per	Low	Mid	High	Source	Date
Orthotist and Prosthetist	Columbia MSA, SC	Y	51980 FQ	80220 MW	131170 TQ	USBLS	5/07
	Tennessee	Y	26790 FQ	43800 MW	58940 TQ	USBLS	5/07
	Memphis MSA, TN-MS-AR	Y	49710 FQ	56700 MW	64640 TQ	USBLS	5/07
	Texas	Y	60970 FQ	72810 MW	81110 TQ	USBLS	5/07
	Dallas-Fort Worth-Arlington MSA, TX	Y	43830 FQ	68130 MW	76980 TQ	USBLS	5/07
	El Paso MSA, TX	Y	86430 FQ	99400 MW	114890 TQ	USBLS	5/07
	Houston-Sugar Land-Baytown MSA, TX	Y	69570 FQ	78040 MW	89280 TQ	USBLS	5/07
	Utah	Y	30770 FQ	37960 MW	48560 TQ	USBLS	5/07
	Virginia	Y	52750 FQ	64730 MW	74820 TQ	USBLS	5/07
	Virginia Beach-Norfolk-Newport News MSA, VA-NC	Y	58020 FQ	65580 MW	71950 TQ	USBLS	5/07
	Washington	H	25.13 FQ	31.48 MW	42.58 TQ	WABLS	3/08
	Seattle-Tacoma-Bellevue MSA, WA	Y	52810 FQ	65310 MW	85620 TQ	USBLS	5/07
	West Virginia	Y	49690 FQ	61013 MW	78611	WVBLS	7/08-9/08
	Wisconsin	Y	38420 FQ	60170 MW	85270 TQ	USBLS	5/07
	Puerto Rico	Y	32260 FQ	46290 MW	59490 TQ	USBLS	5/07
Otolaryngologist	United States	Y	180084 LO	264878 AW	392890 HI	PSEARCH	2008
Outdoor Power Equipment and Other Small Engine Mechanic	Alabama	Y	17640 FQ	23210 MW	29070 TQ	USBLS	5/07
	Birmingham-Hoover MSA, AL	Y	21980 FQ	24680 MW	29100 TQ	USBLS	5/07
	Montgomery MSA, AL	Y	16250 FQ	17550 MW	18850 TQ	USBLS	5/07
	Alaska	Y	27550 FQ	29840 MW	32380 TQ	USBLS	5/07
	Arizona	Y	24600 FQ	28830 MW	35680 TQ	USBLS	5/07
	Phoenix-Mesa-Scottsdale MSA, AZ	Y	25940 FQ	30240 MW	36460 TQ	USBLS	5/07
	Arkansas	Y	16860 FQ	26620 MW	30830 TQ	USBLS	5/07
	Little Rock-North Little Rock MSA, AR	Y	23620 FQ	28130 MW	30880 TQ	USBLS	5/07
	California	H	11.39 FQ	14.53 MW	18.22 TQ	CABLS	1/08-3/08
	Los Angeles-Long Beach-Glendale PMSA, CA	H	12.38 FQ	14.79 MW	17.89 TQ	CABLS	1/08-3/08
	Oakland-Fremont-Hayward MSA, CA	H	14.62 FQ	17.12 MW	19.44 TQ	CABLS	1/08-3/08
	Riverside-San Bernardino-Ontario MSA, CA	H	9.48 FQ	11.46 MW	13.89 TQ	CABLS	1/08-3/08
	Sacramento-Arden Arcade-Roseville MSA, CA	H	10.53 FQ	12.08 MW	17.48 TQ	CABLS	1/08-3/08
	San Diego-Carlsbad-San Marcos MSA, CA	H	15.21 FQ	19.64 MW	22.99 TQ	CABLS	1/08-3/08
	San Francisco-San Mateo-Redwood PMSA, CA	H	12.78 FQ	14.33 MW	20.05 TQ	CABLS	1/08-3/08
	San Jose-Sunnyvale-Santa Clara MSA, CA	H	12.58 FQ	14.12 MW	18.04 TQ	CABLS	1/08-3/08
	Santa Ana-Anaheim-Irvine PMSA, CA	Y	23790 FQ	33080 MW	42160 TQ	USBLS	5/07
	Colorado	Y	26490 FQ	31270 MW	41540 TQ	USBLS	5/07
	Colorado Springs MSA, CO	Y	24020 FQ	27890 MW	30850 TQ	USBLS	5/07
	Denver-Aurora MSA, CO	Y	28990 FQ	32390 MW	41450 TQ	USBLS	5/07
	Connecticut	H	11.48 AE	16.29 MW		CTBLS	1/08-3/08
	Bridgeport-Stamford-Norwalk MSA, CT	Y	23980 FQ	33940 MW	38820 TQ	USBLS	5/07
	Hartford-West Hartford-East Hartford MSA, CT	Y	26460 FQ	32500 MW	42470 TQ	USBLS	5/07
	Delaware	Y	25640 FQ	30960 MW	36210 TQ	USBLS	5/07
	Wilmington PMSA, DE-MD-NJ	Y	27130 FQ	31880 MW	36730 TQ	USBLS	5/07
	Washington-Arlington-Alexandria MSA, DC-VA-MD-WV	Y	30150 FQ	36420 MW	46170 TQ	USBLS	5/07
	Florida	Y	25600 FQ	29750 MW	35540 TQ	USBLS	5/07
	Fort Lauderdale-Pompano Beach-Deerfield Beach PMSA, FL	Y	23130 FQ	27720 MW	30890 TQ	USBLS	5/07
	Jacksonville MSA, FL	Y	27110 FQ	29740 MW	33980 TQ	USBLS	5/07
	Lakeland MSA, FL	Y	27350 FQ	30540 MW	35920 TQ	USBLS	5/07
	Miami-Fort Lauderdale-Miami Beach MSA, FL	Y	25310 FQ	29280 MW	34430 TQ	USBLS	5/07

Occupation/Type/Industry	Location	Per	Low	Mid	High	Source	Date
Outdoor Power Equipment and Other Small Engine Mechanic	Orlando-Kissimmee MSA, FL	Y	25460 FQ	31500 MW	37810 TQ	USBLS	5/07
	Tampa-St. Petersburg-Clearwater MSA, FL	Y	26870 FQ	29940 MW	33050 TQ	USBLS	5/07
	West Palm Beach-Boca Raton-Boynton Beach PMSA, FL	Y	32360 FQ	37010 MW	42980 TQ	USBLS	5/07
	Georgia	Y	23330 FQ	28470 MW	34790 TQ	USBLS	5/07
	Atlanta-Sandy Springs-Marietta MSA, GA	Y	28370 FQ	34730 MW	42250 TQ	USBLS	5/07
	Augusta-Richmond County MSA, GA-SC	Y	22160 FQ	25520 MW	30120 TQ	USBLS	5/07
	Hawaii	Y	24790 FQ	32810 MW	44020 TQ	USBLS	5/07
	Honolulu MSA, HI	Y	20540 FQ	27580 MW	36460 TQ	USBLS	5/07
	Idaho	Y	19930 FQ	22560 MW	28310 TQ	USBLS	5/07
	Illinois	Y	17900 FQ	27790 MW	32720 TQ	USBLS	5/07
	Chicago-Naperville-Joliet MSA, IL-IN-WI	Y	21680 FQ	28440 MW	32820 TQ	USBLS	5/07
	Indiana	Y	23500 FQ	27580 MW	31770 TQ	USBLS	5/07
	Gary PMSA, IN	Y	23530 FQ	27780 MW	31740 TQ	USBLS	5/07
	Indianapolis-Carmel MSA, IN	Y	24050 FQ	29160 MW	35260 TQ	USBLS	5/07
	Terre Haute MSA, IN	Y	23590 FQ	26190 MW	28810 TQ	USBLS	5/07
	Iowa	Y	20700 FQ	26310 MW	32690 TQ	USBLS	5/07
	Des Moines-West Des Moines MSA, IA	Y	18730 FQ	22450 MW	30080 TQ	USBLS	5/07
	Kansas	Y	20650 FQ	25660 MW	33390 TQ	USBLS	5/07
	Kentucky	Y	25150 FQ	28992 MW	32747 TQ	KYBLS	2008
	Louisville-Jefferson County MSA, KY-IN	Y	25950 FQ	28710 MW	31860 TQ	USBLS	5/07
	Louisiana	H	8.85 FQ	12.59 MW	15.19 TQ	LABLS	1/08-3/08
	Maine	Y	20470 FQ	25690 MW	29950 TQ	USBLS	5/07
	Portland-South Portland-Biddeford MSA, ME	Y	25590 FQ	27900 MW	30170 TQ	USBLS	5/07
	Maryland	Y		34225 MW		MDBLS	3/08
	Baltimore-Towson MSA, MD	Y	24870 FQ	31140 MW	37520 TQ	USBLS	5/07
	Bethesda-Gaithersburg-Frederick PMSA, MD	Y	29910 FQ	33930 MW	38180 TQ	USBLS	5/07
	Massachusetts	Y	25990 FQ	33240 MW	37960 TQ	USBLS	5/07
	Barnstable Town MSA, MA	Y	29190 FQ	33390 MW	37590 TQ	USBLS	5/07
	Boston-Cambridge-Quincy NECTA, MA	Y	31620 FQ	36660 MW	42110 TQ	USBLS	5/07
	Worcester MSA, MA-CT	Y	20060 FQ	22880 MW	29890 TQ	USBLS	5/07
	Michigan	Y	22970 FQ	28590 MW	36040 TQ	USBLS	5/07
	Detroit-Warren-Livonia MSA, MI	Y	25410 FQ	29980 MW	38270 TQ	USBLS	5/07
	Grand Rapids-Wyoming MSA, MI	Y	26620 FQ	32950 MW	37230 TQ	USBLS	5/07
	Warren-Troy-Farmington Hills PMSA, MI	Y	20660 FQ	27470 MW	38050 TQ	USBLS	5/07
	Minnesota	Y	25772 FQ	30251 MW	35978 TQ	MNBLS	10/08-12/08
	Duluth-Superior MSA, MN-WI	Y	17213 FQ	20139 MW	29790 TQ	MNBLS	10/08-12/08
	Minneapolis-Saint Paul MSA, MN-WI	Y	27513 FQ	31919 MW	37520 TQ	MNBLS	10/08-12/08
	Mississippi	Y	15620 FQ	19820 MW	25570 TQ	USBLS	5/07
	Gulfport-Biloxi MSA, MS	Y	19130 FQ	24180 MW	31400 TQ	USBLS	5/07
	Missouri	Y	18690 FQ	25940 MW	35430 TQ	USBLS	5/07
	Kansas City MSA, MO-KS	Y	27140 FQ	37530 MW	64860 TQ	USBLS	5/07
	St. Louis MSA, MO-IL	Y	17630 FQ	19750 MW	29450 TQ	USBLS	5/07
	Montana	Y	17290 FQ	24150 MW	30540 TQ	USBLS	5/07
	Billings MSA, MT	Y	13710 FQ	14630 MW	25720 TQ	USBLS	5/07
	Nebraska	Y	22150 FQ	28750 MW	36710 TQ	USBLS	5/07
	Omaha-Council Bluffs MSA, NE-IA	Y	25190 FQ	30530 MW	37790 TQ	USBLS	5/07
	Nevada	H	12.29 FQ	14.62 MW	17.55 TQ	NVBLS	5/08
	Las Vegas-Paradise MSA, NV	H	11.85 FQ	14.68 MW	18.06 TQ	NVBLS	5/08
	New Hampshire	H	11.51 AE	14.12 MW	17.15 AEX	NHBLS	6/08
	New Jersey	Y	25670 FQ	33020 MW	39030 TQ	USBLS	5/07
	Camden PMSA, NJ	Y	22880 FQ	33680 MW	36820 TQ	USBLS	5/07
	Edison PMSA, NJ	Y	32050 FQ	37300 MW	43660 TQ	USBLS	5/07
	Newark-Union PMSA, NJ-PA	Y	22770 FQ	25480 MW	37690 TQ	USBLS	5/07
	New Mexico	Y	18570 FQ	23270 MW	31220 TQ	USBLS	5/07
	Albuquerque MSA, NM	Y	17150 FQ	20840 MW	26810 TQ	USBLS	5/07
	New York	Y	26470 FQ	32030 MW	38520 TQ	USBLS	5/07

AE Average entry wage	**AW** Average wage paid	**FQ** First quartile wage	**LO** Lowest wage paid	**MTC** Median total compensation	**TCC** Total cash compensation
AER Average entry range	**AWR** Average wage range	**H** Hourly	**LR** Low end range	**MW** Median wage paid	**TQ** Third quartile wage
AEX Average experienced wage	**AXR** Average experienced range	**HI** Highest wage paid	**M** Monthly	**MWR** Median wage range	**W** Weekly
ATC Average total compensation	**D** Daily	**HR** High end range	**MCC** Median cash compensation	**S** See annotated source	**Y** Yearly

Outdoor Power Equipment and Other Small Engine Mechanic

Occupation/Type/Industry	Location	Per	Low	Mid	High	Source	Date
Outdoor Power Equipment and Other Small Engine Mechanic	Albany-Schenectady-Troy MSA, NY	Y	21140 FQ	25470 MW	35860 TQ	USBLS	5/07
	Buffalo-Niagara Falls MSA, NY	Y	26690 FQ	30090 MW	34910 TQ	USBLS	5/07
	Nassau-Suffolk PMSA, NY	Y	31080 FQ	35070 MW	41740 TQ	USBLS	5/07
	New York-Northern New Jersey-Long Island MSA, NY-NJ-PA	Y	29960 FQ	37050 MW	45130 TQ	USBLS	5/07
	North Carolina	Y	23650 FQ	27320 MW	31270 TQ	USBLS	5/07
	Charlotte-Gastonia-Concord MSA, NC-SC	Y	22500 FQ	28260 MW	34900 TQ	USBLS	5/07
	North Dakota	Y	19140 FQ	23590 MW	30350 TQ	USBLS	5/07
	Fargo MSA, ND-MN	Y	18800 FQ	21750 MW	24470 TQ	USBLS	5/07
	Ohio	Y	20760 FQ	25950 MW	31600 TQ	USBLS	5/07
	Cincinnati-Middletown MSA, OH-KY-IN	Y	25370 FQ	28990 MW	33940 TQ	USBLS	5/07
	Cleveland-Elyria-Mentor MSA, OH	Y	25270 FQ	27880 MW	34760 TQ	USBLS	5/07
	Columbus MSA, OH	Y	24290 FQ	31170 MW	35740 TQ	USBLS	5/07
	Dayton MSA, OH	Y	23300 FQ	29070 MW	34850 TQ	USBLS	5/07
	Oklahoma	Y	16510 FQ	20750 MW	27880 TQ	USBLS	5/07
	Oklahoma City MSA, OK	Y	15390 FQ	17830 MW	23980 TQ	USBLS	5/07
	Tulsa MSA, OK	Y	17420 FQ	19170 MW	30130 TQ	USBLS	5/07
	Oregon	H	11.41 FQ	14.19 MW	16.97 TQ	ORBLS	5/08
	Portland-Vancouver-Beaverton MSA, OR-WA	Y	27560 FQ	31580 MW	37440 TQ	USBLS	5/07
	Pennsylvania	Y	22420 FQ	28390 MW	34500 TQ	USBLS	5/07
	Allentown-Bethlehem-Easton MSA, PA-NJ	Y	23090 FQ	28410 MW	33230 TQ	USBLS	5/07
	Philadelphia-Camden-Wilmington MSA, PA-NJ-DE-MD	Y	29270 FQ	34070 MW	38390 TQ	USBLS	5/07
	Pittsburgh MSA, PA	Y	23890 FQ	29820 MW	38790 TQ	USBLS	5/07
	Rhode Island	Y	22810 FQ	26200 MW	30530 TQ	USBLS	5/07
	Providence-Fall River-Warwick MSA, RI-MA	Y	23140 FQ	27120 MW	31700 TQ	USBLS	5/07
	South Carolina	Y	24530 FQ	27670 MW	30760 TQ	USBLS	5/07
	Charleston-North Charleston MSA, SC	Y	24950 FQ	30760 MW	34270 TQ	USBLS	5/07
	Columbia MSA, SC	Y	25090 FQ	27470 MW	29980 TQ	USBLS	5/07
	South Dakota	Y	22752 FQ	25068 MW	28718 TQ	SDBLS	7/08-9/08
	Tennessee	Y	19410 FQ	23190 MW	29040 TQ	USBLS	5/07
	Memphis MSA, TN-MS-AR	Y	24240 FQ	33030 MW	43560 TQ	USBLS	5/07
	Nashville-Davidson-Murfreesboro MSA, TN	Y	17400 FQ	19110 MW	23470 TQ	USBLS	5/07
	Texas	Y	20830 FQ	26040 MW	34800 TQ	USBLS	5/07
	Austin-Round Rock MSA, TX	Y	22170 FQ	24470 MW	29690 TQ	USBLS	5/07
	Dallas-Fort Worth-Arlington MSA, TX	Y	24640 FQ	28520 MW	35730 TQ	USBLS	5/07
	Houston-Sugar Land-Baytown MSA, TX	Y	22570 FQ	28420 MW	38470 TQ	USBLS	5/07
	San Antonio MSA, TX	Y	20390 FQ	25860 MW	35050 TQ	USBLS	5/07
	Utah	Y	23570 FQ	27730 MW	34110 TQ	USBLS	5/07
	Salt Lake City MSA, UT	Y	28420 FQ	33960 MW	41910 TQ	USBLS	5/07
	Vermont	Y	22590 FQ	27550 MW	31490 TQ	USBLS	5/07
	Burlington-South Burlington MSA, VT	Y	20550 FQ	24080 MW	31060 TQ	USBLS	5/07
	Virginia	Y	23620 FQ	28960 MW	37060 TQ	USBLS	5/07
	Richmond MSA, VA	Y	23880 FQ	27410 MW	32870 TQ	USBLS	5/07
	Virginia Beach-Norfolk-Newport News MSA, VA-NC	Y	28220 FQ	31220 MW	40650 TQ	USBLS	5/07
	Washington	H	12.06 FQ	14.66 MW	17.97 TQ	WABLS	3/08
	Seattle-Tacoma-Bellevue MSA, WA	Y	27260 FQ	34050 MW	40490 TQ	USBLS	5/07
	West Virginia	Y	15363 FQ	20155 MW	23484 TQ	WVBLS	7/08-9/08
	Wisconsin	Y	22090 FQ	27230 MW	33120 TQ	USBLS	5/07
	Milwaukee-Waukesha-West Allis MSA, WI	Y	22100 FQ	28840 MW	37230 TQ	USBLS	5/07
	Wyoming	Y	24433 FQ	28791 MW	32606 TQ	WYBLS	9/08
	Puerto Rico	Y	14470 FQ	17150 MW	19380 TQ	USBLS	5/07

Occupation/Type/Industry	Location	Per	Low	Mid	High	Source	Date
Outdoor Power Equipment and Other Small Engine Mechanic	San Juan-Caguas-Guaynabo MSA, PR	Y	14840 FQ	17330 MW	19480 TQ	USBLS	5/07
Overseas Production Manager Apparel Industry	United States	Y		82000 MW		247FASH	2009
Packaging and Filling Machine Operator and Tender	Alabama	Y	17440 FQ	21980 MW	29070 TQ	USBLS	5/07
	Birmingham-Hoover MSA, AL	Y	17140 FQ	21050 MW	28850 TQ	USBLS	5/07
	Tuscaloosa MSA, AL	Y	23570 FQ	26350 MW	29110 TQ	USBLS	5/07
	Alaska	Y	15770 FQ	18370 MW	25770 TQ	USBLS	5/07
	Anchorage MSA, AK	Y	19860 FQ	22060 MW	25330 TQ	USBLS	5/07
	Arizona	Y	17880 FQ	22460 MW	30680 TQ	USBLS	5/07
	Phoenix-Mesa-Scottsdale MSA, AZ	Y	18530 FQ	23080 MW	31800 TQ	USBLS	5/07
	Tucson MSA, AZ	Y	20710 FQ	23740 MW	29870 TQ	USBLS	5/07
	Arkansas	Y	19130 FQ	22770 MW	28720 TQ	USBLS	5/07
	Fayetteville-Springdale-Rogers MSA, AR-MO	Y	20410 FQ	23050 MW	27260 TQ	USBLS	5/07
	Jonesboro MSA, AR	Y	17990 FQ	20620 MW	30360 TQ	USBLS	5/07
	Little Rock-North Little Rock MSA, AR	Y	20320 FQ	23070 MW	26700 TQ	USBLS	5/07
	California	H	8.78 FQ	10.81 MW	14.78 TQ	CABLS	1/08-3/08
	Los Angeles-Long Beach-Glendale PMSA, CA	H	8.61 FQ	10.22 MW	15.27 TQ	CABLS	1/08-3/08
	Oakland-Fremont-Hayward MSA, CA	H	9.15 FQ	12.46 MW	16.20 TQ	CABLS	1/08-3/08
	Riverside-San Bernardino-Ontario MSA, CA	H	8.81 FQ	10.33 MW	12.86 TQ	CABLS	1/08-3/08
	Sacramento-Arden Arcade-Roseville MSA, CA	H	9.75 FQ	11.70 MW	15.09 TQ	CABLS	1/08-3/08
	San Diego-Carlsbad-San Marcos MSA, CA	H	8.72 FQ	10.02 MW	13.45 TQ	CABLS	1/08-3/08
	San Francisco-San Mateo-Redwood PMSA, CA	H	9.78 FQ	11.40 MW	16.08 TQ	CABLS	1/08-3/08
	San Jose-Sunnyvale-Santa Clara MSA, CA	H	10.01 FQ	11.18 MW	13.42 TQ	CABLS	1/08-3/08
	Santa Ana-Anaheim-Irvine PMSA, CA	Y	16510 FQ	19590 MW	29080 TQ	USBLS	5/07
	Colorado	Y	20440 FQ	26790 MW	35300 TQ	USBLS	5/07
	Boulder MSA, CO	Y	19130 FQ	22790 MW	28020 TQ	USBLS	5/07
	Colorado Springs MSA, CO	Y	21050 FQ	25450 MW	31670 TQ	USBLS	5/07
	Denver-Aurora MSA, CO	Y	19460 FQ	26150 MW	33100 TQ	USBLS	5/07
	Connecticut	H	9.26 AE	12.64 MW		CTBLS	1/08-3/08
	Bridgeport-Stamford-Norwalk MSA, CT	Y	19010 FQ	26570 MW	36540 TQ	USBLS	5/07
	Hartford-West Hartford-East Hartford MSA, CT	Y	20780 FQ	27090 MW	35270 TQ	USBLS	5/07
	Delaware	Y	19950 FQ	26100 MW	36880 TQ	USBLS	5/07
	Wilmington PMSA, DE-MD-NJ	Y	21930 FQ	30640 MW	43670 TQ	USBLS	5/07
	District of Columbia	Y	16810 FQ	19110 MW	26640 TQ	USBLS	5/07
	Washington-Arlington-Alexandria MSA, DC-VA-MD-WV	Y	18560 FQ	25830 MW	32740 TQ	USBLS	5/07
	Florida	Y	18640 FQ	23060 MW	29400 TQ	USBLS	5/07
	Fort Lauderdale-Pompano Beach-Deerfield Beach PMSA, FL	Y	17480 FQ	21180 MW	25970 TQ	USBLS	5/07
	Jacksonville MSA, FL	Y	21080 FQ	26880 MW	32620 TQ	USBLS	5/07
	Miami-Fort Lauderdale-Miami Beach MSA, FL	Y	15790 FQ	19550 MW	24570 TQ	USBLS	5/07
	Orlando-Kissimmee MSA, FL	Y	19410 FQ	22820 MW	28910 TQ	USBLS	5/07
	Tampa-St. Petersburg-Clearwater MSA, FL	Y	17770 FQ	22600 MW	28140 TQ	USBLS	5/07
	West Palm Beach-Boca Raton-Boynton Beach PMSA, FL	Y	14710 FQ	16930 MW	23580 TQ	USBLS	5/07
	Georgia	Y	18460 FQ	23460 MW	29730 TQ	USBLS	5/07
	Atlanta-Sandy Springs-Marietta MSA, GA	Y	18500 FQ	23670 MW	29090 TQ	USBLS	5/07
	Hawaii	Y	18590 FQ	21840 MW	26550 TQ	USBLS	5/07

AE Average entry wage	**AW** Average wage paid	**FQ** First quartile wage	**LO** Lowest wage paid	**MTC** Median total compensation	**TCC** Total cash compensation
AER Average entry range	**AWR** Average wage range	**H** Hourly	**LR** Low end range	**MW** Median wage paid	**TQ** Third quartile wage
AEX Average experienced wage	**AXR** Average experienced range	**HI** Highest wage paid	**M** Monthly	**MWR** Median wage range	**W** Weekly
ATC Average total compensation	**D** Daily	**HR** High end range	**MCC** Median cash compensation	**S** See annotated source	**Y** Yearly

Occupation/Type/Industry	Location	Per	Low	Mid	High	Source	Date
Packaging and Filling Machine Operator and Tender							
	Honolulu MSA, HI	Y	17990 FQ	21940 MW	27060 TQ	USBLS	5/07
	Idaho	Y	20240 FQ	25040 MW	29900 TQ	USBLS	5/07
	Boise City-Nampa MSA, ID	Y	23150 FQ	28200 MW	32710 TQ	USBLS	5/07
	Illinois	Y	17790 FQ	23790 MW	32030 TQ	USBLS	5/07
	Chicago-Naperville-Joliet MSA, IL-IN-WI	Y	17870 FQ	24250 MW	32970 TQ	USBLS	5/07
	Peoria MSA, IL	Y	18310 FQ	20300 MW	31360 TQ	USBLS	5/07
	Indiana	Y	20180 FQ	27170 MW	35440 TQ	USBLS	5/07
	Gary PMSA, IN	Y	20920 FQ	29720 MW	45160 TQ	USBLS	5/07
	Indianapolis-Carmel MSA, IN	Y	19890 FQ	23850 MW	31660 TQ	USBLS	5/07
	Iowa	Y	20410 FQ	26320 MW	33750 TQ	USBLS	5/07
	Cedar Rapids MSA, IA	Y	18660 FQ	25890 MW	37360 TQ	USBLS	5/07
	Davenport-Moline-Rock Island MSA, IA-IL	Y	19780 FQ	23170 MW	31410 TQ	USBLS	5/07
	Des Moines-West Des Moines MSA, IA	Y	24000 FQ	30610 MW	35590 TQ	USBLS	5/07
	Iowa City MSA, IA	Y	23610 FQ	29160 MW	34350 TQ	USBLS	5/07
	Waterloo-Cedar Falls MSA, IA	Y	23210 FQ	27140 MW	34130 TQ	USBLS	5/07
	Kansas	Y	21600 FQ	27680 MW	32990 TQ	USBLS	5/07
	Topeka MSA, KS	Y	16850 FQ	22230 MW	32500 TQ	USBLS	5/07
	Wichita MSA, KS	Y	18480 FQ	24060 MW	28840 TQ	USBLS	5/07
	Kentucky	Y	19842 FQ	26397 MW	32854 TQ	KYBLS	2008
	Lexington-Fayette MSA, KY	Y	20910 FQ	30570 MW	39170 TQ	USBLS	5/07
	Louisville-Jefferson County MSA, KY-IN	Y	19800 FQ	29020 MW	39000 TQ	USBLS	5/07
	Louisiana	H	7.65 FQ	9.81 MW	12.09 TQ	LABLS	1/08-3/08
	Baton Rouge MSA, LA	Y	15830 FQ	20770 MW	24330 TQ	USBLS	5/07
	New Orleans-Metairie-Kenner MSA, LA	Y	17700 FQ	21170 MW	26350 TQ	USBLS	5/07
	Shreveport-Bossier City MSA, LA	Y	17570 FQ	20740 MW	24970 TQ	USBLS	5/07
	Maine	Y	19840 FQ	24800 MW	29350 TQ	USBLS	5/07
	Bangor MSA, ME	Y	17650 FQ	19340 MW	28370 TQ	USBLS	5/07
	Portland-South Portland-Biddeford MSA, ME	Y	20570 FQ	26060 MW	31090 TQ	USBLS	5/07
	Maryland	Y		25925 MW		MDBLS	3/08
	Baltimore-Towson MSA, MD	Y	19710 FQ	24860 MW	35790 TQ	USBLS	5/07
	Bethesda-Gaithersburg-Frederick PMSA, MD	Y	23140 FQ	29220 MW	35820 TQ	USBLS	5/07
	Hagerstown-Martinsburg MSA, MD-WV	Y	20720 FQ	27700 MW	38450 TQ	USBLS	5/07
	Massachusetts	Y	19030 FQ	23910 MW	30150 TQ	USBLS	5/07
	Boston-Cambridge-Quincy NECTA, MA	Y	19230 FQ	24890 MW	30400 TQ	USBLS	5/07
	Lynn-Peabody-Salem NECTA, MA	Y	20780 FQ	25950 MW	29900 TQ	USBLS	5/07
	Worcester MSA, MA-CT	Y	21960 FQ	26730 MW	32660 TQ	USBLS	5/07
	Michigan	Y	19000 FQ	23500 MW	32240 TQ	USBLS	5/07
	Detroit-Warren-Livonia MSA, MI	Y	20320 FQ	25470 MW	36240 TQ	USBLS	5/07
	Grand Rapids-Wyoming MSA, MI	Y	15940 FQ	20490 MW	25540 TQ	USBLS	5/07
	Warren-Troy-Farmington Hills PMSA, MI	Y	20600 FQ	26490 MW	38130 TQ	USBLS	5/07
	Minnesota	Y	22350 FQ	27295 MW	34573 TQ	MNBLS	10/08-12/08
	Duluth-Superior MSA, MN-WI	Y	20111 FQ	34676 MW	38616 TQ	MNBLS	10/08-12/08
	Minneapolis-Saint Paul MSA, MN-WI	Y	22050 FQ	27005 MW	34013 TQ	MNBLS	10/08-12/08
	Rochester MSA, MN	Y	26867 FQ	33883 MW	43424 TQ	MNBLS	10/08-12/08
	Mississippi	Y	17110 FQ	21450 MW	27030 TQ	USBLS	5/07
	Gulfport-Biloxi MSA, MS	Y	13910 FQ	20420 MW	26100 TQ	USBLS	5/07
	Jackson MSA, MS	Y	15510 FQ	17940 MW	24180 TQ	USBLS	5/07
	Missouri	Y	20300 FQ	24630 MW	33050 TQ	USBLS	5/07
	Joplin MSA, MO	Y	19810 FQ	33090 MW	36670 TQ	USBLS	5/07
	Kansas City MSA, MO-KS	Y	23670 FQ	29070 MW	34640 TQ	USBLS	5/07
	St. Louis MSA, MO-IL	Y	20200 FQ	23580 MW	32530 TQ	USBLS	5/07
	Montana	Y	17280 FQ	22560 MW	33000 TQ	USBLS	5/07
	Billings MSA, MT	Y	17280 FQ	21040 MW	29910 TQ	USBLS	5/07
	Nebraska	Y	20330 FQ	24810 MW	30360 TQ	USBLS	5/07
	Omaha-Council Bluffs MSA, NE-IA	Y	20320 FQ	24280 MW	31610 TQ	USBLS	5/07

AE	Average entry wage	AW	Average wage paid	FQ	First quartile wage	LO	Lowest wage paid	MTC	Median total compensation	TCC	Total cash compensation
AER	Average entry range	AWR	Average wage range	H	Hourly	LR	Low end range	MW	Median wage paid	TQ	Third quartile wage
AEX	Average experienced wage	AXR	Average experienced range	HI	Highest wage paid	M	Monthly	MWR	Median wage range	W	Weekly
ATC	Average total compensation	D	Daily	HR	High end range	MCC	Median cash compensation	S	See annotated source	Y	Yearly

Occupation/Type/Industry	Location	Per	Low	Mid	High	Source	Date
Packaging and Filling Machine Operator and Tender	Nevada	H	10.49 FQ	13.12 MW	15.64 TQ	NVBLS	5/08
	Las Vegas-Paradise MSA, NV	H	10.47 FQ	12.99 MW	15.14 TQ	NVBLS	5/08
	New Hampshire	H	8.59 AE	11.41 MW	16.85 AEX	NHBLS	6/08
	Manchester MSA, NH	Y	19370 FQ	22440 MW	29680 TQ	USBLS	5/07
	Nashua NECTA, NH-MA	Y	18900 FQ	27400 MW	41790 TQ	USBLS	5/07
	New Jersey	Y	16960 FQ	21580 MW	30740 TQ	USBLS	5/07
	Camden PMSA, NJ	Y	17820 FQ	27660 MW	39530 TQ	USBLS	5/07
	Edison PMSA, NJ	Y	17740 FQ	22290 MW	33190 TQ	USBLS	5/07
	Newark-Union PMSA, NJ-PA	Y	16420 FQ	21510 MW	28060 TQ	USBLS	5/07
	New Mexico	Y	13950 FQ	19850 MW	24440 TQ	USBLS	5/07
	Albuquerque MSA, NM	Y	15270 FQ	21200 MW	24370 TQ	USBLS	5/07
	New York	Y	18270 FQ	23740 MW	31750 TQ	USBLS	5/07
	Albany-Schenectady-Troy MSA, NY	Y	21120 FQ	29960 MW	40050 TQ	USBLS	5/07
	Buffalo-Niagara Falls MSA, NY	Y	18260 FQ	24970 MW	35500 TQ	USBLS	5/07
	Nassau-Suffolk PMSA, NY	Y	17600 FQ	21590 MW	28380 TQ	USBLS	5/07
	New York-Northern New Jersey-Long Island MSA, NY-NJ-PA	Y	16950 FQ	21710 MW	30110 TQ	USBLS	5/07
	Syracuse MSA, NY	Y	18610 FQ	21820 MW	25710 TQ	USBLS	5/07
	Utica-Rome MSA, NY	Y	24340 FQ	28700 MW	33620 TQ	USBLS	5/07
	North Carolina	Y	18120 FQ	23810 MW	32170 TQ	USBLS	5/07
	Charlotte-Gastonia-Concord MSA, NC-SC	Y	19220 FQ	23770 MW	27930 TQ	USBLS	5/07
	Raleigh-Cary MSA, NC	Y	19550 FQ	30620 MW	37040 TQ	USBLS	5/07
	North Dakota	Y	19400 FQ	23390 MW	27220 TQ	USBLS	5/07
	Fargo MSA, ND-MN	Y	21200 FQ	23580 MW	26750 TQ	USBLS	5/07
	Grand Forks MSA, ND-MN	Y	19870 FQ	25760 MW	28280 TQ	USBLS	5/07
	Ohio	Y	20620 FQ	26220 MW	33070 TQ	USBLS	5/07
	Cincinnati-Middletown MSA, OH-KY-IN	Y	21310 FQ	26060 MW	32480 TQ	USBLS	5/07
	Cleveland-Elyria-Mentor MSA, OH	Y	18470 FQ	24430 MW	30350 TQ	USBLS	5/07
	Columbus MSA, OH	Y	26190 FQ	33640 MW	40350 TQ	USBLS	5/07
	Dayton MSA, OH	Y	19170 FQ	21750 MW	27210 TQ	USBLS	5/07
	Oklahoma	Y	18140 FQ	22130 MW	27720 TQ	USBLS	5/07
	Oklahoma City MSA, OK	Y	16890 FQ	20710 MW	25860 TQ	USBLS	5/07
	Tulsa MSA, OK	Y	17410 FQ	20030 MW	26370 TQ	USBLS	5/07
	Oregon	H	9.12 FQ	11.00 MW	13.89 TQ	ORBLS	5/08
	Medford MSA, OR	Y	17750 FQ	19280 MW	24770 TQ	USBLS	5/07
	Portland-Vancouver-Beaverton MSA, OR-WA	Y	18790 FQ	22640 MW	29860 TQ	USBLS	5/07
	Pennsylvania	Y	19460 FQ	25760 MW	33640 TQ	USBLS	5/07
	Allentown-Bethlehem-Easton MSA, PA-NJ	Y	18580 FQ	22110 MW	31770 TQ	USBLS	5/07
	Philadelphia-Camden-Wilmington MSA, PA-NJ-DE-MD	Y	18470 FQ	25220 MW	34910 TQ	USBLS	5/07
	Pittsburgh MSA, PA	Y	20070 FQ	28530 MW	35370 TQ	USBLS	5/07
	Rhode Island	Y	17540 FQ	21550 MW	25880 TQ	USBLS	5/07
	Providence-Fall River-Warwick MSA, RI-MA	Y	17680 FQ	21600 MW	25630 TQ	USBLS	5/07
	South Carolina	Y	18370 FQ	22580 MW	28650 TQ	USBLS	5/07
	Charleston-North Charleston MSA, SC	Y	19250 FQ	26960 MW	33990 TQ	USBLS	5/07
	Columbia MSA, SC	Y	19820 FQ	27870 MW	32490 TQ	USBLS	5/07
	South Dakota	Y	21270 FQ	25270 MW	29025	SDBLS	7/08-9/08
	Sioux Falls MSA, SD	Y	24714 FQ	27236 MW	29960 TQ	SDBLS	7/08-9/08
	Tennessee	Y	18710 FQ	24210 MW	29600 TQ	USBLS	5/07
	Clarksville MSA, TN-KY	Y	19730 FQ	27430 MW	34180 TQ	USBLS	5/07
	Memphis MSA, TN-MS-AR	Y	18780 FQ	26170 MW	31710 TQ	USBLS	5/07
	Nashville-Davidson-Murfreesboro MSA, TN	Y	21090 FQ	26600 MW	32790 TQ	USBLS	5/07
	Texas	Y	17540 FQ	21560 MW	28270 TQ	USBLS	5/07
	Austin-Round Rock MSA, TX	Y	20440 FQ	33310 MW	36940 TQ	USBLS	5/07
	Beaumont-Port Arthur MSA, TX	Y	15300 FQ	21770 MW	27310 TQ	USBLS	5/07
	Dallas-Fort Worth-Arlington MSA, TX	Y	17470 FQ	21420 MW	29750 TQ	USBLS	5/07
	El Paso MSA, TX	Y	16540 FQ	22420 MW	28090 TQ	USBLS	5/07

AE	Average entry wage	AW	Average wage paid	FQ	First quartile wage
AER	Average entry range	AWR	Average wage range	H	Hourly
AEX	Average experienced wage	AXR	Average experienced range	HI	Highest wage paid
ATC	Average total salaries compensation	D	Daily	HR	High end range

LO	Lowest wage paid	MTC	Median total compensation	TCC	Total cash compensation
LR	Low end range	MW	Median wage paid	TQ	Third quartile wage
M	Monthly	MWR	Median wage range	W	Weekly
MCC	Median cash compensation	S	See annotated source	Y	Yearly

Occupation/Type/Industry	Location	Per	Low	Mid	High	Source	Date
Packaging and Filling Machine Operator and Tender	Houston-Sugar Land-Baytown MSA, TX	Y	18640 FQ	22600 MW	28590 TQ	USBLS	5/07
	San Antonio MSA, TX	Y	17470 FQ	20590 MW	24130 TQ	USBLS	5/07
	Utah	Y	18070 FQ	22790 MW	27340 TQ	USBLS	5/07
	Salt Lake City MSA, UT	Y	18150 FQ	22150 MW	27940 TQ	USBLS	5/07
	Vermont	Y	22000 FQ	25790 MW	30500 TQ	USBLS	5/07
	Burlington-South Burlington MSA, VT	Y	24140 FQ	28650 MW	34040 TQ	USBLS	5/07
	Virginia	Y	17760 FQ	23210 MW	31220 TQ	USBLS	5/07
	Richmond MSA, VA	Y	16570 FQ	18900 MW	26800 TQ	USBLS	5/07
	Virginia Beach-Norfolk-Newport News MSA, VA-NC	Y	17310 FQ	21640 MW	28520 TQ	USBLS	5/07
	Washington	H	10.02 FQ	12.08 MW	15.35 TQ	WABLS	3/08
	Seattle-Tacoma-Bellevue MSA, WA	Y	22680 FQ	27300 MW	35090 TQ	USBLS	5/07
	West Virginia	Y	17974 FQ	23179 MW	33981 TQ	WVBLS	7/08-9/08
	Charleston MSA, WV	Y	23610 FQ	32890 MW	36610 TQ	USBLS	5/07
	Wisconsin	Y	21420 FQ	26480 MW	32240 TQ	USBLS	5/07
	Milwaukee-Waukesha-West Allis MSA, WI	Y	21560 FQ	25330 MW	29840 TQ	USBLS	5/07
	Wyoming	Y	25216 FQ	32042 MW	35821 TQ	WYBLS	9/08
	Puerto Rico	Y	13380 FQ	16310 MW	24220 TQ	USBLS	5/07
	San Juan-Caguas-Guaynabo MSA, PR	Y	13440 FQ	16630 MW	23600 TQ	USBLS	5/07
	Virgin Islands	Y	15200 FQ	17230 MW	20110 TQ	USBLS	5/07
Packer and Packager							
Hand	Alabama	Y	14060 FQ	17640 MW	22420 TQ	USBLS	5/07
Hand	Birmingham-Hoover MSA, AL	Y	14500 FQ	17460 MW	20280 TQ	USBLS	5/07
Hand	Alaska	Y	16200 FQ	20620 MW	27610 TQ	USBLS	5/07
Hand	Anchorage MSA, AK	Y	16870 FQ	22240 MW	29390 TQ	USBLS	5/07
Hand	Arizona	Y	14660 FQ	15650 MW	21330 TQ	USBLS	5/07
Hand	Phoenix-Mesa-Scottsdale MSA, AZ	Y	14660 FQ	15750 MW	21820 TQ	USBLS	5/07
Hand	Tucson MSA, AZ	Y	14600 FQ	15310 MW	18290 TQ	USBLS	5/07
Hand	Arkansas	Y	15580 FQ	20730 MW	28090 TQ	USBLS	5/07
Hand	Jonesboro MSA, AR	Y	22350 FQ	27110 MW	29700 TQ	USBLS	5/07
Hand	Little Rock-North Little Rock MSA, AR	Y	14330 FQ	15480 MW	19000 TQ	USBLS	5/07
Hand	California	H	8.07 FQ	8.83 MW	9.94 TQ	CABLS	1/08-3/08
Hand	Los Angeles-Long Beach-Glendale PMSA, CA	H	8.00 FQ	8.62 MW	9.58 TQ	CABLS	1/08-3/08
Hand	Oakland-Fremont-Hayward MSA, CA	H	8.48 FQ	9.27 MW	11.09 TQ	CABLS	1/08-3/08
Hand	Riverside-San Bernardino-Ontario MSA, CA	H	8.30 FQ	9.11 MW	10.70 TQ	CABLS	1/08-3/08
Hand	Sacramento-Arden Arcade-Roseville MSA, CA	H	8.38 FQ	9.02 MW	10.00 TQ	CABLS	1/08-3/08
Hand	San Diego-Carlsbad-San Marcos MSA, CA	H	8.04 FQ	8.87 MW	10.04 TQ	CABLS	1/08-3/08
Hand	San Francisco-San Mateo-Redwood PMSA, CA	H	8.31 FQ	9.00 MW	10.04 TQ	CABLS	1/08-3/08
Hand	San Jose-Sunnyvale-Santa Clara MSA, CA	H	8.44 FQ	9.23 MW	11.30 TQ	CABLS	1/08-3/08
Hand	Santa Ana-Anaheim-Irvine PMSA, CA	Y	16660 FQ	18200 MW	21660 TQ	USBLS	5/07
Hand	Santa Rosa-Petaluma MSA, CA	H	8.42 FQ	9.08 MW	10.25 TQ	CABLS	1/08-3/08
Hand	Colorado	Y	15170 FQ	16240 MW	20400 TQ	USBLS	5/07
Hand	Denver-Aurora MSA, CO	Y	15150 FQ	16110 MW	20630 TQ	USBLS	5/07
Hand	Connecticut	H	8.52 AE	9.78 MW		CTBLS	1/08-3/08
Hand	Bridgeport-Stamford-Norwalk MSA, CT	Y	17360 FQ	19230 MW	24140 TQ	USBLS	5/07
Hand	Hartford-West Hartford-East Hartford MSA, CT	Y	17060 FQ	18680 MW	22390 TQ	USBLS	5/07
Hand	District of Columbia	Y	18870 FQ	22010 MW	33170 TQ	USBLS	5/07
Hand	Washington-Arlington-Alexandria MSA, DC-VA-MD-WV	Y	15060 FQ	19970 MW	24340 TQ	USBLS	5/07
Hand	Florida	Y	14960 FQ	17310 MW	21940 TQ	USBLS	5/07

AE Average entry wage	**AW** Average wage paid	**FQ** First quartile wage	**LO** Lowest wage paid	**MTC** Median total compensation	**TCC** Total cash compensation
AER Average entry range	**AWR** Average wage range	**H** Hourly	**LR** Low end range	**MW** Median wage paid	**TQ** Third quartile wage
AEX Average experienced wage	**AXR** Average experienced range	**HI** Highest wage paid	**M** Monthly	**MWR** Median wage range	**W** Weekly
ATC Average total compensation	**D** Daily	**HR** High end range	**MCC** Median cash compensation	**S** See annotated source	**Y** Yearly

Packer and Packager

Occupation/Type/Industry	Location	Per	Low	Mid	High	Source	Date
Hand	Fort Lauderdale-Pompano Beach-Deerfield Beach PMSA, FL	Y	15170 FQ	17920 MW	22710 TQ	USBLS	5/07
Hand	Jacksonville MSA, FL	Y	15360 FQ	18440 MW	24600 TQ	USBLS	5/07
Hand	Miami-Fort Lauderdale-Miami Beach MSA, FL	Y	14880 FQ	17110 MW	22640 TQ	USBLS	5/07
Hand	Orlando-Kissimmee MSA, FL	Y	15580 FQ	19550 MW	24410 TQ	USBLS	5/07
Hand	Tallahassee MSA, FL	Y	14540 FQ	15780 MW	19230 TQ	USBLS	5/07
Hand	Tampa-St. Petersburg-Clearwater MSA, FL	Y	14970 FQ	16900 MW	20800 TQ	USBLS	5/07
Hand	West Palm Beach-Boca Raton-Boynton Beach PMSA, FL	Y	15250 FQ	18080 MW	26250 TQ	USBLS	5/07
Hand	Georgia	Y	14840 FQ	18110 MW	22730 TQ	USBLS	5/07
Hand	Atlanta-Sandy Springs-Marietta MSA, GA	Y	15450 FQ	18570 MW	23090 TQ	USBLS	5/07
Hand	Augusta-Richmond County MSA, GA-SC	Y	13610 FQ	16110 MW	20880 TQ	USBLS	5/07
Hand	Hawaii	Y	15530 FQ	17360 MW	21620 TQ	USBLS	5/07
Hand	Honolulu MSA, HI	Y	15520 FQ	17200 MW	21610 TQ	USBLS	5/07
Hand	Idaho	Y	13190 FQ	15410 MW	21200 TQ	USBLS	5/07
Hand	Boise City-Nampa MSA, ID	Y	13470 FQ	17320 MW	27240 TQ	USBLS	5/07
Hand	Pocatello MSA, ID	Y	12310 FQ	13710 MW	15100 TQ	USBLS	5/07
Hand	Illinois	Y	15260 FQ	17930 MW	23530 TQ	USBLS	5/07
Hand	Chicago-Naperville-Joliet MSA, IL-IN-WI	Y	15230 FQ	17710 MW	22890 TQ	USBLS	5/07
Hand	Indiana	Y	15280 FQ	19570 MW	25910 TQ	USBLS	5/07
Hand	Gary PMSA, IN	Y	13800 FQ	17220 MW	26850 TQ	USBLS	5/07
Hand	Indianapolis-Carmel MSA, IN	Y	16410 FQ	19580 MW	26750 TQ	USBLS	5/07
Hand	Iowa	Y	14540 FQ	17890 MW	22980 TQ	USBLS	5/07
Hand	Des Moines-West Des Moines MSA, IA	Y	14000 FQ	15570 MW	20110 TQ	USBLS	5/07
Hand	Kansas	Y	14550 FQ	19000 MW	23650 TQ	USBLS	5/07
Hand	Wichita MSA, KS	Y	13980 FQ	17110 MW	22890 TQ	USBLS	5/07
Hand	Kentucky	Y	14815 FQ	19131 MW	24099 TQ	KYBLS	2008
Hand	Elizabethtown MSA, KY	Y	19070 FQ	24790 MW	31390 TQ	USBLS	5/07
Hand	Louisville-Jefferson County MSA, KY-IN	Y	14250 FQ	18150 MW	22800 TQ	USBLS	5/07
Hand	Louisiana	H	6.32 FQ	7.37 MW	10.51 TQ	LABLS	1/08-3/08
Hand	Baton Rouge MSA, LA	Y	12650 FQ	14100 MW	17890 TQ	USBLS	5/07
Hand	New Orleans-Metairie-Kenner MSA, LA	Y	13510 FQ	16080 MW	19940 TQ	USBLS	5/07
Hand	Maine	Y	16150 FQ	18580 MW	22490 TQ	USBLS	5/07
Hand	Bangor MSA, ME	Y	15210 FQ	16630 MW	18320 TQ	USBLS	5/07
Hand	Maryland	Y		21950 MW		MDBLS	3/08
Hand	Baltimore-Towson MSA, MD	Y	16650 FQ	21350 MW	28690 TQ	USBLS	5/07
Hand	Bethesda-Gaithersburg-Frederick PMSA, MD	Y	16740 FQ	21160 MW	26890 TQ	USBLS	5/07
Hand	Massachusetts	Y	17300 FQ	19710 MW	23460 TQ	USBLS	5/07
Hand	Barnstable Town MSA, MA	Y	17040 FQ	19770 MW	24080 TQ	USBLS	5/07
Hand	Boston-Cambridge-Quincy NECTA, MA	Y	17260 FQ	19440 MW	23350 TQ	USBLS	5/07
Hand	Worcester MSA, MA-CT	Y	17270 FQ	20100 MW	25760 TQ	USBLS	5/07
Hand	Michigan	Y	15270 FQ	17710 MW	23750 TQ	USBLS	5/07
Hand	Detroit-Warren-Livonia MSA, MI	Y	15330 FQ	17920 MW	26060 TQ	USBLS	5/07
Hand	Grand Rapids-Wyoming MSA, MI	Y	15950 FQ	18970 MW	22780 TQ	USBLS	5/07
Hand	Warren-Troy-Farmington Hills PMSA, MI	Y	15150 FQ	17000 MW	24480 TQ	USBLS	5/07
Hand	Minnesota	Y	16572 FQ	21701 MW	25654 TQ	MNBLS	10/08-12/08
Hand	Duluth-Superior MSA, MN-WI	Y	14960 FQ	16541 MW	18757 TQ	MNBLS	10/08-12/08
Hand	Minneapolis-Saint Paul MSA, MN-WI	Y	18258 FQ	22960 MW	26435 TQ	MNBLS	10/08-12/08
Hand	Rochester MSA, MN	Y	14900 FQ	16239 MW	19913 TQ	MNBLS	10/08-12/08
Hand	Mississippi	Y	13880 FQ	17880 MW	22250 TQ	USBLS	5/07
Hand	Jackson MSA, MS	Y	13060 FQ	15100 MW	19640 TQ	USBLS	5/07
Hand	Missouri	Y	15690 FQ	19260 MW	24030 TQ	USBLS	5/07
Hand	Joplin MSA, MO	Y	15450 FQ	17340 MW	20360 TQ	USBLS	5/07
Hand	Kansas City MSA, MO-KS	Y	15380 FQ	19360 MW	23950 TQ	USBLS	5/07
Hand	St. Louis MSA, MO-IL	Y	15390 FQ	18960 MW	24070 TQ	USBLS	5/07
Hand	Montana	Y	14100 FQ	15630 MW	21490 TQ	USBLS	5/07

AE	Average entry wage	AW	Average wage paid	FQ	First quartile wage	LO	Lowest wage paid	MTC	Median total compensation	TCC	Total cash compensation
AER	Average entry range	AWR	Average wage range	H	Hourly	LR	Low end range	MW	Median wage paid	TQ	Third quartile wage
AEX	Average experienced wage	AXR	Average experienced range	HI	Highest wage paid	M	Monthly	MWR	Median wage range	W	Weekly
ATC	Average total compensation	D	Daily	HR	High end range	MCC	Median cash compensation	S	See annotated source	Y	Yearly

Occupation/Type/Industry	Location	Per	Low	Mid	High	Source	Date
Packer and Packager							
Hand	Billings MSA, MT	Y	15460 FQ	17950 MW	21260 TQ	USBLS	5/07
Hand	Nebraska	Y	15050 FQ	19480 MW	25640 TQ	USBLS	5/07
Hand	Lincoln MSA, NE	Y	15350 FQ	18380 MW	21630 TQ	USBLS	5/07
Hand	Omaha-Council Bluffs MSA, NE-IA	Y	14860 FQ	18170 MW	23840 TQ	USBLS	5/07
Hand	Nevada	H	6.95 FQ	10.18 MW	12.75 TQ	NVBLS	5/08
Hand	Las Vegas-Paradise MSA, NV	H	6.58 FQ	8.29 MW	12.35 TQ	NVBLS	5/08
Hand	New Hampshire	H	7.55 AE	9.18 MW	10.95 AEX	NHBLS	6/08
Hand	Manchester MSA, NH	Y	13620 FQ	16750 MW	18940 TQ	USBLS	5/07
Hand	Nashua NECTA, NH-MA	Y	17100 FQ	20010 MW	26700 TQ	USBLS	5/07
Hand	New Jersey	Y	15490 FQ	17760 MW	23000 TQ	USBLS	5/07
Hand	Camden PMSA, NJ	Y	16520 FQ	20730 MW	24850 TQ	USBLS	5/07
Hand	Edison PMSA, NJ	Y	15490 FQ	17490 MW	22690 TQ	USBLS	5/07
Hand	Newark-Union PMSA, NJ-PA	Y	15480 FQ	17570 MW	22380 TQ	USBLS	5/07
Hand	Ocean City MSA, NJ	Y	15460 FQ	15870 MW	16890 TQ	USBLS	5/07
Hand	New Mexico	Y	12960 FQ	14780 MW	18970 TQ	USBLS	5/07
Hand	Albuquerque MSA, NM	Y	13180 FQ	15330 MW	19700 TQ	USBLS	5/07
Hand	New York	Y	15730 FQ	18510 MW	24210 TQ	USBLS	5/07
Hand	Albany-Schenectady-Troy MSA, NY	Y	16830 FQ	22000 MW	31850 TQ	USBLS	5/07
Hand	Buffalo-Niagara Falls MSA, NY	Y	16580 FQ	18920 MW	23850 TQ	USBLS	5/07
Hand	Kingston MSA, NY	Y	15470 FQ	21520 MW	26250 TQ	USBLS	5/07
Hand	Nassau-Suffolk PMSA, NY	Y	16320 FQ	19410 MW	24950 TQ	USBLS	5/07
Hand	New York-Northern New Jersey-Long Island MSA, NY-NJ-PA	Y	15510 FQ	17720 MW	22650 TQ	USBLS	5/07
Hand	North Carolina	Y	15310 FQ	18090 MW	22240 TQ	USBLS	5/07
Hand	Charlotte-Gastonia-Concord MSA, NC-SC	Y	15930 FQ	18480 MW	22890 TQ	USBLS	5/07
Hand	Raleigh-Cary MSA, NC	Y	16190 FQ	19070 MW	26040 TQ	USBLS	5/07
Hand	North Dakota	Y	13110 FQ	15250 MW	18550 TQ	USBLS	5/07
Hand	Fargo MSA, ND-MN	Y	14160 FQ	16770 MW	18950 TQ	USBLS	5/07
Hand	Grand Forks MSA, ND-MN	Y	13970 FQ	15720 MW	18720 TQ	USBLS	5/07
Hand	Ohio	Y	15650 FQ	20350 MW	26330 TQ	USBLS	5/07
Hand	Canton-Massillon MSA, OH	Y	14860 FQ	18380 MW	22640 TQ	USBLS	5/07
Hand	Cincinnati-Middletown MSA, OH-KY-IN	Y	14960 FQ	18130 MW	23220 TQ	USBLS	5/07
Hand	Cleveland-Elyria-Mentor MSA, OH	Y	17980 FQ	21720 MW	28100 TQ	USBLS	5/07
Hand	Columbus MSA, OH	Y	16360 FQ	21040 MW	25510 TQ	USBLS	5/07
Hand	Dayton MSA, OH	Y	14910 FQ	16070 MW	21200 TQ	USBLS	5/07
Hand	Springfield MSA, OH	Y	15110 FQ	16170 MW	18870 TQ	USBLS	5/07
Hand	Oklahoma	Y	13450 FQ	16040 MW	21230 TQ	USBLS	5/07
Hand	Lawton MSA, OK	Y	13540 FQ	15930 MW	18350 TQ	USBLS	5/07
Hand	Oklahoma City MSA, OK	Y	12760 FQ	14380 MW	18390 TQ	USBLS	5/07
Hand	Tulsa MSA, OK	Y	14870 FQ	18110 MW	22430 TQ	USBLS	5/07
Hand	Medford MSA, OR	Y	17190 FQ	18310 MW	20230 TQ	USBLS	5/07
Hand	Portland-Vancouver-Beaverton MSA, OR-WA	Y	17230 FQ	18410 MW	20300 TQ	USBLS	5/07
Hand	Pennsylvania	Y	15620 FQ	19370 MW	25340 TQ	USBLS	5/07
Hand	Allentown-Bethlehem-Easton MSA, PA-NJ	Y	16410 FQ	22240 MW	30010 TQ	USBLS	5/07
Hand	Erie MSA, PA	Y	16170 FQ	18890 MW	24510 TQ	USBLS	5/07
Hand	Philadelphia-Camden-Wilmington MSA, PA-NJ-DE-MD	Y	15470 FQ	19810 MW	24550 TQ	USBLS	5/07
Hand	Pittsburgh MSA, PA	Y	15660 FQ	18890 MW	23670 TQ	USBLS	5/07
Hand	Reading MSA, PA	Y	16220 FQ	19190 MW	24160 TQ	USBLS	5/07
Hand	Rhode Island	Y	16500 FQ	18380 MW	22720 TQ	USBLS	5/07
Hand	Providence-Fall River-Warwick MSA, RI-MA	Y	16510 FQ	18400 MW	22410 TQ	USBLS	5/07
Hand	South Carolina	Y	13870 FQ	16970 MW	22060 TQ	USBLS	5/07
Hand	Charleston-North Charleston MSA, SC	Y	13740 FQ	16210 MW	18950 TQ	USBLS	5/07
Hand	Columbia MSA, SC	Y	13950 FQ	17040 MW	20510 TQ	USBLS	5/07
Hand	South Dakota	Y	15735 FQ	19407 MW	23987 TQ	SDBLS	7/08-9/08
Hand	Sioux Falls MSA, SD	Y	17415 FQ	20176 MW	24664 TQ	SDBLS	7/08-9/08
Hand	Tennessee	Y	14800 FQ	19020 MW	23940 TQ	USBLS	5/07
Hand	Johnson City MSA, TN	Y	14810 FQ	18820 MW	22390 TQ	USBLS	5/07
Hand	Memphis MSA, TN-MS-AR	Y	15980 FQ	19430 MW	23510 TQ	USBLS	5/07

AE	Average entry wage	**AW**	Average wage paid	**FQ**	First quartile wage	**LO** Lowest wage paid	**MTC** Median total compensation	**TCC** Total cash compensation
AER	Average entry range	**AWR**	Average wage range	**H**	Hourly	**LR** Low end range	**MW** Median wage paid	**TQ** Third quartile wage
AEX	Average experienced wage	**AXR**	Average experienced range	**HI**	Highest wage paid	**M** Monthly	**MWR** Median wage range	**W** Weekly
ATC	Average total compensation	**D**	Daily	**HR**	High end range	**MCC** Median cash compensation	**S** See annotated source	**Y** Yearly

Occupation/Type/Industry	Location	Per	Low	Mid	High	Source	Date
Packer and Packager							
Hand	Nashville-Davidson-Murfreesboro MSA, TN	Y	15170 FQ	19780 MW	24120 TQ	USBLS	5/07
Hand	Texas	Y	13450 FQ	15910 MW	21230 TQ	USBLS	5/07
Hand	Austin-Round Rock MSA, TX	Y	13300 FQ	15480 MW	19830 TQ	USBLS	5/07
Hand	Dallas-Fort Worth-Arlington MSA, TX	Y	13920 FQ	17200 MW	22890 TQ	USBLS	5/07
Hand	El Paso MSA, TX	Y	12530 FQ	13970 MW	15440 TQ	USBLS	5/07
Hand	Houston-Sugar Land-Baytown MSA, TX	Y	13180 FQ	15300 MW	19990 TQ	USBLS	5/07
Hand	San Antonio MSA, TX	Y	15590 FQ	18260 MW	24610 TQ	USBLS	5/07
Hand	Utah	Y	14050 FQ	17640 MW	22930 TQ	USBLS	5/07
Hand	Salt Lake City MSA, UT	Y	15140 FQ	20000 MW	24390 TQ	USBLS	5/07
Hand	Vermont	Y	19380 FQ	22290 MW	26100 TQ	USBLS	5/07
Hand	Burlington-South Burlington MSA, VT	Y	19370 FQ	22400 MW	27840 TQ	USBLS	5/07
Hand	Virginia	Y	14630 FQ	17860 MW	21650 TQ	USBLS	5/07
Hand	Richmond MSA, VA	Y	13290 FQ	15470 MW	18140 TQ	USBLS	5/07
Hand	Roanoke MSA, VA	Y	14010 FQ	16840 MW	19440 TQ	USBLS	5/07
Hand	Virginia Beach-Norfolk-Newport News MSA, VA-NC	Y	14840 FQ	18070 MW	21320 TQ	USBLS	5/07
Hand	Washington	H	8.62 FQ	9.33 MW	11.30 TQ	WABLS	3/08
Hand	Seattle-Tacoma-Bellevue MSA, WA	Y	17750 FQ	19260 MW	24000 TQ	USBLS	5/07
Hand	West Virginia	Y	14435 FQ	16350 MW	19638 TQ	WVBLS	7/08-9/08
Hand	Charleston MSA, WV	Y	13730 FQ	15230 MW	21510 TQ	USBLS	5/07
Hand	Wisconsin	Y	16820 FQ	21930 MW	29140 TQ	USBLS	5/07
Hand	Green Bay MSA, WI	Y	16150 FQ	19080 MW	23650 TQ	USBLS	5/07
Hand	Milwaukee-Waukesha-West Allis MSA, WI	Y	16620 FQ	21640 MW	27560 TQ	USBLS	5/07
Hand	Racine MSA, WI	Y	14840 FQ	18250 MW	23140 TQ	USBLS	5/07
Hand	Wyoming	Y	13686 FQ	16002 MW	20074 TQ	WYBLS	9/08
Hand	Cheyenne MSA, WY	Y	15129 FQ	18556 MW	23144 TQ	WYBLS	9/08
Hand	Puerto Rico	Y	12310 FQ	13460 MW	14620 TQ	USBLS	5/07
Hand	San Juan-Caguas-Guaynabo MSA, PR	Y	12320 FQ	13480 MW	14650 TQ	USBLS	5/07
Hand	Guam	Y	12530 FQ	13990 MW	15770 TQ	USBLS	5/07
Painter							
Construction and Maintenance	Alabama	Y	23530 FQ	27980 MW	32880 TQ	USBLS	5/07
Construction and Maintenance	Birmingham-Hoover MSA, AL	Y	24760 FQ	27380 MW	29900 TQ	USBLS	5/07
Construction and Maintenance	Alaska	Y	28870 FQ	37310 MW	52830 TQ	USBLS	5/07
Construction and Maintenance	Anchorage MSA, AK	Y	28390 FQ	34920 MW	40560 TQ	USBLS	5/07
Construction and Maintenance	Arizona	Y	24270 FQ	29430 MW	34870 TQ	USBLS	5/07
Construction and Maintenance	Phoenix-Mesa-Scottsdale MSA, AZ	Y	24130 FQ	29550 MW	35230 TQ	USBLS	5/07
Construction and Maintenance	Tucson MSA, AZ	Y	25880 FQ	29570 MW	33150 TQ	USBLS	5/07
Construction and Maintenance	Arkansas	Y	24780 FQ	28590 MW	32640 TQ	USBLS	5/07
Construction and Maintenance	Little Rock-North Little Rock MSA, AR	Y	26930 FQ	30830 MW	35700 TQ	USBLS	5/07
Construction and Maintenance	California	H	14.72 FQ	18.71 MW	23.76 TQ	CABLS	1/08-3/08
Construction and Maintenance	Los Angeles-Long Beach-Glendale PMSA, CA	H	14.52 FQ	18.27 MW	23.25 TQ	CABLS	1/08-3/08
Construction and Maintenance	Oakland-Fremont-Hayward MSA, CA	H	16.17 FQ	22.12 MW	26.85 TQ	CABLS	1/08-3/08
Construction and Maintenance	Riverside-San Bernardino-Ontario MSA, CA	H	12.54 FQ	15.35 MW	19.78 TQ	CABLS	1/08-3/08
Construction and Maintenance	Sacramento-Arden Arcade-Roseville MSA, CA	H	16.24 FQ	21.07 MW	25.45 TQ	CABLS	1/08-3/08
Construction and Maintenance	San Diego-Carlsbad-San Marcos MSA, CA	H	15.77 FQ	18.00 MW	20.97 TQ	CABLS	1/08-3/08
Construction and Maintenance	San Francisco-San Mateo-Redwood PMSA, CA	H	20.37 FQ	24.26 MW	28.93 TQ	CABLS	1/08-3/08
Construction and Maintenance	San Jose-Sunnyvale-Santa Clara MSA, CA	H	14.17 FQ	17.46 MW	23.18 TQ	CABLS	1/08-3/08
Construction and Maintenance	Santa Ana-Anaheim-Irvine PMSA, CA	Y	30200 FQ	37200 MW	48050 TQ	USBLS	5/07
Construction and Maintenance	Colorado	Y	26870 FQ	33070 MW	39060 TQ	USBLS	5/07
Construction and Maintenance	Denver-Aurora MSA, CO	Y	30710 FQ	34880 MW	39230 TQ	USBLS	5/07
Construction and Maintenance	Connecticut	H	13.57 AE	18.06 MW		CTBLS	1/08-3/08
Construction and Maintenance	Bridgeport-Stamford-Norwalk MSA, CT	Y	33350 FQ	37060 MW	41380 TQ	USBLS	5/07

AE	Average entry wage	AW	Average wage paid	FQ	First quartile wage	LO	Lowest wage paid	MTC	Median total compensation	TCC	Total cash compensation
AER	Average entry range	AWR	Average wage range	H	Hourly	LR	Low end range	MW	Median wage paid	TQ	Third quartile wage
AEX	Average experienced wage	AXR	Average experienced range	HI	Highest wage paid	M	Monthly	MWR	Median wage range	W	Weekly
ATC	Average total salaries	D	Daily	HR	High end range	MCC	Median cash compensation	S	See annotated source	Y	Yearly

Occupation/Type/Industry	Location	Per	Low	Mid	High	Source	Date
Painter							
Construction and Maintenance	Hartford-West Hartford-East Hartford MSA, CT	Y	29110 FQ	35670 MW	43080 TQ	USBLS	5/07
Construction and Maintenance	New Haven MSA, CT	Y	28910 FQ	35140 MW	45460 TQ	USBLS	5/07
Construction and Maintenance	Delaware	Y	27930 FQ	32880 MW	41400 TQ	USBLS	5/07
Construction and Maintenance	Wilmington PMSA, DE-MD-NJ	Y	28360 FQ	33870 MW	44610 TQ	USBLS	5/07
Construction and Maintenance	District of Columbia	Y	29500 FQ	40300 MW	55870 TQ	USBLS	5/07
Construction and Maintenance	Washington-Arlington-Alexandria MSA, DC-VA-MD-WV	Y	28330 FQ	33160 MW	39920 TQ	USBLS	5/07
Construction and Maintenance	Florida	Y	24880 FQ	29250 MW	35420 TQ	USBLS	5/07
Construction and Maintenance	Fort Lauderdale-Pompano Beach-Deerfield Beach PMSA, FL	Y	24860 FQ	28630 MW	33680 TQ	USBLS	5/07
Construction and Maintenance	Jacksonville MSA, FL	Y	20700 FQ	28270 MW	33770 TQ	USBLS	5/07
Construction and Maintenance	Miami-Fort Lauderdale-Miami Beach MSA, FL	Y	25150 FQ	29340 MW	36050 TQ	USBLS	5/07
Construction and Maintenance	Orlando-Kissimmee MSA, FL	Y	24520 FQ	29890 MW	36740 TQ	USBLS	5/07
Construction and Maintenance	Tallahassee MSA, FL	Y	19590 FQ	27090 MW	30290 TQ	USBLS	5/07
Construction and Maintenance	Tampa-St. Petersburg-Clearwater MSA, FL	Y	26890 FQ	30800 MW	37440 TQ	USBLS	5/07
Construction and Maintenance	West Palm Beach-Boca Raton-Boynton Beach PMSA, FL	Y	26390 FQ	30400 MW	36470 TQ	USBLS	5/07
Construction and Maintenance	Georgia	Y	24430 FQ	29460 MW	37350 TQ	USBLS	5/07
Construction and Maintenance	Atlanta-Sandy Springs-Marietta MSA, GA	Y	26720 FQ	30980 MW	39410 TQ	USBLS	5/07
Construction and Maintenance	Savannah MSA, GA	Y	24540 FQ	28370 MW	31700 TQ	USBLS	5/07
Construction and Maintenance	Hawaii	Y	33480 FQ	42240 MW	57730 TQ	USBLS	5/07
Construction and Maintenance	Honolulu MSA, HI	Y	33940 FQ	46190 MW	61000 TQ	USBLS	5/07
Construction and Maintenance	Idaho	Y	21950 FQ	26990 MW	31890 TQ	USBLS	5/07
Construction and Maintenance	Boise City-Nampa MSA, ID	Y	20540 FQ	25280 MW	29230 TQ	USBLS	5/07
Construction and Maintenance	Illinois	Y	29680 FQ	39540 MW	65640 TQ	USBLS	5/07
Construction and Maintenance	Chicago-Naperville-Joliet MSA, IL-IN-WI	Y	30290 FQ	40010 MW	68330 TQ	USBLS	5/07
Construction and Maintenance	Indiana	Y	27170 FQ	33310 MW	45360 TQ	USBLS	5/07
Construction and Maintenance	Gary PMSA, IN	Y	22040 FQ	35970 MW	52350 TQ	USBLS	5/07
Construction and Maintenance	Indianapolis-Carmel MSA, IN	Y	28760 FQ	34140 MW	44660 TQ	USBLS	5/07
Construction and Maintenance	Iowa	Y	24540 FQ	31230 MW	41000 TQ	USBLS	5/07
Construction and Maintenance	Cedar Rapids MSA, IA	Y	27300 FQ	33170 MW	41550 TQ	USBLS	5/07
Construction and Maintenance	Des Moines-West Des Moines MSA, IA	Y	24420 FQ	33340 MW	45140 TQ	USBLS	5/07
Construction and Maintenance	Kansas	Y	22810 FQ	30420 MW	42360 TQ	USBLS	5/07
Construction and Maintenance	Wichita MSA, KS	Y	20790 FQ	31680 MW	38560 TQ	USBLS	5/07
Construction and Maintenance	Kentucky	Y	24374 FQ	30348 MW	37247 TQ	KYBLS	2008
Construction and Maintenance	Elizabethtown MSA, KY	Y	22300 FQ	24820 MW	28950 TQ	USBLS	5/07
Construction and Maintenance	Louisville-Jefferson County MSA, KY-IN	Y	26930 FQ	31160 MW	38760 TQ	USBLS	5/07
Construction and Maintenance	Louisiana	H	12.38 FQ	14.21 MW	16.82 TQ	LABLS	1/08-3/08
Construction and Maintenance	Baton Rouge MSA, LA	Y	26500 FQ	29190 MW	32560 TQ	USBLS	5/07
Construction and Maintenance	Houma-Bayou Cane-Thibodaux MSA, LA	Y	30700 FQ	34160 MW	37260 TQ	USBLS	5/07
Construction and Maintenance	New Orleans-Metairie-Kenner MSA, LA	Y	25640 FQ	29640 MW	35210 TQ	USBLS	5/07
Construction and Maintenance	Maine	Y	27460 FQ	33730 MW	38710 TQ	USBLS	5/07
Construction and Maintenance	Portland-South Portland-Biddeford MSA, ME	Y	23690 FQ	29390 MW	35290 TQ	USBLS	5/07
Construction and Maintenance	Maryland	Y		35000 MW		MDBLS	3/08
Construction and Maintenance	Baltimore-Towson MSA, MD	Y	29740 FQ	35060 MW	44370 TQ	USBLS	5/07
Construction and Maintenance	Bethesda-Gaithersburg-Frederick PMSA, MD	Y	29600 FQ	35050 MW	41570 TQ	USBLS	5/07
Construction and Maintenance	Massachusetts	Y	28420 FQ	35900 MW	45430 TQ	USBLS	5/07
Construction and Maintenance	Boston-Cambridge-Quincy NECTA, MA	Y	30110 FQ	38330 MW	48320 TQ	USBLS	5/07
Construction and Maintenance	Worcester MSA, MA-CT	Y	28470 FQ	35810 MW	48920 TQ	USBLS	5/07
Construction and Maintenance	Michigan	Y	28960 FQ	37240 MW	48620 TQ	USBLS	5/07
Construction and Maintenance	Detroit-Warren-Livonia MSA, MI	Y	35020 FQ	41840 MW	51050 TQ	USBLS	5/07
Construction and Maintenance	Grand Rapids-Wyoming MSA, MI	Y	25090 FQ	31730 MW	42600 TQ	USBLS	5/07
Construction and Maintenance	Warren-Troy-Farmington Hills PMSA, MI	Y	34830 FQ	40600 MW	51980 TQ	USBLS	5/07

AE	Average entry wage	AW	Average wage paid	FQ	First quartile wage	LO	Lowest wage paid	MTC	Median total compensation	TCC	Total cash compensation
AER	Average entry range	AWR	Average wage range	H	Hourly	LR	Low end range	MW	Median wage paid	TQ	Third quartile wage
AEX	Average experienced wage	AXR	Average experienced range	HI	Highest wage paid	M	Monthly	MWR	Median wage range	W	Weekly
ATC	Average total compensation	D	Daily	HR	High end range	MCC	Median cash compensation	S	See annotated source	Y	Yearly

Painter

Occupation/Type/Industry	Location	Per	Low	Mid	High	Source	Date
Painter							
Construction and Maintenance	Minnesota	Y	32290 FQ	39783 MW	53758 TQ	MNBLS	10/08-12/08
Construction and Maintenance	Duluth-Superior MSA, MN-WI	Y	29571 FQ	45748 MW	60007 TQ	MNBLS	10/08-12/08
Construction and Maintenance	Minneapolis-Saint Paul MSA, MN-WI	Y	32965 FQ	40131 MW	55539 TQ	MNBLS	10/08-12/08
Construction and Maintenance	Rochester MSA, MN	Y	27241 FQ	32470 MW	45794 TQ	MNBLS	10/08-12/08
Construction and Maintenance	Mississippi	Y	22910 FQ	27340 MW	31530 TQ	USBLS	5/07
Construction and Maintenance	Hattiesburg MSA, MS	Y	22170 FQ	24200 MW	28010 TQ	USBLS	5/07
Construction and Maintenance	Jackson MSA, MS	Y	25920 FQ	29250 MW	33720 TQ	USBLS	5/07
Construction and Maintenance	Missouri	Y	27740 FQ	36870 MW	54280 TQ	USBLS	5/07
Construction and Maintenance	Kansas City MSA, MO-KS	Y	24270 FQ	30470 MW	39520 TQ	USBLS	5/07
Construction and Maintenance	St. Louis MSA, MO-IL	Y	35720 FQ	52320 MW	59190 TQ	USBLS	5/07
Construction and Maintenance	Montana	Y	27070 FQ	30430 MW	36610 TQ	USBLS	5/07
Construction and Maintenance	Billings MSA, MT	Y	32030 FQ	36420 MW	41380 TQ	USBLS	5/07
Construction and Maintenance	Nebraska	Y	22840 FQ	27570 MW	32580 TQ	USBLS	5/07
Construction and Maintenance	Omaha-Council Bluffs MSA, NE-IA	Y	23690 FQ	28810 MW	33990 TQ	USBLS	5/07
Construction and Maintenance	Nevada	H	14.35 FQ	17.71 MW	23.51 TQ	NVBLS	5/08
Construction and Maintenance	Las Vegas-Paradise MSA, NV	H	14.44 FQ	17.94 MW	24.64 TQ	NVBLS	5/08
Construction and Maintenance	New Hampshire	H	12.87 AE	15.81 MW	17.90 AEX	NHBLS	6/08
Construction and Maintenance	Manchester MSA, NH	Y	26990 FQ	30130 MW	36050 TQ	USBLS	5/07
Construction and Maintenance	Nashua NECTA, NH-MA	Y	28290 FQ	33310 MW	42820 TQ	USBLS	5/07
Construction and Maintenance	New Jersey	Y	29500 FQ	36510 MW	50980 TQ	USBLS	5/07
Construction and Maintenance	Camden PMSA, NJ	Y	33500 FQ	45040 MW	54440 TQ	USBLS	5/07
Construction and Maintenance	Edison PMSA, NJ	Y	26310 FQ	30890 MW	39960 TQ	USBLS	5/07
Construction and Maintenance	Newark-Union PMSA, NJ-PA	Y	30560 FQ	37710 MW	53040 TQ	USBLS	5/07
Construction and Maintenance	Trenton-Ewing MSA, NJ	Y	35410 FQ	39690 MW	45770 TQ	USBLS	5/07
Construction and Maintenance	New Mexico	Y	21750 FQ	27540 MW	34770 TQ	USBLS	5/07
Construction and Maintenance	Albuquerque MSA, NM	Y	21990 FQ	27730 MW	33500 TQ	USBLS	5/07
Construction and Maintenance	New York	Y	29300 FQ	39900 MW	55830 TQ	USBLS	5/07
Construction and Maintenance	Albany-Schenectady-Troy MSA, NY	Y	35420 FQ	42590 MW	49190 TQ	USBLS	5/07
Construction and Maintenance	Buffalo-Niagara Falls MSA, NY	Y	31050 FQ	46050 MW	56700 TQ	USBLS	5/07
Construction and Maintenance	Nassau-Suffolk PMSA, NY	Y	29400 FQ	38190 MW	53540 TQ	USBLS	5/07
Construction and Maintenance	New York-Northern New Jersey-Long Island MSA, NY-NJ-PA	Y	29380 FQ	39320 MW	58910 TQ	USBLS	5/07
Construction and Maintenance	North Carolina	Y	24260 FQ	28180 MW	31990 TQ	USBLS	5/07
Construction and Maintenance	Charlotte-Gastonia-Concord MSA, NC-SC	Y	27410 FQ	31160 MW	35280 TQ	USBLS	5/07
Construction and Maintenance	Durham MSA, NC	Y	21270 FQ	26040 MW	32110 TQ	USBLS	5/07
Construction and Maintenance	Raleigh-Cary MSA, NC	Y	25840 FQ	28230 MW	30680 TQ	USBLS	5/07
Construction and Maintenance	North Dakota	Y	23630 FQ	27670 MW	32860 TQ	USBLS	5/07
Construction and Maintenance	Fargo MSA, ND-MN	Y	24430 FQ	28000 MW	31710 TQ	USBLS	5/07
Construction and Maintenance	Ohio	Y	26720 FQ	32410 MW	43040 TQ	USBLS	5/07
Construction and Maintenance	Cincinnati-Middletown MSA, OH-KY-IN	Y	28050 FQ	34580 MW	41140 TQ	USBLS	5/07
Construction and Maintenance	Cleveland-Elyria-Mentor MSA, OH	Y	25750 FQ	31190 MW	42870 TQ	USBLS	5/07
Construction and Maintenance	Columbus MSA, OH	Y	27200 FQ	30400 MW	36460 TQ	USBLS	5/07
Construction and Maintenance	Dayton MSA, OH	Y	25540 FQ	29960 MW	35980 TQ	USBLS	5/07
Construction and Maintenance	Mansfield MSA, OH	Y	21470 FQ	26090 MW	39300 TQ	USBLS	5/07
Construction and Maintenance	Oklahoma	Y	22770 FQ	28980 MW	38840 TQ	USBLS	5/07
Construction and Maintenance	Oklahoma City MSA, OK	Y	22120 FQ	30690 MW	41030 TQ	USBLS	5/07
Construction and Maintenance	Tulsa MSA, OK	Y	24510 FQ	29270 MW	36850 TQ	USBLS	5/07
Construction and Maintenance	Oregon	H	12.36 FQ	15.02 MW	18.43 TQ	ORBLS	5/08
Construction and Maintenance	Portland-Vancouver-Beaverton MSA, OR-WA	Y	27100 FQ	33240 MW	40020 TQ	USBLS	5/07
Construction and Maintenance	Pennsylvania	Y	28470 FQ	35160 MW	44590 TQ	USBLS	5/07
Construction and Maintenance	Allentown-Bethlehem-Easton MSA, PA-NJ	Y	27380 FQ	31080 MW	36650 TQ	USBLS	5/07
Construction and Maintenance	Philadelphia-Camden-Wilmington MSA, PA-NJ-DE-MD	Y	32220 FQ	39490 MW	50490 TQ	USBLS	5/07
Construction and Maintenance	Pittsburgh MSA, PA	Y	28850 FQ	35440 MW	48790 TQ	USBLS	5/07
Construction and Maintenance	Rhode Island	Y	27890 FQ	33350 MW	39200 TQ	USBLS	5/07
Construction and Maintenance	Providence-Fall River-Warwick MSA, RI-MA	Y	27470 FQ	33450 MW	39350 TQ	USBLS	5/07
Construction and Maintenance	South Carolina	Y	25870 FQ	29270 MW	33550 TQ	USBLS	5/07
Construction and Maintenance	Charleston-North Charleston MSA, SC	Y	27430 FQ	30820 MW	35240 TQ	USBLS	5/07

AE	Average entry wage	AW	Average wage paid	FQ	First quartile wage
AER	Average entry range	AWR	Average wage range	H	Hourly
AEX	Average experienced wage	AXR	Average experienced range	HI	Highest wage paid
ATC	Average total compensation	D	Daily	HR	High end range

LO	Lowest wage paid	MTC	Median total compensation	TCC Total cash compensation
LR	Low end range	MW	Median wage paid	TQ Third quartile wage
M	Monthly	MWR	Median wage range	W Weekly
		MCC Median cash compensation	S	See annotated source	Y Yearly

Occupation/Type/Industry	Location	Per	Low	Mid	High	Source	Date
Painter							
Construction and Maintenance	Columbia MSA, SC	Y	26030 FQ	31040 MW	37020 TQ	USBLS	5/07
Construction and Maintenance	Florence MSA, SC	Y	21530 FQ	24180 MW	29490 TQ	USBLS	5/07
Construction and Maintenance	South Dakota	Y	21199 FQ	26374 MW	31939 TQ	SDBLS	7/08-9/08
Construction and Maintenance	Rapid City MSA, SD	Y	22493 FQ	26284 MW	30256 TQ	SDBLS	7/08-9/08
Construction and Maintenance	Sioux Falls MSA, SD	Y	20120 FQ	27129 MW	37222 TQ	SDBLS	7/08-9/08
Construction and Maintenance	Tennessee	Y	25340 FQ	29010 MW	33450 TQ	USBLS	5/07
Construction and Maintenance	Clarksville MSA, TN-KY	Y	18890 FQ	26190 MW	30710 TQ	USBLS	5/07
Construction and Maintenance	Memphis MSA, TN-MS-AR	Y	27830 FQ	31500 MW	38150 TQ	USBLS	5/07
Construction and Maintenance	Nashville-Davidson-Murfreesboro MSA, TN	Y	22940 FQ	27370 MW	31330 TQ	USBLS	5/07
Construction and Maintenance	Texas	Y	23620 FQ	27660 MW	31750 TQ	USBLS	5/07
Construction and Maintenance	Austin-Round Rock MSA, TX	Y	19840 FQ	23100 MW	27030 TQ	USBLS	5/07
Construction and Maintenance	Beaumont-Port Arthur MSA, TX	Y	27320 FQ	31280 MW	35950 TQ	USBLS	5/07
Construction and Maintenance	Dallas-Fort Worth-Arlington MSA, TX	Y	24810 FQ	27950 MW	31130 TQ	USBLS	5/07
Construction and Maintenance	El Paso MSA, TX	Y	19370 FQ	22060 MW	25790 TQ	USBLS	5/07
Construction and Maintenance	Houston-Sugar Land-Baytown MSA, TX	Y	25490 FQ	28620 MW	32490 TQ	USBLS	5/07
Construction and Maintenance	San Antonio MSA, TX	Y	21850 FQ	24620 MW	29130 TQ	USBLS	5/07
Construction and Maintenance	Utah	Y	26060 FQ	30440 MW	36360 TQ	USBLS	5/07
Construction and Maintenance	Salt Lake City MSA, UT	Y	26250 FQ	30230 MW	35030 TQ	USBLS	5/07
Construction and Maintenance	Vermont	Y	27420 FQ	30730 MW	35940 TQ	USBLS	5/07
Construction and Maintenance	Burlington-South Burlington MSA, VT	Y	29300 FQ	35330 MW	40170 TQ	USBLS	5/07
Construction and Maintenance	Virginia	Y	26610 FQ	30900 MW	37150 TQ	USBLS	5/07
Construction and Maintenance	Richmond MSA, VA	Y	27810 FQ	31750 MW	37110 TQ	USBLS	5/07
Construction and Maintenance	Virginia Beach-Norfolk-Newport News MSA, VA-NC	Y	26080 FQ	30160 MW	38960 TQ	USBLS	5/07
Construction and Maintenance	Washington	H	13.94 FQ	17.56 MW	22.33 TQ	WABLS	3/08
Construction and Maintenance	Seattle-Tacoma-Bellevue MSA, WA	Y	28320 FQ	35790 MW	45740 TQ	USBLS	5/07
Construction and Maintenance	West Virginia	Y	25312 FQ	30719 MW	39286 TQ	WVBLS	7/08-9/08
Construction and Maintenance	Charleston MSA, WV	Y	28500 FQ	37610 MW	44690 TQ	USBLS	5/07
Construction and Maintenance	Wisconsin	Y	26820 FQ	35240 MW	47070 TQ	USBLS	5/07
Construction and Maintenance	Milwaukee-Waukesha-West Allis MSA, WI	Y	26810 FQ	36330 MW	48350 TQ	USBLS	5/07
Construction and Maintenance	Wyoming	Y	27102 FQ	31467 MW	42988 TQ	WYBLS	9/08
Construction and Maintenance	Casper MSA, WY	Y	28491 FQ	31698 MW	40635 TQ	WYBLS	9/08
Construction and Maintenance	Cheyenne MSA, WY	Y	27034 FQ	29477 MW	32179 TQ	WYBLS	9/08
Construction and Maintenance	Puerto Rico	Y	12860 FQ	14420 MW	17230 TQ	USBLS	5/07
Construction and Maintenance	San Juan-Caguas-Guaynabo MSA, PR	Y	12990 FQ	14710 MW	18320 TQ	USBLS	5/07
Construction and Maintenance	Virgin Islands	Y	27660 FQ	31050 MW	34920 TQ	USBLS	5/07
Construction and Maintenance	Guam	Y	23840 FQ	28200 MW	31650 TQ	USBLS	5/07
Transportation Equipment	Alabama	Y	24260 FQ	30260 MW	39370 TQ	USBLS	5/07
Transportation Equipment	Birmingham-Hoover MSA, AL	Y	27920 FQ	35580 MW	46820 TQ	USBLS	5/07
Transportation Equipment	Huntsville MSA, AL	Y	23200 FQ	30420 MW	36780 TQ	USBLS	5/07
Transportation Equipment	Alaska	Y	31800 FQ	36520 MW	45390 TQ	USBLS	5/07
Transportation Equipment	Arizona	Y	27550 FQ	34040 MW	41270 TQ	USBLS	5/07
Transportation Equipment	Phoenix-Mesa-Scottsdale MSA, AZ	Y	27120 FQ	33580 MW	40290 TQ	USBLS	5/07
Transportation Equipment	Tucson MSA, AZ	Y	37760 FQ	44430 MW	50970 TQ	USBLS	5/07
Transportation Equipment	Arkansas	Y	24530 FQ	29800 MW	36150 TQ	USBLS	5/07
Transportation Equipment	Little Rock-North Little Rock MSA, AR	Y	30230 FQ	34490 MW	38450 TQ	USBLS	5/07
Transportation Equipment	California	H	14.62 FQ	19.69 MW	26.07 TQ	CABLS	1/08-3/08
Transportation Equipment	Bakersfield MSA, CA	H	13.77 FQ	15.47 MW	22.75 TQ	CABLS	1/08-3/08
Transportation Equipment	Los Angeles-Long Beach-Glendale PMSA, CA	H	13.52 FQ	18.17 MW	24.03 TQ	CABLS	1/08-3/08
Transportation Equipment	Oakland-Fremont-Hayward MSA, CA	H	19.74 FQ	26.05 MW	29.67 TQ	CABLS	1/08-3/08
Transportation Equipment	Riverside-San Bernardino-Ontario MSA, CA	H	12.63 FQ	14.55 MW	18.29 TQ	CABLS	1/08-3/08
Transportation Equipment	Sacramento-Arden Arcade-Roseville MSA, CA	H	20.61 FQ	24.50 MW	28.57 TQ	CABLS	1/08-3/08
Transportation Equipment	San Diego-Carlsbad-San Marcos MSA, CA	H	13.55 FQ	19.01 MW	26.92 TQ	CABLS	1/08-3/08
Transportation Equipment	San Francisco-San Mateo-Redwood PMSA, CA	H	17.50 FQ	20.23 MW	28.05 TQ	CABLS	1/08-3/08

AE	Average entry wage	AW	Average wage paid	FQ	First quartile wage
AER	Average entry range	AWR	Average wage range	H	Hourly
AEX	Average experienced wage	AXR	Average experienced range	HI	Highest wage paid
ATC	Average total compensation	D	Daily	HR	High end range

LO	Lowest wage paid	MTC	Median total compensation
LR	Low end range	MW	Median wage paid
M	Monthly	MWR	Median wage range
MCC	Median cash compensation	S	See annotated source

TCC	Total cash compensation
TQ	Third quartile wage
W	Weekly
Y	Yearly

Occupation/Type/Industry	Location	Per	Low	Mid	High	Source	Date
Painter							
Transportation Equipment	San Jose-Sunnyvale-Santa Clara MSA, CA	H	14.31 FQ	16.66 MW	25.57 TQ	CABLS	1/08-3/08
Transportation Equipment	Santa Ana-Anaheim-Irvine PMSA, CA	Y	33380 FQ	42470 MW	56150 TQ	USBLS	5/07
Transportation Equipment	Colorado	Y	33070 FQ	45440 MW	66700 TQ	USBLS	5/07
Transportation Equipment	Denver-Aurora MSA, CO	Y	37810 FQ	48070 MW	69950 TQ	USBLS	5/07
Transportation Equipment	Connecticut	H	12.15 AE	14.46 MW		CTBLS	1/08-3/08
Transportation Equipment	Bridgeport-Stamford-Norwalk MSA, CT	Y	26120 FQ	28820 MW	37040 TQ	USBLS	5/07
Transportation Equipment	Danbury MSA, CT	Y	24380 FQ	41800 MW	48210 TQ	USBLS	5/07
Transportation Equipment	Hartford-West Hartford-East Hartford MSA, CT	Y	25820 FQ	29390 MW	36030 TQ	USBLS	5/07
Transportation Equipment	Delaware	Y	30740 FQ	36940 MW	44840 TQ	USBLS	5/07
Transportation Equipment	Wilmington PMSA, DE-MD-NJ	Y	30230 FQ	36250 MW	43680 TQ	USBLS	5/07
Transportation Equipment	Washington-Arlington-Alexandria MSA, DC-VA-MD-WV	Y	24860 FQ	43940 MW	57970 TQ	USBLS	5/07
Transportation Equipment	Florida	Y	27250 FQ	33950 MW	41270 TQ	USBLS	5/07
Transportation Equipment	Fort Lauderdale-Pompano Beach-Deerfield Beach PMSA, FL	Y	24060 FQ	30150 MW	39490 TQ	USBLS	5/07
Transportation Equipment	Jacksonville MSA, FL	Y	30120 FQ	35230 MW	40020 TQ	USBLS	5/07
Transportation Equipment	Miami-Fort Lauderdale-Miami Beach MSA, FL	Y	26710 FQ	32640 MW	42380 TQ	USBLS	5/07
Transportation Equipment	Orlando-Kissimmee MSA, FL	Y	26760 FQ	32250 MW	38040 TQ	USBLS	5/07
Transportation Equipment	Tallahassee MSA, FL	Y	23280 FQ	30790 MW	36980 TQ	USBLS	5/07
Transportation Equipment	Tampa-St. Petersburg-Clearwater MSA, FL	Y	25590 FQ	33590 MW	44480 TQ	USBLS	5/07
Transportation Equipment	West Palm Beach-Boca Raton-Boynton Beach PMSA, FL	Y	32680 FQ	38960 MW	45800 TQ	USBLS	5/07
Transportation Equipment	Georgia	Y	29380 FQ	34560 MW	42960 TQ	USBLS	5/07
Transportation Equipment	Atlanta-Sandy Springs-Marietta MSA, GA	Y	30720 FQ	34820 MW	44680 TQ	USBLS	5/07
Transportation Equipment	Hawaii	Y	25740 FQ	32060 MW	36380 TQ	USBLS	5/07
Transportation Equipment	Honolulu MSA, HI	Y	26950 FQ	33570 MW	36640 TQ	USBLS	5/07
Transportation Equipment	Idaho	Y	30780 FQ	36700 MW	46880 TQ	USBLS	5/07
Transportation Equipment	Boise City-Nampa MSA, ID	Y	34850 FQ	39430 MW	49690 TQ	USBLS	5/07
Transportation Equipment	Illinois	Y	26100 FQ	40950 MW	56000 TQ	USBLS	5/07
Transportation Equipment	Chicago-Naperville-Joliet MSA, IL-IN-WI	Y	23110 FQ	36310 MW	47260 TQ	USBLS	5/07
Transportation Equipment	Peoria MSA, IL	Y	31810 FQ	35450 MW	39250 TQ	USBLS	5/07
Transportation Equipment	Indiana	Y	27500 FQ	32210 MW	41610 TQ	USBLS	5/07
Transportation Equipment	Gary PMSA, IN	Y	33630 FQ	38800 MW	55710 TQ	USBLS	5/07
Transportation Equipment	Indianapolis-Carmel MSA, IN	Y	27940 FQ	37500 MW	46790 TQ	USBLS	5/07
Transportation Equipment	Iowa	Y	26530 FQ	30490 MW	36100 TQ	USBLS	5/07
Transportation Equipment	Des Moines-West Des Moines MSA, IA	Y	27410 FQ	35730 MW	40050 TQ	USBLS	5/07
Transportation Equipment	Kansas	Y	29310 FQ	38290 MW	49490 TQ	USBLS	5/07
Transportation Equipment	Wichita MSA, KS	Y	39250 FQ	47340 MW	54300 TQ	USBLS	5/07
Transportation Equipment	Kentucky	Y	31881 FQ	42188 MW	54462 TQ	KYBLS	2008
Transportation Equipment	Louisiana	H	13.32 FQ	16.31 MW	19.39 TQ	LABLS	1/08-3/08
Transportation Equipment	Baton Rouge MSA, LA	Y	24220 FQ	29260 MW	35760 TQ	USBLS	5/07
Transportation Equipment	New Orleans-Metairie-Kenner MSA, LA	Y	32740 FQ	38240 MW	53190 TQ	USBLS	5/07
Transportation Equipment	Maine	Y	25480 FQ	32230 MW	38580 TQ	USBLS	5/07
Transportation Equipment	Maryland	Y		33400 MW		MDBLS	3/08
Transportation Equipment	Baltimore-Towson MSA, MD	Y	29370 FQ	39230 MW	55270 TQ	USBLS	5/07
Transportation Equipment	Bethesda-Gaithersburg-Frederick PMSA, MD	Y	22210 FQ	24820 MW	49860 TQ	USBLS	5/07
Transportation Equipment	Massachusetts	Y	31890 FQ	37230 MW	46870 TQ	USBLS	5/07
Transportation Equipment	Boston-Cambridge-Quincy NECTA, MA	Y	35370 FQ	40360 MW	57040 TQ	USBLS	5/07
Transportation Equipment	New Bedford MSA, MA	Y	30820 FQ	35190 MW	44990 TQ	USBLS	5/07
Transportation Equipment	Michigan	Y	32780 FQ	45440 MW	59930 TQ	USBLS	5/07
Transportation Equipment	Detroit-Warren-Livonia MSA, MI	Y	43050 FQ	55220 MW	67720 TQ	USBLS	5/07
Transportation Equipment	Grand Rapids-Wyoming MSA, MI	Y	33290 FQ	37600 MW	56410 TQ	USBLS	5/07
Transportation Equipment	Warren-Troy-Farmington Hills PMSA, MI	Y	45320 FQ	55000 MW	69230 TQ	USBLS	5/07

AE	Average entry wage	AW	Average wage paid	FQ	First quartile wage	LO	Lowest wage paid	MTC	Median total compensation	TCC	Total cash compensation
AER	Average entry range	AWR	Average wage range	H	Hourly	LR	Low end range	MW	Median wage paid	TQ	Third quartile wage
AEX	Average experienced wage	AXR	Average experienced range	HI	Highest wage paid	M	Monthly	MWR	Median wage range	W	Weekly
ATC	Average total salaries	D	Daily	HR	High end range	MCC	Median cash compensation	S	See annotated source	Y	Yearly

Painter

Occupation/Type/Industry	Location	Per	Low	Mid	High	Source	Date
Transportation Equipment	Minnesota	Y	31121 FQ	36439 MW	49667 TQ	MNBLS	10/08-12/08
Transportation Equipment	Duluth-Superior MSA, MN-WI	Y	35910 FQ	38533 MW	41498 TQ	MNBLS	10/08-12/08
Transportation Equipment	Minneapolis-Saint Paul MSA, MN-WI	Y	34801 FQ	43125 MW	63092 TQ	MNBLS	10/08-12/08
Transportation Equipment	Mississippi	Y	26990 FQ	31620 MW	39240 TQ	USBLS	5/07
Transportation Equipment	Jackson MSA, MS	Y	25540 FQ	31550 MW	36640 TQ	USBLS	5/07
Transportation Equipment	Missouri	Y	33270 FQ	44290 MW	56540 TQ	USBLS	5/07
Transportation Equipment	Kansas City MSA, MO-KS	Y	34170 FQ	44950 MW	57980 TQ	USBLS	5/07
Transportation Equipment	St. Louis MSA, MO-IL	Y	37960 FQ	45670 MW	55150 TQ	USBLS	5/07
Transportation Equipment	Montana	Y	23810 FQ	28410 MW	37400 TQ	USBLS	5/07
Transportation Equipment	Nebraska	Y	26030 FQ	31060 MW	41330 TQ	USBLS	5/07
Transportation Equipment	Omaha-Council Bluffs MSA, NE-IA	Y	27320 FQ	32010 MW	52250 TQ	USBLS	5/07
Transportation Equipment	Nevada	H	15.34 FQ	19.35 MW	25.16 TQ	NVBLS	5/08
Transportation Equipment	Las Vegas-Paradise MSA, NV	H	15.81 FQ	20.97 MW	25.56 TQ	NVBLS	5/08
Transportation Equipment	New Hampshire	H	12.59 AE	17.45 MW	20.57 AEX	NHBLS	6/08
Transportation Equipment	Nashua NECTA, NH-MA	Y	27280 FQ	34860 MW	44360 TQ	USBLS	5/07
Transportation Equipment	New Jersey	Y	30680 FQ	39490 MW	45610 TQ	USBLS	5/07
Transportation Equipment	Atlantic City MSA, NJ	Y	29970 FQ	35370 MW	43290 TQ	USBLS	5/07
Transportation Equipment	Camden PMSA, NJ	Y	37200 FQ	41460 MW	45570 TQ	USBLS	5/07
Transportation Equipment	Edison PMSA, NJ	Y	30250 FQ	39240 MW	47790 TQ	USBLS	5/07
Transportation Equipment	Newark-Union PMSA, NJ-PA	Y	27390 FQ	35020 MW	42900 TQ	USBLS	5/07
Transportation Equipment	New Mexico	Y	21080 FQ	23070 MW	32270 TQ	USBLS	5/07
Transportation Equipment	Albuquerque MSA, NM	Y	25310 FQ	34090 MW	40590 TQ	USBLS	5/07
Transportation Equipment	New York	Y	26990 FQ	31880 MW	40060 TQ	USBLS	5/07
Transportation Equipment	Albany-Schenectady-Troy MSA, NY	Y	30470 FQ	40460 MW	48460 TQ	USBLS	5/07
Transportation Equipment	Buffalo-Niagara Falls MSA, NY	Y	26090 FQ	29620 MW	34690 TQ	USBLS	5/07
Transportation Equipment	Nassau-Suffolk PMSA, NY	Y	25600 FQ	28650 MW	34720 TQ	USBLS	5/07
Transportation Equipment	New York-Northern New Jersey-Long Island MSA, NY-NJ-PA	Y	28140 FQ	36260 MW	44230 TQ	USBLS	5/07
Transportation Equipment	North Carolina	Y	29900 FQ	39120 MW	47520 TQ	USBLS	5/07
Transportation Equipment	Charlotte-Gastonia-Concord MSA, NC-SC	Y	39680 FQ	45150 MW	49800 TQ	USBLS	5/07
Transportation Equipment	Raleigh-Cary MSA, NC	Y	36870 FQ	53760 MW	62790 TQ	USBLS	5/07
Transportation Equipment	North Dakota	Y	32550 FQ	35850 MW	38800 TQ	USBLS	5/07
Transportation Equipment	Ohio	Y	27500 FQ	36050 MW	53220 TQ	USBLS	5/07
Transportation Equipment	Cincinnati-Middletown MSA, OH-KY-IN	Y	29140 FQ	37820 MW	45990 TQ	USBLS	5/07
Transportation Equipment	Cleveland-Elyria-Mentor MSA, OH	Y	32580 FQ	52040 MW	65600 TQ	USBLS	5/07
Transportation Equipment	Columbus MSA, OH	Y	28030 FQ	32340 MW	48680 TQ	USBLS	5/07
Transportation Equipment	Dayton MSA, OH	Y	28760 FQ	33830 MW	53740 TQ	USBLS	5/07
Transportation Equipment	Oklahoma	Y	26420 FQ	30800 MW	37280 TQ	USBLS	5/07
Transportation Equipment	Oklahoma City MSA, OK	Y	26130 FQ	29830 MW	36570 TQ	USBLS	5/07
Transportation Equipment	Tulsa MSA, OK	Y	27670 FQ	32550 MW	36950 TQ	USBLS	5/07
Transportation Equipment	Oregon	H	14.48 FQ	17.43 MW	21.80 TQ	ORBLS	5/08
Transportation Equipment	Eugene-Springfield MSA, OR	Y	32410 FQ	35820 MW	39230 TQ	USBLS	5/07
Transportation Equipment	Portland-Vancouver-Beaverton MSA, OR-WA	Y	32180 FQ	39720 MW	51760 TQ	USBLS	5/07
Transportation Equipment	Pennsylvania	Y	32470 FQ	38930 MW	45560 TQ	USBLS	5/07
Transportation Equipment	Allentown-Bethlehem-Easton MSA, PA-NJ	Y	34200 FQ	39120 MW	46290 TQ	USBLS	5/07
Transportation Equipment	Lancaster MSA, PA	Y	33130 FQ	36660 MW	40470 TQ	USBLS	5/07
Transportation Equipment	Philadelphia-Camden-Wilmington MSA, PA-NJ-DE-MD	Y	34200 FQ	41350 MW	46850 TQ	USBLS	5/07
Transportation Equipment	Pittsburgh MSA, PA	Y	31620 FQ	36290 MW	44540 TQ	USBLS	5/07
Transportation Equipment	Rhode Island	Y	28500 FQ	35260 MW	42680 TQ	USBLS	5/07
Transportation Equipment	Providence-Fall River-Warwick MSA, RI-MA	Y	28560 FQ	34560 MW	41670 TQ	USBLS	5/07
Transportation Equipment	South Carolina	Y	27310 FQ	33730 MW	42400 TQ	USBLS	5/07
Transportation Equipment	Charleston-North Charleston MSA, SC	Y	32700 FQ	37340 MW	46850 TQ	USBLS	5/07
Transportation Equipment	Columbia MSA, SC	Y	27390 FQ	30220 MW	40780 TQ	USBLS	5/07
Transportation Equipment	South Dakota	Y	26392 FQ	28677 MW	31272 TQ	SDBLS	7/08-9/08
Transportation Equipment	Sioux Falls MSA, SD	Y	26834 FQ	29326 MW	31980 TQ	SDBLS	7/08-9/08
Transportation Equipment	Tennessee	Y	30610 FQ	46820 MW	57970 TQ	USBLS	5/07
Transportation Equipment	Knoxville MSA, TN	Y	30860 FQ	35180 MW	49170 TQ	USBLS	5/07

AE	Average entry wage	AW	Average wage paid	FQ	First quartile wage	LO Lowest wage paid	MTC Median total compensation	TCC Total cash compensation
AER	Average entry range	AWR	Average wage range	H	Hourly	LR Low end range	MW Median wage paid	TQ Third quartile wage
AEX	Average experienced wage	AXR	Average experienced range	HI	Highest wage paid	M Monthly	MWR Median wage range	W Weekly
ATC	Average total compensation	D	Daily	HR	High end range	MCC Median cash compensation	S See annotated source	Y Yearly

Occupation/Type/Industry	Location	Per	Low	Mid	High	Source	Date
Painter							
Transportation Equipment	Memphis MSA, TN-MS-AR	Y	31550 FQ	43360 MW	49530 TQ	USBLS	5/07
Transportation Equipment	Texas	Y	24020 FQ	30380 MW	39960 TQ	USBLS	5/07
Transportation Equipment	Austin-Round Rock MSA, TX	Y	25280 FQ	34890 MW	38330 TQ	USBLS	5/07
Transportation Equipment	Dallas-Fort Worth-Arlington MSA, TX	Y	26400 FQ	32950 MW	46270 TQ	USBLS	5/07
Transportation Equipment	El Paso MSA, TX	Y	23800 FQ	29600 MW	33410 TQ	USBLS	5/07
Transportation Equipment	Houston-Sugar Land-Baytown MSA, TX	Y	26570 FQ	31090 MW	38910 TQ	USBLS	5/07
Transportation Equipment	San Antonio MSA, TX	Y	19930 FQ	24640 MW	36960 TQ	USBLS	5/07
Transportation Equipment	Utah	Y	31510 FQ	38470 MW	50030 TQ	USBLS	5/07
Transportation Equipment	Salt Lake City MSA, UT	Y	32550 FQ	44520 MW	52830 TQ	USBLS	5/07
Transportation Equipment	Virginia	Y	27690 FQ	36360 MW	52320 TQ	USBLS	5/07
Transportation Equipment	Richmond MSA, VA	Y	31250 FQ	36870 MW	50830 TQ	USBLS	5/07
Transportation Equipment	Virginia Beach-Norfolk-Newport News MSA, VA-NC	Y	26670 FQ	35290 MW	49260 TQ	USBLS	5/07
Transportation Equipment	Washington	H	16.52 FQ	22.69 MW	29.64 TQ	WABLS	3/08
Transportation Equipment	Seattle-Tacoma-Bellevue MSA, WA	Y	39780 FQ	53650 MW	64710 TQ	USBLS	5/07
Transportation Equipment	West Virginia	Y	24357 FQ	28427 MW	38248 TQ	WVBLS	7/08-9/08
Transportation Equipment	Wisconsin	Y	29620 FQ	35660 MW	43440 TQ	USBLS	5/07
Transportation Equipment	Milwaukee-Waukesha-West Allis MSA, WI	Y	26740 FQ	34780 MW	50440 TQ	USBLS	5/07
Transportation Equipment	Wyoming	Y	34547 FQ	39099 MW	43029 TQ	WYBLS	9/08
Painting, Coating, and Decorating Worker							
	Alabama	Y	18550 FQ	21820 MW	25620 TQ	USBLS	5/07
	Birmingham-Hoover MSA, AL	Y	19000 FQ	22180 MW	26680 TQ	USBLS	5/07
	Alaska	Y	21570 FQ	27100 MW	30500 TQ	USBLS	5/07
	Arizona	Y	19490 FQ	23030 MW	28570 TQ	USBLS	5/07
	Phoenix-Mesa-Scottsdale MSA, AZ	Y	19820 FQ	23140 MW	28690 TQ	USBLS	5/07
	Tucson MSA, AZ	Y	18830 FQ	22850 MW	31520 TQ	USBLS	5/07
	Arkansas	Y	16840 FQ	20170 MW	24630 TQ	USBLS	5/07
	California	H	8.79 FQ	10.60 MW	13.81 TQ	CABLS	1/08-3/08
	Los Angeles-Long Beach-Glendale PMSA, CA	H	8.56 FQ	9.74 MW	12.10 TQ	CABLS	1/08-3/08
	Oakland-Fremont-Hayward MSA, CA	H	9.02 FQ	12.73 MW	16.33 TQ	CABLS	1/08-3/08
	Riverside-San Bernardino-Ontario MSA, CA	H	8.61 FQ	10.48 MW	12.80 TQ	CABLS	1/08-3/08
	Sacramento-Arden Arcade-Roseville MSA, CA	H	8.22 FQ	9.48 MW	14.54 TQ	CABLS	1/08-3/08
	San Diego-Carlsbad-San Marcos MSA, CA	H	8.00 FQ	13.68 MW	16.03 TQ	CABLS	1/08-3/08
	San Francisco-San Mateo-Redwood PMSA, CA	H	16.50 FQ	18.96 MW	26.11 TQ	CABLS	1/08-3/08
	San Jose-Sunnyvale-Santa Clara MSA, CA	H	13.62 FQ	15.16 MW	17.39 TQ	CABLS	1/08-3/08
	Santa Ana-Anaheim-Irvine PMSA, CA	Y	20010 FQ	22740 MW	27340 TQ	USBLS	5/07
	Santa Rosa-Petaluma MSA, CA	H	8.89 FQ	10.25 MW	12.29 TQ	CABLS	1/08-3/08
	Colorado	Y	20760 FQ	26360 MW	31020 TQ	USBLS	5/07
	Denver-Aurora MSA, CO	Y	21740 FQ	26640 MW	30900 TQ	USBLS	5/07
	Connecticut	H	10.32 AE	14.66 MW		CTBLS	1/08-3/08
	Bridgeport-Stamford-Norwalk MSA, CT	Y	33280 FQ	36700 MW	40140 TQ	USBLS	5/07
	Hartford-West Hartford-East Hartford MSA, CT	Y	21020 FQ	26670 MW	30580 TQ	USBLS	5/07
	Delaware	Y	20730 FQ	22950 MW	25840 TQ	USBLS	5/07
	Wilmington PMSA, DE-MD-NJ	Y	21050 FQ	23670 MW	26820 TQ	USBLS	5/07
	District of Columbia	Y	23220 FQ	31630 MW	53040 TQ	USBLS	5/07
	Washington-Arlington-Alexandria MSA, DC-VA-MD-WV	Y	24760 FQ	29550 MW	40930 TQ	USBLS	5/07
	Florida	Y	18940 FQ	22610 MW	27410 TQ	USBLS	5/07
	Fort Lauderdale-Pompano Beach-Deerfield Beach PMSA, FL	Y	21130 FQ	24080 MW	27810 TQ	USBLS	5/07
	Jacksonville MSA, FL	Y	19820 FQ	22800 MW	27570 TQ	USBLS	5/07
	Lakeland MSA, FL	Y	18380 FQ	21980 MW	26220 TQ	USBLS	5/07

AE	Average entry wage	**AW**	Average wage paid	**LO**	Lowest wage paid
AER	Average entry range	**AWR**	Average wage range	**LR**	Low end range
AEX	Average experienced wage	**AXR**	Average experienced range	**M**	Monthly
ATC	Average total compensation	**D**	Daily	**MCC**	Median cash compensation

FQ	First quartile wage	**MTC**	Median total compensation
H	Hourly	**MW**	Median wage paid
HI	Highest wage paid	**MWR**	Median wage range
HR	High end range	**S**	See annotated source

TCC	Total cash compensation
TQ	Third quartile wage
W	Weekly
Y	Yearly

Painting, Coating, and Decorating Worker

Occupation/Type/Industry	Location	Per	Low	Mid	High	Source	Date
	Miami-Fort Lauderdale-Miami Beach MSA, FL	Y	20290 FQ	24230 MW	28420 TQ	USBLS	5/07
	Orlando-Kissimmee MSA, FL	Y	17630 FQ	21440 MW	25790 TQ	USBLS	5/07
	Tampa-St. Petersburg-Clearwater MSA, FL	Y	18540 FQ	22100 MW	26580 TQ	USBLS	5/07
	West Palm Beach-Boca Raton-Boynton Beach PMSA, FL	Y	21420 FQ	25940 MW	29270 TQ	USBLS	5/07
	Georgia	Y	20190 FQ	23120 MW	27340 TQ	USBLS	5/07
	Atlanta-Sandy Springs-Marietta MSA, GA	Y	21470 FQ	24240 MW	28990 TQ	USBLS	5/07
	Idaho	Y	18210 FQ	21600 MW	27130 TQ	USBLS	5/07
	Boise City-Nampa MSA, ID	Y	17430 FQ	19640 MW	24050 TQ	USBLS	5/07
	Illinois	Y	21100 FQ	23560 MW	27010 TQ	USBLS	5/07
	Chicago-Naperville-Joliet MSA, IL-IN-WI	Y	21690 FQ	23800 MW	26820 TQ	USBLS	5/07
	Indiana	Y	18850 FQ	22300 MW	26920 TQ	USBLS	5/07
	Gary PMSA, IN	Y	14810 FQ	20980 MW	23780 TQ	USBLS	5/07
	Indianapolis-Carmel MSA, IN	Y	17720 FQ	20240 MW	25640 TQ	USBLS	5/07
	Iowa	Y	18410 FQ	23610 MW	28690 TQ	USBLS	5/07
	Des Moines-West Des Moines MSA, IA	Y	21290 FQ	26020 MW	28890 TQ	USBLS	5/07
	Kansas	Y	17580 FQ	21700 MW	26250 TQ	USBLS	5/07
	Wichita MSA, KS	Y	16790 FQ	18640 MW	24980 TQ	USBLS	5/07
	Kentucky	Y	18348 FQ	21627 MW	27278 TQ	KYBLS	2008
	Louisville-Jefferson County MSA, KY-IN	Y	19280 FQ	22530 MW	28070 TQ	USBLS	5/07
	Louisiana	H	9.10 FQ	10.84 MW	12.93 TQ	LABLS	1/08-3/08
	Maine	Y	17240 FQ	21080 MW	27590 TQ	USBLS	5/07
	Maryland	Y		26775 MW		MDBLS	3/08
	Baltimore-Towson MSA, MD	Y	23160 FQ	26550 MW	30460 TQ	USBLS	5/07
	Massachusetts	Y	24000 FQ	29610 MW	36860 TQ	USBLS	5/07
	Boston-Cambridge-Quincy NECTA, MA	Y	22830 FQ	27840 MW	34710 TQ	USBLS	5/07
	Worcester MSA, MA-CT	Y	29560 FQ	36620 MW	41120 TQ	USBLS	5/07
	Michigan	Y	19220 FQ	22630 MW	28740 TQ	USBLS	5/07
	Detroit-Warren-Livonia MSA, MI	Y	18350 FQ	21670 MW	24710 TQ	USBLS	5/07
	Warren-Troy-Farmington Hills PMSA, MI	Y	17910 FQ	21210 MW	23950 TQ	USBLS	5/07
	Minnesota	Y	20712 FQ	25170 MW	32935 TQ	MNBLS	10/08-12/08
	Duluth-Superior MSA, MN-WI	Y	18079 FQ	22050 MW	25585 TQ	MNBLS	10/08-12/08
	Minneapolis-Saint Paul MSA, MN-WI	Y	20598 FQ	24818 MW	35164 TQ	MNBLS	10/08-12/08
	Mississippi	Y	19330 FQ	26190 MW	37770 TQ	USBLS	5/07
	Jackson MSA, MS	Y	19140 FQ	22490 MW	26570 TQ	USBLS	5/07
	Missouri	Y	18040 FQ	23310 MW	33030 TQ	USBLS	5/07
	Joplin MSA, MO	Y	18900 FQ	26440 MW	32230 TQ	USBLS	5/07
	Kansas City MSA, MO-KS	Y	18110 FQ	22310 MW	25410 TQ	USBLS	5/07
	St. Louis MSA, MO-IL	Y	22060 FQ	30870 MW	37850 TQ	USBLS	5/07
	Springfield MSA, MO	Y	17110 FQ	19520 MW	24520 TQ	USBLS	5/07
	Montana	Y	19990 FQ	25200 MW	32080 TQ	USBLS	5/07
	Nebraska	Y	14130 FQ	21250 MW	27320 TQ	USBLS	5/07
	Omaha-Council Bluffs MSA, NE-IA	Y	22340 FQ	27580 MW	30430 TQ	USBLS	5/07
	Nevada	H	10.53 FQ	13.05 MW	16.07 TQ	NVBLS	5/08
	Las Vegas-Paradise MSA, NV	H	10.94 FQ	14.28 MW	17.64 TQ	NVBLS	5/08
	New Hampshire	H	8.07 AE	9.76 MW	10.92 AEX	NHBLS	6/08
	New Jersey	Y	19640 FQ	25810 MW	34050 TQ	USBLS	5/07
	Camden PMSA, NJ	Y	22260 FQ	25480 MW	28870 TQ	USBLS	5/07
	Edison PMSA, NJ	Y	16610 FQ	22090 MW	31530 TQ	USBLS	5/07
	Newark-Union PMSA, NJ-PA	Y	24280 FQ	29980 MW	36320 TQ	USBLS	5/07
	New Mexico	Y	17930 FQ	21450 MW	25870 TQ	USBLS	5/07
	Albuquerque MSA, NM	Y	19580 FQ	22330 MW	25870 TQ	USBLS	5/07
	New York	Y	19260 FQ	23930 MW	32060 TQ	USBLS	5/07
	Albany-Schenectady-Troy MSA, NY	Y	20030 FQ	24680 MW	29700 TQ	USBLS	5/07
	Buffalo-Niagara Falls MSA, NY	Y	19530 FQ	21370 MW	23240 TQ	USBLS	5/07
	Nassau-Suffolk PMSA, NY	Y	23340 FQ	31480 MW	44780 TQ	USBLS	5/07

AE	Average entry wage	AW	Average wage paid	FQ	First quartile wage	LO	Lowest wage paid	MTC	Median total compensation	TCC	Total cash compensation
AER	Average entry range	AWR	Average wage range	H	Hourly	LR	Low end range	MW	Median wage paid	TQ	Third quartile wage
AEX	Average experienced wage	AXR	Average experienced range	HI	Highest wage paid	M	Monthly	MWR	Median wage range	W	Weekly
ATC	Average total compensation	D	Daily	HR	High end range	MCC	Median cash compensation	S	See annotated source	Y	Yearly

Occupation/Type/Industry	Location	Per	Low	Mid	High	Source	Date
Painting, Coating, and Decorating Worker	New York-Northern New Jersey-Long Island MSA, NY-NJ-PA	Y	19320 FQ	26370 MW	38570 TQ	USBLS	5/07
	North Carolina	Y	18400 FQ	22390 MW	27100 TQ	USBLS	5/07
	Charlotte-Gastonia-Concord MSA, NC-SC	Y	21210 FQ	26040 MW	29370 TQ	USBLS	5/07
	Raleigh-Cary MSA, NC	Y	20770 FQ	23520 MW	26700 TQ	USBLS	5/07
	North Dakota	Y	20870 FQ	24920 MW	33070 TQ	USBLS	5/07
	Ohio	Y	17520 FQ	21690 MW	28450 TQ	USBLS	5/07
	Cincinnati-Middletown MSA, OH-KY-IN	Y	19810 FQ	22910 MW	27130 TQ	USBLS	5/07
	Cleveland-Elyria-Mentor MSA, OH	Y	19570 FQ	23960 MW	29390 TQ	USBLS	5/07
	Columbus MSA, OH	Y	19550 FQ	23240 MW	32990 TQ	USBLS	5/07
	Dayton MSA, OH	Y	16980 FQ	20330 MW	29530 TQ	USBLS	5/07
	Oklahoma	Y	17460 FQ	21850 MW	29700 TQ	USBLS	5/07
	Oklahoma City MSA, OK	Y	16560 FQ	20480 MW	28140 TQ	USBLS	5/07
	Tulsa MSA, OK	Y	20040 FQ	24790 MW	31850 TQ	USBLS	5/07
	Oregon	H	10.10 FQ	12.70 MW	15.69 TQ	ORBLS	5/08
	Portland-Vancouver-Beaverton MSA, OR-WA	Y	22080 FQ	27630 MW	33030 TQ	USBLS	5/07
	Pennsylvania	Y	20690 FQ	25580 MW	30090 TQ	USBLS	5/07
	Allentown-Bethlehem-Easton MSA, PA-NJ	Y	24360 FQ	28440 MW	32270 TQ	USBLS	5/07
	Philadelphia-Camden-Wilmington MSA, PA-NJ-DE-MD	Y	23940 FQ	28210 MW	32190 TQ	USBLS	5/07
	Pittsburgh MSA, PA	Y	18360 FQ	21940 MW	25850 TQ	USBLS	5/07
	Rhode Island	Y	18350 FQ	24490 MW	37400 TQ	USBLS	5/07
	Providence-Fall River-Warwick MSA, RI-MA	Y	19630 FQ	25710 MW	36790 TQ	USBLS	5/07
	South Carolina	Y	19250 FQ	23470 MW	28380 TQ	USBLS	5/07
	Charleston-North Charleston MSA, SC	Y	19220 FQ	22720 MW	26660 TQ	USBLS	5/07
	Columbia MSA, SC	Y	18080 FQ	22480 MW	29090 TQ	USBLS	5/07
	South Dakota	Y	19301 FQ	22788 MW	25889 TQ	SDBLS	7/08-9/08
	Tennessee	Y	18820 FQ	22050 MW	27560 TQ	USBLS	5/07
	Memphis MSA, TN-MS-AR	Y	19200 FQ	22350 MW	26300 TQ	USBLS	5/07
	Nashville-Davidson-Murfreesboro MSA, TN	Y	19470 FQ	22090 MW	27890 TQ	USBLS	5/07
	Texas	Y	17810 FQ	21280 MW	26100 TQ	USBLS	5/07
	Austin-Round Rock MSA, TX	Y	17980 FQ	19920 MW	23080 TQ	USBLS	5/07
	Dallas-Fort Worth-Arlington MSA, TX	Y	19040 FQ	23170 MW	29460 TQ	USBLS	5/07
	El Paso MSA, TX	Y	16590 FQ	19700 MW	23110 TQ	USBLS	5/07
	Houston-Sugar Land-Baytown MSA, TX	Y	17400 FQ	20350 MW	25690 TQ	USBLS	5/07
	San Antonio MSA, TX	Y	19370 FQ	22260 MW	26450 TQ	USBLS	5/07
	Utah	Y	20950 FQ	24600 MW	28100 TQ	USBLS	5/07
	Salt Lake City MSA, UT	Y	21340 FQ	25110 MW	28180 TQ	USBLS	5/07
	Virginia	Y	19920 FQ	23120 MW	28760 TQ	USBLS	5/07
	Richmond MSA, VA	Y	21710 FQ	26660 MW	31970 TQ	USBLS	5/07
	Virginia Beach-Norfolk-Newport News MSA, VA-NC	Y	15330 FQ	20130 MW	26740 TQ	USBLS	5/07
	Washington	H	13.05 FQ	15.84 MW	28.81 TQ	WABLS	3/08
	Seattle-Tacoma-Bellevue MSA, WA	Y	29560 FQ	37050 MW	64570 TQ	USBLS	5/07
	West Virginia	Y	18618 FQ	22247 MW	27428 TQ	WVBLS	7/08-9/08
	Wisconsin	Y	19570 FQ	23610 MW	29510 TQ	USBLS	5/07
	Milwaukee-Waukesha-West Allis MSA, WI	Y	20570 FQ	23750 MW	30350 TQ	USBLS	5/07
	Racine MSA, WI	Y	21270 FQ	29680 MW	34760 TQ	USBLS	5/07
	Wyoming	Y	18203 FQ	21000 MW	32732 TQ	WYBLS	9/08
	Puerto Rico	Y	12680 FQ	14390 MW	18720 TQ	USBLS	5/07
	San Juan-Caguas-Guaynabo MSA, PR	Y	12590 FQ	14210 MW	17990 TQ	USBLS	5/07
Paper Goods Machine Setter, Operator, and Tender	Alabama	Y	30670 FQ	41550 MW	53770 TQ	USBLS	5/07
	Birmingham-Hoover MSA, AL	Y	20970 FQ	27090 MW	30800 TQ	USBLS	5/07

Occupation/Type/Industry	Location	Per	Low	Mid	High	Source	Date
Paper Goods Machine Setter, Operator, and Tender	Arizona	Y	26550 FQ	31550 MW	37270 TQ	USBLS	5/07
	Phoenix-Mesa-Scottsdale MSA, AZ	Y	25140 FQ	29330 MW	35020 TQ	USBLS	5/07
	Arkansas	Y	27860 FQ	32980 MW	37490 TQ	USBLS	5/07
	Little Rock-North Little Rock MSA, AR	Y	23130 FQ	29360 MW	34300 TQ	USBLS	5/07
	California	H	11.23 FQ	15.04 MW	19.32 TQ	CABLS	1/08-3/08
	Los Angeles-Long Beach-Glendale PMSA, CA	H	10.33 FQ	13.69 MW	18.23 TQ	CABLS	1/08-3/08
	Oakland-Fremont-Hayward MSA, CA	H	11.03 FQ	14.78 MW	18.51 TQ	CABLS	1/08-3/08
	Riverside-San Bernardino-Ontario MSA, CA	H	11.15 FQ	14.39 MW	18.00 TQ	CABLS	1/08-3/08
	Sacramento-Arden Arcade-Roseville MSA, CA	H	13.14 FQ	14.62 MW	16.72 TQ	CABLS	1/08-3/08
	San Diego-Carlsbad-San Marcos MSA, CA	H	12.15 FQ	15.55 MW	19.61 TQ	CABLS	1/08-3/08
	San Francisco-San Mateo-Redwood PMSA, CA	H	9.22 FQ	11.52 MW	14.65 TQ	CABLS	1/08-3/08
	San Jose-Sunnyvale-Santa Clara MSA, CA	H	15.08 FQ	17.25 MW	20.16 TQ	CABLS	1/08-3/08
	Santa Ana-Anaheim-Irvine PMSA, CA	Y	23390 FQ	34570 MW	42870 TQ	USBLS	5/07
	Colorado	Y	28160 FQ	34870 MW	41400 TQ	USBLS	5/07
	Denver-Aurora MSA, CO	Y	28490 FQ	33970 MW	38820 TQ	USBLS	5/07
	Connecticut	H	11.74 AE	17.21 MW		CTBLS	1/08-3/08
	Bridgeport-Stamford-Norwalk MSA, CT	Y	30590 FQ	34940 MW	39730 TQ	USBLS	5/07
	Hartford-West Hartford-East Hartford MSA, CT	Y	24030 FQ	30130 MW	37580 TQ	USBLS	5/07
	Washington-Arlington-Alexandria MSA, DC-VA-MD-WV	Y	22340 FQ	28840 MW	35650 TQ	USBLS	5/07
	Florida	Y	20030 FQ	26100 MW	30840 TQ	USBLS	5/07
	Fort Lauderdale-Pompano Beach-Deerfield Beach PMSA, FL	Y	19160 FQ	24170 MW	28720 TQ	USBLS	5/07
	Jacksonville MSA, FL	Y	19600 FQ	24860 MW	30990 TQ	USBLS	5/07
	Miami-Fort Lauderdale-Miami Beach MSA, FL	Y	23230 FQ	27410 MW	30570 TQ	USBLS	5/07
	Orlando-Kissimmee MSA, FL	Y	19310 FQ	24440 MW	29150 TQ	USBLS	5/07
	Tampa-St. Petersburg-Clearwater MSA, FL	Y	20260 FQ	23750 MW	28030 TQ	USBLS	5/07
	Georgia	Y	27570 FQ	33950 MW	41940 TQ	USBLS	5/07
	Atlanta-Sandy Springs-Marietta MSA, GA	Y	25970 FQ	31430 MW	35680 TQ	USBLS	5/07
	Hawaii	Y	19840 FQ	29030 MW	43920 TQ	USBLS	5/07
	Idaho	Y	27500 FQ	32540 MW	36640 TQ	USBLS	5/07
	Illinois	Y	26150 FQ	32540 MW	37860 TQ	USBLS	5/07
	Chicago-Naperville-Joliet MSA, IL-IN-WI	Y	27480 FQ	33620 MW	38940 TQ	USBLS	5/07
	Indiana	Y	26100 FQ	31130 MW	36490 TQ	USBLS	5/07
	Indianapolis-Carmel MSA, IN	Y	26980 FQ	31670 MW	35620 TQ	USBLS	5/07
	Iowa	Y	25660 FQ	30150 MW	34860 TQ	USBLS	5/07
	Cedar Rapids MSA, IA	Y	32730 FQ	35320 MW	37930 TQ	USBLS	5/07
	Des Moines-West Des Moines MSA, IA	Y	25080 FQ	28050 MW	30870 TQ	USBLS	5/07
	Kansas	Y	27520 FQ	33150 MW	41950 TQ	USBLS	5/07
	Kentucky	Y	26297 FQ	33377 MW	41630 TQ	KYBLS	2008
	Louisville-Jefferson County MSA, KY-IN	Y	21480 FQ	25000 MW	35540 TQ	USBLS	5/07
	Louisiana	H	16.38 FQ	20.19 MW	25.28 TQ	LABLS	1/08-3/08
	Maine	Y	31560 FQ	38230 MW	45200 TQ	USBLS	5/07
	Maryland	Y		28450 MW		MDBLS	3/08
	Baltimore-Towson MSA, MD	Y	22460 FQ	28180 MW	34590 TQ	USBLS	5/07
	Bethesda-Gaithersburg-Frederick PMSA, MD	Y	14520 FQ	27870 MW	34030 TQ	USBLS	5/07
	Massachusetts	Y	26220 FQ	32960 MW	39050 TQ	USBLS	5/07
	Boston-Cambridge-Quincy NECTA, MA	Y	26200 FQ	32300 MW	36920 TQ	USBLS	5/07
	Worcester MSA, MA-CT	Y	26450 FQ	31610 MW	35830 TQ	USBLS	5/07

AE	Average entry wage	AW	Average wage paid	FQ	First quartile wage	LO	Lowest wage paid	MTC	Median total compensation	TCC	Total cash compensation
AER	Average entry range	AWR	Average wage range	H	Hourly	LR	Low end range	MW	Median wage paid	TQ	Third quartile wage
AEX	Average experienced wage	AXR	Average experienced range	HI	Highest wage paid	M	Monthly	MWR	Median wage range	W	Weekly
ATC	Average total compensation	D	Daily	HR	High end range	MCC	Median cash compensation	S	See annotated source	Y	Yearly

Occupation/Type/Industry	Location	Per	Low	Mid	High	Source	Date
Paper Goods Machine Setter, Operator, and Tender	Michigan	Y	26980 FQ	34750 MW	42770 TQ	USBLS	5/07
	Detroit-Warren-Livonia MSA, MI	Y	28210 FQ	35530 MW	40290 TQ	USBLS	5/07
	Grand Rapids-Wyoming MSA, MI	Y	31850 FQ	37950 MW	44970 TQ	USBLS	5/07
	Warren-Troy-Farmington Hills PMSA, MI	Y	33290 FQ	36470 MW	39660 TQ	USBLS	5/07
	Minnesota	Y	28830 FQ	36335 MW	48309 TQ	MNBLS	10/08-12/08
	Minneapolis-Saint Paul MSA, MN-WI	Y	29763 FQ	36335 MW	46578 TQ	MNBLS	10/08-12/08
	Mississippi	Y	22750 FQ	30140 MW	36470 TQ	USBLS	5/07
	Jackson MSA, MS	Y	31070 FQ	33340 MW	35520 TQ	USBLS	5/07
	Missouri	Y	24360 FQ	29390 MW	33870 TQ	USBLS	5/07
	Kansas City MSA, MO-KS	Y	25660 FQ	29750 MW	33600 TQ	USBLS	5/07
	St. Louis MSA, MO-IL	Y	22610 FQ	28690 MW	34630 TQ	USBLS	5/07
	Nebraska	Y	23260 FQ	27430 MW	33240 TQ	USBLS	5/07
	Omaha-Council Bluffs MSA, NE-IA	Y	23550 FQ	27450 MW	32360 TQ	USBLS	5/07
	Las Vegas-Paradise MSA, NV	H	9.59 FQ	12.89 MW	15.01 TQ	NVBLS	5/08
	New Hampshire	H	8.88 AE	15.50 MW	17.06 AEX	NHBLS	6/08
	Nashua NECTA, NH-MA	Y	22370 FQ	24710 MW	33370 TQ	USBLS	5/07
	New Jersey	Y	23100 FQ	28650 MW	34370 TQ	USBLS	5/07
	Camden PMSA, NJ	Y	25670 FQ	29580 MW	36170 TQ	USBLS	5/07
	Edison PMSA, NJ	Y	29510 FQ	32570 MW	35820 TQ	USBLS	5/07
	Newark-Union PMSA, NJ-PA	Y	22060 FQ	25780 MW	29360 TQ	USBLS	5/07
	Trenton-Ewing MSA, NJ	Y	23630 FQ	28430 MW	35460 TQ	USBLS	5/07
	New Mexico	Y	20520 FQ	22120 MW	23900 TQ	USBLS	5/07
	Albuquerque MSA, NM	Y	20470 FQ	22020 MW	23650 TQ	USBLS	5/07
	New York	Y	22970 FQ	29500 MW	36740 TQ	USBLS	5/07
	Albany-Schenectady-Troy MSA, NY	Y	27870 FQ	32610 MW	36740 TQ	USBLS	5/07
	Buffalo-Niagara Falls MSA, NY	Y	24390 FQ	28850 MW	33820 TQ	USBLS	5/07
	Nassau-Suffolk PMSA, NY	Y	20940 FQ	26140 MW	33430 TQ	USBLS	5/07
	New York-Northern New Jersey-Long Island MSA, NY-NJ-PA	Y	22020 FQ	28070 MW	34260 TQ	USBLS	5/07
	North Carolina	Y	22350 FQ	28290 MW	34880 TQ	USBLS	5/07
	Charlotte-Gastonia-Concord MSA, NC-SC	Y	22890 FQ	28480 MW	36950 TQ	USBLS	5/07
	Raleigh-Cary MSA, NC	Y	23610 FQ	30900 MW	43590 TQ	USBLS	5/07
	Ohio	Y	25010 FQ	31890 MW	35950 TQ	USBLS	5/07
	Canton-Massillon MSA, OH	Y	24890 FQ	29270 MW	33300 TQ	USBLS	5/07
	Cincinnati-Middletown MSA, OH-KY-IN	Y	26450 FQ	30870 MW	35030 TQ	USBLS	5/07
	Cleveland-Elyria-Mentor MSA, OH	Y	24460 FQ	33350 MW	36980 TQ	USBLS	5/07
	Columbus MSA, OH	Y	28110 FQ	33920 MW	37400 TQ	USBLS	5/07
	Dayton MSA, OH	Y	19470 FQ	26140 MW	32260 TQ	USBLS	5/07
	Mansfield MSA, OH	Y	23520 FQ	31050 MW	34690 TQ	USBLS	5/07
	Oklahoma	Y	24640 FQ	35990 MW	42600 TQ	USBLS	5/07
	Oklahoma City MSA, OK	Y	22730 FQ	31740 MW	38340 TQ	USBLS	5/07
	Tulsa MSA, OK	Y	30470 FQ	37430 MW	44240 TQ	USBLS	5/07
	Oregon	H	12.50 FQ	18.82 MW	22.49 TQ	ORBLS	5/08
	Portland-Vancouver-Beaverton MSA, OR-WA	Y	32880 FQ	42560 MW	50890 TQ	USBLS	5/07
	Pennsylvania	Y	26090 FQ	32680 MW	41410 TQ	USBLS	5/07
	Allentown-Bethlehem-Easton MSA, PA-NJ	Y	25230 FQ	30580 MW	35390 TQ	USBLS	5/07
	Philadelphia-Camden-Wilmington MSA, PA-NJ-DE-MD	Y	29560 FQ	36650 MW	48160 TQ	USBLS	5/07
	Pittsburgh MSA, PA	Y	18780 FQ	30860 MW	34800 TQ	USBLS	5/07
	Rhode Island	Y	21210 FQ	26750 MW	31940 TQ	USBLS	5/07
	Providence-Fall River-Warwick MSA, RI-MA	Y	21680 FQ	27330 MW	33230 TQ	USBLS	5/07
	South Carolina	Y	26960 FQ	33100 MW	43750 TQ	USBLS	5/07
	Columbia MSA, SC	Y	24980 FQ	28750 MW	32030 TQ	USBLS	5/07
	Florence MSA, SC	Y	28850 FQ	35330 MW	43820 TQ	USBLS	5/07
	South Dakota	Y	23332 FQ	27916 MW	32989 TQ	SDBLS	7/08-9/08
	Tennessee	Y	24970 FQ	28970 MW	32970 TQ	USBLS	5/07

AE	Average entry wage	AW	Average wage paid	FQ	First quartile wage	LO	Lowest wage paid	MTC	Median total compensation	TCC	Total cash compensation
AER	Average entry range	AWR	Average wage range	H	Hourly	LR	Low end range	MW	Median wage paid	TQ	Third quartile wage
AEX	Average experienced wage	AXR	Average experienced range	HI	Highest wage paid	M	Monthly	MWR	Median wage range	W	Weekly
ATC	Average total compensation	D	Daily	HR	High end range	MCC	Median cash compensation	S	See annotated source	Y	Yearly

Occupation/Type/Industry	Location	Per	Low	Mid	High	Source	Date
Paper Goods Machine Setter, Operator, and Tender	Kingsport-Bristol-Bristol MSA, TN-VA	Y	21370 FQ	23490 MW	26710 TQ	USBLS	5/07
	Memphis MSA, TN-MS-AR	Y	26160 FQ	29620 MW	34620 TQ	USBLS	5/07
	Nashville-Davidson-Murfreesboro MSA, TN	Y	25070 FQ	29220 MW	32860 TQ	USBLS	5/07
	Texas	Y	22020 FQ	27430 MW	33550 TQ	USBLS	5/07
	Dallas-Fort Worth-Arlington MSA, TX	Y	22550 FQ	27620 MW	32430 TQ	USBLS	5/07
	El Paso MSA, TX	Y	21060 FQ	24440 MW	28000 TQ	USBLS	5/07
	Houston-Sugar Land-Baytown MSA, TX	Y	20800 FQ	27610 MW	34730 TQ	USBLS	5/07
	San Antonio MSA, TX	Y	19290 FQ	23240 MW	27950 TQ	USBLS	5/07
	Utah	Y	20190 FQ	25710 MW	29690 TQ	USBLS	5/07
	Salt Lake City MSA, UT	Y	23900 FQ	27190 MW	31330 TQ	USBLS	5/07
	Vermont	Y	26280 FQ	30060 MW	37320 TQ	USBLS	5/07
	Burlington-South Burlington MSA, VT	Y	24830 FQ	27630 MW	32570 TQ	USBLS	5/07
	Virginia	Y	24110 FQ	29230 MW	37850 TQ	USBLS	5/07
	Richmond MSA, VA	Y	25130 FQ	29510 MW	39440 TQ	USBLS	5/07
	Virginia Beach-Norfolk-Newport News MSA, VA-NC	Y	21290 FQ	27230 MW	37210 TQ	USBLS	5/07
	Washington	H	15.96 FQ	20.50 MW	24.85 TQ	WABLS	3/08
	Seattle-Tacoma-Bellevue MSA, WA	Y	26060 FQ	39400 MW	48230 TQ	USBLS	5/07
	Spokane MSA, WA	Y	25530 FQ	30330 MW	36700 TQ	USBLS	5/07
	West Virginia	Y	19334 FQ	27111 MW	34809 TQ	WVBLS	7/08-9/08
	Wisconsin	Y	29600 FQ	36710 MW	44230 TQ	USBLS	5/07
	Milwaukee-Waukesha-West Allis MSA, WI	Y	25110 FQ	32840 MW	38530 TQ	USBLS	5/07
	Puerto Rico	Y	16970 FQ	24030 MW	31180 TQ	USBLS	5/07
	San Juan-Caguas-Guaynabo MSA, PR	Y	16960 FQ	24010 MW	31180 TQ	USBLS	5/07
Paperhanger	Alabama	Y	16530 FQ	22300 MW	26280 TQ	USBLS	5/07
	California	H	20.43 FQ	26.02 MW	32.83 TQ	CABLS	1/08-3/08
	Colorado	Y	29570 FQ	33960 MW	38160 TQ	USBLS	5/07
	Denver-Aurora MSA, CO	Y	30100 FQ	34620 MW	38950 TQ	USBLS	5/07
	Connecticut	H	13.56 AE	20.26 MW		CTBLS	1/08-3/08
	Florida	Y	23830 FQ	28000 MW	31600 TQ	USBLS	5/07
	Georgia	Y	30790 FQ	33310 MW	35830 TQ	USBLS	5/07
	Atlanta-Sandy Springs-Marietta MSA, GA	Y	31300 FQ	33530 MW	35750 TQ	USBLS	5/07
	Chicago-Naperville-Joliet MSA, IL-IN-WI	Y	29460 FQ	40360 MW	67440 TQ	USBLS	5/07
	Indiana	Y	33470 FQ	44150 MW	49480 TQ	USBLS	5/07
	Indianapolis-Carmel MSA, IN	Y	38160 FQ	45300 MW	49370 TQ	USBLS	5/07
	Iowa	Y	24870 FQ	29910 MW	42210 TQ	USBLS	5/07
	Kansas	Y	21280 FQ	24520 MW	30340 TQ	USBLS	5/07
	Kentucky	Y	35913 FQ	38595 MW	41446 TQ	KYBLS	2008
	Maine	Y	27720 FQ	29550 MW	31390 TQ	USBLS	5/07
	Maryland	Y		32875 MW		MDBLS	3/08
	Baltimore-Towson MSA, MD	Y	30410 FQ	32640 MW	35800 TQ	USBLS	5/07
	Michigan	Y	22400 FQ	31510 MW	44760 TQ	USBLS	5/07
	Detroit-Warren-Livonia MSA, MI	Y	29810 FQ	34480 MW	47030 TQ	USBLS	5/07
	Minnesota	Y	40637 FQ	45590 MW	50617 TQ	MNBLS	10/08-12/08
	Missouri	Y	27750 FQ	30320 MW	39490 TQ	USBLS	5/07
	Kansas City MSA, MO-KS	Y	29190 FQ	38770 MW	44470 TQ	USBLS	5/07
	St. Louis MSA, MO-IL	Y	26740 FQ	28580 MW	30410 TQ	USBLS	5/07
	Nevada	H	21.89 FQ	23.81 MW	25.73 TQ	NVBLS	5/08
	Las Vegas-Paradise MSA, NV	H	21.88 FQ	23.85 MW	25.87 TQ	NVBLS	5/08
	New Jersey	Y	36030 FQ	52990 MW	64200 TQ	USBLS	5/07
	Newark-Union PMSA, NJ-PA	Y	29220 FQ	35550 MW	47360 TQ	USBLS	5/07
	New York	Y	31020 FQ	36850 MW	47970 TQ	USBLS	5/07
	Nassau-Suffolk PMSA, NY	Y	24380 FQ	30200 MW	48550 TQ	USBLS	5/07
	New York-Northern New Jersey-Long Island MSA, NY-NJ-PA	Y	32220 FQ	38390 MW	55270 TQ	USBLS	5/07
	North Carolina	Y	25570 FQ	29600 MW	37240 TQ	USBLS	5/07
	Charlotte-Gastonia-Concord MSA, NC-SC	Y	26240 FQ	29610 MW	37630 TQ	USBLS	5/07

AE	Average entry wage	AW	Average wage paid	FQ	First quartile wage	LO	Lowest wage paid	MTC	Median total compensation	TCC	Total cash compensation
AER	Average entry range	AWR	Average wage range	H	Hourly	LR	Low end range	MW	Median wage paid	TQ	Third quartile wage
AEX	Average experienced wage	AXR	Average experienced range	HI	Highest wage paid	M	Monthly	MWR	Median wage range	W	Weekly
ATC	Average total compensation	D	Daily	HR	High end range	MCC	Median cash compensation	S	See annotated source	Y	Yearly

Occupation/Type/Industry	Location	Per	Low	Mid	High	Source	Date
Paperhanger	Ohio	Y	25710 FQ	34180 MW	43800 TQ	USBLS	5/07
	Cincinnati-Middletown MSA, OH-KY-IN	Y	34460 FQ	42900 MW	48870 TQ	USBLS	5/07
	Dayton MSA, OH	Y	23240 FQ	25140 MW	27680 TQ	USBLS	5/07
	Oklahoma	Y	25440 FQ	33260 MW	40060 TQ	USBLS	5/07
	Oregon	H	15.88 FQ	17.14 MW	18.40 TQ	ORBLS	5/08
	Portland-Vancouver-Beaverton MSA, OR-WA	Y	31960 FQ	34450 MW	36950 TQ	USBLS	5/07
	Pennsylvania	Y	30590 FQ	44030 MW	60390 TQ	USBLS	5/07
	Allentown-Bethlehem-Easton MSA, PA-NJ	Y	24910 FQ	27440 MW	30330 TQ	USBLS	5/07
	Philadelphia-Camden-Wilmington MSA, PA-NJ-DE-MD	Y	43900 FQ	59070 MW	74950 TQ	USBLS	5/07
	Pittsburgh MSA, PA	Y	44050 FQ	48410 MW	51560 TQ	USBLS	5/07
	South Carolina	Y	23830 FQ	26130 MW	29800 TQ	USBLS	5/07
	Texas	Y	15410 FQ	26050 MW	30680 TQ	USBLS	5/07
	Virginia	Y	30060 FQ	34140 MW	40690 TQ	USBLS	5/07
	Virginia Beach-Norfolk-Newport News MSA, VA-NC	Y	29570 FQ	33310 MW	38380 TQ	USBLS	5/07
	West Virginia	Y	25712 FQ	29527 MW	40949 TQ	WVBLS	7/08-9/08
	Wisconsin	Y	32260 FQ	36330 MW	50800 TQ	USBLS	5/07
	Wyoming	Y	21996 FQ	24038 MW	25996 TQ	WYBLS	9/08
Paralegal							
White House Staff	United States	Y			38900-40000 HR	WPOST02	2008
Paralegal and Legal Assistant	Alabama	Y	31990 FQ	40290 MW	47930 TQ	USBLS	5/07
	Birmingham-Hoover MSA, AL	Y	37460 FQ	45080 MW	52810 TQ	USBLS	5/07
	Alaska	Y	41600 FQ	49110 MW	60290 TQ	USBLS	5/07
	Anchorage MSA, AK	Y	43630 FQ	50520 MW	61890 TQ	USBLS	5/07
	Fairbanks MSA, AK	Y	40680 FQ	48500 MW	60860 TQ	USBLS	5/07
	Arizona	Y	37600 FQ	45680 MW	58470 TQ	USBLS	5/07
	Phoenix-Mesa-Scottsdale MSA, AZ	Y	38040 FQ	46380 MW	59330 TQ	USBLS	5/07
	Tucson MSA, AZ	Y	37980 FQ	45460 MW	56330 TQ	USBLS	5/07
	Arkansas	Y	28630 FQ	39240 MW	51420 TQ	USBLS	5/07
	Fort Smith MSA, AR-OK	Y	28120 FQ	32560 MW	46450 TQ	USBLS	5/07
	Jonesboro MSA, AR	Y	25790 FQ	28930 MW	35750 TQ	USBLS	5/07
	Little Rock-North Little Rock MSA, AR	Y	35650 FQ	44720 MW	56000 TQ	USBLS	5/07
	California	H	20.26 FQ	26.07 MW	32.82 TQ	CABLS	1/08-3/08
	Los Angeles-Long Beach-Glendale PMSA, CA	H	19.58 FQ	25.75 MW	33.28 TQ	CABLS	1/08-3/08
	Oakland-Fremont-Hayward MSA, CA	H	23.12 FQ	27.54 MW	32.14 TQ	CABLS	1/08-3/08
	Riverside-San Bernardino-Ontario MSA, CA	H	16.55 FQ	22.35 MW	29.53 TQ	CABLS	1/08-3/08
	Sacramento-Arden Arcade-Roseville MSA, CA	H	18.33 FQ	22.99 MW	27.59 TQ	CABLS	1/08-3/08
	San Diego-Carlsbad-San Marcos MSA, CA	H	20.93 FQ	26.34 MW	31.75 TQ	CABLS	1/08-3/08
	San Francisco-San Mateo-Redwood PMSA, CA	H	23.27 FQ	28.88 MW	37.30 TQ	CABLS	1/08-3/08
	San Jose-Sunnyvale-Santa Clara MSA, CA	H	23.98 FQ	30.97 MW	39.06 TQ	CABLS	1/08-3/08
	Santa Ana-Anaheim-Irvine PMSA, CA	Y	42380 FQ	56450 MW	69010 TQ	USBLS	5/07
	Colorado	Y	36100 FQ	43910 MW	55100 TQ	USBLS	5/07
	Denver-Aurora MSA, CO	Y	38410 FQ	46460 MW	57500 TQ	USBLS	5/07
	Fort Collins-Loveland MSA, CO	Y	28060 FQ	38380 MW	49680 TQ	USBLS	5/07
	Connecticut	H	17.12 AE	22.98 MW		CTBLS	1/08-3/08
	Bridgeport-Stamford-Norwalk MSA, CT	Y	41120 FQ	49820 MW	58490 TQ	USBLS	5/07
	Hartford-West Hartford-East Hartford MSA, CT	Y	39010 FQ	47270 MW	58110 TQ	USBLS	5/07
	Norwich-New London MSA, CT-RI	Y	40420 FQ	44520 MW	48170 TQ	USBLS	5/07
	Waterbury MSA, CT	Y	36710 FQ	41890 MW	47890 TQ	USBLS	5/07
	Delaware	Y	37720 FQ	46460 MW	57960 TQ	USBLS	5/07

AE	Average entry wage	**AW**	Average wage paid	**FQ**	First quartile wage	**LO**	Lowest wage paid	**MTC** Median total compensation **TCC** Total cash compensation
AER	Average entry range	**AWR**	Average wage range	**H**	Hourly	**LR**	Low end range	**MW** Median wage paid **TQ** Third quartile wage
AEX	Average experienced wage	**AXR**	Average experienced range	**HI**	Highest wage paid	**M**	Monthly	**MWR** Median wage range **W** Weekly
ATC	Average total compensation **D**		Daily	**HR**	High end range	**MCC**	Median cash compensation	**S** See annotated source **Y** Yearly

Paralegal and Legal Assistant

Occupation/Type/Industry	Location	Per	Low	Mid	High	Source	Date
Paralegal and Legal Assistant	Wilmington PMSA, DE-MD-NJ	Y	39760 FQ	47930 MW	59890 TQ	USBLS	5/07
	District of Columbia	Y	40830 FQ	53720 MW	71250 TQ	USBLS	5/07
	Washington-Arlington-Alexandria MSA, DC-VA-MD-WV	Y	40150 FQ	51410 MW	66590 TQ	USBLS	5/07
	Florida	Y	33070 FQ	42170 MW	52300 TQ	USBLS	5/07
	Fort Lauderdale-Pompano Beach-Deerfield Beach PMSA, FL	Y	38400 FQ	46450 MW	53960 TQ	USBLS	5/07
	Jacksonville MSA, FL	Y	31260 FQ	37530 MW	46890 TQ	USBLS	5/07
	Miami-Fort Lauderdale-Miami Beach MSA, FL	Y	35000 FQ	45890 MW	55570 TQ	USBLS	5/07
	Orlando-Kissimmee MSA, FL	Y	37410 FQ	44650 MW	52530 TQ	USBLS	5/07
	Pensacola-Ferry Pass-Brent MSA, FL	Y	27350 FQ	33910 MW	38680 TQ	USBLS	5/07
	Tampa-St. Petersburg-Clearwater MSA, FL	Y	36030 FQ	45280 MW	55630 TQ	USBLS	5/07
	West Palm Beach-Boca Raton-Boynton Beach PMSA, FL	Y	38260 FQ	46820 MW	55590 TQ	USBLS	5/07
	Georgia	Y	34740 FQ	45290 MW	59650 TQ	USBLS	5/07
	Atlanta-Sandy Springs-Marietta MSA, GA	Y	37020 FQ	47670 MW	61050 TQ	USBLS	5/07
	Macon MSA, GA	Y	35690 FQ	43910 MW	58060 TQ	USBLS	5/07
	Savannah MSA, GA	Y	33190 FQ	37370 MW	50880 TQ	USBLS	5/07
	Hawaii	Y	36050 FQ	45310 MW	55880 TQ	USBLS	5/07
	Honolulu MSA, HI	Y	35530 FQ	44610 MW	55280 TQ	USBLS	5/07
	Idaho	Y	34670 FQ	40370 MW	50660 TQ	USBLS	5/07
	Boise City-Nampa MSA, ID	Y	37700 FQ	44200 MW	54270 TQ	USBLS	5/07
	Illinois	Y	40390 FQ	49900 MW	60680 TQ	USBLS	5/07
	Chicago-Naperville-Joliet MSA, IL-IN-WI	Y	41460 FQ	50660 MW	61590 TQ	USBLS	5/07
	Indiana	Y	29950 FQ	38240 MW	46870 TQ	USBLS	5/07
	Gary PMSA, IN	Y	28280 FQ	31870 MW	39580 TQ	USBLS	5/07
	Indianapolis-Carmel MSA, IN	Y	33680 FQ	42600 MW	51590 TQ	USBLS	5/07
	Iowa	Y	31650 FQ	39130 MW	50160 TQ	USBLS	5/07
	Des Moines-West Des Moines MSA, IA	Y	40910 FQ	49060 MW	57520 TQ	USBLS	5/07
	Waterloo-Cedar Falls MSA, IA	Y	26510 FQ	28850 MW	31480 TQ	USBLS	5/07
	Kansas	Y	30090 FQ	35760 MW	43130 TQ	USBLS	5/07
	Wichita MSA, KS	Y	28810 FQ	34990 MW	41210 TQ	USBLS	5/07
	Kentucky	Y	27418 FQ	33020 MW	44442 TQ	KYBLS	2008
	Louisville-Jefferson County MSA, KY-IN	Y	27420 FQ	33860 MW	44900 TQ	USBLS	5/07
	Louisiana	H	14.29 FQ	17.87 MW	21.97 TQ	LABLS	1/08-3/08
	Baton Rouge MSA, LA	Y	31060 FQ	37220 MW	42820 TQ	USBLS	5/07
	New Orleans-Metairie-Kenner MSA, LA	Y	32530 FQ	40580 MW	48380 TQ	USBLS	5/07
	Maine	Y	34910 FQ	40260 MW	47840 TQ	USBLS	5/07
	Lewiston-Auburn MSA, ME	Y	36340 FQ	40440 MW	46200 TQ	USBLS	5/07
	Portland-South Portland-Biddeford MSA, ME	Y	36580 FQ	43090 MW	50130 TQ	USBLS	5/07
	Maryland	Y		48275 MW		MDBLS	3/08
	Baltimore-Towson MSA, MD	Y	38630 FQ	49070 MW	58630 TQ	USBLS	5/07
	Bethesda-Gaithersburg-Frederick PMSA, MD	Y	34440 FQ	45400 MW	60410 TQ	USBLS	5/07
	Hagerstown-Martinsburg MSA, MD-WV	Y	33950 FQ	39300 MW	48980 TQ	USBLS	5/07
	Massachusetts	Y	39300 FQ	49320 MW	60660 TQ	USBLS	5/07
	Boston-Cambridge-Quincy NECTA, MA	Y	42160 FQ	52660 MW	65330 TQ	USBLS	5/07
	Worcester MSA, MA-CT	Y	36240 FQ	47270 MW	55770 TQ	USBLS	5/07
	Michigan	Y	39190 FQ	47620 MW	57360 TQ	USBLS	5/07
	Detroit-Warren-Livonia MSA, MI	Y	42750 FQ	49560 MW	58800 TQ	USBLS	5/07
	Grand Rapids-Wyoming MSA, MI	Y	34740 FQ	48730 MW	58330 TQ	USBLS	5/07
	Warren-Troy-Farmington Hills PMSA, MI	Y	41340 FQ	47350 MW	55090 TQ	USBLS	5/07
	Minnesota	Y	38281 FQ	48450 MW	61528 TQ	MNBLS	10/08-12/08
	Duluth-Superior MSA, MN-WI	Y	24450 FQ	37800 MW	47896 TQ	MNBLS	10/08-12/08

AE Average entry wage	**AW** Average wage paid	**FQ** First quartile wage	**LO** Lowest wage paid	**MTC** Median total compensation **TCC** Total cash compensation
AER Average entry range	**AWR** Average wage range	**H** Hourly	**LR** Low end range	**MW** Median wage paid **TQ** Third quartile wage
AEX Average experienced wage	**AXR** Average experienced range	**HI** Highest wage paid	**M** Monthly	**MWR** Median wage range **W** Weekly
ATC Average total compensation	**D** Daily	**HR** High end range	**MCC** Median cash compensation	**S** See annotated source **Y** Yearly

Occupation/Type/Industry	Location	Per	Low	Mid	High	Source	Date
Paralegal and Legal Assistant	Minneapolis-Saint Paul MSA, MN-WI	Y	40248 FQ	51118 MW	63401 TQ	MNBLS	10/08-12/08
	Rochester MSA, MN	Y	34903 FQ	38257 MW	42233 TQ	MNBLS	10/08-12/08
	Mississippi	Y	27920 FQ	33470 MW	43110 TQ	USBLS	5/07
	Jackson MSA, MS	Y	29660 FQ	36010 MW	45950 TQ	USBLS	5/07
	Missouri	Y	30480 FQ	40150 MW	51010 TQ	USBLS	5/07
	Kansas City MSA, MO-KS	Y	33860 FQ	43830 MW	53020 TQ	USBLS	5/07
	St. Louis MSA, MO-IL	Y	31110 FQ	39580 MW	50850 TQ	USBLS	5/07
	Montana	Y	26480 FQ	31050 MW	40010 TQ	USBLS	5/07
	Billings MSA, MT	Y	30340 FQ	39510 MW	49040 TQ	USBLS	5/07
	Nebraska	Y	29630 FQ	36980 MW	46140 TQ	USBLS	5/07
	Omaha-Council Bluffs MSA, NE-IA	Y	32280 FQ	40880 MW	47960 TQ	USBLS	5/07
	Nevada	H	20.09 FQ	22.65 MW	25.40 TQ	NVBLS	5/08
	Las Vegas-Paradise MSA, NV	H	19.74 FQ	22.28 MW	24.99 TQ	NVBLS	5/08
	Reno-Sparks MSA, NV	H	21.85 FQ	24.04 MW	27.33 TQ	NVBLS	5/08
	New Hampshire	H	17.65 AE	21.31 MW	23.75 AEX	NHBLS	6/08
	Manchester MSA, NH	Y	35700 FQ	41110 MW	48400 TQ	USBLS	5/07
	Nashua NECTA, NH-MA	Y	33970 FQ	43900 MW	55650 TQ	USBLS	5/07
	New Jersey	Y	40430 FQ	49530 MW	59740 TQ	USBLS	5/07
	Camden PMSA, NJ	Y	40750 FQ	50150 MW	65330 TQ	USBLS	5/07
	Edison PMSA, NJ	Y	38650 FQ	46350 MW	57050 TQ	USBLS	5/07
	Newark-Union PMSA, NJ-PA	Y	41930 FQ	52560 MW	61020 TQ	USBLS	5/07
	New Mexico	Y	29660 FQ	34620 MW	43160 TQ	USBLS	5/07
	Albuquerque MSA, NM	Y	29820 FQ	34180 MW	42690 TQ	USBLS	5/07
	Las Cruces MSA, NM	Y	29240 FQ	34300 MW	38820 TQ	USBLS	5/07
	New York	Y	42040 FQ	53190 MW	67360 TQ	USBLS	5/07
	Albany-Schenectady-Troy MSA, NY	Y	34950 FQ	41930 MW	49160 TQ	USBLS	5/07
	Buffalo-Niagara Falls MSA, NY	Y	34670 FQ	43310 MW	54240 TQ	USBLS	5/07
	Nassau-Suffolk PMSA, NY	Y	44130 FQ	52850 MW	60750 TQ	USBLS	5/07
	New York-Northern New Jersey-Long Island MSA, NY-NJ-PA	Y	43430 FQ	54830 MW	67890 TQ	USBLS	5/07
	North Carolina	Y	29470 FQ	35520 MW	43570 TQ	USBLS	5/07
	Charlotte-Gastonia-Concord MSA, NC-SC	Y	30270 FQ	37000 MW	46230 TQ	USBLS	5/07
	Durham MSA, NC	Y	34100 FQ	38080 MW	43930 TQ	USBLS	5/07
	Raleigh-Cary MSA, NC	Y	29450 FQ	36110 MW	47010 TQ	USBLS	5/07
	North Dakota	Y	29600 FQ	35290 MW	41780 TQ	USBLS	5/07
	Bismarck MSA, ND	Y	31960 FQ	39620 MW	49230 TQ	USBLS	5/07
	Fargo MSA, ND-MN	Y	34170 FQ	38730 MW	45850 TQ	USBLS	5/07
	Ohio	Y	32350 FQ	41500 MW	53080 TQ	USBLS	5/07
	Cincinnati-Middletown MSA, OH-KY-IN	Y	30390 FQ	37960 MW	51070 TQ	USBLS	5/07
	Cleveland-Elyria-Mentor MSA, OH	Y	36480 FQ	45890 MW	57170 TQ	USBLS	5/07
	Columbus MSA, OH	Y	32110 FQ	44090 MW	55020 TQ	USBLS	5/07
	Dayton MSA, OH	Y	37780 FQ	48980 MW	58240 TQ	USBLS	5/07
	Oklahoma	Y	29750 FQ	37120 MW	45720 TQ	USBLS	5/07
	Oklahoma City MSA, OK	Y	31630 FQ	38340 MW	47290 TQ	USBLS	5/07
	Tulsa MSA, OK	Y	30440 FQ	36010 MW	43550 TQ	USBLS	5/07
	Oregon	H	16.92 FQ	20.10 MW	24.98 TQ	ORBLS	5/08
	Portland-Vancouver-Beaverton MSA, OR-WA	Y	35030 FQ	42750 MW	54730 TQ	USBLS	5/07
	Pennsylvania	Y	33560 FQ	42460 MW	52440 TQ	USBLS	5/07
	Allentown-Bethlehem-Easton MSA, PA-NJ	Y	35880 FQ	44530 MW	56240 TQ	USBLS	5/07
	Philadelphia-Camden-Wilmington MSA, PA-NJ-DE-MD	Y	38430 FQ	46970 MW	58140 TQ	USBLS	5/07
	Pittsburgh MSA, PA	Y	30980 FQ	39720 MW	50250 TQ	USBLS	5/07
	Rhode Island	Y	37870 FQ	45760 MW	54000 TQ	USBLS	5/07
	Providence-Fall River-Warwick MSA, RI-MA	Y	36740 FQ	44580 MW	53130 TQ	USBLS	5/07
	South Carolina	Y	30930 FQ	37550 MW	45430 TQ	USBLS	5/07
	Charleston-North Charleston MSA, SC	Y	33230 FQ	40070 MW	47450 TQ	USBLS	5/07
	Columbia MSA, SC	Y	32620 FQ	38550 MW	46670 TQ	USBLS	5/07
	Spartanburg MSA, SC	Y	29570 FQ	33900 MW	39100 TQ	USBLS	5/07
	South Dakota	Y	34467 FQ	42453 MW	49687 TQ	SDBLS	7/08-9/08

AE	Average entry wage	AW	Average wage paid	FQ	First quartile wage	LO	Lowest wage paid	MTC	Median total compensation	TCC	Total cash compensation
AER	Average entry range	AWR	Average wage range	H	Hourly	LR	Low end range	MW	Median wage paid	TQ	Third quartile wage
AEX	Average experienced wage	AXR	Average experienced range	HI	Highest wage paid	M	Monthly	MWR	Median wage range	W	Weekly
ATC	Average total compensation	D	Daily	HR	High end range	MCC	Median cash compensation	S	See annotated source	Y	Yearly

Occupation/Type/Industry	Location	Per	Low	Mid	High	Source	Date
Paralegal and Legal Assistant	Sioux Falls MSA, SD	Y	35906 FQ	43292 MW	49121 TQ	SDBLS	7/08-9/08
	Tennessee	Y	28770 FQ	36920 MW	48010 TQ	USBLS	5/07
	Memphis MSA, TN-MS-AR	Y	29800 FQ	42630 MW	55060 TQ	USBLS	5/07
	Nashville-Davidson-Murfreesboro MSA, TN	Y	34450 FQ	39770 MW	49040 TQ	USBLS	5/07
	Texas	Y	35480 FQ	45340 MW	57830 TQ	USBLS	5/07
	Austin-Round Rock MSA, TX	Y	40990 FQ	50470 MW	59860 TQ	USBLS	5/07
	Dallas-Fort Worth-Arlington MSA, TX	Y	38620 FQ	49600 MW	61360 TQ	USBLS	5/07
	El Paso MSA, TX	Y	34890 FQ	38850 MW	46980 TQ	USBLS	5/07
	Houston-Sugar Land-Baytown MSA, TX	Y	39400 FQ	48070 MW	60280 TQ	USBLS	5/07
	San Antonio MSA, TX	Y	27180 FQ	36520 MW	46930 TQ	USBLS	5/07
	Utah	Y	34870 FQ	42220 MW	49050 TQ	USBLS	5/07
	Salt Lake City MSA, UT	Y	38070 FQ	44260 MW	50430 TQ	USBLS	5/07
	Vermont	Y	37580 FQ	45360 MW	58790 TQ	USBLS	5/07
	Burlington-South Burlington MSA, VT	Y	38470 FQ	45150 MW	58890 TQ	USBLS	5/07
	Virginia	Y	34360 FQ	43150 MW	55400 TQ	USBLS	5/07
	Richmond MSA, VA	Y	33220 FQ	39660 MW	48790 TQ	USBLS	5/07
	Virginia Beach-Norfolk-Newport News MSA, VA-NC	Y	30990 FQ	38600 MW	46250 TQ	USBLS	5/07
	Washington	H	17.23 FQ	22.32 MW	27.53 TQ	WABLS	3/08
	Olympia MSA, WA	Y	41790 FQ	45930 MW	50110 TQ	USBLS	5/07
	Seattle-Tacoma-Bellevue MSA, WA	Y	39030 FQ	48520 MW	59770 TQ	USBLS	5/07
	West Virginia	Y	29120 FQ	35212 MW	43573 TQ	WVBLS	7/08-9/08
	Charleston MSA, WV	Y	28340 FQ	34360 MW	41560 TQ	USBLS	5/07
	Parkersburg-Marietta-Vienna MSA, WV-OH	Y	28310 FQ	34670 MW	41690 TQ	USBLS	5/07
	Wisconsin	Y	35080 FQ	42290 MW	53630 TQ	USBLS	5/07
	Milwaukee-Waukesha-West Allis MSA, WI	Y	38370 FQ	47640 MW	59060 TQ	USBLS	5/07
	Wyoming	Y	24756 FQ	30337 MW	36573 TQ	WYBLS	9/08
	Cheyenne MSA, WY	Y	22454 FQ	24987 MW	39520 TQ	WYBLS	9/08
	Puerto Rico	Y	26360 FQ	30240 MW	38290 TQ	USBLS	5/07
	San Juan-Caguas-Guaynabo MSA, PR	Y	25880 FQ	29670 MW	36160 TQ	USBLS	5/07
	Virgin Islands	Y	41280 FQ	46000 MW	50530 TQ	USBLS	5/07
	Guam	Y	31240 FQ	38610 MW	51250 TQ	USBLS	5/07
Paramedic	Cherokee County, GA	Y	34212 LO		53029 HI	AREGC	2007
	Fairfax County, VA	Y	57000 LO			WPOST03	2008
Paramedic Coordinator	Cincinnati, OH	Y	53522 LO		71929 HI	COHSS	10/08
Paramedic Training Officer	Cincinnati, OH	Y			60819 HI	COHSS	10/08
Paramilitary Operations Officer U.S. Central Intelligence Agency	District of Columbia	Y	54525 LO		75669 HI	CIA01	2008
Parent Consultant State Government	Ohio	H	20.71 LO		26.11 HI	ODAS	2008
Parent Counselor-Trainer Public Schools	North Carolina	M	2357 LO		3957 HI	NCSS	2008-2009
Parent Facilitator Public Schools	Chicago, IL	H	6.50 LO		12.00 HI	CPSSS	7/1/06
Pari-Mutuel Commissioner Racing and Charitable Gaming Commission	New Hampshire	Y		12379 AW		NHUL03	2008
Park Attendant	Cincinnati, OH	Y	23911 LO		32519 HI	COHSS	10/08
Park Horticulturalist	Seattle, WA	H	34.12 LO		39.67 HI	CSSS	2008
Park Naturalist	Cincinnati, OH	Y	39113 LO		44100 HI	COHSS	10/08
Park Officer Cadet	Ohio	H	16.83 LO		20.17 HI	ODAS	2008
Park Planner	Carlsbad, CA	S	2576 LO		3131 HI	CCSS01	8/5/08

AE	Average entry wage	AW	Average wage paid	FQ	First quartile wage	LO	Lowest wage paid	MTC	Median total compensation	TCC	Total cash compensation
AER	Average entry range	AWR	Average wage range	H	Hourly	LR	Low end range	MW	Median wage paid	TQ	Third quartile wage
AEX	Average experienced wage	AXR	Average experienced range	HI	Highest wage paid	M	Monthly	MWR	Median wage range	W	Weekly
ATC	Average total compensation	D	Daily	HR	High end range	MCC	Median cash compensation	S	See annotated source	Y	Yearly

Occupation/Type/Industry	Location	Per	Low	Mid	High	Source	Date
Park Ranger	Colorado Springs, CO	M	3082 LO			COSPRS	1/1/09
	Rowe, MA	Y			39450 HI	FRCOG	2009
Parking Attendant	Syracuse, NY	H			13.11 HI	PSTAN	2008
Parking Enforcement Worker	Alabama	Y	22570 FQ	27870 MW	35170 TQ	USBLS	5/07
	Arizona	Y	26040 FQ	29840 MW	34460 TQ	USBLS	5/07
	Phoenix-Mesa-Scottsdale MSA, AZ	Y	22850 FQ	27770 MW	33520 TQ	USBLS	5/07
	Tucson MSA, AZ	Y	27130 FQ	30230 MW	33710 TQ	USBLS	5/07
	California	H	16.70 FQ	21.03 MW	23.97 TQ	CABLS	1/08-3/08
	Los Angeles-Long Beach-Glendale PMSA, CA	H	13.72 FQ	18.31 MW	22.60 TQ	CABLS	1/08-3/08
	Oakland-Fremont-Hayward MSA, CA	H	20.15 FQ	22.41 MW	24.60 TQ	CABLS	1/08-3/08
	Riverside-San Bernardino-Ontario MSA, CA	H	16.60 FQ	19.48 MW	23.27 TQ	CABLS	1/08-3/08
	Sacramento-Arden Arcade-Roseville MSA, CA	H	16.98 FQ	18.39 MW	20.00 TQ	CABLS	1/08-3/08
	San Diego-Carlsbad-San Marcos MSA, CA	H	15.68 FQ	17.82 MW	20.91 TQ	CABLS	1/08-3/08
	Santa Ana-Anaheim-Irvine PMSA, CA	Y	34630 FQ	42010 MW	47860 TQ	USBLS	5/07
	Santa Rosa-Petaluma MSA, CA	H	17.24 FQ	18.99 MW	23.00 TQ	CABLS	1/08-3/08
	Colorado	Y	29470 FQ	35660 MW	41350 TQ	USBLS	5/07
	Denver-Aurora MSA, CO	Y	29430 FQ	36020 MW	42520 TQ	USBLS	5/07
	Connecticut	H	12.35 AE	16.04 MW		CTBLS	1/08-3/08
	Bridgeport-Stamford-Norwalk MSA, CT	Y	28760 FQ	37590 MW	44730 TQ	USBLS	5/07
	Delaware	Y	30770 FQ	35030 MW	38920 TQ	USBLS	5/07
	Washington-Arlington-Alexandria MSA, DC-VA-MD-WV	Y	28610 FQ	33480 MW	40680 TQ	USBLS	5/07
	Florida	Y	24690 FQ	29420 MW	36020 TQ	USBLS	5/07
	Fort Lauderdale-Pompano Beach-Deerfield Beach PMSA, FL	Y	28530 FQ	33520 MW	38620 TQ	USBLS	5/07
	Miami-Fort Lauderdale-Miami Beach MSA, FL	Y	28400 FQ	32700 MW	39720 TQ	USBLS	5/07
	Tampa-St. Petersburg-Clearwater MSA, FL	Y	22790 FQ	27040 MW	34830 TQ	USBLS	5/07
	Georgia	Y	20350 FQ	23100 MW	32860 TQ	USBLS	5/07
	Atlanta-Sandy Springs-Marietta MSA, GA	Y	22870 FQ	32200 MW	36170 TQ	USBLS	5/07
	Illinois	Y	24890 FQ	33380 MW	42380 TQ	USBLS	5/07
	Chicago-Naperville-Joliet MSA, IL-IN-WI	Y	27790 FQ	34820 MW	44390 TQ	USBLS	5/07
	Indiana	Y	21160 FQ	25030 MW	31050 TQ	USBLS	5/07
	Iowa	Y	26870 FQ	30100 MW	33560 TQ	USBLS	5/07
	Kansas	Y	23520 FQ	26870 MW	30130 TQ	USBLS	5/07
	Kentucky	Y	21343 FQ	23804 MW	27417 TQ	KYBLS	2008
	Louisville-Jefferson County MSA, KY-IN	Y	21880 FQ	25660 MW	29690 TQ	USBLS	5/07
	Louisiana	H	8.97 FQ	10.35 MW	11.75 TQ	LABLS	1/08-3/08
	Maine	Y	20910 FQ	27760 MW	32150 TQ	USBLS	5/07
	Maryland	Y		28150 MW		MDBLS	3/08
	Baltimore-Towson MSA, MD	Y	18900 FQ	23700 MW	30270 TQ	USBLS	5/07
	Massachusetts	Y	25340 FQ	34060 MW	44410 TQ	USBLS	5/07
	Boston-Cambridge-Quincy NECTA, MA	Y	24860 FQ	34650 MW	45250 TQ	USBLS	5/07
	Michigan	Y	23200 FQ	30040 MW	35530 TQ	USBLS	5/07
	Detroit-Warren-Livonia MSA, MI	Y	29680 FQ	33200 MW	36740 TQ	USBLS	5/07
	Minnesota	Y	28021 FQ	31085 MW	34169 TQ	MNBLS	10/08-12/08
	Duluth-Superior MSA, MN-WI	Y	26191 FQ	29192 MW	31973 TQ	MNBLS	10/08-12/08
	Minneapolis-Saint Paul MSA, MN-WI	Y	28481 FQ	30991 MW	33490 TQ	MNBLS	10/08-12/08
	Mississippi	Y	19350 FQ	21150 MW	23040 TQ	USBLS	5/07
	Missouri	Y	22670 FQ	26320 MW	32640 TQ	USBLS	5/07
	Kansas City MSA, MO-KS	Y	27560 FQ	30640 MW	35880 TQ	USBLS	5/07
	St. Louis MSA, MO-IL	Y	22430 FQ	27770 MW	37830 TQ	USBLS	5/07
	Nevada	H	17.80 FQ	21.34 MW	25.07 TQ	NVBLS	5/08

AE Average entry wage	**AW** Average wage paid	**FQ** First quartile wage	**LO** Lowest wage paid	**MTC** Median total compensation	**TCC** Total cash compensation
AER Average entry range	**AWR** Average wage range	**H** Hourly	**LR** Low end range	**MW** Median wage paid	**TQ** Third quartile wage
AEX Average experienced wage	**AXR** Average experienced range	**HI** Highest wage paid	**M** Monthly	**MWR** Median wage range	**W** Weekly
ATC Average total compensation	**D** Daily	**HR** High end range	**MCC** Median cash compensation	**S** See annotated source	**Y** Yearly

Occupation/Type/Industry	Location	Per	Low	Mid	High	Source	Date
Parking Enforcement Worker	New Hampshire	H	12.86 AE	15.62 MW	17.03 AEX	NHBLS	6/08
	New Jersey	Y	25210 FQ	33980 MW	45010 TQ	USBLS	5/07
	Camden PMSA, NJ	Y	34180 FQ	40950 MW	49690 TQ	USBLS	5/07
	Edison PMSA, NJ	Y	26670 FQ	37510 MW	46360 TQ	USBLS	5/07
	Newark-Union PMSA, NJ-PA	Y	22850 FQ	31470 MW	41290 TQ	USBLS	5/07
	New York	Y	24780 FQ	29970 MW	37630 TQ	USBLS	5/07
	Albany-Schenectady-Troy MSA, NY	Y	22870 FQ	24960 MW	27960 TQ	USBLS	5/07
	Nassau-Suffolk PMSA, NY	Y	24590 FQ	30220 MW	37550 TQ	USBLS	5/07
	New York-Northern New Jersey-Long Island MSA, NY-NJ-PA	Y	27030 FQ	32560 MW	41560 TQ	USBLS	5/07
	North Carolina	Y	21270 FQ	25540 MW	30090 TQ	USBLS	5/07
	Ohio	Y	27180 FQ	33120 MW	37560 TQ	USBLS	5/07
	Cleveland-Elyria-Mentor MSA, OH	Y	27640 FQ	33510 MW	37450 TQ	USBLS	5/07
	Oklahoma	Y	23680 FQ	30130 MW	36930 TQ	USBLS	5/07
	Oregon	H	15.20 FQ	17.81 MW	20.31 TQ	ORBLS	5/08
	Portland-Vancouver-Beaverton MSA, OR-WA	Y	34690 FQ	39800 MW	43550 TQ	USBLS	5/07
	Pennsylvania	Y	18650 FQ	23210 MW	29040 TQ	USBLS	5/07
	Allentown-Bethlehem-Easton MSA, PA-NJ	Y	22590 FQ	28270 MW	31140 TQ	USBLS	5/07
	Philadelphia-Camden-Wilmington MSA, PA-NJ-DE-MD	Y	23150 FQ	33400 MW	41080 TQ	USBLS	5/07
	Pittsburgh MSA, PA	Y	16190 FQ	19280 MW	24490 TQ	USBLS	5/07
	South Carolina	Y	22140 FQ	26460 MW	30420 TQ	USBLS	5/07
	South Dakota	Y	27804 FQ	30251 MW	32700 TQ	SDBLS	7/08-9/08
	Tennessee	Y	29050 FQ	41530 MW	54980 TQ	USBLS	5/07
	Memphis MSA, TN-MS-AR	Y	34830 FQ	43250 MW	48970 TQ	USBLS	5/07
	Texas	Y	22580 FQ	25450 MW	29390 TQ	USBLS	5/07
	Dallas-Fort Worth-Arlington MSA, TX	Y	23940 FQ	27340 MW	30350 TQ	USBLS	5/07
	Houston-Sugar Land-Baytown MSA, TX	Y	21690 FQ	23470 MW	25250 TQ	USBLS	5/07
	Utah	Y	23990 FQ	35150 MW	41220 TQ	USBLS	5/07
	Salt Lake City MSA, UT	Y	23430 FQ	30070 MW	37660 TQ	USBLS	5/07
	Virginia	Y	22530 FQ	26130 MW	34330 TQ	USBLS	5/07
	Virginia Beach-Norfolk-Newport News MSA, VA-NC	Y	21910 FQ	26610 MW	32960 TQ	USBLS	5/07
	Washington	H	16.95 FQ	18.46 MW	19.94 TQ	WABLS	3/08
	Seattle-Tacoma-Bellevue MSA, WA	Y	35360 FQ	37990 MW	40560 TQ	USBLS	5/07
	West Virginia	Y	17690 FQ	20753 MW	24382 TQ	WVBLS	7/08-9/08
	Wisconsin	Y	21960 FQ	30640 MW	38220 TQ	USBLS	5/07
	Milwaukee-Waukesha-West Allis MSA, WI	Y	21600 FQ	33830 MW	37980 TQ	USBLS	5/07
	Wyoming	Y	20769 FQ	26153 MW	32594 TQ	WYBLS	9/08
Parking Lot Attendant	Alabama	Y	13260 FQ	15470 MW	18530 TQ	USBLS	5/07
	Birmingham-Hoover MSA, AL	Y	13750 FQ	15940 MW	18010 TQ	USBLS	5/07
	Alaska	Y	20150 FQ	22030 MW	24350 TQ	USBLS	5/07
	Arizona	Y	15350 FQ	17990 MW	22430 TQ	USBLS	5/07
	Phoenix-Mesa-Scottsdale MSA, AZ	Y	15290 FQ	17900 MW	22590 TQ	USBLS	5/07
	Tucson MSA, AZ	Y	15900 FQ	18420 MW	21670 TQ	USBLS	5/07
	Arkansas	Y	16020 FQ	17720 MW	20740 TQ	USBLS	5/07
	Little Rock-North Little Rock MSA, AR	Y	16280 FQ	17820 MW	20980 TQ	USBLS	5/07
	California	H	8.01 FQ	8.94 MW	10.75 TQ	CABLS	1/08-3/08
	Los Angeles-Long Beach-Glendale PMSA, CA	H	8.00 FQ	8.63 MW	9.51 TQ	CABLS	1/08-3/08
	Oakland-Fremont-Hayward MSA, CA	H	9.53 FQ	11.12 MW	12.44 TQ	CABLS	1/08-3/08
	Riverside-San Bernardino-Ontario MSA, CA	H	8.00 FQ	8.80 MW	11.38 TQ	CABLS	1/08-3/08
	Sacramento-Arden Arcade-Roseville MSA, CA	H	8.25 FQ	8.95 MW	10.03 TQ	CABLS	1/08-3/08
	San Diego-Carlsbad-San Marcos MSA, CA	H	8.00 FQ	8.95 MW	10.62 TQ	CABLS	1/08-3/08

AE Average entry wage
AER Average entry range
AEX Average experienced wage
ATC Average total compensation
AW Average wage paid
AWR Average wage range
AXR Average experienced range
D Daily
FQ First quartile wage
H Hourly
HI Highest wage paid
HR High end range
LO Lowest wage paid
LR Low end range
M Monthly
MCC Median cash compensation
MTC Median total compensation
MW Median wage paid
MWR Median wage range
S See annotated source
TCC Total cash compensation
TQ Third quartile wage
W Weekly
Y Yearly

Occupation/Type/Industry	Location	Per	Low	Mid	High	Source	Date
Parking Lot Attendant	San Francisco-San Mateo-Redwood PMSA, CA	H	9.65 FQ	11.77 MW	15.35 TQ	CABLS	1/08-3/08
	San Jose-Sunnyvale-Santa Clara MSA, CA	H	8.85 FQ	10.84 MW	13.40 TQ	CABLS	1/08-3/08
	Santa Ana-Anaheim-Irvine PMSA, CA	Y	15910 FQ	16920 MW	18530 TQ	USBLS	5/07
	Colorado	Y	15070 FQ	16300 MW	20810 TQ	USBLS	5/07
	Colorado Springs MSA, CO	Y	15450 FQ	17080 MW	19610 TQ	USBLS	5/07
	Denver-Aurora MSA, CO	Y	14980 FQ	15760 MW	20850 TQ	USBLS	5/07
	Connecticut	H	8.53 AE	9.99 MW		CTBLS	1/08-3/08
	Bridgeport-Stamford-Norwalk MSA, CT	Y	19770 FQ	22260 MW	24690 TQ	USBLS	5/07
	Hartford-West Hartford-East Hartford MSA, CT	Y	19880 FQ	22010 MW	24290 TQ	USBLS	5/07
	Delaware	Y	16420 FQ	18630 MW	21390 TQ	USBLS	5/07
	Dover MSA, DE	Y	14880 FQ	16850 MW	19980 TQ	USBLS	5/07
	Wilmington PMSA, DE-MD-NJ	Y	17010 FQ	19050 MW	22260 TQ	USBLS	5/07
	District of Columbia	Y	18100 FQ	21060 MW	23830 TQ	USBLS	5/07
	Washington-Arlington-Alexandria MSA, DC-VA-MD-WV	Y	17520 FQ	20300 MW	23570 TQ	USBLS	5/07
	Florida	Y	14700 FQ	15910 MW	18830 TQ	USBLS	5/07
	Cape Coral-Fort Myers MSA, FL	Y	14660 FQ	15890 MW	17990 TQ	USBLS	5/07
	Fort Lauderdale-Pompano Beach-Deerfield Beach PMSA, FL	Y	14940 FQ	16200 MW	20020 TQ	USBLS	5/07
	Jacksonville MSA, FL	Y	14600 FQ	15460 MW	20620 TQ	USBLS	5/07
	Miami-Fort Lauderdale-Miami Beach MSA, FL	Y	14740 FQ	16050 MW	18940 TQ	USBLS	5/07
	Orlando-Kissimmee MSA, FL	Y	14840 FQ	15960 MW	18500 TQ	USBLS	5/07
	Tampa-St. Petersburg-Clearwater MSA, FL	Y	14430 FQ	15140 MW	17290 TQ	USBLS	5/07
	West Palm Beach-Boca Raton-Boynton Beach PMSA, FL	Y	15810 FQ	18100 MW	21290 TQ	USBLS	5/07
	Georgia	Y	14090 FQ	17850 MW	22460 TQ	USBLS	5/07
	Atlanta-Sandy Springs-Marietta MSA, GA	Y	15050 FQ	18700 MW	23200 TQ	USBLS	5/07
	Savannah MSA, GA	Y	12280 FQ	13430 MW	14590 TQ	USBLS	5/07
	Hawaii	Y	15550 FQ	17120 MW	19970 TQ	USBLS	5/07
	Honolulu MSA, HI	Y	15510 FQ	16880 MW	19300 TQ	USBLS	5/07
	Idaho	Y	14210 FQ	17210 MW	19780 TQ	USBLS	5/07
	Boise City-Nampa MSA, ID	Y	14310 FQ	17460 MW	19900 TQ	USBLS	5/07
	Illinois	Y	16050 FQ	20470 MW	26840 TQ	USBLS	5/07
	Chicago-Naperville-Joliet MSA, IL-IN-WI	Y	16660 FQ	21300 MW	27470 TQ	USBLS	5/07
	Indiana	Y	13270 FQ	15740 MW	20150 TQ	USBLS	5/07
	Gary PMSA, IN	Y	14030 FQ	16620 MW	19830 TQ	USBLS	5/07
	Indianapolis-Carmel MSA, IN	Y	13480 FQ	17750 MW	21580 TQ	USBLS	5/07
	Iowa	Y	14510 FQ	18600 MW	22520 TQ	USBLS	5/07
	Des Moines-West Des Moines MSA, IA	Y	13920 FQ	15570 MW	21510 TQ	USBLS	5/07
	Kansas	Y	14940 FQ	16740 MW	18660 TQ	USBLS	5/07
	Wichita MSA, KS	Y	14020 FQ	16300 MW	18480 TQ	USBLS	5/07
	Kentucky	Y	16886 FQ	18333 MW	19920 TQ	KYBLS	2008
	Louisville-Jefferson County MSA, KY-IN	Y	15590 FQ	17390 MW	19650 TQ	USBLS	5/07
	Louisiana	H	6.39 FQ	7.56 MW	9.13 TQ	LABLS	1/08-3/08
	Baton Rouge MSA, LA	Y	14460 FQ	16930 MW	18600 TQ	USBLS	5/07
	Lake Charles MSA, LA	Y	12620 FQ	14280 MW	16040 TQ	CTBLS	5/07
	New Orleans-Metairie-Kenner MSA, LA	Y	13200 FQ	15520 MW	19440 TQ	USBLS	5/07
	Maine	Y	14670 FQ	17000 MW	23870 TQ	USBLS	5/07
	Portland-South Portland-Biddeford MSA, ME	Y	16390 FQ	19080 MW	25560 TQ	USBLS	5/07
	Maryland	Y		19000 MW		MDBLS	3/08
	Baltimore-Towson MSA, MD	Y	16130 FQ	18440 MW	21710 TQ	USBLS	5/07
	Bethesda-Gaithersburg-Frederick PMSA, MD	Y	15060 FQ	18340 MW	22440 TQ	USBLS	5/07
	Massachusetts	Y	16810 FQ	20210 MW	24190 TQ	USBLS	5/07

Occupation/Type/Industry	Location	Per	Low	Mid	High	Source	Date
Parking Lot Attendant	Boston-Cambridge-Quincy NECTA, MA	Y	16790 FQ	20270 MW	24480 TQ	USBLS	5/07
	New Bedford MSA, MA	Y	20910 FQ	22330 MW	23740 TQ	USBLS	5/07
	Worcester MSA, MA-CT	Y	15710 FQ	17630 MW	21930 TQ	USBLS	5/07
	Michigan	Y	15300 FQ	17360 MW	22020 TQ	USBLS	5/07
	Detroit-Warren-Livonia MSA, MI	Y	15460 FQ	18740 MW	22740 TQ	USBLS	5/07
	Grand Rapids-Wyoming MSA, MI	Y	15300 FQ	16560 MW	18940 TQ	USBLS	5/07
	Warren-Troy-Farmington Hills PMSA, MI	Y	15030 FQ	15760 MW	22720 TQ	USBLS	5/07
	Minnesota	Y	17040 FQ	20879 MW	25582 TQ	MNBLS	10/08-12/08
	Duluth-Superior MSA, MN-WI	Y	15709 FQ	19672 MW	23896 TQ	MNBLS	10/08-12/08
	Minneapolis-Saint Paul MSA, MN-WI	Y	17176 FQ	21025 MW	25602 TQ	MNBLS	10/08-12/08
	Rochester MSA, MN	Y	22299 FQ	29614 MW	33954 TQ	MNBLS	10/08-12/08
	Mississippi	Y	13050 FQ	14870 MW	18630 TQ	USBLS	5/07
	Jackson MSA, MS	Y	13470 FQ	15640 MW	17700 TQ	USBLS	5/07
	Missouri	Y	15620 FQ	17940 MW	20660 TQ	USBLS	5/07
	Kansas City MSA, MO-KS	Y	15080 FQ	17190 MW	20500 TQ	USBLS	5/07
	St. Louis MSA, MO-IL	Y	16190 FQ	18380 MW	21130 TQ	USBLS	5/07
	Montana	Y	13860 FQ	15000 MW	20690 TQ	USBLS	5/07
	Nebraska	Y	14780 FQ	17390 MW	19760 TQ	USBLS	5/07
	Omaha-Council Bluffs MSA, NE-IA	Y	14730 FQ	17280 MW	20050 TQ	USBLS	5/07
	Nevada	H	7.00 FQ	8.76 MW	10.63 TQ	NVBLS	5/08
	Las Vegas-Paradise MSA, NV	H	7.24 FQ	9.08 MW	10.88 TQ	NVBLS	5/08
	New Hampshire	H	8.33 AE	10.38 MW	11.69 AEX	NHBLS	6/08
	Manchester MSA, NH	Y	17360 FQ	19570 MW	23220 TQ	USBLS	5/07
	New Jersey	Y	17170 FQ	19870 MW	23610 TQ	USBLS	5/07
	Camden PMSA, NJ	Y	17110 FQ	19870 MW	24870 TQ	USBLS	5/07
	Edison PMSA, NJ	Y	18500 FQ	21420 MW	24250 TQ	USBLS	5/07
	Newark-Union PMSA, NJ-PA	Y	17150 FQ	19790 MW	24100 TQ	USBLS	5/07
	Trenton-Ewing MSA, NJ	Y	16470 FQ	17920 MW	20860 TQ	USBLS	5/07
	New Mexico	Y	13950 FQ	17620 MW	22330 TQ	USBLS	5/07
	Albuquerque MSA, NM	Y	14360 FQ	18250 MW	22370 TQ	USBLS	5/07
	New York	Y	15840 FQ	18080 MW	21110 TQ	USBLS	5/07
	Albany-Schenectady-Troy MSA, NY	Y	17740 FQ	19920 MW	23940 TQ	USBLS	5/07
	Buffalo-Niagara Falls MSA, NY	Y	15440 FQ	16560 MW	19350 TQ	USBLS	5/07
	Nassau-Suffolk PMSA, NY	Y	14880 FQ	16510 MW	20700 TQ	USBLS	5/07
	New York-Northern New Jersey-Long Island MSA, NY-NJ-PA	Y	16160 FQ	18500 MW	21980 TQ	USBLS	5/07
	North Carolina	Y	15240 FQ	17800 MW	21600 TQ	USBLS	5/07
	Charlotte-Gastonia-Concord MSA, NC-SC	Y	16550 FQ	20690 MW	23420 TQ	USBLS	5/07
	Durham MSA, NC	Y	15540 FQ	17150 MW	18910 TQ	USBLS	5/07
	Raleigh-Cary MSA, NC	Y	14920 FQ	16800 MW	18980 TQ	USBLS	5/07
	North Dakota	Y	13020 FQ	14920 MW	17840 TQ	USBLS	5/07
	Fargo MSA, ND-MN	Y	12800 FQ	14390 MW	17270 TQ	USBLS	5/07
	Ohio	Y	14970 FQ	17220 MW	21010 TQ	USBLS	5/07
	Cincinnati-Middletown MSA, OH-KY-IN	Y	14610 FQ	15870 MW	18770 TQ	USBLS	5/07
	Cleveland-Elyria-Mentor MSA, OH	Y	14900 FQ	16160 MW	18480 TQ	USBLS	5/07
	Columbus MSA, OH	Y	16550 FQ	20670 MW	25580 TQ	USBLS	5/07
	Dayton MSA, OH	Y	14880 FQ	17430 MW	19630 TQ	USBLS	5/07
	Oklahoma	Y	13590 FQ	16250 MW	22590 TQ	USBLS	5/07
	Oklahoma City MSA, OK	Y	14870 FQ	18820 MW	33060 TQ	USBLS	5/07
	Tulsa MSA, OK	Y	13160 FQ	15130 MW	18260 TQ	USBLS	5/07
	Oregon	H	8.58 FQ	9.23 MW	10.10 TQ	ORBLS	5/08
	Portland-Vancouver-Beaverton MSA, OR-WA	Y	17560 FQ	19000 MW	21070 TQ	USBLS	5/07
	Pennsylvania	Y	15030 FQ	17750 MW	21780 TQ	USBLS	5/07
	Allentown-Bethlehem-Easton MSA, PA-NJ	Y	16580 FQ	18790 MW	22570 TQ	USBLS	5/07
	Philadelphia-Camden-Wilmington MSA, PA-NJ-DE-MD	Y	14910 FQ	17440 MW	20840 TQ	USBLS	5/07
	Pittsburgh MSA, PA	Y	15650 FQ	18790 MW	23680 TQ	USBLS	5/07

Occupation/Type/Industry	Location	Per	Low	Mid	High	Source	Date
Parking Lot Attendant	Rhode Island	Y	16700 FQ	18470 MW	20710 TQ	USBLS	5/07
	Providence-Fall River-Warwick MSA, RI-MA	Y	16760 FQ	18720 MW	21590 TQ	USBLS	5/07
	South Carolina	Y	13240 FQ	15760 MW	19920 TQ	USBLS	5/07
	Charleston-North Charleston MSA, SC	Y	12570 FQ	14010 MW	17510 TQ	USBLS	5/07
	Columbia MSA, SC	Y	17050 FQ	20580 MW	25140 TQ	USBLS	5/07
	South Dakota	Y	18416 FQ	21275 MW	24242 TQ	SDBLS	7/08-9/08
	Sioux Falls MSA, SD	Y	20084 FQ	22732 MW	24921 TQ	SDBLS	7/08-9/08
	Tennessee	Y	13920 FQ	16700 MW	19230 TQ	USBLS	5/07
	Memphis MSA, TN-MS-AR	Y	13560 FQ	16610 MW	19170 TQ	USBLS	5/07
	Nashville-Davidson-Murfreesboro MSA, TN	Y	13460 FQ	16130 MW	18900 TQ	USBLS	5/07
	Texas	Y	13870 FQ	16950 MW	20590 TQ	USBLS	5/07
	Austin-Round Rock MSA, TX	Y	14940 FQ	20430 MW	23240 TQ	USBLS	5/07
	Dallas-Fort Worth-Arlington MSA, TX	Y	14700 FQ	17570 MW	21520 TQ	USBLS	5/07
	El Paso MSA, TX	Y	12460 FQ	13720 MW	15270 TQ	USBLS	5/07
	Houston-Sugar Land-Baytown MSA, TX	Y	13350 FQ	16220 MW	19440 TQ	USBLS	5/07
	San Antonio MSA, TX	Y	14140 FQ	16890 MW	20300 TQ	USBLS	5/07
	Utah	Y	15710 FQ	17510 MW	19840 TQ	USBLS	5/07
	Salt Lake City MSA, UT	Y	15540 FQ	17350 MW	19650 TQ	USBLS	5/07
	Vermont	Y	17100 FQ	18430 MW	21770 TQ	USBLS	5/07
	Virginia	Y	16340 FQ	18330 MW	21870 TQ	USBLS	5/07
	Richmond MSA, VA	Y	15560 FQ	17190 MW	18930 TQ	USBLS	5/07
	Virginia Beach-Norfolk-Newport News MSA, VA-NC	Y	15860 FQ	17460 MW	19220 TQ	USBLS	5/07
	Washington	H	8.82 FQ	9.77 MW	13.46 TQ	WABLS	3/08
	Seattle-Tacoma-Bellevue MSA, WA	Y	18150 FQ	20550 MW	28180 TQ	USBLS	5/07
	West Virginia	Y	14219 FQ	15871 MW	19352 TQ	WVBLS	7/08-9/08
	Charleston MSA, WV	Y	15150 FQ	16930 MW	18890 TQ	USBLS	5/07
	Wheeling MSA, WV-OH	Y	13040 FQ	13830 MW	14620 TQ	USBLS	5/07
	Wisconsin	Y	16360 FQ	19020 MW	22730 TQ	USBLS	5/07
	Milwaukee-Waukesha-West Allis MSA, WI	Y	15630 FQ	17460 MW	20070 TQ	USBLS	5/07
	Wyoming	Y	15791 FQ	19449 MW	21607 TQ	WYBLS	9/08
	Puerto Rico	Y	12280 FQ	13480 MW	14680 TQ	USBLS	5/07
	San Juan-Caguas-Guaynabo MSA, PR	Y	12280 FQ	13470 MW	14670 TQ	USBLS	5/07
	Virgin Islands	Y	14220 FQ	16710 MW	20580 TQ	USBLS	5/07
	Guam	Y	12170 FQ	13460 MW	14740 TQ	USBLS	5/07
Parking Meter Collector	Cincinnati, OH	Y	36517 LO		38340 HI	COHSS	10/08
Parking Meter Mechanic	Colorado Springs, CO	M	2646 LO			COSPRS	1/1/09
Parks, Trails, and Open Space Manager	Colorado Springs, CO	M	6687 LO			COSPRS	1/1/09
Parks and Recreation Director	Marietta, MS	Y			200 HI	MML	2008
	Pascagoula, MS	Y			58896 HI	MML	2008
Parks and Recreation Services Manager	Seaside, CA	S	3464 LO		4137 HI	SSSS	8/08
Parks Athletic Fields Scheduler	Seattle, WA	H	19.68 LO		21.97 HI	CSSS	2008
Parks Director	Cincinnati, OH	Y	98374 LO		132805 HI	COHSS	10/08
Parliamentarian							
United States House of Representatives	United States	Y			167800 HI	CRS01	1/08
United States Senate	United States	Y			162515 HI	CRS01	2007
Parole Agent	South Dakota	Y	28194 LO		42290 HI	AFT02	3/1/08
Parole Officer	Georgia	Y	29400 LO		51406 HI	AFT02	3/1/08
	Ohio	H	18.99 LO		23.76 HI	ODAS	2008
Parts Salesperson	Alabama	Y	20180 FQ	25060 MW	32190 TQ	USBLS	5/07
	Birmingham-Hoover MSA, AL	Y	21280 FQ	25430 MW	31410 TQ	USBLS	5/07
	Alaska	Y	24210 FQ	30050 MW	38490 TQ	USBLS	5/07

AE	Average entry wage	AW	Average wage paid	FQ	First quartile wage	LO	Lowest wage paid	MTC	Median total compensation	TCC	Total cash compensation
AER	Average entry range	AWR	Average wage range	H	Hourly	LR	Low end range	MW	Median wage paid	TQ	Third quartile wage
AEX	Average experienced wage	AXR	Average experienced range	HI	Highest wage paid	M	Monthly	MWR	Median wage range	W	Weekly
ATC	Average total compensation	D	Daily	HR	High end range	MCC	Median cash compensation	S	See annotated source	Y	Yearly

Occupation/Type/Industry	Location	Per	Low	Mid	High	Source	Date
Parts Salesperson	Anchorage MSA, AK	Y	24520 FQ	30290 MW	39040 TQ	USBLS	5/07
	Arizona	Y	22290 FQ	29160 MW	39410 TQ	USBLS	5/07
	Phoenix-Mesa-Scottsdale MSA, AZ	Y	24910 FQ	31650 MW	42540 TQ	USBLS	5/07
	Tucson MSA, AZ	Y	20410 FQ	25060 MW	33930 TQ	USBLS	5/07
	Yuma MSA, AZ	Y	15370 FQ	24240 MW	36610 TQ	USBLS	5/07
	Arkansas	Y	18550 FQ	23730 MW	31920 TQ	USBLS	5/07
	Jonesboro MSA, AR	Y	18870 FQ	22880 MW	29650 TQ	USBLS	5/07
	Little Rock-North Little Rock MSA, AR	Y	18080 FQ	24690 MW	36790 TQ	USBLS	5/07
	Pine Bluff MSA, AR	Y	15700 FQ	21660 MW	27340 TQ	USBLS	5/07
	California	H	11.54 FQ	15.31 MW	20.86 TQ	CABLS	1/08-3/08
	Los Angeles-Long Beach-Glendale PMSA, CA	H	11.29 FQ	14.92 MW	19.75 TQ	CABLS	1/08-3/08
	Oakland-Fremont-Hayward MSA, CA	H	13.99 FQ	18.61 MW	24.27 TQ	CABLS	1/08-3/08
	Riverside-San Bernardino-Ontario MSA, CA	H	11.75 FQ	16.19 MW	22.62 TQ	CABLS	1/08-3/08
	Sacramento-Arden Arcade-Roseville MSA, CA	H	13.09 FQ	16.79 MW	22.42 TQ	CABLS	1/08-3/08
	San Diego-Carlsbad-San Marcos MSA, CA	H	11.45 FQ	14.56 MW	20.24 TQ	CABLS	1/08-3/08
	San Francisco-San Mateo-Redwood PMSA, CA	H	11.95 FQ	17.02 MW	24.88 TQ	CABLS	1/08-3/08
	San Jose-Sunnyvale-Santa Clara MSA, CA	H	12.64 FQ	16.17 MW	21.71 TQ	CABLS	1/08-3/08
	Santa Ana-Anaheim-Irvine PMSA, CA	Y	23940 FQ	35900 MW	47850 TQ	USBLS	5/07
	Colorado	Y	25110 FQ	32130 MW	41520 TQ	USBLS	5/07
	Colorado Springs MSA, CO	Y	26110 FQ	30930 MW	39680 TQ	USBLS	5/07
	Denver-Aurora MSA, CO	Y	25430 FQ	34210 MW	44240 TQ	USBLS	5/07
	Connecticut	H	10.95 AE	15.59 MW		CTBLS	1/08-3/08
	Bridgeport-Stamford-Norwalk MSA, CT	Y	32600 FQ	39080 MW	48890 TQ	USBLS	5/07
	Hartford-West Hartford-East Hartford MSA, CT	Y	22750 FQ	27890 MW	37670 TQ	USBLS	5/07
	New Haven MSA, CT	Y	23910 FQ	31060 MW	39940 TQ	USBLS	5/07
	Waterbury MSA, CT	Y	25190 FQ	33910 MW	39930 TQ	USBLS	5/07
	Delaware	Y	21120 FQ	25820 MW	32760 TQ	USBLS	5/07
	Dover MSA, DE	Y	22030 FQ	27580 MW	33170 TQ	USBLS	5/07
	Wilmington PMSA, DE-MD-NJ	Y	21050 FQ	27020 MW	35020 TQ	USBLS	5/07
	District of Columbia	Y	18790 FQ	21940 MW	25170 TQ	USBLS	5/07
	Washington-Arlington-Alexandria MSA, DC-VA-MD-WV	Y	23530 FQ	32500 MW	43650 TQ	USBLS	5/07
	Florida	Y	21300 FQ	26940 MW	35030 TQ	USBLS	5/07
	Cape Coral-Fort Myers MSA, FL	Y	23890 FQ	30460 MW	42050 TQ	USBLS	5/07
	Fort Lauderdale-Pompano Beach-Deerfield Beach PMSA, FL	Y	20180 FQ	27170 MW	32390 TQ	USBLS	5/07
	Jacksonville MSA, FL	Y	20480 FQ	24880 MW	35660 TQ	USBLS	5/07
	Lakeland MSA, FL	Y	19550 FQ	27360 MW	34880 TQ	USBLS	5/07
	Miami-Fort Lauderdale-Miami Beach MSA, FL	Y	21020 FQ	27720 MW	34850 TQ	USBLS	5/07
	Orlando-Kissimmee MSA, FL	Y	22990 FQ	27660 MW	35600 TQ	USBLS	5/07
	Tampa-St. Petersburg-Clearwater MSA, FL	Y	23220 FQ	28260 MW	37500 TQ	USBLS	5/07
	West Palm Beach-Boca Raton-Boynton Beach PMSA, FL	Y	25280 FQ	32830 MW	39360 TQ	USBLS	5/07
	Georgia	Y	22130 FQ	29090 MW	39410 TQ	USBLS	5/07
	Atlanta-Sandy Springs-Marietta MSA, GA	Y	23090 FQ	30400 MW	45240 TQ	USBLS	5/07
	Macon MSA, GA	Y	26160 FQ	33900 MW	40230 TQ	USBLS	5/07
	Hawaii	Y	21780 FQ	27580 MW	35130 TQ	USBLS	5/07
	Honolulu MSA, HI	Y	21760 FQ	28190 MW	36490 TQ	USBLS	5/07
	Idaho	Y	20790 FQ	26210 MW	34190 TQ	USBLS	5/07
	Boise City-Nampa MSA, ID	Y	20710 FQ	26560 MW	34680 TQ	USBLS	5/07
	Coeur d'Alene MSA, ID	Y	26940 FQ	33590 MW	38050 TQ	USBLS	5/07
	Pocatello MSA, ID	Y	22600 FQ	28010 MW	32650 TQ	USBLS	5/07
	Illinois	Y	22680 FQ	29660 MW	38730 TQ	USBLS	5/07

AE	Average entry wage	**AW**	Average wage paid	**FQ**	First quartile wage	**LO**	Lowest wage paid	**MTC**	Median total compensation	**TCC**	Total cash compensation
AER	Average entry range	**AWR**	Average wage range	**H**	Hourly	**LR**	Low end range	**MW**	Median wage paid	**TQ**	Third quartile wage
AEX	Average experienced wage	**AXR**	Average experienced range	**HI**	Highest wage paid	**M**	Monthly	**MWR**	Median wage range	**W**	Weekly
ATC	Average total compensation	**D**	Daily	**HR**	High end range	**MCC**	Median cash compensation	**S**	See annotated source	**Y**	Yearly

Parts Salesperson

Occupation/Type/Industry	Location	Per	Low	Mid	High	Source	Date
Parts Salesperson	Chicago-Naperville-Joliet MSA, IL-IN-WI	Y	22700 FQ	30430 MW	40760 TQ	USBLS	5/07
	Indiana	Y	21070 FQ	26910 MW	35440 TQ	USBLS	5/07
	Evansville MSA, IN-KY	Y	19200 FQ	24060 MW	33350 TQ	USBLS	5/07
	Gary PMSA, IN	Y	19070 FQ	24220 MW	35870 TQ	USBLS	5/07
	Indianapolis-Carmel MSA, IN	Y	25690 FQ	32650 MW	43150 TQ	USBLS	5/07
	Iowa	Y	19900 FQ	26580 MW	34780 TQ	USBLS	5/07
	Cedar Rapids MSA, IA	Y	20500 FQ	27990 MW	33330 TQ	USBLS	5/07
	Davenport-Moline-Rock Island MSA, IA-IL	Y	20450 FQ	26810 MW	34310 TQ	USBLS	5/07
	Des Moines-West Des Moines MSA, IA	Y	23940 FQ	32910 MW	43030 TQ	USBLS	5/07
	Kansas	Y	20280 FQ	26300 MW	33550 TQ	USBLS	5/07
	Wichita MSA, KS	Y	22210 FQ	27870 MW	33960 TQ	USBLS	5/07
	Kentucky	Y	19895 FQ	24732 MW	31002 TQ	KYBLS	2008
	Bowling Green MSA, KY	Y	17840 FQ	22970 MW	27920 TQ	USBLS	5/07
	Louisville-Jefferson County MSA, KY-IN	Y	21400 FQ	26400 MW	32040 TQ	USBLS	5/07
	Louisiana	H	9.20 FQ	12.12 MW	16.86 TQ	LABLS	1/08-3/08
	Baton Rouge MSA, LA	Y	19100 FQ	24650 MW	41480 TQ	USBLS	5/07
	Lafayette MSA, LA	Y	27030 FQ	34770 MW	43810 TQ	USBLS	5/07
	New Orleans-Metairie-Kenner MSA, LA	Y	20270 FQ	30270 MW	39400 TQ	USBLS	5/07
	Maine	Y	22210 FQ	27760 MW	35590 TQ	USBLS	5/07
	Portland-South Portland-Biddeford MSA, ME	Y	27840 FQ	33420 MW	39450 TQ	USBLS	5/07
	Maryland	Y		30400 MW		MDBLS	3/08
	Baltimore-Towson MSA, MD	Y	20450 FQ	27810 MW	37380 TQ	USBLS	5/07
	Bethesda-Gaithersburg-Frederick PMSA, MD	Y	24910 FQ	35200 MW	49050 TQ	USBLS	5/07
	Massachusetts	Y	24610 FQ	31920 MW	40250 TQ	USBLS	5/07
	Boston-Cambridge-Quincy NECTA, MA	Y	25660 FQ	32880 MW	39610 TQ	USBLS	5/07
	Worcester MSA, MA-CT	Y	24890 FQ	31350 MW	39630 TQ	USBLS	5/07
	Michigan	Y	20210 FQ	26850 MW	36560 TQ	USBLS	5/07
	Detroit-Warren-Livonia MSA, MI	Y	23490 FQ	31680 MW	42960 TQ	USBLS	5/07
	Grand Rapids-Wyoming MSA, MI	Y	21070 FQ	28300 MW	38320 TQ	USBLS	5/07
	Warren-Troy-Farmington Hills PMSA, MI	Y	25470 FQ	33300 MW	45760 TQ	USBLS	5/07
	Minnesota	Y	24534 FQ	31506 MW	40420 TQ	MNBLS	10/08-12/08
	Duluth-Superior MSA, MN-WI	Y	23325 FQ	29199 MW	35094 TQ	MNBLS	10/08-12/08
	Minneapolis-Saint Paul MSA, MN-WI	Y	25113 FQ	34759 MW	43824 TQ	MNBLS	10/08-12/08
	Rochester MSA, MN	Y	22759 FQ	28443 MW	34117 TQ	MNBLS	10/08-12/08
	Mississippi	Y	19430 FQ	23840 MW	31390 TQ	USBLS	5/07
	Jackson MSA, MS	Y	23130 FQ	28920 MW	36100 TQ	USBLS	5/07
	Missouri	Y	20340 FQ	26460 MW	36450 TQ	USBLS	5/07
	Kansas City MSA, MO-KS	Y	21500 FQ	27820 MW	37590 TQ	USBLS	5/07
	St. Louis MSA, MO-IL	Y	23550 FQ	31400 MW	41830 TQ	USBLS	5/07
	Montana	Y	24250 FQ	29500 MW	35720 TQ	USBLS	5/07
	Billings MSA, MT	Y	27600 FQ	34050 MW	38520 TQ	USBLS	5/07
	Nebraska	Y	20810 FQ	26990 MW	36410 TQ	USBLS	5/07
	Omaha-Council Bluffs MSA, NE-IA	Y	22120 FQ	29520 MW	39740 TQ	USBLS	5/07
	Nevada	H	12.09 FQ	14.86 MW	18.53 TQ	NVBLS	5/08
	Las Vegas-Paradise MSA, NV	H	12.44 FQ	14.99 MW	18.85 TQ	NVBLS	5/08
	New Hampshire	H	10.70 AE	14.88 MW	18.02 AEX	NHBLS	6/08
	Manchester MSA, NH	Y	29640 FQ	39440 MW	48060 TQ	USBLS	5/07
	Nashua NECTA, NH-MA	Y	20200 FQ	27010 MW	33000 TQ	USBLS	5/07
	New Jersey	Y	22990 FQ	30740 MW	42500 TQ	USBLS	5/07
	Camden PMSA, NJ	Y	24290 FQ	33700 MW	43040 TQ	USBLS	5/07
	Edison PMSA, NJ	Y	25190 FQ	31330 MW	40760 TQ	USBLS	5/07
	Newark-Union PMSA, NJ-PA	Y	23320 FQ	31360 MW	41940 TQ	USBLS	5/07
	New Mexico	Y	21960 FQ	28970 MW	36760 TQ	USBLS	5/07
	Albuquerque MSA, NM	Y	25370 FQ	29750 MW	37400 TQ	USBLS	5/07
	New York	Y	23360 FQ	30720 MW	40660 TQ	USBLS	5/07
	Albany-Schenectady-Troy MSA, NY	Y	27040 FQ	34400 MW	40150 TQ	USBLS	5/07
	Binghamton MSA, NY	Y	19870 FQ	26350 MW	31080 TQ	USBLS	5/07

AE	Average entry wage	AW	Average wage paid	FQ	First quartile wage
AER	Average entry range	AWR	Average wage range	H	Hourly
AEX	Average experienced wage	AXR	Average experienced range	HI	Highest wage paid
ATC	Average total compensation	D	Daily	HR	High end range

LO	Lowest wage paid
LR	Low end range
M	Monthly
MCC	Median cash compensation

MTC	Median total compensation
MW	Median wage paid
MWR	Median wage range
S	See annotated source

TCC	Total cash compensation
TQ	Third quartile wage
W	Weekly
Y	Yearly

Occupation/Type/Industry	Location	Per	Low	Mid	High	Source	Date
Parts Salesperson	Buffalo-Niagara Falls MSA, NY	Y	21320 FQ	25530 MW	33520 TQ	USBLS	5/07
	Nassau-Suffolk PMSA, NY	Y	31970 FQ	41900 MW	54340 TQ	USBLS	5/07
	New York-Northern New Jersey-Long Island MSA, NY-NJ-PA	Y	24210 FQ	32080 MW	45310 TQ	USBLS	5/07
	Utica-Rome MSA, NY	Y	18170 FQ	23610 MW	30350 TQ	USBLS	5/07
	North Carolina	Y	20470 FQ	26090 MW	34360 TQ	USBLS	5/07
	Charlotte-Gastonia-Concord MSA, NC-SC	Y	22410 FQ	28800 MW	37260 TQ	USBLS	5/07
	Durham MSA, NC	Y	22250 FQ	26620 MW	37710 TQ	USBLS	5/07
	Raleigh-Cary MSA, NC	Y	23670 FQ	29030 MW	37180 TQ	USBLS	5/07
	North Dakota	Y	20340 FQ	25500 MW	32850 TQ	USBLS	5/07
	Fargo MSA, ND-MN	Y	22570 FQ	28610 MW	38280 TQ	USBLS	5/07
	Ohio	Y	20080 FQ	25190 MW	33480 TQ	USBLS	5/07
	Cincinnati-Middletown MSA, OH-KY-IN	Y	20640 FQ	26600 MW	35090 TQ	USBLS	5/07
	Cleveland-Elyria-Mentor MSA, OH	Y	20470 FQ	25700 MW	36500 TQ	USBLS	5/07
	Columbus MSA, OH	Y	23620 FQ	30380 MW	37950 TQ	USBLS	5/07
	Dayton MSA, OH	Y	20700 FQ	25880 MW	34050 TQ	USBLS	5/07
	Oklahoma	Y	17260 FQ	22800 MW	30360 TQ	USBLS	5/07
	Oklahoma City MSA, OK	Y	22540 FQ	27500 MW	31770 TQ	USBLS	5/07
	Tulsa MSA, OK	Y	16750 FQ	19650 MW	29830 TQ	USBLS	5/07
	Oregon	H	12.23 FQ	15.34 MW	19.33 TQ	ORBLS	5/08
	Portland-Vancouver-Beaverton MSA, OR-WA	Y	26980 FQ	33950 MW	42760 TQ	USBLS	5/07
	Pennsylvania	Y	21790 FQ	28620 MW	36220 TQ	USBLS	5/07
	Allentown-Bethlehem-Easton MSA, PA-NJ	Y	21430 FQ	27830 MW	34610 TQ	USBLS	5/07
	Philadelphia-Camden-Wilmington MSA, PA-NJ-DE-MD	Y	24850 FQ	31150 MW	40160 TQ	USBLS	5/07
	Pittsburgh MSA, PA	Y	22060 FQ	29080 MW	36140 TQ	USBLS	5/07
	Rhode Island	Y	24390 FQ	29510 MW	37680 TQ	USBLS	5/07
	Providence-Fall River-Warwick MSA, RI-MA	Y	25720 FQ	31660 MW	42440 TQ	USBLS	5/07
	South Carolina	Y	20960 FQ	27530 MW	35850 TQ	USBLS	5/07
	Charleston-North Charleston MSA, SC	Y	22990 FQ	31420 MW	39190 TQ	USBLS	5/07
	Columbia MSA, SC	Y	23570 FQ	30920 MW	37740 TQ	USBLS	5/07
	South Dakota	Y	22250 FQ	27089 MW	33289 TQ	SDBLS	7/08-9/08
	Rapid City MSA, SD	Y	22791 FQ	26965 MW	31716 TQ	SDBLS	7/08-9/08
	Sioux Falls MSA, SD	Y	25927 FQ	31224 MW	36545 TQ	SDBLS	7/08-9/08
	Tennessee	Y	20540 FQ	27850 MW	36500 TQ	USBLS	5/07
	Clarksville MSA, TN-KY	Y	18110 FQ	22080 MW	31610 TQ	USBLS	5/07
	Johnson City MSA, TN	Y	19640 FQ	24040 MW	30520 TQ	USBLS	5/07
	Memphis MSA, TN-MS-AR	Y	21780 FQ	29260 MW	38430 TQ	USBLS	5/07
	Nashville-Davidson-Murfreesboro MSA, TN	Y	19700 FQ	28390 MW	37960 TQ	USBLS	5/07
	Texas	Y	19910 FQ	26850 MW	36950 TQ	USBLS	5/07
	Austin-Round Rock MSA, TX	Y	21710 FQ	29620 MW	39860 TQ	USBLS	5/07
	Corpus Christi MSA, TX	Y	18580 FQ	24970 MW	29020 TQ	USBLS	5/07
	Dallas-Fort Worth-Arlington MSA, TX	Y	20980 FQ	28160 MW	38940 TQ	USBLS	5/07
	El Paso MSA, TX	Y	21440 FQ	26440 MW	34120 TQ	USBLS	5/07
	Houston-Sugar Land-Baytown MSA, TX	Y	23650 FQ	30900 MW	42620 TQ	USBLS	5/07
	San Antonio MSA, TX	Y	17680 FQ	22610 MW	33950 TQ	USBLS	5/07
	Utah	Y	21430 FQ	26040 MW	34760 TQ	USBLS	5/07
	Salt Lake City MSA, UT	Y	22540 FQ	28760 MW	38470 TQ	USBLS	5/07
	Vermont	Y	25620 FQ	29960 MW	35930 TQ	USBLS	5/07
	Burlington-South Burlington MSA, VT	Y	27010 FQ	30440 MW	35130 TQ	USBLS	5/07
	Virginia	Y	22570 FQ	28850 MW	37570 TQ	USBLS	5/07
	Richmond MSA, VA	Y	24400 FQ	29560 MW	37380 TQ	USBLS	5/07
	Virginia Beach-Norfolk-Newport News MSA, VA-NC	Y	22900 FQ	29530 MW	39630 TQ	USBLS	5/07
	Washington	H	11.07 FQ	13.95 MW	17.95 TQ	WABLS	3/08
	Seattle-Tacoma-Bellevue MSA, WA	Y	22670 FQ	29750 MW	39960 TQ	USBLS	5/07
	West Virginia	Y	17262 FQ	23225 MW	30154 TQ	WVBLS	7/08-9/08

AE Average entry wage	**AW** Average wage paid	**FQ** First quartile wage	**LO** Lowest wage paid	**MTC** Median total compensation	**TCC** Total cash compensation
AER Average entry range	**AWR** Average wage range	**H** Hourly	**LR** Low end range	**MW** Median wage paid	**TQ** Third quartile wage
AEX Average experienced wage	**AXR** Average experienced range	**HI** Highest wage paid	**M** Monthly	**MWR** Median wage range	**W** Weekly
ATC Average total compensation	**D** Daily	**HR** High end range	**MCC** Median cash compensation	**S** See annotated source	**Y** Yearly

Occupation/Type/Industry	Location	Per	Low	Mid	High	Source	Date
Parts Salesperson	Charleston MSA, WV	Y	19720 FQ	27040 MW	32800 TQ	USBLS	5/07
	Wisconsin	Y	24170 FQ	30310 MW	37370 TQ	USBLS	5/07
	Milwaukee-Waukesha-West Allis MSA, WI	Y	26060 FQ	32970 MW	40160 TQ	USBLS	5/07
	Wyoming	Y	20568 FQ	26531 MW	33532 TQ	WYBLS	9/08
	Cheyenne MSA, WY	Y	24370 FQ	28224 MW	32812 TQ	WYBLS	9/08
	Puerto Rico	Y	13060 FQ	15080 MW	19380 TQ	USBLS	5/07
	Aguadilla-Isabela-San Sebastian MSA, PR	Y	12530 FQ	13660 MW	14800 TQ	USBLS	5/07
	San Juan-Caguas-Guaynabo MSA, PR	Y	13200 FQ	15380 MW	19930 TQ	USBLS	5/07
	Virgin Islands	Y	17380 FQ	19550 MW	22470 TQ	USBLS	5/07
	Guam	Y	15010 FQ	18710 MW	23850 TQ	USBLS	5/07
Passenger Service Agent	United States	H		8.68 AW		AVJOB01	2009
Pastoral Counselor	United States	Y		47900 AW		HCC04	2009
Pastry Chef	United States	H	9.17 AE		15.57 AEX	CHAROB	2009
Patent Attorney First-Year	United States	Y	100000 LO			NBJ	2008
Patient Care Technician	United States	H		10.00-15.00 AW		FREEP11	2009
Patient Representative	United States	Y		41800 MW		CNNM04	2007
Patrol Officer							
Police Department	Bainbridge, GA	Y	26274 LO		55321 HI	GACTY01	2008
Police Department	Macon, GA	Y	28122 LO		42515 HI	GACTY01	2008
Patternmaker							
Metals and Plastics	Alabama	Y	26640 FQ	33300 MW	39000 TQ	USBLS	5/07
Metals and Plastics	Birmingham-Hoover MSA, AL	Y	25380 FQ	33290 MW	38680 TQ	USBLS	5/07
Metals and Plastics	Arizona	Y	25370 FQ	29130 MW	37640 TQ	USBLS	5/07
Metals and Plastics	Phoenix-Mesa-Scottsdale MSA, AZ	Y	26330 FQ	29750 MW	38980 TQ	USBLS	5/07
Metals and Plastics	California	H	12.84 FQ	18.86 MW	27.35 TQ	CABLS	1/08-3/08
Metals and Plastics	Los Angeles-Long Beach-Glendale PMSA, CA	H	8.00 FQ	15.32 MW	27.80 TQ	CABLS	1/08-3/08
Metals and Plastics	Oakland-Fremont-Hayward MSA, CA	H	20.88 FQ	27.28 MW	30.53 TQ	CABLS	1/08-3/08
Metals and Plastics	Connecticut	H	17.99 AE	28.03 MW		CTBLS	1/08-3/08
Metals and Plastics	Florida	Y	21230 FQ	27660 MW	40650 TQ	USBLS	5/07
Metals and Plastics	Tampa-St. Petersburg-Clearwater MSA, FL	Y	18740 FQ	21640 MW	24720 TQ	USBLS	5/07
Metals and Plastics	Georgia	Y	49610 FQ	53080 MW	56650 TQ	USBLS	5/07
Metals and Plastics	Atlanta-Sandy Springs-Marietta MSA, GA	Y	50280 FQ	53590 MW	56910 TQ	USBLS	5/07
Metals and Plastics	Illinois	Y	26870 FQ	33330 MW	39140 TQ	USBLS	5/07
Metals and Plastics	Chicago-Naperville-Joliet MSA, IL-IN-WI	Y	26240 FQ	33280 MW	38000 TQ	USBLS	5/07
Metals and Plastics	Indiana	Y	35110 FQ	46430 MW	55350 TQ	USBLS	5/07
Metals and Plastics	Iowa	Y	30230 FQ	38090 MW	51490 TQ	USBLS	5/07
Metals and Plastics	Kansas	Y	35620 FQ	49390 MW	57030 TQ	USBLS	5/07
Metals and Plastics	Wichita MSA, KS	Y	48550 FQ	54010 MW	58470 TQ	USBLS	5/07
Metals and Plastics	Massachusetts	Y	32350 FQ	39610 MW	50050 TQ	USBLS	5/07
Metals and Plastics	Michigan	Y	42340 FQ	51080 MW	59040 TQ	USBLS	5/07
Metals and Plastics	Detroit-Warren-Livonia MSA, MI	Y	34620 FQ	40970 MW	48570 TQ	USBLS	5/07
Metals and Plastics	Grand Rapids-Wyoming MSA, MI	Y	45950 FQ	54420 MW	60490 TQ	USBLS	5/07
Metals and Plastics	Warren-Troy-Farmington Hills PMSA, MI	Y	32190 FQ	43440 MW	49790 TQ	USBLS	5/07
Metals and Plastics	Minnesota	Y	34936 FQ	41021 MW	51450 TQ	MNBLS	10/08-12/08
Metals and Plastics	Minneapolis-Saint Paul MSA, MN-WI	Y	42524 FQ	56934 MW	67332 TQ	MNBLS	10/08-12/08
Metals and Plastics	Missouri	Y	30590 FQ	46980 MW	64190 TQ	USBLS	5/07
Metals and Plastics	St. Louis MSA, MO-IL	Y	59580 FQ	64270 MW	70410 TQ	USBLS	5/07
Metals and Plastics	Nevada	H	11.38 FQ	13.47 MW	17.36 TQ	NVBLS	5/08
Metals and Plastics	New York	Y	28150 FQ	35820 MW	45470 TQ	USBLS	5/07

AE	Average entry wage	AW	Average wage paid	FQ	First quartile wage
AER	Average entry range	AWR	Average wage range	H	Hourly
AEX	Average experienced wage	AXR	Average experienced range	HI	Highest wage paid
ATC	Average total compensation	D	Daily	HR	High end range

LO	Lowest wage paid	MTC	Median total compensation	TCC	Total cash compensation
LR	Low end range	MW	Median wage paid	TQ	Third quartile wage
M	Monthly	MWR	Median wage range	W	Weekly
MCC	Median cash compensation	S	See annotated source	Y	Yearly

Occupation/Type/Industry	Location	Per	Low	Mid	High	Source	Date
Patternmaker							
Metals and Plastics	Buffalo-Niagara Falls MSA, NY	Y	32620 FQ	42300 MW	53620 TQ	USBLS	5/07
Metals and Plastics	New York-Northern New Jersey-Long Island MSA, NY-NJ-PA	Y	19030 FQ	24340 MW	38770 TQ	USBLS	5/07
Metals and Plastics	North Carolina	Y	22680 FQ	31510 MW	40120 TQ	USBLS	5/07
Metals and Plastics	Charlotte-Gastonia-Concord MSA, NC-SC	Y	26390 FQ	29370 MW	39810 TQ	USBLS	5/07
Metals and Plastics	Ohio	Y	29850 FQ	42400 MW	72900 TQ	USBLS	5/07
Metals and Plastics	Cincinnati-Middletown MSA, OH-KY-IN	Y	33060 FQ	43410 MW	52510 TQ	USBLS	5/07
Metals and Plastics	Dayton MSA, OH	Y	26760 FQ	34510 MW	43670 TQ	USBLS	5/07
Metals and Plastics	Oklahoma	Y	20350 FQ	26850 MW	40760 TQ	USBLS	5/07
Metals and Plastics	Portland-Vancouver-Beaverton MSA, OR-WA	Y	30320 FQ	35250 MW	55220 TQ	USBLS	5/07
Metals and Plastics	Pennsylvania	Y	23520 FQ	32740 MW	37340 TQ	USBLS	5/07
Metals and Plastics	Allentown-Bethlehem-Easton MSA, PA-NJ	Y	29730 FQ	34010 MW	37450 TQ	USBLS	5/07
Metals and Plastics	Philadelphia-Camden-Wilmington MSA, PA-NJ-DE-MD	Y	34400 FQ	55430 MW	67240 TQ	USBLS	5/07
Metals and Plastics	Rhode Island	Y	30210 FQ	41780 MW	47030 TQ	USBLS	5/07
Metals and Plastics	Providence-Fall River-Warwick MSA, RI-MA	Y	29330 FQ	41040 MW	46660 TQ	USBLS	5/07
Metals and Plastics	South Carolina	Y	25540 FQ	27710 MW	31420 TQ	USBLS	5/07
Metals and Plastics	Tennessee	Y	31900 FQ	39100 MW	44080 TQ	USBLS	5/07
Metals and Plastics	Texas	Y	20300 FQ	26530 MW	35110 TQ	USBLS	5/07
Metals and Plastics	Dallas-Fort Worth-Arlington MSA, TX	Y	23740 FQ	30170 MW	36540 TQ	USBLS	5/07
Metals and Plastics	Houston-Sugar Land-Baytown MSA, TX	Y	20750 FQ	23920 MW	30710 TQ	USBLS	5/07
Metals and Plastics	Virginia	Y	27450 FQ	35780 MW	44210 TQ	USBLS	5/07
Metals and Plastics	Virginia Beach-Norfolk-Newport News MSA, VA-NC	Y	27560 FQ	37740 MW	45830 TQ	USBLS	5/07
Metals and Plastics	Washington	H	12.40 FQ	13.42 MW	14.44 TQ	WABLS	3/08
Metals and Plastics	Seattle-Tacoma-Bellevue MSA, WA	Y	44950 FQ	54690 MW	59910 TQ	USBLS	5/07
Metals and Plastics	Wisconsin	Y	32300 FQ	37330 MW	45790 TQ	USBLS	5/07
Metals and Plastics	Milwaukee-Waukesha-West Allis MSA, WI	Y	35110 FQ	42550 MW	51210 TQ	USBLS	5/07
Wood	Arizona	Y	39570 FQ	44020 MW	47760 TQ	USBLS	5/07
Wood	California	H	11.87 FQ	17.81 MW	23.30 TQ	CABLS	1/08-3/08
Wood	Connecticut	H	12.79 AE	15.53 MW		CTBLS	1/08-3/08
Wood	Georgia	Y	38150 FQ	49510 MW	55090 TQ	USBLS	5/07
Wood	Illinois	Y	22490 FQ	27290 MW	38760 TQ	USBLS	5/07
Wood	Indiana	Y	24760 FQ	32250 MW	45630 TQ	USBLS	5/07
Wood	Iowa	Y	24080 FQ	35250 MW	43630 TQ	USBLS	5/07
Wood	Michigan	Y	43630 FQ	49240 MW	65380 TQ	USBLS	5/07
Wood	Minnesota	Y	25305 FQ	37693 MW	68794 TQ	MNBLS	10/08-12/08
Wood	Missouri	Y	14520 FQ	17300 MW	24110 TQ	USBLS	5/07
Wood	New York	Y	23220 FQ	30980 MW	36940 TQ	USBLS	5/07
Wood	North Carolina	Y	22880 FQ	28190 MW	31890 TQ	USBLS	5/07
Wood	Ohio	Y	30040 FQ	39950 MW	48320 TQ	USBLS	5/07
Wood	Pennsylvania	Y	26080 FQ	32380 MW	37110 TQ	USBLS	5/07
Wood	Texas	Y	19410 FQ	22410 MW	28180 TQ	USBLS	5/07
Wood	Washington	H	14.59 FQ	15.93 MW	17.22 TQ	WABLS	3/08
Wood	Wisconsin	Y	28370 FQ	34230 MW	42780 TQ	USBLS	5/07
Paving, Surfacing, and Tamping Equipment Operator							
	Alabama	Y	22170 FQ	25860 MW	29950 TQ	USBLS	5/07
	Birmingham-Hoover MSA, AL	Y	22340 FQ	27440 MW	31870 TQ	USBLS	5/07
	Montgomery MSA, AL	Y	23030 FQ	25780 MW	28280 TQ	USBLS	5/07
	Arizona	Y	32750 FQ	37440 MW	44050 TQ	USBLS	5/07
	Phoenix-Mesa-Scottsdale MSA, AZ	Y	34730 FQ	40360 MW	49990 TQ	USBLS	5/07
	Tucson MSA, AZ	Y	25550 FQ	33370 MW	40390 TQ	USBLS	5/07
	Arkansas	Y	22920 FQ	27500 MW	33150 TQ	USBLS	5/07
	Little Rock-North Little Rock MSA, AR	Y	25770 FQ	28980 MW	36130 TQ	USBLS	5/07
	California	H	18.45 FQ	22.78 MW	28.91 TQ	CABLS	1/08-3/08

AE Average entry wage	**AW** Average wage paid	**FQ** First quartile wage	**LO** Lowest wage paid	**MTC** Median total compensation	**TCC** Total cash compensation
AER Average entry range	**AWR** Average wage range	**H** Hourly	**LR** Low end range	**MW** Median wage paid	**TQ** Third quartile wage
AEX Average experienced wage	**AXR** Average experienced range	**HI** Highest wage paid	**M** Monthly	**MWR** Median wage range	**W** Weekly
ATC Average total compensation	**D** Daily	**HR** High end range	**MCC** Median cash compensation	**S** See annotated source	**Y** Yearly

Occupation/Type/Industry	Location	Per	Low	Mid	High	Source	Date
Paving, Surfacing, and Tamping Equipment Operator							
	Los Angeles-Long Beach-Glendale PMSA, CA	H	18.01 FQ	22.45 MW	31.29 TQ	CABLS	1/08-3/08
	Oakland-Fremont-Hayward MSA, CA	H	23.28 FQ	28.38 MW	32.84 TQ	CABLS	1/08-3/08
	Riverside-San Bernardino-Ontario MSA, CA	H	17.99 FQ	23.10 MW	29.13 TQ	CABLS	1/08-3/08
	Sacramento-Arden Arcade-Roseville MSA, CA	H	17.09 FQ	21.97 MW	27.19 TQ	CABLS	1/08-3/08
	San Diego-Carlsbad-San Marcos MSA, CA	H	18.59 FQ	23.31 MW	30.95 TQ	CABLS	1/08-3/08
	San Francisco-San Mateo-Redwood PMSA, CA	H	23.04 FQ	30.05 MW	37.18 TQ	CABLS	1/08-3/08
	San Jose-Sunnyvale-Santa Clara MSA, CA	H	18.89 FQ	22.30 MW	25.26 TQ	CABLS	1/08-3/08
	Santa Ana-Anaheim-Irvine PMSA, CA	Y	37170 FQ	43980 MW	53450 TQ	USBLS	5/07
	Colorado	Y	31920 FQ	38040 MW	44280 TQ	USBLS	5/07
	Denver-Aurora MSA, CO	Y	32000 FQ	40110 MW	46470 TQ	USBLS	5/07
	Fort Collins-Loveland MSA, CO	Y	32920 FQ	38610 MW	49900 TQ	USBLS	5/07
	Connecticut	H	12.76 AE	19.66 MW		CTBLS	1/08-3/08
	Bridgeport-Stamford-Norwalk MSA, CT	Y	22230 FQ	35430 MW	50160 TQ	USBLS	5/07
	Hartford-West Hartford-East Hartford MSA, CT	Y	33780 FQ	39770 MW	48520 TQ	USBLS	5/07
	Delaware	Y	31680 FQ	36740 MW	47050 TQ	USBLS	5/07
	Wilmington PMSA, DE-MD-NJ	Y	32110 FQ	36830 MW	47470 TQ	USBLS	5/07
	Washington-Arlington-Alexandria MSA, DC-VA-MD-WV	Y	29070 FQ	33980 MW	38740 TQ	USBLS	5/07
	Florida	Y	24420 FQ	28300 MW	33000 TQ	USBLS	5/07
	Fort Lauderdale-Pompano Beach-Deerfield Beach PMSA, FL	Y	24970 FQ	30300 MW	35540 TQ	USBLS	5/07
	Jacksonville MSA, FL	Y	24560 FQ	29340 MW	38390 TQ	USBLS	5/07
	Miami-Fort Lauderdale-Miami Beach MSA, FL	Y	25320 FQ	29400 MW	34840 TQ	USBLS	5/07
	Orlando-Kissimmee MSA, FL	Y	22710 FQ	26410 MW	31030 TQ	USBLS	5/07
	Tampa-St. Petersburg-Clearwater MSA, FL	Y	25020 FQ	28470 MW	33970 TQ	USBLS	5/07
	West Palm Beach-Boca Raton-Boynton Beach PMSA, FL	Y	25460 FQ	29000 MW	34290 TQ	USBLS	5/07
	Georgia	Y	22310 FQ	27130 MW	31630 TQ	USBLS	5/07
	Atlanta-Sandy Springs-Marietta MSA, GA	Y	25570 FQ	29110 MW	34480 TQ	USBLS	5/07
	Savannah MSA, GA	Y	24950 FQ	28370 MW	31370 TQ	USBLS	5/07
	Hawaii	Y	62020 FQ	68440 MW	74090 TQ	USBLS	5/07
	Honolulu MSA, HI	Y	56350 FQ	67810 MW	73870 TQ	USBLS	5/07
	Idaho	Y	26240 FQ	30390 MW	35350 TQ	USBLS	5/07
	Boise City-Nampa MSA, ID	Y	28260 FQ	33070 MW	37590 TQ	USBLS	5/07
	Illinois	Y	37450 FQ	47960 MW	64850 TQ	USBLS	5/07
	Chicago-Naperville-Joliet MSA, IL-IN-WI	Y	36680 FQ	49180 MW	73260 TQ	USBLS	5/07
	Indiana	Y	27310 FQ	35910 MW	48190 TQ	USBLS	5/07
	Gary PMSA, IN	Y	28640 FQ	34040 MW	40420 TQ	USBLS	5/07
	Indianapolis-Carmel MSA, IN	Y	28300 FQ	38140 MW	51990 TQ	USBLS	5/07
	Iowa	Y	28710 FQ	34390 MW	40000 TQ	USBLS	5/07
	Des Moines-West Des Moines MSA, IA	Y	29180 FQ	32210 MW	48230 TQ	USBLS	5/07
	Dubuque MSA, IA	Y	34400 FQ	38030 MW	46650 TQ	USBLS	5/07
	Kansas	Y	23030 FQ	27720 MW	33470 TQ	USBLS	5/07
	Topeka MSA, KS	Y	24560 FQ	28370 MW	32100 TQ	USBLS	5/07
	Wichita MSA, KS	Y	28240 FQ	32470 MW	35650 TQ	USBLS	5/07
	Kentucky	Y	30929 FQ	35554 MW	40963 TQ	KYBLS	2008
	Louisville-Jefferson County MSA, KY-IN	Y	31390 FQ	37730 MW	44910 TQ	USBLS	5/07
	Louisiana	H	11.18 FQ	13.46 MW	15.76 TQ	LABLS	1/08-3/08
	Baton Rouge MSA, LA	Y	26150 FQ	30160 MW	35400 TQ	USBLS	5/07
	New Orleans-Metairie-Kenner MSA, LA	Y	24190 FQ	28640 MW	33070 TQ	USBLS	5/07

AE	Average entry wage	AW	Average wage paid	FQ	First quartile wage
AER	Average entry range	AWR	Average wage range	H	Hourly
AEX	Average experienced wage	AXR	Average experienced range	HI	Highest wage paid
ATC	Average total compensation	D	Daily	HR	High end range

LO	Lowest wage paid	MTC	Median total compensation	TCC	Total cash compensation
LR	Low end range	MW	Median wage paid	TQ	Third quartile wage
M	Monthly	MWR	Median wage range	W	Weekly
MCC	Median cash compensation	S	See annotated source	Y	Yearly

Occupation/Type/Industry	Location	Per	Low	Mid	High	Source	Date
Paving, Surfacing, and Tamping Equipment Operator	Maine	Y	22010 FQ	25520 MW	30060 TQ	USBLS	5/07
	Portland-South Portland-Biddeford MSA, ME	Y	25950 FQ	30800 MW	37420 TQ	USBLS	5/07
	Maryland	Y		32750 MW		MDBLS	3/08
	Baltimore-Towson MSA, MD	Y	25510 FQ	32060 MW	41000 TQ	USBLS	5/07
	Bethesda-Gaithersburg-Frederick PMSA, MD	Y	28730 FQ	32320 MW	37950 TQ	USBLS	5/07
	Massachusetts	Y	34880 FQ	39810 MW	46910 TQ	USBLS	5/07
	Boston-Cambridge-Quincy NECTA, MA	Y	33630 FQ	39320 MW	48670 TQ	USBLS	5/07
	Worcester MSA, MA-CT	Y	33790 FQ	36020 MW	38410 TQ	USBLS	5/07
	Michigan	Y	27220 FQ	39440 MW	50230 TQ	USBLS	5/07
	Detroit-Warren-Livonia MSA, MI	Y	23990 FQ	40490 MW	49820 TQ	USBLS	5/07
	Grand Rapids-Wyoming MSA, MI	Y	34800 FQ	50010 MW	56920 TQ	USBLS	5/07
	Warren-Troy-Farmington Hills PMSA, MI	Y	22770 FQ	35010 MW	47460 TQ	USBLS	5/07
	Minnesota	Y	36674 FQ	44336 MW	55328 TQ	MNBLS	10/08-12/08
	Duluth-Superior MSA, MN-WI	Y	38108 FQ	58026 MW	63601 TQ	MNBLS	10/08-12/08
	Minneapolis-Saint Paul MSA, MN-WI	Y	38529 FQ	45727 MW	55022 TQ	MNBLS	10/08-12/08
	Mississippi	Y	21450 FQ	25050 MW	28430 TQ	USBLS	5/07
	Hattiesburg MSA, MS	Y	19360 FQ	22520 MW	25560 TQ	USBLS	5/07
	Jackson MSA, MS	Y	19680 FQ	25660 MW	28890 TQ	USBLS	5/07
	Missouri	Y	26420 FQ	36730 MW	46680 TQ	USBLS	5/07
	Kansas City MSA, MO-KS	Y	25270 FQ	31100 MW	41170 TQ	USBLS	5/07
	St. Louis MSA, MO-IL	Y	29800 FQ	44140 MW	52540 TQ	USBLS	5/07
	Springfield MSA, MO	Y	33420 FQ	41010 MW	44770 TQ	USBLS	5/07
	Montana	Y	31170 FQ	35130 MW	40190 TQ	USBLS	5/07
	Nebraska	Y	24040 FQ	27620 MW	31790 TQ	USBLS	5/07
	Omaha-Council Bluffs MSA, NE-IA	Y	26760 FQ	29970 MW	34950 TQ	USBLS	5/07
	Nevada	H	16.59 FQ	20.10 MW	24.20 TQ	NVBLS	5/08
	Las Vegas-Paradise MSA, NV	H	15.75 FQ	19.20 MW	24.27 TQ	NVBLS	5/08
	New Hampshire	H	15.74 AE	18.36 MW	22.17 AEX	NHBLS	6/08
	New Jersey	Y	31240 FQ	41770 MW	52930 TQ	USBLS	5/07
	Camden PMSA, NJ	Y	29010 FQ	37320 MW	44770 TQ	USBLS	5/07
	Edison PMSA, NJ	Y	43570 FQ	51710 MW	61550 TQ	USBLS	5/07
	Newark-Union PMSA, NJ-PA	Y	30310 FQ	40370 MW	52810 TQ	USBLS	5/07
	New Mexico	Y	25470 FQ	28720 MW	32160 TQ	USBLS	5/07
	Albuquerque MSA, NM	Y	25160 FQ	28900 MW	33100 TQ	USBLS	5/07
	New York	Y	37560 FQ	48890 MW	58310 TQ	USBLS	5/07
	Albany-Schenectady-Troy MSA, NY	Y	36410 FQ	40970 MW	55320 TQ	USBLS	5/07
	Buffalo-Niagara Falls MSA, NY	Y	26750 FQ	42520 MW	50730 TQ	USBLS	5/07
	Nassau-Suffolk PMSA, NY	Y	29820 FQ	39180 MW	53080 TQ	USBLS	5/07
	New York-Northern New Jersey-Long Island MSA, NY-NJ-PA	Y	39030 FQ	49680 MW	60080 TQ	USBLS	5/07
	North Carolina	Y	23780 FQ	27560 MW	31080 TQ	USBLS	5/07
	Charlotte-Gastonia-Concord MSA, NC-SC	Y	26070 FQ	30120 MW	34040 TQ	USBLS	5/07
	Raleigh-Cary MSA, NC	Y	25710 FQ	28300 MW	30880 TQ	MDBLS	5/07
	North Dakota	Y	27040 FQ	33490 MW	38530 TQ	USBLS	5/07
	Fargo MSA, ND-MN	Y	23420 FQ	33860 MW	39310 TQ	USBLS	5/07
	Ohio	Y	32160 FQ	39220 MW	48550 TQ	USBLS	5/07
	Cincinnati-Middletown MSA, OH-KY-IN	Y	30340 FQ	39840 MW	50090 TQ	USBLS	5/07
	Cleveland-Elyria-Mentor MSA, OH	Y	37630 FQ	41520 MW	49640 TQ	USBLS	5/07
	Columbus MSA, OH	Y	29830 FQ	36870 MW	46230 TQ	USBLS	5/07
	Dayton MSA, OH	Y	27370 FQ	33330 MW	43940 TQ	USBLS	5/07
	Oklahoma	Y	22740 FQ	26300 MW	30500 TQ	USBLS	5/07
	Oklahoma City MSA, OK	Y	24100 FQ	27960 MW	31910 TQ	USBLS	5/07
	Tulsa MSA, OK	Y	25150 FQ	28800 MW	32780 TQ	USBLS	5/07
	Oregon	H	15.69 FQ	19.47 MW	22.94 TQ	ORBLS	5/08
	Portland-Vancouver-Beaverton MSA, OR-WA	Y	30910 FQ	37650 MW	48630 TQ	USBLS	5/07
	Pennsylvania	Y	26220 FQ	32500 MW	40810 TQ	USBLS	5/07

AE	Average entry wage	AW	Average wage paid	FQ	First quartile wage
AER	Average entry range	AWR	Average wage range	H	Hourly
AEX	Average experienced wage	AXR	Average experienced range	HI	Highest wage paid
ATC	Average total compensation	D	Daily	HR	High end range

LO	Lowest wage paid	MTC	Median total compensation	TCC	Total cash compensation
LR	Low end range	MW	Median wage paid	TQ	Third quartile wage
M	Monthly	MWR	Median wage range	W	Weekly
MCC	Median cash compensation	S	See annotated source	Y	Yearly

Occupation/Type/Industry	Location	Per	Low	Mid	High	Source	Date
Paving, Surfacing, and Tamping Equipment Operator	Allentown-Bethlehem-Easton MSA, PA-NJ	Y	20650 FQ	35660 MW	44550 TQ	USBLS	5/07
	Lancaster MSA, PA	Y	29800 FQ	33920 MW	37800 TQ	USBLS	5/07
	Philadelphia-Camden-Wilmington MSA, PA-NJ-DE-MD	Y	30640 FQ	36320 MW	43400 TQ	USBLS	5/07
	Pittsburgh MSA, PA	Y	29300 FQ	40390 MW	48890 TQ	USBLS	5/07
	Providence-Fall River-Warwick MSA, RI-MA	Y	26510 FQ	39720 MW	46840 TQ	USBLS	5/07
	South Carolina	Y	23570 FQ	27560 MW	31710 TQ	USBLS	5/07
	Charleston-North Charleston MSA, SC	Y	24120 FQ	29710 MW	35710 TQ	USBLS	5/07
	Columbia MSA, SC	Y	23390 FQ	26890 MW	31730 TQ	USBLS	5/07
	Spartanburg MSA, SC	Y	22980 FQ	28190 MW	36010 TQ	USBLS	5/07
	South Dakota	Y	27738 FQ	33828 MW	41550 TQ	SDBLS	7/08-9/08
	Sioux Falls MSA, SD	Y	26671 FQ	32681 MW	38882 TQ	SDBLS	7/08-9/08
	Tennessee	Y	25750 FQ	29380 MW	33800 TQ	USBLS	5/07
	Memphis MSA, TN-MS-AR	Y	25990 FQ	29000 MW	32690 TQ	USBLS	5/07
	Nashville-Davidson-Murfreesboro MSA, TN	Y	27170 FQ	30680 MW	34960 TQ	USBLS	5/07
	Texas	Y	21880 FQ	25840 MW	31310 TQ	USBLS	5/07
	Austin-Round Rock MSA, TX	Y	22500 FQ	25920 MW	32030 TQ	USBLS	5/07
	Dallas-Fort Worth-Arlington MSA, TX	Y	21870 FQ	27550 MW	34390 TQ	USBLS	5/07
	El Paso MSA, TX	Y	20200 FQ	23190 MW	27880 TQ	USBLS	5/07
	Houston-Sugar Land-Baytown MSA, TX	Y	23590 FQ	27300 MW	31750 TQ	USBLS	5/07
	San Antonio MSA, TX	Y	22680 FQ	26120 MW	31700 TQ	USBLS	5/07
	Utah	Y	26140 FQ	30760 MW	40890 TQ	USBLS	5/07
	Salt Lake City MSA, UT	Y	29850 FQ	35430 MW	46020 TQ	USBLS	5/07
	Vermont	Y	26770 FQ	33200 MW	37390 TQ	USBLS	5/07
	Burlington-South Burlington MSA, VT	Y	31990 FQ	35290 MW	38720 TQ	USBLS	5/07
	Virginia	Y	26230 FQ	31430 MW	38320 TQ	USBLS	5/07
	Richmond MSA, VA	Y	24510 FQ	30430 MW	43460 TQ	USBLS	5/07
	Virginia Beach-Norfolk-Newport News MSA, VA-NC	Y	25500 FQ	29250 MW	37760 TQ	USBLS	5/07
	Washington	H	20.31 FQ	24.58 MW	30.29 TQ	WABLS	3/08
	Seattle-Tacoma-Bellevue MSA, WA	Y	40610 FQ	54660 MW	65470 TQ	USBLS	5/07
	West Virginia	Y	25988 FQ	32551 MW	56787 TQ	WVBLS	7/08-9/08
	Charleston MSA, WV	Y	67570 FQ	72260 MW	76950 TQ	USBLS	5/07
	Wisconsin	Y	35660 FQ	40720 MW	48620 TQ	USBLS	5/07
	Milwaukee-Waukesha-West Allis MSA, WI	Y	36470 FQ	41780 MW	47800 TQ	USBLS	5/07
	Wyoming	Y	25900 FQ	30593 MW	37841 TQ	WYBLS	9/08
	Cheyenne MSA, WY	Y	22987 FQ	24657 MW	26330 TQ	WYBLS	9/08
	Puerto Rico	Y	15730 FQ	18580 MW	23210 TQ	USBLS	5/07
	San Juan-Caguas-Guaynabo MSA, PR	Y	15830 FQ	18180 MW	22400 TQ	USBLS	5/07
	Virgin Islands	Y	22310 FQ	26360 MW	30620 TQ	USBLS	5/07
Payroll and Timekeeping Clerk	Alabama	Y	23760 FQ	29420 MW	36160 TQ	USBLS	5/07
	Birmingham-Hoover MSA, AL	Y	25870 FQ	31730 MW	38220 TQ	USBLS	5/07
	Tuscaloosa MSA, AL	Y	26080 FQ	30910 MW	37860 TQ	USBLS	5/07
	Alaska	Y	33450 FQ	39230 MW	47700 TQ	USBLS	5/07
	Anchorage MSA, AK	Y	33480 FQ	39470 MW	48520 TQ	USBLS	5/07
	Arizona	Y	26620 FQ	32790 MW	38720 TQ	USBLS	5/07
	Phoenix-Mesa-Scottsdale MSA, AZ	Y	26890 FQ	33290 MW	39310 TQ	USBLS	5/07
	Tucson MSA, AZ	Y	27280 FQ	33150 MW	38130 TQ	USBLS	5/07
	Arkansas	Y	22930 FQ	28150 MW	34380 TQ	USBLS	5/07
	Little Rock-North Little Rock MSA, AR	Y	26370 FQ	32270 MW	38200 TQ	USBLS	5/07
	California	H	15.25 FQ	18.73 MW	22.62 TQ	CABLS	1/08-3/08
	Los Angeles-Long Beach-Glendale PMSA, CA	H	15.60 FQ	18.94 MW	22.48 TQ	CABLS	1/08-3/08
	Oakland-Fremont-Hayward MSA, CA	H	17.57 FQ	21.63 MW	25.07 TQ	CABLS	1/08-3/08
	Riverside-San Bernardino-Ontario MSA, CA	H	13.90 FQ	17.07 MW	20.12 TQ	CABLS	1/08-3/08

AE	Average entry wage	AW	Average wage paid	FQ	First quartile wage	LO	Lowest wage paid	MTC	Median total compensation	TCC	Total cash compensation
AER	Average entry range	AWR	Average wage range	H	Hourly	LR	Low end range	MW	Median wage paid	TQ	Third quartile wage
AEX	Average experienced wage	AXR	Average experienced range	HI	Highest wage paid	M	Monthly	MWR	Median wage range	W	Weekly
ATC	Average total compensation	D	Daily	HR	High end range	MCC	Median cash compensation	S	See annotated source	Y	Yearly

1197

Occupation/Type/Industry	Location	Per	Low	Mid	High	Source	Date
Payroll and Timekeeping Clerk	Sacramento-Arden Arcade-Roseville MSA, CA	H	16.89 FQ	19.78 MW	22.81 TQ	CABLS	1/08-3/08
	San Diego-Carlsbad-San Marcos MSA, CA	H	15.32 FQ	18.52 MW	22.10 TQ	CABLS	1/08-3/08
	San Francisco-San Mateo-Redwood PMSA, CA	H	19.82 FQ	22.94 MW	25.94 TQ	CABLS	1/08-3/08
	San Jose-Sunnyvale-Santa Clara MSA, CA	H	17.26 FQ	21.35 MW	25.57 TQ	CABLS	1/08-3/08
	Santa Ana-Anaheim-Irvine PMSA, CA	Y	32910 FQ	38930 MW	46290 TQ	USBLS	5/07
	Colorado	Y	31030 FQ	37170 MW	43890 TQ	USBLS	5/07
	Denver-Aurora MSA, CO	Y	33300 FQ	38680 MW	44910 TQ	USBLS	5/07
	Connecticut	H	15.52 AE	19.95 MW		CTBLS	1/08-3/08
	Bridgeport-Stamford-Norwalk MSA, CT	Y	37020 FQ	43470 MW	49830 TQ	USBLS	5/07
	Hartford-West Hartford-East Hartford MSA, CT	Y	35200 FQ	41110 MW	47570 TQ	USBLS	5/07
	New Haven MSA, CT	Y	33820 FQ	38380 MW	44540 TQ	USBLS	5/07
	Delaware	Y	28160 FQ	34780 MW	39820 TQ	USBLS	5/07
	Dover MSA, DE	Y	23040 FQ	30450 MW	39400 TQ	USBLS	5/07
	Wilmington PMSA, DE-MD-NJ	Y	30290 FQ	35770 MW	40760 TQ	USBLS	5/07
	District of Columbia	Y	36470 FQ	43890 MW	49340 TQ	USBLS	5/07
	Washington-Arlington-Alexandria MSA, DC-VA-MD-WV	Y	34510 FQ	41690 MW	47730 TQ	USBLS	5/07
	Florida	Y	27600 FQ	32270 MW	38290 TQ	USBLS	5/07
	Fort Lauderdale-Pompano Beach-Deerfield Beach PMSA, FL	Y	30690 FQ	36210 MW	43240 TQ	USBLS	5/07
	Jacksonville MSA, FL	Y	27110 FQ	31610 MW	37000 TQ	USBLS	5/07
	Miami-Fort Lauderdale-Miami Beach MSA, FL	Y	31000 FQ	35980 MW	41780 TQ	USBLS	5/07
	Orlando-Kissimmee MSA, FL	Y	26360 FQ	32050 MW	37980 TQ	USBLS	5/07
	Tampa-St. Petersburg-Clearwater MSA, FL	Y	27010 FQ	31170 MW	36770 TQ	USBLS	5/07
	West Palm Beach-Boca Raton-Boynton Beach PMSA, FL	Y	31240 FQ	35930 MW	40710 TQ	USBLS	5/07
	Georgia	Y	26410 FQ	32750 MW	39620 TQ	USBLS	5/07
	Atlanta-Sandy Springs-Marietta MSA, GA	Y	28660 FQ	34960 MW	42030 TQ	USBLS	5/07
	Hawaii	Y	30660 FQ	36470 MW	42110 TQ	USBLS	5/07
	Honolulu MSA, HI	Y	31540 FQ	37240 MW	42400 TQ	USBLS	5/07
	Idaho	Y	23240 FQ	28980 MW	33930 TQ	USBLS	5/07
	Boise City-Nampa MSA, ID	Y	24070 FQ	29590 MW	34270 TQ	USBLS	5/07
	Pocatello MSA, ID	Y	17220 FQ	21090 MW	29710 TQ	USBLS	5/07
	Illinois	Y	28190 FQ	35220 MW	43030 TQ	USBLS	5/07
	Chicago-Naperville-Joliet MSA, IL-IN-WI	Y	29810 FQ	36550 MW	45150 TQ	USBLS	5/07
	Rockford MSA, IL	Y	27940 FQ	33020 MW	38960 TQ	USBLS	5/07
	Indiana	Y	26390 FQ	31670 MW	37560 TQ	USBLS	5/07
	Gary PMSA, IN	Y	27470 FQ	32260 MW	40780 TQ	USBLS	5/07
	Indianapolis-Carmel MSA, IN	Y	29000 FQ	34630 MW	40290 TQ	USBLS	5/07
	Iowa	Y	25990 FQ	31870 MW	38080 TQ	USBLS	5/07
	Davenport-Moline-Rock Island MSA, IA-IL	Y	19760 FQ	30910 MW	38050 TQ	USBLS	5/07
	Des Moines-West Des Moines MSA, IA	Y	32450 FQ	37410 MW	42730 TQ	USBLS	5/07
	Dubuque MSA, IA	Y	23680 FQ	30930 MW	35360 TQ	USBLS	5/07
	Sioux City MSA, IA-NE-SD	Y	25810 FQ	29560 MW	35170 TQ	USBLS	5/07
	Kansas	Y	25680 FQ	30940 MW	36780 TQ	USBLS	5/07
	Lawrence MSA, KS	Y	26640 FQ	30710 MW	36790 TQ	USBLS	5/07
	Wichita MSA, KS	Y	26410 FQ	31020 MW	36590 TQ	USBLS	5/07
	Kentucky	Y	26002 FQ	31691 MW	37948 TQ	KYBLS	2008
	Louisville-Jefferson County MSA, KY-IN	Y	27660 FQ	32610 MW	37820 TQ	USBLS	5/07
	Owensboro MSA, KY	Y	24290 FQ	29210 MW	34910 TQ	USBLS	5/07
	Louisiana	H	11.21 FQ	13.58 MW	16.58 TQ	LABLS	1/08-3/08
	Baton Rouge MSA, LA	Y	23430 FQ	28570 MW	34630 TQ	USBLS	5/07
	New Orleans-Metairie-Kenner MSA, LA	Y	24190 FQ	29140 MW	35420 TQ	USBLS	5/07
	Maine	Y	26440 FQ	30470 MW	35970 TQ	USBLS	5/07

AE Average entry wage
AER Average entry range
AEX Average experienced wage
ATC Average total compensation
AW Average wage paid
AWR Average wage range
AXR Average experienced range
D Daily
FQ First quartile wage
H Hourly
HI Highest wage paid
HR High end range
LO Lowest wage paid
LR Low end range
M Monthly
MCC Median cash compensation
MTC Median total compensation
MW Median wage paid
MWR Median wage range
S See annotated source
TCC Total cash compensation
TQ Third quartile wage
W Weekly
Y Yearly

1198

Occupation/Type/Industry	Location	Per	Low	Mid	High	Source	Date
Payroll and Timekeeping Clerk	Portland-South Portland-Biddeford MSA, ME	Y	28290 FQ	33180 MW	38180 TQ	USBLS	5/07
	Maryland	Y		38650 MW		MDBLS	3/08
	Baltimore-Towson MSA, MD	Y	32330 FQ	37970 MW	44970 TQ	USBLS	5/07
	Bethesda-Gaithersburg-Frederick PMSA, MD	Y	33150 FQ	41060 MW	48820 TQ	USBLS	5/07
	Massachusetts	Y	32310 FQ	38600 MW	46090 TQ	USBLS	5/07
	Boston-Cambridge-Quincy NECTA, MA	Y	34830 FQ	40990 MW	48000 TQ	USBLS	5/07
	Springfield MSA, MA-CT	Y	28550 FQ	33310 MW	40240 TQ	USBLS	5/07
	Worcester MSA, MA-CT	Y	27510 FQ	34930 MW	41290 TQ	USBLS	5/07
	Michigan	Y	28340 FQ	34000 MW	39580 TQ	USBLS	5/07
	Detroit-Warren-Livonia MSA, MI	Y	31350 FQ	36030 MW	41900 TQ	USBLS	5/07
	Grand Rapids-Wyoming MSA, MI	Y	27270 FQ	31700 MW	37870 TQ	USBLS	5/07
	Lansing-East Lansing MSA, MI	Y	26690 FQ	32360 MW	37690 TQ	USBLS	5/07
	Muskegon-Norton Shores MSA, MI	Y	29360 FQ	34030 MW	38050 TQ	USBLS	5/07
	Warren-Troy-Farmington Hills PMSA, MI	Y	30980 FQ	36410 MW	43030 TQ	USBLS	5/07
	Minnesota	Y	32098 FQ	37479 MW	43432 TQ	MNBLS	10/08-12/08
	Duluth-Superior MSA, MN-WI	Y	27258 FQ	32462 MW	37614 TQ	MNBLS	10/08-12/08
	Minneapolis-Saint Paul MSA, MN-WI	Y	34294 FQ	39217 MW	45763 TQ	MNBLS	10/08-12/08
	Rochester MSA, MN	Y	31332 FQ	35540 MW	39547 TQ	MNBLS	10/08-12/08
	Mississippi	Y	23600 FQ	28570 MW	34160 TQ	USBLS	5/07
	Jackson MSA, MS	Y	27790 FQ	33460 MW	39900 TQ	USBLS	5/07
	Missouri	Y	26330 FQ	33090 MW	39140 TQ	USBLS	5/07
	Jefferson City MSA, MO	Y	14900 FQ	21290 MW	34280 TQ	USBLS	5/07
	Kansas City MSA, MO-KS	Y	29450 FQ	35010 MW	40290 TQ	USBLS	5/07
	St. Louis MSA, MO-IL	Y	27860 FQ	34480 MW	39890 TQ	USBLS	5/07
	Springfield MSA, MO	Y	20420 FQ	24110 MW	30980 TQ	USBLS	5/07
	Montana	Y	23730 FQ	28690 MW	33870 TQ	USBLS	5/07
	Billings MSA, MT	Y	23050 FQ	28900 MW	35470 TQ	USBLS	5/07
	Nebraska	Y	26570 FQ	31960 MW	39230 TQ	USBLS	5/07
	Lincoln MSA, NE	Y	26780 FQ	32120 MW	37460 TQ	USBLS	5/07
	Omaha-Council Bluffs MSA, NE-IA	Y	28710 FQ	34360 MW	41010 TQ	USBLS	5/07
	Nevada	H	13.69 FQ	16.49 MW	19.30 TQ	NVBLS	5/08
	Las Vegas-Paradise MSA, NV	H	14.04 FQ	16.79 MW	19.34 TQ	NVBLS	5/08
	New Hampshire	H	13.04 AE	16.76 MW	18.99 AEX	NHBLS	6/08
	Manchester MSA, NH	Y	34020 FQ	38800 MW	44160 TQ	USBLS	5/07
	Nashua NECTA, NH-MA	Y	30040 FQ	33390 MW	36560 TQ	USBLS	5/07
	Portsmouth MSA, NH-ME	Y	33470 FQ	38290 MW	51230 TQ	USBLS	5/07
	Rochester-Dover MSA, NH-ME	Y	31930 FQ	37060 MW	43980 TQ	USBLS	5/07
	New Jersey	Y	31810 FQ	38420 MW	46710 TQ	USBLS	5/07
	Camden PMSA, NJ	Y	31930 FQ	36610 MW	42410 TQ	USBLS	5/07
	Edison PMSA, NJ	Y	30920 FQ	36490 MW	44790 TQ	USBLS	5/07
	Newark-Union PMSA, NJ-PA	Y	32310 FQ	39590 MW	47630 TQ	USBLS	5/07
	Ocean City MSA, NJ	Y	24630 FQ	29130 MW	43170 TQ	USBLS	5/07
	Vineland-Millville-Bridgeton MSA, NJ	Y	28820 FQ	33680 MW	42750 TQ	USBLS	5/07
	New Mexico	Y	21560 FQ	27940 MW	33180 TQ	USBLS	5/07
	Albuquerque MSA, NM	Y	20600 FQ	27430 MW	34430 TQ	USBLS	5/07
	Farmington MSA, NM	Y	22190 FQ	30350 MW	35030 TQ	USBLS	5/07
	New York	Y	29730 FQ	35230 MW	42380 TQ	USBLS	5/07
	Albany-Schenectady-Troy MSA, NY	Y	29720 FQ	34610 MW	40290 TQ	USBLS	5/07
	Buffalo-Niagara Falls MSA, NY	Y	27290 FQ	32110 MW	39180 TQ	USBLS	5/07
	Nassau-Suffolk PMSA, NY	Y	33830 FQ	39550 MW	46440 TQ	USBLS	5/07
	New York-Northern New Jersey-Long Island MSA, NY-NJ-PA	Y	31180 FQ	37270 MW	45210 TQ	USBLS	5/07
	Utica-Rome MSA, NY	Y	27390 FQ	32220 MW	37920 TQ	USBLS	5/07
	North Carolina	Y	25910 FQ	31330 MW	37240 TQ	USBLS	5/07
	Charlotte-Gastonia-Concord MSA, NC-SC	Y	27730 FQ	32920 MW	39140 TQ	USBLS	5/07
	Raleigh-Cary MSA, NC	Y	28170 FQ	33630 MW	39420 TQ	USBLS	5/07
	North Dakota	Y	23520 FQ	29430 MW	35460 TQ	USBLS	5/07

AE	Average entry wage	AW	Average wage paid	FQ	First quartile wage	LO	Lowest wage paid
AER	Average entry range	AWR	Average wage range	H	Hourly	LR	Low end range
AEX	Average experienced wage	AXR	Average experienced range	HI	Highest wage paid	M	Monthly
ATC	Average total compensation	D	Daily	HR	High end range	MCC	Median cash compensation

MTC	Median total compensation	TCC	Total cash compensation
MW	Median wage paid	TQ	Third quartile wage
MWR	Median wage range	W	Weekly
S	See annotated source	Y	Yearly

Occupation/Type/Industry	Location	Per	Low	Mid	High	Source	Date
Payroll and Timekeeping Clerk	Bismarck MSA, ND	Y	26790 FQ	31000 MW	36700 TQ	USBLS	5/07
	Fargo MSA, ND-MN	Y	27780 FQ	33030 MW	38270 TQ	USBLS	5/07
	Ohio	Y	27350 FQ	33060 MW	39130 TQ	USBLS	5/07
	Cincinnati-Middletown MSA, OH-KY-IN	Y	28490 FQ	34020 MW	40210 TQ	USBLS	5/07
	Cleveland-Elyria-Mentor MSA, OH	Y	30810 FQ	36200 MW	42140 TQ	USBLS	5/07
	Columbus MSA, OH	Y	29070 FQ	34700 MW	39830 TQ	USBLS	5/07
	Dayton MSA, OH	Y	27450 FQ	32350 MW	38560 TQ	USBLS	5/07
	Springfield MSA, OH	Y	27620 FQ	33870 MW	40540 TQ	USBLS	5/07
	Oklahoma	Y	23450 FQ	28570 MW	34850 TQ	USBLS	5/07
	Oklahoma City MSA, OK	Y	25040 FQ	29680 MW	36790 TQ	USBLS	5/07
	Tulsa MSA, OK	Y	23580 FQ	28620 MW	34310 TQ	USBLS	5/07
	Oregon	H	14.19 FQ	17.00 MW	20.04 TQ	ORBLS	5/08
	Portland-Vancouver-Beaverton MSA, OR-WA	Y	30790 FQ	36750 MW	43410 TQ	USBLS	5/07
	Pennsylvania	Y	26440 FQ	31850 MW	38180 TQ	USBLS	5/07
	Allentown-Bethlehem-Easton MSA, PA-NJ	Y	27440 FQ	31250 MW	36840 TQ	USBLS	5/07
	Philadelphia-Camden-Wilmington MSA, PA-NJ-DE-MD	Y	30490 FQ	35850 MW	41560 TQ	USBLS	5/07
	Pittsburgh MSA, PA	Y	25850 FQ	31800 MW	37980 TQ	USBLS	5/07
	Rhode Island	Y	29220 FQ	34900 MW	40930 TQ	USBLS	5/07
	Providence-Fall River-Warwick MSA, RI-MA	Y	28540 FQ	34250 MW	40610 TQ	USBLS	5/07
	South Carolina	Y	24690 FQ	30240 MW	36730 TQ	USBLS	5/07
	Charleston-North Charleston MSA, SC	Y	26190 FQ	33410 MW	39770 TQ	USBLS	5/07
	Columbia MSA, SC	Y	27140 FQ	32260 MW	37310 TQ	USBLS	5/07
	South Dakota	Y	25350 FQ	28507 MW	31731 TQ	SDBLS	7/08-9/08
	Sioux Falls MSA, SD	Y	26039 FQ	29112 MW	32258 TQ	SDBLS	7/08-9/08
	Tennessee	Y	25810 FQ	30960 MW	37620 TQ	USBLS	5/07
	Memphis MSA, TN-MS-AR	Y	28140 FQ	33830 MW	41700 TQ	USBLS	5/07
	Nashville-Davidson-Murfreesboro MSA, TN	Y	28290 FQ	33720 MW	39700 TQ	USBLS	5/07
	Texas	Y	25820 FQ	31360 MW	38050 TQ	USBLS	5/07
	Austin-Round Rock MSA, TX	Y	25770 FQ	32700 MW	39420 TQ	USBLS	5/07
	Dallas-Fort Worth-Arlington MSA, TX	Y	27470 FQ	33440 MW	39630 TQ	USBLS	5/07
	El Paso MSA, TX	Y	24560 FQ	28860 MW	34030 TQ	USBLS	5/07
	Houston-Sugar Land-Baytown MSA, TX	Y	27560 FQ	33680 MW	40480 TQ	USBLS	5/07
	San Antonio MSA, TX	Y	25270 FQ	31290 MW	37370 TQ	USBLS	5/07
	Utah	Y	26280 FQ	31630 MW	37860 TQ	USBLS	5/07
	Salt Lake City MSA, UT	Y	28050 FQ	33580 MW	39220 TQ	USBLS	5/07
	Vermont	Y	24400 FQ	30290 MW	36540 TQ	USBLS	5/07
	Burlington-South Burlington MSA, VT	Y	28860 FQ	33840 MW	38680 TQ	USBLS	5/07
	Virginia	Y	28470 FQ	35950 MW	43510 TQ	USBLS	5/07
	Richmond MSA, VA	Y	29080 FQ	34410 MW	39930 TQ	USBLS	5/07
	Virginia Beach-Norfolk-Newport News MSA, VA-NC	Y	27340 FQ	33210 MW	39220 TQ	USBLS	5/07
	Washington	H	15.06 FQ	18.18 MW	21.36 TQ	WABLS	3/08
	Bremerton-Silverdale MSA, WA	Y	33800 FQ	37840 MW	43350 TQ	USBLS	5/07
	Seattle-Tacoma-Bellevue MSA, WA	Y	33950 FQ	39580 MW	45510 TQ	USBLS	5/07
	West Virginia	Y	22980 FQ	29168 MW	35680 TQ	WVBLS	7/08-9/08
	Charleston MSA, WV	Y	23820 FQ	27960 MW	33930 TQ	USBLS	5/07
	Wisconsin	Y	27570 FQ	33240 MW	39210 TQ	USBLS	5/07
	Green Bay MSA, WI	Y	29250 FQ	33640 MW	38150 TQ	USBLS	5/07
	Milwaukee-Waukesha-West Allis MSA, WI	Y	30340 FQ	36620 MW	43650 TQ	USBLS	5/07
	Racine MSA, WI	Y	21640 FQ	27830 MW	34960 TQ	USBLS	5/07
	Wyoming	Y	25629 FQ	30828 MW	37491 TQ	WYBLS	9/08
	Cheyenne MSA, WY	Y	27912 FQ	32504 MW	42611 TQ	WYBLS	9/08
	Puerto Rico	Y	16470 FQ	20320 MW	26670 TQ	USBLS	5/07
	San Juan-Caguas-Guaynabo MSA, PR	Y	17540 FQ	21570 MW	27880 TQ	USBLS	5/07
	Virgin Islands	Y	19960 FQ	23040 MW	27260 TQ	USBLS	5/07
	Guam	Y	22510 FQ	26650 MW	31930 TQ	USBLS	5/07

AE Average entry wage	**AW** Average wage paid	**FQ** First quartile wage	**LO** Lowest wage paid	**MTC** Median total compensation	**TCC** Total cash compensation
AER Average entry range	**AWR** Average wage range	**H** Hourly	**LR** Low end range	**MW** Median wage paid	**TQ** Third quartile wage
AEX Average experienced wage	**AXR** Average experienced range	**HI** Highest wage paid	**M** Monthly	**MWR** Median wage range	**W** Weekly
ATC Average total compensation	**D** Daily	**HR** High end range	**MCC** Median cash compensation	**S** See annotated source	**Y** Yearly

Occupation/Type/Industry	Location	Per	Low	Mid	High	Source	Date
Payroll Technician							
Municipal Government	Walnut Creek, CA	Y	52915 LO		63855 HI	WCSWP	7/11/08
Pediatric Dermatologist							
Full-Time	United States	Y		203727 AW		SPDR	2008
Pediatrician	United States	Y		187500 ATC		MEDEC01	2007
General	Alabama	Y	106960 FQ	139610 MW		USBLS	5/07
General	Birmingham-Hoover MSA, AL	Y	88680 FQ	111630 MW		USBLS	5/07
General	Alaska	Y	89400 FQ	135070 MW		USBLS	5/07
General	Arizona	Y	108460 FQ			USBLS	5/07
General	Phoenix-Mesa-Scottsdale MSA, AZ	Y	105050 FQ			USBLS	5/07
General	Tucson MSA, AZ	Y	118410 FQ			USBLS	5/07
General	Arkansas	Y	91630 FQ	106030 MW		USBLS	5/07
General	California	H	59.16 FQ			CABLS	1/08-3/08
General	Los Angeles-Long Beach-Glendale PMSA, CA	H	60.56 FQ			CABLS	1/08-3/08
General	Oakland-Fremont-Hayward MSA, CA	H	55.16 FQ			CABLS	1/08-3/08
General	Oxnard-Thousand Oaks-Ventura MSA, CA	H	62.29 FQ			CABLS	1/08-3/08
General	Riverside-San Bernardino-Ontario MSA, CA	H	59.05 FQ			CABLS	1/08-3/08
General	Sacramento-Arden Arcade-Roseville MSA, CA	H	64.07 FQ			CABLS	1/08-3/08
General	San Diego-Carlsbad-San Marcos MSA, CA	H	58.25 FQ			CABLS	1/08-3/08
General	San Francisco-San Mateo-Redwood PMSA, CA	H	53.92 FQ	65.96 MW		CABLS	1/08-3/08
General	Santa Ana-Anaheim-Irvine PMSA, CA	Y	123520 FQ			USBLS	5/07
General	Colorado	Y	124690 FQ			USBLS	5/07
General	Denver-Aurora MSA, CO	Y	127850 FQ			USBLS	5/07
General	Connecticut	H	35.57 AE	65.25 MW		CTBLS	1/08-3/08
General	Bridgeport-Stamford-Norwalk MSA, CT	Y	108160 FQ			USBLS	5/07
General	Hartford-West Hartford-East Hartford MSA, CT	Y	59460 FQ	125570 MW		USBLS	5/07
General	New Haven MSA, CT	Y	97890 FQ	119620 MW		USBLS	5/07
General	Delaware	Y	117510 FQ	132530 MW		USBLS	5/07
General	Wilmington PMSA, DE-MD-NJ	Y	119030 FQ	133910 MW		USBLS	5/07
General	District of Columbia	Y	64630 FQ	73230 MW	84860 TQ	USBLS	5/07
General	Washington-Arlington-Alexandria MSA, DC-VA-MD-WV	Y	67810 FQ	84480 MW	123360 TQ	USBLS	5/07
General	Florida	Y	111450 FQ			USBLS	5/07
General	Miami-Fort Lauderdale-Miami Beach MSA, FL	Y	49190 FQ	121890 MW		USBLS	5/07
General	Orlando-Kissimmee MSA, FL	Y	123760 FQ			USBLS	5/07
General	Tampa-St. Petersburg-Clearwater MSA, FL	Y	118930 FQ	145510 MW		USBLS	5/07
General	Georgia	Y	45090 FQ	110430 MW		USBLS	5/07
General	Atlanta-Sandy Springs-Marietta MSA, GA	Y	43120 FQ	47640 MW	131380 TQ	USBLS	5/07
General	Hawaii	Y	102070 FQ	136180 MW		USBLS	5/07
General	Honolulu MSA, HI	Y	96940 FQ	124740 MW		USBLS	5/07
General	Idaho	Y	93020 FQ	139430 MW		USBLS	5/07
General	Boise City-Nampa MSA, ID	Y	112420 FQ			USBLS	5/07
General	Illinois	Y	100010 FQ	117130 MW		USBLS	5/07
General	Chicago-Naperville-Joliet MSA, IL-IN-WI	Y	87320 FQ	112580 MW	128830 TQ	USBLS	5/07
General	Indiana	Y	114760 FQ	135470 MW		USBLS	5/07
General	Indianapolis-Carmel MSA, IN	Y	113620 FQ	134280 MW		USBLS	5/07
General	Iowa	Y	99170 FQ			USBLS	5/07
General	Kansas	Y	84740 FQ	134890 MW		USBLS	5/07
General	Lexington-Fayette MSA, KY	Y	142470 FQ			USBLS	5/07
General	Louisiana	Y		170279 AW		LABLS	1/08-3/08
General	New Orleans-Metairie-Kenner MSA, LA	Y	99360 FQ	139740 MW		USBLS	5/07
General	Maine	Y	127280 FQ			USBLS	5/07

Occupation/Type/Industry	Location	Per	Low	Mid	High	Source	Date
Pediatrician							
General	Portland-South Portland-Biddeford MSA, ME	Y	121840 FQ			USBLS	5/07
General	Maryland	Y		117975 MW		MDBLS	3/08
General	Baltimore-Towson MSA, MD	Y	89900 FQ	103990 MW	126660 TQ	USBLS	5/07
General	Bethesda-Gaithersburg-Frederick PMSA, MD	Y	107940 FQ	121730 MW	141580 TQ	USBLS	5/07
General	Massachusetts	Y	114800 FQ	145240 MW		USBLS	5/07
General	Boston-Cambridge-Quincy NECTA, MA	Y	113310 FQ			USBLS	5/07
General	Michigan	Y	103040 FQ	133470 MW		USBLS	5/07
General	Detroit-Warren-Livonia MSA, MI	Y	102750 FQ	132830 MW		USBLS	5/07
General	Grand Rapids-Wyoming MSA, MI	Y	73270 FQ	117070 MW		USBLS	5/07
General	Warren-Troy-Farmington Hills PMSA, MI	Y	63540 FQ	111440 MW		USBLS	5/07
General	Minnesota	Y	137903 FQ	171099 AW		MNBLS	10/08-12/08
General	Minneapolis-Saint Paul MSA, MN-WI	Y	138028 FQ	170587 AW		MNBLS	10/08-12/08
General	Mississippi	Y	102820 FQ			USBLS	5/07
General	Jackson MSA, MS	Y	88230 FQ			USBLS	5/07
General	Missouri	Y	84370 FQ	144540 MW		USBLS	5/07
General	Kansas City MSA, MO-KS	Y	46650 FQ	87880 MW		USBLS	5/07
General	St. Louis MSA, MO-IL	Y	131490 FQ			USBLS	5/07
General	Montana	Y	48150 FQ	99300 MW		USBLS	5/07
General	Nebraska	Y	121870 FQ			USBLS	5/07
General	Nevada	H	65.99 FQ	89.45 AW		NVBLS	5/08
General	Las Vegas-Paradise MSA, NV	H		94.77 AW		NVBLS	5/08
General	New Hampshire	H	47.23 AE	74.68 AW	88.41 AEX	NHBLS	6/08
General	New Jersey	Y	109340 FQ	135270 MW		USBLS	5/07
General	Camden PMSA, NJ	Y	112660 FQ	135060 MW		USBLS	5/07
General	Edison PMSA, NJ	Y	96840 FQ	122740 MW		USBLS	5/07
General	Newark-Union PMSA, NJ-PA	Y	128290 FQ			USBLS	5/07
General	New Mexico	Y	114640 FQ			USBLS	5/07
General	New York	Y	108260 FQ	134110 MW		USBLS	5/07
General	Albany-Schenectady-Troy MSA, NY	Y	111750 FQ	128680 MW		USBLS	5/07
General	Nassau-Suffolk PMSA, NY	Y	124400 FQ			USBLS	5/07
General	New York-Northern New Jersey-Long Island MSA, NY-NJ-PA	Y	107930 FQ	136690 MW		USBLS	5/07
General	North Carolina	Y	124780 FQ			USBLS	5/07
General	Charlotte-Gastonia-Concord MSA, NC-SC	Y	122470 FQ			USBLS	5/07
General	Raleigh-Cary MSA, NC	Y	128190 FQ			USBLS	5/07
General	North Dakota	Y	62160 FQ	126980 MW		USBLS	5/07
General	Ohio	Y	111350 FQ	139690 MW		USBLS	5/07
General	Cincinnati-Middletown MSA, OH-KY-IN	Y	120450 FQ			USBLS	5/07
General	Cleveland-Elyria-Mentor MSA, OH	Y	110330 FQ	141330 MW		USBLS	5/07
General	Columbus MSA, OH	Y	108640 FQ	132700 MW		USBLS	5/07
General	Dayton MSA, OH	Y	124340 FQ			USBLS	5/07
General	Portland-Vancouver-Beaverton MSA, OR-WA	Y	132710 FQ			USBLS	5/07
General	Pennsylvania	Y	88520 FQ	127550 MW		USBLS	5/07
General	Allentown-Bethlehem-Easton MSA, PA-NJ	Y	134980 FQ			USBLS	5/07
General	Philadelphia-Camden-Wilmington MSA, PA-NJ-DE-MD	Y	86460 FQ	122890 MW		USBLS	5/07
General	Rhode Island	Y	116900 FQ	140410 MW		USBLS	5/07
General	Providence-Fall River-Warwick MSA, RI-MA	Y	114980 FQ	138910 MW		USBLS	5/07
General	South Carolina	Y	85560 FQ	137900 MW		USBLS	5/07
General	Columbia MSA, SC	Y	108970 FQ	136210 MW		USBLS	5/07
General	South Dakota	Y	140251 FQ			SDBLS	7/08-9/08
General	Tennessee	Y	115260 FQ			USBLS	5/07
General	Memphis MSA, TN-MS-AR	Y	99630 FQ	140120 MW		USBLS	5/07
General	Nashville-Davidson-Murfreesboro MSA, TN	Y	143210 FQ			USBLS	5/07

AE Average entry wage	**AW** Average wage paid	**FQ** First quartile wage	**LO** Lowest wage paid	**MTC** Median total compensation	**TCC** Total cash compensation
AER Average entry range	**AWR** Average wage range	**H** Hourly	**LR** Low end range	**MW** Median wage paid	**TQ** Third quartile wage
AEX Average experienced wage	**AXR** Average experienced range	**HI** Highest wage paid	**M** Monthly	**MWR** Median wage range	**W** Weekly
ATC Average total compensation	**D** Daily	**HR** High end range	**MCC** Median cash compensation	**S** See annotated source	**Y** Yearly

Occupation/Type/Industry	Location	Per	Low	Mid	High	Source	Date
Pediatrician							
General	Texas	Y	110810 FQ			USBLS	5/07
General	Austin-Round Rock MSA, TX	Y	135840 FQ			USBLS	5/07
General	Dallas-Fort Worth-Arlington MSA, TX	Y	120370 FQ			USBLS	5/07
General	El Paso MSA, TX	Y	104970 FQ			USBLS	5/07
General	Houston-Sugar Land-Baytown MSA, TX	Y	46440 FQ	119130 MW		USBLS	5/07
General	San Antonio MSA, TX	Y	117590 FQ			USBLS	5/07
General	Utah	Y	127920 FQ			USBLS	5/07
General	Salt Lake City MSA, UT	Y	111600 FQ			USBLS	5/07
General	Vermont	Y	65630 FQ	110220 MW		USBLS	5/07
General	Burlington-South Burlington MSA, VT	Y	50330 FQ	109980 MW		USBLS	5/07
General	Virginia	Y	82680 FQ	126910 MW		USBLS	5/07
General	Richmond MSA, VA	Y	116170 FQ			USBLS	5/07
General	Virginia Beach-Norfolk-Newport News MSA, VA-NC	Y	114300 FQ	136800 MW		USBLS	5/07
General	Washington	H	55.51 FQ	63.56 MW		WABLS	3/08
General	Seattle-Tacoma-Bellevue MSA, WA	Y	114680 FQ	127920 MW		USBLS	5/07
General	West Virginia	Y	122429 FQ	169246 AW		WVBLS	7/08-9/08
General	Wisconsin	Y	123440 FQ			USBLS	5/07
General	Milwaukee-Waukesha-West Allis MSA, WI	Y	113860 FQ	140540 MW		USBLS	5/07
General	Wyoming	Y	84460 FQ	114468 MW	132388 TQ	WYBLS	9/08
General	Puerto Rico	Y	57020 FQ	64390 MW	103610 TQ	USBLS	5/07
General	San Juan-Caguas-Guaynabo MSA, PR	Y	57930 FQ	66020 MW	109500 TQ	USBLS	5/07
Pedicab Driver	District of Columbia	H	19.00-23.00 AW			WPOST01	2009
Peer Review Nurse							
State Government	Ohio	H	24.90 LO		34.83 HI	ODAS	2008
Penal Industries Sales Representative	Ohio	H	17.22 LO		21.77 HI	ODAS	2008
Pension Fund Manager							
Municipal Government	Cincinnati, OH	Y	90676 LO		122414 HI	COHSS	10/08
Perfusionist	United States	Y		86400 AW		HCC01	2009
Perinatologist	United States	Y		356576 AW		CEJ01	2008
Perioperative Nurse							
Staff, Large Facility	United States	Y		62300 AW		AORN01	2007
Staff, Small Facility	United States	Y		59400 AW		AORN01	2007
Peripatologist							
State Government	Ohio	H	22.60 LO		30.13 HI	ODAS	2008
Permit Clerk							
County Government	Douglas County, GA	Y	25612 LO		40945 HI	AREGC	2007
Personal and Home Care Aide	Alabama	Y	13320 FQ	15540 MW	18080 TQ	USBLS	5/07
	Birmingham-Hoover MSA, AL	Y	14810 FQ	17020 MW	18910 TQ	USBLS	5/07
	Alaska	Y	23150 FQ	26850 MW	30800 TQ	USBLS	5/07
	Anchorage MSA, AK	Y	22640 FQ	26500 MW	30790 TQ	USBLS	5/07
	Arizona	Y	18090 FQ	20920 MW	23990 TQ	USBLS	5/07
	Phoenix-Mesa-Scottsdale MSA, AZ	Y	18440 FQ	21450 MW	24520 TQ	USBLS	5/07
	Tucson MSA, AZ	Y	17870 FQ	20040 MW	22750 TQ	USBLS	5/07
	Yuma MSA, AZ	Y	17670 FQ	22310 MW	27920 TQ	USBLS	5/07
	Arkansas	Y	14430 FQ	15750 MW	18360 TQ	USBLS	5/07
	Little Rock-North Little Rock MSA, AR	Y	14360 FQ	15550 MW	20010 TQ	USBLS	5/07
	California	H	8.89 FQ	10.11 MW	11.58 TQ	CABLS	1/08-3/08
	Fresno MSA, CA	H	8.12 FQ	8.87 MW	9.81 TQ	CABLS	1/08-3/08
	Los Angeles-Long Beach-Glendale PMSA, CA	H	8.63 FQ	9.56 MW	10.98 TQ	CABLS	1/08-3/08

AE	Average entry wage	AW	Average wage paid	FQ	First quartile wage
AER	Average entry range	AWR	Average wage range	H	Hourly
AEX	Average experienced wage	AXR	Average experienced range	HI	Highest wage paid
ATC	Average total compensation	D	Daily	HR	High end range

LO	Lowest wage paid	MTC	Median total compensation	TCC	Total cash compensation
LR	Low end range	MW	Median wage paid	TQ	Third quartile wage
M	Monthly	MWR	Median wage range	W	Weekly
MCC	Median cash compensation	S	See annotated source	Y	Yearly

Personal and Home Care Aide

Occupation/Type/Industry	Location	Per	Low	Mid	High	Source	Date
Personal and Home Care Aide	Oakland-Fremont-Hayward MSA, CA	H	10.15 FQ	11.76 MW	13.35 TQ	CABLS	1/08-3/08
	Riverside-San Bernardino-Ontario MSA, CA	H	8.67 FQ	9.59 MW	11.07 TQ	CABLS	1/08-3/08
	Sacramento-Arden Arcade-Roseville MSA, CA	H	10.15 FQ	10.98 MW	11.82 TQ	CABLS	1/08-3/08
	San Diego-Carlsbad-San Marcos MSA, CA	H	8.99 FQ	10.14 MW	11.56 TQ	CABLS	1/08-3/08
	San Francisco-San Mateo-Redwood PMSA, CA	H	10.31 FQ	11.23 MW	12.18 TQ	CABLS	1/08-3/08
	San Jose-Sunnyvale-Santa Clara MSA, CA	H	9.84 FQ	11.12 MW	12.39 TQ	CABLS	1/08-3/08
	Santa Ana-Anaheim-Irvine PMSA, CA	Y	19390 FQ	22340 MW	25140 TQ	USBLS	5/07
	Colorado	Y	16950 FQ	18660 MW	21050 TQ	USBLS	5/07
	Denver-Aurora MSA, CO	Y	17210 FQ	19020 MW	21420 TQ	USBLS	5/07
	Connecticut	H	8.76 AE	10.13 MW		CTBLS	1/08-3/08
	Bridgeport-Stamford-Norwalk MSA, CT	Y	17970 FQ	20300 MW	24130 TQ	USBLS	5/07
	Hartford-West Hartford-East Hartford MSA, CT	Y	18000 FQ	20080 MW	23210 TQ	USBLS	5/07
	Delaware	Y	19990 FQ	22530 MW	25580 TQ	USBLS	5/07
	Wilmington PMSA, DE-MD-NJ	Y	20320 FQ	23280 MW	26750 TQ	USBLS	5/07
	District of Columbia	Y	16810 FQ	20570 MW	24210 TQ	USBLS	5/07
	Washington-Arlington-Alexandria MSA, DC-VA-MD-WV	Y	18410 FQ	21350 MW	24500 TQ	USBLS	5/07
	Florida	Y	16580 FQ	18690 MW	22210 TQ	USBLS	5/07
	Fort Lauderdale-Pompano Beach-Deerfield Beach PMSA, FL	Y	15070 FQ	17020 MW	19350 TQ	USBLS	5/07
	Jacksonville MSA, FL	Y	17100 FQ	18540 MW	20360 TQ	USBLS	5/07
	Miami-Fort Lauderdale-Miami Beach MSA, FL	Y	16260 FQ	18050 MW	20450 TQ	USBLS	5/07
	Orlando-Kissimmee MSA, FL	Y	14280 FQ	14690 MW	15220 TQ	USBLS	5/07
	Pensacola-Ferry Pass-Brent MSA, FL	Y	16270 FQ	17480 MW	18690 TQ	USBLS	5/07
	Tampa-St. Petersburg-Clearwater MSA, FL	Y	16830 FQ	18910 MW	21790 TQ	USBLS	5/07
	West Palm Beach-Boca Raton-Boynton Beach PMSA, FL	Y	18100 FQ	19990 MW	22220 TQ	USBLS	5/07
	Georgia	Y	16620 FQ	18750 MW	21930 TQ	USBLS	5/07
	Atlanta-Sandy Springs-Marietta MSA, GA	Y	18440 FQ	21260 MW	23690 TQ	USBLS	5/07
	Hawaii	Y	15500 FQ	18900 MW	23240 TQ	USBLS	5/07
	Honolulu MSA, HI	Y	15610 FQ	16170 MW	22410 TQ	USBLS	5/07
	Idaho	Y	16090 FQ	17670 MW	19330 TQ	USBLS	5/07
	Boise City-Nampa MSA, ID	Y	16440 FQ	17880 MW	19360 TQ	USBLS	5/07
	Illinois	Y	15550 FQ	17390 MW	19500 TQ	USBLS	5/07
	Chicago-Naperville-Joliet MSA, IL-IN-WI	Y	15700 FQ	17490 MW	19420 TQ	USBLS	5/07
	Indiana	Y	17460 FQ	19570 MW	22500 TQ	USBLS	5/07
	Elkhart-Goshen MSA, IN	Y	17360 FQ	19070 MW	21510 TQ	USBLS	5/07
	Gary PMSA, IN	Y	16810 FQ	18480 MW	20700 TQ	USBLS	5/07
	Indianapolis-Carmel MSA, IN	Y	18880 FQ	20890 MW	23580 TQ	USBLS	5/07
	Iowa	Y	17590 FQ	19760 MW	23010 TQ	USBLS	5/07
	Des Moines-West Des Moines MSA, IA	Y	20330 FQ	23130 MW	27470 TQ	USBLS	5/07
	Sioux City MSA, IA-NE-SD	Y	16950 FQ	18410 MW	20020 TQ	USBLS	5/07
	Waterloo-Cedar Falls MSA, IA	Y	18660 FQ	21570 MW	25130 TQ	USBLS	5/07
	Kansas	Y	16590 FQ	18130 MW	19760 TQ	USBLS	5/07
	Topeka MSA, KS	Y	15730 FQ	17550 MW	19720 TQ	USBLS	5/07
	Wichita MSA, KS	Y	16730 FQ	18100 MW	19510 TQ	USBLS	5/07
	Kentucky	Y	15389 FQ	17608 MW	19557 TQ	KYBLS	2008
	Lexington-Fayette MSA, KY	Y	15430 FQ	17510 MW	20120 TQ	USBLS	5/07
	Louisville-Jefferson County MSA, KY-IN	Y	15940 FQ	17570 MW	19170 TQ	USBLS	5/07
	Louisiana	H	6.28 FQ	7.16 MW	8.54 TQ	LABLS	1/08-3/08
	Baton Rouge MSA, LA	Y	13060 FQ	15090 MW	17640 TQ	USBLS	5/07
	Houma-Bayou Cane-Thibodaux MSA, LA	Y	12870 FQ	14260 MW	17220 TQ	USBLS	5/07

AE	Average entry wage	AW	Average wage paid	FQ	First quartile wage
AER	Average entry range	AWR	Average wage range	H	Hourly
AEX	Average experienced wage	AXR	Average experienced range	HI	Highest wage paid
ATC	Average total compensation	D	Daily	HR	High end range

LO	Lowest wage paid	MTC	Median total compensation	TCC	Total cash compensation
LR	Low end range	MW	Median wage paid	TQ	Third quartile wage
M	Monthly	MWR	Median wage range	W	Weekly
MCC	Median cash compensation	S	See annotated source	Y	Yearly

Occupation/Type/Industry	Location	Per	Low	Mid	High	Source	Date
Personal and Home Care Aide	New Orleans-Metairie-Kenner MSA, LA	Y	13200 FQ	15040 MW	17760 TQ	USBLS	5/07
	Maine	Y	17090 FQ	18670 MW	21190 TQ	USBLS	5/07
	Portland-South Portland-Biddeford MSA, ME	Y	16700 FQ	18070 MW	20180 TQ	USBLS	5/07
	Maryland	Y		21900 MW		MDBLS	3/08
	Baltimore-Towson MSA, MD	Y	17450 FQ	20590 MW	23770 TQ	USBLS	5/07
	Bethesda-Gaithersburg-Frederick PMSA, MD	Y	19620 FQ	22210 MW	24930 TQ	USBLS	5/07
	Massachusetts	Y	21300 FQ	23390 MW	25700 TQ	USBLS	5/07
	Boston-Cambridge-Quincy NECTA, MA	Y	21500 FQ	23500 MW	25590 TQ	USBLS	5/07
	Worcester MSA, MA-CT	Y	21500 FQ	23390 MW	25520 TQ	USBLS	5/07
	Michigan	Y	17450 FQ	19650 MW	23270 TQ	USBLS	5/07
	Detroit-Warren-Livonia MSA, MI	Y	17990 FQ	20460 MW	23590 TQ	USBLS	5/07
	Grand Rapids-Wyoming MSA, MI	Y	17170 FQ	18620 MW	20330 TQ	USBLS	5/07
	Warren-Troy-Farmington Hills PMSA, MI	Y	19000 FQ	21640 MW	24700 TQ	USBLS	5/07
	Minnesota	Y	21695 FQ	23818 MW	26108 TQ	MNBLS	10/08-12/08
	Duluth-Superior MSA, MN-WI	Y	18956 FQ	21204 MW	24728 TQ	MNBLS	10/08-12/08
	Minneapolis-Saint Paul MSA, MN-WI	Y	22082 FQ	24069 MW	26223 TQ	MNBLS	10/08-12/08
	Rochester MSA, MN	Y	21340 FQ	23483 MW	25649 TQ	MNBLS	10/08-12/08
	Mississippi	Y	12780 FQ	14300 MW	17290 TQ	USBLS	5/07
	Jackson MSA, MS	Y	12990 FQ	14530 MW	18750 TQ	USBLS	5/07
	Missouri	Y	15830 FQ	17700 MW	19670 TQ	USBLS	5/07
	Kansas City MSA, MO-KS	Y	17190 FQ	19200 MW	21460 TQ	USBLS	5/07
	St. Louis MSA, MO-IL	Y	16580 FQ	18730 MW	20980 TQ	USBLS	5/07
	Springfield MSA, MO	Y	16030 FQ	17200 MW	18400 TQ	USBLS	5/07
	Montana	Y	16630 FQ	18440 MW	20870 TQ	USBLS	5/07
	Billings MSA, MT	Y	19910 FQ	21300 MW	22730 TQ	USBLS	5/07
	Nebraska	Y	16790 FQ	19150 MW	22550 TQ	USBLS	5/07
	Omaha-Council Bluffs MSA, NE-IA	Y	16510 FQ	17980 MW	19410 TQ	USBLS	5/07
	Las Vegas-Paradise MSA, NV	H	9.09 FQ	10.72 MW	12.62 TQ	NVBLS	5/08
	New Hampshire	H	8.67 AE	10.70 MW	11.50 AEX	NHBLS	6/08
	Manchester MSA, NH	Y	17210 FQ	20980 MW	26190 TQ	USBLS	5/07
	Nashua NECTA, NH-MA	Y	20620 FQ	22160 MW	23690 TQ	USBLS	5/07
	New Jersey	Y	19000 FQ	22650 MW	31350 TQ	USBLS	5/07
	Camden PMSA, NJ	Y	19120 FQ	22890 MW	35150 TQ	USBLS	5/07
	Edison PMSA, NJ	Y	20150 FQ	23630 MW	32640 TQ	USBLS	5/07
	Newark-Union PMSA, NJ-PA	Y	18200 FQ	22760 MW	32270 TQ	USBLS	5/07
	New Mexico	Y	16960 FQ	18430 MW	20100 TQ	USBLS	5/07
	Albuquerque MSA, NM	Y	17070 FQ	18560 MW	20490 TQ	USBLS	5/07
	New York	Y	19510 FQ	21600 MW	23550 TQ	USBLS	5/07
	Albany-Schenectady-Troy MSA, NY	Y	19630 FQ	21980 MW	24590 TQ	USBLS	5/07
	Buffalo-Niagara Falls MSA, NY	Y	15790 FQ	17890 MW	20820 TQ	USBLS	5/07
	Nassau-Suffolk PMSA, NY	Y	18460 FQ	20330 MW	22730 TQ	USBLS	5/07
	New York-Northern New Jersey-Long Island MSA, NY-NJ-PA	Y	19820 FQ	21830 MW	23780 TQ	USBLS	5/07
	North Carolina	Y	16230 FQ	17970 MW	19930 TQ	USBLS	5/07
	Charlotte-Gastonia-Concord MSA, NC-SC	Y	15980 FQ	17650 MW	19700 TQ	USBLS	5/07
	Raleigh-Cary MSA, NC	Y	17530 FQ	19930 MW	23170 TQ	USBLS	5/07
	Winston-Salem MSA, NC	Y	17610 FQ	19150 MW	20880 TQ	USBLS	5/07
	North Dakota	Y	17420 FQ	19210 MW	22000 TQ	USBLS	5/07
	Fargo MSA, ND-MN	Y	17190 FQ	18960 MW	21500 TQ	USBLS	5/07
	Ohio	Y	16820 FQ	19030 MW	22070 TQ	USBLS	5/07
	Cincinnati-Middletown MSA, OH-KY-IN	Y	17120 FQ	18950 MW	23050 TQ	USBLS	5/07
	Cleveland-Elyria-Mentor MSA, OH	Y	17230 FQ	18860 MW	21290 TQ	USBLS	5/07
	Columbus MSA, OH	Y	19190 FQ	21470 MW	23700 TQ	USBLS	5/07
	Dayton MSA, OH	Y	17880 FQ	19830 MW	22090 TQ	USBLS	5/07
	Mansfield MSA, OH	Y	17880 FQ	20280 MW	31370 TQ	USBLS	5/07
	Oklahoma	Y	14740 FQ	16840 MW	18670 TQ	USBLS	5/07
	Oklahoma City MSA, OK	Y	13650 FQ	16070 MW	18480 TQ	USBLS	5/07

AE	Average entry wage	AW	Average wage paid	FQ	First quartile wage
AER	Average entry range	AWR	Average wage range	H	Hourly
AEX	Average experienced wage	AXR	Average experienced range	HI	Highest wage paid
ATC	Average total compensation	D	Daily	HR	High end range

LO	Lowest wage paid	MTC	Median total compensation	TCC	Total cash compensation
LR	Low end range	MW	Median wage paid	TQ	Third quartile wage
M	Monthly	MWR	Median wage range	W	Weekly
MCC	Median cash compensation	S	See annotated source	Y	Yearly

Occupation/Type/Industry	Location	Per	Low	Mid	High	Source	Date
Personal and Home Care Aide	Tulsa MSA, OK	Y	15520 FQ	17120 MW	18700 TQ	USBLS	5/07
	Oregon	H	9.15 FQ	10.21 MW	11.57 TQ	ORBLS	5/08
	Portland-Vancouver-Beaverton MSA, OR-WA	Y	18500 FQ	20400 MW	23090 TQ	USBLS	5/07
	Pennsylvania	Y	17110 FQ	19490 MW	22870 TQ	USBLS	5/07
	Allentown-Bethlehem-Easton MSA, PA-NJ	Y	18330 FQ	20520 MW	23470 TQ	USBLS	5/07
	Philadelphia-Camden-Wilmington MSA, PA-NJ-DE-MD	Y	17820 FQ	21060 MW	24840 TQ	USBLS	5/07
	Pittsburgh MSA, PA	Y	17180 FQ	19070 MW	22010 TQ	USBLS	5/07
	Reading MSA, PA	Y	17600 FQ	19480 MW	22280 TQ	USBLS	5/07
	Rhode Island	Y	19970 FQ	22220 MW	24670 TQ	USBLS	5/07
	Providence-Fall River-Warwick MSA, RI-MA	Y	19710 FQ	22100 MW	24590 TQ	USBLS	5/07
	South Carolina	Y	16580 FQ	18120 MW	19960 TQ	USBLS	5/07
	Charleston-North Charleston MSA, SC	Y	17180 FQ	19430 MW	22900 TQ	USBLS	5/07
	Columbia MSA, SC	Y	16600 FQ	17760 MW	18920 TQ	USBLS	5/07
	Myrtle Beach-Conway-North Myrtle Beach MSA, SC	Y	16840 FQ	17940 MW	19030 TQ	USBLS	5/07
	South Dakota	Y	16927 FQ	18901 MW	21442 TQ	SDBLS	7/08-9/08
	Sioux Falls MSA, SD	Y	17804 FQ	19999 MW	22852 TQ	SDBLS	7/08-9/08
	Tennessee	Y	16190 FQ	17960 MW	19740 TQ	USBLS	5/07
	Memphis MSA, TN-MS-AR	Y	16680 FQ	17960 MW	19250 TQ	USBLS	5/07
	Nashville-Davidson-Murfreesboro MSA, TN	Y	17340 FQ	19080 MW	20960 TQ	USBLS	5/07
	Texas	Y	12500 FQ	13780 MW	15080 TQ	USBLS	5/07
	Austin-Round Rock MSA, TX	Y	12740 FQ	14170 MW	15810 TQ	USBLS	5/07
	Beaumont-Port Arthur MSA, TX	Y	12430 FQ	13540 MW	14650 TQ	USBLS	5/07
	Dallas-Fort Worth-Arlington MSA, TX	Y	12610 FQ	13990 MW	15570 TQ	USBLS	5/07
	El Paso MSA, TX	Y	12230 FQ	13400 MW	14560 TQ	USBLS	5/07
	Houston-Sugar Land-Baytown MSA, TX	Y	12590 FQ	14010 MW	15500 TQ	USBLS	5/07
	San Antonio MSA, TX	Y	12520 FQ	13790 MW	15070 TQ	USBLS	5/07
	Utah	Y	16970 FQ	19180 MW	22530 TQ	USBLS	5/07
	Salt Lake City MSA, UT	Y	18810 FQ	20810 MW	23090 TQ	USBLS	5/07
	Burlington-South Burlington MSA, VT	Y	19560 FQ	21110 MW	22740 TQ	USBLS	5/07
	Virginia	Y	13690 FQ	16160 MW	19370 TQ	USBLS	5/07
	Richmond MSA, VA	Y	14110 FQ	16620 MW	19290 TQ	USBLS	5/07
	Virginia Beach-Norfolk-Newport News MSA, VA-NC	Y	13110 FQ	15090 MW	18260 TQ	USBLS	5/07
	Washington	H	9.86 FQ	10.79 MW	11.72 TQ	WABLS	3/08
	Bremerton-Silverdale MSA, WA	Y	19750 FQ	21070 MW	22500 TQ	USBLS	5/07
	Seattle-Tacoma-Bellevue MSA, WA	Y	20830 FQ	22580 MW	24510 TQ	USBLS	5/07
	West Virginia	Y	14319 FQ	15725 MW	17935 TQ	WVBLS	7/08-9/08
	Charleston MSA, WV	Y	14300 FQ	16040 MW	17880 TQ	USBLS	5/07
	Wheeling MSA, WV-OH	Y	14480 FQ	16410 MW	18310 TQ	USBLS	5/07
	Wisconsin	Y	17770 FQ	19910 MW	22600 TQ	USBLS	5/07
	Milwaukee-Waukesha-West Allis MSA, WI	Y	17880 FQ	19620 MW	22140 TQ	USBLS	5/07
	Racine MSA, WI	Y	17360 FQ	19370 MW	22300 TQ	USBLS	5/07
	Wyoming	Y	19939 FQ	21720 MW	23974 TQ	WYBLS	9/08
	Puerto Rico	Y	12300 FQ	13290 MW	14280 TQ	USBLS	5/07
	San Juan-Caguas-Guaynabo MSA, PR	Y	12300 FQ	13260 MW	14220 TQ	USBLS	5/07
Personal Banker	United States	Y		37700 AW		BUS201	2005-2006
Personal Financial Advisor	Alabama	Y	48130 FQ	75540 MW		USBLS	5/07
	Birmingham-Hoover MSA, AL	Y	40850 FQ	73760 MW	136580 TQ	USBLS	5/07
	Alaska	Y	36920 FQ	47030 MW	59930 TQ	USBLS	5/07
	Arizona	Y	35290 FQ	56320 MW	93760 TQ	USBLS	5/07
	Phoenix-Mesa-Scottsdale MSA, AZ	Y	37890 FQ	57820 MW	97550 TQ	USBLS	5/07
	Tucson MSA, AZ	Y	27330 FQ	46330 MW	68860 TQ	USBLS	5/07
	Arkansas	Y	32940 FQ	51620 MW	77030 TQ	USBLS	5/07

AE	Average entry wage	AW	Average wage paid	FQ	First quartile wage	LO	Lowest wage paid	MTC Median total compensation TCC Total cash compensation
AER	Average entry range	AWR	Average wage range	H	Hourly	LR	Low end range	MW Median wage paid TQ Third quartile wage
AEX	Average experienced wage	AXR	Average experienced range	HI	Highest wage paid	M	Monthly	MWR Median wage range W Weekly
ATC	Average total compensation	D	Daily	HR	High end range	MCC	Median cash compensation	S See annotated source Y Yearly

Occupation/Type/Industry	Location	Per	Low	Mid	High	Source	Date
Personal Financial Advisor	Fayetteville-Springdale-Rogers MSA, AR-MO	Y	32430 FQ	65360 MW	138520 TQ	USBLS	5/07
	Little Rock-North Little Rock MSA, AR	Y	44060 FQ	53390 MW	75790 TQ	USBLS	5/07
	California	H	23.15 FQ	32.18 MW	58.05 TQ	CABLS	1/08-3/08
	Fresno MSA, CA	H	25.91 FQ	41.74 MW	50.08 TQ	CABLS	1/08-3/08
	Los Angeles-Long Beach-Glendale PMSA, CA	H	25.62 FQ	33.74 MW	58.53 TQ	CABLS	1/08-3/08
	Oakland-Fremont-Hayward MSA, CA	H	19.41 FQ	29.88 MW	39.38 TQ	CABLS	1/08-3/08
	Oxnard-Thousand Oaks-Ventura MSA, CA	H	27.33 FQ	47.34 MW		CABLS	1/08-3/08
	Riverside-San Bernardino-Ontario MSA, CA	H	27.27 FQ	30.72 MW	37.17 TQ	CABLS	1/08-3/08
	Sacramento-Arden Arcade-Roseville MSA, CA	H	18.09 FQ	21.90 MW	28.23 TQ	CABLS	1/08-3/08
	San Diego-Carlsbad-San Marcos MSA, CA	H	25.61 FQ	30.55 MW	40.04 TQ	CABLS	1/08-3/08
	San Francisco-San Mateo-Redwood PMSA, CA	H	25.69 FQ	38.94 MW		CABLS	1/08-3/08
	San Jose-Sunnyvale-Santa Clara MSA, CA	H	28.66 FQ	44.31 MW		CABLS	1/08-3/08
	Santa Ana-Anaheim-Irvine PMSA, CA	Y	36970 FQ	69690 MW		USBLS	5/07
	Santa Rosa-Petaluma MSA, CA	H	26.61 FQ	32.36 MW	42.31 TQ	CABLS	1/08-3/08
	Colorado	Y	48790 FQ	101890 MW		USBLS	5/07
	Denver-Aurora MSA, CO	Y	53610 FQ	115080 MW		USBLS	5/07
	Connecticut	H	25.14 AE	44.70 MW		CTBLS	1/08-3/08
	Bridgeport-Stamford-Norwalk MSA, CT	Y	63710 FQ	97350 MW		USBLS	5/07
	Hartford-West Hartford-East Hartford MSA, CT	Y	57160 FQ	87220 MW	132060 TQ	USBLS	5/07
	Delaware	Y	54350 FQ	69640 MW	93480 TQ	USBLS	5/07
	Wilmington PMSA, DE-MD-NJ	Y	55290 FQ	69840 MW	94440 TQ	USBLS	5/07
	District of Columbia	Y	48910 FQ	71060 MW	92910 TQ	USBLS	5/07
	Washington-Arlington-Alexandria MSA, DC-VA-MD-WV	Y	47720 FQ	68180 MW	101150 TQ	USBLS	5/07
	Florida	Y	37700 FQ	49660 MW	81520 TQ	USBLS	5/07
	Cape Coral-Fort Myers MSA, FL	Y	38940 FQ	53480 MW	65380 TQ	USBLS	5/07
	Fort Lauderdale-Pompano Beach-Deerfield Beach PMSA, FL	Y	37000 FQ	64030 MW	119690 TQ	USBLS	5/07
	Jacksonville MSA, FL	Y	41130 FQ	61660 MW	92860 TQ	USBLS	5/07
	Miami-Fort Lauderdale-Miami Beach MSA, FL	Y	38660 FQ	50280 MW	88740 TQ	USBLS	5/07
	Orlando-Kissimmee MSA, FL	Y	33780 FQ	43350 MW	70600 TQ	USBLS	5/07
	Tampa-St. Petersburg-Clearwater MSA, FL	Y	40930 FQ	53520 MW	75040 TQ	USBLS	5/07
	West Palm Beach-Boca Raton-Boynton Beach PMSA, FL	Y	37870 FQ	53780 MW	93310 TQ	USBLS	5/07
	Georgia	Y	47860 FQ	63120 MW	93420 TQ	USBLS	5/07
	Atlanta-Sandy Springs-Marietta MSA, GA	Y	48740 FQ	65010 MW	94560 TQ	USBLS	5/07
	Hawaii	Y	30040 FQ	47290 MW	100460 TQ	USBLS	5/07
	Honolulu MSA, HI	Y	26410 FQ	42130 MW	88780 TQ	USBLS	5/07
	Idaho	Y	30410 FQ	45560 MW	65670 TQ	USBLS	5/07
	Boise City-Nampa MSA, ID	Y	42820 FQ	52710 MW	74350 TQ	USBLS	5/07
	Illinois	Y	41970 FQ	65590 MW	99510 TQ	USBLS	5/07
	Chicago-Naperville-Joliet MSA, IL-IN-WI	Y	42500 FQ	67020 MW	103380 TQ	USBLS	5/07
	Indiana	Y	41980 FQ	62500 MW	117820 TQ	USBLS	5/07
	Fort Wayne MSA, IN	Y	18340 FQ	39500 MW	66390 TQ	USBLS	5/07
	Gary PMSA, IN	Y	31690 FQ	50870 MW	118070 TQ	USBLS	5/07
	Indianapolis-Carmel MSA, IN	Y	50030 FQ	96590 MW		USBLS	5/07
	Iowa	Y	38320 FQ	51010 MW	97670 TQ	USBLS	5/07
	Cedar Rapids MSA, IA	Y	56410 FQ	72350 MW	128160 TQ	USBLS	5/07
	Des Moines-West Des Moines MSA, IA	Y	47420 FQ	65540 MW	110790 TQ	USBLS	5/07
	Kansas	Y	38830 FQ	49910 MW	88680 TQ	USBLS	5/07

Occupation/Type/Industry	Location	Per	Low	Mid	High	Source	Date
Personal Financial Advisor	Wichita MSA, KS	Y	42790 FQ	49130 MW	80150 TQ	USBLS	5/07
	Kentucky	Y	30441 FQ	46726 MW	76197 TQ	KYBLS	2008
	Louisville-Jefferson County MSA, KY-IN	Y	33760 FQ	64170 MW	76670 TQ	USBLS	5/07
	Louisiana	H	15.76 FQ	24.99 MW	56.08 TQ	LABLS	1/08-3/08
	Baton Rouge MSA, LA	Y	45800 FQ	60560 MW	82010 TQ	USBLS	5/07
	New Orleans-Metairie-Kenner MSA, LA	Y	45410 FQ	85010 MW	128960 TQ	USBLS	5/07
	Maine	Y	51300 FQ	94100 MW		USBLS	5/07
	Portland-South Portland-Biddeford MSA, ME	Y	67620 FQ	116690 MW		USBLS	5/07
	Maryland	Y		69175 MW		MDBLS	3/08
	Baltimore-Towson MSA, MD	Y	54720 FQ	73880 MW	97680 TQ	USBLS	5/07
	Bethesda-Gaithersburg-Frederick PMSA, MD	Y	44400 FQ	60960 MW	85800 TQ	USBLS	5/07
	Hagerstown-Martinsburg MSA, MD-WV	Y	32580 FQ	36560 MW	60460 TQ	USBLS	5/07
	Massachusetts	Y	59410 FQ	102100 MW		USBLS	5/07
	Boston-Cambridge-Quincy NECTA, MA	Y	65810 FQ	111060 MW		USBLS	5/07
	Worcester MSA, MA-CT	Y	64930 FQ	112350 MW		USBLS	5/07
	Michigan	Y	37510 FQ	57670 MW	103400 TQ	USBLS	5/07
	Detroit-Warren-Livonia MSA, MI	Y	36090 FQ	56080 MW	122850 TQ	USBLS	5/07
	Grand Rapids-Wyoming MSA, MI	Y	38150 FQ	61840 MW	80500 TQ	USBLS	5/07
	Warren-Troy-Farmington Hills PMSA, MI	Y	32640 FQ	57310 MW	127890 TQ	USBLS	5/07
	Minnesota	Y	49818 FQ	71609 MW	88020 TQ	MNBLS	10/08-12/08
	Duluth-Superior MSA, MN-WI	Y	45313 FQ	55271 MW	108529 TQ	MNBLS	10/08-12/08
	Minneapolis-Saint Paul MSA, MN-WI	Y	49734 FQ	72787 MW	89021 TQ	MNBLS	10/08-12/08
	Mississippi	Y	36070 FQ	49170 MW	74110 TQ	USBLS	5/07
	Gulfport-Biloxi MSA, MS	Y	34290 FQ	42820 MW	52300 TQ	USBLS	5/07
	Jackson MSA, MS	Y	37610 FQ	50650 MW	75640 TQ	USBLS	5/07
	Missouri	Y	34840 FQ	58170 MW	93150 TQ	USBLS	5/07
	Kansas City MSA, MO-KS	Y	29850 FQ	55340 MW	86980 TQ	USBLS	5/07
	St. Joseph MSA, MO-KS	Y	35560 FQ	52280 MW	76150 TQ	USBLS	5/07
	St. Louis MSA, MO-IL	Y	44320 FQ	65690 MW	103560 TQ	USBLS	5/07
	Montana	Y	35870 FQ	47230 MW	89930 TQ	USBLS	5/07
	Billings MSA, MT	Y	34040 FQ	68920 MW	105250 TQ	USBLS	5/07
	Missoula MSA, MT	Y	38250 FQ	45100 MW	49760 TQ	USBLS	5/07
	Nebraska	Y	39560 FQ	47050 MW	72540 TQ	USBLS	5/07
	Omaha-Council Bluffs MSA, NE-IA	Y	34640 FQ	44410 MW	67200 TQ	USBLS	5/07
	Nevada	H	19.37 FQ	28.13 MW	46.94 TQ	NVBLS	5/08
	Las Vegas-Paradise MSA, NV	H	19.49 FQ	23.46 MW	46.14 TQ	NVBLS	5/08
	New Hampshire	H	20.38 AE	29.02 MW	47.34 AEX	NHBLS	6/08
	Manchester MSA, NH	Y	40550 FQ	44260 MW	56600 TQ	USBLS	5/07
	Nashua NECTA, NH-MA	Y	51310 FQ	75280 MW	98810 TQ	USBLS	5/07
	Portsmouth MSA, NH-ME	Y	66400 FQ	85210 MW	104740 TQ	USBLS	5/07
	New Jersey	Y	47780 FQ	81750 MW	142960 TQ	USBLS	5/07
	Camden PMSA, NJ	Y	43520 FQ	58420 MW	88180 TQ	USBLS	5/07
	Edison PMSA, NJ	Y	55440 FQ	83250 MW	123040 TQ	USBLS	5/07
	Newark-Union PMSA, NJ-PA	Y	44610 FQ	72410 MW		USBLS	5/07
	New Mexico	Y	42340 FQ	55860 MW	106620 TQ	USBLS	5/07
	Albuquerque MSA, NM	Y	39960 FQ	47290 MW	61160 TQ	USBLS	5/07
	New York	Y	68640 FQ	121560 MW		USBLS	5/07
	Albany-Schenectady-Troy MSA, NY	Y	83070 FQ	115070 MW		USBLS	5/07
	Buffalo-Niagara Falls MSA, NY	Y	42680 FQ	52770 MW	77070 TQ	USBLS	5/07
	Nassau-Suffolk PMSA, NY	Y	65970 FQ	94420 MW		USBLS	5/07
	New York-Northern New Jersey-Long Island MSA, NY-NJ-PA	Y	67990 FQ	119080 MW		USBLS	5/07
	Utica-Rome MSA, NY	Y	52620 FQ	71700 MW		USBLS	5/07
	North Carolina	Y	47560 FQ	61260 MW	79560 TQ	USBLS	5/07
	Charlotte-Gastonia-Concord MSA, NC-SC	Y	51290 FQ	64830 MW	81640 TQ	USBLS	5/07
	Raleigh-Cary MSA, NC	Y	33400 FQ	51910 MW	70090 TQ	USBLS	5/07
	North Dakota	Y	33450 FQ	40800 MW	60260 TQ	USBLS	5/07

AE	Average entry wage	AW	Average wage paid	FQ	First quartile wage	LO	Lowest wage paid	MTC	Median total compensation	TCC	Total cash compensation
AER	Average entry range	AWR	Average wage range	H	Hourly	LR	Low end range	MW	Median wage paid	TQ	Third quartile wage
AEX	Average experienced wage	AXR	Average experienced range	HI	Highest wage paid	M	Monthly	MWR	Median wage range	W	Weekly
ATC	Average total compensation	D	Daily	HR	High end range	MCC	Median cash compensation	S	See annotated source	Y	Yearly

Occupation/Type/Industry	Location	Per	Low	Mid	High	Source	Date
Personal Financial Advisor	Fargo MSA, ND-MN	Y	45360 FQ	69590 MW	100250 TQ	USBLS	5/07
	Grand Forks MSA, ND-MN	Y	34550 FQ	39850 MW	45430 TQ	USBLS	5/07
	Ohio	Y	43860 FQ	69860 MW	110880 TQ	USBLS	5/07
	Cincinnati-Middletown MSA, OH-KY-IN	Y	45230 FQ	69230 MW	109930 TQ	USBLS	5/07
	Cleveland-Elyria-Mentor MSA, OH	Y	56930 FQ	80460 MW	119200 TQ	USBLS	5/07
	Columbus MSA, OH	Y	33330 FQ	59300 MW	111110 TQ	USBLS	5/07
	Dayton MSA, OH	Y	30140 FQ	66880 MW	76060 TQ	USBLS	5/07
	Oklahoma	Y	28350 FQ	44660 MW	95000 TQ	USBLS	5/07
	Oklahoma City MSA, OK	Y	25490 FQ	34260 MW	54360 TQ	USBLS	5/07
	Tulsa MSA, OK	Y	38220 FQ	104700 MW	124660 TQ	USBLS	5/07
	Oregon	H	22.05 FQ	26.48 MW	39.06 TQ	ORBLS	5/08
	Portland-Vancouver-Beaverton MSA, OR-WA	Y	44060 FQ	53690 MW	79390 TQ	USBLS	5/07
	Pennsylvania	Y	45640 FQ	60500 MW	95320 TQ	USBLS	5/07
	Allentown-Bethlehem-Easton MSA, PA-NJ	Y	44420 FQ	51240 MW	72530 TQ	USBLS	5/07
	Philadelphia-Camden-Wilmington MSA, PA-NJ-DE-MD	Y	48540 FQ	62260 MW	94160 TQ	USBLS	5/07
	Pittsburgh MSA, PA	Y	42010 FQ	65930 MW	108120 TQ	USBLS	5/07
	Rhode Island	Y	44630 FQ	64150 MW	91860 TQ	USBLS	5/07
	Providence-Fall River-Warwick MSA, RI-MA	Y	42750 FQ	62710 MW	88130 TQ	USBLS	5/07
	South Carolina	Y	31350 FQ	51600 MW	85440 TQ	USBLS	5/07
	Charleston-North Charleston MSA, SC	Y	32110 FQ	58920 MW	91100 TQ	USBLS	5/07
	Columbia MSA, SC	Y	39120 FQ	58450 MW	92380 TQ	USBLS	5/07
	South Dakota	Y	42668 FQ	54486 MW	73107 TQ	SDBLS	7/08-9/08
	Sioux Falls MSA, SD	Y	43290 FQ	53749 MW	76128 TQ	SDBLS	7/08-9/08
	Tennessee	Y	52020 FQ	64740 MW	90500 TQ	USBLS	5/07
	Memphis MSA, TN-MS-AR	Y	56650 FQ	87200 MW	97760 TQ	USBLS	5/07
	Nashville-Davidson-Murfreesboro MSA, TN	Y	55230 FQ	61630 MW	73720 TQ	USBLS	5/07
	Texas	Y	43770 FQ	63610 MW	112770 TQ	USBLS	5/07
	Austin-Round Rock MSA, TX	Y	39560 FQ	55980 MW	97140 TQ	USBLS	5/07
	Dallas-Fort Worth-Arlington MSA, TX	Y	50280 FQ	75110 MW	139210 TQ	USBLS	5/07
	El Paso MSA, TX	Y	58960 FQ	115300 MW	128340 TQ	USBLS	5/07
	Houston-Sugar Land-Baytown MSA, TX	Y	43520 FQ	60180 MW	108770 TQ	USBLS	5/07
	San Antonio MSA, TX	Y	36130 FQ	49740 MW	95000 TQ	USBLS	5/07
	Utah	Y	42680 FQ	57430 MW	119780 TQ	USBLS	5/07
	Salt Lake City MSA, UT	Y	45250 FQ	57920 MW	126180 TQ	USBLS	5/07
	Vermont	Y	44920 FQ	60080 MW	80230 TQ	USBLS	5/07
	Burlington-South Burlington MSA, VT	Y	41170 FQ	60260 MW	122380 TQ	USBLS	5/07
	Virginia	Y	48110 FQ	76100 MW	118460 TQ	USBLS	5/07
	Charlottesville MSA, VA	Y	41460 FQ	68910 MW	94690 TQ	USBLS	5/07
	Richmond MSA, VA	Y	56620 FQ	93530 MW	122320 TQ	USBLS	5/07
	Virginia Beach-Norfolk-Newport News MSA, VA-NC	Y	44030 FQ	63430 MW	93920 TQ	USBLS	5/07
	Washington	H	25.43 FQ	38.95 MW	51.84 TQ	WABLS	3/08
	Seattle-Tacoma-Bellevue MSA, WA	Y	56060 FQ	84630 MW	110680 TQ	USBLS	5/07
	West Virginia	Y	32911 FQ	45387 MW	54130 TQ	WVBLS	7/08-9/08
	Charleston MSA, WV	Y	41220 FQ	45990 MW	51240 TQ	USBLS	5/07
	Wisconsin	Y	40960 FQ	54010 MW	85030 TQ	USBLS	5/07
	Milwaukee-Waukesha-West Allis MSA, WI	Y	40840 FQ	50570 MW	93600 TQ	USBLS	5/07
	Wyoming	Y	37665 FQ	81522 MW	134804 TQ	WYBLS	9/08
	Puerto Rico	Y	36800 FQ	59710 MW	96870 TQ	USBLS	5/07
	San Juan-Caguas-Guaynabo MSA, PR	Y	36480 FQ	59680 MW	96460 TQ	USBLS	5/07
Personal Lines Manager Insurance Agency	United States	Y	40313 LO		108947 HI	INSJ01	2006
Personnel Analyst Municipal Government	Gresham, OR	Y	52404 LO		68088 HI	GOSS01	7/1/08

AE	Average entry wage	**AW**	Average wage paid	**FQ**	First quartile wage	**LO** Lowest wage paid	**MTC** Median total compensation	**TCC** Total cash compensation
AER	Average entry range	**AWR**	Average wage range	**H**	Hourly	**LR** Low end range	**MW** Median wage paid	**TQ** Third quartile wage
AEX	Average experienced wage	**AXR**	Average experienced range	**HI**	Highest wage paid	**M** Monthly	**MWR** Median wage range	**W** Weekly
ATC	Average total compensation	**D**	Daily	**HR**	High end range	**MCC** Median cash compensation	**S** See annotated source	**Y** Yearly

Occupation/Type/Industry	Location	Per	Low	Mid	High	Source	Date
Personnel Officer							
Municipal Government	Seaside, CA	S			3520 HI	SSSS	8/08
Personnel Specialist							
State Government	West Virginia	Y	22224 LO		41112 HI	AFT02	3/1/08
Pest Control Worker	Alabama	Y	21030 FQ	27400 MW	34530 TQ	USBLS	5/07
	Birmingham-Hoover MSA, AL	Y	25160 FQ	33790 MW	42130 TQ	USBLS	5/07
	Arizona	Y	19450 FQ	26720 MW	31100 TQ	USBLS	5/07
	Phoenix-Mesa-Scottsdale MSA, AZ	Y	20200 FQ	27040 MW	30830 TQ	USBLS	5/07
	Prescott MSA, AZ	Y	20120 FQ	31540 MW	39030 TQ	USBLS	5/07
	Tucson MSA, AZ	Y	16790 FQ	20820 MW	29730 TQ	USBLS	5/07
	Arkansas	Y	21830 FQ	25520 MW	29400 TQ	USBLS	5/07
	Little Rock-North Little Rock MSA, AR	Y	23190 FQ	26060 MW	29040 TQ	USBLS	5/07
	California	H	12.45 FQ	14.57 MW	17.29 TQ	CABLS	1/08-3/08
	Los Angeles-Long Beach-Glendale PMSA, CA	H	11.98 FQ	14.97 MW	17.43 TQ	CABLS	1/08-3/08
	Oakland-Fremont-Hayward MSA, CA	H	12.41 FQ	13.73 MW	14.99 TQ	CABLS	1/08-3/08
	Riverside-San Bernardino-Ontario MSA, CA	H	11.30 FQ	14.74 MW	20.34 TQ	CABLS	1/08-3/08
	Sacramento-Arden Arcade-Roseville MSA, CA	H	14.04 FQ	15.55 MW	17.58 TQ	CABLS	1/08-3/08
	San Diego-Carlsbad-San Marcos MSA, CA	H	12.53 FQ	13.71 MW	15.00 TQ	CABLS	1/08-3/08
	San Francisco-San Mateo-Redwood PMSA, CA	H	15.81 FQ	17.41 MW	18.80 TQ	CABLS	1/08-3/08
	San Jose-Sunnyvale-Santa Clara MSA, CA	H	13.72 FQ	15.12 MW	18.06 TQ	CABLS	1/08-3/08
	Santa Ana-Anaheim-Irvine PMSA, CA	Y	25950 FQ	29910 MW	35500 TQ	USBLS	5/07
	Santa Rosa-Petaluma MSA, CA	H	15.02 FQ	17.56 MW	20.90 TQ	CABLS	1/08-3/08
	Stockton MSA, CA	H	13.78 FQ	16.12 MW	20.22 TQ	CABLS	1/08-3/08
	Colorado	Y	30410 FQ	41840 MW	48600 TQ	USBLS	5/07
	Denver-Aurora MSA, CO	Y	39040 FQ	45410 MW	50640 TQ	USBLS	5/07
	Connecticut	H	9.89 AE	13.98 MW		CTBLS	1/08-3/08
	Bridgeport-Stamford-Norwalk MSA, CT	Y	20220 FQ	29570 MW	40020 TQ	USBLS	5/07
	Hartford-West Hartford-East Hartford MSA, CT	Y	23090 FQ	26970 MW	33010 TQ	USBLS	5/07
	Delaware	Y	25220 FQ	29040 MW	34250 TQ	USBLS	5/07
	Wilmington PMSA, DE-MD-NJ	Y	26140 FQ	29830 MW	36600 TQ	USBLS	5/07
	District of Columbia	Y	21350 FQ	24270 MW	31480 TQ	USBLS	5/07
	Washington-Arlington-Alexandria MSA, DC-VA-MD-WV	Y	23300 FQ	33230 MW	41950 TQ	USBLS	5/07
	Florida	Y	22810 FQ	28130 MW	34430 TQ	USBLS	5/07
	Cape Coral-Fort Myers MSA, FL	Y	24560 FQ	28370 MW	35090 TQ	USBLS	5/07
	Fort Lauderdale-Pompano Beach-Deerfield Beach PMSA, FL	Y	21970 FQ	27050 MW	32600 TQ	USBLS	5/07
	Jacksonville MSA, FL	Y	22810 FQ	28010 MW	32650 TQ	USBLS	5/07
	Miami-Fort Lauderdale-Miami Beach MSA, FL	Y	22930 FQ	28000 MW	35460 TQ	USBLS	5/07
	Orlando-Kissimmee MSA, FL	Y	25070 FQ	31200 MW	37910 TQ	USBLS	5/07
	Pensacola-Ferry Pass-Brent MSA, FL	Y	21210 FQ	24220 MW	29050 TQ	USBLS	5/07
	Tampa-St. Petersburg-Clearwater MSA, FL	Y	21780 FQ	25460 MW	30550 TQ	USBLS	5/07
	West Palm Beach-Boca Raton-Boynton Beach PMSA, FL	Y	27960 FQ	33240 MW	45210 TQ	USBLS	5/07
	Georgia	Y	20470 FQ	28200 MW	35220 TQ	USBLS	5/07
	Atlanta-Sandy Springs-Marietta MSA, GA	Y	20470 FQ	29890 MW	37110 TQ	USBLS	5/07
	Macon MSA, GA	Y	23830 FQ	29800 MW	37640 TQ	USBLS	5/07
	Hawaii	Y	25270 FQ	31820 MW	40570 TQ	USBLS	5/07
	Honolulu MSA, HI	Y	25440 FQ	34320 MW	47300 TQ	USBLS	5/07
	Idaho	Y	22390 FQ	24890 MW	31370 TQ	USBLS	5/07

AE	Average entry wage	AW	Average wage paid	FQ	First quartile wage
AER	Average entry range	AWR	Average wage range	H	Hourly
AEX	Average experienced wage	AXR	Average experienced range	HI	Highest wage paid
ATC	Average total compensation	D	Daily	HR	High end range
LO	Lowest wage paid	MTC	Median total compensation	TCC	Total cash compensation
LR	Low end range	MW	Median wage paid	TQ	Third quartile wage
M	Monthly	MWR	Median wage range	W	Weekly
MCC	Median cash compensation	S	See annotated source	Y	Yearly

Occupation/Type/Industry	Location	Per	Low	Mid	High	Source	Date
Pest Control Worker	Boise City-Nampa MSA, ID	Y	21990 FQ	24260 MW	31260 TQ	USBLS	5/07
	Illinois	Y	21400 FQ	25850 MW	34870 TQ	USBLS	5/07
	Chicago-Naperville-Joliet MSA, IL-IN-WI	Y	21430 FQ	24390 MW	33340 TQ	USBLS	5/07
	Indiana	Y	21950 FQ	26300 MW	32900 TQ	USBLS	5/07
	Gary PMSA, IN	Y	26310 FQ	30290 MW	34730 TQ	USBLS	5/07
	Indianapolis-Carmel MSA, IN	Y	22500 FQ	26020 MW	32740 TQ	USBLS	5/07
	Iowa	Y	20360 FQ	28800 MW	37200 TQ	USBLS	5/07
	Des Moines-West Des Moines MSA, IA	Y	23470 FQ	31240 MW	43880 TQ	USBLS	5/07
	Kansas	Y	25420 FQ	32730 MW	38170 TQ	USBLS	5/07
	Topeka MSA, KS	Y	24670 FQ	31590 MW	37340 TQ	USBLS	5/07
	Wichita MSA, KS	Y	27490 FQ	32890 MW	37270 TQ	USBLS	5/07
	Kentucky	Y	21822 FQ	25787 MW	30678 TQ	KYBLS	2008
	Louisville-Jefferson County MSA, KY-IN	Y	21790 FQ	24310 MW	27510 TQ	USBLS	5/07
	Louisiana	H	9.19 FQ	11.71 MW	15.28 TQ	LABLS	1/08-3/08
	Baton Rouge MSA, LA	Y	20330 FQ	24150 MW	29480 TQ	USBLS	5/07
	Houma-Bayou Cane-Thibodaux MSA, LA	Y	17140 FQ	32960 MW	49140 TQ	USBLS	5/07
	New Orleans-Metairie-Kenner MSA, LA	Y	20100 FQ	25100 MW	34350 TQ	USBLS	5/07
	Maine	Y	28180 FQ	30810 MW	35150 TQ	USBLS	5/07
	Maryland	Y		31800 MW		MDBLS	3/08
	Baltimore-Towson MSA, MD	Y	28130 FQ	32000 MW	36990 TQ	USBLS	5/07
	Bethesda-Gaithersburg-Frederick PMSA, MD	Y	20730 FQ	24330 MW	31150 TQ	USBLS	5/07
	Massachusetts	Y	27610 FQ	32240 MW	37800 TQ	USBLS	5/07
	Boston-Cambridge-Quincy NECTA, MA	Y	27750 FQ	31670 MW	36790 TQ	USBLS	5/07
	Worcester MSA, MA-CT	Y	27780 FQ	31530 MW	35930 TQ	USBLS	5/07
	Michigan	Y	28550 FQ	34360 MW	38670 TQ	USBLS	5/07
	Detroit-Warren-Livonia MSA, MI	Y	30160 FQ	34600 MW	38400 TQ	USBLS	5/07
	Grand Rapids-Wyoming MSA, MI	Y	25820 FQ	32140 MW	38230 TQ	USBLS	5/07
	Warren-Troy-Farmington Hills PMSA, MI	Y	29710 FQ	34180 MW	38240 TQ	USBLS	5/07
	Minnesota	Y	30551 FQ	42074 MW	51317 TQ	MNBLS	10/08-12/08
	Minneapolis-Saint Paul MSA, MN-WI	Y	31817 FQ	44311 MW	52958 TQ	MNBLS	10/08-12/08
	Mississippi	Y	22270 FQ	27800 MW	33690 TQ	USBLS	5/07
	Jackson MSA, MS	Y	27260 FQ	31160 MW	40820 TQ	USBLS	5/07
	Missouri	Y	23560 FQ	30820 MW	40300 TQ	USBLS	5/07
	Kansas City MSA, MO-KS	Y	29950 FQ	36070 MW	41500 TQ	USBLS	5/07
	St. Louis MSA, MO-IL	Y	21300 FQ	29900 MW	40230 TQ	USBLS	5/07
	Montana	Y	15970 FQ	21060 MW	29910 TQ	USBLS	5/07
	Nebraska	Y	27800 FQ	34860 MW	40640 TQ	USBLS	5/07
	Omaha-Council Bluffs MSA, NE-IA	Y	27190 FQ	30910 MW	37440 TQ	USBLS	5/07
	Nevada	H	14.14 FQ	16.91 MW	19.34 TQ	NVBLS	5/08
	Las Vegas-Paradise MSA, NV	H	14.37 FQ	17.14 MW	19.48 TQ	NVBLS	5/08
	New Hampshire	H	10.96 AE	17.18 MW	20.81 AEX	NHBLS	6/08
	Nashua NECTA, NH-MA	Y	37220 FQ	43230 MW	57630 TQ	USBLS	5/07
	New Jersey	Y	26250 FQ	30700 MW	40130 TQ	USBLS	5/07
	Camden PMSA, NJ	Y	26590 FQ	30110 MW	34920 TQ	USBLS	5/07
	Edison PMSA, NJ	Y	26370 FQ	31160 MW	39940 TQ	USBLS	5/07
	Newark-Union PMSA, NJ-PA	Y	26830 FQ	30170 MW	41830 TQ	USBLS	5/07
	New Mexico	Y	25380 FQ	33820 MW	39910 TQ	USBLS	5/07
	Albuquerque MSA, NM	Y	31660 FQ	36240 MW	40440 TQ	USBLS	5/07
	New York	Y	27120 FQ	31800 MW	37810 TQ	USBLS	5/07
	Albany-Schenectady-Troy MSA, NY	Y	19720 FQ	28380 MW	31570 TQ	USBLS	5/07
	Buffalo-Niagara Falls MSA, NY	Y	33190 FQ	40090 MW	46940 TQ	USBLS	5/07
	Nassau-Suffolk PMSA, NY	Y	21550 FQ	31350 MW	42990 TQ	USBLS	5/07
	New York-Northern New Jersey-Long Island MSA, NY-NJ-PA	Y	26650 FQ	31410 MW	39040 TQ	USBLS	5/07
	North Carolina	Y	22330 FQ	27900 MW	33750 TQ	USBLS	5/07
	Charlotte-Gastonia-Concord MSA, NC-SC	Y	24640 FQ	29850 MW	35290 TQ	USBLS	5/07

AE	Average entry wage	AW	Average wage paid	FQ	First quartile wage
AER	Average entry range	AWR	Average wage range	H	Hourly
AEX	Average experienced wage	AXR	Average experienced range	HI	Highest wage paid
ATC	Average total compensation	D	Daily	HR	High end range

LO	Lowest wage paid	MTC	Median total compensation	TCC	Total cash compensation
LR	Low end range	MW	Median wage paid	TQ	Third quartile wage
M	Monthly	MWR	Median wage range	W	Weekly
MCC	Median cash compensation	S	See annotated source	Y	Yearly

Pest Control Worker

Occupation/Type/Industry	Location	Per	Low	Mid	High	Source	Date
Pest Control Worker	Raleigh-Cary MSA, NC	Y	25660 FQ	30660 MW	43150 TQ	USBLS	5/07
	North Dakota	Y	27800 FQ	40700 MW	47630 TQ	USBLS	5/07
	Ohio	Y	23540 FQ	28620 MW	33870 TQ	USBLS	5/07
	Cincinnati-Middletown MSA, OH-KY-IN	Y	24810 FQ	28860 MW	32380 TQ	USBLS	5/07
	Cleveland-Elyria-Mentor MSA, OH	Y	22170 FQ	24470 MW	30830 TQ	USBLS	5/07
	Columbus MSA, OH	Y	26800 FQ	31840 MW	40780 TQ	USBLS	5/07
	Dayton MSA, OH	Y	18900 FQ	30820 MW	47370 TQ	USBLS	5/07
	Oklahoma	Y	20040 FQ	26590 MW	32730 TQ	USBLS	5/07
	Oklahoma City MSA, OK	Y	19190 FQ	26690 MW	32270 TQ	USBLS	5/07
	Tulsa MSA, OK	Y	23350 FQ	29720 MW	37580 TQ	USBLS	5/07
	Oregon	H	12.64 FQ	15.32 MW	18.13 TQ	ORBLS	5/08
	Portland-Vancouver-Beaverton MSA, OR-WA	Y	31410 FQ	37320 MW	45830 TQ	USBLS	5/07
	Pennsylvania	Y	23560 FQ	29010 MW	37190 TQ	USBLS	5/07
	Allentown-Bethlehem-Easton MSA, PA-NJ	Y	22260 FQ	25430 MW	32310 TQ	USBLS	5/07
	Philadelphia-Camden-Wilmington MSA, PA-NJ-DE-MD	Y	25300 FQ	29190 MW	35000 TQ	USBLS	5/07
	Pittsburgh MSA, PA	Y	23350 FQ	35960 MW	50030 TQ	USBLS	5/07
	York-Hanover MSA, PA	Y	26310 FQ	31520 MW	40980 TQ	USBLS	5/07
	Rhode Island	Y	24420 FQ	28860 MW	32470 TQ	USBLS	5/07
	Providence-Fall River-Warwick MSA, RI-MA	Y	24660 FQ	29110 MW	32700 TQ	USBLS	5/07
	South Carolina	Y	23440 FQ	28950 MW	35910 TQ	USBLS	5/07
	Charleston-North Charleston MSA, SC	Y	26670 FQ	32070 MW	38460 TQ	USBLS	5/07
	Columbia MSA, SC	Y	22670 FQ	27190 MW	31950 TQ	USBLS	5/07
	Spartanburg MSA, SC	Y	26700 FQ	30290 MW	36140 TQ	USBLS	5/07
	South Dakota	Y	24559 FQ	39662 MW	45882 TQ	SDBLS	7/08-9/08
	Sioux Falls MSA, SD	Y	26560 FQ	41688 MW	46775 TQ	SDBLS	7/08-9/08
	Tennessee	Y	23390 FQ	27860 MW	33460 TQ	USBLS	5/07
	Memphis MSA, TN-MS-AR	Y	23670 FQ	28060 MW	33790 TQ	USBLS	5/07
	Nashville-Davidson-Murfreesboro MSA, TN	Y	21920 FQ	26580 MW	29820 TQ	USBLS	5/07
	Texas	Y	23890 FQ	29360 MW	36810 TQ	USBLS	5/07
	Austin-Round Rock MSA, TX	Y	24360 FQ	28170 MW	32890 TQ	USBLS	5/07
	Dallas-Fort Worth-Arlington MSA, TX	Y	25900 FQ	34550 MW	47550 TQ	USBLS	5/07
	El Paso MSA, TX	Y	22830 FQ	26950 MW	39880 TQ	USBLS	5/07
	Houston-Sugar Land-Baytown MSA, TX	Y	25070 FQ	28750 MW	34280 TQ	USBLS	5/07
	San Antonio MSA, TX	Y	23140 FQ	28810 MW	35220 TQ	USBLS	5/07
	Utah	Y	22060 FQ	29020 MW	35310 TQ	USBLS	5/07
	Salt Lake City MSA, UT	Y	28440 FQ	33480 MW	38340 TQ	USBLS	5/07
	Vermont	Y	23470 FQ	25990 MW	40590 TQ	USBLS	5/07
	Virginia	Y	22720 FQ	30940 MW	43780 TQ	USBLS	5/07
	Richmond MSA, VA	Y	28230 FQ	35770 MW	45340 TQ	USBLS	5/07
	Virginia Beach-Norfolk-Newport News MSA, VA-NC	Y	18990 FQ	26300 MW	44420 TQ	USBLS	5/07
	Washington	H	13.99 FQ	17.64 MW	21.77 TQ	WABLS	3/08
	Seattle-Tacoma-Bellevue MSA, WA	Y	29750 FQ	37840 MW	46310 TQ	USBLS	5/07
	West Virginia	Y	22315 FQ	27235 MW	31581 TQ	WVBLS	7/08-9/08
	Wisconsin	Y	31230 FQ	37140 MW	43190 TQ	USBLS	5/07
	Wyoming	Y	20035 FQ	25509 MW	37761 TQ	WYBLS	9/08
	Cheyenne MSA, WY	Y	19018 FQ	20923 MW	41891 TQ	WYBLS	9/08
	Puerto Rico	Y	16730 FQ	20650 MW	24150 TQ	USBLS	5/07
	San Juan-Caguas-Guaynabo MSA, PR	Y	16820 FQ	20660 MW	24120 TQ	USBLS	5/07
	Virgin Islands	Y	20090 FQ	21770 MW	23640 TQ	USBLS	5/07
	Guam	Y	15840 FQ	19200 MW	22350 TQ	USBLS	5/07

Pesticide/Fertilizer Inspector

Occupation/Type/Industry	Location	Per	Low	Mid	High	Source	Date
State Government	Ohio	H	18.36 LO		23.87 HI	ODAS	2008

Pesticide Handler, Sprayer, and Applicator

Occupation/Type/Industry	Location	Per	Low	Mid	High	Source	Date
Vegetation	Alabama	Y	21470 FQ	26410 MW	32240 TQ	USBLS	5/07
Vegetation	Birmingham-Hoover MSA, AL	Y	26380 FQ	29220 MW	35040 TQ	USBLS	5/07

AE	Average entry wage	AW	Average wage paid	FQ	First quartile wage	LO	Lowest wage paid	MTC	Median total compensation	TCC	Total cash compensation
AER	Average entry range	AWR	Average wage range	H	Hourly	LR	Low end range	MW	Median wage paid	TQ	Third quartile wage
AEX	Average experienced wage	AXR	Average experienced range	HI	Highest wage paid	M	Monthly	MWR	Median wage range	W	Weekly
ATC	Average total compensation	D	Daily	HR	High end range	MCC	Median cash compensation	S	See annotated source	Y	Yearly

Occupation/Type/Industry	Location	Per	Low	Mid	High	Source	Date
Pesticide Handler, Sprayer, and Applicator							
Vegetation	Arizona	Y	17570 FQ	21040 MW	27040 TQ	USBLS	5/07
Vegetation	Phoenix-Mesa-Scottsdale MSA, AZ	Y	17930 FQ	28710 MW	41720 TQ	USBLS	5/07
Vegetation	Tucson MSA, AZ	Y	20190 FQ	21550 MW	22920 TQ	USBLS	5/07
Vegetation	Arkansas	Y	20420 FQ	24590 MW	29780 TQ	USBLS	5/07
Vegetation	California	H	11.19 FQ	14.59 MW	20.99 TQ	CABLS	1/08-3/08
Vegetation	Fresno MSA, CA	H	8.95 FQ	11.45 MW	13.72 TQ	CABLS	1/08-3/08
Vegetation	Los Angeles-Long Beach-Glendale PMSA, CA	H	15.24 FQ	18.66 MW	23.70 TQ	CABLS	1/08-3/08
Vegetation	Oakland-Fremont-Hayward MSA, CA	H	15.68 FQ	25.19 MW	35.29 TQ	CABLS	1/08-3/08
Vegetation	Riverside-San Bernardino-Ontario MSA, CA	H	10.64 FQ	13.95 MW	18.94 TQ	CABLS	1/08-3/08
Vegetation	Sacramento-Arden Arcade-Roseville MSA, CA	H	14.56 FQ	17.69 MW	21.50 TQ	CABLS	1/08-3/08
Vegetation	San Diego-Carlsbad-San Marcos MSA, CA	H	11.42 FQ	15.38 MW	21.41 TQ	CABLS	1/08-3/08
Vegetation	San Francisco-San Mateo-Redwood PMSA, CA	H	10.14 FQ	17.94 MW	25.41 TQ	CABLS	1/08-3/08
Vegetation	San Jose-Sunnyvale-Santa Clara MSA, CA	H	14.25 FQ	16.60 MW	19.40 TQ	CABLS	1/08-3/08
Vegetation	Santa Ana-Anaheim-Irvine PMSA, CA	Y	29430 FQ	38240 MW	43530 TQ	USBLS	5/07
Vegetation	Colorado	Y	24520 FQ	28980 MW	35130 TQ	USBLS	5/07
Vegetation	Colorado Springs MSA, CO	Y	21320 FQ	23900 MW	29270 TQ	USBLS	5/07
Vegetation	Denver-Aurora MSA, CO	Y	24900 FQ	28740 MW	33930 TQ	USBLS	5/07
Vegetation	Connecticut	H	12.99 AE	17.57 MW		CTBLS	1/08-3/08
Vegetation	Delaware	Y	25410 FQ	29300 MW	35450 TQ	USBLS	5/07
Vegetation	Wilmington PMSA, DE-MD-NJ	Y	25530 FQ	29010 MW	34400 TQ	USBLS	5/07
Vegetation	Washington-Arlington-Alexandria MSA, DC-VA-MD-WV	Y	29050 FQ	36810 MW	41070 TQ	USBLS	5/07
Vegetation	Florida	Y	22880 FQ	27770 MW	32420 TQ	USBLS	5/07
Vegetation	Fort Lauderdale-Pompano Beach-Deerfield Beach PMSA, FL	Y	27100 FQ	29430 MW	31900 TQ	USBLS	5/07
Vegetation	Jacksonville MSA, FL	Y	21400 FQ	25860 MW	29610 TQ	USBLS	5/07
Vegetation	Miami-Fort Lauderdale-Miami Beach MSA, FL	Y	25230 FQ	28980 MW	32770 TQ	USBLS	5/07
Vegetation	Orlando-Kissimmee MSA, FL	Y	23170 FQ	28860 MW	35090 TQ	USBLS	5/07
Vegetation	Tampa-St. Petersburg-Clearwater MSA, FL	Y	20330 FQ	24870 MW	30000 TQ	USBLS	5/07
Vegetation	West Palm Beach-Boca Raton-Boynton Beach PMSA, FL	Y	21760 FQ	28000 MW	33230 TQ	USBLS	5/07
Vegetation	Georgia	Y	21270 FQ	27800 MW	33150 TQ	USBLS	5/07
Vegetation	Atlanta-Sandy Springs-Marietta MSA, GA	Y	24970 FQ	27870 MW	32200 TQ	USBLS	5/07
Vegetation	Idaho	Y	22930 FQ	26400 MW	29680 TQ	USBLS	5/07
Vegetation	Boise City-Nampa MSA, ID	Y	22880 FQ	26070 MW	29350 TQ	USBLS	5/07
Vegetation	Illinois	Y	23580 FQ	32960 MW	60530 TQ	USBLS	5/07
Vegetation	Chicago-Naperville-Joliet MSA, IL-IN-WI	Y	22330 FQ	35200 MW	63060 TQ	USBLS	5/07
Vegetation	Indiana	Y	23720 FQ	28250 MW	33820 TQ	USBLS	5/07
Vegetation	Fort Wayne MSA, IN	Y	20690 FQ	22960 MW	28500 TQ	USBLS	5/07
Vegetation	Indianapolis-Carmel MSA, IN	Y	23950 FQ	27420 MW	35020 TQ	USBLS	5/07
Vegetation	Iowa	Y	24120 FQ	27960 MW	33320 TQ	USBLS	5/07
Vegetation	Des Moines-West Des Moines MSA, IA	Y	23650 FQ	28150 MW	36080 TQ	USBLS	5/07
Vegetation	Kansas	Y	22630 FQ	27500 MW	32760 TQ	USBLS	5/07
Vegetation	Wichita MSA, KS	Y	23410 FQ	28310 MW	32380 TQ	USBLS	5/07
Vegetation	Kentucky	Y	26793 FQ	33601 MW	38361 TQ	KYBLS	2008
Vegetation	Louisville-Jefferson County MSA, KY-IN	Y	31320 FQ	33910 MW	36630 TQ	USBLS	5/07
Vegetation	Louisiana	H	8.38 FQ	10.40 MW	13.41 TQ	LABLS	1/08-3/08
Vegetation	Baton Rouge MSA, LA	Y	17210 FQ	18600 MW	20110 TQ	USBLS	5/07
Vegetation	New Orleans-Metairie-Kenner MSA, LA	Y	13000 FQ	14950 MW	23150 TQ	USBLS	5/07
Vegetation	Maine	Y	17400 FQ	23490 MW	30000 TQ	USBLS	5/07

AE	Average entry wage	AW	Average wage paid	FQ	First quartile wage
AER	Average entry range	AWR	Average wage range	H	Hourly
AEX	Average experienced wage	AXR	Average experienced range	HI	Highest wage paid
ATC	Average total compensation	D	Daily	HR	High end range

LO	Lowest wage paid	MTC	Median total compensation	TCC	Total cash compensation
LR	Low end range	MW	Median wage paid	TQ	Third quartile wage
M	Monthly	MWR	Median wage range	W	Weekly
MCC	Median cash compensation	S	See annotated source	Y	Yearly

Occupation/Type/Industry	Location	Per	Low	Mid	High	Source	Date
Pesticide Handler, Sprayer, and Applicator							
Vegetation	Portland-South Portland-Biddeford MSA, ME	Y	20130 FQ	26650 MW	32620 TQ	USBLS	5/07
Vegetation	Maryland	Y		32325 MW		MDBLS	3/08
Vegetation	Baltimore-Towson MSA, MD	Y	29130 FQ	35920 MW	44330 TQ	USBLS	5/07
Vegetation	Bethesda-Gaithersburg-Frederick PMSA, MD	Y	28640 FQ	34590 MW	40670 TQ	USBLS	5/07
Vegetation	Massachusetts	Y	27500 FQ	32890 MW	40600 TQ	USBLS	5/07
Vegetation	Boston-Cambridge-Quincy NECTA, MA	Y	31470 FQ	38380 MW	46080 TQ	USBLS	5/07
Vegetation	Michigan	Y	26840 FQ	30260 MW	34660 TQ	USBLS	5/07
Vegetation	Detroit-Warren-Livonia MSA, MI	Y	27610 FQ	30210 MW	32860 TQ	USBLS	5/07
Vegetation	Grand Rapids-Wyoming MSA, MI	Y	29790 FQ	34170 MW	38260 TQ	USBLS	5/07
Vegetation	Warren-Troy-Farmington Hills PMSA, MI	Y	27840 FQ	30480 MW	34040 TQ	USBLS	5/07
Vegetation	Minnesota	Y	27028 FQ	29746 MW	32684 TQ	MNBLS	10/08-12/08
Vegetation	Minneapolis-Saint Paul MSA, MN-WI	Y	27258 FQ	30060 MW	33437 TQ	MNBLS	10/08-12/08
Vegetation	Missouri	Y	23140 FQ	27320 MW	32780 TQ	USBLS	5/07
Vegetation	Kansas City MSA, MO-KS	Y	23210 FQ	28410 MW	35540 TQ	USBLS	5/07
Vegetation	St. Louis MSA, MO-IL	Y	25190 FQ	30280 MW	38650 TQ	USBLS	5/07
Vegetation	Montana	Y	15910 FQ	20130 MW	26010 TQ	USBLS	5/07
Vegetation	Nebraska	Y	19140 FQ	24100 MW	31450 TQ	USBLS	5/07
Vegetation	Omaha-Council Bluffs MSA, NE-IA	Y	23100 FQ	30840 MW	35310 TQ	USBLS	5/07
Vegetation	Nevada	H	11.27 FQ	13.20 MW	15.62 TQ	NVBLS	5/08
Vegetation	Las Vegas-Paradise MSA, NV	H	11.19 FQ	12.83 MW	14.72 TQ	NVBLS	5/08
Vegetation	New Jersey	Y	26820 FQ	31770 MW	39390 TQ	USBLS	5/07
Vegetation	Newark-Union PMSA, NJ-PA	Y	26000 FQ	28450 MW	34080 TQ	USBLS	5/07
Vegetation	New Mexico	Y	17240 FQ	19410 MW	26700 TQ	USBLS	5/07
Vegetation	New York	Y	29130 FQ	34820 MW	40970 TQ	USBLS	5/07
Vegetation	Buffalo-Niagara Falls MSA, NY	Y	28110 FQ	31250 MW	38370 TQ	USBLS	5/07
Vegetation	Nassau-Suffolk PMSA, NY	Y	34480 FQ	38080 MW	43310 TQ	USBLS	5/07
Vegetation	New York-Northern New Jersey-Long Island MSA, NY-NJ-PA	Y	31420 FQ	36470 MW	43590 TQ	USBLS	5/07
Vegetation	North Carolina	Y	21940 FQ	26960 MW	34210 TQ	USBLS	5/07
Vegetation	Charlotte-Gastonia-Concord MSA, NC-SC	Y	22470 FQ	26560 MW	30790 TQ	USBLS	5/07
Vegetation	Raleigh-Cary MSA, NC	Y	23900 FQ	30760 MW	37610 TQ	USBLS	5/07
Vegetation	North Dakota	Y	21850 FQ	24300 MW	29230 TQ	USBLS	5/07
Vegetation	Ohio	Y	21150 FQ	24540 MW	32900 TQ	USBLS	5/07
Vegetation	Cincinnati-Middletown MSA, OH-KY-IN	Y	20450 FQ	27420 MW	33520 TQ	USBLS	5/07
Vegetation	Cleveland-Elyria-Mentor MSA, OH	Y	29360 FQ	34190 MW	38320 TQ	USBLS	5/07
Vegetation	Columbus MSA, OH	Y	21010 FQ	23100 MW	25190 TQ	USBLS	5/07
Vegetation	Oklahoma	Y	18470 FQ	24900 MW	32260 TQ	USBLS	5/07
Vegetation	Oklahoma City MSA, OK	Y	23040 FQ	37960 MW	42550 TQ	USBLS	5/07
Vegetation	Oregon	H	12.78 FQ	15.89 MW	19.81 TQ	ORBLS	5/08
Vegetation	Portland-Vancouver-Beaverton MSA, OR-WA	Y	25510 FQ	30290 MW	37790 TQ	USBLS	5/07
Vegetation	Pennsylvania	Y	25330 FQ	32210 MW	37190 TQ	USBLS	5/07
Vegetation	Allentown-Bethlehem-Easton MSA, PA-NJ	Y	34850 FQ	37370 MW	39830 TQ	USBLS	5/07
Vegetation	Philadelphia-Camden-Wilmington MSA, PA-NJ-DE-MD	Y	21340 FQ	27540 MW	35200 TQ	USBLS	5/07
Vegetation	South Carolina	Y	22160 FQ	27580 MW	33750 TQ	USBLS	5/07
Vegetation	Charleston-North Charleston MSA, SC	Y	30690 FQ	35440 MW	39830 TQ	USBLS	5/07
Vegetation	Columbia MSA, SC	Y	18340 FQ	25150 MW	30220 TQ	USBLS	5/07
Vegetation	South Dakota	Y	20757 FQ	24339 MW	28679 TQ	SDBLS	7/08-9/08
Vegetation	Sioux Falls MSA, SD	Y	24530 FQ	29195 MW	33759 TQ	SDBLS	7/08-9/08
Vegetation	Tennessee	Y	20540 FQ	23280 MW	27860 TQ	USBLS	5/07
Vegetation	Memphis MSA, TN-MS-AR	Y	22550 FQ	25140 MW	29280 TQ	USBLS	5/07
Vegetation	Texas	Y	24770 FQ	32780 MW	39580 TQ	USBLS	5/07
Vegetation	Austin-Round Rock MSA, TX	Y	21800 FQ	23920 MW	28400 TQ	USBLS	5/07

AE Average entry wage	**AW** Average wage paid	**FQ** First quartile wage	**LO** Lowest wage paid	**MTC** Median total compensation	**TCC** Total cash compensation
AER Average entry range	**AWR** Average wage range	**H** Hourly	**LR** Low end range	**MW** Median wage paid	**TQ** Third quartile wage
AEX Average experienced wage	**AXR** Average experienced range	**HI** Highest wage paid	**M** Monthly	**MWR** Median wage range	**W** Weekly
ATC Average total compensation	**D** Daily	**HR** High end range	**MCC** Median cash compensation	**S** See annotated source	**Y** Yearly

Occupation/Type/Industry	Location	Per	Low	Mid	High	Source	Date
Pesticide Handler, Sprayer, and Applicator							
Vegetation	Dallas-Fort Worth-Arlington MSA, TX	Y	28950 FQ	35820 MW	42980 TQ	USBLS	5/07
Vegetation	Houston-Sugar Land-Baytown MSA, TX	Y	29080 FQ	35930 MW	43560 TQ	USBLS	5/07
Vegetation	San Antonio MSA, TX	Y	22150 FQ	25470 MW	36970 TQ	USBLS	5/07
Vegetation	Utah	Y	22760 FQ	25950 MW	30950 TQ	USBLS	5/07
Vegetation	Virginia	Y	26450 FQ	36030 MW	40410 TQ	USBLS	5/07
Vegetation	Virginia Beach-Norfolk-Newport News MSA, VA-NC	Y	22760 FQ	27930 MW	37480 TQ	USBLS	5/07
Vegetation	Washington	H	11.55 FQ	14.20 MW	17.58 TQ	WABLS	3/08
Vegetation	Seattle-Tacoma-Bellevue MSA, WA	Y	27010 FQ	32750 MW	38110 TQ	USBLS	5/07
Vegetation	West Virginia	Y	22779 FQ	25118 MW	28051 TQ	WVBLS	7/08-9/08
Vegetation	Wisconsin	Y	23180 FQ	28150 MW	36180 TQ	USBLS	5/07
Vegetation	Milwaukee-Waukesha-West Allis MSA, WI	Y	26690 FQ	34230 MW	46260 TQ	USBLS	5/07
Vegetation	Wyoming	Y	23798 FQ	26816 MW	29914 TQ	WYBLS	9/08
Vegetation	Puerto Rico	Y	12750 FQ	14470 MW	18530 TQ	USBLS	5/07
Vegetation	San Juan-Caguas-Guaynabo MSA, PR	Y	13970 FQ	17270 MW	27250 TQ	USBLS	5/07
Pet Groomer	United States	Y		17077 AW		SUSA01	2008
Pet License Canvasser							
Municipal Government	Seattle, WA	H			15.38 HI	CSSS	2008
Petroleum Engineer	Alabama	Y	66570 FQ	78000 MW	88370 TQ	USBLS	5/07
	Alaska	Y	88550 FQ	115950 MW		USBLS	5/07
	Arizona	Y	67680 FQ	75890 MW	84550 TQ	USBLS	5/07
	California	H	46.12 FQ	55.83 MW		CABLS	1/08-3/08
	Connecticut	H	23.88 AE	49.29 MW		CTBLS	1/08-3/08
	Illinois	Y	50700 FQ	76560 MW	94440 TQ	USBLS	5/07
	Kansas	Y	53700 FQ	68320 MW	87910 TQ	USBLS	5/07
	Kentucky	Y	51134 FQ	73330 MW	95585 TQ	KYBLS	2008
	Louisiana	H	37.36 FQ	44.98 MW	53.36 TQ	LABLS	1/08-3/08
	Michigan	Y	60360 FQ	80230 MW	135450 TQ	USBLS	5/07
	Mississippi	Y	59070 FQ	82130 MW	101160 TQ	USBLS	5/07
	Missouri	Y	69850 FQ	76510 MW	86330 TQ	USBLS	5/07
	Montana	Y	69710 FQ	80030 MW	95540 TQ	USBLS	5/07
	New Mexico	Y	63700 FQ	84510 MW	103450 TQ	USBLS	5/07
	North Dakota	Y	67130 FQ	119700 MW		USBLS	5/07
	Ohio	Y	83130 FQ	90860 MW	98530 TQ	USBLS	5/07
	Oklahoma	Y	63680 FQ	88030 MW	120480 TQ	USBLS	5/07
	Pennsylvania	Y	49850 FQ	66570 MW	97570 TQ	USBLS	5/07
	Texas	Y	85920 FQ	117540 MW		USBLS	5/07
	Utah	Y	74320 FQ	89770 MW	109350 TQ	USBLS	5/07
	Virginia	Y	83870 FQ	100310 MW	118290 TQ	USBLS	5/07
	Washington	H	38.04 FQ	45.68 MW	54.61 TQ	WABLS	3/08
	West Virginia	Y	67998 FQ	89978 MW	120603 TQ	WVBLS	7/08-9/08
Citizen of the United States	United States	Y		142707 AW		SPE	6/08-7/08
Not a Citizen of the United States	United States	Y		126154 AW		SPE	6/08-7/08
Petroleum Geologist	United States	Y	58000-130000 LR	82800-162800 AWR	95000-200000 HR	AAPG	2008
Petroleum Pump System Operator, Refinery Operator, and Gauger	Alabama	Y	43520 FQ	48940 MW	56540 TQ	USBLS	5/07
	Alaska	Y	59090 FQ	75110 MW	84700 TQ	USBLS	5/07
	Arizona	Y	42350 FQ	47820 MW	56380 TQ	USBLS	5/07
	Phoenix-Mesa-Scottsdale MSA, AZ	Y	41470 FQ	47270 MW	56240 TQ	USBLS	5/07
	Tucson MSA, AZ	Y	43850 FQ	47940 MW	54340 TQ	USBLS	5/07
	Arkansas	Y	33930 FQ	39930 MW	55470 TQ	USBLS	5/07
	California	H	24.12 FQ	29.61 MW	35.85 TQ	CABLS	1/08-3/08
	Los Angeles-Long Beach-Glendale PMSA, CA	H	23.54 FQ	31.06 MW	37.01 TQ	CABLS	1/08-3/08
	Oakland-Fremont-Hayward MSA, CA	H	24.09 FQ	29.91 MW	35.87 TQ	CABLS	1/08-3/08

AE	Average entry wage	AW	Average wage paid	FQ First quartile wage
AER	Average entry range	AWR	Average wage range	H Hourly
AEX	Average experienced wage	AXR	Average experienced range	HI Highest wage paid
ATC	Average total compensation	D	Daily	HR High end range

LO	Lowest wage paid	MTC Median total compensation	TCC Total cash compensation
LR	Low end range	MW Median wage paid	TQ Third quartile wage
M	Monthly	MWR Median wage range	W Weekly
MCC Median cash compensation	S See annotated source	Y Yearly	

Occupation/Type/Industry	Location	Per	Low	Mid	High	Source	Date
Petroleum Pump System Operator, Refinery Operator, and Gauger	San Diego-Carlsbad-San Marcos MSA, CA	H	22.99 FQ	27.56 MW	33.68 TQ	CABLS	1/08-3/08
	San Francisco-San Mateo-Redwood PMSA, CA	H	24.18 FQ	26.31 MW	28.43 TQ	CABLS	1/08-3/08
	Santa Ana-Anaheim-Irvine PMSA, CA	Y	46770 FQ	55940 MW	69170 TQ	USBLS	5/07
	Colorado	Y	47700 FQ	61630 MW	69680 TQ	USBLS	5/07
	Denver-Aurora MSA, CO	Y	54630 FQ	63880 MW	70970 TQ	USBLS	5/07
	Connecticut	H	19.93 AE	23.22 MW		CTBLS	1/08-3/08
	Delaware	Y	49320 FQ	57240 MW	63350 TQ	USBLS	5/07
	Wilmington PMSA, DE-MD-NJ	Y	53280 FQ	58680 MW	64070 TQ	USBLS	5/07
	Florida	Y	36870 FQ	45610 MW	52650 TQ	USBLS	5/07
	Georgia	Y	44080 FQ	48510 MW	57300 TQ	USBLS	5/07
	Atlanta-Sandy Springs-Marietta MSA, GA	Y	45250 FQ	51540 MW	67800 TQ	USBLS	5/07
	Hawaii	Y	50800 FQ	57910 MW	65770 TQ	USBLS	5/07
	Honolulu MSA, HI	Y	50430 FQ	58000 MW	66620 TQ	USBLS	5/07
	Illinois	Y	22980 FQ	42580 MW	47490 TQ	USBLS	5/07
	Chicago-Naperville-Joliet MSA, IL-IN-WI	Y	24830 FQ	43950 MW	51500 TQ	USBLS	5/07
	Indiana	Y	36680 FQ	50350 MW	55970 TQ	USBLS	5/07
	Gary PMSA, IN	Y	35700 FQ	51000 MW	56500 TQ	USBLS	5/07
	Iowa	Y	51610 FQ	56010 MW	60430 TQ	USBLS	5/07
	Kansas	Y	44270 FQ	53090 MW	59300 TQ	USBLS	5/07
	Wichita MSA, KS	Y	51430 FQ	55720 MW	59940 TQ	USBLS	5/07
	Kentucky	Y	47210 FQ	55100 MW	61196 TQ	KYBLS	2008
	Louisville-Jefferson County MSA, KY-IN	Y	31510 FQ	46830 MW	56970 TQ	USBLS	5/07
	Louisiana	H	21.86 FQ	26.56 MW	29.95 TQ	LABLS	1/08-3/08
	Baton Rouge MSA, LA	Y	48170 FQ	55720 MW	63050 TQ	USBLS	5/07
	Lafayette MSA, LA	Y	32440 FQ	43810 MW	52750 TQ	USBLS	5/07
	New Orleans-Metairie-Kenner MSA, LA	Y	49330 FQ	57480 MW	64200 TQ	USBLS	5/07
	Maryland	Y		44450 MW		MDBLS	3/08
	Baltimore-Towson MSA, MD	Y	38590 FQ	41880 MW	47080 TQ	USBLS	5/07
	Massachusetts	Y	33890 FQ	39200 MW	45850 TQ	USBLS	5/07
	Michigan	Y	41950 FQ	48180 MW	56370 TQ	USBLS	5/07
	Detroit-Warren-Livonia MSA, MI	Y	43190 FQ	48740 MW	56940 TQ	USBLS	5/07
	Minnesota	Y	44940 FQ	47987 MW	51097 TQ	MNBLS	10/08-12/08
	Minneapolis-Saint Paul MSA, MN-WI	Y	44981 FQ	47894 MW	50797 TQ	MNBLS	10/08-12/08
	Mississippi	Y	53240 FQ	65190 MW	70750 TQ	USBLS	5/07
	St. Louis MSA, MO-IL	Y	42760 FQ	45910 MW	49060 TQ	USBLS	5/07
	Montana	Y	53270 FQ	57400 MW	61700 TQ	USBLS	5/07
	Billings MSA, MT	Y	54870 FQ	58650 MW	62450 TQ	USBLS	5/07
	Nebraska	Y	45840 FQ	54770 MW	61470 TQ	USBLS	5/07
	New Jersey	Y	47720 FQ	56100 MW	66430 TQ	USBLS	5/07
	Camden PMSA, NJ	Y	47650 FQ	56970 MW	66970 TQ	USBLS	5/07
	Edison PMSA, NJ	Y	48810 FQ	55640 MW	65180 TQ	USBLS	5/07
	New Mexico	Y	32740 FQ	48900 MW	60630 TQ	USBLS	5/07
	New York	Y	41990 FQ	47640 MW	52770 TQ	USBLS	5/07
	Nassau-Suffolk PMSA, NY	Y	44560 FQ	48730 MW	53060 TQ	USBLS	5/07
	New York-Northern New Jersey-Long Island MSA, NY-NJ-PA	Y	44760 FQ	51800 MW	60470 TQ	USBLS	5/07
	North Carolina	Y	38950 FQ	45570 MW	52900 TQ	USBLS	5/07
	North Dakota	Y	37670 FQ	43840 MW	50840 TQ	USBLS	5/07
	Ohio	Y	47000 FQ	54080 MW	62760 TQ	USBLS	5/07
	Oklahoma	Y	34800 FQ	46090 MW	58850 TQ	USBLS	5/07
	Tulsa MSA, OK	Y	35680 FQ	53800 MW	66220 TQ	USBLS	5/07
	Oregon	H	21.82 FQ	24.40 MW	27.41 TQ	ORBLS	5/08
	Portland-Vancouver-Beaverton MSA, OR-WA	Y	46330 FQ	50590 MW	56800 TQ	USBLS	5/07
	Pennsylvania	Y	42320 FQ	49290 MW	56000 TQ	USBLS	5/07
	Philadelphia-Camden-Wilmington MSA, PA-NJ-DE-MD	Y	42430 FQ	48770 MW	59570 TQ	USBLS	5/07

AE Average entry wage	**AW** Average wage paid	**FQ** First quartile wage	**LO** Lowest wage paid	**MTC** Median total compensation	**TCC** Total cash compensation
AER Average entry range	**AWR** Average wage range	**H** Hourly	**LR** Low end range	**MW** Median wage paid	**TQ** Third quartile wage
AEX Average experienced wage	**AXR** Average experienced range	**HI** Highest wage paid	**M** Monthly	**MWR** Median wage range	**W** Weekly
ATC Average total compensation	**D** Daily	**HR** High end range	**MCC** Median cash compensation	**S** See annotated source	**Y** Yearly

Occupation/Type/Industry	Location	Per	Low	Mid	High	Source	Date
Petroleum Pump System Operator, Refinery Operator, and Gauger	Pittsburgh MSA, PA	Y	51020 FQ	55260 MW	59330 TQ	USBLS	5/07
	South Dakota	Y	40767 FQ	51093 MW	56364 TQ	SDBLS	7/08-9/08
	Tennessee	Y	37870 FQ	43580 MW	49370 TQ	USBLS	5/07
	Memphis MSA, TN-MS-AR	Y	38250 FQ	44510 MW	50750 TQ	USBLS	5/07
	Texas	Y	41630 FQ	52060 MW	64070 TQ	USBLS	5/07
	Dallas-Fort Worth-Arlington MSA, TX	Y	36320 FQ	46160 MW	55630 TQ	USBLS	5/07
	El Paso MSA, TX	Y	51760 FQ	55950 MW	60130 TQ	USBLS	5/07
	Houston-Sugar Land-Baytown MSA, TX	Y	43120 FQ	53190 MW	65480 TQ	USBLS	5/07
	San Antonio MSA, TX	Y	34850 FQ	43850 MW	55770 TQ	USBLS	5/07
	Utah	Y	40990 FQ	45880 MW	54190 TQ	USBLS	5/07
	Salt Lake City MSA, UT	Y	40370 FQ	43070 MW	45770 TQ	USBLS	5/07
	Washington	H	26.25 FQ	30.08 MW	33.61 TQ	WABLS	3/08
	Seattle-Tacoma-Bellevue MSA, WA	Y	47930 FQ	55600 MW	62400 TQ	USBLS	5/07
	West Virginia	Y	43322 FQ	46956 MW	51433 TQ	WVBLS	7/08-9/08
	Wisconsin	Y	27960 FQ	30960 MW	48610 TQ	USBLS	5/07
	Wyoming	Y	33623 FQ	37590 MW	57598 TQ	WYBLS	9/08
	Cheyenne MSA, WY	Y	56777 FQ	60429 MW	64082 TQ	WYBLS	9/08
	Puerto Rico	Y	26120 FQ	35300 MW	48480 TQ	USBLS	5/07
Petrologist	United States	Y		67470 AW		SUSA03	2008
Pharmaceutical Sales Representative	United States	Y		93700 MW		CNNM02	2007
Pharmacist	Alabama	Y	87550 FQ	99070 MW	115000 TQ	USBLS	5/07
	Birmingham-Hoover MSA, AL	Y	87100 FQ	96830 MW	107720 TQ	USBLS	5/07
	Huntsville MSA, AL	Y	95280 FQ	107420 MW	119750 TQ	USBLS	5/07
	Alaska	Y	99680 FQ	112030 MW	123300 TQ	USBLS	5/07
	Anchorage MSA, AK	Y	99520 FQ	111070 MW	121880 TQ	USBLS	5/07
	Arizona	Y	89230 FQ	105450 MW	118120 TQ	USBLS	5/07
	Phoenix-Mesa-Scottsdale MSA, AZ	Y	91110 FQ	106420 MW	118600 TQ	USBLS	5/07
	Tucson MSA, AZ	Y	73520 FQ	99370 MW	114590 TQ	USBLS	5/07
	Arkansas	Y	84600 FQ	95920 MW	108190 TQ	USBLS	5/07
	Little Rock-North Little Rock MSA, AR	Y	85170 FQ	96660 MW	107780 TQ	USBLS	5/07
	California	H	51.88 FQ	57.17 MW	62.14 TQ	CABLS	1/08-3/08
	Los Angeles-Long Beach-Glendale PMSA, CA	H	49.75 FQ	56.22 MW	61.22 TQ	CABLS	1/08-3/08
	Oakland-Fremont-Hayward MSA, CA	H	51.85 FQ	57.35 MW	62.54 TQ	CABLS	1/08-3/08
	Riverside-San Bernardino-Ontario MSA, CA	H	52.62 FQ	57.11 MW	61.35 TQ	CABLS	1/08-3/08
	Sacramento-Arden Arcade-Roseville MSA, CA	H	52.05 FQ	57.48 MW	62.79 TQ	CABLS	1/08-3/08
	San Diego-Carlsbad-San Marcos MSA, CA	H	52.92 FQ	57.38 MW	61.77 TQ	CABLS	1/08-3/08
	San Francisco-San Mateo-Redwood PMSA, CA	H	51.76 FQ	58.30 MW	65.37 TQ	CABLS	1/08-3/08
	San Jose-Sunnyvale-Santa Clara MSA, CA	H	54.19 FQ	59.20 MW	64.53 TQ	CABLS	1/08-3/08
	Santa Ana-Anaheim-Irvine PMSA, CA	Y	102990 FQ	113920 MW	123270 TQ	USBLS	5/07
	Stockton MSA, CA	H	51.60 FQ	57.03 MW	61.85 TQ	CABLS	1/08-3/08
	Colorado	Y	89360 FQ	100990 MW	114930 TQ	USBLS	5/07
	Denver-Aurora MSA, CO	Y	89280 FQ	101340 MW	115140 TQ	USBLS	5/07
	Pueblo MSA, CO	Y	81790 FQ	93710 MW	105850 TQ	USBLS	5/07
	Connecticut	H	40.25 AE	50.04 MW		CTBLS	1/08-3/08
	Bridgeport-Stamford-Norwalk MSA, CT	Y	93110 FQ	106270 MW	119590 TQ	USBLS	5/07
	Hartford-West Hartford-East Hartford MSA, CT	Y	85350 FQ	100000 MW	114740 TQ	USBLS	5/07
	New Haven MSA, CT	Y	87960 FQ	97360 MW	111640 TQ	USBLS	5/07
	Delaware	Y	81360 FQ	94790 MW	112210 TQ	USBLS	5/07
	Wilmington PMSA, DE-MD-NJ	Y	81250 FQ	92990 MW	110440 TQ	USBLS	5/07

Occupation/Type/Industry	Location	Per	Low	Mid	High	Source	Date
Pharmacist	District of Columbia	Y	76100 FQ	89360 MW	98900 TQ	USBLS	5/07
	Washington-Arlington-Alexandria MSA, DC-VA-MD-WV	Y	86230 FQ	95490 MW	107240 TQ	USBLS	5/07
	Florida	Y	89080 FQ	99690 MW	112440 TQ	USBLS	5/07
	Fort Lauderdale-Pompano Beach-Deerfield Beach PMSA, FL	Y	87880 FQ	99980 MW	116000 TQ	USBLS	5/07
	Jacksonville MSA, FL	Y	89730 FQ	100660 MW	112710 TQ	USBLS	5/07
	Miami-Fort Lauderdale-Miami Beach MSA, FL	Y	90020 FQ	101310 MW	114540 TQ	USBLS	5/07
	Orlando-Kissimmee MSA, FL	Y	90820 FQ	100260 MW	112440 TQ	USBLS	5/07
	Pensacola-Ferry Pass-Brent MSA, FL	Y	87970 FQ	99330 MW	112490 TQ	USBLS	5/07
	Tampa-St. Petersburg-Clearwater MSA, FL	Y	87150 FQ	96060 MW	106340 TQ	USBLS	5/07
	West Palm Beach-Boca Raton-Boynton Beach PMSA, FL	Y	89490 FQ	98680 MW	109270 TQ	USBLS	5/07
	Georgia	Y	88280 FQ	99170 MW	111980 TQ	USBLS	5/07
	Atlanta-Sandy Springs-Marietta MSA, GA	Y	89680 FQ	99360 MW	110000 TQ	USBLS	5/07
	Hawaii	Y	83770 FQ	96000 MW	109270 TQ	USBLS	5/07
	Honolulu MSA, HI	Y	82860 FQ	95160 MW	108230 TQ	USBLS	5/07
	Idaho	Y	83280 FQ	93810 MW	104760 TQ	USBLS	5/07
	Boise City-Nampa MSA, ID	Y	85820 FQ	96660 MW	109100 TQ	USBLS	5/07
	Illinois	Y	86900 FQ	99760 MW	114840 TQ	USBLS	5/07
	Chicago-Naperville-Joliet MSA, IL-IN-WI	Y	86110 FQ	98200 MW	112930 TQ	USBLS	5/07
	Rockford MSA, IL	Y	89420 FQ	102460 MW	115950 TQ	USBLS	5/07
	Indiana	Y	87410 FQ	96210 MW	105750 TQ	USBLS	5/07
	Evansville MSA, IN-KY	Y	86240 FQ	94910 MW	104180 TQ	USBLS	5/07
	Gary PMSA, IN	Y	87430 FQ	94670 MW	101920 TQ	USBLS	5/07
	Indianapolis-Carmel MSA, IN	Y	86380 FQ	95070 MW	104580 TQ	USBLS	5/07
	Terre Haute MSA, IN	Y	94750 FQ	104140 MW	116260 TQ	USBLS	5/07
	Iowa	Y	82810 FQ	92400 MW	101840 TQ	USBLS	5/07
	Des Moines-West Des Moines MSA, IA	Y	75100 FQ	90710 MW	100890 TQ	USBLS	5/07
	Dubuque MSA, IA	Y	86890 FQ	93950 MW	101380 TQ	USBLS	5/07
	Kansas	Y	84820 FQ	94510 MW	106110 TQ	USBLS	5/07
	Wichita MSA, KS	Y	89080 FQ	98020 MW	110790 TQ	USBLS	5/07
	Kentucky	Y	94005 FQ	107413 MW	121776 TQ	KYBLS	2008
	Bowling Green MSA, KY	Y	90500 FQ	99830 MW	110160 TQ	USBLS	5/07
	Louisville-Jefferson County MSA, KY-IN	Y	97370 FQ	109710 MW	121000 TQ	USBLS	5/07
	Louisiana	H	38.65 FQ	44.46 MW	49.95 TQ	LABLS	1/08-3/08
	Baton Rouge MSA, LA	Y	85170 FQ	95340 MW	107470 TQ	USBLS	5/07
	New Orleans-Metairie-Kenner MSA, LA	Y	84620 FQ	94530 MW	105870 TQ	USBLS	5/07
	Maine	Y	100140 FQ	112550 MW	124020 TQ	USBLS	5/07
	Portland-South Portland-Biddeford MSA, ME	Y	94380 FQ	107040 MW	120850 TQ	USBLS	5/07
	Maryland	Y		97925 MW		MDBLS	3/08
	Baltimore-Towson MSA, MD	Y	86880 FQ	96830 MW	110660 TQ	USBLS	5/07
	Bethesda-Gaithersburg-Frederick PMSA, MD	Y	86950 FQ	96570 MW	109250 TQ	USBLS	5/07
	Massachusetts	Y	80360 FQ	91910 MW	102230 TQ	USBLS	5/07
	Boston-Cambridge-Quincy NECTA, MA	Y	73280 FQ	89390 MW	100660 TQ	USBLS	5/07
	Worcester MSA, MA-CT	Y	73310 FQ	89250 MW	99710 TQ	USBLS	5/07
	Michigan	Y	89340 FQ	100280 MW	112230 TQ	USBLS	5/07
	Detroit-Warren-Livonia MSA, MI	Y	89520 FQ	99490 MW	111000 TQ	USBLS	5/07
	Grand Rapids-Wyoming MSA, MI	Y	86520 FQ	99020 MW	110790 TQ	USBLS	5/07
	Muskegon-Norton Shores MSA, MI	Y	88180 FQ	95880 MW	103690 TQ	USBLS	5/07
	Warren-Troy-Farmington Hills PMSA, MI	Y	92240 FQ	102070 MW	113280 TQ	USBLS	5/07
	Minnesota	Y	101274 FQ	115137 MW	126802 TQ	MNBLS	10/08-12/08
	Duluth-Superior MSA, MN-WI	Y	92632 FQ	110565 MW	123758 TQ	MNBLS	10/08-12/08
	Minneapolis-Saint Paul MSA, MN-WI	Y	101672 FQ	115984 MW	127535 TQ	MNBLS	10/08-12/08

AE	Average entry wage	AW	Average wage paid	FQ	First quartile wage
AER	Average entry range	AWR	Average wage range	H	Hourly
AEX	Average experienced wage	AXR	Average experienced range	HI	Highest wage paid
ATC	Average total compensation	D	Daily	HR	High end range

LO	Lowest wage paid	MTC	Median total compensation	TCC	Total cash compensation
LR	Low end range	MW	Median wage paid	TQ	Third quartile wage
M	Monthly	MWR	Median wage range	W	Weekly
MCC	Median cash compensation	S	See annotated source	Y	Yearly

Occupation/Type/Industry	Location	Per	Low	Mid	High	Source	Date
Pharmacist	Rochester MSA, MN	Y	104554 FQ	114297 MW	125010 TQ	MNBLS	10/08-12/08
	Mississippi	Y	82680 FQ	95530 MW	109790 TQ	USBLS	5/07
	Jackson MSA, MS	Y	75570 FQ	90220 MW	104930 TQ	USBLS	5/07
	Missouri	Y	86800 FQ	96510 MW	110110 TQ	USBLS	5/07
	Kansas City MSA, MO-KS	Y	85280 FQ	94150 MW	105980 TQ	USBLS	5/07
	St. Louis MSA, MO-IL	Y	85260 FQ	94460 MW	104970 TQ	USBLS	5/07
	Montana	Y	79870 FQ	89820 MW	98380 TQ	USBLS	5/07
	Billings MSA, MT	Y	84290 FQ	93060 MW	102360 TQ	USBLS	5/07
	Nebraska	Y	81620 FQ	90630 MW	99040 TQ	USBLS	5/07
	Lincoln MSA, NE	Y	85080 FQ	91620 MW	98160 TQ	USBLS	5/07
	Omaha-Council Bluffs MSA, NE-IA	Y	80940 FQ	89620 MW	97440 TQ	USBLS	5/07
	Nevada	H	44.42 FQ	51.26 MW	58.09 TQ	NVBLS	5/08
	Las Vegas-Paradise MSA, NV	H	43.60 FQ	49.81 MW	56.85 TQ	NVBLS	5/08
	New Hampshire	H	42.56 AE	50.52 MW	54.83 AEX	NHBLS	6/08
	Manchester MSA, NH	Y	91230 FQ	101190 MW	113270 TQ	USBLS	5/07
	Nashua NECTA, NH-MA	Y	86930 FQ	99920 MW	114730 TQ	USBLS	5/07
	New Jersey	Y	86510 FQ	97720 MW	110650 TQ	USBLS	5/07
	Atlantic City MSA, NJ	Y	91880 FQ	102270 MW	113100 TQ	USBLS	5/07
	Camden PMSA, NJ	Y	85740 FQ	96630 MW	109150 TQ	USBLS	5/07
	Edison PMSA, NJ	Y	85870 FQ	99440 MW	113400 TQ	USBLS	5/07
	Newark-Union PMSA, NJ-PA	Y	87230 FQ	97960 MW	110640 TQ	USBLS	5/07
	New Mexico	Y	85460 FQ	97410 MW	112600 TQ	USBLS	5/07
	Albuquerque MSA, NM	Y	84550 FQ	95880 MW	109880 TQ	USBLS	5/07
	Farmington MSA, NM	Y	95820 FQ	110540 MW	124830 TQ	USBLS	5/07
	New York	Y	83650 FQ	97050 MW	112080 TQ	USBLS	5/07
	Albany-Schenectady-Troy MSA, NY	Y	80470 FQ	90740 MW	100220 TQ	USBLS	5/07
	Buffalo-Niagara Falls MSA, NY	Y	85970 FQ	95580 MW	105610 TQ	USBLS	5/07
	Nassau-Suffolk PMSA, NY	Y	86230 FQ	99560 MW	115610 TQ	USBLS	5/07
	New York-Northern New Jersey-Long Island MSA, NY-NJ-PA	Y	83400 FQ	97110 MW	111980 TQ	USBLS	5/07
	North Carolina	Y	89880 FQ	103250 MW	117610 TQ	USBLS	5/07
	Charlotte-Gastonia-Concord MSA, NC-SC	Y	89520 FQ	103680 MW	116330 TQ	USBLS	5/07
	Durham MSA, NC	Y	91360 FQ	100850 MW	112300 TQ	USBLS	5/07
	Raleigh-Cary MSA, NC	Y	88550 FQ	98550 MW	112080 TQ	USBLS	5/07
	North Dakota	Y	73580 FQ	86950 MW	98440 TQ	USBLS	5/07
	Fargo MSA, ND-MN	Y	83610 FQ	92290 MW	101850 TQ	USBLS	5/07
	Ohio	Y	87810 FQ	98180 MW	109660 TQ	USBLS	5/07
	Cincinnati-Middletown MSA, OH-KY-IN	Y	88680 FQ	101850 MW	115070 TQ	USBLS	5/07
	Cleveland-Elyria-Mentor MSA, OH	Y	90950 FQ	100430 MW	112680 TQ	USBLS	5/07
	Columbus MSA, OH	Y	85540 FQ	94870 MW	103960 TQ	USBLS	5/07
	Dayton MSA, OH	Y	91380 FQ	101720 MW	114920 TQ	USBLS	5/07
	Springfield MSA, OH	Y	94660 FQ	109510 MW	120690 TQ	USBLS	5/07
	Oklahoma	Y	83810 FQ	93550 MW	104060 TQ	USBLS	5/07
	Oklahoma City MSA, OK	Y	85020 FQ	93460 MW	102630 TQ	USBLS	5/07
	Tulsa MSA, OK	Y	85440 FQ	94960 MW	106990 TQ	USBLS	5/07
	Oregon	H	44.63 FQ	50.48 MW	56.78 TQ	ORBLS	5/08
	Portland-Vancouver-Beaverton MSA, OR-WA	Y	91650 FQ	103510 MW	115820 TQ	USBLS	5/07
	Salem MSA, OR	Y	91990 FQ	104020 MW	118840 TQ	USBLS	5/07
	Pennsylvania	Y	81310 FQ	91850 MW	101820 TQ	USBLS	5/07
	Allentown-Bethlehem-Easton MSA, PA-NJ	Y	82450 FQ	92310 MW	102530 TQ	USBLS	5/07
	Philadelphia-Camden-Wilmington MSA, PA-NJ-DE-MD	Y	83300 FQ	94330 MW	105400 TQ	USBLS	5/07
	Pittsburgh MSA, PA	Y	80930 FQ	90910 MW	99870 TQ	USBLS	5/07
	Rhode Island	Y	85940 FQ	96080 MW	108170 TQ	USBLS	5/07
	Providence-Fall River-Warwick MSA, RI-MA	Y	84640 FQ	94720 MW	106300 TQ	USBLS	5/07
	South Carolina	Y	87920 FQ	100060 MW	113860 TQ	USBLS	5/07
	Charleston-North Charleston MSA, SC	Y	84820 FQ	94460 MW	104310 TQ	USBLS	5/07
	Columbia MSA, SC	Y	88460 FQ	98010 MW	109790 TQ	USBLS	5/07
	South Dakota	Y	82058 FQ	93416 MW	104128 TQ	SDBLS	7/08-9/08
	Sioux Falls MSA, SD	Y	82925 FQ	92251 MW	101139 TQ	SDBLS	7/08-9/08

AE Average entry wage	**AW** Average wage paid	**FQ** First quartile wage	**LO** Lowest wage paid	**MTC** Median total compensation	**TCC** Total cash compensation
AER Average entry range	**AWR** Average wage range	**H** Hourly	**LR** Low end range	**MW** Median wage paid	**TQ** Third quartile wage
AEX Average experienced wage	**AXR** Average experienced range	**HI** Highest wage paid	**M** Monthly	**MWR** Median wage range	**W** Weekly
ATC Average total compensation	**D** Daily	**HR** High end range	**MCC** Median cash compensation	**S** See annotated source	**Y** Yearly

Occupation/Type/Industry	Location	Per	Low	Mid	High	Source	Date
Pharmacist	Tennessee	Y	93850 FQ	107760 MW	120560 TQ	USBLS	5/07
	Knoxville MSA, TN	Y	88820 FQ	101250 MW	114600 TQ	USBLS	5/07
	Memphis MSA, TN-MS-AR	Y	91630 FQ	107330 MW	121330 TQ	USBLS	5/07
	Nashville-Davidson-Murfreesboro MSA, TN	Y	95800 FQ	107690 MW	119970 TQ	USBLS	5/07
	Texas	Y	93270 FQ	105410 MW	118150 TQ	USBLS	5/07
	Austin-Round Rock MSA, TX	Y	89080 FQ	102450 MW	115770 TQ	USBLS	5/07
	Brownsville-Harlingen MSA, TX	Y	94570 FQ	111860 MW	129400 TQ	USBLS	5/07
	Dallas-Fort Worth-Arlington MSA, TX	Y	99270 FQ	110010 MW	120720 TQ	USBLS	5/07
	El Paso MSA, TX	Y	91260 FQ	102540 MW	116020 TQ	USBLS	5/07
	Houston-Sugar Land-Baytown MSA, TX	Y	91030 FQ	101360 MW	113320 TQ	USBLS	5/07
	San Antonio MSA, TX	Y	91620 FQ	102810 MW	116000 TQ	USBLS	5/07
	Utah	Y	91640 FQ	101670 MW	113450 TQ	USBLS	5/07
	Salt Lake City MSA, UT	Y	90250 FQ	99410 MW	111580 TQ	USBLS	5/07
	Vermont	Y	90640 FQ	105080 MW	119000 TQ	USBLS	5/07
	Burlington-South Burlington MSA, VT	Y	91450 FQ	108190 MW	120040 TQ	USBLS	5/07
	Virginia	Y	88490 FQ	99830 MW	113660 TQ	USBLS	5/07
	Richmond MSA, VA	Y	86730 FQ	95590 MW	105580 TQ	USBLS	5/07
	Virginia Beach-Norfolk-Newport News MSA, VA-NC	Y	90870 FQ	101760 MW	113790 TQ	USBLS	5/07
	Washington	H	43.37 FQ	48.57 MW	55.06 TQ	WABLS	3/08
	Bremerton-Silverdale MSA, WA	Y	91770 FQ	107740 MW	120370 TQ	USBLS	5/07
	Olympia MSA, WA	Y	89230 FQ	101450 MW	114190 TQ	USBLS	5/07
	Seattle-Tacoma-Bellevue MSA, WA	Y	89910 FQ	100930 MW	114160 TQ	USBLS	5/07
	Spokane MSA, WA	Y	83030 FQ	92690 MW	102840 TQ	USBLS	5/07
	West Virginia	Y	92490 FQ	106008 MW	121912 TQ	WVBLS	7/08-9/08
	Charleston MSA, WV	Y	99360 FQ	111520 MW	122840 TQ	USBLS	5/07
	Wisconsin	Y	94400 FQ	107630 MW	119310 TQ	USBLS	5/07
	Milwaukee-Waukesha-West Allis MSA, WI	Y	95080 FQ	108110 MW	119300 TQ	USBLS	5/07
	Wyoming	Y	87171 FQ	96758 MW	106833 TQ	WYBLS	9/08
	Cheyenne MSA, WY	Y	89403 FQ	96873 MW	104564 TQ	WYBLS	9/08
	Puerto Rico	Y	44590 FQ	57790 MW	70390 TQ	USBLS	5/07
	San Juan-Caguas-Guaynabo MSA, PR	Y	43890 FQ	57280 MW	68850 TQ	USBLS	5/07
	Virgin Islands	Y	54360 FQ	81090 MW	96530 TQ	USBLS	5/07
	Guam	Y	65050 FQ	83970 MW	94730 TQ	USBLS	5/07
Department of Corrections	New Hampshire	Y		47633 AW		NHUL03	2008
Independent Pharmacy	United States	Y		109618 AW		PCMAN	2008
Pharmacologist							
State Government	Ohio	H	36.56 LO		50.81 HI	ODAS	2008
Pharmacy Aide	Alabama	Y	13990 FQ	16970 MW	20860 TQ	USBLS	5/07
	Birmingham-Hoover MSA, AL	Y	16430 FQ	18760 MW	22550 TQ	USBLS	5/07
	Mobile MSA, AL	Y	16870 FQ	18710 MW	22150 TQ	USBLS	5/07
	Tuscaloosa MSA, AL	Y	12550 FQ	14100 MW	15650 TQ	USBLS	5/07
	Alaska	Y	27200 FQ	32070 MW	38870 TQ	USBLS	5/07
	Arizona	Y	16580 FQ	21910 MW	26450 TQ	USBLS	5/07
	Phoenix-Mesa-Scottsdale MSA, AZ	Y	16670 FQ	21420 MW	26420 TQ	USBLS	5/07
	Tucson MSA, AZ	Y	14630 FQ	19080 MW	21590 TQ	USBLS	5/07
	Arkansas	Y	15580 FQ	18040 MW	22000 TQ	USBLS	5/07
	Little Rock-North Little Rock MSA, AR	Y	16630 FQ	18920 MW	22670 TQ	USBLS	5/07
	California	H	8.96 FQ	10.19 MW	13.20 TQ	CABLS	1/08-3/08
	Los Angeles-Long Beach-Glendale PMSA, CA	H	8.59 FQ	9.39 MW	10.96 TQ	CABLS	1/08-3/08
	Oakland-Fremont-Hayward MSA, CA	H	11.16 FQ	13.80 MW	16.80 TQ	CABLS	1/08-3/08
	Riverside-San Bernardino-Ontario MSA, CA	H	8.73 FQ	9.59 MW	12.57 TQ	CABLS	1/08-3/08
	Sacramento-Arden Arcade-Roseville MSA, CA	H	10.85 FQ	13.20 MW	17.90 TQ	CABLS	1/08-3/08
	San Diego-Carlsbad-San Marcos MSA, CA	H	9.10 FQ	10.12 MW	12.55 TQ	CABLS	1/08-3/08

AE	Average entry wage	**AW**	Average wage paid	**FQ**	First quartile wage	**LO**	Lowest wage paid
AER	Average entry range	**AWR**	Average wage range	**H**	Hourly	**LR**	Low end range
AEX	Average experienced wage	**AXR**	Average experienced range	**HI**	Highest wage paid	**M**	Monthly
ATC	Average total compensation	**D**	Daily	**HR**	High end range	**MCC**	Median cash compensation

MTC	Median total compensation	**TCC**	Total cash compensation
MW	Median wage paid	**TQ**	Third quartile wage
MWR	Median wage range	**W**	Weekly
S	See annotated source	**Y**	Yearly

Occupation/Type/Industry	Location	Per	Low	Mid	High	Source	Date
Pharmacy Aide	San Francisco-San Mateo-Redwood PMSA, CA	H	11.48 FQ	15.88 MW	21.74 TQ	CABLS	1/08-3/08
	San Jose-Sunnyvale-Santa Clara MSA, CA	H	12.15 FQ	13.31 MW	14.42 TQ	CABLS	1/08-3/08
	Santa Ana-Anaheim-Irvine PMSA, CA	Y	17770 FQ	19650 MW	24410 TQ	USBLS	5/07
	Santa Rosa-Petaluma MSA, CA	H	9.19 FQ	10.64 MW	12.28 TQ	CABLS	1/08-3/08
	Stockton MSA, CA	H	8.63 FQ	9.71 MW	11.37 TQ	CABLS	1/08-3/08
	Colorado	Y	19400 FQ	25100 MW	32830 TQ	USBLS	5/07
	Denver-Aurora MSA, CO	Y	19640 FQ	26860 MW	34460 TQ	USBLS	5/07
	Connecticut	H	8.83 AE	10.81 MW		CTBLS	1/08-3/08
	Bridgeport-Stamford-Norwalk MSA, CT	Y	18500 FQ	21320 MW	26180 TQ	USBLS	5/07
	Hartford-West Hartford-East Hartford MSA, CT	Y	19280 FQ	22520 MW	25850 TQ	USBLS	5/07
	District of Columbia	Y	20210 FQ	26820 MW	36020 TQ	USBLS	5/07
	Washington-Arlington-Alexandria MSA, DC-VA-MD-WV	Y	18190 FQ	22960 MW	31710 TQ	USBLS	5/07
	Florida	Y	16360 FQ	18270 MW	20420 TQ	USBLS	5/07
	Fort Lauderdale-Pompano Beach-Deerfield Beach PMSA, FL	Y	17650 FQ	20560 MW	23830 TQ	USBLS	5/07
	Jacksonville MSA, FL	Y	17010 FQ	19450 MW	22500 TQ	USBLS	5/07
	Miami-Fort Lauderdale-Miami Beach MSA, FL	Y	15730 FQ	17980 MW	20510 TQ	USBLS	5/07
	Orlando-Kissimmee MSA, FL	Y	16420 FQ	17860 MW	19480 TQ	USBLS	5/07
	Tampa-St. Petersburg-Clearwater MSA, FL	Y	16510 FQ	18380 MW	20390 TQ	USBLS	5/07
	West Palm Beach-Boca Raton-Boynton Beach PMSA, FL	Y	15550 FQ	17660 MW	19740 TQ	USBLS	5/07
	Georgia	Y	16770 FQ	19070 MW	22650 TQ	USBLS	5/07
	Atlanta-Sandy Springs-Marietta MSA, GA	Y	17170 FQ	19140 MW	22830 TQ	USBLS	5/07
	Hawaii	Y	19050 FQ	22170 MW	25240 TQ	USBLS	5/07
	Honolulu MSA, HI	Y	18450 FQ	21720 MW	25460 TQ	USBLS	5/07
	Idaho	Y	13790 FQ	17080 MW	23660 TQ	USBLS	5/07
	Boise City-Nampa MSA, ID	Y	13800 FQ	17550 MW	22820 TQ	USBLS	5/07
	Illinois	Y	17570 FQ	20970 MW	23850 TQ	USBLS	5/07
	Chicago-Naperville-Joliet MSA, IL-IN-WI	Y	19540 FQ	22100 MW	24540 TQ	USBLS	5/07
	Rockford MSA, IL	Y	20010 FQ	22520 MW	25280 TQ	USBLS	5/07
	Indiana	Y	16980 FQ	19050 MW	21910 TQ	USBLS	5/07
	Gary PMSA, IN	Y	17970 FQ	20630 MW	24440 TQ	USBLS	5/07
	Indianapolis-Carmel MSA, IN	Y	17190 FQ	19440 MW	22100 TQ	USBLS	5/07
	Iowa	Y	18130 FQ	21830 MW	25060 TQ	USBLS	5/07
	Kansas	Y	17240 FQ	20270 MW	24100 TQ	USBLS	5/07
	Lawrence MSA, KS	Y	19170 FQ	22470 MW	26160 TQ	USBLS	5/07
	Wichita MSA, KS	Y	16930 FQ	21640 MW	25630 TQ	USBLS	5/07
	Kentucky	Y	15820 FQ	18676 MW	22185 TQ	KYBLS	2008
	Louisville-Jefferson County MSA, KY-IN	Y	16190 FQ	19420 MW	23790 TQ	USBLS	5/07
	Louisiana	H	7.86 FQ	9.40 MW	10.94 TQ	LABLS	1/08-3/08
	Baton Rouge MSA, LA	Y	13760 FQ	16140 MW	21010 TQ	USBLS	5/07
	Lake Charles MSA, LA	Y	14470 FQ	17860 MW	20570 TQ	USBLS	5/07
	New Orleans-Metairie-Kenner MSA, LA	Y	15980 FQ	19390 MW	23090 TQ	USBLS	5/07
	Shreveport-Bossier City MSA, LA	Y	19970 FQ	22490 MW	25030 TQ	USBLS	5/07
	Maine	Y	17030 FQ	19370 MW	23150 TQ	USBLS	5/07
	Maryland	Y		21900 MW		MDBLS	3/08
	Baltimore-Towson MSA, MD	Y	16740 FQ	19680 MW	26310 TQ	USBLS	5/07
	Bethesda-Gaithersburg-Frederick PMSA, MD	Y	17730 FQ	20580 MW	24730 TQ	USBLS	5/07
	Massachusetts	Y	18310 FQ	21230 MW	24490 TQ	USBLS	5/07
	Boston-Cambridge-Quincy NECTA, MA	Y	18230 FQ	21810 MW	26280 TQ	USBLS	5/07
	Worcester MSA, MA-CT	Y	18810 FQ	21050 MW	23400 TQ	USBLS	5/07
	Michigan	Y	17260 FQ	19510 MW	23190 TQ	USBLS	5/07
	Detroit-Warren-Livonia MSA, MI	Y	17360 FQ	19500 MW	22820 TQ	USBLS	5/07

AE	Average entry wage	AW	Average wage paid	FQ	First quartile wage	LO	Lowest wage paid	MTC	Median total compensation	TCC	Total cash compensation
AER	Average entry range	AWR	Average wage range	H	Hourly	LR	Low end range	MW	Median wage paid	TQ	Third quartile wage
AEX	Average experienced wage	AXR	Average experienced range	HI	Highest wage paid	M	Monthly	MWR	Median wage range	W	Weekly
ATC	Average total compensation	D	Daily	HR	High end range	MCC	Median cash compensation	S	See annotated source	Y	Yearly

Pharmacy Aide

Occupation/Type/Industry	Location	Per	Low	Mid	High	Source	Date
Pharmacy Aide	Grand Rapids-Wyoming MSA, MI	Y	16390 FQ	19880 MW	25040 TQ	USBLS	5/07
	Warren-Troy-Farmington Hills PMSA, MI	Y	17770 FQ	20180 MW	23290 TQ	USBLS	5/07
	Minnesota	Y	18945 FQ	21559 MW	25920 TQ	MNBLS	10/08-12/08
	Duluth-Superior MSA, MN-WI	Y	17879 FQ	19291 MW	21078 TQ	MNBLS	10/08-12/08
	Minneapolis-Saint Paul MSA, MN-WI	Y	18883 FQ	21350 MW	24874 TQ	MNBLS	10/08-12/08
	Rochester MSA, MN	Y	22850 FQ	27368 MW	30350 TQ	MNBLS	10/08-12/08
	Mississippi	Y	13570 FQ	16200 MW	20360 TQ	USBLS	5/07
	Jackson MSA, MS	Y	17510 FQ	21160 MW	24600 TQ	USBLS	5/07
	Missouri	Y	15540 FQ	17960 MW	21770 TQ	USBLS	5/07
	Kansas City MSA, MO-KS	Y	16870 FQ	18650 MW	22870 TQ	USBLS	5/07
	St. Louis MSA, MO-IL	Y	17330 FQ	20240 MW	24470 TQ	USBLS	5/07
	Montana	Y	17720 FQ	20230 MW	23010 TQ	USBLS	5/07
	Nebraska	Y	17490 FQ	19750 MW	23130 TQ	USBLS	5/07
	Omaha-Council Bluffs MSA, NE-IA	Y	16170 FQ	18690 MW	23730 TQ	USBLS	5/07
	Nevada	H	9.97 FQ	11.46 MW	15.38 TQ	NVBLS	5/08
	Las Vegas-Paradise MSA, NV	H	10.68 FQ	12.02 MW	16.70 TQ	NVBLS	5/08
	New Hampshire	H	8.81 AE	11.19 MW	13.16 AEX	NHBLS	6/08
	New Jersey	Y	16420 FQ	18470 MW	22540 TQ	USBLS	5/07
	Camden PMSA, NJ	Y	16210 FQ	18370 MW	22010 TQ	USBLS	5/07
	Edison PMSA, NJ	Y	16700 FQ	18250 MW	20320 TQ	USBLS	5/07
	Newark-Union PMSA, NJ-PA	Y	17290 FQ	21470 MW	25920 TQ	USBLS	5/07
	New Mexico	Y	17170 FQ	21900 MW	28350 TQ	USBLS	5/07
	Albuquerque MSA, NM	Y	17660 FQ	22490 MW	27690 TQ	USBLS	5/07
	New York	Y	17140 FQ	20590 MW	27990 TQ	USBLS	5/07
	Albany-Schenectady-Troy MSA, NY	Y	16870 FQ	18760 MW	23780 TQ	USBLS	5/07
	Buffalo-Niagara Falls MSA, NY	Y	16860 FQ	19230 MW	25280 TQ	USBLS	5/07
	Nassau-Suffolk PMSA, NY	Y	18910 FQ	23750 MW	33490 TQ	USBLS	5/07
	New York-Northern New Jersey-Long Island MSA, NY-NJ-PA	Y	16920 FQ	20270 MW	27980 TQ	USBLS	5/07
	North Carolina	Y	16430 FQ	18260 MW	21030 TQ	USBLS	5/07
	Charlotte-Gastonia-Concord MSA, NC-SC	Y	16950 FQ	18660 MW	21470 TQ	USBLS	5/07
	Durham MSA, NC	Y	18340 FQ	21480 MW	25360 TQ	USBLS	5/07
	Raleigh-Cary MSA, NC	Y	17490 FQ	19380 MW	22430 TQ	USBLS	5/07
	Winston-Salem MSA, NC	Y	15780 FQ	18060 MW	20210 TQ	USBLS	5/07
	North Dakota	Y	18110 FQ	20770 MW	22980 TQ	USBLS	5/07
	Fargo MSA, ND-MN	Y	18450 FQ	20720 MW	22670 TQ	USBLS	5/07
	Ohio	Y	16460 FQ	19120 MW	23220 TQ	USBLS	5/07
	Cincinnati-Middletown MSA, OH-KY-IN	Y	16840 FQ	19290 MW	22400 TQ	USBLS	5/07
	Cleveland-Elyria-Mentor MSA, OH	Y	16590 FQ	18600 MW	22020 TQ	USBLS	5/07
	Columbus MSA, OH	Y	16410 FQ	19790 MW	28930 TQ	USBLS	5/07
	Dayton MSA, OH	Y	17330 FQ	19670 MW	23180 TQ	USBLS	5/07
	Oklahoma	Y	14190 FQ	17430 MW	20640 TQ	USBLS	5/07
	Oklahoma City MSA, OK	Y	15930 FQ	17910 MW	20110 TQ	USBLS	5/07
	Tulsa MSA, OK	Y	13110 FQ	14920 MW	19010 TQ	USBLS	5/07
	Pennsylvania	Y	15350 FQ	18510 MW	24510 TQ	USBLS	5/07
	Allentown-Bethlehem-Easton MSA, PA-NJ	Y	15220 FQ	17720 MW	25980 TQ	USBLS	5/07
	Philadelphia-Camden-Wilmington MSA, PA-NJ-DE-MD	Y	15880 FQ	18140 MW	23200 TQ	USBLS	5/07
	Pittsburgh MSA, PA	Y	16510 FQ	23360 MW	28600 TQ	USBLS	5/07
	Rhode Island	Y	18040 FQ	21380 MW	25650 TQ	USBLS	5/07
	Providence-Fall River-Warwick MSA, RI-MA	Y	18160 FQ	21210 MW	24310 TQ	USBLS	5/07
	South Carolina	Y	16180 FQ	18190 MW	20690 TQ	USBLS	5/07
	Charleston-North Charleston MSA, SC	Y	16850 FQ	19210 MW	23970 TQ	USBLS	5/07
	Columbia MSA, SC	Y	14520 FQ	16830 MW	19570 TQ	USBLS	5/07
	South Dakota	Y	17574 FQ	19141 MW	21752 TQ	SDBLS	7/08-9/08
	Tennessee	Y	16360 FQ	18570 MW	22270 TQ	USBLS	5/07
	Memphis MSA, TN-MS-AR	Y	17420 FQ	19610 MW	24980 TQ	USBLS	5/07

AE	Average entry wage	AW	Average wage paid	FQ	First quartile wage
AER	Average entry range	AWR	Average wage range	H	Hourly
AEX	Average experienced wage	AXR	Average experienced range	HI	Highest wage paid
ATC	Average total compensation	D	Daily	HR	High end range

LO Lowest wage paid
LR Low end range
M Monthly
MCC Median cash compensation

MTC Median total compensation
MW Median wage paid
MWR Median wage range
S See annotated source

TCC Total cash compensation
TQ Third quartile wage
W Weekly
Y Yearly

Occupation/Type/Industry	Location	Per	Low	Mid	High	Source	Date
Pharmacy Aide	Nashville-Davidson-Murfreesboro MSA, TN	Y	15240 FQ	17560 MW	19950 TQ	USBLS	5/07
	Texas	Y	16590 FQ	19580 MW	23360 TQ	USBLS	5/07
	Austin-Round Rock MSA, TX	Y	20590 FQ	22860 MW	25530 TQ	USBLS	5/07
	Dallas-Fort Worth-Arlington MSA, TX	Y	15780 FQ	19090 MW	24140 TQ	USBLS	5/07
	Houston-Sugar Land-Baytown MSA, TX	Y	17430 FQ	19810 MW	23210 TQ	USBLS	5/07
	Utah	Y	18240 FQ	21790 MW	26000 TQ	USBLS	5/07
	Provo-Orem MSA, UT	Y	17490 FQ	19340 MW	21940 TQ	USBLS	5/07
	Salt Lake City MSA, UT	Y	20330 FQ	23250 MW	38310 TQ	USBLS	5/07
	Vermont	Y	19190 FQ	21490 MW	23880 TQ	USBLS	5/07
	Burlington-South Burlington MSA, VT	Y	17940 FQ	20670 MW	24280 TQ	USBLS	5/07
	Virginia	Y	16730 FQ	19250 MW	23260 TQ	USBLS	5/07
	Richmond MSA, VA	Y	16060 FQ	18310 MW	22720 TQ	USBLS	5/07
	Virginia Beach-Norfolk-Newport News MSA, VA-NC	Y	18870 FQ	21290 MW	23970 TQ	USBLS	5/07
	Washington	H	9.72 FQ	11.62 MW	14.28 TQ	WABLS	3/08
	Seattle-Tacoma-Bellevue MSA, WA	Y	19810 FQ	24930 MW	30260 TQ	USBLS	5/07
	West Virginia	Y	14583 FQ	16408 MW	20022 TQ	WVBLS	7/08-9/08
	Charleston MSA, WV	Y	14030 FQ	15830 MW	18570 TQ	USBLS	5/07
	Wisconsin	Y	15480 FQ	18320 MW	22600 TQ	USBLS	5/07
	Milwaukee-Waukesha-West Allis MSA, WI	Y	15540 FQ	18150 MW	23410 TQ	USBLS	5/07
	Wyoming	Y	19145 FQ	24455 MW	29089 TQ	WYBLS	9/08
	Puerto Rico	Y	13060 FQ	15050 MW	17620 TQ	USBLS	5/07
	San Juan-Caguas-Guaynabo MSA, PR	Y	13060 FQ	15060 MW	17710 TQ	USBLS	5/07
Pharmacy Technician	Alabama	Y	18460 FQ	22310 MW	27440 TQ	USBLS	5/07
	Birmingham-Hoover MSA, AL	Y	18130 FQ	21960 MW	27770 TQ	USBLS	5/07
	Alaska	Y	28660 FQ	33990 MW	39020 TQ	USBLS	5/07
	Anchorage MSA, AK	Y	28950 FQ	34410 MW	39350 TQ	USBLS	5/07
	Arizona	Y	24040 FQ	28150 MW	32480 TQ	USBLS	5/07
	Phoenix-Mesa-Scottsdale MSA, AZ	Y	24310 FQ	28380 MW	32680 TQ	USBLS	5/07
	Tucson MSA, AZ	Y	23430 FQ	27380 MW	31340 TQ	USBLS	5/07
	Arkansas	Y	19620 FQ	22640 MW	26360 TQ	USBLS	5/07
	Little Rock-North Little Rock MSA, AR	Y	20680 FQ	23480 MW	27500 TQ	USBLS	5/07
	California	H	14.65 FQ	17.29 MW	19.77 TQ	CABLS	1/08-3/08
	Los Angeles-Long Beach-Glendale PMSA, CA	H	14.03 FQ	16.92 MW	19.47 TQ	CABLS	1/08-3/08
	Modesto MSA, CA	H	16.09 FQ	17.90 MW	19.84 TQ	CABLS	1/08-3/08
	Oakland-Fremont-Hayward MSA, CA	H	16.00 FQ	18.27 MW	21.52 TQ	CABLS	1/08-3/08
	Riverside-San Bernardino-Ontario MSA, CA	H	13.45 FQ	16.29 MW	18.62 TQ	CABLS	1/08-3/08
	Sacramento-Arden Arcade-Roseville MSA, CA	H	16.28 FQ	18.12 MW	20.31 TQ	CABLS	1/08-3/08
	San Diego-Carlsbad-San Marcos MSA, CA	H	14.33 FQ	16.77 MW	19.38 TQ	CABLS	1/08-3/08
	San Francisco-San Mateo-Redwood PMSA, CA	H	17.20 FQ	19.90 MW	24.31 TQ	CABLS	1/08-3/08
	San Jose-Sunnyvale-Santa Clara MSA, CA	H	16.59 FQ	19.41 MW	23.07 TQ	CABLS	1/08-3/08
	Santa Ana-Anaheim-Irvine PMSA, CA	Y	29270 FQ	34380 MW	39130 TQ	USBLS	5/07
	Stockton MSA, CA	H	14.06 FQ	16.87 MW	19.01 TQ	CABLS	1/08-3/08
	Colorado	Y	25940 FQ	30680 MW	35820 TQ	USBLS	5/07
	Denver-Aurora MSA, CO	Y	26610 FQ	32290 MW	37000 TQ	USBLS	5/07
	Fort Collins-Loveland MSA, CO	Y	28410 FQ	34250 MW	37810 TQ	USBLS	5/07
	Pueblo MSA, CO	Y	22530 FQ	27850 MW	31900 TQ	USBLS	5/07
	Connecticut	H	10.78 AE	14.22 MW		CTBLS	1/08-3/08
	Bridgeport-Stamford-Norwalk MSA, CT	Y	23610 FQ	28010 MW	34850 TQ	USBLS	5/07
	Hartford-West Hartford-East Hartford MSA, CT	Y	22820 FQ	27950 MW	35670 TQ	USBLS	5/07
	Delaware	Y	17600 FQ	22790 MW	30840 TQ	USBLS	5/07

AE	Average entry wage	AW	Average wage paid	FQ	First quartile wage	LO	Lowest wage paid	MTC	Median total compensation	TCC	Total cash compensation
AER	Average entry range	AWR	Average wage range	H	Hourly	LR	Low end range	MW	Median wage paid	TQ	Third quartile wage
AEX	Average experienced wage	AXR	Average experienced range	HI	Highest wage paid	M	Monthly	MWR	Median wage range	W	Weekly
ATC	Average total compensation	D	Daily	HR	High end range	MCC	Median cash compensation	S	See annotated source	Y	Yearly

Pharmacy Technician

Occupation/Type/Industry	Location	Per	Low	Mid	High	Source	Date
Pharmacy Technician	Wilmington PMSA, DE-MD-NJ	Y	17630 FQ	24910 MW	32030 TQ	USBLS	5/07
	District of Columbia	Y	27810 FQ	33040 MW	38180 TQ	USBLS	5/07
	Washington-Arlington-Alexandria MSA, DC-VA-MD-WV	Y	23140 FQ	29130 MW	35860 TQ	USBLS	5/07
	Florida	Y	21600 FQ	25820 MW	30790 TQ	USBLS	5/07
	Cape Coral-Fort Myers MSA, FL	Y	20800 FQ	25610 MW	29840 TQ	USBLS	5/07
	Fort Lauderdale-Pompano Beach-Deerfield Beach PMSA, FL	Y	22780 FQ	27830 MW	33900 TQ	USBLS	5/07
	Jacksonville MSA, FL	Y	22140 FQ	27170 MW	32040 TQ	USBLS	5/07
	Miami-Fort Lauderdale-Miami Beach MSA, FL	Y	21770 FQ	26600 MW	31950 TQ	USBLS	5/07
	Orlando-Kissimmee MSA, FL	Y	21830 FQ	25300 MW	30000 TQ	USBLS	5/07
	Tallahassee MSA, FL	Y	20750 FQ	25930 MW	31330 TQ	USBLS	5/07
	Tampa-St. Petersburg-Clearwater MSA, FL	Y	21910 FQ	25820 MW	30800 TQ	USBLS	5/07
	West Palm Beach-Boca Raton-Boynton Beach PMSA, FL	Y	23310 FQ	28150 MW	32680 TQ	USBLS	5/07
	Georgia	Y	20420 FQ	24860 MW	29850 TQ	USBLS	5/07
	Atlanta-Sandy Springs-Marietta MSA, GA	Y	20490 FQ	24890 MW	30060 TQ	USBLS	5/07
	Augusta-Richmond County MSA, GA-SC	Y	21990 FQ	28070 MW	39670 TQ	USBLS	5/07
	Hawaii	Y	29200 FQ	33360 MW	37180 TQ	USBLS	5/07
	Honolulu MSA, HI	Y	30650 FQ	34270 MW	37430 TQ	USBLS	5/07
	Idaho	Y	22840 FQ	26980 MW	30740 TQ	USBLS	5/07
	Boise City-Nampa MSA, ID	Y	24290 FQ	28360 MW	31890 TQ	USBLS	5/07
	Lewiston MSA, ID-WA	Y	19090 FQ	23470 MW	32110 TQ	USBLS	5/07
	Illinois	Y	21890 FQ	25760 MW	30260 TQ	USBLS	5/07
	Chicago-Naperville-Joliet MSA, IL-IN-WI	Y	22820 FQ	26830 MW	30880 TQ	USBLS	5/07
	Indiana	Y	21620 FQ	25460 MW	29720 TQ	USBLS	5/07
	Evansville MSA, IN-KY	Y	19930 FQ	23860 MW	28610 TQ	USBLS	5/07
	Gary PMSA, IN	Y	22330 FQ	26240 MW	29840 TQ	USBLS	5/07
	Indianapolis-Carmel MSA, IN	Y	23290 FQ	27020 MW	31140 TQ	USBLS	5/07
	Iowa	Y	20860 FQ	24610 MW	28980 TQ	USBLS	5/07
	Des Moines-West Des Moines MSA, IA	Y	21870 FQ	25680 MW	29640 TQ	USBLS	5/07
	Kansas	Y	21470 FQ	25190 MW	29650 TQ	USBLS	5/07
	Wichita MSA, KS	Y	21200 FQ	24030 MW	28370 TQ	USBLS	5/07
	Kentucky	Y	19614 FQ	23688 MW	28977 TQ	KYBLS	2008
	Louisville-Jefferson County MSA, KY-IN	Y	19420 FQ	24280 MW	29330 TQ	USBLS	5/07
	Louisiana	H	10.03 FQ	11.50 MW	13.56 TQ	LABLS	1/08-3/08
	Baton Rouge MSA, LA	Y	20630 FQ	23620 MW	27640 TQ	USBLS	5/07
	New Orleans-Metairie-Kenner MSA, LA	Y	21310 FQ	25230 MW	29960 TQ	USBLS	5/07
	Maine	Y	20990 FQ	25500 MW	30040 TQ	USBLS	5/07
	Portland-South Portland-Biddeford MSA, ME	Y	21690 FQ	25570 MW	29870 TQ	USBLS	5/07
	Maryland	Y		28250 MW		MDBLS	3/08
	Baltimore-Towson MSA, MD	Y	23120 FQ	27750 MW	32750 TQ	USBLS	5/07
	Bethesda-Gaithersburg-Frederick PMSA, MD	Y	21990 FQ	28660 MW	37450 TQ	USBLS	5/07
	Cumberland MSA, MD-WV	Y	20810 FQ	23120 MW	26880 TQ	USBLS	5/07
	Hagerstown-Martinsburg MSA, MD-WV	Y	20590 FQ	24590 MW	29680 TQ	USBLS	5/07
	Massachusetts	Y	23470 FQ	28490 MW	34160 TQ	USBLS	5/07
	Barnstable Town MSA, MA	Y	22150 FQ	26590 MW	34320 TQ	USBLS	5/07
	Boston-Cambridge-Quincy NECTA, MA	Y	25320 FQ	30360 MW	36370 TQ	USBLS	5/07
	Worcester MSA, MA-CT	Y	25230 FQ	28750 MW	32930 TQ	USBLS	5/07
	Michigan	Y	22740 FQ	27070 MW	31900 TQ	USBLS	5/07
	Ann Arbor MSA, MI	Y	25060 FQ	29120 MW	33860 TQ	USBLS	5/07
	Detroit-Warren-Livonia MSA, MI	Y	23260 FQ	28030 MW	33160 TQ	USBLS	5/07
	Flint MSA, MI	Y	22000 FQ	25510 MW	29590 TQ	USBLS	5/07
	Grand Rapids-Wyoming MSA, MI	Y	23170 FQ	27420 MW	31530 TQ	USBLS	5/07

AE	Average entry wage	**AW**	Average wage paid	**FQ**	First quartile wage	**LO**	Lowest wage paid	**MTC**	Median total compensation
AER	Average entry range	**AWR**	Average wage range	**H**	Hourly	**LR**	Low end range	**MW**	Median wage paid
AEX	Average experienced wage	**AXR**	Average experienced range	**HI**	Highest wage paid	**M**	Monthly	**MWR**	Median wage range
ATC	Average total compensation	**D**	Daily	**HR**	High end range	**MCC**	Median cash compensation	**S**	See annotated source

TCC	Total cash compensation
TQ	Third quartile wage
W	Weekly
Y	Yearly

Occupation/Type/Industry	Location	Per	Low	Mid	High	Source	Date
Pharmacy Technician	Muskegon-Norton Shores MSA, MI	Y	22700 FQ	26660 MW	30260 TQ	USBLS	5/07
	Warren-Troy-Farmington Hills PMSA, MI	Y	22210 FQ	26650 MW	31280 TQ	USBLS	5/07
	Minnesota	Y	24931 FQ	30099 MW	36251 TQ	MNBLS	10/08-12/08
	Duluth-Superior MSA, MN-WI	Y	21489 FQ	28771 MW	36084 TQ	MNBLS	10/08-12/08
	Minneapolis-Saint Paul MSA, MN-WI	Y	25737 FQ	31167 MW	37747 TQ	MNBLS	10/08-12/08
	Rochester MSA, MN	Y	30137 FQ	34756 MW	40250 TQ	MNBLS	10/08-12/08
	Mississippi	Y	19500 FQ	23180 MW	28030 TQ	USBLS	5/07
	Jackson MSA, MS	Y	19990 FQ	23470 MW	28290 TQ	USBLS	5/07
	Missouri	Y	19360 FQ	22960 MW	27920 TQ	USBLS	5/07
	Joplin MSA, MO	Y	17680 FQ	20930 MW	24130 TQ	USBLS	5/07
	Kansas City MSA, MO-KS	Y	19830 FQ	23680 MW	28880 TQ	USBLS	5/07
	St. Louis MSA, MO-IL	Y	19890 FQ	23740 MW	28990 TQ	USBLS	5/07
	Montana	Y	23900 FQ	27460 MW	31540 TQ	USBLS	5/07
	Billings MSA, MT	Y	22470 FQ	25560 MW	29510 TQ	USBLS	5/07
	Nebraska	Y	21760 FQ	25190 MW	29720 TQ	USBLS	5/07
	Omaha-Council Bluffs MSA, NE-IA	Y	22680 FQ	26270 MW	30000 TQ	USBLS	5/07
	Nevada	H	13.09 FQ	15.48 MW	17.93 TQ	NVBLS	5/08
	Las Vegas-Paradise MSA, NV	H	13.17 FQ	15.61 MW	17.99 TQ	NVBLS	5/08
	Reno-Sparks MSA, NV	H	12.86 FQ	15.08 MW	18.01 TQ	NVBLS	5/08
	New Hampshire	H	9.70 AE	12.27 MW	14.91 AEX	NHBLS	6/08
	Manchester MSA, NH	Y	19760 FQ	22920 MW	29410 TQ	USBLS	5/07
	Nashua NECTA, NH-MA	Y	21020 FQ	23380 MW	27700 TQ	USBLS	5/07
	New Jersey	Y	22130 FQ	26230 MW	32360 TQ	USBLS	5/07
	Camden PMSA, NJ	Y	22040 FQ	25200 MW	29880 TQ	USBLS	5/07
	Edison PMSA, NJ	Y	22450 FQ	26410 MW	30960 TQ	USBLS	5/07
	Newark-Union PMSA, NJ-PA	Y	22250 FQ	27740 MW	35400 TQ	USBLS	5/07
	New Mexico	Y	22600 FQ	27110 MW	31120 TQ	USBLS	5/07
	Albuquerque MSA, NM	Y	23290 FQ	27360 MW	30760 TQ	USBLS	5/07
	New York	Y	21990 FQ	27160 MW	35190 TQ	USBLS	5/07
	Albany-Schenectady-Troy MSA, NY	Y	21800 FQ	26490 MW	35780 TQ	USBLS	5/07
	Buffalo-Niagara Falls MSA, NY	Y	20540 FQ	24520 MW	30300 TQ	USBLS	5/07
	Nassau-Suffolk PMSA, NY	Y	21890 FQ	27820 MW	35750 TQ	USBLS	5/07
	New York-Northern New Jersey-Long Island MSA, NY-NJ-PA	Y	22540 FQ	28140 MW	35960 TQ	USBLS	5/07
	North Carolina	Y	19720 FQ	23940 MW	29060 TQ	USBLS	5/07
	Charlotte-Gastonia-Concord MSA, NC-SC	Y	20370 FQ	25040 MW	29560 TQ	USBLS	5/07
	Raleigh-Cary MSA, NC	Y	20190 FQ	24060 MW	28670 TQ	USBLS	5/07
	North Dakota	Y	23910 FQ	28280 MW	32790 TQ	USBLS	5/07
	Bismarck MSA, ND	Y	23350 FQ	26510 MW	29850 TQ	USBLS	5/07
	Fargo MSA, ND-MN	Y	20580 FQ	28180 MW	33810 TQ	USBLS	5/07
	Ohio	Y	19980 FQ	24260 MW	29400 TQ	USBLS	5/07
	Cincinnati-Middletown MSA, OH-KY-IN	Y	19790 FQ	23790 MW	29010 TQ	USBLS	5/07
	Cleveland-Elyria-Mentor MSA, OH	Y	20430 FQ	25120 MW	30570 TQ	USBLS	5/07
	Columbus MSA, OH	Y	21310 FQ	25000 MW	29860 TQ	USBLS	5/07
	Dayton MSA, OH	Y	21050 FQ	25630 MW	29950 TQ	USBLS	5/07
	Oklahoma	Y	19620 FQ	23060 MW	27750 TQ	USBLS	5/07
	Oklahoma City MSA, OK	Y	20090 FQ	23370 MW	27790 TQ	USBLS	5/07
	Tulsa MSA, OK	Y	20540 FQ	24200 MW	29160 TQ	USBLS	5/07
	Oregon	H	13.27 FQ	15.95 MW	18.20 TQ	ORBLS	5/08
	Portland-Vancouver-Beaverton MSA, OR-WA	Y	29120 FQ	34030 MW	37800 TQ	USBLS	5/07
	Pennsylvania	Y	19900 FQ	24320 MW	29660 TQ	USBLS	5/07
	Allentown-Bethlehem-Easton MSA, PA-NJ	Y	19300 FQ	24560 MW	29320 TQ	USBLS	5/07
	Philadelphia-Camden-Wilmington MSA, PA-NJ-DE-MD	Y	20030 FQ	25500 MW	31230 TQ	USBLS	5/07
	Pittsburgh MSA, PA	Y	19820 FQ	23710 MW	28450 TQ	USBLS	5/07
	York-Hanover MSA, PA	Y	19220 FQ	23040 MW	27570 TQ	USBLS	5/07
	Rhode Island	Y	24210 FQ	29130 MW	35530 TQ	USBLS	5/07
	Providence-Fall River-Warwick MSA, RI-MA	Y	23610 FQ	28720 MW	35210 TQ	USBLS	5/07

AE	Average entry wage	AW	Average wage paid	FQ	First quartile wage
AER	Average entry range	AWR	Average wage range	H	Hourly
AEX	Average experienced wage	AXR	Average experienced range	HI	Highest wage paid
ATC	Average total compensation	D	Daily	HR	High end range

LO	Lowest wage paid	MTC	Median total compensation	TCC	Total cash compensation
LR	Low end range	MW	Median wage paid	TQ	Third quartile wage
M	Monthly	MWR	Median wage range	W	Weekly
MCC	Median cash compensation	S	See annotated source	Y	Yearly

Occupation/Type/Industry	Location	Per	Low	Mid	High	Source	Date
Pharmacy Technician	South Carolina	Y	20300 FQ	23980 MW	28780 TQ	USBLS	5/07
	Charleston-North Charleston MSA, SC	Y	21710 FQ	26560 MW	30640 TQ	USBLS	5/07
	Columbia MSA, SC	Y	20230 FQ	23690 MW	28820 TQ	USBLS	5/07
	South Dakota	Y	23079 FQ	26716 MW	31109 TQ	SDBLS	7/08-9/08
	Sioux Falls MSA, SD	Y	25085 FQ	28412 MW	31689 TQ	SDBLS	7/08-9/08
	Tennessee	Y	21960 FQ	26080 MW	30500 TQ	USBLS	5/07
	Memphis MSA, TN-MS-AR	Y	22450 FQ	26530 MW	31240 TQ	USBLS	5/07
	Nashville-Davidson-Murfreesboro MSA, TN	Y	22860 FQ	27610 MW	32310 TQ	USBLS	5/07
	Texas	Y	23430 FQ	27610 MW	31560 TQ	USBLS	5/07
	Austin-Round Rock MSA, TX	Y	24640 FQ	28410 MW	31990 TQ	USBLS	5/07
	Dallas-Fort Worth-Arlington MSA, TX	Y	24940 FQ	28860 MW	33240 TQ	USBLS	5/07
	El Paso MSA, TX	Y	20730 FQ	23580 MW	27510 TQ	USBLS	5/07
	Houston-Sugar Land-Baytown MSA, TX	Y	25280 FQ	28750 MW	32490 TQ	USBLS	5/07
	San Antonio MSA, TX	Y	24530 FQ	28040 MW	31910 TQ	USBLS	5/07
	Utah	Y	25770 FQ	29220 MW	32750 TQ	USBLS	5/07
	Provo-Orem MSA, UT	Y	25500 FQ	29040 MW	32370 TQ	USBLS	5/07
	Salt Lake City MSA, UT	Y	26140 FQ	29580 MW	33310 TQ	USBLS	5/07
	Vermont	Y	20900 FQ	26420 MW	31890 TQ	USBLS	5/07
	Burlington-South Burlington MSA, VT	Y	23540 FQ	28360 MW	33650 TQ	USBLS	5/07
	Virginia	Y	21210 FQ	25300 MW	30560 TQ	USBLS	5/07
	Charlottesville MSA, VA	Y	23830 FQ	28050 MW	33150 TQ	USBLS	5/07
	Richmond MSA, VA	Y	21390 FQ	25640 MW	30880 TQ	USBLS	5/07
	Virginia Beach-Norfolk-Newport News MSA, VA-NC	Y	20670 FQ	24860 MW	30000 TQ	USBLS	5/07
	Washington	H	15.04 FQ	16.97 MW	18.82 TQ	WABLS	3/08
	Seattle-Tacoma-Bellevue MSA, WA	Y	32000 FQ	35800 MW	39850 TQ	USBLS	5/07
	West Virginia	Y	18874 FQ	22764 MW	26944 TQ	WVBLS	7/08-9/08
	Charleston MSA, WV	Y	18390 FQ	21550 MW	24740 TQ	USBLS	5/07
	Wisconsin	Y	22380 FQ	26450 MW	30620 TQ	USBLS	5/07
	Milwaukee-Waukesha-West Allis MSA, WI	Y	22940 FQ	27130 MW	31500 TQ	USBLS	5/07
	Wyoming	Y	25876 FQ	29654 MW	33686 TQ	WYBLS	9/08
	Cheyenne MSA, WY	Y	27473 FQ	30793 MW	34183 TQ	WYBLS	9/08
	Puerto Rico	Y	13660 FQ	16390 MW	20200 TQ	USBLS	5/07
	Aguadilla-Isabela-San Sebastian MSA, PR	Y	12560 FQ	13600 MW	14640 TQ	USBLS	5/07
	San Juan-Caguas-Guaynabo MSA, PR	Y	13600 FQ	16240 MW	19810 TQ	USBLS	5/07
	Virgin Islands	Y	21370 FQ	23860 MW	27340 TQ	USBLS	5/07
	Guam	Y	18750 FQ	22550 MW	27340 TQ	USBLS	5/07
Philosophy and Religion Teacher							
Postsecondary	Alabama	Y	39440 FQ	52050 MW	63900 TQ	USBLS	5/07
Postsecondary	Arizona	Y	27980 FQ	41760 MW	59480 TQ	USBLS	5/07
Postsecondary	Phoenix-Mesa-Scottsdale MSA, AZ	Y	27430 FQ	35450 MW	51400 TQ	USBLS	5/07
Postsecondary	Arkansas	Y	42490 FQ	51090 MW	60060 TQ	USBLS	5/07
Postsecondary	Little Rock-North Little Rock MSA, AR	Y	36500 FQ	47280 MW	57130 TQ	USBLS	5/07
Postsecondary	California	Y		68132 AW		CABLS	1/08-3/08
Postsecondary	Los Angeles-Long Beach-Glendale PMSA, CA	Y		70532 AW		CABLS	1/08-3/08
Postsecondary	Oakland-Fremont-Hayward MSA, CA	Y		87739 AW		CABLS	1/08-3/08
Postsecondary	Riverside-San Bernardino-Ontario MSA, CA	Y		79853 AW		CABLS	1/08-3/08
Postsecondary	Sacramento-Arden Arcade-Roseville MSA, CA	Y		89421 AW		CABLS	1/08-3/08
Postsecondary	San Diego-Carlsbad-San Marcos MSA, CA	Y		67886 AW		CABLS	1/08-3/08
Postsecondary	San Francisco-San Mateo-Redwood PMSA, CA	Y		71127 AW		CABLS	1/08-3/08
Postsecondary	Santa Ana-Anaheim-Irvine PMSA, CA	Y	31050 FQ	36710 MW	60390 TQ	USBLS	5/07
Postsecondary	Colorado	Y	35830 FQ	51060 MW	68610 TQ	USBLS	5/07
Postsecondary	Denver-Aurora MSA, CO	Y	38220 FQ	50480 MW	63290 TQ	USBLS	5/07

AE	Average entry wage	AW	Average wage paid	FQ	First quartile wage	LO	Lowest wage paid	MTC	Median total compensation	TCC	Total cash compensation
AER	Average entry range	AWR	Average wage range	H	Hourly	LR	Low end range	MW	Median wage paid	TQ	Third quartile wage
AEX	Average experienced wage	AXR	Average experienced range	HI	Highest wage paid	M	Monthly	MWR	Median wage range	W	Weekly
ATC	Average total compensation	D	Daily	HR	High end range	MCC	Median cash compensation	S	See annotated source	Y	Yearly

Philosophy and Religion Teacher

Occupation/Type/Industry	Location	Per	Low	Mid	High	Source	Date
Philosophy and Religion Teacher							
Postsecondary	District of Columbia	Y	50410 FQ	65260 MW	82870 TQ	USBLS	5/07
Postsecondary	Washington-Arlington-Alexandria MSA, DC-VA-MD-WV	Y	44820 FQ	60990 MW	77480 TQ	USBLS	5/07
Postsecondary	Florida	Y	41670 FQ	55550 MW	70840 TQ	USBLS	5/07
Postsecondary	Jacksonville MSA, FL	Y	41460 FQ	52880 MW	62790 TQ	USBLS	5/07
Postsecondary	Miami-Fort Lauderdale-Miami Beach MSA, FL	Y	37540 FQ	50540 MW	70830 TQ	USBLS	5/07
Postsecondary	Orlando-Kissimmee MSA, FL	Y	45240 FQ	54520 MW	61030 TQ	USBLS	5/07
Postsecondary	Tampa-St. Petersburg-Clearwater MSA, FL	Y	44560 FQ	64520 MW	87540 TQ	USBLS	5/07
Postsecondary	West Palm Beach-Boca Raton-Boynton Beach PMSA, FL	Y	43620 FQ	59230 MW	77160 TQ	USBLS	5/07
Postsecondary	Georgia	Y	43850 FQ	57320 MW	76510 TQ	USBLS	5/07
Postsecondary	Atlanta-Sandy Springs-Marietta MSA, GA	Y	46860 FQ	62200 MW	80230 TQ	USBLS	5/07
Postsecondary	Hawaii	Y	41460 FQ	58130 MW	77470 TQ	USBLS	5/07
Postsecondary	Honolulu MSA, HI	Y	40620 FQ	57300 MW	77100 TQ	USBLS	5/07
Postsecondary	Illinois	Y	44180 FQ	55650 MW	71420 TQ	USBLS	5/07
Postsecondary	Chicago-Naperville-Joliet MSA, IL-IN-WI	Y	45350 FQ	56220 MW	71020 TQ	USBLS	5/07
Postsecondary	Indiana	Y	43250 FQ	56230 MW	70310 TQ	USBLS	5/07
Postsecondary	Indianapolis-Carmel MSA, IN	Y	30700 FQ	49340 MW	63550 TQ	USBLS	5/07
Postsecondary	Iowa	Y	44590 FQ	56620 MW	70800 TQ	USBLS	5/07
Postsecondary	Kansas	Y	35800 FQ	53360 MW	75010 TQ	USBLS	5/07
Postsecondary	Kentucky	Y	41408 FQ	55586 MW	72842 TQ	KYBLS	2008
Postsecondary	Louisville-Jefferson County MSA, KY-IN	Y	42520 FQ	52020 MW	68340 TQ	USBLS	5/07
Postsecondary	Louisiana	Y		56987 AW		LABLS	1/08-3/08
Postsecondary	Maine	Y	37850 FQ	49170 MW	72320 TQ	USBLS	5/07
Postsecondary	Portland-South Portland-Biddeford MSA, ME	Y	33990 FQ	40600 MW	57700 TQ	USBLS	5/07
Postsecondary	Maryland	Y		67325 MW		MDBLS	3/08
Postsecondary	Baltimore-Towson MSA, MD	Y	55620 FQ	69090 MW	96930 TQ	USBLS	5/07
Postsecondary	Bethesda-Gaithersburg-Frederick PMSA, MD	Y	57720 FQ	67550 MW	91090 TQ	USBLS	5/07
Postsecondary	Massachusetts	Y	55380 FQ	71610 MW	92330 TQ	USBLS	5/07
Postsecondary	Boston-Cambridge-Quincy NECTA, MA	Y	55260 FQ	71440 MW	90850 TQ	USBLS	5/07
Postsecondary	Worcester MSA, MA-CT	Y	53150 FQ	69270 MW	87490 TQ	USBLS	5/07
Postsecondary	Michigan	Y	45790 FQ	58460 MW	74900 TQ	USBLS	5/07
Postsecondary	Detroit-Warren-Livonia MSA, MI	Y	34670 FQ	46650 MW	68020 TQ	USBLS	5/07
Postsecondary	Warren-Troy-Farmington Hills PMSA, MI	Y	31750 FQ	41900 MW	61610 TQ	USBLS	5/07
Postsecondary	Minnesota	Y	42319 FQ	51934 MW	66048 TQ	MNBLS	10/08-12/08
Postsecondary	Duluth-Superior MSA, MN-WI	Y	39505 FQ	50250 MW	75412 TQ	MNBLS	10/08-12/08
Postsecondary	Minneapolis-Saint Paul MSA, MN-WI	Y	44966 FQ	55742 MW	70578 TQ	MNBLS	10/08-12/08
Postsecondary	Mississippi	Y	45050 FQ	55000 MW	71300 TQ	USBLS	5/07
Postsecondary	Jackson MSA, MS	Y	49860 FQ	58750 MW	76160 TQ	USBLS	5/07
Postsecondary	Missouri	Y	43330 FQ	54220 MW	73340 TQ	USBLS	5/07
Postsecondary	Kansas City MSA, MO-KS	Y	42290 FQ	53980 MW	71560 TQ	USBLS	5/07
Postsecondary	St. Louis MSA, MO-IL	Y	43660 FQ	56610 MW	78060 TQ	USBLS	5/07
Postsecondary	Montana	Y	13940 FQ	15090 MW	16250 TQ	USBLS	5/07
Postsecondary	Nebraska	Y	32680 FQ	36950 MW	51360 TQ	USBLS	5/07
Postsecondary	Lincoln MSA, NE	Y	33560 FQ	52900 MW	60930 TQ	USBLS	5/07
Postsecondary	Omaha-Council Bluffs MSA, NE-IA	Y	31210 FQ	44020 MW	70010 TQ	USBLS	5/07
Postsecondary	New Hampshire	Y	48742 AE	66567 MW	85145 AEX	NHBLS	6/08
Postsecondary	New Jersey	Y	52580 FQ	66890 MW	99960 TQ	USBLS	5/07
Postsecondary	Edison PMSA, NJ	Y	60790 FQ	100140 MW		USBLS	5/07
Postsecondary	Newark-Union PMSA, NJ-PA	Y	51680 FQ	63050 MW	88870 TQ	USBLS	5/07
Postsecondary	New Mexico	Y	47350 FQ	57000 MW	72420 TQ	USBLS	5/07
Postsecondary	New York	Y	53730 FQ	67300 MW	88680 TQ	USBLS	5/07
Postsecondary	Nassau-Suffolk PMSA, NY	Y	48840 FQ	58330 MW	73120 TQ	USBLS	5/07
Postsecondary	New York-Northern New Jersey-Long Island MSA, NY-NJ-PA	Y	53850 FQ	67130 MW	90490 TQ	USBLS	5/07
Postsecondary	North Carolina	Y	43240 FQ	54280 MW	72490 TQ	USBLS	5/07

Occupation/Type/Industry	Location	Per	Low	Mid	High	Source	Date
Philosophy and Religion Teacher							
Postsecondary	Charlotte-Gastonia-Concord MSA, NC-SC	Y	41620 FQ	56090 MW	76380 TQ	USBLS	5/07
Postsecondary	Raleigh-Cary MSA, NC	Y	39490 FQ	46880 MW	58970 TQ	USBLS	5/07
Postsecondary	Fargo MSA, ND-MN	Y	40690 FQ	47920 MW	58960 TQ	USBLS	5/07
Postsecondary	Ohio	Y	43390 FQ	58710 MW	77680 TQ	USBLS	5/07
Postsecondary	Cincinnati-Middletown MSA, OH-KY-IN	Y	39750 FQ	54810 MW	75300 TQ	USBLS	5/07
Postsecondary	Cleveland-Elyria-Mentor MSA, OH	Y	38330 FQ	54980 MW	74630 TQ	USBLS	5/07
Postsecondary	Columbus MSA, OH	Y	52590 FQ	72150 MW	91850 TQ	USBLS	5/07
Postsecondary	Dayton MSA, OH	Y	45370 FQ	58890 MW	81890 TQ	USBLS	5/07
Postsecondary	Oklahoma	Y	31200 FQ	48970 MW	62470 TQ	USBLS	5/07
Postsecondary	Oklahoma City MSA, OK	Y	24290 FQ	51280 MW	70080 TQ	USBLS	5/07
Postsecondary	Tulsa MSA, OK	Y	27170 FQ	47600 MW	56570 TQ	USBLS	5/07
Postsecondary	Portland-Vancouver-Beaverton MSA, OR-WA	Y	41390 FQ	52990 MW	65260 TQ	USBLS	5/07
Postsecondary	Pennsylvania	Y	44270 FQ	56860 MW	74870 TQ	USBLS	5/07
Postsecondary	Allentown-Bethlehem-Easton MSA, PA-NJ	Y	44830 FQ	53280 MW	70450 TQ	USBLS	5/07
Postsecondary	Philadelphia-Camden-Wilmington MSA, PA-NJ-DE-MD	Y	45510 FQ	58920 MW	78150 TQ	USBLS	5/07
Postsecondary	Pittsburgh MSA, PA	Y	40790 FQ	56600 MW	77250 TQ	USBLS	5/07
Postsecondary	Rhode Island	Y	50000 FQ	66230 MW	94690 TQ	USBLS	5/07
Postsecondary	Providence-Fall River-Warwick MSA, RI-MA	Y	50000 FQ	66230 MW	94690 TQ	USBLS	5/07
Postsecondary	South Carolina	Y	42460 FQ	51790 MW	65720 TQ	USBLS	5/07
Postsecondary	Columbia MSA, SC	Y	44890 FQ	51140 MW	62470 TQ	USBLS	5/07
Postsecondary	South Dakota	Y	38915 FQ	46911 MW	59253 TQ	SDBLS	7/08-9/08
Postsecondary	Sioux Falls MSA, SD	Y	37478 FQ	47355 MW	62132 TQ	SDBLS	7/08-9/08
Postsecondary	Tennessee	Y	19800 FQ	44530 MW	60410 TQ	USBLS	5/07
Postsecondary	Memphis MSA, TN-MS-AR	Y	39510 FQ	52360 MW	66900 TQ	USBLS	5/07
Postsecondary	Nashville-Davidson-Murfreesboro MSA, TN	Y	19010 FQ	42350 MW	58430 TQ	USBLS	5/07
Postsecondary	Texas	Y	43050 FQ	56670 MW	78650 TQ	USBLS	5/07
Postsecondary	Austin-Round Rock MSA, TX	Y	35140 FQ	57560 MW	83210 TQ	USBLS	5/07
Postsecondary	Dallas-Fort Worth-Arlington MSA, TX	Y	42310 FQ	52900 MW	78650 TQ	USBLS	5/07
Postsecondary	Houston-Sugar Land-Baytown MSA, TX	Y	49940 FQ	73260 MW	85850 TQ	USBLS	5/07
Postsecondary	San Antonio MSA, TX	Y	42850 FQ	56900 MW	75820 TQ	USBLS	5/07
Postsecondary	Utah	Y	52550 FQ	58400 MW	67110 TQ	USBLS	5/07
Postsecondary	Vermont	Y	47150 FQ	55140 MW	64200 TQ	USBLS	5/07
Postsecondary	Virginia	Y	36660 FQ	51790 MW	65540 TQ	USBLS	5/07
Postsecondary	Richmond MSA, VA	Y	47410 FQ	60130 MW	75090 TQ	USBLS	5/07
Postsecondary	Virginia Beach-Norfolk-Newport News MSA, VA-NC	Y	40440 FQ	54020 MW	72020 TQ	USBLS	5/07
Postsecondary	Washington	Y		61031 AW		WABLS	3/08
Postsecondary	Seattle-Tacoma-Bellevue MSA, WA	Y	48590 FQ	57860 MW	71770 TQ	USBLS	5/07
Postsecondary	West Virginia	Y	40601 FQ	52899 MW	68834 TQ	WVBLS	7/08-9/08
Postsecondary	Wisconsin	Y	43110 FQ	53510 MW	67500 TQ	USBLS	5/07
Postsecondary	Milwaukee-Waukesha-West Allis MSA, WI	Y	48490 FQ	57890 MW	73850 TQ	USBLS	5/07
Postsecondary	Puerto Rico	Y	40420 FQ	57420 MW	67550 TQ	USBLS	5/07
Postsecondary	San Juan-Caguas-Guaynabo MSA, PR	Y	55140 FQ	63860 MW	70760 TQ	USBLS	5/07
Phlebotomist							
State Government	Ohio	H	15.62 LO		18.36 HI	ODAS	2008
Phlebotomy Technician	United States	Y		24500 AW		AAHS	2009
Photogrammetric Technologist	United States	Y		29230 AW		SUSA02	2008
Photographer	Alabama	Y	17160 FQ	20060 MW	26200 TQ	USBLS	5/07
	Birmingham-Hoover MSA, AL	Y	18490 FQ	22100 MW	28050 TQ	USBLS	5/07
	Alaska	Y	33200 FQ	40170 MW	46790 TQ	USBLS	5/07
	Arizona	Y	23770 FQ	32340 MW	41030 TQ	USBLS	5/07
	Phoenix-Mesa-Scottsdale MSA, AZ	Y	24930 FQ	34140 MW	42060 TQ	USBLS	5/07

AE Average entry wage AW Average wage paid FQ First quartile wage LO Lowest wage paid MTC Median total compensation TCC Total cash compensation
AER Average entry range AWR Average wage range H Hourly LR Low end range MW Median wage paid TQ Third quartile wage
AEX Average experienced wage AXR Average experienced range HI Highest wage paid M Monthly MWR Median wage range W Weekly
ATC Average total compensation D Daily HR High end range MCC Median cash compensation S See annotated source Y Yearly

Occupation/Type/Industry	Location	Per	Low	Mid	High	Source	Date
Photographer	Tucson MSA, AZ	Y	22780 FQ	27820 MW	34990 TQ	USBLS	5/07
	Arkansas	Y	21280 FQ	26930 MW	33060 TQ	USBLS	5/07
	Little Rock-North Little Rock MSA, AR	Y	21020 FQ	26620 MW	30170 TQ	USBLS	5/07
	California	H	10.51 FQ	18.60 MW	27.60 TQ	CABLS	1/08-3/08
	Los Angeles-Long Beach-Glendale PMSA, CA	H	9.69 FQ	20.78 MW	26.18 TQ	CABLS	1/08-3/08
	Oakland-Fremont-Hayward MSA, CA	H	9.30 FQ	15.41 MW	22.23 TQ	CABLS	1/08-3/08
	Riverside-San Bernardino-Ontario MSA, CA	H	12.20 FQ	15.69 MW	27.10 TQ	CABLS	1/08-3/08
	Sacramento-Arden Arcade-Roseville MSA, CA	H	11.62 FQ	17.75 MW	26.94 TQ	CABLS	1/08-3/08
	San Diego-Carlsbad-San Marcos MSA, CA	H	9.65 FQ	14.58 MW	20.85 TQ	CABLS	1/08-3/08
	San Francisco-San Mateo-Redwood PMSA, CA	H	20.68 FQ	35.00 MW	38.64 TQ	CABLS	1/08-3/08
	San Jose-Sunnyvale-Santa Clara MSA, CA	H	8.94 FQ	9.97 MW	17.68 TQ	CABLS	1/08-3/08
	Santa Ana-Anaheim-Irvine PMSA, CA	Y	22370 FQ	43080 MW	56690 TQ	USBLS	5/07
	Colorado	Y	16340 FQ	27250 MW	43430 TQ	USBLS	5/07
	Denver-Aurora MSA, CO	Y	15280 FQ	28040 MW	52750 TQ	USBLS	5/07
	Connecticut	H	10.02 AE	14.18 MW		CTBLS	1/08-3/08
	Hartford-West Hartford-East Hartford MSA, CT	Y	27400 FQ	33990 MW	48860 TQ	USBLS	5/07
	Delaware	Y	18030 FQ	24360 MW	33620 TQ	USBLS	5/07
	Wilmington PMSA, DE-MD-NJ	Y	18920 FQ	28290 MW	35040 TQ	USBLS	5/07
	District of Columbia	Y	38860 FQ	49240 MW	58280 TQ	USBLS	5/07
	Washington-Arlington-Alexandria MSA, DC-VA-MD-WV	Y	28130 FQ	37150 MW	58000 TQ	USBLS	5/07
	Florida	Y	18520 FQ	24470 MW	36690 TQ	USBLS	5/07
	Fort Lauderdale-Pompano Beach-Deerfield Beach PMSA, FL	Y	18390 FQ	22160 MW	30460 TQ	USBLS	5/07
	Jacksonville MSA, FL	Y	17430 FQ	22670 MW	30190 TQ	USBLS	5/07
	Miami-Fort Lauderdale-Miami Beach MSA, FL	Y	18910 FQ	25320 MW	38710 TQ	USBLS	5/07
	Orlando-Kissimmee MSA, FL	Y	16380 FQ	20280 MW	34910 TQ	USBLS	5/07
	Tampa-St. Petersburg-Clearwater MSA, FL	Y	21420 FQ	28550 MW	45320 TQ	USBLS	5/07
	West Palm Beach-Boca Raton-Boynton Beach PMSA, FL	Y	14970 FQ	17750 MW	29880 TQ	USBLS	5/07
	Georgia	Y	15600 FQ	19900 MW	29580 TQ	USBLS	5/07
	Atlanta-Sandy Springs-Marietta MSA, GA	Y	14850 FQ	18730 MW	28550 TQ	USBLS	5/07
	Hawaii	Y	18220 FQ	27560 MW	37610 TQ	USBLS	5/07
	Honolulu MSA, HI	Y	17500 FQ	20120 MW	30870 TQ	USBLS	5/07
	Idaho	Y	20830 FQ	24860 MW	29360 TQ	USBLS	5/07
	Boise City-Nampa MSA, ID	Y	22080 FQ	26040 MW	32540 TQ	USBLS	5/07
	Illinois	Y	24490 FQ	36510 MW	56940 TQ	USBLS	5/07
	Chicago-Naperville-Joliet MSA, IL-IN-WI	Y	26130 FQ	39380 MW	63410 TQ	USBLS	5/07
	Indiana	Y	20110 FQ	28830 MW	38420 TQ	USBLS	5/07
	Elkhart-Goshen MSA, IN	Y	17760 FQ	19320 MW	27390 TQ	USBLS	5/07
	Gary PMSA, IN	Y	18220 FQ	20420 MW	29820 TQ	USBLS	5/07
	Indianapolis-Carmel MSA, IN	Y	26600 FQ	31560 MW	40230 TQ	USBLS	5/07
	South Bend-Mishawaka MSA, IN-MI	Y	18120 FQ	24320 MW	37890 TQ	USBLS	5/07
	Iowa	Y	18310 FQ	25560 MW	30550 TQ	USBLS	5/07
	Des Moines-West Des Moines MSA, IA	Y	22890 FQ	27540 MW	30570 TQ	USBLS	5/07
	Kansas	Y	15580 FQ	19060 MW	28760 TQ	USBLS	5/07
	Topeka MSA, KS	Y	16950 FQ	21100 MW	28020 TQ	USBLS	5/07
	Wichita MSA, KS	Y	16700 FQ	18230 MW	22230 TQ	USBLS	5/07
	Kentucky	Y	17544 FQ	21811 MW	28752 TQ	KYBLS	2008
	Louisville-Jefferson County MSA, KY-IN	Y	16290 FQ	20090 MW	25660 TQ	USBLS	5/07
	Louisiana	H	9.99 FQ	11.66 MW	14.74 TQ	LABLS	1/08-3/08
	Baton Rouge MSA, LA	Y	22180 FQ	25660 MW	32420 TQ	USBLS	5/07

AE Average entry wage	**AW** Average wage paid	**FQ** First quartile wage	**LO** Lowest wage paid	**MTC** Median total compensation	**TCC** Total cash compensation
AER Average entry range	**AWR** Average wage range	**H** Hourly	**LR** Low end range	**MW** Median wage paid	**TQ** Third quartile wage
AEX Average experienced wage	**AXR** Average experienced range	**HI** Highest wage paid	**M** Monthly	**MWR** Median wage range	**W** Weekly
ATC Average total compensation	**D** Daily	**HR** High end range	**MCC** Median cash compensation	**S** See annotated source	**Y** Yearly

Photographer

Occupation/Type/Industry	Location	Per	Low	Mid	High	Source	Date
Photographer	New Orleans-Metairie-Kenner MSA, LA	Y	21210 FQ	23890 MW	30520 TQ	USBLS	5/07
	Maine	Y	17950 FQ	22110 MW	35900 TQ	USBLS	5/07
	Portland-South Portland-Biddeford MSA, ME	Y	16850 FQ	18980 MW	45970 TQ	USBLS	5/07
	Maryland	Y		24875 MW		MDBLS	3/08
	Baltimore-Towson MSA, MD	Y	14970 FQ	21870 MW	39180 TQ	USBLS	5/07
	Bethesda-Gaithersburg-Frederick PMSA, MD	Y	15300 FQ	31490 MW	41330 TQ	USBLS	5/07
	Hagerstown-Martinsburg MSA, MD-WV	Y	19850 FQ	25030 MW	33120 TQ	USBLS	5/07
	Massachusetts	Y	20900 FQ	29350 MW	45740 TQ	USBLS	5/07
	Boston-Cambridge-Quincy NECTA, MA	Y	23230 FQ	30440 MW	48470 TQ	USBLS	5/07
	Worcester MSA, MA-CT	Y	20730 FQ	42400 MW	48010 TQ	USBLS	5/07
	Michigan	Y	20520 FQ	27720 MW	37650 TQ	USBLS	5/07
	Detroit-Warren-Livonia MSA, MI	Y	20220 FQ	27580 MW	38870 TQ	USBLS	5/07
	Flint MSA, MI	Y	24510 FQ	27600 MW	30600 TQ	USBLS	5/07
	Grand Rapids-Wyoming MSA, MI	Y	21520 FQ	29260 MW	44000 TQ	USBLS	5/07
	Warren-Troy-Farmington Hills PMSA, MI	Y	19120 FQ	23390 MW	30820 TQ	USBLS	5/07
	Minnesota	Y	30173 FQ	43690 MW	64437 TQ	MNBLS	10/08-12/08
	Duluth-Superior MSA, MN-WI	Y	17607 FQ	19700 MW	26856 TQ	MNBLS	10/08-12/08
	Minneapolis-Saint Paul MSA, MN-WI	Y	36335 FQ	51076 MW	69427 TQ	MNBLS	10/08-12/08
	Rochester MSA, MN	Y	29238 FQ	42669 MW	55360 TQ	MNBLS	10/08-12/08
	Mississippi	Y	19060 FQ	25000 MW	34270 TQ	USBLS	5/07
	Jackson MSA, MS	Y	18190 FQ	22700 MW	29600 TQ	USBLS	5/07
	Missouri	Y	19160 FQ	28430 MW	41570 TQ	USBLS	5/07
	Kansas City MSA, MO-KS	Y	29200 FQ	37440 MW	46910 TQ	USBLS	5/07
	St. Louis MSA, MO-IL	Y	20130 FQ	30040 MW	40000 TQ	USBLS	5/07
	Montana	Y	20980 FQ	25180 MW	36810 TQ	USBLS	5/07
	Nebraska	Y	16660 FQ	22380 MW	30820 TQ	USBLS	5/07
	Omaha-Council Bluffs MSA, NE-IA	Y	17700 FQ	26170 MW	30530 TQ	USBLS	5/07
	Nevada	H	9.81 FQ	15.69 MW	18.28 TQ	NVBLS	5/08
	Carson City MSA, NV	H	13.24 FQ	14.26 MW	15.33 TQ	NVBLS	5/08
	Las Vegas-Paradise MSA, NV	H	9.82 FQ	15.84 MW	18.30 TQ	NVBLS	5/08
	New Jersey	Y	20950 FQ	29930 MW	46920 TQ	USBLS	5/07
	Camden PMSA, NJ	Y	23730 FQ	34610 MW	47320 TQ	USBLS	5/07
	Edison PMSA, NJ	Y	19670 FQ	26730 MW	45960 TQ	USBLS	5/07
	Newark-Union PMSA, NJ-PA	Y	20490 FQ	29550 MW	45790 TQ	USBLS	5/07
	New Mexico	Y	18130 FQ	31920 MW	42770 TQ	USBLS	5/07
	Albuquerque MSA, NM	Y	20070 FQ	32580 MW	41420 TQ	USBLS	5/07
	New York	Y	20350 FQ	33860 MW	53160 TQ	USBLS	5/07
	Albany-Schenectady-Troy MSA, NY	Y	20570 FQ	32930 MW	44950 TQ	USBLS	5/07
	Buffalo-Niagara Falls MSA, NY	Y	17640 FQ	20540 MW	25710 TQ	USBLS	5/07
	Nassau-Suffolk PMSA, NY	Y	16480 FQ	23420 MW	40330 TQ	USBLS	5/07
	New York-Northern New Jersey-Long Island MSA, NY-NJ-PA	Y	23270 FQ	36850 MW	59160 TQ	USBLS	5/07
	North Carolina	Y	20170 FQ	28590 MW	44700 TQ	USBLS	5/07
	Charlotte-Gastonia-Concord MSA, NC-SC	Y	15860 FQ	20890 MW	35750 TQ	USBLS	5/07
	Winston-Salem MSA, NC	Y	37400 FQ	42010 MW	46480 TQ	USBLS	5/07
	North Dakota	Y	20790 FQ	30310 MW	44230 TQ	USBLS	5/07
	Fargo MSA, ND-MN	Y	26170 FQ	40460 MW	44920 TQ	USBLS	5/07
	Ohio	Y	17480 FQ	20990 MW	31110 TQ	USBLS	5/07
	Cincinnati-Middletown MSA, OH-KY-IN	Y	16850 FQ	18510 MW	21470 TQ	USBLS	5/07
	Cleveland-Elyria-Mentor MSA, OH	Y	17350 FQ	21170 MW	28390 TQ	USBLS	5/07
	Columbus MSA, OH	Y	18920 FQ	27660 MW	37420 TQ	USBLS	5/07
	Dayton MSA, OH	Y	28530 FQ	36280 MW	45750 TQ	USBLS	5/07
	Oklahoma	Y	16600 FQ	20490 MW	28200 TQ	USBLS	5/07
	Oklahoma City MSA, OK	Y	16800 FQ	19830 MW	27080 TQ	USBLS	5/07
	Tulsa MSA, OK	Y	14510 FQ	23350 MW	38750 TQ	USBLS	5/07
	Oregon	H	11.04 FQ	13.83 MW	18.29 TQ	ORBLS	5/08

Occupation/Type/Industry	Location	Per	Low	Mid	High	Source	Date
Photographer	Portland-Vancouver-Beaverton MSA, OR-WA	Y	21670 FQ	28610 MW	39520 TQ	USBLS	5/07
	Pennsylvania	Y	21900 FQ	27990 MW	37890 TQ	USBLS	5/07
	Allentown-Bethlehem-Easton MSA, PA-NJ	Y	20870 FQ	30460 MW	43920 TQ	USBLS	5/07
	Philadelphia-Camden-Wilmington MSA, PA-NJ-DE-MD	Y	25730 FQ	31730 MW	41450 TQ	USBLS	5/07
	Pittsburgh MSA, PA	Y	21740 FQ	24190 MW	33650 TQ	USBLS	5/07
	Rhode Island	Y	29180 FQ	36870 MW	53730 TQ	USBLS	5/07
	Providence-Fall River-Warwick MSA, RI-MA	Y	25740 FQ	33450 MW	50310 TQ	USBLS	5/07
	South Carolina	Y	20170 FQ	27220 MW	36910 TQ	USBLS	5/07
	Charleston-North Charleston MSA, SC	Y	21970 FQ	30930 MW	43780 TQ	USBLS	5/07
	Columbia MSA, SC	Y	24640 FQ	27980 MW	31370 TQ	USBLS	5/07
	Spartanburg MSA, SC	Y	28800 FQ	39300 MW	43740 TQ	USBLS	5/07
	South Dakota	Y	21955 FQ	25889 MW	30754 TQ	SDBLS	7/08-9/08
	Sioux Falls MSA, SD	Y	29219 FQ	35698 MW	42079 TQ	SDBLS	7/08-9/08
	Tennessee	Y	18560 FQ	22410 MW	29920 TQ	USBLS	5/07
	Memphis MSA, TN-MS-AR	Y	19730 FQ	23450 MW	30110 TQ	USBLS	5/07
	Nashville-Davidson-Murfreesboro MSA, TN	Y	18120 FQ	21660 MW	29250 TQ	USBLS	5/07
	Texas	Y	17300 FQ	22460 MW	32020 TQ	USBLS	5/07
	Austin-Round Rock MSA, TX	Y	23500 FQ	28150 MW	32320 TQ	USBLS	5/07
	Dallas-Fort Worth-Arlington MSA, TX	Y	17480 FQ	22130 MW	40250 TQ	USBLS	5/07
	El Paso MSA, TX	Y	16070 FQ	18760 MW	23950 TQ	USBLS	5/07
	Houston-Sugar Land-Baytown MSA, TX	Y	18820 FQ	23520 MW	33100 TQ	USBLS	5/07
	San Antonio MSA, TX	Y	13940 FQ	17170 MW	28120 TQ	USBLS	5/07
	Utah	Y	21170 FQ	28110 MW	37780 TQ	USBLS	5/07
	Provo-Orem MSA, UT	Y	18630 FQ	20270 MW	23930 TQ	USBLS	5/07
	Salt Lake City MSA, UT	Y	24680 FQ	29760 MW	41650 TQ	USBLS	5/07
	Vermont	Y	26790 FQ	30260 MW	36520 TQ	USBLS	5/07
	Virginia	Y	21400 FQ	31700 MW	43830 TQ	USBLS	5/07
	Richmond MSA, VA	Y	27350 FQ	32750 MW	45170 TQ	USBLS	5/07
	Virginia Beach-Norfolk-Newport News MSA, VA-NC	Y	15170 FQ	17870 MW	31280 TQ	USBLS	5/07
	Washington	H	11.81 FQ	16.32 MW	25.06 TQ	WABLS	3/08
	Seattle-Tacoma-Bellevue MSA, WA	Y	24850 FQ	34570 MW	53030 TQ	USBLS	5/07
	Spokane MSA, WA	Y	30800 FQ	37630 MW	55050 TQ	USBLS	5/07
	West Virginia	Y	19189 FQ	22108 MW	30938 TQ	WVBLS	7/08-9/08
	Charleston MSA, WV	Y	17910 FQ	19960 MW	29030 TQ	USBLS	5/07
	Wisconsin	Y	22720 FQ	30890 MW	47690 TQ	USBLS	5/07
	Milwaukee-Waukesha-West Allis MSA, WI	Y	22860 FQ	31550 MW	57170 TQ	USBLS	5/07
	Wyoming	Y	26038 FQ	34381 MW	44025 TQ	WYBLS	9/08
	Cheyenne MSA, WY	Y	26164 FQ	36525 MW	42321 TQ	WYBLS	9/08
	Puerto Rico	Y	21570 FQ	26580 MW	34140 TQ	USBLS	5/07
	San Juan-Caguas-Guaynabo MSA, PR	Y	22430 FQ	27190 MW	34740 TQ	USBLS	5/07
	Guam	Y	14700 FQ	23300 MW	28920 TQ	USBLS	5/07
Cruise Ship	United States	M	1800 LO		2100 HI	CRU03	2008
State Highway Patrol	Missouri	S	1081 LO		1498 HI	MSHPSS	7/1/08
Photographic Process Worker	Alabama	Y	16580 FQ	19670 MW	29640 TQ	USBLS	5/07
	Arizona	Y	18930 FQ	25380 MW	29520 TQ	USBLS	5/07
	Phoenix-Mesa-Scottsdale MSA, AZ	Y	18100 FQ	21600 MW	27790 TQ	USBLS	5/07
	Tucson MSA, AZ	Y	25160 FQ	27480 MW	29800 TQ	USBLS	5/07
	Arkansas	Y	18520 FQ	22640 MW	33160 TQ	USBLS	5/07
	Little Rock-North Little Rock MSA, AR	Y	17700 FQ	19510 MW	22990 TQ	USBLS	5/07
	California	H	9.15 FQ	12.35 MW	16.33 TQ	CABLS	1/08-3/08
	Los Angeles-Long Beach-Glendale PMSA, CA	H	8.86 FQ	12.61 MW	19.19 TQ	CABLS	1/08-3/08
	Oakland-Fremont-Hayward MSA, CA	H	10.63 FQ	12.15 MW	15.67 TQ	CABLS	1/08-3/08
	Riverside-San Bernardino-Ontario MSA, CA	H	11.81 FQ	15.19 MW	20.96 TQ	CABLS	1/08-3/08

AE Average entry wage	**AW** Average wage paid	**FQ** First quartile wage	**LO** Lowest wage paid	**MTC** Median total compensation	**TCC** Total cash compensation
AER Average entry range	**AWR** Average wage range	**H** Hourly	**LR** Low end range	**MW** Median wage paid	**TQ** Third quartile wage
AEX Average experienced wage	**AXR** Average experienced range	**HI** Highest wage paid	**M** Monthly	**MWR** Median wage range	**W** Weekly
ATC Average total compensation	**D** Daily	**HR** High end range	**MCC** Median cash compensation	**S** See annotated source	**Y** Yearly

Photographic Process Worker

Occupation/Type/Industry	Location	Per	Low	Mid	High	Source	Date
Photographic Process Worker	Sacramento-Arden Arcade-Roseville MSA, CA	H	10.25 FQ	12.68 MW	15.06 TQ	CABLS	1/08-3/08
	San Diego-Carlsbad-San Marcos MSA, CA	H	9.64 FQ	13.56 MW	15.81 TQ	CABLS	1/08-3/08
	San Francisco-San Mateo-Redwood PMSA, CA	H	13.75 FQ	15.07 MW	16.96 TQ	CABLS	1/08-3/08
	San Jose-Sunnyvale-Santa Clara MSA, CA	H	13.67 FQ	16.27 MW	19.19 TQ	CABLS	1/08-3/08
	Santa Ana-Anaheim-Irvine PMSA, CA	Y	17980 FQ	19840 MW	26300 TQ	USBLS	5/07
	Colorado	Y	18430 FQ	22060 MW	25820 TQ	USBLS	5/07
	Denver-Aurora MSA, CO	Y	18420 FQ	22040 MW	24820 TQ	USBLS	5/07
	Connecticut	H	9.37 AE	11.07 MW		CTBLS	1/08-3/08
	Bridgeport-Stamford-Norwalk MSA, CT	Y	19220 FQ	22010 MW	29150 TQ	USBLS	5/07
	Hartford-West Hartford-East Hartford MSA, CT	Y	19390 FQ	25820 MW	31960 TQ	USBLS	5/07
	New Haven MSA, CT	Y	19710 FQ	21600 MW	23500 TQ	USBLS	5/07
	Delaware	Y	21190 FQ	23450 MW	25780 TQ	USBLS	5/07
	Wilmington PMSA, DE-MD-NJ	Y	20680 FQ	23580 MW	26730 TQ	USBLS	5/07
	District of Columbia	Y	26600 FQ	36760 MW	46550 TQ	USBLS	5/07
	Washington-Arlington-Alexandria MSA, DC-VA-MD-WV	Y	19340 FQ	24460 MW	32140 TQ	USBLS	5/07
	Florida	Y	19960 FQ	24210 MW	31220 TQ	USBLS	5/07
	Fort Lauderdale-Pompano Beach-Deerfield Beach PMSA, FL	Y	21760 FQ	25670 MW	30060 TQ	USBLS	5/07
	Jacksonville MSA, FL	Y	22010 FQ	28510 MW	34210 TQ	USBLS	5/07
	Miami-Fort Lauderdale-Miami Beach MSA, FL	Y	18250 FQ	23220 MW	28960 TQ	USBLS	5/07
	Orlando-Kissimmee MSA, FL	Y	21270 FQ	23960 MW	28810 TQ	USBLS	5/07
	Tampa-St. Petersburg-Clearwater MSA, FL	Y	19640 FQ	22820 MW	31510 TQ	USBLS	5/07
	West Palm Beach-Boca Raton-Boynton Beach PMSA, FL	Y	18840 FQ	22130 MW	28400 TQ	USBLS	5/07
	Georgia	Y	16890 FQ	25810 MW	42910 TQ	USBLS	5/07
	Atlanta-Sandy Springs-Marietta MSA, GA	Y	23940 FQ	31870 MW	50400 TQ	USBLS	5/07
	Hawaii	Y	18080 FQ	22120 MW	28700 TQ	USBLS	5/07
	Honolulu MSA, HI	Y	17600 FQ	21180 MW	27440 TQ	USBLS	5/07
	Idaho	Y	19730 FQ	29920 MW	44200 TQ	USBLS	5/07
	Boise City-Nampa MSA, ID	Y	20220 FQ	42820 MW	60630 TQ	USBLS	5/07
	Illinois	Y	18840 FQ	25490 MW	33950 TQ	USBLS	5/07
	Chicago-Naperville-Joliet MSA, IL-IN-WI	Y	19990 FQ	26910 MW	38290 TQ	USBLS	5/07
	Indiana	Y	18730 FQ	23070 MW	28070 TQ	USBLS	5/07
	Indianapolis-Carmel MSA, IN	Y	18320 FQ	27270 MW	32530 TQ	USBLS	5/07
	Iowa	Y	17790 FQ	21470 MW	28200 TQ	USBLS	5/07
	Kansas	Y	19600 FQ	24460 MW	28790 TQ	USBLS	5/07
	Kentucky	Y	17986 FQ	20414 MW	25360 TQ	KYBLS	2008
	Louisville-Jefferson County MSA, KY-IN	Y	20570 FQ	23540 MW	28480 TQ	USBLS	5/07
	Louisiana	H	9.33 FQ	10.96 MW	17.18 TQ	LABLS	1/08-3/08
	Baton Rouge MSA, LA	Y	18930 FQ	23270 MW	35020 TQ	USBLS	5/07
	New Orleans-Metairie-Kenner MSA, LA	Y	20330 FQ	23400 MW	39220 TQ	USBLS	5/07
	Maine	Y	23910 FQ	28860 MW	36210 TQ	USBLS	5/07
	Portland-South Portland-Biddeford MSA, ME	Y	27790 FQ	33050 MW	39950 TQ	USBLS	5/07
	Maryland	Y		24275 MW		MDBLS	3/08
	Baltimore-Towson MSA, MD	Y	17260 FQ	21520 MW	30680 TQ	USBLS	5/07
	Bethesda-Gaithersburg-Frederick PMSA, MD	Y	17660 FQ	23560 MW	30630 TQ	USBLS	5/07
	Massachusetts	Y	19100 FQ	24240 MW	30250 TQ	USBLS	5/07
	Boston-Cambridge-Quincy NECTA, MA	Y	21310 FQ	25520 MW	29290 TQ	USBLS	5/07
	Worcester MSA, MA-CT	Y	25700 FQ	29250 MW	34140 TQ	USBLS	5/07
	Michigan	Y	20140 FQ	24250 MW	31720 TQ	USBLS	5/07
	Detroit-Warren-Livonia MSA, MI	Y	21100 FQ	26810 MW	34330 TQ	USBLS	5/07

AE	Average entry wage	AW	Average wage paid	FQ	First quartile wage	LO Lowest wage paid	MTC Median total compensation	TCC Total cash compensation
AER	Average entry range	AWR	Average wage range	H	Hourly	LR Low end range	MW Median wage paid	TQ Third quartile wage
AEX	Average experienced wage	AXR	Average experienced range	HI	Highest wage paid	M Monthly	MWR Median wage range	W Weekly
ATC	Average total compensation	D	Daily	HR	High end range	MCC Median cash compensation	S See annotated source	Y Yearly

1232

Occupation/Type/Industry	Location	Per	Low	Mid	High	Source	Date
Photographic Process Worker	Warren-Troy-Farmington Hills PMSA, MI	Y	20700 FQ	27940 MW	34450 TQ	USBLS	5/07
	Minnesota	Y	25792 FQ	30758 MW	41384 TQ	MNBLS	10/08-12/08
	Minneapolis-Saint Paul MSA, MN-WI	Y	29960 FQ	36719 MW	45956 TQ	MNBLS	10/08-12/08
	Mississippi	Y	13940 FQ	18770 MW	31600 TQ	USBLS	5/07
	Missouri	Y	19980 FQ	23910 MW	29500 TQ	USBLS	5/07
	Kansas City MSA, MO-KS	Y	20140 FQ	25190 MW	29580 TQ	USBLS	5/07
	St. Louis MSA, MO-IL	Y	22220 FQ	26130 MW	31050 TQ	USBLS	5/07
	Montana	Y	18990 FQ	29570 MW	39310 TQ	USBLS	5/07
	Nebraska	Y	16720 FQ	18660 MW	25700 TQ	USBLS	5/07
	Nevada	H	11.94 FQ	14.08 MW	17.93 TQ	NVBLS	5/08
	Las Vegas-Paradise MSA, NV	H	12.93 FQ	15.51 MW	22.86 TQ	NVBLS	5/08
	New Hampshire	H	7.91 AE	12.60 MW	20.81 AEX	NHBLS	6/08
	New Jersey	Y	23700 FQ	31310 MW	40150 TQ	USBLS	5/07
	Camden PMSA, NJ	Y	20920 FQ	27100 MW	37290 TQ	USBLS	5/07
	Edison PMSA, NJ	Y	24140 FQ	29760 MW	35530 TQ	USBLS	5/07
	Newark-Union PMSA, NJ-PA	Y	33130 FQ	37730 MW	44340 TQ	USBLS	5/07
	New Mexico	Y	15110 FQ	23460 MW	30000 TQ	USBLS	5/07
	Albuquerque MSA, NM	Y	21160 FQ	25990 MW	30700 TQ	USBLS	5/07
	New York	Y	26900 FQ	36660 MW	54780 TQ	USBLS	5/07
	Buffalo-Niagara Falls MSA, NY	Y	17660 FQ	22020 MW	29180 TQ	USBLS	5/07
	Nassau-Suffolk PMSA, NY	Y	30510 FQ	36780 MW	47860 TQ	USBLS	5/07
	New York-Northern New Jersey-Long Island MSA, NY-NJ-PA	Y	30200 FQ	37980 MW	54540 TQ	USBLS	5/07
	North Carolina	Y	15460 FQ	19530 MW	28760 TQ	USBLS	5/07
	Charlotte-Gastonia-Concord MSA, NC-SC	Y	18150 FQ	20970 MW	24760 TQ	USBLS	5/07
	Durham MSA, NC	Y	15400 FQ	18430 MW	23840 TQ	USBLS	5/07
	Ohio	Y	20070 FQ	28390 MW	37050 TQ	USBLS	5/07
	Cincinnati-Middletown MSA, OH-KY-IN	Y	16010 FQ	18180 MW	22730 TQ	USBLS	5/07
	Cleveland-Elyria-Mentor MSA, OH	Y	22710 FQ	27930 MW	31300 TQ	USBLS	5/07
	Dayton MSA, OH	Y	30730 FQ	33710 MW	36250 TQ	USBLS	5/07
	Oklahoma	Y	13740 FQ	18580 MW	27740 TQ	USBLS	5/07
	Oklahoma City MSA, OK	Y	16060 FQ	23260 MW	33080 TQ	USBLS	5/07
	Tulsa MSA, OK	Y	12610 FQ	13990 MW	16010 TQ	USBLS	5/07
	Oregon	H	10.57 FQ	13.25 MW	15.55 TQ	ORBLS	5/08
	Portland-Vancouver-Beaverton MSA, OR-WA	Y	21800 FQ	26370 MW	31060 TQ	USBLS	5/07
	Pennsylvania	Y	22860 FQ	28360 MW	37790 TQ	USBLS	5/07
	Philadelphia-Camden-Wilmington MSA, PA-NJ-DE-MD	Y	22460 FQ	26360 MW	32360 TQ	USBLS	5/07
	Pittsburgh MSA, PA	Y	20280 FQ	26050 MW	34930 TQ	USBLS	5/07
	Rhode Island	Y	20630 FQ	22710 MW	26360 TQ	USBLS	5/07
	Providence-Fall River-Warwick MSA, RI-MA	Y	20490 FQ	22370 MW	25490 TQ	USBLS	5/07
	South Carolina	Y	21700 FQ	24820 MW	29840 TQ	USBLS	5/07
	South Dakota	Y	19358 FQ	23326 MW	27552 TQ	SDBLS	7/08-9/08
	Sioux Falls MSA, SD	Y	20122 FQ	25075 MW	29684 TQ	SDBLS	7/08-9/08
	Tennessee	Y	19210 FQ	23880 MW	31310 TQ	USBLS	5/07
	Memphis MSA, TN-MS-AR	Y	18340 FQ	21860 MW	25870 TQ	USBLS	5/07
	Nashville-Davidson-Murfreesboro MSA, TN	Y	33390 FQ	38790 MW	46440 TQ	USBLS	5/07
	Texas	Y	18850 FQ	25520 MW	32040 TQ	USBLS	5/07
	Austin-Round Rock MSA, TX	Y	18950 FQ	21570 MW	25600 TQ	USBLS	5/07
	Dallas-Fort Worth-Arlington MSA, TX	Y	17930 FQ	25360 MW	35290 TQ	USBLS	5/07
	Houston-Sugar Land-Baytown MSA, TX	Y	26710 FQ	29060 MW	31500 TQ	USBLS	5/07
	Utah	Y	17280 FQ	22870 MW	30420 TQ	USBLS	5/07
	Salt Lake City MSA, UT	Y	20560 FQ	23460 MW	29770 TQ	USBLS	5/07
	Vermont	Y	21190 FQ	24030 MW	29750 TQ	USBLS	5/07
	Virginia	Y	19550 FQ	23240 MW	29180 TQ	USBLS	5/07
	Richmond MSA, VA	Y	17580 FQ	41210 MW	46170 TQ	USBLS	5/07
	Virginia Beach-Norfolk-Newport News MSA, VA-NC	Y	20490 FQ	23010 MW	26170 TQ	USBLS	5/07
	Washington	H	11.09 FQ	13.26 MW	18.95 TQ	WABLS	3/08

AE	Average entry wage	AW	Average wage paid	FQ	First quartile wage	LO	Lowest wage paid	MTC	Median total compensation	TCC	Total cash compensation
AER	Average entry range	AWR	Average wage range	H	Hourly	LR	Low end range	MW	Median wage paid	TQ	Third quartile wage
AEX	Average experienced wage	AXR	Average experienced range	HI	Highest wage paid	M	Monthly	MWR	Median wage range	W	Weekly
ATC	Average total compensation	D	Daily	HR	High end range	MCC	Median cash compensation	S	See annotated source	Y	Yearly

Occupation/Type/Industry	Location	Per	Low	Mid	High	Source	Date
Photographic Process Worker	West Virginia	Y	15221 FQ	18699 MW	26968 TQ	WVBLS	7/08-9/08
	Wisconsin	Y	19100 FQ	23370 MW	34340 TQ	USBLS	5/07
	Milwaukee-Waukesha-West Allis MSA, WI	Y	19420 FQ	23280 MW	39360 TQ	USBLS	5/07
	Wyoming	Y	21795 FQ	24943 MW	28724 TQ	WYBLS	9/08
	Puerto Rico	Y	16160 FQ	18310 MW	24520 TQ	USBLS	5/07
Photographic Processing Machine Operator							
	Alabama	Y	16840 FQ	19180 MW	22440 TQ	USBLS	5/07
	Birmingham-Hoover MSA, AL	Y	17480 FQ	19940 MW	22820 TQ	USBLS	5/07
	Alaska	Y	20190 FQ	23300 MW	29240 TQ	USBLS	5/07
	Anchorage MSA, AK	Y	19830 FQ	23050 MW	28090 TQ	USBLS	5/07
	Arizona	Y	16100 FQ	20010 MW	25060 TQ	USBLS	5/07
	Phoenix-Mesa-Scottsdale MSA, AZ	Y	15940 FQ	20280 MW	25530 TQ	USBLS	5/07
	Tucson MSA, AZ	Y	17230 FQ	20360 MW	25550 TQ	USBLS	5/07
	California	H	9.08 FQ	10.94 MW	14.28 TQ	CABLS	1/08-3/08
	Los Angeles-Long Beach-Glendale PMSA, CA	H	9.15 FQ	11.38 MW	16.89 TQ	CABLS	1/08-3/08
	Oakland-Fremont-Hayward MSA, CA	H	8.80 FQ	11.19 MW	16.06 TQ	CABLS	1/08-3/08
	Riverside-San Bernardino-Ontario MSA, CA	H	8.92 FQ	10.22 MW	12.66 TQ	CABLS	1/08-3/08
	Sacramento-Arden Arcade-Roseville MSA, CA	H	8.99 FQ	10.76 MW	13.70 TQ	CABLS	1/08-3/08
	San Diego-Carlsbad-San Marcos MSA, CA	H	8.99 FQ	10.76 MW	13.97 TQ	CABLS	1/08-3/08
	San Francisco-San Mateo-Redwood PMSA, CA	H	10.35 FQ	11.89 MW	15.69 TQ	CABLS	1/08-3/08
	San Jose-Sunnyvale-Santa Clara MSA, CA	H	10.78 FQ	12.91 MW	15.17 TQ	CABLS	1/08-3/08
	Santa Ana-Anaheim-Irvine PMSA, CA	Y	18390 FQ	21570 MW	26800 TQ	USBLS	5/07
	Colorado	Y	19080 FQ	22020 MW	25290 TQ	USBLS	5/07
	Denver-Aurora MSA, CO	Y	19920 FQ	22900 MW	26910 TQ	USBLS	5/07
	Fort Collins-Loveland MSA, CO	Y	18130 FQ	21510 MW	24750 TQ	USBLS	5/07
	Connecticut	H	8.70 AE	10.34 MW		CTBLS	1/08-3/08
	Bridgeport-Stamford-Norwalk MSA, CT	Y	18020 FQ	20480 MW	24750 TQ	USBLS	5/07
	Hartford-West Hartford-East Hartford MSA, CT	Y	18570 FQ	22900 MW	31170 TQ	USBLS	5/07
	New Haven MSA, CT	Y	17830 FQ	19680 MW	22980 TQ	USBLS	5/07
	Delaware	Y	18570 FQ	21190 MW	25450 TQ	USBLS	5/07
	Wilmington PMSA, DE-MD-NJ	Y	18760 FQ	21480 MW	29510 TQ	USBLS	5/07
	District of Columbia	Y	19880 FQ	25710 MW	31130 TQ	USBLS	5/07
	Washington-Arlington-Alexandria MSA, DC-VA-MD-WV	Y	18090 FQ	21520 MW	26290 TQ	USBLS	5/07
	Florida	Y	16320 FQ	18410 MW	21870 TQ	USBLS	5/07
	Fort Lauderdale-Pompano Beach-Deerfield Beach PMSA, FL	Y	16740 FQ	19130 MW	23380 TQ	USBLS	5/07
	Jacksonville MSA, FL	Y	16170 FQ	18230 MW	21650 TQ	USBLS	5/07
	Miami-Fort Lauderdale-Miami Beach MSA, FL	Y	15720 FQ	18390 MW	22370 TQ	USBLS	5/07
	Orlando-Kissimmee MSA, FL	Y	17060 FQ	18930 MW	23060 TQ	USBLS	5/07
	Tampa-St. Petersburg-Clearwater MSA, FL	Y	16330 FQ	18150 MW	20750 TQ	USBLS	5/07
	West Palm Beach-Boca Raton-Boynton Beach PMSA, FL	Y	16340 FQ	18770 MW	23060 TQ	USBLS	5/07
	Georgia	Y	16890 FQ	20230 MW	25270 TQ	USBLS	5/07
	Atlanta-Sandy Springs-Marietta MSA, GA	Y	18330 FQ	22380 MW	29850 TQ	USBLS	5/07
	Augusta-Richmond County MSA, GA-SC	Y	15860 FQ	17660 MW	19860 TQ	USBLS	5/07
	Hawaii	Y	20250 FQ	23500 MW	29250 TQ	USBLS	5/07
	Honolulu MSA, HI	Y	20230 FQ	23790 MW	29080 TQ	USBLS	5/07
	Idaho	Y	17220 FQ	19550 MW	23060 TQ	USBLS	5/07
	Illinois	Y	17890 FQ	21470 MW	27630 TQ	USBLS	5/07

AE	Average entry wage	AW	Average wage paid	FQ	First quartile wage	LO	Lowest wage paid	MTC	Median total compensation	TCC	Total cash compensation
AER	Average entry range	AWR	Average wage range	H	Hourly	LR	Low end range	MW	Median wage paid	TQ	Third quartile wage
AEX	Average experienced wage	AXR	Average experienced range	HI	Highest wage paid	M	Monthly	MWR	Median wage range	W	Weekly
ATC	Average total compensation	D	Daily	HR	High end range	MCC	Median cash compensation	S	See annotated source	Y	Yearly

1234

Occupation/Type/Industry	Location	Per	Low	Mid	High	Source	Date
Photographic Processing Machine Operator							
	Chicago-Naperville-Joliet MSA, IL-IN-WI	Y	18290 FQ	21600 MW	26980 TQ	USBLS	5/07
	Indiana	Y	17070 FQ	19640 MW	23660 TQ	USBLS	5/07
	Elkhart-Goshen MSA, IN	Y	17920 FQ	20480 MW	22680 TQ	USBLS	5/07
	Gary PMSA, IN	Y	16310 FQ	19050 MW	22660 TQ	USBLS	5/07
	Indianapolis-Carmel MSA, IN	Y	17540 FQ	20670 MW	26360 TQ	USBLS	5/07
	Iowa	Y	16510 FQ	18680 MW	22010 TQ	USBLS	5/07
	Des Moines-West Des Moines MSA, IA	Y	17820 FQ	20250 MW	24380 TQ	USBLS	5/07
	Kansas	Y	17460 FQ	20420 MW	25280 TQ	USBLS	5/07
	Wichita MSA, KS	Y	17000 FQ	18710 MW	21440 TQ	USBLS	5/07
	Kentucky	Y	16639 FQ	18632 MW	21794 TQ	KYBLS	2008
	Louisville-Jefferson County MSA, KY-IN	Y	16270 FQ	18990 MW	22830 TQ	USBLS	5/07
	Louisiana	H	7.83 FQ	8.92 MW	10.37 TQ	LABLS	1/08-3/08
	Baton Rouge MSA, LA	Y	16100 FQ	18160 MW	20880 TQ	USBLS	5/07
	New Orleans-Metairie-Kenner MSA, LA	Y	17760 FQ	19920 MW	22270 TQ	USBLS	5/07
	Maine	Y	17800 FQ	20170 MW	22990 TQ	USBLS	5/07
	Portland-South Portland-Biddeford MSA, ME	Y	17940 FQ	20060 MW	23230 TQ	USBLS	5/07
	Maryland	Y		19825 MW		MDBLS	3/08
	Baltimore-Towson MSA, MD	Y	16680 FQ	18480 MW	21180 TQ	USBLS	5/07
	Bethesda-Gaithersburg-Frederick PMSA, MD	Y	18950 FQ	22560 MW	28130 TQ	USBLS	5/07
	Massachusetts	Y	17780 FQ	20090 MW	24900 TQ	USBLS	5/07
	Boston-Cambridge-Quincy NECTA, MA	Y	18450 FQ	22190 MW	29460 TQ	USBLS	5/07
	Lynn-Peabody-Salem NECTA, MA	Y	17020 FQ	18960 MW	23660 TQ	USBLS	5/07
	New Bedford MSA, MA	Y	19090 FQ	21230 MW	23690 TQ	USBLS	5/07
	Springfield MSA, MA-CT	Y	17590 FQ	19400 MW	22640 TQ	USBLS	5/07
	Worcester MSA, MA-CT	Y	17540 FQ	19410 MW	22250 TQ	USBLS	5/07
	Michigan	Y	17640 FQ	20240 MW	25200 TQ	USBLS	5/07
	Detroit-Warren-Livonia MSA, MI	Y	17760 FQ	19990 MW	23800 TQ	USBLS	5/07
	Grand Rapids-Wyoming MSA, MI	Y	20480 FQ	23000 MW	25350 TQ	USBLS	5/07
	Lansing-East Lansing MSA, MI	Y	15670 FQ	18350 MW	24010 TQ	USBLS	5/07
	Warren-Troy-Farmington Hills PMSA, MI	Y	17610 FQ	19970 MW	24360 TQ	USBLS	5/07
	Minnesota	Y	18525 FQ	22703 MW	30706 TQ	MNBLS	10/08-12/08
	Duluth-Superior MSA, MN-WI	Y	17219 FQ	21044 MW	25046 TQ	MNBLS	10/08-12/08
	Minneapolis-Saint Paul MSA, MN-WI	Y	19168 FQ	23957 MW	34013 TQ	MNBLS	10/08-12/08
	Mississippi	Y	16180 FQ	18330 MW	21650 TQ	USBLS	5/07
	Gulfport-Biloxi MSA, MS	Y	16560 FQ	18330 MW	21760 TQ	USBLS	5/07
	Missouri	Y	16550 FQ	19210 MW	23430 TQ	USBLS	5/07
	Kansas City MSA, MO-KS	Y	19180 FQ	23100 MW	28070 TQ	USBLS	5/07
	St. Louis MSA, MO-IL	Y	17490 FQ	20150 MW	25110 TQ	USBLS	5/07
	Springfield MSA, MO	Y	16080 FQ	18330 MW	21830 TQ	USBLS	5/07
	Montana	Y	16870 FQ	19370 MW	23760 TQ	USBLS	5/07
	Nebraska	Y	16640 FQ	18470 MW	21600 TQ	USBLS	5/07
	Omaha-Council Bluffs MSA, NE-IA	Y	17850 FQ	20390 MW	23780 TQ	USBLS	5/07
	Nevada	H	8.96 FQ	10.61 MW	12.65 TQ	NVBLS	5/08
	Las Vegas-Paradise MSA, NV	H	8.95 FQ	10.68 MW	12.66 TQ	NVBLS	5/08
	New Hampshire	H	8.19 AE	10.38 MW	11.54 AEX	NHBLS	6/08
	Manchester MSA, NH	Y	17880 FQ	19950 MW	23250 TQ	USBLS	5/07
	Nashua NECTA, NH-MA	Y	15740 FQ	18450 MW	23070 TQ	USBLS	5/07
	New Jersey	Y	17220 FQ	19640 MW	23210 TQ	USBLS	5/07
	Camden PMSA, NJ	Y	17550 FQ	19860 MW	23200 TQ	USBLS	5/07
	Edison PMSA, NJ	Y	17410 FQ	20030 MW	23820 TQ	USBLS	5/07
	Newark-Union PMSA, NJ-PA	Y	17400 FQ	20240 MW	24270 TQ	USBLS	5/07
	New Mexico	Y	14990 FQ	17540 MW	21020 TQ	USBLS	5/07
	Albuquerque MSA, NM	Y	14400 FQ	17230 MW	20550 TQ	USBLS	5/07
	New York	Y	16940 FQ	19810 MW	25330 TQ	USBLS	5/07
	Albany-Schenectady-Troy MSA, NY	Y	16850 FQ	19090 MW	21880 TQ	USBLS	5/07
	Buffalo-Niagara Falls MSA, NY	Y	15600 FQ	17700 MW	20360 TQ	USBLS	5/07

AE	Average entry wage	AW	Average wage paid	FQ	First quartile wage	LO	Lowest wage paid	MTC	Median total compensation	TCC	Total cash compensation
AER	Average entry range	AWR	Average wage range	H	Hourly	LR	Low end range	MW	Median wage paid	TQ	Third quartile wage
AEX	Average experienced wage	AXR	Average experienced range	HI	Highest wage paid	M	Monthly	MWR	Median wage range	W	Weekly
ATC	Average total compensation	D	Daily	HR	High end range	MCC	Median cash compensation	S	See annotated source	Y	Yearly

Photographic Processing Machine Operator

Occupation/Type/Industry	Location	Per	Low	Mid	High	Source	Date
	Nassau-Suffolk PMSA, NY	Y	17570 FQ	21740 MW	31080 TQ	USBLS	5/07
	New York-Northern New Jersey-Long Island MSA, NY-NJ-PA	Y	17280 FQ	20510 MW	26880 TQ	USBLS	5/07
	North Carolina	Y	16480 FQ	19050 MW	22470 TQ	USBLS	5/07
	Charlotte-Gastonia-Concord MSA, NC-SC	Y	17520 FQ	19750 MW	22850 TQ	USBLS	5/07
	Raleigh-Cary MSA, NC	Y	17920 FQ	20110 MW	23090 TQ	USBLS	5/07
	North Dakota	Y	16490 FQ	18530 MW	20710 TQ	USBLS	5/07
	Fargo MSA, ND-MN	Y	18280 FQ	19980 MW	22620 TQ	USBLS	5/07
	Ohio	Y	16990 FQ	19100 MW	22550 TQ	USBLS	5/07
	Cincinnati-Middletown MSA, OH-KY-IN	Y	16940 FQ	18930 MW	21910 TQ	USBLS	5/07
	Cleveland-Elyria-Mentor MSA, OH	Y	17240 FQ	19610 MW	22850 TQ	USBLS	5/07
	Columbus MSA, OH	Y	17270 FQ	19460 MW	25710 TQ	USBLS	5/07
	Dayton MSA, OH	Y	17500 FQ	20070 MW	24370 TQ	USBLS	5/07
	Oklahoma	Y	16260 FQ	18440 MW	21240 TQ	USBLS	5/07
	Oklahoma City MSA, OK	Y	16080 FQ	18330 MW	21220 TQ	USBLS	5/07
	Tulsa MSA, OK	Y	16950 FQ	19000 MW	21530 TQ	USBLS	5/07
	Oregon	H	9.41 FQ	11.18 MW	13.67 TQ	ORBLS	5/08
	Portland-Vancouver-Beaverton MSA, OR-WA	Y	20800 FQ	24620 MW	30120 TQ	USBLS	5/07
	Pennsylvania	Y	15740 FQ	18180 MW	22760 TQ	USBLS	5/07
	Allentown-Bethlehem-Easton MSA, PA-NJ	Y	14680 FQ	17380 MW	22940 TQ	USBLS	5/07
	Philadelphia-Camden-Wilmington MSA, PA-NJ-DE-MD	Y	16180 FQ	18650 MW	23380 TQ	USBLS	5/07
	Pittsburgh MSA, PA	Y	16780 FQ	18700 MW	22710 TQ	USBLS	5/07
	Rhode Island	Y	17120 FQ	19420 MW	22310 TQ	USBLS	5/07
	Providence-Fall River-Warwick MSA, RI-MA	Y	17100 FQ	19110 MW	22170 TQ	USBLS	5/07
	South Carolina	Y	15870 FQ	18420 MW	22210 TQ	USBLS	5/07
	Charleston-North Charleston MSA, SC	Y	15230 FQ	18690 MW	22410 TQ	USBLS	5/07
	Columbia MSA, SC	Y	15340 FQ	18570 MW	22810 TQ	USBLS	5/07
	South Dakota	Y	17575 FQ	19315 MW	21760 TQ	SDBLS	7/08-9/08
	Sioux Falls MSA, SD	Y	19155 FQ	21380 MW	24328 TQ	SDBLS	7/08-9/08
	Tennessee	Y	16340 FQ	18920 MW	22940 TQ	USBLS	5/07
	Memphis MSA, TN-MS-AR	Y	16750 FQ	19460 MW	22790 TQ	USBLS	5/07
	Nashville-Davidson-Murfreesboro MSA, TN	Y	17050 FQ	20610 MW	25640 TQ	USBLS	5/07
	Texas	Y	16260 FQ	18810 MW	23280 TQ	USBLS	5/07
	Austin-Round Rock MSA, TX	Y	17950 FQ	21360 MW	32240 TQ	USBLS	5/07
	Dallas-Fort Worth-Arlington MSA, TX	Y	16960 FQ	20280 MW	25470 TQ	USBLS	5/07
	El Paso MSA, TX	Y	14930 FQ	17400 MW	20010 TQ	USBLS	5/07
	Houston-Sugar Land-Baytown MSA, TX	Y	16150 FQ	18360 MW	22110 TQ	USBLS	5/07
	Utah	Y	18280 FQ	21500 MW	25120 TQ	USBLS	5/07
	Salt Lake City MSA, UT	Y	18300 FQ	21240 MW	24270 TQ	USBLS	5/07
	Vermont	Y	17810 FQ	19410 MW	21780 TQ	USBLS	5/07
	Virginia	Y	17100 FQ	19800 MW	23850 TQ	USBLS	5/07
	Richmond MSA, VA	Y	19020 FQ	21690 MW	24870 TQ	USBLS	5/07
	Virginia Beach-Norfolk-Newport News MSA, VA-NC	Y	16810 FQ	19490 MW	24920 TQ	USBLS	5/07
	Washington	H	9.09 FQ	10.66 MW	12.56 TQ	WABLS	3/08
	Seattle-Tacoma-Bellevue MSA, WA	Y	18130 FQ	21520 MW	29370 TQ	USBLS	5/07
	West Virginia	Y	16314 FQ	18071 MW	20064 TQ	WVBLS	7/08-9/08
	Charleston MSA, WV	Y	16190 FQ	17440 MW	18700 TQ	USBLS	5/07
	Wisconsin	Y	16880 FQ	19660 MW	23680 TQ	USBLS	5/07
	Appleton MSA, WI	Y	16490 FQ	18980 MW	22590 TQ	USBLS	5/07
	Milwaukee-Waukesha-West Allis MSA, WI	Y	16670 FQ	20070 MW	24320 TQ	USBLS	5/07
	Wyoming	Y	18884 FQ	21903 MW	24338 TQ	WYBLS	9/08
	Puerto Rico	Y	16260 FQ	18340 MW	20820 TQ	USBLS	5/07
	San Juan-Caguas-Guaynabo MSA, PR	Y	16320 FQ	18320 MW	20640 TQ	USBLS	5/07

AE	Average entry wage	AW	Average wage paid	FQ	First quartile wage
AER	Average entry range	AWR	Average wage range	H	Hourly
AEX	Average experienced wage	AXR	Average experienced range	HI	Highest wage paid
ATC	Average total compensation	D	Daily	HR	High end range

LO Lowest wage paid
LR Low end range
M Monthly
MCC Median cash compensation

MTC Median total compensation
MW Median wage paid
MWR Median wage range
S See annotated source

TCC Total cash compensation
TQ Third quartile wage
W Weekly
Y Yearly

Occupation/Type/Industry	Location	Per	Low	Mid	High	Source	Date
Photojournalist							
State Government	Ohio	H	17.22 LO		21.77 HI	ODAS	2008
Physical Therapist	Alabama	Y	58630 FQ	70880 MW	82750 TQ	USBLS	5/07
	Birmingham-Hoover MSA, AL	Y	63660 FQ	75450 MW	87020 TQ	USBLS	5/07
	Alaska	Y	65120 FQ	74430 MW	86370 TQ	USBLS	5/07
	Anchorage MSA, AK	Y	66100 FQ	76160 MW	98800 TQ	USBLS	5/07
	Arizona	Y	51090 FQ	64850 MW	78350 TQ	USBLS	5/07
	Phoenix-Mesa-Scottsdale MSA, AZ	Y	49860 FQ	62970 MW	76090 TQ	USBLS	5/07
	Tucson MSA, AZ	Y	54440 FQ	69590 MW	86360 TQ	USBLS	5/07
	Arkansas	Y	54450 FQ	67550 MW	84250 TQ	USBLS	5/07
	Little Rock-North Little Rock MSA, AR	Y	48430 FQ	63770 MW	84770 TQ	USBLS	5/07
	California	H	31.35 FQ	37.94 MW	45.41 TQ	CABLS	1/08-3/08
	Bakersfield MSA, CA	H	33.39 FQ	38.74 MW	45.30 TQ	CABLS	1/08-3/08
	Los Angeles-Long Beach-Glendale PMSA, CA	H	28.69 FQ	36.92 MW	44.11 TQ	CABLS	1/08-3/08
	Oakland-Fremont-Hayward MSA, CA	H	36.70 FQ	42.65 MW	48.38 TQ	CABLS	1/08-3/08
	Riverside-San Bernardino-Ontario MSA, CA	H	31.83 FQ	38.56 MW	47.95 TQ	CABLS	1/08-3/08
	Sacramento-Arden Arcade-Roseville MSA, CA	H	33.80 FQ	39.94 MW	45.96 TQ	CABLS	1/08-3/08
	San Diego-Carlsbad-San Marcos MSA, CA	H	30.85 FQ	36.89 MW	42.72 TQ	CABLS	1/08-3/08
	San Francisco-San Mateo-Redwood PMSA, CA	H	34.58 FQ	39.76 MW	48.18 TQ	CABLS	1/08-3/08
	San Jose-Sunnyvale-Santa Clara MSA, CA	H	34.34 FQ	39.80 MW	45.23 TQ	CABLS	1/08-3/08
	Santa Ana-Anaheim-Irvine PMSA, CA	Y	67720 FQ	77910 MW	96980 TQ	USBLS	5/07
	Santa Rosa-Petaluma MSA, CA	H	31.93 FQ	35.74 MW	39.85 TQ	CABLS	1/08-3/08
	Colorado	Y	53800 FQ	60840 MW	71320 TQ	USBLS	5/07
	Denver-Aurora MSA, CO	Y	53070 FQ	60170 MW	70790 TQ	USBLS	5/07
	Connecticut	H	26.14 AE	34.25 MW		CTBLS	1/08-3/08
	Bridgeport-Stamford-Norwalk MSA, CT	Y	61350 FQ	73390 MW	90010 TQ	USBLS	5/07
	Hartford-West Hartford-East Hartford MSA, CT	Y	59660 FQ	69110 MW	82550 TQ	USBLS	5/07
	Delaware	Y	57130 FQ	69280 MW	79830 TQ	USBLS	5/07
	Wilmington PMSA, DE-MD-NJ	Y	57190 FQ	69530 MW	79510 TQ	USBLS	5/07
	District of Columbia	Y	50920 FQ	67800 MW	79510 TQ	USBLS	5/07
	Washington-Arlington-Alexandria MSA, DC-VA-MD-WV	Y	61300 FQ	74110 MW	85980 TQ	USBLS	5/07
	Florida	Y	59670 FQ	71280 MW	82900 TQ	USBLS	5/07
	Fort Lauderdale-Pompano Beach-Deerfield Beach PMSA, FL	Y	65550 FQ	74450 MW	85970 TQ	USBLS	5/07
	Jacksonville MSA, FL	Y	61540 FQ	72270 MW	85730 TQ	USBLS	5/07
	Miami-Fort Lauderdale-Miami Beach MSA, FL	Y	60510 FQ	72700 MW	85970 TQ	USBLS	5/07
	Orlando-Kissimmee MSA, FL	Y	59290 FQ	68790 MW	77540 TQ	USBLS	5/07
	Tallahassee MSA, FL	Y	51910 FQ	66070 MW	76210 TQ	USBLS	5/07
	Tampa-St. Petersburg-Clearwater MSA, FL	Y	61150 FQ	73690 MW	89220 TQ	USBLS	5/07
	West Palm Beach-Boca Raton-Boynton Beach PMSA, FL	Y	61030 FQ	69690 MW	81750 TQ	USBLS	5/07
	Georgia	Y	58500 FQ	71330 MW	83940 TQ	USBLS	5/07
	Athens-Clarke County MSA, GA	Y	42380 FQ	62590 MW	75690 TQ	USBLS	5/07
	Atlanta-Sandy Springs-Marietta MSA, GA	Y	61390 FQ	74210 MW	86250 TQ	USBLS	5/07
	Hawaii	Y	39240 FQ	55460 MW	68920 TQ	USBLS	5/07
	Honolulu MSA, HI	Y	38360 FQ	55460 MW	69370 TQ	USBLS	5/07
	Idaho	Y	55930 FQ	64700 MW	76590 TQ	USBLS	5/07
	Boise City-Nampa MSA, ID	Y	57850 FQ	65680 MW	75770 TQ	USBLS	5/07
	Coeur d'Alene MSA, ID	Y	60580 FQ	68730 MW	75790 TQ	USBLS	5/07
	Illinois	Y	59760 FQ	73020 MW	91000 TQ	USBLS	5/07

AE Average entry wage	**AW** Average wage paid	**FQ** First quartile wage	**LO** Lowest wage paid	**MTC** Median total compensation	**TCC** Total cash compensation
AER Average entry range	**AWR** Average wage range	**H** Hourly	**LR** Low end range	**MW** Median wage paid	**TQ** Third quartile wage
AEX Average experienced wage	**AXR** Average experienced range	**HI** Highest wage paid	**M** Monthly	**MWR** Median wage range	**W** Weekly
ATC Average total compensation	**D** Daily	**HR** High end range	**MCC** Median cash compensation	**S** See annotated source	**Y** Yearly

Physical Therapist

Occupation/Type/Industry	Location	Per	Low	Mid	High	Source	Date
Physical Therapist	Chicago-Naperville-Joliet MSA, IL-IN-WI	Y	60670 FQ	73550 MW	93130 TQ	USBLS	5/07
	Peoria MSA, IL	Y	57630 FQ	71530 MW	85250 TQ	USBLS	5/07
	Indiana	Y	56360 FQ	68410 MW	79940 TQ	USBLS	5/07
	Gary PMSA, IN	Y	59670 FQ	72730 MW	90900 TQ	USBLS	5/07
	Indianapolis-Carmel MSA, IN	Y	59240 FQ	68920 MW	79880 TQ	USBLS	5/07
	Iowa	Y	55150 FQ	64560 MW	75370 TQ	USBLS	5/07
	Cedar Rapids MSA, IA	Y	48240 FQ	60000 MW	70170 TQ	USBLS	5/07
	Davenport-Moline-Rock Island MSA, IA-IL	Y	54490 FQ	67030 MW	87390 TQ	USBLS	5/07
	Des Moines-West Des Moines MSA, IA	Y	54670 FQ	63010 MW	72640 TQ	USBLS	5/07
	Dubuque MSA, IA	Y	62050 FQ	69690 MW	77470 TQ	USBLS	5/07
	Iowa City MSA, IA	Y	58040 FQ	69530 MW	78840 TQ	USBLS	5/07
	Kansas	Y	55800 FQ	65630 MW	77000 TQ	USBLS	5/07
	Wichita MSA, KS	Y	56730 FQ	67600 MW	77280 TQ	USBLS	5/07
	Kentucky	Y	62614 FQ	72112 MW	82887 TQ	KYBLS	2008
	Bowling Green MSA, KY	Y	73390 FQ	82030 MW	94440 TQ	USBLS	5/07
	Louisville-Jefferson County MSA, KY-IN	Y	60780 FQ	70120 MW	81710 TQ	USBLS	5/07
	Louisiana	H	28.30 FQ	35.23 MW	42.82 TQ	LABLS	1/08-3/08
	Baton Rouge MSA, LA	Y	59350 FQ	74820 MW	90340 TQ	USBLS	5/07
	New Orleans-Metairie-Kenner MSA, LA	Y	54280 FQ	68480 MW	81990 TQ	USBLS	5/07
	Shreveport-Bossier City MSA, LA	Y	62320 FQ	72830 MW	83050 TQ	USBLS	5/07
	Maine	Y	53080 FQ	59130 MW	66030 TQ	USBLS	5/07
	Lewiston-Auburn MSA, ME	Y	52920 FQ	58790 MW	64820 TQ	USBLS	5/07
	Portland-South Portland-Biddeford MSA, ME	Y	54500 FQ	60440 MW	67870 TQ	USBLS	5/07
	Maryland	Y		77025 MW		MDBLS	3/08
	Baltimore-Towson MSA, MD	Y	60160 FQ	74830 MW	88630 TQ	USBLS	5/07
	Bethesda-Gaithersburg-Frederick PMSA, MD	Y	68250 FQ	77600 MW	87880 TQ	USBLS	5/07
	Massachusetts	Y	57420 FQ	68180 MW	78660 TQ	USBLS	5/07
	Boston-Cambridge-Quincy NECTA, MA	Y	58370 FQ	68850 MW	79850 TQ	USBLS	5/07
	Springfield MSA, MA-CT	Y	57570 FQ	68390 MW	78000 TQ	USBLS	5/07
	Worcester MSA, MA-CT	Y	51580 FQ	61650 MW	73930 TQ	USBLS	5/07
	Michigan	Y	57840 FQ	69020 MW	79790 TQ	USBLS	5/07
	Ann Arbor MSA, MI	Y	55120 FQ	67060 MW	75570 TQ	USBLS	5/07
	Detroit-Warren-Livonia MSA, MI	Y	59450 FQ	70640 MW	81400 TQ	USBLS	5/07
	Grand Rapids-Wyoming MSA, MI	Y	55280 FQ	62860 MW	73830 TQ	USBLS	5/07
	Warren-Troy-Farmington Hills PMSA, MI	Y	57100 FQ	70420 MW	88780 TQ	USBLS	5/07
	Minnesota	Y	60220 FQ	68883 MW	77807 TQ	MNBLS	10/08-12/08
	Duluth-Superior MSA, MN-WI	Y	58358 FQ	67000 MW	76719 TQ	MNBLS	10/08-12/08
	Minneapolis-Saint Paul MSA, MN-WI	Y	60534 FQ	69270 MW	77609 TQ	MNBLS	10/08-12/08
	Rochester MSA, MN	Y	64935 FQ	74535 MW	82421 TQ	MNBLS	10/08-12/08
	Mississippi	Y	56270 FQ	70030 MW	84670 TQ	USBLS	5/07
	Jackson MSA, MS	Y	53520 FQ	62700 MW	77340 TQ	USBLS	5/07
	Missouri	Y	50120 FQ	62020 MW	75000 TQ	USBLS	5/07
	Joplin MSA, MO	Y	47330 FQ	59220 MW	73450 TQ	USBLS	5/07
	Kansas City MSA, MO-KS	Y	55100 FQ	63070 MW	73230 TQ	USBLS	5/07
	St. Louis MSA, MO-IL	Y	46870 FQ	59220 MW	72580 TQ	USBLS	5/07
	Montana	Y	46540 FQ	56820 MW	64230 TQ	USBLS	5/07
	Billings MSA, MT	Y	54050 FQ	61760 MW	70180 TQ	USBLS	5/07
	Nebraska	Y	53010 FQ	64380 MW	76070 TQ	USBLS	5/07
	Omaha-Council Bluffs MSA, NE-IA	Y	54490 FQ	62680 MW	72580 TQ	USBLS	5/07
	Nevada	H	32.15 FQ	36.99 MW	44.02 TQ	NVBLS	5/08
	Las Vegas-Paradise MSA, NV	H	31.96 FQ	38.12 MW	47.75 TQ	NVBLS	5/08
	New Hampshire	H	25.75 AE	32.05 MW	36.89 AEX	NHBLS	6/08
	Manchester MSA, NH	Y	55910 FQ	63750 MW	72790 TQ	USBLS	5/07
	Nashua NECTA, NH-MA	Y	54370 FQ	62410 MW	74990 TQ	USBLS	5/07
	Rochester-Dover MSA, NH-ME	Y	54920 FQ	64230 MW	73010 TQ	USBLS	5/07
	New Jersey	Y	64090 FQ	75830 MW	90990 TQ	USBLS	5/07
	Camden PMSA, NJ	Y	59820 FQ	70830 MW	83000 TQ	USBLS	5/07

Physical Therapist

Occupation/Type/Industry	Location	Per	Low	Mid	High	Source	Date
Physical Therapist	Edison PMSA, NJ	Y	63630 FQ	75210 MW	89030 TQ	USBLS	5/07
	Newark-Union PMSA, NJ-PA	Y	66350 FQ	79930 MW	104140 TQ	USBLS	5/07
	New Mexico	Y	41410 FQ	59030 MW	75720 TQ	USBLS	5/07
	Albuquerque MSA, NM	Y	37390 FQ	57400 MW	74400 TQ	USBLS	5/07
	Farmington MSA, NM	Y	36320 FQ	63000 MW	76080 TQ	USBLS	5/07
	New York	Y	56900 FQ	66420 MW	80920 TQ	USBLS	5/07
	Albany-Schenectady-Troy MSA, NY	Y	52300 FQ	60740 MW	70560 TQ	USBLS	5/07
	Buffalo-Niagara Falls MSA, NY	Y	51980 FQ	58540 MW	69120 TQ	USBLS	5/07
	Nassau-Suffolk PMSA, NY	Y	59320 FQ	70210 MW	82850 TQ	USBLS	5/07
	New York-Northern New Jersey-Long Island MSA, NY-NJ-PA	Y	61570 FQ	73140 MW	88130 TQ	USBLS	5/07
	North Carolina	Y	59600 FQ	69980 MW	81920 TQ	USBLS	5/07
	Charlotte-Gastonia-Concord MSA, NC-SC	Y	58810 FQ	69550 MW	82950 TQ	USBLS	5/07
	Durham MSA, NC	Y	59560 FQ	68640 MW	77600 TQ	USBLS	5/07
	Raleigh-Cary MSA, NC	Y	55420 FQ	68340 MW	84400 TQ	USBLS	5/07
	North Dakota	Y	51180 FQ	58980 MW	70310 TQ	USBLS	5/07
	Fargo MSA, ND-MN	Y	56220 FQ	63900 MW	75820 TQ	USBLS	5/07
	Ohio	Y	61550 FQ	71570 MW	81430 TQ	USBLS	5/07
	Cincinnati-Middletown MSA, OH-KY-IN	Y	59860 FQ	70520 MW	82290 TQ	USBLS	5/07
	Cleveland-Elyria-Mentor MSA, OH	Y	64830 FQ	72460 MW	80660 TQ	USBLS	5/07
	Columbus MSA, OH	Y	58110 FQ	68840 MW	80760 TQ	USBLS	5/07
	Dayton MSA, OH	Y	59480 FQ	69530 MW	79450 TQ	USBLS	5/07
	Oklahoma	Y	55460 FQ	67320 MW	78300 TQ	USBLS	5/07
	Oklahoma City MSA, OK	Y	57860 FQ	70140 MW	80500 TQ	USBLS	5/07
	Tulsa MSA, OK	Y	53480 FQ	63190 MW	73860 TQ	USBLS	5/07
	Oregon	H	28.94 FQ	32.73 MW	37.14 TQ	ORBLS	5/08
	Portland-Vancouver-Beaverton MSA, OR-WA	Y	58460 FQ	66160 MW	74770 TQ	USBLS	5/07
	Salem MSA, OR	Y	58590 FQ	68890 MW	77170 TQ	USBLS	5/07
	Pennsylvania	Y	56260 FQ	68010 MW	81080 TQ	USBLS	5/07
	Allentown-Bethlehem-Easton MSA, PA-NJ	Y	58950 FQ	68520 MW	79610 TQ	USBLS	5/07
	Philadelphia-Camden-Wilmington MSA, PA-NJ-DE-MD	Y	57310 FQ	69200 MW	82570 TQ	USBLS	5/07
	Pittsburgh MSA, PA	Y	53510 FQ	66870 MW	78070 TQ	USBLS	5/07
	Rhode Island	Y	60490 FQ	74720 MW	95590 TQ	USBLS	5/07
	Providence-Fall River-Warwick MSA, RI-MA	Y	59280 FQ	72300 MW	90840 TQ	USBLS	5/07
	South Carolina	Y	55880 FQ	68950 MW	82660 TQ	USBLS	5/07
	Charleston-North Charleston MSA, SC	Y	52700 FQ	60220 MW	74300 TQ	USBLS	5/07
	Columbia MSA, SC	Y	60620 FQ	73400 MW	84720 TQ	USBLS	5/07
	Florence MSA, SC	Y	59000 FQ	74720 MW	93860 TQ	USBLS	5/07
	South Dakota	Y	54994 FQ	63053 MW	73489 TQ	SDBLS	7/08-9/08
	Sioux Falls MSA, SD	Y	54238 FQ	62844 MW	72533 TQ	SDBLS	7/08-9/08
	Tennessee	Y	60180 FQ	71670 MW	83710 TQ	USBLS	5/07
	Knoxville MSA, TN	Y	55720 FQ	65100 MW	76430 TQ	USBLS	5/07
	Memphis MSA, TN-MS-AR	Y	61680 FQ	73690 MW	90290 TQ	USBLS	5/07
	Nashville-Davidson-Murfreesboro MSA, TN	Y	61890 FQ	71280 MW	79690 TQ	USBLS	5/07
	Texas	Y	61050 FQ	73920 MW	90940 TQ	USBLS	5/07
	Austin-Round Rock MSA, TX	Y	52760 FQ	60500 MW	70830 TQ	USBLS	5/07
	Corpus Christi MSA, TX	Y	62050 FQ	71610 MW	80850 TQ	USBLS	5/07
	Dallas-Fort Worth-Arlington MSA, TX	Y	63960 FQ	76370 MW	93250 TQ	USBLS	5/07
	El Paso MSA, TX	Y	65110 FQ	80790 MW	105840 TQ	USBLS	5/07
	Houston-Sugar Land-Baytown MSA, TX	Y	63690 FQ	73950 MW	86460 TQ	USBLS	5/07
	San Antonio MSA, TX	Y	60320 FQ	75430 MW	94930 TQ	USBLS	5/07
	Utah	Y	56120 FQ	65340 MW	77160 TQ	USBLS	5/07
	Salt Lake City MSA, UT	Y	57840 FQ	67010 MW	79250 TQ	USBLS	5/07
	Vermont	Y	50880 FQ	58650 MW	68050 TQ	USBLS	5/07
	Burlington-South Burlington MSA, VT	Y	47430 FQ	55610 MW	64600 TQ	USBLS	5/07
	Virginia	Y	57660 FQ	70770 MW	82190 TQ	USBLS	5/07

AE	Average entry wage	AW	Average wage paid	FQ	First quartile wage
AER	Average entry range	AWR	Average wage range	H	Hourly
AEX	Average experienced wage	AXR	Average experienced range	HI	Highest wage paid
ATC	Average total compensation	D	Daily	HR	High end range

LO	Lowest wage paid	MTC	Median total compensation	TCC	Total cash compensation
LR	Low end range	MW	Median wage paid	TQ	Third quartile wage
M	Monthly	MWR	Median wage range	W	Weekly
MCC	Median cash compensation	S	See annotated source	Y	Yearly

Occupation/Type/Industry	Location	Per	Low	Mid	High	Source	Date
Physical Therapist	Richmond MSA, VA	Y	53900 FQ	69240 MW	82790 TQ	USBLS	5/07
	Roanoke MSA, VA	Y	60420 FQ	70430 MW	79320 TQ	USBLS	5/07
	Virginia Beach-Norfolk-Newport News MSA, VA-NC	Y	63950 FQ	73700 MW	81700 TQ	USBLS	5/07
	Washington	H	29.35 FQ	34.09 MW	38.32 TQ	WABLS	3/08
	Seattle-Tacoma-Bellevue MSA, WA	Y	60930 FQ	70730 MW	79030 TQ	USBLS	5/07
	West Virginia	Y	63289 FQ	76029 TQ	91217 TQ	WVBLS	7/08-9/08
	Charleston MSA, WV	Y	60770 FQ	71930 MW	94210 TQ	USBLS	5/07
	Wheeling MSA, WV-OH	Y	58140 FQ	69480 MW	81530 TQ	USBLS	5/07
	Wisconsin	Y	58750 FQ	68690 MW	77390 TQ	USBLS	5/07
	Milwaukee-Waukesha-West Allis MSA, WI	Y	57060 FQ	68920 MW	77660 TQ	USBLS	5/07
	Wyoming	Y	58087 FQ	65452 MW	74390 TQ	WYBLS	9/08
	Casper MSA, WY	Y	59013 FQ	65202 MW	70495 TQ	WYBLS	9/08
	Cheyenne MSA, WY	Y	58500 FQ	63176 MW	67522 TQ	WYBLS	9/08
	Puerto Rico	Y	20290 FQ	28020 MW	39430 TQ	USBLS	5/07
	San Juan-Caguas-Guaynabo MSA, PR	Y	21780 FQ	28990 MW	40730 TQ	USBLS	5/07
	Guam	Y	19830 FQ	46660 MW	82060 TQ	USBLS	5/07
Physical Therapist Aide	Alabama	Y	17100 FQ	19260 MW	22510 TQ	USBLS	5/07
	Birmingham-Hoover MSA, AL	Y	17870 FQ	19740 MW	22650 TQ	USBLS	5/07
	Arizona	Y	19920 FQ	23050 MW	27440 TQ	USBLS	5/07
	Phoenix-Mesa-Scottsdale MSA, AZ	Y	19780 FQ	22730 MW	26880 TQ	USBLS	5/07
	Tucson MSA, AZ	Y	20870 FQ	25530 MW	29480 TQ	USBLS	5/07
	Arkansas	Y	17140 FQ	19720 MW	23290 TQ	USBLS	5/07
	Fayetteville-Springdale-Rogers MSA, AR-MO	Y	21350 FQ	24320 MW	28730 TQ	USBLS	5/07
	Little Rock-North Little Rock MSA, AR	Y	18940 FQ	21500 MW	24080 TQ	USBLS	5/07
	California	H	10.70 FQ	12.35 MW	14.70 TQ	CABLS	1/08-3/08
	Bakersfield MSA, CA	H	10.71 FQ	11.63 MW	12.77 TQ	CABLS	1/08-3/08
	Los Angeles-Long Beach-Glendale PMSA, CA	H	10.54 FQ	12.17 MW	14.20 TQ	CABLS	1/08-3/08
	Oakland-Fremont-Hayward MSA, CA	H	13.42 FQ	16.20 MW	18.43 TQ	CABLS	1/08-3/08
	Riverside-San Bernardino-Ontario MSA, CA	H	10.99 FQ	12.12 MW	14.04 TQ	CABLS	1/08-3/08
	Sacramento-Arden Arcade-Roseville MSA, CA	H	10.85 FQ	11.97 MW	13.86 TQ	CABLS	1/08-3/08
	San Diego-Carlsbad-San Marcos MSA, CA	H	9.72 FQ	11.11 MW	13.19 TQ	CABLS	1/08-3/08
	San Francisco-San Mateo-Redwood PMSA, CA	H	10.53 FQ	13.92 MW	15.99 TQ	CABLS	1/08-3/08
	San Jose-Sunnyvale-Santa Clara MSA, CA	H	11.59 FQ	13.55 MW	18.62 TQ	CABLS	1/08-3/08
	Santa Ana-Anaheim-Irvine PMSA, CA	Y	20930 FQ	25930 MW	30710 TQ	USBLS	5/07
	Colorado	Y	23560 FQ	29880 MW	35480 TQ	USBLS	5/07
	Denver-Aurora MSA, CO	Y	25760 FQ	31630 MW	35690 TQ	USBLS	5/07
	Connecticut	H	10.04 AE	13.62 MW		CTBLS	1/08-3/08
	Bridgeport-Stamford-Norwalk MSA, CT	Y	25950 FQ	29520 MW	33910 TQ	USBLS	5/07
	Hartford-West Hartford-East Hartford MSA, CT	Y	21860 FQ	28190 MW	35390 TQ	USBLS	5/07
	Waterbury MSA, CT	Y	20480 FQ	22810 MW	28330 TQ	USBLS	5/07
	Delaware	Y	19750 FQ	25290 MW	36250 TQ	USBLS	5/07
	Wilmington PMSA, DE-MD-NJ	Y	19960 FQ	26390 MW	35540 TQ	USBLS	5/07
	District of Columbia	Y	24180 FQ	30240 MW	35840 TQ	USBLS	5/07
	Washington-Arlington-Alexandria MSA, DC-VA-MD-WV	Y	21060 FQ	25780 MW	33250 TQ	USBLS	5/07
	Florida	Y	19860 FQ	22660 MW	25840 TQ	USBLS	5/07
	Fort Lauderdale-Pompano Beach-Deerfield Beach PMSA, FL	Y	21030 FQ	23140 MW	25930 TQ	USBLS	5/07
	Jacksonville MSA, FL	Y	21890 FQ	25030 MW	32530 TQ	USBLS	5/07
	Miami-Fort Lauderdale-Miami Beach MSA, FL	Y	20680 FQ	23180 MW	27720 TQ	USBLS	5/07

AE	Average entry wage	AW	Average wage paid	FQ	First quartile wage
AER	Average entry range	AWR	Average wage range	H	Hourly
AEX	Average experienced wage	AXR	Average experienced range	HI	Highest wage paid
ATC	Average total compensation	D	Daily	HR	High end range

LO	Lowest wage paid	MTC	Median total compensation
LR	Low end range	MW	Median wage paid
M	Monthly	MWR	Median wage range
MCC	Median cash compensation	S	See annotated source

TCC	Total cash compensation
TQ	Third quartile wage
W	Weekly
Y	Yearly

Occupation/Type/Industry	Location	Per	Low	Mid	High	Source	Date
Physical Therapist Aide	Orlando-Kissimmee MSA, FL	Y	18650 FQ	21170 MW	23800 TQ	USBLS	5/07
	Tampa-St. Petersburg-Clearwater MSA, FL	Y	20000 FQ	22800 MW	25680 TQ	USBLS	5/07
	West Palm Beach-Boca Raton-Boynton Beach PMSA, FL	Y	21370 FQ	24030 MW	27430 TQ	USBLS	5/07
	Georgia	Y	17000 FQ	21070 MW	26560 TQ	USBLS	5/07
	Atlanta-Sandy Springs-Marietta MSA, GA	Y	19980 FQ	24350 MW	29240 TQ	USBLS	5/07
	Hawaii	Y	23290 FQ	25910 MW	30130 TQ	USBLS	5/07
	Honolulu MSA, HI	Y	23190 FQ	25790 MW	30830 TQ	USBLS	5/07
	Idaho	Y	18410 FQ	21930 MW	25510 TQ	USBLS	5/07
	Boise City-Nampa MSA, ID	Y	20110 FQ	23850 MW	27390 TQ	USBLS	5/07
	Coeur d'Alene MSA, ID	Y	18950 FQ	21740 MW	23820 TQ	USBLS	5/07
	Illinois	Y	20410 FQ	24710 MW	30200 TQ	USBLS	5/07
	Chicago-Naperville-Joliet MSA, IL-IN-WI	Y	20230 FQ	24570 MW	30200 TQ	USBLS	5/07
	Indiana	Y	18330 FQ	21810 MW	26030 TQ	USBLS	5/07
	Gary PMSA, IN	Y	18200 FQ	24770 MW	29030 TQ	USBLS	5/07
	Indianapolis-Carmel MSA, IN	Y	17310 FQ	19180 MW	23160 TQ	USBLS	5/07
	Iowa	Y	18580 FQ	22270 MW	26720 TQ	USBLS	5/07
	Des Moines-West Des Moines MSA, IA	Y	21790 FQ	27240 MW	31790 TQ	USBLS	5/07
	Kansas	Y	17860 FQ	21510 MW	25250 TQ	USBLS	5/07
	Topeka MSA, KS	Y	20000 FQ	24960 MW	28080 TQ	USBLS	5/07
	Wichita MSA, KS	Y	17640 FQ	20570 MW	24200 TQ	USBLS	5/07
	Kentucky	Y	19469 FQ	22799 MW	26851 TQ	KYBLS	2008
	Louisville-Jefferson County MSA, KY-IN	Y	20930 FQ	23310 MW	26920 TQ	USBLS	5/07
	Louisiana	H	8.26 FQ	9.36 MW	11.36 TQ	LABLS	1/08-3/08
	Baton Rouge MSA, LA	Y	16570 FQ	18550 MW	21060 TQ	USBLS	5/07
	Lafayette MSA, LA	Y	17130 FQ	18400 MW	19700 TQ	USBLS	5/07
	New Orleans-Metairie-Kenner MSA, LA	Y	19290 FQ	23690 MW	27860 TQ	USBLS	5/07
	Maine	Y	19770 FQ	22800 MW	27030 TQ	USBLS	5/07
	Maryland	Y		23850 MW		MDBLS	3/08
	Baltimore-Towson MSA, MD	Y	17900 FQ	21520 MW	32120 TQ	USBLS	5/07
	Bethesda-Gaithersburg-Frederick PMSA, MD	Y	22360 FQ	26570 MW	34730 TQ	USBLS	5/07
	Massachusetts	Y	24460 FQ	27920 MW	32090 TQ	USBLS	5/07
	Boston-Cambridge-Quincy NECTA, MA	Y	25970 FQ	29200 MW	33250 TQ	USBLS	5/07
	Worcester MSA, MA-CT	Y	22020 FQ	24220 MW	29180 TQ	USBLS	5/07
	Michigan	Y	20660 FQ	24720 MW	30150 TQ	USBLS	5/07
	Detroit-Warren-Livonia MSA, MI	Y	19010 FQ	22920 MW	26900 TQ	USBLS	5/07
	Grand Rapids-Wyoming MSA, MI	Y	22200 FQ	25490 MW	29440 TQ	USBLS	5/07
	Warren-Troy-Farmington Hills PMSA, MI	Y	18870 FQ	23110 MW	28040 TQ	USBLS	5/07
	Minnesota	Y	23745 FQ	27802 MW	31681 TQ	MNBLS	10/08-12/08
	Duluth-Superior MSA, MN-WI	Y	25899 FQ	31001 MW	37776 TQ	MNBLS	10/08-12/08
	Minneapolis-Saint Paul MSA, MN-WI	Y	25606 FQ	29192 MW	33636 TQ	MNBLS	10/08-12/08
	Mississippi	Y	16710 FQ	18720 MW	21740 TQ	USBLS	5/07
	Hattiesburg MSA, MS	Y	16570 FQ	18080 MW	19760 TQ	USBLS	5/07
	Jackson MSA, MS	Y	16810 FQ	19000 MW	22640 TQ	USBLS	5/07
	Missouri	Y	17650 FQ	21040 MW	24960 TQ	USBLS	5/07
	Kansas City MSA, MO-KS	Y	20220 FQ	23570 MW	28030 TQ	USBLS	5/07
	St. Louis MSA, MO-IL	Y	17660 FQ	21190 MW	25320 TQ	USBLS	5/07
	Montana	Y	19410 FQ	22720 MW	27570 TQ	USBLS	5/07
	Nebraska	Y	17830 FQ	21020 MW	24490 TQ	USBLS	5/07
	Omaha-Council Bluffs MSA, NE-IA	Y	18940 FQ	22390 MW	27980 TQ	USBLS	5/07
	Nevada	H	9.60 FQ	11.79 MW	14.19 TQ	NVBLS	5/08
	Las Vegas-Paradise MSA, NV	H	9.36 FQ	12.33 MW	14.33 TQ	NVBLS	5/08
	Reno-Sparks MSA, NV	H	9.92 FQ	11.44 MW	14.35 TQ	NVBLS	5/08
	New Hampshire	H	10.63 AE	13.63 MW	15.76 AEX	NHBLS	6/08
	New Jersey	Y	19530 FQ	22510 MW	25990 TQ	USBLS	5/07
	Camden PMSA, NJ	Y	21490 FQ	23670 MW	26750 TQ	USBLS	5/07
	Edison PMSA, NJ	Y	17330 FQ	19800 MW	23350 TQ	USBLS	5/07
	Newark-Union PMSA, NJ-PA	Y	21050 FQ	23550 MW	28120 TQ	USBLS	5/07
	New Mexico	Y	21100 FQ	24610 MW	34860 TQ	USBLS	5/07

AE	Average entry wage	**AW**	Average wage paid	**FQ**	First quartile wage	**LO** Lowest wage paid	**MTC** Median total compensation	**TCC** Total cash compensation
AER	Average entry range	**AWR**	Average wage range	**H**	Hourly	**LR** Low end range	**MW** Median wage paid	**TQ** Third quartile wage
AEX	Average experienced wage	**AXR**	Average experienced range	**HI**	Highest wage paid	**M** Monthly	**MWR** Median wage range	**W** Weekly
ATC	Average total compensation	**D**	Daily	**HR**	High end range	**MCC** Median cash compensation	**S** See annotated source	**Y** Yearly

Occupation/Type/Industry	Location	Per	Low	Mid	High	Source	Date
Physical Therapist Aide	Albuquerque MSA, NM	Y	20930 FQ	26780 MW	34690 TQ	USBLS	5/07
	New York	Y	21310 FQ	24320 MW	30000 TQ	USBLS	5/07
	Albany-Schenectady-Troy MSA, NY	Y	24150 FQ	27460 MW	30730 TQ	USBLS	5/07
	Buffalo-Niagara Falls MSA, NY	Y	23550 FQ	26680 MW	29560 TQ	USBLS	5/07
	Nassau-Suffolk PMSA, NY	Y	20250 FQ	22900 MW	27430 TQ	USBLS	5/07
	New York-Northern New Jersey-Long Island MSA, NY-NJ-PA	Y	20400 FQ	23340 MW	28600 TQ	USBLS	5/07
	North Carolina	Y	20220 FQ	23140 MW	26630 TQ	USBLS	5/07
	Charlotte-Gastonia-Concord MSA, NC-SC	Y	19430 FQ	22910 MW	27340 TQ	USBLS	5/07
	Durham MSA, NC	Y	21560 FQ	25190 MW	29030 TQ	USBLS	5/07
	North Dakota	Y	19170 FQ	22250 MW	25510 TQ	USBLS	5/07
	Ohio	Y	20170 FQ	23680 MW	28070 TQ	USBLS	5/07
	Canton-Massillon MSA, OH	Y	18470 FQ	22320 MW	27470 TQ	USBLS	5/07
	Cincinnati-Middletown MSA, OH-KY-IN	Y	19360 FQ	22820 MW	28320 TQ	USBLS	5/07
	Cleveland-Elyria-Mentor MSA, OH	Y	21760 FQ	24650 MW	28550 TQ	USBLS	5/07
	Columbus MSA, OH	Y	18390 FQ	20620 MW	24690 TQ	USBLS	5/07
	Dayton MSA, OH	Y	20220 FQ	22810 MW	25830 TQ	USBLS	5/07
	Oklahoma	Y	16190 FQ	18860 MW	21580 TQ	USBLS	5/07
	Oklahoma City MSA, OK	Y	15240 FQ	18110 MW	20340 TQ	USBLS	5/07
	Tulsa MSA, OK	Y	19270 FQ	21310 MW	23270 TQ	USBLS	5/07
	Oregon	H	10.33 FQ	11.51 MW	13.23 TQ	ORBLS	5/08
	Eugene-Springfield MSA, OR	Y	18860 FQ	21000 MW	24320 TQ	USBLS	5/07
	Portland-Vancouver-Beaverton MSA, OR-WA	Y	21920 FQ	24410 MW	28280 TQ	USBLS	5/07
	Pennsylvania	Y	20030 FQ	23960 MW	28780 TQ	USBLS	5/07
	Allentown-Bethlehem-Easton MSA, PA-NJ	Y	25110 FQ	27820 MW	30270 TQ	USBLS	5/07
	Lancaster MSA, PA	Y	25260 FQ	29330 MW	35280 TQ	USBLS	5/07
	Philadelphia-Camden-Wilmington MSA, PA-NJ-DE-MD	Y	20180 FQ	23470 MW	29050 TQ	USBLS	5/07
	Pittsburgh MSA, PA	Y	19390 FQ	23530 MW	27650 TQ	USBLS	5/07
	Rhode Island	Y	21110 FQ	24510 MW	27530 TQ	USBLS	5/07
	Providence-Fall River-Warwick MSA, RI-MA	Y	21090 FQ	24940 MW	28330 TQ	USBLS	5/07
	South Carolina	Y	17780 FQ	20620 MW	23870 TQ	USBLS	5/07
	Charleston-North Charleston MSA, SC	Y	22060 FQ	24640 MW	28600 TQ	USBLS	5/07
	Columbia MSA, SC	Y	17580 FQ	19560 MW	22560 TQ	USBLS	5/07
	South Dakota	Y	22006 FQ	24161 MW	26731 TQ	SDBLS	7/08-9/08
	Tennessee	Y	18300 FQ	21310 MW	24640 TQ	USBLS	5/07
	Memphis MSA, TN-MS-AR	Y	17390 FQ	19800 MW	24240 TQ	USBLS	5/07
	Nashville-Davidson-Murfreesboro MSA, TN	Y	19930 FQ	23120 MW	27030 TQ	USBLS	5/07
	Texas	Y	17200 FQ	20300 MW	23840 TQ	USBLS	5/07
	Austin-Round Rock MSA, TX	Y	18430 FQ	21520 MW	24140 TQ	USBLS	5/07
	Dallas-Fort Worth-Arlington MSA, TX	Y	16800 FQ	21070 MW	24100 TQ	USBLS	5/07
	El Paso MSA, TX	Y	17830 FQ	19970 MW	23560 TQ	USBLS	5/07
	Houston-Sugar Land-Baytown MSA, TX	Y	18330 FQ	22400 MW	27400 TQ	USBLS	5/07
	San Antonio MSA, TX	Y	17700 FQ	19620 MW	23130 TQ	USBLS	5/07
	Utah	Y	15740 FQ	18110 MW	20500 TQ	USBLS	5/07
	Salt Lake City MSA, UT	Y	17560 FQ	19480 MW	21860 TQ	USBLS	5/07
	Vermont	Y	22350 FQ	25310 MW	28930 TQ	USBLS	5/07
	Virginia	Y	20490 FQ	23220 MW	27540 TQ	USBLS	5/07
	Richmond MSA, VA	Y	20590 FQ	23420 MW	28940 TQ	USBLS	5/07
	Virginia Beach-Norfolk-Newport News MSA, VA-NC	Y	18510 FQ	22040 MW	24510 TQ	USBLS	5/07
	Washington	H	10.30 FQ	11.79 MW	13.86 TQ	WABLS	3/08
	Seattle-Tacoma-Bellevue MSA, WA	Y	21620 FQ	24460 MW	29870 TQ	USBLS	5/07
	West Virginia	Y	19295 FQ	22969 MW	26375 TQ	WVBLS	7/08-9/08
	Wisconsin	Y	21790 FQ	24300 MW	28040 TQ	USBLS	5/07
	Milwaukee-Waukesha-West Allis MSA, WI	Y	22370 FQ	24720 MW	28460 TQ	USBLS	5/07

AE Average entry wage	**AW** Average wage paid	**FQ** First quartile wage	**LO** Lowest wage paid	**MTC** Median total compensation	**TCC** Total cash compensation
AER Average entry range	**AWR** Average wage range	**H** Hourly	**LR** Low end range	**MW** Median wage paid	**TQ** Third quartile wage
AEX Average experienced wage	**AXR** Average experienced range	**HI** Highest wage paid	**M** Monthly	**MWR** Median wage range	**W** Weekly
ATC Average total compensation	**D** Daily	**HR** High end range	**MCC** Median cash compensation	**S** See annotated source	**Y** Yearly

Occupation/Type/Industry	Location	Per	Low	Mid	High	Source	Date
Physical Therapist Aide	Wyoming	Y	19386 FQ	22588 MW	28081 TQ	WYBLS	9/08
	Cheyenne MSA, WY	Y	21426 FQ	28006 MW	31444 TQ	WYBLS	9/08
	Puerto Rico	Y	14320 FQ	17320 MW	20050 TQ	USBLS	5/07
Physical Therapist Assistant	Alabama	Y	36600 FQ	44040 MW	50420 TQ	USBLS	5/07
	Birmingham-Hoover MSA, AL	Y	42360 FQ	47780 MW	53310 TQ	USBLS	5/07
	Alaska	Y	40120 FQ	43610 MW	47100 TQ	USBLS	5/07
	Anchorage MSA, AK	Y	39630 FQ	42770 MW	45900 TQ	USBLS	5/07
	Arizona	Y	21090 FQ	32970 MW	42320 TQ	USBLS	5/07
	Phoenix-Mesa-Scottsdale MSA, AZ	Y	20960 FQ	30990 MW	39350 TQ	USBLS	5/07
	Tucson MSA, AZ	Y	21140 FQ	42110 MW	49110 TQ	USBLS	5/07
	Arkansas	Y	35020 FQ	43450 MW	51330 TQ	USBLS	5/07
	Little Rock-North Little Rock MSA, AR	Y	23710 FQ	37910 MW	51060 TQ	USBLS	5/07
	California	H	21.96 FQ	27.10 MW	30.94 TQ	CABLS	1/08-3/08
	Los Angeles-Long Beach-Glendale PMSA, CA	H	23.50 FQ	28.07 MW	31.55 TQ	CABLS	1/08-3/08
	Oakland-Fremont-Hayward MSA, CA	H	25.65 FQ	29.04 MW	32.74 TQ	CABLS	1/08-3/08
	Riverside-San Bernardino-Ontario MSA, CA	H	22.24 FQ	26.73 MW	29.98 TQ	CABLS	1/08-3/08
	Sacramento-Arden Arcade-Roseville MSA, CA	H	21.03 FQ	26.56 MW	30.01 TQ	CABLS	1/08-3/08
	San Diego-Carlsbad-San Marcos MSA, CA	H	23.04 FQ	26.14 MW	29.09 TQ	CABLS	1/08-3/08
	San Francisco-San Mateo-Redwood PMSA, CA	H	24.96 FQ	29.15 MW	32.82 TQ	CABLS	1/08-3/08
	San Jose-Sunnyvale-Santa Clara MSA, CA	H	18.80 FQ	22.98 MW	31.80 TQ	CABLS	1/08-3/08
	Santa Ana-Anaheim-Irvine PMSA, CA	Y	44830 FQ	55940 MW	62600 TQ	USBLS	5/07
	Stockton MSA, CA	H	18.26 FQ	22.06 MW	27.50 TQ	CABLS	1/08-3/08
	Colorado	Y	29930 FQ	36060 MW	42320 TQ	USBLS	5/07
	Denver-Aurora MSA, CO	Y	32410 FQ	37360 MW	43250 TQ	USBLS	5/07
	Connecticut	H	14.34 AE	22.14 MW		CTBLS	1/08-3/08
	Bridgeport-Stamford-Norwalk MSA, CT	Y	35440 FQ	44080 MW	52740 TQ	USBLS	5/07
	Hartford-West Hartford-East Hartford MSA, CT	Y	44100 FQ	52890 MW	61150 TQ	USBLS	5/07
	Delaware	Y	34890 FQ	42940 MW	52110 TQ	USBLS	5/07
	Wilmington PMSA, DE-MD-NJ	Y	33760 FQ	40940 MW	52780 TQ	USBLS	5/07
	District of Columbia	Y	35800 FQ	42540 MW	48050 TQ	USBLS	5/07
	Washington-Arlington-Alexandria MSA, DC-VA-MD-WV	Y	24690 FQ	37770 MW	50050 TQ	USBLS	5/07
	Florida	Y	42510 FQ	49620 MW	57440 TQ	USBLS	5/07
	Fort Lauderdale-Pompano Beach-Deerfield Beach PMSA, FL	Y	47780 FQ	53520 MW	60160 TQ	USBLS	5/07
	Jacksonville MSA, FL	Y	25710 FQ	46610 MW	52710 TQ	USBLS	5/07
	Miami-Fort Lauderdale-Miami Beach MSA, FL	Y	44520 FQ	51720 MW	58660 TQ	USBLS	5/07
	Orlando-Kissimmee MSA, FL	Y	43760 FQ	49490 MW	55850 TQ	USBLS	5/07
	Sarasota-Bradenton-Venice MSA, FL	Y	41190 FQ	47490 MW	53830 TQ	USBLS	5/07
	Tampa-St. Petersburg-Clearwater MSA, FL	Y	42940 FQ	49410 MW	58740 TQ	USBLS	5/07
	West Palm Beach-Boca Raton-Boynton Beach PMSA, FL	Y	46190 FQ	53650 MW	59210 TQ	USBLS	5/07
	Georgia	Y	35260 FQ	44320 MW	53240 TQ	USBLS	5/07
	Atlanta-Sandy Springs-Marietta MSA, GA	Y	35770 FQ	46870 MW	58420 TQ	USBLS	5/07
	Hawaii	Y	33360 FQ	37490 MW	42430 TQ	USBLS	5/07
	Honolulu MSA, HI	Y	34180 FQ	37950 MW	42870 TQ	USBLS	5/07
	Idaho	Y	33370 FQ	41750 MW	48130 TQ	USBLS	5/07
	Boise City-Nampa MSA, ID	Y	27350 FQ	38270 MW	45830 TQ	USBLS	5/07
	Illinois	Y	36540 FQ	45590 MW	53880 TQ	USBLS	5/07
	Chicago-Naperville-Joliet MSA, IL-IN-WI	Y	37640 FQ	46660 MW	55030 TQ	USBLS	5/07
	Indiana	Y	39200 FQ	46690 MW	55040 TQ	USBLS	5/07

AE	Average entry wage	AW	Average wage paid	FQ	First quartile wage
AER	Average entry range	AWR	Average wage range	H	Hourly
AEX	Average experienced wage	AXR	Average experienced range	HI	Highest wage paid
ATC	Average total compensation	D	Daily	HR	High end range

LO	Lowest wage paid	MTC	Median total compensation	TCC	Total cash compensation
LR	Low end range	MW	Median wage paid	TQ	Third quartile wage
M	Monthly	MWR	Median wage range	W	Weekly
MCC	Median cash compensation	S	See annotated source	Y	Yearly

Occupation/Type/Industry	Location	Per	Low	Mid	High	Source	Date
Physical Therapist Assistant	Fort Wayne MSA, IN	Y	34420 FQ	39940 MW	48260 TQ	USBLS	5/07
	Gary PMSA, IN	Y	37710 FQ	44080 MW	51390 TQ	USBLS	5/07
	Indianapolis-Carmel MSA, IN	Y	42750 FQ	51420 MW	59350 TQ	USBLS	5/07
	South Bend-Mishawaka MSA, IN-MI	Y	36430 FQ	42600 MW	49910 TQ	USBLS	5/07
	Iowa	Y	24330 FQ	33340 MW	40470 TQ	USBLS	5/07
	Des Moines-West Des Moines MSA, IA	Y	34290 FQ	38650 MW	44290 TQ	USBLS	5/07
	Kansas	Y	37120 FQ	43040 MW	49620 TQ	USBLS	5/07
	Wichita MSA, KS	Y	36870 FQ	43120 MW	49380 TQ	USBLS	5/07
	Kentucky	Y	37310 FQ	43399 MW	51491 TQ	KYBLS	2008
	Louisville-Jefferson County MSA, KY-IN	Y	40580 FQ	49970 MW	56610 TQ	USBLS	5/07
	Louisiana	H	13.71 FQ	19.37 MW	25.33 TQ	LABLS	1/08-3/08
	Baton Rouge MSA, LA	Y	33640 FQ	45380 MW	55200 TQ	USBLS	5/07
	Lafayette MSA, LA	Y	17280 FQ	27630 MW	53710 TQ	USBLS	5/07
	New Orleans-Metairie-Kenner MSA, LA	Y	31870 FQ	43990 MW	57430 TQ	USBLS	5/07
	Maine	Y	34750 FQ	38770 MW	43900 TQ	USBLS	5/07
	Portland-South Portland-Biddeford MSA, ME	Y	33940 FQ	37950 MW	45510 TQ	USBLS	5/07
	Maryland	Y		43550 MW		MDBLS	3/08
	Baltimore-Towson MSA, MD	Y	41110 FQ	49640 MW	58540 TQ	USBLS	5/07
	Bethesda-Gaithersburg-Frederick PMSA, MD	Y	22770 FQ	25030 MW	33140 TQ	USBLS	5/07
	Massachusetts	Y	41600 FQ	46720 MW	52770 TQ	USBLS	5/07
	Boston-Cambridge-Quincy NECTA, MA	Y	40460 FQ	46290 MW	52760 TQ	USBLS	5/07
	Worcester MSA, MA-CT	Y	39130 FQ	44770 MW	51780 TQ	USBLS	5/07
	Michigan	Y	31060 FQ	37880 MW	45240 TQ	USBLS	5/07
	Detroit-Warren-Livonia MSA, MI	Y	28530 FQ	35330 MW	45460 TQ	USBLS	5/07
	Flint MSA, MI	Y	35020 FQ	39750 MW	44710 TQ	USBLS	5/07
	Grand Rapids-Wyoming MSA, MI	Y	34860 FQ	38920 MW	44190 TQ	USBLS	5/07
	Warren-Troy-Farmington Hills PMSA, MI	Y	28370 FQ	33460 MW	43980 TQ	USBLS	5/07
	Minnesota	Y	35413 FQ	41279 MW	47323 TQ	MNBLS	10/08-12/08
	Duluth-Superior MSA, MN-WI	Y	35497 FQ	40296 MW	45911 TQ	MNBLS	10/08-12/08
	Minneapolis-Saint Paul MSA, MN-WI	Y	34817 FQ	42032 MW	48138 TQ	MNBLS	10/08-12/08
	Rochester MSA, MN	Y	38766 FQ	43765 MW	49329 TQ	MNBLS	10/08-12/08
	Mississippi	Y	32750 FQ	41700 MW	50660 TQ	USBLS	5/07
	Jackson MSA, MS	Y	33290 FQ	37630 MW	45070 TQ	USBLS	5/07
	Missouri	Y	35600 FQ	42240 MW	47780 TQ	USBLS	5/07
	Kansas City MSA, MO-KS	Y	38500 FQ	43920 MW	49390 TQ	USBLS	5/07
	St. Louis MSA, MO-IL	Y	38070 FQ	43950 MW	49550 TQ	USBLS	5/07
	Montana	Y	32560 FQ	35610 MW	39080 TQ	USBLS	5/07
	Nebraska	Y	31620 FQ	37030 MW	43760 TQ	USBLS	5/07
	Lincoln MSA, NE	Y	34870 FQ	40070 MW	46020 TQ	USBLS	5/07
	Omaha-Council Bluffs MSA, NE-IA	Y	27370 FQ	35530 MW	42620 TQ	USBLS	5/07
	Nevada	H	18.60 FQ	23.87 MW	27.64 TQ	NVBLS	5/08
	Las Vegas-Paradise MSA, NV	H	18.66 FQ	24.13 MW	27.90 TQ	NVBLS	5/08
	Reno-Sparks MSA, NV	H	16.27 FQ	23.14 MW	26.50 TQ	NVBLS	5/08
	New Hampshire	H	16.65 AE	21.06 MW	23.07 AEX	NHBLS	6/08
	Manchester MSA, NH	Y	34310 FQ	42180 MW	46900 TQ	USBLS	5/07
	New Jersey	Y	29280 FQ	43930 MW	52960 TQ	USBLS	5/07
	Camden PMSA, NJ	Y	39740 FQ	43990 MW	47980 TQ	USBLS	5/07
	Edison PMSA, NJ	Y	35390 FQ	50370 MW	59040 TQ	USBLS	5/07
	Newark-Union PMSA, NJ-PA	Y	22860 FQ	31640 MW	49370 TQ	USBLS	5/07
	New Mexico	Y	25300 FQ	38980 MW	49410 TQ	USBLS	5/07
	Albuquerque MSA, NM	Y	27860 FQ	41600 MW	51690 TQ	USBLS	5/07
	New York	Y	35400 FQ	42930 MW	50880 TQ	USBLS	5/07
	Albany-Schenectady-Troy MSA, NY	Y	32260 FQ	35860 MW	39610 TQ	USBLS	5/07
	Binghamton MSA, NY	Y	32600 FQ	37540 MW	43680 TQ	USBLS	5/07
	Buffalo-Niagara Falls MSA, NY	Y	31580 FQ	35970 MW	41540 TQ	USBLS	5/07
	Nassau-Suffolk PMSA, NY	Y	42140 FQ	48640 MW	55310 TQ	USBLS	5/07

AE	Average entry wage	AW	Average wage paid	FQ	First quartile wage	LO	Lowest wage paid	MTC	Median total compensation	TCC	Total cash compensation
AER	Average entry range	AWR	Average wage range	H	Hourly	LR	Low end range	MW	Median wage paid	TQ	Third quartile wage
AEX	Average experienced wage	AXR	Average experienced range	HI	Highest wage paid	M	Monthly	MWR	Median wage range	W	Weekly
ATC	Average total compensation	D	Daily	HR	High end range	MCC	Median cash compensation	S	See annotated source	Y	Yearly

Occupation/Type/Industry	Location	Per	Low	Mid	High	Source	Date
Physical Therapist Assistant	New York-Northern New Jersey-Long Island MSA, NY-NJ-PA	Y	37170 FQ	46410 MW	54520 TQ	USBLS	5/07
	North Carolina	Y	39230 FQ	45410 MW	52290 TQ	USBLS	5/07
	Charlotte-Gastonia-Concord MSA, NC-SC	Y	39820 FQ	48550 MW	58100 TQ	USBLS	5/07
	Raleigh-Cary MSA, NC	Y	30910 FQ	44470 MW	54370 TQ	USBLS	5/07
	Winston-Salem MSA, NC	Y	42100 FQ	51760 MW	60740 TQ	USBLS	5/07
	North Dakota	Y	27530 FQ	30490 MW	34450 TQ	USBLS	5/07
	Ohio	Y	40670 FQ	46520 MW	54300 TQ	USBLS	5/07
	Cincinnati-Middletown MSA, OH-KY-IN	Y	41190 FQ	48050 MW	56200 TQ	USBLS	5/07
	Cleveland-Elyria-Mentor MSA, OH	Y	42400 FQ	48610 MW	56440 TQ	USBLS	5/07
	Columbus MSA, OH	Y	41860 FQ	46240 MW	51920 TQ	USBLS	5/07
	Dayton MSA, OH	Y	40320 FQ	46680 MW	53590 TQ	USBLS	5/07
	Oklahoma	Y	29940 FQ	39630 MW	48400 TQ	USBLS	5/07
	Oklahoma City MSA, OK	Y	24380 FQ	41070 MW	49280 TQ	USBLS	5/07
	Tulsa MSA, OK	Y	26910 FQ	32540 MW	39630 TQ	USBLS	5/07
	Oregon	H	18.41 FQ	20.92 MW	23.25 TQ	ORBLS	5/08
	Portland-Vancouver-Beaverton MSA, OR-WA	Y	38340 FQ	44260 MW	50150 TQ	USBLS	5/07
	Pennsylvania	Y	32900 FQ	38120 MW	45090 TQ	USBLS	5/07
	Allentown-Bethlehem-Easton MSA, PA-NJ	Y	34940 FQ	39820 MW	45690 TQ	USBLS	5/07
	Philadelphia-Camden-Wilmington MSA, PA-NJ-DE-MD	Y	35820 FQ	43100 MW	51900 TQ	USBLS	5/07
	Pittsburgh MSA, PA	Y	33580 FQ	37330 MW	41480 TQ	USBLS	5/07
	Providence-Fall River-Warwick MSA, RI-MA	Y	42580 FQ	47360 MW	54110 TQ	USBLS	5/07
	South Carolina	Y	39940 FQ	46070 MW	52990 TQ	USBLS	5/07
	Charleston-North Charleston MSA, SC	Y	39830 FQ	45340 MW	53680 TQ	USBLS	5/07
	Columbia MSA, SC	Y	40830 FQ	47400 MW	54980 TQ	USBLS	5/07
	South Dakota	Y	28124 FQ	31911 MW	36808 TQ	SDBLS	7/08-9/08
	Sioux Falls MSA, SD	Y	26932 FQ	30281 MW	33553 TQ	SDBLS	7/08-9/08
	Tennessee	Y	37190 FQ	45920 MW	55250 TQ	USBLS	5/07
	Memphis MSA, TN-MS-AR	Y	22500 FQ	39860 MW	50390 TQ	USBLS	5/07
	Nashville-Davidson-Murfreesboro MSA, TN	Y	44730 FQ	53980 MW	71750 TQ	USBLS	5/07
	Texas	Y	41660 FQ	49080 MW	59150 TQ	USBLS	5/07
	Austin-Round Rock MSA, TX	Y	38130 FQ	43760 MW	52730 TQ	USBLS	5/07
	Brownsville-Harlingen MSA, TX	Y	17860 FQ	23890 MW	45700 TQ	USBLS	5/07
	Dallas-Fort Worth-Arlington MSA, TX	Y	42610 FQ	50520 MW	63010 TQ	USBLS	5/07
	El Paso MSA, TX	Y	34290 FQ	46700 MW	56880 TQ	USBLS	5/07
	Houston-Sugar Land-Baytown MSA, TX	Y	39680 FQ	46420 MW	53900 TQ	USBLS	5/07
	San Antonio MSA, TX	Y	47810 FQ	53620 MW	60100 TQ	USBLS	5/07
	Utah	Y	34370 FQ	39060 MW	45040 TQ	USBLS	5/07
	Salt Lake City MSA, UT	Y	34850 FQ	40240 MW	46540 TQ	USBLS	5/07
	Vermont	Y	35970 FQ	42200 MW	46780 TQ	USBLS	5/07
	Virginia	Y	35300 FQ	46770 MW	57490 TQ	USBLS	5/07
	Lynchburg MSA, VA	Y	39500 FQ	45410 MW	52130 TQ	USBLS	5/07
	Richmond MSA, VA	Y	28820 FQ	40690 MW	53000 TQ	USBLS	5/07
	Virginia Beach-Norfolk-Newport News MSA, VA-NC	Y	45960 FQ	56740 MW	63310 TQ	USBLS	5/07
	Washington	H	19.62 FQ	22.40 MW	25.11 TQ	WABLS	3/08
	Seattle-Tacoma-Bellevue MSA, WA	Y	41030 FQ	46470 MW	51800 TQ	USBLS	5/07
	West Virginia	Y	33216 FQ	39384 MW	46409 TQ	WVBLS	7/08-9/08
	Charleston MSA, WV	Y	22410 FQ	34070 MW	40080 TQ	USBLS	5/07
	Milwaukee-Waukesha-West Allis MSA, WI	Y	34720 FQ	41340 MW	47100 TQ	USBLS	5/07
	Wyoming	Y	31606 FQ	38400 MW	43000 TQ	WYBLS	9/08
	Casper MSA, WY	Y	25274 FQ	36536 MW	41161 TQ	WYBLS	9/08
	Cheyenne MSA, WY	Y	24517 FQ	34300 MW	42077 TQ	WYBLS	9/08
	Puerto Rico	Y	14330 FQ	16790 MW	20260 TQ	USBLS	5/07
	San Juan-Caguas-Guaynabo MSA, PR	Y	14410 FQ	16930 MW	20760 TQ	USBLS	5/07

AE Average entry wage	**AW** Average wage paid	**FQ** First quartile wage	**LO** Lowest wage paid	**MTC** Median total compensation	**TCC** Total cash compensation
AER Average entry range	**AWR** Average wage range	**H** Hourly	**LR** Low end range	**MW** Median wage paid	**TQ** Third quartile wage
AEX Average experienced wage	**AXR** Average experienced range	**HI** Highest wage paid	**M** Monthly	**MWR** Median wage range	**W** Weekly
ATC Average total compensation	**D** Daily	**HR** High end range	**MCC** Median cash compensation	**S** See annotated source	**Y** Yearly

Occupation/Type/Industry	Location	Per	Low	Mid	High	Source	Date
Physician							
Veterans Health Administration	United States	Y	93818 LO		137596 HI	OPM01	1/1/08
Physician Assistant	United States	Y		86214 ATC		MODPHY	2007
	Alabama	Y	42510 FQ	68820 MW	83880 TQ	USBLS	5/07
	Birmingham-Hoover MSA, AL	Y	28600 FQ	66090 MW	81870 TQ	USBLS	5/07
	Mobile MSA, AL	Y	56340 FQ	65110 MW	77640 TQ	USBLS	5/07
	Alaska	Y	70440 FQ	87660 MW	111000 TQ	USBLS	5/07
	Anchorage MSA, AK	Y	82420 FQ	97840 MW	119200 TQ	USBLS	5/07
	Arizona	Y	70600 FQ	82920 MW	93110 TQ	USBLS	5/07
	Phoenix-Mesa-Scottsdale MSA, AZ	Y	72370 FQ	84590 MW	93540 TQ	USBLS	5/07
	Tucson MSA, AZ	Y	68830 FQ	77790 MW	89930 TQ	USBLS	5/07
	Arkansas	Y	63040 FQ	71480 MW	79390 TQ	USBLS	5/07
	Little Rock-North Little Rock MSA, AR	Y	22750 FQ	25360 MW	59280 TQ	USBLS	5/07
	California	H	30.30 FQ	40.29 MW	47.93 TQ	CABLS	1/08-3/08
	Los Angeles-Long Beach-Glendale PMSA, CA	H	34.77 FQ	43.39 MW	49.57 TQ	CABLS	1/08-3/08
	Oakland-Fremont-Hayward MSA, CA	H	34.98 FQ	42.90 MW	49.70 TQ	CABLS	1/08-3/08
	Riverside-San Bernardino-Ontario MSA, CA	H	21.06 FQ	28.06 MW	39.30 TQ	CABLS	1/08-3/08
	Sacramento-Arden Arcade-Roseville MSA, CA	H	32.90 FQ	41.88 MW	48.38 TQ	CABLS	1/08-3/08
	San Diego-Carlsbad-San Marcos MSA, CA	H	31.06 FQ	36.16 MW	41.96 TQ	CABLS	1/08-3/08
	San Francisco-San Mateo-Redwood PMSA, CA	H	33.22 FQ	40.80 MW	46.65 TQ	CABLS	1/08-3/08
	San Jose-Sunnyvale-Santa Clara MSA, CA	H	41.23 FQ	47.46 MW	52.90 TQ	CABLS	1/08-3/08
	Santa Ana-Anaheim-Irvine PMSA, CA	Y	41270 FQ	69590 MW	90480 TQ	USBLS	5/07
	Santa Rosa-Petaluma MSA, CA	H	19.06 FQ	35.41 MW	42.06 TQ	CABLS	1/08-3/08
	Colorado	Y	65890 FQ	77270 MW	90390 TQ	USBLS	5/07
	Boulder MSA, CO	Y	57390 FQ	66620 MW	77040 TQ	USBLS	5/07
	Denver-Aurora MSA, CO	Y	69070 FQ	80040 MW	91770 TQ	USBLS	5/07
	Connecticut	H	35.84 AE	44.99 MW		CTBLS	1/08-3/08
	Bridgeport-Stamford-Norwalk MSA, CT	Y	82140 FQ	92030 MW	101690 TQ	USBLS	5/07
	Hartford-West Hartford-East Hartford MSA, CT	Y	84930 FQ	96570 MW	110070 TQ	USBLS	5/07
	Delaware	Y	73130 FQ	82790 MW	93320 TQ	USBLS	5/07
	Wilmington PMSA, DE-MD-NJ	Y	72250 FQ	81630 MW	93100 TQ	USBLS	5/07
	District of Columbia	Y	65060 FQ	76620 MW	90750 TQ	USBLS	5/07
	Washington-Arlington-Alexandria MSA, DC-VA-MD-WV	Y	65020 FQ	81650 MW	96140 TQ	USBLS	5/07
	Florida	Y	67250 FQ	80960 MW	98670 TQ	USBLS	5/07
	Fort Lauderdale-Pompano Beach-Deerfield Beach PMSA, FL	Y	70310 FQ	80390 MW	93980 TQ	USBLS	5/07
	Jacksonville MSA, FL	Y	77930 FQ	102480 MW	112850 TQ	USBLS	5/07
	Miami-Fort Lauderdale-Miami Beach MSA, FL	Y	65660 FQ	76680 MW	92650 TQ	USBLS	5/07
	Orlando-Kissimmee MSA, FL	Y	74470 FQ	84350 MW	98300 TQ	USBLS	5/07
	Tallahassee MSA, FL	Y	71170 FQ	79510 MW	92480 TQ	USBLS	5/07
	Tampa-St. Petersburg-Clearwater MSA, FL	Y	57940 FQ	77890 MW	93820 TQ	USBLS	5/07
	West Palm Beach-Boca Raton-Boynton Beach PMSA, FL	Y	47760 FQ	72780 MW	86150 TQ	USBLS	5/07
	Georgia	Y	67100 FQ	81380 MW	96500 TQ	USBLS	5/07
	Atlanta-Sandy Springs-Marietta MSA, GA	Y	72540 FQ	86230 MW	100210 TQ	USBLS	5/07
	Hawaii	Y	53440 FQ	62770 MW	81630 TQ	USBLS	5/07
	Honolulu MSA, HI	Y	55260 FQ	61640 MW	83820 TQ	USBLS	5/07
	Idaho	Y	37690 FQ	68840 MW	82150 TQ	USBLS	5/07
	Boise City-Nampa MSA, ID	Y	37900 FQ	69360 MW	84290 TQ	USBLS	5/07
	Illinois	Y	37830 FQ	63350 MW	82670 TQ	USBLS	5/07
	Chicago-Naperville-Joliet MSA, IL-IN-WI	Y	37280 FQ	58830 MW	77540 TQ	USBLS	5/07

AE	Average entry wage	AW	Average wage paid	FQ	First quartile wage	LO	Lowest wage paid	MTC	Median total compensation	TCC	Total cash compensation
AER	Average entry range	AWR	Average wage range	H	Hourly	LR	Low end range	MW	Median wage paid	TQ	Third quartile wage
AEX	Average experienced wage	AXR	Average experienced range	M	Monthly	MWR	Median wage range	W	Weekly
ATC	Average total compensation	D	Daily	HR	High end range	MCC	Median cash compensation	S	See annotated source	Y	Yearly

Physician Assistant

Occupation/Type/Industry	Location	Per	Low	Mid	High	Source	Date
Physician Assistant	Indiana	Y	58140 FQ	72040 MW	82470 TQ	USBLS	5/07
	Gary PMSA, IN	Y	44780 FQ	64120 MW	74940 TQ	USBLS	5/07
	Indianapolis-Carmel MSA, IN	Y	63340 FQ	73040 MW	82100 TQ	USBLS	5/07
	Iowa	Y	65200 FQ	75770 MW	88030 TQ	USBLS	5/07
	Des Moines-West Des Moines MSA, IA	Y	68900 FQ	76790 MW	87070 TQ	USBLS	5/07
	Kansas	Y	68930 FQ	77590 MW	89780 TQ	USBLS	5/07
	Wichita MSA, KS	Y	66620 FQ	74160 MW	82400 TQ	USBLS	5/07
	Kentucky	Y	64065 FQ	73775 MW	83944 TQ	KYBLS	2008
	Louisville-Jefferson County MSA, KY-IN	Y	69100 FQ	80100 MW	130580 TQ	USBLS	5/07
	Louisiana	H	14.78 FQ	28.80 MW	37.76 TQ	LABLS	1/08-3/08
	Baton Rouge MSA, LA	Y	23720 FQ	47600 MW	72870 TQ	USBLS	5/07
	New Orleans-Metairie-Kenner MSA, LA	Y	67470 FQ	78340 MW	88270 TQ	USBLS	5/07
	Maine	Y	69810 FQ	79010 MW	93530 TQ	USBLS	5/07
	Portland-South Portland-Biddeford MSA, ME	Y	70960 FQ	77580 MW	87230 TQ	USBLS	5/07
	Maryland	Y		87525 MW		MDBLS	3/08
	Baltimore-Towson MSA, MD	Y	68040 FQ	81630 MW	97000 TQ	USBLS	5/07
	Bethesda-Gaithersburg-Frederick PMSA, MD	Y	84930 FQ	94920 MW	104260 TQ	USBLS	5/07
	Massachusetts	Y	69340 FQ	82110 MW	97170 TQ	USBLS	5/07
	Boston-Cambridge-Quincy NECTA, MA	Y	71220 FQ	83150 MW	99000 TQ	USBLS	5/07
	Worcester MSA, MA-CT	Y	38830 FQ	57930 MW	91600 TQ	USBLS	5/07
	Michigan	Y	68970 FQ	78210 MW	91120 TQ	USBLS	5/07
	Detroit-Warren-Livonia MSA, MI	Y	68960 FQ	78620 MW	90480 TQ	USBLS	5/07
	Grand Rapids-Wyoming MSA, MI	Y	70200 FQ	80040 MW	93910 TQ	USBLS	5/07
	Warren-Troy-Farmington Hills PMSA, MI	Y	63050 FQ	77190 MW	89020 TQ	USBLS	5/07
	Minnesota	Y	77169 FQ	87778 MW	99161 TQ	MNBLS	10/08-12/08
	Duluth-Superior MSA, MN-WI	Y	83467 FQ	90990 MW	98837 TQ	MNBLS	10/08-12/08
	Minneapolis-Saint Paul MSA, MN-WI	Y	76165 FQ	87391 MW	99318 TQ	MNBLS	10/08-12/08
	Rochester MSA, MN	Y	82197 FQ	93828 MW	103259 TQ	MNBLS	10/08-12/08
	Mississippi	Y	27590 FQ	32490 MW	55770 TQ	USBLS	5/07
	Missouri	Y	33590 FQ	62670 MW	79150 TQ	USBLS	5/07
	Kansas City MSA, MO-KS	Y	48210 FQ	75830 MW	93150 TQ	USBLS	5/07
	St. Louis MSA, MO-IL	Y	29610 FQ	60630 MW	76320 TQ	USBLS	5/07
	Montana	Y	52860 FQ	62620 MW	74250 TQ	USBLS	5/07
	Nebraska	Y	67390 FQ	76090 MW	86860 TQ	USBLS	5/07
	Omaha-Council Bluffs MSA, NE-IA	Y	68520 FQ	74720 MW	81330 TQ	USBLS	5/07
	Nevada	H	21.70 FQ	36.29 MW	46.34 TQ	NVBLS	5/08
	Las Vegas-Paradise MSA, NV	H	21.73 FQ	36.98 MW	49.18 TQ	NVBLS	5/08
	New Hampshire	H	33.21 AE	40.18 MW	43.68 AEX	NHBLS	6/08
	Manchester MSA, NH	Y	75890 FQ	83830 MW	93130 TQ	USBLS	5/07
	Nashua NECTA, NH-MA	Y	72070 FQ	82790 MW	94260 TQ	USBLS	5/07
	New Jersey	Y	75240 FQ	89130 MW	102420 TQ	USBLS	5/07
	Camden PMSA, NJ	Y	67580 FQ	81030 MW	101470 TQ	USBLS	5/07
	Edison PMSA, NJ	Y	76470 FQ	89120 MW	100560 TQ	USBLS	5/07
	Newark-Union PMSA, NJ-PA	Y	78550 FQ	91370 MW	104300 TQ	USBLS	5/07
	New Mexico	Y	27190 FQ	47870 MW	66020 TQ	USBLS	5/07
	Albuquerque MSA, NM	Y	28750 FQ	42030 MW	63210 TQ	USBLS	5/07
	New York	Y	72620 FQ	83990 MW	95460 TQ	USBLS	5/07
	Albany-Schenectady-Troy MSA, NY	Y	69200 FQ	77750 MW	92640 TQ	USBLS	5/07
	Buffalo-Niagara Falls MSA, NY	Y	65430 FQ	75400 MW	89140 TQ	USBLS	5/07
	Nassau-Suffolk PMSA, NY	Y	79980 FQ	89070 MW	97420 TQ	USBLS	5/07
	New York-Northern New Jersey-Long Island MSA, NY-NJ-PA	Y	77410 FQ	87850 MW	97630 TQ	USBLS	5/07
	North Carolina	Y	69190 FQ	78030 MW	90590 TQ	USBLS	5/07
	Charlotte-Gastonia-Concord MSA, NC-SC	Y	70080 FQ	79960 MW	95460 TQ	USBLS	5/07
	Raleigh-Cary MSA, NC	Y	68990 FQ	75830 MW	84840 TQ	USBLS	5/07
	North Dakota	Y	58300 FQ	70090 MW	81610 TQ	USBLS	5/07
	Fargo MSA, ND-MN	Y	67860 FQ	75930 MW	88060 TQ	USBLS	5/07

Occupation/Type/Industry	Location	Per	Low	Mid	High	Source	Date
Physician Assistant	Ohio	Y	68100 FQ	77100 MW	88790 TQ	USBLS	5/07
	Cincinnati-Middletown MSA, OH-KY-IN	Y	65570 FQ	77450 MW	90260 TQ	USBLS	5/07
	Cleveland-Elyria-Mentor MSA, OH	Y	68540 FQ	76180 MW	86560 TQ	USBLS	5/07
	Columbus MSA, OH	Y	72540 FQ	80970 MW	92450 TQ	USBLS	5/07
	Dayton MSA, OH	Y	70960 FQ	79020 MW	89960 TQ	USBLS	5/07
	Mansfield MSA, OH	Y	88270 FQ	95170 MW	102070 TQ	USBLS	5/07
	Oklahoma	Y	68840 FQ	78920 MW	93920 TQ	USBLS	5/07
	Oklahoma City MSA, OK	Y	67430 FQ	77440 MW	93620 TQ	USBLS	5/07
	Tulsa MSA, OK	Y	69210 FQ	76590 MW	86780 TQ	USBLS	5/07
	Oregon	H	33.88 FQ	39.55 MW	46.81 TQ	ORBLS	5/08
	Eugene-Springfield MSA, OR	Y	63590 FQ	79930 MW	96510 TQ	USBLS	5/07
	Portland-Vancouver-Beaverton MSA, OR-WA	Y	73290 FQ	88790 MW	108780 TQ	USBLS	5/07
	Pennsylvania	Y	56240 FQ	67630 MW	78260 TQ	USBLS	5/07
	Allentown-Bethlehem-Easton MSA, PA-NJ	Y	58720 FQ	67710 MW	78800 TQ	USBLS.	5/07
	Philadelphia-Camden-Wilmington MSA, PA-NJ-DE-MD	Y	53620 FQ	73580 MW	88740 TQ	USBLS	5/07
	Pittsburgh MSA, PA	Y	57150 FQ	67450 MW	77170 TQ	USBLS	5/07
	Rhode Island	Y	61140 FQ	74480 MW	89810 TQ	USBLS	5/07
	Providence-Fall River-Warwick MSA, RI-MA	Y	62260 FQ	75970 MW	90030 TQ	USBLS	5/07
	South Carolina	Y	61650 FQ	74650 MW	92070 TQ	USBLS	5/07
	Charleston-North Charleston MSA, SC	Y	62470 FQ	70390 MW	86760 TQ	USBLS	5/07
	Columbia MSA, SC	Y	63240 FQ	83450 MW	96600 TQ	USBLS	5/07
	South Dakota	Y	71507 FQ	81112 MW	92705 TQ	SDBLS	7/08-9/08
	Sioux Falls MSA, SD	Y	74992 FQ	85028 MW	96177 TQ	SDBLS	7/08-9/08
	Tennessee	Y	61390 FQ	73460 MW	87110 TQ	USBLS	5/07
	Clarksville MSA, TN-KY	Y	63310 FQ	71260 MW	81910 TQ	USBLS	5/07
	Memphis MSA, TN-MS-AR	Y	36300 FQ	62450 MW	78420 TQ	USBLS	5/07
	Nashville-Davidson-Murfreesboro MSA, TN	Y	54340 FQ	69070 MW	89330 TQ	USBLS	5/07
	Texas	Y	68110 FQ	81250 MW	95930 TQ	USBLS	5/07
	Austin-Round Rock MSA, TX	Y	56280 FQ	66540 MW	80170 TQ	USBLS	5/07
	Brownsville-Harlingen MSA, TX	Y	90280 FQ	111850 MW	129200 TQ	USBLS	5/07
	Dallas-Fort Worth-Arlington MSA, TX	Y	69950 FQ	80770 MW	97760 TQ	USBLS	5/07
	El Paso MSA, TX	Y	69840 FQ	75850 MW	82350 TQ	USBLS	5/07
	Houston-Sugar Land-Baytown MSA, TX	Y	64010 FQ	81860 MW	97470 TQ	USBLS	5/07
	San Antonio MSA, TX	Y	72760 FQ	83140 MW	93990 TQ	USBLS	5/07
	Utah	Y	70640 FQ	83710 MW	97540 TQ	USBLS	5/07
	Salt Lake City MSA, UT	Y	75660 FQ	87500 MW	97360 TQ	USBLS	5/07
	Vermont	Y	67270 FQ	80630 MW	94730 TQ	USBLS	5/07
	Burlington-South Burlington MSA, VT	Y	70530 FQ	81590 MW	95810 TQ	USBLS	5/07
	Virginia	Y	45340 FQ	65050 MW	82750 TQ	USBLS	5/07
	Richmond MSA, VA	Y	65000 FQ	80160 MW	90320 TQ	USBLS	5/07
	Virginia Beach-Norfolk-Newport News MSA, VA-NC	Y	50040 FQ	64260 MW	77900 TQ	USBLS	5/07
	Washington	H	35.95 FQ	41.27 MW	48.00 TQ	WABLS	3/08
	Seattle-Tacoma-Bellevue MSA, WA	Y	73630 FQ	84300 MW	97060 TQ	USBLS	5/07
	Spokane MSA, WA	Y	70990 FQ	79670 MW	100720 TQ	USBLS	5/07
	West Virginia	Y	67235 FQ	76672 MW	86956 TQ	WVBLS	7/08-9/08
	Charleston MSA, WV	Y	65980 FQ	74640 MW	86220 TQ	USBLS	5/07
	Huntington-Ashland MSA, WV-KY-OH	Y	65700 FQ	74440 MW	85120 TQ	USBLS	5/07
	Wisconsin	Y	69350 FQ	80430 MW	93430 TQ	USBLS	5/07
	Green Bay MSA, WI	Y	71650 FQ	80830 MW	97370 TQ	USBLS	5/07
	Milwaukee-Waukesha-West Allis MSA, WI	Y	71870 FQ	84570 MW	94430 TQ	USBLS	5/07
	Wyoming	Y	58137 FQ	67690 MW	79040 TQ	WYBLS	9/08
	Cheyenne MSA, WY	Y	64275 FQ	76660 MW	94322 TQ	WYBLS	9/08
	Puerto Rico	Y	20250 FQ	51280 MW	80640 TQ	USBLS	5/07
	San Juan-Caguas-Guaynabo MSA, PR	Y	19190 FQ	47910 MW	83070 TQ	USBLS	5/07

AE	Average entry wage	AW	Average wage paid	FQ	First quartile wage	LO	Lowest wage paid	MTC	Median total compensation	TCC	Total cash compensation
AER	Average entry range	AWR	Average wage range	H	Hourly	LR	Low end range	MW	Median wage paid	TQ	Third quartile wage
AEX	Average experienced wage	AXR	Average experienced range	HI	Highest wage paid	M	Monthly	MWR	Median wage range	W	Weekly
ATC	Average total compensation	D	Daily	HR	High end range	MCC	Median cash compensation	S	See annotated source	Y	Yearly

Occupation/Type/Industry	Location	Per	Low	Mid	High	Source	Date
Physician Assistant	Guam	Y	24070 FQ	28650 MW	33230 TQ	USBLS	5/07
Physicist	Alabama	Y	83110 FQ	102060 MW	124960 TQ	USBLS	5/07
	Phoenix-Mesa-Scottsdale MSA, AZ	Y	109900 FQ	125960 MW		USBLS	5/07
	Arkansas	Y	40910 FQ	46830 MW	56420 TQ	USBLS	5/07
	California	H	36.72 FQ	47.01 MW	58.31 TQ	CABLS	1/08-3/08
	Los Angeles-Long Beach-Glendale PMSA, CA	H	36.76 FQ	44.39 MW	54.35 TQ	CABLS	1/08-3/08
	Oakland-Fremont-Hayward MSA, CA	H	35.30 FQ	51.82 MW	63.15 TQ	CABLS	1/08-3/08
	Riverside-San Bernardino-Ontario MSA, CA	H	40.89 FQ	47.20 MW	57.98 TQ	CABLS	1/08-3/08
	Sacramento-Arden Arcade-Roseville MSA, CA	H	34.97 FQ	40.98 MW	50.78 TQ	CABLS	1/08-3/08
	San Diego-Carlsbad-San Marcos MSA, CA	H	29.00 FQ	49.77 MW	60.52 TQ	CABLS	1/08-3/08
	San Francisco-San Mateo-Redwood PMSA, CA	H	41.47 FQ	49.96 MW	60.34 TQ	CABLS	1/08-3/08
	San Jose-Sunnyvale-Santa Clara MSA, CA	H	36.16 FQ	50.67 MW	63.68 TQ	CABLS	1/08-3/08
	Santa Rosa-Petaluma MSA, CA	H	44.84 FQ	53.80 MW	60.37 TQ	CABLS	1/08-3/08
	Colorado	Y	80010 FQ	105160 MW	131970 TQ	USBLS	5/07
	Delaware	Y	45430 FQ	65850 MW	101310 TQ	USBLS	5/07
	Wilmington PMSA, DE-MD-NJ	Y	44950 FQ	64070 MW	100520 TQ	USBLS	5/07
	District of Columbia	Y	91370 FQ	111380 MW	140400 TQ	USBLS	5/07
	Washington-Arlington-Alexandria MSA, DC-VA-MD-WV	Y	90320 FQ	113130 MW	141040 TQ	USBLS	5/07
	Florida	Y	83130 FQ	99910 MW	140060 TQ	USBLS	5/07
	Fort Lauderdale-Pompano Beach-Deerfield Beach PMSA, FL	Y	90490 FQ	100160 MW	109630 TQ	USBLS	5/07
	Miami-Fort Lauderdale-Miami Beach MSA, FL	Y	92010 FQ	104060 MW		USBLS	5/07
	Tampa-St. Petersburg-Clearwater MSA, FL	Y	67970 FQ	105260 MW	138430 TQ	USBLS	5/07
	Georgia	Y	60740 FQ	90960 MW	105310 TQ	USBLS	5/07
	Hawaii	Y	61220 FQ	87060 MW	95790 TQ	USBLS	5/07
	Honolulu MSA, HI	Y	68260 FQ	87550 MW	95760 TQ	USBLS	5/07
	Idaho	Y	57650 FQ	95350 MW	118200 TQ	USBLS	5/07
	Illinois	Y	83340 FQ	97180 MW	111850 TQ	USBLS	5/07
	Chicago-Naperville-Joliet MSA, IL-IN-WI	Y	82010 FQ	97610 MW	113740 TQ	USBLS	5/07
	Indiana	Y	86250 FQ	118140 MW		USBLS	5/07
	Kansas	Y	52100 FQ	56230 MW	60350 TQ	USBLS	5/07
	Kentucky	Y	78199 FQ	122599 MW		KYBLS	2008
	Louisiana	H	29.11 FQ	35.12 MW	48.05 TQ	LABLS	1/08-3/08
	Maine	Y	85660 FQ	93210 MW	101070 TQ	USBLS	5/07
	Maryland	Y		111575 MW		MDBLS	3/08
	Baltimore-Towson MSA, MD	Y	82440 FQ	99880 MW	131990 TQ	USBLS	5/07
	Bethesda-Gaithersburg-Frederick PMSA, MD	Y	87180 FQ	111200 MW	138960 TQ	USBLS	5/07
	Massachusetts	Y	84630 FQ	107240 MW	138730 TQ	USBLS	5/07
	Boston-Cambridge-Quincy NECTA, MA	Y	83800 FQ	105910 MW	137890 TQ	USBLS	5/07
	Michigan	Y	54090 FQ	78620 MW	108800 TQ	USBLS	5/07
	Detroit-Warren-Livonia MSA, MI	Y	76780 FQ	105820 MW	129200 TQ	USBLS	5/07
	Minnesota	Y	81040 FQ	101201 MW	127325 TQ	MNBLS	10/08-12/08
	Duluth-Superior MSA, MN-WI	Y	121247 FQ	144734 MW		MNBLS	10/08-12/08
	Minneapolis-Saint Paul MSA, MN-WI	Y	72691 FQ	94149 MW	110261 TQ	MNBLS	10/08-12/08
	Mississippi	Y	57750 FQ	88450 MW	130180 TQ	USBLS	5/07
	Missouri	Y	71530 FQ	87740 MW	122460 TQ	USBLS	5/07
	St. Louis MSA, MO-IL	Y	73100 FQ	86430 MW	101170 TQ	USBLS	5/07
	Nebraska	Y	36250 FQ	49370 MW	101920 TQ	USBLS	5/07
	Nevada	H	26.45 FQ	35.50 MW	47.48 TQ	NVBLS	5/08
	Las Vegas-Paradise MSA, NV	H	28.64 FQ	41.21 MW	54.32 TQ	NVBLS	5/08
	New Hampshire	H	27.00 AE	46.90 MW	57.42 AEX	NHBLS	6/08
	New Jersey	Y	91690 FQ	110540 MW	126890 TQ	USBLS	5/07

AE	Average entry wage	**AW**	Average wage paid	**FQ**	First quartile wage
AER	Average entry range	**AWR**	Average wage range	**H**	Hourly
AEX	Average experienced wage	**AXR**	Average experienced range	**HI**	Highest wage paid
ATC	Average total compensation	**D**	Daily	**HR**	High end range

LO	Lowest wage paid	**MTC**	Median total compensation	**TCC**	Total cash compensation
LR	Low end range	**MW**	Median wage paid	**TQ**	Third quartile wage
M	Monthly	**MWR**	Median wage range	**W**	Weekly
MCC	Median cash compensation	**S**	See annotated source	**Y**	Yearly

Occupation/Type/Industry	Location	Per	Low	Mid	High	Source	Date
Physicist	Edison PMSA, NJ	Y	87980 FQ	108240 MW	124070 TQ	USBLS	5/07
	Newark-Union PMSA, NJ-PA	Y	93680 FQ	111830 MW	127600 TQ	USBLS	5/07
	Trenton-Ewing MSA, NJ	Y	94710 FQ	111330 MW	130880 TQ	USBLS	5/07
	New Mexico	Y	97840 FQ	119440 MW	141630 TQ	USBLS	5/07
	New York	Y	79970 FQ	106670 MW	140600 TQ	USBLS	5/07
	Nassau-Suffolk PMSA, NY	Y	78590 FQ	105850 MW	137740 TQ	USBLS	5/07
	New York-Northern New Jersey-Long Island MSA, NY-NJ-PA	Y	84730 FQ	109600 MW	134020 TQ	USBLS	5/07
	North Carolina	Y	54630 FQ	77790 MW	106300 TQ	USBLS	5/07
	Ohio	Y	69020 FQ	92230 MW	115650 TQ	USBLS	5/07
	Cincinnati-Middletown MSA, OH-KY-IN	Y	62460 FQ	79360 MW	94680 TQ	USBLS	5/07
	Cleveland-Elyria-Mentor MSA, OH	Y	64910 FQ	96940 MW	122890 TQ	USBLS	5/07
	Columbus MSA, OH	Y	75130 FQ	96580 MW	121630 TQ	USBLS	5/07
	Dayton MSA, OH	Y	74850 FQ	93830 MW	110480 TQ	USBLS	5/07
	Portland-Vancouver-Beaverton MSA, OR-WA	Y	97410 FQ			USBLS	5/07
	Pennsylvania	Y	86320 FQ	102010 MW	132150 TQ	USBLS	5/07
	Philadelphia-Camden-Wilmington MSA, PA-NJ-DE-MD	Y	64850 FQ	91510 MW	114520 TQ	USBLS	5/07
	South Carolina	Y	23980 FQ	67280 MW	89870 TQ	USBLS	5/07
	Tennessee	Y	77770 FQ	93570 MW	120570 TQ	USBLS	5/07
	Memphis MSA, TN-MS-AR	Y	85890 FQ	104160 MW	135310 TQ	USBLS	5/07
	Texas	Y	50050 FQ	88710 MW	121110 TQ	USBLS	5/07
	Austin-Round Rock MSA, TX	Y	36910 FQ	41160 MW	61170 TQ	USBLS	5/07
	Dallas-Fort Worth-Arlington MSA, TX	Y	91350 FQ	103690 MW		USBLS	5/07
	Houston-Sugar Land-Baytown MSA, TX	Y	55850 FQ	88610 MW	124890 TQ	USBLS	5/07
	San Antonio MSA, TX	Y	86220 FQ	104130 MW	125590 TQ	USBLS	5/07
	Utah	Y	61190 FQ	88850 MW	116800 TQ	USBLS	5/07
	Virginia	Y	75960 FQ	94200 MW	122280 TQ	USBLS	5/07
	Richmond MSA, VA	Y	47950 FQ	88510 MW	102160 TQ	USBLS	5/07
	Virginia Beach-Norfolk-Newport News MSA, VA-NC	Y	71500 FQ	81160 MW	101220 TQ	USBLS	5/07
	Washington	H	30.43 FQ	40.65 MW	50.48 TQ	WABLS	3/08
	Seattle-Tacoma-Bellevue MSA, WA	Y	49220 FQ	74690 MW	108790 TQ	USBLS	5/07
	West Virginia	Y	91611 FQ	121441 MW		WVBLS	7/08-9/08
	Wisconsin	Y	42970 FQ	49100 MW	82810 TQ	USBLS	5/07
	Milwaukee-Waukesha-West Allis MSA, WI	Y	53140 FQ	115980 MW		USBLS	5/07
Physics Teacher							
Postsecondary	Alabama	Y	51370 FQ	68700 MW	87670 TQ	USBLS	5/07
Postsecondary	Arizona	Y	48820 FQ	64340 MW	90740 TQ	USBLS	5/07
Postsecondary	Phoenix-Mesa-Scottsdale MSA, AZ	Y	31780 FQ	49920 MW	61570 TQ	USBLS	5/07
Postsecondary	California	Y		97071 AW		CABLS	1/08-3/08
Postsecondary	Los Angeles-Long Beach-Glendale PMSA, CA	Y		102373 AW		CABLS	1/08-3/08
Postsecondary	Oakland-Fremont-Hayward MSA, CA	Y		98568 AW		CABLS	1/08-3/08
Postsecondary	Riverside-San Bernardino-Ontario MSA, CA	Y		94087 AW		CABLS	1/08-3/08
Postsecondary	Sacramento-Arden Arcade-Roseville MSA, CA	Y		87042 AW		CABLS	1/08-3/08
Postsecondary	San Diego-Carlsbad-San Marcos MSA, CA	Y		86355 AW		CABLS	1/08-3/08
Postsecondary	San Francisco-San Mateo-Redwood PMSA, CA	Y		113520 AW		CABLS	1/08-3/08
Postsecondary	Santa Ana-Anaheim-Irvine PMSA, CA	Y	66540 FQ	82680 MW	106740 TQ	USBLS	5/07
Postsecondary	Colorado	Y	51260 FQ	77120 MW	126090 TQ	USBLS	5/07
Postsecondary	Denver-Aurora MSA, CO	Y	51540 FQ	73950 MW	121990 TQ	USBLS	5/07
Postsecondary	Wilmington PMSA, DE-MD-NJ	Y	48850 FQ	68730 MW	102610 TQ	USBLS	5/07
Postsecondary	District of Columbia	Y	60280 FQ	78120 MW	106690 TQ	USBLS	5/07

AE	Average entry wage	**AW**	Average wage paid	**LO**	Lowest wage paid
AER	Average entry range	**AWR**	Average wage range	**LR**	Low end range
AEX	Average experienced wage	**AXR**	Average experienced range	**HI**	Highest wage paid
ATC	Average total compensation	**D**	Daily	**HR**	High end range

FQ	First quartile wage	**MTC**	Median total compensation	**TCC**	Total cash compensation
H	Hourly	**MW**	Median wage paid	**TQ**	Third quartile wage
M	Monthly	**MWR**	Median wage range	**W**	Weekly
MCC	Median cash compensation	**S**	See annotated source	**Y**	Yearly

Physics Teacher

Occupation/Type/Industry	Location	Per	Low	Mid	High	Source	Date
Physics Teacher							
Postsecondary	Washington-Arlington-Alexandria MSA, DC-VA-MD-WV	Y	57210 FQ	75850 MW	103760 TQ	USBLS	5/07
Postsecondary	Florida	Y	52300 FQ	68120 MW	81160 TQ	USBLS	5/07
Postsecondary	Miami-Fort Lauderdale-Miami Beach MSA, FL	Y	50570 FQ	66570 MW	78230 TQ	USBLS	5/07
Postsecondary	Orlando-Kissimmee MSA, FL	Y	49130 FQ	59910 MW	74160 TQ	USBLS	5/07
Postsecondary	West Palm Beach-Boca Raton-Boynton Beach PMSA, FL	Y	50010 FQ	61620 MW	79200 TQ	USBLS	5/07
Postsecondary	Georgia	Y	48340 FQ	63300 MW	78970 TQ	USBLS	5/07
Postsecondary	Atlanta-Sandy Springs-Marietta MSA, GA	Y	50620 FQ	68160 MW	84110 TQ	USBLS	5/07
Postsecondary	Illinois	Y	51120 FQ	64490 MW	86780 TQ	USBLS	5/07
Postsecondary	Chicago-Naperville-Joliet MSA, IL-IN-WI	Y	52060 FQ	61940 MW	82710 TQ	USBLS	5/07
Postsecondary	Indiana	Y	56440 FQ	72250 MW	90050 TQ	USBLS	5/07
Postsecondary	Iowa	Y	58050 FQ	83200 MW	101830 TQ	USBLS	5/07
Postsecondary	Kansas	Y	43300 FQ	61220 MW	93290 TQ	USBLS	5/07
Postsecondary	Kentucky	Y	51241 FQ	64443 MW	82810 TQ	KYBLS	2008
Postsecondary	Louisville-Jefferson County MSA, KY-IN	Y	50900 FQ	69380 MW	87570 TQ	USBLS	5/07
Postsecondary	Louisiana	Y		70971 AW		LABLS	1/08-3/08
Postsecondary	Baton Rouge MSA, LA	Y	69210 FQ	79740 MW	92390 TQ	USBLS	5/07
Postsecondary	Maine	Y	54190 FQ	68770 MW	90780 TQ	USBLS	5/07
Postsecondary	Maryland	Y		90000 MW		MDBLS	3/08
Postsecondary	Baltimore-Towson MSA, MD	Y	62850 FQ	88770 MW	120740 TQ	USBLS	5/07
Postsecondary	Massachusetts	Y	67210 FQ	86500 MW	115660 TQ	USBLS	5/07
Postsecondary	Boston-Cambridge-Quincy NECTA, MA	Y	67770 FQ	88190 MW	122890 TQ	USBLS	5/07
Postsecondary	Michigan	Y	56380 FQ	71120 MW	90800 TQ	USBLS	5/07
Postsecondary	Detroit-Warren-Livonia MSA, MI	Y	58520 FQ	71380 MW	87870 TQ	USBLS	5/07
Postsecondary	Minnesota	Y	45971 FQ	60681 MW	85068 TQ	MNBLS	10/08-12/08
Postsecondary	Duluth-Superior MSA, MN-WI	Y	54288 FQ	62668 MW	76897 TQ	MNBLS	10/08-12/08
Postsecondary	Minneapolis-Saint Paul MSA, MN-WI	Y	53158 FQ	71676 MW	105323 TQ	MNBLS	10/08-12/08
Postsecondary	Mississippi	Y	51010 FQ	62600 MW	78560 TQ	USBLS	5/07
Postsecondary	Missouri	Y	39800 FQ	55850 MW	73860 TQ	USBLS	5/07
Postsecondary	Kansas City MSA, MO-KS	Y	44420 FQ	57610 MW	81420 TQ	USBLS	5/07
Postsecondary	St. Louis MSA, MO-IL	Y	43270 FQ	59290 MW	77730 TQ	USBLS	5/07
Postsecondary	Montana	Y	44120 FQ	58080 MW	78370 TQ	USBLS	5/07
Postsecondary	Nebraska	Y	41360 FQ	60340 MW	79370 TQ	USBLS	5/07
Postsecondary	Omaha-Council Bluffs MSA, NE-IA	Y	41130 FQ	58750 MW	75520 TQ	USBLS	5/07
Postsecondary	New Hampshire	Y	47535 AE	72810 MW	92648 AEX	NHBLS	6/08
Postsecondary	New Jersey	Y	57390 FQ	81830 MW	116280 TQ	USBLS	5/07
Postsecondary	Edison PMSA, NJ	Y	61530 FQ	96900 MW	127170 TQ	USBLS	5/07
Postsecondary	New Mexico	Y	63680 FQ	72400 MW	87660 TQ	USBLS	5/07
Postsecondary	New York	Y	66360 FQ	85780 MW	109650 TQ	USBLS	5/07
Postsecondary	New York-Northern New Jersey-Long Island MSA, NY-NJ-PA	Y	63960 FQ	82230 MW	104090 TQ	USBLS	5/07
Postsecondary	North Carolina	Y	52610 FQ	69600 MW	91640 TQ	USBLS	5/07
Postsecondary	Charlotte-Gastonia-Concord MSA, NC-SC	Y	63920 FQ	74540 MW	93440 TQ	USBLS	5/07
Postsecondary	Durham MSA, NC	Y	60170 FQ	76050 MW	98750 TQ	USBLS	5/07
Postsecondary	Raleigh-Cary MSA, NC	Y	66800 FQ	83510 MW	104900 TQ	USBLS	5/07
Postsecondary	North Dakota	Y	39880 FQ	54350 MW	72980 TQ	USBLS	5/07
Postsecondary	Ohio	Y	57630 FQ	77080 MW	99620 TQ	USBLS	5/07
Postsecondary	Cincinnati-Middletown MSA, OH-KY-IN	Y	51470 FQ	73280 MW	93090 TQ	USBLS	5/07
Postsecondary	Cleveland-Elyria-Mentor MSA, OH	Y	51220 FQ	73260 MW	96720 TQ	USBLS	5/07
Postsecondary	Columbus MSA, OH	Y	78200 FQ	94400 MW	115570 TQ	USBLS	5/07
Postsecondary	Dayton MSA, OH	Y	52820 FQ	78380 MW	104110 TQ	USBLS	5/07
Postsecondary	Oklahoma	Y	41470 FQ	46110 MW	58620 TQ	USBLS	5/07
Postsecondary	Tulsa MSA, OK	Y	41920 FQ	45400 MW	49830 TQ	USBLS	5/07
Postsecondary	Portland-Vancouver-Beaverton MSA, OR-WA	Y	58870 FQ	77600 MW	98270 TQ	USBLS	5/07
Postsecondary	Pennsylvania	Y	52750 FQ	72520 MW	98380 TQ	USBLS	5/07

Occupation/Type/Industry	Location	Per	Low	Mid	High	Source	Date
Physics Teacher							
Postsecondary	Allentown-Bethlehem-Easton MSA, PA-NJ	Y	57880 FQ	72150 MW	88550 TQ	USBLS	5/07
Postsecondary	Philadelphia-Camden-Wilmington MSA, PA-NJ-DE-MD	Y	54240 FQ	75260 MW	104840 TQ	USBLS	5/07
Postsecondary	Pittsburgh MSA, PA	Y	50450 FQ	70270 MW	92750 TQ	USBLS	5/07
Postsecondary	Rhode Island	Y	56980 FQ	75610 MW	98210 TQ	USBLS	5/07
Postsecondary	Providence-Fall River-Warwick MSA, RI-MA	Y	56980 FQ	75610 MW	98210 TQ	USBLS	5/07
Postsecondary	South Carolina	Y	45140 FQ	61110 MW	78890 TQ	USBLS	5/07
Postsecondary	South Dakota	Y	52113 FQ	61271 MW	70767 TQ	SDBLS	7/08-9/08
Postsecondary	Tennessee	Y	44770 FQ	53340 MW	76990 TQ	USBLS	5/07
Postsecondary	Memphis MSA, TN-MS-AR	Y	45890 FQ	55640 MW	73160 TQ	USBLS	5/07
Postsecondary	Nashville-Davidson-Murfreesboro MSA, TN	Y	46750 FQ	62750 MW	87390 TQ	USBLS	5/07
Postsecondary	Texas	Y	46900 FQ	65420 MW	92990 TQ	USBLS	5/07
Postsecondary	Austin-Round Rock MSA, TX	Y	40500 FQ	83520 MW	107600 TQ	USBLS	5/07
Postsecondary	Dallas-Fort Worth-Arlington MSA, TX	Y	48760 FQ	69190 MW	94050 TQ	USBLS	5/07
Postsecondary	El Paso MSA, TX	Y	39450 FQ	58010 MW	73350 TQ	USBLS	5/07
Postsecondary	Houston-Sugar Land-Baytown MSA, TX	Y	49870 FQ	81820 MW	112270 TQ	USBLS	5/07
Postsecondary	San Antonio MSA, TX	Y	42870 FQ	55850 MW	67530 TQ	USBLS	5/07
Postsecondary	Utah	Y	50510 FQ	65500 MW	94470 TQ	USBLS	5/07
Postsecondary	Vermont	Y	52640 FQ	63990 MW	77170 TQ	USBLS	5/07
Postsecondary	Virginia	Y	43860 FQ	62310 MW	83730 TQ	USBLS	5/07
Postsecondary	Richmond MSA, VA	Y	49770 FQ	67540 MW	92140 TQ	USBLS	5/07
Postsecondary	Virginia Beach-Norfolk-Newport News MSA, VA-NC	Y	41970 FQ	69680 MW	86960 TQ	USBLS	5/07
Postsecondary	Washington	Y		74949 AW		WABLS	3/08
Postsecondary	West Virginia	Y	48804 FQ	63213 MW	80480 TQ	WVBLS	7/08-9/08
Postsecondary	Wisconsin	Y	47360 FQ	62720 MW	90740 TQ	USBLS	5/07
Postsecondary	Milwaukee-Waukesha-West Allis MSA, WI	Y	46560 FQ	59120 MW	76180 TQ	USBLS	5/07
Postsecondary	Wyoming	Y	42861 FQ	60201 MW	78195 TQ	WYBLS	9/08
Postsecondary	Puerto Rico	Y	50020 FQ	59670 MW	73350 TQ	USBLS	5/07
Pikes Peak Highway Manager	Colorado Springs, CO	M	6194 LO			COSPRS	1/1/09
Pile-Driver Operator	Alabama	Y	34030 FQ	42580 MW	52170 TQ	USBLS	5/07
	Alaska	Y	36870 FQ	45530 MW	63880 TQ	USBLS	5/07
	Arizona	Y	47690 FQ	58270 MW	63830 TQ	USBLS	5/07
	Phoenix-Mesa-Scottsdale MSA, AZ	Y	47690 FQ	58270 MW	63830 TQ	USBLS	5/07
	California	H	32.15 FQ	35.53 MW	38.62 TQ	CABLS	1/08-3/08
	Los Angeles-Long Beach-Glendale PMSA, CA	H	33.40 FQ	36.28 MW	40.48 TQ	CABLS	1/08-3/08
	Oakland-Fremont-Hayward MSA, CA	H	33.96 FQ	36.54 MW	39.14 TQ	CABLS	1/08-3/08
	Washington-Arlington-Alexandria MSA, DC-VA-MD-WV	Y	39450 FQ	44130 MW	49600 TQ	USBLS	5/07
	Florida	Y	32400 FQ	36740 MW	43070 TQ	USBLS	5/07
	Fort Lauderdale-Pompano Beach-Deerfield Beach PMSA, FL	Y	33330 FQ	36560 MW	41490 TQ	USBLS	5/07
	Jacksonville MSA, FL	Y	30260 FQ	35680 MW	38890 TQ	USBLS	5/07
	Miami-Fort Lauderdale-Miami Beach MSA, FL	Y	32890 FQ	37180 MW	44590 TQ	USBLS	5/07
	Tampa-St. Petersburg-Clearwater MSA, FL	Y	34420 FQ	38500 MW	44290 TQ	USBLS	5/07
	Georgia	Y	22770 FQ	25170 MW	30090 TQ	USBLS	5/07
	Illinois	Y	60730 FQ	82280 MW	90560 TQ	USBLS	5/07
	Chicago-Naperville-Joliet MSA, IL-IN-WI	Y	81270 FQ	86940 MW	92630 TQ	USBLS	5/07
	Indiana	Y	78010 FQ	84940 MW	91880 TQ	USBLS	5/07
	Kansas	Y	21740 FQ	24760 MW	42720 TQ	USBLS	5/07
	Kentucky	Y	27759 FQ	33390 MW	39755 TQ	KYBLS	2008
	Louisiana	H	15.46 FQ	18.41 MW	28.87 TQ	LABLS	1/08-3/08
	Baton Rouge MSA, LA	Y	30550 FQ	35180 MW	39620 TQ	USBLS	5/07

AE	Average entry wage	AW	Average wage paid	FQ	First quartile wage
AER	Average entry range	AWR	Average wage range	H	Hourly
AEX	Average experienced wage	AXR	Average experienced range	HI	Highest wage paid
ATC	Average total compensation	D	Daily	HR	High end range

LO	Lowest wage paid	MTC	Median total compensation	TCC	Total cash compensation
LR	Low end range	MW	Median wage paid	TQ	Third quartile wage
M	Monthly	MWR	Median wage range	W	Weekly
MCC	Median cash compensation	S	See annotated source	Y	Yearly

Occupation/Type/Industry	Location	Per	Low	Mid	High	Source	Date
Pile-Driver Operator	New Orleans-Metairie-Kenner MSA, LA	Y	28660 FQ	35460 MW	54070 TQ	USBLS	5/07
	Massachusetts	Y	61530 FQ	67710 MW	75860 TQ	USBLS	5/07
	Boston-Cambridge-Quincy NECTA, MA	Y	62090 FQ	67650 MW	75680 TQ	USBLS	5/07
	Michigan	Y	36240 FQ	42230 MW	47290 TQ	USBLS	5/07
	Minnesota	Y	58985 FQ	67521 MW	77512 TQ	MNBLS	10/08-12/08
	Minneapolis-Saint Paul MSA, MN-WI	Y	62284 FQ	68270 MW	76321 TQ	MNBLS	10/08-12/08
	Mississippi	Y	28770 FQ	54950 MW	61590 TQ	USBLS	5/07
	New Hampshire	H	16.99 AE	28.30 MW	32.85 AEX	NHBLS	6/08
	New Jersey	Y	47070 FQ	62480 MW	73460 TQ	USBLS	5/07
	Edison PMSA, NJ	Y	50580 FQ	65550 MW	75740 TQ	USBLS	5/07
	Newark-Union PMSA, NJ-PA	Y	44070 FQ	48330 MW	65820 TQ	USBLS	5/07
	New York-Northern New Jersey-Long Island MSA, NY-NJ-PA	Y	48900 FQ	68410 MW	79530 TQ	USBLS	5/07
	North Carolina	Y	23810 FQ	32550 MW	39930 TQ	USBLS	5/07
	Ohio	Y	53330 FQ	57970 MW	62520 TQ	USBLS	5/07
	Oregon	H	22.84 FQ	26.70 MW	30.19 TQ	ORBLS	5/08
	Pennsylvania	Y	62060 FQ	66770 MW	71940 TQ	USBLS	5/07
	Philadelphia-Camden-Wilmington MSA, PA-NJ-DE-MD	Y	64580 FQ	68740 MW	72910 TQ	USBLS	5/07
	Tennessee	Y	28960 FQ	34950 MW	40610 TQ	USBLS	5/07
	Nashville-Davidson-Murfreesboro MSA, TN	Y	26320 FQ	34040 MW	38360 TQ	USBLS	5/07
	Texas	Y	32440 FQ	37370 MW	45000 TQ	USBLS	5/07
	Houston-Sugar Land-Baytown MSA, TX	Y	33050 FQ	36860 MW	41640 TQ	USBLS	5/07
	Virginia	Y	35010 FQ	39680 MW	45870 TQ	USBLS	5/07
	Virginia Beach-Norfolk-Newport News MSA, VA-NC	Y	35190 FQ	40840 MW	46810 TQ	USBLS	5/07
	Washington	H	23.88 FQ	30.88 MW	37.13 TQ	WABLS	3/08
	Seattle-Tacoma-Bellevue MSA, WA	Y	46620 FQ	67740 MW	81350 TQ	USBLS	5/07
Pipelayer	Alabama	Y	22910 FQ	28420 MW	35680 TQ	USBLS	5/07
	Birmingham-Hoover MSA, AL	Y	25540 FQ	33610 MW	41350 TQ	USBLS	5/07
	Arizona	Y	27640 FQ	33310 MW	38740 TQ	USBLS	5/07
	Phoenix-Mesa-Scottsdale MSA, AZ	Y	27800 FQ	33360 MW	39060 TQ	USBLS	5/07
	Tucson MSA, AZ	Y	29860 FQ	34910 MW	38340 TQ	USBLS	5/07
	Arkansas	Y	20950 FQ	27440 MW	35490 TQ	USBLS	5/07
	Fort Smith MSA, AR-OK	Y	19980 FQ	24490 MW	29260 TQ	USBLS	5/07
	Little Rock-North Little Rock MSA, AR	Y	27620 FQ	32260 MW	39380 TQ	USBLS	5/07
	Pine Bluff MSA, AR	Y	17740 FQ	19520 MW	28020 TQ	USBLS	5/07
	California	H	17.19 FQ	23.02 MW	28.31 TQ	CABLS	1/08-3/08
	Los Angeles-Long Beach-Glendale PMSA, CA	H	19.38 FQ	25.80 MW	28.83 TQ	CABLS	1/08-3/08
	Oakland-Fremont-Hayward MSA, CA	H	22.37 FQ	26.05 MW	28.76 TQ	CABLS	1/08-3/08
	Riverside-San Bernardino-Ontario MSA, CA	H	19.91 FQ	23.66 MW	29.65 TQ	CABLS	1/08-3/08
	Sacramento-Arden Arcade-Roseville MSA, CA	H	20.58 FQ	23.49 MW	27.13 TQ	CABLS	1/08-3/08
	San Diego-Carlsbad-San Marcos MSA, CA	H	18.59 FQ	22.31 MW	28.05 TQ	CABLS	1/08-3/08
	San Francisco-San Mateo-Redwood PMSA, CA	H	21.63 FQ	27.20 MW	30.66 TQ	CABLS	1/08-3/08
	San Jose-Sunnyvale-Santa Clara MSA, CA	H	24.16 FQ	26.30 MW	28.55 TQ	CABLS	1/08-3/08
	Santa Ana-Anaheim-Irvine PMSA, CA	Y	31160 FQ	39770 MW	53310 TQ	USBLS	5/07
	Colorado	Y	28510 FQ	33720 MW	43630 TQ	USBLS	5/07
	Denver-Aurora MSA, CO	Y	29690 FQ	34390 MW	43740 TQ	USBLS	5/07
	Pueblo MSA, CO	Y	22160 FQ	25850 MW	29820 TQ	USBLS	5/07
	Connecticut	H	20.22 AE	24.35 MW		CTBLS	1/08-3/08
	Bridgeport-Stamford-Norwalk MSA, CT	Y	45880 FQ	53570 MW	61390 TQ	USBLS	5/07

AE	Average entry wage	AW	Average wage paid	FQ	First quartile wage	LO	Lowest wage paid	MTC	Median total compensation	TCC	Total cash compensation
AER	Average entry range	AWR	Average wage range	H	Hourly	LR	Low end range	MW	Median wage paid	TQ	Third quartile wage
AEX	Average experienced wage	AXR	Average experienced range	HI	Highest wage paid	M	Monthly	MWR	Median wage range	W	Weekly
ATC	Average total compensation	D	Daily	HR	High end range	MCC	Median cash compensation	S	See annotated source	Y	Yearly

Occupation/Type/Industry	Location	Per	Low	Mid	High	Source	Date
Pipelayer	Hartford-West Hartford-East Hartford MSA, CT	Y	41060 FQ	46160 MW	52820 TQ	USBLS	5/07
	Delaware	Y	28350 FQ	35300 MW	41070 TQ	USBLS	5/07
	Wilmington PMSA, DE-MD-NJ	Y	30290 FQ	36020 MW	41960 TQ	USBLS	5/07
	Washington-Arlington-Alexandria MSA, DC-VA-MD-WV	Y	30470 FQ	35640 MW	41390 TQ	USBLS	5/07
	Florida	Y	25250 FQ	29060 MW	33950 TQ	USBLS	5/07
	Fort Lauderdale-Pompano Beach-Deerfield Beach PMSA, FL	Y	25370 FQ	29050 MW	33960 TQ	USBLS	5/07
	Jacksonville MSA, FL	Y	24500 FQ	28440 MW	32160 TQ	USBLS	5/07
	Miami-Fort Lauderdale-Miami Beach MSA, FL	Y	26420 FQ	30510 MW	36690 TQ	USBLS	5/07
	Orlando-Kissimmee MSA, FL	Y	25460 FQ	28260 MW	31380 TQ	USBLS	5/07
	Tampa-St. Petersburg-Clearwater MSA, FL	Y	25520 FQ	29260 MW	33400 TQ	USBLS	5/07
	West Palm Beach-Boca Raton-Boynton Beach PMSA, FL	Y	27310 FQ	31480 MW	37020 TQ	USBLS	5/07
	Georgia	Y	22680 FQ	27640 MW	34310 TQ	USBLS	5/07
	Atlanta-Sandy Springs-Marietta MSA, GA	Y	24000 FQ	29230 MW	36420 TQ	USBLS	5/07
	Hawaii	Y	33760 FQ	47440 MW	60410 TQ	USBLS	5/07
	Idaho	Y	27060 FQ	29630 MW	34160 TQ	USBLS	5/07
	Boise City-Nampa MSA, ID	Y	26920 FQ	28930 MW	30930 TQ	USBLS	5/07
	Coeur d'Alene MSA, ID	Y	26330 FQ	37480 MW	45130 TQ	USBLS	5/07
	Illinois	Y	47910 FQ	59920 MW	72070 TQ	USBLS	5/07
	Chicago-Naperville-Joliet MSA, IL-IN-WI	Y	53600 FQ	64220 MW	74530 TQ	USBLS	5/07
	Indiana	Y	35010 FQ	42570 MW	51740 TQ	USBLS	5/07
	Gary PMSA, IN	Y	47760 FQ	52830 MW	58910 TQ	USBLS	5/07
	Indianapolis-Carmel MSA, IN	Y	33840 FQ	39660 MW	51890 TQ	USBLS	5/07
	Iowa	Y	28810 FQ	37470 MW	45580 TQ	USBLS	5/07
	Des Moines-West Des Moines MSA, IA	Y	35650 FQ	41920 MW	46850 TQ	USBLS	5/07
	Kansas	Y	26190 FQ	36040 MW	52040 TQ	USBLS	5/07
	Wichita MSA, KS	Y	22670 FQ	30950 MW	49780 TQ	USBLS	5/07
	Kentucky	Y	28559 FQ	35025 MW	41634 TQ	KYBLS	2008
	Louisville-Jefferson County MSA, KY-IN	Y	31100 FQ	35390 MW	39440 TQ	USBLS	5/07
	Louisiana	H	10.79 FQ	13.11 MW	16.69 TQ	LABLS	1/08-3/08
	Baton Rouge MSA, LA	Y	22160 FQ	27070 MW	35630 TQ	USBLS	5/07
	New Orleans-Metairie-Kenner MSA, LA	Y	20830 FQ	24830 MW	29360 TQ	USBLS	5/07
	Shreveport-Bossier City MSA, LA	Y	23180 FQ	26990 MW	30060 TQ	USBLS	5/07
	Maine	Y	27430 FQ	33170 MW	37190 TQ	USBLS	5/07
	Maryland	Y		35775 MW		MDBLS	3/08
	Baltimore-Towson MSA, MD	Y	28560 FQ	33640 MW	38680 TQ	USBLS	5/07
	Bethesda-Gaithersburg-Frederick PMSA, MD	Y	27120 FQ	32820 MW	39530 TQ	USBLS	5/07
	Hagerstown-Martinsburg MSA, MD-WV	Y	23540 FQ	30190 MW	35740 TQ	USBLS	5/07
	Massachusetts	Y	36510 FQ	42700 MW	55020 TQ	USBLS	5/07
	Boston-Cambridge-Quincy NECTA, MA	Y	36250 FQ	41040 MW	54860 TQ	USBLS	5/07
	Worcester MSA, MA-CT	Y	42510 FQ	51580 MW	60320 TQ	USBLS	5/07
	Michigan	Y	32390 FQ	37550 MW	45350 TQ	USBLS	5/07
	Detroit-Warren-Livonia MSA, MI	Y	33490 FQ	38880 MW	47050 TQ	USBLS	5/07
	Grand Rapids-Wyoming MSA, MI	Y	30640 FQ	33750 MW	40820 TQ	USBLS	5/07
	Warren-Troy-Farmington Hills PMSA, MI	Y	35600 FQ	44110 MW	50240 TQ	USBLS	5/07
	Minnesota	Y	44557 FQ	55254 MW	63295 TQ	MNBLS	10/08-12/08
	Duluth-Superior MSA, MN-WI	Y	54980 FQ	59881 MW	64402 TQ	MNBLS	10/08-12/08
	Minneapolis-Saint Paul MSA, MN-WI	Y	49005 FQ	57488 MW	64950 TQ	MNBLS	10/08-12/08
	Rochester MSA, MN	Y	36547 FQ	40320 MW	48057 TQ	MNBLS	10/08-12/08
	Mississippi	Y	22030 FQ	25120 MW	29530 TQ	USBLS	5/07
	Jackson MSA, MS	Y	21420 FQ	23330 MW	25740 TQ	USBLS	5/07

Occupation/Type/Industry	Location	Per	Low	Mid	High	Source	Date
Pipelayer	Missouri	Y	26760 FQ	34920 MW	48320 TQ	USBLS	5/07
	Kansas City MSA, MO-KS	Y	34520 FQ	51390 MW	58070 TQ	USBLS	5/07
	St. Louis MSA, MO-IL	Y	36180 FQ	44590 MW	57870 TQ	USBLS	5/07
	Montana	Y	25520 FQ	31610 MW	42440 TQ	USBLS	5/07
	Billings MSA, MT	Y	33330 FQ	39650 MW	45600 TQ	USBLS	5/07
	Nebraska	Y	25640 FQ	31230 MW	39410 TQ	USBLS	5/07
	Omaha-Council Bluffs MSA, NE-IA	Y	29390 FQ	35670 MW	43660 TQ	USBLS	5/07
	Nevada	H	14.43 FQ	19.10 MW	24.84 TQ	NVBLS	5/08
	Las Vegas-Paradise MSA, NV	H	13.68 FQ	18.04 MW	23.62 TQ	NVBLS	5/08
	New Hampshire	H	13.61 AE	18.07 MW	20.14 AEX	NHBLS	6/08
	Nashua NECTA, NH-MA	Y	37800 FQ	41480 MW	44970 TQ	USBLS	5/07
	New Jersey	Y	37980 FQ	50350 MW	56830 TQ	USBLS	5/07
	Edison PMSA, NJ	Y	39250 FQ	50010 MW	57350 TQ	USBLS	5/07
	Newark-Union PMSA, NJ-PA	Y	39380 FQ	50660 MW	56780 TQ	USBLS	5/07
	New Mexico	Y	25580 FQ	29370 MW	46080 TQ	USBLS	5/07
	New York	Y	35840 FQ	45900 MW	57390 TQ	USBLS	5/07
	Buffalo-Niagara Falls MSA, NY	Y	37260 FQ	44480 MW	50710 TQ	USBLS	5/07
	Nassau-Suffolk PMSA, NY	Y	54690 FQ	66940 MW	86380 TQ	USBLS	5/07
	New York-Northern New Jersey-Long Island MSA, NY-NJ-PA	Y	37940 FQ	49870 MW	58440 TQ	USBLS	5/07
	Syracuse MSA, NY	Y	43800 FQ	48370 MW	51830 TQ	USBLS	5/07
	North Carolina	Y	22500 FQ	26420 MW	30680 TQ	USBLS	5/07
	Asheville MSA, NC	Y	22450 FQ	26690 MW	31220 TQ	USBLS	5/07
	Charlotte-Gastonia-Concord MSA, NC-SC	Y	23600 FQ	27560 MW	32110 TQ	USBLS	5/07
	Raleigh-Cary MSA, NC	Y	21080 FQ	25170 MW	29850 TQ	USBLS	5/07
	North Dakota	Y	22860 FQ	27510 MW	31100 TQ	USBLS	5/07
	Fargo MSA, ND-MN	Y	24420 FQ	27820 MW	31700 TQ	USBLS	5/07
	Grand Forks MSA, ND-MN	Y	27470 FQ	30700 MW	33100 TQ	USBLS	5/07
	Ohio	Y	31160 FQ	37990 MW	46950 TQ	USBLS	5/07
	Cincinnati-Middletown MSA, OH-KY-IN	Y	30570 FQ	37540 MW	45940 TQ	USBLS	5/07
	Cleveland-Elyria-Mentor MSA, OH	Y	33460 FQ	41670 MW	51080 TQ	USBLS	5/07
	Columbus MSA, OH	Y	30990 FQ	39050 MW	46790 TQ	USBLS	5/07
	Dayton MSA, OH	Y	39360 FQ	51340 MW	63100 TQ	USBLS	5/07
	Oklahoma	Y	20200 FQ	23170 MW	26890 TQ	USBLS	5/07
	Oklahoma City MSA, OK	Y	21380 FQ	23830 MW	28400 TQ	USBLS	5/07
	Tulsa MSA, OK	Y	14580 FQ	21720 MW	26850 TQ	USBLS	5/07
	Oregon	H	16.18 FQ	19.80 MW	24.18 TQ	ORBLS	5/08
	Portland-Vancouver-Beaverton MSA, OR-WA	Y	33290 FQ	40870 MW	50570 TQ	USBLS	5/07
	Pennsylvania	Y	29690 FQ	36190 MW	45430 TQ	USBLS	5/07
	Allentown-Bethlehem-Easton MSA, PA-NJ	Y	28550 FQ	34280 MW	44330 TQ	USBLS	5/07
	Philadelphia-Camden-Wilmington MSA, PA-NJ-DE-MD	Y	30530 FQ	35940 MW	41870 TQ	USBLS	5/07
	Pittsburgh MSA, PA	Y	36420 FQ	46250 MW	54500 TQ	USBLS	5/07
	Rhode Island	Y	43950 FQ	52070 MW	57310 TQ	USBLS	5/07
	Providence-Fall River-Warwick MSA, RI-MA	Y	48650 FQ	52860 MW	57710 TQ	USBLS	5/07
	South Carolina	Y	24500 FQ	28930 MW	34000 TQ	USBLS	5/07
	Charleston-North Charleston MSA, SC	Y	24120 FQ	28000 MW	31880 TQ	USBLS	5/07
	Columbia MSA, SC	Y	28610 FQ	32610 MW	38660 TQ	USBLS	5/07
	South Dakota	Y	24834 FQ	29370 MW	35708 TQ	SDBLS	7/08-9/08
	Sioux Falls MSA, SD	Y	26243 FQ	32406 MW	40692 TQ	SDBLS	7/08-9/08
	Tennessee	Y	23890 FQ	28520 MW	35650 TQ	USBLS	5/07
	Memphis MSA, TN-MS-AR	Y	22700 FQ	26630 MW	35910 TQ	USBLS	5/07
	Nashville-Davidson-Murfreesboro MSA, TN	Y	24570 FQ	28120 MW	31610 TQ	USBLS	5/07
	Texas	Y	21670 FQ	25340 MW	29790 TQ	USBLS	5/07
	Austin-Round Rock MSA, TX	Y	21370 FQ	24950 MW	28100 TQ	USBLS	5/07
	Dallas-Fort Worth-Arlington MSA, TX	Y	21840 FQ	25770 MW	29680 TQ	USBLS	5/07
	El Paso MSA, TX	Y	21930 FQ	24130 MW	28590 TQ	USBLS	5/07
	Houston-Sugar Land-Baytown MSA, TX	Y	22540 FQ	26030 MW	30050 TQ	USBLS	5/07

AE	Average entry wage	**AW**	Average wage paid	**FQ**	First quartile wage	**LO**	Lowest wage paid	**MTC** Median total compensation **TCC** Total cash compensation
AER	Average entry range	**AWR**	Average wage range	**H**	Hourly	**LR**	Low end range	**MW** Median wage paid **TQ** Third quartile wage
AEX	Average experienced wage	**AXR**	Average experienced range	**HI**	Highest wage paid	**M**	Monthly	**MWR** Median wage range **W** Weekly
ATC	Average total compensation	**D**	Daily	**HR**	High end range	**MCC**	Median cash compensation	**S** See annotated source **Y** Yearly

Occupation/Type/Industry	Location	Per	Low	Mid	High	Source	Date
Pipelayer	Midland MSA, TX	Y	32520 FQ	35680 MW	38610 TQ	USBLS	5/07
	San Antonio MSA, TX	Y	22530 FQ	25250 MW	29720 TQ	USBLS	5/07
	Utah	Y	25140 FQ	29070 MW	34800 TQ	USBLS	5/07
	Ogden-Clearfield MSA, UT	Y	22100 FQ	26080 MW	31610 TQ	USBLS	5/07
	Salt Lake City MSA, UT	Y	26590 FQ	29950 MW	35710 TQ	USBLS	5/07
	Vermont	Y	30040 FQ	35940 MW	47410 TQ	USBLS	5/07
	Virginia	Y	25630 FQ	30040 MW	36540 TQ	USBLS	5/07
	Richmond MSA, VA	Y	25800 FQ	29190 MW	33880 TQ	USBLS	5/07
	Roanoke MSA, VA	Y	24020 FQ	26580 MW	31780 TQ	USBLS	5/07
	Virginia Beach-Norfolk- Newport News MSA, VA-NC	Y	22740 FQ	26910 MW	31240 TQ	USBLS	5/07
	Washington	H	19.39 FQ	23.92 MW	28.32 TQ	WABLS	3/08
	Seattle-Tacoma-Bellevue MSA, WA	Y	38740 FQ	48700 MW	57330 TQ	USBLS	5/07
	West Virginia	Y	24075 FQ	30220 MW	39388 TQ	WVBLS	7/08-9/08
	Wisconsin	Y	39900 FQ	48790 MW	57370 TQ	USBLS	5/07
	Green Bay MSA, WI	Y	46500 FQ	55680 MW	63990 TQ	USBLS	5/07
	Milwaukee-Waukesha-West Allis MSA, WI	Y	42950 FQ	52200 MW	60030 TQ	USBLS	5/07
	Wyoming	Y	26988 FQ	28812 MW	30622 TQ	WYBLS	9/08
	Puerto Rico	Y	19730 FQ	28200 MW	33210 TQ	USBLS	5/07
	San Juan-Caguas-Guaynabo MSA, PR	Y	25600 FQ	29490 MW	34750 TQ	USBLS	5/07
Plan Check Engineer Municipal Government	Walnut Creek, CA	Y	98480 LO		119692 HI	WCSWP	7/11/08
Planetarium Director Christa McAuliffe Planetarium	New Hampshire	Y			79785 HI	NHUL03	2008
Planner	California	Y		86400 MW		APA01	2008
	Illinois	Y		70000 MW		APA01	2008
	New Jersey	Y		83000 MW		APA01	2008
Plant Food Safety/HACCP Manager	United States	Y		80600 MCC		MANDP	2008
Plant Manager	United States	Y		99987 AW		PLANTE	2007
Plant Operator Waste Water Treatment Facility	Montague, MA	H			17.99 HI	FRCOG	2009
Plant Pathologist State Government	Ohio	H	21.77 LO		31.86 HI	ODAS	2008
Plant Pest Control Specialist State Government	Ohio	H	18.36 LO		23.87 HI	ODAS	2008
Plasterer and Stucco Mason	Alabama	Y	29010 FQ	33110 MW	36950 TQ	USBLS	5/07
	Arizona	Y	22780 FQ	28570 MW	34580 TQ	USBLS	5/07
	Phoenix-Mesa-Scottsdale MSA, AZ	Y	22830 FQ	28650 MW	34910 TQ	USBLS	5/07
	Tucson MSA, AZ	Y	24620 FQ	29060 MW	34010 TQ	USBLS	5/07
	Arkansas	Y	29340 FQ	37380 MW	45440 TQ	USBLS	5/07
	Little Rock-North Little Rock MSA, AR	Y	33490 FQ	43380 MW	47740 TQ	USBLS	5/07
	California	H	16.64 FQ	19.98 MW	25.10 TQ	CABLS	1/08-3/08
	Los Angeles-Long Beach- Glendale PMSA, CA	H	16.58 FQ	18.35 MW	20.71 TQ	CABLS	1/08-3/08
	Modesto MSA, CA	H	23.89 FQ	30.21 MW	35.51 TQ	CABLS	1/08-3/08
	Oakland-Fremont-Hayward MSA, CA	H	17.70 FQ	20.46 MW	27.70 TQ	CABLS	1/08-3/08
	Riverside-San Bernardino- Ontario MSA, CA	H	16.82 FQ	20.94 MW	25.79 TQ	CABLS	1/08-3/08
	Sacramento-Arden Arcade- Roseville MSA, CA	H	14.43 FQ	17.64 MW	22.07 TQ	CABLS	1/08-3/08
	San Diego-Carlsbad-San Marcos MSA, CA	H	16.08 FQ	19.19 MW	22.91 TQ	CABLS	1/08-3/08
	San Francisco-San Mateo- Redwood PMSA, CA	H	16.10 FQ	19.79 MW	24.28 TQ	CABLS	1/08-3/08
	San Jose-Sunnyvale-Santa Clara MSA, CA	H	19.39 FQ	22.56 MW	25.34 TQ	CABLS	1/08-3/08

AE	Average entry wage	**AW**	Average wage paid	**FQ**	First quartile wage	**LO**	Lowest wage paid	**MTC** Median total compensation	**TCC** Total cash compensation
AER	Average entry range	**AWR**	Average wage range	**H**	Hourly	**LR**	Low end range	**MW** Median wage paid	**TQ** Third quartile wage
AEX	Average experienced wage	**AXR**	Average experienced range	**HI**	Highest wage paid	**M**	Monthly	**MWR** Median wage range	**W** Weekly
ATC	Average total compensation	**D**	Daily	**HR**	High end range	**MCC**	Median cash compensation	**S** See annotated source	**Y** Yearly

Occupation/Type/Industry	Location	Per	Low	Mid	High	Source	Date
Plasterer and Stucco Mason	Santa Ana-Anaheim-Irvine PMSA, CA	Y	39050 FQ	47320 MW	57210 TQ	USBLS	5/07
	Colorado	Y	27060 FQ	30350 MW	36890 TQ	USBLS	5/07
	Denver-Aurora MSA, CO	Y	27350 FQ	29970 MW	33950 TQ	USBLS	5/07
	Fort Collins-Loveland MSA, CO	Y	26860 FQ	29550 MW	32990 TQ	USBLS	5/07
	Delaware	Y	33860 FQ	40160 MW	49190 TQ	USBLS	5/07
	Wilmington PMSA, DE-MD-NJ	Y	28500 FQ	37400 MW	45800 TQ	USBLS	5/07
	District of Columbia	Y	31220 FQ	38380 MW	45320 TQ	USBLS	5/07
	Washington-Arlington-Alexandria MSA, DC-VA-MD-WV	Y	26480 FQ	31970 MW	38870 TQ	USBLS	5/07
	Florida	Y	30200 FQ	36160 MW	41760 TQ	USBLS	5/07
	Fort Lauderdale-Pompano Beach-Deerfield Beach PMSA, FL	Y	28620 FQ	35270 MW	41240 TQ	USBLS	5/07
	Jacksonville MSA, FL	Y	35650 FQ	38010 MW	40410 TQ	USBLS	5/07
	Miami-Fort Lauderdale-Miami Beach MSA, FL	Y	33180 FQ	37790 MW	44000 TQ	USBLS	5/07
	Orlando-Kissimmee MSA, FL	Y	29830 FQ	35960 MW	43540 TQ	USBLS	5/07
	Tampa-St. Petersburg-Clearwater MSA, FL	Y	31550 FQ	35630 MW	40310 TQ	USBLS	5/07
	West Palm Beach-Boca Raton-Boynton Beach PMSA, FL	Y	36550 FQ	40220 MW	46010 TQ	USBLS	5/07
	Georgia	Y	26990 FQ	31320 MW	36060 TQ	USBLS	5/07
	Hawaii	Y	48600 FQ	57160 MW	62760 TQ	USBLS	5/07
	Honolulu MSA, HI	Y	53640 FQ	59290 MW	64880 TQ	USBLS	5/07
	Idaho	Y	24630 FQ	28450 MW	31630 TQ	USBLS	5/07
	Illinois	Y	49460 FQ	56970 MW	67090 TQ	USBLS	5/07
	Chicago-Naperville-Joliet MSA, IL-IN-WI	Y	54140 FQ	65660 MW	82440 TQ	USBLS	5/07
	Indiana	Y	32310 FQ	41140 MW	53130 TQ	USBLS	5/07
	Indianapolis-Carmel MSA, IN	Y	34910 FQ	42000 MW	52390 TQ	USBLS	5/07
	Iowa	Y	28940 FQ	35260 MW	44920 TQ	USBLS	5/07
	Kansas	Y	27290 FQ	34420 MW	41390 TQ	USBLS	5/07
	Wichita MSA, KS	Y	27970 FQ	32890 MW	39270 TQ	USBLS	5/07
	Kentucky	Y	29751 FQ	34806 MW	41900 TQ	KYBLS	2008
	Louisville-Jefferson County MSA, KY-IN	Y	23300 FQ	30960 MW	45140 TQ	USBLS	5/07
	Louisiana	H	13.74 FQ	16.59 MW	19.27 TQ	LABLS	1/08-3/08
	New Orleans-Metairie-Kenner MSA, LA	Y	30580 FQ	36590 MW	41960 TQ	USBLS	5/07
	Shreveport-Bossier City MSA, LA	Y	32590 FQ	35960 MW	40900 TQ	USBLS	5/07
	Maryland	Y		33800 MW		MDBLS	3/08
	Baltimore-Towson MSA, MD	Y	30570 FQ	36000 MW	40510 TQ	USBLS	5/07
	Bethesda-Gaithersburg-Frederick PMSA, MD	Y	24860 FQ	30400 MW	36220 TQ	USBLS	5/07
	Massachusetts	Y	40830 FQ	51310 MW	59920 TQ	USBLS	5/07
	Boston-Cambridge-Quincy NECTA, MA	Y	42550 FQ	57150 MW	71030 TQ	USBLS	5/07
	Michigan	Y	40850 FQ	57660 MW	65880 TQ	USBLS	5/07
	Detroit-Warren-Livonia MSA, MI	Y	56440 FQ	63480 MW	69230 TQ	USBLS	5/07
	Grand Rapids-Wyoming MSA, MI	Y	34830 FQ	43840 MW	52450 TQ	USBLS	5/07
	Warren-Troy-Farmington Hills PMSA, MI	Y	56350 FQ	63400 MW	69050 TQ	USBLS	5/07
	Minnesota	Y	43272 FQ	56666 MW	65888 TQ	MNBLS	10/08-12/08
	Minneapolis-Saint Paul MSA, MN-WI	Y	48130 FQ	60903 MW	68733 TQ	MNBLS	10/08-12/08
	Mississippi	Y	22190 FQ	28610 MW	34570 TQ	USBLS	5/07
	Jackson MSA, MS	Y	28330 FQ	34970 MW	44320 TQ	USBLS	5/07
	Missouri	Y	33990 FQ	38670 MW	45240 TQ	USBLS	5/07
	Kansas City MSA, MO-KS	Y	29010 FQ	37400 MW	46530 TQ	USBLS	5/07
	St. Louis MSA, MO-IL	Y	41820 FQ	52030 MW	58940 TQ	USBLS	5/07
	Montana	Y	32970 FQ	36550 MW	41110 TQ	USBLS	5/07
	Nebraska	Y	28440 FQ	35130 MW	45180 TQ	USBLS	5/07
	Omaha-Council Bluffs MSA, NE-IA	Y	27280 FQ	31100 MW	38560 TQ	USBLS	5/07
	Nevada	H	14.84 FQ	17.68 MW	23.42 TQ	NVBLS	5/08

AE Average entry wage	**AW** Average wage paid	**FQ** First quartile wage	**LO** Lowest wage paid	**MTC** Median total compensation	**TCC** Total cash compensation
AER Average entry range	**AWR** Average wage range	**H** Hourly	**LR** Low end range	**MW** Median wage paid	**TQ** Third quartile wage
AEX Average experienced wage	**AXR** Average experienced range	**HI** Highest wage paid	**M** Monthly	**MWR** Median wage range	**W** Weekly
ATC Average total compensation	**D** Daily	**HR** High end range	**MCC** Median cash compensation	**S** See annotated source	**Y** Yearly

Occupation/Type/Industry	Location	Per	Low	Mid	High	Source	Date
Plasterer and Stucco Mason	Las Vegas-Paradise MSA, NV	H	15.32 FQ	18.27 MW	24.27 TQ	NVBLS	5/08
	New Jersey	Y	29080 FQ	32800 MW	48730 TQ	USBLS	5/07
	Edison PMSA, NJ	Y	28030 FQ	30470 MW	35980 TQ	USBLS	5/07
	Newark-Union PMSA, NJ-PA	Y	28660 FQ	30940 MW	33150 TQ	USBLS	5/07
	New Mexico	Y	23660 FQ	28990 MW	37740 TQ	USBLS	5/07
	Albuquerque MSA, NM	Y	25340 FQ	30680 MW	40130 TQ	USBLS	5/07
	New York	Y	37800 FQ	54500 MW	65410 TQ	USBLS	5/07
	Buffalo-Niagara Falls MSA, NY	Y	32500 FQ	37600 MW	49080 TQ	USBLS	5/07
	Nassau-Suffolk PMSA, NY	Y	32930 FQ	41790 MW	55260 TQ	USBLS	5/07
	New York-Northern New Jersey-Long Island MSA, NY-NJ-PA	Y	33080 FQ	51530 MW	64220 TQ	USBLS	5/07
	North Carolina	Y	25380 FQ	30740 MW	35110 TQ	USBLS	5/07
	Charlotte-Gastonia-Concord MSA, NC-SC	Y	30110 FQ	35120 MW	40090 TQ	USBLS	5/07
	North Dakota	Y	28350 FQ	31620 MW	41730 TQ	USBLS	5/07
	Fargo MSA, ND-MN	Y	31440 FQ	40270 MW	46380 TQ	USBLS	5/07
	Ohio	Y	28980 FQ	38320 MW	45340 TQ	USBLS	5/07
	Cincinnati-Middletown MSA, OH-KY-IN	Y	41020 FQ	44350 MW	47760 TQ	USBLS	5/07
	Cleveland-Elyria-Mentor MSA, OH	Y	36170 FQ	40710 MW	45700 TQ	USBLS	5/07
	Columbus MSA, OH	Y	19320 FQ	29770 MW	41650 TQ	USBLS	5/07
	Oklahoma	Y	34530 FQ	38310 MW	42120 TQ	USBLS	5/07
	Oklahoma City MSA, OK	Y	35370 FQ	38670 MW	41810 TQ	USBLS	5/07
	Oregon	H	16.39 FQ	18.38 MW	24.63 TQ	ORBLS	5/08
	Portland-Vancouver-Beaverton MSA, OR-WA	Y	24490 FQ	38740 MW	51600 TQ	USBLS	5/07
	Pennsylvania	Y	36050 FQ	44060 MW	53950 TQ	USBLS	5/07
	Philadelphia-Camden-Wilmington MSA, PA-NJ-DE-MD	Y	30310 FQ	43280 MW	65380 TQ	USBLS	5/07
	Pittsburgh MSA, PA	Y	40480 FQ	44290 MW	48060 TQ	USBLS	5/07
	Rhode Island	Y	34110 FQ	38270 MW	51600 TQ	USBLS	5/07
	Providence-Fall River-Warwick MSA, RI-MA	Y	34720 FQ	38860 MW	49060 TQ	USBLS	5/07
	South Carolina	Y	27760 FQ	32510 MW	38690 TQ	USBLS	5/07
	South Dakota	Y	22365 FQ	24842 MW	38537 TQ	SDBLS	7/08-9/08
	Tennessee	Y	27200 FQ	30290 MW	33530 TQ	USBLS	5/07
	Knoxville MSA, TN	Y	28790 FQ	31210 MW	33580 TQ	USBLS	5/07
	Texas	Y	26700 FQ	30640 MW	35540 TQ	USBLS	5/07
	Austin-Round Rock MSA, TX	Y	21840 FQ	27810 MW	32690 TQ	USBLS	5/07
	Dallas-Fort Worth-Arlington MSA, TX	Y	28770 FQ	32680 MW	37520 TQ	USBLS	5/07
	El Paso MSA, TX	Y	26950 FQ	31410 MW	39380 TQ	USBLS	5/07
	Houston-Sugar Land-Baytown MSA, TX	Y	26140 FQ	29840 MW	35700 TQ	USBLS	5/07
	San Antonio MSA, TX	Y	27600 FQ	30510 MW	34110 TQ	USBLS	5/07
	Utah	Y	20650 FQ	28040 MW	34160 TQ	USBLS	5/07
	Salt Lake City MSA, UT	Y	17790 FQ	24150 MW	31570 TQ	USBLS	5/07
	Richmond MSA, VA	Y	28170 FQ	32610 MW	37150 TQ	USBLS	5/07
	Washington	H	21.50 FQ	29.29 MW	41.68 TQ	WABLS	3/08
	West Virginia	Y	32323 FQ	43004 MW	50501 TQ	WVBLS	7/08-9/08
	Charleston MSA, WV	Y	29580 FQ	34770 MW	44330 TQ	USBLS	5/07
	Wisconsin	Y	31070 FQ	38880 MW	50540 TQ	USBLS	5/07
	Milwaukee-Waukesha-West Allis MSA, WI	Y	43640 FQ	53450 MW	62130 TQ	USBLS	5/07
	Puerto Rico	Y	15410 FQ	18470 MW	29030 TQ	USBLS	5/07
	San Juan-Caguas-Guaynabo MSA, PR	Y	16050 FQ	19600 MW	30540 TQ	USBLS	5/07
	Guam	Y	21020 FQ	22700 MW	24560 TQ	USBLS	5/07
Plating and Coating Machine Setter, Operator, and Tender							
Metals and Plastics	Alabama	Y	26150 FQ	32110 MW	38030 TQ	USBLS	5/07
Metals and Plastics	Birmingham-Hoover MSA, AL	Y	28630 FQ	34400 MW	39010 TQ	USBLS	5/07
Metals and Plastics	Arizona	Y	19850 FQ	23130 MW	28470 TQ	USBLS	5/07
Metals and Plastics	Phoenix-Mesa-Scottsdale MSA, AZ	Y	19540 FQ	22740 MW	28510 TQ	USBLS	5/07
Metals and Plastics	Tucson MSA, AZ	Y	19900 FQ	23160 MW	26840 TQ	USBLS	5/07
Metals and Plastics	Arkansas	Y	23890 FQ	30410 MW	35350 TQ	USBLS	5/07

AE	Average entry wage	AW	Average wage paid	FQ	First quartile wage	LO Lowest wage paid	MTC Median total compensation	TCC Total cash compensation
AER	Average entry range	AWR	Average wage range	H	Hourly	LR Low end range	MW Median wage paid	TQ Third quartile wage
AEX	Average experienced wage	AXR	Average experienced range	HI	Highest wage paid	M Monthly	MWR Median wage range	W Weekly
ATC	Average total compensation	D	Daily	HR	High end range	MCC Median cash compensation	S See annotated source	Y Yearly

Plating and Coating Machine Setter, Operator, and Tender

Occupation/Type/Industry	Location	Per	Low	Mid	High	Source	Date
Metals and Plastics	Little Rock-North Little Rock MSA, AR	Y	29160 FQ	32250 MW	35250 TQ	USBLS	5/07
Metals and Plastics	California	H	9.49 FQ	11.74 MW	15.91 TQ	CABLS	1/08-3/08
Metals and Plastics	Los Angeles-Long Beach-Glendale PMSA, CA	H	9.31 FQ	11.29 MW	15.98 TQ	CABLS	1/08-3/08
Metals and Plastics	Oakland-Fremont-Hayward MSA, CA	H	10.04 FQ	12.40 MW	15.89 TQ	CABLS	1/08-3/08
Metals and Plastics	Sacramento-Arden Arcade-Roseville MSA, CA	H	8.54 FQ	10.20 MW	13.07 TQ	CABLS	1/08-3/08
Metals and Plastics	San Diego-Carlsbad-San Marcos MSA, CA	H	8.03 FQ	10.43 MW	14.72 TQ	CABLS	1/08-3/08
Metals and Plastics	San Francisco-San Mateo-Redwood PMSA, CA	H	11.91 FQ	14.05 MW	16.75 TQ	CABLS	1/08-3/08
Metals and Plastics	San Jose-Sunnyvale-Santa Clara MSA, CA	H	10.69 FQ	13.47 MW	17.09 TQ	CABLS	1/08-3/08
Metals and Plastics	Santa Ana-Anaheim-Irvine PMSA, CA	Y	18650 FQ	21940 MW	28080 TQ	USBLS	5/07
Metals and Plastics	Colorado	Y	22370 FQ	27040 MW	32510 TQ	USBLS	5/07
Metals and Plastics	Denver-Aurora MSA, CO	Y	22250 FQ	26420 MW	32090 TQ	USBLS	5/07
Metals and Plastics	Connecticut	H	10.50 AE	13.75 MW		CTBLS	1/08-3/08
Metals and Plastics	Bridgeport-Stamford-Norwalk MSA, CT	Y	22820 FQ	28800 MW	38440 TQ	USBLS	5/07
Metals and Plastics	Hartford-West Hartford-East Hartford MSA, CT	Y	23350 FQ	28160 MW	34750 TQ	USBLS	5/07
Metals and Plastics	New Haven MSA, CT	Y	21510 FQ	25520 MW	30550 TQ	USBLS	5/07
Metals and Plastics	Florida	Y	18710 FQ	23420 MW	32760 TQ	USBLS	5/07
Metals and Plastics	Fort Lauderdale-Pompano Beach-Deerfield Beach PMSA, FL	Y	21070 FQ	27820 MW	44230 TQ	USBLS	5/07
Metals and Plastics	Miami-Fort Lauderdale-Miami Beach MSA, FL	Y	19200 FQ	26360 MW	36210 TQ	USBLS	5/07
Metals and Plastics	Orlando-Kissimmee MSA, FL	Y	20860 FQ	22880 MW	27330 TQ	USBLS	5/07
Metals and Plastics	Tampa-St. Petersburg-Clearwater MSA, FL	Y	17570 FQ	19350 MW	23140 TQ	USBLS	5/07
Metals and Plastics	West Palm Beach-Boca Raton-Boynton Beach PMSA, FL	Y	17910 FQ	19940 MW	28550 TQ	USBLS	5/07
Metals and Plastics	Georgia	Y	18890 FQ	26210 MW	30820 TQ	USBLS	5/07
Metals and Plastics	Atlanta-Sandy Springs-Marietta MSA, GA	Y	20150 FQ	27030 MW	30020 TQ	USBLS	5/07
Metals and Plastics	Idaho	Y	18460 FQ	21540 MW	34020 TQ	USBLS	5/07
Metals and Plastics	Illinois	Y	23200 FQ	28290 MW	35480 TQ	USBLS	5/07
Metals and Plastics	Chicago-Naperville-Joliet MSA, IL-IN-WI	Y	22290 FQ	27280 MW	33900 TQ	USBLS	5/07
Metals and Plastics	Indiana	Y	22450 FQ	30480 MW	46290 TQ	USBLS	5/07
Metals and Plastics	Evansville MSA, IN-KY	Y	25910 FQ	33070 MW	36990 TQ	USBLS	5/07
Metals and Plastics	Gary PMSA, IN	Y	23920 FQ	31000 MW	37830 TQ	USBLS	5/07
Metals and Plastics	Indianapolis-Carmel MSA, IN	Y	23850 FQ	28180 MW	44060 TQ	USBLS	5/07
Metals and Plastics	Iowa	Y	26440 FQ	33720 MW	37500 TQ	USBLS	5/07
Metals and Plastics	Davenport-Moline-Rock Island MSA, IA-IL	Y	23100 FQ	33870 MW	37180 TQ	USBLS	5/07
Metals and Plastics	Kansas	Y	22290 FQ	27680 MW	33620 TQ	USBLS	5/07
Metals and Plastics	Wichita MSA, KS	Y	22520 FQ	27280 MW	33290 TQ	USBLS	5/07
Metals and Plastics	Kentucky	Y	21473 FQ	28638 MW	35593 TQ	KYBLS	2008
Metals and Plastics	Louisville-Jefferson County MSA, KY-IN	Y	18950 FQ	24020 MW	33060 TQ	USBLS	5/07
Metals and Plastics	Louisiana	H	10.46 FQ	13.92 MW	16.28 TQ	LABLS	1/08-3/08
Metals and Plastics	Baton Rouge MSA, LA	Y	17980 FQ	20600 MW	27430 TQ	USBLS	5/07
Metals and Plastics	Maine	Y	24620 FQ	32160 MW	36780 TQ	USBLS	5/07
Metals and Plastics	Portland-South Portland-Biddeford MSA, ME	Y	24100 FQ	31640 MW	36260 TQ	USBLS	5/07
Metals and Plastics	Maryland	Y		28000 MW		MDBLS	3/08
Metals and Plastics	Baltimore-Towson MSA, MD	Y	23610 FQ	27340 MW	30650 TQ	USBLS	5/07
Metals and Plastics	Massachusetts	Y	26850 FQ	33840 MW	40490 TQ	USBLS	5/07
Metals and Plastics	Boston-Cambridge-Quincy NECTA, MA	Y	33150 FQ	39120 MW	43910 TQ	USBLS	5/07
Metals and Plastics	Worcester MSA, MA-CT	Y	30140 FQ	37250 MW	44150 TQ	USBLS	5/07
Metals and Plastics	Michigan	Y	23020 FQ	30350 MW	38360 TQ	USBLS	5/07
Metals and Plastics	Detroit-Warren-Livonia MSA, MI	Y	22870 FQ	31700 MW	39340 TQ	USBLS	5/07

AE	Average entry wage	AW	Average wage paid	FQ	First quartile wage
AER	Average entry range	AWR	Average wage range	H	Hourly
AEX	Average experienced wage	AXR	Average experienced range	HI	Highest wage paid
ATC	Average total compensation	D	Daily	HR	High end range

LO	Lowest wage paid	MTC	Median total compensation
LR	Low end range	MW	Median wage paid
M	Monthly	MWR	Median wage range
MCC	Median cash compensation	S	See annotated source

TCC	Total cash compensation		
TQ	Third quartile wage		
W	Weekly		
Y	Yearly		

Occupation/Type/Industry	Location	Per	Low	Mid	High	Source	Date
Plating and Coating Machine Setter, Operator, and Tender							
Metals and Plastics	Grand Rapids-Wyoming MSA, MI	Y	23500 FQ	30050 MW	38460 TQ	USBLS	5/07
Metals and Plastics	Warren-Troy-Farmington Hills PMSA, MI	Y	19870 FQ	26930 MW	37420 TQ	USBLS	5/07
Metals and Plastics	Minnesota	Y	26881 FQ	32095 MW	38015 TQ	MNBLS	10/08-12/08
Metals and Plastics	Minneapolis-Saint Paul MSA, MN-WI	Y	28125 FQ	33495 MW	38616 TQ	MNBLS	10/08-12/08
Metals and Plastics	Mississippi	Y	25720 FQ	30510 MW	34480 TQ	USBLS	5/07
Metals and Plastics	Jackson MSA, MS	Y	29860 FQ	33160 MW	36070 TQ	USBLS	5/07
Metals and Plastics	Missouri	Y	21850 FQ	27450 MW	35240 TQ	USBLS	5/07
Metals and Plastics	Kansas City MSA, MO-KS	Y	22340 FQ	28380 MW	33110 TQ	USBLS	5/07
Metals and Plastics	St. Louis MSA, MO-IL	Y	25030 FQ	30950 MW	39410 TQ	USBLS	5/07
Metals and Plastics	Nebraska	Y	23650 FQ	28490 MW	32650 TQ	USBLS	5/07
Metals and Plastics	Nevada	H	9.68 FQ	11.12 MW	15.45 TQ	NVBLS	5/08
Metals and Plastics	Las Vegas-Paradise MSA, NV	H	9.95 FQ	10.67 MW	11.40 TQ	NVBLS	5/08
Metals and Plastics	Nashua NECTA, NH-MA	Y	28240 FQ	32320 MW	36290 TQ	USBLS	5/07
Metals and Plastics	New Jersey	Y	18850 FQ	26110 MW	33760 TQ	USBLS	5/07
Metals and Plastics	Camden PMSA, NJ	Y	17490 FQ	25420 MW	31680 TQ	USBLS	5/07
Metals and Plastics	Edison PMSA, NJ	Y	20910 FQ	30470 MW	36560 TQ	USBLS	5/07
Metals and Plastics	Newark-Union PMSA, NJ-PA	Y	21130 FQ	27950 MW	35190 TQ	USBLS	5/07
Metals and Plastics	New York	Y	21500 FQ	26990 MW	34560 TQ	USBLS	5/07
Metals and Plastics	Buffalo-Niagara Falls MSA, NY	Y	22400 FQ	27860 MW	34930 TQ	USBLS	5/07
Metals and Plastics	Nassau-Suffolk PMSA, NY	Y	23440 FQ	29980 MW	36410 TQ	USBLS	5/07
Metals and Plastics	New York-Northern New Jersey-Long Island MSA, NY-NJ-PA	Y	20810 FQ	28310 MW	35610 TQ	USBLS	5/07
Metals and Plastics	North Carolina	Y	23900 FQ	28220 MW	32350 TQ	USBLS	5/07
Metals and Plastics	Charlotte-Gastonia-Concord MSA, NC-SC	Y	21380 FQ	25090 MW	30820 TQ	USBLS	5/07
Metals and Plastics	North Dakota	Y	20530 FQ	26360 MW	38870 TQ	USBLS	5/07
Metals and Plastics	Fargo MSA, ND-MN	Y	19250 FQ	23380 MW	28370 TQ	USBLS	5/07
Metals and Plastics	Ohio	Y	22660 FQ	28290 MW	34770 TQ	USBLS	5/07
Metals and Plastics	Cincinnati-Middletown MSA, OH-KY-IN	Y	22860 FQ	28580 MW	43470 TQ	USBLS	5/07
Metals and Plastics	Cleveland-Elyria-Mentor MSA, OH	Y	23110 FQ	27300 MW	31710 TQ	USBLS	5/07
Metals and Plastics	Dayton MSA, OH	Y	20670 FQ	25660 MW	31270 TQ	USBLS	5/07
Metals and Plastics	Oklahoma	Y	23150 FQ	29760 MW	42480 TQ	USBLS	5/07
Metals and Plastics	Oklahoma City MSA, OK	Y	26580 FQ	31750 MW	44740 TQ	USBLS	5/07
Metals and Plastics	Tulsa MSA, OK	Y	19530 FQ	26250 MW	34950 TQ	USBLS	5/07
Metals and Plastics	Oregon	H	12.56 FQ	14.73 MW	18.37 TQ	ORBLS	5/08
Metals and Plastics	Portland-Vancouver-Beaverton MSA, OR-WA	Y	26250 FQ	30920 MW	38890 TQ	USBLS	5/07
Metals and Plastics	Pennsylvania	Y	25550 FQ	32280 MW	38030 TQ	USBLS	5/07
Metals and Plastics	Allentown-Bethlehem-Easton MSA, PA-NJ	Y	25240 FQ	33130 MW	38050 TQ	USBLS	5/07
Metals and Plastics	Philadelphia-Camden-Wilmington MSA, PA-NJ-DE-MD	Y	25180 FQ	32030 MW	37680 TQ	USBLS	5/07
Metals and Plastics	Pittsburgh MSA, PA	Y	23840 FQ	30900 MW	38620 TQ	USBLS	5/07
Metals and Plastics	Rhode Island	Y	23870 FQ	30450 MW	40540 TQ	USBLS	5/07
Metals and Plastics	Providence-Fall River-Warwick MSA, RI-MA	Y	24190 FQ	30850 MW	40840 TQ	USBLS	5/07
Metals and Plastics	South Carolina	Y	20470 FQ	24810 MW	31670 TQ	USBLS	5/07
Metals and Plastics	Charleston-North Charleston MSA, SC	Y	22010 FQ	26860 MW	36330 TQ	USBLS	5/07
Metals and Plastics	Spartanburg MSA, SC	Y	21210 FQ	30080 MW	36320 TQ	USBLS	5/07
Metals and Plastics	South Dakota	Y	22334 FQ	25249 MW	28767 TQ	SDBLS	7/08-9/08
Metals and Plastics	Rapid City MSA, SD	Y	21016 FQ	23757 MW	26786 TQ	SDBLS	7/08-9/08
Metals and Plastics	Tennessee	Y	19770 FQ	22830 MW	28460 TQ	USBLS	5/07
Metals and Plastics	Nashville-Davidson-Murfreesboro MSA, TN	Y	20390 FQ	22290 MW	27410 TQ	USBLS	5/07
Metals and Plastics	Texas	Y	19350 FQ	23840 MW	31140 TQ	USBLS	5/07
Metals and Plastics	Austin-Round Rock MSA, TX	Y	19930 FQ	24540 MW	28460 TQ	USBLS	5/07
Metals and Plastics	Dallas-Fort Worth-Arlington MSA, TX	Y	18640 FQ	22630 MW	27970 TQ	USBLS	5/07
Metals and Plastics	El Paso MSA, TX	Y	13620 FQ	16040 MW	19110 TQ	USBLS	5/07

AE Average entry wage	**AW** Average wage paid	**FQ** First quartile wage	**LO** Lowest wage paid	**MTC** Median total compensation	**TCC** Total cash compensation
AER Average entry range	**AWR** Average wage range	**H** Hourly	**LR** Low end range	**MW** Median wage paid	**TQ** Third quartile wage
AEX Average experienced wage	**AXR** Average experienced range	**HI** Highest wage paid	**M** Monthly	**MWR** Median wage range	**W** Weekly
ATC Average total compensation	**D** Daily	**HR** High end range	**MCC** Median cash compensation	**S** See annotated source	**Y** Yearly

Occupation/Type/Industry	Location	Per	Low	Mid	High	Source	Date
Plating and Coating Machine Setter, Operator, and Tender							
Metals and Plastics	Houston-Sugar Land-Baytown MSA, TX	Y	19860 FQ	24760 MW	34330 TQ	USBLS	5/07
Metals and Plastics	San Antonio MSA, TX	Y	21170 FQ	24950 MW	30270 TQ	USBLS	5/07
Metals and Plastics	Utah	Y	22740 FQ	30260 MW	40910 TQ	USBLS	5/07
Metals and Plastics	Salt Lake City MSA, UT	Y	21910 FQ	28850 MW	36910 TQ	USBLS	5/07
Metals and Plastics	Virginia	Y	21940 FQ	26720 MW	33900 TQ	USBLS	5/07
Metals and Plastics	Richmond MSA, VA	Y	19710 FQ	25080 MW	32640 TQ	USBLS	5/07
Metals and Plastics	Virginia Beach-Norfolk-Newport News MSA, VA-NC	Y	25980 FQ	31450 MW	36620 TQ	USBLS	5/07
Metals and Plastics	Washington	H	11.14 FQ	14.06 MW	17.81 TQ	WABLS	3/08
Metals and Plastics	Seattle-Tacoma-Bellevue MSA, WA	Y	22640 FQ	28080 MW	35050 TQ	USBLS	5/07
Metals and Plastics	West Virginia	Y	33848 FQ	41685 MW	46470 TQ	WVBLS	7/08-9/08
Metals and Plastics	Wisconsin	Y	21950 FQ	26360 MW	31450 TQ	USBLS	5/07
Metals and Plastics	Milwaukee-Waukesha-West Allis MSA, WI	Y	22180 FQ	26300 MW	31300 TQ	USBLS	5/07
Metals and Plastics	Wyoming	Y	24848 FQ	29341 MW	33050 TQ	WYBLS	9/08
Metals and Plastics	Puerto Rico	Y	12520 FQ	13650 MW	14780 TQ	USBLS	5/07
Plumber, Pipefitter, and Steamfitter							
	Alabama	Y	26560 FQ	33130 MW	41340 TQ	USBLS	5/07
	Birmingham-Hoover MSA, AL	Y	28210 FQ	34450 MW	41700 TQ	USBLS	5/07
	Huntsville MSA, AL	Y	26150 FQ	31740 MW	41800 TQ	USBLS	5/07
	Tuscaloosa MSA, AL	Y	30370 FQ	34920 MW	41220 TQ	USBLS	5/07
	Alaska	Y	48650 FQ	61900 MW	72560 TQ	USBLS	5/07
	Anchorage MSA, AK	Y	47920 FQ	61210 MW	72190 TQ	USBLS	5/07
	Fairbanks MSA, AK	Y	56520 FQ	67070 MW	76600 TQ	USBLS	5/07
	Arizona	Y	29970 FQ	37840 MW	48470 TQ	USBLS	5/07
	Phoenix-Mesa-Scottsdale MSA, AZ	Y	29760 FQ	37990 MW	48830 TQ	USBLS	5/07
	Tucson MSA, AZ	Y	34570 FQ	39280 MW	47380 TQ	USBLS	5/07
	Yuma MSA, AZ	Y	20180 FQ	27080 MW	33430 TQ	USBLS	5/07
	Arkansas	Y	27280 FQ	34390 MW	41300 TQ	USBLS	5/07
	Fort Smith MSA, AR-OK	Y	27380 FQ	34000 MW	38640 TQ	USBLS	5/07
	Little Rock-North Little Rock MSA, AR	Y	29560 FQ	38470 MW	44380 TQ	USBLS	5/07
	California	H	17.19 FQ	23.10 MW	30.68 TQ	CABLS	1/08-3/08
	Los Angeles-Long Beach-Glendale PMSA, CA	H	15.86 FQ	21.55 MW	28.64 TQ	CABLS	1/08-3/08
	Oakland-Fremont-Hayward MSA, CA	H	21.67 FQ	28.57 MW	37.43 TQ	CABLS	1/08-3/08
	Riverside-San Bernardino-Ontario MSA, CA	H	14.66 FQ	19.02 MW	24.67 TQ	CABLS	1/08-3/08
	Sacramento-Arden Arcade-Roseville MSA, CA	H	17.43 FQ	23.06 MW	30.07 TQ	CABLS	1/08-3/08
	San Diego-Carlsbad-San Marcos MSA, CA	H	19.23 FQ	23.90 MW	30.59 TQ	CABLS	1/08-3/08
	San Francisco-San Mateo-Redwood PMSA, CA	H	20.70 FQ	29.96 MW	38.95 TQ	CABLS	1/08-3/08
	San Jose-Sunnyvale-Santa Clara MSA, CA	H	22.75 FQ	33.90 MW	44.10 TQ	CABLS	1/08-3/08
	Santa Ana-Anaheim-Irvine PMSA, CA	Y	34350 FQ	44680 MW	56610 TQ	USBLS	5/07
	Colorado	Y	34070 FQ	43260 MW	54740 TQ	USBLS	5/07
	Denver-Aurora MSA, CO	Y	34010 FQ	43090 MW	55330 TQ	USBLS	5/07
	Pueblo MSA, CO	Y	29810 FQ	43640 MW	49860 TQ	USBLS	5/07
	Connecticut	H	18.88 AE	27.45 MW		CTBLS	1/08-3/08
	Bridgeport-Stamford-Norwalk MSA, CT	Y	40490 FQ	55290 MW	64220 TQ	USBLS	5/07
	Hartford-West Hartford-East Hartford MSA, CT	Y	44230 FQ	52370 MW	63270 TQ	USBLS	5/07
	Delaware	Y	37780 FQ	48770 MW	64450 TQ	USBLS	5/07
	Dover MSA, DE	Y	34560 FQ	40160 MW	64520 TQ	USBLS	5/07
	Wilmington PMSA, DE-MD-NJ	Y	41660 FQ	53440 MW	69220 TQ	USBLS	5/07
	District of Columbia	Y	45000 FQ	54890 MW	66730 TQ	USBLS	5/07
	Washington-Arlington-Alexandria MSA, DC-VA-MD-WV	Y	38780 FQ	48050 MW	60640 TQ	USBLS	5/07

AE	Average entry wage	AW	Average wage paid	FQ	First quartile wage
AER	Average entry range	AWR	Average wage range	H	Hourly
AEX	Average experienced wage	AXR	Average experienced range	HI	Highest wage paid
ATC	Average total compensation	D	Daily	HR	High end range

LO	Lowest wage paid	MTC	Median total compensation
LR	Low end range	MW	Median wage paid
M	Monthly	MWR	Median wage range
MCC	Median cash compensation	S	See annotated source

TCC	Total cash compensation
TQ	Third quartile wage
W	Weekly
Y	Yearly

Occupation/Type/Industry	Location	Per	Low	Mid	High	Source	Date
Plumber, Pipefitter, and Steamfitter	Florida	Y	28590 FQ	35230 MW	42240 TQ	USBLS	5/07
	Cape Coral-Fort Myers MSA, FL	Y	29630 FQ	36450 MW	44130 TQ	USBLS	5/07
	Fort Lauderdale-Pompano Beach-Deerfield Beach PMSA, FL	Y	27260 FQ	36860 MW	47260 TQ	USBLS	5/07
	Jacksonville MSA, FL	Y	28890 FQ	35600 MW	41760 TQ	USBLS	5/07
	Miami-Fort Lauderdale-Miami Beach MSA, FL	Y	28760 FQ	37390 MW	46530 TQ	USBLS	5/07
	Orlando-Kissimmee MSA, FL	Y	28950 FQ	34760 MW	40110 TQ	USBLS	5/07
	Tampa-St. Petersburg-Clearwater MSA, FL	Y	27470 FQ	34390 MW	39660 TQ	USBLS	5/07
	West Palm Beach-Boca Raton-Boynton Beach PMSA, FL	Y	28160 FQ	35580 MW	44630 TQ	USBLS	5/07
	Georgia	Y	28410 FQ	35690 MW	46150 TQ	USBLS	5/07
	Atlanta-Sandy Springs-Marietta MSA, GA	Y	30170 FQ	37220 MW	50140 TQ	USBLS	5/07
	Macon MSA, GA	Y	36890 FQ	41400 MW	46590 TQ	USBLS	5/07
	Hawaii	Y	36080 FQ	47410 MW	60760 TQ	USBLS	5/07
	Honolulu MSA, HI	Y	38090 FQ	48240 MW	61570 TQ	USBLS	5/07
	Idaho	Y	28650 FQ	38080 MW	48930 TQ	USBLS	5/07
	Boise City-Nampa MSA, ID	Y	29520 FQ	37880 MW	50760 TQ	USBLS	5/07
	Illinois	Y	49230 FQ	69330 MW	81370 TQ	USBLS	5/07
	Chicago-Naperville-Joliet MSA, IL-IN-WI	Y	51010 FQ	70820 MW	82490 TQ	USBLS	5/07
	Peoria MSA, IL	Y	49210 FQ	64840 MW	75780 TQ	USBLS	5/07
	Indiana	Y	38040 FQ	50770 MW	62030 TQ	USBLS	5/07
	Gary PMSA, IN	Y	52110 FQ	62240 MW	75020 TQ	USBLS	5/07
	Indianapolis-Carmel MSA, IN	Y	38460 FQ	48630 MW	58200 TQ	USBLS	5/07
	South Bend-Mishawaka MSA, IN-MI	Y	40010 FQ	53620 MW	61340 TQ	USBLS	5/07
	Iowa	Y	31370 FQ	41970 MW	56590 TQ	USBLS	5/07
	Des Moines-West Des Moines MSA, IA	Y	32040 FQ	42480 MW	61180 TQ	USBLS	5/07
	Kansas	Y	32980 FQ	42280 MW	56920 TQ	USBLS	5/07
	Wichita MSA, KS	Y	33870 FQ	42240 MW	54280 TQ	USBLS	5/07
	Kentucky	Y	33736 FQ	42394 MW	56963 TQ	KYBLS	2008
	Louisville-Jefferson County MSA, KY-IN	Y	34750 FQ	43070 MW	58810 TQ	USBLS	5/07
	Louisiana	H	16.80 FQ	20.34 MW	23.03 TQ	LABLS	1/08-3/08
	Baton Rouge MSA, LA	Y	39480 FQ	44270 MW	48830 TQ	USBLS	5/07
	New Orleans-Metairie-Kenner MSA, LA	Y	30460 FQ	38720 MW	45550 TQ	USBLS	5/07
	Maine	Y	34060 FQ	42430 MW	48200 TQ	USBLS	5/07
	Portland-South Portland-Biddeford MSA, ME	Y	31530 FQ	39280 MW	46280 TQ	USBLS	5/07
	Maryland	Y		49500 MW		MDBLS	3/08
	Baltimore-Towson MSA, MD	Y	39090 FQ	47760 MW	58740 TQ	USBLS	5/07
	Bethesda-Gaithersburg-Frederick PMSA, MD	Y	36520 FQ	46210 MW	58240 TQ	USBLS	5/07
	Massachusetts	Y	41510 FQ	55980 MW	70450 TQ	USBLS	5/07
	Boston-Cambridge-Quincy NECTA, MA	Y	46430 FQ	62450 MW	83520 TQ	USBLS	5/07
	Worcester MSA, MA-CT	Y	39370 FQ	48620 MW	57770 TQ	USBLS	5/07
	Michigan	Y	39120 FQ	55700 MW	69420 TQ	USBLS	5/07
	Detroit-Warren-Livonia MSA, MI	Y	46270 FQ	63270 MW	74170 TQ	USBLS	5/07
	Grand Rapids-Wyoming MSA, MI	Y	36250 FQ	50620 MW	59260 TQ	USBLS	5/07
	Lansing-East Lansing MSA, MI	Y	43440 FQ	59840 MW	69380 TQ	USBLS	5/07
	Warren-Troy-Farmington Hills PMSA, MI	Y	43960 FQ	61600 MW	73310 TQ	USBLS	5/07
	Minnesota	Y	43862 FQ	62484 MW	77206 TQ	MNBLS	10/08-12/08
	Duluth-Superior MSA, MN-WI	Y	34524 FQ	48625 MW	70883 TQ	MNBLS	10/08-12/08
	Minneapolis-Saint Paul MSA, MN-WI	Y	52598 FQ	70272 MW	80041 TQ	MNBLS	10/08-12/08
	Rochester MSA, MN	Y	40757 FQ	64915 MW	77246 TQ	MNBLS	10/08-12/08
	Mississippi	Y	25750 FQ	31470 MW	41030 TQ	USBLS	5/07
	Gulfport-Biloxi MSA, MS	Y	28770 FQ	34590 MW	42700 TQ	USBLS	5/07
	Jackson MSA, MS	Y	22340 FQ	27990 MW	36560 TQ	USBLS	5/07
	Missouri	Y	37480 FQ	53140 MW	67950 TQ	USBLS	5/07

AE	Average entry wage	AW	Average wage paid	FQ	First quartile wage	LO	Lowest wage paid	MTC	Median total compensation	TCC	Total cash compensation
AER	Average entry range	AWR	Average wage range	H	Hourly	LR	Low end range	MW	Median wage paid	TQ	Third quartile wage
AEX	Average experienced wage	AXR	Average experienced range	HI	Highest wage paid	M	Monthly	MWR	Median wage range	W	Weekly
ATC	Average total compensation	D	Daily	HR	High end range	MCC	Median cash compensation	S	See annotated source	Y	Yearly

Occupation/Type/Industry	Location	Per	Low	Mid	High	Source	Date
Plumber, Pipefitter, and Steamfitter	Kansas City MSA, MO-KS	Y	38510 FQ	53880 MW	70760 TQ	USBLS	5/07
	St. Louis MSA, MO-IL	Y	50750 FQ	63810 MW	72590 TQ	USBLS	5/07
	Montana	Y	34560 FQ	44610 MW	53040 TQ	USBLS	5/07
	Billings MSA, MT	Y	38550 FQ	44890 MW	50410 TQ	USBLS	5/07
	Great Falls MSA, MT	Y	33050 FQ	40890 MW	47670 TQ	USBLS	5/07
	Nebraska	Y	34520 FQ	47770 MW	58440 TQ	USBLS	5/07
	Omaha-Council Bluffs MSA, NE-IA	Y	44900 FQ	55170 MW	61830 TQ	USBLS	5/07
	Nevada	H	17.99 FQ	22.92 MW	32.57 TQ	NVBLS	5/08
	Carson City MSA, NV	H	20.83 FQ	27.02 MW	35.45 TQ	NVBLS	5/08
	Las Vegas-Paradise MSA, NV	H	17.86 FQ	22.52 MW	32.12 TQ	NVBLS	5/08
	New Hampshire	H	15.27 AE	20.62 MW	24.49 AEX	NHBLS	6/08
	Manchester MSA, NH	Y	36840 FQ	49660 MW	57580 TQ	USBLS	5/07
	Nashua NECTA, NH-MA	Y	33470 FQ	40600 MW	55500 TQ	USBLS	5/07
	New Jersey	Y	41050 FQ	54370 MW	76300 TQ	USBLS	5/07
	Camden PMSA, NJ	Y	43070 FQ	56650 MW	77980 TQ	USBLS	5/07
	Edison PMSA, NJ	Y	45830 FQ	58880 MW	86410 TQ	USBLS	5/07
	Newark-Union PMSA, NJ-PA	Y	41390 FQ	54810 MW	71430 TQ	USBLS	5/07
	New Mexico	Y	28320 FQ	36510 MW	49070 TQ	USBLS	5/07
	Albuquerque MSA, NM	Y	29310 FQ	39450 MW	53960 TQ	USBLS	5/07
	New York	Y	38610 FQ	54950 MW	73950 TQ	USBLS	5/07
	Albany-Schenectady-Troy MSA, NY	Y	37090 FQ	48410 MW	60420 TQ	USBLS	5/07
	Buffalo-Niagara Falls MSA, NY	Y	39270 FQ	52460 MW	60890 TQ	USBLS	5/07
	Nassau-Suffolk PMSA, NY	Y	39980 FQ	59880 MW	88370 TQ	USBLS	5/07
	New York-Northern New Jersey-Long Island MSA, NY-NJ-PA	Y	40440 FQ	57050 MW	80150 TQ	USBLS	5/07
	North Carolina	Y	28980 FQ	34850 MW	41200 TQ	USBLS	5/07
	Charlotte-Gastonia-Concord MSA, NC-SC	Y	30330 FQ	35890 MW	42170 TQ	USBLS	5/07
	Raleigh-Cary MSA, NC	Y	33620 FQ	39460 MW	48110 TQ	USBLS	5/07
	North Dakota	Y	32400 FQ	43790 MW	54310 TQ	USBLS	5/07
	Fargo MSA, ND-MN	Y	39220 FQ	45100 MW	51440 TQ	USBLS	5/07
	Ohio	Y	34480 FQ	46580 MW	61820 TQ	USBLS	5/07
	Cincinnati-Middletown MSA, OH-KY-IN	Y	34590 FQ	45390 MW	56610 TQ	USBLS	5/07
	Cleveland-Elyria-Mentor MSA, OH	Y	39220 FQ	58520 MW	73230 TQ	USBLS	5/07
	Columbus MSA, OH	Y	35010 FQ	43750 MW	56380 TQ	USBLS	5/07
	Dayton MSA, OH	Y	36490 FQ	46630 MW	57980 TQ	USBLS	5/07
	Mansfield MSA, OH	Y	42140 FQ	57070 MW	68500 TQ	USBLS	5/07
	Oklahoma	Y	27450 FQ	36190 MW	45270 TQ	USBLS	5/07
	Oklahoma City MSA, OK	Y	30750 FQ	40060 MW	48370 TQ	USBLS	5/07
	Tulsa MSA, OK	Y	26740 FQ	35910 MW	43680 TQ	USBLS	5/07
	Oregon	H	21.35 FQ	28.83 MW	36.34 TQ	ORBLS	5/08
	Portland-Vancouver-Beaverton MSA, OR-WA	Y	41900 FQ	60470 MW	75010 TQ	USBLS	5/07
	Pennsylvania	Y	39670 FQ	50860 MW	65160 TQ	USBLS	5/07
	Allentown-Bethlehem-Easton MSA, PA-NJ	Y	47190 FQ	64840 MW	73170 TQ	USBLS	5/07
	Philadelphia-Camden-Wilmington MSA, PA-NJ-DE-MD	Y	42090 FQ	54020 MW	71930 TQ	USBLS	5/07
	Pittsburgh MSA, PA	Y	46400 FQ	57810 MW	68440 TQ	USBLS	5/07
	Rhode Island	Y	41750 FQ	49570 MW	62150 TQ	USBLS	5/07
	Providence-Fall River-Warwick MSA, RI-MA	Y	41650 FQ	50200 MW	62590 TQ	USBLS	5/07
	South Carolina	Y	29200 FQ	34670 MW	39910 TQ	USBLS	5/07
	Charleston-North Charleston MSA, SC	Y	29210 FQ	34700 MW	39110 TQ	USBLS	5/07
	Columbia MSA, SC	Y	31940 FQ	36060 MW	39960 TQ	USBLS	5/07
	South Dakota	Y	29951 FQ	36139 MW	43893 TQ	SDBLS	7/08-9/08
	Sioux Falls MSA, SD	Y	31206 FQ	37537 MW	44279 TQ	SDBLS	7/08-9/08
	Tennessee	Y	27500 FQ	36360 MW	47020 TQ	USBLS	5/07
	Johnson City MSA, TN	Y	25970 FQ	31010 MW	36360 TQ	USBLS	5/07
	Memphis MSA, TN-MS-AR	Y	28300 FQ	36560 MW	48070 TQ	USBLS	5/07
	Nashville-Davidson-Murfreesboro MSA, TN	Y	26940 FQ	36980 MW	46780 TQ	USBLS	5/07
	Texas	Y	31140 FQ	39690 MW	49190 TQ	USBLS	5/07

AE Average entry wage	AW Average wage paid	FQ First quartile wage	LO Lowest wage paid	MTC Median total compensation	TCC Total cash compensation
AER Average entry range	AWR Average wage range	H Hourly	LR Low end range	MW Median wage paid	TQ Third quartile wage
AEX Average experienced wage	AXR Average experienced range	HI Highest wage paid	M Monthly	MWR Median wage range	W Weekly
ATC Average total compensation	D Daily	HR High end range	MCC Median cash compensation	S See annotated source	Y Yearly

Occupation/Type/Industry	Location	Per	Low	Mid	High	Source	Date
Plumber, Pipefitter, and Steamfitter	Austin-Round Rock MSA, TX	Y	33590 FQ	42460 MW	52910 TQ	USBLS	5/07
	Corpus Christi MSA, TX	Y	28840 FQ	35050 MW	44190 TQ	USBLS	5/07
	Dallas-Fort Worth-Arlington MSA, TX	Y	31810 FQ	42370 MW	53180 TQ	USBLS	5/07
	El Paso MSA, TX	Y	26540 FQ	30580 MW	35880 TQ	USBLS	5/07
	Houston-Sugar Land-Baytown MSA, TX	Y	35550 FQ	43160 MW	50700 TQ	USBLS	5/07
	San Antonio MSA, TX	Y	29950 FQ	36120 MW	41930 TQ	USBLS	5/07
	Utah	Y	35200 FQ	44180 MW	54370 TQ	USBLS	5/07
	St. George MSA, UT	Y	32630 FQ	43040 MW	48250 TQ	USBLS	5/07
	Salt Lake City MSA, UT	Y	34520 FQ	44820 MW	54830 TQ	USBLS	5/07
	Vermont	Y	32930 FQ	39540 MW	48190 TQ	USBLS	5/07
	Burlington-South Burlington MSA, VT	Y	35130 FQ	43520 MW	51420 TQ	USBLS	5/07
	Virginia	Y	32600 FQ	39190 MW	47290 TQ	USBLS	5/07
	Lynchburg MSA, VA	Y	21790 FQ	33830 MW	37930 TQ	USBLS	5/07
	Richmond MSA, VA	Y	33140 FQ	38810 MW	46180 TQ	USBLS	5/07
	Virginia Beach-Norfolk-Newport News MSA, VA-NC	Y	32100 FQ	38060 MW	45170 TQ	USBLS	5/07
	Washington	H	18.27 FQ	24.70 MW	31.52 TQ	WABLS	3/08
	Seattle-Tacoma-Bellevue MSA, WA	Y	40750 FQ	53470 MW	69400 TQ	USBLS	5/07
	West Virginia	Y	30671 FQ	39706 MW	58316 TQ	WVBLS	7/08-9/08
	Charleston MSA, WV	Y	37310 FQ	54410 MW	62180 TQ	USBLS	5/07
	Wisconsin	Y	42310 FQ	58050 MW	69470 TQ	USBLS	5/07
	Milwaukee-Waukesha-West Allis MSA, WI	Y	51550 FQ	65660 MW	74310 TQ	USBLS	5/07
	Wyoming	Y	30690 FQ	38254 MW	50387 TQ	WYBLS	9/08
	Cheyenne MSA, WY	Y	28982 FQ	32028 MW	37932 TQ	WYBLS	9/08
	Puerto Rico	Y	15480 FQ	17820 MW	20540 TQ	USBLS	5/07
	Aguadilla-Isabela-San Sebastian MSA, PR	Y	13720 FQ	16230 MW	18190 TQ	USBLS	5/07
	San Juan-Caguas-Guaynabo MSA, PR	Y	15810 FQ	18230 MW	22170 TQ	USBLS	5/07
	Virgin Islands	Y	34560 FQ	42150 MW	48730 TQ	USBLS	5/07
	Guam	Y	26110 FQ	28600 MW	31280 TQ	USBLS	5/07
Podiatrist	Alabama	Y	93790 FQ	126710 MW		USBLS	5/07
	Arizona	Y	63640 FQ	111630 MW	126750 TQ	USBLS	5/07
	Phoenix-Mesa-Scottsdale MSA, AZ	Y	103870 FQ	118350 MW	129710 TQ	USBLS	5/07
	Tucson MSA, AZ	Y	45070 FQ	50740 MW	63450 TQ	USBLS	5/07
	California	H	26.68 FQ	42.65 MW		CABLS	1/08-3/08
	Los Angeles-Long Beach-Glendale PMSA, CA	H	26.40 FQ	30.18 MW	48.16 TQ	CABLS	1/08-3/08
	Oakland-Fremont-Hayward MSA, CA	H	49.37 FQ	56.50 MW		CABLS	1/08-3/08
	Sacramento-Arden Arcade-Roseville MSA, CA	H	32.45 FQ	44.73 MW	50.88 TQ	CABLS	1/08-3/08
	San Diego-Carlsbad-San Marcos MSA, CA	H	22.54 FQ	30.54 MW	66.32 TQ	CABLS	1/08-3/08
	San Jose-Sunnyvale-Santa Clara MSA, CA	H	43.30 FQ	61.69 MW		CABLS	1/08-3/08
	Santa Ana-Anaheim-Irvine PMSA, CA	Y	88260 FQ	121650 MW		USBLS	5/07
	Colorado	Y	48810 FQ	112840 MW		USBLS	5/07
	Connecticut	H	27.00 AE	61.85 MW		CTBLS	1/08-3/08
	Bridgeport-Stamford-Norwalk MSA, CT	Y	66990 FQ	141950 MW		USBLS	5/07
	Hartford-West Hartford-East Hartford MSA, CT	Y	41100 FQ	46570 MW	117260 TQ	USBLS	5/07
	Delaware	Y	70250 FQ	78620 MW	109880 TQ	USBLS	5/07
	Wilmington PMSA, DE-MD-NJ	Y	69980 FQ	79800 MW	111910 TQ	USBLS	5/07
	Washington-Arlington-Alexandria MSA, DC-VA-MD-WV	Y	89260 FQ	116410 MW		USBLS	5/07
	Florida	Y	53520 FQ	103570 MW		USBLS	5/07
	Jacksonville MSA, FL	Y	89370 FQ	116400 MW		USBLS	5/07
	Miami-Fort Lauderdale-Miami Beach MSA, FL	Y	36050 FQ	90720 MW	136340 TQ	USBLS	5/07

AE	Average entry wage	AW	Average wage paid	FQ	First quartile wage
AER	Average entry range	AWR	Average wage range	H	Hourly
AEX	Average experienced wage	AXR	Average experienced range	HI	Highest wage paid
ATC	Average total compensation	D	Daily	HR	High end range

LO	Lowest wage paid	MTC	Median total compensation
LR	Low end range	MW	Median wage paid
M	Monthly	MWR	Median wage range
MCC	Median cash compensation	S	See annotated source

TCC	Total cash compensation
TQ	Third quartile wage
W	Weekly
Y	Yearly

Occupation/Type/Industry	Location	Per	Low	Mid	High	Source	Date
Podiatrist	Tampa-St. Petersburg-Clearwater MSA, FL	Y	78460 FQ	98520 MW	131260 TQ	USBLS	5/07
	West Palm Beach-Boca Raton-Boynton Beach PMSA, FL	Y	111340 FQ			USBLS	5/07
	Georgia	Y	95180 FQ			USBLS	5/07
	Augusta-Richmond County MSA, GA-SC	Y	72060 FQ	78680 MW	88930 TQ	USBLS	5/07
	Illinois	Y	82570 FQ	104380 MW	127230 TQ	USBLS	5/07
	Chicago-Naperville-Joliet MSA, IL-IN-WI	Y	66380 FQ	108260 MW	132370 TQ	USBLS	5/07
	Indiana	Y	86950 FQ	116270 MW		USBLS	5/07
	Iowa	Y	66620 FQ	102130 MW	143640 TQ	USBLS	5/07
	Kansas	Y	111120 FQ	130710 MW		USBLS	5/07
	Kentucky	Y	139378 FQ			KYBLS	2008
	Louisville-Jefferson County MSA, KY-IN	Y	118230 FQ			USBLS	5/07
	Louisiana	Y		162922 AW		LABLS	1/08-3/08
	Maine	Y	87620 FQ	101210 MW	140820 TQ	USBLS	5/07
	Maryland	Y		138300 MW		MDBLS	3/08
	Baltimore-Towson MSA, MD	Y	97680 FQ	130100 MW		USBLS	5/07
	Massachusetts	Y	77170 FQ	98020 MW	142370 TQ	USBLS	5/07
	Boston-Cambridge-Quincy NECTA, MA	Y	80940 FQ	101230 MW		USBLS	5/07
	Michigan	Y	131080 FQ			USBLS	5/07
	Minnesota	Y	117166 FQ	164989 AW		MNBLS	10/08-12/08
	Minneapolis-Saint Paul MSA, MN-WI	Y		187557 AW		MNBLS	10/08-12/08
	Missouri	Y	93520 FQ	119160 MW		USBLS	5/07
	St. Louis MSA, MO-IL	Y	91810 FQ	99390 MW	144740 TQ	USBLS	5/07
	Montana	Y	76970 FQ			USBLS	5/07
	Nebraska	Y	70750 FQ	83120 MW		USBLS	5/07
	Nevada	H	35.89 FQ	56.62 MW	64.13 TQ	NVBLS	5/08
	Las Vegas-Paradise MSA, NV	H	54.08 FQ	59.39 MW	64.69 TQ	NVBLS	5/08
	New Jersey	Y	83570 FQ	102240 MW		USBLS	5/07
	Camden PMSA, NJ	Y	88420 FQ	122850 MW		USBLS	5/07
	Edison PMSA, NJ	Y	83550 FQ	107330 MW	129880 TQ	USBLS	5/07
	Newark-Union PMSA, NJ-PA	Y	98110 FQ			USBLS	5/07
	New Mexico	Y	46250 FQ	79960 MW		USBLS	5/07
	New York	Y	95810 FQ	123490 MW		USBLS	5/07
	Albany-Schenectady-Troy MSA, NY	Y	90250 FQ	129170 MW		USBLS	5/07
	Nassau-Suffolk PMSA, NY	Y	99420 FQ			USBLS	5/07
	New York-Northern New Jersey-Long Island MSA, NY-NJ-PA	Y	92750 FQ	122140 MW		USBLS	5/07
	North Carolina	Y	93430 FQ	114850 MW		USBLS	5/07
	Ohio	Y	85130 FQ	107080 MW	122950 TQ	USBLS	5/07
	Cincinnati-Middletown MSA, OH-KY-IN	Y	92400 FQ	114160 MW		USBLS	5/07
	Cleveland-Elyria-Mentor MSA, OH	Y	94060 FQ	109150 MW	121150 TQ	USBLS	5/07
	Columbus MSA, OH	Y	90840 FQ	100960 MW	113020 TQ	USBLS	5/07
	Oklahoma	Y	35480 FQ	104760 MW		USBLS	5/07
	Pennsylvania	Y	46840 FQ	77180 MW	129240 TQ	USBLS	5/07
	Allentown-Bethlehem-Easton MSA, PA-NJ	Y	113280 FQ			USBLS	5/07
	Philadelphia-Camden-Wilmington MSA, PA-NJ-DE-MD	Y	48790 FQ	81640 MW	138830 TQ	USBLS	5/07
	Pittsburgh MSA, PA	Y	45290 FQ	50570 MW	97250 TQ	USBLS	5/07
	Providence-Fall River-Warwick MSA, RI-MA	Y	52930 FQ	77500 MW	128560 TQ	USBLS	5/07
	South Carolina	Y	75760 FQ	99270 MW	139020 TQ	USBLS	5/07
	Columbia MSA, SC	Y	100940 FQ	125610 MW	142040 TQ	USBLS	5/07
	South Dakota	Y	88152 FQ	101584 MW	133987 TQ	SDBLS	7/08-9/08
	Tennessee	Y	40010 FQ	119090 MW		USBLS	5/07
	Texas	Y	97920 FQ	113650 MW	137570 TQ	USBLS	5/07
	Austin-Round Rock MSA, TX	Y	38340 FQ	115980 MW	133510 TQ	USBLS	5/07
	Dallas-Fort Worth-Arlington MSA, TX	Y	100620 FQ	143630 MW		USBLS	5/07
	Houston-Sugar Land-Baytown MSA, TX	Y	79130 FQ	115650 MW		USBLS	5/07

AE Average entry wage	**AW** Average wage paid	**FQ** First quartile wage	**LO** Lowest wage paid	**MTC** Median total compensation	**TCC** Total cash compensation
AER Average entry range	**AWR** Average wage range	**H** Hourly	**LR** Low end range	**MW** Median wage paid	**TQ** Third quartile wage
AEX Average experienced wage	**AXR** Average experienced range	**HI** Highest wage paid	**M** Monthly	**MWR** Median wage range	**W** Weekly
ATC Average total compensation	**D** Daily	**HR** High end range	**MCC** Median cash compensation	**S** See annotated source	**Y** Yearly

Occupation/Type/Industry	Location	Per	Low	Mid	High	Source	Date
Podiatrist	San Antonio MSA, TX	Y	100800 FQ	108850 MW	118390 TQ	USBLS	5/07
	Utah	Y	43470 FQ	48560 MW	58810 TQ	USBLS	5/07
	Salt Lake City MSA, UT	Y	49700 FQ	54040 MW	58520 TQ	USBLS	5/07
	Virginia	Y	89660 FQ	112100 MW		USBLS	5/07
	Virginia Beach-Norfolk- Newport News MSA, VA-NC	Y	136610 FQ			USBLS	5/07
	Washington	H	56.04 FQ	66.41 MW		WABLS	3/08
	Seattle-Tacoma-Bellevue MSA, WA	Y	113130 FQ	130390 MW		USBLS	5/07
	Wisconsin	Y	83590 FQ	137810 MW		USBLS	5/07
	Milwaukee-Waukesha-West Allis MSA, WI	Y	81900 FQ	117240 MW		USBLS	5/07
	Wyoming	Y	101041 FQ	114208 MW	137741 TQ	WYBLS	9/08
Police, Fire, and Ambulance Dispatcher	Alabama	Y	20180 FQ	25090 MW	31120 TQ	USBLS	5/07
	Birmingham-Hoover MSA, AL	Y	16240 FQ	26050 MW	33290 TQ	USBLS	5/07
	Alaska	Y	34890 FQ	38820 MW	44060 TQ	USBLS	5/07
	Anchorage MSA, AK	Y	35320 FQ	38260 MW	40960 TQ	USBLS	5/07
	Arizona	Y	29180 FQ	34960 MW	41120 TQ	USBLS	5/07
	Phoenix-Mesa-Scottsdale MSA, AZ	Y	32040 FQ	36940 MW	43160 TQ	USBLS	5/07
	Tucson MSA, AZ	Y	32250 FQ	36690 MW	42770 TQ	USBLS	5/07
	Yuma MSA, AZ	Y	23700 FQ	27370 MW	33050 TQ	USBLS	5/07
	Arkansas	Y	19060 FQ	22920 MW	27810 TQ	USBLS	5/07
	Little Rock-North Little Rock MSA, AR	Y	22440 FQ	26190 MW	31190 TQ	USBLS	5/07
	California	H	18.46 FQ	24.00 MW	29.52 TQ	CABLS	1/08-3/08
	Fresno MSA, CA	H	13.99 FQ	17.37 MW	20.69 TQ	CABLS	1/08-3/08
	Los Angeles-Long Beach- Glendale PMSA, CA	H	18.53 FQ	22.91 MW	28.44 TQ	CABLS	1/08-3/08
	Oakland-Fremont-Hayward MSA, CA	H	22.99 FQ	29.91 MW	34.80 TQ	CABLS	1/08-3/08
	Riverside-San Bernardino- Ontario MSA, CA	H	16.45 FQ	21.02 MW	24.20 TQ	CABLS	1/08-3/08
	Sacramento-Arden Arcade- Roseville MSA, CA	H	20.30 FQ	23.37 MW	26.90 TQ	CABLS	1/08-3/08
	San Diego-Carlsbad-San Marcos MSA, CA	H	19.34 FQ	23.74 MW	28.00 TQ	CABLS	1/08-3/08
	San Francisco-San Mateo- Redwood PMSA, CA	H	22.76 FQ	26.34 MW	33.21 TQ	CABLS	1/08-3/08
	San Jose-Sunnyvale-Santa Clara MSA, CA	H	27.48 FQ	34.08 MW	40.18 TQ	CABLS	1/08-3/08
	Santa Ana-Anaheim-Irvine PMSA, CA	Y	42950 FQ	54280 MW	60330 TQ	USBLS	5/07
	Colorado	Y	33790 FQ	38930 MW	46120 TQ	USBLS	5/07
	Denver-Aurora MSA, CO	Y	35290 FQ	40560 MW	47190 TQ	USBLS	5/07
	Connecticut	H	14.56 AE	19.16 MW		CTBLS	1/08-3/08
	Bridgeport-Stamford-Norwalk MSA, CT	Y	35700 FQ	41820 MW	47330 TQ	USBLS	5/07
	Hartford-West Hartford-East Hartford MSA, CT	Y	31650 FQ	42230 MW	48540 TQ	USBLS	5/07
	New Haven MSA, CT	Y	33790 FQ	38040 MW	43690 TQ	USBLS	5/07
	Waterbury MSA, CT	Y	34620 FQ	37560 MW	41930 TQ	USBLS	5/07
	Delaware	Y	29620 FQ	33980 MW	40700 TQ	USBLS	5/07
	Wilmington PMSA, DE-MD- NJ	Y	30250 FQ	35150 MW	42910 TQ	USBLS	5/07
	District of Columbia	Y	35780 FQ	43960 MW	56730 TQ	USBLS	5/07
	Washington-Arlington- Alexandria MSA, DC-VA- MD-WV	Y	33930 FQ	40130 MW	51200 TQ	USBLS	5/07
	Florida	Y	27770 FQ	33150 MW	40950 TQ	USBLS	5/07
	Fort Lauderdale-Pompano Beach-Deerfield Beach PMSA, FL	Y	32780 FQ	38750 MW	46810 TQ	USBLS	5/07
	Jacksonville MSA, FL	Y	27890 FQ	31570 MW	37150 TQ	USBLS	5/07
	Lakeland MSA, FL	Y	25290 FQ	28910 MW	34010 TQ	USBLS	5/07
	Miami-Fort Lauderdale-Miami Beach MSA, FL	Y	34250 FQ	40620 MW	49950 TQ	USBLS	5/07
	Orlando-Kissimmee MSA, FL	Y	27270 FQ	31880 MW	38710 TQ	USBLS	5/07
	Tampa-St. Petersburg- Clearwater MSA, FL	Y	28300 FQ	32660 MW	40560 TQ	USBLS	5/07

AE	Average entry wage	AW	Average wage paid	FQ	First quartile wage
AER	Average entry range	AWR	Average wage range	H	Hourly
AEX	Average experienced wage	AXR	Average experienced range	HI	Highest wage paid
ATC	Average total compensation	D	Daily	HR	High end range

LO	Lowest wage paid	MTC	Median total compensation	TCC	Total cash compensation
LR	Low end range	MW	Median wage paid	TQ	Third quartile wage
M	Monthly	MWR	Median wage range	W	Weekly
MCC	Median cash compensation	S	See annotated source	Y	Yearly

Occupation/Type/Industry	Location	Per	Low	Mid	High	Source	Date
Police, Fire, and Ambulance Dispatcher	West Palm Beach-Boca Raton-Boynton Beach PMSA, FL	Y	34590 FQ	41580 MW	50290 TQ	USBLS	5/07
	Georgia	Y	22270 FQ	27220 MW	31800 TQ	USBLS	5/07
	Atlanta-Sandy Springs-Marietta MSA, GA	Y	26340 FQ	30340 MW	35150 TQ	USBLS	5/07
	Augusta-Richmond County MSA, GA-SC	Y	22640 FQ	26750 MW	30310 TQ	USBLS	5/07
	Hawaii	Y	30750 FQ	37690 MW	44690 TQ	USBLS	5/07
	Honolulu MSA, HI	Y	34180 FQ	39480 MW	45910 TQ	USBLS	5/07
	Idaho	Y	26460 FQ	31750 MW	41530 TQ	USBLS	5/07
	Boise City-Nampa MSA, ID	Y	29760 FQ	37740 MW	47600 TQ	USBLS	5/07
	Illinois	Y	29800 FQ	39560 MW	47530 TQ	USBLS	5/07
	Chicago-Naperville-Joliet MSA, IL-IN-WI	Y	31330 FQ	41390 MW	49250 TQ	USBLS	5/07
	Peoria MSA, IL	Y	27150 FQ	39640 MW	48060 TQ	USBLS	5/07
	Indiana	Y	23360 FQ	28370 MW	33540 TQ	USBLS	5/07
	Gary PMSA, IN	Y	18230 FQ	25370 MW	31010 TQ	USBLS	5/07
	Indianapolis-Carmel MSA, IN	Y	25690 FQ	30520 MW	36700 TQ	USBLS	5/07
	Iowa	Y	26890 FQ	31280 MW	37600 TQ	USBLS	5/07
	Des Moines-West Des Moines MSA, IA	Y	27950 FQ	35070 MW	48420 TQ	USBLS	5/07
	Kansas	Y	23050 FQ	27830 MW	33100 TQ	USBLS	5/07
	Wichita MSA, KS	Y	26210 FQ	29100 MW	32400 TQ	USBLS	5/07
	Kentucky	Y	22025 FQ	27997 MW	36943 TQ	KYBLS	2008
	Louisville-Jefferson County MSA, KY-IN	Y	27040 FQ	33560 MW	41450 TQ	USBLS	5/07
	Louisiana	H	9.36 FQ	11.72 MW	14.74 TQ	LABLS	1/08-3/08
	Baton Rouge MSA, LA	Y	20380 FQ	26470 MW	34560 TQ	USBLS	5/07
	Houma-Bayou Cane-Thibodaux MSA, LA	Y	20430 FQ	23810 MW	28630 TQ	USBLS	5/07
	New Orleans-Metairie-Kenner MSA, LA	Y	22950 FQ	28370 MW	34350 TQ	USBLS	5/07
	Maine	Y	27230 FQ	32680 MW	37600 TQ	USBLS	5/07
	Portland-South Portland-Biddeford MSA, ME	Y	31490 FQ	35780 MW	39500 TQ	USBLS	5/07
	Maryland	Y		36300 MW		MDBLS	3/08
	Baltimore-Towson MSA, MD	Y	30040 FQ	35220 MW	41290 TQ	USBLS	5/07
	Bethesda-Gaithersburg-Frederick PMSA, MD	Y	35580 FQ	40800 MW	48230 TQ	USBLS	5/07
	Hagerstown-Martinsburg MSA, MD-WV	Y	22990 FQ	27220 MW	30880 TQ	USBLS	5/07
	Massachusetts	Y	31560 FQ	36230 MW	41460 TQ	USBLS	5/07
	Boston-Cambridge-Quincy NECTA, MA	Y	34340 FQ	39140 MW	46100 TQ	USBLS	5/07
	Worcester MSA, MA-CT	Y	30180 FQ	33040 MW	36640 TQ	USBLS	5/07
	Michigan	Y	32420 FQ	37770 MW	43750 TQ	USBLS	5/07
	Detroit-Warren-Livonia MSA, MI	Y	35770 FQ	41130 MW	46340 TQ	USBLS	5/07
	Grand Rapids-Wyoming MSA, MI	Y	32870 FQ	37540 MW	44280 TQ	USBLS	5/07
	Warren-Troy-Farmington Hills PMSA, MI	Y	35730 FQ	40990 MW	46330 TQ	USBLS	5/07
	Minnesota	Y	36063 FQ	42121 MW	49104 TQ	MNBLS	10/08-12/08
	Duluth-Superior MSA, MN-WI	Y	40153 FQ	45607 MW	50832 TQ	MNBLS	10/08-12/08
	Minneapolis-Saint Paul MSA, MN-WI	Y	39071 FQ	46086 MW	52372 TQ	MNBLS	10/08-12/08
	Mississippi	Y	19330 FQ	22620 MW	25920 TQ	USBLS	5/07
	Jackson MSA, MS	Y	21570 FQ	23580 MW	25800 TQ	USBLS	5/07
	Missouri	Y	20540 FQ	27280 MW	35210 TQ	USBLS	5/07
	Joplin MSA, MO	Y	22120 FQ	25270 MW	31320 TQ	USBLS	5/07
	Kansas City MSA, MO-KS	Y	27090 FQ	32850 MW	40200 TQ	USBLS	5/07
	St. Louis MSA, MO-IL	Y	29880 FQ	35040 MW	40350 TQ	USBLS	5/07
	Montana	Y	23260 FQ	27360 MW	31750 TQ	USBLS	5/07
	Billings MSA, MT	Y	27790 FQ	33730 MW	40320 TQ	USBLS	5/07
	Nebraska	Y	22110 FQ	25880 MW	31280 TQ	USBLS	5/07
	Lincoln MSA, NE	Y	28060 FQ	34370 MW	40300 TQ	USBLS	5/07
	Omaha-Council Bluffs MSA, NE-IA	Y	26100 FQ	29460 MW	35230 TQ	USBLS	5/07
	Nevada	H	18.52 FQ	22.97 MW	28.51 TQ	NVBLS	5/08
	Las Vegas-Paradise MSA, NV	H	19.89 FQ	24.77 MW	30.31 TQ	NVBLS	5/08
	Reno-Sparks MSA, NV	H	20.26 FQ	23.50 MW	27.49 TQ	NVBLS	5/08

AE Average entry wage	**AW** Average wage paid	**FQ** First quartile wage	**LO** Lowest wage paid	**MTC** Median total compensation **TCC** Total cash compensation
AER Average entry range	**AWR** Average wage range	**H** Hourly	**LR** Low end range	**MW** Median wage paid **TQ** Third quartile wage
AEX Average experienced wage	**AXR** Average experienced range	**HI** Highest wage paid	**M** Monthly	**MWR** Median wage range **W** Weekly
ATC Average total compensation **D** Daily		**HR** High end range	**MCC** Median cash compensation	**S** See annotated source **Y** Yearly

Occupation/Type/Industry	Location	Per	Low	Mid	High	Source	Date
Police, Fire, and Ambulance Dispatcher	New Hampshire	H	13.70 AE	16.57 MW	18.30 AEX	NHBLS	6/08
	Nashua NECTA, NH-MA	Y	32660 FQ	36490 MW	41680 TQ	USBLS	5/07
	New Jersey	Y	30080 FQ	36690 MW	44270 TQ	USBLS	5/07
	Camden PMSA, NJ	Y	31580 FQ	38160 MW	44880 TQ	USBLS	5/07
	Edison PMSA, NJ	Y	29590 FQ	35740 MW	42710 TQ	USBLS	5/07
	Newark-Union PMSA, NJ-PA	Y	30630 FQ	37500 MW	44380 TQ	USBLS	5/07
	New Mexico	Y	22690 FQ	27120 MW	30820 TQ	USBLS	5/07
	Albuquerque MSA, NM	Y	23630 FQ	27940 MW	31150 TQ	USBLS	5/07
	New York	Y	32140 FQ	37640 MW	43930 TQ	USBLS	5/07
	Albany-Schenectady-Troy MSA, NY	Y	31100 FQ	36170 MW	40740 TQ	USBLS	5/07
	Buffalo-Niagara Falls MSA, NY	Y	29370 FQ	35280 MW	45040 TQ	USBLS	5/07
	Nassau-Suffolk PMSA, NY	Y	34060 FQ	43260 MW	49900 TQ	USBLS	5/07
	New York-Northern New Jersey-Long Island MSA, NY-NJ-PA	Y	32300 FQ	38140 MW	45140 TQ	USBLS	5/07
	North Carolina	Y	24690 FQ	28320 MW	32120 TQ	USBLS	5/07
	Charlotte-Gastonia-Concord MSA, NC-SC	Y	25370 FQ	29140 MW	35050 TQ	USBLS	5/07
	Raleigh-Cary MSA, NC	Y	28470 FQ	31790 MW	36810 TQ	USBLS	5/07
	North Dakota	Y	25710 FQ	30680 MW	36270 TQ	USBLS	5/07
	Ohio	Y	29940 FQ	36060 MW	41950 TQ	USBLS	5/07
	Cincinnati-Middletown MSA, OH-KY-IN	Y	32850 FQ	37430 MW	43420 TQ	USBLS	5/07
	Cleveland-Elyria-Mentor MSA, OH	Y	32220 FQ	37500 MW	43110 TQ	USBLS	5/07
	Columbus MSA, OH	Y	35390 FQ	40180 MW	46640 TQ	USBLS	5/07
	Dayton MSA, OH	Y	31300 FQ	37600 MW	44360 TQ	USBLS	5/07
	Oklahoma	Y	18400 FQ	23410 MW	29080 TQ	USBLS	5/07
	Oklahoma City MSA, OK	Y	19030 FQ	25950 MW	31720 TQ	USBLS	5/07
	Tulsa MSA, OK	Y	21340 FQ	27180 MW	32030 TQ	USBLS	5/07
	Oregon	H	16.74 FQ	19.66 MW	23.05 TQ	ORBLS	5/08
	Portland-Vancouver-Beaverton MSA, OR-WA	Y	36430 FQ	44000 MW	50520 TQ	USBLS	5/07
	Pennsylvania	Y	27010 FQ	32850 MW	38040 TQ	USBLS	5/07
	Allentown-Bethlehem-Easton MSA, PA-NJ	Y	30930 FQ	34360 MW	37890 TQ	USBLS	5/07
	Philadelphia-Camden-Wilmington MSA, PA-NJ-DE-MD	Y	31870 FQ	36900 MW	43440 TQ	USBLS	5/07
	Pittsburgh MSA, PA	Y	25090 FQ	30150 MW	35590 TQ	USBLS	5/07
	Rhode Island	Y	32340 FQ	36680 MW	41460 TQ	USBLS	5/07
	Providence-Fall River-Warwick MSA, RI-MA	Y	31370 FQ	36050 MW	40510 TQ	USBLS	5/07
	South Carolina	Y	22740 FQ	26820 MW	30270 TQ	USBLS	5/07
	Charleston-North Charleston MSA, SC	Y	25350 FQ	28400 MW	31520 TQ	USBLS	5/07
	Columbia MSA, SC	Y	24930 FQ	28070 MW	31550 TQ	USBLS	5/07
	South Dakota	Y	23882 FQ	27933 MW	32002 TQ	SDBLS	7/08-9/08
	Tennessee	Y	23400 FQ	28170 MW	34040 TQ	USBLS	5/07
	Memphis MSA, TN-MS-AR	Y	24440 FQ	36050 MW	45970 TQ	USBLS	5/07
	Nashville-Davidson-Murfreesboro MSA, TN	Y	25540 FQ	29170 MW	35440 TQ	USBLS	5/07
	Texas	Y	24310 FQ	29380 MW	35060 TQ	USBLS	5/07
	Austin-Round Rock MSA, TX	Y	23950 FQ	27560 MW	31190 TQ	USBLS	5/07
	Dallas-Fort Worth-Arlington MSA, TX	Y	28990 FQ	35090 MW	39900 TQ	USBLS	5/07
	El Paso MSA, TX	Y	28060 FQ	31330 MW	35970 TQ	USBLS	5/07
	Houston-Sugar Land-Baytown MSA, TX	Y	28300 FQ	32300 MW	37730 TQ	USBLS	5/07
	San Antonio MSA, TX	Y	27180 FQ	29710 MW	32360 TQ	USBLS	5/07
	Utah	Y	26560 FQ	31020 MW	36690 TQ	USBLS	5/07
	Ogden-Clearfield MSA, UT	Y	26760 FQ	31230 MW	36830 TQ	USBLS	5/07
	Salt Lake City MSA, UT	Y	28520 FQ	32830 MW	38140 TQ	USBLS	5/07
	Vermont	Y	30800 FQ	35100 MW	38820 TQ	USBLS	5/07
	Burlington-South Burlington MSA, VT	Y	30370 FQ	34580 MW	38130 TQ	USBLS	5/07
	Virginia	Y	26520 FQ	31460 MW	38940 TQ	USBLS	5/07
	Richmond MSA, VA	Y	28010 FQ	33360 MW	39340 TQ	USBLS	5/07

AE Average entry wage	**AW** Average wage paid	**FQ** First quartile wage	**LO** Lowest wage paid	**MTC** Median total compensation	**TCC** Total cash compensation
AER Average entry range	**AWR** Average wage range	**H** Hourly	**LR** Low end range	**MW** Median wage paid	**TQ** Third quartile wage
AEX Average experienced wage	**AXR** Average experienced range	**HI** Highest wage paid	**M** Monthly	**MWR** Median wage range	**W** Weekly
ATC Average total compensation	**D** Daily	**HR** High end range	**MCC** Median cash compensation	**S** See annotated source	**Y** Yearly

Occupation/Type/Industry	Location	Per	Low	Mid	High	Source	Date
Police, Fire, and Ambulance Dispatcher	Virginia Beach-Norfolk-Newport News MSA, VA-NC	Y	28340 FQ	33200 MW	39730 TQ	USBLS	5/07
	Washington	H	18.61 FQ	21.64 MW	24.20 TQ	WABLS	3/08
	Seattle-Tacoma-Bellevue MSA, WA	Y	42460 FQ	46740 MW	51220 TQ	USBLS	5/07
	West Virginia	Y	18340 FQ	21218 MW	24853 TQ	WVBLS	7/08-9/08
	Charleston MSA, WV	Y	16700 FQ	18990 MW	22040 TQ	USBLS	5/07
	Huntington-Ashland MSA, WV-KY-OH	Y	20360 FQ	24820 MW	30020 TQ	USBLS	5/07
	Parkersburg-Marietta-Vienna MSA, WV-OH	Y	27190 FQ	33410 MW	38110 TQ	USBLS	5/07
	Wisconsin	Y	33120 FQ	37400 MW	42900 TQ	USBLS	5/07
	Milwaukee-Waukesha-West Allis MSA, WI	Y	34520 FQ	39710 MW	46180 TQ	USBLS	5/07
	Cheyenne MSA, WY	Y	33805 FQ	36823 MW	39855 TQ	WYBLS	9/08
	Puerto Rico	Y	14210 FQ	17450 MW	20990 TQ	USBLS	5/07
	San Juan-Caguas-Guaynabo MSA, PR.	Y	15040 FQ	18640 MW	21940 TQ	USBLS	5/07
Police and Sheriff's Patrol Officer	Alabama	Y	27840 FQ	34530 MW	43460 TQ	USBLS	5/07
	Birmingham-Hoover MSA, AL	Y	30230 FQ	38650 MW	49090 TQ	USBLS	5/07
	Alaska	Y	48420 FQ	58980 MW	70420 TQ	USBLS	5/07
	Anchorage MSA, AK	Y	53780 FQ	63360 MW	74020 TQ	USBLS	5/07
	Arizona	Y	43690 FQ	50620 MW	58900 TQ	USBLS	5/07
	Flagstaff MSA, AZ	Y	43790 FQ	48810 MW	55160 TQ	USBLS	5/07
	Phoenix-Mesa-Scottsdale MSA, AZ	Y	45070 FQ	51460 MW	59630 TQ	USBLS	5/07
	Tucson MSA, AZ	Y	46490 FQ	53810 MW	60650 TQ	USBLS	5/07
	Arkansas	Y	26600 FQ	32740 MW	42590 TQ	USBLS	5/07
	Fort Smith MSA, AR-OK	Y	25370 FQ	31330 MW	42210 TQ	USBLS	5/07
	Little Rock-North Little Rock MSA, AR	Y	31900 FQ	40680 MW	47610 TQ	USBLS	5/07
	Pine Bluff MSA, AR	Y	29060 FQ	35190 MW	42580 TQ	USBLS	5/07
	California	H	29.54 FQ	35.34 MW	40.26 TQ	CABLS	1/08-3/08
	Los Angeles-Long Beach-Glendale PMSA, CA	H	32.06 FQ	36.84 MW	41.46 TQ	CABLS	1/08-3/08
	Oakland-Fremont-Hayward MSA, CA	H	34.88 FQ	38.90 MW	45.28 TQ	CABLS	1/08-3/08
	Riverside-San Bernardino-Ontario MSA, CA	H	27.84 FQ	34.10 MW	38.99 TQ	CABLS	1/08-3/08
	Sacramento-Arden Arcade-Roseville MSA, CA	H	25.51 FQ	29.02 MW	32.30 TQ	CABLS	1/08-3/08
	San Diego-Carlsbad-San Marcos MSA, CA	H	30.04 FQ	34.79 MW	38.48 TQ	CABLS	1/08-3/08
	San Jose-Sunnyvale-Santa Clara MSA, CA	H	36.01 FQ	42.61 MW	49.13 TQ	CABLS	1/08-3/08
	Santa Ana-Anaheim-Irvine PMSA, CA	Y	68880 FQ	75400 MW	81580 TQ	USBLS	5/07
	Santa Rosa-Petaluma MSA, CA	H	30.35 FQ	36.01 MW	39.92 TQ	CABLS	1/08-3/08
	Colorado	Y	45890 FQ	56380 MW	65980 TQ	USBLS	5/07
	Colorado Springs MSA, CO	Y	43290 FQ	50070 MW	60170 TQ	USBLS	5/07
	Denver-Aurora MSA, CO	Y	51490 FQ	60500 MW	69450 TQ	USBLS	5/07
	Connecticut	H	21.32 AE	27.81 MW		CTBLS	1/08-3/08
	Bridgeport-Stamford-Norwalk MSA, CT	Y	50100 FQ	58400 MW	65090 TQ	USBLS	5/07
	Hartford-West Hartford-East Hartford MSA, CT	Y	48260 FQ	56860 MW	63660 TQ	USBLS	5/07
	Delaware	Y	45110 FQ	56000 MW	65090 TQ	USBLS	5/07
	Wilmington PMSA, DE-MD-NJ	Y	47910 FQ	57890 MW	67510 TQ	USBLS	5/07
	District of Columbia	Y	54240 FQ	62320 MW	74320 TQ	USBLS	5/07
	Washington-Arlington-Alexandria MSA, DC-VA-MD-WV	Y	47390 FQ	57650 MW	70170 TQ	USBLS	5/07
	Florida	Y	38420 FQ	47960 MW	59620 TQ	USBLS	5/07
	Fort Lauderdale-Pompano Beach-Deerfield Beach PMSA, FL	Y	52920 FQ	60790 MW	69120 TQ	USBLS	5/07
	Miami-Fort Lauderdale-Miami Beach MSA, FL	Y	47600 FQ	57960 MW	67100 TQ	USBLS	5/07
	Orlando-Kissimmee MSA, FL	Y	37090 FQ	44580 MW	55620 TQ	USBLS	5/07

AE	Average entry wage	AW	Average wage paid	FQ	First quartile wage	LO	Lowest wage paid	MTC	Median total compensation	TCC	Total cash compensation
AER	Average entry range	AWR	Average wage range	H	Hourly	LR	Low end range	MW	Median wage paid	TQ	Third quartile wage
AEX	Average experienced wage	AXR	Average experienced range	HI	Highest wage paid	M	Monthly	MWR	Median wage range	W	Weekly
ATC	Average total compensation	D	Daily	HR	High end range	MCC	Median cash compensation	S	See annotated source	Y	Yearly

Occupation/Type/Industry	Location	Per	Low	Mid	High	Source	Date
Police and Sheriff's Patrol Officer	Tampa-St. Petersburg-Clearwater MSA, FL	Y	42180 FQ	49240 MW	57930 TQ	USBLS	5/07
	West Palm Beach-Boca Raton-Boynton Beach PMSA, FL	Y	44090 FQ	54510 MW	66140 TQ	USBLS	5/07
	Georgia	Y	30170 FQ	36310 MW	43150 TQ	USBLS	5/07
	Atlanta-Sandy Springs-Marietta MSA, GA	Y	34790 FQ	39830 MW	47730 TQ	USBLS	5/07
	Savannah MSA, GA	Y	29090 FQ	34220 MW	40470 TQ	USBLS	5/07
	Hawaii	Y	43610 FQ	48060 MW	53510 TQ	USBLS	5/07
	Honolulu MSA, HI	Y	43930 FQ	48200 MW	53480 TQ	USBLS	5/07
	Idaho	Y	35690 FQ	42950 MW	54120 TQ	USBLS	5/07
	Boise City-Nampa MSA, ID	Y	39270 FQ	50110 MW	59070 TQ	USBLS	5/07
	Lewiston MSA, ID-WA	Y	35000 FQ	45840 MW	56360 TQ	USBLS	5/07
	Illinois	Y	46950 FQ	63630 MW	72770 TQ	USBLS	5/07
	Chicago-Naperville-Joliet MSA, IL-IN-WI	Y	53440 FQ	66050 MW	73990 TQ	USBLS	5/07
	Indiana	Y	35950 FQ	42810 MW	50310 TQ	USBLS	5/07
	Gary PMSA, IN	Y	38120 FQ	43060 MW	47180 TQ	USBLS	5/07
	Indianapolis-Carmel MSA, IN	Y	39930 FQ	51930 MW	58300 TQ	USBLS	5/07
	Iowa	Y	35010 FQ	42840 MW	51260 TQ	USBLS	5/07
	Des Moines-West Des Moines MSA, IA	Y	41240 FQ	51240 MW	59070 TQ	USBLS	5/07
	Dubuque MSA, IA	Y	42060 FQ	45520 MW	49190 TQ	USBLS	5/07
	Kansas	Y	30040 FQ	37520 MW	48890 TQ	USBLS	5/07
	Wichita MSA, KS	Y	30090 FQ	34340 MW	40360 TQ	USBLS	5/07
	Kentucky	Y	32581 FQ	38326 MW	44500 TQ	KYBLS	2008
	Louisville-Jefferson County MSA, KY-IN	Y	35700 FQ	40800 MW	46600 TQ	USBLS	5/07
	Louisiana	H	12.20 FQ	14.92 MW	18.38 TQ	LABLS	1/08-3/08
	Baton Rouge MSA, LA	Y	26710 FQ	33240 MW	41000 TQ	USBLS	5/07
	Lake Charles MSA, LA	Y	25400 FQ	29790 MW	35720 TQ	USBLS	5/07
	New Orleans-Metairie-Kenner MSA, LA	Y	29140 FQ	34080 MW	39250 TQ	USBLS	5/07
	Shreveport-Bossier City MSA, LA	Y	30270 FQ	37640 MW	44850 TQ	USBLS	5/07
	Maine	Y	31200 FQ	38200 MW	44670 TQ	USBLS	5/07
	Lewiston-Auburn MSA, ME	Y	34110 FQ	38740 MW	45680 TQ	USBLS	5/07
	Portland-South Portland-Biddeford MSA, ME	Y	36020 FQ	40990 MW	46040 TQ	USBLS	5/07
	Maryland	Y		52575 MW		MDBLS	3/08
	Baltimore-Towson MSA, MD	Y	44630 FQ	52110 MW	60180 TQ	USBLS	5/07
	Bethesda-Gaithersburg-Frederick PMSA, MD	Y	49500 FQ	61400 MW	74390 TQ	USBLS	5/07
	Massachusetts	Y	44360 FQ	51590 MW	61990 TQ	USBLS	5/07
	Boston-Cambridge-Quincy NECTA, MA	Y	46870 FQ	54320 MW	62820 TQ	USBLS	5/07
	New Bedford MSA, MA	Y	46740 FQ	56830 MW	67540 TQ	USBLS	5/07
	Worcester MSA, MA-CT	Y	43570 FQ	50980 MW	67140 TQ	USBLS	5/07
	Michigan	Y	43670 FQ	52700 MW	59420 TQ	USBLS	5/07
	Detroit-Warren-Livonia MSA, MI	Y	47870 FQ	54370 MW	60040 TQ	USBLS	5/07
	Grand Rapids-Wyoming MSA, MI	Y	50730 FQ	56210 MW	61250 TQ	USBLS	5/07
	Warren-Troy-Farmington Hills PMSA, MI	Y	46300 FQ	55370 MW	62050 TQ	USBLS	5/07
	Minnesota	Y	42837 FQ	53356 MW	62640 TQ	MNBLS	10/08-12/08
	Duluth-Superior MSA, MN-WI	Y	43632 FQ	48389 MW	54307 TQ	MNBLS	10/08-12/08
	Minneapolis-Saint Paul MSA, MN-WI	Y	51662 FQ	60058 MW	66614 TQ	MNBLS	10/08-12/08
	Mississippi	Y	24180 FQ	28960 MW	33840 TQ	USBLS	5/07
	Gulfport-Biloxi MSA, MS	Y	26480 FQ	31520 MW	35740 TQ	USBLS	5/07
	Hattiesburg MSA, MS	Y	25090 FQ	28590 MW	33290 TQ	USBLS	5/07
	Jackson MSA, MS	Y	26710 FQ	30300 MW	35190 TQ	USBLS	5/07
	Missouri	Y	26830 FQ	36540 MW	47480 TQ	USBLS	5/07
	Kansas City MSA, MO-KS	Y	29770 FQ	40880 MW	53030 TQ	USBLS	5/07
	St. Louis MSA, MO-IL	Y	37850 FQ	46060 MW	54330 TQ	USBLS	5/07
	Montana	Y	33300 FQ	40180 MW	47430 TQ	USBLS	5/07
	Missoula MSA, MT	Y	35450 FQ	39300 MW	45060 TQ	USBLS	5/07
	Nebraska	Y	35070 FQ	43520 MW	50050 TQ	USBLS	5/07
	Omaha-Council Bluffs MSA, NE-IA	Y	41790 FQ	46360 MW	51080 TQ	USBLS	5/07
	Nevada	H	24.39 FQ	29.45 MW	34.88 TQ	NVBLS	5/08

AE Average entry wage	**AW** Average wage paid	**FQ** First quartile wage	**LO** Lowest wage paid	**MTC** Median total compensation	**TCC** Total cash compensation
AER Average entry range	**AWR** Average wage range	**H** Hourly	**LR** Low end range	**MW** Median wage paid	**TQ** Third quartile wage
AEX Average experienced wage	**AXR** Average experienced range	**HI** Highest wage paid	**M** Monthly	**MWR** Median wage range	**W** Weekly
ATC Average total compensation	**D** Daily	**HR** High end range	**MCC** Median cash compensation	**S** See annotated source	**Y** Yearly

Occupation/Type/Industry	Location	Per	Low	Mid	High	Source	Date
Police and Sheriff's Patrol Officer	Las Vegas-Paradise MSA, NV	H	26.78 FQ	31.52 MW	36.68 TQ	NVBLS	5/08
	New Hampshire	H	15.33 AE	20.81 MW	24.24 AEX	NHBLS	6/08
	Manchester MSA, NH	Y	38640 FQ	47260 MW	57590 TQ	USBLS	5/07
	Nashua NECTA, NH-MA	Y	39430 FQ	50430 MW	58000 TQ	USBLS	5/07
	New Jersey	Y	59100 FQ	73980 MW	88750 TQ	USBLS	5/07
	Camden PMSA, NJ	Y	50440 FQ	63930 MW	77380 TQ	USBLS	5/07
	Edison PMSA, NJ	Y	59760 FQ	77080 MW	90170 TQ	USBLS	5/07
	Newark-Union PMSA, NJ-PA	Y	59610 FQ	70620 MW	81610 TQ	USBLS	5/07
	New Mexico	Y	32780 FQ	38030 MW	45490 TQ	USBLS	5/07
	Albuquerque MSA, NM	Y	35290 FQ	39980 MW	46850 TQ	USBLS	5/07
	New York	Y	45610 FQ	55700 MW	64110 TQ	USBLS	5/07
	Albany-Schenectady-Troy MSA, NY	Y	39530 FQ	52820 MW	59760 TQ	USBLS	5/07
	Buffalo-Niagara Falls MSA, NY	Y	48750 FQ	56080 MW	61840 TQ	USBLS	5/07
	Glens Falls MSA, NY	Y	30220 FQ	36670 MW	46020 TQ	USBLS	5/07
	Ithaca MSA, NY	Y	45020 FQ	54130 MW	60460 TQ	USBLS	5/07
	Nassau-Suffolk PMSA, NY	Y	64750 FQ	77500 MW	91400 TQ	USBLS	5/07
	New York-Northern New Jersey-Long Island MSA, NY-NJ-PA	Y	50000 FQ	60920 MW	74230 TQ	USBLS	5/07
	North Carolina	Y	31730 FQ	37540 MW	46870 TQ	USBLS	5/07
	Asheville MSA, NC	Y	29350 FQ	34420 MW	41410 TQ	USBLS	5/07
	Charlotte-Gastonia-Concord MSA, NC-SC	Y	35430 FQ	42730 MW	51950 TQ	USBLS	5/07
	Raleigh-Cary MSA, NC	Y	35290 FQ	40990 MW	51830 TQ	USBLS	5/07
	North Dakota	Y	32300 FQ	40030 MW	48350 TQ	USBLS	5/07
	Fargo MSA, ND-MN	Y	41740 FQ	47100 MW	52600 TQ	USBLS	5/07
	Ohio	Y	37510 FQ	49570 MW	59070 TQ	USBLS	5/07
	Cincinnati-Middletown MSA, OH-KY-IN	Y	45540 FQ	54390 MW	61040 TQ	USBLS	5/07
	Cleveland-Elyria-Mentor MSA, OH	Y	42810 FQ	55870 MW	62080 TQ	USBLS	5/07
	Columbus MSA, OH	Y	42450 FQ	55810 MW	61770 TQ	USBLS	5/07
	Dayton MSA, OH	Y	45540 FQ	54560 MW	61220 TQ	USBLS	5/07
	Oklahoma	Y	23920 FQ	31720 MW	45710 TQ	USBLS	5/07
	Oklahoma City MSA, OK	Y	30130 FQ	43480 MW	55650 TQ	USBLS	5/07
	Tulsa MSA, OK	Y	20220 FQ	34800 MW	49140 TQ	USBLS	5/07
	Oregon	H	22.85 FQ	26.84 MW	30.54 MW	ORBLS	5/08
	Portland-Vancouver-Beaverton MSA, OR-WA	Y	51510 FQ	59630 MW	67100 TQ	USBLS	5/07
	Pennsylvania	Y	42000 FQ	55450 MW	63520 TQ	USBLS	5/07
	Allentown-Bethlehem-Easton MSA, PA-NJ	Y	40290 FQ	50730 MW	62630 TQ	USBLS	5/07
	Philadelphia-Camden-Wilmington MSA, PA-NJ-DE-MD	Y	52430 FQ	59450 MW	66130 TQ	USBLS	5/07
	Pittsburgh MSA, PA	Y	36160 FQ	54630 MW	63090 TQ	USBLS	5/07
	Reading MSA, PA	Y	44400 FQ	51620 MW	61680 TQ	USBLS	5/07
	Rhode Island	Y	44430 FQ	49790 MW	57190 TQ	USBLS	5/07
	Providence-Fall River-Warwick MSA, RI-MA	Y	44600 FQ	49830 MW	57080 TQ	USBLS	5/07
	South Carolina	Y	29670 FQ	34900 MW	41090 TQ	USBLS	5/07
	Charleston-North Charleston MSA, SC	Y	31830 FQ	36410 MW	41090 TQ	USBLS	5/07
	Columbia MSA, SC	Y	30720 FQ	36920 MW	45310 TQ	USBLS	5/07
	Myrtle Beach-Conway-North Myrtle Beach MSA, SC	Y	28370 FQ	32080 MW	39560 TQ	USBLS	5/07
	South Dakota	Y	29428 FQ	35739 MW	45011 TQ	SDBLS	7/08-9/08
	Tennessee	Y	28660 FQ	34480 MW	43110 TQ	USBLS	5/07
	Nashville-Davidson-Murfreesboro MSA, TN	Y	33730 FQ	42720 MW	54400 TQ	USBLS	5/07
	Texas	Y	36440 FQ	45940 MW	56430 TQ	USBLS	5/07
	Austin-Round Rock MSA, TX	Y	31210 FQ	38070 MW	49730 TQ	USBLS	5/07
	Dallas-Fort Worth-Arlington MSA, TX	Y	43010 FQ	51370 MW	61020 TQ	USBLS	5/07
	Houston-Sugar Land-Baytown MSA, TX	Y	41090 FQ	49380 MW	59130 TQ	USBLS	5/07
	San Antonio MSA, TX	Y	38360 FQ	45860 MW	52570 TQ	USBLS	5/07
	Utah	Y	35900 FQ	41570 MW	50130 TQ	USBLS	5/07
	Salt Lake City MSA, UT	Y	39490 FQ	46440 MW	53670 TQ	USBLS	5/07
	Vermont	Y	29470 FQ	36690 MW	45490 TQ	USBLS	5/07

AE	Average entry wage	AW	Average wage paid	FQ	First quartile wage
AER	Average entry range	AWR	Average wage range	H	Hourly
AEX	Average experienced wage	AXR	Average experienced range	HI	Highest wage paid
ATC	Average total compensation	D	Daily	HR	High end range

LO	Lowest wage paid	MTC	Median total compensation
LR	Low end range	MW	Median wage paid
M	Monthly	MWR	Median wage range
		MCC	Median cash compensation
		S	See annotated source

TCC	Total cash compensation		
TQ	Third quartile wage		
W	Weekly		
Y	Yearly		

Occupation/Type/Industry	Location	Per	Low	Mid	High	Source	Date
Police and Sheriff's Patrol Officer	Burlington-South Burlington MSA, VT	Y	36060 FQ	43680 MW	51300 TQ	USBLS	5/07
	Virginia	Y	36390 FQ	44610 MW	56020 TQ	USBLS	5/07
	Richmond MSA, VA	Y	36900 FQ	43870 MW	51610 TQ	USBLS	5/07
	Virginia Beach-Norfolk-Newport News MSA, VA-NC	Y	36540 FQ	41600 MW	50650 TQ	USBLS	5/07
	Washington	H	26.24 FQ	29.90 MW	34.35 TQ	WABLS	3/08
	Olympia MSA, WA	Y	55840 FQ	65100 MW	72820 TQ	USBLS	5/07
	Seattle-Tacoma-Bellevue MSA, WA	Y	55880 FQ	63820 MW	73230 TQ	USBLS	5/07
	West Virginia	Y	28629 FQ	35622 MW	41850 TQ	WVBLS	7/08-9/08
	Charleston MSA, WV	Y	32700 FQ	37570 MW	43530 TQ	USBLS	5/07
	Wisconsin	Y	40820 FQ	50850 MW	59300 TQ	USBLS	5/07
	Green Bay MSA, WI	Y	40080 FQ	54720 MW	61250 TQ	USBLS	5/07
	Milwaukee-Waukesha-West Allis MSA, WI	Y	53940 FQ	58550 MW	63220 TQ	USBLS	5/07
	Wyoming	Y	37926 FQ	43982 MW	50657 TQ	WYBLS	9/08
	Cheyenne MSA, WY	Y	36968 FQ	40567 MW	46684 TQ	WYBLS	9/08
	Puerto Rico	Y	26270 FQ	28430 MW	30580 TQ	USBLS	5/07
	San Juan-Caguas-Guaynabo MSA, PR	Y	26730 FQ	28720 MW	30720 TQ	USBLS	5/07
Police Assistant	Walnut Creek, CA	Y	57249 LO		68904 HI	WCSWP	9/21/07
Police Chief	Hinesville, GA	Y	64666 LO		122884 HI	GACTY01	2008
	Macon, GA	Y	69701 LO		105269 HI	GACTY01	2008
	Biloxi, MS	Y			83447 HI	MML	2008
	Carthage, MS	Y			46063 HI	MML	2008
	Macon, MS	Y			42042 HI	MML	2008
	Tupelo, MS	Y			76385 HI	MML	2008
	Bismarck, ND	M			6836 HI	NDLC01	2008
	Elgin, ND	M			1800 HI	NDLC02	2008
	Grand Forks, ND	M			8233 HI	NDLC01	2008
	Oakes, ND	M			3738 HI	NDLC01	2008
	Powers Lake, ND	M			2000 HI	NDLC02	2008
Police Commander	Seaside, CA	S	3743 LO		4596 HI	SSSS	8/08
	Colorado Springs, CO	M			9117 HI	COSPRS	1/1/09
Police Corporal	Griffin, GA	Y	33238 LO		50398 HI	GACTY01	2008
	Tyrone, GA	Y	36973 LO		52222 HI	GACTY01	2008
Police Court Liason	Colorado Springs, CO	M	3488 LO			COSPRS	1/1/09
Police Criminalist	Cincinnati, OH	Y	38076 LO		51171 HI	COHSS	10/08
Police Evidence Supervisor	Colorado Springs, CO	M	4442 LO			COSPRS	1/1/09
Police Logistics Support Manager	Colorado Springs, CO	M	5606 LO			COSPRS	1/1/09
Police Property Coordinator	Colorado Springs, CO	M	2891 LO			COSPRS	1/1/09
Police Psychologist	Colorado Springs, CO	M	5939 LO			COSPRS	1/1/09
Police Records Manager	Gresham, OR	Y	57996 LO		75420 HI	GOSS01	7/1/08
Police Records Supervisor	Seaside, CA	S	2230 LO		2710 HI	SSSS	8/08
Police Records Technician	Walnut Creek, CA	Y	48140 LO		57919 HI	WCSWP	9/21/07
Police Recruit	New York, NY	Y	41975 LO			NYDN	2008
	Cincinnati, OH	Y			31320 HI	COHSS	10/08
Police Services Officer	Walnut Creek, CA	Y	48140 LO		57919 HI	WCSWP	9/21/07
Police Technician	Cincinnati, OH	Y	34874 LO		36962 HI	COHSS	10/08
Police Training Coordinator	Carlsbad, CA	S	1800 LO		2188 HI	CCSS01	8/5/08
Police Training Specialist	Colorado Springs, CO	M	4006 LO			COSPRS	1/1/09
Policy Expert on Cyberterrorism	Wisconsin	Y			107258 HI	MJSENT	2009
Political Science Teacher Postsecondary	Alabama	Y	40260 FQ	54710 MW	70260 TQ	USBLS	5/07

AE	Average entry wage	AW	Average wage paid	FQ	First quartile wage	LO	Lowest wage paid	MTC	Median total compensation	TCC	Total cash compensation
AER	Average entry range	AWR	Average wage range	H	Hourly	LR	Low end range	MW	Median wage paid	TQ	Third quartile wage
AEX	Average experienced wage	AXR	Average experienced range	HI	Highest wage paid	M	Monthly	MWR	Median wage range	W	Weekly
ATC	Average total compensation	D	Daily	HR	High end range	MCC	Median cash compensation	S	See annotated source	Y	Yearly

Political Science Teacher

Occupation/Type/Industry	Location	Per	Low	Mid	High	Source	Date
Political Science Teacher							
Postsecondary	Alaska	Y	28650 FQ	59500 MW	83400 TQ	USBLS	5/07
Postsecondary	Anchorage MSA, AK	Y	27350 FQ	57200 MW	83010 TQ	USBLS	5/07
Postsecondary	Arizona	Y	35950 FQ	47800 MW	67260 TQ	USBLS	5/07
Postsecondary	Phoenix-Mesa-Scottsdale MSA, AZ	Y	32630 FQ	43320 MW	55690 TQ	USBLS	5/07
Postsecondary	Arkansas	Y	41700 FQ	52110 MW	63370 TQ	USBLS	5/07
Postsecondary	California	Y		85852 AW		CABLS	1/08-3/08
Postsecondary	Los Angeles-Long Beach-Glendale PMSA, CA	Y		89913 AW		CABLS	1/08-3/08
Postsecondary	Oakland-Fremont-Hayward MSA, CA	Y		82848 AW		CABLS	1/08-3/08
Postsecondary	Riverside-San Bernardino-Ontario MSA, CA	Y		78756 AW		CABLS	1/08-3/08
Postsecondary	Sacramento-Arden Arcade-Roseville MSA, CA	Y		84048 AW		CABLS	1/08-3/08
Postsecondary	San Diego-Carlsbad-San Marcos MSA, CA	Y		91944 AW		CABLS	1/08-3/08
Postsecondary	San Francisco-San Mateo-Redwood PMSA, CA	Y		84960 AW		CABLS	1/08-3/08
Postsecondary	Santa Ana-Anaheim-Irvine PMSA, CA	Y	67750 FQ	80040 MW	97750 TQ	USBLS	5/07
Postsecondary	Colorado	Y	47790 FQ	59590 MW	76600 TQ	USBLS	5/07
Postsecondary	Denver-Aurora MSA, CO	Y	42860 FQ	57580 MW	71930 TQ	USBLS	5/07
Postsecondary	Wilmington PMSA, DE-MD-NJ	Y	53070 FQ	70590 MW	97330 TQ	USBLS	5/07
Postsecondary	District of Columbia	Y	49230 FQ	60830 MW	74480 TQ	USBLS	5/07
Postsecondary	Washington-Arlington-Alexandria MSA, DC-VA-MD-WV	Y	51430 FQ	64780 MW	86700 TQ	USBLS	5/07
Postsecondary	Florida	Y	44170 FQ	58960 MW	77590 TQ	USBLS	5/07
Postsecondary	Miami-Fort Lauderdale-Miami Beach MSA, FL	Y	45530 FQ	65110 MW	78470 TQ	USBLS	5/07
Postsecondary	Orlando-Kissimmee MSA, FL	Y	32820 FQ	46380 MW	61270 TQ	USBLS	5/07
Postsecondary	Tampa-St. Petersburg-Clearwater MSA, FL	Y	52550 FQ	66280 MW	86370 TQ	USBLS	5/07
Postsecondary	Georgia	Y	46760 FQ	59550 MW	73800 TQ	USBLS	5/07
Postsecondary	Atlanta-Sandy Springs-Marietta MSA, GA	Y	50140 FQ	63370 MW	77090 TQ	USBLS	5/07
Postsecondary	Hawaii	Y	52540 FQ	67210 MW	84830 TQ	USBLS	5/07
Postsecondary	Honolulu MSA, HI	Y	56760 FQ	70400 MW	87840 TQ	USBLS	5/07
Postsecondary	Illinois	Y	45770 FQ	60880 MW	81270 TQ	USBLS	5/07
Postsecondary	Chicago-Naperville-Joliet MSA, IL-IN-WI	Y	48990 FQ	64810 MW	88390 TQ	USBLS	5/07
Postsecondary	Indiana	Y	50240 FQ	64430 MW	79770 TQ	USBLS	5/07
Postsecondary	Indianapolis-Carmel MSA, IN	Y	47880 FQ	59000 MW	75650 TQ	USBLS	5/07
Postsecondary	Iowa	Y	46600 FQ	62830 MW	85550 TQ	USBLS	5/07
Postsecondary	Kansas	Y	42500 FQ	64790 MW	79560 TQ	USBLS	5/07
Postsecondary	Kentucky	Y	35082 FQ	53414 MW	76556 TQ	KYBLS	2008
Postsecondary	Louisiana	Y		58131 AW		LABLS	1/08-3/08
Postsecondary	Maine	Y	55530 FQ	63650 MW	76620 TQ	USBLS	5/07
Postsecondary	Maryland	Y		69700 MW		MDBLS	3/08
Postsecondary	Baltimore-Towson MSA, MD	Y	53910 FQ	61220 MW	91770 TQ	USBLS	5/07
Postsecondary	Bethesda-Gaithersburg-Frederick PMSA, MD	Y	56220 FQ	74860 MW	106460 TQ	USBLS	5/07
Postsecondary	Massachusetts	Y	64800 FQ	82900 MW	111550 TQ	USBLS	5/07
Postsecondary	Boston-Cambridge-Quincy NECTA, MA	Y	66120 FQ	85760 MW	119430 TQ	USBLS	5/07
Postsecondary	Michigan	Y	48680 FQ	61910 MW	80370 TQ	USBLS	5/07
Postsecondary	Detroit-Warren-Livonia MSA, MI	Y	37770 FQ	60850 MW	84310 TQ	USBLS	5/07
Postsecondary	Warren-Troy-Farmington Hills PMSA, MI	Y	34170 FQ	47010 MW	80570 TQ	USBLS	5/07
Postsecondary	Minnesota	Y	50605 FQ	64719 MW	91555 TQ	MNBLS	10/08-12/08
Postsecondary	Minneapolis-Saint Paul MSA, MN-WI	Y	54079 FQ	75056 MW	113076 TQ	MNBLS	10/08-12/08
Postsecondary	Mississippi	Y	52240 FQ	60290 MW	73860 TQ	USBLS	5/07
Postsecondary	Missouri	Y	44820 FQ	58260 MW	73320 TQ	USBLS	5/07
Postsecondary	Kansas City MSA, MO-KS	Y	44220 FQ	59030 MW	76810 TQ	USBLS	5/07
Postsecondary	St. Louis MSA, MO-IL	Y	48750 FQ	63280 MW	79980 TQ	USBLS	5/07
Postsecondary	Montana	Y	42510 FQ	52980 MW	70540 TQ	USBLS	5/07
Postsecondary	Nebraska	Y	48410 FQ	63150 MW	79000 TQ	USBLS	5/07

AE	Average entry wage	AW	Average wage paid	FQ	First quartile wage
AER	Average entry range	AWR	Average wage range	H	Hourly
AEX	Average experienced wage	AXR	Average experienced range	HI	Highest wage paid
ATC	Average total compensation	D	Daily	HR	High end range

LO	Lowest wage paid	MTC	Median total compensation	TCC	Total cash compensation
LR	Low end range	MW	Median wage paid	TQ	Third quartile wage
M	Monthly	MWR	Median wage range	W	Weekly
MCC	Median cash compensation	S	See annotated source	Y	Yearly

Occupation/Type/Industry	Location	Per	Low	Mid	High	Source	Date
Political Science Teacher							
Postsecondary	New Hampshire	Y	53904 AE	66961 MW	82309 AEX	NHBLS	6/08
Postsecondary	New Jersey	Y	56240 FQ	75600 MW	107100 TQ	USBLS	5/07
Postsecondary	Edison PMSA, NJ	Y	59100 FQ	81600 MW	121660 TQ	USBLS	5/07
Postsecondary	Newark-Union PMSA, NJ-PA	Y	55160 FQ	74950 MW	103140 TQ	USBLS	5/07
Postsecondary	New Mexico	Y	57120 FQ	70660 MW	88090 TQ	USBLS	5/07
Postsecondary	New York	Y	58160 FQ	75220 MW	99680 TQ	USBLS	5/07
Postsecondary	New York-Northern New Jersey-Long Island MSA, NY-NJ-PA	Y	57500 FQ	74200 MW	101410 TQ	USBLS	5/07
Postsecondary	North Carolina	Y	46780 FQ	60120 MW	82700 TQ	USBLS	5/07
Postsecondary	Charlotte-Gastonia-Concord MSA, NC-SC	Y	49020 FQ	57080 MW	86640 TQ	USBLS	5/07
Postsecondary	Raleigh-Cary MSA, NC	Y	34800 FQ	43430 MW	58840 TQ	USBLS	5/07
Postsecondary	North Dakota	Y	49890 FQ	59150 MW	75680 TQ	USBLS	5/07
Postsecondary	Fargo MSA, ND-MN	Y	50190 FQ	55440 MW	60700 TQ	USBLS	5/07
Postsecondary	Ohio	Y	40460 FQ	60910 MW	85000 TQ	USBLS	5/07
Postsecondary	Cincinnati-Middletown MSA, OH-KY-IN	Y	29400 FQ	45790 MW	64580 TQ	USBLS	5/07
Postsecondary	Cleveland-Elyria-Mentor MSA, OH	Y	35970 FQ	47770 MW	70720 TQ	USBLS	5/07
Postsecondary	Columbus MSA, OH	Y	66750 FQ	80770 MW	106830 TQ	USBLS	5/07
Postsecondary	Dayton MSA, OH	Y	45830 FQ	64470 MW	88880 TQ	USBLS	5/07
Postsecondary	Oklahoma	Y	30610 FQ	36910 MW	49260 TQ	USBLS	5/07
Postsecondary	Oklahoma City MSA, OK	Y	28240 FQ	33380 MW	53030 TQ	USBLS	5/07
Postsecondary	Tulsa MSA, OK	Y	32300 FQ	38330 MW	55130 TQ	USBLS	5/07
Postsecondary	Portland-Vancouver-Beaverton MSA, OR-WA	Y	49220 FQ	64230 MW	94650 TQ	USBLS	5/07
Postsecondary	Pennsylvania	Y	54410 FQ	71460 MW	96250 TQ	USBLS	5/07
Postsecondary	Philadelphia-Camden-Wilmington MSA, PA-NJ-DE-MD	Y	53990 FQ	73540 MW	104430 TQ	USBLS	5/07
Postsecondary	Pittsburgh MSA, PA	Y	53920 FQ	74650 MW	97360 TQ	USBLS	5/07
Postsecondary	Rhode Island	Y	56730 FQ	79150 MW	100550 TQ	USBLS	5/07
Postsecondary	Providence-Fall River-Warwick MSA, RI-MA	Y	56730 FQ	79150 MW	100550 TQ	USBLS	5/07
Postsecondary	South Carolina	Y	47020 FQ	59970 MW	78630 TQ	USBLS	5/07
Postsecondary	South Dakota	Y	46425 FQ	60465 MW	79261 TQ	SDBLS	7/08-9/08
Postsecondary	Tennessee	Y	44250 FQ	50130 MW	63000 TQ	USBLS	5/07
Postsecondary	Memphis MSA, TN-MS-AR	Y	47940 FQ	61270 MW	78740 TQ	USBLS	5/07
Postsecondary	Nashville-Davidson-Murfreesboro MSA, TN	Y	44930 FQ	50830 MW	62540 TQ	USBLS	5/07
Postsecondary	Texas	Y	42770 FQ	58660 MW	78210 TQ	USBLS	5/07
Postsecondary	Austin-Round Rock MSA, TX	Y	32250 FQ	71910 MW	96730 TQ	USBLS	5/07
Postsecondary	Dallas-Fort Worth-Arlington MSA, TX	Y	32040 FQ	54090 MW	74710 TQ	USBLS	5/07
Postsecondary	El Paso MSA, TX	Y	52940 FQ	62070 MW	74740 TQ	USBLS	5/07
Postsecondary	Houston-Sugar Land-Baytown MSA, TX	Y	49510 FQ	70110 MW	109180 TQ	USBLS	5/07
Postsecondary	San Antonio MSA, TX	Y	34960 FQ	51650 MW	63190 TQ	USBLS	5/07
Postsecondary	Utah	Y	48490 FQ	60170 MW	80130 TQ	USBLS	5/07
Postsecondary	Vermont	Y	46830 FQ	57380 MW	74410 TQ	USBLS	5/07
Postsecondary	Burlington-South Burlington MSA, VT	Y	49950 FQ	57710 MW	71420 TQ	USBLS	5/07
Postsecondary	Virginia	Y	46510 FQ	61570 MW	85590 TQ	USBLS	5/07
Postsecondary	Richmond MSA, VA	Y	50760 FQ	61100 MW	83130 TQ	USBLS	5/07
Postsecondary	Virginia Beach-Norfolk-Newport News MSA, VA-NC	Y	52230 FQ	65020 MW	82950 TQ	USBLS	5/07
Postsecondary	Washington	Y		72312 AW		WABLS	3/08
Postsecondary	West Virginia	Y	42665 FQ	53062 MW	75319 TQ	WVBLS	7/08-9/08
Postsecondary	Wisconsin	Y	44670 FQ	57640 MW	75570 TQ	USBLS	5/07
Postsecondary	Milwaukee-Waukesha-West Allis MSA, WI	Y	46290 FQ	60660 MW	81220 TQ	USBLS	5/07
Postsecondary	Wyoming	Y	50150 FQ	61178 MW	73327 TQ	WYBLS	9/08
Political Scientist	District of Columbia	Y	75160 FQ	98500 MW	121270 TQ	USBLS	5/07
	Illinois	Y	32140 FQ	41510 MW	62270 TQ	USBLS	5/07
	Maryland	Y		104800 MW		MDBLS	3/08
	New York	Y	45060 FQ	64210 MW	95330 TQ	USBLS	5/07
	Pennsylvania	Y	68370 FQ	81320 MW	115260 TQ	USBLS	5/07
	Texas	Y	27840 FQ	32640 MW	38480 TQ	USBLS	5/07
	Virginia	Y	90900 FQ	110140 MW	144720 TQ	USBLS	5/07

AE	Average entry wage	AW	Average wage paid	FQ	First quartile wage	LO	Lowest wage paid	MTC	Median total compensation	TCC	Total cash compensation
AER	Average entry range	AWR	Average wage range	H	Hourly	LR	Low end range	MW	Median wage paid	TQ	Third quartile wage
AEX	Average experienced wage	AXR	Average experienced range	HI	Highest wage paid	M	Monthly	MWR	Median wage range	W	Weekly
ATC	Average total compensation	D	Daily	HR	High end range	MCC	Median cash compensation	S	See annotated source	Y	Yearly

Occupation/Type/Industry	Location	Per	Low	Mid	High	Source	Date
Political Scientist	Washington	H	18.31 FQ	31.74 MW	41.66 TQ	WABLS	3/08
Polygraph Examiner U.S. Central Intelligence Agency	District of Columbia	Y	54252 LO		107854 HI	CIA03	2008
Pool Maintenance Worker Municipal Government	Seattle, WA	H	20.23 LO		21.82 HI	CSSS	2007
Pool Manager Municipal Government Municipal Government	Seaside, CA Cincinnati, OH	S Y	1200 LO 20880 LO		1380 HI 27144 HI	SSSS COHSS	8/08 10/08
Port Director	West Coast	Y		254535 ATC		PCMEM	2008
Postal Service Clerk	Alabama	Y	41600 FQ	44740 MW	47890 TQ	USBLS	5/07
	Birmingham-Hoover MSA, AL	Y	42220 FQ	45170 MW	48120 TQ	USBLS	5/07
	Alaska	Y	41780 FQ	44840 MW	47900 TQ	USBLS	5/07
	Arizona	Y	42050 FQ	45020 MW	48000 TQ	USBLS	5/07
	Flagstaff MSA, AZ	Y	41540 FQ	44680 MW	47820 TQ	USBLS	5/07
	Phoenix-Mesa-Scottsdale MSA, AZ	Y	42300 FQ	45190 MW	48080 TQ	USBLS	5/07
	Tucson MSA, AZ	Y	42370 FQ	45230 MW	48100 TQ	USBLS	5/07
	Arkansas	Y	40870 FQ	44250 MW	47620 TQ	USBLS	5/07
	Fort Smith MSA, AR-OK	Y	40750 FQ	44150 MW	47560 TQ	USBLS	5/07
	Little Rock-North Little Rock MSA, AR	Y	40920 FQ	44270 MW	47620 TQ	USBLS	5/07
	California	H	20.58 FQ	22.07 MW	23.56 TQ	CABLS	1/08-3/08
	Los Angeles-Long Beach-Glendale PMSA, CA	H	20.83 FQ	22.23 MW	23.63 TQ	CABLS	1/08-3/08
	Oakland-Fremont-Hayward MSA, CA	H	20.63 FQ	22.10 MW	23.56 TQ	CABLS	1/08-3/08
	Riverside-San Bernardino-Ontario MSA, CA	H	20.32 FQ	21.90 MW	23.47 TQ	CABLS	1/08-3/08
	Sacramento-Arden Arcade-Roseville MSA, CA	H	20.51 FQ	22.05 MW	23.58 TQ	CABLS	1/08-3/08
	San Diego-Carlsbad-San Marcos MSA, CA	H	20.36 FQ	21.93 MW	23.48 TQ	CABLS	1/08-3/08
	San Francisco-San Mateo-Redwood PMSA, CA	H	20.83 FQ	22.23 MW	23.63 TQ	CABLS	1/08-3/08
	San Jose-Sunnyvale-Santa Clara MSA, CA	H	20.62 FQ	22.09 MW	23.56 TQ	CABLS	1/08-3/08
	Santa Ana-Anaheim-Irvine PMSA, CA	Y	41310 FQ	44540 MW	47770 TQ	USBLS	5/07
	Colorado	Y	41840 FQ	44890 MW	47930 TQ	USBLS	5/07
	Denver-Aurora MSA, CO	Y	42410 FQ	45260 MW	48120 TQ	USBLS	5/07
	Connecticut	H	21.32 AE	22.19 MW		CTBLS	1/08-3/08
	Bridgeport-Stamford-Norwalk MSA, CT	Y	42480 FQ	45310 MW	48130 TQ	USBLS	5/07
	Hartford-West Hartford-East Hartford MSA, CT	Y	42060 FQ	45030 MW	47990 TQ	USBLS	5/07
	Delaware	Y	41910 FQ	44940 MW	47980 TQ	USBLS	5/07
	Dover MSA, DE	Y	42330 FQ	45320 MW	48320 TQ	USBLS	5/07
	Wilmington PMSA, DE-MD-NJ	Y	42150 FQ	45090 MW	48020 TQ	USBLS	5/07
	District of Columbia	Y	42770 FQ	45500 MW	48230 TQ	USBLS	5/07
	Washington-Arlington-Alexandria MSA, DC-VA-MD-WV	Y	42370 FQ	45250 MW	48120 TQ	USBLS	5/07
	Florida	Y	42190 FQ	45130 MW	48070 TQ	USBLS	5/07
	Fort Lauderdale-Pompano Beach-Deerfield Beach PMSA, FL	Y	42450 FQ	45290 MW	48120 TQ	USBLS	5/07
	Jacksonville MSA, FL	Y	42510 FQ	45320 MW	48140 TQ	USBLS	5/07
	Miami-Fort Lauderdale-Miami Beach MSA, FL	Y	42490 FQ	45310 MW	48140 TQ	USBLS	5/07
	Orlando-Kissimmee MSA, FL	Y	42400 FQ	45260 MW	48120 TQ	USBLS	5/07
	Tampa-St. Petersburg-Clearwater MSA, FL	Y	41910 FQ	44980 MW	48040 TQ	USBLS	5/07
	West Palm Beach-Boca Raton-Boynton Beach PMSA, FL	Y	42180 FQ	45120 MW	48060 TQ	USBLS	5/07
	Georgia	Y	42530 FQ	45350 MW	48170 TQ	USBLS	5/07

AE	Average entry wage	AW	Average wage paid	FQ	First quartile wage
AER	Average entry range	AWR	Average wage range	H	Hourly
AEX	Average experienced wage	AXR	Average experienced range	HI	Highest wage paid
ATC	Average total compensation	D	Daily	HR	High end range

LO Lowest wage paid
LR Low end range
M Monthly
MCC Median cash compensation

MTC Median total compensation
MW Median wage paid
MWR Median wage range
S See annotated source

TCC Total cash compensation
TQ Third quartile wage
W Weekly
Y Yearly

Occupation/Type/Industry	Location	Per	Low	Mid	High	Source	Date
Postal Service Clerk	Atlanta-Sandy Springs- Marietta MSA, GA	Y	42710 FQ	45470 MW	48230 TQ	USBLS	5/07
	Hawaii	Y	41370 FQ	44570 MW	47760 TQ	USBLS	5/07
	Honolulu MSA, HI	Y	41330 FQ	44540 MW	47750 TQ	USBLS	5/07
	Idaho	Y	41320 FQ	44540 MW	47770 TQ	USBLS	5/07
	Boise City-Nampa MSA, ID	Y	42100 FQ	45050 MW	48010 TQ	USBLS	5/07
	Illinois	Y	42510 FQ	45340 MW	48170 TQ	USBLS	5/07
	Chicago-Naperville-Joliet MSA, IL-IN-WI	Y	42590 FQ	45390 MW	48180 TQ	USBLS	5/07
	Indiana	Y	42440 FQ	45300 MW	48150 TQ	USBLS	5/07
	Gary PMSA, IN	Y	42510 FQ	45340 MW	48180 TQ	USBLS	5/07
	Indianapolis-Carmel MSA, IN	Y	42430 FQ	45280 MW	48130 TQ	USBLS	5/07
	Iowa	Y	42490 FQ	45320 MW	48150 TQ	USBLS	5/07
	Des Moines-West Des Moines MSA, IA	Y	42690 FQ	45450 MW	48200 TQ	USBLS	5/07
	Kansas	Y	42190 FQ	45110 MW	48040 TQ	USBLS	5/07
	Wichita MSA, KS	Y	42050 FQ	45020 MW	47990 TQ	USBLS	5/07
	Kentucky	Y	42975 FQ	46153 MW	49329 TQ	KYBLS	2008
	Louisville-Jefferson County MSA, KY-IN	Y	41930 FQ	44940 MW	47950 TQ	USBLS	5/07
	Louisiana	H	20.16 FQ	21.62 MW	23.07 TQ	LABLS	1/08-3/08
	Baton Rouge MSA, LA	Y	41920 FQ	44950 MW	47980 TQ	USBLS	5/07
	Lafayette MSA, LA	Y	42630 FQ	45410 MW	48180 TQ	USBLS	5/07
	New Orleans-Metairie-Kenner MSA, LA	Y	42290 FQ	45200 MW	48100 TQ	USBLS	5/07
	Maine	Y	41640 FQ	44780 MW	47910 TQ	USBLS	5/07
	Portland-South Portland- Biddeford MSA, ME	Y	42290 FQ	45180 MW	48070 TQ	USBLS	5/07
	Maryland	Y		46300 MW		MDBLS	3/08
	Baltimore-Towson MSA, MD	Y	42420 FQ	45280 MW	48140 TQ	USBLS	5/07
	Bethesda-Gaithersburg- Frederick PMSA, MD	Y	42530 FQ	45360 MW	48190 TQ	USBLS	5/07
	Massachusetts	Y	42300 FQ	45190 MW	48080 TQ	USBLS	5/07
	Boston-Cambridge-Quincy NECTA, MA	Y	42550 FQ	45360 MW	48170 TQ	USBLS	5/07
	Springfield MSA, MA-CT	Y	42290 FQ	45180 MW	48070 TQ	USBLS	5/07
	Worcester MSA, MA-CT	Y	41930 FQ	44940 MW	47950 TQ	USBLS	5/07
	Michigan	Y	42490 FQ	45320 MW	48140 TQ	USBLS	5/07
	Detroit-Warren-Livonia MSA, MI	Y	42630 FQ	45410 MW	48190 TQ	USBLS	5/07
	Grand Rapids-Wyoming MSA, MI	Y	42670 FQ	45430 MW	48200 TQ	USBLS	5/07
	Lansing-East Lansing MSA, MI	Y	42410 FQ	45300 MW	48180 TQ	USBLS	5/07
	Warren-Troy-Farmington Hills PMSA, MI	Y	42580 FQ	45370 MW	48170 TQ	USBLS	5/07
	Minnesota	Y	43463 FQ	46658 MW	49864 TQ	MNBLS	10/08-12/08
	Duluth-Superior MSA, MN-WI	Y	44161 FQ	47116 MW	50083 TQ	MNBLS	10/08-12/08
	Minneapolis-Saint Paul MSA, MN-WI	Y	43775 FQ	46867 MW	49958 TQ	MNBLS	10/08-12/08
	Rochester MSA, MN	Y	43252 FQ	46514 MW	49777 TQ	MNBLS	10/08-12/08
	Mississippi	Y	41930 FQ	44960 MW	48000 TQ	USBLS	5/07
	Jackson MSA, MS	Y	42480 FQ	45310 MW	48130 TQ	USBLS	5/07
	Missouri	Y	42030 FQ	45020 MW	48010 TQ	USBLS	5/07
	Kansas City MSA, MO-KS	Y	42600 FQ	45390 MW	48180 TQ	USBLS	5/07
	St. Louis MSA, MO-IL	Y	41650 FQ	44790 MW	47920 TQ	USBLS	5/07
	Springfield MSA, MO	Y	41670 FQ	44770 MW	47860 TQ	USBLS	5/07
	Montana	Y	42050 FQ	45030 MW	48010 TQ	USBLS	5/07
	Billings MSA, MT	Y	42600 FQ	45390 MW	48170 TQ	USBLS	5/07
	Nebraska	Y	42300 FQ	45190 MW	48090 TQ	USBLS	5/07
	Omaha-Council Bluffs MSA, NE-IA	Y	42620 FQ	45400 MW	48180 TQ	USBLS	5/07
	Nevada	H	20.45 FQ	21.98 MW	23.50 TQ	NVBLS	5/08
	Las Vegas-Paradise MSA, NV	H	20.21 FQ	21.82 MW	23.43 TQ	NVBLS	5/08
	New Hampshire	H	20.52 AE	22.13 MW	22.32 AEX	NHBLS	6/08
	Manchester MSA, NH	Y	42770 FQ	45500 MW	48230 TQ	USBLS	5/07
	Nashua NECTA, NH-MA	Y	41850 FQ	44930 MW	48000 TQ	USBLS	5/07
	Portsmouth MSA, NH-ME	Y	41010 FQ	44440 MW	47880 TQ	USBLS	5/07
	New Jersey	Y	42320 FQ	45200 MW	48090 TQ	USBLS	5/07
	Camden PMSA, NJ	Y	42110 FQ	45060 MW	48010 TQ	USBLS	5/07
	Edison PMSA, NJ	Y	42560 FQ	45370 MW	48190 TQ	USBLS	5/07
	Newark-Union PMSA, NJ-PA	Y	42610 FQ	45390 MW	48180 TQ	USBLS	5/07
	New Mexico	Y	41460 FQ	44630 MW	47810 TQ	USBLS	5/07

AE	Average entry wage	AW	Average wage paid	FQ	First quartile wage
AER	Average entry range	AWR	Average wage range	H	Hourly
AEX	Average experienced wage	AXR	Average experienced range	HI	Highest wage paid
ATC	Average total compensation	D	Daily	HR	High end range

LO	Lowest wage paid	MTC	Median total compensation	TCC	Total cash compensation
LR	Low end range	MW	Median wage paid	TQ	Third quartile wage
M	Monthly	MWR	Median wage range	W	Weekly
MCC	Median cash compensation	S	See annotated source	Y	Yearly

Occupation/Type/Industry	Location	Per	Low	Mid	High	Source	Date
Postal Service Clerk	Albuquerque MSA, NM	Y	42350 FQ	45230 MW	48120 TQ	USBLS	5/07
	Santa Fe MSA, NM	Y	41980 FQ	44970 MW	47970 TQ	USBLS	5/07
	New York	Y	42330 FQ	45210 MW	48090 TQ	USBLS	5/07
	Albany-Schenectady-Troy MSA, NY	Y	41850 FQ	44880 MW	47920 TQ	USBLS	5/07
	Buffalo-Niagara Falls MSA, NY	Y	41610 FQ	44770 MW	47940 TQ	USBLS	5/07
	Kingston MSA, NY	Y	41930 FQ	44940 MW	47950 TQ	USBLS	5/07
	Nassau-Suffolk PMSA, NY	Y	42590 FQ	45390 MW	48180 TQ	USBLS	5/07
	New York-Northern New Jersey-Long Island MSA, NY-NJ-PA	Y	42530 FQ	45340 MW	48160 TQ	USBLS	5/07
	Syracuse MSA, NY	Y	42280 FQ	45190 MW	48100 TQ	USBLS	5/07
	North Carolina	Y	41190 FQ	44460 MW	47730 TQ	USBLS	5/07
	Charlotte-Gastonia-Concord MSA, NC-SC	Y	41650 FQ	44760 MW	47880 TQ	USBLS	5/07
	Raleigh-Cary MSA, NC	Y	42200 FQ	45140 MW	48080 TQ	USBLS	5/07
	North Dakota	Y	41690 FQ	44780 MW	47870 TQ	USBLS	5/07
	Fargo MSA, ND-MN	Y	41770 FQ	44830 MW	47900 TQ	USBLS	5/07
	Ohio	Y	42450 FQ	45290 MW	48140 TQ	USBLS	5/07
	Cincinnati-Middletown MSA, OH-KY-IN	Y	42470 FQ	45310 MW	48150 TQ	USBLS	5/07
	Cleveland-Elyria-Mentor MSA, OH	Y	42690 FQ	45450 MW	48210 TQ	USBLS	5/07
	Columbus MSA, OH	Y	42420 FQ	45280 MW	48130 TQ	USBLS	5/07
	Dayton MSA, OH	Y	42460 FQ	45290 MW	48130 TQ	USBLS	5/07
	Oklahoma	Y	41670 FQ	44770 MW	47870 TQ	USBLS	5/07
	Oklahoma City MSA, OK	Y	42140 FQ	45080 MW	48020 TQ	USBLS	5/07
	Tulsa MSA, OK	Y	42240 FQ	45150 MW	48060 TQ	USBLS	5/07
	Oregon	H	20.32 FQ	21.90 MW	23.46 TQ	ORBLS	5/08
	Portland-Vancouver-Beaverton MSA, OR-WA	Y	41350 FQ	44560 MW	47760 TQ	USBLS	5/07
	Pennsylvania	Y	42330 FQ	45210 MW	48090 TQ	USBLS	5/07
	Allentown-Bethlehem-Easton MSA, PA-NJ	Y	42670 FQ	45430 MW	48200 TQ	USBLS	5/07
	Lancaster MSA, PA	Y	41000 FQ	44320 MW	47640 TQ	USBLS	5/07
	Philadelphia-Camden-Wilmington MSA, PA-NJ-DE-MD	Y	42480 FQ	45310 MW	48130 TQ	USBLS	5/07
	Pittsburgh MSA, PA	Y	42210 FQ	45130 MW	48040 TQ	USBLS	5/07
	Rhode Island	Y	42400 FQ	45270 MW	48130 TQ	USBLS	5/07
	Providence-Fall River-Warwick MSA, RI-MA	Y	42290 FQ	45200 MW	48110 TQ	USBLS	5/07
	South Carolina	Y	42070 FQ	45050 MW	48020 TQ	USBLS	5/07
	Charleston-North Charleston MSA, SC	Y	42000 FQ	44990 MW	47970 TQ	USBLS	5/07
	Columbia MSA, SC	Y	41950 FQ	44980 MW	48010 TQ	USBLS	5/07
	Myrtle Beach-Conway-North Myrtle Beach MSA, SC	Y	41810 FQ	44860 MW	47910 TQ	USBLS	5/07
	South Dakota	Y	42711 FQ	46073 MW	49435 TQ	SDBLS	7/08-9/08
	Sioux Falls MSA, SD	Y	43395 FQ	46529 MW	49663 TQ	SDBLS	7/08-9/08
	Tennessee	Y	42100 FQ	45070 MW	48040 TQ	USBLS	5/07
	Memphis MSA, TN-MS-AR	Y	42450 FQ	45300 MW	48150 TQ	USBLS	5/07
	Nashville-Davidson-Murfreesboro MSA, TN	Y	42220 FQ	45170 MW	48110 TQ	USBLS	5/07
	Texas	Y	42200 FQ	45140 MW	48080 TQ	USBLS	5/07
	Austin-Round Rock MSA, TX	Y	42370 FQ	45230 MW	48100 TQ	USBLS	5/07
	Dallas-Fort Worth-Arlington MSA, TX	Y	42440 FQ	45310 MW	48190 TQ	USBLS	5/07
	El Paso MSA, TX	Y	42550 FQ	45350 MW	48160 TQ	USBLS	5/07
	Houston-Sugar Land-Baytown MSA, TX	Y	42420 FQ	45300 MW	48190 TQ	USBLS	5/07
	San Antonio MSA, TX	Y	42620 FQ	45400 MW	48180 TQ	USBLS	5/07
	Utah	Y	41510 FQ	44660 MW	47810 TQ	USBLS	5/07
	Salt Lake City MSA, UT	Y	41390 FQ	44580 MW	47770 TQ	USBLS	5/07
	Vermont	Y	41170 FQ	44450 MW	47720 TQ	USBLS	5/07
	Burlington-South Burlington MSA, VT	Y	42120 FQ	45060 MW	48010 TQ	USBLS	5/07
	Virginia	Y	41800 FQ	44860 MW	47920 TQ	USBLS	5/07
	Charlottesville MSA, VA	Y	41830 FQ	44870 MW	47920 TQ	USBLS	5/07
	Richmond MSA, VA	Y	42320 FQ	45200 MW	48080 TQ	USBLS	5/07

Occupation/Type/Industry	Location	Per	Low	Mid	High	Source	Date
Postal Service Clerk	Virginia Beach-Norfolk-Newport News MSA, VA-NC	Y	41810 FQ	44870 MW	47930 TQ	USBLS	5/07
	Washington	H	20.22 FQ	21.76 MW	23.28 TQ	WABLS	3/08
	Seattle-Tacoma-Bellevue MSA, WA	Y	41650 FQ	44760 MW	47870 TQ	USBLS	5/07
	West Virginia	Y	43057 FQ	46313 MW	49569 TQ	WVBLS	7/08-9/08
	Charleston MSA, WV	Y	40960 FQ	44290 MW	47630 TQ	USBLS	5/07
	Wisconsin	Y	42080 FQ	45060 MW	48030 TQ	USBL'S	5/07
	Milwaukee-Waukesha-West Allis MSA, WI	Y	42350 FQ	45240 MW	48130 TQ	USBLS	5/07
	Wyoming	Y	42534 FQ	45977 MW	49420 TQ	WYBLS	9/08
	Puerto Rico	Y	42380 FQ	45250 MW	48110 TQ	USBLS	5/07
	Virgin Islands	Y	42620 FQ	45400 MW	48180 TQ	USBLS	5/07
	Guam	Y	41250 FQ	44490 MW	47720 TQ	USBLS	5/07
Postal Service Mail Carrier	Alabama	Y	37240 FQ	43580 MW	49870 TQ	USBLS	5/07
	Birmingham-Hoover MSA, AL	Y	38080 FQ	43940 MW	49310 TQ	USBLS	5/07
	Alaska	Y	41830 FQ	44990 MW	48150 TQ	USBLS	5/07
	Arizona	Y	40440 FQ	44400 MW	48360 TQ	USBLS	5/07
	Phoenix-Mesa-Scottsdale MSA, AZ	Y	40590 FQ	44450 MW	48310 TQ	USBLS	5/07
	Tucson MSA, AZ	Y	41080 FQ	44760 MW	48450 TQ	USBLS	5/07
	Arkansas	Y	37130 FQ	43150 MW	49130 TQ	USBLS	5/07
	Fort Smith MSA, AR-OK	Y	37400 FQ	43250 MW	48710 TQ	USBLS	5/07
	Little Rock-North Little Rock MSA, AR	Y	39090 FQ	44130 MW	48800 TQ	USBLS	5/07
	California	H	20.40 FQ	22.01 MW	23.62 TQ	CABLS	1/08-3/08
	Los Angeles-Long Beach-Glendale PMSA, CA	H	20.69 FQ	22.15 MW	23.60 TQ	CABLS	1/08-3/08
	Oakland-Fremont-Hayward MSA, CA	H	20.48 FQ	22.02 MW	23.56 TQ	CABLS	1/08-3/08
	Riverside-San Bernardino-Ontario MSA, CA	H	20.02 FQ	21.88 MW	23.73 TQ	CABLS	1/08-3/08
	Sacramento-Arden Arcade-Roseville MSA, CA	H	19.85 FQ	21.76 MW	23.68 TQ	CABLS	1/08-3/08
	San Diego-Carlsbad-San Marcos MSA, CA	H	20.34 FQ	21.97 MW	23.59 TQ	CABLS	1/08-3/08
	San Francisco-San Mateo-Redwood PMSA, CA	H	20.80 FQ	22.22 MW	23.64 TQ	CABLS	1/08-3/08
	San Jose-Sunnyvale-Santa Clara MSA, CA	H	20.54 FQ	22.06 MW	23.58 TQ	CABLS	1/08-3/08
	Santa Ana-Anaheim-Irvine PMSA, CA	Y	41890 FQ	44920 MW	47960 TQ	USBLS	5/07
	Stockton MSA, CA	H	19.74 FQ	21.65 MW	23.56 TQ	CABLS	1/08-3/08
	Colorado	Y	41060 FQ	44630 MW	48190 TQ	USBLS	5/07
	Denver-Aurora MSA, CO	Y	41730 FQ	44940 MW	48150 TQ	USBLS	5/07
	Connecticut	H	19.81 AE	22.07 MW		CTBLS	1/08-3/08
	Bridgeport-Stamford-Norwalk MSA, CT	Y	41820 FQ	45130 MW	48430 TQ	USBLS	5/07
	Hartford-West Hartford-East Hartford MSA, CT	Y	40960 FQ	44790 MW	48620 TQ	USBLS	5/07
	Delaware	Y	39810 FQ	44270 MW	48620 TQ	USBLS	5/07
	Wilmington PMSA, DE-MD-NJ	Y	41240 FQ	44990 MW	48750 TQ	USBLS	5/07
	District of Columbia	Y	41470 FQ	44630 MW	47800 TQ	USBLS	5/07
	Washington-Arlington-Alexandria MSA, DC-VA-MD-WV	Y	41020 FQ	44720 MW	48420 TQ	USBLS	5/07
	Florida	Y	40510 FQ	44540 MW	48570 TQ	USBLS	5/07
	Fort Lauderdale-Pompano Beach-Deerfield Beach PMSA, FL	Y	41940 FQ	45050 MW	48170 TQ	USBLS	5/07
	Jacksonville MSA, FL	Y	40110 FQ	44420 MW	48740 TQ	USBLS	5/07
	Miami-Fort Lauderdale-Miami Beach MSA, FL	Y	41880 FQ	45020 MW	48150 TQ	USBLS	5/07
	Orlando-Kissimmee MSA, FL	Y	40640 FQ	44670 MW	48700 TQ	USBLS	5/07
	Pensacola-Ferry Pass-Brent MSA, FL	Y	39120 FQ	44180 MW	48840 TQ	USBLS	5/07
	Tampa-St. Petersburg-Clearwater MSA, FL	Y	40100 FQ	44400 MW	48700 TQ	USBLS	5/07
	West Palm Beach-Boca Raton-Boynton Beach PMSA, FL	Y	41130 FQ	44610 MW	48080 TQ	USBLS	5/07

AE Average entry wage	**AW** Average wage paid	**FQ** First quartile wage	**LO** Lowest wage paid	**MTC** Median total compensation	**TCC** Total cash compensation
AER Average entry range	**AWR** Average wage range	**H** Hourly	**LR** Low end range	**MW** Median wage paid	**TQ** Third quartile wage
AEX Average experienced wage	**AXR** Average experienced range	**HI** Highest wage paid	**M** Monthly	**MWR** Median wage range	**W** Weekly
ATC Average total compensation	**D** Daily	**HR** High end range	**MCC** Median cash compensation	**S** See annotated source	**Y** Yearly

Postal Service Mail Carrier

Occupation/Type/Industry	Location	Per	Low	Mid	High	Source	Date
Postal Service Mail Carrier	Georgia	Y	37990 FQ	43810 MW	49120 TQ	USBLS	5/07
	Athens-Clarke County MSA, GA	Y	36860 FQ	42910 MW	48660 TQ	USBLS	5/07
	Atlanta-Sandy Springs-Marietta MSA, GA	Y	39190 FQ	44270 MW	48970 TQ	USBLS	5/07
	Hawaii	Y	41740 FQ	45050 MW	48350 TQ	USBLS	5/07
	Honolulu MSA, HI	Y	42080 FQ	45080 MW	48080 TQ	USBLS	5/07
	Idaho	Y	37290 FQ	43280 MW	48420 TQ	USBLS	5/07
	Boise City-Nampa MSA, ID	Y	38540 FQ	43850 MW	48560 TQ	USBLS	5/07
	Illinois	Y	41010 FQ	44730 MW	48440 TQ	USBLS	5/07
	Chicago-Naperville-Joliet MSA, IL-IN-WI	Y	41670 FQ	45010 MW	48350 TQ	USBLS	5/07
	Rockford MSA, IL	Y	40620 FQ	44600 MW	48590 TQ	USBLS	5/07
	Indiana	Y	39370 FQ	44240 MW	48800 TQ	USBLS	5/07
	Gary PMSA, IN	Y	41020 FQ	44850 MW	48680 TQ	USBLS	5/07
	Indianapolis-Carmel MSA, IN	Y	40460 FQ	44550 MW	48650 TQ	USBLS	5/07
	Iowa	Y	39070 FQ	44340 MW	49250 TQ	USBLS	5/07
	Des Moines-West Des Moines MSA, IA	Y	40800 FQ	44720 MW	48640 TQ	USBLS	5/07
	Sioux City MSA, IA-NE-SD	Y	39940 FQ	44390 MW	48790 TQ	USBLS	5/07
	Kansas	Y	39260 FQ	44080 MW	48530 TQ	USBLS	5/07
	Wichita MSA, KS	Y	40630 FQ	44530 MW	48430 TQ	USBLS	5/07
	Kentucky	Y	39248 FQ	45269 MW	50807 TQ	KYBLS	2008
	Lexington-Fayette MSA, KY	Y	41160 FQ	44870 MW	48570 TQ	USBLS	5/07
	Louisville-Jefferson County MSA, KY-IN	Y	40080 FQ	44360 MW	48650 TQ	USBLS	5/07
	Louisiana	H	19.14 FQ	21.39 MW	23.58 TQ	LABLS	1/08-3/08
	Baton Rouge MSA, LA	Y	39240 FQ	44310 MW	48990 TQ	USBLS	5/07
	Houma-Bayou Cane-Thibodaux MSA, LA	Y	38220 FQ	44530 MW	50150 TQ	USBLS	5/07
	New Orleans-Metairie-Kenner MSA, LA	Y	41790 FQ	45100 MW	48420 TQ	USBLS	5/07
	Maine	Y	36940 FQ	43190 MW	48550 TQ	USBLS	5/07
	Lewiston-Auburn MSA, ME	Y	37230 FQ	43510 MW	49140 TQ	USBLS	5/07
	Portland-South Portland-Biddeford MSA, ME	Y	40570 FQ	44830 MW	49080 TQ	USBLS	5/07
	Maryland	Y		45600 MW		MDBLS	3/08
	Baltimore-Towson MSA, MD	Y	40560 FQ	44490 MW	48420 TQ	USBLS	5/07
	Bethesda-Gaithersburg-Frederick PMSA, MD	Y	41430 FQ	44940 MW	48450 TQ	USBLS	5/07
	Salisbury MSA, MD	Y	37140 FQ	43650 MW	49490 TQ	USBLS	5/07
	Massachusetts	Y	41490 FQ	44920 MW	48340 TQ	USBLS	5/07
	Boston-Cambridge-Quincy NECTA, MA	Y	41890 FQ	45040 MW	48190 TQ	USBLS	5/07
	Worcester MSA, MA-CT	Y	40330 FQ	44320 MW	48320 TQ	USBLS	5/07
	Michigan	Y	40530 FQ	44580 MW	48640 TQ	USBLS	5/07
	Ann Arbor MSA, MI	Y	40570 FQ	44590 MW	48610 TQ	USBLS	5/07
	Detroit-Warren-Livonia MSA, MI	Y	41900 FQ	45150 MW	48400 TQ	USBLS	5/07
	Grand Rapids-Wyoming MSA, MI	Y	39660 FQ	44280 MW	48710 TQ	USBLS	5/07
	Warren-Troy-Farmington Hills PMSA, MI	Y	41540 FQ	45050 MW	48560 TQ	USBLS	5/07
	Minnesota	Y	40851 FQ	45982 MW	50738 TQ	MNBLS	10/08-12/08
	Duluth-Superior MSA, MN-WI	Y	42402 FQ	46481 MW	50572 TQ	MNBLS	10/08-12/08
	Minneapolis-Saint Paul MSA, MN-WI	Y	42318 FQ	46367 MW	50426 TQ	MNBLS	10/08-12/08
	Rochester MSA, MN	Y	40407 FQ	45784 MW	50660 TQ	MNBLS	10/08-12/08
	Mississippi	Y	36850 FQ	43300 MW	50170 TQ	USBLS	5/07
	Gulfport-Biloxi MSA, MS	Y	37670 FQ	43710 MW	49450 TQ	USBLS	5/07
	Jackson MSA, MS	Y	38170 FQ	43880 MW	49040 TQ	USBLS	5/07
	Pascagoula MSA, MS	Y	38010 FQ	44050 MW	49720 TQ	USBLS	5/07
	Missouri	Y	39390 FQ	44190 MW	48680 TQ	USBLS	5/07
	Joplin MSA, MO	Y	36940 FQ	43030 MW	49320 TQ	USBLS	5/07
	Kansas City MSA, MO-KS	Y	40920 FQ	44740 MW	48560 TQ	USBLS	5/07
	St. Louis MSA, MO-IL	Y	40900 FQ	44680 MW	48460 TQ	USBLS	5/07
	Springfield MSA, MO	Y	37290 FQ	43270 MW	49130 TQ	USBLS	5/07
	Montana	Y	38740 FQ	43900 MW	48440 TQ	USBLS	5/07
	Billings MSA, MT	Y	40590 FQ	44550 MW	48510 TQ	USBLS	5/07
	Nebraska	Y	38950 FQ	44070 MW	48760 TQ	USBLS	5/07
	Lincoln MSA, NE	Y	40480 FQ	44510 MW	48550 TQ	USBLS	5/07

AE	Average entry wage	AW	Average wage paid	FQ	First quartile wage	LO	Lowest wage paid	MTC	Median total compensation	TCC	Total cash compensation
AER	Average entry range	AWR	Average wage range	H	Hourly	LR	Low end range	MW	Median wage paid	TQ	Third quartile wage
AEX	Average experienced wage	AXR	Average experienced range	HI	Highest wage paid	M	Monthly	MWR	Median wage range	W	Weekly
ATC	Average total compensation	D	Daily	HR	High end range	MCC	Median cash compensation	S	See annotated source	Y	Yearly

Occupation/Type/Industry	Location	Per	Low	Mid	High	Source	Date
Postal Service Mail Carrier	Omaha-Council Bluffs MSA, NE-IA	Y	41170 FQ	45100 MW	49040 TQ	USBLS	5/07
	Nevada	H	20.07 FQ	21.81 MW	23.55 TQ	NVBLS	5/08
	Carson City MSA, NV	H	20.56 FQ	22.05 MW	23.54 TQ	NVBLS	5/08
	Las Vegas-Paradise MSA, NV	H	20.18 FQ	21.86 MW	23.53 TQ	NVBLS	5/08
	New Hampshire	H	17.69 AE	21.88 MW	23.77 AEX	NHBLS	6/08
	Manchester MSA, NH	Y	41720 FQ	45360 MW	49000 TQ	USBLS	5/07
	Nashua NECTA, NH-MA	Y	38530 FQ	44310 MW	49680 TQ	USBLS	5/07
	New Jersey	Y	41210 FQ	44720 MW	48230 TQ	USBLS	5/07
	Camden PMSA, NJ	Y	41060 FQ	44740 MW	48410 TQ	USBLS	5/07
	Edison PMSA, NJ	Y	41350 FQ	44840 MW	48340 TQ	USBLS	5/07
	Newark-Union PMSA, NJ-PA	Y	41040 FQ	44630 MW	48220 TQ	USBLS	5/07
	New Mexico	Y	40170 FQ	44180 MW	48190 TQ	USBLS	5/07
	Albuquerque MSA, NM	Y	40310 FQ	44230 MW	48150 TQ	USBLS	5/07
	New York	Y	41000 FQ	44580 MW	48150 TQ	USBLS	5/07
	Albany-Schenectady-Troy MSA, NY	Y	40060 FQ	44270 MW	48480 TQ	USBLS	5/07
	Buffalo-Niagara Falls MSA, NY	Y	41440 FQ	44890 MW	48330 TQ	USBLS	5/07
	Nassau-Suffolk PMSA, NY	Y	41260 FQ	44570 MW	47880 TQ	USBLS	5/07
	New York-Northern New Jersey-Long Island MSA, NY-NJ-PA	Y	41420 FQ	44700 MW	47990 TQ	USBLS	5/07
	Utica-Rome MSA, NY	Y	39930 FQ	44330 MW	48670 TQ	USBLS	5/07
	North Carolina	Y	37780 FQ	43750 MW	49260 TQ	USBLS	5/07
	Charlotte-Gastonia-Concord MSA, NC-SC	Y	38560 FQ	43920 MW	48770 TQ	USBLS	5/07
	Raleigh-Cary MSA, NC	Y	38660 FQ	44110 MW	49060 TQ	USBLS	5/07
	North Dakota	Y	37920 FQ	43710 MW	49070 TQ	USBLS	5/07
	Fargo MSA, ND-MN	Y	40190 FQ	44520 MW	48860 TQ	USBLS	5/07
	Ohio	Y	40730 FQ	44650 MW	48570 TQ	USBLS	5/07
	Cincinnati-Middletown MSA, OH-KY-IN	Y	40530 FQ	44460 MW	48390 TQ	USBLS	5/07
	Cleveland-Elyria-Mentor MSA, OH	Y	42080 FQ	45180 MW	48290 TQ	USBLS	5/07
	Columbus MSA, OH	Y	40530 FQ	44620 MW	48720 TQ	USBLS	5/07
	Dayton MSA, OH	Y	41490 FQ	44880 MW	48270 TQ	USBLS	5/07
	Mansfield MSA, OH	Y	40930 FQ	44870 MW	48810 TQ	USBLS	5/07
	Springfield MSA, OH	Y	41220 FQ	44940 MW	48650 TQ	USBLS	5/07
	Oklahoma	Y	38620 FQ	44120 MW	49080 TQ	USBLS	5/07
	Oklahoma City MSA, OK	Y	40060 FQ	44410 MW	48760 TQ	USBLS	5/07
	Tulsa MSA, OK	Y	40520 FQ	44690 MW	48860 TQ	USBLS	5/07
	Oregon	H	19.97 FQ	21.88 MW	23.79 TQ	ORBLS	5/08
	Medford MSA, OR	Y	40570 FQ	44520 MW	48470 TQ	USBLS	5/07
	Portland-Vancouver-Beaverton MSA, OR-WA	Y	40970 FQ	44680 MW	48390 TQ	USBLS	5/07
	Salem MSA, OR	Y	40200 FQ	44230 MW	48270 TQ	USBLS	5/07
	Pennsylvania	Y	40880 FQ	44830 MW	48780 TQ	USBLS	5/07
	Allentown-Bethlehem-Easton MSA, PA-NJ	Y	40550 FQ	44790 MW	49020 TQ	USBLS	5/07
	Philadelphia-Camden-Wilmington MSA, PA-NJ-DE-MD	Y	41680 FQ	45030 MW	48390 TQ	USBLS	5/07
	Pittsburgh MSA, PA	Y	41300 FQ	44990 MW	48680 TQ	USBLS	5/07
	Rhode Island	Y	41440 FQ	44950 MW	48470 TQ	USBLS	5/07
	Providence-Fall River-Warwick MSA, RI-MA	Y	41350 FQ	44930 MW	48510 TQ	USBLS	5/07
	South Carolina	Y	37650 FQ	43710 MW	49550 TQ	USBLS	5/07
	Charleston-North Charleston MSA, SC	Y	37650 FQ	43610 MW	49360 TQ	USBLS	5/07
	Columbia MSA, SC	Y	39090 FQ	44370 MW	49310 TQ	USBLS	5/07
	South Dakota	Y	39086 FQ	45225 MW	51028 TQ	SDBLS	7/08-9/08
	Sioux Falls MSA, SD	Y	40000 FQ	45689 MW	50881 TQ	SDBLS	7/08-9/08
	Tennessee	Y	38020 FQ	44310 MW	50220 TQ	USBLS	5/07
	Kingsport-Bristol-Bristol MSA, TN-VA	Y	37470 FQ	44010 MW	50470 TQ	USBLS	5/07
	Memphis MSA, TN-MS-AR	Y	40470 FQ	44690 MW	48900 TQ	USBLS	5/07
	Nashville-Davidson-Murfreesboro MSA, TN	Y	38580 FQ	44430 MW	49800 TQ	USBLS	5/07
	Texas	Y	40610 FQ	44730 MW	48860 TQ	USBLS	5/07
	Austin-Round Rock MSA, TX	Y	40610 FQ	45010 MW	49410 TQ	USBLS	5/07

AE	Average entry wage	AW	Average wage paid	FQ	First quartile wage	LO	Lowest wage paid	MTC	Median total compensation	TCC	Total cash compensation
AER	Average entry range	AWR	Average wage range	H	Hourly	LR	Low end range	MW	Median wage paid	TQ	Third quartile wage
AEX	Average experienced wage	AXR	Average experienced range	HI	Highest wage paid	M	Monthly	MWR	Median wage range	W	Weekly
ATC	Average total compensation	D	Daily	HR	High end range	MCC	Median cash compensation	S	See annotated source	Y	Yearly

Occupation/Type/Industry	Location	Per	Low	Mid	High	Source	Date
Postal Service Mail Carrier	Dallas-Fort Worth-Arlington MSA, TX	Y	40830 FQ	44840 MW	48860 TQ	USBLS	5/07
	El Paso MSA, TX	Y	41970 FQ	45120 MW	48260 TQ	USBLS	5/07
	Houston-Sugar Land-Baytown MSA, TX	Y	41470 FQ	45020 MW	48570 TQ	USBLS	5/07
	San Antonio MSA, TX	Y	41310 FQ	44990 MW	48670 TQ	USBLS	5/07
	Utah	Y	40860 FQ	44670 MW	48470 TQ	USBLS	5/07
	St. George MSA, UT	Y	37560 FQ	43030 MW	47330 TQ	USBLS	5/07
	Salt Lake City MSA, UT	Y	41500 FQ	44910 MW	48310 TQ	USBLS	5/07
	Vermont	Y	36210 FQ	43000 MW	49390 TQ	USBLS	5/07
	Burlington-South Burlington MSA, VT	Y	38770 FQ	44340 MW	49410 TQ	USBLS	5/07
	Virginia	Y	39450 FQ	44320 MW	48920 TQ	USBLS	5/07
	Charlottesville MSA, VA	Y	38550 FQ	44700 MW	50430 TQ	USBLS	5/07
	Richmond MSA, VA	Y	38750 FQ	44150 MW	49010 TQ	USBLS	5/07
	Virginia Beach-Norfolk-Newport News MSA, VA-NC	Y	41220 FQ	44720 MW	48220 TQ	USBLS	5/07
	Washington	H	19.58 FQ	21.56 MW	23.54 TQ	WABLS	3/08
	Seattle-Tacoma-Bellevue MSA, WA	Y	40840 FQ	44480 MW	48130 TQ	USBLS	5/07
	Spokane MSA, WA	Y	40060 FQ	44170 MW	48280 TQ	USBLS	5/07
	West Virginia	Y	39329 FQ	45287 MW	50639 TQ	WVBLS	7/08-9/08
	Charleston MSA, WV	Y	40310 FQ	44590 MW	48860 TQ	USBLS	5/07
	Wisconsin	Y	38720 FQ	44140 MW	49080 TQ	USBLS	5/07
	Milwaukee-Waukesha-West Allis MSA, WI	Y	41490 FQ	44970 MW	48450 TQ	USBLS	5/07
	Wyoming	Y	42197 FQ	46097 MW	49997 TQ	WYBLS	9/08
	Casper MSA, WY	Y	44025 FQ	47059 MW	50092 TQ	WYBLS	9/08
	Puerto Rico	Y	42420 FQ	45410 MW	48400 TQ	USBLS	5/07
	Virgin Islands	Y	42560 FQ	45360 MW	48160 TQ	USBLS	5/07
	Guam	Y	41560 FQ	44690 MW	47830 TQ	USBLS	5/07
Postal Service Mail Sorter, Processor, and Processing Machine Operator	Alabama	Y	34380 FQ	42920 MW	47000 TQ	USBLS	5/07
	Birmingham-Hoover MSA, AL	Y	40330 FQ	43900 MW	47470 TQ	USBLS	5/07
	Montgomery MSA, AL	Y	40050 FQ	43690 MW	47320 TQ	USBLS	5/07
	Alaska	Y	23780 FQ	38590 MW	45300 TQ	USBLS	5/07
	Arizona	Y	40120 FQ	43740 MW	47350 TQ	USBLS	5/07
	Phoenix-Mesa-Scottsdale MSA, AZ	Y	40490 FQ	43990 MW	47480 TQ	USBLS	5/07
	Tucson MSA, AZ	Y	40400 FQ	43920 MW	47440 TQ	USBLS	5/07
	Arkansas	Y	29800 FQ	41300 MW	46150 TQ	USBLS	5/07
	Little Rock-North Little Rock MSA, AR	Y	39470 FQ	43620 MW	47320 TQ	USBLS	5/07
	California	H	19.50 FQ	21.44 MW	23.25 TQ	CABLS	1/08-3/08
	Los Angeles-Long Beach-Glendale PMSA, CA	H	19.68 FQ	21.48 MW	23.27 TQ	CABLS	1/08-3/08
	Modesto MSA, CA	H	13.43 FQ	15.26 MW	22.25 TQ	CABLS	1/08-3/08
	Oakland-Fremont-Hayward MSA, CA	H	19.82 FQ	21.57 MW	23.31 TQ	CABLS	1/08-3/08
	Riverside-San Bernardino-Ontario MSA, CA	H	18.22 FQ	21.19 MW	23.12 TQ	CABLS	1/08-3/08
	Sacramento-Arden Arcade-Roseville MSA, CA	H	17.38 FQ	20.97 MW	23.03 TQ	CABLS	1/08-3/08
	San Diego-Carlsbad-San Marcos MSA, CA	H	18.91 FQ	21.24 MW	23.14 TQ	CABLS	1/08-3/08
	San Francisco-San Mateo-Redwood PMSA, CA	H	20.49 FQ	22.00 MW	23.52 TQ	CABLS	1/08-3/08
	San Jose-Sunnyvale-Santa Clara MSA, CA	H	19.89 FQ	21.60 MW	23.32 TQ	CABLS	1/08-3/08
	Santa Ana-Anaheim-Irvine PMSA, CA	Y	38290 FQ	43440 MW	47210 TQ	USBLS	5/07
	Stockton MSA, CA	H	20.22 FQ	21.83 MW	23.43 TQ	CABLS	1/08-3/08
	Colorado	Y	39790 FQ	43670 MW	47330 TQ	USBLS	5/07
	Denver-Aurora MSA, CO	Y	40760 FQ	44180 MW	47590 TQ	USBLS	5/07
	Connecticut	H	17.18 AE	21.81 MW		CTBLS	1/08-3/08
	Bridgeport-Stamford-Norwalk MSA, CT	Y	41220 FQ	44470 MW	47710 TQ	USBLS	5/07
	Hartford-West Hartford-East Hartford MSA, CT	Y	41230 FQ	44480 MW	47730 TQ	USBLS	5/07

AE	Average entry wage	**AW**	Average wage paid	**FQ**	First quartile wage	**LO**	Lowest wage paid	**MTC** Median total compensation	**TCC** Total cash compensation
AER	Average entry range	**AWR**	Average wage range	**H**	Hourly	**LR**	Low end range	**MW** Median wage paid	**TQ** Third quartile wage
AEX	Average experienced wage	**AXR**	Average experienced range	**HI**	Highest wage paid	**M**	Monthly	**MWR** Median wage range	**W** Weekly
ATC	Average total compensation	**D**	Daily	**HR**	High end range	**MCC**	Median cash compensation	**S** See annotated source	**Y** Yearly

Occupation/Type/Industry	Location	Per	Low	Mid	High	Source	Date
Postal Service Mail Sorter, Processor, and Processing Machine Operator	Delaware	Y	40250 FQ	43830 MW	47410 TQ	USBLS	5/07
	Wilmington PMSA, DE-MD-NJ	Y	40230 FQ	43810 MW	47400 TQ	USBLS	5/07
	District of Columbia	Y	41500 FQ	44660 MW	47810 TQ	USBLS	5/07
	Washington-Arlington-Alexandria MSA, DC-VA-MD-WV	Y	41260 FQ	44510 MW	47750 TQ	USBLS	5/07
	Florida	Y	40480 FQ	43990 MW	47500 TQ	USBLS	5/07
	Fort Lauderdale-Pompano Beach-Deerfield Beach PMSA, FL	Y	40130 FQ	43740 MW	47350 TQ	USBLS	5/07
	Jacksonville MSA, FL	Y	40720 FQ	44150 MW	47580 TQ	USBLS	5/07
	Miami-Fort Lauderdale-Miami Beach MSA, FL	Y	40460 FQ	43960 MW	47460 TQ	USBLS	5/07
	Orlando-Kissimmee MSA, FL	Y	40860 FQ	44240 MW	47610 TQ	USBLS	5/07
	Tampa-St. Petersburg-Clearwater MSA, FL	Y	40300 FQ	43870 MW	47440 TQ	USBLS	5/07
	West Palm Beach-Boca Raton-Boynton Beach PMSA, FL	Y	40750 FQ	44160 MW	47570 TQ	USBLS	5/07
	Georgia	Y	40660 FQ	44120 MW	47580 TQ	USBLS	5/07
	Atlanta-Sandy Springs-Marietta MSA, GA	Y	41250 FQ	44510 MW	47760 TQ	USBLS	5/07
	Hawaii	Y	35840 FQ	42320 MW	46640 TQ	USBLS	5/07
	Honolulu MSA, HI	Y	36420 FQ	42520 MW	46740 TQ	USBLS	5/07
	Idaho	Y	24520 FQ	41030 MW	45990 TQ	USBLS	5/07
	Boise City-Nampa MSA, ID	Y	34950 FQ	42470 MW	46710 TQ	USBLS	5/07
	Illinois	Y	40700 FQ	44130 MW	47560 TQ	USBLS	5/07
	Chicago-Naperville-Joliet MSA, IL-IN-WI	Y	41090 FQ	44390 MW	47690 TQ	USBLS	5/07
	Rockford MSA, IL	Y	41700 FQ	44780 MW	47870 TQ	USBLS	5/07
	Indiana	Y	36130 FQ	43450 MW	47230 TQ	USBLS	5/07
	Gary PMSA, IN	Y	31490 FQ	43170 MW	47110 TQ	USBLS	5/07
	Indianapolis-Carmel MSA, IN	Y	40900 FQ	44270 MW	47640 TQ	USBLS	5/07
	Terre Haute MSA, IN	Y	35270 FQ	42860 MW	46910 TQ	USBLS	5/07
	Iowa	Y	35220 FQ	42980 MW	47000 TQ	USBLS	5/07
	Des Moines-West Des Moines MSA, IA	Y	41270 FQ	44530 MW	47790 TQ	USBLS	5/07
	Sioux City MSA, IA-NE-SD	Y	36090 FQ	43250 MW	47100 TQ	USBLS	5/07
	Kansas	Y	33350 FQ	42740 MW	46870 TQ	USBLS	5/07
	Wichita MSA, KS	Y	37220 FQ	43170 MW	47070 TQ	USBLS	5/07
	Kentucky	Y	30140 FQ	43087 MW	47805 TQ	KYBLS	2008
	Louisville-Jefferson County MSA, KY-IN	Y	39400 FQ	43620 MW	47300 TQ	USBLS	5/07
	Louisiana	H	17.25 FQ	20.62 MW	22.57 TQ	LABLS	1/08-3/08
	Baton Rouge MSA, LA	Y	34250 FQ	40990 MW	46020 TQ	USBLS	5/07
	Lafayette MSA, LA	Y	37770 FQ	43240 MW	47100 TQ	USBLS	5/07
	New Orleans-Metairie-Kenner MSA, LA	Y	41030 FQ	44340 MW	47660 TQ	USBLS	5/07
	Maine	Y	28730 FQ	41950 MW	46460 TQ	USBLS	5/07
	Portland-South Portland-Biddeford MSA, ME	Y	40730 FQ	44140 MW	47550 TQ	USBLS	5/07
	Maryland	Y		45250 MW		MDBLS	3/08
	Baltimore-Towson MSA, MD	Y	41230 FQ	44480 MW	47730 TQ	USBLS	5/07
	Bethesda-Gaithersburg-Frederick PMSA, MD	Y	41090 FQ	44380 MW	47680 TQ	USBLS	5/07
	Massachusetts	Y	40830 FQ	44220 MW	47600 TQ	USBLS	5/07
	Boston-Cambridge-Quincy NECTA, MA	Y	41330 FQ	44540 MW	47750 TQ	USBLS	5/07
	Springfield MSA, MA-CT	Y	40360 FQ	43910 MW	47460 TQ	USBLS	5/07
	Worcester MSA, MA-CT	Y	40360 FQ	43900 MW	47430 TQ	USBLS	5/07
	Michigan	Y	40820 FQ	44210 MW	47600 TQ	USBLS	5/07
	Detroit-Warren-Livonia MSA, MI	Y	41580 FQ	44720 MW	47860 TQ	USBLS	5/07
	Grand Rapids-Wyoming MSA, MI	Y	40150 FQ	43760 MW	47370 TQ	USBLS	5/07
	Warren-Troy-Farmington Hills PMSA, MI	Y	41180 FQ	44450 MW	47720 TQ	USBLS	5/07
	Minnesota	Y	42235 FQ	45847 MW	49458 TQ	MNBLS	10/08-12/08
	Duluth-Superior MSA, MN-WI	Y	42079 FQ	45732 MW	49385 TQ	MNBLS	10/08-12/08

AE	Average entry wage	AW	Average wage paid	FQ	First quartile wage	LO	Lowest wage paid	MTC	Median total compensation	TCC	Total cash compensation
AER	Average entry range	AWR	Average wage range	H	Hourly	LR	Low end range	MW	Median wage paid	TQ	Third quartile wage
AEX	Average experienced wage	AXR	Average experienced range	HI	Highest wage paid	M	Monthly	MWR	Median wage range	W	Weekly
ATC	Average total compensation	D	Daily	HR	High end range	MCC	Median cash compensation	S	See annotated source	Y	Yearly

Occupation/Type/Industry	Location	Per	Low	Mid	High	Source	Date
Postal Service Mail Sorter, Processor, and Processing Machine Operator	Minneapolis-Saint Paul MSA, MN-WI	Y	43234 FQ	46513 MW	49781 TQ	MNBLS	10/08-12/08
	Rochester MSA, MN	Y	37343 FQ	44479 MW	48759 TQ	MNBLS	10/08-12/08
	Mississippi	Y	27200 FQ	42000 MW	46480 TQ	USBLS	5/07
	Hattiesburg MSA, MS	Y	40430 FQ	43940 MW	47450 TQ	USBLS	5/07
	Jackson MSA, MS	Y	40210 FQ	43800 MW	47380 TQ	USBLS	5/07
	Missouri	Y	37180 FQ	43340 MW	47160 TQ	USBLS	5/07
	Kansas City MSA, MO-KS	Y	41060 FQ	44370 MW	47690 TQ	USBLS	5/07
	St. Louis MSA, MO-IL	Y	37100 FQ	43260 MW	47120 TQ	USBLS	5/07
	Montana	Y	23650 FQ	37970 MW	44840 TQ	USBLS	5/07
	Billings MSA, MT	Y	34590 FQ	41320 MW	46140 TQ	USBLS	5/07
	Nebraska	Y	32900 FQ	42760 MW	46870 TQ	USBLS	5/07
	Omaha-Council Bluffs MSA, NE-IA	Y	40800 FQ	44200 MW	47590 TQ	USBLS	5/07
	Nevada	H	17.44 FQ	21.10 MW	23.07 TQ	NVBLS	5/08
	Las Vegas-Paradise MSA, NV	H	18.25 FQ	21.23 MW	23.13 AEX	NVBLS	5/08
	New Hampshire	H	15.34 AE	21.33 MW	22.33 AEX	NHBLS	6/08
	Manchester MSA, NH	Y	41540 FQ	44690 MW	47840 TQ	USBLS	5/07
	Nashua NECTA, NH-MA	Y	37990 FQ	43160 MW	47080 TQ	USBLS	5/07
	New Jersey	Y	40600 FQ	44070 MW	47540 TQ	USBLS	5/07
	Camden PMSA, NJ	Y	40390 FQ	43990 MW	47560 TQ	USBLS	5/07
	Edison PMSA, NJ	Y	40480 FQ	43970 MW	47470 TQ	USBLS	5/07
	Newark-Union PMSA, NJ-PA	Y	41140 FQ	44420 MW	47700 TQ	USBLS	5/07
	New Mexico	Y	29700 FQ	41340 MW	46150 TQ	USBLS	5/07
	Albuquerque MSA, NM	Y	36280 FQ	42870 MW	46910 TQ	USBLS	5/07
	Santa Fe MSA, NM	Y	40040 FQ	43680 MW	47320 TQ	USBLS	5/07
	New York	Y	40630 FQ	44080 MW	47540 TQ	USBLS	5/07
	Albany-Schenectady-Troy MSA, NY	Y	41120 FQ	44420 MW	47720 TQ	USBLS	5/07
	Buffalo-Niagara Falls MSA, NY	Y	41220 FQ	44470 MW	47720 TQ	USBLS	5/07
	Nassau-Suffolk PMSA, NY	Y	40170 FQ	43770 MW	47360 TQ	USBLS	5/07
	New York-Northern New Jersey-Long Island MSA, NY-NJ-PA	Y	40890 FQ	44260 MW	47630 TQ	USBLS	5/07
	North Carolina	Y	36930 FQ	43330 MW	47170 TQ	USBLS	5/07
	Charlotte-Gastonia-Concord MSA, NC-SC	Y	39280 FQ	43590 MW	47290 TQ	USBLS	5/07
	Durham MSA, NC	Y	41000 FQ	44320 MW	47640 TQ	USBLS	5/07
	Raleigh-Cary MSA, NC	Y	40410 FQ	43940 MW	47470 TQ	USBLS	5/07
	North Dakota	Y	24520 FQ	39650 MW	45430 TQ	USBLS	5/07
	Fargo MSA, ND-MN	Y	40140 FQ	43750 MW	47350 TQ	USBLS	5/07
	Ohio	Y	40500 FQ	44000 MW	47500 TQ	USBLS	5/07
	Cincinnati-Middletown MSA, OH-KY-IN	Y	40880 FQ	44270 MW	47650 TQ	USBLS	5/07
	Cleveland-Elyria-Mentor MSA, OH	Y	41320 FQ	44540 MW	47750 TQ	USBLS	5/07
	Columbus MSA, OH	Y	40520 FQ	44010 MW	47500 TQ	USBLS	5/07
	Dayton MSA, OH	Y	40420 FQ	43950 MW	47480 TQ	USBLS	5/07
	Oklahoma	Y	35520 FQ	43110 MW	47140 TQ	USBLS	5/07
	Oklahoma City MSA, OK	Y	40510 FQ	44050 MW	47600 TQ	USBLS	5/07
	Tulsa MSA, OK	Y	40540 FQ	44070 MW	47610 TQ	USBLS	5/07
	Oregon	H	17.89 FQ	21.12 MW	23.08 TQ	ORBLS	5/08
	Portland-Vancouver-Beaverton MSA, OR-WA	Y	40310 FQ	43860 MW	47420 TQ	USBLS	5/07
	Pennsylvania	Y	38050 FQ	43480 MW	47240 TQ	USBLS	5/07
	Allentown-Bethlehem-Easton MSA, PA-NJ	Y	40220 FQ	43810 MW	47400 TQ	USBLS	5/07
	Philadelphia-Camden-Wilmington MSA, PA-NJ-DE-MD	Y	40560 FQ	44050 MW	47540 TQ	USBLS	5/07
	Pittsburgh MSA, PA	Y	37660 FQ	43260 MW	47130 TQ	USBLS	5/07
	Rhode Island	Y	41250 FQ	44500 MW	47740 TQ	USBLS	5/07
	Providence-Fall River-Warwick MSA, RI-MA	Y	41190 FQ	44460 MW	47730 TQ	USBLS	5/07
	South Carolina	Y	36100 FQ	43170 MW	47120 TQ	USBLS	5/07
	Charleston-North Charleston MSA, SC	Y	37880 FQ	43410 MW	47300 TQ	USBLS	5/07
	Columbia MSA, SC	Y	40580 FQ	44060 MW	47540 TQ	USBLS	5/07

AE	Average entry wage	AW	Average wage paid	FQ	First quartile wage
AER	Average entry range	AWR	Average wage range	H	Hourly
AEX	Average experienced wage	AXR	Average experienced range	HI	Highest wage paid
ATC	Average total compensation	D	Daily	HR	High end range

LO	Lowest wage paid	MTC	Median total compensation
LR	Low end range	MW	Median wage paid
M	Monthly	MWR	Median wage range
		MCC	Median cash compensation

TCC	Total cash compensation	
TQ	Third quartile wage	
W	Weekly	
S	See annotated source	Y	Yearly

Occupation/Type/Industry	Location	Per	Low	Mid	High	Source	Date
Postal Service Mail Sorter, Processor, and Processing Machine Operator							
	South Dakota	Y	26030 FQ	41536 MW	47166 TQ	SDBLS	7/08-9/08
	Sioux Falls MSA, SD	Y	35737 FQ	44074 MW	48435 TQ	SDBLS	7/08-9/08
	Tennessee	Y	40260 FQ	43850 MW	47450 TQ	USBLS	5/07
	Memphis MSA, TN-MS-AR	Y	41780 FQ	44860 MW	47940 TQ	USBLS	5/07
	Nashville-Davidson-Murfreesboro MSA, TN	Y	38110 FQ	43280 MW	47150 TQ	USBLS	5/07
	Texas	Y	40720 FQ	44150 MW	47570 TQ	USBLS	5/07
	Austin-Round Rock MSA, TX	Y	40960 FQ	44300 MW	47630 TQ	USBLS	5/07
	Dallas-Fort Worth-Arlington MSA, TX	Y	41190 FQ	44460 MW	47730 TQ	USBLS	5/07
	El Paso MSA, TX	Y	36450 FQ	43300 MW	47200 TQ	USBLS	5/07
	Houston-Sugar Land-Baytown MSA, TX	Y	41700 FQ	44810 MW	47920 TQ	USBLS	5/07
	San Antonio MSA, TX	Y	40760 FQ	44160 MW	47560 TQ	USBLS	5/07
	Utah	Y	32170 FQ	41420 MW	46190 TQ	USBLS	5/07
	Salt Lake City MSA, UT	Y	35620 FQ	42530 MW	46750 TQ	USBLS	5/07
	Vermont	Y	27660 FQ	40820 MW	45890 TQ	USBLS	5/07
	Burlington-South Burlington MSA, VT	Y	35500 FQ	42740 MW	46850 TQ	USBLS	5/07
	Virginia	Y	40040 FQ	43700 MW	47360 TQ	USBLS	5/07
	Charlottesville MSA, VA	Y	40810 FQ	44190 MW	47580 TQ	USBLS	5/07
	Richmond MSA, VA	Y	35060 FQ	43510 MW	47250 TQ	USBLS	5/07
	Virginia Beach-Norfolk-Newport News MSA, VA-NC	Y	40120 FQ	43740 MW	47350 TQ	USBLS	5/07
	Washington	H	19.54 FQ	21.30 MW	23.06 TQ	WABLS	3/08
	Seattle-Tacoma-Bellevue MSA, WA	Y	40910 FQ	44280 MW	47650 TQ	USBLS	5/07
	Spokane MSA, WA	Y	32390 FQ	42620 MW	46790 TQ	USBLS	5/07
	West Virginia	Y	23964 FQ	39498 MW	46694 TQ	WVBLS	7/08-9/08
	Charleston MSA, WV	Y	33800 FQ	42590 MW	46770 TQ	USBLS	5/07
	Wisconsin	Y	38940 FQ	43610 MW	47310 TQ	USBLS	5/07
	Milwaukee-Waukesha-West Allis MSA, WI	Y	41070 FQ	44390 MW	47710 TQ	USBLS	5/07
	Wyoming	Y	23968 FQ	41388 MW	47127 TQ	WYBLS	9/08
	Puerto Rico	Y	18610 FQ	42310 MW	46640 TQ	USBLS	5/07
	Virgin Islands	Y	42220 FQ	45140 MW	48050 TQ	USBLS	5/07
Postmaster and Mail Superintendent							
	Alabama	Y	51750 FQ	59390 MW	69480 TQ	USBLS	5/07
	Birmingham-Hoover MSA, AL	Y	53130 FQ	61190 MW	72350 TQ	USBLS	5/07
	Alaska	Y	34550 FQ	44350 MW	56030 TQ	USBLS	5/07
	Arizona	Y	52280 FQ	60620 MW	72900 TQ	USBLS	5/07
	Phoenix-Mesa-Scottsdale MSA, AZ	Y	62600 FQ	72670 MW	82320 TQ	USBLS	5/07
	Arkansas	Y	43530 FQ	53700 MW	63340 TQ	USBLS	5/07
	Little Rock-North Little Rock MSA, AR	Y	50460 FQ	62550 MW	77350 TQ	USBLS	5/07
	California	H	25.89 FQ	31.89 MW	38.43 TQ	CABLS	1/08-3/08
	Los Angeles-Long Beach-Glendale PMSA, CA	H	35.95 FQ	41.77 MW	46.63 TQ	CABLS	1/08-3/08
	Oakland-Fremont-Hayward MSA, CA	H	33.32 FQ	37.67 MW	43.36 TQ	CABLS	1/08-3/08
	Riverside-San Bernardino-Ontario MSA, CA	H	29.41 FQ	34.74 MW	39.05 TQ	CABLS	1/08-3/08
	Sacramento-Arden Arcade-Roseville MSA, CA	H	26.36 FQ	32.74 MW	38.53 TQ	CABLS	1/08-3/08
	San Diego-Carlsbad-San Marcos MSA, CA	H	31.17 FQ	37.16 MW	43.91 TQ	CABLS	1/08-3/08
	San Francisco-San Mateo-Redwood PMSA, CA	H	26.48 FQ	31.17 MW	39.29 TQ	CABLS	1/08-3/08
	San Jose-Sunnyvale-Santa Clara MSA, CA	H	30.54 FQ	39.41 MW	45.94 TQ	CABLS	1/08-3/08
	Santa Ana-Anaheim-Irvine PMSA, CA	Y	72350 FQ	86550 MW	95020 TQ	USBLS	5/07
	Colorado	Y	45060 FQ	56290 MW	68550 TQ	USBLS	5/07
	Denver-Aurora MSA, CO	Y	54550 FQ	68010 MW	84190 TQ	USBLS	5/07
	Connecticut	H	25.97 AE	32.46 MW		CTBLS	1/08-3/08
	Hartford-West Hartford-East Hartford MSA, CT	Y	56510 FQ	66090 MW	76550 TQ	USBLS	5/07

AE	Average entry wage	**AW**	Average wage paid	**FQ**	First quartile wage	
AER	Average entry range	**AWR**	Average wage range	**H**	Hourly	
AEX	Average experienced wage	**AXR**	Average experienced range	**HI**	Highest wage paid	
ATC	Average total compensation	**D**	Daily	**HR**	High end range	

LO	Lowest wage paid	**MTC**	Median total compensation
LR	Low end range	**MW**	Median wage paid
M	Monthly	**MWR**	Median wage range
MCC	Median cash compensation	**S**	See annotated source

TCC	Total cash compensation
TQ	Third quartile wage
W	Weekly
Y	Yearly

Occupation/Type/Industry	Location	Per	Low	Mid	High	Source	Date
Postmaster and Mail Superintendent	Delaware	Y	58100 FQ	67120 MW	75370 TQ	USBLS	5/07
	Wilmington PMSA, DE-MD-NJ	Y	54340 FQ	61580 MW	71720 TQ	USBLS	5/07
	Washington-Arlington-Alexandria MSA, DC-VA-MD-WV	Y	52560 FQ	63500 MW	76060 TQ	USBLS	5/07
	Florida	Y	56960 FQ	67810 MW	79480 TQ	USBLS	5/07
	Orlando-Kissimmee MSA, FL	Y	59300 FQ	70680 MW	83130 TQ	USBLS	5/07
	Tampa-St. Petersburg-Clearwater MSA, FL	Y	60760 FQ	73060 MW	86260 TQ	USBLS	5/07
	Georgia	Y	53230 FQ	61820 MW	73610 TQ	USBLS	5/07
	Atlanta-Sandy Springs-Marietta MSA, GA	Y	58500 FQ	69700 MW	80720 TQ	USBLS	5/07
	Hawaii	Y	55810 FQ	63800 MW	74810 TQ	USBLS	5/07
	Idaho	Y	45510 FQ	55580 MW	65530 TQ	USBLS	5/07
	Illinois	Y	47640 FQ	57280 MW	67620 TQ	USBLS	5/07
	Chicago-Naperville-Joliet MSA, IL-IN-WI	Y	59890 FQ	71140 MW	80970 TQ	USBLS	5/07
	Indiana	Y	47910 FQ	57430 MW	67020 TQ	USBLS	5/07
	Evansville MSA, IN-KY	Y	47780 FQ	58140 MW	68770 TQ	USBLS	5/07
	Gary PMSA, IN	Y	52190 FQ	63250 MW	75040 TQ	USBLS	5/07
	Indianapolis-Carmel MSA, IN	Y	54480 FQ	64800 MW	76400 TQ	USBLS	5/07
	Terre Haute MSA, IN	Y	42090 FQ	49600 MW	59070 TQ	USBLS	5/07
	Iowa	Y	44280 FQ	54130 MW	61940 TQ	USBLS	5/07
	Davenport-Moline-Rock Island MSA, IA-IL	Y	51310 FQ	57720 MW	64130 TQ	USBLS	5/07
	Des Moines-West Des Moines MSA, IA	Y	42500 FQ	56540 MW	69080 TQ	USBLS	5/07
	Sioux City MSA, IA-NE-SD	Y	47210 FQ	54870 MW	60740 TQ	USBLS	5/07
	Kansas	Y	42220 FQ	53480 MW	62440 TQ	USBLS	5/07
	Wichita MSA, KS	Y	48570 FQ	58850 MW	69910 TQ	USBLS	5/07
	Kentucky	Y	44886 FQ	55965 MW	65838 TQ	KYBLS	2008
	Louisville-Jefferson County MSA, KY-IN	Y	49700 FQ	59970 MW	73810 TQ	USBLS	5/07
	Louisiana	H	25.19 FQ	28.95 MW	34.17 TQ	LABLS	1/08-3/08
	Baton Rouge MSA, LA	Y	52780 FQ	60320 MW	70680 TQ	USBLS	5/07
	New Orleans-Metairie-Kenner MSA, LA	Y	57720 FQ	69900 MW	81640 TQ	USBLS	5/07
	Maine	Y	46400 FQ	55200 MW	62540 TQ	USBLS	5/07
	Bangor MSA, ME	Y	47140 FQ	54570 MW	61330 TQ	USBLS	5/07
	Portland-South Portland-Biddeford MSA, ME	Y	52440 FQ	62370 MW	73820 TQ	USBLS	5/07
	Maryland	Y		61625 MW		MDBLS	3/08
	Baltimore-Towson MSA, MD	Y	55670 FQ	65090 MW	75820 TQ	USBLS	5/07
	Bethesda-Gaithersburg-Frederick PMSA, MD	Y	52890 FQ	63510 MW	75210 TQ	USBLS	5/07
	Massachusetts	Y	57400 FQ	67280 MW	76480 TQ	USBLS	5/07
	Boston-Cambridge-Quincy NECTA, MA	Y	64000 FQ	71710 MW	79200 TQ	USBLS	5/07
	Worcester MSA, MA-CT	Y	59110 FQ	68080 MW	75410 TQ	USBLS	5/07
	Michigan	Y	53030 FQ	61780 MW	72630 TQ	USBLS	5/07
	Detroit-Warren-Livonia MSA, MI	Y	64660 FQ	72890 MW	81120 TQ	USBLS	5/07
	Grand Rapids-Wyoming MSA, MI	Y	58000 FQ	68580 MW	76980 TQ	USBLS	5/07
	Warren-Troy-Farmington Hills PMSA, MI	Y	61100 FQ	70970 MW	79550 TQ	USBLS	5/07
	Minnesota	Y	52059 FQ	60317 MW	69096 TQ	MNBLS	10/08-12/08
	Duluth-Superior MSA, MN-WI	Y	53842 FQ	60745 MW	68450 TQ	MNBLS	10/08-12/08
	Minneapolis-Saint Paul MSA, MN-WI	Y	59733 FQ	70212 MW	79710 TQ	MNBLS	10/08-12/08
	Rochester MSA, MN	Y	56016 FQ	62744 MW	72448 TQ	MNBLS	10/08-12/08
	Mississippi	Y	51830 FQ	59120 MW	68650 TQ	USBLS	5/07
	Jackson MSA, MS	Y	56030 FQ	67540 MW	78270 TQ	USBLS	5/07
	Missouri	Y	43870 FQ	55010 MW	63100 TQ	USBLS	5/07
	Kansas City MSA, MO-KS	Y	50820 FQ	60550 MW	73970 TQ	USBLS	5/07
	St. Louis MSA, MO-IL	Y	51050 FQ	60040 MW	71990 TQ	USBLS	5/07
	Montana	Y	38980 FQ	48260 MW	59030 TQ	USBLS	5/07
	Nebraska	Y	44600 FQ	53870 MW	61850 TQ	USBLS	5/07
	Omaha-Council Bluffs MSA, NE-IA	Y	49440 FQ	58620 MW	71920 TQ	USBLS	5/07

AE	Average entry wage	AW	Average wage paid	FQ	First quartile wage	LO	Lowest wage paid	MTC	Median total compensation	TCC	Total cash compensation
AER	Average entry range	AWR	Average wage range	H	Hourly	LR	Low end range	MW	Median wage paid	TQ	Third quartile wage
AEX	Average experienced wage	AXR	Average experienced range	HI	Highest wage paid	M	Monthly	MWR	Median wage range	W	Weekly
ATC	Average total compensation	D	Daily	HR	High end range	MCC	Median cash compensation	S	See annotated source	Y	Yearly

Postmaster and Mail Superintendent

Occupation/Type/Industry	Location	Per	Low	Mid	High	Source	Date
	Nevada	H	22.49 FQ	27.72 MW	34.31 TQ	NVBLS	5/08
	Las Vegas-Paradise MSA, NV	H	27.79 FQ	33.49 MW	40.25 TQ	NVBLS	5/08
	New Hampshire	H	23.23 AE	29.71 MW	32.95 AEX	NHBLS	6/08
	New Jersey	Y	60720 FQ	70690 MW	79290 TQ	USBLS	5/07
	Camden PMSA, NJ	Y	58500 FQ	68770 MW	78540 TQ	USBLS	5/07
	Edison PMSA, NJ	Y	65130 FQ	72830 MW	80520 TQ	USBLS	5/07
	Newark-Union PMSA, NJ-PA	Y	60110 FQ	69800 MW	77770 TQ	USBLS	5/07
	New Mexico	Y	38250 FQ	49260 MW	60110 TQ	USBLS	5/07
	Albuquerque MSA, NM	Y	51810 FQ	60540 MW	76640 TQ	USBLS	5/07
	New York	Y	50900 FQ	59440 MW	70730 TQ	USBLS	5/07
	Albany-Schenectady-Troy MSA, NY	Y	51360 FQ	61700 MW	74670 TQ	USBLS	5/07
	Buffalo-Niagara Falls MSA, NY	Y	52920 FQ	63410 MW	74820 TQ	USBLS	5/07
	Nassau-Suffolk PMSA, NY	Y	66100 FQ	73790 MW	81480 TQ	USBLS	5/07
	New York-Northern New Jersey-Long Island MSA, NY-NJ-PA	Y	64800 FQ	72790 MW	80780 TQ	USBLS	5/07
	North Carolina	Y	52430 FQ	60070 MW	70480 TQ	USBLS	5/07
	Charlotte-Gastonia-Concord MSA, NC-SC	Y	55760 FQ	64120 MW	77350 TQ	USBLS	5/07
	North Dakota	Y	36170 FQ	46330 MW	56330 TQ	USBLS	5/07
	Ohio	Y	51340 FQ	59220 MW	69870 TQ	USBLS	5/07
	Cincinnati-Middletown MSA, OH-KY-IN	Y	53960 FQ	62380 MW	75080 TQ	USBLS	5/07
	Cleveland-Elyria-Mentor MSA, OH	Y	58170 FQ	69160 MW	79300 TQ	USBLS	5/07
	Columbus MSA, OH	Y	52600 FQ	62080 MW	75210 TQ	USBLS	5/07
	Dayton MSA, OH	Y	55060 FQ	64990 MW	75330 TQ	USBLS	5/07
	Oklahoma	Y	44550 FQ	55210 MW	63610 TQ	USBLS	5/07
	Oklahoma City MSA, OK	Y	53460 FQ	62420 MW	75680 TQ	USBLS	5/07
	Tulsa MSA, OK	Y	46870 FQ	59140 MW	71130 TQ	USBLS	5/07
	Oregon	H	23.86 FQ	28.90 MW	34.78 TQ	ORBLS	5/08
	Portland-Vancouver-Beaverton MSA, OR-WA	Y	60260 FQ	71120 MW	80530 TQ	USBLS	5/07
	Pennsylvania	Y	47950 FQ	57240 MW	66640 TQ	USBLS	5/07
	Allentown-Bethlehem-Easton MSA, PA-NJ	Y	52410 FQ	60040 MW	70380 TQ	USBLS	5/07
	Philadelphia-Camden-Wilmington MSA, PA-NJ-DE-MD	Y	56200 FQ	64380 MW	76450 TQ	USBLS	5/07
	Pittsburgh MSA, PA	Y	49090 FQ	58250 MW	68870 TQ	USBLS	5/07
	Reading MSA, PA	Y	52410 FQ	59010 MW	67210 TQ	USBLS	5/07
	Rhode Island	Y	56030 FQ	65840 MW	77350 TQ	USBLS	5/07
	Providence-Fall River-Warwick MSA, RI-MA	Y	57340 FQ	67910 MW	77870 TQ	USBLS	5/07
	South Carolina	Y	52050 FQ	60970 MW	72100 TQ	USBLS	5/07
	Charleston-North Charleston MSA, SC	Y	52750 FQ	59310 MW	68230 TQ	USBLS	5/07
	Columbia MSA, SC	Y	53210 FQ	63350 MW	76960 TQ	USBLS	5/07
	South Dakota	Y	40727 FQ	53098 MW	62306 TQ	SDBLS	7/08-9/08
	Sioux Falls MSA, SD	Y	55449 FQ	62127 MW	78199 TQ	SDBLS	7/08-9/08
	Tennessee	Y	53550 FQ	61920 MW	73320 TQ	USBLS	5/07
	Memphis MSA, TN-MS-AR	Y	49070 FQ	60110 MW	72350 TQ	USBLS	5/07
	Nashville-Davidson-Murfreesboro MSA, TN	Y	57860 FQ	69630 MW	83870 TQ	USBLS	5/07
	Texas	Y	48440 FQ	58750 MW	70450 TQ	USBLS	5/07
	Austin-Round Rock MSA, TX	Y	57960 FQ	67480 MW	76280 TQ	USBLS	5/07
	Dallas-Fort Worth-Arlington MSA, TX	Y	58570 FQ	70350 MW	79910 TQ	USBLS	5/07
	Houston-Sugar Land-Baytown MSA, TX	Y	60050 FQ	70560 MW	80030 TQ	USBLS	5/07
	San Antonio MSA, TX	Y	52380 FQ	62350 MW	75580 TQ	USBLS	5/07
	Utah	Y	47550 FQ	57950 MW	70550 TQ	USBLS	5/07
	Vermont	Y	45910 FQ	54390 MW	61390 TQ	USBLS	5/07
	Burlington-South Burlington MSA, VT	Y	53630 FQ	59140 MW	65090 TQ	USBLS	5/07
	Virginia	Y	47010 FQ	56540 MW	65110 TQ	USBLS	5/07
	Richmond MSA, VA	Y	51270 FQ	59770 MW	72420 TQ	USBLS	5/07
	Virginia Beach-Norfolk-Newport News MSA, VA-NC	Y	41100 FQ	51280 MW	62070 TQ	USBLS	5/07

AE	Average entry wage	AW	Average wage paid	FQ	First quartile wage	LO	Lowest wage paid	MTC	Median total compensation
AER	Average entry range	AWR	Average wage range	H	Hourly	LR	Low end range	MW	Median wage paid
AEX	Average experienced wage	AXR	Average experienced range	HI	Highest wage paid	M	Monthly	MWR	Median wage range
ATC	Average total compensation	D	Daily	HR	High end range	MCC	Median cash compensation	S	See annotated source

TCC Total cash compensation
TQ Third quartile wage
W Weekly
Y Yearly

Occupation/Type/Industry	Location	Per	Low	Mid	High	Source	Date
Postmaster and Mail Superintendent	Washington	H	23.86 FQ	29.07 MW	35.05 TQ	WABLS	3/08
	Seattle-Tacoma-Bellevue MSA, WA	Y	59220 FQ	71340 MW	82850 TQ	USBLS	5/07
	West Virginia	Y	41874 FQ	52327 MW	62419 TQ	WVBLS	7/08-9/08
	Charleston MSA, WV	Y	40150 FQ	51930 MW	62450 TQ	USBLS	5/07
	Wisconsin	Y	51970 FQ	59740 MW	69940 TQ	USBLS	5/07
	Milwaukee-Waukesha-West Allis MSA, WI	Y	62140 FQ	71990 MW	81100 TQ	USBLS	5/07
	Wyoming	Y	40673 FQ	51002 MW	62361 TQ	WYBLS	9/08
	Casper MSA, WY	Y	44473 FQ	51096 MW	69277 TQ	WYBLS	9/08
	Puerto Rico	Y	56930 FQ	63540 MW	74440 TQ	USBLS	5/07
Postmaster General							
United States Postal Service	United States	Y			263575 HI	CNN01	2008
Poultry Products Inspector							
State Government	Ohio	H	15.09 LO		17.03 HI	ODAS	2008
Pourer and Caster							
Metals	Alabama	Y	23650 FQ	30110 MW	39120 TQ	USBLS	5/07
Metals	Birmingham-Hoover MSA, AL	Y	26570 FQ	34370 MW	44820 TQ	USBLS	5/07
Metals	Arizona	Y	23160 FQ	29910 MW	38500 TQ	USBLS	5/07
Metals	Phoenix-Mesa-Scottsdale MSA, AZ	Y	25380 FQ	29310 MW	35720 TQ	USBLS	5/07
Metals	Arkansas	Y	24190 FQ	31730 MW	37610 TQ	USBLS	5/07
Metals	California	H	10.55 FQ	12.68 MW	15.11 TQ	CABLS	1/08-3/08
Metals	Los Angeles-Long Beach-Glendale PMSA, CA	H	9.67 FQ	11.64 MW	14.32 TQ	CABLS	1/08-3/08
Metals	Oakland-Fremont-Hayward MSA, CA	H	11.96 FQ	13.87 MW	15.47 TQ	CABLS	1/08-3/08
Metals	Riverside-San Bernardino-Ontario MSA, CA	H	11.92 FQ	20.89 MW	23.23 TQ	CABLS	1/08-3/08
Metals	San Diego-Carlsbad-San Marcos MSA, CA	H	9.98 FQ	11.26 MW	14.12 TQ	CABLS	1/08-3/08
Metals	Colorado	Y	28120 FQ	33260 MW	46180 TQ	USBLS	5/07
Metals	Connecticut	H	10.73 AE	16.47 MW		CTBLS	1/08-3/08
Metals	Hartford-West Hartford-East Hartford MSA, CT	Y	21830 FQ	24580 MW	35350 TQ	USBLS	5/07
Metals	Florida	Y	21140 FQ	26460 MW	32990 TQ	USBLS	5/07
Metals	Jacksonville MSA, FL	Y	33020 FQ	41350 MW	45810 TQ	USBLS	5/07
Metals	Miami-Fort Lauderdale-Miami Beach MSA, FL	Y	18760 FQ	24340 MW	28630 TQ	USBLS	5/07
Metals	Tampa-St. Petersburg-Clearwater MSA, FL	Y	22320 FQ	25930 MW	29180 TQ	USBLS	5/07
Metals	Georgia	Y	21560 FQ	26800 MW	30730 TQ	USBLS	5/07
Metals	Atlanta-Sandy Springs-Marietta MSA, GA	Y	19360 FQ	25740 MW	29690 TQ	USBLS	5/07
Metals	Illinois	Y	25270 FQ	29310 MW	40150 TQ	USBLS	5/07
Metals	Chicago-Naperville-Joliet MSA, IL-IN-WI	Y	27330 FQ	38530 MW	60620 TQ	USBLS	5/07
Metals	Indiana	Y	27680 FQ	38580 MW	50130 TQ	USBLS	5/07
Metals	Gary PMSA, IN	Y	49030 FQ	58200 MW	68310 TQ	USBLS	5/07
Metals	Indianapolis-Carmel MSA, IN	Y	35590 FQ	41280 MW	45630 TQ	USBLS	5/07
Metals	Iowa	Y	26670 FQ	32610 MW	37960 TQ	USBLS	5/07
Metals	Kansas	Y	19980 FQ	22490 MW	26320 TQ	USBLS	5/07
Metals	Kentucky	Y	22577 FQ	29669 MW	35336 TQ	KYBLS	2008
Metals	Massachusetts	Y	25160 FQ	30030 MW	37320 TQ	USBLS	5/07
Metals	Boston-Cambridge-Quincy NECTA, MA	Y	28460 FQ	33400 MW	41710 TQ	USBLS	5/07
Metals	Michigan	Y	27710 FQ	32250 MW	38000 TQ	USBLS	5/07
Metals	Detroit-Warren-Livonia MSA, MI	Y	32500 FQ	37110 MW	42750 TQ	USBLS	5/07
Metals	Grand Rapids-Wyoming MSA, MI	Y	25830 FQ	28910 MW	31650 TQ	USBLS	5/07
Metals	Warren-Troy-Farmington Hills PMSA, MI	Y	29120 FQ	33550 MW	41430 TQ	USBLS	5/07
Metals	Minnesota	Y	31629 FQ	36107 MW	41208 TQ	MNBLS	10/08-12/08
Metals	Minneapolis-Saint Paul MSA, MN-WI	Y	33059 FQ	38025 MW	43654 TQ	MNBLS	10/08-12/08
Metals	Missouri	Y	28050 FQ	33250 MW	36730 TQ	USBLS	5/07
Metals	St. Louis MSA, MO-IL	Y	28140 FQ	34470 MW	39800 TQ	USBLS	5/07

AE	Average entry wage	AW	Average wage paid	FQ	First quartile wage
AER	Average entry range	AWR	Average wage range	H	Hourly
AEX	Average experienced wage	AXR	Average experienced range	HI	Highest wage paid
ATC	Average total compensation	D	Daily	HR	High end range

LO	Lowest wage paid	MTC	Median total compensation	TCC	Total cash compensation
LR	Low end range	MW	Median wage paid	TQ	Third quartile wage
M	Monthly	MWR	Median wage range	W	Weekly
MCC	Median cash compensation	S	See annotated source	Y	Yearly

Pourer and Caster

Occupation/Type/Industry	Location	Per	Low	Mid	High	Source	Date
Pourer and Caster							
Metals	New Hampshire	H	12.45 AE	15.82 MW	17.31 AEX	NHBLS	6/08
Metals	Nashua NECTA, NH-MA	Y	28190 FQ	31840 MW	34790 TQ	USBLS	5/07
Metals	New Jersey	Y	24090 FQ	26750 MW	29570 TQ	USBLS	5/07
Metals	Newark-Union PMSA, NJ-PA	Y	24740 FQ	26690 MW	28630 TQ	USBLS	5/07
Metals	New York	Y	24050 FQ	32430 MW	41060 TQ	USBLS	5/07
Metals	New York-Northern New Jersey-Long Island MSA, NY-NJ-PA	Y	23900 FQ	26950 MW	30780 TQ	USBLS	5/07
Metals	North Carolina	Y	24720 FQ	30260 MW	34700 TQ	USBLS	5/07
Metals	Charlotte-Gastonia-Concord MSA, NC-SC	Y	26130 FQ	31000 MW	34750 TQ	USBLS	5/07
Metals	Ohio	Y	24490 FQ	30400 MW	37980 TQ	USBLS	5/07
Metals	Cincinnati-Middletown MSA, OH-KY-IN	Y	24000 FQ	30160 MW	38280 TQ	USBLS	5/07
Metals	Cleveland-Elyria-Mentor MSA, OH	Y	24130 FQ	28720 MW	38460 TQ	USBLS	5/07
Metals	Columbus MSA, OH	Y	30700 FQ	35270 MW	38550 TQ	USBLS	5/07
Metals	Dayton MSA, OH	Y	23690 FQ	27890 MW	33500 TQ	USBLS	5/07
Metals	Oklahoma	Y	25710 FQ	28250 MW	31150 TQ	USBLS	5/07
Metals	Tulsa MSA, OK	Y	26160 FQ	28550 MW	30970 TQ	USBLS	5/07
Metals	Oregon	H	12.08 FQ	14.49 MW	17.43 TQ	ORBLS	5/08
Metals	Portland-Vancouver-Beaverton MSA, OR-WA	Y	25380 FQ	30360 MW	36050 TQ	USBLS	5/07
Metals	Pennsylvania	Y	27000 FQ	30850 MW	35720 TQ	USBLS	5/07
Metals	Allentown-Bethlehem-Easton MSA, PA-NJ	Y	28030 FQ	30660 MW	33610 TQ	USBLS	5/07
Metals	Philadelphia-Camden-Wilmington MSA, PA-NJ-DE-MD	Y	35260 FQ	40030 MW	46750 TQ	USBLS	5/07
Metals	Pittsburgh MSA, PA	Y	27270 FQ	30710 MW	35280 TQ	USBLS	5/07
Metals	Rhode Island	Y	21300 FQ	26140 MW	30470 TQ	USBLS	5/07
Metals	Providence-Fall River-Warwick MSA, RI-MA	Y	21480 FQ	26000 MW	30300 TQ	USBLS	5/07
Metals	South Carolina	Y	27750 FQ	39530 MW	44740 TQ	USBLS	5/07
Metals	Charleston-North Charleston MSA, SC	Y	41460 FQ	44140 MW	46830 TQ	USBLS	5/07
Metals	South Dakota	Y	21883 FQ	24123 MW	29059 TQ	SDBLS	7/08-9/08
Metals	Tennessee	Y	30210 FQ	35160 MW	38710 TQ	USBLS	5/07
Metals	Texas	Y	21130 FQ	32870 MW	40160 TQ	USBLS	5/07
Metals	Beaumont-Port Arthur MSA, TX	Y	42620 FQ	45630 MW	48650 TQ	USBLS	5/07
Metals	Dallas-Fort Worth-Arlington MSA, TX	Y	17570 FQ	20240 MW	31740 TQ	USBLS	5/07
Metals	El Paso MSA, TX	Y	29000 FQ	34450 MW	38120 TQ	USBLS	5/07
Metals	Houston-Sugar Land-Baytown MSA, TX	Y	18210 FQ	21980 MW	32960 TQ	USBLS	5/07
Metals	Utah	Y	21490 FQ	24490 MW	27950 TQ	USBLS	5/07
Metals	Virginia	Y	23870 FQ	28060 MW	31620 TQ	USBLS	5/07
Metals	Washington	H	13.33 FQ	15.08 MW	17.96 TQ	WABLS	3/08
Metals	Seattle-Tacoma-Bellevue MSA, WA	Y	27330 FQ	31770 MW	37010 TQ	USBLS	5/07
Metals	West Virginia	Y	34889 FQ	37114 MW	39340 TQ	WVBLS	7/08-9/08
Metals	Wisconsin	Y	25020 FQ	30740 MW	35390 TQ	USBLS	5/07
Metals	Milwaukee-Waukesha-West Allis MSA, WI	Y	24470 FQ	30430 MW	36050 TQ	USBLS	5/07
Power Distributor and Dispatcher	Alabama	Y	56550 FQ	65520 MW	76220 TQ	USBLS	5/07
	Alaska	Y	64020 FQ	71370 MW	80210 TQ	USBLS	5/07
	Arizona	Y	52620 FQ	60120 MW	69910 TQ	USBLS	5/07
	Arkansas	Y	41760 FQ	54690 MW	67570 TQ	USBLS	5/07
	California	H	27.94 FQ	36.68 MW	43.61 TQ	CABLS	1/08-3/08
	Colorado	Y	58940 FQ	65320 MW	74180 TQ	USBLS	5/07
	Connecticut	H	23.97 AE	33.66 MW		CTBLS	1/08-3/08
	Delaware	Y	62550 FQ	71250 MW	77910 TQ	USBLS	5/07
	Florida	Y	48480 FQ	60410 MW	72270 TQ	USBLS	5/07
	Georgia	Y	54480 FQ	59910 MW	65370 TQ	USBLS	5/07
	Illinois	Y	57270 FQ	65340 MW	76150 TQ	USBLS	5/07
	Indiana	Y	53070 FQ	66130 MW	74520 TQ	USBLS	5/07
	Iowa	Y	51300 FQ	57260 MW	63390 TQ	USBLS	5/07
	Kansas	Y	52050 FQ	62620 MW	70720 TQ	USBLS	5/07
	Kentucky	Y	57816 FQ	64840 MW	72658 TQ	KYBLS	2008

AE	Average entry wage	AW	Average wage paid	FQ	First quartile wage	LO	Lowest wage paid	MTC	Median total compensation	TCC	Total cash compensation
AER	Average entry range	AWR	Average wage range	H	Hourly	LR	Low end range	MW	Median wage paid	TQ	Third quartile wage
AEX	Average experienced wage	AXR	Average experienced range	HI	Highest wage paid	M	Monthly	MWR	Median wage range	W	Weekly
ATC	Average total compensation	D	Daily	HR	High end range	MCC	Median cash compensation	S	See annotated source	Y	Yearly

Occupation/Type/Industry	Location	Per	Low	Mid	High	Source	Date
Power Distributor and Dispatcher	Maine	Y	44030 FQ	47720 MW	51320 TQ	USBLS	5/07
	Maryland	Y		71625 MW		MDBLS	3/08
	Massachusetts	Y	57070 FQ	65450 MW	73740 TQ	USBLS	5/07
	Michigan	Y	56480 FQ	65090 MW	72670 TQ	USBLS	5/07
	Minnesota	Y	57421 FQ	73106 MW	81866 TQ	MNBLS	10/08-12/08
	Missouri	Y	50360 FQ	58390 MW	68210 TQ	USBLS	5/07
	Montana	Y	70080 FQ	77270 MW	88360 TQ	USBLS	5/07
	Nebraska	Y	57280 FQ	69630 MW	78300 TQ	USBLS	5/07
	New Jersey	Y	54910 FQ	61410 MW	69780 TQ	USBLS	5/07
	New York	Y	46230 FQ	68850 MW	78230 TQ	USBLS	5/07
	North Carolina	Y	38710 FQ	47280 MW	63130 TQ	USBLS	5/07
	Ohio	Y	43580 FQ	54060 MW	60740 TQ	USBLS	5/07
	Oklahoma	Y	54500 FQ	62660 MW	73100 TQ	USBLS	5/07
	Oregon	H	33.04 FQ	36.52 MW	40.90 TQ	ORBLS	5/08
	Pennsylvania	Y	56440 FQ	66860 MW	77580 TQ	USBLS	5/07
	South Carolina	Y	57530 FQ	70040 MW	78050 TQ	USBLS	5/07
	South Dakota	Y	64354 FQ	71469 MW	77296 TQ	SDBLS	7/08-9/08
	Tennessee	Y	35790 FQ	58280 MW	68540 TQ	USBLS	5/07
	Texas	Y	43100 FQ	53370 MW	63850 TQ	USBLS	5/07
	Utah	Y	59800 FQ	71890 MW	84290 TQ	USBLS	5/07
	Virginia	Y	47010 FQ	54500 MW	61320 TQ	USBLS	5/07
	Washington	H	33.15 FQ	36.76 MW	41.68 TQ	WABLS	3/08
	West Virginia	Y	71974 FQ	78185 MW	84394 TQ	WVBLS	7/08-9/08
	Wisconsin	Y	55630 FQ	62130 MW	71330 TQ	USBLS	5/07
	Wyoming	Y	56610 FQ	61557 MW	66504 TQ	WYBLS	9/08
Power Plant Operator	Alabama	Y	43090 FQ	50510 MW	59070 TQ	USBLS	5/07
	Alaska	Y	30710 FQ	36080 MW	65790 TQ	USBLS	5/07
	Arizona	Y	38310 FQ	44780 MW	53590 TQ	USBLS	5/07
	Tucson MSA, AZ	Y	35950 FQ	40910 MW	45560 TQ	USBLS	5/07
	Arkansas	Y	54090 FQ	59720 MW	73420 TQ	USBLS	5/07
	California	H	27.32 FQ	32.64 MW	37.64 TQ	CABLS	1/08-3/08
	Los Angeles-Long Beach-Glendale PMSA, CA	H	28.32 FQ	32.10 MW	35.85 TQ	CABLS	1/08-3/08
	Oakland-Fremont-Hayward MSA, CA	H	28.39 FQ	32.92 MW	37.77 TQ	CABLS	1/08-3/08
	Riverside-San Bernardino-Ontario MSA, CA	H	28.31 FQ	32.14 MW	36.32 TQ	CABLS	1/08-3/08
	Sacramento-Arden Arcade-Roseville MSA, CA	H	27.79 FQ	30.16 MW	32.92 TQ	CABLS	1/08-3/08
	San Diego-Carlsbad-San Marcos MSA, CA	H	34.16 FQ	36.50 MW	38.85 TQ	CABLS	1/08-3/08
	San Jose-Sunnyvale-Santa Clara MSA, CA	H	30.28 FQ	34.90 MW	39.40 TQ	CABLS	1/08-3/08
	Santa Ana-Anaheim-Irvine PMSA, CA	Y	47120 FQ	66500 MW	75800 TQ	USBLS	5/07
	Colorado	Y	45160 FQ	54850 MW	61550 TQ	USBLS	5/07
	Denver-Aurora MSA, CO	Y	52310 FQ	56640 MW	61060 TQ	USBLS	5/07
	Connecticut	H	24.79 AE	30.51 MW		CTBLS	1/08-3/08
	Bridgeport-Stamford-Norwalk MSA, CT	Y	53850 FQ	60290 MW	68910 TQ	USBLS	5/07
	Delaware	Y	58730 FQ	63590 MW	69690 TQ	USBLS	5/07
	Wilmington PMSA, DE-MD-NJ	Y	53340 FQ	60300 MW	68480 TQ	USBLS	5/07
	Washington-Arlington-Alexandria MSA, DC-VA-MD-WV	Y	48080 FQ	55810 MW	63490 TQ	USBLS	5/07
	Florida	Y	46680 FQ	54470 MW	63130 TQ	USBLS	5/07
	Fort Lauderdale-Pompano Beach-Deerfield Beach PMSA, FL	Y	46820 FQ	53520 MW	63960 TQ	USBLS	5/07
	Jacksonville MSA, FL	Y	50740 FQ	57620 MW	63730 TQ	USBLS	5/07
	Miami-Fort Lauderdale-Miami Beach MSA, FL	Y	51240 FQ	59500 MW	69570 TQ	USBLS	5/07
	Orlando-Kissimmee MSA, FL	Y	45260 FQ	54820 MW	64030 TQ	USBLS	5/07
	Tampa-St. Petersburg-Clearwater MSA, FL	Y	46240 FQ	54660 MW	62770 TQ	USBLS	5/07
	Georgia	Y	42950 FQ	49390 MW	58230 TQ	USBLS	5/07
	Atlanta-Sandy Springs-Marietta MSA, GA	Y	42660 FQ	51540 MW	63080 TQ	USBLS	5/07
	Hawaii	Y	54260 FQ	65150 MW	71910 TQ	USBLS	5/07
	Idaho	Y	49030 FQ	65090 MW	73290 TQ	USBLS	5/07

AE	Average entry wage	AW	Average wage paid	FQ	First quartile wage	LO	Lowest wage paid	MTC	Median total compensation	TCC	Total cash compensation
AER	Average entry range	AWR	Average wage range	H	Hourly	LR	Low end range	MW	Median wage paid	TQ	Third quartile wage
AEX	Average experienced wage	AXR	Average experienced range	HI	Highest wage paid	M	Monthly	MWR	Median wage range	W	Weekly
ATC	Average total compensation	D	Daily	HR	High end range	MCC	Median cash compensation	S	See annotated source	Y	Yearly

Occupation/Type/Industry	Location	Per	Low	Mid	High	Source	Date
Power Plant Operator	Boise City-Nampa MSA, ID	Y	55860 FQ	64590 MW	70120 TQ	USBLS	5/07
	Illinois	Y	48340 FQ	55400 MW	61340 TQ	USBLS	5/07
	Chicago-Naperville-Joliet MSA, IL-IN-WI	Y	48620 FQ	56750 MW	63450 TQ	USBLS	5/07
	Indiana	Y	50620 FQ	57340 MW	63340 TQ	USBLS	5/07
	Indianapolis-Carmel MSA, IN	Y	51140 FQ	61010 MW	73610 TQ	USBLS	5/07
	Terre Haute MSA, IN	Y	54170 FQ	59190 MW	64200 TQ	USBLS	5/07
	Iowa	Y	42180 FQ	49430 MW	58630 TQ	USBLS	5/07
	Des Moines-West Des Moines MSA, IA	Y	38670 FQ	46020 MW	54930 TQ	USBLS	5/07
	Kansas	Y	31900 FQ	45450 MW	56980 TQ	USBLS	5/07
	Topeka MSA, KS	Y	28140 FQ	52810 MW	61190 TQ	USBLS	5/07
	Wichita MSA, KS	Y	31020 FQ	36510 MW	54290 TQ	USBLS	5/07
	Kentucky	Y	50328 FQ	57875 MW	66352 TQ	KYBLS	2008
	Lexington-Fayette MSA, KY	Y	28420 FQ	52330 MW	67980 TQ	USBLS	5/07
	Louisville-Jefferson County MSA, KY-IN	Y	54200 FQ	58120 MW	63210 TQ	USBLS	5/07
	Louisiana	H	15.17 FQ	18.35 MW	24.84 TQ	LABLS	1/08-3/08
	New Orleans-Metairie-Kenner MSA, LA	Y	30610 FQ	36290 MW	44890 TQ	USBLS	5/07
	Maine	Y	34990 FQ	50240 MW	65220 TQ	USBLS	5/07
	Portland-South Portland-Biddeford MSA, ME	Y	21920 FQ	34370 MW	43700 TQ	USBLS	5/07
	Maryland	Y		57500 MW		MDBLS	3/08
	Baltimore-Towson MSA, MD	Y	46700 FQ	54620 MW	61660 TQ	USBLS	5/07
	Massachusetts	Y	48960 FQ	56520 MW	64070 TQ	USBLS	5/07
	Boston-Cambridge-Quincy NECTA, MA	Y	47750 FQ	55390 MW	61130 TQ	USBLS	5/07
	Worcester MSA, MA-CT	Y	36650 FQ	44450 MW	51590 TQ	USBLS	5/07
	Michigan	Y	49520 FQ	56810 MW	62960 TQ	USBLS	5/07
	Detroit-Warren-Livonia MSA, MI	Y	53580 FQ	58960 MW	64570 TQ	USBLS	5/07
	Grand Rapids-Wyoming MSA, MI	Y	41280 FQ	47110 MW	54200 TQ	USBLS	5/07
	Minnesota	Y	51284 FQ	59474 MW	67280 TQ	MNBLS	10/08-12/08
	Duluth-Superior MSA, MN-WI	Y	53886 FQ	58904 MW	64823 TQ	MNBLS	10/08-12/08
	Minneapolis-Saint Paul MSA, MN-WI	Y	53896 FQ	63061 MW	70639 TQ	MNBLS	10/08-12/08
	Rochester MSA, MN	Y	51140 FQ	55794 MW	60605 TQ	MNBLS	10/08-12/08
	Mississippi	Y	40930 FQ	52260 MW	67210 TQ	USBLS	5/07
	Jackson MSA, MS	Y	33820 FQ	48990 MW	60290 TQ	USBLS	5/07
	Missouri	Y	38130 FQ	52230 MW	63250 TQ	USBLS	5/07
	Kansas City MSA, MO-KS	Y	47290 FQ	56850 MW	65670 TQ	USBLS	5/07
	St. Louis MSA, MO-IL	Y	36540 FQ	48550 MW	62760 TQ	USBLS	5/07
	Montana	Y	55250 FQ	61780 MW	72450 TQ	USBLS	5/07
	Nebraska	Y	39550 FQ	50090 MW	61660 TQ	USBLS	5/07
	Nevada	H	27.39 FQ	31.77 MW	36.33 TQ	NVBLS	5/08
	Las Vegas-Paradise MSA, NV	H	28.14 FQ	32.32 MW	37.24 TQ	NVBLS	5/08
	New Hampshire	H	15.83 AE	22.28 MW	27.02 AEX	NHBLS	6/08
	New Jersey	Y	49340 FQ	59400 MW	71820 TQ	USBLS	5/07
	Camden PMSA, NJ	Y	54380 FQ	65110 MW	82170 TQ	USBLS	5/07
	Edison PMSA, NJ	Y	57100 FQ	67080 MW	79390 TQ	USBLS	5/07
	Newark-Union PMSA, NJ-PA	Y	48060 FQ	56350 MW	65190 TQ	USBLS	5/07
	New York	Y	54880 FQ	68570 MW	80970 TQ	USBLS	5/07
	Albany-Schenectady-Troy MSA, NY	Y	60400 FQ	72820 MW	83500 TQ	USBLS	5/07
	Buffalo-Niagara Falls MSA, NY	Y	56340 FQ	74370 MW	84960 TQ	USBLS	5/07
	Nassau-Suffolk PMSA, NY	Y	62380 FQ	73070 MW	82250 TQ	USBLS	5/07
	New York-Northern New Jersey-Long Island MSA, NY-NJ-PA	Y	53380 FQ	66070 MW	79200 TQ	USBLS	5/07
	North Carolina	Y	43420 FQ	55170 MW	63770 TQ	USBLS	5/07
	Charlotte-Gastonia-Concord MSA, NC-SC	Y	44680 FQ	54480 MW	60980 TQ	USBLS	5/07
	Durham MSA, NC	Y	38480 FQ	52880 MW	59540 TQ	USBLS	5/07
	North Dakota	Y	55870 FQ	61560 MW	70220 TQ	USBLS	5/07
	Ohio	Y	51840 FQ	56880 MW	62140 TQ	USBLS	5/07
	Cincinnati-Middletown MSA, OH-KY-IN	Y	53560 FQ	57810 MW	62100 TQ	USBLS	5/07
	Cleveland-Elyria-Mentor MSA, OH	Y	52120 FQ	56130 MW	60130 TQ	USBLS	5/07

AE Average entry wage	**AW** Average wage paid	**FQ** First quartile wage	**LO** Lowest wage paid	**MTC** Median total compensation	**TCC** Total cash compensation
AER Average entry range	**AWR** Average wage range	**H** Hourly	**LR** Low end range	**MW** Median wage paid	**TQ** Third quartile wage
AEX Average experienced wage	**AXR** Average experienced range	**HI** Highest wage paid	**M** Monthly	**MWR** Median wage range	**W** Weekly
ATC Average total compensation	**D** Daily	**HR** High end range	**MCC** Median cash compensation	**S** See annotated source	**Y** Yearly

Occupation/Type/Industry	Location	Per	Low	Mid	High	Source	Date
Power Plant Operator	Columbus MSA, OH	Y	41490 FQ	45740 MW	56500 TQ	USBLS	5/07
	Oklahoma	Y	49970 FQ	55930 MW	62330 TQ	USBLS	5/07
	Oklahoma City MSA, OK	Y	54440 FQ	60920 MW	68740 TQ	USBLS	5/07
	Tulsa MSA, OK	Y	49440 FQ	54980 MW	60180 TQ	USBLS	5/07
	Oregon	H	20.24 FQ	24.28 MW	32.78 TQ	ORBLS	5/08
	Pennsylvania	Y	45690 FQ	54940 MW	66280 TQ	USBLS	5/07
	Allentown-Bethlehem-Easton MSA, PA-NJ	Y	60660 FQ	77960 MW	87230 TQ	USBLS	5/07
	Erie MSA, PA	Y	44600 FQ	51210 MW	57790 TQ	USBLS	5/07
	Philadelphia-Camden-Wilmington MSA, PA-NJ-DE-MD	Y	48170 FQ	57180 MW	66680 TQ	USBLS	5/07
	Pittsburgh MSA, PA	Y	45260 FQ	52180 MW	62610 TQ	USBLS	5/07
	Rhode Island	Y	49870 FQ	58520 MW	66360 TQ	USBLS	5/07
	Providence-Fall River-Warwick MSA, RI-MA	Y	49600 FQ	58350 MW	66230 TQ	USBLS	5/07
	South Carolina	Y	51370 FQ	65030 MW	81130 TQ	USBLS	5/07
	Columbia MSA, SC	Y	51990 FQ	58730 MW	66550 TQ	USBLS	5/07
	South Dakota	Y	49418 FQ	56708 MW	66460 TQ	SDBLS	7/08-9/08
	Tennessee	Y	37290 FQ	51140 MW	58970 TQ	USBLS	5/07
	Memphis MSA, TN-MS-AR	Y	39400 FQ	45320 MW	53390 TQ	USBLS	5/07
	Nashville-Davidson-Murfreesboro MSA, TN	Y	26770 FQ	32900 MW	40560 TQ	USBLS	5/07
	Texas	Y	42720 FQ	53650 MW	63860 TQ	USBLS	5/07
	Dallas-Fort Worth-Arlington MSA, TX	Y	37820 FQ	48020 MW	58960 TQ	USBLS	5/07
	Houston-Sugar Land-Baytown MSA, TX	Y	47060 FQ	57910 MW	71240 TQ	USBLS	5/07
	Utah	Y	37330 FQ	46400 MW	56230 TQ	USBLS	5/07
	Salt Lake City MSA, UT	Y	25100 FQ	42950 MW	50040 TQ	USBLS	5/07
	Vermont	Y	27220 FQ	32600 MW	45190 TQ	USBLS	5/07
	Virginia	Y	36630 FQ	43740 MW	52830 TQ	USBLS	5/07
	Richmond MSA, VA	Y	34330 FQ	40970 MW	53780 TQ	USBLS	5/07
	Washington	H	27.41 FQ	31.93 MW	38.81 TQ	WABLS	3/08
	Seattle-Tacoma-Bellevue MSA, WA	Y	61970 FQ	71220 MW		USBLS	5/07
	West Virginia	Y	52638 FQ	60614 MW	72944 TQ	WVBLS	7/08-9/08
	Wisconsin	Y	40400 FQ	52520 MW	71150 TQ	USBLS	5/07
	Milwaukee-Waukesha-West Allis MSA, WI	Y	44790 FQ	60510 MW	73550 TQ	USBLS	5/07
	Wyoming	Y	52764 FQ	61002 MW	69128 TQ	WYBLS	9/08
	Guam	Y	32460 FQ	36430 MW	40940 TQ	USBLS	5/07
Preaching Minister Church of Christ	United States	Y	13000-80000 LR	53710-131125 AWR	90000-175000 HR	ACU	2008
Preneed Manager	United States	Y		41157 MW		NFDA	2006
Prep Department Foreman Printing Industry	United States	Y		44761 AW		GRAM	2006
Prepress Systems Operator	United States	Y		42313 ATC		CVERT	2007
Prepress Technician and Worker	Alabama	Y	21360 FQ	27930 MW	35030 TQ	USBLS	5/07
	Birmingham-Hoover MSA, AL	Y	25510 FQ	31360 MW	40770 TQ	USBLS	5/07
	Alaska	Y	27060 FQ	30600 MW	39190 TQ	USBLS	5/07
	Anchorage MSA, AK	Y	26590 FQ	29280 MW	34450 TQ	USBLS	5/07
	Arizona	Y	21480 FQ	27040 MW	34640 TQ	USBLS	5/07
	Phoenix-Mesa-Scottsdale MSA, AZ	Y	22320 FQ	28770 MW	35790 TQ	USBLS	5/07
	Tucson MSA, AZ	Y	18350 FQ	22320 MW	27590 TQ	USBLS	5/07
	Arkansas	Y	24590 FQ	29080 MW	35010 TQ	USBLS	5/07
	Little Rock-North Little Rock MSA, AR	Y	25660 FQ	29470 MW	34810 TQ	USBLS	5/07
	California	H	14.57 FQ	19.23 MW	25.60 TQ	CABLS	1/08-3/08
	Bakersfield MSA, CA	H	8.27 FQ	8.89 MW	15.98 TQ	CABLS	1/08-3/08
	Fresno MSA, CA	H	13.92 FQ	19.22 MW	24.56 TQ	CABLS	1/08-3/08
	Los Angeles-Long Beach-Glendale PMSA, CA	H	13.81 FQ	19.79 MW	27.21 TQ	CABLS	1/08-3/08
	Modesto MSA, CA	H	16.37 FQ	18.32 MW	22.05 TQ	CABLS	1/08-3/08
	Oakland-Fremont-Hayward MSA, CA	H	16.46 FQ	19.86 MW	29.11 TQ	CABLS	1/08-3/08

AE	Average entry wage	AW	Average wage paid	FQ	First quartile wage	LO	Lowest wage paid	MTC	Median total compensation
AER	Average entry range	AWR	Average wage range	H	Hourly	LR	Low end range	MW	Median wage paid
AEX	Average experienced wage	AXR	Average experienced range	HI	Highest wage paid	M	Monthly	MWR	Median wage range
ATC	Average total compensation	D	Daily	HR	High end range	MCC	Median cash compensation	S	See annotated source

TCC	Total cash compensation
TQ	Third quartile wage
W	Weekly
Y	Yearly

Occupation/Type/Industry	Location	Per	Low	Mid	High	Source	Date
Prepress Technician and Worker	Riverside-San Bernardino-Ontario MSA, CA	H	13.44 FQ	17.53 MW	22.74 TQ	CABLS	1/08-3/08
	Sacramento-Arden Arcade-Roseville MSA, CA	H	16.94 FQ	18.70 MW	21.16 TQ	CABLS	1/08-3/08
	San Diego-Carlsbad-San Marcos MSA, CA	H	12.22 FQ	17.98 MW	24.48 TQ	CABLS	1/08-3/08
	San Francisco-San Mateo-Redwood PMSA, CA	H	19.82 FQ	24.30 MW	31.13 TQ	CABLS	1/08-3/08
	San Jose-Sunnyvale-Santa Clara MSA, CA	H	15.43 FQ	19.96 MW	25.14 TQ	CABLS	1/08-3/08
	Santa Ana-Anaheim-Irvine PMSA, CA	Y	28050 FQ	36370 MW	49730 TQ	USBLS	5/07
	Colorado	Y	30590 FQ	37350 MW	48060 TQ	USBLS	5/07
	Denver-Aurora MSA, CO	Y	33820 FQ	42300 MW	51650 TQ	USBLS	5/07
	Connecticut	H	14.31 AE	19.18 MW		CTBLS	1/08-3/08
	Bridgeport-Stamford-Norwalk MSA, CT	Y	38150 FQ	47860 MW	63960 TQ	USBLS	5/07
	Hartford-West Hartford-East Hartford MSA, CT	Y	30850 FQ	36060 MW	43870 TQ	USBLS	5/07
	Delaware	Y	27260 FQ	36180 MW	45050 TQ	USBLS	5/07
	Wilmington PMSA, DE-MD-NJ	Y	21300 FQ	41260 MW	49850 TQ	USBLS	5/07
	District of Columbia	Y	39670 FQ	56200 MW	67060 TQ	USBLS	5/07
	Washington-Arlington-Alexandria MSA, DC-VA-MD-WV	Y	27510 FQ	41940 MW	55040 TQ	USBLS	5/07
	Florida	Y	24230 FQ	29900 MW	37660 TQ	USBLS	5/07
	Fort Lauderdale-Pompano Beach-Deerfield Beach PMSA, FL	Y	21050 FQ	28390 MW	38990 TQ	USBLS	5/07
	Jacksonville MSA, FL	Y	30670 FQ	35250 MW	40700 TQ	USBLS	5/07
	Miami-Fort Lauderdale-Miami Beach MSA, FL	Y	24200 FQ	31430 MW	42120 TQ	USBLS	5/07
	Orlando-Kissimmee MSA, FL	Y	27150 FQ	32580 MW	37410 TQ	USBLS	5/07
	Tallahassee MSA, FL	Y	21490 FQ	25880 MW	31620 TQ	USBLS	5/07
	Tampa-St. Petersburg-Clearwater MSA, FL	Y	24260 FQ	28910 MW	35180 TQ	USBLS	5/07
	West Palm Beach-Boca Raton-Boynton Beach PMSA, FL	Y	25840 FQ	33090 MW	40410 TQ	USBLS	5/07
	Georgia	Y	25380 FQ	32990 MW	43160 TQ	USBLS	5/07
	Atlanta-Sandy Springs-Marietta MSA, GA	Y	28590 FQ	35690 MW	45480 TQ	USBLS	5/07
	Hawaii	Y	26090 FQ	33870 MW	44220 TQ	USBLS	5/07
	Honolulu MSA, HI	Y	25140 FQ	32580 MW	40920 TQ	USBLS	5/07
	Idaho	Y	13610 FQ	15910 MW	23410 TQ	USBLS	5/07
	Boise City-Nampa MSA, ID	Y	13160 FQ	15230 MW	22660 TQ	USBLS	5/07
	Illinois	Y	28640 FQ	35720 MW	46960 TQ	USBLS	5/07
	Chicago-Naperville-Joliet MSA, IL-IN-WI	Y	30070 FQ	36980 MW	49050 TQ	USBLS	5/07
	Peoria MSA, IL	Y	30880 FQ	35790 MW	41140 TQ	USBLS	5/07
	Indiana	Y	26700 FQ	34480 MW	42750 TQ	USBLS	5/07
	Evansville MSA, IN-KY	Y	25580 FQ	32520 MW	38910 TQ	USBLS	5/07
	Gary PMSA, IN	Y	24510 FQ	36320 MW	53580 TQ	USBLS	5/07
	Indianapolis-Carmel MSA, IN	Y	29390 FQ	36320 MW	44000 TQ	USBLS	5/07
	Iowa	Y	24130 FQ	32740 MW	41700 TQ	USBLS	5/07
	Des Moines-West Des Moines MSA, IA	Y	35600 FQ	43230 MW	50360 TQ	USBLS	5/07
	Kansas	Y	22950 FQ	30440 MW	39250 TQ	USBLS	5/07
	Wichita MSA, KS	Y	20580 FQ	27030 MW	40620 TQ	USBLS	5/07
	Kentucky	Y	24819 FQ	32810 MW	40800 TQ	KYBLS	2008
	Louisville-Jefferson County MSA, KY-IN	Y	29530 FQ	36130 MW	43950 TQ	USBLS	5/07
	Louisiana	H	11.54 FQ	14.15 MW	16.61 TQ	LABLS	1/08-3/08
	Baton Rouge MSA, LA	Y	27090 FQ	31750 MW	39630 TQ	USBLS	5/07
	New Orleans-Metairie-Kenner MSA, LA	Y	22290 FQ	27600 MW	31090 TQ	USBLS	5/07
	Maine	Y	25670 FQ	30620 MW	35650 TQ	USBLS	5/07
	Portland-South Portland-Biddeford MSA, ME	Y	24020 FQ	30290 MW	36270 TQ	USBLS	5/07
	Maryland	Y		41450 MW		MDBLS	3/08
	Baltimore-Towson MSA, MD	Y	32170 FQ	39390 MW	46280 TQ	USBLS	5/07

AE	Average entry wage	**AW**	Average wage paid	**FQ**	First quartile wage
AER	Average entry range	**AWR**	Average wage range	**H**	Hourly
AEX	Average experienced wage	**AXR**	Average experienced range	**HI**	Highest wage paid
ATC	Average total compensation	**D**	Daily	**HR**	High end range

LO	Lowest wage paid	**MTC**	Median total compensation	**TCC**	Total cash compensation
LR	Low end range	**MW**	Median wage paid	**TQ**	Third quartile wage
M	Monthly	**MWR**	Median wage range	**W**	Weekly
MCC	Median cash compensation	**S**	See annotated source	**Y**	Yearly

Occupation/Type/Industry	Location	Per	Low	Mid	High	Source	Date
Prepress Technician and Worker	Bethesda-Gaithersburg-Frederick PMSA, MD	Y	35010 FQ	41560 MW	47870 TQ	USBLS	5/07
	Massachusetts	Y	23490 FQ	35010 MW	46790 TQ	USBLS	5/07
	Boston-Cambridge-Quincy NECTA, MA	Y	23580 FQ	41640 MW	51600 TQ	USBLS	5/07
	Worcester MSA, MA-CT	Y	32170 FQ	40740 MW	51750 TQ	USBLS	5/07
	Michigan	Y	26410 FQ	34930 MW	42320 TQ	USBLS	5/07
	Detroit-Warren-Livonia MSA, MI	Y	26950 FQ	36840 MW	45800 TQ	USBLS	5/07
	Grand Rapids-Wyoming MSA, MI	Y	33870 FQ	39210 MW	44960 TQ	USBLS	5/07
	Warren-Troy-Farmington Hills PMSA, MI	Y	28410 FQ	37930 MW	48050 TQ	USBLS	5/07
	Minnesota	Y	32116 FQ	41591 MW	51761 TQ	MNBLS	10/08-12/08
	Duluth-Superior MSA, MN-WI	Y	36273 FQ	42109 MW	46899 TQ	MNBLS	10/08-12/08
	Minneapolis-Saint Paul MSA, MN-WI	Y	37704 FQ	46671 MW	56042 TQ	MNBLS	10/08-12/08
	Mississippi	Y	20610 FQ	26140 MW	31600 TQ	USBLS	5/07
	Jackson MSA, MS	Y	21790 FQ	28290 MW	32870 TQ	USBLS	5/07
	Missouri	Y	22290 FQ	30850 MW	44580 TQ	USBLS	5/07
	Jefferson City MSA, MO	Y	28410 FQ	34430 MW	41150 TQ	USBLS	5/07
	Kansas City MSA, MO-KS	Y	26050 FQ	33810 MW	42910 TQ	USBLS	5/07
	St. Joseph MSA, MO-KS	Y	26800 FQ	29140 MW	33800 TQ	USBLS	5/07
	St. Louis MSA, MO-IL	Y	23970 FQ	39310 MW	49530 TQ	USBLS	5/07
	Montana	Y	19420 FQ	24600 MW	32950 TQ	USBLS	5/07
	Billings MSA, MT	Y	24420 FQ	30190 MW	36720 TQ	USBLS	5/07
	Nebraska	Y	22460 FQ	29310 MW	37040 TQ	USBLS	5/07
	Omaha-Council Bluffs MSA, NE-IA	Y	22480 FQ	28530 MW	35580 TQ	USBLS	5/07
	Nevada	H	8.64 FQ	14.40 MW	18.93 TQ	NVBLS	5/08
	Las Vegas-Paradise MSA, NV	H	8.36 FQ	12.75 MW	16.46 TQ	NVBLS	5/08
	New Hampshire	H	10.86 AE	13.46 MW	16.87 AEX	NHBLS	6/08
	Manchester MSA, NH	Y	21670 FQ	26850 MW	41970 TQ	USBLS	5/07
	Nashua NECTA, NH-MA	Y	23750 FQ	25990 MW	28300 TQ	USBLS	5/07
	New Jersey	Y	31330 FQ	41650 MW	52270 TQ	USBLS	5/07
	Camden PMSA, NJ	Y	30890 FQ	39520 MW	52800 TQ	USBLS	5/07
	Edison PMSA, NJ	Y	26830 FQ	40890 MW	51590 TQ	USBLS	5/07
	Newark-Union PMSA, NJ-PA	Y	37630 FQ	44120 MW	53330 TQ	USBLS	5/07
	New Mexico	Y	21110 FQ	26580 MW	30930 TQ	USBLS	5/07
	Albuquerque MSA, NM	Y	20910 FQ	26100 MW	29650 TQ	USBLS	5/07
	New York	Y	29210 FQ	39920 MW	51230 TQ	USBLS	5/07
	Albany-Schenectady-Troy MSA, NY	Y	30660 FQ	34790 MW	39560 TQ	USBLS	5/07
	Buffalo-Niagara Falls MSA, NY	Y	24880 FQ	33890 MW	45780 TQ	USBLS	5/07
	Nassau-Suffolk PMSA, NY	Y	25550 FQ	40200 MW	49640 TQ	USBLS	5/07
	New York-Northern New Jersey-Long Island MSA, NY-NJ-PA	Y	32290 FQ	43760 MW	54740 TQ	USBLS	5/07
	Syracuse MSA, NY	Y	23330 FQ	35790 MW	45530 TQ	USBLS	5/07
	North Carolina	Y	26190 FQ	33260 MW	40870 TQ	USBLS	5/07
	Charlotte-Gastonia-Concord MSA, NC-SC	Y	31040 FQ	39250 MW	45390 TQ	USBLS	5/07
	Durham MSA, NC	Y	32010 FQ	36920 MW	42530 TQ	USBLS	5/07
	Raleigh-Cary MSA, NC	Y	26680 FQ	32880 MW	41290 TQ	USBLS	5/07
	North Dakota	Y	19350 FQ	22460 MW	30050 TQ	USBLS	5/07
	Fargo MSA, ND-MN	Y	24090 FQ	29380 MW	34690 TQ	USBLS	5/07
	Ohio	Y	26390 FQ	34270 MW	42220 TQ	USBLS	5/07
	Cincinnati-Middletown MSA, OH-KY-IN	Y	27780 FQ	36170 MW	44560 TQ	USBLS	5/07
	Cleveland-Elyria-Mentor MSA, OH	Y	32030 FQ	38030 MW	46060 TQ	USBLS	5/07
	Columbus MSA, OH	Y	29710 FQ	35560 MW	42730 TQ	USBLS	5/07
	Dayton MSA, OH	Y	22560 FQ	31770 MW	44870 TQ	USBLS	5/07
	Oklahoma	Y	19220 FQ	27570 MW	35720 TQ	USBLS	5/07
	Oklahoma City MSA, OK	Y	20360 FQ	31490 MW	37860 TQ	USBLS	5/07
	Tulsa MSA, OK	Y	26080 FQ	30170 MW	38050 TQ	USBLS	5/07
	Oregon	H	13.54 FQ	17.48 MW	21.88 TQ	ORBLS	5/08
	Portland-Vancouver-Beaverton MSA, OR-WA	Y	27530 FQ	37310 MW	46140 TQ	USBLS	5/07
	Pennsylvania	Y	26600 FQ	34960 MW	44180 TQ	USBLS	5/07

AE	Average entry wage	AW	Average wage paid	FQ	First quartile wage	LO	Lowest wage paid	MTC	Median total compensation	TCC	Total cash compensation
AER	Average entry range	AWR	Average wage range	H	Hourly	LR	Low end range	MW	Median wage paid	TQ	Third quartile wage
AEX	Average experienced wage	AXR	Average experienced range	HI	Highest wage paid	M	Monthly	MWR	Median wage range	W	Weekly
ATC	Average total compensation	D	Daily	HR	High end range	MCC	Median cash compensation	S	See annotated source	Y	Yearly

Occupation/Type/Industry	Location	Per	Low	Mid	High	Source	Date
Prepress Technician and Worker	Allentown-Bethlehem-Easton MSA, PA-NJ	Y	25830 FQ	33610 MW	43430 TQ	USBLS	5/07
	Philadelphia-Camden-Wilmington MSA, PA-NJ-DE-MD	Y	27160 FQ	37720 MW	48360 TQ	USBLS	5/07
	Pittsburgh MSA, PA	Y	26110 FQ	35690 MW	48010 TQ	USBLS	5/07
	York-Hanover MSA, PA	Y	28160 FQ	36460 MW	42570 TQ	USBLS	5/07
	Rhode Island	Y	28240 FQ	35520 MW	43570 TQ	USBLS	5/07
	Providence-Fall River-Warwick MSA, RI-MA	Y	28090 FQ	35620 MW	43760 TQ	USBLS	5/07
	South Carolina	Y	22320 FQ	27620 MW	33590 TQ	USBLS	5/07
	Columbia MSA, SC	Y	22520 FQ	27200 MW	32120 TQ	USBLS	5/07
	Spartanburg MSA, SC	Y	27710 FQ	32480 MW	37130 TQ	USBLS	5/07
	South Dakota	Y	21621 FQ	25967 MW	30890 TQ	SDBLS	7/08-9/08
	Rapid City MSA, SD	Y	19151 FQ	22177 MW	26104 TQ	SDBLS	7/08-9/08
	Sioux Falls MSA, SD	Y	24947 FQ	29207 MW	33295 TQ	SDBLS	7/08-9/08
	Tennessee	Y	26840 FQ	34610 MW	40980 TQ	USBLS	5/07
	Memphis MSA, TN-MS-AR	Y	32720 FQ	37010 MW	44920 TQ	USBLS	5/07
	Nashville-Davidson-Murfreesboro MSA, TN	Y	23950 FQ	34670 MW	41600 TQ	USBLS	5/07
	Texas	Y	21870 FQ	28220 MW	36400 TQ	USBLS	5/07
	Austin-Round Rock MSA, TX	Y	21590 FQ	30340 MW	37860 TQ	USBLS	5/07
	Dallas-Fort Worth-Arlington MSA, TX	Y	24650 FQ	30880 MW	40100 TQ	USBLS	5/07
	El Paso MSA, TX	Y	12640 FQ	14010 MW	21870 TQ	USBLS	5/07
	Houston-Sugar Land-Baytown MSA, TX	Y	22980 FQ	28510 MW	36330 TQ	USBLS	5/07
	San Antonio MSA, TX	Y	22000 FQ	28020 MW	35080 TQ	USBLS	5/07
	Utah	Y	23870 FQ	28910 MW	35360 TQ	USBLS	5/07
	Salt Lake City MSA, UT	Y	23910 FQ	29770 MW	37090 TQ	USBLS	5/07
	Vermont	Y	29920 FQ	35410 MW	42870 TQ	USBLS	5/07
	Burlington-South Burlington MSA, VT	Y	30750 FQ	36980 MW	44850 TQ	USBLS	5/07
	Virginia	Y	24330 FQ	32460 MW	42390 TQ	USBLS	5/07
	Richmond MSA, VA	Y	32610 FQ	37760 MW	42560 TQ	USBLS	5/07
	Virginia Beach-Norfolk-Newport News MSA, VA-NC	Y	21320 FQ	28630 MW	39490 TQ	USBLS	5/07
	Washington	H	14.95 FQ	18.81 MW	23.22 TQ	WABLS	3/08
	Seattle-Tacoma-Bellevue MSA, WA	Y	33280 FQ	41130 MW	49510 TQ	USBLS	5/07
	West Virginia	Y	18317 FQ	21789 MW	30134 TQ	WVBLS	7/08-9/08
	Wisconsin	Y	29990 FQ	37300 MW	45390 TQ	USBLS	5/07
	Milwaukee-Waukesha-West Allis MSA, WI	Y	31150 FQ	38580 MW	46450 TQ	USBLS	5/07
	Wyoming	Y	17856 FQ	22047 MW	29077 TQ	WYBLS	9/08
	Puerto Rico	Y	16510 FQ	21140 MW	26700 TQ	USBLS	5/07
	San Juan-Caguas-Guaynabo MSA, PR	Y	17140 FQ	21480 MW	26760 TQ	USBLS	5/07
Preschool Instructor	Carlsbad, CA	H	14.00 LO		22.00 HI	CCSS	1/1/08
Preschool Teacher							
Except Special Education	Alabama	Y	15710 FQ	20020 MW	25870 TQ	USBLS	5/07
Except Special Education	Birmingham-Hoover MSA, AL	Y	17540 FQ	20330 MW	24270 TQ	USBLS	5/07
Except Special Education	Alaska	Y	21320 FQ	24820 MW	31540 TQ	USBLS	5/07
Except Special Education	Anchorage MSA, AK	Y	21040 FQ	23440 MW	28370 TQ	USBLS	5/07
Except Special Education	Arizona	Y	17250 FQ	20450 MW	24950 TQ	USBLS	5/07
Except Special Education	Phoenix-Mesa-Scottsdale MSA, AZ	Y	17120 FQ	20060 MW	24310 TQ	USBLS	5/07
Except Special Education	Prescott MSA, AZ	Y	15930 FQ	17550 MW	19280 TQ	USBLS	5/07
Except Special Education	Tucson MSA, AZ	Y	19060 FQ	22610 MW	28570 TQ	USBLS	5/07
Except Special Education	Arkansas	Y	16230 FQ	19800 MW	28780 TQ	USBLS	5/07
Except Special Education	Little Rock-North Little Rock MSA, AR	Y	16790 FQ	19830 MW	30590 TQ	USBLS	5/07
Except Special Education	Pine Bluff MSA, AR	Y	16800 FQ	19970 MW	30340 TQ	USBLS	5/07
Except Special Education	California	Y		29390 AW		CABLS	1/08-3/08
Except Special Education	Bakersfield MSA, CA	H	9.54 FQ	11.96 MW	16.06 TQ	CABLS	1/08-3/08
Except Special Education	Los Angeles-Long Beach-Glendale PMSA, CA	H	10.64 FQ	12.93 MW	16.67 TQ	CABLS	1/08-3/08
Except Special Education	Oakland-Fremont-Hayward MSA, CA	H	12.45 FQ	14.22 MW	16.67 TQ	CABLS	1/08-3/08

AE Average entry wage	**AW** Average wage paid	**FQ** First quartile wage	**LO** Lowest wage paid	**MTC** Median total compensation	**TCC** Total cash compensation
AER Average entry range	**AWR** Average wage range	**H** Hourly	**LR** Low end range	**MW** Median wage paid	**TQ** Third quartile wage
AEX Average experienced wage	**AXR** Average experienced range	**HI** Highest wage paid	**M** Monthly	**MWR** Median wage range	**W** Weekly
ATC Average total compensation	**D** Daily	**HR** High end range	**MCC** Median cash compensation	**S** See annotated source	**Y** Yearly

Preschool Teacher

Occupation/Type/Industry	Location	Per	Low	Mid	High	Source	Date
Preschool Teacher							
Except Special Education	Riverside-San Bernardino-Ontario MSA, CA	H	9.54 FQ	11.09 MW	12.74 TQ	CABLS	1/08-3/08
Except Special Education	Sacramento-Arden Arcade-Roseville MSA, CA	H	9.77 FQ	11.69 MW	14.06 TQ	CABLS	1/08-3/08
Except Special Education	San Diego-Carlsbad-San Marcos MSA, CA	H	10.88 FQ	12.82 MW	15.52 TQ	CABLS	1/08-3/08
Except Special Education	San Francisco-San Mateo-Redwood PMSA, CA	H	13.75 FQ	16.13 MW	19.07 TQ	CABLS	1/08-3/08
Except Special Education	San Jose-Sunnyvale-Santa Clara MSA, CA	H	12.78 FQ	15.31 MW	19.00 TQ	CABLS	1/08-3/08
Except Special Education	Santa Ana-Anaheim-Irvine PMSA, CA	Y	22760 FQ	27230 MW	32550 TQ	USBLS	5/07
Except Special Education	Colorado	Y	19040 FQ	24180 MW	29240 TQ	USBLS	5/07
Except Special Education	Boulder MSA, CO	Y	21800 FQ	25080 MW	29210 TQ	USBLS	5/07
Except Special Education	Denver-Aurora MSA, CO	Y	17080 FQ	24060 MW	28820 TQ	USBLS	5/07
Except Special Education	Connecticut	H	10.03 AE	13.06 MW		CTBLS	1/08-3/08
Except Special Education	Bridgeport-Stamford-Norwalk MSA, CT	Y	22480 FQ	27540 MW	32950 TQ	USBLS	5/07
Except Special Education	Danbury MSA, CT	Y	22850 FQ	27180 MW	30690 TQ	USBLS	5/07
Except Special Education	Hartford-West Hartford-East Hartford MSA, CT	Y	20870 FQ	24980 MW	30150 TQ	USBLS	5/07
Except Special Education	Delaware	Y	19290 FQ	23210 MW	28940 TQ	USBLS	5/07
Except Special Education	Wilmington PMSA, DE-MD-NJ	Y	20350 FQ	24160 MW	30130 TQ	USBLS	5/07
Except Special Education	District of Columbia	Y	23160 FQ	28640 MW	36960 TQ	USBLS	5/07
Except Special Education	Washington-Arlington-Alexandria MSA, DC-VA-MD-WV	Y	20700 FQ	26400 MW	33090 TQ	USBLS	5/07
Except Special Education	Florida	Y	17790 FQ	21660 MW	28080 TQ	USBLS	5/07
Except Special Education	Cape Coral-Fort Myers MSA, FL	Y	18190 FQ	21940 MW	28120 TQ	USBLS	5/07
Except Special Education	Fort Lauderdale-Pompano Beach-Deerfield Beach PMSA, FL	Y	20390 FQ	23470 MW	28650 TQ	USBLS	5/07
Except Special Education	Jacksonville MSA, FL	Y	17810 FQ	20180 MW	23270 TQ	USBLS	5/07
Except Special Education	Miami-Fort Lauderdale-Miami Beach MSA, FL	Y	17730 FQ	21970 MW	28540 TQ	USBLS	5/07
Except Special Education	Orlando-Kissimmee MSA, FL	Y	19000 FQ	23320 MW	29560 TQ	USBLS	5/07
Except Special Education	Sarasota-Bradenton-Venice MSA, FL	Y	18950 FQ	23620 MW	30980 TQ	USBLS	5/07
Except Special Education	Tampa-St. Petersburg-Clearwater MSA, FL	Y	18440 FQ	22290 MW	29490 TQ	USBLS	5/07
Except Special Education	West Palm Beach-Boca Raton-Boynton Beach PMSA, FL	Y	18380 FQ	21730 MW	27210 TQ	USBLS	5/07
Except Special Education	Georgia	Y	15000 FQ	18490 MW	25010 TQ	USBLS	5/07
Except Special Education	Atlanta-Sandy Springs-Marietta MSA, GA	Y	15600 FQ	18660 MW	24100 TQ	USBLS	5/07
Except Special Education	Hawaii	Y	21340 FQ	26190 MW	32540 TQ	USBLS	5/07
Except Special Education	Honolulu MSA, HI	Y	20600 FQ	25760 MW	31720 TQ	USBLS	5/07
Except Special Education	Idaho	Y	16080 FQ	19640 MW	23360 TQ	USBLS	5/07
Except Special Education	Boise City-Nampa MSA, ID	Y	20460 FQ	22450 MW	25390 TQ	USBLS	5/07
Except Special Education	Illinois	Y	20460 FQ	25900 MW	33190 TQ	USBLS	5/07
Except Special Education	Chicago-Naperville-Joliet MSA, IL-IN-WI	Y	22120 FQ	27220 MW	34610 TQ	USBLS	5/07
Except Special Education	Indiana	Y	17840 FQ	21910 MW	27070 TQ	USBLS	5/07
Except Special Education	Elkhart-Goshen MSA, IN	Y	17610 FQ	19800 MW	24120 TQ	USBLS	5/07
Except Special Education	Gary PMSA, IN	Y	20700 FQ	29320 MW	44310 TQ	USBLS	5/07
Except Special Education	Indianapolis-Carmel MSA, IN	Y	18260 FQ	21750 MW	24920 TQ	USBLS	5/07
Except Special Education	Iowa	Y	16520 FQ	19770 MW	25900 TQ	USBLS	5/07
Except Special Education	Des Moines-West Des Moines MSA, IA	Y	17790 FQ	20660 MW	26710 TQ	USBLS	5/07
Except Special Education	Sioux City MSA, IA-NE-SD	Y	17060 FQ	22090 MW	25070 TQ	USBLS	5/07
Except Special Education	Kansas	Y	17460 FQ	22010 MW	29240 TQ	USBLS	5/07
Except Special Education	Wichita MSA, KS	Y	17330 FQ	19900 MW	28450 TQ	USBLS	5/07
Except Special Education	Kentucky	Y	16797 FQ	21583 MW	33101 TQ	KYBLS	2008
Except Special Education	Louisville-Jefferson County MSA, KY-IN	Y	16440 FQ	18850 MW	25870 TQ	USBLS	5/07
Except Special Education	Louisiana	H	6.85 FQ	8.37 MW	10.40 TQ	LABLS	1/08-3/08
Except Special Education	Baton Rouge MSA, LA	Y	13850 FQ	16660 MW	20660 TQ	USBLS	5/07
Except Special Education	New Orleans-Metairie-Kenner MSA, LA	Y	16940 FQ	20790 MW	25670 TQ	USBLS	5/07

AE	Average entry wage	**AW**	Average wage paid	**FQ**	First quartile wage	**LO**	Lowest wage paid	**MTC** Median total compensation	**TCC** Total cash compensation
AER	Average entry range	**AWR**	Average wage range	**H**	Hourly	**LR**	Low end range	**MW** Median wage paid	**TQ** Third quartile wage
AEX	Average experienced wage	**AXR**	Average experienced range	**HI**	Highest wage paid	**M**	Monthly	**MWR** Median wage range	**W** Weekly
ATC	Average total compensation	**D**	Daily	**HR**	High end range	**MCC**	Median cash compensation	**S** See annotated source	**Y** Yearly

Occupation/Type/Industry	Location	Per	Low	Mid	High	Source	Date
Preschool Teacher							
Except Special Education	Maine	Y	22120 FQ	25500 MW	30310 TQ	USBLS	5/07
Except Special Education	Portland-South Portland-Biddeford MSA, ME	Y	22150 FQ	24770 MW	28570 TQ	USBLS	5/07
Except Special Education	Maryland	Y		26425 MW		MDBLS	3/08
Except Special Education	Baltimore-Towson MSA, MD	Y	20890 FQ	25060 MW	33900 TQ	USBLS	5/07
Except Special Education	Bethesda-Gaithersburg-Frederick PMSA, MD	Y	21640 FQ	25440 MW	31530 TQ	USBLS	5/07
Except Special Education	Cumberland MSA, MD-WV	Y	22130 FQ	25460 MW	33090 TQ	USBLS	5/07
Except Special Education	Massachusetts	Y	23300 FQ	27700 MW	32990 TQ	USBLS	5/07
Except Special Education	Boston-Cambridge-Quincy NECTA, MA	Y	24810 FQ	28450 MW	33600 TQ	USBLS	5/07
Except Special Education	Worcester MSA, MA-CT	Y	24760 FQ	29390 MW	37330 TQ	USBLS	5/07
Except Special Education	Michigan	Y	20120 FQ	28410 MW	39390 TQ	USBLS	5/07
Except Special Education	Detroit-Warren-Livonia MSA, MI	Y	22710 FQ	29800 MW	39690 TQ	USBLS	5/07
Except Special Education	Grand Rapids-Wyoming MSA, MI	Y	25130 FQ	40090 MW	54580 TQ	USBLS	5/07
Except Special Education	Muskegon-Norton Shores MSA, MI	Y	22650 FQ	27050 MW	52620 TQ	USBLS	5/07
Except Special Education	Warren-Troy-Farmington Hills PMSA, MI	Y	21920 FQ	27960 MW	35830 TQ	USBLS	5/07
Except Special Education	Minnesota	Y	24157 FQ	29493 MW	36659 TQ	MNBLS	10/08-12/08
Except Special Education	Duluth-Superior MSA, MN-WI	Y	21081 FQ	31324 MW	43449 TQ	MNBLS	10/08-12/08
Except Special Education	Minneapolis-Saint Paul MSA, MN-WI	Y	24680 FQ	29221 MW	34787 TQ	MNBLS	10/08-12/08
Except Special Education	Rochester MSA, MN	Y	25453 FQ	31428 MW	39552 TQ	MNBLS	10/08-12/08
Except Special Education	Mississippi	Y	14750 FQ	20220 MW	27020 TQ	USBLS	5/07
Except Special Education	Jackson MSA, MS	Y	14130 FQ	20350 MW	29820 TQ	USBLS	5/07
Except Special Education	Missouri	Y	17620 FQ	22210 MW	29070 TQ	USBLS	5/07
Except Special Education	Kansas City MSA, MO-KS	Y	18700 FQ	23070 MW	31920 TQ	USBLS	5/07
Except Special Education	St. Louis MSA, MO-IL	Y	18230 FQ	22470 MW	29190 TQ	USBLS	5/07
Except Special Education	Montana	Y	16340 FQ	18930 MW	23950 TQ	USBLS	5/07
Except Special Education	Billings MSA, MT	Y	15070 FQ	17880 MW	26080 TQ	USBLS	5/07
Except Special Education	Great Falls MSA, MT	Y	15960 FQ	18090 MW	21410 TQ	USBLS	5/07
Except Special Education	Nebraska	Y	16570 FQ	20040 MW	27230 TQ	USBLS	5/07
Except Special Education	Omaha-Council Bluffs MSA, NE-IA	Y	17350 FQ	21290 MW	27940 TQ	USBLS	5/07
Except Special Education	Nevada	H	8.80 FQ	10.42 MW	13.30 TQ	NVBLS	5/08
Except Special Education	Las Vegas-Paradise MSA, NV	H	8.60 FQ	10.09 MW	12.82 TQ	NVBLS	5/08
Except Special Education	New Hampshire	H	10.28 AE	12.50 MW	14.35 AEX	NHBLS	6/08
Except Special Education	Manchester MSA, NH	Y	21170 FQ	24270 MW	27970 TQ	USBLS	5/07
Except Special Education	Nashua NECTA, NH-MA	Y	22360 FQ	25750 MW	29070 TQ	USBLS	5/07
Except Special Education	New Jersey	Y	22930 FQ	29640 MW	41670 TQ	USBLS	5/07
Except Special Education	Camden PMSA, NJ	Y	19660 FQ	23670 MW	33010 TQ	USBLS	5/07
Except Special Education	Edison PMSA, NJ	Y	22840 FQ	27990 MW	35760 TQ	USBLS	5/07
Except Special Education	Newark-Union PMSA, NJ-PA	Y	24380 FQ	32850 MW	44630 TQ	USBLS	5/07
Except Special Education	Ocean City MSA, NJ	Y	21170 FQ	24150 MW	36390 TQ	USBLS	5/07
Except Special Education	New Mexico	Y	16300 FQ	21500 MW	29950 TQ	USBLS	5/07
Except Special Education	Albuquerque MSA, NM	Y	16140 FQ	19530 MW	24980 TQ	USBLS	5/07
Except Special Education	Las Cruces MSA, NM	Y	22360 FQ	27060 MW	30360 TQ	USBLS	5/07
Except Special Education	New York	Y	21330 FQ	27680 MW	36520 TQ	USBLS	5/07
Except Special Education	Albany-Schenectady-Troy MSA, NY	Y	19670 FQ	23080 MW	27860 TQ	USBLS	5/07
Except Special Education	Buffalo-Niagara Falls MSA, NY	Y	17220 FQ	20320 MW	25640 TQ	USBLS	5/07
Except Special Education	Glens Falls MSA, NY	Y	18600 FQ	20790 MW	25870 TQ	USBLS	5/07
Except Special Education	Nassau-Suffolk PMSA, NY	Y	22110 FQ	26580 MW	30590 TQ	USBLS	5/07
Except Special Education	New York-Northern New Jersey-Long Island MSA, NY-NJ-PA	Y	24170 FQ	30180 MW	39730 TQ	USBLS	5/07
Except Special Education	North Carolina	Y	16660 FQ	19240 MW	23790 TQ	USBLS	5/07
Except Special Education	Charlotte-Gastonia-Concord MSA, NC-SC	Y	17650 FQ	20150 MW	23940 TQ	USBLS	5/07
Except Special Education	Raleigh-Cary MSA, NC	Y	17370 FQ	20540 MW	24210 TQ	USBLS	5/07
Except Special Education	North Dakota	Y	17830 FQ	22480 MW	28010 TQ	USBLS	5/07
Except Special Education	Fargo MSA, ND-MN	Y	17170 FQ	19790 MW	24810 TQ	USBLS	5/07
Except Special Education	Grand Forks MSA, ND-MN	Y	24740 FQ	27270 MW	29730 TQ	USBLS	5/07
Except Special Education	Ohio	Y	17280 FQ	20160 MW	24310 TQ	USBLS	5/07
Except Special Education	Canton-Massillon MSA, OH	Y	17750 FQ	19940 MW	23170 TQ	USBLS	5/07
Except Special Education	Cincinnati-Middletown MSA, OH-KY-IN	Y	17810 FQ	20730 MW	24840 TQ	USBLS	5/07

AE	Average entry wage	AW	Average wage paid	FQ	First quartile wage
AER	Average entry range	AWR	Average wage range	H	Hourly
AEX	Average experienced wage	AXR	Average experienced range	HI	Highest wage paid
ATC	Average total compensation	D	Daily	HR	High end range

LO	Lowest wage paid	MTC	Median total compensation	TCC	Total cash compensation
LR	Low end range	MW	Median wage paid	TQ	Third quartile wage
M	Monthly	MWR	Median wage range	W	Weekly
MCC	Median cash compensation	S	See annotated source	Y	Yearly

Preschool Teacher

Occupation/Type/Industry	Location	Per	Low	Mid	High	Source	Date
Except Special Education	Cleveland-Elyria-Mentor MSA, OH	Y	17520 FQ	20710 MW	25190 TQ	USBLS	5/07
Except Special Education	Columbus MSA, OH	Y	17630 FQ	20590 MW	24650 TQ	USBLS	5/07
Except Special Education	Dayton MSA, OH	Y	18280 FQ	21420 MW	24900 TQ	USBLS	5/07
Except Special Education	Oklahoma	Y	15010 FQ	19000 MW	28160 TQ	USBLS	5/07
Except Special Education	Oklahoma City MSA, OK	Y	16170 FQ	19700 MW	28020 TQ	USBLS	5/07
Except Special Education	Tulsa MSA, OK	Y	14190 FQ	17890 MW	24170 TQ	USBLS	5/07
Except Special Education	Oregon	H	9.42 FQ	10.99 MW	13.44 TQ	ORBLS	5/08
Except Special Education	Eugene-Springfield MSA, OR	Y	19100 FQ	21910 MW	27310 TQ	USBLS	5/07
Except Special Education	Portland-Vancouver-Beaverton MSA, OR-WA	Y	19670 FQ	23050 MW	28280 TQ	USBLS	5/07
Except Special Education	Pennsylvania	Y	17770 FQ	22110 MW	28000 TQ	USBLS	5/07
Except Special Education	Allentown-Bethlehem-Easton MSA, PA-NJ	Y	19210 FQ	22640 MW	29830 TQ	USBLS	5/07
Except Special Education	Erie MSA, PA	Y	16210 FQ	17620 MW	19100 TQ	USBLS	5/07
Except Special Education	Philadelphia-Camden-Wilmington MSA, PA-NJ-DE-MD	Y	19430 FQ	23400 MW	29020 TQ	USBLS	5/07
Except Special Education	Pittsburgh MSA, PA	Y	15290 FQ	19800 MW	24650 TQ	USBLS	5/07
Except Special Education	Rhode Island	Y	23050 FQ	28500 MW	34640 TQ	USBLS	5/07
Except Special Education	Providence-Fall River-Warwick MSA, RI-MA	Y	20900 FQ	26180 MW	32510 TQ	USBLS	5/07
Except Special Education	South Carolina	Y	16380 FQ	20370 MW	30600 TQ	USBLS	5/07
Except Special Education	Charleston-North Charleston MSA, SC	Y	18720 FQ	22310 MW	28030 TQ	USBLS	5/07
Except Special Education	Columbia MSA, SC	Y	17170 FQ	23160 MW	37310 TQ	USBLS	5/07
Except Special Education	South Dakota	Y	23631 FQ	27377 MW	31543 TQ	SDBLS	7/08-9/08
Except Special Education	Sioux Falls MSA, SD	Y	23252 FQ	27955 MW	31937 TQ	SDBLS	7/08-9/08
Except Special Education	Tennessee	Y	14820 FQ	17730 MW	22090 TQ	USBLS	5/07
Except Special Education	Memphis MSA, TN-MS-AR	Y	14620 FQ	17280 MW	20300 TQ	USBLS	5/07
Except Special Education	Nashville-Davidson-Murfreesboro MSA, TN	Y	16040 FQ	18480 MW	22150 TQ	USBLS	5/07
Except Special Education	Texas	Y	15400 FQ	18840 MW	26350 TQ	USBLS	5/07
Except Special Education	Austin-Round Rock MSA, TX	Y	17100 FQ	19740 MW	27690 TQ	USBLS	5/07
Except Special Education	Dallas-Fort Worth-Arlington MSA, TX	Y	16480 FQ	19010 MW	23960 TQ	USBLS	5/07
Except Special Education	El Paso MSA, TX	Y	13950 FQ	16500 MW	41670 TQ	USBLS	5/07
Except Special Education	Houston-Sugar Land-Baytown MSA, TX	Y	15120 FQ	18360 MW	24840 TQ	USBLS	5/07
Except Special Education	San Antonio MSA, TX	Y	14490 FQ	18400 MW	23720 TQ	USBLS	5/07
Except Special Education	Utah	Y	17320 FQ	21110 MW	27240 TQ	USBLS	5/07
Except Special Education	Salt Lake City MSA, UT	Y	16790 FQ	20000 MW	25860 TQ	USBLS	5/07
Except Special Education	Vermont	Y	21690 FQ	27360 MW	33690 TQ	USBLS	5/07
Except Special Education	Burlington-South Burlington MSA, VT	Y	19530 FQ	23510 MW	31190 TQ	USBLS	5/07
Except Special Education	Virginia	Y	17880 FQ	22670 MW	31450 TQ	USBLS	5/07
Except Special Education	Richmond MSA, VA	Y	18450 FQ	22140 MW	30810 TQ	USBLS	5/07
Except Special Education	Virginia Beach-Norfolk-Newport News MSA, VA-NC	Y	15860 FQ	18750 MW	24450 TQ	USBLS	5/07
Except Special Education	Washington	H	10.43 FQ	12.24 MW	15.07 TQ	WABLS	3/08
Except Special Education	Seattle-Tacoma-Bellevue MSA, WA	Y	21790 FQ	25260 MW	31730 TQ	USBLS	5/07
Except Special Education	West Virginia	Y	15799 FQ	20572 MW	30507 TQ	WVBLS	7/08-9/08
Except Special Education	Charleston MSA, WV	Y	15330 FQ	18970 MW	27000 TQ	USBLS	5/07
Except Special Education	Parkersburg-Marietta-Vienna MSA, WV-OH	Y	13910 FQ	15590 MW	19620 TQ	USBLS	5/07
Except Special Education	Wisconsin	Y	18110 FQ	21200 MW	25510 TQ	USBLS	5/07
Except Special Education	Milwaukee-Waukesha-West Allis MSA, WI	Y	18130 FQ	20720 MW	24800 TQ	USBLS	5/07
Except Special Education	Wyoming	Y	17875 FQ	21480 MW	28102 TQ	WYBLS	9/08
Except Special Education	Cheyenne MSA, WY	Y	19819 FQ	22022 MW	24522 TQ	WYBLS	9/08
Except Special Education	Puerto Rico	Y	14530 FQ	20380 MW	23810 TQ	USBLS	5/07
Except Special Education	San Juan-Caguas-Guaynabo MSA, PR	Y	14660 FQ	20420 MW	23780 TQ	USBLS	5/07
Except Special Education	Virgin Islands	Y	18680 FQ	24530 MW	29510 TQ	USBLS	5/07
Except Special Education	Guam	Y	15890 FQ	19460 MW	24090 TQ	USBLS	5/07

President

Occupation/Type/Industry	Location	Per	Low	Mid	High	Source	Date
Large Private University	United States	Y		527000 MW		USNEWS05	2006
Loyola College	Baltimore, MD	Y			0 HI	BMAG	2009
Public University	United States	Y		427400 MW		BWEEK03	2007-2008

AE Average entry wage	**AW** Average wage paid	**FQ** First quartile wage	**LO** Lowest wage paid	**MTC** Median total compensation **TCC** Total cash compensation
AER Average entry range	**AWR** Average wage range	**H** Hourly	**LR** Low end range	**MW** Median wage paid **TQ** Third quartile wage
AEX Average experienced wage	**AXR** Average experienced range	**HI** Highest wage paid	**M** Monthly	**MWR** Median wage range **W** Weekly
ATC Average total compensation	**D** Daily	**HR** High end range	**MCC** Median cash compensation	**S** See annotated source **Y** Yearly

Occupation/Type/Industry	Location	Per	Low	Mid	High	Source	Date
President							
University of Baltimore	Baltimore, MD	Y			278700 HI	BMAG	2009
University of California	California	Y			434166 HI	LAT02	2006-2007
University of Michigan	Ann Arbor, MI	Y			743151 HI	LAT02	2006-2007
Yale University	New Haven, CT	Y			869026 HI	LAT02	2005-2006
President of the United States	United States	Y			400000 HI	IPL	2008
Press Secretary/Communications Director							
For United States Representative	United States	Y			55000 HI	WPOST	2006
Presser							
Textile, Garment, and Related Materials	Alabama	Y	13120 FQ	15330 MW	19060 TQ	USBLS	5/07
Textile, Garment, and Related Materials	Birmingham-Hoover MSA, AL	Y	13180 FQ	15360 MW	18820 TQ	USBLS	5/07
Textile, Garment, and Related Materials	Alaska	Y	16680 FQ	18690 MW	33100 TQ	USBLS	5/07
Textile, Garment, and Related Materials	Anchorage MSA, AK	Y	16260 FQ	18550 MW	34520 TQ	USBLS	5/07
Textile, Garment, and Related Materials	Arizona	Y	15280 FQ	18440 MW	23870 TQ	USBLS	5/07
Textile, Garment, and Related Materials	Phoenix-Mesa-Scottsdale MSA, AZ	Y	15570 FQ	20160 MW	25590 TQ	USBLS	5/07
Textile, Garment, and Related Materials	Tucson MSA, AZ	Y	14580 FQ	16000 MW	18270 TQ	USBLS	5/07
Textile, Garment, and Related Materials	Arkansas	Y	15010 FQ	16870 MW	18580 TQ	USBLS	5/07
Textile, Garment, and Related Materials	Little Rock-North Little Rock MSA, AR	Y	15880 FQ	17380 MW	18980 TQ	USBLS	5/07
Textile, Garment, and Related Materials	California	H	8.28 FQ	9.12 MW	10.43 TQ	CABLS	1/08-3/08
Textile, Garment, and Related Materials	Fresno MSA, CA	H	8.92 FQ	9.63 MW	10.45 TQ	CABLS	1/08-3/08
Textile, Garment, and Related Materials	Los Angeles-Long Beach-Glendale PMSA, CA	H	8.00 FQ	8.74 MW	9.64 TQ	CABLS	1/08-3/08
Textile, Garment, and Related Materials	Oakland-Fremont-Hayward MSA, CA	H	8.94 FQ	10.19 MW	11.97 TQ	CABLS	1/08-3/08
Textile, Garment, and Related Materials	Riverside-San Bernardino-Ontario MSA, CA	H	8.50 FQ	9.47 MW	11.23 TQ	CABLS	1/08-3/08
Textile, Garment, and Related Materials	Sacramento-Arden Arcade-Roseville MSA, CA	H	8.49 FQ	9.39 MW	10.89 TQ	CABLS	1/08-3/08
Textile, Garment, and Related Materials	San Diego-Carlsbad-San Marcos MSA, CA	H	8.49 FQ	9.17 MW	9.94 TQ	CABLS	1/08-3/08
Textile, Garment, and Related Materials	San Francisco-San Mateo-Redwood PMSA, CA	H	9.05 FQ	10.27 MW	11.67 TQ	CABLS	1/08-3/08
Textile, Garment, and Related Materials	San Jose-Sunnyvale-Santa Clara MSA, CA	H	8.10 FQ	9.31 MW	10.58 TQ	CABLS	1/08-3/08
Textile, Garment, and Related Materials	Santa Ana-Anaheim-Irvine PMSA, CA	Y	17360 FQ	19280 MW	22450 TQ	USBLS	5/07
Textile, Garment, and Related Materials	Colorado	Y	17270 FQ	19640 MW	22250 TQ	USBLS	5/07
Textile, Garment, and Related Materials	Denver-Aurora MSA, CO	Y	17650 FQ	19940 MW	22630 TQ	USBLS	5/07
Textile, Garment, and Related Materials	Connecticut	H	8.79 AE	10.42 MW		CTBLS	1/08-3/08
Textile, Garment, and Related Materials	Bridgeport-Stamford-Norwalk MSA, CT	Y	19270 FQ	21900 MW	24830 TQ	USBLS	5/07
Textile, Garment, and Related Materials	Hartford-West Hartford-East Hartford MSA, CT	Y	17570 FQ	19340 MW	23500 TQ	USBLS	5/07
Textile, Garment, and Related Materials	Delaware	Y	15670 FQ	18510 MW	25110 TQ	USBLS	5/07
Textile, Garment, and Related Materials	District of Columbia	Y	20880 FQ	26350 MW	29780 TQ	USBLS	5/07
Textile, Garment, and Related Materials	Washington-Arlington-Alexandria MSA, DC-VA-MD-WV	Y	16810 FQ	19450 MW	23690 TQ	USBLS	5/07
Textile, Garment, and Related Materials	Florida	Y	16100 FQ	18920 MW	22800 TQ	USBLS	5/07
Textile, Garment, and Related Materials	Fort Lauderdale-Pompano Beach-Deerfield Beach PMSA, FL	Y	16830 FQ	20960 MW	23010 TQ	USBLS	5/07
Textile, Garment, and Related Materials	Jacksonville MSA, FL	Y	15990 FQ	17730 MW	20110 TQ	USBLS	5/07
Textile, Garment, and Related Materials	Miami-Fort Lauderdale-Miami Beach MSA, FL	Y	15980 FQ	20890 MW	23500 TQ	USBLS	5/07
Textile, Garment, and Related Materials	Orlando-Kissimmee MSA, FL	Y	17540 FQ	19750 MW	24690 TQ	USBLS	5/07
Textile, Garment, and Related Materials	Pensacola-Ferry Pass-Brent MSA, FL	Y	14410 FQ	14950 MW	15470 TQ	USBLS	5/07
Textile, Garment, and Related Materials	Tampa-St. Petersburg-Clearwater MSA, FL	Y	15330 FQ	17620 MW	21170 TQ	USBLS	5/07
Textile, Garment, and Related Materials	West Palm Beach-Boca Raton-Boynton Beach PMSA, FL	Y	21220 FQ	23290 MW	25680 TQ	USBLS	5/07
Textile, Garment, and Related Materials	Georgia	Y	16130 FQ	17650 MW	19270 TQ	USBLS	5/07
Textile, Garment, and Related Materials	Atlanta-Sandy Springs-Marietta MSA, GA	Y	16860 FQ	18100 MW	19390 TQ	USBLS	5/07
Textile, Garment, and Related Materials	Hawaii	Y	16440 FQ	18120 MW	19690 TQ	USBLS	5/07

AE	Average entry wage	AW	Average wage paid	FQ	First quartile wage	LO	Lowest wage paid	MTC	Median total compensation	TCC	Total cash compensation
AER	Average entry range	AWR	Average wage range	H	Hourly	LR	Low end range	MW	Median wage paid	TQ	Third quartile wage
AEX	Average experienced wage	AXR	Average experienced range	HI	Highest wage paid	M	Monthly	MWR	Median wage range	W	Weekly
ATC	Average total compensation	D	Daily	HR	High end range	MCC	Median cash compensation	S	See annotated source	Y	Yearly

1298

Presser

Occupation/Type/Industry	Location	Per	Low	Mid	High	Source	Date
Textile, Garment, and Related Materials	Honolulu MSA, HI	Y	16360 FQ	17860 MW	19360 TQ	USBLS	5/07
Textile, Garment, and Related Materials	Idaho	Y	14480 FQ	17590 MW	20460 TQ	USBLS	5/07
Textile, Garment, and Related Materials	Boise City-Nampa MSA, ID	Y	13950 FQ	17070 MW	19820 TQ	USBLS	5/07
Textile, Garment, and Related Materials	Illinois	Y	16870 FQ	18590 MW	21530 TQ	USBLS	5/07
Textile, Garment, and Related Materials	Chicago-Naperville-Joliet MSA, IL-IN-WI	Y	16810 FQ	18410 MW	21150 TQ	USBLS	5/07
Textile, Garment, and Related Materials	Indiana	Y	15290 FQ	18230 MW	22220 TQ	USBLS	5/07
Textile, Garment, and Related Materials	Indianapolis-Carmel MSA, IN	Y	15980 FQ	19070 MW	24040 TQ	USBLS	5/07
Textile, Garment, and Related Materials	Iowa	Y	16500 FQ	18840 MW	21770 TQ	USBLS	5/07
Textile, Garment, and Related Materials	Des Moines-West Des Moines MSA, IA	Y	18100 FQ	20650 MW	23380 TQ	USBLS	5/07
Textile, Garment, and Related Materials	Kansas	Y	13690 FQ	17140 MW	20640 TQ	USBLS	5/07
Textile, Garment, and Related Materials	Wichita MSA, KS	Y	13680 FQ	16430 MW	19350 TQ	USBLS	5/07
Textile, Garment, and Related Materials	Kentucky	Y	16788 FQ	18989 MW	21926 TQ	KYBLS	2008
Textile, Garment, and Related Materials	Louisville-Jefferson County MSA, KY-IN	Y	17180 FQ	19290 MW	22120 TQ	USBLS	5/07
Textile, Garment, and Related Materials	Louisiana	H	7.43 FQ	8.58 MW	10.24 TQ	LABLS	1/08-3/08
Textile, Garment, and Related Materials	Baton Rouge MSA, LA	Y	14500 FQ	16960 MW	19720 TQ	USBLS	5/07
Textile, Garment, and Related Materials	New Orleans-Metairie-Kenner MSA, LA	Y	18670 FQ	21560 MW	23630 TQ	USBLS	5/07
Textile, Garment, and Related Materials	Maine	Y	18450 FQ	20910 MW	23010 TQ	USBLS	5/07
Textile, Garment, and Related Materials	Portland-South Portland-Biddeford MSA, ME	Y	19360 FQ	21240 MW	23010 TQ	USBLS	5/07
Textile, Garment, and Related Materials	Maryland	Y		20600 MW		MDBLS	3/08
Textile, Garment, and Related Materials	Baltimore-Towson MSA, MD	Y	16750 FQ	23920 MW	27340 TQ	USBLS	5/07
Textile, Garment, and Related Materials	Bethesda-Gaithersburg-Frederick PMSA, MD	Y	16690 FQ	19670 MW	22880 TQ	USBLS	5/07
Textile, Garment, and Related Materials	Massachusetts	Y	18670 FQ	22090 MW	25580 TQ	USBLS	5/07
Textile, Garment, and Related Materials	Boston-Cambridge-Quincy NECTA, MA	Y	18910 FQ	21530 MW	23870 TQ	USBLS	5/07
Textile, Garment, and Related Materials	Michigan	Y	15890 FQ	19010 MW	24240 TQ	USBLS	5/07
Textile, Garment, and Related Materials	Detroit-Warren-Livonia MSA, MI	Y	15590 FQ	20430 MW	25310 TQ	USBLS	5/07
Textile, Garment, and Related Materials	Grand Rapids-Wyoming MSA, MI	Y	15220 FQ	17700 MW	22710 TQ	USBLS	5/07
Textile, Garment, and Related Materials	Warren-Troy-Farmington Hills PMSA, MI	Y	15540 FQ	20370 MW	25570 TQ	USBLS	5/07
Textile, Garment, and Related Materials	Minnesota	Y	20640 FQ	23708 MW	26860 TQ	MNBLS	10/08-12/08
Textile, Garment, and Related Materials	Minneapolis-Saint Paul MSA, MN-WI	Y	21604 FQ	24828 MW	28042 TQ	MNBLS	10/08-12/08
Textile, Garment, and Related Materials	Mississippi	Y	13220 FQ	15600 MW	18620 TQ	USBLS	5/07
Textile, Garment, and Related Materials	Jackson MSA, MS	Y	12750 FQ	14340 MW	17470 TQ	USBLS	5/07
Textile, Garment, and Related Materials	Missouri	Y	16140 FQ	18650 MW	22160 TQ	USBLS	5/07
Textile, Garment, and Related Materials	Kansas City MSA, MO-KS	Y	16160 FQ	19030 MW	22730 TQ	USBLS	5/07
Textile, Garment, and Related Materials	St. Louis MSA, MO-IL	Y	16580 FQ	19630 MW	23160 TQ	USBLS	5/07
Textile, Garment, and Related Materials	Springfield MSA, MO	Y	16480 FQ	17660 MW	18870 TQ	USBLS	5/07
Textile, Garment, and Related Materials	Montana	Y	15080 FQ	16930 MW	19110 TQ	USBLS	5/07
Textile, Garment, and Related Materials	Billings MSA, MT	Y	15550 FQ	16770 MW	18020 TQ	USBLS	5/07
Textile, Garment, and Related Materials	Nebraska	Y	14450 FQ	16760 MW	19080 TQ	USBLS	5/07
Textile, Garment, and Related Materials	Omaha-Council Bluffs MSA, NE-IA	Y	14360 FQ	17200 MW	19660 TQ	USBLS	5/07
Textile, Garment, and Related Materials	Nevada	H	9.35 FQ	10.36 MW	11.34 TQ	NVBLS	5/08
Textile, Garment, and Related Materials	Las Vegas-Paradise MSA, NV	H	9.42 FQ	10.33 MW	11.19 TQ	NVBLS	5/08
Textile, Garment, and Related Materials	New Hampshire	H	9.12 AE	10.87 MW	12.20 AEX	NHBLS	6/08
Textile, Garment, and Related Materials	Manchester MSA, NH	Y	20680 FQ	23550 MW	26580 TQ	USBLS	5/07
Textile, Garment, and Related Materials	New Jersey	Y	16910 FQ	20430 MW	25000 TQ	USBLS	5/07
Textile, Garment, and Related Materials	Camden PMSA, NJ	Y	20310 FQ	22120 MW	23950 TQ	USBLS	5/07
Textile, Garment, and Related Materials	Edison PMSA, NJ	Y	16090 FQ	18460 MW	24710 TQ	USBLS	5/07
Textile, Garment, and Related Materials	Newark-Union PMSA, NJ-PA	Y	17600 FQ	23380 MW	29990 TQ	USBLS	5/07
Textile, Garment, and Related Materials	New Mexico	Y	13610 FQ	16800 MW	18980 TQ	USBLS	5/07
Textile, Garment, and Related Materials	Albuquerque MSA, NM	Y	16880 FQ	18310 MW	19830 TQ	USBLS	5/07
Textile, Garment, and Related Materials	New York	Y	15790 FQ	18670 MW	23710 TQ	USBLS	5/07
Textile, Garment, and Related Materials	Albany-Schenectady-Troy MSA, NY	Y	16610 FQ	18870 MW	23560 TQ	USBLS	5/07
Textile, Garment, and Related Materials	Buffalo-Niagara Falls MSA, NY	Y	17600 FQ	20030 MW	23930 TQ	USBLS	5/07
Textile, Garment, and Related Materials	Nassau-Suffolk PMSA, NY	Y	25580 FQ	27790 MW	30120 TQ	USBLS	5/07
Textile, Garment, and Related Materials	New York-Northern New Jersey-Long Island MSA, NY-NJ-PA	Y	15790 FQ	18580 MW	24450 TQ	USBLS	5/07
Textile, Garment, and Related Materials	North Carolina	Y	16080 FQ	18510 MW	22150 TQ	USBLS	5/07

AE	Average entry wage	AW	Average wage paid	FQ	First quartile wage
AER	Average entry range	AWR	Average wage range	H	Hourly
AEX	Average experienced wage	AXR	Average experienced range	HI	Highest wage paid
ATC	Average total compensation	D	Daily	HR	High end range

LO	Lowest wage paid	MTC	Median total compensation	TCC	Total cash compensation
LR	Low end range	MW	Median wage paid	TQ	Third quartile wage
M	Monthly	MWR	Median wage range	W	Weekly
MCC	Median cash compensation	S	See annotated source	Y	Yearly

Occupation/Type/Industry	Location	Per	Low	Mid	High	Source	Date
Presser							
Textile, Garment, and Related Materials	Charlotte-Gastonia-Concord MSA, NC-SC	Y	15420 FQ	18660 MW	21280 TQ	USBLS	5/07
Textile, Garment, and Related Materials	Durham MSA, NC	Y	16160 FQ	20310 MW	24740 TQ	USBLS	5/07
Textile, Garment, and Related Materials	Raleigh-Cary MSA, NC	Y	18330 FQ	21620 MW	24760 TQ	USBLS	5/07
Textile, Garment, and Related Materials	Winston-Salem MSA, NC	Y	16070 FQ	20100 MW	22860 TQ	USBLS	5/07
Textile, Garment, and Related Materials	North Dakota	Y	16630 FQ	19300 MW	21660 TQ	USBLS	5/07
Textile, Garment, and Related Materials	Ohio	Y	16730 FQ	18900 MW	22230 TQ	USBLS	5/07
Textile, Garment, and Related Materials	Cincinnati-Middletown MSA, OH-KY-IN	Y	16810 FQ	18560 MW	21650 TQ	USBLS	5/07
Textile, Garment, and Related Materials	Cleveland-Elyria-Mentor MSA, OH	Y	16800 FQ	19160 MW	21910 TQ	USBLS	5/07
Textile, Garment, and Related Materials	Columbus MSA, OH	Y	19780 FQ	22270 MW	24810 TQ	USBLS	5/07
Textile, Garment, and Related Materials	Dayton MSA, OH	Y	15790 FQ	18180 MW	21870 TQ	USBLS	5/07
Textile, Garment, and Related Materials	Oklahoma	Y	15490 FQ	20530 MW	26940 TQ	USBLS	5/07
Textile, Garment, and Related Materials	Oklahoma City MSA, OK	Y	18830 FQ	22610 MW	29380 TQ	USBLS	5/07
Textile, Garment, and Related Materials	Tulsa MSA, OK	Y	14280 FQ	17610 MW	20100 TQ	USBLS	5/07
Textile, Garment, and Related Materials	Oregon	H	8.70 FQ	9.54 MW	11.12 TQ	ORBLS	5/08
Textile, Garment, and Related Materials	Portland-Vancouver-Beaverton MSA, OR-WA	Y	18490 FQ	20780 MW	23990 TQ	USBLS	5/07
Textile, Garment, and Related Materials	Pennsylvania	Y	15820 FQ	19420 MW	23230 TQ	USBLS	5/07
Textile, Garment, and Related Materials	Allentown-Bethlehem-Easton MSA, PA-NJ	Y	16910 FQ	20550 MW	24040 TQ	USBLS	5/07
Textile, Garment, and Related Materials	Philadelphia-Camden-Wilmington MSA, PA-NJ-DE-MD	Y	18950 FQ	21850 MW	24600 TQ	USBLS	5/07
Textile, Garment, and Related Materials	Pittsburgh MSA, PA	Y	14470 FQ	16830 MW	20150 TQ	USBLS	5/07
Textile, Garment, and Related Materials	Rhode Island	Y	15530 FQ	17900 MW	23120 TQ	USBLS	5/07
Textile, Garment, and Related Materials	Providence-Fall River-Warwick MSA, RI-MA	Y	15570 FQ	19240 MW	24160 TQ	USBLS	5/07
Textile, Garment, and Related Materials	South Carolina	Y	15280 FQ	17690 MW	19900 TQ	USBLS	5/07
Textile, Garment, and Related Materials	Charleston-North Charleston MSA, SC	Y	16310 FQ	17870 MW	19460 TQ	USBLS	5/07
Textile, Garment, and Related Materials	Columbia MSA, SC	Y	16090 FQ	18200 MW	21740 TQ	USBLS	5/07
Textile, Garment, and Related Materials	South Dakota	Y	14250 FQ	16598 MW	18667 TQ	SDBLS	7/08-9/08
Textile, Garment, and Related Materials	Tennessee	Y	15500 FQ	17890 MW	20420 TQ	USBLS	5/07
Textile, Garment, and Related Materials	Kingsport-Bristol-Bristol MSA, TN-VA	Y	12620 FQ	14430 MW	15920 TQ	USBLS	5/07
Textile, Garment, and Related Materials	Memphis MSA, TN-MS-AR	Y	16340 FQ	17980 MW	19910 TQ	USBLS	5/07
Textile, Garment, and Related Materials	Nashville-Davidson-Murfreesboro MSA, TN	Y	15000 FQ	18780 MW	22460 TQ	USBLS	5/07
Textile, Garment, and Related Materials	Texas	Y	13550 FQ	16040 MW	19040 TQ	USBLS	5/07
Textile, Garment, and Related Materials	Austin-Round Rock MSA, TX	Y	16260 FQ	17760 MW	19350 TQ	USBLS	5/07
Textile, Garment, and Related Materials	Beaumont-Port Arthur MSA, TX	Y	13260 FQ	15420 MW	17930 TQ	USBLS	5/07
Textile, Garment, and Related Materials	Dallas-Fort Worth-Arlington MSA, TX	Y	13700 FQ	16580 MW	20200 TQ	USBLS	5/07
Textile, Garment, and Related Materials	El Paso MSA, TX	Y	12210 FQ	13270 MW	14340 TQ	USBLS	5/07
Textile, Garment, and Related Materials	Houston-Sugar Land-Baytown MSA, TX	Y	14250 FQ	16780 MW	19720 TQ	USBLS	5/07
Textile, Garment, and Related Materials	San Antonio MSA, TX	Y	14130 FQ	17180 MW	20200 TQ	USBLS	5/07
Textile, Garment, and Related Materials	Utah	Y	14160 FQ	17930 MW	20560 TQ	USBLS	5/07
Textile, Garment, and Related Materials	Ogden-Clearfield MSA, UT	Y	15110 FQ	19050 MW	21080 TQ	USBLS	5/07
Textile, Garment, and Related Materials	Salt Lake City MSA, UT	Y	14760 FQ	17580 MW	20140 TQ	USBLS	5/07
Textile, Garment, and Related Materials	Vermont	Y	17000 FQ	18590 MW	20600 TQ	USBLS	5/07
Textile, Garment, and Related Materials	Virginia	Y	16590 FQ	18520 MW	21110 TQ	USBLS	5/07
Textile, Garment, and Related Materials	Richmond MSA, VA	Y	15990 FQ	17830 MW	20030 TQ	USBLS	5/07
Textile, Garment, and Related Materials	Virginia Beach-Norfolk-Newport News MSA, VA-NC	Y	17020 FQ	19160 MW	22280 TQ	USBLS	5/07
Textile, Garment, and Related Materials	Washington	H	8.84 FQ	9.67 MW	11.45 TQ	WABLS	3/08
Textile, Garment, and Related Materials	Olympia MSA, WA	Y	17680 FQ	18840 MW	19920 TQ	USBLS	5/07
Textile, Garment, and Related Materials	Seattle-Tacoma-Bellevue MSA, WA	Y	18790 FQ	21580 MW	26100 TQ	USBLS	5/07
Textile, Garment, and Related Materials	West Virginia	Y	16423 FQ	18429 MW	21087 TQ	WVBLS	7/08-9/08
Textile, Garment, and Related Materials	Charleston MSA, WV	Y	16040 FQ	17890 MW	20140 TQ	USBLS	5/07
Textile, Garment, and Related Materials	Huntington-Ashland MSA, WV-KY-OH	Y	13120 FQ	15080 MW	17850 TQ	USBLS	5/07
Textile, Garment, and Related Materials	Wisconsin	Y	17880 FQ	21150 MW	25680 TQ	USBLS	5/07
Textile, Garment, and Related Materials	Milwaukee-Waukesha-West Allis MSA, WI	Y	18960 FQ	23710 MW	28040 TQ	USBLS	5/07
Textile, Garment, and Related Materials	Wyoming	Y	16949 FQ	18634 MW	21411 TQ	WYBLS	9/08
Textile, Garment, and Related Materials	Puerto Rico	Y	12370 FQ	13610 MW	14890 TQ	USBLS	5/07

AE	Average entry wage	AW	Average wage paid	FQ	First quartile wage	LO	Lowest wage paid	MTC	Median total compensation	TCC	Total cash compensation
AER	Average entry range	AWR	Average wage range	H	Hourly	LR	Low end range	MW	Median wage paid	TQ	Third quartile wage
AEX	Average experienced wage	AXR	Average experienced range	HI	Highest wage paid	M	Monthly	MWR	Median wage range	W	Weekly
ATC	Average total compensation	D	Daily	HR	High end range	MCC	Median cash compensation	S	See annotated source	Y	Yearly

Occupation/Type/Industry	Location	Per	Low	Mid	High	Source	Date
Presser							
Textile, Garment, and Related Materials	San Juan-Caguas-Guaynabo MSA, PR	Y	12490 FQ	13870 MW	15480 TQ	USBLS	5/07
Textile, Garment, and Related Materials	Virgin Islands	Y	14060 FQ	15300 MW	18060 TQ	USBLS	5/07
Pretreatment Specialist							
Municipal Government	Cincinnati, OH	Y	38340 LO		44936 HI	COHSS	10/08
Principal							
Public Schools	Kansas	Y		80608 AW		KLIB	2007-2008
Principal City Planner	Gresham, OR	Y	67620 LO		87924 HI	GOSS01	7/1/08
Principal Engineer							
Department of Transportation	New Hampshire	Y		80720 AW		NHUL03	2008
Print Production Artist	United States	Y	36000 FQ	45000 MW	53000 TQ	AIGA01	2008
Print Production Manager	United States	Y	46000 AE			CCRUN02	2008
Printer and Photograph Coordinator							
White House Staff	United States	Y			54525 HI	WPOST02	2008
Printing Machine Operator	Alabama	Y	19970 FQ	25520 MW	33850 TQ	USBLS	5/07
	Birmingham-Hoover MSA, AL	Y	23800 FQ	30220 MW	38760 TQ	USBLS	5/07
	Alaska	Y	34080 FQ	40660 MW	53070 TQ	USBLS	5/07
	Anchorage MSA, AK	Y	32920 FQ	40120 MW	54740 TQ	USBLS	5/07
	Arizona	Y	22620 FQ	28760 MW	35990 TQ	USBLS	5/07
	Phoenix-Mesa-Scottsdale MSA, AZ	Y	22140 FQ	28860 MW	36670 TQ	USBLS	5/07
	Tucson MSA, AZ	Y	25880 FQ	28910 MW	32360 TQ	USBLS	5/07
	Arkansas	Y	20630 FQ	27770 MW	35210 TQ	USBLS	5/07
	Little Rock-North Little Rock MSA, AR	Y	24840 FQ	28570 MW	32470 TQ	USBLS	5/07
	California	H	11.64 FQ	15.73 MW	20.98 TQ	CABLS	1/08-3/08
	Los Angeles-Long Beach-Glendale PMSA, CA	H	10.19 FQ	14.27 MW	19.21 TQ	CABLS	1/08-3/08
	Oakland-Fremont-Hayward MSA, CA	H	12.16 FQ	17.10 MW	23.66 TQ	CABLS	1/08-3/08
	Riverside-San Bernardino-Ontario MSA, CA	H	13.23 FQ	16.90 MW	21.49 TQ	CABLS	1/08-3/08
	Sacramento-Arden Arcade-Roseville MSA, CA	H	13.76 FQ	17.57 MW	21.23 TQ	CABLS	1/08-3/08
	San Diego-Carlsbad-San Marcos MSA, CA	H	10.29 FQ	13.68 MW	17.34 TQ	CABLS	1/08-3/08
	San Francisco-San Mateo-Redwood PMSA, CA	H	17.55 FQ	22.74 MW	28.38 TQ	CABLS	1/08-3/08
	San Jose-Sunnyvale-Santa Clara MSA, CA	H	13.43 FQ	17.80 MW	23.09 TQ	CABLS	1/08-3/08
	Santa Ana-Anaheim-Irvine PMSA, CA	Y	24900 FQ	31710 MW	42140 TQ	USBLS	5/07
	Colorado	Y	25580 FQ	32200 MW	40890 TQ	USBLS	5/07
	Colorado Springs MSA, CO	Y	23920 FQ	28200 MW	34410 TQ	USBLS	5/07
	Denver-Aurora MSA, CO	Y	26730 FQ	34240 MW	43080 TQ	USBLS	5/07
	Fort Collins-Loveland MSA, CO	Y	23320 FQ	32780 MW	46610 TQ	USBLS	5/07
	Connecticut	H	11.06 AE	15.97 MW		CTBLS	1/08-3/08
	Bridgeport-Stamford-Norwalk MSA, CT	Y	22020 FQ	30680 MW	42160 TQ	USBLS	5/07
	Hartford-West Hartford-East Hartford MSA, CT	Y	24240 FQ	31250 MW	41260 TQ	USBLS	5/07
	Delaware	Y	24440 FQ	31260 MW	39270 TQ	USBLS	5/07
	Wilmington PMSA, DE-MD-NJ	Y	24080 FQ	30190 MW	39650 TQ	USBLS	5/07
	District of Columbia	Y	41430 FQ	52460 MW	79250 TQ	USBLS	5/07
	Washington-Arlington-Alexandria MSA, DC-VA-MD-WV	Y	30420 FQ	43490 MW	57460 TQ	USBLS	5/07
	Florida	Y	23460 FQ	30200 MW	38650 TQ	USBLS	5/07

AE	Average entry wage	AW	Average wage paid	FQ	First quartile wage	LO	Lowest wage paid	MTC	Median total compensation	TCC	Total cash compensation
AER	Average entry range	AWR	Average wage range	H	Hourly	LR	Low end range	MW	Median wage paid	TQ	Third quartile wage
AEX	Average experienced wage	AXR	Average experienced range	HI	Highest wage paid	M	Monthly	MWR	Median wage range	W	Weekly
ATC	Average total compensation	D	Daily	HR	High end range	MCC	Median cash compensation	S	See annotated source	Y	Yearly

Occupation/Type/Industry	Location	Per	Low	Mid	High	Source	Date
Printing Machine Operator	Fort Lauderdale-Pompano Beach-Deerfield Beach PMSA, FL	Y	21890 FQ	28830 MW	39460 TQ	USBLS	5/07
	Jacksonville MSA, FL	Y	26500 FQ	32440 MW	39640 TQ	USBLS	5/07
	Miami-Fort Lauderdale-Miami Beach MSA, FL	Y	22480 FQ	29540 MW	37680 TQ	USBLS	5/07
	Orlando-Kissimmee MSA, FL	Y	24950 FQ	31960 MW	41180 TQ	USBLS	5/07
	Tampa-St. Petersburg-Clearwater MSA, FL	Y	23150 FQ	31120 MW	39510 TQ	USBLS	5/07
	West Palm Beach-Boca Raton-Boynton Beach PMSA, FL	Y	24470 FQ	31720 MW	38690 TQ	USBLS	5/07
	Georgia	Y	26320 FQ	33840 MW	41020 TQ	USBLS	5/07
	Atlanta-Sandy Springs-Marietta MSA, GA	Y	28820 FQ	35510 MW	42870 TQ	USBLS	5/07
	Savannah MSA, GA	Y	21810 FQ	26060 MW	33560 TQ	USBLS	5/07
	Hawaii	Y	21730 FQ	27450 MW	44230 TQ	USBLS	5/07
	Honolulu MSA, HI	Y	21630 FQ	27430 MW	47370 TQ	USBLS	5/07
	Idaho	Y	20080 FQ	28000 MW	35180 TQ	USBLS	5/07
	Boise City-Nampa MSA, ID	Y	19280 FQ	26310 MW	30300 TQ	USBLS	5/07
	Illinois	Y	22180 FQ	29970 MW	39250 TQ	USBLS	5/07
	Chicago-Naperville-Joliet MSA, IL-IN-WI	Y	22310 FQ	30450 MW	40560 TQ	USBLS	5/07
	Indiana	Y	23930 FQ	31400 MW	40190 TQ	USBLS	5/07
	Elkhart-Goshen MSA, IN	Y	22350 FQ	26420 MW	36250 TQ	USBLS	5/07
	Evansville MSA, IN-KY	Y	19260 FQ	27030 MW	42790 TQ	USBLS	5/07
	Gary PMSA, IN	Y	21510 FQ	30920 MW	44690 TQ	USBLS	5/07
	Indianapolis-Carmel MSA, IN	Y	24270 FQ	31970 MW	42170 TQ	USBLS	5/07
	Iowa	Y	23800 FQ	29630 MW	37950 TQ	USBLS	5/07
	Des Moines-West Des Moines MSA, IA	Y	24940 FQ	33010 MW	44420 TQ	USBLS	5/07
	Kansas	Y	24000 FQ	32110 MW	40640 TQ	USBLS	5/07
	Wichita MSA, KS	Y	28880 FQ	37190 MW	46090 TQ	USBLS	5/07
	Kentucky	Y	23867 FQ	32888 MW	40935 TQ	KYBLS	2008
	Louisville-Jefferson County MSA, KY-IN	Y	23890 FQ	31410 MW	42320 TQ	USBLS	5/07
	Louisiana	H	10.05 FQ	12.72 MW	15.67 TQ	LABLS	1/08-3/08
	Baton Rouge MSA, LA	Y	19220 FQ	24100 MW	31670 TQ	USBLS	5/07
	New Orleans-Metairie-Kenner MSA, LA	Y	22180 FQ	27650 MW	34390 TQ	USBLS	5/07
	Maine	Y	24910 FQ	29710 MW	36080 TQ	USBLS	5/07
	Lewiston-Auburn MSA, ME	Y	24590 FQ	30320 MW	37760 TQ	USBLS	5/07
	Portland-South Portland-Biddeford MSA, ME	Y	25420 FQ	30020 MW	38730 TQ	USBLS	5/07
	Maryland	Y		36900 MW		MDBLS	3/08
	Baltimore-Towson MSA, MD	Y	26240 FQ	33350 MW	46440 TQ	USBLS	5/07
	Bethesda-Gaithersburg-Frederick PMSA, MD	Y	27080 FQ	35360 MW	45630 TQ	USBLS	5/07
	Massachusetts	Y	26490 FQ	35080 MW	44510 TQ	USBLS	5/07
	Boston-Cambridge-Quincy NECTA, MA	Y	24210 FQ	34790 MW	45940 TQ	USBLS	5/07
	Lynn-Peabody-Salem NECTA, MA	Y	29830 FQ	37390 MW	44780 TQ	USBLS	5/07
	Worcester MSA, MA-CT	Y	27490 FQ	31840 MW	37380 TQ	USBLS	5/07
	Michigan	Y	24850 FQ	32000 MW	40970 TQ	USBLS	5/07
	Detroit-Warren-Livonia MSA, MI	Y	25950 FQ	31780 MW	41850 TQ	USBLS	5/07
	Grand Rapids-Wyoming MSA, MI	Y	31750 FQ	39490 MW	46030 TQ	USBLS	5/07
	Muskegon-Norton Shores MSA, MI	Y	25420 FQ	35590 MW	41990 TQ	USBLS	5/07
	Warren-Troy-Farmington Hills PMSA, MI	Y	25390 FQ	31130 MW	41440 TQ	USBLS	5/07
	Minnesota	Y	29151 FQ	39839 MW	50589 TQ	MNBLS	10/08-12/08
	Duluth-Superior MSA, MN-WI	Y	23615 FQ	29400 MW	39549 TQ	MNBLS	10/08-12/08
	Minneapolis-Saint Paul MSA, MN-WI	Y	35205 FQ	43758 MW	53938 TQ	MNBLS	10/08-12/08
	Rochester MSA, MN	Y	30958 FQ	36789 MW	43736 TQ	MNBLS	10/08-12/08
	Mississippi	Y	21320 FQ	26880 MW	31660 TQ	USBLS	5/07
	Jackson MSA, MS	Y	23720 FQ	27800 MW	31530 TQ	USBLS	5/07
	Missouri	Y	21780 FQ	29110 MW	40390 TQ	USBLS	5/07
	Kansas City MSA, MO-KS	Y	24520 FQ	32930 MW	42940 TQ	USBLS	5/07
	St. Louis MSA, MO-IL	Y	23710 FQ	30580 MW	42490 TQ	USBLS	5/07

AE	Average entry wage	AW	Average wage paid	FQ	First quartile wage
AER	Average entry range	AWR	Average wage range	H	Hourly
AEX	Average experienced wage	AXR	Average experienced range	HI	Highest wage paid
ATC	Average total compensation	D	Daily	HR	High end range

LO	Lowest wage paid	MTC	Median total compensation
LR	Low end range	MW	Median wage paid
M	Monthly	MWR	Median wage range
MCC	Median cash compensation	S	See annotated source

TCC	Total cash compensation
TQ	Third quartile wage
W	Weekly
Y	Yearly

Occupation/Type/Industry	Location	Per	Low	Mid	High	Source	Date
Printing Machine Operator	Montana	Y	18670 FQ	23370 MW	31010 TQ	USBLS	5/07
	Billings MSA, MT	Y	17160 FQ	22110 MW	32510 TQ	USBLS	5/07
	Nebraska	Y	21660 FQ	26550 MW	33580 TQ	USBLS	5/07
	Omaha-Council Bluffs MSA, NE-IA	Y	22550 FQ	27520 MW	34470 TQ	USBLS	5/07
	Nevada	H	13.62 FQ	17.02 MW	21.43 TQ	NVBLS	5/08
	Carson City MSA, NV	H	13.47 FQ	21.10 MW	23.52 TQ	NVBLS	5/08
	Las Vegas-Paradise MSA, NV	H	12.81 FQ	16.06 MW	20.18 TQ	NVBLS	5/08
	New Hampshire	H	11.17 AE	15.76 MW	19.13 AEX	NHBLS	6/08
	Manchester MSA, NH	Y	28060 FQ	33210 MW	41420 TQ	USBLS	5/07
	Nashua NECTA, NH-MA	Y	30090 FQ	38290 MW	48360 TQ	USBLS	5/07
	New Jersey	Y	23140 FQ	37100 MW	49490 TQ	USBLS	5/07
	Camden PMSA, NJ	Y	22890 FQ	37140 MW	48560 TQ	USBLS	5/07
	Edison PMSA, NJ	Y	28410 FQ	39510 MW	53050 TQ	USBLS	5/07
	Newark-Union PMSA, NJ-PA	Y	21640 FQ	36540 MW	47000 TQ	USBLS	5/07
	New Mexico	Y	19550 FQ	25540 MW	34910 TQ	USBLS	5/07
	Albuquerque MSA, NM	Y	22900 FQ	28730 MW	38790 TQ	USBLS	5/07
	New York	Y	23960 FQ	32340 MW	43190 TQ	USBLS	5/07
	Albany-Schenectady-Troy MSA, NY	Y	33050 FQ	38660 MW	47380 TQ	USBLS	5/07
	Buffalo-Niagara Falls MSA, NY	Y	29050 FQ	35410 MW	41840 TQ	USBLS	5/07
	Nassau-Suffolk PMSA, NY	Y	24400 FQ	33320 MW	44400 TQ	USBLS	5/07
	New York-Northern New Jersey-Long Island MSA, NY-NJ-PA	Y	23340 FQ	34450 MW	48030 TQ	USBLS	5/07
	North Carolina	Y	22570 FQ	30040 MW	39570 TQ	USBLS	5/07
	Charlotte-Gastonia-Concord MSA, NC-SC	Y	26470 FQ	34490 MW	43450 TQ	USBLS	5/07
	Raleigh-Cary MSA, NC	Y	27250 FQ	36130 MW	44550 TQ	USBLS	5/07
	North Dakota	Y	20740 FQ	25950 MW	32090 TQ	USBLS	5/07
	Fargo MSA, ND-MN	Y	19330 FQ	27420 MW	33790 TQ	USBLS	5/07
	Ohio	Y	23850 FQ	31360 MW	39440 TQ	USBLS	5/07
	Cincinnati-Middletown MSA, OH-KY-IN	Y	27610 FQ	34980 MW	41450 TQ	USBLS	5/07
	Cleveland-Elyria-Mentor MSA, OH	Y	22900 FQ	29840 MW	38880 TQ	USBLS	5/07
	Columbus MSA, OH	Y	27280 FQ	35820 MW	43010 TQ	USBLS	5/07
	Dayton MSA, OH	Y	25570 FQ	31110 MW	38650 TQ	USBLS	5/07
	Mansfield MSA, OH	Y	20930 FQ	25190 MW	29720 TQ	USBLS	5/07
	Oklahoma	Y	19830 FQ	24530 MW	31600 TQ	USBLS	5/07
	Oklahoma City MSA, OK	Y	21000 FQ	24610 MW	30670 TQ	USBLS	5/07
	Tulsa MSA, OK	Y	21290 FQ	27150 MW	34510 TQ	USBLS	5/07
	Oregon	H	11.76 FQ	17.06 MW	21.81 TQ	ORBLS	5/08
	Portland-Vancouver-Beaverton MSA, OR-WA	Y	25500 FQ	37270 MW	46540 TQ	USBLS	5/07
	Pennsylvania	Y	26980 FQ	33960 MW	43810 TQ	USBLS	5/07
	Allentown-Bethlehem-Easton MSA, PA-NJ	Y	25640 FQ	31760 MW	41320 TQ	USBLS	5/07
	Philadelphia-Camden-Wilmington MSA, PA-NJ-DE-MD	Y	26910 FQ	35680 MW	47670 TQ	USBLS	5/07
	Pittsburgh MSA, PA	Y	24180 FQ	31300 MW	39930 TQ	USBLS	5/07
	Rhode Island	Y	26580 FQ	31820 MW	39170 TQ	USBLS	5/07
	Providence-Fall River-Warwick MSA, RI-MA	Y	25700 FQ	31710 MW	39410 TQ	USBLS	5/07
	South Carolina	Y	22080 FQ	27700 MW	34920 TQ	USBLS	5/07
	Charleston-North Charleston MSA, SC	Y	19820 FQ	23630 MW	29150 TQ	USBLS	5/07
	Columbia MSA, SC	Y	24570 FQ	29710 MW	39340 TQ	USBLS	5/07
	South Dakota	Y	24682 FQ	29091 MW	35676 TQ	SDBLS	7/08-9/08
	Sioux Falls MSA, SD	Y	27314 FQ	32309 MW	40182 TQ	SDBLS	7/08-9/08
	Tennessee	Y	21360 FQ	27420 MW	37190 TQ	USBLS	5/07
	Memphis MSA, TN-MS-AR	Y	26620 FQ	36030 MW	45120 TQ	USBLS	5/07
	Nashville-Davidson-Murfreesboro MSA, TN	Y	28170 FQ	35580 MW	45240 TQ	USBLS	5/07
	Texas	Y	21420 FQ	27890 MW	36680 TQ	USBLS	5/07
	Austin-Round Rock MSA, TX	Y	23980 FQ	29020 MW	35400 TQ	USBLS	5/07
	Dallas-Fort Worth-Arlington MSA, TX	Y	24730 FQ	32100 MW	40370 TQ	USBLS	5/07
	El Paso MSA, TX	Y	16630 FQ	20960 MW	25070 TQ	USBLS	5/07

AE Average entry wage	**AW** Average wage paid	**FQ** First quartile wage	**LO** Lowest wage paid	**MTC** Median total compensation	**TCC** Total cash compensation
AER Average entry range	**AWR** Average wage range	**H** Hourly	**LR** Low end range	**MW** Median wage paid	**TQ** Third quartile wage
AEX Average experienced wage	**AXR** Average experienced range	**HI** Highest wage paid	**M** Monthly	**MWR** Median wage range	**W** Weekly
ATC Average total compensation	**D** Daily	**HR** High end range	**MCC** Median cash compensation	**S** See annotated source	**Y** Yearly

Occupation/Type/Industry	Location	Per	Low	Mid	High	Source	Date
Printing Machine Operator	Houston-Sugar Land-Baytown						
	MSA, TX	Y	19500 FQ	26290 MW	35670 TQ	USBLS	5/07
	San Antonio MSA, TX	Y	23210 FQ	29330 MW	36590 TQ	USBLS	5/07
	Utah	Y	17160 FQ	22250 MW	31310 TQ	USBLS	5/07
	Provo-Orem MSA, UT	Y	16420 FQ	19250 MW	24490 TQ	USBLS	5/07
	Salt Lake City MSA, UT	Y	19800 FQ	24700 MW	35720 TQ	USBLS	5/07
	Vermont	Y	24590 FQ	31340 MW	39020 TQ	USBLS	5/07
	Burlington-South Burlington						
	MSA, VT	Y	27550 FQ	34420 MW	42140 TQ	USBLS	5/07
	Virginia	Y	24260 FQ	32350 MW	42830 TQ	USBLS	5/07
	Lynchburg MSA, VA	Y	25160 FQ	31690 MW	39260 TQ	USBLS	5/07
	Richmond MSA, VA	Y	27810 FQ	34680 MW	41240 TQ	USBLS	5/07
	Virginia Beach-Norfolk-						
	Newport News MSA, VA-NC	Y	19060 FQ	26030 MW	34380 TQ	USBLS	5/07
	Washington	H	13.48 FQ	17.94 MW	22.26 TQ	WABLS	3/08
	Seattle-Tacoma-Bellevue						
	MSA, WA	Y	28180 FQ	38180 MW	46920 TQ	USBLS	5/07
	West Virginia	Y	20522 FQ	24897 MW	32956 TQ	WVBLS	7/08-9/08
	Charleston MSA, WV	Y	21200 FQ	23390 MW	26540 TQ	USBLS	5/07
	Wisconsin	Y	27100 FQ	35470 MW	44020 TQ	USBLS	5/07
	Appleton MSA, WI	Y	33150 FQ	39250 MW	43950 TQ	USBLS	5/07
	Milwaukee-Waukesha-West						
	Allis MSA, WI	Y	24140 FQ	34110 MW	43900 TQ	USBLS	5/07
	Wyoming	Y	20692 FQ	25441 MW	30138 TQ	WYBLS	9/08
	Casper MSA, WY	Y	24141 FQ	27442 MW	31939 TQ	WYBLS	9/08
	Cheyenne MSA, WY	Y	22394 FQ	24061 MW	25727 TQ	WYBLS	9/08
	Puerto Rico	Y	14000 FQ	17480 MW	24920 TQ	USBLS	5/07
	San Juan-Caguas-Guaynabo						
	MSA, PR	Y	13980 FQ	18470 MW	27360 TQ	USBLS	5/07
Private							
U.S. Army, Active Duty, Pay Grade E-2	United States	M		1569 AW		DOD1	2009
Private 1st Class							
U.S. Army, Active Duty, Pay Grade E-3	United States	M	1650 LO		1860 HI	DOD1	2009
U.S. Marines, Active Duty, Pay Grade E-2	United States	M		1569 AW		DOD1	2009
Private Contractor for the United States Military							
Working in Iraq	United States	D			1000 HI	LAT03	2007
Private Detective and Investigator	Alabama	Y	28910 FQ	38660 MW	47310 TQ	USBLS	5/07
	Birmingham-Hoover MSA, AL	Y	28260 FQ	37900 MW	45290 TQ	USBLS	5/07
	Arizona	Y	29330 FQ	40960 MW	62990 TQ	USBLS	5/07
	Phoenix-Mesa-Scottsdale						
	MSA, AZ	Y	31720 FQ	48230 MW	69560 TQ	USBLS	5/07
	Tucson MSA, AZ	Y	26190 FQ	29970 MW	37410 TQ	USBLS	5/07
	Arkansas	Y	28570 FQ	34330 MW	51650 TQ	USBLS	5/07
	Little Rock-North Little Rock						
	MSA, AR	Y	28060 FQ	31920 MW	55980 TQ	USBLS	5/07
	California	H	17.14 FQ	25.12 MW	32.98 TQ	CABLS	1/08-3/08
	Bakersfield MSA, CA	H	13.17 FQ	23.72 MW	26.66 TQ	CABLS	1/08-3/08
	Fresno MSA, CA	H	20.78 FQ	23.52 MW	33.32 TQ	CABLS	1/08-3/08
	Los Angeles-Long Beach-						
	Glendale PMSA, CA	H	19.34 FQ	22.96 MW	29.41 TQ	CABLS	1/08-3/08
	Oakland-Fremont-Hayward						
	MSA, CA	H	23.06 FQ	32.18 MW	41.70 TQ	CABLS	1/08-3/08
	Riverside-San Bernardino-						
	Ontario MSA, CA	H	11.65 FQ	16.34 MW	32.85 TQ	CABLS	1/08-3/08
	Sacramento-Arden Arcade-						
	Roseville MSA, CA	H	14.43 FQ	21.17 MW	27.02 TQ	CABLS	1/08-3/08
	San Francisco-San Mateo-						
	Redwood PMSA, CA	H	26.29 FQ	28.95 MW	31.63 TQ	CABLS	1/08-3/08
	San Jose-Sunnyvale-Santa						
	Clara MSA, CA	H	32.63 FQ	35.72 MW	38.95 TQ	CABLS	1/08-3/08
	Santa Ana-Anaheim-Irvine						
	PMSA, CA	Y	35970 FQ	57920 MW	74670 TQ	USBLS	5/07
	Colorado	Y	32910 FQ	37550 MW	44940 TQ	USBLS	5/07
	Denver-Aurora MSA, CO	Y	33680 FQ	38150 MW	46810 TQ	USBLS	5/07
	Connecticut	H	12.83 AE	21.98 MW		CTBLS	1/08-3/08
	Bridgeport-Stamford-Norwalk						
	MSA, CT	Y	29600 FQ	61140 MW	68920 TQ	USBLS	5/07

AE	Average entry wage	AW	Average wage paid	FQ	First quartile wage	
AER	Average entry range	AWR	Average wage range	H	Hourly	
AEX	Average experienced wage	AXR	Average experienced range	HI	Highest wage paid	
ATC	Average total compensation	D	Daily	HR	High end range	

LO	Lowest wage paid	MTC	Median total compensation	TCC	Total cash compensation
LR	Low end range	MW	Median wage paid	TQ	Third quartile wage
M	Monthly	MWR	Median wage range	W	Weekly
MCC	Median cash compensation	S	See annotated source	Y	Yearly

Occupation/Type/Industry	Location	Per	Low	Mid	High	Source	Date
Private Detective and Investigator	Hartford-West Hartford-East Hartford MSA, CT	Y	26720 FQ	32710 MW	53210 TQ	USBLS	5/07
	Delaware	Y	28570 FQ	45010 MW	53160 TQ	USBLS	5/07
	Wilmington PMSA, DE-MD-NJ	Y	41910 FQ	49330 MW	61430 TQ	USBLS	5/07
	Florida	Y	24910 FQ	36060 MW	45610 TQ	USBLS	5/07
	Fort Lauderdale-Pompano Beach-Deerfield Beach PMSA, FL	Y	35260 FQ	39600 MW	51110 TQ	USBLS	5/07
	Jacksonville MSA, FL	Y	17670 FQ	19700 MW	23870 TQ	USBLS	5/07
	Miami-Fort Lauderdale-Miami Beach MSA, FL	Y	33360 FQ	39540 MW	52070 TQ	USBLS	5/07
	Orlando-Kissimmee MSA, FL	Y	23410 FQ	34020 MW	41990 TQ	USBLS	5/07
	Sarasota-Bradenton-Venice MSA, FL	Y	35950 FQ	44240 MW	51070 TQ	USBLS	5/07
	Tampa-St. Petersburg-Clearwater MSA, FL	Y	30870 FQ	37800 MW	44820 TQ	USBLS	5/07
	West Palm Beach-Boca Raton-Boynton Beach PMSA, FL	Y	29340 FQ	34510 MW	41530 TQ	USBLS	5/07
	Georgia	Y	20170 FQ	29170 MW	53630 TQ	USBLS	5/07
	Atlanta-Sandy Springs-Marietta MSA, GA	Y	19630 FQ	35990 MW	56510 TQ	USBLS	5/07
	Idaho	Y	22030 FQ	25050 MW	29720 TQ	USBLS	5/07
	Illinois	Y	23540 FQ	33420 MW	45340 TQ	USBLS	5/07
	Chicago-Naperville-Joliet MSA, IL-IN-WI	Y	24430 FQ	34830 MW	47420 TQ	USBLS	5/07
	Indiana	Y	23210 FQ	33110 MW	53170 TQ	USBLS	5/07
	Indianapolis-Carmel MSA, IN	Y	28450 FQ	42570 MW	54090 TQ	USBLS	5/07
	Iowa	Y	23060 FQ	32280 MW	47200 TQ	USBLS	5/07
	Des Moines-West Des Moines MSA, IA	Y	24860 FQ	32780 MW	46660 TQ	USBLS	5/07
	Kansas	Y	16570 FQ	27920 MW	40270 TQ	USBLS	5/07
	Kentucky	Y	21420 FQ	27047 MW	33009 TQ	KYBLS	2008
	Louisiana	H	11.54 FQ	13.95 MW	17.45 TQ	LABLS	1/08-3/08
	Baton Rouge MSA, LA	Y	24460 FQ	28410 MW	33410 TQ	USBLS	5/07
	New Orleans-Metairie-Kenner MSA, LA	Y	24800 FQ	28880 MW	34380 TQ	USBLS	5/07
	Maine	Y	26100 FQ	30000 MW	36880 TQ	USBLS	5/07
	Maryland	Y		36325 MW		MDBLS	3/08
	Baltimore-Towson MSA, MD	Y	32070 FQ	38180 MW	46680 TQ	USBLS	5/07
	Bethesda-Gaithersburg-Frederick PMSA, MD	Y	24940 FQ	29470 MW	38800 TQ	USBLS	5/07
	Massachusetts	Y	20780 FQ	33920 MW	41450 TQ	USBLS	5/07
	Michigan	Y	31640 FQ	39830 MW	52960 TQ	USBLS	5/07
	Ann Arbor MSA, MI	Y	29430 FQ	35630 MW	47260 TQ	USBLS	5/07
	Detroit-Warren-Livonia MSA, MI	Y	34270 FQ	42650 MW	57630 TQ	USBLS	5/07
	Warren-Troy-Farmington Hills PMSA, MI	Y	37400 FQ	52050 MW	75870 TQ	USBLS	5/07
	Minnesota	Y	27822 FQ	32538 MW	44667 TQ	MNBLS	10/08-12/08
	Minneapolis-Saint Paul MSA, MN-WI	Y	28764 FQ	34033 MW	45733 TQ	MNBLS	10/08-12/08
	Mississippi	Y	31760 FQ	37640 MW	55850 TQ	USBLS	5/07
	Jackson MSA, MS	Y	27700 FQ	37510 MW	47150 TQ	USBLS	5/07
	Missouri	Y	24900 FQ	34700 MW	40970 TQ	USBLS	5/07
	Kansas City MSA, MO-KS	Y	29670 FQ	35770 MW	39900 TQ	USBLS	5/07
	St. Louis MSA, MO-IL	Y	28610 FQ	39720 MW	66010 TQ	USBLS	5/07
	Montana	Y	21810 FQ	30080 MW	64930 TQ	USBLS	5/07
	Nebraska	Y	26950 FQ	35530 MW	71600 TQ	USBLS	5/07
	Nevada	H	15.14 FQ	22.30 MW	28.33 TQ	NVBLS	5/08
	Las Vegas-Paradise MSA, NV	H	14.60 FQ	21.54 MW	27.06 TQ	NVBLS	5/08
	New Hampshire	H	10.56 AE	12.53 MW	14.48 AEX	NHBLS	6/08
	Manchester MSA, NH	Y	24060 FQ	26340 MW	28490 TQ	USBLS	5/07
	New Jersey	Y	41160 FQ	60470 MW	75150 TQ	USBLS	5/07
	Edison PMSA, NJ	Y	33960 FQ	49880 MW	74340 TQ	USBLS	5/07
	Newark-Union PMSA, NJ-PA	Y	46060 FQ	60700 MW	74170 TQ	USBLS	5/07
	New Mexico	Y	22310 FQ	28790 MW	66800 TQ	USBLS	5/07
	Albuquerque MSA, NM	Y	21780 FQ	27760 MW	67100 TQ	USBLS	5/07
	New York	Y	26740 FQ	43050 MW	59060 TQ	USBLS	5/07
	Buffalo-Niagara Falls MSA, NY	Y	32470 FQ	35610 MW	38870 TQ	USBLS	5/07
	Nassau-Suffolk PMSA, NY	Y	28920 FQ	45120 MW	51480 TQ	USBLS	5/07

AE Average entry wage	**AW** Average wage paid	**FQ** First quartile wage	**LO** Lowest wage paid	**MTC** Median total compensation	**TCC** Total cash compensation
AER Average entry range	**AWR** Average wage range	**H** Hourly	**LR** Low end range	**MW** Median wage paid	**TQ** Third quartile wage
AEX Average experienced wage	**AXR** Average experienced range	**HI** Highest wage paid	**M** Monthly	**MWR** Median wage range	**W** Weekly
ATC Average total compensation	**D** Daily	**HR** High end range	**MCC** Median cash compensation	**S** See annotated source	**Y** Yearly

Occupation/Type/Industry	Location	Per	Low	Mid	High	Source	Date
Private Detective and Investigator	New York-Northern New Jersey-Long Island MSA, NY-NJ-PA	Y	35790 FQ	52180 MW	69400 TQ	USBLS	5/07
	North Carolina	Y	28440 FQ	42620 MW	54060 TQ	USBLS	5/07
	Charlotte-Gastonia-Concord MSA, NC-SC	Y	49590 FQ	53940 MW	58200 TQ	USBLS	5/07
	Raleigh-Cary MSA, NC	Y	27300 FQ	31280 MW	42650 TQ	USBLS	5/07
	North Dakota	Y	19440 FQ	24820 MW	43490 TQ	USBLS	5/07
	Ohio	Y	25790 FQ	33190 MW	53780 TQ	USBLS	5/07
	Cincinnati-Middletown MSA, OH-KY-IN	Y	26090 FQ	29560 MW	37030 TQ	USBLS	5/07
	Cleveland-Elyria-Mentor MSA, OH	Y	28700 FQ	42860 MW	58730 TQ	USBLS	5/07
	Columbus MSA, OH	Y	24400 FQ	29920 MW	61960 TQ	USBLS	5/07
	Dayton MSA, OH	Y	23880 FQ	30110 MW	39980 TQ	USBLS	5/07
	Oklahoma	Y	31210 FQ	42980 MW	51140 TQ	USBLS	5/07
	Oregon	H	10.62 FQ	15.42 MW	23.85 TQ	ORBLS	5/08
	Portland-Vancouver-Beaverton MSA, OR-WA	Y	24740 FQ	35990 MW	54010 TQ	USBLS	5/07
	Pennsylvania	Y	23780 FQ	29990 MW	43990 TQ	USBLS	5/07
	Allentown-Bethlehem-Easton MSA, PA-NJ	Y	21700 FQ	25640 MW	35980 TQ	USBLS	5/07
	Philadelphia-Camden-Wilmington MSA, PA-NJ-DE-MD	Y	22540 FQ	30190 MW	47690 TQ	USBLS	5/07
	Pittsburgh MSA, PA	Y	26150 FQ	30300 MW	39430 TQ	USBLS	5/07
	Rhode Island	Y	33640 FQ	37800 MW	45240 TQ	USBLS	5/07
	Providence-Fall River-Warwick MSA, RI-MA	Y	33300 FQ	37590 MW	44200 TQ	USBLS	5/07
	South Carolina	Y	30000 FQ	49330 MW	56060 TQ	USBLS	5/07
	Charleston-North Charleston MSA, SC	Y	25310 FQ	32400 MW	41180 TQ	USBLS	5/07
	Columbia MSA, SC	Y	25060 FQ	33400 MW	49610 TQ	USBLS	5/07
	South Dakota	Y	21610 FQ	23375 MW	25951 TQ	SDBLS	7/08-9/08
	Tennessee	Y	15530 FQ	26920 MW	46680 TQ	USBLS	5/07
	Memphis MSA, TN-MS-AR	Y	23440 FQ	37490 MW	59980 TQ	USBLS	5/07
	Nashville-Davidson-Murfreesboro MSA, TN	Y	23420 FQ	29290 MW	42590 TQ	USBLS	5/07
	Texas	Y	29650 FQ	38290 MW	57090 TQ	USBLS	5/07
	Austin-Round Rock MSA, TX	Y	32200 FQ	39260 MW	58120 TQ	USBLS	5/07
	Dallas-Fort Worth-Arlington MSA, TX	Y	30320 FQ	39850 MW	57220 TQ	USBLS	5/07
	El Paso MSA, TX	Y	25590 FQ	29780 MW	36690 TQ	USBLS	5/07
	Houston-Sugar Land-Baytown MSA, TX	Y	28620 FQ	36990 MW	57130 TQ	USBLS	5/07
	San Antonio MSA, TX	Y	28360 FQ	39430 MW	60440 TQ	USBLS	5/07
	Utah	Y	26610 FQ	32880 MW	41540 TQ	USBLS	5/07
	Salt Lake City MSA, UT	Y	30240 FQ	35710 MW	47610 TQ	USBLS	5/07
	Virginia	Y	36680 FQ	54190 MW	81120 TQ	USBLS	5/07
	Richmond MSA, VA	Y	24210 FQ	33870 MW	39740 TQ	USBLS	5/07
	Washington	H	15.30 FQ	17.97 MW	26.18 TQ	WABLS	3/08
	Seattle-Tacoma-Bellevue MSA, WA	Y	33570 FQ	38280 MW	52550 TQ	USBLS	5/07
	West Virginia	Y	28551 FQ	48439 MW	59473 TQ	WVBLS	7/08-9/08
	Wisconsin	Y	25100 FQ	31540 MW	46050 TQ	USBLS	5/07
	Milwaukee-Waukesha-West Allis MSA, WI	Y	22710 FQ	29270 MW	36630 TQ	USBLS	5/07
	Wyoming	Y	27408 FQ	35510 MW	44808 TQ	WYBLS	9/08
	Puerto Rico	Y	20290 FQ	25800 MW	31260 TQ	USBLS	5/07
	San Juan-Caguas-Guaynabo MSA, PR	Y	21980 FQ	26970 MW	32180 TQ	USBLS	5/07
Prize Analyst State Lottery	Tennessee	Y			21184 HI	THETN	2008
Probation Officer and Correctional Treatment Specialist	Alabama	Y	32950 FQ	39110 MW	49270 TQ	USBLS	5/07
	Birmingham-Hoover MSA, AL	Y	32960 FQ	40810 MW	50960 TQ	USBLS	5/07
	Alaska	Y	44530 FQ	50950 MW	59630 TQ	USBLS	5/07
	Anchorage MSA, AK	Y	44240 FQ	49970 MW	57800 TQ	USBLS	5/07
	Arizona	Y	34290 FQ	39480 MW	46980 TQ	USBLS	5/07

AE Average entry wage	**AW** Average wage paid	**FQ** First quartile wage	**LO** Lowest wage paid	**MTC** Median total compensation	**TCC** Total cash compensation
AER Average entry range	**AWR** Average wage range	**H** Hourly	**LR** Low end range	**MW** Median wage paid	**TQ** Third quartile wage
AEX Average experienced wage	**AXR** Average experienced range	**HI** Highest wage paid	**M** Monthly	**MWR** Median wage range	**W** Weekly
ATC Average total compensation	**D** Daily	**HR** High end range	**MCC** Median cash compensation	**S** See annotated source	**Y** Yearly

Occupation/Type/Industry	Location	Per	Low	Mid	High	Source	Date
Probation Officer and Correctional Treatment Specialist							
	Phoenix-Mesa-Scottsdale MSA, AZ	Y	37150 FQ	41010 MW	48780 TQ	USBLS	5/07
	Tucson MSA, AZ	Y	34580 FQ	40650 MW	47790 TQ	USBLS	5/07
	Arkansas	Y	27250 FQ	29830 MW	32890 TQ	USBLS	5/07
	Fayetteville-Springdale-Rogers MSA, AR-MO	Y	27810 FQ	30180 MW	32810 TQ	USBLS	5/07
	Jonesboro MSA, AR	Y	27660 FQ	29630 MW	31600 TQ	USBLS	5/07
	Little Rock-North Little Rock MSA, AR	Y	28470 FQ	31900 MW	38930 TQ	USBLS	5/07
	California	H	28.19 FQ	36.18 MW	43.15 TQ	CABLS	1/08-3/08
	Oakland-Fremont-Hayward MSA, CA	H	35.80 FQ	39.48 MW	43.71 TQ	CABLS	1/08-3/08
	Riverside-San Bernardino-Ontario MSA, CA	H	29.38 FQ	39.38 MW	46.45 TQ	CABLS	1/08-3/08
	San Diego-Carlsbad-San Marcos MSA, CA	H	23.17 FQ	28.20 MW	33.55 TQ	CABLS	1/08-3/08
	San Francisco-San Mateo-Redwood PMSA, CA	H	36.16 FQ	39.63 MW	43.35 TQ	CABLS	1/08-3/08
	Colorado	Y	44300 FQ	54470 MW	65220 TQ	USBLS	5/07
	Denver-Aurora MSA, CO	Y	44800 FQ	54280 MW	65650 TQ	USBLS	5/07
	Connecticut	H	23.40 AE	31.50 MW		CTBLS	1/08-3/08
	Hartford-West Hartford-East Hartford MSA, CT	Y	52890 FQ	65320 MW	78620 TQ	USBLS	5/07
	Norwich-New London MSA, CT-RI	Y	52080 FQ	60990 MW	76250 TQ	USBLS	5/07
	Delaware	Y	42530 FQ	46690 MW	50850 TQ	USBLS	5/07
	Washington-Arlington-Alexandria MSA, DC-VA-MD-WV	Y	34340 FQ	44990 MW	59330 TQ	USBLS	5/07
	Florida	Y	31960 FQ	37250 MW	44270 TQ	USBLS	5/07
	Jacksonville MSA, FL	Y	32220 FQ	37890 MW	45790 TQ	USBLS	5/07
	Orlando-Kissimmee MSA, FL	Y	32720 FQ	37530 MW	43920 TQ	USBLS	5/07
	Tallahassee MSA, FL	Y	32950 FQ	37630 MW	44450 TQ	USBLS	5/07
	Georgia	Y	30160 FQ	35250 MW	40150 TQ	USBLS	5/07
	Atlanta-Sandy Springs-Marietta MSA, GA	Y	31610 FQ	36170 MW	40690 TQ	USBLS	5/07
	Hawaii	Y	45470 FQ	52140 MW	60170 TQ	USBLS	5/07
	Idaho	Y	30860 FQ	36060 MW	41290 TQ	USBLS	5/07
	Boise City-Nampa MSA, ID	Y	32880 FQ	37180 MW	41780 TQ	USBLS	5/07
	Illinois	Y	43680 FQ	53350 MW	63090 TQ	USBLS	5/07
	Chicago-Naperville-Joliet MSA, IL-IN-WI	Y	42750 FQ	50540 MW	61330 TQ	USBLS	5/07
	Indiana	Y	30570 FQ	36810 MW	43750 TQ	USBLS	5/07
	Gary PMSA, IN	Y	31380 FQ	37110 MW	43590 TQ	USBLS	5/07
	Indianapolis-Carmel MSA, IN	Y	29880 FQ	35090 MW	40520 TQ	USBLS	5/07
	Iowa	Y	45650 FQ	54320 MW	61790 TQ	USBLS	5/07
	Kansas	Y	32770 FQ	38210 MW	45890 TQ	USBLS	5/07
	Wichita MSA, KS	Y	32660 FQ	38070 MW	45200 TQ	USBLS	5/07
	Louisville-Jefferson County MSA, KY-IN	Y	30360 FQ	34900 MW	39690 TQ	USBLS	5/07
	Louisiana	H	14.02 FQ	17.91 MW	23.12 TQ	LABLS	1/08-3/08
	New Orleans-Metairie-Kenner MSA, LA	Y	31930 FQ	39930 MW	49500 TQ	USBLS	5/07
	Maryland	Y		53700 MW		MDBLS	3/08
	Baltimore-Towson MSA, MD	Y	44800 FQ	52830 MW	59310 TQ	USBLS	5/07
	Massachusetts	Y	54730 FQ	67610 MW	75720 TQ	USBLS	5/07
	Barnstable Town MSA, MA	Y	63360 FQ	71230 MW	77370 TQ	USBLS	5/07
	Worcester MSA, MA-CT	Y	62420 FQ	71040 MW	77410 TQ	USBLS	5/07
	Michigan	Y	46690 FQ	55110 MW	61310 TQ	USBLS	5/07
	Detroit-Warren-Livonia MSA, MI	Y	47620 FQ	55610 MW	61700 TQ	USBLS	5/07
	Grand Rapids-Wyoming MSA, MI	Y	52020 FQ	57340 MW	62560 TQ	USBLS	5/07
	Warren-Troy-Farmington Hills PMSA, MI	Y	50830 FQ	56750 MW	62030 TQ	USBLS	5/07
	Minnesota	Y	51296 FQ	63066 MW	74731 TQ	MNBLS	10/08-12/08
	Duluth-Superior MSA, MN-WI	Y	44956 FQ	53650 MW	62616 TQ	MNBLS	10/08-12/08
	Minneapolis-Saint Paul MSA, MN-WI	Y	55805 FQ	66895 MW	77891 TQ	MNBLS	10/08-12/08

Occupation/Type/Industry	Location	Per	Low	Mid	High	Source	Date
Probation Officer and Correctional Treatment Specialist							
	Mississippi	Y	21830 FQ	26970 MW	32880 TQ	USBLS	5/07
	Missouri	Y	29830 FQ	34050 MW	37940 TQ	USBLS	5/07
	Kansas City MSA, MO-KS	Y	30850 FQ	35110 MW	39710 TQ	USBLS	5/07
	St. Joseph MSA, MO-KS	Y	30780 FQ	34630 MW	37990 TQ	USBLS	5/07
	St. Louis MSA, MO-IL	Y	30910 FQ	35840 MW	40470 TQ	USBLS	5/07
	Montana	Y	32760 FQ	37840 MW	44370 TQ	USBLS	5/07
	Nebraska	Y	28450 FQ	35370 MW	41090 TQ	USBLS	5/07
	Omaha-Council Bluffs MSA, NE-IA	Y	34090 FQ	41530 MW	49520 TQ	USBLS	5/07
	Nevada	H	23.75 FQ	28.76 MW	34.09 TQ	NVBLS	5/08
	New Hampshire	H	21.23 AE	23.50 MW	24.98 AEX	NHBLS	6/08
	New Jersey	Y	47420 FQ	61250 MW	74550 TQ	USBLS	5/07
	Camden PMSA, NJ	Y	49340 FQ	61020 MW	73470 TQ	USBLS	5/07
	Edison PMSA, NJ	Y	45910 FQ	58890 MW	73900 TQ	USBLS	5/07
	Newark-Union PMSA, NJ-PA	Y	45920 FQ	60400 MW	73030 TQ	USBLS	5/07
	New Mexico	Y	28120 FQ	32120 MW	38250 TQ	USBLS	5/07
	Albuquerque MSA, NM	Y	29670 FQ	35010 MW	43080 TQ	USBLS	5/07
	New York	Y	49100 FQ	56740 MW	63750 TQ	USBLS	5/07
	Albany-Schenectady-Troy MSA, NY	Y	43090 FQ	50650 MW	59480 TQ	USBLS	5/07
	New York-Northern New Jersey-Long Island MSA, NY-NJ-PA	Y	48720 FQ	58210 MW	69310 TQ	USBLS	5/07
	North Carolina	Y	33310 FQ	36260 MW	39220 TQ	USBLS	5/07
	Charlotte-Gastonia-Concord MSA, NC-SC	Y	33140 FQ	36270 MW	39420 TQ	USBLS	5/07
	Raleigh-Cary MSA, NC	Y	32580 FQ	35740 MW	38880 TQ	USBLS	5/07
	Ohio	Y	34760 FQ	42490 MW	51060 TQ	USBLS	5/07
	Cincinnati-Middletown MSA, OH-KY-IN	Y	30930 FQ	37790 MW	46750 TQ	USBLS	5/07
	Cleveland-Elyria-Mentor MSA, OH	Y	39770 FQ	46460 MW	54130 TQ	USBLS	5/07
	Columbus MSA, OH	Y	33360 FQ	42600 MW	52270 TQ	USBLS	5/07
	Oklahoma	Y	24120 FQ	29540 MW	36030 TQ	USBLS	5/07
	Tulsa MSA, OK	Y	20370 FQ	26860 MW	35800 TQ	USBLS	5/07
	Oregon	H	18.94 FQ	22.89 MW	28.84 TQ	ORBLS	5/08
	Portland-Vancouver-Beaverton MSA, OR-WA	Y	46170 FQ	52730 MW	58790 TQ	USBLS	5/07
	Pennsylvania	Y	37030 FQ	44740 MW	51780 TQ	USBLS	5/07
	Allentown-Bethlehem-Easton MSA, PA-NJ	Y	36560 FQ	45590 MW	54830 TQ	USBLS	5/07
	Philadelphia-Camden-Wilmington MSA, PA-NJ-DE-MD	Y	42480 FQ	48790 MW	58620 TQ	USBLS	5/07
	Pittsburgh MSA, PA	Y	37860 FQ	46470 MW	53550 TQ	USBLS	5/07
	South Carolina	Y	29380 FQ	34360 MW	39360 TQ	USBLS	5/07
	Columbia MSA, SC	Y	27030 FQ	31870 MW	37850 TQ	USBLS	5/07
	South Dakota	Y	31082 FQ	37368 MW	44364 TQ	SDBLS	7/08-9/08
	Tennessee	Y	27540 FQ	32240 MW	38260 TQ	USBLS	5/07
	Kingsport-Bristol-Bristol MSA, TN-VA	Y	27110 FQ	32960 MW	40790 TQ	USBLS	5/07
	Knoxville MSA, TN	Y	25630 FQ	29560 MW	35870 TQ	USBLS	5/07
	Memphis MSA, TN-MS-AR	Y	27820 FQ	31570 MW	36440 TQ	USBLS	5/07
	Nashville-Davidson-Murfreesboro MSA, TN	Y	28650 FQ	34180 MW	39990 TQ	USBLS	5/07
	Texas	Y	27790 FQ	31370 MW	37570 TQ	USBLS	5/07
	Dallas-Fort Worth-Arlington MSA, TX	Y	27690 FQ	31230 MW	36790 TQ	USBLS	5/07
	San Antonio MSA, TX	Y	27220 FQ	30550 MW	36320 TQ	USBLS	5/07
	Vermont	Y	38720 FQ	46020 MW	51990 TQ	USBLS	5/07
	Burlington-South Burlington MSA, VT	Y	39250 FQ	45810 MW	51250 TQ	USBLS	5/07
	Virginia	Y	33820 FQ	40600 MW	50490 TQ	USBLS	5/07
	Richmond MSA, VA	Y	33670 FQ	39990 MW	48700 TQ	USBLS	5/07
	Virginia Beach-Norfolk-Newport News MSA, VA-NC	Y	33990 FQ	41080 MW	50860 TQ	USBLS	5/07
	Washington	H	20.79 FQ	23.43 MW	27.06 TQ	WABLS	3/08
	Seattle-Tacoma-Bellevue MSA, WA	Y	41340 FQ	48370 MW	57860 TQ	USBLS	5/07

AE	Average entry wage	AW	Average wage paid	FQ	First quartile wage
AER	Average entry range	AWR	Average wage range	H	Hourly
AEX	Average experienced wage	AXR	Average experienced range	HI	Highest wage paid
ATC	Average total compensation	D	Daily	HR	High end range

LO	Lowest wage paid	MTC	Median total compensation
LR	Low end range	MW	Median wage paid
M	Monthly	MWR	Median wage range
MCC	Median cash compensation	S	See annotated source

TCC	Total cash compensation
TQ	Third quartile wage
W	Weekly
Y	Yearly

Occupation/Type/Industry	Location	Per	Low	Mid	High	Source	Date
Probation Officer and Correctional Treatment Specialist	West Virginia	Y	22181 FQ	25508 MW	29788 TQ	WVBLS	7/08-9/08
	Charleston MSA, WV	Y	23260 FQ	26540 MW	29890 TQ	USBLS	5/07
	Huntington-Ashland MSA, WV-KY-OH	Y	26800 FQ	32260 MW	38110 TQ	USBLS	5/07
	Milwaukee-Waukesha-West Allis MSA, WI	Y	41820 FQ	45780 MW	49740 TQ	USBLS	5/07
	Wyoming	Y	36413 FQ	40095 MW	46590 TQ	WYBLS	9/08
Probation/Parole Supervisor	Alabama	Y	37961 LO		60415 HI	AFT02	3/1/08
Process Engineer	United States	Y		68125 AW		AUTOM	2008
Procurement Clerk	Alabama	Y	23640 FQ	31300 MW	38890 TQ	USBLS	5/07
	Birmingham-Hoover MSA, AL	Y	23980 FQ	29180 MW	38450 TQ	USBLS	5/07
	Mobile MSA, AL	Y	23200 FQ	29440 MW	37140 TQ	USBLS	5/07
	Alaska	Y	34120 FQ	40380 MW	47320 TQ	USBLS	5/07
	Anchorage MSA, AK	Y	35450 FQ	40520 MW	47450 TQ	USBLS	5/07
	Arizona	Y	29320 FQ	35240 MW	42890 TQ	USBLS	5/07
	Phoenix-Mesa-Scottsdale MSA, AZ	Y	30260 FQ	36750 MW	44370 TQ	USBLS	5/07
	Tucson MSA, AZ	Y	29110 FQ	35940 MW	44500 TQ	USBLS	5/07
	Arkansas	Y	23830 FQ	30550 MW	37950 TQ	USBLS	5/07
	Fort Smith MSA, AR-OK	Y	22960 FQ	29640 MW	35750 TQ	USBLS	5/07
	Little Rock-North Little Rock MSA, AR	Y	27670 FQ	35010 MW	40260 TQ	USBLS	5/07
	Pine Bluff MSA, AR	Y	30540 FQ	38300 MW	45030 TQ	USBLS	5/07
	California	H	14.48 FQ	18.27 MW	22.35 TQ	CABLS	1/08-3/08
	Los Angeles-Long Beach-Glendale PMSA, CA	H	13.39 FQ	16.49 MW	21.16 TQ	CABLS	1/08-3/08
	Oakland-Fremont-Hayward MSA, CA	H	18.34 FQ	22.06 MW	25.84 TQ	CABLS	1/08-3/08
	Oxnard-Thousand Oaks-Ventura MSA, CA	H	14.63 FQ	18.14 MW	21.80 TQ	CABLS	1/08-3/08
	Riverside-San Bernardino-Ontario MSA, CA	H	13.92 FQ	17.06 MW	20.77 TQ	CABLS	1/08-3/08
	Sacramento-Arden Arcade-Roseville MSA, CA	H	14.61 FQ	17.94 MW	21.10 TQ	CABLS	1/08-3/08
	San Diego-Carlsbad-San Marcos MSA, CA	H	14.78 FQ	18.82 MW	22.39 TQ	CABLS	1/08-3/08
	San Francisco-San Mateo-Redwood PMSA, CA	H	18.20 FQ	23.05 MW	27.90 TQ	CABLS	1/08-3/08
	San Jose-Sunnyvale-Santa Clara MSA, CA	H	17.13 FQ	20.49 MW	24.89 TQ	CABLS	1/08-3/08
	Santa Ana-Anaheim-Irvine PMSA, CA	Y	31100 FQ	38040 MW	45550 TQ	USBLS	5/07
	Stockton MSA, CA	H	18.59 FQ	21.93 MW	24.59 TQ	CABLS	1/08-3/08
	Colorado	Y	30140 FQ	36430 MW	44650 TQ	USBLS	5/07
	Denver-Aurora MSA, CO	Y	31720 FQ	38580 MW	46350 TQ	USBLS	5/07
	Connecticut	H	14.19 AE	18.49 MW		CTBLS	1/08-3/08
	Bridgeport-Stamford-Norwalk MSA, CT	Y	33430 FQ	39240 MW	46040 TQ	USBLS	5/07
	Hartford-West Hartford-East Hartford MSA, CT	Y	30950 FQ	36340 MW	43180 TQ	USBLS	5/07
	Delaware	Y	29640 FQ	36040 MW	43160 TQ	USBLS	5/07
	Wilmington PMSA, DE-MD-NJ	Y	31770 FQ	37530 MW	45120 TQ	USBLS	5/07
	District of Columbia	Y	37750 FQ	43370 MW	47880 TQ	USBLS	5/07
	Washington-Arlington-Alexandria MSA, DC-VA-MD-WV	Y	34570 FQ	41800 MW	47730 TQ	USBLS	5/07
	Florida	Y	25660 FQ	30620 MW	37330 TQ	USBLS	5/07
	Fort Lauderdale-Pompano Beach-Deerfield Beach PMSA, FL	Y	25260 FQ	28860 MW	34040 TQ	USBLS	5/07
	Jacksonville MSA, FL	Y	25820 FQ	32630 MW	38350 TQ	USBLS	5/07
	Miami-Fort Lauderdale-Miami Beach MSA, FL	Y	25940 FQ	30380 MW	37480 TQ	USBLS	5/07
	Orlando-Kissimmee MSA, FL	Y	24690 FQ	30510 MW	36460 TQ	USBLS	5/07
	Tampa-St. Petersburg-Clearwater MSA, FL	Y	25910 FQ	31640 MW	38620 TQ	USBLS	5/07

AE	Average entry wage	AW	Average wage paid	FQ	First quartile wage	LO	Lowest wage paid
AER	Average entry range	AWR	Average wage range	H	Hourly	LR	Low end range
AEX	Average experienced wage	AXR	Average experienced range	HI	Highest wage paid	M	Monthly
ATC	Average total compensation	D	Daily	HR	High end range	MCC	Median cash compensation

MTC	Median total compensation	TCC	Total cash compensation
MW	Median wage paid	TQ	Third quartile wage
MWR	Median wage range	W	Weekly
S	See annotated source	Y	Yearly

Occupation/Type/Industry	Location	Per	Low	Mid	High	Source	Date
Procurement Clerk	West Palm Beach-Boca Raton-Boynton Beach PMSA, FL	Y	25670 FQ	29890 MW	36900 TQ	USBLS	5/07
	Georgia	Y	27160 FQ	33030 MW	39760 TQ	USBLS	5/07
	Athens-Clarke County MSA, GA	Y	26080 FQ	29320 MW	35230 TQ	USBLS	5/07
	Atlanta-Sandy Springs-Marietta MSA, GA	Y	27240 FQ	31790 MW	39150 TQ	USBLS	5/07
	Macon MSA, GA	Y	29920 FQ	35290 MW	41710 TQ	USBLS	5/07
	Hawaii	Y	30770 FQ	37560 MW	45420 TQ	USBLS	5/07
	Honolulu MSA, HI	Y	31060 FQ	38120 MW	45980 TQ	USBLS	5/07
	Idaho	Y	29190 FQ	33870 MW	38250 TQ	USBLS	5/07
	Boise City-Nampa MSA, ID	Y	29370 FQ	33820 MW	38070 TQ	USBLS	5/07
	Illinois	Y	29050 FQ	35840 MW	42590 TQ	USBLS	5/07
	Chicago-Naperville-Joliet MSA, IL-IN-WI	Y	29440 FQ	36350 MW	43270 TQ	USBLS	5/07
	Indiana	Y	25480 FQ	30330 MW	36230 TQ	USBLS	5/07
	Evansville MSA, IN-KY	Y	22630 FQ	25990 MW	30260 TQ	USBLS	5/07
	Fort Wayne MSA, IN	Y	27430 FQ	33030 MW	38990 TQ	USBLS	5/07
	Gary PMSA, IN	Y	24380 FQ	30780 MW	37000 TQ	USBLS	5/07
	Indianapolis-Carmel MSA, IN	Y	27590 FQ	32530 MW	37880 TQ	USBLS	5/07
	Iowa	Y	22810 FQ	30850 MW	37190 TQ	USBLS	5/07
	Davenport-Moline-Rock Island MSA, IA-IL	Y	28000 FQ	35350 MW	41950 TQ	USBLS	5/07
	Des Moines-West Des Moines MSA, IA	Y	29020 FQ	34810 MW	39420 TQ	USBLS	5/07
	Kansas	Y	24710 FQ	31390 MW	39070 TQ	USBLS	5/07
	Wichita MSA, KS	Y	26840 FQ	32970 MW	41030 TQ	USBLS	5/07
	Kentucky	Y	27120 FQ	34252 MW	41175 TQ	KYBLS	2008
	Louisville-Jefferson County MSA, KY-IN	Y	24800 FQ	29600 MW	38040 TQ	USBLS	5/07
	Louisiana	H	10.90 FQ	14.39 MW	18.19 TQ	LABLS	1/08-3/08
	Baton Rouge MSA, LA	Y	27430 FQ	34130 MW	40580 TQ	USBLS	5/07
	New Orleans-Metairie-Kenner MSA, LA	Y	21830 FQ	28380 MW	36860 TQ	USBLS	5/07
	Shreveport-Bossier City MSA, LA	Y	26720 FQ	35130 MW	43420 TQ	USBLS	5/07
	Maine	Y	26940 FQ	33300 MW	41460 TQ	USBLS	5/07
	Portland-South Portland-Biddeford MSA, ME	Y	27250 FQ	32110 MW	38240 TQ	USBLS	5/07
	Maryland	Y		38950 MW		MDBLS	3/08
	Baltimore-Towson MSA, MD	Y	33460 FQ	38600 MW	44570 TQ	USBLS	5/07
	Bethesda-Gaithersburg-Frederick PMSA, MD	Y	33260 FQ	39690 MW	47000 TQ	USBLS	5/07
	Hagerstown-Martinsburg MSA, MD-WV	Y	24580 FQ	33160 MW	39760 TQ	USBLS	5/07
	Salisbury MSA, MD	Y	27590 FQ	33940 MW	43860 TQ	USBLS	5/07
	Massachusetts	Y	29000 FQ	35650 MW	44720 TQ	USBLS	5/07
	Boston-Cambridge-Quincy NECTA, MA	Y	29290 FQ	36930 MW	46450 TQ	USBLS	5/07
	Worcester MSA, MA-CT	Y	26600 FQ	33960 MW	40940 TQ	USBLS	5/07
	Michigan	Y	28660 FQ	34460 MW	41610 TQ	USBLS	5/07
	Detroit-Warren-Livonia MSA, MI	Y	29910 FQ	35320 MW	42500 TQ	USBLS	5/07
	Grand Rapids-Wyoming MSA, MI	Y	30810 FQ	35820 MW	40140 TQ	USBLS	5/07
	Warren-Troy-Farmington Hills PMSA, MI	Y	29220 FQ	34060 MW	41920 TQ	USBLS	5/07
	Minnesota	Y	27497 FQ	33357 MW	39914 TQ	MNBLS	10/08-12/08
	Duluth-Superior MSA, MN-WI	Y	31567 FQ	36355 MW	40205 TQ	MNBLS	10/08-12/08
	Minneapolis-Saint Paul MSA, MN-WI	Y	28684 FQ	34835 MW	41090 TQ	MNBLS	10/08-12/08
	Rochester MSA, MN	Y	29880 FQ	36163 MW	41530 TQ	MNBLS	10/08-12/08
	Mississippi	Y	24940 FQ	32990 MW	40050 TQ	USBLS	5/07
	Jackson MSA, MS	Y	24950 FQ	35410 MW	42760 TQ	USBLS	5/07
	Missouri	Y	22980 FQ	29440 MW	36920 TQ	USBLS	5/07
	Joplin MSA, MO	Y	21780 FQ	24140 MW	27650 TQ	USBLS	5/07
	Kansas City MSA, MO-KS	Y	26710 FQ	34280 MW	42100 TQ	USBLS	5/07
	St. Louis MSA, MO-IL	Y	26350 FQ	32720 MW	39330 TQ	USBLS	5/07
	Montana	Y	25530 FQ	32000 MW	37580 TQ	USBLS	5/07
	Nebraska	Y	23540 FQ	30120 MW	36590 TQ	USBLS	5/07
	Lincoln MSA, NE	Y	26390 FQ	30980 MW	39200 TQ	USBLS	5/07

AE Average entry wage / AER Average entry range / AEX Average experienced wage / ATC Average total compensation / AW Average wage paid / AWR Average wage range / AXR Average experienced range / D Daily / FQ First quartile wage / H Hourly / HI Highest wage paid / HR High end range / LO Lowest wage paid / LR Low end range / M Monthly / MCC Median cash compensation / MTC Median total compensation / MW Median wage paid / MWR Median wage range / S See annotated source / TCC Total cash compensation / TQ Third quartile wage / W Weekly / Y Yearly

Occupation/Type/Industry	Location	Per	Low	Mid	High	Source	Date
Procurement Clerk	Omaha-Council Bluffs MSA, NE-IA	Y	26710 FQ	32280 MW	37510 TQ	USBLS	5/07
	Nevada	H	13.90 FQ	16.86 MW	19.16 TQ	NVBLS	5/08
	Carson City MSA, NV	H	15.48 FQ	18.59 MW	21.95 TQ	NVBLS	5/08
	Las Vegas-Paradise MSA, NV	H	14.14 FQ	16.96 MW	19.07 TQ	NVBLS	5/08
	Reno-Sparks MSA, NV	H	11.91 FQ	15.50 MW	19.40 TQ	NVBLS	5/08
	New Hampshire	H	12.01 AE	14.96 MW	17.92 AEX	NHBLS	6/08
	Manchester MSA, NH	Y	26620 FQ	30490 MW	35960 TQ	USBLS	5/07
	Nashua NECTA, NH-MA	Y	25140 FQ	32020 MW	42820 TQ	USBLS	5/07
	New Jersey	Y	31720 FQ	37900 MW	44850 TQ	USBLS	5/07
	Camden PMSA, NJ	Y	33080 FQ	38780 MW	44640 TQ	USBLS	5/07
	Edison PMSA, NJ	Y	30760 FQ	37790 MW	45200 TQ	USBLS	5/07
	Newark-Union PMSA, NJ-PA	Y	33470 FQ	39160 MW	46190 TQ	USBLS	5/07
	New Mexico	Y	28050 FQ	36030 MW	42830 TQ	USBLS	5/07
	Albuquerque MSA, NM	Y	33440 FQ	39280 MW	45550 TQ	USBLS	5/07
	New York	Y	28400 FQ	35220 MW	43340 TQ	USBLS	5/07
	Albany-Schenectady-Troy MSA, NY	Y	28210 FQ	31960 MW	39400 TQ	USBLS	5/07
	Buffalo-Niagara Falls MSA, NY	Y	25920 FQ	30120 MW	35870 TQ	USBLS	5/07
	Nassau-Suffolk PMSA, NY	Y	33780 FQ	40330 MW	46820 TQ	USBLS	5/07
	New York-Northern New Jersey-Long Island MSA, NY-NJ-PA	Y	31520 FQ	37760 MW	45570 TQ	USBLS	5/07
	North Carolina	Y	29150 FQ	35080 MW	40910 TQ	USBLS	5/07
	Charlotte-Gastonia-Concord MSA, NC-SC	Y	30410 FQ	37350 MW	44360 TQ	USBLS	5/07
	Raleigh-Cary MSA, NC	Y	31550 FQ	36190 MW	41780 TQ	USBLS	5/07
	Winston-Salem MSA, NC	Y	28560 FQ	33560 MW	38470 TQ	USBLS	5/07
	North Dakota	Y	24880 FQ	32170 MW	36750 TQ	USBLS	5/07
	Bismarck MSA, ND	Y	24710 FQ	32560 MW	37180 TQ	USBLS	5/07
	Fargo MSA, ND-MN	Y	26870 FQ	32180 MW	36030 TQ	USBLS	5/07
	Ohio	Y	25710 FQ	32130 MW	39460 TQ	USBLS	5/07
	Cincinnati-Middletown MSA, OH-KY-IN	Y	26930 FQ	33040 MW	38930 TQ	USBLS	5/07
	Cleveland-Elyria-Mentor MSA, OH	Y	27630 FQ	32340 MW	38970 TQ	USBLS	5/07
	Columbus MSA, OH	Y	30880 FQ	37250 MW	44120 TQ	USBLS	5/07
	Dayton MSA, OH	Y	26050 FQ	34370 MW	44300 TQ	USBLS	5/07
	Oklahoma	Y	27120 FQ	33840 MW	40960 TQ	USBLS	5/07
	Oklahoma City MSA, OK	Y	32620 FQ	37990 MW	44430 TQ	USBLS	5/07
	Tulsa MSA, OK	Y	25470 FQ	29160 MW	34880 TQ	USBLS	5/07
	Oregon	H	14.32 FQ	16.88 MW	19.67 TQ	ORBLS	5/08
	Portland-Vancouver-Beaverton MSA, OR-WA	Y	29620 FQ	35180 MW	41360 TQ	USBLS	5/07
	Pennsylvania	Y	27430 FQ	35180 MW	43480 TQ	USBLS	5/07
	Allentown-Bethlehem-Easton MSA, PA-NJ	Y	26310 FQ	32350 MW	43910 TQ	USBLS	5/07
	Philadelphia-Camden-Wilmington MSA, PA-NJ-DE-MD	Y	28710 FQ	36800 MW	44470 TQ	USBLS	5/07
	Pittsburgh MSA, PA	Y	26580 FQ	32430 MW	39140 TQ	USBLS	5/07
	Rhode Island	Y	28220 FQ	33590 MW	40650 TQ	USBLS	5/07
	Providence-Fall River-Warwick MSA, RI-MA	Y	28250 FQ	33680 MW	40160 TQ	USBLS	5/07
	South Carolina	Y	25520 FQ	31850 MW	37460 TQ	USBLS	5/07
	Charleston-North Charleston MSA, SC	Y	25510 FQ	31290 MW	38920 TQ	USBLS	5/07
	Columbia MSA, SC	Y	27750 FQ	34200 MW	38730 TQ	USBLS	5/07
	South Dakota	Y	23815 FQ	28365 MW	35222 TQ	SDBLS	7/08-9/08
	Sioux Falls MSA, SD	Y	24025 FQ	27919 MW	31874 TQ	SDBLS	7/08-9/08
	Tennessee	Y	25120 FQ	30810 MW	37820 TQ	USBLS	5/07
	Clarksville MSA, TN-KY	Y	32770 FQ	36210 MW	40160 TQ	USBLS	5/07
	Kingsport-Bristol-Bristol MSA, TN-VA	Y	21680 FQ	25280 MW	34110 TQ	USBLS	5/07
	Memphis MSA, TN-MS-AR	Y	27240 FQ	32270 MW	38620 TQ	USBLS	5/07
	Nashville-Davidson-Murfreesboro MSA, TN	Y	26820 FQ	32900 MW	40810 TQ	USBLS	5/07
	Texas	Y	25380 FQ	32160 MW	39750 TQ	USBLS	5/07
	Austin-Round Rock MSA, TX	Y	25660 FQ	32920 MW	40990 TQ	USBLS	5/07
	Beaumont-Port Arthur MSA, TX	Y	25280 FQ	29450 MW	39500 TQ	USBLS	5/07

AE	Average entry wage	AW	Average wage paid	FQ	First quartile wage	LO	Lowest wage paid	MTC Median total compensation TCC Total cash compensation
AER	Average entry range	AWR	Average wage range	H	Hourly	LR	Low end range	MW Median wage paid TQ Third quartile wage
AEX	Average experienced wage	AXR	Average experienced range	HI	Highest wage paid	M	Monthly	MWR Median wage range W Weekly
ATC	Average total compensation	D	Daily	HR	High end range	MCC	Median cash compensation S	See annotated source Y Yearly

Occupation/Type/Industry	Location	Per	Low	Mid	High	Source	Date
Procurement Clerk	Corpus Christi MSA, TX	Y	24820 FQ	33790 MW	41230 TQ	USBLS	5/07
	Dallas-Fort Worth-Arlington MSA, TX	Y	27880 FQ	34550 MW	44050 TQ	USBLS	5/07
	El Paso MSA, TX	Y	24310 FQ	30790 MW	36830 TQ	USBLS	5/07
	Houston-Sugar Land-Baytown MSA, TX	Y	24170 FQ	30810 MW	39320 TQ	USBLS	5/07
	Midland MSA, TX	Y	25770 FQ	28800 MW	32820 TQ	USBLS	5/07
	San Antonio MSA, TX	Y	26420 FQ	33820 MW	39660 TQ	USBLS	5/07
	Utah	Y	25160 FQ	32720 MW	38820 TQ	USBLS	5/07
	Ogden-Clearfield MSA, UT	Y	31360 FQ	35680 MW	39770 TQ	USBLS	5/07
	Salt Lake City MSA, UT	Y	25520 FQ	33220 MW	40260 TQ	USBLS	5/07
	Vermont	Y	29100 FQ	34380 MW	40370 TQ	USBLS	5/07
	Burlington-South Burlington MSA, VT	Y	31350 FQ	35140 MW	39110 TQ	USBLS	5/07
	Virginia	Y	30690 FQ	37420 MW	44920 TQ	USBLS	5/07
	Richmond MSA, VA	Y	31760 FQ	36690 MW	42930 TQ	USBLS	5/07
	Roanoke MSA, VA	Y	22920 FQ	27800 MW	34660 TQ	USBLS	5/07
	Virginia Beach-Norfolk-Newport News MSA, VA-NC	Y	28940 FQ	35550 MW	41940 TQ	USBLS	5/07
	Washington	H	14.95 FQ	17.90 MW	20.94 TQ	WABLS	3/08
	Olympia MSA, WA	Y	32160 FQ	35380 MW	38530 TQ	USBLS	5/07
	Seattle-Tacoma-Bellevue MSA, WA	Y	32020 FQ	37530 MW	43130 TQ	USBLS	5/07
	West Virginia	Y	21622 FQ	30869 MW	40407 TQ	WVBLS	7/08-9/08
	Charleston MSA, WV	Y	23040 FQ	30270 MW	36790 TQ	USBLS	5/07
	Wisconsin	Y	27670 FQ	32760 MW	38360 TQ	USBLS	5/07
	Milwaukee-Waukesha-West Allis MSA, WI	Y	28010 FQ	33360 MW	38570 TQ	USBLS	5/07
	Wyoming	Y	31576 FQ	37490 MW	43780 TQ	WYBLS	9/08
	Casper MSA, WY	Y	26472 FQ	32108 MW	41133 TQ	WYBLS	9/08
	Puerto Rico	Y	13720 FQ	17240 MW	25380 TQ	USBLS	5/07
	San Juan-Caguas-Guaynabo MSA, PR	Y	13410 FQ	15840 MW	22030 TQ	USBLS	5/07
	Guam	Y	18990 FQ	32070 MW	42720 TQ	USBLS	5/07
Producer and Director	Alabama	Y	32940 FQ	42350 MW	55510 TQ	USBLS	5/07
	Birmingham-Hoover MSA, AL	Y	33600 FQ	40530 MW	55440 TQ	USBLS	5/07
	Arizona	Y	36070 FQ	45140 MW	59920 TQ	USBLS	5/07
	Phoenix-Mesa-Scottsdale MSA, AZ	Y	32580 FQ	45050 MW	63110 TQ	USBLS	5/07
	Tucson MSA, AZ	Y	40830 FQ	45810 MW	55130 TQ	USBLS	5/07
	Arkansas	Y	23470 FQ	35040 MW	50350 TQ	USBLS	5/07
	Little Rock-North Little Rock MSA, AR	Y	27820 FQ	36500 MW	49110 TQ	USBLS	5/07
	California	H	24.87 FQ	42.13 MW	60.58 TQ	CABLS	1/08-3/08
	Bakersfield MSA, CA	H	19.20 FQ	27.57 MW	40.45 TQ	CABLS	1/08-3/08
	Fresno MSA, CA	H	15.08 FQ	18.75 MW	23.75 TQ	CABLS	1/08-3/08
	Los Angeles-Long Beach-Glendale PMSA, CA	H	27.86 FQ	46.32 MW	65.86 TQ	CABLS	1/08-3/08
	Modesto MSA, CA	H	14.94 FQ	17.75 MW	31.27 TQ	CABLS	1/08-3/08
	Oakland-Fremont-Hayward MSA, CA	H	23.17 FQ	31.78 MW	46.14 TQ	CABLS	1/08-3/08
	Riverside-San Bernardino-Ontario MSA, CA	H	17.32 FQ	27.02 MW	33.98 TQ	CABLS	1/08-3/08
	Sacramento-Arden Arcade-Roseville MSA, CA	H	19.31 FQ	28.27 MW	34.58 TQ	CABLS	1/08-3/08
	San Diego-Carlsbad-San Marcos MSA, CA	H	19.92 FQ	25.38 MW	34.30 TQ	CABLS	1/08-3/08
	San Francisco-San Mateo-Redwood PMSA, CA	H	25.42 FQ	37.94 MW	55.03 TQ	CABLS	1/08-3/08
	San Jose-Sunnyvale-Santa Clara MSA, CA	H	23.30 FQ	35.51 MW	51.26 TQ	CABLS	1/08-3/08
	Santa Ana-Anaheim-Irvine PMSA, CA	Y	54160 FQ	67480 MW	89060 TQ	USBLS	5/07
	Stockton MSA, CA	H	20.36 FQ	22.02 MW	23.81 TQ	CABLS	1/08-3/08
	Colorado	Y	35440 FQ	49280 MW	78070 TQ	USBLS	5/07
	Boulder MSA, CO	Y	42410 FQ	47920 MW	66330 TQ	USBLS	5/07
	Denver-Aurora MSA, CO	Y	39170 FQ	55280 MW	85820 TQ	USBLS	5/07
	Bridgeport-Stamford-Norwalk MSA, CT	Y	53410 FQ	97660 MW	113410 TQ	USBLS	5/07
	Hartford-West Hartford-East Hartford MSA, CT	Y	29310 FQ	58730 MW	85050 TQ	USBLS	5/07

AE Average entry wage	**AW** Average wage paid	**FQ** First quartile wage	**LO** Lowest wage paid	**MTC** Median total compensation	**TCC** Total cash compensation
AER Average entry range	**AWR** Average wage range	**H** Hourly	**LR** Low end range	**MW** Median wage paid	**TQ** Third quartile wage
AEX Average experienced wage	**AXR** Average experienced range	**HI** Highest wage paid	**M** Monthly	**MWR** Median wage range	**W** Weekly
ATC Average total compensation	**D** Daily	**HR** High end range	**MCC** Median cash compensation	**S** See annotated source	**Y** Yearly

Occupation/Type/Industry	Location	Per	Low	Mid	High	Source	Date
Producer and Director	District of Columbia	Y	55660 FQ	76250 MW	92450 TQ	USBLS	5/07
	Washington-Arlington-Alexandria MSA, DC-VA-MD-WV	Y	51540 FQ	71070 MW	89960 TQ	USBLS	5/07
	Florida	Y	33370 FQ	49620 MW	76550 TQ	USBLS	5/07
	Fort Lauderdale-Pompano Beach-Deerfield Beach PMSA, FL	Y	37980 FQ	62810 MW	80220 TQ	USBLS	5/07
	Jacksonville MSA, FL	Y	38440 FQ	52710 MW	91030 TQ	USBLS	5/07
	Miami-Fort Lauderdale-Miami Beach MSA, FL	Y	33030 FQ	54580 MW	82120 TQ	USBLS	5/07
	Orlando-Kissimmee MSA, FL	Y	37270 FQ	63190 MW	101320 TQ	USBLS	5/07
	Tampa-St. Petersburg-Clearwater MSA, FL	Y	30830 FQ	43140 MW	54770 TQ	USBLS	5/07
	West Palm Beach-Boca Raton-Boynton Beach PMSA, FL	Y	42740 FQ	71970 MW		USBLS	5/07
	Georgia	Y	49170 FQ	70970 MW	94610 TQ	USBLS	5/07
	Atlanta-Sandy Springs-Marietta MSA, GA	Y	50880 FQ	72550 MW	96940 TQ	USBLS	5/07
	Augusta-Richmond County MSA, GA-SC	Y	25950 FQ	51830 MW	72990 TQ	USBLS	5/07
	Hawaii	Y	24970 FQ	47470 MW	68000 TQ	USBLS	5/07
	Idaho	Y	28290 FQ	35420 MW	45680 TQ	USBLS	5/07
	Boise City-Nampa MSA, ID	Y	29380 FQ	36680 MW	47750 TQ	USBLS	5/07
	Illinois	Y	35890 FQ	51360 MW	88550 TQ	USBLS	5/07
	Chicago-Naperville-Joliet MSA, IL-IN-WI	Y	40000 FQ	58750 MW	93680 TQ	USBLS	5/07
	Indiana	Y	31120 FQ	42780 MW	56400 TQ	USBLS	5/07
	Indianapolis-Carmel MSA, IN	Y	35550 FQ	46980 MW	62970 TQ	USBLS	5/07
	Iowa	Y	29350 FQ	36730 MW	48580 TQ	USBLS	5/07
	Des Moines-West Des Moines MSA, IA	Y	29510 FQ	36990 MW	51450 TQ	USBLS	5/07
	Kansas	Y	28600 FQ	40650 MW	57630 TQ	USBLS	5/07
	Wichita MSA, KS	Y	31220 FQ	34650 MW	38550 TQ	USBLS	5/07
	Kentucky	Y	29286 FQ	38536 MW	47821 TQ	KYBLS	2008
	Louisville-Jefferson County MSA, KY-IN	Y	24770 FQ	37890 MW	46890 TQ	USBLS	5/07
	Louisiana	H	10.60 FQ	17.40 MW	23.56 TQ	LABLS	1/08-3/08
	Baton Rouge MSA, LA	Y	38120 FQ	43330 MW	51440 TQ	USBLS	5/07
	New Orleans-Metairie-Kenner MSA, LA	Y	19350 FQ	29530 MW	51340 TQ	USBLS	5/07
	Maine	Y	32920 FQ	38260 MW	56080 TQ	USBLS	5/07
	Portland-South Portland-Biddeford MSA, ME	Y	37510 FQ	53290 MW	63900 TQ	USBLS	5/07
	Maryland	Y		68550 MW		MDBLS	3/08
	Baltimore-Towson MSA, MD	Y	34520 FQ	47180 MW	66910 TQ	USBLS	5/07
	Bethesda-Gaithersburg-Frederick PMSA, MD	Y	61420 FQ	76940 MW	91850 TQ	USBLS	5/07
	Massachusetts	Y	36570 FQ	51170 MW	81580 TQ	USBLS	5/07
	Boston-Cambridge-Quincy NECTA, MA	Y	35940 FQ	50150 MW	80190 TQ	USBLS	5/07
	Michigan	Y	40630 FQ	54010 MW	75000 TQ	USBLS	5/07
	Detroit-Warren-Livonia MSA, MI	Y	45280 FQ	61660 MW	79590 TQ	USBLS	5/07
	Grand Rapids-Wyoming MSA, MI	Y	33960 FQ	45240 MW	58990 TQ	USBLS	5/07
	Lansing-East Lansing MSA, MI	Y	28510 FQ	42390 MW	51510 TQ	USBLS	5/07
	Warren-Troy-Farmington Hills PMSA, MI	Y	44980 FQ	64610 MW	82850 TQ	USBLS	5/07
	Minnesota	Y	44569 FQ	59530 MW	73570 TQ	MNBLS	10/08-12/08
	Duluth-Superior MSA, MN-WI	Y	26783 FQ	42068 MW	48743 TQ	MNBLS	10/08-12/08
	Minneapolis-Saint Paul MSA, MN-WI	Y	48231 FQ	61204 MW	74899 TQ	MNBLS	10/08-12/08
	Rochester MSA, MN	Y	53310 FQ	70574 MW	82525 TQ	MNBLS	10/08-12/08
	Mississippi	Y	27330 FQ	34410 MW	41950 TQ	USBLS	5/07
	Jackson MSA, MS	Y	22030 FQ	29460 MW	35780 TQ	USBLS	5/07
	Missouri	Y	30740 FQ	47430 MW	66320 TQ	USBLS	5/07
	Kansas City MSA, MO-KS	Y	35130 FQ	49880 MW	62610 TQ	USBLS	5/07
	St. Louis MSA, MO-IL	Y	35240 FQ	59920 MW	76210 TQ	USBLS	5/07
	Montana	Y	27590 FQ	32470 MW	41750 TQ	USBLS	5/07
	Billings MSA, MT	Y	29120 FQ	36970 MW	46100 TQ	USBLS	5/07
	Nebraska	Y	28840 FQ	37420 MW	49550 TQ	USBLS	5/07

AE	Average entry wage	AW	Average wage paid	FQ	First quartile wage
AER	Average entry range	AWR	Average wage range	H	Hourly
AEX	Average experienced wage	AXR	Average experienced range	HI	Highest wage paid
ATC	Average total compensation	D	Daily	HR	High end range

LO	Lowest wage paid	MTC	Median total compensation	TCC	Total cash compensation
LR	Low end range	MW	Median wage paid	TQ	Third quartile wage
		MWR	Median wage range	W	Weekly
M	Monthly	S	See annotated source	Y	Yearly
MCC	Median cash compensation				

Occupation/Type/Industry	Location	Per	Low	Mid	High	Source	Date
Producer and Director	Lincoln MSA, NE	Y	27800 FQ	37860 MW	50390 TQ	USBLS	5/07
	Omaha-Council Bluffs MSA, NE-IA	Y	30090 FQ	38980 MW	50500 TQ	USBLS	5/07
	Nevada	Y	42009 FQ	56834 MW	67250 TQ	NVBLS	5/08
	Las Vegas-Paradise MSA, NV	Y	43876 FQ	56912 MW	65603 TQ	NVBLS	5/08
	New Hampshire	H	16.39 AE	25.94 MW	34.47 AEX	NHBLS	6/08
	New Jersey	Y	41620 FQ	65910 MW	96300 TQ	USBLS	5/07
	Camden PMSA, NJ	Y	15740 FQ	16320 MW	20010 TQ	USBLS	5/07
	Edison PMSA, NJ	Y	23430 FQ	47140 MW	68420 TQ	USBLS	5/07
	Newark-Union PMSA, NJ-PA	Y	43470 FQ	71110 MW	98590 TQ	USBLS	5/07
	New Mexico	Y	32320 FQ	46100 MW	78050 TQ	USBLS	5/07
	Albuquerque MSA, NM	Y	31690 FQ	47750 MW	82450 TQ	USBLS	5/07
	New York	Y	56470 FQ	92890 MW		USBLS	5/07
	Albany-Schenectady-Troy MSA, NY	Y	44410 FQ	65020 MW	85940 TQ	USBLS	5/07
	Buffalo-Niagara Falls MSA, NY	Y	34500 FQ	45510 MW	71680 TQ	USBLS	5/07
	Nassau-Suffolk PMSA, NY	Y	62830 FQ	100800 MW		USBLS	5/07
	New York-Northern New Jersey-Long Island MSA, NY-NJ-PA	Y	59110 FQ	94960 MW		USBLS	5/07
	North Carolina	Y	31170 FQ	44100 MW	61220 TQ	USBLS	5/07
	Charlotte-Gastonia-Concord MSA, NC-SC	Y	41900 FQ	58940 MW	76570 TQ	USBLS	5/07
	Raleigh-Cary MSA, NC	Y	42230 FQ	51800 MW	84210 TQ	USBLS	5/07
	North Dakota	Y	29630 FQ	44800 MW	50240 TQ	USBLS	5/07
	Fargo MSA, ND-MN	Y	31130 FQ	45430 MW	50280 TQ	USBLS	5/07
	Ohio	Y	39280 FQ	54580 MW	73150 TQ	USBLS	5/07
	Canton-Massillon MSA, OH	Y	24110 FQ	36730 MW	55970 TQ	USBLS	5/07
	Cincinnati-Middletown MSA, OH-KY-IN	Y	43910 FQ	66640 MW	78720 TQ	USBLS	5/07
	Cleveland-Elyria-Mentor MSA, OH	Y	41370 FQ	56420 MW	74000 TQ	USBLS	5/07
	Columbus MSA, OH	Y	41370 FQ	55520 MW	69470 TQ	USBLS	5/07
	Dayton MSA, OH	Y	45060 FQ	59860 MW	74720 TQ	USBLS	5/07
	Oklahoma	Y	29280 FQ	37250 MW	47730 TQ	USBLS	5/07
	Oklahoma City MSA, OK	Y	29030 FQ	37460 MW	53860 TQ	USBLS	5/07
	Tulsa MSA, OK	Y	32360 FQ	37610 MW	46930 TQ	USBLS	5/07
	Portland-Vancouver-Beaverton MSA, OR-WA	Y	38560 FQ	54590 MW	98120 TQ	USBLS	5/07
	Pennsylvania	Y	31110 FQ	45100 MW	61590 TQ	USBLS	5/07
	Allentown-Bethlehem-Easton MSA, PA-NJ	Y	15990 FQ	37730 MW	60030 TQ	USBLS	5/07
	Lancaster MSA, PA	Y	27320 FQ	33340 MW	47560 TQ	USBLS	5/07
	Philadelphia-Camden-Wilmington MSA, PA-NJ-DE-MD	Y	28040 FQ	39340 MW	53190 TQ	USBLS	5/07
	Pittsburgh MSA, PA	Y	38190 FQ	54910 MW	65210 TQ	USBLS	5/07
	Rhode Island	Y	52420 FQ	66690 MW	81550 TQ	USBLS	5/07
	Providence-Fall River-Warwick MSA, RI-MA	Y	52360 FQ	66420 MW	81440 TQ	USBLS	5/07
	South Carolina	Y	22220 FQ	29820 MW	42790 TQ	USBLS	5/07
	Charleston-North Charleston MSA, SC	Y	23470 FQ	28600 MW	40840 TQ	USBLS	5/07
	Columbia MSA, SC	Y	13330 FQ	16800 MW	31850 TQ	USBLS	5/07
	South Dakota	Y	37459 FQ	50877 MW	59683 TQ	SDBLS	7/08-9/08
	Sioux Falls MSA, SD	Y	42898 FQ	53175 MW	59356 TQ	SDBLS	7/08-9/08
	Tennessee	Y	32870 FQ	52380 MW	86180 TQ	USBLS	5/07
	Knoxville MSA, TN	Y	44090 FQ	65270 MW	103470 TQ	USBLS	5/07
	Memphis MSA, TN-MS-AR	Y	26070 FQ	37350 MW	60220 TQ	USBLS	5/07
	Nashville-Davidson-Murfreesboro MSA, TN	Y	35880 FQ	55100 MW	105680 TQ	USBLS	5/07
	Texas	Y	36360 FQ	55770 MW	77960 TQ	USBLS	5/07
	Austin-Round Rock MSA, TX	Y	32100 FQ	52660 MW	68170 TQ	USBLS	5/07
	Dallas-Fort Worth-Arlington MSA, TX	Y	46170 FQ	62890 MW	80290 TQ	USBLS	5/07
	El Paso MSA, TX	Y	32270 FQ	51900 MW	61150 TQ	USBLS	5/07
	Houston-Sugar Land-Baytown MSA, TX	Y	38800 FQ	61340 MW	89430 TQ	USBLS	5/07
	San Antonio MSA, TX	Y	39370 FQ	55220 MW	76120 TQ	USBLS	5/07
	Utah	Y	36500 FQ	52920 MW	66570 TQ	USBLS	5/07
	Salt Lake City MSA, UT	Y	38610 FQ	54820 MW	66640 TQ	USBLS	5/07

AE Average entry wage	AW Average wage paid	FQ First quartile wage	LO Lowest wage paid	MTC Median total compensation	TCC Total cash compensation
AER Average entry range	AWR Average wage range	H Hourly	LR Low end range	MW Median wage paid	TQ Third quartile wage
AEX Average experienced wage	AXR Average experienced range	HI Highest wage paid	M Monthly	MWR Median wage range	W Weekly
ATC Average total compensation	D Daily	HR High end range	MCC Median cash compensation	S See annotated source	Y Yearly

Occupation/Type/Industry	Location	Per	Low	Mid	High	Source	Date
Producer and Director	Vermont	Y	29190 FQ	32380 MW	41280 TQ	USBLS	5/07
	Burlington-South Burlington MSA, VT	Y	29330 FQ	32200 MW	40090 TQ	USBLS	5/07
	Virginia	Y	39680 FQ	54520 MW	73760 TQ	USBLS	5/07
	Richmond MSA, VA	Y	33590 FQ	46970 MW	64960 TQ	USBLS	5/07
	Roanoke MSA, VA	Y	34370 FQ	41040 MW	53710 TQ	USBLS	5/07
	Virginia Beach-Norfolk-Newport News MSA, VA-NC	Y	35850 FQ	52970 MW	70730 TQ	USBLS	5/07
	Washington	H	20.32 FQ	24.06 MW	34.30 TQ	WABLS	3/08
	Seattle-Tacoma-Bellevue MSA, WA	Y	42390 FQ	50770 MW	73410 TQ	USBLS	5/07
	West Virginia	Y	29782 FQ	37412 MW	70122 TQ	WVBLS	7/08-9/08
	Wisconsin	Y	37060 FQ	46600 MW	59080 TQ	USBLS	5/07
	Milwaukee-Waukesha-West Allis MSA, WI	Y	42570 FQ	56900 MW	71390 TQ	USBLS	5/07
	Wyoming	Y	29924 FQ	41570 MW	50568 TQ	WYBLS	9/08
	Puerto Rico	Y	24240 FQ	31770 MW	44850 TQ	USBLS	5/07
	San Juan-Caguas-Guaynabo MSA, PR	Y	24260 FQ	31830 MW	44860 TQ	USBLS	5/07
Production, Planning, and Expediting Clerk	Alabama	Y	27770 FQ	35990 MW	46350 TQ	USBLS	5/07
	Birmingham-Hoover MSA, AL	Y	29680 FQ	38430 MW	47570 TQ	USBLS	5/07
	Tuscaloosa MSA, AL	Y	28510 FQ	37140 MW	50510 TQ	USBLS	5/07
	Alaska	Y	35540 FQ	45660 MW	59130 TQ	USBLS	5/07
	Anchorage MSA, AK	Y	34460 FQ	43710 MW	56180 TQ	USBLS	5/07
	Arizona	Y	28700 FQ	37210 MW	47300 TQ	USBLS	5/07
	Phoenix-Mesa-Scottsdale MSA, AZ	Y	29050 FQ	37600 MW	47560 TQ	USBLS	5/07
	Prescott MSA, AZ	Y	26730 FQ	32720 MW	38840 TQ	USBLS	5/07
	Tucson MSA, AZ	Y	27930 FQ	37810 MW	48650 TQ	USBLS	5/07
	Arkansas	Y	28540 FQ	35870 MW	44650 TQ	USBLS	5/07
	Fort Smith MSA, AR-OK	Y	31670 FQ	37400 MW	41870 TQ	USBLS	5/07
	Little Rock-North Little Rock MSA, AR	Y	29170 FQ	36990 MW	45790 TQ	USBLS	5/07
	California	H	16.37 FQ	21.32 MW	26.07 TQ	CABLS	1/08-3/08
	Los Angeles-Long Beach-Glendale PMSA, CA	H	15.77 FQ	20.77 MW	25.59 TQ	CABLS	1/08-3/08
	Modesto MSA, CA	H	15.91 FQ	19.89 MW	24.36 TQ	CABLS	1/08-3/08
	Oakland-Fremont-Hayward MSA, CA	H	17.86 FQ	22.01 MW	25.06 TQ	CABLS	1/08-3/08
	Riverside-San Bernardino-Ontario MSA, CA	H	13.99 FQ	18.46 MW	23.93 TQ	CABLS	1/08-3/08
	Sacramento-Arden Arcade-Roseville MSA, CA	H	18.46 FQ	21.90 MW	24.43 TQ	CABLS	1/08-3/08
	San Diego-Carlsbad-San Marcos MSA, CA	H	17.13 FQ	22.39 MW	27.68 TQ	CABLS	1/08-3/08
	San Francisco-San Mateo-Redwood PMSA, CA	H	19.03 FQ	22.90 MW	27.43 TQ	CABLS	1/08-3/08
	San Jose-Sunnyvale-Santa Clara MSA, CA	H	18.71 FQ	23.72 MW	29.65 TQ	CABLS	1/08-3/08
	Santa Ana-Anaheim-Irvine PMSA, CA	Y	32850 FQ	42250 MW	53720 TQ	USBLS	5/07
	Santa Rosa-Petaluma MSA, CA	H	19.34 FQ	23.85 MW	30.58 TQ	CABLS	1/08-3/08
	Colorado	Y	33650 FQ	42590 MW	50110 TQ	USBLS	5/07
	Denver-Aurora MSA, CO	Y	33440 FQ	42760 MW	49500 TQ	USBLS	5/07
	Connecticut	H	15.18 AE	21.55 MW		CTBLS	1/08-3/08
	Bridgeport-Stamford-Norwalk MSA, CT	Y	36110 FQ	45050 MW	59480 TQ	USBLS	5/07
	Hartford-West Hartford-East Hartford MSA, CT	Y	32770 FQ	41590 MW	54750 TQ	USBLS	5/07
	New Haven MSA, CT	Y	34730 FQ	44290 MW	54110 TQ	USBLS	5/07
	Delaware	Y	31520 FQ	43760 MW	53130 TQ	USBLS	5/07
	Wilmington PMSA, DE-MD-NJ	Y	35530 FQ	47940 MW	58710 TQ	USBLS	5/07
	District of Columbia	Y	37090 FQ	44680 MW	52660 TQ	USBLS	5/07
	Washington-Arlington-Alexandria MSA, DC-VA-MD-WV	Y	36720 FQ	45340 MW	54860 TQ	USBLS	5/07
	Florida	Y	28210 FQ	35750 MW	45380 TQ	USBLS	5/07

AE	Average entry wage	AW	Average wage paid	FQ	First quartile wage	LO	Lowest wage paid	MTC	Median total compensation	TCC	Total cash compensation
AER	Average entry range	AWR	Average wage range	H	Hourly	LR	Low end range	MW	Median wage paid	TQ	Third quartile wage
AEX	Average experienced wage	AXR	Average experienced range	HI	Highest wage paid	M	Monthly	MWR	Median wage range	W	Weekly
ATC	Average total compensation	D	Daily	HR	High end range	MCC	Median cash compensation	S	See annotated source	Y	Yearly.

1315

Occupation/Type/Industry	Location	Per	Low	Mid	High	Source	Date
Production, Planning, and Expediting Clerk	Fort Lauderdale-Pompano Beach-Deerfield Beach PMSA, FL	Y	27900 FQ	36160 MW	47940 TQ	USBLS	5/07
	Jacksonville MSA, FL	Y	29210 FQ	36800 MW	46700 TQ	USBLS	5/07
	Lakeland MSA, FL	Y	29720 FQ	38230 MW	47490 TQ	USBLS	5/07
	Miami-Fort Lauderdale-Miami Beach MSA, FL	Y	27500 FQ	35090 MW	46280 TQ	USBLS	5/07
	Orlando-Kissimmee MSA, FL	Y	27720 FQ	34670 MW	43140 TQ	USBLS	5/07
	Pensacola-Ferry Pass-Brent MSA, FL	Y	29960 FQ	41220 MW	50050 TQ	USBLS	5/07
	Tampa-St. Petersburg-Clearwater MSA, FL	Y	28520 FQ	35600 MW	44200 TQ	USBLS	5/07
	West Palm Beach-Boca Raton-Boynton Beach PMSA, FL	Y	30050 FQ	36700 MW	46170 TQ	USBLS	5/07
	Georgia	Y	28740 FQ	36600 MW	46580 TQ	USBLS	5/07
	Atlanta-Sandy Springs-Marietta MSA, GA	Y	28860 FQ	37070 MW	46780 TQ	USBLS	5/07
	Hawaii	Y	29350 FQ	38300 MW	49870 TQ	USBLS	5/07
	Honolulu MSA, HI	Y	30500 FQ	39520 MW	50410 TQ	USBLS	5/07
	Idaho	Y	25550 FQ	36670 MW	46110 TQ	USBLS	5/07
	Boise City-Nampa MSA, ID	Y	23520 FQ	35100 MW	44610 TQ	USBLS	5/07
	Illinois	Y	30580 FQ	40440 MW	51590 TQ	USBLS	5/07
	Chicago-Naperville-Joliet MSA, IL-IN-WI	Y	32870 FQ	42520 MW	53600 TQ	USBLS	5/07
	Rockford MSA, IL	Y	30260 FQ	37810 MW	46570 TQ	USBLS	5/07
	Indiana	Y	27910 FQ	36180 MW	46840 TQ	USBLS	5/07
	Gary PMSA, IN	Y	31400 FQ	42820 MW	53110 TQ	USBLS	5/07
	Indianapolis-Carmel MSA, IN	Y	29090 FQ	37840 MW	49090 TQ	USBLS	5/07
	Iowa	Y	24770 FQ	31520 MW	41120 TQ	USBLS	5/07
	Des Moines-West Des Moines MSA, IA	Y	29580 FQ	36880 MW	48090 TQ	USBLS	5/07
	Kansas	Y	30200 FQ	40080 MW	48800 TQ	USBLS	5/07
	Wichita MSA, KS	Y	36700 FQ	45340 MW	51200 TQ	USBLS	5/07
	Kentucky	Y	30705 FQ	38773 MW	48267 TQ	KYBLS	2008
	Louisville-Jefferson County MSA, KY-IN	Y	28540 FQ	37070 MW	47940 TQ	USBLS	5/07
	Louisiana	H	14.87 FQ	20.19 MW	25.27 TQ	LABLS	1/08-3/08
	Baton Rouge MSA, LA	Y	37010 FQ	44890 MW	54560 TQ	USBLS	5/07
	New Orleans-Metairie-Kenner MSA, LA	Y	30860 FQ	42800 MW	52820 TQ	USBLS	5/07
	Maine	Y	33360 FQ	38490 MW	47000 TQ	USBLS	5/07
	Bangor MSA, ME	Y	30070 FQ	35650 MW	44980 TQ	USBLS	5/07
	Portland-South Portland-Biddeford MSA, ME	Y	32030 FQ	38390 MW	48250 TQ	USBLS	5/07
	Maryland	Y		45025 MW		MDBLS	3/08
	Baltimore-Towson MSA, MD	Y	35350 FQ	44350 MW	54860 TQ	USBLS	
	Bethesda-Gaithersburg-Frederick PMSA, MD	Y	35940 FQ	45390 MW	55430 TQ	USBLS	5/07
	Massachusetts	Y	36520 FQ	45670 MW	56410 TQ	USBLS	5/07
	Boston-Cambridge-Quincy NECTA, MA	Y	37980 FQ	46360 MW	56300 TQ	USBLS	5/07
	Worcester MSA, MA-CT	Y	34790 FQ	42070 MW	50850 TQ	USBLS	5/07
	Michigan	Y	32500 FQ	41150 MW	50470 TQ	USBLS	5/07
	Detroit-Warren-Livonia MSA, MI	Y	33010 FQ	42560 MW	51680 TQ	USBLS	5/07
	Grand Rapids-Wyoming MSA, MI	Y	35370 FQ	42610 MW	52100 TQ	USBLS	5/07
	Warren-Troy-Farmington Hills PMSA, MI	Y	32600 FQ	42200 MW	51820 TQ	USBLS	5/07
	Minnesota	Y	35106 FQ	43005 MW	50936 TQ	MNBLS	10/08-12/08
	Duluth-Superior MSA, MN-WI	Y	31421 FQ	39883 MW	56130 TQ	MNBLS	10/08-12/08
	Minneapolis-Saint Paul MSA, MN-WI	Y	37166 FQ	44660 MW	51925 TQ	MNBLS	10/08-12/08
	Rochester MSA, MN	Y	35561 FQ	43739 MW	49761 TQ	MNBLS	10/08-12/08
	Mississippi	Y	27140 FQ	33580 MW	44880 TQ	USBLS	5/07
	Jackson MSA, MS	Y	29120 FQ	37590 MW	45460 TQ	USBLS	5/07
	Missouri	Y	28410 FQ	37020 MW	46640 TQ	USBLS	5/07
	Kansas City MSA, MO-KS	Y	28810 FQ	37910 MW	47260 TQ	USBLS	5/07
	St. Louis MSA, MO-IL	Y	31790 FQ	40630 MW	50070 TQ	USBLS	5/07
	Montana	Y	27080 FQ	37820 MW	49040 TQ	USBLS	5/07
	Billings MSA, MT	Y	25100 FQ	30570 MW	44570 TQ	USBLS	5/07

AE	Average entry wage	AW	Average wage paid	FQ	First quartile wage	LO	Lowest wage paid
AER	Average entry range	AWR	Average wage range	H	Hourly	LR	Low end range
AEX	Average experienced wage	AXR	Average experienced range	HI	Highest wage paid	M	Monthly
ATC	Average total compensation	D	Daily	HR	High end range	MCC	Median cash compensation

MTC Median total compensation   TCC Total cash compensation
MW Median wage paid   TQ Third quartile wage
MWR Median wage range   W Weekly
S See annotated source   Y Yearly

Occupation/Type/Industry	Location	Per	Low	Mid	High	Source	Date
Production, Planning, and Expediting Clerk	Nebraska	Y	26020 FQ	32790 MW	41300 TQ	USBLS	5/07
	Omaha-Council Bluffs MSA, NE-IA	Y	26760 FQ	33700 MW	41630 TQ	USBLS	5/07
	Nevada	H	14.34 FQ	17.85 MW	22.16 TQ	NVBLS	5/08
	Las Vegas-Paradise MSA, NV	H	14.66 FQ	18.39 MW	22.33 TQ	NVBLS	5/08
	New Hampshire	H	14.84 AE	20.33 MW	23.78 AEX	NHBLS	6/08
	Manchester MSA, NH	Y	35500 FQ	42830 MW	50310 TQ	USBLS	5/07
	Nashua NECTA, NH-MA	Y	35030 FQ	43520 MW	52910 TQ	USBLS	5/07
	Portsmouth MSA, NH-ME	Y	36500 FQ	50650 MW	68990 TQ	USBLS	5/07
	New Jersey	Y	35190 FQ	43640 MW	50940 TQ	USBLS	5/07
	Camden PMSA, NJ	Y	32070 FQ	41440 MW	50000 TQ	USBLS	5/07
	Edison PMSA, NJ	Y	36450 FQ	44390 MW	52140 TQ	USBLS	5/07
	Newark-Union PMSA, NJ-PA	Y	35190 FQ	43670 MW	50590 TQ	USBLS	5/07
	Vineland-Millville-Bridgeton MSA, NJ	Y	35800 FQ	41010 MW	46670 TQ	USBLS	5/07
	New Mexico	Y	31280 FQ	41850 MW	52220 TQ	USBLS	5/07
	Albuquerque MSA, NM	Y	32850 FQ	42290 MW	52220 TQ	USBLS	5/07
	New York	Y	34170 FQ	43210 MW	53560 TQ	USBLS	5/07
	Albany-Schenectady-Troy MSA, NY	Y	34880 FQ	42950 MW	51410 TQ	USBLS	5/07
	Buffalo-Niagara Falls MSA, NY	Y	32710 FQ	42170 MW	52200 TQ	USBLS	5/07
	Nassau-Suffolk PMSA, NY	Y	34520 FQ	45160 MW	56970 TQ	USBLS	5/07
	New York-Northern New Jersey-Long Island MSA, NY-NJ-PA	Y	35570 FQ	44290 MW	53730 TQ	USBLS	5/07
	North Carolina	Y	28110 FQ	35340 MW	44720 TQ	USBLS	5/07
	Charlotte-Gastonia-Concord MSA, NC-SC	Y	29000 FQ	36560 MW	45750 TQ	USBLS	5/07
	Raleigh-Cary MSA, NC	Y	31270 FQ	38390 MW	47190 TQ	USBLS	5/07
	North Dakota	Y	30100 FQ	38300 MW	47580 TQ	USBLS	5/07
	Fargo MSA, ND-MN	Y	28620 FQ	38580 MW	50870 TQ	USBLS	5/07
	Ohio	Y	29860 FQ	37890 MW	48040 TQ	USBLS	5/07
	Canton-Massillon MSA, OH	Y	26870 FQ	32260 MW	37660 TQ	USBLS	5/07
	Cincinnati-Middletown MSA, OH-KY-IN	Y	30940 FQ	38600 MW	48050 TQ	USBLS	5/07
	Cleveland-Elyria-Mentor MSA, OH	Y	33160 FQ	41120 MW	50840 TQ	USBLS	5/07
	Columbus MSA, OH	Y	29490 FQ	37680 MW	47880 TQ	USBLS	5/07
	Dayton MSA, OH	Y	29210 FQ	37170 MW	46200 TQ	USBLS	5/07
	Oklahoma	Y	27430 FQ	40120 MW	52420 TQ	USBLS	5/07
	Oklahoma City MSA, OK	Y	32380 FQ	46320 MW	56960 TQ	USBLS	5/07
	Tulsa MSA, OK	Y	23210 FQ	35220 MW	47800 TQ	USBLS	5/07
	Oregon	H	15.20 FQ	18.76 MW	23.03 TQ	ORBLS	5/08
	Portland-Vancouver-Beaverton MSA, OR-WA	Y	32920 FQ	40040 MW	48560 TQ	USBLS	5/07
	Pennsylvania	Y	31080 FQ	39780 MW	49450 TQ	USBLS	5/07
	Allentown-Bethlehem-Easton MSA, PA-NJ	Y	33990 FQ	41000 MW	50850 TQ	USBLS	5/07
	Philadelphia-Camden-Wilmington MSA, PA-NJ-DE-MD	Y	33520 FQ	42200 MW	51810 TQ	USBLS	5/07
	Pittsburgh MSA, PA	Y	29390 FQ	38630 MW	49170 TQ	USBLS	5/07
	Reading MSA, PA	Y	28040 FQ	37600 MW	45710 TQ	USBLS	5/07
	Rhode Island	Y	29450 FQ	38200 MW	48050 TQ	USBLS	5/07
	Providence-Fall River-Warwick MSA, RI-MA	Y	29070 FQ	37410 MW	47150 TQ	USBLS	5/07
	South Carolina	Y	29240 FQ	37840 MW	49630 TQ	USBLS	5/07
	Charleston-North Charleston MSA, SC	Y	31310 FQ	43360 MW	55380 TQ	USBLS	5/07
	Columbia MSA, SC	Y	30620 FQ	40130 MW	49150 TQ	USBLS	5/07
	Florence MSA, SC	Y	33190 FQ	42770 MW	51660 TQ	USBLS	5/07
	South Dakota	Y	27371 FQ	31103 MW	37728 TQ	SDBLS	7/08-9/08
	Sioux Falls MSA, SD	Y	28149 FQ	31485 MW	37997 TQ	SDBLS	7/08-9/08
	Tennessee	Y	27740 FQ	36270 MW	45920 TQ	USBLS	5/07
	Clarksville MSA, TN-KY	Y	26620 FQ	35080 MW	40580 TQ	USBLS	5/07
	Kingsport-Bristol-Bristol MSA, TN-VA	Y	28360 FQ	41120 MW	48100 TQ	USBLS	5/07
	Memphis MSA, TN-MS-AR	Y	31930 FQ	40320 MW	49120 TQ	USBLS	5/07
	Nashville-Davidson-Murfreesboro MSA, TN	Y	28090 FQ	36450 MW	45240 TQ	USBLS	5/07

AE	Average entry wage	AW	Average wage paid	FQ	First quartile wage
AER	Average entry range	AWR	Average wage range	H	Hourly
AEX	Average experienced wage	AXR	Average experienced range	HI	Highest wage paid
ATC	Average total compensation	D	Daily	HR	High end range

LO	Lowest wage paid	MTC	Median total compensation	TCC	Total cash compensation
LR	Low end range	MW	Median wage paid	TQ	Third quartile wage
M	Monthly	MWR	Median wage range	W	Weekly
MCC	Median cash compensation	S	See annotated source	Y	Yearly

Occupation/Type/Industry	Location	Per	Low	Mid	High	Source	Date
Production, Planning, and Expediting Clerk	Texas	Y	29030 FQ	36950 MW	47280 TQ	USBLS	5/07
	Austin-Round Rock MSA, TX	Y	27410 FQ	35930 MW	46190 TQ	USBLS	5/07
	Beaumont-Port Arthur MSA, TX	Y	28630 FQ	37100 MW	49160 TQ	USBLS	5/07
	Brownsville-Harlingen MSA, TX	Y	18620 FQ	26990 MW	33500 TQ	USBLS	5/07
	Dallas-Fort Worth-Arlington MSA, TX	Y	29960 FQ	38010 MW	49140 TQ	USBLS	5/07
	El Paso MSA, TX	Y	21410 FQ	30320 MW	39810 TQ	USBLS	5/07
	Houston-Sugar Land-Baytown MSA, TX	Y	30230 FQ	37140 MW	46830 TQ	USBLS	5/07
	San Antonio MSA, TX	Y	30860 FQ	37270 MW	45660 TQ	USBLS	5/07
	Utah	Y	24220 FQ	28970 MW	39850 TQ	USBLS	5/07
	Salt Lake City MSA, UT	Y	25770 FQ	33750 MW	45110 TQ	USBLS	5/07
	Vermont	Y	31130 FQ	37220 MW	45430 TQ	USBLS	5/07
	Burlington-South Burlington MSA, VT	Y	34710 FQ	41080 MW	50130 TQ	USBLS	5/07
	Virginia	Y	33220 FQ	42890 MW	52570 TQ	USBLS	5/07
	Richmond MSA, VA	Y	34920 FQ	41850 MW	50290 TQ	USBLS	5/07
	Virginia Beach-Norfolk-Newport News MSA, VA-NC	Y	33650 FQ	45670 MW	56670 TQ	USBLS	5/07
	Washington	H	16.78 FQ	20.79 MW	24.55 TQ	WABLS	3/08
	Olympia MSA, WA	Y	39400 FQ	44930 MW	49570 TQ	USBLS	5/07
	Seattle-Tacoma-Bellevue MSA, WA	Y	35450 FQ	42930 MW	49560 TQ	USBLS	5/07
	West Virginia	Y	24986 FQ	35166 MW	48879 TQ	WVBLS	7/08-9/08
	Charleston MSA, WV	Y	29070 FQ	41560 MW	48480 TQ	USBLS	5/07
	Parkersburg-Marietta-Vienna MSA, WV-OH	Y	27880 FQ	35850 MW	45370 TQ	USBLS	5/07
	Wisconsin	Y	32050 FQ	39730 MW	48210 TQ	USBLS	5/07
	Appleton MSA, WI	Y	33580 FQ	40210 MW	46920 TQ	USBLS	5/07
	Milwaukee-Waukesha-West Allis MSA, WI	Y	32550 FQ	41660 MW	49380 TQ	USBLS	5/07
	Wyoming	Y	27262 FQ	36966 MW	47217 TQ	WYBLS	9/08
	Cheyenne MSA, WY	Y	20296 FQ	30125 MW	41485 TQ	WYBLS	9/08
	Puerto Rico	Y	20200 FQ	29250 MW	39220 TQ	USBLS	5/07
	San Juan-Caguas-Guaynabo MSA, PR	Y	19860 FQ	27850 MW	38770 TQ	USBLS	5/07
	Virgin Islands	Y	26620 FQ	33960 MW	49750 TQ	USBLS	5/07
	Guam	Y	32850 FQ	38270 MW	45440 TQ	USBLS	5/07
Production Supervisor							
Semi-Skilled Operation	Southeast, MI	Y		45549 AW		MIOAKL02	2007
Unskilled Operation	Southeast, MI	Y		48962 AW		MIOAKL02	2007
Professional Organizer							
Independent	United States	H		50.00-150.00 AWR		WSJ07	2008
Professional Racing Sailor	Rhode Island	Y		65000-83000 AWR		RIM01	2009
Professional Skateboarder							
Celebrity	United States	Y	500000 LO		1000000 HI	ASPORT	2009
Mid-Level	United States	Y	50000 LO		100000 HI	ASPORT	2009
Professor							
Area, Ethnic, Cultural, and Gender Studies	United States	Y		94700 AW		CHE	2007-2008
Broadcast Education	United States	Y		84861 AW		BEA	9/07-12/07
Business, Management, Marketing, and Related Support Activities	United States	Y		102965 AW		CHE	2007-2008
Engineering	United States	Y		107134 AW		CHE	2007-2008
Family and Consumer Sciences/Human Sciences	United States	Y		81482 MW		HED01	2007-2008
Legal Professions and Studies	United States	Y		129527 AW		CHE	2007-2008
Natural Resources and Conservation	United States	Y		87676 MW		HED01	2007-2008
Parks, Recreation, Leisure, and Fitness Studies	United States	Y		76038 AW		CHE	2007-2008
Theology and Religious Vocations	United States	Y		69855 MW		HED01	2007-2008

AE	Average entry wage	AW	Average wage paid	FQ	First quartile wage	LO	Lowest wage paid	MTC	Median total compensation	TCC	Total cash compensation
AER	Average entry range	AWR	Average wage range	H	Hourly	LR	Low end range	MW	Median wage paid	TQ	Third quartile wage
AEX	Average experienced wage	AXR	Average experienced range	HI	Highest wage paid	M	Monthly	MWR	Median wage range	W	Weekly
ATC	Average total compensation	D	Daily	HR	High end range	MCC	Median cash compensation	S	See annotated source	Y	Yearly

Occupation/Type/Industry	Location	Per	Low	Mid	High	Source	Date
Program Specialist							
Municipal Government	Walnut Creek, CA	Y	55240 LO		66542 HI	WCSWP	6/27/08
Programming Project Leader	United States	Y		84004 AW		ADT01	2007
Project Coordinator							
Department of Environmental Quality	Oregon	M	3386 LO		4951 HI	ODEQSS	11/1/08
Promotional Marketer	United States	Y		79926 AW		PROMO	5/9/07-5/23/07
Proofreader and Copy Marker	Alabama	Y	16910 FQ	18930 MW	24250 TQ	USBLS	5/07
	Birmingham-Hoover MSA, AL	Y	16910 FQ	18490 MW	20220 TQ	USBLS	5/07
	Arizona	Y	14760 FQ	15490 MW	20690 TQ	USBLS	5/07
	Phoenix-Mesa-Scottsdale MSA, AZ	Y	14750 FQ	15460 MW	20010 TQ	USBLS	5/07
	Arkansas	Y	20500 FQ	24470 MW	28990 TQ	USBLS	5/07
	Little Rock-North Little Rock MSA, AR	Y	22100 FQ	24250 MW	28000 TQ	USBLS	5/07
	California	H	12.59 FQ	15.66 MW	19.98 TQ	CABLS	1/08-3/08
	Los Angeles-Long Beach-Glendale PMSA, CA	H	13.39 FQ	17.20 MW	19.57 TQ	CABLS	1/08-3/08
	Oakland-Fremont-Hayward MSA, CA	H	13.78 FQ	16.01 MW	21.03 TQ	CABLS	1/08-3/08
	Oxnard-Thousand Oaks-Ventura MSA, CA	H	10.53 FQ	11.68 MW	14.05 TQ	CABLS	1/08-3/08
	Riverside-San Bernardino-Ontario MSA, CA	H	13.86 FQ	15.38 MW	18.44 TQ	CABLS	1/08-3/08
	Sacramento-Arden Arcade-Roseville MSA, CA	H	13.26 FQ	15.12 MW	19.01 TQ	CABLS	1/08-3/08
	San Diego-Carlsbad-San Marcos MSA, CA	H	9.29 FQ	11.09 MW	13.73 TQ	CABLS	1/08-3/08
	San Francisco-San Mateo-Redwood PMSA, CA	H	14.88 FQ	21.18 MW	28.82 TQ	CABLS	1/08-3/08
	San Jose-Sunnyvale-Santa Clara MSA, CA	H	12.74 FQ	15.39 MW	21.45 TQ	CABLS	1/08-3/08
	Santa Ana-Anaheim-Irvine PMSA, CA	Y	29430 FQ	35170 MW	52750 TQ	USBLS	5/07
	Colorado	Y	20650 FQ	24950 MW	37640 TQ	USBLS	5/07
	Denver-Aurora MSA, CO	Y	19760 FQ	22890 MW	40300 TQ	USBLS	5/07
	Connecticut	H	11.28 AE	16.25 MW		CTBLS	1/08-3/08
	Bridgeport-Stamford-Norwalk MSA, CT	Y	24640 FQ	32790 MW	41840 TQ	USBLS	5/07
	Hartford-West Hartford-East Hartford MSA, CT	Y	28320 FQ	34990 MW	40650 TQ	USBLS	5/07
	District of Columbia	Y	30310 FQ	35890 MW	43310 TQ	USBLS	5/07
	Washington-Arlington-Alexandria MSA, DC-VA-MD-WV	Y	27690 FQ	33840 MW	39780 TQ	USBLS	5/07
	Florida	Y	19610 FQ	25980 MW	32520 TQ	USBLS	5/07
	Fort Lauderdale-Pompano Beach-Deerfield Beach PMSA, FL	Y	27930 FQ	34340 MW	38830 TQ	USBLS	5/07
	Miami-Fort Lauderdale-Miami Beach MSA, FL	Y	24010 FQ	31310 MW	38760 TQ	USBLS	5/07
	Tampa-St. Petersburg-Clearwater MSA, FL	Y	22150 FQ	27670 MW	32690 TQ	USBLS	5/07
	Georgia	Y	19730 FQ	24710 MW	33060 TQ	USBLS	5/07
	Atlanta-Sandy Springs-Marietta MSA, GA	Y	19970 FQ	24790 MW	36160 TQ	USBLS	5/07
	Illinois	Y	21860 FQ	31580 MW	41270 TQ	USBLS	5/07
	Indiana	Y	19990 FQ	26830 MW	32200 TQ	USBLS	5/07
	Gary PMSA, IN	Y	22870 FQ	28850 MW	35430 TQ	USBLS	5/07
	Indianapolis-Carmel MSA, IN	Y	19680 FQ	27920 MW	33120 TQ	USBLS	5/07
	Iowa	Y	18310 FQ	23620 MW	30240 TQ	USBLS	5/07
	Kansas	Y	16520 FQ	19440 MW	27940 TQ	USBLS	5/07
	Kentucky	Y	23209 FQ	28712 MW	33963 TQ	KYBLS	2008
	Louisville-Jefferson County MSA, KY-IN	Y	23660 FQ	28070 MW	32330 TQ	USBLS	5/07
	Maine	Y	21360 FQ	23660 MW	28450 TQ	USBLS	5/07
	Maryland	Y		32925 MW		MDBLS	3/08
	Baltimore-Towson MSA, MD	Y	26360 FQ	32900 MW	39130 TQ	USBLS	5/07

AE	Average entry wage	**AW**	Average wage paid	**LO** Lowest wage paid	**MTC** Median total compensation	**TCC** Total cash compensation
AER	Average entry range	**AWR**	Average wage range	**LR** Low end range	**MW** Median wage paid	**TQ** Third quartile wage
AEX	Average experienced wage	**AXR**	Average experienced range	**HI** Highest wage paid	**MWR** Median wage range	**W** Weekly
ATC	Average total compensation **D**	Daily	**HR** High end range	**MCC** Median cash compensation	**S** See annotated source	**Y** Yearly

Occupation/Type/Industry	Location	Per	Low	Mid	High	Source	Date
Proofreader and Copy Marker	Bethesda-Gaithersburg-Frederick PMSA, MD	Y	26870 FQ	32870 MW	36180 TQ	USBLS	5/07
	Massachusetts	Y	27260 FQ	34750 MW	46370 TQ	USBLS	5/07
	Boston-Cambridge-Quincy NECTA, MA	Y	27380 FQ	34900 MW	46250 TQ	USBLS	5/07
	Michigan	Y	24980 FQ	33710 MW	41410 TQ	USBLS	5/07
	Detroit-Warren-Livonia MSA, MI	Y	27560 FQ	36370 MW	45160 TQ	USBLS	5/07
	Grand Rapids-Wyoming MSA, MI	Y	25600 FQ	34040 MW	38830 TQ	USBLS	5/07
	Warren-Troy-Farmington Hills PMSA, MI	Y	25850 FQ	36540 MW	44740 TQ	USBLS	5/07
	Minnesota	Y	25478 FQ	35730 MW	43172 TQ	MNBLS	10/08-12/08
	Minneapolis-Saint Paul MSA, MN-WI	Y	36146 FQ	41309 MW	46648 TQ	MNBLS	10/08-12/08
	Mississippi	Y	20650 FQ	23920 MW	28470 TQ	USBLS	5/07
	Jackson MSA, MS	Y	22460 FQ	26470 MW	30130 TQ	USBLS	5/07
	Missouri	Y	19720 FQ	26950 MW	38180 TQ	USBLS	5/07
	Kansas City MSA, MO-KS	Y	27210 FQ	31530 MW	36840 TQ	USBLS	5/07
	St. Louis MSA, MO-IL	Y	27570 FQ	36650 MW	49910 TQ	USBLS	5/07
	Nebraska	Y	18180 FQ	22540 MW	29010 TQ	USBLS	5/07
	Omaha-Council Bluffs MSA, NE-IA	Y	19760 FQ	23810 MW	29900 TQ	USBLS	5/07
	Nevada	H	9.35 FQ	13.36 MW	16.59 TQ	NVBLS	5/08
	Las Vegas-Paradise MSA, NV	H	7.08 FQ	10.76 MW	13.15 TQ	NVBLS	5/08
	New Hampshire	H	10.48 AE	13.29 MW	14.83 AEX	NHBLS	6/08
	New Jersey	Y	28160 FQ	36110 MW	43350 TQ	USBLS	5/07
	Camden PMSA, NJ	Y	21880 FQ	27750 MW	32240 TQ	USBLS	5/07
	Edison PMSA, NJ	Y	26300 FQ	36270 MW	45620 TQ	USBLS	5/07
	Newark-Union PMSA, NJ-PA	Y	30190 FQ	36740 MW	44170 TQ	USBLS	5/07
	New York	Y	28880 FQ	38820 MW	46200 TQ	USBLS	5/07
	Albany-Schenectady-Troy MSA, NY	Y	23250 FQ	26490 MW	33540 TQ	USBLS	5/07
	Buffalo-Niagara Falls MSA, NY	Y	19970 FQ	30190 MW	44120 TQ	USBLS	5/07
	Nassau-Suffolk PMSA, NY	Y	24780 FQ	31750 MW	45020 TQ	USBLS	5/07
	New York-Northern New Jersey Long Island MSA, NY-NJ-PA	Y	30540 FQ	39140 MW	46240 TQ	USBLS	5/07
	North Carolina	Y	21170 FQ	25760 MW	33560 TQ	USBLS	5/07
	Ohio	Y	20940 FQ	29150 MW	37880 TQ	USBLS	5/07
	Cincinnati-Middletown MSA, OH-KY-IN	Y	25920 FQ	34030 MW	44230 TQ	USBLS	5/07
	Cleveland-Elyria-Mentor MSA, OH	Y	18880 FQ	28940 MW	39600 TQ	USBLS	5/07
	Columbus MSA, OH	Y	26700 FQ	32710 MW	39650 TQ	USBLS	5/07
	Oklahoma	Y	17890 FQ	20670 MW	23800 TQ	USBLS	5/07
	Oklahoma City MSA, OK	Y	17550 FQ	19510 MW	25810 TQ	USBLS	5/07
	Oregon	H	15.23 FQ	17.45 MW	19.53 TQ	ORBLS	5/08
	Portland-Vancouver-Beaverton MSA, OR-WA	Y	33110 FQ	36950 MW	42740 TQ	USBLS	5/07
	Pennsylvania	Y	22490 FQ	27150 MW	32360 TQ	USBLS	5/07
	Philadelphia-Camden-Wilmington MSA, PA-NJ-DE-MD	Y	24100 FQ	28370 MW	35070 TQ	USBLS	5/07
	Pittsburgh MSA, PA	Y	25390 FQ	27540 MW	29800 TQ	USBLS	5/07
	Rhode Island	Y	36370 FQ	43410 MW	48340 TQ	USBLS	5/07
	Providence-Fall River-Warwick MSA, RI-MA	Y	35540 FQ	43090 MW	48180 TQ	USBLS	5/07
	South Carolina	Y	26870 FQ	33190 MW	41730 TQ	USBLS	5/07
	Charleston-North Charleston MSA, SC	Y	28510 FQ	32090 MW	36690 TQ	USBLS	5/07
	South Dakota	Y	18595 FQ	21889 MW	24653 TQ	SDBLS	7/08-9/08
	Sioux Falls MSA, SD	Y	20915 FQ	23361 MW	25638 TQ	SDBLS	7/08-9/08
	Tennessee	Y	22630 FQ	27240 MW	32190 TQ	USBLS	5/07
	Memphis MSA, TN-MS-AR	Y	26570 FQ	30080 MW	36300 TQ	USBLS	5/07
	Nashville-Davidson-Murfreesboro MSA, TN	Y	23270 FQ	29840 MW	35190 TQ	USBLS	5/07
	Texas	Y	19330 FQ	28480 MW	36390 TQ	USBLS	5/07
	Dallas-Fort Worth-Arlington MSA, TX	Y	25270 FQ	32210 MW	38930 TQ	USBLS	5/07

AE Average entry wage	**AW** Average wage paid	**FQ** First quartile wage	**LO** Lowest wage paid	**MTC** Median total compensation	**TCC** Total cash compensation
AER Average entry range	**AWR** Average wage range	**H** Hourly	**LR** Low end range	**MW** Median wage paid	**TQ** Third quartile wage
AEX Average experienced wage	**AXR** Average experienced range	**HI** Highest wage paid	**M** Monthly	**MWR** Median wage range	**W** Weekly
ATC Average total compensation	**D** Daily	**HR** High end range	**MCC** Median cash compensation	**S** See annotated source	**Y** Yearly

Occupation/Type/Industry	Location	Per	Low	Mid	High	Source	Date
Proofreader and Copy Marker	Houston-Sugar Land-Baytown MSA, TX	Y	21320 FQ	31760 MW	39130 TQ	USBLS	5/07
	San Antonio MSA, TX	Y	14000 FQ	21820 MW	32580 TQ	USBLS	5/07
	Utah	Y	21550 FQ	25340 MW	30830 TQ	USBLS	5/07
	Salt Lake City MSA, UT	Y	22290 FQ	26390 MW	33430 TQ	USBLS	5/07
	Virginia	Y	17800 FQ	23390 MW	32430 TQ	USBLS	5/07
	Richmond MSA, VA	Y	17380 FQ	19390 MW	26520 TQ	USBLS	5/07
	Virginia Beach-Norfolk-Newport News MSA, VA-NC	Y	16650 FQ	18130 MW	22180 TQ	USBLS	5/07
	Washington	H	13.23 FQ	16.33 MW	23.00 TQ	WABLS	3/08
	Seattle-Tacoma-Bellevue MSA, WA	Y	30510 FQ	37090 MW	63220 TQ	USBLS	5/07
	West Virginia	Y	20169 FQ	26375 MW	34341 TQ	WVBLS	7/08-9/08
	Wisconsin	Y	22460 FQ	28040 MW	34240 TQ	USBLS	5/07
	Milwaukee-Waukesha-West Allis MSA, WI	Y	24860 FQ	29380 MW	35010 TQ	USBLS	5/07
Property, Real Estate, and Community Association Manager	Alabama	Y	40310 FQ	52710 MW	74750 TQ	USBLS	5/07
	Birmingham-Hoover MSA, AL	Y	45280 FQ	53280 MW	84290 TQ	USBLS	5/07
	Alaska	Y	34940 FQ	48000 MW	70640 TQ	USBLS	5/07
	Anchorage MSA, AK	Y	37350 FQ	49670 MW	80220 TQ	USBLS	5/07
	Arizona	Y	33530 FQ	42390 MW	58660 TQ	USBLS	5/07
	Phoenix-Mesa-Scottsdale MSA, AZ	Y	34990 FQ	43520 MW	62740 TQ	USBLS	5/07
	Tucson MSA, AZ	Y	31020 FQ	39100 MW	53000 TQ	USBLS	5/07
	Arkansas	Y	21610 FQ	28390 MW	44110 TQ	USBLS	5/07
	Jonesboro MSA, AR	Y	28770 FQ	34510 MW	39730 TQ	USBLS	5/07
	Little Rock-North Little Rock MSA, AR	Y	22250 FQ	31680 MW	47480 TQ	USBLS	5/07
	California	H	10.98 FQ	17.40 MW	29.39 TQ	CABLS	1/08-3/08
	Los Angeles-Long Beach-Glendale PMSA, CA	H	8.79 FQ	14.44 MW	26.29 TQ	CABLS	1/08-3/08
	Oakland-Fremont-Hayward MSA, CA	H	11.68 FQ	20.88 MW	31.07 TQ	CABLS	1/08-3/08
	Riverside-San Bernardino-Ontario MSA, CA	H	9.68 FQ	14.06 MW	24.50 TQ	CABLS	1/08-3/08
	Sacramento-Arden Arcade-Roseville MSA, CA	H	12.05 FQ	18.17 MW	30.11 TQ	CABLS	1/08-3/08
	San Diego-Carlsbad-San Marcos MSA, CA	H	10.18 FQ	17.60 MW	24.89 TQ	CABLS	1/08-3/08
	San Francisco-San Mateo-Redwood PMSA, CA	H	14.83 FQ	23.69 MW	38.69 TQ	CABLS	1/08-3/08
	San Jose-Sunnyvale-Santa Clara MSA, CA	H	15.10 FQ	18.64 MW	38.32 TQ	CABLS	1/08-3/08
	Santa Ana-Anaheim-Irvine PMSA, CA	Y	27120 FQ	40670 MW	63880 TQ	USBLS	5/07
	Stockton MSA, CA	H	9.49 FQ	18.33 MW	32.28 TQ	CABLS	1/08-3/08
	Colorado	Y	37830 FQ	53660 MW	82960 TQ	USBLS	5/07
	Denver-Aurora MSA, CO	Y	39110 FQ	62580 MW	93740 TQ	USBLS	5/07
	Connecticut	H	18.15 AE	26.32 MW		CTBLS	1/08-3/08
	Bridgeport-Stamford-Norwalk MSA, CT	Y	49470 FQ	67210 MW	92320 TQ	USBLS	5/07
	Hartford-West Hartford-East Hartford MSA, CT	Y	38670 FQ	53520 MW	84590 TQ	USBLS	5/07
	New Haven MSA, CT	Y	41600 FQ	47300 MW	83600 TQ	USBLS	5/07
	Delaware	Y	40370 FQ	54690 MW	82660 TQ	USBLS	5/07
	Wilmington PMSA, DE-MD-NJ	Y	44200 FQ	55550 MW	83210 TQ	USBLS	5/07
	District of Columbia	Y	44280 FQ	59860 MW	80730 TQ	USBLS	5/07
	Washington-Arlington-Alexandria MSA, DC-VA-MD-WV	Y	47030 FQ	63810 MW	88450 TQ	USBLS	5/07
	Florida	Y	35990 FQ	49030 MW	75360 TQ	USBLS	5/07
	Fort Lauderdale-Pompano Beach-Deerfield Beach PMSA, FL	Y	41740 FQ	48300 MW	87940 TQ	USBLS	5/07
	Jacksonville MSA, FL	Y	41470 FQ	55740 MW	91840 TQ	USBLS	5/07
	Lakeland MSA, FL	Y	53810 FQ	73800 MW	85470 TQ	USBLS	5/07

AE	Average entry wage	**AW**	Average wage paid	**FQ**	First quartile wage	**LO**	Lowest wage paid	**MTC** Median total compensation **TCC** Total cash compensation
AER	Average entry range	**AWR**	Average wage range	**H**	Hourly	**LR**	Low end range	**MW** Median wage paid **TQ** Third quartile wage
AEX	Average experienced wage	**AXR**	Average experienced range	**HI**	Highest wage paid	**M**	Monthly	**MWR** Median wage range **W** Weekly
ATC	Average total compensation	**D**	Daily	**HR**	High end range	**MCC**	Median cash compensation	**S** See annotated source **Y** Yearly

Occupation/Type/Industry	Location	Per	Low	Mid	High	Source	Date
Property, Real Estate, and Community Association Manager							
	Miami-Fort Lauderdale-Miami Beach MSA, FL	Y	36460 FQ	47580 MW	72620 TQ	USBLS	5/07
	Orlando-Kissimmee MSA, FL	Y	34320 FQ	44260 MW	76310 TQ	USBLS	5/07
	Pensacola-Ferry Pass-Brent MSA, FL	Y	19850 FQ	41960 MW	57210 TQ	USBLS	5/07
	Tallahassee MSA, FL	Y	33740 FQ	43890 MW	69910 TQ	USBLS	5/07
	Tampa-St. Petersburg-Clearwater MSA, FL	Y	35090 FQ	49370 MW	74510 TQ	USBLS	5/07
	West Palm Beach-Boca Raton-Boynton Beach PMSA, FL	Y	36460 FQ	50920 MW	72820 TQ	USBLS	5/07
	Georgia	Y	39580 FQ	50180 MW	60440 TQ	USBLS	5/07
	Athens-Clarke County MSA, GA	Y	32980 FQ	37750 MW	54300 TQ	USBLS	5/07
	Atlanta-Sandy Springs-Marietta MSA, GA	Y	40280 FQ	50820 MW	60610 TQ	USBLS	5/07
	Augusta-Richmond County MSA, GA-SC	Y	43650 FQ	52090 MW	100720 TQ	USBLS	5/07
	Hawaii	Y	31830 FQ	41680 MW	58770 TQ	USBLS	5/07
	Honolulu MSA, HI	Y	31780 FQ	41250 MW	62540 TQ	USBLS	5/07
	Idaho	Y	19930 FQ	24770 MW	40050 TQ	USBLS	5/07
	Boise City-Nampa MSA, ID	Y	19860 FQ	24280 MW	39900 TQ	USBLS	5/07
	Idaho Falls MSA, ID	Y	22400 FQ	33510 MW	37240 TQ	USBLS	5/07
	Illinois	Y	36230 FQ	54580 MW	78170 TQ	USBLS	5/07
	Chicago-Naperville-Joliet MSA, IL-IN-WI	Y	40790 FQ	56610 MW	80610 TQ	USBLS	5/07
	Peoria MSA, IL	Y	35490 FQ	52120 MW		USBLS	5/07
	Indiana	Y	38090 FQ	48070 MW	63870 TQ	USBLS	5/07
	Gary PMSA, IN	Y	43170 FQ	48410 MW	61000 TQ	USBLS	5/07
	Indianapolis-Carmel MSA, IN	Y	37810 FQ	49600 MW	77920 TQ	USBLS	5/07
	Iowa	Y	30560 FQ	39150 MW	56460 TQ	USBLS	5/07
	Des Moines-West Des Moines MSA, IA	Y	33340 FQ	38630 MW	57640 TQ	USBLS	5/07
	Kansas	Y	32730 FQ	49640 MW	79480 TQ	USBLS	5/07
	Wichita MSA, KS	Y	43990 FQ	52260 MW	62420 TQ	USBLS	5/07
	Kentucky	Y	28165 FQ	39886 MW	60468 TQ	KYBLS	2008
	Louisville-Jefferson County MSA, KY-IN	Y	28170 FQ	39770 MW	58120 TQ	USBLS	5/07
	Louisiana	H	10.73 FQ	16.11 MW	21.50 TQ	LABLS	1/08-3/08
	Baton Rouge MSA, LA	Y	14380 FQ	28370 MW	36210 TQ	USBLS	5/07
	New Orleans-Metairie-Kenner MSA, LA	Y	27870 FQ	40410 MW	53500 TQ	USBLS	5/07
	Maine	Y	34400 FQ	43920 MW	53680 TQ	USBLS	5/07
	Portland-South Portland-Biddeford MSA, ME	Y	31330 FQ	45670 MW	55320 TQ	USBLS	5/07
	Baltimore-Towson MSA, MD	Y	46870 FQ	64130 MW	95010 TQ	USBLS	5/07
	Bethesda-Gaithersburg-Frederick PMSA, MD	Y	54460 FQ	65680 MW	84920 TQ	USBLS	5/07
	Massachusetts	Y	45780 FQ	60700 MW	78570 TQ	USBLS	5/07
	Boston-Cambridge-Quincy NECTA, MA	Y	50130 FQ	63670 MW	79600 TQ	USBLS	5/07
	Worcester MSA, MA-CT	Y	25630 FQ	58430 MW	80100 TQ	USBLS	5/07
	Michigan	Y	31900 FQ	43560 MW	65420 TQ	USBLS	5/07
	Detroit-Warren-Livonia MSA, MI	Y	33890 FQ	44400 MW	67620 TQ	USBLS	5/07
	Grand Rapids-Wyoming MSA, MI	Y	23450 FQ	36900 MW	58460 TQ	USBLS	5/07
	Warren-Troy-Farmington Hills PMSA, MI	Y	32090 FQ	43480 MW	65060 TQ	USBLS	5/07
	Minnesota	Y	32509 FQ	44667 MW	66135 TQ	MNBLS	10/08-12/08
	Duluth-Superior MSA, MN-WI	Y	43061 FQ	50641 MW	73413 TQ	MNBLS	10/08-12/08
	Minneapolis-Saint Paul MSA, MN-WI	Y	35888 FQ	48264 MW	73079 TQ	MNBLS	10/08-12/08
	Rochester MSA, MN	Y	26055 FQ	30956 MW	40377 TQ	MNBLS	10/08-12/08
	Mississippi	Y	25130 FQ	31340 MW	40150 TQ	USBLS	5/07
	Jackson MSA, MS	Y	29340 FQ	36710 MW	47520 TQ	USBLS	5/07
	Pascagoula MSA, MS	Y	24530 FQ	31490 MW	43370 TQ	USBLS	5/07
	Missouri	Y	37310 FQ	51570 MW	74360 TQ	USBLS	5/07
	Kansas City MSA, MO-KS	Y	41040 FQ	52280 MW	82670 TQ	USBLS	5/07
	St. Louis MSA, MO-IL	Y	34150 FQ	52050 MW	80430 TQ	USBLS	5/07

AE Average entry wage	**AW** Average wage paid	**FQ** First quartile wage	**LO** Lowest wage paid	**MTC** Median total compensation	**TCC** Total cash compensation
AER Average entry range	**AWR** Average wage range	**H** Hourly	**LR** Low end range	**MW** Median wage paid	**TQ** Third quartile wage
AEX Average experienced wage	**AXR** Average experienced range	**HI** Highest wage paid	**M** Monthly	**MWR** Median wage range	**W** Weekly
ATC Average total compensation	**D** Daily	**HR** High end range	**MCC** Median cash compensation	**S** See annotated source	**Y** Yearly

Occupation/Type/Industry	Location	Per	Low	Mid	High	Source	Date
Property, Real Estate, and Community Association Manager	Montana	Y	19060 FQ	26160 MW	31560 TQ	USBLS	5/07
	Billings MSA, MT	Y	21110 FQ	26270 MW	42820 TQ	USBLS	5/07
	Nebraska	Y	46380 FQ	61920 MW	78120 TQ	USBLS	5/07
	Omaha-Council Bluffs MSA, NE-IA	Y	47260 FQ	63390 MW	78740 TQ	USBLS	5/07
	Nevada	H	13.40 FQ	18.91 MW	29.40 TQ	NVBLS	5/08
	Las Vegas-Paradise MSA, NV	H	13.97 FQ	20.76 MW	31.78 TQ	NVBLS	5/08
	New Hampshire	H	16.50 AE	24.62 MW	35.19 AEX	NHBLS	6/08
	Manchester MSA, NH	Y	29800 FQ	47490 MW	55430 TQ	USBLS	5/07
	Nashua NECTA, NH-MA	Y	43030 FQ	51370 MW	59930 TQ	USBLS	5/07
	New Jersey	Y	46370 FQ	59490 MW	81560 TQ	USBLS	5/07
	Camden PMSA, NJ	Y	43150 FQ	49850 MW	61300 TQ	USBLS	5/07
	Edison PMSA, NJ	Y	48240 FQ	58760 MW	81630 TQ	USBLS	5/07
	Newark-Union PMSA, NJ-PA	Y	44550 FQ	61990 MW	83340 TQ	USBLS	5/07
	New Mexico	Y	27610 FQ	40720 MW	53070 TQ	USBLS	5/07
	Albuquerque MSA, NM	Y	38150 FQ	44450 MW	51350 TQ	USBLS	5/07
	New York	Y	57880 FQ	71840 MW	103120 TQ	USBLS	5/07
	Albany-Schenectady-Troy MSA, NY	Y	59410 FQ	78460 MW	96430 TQ	USBLS	5/07
	Buffalo-Niagara Falls MSA, NY	Y	52450 FQ	60150 MW	75630 TQ	USBLS	5/07
	Nassau-Suffolk PMSA, NY	Y	92460 FQ			USBLS	5/07
	New York-Northern New Jersey-Long Island MSA, NY-NJ-PA	Y	54170 FQ	68440 MW	94700 TQ	USBLS	5/07
	Syracuse MSA, NY	Y	38070 FQ	46070 MW	62910 TQ	USBLS	5/07
	North Carolina	Y	45110 FQ	57110 MW	86000 TQ	USBLS	5/07
	Asheville MSA, NC	Y	36820 FQ	58100 MW	79630 TQ	USBLS	5/07
	Charlotte-Gastonia-Concord MSA, NC-SC	Y	51620 FQ	65600 MW	104580 TQ	USBLS	5/07
	Raleigh-Cary MSA, NC	Y	44880 FQ	52670 MW	70720 TQ	USBLS	5/07
	North Dakota	Y	30310 FQ	36730 MW	50400 TQ	USBLS	5/07
	Fargo MSA, ND-MN	Y	28780 FQ	32940 MW	38700 TQ	USBLS	5/07
	Ohio	Y	39700 FQ	56400 MW	79460 TQ	USBLS	5/07
	Cincinnati-Middletown MSA, OH-KY-IN	Y	29660 FQ	51880 MW	81550 TQ	USBLS	5/07
	Cleveland-Elyria-Mentor MSA, OH	Y	39310 FQ	59910 MW	88040 TQ	USBLS	5/07
	Columbus MSA, OH	Y	44800 FQ	59040 MW	75770 TQ	USBLS	5/07
	Dayton MSA, OH	Y	35860 FQ	43320 MW	50940 TQ	USBLS	5/07
	Oklahoma	Y	24850 FQ	33600 MW	49510 TQ	USBLS	5/07
	Lawton MSA, OK	Y	19550 FQ	24670 MW	29000 TQ	USBLS	5/07
	Oklahoma City MSA, OK	Y	27990 FQ	36320 MW	56630 TQ	USBLS	5/07
	Tulsa MSA, OK	Y	24490 FQ	35210 MW	48620 TQ	USBLS	5/07
	Oregon	H	14.29 FQ	19.63 MW	27.25 TQ	ORBLS	5/08
	Portland-Vancouver-Beaverton MSA, OR-WA	Y	33850 FQ	46270 MW	61660 TQ	USBLS	5/07
	Pennsylvania	Y	38370 FQ	50220 MW	75780 TQ	USBLS	5/07
	Allentown-Bethlehem-Easton MSA, PA-NJ	Y	41730 FQ	63760 MW	75460 TQ	USBLS	5/07
	Philadelphia-Camden-Wilmington MSA, PA-NJ-DE-MD	Y	45540 FQ	57460 MW	86650 TQ	USBLS	5/07
	Pittsburgh MSA, PA	Y	38090 FQ	45470 MW	72540 TQ	USBLS	5/07
	Rhode Island	Y	41670 FQ	49720 MW	63950 TQ	USBLS	5/07
	Providence-Fall River-Warwick MSA, RI-MA	Y	40760 FQ	49350 MW	63890 TQ	USBLS	5/07
	South Carolina	Y	34640 FQ	46080 MW	60690 TQ	USBLS	5/07
	Charleston-North Charleston MSA, SC	Y	35190 FQ	48200 MW	63740 TQ	USBLS	5/07
	Columbia MSA, SC	Y	39880 FQ	54470 MW	73340 TQ	USBLS	5/07
	South Dakota	Y	27117 FQ	29991 MW	34444 TQ	SDBLS	7/08-9/08
	Sioux Falls MSA, SD	Y	27489 FQ	29905 MW	32967 TQ	SDBLS	7/08-9/08
	Tennessee	Y	27210 FQ	37100 MW	51020 TQ	USBLS	5/07
	Memphis MSA, TN-MS-AR	Y	29040 FQ	38630 MW	55130 TQ	USBLS	5/07
	Nashville-Davidson-Murfreesboro MSA, TN	Y	30180 FQ	39380 MW	51980 TQ	USBLS	5/07
	Texas	Y	26430 FQ	35240 MW	49110 TQ	USBLS	5/07
	Austin-Round Rock MSA, TX	Y	30840 FQ	42290 MW	57600 TQ	USBLS	5/07

AE	Average entry wage	AW	Average wage paid	FQ	First quartile wage
AER	Average entry range	AWR	Average wage range	H	Hourly
AEX	Average experienced wage	AXR	Average experienced range	HI	Highest wage paid
ATC	Average total compensation	D	Daily	HR	High end range

LO	Lowest wage paid	MTC	Median total compensation
LR	Low end range	MW	Median wage paid
M	Monthly	MWR	Median wage range
MCC	Median cash compensation	S	See annotated source

TCC	Total cash compensation
TQ	Third quartile wage
W	Weekly
Y	Yearly

Occupation/Type/Industry	Location	Per	Low	Mid	High	Source	Date
Property, Real Estate, and Community Association Manager	Dallas-Fort Worth-Arlington MSA, TX	Y	28240 FQ	37670 MW	51140 TQ	USBLS	5/07
	El Paso MSA, TX	Y	26020 FQ	30990 MW	37390 TQ	USBLS	5/07
	Houston-Sugar Land-Baytown MSA, TX	Y	24720 FQ	32280 MW	46350 TQ	USBLS	5/07
	San Antonio MSA, TX	Y	25630 FQ	34960 MW	47570 TQ	USBLS	5/07
	Utah	Y	36020 FQ	53770 MW	73600 TQ	USBLS	5/07
	Salt Lake City MSA, UT	Y	41680 FQ	64250 MW	80390 TQ	USBLS	5/07
	Vermont	Y	32150 FQ	39270 MW	56430 TQ	USBLS	5/07
	Burlington-South Burlington MSA, VT	Y	33040 FQ	37400 MW	50450 TQ	USBLS	5/07
	Virginia	Y	44490 FQ	70150 MW	98630 TQ	USBLS	5/07
	Richmond MSA, VA	Y	50290 FQ	70720 MW	102360 TQ	USBLS	5/07
	Virginia Beach-Norfolk-Newport News MSA, VA-NC	Y	46390 FQ	66870 MW	95800 TQ	USBLS	5/07
	Washington	H	21.89 FQ	27.14 MW	35.72 TQ	WABLS	3/08
	Seattle-Tacoma-Bellevue MSA, WA	Y	46880 FQ	57030 MW	74290 TQ	USBLS	5/07
	West Virginia	Y	28890 FQ	35856 MW	70008 TQ	WVBLS	7/08-9/08
	Charleston MSA, WV	Y	25770 FQ	28790 MW	62340 TQ	USBLS	5/07
	Wisconsin	Y	39120 FQ	52870 MW	85720 TQ	USBLS	5/07
	Milwaukee-Waukesha-West Allis MSA, WI	Y	38730 FQ	55930 MW	95310 TQ	USBLS	5/07
	Wyoming	Y	27269 FQ	36778 MW	54859 TQ	WYBLS	9/08
	Cheyenne MSA, WY	Y	21978 FQ	29242 MW	35970 TQ	WYBLS	9/08
	Puerto Rico	Y	23440 FQ	27930 MW	34740 TQ	USBLS	5/07
	San Juan-Caguas-Guaynabo MSA, PR	Y	23710 FQ	28190 MW	34770 TQ	USBLS	5/07
	Virgin Islands	Y	49040 FQ	58660 MW	77560 TQ	USBLS	5/07
	Guam	Y	21240 FQ	29770 MW	39580 TQ	USBLS	5/07
Property Analyst Department of Transportation	Michigan	H	17.43 LO		29.50 HI	MDOT	10/1/07
Property Appraiser	Bismarck, ND	M	2737 LO		4585 HI	NDLC01	2008
Property Inventory Controller State Highway Patrol	Missouri	S	1192 LO		1676 HI	MSHPSS	7/1/08
Property Manager	United States	Y		75000 MW		BOM	5/08-7/08
Prosecutor	Livingston County, MI	Y			131153 HI	LCPP	2009
Prosthodontist	Maryland	Y		196950 AW		MDBLS	3/08
Protection and Safety Worker State Government	Nebraska	Y	31579 LO		45735 HI	AFT02	3/1/08
Prothonotary	Luzerne County, PA	Y			36500 HI	CVOICE	2008
Psychiatric Aide	Alabama	Y	20440 FQ	22580 MW	24720 TQ	USBLS	5/07
	Birmingham-Hoover MSA, AL	Y	15540 FQ	23050 MW	27520 TQ	USBLS	5/07
	Alaska	Y	29730 FQ	34430 MW	40580 TQ	USBLS	5/07
	Arizona	Y	21110 FQ	23580 MW	27610 TQ	USBLS	5/07
	Phoenix-Mesa-Scottsdale MSA, AZ	Y	20920 FQ	22900 MW	25100 TQ	USBLS	5/07
	Arkansas	Y	17240 FQ	19000 MW	21990 TQ	USBLS	5/07
	Little Rock-North Little Rock MSA, AR	Y	17570 FQ	19040 MW	20940 TQ	USBLS	5/07
	California	H	10.31 FQ	12.97 MW	15.17 TQ	CABLS	1/08-3/08
	Los Angeles-Long Beach-Glendale PMSA, CA	H	10.63 FQ	12.79 MW	14.78 TQ	CABLS	1/08-3/08
	Oakland-Fremont-Hayward MSA, CA	H	9.86 FQ	11.49 MW	12.94 TQ	CABLS	1/08-3/08
	Riverside-San Bernardino-Ontario MSA, CA	H	8.97 FQ	11.05 MW	14.82 TQ	CABLS	1/08-3/08
	San Diego-Carlsbad-San Marcos MSA, CA	H	13.75 FQ	14.71 MW	15.68 TQ	CABLS	1/08-3/08
	San Francisco-San Mateo-Redwood PMSA, CA	H	14.92 FQ	21.29 MW	23.59 TQ	CABLS	1/08-3/08

AE	Average entry wage	AW	Average wage paid	FQ	First quartile wage	LO	Lowest wage paid	MTC	Median total compensation	TCC	Total cash compensation
AER	Average entry range	AWR	Average wage range	H	Hourly	LR	Low end range	MW	Median wage paid	TQ	Third quartile wage
AEX	Average experienced wage	AXR	Average experienced range	HI	Highest wage paid	M	Monthly	MWR	Median wage range	W	Weekly
ATC	Average total compensation	D	Daily	HR	High end range	MCC	Median cash compensation	S	See annotated source	Y	Yearly

Psychiatric Aide

Occupation/Type/Industry	Location	Per	Low	Mid	High	Source	Date
Psychiatric Aide	Santa Ana-Anaheim-Irvine						
	PMSA, CA	Y	22800 FQ	24960 MW	27870 TQ	USBLS	5/07
	Colorado	Y	21320 FQ	24280 MW	28540 TQ	USBLS	5/07
	Denver-Aurora MSA, CO	Y	20320 FQ	22570 MW	26790 TQ	USBLS	5/07
	Connecticut	H	9.88 AE	11.74 MW		CTBLS	1/08-3/08
	Hartford-West Hartford-East						
	Hartford MSA, CT	Y	27250 FQ	30130 MW	34990 TQ	USBLS	5/07
	District of Columbia	Y	26220 FQ	34810 MW	43050 TQ	USBLS	5/07
	Washington-Arlington-						
	Alexandria MSA, DC-VA-						
	MD-WV	Y	25430 FQ	33110 MW	42130 TQ	USBLS	5/07
	Florida	Y	20700 FQ	23310 MW	26950 TQ	USBLS	5/07
	Miami-Fort Lauderdale-Miami						
	Beach MSA, FL	Y	20630 FQ	23240 MW	27150 TQ	USBLS	5/07
	Tampa-St. Petersburg-						
	Clearwater MSA, FL	Y	18100 FQ	20650 MW	24310 TQ	USBLS	5/07
	West Palm Beach-Boca Raton-						
	Boynton Beach PMSA, FL	Y	21190 FQ	23180 MW	25910 TQ	USBLS	5/07
	Georgia	Y	20260 FQ	23290 MW	29790 TQ	USBLS	5/07
	Hawaii	Y	26720 FQ	31050 MW	34540 TQ	USBLS	5/07
	Honolulu MSA, HI	Y	30280 FQ	32750 MW	35480 TQ	USBLS	5/07
	Idaho	Y	19940 FQ	23320 MW	29160 TQ	USBLS	5/07
	Illinois	Y	20460 FQ	24620 MW	30870 TQ	USBLS	5/07
	Chicago-Naperville-Joliet						
	MSA, IL-IN-WI	Y	22080 FQ	25370 MW	30020 TQ	USBLS	5/07
	Indiana	Y	20890 FQ	23260 MW	27940 TQ	USBLS	5/07
	Iowa	Y	23840 FQ	27800 MW	33050 TQ	USBLS	5/07
	Kansas	Y	20430 FQ	22250 MW	24120 TQ	USBLS	5/07
	Kentucky	Y	22244 FQ	25536 MW	30332 TQ	KYBLS	2008
	Louisville-Jefferson County						
	MSA, KY-IN	Y	22140 FQ	24950 MW	28820 TQ	USBLS	5/07
	Louisiana	H	7.19 FQ	8.66 MW	11.02 TQ	LABLS	1/08-3/08
	Baton Rouge MSA, LA	Y	17920 FQ	20590 MW	27410 TQ	USBLS	5/07
	Lake Charles MSA, LA	Y	17010 FQ	19260 MW	23340 TQ	USBLS	5/07
	New Orleans-Metairie-Kenner						
	MSA, LA	Y	15330 FQ	18480 MW	24490 TQ	USBLS	5/07
	Maine	Y	26260 FQ	29060 MW	31860 TQ	USBLS	5/07
	Maryland	Y		27300 MW		MDBLS	3/08
	Massachusetts	Y	26690 FQ	29250 MW	31840 TQ	USBLS	5/07
	Boston-Cambridge-Quincy						
	NECTA, MA	Y	26130 FQ	29240 MW	32370 TQ	USBLS	5/07
	Michigan	Y	26090 FQ	34580 MW	38980 TQ	USBLS	5/07
	Detroit-Warren-Livonia MSA,						
	MI	Y	27300 FQ	34260 MW	37530 TQ	USBLS	5/07
	Warren-Troy-Farmington Hills						
	PMSA, MI	Y	22250 FQ	24510 MW	28800 TQ	USBLS	5/07
	Minnesota	Y	28502 FQ	35173 MW	39219 TQ	MNBLS	10/08-12/08
	Minneapolis-Saint Paul MSA,						
	MN-WI	Y	28962 FQ	35466 MW	39387 TQ	MNBLS	10/08-12/08
	Mississippi	Y	16770 FQ	18140 MW	19540 TQ	USBLS	5/07
	Jackson MSA, MS	Y	16860 FQ	18240 MW	19650 TQ	USBLS	5/07
	Missouri	Y	14940 FQ	18070 MW	23850 TQ	USBLS	5/07
	Kansas City MSA, MO-KS	Y	16970 FQ	22160 MW	26780 TQ	USBLS	5/07
	St. Louis MSA, MO-IL	Y	19690 FQ	22940 MW	28540 TQ	USBLS	5/07
	Montana	Y	21370 FQ	24580 MW	29500 TQ	USBLS	5/07
	Nevada	H	14.01 FQ	15.72 MW	20.95 TQ	NVBLS	5/08
	New Hampshire	H	11.56 AE	13.77 MW	14.84 AEX	NHBLS	6/08
	New Jersey	Y	25570 FQ	30080 MW	38920 TQ	USBLS	5/07
	Camden PMSA, NJ	Y	25040 FQ	28490 MW	35690 TQ	USBLS	5/07
	Edison PMSA, NJ	Y	23990 FQ	28440 MW	33900 TQ	USBLS	5/07
	Newark-Union PMSA, NJ-PA	Y	27280 FQ	32390 MW	40040 TQ	USBLS	5/07
	New Mexico	Y	19150 FQ	23140 MW	29350 TQ	USBLS	5/07
	Albuquerque MSA, NM	Y	20440 FQ	25020 MW	32430 TQ	USBLS	5/07
	New York	Y	28670 FQ	33030 MW	36630 TQ	USBLS	5/07
	Albany-Schenectady-Troy						
	MSA, NY	Y	22980 FQ	25870 MW	32180 TQ	USBLS	5/07
	New York-Northern New						
	Jersey-Long Island MSA, NY-						
	NJ-PA	Y	28230 FQ	32600 MW	36710 TQ	USBLS	5/07
	North Carolina	Y	20770 FQ	24000 MW	28530 TQ	USBLS	5/07
	North Dakota	Y	20400 FQ	22810 MW	26620 TQ	USBLS	5/07
	Ohio	Y	20980 FQ	24710 MW	29240 TQ	USBLS	5/07

AE	Average entry wage	AW	Average wage paid	FQ	First quartile wage
AER	Average entry range	AWR	Average wage range	H	Hourly
AEX	Average experienced wage	AXR	Average experienced range	HI	Highest wage paid
ATC	Average total compensation	D	Daily	HR	High end range

LO	Lowest wage paid	MTC	Median total compensation	TCC	Total cash compensation
LR	Low end range	MW	Median wage paid	TQ	Third quartile wage
M	Monthly	MWR	Median wage range	W	Weekly
MCC	Median cash compensation	S	See annotated source	Y	Yearly

Occupation/Type/Industry	Location	Per	Low	Mid	High	Source	Date
Psychiatric Aide	Cincinnati-Middletown MSA, OH-KY-IN	Y	22750 FQ	25480 MW	33220 TQ	USBLS	5/07
	Columbus MSA, OH	Y	23870 FQ	27110 MW	29960 TQ	USBLS	5/07
	Dayton MSA, OH	Y	26450 FQ	29510 MW	35300 TQ	USBLS	5/07
	Oklahoma	Y	18880 FQ	21030 MW	23340 TQ	USBLS	5/07
	Oklahoma City MSA, OK	Y	17990 FQ	20820 MW	23160 TQ	USBLS	5/07
	Tulsa MSA, OK	Y	19060 FQ	20440 MW	22460 TQ	USBLS	5/07
	Oregon	H	10.14 FQ	12.25 MW	15.07 TQ	ORBLS	5/08
	Portland-Vancouver-Beaverton MSA, OR-WA	Y	20770 FQ	22950 MW	26350 TQ	USBLS	5/07
	Salem MSA, OR	Y	26840 FQ	29410 MW	32580 TQ	USBLS	5/07
	Pennsylvania	Y	22380 FQ	26550 MW	32380 TQ	USBLS	5/07
	Allentown-Bethlehem-Easton MSA, PA-NJ	Y	25000 FQ	28590 MW	31510 TQ	USBLS	5/07
	Philadelphia-Camden-Wilmington MSA, PA-NJ-DE-MD	Y	23590 FQ	27710 MW	35380 TQ	USBLS	5/07
	Pittsburgh MSA, PA	Y	23550 FQ	27920 MW	34970 TQ	USBLS	5/07
	Providence-Fall River-Warwick MSA, RI-MA	Y	23360 FQ	26090 MW	29980 TQ	USBLS	5/07
	South Carolina	Y	17240 FQ	18920 MW	21650 TQ	USBLS	5/07
	South Dakota	Y	20112 FQ	23217 MW	26174 TQ	SDBLS	7/08-9/08
	Tennessee	Y	16250 FQ	18470 MW	21700 TQ	USBLS	5/07
	Memphis MSA, TN-MS-AR	Y	14280 FQ	16850 MW	18960 TQ	USBLS	5/07
	Texas	Y	18480 FQ	21650 MW	25960 TQ	USBLS	5/07
	Dallas-Fort Worth-Arlington MSA, TX	Y	19340 FQ	21560 MW	24030 TQ	USBLS	5/07
	Houston-Sugar Land-Baytown MSA, TX	Y	22830 FQ	26990 MW	30280 TQ	USBLS	5/07
	Virginia	Y	16930 FQ	19380 MW	22670 TQ	USBLS	5/07
	Virginia Beach-Norfolk-Newport News MSA, VA-NC	Y	20140 FQ	23270 MW	27160 TQ	USBLS	5/07
	Washington	H	13.73 FQ	16.20 MW	18.40 TQ	WABLS	3/08
	West Virginia	Y	15368 FQ	17560 MW	20221 TQ	WVBLS	7/08-9/08
	Charleston MSA, WV	Y	14910 FQ	16540 MW	19250 TQ	USBLS	5/07
	Wisconsin	Y	18970 FQ	20950 MW	23020 TQ	USBLS	5/07
	Puerto Rico	Y	14140 FQ	16780 MW	18770 TQ	USBLS	5/07
	San Juan-Caguas-Guaynabo MSA, PR	Y	14140 FQ	16780 MW	18770 TQ	USBLS	5/07
Psychiatric Social Worker							
Department of Corrections	New Hampshire	Y		26107 AW		NHUL03	2008
New Hampshire Hospital	New Hampshire	Y		40251 AW		NHUL03	2008
Psychiatric Technician	Alabama	Y	17900 FQ	22020 MW	28840 TQ	USBLS	5/07
	Birmingham-Hoover MSA, AL	Y	23800 FQ	31750 MW	40830 TQ	USBLS	5/07
	Arizona	Y	26010 FQ	30640 MW	34540 TQ	USBLS	5/07
	Phoenix-Mesa-Scottsdale MSA, AZ	Y	26620 FQ	31100 MW	34540 TQ	USBLS	5/07
	Tucson MSA, AZ	Y	26080 FQ	29500 MW	34480 TQ	USBLS	5/07
	Arkansas	Y	18700 FQ	22290 MW	27920 TQ	USBLS	5/07
	Little Rock-North Little Rock MSA, AR	Y	19770 FQ	22320 MW	26550 TQ	USBLS	5/07
	California	H	17.13 FQ	20.60 MW	23.62 TQ	CABLS	1/08-3/08
	Los Angeles-Long Beach-Glendale PMSA, CA	H	17.64 FQ	20.88 MW	23.57 TQ	CABLS	1/08-3/08
	Oakland-Fremont-Hayward MSA, CA	H	16.98 FQ	22.38 MW	28.09 TQ	CABLS	1/08-3/08
	Riverside-San Bernardino-Ontario MSA, CA	H	17.57 FQ	20.49 MW	23.19 TQ	CABLS	1/08-3/08
	Sacramento-Arden Arcade-Roseville MSA, CA	H	18.33 FQ	25.57 MW	29.54 TQ	CABLS	1/08-3/08
	San Diego-Carlsbad-San Marcos MSA, CA	H	14.40 FQ	18.42 MW	22.02 TQ	CABLS	1/08-3/08
	San Jose-Sunnyvale-Santa Clara MSA, CA	H	21.21 FQ	23.68 MW	26.30 TQ	CABLS	1/08-3/08
	Santa Ana-Anaheim-Irvine PMSA, CA	Y	37720 FQ	43830 MW	48820 TQ	USBLS	5/07
	Colorado	Y	24200 FQ	29760 MW	37040 TQ	USBLS	5/07
	Denver-Aurora MSA, CO	Y	27330 FQ	30950 MW	35900 TQ	USBLS	5/07
	Connecticut	H	17.19 AE	22.65 MW		CTBLS	1/08-3/08
	Delaware	Y	28230 FQ	31220 MW	35540 TQ	USBLS	5/07

AE	Average entry wage	AW	Average wage paid	FQ	First quartile wage
AER	Average entry range	AWR	Average wage range	H	Hourly
AEX	Average experienced wage	AXR	Average experienced range	HI	Highest wage paid
ATC	Average total compensation	D	Daily	HR	High end range

LO	Lowest wage paid	MTC	Median total compensation
LR	Low end range	MW	Median wage paid
M	Monthly	MWR	Median wage range
MCC	Median cash compensation	S	See annotated source

TCC	Total cash compensation
TQ	Third quartile wage
W	Weekly
Y	Yearly

Psychiatric Technician

Occupation/Type/Industry	Location	Per	Low	Mid	High	Source	Date
Psychiatric Technician	Wilmington PMSA, DE-MD-NJ	Y	28930 FQ	31820 MW	36190 TQ	USBLS	5/07
	District of Columbia	Y	28410 FQ	39280 MW	45520 TQ	USBLS	5/07
	Washington-Arlington-Alexandria MSA, DC-VA-MD-WV	Y	26720 FQ	33140 MW	42150 TQ	USBLS	5/07
	Florida	Y	20550 FQ	23750 MW	28550 TQ	USBLS	5/07
	Fort Lauderdale-Pompano Beach-Deerfield Beach PMSA, FL	Y	21960 FQ	24150 MW	27260 TQ	USBLS	5/07
	Jacksonville MSA, FL	Y	20110 FQ	22760 MW	27620 TQ	USBLS	5/07
	Miami-Fort Lauderdale-Miami Beach MSA, FL	Y	21690 FQ	24810 MW	29690 TQ	USBLS	5/07
	Orlando-Kissimmee MSA, FL	Y	18650 FQ	21260 MW	24990 TQ	USBLS	5/07
	Sarasota-Bradenton-Venice MSA, FL	Y	21280 FQ	24990 MW	28570 TQ	USBLS	5/07
	Tampa-St. Petersburg-Clearwater MSA, FL	Y	19860 FQ	22310 MW	25020 TQ	USBLS	5/07
	West Palm Beach-Boca Raton-Boynton Beach PMSA, FL	Y	20700 FQ	22970 MW	26830 TQ	USBLS	5/07
	Georgia	Y	21490 FQ	25170 MW	29930 TQ	USBLS	5/07
	Atlanta-Sandy Springs-Marietta MSA, GA	Y	19250 FQ	21670 MW	24360 TQ	USBLS	5/07
	Augusta-Richmond County MSA, GA-SC	Y	21730 FQ	24230 MW	27260 TQ	USBLS	5/07
	Idaho	Y	23220 FQ	29030 MW	34130 TQ	USBLS	5/07
	Boise City-Nampa MSA, ID	Y	22530 FQ	28030 MW	32160 TQ	USBLS	5/07
	Illinois	Y	28210 FQ	32690 MW	37160 TQ	USBLS	5/07
	Chicago-Naperville-Joliet MSA, IL-IN-WI	Y	29040 FQ	33860 MW	38050 TQ	USBLS	5/07
	Indiana	Y	22430 FQ	25620 MW	30430 TQ	USBLS	5/07
	Indianapolis-Carmel MSA, IN	Y	23670 FQ	28230 MW	38460 TQ	USBLS	5/07
	Iowa	Y	20410 FQ	24770 MW	28740 TQ	USBLS	5/07
	Kansas	Y	23470 FQ	27600 MW	30730 TQ	USBLS	5/07
	Wichita MSA, KS	Y	21510 FQ	23300 MW	26050 TQ	USBLS	5/07
	Kentucky	Y	21279 FQ	23568 MW	27105 TQ	KYBLS	2008
	Louisville-Jefferson County MSA, KY-IN	Y	21660 FQ	23980 MW	27690 TQ	USBLS	5/07
	Louisiana	H	8.10 FQ	10.26 MW	12.78 TQ	LABLS	1/08-3/08
	New Orleans-Metairie-Kenner MSA, LA	Y	16820 FQ	22300 MW	27590 TQ	USBLS	5/07
	Maine	Y	21760 FQ	25130 MW	29130 TQ	USBLS	5/07
	Maryland	Y		32225 MW		MDBLS	3/08
	Baltimore-Towson MSA, MD	Y	29500 FQ	33130 MW	37020 TQ	USBLS	5/07
	Massachusetts	Y	28620 FQ	34340 MW	39750 TQ	USBLS	5/07
	Boston-Cambridge-Quincy NECTA, MA	Y	33760 FQ	37030 MW	41400 TQ	USBLS	5/07
	Michigan	Y	25720 FQ	30900 MW	37240 TQ	USBLS	5/07
	Detroit-Warren-Livonia MSA, MI	Y	26060 FQ	31900 MW	36390 TQ	USBLS	5/07
	Warren-Troy-Farmington Hills PMSA, MI	Y	22930 FQ	29940 MW	35360 TQ	USBLS	5/07
	Minnesota	Y	30706 FQ	33688 MW	38229 TQ	MNBLS	10/08-12/08
	Mississippi	Y	19850 FQ	23240 MW	27040 TQ	USBLS	5/07
	Jackson MSA, MS	Y	23150 FQ	27040 MW	30300 TQ	USBLS	5/07
	Missouri	Y	18430 FQ	21260 MW	24740 TQ	USBLS	5/07
	Kansas City MSA, MO-KS	Y	20280 FQ	23510 MW	27290 TQ	USBLS	5/07
	St. Louis MSA, MO-IL	Y	18290 FQ	20900 MW	24660 TQ	USBLS	5/07
	Montana	Y	20990 FQ	23010 MW	27370 TQ	USBLS	5/07
	Nebraska	Y	22210 FQ	24910 MW	28790 TQ	USBLS	5/07
	Nevada	H	11.24 FQ	13.21 MW	15.36 TQ	NVBLS	5/08
	Las Vegas-Paradise MSA, NV	H	11.24 FQ	13.21 MW	15.36 TQ	NVBLS	5/08
	New Hampshire	H	10.62 AE	15.73 MW	17.82 AEX	NHBLS	6/08
	New Jersey	Y	34050 FQ	43420 MW	50010 TQ	USBLS	5/07
	Camden PMSA, NJ	Y	31670 FQ	43330 MW	50940 TQ	USBLS	5/07
	Edison PMSA, NJ	Y	35610 FQ	40820 MW	49190 TQ	USBLS	5/07
	Newark-Union PMSA, NJ-PA	Y	40260 FQ	44960 MW	50470 TQ	USBLS	5/07
	New Mexico	Y	21900 FQ	26020 MW	29650 TQ	USBLS	5/07
	Albuquerque MSA, NM	Y	25570 FQ	28360 MW	31420 TQ	USBLS	5/07
	New York	Y	28430 FQ	34600 MW	40870 TQ	USBLS	5/07
	Albany-Schenectady-Troy MSA, NY	Y	21000 FQ	25090 MW	31440 TQ	USBLS	5/07

AE	Average entry wage	AW	Average wage paid	FQ	First quartile wage	LO	Lowest wage paid	MTC	Median total compensation	TCC	Total cash compensation
AER	Average entry range	AWR	Average wage range	H	Hourly	LR	Low end range	MW	Median wage paid	TQ	Third quartile wage
AEX	Average experienced wage	AXR	Average experienced range	HI	Highest wage paid	M	Monthly	MWR	Median wage range	W	Weekly
ATC	Average total compensation	D	Daily	HR	High end range	MCC	Median cash compensation	S	See annotated source	Y	Yearly

Occupation/Type/Industry	Location	Per	Low	Mid	High	Source	Date
Psychiatric Technician	Nassau-Suffolk PMSA, NY	Y	32760 FQ	35640 MW	38500 TQ	USBLS	5/07
	New York-Northern New Jersey-Long Island MSA, NY-NJ-PA	Y	33510 FQ	39830 MW	46430 TQ	USBLS	5/07
	North Carolina	Y	20960 FQ	24720 MW	29720 TQ	USBLS	5/07
	North Dakota	Y	19690 FQ	23020 MW	26230 TQ	USBLS	5/07
	Ohio	Y	25590 FQ	32690 MW	37750 TQ	USBLS	5/07
	Cincinnati-Middletown MSA, OH-KY-IN	Y	24620 FQ	29630 MW	34790 TQ	USBLS	5/07
	Cleveland-Elyria-Mentor MSA, OH	Y	27870 FQ	34770 MW	42870 TQ	USBLS	5/07
	Columbus MSA, OH	Y	27550 FQ	33480 MW	37630 TQ	USBLS	5/07
	Oklahoma	Y	19360 FQ	22520 MW	25680 TQ	USBLS	5/07
	Oklahoma City MSA, OK	Y	20380 FQ	23160 MW	25800 TQ	USBLS	5/07
	Tulsa MSA, OK	Y	20130 FQ	22910 MW	25650 TQ	USBLS	5/07
	Oregon	H	15.23 FQ	18.42 MW	21.02 TQ	ORBLS	5/08
	Portland-Vancouver-Beaverton MSA, OR-WA	Y	22520 FQ	28370 MW	38650 TQ	USBLS	5/07
	Pennsylvania	Y	25490 FQ	29430 MW	35490 TQ	USBLS	5/07
	Allentown-Bethlehem-Easton MSA, PA-NJ	Y	32840 FQ	41660 MW	47060 TQ	USBLS	5/07
	Philadelphia-Camden-Wilmington MSA, PA-NJ-DE-MD	Y	28240 FQ	32300 MW	40050 TQ	USBLS	5/07
	Pittsburgh MSA, PA	Y	27780 FQ	30860 MW	34050 TQ	USBLS	5/07
	Rhode Island	Y	31460 FQ	35990 MW	41810 TQ	USBLS	5/07
	Providence-Fall River-Warwick MSA, RI-MA	Y	31480 FQ	36030 MW	41940 TQ	USBLS	5/07
	South Carolina	Y	20510 FQ	22590 MW	25460 TQ	USBLS	5/07
	Tennessee	Y	20790 FQ	23060 MW	27670 TQ	USBLS	5/07
	Memphis MSA, TN-MS-AR	Y	20420 FQ	22510 MW	25040 TQ	USBLS	5/07
	Texas	Y	21190 FQ	25270 MW	30480 TQ	USBLS	5/07
	Dallas-Fort Worth-Arlington MSA, TX	Y	23560 FQ	27330 MW	30890 TQ	USBLS	5/07
	Houston-Sugar Land-Baytown MSA, TX	Y	20570 FQ	24310 MW	29920 TQ	USBLS	5/07
	Vermont	Y	27970 FQ	31350 MW	37700 TQ	USBLS	5/07
	Virginia	Y	22050 FQ	25040 MW	30670 TQ	USBLS	5/07
	Richmond MSA, VA	Y	21960 FQ	24070 MW	28600 TQ	USBLS	5/07
	Virginia Beach-Norfolk-Newport News MSA, VA-NC	Y	22280 FQ	25700 MW	29870 TQ	USBLS	5/07
	Washington	H	12.95 FQ	16.27 MW	18.67 TQ	WABLS	3/08
	Wisconsin	Y	25090 FQ	29600 MW	35940 TQ	USBLS	5/07
	Milwaukee-Waukesha-West Allis MSA, WI	Y	26050 FQ	28800 MW	33300 TQ	USBLS	5/07
	Wyoming	Y	24905 FQ	28689 MW	33403 TQ	WYBLS	9/08
	Puerto Rico	Y	13730 FQ	16450 MW	25240 TQ	USBLS	5/07
	San Juan-Caguas-Guaynabo MSA, PR	Y	15460 FQ	19490 MW	34710 TQ	USBLS	5/07
Psychiatrist	Arizona	Y	137240 FQ			USBLS	5/07
	Phoenix-Mesa-Scottsdale MSA, AZ	Y	142260 FQ			USBLS	5/07
	Tucson MSA, AZ	Y	133170 FQ			USBLS	5/07
	Arkansas	Y	123570 FQ			USBLS	5/07
	California	H	46.04 FQ			CABLS	1/08-3/08
	Los Angeles-Long Beach-Glendale PMSA, CA	H	44.31 FQ	68.06 MW		CABLS	1/08-3/08
	Sacramento-Arden Arcade-Roseville MSA, CA	H	46.43 FQ			CABLS	1/08-3/08
	San Diego-Carlsbad-San Marcos MSA, CA	H	26.45 FQ	46.23 MW		CABLS	1/08-3/08
	San Francisco-San Mateo-Redwood PMSA, CA	H	50.38 FQ			CABLS	1/08-3/08
	Connecticut	H	48.15 AE	80.01 AW		CTBLS	1/08-3/08
	Hartford-West Hartford-East Hartford MSA, CT	Y	116980 FQ			USBLS	5/07
	Delaware	Y	118220 FQ			USBLS	5/07
	Wilmington PMSA, DE-MD-NJ	Y	114650 FQ			USBLS	5/07
	District of Columbia	Y	74600 FQ	139570 MW		USBLS	5/07

Occupation/Type/Industry	Location	Per	Low	Mid	High	Source	Date
Psychiatrist	Washington-Arlington-Alexandria MSA, DC-VA-MD-WV	Y	70060 FQ	141820 MW		USBLS	5/07
	Florida	Y	116410 FQ	145030 MW		USBLS	5/07
	Fort Lauderdale-Pompano Beach-Deerfield Beach PMSA, FL	Y	125630 FQ			USBLS	5/07
	Miami-Fort Lauderdale-Miami Beach MSA, FL	Y	116470 FQ	141190 MW		USBLS	5/07
	Tampa-St. Petersburg-Clearwater MSA, FL	Y	135370 FQ			USBLS	5/07
	West Palm Beach-Boca Raton-Boynton Beach PMSA, FL	Y	70060 FQ	115700 MW	127950 TQ	USBLS	5/07
	Georgia	Y	105630 FQ	128810 MW		USBLS	5/07
	Atlanta-Sandy Springs-Marietta MSA, GA	Y	110330 FQ	130570 MW		USBLS	5/07
	Hawaii	Y	114330 FQ	145480 MW		USBLS	5/07
	Honolulu MSA, HI	Y	133130 FQ			USBLS	5/07
	Illinois	Y	56850 FQ	66460 MW	137540 TQ	USBLS	5/07
	Chicago-Naperville-Joliet MSA, IL-IN-WI	Y	57370 FQ	87600 MW		USBLS	5/07
	Indiana	Y	121560 FQ			USBLS	5/07
	Louisville-Jefferson County MSA, KY-IN	Y	143350 FQ			USBLS	5/07
	Louisiana	Y		106396 AW		LABLS	1/08-3/08
	New Orleans-Metairie-Kenner MSA, LA	Y	31510 FQ	37940 MW		USBLS	5/07
	Maine	Y	122890 FQ			USBLS	5/07
	Bangor MSA, ME	Y	141370 FQ			USBLS	5/07
	Portland-South Portland-Biddeford MSA, ME	Y	139820 FQ			USBLS	5/07
	Maryland	Y		140050 MW		MDBLS	3/08
	Baltimore-Towson MSA, MD	Y	79440 FQ	136940 MW		USBLS	5/07
	Massachusetts	Y	137990 FQ			USBLS	5/07
	Boston-Cambridge-Quincy NECTA, MA	Y	136080 FQ			USBLS	5/07
	Michigan	Y	138650 FQ			USBLS	5/07
	Detroit-Warren-Livonia MSA, MI	Y	141120 FQ			USBLS	5/07
	Grand Rapids-Wyoming MSA, MI	Y	95190 FQ			USBLS	5/07
	Warren-Troy-Farmington Hills PMSA, MI	Y	141860 FQ			USBLS	5/07
	Minnesota	Y	111998 FQ	166444 AW		MNBLS	10/08-12/08
	Duluth-Superior MSA, MN-WI	Y		178862 AW		MNBLS	10/08-12/08
	Minneapolis-Saint Paul MSA, MN-WI	Y	104015 FQ	152278 MW		MNBLS	10/08-12/08
	Mississippi	Y	97110 FQ	142060 MW		USBLS	5/07
	Jackson MSA, MS	Y	134610 FQ			USBLS	5/07
	Missouri	Y	111910 FQ	142050 MW		USBLS	5/07
	Kansas City MSA, MO-KS	Y	131500 FQ			USBLS	5/07
	St. Louis MSA, MO-IL	Y	99070 FQ	144660 MW		USBLS	5/07
	Montana	Y	142010 FQ			USBLS	5/07
	Nebraska	Y	60820 FQ	99200 MW		USBLS	5/07
	Omaha-Council Bluffs MSA, NE-IA	Y	57180 FQ	73040 MW	143960 TQ	USBLS	5/07
	Nevada	H		76.75 AW		NVBLS	5/08
	Las Vegas-Paradise MSA, NV	H		77.56 AW		NVBLS	5/08
	New Hampshire	H	31.87 AE	65.02 MW	72.49 AEX	NHBLS	6/08
	Newark-Union PMSA, NJ-PA	Y	144130 FQ			USBLS	5/07
	New Mexico	Y	137620 FQ			USBLS	5/07
	New York	Y	107530 FQ	140090 MW		USBLS	5/07
	Albany-Schenectady-Troy MSA, NY	Y	142490 FQ			USBLS	5/07
	Buffalo-Niagara Falls MSA, NY	Y	132180 FQ	143990 MW		USBLS	5/07
	Nassau-Suffolk PMSA, NY	Y	140300 FQ			USBLS	5/07
	New York-Northern New Jersey-Long Island MSA, NY-NJ-PA	Y	105080 FQ	143460 MW		USBLS	5/07
	North Carolina	Y	131790 FQ			USBLS	5/07

AE	Average entry wage	AW	Average wage paid	FQ	First quartile wage	LO	Lowest wage paid	MTC	Median total compensation	TCC	Total cash compensation
AER	Average entry range	AWR	Average wage range	H	Hourly	LR	Low end range	MW	Median wage paid	TQ	Third quartile wage
AEX	Average experienced wage	AXR	Average experienced range	HI	Highest wage paid	M	Monthly	MWR	Median wage range	W	Weekly
ATC	Average total compensation	D	Daily	HR	High end range	MCC	Median cash compensation	S	See annotated source	Y	Yearly

Occupation/Type/Industry	Location	Per	Low	Mid	High	Source	Date
Psychiatrist	Charlotte-Gastonia-Concord MSA, NC-SC	Y	140300 FQ			USBLS	5/07
	Winston-Salem MSA, NC	Y	104250 FQ	112100 MW	120230 TQ	USBLS	5/07
	North Dakota	Y	118860 FQ			USBLS	5/07
	Ohio	Y	134770 FQ			USBLS	5/07
	Cincinnati-Middletown MSA, OH-KY-IN	Y	91310 FQ	133840 MW		USBLS	5/07
	Cleveland-Elyria-Mentor MSA, OH	Y	128940 FQ			USBLS	5/07
	Columbus MSA, OH	Y	133740 FQ			USBLS	5/07
	Dayton MSA, OH	Y	142730 FQ			USBLS	5/07
	Oklahoma	Y	138970 FQ			USBLS	5/07
	Oklahoma City MSA, OK	Y	131280 FQ			USBLS	5/07
	Portland-Vancouver-Beaverton MSA, OR-WA	Y	136730 FQ			USBLS	5/07
	Pennsylvania	Y	58430 FQ	130530 MW		USBLS	5/07
	Allentown-Bethlehem-Easton MSA, PA-NJ	Y	54580 FQ	99590 MW		USBLS	5/07
	Philadelphia-Camden-Wilmington MSA, PA-NJ-DE-MD	Y	67400 FQ			USBLS	5/07
	Pittsburgh MSA, PA	Y	91160 FQ	143840 MW		USBLS	5/07
	Rhode Island	Y	134400 FQ			USBLS	5/07
	Providence-Fall River-Warwick MSA, RI-MA	Y	139930 FQ			USBLS	5/07
	South Carolina	Y	82260 FQ	140190 MW		USBLS	5/07
	Columbia MSA, SC	Y	71610 FQ	127210 MW		USBLS	5/07
	South Dakota	Y	149121 FQ			SDBLS	7/08-9/08
	Tennessee	Y	131520 FQ			USBLS	5/07
	Memphis MSA, TN-MS-AR	Y	101810 FQ	134640 MW		USBLS	5/07
	Nashville-Davidson-Murfreesboro MSA, TN	Y	129500 FQ			USBLS	5/07
	Texas	Y	65790 FQ	126420 MW		USBLS	5/07
	Austin-Round Rock MSA, TX	Y	61500 FQ	114400 MW	130150 TQ	USBLS	5/07
	Dallas-Fort Worth-Arlington MSA, TX	Y	100120 FQ	142570 MW		USBLS	5/07
	Houston-Sugar Land-Baytown MSA, TX	Y	43400 FQ	55050 MW	144470 TQ	USBLS	5/07
	San Antonio MSA, TX	Y	140960 FQ			USBLS	5/07
	Utah	Y	112250 FQ	138200 MW		USBLS	5/07
	Salt Lake City MSA, UT	Y	116890 FQ	138030 MW		USBLS	5/07
	Vermont	Y	88620 FQ	134920 MW		USBLS	5/07
	Burlington-South Burlington MSA, VT	Y	47420 FQ	86220 MW	121550 TQ	USBLS	5/07
	Virginia	Y	134300 FQ			USBLS	5/07
	Richmond MSA, VA	Y	140230 FQ			USBLS	5/07
	Virginia Beach-Norfolk-Newport News MSA, VA-NC	Y	81780 FQ			USBLS	5/07
	Washington	H	50.95 FQ	70.60 MW		WABLS	3/08
	Seattle-Tacoma-Bellevue MSA, WA	Y	133640 FQ			USBLS	5/07
	West Virginia	Y	85320 FQ	147575 AW		WVBLS	7/08-9/08
	Wisconsin	Y	73790 FQ			USBLS	5/07
	Puerto Rico	Y	77050 FQ	115640 MW	135210 TQ	USBLS	5/07
	San Juan-Caguas-Guaynabo MSA, PR	Y	110500 FQ	125400 MW	138300 TQ	USBLS	5/07
Health and Human Services	Nebraska	Y			179999-212591 HR	NEST	2008
Psychologist							
Health Service Administration	United States	Y		85000 MW		APACWS	2007
Research Administration	United States	Y		110000 MW		APACWS	2007
Psychology Teacher							
Postsecondary	Alabama	Y	44840 FQ	57340 MW	75160 TQ	USBLS	5/07
Postsecondary	Birmingham-Hoover MSA, AL	Y	50510 FQ	61830 MW	81330 TQ	USBLS	5/07
Postsecondary	Alaska	Y	62150 FQ	76720 MW	94620 TQ	USBLS	5/07
Postsecondary	Anchorage MSA, AK	Y	60290 FQ	79720 MW	98690 TQ	USBLS	5/07
Postsecondary	Arizona	Y	37500 FQ	48650 MW	57750 TQ	USBLS	5/07
Postsecondary	Phoenix-Mesa-Scottsdale MSA, AZ	Y	35170 FQ	46040 MW	54250 TQ	USBLS	5/07
Postsecondary	Arkansas	Y	37400 FQ	50330 MW	60130 TQ	USBLS	5/07

AE	Average entry wage	AW	Average wage paid	FQ	First quartile wage	LO	Lowest wage paid	MTC	Median total compensation	TCC	Total cash compensation
AER	Average entry range	AWR	Average wage range	H	Hourly	LR	Low end range	MW	Median wage paid	TQ	Third quartile wage
AEX	Average experienced wage	AXR	Average experienced range	HI	Highest wage paid	M	Monthly	MWR	Median wage range	W	Weekly
ATC	Average total compensation	D	Daily	HR	High end range	MCC	Median cash compensation	S	See annotated source	Y	Yearly

Psychology Teacher

Occupation/Type/Industry	Location	Per	Low	Mid	High	Source	Date
Psychology Teacher							
Postsecondary	California	Y		80643 AW		CABLS	1/08-3/08
Postsecondary	Fresno MSA, CA	Y		61569 AW		CABLS	1/08-3/08
Postsecondary	Los Angeles-Long Beach-Glendale PMSA, CA	Y		74788 AW		CABLS	1/08-3/08
Postsecondary	Oakland-Fremont-Hayward MSA, CA	Y		78613 AW		CABLS	1/08-3/08
Postsecondary	Riverside-San Bernardino-Ontario MSA, CA	Y		78787 AW		CABLS	1/08-3/08
Postsecondary	Sacramento-Arden Arcade-Roseville MSA, CA	Y		95769 AW		CABLS	1/08-3/08
Postsecondary	San Diego-Carlsbad-San Marcos MSA, CA	Y		90970 AW		CABLS	1/08-3/08
Postsecondary	San Francisco-San Mateo-Redwood PMSA, CA	Y		77259 AW		CABLS	1/08-3/08
Postsecondary	San Jose-Sunnyvale-Santa Clara MSA, CA	Y		72891 AW		CABLS	1/08-3/08
Postsecondary	Santa Ana-Anaheim-Irvine PMSA, CA	Y	55920 FQ	73940 MW	94090 TQ	USBLS	5/07
Postsecondary	Colorado	Y	46020 FQ	60090 MW	78720 TQ	USBLS	5/07
Postsecondary	Denver-Aurora MSA, CO	Y	45650 FQ	64160 MW	87220 TQ	USBLS	5/07
Postsecondary	Delaware	Y	54890 FQ	66890 MW	98050 TQ	USBLS	5/07
Postsecondary	District of Columbia	Y	41870 FQ	57010 MW	75230 TQ	USBLS	5/07
Postsecondary	Washington-Arlington-Alexandria MSA, DC-VA-MD-WV	Y	45450 FQ	59260 MW	74580 TQ	USBLS	5/07
Postsecondary	Florida	Y	44410 FQ	62620 MW	77210 TQ	USBLS	5/07
Postsecondary	Fort Lauderdale-Pompano Beach-Deerfield Beach PMSA, FL	Y	59970 FQ	72210 MW	79270 TQ	USBLS	5/07
Postsecondary	Orlando-Kissimmee MSA, FL	Y	33510 FQ	45160 MW	70970 TQ	USBLS	5/07
Postsecondary	Tampa-St. Petersburg-Clearwater MSA, FL	Y	50150 FQ	61070 MW	77270 TQ	USBLS	5/07
Postsecondary	Georgia	Y	41800 FQ	56810 MW	75820 TQ	USBLS	5/07
Postsecondary	Atlanta-Sandy Springs-Marietta MSA, GA	Y	42570 FQ	57350 MW	73860 TQ	USBLS	5/07
Postsecondary	Hawaii	Y	37460 FQ	52700 MW	75910 TQ	USBLS	5/07
Postsecondary	Honolulu MSA, HI	Y	37530 FQ	53700 MW	77000 TQ	USBLS	5/07
Postsecondary	Illinois	Y	39960 FQ	54900 MW	71600 TQ	USBLS	5/07
Postsecondary	Chicago-Naperville-Joliet MSA, IL-IN-WI	Y	40320 FQ	54810 MW	71340 TQ	USBLS	5/07
Postsecondary	Indiana	Y	48420 FQ	59040 MW	78880 TQ	USBLS	5/07
Postsecondary	Indianapolis-Carmel MSA, IN	Y	44180 FQ	57490 MW	76320 TQ	USBLS	5/07
Postsecondary	Iowa	Y	47870 FQ	61850 MW	82020 TQ	USBLS	5/07
Postsecondary	Des Moines-West Des Moines MSA, IA	Y	41660 FQ	57780 MW	83400 TQ	USBLS	5/07
Postsecondary	Kansas	Y	31420 FQ	53810 MW	81580 TQ	USBLS	5/07
Postsecondary	Wichita MSA, KS	Y	66710 FQ	81900 MW	95000 TQ	USBLS	5/07
Postsecondary	Kentucky	Y	40563 FQ	57110 MW	73514 TQ	KYBLS	2008
Postsecondary	Louisville-Jefferson County MSA, KY-IN	Y	42970 FQ	59050 MW	80880 TQ	USBLS	5/07
Postsecondary	Louisiana	Y		54659 AW		LABLS	1/08-3/08
Postsecondary	Maine	Y	50250 FQ	59400 MW	75390 TQ	USBLS	5/07
Postsecondary	Portland-South Portland-Biddeford MSA, ME	Y	45760 FQ	55220 MW	64880 TQ	USBLS	5/07
Postsecondary	Maryland	Y		69575 MW		MDBLS	3/08
Postsecondary	Baltimore-Towson MSA, MD	Y	52590 FQ	69620 MW	94590 TQ	USBLS	5/07
Postsecondary	Massachusetts	Y	53980 FQ	70660 MW	93780 TQ	USBLS	5/07
Postsecondary	Boston-Cambridge-Quincy NECTA, MA	Y	51510 FQ	69520 MW	93160 TQ	USBLS	5/07
Postsecondary	Worcester MSA, MA-CT	Y	53790 FQ	68890 MW	87990 TQ	USBLS	5/07
Postsecondary	Michigan	Y	36890 FQ	59400 MW	77570 TQ	USBLS	5/07
Postsecondary	Detroit-Warren-Livonia MSA, MI	Y	35030 FQ	57450 MW	81720 TQ	USBLS	5/07
Postsecondary	Warren-Troy-Farmington Hills PMSA, MI	Y	33140 FQ	56400 MW	94650 TQ	USBLS	5/07
Postsecondary	Minnesota	Y	44642 FQ	55690 MW	72890 TQ	MNBLS	10/08-12/08
Postsecondary	Duluth-Superior MSA, MN-WI	Y	46787 FQ	58546 MW	77106 TQ	MNBLS	10/08-12/08
Postsecondary	Minneapolis-Saint Paul MSA, MN-WI	Y	45950 FQ	58149 MW	77169 TQ	MNBLS	10/08-12/08
Postsecondary	Mississippi	Y	49300 FQ	57690 MW	68350 TQ	USBLS	5/07
Postsecondary	Jackson MSA, MS	Y	47630 FQ	55480 MW	62680 TQ	USBLS	5/07

AE	Average entry wage	AW	Average wage paid	FQ	First quartile wage	LO	Lowest wage paid	MTC	Median total compensation	TCC	Total cash compensation
AER	Average entry range	AWR	Average wage range	H	Hourly	LR	Low end range	MW	Median wage paid	TQ	Third quartile wage
AEX	Average experienced wage	AXR	Average experienced range	HI	Highest wage paid	M	Monthly	MWR	Median wage range	W	Weekly
ATC	Average total compensation	D	Daily	HR	High end range	MCC	Median cash compensation	S	See annotated source	Y	Yearly

Psychology Teacher

Occupation/Type/Industry	Location	Per	Low	Mid	High	Source	Date
Psychology Teacher							
Postsecondary	Missouri	Y	44030 FQ	59460 MW	83480 TQ	USBLS	5/07
Postsecondary	Kansas City MSA, MO-KS	Y	41690 FQ	59790 MW	84370 TQ	USBLS	5/07
Postsecondary	St. Louis MSA, MO-IL	Y	36580 FQ	57130 MW	84740 TQ	USBLS	5/07
Postsecondary	Nebraska	Y	39650 FQ	52710 MW	70710 TQ	USBLS	5/07
Postsecondary	Omaha-Council Bluffs MSA, NE-IA	Y	37180 FQ	52000 MW	69890 TQ	USBLS	5/07
Postsecondary	New Hampshire	Y	35395 AE	55121 MW	71496 AEX	NHBLS	6/08
Postsecondary	Manchester MSA, NH	Y	46600 FQ	56960 MW	76220 TQ	USBLS	5/07
Postsecondary	New Jersey	Y	53610 FQ	74790 MW	99190 TQ	USBLS	5/07
Postsecondary	Camden PMSA, NJ	Y	51790 FQ	74690 MW	103040 TQ	USBLS	5/07
Postsecondary	Edison PMSA, NJ	Y	53260 FQ	75990 MW	107540 TQ	USBLS	5/07
Postsecondary	Newark-Union PMSA, NJ-PA	Y	56350 FQ	76440 MW	97360 TQ	USBLS	5/07
Postsecondary	New Mexico	Y	45150 FQ	57620 MW	75760 TQ	USBLS	5/07
Postsecondary	Albuquerque MSA, NM	Y	40520 FQ	52840 MW	67220 TQ	USBLS	5/07
Postsecondary	New York	Y	47440 FQ	65610 MW	91370 TQ	USBLS	5/07
Postsecondary	Buffalo-Niagara Falls MSA, NY	Y	42570 FQ	49380 MW	59580 TQ	USBLS	5/07
Postsecondary	Nassau-Suffolk PMSA, NY	Y	45680 FQ	56590 MW	77930 TQ	USBLS	5/07
Postsecondary	New York-Northern New Jersey-Long Island MSA, NY-NJ-PA	Y	52510 FQ	73190 MW	98420 TQ	USBLS	5/07
Postsecondary	Utica-Rome MSA, NY	Y	42470 FQ	52510 MW	66400 TQ	USBLS	5/07
Postsecondary	North Carolina	Y	45080 FQ	54840 MW	68540 TQ	USBLS	5/07
Postsecondary	Charlotte-Gastonia-Concord MSA, NC-SC	Y	44590 FQ	54970 MW	68330 TQ	USBLS	5/07
Postsecondary	Raleigh-Cary MSA, NC	Y	46700 FQ	57510 MW	75130 TQ	USBLS	5/07
Postsecondary	North Dakota	Y	49290 FQ	57790 MW	75370 TQ	USBLS	5/07
Postsecondary	Fargo MSA, ND-MN	Y	46040 FQ	54560 MW	62620 TQ	USBLS	5/07
Postsecondary	Ohio	Y	45190 FQ	59820 MW	83200 TQ	USBLS	5/07
Postsecondary	Cincinnati-Middletown MSA, OH-KY-IN	Y	43790 FQ	57680 MW	79820 TQ	USBLS	5/07
Postsecondary	Cleveland-Elyria-Mentor MSA, OH	Y	43600 FQ	56360 MW	78840 TQ	USBLS	5/07
Postsecondary	Columbus MSA, OH	Y	56160 FQ	78190 MW	100270 TQ	USBLS	5/07
Postsecondary	Dayton MSA, OH	Y	40670 FQ	55860 MW	80380 TQ	USBLS	5/07
Postsecondary	Oklahoma	Y	34840 FQ	51390 MW	84250 TQ	USBLS	5/07
Postsecondary	Oklahoma City MSA, OK	Y	41920 FQ	72450 MW	103240 TQ	USBLS	5/07
Postsecondary	Tulsa MSA, OK	Y	34360 FQ	41660 MW	54420 TQ	USBLS	5/07
Postsecondary	Portland-Vancouver-Beaverton MSA, OR-WA	Y	51450 FQ	70510 MW	102260 TQ	USBLS	5/07
Postsecondary	Pennsylvania	Y	48620 FQ	62080 MW	80990 TQ	USBLS	5/07
Postsecondary	Allentown-Bethlehem-Easton MSA, PA-NJ	Y	53490 FQ	61270 MW	73190 TQ	USBLS	5/07
Postsecondary	Pittsburgh MSA, PA	Y	48160 FQ	61870 MW	79540 TQ	USBLS	5/07
Postsecondary	Rhode Island	Y	52990 FQ	71560 MW	95980 TQ	USBLS	5/07
Postsecondary	Providence-Fall River-Warwick MSA, RI-MA	Y	53270 FQ	70340 MW	95410 TQ	USBLS	5/07
Postsecondary	South Carolina	Y	47090 FQ	57000 MW	71910 TQ	USBLS	5/07
Postsecondary	Charleston-North Charleston MSA, SC	Y	52460 FQ	58470 MW	65560 TQ	USBLS	5/07
Postsecondary	Columbia MSA, SC	Y	55860 FQ	70950 MW	99200 TQ	USBLS	5/07
Postsecondary	South Dakota	Y	44952 FQ	57661 MW	75882 TQ	SDBLS	7/08-9/08
Postsecondary	Sioux Falls MSA, SD	Y	43767 FQ	52656 MW	59214 TQ	SDBLS	7/08-9/08
Postsecondary	Tennessee	Y	41210 FQ	54860 MW	73270 TQ	USBLS	5/07
Postsecondary	Memphis MSA, TN-MS-AR	Y	41430 FQ	58820 MW	80430 TQ	USBLS	5/07
Postsecondary	Nashville-Davidson-Murfreesboro MSA, TN	Y	44600 FQ	58450 MW	77480 TQ	USBLS	5/07
Postsecondary	Texas	Y	43340 FQ	60410 MW	83420 TQ	USBLS	5/07
Postsecondary	Austin-Round Rock MSA, TX	Y	27430 FQ	62550 MW	86870 TQ	USBLS	5/07
Postsecondary	Dallas-Fort Worth-Arlington MSA, TX	Y	42030 FQ	60090 MW	98050 TQ	USBLS	5/07
Postsecondary	El Paso MSA, TX	Y	43450 FQ	58640 MW	69750 TQ	USBLS	5/07
Postsecondary	Houston-Sugar Land-Baytown MSA, TX	Y	54010 FQ	76210 MW	112980 TQ	USBLS	5/07
Postsecondary	San Antonio MSA, TX	Y	44960 FQ	58340 MW	75990 TQ	USBLS	5/07
Postsecondary	Utah	Y	49700 FQ	60680 MW	78200 TQ	USBLS	5/07
Postsecondary	Salt Lake City MSA, UT	Y	53760 FQ	64240 MW	77620 TQ	USBLS	5/07
Postsecondary	Vermont	Y	43470 FQ	56820 MW	69010 TQ	USBLS	5/07
Postsecondary	Burlington-South Burlington MSA, VT	Y	44100 FQ	61110 MW	75390 TQ	USBLS	5/07
Postsecondary	Virginia	Y	40470 FQ	55660 MW	65670 TQ	USBLS	5/07

AE	Average entry wage	**AW**	Average wage paid	**FQ**	First quartile wage	**LO** Lowest wage paid	**MTC** Median total compensation	**TCC** Total cash compensation
AER	Average entry range	**AWR**	Average wage range	**H**	Hourly	**LR** Low end range	**MW** Median wage paid	**TQ** Third quartile wage
AEX	Average experienced wage	**AXR**	Average experienced range	**HI**	Highest wage paid	**M** Monthly	**MWR** Median wage range	**W** Weekly
ATC	Average total compensation	**D**	Daily	**HR**	High end range	**MCC** Median cash compensation	**S** See annotated source	**Y** Yearly

Occupation/Type/Industry	Location	Per	Low	Mid	High	Source	Date
Psychology Teacher							
Postsecondary	Richmond MSA, VA	Y	38810 FQ	55080 MW	71920 TQ	USBLS	5/07
Postsecondary	Virginia Beach-Norfolk-Newport News MSA, VA-NC	Y	38380 FQ	55980 MW	68590 TQ	USBLS	5/07
Postsecondary	Washington	Y		64575 AW		WABLS	3/08
Postsecondary	Seattle-Tacoma-Bellevue MSA, WA	Y	46080 FQ	57700 MW	74260 TQ	USBLS	5/07
Postsecondary	West Virginia	Y	46292 FQ	60838 MW	77394 TQ	WVBLS	7/08-9/08
Postsecondary	Wisconsin	Y	42180 FQ	54660 MW	67980 TQ	USBLS	5/07
Postsecondary	Milwaukee-Waukesha-West Allis MSA, WI	Y	39480 FQ	53760 MW	67290 TQ	USBLS	5/07
Postsecondary	Wyoming	Y	47371 FQ	60398 MW	66913 TQ	WYBLS	9/08
Postsecondary	Puerto Rico	Y	42260 FQ	49220 MW	64730 TQ	USBLS	5/07
Postsecondary	San Juan-Caguas-Guaynabo MSA, PR	Y	43920 FQ	51320 MW	70130 TQ	USBLS	5/07
Public Address System and Other Announcer							
	Alabama	Y	14820 FQ	21900 MW	25850 TQ	USBLS	5/07
	Arizona	Y	18110 FQ	20770 MW	37290 TQ	USBLS	5/07
	Tucson MSA, AZ	Y	17410 FQ	18750 MW	20450 TQ	USBLS	5/07
	Arkansas	Y	16450 FQ	18640 MW	23180 TQ	USBLS	5/07
	Little Rock-North Little Rock MSA, AR	Y	16110 FQ	18720 MW	40130 TQ	USBLS	5/07
	California	H	9.23 FQ	13.17 MW	21.26 TQ	CABLS	1/08-3/08
	Los Angeles-Long Beach-Glendale PMSA, CA	H	8.87 FQ	12.91 MW	16.15 TQ	CABLS	1/08-3/08
	Riverside-San Bernardino-Ontario MSA, CA	H	8.10 FQ	12.34 MW	19.99 TQ	CABLS	1/08-3/08
	Sacramento-Arden Arcade-Roseville MSA, CA	H	9.03 FQ	12.78 MW	21.42 TQ	CABLS	1/08-3/08
	San Francisco-San Mateo-Redwood PMSA, CA	H	11.52 FQ	19.17 MW	23.64 TQ	CABLS	1/08-3/08
	Colorado	Y	15780 FQ	20100 MW	39780 TQ	USBLS	5/07
	Denver-Aurora MSA, CO	Y	16650 FQ	20730 MW	45820 TQ	USBLS	5/07
	Connecticut	H	8.02 AE	12.85 MW		CTBLS	1/08-3/08
	Florida	Y	16520 FQ	24620 MW	42790 TQ	USBLS	5/07
	Miami-Fort Lauderdale-Miami Beach MSA, FL	Y	16790 FQ	19430 MW	39690 TQ	USBLS	5/07
	Tampa-St. Petersburg-Clearwater MSA, FL	Y	33850 FQ	49050 MW	54380 TQ	USBLS	5/07
	Georgia	Y	19280 FQ	24270 MW	43090 TQ	USBLS	5/07
	Hawaii	Y	20650 FQ	27150 MW	32260 TQ	USBLS	5/07
	Honolulu MSA, HI	Y	20650 FQ	27150 MW	32260 TQ	USBLS	5/07
	Idaho	Y	13290 FQ	15200 MW	17830 TQ	USBLS	5/07
	Illinois	Y	22020 FQ	37840 MW	85550 TQ	USBLS	5/07
	Chicago-Naperville-Joliet MSA, IL-IN-WI	Y	23560 FQ	41270 MW	87200 TQ	USBLS	5/07
	Indiana	Y	16220 FQ	18550 MW	27400 TQ	USBLS	5/07
	Indianapolis-Carmel MSA, IN	Y	14150 FQ	20270 MW	30240 TQ	USBLS	5/07
	Iowa	Y	20170 FQ	30990 MW	35710 TQ	USBLS	5/07
	Des Moines-West Des Moines MSA, IA	Y	31060 FQ	34040 MW	37090 TQ	USBLS	5/07
	Kansas	Y	21960 FQ	26350 MW	31460 TQ	USBLS	5/07
	Kentucky	Y	16979 FQ	18872 MW	24365 TQ	KYBLS	2008
	Louisville-Jefferson County MSA, KY-IN	Y	16540 FQ	18230 MW	22370 TQ	USBLS	5/07
	Baton Rouge MSA, LA	Y	14370 FQ	16670 MW	19030 TQ	USBLS	5/07
	New Orleans-Metairie-Kenner MSA, LA	Y	16330 FQ	19760 MW	24280 TQ	USBLS	5/07
	Maryland	Y		24750 MW		MDBLS	3/08
	Baltimore-Towson MSA, MD	Y	19460 FQ	26100 MW	34860 TQ	USBLS	5/07
	Massachusetts	Y	20920 FQ	33470 MW	42680 TQ	USBLS	5/07
	Boston-Cambridge-Quincy NECTA, MA	Y	19770 FQ	36110 MW	48210 TQ	USBLS	5/07
	Michigan	Y	18130 FQ	22480 MW	61930 TQ	USBLS	5/07
	Detroit-Warren-Livonia MSA, MI	Y	19680 FQ	42860 MW	57690 TQ	USBLS	5/07
	Minnesota	Y	22703 FQ	33416 MW	54571 TQ	MNBLS	10/08-12/08
	Minneapolis-Saint Paul MSA, MN-WI	Y	25894 FQ	41200 MW	72377 TQ	MNBLS	10/08-12/08
	Missouri	Y	23760 FQ	37020 MW	56090 TQ	USBLS	5/07
	Kansas City MSA, MO-KS	Y	27350 FQ	37970 MW	57160 TQ	USBLS	5/07

AE	Average entry wage	AW	Average wage paid	FQ	First quartile wage
AER	Average entry range	AWR	Average wage range	H	Hourly
AEX	Average experienced wage	AXR	Average experienced range	HI	Highest wage paid
ATC	Average total compensation	D	Daily	HR	High end range

LO	Lowest wage paid	MTC	Median total compensation	TCC	Total cash compensation
LR	Low end range	MW	Median wage paid	TQ	Third quartile wage
M	Monthly	MWR	Median wage range	W	Weekly
MCC	Median cash compensation	S	See annotated source	Y	Yearly

Occupation/Type/Industry	Location	Per	Low	Mid	High	Source	Date
Public Address System and Other Announcer	St. Louis MSA, MO-IL	Y	15650 FQ	25270 MW	54800 TQ	USBLS	5/07
	Montana	Y	16810 FQ	18500 MW	27560 TQ	USBLS	5/07
	Billings MSA, MT	Y	16810 FQ	18020 MW	19210 TQ	USBLS	5/07
	Nebraska	Y	13670 FQ	18550 MW	26760 TQ	USBLS	5/07
	Omaha-Council Bluffs MSA, NE-IA	Y	14150 FQ	22050 MW	29870 TQ	USBLS	5/07
	Nevada	H	9.31 FQ	13.50 MW	20.19 TQ	NVBLS	5/08
	Las Vegas-Paradise MSA, NV	H	11.09 FQ	13.90 MW	22.53 TQ	NVBLS	5/08
	New Jersey	Y	23660 FQ	61450 MW	77120 TQ	USBLS	5/07
	Edison PMSA, NJ	Y	50640 FQ	70270 MW	80240 TQ	USBLS	5/07
	New York	Y	17610 FQ	23730 MW	63230 TQ	USBLS	5/07
	Buffalo-Niagara Falls MSA, NY	Y	18450 FQ	26350 MW	49130 TQ	USBLS	5/07
	New York-Northern New Jersey-Long Island MSA, NY-NJ-PA	Y	19400 FQ	51720 MW	80850 TQ	USBLS	5/07
	North Dakota	Y	17660 FQ	23760 MW	29060 TQ	USBLS	5/07
	Fargo MSA, ND-MN	Y	17640 FQ	24260 MW	29120 TQ	USBLS	5/07
	Ohio	Y	16050 FQ	19050 MW	40170 TQ	USBLS	5/07
	Columbus MSA, OH	Y	16310 FQ	26370 MW	54300 TQ	USBLS	5/07
	Oklahoma City MSA, OK	Y	13350 FQ	21650 MW	34680 TQ	USBLS	5/07
	Portland-Vancouver-Beaverton MSA, OR-WA	Y	21100 FQ	22930 MW	32540 TQ	USBLS	5/07
	Pennsylvania	Y	20840 FQ	25010 MW	36350 TQ	USBLS	5/07
	Philadelphia-Camden-Wilmington MSA, PA-NJ-DE-MD	Y	22730 FQ	26960 MW	34800 TQ	USBLS	5/07
	Providence-Fall River-Warwick MSA, RI-MA	Y	35550 FQ	38770 MW	42070 TQ	USBLS	5/07
	South Carolina	Y	19700 FQ	33030 MW	69240 TQ	USBLS	5/07
	South Dakota	Y	18362 FQ	22689 MW	25578 TQ	SDBLS	7/08-9/08
	Sioux Falls MSA, SD	Y	21516 FQ	23541 MW	25611 TQ	SDBLS	7/08-9/08
	Tennessee	Y	13640 FQ	18080 MW	33800 TQ	USBLS	5/07
	Memphis MSA, TN-MS-AR	Y	13080 FQ	14940 MW	35660 TQ	USBLS	5/07
	Texas	Y	18110 FQ	23970 MW	31150 TQ	USBLS	5/07
	Dallas-Fort Worth-Arlington MSA, TX	Y	15050 FQ	23200 MW	31310 TQ	USBLS	5/07
	Houston-Sugar Land-Baytown MSA, TX	Y	20070 FQ	23620 MW	29540 TQ	USBLS	5/07
	San Antonio MSA, TX	Y	18630 FQ	23410 MW	28150 TQ	USBLS	5/07
	Utah	Y	14580 FQ	18040 MW	34580 TQ	USBLS	5/07
	Salt Lake City MSA, UT	Y	14140 FQ	16370 MW	20670 TQ	USBLS	5/07
	Richmond MSA, VA	Y	12190 FQ	13660 MW	15130 TQ	USBLS	5/07
	Washington	H	11.80 FQ	16.15 MW	18.62 TQ	WABLS	3/08
	Seattle-Tacoma-Bellevue MSA, WA	Y	28300 FQ	34540 MW	38660 TQ	USBLS	5/07
	West Virginia	Y	27158 FQ	33292 MW	38171 TQ	WVBLS	7/08-9/08
	Wisconsin	Y	26260 FQ	36740 MW	47690 TQ	USBLS	5/07
	Milwaukee-Waukesha-West Allis MSA, WI	Y	35440 FQ	41730 MW	52310 TQ	USBLS	5/07
	Wyoming	Y	24353 FQ	27190 MW	31705 TQ	WYBLS	9/08
Public Defender	Maryland	Y			52950-85017 HR	BMAG	2009
	Ohio	H	35.44 LO		75.94 HI	ODAS	2008
Public Health Educator	Cincinnati, OH	Y	40186 LO		54007 HI	COHSS	10/08
Public Health Informatics Specialist							
Federal Government	United States	Y		87200 AW		BHM	2006
Hospital	United States	Y		72000 AW		BHM	2006
Public Health Internist	Cincinnati, OH	Y	118283 LO		159683 HI	COHSS	10/08
Public Health Pediatrician	Cincinnati, OH	Y	118283 LO		159683 HI	COHSS	10/08
Public Inquiries Officer							
State Government	Ohio	H	20.89 LO		26.11 HI	ODAS	2008

AE Average entry wage	**AW** Average wage paid	**FQ** First quartile wage	**LO** Lowest wage paid	**MTC** Median total compensation **TCC** Total cash compensation
AER Average entry range	**AWR** Average wage range	**H** Hourly	**LR** Low end range	**MW** Median wage paid **TQ** Third quartile wage
AEX Average experienced wage	**AXR** Average experienced range	**HI** Highest wage paid	**M** Monthly	**MWR** Median wage range **W** Weekly
ATC Average total compensation	**D** Daily	**HR** High end range	**MCC** Median cash compensation	**S** See annotated source **Y** Yearly

Occupation/Type/Industry	Location	Per	Low	Mid	High	Source	Date
Public Printer							
Federal Government	United States	Y			172200 HI	CRS02	1/08
Public Relations Manager	Alabama	Y	49090 FQ	64840 MW	92550 TQ	USBLS	5/07
	Birmingham-Hoover MSA, AL	Y	60290 FQ	80830 MW	111260 TQ	USBLS	5/07
	Alaska	Y	44800 FQ	55040 MW	74900 TQ	USBLS	5/07
	Anchorage MSA, AK	Y	46470 FQ	59530 MW	79160 TQ	USBLS	5/07
	Fairbanks MSA, AK	Y	40150 FQ	49640 MW	60570 TQ	USBLS	5/07
	Arizona	Y	47010 FQ	65060 MW	89950 TQ	USBLS	5/07
	Phoenix-Mesa-Scottsdale MSA, AZ	Y	47780 FQ	67680 MW	91430 TQ	USBLS	5/07
	Tucson MSA, AZ	Y	46740 FQ	59350 MW	86060 TQ	USBLS	5/07
	Arkansas	Y	44090 FQ	63770 MW	77010 TQ	USBLS	5/07
	Little Rock-North Little Rock MSA, AR	Y	51100 FQ	66070 MW	74820 TQ	USBLS	5/07
	California	H	33.70 FQ	46.72 MW	66.40 TQ	CABLS	1/08-3/08
	Los Angeles-Long Beach-Glendale PMSA, CA	H	32.84 FQ	46.17 MW	63.90 TQ	CABLS	1/08-3/08
	Oakland-Fremont-Hayward MSA, CA	H	35.20 FQ	44.62 MW	58.28 TQ	CABLS	1/08-3/08
	Riverside-San Bernardino-Ontario MSA, CA	H	30.46 FQ	42.63 MW	50.58 TQ	CABLS	1/08-3/08
	Sacramento-Arden Arcade-Roseville MSA, CA	H	36.36 FQ	47.36 MW	66.78 TQ	CABLS	1/08-3/08
	San Diego-Carlsbad-San Marcos MSA, CA	H	24.89 FQ	38.31 MW	54.67 TQ	CABLS	1/08-3/08
	San Francisco-San Mateo-Redwood PMSA, CA	H	39.11 FQ	56.07 MW		CABLS	1/08-3/08
	San Jose-Sunnyvale-Santa Clara MSA, CA	H	48.53 FQ			CABLS	1/08-3/08
	Santa Ana-Anaheim-Irvine PMSA, CA	Y	58440 FQ	95100 MW	128270 TQ	USBLS	5/07
	Stockton MSA, CA	H	30.43 FQ	41.21 MW	68.58 TQ	CABLS	1/08-3/08
	Colorado	Y	65020 FQ	87090 MW	120360 TQ	USBLS	5/07
	Colorado Springs MSA, CO	Y	50840 FQ	71390 MW	93150 TQ	USBLS	5/07
	Denver-Aurora MSA, CO	Y	71280 FQ	93350 MW	130560 TQ	USBLS	5/07
	Connecticut	H	27.12 AE	40.55 MW		CTBLS	1/08-3/08
	Bridgeport-Stamford-Norwalk MSA, CT	Y	72190 FQ	103430 MW		USBLS	5/07
	Hartford-West Hartford-East Hartford MSA, CT	Y	60510 FQ	81710 MW	117380 TQ	USBLS	5/07
	Delaware	Y	68230 FQ	90790 MW	121710 TQ	USBLS	5/07
	Wilmington PMSA, DE-MD-NJ	Y	71730 FQ	94270 MW	125320 TQ	USBLS	5/07
	District of Columbia	Y	88090 FQ	121200 MW		USBLS	5/07
	Washington-Arlington-Alexandria MSA, DC-VA-MD-WV	Y	92210 FQ	125120 MW		USBLS	5/07
	Florida	Y	71860 FQ	95100 MW	124700 TQ	USBLS	5/07
	Fort Lauderdale-Pompano Beach-Deerfield Beach PMSA, FL	Y	80110 FQ	98600 MW	129550 TQ	USBLS	5/07
	Jacksonville MSA, FL	Y	79480 FQ	93430 MW	116950 TQ	USBLS	5/07
	Miami-Fort Lauderdale-Miami Beach MSA, FL	Y	79590 FQ	107990 MW	132610 TQ	USBLS	5/07
	Orlando-Kissimmee MSA, FL	Y	57440 FQ	84720 MW	127040 TQ	USBLS	5/07
	Tampa-St. Petersburg-Clearwater MSA, FL	Y	61820 FQ	85670 MW	114730 TQ	USBLS	5/07
	West Palm Beach-Boca Raton-Boynton Beach PMSA, FL	Y	63820 FQ	80390 MW	123080 TQ	USBLS	5/07
	Georgia	Y	55580 FQ	74780 MW	99350 TQ	USBLS	5/07
	Atlanta-Sandy Springs-Marietta MSA, GA	Y	58180 FQ	78290 MW	103680 TQ	USBLS	5/07
	Hawaii	Y	41640 FQ	62010 MW	77630 TQ	USBLS	5/07
	Honolulu MSA, HI	Y	45790 FQ	61640 MW	80670 TQ	USBLS	5/07
	Idaho	Y	29820 FQ	43680 MW	62600 TQ	USBLS	5/07
	Boise City-Nampa MSA, ID	Y	37580 FQ	48960 MW	66340 TQ	USBLS	5/07
	Illinois	Y	54820 FQ	73820 MW	103190 TQ	USBLS	5/07
	Chicago-Naperville-Joliet MSA, IL-IN-WI	Y	57990 FQ	77150 MW	113830 TQ	USBLS	5/07
	Indiana	Y	47710 FQ	65590 MW	86380 TQ	USBLS	5/07
	Evansville MSA, IN-KY	Y	44120 FQ	59080 MW	103890 TQ	USBLS	5/07

AE	Average entry wage	AW	Average wage paid	FQ	First quartile wage	LO	Lowest wage paid	MTC Median total compensation TCC Total cash compensation
AER	Average entry range	AWR	Average wage range	H	Hourly	LR	Low end range	MW Median wage paid TQ Third quartile wage
AEX	Average experienced wage	AXR	Average experienced range	HI	Highest wage paid	M	Monthly	MWR Median wage range W Weekly
ATC	Average total compensation	D	Daily	HR	High end range	MCC	Median cash compensation	S See annotated source Y Yearly

Occupation/Type/Industry	Location	Per	Low	Mid	High	Source	Date
Public Relations Manager	Gary PMSA, IN	Y	47220 FQ	68740 MW	85030 TQ	USBLS	5/07
	Indianapolis-Carmel MSA, IN	Y	50080 FQ	67730 MW	86120 TQ	USBLS	5/07
	Iowa	Y	49260 FQ	68790 MW	88470 TQ	USBLS	5/07
	Des Moines-West Des Moines MSA, IA	Y	63880 FQ	76690 MW	97450 TQ	USBLS	5/07
	Kansas	Y	59440 FQ	78340 MW	110470 TQ	USBLS	5/07
	Wichita MSA, KS	Y	51050 FQ	71930 MW	99710 TQ	USBLS	5/07
	Kentucky	Y	51230 FQ	67379 MW	92069 TQ	KYBLS	2008
	Louisville-Jefferson County MSA, KY-IN	Y	51220 FQ	71020 MW	96120 TQ	USBLS	5/07
	Louisiana	H	18.65 FQ	23.93 MW	30.77 TQ	LABLS	1/08-3/08
	Baton Rouge MSA, LA	Y	44130 FQ	52270 MW	67200 TQ	USBLS	5/07
	New Orleans-Metairie-Kenner MSA, LA	Y	38080 FQ	50720 MW	63730 TQ	USBLS	5/07
	Shreveport-Bossier City MSA, LA	Y	38210 FQ	47760 MW	65270 TQ	USBLS	5/07
	Maine	Y	52680 FQ	71020 MW	97600 TQ	USBLS	5/07
	Portland-South Portland-Biddeford MSA, ME	Y	52480 FQ	65410 MW	94030 TQ	USBLS	5/07
	Maryland	Y		94825 MW		MDBLS	3/08
	Baltimore-Towson MSA, MD	Y	66260 FQ	84970 MW	107890 TQ	USBLS	5/07
	Bethesda-Gaithersburg-Frederick PMSA, MD	Y	71120 FQ	112620 MW		USBLS	5/07
	Massachusetts	Y	78220 FQ	102170 MW	133750 TQ	USBLS	5/07
	Boston-Cambridge-Quincy NECTA, MA	Y	83020 FQ	106140 MW	139480 TQ	USBLS	5/07
	Worcester MSA, MA-CT	Y	64920 FQ	79060 MW	110360 TQ	USBLS	5/07
	Michigan	Y	60370 FQ	83840 MW	116030 TQ	USBLS	5/07
	Detroit-Warren-Livonia MSA, MI	Y	67390 FQ	91980 MW	121020 TQ	USBLS	5/07
	Grand Rapids-Wyoming MSA, MI	Y	47280 FQ	75420 MW	125210 TQ	USBLS	5/07
	Lansing-East Lansing MSA, MI	Y	70750 FQ	89520 MW	117950 TQ	USBLS	5/07
	Warren-Troy-Farmington Hills PMSA, MI	Y	58730 FQ	93940 MW	121170 TQ	USBLS	5/07
	Minnesota	Y	80941 FQ	103817 MW	140758 TQ	MNBLS	10/08-12/08
	Duluth-Superior MSA, MN-WI	Y	72506 FQ	82004 MW	98489 TQ	MNBLS	10/08-12/08
	Minneapolis-Saint Paul MSA, MN-WI	Y	83089 FQ	106726 MW	144887 TQ	MNBLS	10/08-12/08
	Rochester MSA, MN	Y	81292 FQ	107296 MW	129633 TQ	MNBLS	10/08-12/08
	Mississippi	Y	43270 FQ	57480 MW	77120 TQ	USBLS	5/07
	Missouri	Y	60100 FQ	79940 MW	103350 TQ	USBLS	5/07
	Kansas City MSA, MO-KS	Y	63170 FQ	83530 MW	120930 TQ	USBLS	5/07
	St. Louis MSA, MO-IL	Y	66660 FQ	82620 MW	106340 TQ	USBLS	5/07
	Springfield MSA, MO	Y	49220 FQ	59130 MW	85820 TQ	USBLS	5/07
	Montana	Y	34620 FQ	48080 MW	68990 TQ	USBLS	5/07
	Billings MSA, MT	Y	30350 FQ	39410 MW	65410 TQ	USBLS	5/07
	Nebraska	Y	52910 FQ	73780 MW	97410 TQ	USBLS	5/07
	Omaha-Council Bluffs MSA, NE-IA	Y	57670 FQ	80290 MW	100140 TQ	USBLS	5/07
	Nevada	H	30.70 FQ	44.08 MW	53.48 TQ	NVBLS	5/08
	Las Vegas-Paradise MSA, NV	H	32.62 FQ	44.87 MW	53.19 TQ	NVBLS	5/08
	New Hampshire	H	27.54 AE	36.51 MW	47.41 AEX	NHBLS	6/08
	Manchester MSA, NH	Y	59060 FQ	67270 MW	83100 TQ	USBLS	5/07
	New Jersey	Y	81930 FQ	110790 MW		USBLS	5/07
	Camden PMSA, NJ	Y	73290 FQ	95680 MW	139490 TQ	USBLS	5/07
	Edison PMSA, NJ	Y	88070 FQ	117570 MW		USBLS	5/07
	Newark-Union PMSA, NJ-PA	Y	74010 FQ	109610 MW		USBLS	5/07
	New Mexico	Y	39690 FQ	54930 MW	76520 TQ	USBLS	5/07
	Albuquerque MSA, NM	Y	39490 FQ	53080 MW	83280 TQ	USBLS	5/07
	New York	Y	84200 FQ	109830 MW		USBLS	5/07
	Albany-Schenectady-Troy MSA, NY	Y	59820 FQ	82790 MW	107400 TQ	USBLS	5/07
	Buffalo-Niagara Falls MSA, NY	Y	41740 FQ	51880 MW	89860 TQ	USBLS	5/07
	Nassau-Suffolk PMSA, NY	Y	73160 FQ	92130 MW	116340 TQ	USBLS	5/07
	New York-Northern New Jersey-Long Island MSA, NY-NJ-PA	Y	89260 FQ	115730 MW		USBLS	5/07
	Utica-Rome MSA, NY	Y	46990 FQ	67540 MW	90330 TQ	USBLS	5/07
	North Carolina	Y	59920 FQ	78790 MW	103060 TQ	USBLS	5/07

AE	Average entry wage	AW	Average wage paid	FQ	First quartile wage
AER	Average entry range	AWR	Average wage range	H	Hourly
AEX	Average experienced wage	AXR	Average experienced range	HI	Highest wage paid
ATC	Average total compensation	D	Daily	HR	High end range

LO	Lowest wage paid	MTC	Median total compensation	TCC	Total cash compensation
LR	Low end range	MW	Median wage paid	TQ	Third quartile wage
M	Monthly	MWR	Median wage range	W	Weekly
MCC	Median cash compensation	S	See annotated source	Y	Yearly

Occupation/Type/Industry	Location	Per	Low	Mid	High	Source	Date
Public Relations Manager	Charlotte-Gastonia-Concord MSA, NC-SC	Y	63190 FQ	83540 MW	104840 TQ	USBLS	5/07
	Raleigh-Cary MSA, NC	Y	66300 FQ	80170 MW	102530 TQ	USBLS	5/07
	North Dakota	Y	42260 FQ	54870 MW	73700 TQ	USBLS	5/07
	Fargo MSA, ND-MN	Y	48680 FQ	62100 MW	76990 TQ	USBLS	5/07
	Ohio	Y	61610 FQ	82720 MW	105050 TQ	USBLS	5/07
	Cincinnati-Middletown MSA, OH-KY-IN	Y	58060 FQ	78430 MW	103740 TQ	USBLS	5/07
	Cleveland-Elyria-Mentor MSA, OH	Y	65930 FQ	85310 MW	108940 TQ	USBLS	5/07
	Columbus MSA, OH	Y	65460 FQ	87060 MW	106860 TQ	USBLS	5/07
	Dayton MSA, OH	Y	59850 FQ	77230 MW	100060 TQ	USBLS	5/07
	Oklahoma	Y	38860 FQ	54320 MW	76580 TQ	USBLS	5/07
	Oklahoma City MSA, OK	Y	47960 FQ	65790 MW	85610 TQ	USBLS	5/07
	Tulsa MSA, OK	Y	38910 FQ	50150 MW	76360 TQ	USBLS	5/07
	Oregon	H	23.31 FQ	32.41 MW	45.24 TQ	ORBLS	5/08
	Medford MSA, OR	Y	38300 FQ	50120 MW	70300 TQ	USBLS	5/07
	Portland-Vancouver-Beaverton MSA, OR-WA	Y	50650 FQ	72270 MW	97330 TQ	USBLS	5/07
	Pennsylvania	Y	51380 FQ	72270 MW	101560 TQ	USBLS	5/07
	Allentown-Bethlehem-Easton MSA, PA-NJ	Y	45880 FQ	68300 MW	100980 TQ	USBLS	5/07
	Philadelphia-Camden-Wilmington MSA, PA-NJ-DE-MD	Y	60470 FQ	85340 MW	122250 TQ	USBLS	5/07
	Pittsburgh MSA, PA	Y	51240 FQ	71760 MW	94030 TQ	USBLS	5/07
	Rhode Island	Y	69670 FQ	90870 MW	120060 TQ	USBLS	5/07
	Providence-Fall River-Warwick MSA, RI-MA	Y	70020 FQ	91990 MW	120960 TQ	USBLS	5/07
	South Carolina	Y	48540 FQ	62320 MW	80730 TQ	USBLS	5/07
	Charleston-North Charleston MSA, SC	Y	49970 FQ	70610 MW	88690 TQ	USBLS	5/07
	Columbia MSA, SC	Y	48830 FQ	59780 MW	73570 TQ	USBLS	5/07
	South Dakota	Y	60227 FQ	77098 MW	95146 TQ	SDBLS	7/08-9/08
	Sioux Falls MSA, SD	Y	55924 FQ	87322 MW	100411 TQ	SDBLS	7/08-9/08
	Tennessee	Y	39570 FQ	60550 MW	90400 TQ	USBLS	5/07
	Memphis MSA, TN-MS-AR	Y	43670 FQ	73040 MW	93710 TQ	USBLS	5/07
	Nashville-Davidson-Murfreesboro MSA, TN	Y	39660 FQ	61920 MW	92270 TQ	USBLS	5/07
	Texas	Y	64600 FQ	88270 MW	121580 TQ	USBLS	5/07
	Austin-Round Rock MSA, TX	Y	67380 FQ	99410 MW		USBLS	5/07
	Dallas-Fort Worth-Arlington MSA, TX	Y	73210 FQ	96590 MW	124790 TQ	USBLS	5/07
	Houston-Sugar Land-Baytown MSA, TX	Y	66890 FQ	87970 MW	126790 TQ	USBLS	5/07
	San Antonio MSA, TX	Y	56070 FQ	74130 MW	98650 TQ	USBLS	5/07
	Utah	Y	57870 FQ	74620 MW	96870 TQ	USBLS	5/07
	Salt Lake City MSA, UT	Y	57830 FQ	75300 MW	97430 TQ	USBLS	5/07
	Vermont	Y	56900 FQ	65670 MW	95020 TQ	USBLS	5/07
	Burlington-South Burlington MSA, VT	Y	58690 FQ	65430 MW	91860 TQ	USBLS	5/07
	Virginia	Y	85980 FQ	119400 MW		USBLS	5/07
	Richmond MSA, VA	Y	64030 FQ	86490 MW	108640 TQ	USBLS	5/07
	Virginia Beach-Norfolk-Newport News MSA, VA-NC	Y	64000 FQ	90710 MW	113320 TQ	USBLS	5/07
	Washington	H	39.85 FQ	48.14 MW	60.00 TQ	WABLS	3/08
	Seattle-Tacoma-Bellevue MSA, WA	Y	85130 FQ	102910 MW	126780 TQ	USBLS	5/07
	West Virginia	Y	53118 FQ	76244 MW	106218 TQ	WVBLS	7/08-9/08
	Wisconsin	Y	51640 FQ	72700 MW	103280 TQ	USBLS	5/07
	Milwaukee-Waukesha-West Allis MSA, WI	Y	63880 FQ	81790 MW	118120 TQ	USBLS	5/07
	Wyoming	Y	40464 FQ	52212 MW	68287 TQ	WYBLS	9/08
	Puerto Rico	Y	34080 FQ	48530 MW	66340 TQ	USBLS	5/07
	San Juan-Caguas-Guaynabo MSA, PR	Y	35920 FQ	49720 MW	67950 TQ	USBLS	5/07
Public Relations Specialist	Alabama	Y	31520 FQ	39470 MW	50120 TQ	USBLS	5/07
	Birmingham-Hoover MSA, AL	Y	34050 FQ	41390 MW	51890 TQ	USBLS	5/07
	Huntsville MSA, AL	Y	31280 FQ	41900 MW	51430 TQ	USBLS	5/07
	Montgomery MSA, AL	Y	30500 FQ	40670 MW	50900 TQ	USBLS	5/07
	Alaska	Y	49520 FQ	65310 MW	84460 TQ	USBLS	5/07

AE Average entry wage	**AW** Average wage paid	**FQ** First quartile wage	**LO** Lowest wage paid	**MTC** Median total compensation	**TCC** Total cash compensation
AER Average entry range	**AWR** Average wage range	**H** Hourly	**LR** Low end range	**MW** Median wage paid	**TQ** Third quartile wage
AEX Average experienced wage	**AXR** Average experienced range	**HI** Highest wage paid	**M** Monthly	**MWR** Median wage range	**W** Weekly
ATC Average total compensation	**D** Daily	**HR** High end range	**MCC** Median cash compensation	**S** See annotated source	**Y** Yearly

Occupation/Type/Industry	Location	Per	Low	Mid	High	Source	Date
Public Relations Specialist	Anchorage MSA, AK	Y	53600 FQ	78160 MW	88590 TQ	USBLS	5/07
	Fairbanks MSA, AK	Y	43210 FQ	51240 MW	63260 TQ	USBLS	5/07
	Arizona	Y	32330 FQ	42310 MW	58160 TQ	USBLS	5/07
	Flagstaff MSA, AZ	Y	37390 FQ	46710 MW	60750 TQ	USBLS	5/07
	Phoenix-Mesa-Scottsdale MSA, AZ	Y	31850 FQ	41950 MW	58480 TQ	USBLS	5/07
	Tucson MSA, AZ	Y	33760 FQ	40870 MW	52430 TQ	USBLS	5/07
	Arkansas	Y	30950 FQ	36710 MW	47820 TQ	USBLS	5/07
	Fort Smith MSA, AR-OK	Y	28710 FQ	32760 MW	41910 TQ	USBLS	5/07
	Little Rock-North Little Rock MSA, AR	Y	33560 FQ	38500 MW	52830 TQ	USBLS	5/07
	California	H	19.63 FQ	27.57 MW	39.31 TQ	CABLS	1/08-3/08
	Los Angeles-Long Beach-Glendale PMSA, CA	H	18.63 FQ	24.28 MW	35.68 TQ	CABLS	1/08-3/08
	Oakland-Fremont-Hayward MSA, CA	H	20.29 FQ	29.14 MW	38.67 TQ	CABLS	1/08-3/08
	Riverside-San Bernardino-Ontario MSA, CA	H	16.36 FQ	21.69 MW	30.05 TQ	CABLS	1/08-3/08
	Sacramento-Arden Arcade-Roseville MSA, CA	H	21.97 FQ	31.59 MW	39.60 TQ	CABLS	1/08-3/08
	San Diego-Carlsbad-San Marcos MSA, CA	H	17.83 FQ	23.81 MW	33.12 TQ	CABLS	1/08-3/08
	San Francisco-San Mateo-Redwood PMSA, CA	H	22.80 FQ	34.19 MW	44.18 TQ	CABLS	1/08-3/08
	San Jose-Sunnyvale-Santa Clara MSA, CA	H	29.58 FQ	42.85 MW	56.35 TQ	CABLS	1/08-3/08
	Santa Ana-Anaheim-Irvine PMSA, CA	Y	42810 FQ	59050 MW	76620 TQ	USBLS	5/07
	Santa Rosa-Petaluma MSA, CA	H	17.85 FQ	20.76 MW	28.33 TQ	CABLS	1/08-3/08
	Stockton MSA, CA	H	15.92 FQ	24.96 MW	34.30 TQ	CABLS	1/08-3/08
	Colorado	Y	37900 FQ	50540 MW	72160 TQ	USBLS	5/07
	Denver-Aurora MSA, CO	Y	40970 FQ	54150 MW	77560 TQ	USBLS	5/07
	Connecticut	H	17.23 AE	25.73 MW		CTBLS	1/08-3/08
	Bridgeport-Stamford-Norwalk MSA, CT	Y	39400 FQ	52680 MW	66890 TQ	USBLS	5/07
	Hartford-West Hartford-East Hartford MSA, CT	Y	41860 FQ	53740 MW	69050 TQ	USBLS	5/07
	Waterbury MSA, CT	Y	37550 FQ	45270 MW	56980 TQ	USBLS	5/07
	Delaware	Y	40670 FQ	49750 MW	63920 TQ	USBLS	5/07
	Wilmington PMSA, DE-MD-NJ	Y	41210 FQ	51480 MW	66830 TQ	USBLS	5/07
	District of Columbia	Y	58380 FQ	79050 MW	109860 TQ	USBLS	5/07
	Washington-Arlington-Alexandria MSA, DC-VA-MD-WV	Y	54780 FQ	75520 MW	102340 TQ	USBLS	5/07
	Florida	Y	37060 FQ	48230 MW	63460 TQ	USBLS	5/07
	Fort Lauderdale-Pompano Beach-Deerfield Beach PMSA, FL	Y	41500 FQ	51610 MW	68800 TQ	USBLS	5/07
	Jacksonville MSA, FL	Y	40240 FQ	50940 MW	69370 TQ	USBLS	5/07
	Miami-Fort Lauderdale-Miami Beach MSA, FL	Y	38250 FQ	49420 MW	65120 TQ	USBLS	5/07
	Orlando-Kissimmee MSA, FL	Y	36760 FQ	46930 MW	63120 TQ	USBLS	5/07
	Tallahassee MSA, FL	Y	35000 FQ	48240 MW	67130 TQ	USBLS	5/07
	Tampa-St. Petersburg-Clearwater MSA, FL	Y	34710 FQ	46910 MW	62180 TQ	USBLS	5/07
	West Palm Beach-Boca Raton-Boynton Beach PMSA, FL	Y	39600 FQ	49830 MW	67350 TQ	USBLS	5/07
	Georgia	Y	35950 FQ	44840 MW	59600 TQ	USBLS	5/07
	Atlanta-Sandy Springs-Marietta MSA, GA	Y	37440 FQ	46280 MW	63190 TQ	USBLS	5/07
	Hawaii	Y	38360 FQ	47390 MW	60490 TQ	USBLS	5/07
	Honolulu MSA, HI	Y	39270 FQ	48830 MW	62390 TQ	USBLS	5/07
	Idaho	Y	40900 FQ	51300 MW	75760 TQ	USBLS	5/07
	Boise City-Nampa MSA, ID	Y	42140 FQ	55520 MW	83340 TQ	USBLS	5/07
	Idaho Falls MSA, ID	Y	42100 FQ	46130 MW	50160 TQ	USBLS	5/07
	Illinois	Y	35970 FQ	46740 MW	65320 TQ	USBLS	5/07
	Chicago-Naperville-Joliet MSA, IL-IN-WI	Y	36110 FQ	46490 MW	65180 TQ	USBLS	5/07
	Indiana	Y	31080 FQ	40620 MW	53530 TQ	USBLS	5/07
	Gary PMSA, IN	Y	31710 FQ	38050 MW	47490 TQ	USBLS	5/07
	Indianapolis-Carmel MSA, IN	Y	34550 FQ	44720 MW	61360 TQ	USBLS	5/07

AE	Average entry wage	AW	Average wage paid	FQ	First quartile wage	LO	Lowest wage paid	MTC	Median total compensation	TCC	Total cash compensation
AER	Average entry range	AWR	Average wage range	H	Hourly	LR	Low end range	MW	Median wage paid	TQ	Third quartile wage
AEX	Average experienced wage	AXR	Average experienced range	HI	Highest wage paid	M	Monthly	MWR	Median wage range	W	Weekly
ATC	Average total compensation	D	Daily	HR	High end range	MCC	Median cash compensation	S	See annotated source	Y	Yearly

Occupation/Type/Industry	Location	Per	Low	Mid	High	Source	Date
Public Relations Specialist	Iowa	Y	33070 FQ	43540 MW	54860 TQ	USBLS	5/07
	Des Moines-West Des Moines MSA, IA	Y	35820 FQ	47210 MW	71370 TQ	USBLS	5/07
	Kansas	Y	33100 FQ	42210 MW	56270 TQ	USBLS	5/07
	Lawrence MSA, KS	Y	23710 FQ	38710 MW	47300 TQ	USBLS	5/07
	Wichita MSA, KS	Y	30680 FQ	39500 MW	48730 TQ	USBLS	5/07
	Kentucky	Y	31923 FQ	41227 MW	53886 TQ	KYBLS	2008
	Bowling Green MSA, KY	Y	23040 FQ	33090 MW	39470 TQ	USBLS	5/07
	Louisville-Jefferson County MSA, KY-IN	Y	33100 FQ	42460 MW	54700 TQ	USBLS	5/07
	Louisiana	H	14.76 FQ	19.50 MW	25.10 TQ	LABLS	1/08-3/08
	Baton Rouge MSA, LA	Y	33810 FQ	42030 MW	53390 TQ	USBLS	5/07
	New Orleans-Metairie-Kenner MSA, LA	Y	33510 FQ	43740 MW	57550 TQ	USBLS	5/07
	Maine	Y	37650 FQ	48070 MW	64870 TQ	USBLS	5/07
	Lewiston-Auburn MSA, ME	Y	40440 FQ	46220 MW	67420 TQ	USBLS	5/07
	Portland-South Portland-Biddeford MSA, ME	Y	37250 FQ	52060 MW	65320 TQ	USBLS	5/07
	Maryland	Y		56075 MW		MDBLS	3/08
	Baltimore-Towson MSA, MD	Y	37410 FQ	49050 MW	64710 TQ	USBLS	5/07
	Bethesda-Gaithersburg-Frederick PMSA, MD	Y	51040 FQ	72350 MW	91260 TQ	USBLS	5/07
	Massachusetts	Y	41770 FQ	53010 MW	73380 TQ	USBLS	5/07
	Boston-Cambridge-Quincy NECTA, MA	Y	42070 FQ	53170 MW	72420 TQ	USBLS	5/07
	Worcester MSA, MA-CT	Y	40250 FQ	48830 MW	62060 TQ	USBLS	5/07
	Michigan	Y	36540 FQ	49440 MW	66570 TQ	USBLS	5/07
	Detroit-Warren-Livonia MSA, MI	Y	39700 FQ	53980 MW	73350 TQ	USBLS	5/07
	Grand Rapids-Wyoming MSA, MI	Y	33240 FQ	45770 MW	62920 TQ	USBLS	5/07
	Warren-Troy-Farmington Hills PMSA, MI	Y	39720 FQ	53650 MW	75790 TQ	USBLS	5/07
	Minnesota	Y	43951 FQ	54581 MW	71174 TQ	MNBLS	10/08-12/08
	Duluth-Superior MSA, MN-WI	Y	39003 FQ	50020 MW	65420 TQ	MNBLS	10/08-12/08
	Minneapolis-Saint Paul MSA, MN-WI	Y	44621 FQ	54843 MW	72241 TQ	MNBLS	10/08-12/08
	Rochester MSA, MN	Y	45208 FQ	64792 MW	97632 TQ	MNBLS	10/08-12/08
	Mississippi	Y	28500 FQ	35370 MW	43420 TQ	USBLS	5/07
	Jackson MSA, MS	Y	30360 FQ	36180 MW	42530 TQ	USBLS	5/07
	Missouri	Y	34470 FQ	44320 MW	58520 TQ	USBLS	5/07
	Jefferson City MSA, MO	Y	34190 FQ	46280 MW	60710 TQ	USBLS	5/07
	Joplin MSA, MO	Y	32050 FQ	36940 MW	44670 TQ	USBLS	5/07
	Kansas City MSA, MO-KS	Y	37150 FQ	47100 MW	62270 TQ	USBLS	5/07
	St. Louis MSA, MO-IL	Y	37030 FQ	47900 MW	66590 TQ	USBLS	5/07
	Montana	Y	34380 FQ	41270 MW	54810 TQ	USBLS	5/07
	Billings MSA, MT	Y	34770 FQ	39640 MW	59410 TQ	USBLS	5/07
	Nebraska	Y	30190 FQ	38600 MW	51420 TQ	USBLS	5/07
	Lincoln MSA, NE	Y	34820 FQ	45000 MW	66440 TQ	USBLS	5/07
	Omaha-Council Bluffs MSA, NE-IA	Y	31450 FQ	38410 MW	47840 TQ	USBLS	5/07
	Nevada	H	23.39 FQ	29.41 MW	37.79 TQ	NVBLS	5/08
	Las Vegas-Paradise MSA, NV	H	24.84 FQ	29.82 MW	38.00 TQ	NVBLS	6/08
	New Hampshire	H	16.77 AE	21.49 MW	26.16 AEX	NHBLS	6/08
	Manchester MSA, NH	Y	37750 FQ	44220 MW	50080 TQ	USBLS	5/07
	Nashua NECTA, NH-MA	Y	29290 FQ	49590 MW	75050 TQ	USBLS	5/07
	New Jersey	Y	42400 FQ	57200 MW	75250 TQ	USBLS	5/07
	Camden PMSA, NJ	Y	42460 FQ	52270 MW	62670 TQ	USBLS	5/07
	Edison PMSA, NJ	Y	45740 FQ	60770 MW	79020 TQ	USBLS	5/07
	Newark-Union PMSA, NJ-PA	Y	38910 FQ	57140 MW	75700 TQ	USBLS	5/07
	New Mexico	Y	36320 FQ	47600 MW	62900 TQ	USBLS	5/07
	Albuquerque MSA, NM	Y	39070 FQ	49380 MW	65240 TQ	USBLS	5/07
	New York	Y	40870 FQ	54640 MW	72560 TQ	USBLS	5/07
	Albany-Schenectady-Troy MSA, NY	Y	36620 FQ	50010 MW	62430 TQ	USBLS	5/07
	Buffalo-Niagara Falls MSA, NY	Y	34410 FQ	40940 MW	53010 TQ	USBLS	5/07
	Nassau-Suffolk PMSA, NY	Y	45060 FQ	59380 MW	80120 TQ	USBLS	5/07
	New York-Northern New Jersey-Long Island MSA, NY-NJ-PA	Y	42750 FQ	57640 MW	75770 TQ	USBLS	5/07
	North Carolina	Y	35580 FQ	45730 MW	60220 TQ	USBLS	5/07

AE Average entry wage	**AW** Average wage paid	**FQ** First quartile wage	**LO** Lowest wage paid	**MTC** Median total compensation	**TCC** Total cash compensation
AER Average entry range	**AWR** Average wage range	**H** Hourly	**LR** Low end range	**MW** Median wage paid	**TQ** Third quartile wage
AEX Average experienced wage	**AXR** Average experienced range	**HI** Highest wage paid	**M** Monthly	**MWR** Median wage range	**W** Weekly
ATC Average total compensation	**D** Daily	**HR** High end range	**MCC** Median cash compensation	**S** See annotated source	**Y** Yearly

Occupation/Type/Industry	Location	Per	Low	Mid	High	Source	Date
Public Relations Specialist	Charlotte-Gastonia-Concord MSA, NC-SC	Y	36530 FQ	46400 MW	58170 TQ	USBLS	5/07
	Raleigh-Cary MSA, NC	Y	36610 FQ	49550 MW	69590 TQ	USBLS	5/07
	North Dakota	Y	32380 FQ	39260 MW	48930 TQ	USBLS	5/07
	Fargo MSA, ND-MN	Y	32860 FQ	39660 MW	47820 TQ	USBLS	5/07
	Ohio	Y	38980 FQ	49480 MW	62420 TQ	USBLS	5/07
	Cincinnati-Middletown MSA, OH-KY-IN	Y	39300 FQ	49280 MW	64410 TQ	USBLS	5/07
	Cleveland-Elyria-Mentor MSA, OH	Y	40470 FQ	51070 MW	63370 TQ	USBLS	5/07
	Columbus MSA, OH	Y	41840 FQ	52520 MW	68210 TQ	USBLS	5/07
	Dayton MSA, OH	Y	38290 FQ	48030 MW	62170 TQ	USBLS	5/07
	Springfield MSA, OH	Y	41890 FQ	47170 MW	52250 TQ	USBLS	5/07
	Oklahoma	Y	29930 FQ	39610 MW	55030 TQ	USBLS	5/07
	Oklahoma City MSA, OK	Y	30160 FQ	39220 MW	54070 TQ	USBLS	5/07
	Tulsa MSA, OK	Y	33410 FQ	44060 MW	64430 TQ	USBLS	5/07
	Oregon	H	18.58 FQ	24.43 MW	31.54 TQ	ORBLS	5/08
	Portland-Vancouver-Beaverton MSA, OR-WA	Y	38610 FQ	51470 MW	66130 TQ	USBLS	5/07
	Salem MSA, OR	Y	41230 FQ	50080 MW	62740 TQ	USBLS	5/07
	Pennsylvania	Y	38010 FQ	49450 MW	69810 TQ	USBLS	5/07
	Allentown-Bethlehem-Easton MSA, PA-NJ	Y	37600 FQ	48080 MW	64350 TQ	USBLS	5/07
	Erie MSA, PA	Y	26420 FQ	37710 MW	50740 TQ	USBLS	5/07
	Philadelphia-Camden-Wilmington MSA, PA-NJ-DE-MD	Y	41820 FQ	55380 MW	79090 TQ	USBLS	5/07
	Pittsburgh MSA, PA	Y	39150 FQ	51990 MW	74230 TQ	USBLS	5/07
	Reading MSA, PA	Y	40360 FQ	44380 MW	49280 TQ	USBLS	5/07
	Rhode Island	Y	41680 FQ	49500 MW	63070 TQ	USBLS	5/07
	Providence-Fall River-Warwick MSA, RI-MA	Y	41660 FQ	49830 MW	63190 TQ	USBLS	5/07
	South Carolina	Y	32310 FQ	40620 MW	53270 TQ	USBLS	5/07
	Charleston-North Charleston MSA, SC	Y	28710 FQ	36880 MW	46940 TQ	USBLS	5/07
	Columbia MSA, SC	Y	35880 FQ	45220 MW	69340 TQ	USBLS	5/07
	Myrtle Beach-Conway-North Myrtle Beach MSA, SC	Y	17600 FQ	29570 MW	38800 TQ	USBLS	5/07
	South Dakota	Y	29435 FQ	37449 MW	47059 TQ	SDBLS	7/08-9/08
	Sioux Falls MSA, SD	Y	25121 FQ	34247 MW	44406 TQ	SDBLS	7/08-9/08
	Tennessee	Y	29870 FQ	38820 MW	53180 TQ	USBLS	5/07
	Memphis MSA, TN-MS-AR	Y	30230 FQ	40720 MW	54260 TQ	USBLS	5/07
	Nashville-Davidson-Murfreesboro MSA, TN	Y	33090 FQ	42620 MW	55760 TQ	USBLS	5/07
	Texas	Y	36160 FQ	48320 MW	66980 TQ	USBLS	5/07
	Austin-Round Rock MSA, TX	Y	35380 FQ	46940 MW	70780 TQ	USBLS	5/07
	Brownsville-Harlingen MSA, TX	Y	23060 FQ	31340 MW	49580 TQ	USBLS	5/07
	Dallas-Fort Worth-Arlington MSA, TX	Y	39230 FQ	51760 MW	72950 TQ	USBLS	5/07
	El Paso MSA, TX	Y	23370 FQ	34300 MW	45920 TQ	USBLS	5/07
	Houston-Sugar Land-Baytown MSA, TX	Y	39390 FQ	52520 MW	70300 TQ	USBLS	5/07
	San Antonio MSA, TX	Y	36390 FQ	46710 MW	62500 TQ	USBLS	5/07
	Utah	Y	34010 FQ	44910 MW	56780 TQ	USBLS	5/07
	Ogden-Clearfield MSA, UT	Y	39140 FQ	45570 MW	51210 TQ	USBLS	5/07
	Salt Lake City MSA, UT	Y	33230 FQ	45060 MW	57600 TQ	USBLS	5/07
	Vermont	Y	35310 FQ	43430 MW	54470 TQ	USBLS	5/07
	Burlington-South Burlington MSA, VT	Y	36020 FQ	42730 MW	51470 TQ	USBLS	5/07
	Virginia	Y	38350 FQ	53840 MW	79660 TQ	USBLS	5/07
	Richmond MSA, VA	Y	33900 FQ	46100 MW	62930 TQ	USBLS	5/07
	Virginia Beach-Norfolk-Newport News MSA, VA-NC	Y	37980 FQ	49240 MW	66740 TQ	USBLS	5/07
	Washington	H	21.75 FQ	27.84 MW	35.37 TQ	WABLS	3/08
	Seattle-Tacoma-Bellevue MSA, WA	Y	44760 FQ	57710 MW	74420 TQ	USBLS	5/07
	West Virginia	Y	25587 FQ	35687 MW	51400 TQ	WVBLS	7/08-9/08
	Charleston MSA, WV	Y	29480 FQ	37270 MW	53970 TQ	USBLS	5/07
	Wisconsin	Y	34000 FQ	43160 MW	57190 TQ	USBLS	5/07
	Green Bay MSA, WI	Y	32130 FQ	41200 MW	50110 TQ	USBLS	5/07

AE Average entry wage	**AW** Average wage paid	**FQ** First quartile wage	**LO** Lowest wage paid	**MTC** Median total compensation	**TCC** Total cash compensation
AER Average entry range	**AWR** Average wage range	**H** Hourly	**LR** Low end range	**MW** Median wage paid	**TQ** Third quartile wage
AEX Average experienced wage	**AXR** Average experienced range	**HI** Highest wage paid	**M** Monthly	**MWR** Median wage range	**W** Weekly
ATC Average total compensation	**D** Daily	**HR** High end range	**MCC** Median cash compensation	**S** See annotated source	**Y** Yearly

Occupation/Type/Industry	Location	Per	Low	Mid	High	Source	Date
Public Relations Specialist	Milwaukee-Waukesha-West Allis MSA, WI	Y	36410 FQ	46040 MW	63350 TQ	USBLS	5/07
	Wyoming	Y	33579 FQ	40002 MW	50516 TQ	WYBLS	9/08
	Cheyenne MSA, WY	Y	36760 FQ	43551 MW	53825 TQ	WYBLS	9/08
	Puerto Rico	Y	17660 FQ	27350 MW	36030 TQ	USBLS	5/07
	San Juan-Caguas-Guaynabo MSA, PR	Y	17930 FQ	28020 MW	36390 TQ	USBLS	5/07
Public Safety Director	Perry, GA	Y	67800 LO		98000 HI	GACTY01	2008
Public Safety Officer	Berkley, MI	Y	37522 LO		59849 HI	HLIFE01	7/1/08
Public Television President and CEO	Maryland	Y			198048 HI	BMAG	2009
Public Vehicle Investigator Municipal Government	Cincinnati, OH	Y	39113 LO		41597 HI	COHSS	10/08
Public Works Director	Hampton, GA	Y	57112 LO		88524 HI	AREGC	2007
Public Works Inspector Highway Department	Greenfield, MA	H			13.71 HI	FRCOG	2009
Public Works Superintendent	Baldwin County, GA	Y	58114 LO		88428 HI	GACTY03	2008
Publications Attorney and Editor State Supreme Court	Michigan	Y			70073 HI	LSJ02	7/11/07
Publications Editor State Government	Ohio	H	19.88 LO		26.28 HI	ODAS	2008
Publicist	Maryland	Y		80000 AW		WTGMD	2009
Pump Operator							
Except Wellhead Pumpers	Alabama	Y	27840 FQ	37550 MW	61130 TQ	USBLS	5/07
Except Wellhead Pumpers	Alaska	Y	45680 FQ	60320 MW	70290 TQ	USBLS	5/07
Except Wellhead Pumpers	Arkansas	Y	21300 FQ	28390 MW	33510 TQ	USBLS	5/07
Except Wellhead Pumpers	California	H	16.14 FQ	21.86 MW	26.74 TQ	CABLS	1/08-3/08
Except Wellhead Pumpers	Colorado	Y	25590 FQ	36070 MW	47960 TQ	USBLS	5/07
Except Wellhead Pumpers	Florida	Y	24590 FQ	31070 MW	39010 TQ	USBLS	5/07
Except Wellhead Pumpers	Georgia	Y	22200 FQ	25020 MW	30550 TQ	USBLS	5/07
Except Wellhead Pumpers	Hawaii	Y	31190 FQ	46070 MW	59090 TQ	USBLS	5/07
Except Wellhead Pumpers	Illinois	Y	22210 FQ	36140 MW	47740 TQ	USBLS	5/07
Except Wellhead Pumpers	Indiana	Y	32980 FQ	48300 MW	53300 TQ	USBLS	5/07
Except Wellhead Pumpers	Iowa	Y	19460 FQ	27100 MW	32880 TQ	USBLS	5/07
Except Wellhead Pumpers	Kansas	Y	32980 FQ	37740 MW	44190 TQ	USBLS	5/07
Except Wellhead Pumpers	Louisiana	H	15.26 FQ	20.23 MW	26.50 TQ	LABLS	1/08-3/08
Except Wellhead Pumpers	Massachusetts	Y	33220 FQ	45270 MW	57230 TQ	USBLS	5/07
Except Wellhead Pumpers	Michigan	Y	30070 FQ	37910 MW	46540 TQ	USBLS	5/07
Except Wellhead Pumpers	Mississippi	Y	34490 FQ	38150 MW	42450 TQ	USBLS	5/07
Except Wellhead Pumpers	Nebraska	Y	20390 FQ	23670 MW	30630 TQ	USBLS	5/07
Except Wellhead Pumpers	Nevada	H	13.12 FQ	14.18 MW	15.46 TQ	NVBLS	5/08
Except Wellhead Pumpers	New Jersey	Y	29640 FQ	39470 MW	50970 TQ	USBLS	5/07
Except Wellhead Pumpers	New Mexico	Y	37280 FQ	49110 MW	68400 TQ	USBLS	5/07
Except Wellhead Pumpers	New York	Y	33280 FQ	38860 MW	63040 TQ	USBLS	5/07
Except Wellhead Pumpers	North Carolina	Y	33000 FQ	37720 MW	44320 TQ	USBLS	5/07
Except Wellhead Pumpers	Ohio	Y	37980 FQ	53210 MW	63430 TQ	USBLS	5/07
Except Wellhead Pumpers	Oklahoma	Y	32000 FQ	39000 MW	46630 TQ	USBLS	5/07
Except Wellhead Pumpers	Oregon	H	14.34 FQ	17.99 MW	20.35 TQ	ORBLS	5/08
Except Wellhead Pumpers	Pennsylvania	Y	22480 FQ	25000 MW	44900 TQ	USBLS	5/07
Except Wellhead Pumpers	South Carolina	Y	28790 FQ	37870 MW	44930 TQ	USBLS	5/07
Except Wellhead Pumpers	Tennessee	Y	31650 FQ	37810 MW	51990 TQ	USBLS	5/07*
Except Wellhead Pumpers	Texas	Y	33580 FQ	42020 MW	49790 TQ	USBLS	5/07
Except Wellhead Pumpers	Utah	Y	31740 FQ	37270 MW	43760 TQ	USBLS	5/07
Except Wellhead Pumpers	Virginia	Y	33490 FQ	41230 MW	47030 TQ	USBLS	5/07
Except Wellhead Pumpers	Wisconsin	Y	26790 FQ	30970 MW	34740 TQ	USBLS	5/07
Except Wellhead Pumpers	Wyoming	Y	26051 FQ	38437 MW	49670 TQ	WYBLS	9/08
Except Wellhead Pumpers	Puerto Rico	Y	20310 FQ	22800 MW	25520 TQ	USBLS	5/07
Purchasing Agent							
District Government	District of Columbia	Y	40543 LO		57006 HI	AFT02	3/1/08
Except Wholesale, Retail, and Farm	Alabama	Y	38860 FQ	51920 MW	70290 TQ	USBLS	5/07
Except Wholesale, Retail, and Farm	Birmingham-Hoover MSA, AL	Y	38570 FQ	49100 MW	61990 TQ	USBLS	5/07

AE	Average entry wage	AW	Average wage paid	FQ	First quartile wage	LO	Lowest wage paid	MTC	Median total compensation	TCC	Total cash compensation
AER	Average entry range	AWR	Average wage range	H	Hourly	LR	Low end range	MW	Median wage paid	TQ	Third quartile wage
AEX	Average experienced wage	AXR	Average experienced range	HI	Highest wage paid	M	Monthly	MWR	Median wage range	W	Weekly
ATC	Average total compensation	D	Daily	HR	High end range	MCC	Median cash compensation	S	See annotated source	Y	Yearly

Purchasing Agent

Occupation/Type/Industry	Location	Per	Low	Mid	High	Source	Date
Purchasing Agent							
Except Wholesale, Retail, and Farm	Montgomery MSA, AL	Y	39270 FQ	48630 MW	60760 TQ	USBLS	5/07
Except Wholesale, Retail, and Farm	Tuscaloosa MSA, AL	Y	29290 FQ	39360 MW	50790 TQ	USBLS	5/07
Except Wholesale, Retail, and Farm	Alaska	Y	45570 FQ	56290 MW	68250 TQ	USBLS	5/07
Except Wholesale, Retail, and Farm	Anchorage MSA, AK	Y	46740 FQ	57830 MW	69790 TQ	USBLS	5/07
Except Wholesale, Retail, and Farm	Arizona	Y	36450 FQ	47210 MW	61680 TQ	USBLS	5/07
Except Wholesale, Retail, and Farm	Phoenix-Mesa-Scottsdale MSA, AZ	Y	35750 FQ	46490 MW	60330 TQ	USBLS	5/07
Except Wholesale, Retail, and Farm	Tucson MSA, AZ	Y	38800 FQ	51140 MW	64500 TQ	USBLS	5/07
Except Wholesale, Retail, and Farm	Arkansas	Y	32750 FQ	42090 MW	53380 TQ	USBLS	5/07
Except Wholesale, Retail, and Farm	Little Rock-North Little Rock MSA, AR	Y	32450 FQ	40330 MW	51620 TQ	USBLS	5/07
Except Wholesale, Retail, and Farm	Pine Bluff MSA, AR	Y	35730 FQ	44280 MW	64720 TQ	USBLS	5/07
Except Wholesale, Retail, and Farm	California	H	21.81 FQ	28.10 MW	36.26 TQ	CABLS	1/08-3/08
Except Wholesale, Retail, and Farm	Fresno MSA, CA	H	16.67 FQ	22.31 MW	27.78 TQ	CABLS	1/08-3/08
Except Wholesale, Retail, and Farm	Los Angeles-Long Beach-Glendale PMSA, CA	H	21.46 FQ	27.82 MW	36.54 TQ	CABLS	1/08-3/08
Except Wholesale, Retail, and Farm	Oakland-Fremont-Hayward MSA, CA	H	24.02 FQ	29.72 MW	37.27 TQ	CABLS	1/08-3/08
Except Wholesale, Retail, and Farm	Riverside-San Bernardino-Ontario MSA, CA	H	18.82 FQ	23.05 MW	30.39 TQ	CABLS	1/08-3/08
Except Wholesale, Retail, and Farm	Sacramento-Arden Arcade-Roseville MSA, CA	H	20.63 FQ	25.48 MW	33.48 TQ	CABLS	1/08-3/08
Except Wholesale, Retail, and Farm	San Diego-Carlsbad-San Marcos MSA, CA	H	22.18 FQ	27.99 MW	35.97 TQ	CABLS	1/08-3/08
Except Wholesale, Retail, and Farm	San Francisco-San Mateo-Redwood PMSA, CA	H	24.26 FQ	31.19 MW	40.15 TQ	CABLS	1/08-3/08
Except Wholesale, Retail, and Farm	San Jose-Sunnyvale-Santa Clara MSA, CA	H	26.19 FQ	32.90 MW	40.43 TQ	CABLS	1/08-3/08
Except Wholesale, Retail, and Farm	Santa Ana-Anaheim-Irvine PMSA, CA	Y	45530 FQ	57020 MW	70840 TQ	USBLS	5/07
Except Wholesale, Retail, and Farm	Colorado	Y	42860 FQ	55990 MW	72230 TQ	USBLS	5/07
Except Wholesale, Retail, and Farm	Boulder MSA, CO	Y	40550 FQ	53960 MW	69640 TQ	USBLS	5/07
Except Wholesale, Retail, and Farm	Denver-Aurora MSA, CO	Y	43960 FQ	57310 MW	74110 TQ	USBLS	5/07
Except Wholesale, Retail, and Farm	Connecticut	H	19.97 AE	29.13 MW		CTBLS	1/08-3/08
Except Wholesale, Retail, and Farm	Bridgeport-Stamford-Norwalk MSA, CT	Y	45750 FQ	61440 MW	78140 TQ	USBLS	5/07
Except Wholesale, Retail, and Farm	Hartford-West Hartford-East Hartford MSA, CT	Y	48010 FQ	60460 MW	74150 TQ	USBLS	5/07
Except Wholesale, Retail, and Farm	Delaware	Y	45110 FQ	57030 MW	72210 TQ	USBLS	5/07
Except Wholesale, Retail, and Farm	Wilmington PMSA, DE-MD-NJ	Y	47860 FQ	59470 MW	75450 TQ	USBLS	5/07
Except Wholesale, Retail, and Farm	District of Columbia	Y	57540 FQ	76260 MW	94050 TQ	USBLS	5/07
Except Wholesale, Retail, and Farm	Washington-Arlington-Alexandria MSA, DC-VA-MD-WV	Y	52250 FQ	69780 MW	89550 TQ	USBLS	5/07
Except Wholesale, Retail, and Farm	Florida	Y	37040 FQ	47540 MW	62760 TQ	USBLS	5/07
Except Wholesale, Retail, and Farm	Fort Lauderdale-Pompano Beach-Deerfield Beach PMSA, FL	Y	38940 FQ	47340 MW	59630 TQ	USBLS	5/07
Except Wholesale, Retail, and Farm	Jacksonville MSA, FL	Y	38180 FQ	47610 MW	61520 TQ	USBLS	5/07
Except Wholesale, Retail, and Farm	Miami-Fort Lauderdale-Miami Beach MSA, FL	Y	37050 FQ	47650 MW	61590 TQ	USBLS	5/07
Except Wholesale, Retail, and Farm	Orlando-Kissimmee MSA, FL	Y	37260 FQ	48120 MW	66000 TQ	USBLS	5/07
Except Wholesale, Retail, and Farm	Tallahassee MSA, FL	Y	33080 FQ	41270 MW	51790 TQ	USBLS	5/07
Except Wholesale, Retail, and Farm	Tampa-St. Petersburg-Clearwater MSA, FL	Y	37050 FQ	47960 MW	64090 TQ	USBLS	5/07
Except Wholesale, Retail, and Farm	West Palm Beach-Boca Raton-Boynton Beach PMSA, FL	Y	38050 FQ	50210 MW	65200 TQ	USBLS	5/07
Except Wholesale, Retail, and Farm	Georgia	Y	39120 FQ	50360 MW	65870 TQ	USBLS	5/07
Except Wholesale, Retail, and Farm	Atlanta-Sandy Springs-Marietta MSA, GA	Y	40470 FQ	51090 MW	66770 TQ	USBLS	5/07
Except Wholesale, Retail, and Farm	Hawaii	Y	41610 FQ	55450 MW	74290 TQ	USBLS	5/07
Except Wholesale, Retail, and Farm	Honolulu MSA, HI	Y	42250 FQ	58510 MW	76140 TQ	USBLS	5/07
Except Wholesale, Retail, and Farm	Idaho	Y	34680 FQ	44340 MW	56430 TQ	USBLS	5/07
Except Wholesale, Retail, and Farm	Boise City-Nampa MSA, ID	Y	35510 FQ	45420 MW	57000 TQ	USBLS	5/07
Except Wholesale, Retail, and Farm	Illinois	Y	42570 FQ	54670 MW	71940 TQ	USBLS	5/07
Except Wholesale, Retail, and Farm	Chicago-Naperville-Joliet MSA, IL-IN-WI	Y	43100 FQ	54980 MW	71930 TQ	USBLS	5/07
Except Wholesale, Retail, and Farm	Indiana	Y	37220 FQ	47200 MW	60410 TQ	USBLS	5/07
Except Wholesale, Retail, and Farm	Fort Wayne MSA, IN	Y	36690 FQ	49270 MW	65930 TQ	USBLS	5/07
Except Wholesale, Retail, and Farm	Gary PMSA, IN	Y	35090 FQ	46040 MW	58530 TQ	USBLS	5/07

AE Average entry wage	AW Average wage paid	FQ First quartile wage	LO Lowest wage paid	MTC Median total compensation	TCC Total cash compensation
AER Average entry range	AWR Average wage range	H Hourly	LR Low end range	MW Median wage paid	TQ Third quartile wage
AEX Average experienced wage	AXR Average experienced range	HI Highest wage paid	M Monthly	MWR Median wage range	W Weekly
ATC Average total compensation	D Daily	HR High end range	MCC Median cash compensation	S See annotated source	Y Yearly

Purchasing Agent

Occupation/Type/Industry	Location	Per	Low	Mid	High	Source	Date
Except Wholesale, Retail, and Farm	Indianapolis-Carmel MSA, IN	Y	39500 FQ	49460 MW	62600 TQ	USBLS	5/07
Except Wholesale, Retail, and Farm	Iowa	Y	34450 FQ	43250 MW	55450 TQ	USBLS	5/07
Except Wholesale, Retail, and Farm	Des Moines-West Des Moines MSA, IA	Y	34540 FQ	42500 MW	53160 TQ	USBLS	5/07
Except Wholesale, Retail, and Farm	Kansas	Y	39470 FQ	50170 MW	64260 TQ	USBLS	5/07
Except Wholesale, Retail, and Farm	Topeka MSA, KS	Y	43220 FQ	53520 MW	72840 TQ	USBLS	5/07
Except Wholesale, Retail, and Farm	Wichita MSA, KS	Y	43780 FQ	53740 MW	67230 TQ	USBLS	5/07
Except Wholesale, Retail, and Farm	Kentucky	Y	37447 FQ	47772 MW	61223 TQ	KYBLS	2008
Except Wholesale, Retail, and Farm	Elizabethtown MSA, KY	Y	44040 FQ	56750 MW	71140 TQ	USBLS	5/07
Except Wholesale, Retail, and Farm	Louisville-Jefferson County MSA, KY-IN	Y	37380 FQ	48300 MW	61330 TQ	USBLS	5/07
Except Wholesale, Retail, and Farm	Louisiana	H	15.97 FQ	20.66 MW	27.19 TQ	LABLS	1/08-3/08
Except Wholesale, Retail, and Farm	Baton Rouge MSA, LA	Y	36610 FQ	45770 MW	58390 TQ	USBLS	5/07
Except Wholesale, Retail, and Farm	Houma-Bayou Cane-Thibodaux MSA, LA	Y	29000 FQ	35970 MW	44510 TQ	USBLS	5/07
Except Wholesale, Retail, and Farm	New Orleans-Metairie-Kenner MSA, LA	Y	33720 FQ	43550 MW	59080 TQ	USBLS	5/07
Except Wholesale, Retail, and Farm	Maine	Y	36710 FQ	45210 MW	57570 TQ	USBLS	5/07
Except Wholesale, Retail, and Farm	Portland-South Portland-Biddeford MSA, ME	Y	37390 FQ	47160 MW	58090 TQ	USBLS	5/07
Except Wholesale, Retail, and Farm	Maryland	Y		63550 MW		MDBLS	3/08
Except Wholesale, Retail, and Farm	Baltimore-Towson MSA, MD	Y	44620 FQ	57920 MW	77400 TQ	USBLS	5/07
Except Wholesale, Retail, and Farm	Bethesda-Gaithersburg-Frederick PMSA, MD	Y	49710 FQ	62930 MW	82120 TQ	USBLS	5/07
Except Wholesale, Retail, and Farm	Massachusetts	Y	48140 FQ	60120 MW	75590 TQ	USBLS	5/07
Except Wholesale, Retail, and Farm	Boston-Cambridge-Quincy NECTA, MA	Y	50420 FQ	62520 MW	78310 TQ	USBLS	5/07
Except Wholesale, Retail, and Farm	Worcester MSA, MA-CT	Y	45360 FQ	54930 MW	66130 TQ	USBLS	5/07
Except Wholesale, Retail, and Farm	Michigan	Y	43390 FQ	58210 MW	78150 TQ	USBLS	5/07
Except Wholesale, Retail, and Farm	Detroit-Warren-Livonia MSA, MI	Y	49060 FQ	67210 MW	86900 TQ	USBLS	5/07
Except Wholesale, Retail, and Farm	Grand Rapids-Wyoming MSA, MI	Y	37410 FQ	46390 MW	60520 TQ	USBLS	5/07
Except Wholesale, Retail, and Farm	Warren-Troy-Farmington Hills PMSA, MI	Y	48950 FQ	64610 MW	81290 TQ	USBLS	5/07
Except Wholesale, Retail, and Farm	Minnesota	Y	46012 FQ	55823 MW	67626 TQ	MNBLS	10/08-12/08
Except Wholesale, Retail, and Farm	Duluth-Superior MSA, MN-WI	Y	44667 FQ	52341 MW	60004 TQ	MNBLS	10/08-12/08
Except Wholesale, Retail, and Farm	Minneapolis-Saint Paul MSA, MN-WI	Y	47972 FQ	58180 MW	70295 TQ	MNBLS	10/08-12/08
Except Wholesale, Retail, and Farm	Rochester MSA, MN	Y	46922 FQ	58345 MW	69400 TQ	MNBLS	10/08-12/08
Except Wholesale, Retail, and Farm	Mississippi	Y	30040 FQ	39220 MW	55780 TQ	USBLS	5/07
Except Wholesale, Retail, and Farm	Jackson MSA, MS	Y	32070 FQ	39540 MW	50910 TQ	USBLS	5/07
Except Wholesale, Retail, and Farm	Pascagoula MSA, MS	Y	37360 FQ	61480 MW	75030 TQ	USBLS	5/07
Except Wholesale, Retail, and Farm	Missouri	Y	36740 FQ	48490 MW	64690 TQ	USBLS	5/07
Except Wholesale, Retail, and Farm	Kansas City MSA, MO-KS	Y	39880 FQ	51110 MW	65870 TQ	USBLS	5/07
Except Wholesale, Retail, and Farm	St. Louis MSA, MO-IL	Y	42150 FQ	55990 MW	73110 TQ	USBLS	5/07
Except Wholesale, Retail, and Farm	Montana	Y	32610 FQ	42200 MW	57760 TQ	USBLS	5/07
Except Wholesale, Retail, and Farm	Billings MSA, MT	Y	36130 FQ	46680 MW	61030 TQ	USBLS	5/07
Except Wholesale, Retail, and Farm	Nebraska	Y	36800 FQ	47470 MW	61630 TQ	USBLS	5/07
Except Wholesale, Retail, and Farm	Omaha-Council Bluffs MSA, NE-IA	Y	37470 FQ	49140 MW	64470 TQ	USBLS	5/07
Except Wholesale, Retail, and Farm	Nevada	H	18.79 FQ	23.41 MW	29.69 TQ	NVBLS	5/08
Except Wholesale, Retail, and Farm	Las Vegas-Paradise MSA, NV	H	18.83 FQ	23.28 MW	30.17 TQ	NVBLS	5/08
Except Wholesale, Retail, and Farm	New Hampshire	H	19.02 AE	25.45 MW	29.71 AEX	NHBLS	6/08
Except Wholesale, Retail, and Farm	Manchester MSA, NH	Y	42330 FQ	50830 MW	59730 TQ	USBLS	5/07
Except Wholesale, Retail, and Farm	Nashua NECTA, NH-MA	Y	48910 FQ	57190 MW	69960 TQ	USBLS	5/07
Except Wholesale, Retail, and Farm	New Jersey	Y	48200 FQ	62880 MW	80450 TQ	USBLS	5/07
Except Wholesale, Retail, and Farm	Atlantic City MSA, NJ	Y	46750 FQ	56470 MW	79680 TQ	USBLS	5/07
Except Wholesale, Retail, and Farm	Camden PMSA, NJ	Y	45720 FQ	61390 MW	73990 TQ	USBLS	5/07
Except Wholesale, Retail, and Farm	Edison PMSA, NJ	Y	50550 FQ	67690 MW	86580 TQ	USBLS	5/07
Except Wholesale, Retail, and Farm	Newark-Union PMSA, NJ-PA	Y	49020 FQ	62830 MW	80910 TQ	USBLS	5/07
Except Wholesale, Retail, and Farm	New Mexico	Y	38930 FQ	52370 MW	72520 TQ	USBLS	5/07
Except Wholesale, Retail, and Farm	Albuquerque MSA, NM	Y	40260 FQ	58350 MW	76830 TQ	LABLS	1/08-3/08
Except Wholesale, Retail, and Farm	Santa Fe MSA, NM	Y	34890 FQ	43980 MW	52550 TQ	USBLS	5/07
Except Wholesale, Retail, and Farm	New York	Y	43380 FQ	55800 MW	72200 TQ	USBLS	5/07
Except Wholesale, Retail, and Farm	Albany-Schenectady-Troy MSA, NY	Y	39540 FQ	50180 MW	63240 TQ	USBLS	5/07
Except Wholesale, Retail, and Farm	Buffalo-Niagara Falls MSA, NY	Y	39780 FQ	49220 MW	61120 TQ	USBLS	5/07
Except Wholesale, Retail, and Farm	Nassau-Suffolk PMSA, NY	Y	43700 FQ	57100 MW	73930 TQ	USBLS	5/07

AE	Average entry wage	AW	Average wage paid	FQ	First quartile wage	LO Lowest wage paid	MTC Median total compensation	TCC Total cash compensation
AER	Average entry range	AWR	Average wage range	H	Hourly	LR Low end range	MW Median wage paid	TQ Third quartile wage
AEX	Average experienced wage	AXR	Average experienced range	HI	Highest wage paid	M Monthly	MWR Median wage range	W Weekly
ATC	Average total compensation	D	Daily	HR	High end range	MCC Median cash compensation	S See annotated source	Y Yearly

Purchasing Agent

Occupation/Type/Industry	Location	Per	Low	Mid	High	Source	Date
Purchasing Agent							
Except Wholesale, Retail, and Farm	New York-Northern New Jersey-Long Island MSA, NY-NJ-PA	Y	47800 FQ	61750 MW	79460 TQ	USBLS	5/07
Except Wholesale, Retail, and Farm	North Carolina	Y	38190 FQ	48190 MW	61650 TQ	USBLS	5/07
Except Wholesale, Retail, and Farm	Charlotte-Gastonia-Concord MSA, NC-SC	Y	39520 FQ	48220 MW	60000 TQ	USBLS	5/07
Except Wholesale, Retail, and Farm	Raleigh-Cary MSA, NC	Y	40310 FQ	50730 MW	62380 TQ	USBLS	5/07
Except Wholesale, Retail, and Farm	North Dakota	Y	38360 FQ	48620 MW	62080 TQ	USBLS	5/07
Except Wholesale, Retail, and Farm	Fargo MSA, ND-MN	Y	37360 FQ	45070 MW	61090 TQ	USBLS	5/07
Except Wholesale, Retail, and Farm	Ohio	Y	40720 FQ	52070 MW	67810 TQ	USBLS	5/07
Except Wholesale, Retail, and Farm	Cincinnati-Middletown MSA, OH-KY-IN	Y	41780 FQ	53800 MW	70000 TQ	USBLS	5/07
Except Wholesale, Retail, and Farm	Cleveland-Elyria-Mentor MSA, OH	Y	40390 FQ	50000 MW	63480 TQ	USBLS	5/07
Except Wholesale, Retail, and Farm	Columbus MSA, OH	Y	45230 FQ	56890 MW	70700 TQ	USBLS	5/07
Except Wholesale, Retail, and Farm	Dayton MSA, OH	Y	47820 FQ	66120 MW	83050 TQ	USBLS	5/07
Except Wholesale, Retail, and Farm	Oklahoma	Y	34830 FQ	47200 MW	63670 TQ	USBLS	5/07
Except Wholesale, Retail, and Farm	Lawton MSA, OK	Y	37960 FQ	49420 MW	61250 TQ	USBLS	5/07
Except Wholesale, Retail, and Farm	Oklahoma City MSA, OK	Y	37790 FQ	53570 MW	71320 TQ	USBLS	5/07
Except Wholesale, Retail, and Farm	Tulsa MSA, OK	Y	36050 FQ	45850 MW	57710 TQ	USBLS	5/07
Except Wholesale, Retail, and Farm	Oregon	H	18.69 FQ	23.28 MW	29.82 TQ	ORBLS	5/08
Except Wholesale, Retail, and Farm	Medford MSA, OR	Y	35000 FQ	40530 MW	47860 TQ	USBLS	5/07
Except Wholesale, Retail, and Farm	Portland-Vancouver-Beaverton MSA, OR-WA	Y	40500 FQ	51300 MW	64120 TQ	USBLS	5/07
Except Wholesale, Retail, and Farm	Pennsylvania	Y	39590 FQ	50830 MW	67270 TQ	USBLS	5/07
Except Wholesale, Retail, and Farm	Allentown-Bethlehem-Easton MSA, PA-NJ	Y	40540 FQ	49820 MW	64050 TQ	USBLS	5/07
Except Wholesale, Retail, and Farm	Philadelphia-Camden-Wilmington MSA, PA-NJ-DE-MD	Y	45100 FQ	58670 MW	74350 TQ	USBLS	5/07
Except Wholesale, Retail, and Farm	Pittsburgh MSA, PA	Y	38350 FQ	48480 MW	64170 TQ	USBLS	5/07
Except Wholesale, Retail, and Farm	Reading MSA, PA	Y	39020 FQ	48230 MW	58200 TQ	USBLS	5/07
Except Wholesale, Retail, and Farm	Rhode Island	Y	45740 FQ	56810 MW	71700 TQ	USBLS	5/07
Except Wholesale, Retail, and Farm	Providence-Fall River-Warwick MSA, RI-MA	Y	44630 FQ	55830 MW	70890 TQ	USBLS	5/07
Except Wholesale, Retail, and Farm	South Carolina	Y	37250 FQ	48190 MW	63740 TQ	USBLS	5/07
Except Wholesale, Retail, and Farm	Charleston-North Charleston MSA, SC	Y	38930 FQ	50840 MW	69790 TQ	USBLS	5/07
Except Wholesale, Retail, and Farm	Columbia MSA, SC	Y	36060 FQ	44850 MW	57970 TQ	USBLS	5/07
Except Wholesale, Retail, and Farm	South Dakota	Y	37342 FQ	43839 MW	53542 TQ	SDBLS	7/08-9/08
Except Wholesale, Retail, and Farm	Sioux Falls MSA, SD	Y	37273 FQ	42791 MW	51455 TQ	SDBLS	7/08-9/08
Except Wholesale, Retail, and Farm	Tennessee	Y	34210 FQ	44360 MW	59350 TQ	USBLS	5/07
Except Wholesale, Retail, and Farm	Johnson City MSA, TN	Y	35830 FQ	44270 MW	57090 TQ	USBLS	5/07
Except Wholesale, Retail, and Farm	Kingsport-Bristol-Bristol MSA, TN-VA	Y	32920 FQ	43260 MW	57670 TQ	USBLS	5/07
Except Wholesale, Retail, and Farm	Memphis MSA, TN-MS-AR	Y	33420 FQ	45120 MW	62460 TQ	USBLS	5/07
Except Wholesale, Retail, and Farm	Nashville-Davidson-Murfreesboro MSA, TN	Y	35590 FQ	43070 MW	55550 TQ	USBLS	5/07
Except Wholesale, Retail, and Farm	Texas	Y	38370 FQ	49930 MW	65760 TQ	USBLS	5/07
Except Wholesale, Retail, and Farm	Austin-Round Rock MSA, TX	Y	38940 FQ	52050 MW	66070 TQ	USBLS	5/07
Except Wholesale, Retail, and Farm	Dallas-Fort Worth-Arlington MSA, TX	Y	40180 FQ	51920 MW	68610 TQ	USBLS	5/07
Except Wholesale, Retail, and Farm	El Paso MSA, TX	Y	32160 FQ	41580 MW	55810 TQ	USBLS	5/07
Except Wholesale, Retail, and Farm	Houston-Sugar Land-Baytown MSA, TX	Y	39130 FQ	49990 MW	66810 TQ	USBLS	5/07
Except Wholesale, Retail, and Farm	San Antonio MSA, TX	Y	40550 FQ	58070 MW	74020 TQ	USBLS	5/07
Except Wholesale, Retail, and Farm	Utah	Y	37380 FQ	47460 MW	61360 TQ	USBLS	5/07
Except Wholesale, Retail, and Farm	Salt Lake City MSA, UT	Y	35950 FQ	44960 MW	56650 TQ	USBLS	5/07
Except Wholesale, Retail, and Farm	Vermont	Y	36770 FQ	45800 MW	58010 TQ	USBLS	5/07
Except Wholesale, Retail, and Farm	Burlington-South Burlington MSA, VT	Y	43390 FQ	53260 MW	67190 TQ	USBLS	5/07
Except Wholesale, Retail, and Farm	Virginia	Y	44030 FQ	59060 MW	78760 TQ	USBLS	5/07
Except Wholesale, Retail, and Farm	Richmond MSA, VA	Y	46510 FQ	58670 MW	73610 TQ	USBLS	5/07
Except Wholesale, Retail, and Farm	Virginia Beach-Norfolk-Newport News MSA, VA-NC	Y	40890 FQ	51780 MW	70280 TQ	USBLS	5/07
Except Wholesale, Retail, and Farm	Washington	H	22.58 FQ	28.62 MW	36.15 TQ	WABLS	3/08
Except Wholesale, Retail, and Farm	Seattle-Tacoma-Bellevue MSA, WA	Y	48650 FQ	61230 MW	75660 TQ	USBLS	5/07
Except Wholesale, Retail, and Farm	West Virginia	Y	33131 FQ	42912 MW	55739 TQ	WVBLS	7/08-9/08
Except Wholesale, Retail, and Farm	Charleston MSA, WV	Y	23140 FQ	34090 MW	48780 TQ	USBLS	5/07
Except Wholesale, Retail, and Farm	Wisconsin	Y	38020 FQ	46890 MW	59360 TQ	USBLS	5/07

AE	Average entry wage	AW	Average wage paid	FQ	First quartile wage	LO	Lowest wage paid	MTC	Median total compensation	TCC	Total cash compensation
AER	Average entry range	AWR	Average wage range	H	Hourly	LR	Low end range	MW	Median wage paid	TQ	Third quartile wage
AEX	Average experienced wage	AXR	Average experienced range	HI	Highest wage paid	M	Monthly	MWR	Median wage range	W	Weekly
ATC	Average total compensation	D	Daily	HR	High end range	MCC	Median cash compensation	S	See annotated source	Y	Yearly

Occupation/Type/Industry	Location	Per	Low	Mid	High	Source	Date
Purchasing Agent							
Except Wholesale, Retail, and Farm	Milwaukee-Waukesha-West Allis MSA, WI	Y	40190 FQ	48880 MW	62110 TQ	USBLS	5/07
Except Wholesale, Retail, and Farm	Wyoming	Y	36849 FQ	46710 MW	62601 TQ	WYBLS	9/08
Except Wholesale, Retail, and Farm	Casper MSA, WY	Y	37097 FQ	54753 MW	67190 TQ	WYBLS	9/08
Except Wholesale, Retail, and Farm	Cheyenne MSA, WY	Y	38921 FQ	48339 MW	60016 TQ	WYBLS	9/08
Except Wholesale, Retail, and Farm	Puerto Rico	Y	21590 FQ	28870 MW	40250 TQ	USBLS	5/07
Except Wholesale, Retail, and Farm	Aguadilla-Isabela-San Sebastian MSA, PR	Y	17180 FQ	30280 MW	47500 TQ	USBLS	5/07
Except Wholesale, Retail, and Farm	Guayama MSA, PR	Y	23690 FQ	40830 MW	76420 TQ	USBLS	5/07
Except Wholesale, Retail, and Farm	San Juan-Caguas-Guaynabo MSA, PR	Y	21710 FQ	27970 MW	38470 TQ	USBLS	5/07
Except Wholesale, Retail, and Farm	Guam	Y	23320 FQ	35190 MW	53820 TQ	USBLS	5/07
Municipal Government	Gresham, OR	Y	49920 LO		63792 HI	GOSS	1/1/09
Purchasing Agent and Buyer							
Farm Products	Alabama	Y	43040 FQ	56920 MW	79430 TQ	USBLS	5/07
Farm Products	Birmingham-Hoover MSA, AL	Y	43890 FQ	82540 MW	93010 TQ	USBLS	5/07
Farm Products	Arizona	Y	34520 FQ	46920 MW	65520 TQ	USBLS	5/07
Farm Products	Phoenix-Mesa-Scottsdale MSA, AZ	Y	41900 FQ	53540 MW	73110 TQ	USBLS	5/07
Farm Products	Tucson MSA, AZ	Y	29420 FQ	40650 MW	56410 TQ	USBLS	5/07
Farm Products	Arkansas	Y	39520 FQ	47240 MW	59180 TQ	USBLS	5/07
Farm Products	California	H	20.34 FQ	26.88 MW	36.59 TQ	CABLS	1/08-3/08
Farm Products	Los Angeles-Long Beach-Glendale PMSA, CA	H	22.00 FQ	33.25 MW	46.39 TQ	CABLS	1/08-3/08
Farm Products	Modesto MSA, CA	H	21.81 FQ	24.43 MW	28.30 TQ	CABLS	1/08-3/08
Farm Products	Oakland-Fremont-Hayward MSA, CA	H	21.66 FQ	28.44 MW	36.02 TQ	CABLS	1/08-3/08
Farm Products	Riverside-San Bernardino-Ontario MSA, CA	H	21.82 FQ	25.41 MW	36.40 TQ	CABLS	1/08-3/08
Farm Products	Sacramento-Arden Arcade-Roseville MSA, CA	H	21.08 FQ	24.97 MW	34.39 TQ	CABLS	1/08-3/08
Farm Products	San Diego-Carlsbad-San Marcos MSA, CA	H	21.64 FQ	24.80 MW	30.30 TQ	CABLS	1/08-3/08
Farm Products	San Francisco-San Mateo-Redwood PMSA, CA	H	23.79 FQ	28.77 MW	33.13 TQ	CABLS	1/08-3/08
Farm Products	San Jose-Sunnyvale-Santa Clara MSA, CA	H	17.74 FQ	20.09 MW	31.89 TQ	CABLS	1/08-3/08
Farm Products	Santa Ana-Anaheim-Irvine PMSA, CA	Y	22280 FQ	28500 MW	50930 TQ	USBLS	5/07
Farm Products	Colorado	Y	23710 FQ	35030 MW	60010 TQ	USBLS	5/07
Farm Products	Denver-Aurora MSA, CO	Y	42600 FQ	61700 MW	76500 TQ	USBLS	5/07
Farm Products	Connecticut	H	18.38 AE	35.14 MW		CTBLS	1/08-3/08
Farm Products	Bridgeport-Stamford-Norwalk MSA, CT	Y	81720 FQ	89330 MW	96900 TQ	USBLS	5/07
Farm Products	Hartford-West Hartford-East Hartford MSA, CT	Y	31360 FQ	56240 MW	74830 TQ	USBLS	5/07
Farm Products	District of Columbia	Y	47400 FQ	63190 MW	74910 TQ	USBLS	5/07
Farm Products	Washington-Arlington-Alexandria MSA, DC-VA-MD-WV	Y	44070 FQ	58800 MW	74630 TQ	USBLS	5/07
Farm Products	Florida	Y	37940 FQ	50490 MW	62460 TQ	USBLS	5/07
Farm Products	Jacksonville MSA, FL	Y	39380 FQ	47780 MW	58560 TQ	USBLS	5/07
Farm Products	Miami-Fort Lauderdale-Miami Beach MSA, FL	Y	40630 FQ	54160 MW	61320 TQ	USBLS	5/07
Farm Products	West Palm Beach-Boca Raton-Boynton Beach PMSA, FL	Y	37690 FQ	44430 MW	54590 TQ	USBLS	5/07
Farm Products	Georgia	Y	30820 FQ	42990 MW	77040 TQ	USBLS	5/07
Farm Products	Atlanta-Sandy Springs-Marietta MSA, GA	Y	30100 FQ	36860 MW	79610 TQ	USBLS	5/07
Farm Products	Hawaii	Y	26670 FQ	44490 MW	54530 TQ	USBLS	5/07
Farm Products	Honolulu MSA, HI	Y	23710 FQ	47490 MW	58050 TQ	USBLS	5/07
Farm Products	Idaho	Y	22860 FQ	39440 MW	53380 TQ	USBLS	5/07
Farm Products	Illinois	Y	37900 FQ	47210 MW	60480 TQ	USBLS	5/07
Farm Products	Chicago-Naperville-Joliet MSA, IL-IN-WI	Y	38010 FQ	50210 MW	65060 TQ	USBLS	5/07
Farm Products	Indiana	Y	42950 FQ	52860 MW	62500 TQ	USBLS	5/07
Farm Products	Indianapolis-Carmel MSA, IN	Y	44770 FQ	53380 MW	61200 TQ	USBLS	5/07
Farm Products	Iowa	Y	35050 FQ	43530 MW	51510 TQ	USBLS	5/07
Farm Products	Iowa City MSA, IA	Y	35320 FQ	48630 MW	55200 TQ	USBLS	5/07
Farm Products	Kansas	Y	34430 FQ	49200 MW	76540 TQ	USBLS	5/07

AE	Average entry wage	AW	Average wage paid	FQ	First quartile wage
AER	Average entry range	AWR	Average wage range	H	Hourly
AEX	Average experienced wage	AXR	Average experienced range	HI	Highest wage paid
ATC	Average total compensation	D	Daily	HR	High end range

LO	Lowest wage paid	MTC	Median total compensation	TCC	Total cash compensation
LR	Low end range	MW	Median wage paid	TQ	Third quartile wage
M	Monthly	MWR	Median wage range	W	Weekly
MCC	Median cash compensation	S	See annotated source	Y	Yearly

Occupation/Type/Industry	Location	Per	Low	Mid	High	Source	Date
Purchasing Agent and Buyer							
Farm Products	Kentucky	Y	39246 FQ	50852 MW	65982 TQ	KYBLS	2008
Farm Products	Louisville-Jefferson County MSA, KY-IN	Y	44410 FQ	54790 MW	62570 TQ	USBLS	5/07
Farm Products	Louisiana	H	13.86 FQ	17.89 MW	24.13 TQ	LABLS	1/08-3/08
Farm Products	Baton Rouge MSA, LA	Y	29380 FQ	33440 MW	44660 TQ	USBLS	5/07
Farm Products	New Orleans-Metairie-Kenner MSA, LA	Y	33650 FQ	42700 MW	53300 TQ	USBLS	5/07
Farm Products	Maine	Y	30700 FQ	40470 MW	52710 TQ	USBLS	5/07
Farm Products	Maryland	Y		47975 MW		MDBLS	3/08
Farm Products	Baltimore-Towson MSA, MD	Y	35930 FQ	45200 MW	57600 TQ	USBLS	5/07
Farm Products	Massachusetts	Y	41670 FQ	62940 MW	85480 TQ	USBLS	5/07
Farm Products	Boston-Cambridge-Quincy NECTA, MA	Y	40580 FQ	63770 MW	82450 TQ	USBLS	5/07
Farm Products	Springfield MSA, MA-CT	Y	46580 FQ	69400 MW	90590 TQ	USBLS	5/07
Farm Products	Michigan	Y	36940 FQ	48750 MW	62810 TQ	USBLS	5/07
Farm Products	Detroit-Warren-Livonia MSA, MI	Y	36550 FQ	45050 MW	52440 TQ	USBLS	5/07
Farm Products	Grand Rapids-Wyoming MSA, MI	Y	41980 FQ	52940 MW	65200 TQ	USBLS	5/07
Farm Products	Warren-Troy-Farmington Hills PMSA, MI	Y	35000 FQ	42950 MW	50660 TQ	USBLS	5/07
Farm Products	Minnesota	Y	48608 FQ	57554 MW	72360 TQ	MNBLS	10/08-12/08
Farm Products	Minneapolis-Saint Paul MSA, MN-WI	Y	50787 FQ	62215 MW	75654 TQ	MNBLS	10/08-12/08
Farm Products	Mississippi	Y	27990 FQ	40120 MW	56770 TQ	USBLS	5/07
Farm Products	Missouri	Y	29640 FQ	40940 MW	52000 TQ	USBLS	5/07
Farm Products	Kansas City MSA, MO-KS	Y	45130 FQ	59650 MW	76090 TQ	USBLS	5/07
Farm Products	St. Louis MSA, MO-IL	Y	33220 FQ	43320 MW	54770 TQ	USBLS	5/07
Farm Products	Montana	Y	36160 FQ	43060 MW	47920 TQ	USBLS	5/07
Farm Products	Billings MSA, MT	Y	43470 FQ	46570 MW	49780 TQ	USBLS	5/07
Farm Products	Nebraska	Y	42130 FQ	51610 MW	71030 TQ	USBLS	5/07
Farm Products	Omaha-Council Bluffs MSA, NE-IA	Y	40310 FQ	47780 MW	68630 TQ	USBLS	5/07
Farm Products	Nevada	H	19.04 FQ	24.35 MW	29.91 TQ	NVBLS	5/08
Farm Products	Las Vegas-Paradise MSA, NV	H	17.86 FQ	21.05 MW	26.41 TQ	NVBLS	5/08
Farm Products	New Jersey	Y	45270 FQ	52610 MW	65290 TQ	USBLS	5/07
Farm Products	New York	Y	44980 FQ	73310 MW	94100 TQ	USBLS	5/07
Farm Products	Nassau-Suffolk PMSA, NY	Y	49100 FQ	55940 MW	79970 TQ	USBLS	5/07
Farm Products	New York-Northern New Jersey-Long Island MSA, NY-NJ-PA	Y	51310 FQ	81770 MW	94490 TQ	USBLS	5/07
Farm Products	North Carolina	Y	34900 FQ	43620 MW	57420 TQ	USBLS	5/07
Farm Products	Charlotte-Gastonia-Concord MSA, NC-SC	Y	29410 FQ	35840 MW	45360 TQ	USBLS	5/07
Farm Products	Raleigh-Cary MSA, NC	Y	36790 FQ	42900 MW	52950 TQ	USBLS	5/07
Farm Products	North Dakota	Y	39730 FQ	53580 MW	71340 TQ	USBLS	5/07
Farm Products	Ohio	Y	39660 FQ	49260 MW	65560 TQ	USBLS	5/07
Farm Products	Cincinnati-Middletown MSA, OH-KY-IN	Y	42710 FQ	48190 MW	55930 TQ	USBLS	5/07
Farm Products	Cleveland-Elyria-Mentor MSA, OH	Y	37310 FQ	41750 MW	66480 TQ	USBLS	5/07
Farm Products	Columbus MSA, OH	Y	49270 FQ	61680 MW	69540 TQ	USBLS	5/07
Farm Products	Oklahoma	Y	28660 FQ	35710 MW	44290 TQ	USBLS	5/07
Farm Products	Tulsa MSA, OK	Y	28310 FQ	38920 MW	55910 TQ	USBLS	5/07
Farm Products	Oregon	H	19.98 FQ	24.89 MW	28.60 TQ	ORBLS	5/08
Farm Products	Portland-Vancouver-Beaverton MSA, OR-WA	Y	49290 FQ	54000 MW	58540 TQ	USBLS	5/07
Farm Products	Pennsylvania	Y	34740 FQ	43960 MW	54820 TQ	USBLS	5/07
Farm Products	Philadelphia-Camden-Wilmington MSA, PA-NJ-DE-MD	Y	39180 FQ	46020 MW	56070 TQ	USBLS	5/07
Farm Products	Pittsburgh MSA, PA	Y	21100 FQ	28060 MW	43140 TQ	USBLS	5/07
Farm Products	South Carolina	Y	35160 FQ	43680 MW	65340 TQ	USBLS	5/07
Farm Products	Columbia MSA, SC	Y	60350 FQ	67300 MW	73160 TQ	USBLS	5/07
Farm Products	South Dakota	Y	40144 FQ	47592 MW	59428 TQ	SDBLS	7/08-9/08
Farm Products	Sioux Falls MSA, SD	Y	40145 FQ	48666 MW	59756 TQ	SDBLS	7/08-9/08
Farm Products	Tennessee	Y	34780 FQ	42530 MW	52180 TQ	USBLS	5/07
Farm Products	Nashville-Davidson-Murfreesboro MSA, TN	Y	37610 FQ	44930 MW	57600 TQ	USBLS	5/07
Farm Products	Texas	Y	29750 FQ	50440 MW	79990 TQ	USBLS	5/07

AE	Average entry wage	AW	Average wage paid	FQ	First quartile wage
AER	Average entry range	AWR	Average wage range	H	Hourly
AEX	Average experienced wage	AXR	Average experienced range	HI	Highest wage paid
ATC	Average total compensation	D	Daily	HR	High end range

LO	Lowest wage paid	MTC	Median total compensation	TCC	Total cash compensation
LR	Low end range	MW	Median wage paid	TQ	Third quartile wage
M	Monthly	MWR	Median wage range	W	Weekly
MCC	Median cash compensation	S	See annotated source	Y	Yearly

Occupation/Type/Industry	Location	Per	Low	Mid	High	Source	Date
Purchasing Agent and Buyer							
Farm Products	Dallas-Fort Worth-Arlington MSA, TX	Y	31930 FQ	65050 MW	104390 TQ	USBLS	5/07
Farm Products	Houston-Sugar Land-Baytown MSA, TX	Y	25750 FQ	47340 MW	77340 TQ	USBLS	5/07
Farm Products	Utah	Y	31730 FQ	40800 MW	58490 TQ	USBLS	5/07
Farm Products	Vermont	Y	27500 FQ	42990 MW	61050 TQ	USBLS	5/07
Farm Products	Virginia	Y	42340 FQ	63410 MW	74380 TQ	USBLS	5/07
Farm Products	Richmond MSA, VA	Y	41440 FQ	50040 MW	70760 TQ	USBLS	5/07
Farm Products	Washington	H	24.06 FQ	28.38 MW	33.20 TQ	WABLS	3/08
Farm Products	Seattle-Tacoma-Bellevue MSA, WA	Y	52650 FQ	59690 MW	71570 TQ	USBLS	5/07
Farm Products	Wisconsin	Y	30080 FQ	36960 MW	44780 TQ	USBLS	5/07
Farm Products	Milwaukee-Waukesha-West Allis MSA, WI	Y	34940 FQ	37580 MW	40880 TQ	USBLS	5/07
Farm Products	Wyoming	Y	22269 FQ	24847 MW	31805 TQ	WYBLS	9/08
Farm Products	Puerto Rico	Y	26610 FQ	31810 MW	42540 TQ	USBLS	5/07
Farm Products	San Juan-Caguas-Guaynabo MSA, PR	Y	27450 FQ	31740 MW	43360 TQ	USBLS	5/07
Purchasing Manager	Alabama	Y	64790 FQ	83460 MW	103600 TQ	USBLS	5/07
	Birmingham-Hoover MSA, AL	Y	66340 FQ	83140 MW	105230 TQ	USBLS	5/07
	Alaska	Y	60100 FQ	79190 MW	99610 TQ	USBLS	5/07
	Anchorage MSA, AK	Y	63860 FQ	79880 MW	100120 TQ	USBLS	5/07
	Arizona	Y	53800 FQ	74290 MW	99140 TQ	USBLS	5/07
	Phoenix-Mesa-Scottsdale MSA, AZ	Y	53050 FQ	73410 MW	96940 TQ	USBLS	5/07
	Tucson MSA, AZ	Y	60820 FQ	85560 MW	117200 TQ	USBLS	5/07
	Arkansas	Y	58260 FQ	72040 MW	92290 TQ	USBLS	5/07
	Fort Smith MSA, AR-OK	Y	61690 FQ	83040 MW	128920 TQ	USBLS	5/07
	Little Rock-North Little Rock MSA, AR	Y	53430 FQ	71620 MW	95360 TQ	USBLS	5/07
	California	H	34.18 FQ	44.79 MW	57.33 TQ	CABLS	1/08-3/08
	Los Angeles-Long Beach-Glendale PMSA, CA	H	34.36 FQ	44.44 MW	57.81 TQ	CABLS	1/08-3/08
	Oakland-Fremont-Hayward MSA, CA	H	36.13 FQ	47.33 MW	59.48 TQ	CABLS	1/08-3/08
	Riverside-San Bernardino-Ontario MSA, CA	H	30.25 FQ	38.51 MW	49.93 TQ	CABLS	1/08-3/08
	Sacramento-Arden Arcade-Roseville MSA, CA	H	32.93 FQ	42.52 MW	53.79 TQ	CABLS	1/08-3/08
	San Diego-Carlsbad-San Marcos MSA, CA	H	34.70 FQ	44.54 MW	56.95 TQ	CABLS	1/08-3/08
	San Francisco-San Mateo-Redwood PMSA, CA	H	31.82 FQ	45.71 MW	58.03 TQ	CABLS	1/08-3/08
	San Jose-Sunnyvale-Santa Clara MSA, CA	H	43.51 FQ	52.71 MW	64.97 TQ	CABLS	1/08-3/08
	Santa Ana-Anaheim-Irvine PMSA, CA	Y	73100 FQ	89490 MW	110720 TQ	USBLS	5/07
	Colorado	Y	64590 FQ	84990 MW	108320 TQ	USBLS	5/07
	Denver-Aurora MSA, CO	Y	62200 FQ	85370 MW	107050 TQ	USBLS	5/07
	Connecticut	H	28.00 AE	42.06 MW		CTBLS	1/08-3/08
	Bridgeport-Stamford-Norwalk MSA, CT	Y	77880 FQ	99390 MW	130290 TQ	USBLS	5/07
	Hartford-West Hartford-East Hartford MSA, CT	Y	66720 FQ	85380 MW	103710 TQ	USBLS	5/07
	Delaware	Y	87080 FQ	109180 MW	128770 TQ	USBLS	5/07
	Wilmington PMSA, DE-MD-NJ	Y	88610 FQ	110510 MW	130460 TQ	USBLS	5/07
	District of Columbia	Y	98100 FQ	112930 MW	126020 TQ	USBLS	5/07
	Washington-Arlington-Alexandria MSA, DC-VA-MD-WV	Y	93560 FQ	110990 MW	125970 TQ	USBLS	5/07
	Florida	Y	70210 FQ	90830 MW	120150 TQ	USBLS	5/07
	Fort Lauderdale-Pompano Beach-Deerfield Beach PMSA, FL	Y	63840 FQ	84410 MW	101020 TQ	USBLS	5/07
	Jacksonville MSA, FL	Y	76490 FQ	93180 MW	119350 TQ	USBLS	5/07
	Miami-Fort Lauderdale-Miami Beach MSA, FL	Y	74080 FQ	93280 MW	122950 TQ	USBLS	5/07
	Orlando-Kissimmee MSA, FL	Y	62000 FQ	80520 MW	107220 TQ	USBLS	5/07

AE	Average entry wage	AW	Average wage paid	FQ	First quartile wage
AER	Average entry range	AWR	Average wage range	H	Hourly
AEX	Average experienced wage	AXR	Average experienced range	HI	Highest wage paid
ATC	Average total compensation	D	Daily	HR	High end range

LO	Lowest wage paid	MTC	Median total compensation	TCC	Total cash compensation
LR	Low end range	MW	Median wage paid	TQ	Third quartile wage
M	Monthly	MWR	Median wage range	W	Weekly
MCC	Median cash compensation	S	See annotated source	Y	Yearly

Purchasing Manager

Occupation/Type/Industry	Location	Per	Low	Mid	High	Source	Date
Purchasing Manager	Tampa-St. Petersburg-Clearwater MSA, FL	Y	71900 FQ	96210 MW	132160 TQ	USBLS	5/07
	West Palm Beach-Boca Raton-Boynton Beach PMSA, FL	Y	82530 FQ	101930 MW	130820 TQ	USBLS	5/07
	Georgia	Y	63800 FQ	81570 MW	103130 TQ	USBLS	5/07
	Atlanta-Sandy Springs-Marietta MSA, GA	Y	65390 FQ	83760 MW	105970 TQ	USBLS	5/07
	Hawaii	Y	50620 FQ	61890 MW	81790 TQ	USBLS	5/07
	Honolulu MSA, HI	Y	50560 FQ	62550 MW	85920 TQ	USBLS	5/07
	Idaho	Y	44880 FQ	66960 MW	94140 TQ	USBLS	5/07
	Boise City-Nampa MSA, ID	Y	62260 FQ	82470 MW	102480 TQ	USBLS	5/07
	Illinois	Y	58840 FQ	78410 MW	101240 TQ	USBLS	5/07
	Chicago-Naperville-Joliet MSA, IL-IN-WI	Y	61710 FQ	80830 MW	104230 TQ	USBLS	5/07
	Indiana	Y	59220 FQ	75800 MW	95350 TQ	USBLS	5/07
	Gary PMSA, IN	Y	58810 FQ	74460 MW	103350 TQ	USBLS	5/07
	Indianapolis-Carmel MSA, IN	Y	60830 FQ	80500 MW	101190 TQ	USBLS	5/07
	Iowa	Y	61060 FQ	76970 MW	94290 TQ	USBLS	5/07
	Des Moines-West Des Moines MSA, IA	Y	54980 FQ	68500 MW	81470 TQ	USBLS	5/07
	Kansas	Y	58020 FQ	75470 MW	96640 TQ	USBLS	5/07
	Wichita MSA, KS	Y	62620 FQ	84040 MW	100420 TQ	USBLS	5/07
	Kentucky	Y	59049 FQ	74375 MW	99606 TQ	KYBLS	2008
	Louisville-Jefferson County MSA, KY-IN	Y	58000 FQ	71380 MW	94190 TQ	USBLS	5/07
	Louisiana	H	21.40 FQ	27.99 MW	35.40 TQ	LABLS	1/08-3/08
	Baton Rouge MSA, LA	Y	45740 FQ	61160 MW	75170 TQ	USBLS	5/07
	New Orleans-Metairie-Kenner MSA, LA	Y	44370 FQ	56110 MW	70240 TQ	USBLS	5/07
	Maine	Y	54540 FQ	72560 MW	88750 TQ	USBLS	5/07
	Portland-South Portland-Biddeford MSA, ME	Y	56600 FQ	78920 MW	92130 TQ	USBLS	5/07
	Maryland	Y		106925 MW		MDBLS	3/08
	Baltimore-Towson MSA, MD	Y	75360 FQ	96870 MW	119400 TQ	USBLS	5/07
	Bethesda-Gaithersburg-Frederick PMSA, MD	Y	93770 FQ	111550 MW	127810 TQ	USBLS	5/07
	Massachusetts	Y	71020 FQ	94130 MW	122620 TQ	USBLS	5/07
	Boston-Cambridge-Quincy NECTA, MA	Y	73960 FQ	98130 MW	125050 TQ	USBLS	5/07
	Worcester MSA, MA-CT	Y	55550 FQ	75210 MW	90760 TQ	USBLS	5/07
	Michigan	Y	64010 FQ	82540 MW	106490 TQ	USBLS	5/07
	Ann Arbor MSA, MI	Y	69310 FQ	88020 MW	110820 TQ	USBLS	5/07
	Detroit-Warren-Livonia MSA, MI	Y	70160 FQ	89950 MW	117740 TQ	USBLS	5/07
	Grand Rapids-Wyoming MSA, MI	Y	54420 FQ	73220 MW	93580 TQ	USBLS	5/07
	Warren-Troy-Farmington Hills PMSA, MI	Y	65160 FQ	81770 MW	111400 TQ	USBLS	5/07
	Minnesota	Y	78939 FQ	98426 MW	126526 TQ	MNBLS	10/08-12/08
	Duluth-Superior MSA, MN-WI	Y	67803 FQ	84538 MW	110823 TQ	MNBLS	10/08-12/08
	Minneapolis-Saint Paul MSA, MN-WI	Y	82943 FQ	101888 MW	130237 TQ	MNBLS	10/08-12/08
	Rochester MSA, MN	Y	73313 FQ	102151 MW	127456 TQ	MNBLS	10/08-12/08
	Mississippi	Y	49390 FQ	64130 MW	87050 TQ	USBLS	5/07
	Jackson MSA, MS	Y	46550 FQ	58490 MW	79310 TQ	USBLS	5/07
	Missouri	Y	66650 FQ	85020 MW	109350 TQ	USBLS	5/07
	Kansas City MSA, MO-KS	Y	67040 FQ	85280 MW	104520 TQ	USBLS	5/07
	St. Louis MSA, MO-IL	Y	72670 FQ	89940 MW	117140 TQ	USBLS	5/07
	Montana	Y	32630 FQ	56200 MW	73060 TQ	USBLS	5/07
	Nebraska	Y	60280 FQ	82940 MW	105770 TQ	USBLS	5/07
	Lincoln MSA, NE	Y	59050 FQ	76550 MW	92230 TQ	USBLS	5/07
	Omaha-Council Bluffs MSA, NE-IA	Y	60660 FQ	89320 MW	111370 TQ	USBLS	5/07
	Nevada	H	26.66 FQ	36.58 MW	45.37 TQ	NVBLS	5/08
	Las Vegas-Paradise MSA, NV	H	25.92 FQ	37.28 MW	45.80 TQ	NVBLS	5/08
	New Hampshire	H	29.97 AE	42.17 MW	50.44 AEX	NHBLS	6/08
	Manchester MSA, NH	Y	68810 FQ	79710 MW	93410 TQ	USBLS	5/07
	Nashua NECTA, NH-MA	Y	80090 FQ	96190 MW	112730 TQ	USBLS	5/07
	Portsmouth MSA, NH-ME	Y	85570 FQ	99960 MW	118490 TQ	USBLS	5/07
	New Jersey	Y	83320 FQ	107430 MW	136600 TQ	USBLS	5/07
	Camden PMSA, NJ	Y	68190 FQ	88110 MW	120830 TQ	USBLS	5/07
	Edison PMSA, NJ	Y	84040 FQ	105620 MW	125860 TQ	USBLS	5/07

Occupation/Type/Industry	Location	Per	Low	Mid	High	Source	Date
Purchasing Manager	Newark-Union PMSA, NJ-PA	Y	87420 FQ	112880 MW	144060 TQ	USBLS	5/07
	New Mexico	Y	50160 FQ	78690 MW	100740 TQ	USBLS	5/07
	Albuquerque MSA, NM	Y	66040 FQ	87630 MW	107620 TQ	USBLS	5/07
	New York	Y	71430 FQ	96230 MW	131090 TQ	USBLS	5/07
	Albany-Schenectady-Troy MSA, NY	Y	61690 FQ	78830 MW	105840 TQ	USBLS	5/07
	Buffalo-Niagara Falls MSA, NY	Y	61870 FQ	80130 MW	103930 TQ	USBLS	5/07
	Nassau-Suffolk PMSA, NY	Y	78880 FQ	96760 MW	121830 TQ	USBLS	5/07
	New York-Northern New Jersey-Long Island MSA, NY-NJ-PA	Y	83360 FQ	107690 MW	141820 TQ	USBLS	5/07
	North Carolina	Y	63440 FQ	81190 MW	101860 TQ	USBLS	5/07
	Charlotte-Gastonia-Concord MSA, NC-SC	Y	63180 FQ	79080 MW	98120 TQ	USBLS	5/07
	Raleigh-Cary MSA, NC	Y	67750 FQ	82830 MW	112970 TQ	USBLS	5/07
	North Dakota	Y	53730 FQ	72070 MW	93160 TQ	USBLS	5/07
	Fargo MSA, ND-MN	Y	61440 FQ	80190 MW	99590 TQ	USBLS	5/07
	Ohio	Y	59490 FQ	77400 MW	98780 TQ	USBLS	5/07
	Cincinnati-Middletown MSA, OH-KY-IN	Y	64180 FQ	88690 MW	113360 TQ	USBLS	5/07
	Cleveland-Elyria-Mentor MSA, OH	Y	65850 FQ	80440 MW	96190 TQ	USBLS	5/07
	Columbus MSA, OH	Y	56640 FQ	74110 MW	102260 TQ	USBLS	5/07
	Dayton MSA, OH	Y	68300 FQ	87090 MW	112430 TQ	USBLS	5/07
	Oklahoma	Y	46730 FQ	60910 MW	80190 TQ	USBLS	5/07
	Oklahoma City MSA, OK	Y	48540 FQ	61850 MW	78130 TQ	USBLS	5/07
	Tulsa MSA, OK	Y	50090 FQ	62960 MW	87280 TQ	USBLS	5/07
	Oregon	H	29.68 FQ	37.90 MW	48.18 TQ	ORBLS	5/08
	Portland-Vancouver-Beaverton MSA, OR-WA	Y	66650 FQ	82870 MW	102770 TQ	USBLS	5/07
	Pennsylvania	Y	64030 FQ	86170 MW	108860 TQ	USBLS	5/07
	Allentown-Bethlehem-Easton MSA, PA-NJ	Y	62720 FQ	89380 MW	106380 TQ	USBLS	5/07
	Philadelphia-Camden-Wilmington MSA, PA-NJ-DE-MD	Y	73720 FQ	95070 MW	124480 TQ	USBLS	5/07
	Pittsburgh MSA, PA	Y	60150 FQ	82820 MW	106530 TQ	USBLS	5/07
	Rhode Island	Y	74850 FQ	91750 MW	115270 TQ	USBLS	5/07
	Providence-Fall River-Warwick MSA, RI-MA	Y	72600 FQ	89270 MW	112840 TQ	USBLS	5/07
	South Carolina	Y	60460 FQ	76230 MW	94250 TQ	USBLS	5/07
	Charleston-North Charleston MSA, SC	Y	72920 FQ	86060 MW	95680 TQ	USBLS	5/07
	Columbia MSA, SC	Y	55670 FQ	66260 MW	78600 TQ	USBLS	5/07
	South Dakota	Y	68485 FQ	84810 MW	99051 TQ	SDBLS	7/08-9/08
	Sioux Falls MSA, SD	Y	63484 FQ	78257 MW	93870 TQ	SDBLS	7/08-9/08
	Tennessee	Y	44190 FQ	62280 MW	87540 TQ	USBLS	5/07
	Memphis MSA, TN-MS-AR	Y	47500 FQ	72180 MW	107520 TQ	USBLS	5/07
	Nashville-Davidson-Murfreesboro MSA, TN	Y	46810 FQ	64290 MW	86530 TQ	USBLS	5/07
	Texas	Y	68520 FQ	92570 MW	121340 TQ	USBLS	5/07
	Austin-Round Rock MSA, TX	Y	82500 FQ	113630 MW		USBLS	
	Dallas-Fort Worth-Arlington MSA, TX	Y	71180 FQ	96010 MW	123180 TQ	USBLS	5/07
	El Paso MSA, TX	Y	45830 FQ	67820 MW	88890 TQ	USBLS	5/07
	Houston-Sugar Land-Baytown MSA, TX	Y	71070 FQ	95450 MW	122120 TQ	USBLS	5/07
	Midland MSA, TX	Y	63560 FQ	101740 MW	145400 TQ	USBLS	5/07
	San Antonio MSA, TX	Y	68370 FQ	86470 MW	105050 TQ	USBLS	5/07
	Utah	Y	64090 FQ	77370 MW	96060 TQ	USBLS	5/07
	Ogden-Clearfield MSA, UT	Y	71420 FQ	81320 MW	90620 TQ	USBLS	5/07
	Salt Lake City MSA, UT	Y	64060 FQ	78890 MW	101610 TQ	USBLS	5/07
	Vermont	Y	60710 FQ	73620 MW	87170 TQ	USBLS	5/07
	Virginia	Y	79140 FQ	102130 MW	122910 TQ	USBLS	5/07
	Richmond MSA, VA	Y	67600 FQ	89850 MW	127650 TQ	USBLS	5/07
	Virginia Beach-Norfolk-Newport News MSA, VA-NC	Y	81510 FQ	98820 MW	117580 TQ	USBLS	5/07
	Washington	H	37.54 FQ	44.85 MW	54.04 TQ	WABLS	3/08
	Seattle-Tacoma-Bellevue MSA, WA	Y	78080 FQ	92650 MW	111840 TQ	USBLS	5/07
	West Virginia	Y	64106 FQ	76918 MW	97237 TQ	WVBLS	7/08-9/08

AE Average entry wage	**AW** Average wage paid	**FQ** First quartile wage	**LO** Lowest wage paid	**MTC** Median total compensation	**TCC** Total cash compensation
AER Average entry range	**AWR** Average wage range	**H** Hourly	**LR** Low end range	**MW** Median wage paid	**TQ** Third quartile wage
AEX Average experienced wage	**AXR** Average experienced range	**HI** Highest wage paid	**M** Monthly	**MWR** Median wage range	**W** Weekly
ATC Average total compensation	**D** Daily	**HR** High end range	**MCC** Median cash compensation	**S** See annotated source	**Y** Yearly

Occupation/Type/Industry	Location	Per	Low	Mid	High	Source	Date
Purchasing Manager	Charleston MSA, WV	Y	52350 FQ	59030 MW	77990 TQ	USBLS	5/07
	Wisconsin	Y	58770 FQ	77650 MW	96810 TQ	USBLS	5/07
	Milwaukee-Waukesha-West Allis MSA, WI	Y	61830 FQ	82350 MW	103380 TQ	USBLS	5/07
	Wyoming	Y	45606 FQ	61028 MW	76120 TQ	WYBLS	9/08
	Puerto Rico	Y	44530 FQ	65720 MW	91140 TQ	USBLS	5/07
	San Juan-Caguas-Guaynabo MSA, PR	Y	44540 FQ	63560 MW	89060 TQ	USBLS	5/07
	Virgin Islands	Y	42370 FQ	51130 MW	60850 TQ	USBLS	5/07
	Guam	Y	26360 FQ	35740 MW	47730 TQ	USBLS	5/07
Purchasing Technician							
State Government	Montana	Y	22350 LO		33524 HI	AFT02	3/1/08
Quahogger							
Summer	Rhode Island	D		200-250 AW		RIM01	2009
Winter	Rhode Island	D		100 AW		RIM01	2009
Quality Assurance Specialist							
Department of Education	New Hampshire	Y			50656 HI	NHUL03	2008
Quality Control Inspector							
Airline	United States	H		27.00 AW		AVJOB07	2009
Quality Control Specialist							
Contractor Management	United States	Y		62074 ATC		ENR01	2007
General Contractor	United States	Y		62953 ATC		ENR01	2007
Quality Engineer							
Electrical Equipment, Appliance, and Component Manufacturing	United States	Y		76925 AW		QDIG	2008
Fabricated Metal Product Manufacturing	United States	Y		62027 AW		QDIG	2008
Quality Professional	Midwest	Y		74704 AW		QUAL	2008
	Northeast	Y		77775 AW		QUAL	2008
	South	Y		76937 AW		QUAL	2008
	West	Y		83518 AW		QUAL	2008
Quality Specialist							
Professional, Scientific, and Technical Services	United States	Y		155518 AW		QDIG	2008
Racing Enforcement Supervisor							
Racing and Charitable Gaming Commission	New Hampshire	Y			58854 HI	NHUL03	2008
Racing Inspector							
State Government	Ohio	H	15.62 LO		18.36 HI	ODAS	2008
Radiation Therapist	United States	Y			95100 TQ	FORB02	2009
	Alabama	Y	53380 FQ	62010 MW	73790 TQ	USBLS	5/07
	Birmingham-Hoover MSA, AL	Y	54870 FQ	66440 MW	78070 TQ	USBLS	5/07
	Alaska	Y	65810 FQ	75600 MW	84890 TQ	USBLS	5/07
	Arizona	Y	61900 FQ	70970 MW	81110 TQ	USBLS	5/07
	Phoenix-Mesa-Scottsdale MSA, AZ	Y	61240 FQ	70940 MW	81340 TQ	USBLS	5/07
	Arkansas	Y	57710 FQ	67910 MW	78620 TQ	USBLS	5/07
	Little Rock-North Little Rock MSA, AR	Y	58700 FQ	68900 MW	79180 TQ	USBLS	5/07
	California	H	33.77 FQ	40.21 MW	46.71 TQ	CABLS	1/08-3/08
	Los Angeles-Long Beach-Glendale PMSA, CA	H	36.18 FQ	41.87 MW	47.89 TQ	CABLS	1/08-3/08
	Oakland-Fremont-Hayward MSA, CA	H	37.59 FQ	42.73 MW	47.48 TQ	CABLS	1/08-3/08
	Riverside-San Bernardino-Ontario MSA, CA	H	29.47 FQ	35.97 MW	43.01 TQ	CABLS	1/08-3/08
	Sacramento-Arden Arcade-Roseville MSA, CA	H	35.77 FQ	41.41 MW	50.50 TQ	CABLS	1/08-3/08
	San Diego-Carlsbad-San Marcos MSA, CA	H	23.82 FQ	31.06 MW	41.92 TQ	CABLS	1/08-3/08
	San Jose-Sunnyvale-Santa Clara MSA, CA	H	39.28 FQ	45.53 MW	50.89 TQ	CABLS	1/08-3/08

AE	Average entry wage	AW	Average wage paid	FQ	First quartile wage
AER	Average entry range	AWR	Average wage range	H	Hourly
AEX	Average experienced wage	AXR	Average experienced range	HI	Highest wage paid
ATC	Average total compensation	D	Daily	HR	High end range

LO	Lowest wage paid	MTC	Median total compensation
LR	Low end range	MW	Median wage paid
M	Monthly	MWR	Median wage range
MCC	Median cash compensation	S	See annotated source

TCC	Total cash compensation		
TQ	Third quartile wage		
W	Weekly		
Y	Yearly		

Occupation/Type/Industry	Location	Per	Low	Mid	High	Source	Date
Radiation Therapist	Santa Ana-Anaheim-Irvine PMSA, CA	Y	70130 FQ	84760 MW	96920 TQ	USBLS	5/07
	Colorado	Y	58500 FQ	73540 MW	88300 TQ	USBLS	5/07
	Denver-Aurora MSA, CO	Y	66060 FQ	79350 MW	91190 TQ	USBLS	5/07
	Connecticut	H	29.41 AE	38.44 MW		CTBLS	1/08-3/08
	Hartford-West Hartford-East Hartford MSA, CT	Y	69630 FQ	80720 MW	91650 TQ	USBLS	5/07
	Delaware	Y	60720 FQ	73090 MW	90520 TQ	USBLS	5/07
	District of Columbia	Y	48770 FQ	57530 MW	70850 TQ	USBLS	5/07
	Washington-Arlington-Alexandria MSA, DC-VA-MD-WV	Y	53800 FQ	66670 MW	81750 TQ	USBLS	5/07
	Florida	Y	58270 FQ	69020 MW	80910 TQ	USBLS	5/07
	Fort Lauderdale-Pompano Beach-Deerfield Beach PMSA, FL	Y	70740 FQ	82020 MW	101090 TQ	USBLS	5/07
	Jacksonville MSA, FL	Y	57680 FQ	67330 MW	78920 TQ	USBLS	5/07
	Miami-Fort Lauderdale-Miami Beach MSA, FL	Y	59360 FQ	71880 MW	87130 TQ	USBLS	5/07
	Orlando-Kissimmee MSA, FL	Y	57280 FQ	65160 MW	82210 TQ	USBLS	5/07
	Tampa-St. Petersburg-Clearwater MSA, FL	Y	57140 FQ	67240 MW	78290 TQ	USBLS	5/07
	West Palm Beach-Boca Raton-Boynton Beach PMSA, FL	Y	54930 FQ	64450 MW	79480 TQ	USBLS	5/07
	Georgia	Y	50950 FQ	59630 MW	68660 TQ	USBLS	5/07
	Atlanta-Sandy Springs-Marietta MSA, GA	Y	52170 FQ	62300 MW	76240 TQ	USBLS	5/07
	Idaho	Y	35780 FQ	46500 MW	65450 TQ	USBLS	5/07
	Boise City-Nampa MSA, ID	Y	35210 FQ	39680 MW	63710 TQ	USBLS	5/07
	Illinois	Y	54750 FQ	68430 MW	83830 TQ	USBLS	5/07
	Chicago-Naperville-Joliet MSA, IL-IN-WI	Y	52920 FQ	68160 MW	84260 TQ	USBLS	5/07
	Indiana	Y	58340 FQ	67880 MW	78020 TQ	USBLS	5/07
	Indianapolis-Carmel MSA, IN	Y	62380 FQ	69540 MW	76970 TQ	USBLS	5/07
	Iowa	Y	50260 FQ	59000 MW	71140 TQ	USBLS	5/07
	Kansas	Y	55790 FQ	64050 MW	75510 TQ	USBLS	5/07
	Kentucky	Y	56578 FQ	64262 MW	76470 TQ	KYBLS	2008
	Louisville-Jefferson County MSA, KY-IN	Y	54990 FQ	61980 MW	75450 TQ	USBLS	5/07
	Louisiana	H	23.20 FQ	27.80 MW	32.02 TQ	LABLS	1/08-3/08
	Baton Rouge MSA, LA	Y	42310 FQ	46570 MW	53970 TQ	USBLS	5/07
	Maine	Y	50380 FQ	60270 MW	71580 TQ	USBLS	5/07
	Maryland	Y		68825 MW		MDBLS	3/08
	Baltimore-Towson MSA, MD	Y	56100 FQ	64140 MW	77840 TQ	USBLS	5/07
	Massachusetts	Y	61960 FQ	75830 MW	89200 TQ	USBLS	5/07
	Boston-Cambridge-Quincy NECTA, MA	Y	59420 FQ	74180 MW	88550 TQ	USBLS	5/07
	Michigan	Y	53650 FQ	62980 MW	73850 TQ	USBLS	5/07
	Detroit-Warren-Livonia MSA, MI	Y	57400 FQ	66030 MW	75790 TQ	USBLS	5/07
	Warren-Troy-Farmington Hills PMSA, MI	Y	51010 FQ	60610 MW	71660 TQ	USBLS	5/07
	Minnesota	Y	60597 FQ	70536 MW	84127 TQ	MNBLS	10/08-12/08
	Minneapolis-Saint Paul MSA, MN-WI	Y	59436 FQ	70630 MW	88929 TQ	MNBLS	10/08-12/08
	Mississippi	Y	53080 FQ	62030 MW	71790 TQ	USBLS	5/07
	Jackson MSA, MS	Y	39150 FQ	55250 MW	63000 TQ	USBLS	5/07
	Missouri	Y	50950 FQ	63330 MW	76630 TQ	USBLS	5/07
	Kansas City MSA, MO-KS	Y	57800 FQ	67910 MW	77600 TQ	USBLS	5/07
	St. Louis MSA, MO-IL	Y	55690 FQ	65640 MW	77850 TQ	USBLS	5/07
	Montana	Y	61240 FQ	78560 MW	106070 TQ	USBLS	5/07
	Nebraska	Y	50130 FQ	64210 MW	81830 TQ	USBLS	5/07
	Omaha-Council Bluffs MSA, NE-IA	Y	49450 FQ	59900 MW	73930 TQ	USBLS	5/07
	Nevada	H	30.55 FQ	36.90 MW	42.29 TQ	NVBLS	5/08
	New Hampshire	H	30.41 AE	38.31 MW	41.42 AEX	NHBLS	6/08
	New Jersey	Y	77100 FQ	88870 MW	99740 TQ	USBLS	5/07
	Camden PMSA, NJ	Y	86060 FQ	94600 MW	103150 TQ	USBLS	5/07
	Edison PMSA, NJ	Y	73370 FQ	85820 MW	97340 TQ	USBLS	5/07
	Newark-Union PMSA, NJ-PA	Y	81060 FQ	93310 MW	107280 TQ	USBLS	5/07
	New Mexico	Y	58470 FQ	70530 MW	82170 TQ	USBLS	5/07
	Albuquerque MSA, NM	Y	53350 FQ	64960 MW	77730 TQ	USBLS	5/07

AE	Average entry wage	AW	Average wage paid	FQ	First quartile wage
AER	Average entry range	AWR	Average wage range	H	Hourly
AEX	Average experienced wage	AXR	Average experienced range	HI	Highest wage paid
ATC	Average total compensation	D	Daily	HR	High end range

LO	Lowest wage paid	MTC	Median total compensation
LR	Low end range	MW	Median wage paid
M	Monthly	MWR	Median wage range
MCC	Median cash compensation	S	See annotated source

TCC	Total cash compensation
TQ	Third quartile wage
W	Weekly
Y	Yearly

Occupation/Type/Industry	Location	Per	Low	Mid	High	Source	Date
Radiation Therapist	New York	Y	64530 FQ	77340 MW	88170 TQ	USBLS	5/07
	Albany-Schenectady-Troy MSA, NY	Y	67450 FQ	74940 MW	82580 TQ	USBLS	5/07
	Nassau-Suffolk PMSA, NY	Y	67520 FQ	82650 MW	94350 TQ	USBLS	5/07
	New York-Northern New Jersey-Long Island MSA, NY-NJ-PA	Y	73210 FQ	83330 MW	95160 TQ	USBLS	5/07
	North Carolina	Y	57710 FQ	66950 MW	76730 TQ	USBLS	5/07
	Charlotte-Gastonia-Concord MSA, NC-SC	Y	53820 FQ	63230 MW	70650 TQ	USBLS	5/07
	North Dakota	Y	56790 FQ	66700 MW	75010 TQ	USBLS	5/07
	Ohio	Y	54420 FQ	60750 MW	71310 TQ	USBLS	5/07
	Cincinnati-Middletown MSA, OH-KY-IN	Y	55940 FQ	63610 MW	74220 TQ	USBLS	5/07
	Cleveland-Elyria-Mentor MSA, OH	Y	53370 FQ	60630 MW	70930 TQ	USBLS	5/07
	Columbus MSA, OH	Y	57680 FQ	65900 MW	78330 TQ	USBLS	5/07
	Oklahoma	Y	45760 FQ	54830 MW	66350 TQ	USBLS	5/07
	Oklahoma City MSA, OK	Y	43130 FQ	51240 MW	64370 TQ	USBLS	5/07
	Tulsa MSA, OK	Y	49920 FQ	57330 MW	70220 TQ	USBLS	5/07
	Oregon	H	33.81 FQ	38.79 MW	45.19 TQ	ORBLS	5/08
	Portland-Vancouver-Beaverton MSA, OR-WA	Y	69040 FQ	78200 MW	91200 TQ	USBLS	5/07
	Pennsylvania	Y	55980 FQ	69090 MW	81550 TQ	USBLS	5/07
	Pittsburgh MSA, PA	Y	51210 FQ	59120 MW	67940 TQ	USBLS	5/07
	South Carolina	Y	52400 FQ	61380 MW	74270 TQ	USBLS	5/07
	South Dakota	Y	44460 FQ	53391 MW	65573 TQ	SDBLS	7/08-9/08
	Tennessee	Y	56820 FQ	67320 MW	123020 TQ	USBLS	5/07
	Knoxville MSA, TN	Y	52140 FQ	60250 MW	120190 TQ	USBLS	5/07
	Memphis MSA, TN-MS-AR	Y	56550 FQ	63900 MW	72890 TQ	USBLS	5/07
	Nashville-Davidson-Murfreesboro MSA, TN	Y	61100 FQ	70060 MW	92950 TQ	USBLS	5/07
	Texas	Y	65330 FQ	77730 MW	89070 TQ	USBLS	5/07
	Austin-Round Rock MSA, TX	Y	65850 FQ	79780 MW	89700 TQ	USBLS	5/07
	Corpus Christi MSA, TX	Y	66740 FQ	74550 MW	83540 TQ	USBLS	5/07
	Dallas-Fort Worth-Arlington MSA, TX	Y	63950 FQ	75330 MW	85460 TQ	USBLS	5/07
	Houston-Sugar Land-Baytown MSA, TX	Y	72640 FQ	81350 MW	91700 TQ	USBLS	5/07
	Utah	Y	57690 FQ	65740 MW	78820 TQ	USBLS	5/07
	Vermont	Y	55020 FQ	64180 MW	76010 TQ	USBLS	5/07
	Virginia	Y	49860 FQ	63170 MW	80160 TQ	USBLS	5/07
	Richmond MSA, VA	Y	44980 FQ	56890 MW	75220 TQ	USBLS	5/07
	Virginia Beach-Norfolk-Newport News MSA, VA-NC	Y	57120 FQ	69100 MW	83540 TQ	USBLS	5/07
	Washington	H	35.69 FQ	42.11 MW	47.45 TQ	WABLS	3/08
	Seattle-Tacoma-Bellevue MSA, WA	Y	73090 FQ	86680 MW	100350 TQ	USBLS	5/07
	West Virginia	Y	53598 FQ	62569 MW	76714 TQ	WVBLS	7/08-9/08
	Wisconsin	Y	63990 FQ	73740 MW	84460 TQ	USBLS	5/07
	Milwaukee-Waukesha-West Allis MSA, WI	Y	68020 FQ	79600 MW	90190 TQ	USBLS	5/07
	Wyoming	Y	57549 FQ	67592 MW	79180 TQ	WYBLS	9/08
	Puerto Rico	Y	19900 FQ	23360 MW	30360 TQ	USBLS	5/07
	San Juan-Caguas-Guaynabo MSA, PR	Y	19350 FQ	23600 MW	31360 TQ	USBLS	5/07
Radio and Communications Technician							
Department of Transportation	Michigan	H	13.88 LO		27.47 HI	MDOT	10/1/07
Radio and Television Announcer	Alabama	Y	16480 FQ	20070 MW	29540 TQ	USBLS	5/07
	Birmingham-Hoover MSA, AL	Y	17470 FQ	19830 MW	40980 TQ	USBLS	5/07
	Alaska	Y	24110 FQ	32630 MW	40660 TQ	USBLS	5/07
	Anchorage MSA, AK	Y	26400 FQ	35660 MW	41800 TQ	USBLS	5/07
	Arizona	Y	17430 FQ	25590 MW	51130 TQ	USBLS	5/07
	Phoenix-Mesa-Scottsdale MSA, AZ	Y	19900 FQ	28690 MW	58060 TQ	USBLS	5/07
	Tucson MSA, AZ	Y	14960 FQ	23510 MW	42040 TQ	USBLS	5/07
	Arkansas	Y	16340 FQ	23360 MW	30140 TQ	USBLS	5/07
	Little Rock-North Little Rock MSA, AR	Y	20290 FQ	28070 MW	47210 TQ	USBLS	5/07

AE	Average entry wage	AW	Average wage paid	FQ	First quartile wage
AER	Average entry range	AWR	Average wage range	H	Hourly
AEX	Average experienced wage	AXR	Average experienced range	HI	Highest wage paid
ATC	Average total compensation	D	Daily	HR	High end range

LO	Lowest wage paid	MTC	Median total compensation
LR	Low end range	MW	Median wage paid
M	Monthly	MWR	Median wage range
MCC	Median cash compensation	S	See annotated source

TCC	Total cash compensation
TQ	Third quartile wage
W	Weekly
Y	Yearly

Occupation/Type/Industry	Location	Per	Low	Mid	High	Source	Date
Radio and Television Announcer	California	H	11.81 FQ	15.60 MW	24.09 TQ	CABLS	1/08-3/08
	Los Angeles-Long Beach-Glendale PMSA, CA	H	12.22 FQ	16.68 MW	29.55 TQ	CABLS	1/08-3/08
	Riverside-San Bernardino-Ontario MSA, CA	H	10.11 FQ	12.14 MW	16.41 TQ	CABLS	1/08-3/08
	Sacramento-Arden Arcade-Roseville MSA, CA	H	11.68 FQ	15.08 MW	24.96 TQ	CABLS	1/08-3/08
	San Diego-Carlsbad-San Marcos MSA, CA	H	14.05 FQ	18.28 MW	38.09 TQ	CABLS	1/08-3/08
	San Francisco-San Mateo-Redwood PMSA, CA	H	10.59 FQ	14.04 MW	22.61 TQ	CABLS	1/08-3/08
	San Jose-Sunnyvale-Santa Clara MSA, CA	H	13.70 FQ	19.91 MW	24.16 TQ	CABLS	1/08-3/08
	Santa Ana-Anaheim-Irvine PMSA, CA	Y	25260 FQ	31790 MW	44800 TQ	USBLS	5/07
	Denver-Aurora MSA, CO	Y	27930 FQ	35630 MW	53910 TQ	USBLS	5/07
	Connecticut	H	9.32 AE	14.58 MW		CTBLS	1/08-3/08
	Hartford-West Hartford-East Hartford MSA, CT	Y	24550 FQ	33480 MW	41020 TQ	USBLS	5/07
	Wilmington PMSA, DE-MD-NJ	Y	21370 FQ	26140 MW	48150 TQ	USBLS	5/07
	Florida	Y	18140 FQ	28280 MW	51640 TQ	USBLS	5/07
	Jacksonville MSA, FL	Y	20150 FQ	51860 MW	76230 TQ	USBLS	5/07
	Miami-Fort Lauderdale-Miami Beach MSA, FL	Y	18800 FQ	30240 MW	44690 TQ	USBLS	5/07
	Orlando-Kissimmee MSA, FL	Y	27740 FQ	57510 MW	93500 TQ	USBLS	5/07
	Tampa-St. Petersburg-Clearwater MSA, FL	Y	16340 FQ	23000 MW	38740 TQ	USBLS	5/07
	West Palm Beach-Boca Raton-Boynton Beach PMSA, FL	Y	18640 FQ	29310 MW	39700 TQ	USBLS	5/07
	Georgia	Y	19430 FQ	30940 MW	46430 TQ	USBLS	5/07
	Atlanta-Sandy Springs-Marietta MSA, GA	Y	21240 FQ	34040 MW	77150 TQ	USBLS	5/07
	Hawaii	Y	17060 FQ	23000 MW	34800 TQ	USBLS	5/07
	Honolulu MSA, HI	Y	18670 FQ	24160 MW	42200 TQ	USBLS	5/07
	Idaho	Y	17260 FQ	27770 MW	46950 TQ	USBLS	5/07
	Indiana	Y	15530 FQ	21150 MW	32680 TQ	USBLS	5/07
	Indianapolis-Carmel MSA, IN	Y	17910 FQ	25790 MW	45540 TQ	USBLS	5/07
	Iowa	Y	15150 FQ	20940 MW	25730 TQ	USBLS	5/07
	Des Moines-West Des Moines MSA, IA	Y	14030 FQ	15280 MW	24280 TQ	USBLS	5/07
	Kansas	Y	17320 FQ	24260 MW	36400 TQ	USBLS	5/07
	Wichita MSA, KS	Y	18470 FQ	27310 MW	47070 TQ	USBLS	5/07
	Kentucky	Y	14921 FQ	18668 MW	28038 TQ	KYBLS	2008
	Louisville-Jefferson County MSA, KY-IN	Y	14370 FQ	23000 MW	60410 TQ	USBLS	5/07
	Louisiana	H	8.22 FQ	10.57 MW	14.92 TQ	LABLS	1/08-3/08
	Maine	Y	17370 FQ	23750 MW	35750 TQ	USBLS	5/07
	Portland-South Portland-Biddeford MSA, ME	Y	19400 FQ	26810 MW	41100 TQ	USBLS	5/07
	Maryland	Y		35550 MW		MDBLS	3/08
	Baltimore-Towson MSA, MD	Y	27840 FQ	37730 MW	47720 TQ	USBLS	5/07
	Bethesda-Gaithersburg-Frederick PMSA, MD	Y	24960 FQ	31330 MW	48470 TQ	USBLS	5/07
	Massachusetts	Y	25090 FQ	37060 MW	61880 TQ	USBLS	5/07
	Barnstable Town MSA, MA	Y	18530 FQ	25330 MW	36830 TQ	USBLS	5/07
	Michigan	Y	16140 FQ	20010 MW	32410 TQ	USBLS	5/07
	Ann Arbor MSA, MI	Y	15270 FQ	17850 MW	30860 TQ	USBLS	5/07
	Minnesota	Y	17775 FQ	25475 MW	39128 TQ	MNBLS	10/08-12/08
	Duluth-Superior MSA, MN-WI	Y	18832 FQ	22431 MW	26176 TQ	MNBLS	10/08-12/08
	Minneapolis-Saint Paul MSA, MN-WI	Y	35749 FQ	58860 MW	127294 TQ	MNBLS	10/08-12/08
	Rochester MSA, MN	Y	19561 FQ	29563 MW	36321 TQ	MNBLS	10/08-12/08
	Mississippi	Y	14130 FQ	18000 MW	27200 TQ	USBLS	5/07
	Jackson MSA, MS	Y	15040 FQ	19840 MW	30250 TQ	USBLS	5/07
	Missouri	Y	15150 FQ	19630 MW	28380 TQ	USBLS	5/07
	Kansas City MSA, MO-KS	Y	21470 FQ	29790 MW	53050 TQ	USBLS	5/07
	St. Louis MSA, MO-IL	Y	16170 FQ	19840 MW	29630 TQ	USBLS	5/07
	Montana	Y	16020 FQ	19530 MW	28150 TQ	USBLS	5/07
	Billings MSA, MT	Y	16120 FQ	19320 MW	31210 TQ	USBLS	5/07
	Nebraska	Y	15870 FQ	24530 MW	35540 TQ	USBLS	5/07

AE	Average entry wage	AW	Average wage paid	FQ First quartile wage
AER	Average entry range	AWR	Average wage range	H Hourly
AEX	Average experienced wage	AXR	Average experienced range	HI Highest wage paid
ATC	Average total compensation	D	Daily	HR High end range

LO	Lowest wage paid	MTC Median total compensation	TCC Total cash compensation
LR	Low end range	MW Median wage paid	TQ Third quartile wage
M	Monthly	MWR Median wage range	W Weekly
MCC	Median cash compensation	S See annotated source	Y Yearly

Occupation/Type/Industry	Location	Per	Low	Mid	High	Source	Date
Radio and Television Announcer	Omaha-Council Bluffs MSA, NE-IA	Y	23150 FQ	35340 MW	51700 TQ	USBLS	5/07
	Nevada	H	9.64 FQ	16.95 MW	27.14 TQ	NVBLS	5/08
	Las Vegas-Paradise MSA, NV	H	12.10 FQ	19.04 MW	29.38 TQ	NVBLS	5/08
	New Hampshire	H	9.88 AE	13.64 MW	16.77 AEX	NHBLS	6/08
	New Jersey	Y	26380 FQ	44230 MW	110550 TQ	USBLS	5/07
	New Mexico	Y	14280 FQ	20380 MW	36660 TQ	USBLS	5/07
	Albuquerque MSA, NM	Y	22900 FQ	38130 MW	49820 TQ	USBLS	5/07
	Farmington MSA, NM	Y	13730 FQ	22350 MW	32340 TQ	USBLS	5/07
	New York	Y	26440 FQ	38400 MW	63110 TQ	USBLS	5/07
	Buffalo-Niagara Falls MSA, NY	Y	21050 FQ	34070 MW	67900 TQ	USBLS	5/07
	Nassau-Suffolk PMSA, NY	Y	36050 FQ	52520 MW	59390 TQ	USBLS	5/07
	North Carolina	Y	15400 FQ	22620 MW	31360 TQ	USBLS	5/07
	Charlotte-Gastonia-Concord MSA, NC-SC	Y	16910 FQ	27040 MW	36490 TQ	USBLS	5/07
	Raleigh-Cary MSA, NC	Y	15850 FQ	24670 MW	46520 TQ	USBLS	5/07
	North Dakota	Y	16230 FQ	27720 MW	35710 TQ	USBLS	5/07
	Fargo MSA, ND-MN	Y	30190 FQ	35080 MW	40540 TQ	USBLS	5/07
	Ohio	Y	15750 FQ	23420 MW	36300 TQ	USBLS	5/07
	Cincinnati-Middletown MSA, OH-KY-IN	Y	16740 FQ	23690 MW	37450 TQ	USBLS	5/07
	Cleveland-Elyria-Mentor MSA, OH	Y	16340 FQ	24630 MW	38780 TQ	USBLS	5/07
	Columbus MSA, OH	Y	16460 FQ	23110 MW	32240 TQ	USBLS	5/07
	Dayton MSA, OH	Y	15330 FQ	16430 MW	32220 TQ	USBLS	5/07
	Oklahoma	Y	15610 FQ	18390 MW	24470 TQ	USBLS	5/07
	Oklahoma City MSA, OK	Y	15330 FQ	18040 MW	25830 TQ	USBLS	5/07
	Tulsa MSA, OK	Y	17190 FQ	20710 MW	26200 TQ	USBLS	5/07
	Oregon	H	10.40 FQ	13.69 MW	18.07 TQ	ORBLS	5/08
	Pennsylvania	Y	15700 FQ	24570 MW	45570 TQ	USBLS	5/07
	Allentown-Bethlehem-Easton MSA, PA-NJ	Y	14470 FQ	15420 MW	16360 TQ	USBLS	5/07
	Philadelphia-Camden-Wilmington MSA, PA-NJ-DE-MD	Y	19660 FQ	43800 MW	63900 TQ	USBLS	5/07
	Pittsburgh MSA, PA	Y	16370 FQ	25260 MW	40140 TQ	USBLS	5/07
	Providence-Fall River-Warwick MSA, RI-MA	Y	18270 FQ	28530 MW	45300 TQ	USBLS	5/07
	South Carolina	Y	18530 FQ	27050 MW	44880 TQ	USBLS	5/07
	Charleston-North Charleston MSA, SC	Y	23550 FQ	33020 MW	63420 TQ	USBLS	5/07
	Columbia MSA, SC	Y	27280 FQ	35470 MW	61560 TQ	USBLS	5/07
	South Dakota	Y	21599 FQ	24781 MW	30698 TQ	SDBLS	7/08-9/08
	Sioux Falls MSA, SD	Y	23131 FQ	28378 MW	37994 TQ	SDBLS	7/08-9/08
	Tennessee	Y	15010 FQ	20690 MW	30990 TQ	USBLS	5/07
	Nashville-Davidson-Murfreesboro MSA, TN	Y	17920 FQ	27310 MW	47900 TQ	USBLS	5/07
	Texas	Y	18680 FQ	25410 MW	40880 TQ	USBLS	5/07
	Austin-Round Rock MSA, TX	Y	23560 FQ	31610 MW	45240 TQ	USBLS	5/07
	Dallas-Fort Worth-Arlington MSA, TX	Y	19450 FQ	25690 MW	58660 TQ	USBLS	5/07
	Houston-Sugar Land-Baytown MSA, TX	Y	19060 FQ	28140 MW	48220 TQ	USBLS	5/07
	San Antonio MSA, TX	Y	21890 FQ	31320 MW	58200 TQ	USBLS	5/07
	Utah	Y	22610 FQ	32150 MW	55710 TQ	USBLS	5/07
	Salt Lake City MSA, UT	Y	24620 FQ	35850 MW	63750 TQ	USBLS	5/07
	Vermont	Y	18840 FQ	25520 MW	36190 TQ	USBLS	5/07
	Burlington-South Burlington MSA, VT	Y	18610 FQ	26350 MW	41630 TQ	USBLS	5/07
	Virginia	Y	18540 FQ	25060 MW	35600 TQ	USBLS	5/07
	Richmond MSA, VA	Y	19350 FQ	29930 MW	36700 TQ	USBLS	5/07
	Virginia Beach-Norfolk-Newport News MSA, VA-NC	Y	20610 FQ	29390 MW	48780 TQ	USBLS	5/07
	Washington	H	9.16 FQ	13.51 MW	24.51 TQ	WABLS	3/08
	Seattle-Tacoma-Bellevue MSA, WA	Y	35010 FQ	58330 MW	100550 TQ	USBLS	5/07
	West Virginia	Y	15782 FQ	20044 MW	29698 TQ	WVBLS	7/08-9/08
	Wisconsin	Y	19020 FQ	22820 MW	31120 TQ	USBLS	5/07
	Milwaukee-Waukesha-West Allis MSA, WI	Y	19580 FQ	24300 MW	44300 TQ	USBLS	5/07
	Wyoming	Y	18306 FQ	26338 MW	30155 TQ	WYBLS	9/08

AE	Average entry wage	AW	Average wage paid	FQ	First quartile wage
AER	Average entry range	AWR	Average wage range	H	Hourly
AEX	Average experienced wage	AXR	Average experienced range	HI	Highest wage paid
ATC	Average total compensation	D	Daily	HR	High end range

LO	Lowest wage paid	MTC	Median total compensation
LR	Low end range	MW	Median wage paid
M	Monthly	MWR	Median wage range
MCC	Median cash compensation	S	See annotated source

TCC	Total cash compensation
TQ	Third quartile wage
W	Weekly
Y	Yearly

Occupation/Type/Industry	Location	Per	Low	Mid	High	Source	Date
Radio and Television Announcer	Puerto Rico	Y	13540 FQ	16210 MW	32100 TQ	USBLS	5/07
	San Juan-Caguas-Guaynabo MSA, PR	Y	15100 FQ	24440 MW	35800 TQ	USBLS	5/07
	Guam	Y	13500 FQ	15800 MW	20330 TQ	USBLS	5/07
Radio Disc Jockey							
First Year	Rhode Island	Y	·	30000 AW		RIM01	2009
Radio Dispatcher							
Department of Transportation	New Hampshire	Y		11667 AW		NHUL03	2008
Radio Mechanic	Alabama	Y	32340 FQ	40370 MW	53550 TQ	USBLS	5/07
	Arkansas	Y	22740 FQ	32310 MW	38920 TQ	USBLS	5/07
	Little Rock-North Little Rock MSA, AR	Y	32120 FQ	38660 MW	43020 TQ	USBLS	5/07
	California	H	16.15 FQ	20.88 MW	44.73 TQ	CABLS	1/08-3/08
	Los Angeles-Long Beach-Glendale PMSA, CA	H	15.83 FQ	17.04 MW	18.25 TQ	CABLS	1/08-3/08
	San Diego-Carlsbad-San Marcos MSA, CA	H	21.69 FQ	24.58 MW	28.27 TQ	CABLS	1/08-3/08
	Colorado	Y	27800 FQ	33940 MW	46930 TQ	USBLS	5/07
	Connecticut	H	13.45 AE	18.97 MW		CTBLS	1/08-3/08
	Florida	Y	36160 FQ	46270 MW	57030 TQ	USBLS	5/07
	Miami-Fort Lauderdale-Miami Beach MSA, FL	Y	45590 FQ	53690 MW	61750 TQ	USBLS	5/07
	Orlando-Kissimmee MSA, FL	Y	35280 FQ	41530 MW	47650 TQ	USBLS	5/07
	Tampa-St. Petersburg-Clearwater MSA, FL	Y	39590 FQ	47540 MW	57250 TQ	USBLS	5/07
	Georgia	Y	29290 FQ	40270 MW	46060 TQ	USBLS	5/07
	Idaho	Y	40400 FQ	44530 MW	50000 TQ	USBLS	5/07
	Illinois	Y	28670 FQ	33770 MW	41280 TQ	USBLS	5/07
	Chicago-Naperville-Joliet MSA, IL-IN-WI	Y	28780 FQ	34030 MW	42020 TQ	USBLS	5/07
	Indiana	Y	34340 FQ	39960 MW	50080 TQ	USBLS	5/07
	Iowa	Y	25980 FQ	30760 MW	38710 TQ	USBLS	5/07
	Kansas	Y	33680 FQ	43130 MW	52560 TQ	USBLS	5/07
	Kentucky	Y	36095 FQ	42498 MW	52576 TQ	KYBLS	2008
	Louisville-Jefferson County MSA, KY-IN	Y	40360 FQ	49480 MW	55440 TQ	USBLS	5/07
	Maryland	Y		50650 MW		MDBLS	3/08
	Baltimore-Towson MSA, MD	Y	38020 FQ	48040 MW	63670 TQ	USBLS	5/07
	Massachusetts	Y	34960 FQ	40100 MW	48660 TQ	USBLS	5/07
	Michigan	Y	28800 FQ	41480 MW	46600 TQ	USBLS	5/07
	Detroit-Warren-Livonia MSA, MI	Y	27820 FQ	40940 MW	45990 TQ	USBLS	5/07
	Warren-Troy-Farmington Hills PMSA, MI	Y	27030 FQ	40230 MW	45950 TQ	USBLS	5/07
	Minnesota	Y	43310 FQ	51482 MW	63198 TQ	MNBLS	10/08-12/08
	Minneapolis-Saint Paul MSA, MN-WI	Y	53527 FQ	62296 MW	70646 TQ	MNBLS	10/08-12/08
	Missouri	Y	28630 FQ	34240 MW	40590 TQ	USBLS	5/07
	St. Louis MSA, MO-IL	Y	27250 FQ	31450 MW	36160 TQ	USBLS	5/07
	Nevada	H	19.75 FQ	22.01 MW	24.35 TQ	NVBLS	5/08
	New Hampshire	H	16.25 AE	19.91 MW	21.76 AEX	NHBLS	6/08
	New Jersey	Y	38710 FQ	45990 MW	55200 TQ	USBLS	5/07
	New York	Y	34120 FQ	55360 MW	62670 TQ	USBLS	5/07
	New York-Northern New Jersey-Long Island MSA, NY-NJ-PA	Y	55060 FQ	60010 MW	65020 TQ	USBLS	5/07
	North Carolina	Y	31440 FQ	34820 MW	38410 TQ	USBLS	5/07
	Ohio	Y	30470 FQ	42910 MW	50920 TQ	USBLS	5/07
	Oklahoma	Y	22410 FQ	34840 MW	49200 TQ	USBLS	5/07
	Oregon	H	13.85 FQ	18.04 MW	24.94 TQ	ORBLS	5/08
	Portland-Vancouver-Beaverton MSA, OR-WA	Y	42690 FQ	51210 MW	59140 TQ	USBLS	5/07
	Pennsylvania	Y	21980 FQ	28330 MW	34200 TQ	USBLS	5/07
	South Carolina	Y	28150 FQ	32020 MW	36790 TQ	USBLS	5/07
	Tennessee	Y	32680 FQ	42570 MW	51680 TQ	USBLS	5/07
	Texas	Y	26600 FQ	32290 MW	41200 TQ	USBLS	5/07
	Dallas-Fort Worth-Arlington MSA, TX	Y	32330 FQ	39850 MW	45870 TQ	USBLS	5/07

AE	Average entry wage	**AW**	Average wage paid	**FQ**	First quartile wage	**LO**	Lowest wage paid	**MTC**	Median total compensation	**TCC**	Total cash compensation
AER	Average entry range	**AWR**	Average wage range	**H**	Hourly	**LR**	Low end range	**MW**	Median wage paid	**TQ**	Third quartile wage
AEX	Average experienced wage	**AXR**	Average experienced range	**HI**	Highest wage paid	**M**	Monthly	**MWR**	Median wage range	**W**	Weekly
ATC	Average total compensation	**D**	Daily	**HR**	High end range	**MCC**	Median cash compensation	**S**	See annotated source	**Y**	Yearly

Occupation/Type/Industry	Location	Per	Low	Mid	High	Source	Date
Radio Mechanic	Houston-Sugar Land-Baytown MSA, TX	Y	24410 FQ	29080 MW	34300 TQ	USBLS	5/07
	Virginia	Y	33230 FQ	40870 MW	50400 TQ	USBLS	5/07
	Richmond MSA, VA	Y	28930 FQ	32590 MW	37320 TQ	USBLS	5/07
	Virginia Beach-Norfolk-Newport News MSA, VA-NC	Y	35700 FQ	44450 MW	53620 TQ	USBLS	5/07
	Washington	H	22.38 FQ	27.71 MW	35.38 TQ	WABLS	3/08
	Seattle-Tacoma-Bellevue MSA, WA	Y	56070 FQ	69210 MW	77010 TQ	USBLS	5/07
	West Virginia	Y	24242 FQ	27842 MW	32988 TQ	WVBLS	7/08-9/08
	Wisconsin	Y	32130 FQ	36790 MW	41900 TQ	USBLS	5/07
	Wyoming	Y	25405 FQ	34242 MW	41474 TQ	WYBLS	9/08
Radio Officer							
Cruise Ship	United States	M	1900 LO		2500 HI	CRU02	2008
Radio Operator	California	H	17.38 FQ	18.68 MW	19.94 TQ	CABLS	1/08-3/08
	Connecticut	H	15.49 AE	18.17 MW		CTBLS	1/08-3/08
	Illinois	Y	30910 FQ	43310 MW	56330 TQ	USBLS	5/07
	Chicago-Naperville-Joliet MSA, IL-IN-WI	Y	41970 FQ	46970 MW	57520 TQ	USBLS	5/07
	Louisiana	H	10.61 FQ	13.32 MW	15.91 TQ	LABLS	1/08-3/08
	Michigan	Y	48000 FQ	52760 MW	57910 TQ	USBLS	5/07
	Minnesota	Y	42026 FQ	48806 MW	57228 TQ	MNBLS	10/08-12/08
	New York	Y	20440 FQ	30090 MW	53340 TQ	USBLS	5/07
	New York-Northern New Jersey-Long Island MSA, NY-NJ-PA	Y	20540 FQ	30990 MW	53030 TQ	USBLS	5/07
	North Carolina	Y	30570 FQ	36320 MW	43110 TQ	USBLS	5/07
	Pennsylvania	Y	19110 FQ	27860 MW	42450 TQ	USBLS	5/07
	Utah	Y	39550 FQ	42610 MW	45660 TQ	USBLS	5/07
	Salt Lake City MSA, UT	Y	40500 FQ	43260 MW	46010 TQ	USBLS	5/07
	Puerto Rico	Y	13190 FQ	15110 MW	20890 TQ	USBLS	5/07
	San Juan-Caguas-Guaynabo MSA, PR	Y	13370 FQ	15520 MW	21450 TQ	USBLS	5/07
Highway Patrol	Ohio	H	15.77 LO		18.30 HI	ODAS	2008
Radiographer	United States	Y		45261 MW		RTODAY	2007
State Government	Ohio	H	18.36 LO		23.87 HI	ODAS	2008
Radiologic Technologist and Technician	Alabama	Y	35520 FQ	42090 MW	50090 TQ	USBLS	5/07
	Birmingham-Hoover MSA, AL	Y	36040 FQ	41860 MW	48700 TQ	USBLS	5/07
	Huntsville MSA, AL	Y	38590 FQ	46730 MW	57000 TQ	USBLS	5/07
	Tuscaloosa MSA, AL	Y	37490 FQ	45980 MW	54430 TQ	USBLS	5/07
	Alaska	Y	49300 FQ	57160 MW	65280 TQ	USBLS	5/07
	Anchorage MSA, AK	Y	50830 FQ	57730 MW	65370 TQ	USBLS	5/07
	Arizona	Y	39290 FQ	48580 MW	58800 TQ	USBLS	5/07
	Phoenix-Mesa-Scottsdale MSA, AZ	Y	38220 FQ	48350 MW	58340 TQ	USBLS	5/07
	Prescott MSA, AZ	Y	48010 FQ	55780 MW	64500 TQ	USBLS	5/07
	Tucson MSA, AZ	Y	38740 FQ	45630 MW	54930 TQ	USBLS	5/07
	Arkansas	Y	34850 FQ	42010 MW	50200 TQ	USBLS	5/07
	Little Rock-North Little Rock MSA, AR	Y	40250 FQ	47040 MW	54810 TQ	USBLS	5/07
	California	H	23.27 FQ	29.12 MW	35.29 TQ	CABLS	1/08-3/08
	Los Angeles-Long Beach-Glendale PMSA, CA	H	21.32 FQ	27.39 MW	33.48 TQ	CABLS	1/08-3/08
	Oakland-Fremont-Hayward MSA, CA	H	25.79 FQ	35.25 MW	44.48 TQ	CABLS	1/08-3/08
	Riverside-San Bernardino-Ontario MSA, CA	H	22.48 FQ	27.85 MW	32.13 TQ	CABLS	1/08-3/08
	Sacramento-Arden Arcade-Roseville MSA, CA	H	24.46 FQ	30.60 MW	36.42 TQ	CABLS	1/08-3/08
	San Diego-Carlsbad-San Marcos MSA, CA	H	25.63 FQ	29.84 MW	34.03 TQ	CABLS	1/08-3/08
	San Francisco-San Mateo-Redwood PMSA, CA	H	24.83 FQ	30.92 MW	38.26 TQ	CABLS	1/08-3/08
	San Jose-Sunnyvale-Santa Clara MSA, CA	H	29.69 FQ	36.23 MW	42.66 TQ	CABLS	1/08-3/08
	Santa Ana-Anaheim-Irvine PMSA, CA	Y	37480 FQ	55690 MW	70590 TQ	USBLS	5/07

AE	Average entry wage	**AW**	Average wage paid	**FQ**	First quartile wage
AER	Average entry range	**AWR**	Average wage range	**H**	Hourly
AEX	Average experienced wage	**AXR**	Average experienced range	**HI**	Highest wage paid
ATC	Average total compensation	**D**	Daily	**HR**	High end range

LO	Lowest wage paid	**MTC**	Median total compensation	**TCC**	Total cash compensation
LR	Low end range	**MW**	Median wage paid	**TQ**	Third quartile wage
M	Monthly	**MWR**	Median wage range	**W**	Weekly
MCC	Median cash compensation	**S**	See annotated source	**Y**	Yearly

Occupation/Type/Industry	Location	Per	Low	Mid	High	Source	Date
Radiologic Technologist and Technician	Colorado	Y	42470 FQ	51710 MW	61220 TQ	USBLS	5/07
	Denver-Aurora MSA, CO	Y	43180 FQ	53820 MW	62710 TQ	USBLS	5/07
	Connecticut	H	22.81 AE	28.55 MW		CTBLS	1/08-3/08
	Bridgeport-Stamford-Norwalk MSA, CT	Y	48120 FQ	57710 MW	67130 TQ	USBLS	5/07
	Hartford-West Hartford-East Hartford MSA, CT	Y	52310 FQ	58710 MW	66180 TQ	USBLS	5/07
	Delaware	Y	43400 FQ	51450 MW	58470 TQ	USBLS	5/07
	Wilmington PMSA, DE-MD-NJ	Y	44730 FQ	53240 MW	60090 TQ	USBLS	5/07
	District of Columbia	Y	48620 FQ	56970 MW	67700 TQ	USBLS	5/07
	Washington-Arlington-Alexandria MSA, DC-VA-MD-WV	Y	50100 FQ	60900 MW	72420 TQ	USBLS	5/07
	Florida	Y	41010 FQ	48770 MW	58210 TQ	USBLS	5/07
	Fort Lauderdale-Pompano Beach-Deerfield Beach PMSA, FL	Y	44780 FQ	53730 MW	62430 TQ	USBLS	5/07
	Jacksonville MSA, FL	Y	41140 FQ	47580 MW	54640 TQ	USBLS	5/07
	Miami-Fort Lauderdale-Miami Beach MSA, FL	Y	42960 FQ	50950 MW	60950 TQ	USBLS	5/07
	Orlando-Kissimmee MSA, FL	Y	38160 FQ	44930 MW	51450 TQ	USBLS	5/07
	Tampa-St. Petersburg-Clearwater MSA, FL	Y	40840 FQ	51830 MW	60300 TQ	USBLS	5/07
	West Palm Beach-Boca Raton-Boynton Beach PMSA, FL	Y	42680 FQ	48620 MW	57090 TQ	USBLS	5/07
	Georgia	Y	38530 FQ	46420 MW	55890 TQ	USBLS	5/07
	Atlanta-Sandy Springs-Marietta MSA, GA	Y	41750 FQ	49750 MW	59050 TQ	USBLS	5/07
	Hawaii	Y	52430 FQ	58980 MW	65660 TQ	USBLS	5/07
	Honolulu MSA, HI	Y	54850 FQ	59950 MW	65820 TQ	USBLS	5/07
	Idaho	Y	39580 FQ	44700 MW	52340 TQ	USBLS	5/07
	Boise City-Nampa MSA, ID	Y	41580 FQ	46830 MW	54650 TQ	USBLS	5/07
	Illinois	Y	40470 FQ	52190 MW	62350 TQ	USBLS	5/07
	Chicago-Naperville-Joliet MSA, IL-IN-WI	Y	44910 FQ	55400 MW	64090 TQ	USBLS	5/07
	Indiana	Y	41240 FQ	48100 MW	56680 TQ	USBLS	5/07
	Elkhart-Goshen MSA, IN	Y	40720 FQ	45620 MW	51720 TQ	USBLS	5/07
	Fort Wayne MSA, IN	Y	38950 FQ	46190 MW	55090 TQ	USBLS	5/07
	Gary PMSA, IN	Y	42210 FQ	49430 MW	57250 TQ	USBLS	5/07
	Indianapolis-Carmel MSA, IN	Y	44090 FQ	51290 MW	60140 TQ	USBLS	5/07
	Iowa	Y	36460 FQ	42520 MW	49400 TQ	USBLS	5/07
	Des Moines-West Des Moines MSA, IA	Y	37240 FQ	43960 MW	51540 TQ	USBLS	5/07
	Waterloo-Cedar Falls MSA, IA	Y	37130 FQ	43450 MW	50140 TQ	USBLS	5/07
	Kansas	Y	35750 FQ	42660 MW	50270 TQ	USBLS	5/07
	Wichita MSA, KS	Y	35470 FQ	40950 MW	48290 TQ	USBLS	5/07
	Kentucky	Y	37761 FQ	45270 MW	53288 TQ	KYBLS	2008
	Elizabethtown MSA, KY	Y	41610 FQ	49090 MW	58210 TQ	USBLS	5/07
	Louisville-Jefferson County MSA, KY-IN	Y	36670 FQ	44840 MW	54480 TQ	USBLS	5/07
	Louisiana	H	18.06 FQ	21.32 MW	24.79 TQ	LABLS	1/08-3/08
	Baton Rouge MSA, LA	Y	39480 FQ	45250 MW	52010 TQ	USBLS	5/07
	Lafayette MSA, LA	Y	36300 FQ	42680 MW	51320 TQ	USBLS	5/07
	New Orleans-Metairie-Kenner MSA, LA	Y	39520 FQ	45940 MW	53130 TQ	USBLS	5/07
	Maine	Y	43510 FQ	49620 MW	58420 TQ	USBLS	5/07
	Portland-South Portland-Biddeford MSA, ME	Y	46160 FQ	53290 MW	62680 TQ	USBLS	5/07
	Maryland	Y		60800 MW		MDBLS	3/08
	Baltimore-Towson MSA, MD	Y	50030 FQ	58150 MW	67720 TQ	USBLS	5/07
	Bethesda-Gaithersburg-Frederick PMSA, MD	Y	57060 FQ	66450 MW	75790 TQ	USBLS	5/07
	Massachusetts	Y	52600 FQ	64130 MW	74910 TQ	USBLS	5/07
	Boston-Cambridge-Quincy NECTA, MA	Y	56230 FQ	67140 MW	76570 TQ	USBLS	5/07
	Lynn-Peabody-Salem NECTA, MA	Y	58840 FQ	70380 MW	78910 TQ	USBLS	5/07
	Springfield MSA, MA-CT	Y	45000 FQ	52080 MW	62010 TQ	USBLS	5/07
	Worcester MSA, MA-CT	Y	54280 FQ	61680 MW	72660 TQ	USBLS	5/07
	Michigan	Y	40440 FQ	48200 MW	56460 TQ	USBLS	5/07

AE	Average entry wage	**AW**	Average wage paid	**FQ**	First quartile wage	**LO** Lowest wage paid	**MTC** Median total compensation	**TCC** Total cash compensation
AER	Average entry range	**AWR**	Average wage range	**H**	Hourly	**LR** Low end range	**MW** Median wage paid	**TQ** Third quartile wage
AEX	Average experienced wage	**AXR**	Average experienced range	**HI**	Highest wage paid	**M** Monthly	**MWR** Median wage range	**W** Weekly
ATC	Average total compensation	**D**	Daily	**HR**	High end range	**MCC** Median cash compensation	**S** See annotated source	**Y** Yearly

Occupation/Type/Industry	Location	Per	Low	Mid	High	Source	Date
Radiologic Technologist and Technician	Detroit-Warren-Livonia MSA, MI	Y	45130 FQ	52810 MW	59430 TQ	USBLS	5/07
	Grand Rapids-Wyoming MSA, MI	Y	36390 FQ	43460 MW	51940 TQ	USBLS	5/07
	Warren-Troy-Farmington Hills PMSA, MI	Y	43360 FQ	51960 MW	59110 TQ	USBLS	5/07
	Minnesota	Y	46086 FQ	55701 MW	65598 TQ	MNBLS	10/08-12/08
	Duluth-Superior MSA, MN-WI	Y	45249 FQ	53901 MW	64217 TQ	MNBLS	10/08-12/08
	Minneapolis-Saint Paul MSA, MN-WI	Y	46808 FQ	57416 MW	66623 TQ	MNBLS	10/08-12/08
	Rochester MSA, MN	Y	52205 FQ	62528 MW	74391 TQ	MNBLS	10/08-12/08
	Mississippi	Y	34550 FQ	41580 MW	50590 TQ	USBLS	5/07
	Hattiesburg MSA, MS	Y	33200 FQ	38330 MW	49170 TQ	USBLS	5/07
	Jackson MSA, MS	Y	34510 FQ	43260 MW	52990 TQ	USBLS	5/07
	Pascagoula MSA, MS	Y	29250 FQ	36200 MW	45510 TQ	USBLS	5/07
	Missouri	Y	38610 FQ	46560 MW	55500 TQ	USBLS	5/07
	Kansas City MSA, MO-KS	Y	40420 FQ	48020 MW	56500 TQ	USBLS	5/07
	St. Louis MSA, MO-IL	Y	39350 FQ	48360 MW	57290 TQ	USBLS	5/07
	Montana	Y	39460 FQ	46590 MW	55730 TQ	USBLS	5/07
	Billings MSA, MT	Y	43380 FQ	50590 MW	60350 TQ	USBLS	5/07
	Nebraska	Y	37700 FQ	45460 MW	54680 TQ	USBLS	5/07
	Omaha-Council Bluffs MSA, NE-IA	Y	38090 FQ	44760 MW	52620 TQ	USBLS	5/07
	Nevada	H	24.46 FQ	28.59 MW	33.51 TQ	NVBLS	5/08
	Las Vegas-Paradise MSA, NV	H	24.26 FQ	28.77 MW	34.28 TQ	NVBLS	5/08
	New Hampshire	H	21.35 AE	26.57 MW	29.08 AEX	NHBLS	6/08
	Manchester MSA, NH	Y	44870 FQ	53840 MW	61430 TQ	USBLS	5/07
	Nashua NECTA, NH-MA	Y	48600 FQ	56380 MW	63480 TQ	USBLS	5/07
	New Jersey	Y	52760 FQ	59780 MW	69380 TQ	USBLS	5/07
	Camden PMSA, NJ	Y	49930 FQ	57020 MW	63270 TQ	USBLS	5/07
	Edison PMSA, NJ	Y	54430 FQ	61660 MW	71190 TQ	USBLS	5/07
	Newark-Union PMSA, NJ-PA	Y	52060 FQ	58080 MW	65360 TQ	USBLS	5/07
	Vineland-Millville-Bridgeton MSA, NJ	Y	51290 FQ	56740 MW	63250 TQ	USBLS	5/07
	New Mexico	Y	41940 FQ	49490 MW	57920 TQ	USBLS	5/07
	Albuquerque MSA, NM	Y	44340 FQ	50080 MW	57540 TQ	USBLS	5/07
	New York	Y	50090 FQ	59620 MW	70070 TQ	USBLS	5/07
	Albany-Schenectady-Troy MSA, NY	Y	44950 FQ	52120 MW	60170 TQ	USBLS	5/07
	Buffalo-Niagara Falls MSA, NY	Y	41280 FQ	46210 MW	52010 TQ	USBLS	5/07
	Ithaca MSA, NY	Y	44710 FQ	52240 MW	58710 TQ	USBLS	5/07
	Kingston MSA, NY	Y	55850 FQ	64590 MW	73840 TQ	USBLS	5/07
	Nassau-Suffolk PMSA, NY	Y	58130 FQ	65840 MW	74360 TQ	USBLS	5/07
	New York-Northern New Jersey-Long Island MSA, NY-NJ-PA	Y	55440 FQ	63190 MW	72950 TQ	USBLS	5/07
	North Carolina	Y	41630 FQ	48760 MW	57260 TQ	USBLS	5/07
	Charlotte-Gastonia-Concord MSA, NC-SC	Y	44380 FQ	51800 MW	59050 TQ	USBLS	5/07
	Raleigh-Cary MSA, NC	Y	41910 FQ	48010 MW	55370 TQ	USBLS	5/07
	North Dakota	Y	35510 FQ	43430 MW	50790 TQ	USBLS	5/07
	Fargo MSA, ND-MN	Y	32800 FQ	42330 MW	47810 TQ	USBLS	5/07
	Ohio	Y	41540 FQ	47150 MW	53660 TQ	USBLS	5/07
	Cincinnati-Middletown MSA, OH-KY-IN	Y	42300 FQ	47760 MW	54730 TQ	USBLS	5/07
	Cleveland-Elyria-Mentor MSA, OH	Y	43180 FQ	48000 MW	53610 TQ	USBLS	5/07
	Columbus MSA, OH	Y	43240 FQ	49920 MW	58100 TQ	USBLS	5/07
	Dayton MSA, OH	Y	41780 FQ	47700 MW	55510 TQ	USBLS	5/07
	Oklahoma	Y	35210 FQ	42550 MW	51200 TQ	USBLS	5/07
	Oklahoma City MSA, OK	Y	36710 FQ	44220 MW	54910 TQ	USBLS	5/07
	Tulsa MSA, OK	Y	38430 FQ	44570 MW	51530 TQ	USBLS	5/07
	Oregon	H	22.58 FQ	27.99 MW	32.62 TQ	ORBLS	5/08
	Eugene-Springfield MSA, OR	Y	48970 FQ	56900 MW	67770 TQ	USBLS	5/07
	Portland-Vancouver-Beaverton MSA, OR-WA	Y	47200 FQ	58850 MW	67840 TQ	USBLS	5/07
	Pennsylvania	Y	36810 FQ	45790 MW	55430 TQ	USBLS	5/07
	Allentown-Bethlehem-Easton MSA, PA-NJ	Y	41750 FQ	48480 MW	57360 TQ	USBLS	5/07

AE	Average entry wage	AW	Average wage paid	FQ	First quartile wage	LO	Lowest wage paid	MTC	Median total compensation	TCC	Total cash compensation
AER	Average entry range	AWR	Average wage range	H	Hourly	LR	Low end range	MW	Median wage paid	TQ	Third quartile wage
AEX	Average experienced wage	AXR	Average experienced range	HI	Highest wage paid	M	Monthly	MWR	Median wage range	W	Weekly
ATC	Average total compensation	D	Daily	HR	High end range	MCC	Median cash compensation	S	See annotated source	Y	Yearly

1358

Occupation/Type/Industry	Location	Per	Low	Mid	High	Source	Date
Radiologic Technologist and Technician	Philadelphia-Camden-Wilmington MSA, PA-NJ-DE-MD	Y	40440 FQ	51720 MW	60770 TQ	USBLS	5/07
	Pittsburgh MSA, PA	Y	35080 FQ	42530 MW	49870 TQ	USBLS	5/07
	Rhode Island	Y	49700 FQ	56750 MW	64730 TQ	USBLS	5/07
	Providence-Fall River-Warwick MSA, RI-MA	Y	47970 FQ	56240 MW	65080 TQ	USBLS	5/07
	South Carolina	Y	38710 FQ	46100 MW	54660 TQ	USBLS	5/07
	Charleston-North Charleston MSA, SC	Y	37390 FQ	43990 MW	51310 TQ	USBLS	5/07
	Columbia MSA, SC	Y	39930 FQ	47430 MW	56290 TQ	USBLS	5/07
	South Dakota	Y	35743 FQ	43651 MW	53048 TQ	SDBLS	7/08-9/08
	Sioux Falls MSA, SD	Y	39099 FQ	47301 MW	57090 TQ	SDBLS	7/08-9/08
	Tennessee	Y	38870 FQ	46700 MW	55810 TQ	USBLS	5/07
	Johnson City MSA, TN	Y	36580 FQ	43730 MW	49450 TQ	USBLS	5/07
	Memphis MSA, TN-MS-AR	Y	40610 FQ	48320 MW	56320 TQ	USBLS	5/07
	Nashville-Davidson-Murfreesboro MSA, TN	Y	41200 FQ	49300 MW	59080 TQ	USBLS	5/07
	Texas	Y	39410 FQ	48190 MW	58000 TQ	USBLS	5/07
	Austin-Round Rock MSA, TX	Y	42840 FQ	49500 MW	57880 TQ	USBLS	5/07
	Dallas-Fort Worth-Arlington MSA, TX	Y	44170 FQ	53580 MW	61470 TQ	USBLS	5/07
	El Paso MSA, TX	Y	36270 FQ	43990 MW	55630 TQ	USBLS	5/07
	Houston-Sugar Land-Baytown MSA, TX	Y	41250 FQ	49850 MW	59230 TQ	USBLS	5/07
	San Antonio MSA, TX	Y	38770 FQ	46520 MW	55990 TQ	USBLS	5/07
	Utah	Y	34950 FQ	43820 MW	54020 TQ	USBLS	5/07
	Salt Lake City MSA, UT	Y	34640 FQ	44290 MW	54710 TQ	USBLS	5/07
	Vermont	Y	43080 FQ	50040 MW	59760 TQ	USBLS	5/07
	Burlington-South Burlington MSA, VT	Y	41680 FQ	49630 MW	61620 TQ	USBLS	5/07
	Virginia	Y	40110 FQ	49510 MW	60110 TQ	USBLS	5/07
	Richmond MSA, VA	Y	41280 FQ	49410 MW	58230 TQ	USBLS	5/07
	Virginia Beach-Norfolk-Newport News MSA, VA-NC	Y	42270 FQ	49470 MW	57250 TQ	USBLS	5/07
	Washington	H	23.71 FQ	28.23 MW	33.16 TQ	WABLS	3/08
	Seattle-Tacoma-Bellevue MSA, WA	Y	51650 FQ	61690 MW	73080 TQ	USBLS	5/07
	West Virginia	Y	33640 FQ	41796 MW	49911 TQ	WVBLS	7/08-9/08
	Charleston MSA, WV	Y	29480 FQ	37270 MW	46410 TQ	USBLS	5/07
	Parkersburg-Marietta-Vienna MSA, WV-OH	Y	32760 FQ	37260 MW	45160 TQ	USBLS	5/07
	Wisconsin	Y	42800 FQ	49280 MW	57410 TQ	USBLS	5/07
	Appleton MSA, WI	Y	39770 FQ	46820 MW	54940 TQ	USBLS	5/07
	Milwaukee-Waukesha-West Allis MSA, WI	Y	44420 FQ	51260 MW	59840 TQ	USBLS	5/07
	Racine MSA, WI	Y	42570 FQ	48560 MW	56640 TQ	USBLS	5/07
	Wyoming	Y	37082 FQ	45947 MW	54217 TQ	WYBLS	9/08
	Cheyenne MSA, WY	Y	35007 FQ	39240 MW	45738 TQ	WYBLS	9/08
	Puerto Rico	Y	17540 FQ	20930 MW	25430 TQ	USBLS	5/07
	San Juan-Caguas-Guaynabo MSA, PR	Y	18590 FQ	21950 MW	26090 TQ	USBLS	5/07
	Guam	Y	25240 FQ	28930 MW	34080 TQ	USBLS	5/07
Radiologist	United States	Y	350000 AE			USATOD02	2007
Radiosurgeon	United States	Y	200000 LO		800000 HI	BUS202	2007
Rail Car Repairer	Alabama	Y	26190 FQ	40420 MW	46510 TQ	USBLS	5/07
	California	H	21.47 FQ	26.94 MW	30.92 TQ	CABLS	1/08-3/08
	Colorado	Y	34610 FQ	46770 MW	55510 TQ	USBLS	5/07
	Delaware	Y	38180 FQ	42020 MW	45720 TQ	USBLS	5/07
	Florida	Y	32260 FQ	44020 MW	50170 TQ	USBLS	5/07
	Georgia	Y	32510 FQ	36270 MW	40210 TQ	USBLS	5/07
	Illinois	Y	34280 FQ	41360 MW	49560 TQ	USBLS	5/07
	Indiana	Y	40430 FQ	45540 MW	55130 TQ	USBLS	5/07
	Iowa	Y	26190 FQ	31870 MW	43310 TQ	USBLS	5/07
	Kansas	Y	38860 FQ	46860 MW	58110 TQ	USBLS	5/07
	Kentucky	Y	29114 FQ	33550 MW	42422 TQ	KYBLS	2008
	Louisiana	H	15.62 FQ	19.06 MW	22.26 TQ	LABLS	1/08-3/08
	Maryland	Y		43025 MW		MDBLS	3/08

AE	Average entry wage	**AW**	Average wage paid	**FQ**	First quartile wage	**LO**	Lowest wage paid	**MTC**	Median total compensation	**TCC**	Total cash compensation
AER	Average entry range	**AWR**	Average wage range	**H**	Hourly	**LR**	Low end range	**MW**	Median wage paid	**TQ**	Third quartile wage
AEX	Average experienced wage	**AXR**	Average experienced range	**HI**	Highest wage paid	**M**	Monthly	**MWR**	Median wage range	**W**	Weekly
ATC	Average total compensation	**D**	Daily	**HR**	High end range	**MCC**	Median cash compensation	**S**	See annotated source	**Y**	Yearly

Occupation/Type/Industry	Location	Per	Low	Mid	High	Source	Date
Rail Car Repairer	Michigan	Y	37080 FQ	44540 MW	50000 TQ	USBLS	5/07
	Minnesota	Y	40164 FQ	46971 MW	58342 TQ	MNBLS	10/08-12/08
	Mississippi	Y	23120 FQ	38540 MW	47330 TQ	USBLS	5/07
	Missouri	Y	30340 FQ	38240 MW	48810 TQ	USBLS	5/07
	Nebraska	Y	42970 FQ	49360 MW	61940 TQ	USBLS	5/07
	Nevada	H	18.85 FQ	20.95 MW	23.06 TQ	NVBLS	5/08
	New Jersey	Y	43000 FQ	49290 MW	58160 TQ	USBLS	5/07
	North Carolina	Y	26190 FQ	31830 MW	44240 TQ	USBLS	5/07
	North Dakota	Y	43040 FQ	48320 MW	58860 TQ	USBLS	5/07
	Ohio	Y	34930 FQ	42970 MW	48500 TQ	USBLS	5/07
	Oregon	H	19.02 FQ	21.43 MW	24.27 TQ	ORBLS	5/08
	Pennsylvania	Y	32540 FQ	41550 MW	50940 TQ	USBLS	5/07
	South Carolina	Y	29010 FQ	38860 MW	46960 TQ	USBLS	5/07
	Tennessee	Y	43540 FQ	50730 MW	58530 TQ	USBLS	5/07
	Texas	Y	28950 FQ	36870 MW	47130 TQ	USBLS	5/07
	Virginia	Y	40010 FQ	46230 MW	55350 TQ	USBLS	5/07
	West Virginia	Y	28211 FQ	46510 MW	57807 TQ	WVBLS	7/08-9/08
	Wisconsin	Y	41600 FQ	46940 MW	54240 TQ	USBLS	5/07
	Wyoming	Y	32116 FQ	37772 MW	45666 TQ	WYBLS	9/08
Rail-Track Laying and Maintenance Equipment Operator	Alabama	Y	32230 FQ	37140 MW	43340 TQ	USBLS	5/07
	Arkansas	Y	34350 FQ	40430 MW	44610 TQ	USBLS	5/07
	California	H	19.26 FQ	21.75 MW	24.63 TQ	CABLS	1/08-3/08
	Colorado	Y	40280 FQ	44740 MW	49360 TQ	USBLS	5/07
	Florida	Y	41410 FQ	45170 MW	48930 TQ	USBLS	5/07
	Georgia	Y	27200 FQ	32990 MW	41080 TQ	USBLS	5/07
	Illinois	Y	36840 FQ	42350 MW	47350 TQ	USBLS	5/07
	Indiana	Y	42520 FQ	50600 MW	58370 TQ	USBLS	5/07
	Iowa	Y	37140 FQ	41700 MW	47950 TQ	USBLS	5/07
	Kentucky	Y	37724 FQ	44052 MW	49470 TQ	KYBLS	2008
	Louisiana	H	14.24 FQ	19.78 MW	22.53 TQ	LABLS	1/08-3/08
	Maine	Y	30510 FQ	36960 MW	43700 TQ	USBLS	5/07
	Maryland	Y		32375 MW		MDBLS	3/08
	Massachusetts	Y	37660 FQ	42430 MW	47930 TQ	USBLS	5/07
	Michigan	Y	34920 FQ	40930 MW	46910 TQ	USBLS	5/07
	Minnesota	Y	40437 FQ	46212 MW	53052 TQ	MNBLS	10/08-12/08
	Mississippi	Y	29280 FQ	39970 MW	45980 TQ	USBLS	5/07
	Missouri	Y	39280 FQ	44070 MW	48980 TQ	USBLS	5/07
	Nebraska	Y	40740 FQ	45330 MW	50340 TQ	USBLS	5/07
	Nevada	H	19.78 FQ	21.27 MW	22.85 TQ	NVBLS	5/08
	New Jersey	Y	35850 FQ	39130 MW	42800 TQ	USBLS	5/07
	New Mexico	Y	39560 FQ	45810 MW	53830 TQ	USBLS	5/07
	New York	Y	36860 FQ	44210 MW	51310 TQ	USBLS	5/07
	North Carolina	Y	26870 FQ	31520 MW	37720 TQ	USBLS	5/07
	Ohio	Y	39200 FQ	45420 MW	50670 TQ	USBLS	5/07
	Oklahoma	Y	33430 FQ	42560 MW	52380 TQ	USBLS	5/07
	Oregon	H	19.22 FQ	21.29 MW	23.38 TQ	ORBLS	5/08
	Pennsylvania	Y	36240 FQ	43110 MW	48750 TQ	USBLS	5/07
	South Carolina	Y	32490 FQ	43490 MW	48600 TQ	USBLS	5/07
	Tennessee	Y	32420 FQ	41320 MW	47860 TQ	USBLS	5/07
	Texas	Y	22460 FQ	35740 MW	44460 TQ	USBLS	5/07
	Virginia	Y	38410 FQ	43230 MW	48270 TQ	USBLS	5/07
	Wisconsin	Y	32850 FQ	42900 MW	49900 TQ	USBLS	5/07
	Wyoming	Y	34851 FQ	41477 MW	50591 TQ	WYBLS	9/08
Rail Yard Engineer, Dinkey Operator, and Hostler	Alabama	Y	39540 FQ	42890 MW	46020 TQ	USBLS	5/07
	California	H	12.47 FQ	14.44 MW	17.35 TQ	CABLS	1/08-3/08
	Colorado	Y	30940 FQ	38940 MW	44580 TQ	USBLS	5/07
	Florida	Y	39920 FQ	44380 MW	48700 TQ	USBLS	5/07
	Georgia	Y	26600 FQ	42530 MW	47740 TQ	USBLS	5/07
	Illinois	Y	28440 FQ	31200 MW	34130 TQ	USBLS	5/07
	Kentucky	Y	28357 FQ	38404 MW	47151 TQ	KYBLS	2008
	Louisiana	H	12.97 FQ	14.80 MW	16.84 TQ	LABLS	1/08-3/08
	Mississippi	Y	33740 FQ	46290 MW	80210 TQ	USBLS	5/07
	Missouri	Y	32110 FQ	39490 MW	46860 TQ	USBLS	5/07
	Nebraska	Y	13860 FQ	20820 MW	32020 TQ	USBLS	5/07
	New Jersey	Y	43750 FQ	57960 MW	68680 TQ	USBLS	5/07
	Ohio	Y	24340 FQ	29340 MW	34290 TQ	USBLS	5/07

AE Average entry wage	**AW** Average wage paid	**FQ** First quartile wage	**LO** Lowest wage paid	**MTC** Median total compensation	**TCC** Total cash compensation
AER Average entry range	**AWR** Average wage range	**H** Hourly	**LR** Low end range	**MW** Median wage paid	**TQ** Third quartile wage
AEX Average experienced wage	**AXR** Average experienced range	**HI** Highest wage paid	**M** Monthly	**MWR** Median wage range	**W** Weekly
ATC Average total compensation	**D** Daily	**HR** High end range	**MCC** Median cash compensation	**S** See annotated source	**Y** Yearly

Occupation/Type/Industry	Location	Per	Low	Mid	High	Source	Date
Rail Yard Engineer, Dinkey Operator, and Hostler	Oregon	H	13.76 FQ	19.49 MW	22.44 TQ	ORBLS	5/08
	Pennsylvania	Y	43750 FQ	50420 MW	55140 MW	USBLS	5/07
	Texas	Y	25060 FQ	28490 MW	35280 TQ	USBLS	5/07
	Wisconsin	Y	31910 FQ	40420 MW	46630 TQ	USBLS	5/07
Railroad Brake, Signal, and Switch Operator	Alabama	Y	37400 FQ	43590 MW	48690 TQ	USBLS	5/07
	Arizona	Y	42950 FQ	46840 MW	50600 TQ	USBLS	5/07
	Arkansas	Y	46750 FQ	59670 MW	71240 TQ	USBLS	5/07
	California	H	20.74 FQ	22.69 MW	26.08 TQ	CABLS	1/08-3/08
	Colorado	Y	43010 FQ	47900 MW	57130 TQ	USBLS	5/07
	Georgia	Y	43360 FQ	46390 MW	49440 TQ	USBLS	5/07
	Idaho	Y	41980 FQ	45720 MW	49460 TQ	USBLS	5/07
	Illinois	Y	46770 FQ	57900 MW	68950 TQ	USBLS	5/07
	Indiana	Y	35340 FQ	40410 MW	48740 TQ	USBLS	5/07
	Iowa	Y	41180 FQ	46160 MW	53390 TQ	USBLS	5/07
	Kansas	Y	51180 FQ	63420 MW	73790 TQ	USBLS	5/07
	Kentucky	Y	42002 FQ	47587 MW	53082 TQ	KYBLS	2008
	Louisiana	H	18.88 FQ	23.58 MW	32.51 TQ	LABLS	1/08-3/08
	Massachusetts	Y	42300 FQ	45770 MW	49240 TQ	USBLS	5/07
	Michigan	Y	45700 FQ	57830 MW	70600 TQ	USBLS	5/07
	Minnesota	Y	45900 FQ	53005 MW	70358 TQ	MNBLS	10/08-12/08
	Mississippi	Y	51450 FQ	64980 MW	78790 TQ	USBLS	5/07
	Missouri	Y	51330 FQ	64080 MW	75540 TQ	USBLS	5/07
	Nebraska	Y	51080 FQ	59370 MW	70110 TQ	USBLS	5/07
	Nevada	H	25.38 FQ	31.64 MW	36.34 TQ	NVBLS	5/08
	New Jersey	Y	42770 FQ	47380 MW	52080 TQ	USBLS	5/07
	New York	Y	41090 FQ	45060 MW	51400 TQ	USBLS	5/07
	Ohio	Y	30600 FQ	36990 MW	44950 TQ	USBLS	5/07
	Pennsylvania	Y	40800 FQ	45260 MW	60410 TQ	USBLS	5/07
	South Carolina	Y	43130 FQ	45930 MW	48790 TQ	USBLS	5/07
	Tennessee	Y	46540 FQ	60000 MW	71620 TQ	USBLS	5/07
	Texas	Y	43480 FQ	59980 MW	72840 TQ	USBLS	5/07
	Utah	Y	43410 FQ	46330 MW	49210 TQ	USBLS	5/07
	Virginia	Y	29170 FQ	32580 MW	35660 TQ	USBLS	5/07
	Wisconsin	Y	44370 FQ	53730 MW	65910 TQ	USBLS	5/07
	Wyoming	Y	62360 FQ	71046 MW	81392 TQ	WYBLS	9/08
Railroad Conductor and Yardmaster	Alabama	Y	37880 FQ	47380 MW	60000 TQ	USBLS	5/07
	Arkansas	Y	51630 FQ	60060 MW	81270 TQ	USBLS	5/07
	California	H	21.60 FQ	26.89 MW	31.34 TQ	CABLS	1/08-3/08
	Colorado	Y	44270 FQ	59690 MW	79610 TQ	USBLS	5/07
	Delaware	Y	39990 FQ	44440 MW	63540 TQ	USBLS	5/07
	Florida	Y	40980 FQ	47920 MW	58360 TQ	USBLS	5/07
	Georgia	Y	37440 FQ	45310 MW	52130 TQ	USBLS	5/07
	Illinois	Y	48150 FQ	63310 MW	82240 TQ	USBLS	5/07
	Indiana	Y	44410 FQ	52400 MW	58730 TQ	USBLS	5/07
	Iowa	Y	45280 FQ	56750 MW	74000 TQ	USBLS	5/07
	Kansas	Y	57940 FQ	73060 MW	87580 TQ	USBLS	5/07
	Kentucky	Y	55815 FQ	69884 MW	88144 TQ	KYBLS	2008
	Louisiana	H	20.55 FQ	26.35 MW	36.94 TQ	LABLS	1/08-3/08
	Maine	Y	47140 FQ	59970 MW	78640 TQ	USBLS	5/07
	Maryland	Y		72400 MW		MDBLS	3/08
	Massachusetts	Y	44970 FQ	49330 MW	56080 TQ	USBLS	5/07
	Michigan	Y	38440 FQ	49770 MW	71320 TQ	USBLS	5/07
	Minnesota	Y	43871 FQ	50623 MW	76538 TQ	MNBLS	10/08-12/08
	Mississippi	Y	51830 FQ	64690 MW	82020 TQ	USBLS	5/07
	Missouri	Y	56910 FQ	69130 MW	84350 TQ	USBLS	5/07
	Nebraska	Y	58630 FQ	71810 MW	87170 TQ	USBLS	5/07
	Nevada	H	27.55 FQ	34.97 MW	42.90 TQ	NVBLS	5/08
	New Jersey	Y	42680 FQ	51420 MW	66020 TQ	USBLS	5/07
	New York	Y	42970 FQ	53080 MW	67740 TQ	USBLS	5/07
	North Carolina	Y	26700 FQ	38210 MW	47410 TQ	USBLS	5/07
	Ohio	Y	36640 FQ	41430 MW	45850 TQ	USBLS	5/07
	Oklahoma	Y	53220 FQ	66300 MW	80010 TQ	USBLS	5/07
	Oregon	H	25.16 FQ	33.16 MW	40.87 TQ	ORBLS	5/08
	Pennsylvania	Y	38550 FQ	46880 MW	65920 TQ	USBLS	5/07
	South Carolina	Y	39930 FQ	46840 MW	60290 TQ	USBLS	5/07
	Tennessee	Y	55980 FQ	70690 MW	86710 TQ	USBLS	5/07

AE	Average entry wage	AW	Average wage paid	FQ	First quartile wage	LO	Lowest wage paid	MTC	Median total compensation	TCC	Total cash compensation
AER	Average entry range	AWR	Average wage range	H	Hourly	LR	Low end range	MW	Median wage paid	TQ	Third quartile wage
AEX	Average experienced wage	AXR	Average experienced range	HI	Highest wage paid	M	Monthly	MWR	Median wage range	W	Weekly
ATC	Average total compensation	D	Daily	HR	High end range	MCC	Median cash compensation	S	See annotated source	Y	Yearly

Occupation/Type/Industry	Location	Per	Low	Mid	High	Source	Date
Railroad Conductor and Yardmaster	Texas	Y	55330 FQ	72790 MW	88840 TQ	USBLS	5/07
	Virginia	Y	56290 FQ	70860 MW	87160 TQ	USBLS	5/07
	Wisconsin	Y	52620 FQ	58000 MW	75430 TQ	USBLS	5/07
	Wyoming	Y	61613 FQ	76786 MW	92184 TQ	WYBLS	9/08
Railroad Inspection Manager							
State Government	Ohio	H	27.93 LO		36.59 HI	ODAS	2008
Railroad Inspector/Investigator							
Department of Transportation	New Hampshire	Y			51953 HI	NHUL03	2008
Railroad Safety Inspector							
Department of Transportation	Michigan	H	17.84 LO		26.69 HI	MDOT	10/1/07
Ramp Agent							
Southwest Airlines	Rhode Island	Y	20360 LO			RIM01	2009
Ramp Service Agent	United States	H		10.12 AW		AVJOB03	2009
R&D/Technical Director							
Coatings Industry	United States	Y		110000 ATC		CWRLD01	2008
Real-Bearded Santa	United States	H			125.00 HI	ABCN	12/08
Real Estate Appraiser							
Department of Revenue Administration	New Hampshire	Y		44807 AW		NHUL03	2008
Real Estate Broker	United States	Y			151000 TQ	FORB02	2009
	Alabama	Y	41550 FQ	76710 MW		USBLS	5/07
	Birmingham-Hoover MSA, AL	Y	60280 FQ	80900 MW		USBLS	5/07
	Alaska	Y	54700 FQ	59350 MW	64110 TQ	USBLS	5/07
	Anchorage MSA, AK	Y	56960 FQ	60990 MW	65030 TQ	USBLS	5/07
	Phoenix-Mesa-Scottsdale MSA, AZ	Y	34660 FQ	42740 MW	114360 TQ	USBLS	5/07
	Tucson MSA, AZ	Y	33990 FQ	37670 MW	41540 TQ	USBLS	5/07
	Arkansas	Y	26780 FQ	46260 MW	73850 TQ	USBLS	5/07
	Little Rock-North Little Rock MSA, AR	Y	50840 FQ	74320 MW	85900 TQ	USBLS	5/07
	California	H	24.27 FQ	34.16 MW	63.19 TQ	CABLS	1/08-3/08
	Los Angeles-Long Beach-Glendale PMSA, CA	H	23.87 FQ	29.11 MW	47.28 TQ	CABLS	1/08-3/08
	Oakland-Fremont-Hayward MSA, CA	H	23.59 FQ	43.90 MW		CABLS	1/08-3/08
	Riverside-San Bernardino-Ontario MSA, CA	H	24.75 FQ	28.78 MW	39.76 TQ	CABLS	1/08-3/08
	Sacramento-Arden Arcade-Roseville MSA, CA	H	25.80 FQ	36.55 MW		CABLS	1/08-3/08
	San Diego-Carlsbad-San Marcos MSA, CA	H	23.48 FQ	38.62 MW		CABLS	1/08-3/08
	San Francisco-San Mateo-Redwood PMSA, CA	H	49.30 FQ	66.02 MW		CABLS	1/08-3/08
	San Jose-Sunnyvale-Santa Clara MSA, CA	H	28.44 FQ	41.88 MW	51.25 TQ	CABLS	1/08-3/08
	Santa Ana-Anaheim-Irvine PMSA, CA	Y	44300 FQ	64360 MW	116210 TQ	USBLS	5/07
	Colorado	Y	30180 FQ	63490 MW	98310 TQ	USBLS	5/07
	Colorado Springs MSA, CO	Y	41160 FQ	46320 MW	51470 TQ	USBLS	5/07
	Denver-Aurora MSA, CO	Y	27690 FQ	64820 MW	96210 TQ	USBLS	5/07
	Connecticut	H	14.89 AE	42.15 MW		CTBLS	1/08-3/08
	Delaware	Y	47560 FQ	64970 MW	87170 TQ	USBLS	5/07
	Wilmington PMSA, DE-MD-NJ	Y	44060 FQ	78520 MW	92250 TQ	USBLS	5/07
	District of Columbia	Y	42550 FQ	53500 MW	69270 TQ	USBLS	5/07
	Washington-Arlington-Alexandria MSA, DC-VA-MD-WV	Y	45560 FQ	59690 MW	87010 TQ	USBLS	5/07
	Florida	Y	38140 FQ	61730 MW	110670 TQ	USBLS	5/07
	Fort Lauderdale-Pompano Beach-Deerfield Beach PMSA, FL	Y	33950 FQ	47780 MW	79560 TQ	USBLS	5/07
	Jacksonville MSA, FL	Y	41140 FQ	132150 MW		USBLS	5/07

AE	Average entry wage	AW	Average wage paid	FQ	First quartile wage
AER	Average entry range	AWR	Average wage range	H	Hourly
AEX	Average experienced wage	AXR	Average experienced range	HI	Highest wage paid
ATC	Average total compensation	D	Daily	HR	High end range

LO	Lowest wage paid	MTC	Median total compensation	TCC	Total cash compensation
LR	Low end range	MW	Median wage paid	TQ	Third quartile wage
M	Monthly	MWR	Median wage range	W	Weekly
MCC	Median cash compensation	S	See annotated source	Y	Yearly

Occupation/Type/Industry	Location	Per	Low	Mid	High	Source	Date
Real Estate Broker	Miami-Fort Lauderdale-Miami Beach MSA, FL	Y	37590 FQ	75940 MW	121620 TQ	USBLS	5/07
	Orlando-Kissimmee MSA, FL	Y	34500 FQ	55840 MW	99340 TQ	USBLS	5/07
	Tampa-St. Petersburg-Clearwater MSA, FL	Y	43110 FQ	53420 MW	65230 TQ	USBLS	5/07
	West Palm Beach-Boca Raton-Boynton Beach PMSA, FL	Y	84570 FQ	111020 MW		USBLS	5/07
	Georgia	Y	39090 FQ	58130 MW	118210 TQ	USBLS	5/07
	Atlanta-Sandy Springs-Marietta MSA, GA	Y	49210 FQ	75190 MW	127100 TQ	USBLS	5/07
	Idaho	Y	22240 FQ	24760 MW	40700 TQ	USBLS	5/07
	Boise City-Nampa MSA, ID	Y	22550 FQ	24820 MW	41080 TQ	USBLS	5/07
	Illinois	Y	35810 FQ	56670 MW	79130 TQ	USBLS	5/07
	Chicago-Naperville-Joliet MSA, IL-IN-WI	Y	35190 FQ	58320 MW	81380 TQ	USBLS	5/07
	Rockford MSA, IL	Y	36100 FQ	44350 MW	50350 TQ	USBLS	5/07
	Indiana	Y	28850 FQ	56340 MW	84560 TQ	USBLS	5/07
	Indianapolis-Carmel MSA, IN	Y	51750 FQ	60370 MW	120310 TQ	USBLS	5/07
	Iowa	Y	36160 FQ	47950 MW	61270 TQ	USBLS	5/07
	Des Moines-West Des Moines MSA, IA	Y	43570 FQ	54970 MW	71900 TQ	USBLS	5/07
	Louisiana	H	20.10 FQ	22.48 MW	25.12 TQ	LABLS	1/08-3/08
	Maine	Y	42190 FQ	61300 MW	133740 TQ	USBLS	5/07
	Portland-South Portland-Biddeford MSA, ME	Y	41000 FQ	71270 MW	136120 TQ	USBLS	5/07
	Maryland	Y		56450 MW		MDBLS	3/08
	Baltimore-Towson MSA, MD	Y	20600 FQ	43790 MW	65840 TQ	USBLS	5/07
	Bethesda-Gaithersburg-Frederick PMSA, MD	Y	48160 FQ	62430 MW	89430 TQ	USBLS	5/07
	Massachusetts	Y	27340 FQ	53550 MW	87110 TQ	USBLS	5/07
	Boston-Cambridge-Quincy NECTA, MA	Y	27250 FQ	53230 MW	80980 TQ	USBLS	5/07
	Warren-Troy-Farmington Hills PMSA, MI	Y	53560 FQ	61010 MW	108470 TQ	USBLS	5/07
	Minnesota	Y	66479 FQ	100658 MW	132531 TQ	MNBLS	10/08-12/08
	Duluth-Superior MSA, MN-WI	Y	42686 FQ	47178 MW	51660 TQ	MNBLS	10/08-12/08
	Minneapolis-Saint Paul MSA, MN-WI	Y	75900 FQ	107864 MW	134472 TQ	MNBLS	10/08-12/08
	Mississippi	Y	27700 FQ	48310 MW	106880 TQ	USBLS	5/07
	Missouri	Y	31700 FQ	43810 MW	62240 TQ	USBLS	5/07
	Kansas City MSA, MO-KS	Y	28900 FQ	33520 MW	60730 TQ	USBLS	5/07
	St. Louis MSA, MO-IL	Y	36870 FQ	75670 MW	113900 TQ	USBLS	5/07
	Montana	Y	54360 FQ	60310 MW	67860 TQ	USBLS	5/07
	Nebraska	Y	23220 FQ	39850 MW	75050 TQ	USBLS	5/07
	Omaha-Council Bluffs MSA, NE-IA	Y	24340 FQ	34610 MW	62050 TQ	USBLS	5/07
	Nevada	H	14.66 FQ	18.82 MW	37.19 TQ	NVBLS	5/08
	Carson City MSA, NV	H	32.68 FQ	35.21 MW	37.75 TQ	NVBLS	5/08
	New Jersey	Y	55490 FQ	78080 MW	104270 TQ	USBLS	5/07
	Camden PMSA, NJ	Y	58470 FQ	65300 MW		USBLS	5/07
	Edison PMSA, NJ	Y	58680 FQ	93530 MW	119560 TQ	USBLS	5/07
	Newark-Union PMSA, NJ-PA	Y	39240 FQ	53780 MW	82410 TQ	USBLS	5/07
	New Mexico	Y	27110 FQ	76590 MW	112110 TQ	USBLS	5/07
	Albany-Schenectady-Troy MSA, NY	Y	36420 FQ	44710 MW	70690 TQ	USBLS	5/07
	Buffalo-Niagara Falls MSA, NY	Y	37500 FQ	48590 MW	120540 TQ	USBLS	5/07
	Nassau-Suffolk PMSA, NY	Y	52320 FQ	61270 MW	87890 TQ	USBLS	5/07
	New York-Northern New Jersey-Long Island MSA, NY-NJ-PA	Y	62280 FQ	93880 MW		USBLS	5/07
	North Carolina	Y	26840 FQ	32210 MW	49760 TQ	USBLS	5/07
	Charlotte-Gastonia-Concord MSA, NC-SC	Y	29890 FQ	38850 MW	74830 TQ	USBLS	5/07
	Greensboro-High Point MSA, NC	Y	23900 FQ	29560 MW	38860 TQ	USBLS	5/07
	Raleigh-Cary MSA, NC	Y	27750 FQ	35110 MW	52960 TQ	USBLS	5/07
	Ohio	Y	39600 FQ	46480 MW	60170 TQ	USBLS	5/07
	Cincinnati-Middletown MSA, OH-KY-IN	Y	42720 FQ	49620 MW	76090 TQ	USBLS	5/07
	Cleveland-Elyria-Mentor MSA, OH	Y	41430 FQ	46090 MW	54080 TQ	USBLS	5/07

AE	Average entry wage	AW	Average wage paid	FQ	First quartile wage	LO	Lowest wage paid	MTC	Median total compensation	TCC	Total cash compensation
AER	Average entry range	AWR	Average wage range	H	Hourly	LR	Low end range	MW	Median wage paid	TQ	Third quartile wage
AEX	Average experienced wage	AXR	Average experienced range	HI	Highest wage paid	M	Monthly	MWR	Median wage range	W	Weekly
ATC	Average total compensation	D	Daily	HR	High end range	MCC	Median cash compensation	S	See annotated source	Y	Yearly

Occupation/Type/Industry	Location	Per	Low	Mid	High	Source	Date
Real Estate Broker	Columbus MSA, OH	Y	41760 FQ	47190 MW	95660 TQ	USBLS	5/07
	Oklahoma	Y	40580 FQ	58060 MW	97660 TQ	USBLS	5/07
	Tulsa MSA, OK	Y	58610 FQ	85650 MW	99720 TQ	USBLS	5/07
	Portland-Vancouver-Beaverton MSA, OR-WA	Y	38150 FQ	49890 MW		USBLS	5/07
	Allentown-Bethlehem-Easton MSA, PA-NJ	Y	43500 FQ	60390 MW	137870 TQ	USBLS	5/07
	South Carolina	Y	46700 FQ	60960 MW	80150 TQ	USBLS	5/07
	Charleston-North Charleston MSA, SC	Y	48920 FQ	114320 MW		USBLS	5/07
	Columbia MSA, SC	Y	42440 FQ	59420 MW	76000 TQ	USBLS	5/07
	South Dakota	Y	41900 FQ	45593 MW	49493 TQ	SDBLS	7/08-9/08
	Tennessee	Y	30710 FQ	47010 MW	70030 TQ	USBLS	5/07
	Nashville-Davidson-Murfreesboro MSA, TN	Y	43240 FQ	52340 MW	62600 TQ	USBLS	5/07
	Texas	Y	59250 FQ	83350 MW	105280 TQ	USBLS	5/07
	Austin-Round Rock MSA, TX	Y	63960 FQ	69050 MW	74190 TQ	USBLS	5/07
	Dallas-Fort Worth-Arlington MSA, TX	Y	65710 FQ	93900 MW	116140 TQ	USBLS	5/07
	Houston-Sugar Land-Baytown MSA, TX	Y	55720 FQ	90610 MW	104880 TQ	USBLS	5/07
	San Antonio MSA, TX	Y	41750 FQ	69110 MW	97290 TQ	USBLS	5/07
	Utah	Y	51010 FQ	60500 MW	75360 TQ	USBLS	5/07
	Salt Lake City MSA, UT	Y	49220 FQ	56480 MW	68740 TQ	USBLS	5/07
	Burlington-South Burlington MSA, VT	Y	31270 FQ	34840 MW	38380 TQ	USBLS	5/07
	Virginia	Y	42140 FQ	52910 MW	92740 TQ	USBLS	5/07
	Richmond MSA, VA	Y	48800 FQ	59190 MW	83870 TQ	USBLS	5/07
	Virginia Beach-Norfolk-Newport News MSA, VA-NC	Y	44080 FQ	50640 MW	139890 TQ	USBLS	5/07
	Washington	H	22.87 FQ	32.10 MW	61.62 TQ	WABLS	3/08
	Seattle-Tacoma-Bellevue MSA, WA	Y	48830 FQ	67060 MW	126520 TQ	USBLS	5/07
	West Virginia	Y	33845 FQ	55425 MW	76130 TQ	WVBLS	7/08-9/08
	Wisconsin	Y	34690 FQ	46620 MW	70720 TQ	USBLS	5/07
	Puerto Rico	Y	36540 FQ	64650 MW	70580 TQ	USBLS	5/07
	San Juan-Caguas-Guaynabo MSA, PR	Y	36540 FQ	64650 MW	70580 TQ	USBLS	5/07
	Virgin Islands	Y	32190 FQ	36450 MW	41340 TQ	USBLS	5/07
Real Estate Management Professional							
Accredited Residential Manager Certification	United States	Y		57893 ATC		IREM01	2006
Real Estate Sales Agent	Alabama	Y	35350 FQ	48170 MW	72050 TQ	USBLS	5/07
	Birmingham-Hoover MSA, AL	Y	38430 FQ	48640 MW	77120 TQ	USBLS	5/07
	Huntsville MSA, AL	Y	44560 FQ	53180 MW	79820 TQ	USBLS	5/07
	Alaska	Y	43530 FQ	61590 MW	74610 TQ	USBLS	5/07
	Arizona	Y	34140 FQ	45550 MW	72510 TQ	USBLS	5/07
	Phoenix-Mesa-Scottsdale MSA, AZ	Y	34950 FQ	45780 MW	72020 TQ	USBLS	5/07
	Arkansas	Y	22890 FQ	35640 MW	46110 TQ	USBLS	5/07
	Little Rock-North Little Rock MSA, AR	Y	25770 FQ	37460 MW	48400 TQ	USBLS	5/07
	California	H	16.50 FQ	25.87 MW	40.61 TQ	CABLS	1/08-3/08
	Modesto MSA, CA	H	18.95 FQ	31.32 MW	34.72 TQ	CABLS	1/08-3/08
	Oakland-Fremont-Hayward MSA, CA	H	15.67 FQ	19.28 MW	29.42 TQ	CABLS	1/08-3/08
	Riverside-San Bernardino-Ontario MSA, CA	H	18.67 FQ	26.48 MW	31.67 TQ	CABLS	1/08-3/08
	Sacramento-Arden Arcade-Roseville MSA, CA	H	15.35 FQ	26.23 MW	34.01 TQ	CABLS	1/08-3/08
	San Diego-Carlsbad-San Marcos MSA, CA	H	31.90 FQ	49.29 MW		CABLS	1/08-3/08
	San Francisco-San Mateo-Redwood PMSA, CA	H	16.03 FQ	22.91 MW	40.10 TQ	CABLS	1/08-3/08
	San Jose-Sunnyvale-Santa Clara MSA, CA	H	18.88 FQ	31.55 MW	39.25 TQ	CABLS	1/08-3/08
	Santa Ana-Anaheim-Irvine PMSA, CA	Y	38680 FQ	67000 MW	94290 TQ	USBLS	5/07
	Colorado	Y	29550 FQ	50270 MW	76460 TQ	USBLS	5/07

AE	Average entry wage	AW	Average wage paid	FQ	First quartile wage	LO	Lowest wage paid	MTC	Median total compensation	TCC	Total cash compensation
AER	Average entry range	AWR	Average wage range	H	Hourly	LR	Low end range	MW	Median wage paid	TQ	Third quartile wage
AEX	Average experienced wage	AXR	Average experienced range	HI	Highest wage paid	M	Monthly	MWR	Median wage range	W	Weekly
ATC	Average total compensation	D	Daily	HR	High end range	MCC	Median cash compensation	S	See annotated source	Y	Yearly

1364

Occupation/Type/Industry	Location	Per	Low	Mid	High	Source	Date
Real Estate Sales Agent	Denver-Aurora MSA, CO	Y	30530 FQ	58420 MW	91990 TQ	USBLS	5/07
	Pueblo MSA, CO	Y	29800 FQ	44980 MW	127260 TQ	USBLS	5/07
	Connecticut	H	15.23 AE	27.66 MW		CTBLS	1/08-3/08
	Bridgeport-Stamford-Norwalk MSA, CT	Y	44810 FQ	59900 MW	75510 TQ	USBLS	5/07
	Hartford-West Hartford-East Hartford MSA, CT	Y	39900 FQ	52420 MW	86070 TQ	USBLS	5/07
	Delaware	Y	31130 FQ	40950 MW	74880 TQ	USBLS	5/07
	Dover MSA, DE	Y	29750 FQ	47670 MW	90210 TQ	USBLS	5/07
	Wilmington PMSA, DE-MD-NJ	Y	25850 FQ	35550 MW	45170 TQ	USBLS	5/07
	District of Columbia	Y	34680 FQ	54840 MW	97180 TQ	USBLS	5/07
	Washington-Arlington-Alexandria MSA, DC-VA-MD-WV	Y	32910 FQ	45320 MW	76740 TQ	USBLS	5/07
	Florida	Y	25340 FQ	36140 MW	54460 TQ	USBLS	5/07
	Fort Lauderdale-Pompano Beach-Deerfield Beach PMSA, FL	Y	31570 FQ	44230 MW	72650 TQ	USBLS	5/07
	Jacksonville MSA, FL	Y	24420 FQ	33060 MW	47260 TQ	USBLS	5/07
	Miami-Fort Lauderdale-Miami Beach MSA, FL	Y	26860 FQ	38190 MW	67450 TQ	USBLS	5/07
	Orlando-Kissimmee MSA, FL	Y	26460 FQ	34760 MW	50300 TQ	USBLS	5/07
	Tampa-St. Petersburg-Clearwater MSA, FL	Y	24650 FQ	40010 MW	56940 TQ	USBLS	5/07
	West Palm Beach-Boca Raton-Boynton Beach PMSA, FL	Y	26410 FQ	37010 MW	49470 TQ	USBLS	5/07
	Georgia	Y	23670 FQ	29220 MW	44540 TQ	USBLS	5/07
	Atlanta-Sandy Springs-Marietta MSA, GA	Y	24610 FQ	29610 MW	51310 TQ	USBLS	5/07
	Augusta-Richmond County MSA, GA-SC	Y	25420 FQ	36500 MW	55980 TQ	USBLS	5/07
	Macon MSA, GA	Y	29300 FQ	33560 MW	39940 TQ	USBLS	5/07
	Hawaii	Y	48860 FQ	66020 MW	97920 TQ	USBLS	5/07
	Idaho	Y	30890 FQ	40760 MW	57570 TQ	USBLS	5/07
	Boise City-Nampa MSA, ID	Y	34150 FQ	49930 MW	58960 TQ	USBLS	5/07
	Illinois	Y	30790 FQ	41120 MW	57850 TQ	USBLS	5/07
	Champaign-Urbana MSA, IL	Y	28020 FQ	30920 MW	39930 TQ	USBLS	5/07
	Chicago-Naperville-Joliet MSA, IL-IN-WI	Y	32120 FQ	42210 MW	58390 TQ	USBLS	5/07
	Indiana	Y	21970 FQ	34500 MW	54850 TQ	USBLS	5/07
	Gary PMSA, IN	Y	42530 FQ	46610 MW	50740 TQ	USBLS	5/07
	Indianapolis-Carmel MSA, IN	Y	21120 FQ	40630 MW	66790 TQ	USBLS	5/07
	Iowa	Y	21570 FQ	35240 MW	53000 TQ	USBLS	5/07
	Davenport-Moline-Rock Island MSA, IA-IL	Y	34980 FQ	45150 MW	61810 TQ	USBLS	5/07
	Des Moines-West Des Moines MSA, IA	Y	26180 FQ	36940 MW	54600 TQ	USBLS	5/07
	Kansas	Y	36110 FQ	44920 MW	66820 TQ	USBLS	5/07
	Wichita MSA, KS	Y	22600 FQ	40150 MW	67700 TQ	USBLS	5/07
	Kentucky	Y	19417 FQ	25242 MW	34601 TQ	KYBLS	2008
	Lexington-Fayette MSA, KY	Y	18870 FQ	21990 MW	26980 TQ	USBLS	5/07
	Louisville-Jefferson County MSA, KY-IN	Y	24530 FQ	28290 MW	38370 TQ	USBLS	5/07
	Louisiana	H	11.53 FQ	16.32 MW	22.89 TQ	LABLS	1/08-3/08
	Baton Rouge MSA, LA	Y	14400 FQ	41690 MW	51130 TQ	USBLS	5/07
	Lake Charles MSA, LA	Y	24950 FQ	32120 MW	37200 TQ	USBLS	5/07
	New Orleans-Metairie-Kenner MSA, LA	Y	25350 FQ	34940 MW	45680 TQ	USBLS	5/07
	Maryland	Y		53175 MW		MDBLS	3/08
	Baltimore-Towson MSA, MD	Y	37960 FQ	56420 MW	77210 TQ	USBLS	5/07
	Bethesda-Gaithersburg-Frederick PMSA, MD	Y	36270 FQ	50730 MW	70940 TQ	USBLS	5/07
	Cumberland MSA, MD-WV	Y	26040 FQ	32990 MW	43820 TQ	USBLS	5/07
	Massachusetts	Y	35490 FQ	51300 MW	82750 TQ	USBLS	5/07
	Boston-Cambridge-Quincy NECTA, MA	Y	42020 FQ	72930 MW	136520 TQ	USBLS	5/07
	Worcester MSA, MA-CT	Y	33950 FQ	37020 MW	54210 TQ	USBLS	5/07
	Michigan	Y	26790 FQ	38490 MW	54190 TQ	USBLS	5/07
	Detroit-Warren-Livonia MSA, MI	Y	28590 FQ	39490 MW	56390 TQ	USBLS	5/07

AE	Average entry wage	AW	Average wage paid	FQ	First quartile wage
AER	Average entry range	AWR	Average wage range	H	Hourly
AEX	Average experienced wage	AXR	Average experienced range	HI	Highest wage paid
ATC	Average total compensation	D	Daily	HR	High end range

LO	Lowest wage paid	
LR	Low end range	
M	Monthly	
MCC	Median cash compensation	

MTC	Median total compensation	
MW	Median wage paid	
MWR	Median wage range	
S	See annotated source	

TCC	Total cash compensation
TQ	Third quartile wage
W	Weekly
Y	Yearly

Real Estate Sales Agent

Occupation/Type/Industry	Location	Per	Low	Mid	High	Source	Date
Real Estate Sales Agent	Grand Rapids-Wyoming MSA, MI	Y	15560 FQ	27760 MW	40060 TQ	USBLS	5/07
	Warren-Troy-Farmington Hills PMSA, MI	Y	27800 FQ	38550 MW	56610 TQ	USBLS	5/07
	Minnesota	Y	26181 FQ	34311 MW	49445 TQ	MNBLS	10/08-12/08
	Duluth-Superior MSA, MN-WI	Y	49333 FQ	54587 MW	59293 TQ	MNBLS	10/08-12/08
	Minneapolis-Saint Paul MSA, MN-WI	Y	25866 FQ	32797 MW	46904 TQ	MNBLS	10/08-12/08
	Rochester MSA, MN	Y	24921 FQ	29250 MW	38695 TQ	MNBLS	10/08-12/08
	Mississippi	Y	22820 FQ	33820 MW	43610 TQ	USBLS	5/07
	Jackson MSA, MS	Y	25570 FQ	33860 MW	38240 TQ	USBLS	5/07
	Missouri	Y	24740 FQ	33640 MW	57140 TQ	USBLS	5/07
	Kansas City MSA, MO-KS	Y	31040 FQ	42910 MW	74370 TQ	USBLS	5/07
	St. Louis MSA, MO-IL	Y	25700 FQ	36390 MW	71560 TQ	USBLS	5/07
	Montana	Y	19560 FQ	36970 MW	61920 TQ	USBLS	5/07
	Billings MSA, MT	Y	36560 FQ	42450 MW	49930 TQ	USBLS	5/07
	Nebraska	Y	27900 FQ	40130 MW	48580 TQ	USBLS	5/07
	Omaha-Council Bluffs MSA, NE-IA	Y	33680 FQ	43040 MW	50500 TQ	USBLS	5/07
	Nevada	H	14.27 FQ	21.84 MW	40.50 TQ	NVBLS	5/08
	Las Vegas-Paradise MSA, NV	H	14.05 FQ	22.07 MW	44.53 TQ	NVBLS	5/08
	Reno-Sparks MSA, NV	H	16.62 FQ	18.56 MW	21.51 TQ	NVBLS	5/08
	New Hampshire	H	12.86 AE	15.40 MW	24.94 AEX	NHBLS	6/08
	Manchester MSA, NH	Y	28010 FQ	31610 MW	38600 TQ	USBLS	5/07
	Nashua NECTA, NH-MA	Y	25340 FQ	37890 MW	57210 TQ	USBLS	5/07
	New Jersey	Y	24790 FQ	36690 MW	54720 TQ	USBLS	5/07
	Camden PMSA, NJ	Y	24400 FQ	32380 MW	42760 TQ	USBLS	5/07
	Edison PMSA, NJ	Y	31640 FQ	40450 MW	56590 TQ	USBLS	5/07
	Newark-Union PMSA, NJ-PA	Y	22390 FQ	30700 MW	51090 TQ	USBLS	5/07
	New Mexico	Y	28860 FQ	43620 MW	74200 TQ	USBLS	5/07
	Albuquerque MSA, NM	Y	33810 FQ	58640 MW	102350 TQ	USBLS	5/07
	New York	Y	41670 FQ	60800 MW	95440 TQ	USBLS	5/07
	Albany-Schenectady-Troy MSA, NY	Y	30180 FQ	45660 MW	74890 TQ	USBLS	5/07
	Buffalo-Niagara Falls MSA, NY	Y	27510 FQ	33410 MW	52910 TQ	USBLS	5/07
	Nassau-Suffolk PMSA, NY	Y	46430 FQ	72960 MW	122480 TQ	USBLS	5/07
	New York-Northern New Jersey-Long Island MSA, NY-NJ-PA	Y	42470 FQ	61580 MW	97220 TQ	USBLS	5/07
	North Carolina	Y	32150 FQ	47750 MW	70740 TQ	USBLS	5/07
	Charlotte-Gastonia-Concord MSA, NC-SC	Y	31760 FQ	55510 MW	79180 TQ	USBLS	5/07
	Raleigh-Cary MSA, NC	Y	30990 FQ	49360 MW	75840 TQ	USBLS	5/07
	North Dakota	Y	28500 FQ	41080 MW	61660 TQ	USBLS	5/07
	Fargo MSA, ND-MN	Y	27750 FQ	38630 MW	50770 TQ	USBLS	5/07
	Ohio	Y	30350 FQ	44030 MW	70960 TQ	USBLS	5/07
	Cincinnati-Middletown MSA, OH-KY-IN	Y	28820 FQ	35400 MW	62120 TQ	USBLS	5/07
	Cleveland-Elyria-Mentor MSA, OH	Y	31030 FQ	58290 MW	76020 TQ	USBLS	5/07
	Columbus MSA, OH	Y	30610 FQ	43410 MW	61380 TQ	USBLS	5/07
	Dayton MSA, OH	Y	24090 FQ	35180 MW	95490 TQ	USBLS	5/07
	Oklahoma	Y	24830 FQ	39860 MW	57710 TQ	USBLS	5/07
	Oklahoma City MSA, OK	Y	27810 FQ	39490 MW	59640 TQ	USBLS	5/07
	Tulsa MSA, OK	Y	24810 FQ	44000 MW	56980 TQ	USBLS	5/07
	Portland-Vancouver-Beaverton MSA, OR-WA	Y	33810 FQ	50120 MW	69520 TQ	USBLS	5/07
	Pennsylvania	Y	29630 FQ	41880 MW	56350 TQ	USBLS	5/07
	Allentown-Bethlehem-Easton MSA, PA-NJ	Y	23530 FQ	36530 MW	58640 TQ	USBLS	5/07
	Lancaster MSA, PA	Y	28320 FQ	40990 MW	49610 TQ	USBLS	5/07
	Philadelphia-Camden-Wilmington MSA, PA-NJ-DE-MD	Y	30600 FQ	44160 MW	58900 TQ	USBLS	5/07
	Pittsburgh MSA, PA	Y	23680 FQ	36420 MW	49950 TQ	USBLS	5/07
	Reading MSA, PA	Y	31140 FQ	41730 MW	48810 TQ	USBLS	5/07
	Providence-Fall River-Warwick MSA, RI-MA	Y	33690 FQ	39110 MW	62630 TQ	USBLS	5/07
	South Carolina	Y	25350 FQ	33690 MW	58140 TQ	USBLS	5/07
	Charleston-North Charleston MSA, SC	Y	30990 FQ	35580 MW	63060 TQ	USBLS	5/07

AE	Average entry wage	AW	Average wage paid	FQ	First quartile wage
AER	Average entry range	AWR	Average wage range	H	Hourly
AEX	Average experienced wage	AXR	Average experienced range	HI	Highest wage paid
ATC	Average total compensation	D	Daily	HR	High end range

LO	Lowest wage paid	MTC	Median total compensation	TCC	Total cash compensation
LR	Low end range	MW	Median wage paid	TQ	Third quartile wage
M	Monthly	MWR	Median wage range	W	Weekly
MCC	Median cash compensation	S	See annotated source	Y	Yearly

Occupation/Type/Industry	Location	Per	Low	Mid	High	Source	Date
Real Estate Sales Agent	Columbia MSA, SC	Y	24260 FQ	32900 MW	44250 TQ	USBLS	5/07
	South Dakota	Y	38083 FQ	45694 MW	60016 TQ	SDBLS	7/08-9/08
	Sioux Falls MSA, SD	Y	39759 FQ	52594 MW	70973 TQ	SDBLS	7/08-9/08
	Tennessee	Y	24500 FQ	29350 MW	47100 TQ	USBLS	5/07
	Kingsport-Bristol-Bristol MSA, TN-VA	Y	21610 FQ	26290 MW	29820 TQ	USBLS	5/07
	Memphis MSA, TN-MS-AR	Y	22670 FQ	26870 MW	30860 TQ	USBLS	5/07
	Nashville-Davidson-Murfreesboro MSA, TN	Y	24240 FQ	30650 MW	47390 TQ	USBLS	5/07
	Texas	Y	23250 FQ	32720 MW	65540 TQ	USBLS	5/07
	Austin-Round Rock MSA, TX	Y	22870 FQ	29670 MW	72830 TQ	USBLS	5/07
	Beaumont-Port Arthur MSA, TX	Y	20630 FQ	22860 MW	25710 TQ	USBLS	5/07
	Dallas-Fort Worth-Arlington MSA, TX	Y	24240 FQ	32660 MW	69950 TQ	USBLS	5/07
	El Paso MSA, TX	Y	23350 FQ	34800 MW	80550 TQ	USBLS	5/07
	Houston-Sugar Land-Baytown MSA, TX	Y	23800 FQ	36100 MW	66650 TQ	USBLS	5/07
	San Antonio MSA, TX	Y	21610 FQ	25260 MW	44000 TQ	USBLS	5/07
	Utah	Y	29370 FQ	40890 MW	66220 TQ	USBLS	5/07
	Salt Lake City MSA, UT	Y	36890 FQ	46510 MW	112350 TQ	USBLS	5/07
	Vermont	Y	48810 FQ	63790 MW	95060 TQ	USBLS	5/07
	Burlington-South Burlington MSA, VT	Y	57740 FQ	64790 MW	112100 TQ	USBLS	5/07
	Virginia	Y	27020 FQ	37140 MW	58330 TQ	USBLS	5/07
	Richmond MSA, VA	Y	30220 FQ	39050 MW	59800 TQ	USBLS	5/07
	Virginia Beach-Norfolk-Newport News MSA, VA-NC	Y	26930 FQ	37000 MW	63200 TQ	USBLS	5/07
	Washington	H	14.66 FQ	21.82 MW	30.46 TQ	WABLS	3/08
	Seattle-Tacoma-Bellevue MSA, WA	Y	29500 FQ	44380 MW	64790 TQ	USBLS	5/07
	West Virginia	Y	22276 FQ	36389 MW	58778 TQ	WVBLS	7/08-9/08
	Charleston MSA, WV	Y	19700 FQ	33500 MW	58070 TQ	USBLS	5/07
	Wisconsin	Y	32160 FQ	37760 MW	55620 TQ	USBLS	5/07
	Milwaukee-Waukesha-West Allis MSA, WI	Y	27320 FQ	34150 MW	41240 TQ	USBLS	5/07
	Wyoming	Y	34842 FQ	47129 MW	63425 TQ	WYBLS	9/08
	Cheyenne MSA, WY	Y	58572 FQ	88313 MW	97813 TQ	WYBLS	9/08
	Puerto Rico	Y	22450 FQ	28440 MW	56690 TQ	USBLS	5/07
	San Juan-Caguas-Guaynabo MSA, PR	Y	22320 FQ	26950 MW	55900 TQ	USBLS	5/07
	Virgin Islands	Y	32930 FQ	35810 MW	38810 TQ	USBLS	5/07
Real Property Agent							
Municipal Government	Seattle, WA	H	24.82 LO		29.03 HI	CSSS	2007
Receptionist and Information Clerk	Alabama	Y	17540 FQ	21080 MW	24800 TQ	USBLS	5/07
	Birmingham-Hoover MSA, AL	Y	19690 FQ	22960 MW	26730 TQ	USBLS	5/07
	Montgomery MSA, AL	Y	17140 FQ	20810 MW	23940 TQ	USBLS	5/07
	Alaska	Y	23110 FQ	28510 MW	33930 TQ	USBLS	5/07
	Anchorage MSA, AK	Y	22900 FQ	28210 MW	33240 TQ	USBLS	5/07
	Arizona	Y	19800 FQ	23950 MW	29100 TQ	USBLS	5/07
	Phoenix-Mesa-Scottsdale MSA, AZ	Y	19990 FQ	24400 MW	29730 TQ	USBLS	5/07
	Tucson MSA, AZ	Y	20140 FQ	23180 MW	26990 TQ	USBLS	5/07
	Arkansas	Y	16990 FQ	20230 MW	23520 TQ	USBLS	5/07
	Fayetteville-Springdale-Rogers MSA, AR-MO	Y	18190 FQ	21560 MW	24310 TQ	USBLS	5/07
	Little Rock-North Little Rock MSA, AR	Y	18120 FQ	21390 MW	24250 TQ	USBLS	5/07
	California	H	10.18 FQ	12.53 MW	15.29 TQ	CABLS	1/08-3/08
	Los Angeles-Long Beach-Glendale PMSA, CA	H	10.02 FQ	12.26 MW	14.79 TQ	CABLS	1/08-3/08
	Oakland-Fremont-Hayward MSA, CA	H	11.43 FQ	14.31 MW	17.66 TQ	CABLS	1/08-3/08
	Riverside-San Bernardino-Ontario MSA, CA	H	9.68 FQ	11.44 MW	13.96 TQ	CABLS	1/08-3/08
	Sacramento-Arden Arcade-Roseville MSA, CA	H	10.32 FQ	12.86 MW	15.67 TQ	CABLS	1/08-3/08
	San Diego-Carlsbad-San Marcos MSA, CA	H	10.04 FQ	12.19 MW	14.65 TQ	CABLS	1/08-3/08

Occupation/Type/Industry	Location	Per	Low	Mid	High	Source	Date
Receptionist and Information Clerk							
	San Francisco-San Mateo-Redwood PMSA, CA	H	11.86 FQ	15.06 MW	18.22 TQ	CABLS	1/08-3/08
	San Jose-Sunnyvale-Santa Clara MSA, CA	H	11.81 FQ	14.73 MW	18.06 TQ	CABLS	1/08-3/08
	Santa Ana-Anaheim-Irvine PMSA, CA	Y	21790 FQ	26830 MW	31530 TQ	USBLS	5/07
	Santa Rosa-Petaluma MSA, CA	H	10.90 FQ	13.01 MW	15.36 TQ	CABLS	1/08-3/08
	Stockton MSA, CA	H	10.09 FQ	11.59 MW	13.92 TQ	CABLS	1/08-3/08
	Colorado	Y	21250 FQ	25840 MW	30730 TQ	USBLS	5/07
	Denver-Aurora MSA, CO	Y	21880 FQ	26930 MW	31540 TQ	USBLS	5/07
	Fort Collins-Loveland MSA, CO	Y	19700 FQ	24010 MW	28830 TQ	USBLS	5/07
	Connecticut	H	10.38 AE	13.98 MW		CTBLS	1/08-3/08
	Bridgeport-Stamford-Norwalk MSA, CT	Y	24790 FQ	29430 MW	35600 TQ	USBLS	5/07
	Hartford-West Hartford-East Hartford MSA, CT	Y	22860 FQ	28080 MW	32830 TQ	USBLS	5/07
	Norwich-New London MSA, CT-RI	Y	20900 FQ	25950 MW	29700 TQ	USBLS	5/07
	Waterbury MSA, CT	Y	20630 FQ	26500 MW	30680 TQ	USBLS	5/07
	Delaware	Y	20460 FQ	24300 MW	29960 TQ	USBLS	5/07
	Wilmington PMSA, DE-MD-NJ	Y	20740 FQ	24850 MW	30410 TQ	USBLS	5/07
	District of Columbia	Y	24940 FQ	29140 MW	34590 TQ	USBLS	5/07
	Washington-Arlington-Alexandria MSA, DC-VA-MD-WV	Y	21810 FQ	27570 MW	33180 TQ	USBLS	5/07
	Florida	Y	19260 FQ	22860 MW	27320 TQ	USBLS	5/07
	Cape Coral-Fort Myers MSA, FL	Y	19990 FQ	23580 MW	27790 TQ	USBLS	5/07
	Fort Lauderdale-Pompano Beach-Deerfield Beach PMSA, FL	Y	20510 FQ	24120 MW	28840 TQ	USBLS	5/07
	Jacksonville MSA, FL	Y	18890 FQ	22230 MW	26750 TQ	USBLS	5/07
	Miami-Fort Lauderdale-Miami Beach MSA, FL	Y	19900 FQ	23550 MW	28190 TQ	USBLS	5/07
	Orlando-Kissimmee MSA, FL	Y	19060 FQ	22340 MW	26270 TQ	USBLS	5/07
	Tampa-St. Petersburg-Clearwater MSA, FL	Y	19660 FQ	23200 MW	27880 TQ	USBLS	5/07
	West Palm Beach-Boca Raton-Boynton Beach PMSA, FL	Y	20840 FQ	24520 MW	29120 TQ	USBLS	5/07
	Georgia	Y	19600 FQ	24010 MW	29140 TQ	USBLS	5/07
	Atlanta-Sandy Springs-Marietta MSA, GA	Y	21550 FQ	26200 MW	30770 TQ	USBLS	5/07
	Hawaii	Y	20370 FQ	25720 MW	30920 TQ	USBLS	5/07
	Honolulu MSA, HI	Y	19770 FQ	25360 MW	30530 TQ	USBLS	5/07
	Idaho	Y	18340 FQ	21880 MW	26390 TQ	USBLS	5/07
	Boise City-Nampa MSA, ID	Y	19240 FQ	22460 MW	27530 TQ	USBLS	5/07
	Pocatello MSA, ID	Y	16970 FQ	20560 MW	24660 TQ	USBLS	5/07
	Illinois	Y	19910 FQ	24460 MW	29810 TQ	USBLS	5/07
	Chicago-Naperville-Joliet MSA, IL-IN-WI	Y	20860 FQ	25630 MW	30680 TQ	USBLS	5/07
	Peoria MSA, IL	Y	18450 FQ	21480 MW	24770 TQ	USBLS	5/07
	Rockford MSA, IL	Y	19840 FQ	23390 MW	28740 TQ	USBLS	5/07
	Indiana	Y	18330 FQ	22460 MW	26940 TQ	USBLS	5/07
	Evansville MSA, IN-KY	Y	17270 FQ	21150 MW	24450 TQ	USBLS	5/07
	Gary PMSA, IN	Y	17860 FQ	21920 MW	26440 TQ	USBLS	5/07
	Indianapolis-Carmel MSA, IN	Y	19920 FQ	24340 MW	28950 TQ	USBLS	5/07
	Iowa	Y	18050 FQ	22120 MW	26230 TQ	USBLS	5/07
	Des Moines-West Des Moines MSA, IA	Y	19120 FQ	23480 MW	28380 TQ	USBLS	5/07
	Waterloo-Cedar Falls MSA, IA	Y	20050 FQ	23210 MW	26480 TQ	USBLS	5/07
	Kansas	Y	18180 FQ	21920 MW	26070 TQ	USBLS	5/07
	Wichita MSA, KS	Y	18700 FQ	21830 MW	25300 TQ	USBLS	5/07
	Kentucky	Y	18138 FQ	22100 MW	26473 TQ	KYBLS	2008
	Louisville-Jefferson County MSA, KY-IN	Y	19160 FQ	23170 MW	27680 TQ	USBLS	5/07
	Louisiana	H	7.96 FQ	9.52 MW	11.37 TQ	LABLS	1/08-3/08
	Baton Rouge MSA, LA	Y	17030 FQ	20080 MW	23930 TQ	USBLS	5/07
	Houma-Bayou Cane-Thibodaux MSA, LA	Y	16850 FQ	19720 MW	23760 TQ	USBLS	5/07

AE	Average entry wage	**AW**	Average wage paid	**FQ**	First quartile wage
AER	Average entry range	**AWR**	Average wage range	**H**	Hourly
AEX	Average experienced wage	**AXR**	Average experienced range	**HI**	Highest wage paid
ATC	Average total compensation	**D**	Daily	**HR**	High end range

LO	Lowest wage paid	**MTC**	Median total compensation	**TCC**	Total cash compensation
LR	Low end range	**MW**	Median wage paid	**TQ**	Third quartile wage
M	Monthly	**MWR**	Median wage range	**W**	Weekly
MCC	Median cash compensation	**S**	See annotated source	**Y**	Yearly

Receptionist and Information Clerk

Occupation/Type/Industry	Location	Per	Low	Mid	High	Source	Date
Receptionist and Information Clerk	Lafayette MSA, LA	Y	15070 FQ	18510 MW	22840 TQ	USBLS	5/07
	New Orleans-Metairie-Kenner MSA, LA	Y	17900 FQ	21420 MW	24970 TQ	USBLS	5/07
	Maine	Y	19450 FQ	23230 MW	27640 TQ	USBLS	5/07
	Portland-South Portland-Biddeford MSA, ME	Y	21540 FQ	26010 MW	29570 TQ	USBLS	5/07
	Maryland	Y		25500 MW		MDBLS	3/08
	Baltimore-Towson MSA, MD	Y	20440 FQ	24700 MW	30460 TQ	USBLS	5/07
	Bethesda-Gaithersburg-Frederick PMSA, MD	Y	21420 FQ	27230 MW	33030 TQ	USBLS	5/07
	Cumberland MSA, MD-WV	Y	18810 FQ	22010 MW	25150 TQ	USBLS	5/07
	Massachusetts	Y	20690 FQ	25760 MW	31500 TQ	USBLS	5/07
	Barnstable Town MSA, MA	Y	22040 FQ	27190 MW	31910 TQ	USBLS	5/07
	Boston-Cambridge-Quincy NECTA, MA	Y	20110 FQ	26030 MW	32180 TQ	USBLS	5/07
	Worcester MSA, MA-CT	Y	20900 FQ	25130 MW	29860 TQ	USBLS	5/07
	Michigan	Y	20570 FQ	24660 MW	29680 TQ	USBLS	5/07
	Detroit-Warren-Livonia MSA, MI	Y	21260 FQ	25440 MW	30320 TQ	USBLS	5/07
	Grand Rapids-Wyoming MSA, MI	Y	20510 FQ	24640 MW	30220 TQ	USBLS	5/07
	Warren-Troy-Farmington Hills PMSA, MI	Y	21480 FQ	25550 MW	30670 TQ	USBLS	5/07
	Minnesota	Y	22470 FQ	27529 MW	32337 TQ	MNBLS	10/08-12/08
	Duluth-Superior MSA, MN-WI	Y	17485 FQ	21232 MW	26436 TQ	MNBLS	10/08-12/08
	Minneapolis-Saint Paul MSA, MN-WI	Y	23698 FQ	28705 MW	33107 TQ	MNBLS	10/08-12/08
	Rochester MSA, MN	Y	19804 FQ	24866 MW	31215 TQ	MNBLS	10/08-12/08
	Mississippi	Y	17120 FQ	20020 MW	23450 TQ	USBLS	5/07
	Jackson MSA, MS	Y	17300 FQ	20110 MW	24700 TQ	USBLS	5/07
	Missouri	Y	17820 FQ	21800 MW	26490 TQ	USBLS	5/07
	Kansas City MSA, MO-KS	Y	20830 FQ	24450 MW	29150 TQ	USBLS	5/07
	St. Louis MSA, MO-IL	Y	18440 FQ	22610 MW	27390 TQ	USBLS	5/07
	Montana	Y	18130 FQ	21770 MW	25450 TQ	USBLS	5/07
	Billings MSA, MT	Y	19020 FQ	22740 MW	27230 TQ	USBLS	5/07
	Nebraska	Y	17990 FQ	22070 MW	26550 TQ	USBLS	5/07
	Omaha-Council Bluffs MSA, NE-IA	Y	19690 FQ	23630 MW	28340 TQ	USBLS	5/07
	Nevada	H	10.28 FQ	12.09 MW	14.52 TQ	NVBLS	5/08
	Las Vegas-Paradise MSA, NV	H	10.30 FQ	12.00 MW	14.42 TQ	NVBLS	5/08
	New Hampshire	H	9.49 AE	12.54 MW	14.05 AEX	NHBLS	6/08
	Manchester MSA, NH	Y	23290 FQ	27370 MW	31350 TQ	USBLS	5/07
	Nashua NECTA, NH-MA	Y	20920 FQ	24770 MW	29090 TQ	USBLS	5/07
	New Jersey	Y	20910 FQ	25170 MW	29990 TQ	USBLS	5/07
	Camden PMSA, NJ	Y	21080 FQ	24630 MW	29040 TQ	USBLS	5/07
	Edison PMSA, NJ	Y	21200 FQ	25610 MW	30270 TQ	USBLS	5/07
	Newark-Union PMSA, NJ-PA	Y	20860 FQ	25250 MW	30390 TQ	USBLS	5/07
	Ocean City MSA, NJ	Y	19710 FQ	22270 MW	24650 TQ	USBLS	5/07
	Trenton-Ewing MSA, NJ	Y	20850 FQ	25490 MW	30030 TQ	USBLS	5/07
	New Mexico	Y	17160 FQ	20980 MW	25680 TQ	USBLS	5/07
	Albuquerque MSA, NM	Y	17460 FQ	21870 MW	26890 TQ	USBLS	5/07
	New York	Y	21790 FQ	26450 MW	32030 TQ	USBLS	5/07
	Albany-Schenectady-Troy MSA, NY	Y	21230 FQ	24890 MW	29560 TQ	USBLS	5/07
	Buffalo-Niagara Falls MSA, NY	Y	20360 FQ	23490 MW	28250 TQ	USBLS	5/07
	Kingston MSA, NY	Y	19270 FQ	23320 MW	27340 TQ	USBLS	5/07
	Nassau-Suffolk PMSA, NY	Y	22890 FQ	28190 MW	33900 TQ	USBLS	5/07
	New York-Northern New Jersey-Long Island MSA, NY-NJ-PA	Y	22270 FQ	27290 MW	32720 TQ	USBLS	5/07
	Utica-Rome MSA, NY	Y	18530 FQ	22100 MW	25410 TQ	USBLS	5/07
	North Carolina	Y	19090 FQ	22900 MW	27510 TQ	USBLS	5/07
	Charlotte-Gastonia-Concord MSA, NC-SC	Y	20240 FQ	24630 MW	29350 TQ	USBLS	5/07
	Durham MSA, NC	Y	20210 FQ	24210 MW	29010 TQ	USBLS	5/07
	Raleigh-Cary MSA, NC	Y	20630 FQ	25050 MW	29770 TQ	USBLS	5/07
	North Dakota	Y	18120 FQ	21460 MW	24610 TQ	USBLS	5/07
	Fargo MSA, ND-MN	Y	19200 FQ	22590 MW	26810 TQ	USBLS	5/07
	Ohio	Y	18580 FQ	22630 MW	27180 TQ	USBLS	5/07
	Canton-Massillon MSA, OH	Y	17050 FQ	20580 MW	24420 TQ	USBLS	5/07

AE	Average entry wage	AW	Average wage paid	FQ First quartile wage
AER	Average entry range	AWR	Average wage range	H Hourly
AEX	Average experienced wage	AXR	Average experienced range	HI Highest wage paid
ATC	Average total compensation	D	Daily	HR High end range

LO	Lowest wage paid	MTC	Median total compensation	TCC	Total cash compensation
LR	Low end range	MW	Median wage paid	TQ	Third quartile wage
M	Monthly	MWR	Median wage range	W	Weekly
MCC	Median cash compensation	S	See annotated source	Y	Yearly

Occupation/Type/Industry	Location	Per	Low	Mid	High	Source	Date
Receptionist and Information Clerk							
	Cincinnati-Middletown MSA, OH-KY-IN	Y	18950 FQ	22990 MW	27660 TQ	USBLS	5/07
	Cleveland-Elyria-Mentor MSA, OH	Y	19730 FQ	24260 MW	29280 TQ	USBLS	5/07
	Columbus MSA, OH	Y	19420 FQ	23660 MW	28330 TQ	USBLS	5/07
	Dayton MSA, OH	Y	18890 FQ	22700 MW	26790 TQ	USBLS	5/07
	Mansfield MSA, OH	Y	18900 FQ	22150 MW	25450 TQ	USBLS	5/07
	Oklahoma	Y	17490 FQ	21330 MW	25240 TQ	USBLS	5/07
	Oklahoma City MSA, OK	Y	18800 FQ	22200 MW	25860 TQ	USBLS	5/07
	Tulsa MSA, OK	Y	18960 FQ	22750 MW	27190 TQ	USBLS	5/07
	Oregon	H	10.15 FQ	12.07 MW	14.52 TQ	ORBLS	5/08
	Portland-Vancouver-Beaverton MSA, OR-WA	Y	21480 FQ	25660 MW	30390 TQ	USBLS	5/07
	Pennsylvania	Y	18960 FQ	22880 MW	27840 TQ	USBLS	5/07
	Allentown-Bethlehem-Easton MSA, PA-NJ	Y	19680 FQ	23080 MW	27570 TQ	USBLS	5/07
	Philadelphia-Camden-Wilmington MSA, PA-NJ-DE-MD	Y	20680 FQ	24990 MW	30050 TQ	USBLS	5/07
	Pittsburgh MSA, PA	Y	18500 FQ	22060 MW	25540 TQ	USBLS	5/07
	Rhode Island	Y	20880 FQ	24800 MW	29870 TQ	USBLS	5/07
	Providence-Fall River-Warwick MSA, RI-MA	Y	20700 FQ	24680 MW	29690 TQ	USBLS	5/07
	South Carolina	Y	19550 FQ	22880 MW	27060 TQ	USBLS	5/07
	Charleston-North Charleston MSA, SC	Y	19680 FQ	22770 MW	26430 TQ	USBLS	5/07
	Columbia MSA, SC	Y	20420 FQ	24200 MW	28850 TQ	USBLS	5/07
	South Dakota	Y	18757 FQ	21869 MW	24820 TQ	SDBLS	7/08-9/08
	Sioux Falls MSA, SD	Y	20085 FQ	22958 MW	25788 TQ	SDBLS	7/08-9/08
	Tennessee	Y	19310 FQ	22980 MW	27390 TQ	USBLS	5/07
	Clarksville MSA, TN-KY	Y	16750 FQ	20510 MW	24000 TQ	USBLS	5/07
	Memphis MSA, TN-MS-AR	Y	19350 FQ	22990 MW	26950 TQ	USBLS	5/07
	Nashville-Davidson-Murfreesboro MSA, TN	Y	20850 FQ	25010 MW	29730 TQ	USBLS	5/07
	Texas	Y	17770 FQ	22200 MW	27600 TQ	USBLS	5/07
	Austin-Round Rock MSA, TX	Y	20240 FQ	25580 MW	30640 TQ	USBLS	5/07
	Dallas-Fort Worth-Arlington MSA, TX	Y	20560 FQ	25270 MW	29890 TQ	USBLS	5/07
	El Paso MSA, TX	Y	14480 FQ	17640 MW	21750 TQ	USBLS	5/07
	Houston-Sugar Land-Baytown MSA, TX	Y	18920 FQ	22720 MW	27880 TQ	USBLS	5/07
	San Antonio MSA, TX	Y	16490 FQ	21060 MW	26030 TQ	USBLS	5/07
	Utah	Y	17390 FQ	20930 MW	24710 TQ	USBLS	5/07
	Salt Lake City MSA, UT	Y	17970 FQ	21620 MW	25090 TQ	USBLS	5/07
	Vermont	Y	20960 FQ	24680 MW	29440 TQ	USBLS	5/07
	Burlington-South Burlington MSA, VT	Y	20840 FQ	25090 MW	30280 TQ	USBLS	5/07
	Virginia	Y	19360 FQ	23740 MW	29430 TQ	USBLS	5/07
	Lynchburg MSA, VA	Y	16890 FQ	20350 MW	25230 TQ	USBLS	5/07
	Richmond MSA, VA	Y	19260 FQ	23160 MW	27830 TQ	USBLS	5/07
	Virginia Beach-Norfolk-Newport News MSA, VA-NC	Y	18370 FQ	21890 MW	25460 TQ	USBLS	5/07
	Washington	H	10.15 FQ	12.00 MW	14.34 TQ	WABLS	3/08
	Olympia MSA, WA	Y	20700 FQ	23500 MW	27800 TQ	USBLS	5/07
	Seattle-Tacoma-Bellevue MSA, WA	Y	21620 FQ	26270 MW	30720 TQ	USBLS	5/07
	Spokane MSA, WA	Y	20100 FQ	22750 MW	26560 TQ	USBLS	5/07
	West Virginia	Y	17062 FQ	20116 MW	23964 TQ	WVBLS	7/08-9/08
	Charleston MSA, WV	Y	17560 FQ	20410 MW	23910 TQ	USBLS	5/07
	Huntington-Ashland MSA, WV-KY-OH	Y	16420 FQ	19070 MW	23580 TQ	USBLS	5/07
	Wisconsin	Y	20420 FQ	24450 MW	29130 TQ	USBLS	5/07
	Milwaukee-Waukesha-West Allis MSA, WI	Y	21080 FQ	25340 MW	30240 TQ	USBLS	5/07
	Wyoming	Y	18535 FQ	21997 MW	25197 TQ	WYBLS	9/08
	Cheyenne MSA, WY	Y	18660 FQ	22466 MW	26667 TQ	WYBLS	9/08
	Puerto Rico	Y	13100 FQ	15060 MW	18040 TQ	USBLS	5/07
	San Juan-Caguas-Guaynabo MSA, PR	Y	13210 FQ	15310 MW	18340 TQ	USBLS	5/07
	Virgin Islands	Y	18730 FQ	22010 MW	25310 TQ	USBLS	5/07
	Guam	Y	13250 FQ	15440 MW	20210 TQ	USBLS	5/07

AE Average entry wage	**AW** Average wage paid	**FQ** First quartile wage	**LO** Lowest wage paid	**MTC** Median total compensation	**TCC** Total cash compensation
AER Average entry range	**AWR** Average wage range	**H** Hourly	**LR** Low end range	**MW** Median wage paid	**TQ** Third quartile wage
AEX Average experienced wage	**AXR** Average experienced range	**HI** Highest wage paid	**M** Monthly	**MWR** Median wage range	**W** Weekly
ATC Average total compensation	**D** Daily	**HR** High end range	**MCC** Median cash compensation	**S** See annotated source	**Y** Yearly

Occupation/Type/Industry	Location	Per	Low	Mid	High	Source	Date
Reclamation Inspector							
State Government	Ohio	H	19.88 LO		26.28 HI	ODAS	2008
Recording Machine Operator							
Independent Motion Picture	East Coast	W			1468 HI	MPEG05	8/1/08-7/31/09
Recordist							
Journeyman, Independent Motion Picture	West Coast	H			34.94-38.84 HR	MPEG02	8/3/08-7/31/09
Records Analyst							
White House Staff	United States	Y			35392 HI	WPOST02	2008
Records Clerk	Americus, GA	Y	21230 LO		29721 HI	GACTY01	2008
	Atlanta, GA	Y	27475 LO		40113 HI	GACTY01	2008
State Court of Appeals	Michigan	Y		41767 AW		LSJ02	7/11/07
Recreation and Fitness Studies Teacher							
Postsecondary	Alabama	Y	43590 FQ	57980 MW	71980 TQ	USBLS	5/07
Postsecondary	Birmingham-Hoover MSA, AL	Y	37100 FQ	61080 MW	74500 TQ	USBLS	5/07
Postsecondary	Tucson MSA, AZ	Y	49600 FQ	53280 MW	57730 TQ	USBLS	5/07
Postsecondary	Arkansas	Y	29590 FQ	44960 MW	59350 TQ	USBLS	5/07
Postsecondary	California	Y		90139 AW		CABLS	1/08-3/08
Postsecondary	Los Angeles-Long Beach-Glendale PMSA, CA	Y		90672 AW		CABLS	1/08-3/08
Postsecondary	Oakland-Fremont-Hayward MSA, CA	Y		78818 AW		CABLS	1/08-3/08
Postsecondary	Riverside-San Bernardino-Ontario MSA, CA	Y		84099 AW		CABLS	1/08-3/08
Postsecondary	Sacramento-Arden Arcade-Roseville MSA, CA	Y		95338 AW		CABLS	1/08-3/08
Postsecondary	San Diego-Carlsbad-San Marcos MSA, CA	Y		93246 AW		CABLS	1/08-3/08
Postsecondary	San Francisco-San Mateo-Redwood PMSA, CA	Y		112535 AW		CABLS	1/08-3/08
Postsecondary	Santa Ana-Anaheim-Irvine PMSA, CA	Y	47770 FQ	70530 MW	91710 TQ	USBLS	5/07
Postsecondary	Colorado	Y	37790 FQ	46780 MW	62200 TQ	USBLS	5/07
Postsecondary	Denver-Aurora MSA, CO	Y	38060 FQ	43340 MW	57870 TQ	USBLS	5/07
Postsecondary	Norwich-New London MSA, CT-RI	Y	47970 FQ	57180 MW	68980 TQ	USBLS	5/07
Postsecondary	Delaware	Y	45950 FQ	63170 MW	78150 TQ	USBLS	5/07
Postsecondary	District of Columbia	Y	51910 FQ	63940 MW	74360 TQ	USBLS	5/07
Postsecondary	Washington-Arlington-Alexandria MSA, DC-VA-MD-WV	Y	43940 FQ	57720 MW	71690 TQ	USBLS	5/07
Postsecondary	Florida	Y	42120 FQ	57230 MW	73340 TQ	USBLS	5/07
Postsecondary	Miami-Fort Lauderdale-Miami Beach MSA, FL	Y	44760 FQ	63920 MW	76710 TQ	USBLS	5/07
Postsecondary	Orlando-Kissimmee MSA, FL	Y	33880 FQ	49050 MW	72260 TQ	USBLS	5/07
Postsecondary	Georgia	Y	32280 FQ	41710 MW	55950 TQ	USBLS	5/07
Postsecondary	Atlanta-Sandy Springs-Marietta MSA, GA	Y	33660 FQ	46290 MW	61130 TQ	USBLS	5/07
Postsecondary	Illinois	Y	32350 FQ	51010 MW	67630 TQ	USBLS	5/07
Postsecondary	Chicago-Naperville-Joliet MSA, IL-IN-WI	Y	33510 FQ	52750 MW	74130 TQ	USBLS	5/07
Postsecondary	Indiana	Y	26060 FQ	41560 MW	60490 TQ	USBLS	5/07
Postsecondary	Indianapolis-Carmel MSA, IN	Y	16680 FQ	20690 MW	49010 TQ	USBLS	5/07
Postsecondary	Iowa	Y	36110 FQ	48790 MW	65020 TQ	USBLS	5/07
Postsecondary	Kansas	Y	26760 FQ	37110 MW	56450 TQ	USBLS	5/07
Postsecondary	Kentucky	Y	37737 FQ	50086 MW	65553 TQ	KYBLS	2008
Postsecondary	Louisiana	Y		48302 AW		LABLS	1/08-3/08
Postsecondary	Baton Rouge MSA, LA	Y	52380 FQ	66420 MW	74140 TQ	USBLS	5/07
Postsecondary	New Orleans-Metairie-Kenner MSA, LA	Y	33330 FQ	39270 MW	53460 TQ	USBLS	5/07
Postsecondary	Maine	Y	42180 FQ	53100 MW	62190 TQ	USBLS	5/07
Postsecondary	Maryland	Y		64750 MW		MDBLS	3/08
Postsecondary	Baltimore-Towson MSA, MD	Y	52370 FQ	63650 MW	79060 TQ	USBLS	5/07
Postsecondary	Massachusetts	Y	38590 FQ	56410 MW	74060 TQ	USBLS	5/07
Postsecondary	Boston-Cambridge-Quincy NECTA, MA	Y	41740 FQ	54910 MW	68740 TQ	USBLS	5/07

AE	Average entry wage	AW	Average wage paid	FQ	First quartile wage	LO	Lowest wage paid	MTC	Median total compensation	TCC	Total cash compensation
AER	Average entry range	AWR	Average wage range	H	Hourly	LR	Low end range	MW	Median wage paid	TQ	Third quartile wage
AEX	Average experienced wage	AXR	Average experienced range	HI	Highest wage paid	M	Monthly	MWR	Median wage range	W	Weekly
ATC	Average total compensation	D	Daily	HR	High end range	MCC	Median cash compensation	S	See annotated source	Y	Yearly

Recreation and Fitness Studies Teacher

Occupation/Type/Industry	Location	Per	Low	Mid	High	Source	Date
Recreation and Fitness Studies Teacher							
Postsecondary	Michigan	Y	44480 FQ	64430 MW	81310 TQ	USBLS	5/07
Postsecondary	Detroit-Warren-Livonia MSA, MI	Y	44660 FQ	68430 MW	92510 TQ	USBLS	5/07
Postsecondary	Lansing-East Lansing MSA, MI	Y	67600 FQ	80890 MW	99510 TQ	USBLS	5/07
Postsecondary	Warren-Troy-Farmington Hills PMSA, MI	Y	29810 FQ	77990 MW	96720 TQ	USBLS	5/07
Postsecondary	Minnesota	Y	42047 FQ	53786 MW	68454 TQ	MNBLS	10/08-12/08
Postsecondary	Duluth-Superior MSA, MN-WI	Y	45029 FQ	52112 MW	65880 TQ	MNBLS	10/08-12/08
Postsecondary	Minneapolis-Saint Paul MSA, MN-WI	Y	43564 FQ	56360 MW	74323 TQ	MNBLS	10/08-12/08
Postsecondary	Mississippi	Y	38070 FQ	50540 MW	62920 TQ	USBLS	5/07
Postsecondary	Missouri	Y	35380 FQ	46510 MW	58840 TQ	USBLS	5/07
Postsecondary	Kansas City MSA, MO-KS	Y	34980 FQ	49150 MW	63840 TQ	USBLS	5/07
Postsecondary	St. Louis MSA, MO-IL	Y	32240 FQ	49500 MW	64950 TQ	USBLS	5/07
Postsecondary	Montana	Y	15370 FQ	18870 MW	42810 TQ	USBLS	5/07
Postsecondary	Nebraska	Y	35930 FQ	43870 MW	54610 TQ	USBLS	5/07
Postsecondary	Omaha-Council Bluffs MSA, NE-IA	Y	30240 FQ	41590 MW	53980 TQ	USBLS	5/07
Postsecondary	Nevada	Y	31784 FQ	45303 MW	51361 TQ	NVBLS	5/08
Postsecondary	New Hampshire	Y	51037 AE	66514 MW	80253 AEX	NHBLS	6/08
Postsecondary	New Jersey	Y	35910 FQ	51390 MW	69220 TQ	USBLS	5/07
Postsecondary	Edison PMSA, NJ	Y	27360 FQ	43720 MW	64410 TQ	USBLS	5/07
Postsecondary	New Mexico	Y	42870 FQ	48070 MW	59380 TQ	USBLS	5/07
Postsecondary	New York	Y	36760 FQ	50400 MW	71150 TQ	USBLS	5/07
Postsecondary	New York-Northern New Jersey-Long Island MSA, NY-NJ-PA	Y	42460 FQ	58170 MW	80450 TQ	USBLS	5/07
Postsecondary	North Carolina	Y	38330 FQ	48520 MW	59930 TQ	USBLS	5/07
Postsecondary	Charlotte-Gastonia-Concord MSA, NC-SC	Y	35990 FQ	41590 MW	50490 TQ	USBLS	5/07
Postsecondary	Raleigh-Cary MSA, NC	Y	36280 FQ	42830 MW	51740 TQ	USBLS	5/07
Postsecondary	North Dakota	Y	39580 FQ	48750 MW	61190 TQ	USBLS	5/07
Postsecondary	Fargo MSA, ND-MN	Y	38080 FQ	47860 MW	60760 TQ	USBLS	5/07
Postsecondary	Ohio	Y	36000 FQ	51190 MW	69620 TQ	USBLS	5/07
Postsecondary	Cincinnati-Middletown MSA, OH-KY-IN	Y	28380 FQ	47960 MW	60690 TQ	USBLS	5/07
Postsecondary	Cleveland-Elyria-Mentor MSA, OH	Y	35250 FQ	50250 MW	66810 TQ	USBLS	5/07
Postsecondary	Columbus MSA, OH	Y	40700 FQ	60610 MW	87940 TQ	USBLS	5/07
Postsecondary	Dayton MSA, OH	Y	28330 FQ	36950 MW	58260 TQ	USBLS	5/07
Postsecondary	Oklahoma	Y	27970 FQ	36450 MW	51790 TQ	USBLS	5/07
Postsecondary	Oklahoma City MSA, OK	Y	28120 FQ	35130 MW	54760 TQ	USBLS	5/07
Postsecondary	Portland-Vancouver-Beaverton MSA, OR-WA	Y	35050 FQ	51110 MW	77610 TQ	USBLS	5/07
Postsecondary	Pennsylvania	Y	39760 FQ	50980 MW	67010 TQ	USBLS	5/07
Postsecondary	Allentown-Bethlehem-Easton MSA, PA-NJ	Y	37960 FQ	55460 MW	73450 TQ	USBLS	5/07
Postsecondary	Philadelphia-Camden-Wilmington MSA, PA-NJ-DE-MD	Y	33740 FQ	45080 MW	66730 TQ	USBLS	5/07
Postsecondary	Pittsburgh MSA, PA	Y	47240 FQ	52760 MW	64950 TQ	USBLS	5/07
Postsecondary	South Carolina	Y	36970 FQ	50660 MW	70350 TQ	USBLS	5/07
Postsecondary	South Dakota	Y	40320 FQ	47731 MW	59537 TQ	SDBLS	7/08-9/08
Postsecondary	Sioux Falls MSA, SD	Y	36539 FQ	43030 MW	49821 TQ	SDBLS	7/08-9/08
Postsecondary	Tennessee	Y	31430 FQ	42990 MW	52180 TQ	USBLS	5/07
Postsecondary	Nashville-Davidson-Murfreesboro MSA, TN	Y	19570 FQ	35310 MW	50750 TQ	USBLS	5/07
Postsecondary	Texas	Y	33320 FQ	47770 MW	63370 TQ	USBLS	5/07
Postsecondary	Austin-Round Rock MSA, TX	Y	15530 FQ	53960 MW	85270 TQ	USBLS	5/07
Postsecondary	Dallas-Fort Worth-Arlington MSA, TX	Y	35470 FQ	48230 MW	60160 TQ	USBLS	5/07
Postsecondary	El Paso MSA, TX	Y	28170 FQ	39410 MW	58530 TQ	USBLS	5/07
Postsecondary	Houston-Sugar Land-Baytown MSA, TX	Y	40770 FQ	56000 MW	71730 TQ	USBLS	5/07
Postsecondary	San Antonio MSA, TX	Y	19640 FQ	36990 MW	55810 TQ	USBLS	5/07
Postsecondary	Utah	Y	44900 FQ	52520 MW	60040 TQ	USBLS	5/07
Postsecondary	Vermont	Y	31040 FQ	42720 MW	50700 TQ	USBLS	5/07
Postsecondary	Virginia	Y	34150 FQ	47450 MW	62240 TQ	USBLS	5/07
Postsecondary	Richmond MSA, VA	Y	28430 FQ	30900 MW	43550 TQ	USBLS	5/07

AE	Average entry wage	AW	Average wage paid	FQ	First quartile wage
AER	Average entry range	AWR	Average wage range	H	Hourly
AEX	Average experienced wage	AXR	Average experienced range	HI	Highest wage paid
ATC	Average total compensation	D	Daily	HR	High end range

LO	Lowest wage paid	MTC	Median total compensation	TCC	Total cash compensation
LR	Low end range	MW	Median wage paid	TQ	Third quartile wage
M	Monthly	MWR	Median wage range	W	Weekly
MCC	Median cash compensation	S	See annotated source	Y	Yearly

Occupation/Type/Industry	Location	Per	Low	Mid	High	Source	Date
Recreation and Fitness Studies Teacher							
Postsecondary	Virginia Beach-Norfolk-Newport News MSA, VA-NC	Y	39450 FQ	52970 MW	67290 TQ	USBLS	5/07
Postsecondary	Washington	Y		44580 AW		WABLS	3/08
Postsecondary	Seattle-Tacoma-Bellevue MSA, WA	Y	36920 FQ	43290 MW	50730 TQ	USBLS	5/07
Postsecondary	West Virginia	Y	35724 FQ	41829 MW	51423 TQ	WVBLS	7/08-9/08
Postsecondary	Milwaukee-Waukesha-West Allis MSA, WI	Y	40290 FQ	56520 MW	68820 TQ	USBLS	5/07
Postsecondary	Wyoming	Y	46491 FQ	58370 MW	74027 TQ	WYBLS	9/08
Postsecondary	Puerto Rico	Y	35490 FQ	49310 MW	63000 TQ	USBLS	5/07
Postsecondary	San Juan-Caguas-Guaynabo MSA, PR	Y	36540 FQ	53760 MW	64260 TQ	USBLS	5/07
Recreation Director	Hillsboro, ND	M			825 HI	NDLC01	2008
	Minot, ND	M			5132 HI	NDLC01	2008
	Valley City, ND	M			2306 HI	NDLC01	2008
Recreation Program Coordinator	Seattle, WA	H	24.65 LO		28.79 HI	CSSS	2007
Recreation Program Specialist	Walnut Creek, CA	Y	55240 LO		66542 HI	WCSWP	6/27/08
Recreation Specialist	Carlsbad, CA	S	1475 LO		1793 HI	CCSS01	8/5/08
Recreation Worker	Alabama	Y	14240 FQ	19630 MW	24730 TQ	USBLS	5/07
	Birmingham-Hoover MSA, AL	Y	15080 FQ	18980 MW	23240 TQ	USBLS	5/07
	Tuscaloosa MSA, AL	Y	18480 FQ	22850 MW	26680 TQ	USBLS	5/07
	Alaska	Y	20780 FQ	28220 MW	38570 TQ	USBLS	5/07
	Anchorage MSA, AK	Y	21600 FQ	27500 MW	36390 TQ	USBLS	5/07
	Arizona	Y	16180 FQ	21320 MW	29630 TQ	USBLS	5/07
	Phoenix-Mesa-Scottsdale MSA, AZ	Y	15820 FQ	20170 MW	28650 TQ	USBLS	5/07
	Tucson MSA, AZ	Y	19030 FQ	26250 MW	32130 TQ	USBLS	5/07
	Arkansas	Y	15190 FQ	18230 MW	23060 TQ	USBLS	5/07
	Fayetteville-Springdale-Rogers MSA, AR-MO	Y	14660 FQ	16700 MW	20690 TQ	USBLS	5/07
	Little Rock-North Little Rock MSA, AR	Y	15830 FQ	21290 MW	25950 TQ	USBLS	5/07
	California	H	8.99 FQ	10.84 MW	13.88 TQ	CABLS	1/08-3/08
	Los Angeles-Long Beach-Glendale PMSA, CA	H	9.02 FQ	10.83 MW	12.89 TQ	CABLS	1/08-3/08
	Oakland-Fremont-Hayward MSA, CA	H	9.89 FQ	12.52 MW	15.78 TQ	CABLS	1/08-3/08
	Oxnard-Thousand Oaks-Ventura MSA, CA	H	9.04 FQ	11.35 MW	14.67 TQ	CABLS	1/08-3/08
	Riverside-San Bernardino-Ontario MSA, CA	H	8.61 FQ	9.74 MW	12.10 TQ	CABLS	1/08-3/08
	Sacramento-Arden Arcade-Roseville MSA, CA	H	8.72 FQ	9.93 MW	12.03 TQ	CABLS	1/08-3/08
	San Diego-Carlsbad-San Marcos MSA, CA	H	9.12 FQ	10.84 MW	13.82 TQ	CABLS	1/08-3/08
	San Francisco-San Mateo-Redwood PMSA, CA	H	10.01 FQ	13.36 MW	17.71 TQ	CABLS	1/08-3/08
	San Jose-Sunnyvale-Santa Clara MSA, CA	H	11.91 FQ	14.48 MW	18.01 TQ	CABLS	1/08-3/08
	Santa Ana-Anaheim-Irvine PMSA, CA	Y	18020 FQ	20410 MW	23760 TQ	USBLS	5/07
	Colorado	Y	18050 FQ	22270 MW	30100 TQ	USBLS	5/07
	Denver-Aurora MSA, CO	Y	17750 FQ	22270 MW	29930 TQ	USBLS	5/07
	Fort Collins-Loveland MSA, CO	Y	17050 FQ	19460 MW	24370 TQ	USBLS	5/07
	Connecticut	H	8.87 AE	11.97 MW		CTBLS	1/08-3/08
	Bridgeport-Stamford-Norwalk MSA, CT	Y	19080 FQ	24740 MW	36590 TQ	USBLS	5/07
	Hartford-West Hartford-East Hartford MSA, CT	Y	19310 FQ	24120 MW	35780 TQ	USBLS	5/07
	Norwich-New London MSA, CT-RI	Y	21830 FQ	28390 MW	38380 TQ	USBLS	5/07
	Delaware	Y	19370 FQ	24840 MW	31950 TQ	USBLS	5/07
	Wilmington PMSA, DE-MD-NJ	Y	20540 FQ	26200 MW	32390 TQ	USBLS	5/07

AE	Average entry wage	AW	Average wage paid	FQ	First quartile wage
AER	Average entry range	AWR	Average wage range	H	Hourly
AEX	Average experienced wage	AXR	Average experienced range	HI	Highest wage paid
ATC	Average total compensation	D	Daily	HR	High end range

LO	Lowest wage paid
LR	Low end range
M	Monthly
MCC	Median cash compensation

MTC	Median total compensation
MW	Median wage paid
MWR	Median wage range
S	See annotated source

TCC	Total cash compensation
TQ	Third quartile wage
W	Weekly
Y	Yearly

Recreation Worker

Occupation/Type/Industry	Location	Per	Low	Mid	High	Source	Date
Recreation Worker	District of Columbia	Y	27210 FQ	34240 MW	43810 TQ	USBLS	5/07
	Washington-Arlington-Alexandria MSA, DC-VA-MD-WV	Y	18530 FQ	23050 MW	30640 TQ	USBLS	5/07
	Florida	Y	17200 FQ	21300 MW	26150 TQ	USBLS	5/07
	Fort Lauderdale-Pompano Beach-Deerfield Beach PMSA, FL	Y	16930 FQ	20200 MW	25510 TQ	USBLS	5/07
	Jacksonville MSA, FL	Y	15650 FQ	19300 MW	23310 TQ	USBLS	5/07
	Miami-Fort Lauderdale-Miami Beach MSA, FL	Y	18270 FQ	22170 MW	27570 TQ	USBLS	5/07
	Orlando-Kissimmee MSA, FL	Y	16420 FQ	20510 MW	27100 TQ	USBLS	5/07
	Tampa-St. Petersburg-Clearwater MSA, FL	Y	17490 FQ	22250 MW	26770 TQ	USBLS	5/07
	West Palm Beach-Boca Raton-Boynton Beach PMSA, FL	Y	18840 FQ	22550 MW	27950 TQ	USBLS	5/07
	Georgia	Y	15970 FQ	22080 MW	29740 TQ	USBLS	5/07
	Atlanta-Sandy Springs-Marietta MSA, GA	Y	15050 FQ	22660 MW	30050 TQ	USBLS	5/07
	Augusta-Richmond County MSA, GA-SC	Y	17530 FQ	19770 MW	26200 TQ	USBLS	5/07
	Macon MSA, GA	Y	17750 FQ	24030 MW	28830 TQ	USBLS	5/07
	Hawaii	Y	19120 FQ	26750 MW	35950 TQ	USBLS	5/07
	Honolulu MSA, HI	Y	18050 FQ	23540 MW	35430 TQ	USBLS	5/07
	Idaho	Y	16210 FQ	20010 MW	25290 TQ	USBLS	5/07
	Boise City-Nampa MSA, ID	Y	15630 FQ	18730 MW	24270 TQ	USBLS	5/07
	Illinois	Y	15990 FQ	19280 MW	25120 TQ	USBLS	5/07
	Chicago-Naperville-Joliet MSA, IL-IN-WI	Y	16310 FQ	19920 MW	26550 TQ	USBLS	5/07
	Indiana	Y	16110 FQ	19430 MW	27230 TQ	USBLS	5/07
	Gary PMSA, IN	Y	15040 FQ	17980 MW	22360 TQ	USBLS	5/07
	Indianapolis-Carmel MSA, IN	Y	17010 FQ	25550 MW	30530 TQ	USBLS	5/07
	Iowa	Y	15640 FQ	18600 MW	25300 TQ	USBLS	5/07
	Des Moines-West Des Moines MSA, IA	Y	14650 FQ	17910 MW	25980 TQ	USBLS	5/07
	Sioux City MSA, IA-NE-SD	Y	17990 FQ	21480 MW	26300 TQ	USBLS	5/07
	Kansas	Y	16940 FQ	22280 MW	28050 TQ	USBLS	5/07
	Wichita MSA, KS	Y	18660 FQ	23680 MW	27930 TQ	USBLS	5/07
	Kentucky	Y	17167 FQ	23659 MW	31504 TQ	KYBLS	2008
	Louisville-Jefferson County MSA, KY-IN	Y	18340 FQ	24460 MW	32290 TQ	USBLS	5/07
	Owensboro MSA, KY	Y	15850 FQ	19700 MW	25080 TQ	USBLS	5/07
	Louisiana	H	6.86 FQ	8.56 MW	11.23 TQ	LABLS	1/08-3/08
	Baton Rouge MSA, LA	Y	14950 FQ	18010 MW	22500 TQ	USBLS	5/07
	New Orleans-Metairie-Kenner MSA, LA	Y	13830 FQ	17220 MW	24630 TQ	USBLS	5/07
	Shreveport-Bossier City MSA, LA	Y	17050 FQ	21860 MW	26670 TQ	USBLS	5/07
	Maine	Y	18220 FQ	23380 MW	28980 TQ	USBLS	5/07
	Portland-South Portland-Biddeford MSA, ME	Y	19100 FQ	24670 MW	30550 TQ	USBLS	5/07
	Maryland	Y		22775 MW		MDBLS	3/08
	Baltimore-Towson MSA, MD	Y	18850 FQ	27110 MW	34120 TQ	USBLS	5/07
	Bethesda-Gaithersburg-Frederick PMSA, MD	Y	19230 FQ	24400 MW	33510 TQ	USBLS	5/07
	Massachusetts	Y	18870 FQ	23390 MW	29680 TQ	USBLS	5/07
	Boston-Cambridge-Quincy NECTA, MA	Y	19790 FQ	24760 MW	31410 TQ	USBLS	5/07
	Worcester MSA, MA-CT	Y	17210 FQ	20160 MW	25330 TQ	USBLS	5/07
	Michigan	Y	16810 FQ	20730 MW	27040 TQ	USBLS	5/07
	Detroit-Warren-Livonia MSA, MI	Y	17020 FQ	20820 MW	26410 TQ	USBLS	5/07
	Grand Rapids-Wyoming MSA, MI	Y	17740 FQ	22260 MW	29410 TQ	USBLS	5/07
	Warren-Troy-Farmington Hills PMSA, MI	Y	17830 FQ	21800 MW	26750 TQ	USBLS	5/07
	Minnesota	Y	19468 FQ	24027 MW	30917 TQ	MNBLS	10/08-12/08
	Duluth-Superior MSA, MN-WI	Y	17743 FQ	21654 MW	29339 TQ	MNBLS	10/08-12/08
	Minneapolis-Saint Paul MSA, MN-WI	Y	20043 FQ	25407 MW	32611 TQ	MNBLS	10/08-12/08
	Rochester MSA, MN	Y	21065 FQ	27736 MW	33053 TQ	MNBLS	10/08-12/08
	Mississippi	Y	15570 FQ	19100 MW	24630 TQ	USBLS	5/07

AE	Average entry wage	AW	Average wage paid	FQ	First quartile wage
AER	Average entry range	AWR	Average wage range	H	Hourly
AEX	Average experienced wage	AXR	Average experienced range	HI	Highest wage paid
ATC	Average total compensation	D	Daily	HR	High end range

LO	Lowest wage paid	MTC	Median total compensation	TCC	Total cash compensation
LR	Low end range	MW	Median wage paid	TQ	Third quartile wage
M	Monthly	MWR	Median wage range	W	Weekly
MCC	Median cash compensation	S	See annotated source	Y	Yearly

Recreation Worker

Occupation/Type/Industry	Location	Per	Low	Mid	High	Source	Date
Recreation Worker	Jackson MSA, MS	Y	16000 FQ	21110 MW	27720 TQ	USBLS	5/07
	Missouri	Y	16270 FQ	19650 MW	24660 TQ	USBLS	5/07
	Kansas City MSA, MO-KS	Y	19460 FQ	24140 MW	30750 TQ	USBLS	5/07
	St. Louis MSA, MO-IL	Y	16580 FQ	19540 MW	24400 TQ	USBLS	5/07
	Montana	Y	16210 FQ	18950 MW	26020 TQ	USBLS	5/07
	Billings MSA, MT	Y	18850 FQ	23120 MW	29650 TQ	USBLS	5/07
	Nebraska	Y	14850 FQ	18800 MW	24490 TQ	USBLS	5/07
	Omaha-Council Bluffs MSA, NE-IA	Y	16450 FQ	20160 MW	25890 TQ	USBLS	5/07
	Las Vegas-Paradise MSA, NV	H	9.86 FQ	12.53 MW	15.95 TQ	NVBLS	5/08
	New Hampshire	H	7.95 AE	11.19 MW	13.76 AEX	NHBLS	6/08
	Manchester MSA, NH	Y	15340 FQ	23420 MW	29830 TQ	USBLS	5/07
	Nashua NECTA, NH-MA	Y	20250 FQ	23620 MW	28720 TQ	USBLS	5/07
	New Jersey	Y	17770 FQ	21860 MW	27620 TQ	USBLS	5/07
	Camden PMSA, NJ	Y	17400 FQ	22360 MW	28120 TQ	USBLS	5/07
	Edison PMSA, NJ	Y	17440 FQ	21040 MW	26920 TQ	USBLS	5/07
	Newark-Union PMSA, NJ-PA	Y	18290 FQ	21930 MW	27700 TQ	USBLS	5/07
	Trenton-Ewing MSA, NJ	Y	18450 FQ	23450 MW	28340 TQ	USBLS	5/07
	New Mexico	Y	14250 FQ	17930 MW	25620 TQ	USBLS	5/07
	Albuquerque MSA, NM	Y	14490 FQ	18540 MW	27340 TQ	USBLS	5/07
	New York	Y	17680 FQ	22460 MW	29800 TQ	USBLS	5/07
	Albany-Schenectady-Troy MSA, NY	Y	17720 FQ	21830 MW	25710 TQ	USBLS	5/07
	Buffalo-Niagara Falls MSA, NY	Y	15750 FQ	18670 MW	22540 TQ	USBLS	5/07
	Kingston MSA, NY	Y	17420 FQ	20020 MW	26120 TQ	USBLS	5/07
	Nassau-Suffolk PMSA, NY	Y	18550 FQ	23020 MW	30360 TQ	USBLS	5/07
	New York-Northern New Jersey-Long Island MSA, NY-NJ-PA	Y	18380 FQ	23080 MW	30230 TQ	USBLS	5/07
	North Carolina	Y	16600 FQ	20910 MW	29120 TQ	USBLS	5/07
	Charlotte-Gastonia-Concord MSA, NC-SC	Y	15450 FQ	19190 MW	26480 TQ	USBLS	5/07
	Raleigh-Cary MSA, NC	Y	16030 FQ	19370 MW	25400 TQ	USBLS	5/07
	North Dakota	Y	15030 FQ	18900 MW	25670 TQ	USBLS	5/07
	Fargo MSA, ND-MN	Y	14000 FQ	16870 MW	19630 TQ	USBLS	5/07
	Ohio	Y	16170 FQ	19860 MW	25460 TQ	USBLS	5/07
	Cincinnati-Middletown MSA, OH-KY-IN	Y	15270 FQ	18630 MW	24230 TQ	USBLS	5/07
	Cleveland-Elyria-Mentor MSA, OH	Y	15860 FQ	19660 MW	25760 TQ	USBLS	5/07
	Columbus MSA, OH	Y	17890 FQ	20240 MW	25270 TQ	USBLS	5/07
	Dayton MSA, OH	Y	15830 FQ	21290 MW	29780 TQ	USBLS	5/07
	Oklahoma	Y	13790 FQ	16250 MW	21640 TQ	USBLS	5/07
	Oklahoma City MSA, OK	Y	14380 FQ	18720 MW	27430 TQ	USBLS	5/07
	Tulsa MSA, OK	Y	17390 FQ	22300 MW	29200 TQ	USBLS	5/07
	Oregon	H	9.95 FQ	12.97 MW	17.51 TQ	ORBLS	5/08
	Portland-Vancouver-Beaverton MSA, OR-WA	Y	21230 FQ	28930 MW	37920 TQ	USBLS	5/07
	Pennsylvania	Y	17240 FQ	21900 MW	28770 TQ	USBLS	5/07
	Allentown-Bethlehem-Easton MSA, PA-NJ	Y	18400 FQ	22300 MW	26470 TQ	USBLS	5/07
	Philadelphia-Camden-Wilmington MSA, PA-NJ-DE-MD	Y	18830 FQ	23440 MW	30860 TQ	USBLS	5/07
	Pittsburgh MSA, PA	Y	17160 FQ	21870 MW	28650 TQ	USBLS	5/07
	Rhode Island	Y	16980 FQ	19470 MW	24360 TQ	USBLS	5/07
	Providence-Fall River-Warwick MSA, RI-MA	Y	17270 FQ	20330 MW	25760 TQ	USBLS	5/07
	South Carolina	Y	16560 FQ	19590 MW	26220 TQ	USBLS	5/07
	Charleston-North Charleston MSA, SC	Y	16830 FQ	19270 MW	26710 TQ	USBLS	5/07
	Columbia MSA, SC	Y	17370 FQ	19670 MW	25320 TQ	USBLS	5/07
	South Dakota	Y	19433 FQ	22932 MW	26732 TQ	SDBLS	7/08-9/08
	Sioux Falls MSA, SD	Y	18995 FQ	22280 MW	25685 TQ	SDBLS	7/08-9/08
	Tennessee	Y	16150 FQ	21040 MW	26990 TQ	USBLS	5/07
	Johnson City MSA, TN	Y	20010 FQ	22550 MW	25470 TQ	USBLS	5/07
	Memphis MSA, TN-MS-AR	Y	17800 FQ	22140 MW	27820 TQ	USBLS	5/07
	Nashville-Davidson-Murfreesboro MSA, TN	Y	17500 FQ	22210 MW	29890 TQ	USBLS	5/07
	Texas	Y	14540 FQ	18130 MW	23610 TQ	USBLS	5/07
	Austin-Round Rock MSA, TX	Y	14100 FQ	18610 MW	24920 TQ	USBLS	5/07

AE	Average entry wage	AW	Average wage paid	FQ	First quartile wage	LO	Lowest wage paid	MTC	Median total compensation	TCC	Total cash compensation
AER	Average entry range	AWR	Average wage range	H	Hourly	LR	Low end range	MW	Median wage paid	TQ	Third quartile wage
AEX	Average experienced wage	AXR	Average experienced range	HI	Highest wage paid	M	Monthly	MWR	Median wage range	W	Weekly
ATC	Average total compensation	D	Daily	HR	High end range	MCC	Median cash compensation	S	See annotated source	Y	Yearly

Occupation/Type/Industry	Location	Per	Low	Mid	High	Source	Date
Recreation Worker	Dallas-Fort Worth-Arlington MSA, TX	Y	16460 FQ	19720 MW	27170 TQ	USBLS	5/07
	El Paso MSA, TX	Y	13230 FQ	15260 MW	20510 TQ	USBLS	5/07
	Houston-Sugar Land-Baytown MSA, TX	Y	14530 FQ	17500 MW	20020 TQ	USBLS	5/07
	San Antonio MSA, TX	Y	14480 FQ	17080 MW	19990 TQ	USBLS	5/07
	Utah	Y	15920 FQ	20220 MW	26940 TQ	USBLS	5/07
	Salt Lake City MSA, UT	Y	18390 FQ	22370 MW	28560 TQ	USBLS	5/07
	Vermont	Y	19510 FQ	23510 MW	30110 TQ	USBLS	5/07
	Burlington-South Burlington MSA, VT	Y	20290 FQ	23710 MW	28600 TQ	USBLS	5/07
	Virginia	Y	17010 FQ	22270 MW	31100 TQ	USBLS	5/07
	Lynchburg MSA, VA	Y	17630 FQ	19870 MW	24410 TQ	USBLS	5/07
	Richmond MSA, VA	Y	14460 FQ	19120 MW	26760 TQ	USBLS	5/07
	Virginia Beach-Norfolk-Newport News MSA, VA-NC	Y	16390 FQ	20210 MW	31490 TQ	USBLS	5/07
	Washington	H	9.07 FQ	10.67 MW	13.34 TQ	WABLS	3/08
	Seattle-Tacoma-Bellevue MSA, WA	Y	19010 FQ	22850 MW	28820 TQ	USBLS	5/07
	West Virginia	Y	16369 FQ	21194 MW	26330 TQ	WVBLS	7/08-9/08
	Charleston MSA, WV	Y	14420 FQ	17360 MW	26880 TQ	USBLS	5/07
	Wisconsin	Y	17260 FQ	21300 MW	26720 TQ	USBLS	5/07
	Appleton MSA, WI	Y	18490 FQ	22020 MW	27010 TQ	USBLS	5/07
	Milwaukee-Waukesha-West Allis MSA, WI	Y	18600 FQ	22340 MW	27750 TQ	USBLS	5/07
	Wyoming	Y	17495 FQ	20327 MW	26439 TQ	WYBLS	9/08
	Casper MSA, WY	Y	22116 FQ	27273 MW	35959 TQ	WYBLS	9/08
	Cheyenne MSA, WY	Y	17792 FQ	19114 MW	20426 TQ	WYBLS	9/08
	Puerto Rico	Y	12920 FQ	14670 MW	17870 TQ	USBLS	5/07
	San Juan-Caguas-Guaynabo MSA, PR	Y	13100 FQ	15040 MW	18860 TQ	USBLS	5/07
	Virgin Islands	Y	17160 FQ	19380 MW	22680 TQ	USBLS	5/07
Recreational Therapist	Alabama	Y	23110 FQ	30090 MW	38340 TQ	USBLS	5/07
	Birmingham-Hoover MSA, AL	Y	28680 FQ	33790 MW	41000 TQ	USBLS	5/07
	Montgomery MSA, AL	Y	22420 FQ	26900 MW	32890 TQ	USBLS	5/07
	Arizona	Y	28820 FQ	35730 MW	42010 TQ	USBLS	5/07
	Phoenix-Mesa-Scottsdale MSA, AZ	Y	29690 FQ	36130 MW	41570 TQ	USBLS	5/07
	Tucson MSA, AZ	Y	24360 FQ	32950 MW	41070 TQ	USBLS	5/07
	Arkansas	Y	25760 FQ	35620 MW	45150 TQ	USBLS	5/07
	Little Rock-North Little Rock MSA, AR	Y	31240 FQ	41910 MW	49750 TQ	USBLS	5/07
	California	H	17.73 FQ	22.55 MW	27.87 TQ	CABLS	1/08-3/08
	Los Angeles-Long Beach-Glendale PMSA, CA	H	18.15 FQ	23.06 MW	28.93 TQ	CABLS	1/08-3/08
	Oakland-Fremont-Hayward MSA, CA	H	18.37 FQ	25.11 MW	31.17 TQ	CABLS	1/08-3/08
	Riverside-San Bernardino-Ontario MSA, CA	H	9.13 FQ	16.58 MW	23.26 TQ	CABLS	1/08-3/08
	Sacramento-Arden Arcade-Roseville MSA, CA	H	18.74 FQ	21.33 MW	23.75 TQ	CABLS	1/08-3/08
	San Diego-Carlsbad-San Marcos MSA, CA	H	17.28 FQ	22.19 MW	26.14 TQ	CABLS	1/08-3/08
	San Francisco-San Mateo-Redwood PMSA, CA	H	20.68 FQ	27.12 MW	31.26 TQ	CABLS	1/08-3/08
	San Jose-Sunnyvale-Santa Clara MSA, CA	H	22.53 FQ	28.04 MW	33.02 TQ	CABLS	1/08-3/08
	Santa Ana-Anaheim-Irvine PMSA, CA	Y	36450 FQ	43360 MW	49560 TQ	USBLS	5/07
	Santa Rosa-Petaluma MSA, CA	H	16.95 FQ	21.25 MW	23.93 TQ	CABLS	1/08-3/08
	Colorado	Y	28770 FQ	36720 MW	44870 TQ	USBLS	5/07
	Denver-Aurora MSA, CO	Y	31490 FQ	39830 MW	48700 TQ	USBLS	5/07
	Connecticut	H	15.36 AE	19.39 MW		CTBLS	1/08-3/08
	Bridgeport-Stamford-Norwalk MSA, CT	Y	31540 FQ	37850 MW	46730 TQ	USBLS	5/07
	Hartford-West Hartford-East Hartford MSA, CT	Y	34920 FQ	41050 MW	62560 TQ	USBLS	5/07
	Waterbury MSA, CT	Y	32680 FQ	39740 MW	47190 TQ	USBLS	5/07
	Delaware	Y	30500 FQ	37000 MW	45410 TQ	USBLS	5/07
	Wilmington PMSA, DE-MD-NJ	Y	30260 FQ	37640 MW	47720 TQ	USBLS	5/07

AE Average entry wage	**AW** Average wage paid	**FQ** First quartile wage	**LO** Lowest wage paid	**MTC** Median total compensation	**TCC** Total cash compensation
AER Average entry range	**AWR** Average wage range	**H** Hourly	**LR** Low end range	**MW** Median wage paid	**TQ** Third quartile wage
AEX Average experienced wage	**AXR** Average experienced range	**HI** Highest wage paid	**M** Monthly	**MWR** Median wage range	**W** Weekly
ATC Average total compensation	**D** Daily	**HR** High end range	**MCC** Median cash compensation	**S** See annotated source	**Y** Yearly

Occupation/Type/Industry	Location	Per	Low	Mid	High	Source	Date
Recreational Therapist	District of Columbia	Y	39080 FQ	46410 MW	58460 TQ	USBLS	5/07
	Washington-Arlington- Alexandria MSA, DC-VA- MD-WV	Y	35250 FQ	42910 MW	53280 TQ	USBLS	5/07
	Florida	Y	29460 FQ	37590 MW	48020 TQ	USBLS	5/07
	Fort Lauderdale-Pompano Beach-Deerfield Beach PMSA, FL	Y	27280 FQ	36440 MW	45400 TQ	USBLS	5/07
	Jacksonville MSA, FL	Y	28380 FQ	30760 MW	33040 TQ	USBLS	5/07
	Miami-Fort Lauderdale-Miami Beach MSA, FL	Y	34540 FQ	42490 MW	53340 TQ	USBLS	5/07
	Tampa-St. Petersburg- Clearwater MSA, FL	Y	28130 FQ	35310 MW	45440 TQ	USBLS	5/07
	West Palm Beach-Boca Raton- Boynton Beach PMSA, FL	Y	34680 FQ	40230 MW	48670 TQ	USBLS	5/07
	Georgia	Y	25330 FQ	33330 MW	42570 TQ	USBLS	5/07
	Atlanta-Sandy Springs- Marietta MSA, GA	Y	25630 FQ	34200 MW	42910 TQ	USBLS	5/07
	Hawaii	Y	38090 FQ	45630 MW	57990 TQ	USBLS	5/07
	Honolulu MSA, HI	Y	38890 FQ	46590 MW	59530 TQ	USBLS	5/07
	Idaho	Y	23200 FQ	38030 MW	48380 TQ	USBLS	5/07
	Boise City-Nampa MSA, ID	Y	23230 FQ	39980 MW	48910 TQ	USBLS	5/07
	Illinois	Y	22000 FQ	29730 MW	46320 TQ	USBLS	5/07
	Chicago-Naperville-Joliet MSA, IL-IN-WI	Y	23860 FQ	33970 MW	47790 TQ	USBLS	5/07
	Indiana	Y	25430 FQ	33120 MW	40470 TQ	USBLS	5/07
	Gary PMSA, IN	Y	18640 FQ	31380 MW	39360 TQ	USBLS	5/07
	Indianapolis-Carmel MSA, IN	Y	32720 FQ	38420 MW	45880 TQ	USBLS	5/07
	Iowa	Y	24610 FQ	30970 MW	40960 TQ	USBLS	5/07
	Des Moines-West Des Moines MSA, IA	Y	31530 FQ	39980 MW	53960 TQ	USBLS	5/07
	Kansas	Y	23140 FQ	32890 MW	41010 TQ	USBLS	5/07
	Wichita MSA, KS	Y	23590 FQ	34370 MW	40760 TQ	USBLS	5/07
	Kentucky	Y	30249 FQ	35914 MW	42190 TQ	KYBLS	2008
	Louisville-Jefferson County MSA, KY-IN	Y	30160 FQ	35390 MW	41380 TQ	USBLS	5/07
	Louisiana	H	12.23 FQ	15.75 MW	20.23 TQ	LABLS	1/08-3/08
	Baton Rouge MSA, LA	Y	24770 FQ	32350 MW	38480 TQ	USBLS	5/07
	New Orleans-Metairie-Kenner MSA, LA	Y	26800 FQ	30640 MW	35560 TQ	USBLS	5/07
	Maine	Y	28100 FQ	35040 MW	39840 TQ	USBLS	5/07
	Portland-South Portland- Biddeford MSA, ME	Y	23380 FQ	31180 MW	35490 TQ	USBLS	5/07
	Maryland	Y		35925 MW		MDBLS	3/08
	Baltimore-Towson MSA, MD	Y	22880 FQ	33850 MW	41590 TQ	USBLS	5/07
	Bethesda-Gaithersburg- Frederick PMSA, MD	Y	28070 FQ	39350 MW	50250 TQ	USBLS	5/07
	Massachusetts	Y	31020 FQ	38010 MW	46240 TQ	USBLS	5/07
	Boston-Cambridge-Quincy NECTA, MA	Y	33640 FQ	41070 MW	47930 TQ	USBLS	5/07
	Worcester MSA, MA-CT	Y	32860 FQ	37170 MW	42270 TQ	USBLS	5/07
	Michigan	Y	33680 FQ	42510 MW	49530 TQ	USBLS	5/07
	Detroit-Warren-Livonia MSA, MI	Y	35790 FQ	44220 MW	50820 TQ	USBLS	5/07
	Grand Rapids-Wyoming MSA, MI	Y	34990 FQ	41690 MW	49260 TQ	USBLS	5/07
	Warren-Troy-Farmington Hills PMSA, MI	Y	32120 FQ	40670 MW	50730 TQ	USBLS	5/07
	Minnesota	Y	35519 FQ	40959 MW	49381 TQ	MNBLS	10/08-12/08
	Duluth-Superior MSA, MN-WI	Y	38678 FQ	45395 MW	51097 TQ	MNBLS	10/08-12/08
	Minneapolis-Saint Paul MSA, MN-WI	Y	35027 FQ	40258 MW	48461 TQ	MNBLS	10/08-12/08
	Rochester MSA, MN	Y	34945 FQ	54399 MW	61774 TQ	MNBLS	10/08-12/08
	Mississippi	Y	24250 FQ	28400 MW	37420 TQ	USBLS	5/07
	Jackson MSA, MS	Y	25790 FQ	28790 MW	35160 TQ	USBLS	5/07
	Missouri	Y	24150 FQ	32100 MW	38530 TQ	USBLS	5/07
	Kansas City MSA, MO-KS	Y	29890 FQ	36070 MW	42200 TQ	USBLS	5/07
	St. Louis MSA, MO-IL	Y	23620 FQ	31880 MW	39580 TQ	USBLS	5/07
	Montana	Y	19500 FQ	27480 MW	36660 TQ	USBLS	5/07
	Nebraska	Y	19820 FQ	27350 MW	34930 TQ	USBLS	5/07
	Omaha-Council Bluffs MSA, NE-IA	Y	18670 FQ	30260 MW	41670 TQ	USBLS	5/07

AE Average entry wage	**AW** Average wage paid	**FQ** First quartile wage	**LO** Lowest wage paid	**MTC** Median total compensation **TCC** Total cash compensation
AER Average entry range	**AWR** Average wage range	**H** Hourly	**LR** Low end range	**MW** Median wage paid **TQ** Third quartile wage
AEX Average experienced wage	**AXR** Average experienced range	**HI** Highest wage paid	**M** Monthly	**MWR** Median wage range **W** Weekly
ATC Average total compensation **D** Daily		**HR** High end range	**MCC** Median cash compensation **S** See annotated source	**Y** Yearly

Occupation/Type/Industry	Location	Per	Low	Mid	High	Source	Date
Recreational Therapist	Nevada	H	11.41 FQ	15.86 MW	18.50 TQ	NVBLS	5/08
	Las Vegas-Paradise MSA, NV	H	11.40 FQ	16.03 MW	18.57 TQ	NVBLS	5/08
	New Hampshire	H	17.07 AE	19.63 MW	21.34 AEX	NHBLS	6/08
	New Jersey	Y	29500 FQ	41030 MW	52020 TQ	USBLS	5/07
	Camden PMSA, NJ	Y	34500 FQ	45100 MW	53050 TQ	USBLS	5/07
	Edison PMSA, NJ	Y	38920 FQ	47610 MW	57110 TQ	USBLS	5/07
	Newark-Union PMSA, NJ-PA	Y	25450 FQ	40700 MW	52550 TQ	USBLS	5/07
	New Mexico	Y	25370 FQ	29110 MW	35580 TQ	USBLS	5/07
	New York	Y	35830 FQ	44660 MW	54340 TQ	USBLS	5/07
	Albany-Schenectady-Troy MSA, NY	Y	32000 FQ	39370 MW	47620 TQ	USBLS	5/07
	Buffalo-Niagara Falls MSA, NY	Y	28240 FQ	40830 MW	53630 TQ	USBLS	5/07
	Nassau-Suffolk PMSA, NY	Y	37080 FQ	43960 MW	51380 TQ	USBLS	5/07
	New York-Northern New Jersey-Long Island MSA, NY-NJ-PA	Y	36020 FQ	44920 MW	54670 TQ	USBLS	5/07
	North Carolina	Y	31790 FQ	36950 MW	43850 TQ	USBLS	5/07
	Charlotte-Gastonia-Concord MSA, NC-SC	Y	28700 FQ	34220 MW	40850 TQ	USBLS	5/07
	North Dakota	Y	23180 FQ	33240 MW	39480 TQ	USBLS	5/07
	Fargo MSA, ND-MN	Y	33740 FQ	36980 MW	40580 TQ	USBLS	5/07
	Ohio	Y	33870 FQ	38180 MW	45230 TQ	USBLS	5/07
	Cincinnati-Middletown MSA, OH-KY-IN	Y	33160 FQ	37690 MW	44860 TQ	USBLS	5/07
	Cleveland-Elyria-Mentor MSA, OH	Y	35340 FQ	40750 MW	47510 TQ	USBLS	5/07
	Columbus MSA, OH	Y	32910 FQ	38890 MW	46630 TQ	USBLS	5/07
	Dayton MSA, OH	Y	35100 FQ	39460 MW	49070 TQ	USBLS	5/07
	Oklahoma	Y	24730 FQ	33520 MW	42880 TQ	USBLS	5/07
	Oklahoma City MSA, OK	Y	27980 FQ	34780 MW	41350 TQ	USBLS	5/07
	Tulsa MSA, OK	Y	25490 FQ	36140 MW	53080 TQ	USBLS	5/07
	Oregon	H	16.55 FQ	21.39 MW	25.33 TQ	ORBLS	5/08
	Portland-Vancouver-Beaverton MSA, OR-WA	Y	32310 FQ	44940 MW	58620 TQ	USBLS	5/07
	Pennsylvania	Y	28700 FQ	36660 MW	47810 TQ	USBLS	5/07
	Allentown-Bethlehem-Easton MSA, PA-NJ	Y	33790 FQ	42610 MW	53940 TQ	USBLS	5/07
	Philadelphia-Camden-Wilmington MSA, PA-NJ-DE-MD	Y	32230 FQ	38950 MW	49520 TQ	USBLS	5/07
	Pittsburgh MSA, PA	Y	31830 FQ	38100 MW	51700 TQ	USBLS	5/07
	Rhode Island	Y	23360 FQ	36230 MW	51380 TQ	USBLS	5/07
	Providence-Fall River-Warwick MSA, RI-MA	Y	28200 FQ	38750 MW	49650 TQ	USBLS	5/07
	South Carolina	Y	21100 FQ	28460 MW	36240 TQ	USBLS	5/07
	Charleston-North Charleston MSA, SC	Y	26590 FQ	32210 MW	45640 TQ	USBLS	5/07
	Columbia MSA, SC	Y	21790 FQ	27630 MW	32400 TQ	USBLS	5/07
	South Dakota	Y	32516 FQ	38855 MW	48932 TQ	SDBLS	7/08-9/08
	Tennessee	Y	26350 FQ	31670 MW	38810 TQ	USBLS	5/07
	Memphis MSA, TN-MS-AR	Y	27260 FQ	32940 MW	40510 TQ	USBLS	5/07
	Nashville-Davidson-Murfreesboro MSA, TN	Y	27320 FQ	31300 MW	40060 TQ	USBLS	5/07
	Texas	Y	24930 FQ	33000 MW	44260 TQ	USBLS	5/07
	Austin-Round Rock MSA, TX	Y	26660 FQ	32140 MW	37710 TQ	USBLS	5/07
	Dallas-Fort Worth-Arlington MSA, TX	Y	29940 FQ	37140 MW	50250 TQ	USBLS	5/07
	Houston-Sugar Land-Baytown MSA, TX	Y	26110 FQ	37850 MW	47390 TQ	USBLS	5/07
	San Antonio MSA, TX	Y	33540 FQ	37250 MW	43940 TQ	USBLS	5/07
	Utah	Y	27730 FQ	33840 MW	40560 TQ	USBLS	5/07
	Salt Lake City MSA, UT	Y	27880 FQ	33510 MW	41690 TQ	USBLS	5/07
	Vermont	Y	22240 FQ	28980 MW	41920 TQ	USBLS	5/07
	Virginia	Y	30950 FQ	34900 MW	40780 TQ	USBLS	5/07
	Richmond MSA, VA	Y	31290 FQ	34320 MW	37350 TQ	USBLS	5/07
	Virginia Beach-Norfolk-Newport News MSA, VA-NC	Y	31900 FQ	36860 MW	47530 TQ	USBLS	5/07
	Washington	H	21.36 FQ	24.34 MW	28.27 TQ	WABLS	3/08
	Seattle-Tacoma-Bellevue MSA, WA	Y	44710 FQ	51410 MW	60110 TQ	USBLS	5/07
	West Virginia	Y	27367 FQ	31601 MW	43695 TQ	WVBLS	7/08-9/08

Occupation/Type/Industry	Location	Per	Low	Mid	High	Source	Date
Recreational Therapist	Wisconsin	Y	27250 FQ	36660 MW	46160 TQ	USBLS	5/07
	Milwaukee-Waukesha-West Allis MSA, WI	Y	30290 FQ	37770 MW	46430 TQ	USBLS	5/07
	Wyoming	Y	29599 FQ	37777 MW	44060 TQ	WYBLS	9/08
Recreational Vehicle Service Technician							
	Alabama	Y	20380 FQ	28490 MW	36110 TQ	USBLS	5/07
	Huntsville MSA, AL	Y	22870 FQ	28020 MW	35600 TQ	USBLS	5/07
	Alaska	Y	16000 FQ	25930 MW	39370 TQ	USBLS	5/07
	Arizona	Y	22870 FQ	30300 MW	41100 TQ	USBLS	5/07
	Phoenix-Mesa-Scottsdale MSA, AZ	Y	20880 FQ	24760 MW	41620 TQ	USBLS	5/07
	Tucson MSA, AZ	Y	28000 FQ	35370 MW	41460 TQ	USBLS	5/07
	Arkansas	Y	22230 FQ	25830 MW	30130 TQ	USBLS	5/07
	Little Rock-North Little Rock MSA, AR	Y	22070 FQ	25450 MW	29550 TQ	USBLS	5/07
	California	H	13.23 FQ	16.40 MW	22.05 TQ	CABLS	1/08-3/08
	Los Angeles-Long Beach-Glendale PMSA, CA	H	13.40 FQ	18.78 MW	22.85 TQ	CABLS	1/08-3/08
	Oakland-Fremont-Hayward MSA, CA	H	14.09 FQ	15.60 MW	23.30 TQ	CABLS	1/08-3/08
	Riverside-San Bernardino-Ontario MSA, CA	H	13.25 FQ	15.06 MW	23.41 TQ	CABLS	1/08-3/08
	Sacramento-Arden Arcade-Roseville MSA, CA	H	14.32 FQ	17.54 MW	21.35 TQ	CABLS	1/08-3/08
	San Diego-Carlsbad-San Marcos MSA, CA	H	11.12 FQ	12.82 MW	18.97 TQ	CABLS	1/08-3/08
	San Jose-Sunnyvale-Santa Clara MSA, CA	H	10.60 FQ	12.59 MW	22.99 TQ	CABLS	1/08-3/08
	Santa Ana-Anaheim-Irvine PMSA, CA	Y	30160 FQ	35170 MW	38920 TQ	USBLS	5/07
	Colorado	Y	28140 FQ	37900 MW	46240 TQ	USBLS	5/07
	Denver-Aurora MSA, CO	Y	34710 FQ	41530 MW	47400 TQ	USBLS	5/07
	Connecticut	H	13.26 AE	17.41 MW		CTBLS	1/08-3/08
	Delaware	Y	31620 FQ	34840 MW	38440 TQ	USBLS	5/07
	Wilmington PMSA, DE-MD-NJ	Y	31910 FQ	35090 MW	39800 TQ	USBLS	5/07
	Florida	Y	27880 FQ	34600 MW	41630 TQ	USBLS	5/07
	Jacksonville MSA, FL	Y	26020 FQ	34990 MW	45230 TQ	USBLS	5/07
	Orlando-Kissimmee MSA, FL	Y	27390 FQ	31750 MW	41080 TQ	USBLS	5/07
	Tampa-St. Petersburg-Clearwater MSA, FL	Y	31390 FQ	36180 MW	41370 TQ	USBLS	5/07
	Georgia	Y	19990 FQ	29460 MW	38290 TQ	USBLS	5/07
	Atlanta-Sandy Springs-Marietta MSA, GA	Y	18390 FQ	24090 MW	36640 TQ	USBLS	5/07
	Idaho	Y	21790 FQ	32180 MW	40420 TQ	USBLS	5/07
	Boise City-Nampa MSA, ID	Y	29160 FQ	37430 MW	45570 TQ	USBLS	5/07
	Illinois	Y	22960 FQ	28240 MW	42320 TQ	USBLS	5/07
	Chicago-Naperville-Joliet MSA, IL-IN-WI	Y	23950 FQ	33350 MW	46070 TQ	USBLS	5/07
	Indiana	Y	26470 FQ	32410 MW	39510 TQ	USBLS	5/07
	Indianapolis-Carmel MSA, IN	Y	25140 FQ	29380 MW	38610 TQ	USBLS	5/07
	Iowa	Y	24470 FQ	30640 MW	36380 TQ	USBLS	5/07
	Kansas	Y	20730 FQ	24780 MW	30610 TQ	USBLS	5/07
	Wichita MSA, KS	Y	17940 FQ	20280 MW	24120 TQ	USBLS	5/07
	Kentucky	Y	25496 FQ	33444 MW	40143 TQ	KYBLS	2008
	Louisville-Jefferson County MSA, KY-IN	Y	31470 FQ	39290 MW	44520 TQ	USBLS	5/07
	Louisiana	H	11.98 FQ	14.28 MW	16.05 TQ	LABLS	1/08-3/08
	Maine	Y	25140 FQ	29640 MW	34510 TQ	USBLS	5/07
	Maryland	Y		22225 MW		MDBLS	3/08
	Baltimore-Towson MSA, MD	Y	14970 FQ	18070 MW	29850 TQ	USBLS	5/07
	Massachusetts	Y	26980 FQ	31300 MW	39920 TQ	USBLS	5/07
	Michigan	Y	26020 FQ	29580 MW	34480 TQ	USBLS	5/07
	Detroit-Warren-Livonia MSA, MI	Y	25320 FQ	28390 MW	31510 TQ	USBLS	5/07
	Grand Rapids-Wyoming MSA, MI	Y	27900 FQ	32250 MW	36200 TQ	USBLS	5/07
	Warren-Troy-Farmington Hills PMSA, MI	Y	25650 FQ	28050 MW	30490 TQ	USBLS	5/07
	Minnesota	Y	29055 FQ	35915 MW	43898 TQ	MNBLS	10/08-12/08
	Duluth-Superior MSA, MN-WI	Y	28111 FQ	31604 MW	36377 TQ	MNBLS	10/08-12/08

AE	Average entry wage	AW	Average wage paid	FQ	First quartile wage	LO	Lowest wage paid	MTC	Median total compensation	TCC	Total cash compensation
AER	Average entry range	AWR	Average wage range	H	Hourly	LR	Low end range	MW	Median wage paid	TQ	Third quartile wage
AEX	Average experienced wage	AXR	Average experienced range	HI	Highest wage paid	M	Monthly	MWR	Median wage range	W	Weekly
ATC	Average total compensation	D	Daily	HR	High end range	MCC	Median cash compensation	S	See annotated source	Y	Yearly

Occupation/Type/Industry	Location	Per	Low	Mid	High	Source	Date
Recreational Vehicle Service Technician	Minneapolis-Saint Paul MSA, MN-WI	Y	32611 FQ	41433 MW	50538 TQ	MNBLS	10/08-12/08
	Rochester MSA, MN	Y	21910 FQ	26929 MW	34476 TQ	MNBLS	10/08-12/08
	Mississippi	Y	25750 FQ	28620 MW	32010 TQ	USBLS	5/07
	Jackson MSA, MS	Y	26780 FQ	28470 MW	30170 TQ	USBLS	5/07
	Missouri	Y	21400 FQ	24490 MW	28440 TQ	USBLS	5/07
	Kansas City MSA, MO-KS	Y	24390 FQ	31430 MW	41920 TQ	USBLS	5/07
	Montana	Y	25090 FQ	30300 MW	36950 TQ	USBLS	5/07
	Nebraska	Y	21420 FQ	24610 MW	31130 TQ	USBLS	5/07
	Nevada	H	14.60 FQ	17.45 MW	20.97 TQ	NVBLS	5/08
	Las Vegas-Paradise MSA, NV	H	15.37 FQ	19.09 MW	22.53 TQ	NVBLS	5/08
	New Hampshire	H	14.33 AE	16.06 MW	17.85 AEX	NHBLS	6/08
	New Jersey	Y	32150 FQ	36340 MW	43660 TQ	USBLS	5/07
	Camden PMSA, NJ	Y	23700 FQ	32650 MW	39850 TQ	USBLS	5/07
	Newark-Union PMSA, NJ-PA	Y	31270 FQ	34050 MW	36580 TQ	USBLS	5/07
	New Mexico	Y	28060 FQ	34180 MW	47080 TQ	USBLS	5/07
	New York	Y	22610 FQ	29130 MW	37050 TQ	USBLS	5/07
	Nassau-Suffolk PMSA, NY	Y	35050 FQ	39390 MW	53970 TQ	USBLS	5/07
	New York-Northern New Jersey-Long Island MSA, NY-NJ-PA	Y	34110 FQ	37820 MW	46570 TQ	USBLS	5/07
	North Carolina	Y	26060 FQ	30960 MW	37470 TQ	USBLS	5/07
	North Dakota	Y	27640 FQ	30820 MW	33890 TQ	USBLS	5/07
	Ohio	Y	24880 FQ	29950 MW	36520 TQ	USBLS	5/07
	Cincinnati-Middletown MSA, OH-KY-IN	Y	26810 FQ	32610 MW	36670 TQ	USBLS	5/07
	Cleveland-Elyria-Mentor MSA, OH	Y	26530 FQ	31780 MW	36240 TQ	USBLS	5/07
	Dayton MSA, OH	Y	33860 FQ	37020 MW	40170 TQ	USBLS	5/07
	Oklahoma	Y	22300 FQ	27030 MW	33210 TQ	USBLS	5/07
	Tulsa MSA, OK	Y	24300 FQ	28660 MW	33390 TQ	USBLS	5/07
	Oregon	H	17.00 FQ	19.79 MW	22.97 TQ	ORBLS	5/08
	Portland-Vancouver-Beaverton MSA, OR-WA	Y	38870 FQ	43770 MW	51130 TQ	USBLS	5/07
	Pennsylvania	Y	25830 FQ	31510 MW	39690 TQ	USBLS	5/07
	Allentown-Bethlehem-Easton MSA, PA-NJ	Y	29450 FQ	33170 MW	43250 TQ	USBLS	5/07
	Philadelphia-Camden-Wilmington MSA, PA-NJ-DE-MD	Y	30640 FQ	36180 MW	44540 TQ	USBLS	5/07
	Pittsburgh MSA, PA	Y	22850 FQ	28430 MW	34870 TQ	USBLS	5/07
	Rhode Island	Y	27160 FQ	29970 MW	34280 TQ	USBLS	5/07
	Providence-Fall River-Warwick MSA, RI-MA	Y	27160 FQ	29970 MW	34280 TQ	USBLS	5/07
	South Carolina	Y	27820 FQ	35680 MW	45300 TQ	USBLS	5/07
	Myrtle Beach-Conway-North Myrtle Beach MSA, SC	Y	32470 FQ	44060 MW	48690 TQ	USBLS	5/07
	South Dakota	Y	24413 FQ	27345 MW	30595 TQ	SDBLS	7/08-9/08
	Sioux Falls MSA, SD	Y	24904 FQ	28937 MW	33411 TQ	SDBLS	7/08-9/08
	Tennessee	Y	25570 FQ	29390 MW	35460 TQ	USBLS	5/07
	Memphis MSA, TN-MS-AR	Y	25590 FQ	42130 MW	56060 TQ	USBLS	5/07
	Nashville-Davidson-Murfreesboro MSA, TN	Y	26260 FQ	28700 MW	32000 TQ	USBLS	5/07
	Texas	Y	23960 FQ	33000 MW	39450 TQ	USBLS	5/07
	Austin-Round Rock MSA, TX	Y	27080 FQ	37530 MW	46980 TQ	USBLS	5/07
	Dallas-Fort Worth-Arlington MSA, TX	Y	31220 FQ	35900 MW	40540 TQ	USBLS	5/07
	Houston-Sugar Land-Baytown MSA, TX	Y	24120 FQ	34170 MW	42560 TQ	USBLS	5/07
	San Antonio MSA, TX	Y	25060 FQ	30830 MW	39800 TQ	USBLS	5/07
	Utah	Y	27280 FQ	35550 MW	45100 TQ	USBLS	5/07
	Ogden-Clearfield MSA, UT	Y	30310 FQ	38340 MW	44700 TQ	USBLS	5/07
	Salt Lake City MSA, UT	Y	28030 FQ	31850 MW	53340 TQ	USBLS	5/07
	Virginia	Y	26560 FQ	35610 MW	94590 TQ	USBLS	5/07
	Washington	H	14.04 FQ	16.55 MW	19.59 TQ	WABLS	3/08
	Seattle-Tacoma-Bellevue MSA, WA	Y	30920 FQ	35510 MW	45710 TQ	USBLS	5/07
	West Virginia	Y	25087 FQ	28910 MW	32999 TQ	WVBLS	7/08-9/08
	Wisconsin	Y	23790 FQ	31330 MW	39750 TQ	USBLS	5/07
	Wyoming	Y	21222 FQ	26864 MW	35599 TQ	WYBLS	9/08

AE	Average entry wage	AW	Average wage paid	FQ	First quartile wage	LO	Lowest wage paid	MTC	Median total compensation	TCC	Total cash compensation
AER	Average entry range	AWR	Average wage range	H	Hourly	LR	Low end range	MW	Median wage paid	TQ	Third quartile wage
AEX	Average experienced wage	AXR	Average experienced range	HI	Highest wage paid	M	Monthly	MWR	Median wage range	W	Weekly
ATC	Average total compensation	D	Daily	HR	High end range	MCC	Median cash compensation	S	See annotated source	Y	Yearly

Occupation/Type/Industry	Location	Per	Low	Mid	High	Source	Date
Recycling Coordinator	Shutesbury, MA	Y			1852 HI	FRCOG	2009
Recycling Manager/Supervisor	Cherokee County, GA	Y	32583 LO		50503 HI	GACTY03	2008
	Liberty County, GA	Y	27997 LO		45885 HI	GACTY03	2008
	Pickens County, GA	Y	27833 LO		42351 HI	GACTY03	2008
Recycling Processing Worker	United States	H	8.25 LO		29.50 HI	CHTW	2008
Recycling Program Specialist	Seattle, WA	H	18.96 LO		22.01 HI	CSSS	2007
Red Hat Certified Engineer	United States	Y		86020 AW		CERT03	2008
Redevelopment Project Manager	Seaside, CA	S	2739 LO		3329 HI	SSSS	8/08
Referee							
Judicial Branch, State Government	New Hampshire	Y		93549 AW		NHUL03	2008
Reference Librarian	Carlsbad, CA	H	20.00 LO		26.00 HI	CCSS	1/1/08
Refractory Materials Repairer							
Except Brickmasons	Alabama	Y	25780 FQ	34640 MW	40320 TQ	USBLS	5/07
Except Brickmasons	Arkansas	Y	34180 FQ	38350 MW	43860 TQ	USBLS	5/07
Except Brickmasons	California	H	15.62 FQ	19.16 MW	22.54 TQ	CABLS	1/08-3/08
Except Brickmasons	Georgia	Y	28510 FQ	31400 MW	39230 TQ	USBLS	5/07
Except Brickmasons	Illinois	Y	27020 FQ	35790 MW	45250 TQ	USBLS	5/07
Except Brickmasons	Indiana	Y	33700 FQ	39180 MW	44650 TQ	USBLS	5/07
Except Brickmasons	Louisiana	H	14.21 FQ	18.66 MW	20.91 TQ	LABLS	1/08-3/08
Except Brickmasons	Massachusetts	Y	32160 FQ	37880 MW	47110 TQ	USBLS	5/07
Except Brickmasons	Michigan	Y	46130 FQ	60750 MW	68060 TQ	USBLS	5/07
Except Brickmasons	New Jersey	Y	33110 FQ	43050 MW	47260 TQ	USBLS	5/07
Except Brickmasons	New York	Y	35830 FQ	43000 MW	56260 TQ	USBLS	5/07
Except Brickmasons	North Carolina	Y	31260 FQ	41330 MW	47750 TQ	USBLS	5/07
Except Brickmasons	Ohio	Y	34370 FQ	44140 MW	52060 TQ	USBLS	5/07
Except Brickmasons	Oklahoma	Y	25630 FQ	30280 MW	35820 TQ	USBLS	5/07
Except Brickmasons	Pennsylvania	Y	33780 FQ	42760 MW	55430 TQ	USBLS	5/07
Except Brickmasons	South Carolina	Y	28020 FQ	35020 MW	39690 TQ	USBLS	5/07
Except Brickmasons	Tennessee	Y	32890 FQ	39750 MW	46770 TQ	USBLS	5/07
Except Brickmasons	Texas	Y	32180 FQ	41120 MW	46540 TQ	USBLS	5/07
Except Brickmasons	Virginia	Y	26460 FQ	44130 MW	50580 TQ	USBLS	5/07
Except Brickmasons	Wisconsin	Y	41710 FQ	47240 MW	55620 TQ	USBLS	5/07
Refrigeration Mechanic							
Public Schools	North Carolina	M	2201 LO		3672 HI	NCSS	2008-2009
Refuse and Recyclable Material Collector							
	Alabama	Y	17790 FQ	22360 MW	27130 TQ	USBLS	5/07
	Birmingham-Hoover MSA, AL	Y	19250 FQ	23810 MW	29290 TQ	USBLS	5/07
	Alaska	Y	29330 FQ	38320 MW	52000 TQ	USBLS	5/07
	Anchorage MSA, AK	Y	40300 FQ	51200 MW	57600 TQ	USBLS	5/07
	Arizona	Y	26420 FQ	33060 MW	40140 TQ	USBLS	5/07
	Phoenix-Mesa-Scottsdale MSA, AZ	Y	28390 FQ	35570 MW	42670 TQ	USBLS	5/07
	Arkansas	Y	18220 FQ	21650 MW	26550 TQ	USBLS	5/07
	Jonesboro MSA, AR	Y	16260 FQ	22200 MW	28370 TQ	USBLS	5/07
	Little Rock-North Little Rock MSA, AR	Y	18690 FQ	22190 MW	27370 TQ	USBLS	5/07
	California	H	15.94 FQ	18.25 MW	22.36 TQ	CABLS	1/08-3/08
	Los Angeles-Long Beach-Glendale PMSA, CA	H	15.93 FQ	17.61 MW	19.62 TQ	CABLS	1/08-3/08
	Oakland-Fremont-Hayward MSA, CA	H	17.22 FQ	20.39 MW	23.88 TQ	CABLS	1/08-3/08
	Riverside-San Bernardino-Ontario MSA, CA	H	13.93 FQ	16.83 MW	19.56 TQ	CABLS	1/08-3/08
	Sacramento-Arden Arcade-Roseville MSA, CA	H	17.41 FQ	20.42 MW	22.84 TQ	CABLS	1/08-3/08
	San Diego-Carlsbad-San Marcos MSA, CA	H	16.40 FQ	18.01 MW	20.11 TQ	CABLS	1/08-3/08
	San Francisco-San Mateo-Redwood PMSA, CA	H	18.10 FQ	21.67 MW	24.84 TQ	CABLS	1/08-3/08
	San Jose-Sunnyvale-Santa Clara MSA, CA	H	22.69 FQ	27.71 MW	33.88 TQ	CABLS	1/08-3/08
	Santa Ana-Anaheim-Irvine PMSA, CA	Y	29360 FQ	33630 MW	37440 TQ	USBLS	5/07

AE Average entry wage	**AW** Average wage paid	**FQ** First quartile wage	**LO** Lowest wage paid	**MTC** Median total compensation	**TCC** Total cash compensation
AER Average entry range	**AWR** Average wage range	**H** Hourly	**LR** Low end range	**MW** Median wage paid	**TQ** Third quartile wage
AEX Average experienced wage	**AXR** Average experienced range	**HI** Highest wage paid	**M** Monthly	**MWR** Median wage range	**W** Weekly
ATC Average total compensation	**D** Daily	**HR** High end range	**MCC** Median cash compensation	**S** See annotated source	**Y** Yearly

Occupation/Type/Industry	Location	Per	Low	Mid	High	Source	Date
Refuse and Recyclable Material Collector							
	Stockton MSA, CA	H	16.00 FQ	19.71 MW	22.22 TQ	CABLS	1/08-3/08
	Colorado	Y	25830 FQ	30380 MW	37170 MW	USBLS	5/07
	Denver-Aurora MSA, CO	Y	25580 FQ	30890 MW	36670 TQ	USBLS	5/07
	Fort Collins-Loveland MSA, CO	Y	26860 FQ	31100 MW	36940 TQ	USBLS	5/07
	Connecticut	H	11.16 AE	15.08 MW		CTBLS	1/08-3/08
	Bridgeport-Stamford-Norwalk MSA, CT	Y	26880 FQ	32930 MW	43460 TQ	USBLS	5/07
	Hartford-West Hartford-East Hartford MSA, CT	Y	22230 FQ	29410 MW	37700 TQ	USBLS	5/07
	Delaware	Y	27430 FQ	32680 MW	37010 TQ	USBLS	5/07
	Wilmington PMSA, DE-MD-NJ	Y	28650 FQ	34120 MW	39570 TQ	USBLS	5/07
	District of Columbia	Y	28870 FQ	35260 MW	43530 TQ	USBLS	5/07
	Washington-Arlington-Alexandria MSA, DC-VA-MD-WV	Y	22550 FQ	29970 MW	37800 TQ	USBLS	5/07
	Florida	Y	20910 FQ	25970 MW	31540 TQ	USBLS	5/07
	Fort Lauderdale-Pompano Beach-Deerfield Beach PMSA, FL	Y	18140 FQ	21740 MW	27220 TQ	USBLS	5/07
	Jacksonville MSA, FL	Y	19020 FQ	22810 MW	28580 TQ	USBLS	5/07
	Miami-Fort Lauderdale-Miami Beach MSA, FL	Y	21220 FQ	26940 MW	33940 TQ	USBLS	5/07
	Orlando-Kissimmee MSA, FL	Y	22160 FQ	26500 MW	31500 TQ	USBLS	5/07
	Tampa-St. Petersburg-Clearwater MSA, FL	Y	22540 FQ	27150 MW	31550 TQ	USBLS	5/07
	West Palm Beach-Boca Raton-Boynton Beach PMSA, FL	Y	22740 FQ	27030 MW	32530 TQ	USBLS	5/07
	Georgia	Y	18020 FQ	22810 MW	28760 TQ	USBLS	5/07
	Atlanta-Sandy Springs-Marietta MSA, GA	Y	21070 FQ	25740 MW	31870 TQ	USBLS	5/07
	Augusta-Richmond County MSA, GA-SC	Y	14780 FQ	17600 MW	22940 TQ	USBLS	5/07
	Hawaii	Y	31460 FQ	35020 MW	38800 TQ	USBLS	5/07
	Honolulu MSA, HI	Y	32690 FQ	35600 MW	39600 TQ	USBLS	5/07
	Idaho	Y	24170 FQ	28110 MW	31900 TQ	USBLS	5/07
	Boise City-Nampa MSA, ID	Y	24940 FQ	27780 MW	30730 TQ	USBLS	5/07
	Coeur d'Alene MSA, ID	Y	27510 FQ	34000 MW	41860 TQ	USBLS	5/07
	Illinois	Y	25780 FQ	37930 MW	49910 TQ	USBLS	5/07
	Chicago-Naperville-Joliet MSA, IL-IN-WI	Y	28700 FQ	42430 MW	51430 TQ	USBLS	5/07
	Indiana	Y	22110 FQ	27220 MW	32820 TQ	USBLS	5/07
	Fort Wayne MSA, IN	Y	23790 FQ	26390 MW	28680 TQ	USBLS	5/07
	Gary PMSA, IN	Y	25840 FQ	34770 MW	43680 TQ	USBLS	5/07
	Indianapolis-Carmel MSA, IN	Y	13820 FQ	25130 MW	32330 TQ	USBLS	5/07
	Iowa	Y	19110 FQ	24690 MW	32290 TQ	USBLS	5/07
	Des Moines-West Des Moines MSA, IA	Y	19350 FQ	28210 MW	34560 TQ	USBLS	5/07
	Kansas	Y	20550 FQ	24800 MW	29280 TQ	USBLS	5/07
	Wichita MSA, KS	Y	25710 FQ	30790 MW	37290 TQ	USBLS	5/07
	Kentucky	Y	17905 FQ	22210 MW	28810 TQ	KYBLS	2008
	Louisville-Jefferson County MSA, KY-IN	Y	21050 FQ	24980 MW	31770 TQ	USBLS	5/07
	Louisiana	H	7.53 FQ	9.45 MW	12.37 TQ	LABLS	1/08-3/08
	New Orleans-Metairie-Kenner MSA, LA	Y	16710 FQ	25180 MW	30080 TQ	USBLS	5/07
	Maine	Y	18020 FQ	22780 MW	28570 TQ	USBLS	5/07
	Portland-South Portland-Biddeford MSA, ME	Y	22970 FQ	27970 MW	32990 TQ	USBLS	5/07
	Maryland	Y		28650 MW		MDBLS	3/08
	Baltimore-Towson MSA, MD	Y	19710 FQ	28020 MW	33860 TQ	USBLS	5/07
	Bethesda-Gaithersburg-Frederick PMSA, MD	Y	24220 FQ	32380 MW	36980 TQ	USBLS	5/07
	Massachusetts	Y	28650 FQ	36290 MW	40970 TQ	USBLS	5/07
	Boston-Cambridge-Quincy NECTA, MA	Y	35050 FQ	39350 MW	43860 TQ	USBLS	5/07
	Worcester MSA, MA-CT	Y	22960 FQ	29570 MW	34830 TQ	USBLS	5/07
	Michigan	Y	23190 FQ	32260 MW	38120 TQ	USBLS	5/07
	Detroit-Warren-Livonia MSA, MI	Y	23990 FQ	32310 MW	37540 TQ	USBLS	5/07

AE	Average entry wage	AW	Average wage paid	FQ	First quartile wage	LO	Lowest wage paid	MTC	Median total compensation	TCC	Total cash compensation
AER	Average entry range	AWR	Average wage range	H	Hourly	LR	Low end range	MW	Median wage paid	TQ	Third quartile wage
AEX	Average experienced wage	AXR	Average experienced range	HI	Highest wage paid	M	Monthly	MWR	Median wage range	W	Weekly
ATC	Average total compensation	D	Daily	HR	High end range	MCC	Median cash compensation	S	See annotated source	Y	Yearly

1382

Occupation/Type/Industry	Location	Per	Low	Mid	High	Source	Date
Refuse and Recyclable Material Collector	Grand Rapids-Wyoming MSA, MI	Y	30700 FQ	34630 MW	41020 TQ	USBLS	5/07
	Warren-Troy-Farmington Hills PMSA, MI	Y	27230 FQ	34110 MW	39560 TQ	USBLS	5/07
	Minnesota	Y	28557 FQ	34778 MW	41364 TQ	MNBLS	10/08-12/08
	Duluth-Superior MSA, MN-WI	Y	24812 FQ	33675 MW	38638 TQ	MNBLS	10/08-12/08
	Minneapolis-Saint Paul MSA, MN-WI	Y	32157 FQ	37795 MW	44807 TQ	MNBLS	10/08-12/08
	Mississippi	Y	19340 FQ	22040 MW	24920 TQ	USBLS	5/07
	Jackson MSA, MS	Y	16560 FQ	21300 MW	25880 TQ	USBLS	5/07
	Missouri	Y	17400 FQ	24570 MW	32470 TQ	USBLS	5/07
	Jefferson City MSA, MO	Y	14570 FQ	16650 MW	19520 TQ	USBLS	5/07
	Kansas City MSA, MO-KS	Y	19280 FQ	24180 MW	28850 TQ	USBLS	5/07
	St. Louis MSA, MO-IL	Y	27160 FQ	33180 MW	41000 TQ	USBLS	5/07
	Montana	Y	24460 FQ	31540 MW	35520 TQ	USBLS	5/07
	Nebraska	Y	20210 FQ	23880 MW	30880 TQ	USBLS	5/07
	Omaha-Council Bluffs MSA, NE-IA	Y	20380 FQ	22780 MW	32000 TQ	USBLS	5/07
	Nevada	H	7.16 FQ	12.53 MW	18.11 TQ	NVBLS	5/08
	Las Vegas-Paradise MSA, NV	H	6.73 FQ	12.58 MW	18.83 TQ	NVBLS	5/08
	New Hampshire	H	9.64 AE	13.27 MW	15.53 AEX	NHBLS	6/08
	Manchester MSA, NH	Y	29590 FQ	36430 MW	42640 TQ	USBLS	5/07
	Nashua NECTA, NH-MA	Y	23730 FQ	28990 MW	34860 TQ	USBLS	5/07
	New Jersey	Y	28250 FQ	36010 MW	44700 TQ	USBLS	5/07
	Camden PMSA, NJ	Y	24960 FQ	33270 MW	39060 TQ	USBLS	5/07
	Edison PMSA, NJ	Y	32670 FQ	41200 MW	48950 TQ	USBLS	5/07
	Newark-Union PMSA, NJ-PA	Y	26680 FQ	29840 MW	35040 TQ	USBLS	5/07
	New Mexico	Y	20670 FQ	26320 MW	33550 TQ	USBLS	5/07
	New York	Y	33600 FQ	44530 MW	58450 TQ	USBLS	5/07
	Albany-Schenectady-Troy MSA, NY	Y	25620 FQ	28370 MW	31380 TQ	USBLS	5/07
	Binghamton MSA, NY	Y	18390 FQ	22510 MW	28340 TQ	USBLS	5/07
	Buffalo-Niagara Falls MSA, NY	Y	28160 FQ	31480 MW	37120 TQ	USBLS	5/07
	Nassau-Suffolk PMSA, NY	Y	31660 FQ	40840 MW	50010 TQ	USBLS	5/07
	New York-Northern New Jersey-Long Island MSA, NY-NJ-PA	Y	36080 FQ	47570 MW	58840 TQ	USBLS	5/07
	North Carolina	Y	18450 FQ	23020 MW	28150 TQ	USBLS	5/07
	Charlotte-Gastonia-Concord MSA, NC-SC	Y	15130 FQ	25270 MW	30160 TQ	USBLS	5/07
	Raleigh-Cary MSA, NC	Y	21850 FQ	24740 MW	29270 TQ	USBLS	5/07
	North Dakota	Y	16840 FQ	24130 MW	31060 TQ	USBLS	5/07
	Bismarck MSA, ND	Y	23960 FQ	27380 MW	30910 TQ	USBLS	5/07
	Fargo MSA, ND-MN	Y	29620 FQ	34860 MW	38750 TQ	USBLS	5/07
	Ohio	Y	24090 FQ	29840 MW	35590 TQ	USBLS	5/07
	Cincinnati-Middletown MSA, OH-KY-IN	Y	26750 FQ	30300 MW	35700 TQ	USBLS	5/07
	Cleveland-Elyria-Mentor MSA, OH	Y	22620 FQ	29530 MW	35690 TQ	USBLS	5/07
	Columbus MSA, OH	Y	26000 FQ	32400 MW	36430 TQ	USBLS	5/07
	Dayton MSA, OH	Y	27820 FQ	32090 MW	46140 TQ	USBLS	5/07
	Oklahoma	Y	18820 FQ	23260 MW	28740 TQ	USBLS	5/07
	Oklahoma City MSA, OK	Y	25500 FQ	30430 MW	36150 TQ	USBLS	5/07
	Tulsa MSA, OK	Y	17010 FQ	18680 MW	23570 TQ	USBLS	5/07
	Oregon	H	14.73 FQ	17.94 MW	20.61 TQ	ORBLS	5/08
	Portland-Vancouver-Beaverton MSA, OR-WA	Y	34970 FQ	39840 MW	44610 TQ	USBLS	5/07
	Pennsylvania	Y	22670 FQ	28490 MW	38060 TQ	USBLS	5/07
	Allentown-Bethlehem-Easton MSA, PA-NJ	Y	21340 FQ	26360 MW	30120 TQ	USBLS	5/07
	Philadelphia-Camden-Wilmington MSA, PA-NJ-DE-MD	Y	25280 FQ	33370 MW	41450 TQ	USBLS	5/07
	Pittsburgh MSA, PA	Y	27000 FQ	33780 MW	44380 TQ	USBLS	5/07
	Rhode Island	Y	30920 FQ	34780 MW	38410 TQ	USBLS	5/07
	Providence-Fall River-Warwick MSA, RI-MA	Y	31660 FQ	35880 MW	39880 TQ	USBLS	5/07
	South Carolina	Y	15780 FQ	20900 MW	26340 TQ	USBLS	5/07
	Charleston-North Charleston MSA, SC	Y	21170 FQ	24520 MW	31120 TQ	USBLS	5/07

AE	Average entry wage	AW	Average wage paid	FQ	First quartile wage
AER	Average entry range	AWR	Average wage range	H	Hourly
AEX	Average experienced wage	AXR	Average experienced range	HI	Highest wage paid
ATC	Average total compensation	D	Daily	HR	High end range

LO	Lowest wage paid	MTC	Median total compensation
LR	Low end range	MW	Median wage paid
M	Monthly	MWR	Median wage range
MCC	Median cash compensation	S	See annotated source

TCC	Total cash compensation		
TQ	Third quartile wage		
W	Weekly		
Y	Yearly		

Occupation/Type/Industry	Location	Per	Low	Mid	High	Source	Date
Refuse and Recyclable Material Collector	Columbia MSA, SC	Y	20160 FQ	25140 MW	33200 TQ	USBLS	5/07
	Spartanburg MSA, SC	Y	18690 FQ	21690 MW	25260 TQ	USBLS	5/07
	South Dakota	Y	20904 FQ	24124 MW	28155 TQ	SDBLS	7/08-9/08
	Sioux Falls MSA, SD	Y	23302 FQ	26492 MW	29537 TQ	SDBLS	7/08-9/08
	Tennessee	Y	16760 FQ	21860 MW	28010 TQ	USBLS	5/07
	Memphis MSA, TN-MS-AR	Y	19640 FQ	24170 MW	29210 TQ	USBLS	5/07
	Nashville-Davidson-Murfreesboro MSA, TN	Y	14600 FQ	21860 MW	29050 TQ	USBLS	5/07
	Texas	Y	19200 FQ	24290 MW	30990 TQ	USBLS	5/07
	Austin-Round Rock MSA, TX	Y	20130 FQ	24430 MW	30090 TQ	USBLS	5/07
	Dallas-Fort Worth-Arlington MSA, TX	Y	15220 FQ	25610 MW	39760 TQ	USBLS	5/07
	Houston-Sugar Land-Baytown MSA, TX	Y	19980 FQ	26230 MW	37040 TQ	USBLS	5/07
	San Antonio MSA, TX	Y	21990 FQ	24860 MW	29000 TQ	USBLS	5/07
	Utah	Y	23950 FQ	29450 MW	36140 TQ	USBLS	5/07
	Salt Lake City MSA, UT	Y	22940 FQ	30630 MW	36810 TQ	USBLS	5/07
	Vermont	Y	22010 FQ	26000 MW	30200 TQ	USBLS	5/07
	Burlington-South Burlington MSA, VT	Y	22920 FQ	26460 MW	30400 TQ	USBLS	5/07
	Virginia	Y	19470 FQ	24460 MW	31210 TQ	USBLS	5/07
	Richmond MSA, VA	Y	15410 FQ	25410 MW	30820 TQ	USBLS	5/07
	Virginia Beach-Norfolk-Newport News MSA, VA-NC	Y	22630 FQ	27650 MW	33210 TQ	USBLS	5/07
	Washington	H	15.04 FQ	18.93 MW	22.62 TQ	WABLS	3/08
	Seattle-Tacoma-Bellevue MSA, WA	Y	29520 FQ	40160 MW	50630 TQ	USBLS	5/07
	Spokane MSA, WA	Y	30690 FQ	37750 MW	43010 TQ	USBLS	5/07
	West Virginia	Y	15710 FQ	19158 MW	24052 TQ	WVBLS	7/08-9/08
	Charleston MSA, WV	Y	16430 FQ	19860 MW	24090 TQ	USBLS	5/07
	Wisconsin	Y	23480 FQ	36680 MW	54500 TQ	USBLS	5/07
	Milwaukee-Waukesha-West Allis MSA, WI	Y	39740 FQ	54940 MW	60820 TQ	USBLS	5/07
	Wyoming	Y	25481 FQ	31821 MW	37229 TQ	WYBLS	9/08
	Cheyenne MSA, WY	Y	22857 FQ	24915 MW	28674 TQ	WYBLS	9/08
	Puerto Rico	Y	13440 FQ	16400 MW	18540 TQ	USBLS	5/07
	San Juan-Caguas-Guaynabo MSA, PR	Y	13690 FQ	16730 MW	18650 TQ	USBLS	5/07
	Guam	Y	17000 FQ	19350 MW	23450 TQ	USBLS	5/07
Refuse and Recycling Collection Supervisor	Lumpkin County, GA	Y	28412 LO		43233 HI	GACTY03	2008
	Paulding County, GA	Y	29675 LO		45718 HI	GACTY03	2008
	Putnam County, GA	Y	29598 LO		46114 HI	GACTY03	2008
Refuse and Recycling Route Supervisor and Lead Truck Driver	Polk County, GA	Y	20939 LO		31863 HI	GACTY03	2008
Refuse and Recycling Truck Driver	Elbert County, GA	Y	20800 LO		27955 HI	GACTY03	2008
	Floyd County, GA	Y	22984 LO		37482 HI	GACTY03	2008
	Laurens County, GA	Y	25397 LO		29099 HI	GACTY03	2008
Regional Sales Manager Small Organization	United States	Y	88225 FQ	98575 MW	108925 TQ	ALA02	2008
Register of Copyrights Federal Government	United States	Y			158500 HI	CRS02	1/08
Registered Dietitian Working in Field for 5 Years or Less	United States	Y		42000-55000 MW		ADA01	2007
Registered Nurse	Alabama	Y	44270 FQ	51830 MW	60070 TQ	USBLS	5/07
	Birmingham-Hoover MSA, AL	Y	45990 FQ	54400 MW	62610 TQ	USBLS	5/07
	Tuscaloosa MSA, AL	Y	44970 FQ	52620 MW	60450 TQ	USBLS	5/07
	Alaska	Y	58740 FQ	69630 MW	80300 TQ	USBLS	5/07
	Anchorage MSA, AK	Y	59600 FQ	70870 MW	81060 TQ	USBLS	5/07
	Arizona	Y	50780 FQ	60670 MW	71890 TQ	USBLS	5/07

AE Average entry wage	**AW** Average wage paid	**FQ** First quartile wage	**LO** Lowest wage paid	**MTC** Median total compensation	**TCC** Total cash compensation
AER Average entry range	**AWR** Average wage range	**H** Hourly	**LR** Low end range	**MW** Median wage paid	**TQ** Third quartile wage
AEX Average experienced wage	**AXR** Average experienced range	**HI** Highest wage paid	**M** Monthly	**MWR** Median wage range	**W** Weekly
ATC Average total compensation	**D** Daily	**HR** High end range	**MCC** Median cash compensation	**S** See annotated source	**Y** Yearly

Occupation/Type/Industry	Location	Per	Low	Mid	High	Source	Date
Registered Nurse	Flagstaff MSA, AZ	Y	57330 FQ	67180 MW	76000 TQ	USBLS	5/07
	Phoenix-Mesa-Scottsdale MSA, AZ	Y	50130 FQ	60830 MW	72080 TQ	USBLS	5/07
	Tucson MSA, AZ	Y	51230 FQ	59690 MW	70500 TQ	USBLS	5/07
	Arkansas	Y	41880 FQ	50260 MW	60280 TQ	USBLS	5/07
	Little Rock-North Little Rock MSA, AR	Y	45560 FQ	54830 MW	63600 TQ	USBLS	5/07
	California	H	32.28 FQ	37.71 MW	45.32 TQ	CABLS	1/08-3/08
	Los Angeles-Long Beach-Glendale PMSA, CA	H	32.16 FQ	37.16 MW	43.47 TQ	CABLS	1/08-3/08
	Oakland-Fremont-Hayward MSA, CA	H	35.94 FQ	45.03 MW	55.57 TQ	CABLS	1/08-3/08
	Riverside-San Bernardino-Ontario MSA, CA	H	30.90 FQ	35.31 MW	39.45 TQ	CABLS	1/08-3/08
	Sacramento-Arden Arcade-Roseville MSA, CA	H	33.11 FQ	40.35 MW	47.08 TQ	CABLS	1/08-3/08
	San Diego-Carlsbad-San Marcos MSA, CA	H	31.73 FQ	36.37 MW	41.26 TQ	CABLS	1/08-3/08
	San Francisco-San Mateo-Redwood PMSA, CA	H	35.27 FQ	45.07 MW	54.05 TQ	CABLS	1/08-3/08
	San Jose-Sunnyvale-Santa Clara MSA, CA	H	38.48 FQ	47.86 MW	57.68 TQ	CABLS	1/08-3/08
	Santa Ana-Anaheim-Irvine PMSA, CA	Y	64960 FQ	73710 MW	83200 TQ	USBLS	5/07
	Colorado	Y	52340 FQ	61750 MW	72280 TQ	USBLS	5/07
	Colorado Springs MSA, CO	Y	48200 FQ	57350 MW	65890 TQ	USBLS	5/07
	Denver-Aurora MSA, CO	Y	54960 FQ	64560 MW	74290 TQ	USBLS	5/07
	Connecticut	H	25.66 AE	32.77 MW		CTBLS	1/08-3/08
	Bridgeport-Stamford-Norwalk MSA, CT	Y	55640 FQ	64350 MW	73960 TQ	USBLS	5/07
	Hartford-West Hartford-East Hartford MSA, CT	Y	58680 FQ	68300 MW	77930 TQ	USBLS	5/07
	Delaware	Y	55580 FQ	64140 MW	74080 TQ	USBLS	5/07
	Wilmington PMSA, DE-MD-NJ	Y	55980 FQ	64810 MW	74540 TQ	USBLS	5/07
	District of Columbia	Y	55530 FQ	67060 MW	76740 TQ	USBLS	5/07
	Washington-Arlington-Alexandria MSA, DC-VA-MD-WV	Y	58950 FQ	71140 MW	83790 TQ	USBLS	5/07
	Florida	Y	48130 FQ	57060 MW	67090 TQ	USBLS	5/07
	Fort Lauderdale-Pompano Beach-Deerfield Beach PMSA, FL	Y	51960 FQ	61630 MW	72710 TQ	USBLS	5/07
	Jacksonville MSA, FL	Y	46140 FQ	53980 MW	62150 TQ	USBLS	5/07
	Miami-Fort Lauderdale-Miami Beach MSA, FL	Y	52530 FQ	62220 MW	74540 TQ	USBLS	5/07
	Orlando-Kissimmee MSA, FL	Y	47580 FQ	55060 MW	62670 TQ	USBLS	5/07
	Sarasota-Bradenton-Venice MSA, FL	Y	46430 FQ	54420 MW	61960 TQ	USBLS	5/07
	Tallahassee MSA, FL	Y	44810 FQ	54070 MW	62100 TQ	USBLS	5/07
	Tampa-St. Petersburg-Clearwater MSA, FL	Y	47980 FQ	56590 MW	65470 TQ	USBLS	5/07
	West Palm Beach-Boca Raton-Boynton Beach PMSA, FL	Y	53980 FQ	61800 MW	72910 TQ	USBLS	5/07
	Georgia	Y	47650 FQ	56730 MW	65510 TQ	USBLS	5/07
	Atlanta-Sandy Springs-Marietta MSA, GA	Y	50030 FQ	58590 MW	67640 TQ	USBLS	5/07
	Hawaii	Y	63480 FQ	73580 MW	85600 TQ	USBLS	5/07
	Honolulu MSA, HI	Y	64310 FQ	75060 MW	88180 TQ	USBLS	5/07
	Idaho	Y	44530 FQ	52530 MW	61690 TQ	USBLS	5/07
	Boise City-Nampa MSA, ID	Y	44950 FQ	53410 MW	61260 TQ	USBLS	5/07
	Lewiston MSA, ID-WA	Y	44160 FQ	49970 MW	58610 TQ	USBLS	5/07
	Illinois	Y	49960 FQ	59900 MW	71720 TQ	USBLS	5/07
	Chicago-Naperville-Joliet MSA, IL-IN-WI	Y	54070 FQ	62940 MW	74830 TQ	USBLS	5/07
	Indiana	Y	45260 FQ	54400 MW	63910 TQ	USBLS	5/07
	Fort Wayne MSA, IN	Y	41630 FQ	50010 MW	59240 TQ	USBLS	5/07
	Gary PMSA, IN	Y	48300 FQ	58570 MW	68970 TQ	USBLS	5/07
	Indianapolis-Carmel MSA, IN	Y	49560 FQ	59330 MW	70630 TQ	USBLS	5/07
	South Bend-Mishawaka MSA, IN-MI	Y	45850 FQ	53440 MW	60870 TQ	USBLS	5/07
	Terre Haute MSA, IN	Y	45560 FQ	54400 MW	61610 TQ	USBLS	5/07

AE	Average entry wage	AW	Average wage paid	FQ	First quartile wage	*LO	Lowest wage paid	MTC	Median total compensation	TCC	Total cash compensation
AER	Average entry range	AWR	Average wage range	H	Hourly	LR	Low end range	MW	Median wage paid	TQ	Third quartile wage
AEX	Average experienced wage	AXR	Average experienced range	HI	Highest wage paid	M	Monthly	MWR	Median wage range	W	Weekly
ATC	Average total compensation	D	Daily	HR	High end range	MCC	Median cash compensation	S	See annotated source	Y	Yearly

Occupation/Type/Industry	Location	Per	Low	Mid	High	Source	Date
Registered Nurse	Iowa	Y	41240 FQ	47920 MW	56230 TQ	USBLS	5/07
	Des Moines-West Des Moines MSA, IA	Y	43210 FQ	49600 MW	58500 TQ	USBLS	5/07
	Kansas	Y	43250 FQ	50610 MW	59830 TQ	USBLS	5/07
	Wichita MSA, KS	Y	42690 FQ	49410 MW	58230 TQ	USBLS	5/07
	Kentucky	Y	46712 FQ	55009 MW	63766 TQ	KYBLS	2008
	Louisville-Jefferson County MSA, KY-IN	Y	47420 FQ	55990 MW	64230 TQ	USBLS	5/07
	Louisiana	H	21.46 FQ	25.67 MW	30.17 TQ	LABLS	1/08-3/08
	Baton Rouge MSA, LA	Y	43570 FQ	51950 MW	63080 TQ	USBLS	5/07
	New Orleans-Metairie-Kenner MSA, LA	Y	49350 FQ	57930 MW	67170 TQ	USBLS	5/07
	Shreveport-Bossier City MSA, LA	Y	43170 FQ	51870 MW	61590 TQ	USBLS	5/07
	Maine	Y	47750 FQ	56420 MW	66170 TQ	USBLS	5/07
	Portland-South Portland-Biddeford MSA, ME	Y	52480 FQ	61240 MW	72160 TQ	USBLS	5/07
	Maryland	Y		71850 MW		MDBLS	3/08
	Baltimore-Towson MSA, MD	Y	58830 FQ	70670 MW	82830 TQ	USBLS	5/07
	Bethesda-Gaithersburg-Frederick PMSA, MD	Y	63270 FQ	76730 MW	93560 TQ	USBLS	5/07
	Massachusetts	Y	58930 FQ	71970 MW	90510 TQ	USBLS	5/07
	Boston-Cambridge-Quincy NECTA, MA	Y	62800 FQ	78480 MW	96960 TQ	USBLS	5/07
	Worcester MSA, MA-CT	Y	55330 FQ	65830 MW	87350 TQ	USBLS	5/07
	Michigan	Y	52070 FQ	59840 MW	68930 TQ	USBLS	5/07
	Ann Arbor MSA, MI	Y	54210 FQ	64820 MW	75100 TQ	USBLS	5/07
	Detroit-Warren-Livonia MSA, MI	Y	55300 FQ	63260 MW	72220 TQ	USBLS	5/07
	Grand Rapids-Wyoming MSA, MI	Y	47410 FQ	55120 MW	61560 TQ	USBLS	5/07
	Warren-Troy-Farmington Hills PMSA, MI	Y	55390 FQ	63320 MW	72420 TQ	USBLS	5/07
	Minnesota	Y	57919 FQ	69333 MW	81427 TQ	MNBLS	10/08-12/08
	Duluth-Superior MSA, MN-WI	Y	49224 FQ.	59676 MW	75621 TQ	MNBLS	10/08-12/08
	Minneapolis-Saint Paul MSA, MN-WI	Y	60995 FQ	72053 MW	83352 TQ	MNBLS	10/08-12/08
	Rochester MSA, MN	Y	65188 FQ	74645 MW	84559 TQ	MNBLS	10/08-12/08
	Mississippi	Y	43000 FQ	50460 MW	60580 TQ	USBLS	5/07
	Hattiesburg MSA, MS	Y	46110 FQ	55030 MW	65480 TQ	USBLS	5/07
	Jackson MSA, MS	Y	43450 FQ	54250 MW	64990 TQ	USBLS	5/07
	Pascagoula MSA, MS	Y	44520 FQ	49910 MW	61220 TQ	USBLS	5/07
	Missouri	Y	44430 FQ	53230 MW	63110 TQ	USBLS	5/07
	Kansas City MSA, MO-KS	Y	48200 FQ	56530 MW	65240 TQ	USBLS	5/07
	St. Joseph MSA, MO-KS	Y	45850 FQ	55630 MW	65000 TQ	USBLS	5/07
	St. Louis MSA, MO-IL	Y	44970 FQ	54460 MW	64760 TQ	USBLS	5/07
	Montana	Y	44460 FQ	52450 MW	61360 TQ	USBLS	5/07
	Billings MSA, MT	Y	48950 FQ	56820 MW	66100 TQ	USBLS	5/07
	Nebraska	Y	43210 FQ	50910 MW	60980 TQ	USBLS	5/07
	Lincoln MSA, NE	Y	42370 FQ	49340 MW	58520 TQ	USBLS	5/07
	Omaha-Council Bluffs MSA, NE-IA	Y	44600 FQ	53820 MW	64760 TQ	USBLS	5/07
	Nevada	H	28.60 FQ	33.56 MW	38.19 TQ	NVBLS	5/08
	Las Vegas-Paradise MSA, NV	H	28.75 FQ	33.69 MW	38.14 TQ	NVBLS	5/08
	New Hampshire	H	22.23 AE	28.65 MW	32.77 AEX	NHBLS	6/08
	Manchester MSA, NH	Y	52280 FQ	61440 MW	72440 TQ	USBLS	5/07
	Nashua NECTA, NH-MA	Y	49630 FQ	59240 MW	70860 TQ	USBLS	5/07
	New Jersey	Y	60760 FQ	70760 MW	80930 TQ	USBLS	5/07
	Camden PMSA, NJ	Y	56620 FQ	66030 MW	75160 TQ	USBLS	5/07
	Edison PMSA, NJ	Y	59990 FQ	69710 MW	78970 TQ	USBLS	5/07
	Newark-Union PMSA, NJ-PA	Y	63760 FQ	74350 MW	85280 TQ	USBLS	5/07
	Vineland-Millville-Bridgeton MSA, NJ	Y	55540 FQ	63610 MW	71830 TQ	USBLS	5/07
	New Mexico	Y	49750 FQ	59540 MW	69960 TQ	USBLS	5/07
	Albuquerque MSA, NM	Y	52680 FQ	62630 MW	71820 TQ	USBLS	5/07
	Farmington MSA, NM	Y	52540 FQ	58590 MW	64700 TQ	USBLS	5/07
	Las Cruces MSA, NM	Y	46910 FQ	52870 MW	70760 TQ	USBLS	5/07
	New York	Y	54160 FQ	67460 MW	82970 TQ	USBLS	5/07
	Albany-Schenectady-Troy MSA, NY	Y	46360 FQ	54900 MW	64660 TQ	USBLS	5/07
	Buffalo-Niagara Falls MSA, NY	Y	46220 FQ	55890 MW	65590 TQ	USBLS	5/07

AE	Average entry wage	AW	Average wage paid	FQ	First quartile wage	LO	Lowest wage paid	MTC	Median total compensation	TCC	Total cash compensation
AER	Average entry range	AWR	Average wage range	H	Hourly	LR	Low end range	MW	Median wage paid	TQ	Third quartile wage
AEX	Average experienced wage	AXR	Average experienced range	HI	Highest wage paid	M	Monthly	MWR	Median wage range	W	Weekly
ATC	Average total compensation	D	Daily	HR	High end range	MCC	Median cash compensation	S	See annotated source	Y	Yearly

Occupation/Type/Industry	Location	Per	Low	Mid	High	Source	Date
Registered Nurse	Kingston MSA, NY	Y	46390 FQ	55140 MW	63400 TQ	USBLS	5/07
	Nassau-Suffolk PMSA, NY	Y	63050 FQ	74580 MW	86210 TQ	USBLS	5/07
	New York-Northern New Jersey-Long Island MSA, NY-NJ-PA	Y	63620 FQ	74930 MW	88370 TQ	USBLS	5/07
	Utica-Rome MSA, NY	Y	44700 FQ	51430 MW	59590 TQ	USBLS	5/07
	North Carolina	Y	46310 FQ	54120 MW	62520 TQ	USBLS	5/07
	Charlotte-Gastonia-Concord MSA, NC-SC	Y	46590 FQ	54390 MW	62680 TQ	USBLS	5/07
	Raleigh-Cary MSA, NC	Y	49110 FQ	56260 MW	63900 TQ	USBLS	5/07
	Winston-Salem MSA, NC	Y	46820 FQ	54570 MW	63330 TQ	USBLS	5/07
	North Dakota	Y	44010 FQ	51400 MW	60440 TQ	USBLS	5/07
	Fargo MSA, ND-MN	Y	45940 FQ	53540 MW	60260 TQ	USBLS	5/07
	Grand Forks MSA, ND-MN	Y	50450 FQ	60770 MW	73720 TQ	USBLS	5/07
	Ohio	Y	48430 FQ	55990 MW	63400 TQ	USBLS	5/07
	Cincinnati-Middletown MSA, OH-KY-IN	Y	49360 FQ	57060 MW	64950 TQ	USBLS	5/07
	Cleveland-Elyria-Mentor MSA, OH	Y	52910 FQ	59260 MW	66440 TQ	USBLS	5/07
	Columbus MSA, OH	Y	47910 FQ	55580 MW	62790 TQ	USBLS	5/07
	Dayton MSA, OH	Y	47730 FQ	55770 MW	63870 TQ	USBLS	5/07
	Mansfield MSA, OH	Y	45030 FQ	53320 MW	61180 TQ	USBLS	5/07
	Springfield MSA, OH	Y	42730 FQ	50030 MW	58780 TQ	USBLS	5/07
	Oklahoma	Y	42200 FQ	49510 MW	58240 TQ	USBLS	5/07
	Lawton MSA, OK	Y	48740 FQ	55630 MW	61410 TQ	USBLS	5/07
	Oklahoma City MSA, OK	Y	42780 FQ	51170 MW	59770 TQ	USBLS	5/07
	Tulsa MSA, OK	Y	42770 FQ	50040 MW	58530 TQ	USBLS	5/07
	Oregon	H	28.19 FQ	33.18 MW	37.69 TQ	ORBLS	5/08
	Portland-Vancouver-Beaverton MSA, OR-WA	Y	59640 FQ	68970 MW	77820 TQ	USBLS	5/07
	Pennsylvania	Y	48670 FQ	58100 MW	68640 TQ	USBLS	5/07
	Allentown-Bethlehem-Easton MSA, PA-NJ	Y	52190 FQ	59670 MW	69050 TQ	USBLS	5/07
	Philadelphia-Camden-Wilmington MSA, PA-NJ-DE-MD	Y	56270 FQ	65900 MW	76830 TQ	USBLS	5/07
	Pittsburgh MSA, PA	Y	46540 FQ	55040 MW	63360 TQ	USBLS	5/07
	Rhode Island	Y	55140 FQ	65380 MW	75140 TQ	USBLS	5/07
	Providence-Fall River-Warwick MSA, RI-MA	Y	55110 FQ	64860 MW	74760 TQ	USBLS	5/07
	South Carolina	Y	46040 FQ	54280 MW	62740 TQ	USBLS	5/07
	Charleston-North Charleston MSA, SC	Y	47130 FQ	54940 MW	61860 TQ	USBLS	5/07
	Columbia MSA, SC	Y	45070 FQ	53200 MW	63840 TQ	USBLS	5/07
	South Dakota	Y	43517 FQ	50868 MW	60643 TQ	SDBLS	7/08-9/08
	Sioux Falls MSA, SD	Y	45808 FQ	52607 MW	62861 TQ	SDBLS	7/08-9/08
	Tennessee	Y	45540 FQ	53980 MW	62930 TQ	USBLS	5/07
	Johnson City MSA, TN	Y	44570 FQ	53090 MW	60850 TQ	USBLS	5/07
	Memphis MSA, TN-MS-AR	Y	49810 FQ	58000 MW	65760 TQ	USBLS	5/07
	Nashville-Davidson-Murfreesboro MSA, TN	Y	48040 FQ	57230 MW	66590 TQ	USBLS	5/07
	Texas	Y	48960 FQ	58240 MW	68490 TQ	USBLS	5/07
	Austin-Round Rock MSA, TX	Y	49410 FQ	56940 MW	65660 TQ	USBLS	5/07
	Dallas-Fort Worth-Arlington MSA, TX	Y	51490 FQ	59870 MW	71210 TQ	USBLS	5/07
	El Paso MSA, TX	Y	43740 FQ	54150 MW	64610 TQ	USBLS	5/07
	Houston-Sugar Land-Baytown MSA, TX	Y	54490 FQ	63460 MW	73980 TQ	USBLS	5/07
	San Antonio MSA, TX	Y	49410 FQ	56570 MW	63690 TQ	USBLS	5/07
	Utah	Y	46960 FQ	54810 MW	63950 TQ	USBLS	5/07
	Logan MSA, UT-ID	Y	43690 FQ	50150 MW	60660 TQ	USBLS	5/07
	Salt Lake City MSA, UT	Y	48800 FQ	57120 MW	66490 TQ	USBLS	5/07
	Vermont	Y	47820 FQ	57770 MW	69770 TQ	USBLS	5/07
	Burlington-South Burlington MSA, VT	Y	52920 FQ	66580 MW	76690 TQ	USBLS	5/07
	Virginia	Y	47130 FQ	57380 MW	68770 TQ	USBLS	5/07
	Richmond MSA, VA	Y	48820 FQ	57320 MW	65620 TQ	USBLS	5/07
	Virginia Beach-Norfolk-Newport News MSA, VA-NC	Y	47440 FQ	55570 MW	63380 TQ	USBLS	5/07
	Washington	H	26.79 FQ	32.51 MW	38.73 TQ	WABLS	3/08
	Olympia MSA, WA	Y	57740 FQ	69120 MW	78940 TQ	USBLS	5/07

AE	Average entry wage	AW	Average wage paid	FQ	First quartile wage	LO	Lowest wage paid	MTC Median total compensation TCC Total cash compensation
AER	Average entry range	AWR	Average wage range	H	Hourly	LR	Low end range	MW Median wage paid TQ Third quartile wage
AEX	Average experienced wage	AXR	Average experienced range	HI	Highest wage paid	M	Monthly	MWR Median wage range W Weekly
ATC	Average total compensation	D	Daily	HR	High end range	MCC	Median cash compensation	S See annotated source Y Yearly

Occupation/Type/Industry	Location	Per	Low	Mid	High	Source	Date
Registered Nurse	Seattle-Tacoma-Bellevue MSA, WA	Y	59240 FQ	71750 MW	84000 TQ	USBLS	5/07
	West Virginia	Y	42997 FQ	50519 MW	61343 TQ	WVBLS	7/08-9/08
	Charleston MSA, WV	Y	43260 FQ	50560 MW	60500 TQ	USBLS	5/07
	Wisconsin	Y	50950 FQ	58710 MW	67990 TQ	USBLS	5/07
	Appleton MSA, WI	Y	50370 FQ	56430 MW	62620 TQ	USBLS	5/07
	Milwaukee-Waukesha-West Allis MSA, WI	Y	51600 FQ	60070 MW	69600 TQ	USBLS	5/07
	Wyoming	Y	45641 FQ	53563 MW	62981 TQ	WYBLS	9/08
	Cheyenne MSA, WY	Y	49255 FQ	58761 MW	66870 TQ	WYBLS	9/08
	Puerto Rico	Y	19240 FQ	24020 MW	29860 TQ	USBLS	5/07
	San German-Cabo Rojo MSA, PR	Y	18030 FQ	20990 MW	24440 TQ	USBLS	5/07
	San Juan-Caguas-Guaynabo MSA, PR	Y	20320 FQ	25160 MW	30310 TQ	USBLS	5/07
	Guam	Y	34820 FQ	47800 MW	60450 TQ	USBLS	5/07
Veterans Home	Vermont	Y	46432 LO		72284 HI	AFT02	3/1/08
Registered Nurse Substitute							
Public Schools	Baldwin County, AL	H			13.00 HI	BCPSSS	2008-2009
Registered Polysomnographic Technologist	New England	Y		56830 AW		SLEEP	2008
	Pacific	Y		59063 AW		SLEEP	2008
Registrar							
Department of Regional Community Technical Colleges	New Hampshire	Y		42478 AW		NHUL03	2008
Regulatory Compliance Specialist							
Environmental Protection	United States	Y		70083 AW		EPROT	2008
Regulatory Economist							
State Government	Missouri	Y	49668 LO		70944 HI	AFT02	3/1/08
Rehabilitation Counselor	Alabama	Y	27370 FQ	34850 MW	48760 TQ	USBLS	5/07
	Birmingham-Hoover MSA, AL	Y	25660 FQ	31250 MW	47200 TQ	USBLS	5/07
	Mobile MSA, AL	Y	34930 FQ	41460 MW	51830 TQ	USBLS	5/07
	Arizona	Y	22240 FQ	28640 MW	37470 TQ	USBLS	5/07
	Phoenix-Mesa-Scottsdale MSA, AZ	Y	21800 FQ	25220 MW	35150 TQ	USBLS	5/07
	Tucson MSA, AZ	Y	25020 FQ	34900 MW	39070 TQ	USBLS	5/07
	Arkansas	Y	24440 FQ	30520 MW	38190 TQ	USBLS	5/07
	Little Rock-North Little Rock MSA, AR	Y	26260 FQ	33380 MW	39690 TQ	USBLS	5/07
	California	H	13.96 FQ	19.01 MW	26.07 TQ	CABLS	1/08-3/08
	Los Angeles-Long Beach-Glendale PMSA, CA	H	15.88 FQ	23.01 MW	28.51 TQ	CABLS	1/08-3/08
	Oakland-Fremont-Hayward MSA, CA	H	15.01 FQ	19.43 MW	30.17 TQ	CABLS	1/08-3/08
	Oxnard-Thousand Oaks-Ventura MSA, CA	H	13.97 FQ	15.74 MW	24.43 TQ	CABLS	1/08-3/08
	Riverside-San Bernardino-Ontario MSA, CA	H	15.00 FQ	20.34 MW	26.83 TQ	CABLS	1/08-3/08
	Sacramento-Arden Arcade-Roseville MSA, CA	H	11.34 FQ	14.44 MW	22.39 TQ	CABLS	1/08-3/08
	San Diego-Carlsbad-San Marcos MSA, CA	H	13.28 FQ	17.93 MW	23.36 TQ	CABLS	1/08-3/08
	San Francisco-San Mateo-Redwood PMSA, CA	H	14.77 FQ	17.46 MW	29.56 TQ	CABLS	1/08-3/08
	San Jose-Sunnyvale-Santa Clara MSA, CA	H	18.80 FQ	21.03 MW	23.58 TQ	CABLS	1/08-3/08
	Santa Ana-Anaheim-Irvine PMSA, CA	Y	27550 FQ	35910 MW	57090 TQ	USBLS	5/07
	Colorado	Y	25020 FQ	31580 MW	40730 TQ	USBLS	5/07
	Denver-Aurora MSA, CO	Y	24130 FQ	31970 MW	44790 TQ	USBLS	5/07
	Connecticut	H	12.97 AE	17.10 MW		CTBLS	1/08-3/08
	Bridgeport-Stamford-Norwalk MSA, CT	Y	29590 FQ	36060 MW	56410 TQ	USBLS	5/07
	Hartford-West Hartford-East Hartford MSA, CT	Y	31650 FQ	39730 MW	55580 TQ	USBLS	5/07
	Delaware	Y	27790 FQ	33950 MW	42450 TQ	USBLS	5/07

AE	Average entry wage	**AW**	Average wage paid	**FQ**	First quartile wage
AER	Average entry range	**AWR**	Average wage range	**H**	Hourly
AEX	Average experienced wage	**AXR**	Average experienced range	**HI**	Highest wage paid
ATC	Average total compensation	**D**	Daily	**HR**	High end range

LO	Lowest wage paid	**MTC**	Median total compensation	**TCC** Total cash compensation
LR	Low end range	**MW**	Median wage paid	**TQ** Third quartile wage
M	Monthly	**MWR**	Median wage range	**W** Weekly
MCC	Median cash compensation	**S**	See annotated source	**Y** Yearly

Rehabilitation Counselor

Occupation/Type/Industry	Location	Per	Low	Mid	High	Source	Date
Rehabilitation Counselor	Wilmington PMSA, DE-MD-NJ	Y	25230 FQ	32620 MW	41420 TQ	USBLS	5/07
	District of Columbia	Y	21550 FQ	27440 MW	47090 TQ	USBLS	5/07
	Washington-Arlington-Alexandria MSA, DC-VA-MD-WV	Y	23010 FQ	29000 MW	38990 TQ	USBLS	5/07
	Florida	Y	26950 FQ	32370 MW	39600 TQ	USBLS	5/07
	Fort Lauderdale-Pompano Beach-Deerfield Beach PMSA, FL	Y	21020 FQ	28940 MW	37370 TQ	USBLS	5/07
	Jacksonville MSA, FL	Y	23640 FQ	31130 MW	40280 TQ	USBLS	5/07
	Miami-Fort Lauderdale-Miami Beach MSA, FL	Y	26840 FQ	32410 MW	41220 TQ	USBLS	5/07
	Orlando-Kissimmee MSA, FL	Y	28420 FQ	33130 MW	38620 TQ	USBLS	5/07
	Tampa-St. Petersburg-Clearwater MSA, FL	Y	29720 FQ	35170 MW	40460 TQ	USBLS	5/07
	West Palm Beach-Boca Raton-Boynton Beach PMSA, FL	Y	28270 FQ	36980 MW	45570 TQ	USBLS	5/07
	Georgia	Y	26380 FQ	36760 MW	46630 TQ	USBLS	5/07
	Atlanta-Sandy Springs-Marietta MSA, GA	Y	28410 FQ	38720 MW	47120 TQ	USBLS	5/07
	Hawaii	Y	30430 FQ	40680 MW	56930 TQ	USBLS	5/07
	Honolulu MSA, HI	Y	29330 FQ	34910 MW	54670 TQ	USBLS	5/07
	Idaho	Y	24120 FQ	35150 MW	43420 TQ	USBLS	5/07
	Boise City-Nampa MSA, ID	Y	27330 FQ	36460 MW	44180 TQ	USBLS	5/07
	Illinois	Y	22870 FQ	29270 MW	39970 TQ	USBLS	5/07
	Chicago-Naperville-Joliet MSA, IL-IN-WI	Y	26460 FQ	32290 MW	44070 TQ	USBLS	5/07
	Indiana	Y	22420 FQ	27660 MW	37620 TQ	USBLS	5/07
	Gary PMSA, IN	Y	22540 FQ	35930 MW	55350 TQ	USBLS	5/07
	Indianapolis-Carmel MSA, IN	Y	23330 FQ	27970 MW	40110 TQ	USBLS	5/07
	South Bend-Mishawaka MSA, IN-MI	Y	27560 FQ	32000 MW	41530 TQ	USBLS	5/07
	Iowa	Y	19510 FQ	26340 MW	35660 TQ	USBLS	5/07
	Des Moines-West Des Moines MSA, IA	Y	19950 FQ	24840 MW	37140 TQ	USBLS	5/07
	Sioux City MSA, IA-NE-SD	Y	22610 FQ	32900 MW	36470 TQ	USBLS	5/07
	Kansas	Y	20750 FQ	25340 MW	32380 TQ	USBLS	5/07
	Kentucky	Y	25092 FQ	30407 MW	39039 TQ	KYBLS	2008
	Louisville-Jefferson County MSA, KY-IN	Y	24520 FQ	28770 MW	35510 TQ	USBLS	5/07
	Louisiana	H	13.79 FQ	17.78 MW	22.49 TQ	LABLS	1/08-3/08
	Baton Rouge MSA, LA	Y	27260 FQ	32040 MW	37820 TQ	USBLS	5/07
	Lafayette MSA, LA	Y	44440 FQ	51360 MW	64340 TQ	USBLS	5/07
	New Orleans-Metairie-Kenner MSA, LA	Y	29780 FQ	39010 MW	50430 TQ	USBLS	5/07
	Maine	Y	23780 FQ	35640 MW	46670 TQ	USBLS	5/07
	Lewiston-Auburn MSA, ME	Y	22020 FQ	33260 MW	73280 TQ	USBLS	5/07
	Portland-South Portland-Biddeford MSA, ME	Y	21460 FQ	23730 MW	39590 TQ	USBLS	5/07
	Maryland	Y		25550 MW		MDBLS	3/08
	Baltimore-Towson MSA, MD	Y	22220 FQ	25910 MW	38190 TQ	USBLS	5/07
	Bethesda-Gaithersburg-Frederick PMSA, MD	Y	22160 FQ	25850 MW	31980 TQ	USBLS	5/07
	Massachusetts	Y	26340 FQ	31990 MW	44750 TQ	USBLS	5/07
	Boston-Cambridge-Quincy NECTA, MA	Y	26730 FQ	33300 MW	44010 TQ	USBLS	5/07
	Worcester MSA, MA-CT	Y	24340 FQ	40430 MW	59830 TQ	USBLS	5/07
	Michigan	Y	31070 FQ	46260 MW	59270 TQ	USBLS	5/07
	Detroit-Warren-Livonia MSA, MI	Y	27610 FQ	44900 MW	59000 TQ	USBLS	5/07
	Grand Rapids-Wyoming MSA, MI	Y	50020 FQ	57780 MW	65140 TQ	USBLS	5/07
	Warren-Troy-Farmington Hills PMSA, MI	Y	25190 FQ	36200 MW	56780 TQ	USBLS	5/07
	Minnesota	Y	32443 FQ	38134 MW	47885 TQ	MNBLS	10/08-12/08
	Duluth-Superior MSA, MN-WI	Y	29315 FQ	32977 MW	45814 TQ	MNBLS	10/08-12/08
	Minneapolis-Saint Paul MSA, MN-WI	Y	32610 FQ	37392 MW	45353 TQ	MNBLS	10/08-12/08
	Rochester MSA, MN	Y	31324 FQ	36417 MW	46458 TQ	MNBLS	10/08-12/08
	Mississippi	Y	25250 FQ	31970 MW	40960 TQ	USBLS	5/07
	Jackson MSA, MS	Y	28620 FQ	37240 MW	45380 TQ	USBLS	5/07

AE	Average entry wage	AW	Average wage paid	FQ First quartile wage
AER	Average entry range	AWR	Average wage range	H Hourly
AEX	Average experienced wage	AXR	Average experienced range	HI Highest wage paid
ATC	Average total compensation	D	Daily	HR High end range

LO	Lowest wage paid	MTC	Median total compensation	TCC	Total cash compensation
LR	Low end range	MW	Median wage paid	TQ	Third quartile wage
M	Monthly	MWR	Median wage range	W	Weekly
MCC	Median cash compensation	S	See annotated source	Y	Yearly

Occupation/Type/Industry	Location	Per	Low	Mid	High	Source	Date
Rehabilitation Counselor	Missouri	Y	26710 FQ	30350 MW	36110 TQ	USBLS	5/07
	Kansas City MSA, MO-KS	Y	25580 FQ	29850 MW	35750 TQ	USBLS	5/07
	St. Louis MSA, MO-IL	Y	25480 FQ	29320 MW	34910 TQ	USBLS	5/07
	Montana	Y	23310 FQ	29360 MW	36550 TQ	USBLS	5/07
	Billings MSA, MT	Y	29080 FQ	33630 MW	44000 TQ	USBLS	5/07
	Nebraska	Y	20950 FQ	24310 MW	30600 TQ	USBLS	5/07
	Omaha-Council Bluffs MSA, NE-IA	Y	21830 FQ	24730 MW	30980 TQ	USBLS	5/07
	Nevada	H	13.09 FQ	15.12 MW	20.53 TQ	NVBLS	5/08
	Las Vegas-Paradise MSA, NV	H	12.90 FQ	15.02 MW	19.78 TQ	NVBLS	5/08
	New Hampshire	H	11.41 AE	14.45 MW	20.99 AEX	NHBLS	6/08
	Manchester MSA, NH	Y	40410 FQ	55020 MW	66790 TQ	USBLS	5/07
	Rochester-Dover MSA, NH-ME	Y	23410 FQ	26600 MW	30060 TQ	USBLS	5/07
	New Jersey	Y	26310 FQ	34840 MW	45790 TQ	USBLS	5/07
	Camden PMSA, NJ	Y	28270 FQ	38820 MW	54140 TQ	USBLS	5/07
	Edison PMSA, NJ	Y	23930 FQ	31320 MW	41750 TQ	USBLS	5/07
	Newark-Union PMSA, NJ-PA	Y	29920 FQ	35550 MW	44000 TQ	USBLS	5/07
	Vineland-Millville-Bridgeton MSA, NJ	Y	21720 FQ	24070 MW	27740 TQ	USBLS	5/07
	New Mexico	Y	25330 FQ	32630 MW	43830 TQ	USBLS	5/07
	Albuquerque MSA, NM	Y	24270 FQ	33030 MW	41490 TQ	USBLS	5/07
	New York	Y	21190 FQ	24390 MW	29460 TQ	USBLS	5/07
	Albany-Schenectady-Troy MSA, NY	Y	21050 FQ	22710 MW	24490 TQ	USBLS	5/07
	Buffalo-Niagara Falls MSA, NY	Y	20190 FQ	22760 MW	25740 TQ	USBLS	5/07
	Nassau-Suffolk PMSA, NY	Y	22190 FQ	24950 MW	29870 TQ	USBLS	5/07
	New York-Northern New Jersey-Long Island MSA, NY-NJ-PA	Y	22920 FQ	27380 MW	33330 TQ	USBLS	5/07
	North Carolina	Y	23700 FQ	30380 MW	37650 TQ	USBLS	5/07
	Charlotte-Gastonia-Concord MSA, NC-SC	Y	23120 FQ	32790 MW	45670 TQ	USBLS	5/07
	Raleigh-Cary MSA, NC	Y	30240 FQ	34410 MW	39070 TQ	USBLS	5/07
	North Dakota	Y	24440 FQ	35760 MW	43240 TQ	USBLS	5/07
	Fargo MSA, ND-MN	Y	31180 FQ	37140 MW	45650 TQ	USBLS	5/07
	Ohio	Y	27930 FQ	37720 MW	49940 TQ	USBLS	5/07
	Cincinnati-Middletown MSA, OH-KY-IN	Y	28600 FQ	37680 MW	49410 TQ	USBLS	5/07
	Cleveland-Elyria-Mentor MSA, OH	Y	33470 FQ	42880 MW	53730 TQ	USBLS	5/07
	Columbus MSA, OH	Y	30070 FQ	40050 MW	52600 TQ	USBLS	5/07
	Dayton MSA, OH	Y	30350 FQ	37800 MW	50380 TQ	USBLS	5/07
	Oklahoma	Y	17450 FQ	21930 MW	29300 TQ	USBLS	5/07
	Oklahoma City MSA, OK	Y	19310 FQ	23490 MW	29990 TQ	USBLS	5/07
	Tulsa MSA, OK	Y	16820 FQ	18630 MW	23850 TQ	USBLS	5/07
	Oregon	H	10.87 FQ	13.95 MW	20.58 TQ	ORBLS	5/08
	Portland-Vancouver-Beaverton MSA, OR-WA	Y	22510 FQ	30010 MW	37250 TQ	USBLS	5/07
	Pennsylvania	Y	23420 FQ	29390 MW	42860 TQ	USBLS	5/07
	Allentown-Bethlehem-Easton MSA, PA-NJ	Y	24890 FQ	29230 MW	36760 TQ	USBLS	5/07
	Philadelphia-Camden-Wilmington MSA, PA-NJ-DE-MD	Y	23350 FQ	29050 MW	42560 TQ	USBLS	5/07
	Pittsburgh MSA, PA	Y	23530 FQ	32220 MW	45250 TQ	USBLS	5/07
	Reading MSA, PA	Y	27940 FQ	35980 MW	48090 TQ	USBLS	5/07
	Rhode Island	Y	36250 FQ	48800 MW	58180 TQ	USBLS	5/07
	Providence-Fall River-Warwick MSA, RI-MA	Y	32640 FQ	44280 MW	56780 TQ	USBLS	5/07
	South Carolina	Y	23730 FQ	32170 MW	39410 TQ	USBLS	5/07
	Columbia MSA, SC	Y	29860 FQ	36220 MW	43520 TQ	USBLS	5/07
	South Dakota	Y	28282 FQ	32764 MW	38500 TQ	SDBLS	7/08-9/08
	Sioux Falls MSA, SD	Y	28289 FQ	34016 MW	39069 TQ	SDBLS	7/08-9/08
	Tennessee	Y	17770 FQ	21720 MW	31100 TQ	USBLS	5/07
	Memphis MSA, TN-MS-AR	Y	31310 FQ	35840 MW	40500 TQ	USBLS	5/07
	Nashville-Davidson-Murfreesboro MSA, TN	Y	17350 FQ	19370 MW	27480 TQ	USBLS	5/07
	Texas	Y	24440 FQ	31770 MW	38520 TQ	USBLS	5/07
	Austin-Round Rock MSA, TX	Y	28540 FQ	34920 MW	41720 TQ	USBLS	5/07

AE Average entry wage	AW Average wage paid	FQ First quartile wage	LO Lowest wage paid	MTC Median total compensation	TCC Total cash compensation
AER Average entry range	AWR Average wage range	H Hourly	LR Low end range	MW Median wage paid	TQ Third quartile wage
AEX Average experienced wage	AXR Average experienced range	HI Highest wage paid	M Monthly	MWR Median wage range	W Weekly
ATC Average total compensation	D Daily	HR High end range	MCC Median cash compensation	S See annotated source	Y Yearly

Occupation/Type/Industry	Location	Per	Low	Mid	High	Source	Date
Rehabilitation Counselor	Dallas-Fort Worth-Arlington MSA, TX	Y	25020 FQ	32810 MW	39190 TQ	USBLS	5/07
	El Paso MSA, TX	Y	18310 FQ	23510 MW	30540 TQ	USBLS	5/07
	Houston-Sugar Land-Baytown MSA, TX	Y	29900 FQ	34810 MW	39560 TQ	USBLS	5/07
	San Antonio MSA, TX	Y	26470 FQ	34830 MW	50810 TQ	USBLS	5/07
	Vermont	Y	38640 FQ	46190 MW	53430 TQ	USBLS	5/07
	Burlington-South Burlington MSA, VT	Y	42570 FQ	49440 MW	56650 TQ	USBLS	5/07
	Virginia	Y	22270 FQ	28430 MW	38010 TQ	USBLS	5/07
	Richmond MSA, VA	Y	22730 FQ	29540 MW	40550 TQ	USBLS	5/07
	Virginia Beach-Norfolk-Newport News MSA, VA-NC	Y	20400 FQ	24550 MW	31810 TQ	USBLS	5/07
	Washington	H	12.83 FQ	17.25 MW	21.93 TQ	WABLS	3/08
	Seattle-Tacoma-Bellevue MSA, WA	Y	25290 FQ	34420 MW	42760 TQ	USBLS	5/07
	West Virginia	Y	28208 FQ	35513 MW	42232 TQ	WVBLS	7/08-9/08
	Charleston MSA, WV	Y	33770 FQ	39210 MW	47950 TQ	USBLS	5/07
	Wisconsin	Y	25070 FQ	32730 MW	42840 TQ	USBLS	5/07
	Milwaukee-Waukesha-West Allis MSA, WI	Y	25110 FQ	33800 MW	45920 TQ	USBLS	5/07
	Wyoming	Y	34671 FQ	38431 MW	44690 TQ	WYBLS	9/08
	Puerto Rico	Y	27230 FQ	33160 MW	38970 TQ	USBLS	5/07
	San Juan-Caguas-Guaynabo MSA, PR	Y	27730 FQ	33490 MW	39190 TQ	USBLS	5/07
Reimbursement Analyst	Virginia	Y	40959-53510 LR		84062-109818 HR	VACG05	11/25/07
Reinforcing Iron and Rebar Worker	Alabama	Y	25650 FQ	29770 MW	38000 TQ	USBLS	5/07
	Birmingham-Hoover MSA, AL	Y	25330 FQ	30350 MW	41100 TQ	USBLS	5/07
	Alaska	Y	63370 FQ	67940 MW	72900 TQ	USBLS	5/07
	Arizona	Y	23730 FQ	32270 MW	45090 TQ	USBLS	5/07
	Phoenix-Mesa-Scottsdale MSA, AZ	Y	26370 FQ	33380 MW	50550 TQ	USBLS	5/07
	Tucson MSA, AZ	Y	16110 FQ	21820 MW	35160 TQ	USBLS	5/07
	Arkansas	Y	24520 FQ	29190 MW	35960 TQ	USBLS	5/07
	California	H	15.40 FQ	24.50 MW	32.16 TQ	CABLS	1/08-3/08
	Los Angeles-Long Beach-Glendale PMSA, CA	H	10.27 FQ	17.07 MW	31.59 TQ	CABLS	1/08-3/08
	Oakland-Fremont-Hayward MSA, CA	H	28.24 FQ	32.32 MW	36.66 TQ	CABLS	1/08-3/08
	Riverside-San Bernardino-Ontario MSA, CA	H	15.92 FQ	26.00 MW	33.95 TQ	CABLS	1/08-3/08
	Sacramento-Arden Arcade-Roseville MSA, CA	H	13.25 FQ	17.64 MW	26.68 TQ	CABLS	1/08-3/08
	San Diego-Carlsbad-San Marcos MSA, CA	H	18.25 FQ	26.51 MW	32.38 TQ	CABLS	1/08-3/08
	San Francisco-San Mateo-Redwood PMSA, CA	H	27.09 FQ	29.23 MW	31.37 TQ	CABLS	1/08-3/08
	San Jose-Sunnyvale-Santa Clara MSA, CA	H	14.15 FQ	18.58 MW	21.78 TQ	CABLS	1/08-3/08
	Santa Ana-Anaheim-Irvine PMSA, CA	Y	31530 FQ	47810 MW	61700 TQ	USBLS	5/07
	Colorado	Y	32180 FQ	41740 MW	47120 TQ	USBLS	5/07
	Denver-Aurora MSA, CO	Y	28980 FQ	35300 MW	53010 TQ	USBLS	5/07
	Delaware	Y	32520 FQ	35500 MW	54560 TQ	USBLS	5/07
	Wilmington PMSA, DE-MD-NJ	Y	33500 FQ	37970 MW	56940 TQ	USBLS	5/07
	Washington-Arlington-Alexandria MSA, DC-VA-MD-WV	Y	37120 FQ	43670 MW	49180 TQ	USBLS	5/07
	Florida	Y	26610 FQ	32480 MW	36680 TQ	USBLS	5/07
	Cape Coral-Fort Myers MSA, FL	Y	20380 FQ	21760 MW	23140 TQ	USBLS	5/07
	Fort Lauderdale-Pompano Beach-Deerfield Beach PMSA, FL	Y	29730 FQ	33290 MW	36590 TQ	USBLS	5/07
	Jacksonville MSA, FL	Y	24790 FQ	29240 MW	34280 TQ	USBLS	5/07
	Miami-Fort Lauderdale-Miami Beach MSA, FL	Y	28570 FQ	33220 MW	36920 TQ	USBLS	5/07

AE	Average entry wage	AW	Average wage paid	FQ	First quartile wage	LO	Lowest wage paid	MTC	Median total compensation	TCC	Total cash compensation
AER	Average entry range	AWR	Average wage range	H	Hourly	LR	Low end range	MW	Median wage paid	TQ	Third quartile wage
AEX	Average experienced wage	AXR	Average experienced range	HI	Highest wage paid	M	Monthly	MWR	Median wage range	W	Weekly
ATC	Average total compensation	D	Daily	HR	High end range	MCC	Median cash compensation	S	See annotated source	Y	Yearly

1391

Occupation/Type/Industry	Location	Per	Low	Mid	High	Source	Date
Reinforcing Iron and Rebar Worker	Orlando-Kissimmee MSA, FL	Y	32120 FQ	34930 MW	37780 TQ	USBLS	~5/07
	Tampa-St. Petersburg-Clearwater MSA, FL	Y	30960 FQ	34340 MW	37330 TQ	USBLS	5/07
	Georgia	Y	27520 FQ	31220 MW	39240 TQ	USBLS	5/07
	Atlanta-Sandy Springs-Marietta MSA, GA	Y	27930 FQ	31380 MW	40270 TQ	USBLS	5/07
	Hawaii	Y	34480 FQ	44200 MW	67430 TQ	USBLS	5/07
	Honolulu MSA, HI	Y	34460 FQ	44250 MW	67560 TQ	USBLS	5/07
	Idaho	Y	37750 FQ	45730 MW	49720 TQ	USBLS	5/07
	Illinois	Y	69560 FQ	77560 MW	84870 TQ	USBLS	5/07
	Chicago-Naperville-Joliet MSA, IL-IN-WI	Y	71000 FQ	79530 MW	87920 TQ	USBLS	5/07
	Indiana	Y	30980 FQ	43810 MW	53410 TQ	USBLS	5/07
	Gary PMSA, IN	Y	37390 FQ	47010 MW	61030 TQ	USBLS	5/07
	Indianapolis-Carmel MSA, IN	Y	30550 FQ	42150 MW	51370 TQ	USBLS	5/07
	Iowa	Y	34970 FQ	42060 MW	47760 TQ	USBLS	5/07
	Kansas	Y	20250 FQ	34310 MW	41500 TQ	USBLS	5/07
	Kentucky	Y	30882 FQ	37814 MW	47089 TQ	KYBLS	2008
	Louisville-Jefferson County MSA, KY-IN	Y	32480 FQ	36580 MW	44430 TQ	USBLS	5/07
	Louisiana	H	15.82 FQ	20.88 MW	23.41 TQ	LABLS	1/08-3/08
	Baton Rouge MSA, LA	Y	38760 FQ	44940 MW	49200 TQ	USBLS	5/07
	Maryland	Y		42250 MW		MDBLS	3/08
	Baltimore-Towson MSA, MD	Y	33910 FQ	39490 MW	50070 TQ	USBLS	5/07
	Bethesda-Gaithersburg-Frederick PMSA, MD	Y	36150 FQ	41560 MW	48190 TQ	USBLS	5/07
	Massachusetts	Y	32100 FQ	53750 MW	63370 TQ	USBLS	5/07
	Boston-Cambridge-Quincy NECTA, MA	Y	33150 FQ	55350 MW	64470 TQ	USBLS	5/07
	Michigan	Y	34010 FQ	53450 MW	58970 TQ	USBLS	5/07
	Detroit-Warren-Livonia MSA, MI	Y	34470 FQ	52100 MW	58400 TQ	USBLS	5/07
	Minnesota	Y	56909 FQ	62326 MW	67859 TQ	MNBLS	10/08-12/08
	Duluth-Superior MSA, MN-WI	Y	38550 FQ	56877 MW	64444 TQ	MNBLS	10/08-12/08
	Minneapolis-Saint Paul MSA, MN-WI	Y	59259 FQ	64022 MW	68512 TQ	MNBLS	10/08-12/08
	Mississippi	Y	23610 FQ	28020 MW	31910 TQ	USBLS	5/07
	Missouri	Y	34090 FQ	48070 MW	62550 TQ	USBLS	5/07
	Kansas City MSA, MO-KS	Y	28850 FQ	37970 MW	60230 TQ	USBLS	5/07
	St. Louis MSA, MO-IL	Y	51020 FQ	59020 MW	65900 TQ	USBLS	5/07
	Nebraska	Y	34280 FQ	40950 MW	48570 TQ	USBLS	5/07
	Omaha-Council Bluffs MSA, NE-IA	Y	36660 FQ	43630 MW	50500 TQ	USBLS	5/07
	Nevada	H	16.04 FQ	24.13 MW	30.81 TQ	NVBLS	5/08
	Las Vegas-Paradise MSA, NV	H	16.52 FQ	24.81 MW	30.85 TQ	NVBLS	5/08
	Reno-Sparks MSA, NV	H	17.65 FQ	26.93 MW	33.25 TQ	NVBLS	5/08
	New Hampshire	H	13.23 AE	18.24 MW	23.63 AEX	NHBLS	6/08
	New Jersey	Y	33910 FQ	65210 MW	73960 TQ	USBLS	5/07
	Camden PMSA, NJ	Y	70570 FQ	75750 MW	81210 TQ	USBLS	5/07
	Edison PMSA, NJ	Y	28080 FQ	37830 MW	65960 TQ	USBLS	5/07
	New Mexico	Y	21320 FQ	23280 MW	26060 TQ	USBLS	5/07
	Albuquerque MSA, NM	Y	20890 FQ	22790 MW	27450 TQ	USBLS	5/07
	New York	Y	50190 FQ	63380 MW	85870 TQ	USBLS	5/07
	Nassau-Suffolk PMSA, NY	Y	54590 FQ	63260 MW	90740 TQ	USBLS	5/07
	New York-Northern New Jersey-Long Island MSA, NY-NJ-PA	Y	45130 FQ	64640 MW	78920 TQ	USBLS	5/07
	North Carolina	Y	26440 FQ	33910 MW	39770 TQ	USBLS	5/07
	Charlotte-Gastonia-Concord MSA, NC-SC	Y	24530 FQ	30410 MW	36650 TQ	USBLS	5/07
	North Dakota	Y	27360 FQ	32660 MW	42080 TQ	USBLS	5/07
	Ohio	Y	39640 FQ	54440 MW	60270 TQ	USBLS	5/07
	Cincinnati-Middletown MSA, OH-KY-IN	Y	28790 FQ	48690 MW	54710 TQ	USBLS	5/07
	Cleveland-Elyria-Mentor MSA, OH	Y	35110 FQ	53520 MW	61390 TQ	USBLS	5/07
	Oklahoma	Y	25490 FQ	30310 MW	33970 TQ	USBLS	5/07
	Tulsa MSA, OK	Y	25610 FQ	30710 MW	34400 TQ	USBLS	5/07
	Oregon	H	23.90 FQ	29.63 MW	34.40 TQ	ORBLS	5/08
	Portland-Vancouver-Beaverton MSA, OR-WA	Y	48270 FQ	61020 MW	70060 TQ	USBLS	5/07

AE	Average entry wage	AW	Average wage paid	FQ	First quartile wage	LO	Lowest wage paid	MTC	Median total compensation	TCC	Total cash compensation
AER	Average entry range	AWR	Average wage range	H	Hourly	LR	Low end range	MW	Median wage paid	TQ	Third quartile wage
AEX	Average experienced wage	AXR	Average experienced range	HI	Highest wage paid	M	Monthly	MWR	Median wage range	W	Weekly
ATC	Average total compensation	D	Daily	HR	High end range	MCC	Median cash compensation	S	See annotated source	Y	Yearly

Occupation/Type/Industry	Location	Per	Low	Mid	High	Source	Date
Reinforcing Iron and Rebar Worker	Pennsylvania	Y	39380 FQ	57520 MW	63980 TQ	USBLS	5/07
	Philadelphia-Camden-Wilmington MSA, PA-NJ-DE-MD	Y	36340 FQ	61300 MW	74960 TQ	USBLS	5/07
	Pittsburgh MSA, PA	Y	53890 FQ	59320 MW	64670 TQ	USBLS	5/07
	South Carolina	Y	28320 FQ	31860 MW	36630 TQ	USBLS	5/07
	Columbia MSA, SC	Y	26540 FQ	29460 MW	32480 TQ	USBLS	5/07
	South Dakota	Y	24943 FQ	29249 MW	33085 TQ	SDBLS	7/08-9/08
	Sioux Falls MSA, SD	Y	28170 FQ	30583 MW	32995 TQ	SDBLS	7/08-9/08
	Tennessee	Y	26450 FQ	30420 MW	36380 TQ	USBLS	5/07
	Memphis MSA, TN-MS-AR	Y	26060 FQ	28820 MW	31590 TQ	USBLS	5/07
	Texas	Y	24440 FQ	28040 MW	31940 TQ	USBLS	5/07
	Austin-Round Rock MSA, TX	Y	23350 FQ	26780 MW	30800 TQ	USBLS	5/07
	Dallas-Fort Worth-Arlington MSA, TX	Y	23110 FQ	26910 MW	30660 TQ	USBLS	5/07
	El Paso MSA, TX	Y	27810 FQ	31720 MW	37570 TQ	USBLS	5/07
	Houston-Sugar Land-Baytown MSA, TX	Y	25220 FQ	28700 MW	33330 TQ	USBLS	5/07
	San Antonio MSA, TX	Y	25190 FQ	29040 MW	33020 TQ	USBLS	5/07
	Utah	Y	27410 FQ	43170 MW	51070 TQ	USBLS	5/07
	Salt Lake City MSA, UT	Y	34270 FQ	46010 MW	51210 TQ	USBLS	5/07
	Virginia	Y	33720 FQ	39270 MW	47990 TQ	USBLS	5/07
	Richmond MSA, VA	Y	35580 FQ	40310 MW	50050 TQ	USBLS	5/07
	Virginia Beach-Norfolk-Newport News MSA, VA-NC	Y	36620 FQ	45250 MW	50270 TQ	USBLS	5/07
	West Virginia	Y	45569 FQ	56598 MW	63164 TQ	WVBLS	7/08-9/08
	Charleston MSA, WV	Y	49450 FQ	54150 MW	60320 TQ	USBLS	5/07
	Wisconsin	Y	34590 FQ	50250 MW	58390 TQ	USBLS	5/07
	Puerto Rico	Y	14140 FQ	16340 MW	18220 TQ	USBLS	5/07
	San Juan-Caguas-Guaynabo MSA, PR	Y	15560 FQ	17120 MW	18600 TQ	USBLS	5/07
	Virgin Islands	Y	28030 FQ	33650 MW	38420 TQ	USBLS	5/07
	Guam	Y	22400 FQ	24660 MW	27880 TQ	USBLS	5/07
Religious Services Administrator State Government	Ohio	H	25.40 LO		33.16 HI	ODAS	2008
Rental Housing Inspector Municipal Government	Gresham, OR	Y	47892 LO		60576 HI	GOSS	1/1/09
Reporter							
Catholic News Service	United States	W	1268 LO			NEWG	2008
Consumer Reports	United States	W	1804 LO			NEWG	2008
Detroit Free Press	United States	W	910 LO			NEWG	2008
Detroit News	United States	W	841 LO			NEWG	2008
El Vocero de Puerto Rico	San Juan, PR	W	715 LO			NEWG	2008
New York Times	United States	W	1675 LO			NEWG	2008
New York Times Digital	United States	W	1140 LO			NEWG	2008
Newsweek	United States	W	741 LO			NEWG	2008
Scholastic Magazine	United States	W	576 LO			NEWG	2008
Time	United States	W	882 LO			NEWG	2008
Wall Street Journal	United States	W	1258 LO			NEWG	2008
Reporter and Correspondent	Alabama	Y	19570 FQ	24680 MW	36580 TQ	USBLS	5/07
	Birmingham-Hoover MSA, AL	Y	22900 FQ	35580 MW	47810 TQ	USBLS	5/07
	Alaska	Y	30060 FQ	35290 MW	40570 TQ	USBLS	5/07
	Anchorage MSA, AK	Y	29500 FQ	35650 MW	48240 TQ	USBLS	5/07
	Arizona	Y	26000 FQ	29180 MW	32730 TQ	USBLS	5/07
	Phoenix-Mesa-Scottsdale MSA, AZ	Y	26950 FQ	29640 MW	32380 TQ	USBLS	5/07
	Tucson MSA, AZ	Y	25220 FQ	30800 MW	44380 TQ	USBLS	5/07
	Arkansas	Y	20660 FQ	25680 MW	32780 TQ	USBLS	5/07
	Little Rock-North Little Rock MSA, AR	Y	21830 FQ	31980 MW	43200 TQ	USBLS	5/07
	California	H	14.96 FQ	21.02 MW	29.82 TQ	CABLS	1/08-3/08
	Los Angeles-Long Beach-Glendale PMSA, CA	H	15.70 FQ	22.16 MW	35.82 TQ	CABLS	1/08-3/08
	Oakland-Fremont-Hayward MSA, CA	H	13.65 FQ	18.56 MW	24.35 TQ	CABLS	1/08-3/08
	Riverside-San Bernardino-Ontario MSA, CA	H	13.91 FQ	17.67 MW	26.60 TQ	CABLS	1/08-3/08

AE Average entry wage	**AW** Average wage paid	**FQ** First quartile wage	**LO** Lowest wage paid	**MTC** Median total compensation	**TCC** Total cash compensation
AER Average entry range	**AWR** Average wage range	**H** Hourly	**LR** Low end range	**MW** Median wage paid	**TQ** Third quartile wage
AEX Average experienced wage	**AXR** Average experienced range	**HI** Highest wage paid	**M** Monthly	**MWR** Median wage range	**W** Weekly
ATC Average total compensation	**D** Daily	**HR** High end range	**MCC** Median cash compensation	**S** See annotated source	**Y** Yearly

Occupation/Type/Industry	Location	Per	Low	Mid	High	Source	Date
Reporter and Correspondent	Sacramento-Arden Arcade-Roseville MSA, CA	H	15.36 FQ	22.12 MW	28.17 TQ	CABLS	1/08-3/08
	San Diego-Carlsbad-San Marcos MSA, CA	H	17.22 FQ	19.82 MW	28.02 TQ	CABLS	1/08-3/08
	San Francisco-San Mateo-Redwood PMSA, CA	H	17.65 FQ	26.57 MW	33.86 TQ	CABLS	1/08-3/08
	Santa Ana-Anaheim-Irvine PMSA, CA	Y	30450 FQ	41120 MW	56170 TQ	USBLS	5/07
	Colorado	Y	26960 FQ	36450 MW	64530 TQ	USBLS	5/07
	Denver-Aurora MSA, CO	Y	29730 FQ	49530 MW	73260 TQ	USBLS	5/07
	Connecticut	H	12.98 AE	19.48 MW		CTBLS	1/08-3/08
	Bridgeport-Stamford-Norwalk MSA, CT	Y	30720 FQ	37460 MW	48160 TQ	USBLS	5/07
	Hartford-West Hartford-East Hartford MSA, CT	Y	32730 FQ	45030 MW	60140 TQ	USBLS	5/07
	Delaware	Y	27230 FQ	31640 MW	42620 TQ	USBLS	5/07
	Wilmington PMSA, DE-MD-NJ	Y	27740 FQ	31850 MW	49400 TQ	USBLS	5/07
	District of Columbia	Y	39760 FQ	58680 MW	81850 TQ	USBLS	5/07
	Washington-Arlington-Alexandria MSA, DC-VA-MD-WV	Y	34850 FQ	50780 MW	75820 TQ	USBLS	5/07
	Florida	Y	26780 FQ	37890 MW	54530 TQ	USBLS	5/07
	Fort Lauderdale-Pompano Beach-Deerfield Beach PMSA, FL	Y	22220 FQ	30690 MW	38790 TQ	USBLS	5/07
	Jacksonville MSA, FL	Y	15380 FQ	32020 MW	39790 TQ	USBLS	5/07
	Miami-Fort Lauderdale-Miami Beach MSA, FL	Y	31760 FQ	47010 MW	71560 TQ	USBLS	5/07
	Orlando-Kissimmee MSA, FL	Y	42390 FQ	52240 MW	68200 TQ	USBLS	5/07
	West Palm Beach-Boca Raton-Boynton Beach PMSA, FL	Y	31370 FQ	44020 MW	57350 TQ	USBLS	5/07
	Georgia	Y	23260 FQ	31260 MW	48350 TQ	USBLS	5/07
	Atlanta-Sandy Springs-Marietta MSA, GA	Y	28180 FQ	37290 MW	63050 TQ	USBLS	5/07
	Hawaii	Y	36970 FQ	46760 MW	59400 TQ	USBLS	5/07
	Honolulu MSA, HI	Y	38360 FQ	47930 MW	68180 TQ	USBLS	5/07
	Idaho	Y	24600 FQ	31300 MW	42640 TQ	USBLS	5/07
	Boise City-Nampa MSA, ID	Y	28730 FQ	35490 MW	47340 TQ	USBLS	5/07
	Illinois	Y	17800 FQ	27720 MW	38850 TQ	USBLS	5/07
	Chicago-Naperville-Joliet MSA, IL-IN-WI	Y	18500 FQ	29340 MW	45130 TQ	USBLS	5/07
	Indiana	Y	22800 FQ	30120 MW	43350 TQ	USBLS	5/07
	Elkhart-Goshen MSA, IN	Y	20040 FQ	25630 MW	31230 TQ	USBLS	5/07
	Gary PMSA, IN	Y	23620 FQ	32240 MW	41000 TQ	USBLS	5/07
	Indianapolis-Carmel MSA, IN	Y	27120 FQ	42920 MW	59360 TQ	USBLS	5/07
	Iowa	Y	20230 FQ	26670 MW	38250 TQ	USBLS	5/07
	Des Moines-West Des Moines MSA, IA	Y	33630 FQ	47670 MW	64240 TQ	USBLS	5/07
	Kansas	Y	17420 FQ	22770 MW	31430 TQ	USBLS	5/07
	Wichita MSA, KS	Y	16740 FQ	26090 MW	46330 TQ	USBLS	5/07
	Kentucky	Y	20513 FQ	30039 MW	53443 TQ	KYBLS	2008
	Louisville-Jefferson County MSA, KY-IN	Y	25750 FQ	46460 MW	65970 TQ	USBLS	5/07
	Louisiana	H	12.46 FQ	16.42 MW	21.25 TQ	LABLS	1/08-3/08
	Baton Rouge MSA, LA	Y	29850 FQ	36570 MW	43450 TQ	USBLS	5/07
	Maine	Y	24520 FQ	30250 MW	40460 TQ	USBLS	5/07
	Bangor MSA, ME	Y	21820 FQ	24170 MW	30810 TQ	USBLS	5/07
	Portland-South Portland-Biddeford MSA, ME	Y	32980 FQ	53000 MW	59360 TQ	USBLS	5/07
	Maryland	Y		47125 MW		MDBLS	3/08
	Baltimore-Towson MSA, MD	Y	36020 FQ	65150 MW	76070 TQ	USBLS	5/07
	Bethesda-Gaithersburg-Frederick PMSA, MD	Y	31690 FQ	39980 MW	61600 TQ	USBLS	5/07
	Massachusetts	Y	27650 FQ	37070 MW	53850 TQ	USBLS	5/07
	Boston-Cambridge-Quincy NECTA, MA	Y	26450 FQ	39420 MW	59830 TQ	USBLS	5/07
	Worcester MSA, MA-CT	Y	22390 FQ	24860 MW	28520 TQ	USBLS	5/07
	Michigan	Y	25070 FQ	33050 MW	47410 TQ	USBLS	5/07
	Detroit-Warren-Livonia MSA, MI	Y	26170 FQ	34000 MW	55910 TQ	USBLS	5/07

AE	Average entry wage	**AW**	Average wage paid	**FQ**	First quartile wage	**LO** Lowest wage paid	**MTC** Median total compensation **TCC** Total cash compensation
AER	Average entry range	**AWR**	Average wage range	**H**	Hourly	**LR** Low end range	**MW** Median wage paid **TQ** Third quartile wage
AEX	Average experienced wage	**AXR**	Average experienced range	**HI**	Highest wage paid	**M** Monthly	**MWR** Median wage range **W** Weekly
ATC	Average total compensation	**D**	Daily	**HR**	High end range	**MCC** Median cash compensation	**S** See annotated source **Y** Yearly

Occupation/Type/Industry	Location	Per	Low	Mid	High	Source	Date
Reporter and Correspondent	Grand Rapids-Wyoming MSA, MI	Y	33640 FQ	43660 MW	65500 TQ	USBLS	5/07
	Warren-Troy-Farmington Hills PMSA, MI	Y	25800 FQ	33140 MW	60000 TQ	USBLS	5/07
	Minnesota	Y	26417 FQ	38794 MW	73099 TQ	MNBLS	10/08-12/08
	Duluth-Superior MSA, MN-WI	Y	21489 FQ	29189 MW	46494 TQ	MNBLS	10/08-12/08
	Minneapolis-Saint Paul MSA, MN-WI	Y	37685 FQ	64918 MW	83112 TQ	MNBLS	10/08-12/08
	Mississippi	Y	23900 FQ	28910 MW	37120 TQ	USBLS	5/07
	Jackson MSA, MS	Y	29760 FQ	36670 MW	47370 TQ	USBLS	5/07
	Missouri	Y	21070 FQ	28480 MW	52390 TQ	USBLS	5/07
	Kansas City MSA, MO-KS	Y	21960 FQ	32380 MW	53130 TQ	USBLS	5/07
	St. Louis MSA, MO-IL	Y	16180 FQ	26880 MW	65730 TQ	USBLS	5/07
	Montana	Y	21010 FQ	26070 MW	36230 TQ	USBLS	5/07
	Billings MSA, MT	Y	24380 FQ	30540 MW	42520 TQ	USBLS	5/07
	Nebraska	Y	22340 FQ	28490 MW	38050 TQ	USBLS	5/07
	Omaha-Council Bluffs MSA, NE-IA	Y	28380 FQ	36340 MW	47640 TQ	USBLS	5/07
	Nevada	H	14.17 FQ	18.87 MW	25.70 TQ	NVBLS	5/08
	Las Vegas-Paradise MSA, NV	H	15.03 FQ	21.31 MW	26.85 TQ	NVBLS	5/08
	New Hampshire	H	12.07 AE	16.13 MW	24.10 AEX	NHBLS	6/08
	Nashua NECTA, NH-MA	Y	25600 FQ	31850 MW	43970 TQ	USBLS	5/07
	New Jersey	Y	29000 FQ	41120 MW	54770 TQ	USBLS	5/07
	Atlantic City MSA, NJ	Y	23160 FQ	37720 MW	53960 TQ	USBLS	5/07
	Camden PMSA, NJ	Y	34070 FQ	44310 MW	54060 TQ	USBLS	5/07
	Edison PMSA, NJ	Y	25960 FQ	38650 MW	49470 TQ	USBLS	5/07
	Newark-Union PMSA, NJ-PA	Y	28330 FQ	36960 MW	52670 TQ	USBLS	5/07
	New Mexico	Y	22390 FQ	28140 MW	34890 TQ	USBLS	5/07
	Albuquerque MSA, NM	Y	27700 FQ	31240 MW	38440 TQ	USBLS	5/07
	New York	Y	30600 FQ	44120 MW	71070 TQ	USBLS	5/07
	Albany-Schenectady-Troy MSA, NY	Y	29830 FQ	38680 MW	48890 TQ	USBLS	5/07
	Buffalo-Niagara Falls MSA, NY	Y	36510 FQ	53080 MW	61740 TQ	USBLS	5/07
	Nassau-Suffolk PMSA, NY	Y	26750 FQ	37150 MW	49710 TQ	USBLS	5/07
	New York-Northern New Jersey-Long Island MSA, NY-NJ-PA	Y	32090 FQ	46090 MW	71510 TQ	USBLS	5/07
	North Carolina	Y	24660 FQ	30250 MW	40620 TQ	USBLS	5/07
	Charlotte-Gastonia-Concord MSA, NC-SC	Y	30710 FQ	41220 MW	56740 TQ	USBLS	5/07
	Raleigh-Cary MSA, NC	Y	25220 FQ	28930 MW	37170 TQ	USBLS	5/07
	North Dakota	Y	20330 FQ	24930 MW	33310 TQ	USBLS	5/07
	Fargo MSA, ND-MN	Y	20790 FQ	30380 MW	36110 TQ	USBLS	5/07
	Ohio	Y	23900 FQ	31830 MW	47040 TQ	USBLS	5/07
	Canton-Massillon MSA, OH	Y	28160 FQ	42610 MW	47850 TQ	USBLS	5/07
	Cincinnati-Middletown MSA, OH-KY-IN	Y	29250 FQ	51050 MW	67560 TQ	USBLS	5/07
	Cleveland-Elyria-Mentor MSA, OH	Y	27720 FQ	36650 MW	62800 TQ	USBLS	5/07
	Columbus MSA, OH	Y	24710 FQ	29880 MW	38140 TQ	USBLS	5/07
	Dayton MSA, OH	Y	23670 FQ	28760 MW	46900 TQ	USBLS	5/07
	Oklahoma	Y	21300 FQ	31030 MW	40580 TQ	USBLS	5/07
	Oklahoma City MSA, OK	Y	28020 FQ	36570 MW	46990 TQ	USBLS	5/07
	Tulsa MSA, OK	Y	28540 FQ	35160 MW	45290 TQ	USBLS	5/07
	Oregon	H	11.93 FQ	14.42 MW	19.36 TQ	ORBLS	5/08
	Medford MSA, OR	Y	25460 FQ	31810 MW	42990 TQ	USBLS	5/07
	Portland-Vancouver-Beaverton MSA, OR-WA	Y	25240 FQ	31810 MW	44890 TQ	USBLS	5/07
	Salem MSA, OR	Y	27600 FQ	33470 MW	46600 TQ	USBLS	5/07
	Pennsylvania	Y	24390 FQ	33920 MW	48590 TQ	USBLS	5/07
	Allentown-Bethlehem-Easton MSA, PA-NJ	Y	25660 FQ	33530 MW	45190 TQ	USBLS	5/07
	Philadelphia-Camden-Wilmington MSA, PA-NJ-DE-MD	Y	27670 FQ	37070 MW	61860 TQ	USBLS	5/07
	Pittsburgh MSA, PA	Y	27260 FQ	38350 MW	49970 TQ	USBLS	5/07
	Rhode Island	Y	33950 FQ	58910 MW	72790 TQ	USBLS	5/07
	Providence-Fall River-Warwick MSA, RI-MA	Y	32970 FQ	40650 MW	67530 TQ	USBLS	5/07
	South Carolina	Y	23480 FQ	30280 MW	38770 TQ	USBLS	5/07

AE	Average entry wage	AW	Average wage paid	FQ	First quartile wage
AER	Average entry range	AWR	Average wage range	H	Hourly
AEX	Average experienced wage	AXR	Average experienced range	HI	Highest wage paid
ATC	Average total compensation	D	Daily	HR	High end range

LO Lowest wage paid · LR Low end range · M Monthly · MCC Median cash compensation · MTC Median total compensation · MW Median wage paid · MWR Median wage range · S See annotated source · TCC Total cash compensation · TQ Third quartile wage · W Weekly · Y Yearly

Occupation/Type/Industry	Location	Per	Low	Mid	High	Source	Date
Reporter and Correspondent	Charleston-North Charleston						
	MSA, SC	Y	26150 FQ	34660 MW	41830 TQ	USBLS	5/07
	Columbia MSA, SC	Y	24330 FQ	29080 MW	35950 TQ	USBLS	5/07
	South Dakota	Y	21259 FQ	24387 MW	29547 TQ	SDBLS	7/08-9/08
	Sioux Falls MSA, SD	Y	25132 FQ	30043 MW	38205 TQ	SDBLS	7/08-9/08
	Tennessee	Y	24910 FQ	35180 MW	47290 TQ	USBLS	5/07
	Memphis MSA, TN-MS-AR	Y	29630 FQ	55040 MW	61900 TQ	USBLS	5/07
	Texas	Y	24460 FQ	34590 MW	50540 TQ	USBLS	5/07
	Austin-Round Rock MSA, TX	Y	28810 FQ	44440 MW	69670 TQ	USBLS	5/07
	Dallas-Fort Worth-Arlington						
	MSA, TX	Y	33100 FQ	45400 MW	66460 TQ	USBLS	5/07
	El Paso MSA, TX	Y	26440 FQ	35600 MW	46630 TQ	USBLS	5/07
	Houston-Sugar Land-Baytown						
	MSA, TX	Y	28490 FQ	37560 MW	50620 TQ	USBLS	5/07
	San Antonio MSA, TX	Y	28090 FQ	43490 MW	56040 TQ	USBLS	5/07
	Utah	Y	31480 FQ	47130 MW	65410 TQ	USBLS	5/07
	Salt Lake City MSA, UT	Y	36450 FQ	51240 MW	66000 TQ	USBLS	5/07
	Vermont	Y	25740 FQ	30840 MW	37670 TQ	USBLS	5/07
	Burlington-South Burlington						
	MSA, VT	Y	27760 FQ	33050 MW	43700 TQ	USBLS	5/07
	Virginia	Y	27130 FQ	34560 MW	44430 TQ	USBLS	5/07
	Richmond MSA, VA	Y	28550 FQ	34260 MW	43750 TQ	USBLS	5/07
	Washington	H	13.42 FQ	19.28 MW	29.79 TQ	WABLS	3/08
	Seattle-Tacoma-Bellevue						
	MSA, WA	Y	31960 FQ	55100 MW	68650 TQ	USBLS	5/07
	Spokane MSA, WA	Y	27800 FQ	35500 MW	52560 TQ	USBLS	5/07
	West Virginia	Y	20316 FQ	27608 MW	38113 TQ	WVBLS	7/08-9/08
	Wisconsin	Y	22530 FQ	29960 MW	44410 TQ	USBLS	5/07
	Green Bay MSA, WI	Y	25280 FQ	31270 MW	37940 TQ	USBLS	5/07
	Milwaukee-Waukesha-West						
	Allis MSA, WI	Y	31330 FQ	51160 MW	70140 TQ	USBLS	5/07
	Wyoming	Y	22601 FQ	25697 MW	30707 TQ	WYBLS	9/08
	Puerto Rico	Y	23400 FQ	33550 MW	44690 TQ	USBLS	5/07
	San Juan-Caguas-Guaynabo						
	MSA, PR	Y	23610 FQ	34120 MW	45210 TQ	USBLS	5/07
Reporter of Decisions							
State Supreme Court	Michigan	Y			103586 HI	LSJ02	7/11/07
Reproduction Equipment Supervisor							
State Government	Ohio	H	15.77 LO		18.30 HI	ODAS	2008
Reproductive Endocrinologist	United States	Y		297150 AW		CEJ01	2008
Research Analyst							
Department of Environmental Quality	Oregon	M	2480 LO		5986 HI	ODEQSS	11/1/08
State Government	Connecticut	Y	54396 LO		68344 HI	AFT02	3/1/08
Research Attorney							
State Supreme Court	Michigan	Y			53014 HI	LSJ02	7/11/07
Research Geologist							
Department of Transportation	New Hampshire	Y			71051 HI	NHUL03	2008
State Government	Arizona	Y	43240 LO		73779 HI	AFT02	3/1/08
Research Psychologist	United States	Y		90000 MW		APACWS	2007
Research Specialist							
State Government	Kentucky	Y	29129 LO		38589 HI	AFT02	3/1/08
Research Technician							
State Government	Rhode Island	Y	34510 LO		37216 HI	AFT02	3/1/08
Reservation and Transportation Ticket Agent and Travel Clerk							
	Alabama	Y	21140 FQ	24040 MW	31240 TQ	USBLS	5/07
	Birmingham-Hoover MSA, AL	Y	22150 FQ	27960 MW	34660 TQ	USBLS	5/07
	Alaska	Y	24540 FQ	30740 MW	41170 TQ	USBLS	5/07
	Anchorage MSA, AK	Y	23510 FQ	30400 MW	42230 TQ	USBLS	5/07
	Arizona	Y	17880 FQ	22100 MW	30870 TQ	USBLS	5/07
	Phoenix-Mesa-Scottsdale						
	MSA, AZ	Y	17800 FQ	21950 MW	30420 TQ	USBLS	5/07

AE	Average entry wage	AW	Average wage paid	FQ	First quartile wage
AER	Average entry range	AWR	Average wage range	H	Hourly
AEX	Average experienced wage	AXR	Average experienced range	HI	Highest wage paid
ATC	Average total compensation	D	Daily	HR	High end range

LO	Lowest wage paid	MTC	Median total compensation	TCC	Total cash compensation
LR	Low end range	MW	Median wage paid	TQ	Third quartile wage
M	Monthly	MWR	Median wage range	W	Weekly
MCC	Median cash compensation	S	See annotated source	Y	Yearly

Occupation/Type/Industry	Location	Per	Low	Mid	High	Source	Date
Reservation and Transportation Ticket Agent and Travel Clerk	Tucson MSA, AZ	Y	18610 FQ	23220 MW	37340 TQ	USBLS	5/07
	Arkansas	Y	17770 FQ	24620 MW	34140 TQ	USBLS	5/07
	Fayetteville-Springdale-Rogers MSA, AR-MO	Y	17690 FQ	25640 MW	35760 TQ	USBLS	5/07
	California	H	11.48 FQ	14.31 MW	19.23 TQ	CABLS	1/08-3/08
	Los Angeles-Long Beach-Glendale PMSA, CA	H	11.86 FQ	14.82 MW	19.59 TQ	CABLS	1/08-3/08
	Oakland-Fremont-Hayward MSA, CA	H	11.41 FQ	13.37 MW	16.22 TQ	CABLS	1/08-3/08
	Riverside-San Bernardino-Ontario MSA, CA	H	8.88 FQ	10.06 MW	12.79 TQ	CABLS	1/08-3/08
	Sacramento-Arden Arcade-Roseville MSA, CA	H	11.59 FQ	14.06 MW	17.44 TQ	CABLS	1/08-3/08
	San Diego-Carlsbad-San Marcos MSA, CA	H	12.06 FQ	16.17 MW	20.54 TQ	CABLS	1/08-3/08
	San Francisco-San Mateo-Redwood PMSA, CA	H	12.58 FQ	15.44 MW	19.96 TQ	CABLS	1/08-3/08
	San Jose-Sunnyvale-Santa Clara MSA, CA	H	12.66 FQ	15.05 MW	20.57 TQ	CABLS	1/08-3/08
	Santa Ana-Anaheim-Irvine PMSA, CA	Y	22300 FQ	27310 MW	39640 TQ	USBLS	5/07
	Santa Rosa-Petaluma MSA, CA	H	12.57 FQ	18.99 MW	26.81 TQ	CABLS	1/08-3/08
	Colorado	Y	21840 FQ	26230 MW	35270 TQ	USBLS	5/07
	Boulder MSA, CO	Y	23080 FQ	27880 MW	30950 TQ	USBLS	5/07
	Colorado Springs MSA, CO	Y	22570 FQ	25390 MW	30420 TQ	USBLS	5/07
	Denver-Aurora MSA, CO	Y	23730 FQ	28940 MW	42370 TQ	USBLS	5/07
	Connecticut	H	12.54 AE	19.59 MW		CTBLS	1/08-3/08
	Bridgeport-Stamford-Norwalk MSA, CT	Y	27370 FQ	31630 MW	41530 TQ	USBLS	5/07
	Hartford-West Hartford-East Hartford MSA, CT	Y	26330 FQ	28960 MW	31960 TQ	USBLS	5/07
	Delaware	Y	18320 FQ	26400 MW	32570 TQ	USBLS	5/07
	Wilmington PMSA, DE-MD-NJ	Y	25180 FQ	29840 MW	35810 TQ	USBLS	5/07
	District of Columbia	Y	26770 FQ	30850 MW	37240 TQ	USBLS	5/07
	Washington-Arlington-Alexandria MSA, DC-VA-MD-WV	Y	23320 FQ	29060 MW	38020 TQ	USBLS	5/07
	Florida	Y	22240 FQ	29530 MW	40260 TQ	USBLS	5/07
	Fort Lauderdale-Pompano Beach-Deerfield Beach PMSA, FL	Y	20650 FQ	27990 MW	37990 TQ	USBLS	5/07
	Jacksonville MSA, FL	Y	21260 FQ	27650 MW	38200 TQ	USBLS	5/07
	Miami-Fort Lauderdale-Miami Beach MSA, FL	Y	23610 FQ	32010 MW	43680 TQ	USBLS	5/07
	Orlando-Kissimmee MSA, FL	Y	19570 FQ	26040 MW	34600 TQ	USBLS	5/07
	Tampa-St. Petersburg-Clearwater MSA, FL	Y	24070 FQ	33800 MW	39300 TQ	USBLS	5/07
	West Palm Beach-Boca Raton-Boynton Beach PMSA, FL	Y	26270 FQ	33710 MW	38640 TQ	USBLS	5/07
	Hawaii	Y	20520 FQ	29860 MW	39070 TQ	USBLS	5/07
	Honolulu MSA, HI	Y	20640 FQ	30100 MW	39790 TQ	USBLS	5/07
	Idaho	Y	27330 FQ	34050 MW	39280 TQ	USBLS	5/07
	Boise City-Nampa MSA, ID	Y	29860 FQ	35580 MW	39930 TQ	USBLS	5/07
	Illinois	Y	27100 FQ	41030 MW	46700 TQ	USBLS	5/07
	Chicago-Naperville-Joliet MSA, IL-IN-WI	Y	27730 FQ	41360 MW	46760 TQ	USBLS	5/07
	Indiana	Y	23490 FQ	32100 MW	37830 TQ	USBLS	5/07
	Indianapolis-Carmel MSA, IN	Y	23620 FQ	33000 MW	38340 TQ	USBLS	5/07
	Iowa	Y	20870 FQ	24010 MW	29250 TQ	USBLS	5/07
	Kansas	Y	23000 FQ	27980 MW	36530 TQ	USBLS	5/07
	Wichita MSA, KS	Y	22920 FQ	27840 MW	36350 TQ	USBLS	5/07
	Louisville-Jefferson County MSA, KY-IN	Y	19600 FQ	25980 MW	34480 TQ	USBLS	5/07
	Louisiana	H	10.18 FQ	12.25 MW	17.55 TQ	LABLS	1/08-3/08
	Baton Rouge MSA, LA	Y	23820 FQ	30490 MW	40750 TQ	USBLS	5/07
	New Orleans-Metairie-Kenner MSA, LA	Y	23000 FQ	31750 MW	43180 TQ	USBLS	5/07
	Maine	Y	21920 FQ	24790 MW	31230 TQ	USBLS	5/07
	Portland-South Portland-Biddeford MSA, ME	Y	21610 FQ	23630 MW	27070 TQ	USBLS	5/07

Occupation/Type/Industry	Location	Per	Low	Mid	High	Source	Date
Reservation and Transportation Ticket Agent and Travel Clerk	Maryland	Y		31400 MW		MDBLS	3/08
	Baltimore-Towson MSA, MD	Y	23930 FQ	31570 MW	37270 TQ	USBLS	5/07
	Massachusetts	Y	23770 FQ	32910 MW	42280 TQ	USBLS	5/07
	Boston-Cambridge-Quincy NECTA, MA	Y	25500 FQ	34590 MW	43050 TQ	USBLS	5/07
	Michigan	Y	24080 FQ	32720 MW	40310 TQ	USBLS	5/07
	Detroit-Warren-Livonia MSA, MI	Y	25710 FQ	34330 MW	40880 TQ	USBLS	5/07
	Grand Rapids-Wyoming MSA, MI	Y	25960 FQ	28940 MW	31900 TQ	USBLS	5/07
	Warren-Troy-Farmington Hills PMSA, MI	Y	19220 FQ	22060 MW	25670 TQ	USBLS	5/07
	Minnesota	Y	27206 FQ	36479 MW	46742 TQ	MNBLS	10/08-12/08
	Minneapolis-Saint Paul MSA, MN-WI	Y	30120 FQ	38551 MW	50863 TQ	MNBLS	10/08-12/08
	Mississippi	Y	19600 FQ	23400 MW	33250 TQ	USBLS	5/07
	Jackson MSA, MS	Y	19890 FQ	23940 MW	34270 TQ	USBLS	5/07
	Missouri	Y	21980 FQ	27610 MW	43560 TQ	USBLS	5/07
	Kansas City MSA, MO-KS	Y	23160 FQ	31950 MW	44290 TQ	USBLS	5/07
	St. Louis MSA, MO-IL	Y	22420 FQ	28020 MW	44190 TQ	USBLS	5/07
	Montana	Y	19380 FQ	25040 MW	38010 TQ	USBLS	5/07
	Billings MSA, MT	Y	32640 FQ	39620 MW	43670 TQ	USBLS	5/07
	Nebraska	Y	18590 FQ	21270 MW	25510 TQ	USBLS	5/07
	Omaha-Council Bluffs MSA, NE-IA	Y	19050 FQ	21770 MW	25870 TQ	USBLS	5/07
	Nevada	H	10.11 FQ	13.22 MW	16.34 TQ	NVBLS	5/08
	Las Vegas-Paradise MSA, NV	H	10.62 FQ	13.99 MW	16.84 TQ	NVBLS	5/08
	New Hampshire	H	11.33 AE	18.74 MW	19.88 AEX	NHBLS	6/08
	Manchester MSA, NH	Y	28860 FQ	38930 MW	43390 TQ	USBLS	5/07
	New Jersey	Y	22660 FQ	29570 MW	43690 TQ	USBLS	5/07
	Camden PMSA, NJ	Y	18520 FQ	21550 MW	26090 TQ	USBLS	5/07
	Edison PMSA, NJ	Y	22160 FQ	25780 MW	39600 TQ	USBLS	5/07
	Newark-Union PMSA, NJ-PA	Y	23020 FQ	32410 MW	44760 TQ	USBLS	5/07
	New Mexico	Y	23120 FQ	35240 MW	44430 TQ	USBLS	5/07
	Albuquerque MSA, NM	Y	28600 FQ	39540 MW	45810 TQ	USBLS	5/07
	New York	Y	23810 FQ	32030 MW	41580 TQ	USBLS	5/07
	Albany-Schenectady-Troy MSA, NY	Y	17100 FQ	21340 MW	33900 TQ	USBLS	5/07
	Nassau-Suffolk PMSA, NY	Y	25960 FQ	33410 MW	43150 TQ	USBLS	5/07
	New York-Northern New Jersey-Long Island MSA, NY-NJ-PA	Y	23850 FQ	33060 MW	43430 TQ	USBLS	5/07
	Syracuse MSA, NY	Y	31260 FQ	33800 MW	36280 TQ	USBLS	5/07
	North Carolina	Y	27420 FQ	33740 MW	39120 TQ	USBLS	5/07
	Charlotte-Gastonia-Concord MSA, NC-SC	Y	25040 FQ	32240 MW	36230 TQ	USBLS	5/07
	Raleigh-Cary MSA, NC	Y	27380 FQ	38720 MW	43910 TQ	USBLS	5/07
	North Dakota	Y	17610 FQ	19710 MW	25650 TQ	USBLS	5/07
	Ohio	Y	23270 FQ	31700 MW	40920 TQ	USBLS	5/07
	Cleveland-Elyria-Mentor MSA, OH	Y	23550 FQ	31440 MW	44520 TQ	USBLS	5/07
	Columbus MSA, OH	Y	24020 FQ	33320 MW	39170 TQ	USBLS	3/08
	Dayton MSA, OH	Y	19190 FQ	27540 MW	40000 TQ	USBLS	5/07
	Oklahoma	Y	21660 FQ	30220 MW	40290 TQ	USBLS	5/07
	Tulsa MSA, OK	Y	22450 FQ	28190 MW	38570 TQ	USBLS	5/07
	Oregon	H	10.94 FQ	13.74 MW	17.46 TQ	ORBLS	5/08
	Portland-Vancouver-Beaverton MSA, OR-WA	Y	24250 FQ	29220 MW	36540 TQ	USBLS	5/07
	Pennsylvania	Y	19640 FQ	23980 MW	33410 TQ	USBLS	5/07
	Allentown-Bethlehem-Easton MSA, PA-NJ	Y	21590 FQ	24820 MW	33000 TQ	USBLS	5/07
	Philadelphia-Camden-Wilmington MSA, PA-NJ-DE-MD	Y	20790 FQ	25370 MW	35570 TQ	USBLS	5/07
	Rhode Island	Y	22900 FQ	27150 MW	33270 TQ	USBLS	5/07
	Providence-Fall River-Warwick MSA, RI-MA	Y	22880 FQ	27120 MW	33230 TQ	USBLS	5/07
	South Carolina	Y	18350 FQ	22890 MW	32910 TQ	USBLS	5/07
	Charleston-North Charleston MSA, SC	Y	18120 FQ	22380 MW	32510 TQ	USBLS	5/07
	Columbia MSA, SC	Y	18550 FQ	24390 MW	36630 TQ	USBLS	5/07

AE Average entry wage	**AW** Average wage paid	**FQ** First quartile wage	**LO** Lowest wage paid	**MTC** Median total compensation	**TCC** Total cash compensation
AER Average entry range	**AWR** Average wage range	**H** Hourly	**LR** Low end range	**MW** Median wage paid	**TQ** Third quartile wage
AEX Average experienced wage	**AXR** Average experienced range	**HI** Highest wage paid	**M** Monthly	**MWR** Median wage range	**W** Weekly
ATC Average total compensation	**D** Daily	**HR** High end range	**MCC** Median cash compensation	**S** See annotated source	**Y** Yearly

Occupation/Type/Industry	Location	Per	Low	Mid	High	Source	Date
Reservation and Transportation Ticket Agent and Travel Clerk	South Dakota	Y	20529 FQ	24372 MW	29753 TQ	SDBLS	7/08-9/08
	Sioux Falls MSA, SD	Y	21761 FQ	25704 MW	32634 TQ	SDBLS	7/08-9/08
	Tennessee	Y	17550 FQ	20860 MW	30180 TQ	USBLS	5/07
	Memphis MSA, TN-MS-AR	Y	17100 FQ	20210 MW	25620 TQ	USBLS	5/07
	Nashville-Davidson-Murfreesboro MSA, TN	Y	18490 FQ	22660 MW	34440 TQ	USBLS	5/07
	Texas	Y	25310 FQ	34670 MW	45280 TQ	USBLS	5/07
	Dallas-Fort Worth-Arlington MSA, TX	Y	26880 FQ	40420 MW	46660 TQ	USBLS	5/07
	El Paso MSA, TX	Y	20750 FQ	25750 MW	42930 TQ	USBLS	5/07
	Houston-Sugar Land-Baytown MSA, TX	Y	24320 FQ	30910 MW	40810 TQ	USBLS	5/07
	San Antonio MSA, TX	Y	25470 FQ	40760 MW	46170 TQ	USBLS	5/07
	Utah	Y	18560 FQ	23440 MW	35210 TQ	USBLS	5/07
	Salt Lake City MSA, UT	Y	18550 FQ	23430 MW	35260 TQ	USBLS	5/07
	Virginia	Y	22360 FQ	28130 MW	37330 TQ	USBLS	5/07
	Richmond MSA, VA	Y	21760 FQ	27820 MW	36640 TQ	USBLS	5/07
	Roanoke MSA, VA	Y	16920 FQ	20020 MW	33390 TQ	USBLS	5/07
	Virginia Beach-Norfolk-Newport News MSA, VA-NC	Y	22320 FQ	28320 MW	38050 TQ	USBLS	5/07
	Washington	H	12.36 FQ	15.68 MW	20.62 TQ	WABLS	3/08
	Seattle-Tacoma-Bellevue MSA, WA	Y	27490 FQ	35130 MW	43660 TQ	USBLS	5/07
	West Virginia	Y	21056 FQ	24302 MW	29820 TQ	WVBLS	7/08-9/08
	Charleston MSA, WV	Y	20780 FQ	23320 MW	34780 TQ	USBLS	5/07
	Wisconsin	Y	19340 FQ	22710 MW	26900 TQ	USBLS	5/07
	Milwaukee-Waukesha-West Allis MSA, WI	Y	21390 FQ	23920 MW	28390 TQ	USBLS	5/07
	Wyoming	Y	15466 FQ	19923 MW	28207 TQ	WYBLS	9/08
	Puerto Rico	Y	22480 FQ	33540 MW	44670 TQ	USBLS	5/07
	San Juan-Caguas-Guaynabo MSA, PR	Y	22630 FQ	33640 MW	44740 TQ	USBLS	5/07
	Virgin Islands	Y	16630 FQ	19500 MW	23800 TQ	USBLS	5/07
	Guam	Y	14940 FQ	21280 MW	30170 TQ	USBLS	5/07
Residential Advisor	Alabama	Y	14600 FQ	18170 MW	26070 TQ	USBLS	5/07
	Birmingham-Hoover MSA, AL	Y	13320 FQ	15470 MW	27110 TQ	USBLS	5/07
	Mobile MSA, AL	Y	17410 FQ	24740 MW	30220 TQ	USBLS	5/07
	Alaska	Y	27590 FQ	30720 MW	36650 TQ	USBLS	5/07
	Arizona	Y	22720 FQ	27530 MW	34260 TQ	USBLS	5/07
	Phoenix-Mesa-Scottsdale MSA, AZ	Y	25140 FQ	29270 MW	35130 TQ	USBLS	5/07
	Tucson MSA, AZ	Y	21660 FQ	24280 MW	31450 TQ	USBLS	5/07
	Arkansas	Y	16840 FQ	21230 MW	25880 TQ	USBLS	5/07
	Fort Smith MSA, AR-OK	Y	17960 FQ	19830 MW	21760 TQ	USBLS	5/07
	Little Rock-North Little Rock MSA, AR	Y	19230 FQ	23110 MW	27450 TQ	USBLS	5/07
	California	H	11.29 FQ	14.39 MW	19.08 TQ	CABLS	1/08-3/08
	Los Angeles-Long Beach-Glendale PMSA, CA	H	11.88 FQ	14.87 MW	20.15 TQ	CABLS	1/08-3/08
	Oakland-Fremont-Hayward MSA, CA	H	9.59 FQ	11.82 MW	14.83 TQ	CABLS	1/08-3/08
	Riverside-San Bernardino-Ontario MSA, CA	H	11.92 FQ	14.33 MW	17.91 TQ	CABLS	1/08-3/08
	Sacramento-Arden Arcade-Roseville MSA, CA	H	11.65 FQ	15.78 MW	18.55 TQ	CABLS	1/08-3/08
	San Diego-Carlsbad-San Marcos MSA, CA	H	13.06 FQ	16.23 MW	19.66 TQ	CABLS	1/08-3/08
	San Francisco-San Mateo-Redwood PMSA, CA	H	8.91 FQ	10.99 MW	13.55 TQ	CABLS	1/08-3/08
	Santa Ana-Anaheim-Irvine PMSA, CA	Y	18470 FQ	25390 MW	34020 TQ	USBLS	5/07
	Colorado	Y	20360 FQ	24540 MW	29450 TQ	USBLS	5/07
	Denver-Aurora MSA, CO	Y	20600 FQ	26610 MW	32020 TQ	USBLS	5/07
	Pueblo MSA, CO	Y	17470 FQ	20820 MW	25610 TQ	USBLS	5/07
	Connecticut	H	10.69 AE	12.74 MW		CTBLS	1/08-3/08
	Bridgeport-Stamford-Norwalk MSA, CT	Y	21640 FQ	23370 MW	25090 TQ	USBLS	5/07
	Hartford-West Hartford-East Hartford MSA, CT	Y	23920 FQ	28390 MW	34550 TQ	USBLS	5/07
	Delaware	Y	22670 FQ	28060 MW	34810 TQ	USBLS	5/07

AE	Average entry wage	**AW**	Average wage paid	**FQ**	First quartile wage	**LO** Lowest wage paid
AER	Average entry range	**AWR**	Average wage range	**H**	Hourly	**LR** Low end range
AEX	Average experienced wage	**AXR**	Average experienced range	**HI**	Highest wage paid	**M** Monthly
ATC	Average total compensation	**D**	Daily	**HR**	High end range	**MCC** Median cash compensation

MTC Median total compensation	**TCC** Total cash compensation
MW Median wage paid	**TQ** Third quartile wage
MWR Median wage range	**W** Weekly
S See annotated source	**Y** Yearly

Occupation/Type/Industry	Location	Per	Low	Mid	High	Source	Date
Residential Advisor	Wilmington PMSA, DE-MD-NJ	Y	23960 FQ	29370 MW	36140 TQ	USBLS	5/07
	District of Columbia	Y	19910 FQ	23730 MW	29300 TQ	USBLS	5/07
	Washington-Arlington-Alexandria MSA, DC-VA-MD-WV	Y	19520 FQ	24080 MW	30590 TQ	USBLS	5/07
	Florida	Y	18200 FQ	21310 MW	26630 TQ	USBLS	5/07
	Fort Lauderdale-Pompano Beach-Deerfield Beach PMSA, FL	Y	20470 FQ	22550 MW	26730 TQ	USBLS	5/07
	Jacksonville MSA, FL	Y	20560 FQ	24140 MW	29840 TQ	USBLS	5/07
	Miami-Fort Lauderdale-Miami Beach MSA, FL	Y	18950 FQ	21270 MW	25910 TQ	USBLS	5/07
	Orlando-Kissimmee MSA, FL	Y	18750 FQ	21270 MW	23700 TQ	USBLS	5/07
	Tampa-St. Petersburg-Clearwater MSA, FL	Y	17050 FQ	18600 MW	23970 TQ	USBLS	5/07
	West Palm Beach-Boca Raton-Boynton Beach PMSA, FL	Y	19740 FQ	24500 MW	30250 TQ	USBLS	5/07
	Georgia	Y	16860 FQ	18660 MW	23000 TQ	USBLS	5/07
	Atlanta-Sandy Springs-Marietta MSA, GA	Y	17350 FQ	19840 MW	25490 TQ	USBLS	5/07
	Hawaii	Y	20560 FQ	23060 MW	28890 TQ	USBLS	5/07
	Honolulu MSA, HI	Y	20870 FQ	24400 MW	30160 TQ	USBLS	5/07
	Idaho	Y	17710 FQ	19960 MW	32860 TQ	USBLS	5/07
	Boise City-Nampa MSA, ID	Y	16920 FQ	18170 MW	19540 TQ	USBLS	5/07
	Illinois	Y	20980 FQ	25290 MW	35080 TQ	USBLS	5/07
	Chicago-Naperville-Joliet MSA, IL-IN-WI	Y	22120 FQ	28250 MW	37840 TQ	USBLS	5/07
	Indiana	Y	20600 FQ	23640 MW	29930 TQ	USBLS	5/07
	Indianapolis-Carmel MSA, IN	Y	21680 FQ	24140 MW	28640 TQ	USBLS	5/07
	Iowa	Y	16360 FQ	23090 MW	29580 TQ	USBLS	5/07
	Des Moines-West Des Moines MSA, IA	Y	18540 FQ	21540 MW	24460 TQ	USBLS	5/07
	Kansas	Y	16440 FQ	21570 MW	25420 TQ	USBLS	5/07
	Wichita MSA, KS	Y	17390 FQ	19630 MW	24570 TQ	USBLS	5/07
	Kentucky	Y	17142 FQ	19436 MW	22361 TQ	KYBLS	2008
	Louisville-Jefferson County MSA, KY-IN	Y	17920 FQ	20380 MW	22840 TQ	USBLS	5/07
	Louisiana	H	10.42 FQ	14.68 MW	16.39 TQ	LABLS	1/08-3/08
	Baton Rouge MSA, LA	Y	14290 FQ	17120 MW	21300 TQ	USBLS	5/07
	Shreveport-Bossier City MSA, LA	Y	21990 FQ	28170 MW	31410 TQ	USBLS	5/07
	Maine	Y	17070 FQ	20760 MW	24670 TQ	USBLS	5/07
	Maryland	Y		28100 MW		MDBLS	3/08
	Baltimore-Towson MSA, MD	Y	23360 FQ	28000 MW	32540 TQ	USBLS	5/07
	Bethesda-Gaithersburg-Frederick PMSA, MD	Y	21900 FQ	26580 MW	35100 TQ	USBLS	5/07
	Massachusetts	Y	23560 FQ	27340 MW	32680 TQ	USBLS	5/07
	Boston-Cambridge-Quincy NECTA, MA	Y	23750 FQ	28000 MW	33380 TQ	USBLS	5/07
	Michigan	Y	21510 FQ	26080 MW	32560 TQ	USBLS	5/07
	Detroit-Warren-Livonia MSA, MI	Y	21300 FQ	25290 MW	31830 TQ	USBLS	5/07
	Grand Rapids-Wyoming MSA, MI	Y	22330 FQ	27410 MW	31820 TQ	USBLS	5/07
	Warren-Troy-Farmington Hills PMSA, MI	Y	20940 FQ	28940 MW	35880 TQ	USBLS	5/07
	Minnesota	Y	30039 FQ	35340 MW	40485 TQ	MNBLS	10/08-12/08
	Duluth-Superior MSA, MN-WI	Y	15464 FQ	16467 MW	28847 TQ	MNBLS	10/08-12/08
	Minneapolis-Saint Paul MSA, MN-WI	Y	30938 FQ	36260 MW	40986 TQ	MNBLS	10/08-12/08
	Mississippi	Y	16530 FQ	19270 MW	24350 TQ	USBLS	5/07
	Jackson MSA, MS	Y	17310 FQ	19850 MW	25140 TQ	USBLS	5/07
	Missouri	Y	18150 FQ	24200 MW	30660 TQ	USBLS	5/07
	Jefferson City MSA, MO	Y	23110 FQ	26800 MW	31530 TQ	USBLS	5/07
	Kansas City MSA, MO-KS	Y	20930 FQ	23360 MW	29080 TQ	USBLS	5/07
	St. Louis MSA, MO-IL	Y	19420 FQ	25750 MW	31760 TQ	USBLS	5/07
	Montana	Y	16880 FQ	19150 MW	22780 TQ	USBLS	5/07
	Nebraska	Y	20120 FQ	26890 MW	31110 TQ	USBLS	5/07
	Las Vegas-Paradise MSA, NV	H	10.75 FQ	11.65 MW	13.10 TQ	NVBLS	5/08
	New Hampshire	H	9.23 AE	12.02 MW	13.80 AEX	NHBLS	6/08
	Manchester MSA, NH	Y	22040 FQ	27080 MW	32140 TQ	USBLS	5/07

AE	Average entry wage	AW	Average wage paid	FQ	First quartile wage
AER	Average entry range	AWR	Average wage range	H	Hourly
AEX	Average experienced wage	AXR	Average experienced range	HI	Highest wage paid
ATC	Average total compensation	D	Daily	HR	High end range

LO	Lowest wage paid	MTC	Median total compensation
LR	Low end range	MW	Median wage paid
M	Monthly	MWR	Median wage range
MCC	Median cash compensation	S	See annotated source

TCC	Total cash compensation
TQ	Third quartile wage
W	Weekly
Y	Yearly

Occupation/Type/Industry	Location	Per	Low	Mid	High	Source	Date
Residential Advisor	Nashua NECTA, NH-MA	Y	22080 FQ	23910 MW	26260 TQ	USBLS	5/07
	New Jersey	Y	24610 FQ	33160 MW	43730 TQ	USBLS	5/07
	Camden PMSA, NJ	Y	32430 FQ	41620 MW	55520 TQ	USBLS	5/07
	Edison PMSA, NJ	Y	25160 FQ	33230 MW	41390 TQ	USBLS	5/07
	Newark-Union PMSA, NJ-PA	Y	30840 FQ	36280 MW	49510 TQ	USBLS	5/07
	New Mexico	Y	19170 FQ	23180 MW	27800 TQ	USBLS	5/07
	Albuquerque MSA, NM	Y	17780 FQ	21420 MW	26260 TQ	USBLS	5/07
	New York	Y	24700 FQ	29460 MW	35110 TQ	USBLS	5/07
	Albany-Schenectady-Troy MSA, NY	Y	23210 FQ	28240 MW	32520 TQ	USBLS	5/07
	Buffalo-Niagara Falls MSA, NY	Y	24080 FQ	31040 MW	37690 TQ	USBLS	5/07
	Nassau-Suffolk PMSA, NY	Y	24800 FQ	28370 MW	32160 TQ	USBLS	5/07
	New York-Northern New Jersey-Long Island MSA, NY-NJ-PA	Y	26940 FQ	31750 MW	38870 TQ	USBLS	5/07
	North Carolina	Y	14660 FQ	20160 MW	25300 TQ	USBLS	5/07
	Charlotte-Gastonia-Concord MSA, NC-SC	Y	21410 FQ	23490 MW	26610 TQ	USBLS	5/07
	Raleigh-Cary MSA, NC	Y	13580 FQ	14370 MW	16690 TQ	USBLS	5/07
	North Dakota	Y	17290 FQ	19630 MW	24070 TQ	USBLS	5/07
	Fargo MSA, ND-MN	Y	16920 FQ	24460 MW	29060 TQ	USBLS	5/07
	Ohio	Y	21120 FQ	27750 MW	34310 TQ	USBLS	5/07
	Canton-Massillon MSA, OH	Y	27230 FQ	31940 MW	43350 TQ	USBLS	5/07
	Cincinnati-Middletown MSA, OH-KY-IN	Y	15310 FQ	22580 MW	32620 TQ	USBLS	5/07
	Cleveland-Elyria-Mentor MSA, OH	Y	16020 FQ	27910 MW	38880 TQ	USBLS	5/07
	Columbus MSA, OH	Y	20680 FQ	25430 MW	30530 TQ	USBLS	5/07
	Dayton MSA, OH	Y	26790 FQ	30240 MW	33540 TQ	USBLS	5/07
	Oklahoma	Y	14550 FQ	19490 MW	23660 TQ	USBLS	5/07
	Oklahoma City MSA, OK	Y	17930 FQ	21200 MW	23590 TQ	USBLS	5/07
	Tulsa MSA, OK	Y	23470 FQ	28600 MW	32950 TQ	USBLS	5/07
	Oregon	H	9.53 FQ	11.14 MW	13.32 TQ	ORBLS	5/08
	Portland-Vancouver-Beaverton MSA, OR-WA	Y	19520 FQ	23530 MW	29640 TQ	USBLS	5/07
	Pennsylvania	Y	19940 FQ	23040 MW	29830 TQ	USBLS	5/07
	Allentown-Bethlehem-Easton MSA, PA-NJ	Y	20440 FQ	25320 MW	29140 TQ	USBLS	5/07
	Philadelphia-Camden-Wilmington MSA, PA-NJ-DE-MD	Y	21160 FQ	24610 MW	34760 TQ	USBLS	5/07
	Pittsburgh MSA, PA	Y	19260 FQ	21630 MW	24760 TQ	USBLS	5/07
	Rhode Island	Y	26040 FQ	30140 MW	34960 TQ	USBLS	5/07
	Providence-Fall River-Warwick MSA, RI-MA	Y	27520 FQ	32840 MW	48460 TQ	USBLS	5/07
	South Carolina	Y	18090 FQ	20690 MW	23890 TQ	USBLS	5/07
	Charleston-North Charleston MSA, SC	Y	19260 FQ	20690 MW	22820 TQ	USBLS	5/07
	Columbia MSA, SC	Y	20890 FQ	22850 MW	26530 TQ	USBLS	5/07
	South Dakota	Y	19065 FQ	21675 MW	24459 TQ	SDBLS	7/08-9/08
	Sioux Falls MSA, SD	Y	20246 FQ	22830 MW	25534 TQ	SDBLS	7/08-9/08
	Tennessee	Y	17070 FQ	18850 MW	22380 TQ	USBLS	5/07
	Memphis MSA, TN-MS-AR	Y	17480 FQ	19260 MW	23700 TQ	USBLS	5/07
	Nashville-Davidson-Murfreesboro MSA, TN	Y	17370 FQ	19800 MW	23620 TQ	USBLS	5/07
	Texas	Y	14230 FQ	18840 MW	24030 TQ	USBLS	5/07
	Austin-Round Rock MSA, TX	Y	15960 FQ	21140 MW	24510 TQ	USBLS	5/07
	Dallas-Fort Worth-Arlington MSA, TX	Y	13610 FQ	17500 MW	23720 TQ	USBLS	5/07
	Houston-Sugar Land-Baytown MSA, TX	Y	14920 FQ	21360 MW	25740 TQ	USBLS	5/07
	San Antonio MSA, TX	Y	13230 FQ	15070 MW	23430 TQ	USBLS	5/07
	Utah	Y	17270 FQ	19480 MW	23480 TQ	USBLS	5/07
	Salt Lake City MSA, UT	Y	17510 FQ	19280 MW	22260 TQ	USBLS	5/07
	Vermont	Y	21360 FQ	24460 MW	29830 TQ	USBLS	5/07
	Burlington-South Burlington MSA, VT	Y	18790 FQ	26270 MW	32440 TQ	USBLS	5/07
	Virginia	Y	17080 FQ	22800 MW	28850 TQ	USBLS	5/07
	Richmond MSA, VA	Y	24530 FQ	31560 MW	40020 TQ	USBLS	5/07
	Virginia Beach-Norfolk-Newport News MSA, VA-NC	Y	22180 FQ	24640 MW	28040 TQ	USBLS	5/07

AE	Average entry wage	AW	Average wage paid	FQ	First quartile wage	LO	Lowest wage paid	MTC	Median total compensation	TCC	Total cash compensation
AER	Average entry range	AWR	Average wage range	H	Hourly	LR	Low end range	MW	Median wage paid	TQ	Third quartile wage
AEX	Average experienced wage	AXR	Average experienced range	HI	Highest wage paid	M	Monthly	MWR	Median wage range	W	Weekly
ATC	Average total compensation	D	Daily	HR	High end range	MCC	Median cash compensation	S	See annotated source	Y	Yearly

Occupation/Type/Industry	Location	Per	Low	Mid	High	Source	Date
Residential Advisor	Washington	H	13.37 FQ	15.87 MW	18.29 TQ	WABLS	3/08
	Seattle-Tacoma-Bellevue MSA, WA	Y	28980 FQ	33810 MW	38580 TQ	USBLS	5/07
	West Virginia	Y	15676 FQ	22187 MW	28667 TQ	WVBLS	7/08-9/08
	Charleston MSA, WV	Y	16060 FQ	22920 MW	29940 TQ	USBLS	5/07
	Huntington-Ashland MSA, WV-KY-OH	Y	13170 FQ	15290 MW	18980 TQ	USBLS	5/07
	Wisconsin	Y	22210 FQ	27340 MW	33850 TQ	USBLS	5/07
	Milwaukee-Waukesha-West Allis MSA, WI	Y	23900 FQ	27210 MW	31800 TQ	USBLS	5/07
	Racine MSA, WI	Y	19780 FQ	21420 MW	23070 TQ	USBLS	5/07
	Wyoming	Y	19358 FQ	23055 MW	27479 TQ	WYBLS	9/08
	Cheyenne MSA, WY	Y	18025 FQ	19789 MW	25175 TQ	WYBLS	9/08
	Puerto Rico	Y	19070 FQ	21040 MW	23010 TQ	USBLS	5/07
Residential Unit Manager							
Youth Services	Ohio	H	24.90 LO		34.83 HI	ODAS	2008
Resources Forester							
State Government	Missouri	Y	33360 LO		58500 HI	AFT02	3/1/08
Respiratory Therapist	United States	Y		48705 AW		HOMECARE	8/25/08-9/24/08
	Alabama	Y	38750 FQ	42950 MW	47160 TQ	USBLS	5/07
	Birmingham-Hoover MSA, AL	Y	38770 FQ	44670 MW	50560 TQ	USBLS	5/07
	Alaska	Y	52240 FQ	59240 MW	66770 TQ	USBLS	5/07
	Arizona	Y	39050 FQ	45540 MW	52630 TQ	USBLS	5/07
	Phoenix-Mesa-Scottsdale MSA, AZ	Y	39640 FQ	46010 MW	53190 TQ	USBLS	5/07
	Tucson MSA, AZ	Y	30520 FQ	40800 MW	47280 TQ	USBLS	5/07
	Arkansas	Y	38090 FQ	44690 MW	52640 TQ	USBLS	5/07
	Little Rock-North Little Rock MSA, AR	Y	41620 FQ	49000 MW	57670 TQ	USBLS	5/07
	California	H	26.29 FQ	29.82 MW	35.02 TQ	CABLS	1/08-3/08
	Bakersfield MSA, CA	H	18.42 FQ	23.47 MW	28.24 TQ	CABLS	1/08-3/08
	Los Angeles-Long Beach-Glendale PMSA, CA	H	26.57 FQ	29.78 MW	34.73 TQ	CABLS	1/08-3/08
	Oakland-Fremont-Hayward MSA, CA	H	27.13 FQ	32.55 MW	39.59 TQ	CABLS	1/08-3/08
	Oxnard-Thousand Oaks-Ventura MSA, CA	H	26.68 FQ	31.56 MW	35.15 TQ	CABLS	1/08-3/08
	Riverside-San Bernardino-Ontario MSA, CA	H	25.61 FQ	28.21 MW	30.85 TQ	CABLS	1/08-3/08
	Sacramento-Arden Arcade-Roseville MSA, CA	H	27.09 FQ	30.50 MW	34.65 TQ	CABLS	1/08-3/08
	San Diego-Carlsbad-San Marcos MSA, CA	H	26.45 FQ	30.13 MW	35.53 TQ	CABLS	1/08-3/08
	San Francisco-San Mateo-Redwood PMSA, CA	H	25.74 FQ	29.87 MW	35.32 TQ	CABLS	1/08-3/08
	San Jose-Sunnyvale-Santa Clara MSA, CA	H	33.75 FQ	37.26 MW	41.60 TQ	CABLS	1/08-3/08
	Santa Ana-Anaheim-Irvine PMSA, CA	Y	54740 FQ	61950 MW	72540 TQ	USBLS	5/07
	Colorado	Y	43380 FQ	49930 MW	57030 TQ	USBLS	5/07
	Denver-Aurora MSA, CO	Y	43840 FQ	50110 MW	56790 TQ	USBLS	5/07
	Connecticut	H	23.48 AE	28.08 MW		CTBLS	1/08-3/08
	Hartford-West Hartford-East Hartford MSA, CT	Y	51300 FQ	56700 MW	62080 TQ	USBLS	5/07
	Delaware	Y	50690 FQ	55750 MW	60680 TQ	USBLS	5/07
	Wilmington PMSA, DE-MD-NJ	Y	52270 FQ	56670 MW	61040 TQ	USBLS	5/07
	District of Columbia	Y	40720 FQ	46170 MW	52640 TQ	USBLS	5/07
	Washington-Arlington-Alexandria MSA, DC-VA-MD-WV	Y	49210 FQ	58920 MW	69890 TQ	USBLS	5/07
	Florida	Y	40420 FQ	46350 MW	53390 TQ	USBLS	5/07
	Fort Lauderdale-Pompano Beach-Deerfield Beach PMSA, FL	Y	43790 FQ	51060 MW	59630 TQ	USBLS	5/07
	Jacksonville MSA, FL	Y	38920 FQ	45110 MW	50810 TQ	USBLS	5/07
	Miami-Fort Lauderdale-Miami Beach MSA, FL	Y	42700 FQ	48680 MW	57800 TQ	USBLS	5/07
	Orlando-Kissimmee MSA, FL	Y	41260 FQ	46810 MW	53740 TQ	USBLS	5/07

AE Average entry wage	**AW** Average wage paid	**FQ** First quartile wage	**LO** Lowest wage paid	**MTC** Median total compensation	**TCC** Total cash compensation
AER Average entry range	**AWR** Average wage range	**H** Hourly	**LR** Low end range	**MW** Median wage paid	**TQ** Third quartile wage
AEX Average experienced wage	**AXR** Average experienced range	**HI** Highest wage paid	**M** Monthly	**MWR** Median wage range	**W** Weekly
ATC Average total compensation	**D** Daily	**HR** High end range	**MCC** Median cash compensation	**S** See annotated source	**Y** Yearly

Respiratory Therapist

Occupation/Type/Industry	Location	Per	Low	Mid	High	Source	Date
Respiratory Therapist	Tampa-St. Petersburg-Clearwater MSA, FL	Y	36890 FQ	44310 MW	51780 TQ	USBLS	5/07
	West Palm Beach-Boca Raton-Boynton Beach PMSA, FL	Y	43240 FQ	48030 MW	53130 TQ	USBLS	5/07
	Georgia	Y	41290 FQ	47220 MW	54550 TQ	USBLS	5/07
	Atlanta-Sandy Springs-Marietta MSA, GA	Y	43760 FQ	49930 MW	57520 TQ	USBLS	5/07
	Hawaii	Y	55230 FQ	60300 MW	65380 TQ	USBLS	5/07
	Honolulu MSA, HI	Y	55310 FQ	60460 MW	65510 TQ	USBLS	5/07
	Boise City-Nampa MSA, ID	Y	34400 FQ	41740 MW	50410 TQ	USBLS	5/07
	Coeur d'Alene MSA, ID	Y	40490 FQ	45060 MW	51200 TQ	USBLS	5/07
	Illinois	Y	41590 FQ	48690 MW	56610 TQ	USBLS	5/07
	Chicago-Naperville-Joliet MSA, IL-IN-WI	Y	43580 FQ	50350 MW	57930 TQ	USBLS	5/07
	Rockford MSA, IL	Y	38290 FQ	45460 MW	54400 TQ	USBLS	5/07
	Indiana	Y	42250 FQ	48160 MW	55060 TQ	USBLS	5/07
	Gary PMSA, IN	Y	43000 FQ	48330 MW	55690 TQ	USBLS	5/07
	Indianapolis-Carmel MSA, IN	Y	43830 FQ	51240 MW	58310 TQ	USBLS	5/07
	Iowa	Y	37760 FQ	43330 MW	48740 TQ	USBLS	5/07
	Cedar Rapids MSA, IA	Y	37370 FQ	42780 MW	48660 TQ	USBLS	5/07
	Davenport-Moline-Rock Island MSA, IA-IL	Y	41240 FQ	47000 MW	54430 TQ	USBLS	5/07
	Des Moines-West Des Moines MSA, IA	Y	38920 FQ	44390 MW	49240 TQ	USBLS	5/07
	Iowa City MSA, IA	Y	38410 FQ	43780 MW	49680 TQ	USBLS	5/07
	Kansas	Y	39070 FQ	45810 MW	52670 TQ	USBLS	5/07
	Wichita MSA, KS	Y	39430 FQ	46310 MW	52950 TQ	USBLS	5/07
	Kentucky	Y	37599 FQ	43994 MW	50732 TQ	KYBLS	2008
	Elizabethtown MSA, KY	Y	38590 FQ	43010 MW	47270 TQ	USBLS	5/07
	Louisville-Jefferson County MSA, KY-IN	Y	41810 FQ	46790 MW	51770 TQ	USBLS	5/07
	Louisiana	H	18.90 FQ	21.68 MW	24.54 TQ	LABLS	1/08-3/08
	Baton Rouge MSA, LA	Y	40120 FQ	45590 MW	52550 TQ	USBLS	5/07
	Lafayette MSA, LA	Y	38590 FQ	45950 MW	53570 TQ	USBLS	5/07
	New Orleans-Metairie-Kenner MSA, LA	Y	42200 FQ	46810 MW	51730 TQ	USBLS	5/07
	Maine	Y	43430 FQ	49140 MW	56500 TQ	USBLS	5/07
	Portland-South Portland-Biddeford MSA, ME	Y	42040 FQ	50170 MW	58290 TQ	USBLS	5/07
	Maryland	Y		60925 MW		MDBLS	3/08
	Baltimore-Towson MSA, MD	Y	54300 FQ	58710 MW	63360 TQ	USBLS	5/07
	Bethesda-Gaithersburg-Frederick PMSA, MD	Y	66840 FQ	72900 MW	78310 TQ	USBLS	5/07
	Massachusetts	Y	50520 FQ	57400 MW	64440 TQ	USBLS	5/07
	Boston-Cambridge-Quincy NECTA, MA	Y	51950 FQ	58480 MW	65750 TQ	USBLS	5/07
	Worcester MSA, MA-CT	Y	53890 FQ	59850 MW	66210 TQ	USBLS	5/07
	Michigan	Y	43510 FQ	48950 MW	55770 TQ	USBLS	5/07
	Detroit-Warren-Livonia MSA, MI	Y	44390 FQ	49340 MW	55690 TQ	USBLS	5/07
	Grand Rapids-Wyoming MSA, MI	Y	40920 FQ	46690 MW	52510 TQ	USBLS	5/07
	Warren-Troy-Farmington Hills PMSA, MI	Y	44300 FQ	48900 MW	54770 TQ	USBLS	5/07
	Minnesota	Y	52123 FQ	59498 MW	66362 TQ	MNBLS	10/08-12/08
	Duluth-Superior MSA, MN-WI	Y	51129 FQ	57040 MW	62208 TQ	MNBLS	10/08-12/08
	Minneapolis-Saint Paul MSA, MN-WI	Y	54152 FQ	60252 MW	66278 TQ	MNBLS	10/08-12/08
	Rochester MSA, MN	Y	54284 FQ	62043 MW	69389 TQ	MNBLS	10/08-12/08
	Mississippi	Y	35630 FQ	40870 MW	47590 TQ	USBLS	5/07
	Jackson MSA, MS	Y	36690 FQ	43420 MW	50570 TQ	USBLS	5/07
	Missouri	Y	38520 FQ	44810 MW	51130 TQ	USBLS	5/07
	Kansas City MSA, MO-KS	Y	41080 FQ	46730 MW	52580 TQ	USBLS	5/07
	St. Louis MSA, MO-IL	Y	40690 FQ	46890 MW	53860 TQ	USBLS	5/07
	Montana	Y	40530 FQ	45030 MW	49560 TQ	USBLS	5/07
	Billings MSA, MT	Y	42610 FQ	46860 MW	52640 TQ	USBLS	5/07
	Nebraska	Y	41190 FQ	47640 MW	54620 TQ	USBLS	5/07
	Omaha-Council Bluffs MSA, NE-IA	Y	41810 FQ	48140 MW	55150 TQ	USBLS	5/07
	Nevada	H	26.63 FQ	29.90 MW	33.13 TQ	NVBLS	5/08
	Las Vegas-Paradise MSA, NV	H	27.21 FQ	30.44 MW	33.60 TQ	NVBLS	5/08
	New Hampshire	H	23.39 AE	27.68 MW	29.10 AEX	NHBLS	6/08

Occupation/Type/Industry	Location	Per	Low	Mid	High	Source	Date
Respiratory Therapist	Nashua NECTA, NH-MA	Y	47480 FQ	54690 MW	59970 TQ	USBLS	5/07
	New Jersey	Y	54790 FQ	60170 MW	66690 TQ	USBLS	5/07
	Camden PMSA, NJ	Y	54870 FQ	59940 MW	65700 TQ	USBLS	5/07
	Edison PMSA, NJ	Y	55150 FQ	61890 MW	69960 TQ	USBLS	5/07
	Newark-Union PMSA, NJ-PA	Y	54510 FQ	59160 MW	64680 TQ	USBLS	5/07
	New Mexico	Y	30700 FQ	43560 MW	52160 TQ	USBLS	5/07
	Albuquerque MSA, NM	Y	28550 FQ	41190 MW	53030 TQ	USBLS	5/07
	New York	Y	51710 FQ	60140 MW	68750 TQ	USBLS	5/07
	Albany-Schenectady-Troy MSA, NY	Y	45360 FQ	51370 MW	57640 TQ	USBLS	5/07
	Buffalo-Niagara Falls MSA, NY	Y	43520 FQ	51200 MW	58640 TQ	USBLS	5/07
	Kingston MSA, NY	Y	55600 FQ	60720 MW	66340 TQ	USBLS	5/07
	Nassau-Suffolk PMSA, NY	Y	57870 FQ	64120 MW	71600 TQ	USBLS	5/07
	New York-Northern New Jersey-Long Island MSA, NY-NJ-PA	Y	56390 FQ	62960 MW	70960 TQ	USBLS	5/07
	North Carolina	Y	41740 FQ	47440 MW	54640 TQ	USBLS	5/07
	Charlotte-Gastonia-Concord MSA, NC-SC	Y	42250 FQ	47000 MW	53600 TQ	USBLS	5/07
	Raleigh-Cary MSA, NC	Y	42850 FQ	48540 MW	55350 TQ	USBLS	5/07
	North Dakota	Y	35600 FQ	41090 MW	47410 TQ	USBLS	5/07
	Fargo MSA, ND-MN	Y	35320 FQ	42090 MW	47770 TQ	USBLS	5/07
	Ohio	Y	42070 FQ	47270 MW	52800 TQ	USBLS	5/07
	Cincinnati-Middletown MSA, OH-KY-IN	Y	41640 FQ	47660 MW	54120 TQ	USBLS	5/07
	Cleveland-Elyria-Mentor MSA, OH	Y	44120 FQ	50030 MW	56130 TQ	USBLS	5/07
	Columbus MSA, OH	Y	42560 FQ	47570 MW	54270 TQ	USBLS	5/07
	Dayton MSA, OH	Y	41830 FQ	47870 MW	54390 TQ	USBLS	5/07
	Mansfield MSA, OH	Y	38770 FQ	43770 MW	48110 TQ	USBLS	5/07
	Oklahoma	Y	38800 FQ	44790 MW	51860 TQ	USBLS	5/07
	Oklahoma City MSA, OK	Y	39410 FQ	44920 MW	51190 TQ	USBLS	5/07
	Tulsa MSA, OK	Y	38890 FQ	45970 MW	58430 TQ	USBLS	5/07
	Oregon	H	22.60 FQ	25.86 MW	28.95 TQ	ORBLS	5/08
	Portland-Vancouver-Beaverton MSA, OR-WA	Y	48290 FQ	54550 MW	59990 TQ	USBLS	5/07
	Pennsylvania	Y	43670 FQ	50170 MW	58630 TQ	USBLS	5/07
	Allentown-Bethlehem-Easton MSA, PA-NJ	Y	48140 FQ	55060 MW	61640 TQ	USBLS	5/07
	Philadelphia-Camden-Wilmington MSA, PA-NJ-DE-MD	Y	50940 FQ	57450 MW	63360 TQ	USBLS	5/07
	Pittsburgh MSA, PA	Y	41730 FQ	46390 MW	51160 TQ	USBLS	5/07
	Rhode Island	Y	48070 FQ	54430 MW	60120 TQ	USBLS	5/07
	Providence-Fall River-Warwick MSA, RI-MA	Y	47660 FQ	54170 MW	60180 TQ	USBLS	5/07
	South Carolina	Y	39170 FQ	45240 MW	51560 TQ	USBLS	5/07
	Charleston-North Charleston MSA, SC	Y	39200 FQ	45090 MW	51730 TQ	USBLS	5/07
	Columbia MSA, SC	Y	39720 FQ	45890 MW	51910 TQ	USBLS	5/07
	South Dakota	Y	40483 FQ	48017 MW	56683 TQ	SDBLS	7/08-9/08
	Sioux Falls MSA, SD	Y	40577 FQ	48572 MW	57801 TQ	SDBLS	7/08-9/08
	Tennessee	Y	38060 FQ	44620 MW	51080 TQ	USBLS	5/07
	Memphis MSA, TN-MS-AR	Y	39810 FQ	45220 MW	50310 TQ	USBLS	5/07
	Nashville-Davidson-Murfreesboro MSA, TN	Y	41080 FQ	48620 MW	55700 TQ	USBLS	5/07
	Texas	Y	41680 FQ	47230 MW	53670 TQ	USBLS	5/07
	Austin-Round Rock MSA, TX	Y	40270 FQ	46710 MW	53740 TQ	USBLS	5/07
	Dallas-Fort Worth-Arlington MSA, TX	Y	43760 FQ	48960 MW	56190 TQ	USBLS	5/07
	El Paso MSA, TX	Y	36760 FQ	43530 MW	51910 TQ	USBLS	5/07
	Houston-Sugar Land-Baytown MSA, TX	Y	44090 FQ	49340 MW	55970 TQ	USBLS	5/07
	San Antonio MSA, TX	Y	39890 FQ	45700 MW	51510 TQ	USBLS	5/07
	Utah	Y	44750 FQ	52240 MW	58760 TQ	USBLS	5/07
	Salt Lake City MSA, UT	Y	47190 FQ	53450 MW	58890 TQ	USBLS	5/07
	Vermont	Y	44380 FQ	50320 MW	58340 TQ	USBLS	5/07
	Burlington-South Burlington MSA, VT	Y	43900 FQ	48920 MW	55970 TQ	USBLS	5/07
	Virginia	Y	43740 FQ	52540 MW	60570 TQ	USBLS	5/07
	Richmond MSA, VA	Y	40380 FQ	49340 MW	58540 TQ	USBLS	5/07

AE Average entry wage	**AW** Average wage paid	**FQ** First quartile wage	**LO** Lowest wage paid	**MTC** Median total compensation	**TCC** Total cash compensation
AER Average entry range	**AWR** Average wage range	**H** Hourly	**LR** Low end range	**MW** Median wage paid	**TQ** Third quartile wage
AEX Average experienced wage	**AXR** Average experienced range	**HI** Highest wage paid	**M** Monthly	**MWR** Median wage range	**W** Weekly
ATC Average total compensation	**D** Daily	**HR** High end range	**MCC** Median cash compensation	**S** See annotated source	**Y** Yearly

Occupation/Type/Industry	Location	Per	Low	Mid	High	Source	Date
Respiratory Therapist	Roanoke MSA, VA	Y	38150 FQ	44940 MW	52700 TQ	USBLS	5/07
	Virginia Beach-Norfolk-Newport News MSA, VA-NC	Y	44520 FQ	50410 MW	57570 TQ	USBLS	5/07
	Washington	H	24.16 FQ	27.33 MW	30.82 TQ	WABLS	3/08
	Seattle-Tacoma-Bellevue MSA, WA	Y	50290 FQ	57190 MW	65030 TQ	USBLS	5/07
	West Virginia	Y	38507 FQ	44469 MW	50702 TQ	WVBLS	7/08-9/08
	Charleston MSA, WV	Y	34700 FQ	41070 MW	48720 TQ	USBLS	5/07
	Wisconsin	Y	44400 FQ	50950 MW	58130 TQ	USBLS	5/07
	Milwaukee-Waukesha-West Allis MSA, WI	Y	48860 FQ	54940 MW	60840 TQ	USBLS	5/07
	Wyoming	Y	44585 FQ	50657 MW	58708 TQ	WYBLS	9/08
	Puerto Rico	Y	13560 FQ	16230 MW	21540 TQ	USBLS	5/07
	San Juan-Caguas-Guaynabo MSA, PR	Y	14250 FQ	18340 MW	22560 TQ	USBLS	5/07
Respiratory Therapy Technician	Alabama	Y	27390 FQ	34740 MW	42030 TQ	USBLS	5/07
	Birmingham-Hoover MSA, AL	Y	32070 FQ	37680 MW	45080 TQ	USBLS	5/07
	Arizona	Y	29530 FQ	33140 MW	39240 TQ	USBLS	5/07
	Phoenix-Mesa-Scottsdale MSA, AZ	Y	31080 FQ	34550 MW	40850 TQ	USBLS	5/07
	Arkansas	Y	25510 FQ	31850 MW	37670 TQ	USBLS	5/07
	Little Rock-North Little Rock MSA, AR	Y	23340 FQ	27240 MW	32700 TQ	USBLS	5/07
	California	H	22.37 FQ	26.69 MW	30.83 TQ	CABLS	1/08-3/08
	Los Angeles-Long Beach-Glendale PMSA, CA	H	22.68 FQ	26.52 MW	31.34 TQ	CABLS	1/08-3/08
	Riverside-San Bernardino-Ontario MSA, CA	H	20.98 FQ	25.35 MW	28.92 TQ	CABLS	1/08-3/08
	Sacramento-Arden Arcade-Roseville MSA, CA	H	18.18 FQ	23.41 MW	28.51 TQ	CABLS	1/08-3/08
	San Diego-Carlsbad-San Marcos MSA, CA	H	24.11 FQ	26.36 MW	28.86 TQ	CABLS	1/08-3/08
	San Jose-Sunnyvale-Santa Clara MSA, CA	H	27.44 FQ	33.08 MW	37.55 TQ	CABLS	1/08-3/08
	Santa Ana-Anaheim-Irvine PMSA, CA	Y	49700 FQ	55410 MW	60160 TQ	USBLS	5/07
	Colorado	Y	30890 FQ	37290 MW	45230 TQ	USBLS	5/07
	Connecticut	H	15.00 AE	20.82 MW		CTBLS	1/08-3/08
	Bridgeport-Stamford-Norwalk MSA, CT	Y	32070 FQ	40050 MW	50010 TQ	USBLS	5/07
	District of Columbia	Y	34130 FQ	40800 MW	48870 TQ	USBLS	5/07
	Washington-Arlington-Alexandria MSA, DC-VA-MD-WV	Y	37280 FQ	47850 MW	57710 TQ	USBLS	5/07
	Florida	Y	35510 FQ	40060 MW	45730 TQ	USBLS	5/07
	Fort Lauderdale-Pompano Beach-Deerfield Beach PMSA, FL	Y	37560 FQ	41600 MW	46540 TQ	USBLS	5/07
	Jacksonville MSA, FL	Y	36000 FQ	41920 MW	47190 TQ	USBLS	5/07
	Miami-Fort Lauderdale-Miami Beach MSA, FL	Y	36030 FQ	39930 MW	45160 TQ	USBLS	5/07
	Orlando-Kissimmee MSA, FL	Y	35480 FQ	39630 MW	46050 TQ	USBLS	5/07
	Tampa-St. Petersburg-Clearwater MSA, FL	Y	31610 FQ	37700 MW	43270 TQ	USBLS	5/07
	West Palm Beach-Boca Raton-Boynton Beach PMSA, FL	Y	36590 FQ	40550 MW	45090 TQ	USBLS	5/07
	Georgia	Y	35270 FQ	41190 MW	47620 TQ	USBLS	5/07
	Atlanta-Sandy Springs-Marietta MSA, GA	Y	38730 FQ	44370 MW	49830 TQ	USBLS	5/07
	Hawaii	Y	39170 FQ	46740 MW	53620 TQ	USBLS	5/07
	Idaho	Y	32010 FQ	39360 MW	48070 TQ	USBLS	5/07
	Illinois	Y	31700 FQ	37730 MW	46060 TQ	USBLS	5/07
	Chicago-Naperville-Joliet MSA, IL-IN-WI	Y	33150 FQ	38900 MW	47280 TQ	USBLS	5/07
	Indiana	Y	38880 FQ	45520 MW	52770 TQ	USBLS	5/07
	Gary PMSA, IN	Y	38400 FQ	43820 MW	50040 TQ	USBLS	5/07
	Indianapolis-Carmel MSA, IN	Y	45040 FQ	52580 MW	60720 TQ	USBLS	5/07
	Iowa	Y	28050 FQ	34030 MW	38940 TQ	USBLS	5/07
	Kansas	Y	25850 FQ	32860 MW	41670 TQ	USBLS	5/07
	Wichita MSA, KS	Y	25040 FQ	30860 MW	44090 TQ	USBLS	5/07
	Kentucky	Y	32798 FQ	37399 MW	42391 TQ	KYBLS	2008

AE Average entry wage	**AW** Average wage paid	**FQ** First quartile wage	**LO** Lowest wage paid	**MTC** Median total compensation	**TCC** Total cash compensation
AER Average entry range	**AWR** Average wage range	**H** Hourly	**LR** Low end range	**MW** Median wage paid	**TQ** Third quartile wage
AEX Average experienced wage	**AXR** Average experienced range	**HI** Highest wage paid	**M** Monthly	**MWR** Median wage range	**W** Weekly
ATC Average total compensation	**D** Daily	**HR** High end range	**MCC** Median cash compensation	**S** See annotated source	**Y** Yearly

1405

Occupation/Type/Industry	Location	Per	Low	Mid	High	Source	Date
Respiratory Therapy Technician	Louisville-Jefferson County MSA, KY-IN	Y	29670 FQ	36190 MW	43790 TQ	USBLS	5/07
	Louisiana	H	17.02 FQ	19.33 MW	21.89 TQ	LABLS	1/08-3/08
	Baton Rouge MSA, LA	Y	32450 FQ	35930 MW	39120 TQ	USBLS	5/07
	Lafayette MSA, LA	Y	35700 FQ	40190 MW	45250 TQ	USBLS	5/07
	New Orleans-Metairie-Kenner MSA, LA	Y	35360 FQ	41500 MW	46010 TQ	USBLS	5/07
	Maine	Y	40020 FQ	44160 MW	48200 TQ	USBLS	5/07
	Maryland	Y		58750 MW		MDBLS	3/08
	Baltimore-Towson MSA, MD	Y	49890 FQ	56920 MW	62730 TQ	USBLS	5/07
	Bethesda-Gaithersburg-Frederick PMSA, MD	Y	55030 FQ	58790 MW	62770 TQ	USBLS	5/07
	Massachusetts	Y	33440 FQ	45420 MW	57270 TQ	USBLS	5/07
	Boston-Cambridge-Quincy NECTA, MA	Y	32440 FQ	39440 MW	57590 TQ	USBLS	5/07
	Worcester MSA, MA-CT	Y	43070 FQ	48190 MW	52810 TQ	USBLS	5/07
	Michigan	Y	29850 FQ	38770 MW	47080 TQ	USBLS	5/07
	Detroit-Warren-Livonia MSA, MI	Y	34180 FQ	43980 MW	51170 TQ	USBLS	5/07
	Warren-Troy-Farmington Hills PMSA, MI	Y	34040 FQ	44120 MW	49220 TQ	USBLS	5/07
	Minnesota	Y	42884 FQ	53106 MW	61340 TQ	MNBLS	10/08-12/08
	Minneapolis-Saint Paul MSA, MN-WI	Y	49863 FQ	58295 MW	63464 TQ	MNBLS	10/08-12/08
	Mississippi	Y	27580 FQ	32460 MW	37170 TQ	USBLS	5/07
	Missouri	Y	27550 FQ	32690 MW	38480 TQ	USBLS	5/07
	Kansas City MSA, MO-KS	Y	26490 FQ	29660 MW	33540 TQ	USBLS	5/07
	St. Louis MSA, MO-IL	Y	29870 FQ	35650 MW	42310 TQ	USBLS	5/07
	Montana	Y	25960 FQ	38030 MW	45540 TQ	USBLS	5/07
	Nebraska	Y	34090 FQ	39540 MW	47380 TQ	USBLS	5/07
	Omaha-Council Bluffs MSA, NE-IA	Y	35100 FQ	41100 MW	47980 TQ	USBLS	5/07
	Nevada	H	23.53 FQ	29.67 MW	34.45 TQ	NVBLS	5/08
	Las Vegas-Paradise MSA, NV	H	22.19 FQ	28.89 MW	34.01 TQ	NVBLS	5/08
	New Hampshire	H	21.98 AE	27.97 MW	29.38 AEX	NHBLS	6/08
	New Jersey	Y	44630 FQ	53960 MW	60420 TQ	USBLS	5/07
	Camden PMSA, NJ	Y	48310 FQ	54970 MW	59590 TQ	USBLS	5/07
	Edison PMSA, NJ	Y	43500 FQ	54300 MW	61100 TQ	USBLS	5/07
	Newark-Union PMSA, NJ-PA	Y	44640 FQ	52920 MW	60430 TQ	USBLS	5/07
	New Mexico	Y	33340 FQ	41780 MW	48400 TQ	USBLS	5/07
	Albuquerque MSA, NM	Y	29750 FQ	44200 MW	50690 TQ	USBLS	5/07
	New York	Y	43350 FQ	52550 MW	60250 TQ	USBLS	5/07
	Buffalo-Niagara Falls MSA, NY	Y	39420 FQ	47220 MW	59590 TQ	USBLS	5/07
	Nassau-Suffolk PMSA, NY	Y	40470 FQ	52980 MW	58880 TQ	USBLS	5/07
	New York-Northern New Jersey-Long Island MSA, NY-NJ-PA	Y	44970 FQ	54260 MW	60970 TQ	USBLS	5/07
	North Carolina	Y	31690 FQ	39010 MW	46380 TQ	USBLS	5/07
	Charlotte-Gastonia-Concord MSA, NC-SC	Y	27220 FQ	31160 MW	43380 TQ	USBLS	5/07
	Ohio	Y	34370 FQ	39380 MW	44430 TQ	USBLS	5/07
	Cincinnati-Middletown MSA, OH-KY-IN	Y	35100 FQ	40380 MW	45670 TQ	USBLS	5/07
	Cleveland-Elyria-Mentor MSA, OH	Y	32830 FQ	37470 MW	41030 TQ	USBLS	5/07
	Dayton MSA, OH	Y	39680 FQ	42780 MW	45920 TQ	USBLS	5/07
	Oklahoma	Y	29460 FQ	35590 MW	41890 TQ	USBLS	5/07
	Oklahoma City MSA, OK	Y	28360 FQ	34060 MW	43470 TQ	USBLS	5/07
	Tulsa MSA, OK	Y	29840 FQ	36360 MW	42120 TQ	USBLS	5/07
	Pennsylvania	Y	33870 FQ	40300 MW	47780 TQ	USBLS	5/07
	Allentown-Bethlehem-Easton MSA, PA-NJ	Y	40110 FQ	45960 MW	53220 TQ	USBLS	5/07
	Philadelphia-Camden-Wilmington MSA, PA-NJ-DE-MD	Y	33460 FQ	43220 MW	52110 TQ	USBLS	5/07
	Pittsburgh MSA, PA	Y	28940 FQ	38140 MW	44580 TQ	USBLS	5/07
	South Carolina	Y	28450 FQ	36820 MW	45200 TQ	USBLS	5/07
	Charleston-North Charleston MSA, SC	Y	30240 FQ	42520 MW	48870 TQ	USBLS	5/07
	South Dakota	Y	23843 FQ	26277 MW	35063 TQ	SDBLS	7/08-9/08
	Sioux Falls MSA, SD	Y	23276 FQ	25444 MW	29779 TQ	SDBLS	7/08-9/08

AE	Average entry wage	AW	Average wage paid	FQ	First quartile wage	LO	Lowest wage paid	MTC	Median total compensation	TCC	Total cash compensation
AER	Average entry range	AWR	Average wage range	H	Hourly	LR	Low end range	MW	Median wage paid	TQ	Third quartile wage
AEX	Average experienced wage	AXR	Average experienced range	HI	Highest wage paid	M	Monthly	MWR	Median wage range	W	Weekly
ATC	Average total compensation	D	Daily	HR	High end range	MCC	Median cash compensation	S	See annotated source	Y	Yearly

Occupation/Type/Industry	Location	Per	Low	Mid	High	Source	Date
Respiratory Therapy Technician	Tennessee	Y	30890 FQ	36540 MW	41610 TQ	USBLS	5/07
	Memphis MSA, TN-MS-AR	Y	29680 FQ	35570 MW	39880 TQ	USBLS	5/07
	Nashville-Davidson-Murfreesboro MSA, TN	Y	35550 FQ	40720 MW	45130 TQ	USBLS	5/07
	Texas	Y	32610 FQ	40290 MW	48640 TQ	USBLS	5/07
	Dallas-Fort Worth-Arlington MSA, TX	Y	35720 FQ	43410 MW	52450 TQ	USBLS	5/07
	Houston-Sugar Land-Baytown MSA, TX	Y	30770 FQ	41440 MW	49990 TQ	USBLS	5/07
	San Antonio MSA, TX	Y	36700 FQ	42460 MW	49040 TQ	USBLS	5/07
	Utah	Y	24820 FQ	28500 MW	35160 TQ	USBLS	5/07
	Virginia	Y	37160 FQ	45070 MW	53770 TQ	USBLS	5/07
	Richmond MSA, VA	Y	38630 FQ	46600 MW	54980 TQ	USBLS	5/07
	Washington	H	16.51 FQ	20.13 MW	23.53 TQ	WABLS	3/08
	West Virginia	Y	30554 FQ	35969 MW	41670 TQ	WVBLS	7/08-9/08
	Wisconsin	Y	28770 FQ	35740 MW	42920 TQ	USBLS	5/07
	Wyoming	Y	22980 FQ	33777 MW	47615 TQ	WYBLS	9/08
	Puerto Rico	Y	13510 FQ	16040 MW	19820 TQ	USBLS	5/07
	San Juan-Caguas-Guaynabo MSA, PR	Y	13610 FQ	16370 MW	20310 TQ	USBLS	5/07
Retail Marketing Director							
Apparel Industry	United States	Y		237500 MW		247FASH	2009
Retail Salesperson	Alabama	Y	15300 FQ	18770 MW	24840 TQ	USBLS	5/07
	Birmingham-Hoover MSA, AL	Y	16540 FQ	20130 MW	27440 TQ	USBLS	5/07
	Montgomery MSA, AL	Y	15810 FQ	19150 MW	26430 TQ	USBLS	5/07
	Alaska	Y	19200 FQ	23180 MW	29250 TQ	USBLS	5/07
	Anchorage MSA, AK	Y	18720 FQ	22780 MW	28650 TQ	USBLS	5/07
	Arizona	Y	16970 FQ	21280 MW	28950 TQ	USBLS	5/07
	Phoenix-Mesa-Scottsdale MSA, AZ	Y	17170 FQ	21630 MW	29190 TQ	USBLS	5/07
	Tucson MSA, AZ	Y	16900 FQ	21160 MW	29720 TQ	USBLS	5/07
	Arkansas	Y	15000 FQ	17900 MW	22940 TQ	USBLS	5/07
	Little Rock-North Little Rock MSA, AR	Y	15430 FQ	18550 MW	23440 TQ	USBLS	5/07
	California	H	8.64 FQ	10.18 MW	13.58 TQ	CABLS	1/08-3/08
	Los Angeles-Long Beach-Glendale PMSA, CA	H	8.55 FQ	10.01 MW	13.53 TQ	CABLS	1/08-3/08
	Oakland-Fremont-Hayward MSA, CA	H	8.90 FQ	10.76 MW	14.16 TQ	CABLS	1/08-3/08
	Riverside-San Bernardino-Ontario MSA, CA	H	8.56 FQ	9.85 MW	13.30 TQ	CABLS	1/08-3/08
	Sacramento-Arden Arcade-Roseville MSA, CA	H	8.63 FQ	9.95 MW	12.91 TQ	CABLS	1/08-3/08
	San Diego-Carlsbad-San Marcos MSA, CA	H	8.56 FQ	10.03 MW	13.70 TQ	CABLS	1/08-3/08
	San Francisco-San Mateo-Redwood PMSA, CA	H	9.51 FQ	11.79 MW	15.27 TQ	CABLS	1/08-3/08
	San Jose-Sunnyvale-Santa Clara MSA, CA	H	8.89 FQ	10.66 MW	13.84 TQ	CABLS	1/08-3/08
	Santa Ana-Anaheim-Irvine PMSA, CA	Y	17660 FQ	20460 MW	28200 TQ	USBLS	5/07
	Stockton MSA, CA	H	8.53 FQ	9.79 MW	12.43 TQ	CABLS	1/08-3/08
	Colorado	Y	17340 FQ	21520 MW	28710 TQ	USBLS	5/07
	Denver-Aurora MSA, CO	Y	17530 FQ	21840 MW	29250 TQ	USBLS	5/07
	Pueblo MSA, CO	Y	16020 FQ	19360 MW	24810 TQ	USBLS	5/07
	Connecticut	H	8.61 AE	11.09 MW		CTBLS	1/08-3/08
	Bridgeport-Stamford-Norwalk MSA, CT	Y	18650 FQ	23610 MW	33490 TQ	USBLS	5/07
	Hartford-West Hartford-East Hartford MSA, CT	Y	18480 FQ	22420 MW	29940 TQ	USBLS	5/07
	Delaware	Y	16960 FQ	20140 MW	27610 TQ	USBLS	5/07
	Wilmington PMSA, DE-MD-NJ	Y	16960 FQ	20440 MW	28170 TQ	USBLS	5/07
	District of Columbia	Y	19680 FQ	23410 MW	28750 TQ	USBLS	5/07
	Washington-Arlington-Alexandria MSA, DC-VA-MD-WV	Y	17130 FQ	21200 MW	28620 TQ	USBLS	5/07
	Florida	Y	17550 FQ	22080 MW	30570 TQ	USBLS	5/07

AE	Average entry wage	AW	Average wage paid	FQ	First quartile wage
AER	Average entry range	AWR	Average wage range	H	Hourly
AEX	Average experienced wage	AXR	Average experienced range	HI	Highest wage paid
ATC	Average total salaries	D	Daily	HR	High end range

LO	Lowest wage paid	MTC	Median total compensation	TCC	Total cash compensation
LR	Low end range	MW	Median wage paid	TQ	Third quartile wage
M	Monthly	MWR	Median wage range	W	Weekly
MCC	Median cash compensation	S	See annotated source	Y	Yearly

Occupation/Type/Industry	Location	Per	Low	Mid	High	Source	Date
Retail Salesperson	Fort Lauderdale-Pompano Beach-Deerfield Beach PMSA, FL	Y	18180 FQ	23400 MW	33430 TQ	USBLS	5/07
	Jacksonville MSA, FL	Y	17200 FQ	20990 MW	28260 TQ	USBLS	5/07
	Miami-Fort Lauderdale-Miami Beach MSA, FL	Y	18200 FQ	23250 MW	32080 TQ	USBLS	5/07
	Orlando-Kissimmee MSA, FL	Y	17210 FQ	21170 MW	29340 TQ	USBLS	5/07
	Tampa-St. Petersburg-Clearwater MSA, FL	Y	17120 FQ	21340 MW	29600 TQ	USBLS	5/07
	West Palm Beach-Boca Raton-Boynton Beach PMSA, FL	Y	19200 FQ	24280 MW	34310 TQ	USBLS	5/07
	Georgia	Y	15860 FQ	19300 MW	25520 TQ	USBLS	5/07
	Atlanta-Sandy Springs-Marietta MSA, GA	Y	16760 FQ	20130 MW	27010 TQ	USBLS	5/07
	Hawaii	Y	17470 FQ	20960 MW	25410 TQ	USBLS	5/07
	Honolulu MSA, HI	Y	17070 FQ	20220 MW	24450 TQ	USBLS	5/07
	Idaho	Y	16270 FQ	19600 MW	25790 TQ	USBLS	5/07
	Boise City-Nampa MSA, ID	Y	16810 FQ	19690 MW	26140 TQ	USBLS	5/07
	Coeur d'Alene MSA, ID	Y	17190 FQ	21880 MW	28310 TQ	USBLS	5/07
	Illinois	Y	16700 FQ	20280 MW	27420 TQ	USBLS	5/07
	Champaign-Urbana MSA, IL	Y	17130 FQ	20370 MW	24980 TQ	USBLS	5/07
	Chicago-Naperville-Joliet MSA, IL-IN-WI	Y	16920 FQ	20670 MW	27970 TQ	USBLS	5/07
	Indiana	Y	15460 FQ	18910 MW	25080 TQ	USBLS	5/07
	Fort Wayne MSA, IN	Y	15840 FQ	19200 MW	25270 TQ	USBLS	5/07
	Gary PMSA, IN	Y	15330 FQ	18980 MW	25520 TQ	USBLS	5/07
	Indianapolis-Carmel MSA, IN	Y	16400 FQ	19950 MW	26710 TQ	USBLS	5/07
	Iowa	Y	15590 FQ	19000 MW	25870 TQ	USBLS	5/07
	Des Moines-West Des Moines MSA, IA	Y	16290 FQ	20080 MW	26890 TQ	USBLS	5/07
	Waterloo-Cedar Falls MSA, IA	Y	14930 FQ	17630 MW	22520 TQ	USBLS	5/07
	Kansas	Y	15270 FQ	18770 MW	25680 TQ	USBLS	5/07
	Wichita MSA, KS	Y	15010 FQ	18830 MW	25070 TQ	USBLS	5/07
	Kentucky	Y	14990 FQ	18591 MW	24244 TQ	KYBLS	2008
	Bowling Green MSA, KY	Y	13860 FQ	16790 MW	20600 TQ	USBLS	5/07
	Louisville-Jefferson County MSA, KY-IN	Y	15740 FQ	19200 MW	25240 TQ	USBLS	5/07
	Louisiana	H	7.39 FQ	9.33 MW	12.83 TQ	LABLS	1/08-3/08
	Baton Rouge MSA, LA	Y	14940 FQ	18680 MW	24900 TQ	USBLS	5/07
	New Orleans-Metairie-Kenner MSA, LA	Y	16240 FQ	20450 MW	27800 TQ	USBLS	5/07
	Maine	Y	17870 FQ	22050 MW	28460 TQ	USBLS	5/07
	Portland-South Portland-Biddeford MSA, ME	Y	18660 FQ	22910 MW	29090 TQ	USBLS	5/07
	Maryland	Y		20325 MW		MDBLS	3/08
	Baltimore-Towson MSA, MD	Y	16320 FQ	20120 MW	27530 TQ	USBLS	5/07
	Bethesda-Gaithersburg-Frederick PMSA, MD	Y	16930 FQ	20940 MW	28730 TQ	USBLS	5/07
	Cumberland MSA, MD-WV	Y	14810 FQ	17620 MW	22390 TQ	USBLS	5/07
	Massachusetts	Y	17850 FQ	21170 MW	27740 TQ	USBLS	5/07
	Boston-Cambridge-Quincy NECTA, MA	Y	18040 FQ	21670 MW	28310 TQ	USBLS	5/07
	Springfield MSA, MA-CT	Y	17560 FQ	20280 MW	27550 TQ	USBLS	5/07
	Worcester MSA, MA-CT	Y	18030 FQ	22060 MW	30170 TQ	USBLS	5/07
	Michigan	Y	16060 FQ	20070 MW	27260 TQ	USBLS	5/07
	Detroit-Warren-Livonia MSA, MI	Y	16040 FQ	20190 MW	27970 TQ	USBLS	5/07
	Grand Rapids-Wyoming MSA, MI	Y	15950 FQ	20390 MW	28530 TQ	USBLS	5/07
	Warren-Troy-Farmington Hills PMSA, MI	Y	16070 FQ	20520 MW	28740 TQ	USBLS	5/07
	Minnesota	Y	17135 FQ	20154 MW	26109 TQ	MNBLS	10/08-12/08
	Duluth-Superior MSA, MN-WI	Y	15905 FQ	18782 MW	24036 TQ	MNBLS	10/08-12/08
	Minneapolis-Saint Paul MSA, MN-WI	Y	17613 FQ	20824 MW	27278 TQ	MNBLS	10/08-12/08
	Rochester MSA, MN	Y	16760 FQ	20025 MW	25832 TQ	MNBLS	10/08-12/08
	Mississippi	Y	15810 FQ	19590 MW	26110 TQ	USBLS	5/07
	Hattiesburg MSA, MS	Y	16080 FQ	19150 MW	32330 TQ	USBLS	5/07
	Jackson MSA, MS	Y	15910 FQ	20100 MW	28660 TQ	USBLS	5/07
	Missouri	Y	16000 FQ	19230 MW	26520 TQ	USBLS	5/07
	Kansas City MSA, MO-KS	Y	16550 FQ	20020 MW	27730 TQ	USBLS	5/07
	St. Louis MSA, MO-IL	Y	16180 FQ	19470 MW	26900 TQ	USBLS	5/07

AE	Average entry wage	AW	Average wage paid	FQ	First quartile wage	LO	Lowest wage paid	MTC Median total compensation	TCC Total cash compensation
AER	Average entry range	AWR	Average wage range	H	Hourly	LR	Low end range	MW Median wage paid	TQ Third quartile wage
AEX	Average experienced wage	AXR	Average experienced range	HI	Highest wage paid	M	Monthly	MWR Median wage range	W Weekly
ATC	Average total compensation	D	Daily	HR	High end range	MCC	Median cash compensation	S See annotated source	Y Yearly

Retail Salesperson

Occupation/Type/Industry	Location	Per	Low	Mid	High	Source	Date
Retail Salesperson	Montana	Y	15690 FQ	19400 MW	27380 TQ	USBLS	5/07
	Billings MSA, MT	Y	15640 FQ	20200 MW	28200 TQ	USBLS	5/07
	Nebraska	Y	15090 FQ	18620 MW	25750 TQ	USBLS	5/07
	Omaha-Council Bluffs MSA, NE-IA	Y	16330 FQ	19970 MW	27880 TQ	USBLS	5/07
	Nevada	H	8.31 FQ	10.15 MW	13.35 TQ	NVBLS	5/08
	Las Vegas-Paradise MSA, NV	H	8.21 FQ	10.03 MW	13.27 TQ	NVBLS	5/08
	Reno-Sparks MSA, NV	H	8.62 FQ	10.40 MW	13.51 TQ	NVBLS	5/08
	New Hampshire	H	7.94 AE	10.49 MW	14.28 AEX	NHBLS	6/08
	Manchester MSA, NH	Y	16280 FQ	19560 MW	28580 TQ	USBLS	5/07
	Nashua NECTA, NH-MA	Y	17210 FQ	21090 MW	26770 TQ	USBLS	5/07
	New Jersey	Y	16980 FQ	20920 MW	28960 TQ	USBLS	5/07
	Camden PMSA, NJ	Y	16720 FQ	20860 MW	29440 TQ	USBLS	5/07
	Edison PMSA, NJ	Y	17280 FQ	21210 MW	28770 TQ	USBLS	5/07
	Newark-Union PMSA, NJ-PA	Y	16970 FQ	20910 MW	29380 TQ	USBLS	5/07
	Vineland-Millville-Bridgeton MSA, NJ	Y	16760 FQ	19970 MW	26240 TQ	USBLS	5/07
	New Mexico	Y	15370 FQ	19120 MW	24970 TQ	USBLS	5/07
	Albuquerque MSA, NM	Y	15600 FQ	19730 MW	27010 TQ	USBLS	5/07
	New York	Y	16930 FQ	20970 MW	29070 TQ	USBLS	5/07
	Albany-Schenectady-Troy MSA, NY	Y	16780 FQ	20780 MW	28510 TQ	USBLS	5/07
	Binghamton MSA, NY	Y	15920 FQ	19380 MW	26180 TQ	USBLS	5/07
	Buffalo-Niagara Falls MSA, NY	Y	15800 FQ	18640 MW	24130 TQ	USBLS	5/07
	Nassau-Suffolk PMSA, NY	Y	17660 FQ	22340 MW	31430 TQ	USBLS	5/07
	New York-Northern New Jersey-Long Island MSA, NY-NJ-PA	Y	17220 FQ	21460 MW	29660 TQ	USBLS	5/07
	North Carolina	Y	16030 FQ	19520 MW	26010 TQ	USBLS	5/07
	Charlotte-Gastonia-Concord MSA, NC-SC	Y	16380 FQ	19830 MW	27270 TQ	USBLS	5/07
	Durham MSA, NC	Y	15710 FQ	19620 MW	25650 TQ	USBLS	5/07
	Raleigh-Cary MSA, NC	Y	16360 FQ	19410 MW	26030 TQ	USBLS	5/07
	North Dakota	Y	15370 FQ	18820 MW	26250 TQ	USBLS	5/07
	Fargo MSA, ND-MN	Y	15160 FQ	19000 MW	25180 TQ	USBLS	5/07
	Ohio	Y	16180 FQ	19570 MW	26320 TQ	USBLS	5/07
	Cincinnati-Middletown MSA, OH-KY-IN	Y	16250 FQ	19480 MW	25990 TQ	USBLS	5/07
	Cleveland-Elyria-Mentor MSA, OH	Y	16370 FQ	19910 MW	27510 TQ	USBLS	5/07
	Columbus MSA, OH	Y	16880 FQ	19900 MW	26000 TQ	USBLS	5/07
	Dayton MSA, OH	Y	16160 FQ	19410 MW	25810 TQ	USBLS	5/07
	Oklahoma	Y	14960 FQ	18570 MW	24830 TQ	USBLS	5/07
	Oklahoma City MSA, OK	Y	15330 FQ	18910 MW	24730 TQ	USBLS	5/07
	Tulsa MSA, OK	Y	15920 FQ	19720 MW	28060 TQ	USBLS	5/07
	Oregon	H	9.00 FQ	10.65 MW	13.76 TQ	ORBLS	5/08
	Portland-Vancouver-Beaverton MSA, OR-WA	Y	18660 FQ	22600 MW	29230 TQ	USBLS	5/07
	Pennsylvania	Y	16220 FQ	20060 MW	27520 TQ	USBLS	5/07
	Allentown-Bethlehem-Easton MSA, PA-NJ	Y	17210 FQ	21910 MW	30870 TQ	USBLS	5/07
	Lancaster MSA, PA	Y	17030 FQ	20940 MW	29010 TQ	USBLS	5/07
	Philadelphia-Camden-Wilmington MSA, PA-NJ-DE-MD	Y	16920 FQ	21070 MW	29000 TQ	USBLS	5/07
	Pittsburgh MSA, PA	Y	15720 FQ	19170 MW	25760 TQ	USBLS	5/07
	Rhode Island	Y	18260 FQ	21940 MW	27860 TQ	USBLS	5/07
	Providence-Fall River-Warwick MSA, RI-MA	Y	17880 FQ	21250 MW	27110 TQ	USBLS	5/07
	South Carolina	Y	16160 FQ	19590 MW	25740 TQ	USBLS	5/07
	Charleston-North Charleston MSA, SC	Y	16420 FQ	19610 MW	26720 TQ	USBLS	5/07
	Columbia MSA, SC	Y	16820 FQ	21070 MW	28030 TQ	USBLS	5/07
	South Dakota	Y	15862 FQ	19087 MW	24796 TQ	SDBLS	7/08-9/08
	Sioux Falls MSA, SD	Y	16153 FQ	19719 MW	27143 TQ	SDBLS	7/08-9/08
	Tennessee	Y	16250 FQ	19320 MW	25370 TQ	USBLS	5/07
	Memphis MSA, TN-MS-AR	Y	16420 FQ	19470 MW	25630 TQ	USBLS	5/07
	Nashville-Davidson-Murfreesboro MSA, TN	Y	16770 FQ	19650 MW	25860 TQ	USBLS	5/07
	Texas	Y	15490 FQ	18890 MW	24730 TQ	USBLS	5/07
	Austin-Round Rock MSA, TX	Y	16190 FQ	19370 MW	25500 TQ	USBLS	5/07

AE Average entry wage	**AW** Average wage paid	**FQ** First quartile wage	**LO** Lowest wage paid	**MTC** Median total compensation	**TCC** Total cash compensation
AER Average entry range	**AWR** Average wage range	**H** Hourly	**LR** Low end range	**MW** Median wage paid	**TQ** Third quartile wage
AEX Average experienced wage	**AXR** Average experienced range	**HI** Highest wage paid	**M** Monthly	**MWR** Median wage range	**W** Weekly
ATC Average total compensation	**D** Daily	**HR** High end range	**MCC** Median cash compensation	**S** See annotated source	**Y** Yearly

Occupation/Type/Industry	Location	Per	Low	Mid	High	Source	Date
Retail Salesperson	Dallas-Fort Worth-Arlington MSA, TX	Y	16420 FQ	20010 MW	26400 TQ	USBLS	5/07
	El Paso MSA, TX	Y	14120 FQ	17250 MW	23030 TQ	USBLS	5/07
	Houston-Sugar Land-Baytown MSA, TX	Y	16080 FQ	19220 MW	25250 TQ	USBLS	5/07
	San Antonio MSA, TX	Y	15330 FQ	18760 MW	24070 TQ	USBLS	5/07
	Utah	Y	16500 FQ	19840 MW	25540 TQ	USBLS	5/07
	Salt Lake City MSA, UT	Y	17360 FQ	20840 MW	26810 TQ	USBLS	5/07
	Vermont	Y	18350 FQ	22120 MW	29220 TQ	USBLS	5/07
	Burlington-South Burlington MSA, VT	Y	18140 FQ	21480 MW	28930 TQ	USBLS	5/07
	Virginia	Y	16390 FQ	19820 MW	26740 TQ	USBLS	5/07
	Richmond MSA, VA	Y	16530 FQ	19990 MW	25620 TQ	USBLS	5/07
	Virginia Beach-Norfolk-Newport News MSA, VA-NC	Y	15520 FQ	18640 MW	24770 TQ	USBLS	5/07
	Washington	H	9.46 FQ	11.55 MW	15.10 TQ	WABLS	3/08
	Seattle-Tacoma-Bellevue MSA, WA	Y	19980 FQ	24540 MW	31640 TQ	USBLS	5/07
	West Virginia	Y	14902 FQ	18104 MW	24344 TQ	WVBLS	7/08-9/08
	Charleston MSA, WV	Y	14840 FQ	18610 MW	26450 TQ	USBLS	5/07
	Parkersburg-Marietta-Vienna MSA, WV-OH	Y	14520 FQ	16980 MW	23340 TQ	USBLS	5/07
	Wisconsin	Y	16390 FQ	19350 MW	25530 TQ	USBLS	5/07
	Milwaukee-Waukesha-West Allis MSA, WI	Y	16740 FQ	19370 MW	25520 TQ	USBLS	5/07
	Wyoming	Y	15619 FQ	19171 MW	24906 TQ	WYBLS	9/08
	Cheyenne MSA, WY	Y	14624 FQ	18128 MW	24044 TQ	WYBLS	9/08
	Puerto Rico	Y	12590 FQ	14020 MW	15760 TQ	USBLS	5/07
	San Juan-Caguas-Guaynabo MSA, PR	Y	12630 FQ	14070 MW	15940 TQ	USBLS	5/07
	Virgin Islands	Y	17230 FQ	20500 MW	24750 TQ	USBLS	5/07
	Guam	Y	13300 FQ	15700 MW	21570 TQ	USBLS	5/07
Retailer Account Analyst State Lottery	Tennessee	Y			27006 HI	THETN	2008
Revenue Auditor State Government	South Dakota	Y	28194 LO		42290 HI	AFT02	3/1/08
Revenue Collection Coordinator Municipal Government	Walnut Creek, CA	Y	53358 LO		64389 HI	WCSWP	6/27/08
Revenue Officer United States Internal Revenue Service	Phoenix, AZ	Y	38860 LO			AZREP	2009
RFID Strategist	United States	Y	250000 LO			RFIDU	2005
Rigger	Alabama	Y	21950 FQ	27960 MW	36520 TQ	USBLS	5/07
	California	H	20.34 FQ	25.12 MW	29.80 TQ	CABLS	1/08-3/08
	Los Angeles-Long Beach-Glendale PMSA, CA	H	22.71 FQ	26.99 MW	32.01 TQ	CABLS	1/08-3/08
	San Diego-Carlsbad-San Marcos MSA, CA	H	17.08 FQ	23.08 MW	26.95 TQ	CABLS	1/08-3/08
	San Francisco-San Mateo-Redwood PMSA, CA	H	23.59 FQ	31.13 MW	36.20 TQ	CABLS	1/08-3/08
	Santa Ana-Anaheim-Irvine PMSA, CA	Y	42460 FQ	46330 MW	50000 TQ	USBLS	5/07
	Colorado	Y	35930 FQ	42620 MW	50650 TQ	USBLS	5/07
	Denver-Aurora MSA, CO	Y	34810 FQ	41180 MW	47280 TQ	USBLS	5/07
	Connecticut	H	13.24 AE	20.41 MW		CTBLS	1/08-3/08
	Washington-Arlington-Alexandria MSA, DC-VA-MD-WV	Y	28960 FQ	39780 MW	45850 TQ	USBLS	5/07
	Florida	Y	26140 FQ	34710 MW	46060 TQ	USBLS	5/07
	Miami-Fort Lauderdale-Miami Beach MSA, FL	Y	22290 FQ	34350 MW	50580 TQ	USBLS	5/07
	Orlando-Kissimmee MSA, FL	Y	41110 FQ	45250 MW	49400 TQ	USBLS	5/07
	Tampa-St. Petersburg-Clearwater MSA, FL	Y	25320 FQ	30500 MW	44000 TQ	USBLS	5/07
	West Palm Beach-Boca Raton-Boynton Beach PMSA, FL	Y	41910 FQ	50340 MW	55860 TQ	USBLS	5/07
	Georgia	Y	29870 FQ	39350 MW	47330 TQ	USBLS	5/07

AE	Average entry wage	AW	Average wage paid	FQ	First quartile wage	LO	Lowest wage paid	MTC	Median total compensation	TCC	Total cash compensation
AER	Average entry range	AWR	Average wage range	H	Hourly	LR	Low end range	MW	Median wage paid	TQ	Third quartile wage
AEX	Average experienced wage	AXR	Average experienced range	HI	Highest wage paid	M	Monthly	MWR	Median wage range	W	Weekly
ATC	Average total compensation	D	Daily	HR	High end range	MCC	Median cash compensation	S	See annotated source	Y	Yearly

Occupation/Type/Industry	Location	Per	Low	Mid	High	Source	Date
Rigger	Atlanta-Sandy Springs-Marietta MSA, GA	Y	23400 FQ	27190 MW	31030 TQ	USBLS	5/07
	Illinois	Y	33400 FQ	54490 MW	61280 TQ	USBLS	5/07
	Chicago-Naperville-Joliet MSA, IL-IN-WI	Y	51060 FQ	57120 MW	62640 TQ	USBLS	5/07
	Indiana	Y	22950 FQ	31090 MW	42320 TQ	USBLS	5/07
	Iowa	Y	32070 FQ	35000 MW	38060 TQ	USBLS	5/07
	Kentucky	Y	19397 FQ	39746 MW	48750 TQ	KYBLS	2008
	Louisiana	H	10.51 FQ	13.47 MW	17.55 TQ	LABLS	1/08-3/08
	Baton Rouge MSA, LA	Y	42320 FQ	46190 MW	50050 TQ	USBLS	5/07
	New Orleans-Metairie-Kenner MSA, LA	Y	22160 FQ	28330 MW	35140 TQ	USBLS	5/07
	Maine	Y	35050 FQ	39140 MW	45120 TQ	USBLS	5/07
	Maryland	Y		52625 MW		MDBLS	3/08
	Baltimore-Towson MSA, MD	Y	47280 FQ	51770 MW	56190 TQ	USBLS	5/07
	Massachusetts	Y	38620 FQ	44870 MW	51560 TQ	USBLS	5/07
	Boston-Cambridge-Quincy NECTA, MA	Y	40930 FQ	46880 MW	53910 TQ	USBLS	5/07
	Michigan	Y	21800 FQ	28610 MW	55940 TQ	USBLS	5/07
	Detroit-Warren-Livonia MSA, MI	Y	27750 FQ	53290 MW	72430 TQ	USBLS	5/07
	Minnesota	Y	29506 FQ	48933 MW	67856 TQ	MNBLS	10/08-12/08
	Minneapolis-Saint Paul MSA, MN-WI	Y	30251 FQ	46583 MW	67656 TQ	MNBLS	10/08-12/08
	Mississippi	Y	22070 FQ	24190 MW	27410 TQ	USBLS	5/07
	Missouri	Y	25790 FQ	29710 MW	37370 TQ	USBLS	5/07
	Nebraska	Y	26820 FQ	28820 MW	30810 TQ	USBLS	5/07
	Nevada	H	25.60 FQ	28.64 MW	31.82 TQ	NVBLS	5/08
	Las Vegas-Paradise MSA, NV	H	25.63 FQ	28.66 MW	31.85 TQ	NVBLS	5/08
	New Jersey	Y	38710 FQ	48210 MW	56360 TQ	USBLS	5/07
	New York	Y	42320 FQ	47020 MW	55280 TQ	USBLS	5/07
	Nassau-Suffolk PMSA, NY	Y	42050 FQ	45530 MW	51550 TQ	USBLS	5/07
	New York-Northern New Jersey-Long Island MSA, NY-NJ-PA	Y	42410 FQ	47070 MW	56470 TQ	USBLS	5/07
	North Carolina	Y	24200 FQ	30570 MW	41710 TQ	USBLS	5/07
	Ohio	Y	32260 FQ	38380 MW	51080 TQ	USBLS	5/07
	Cincinnati-Middletown MSA, OH-KY-IN	Y	32790 FQ	36040 MW	41970 TQ	USBLS	5/07
	Oregon	H	17.20 FQ	21.37 MW	31.77 TQ	ORBLS	5/08
	Portland-Vancouver-Beaverton MSA, OR-WA	Y	33670 FQ	43270 MW	67650 TQ	USBLS	5/07
	Pennsylvania	Y	31210 FQ	37810 MW	46770 TQ	USBLS	5/07
	Rhode Island	Y	32500 FQ	36520 MW	43940 TQ	USBLS	5/07
	Providence-Fall River-Warwick MSA, RI-MA	Y	32500 FQ	36520 MW	43940 TQ	USBLS	5/07
	South Carolina	Y	25780 FQ	36840 MW	54110 TQ	USBLS	5/07
	Charleston-North-Charleston MSA, SC	Y	23870 FQ	27620 MW	31530 TQ	USBLS	5/07
	Columbia MSA, SC	Y	25770 FQ	34160 MW	42910 TQ	USBLS	5/07
	Tennessee	Y	32160 FQ	42580 MW	47660 TQ	USBLS	5/07
	Texas	Y	30160 FQ	36660 MW	47490 TQ	USBLS	5/07
	Dallas-Fort Worth-Arlington MSA, TX	Y	32120 FQ	36870 MW	48520 TQ	USBLS	5/07
	Houston-Sugar Land-Baytown MSA, TX	Y	29810 FQ	36090 MW	43410 TQ	USBLS	5/07
	Virginia	Y	34580 FQ	42180 MW	47020 TQ	USBLS	5/07
	Richmond MSA, VA	Y	31460 FQ	40810 MW	47080 TQ	USBLS	5/07
	Virginia Beach-Norfolk-Newport News MSA, VA-NC	Y	36890 FQ	43260 MW	47640 TQ	USBLS	5/07
	Washington	H	19.55 FQ	25.27 MW	28.73 TQ	WABLS	3/08
	Seattle-Tacoma-Bellevue MSA, WA	Y	32140 FQ	40530 MW	45670 TQ	USBLS	5/07
	West Virginia	Y	22001 FQ	25406 MW	31041 TQ	WVBLS	7/08-9/08
	Wisconsin	Y	22570 FQ	26920 MW	34270 TQ	USBLS	5/07
	Wyoming	Y	29955 FQ	34517 MW	37713 TQ	WYBLS	9/08
	Puerto Rico	Y	17890 FQ	22630 MW	52860 TQ	USBLS	5/07
Rights-Of-Way Maintenance Worker Municipal Government	Seattle, WA	H	22.64 LO		23.51 HI	CSSS	2007

AE Average entry wage	**AW** Average wage paid	**FQ** First quartile wage	**LO** Lowest wage paid	**MTC** Median total compensation	**TCC** Total cash compensation
AER Average entry range	**AWR** Average wage range	**H** Hourly	**LR** Low end range	**MW** Median wage paid	**TQ** Third quartile wage
AEX Average experienced wage	**AXR** Average experienced range	**HI** Highest wage paid	**M** Monthly	**MWR** Median wage range	**W** Weekly
ATC Average total compensation	**D** Daily	**HR** High end range	**MCC** Median cash compensation	**S** See annotated source	**Y** Yearly

Occupation/Type/Industry	Location	Per	Low	Mid	High	Source	Date
Risk Management Analyst	United States	Y		64100 AW		RIMS	5/5/08-6/30/08
Risk Manager							
Municipal Government	Hattiesburg, MS	Y			47960 HI	MML	2008
Municipal Government	Vicksburg, MS	Y			50614 HI	MML	2008
Municipal Government	Cincinnati, OH	Y	67078 LO		90555 HI	COHSS	10/08
Road Commissioner	Oakland County, MI	Y			10000 HI	SPO01	2009
Road Crew Supervisor	Camden County, GA	Y	32885 LO		50670 HI	GACTY03	2008
	Coweta County, GA	Y	29267 LO		43902 HI	GACTY03	2008
Roads and Bridges Superintendent	Glynn County, GA	Y	42806 LO		68490 HI	GACTY03	2008
	Peach County, GA	Y	43761 LO		65642 HI	GACTY03	2008
Roadside Park Caretaker	Ohio	H	14.36 LO		18.36 HI	ODAS	2008
Rock Splitter							
Quarry	Arkansas	Y	21740 FQ	24710 MW	30150 TQ	USBLS	5/07
Quarry	Colorado	Y	22790 FQ	25740 MW	32370 TQ	USBLS	5/07
Quarry	Connecticut	H	9.92 AE	17.10 MW		CTBLS	1/08-3/08
Quarry	Georgia	Y	27220 FQ	29740 MW	33590 TQ	USBLS	5/07
Quarry	Illinois	Y	21110 FQ	24910 MW	34170 TQ	USBLS	5/07
Quarry	Indiana	Y	33340 FQ	36250 MW	39140 TQ	USBLS	5/07
Quarry	Iowa	Y	24590 FQ	30820 MW	36480 TQ	USBLS	5/07
Quarry	Kansas	Y	24870 FQ	28430 MW	43400 TQ	USBLS	5/07
Quarry	Maine	Y	20350 FQ	21710 MW	23060 TQ	USBLS	5/07
Quarry	Missouri	Y	24850 FQ	31260 MW	34370 TQ	USBLS	5/07
Quarry	Nevada	H	9.86 FQ	12.26 MW	14.32 TQ	NVBLS	5/08
Quarry	New York	Y	21630 FQ	23620 MW	27210 TQ	USBLS	5/07
Quarry	North Carolina	Y	20480 FQ	23430 MW	26330 TQ	USBLS	5/07
Quarry	Ohio	Y	22630 FQ	30470 MW	35470 TQ	USBLS	5/07
Quarry	Oklahoma	Y	17070 FQ	21470 MW	29430 TQ	USBLS	5/07
Quarry	Pennsylvania	Y	25450 FQ	31860 MW	38850 TQ	USBLS	5/07
Quarry	South Carolina	Y	27490 FQ	31790 MW	35160 TQ	USBLS	5/07
Quarry	Tennessee	Y	13620 FQ	24500 MW	30920 TQ	USBLS	5/07
Quarry	Texas	Y	21430 FQ	24790 MW	32620 TQ	USBLS	5/07
Quarry	Utah	Y	22170 FQ	26420 MW	29660 TQ	USBLS	5/07
Quarry	Wisconsin	Y	22720 FQ	26870 MW	30520 TQ	USBLS	5/07
Rodeo Clown	United States	Y		31054 AW		CBUILD	2008
Rodeo Steer Wrestler	Wisconsin	Y			178000 HI	PRN02	2008
Rolling Machine Setter, Operator, and Tender							
Metals and Plastics	Alabama	Y	30620 FQ	34800 MW	43330 TQ	USBLS	5/07
Metals and Plastics	Birmingham-Hoover MSA, AL	Y	38320 FQ	45350 MW	50420 TQ	USBLS	5/07
Metals and Plastics	Arizona	Y	21950 FQ	27070 MW	31270 TQ	USBLS	5/07
Metals and Plastics	Phoenix-Mesa-Scottsdale MSA, AZ	Y	21240 FQ	26390 MW	31060 TQ	USBLS	5/07
Metals and Plastics	Arkansas	Y	24410 FQ	27960 MW	35290 TQ	USBLS	5/07
Metals and Plastics	Little Rock-North Little Rock MSA, AR	Y	23260 FQ	27150 MW	31030 TQ	USBLS	5/07
Metals and Plastics	California	H	11.11 FQ	15.57 MW	20.22 TQ	CABLS	1/08-3/08
Metals and Plastics	Los Angeles-Long Beach-Glendale PMSA, CA	H	9.46 FQ	13.15 MW	17.87 TQ	CABLS	1/08-3/08
Metals and Plastics	Modesto MSA, CA	H	13.81 FQ	15.07 MW	19.25 TQ	CABLS	1/08-3/08
Metals and Plastics	Oakland-Fremont-Hayward MSA, CA	H	12.64 FQ	16.15 MW	19.99 TQ	CABLS	1/08-3/08
Metals and Plastics	Riverside-San Bernardino-Ontario MSA, CA	H	11.48 FQ	16.78 MW	23.52 TQ	CABLS	1/08-3/08
Metals and Plastics	Sacramento-Arden Arcade-Roseville MSA, CA	H	12.68 FQ	14.62 MW	17.42 TQ	CABLS	1/08-3/08
Metals and Plastics	San Diego-Carlsbad-San Marcos MSA, CA	H	12.50 FQ	18.39 MW	22.22 TQ	CABLS	1/08-3/08
Metals and Plastics	San Jose-Sunnyvale-Santa Clara MSA, CA	H	13.10 FQ	16.59 MW	18.99 TQ	CABLS	1/08-3/08
Metals and Plastics	Santa Ana-Anaheim-Irvine PMSA, CA	Y	33350 FQ	39490 MW	48360 TQ	USBLS	5/07
Metals and Plastics	Colorado	Y	25460 FQ	35120 MW	45870 TQ	USBLS	5/07
Metals and Plastics	Denver-Aurora MSA, CO	Y	27290 FQ	32570 MW	36720 TQ	USBLS	5/07

AE	Average entry wage	AW	Average wage paid	FQ	First quartile wage	LO	Lowest wage paid	MTC	Median total compensation	TCC	Total cash compensation
AER	Average entry range	AWR	Average wage range	H	Hourly	LR	Low end range	MW	Median wage paid	TQ	Third quartile wage
AEX	Average experienced wage	AXR	Average experienced range	HI	Highest wage paid	M	Monthly	MWR	Median wage range	W	Weekly
ATC	Average total compensation	D	Daily	HR	High end range	MCC	Median cash compensation	S	See annotated source	Y	Yearly

1412

Occupation/Type/Industry	Location	Per	Low	Mid	High	Source	Date
Rolling Machine Setter, Operator, and Tender							
Metals and Plastics	Pueblo MSA, CO	Y	27100 FQ	43970 MW	48720 TQ	USBLS	5/07
Metals and Plastics	Connecticut	H	11.23 AE	16.89 MW		CTBLS	1/08-3/08
Metals and Plastics	Bridgeport-Stamford-Norwalk MSA, CT	Y	28140 FQ	33400 MW	37590 TQ	USBLS	5/07
Metals and Plastics	Hartford-West Hartford-East Hartford MSA, CT	Y	31980 FQ	37900 MW	45270 TQ	USBLS	5/07
Metals and Plastics	Washington-Arlington-Alexandria MSA, DC-VA-MD-WV	Y	24590 FQ	29480 MW	35390 TQ	USBLS	5/07
Metals and Plastics	Florida	Y	20620 FQ	25200 MW	30840 TQ	USBLS	5/07
Metals and Plastics	Fort Lauderdale-Pompano Beach-Deerfield Beach PMSA, FL	Y	21000 FQ	23730 MW	28710 TQ	USBLS	5/07
Metals and Plastics	Jacksonville MSA, FL	Y	26470 FQ	32790 MW	44600 TQ	USBLS	5/07
Metals and Plastics	Miami-Fort Lauderdale-Miami Beach MSA, FL	Y	17120 FQ	20890 MW	25210 TQ	USBLS	5/07
Metals and Plastics	Orlando-Kissimmee MSA, FL	Y	26090 FQ	28800 MW	31560 TQ	USBLS	5/07
Metals and Plastics	Tampa-St. Petersburg-Clearwater MSA, FL	Y	20440 FQ	24150 MW	30510 TQ	USBLS	5/07
Metals and Plastics	Georgia	Y	22160 FQ	26850 MW	33480 TQ	USBLS	5/07
Metals and Plastics	Atlanta-Sandy Springs-Marietta MSA, GA	Y	22150 FQ	26010 MW	31260 TQ	USBLS	5/07
Metals and Plastics	Idaho	Y	17090 FQ	19270 MW	22330 TQ	USBLS	5/07
Metals and Plastics	Illinois	Y	25400 FQ	32660 MW	38190 TQ	USBLS	5/07
Metals and Plastics	Chicago-Naperville-Joliet MSA, IL-IN-WI	Y	37420 FQ	45780 MW	53440 TQ	USBLS	5/07
Metals and Plastics	Peoria MSA, IL	Y	34640 FQ	47990 MW	54110 TQ	USBLS	5/07
Metals and Plastics	Indiana	Y	35460 FQ	44290 MW	51000 TQ	USBLS	5/07
Metals and Plastics	Fort Wayne MSA, IN	Y	37540 FQ	44800 MW	50060 TQ	USBLS	5/07
Metals and Plastics	Gary PMSA, IN	Y	43830 FQ	49000 MW	57240 TQ	USBLS	5/07
Metals and Plastics	Indianapolis-Carmel MSA, IN	Y	26670 FQ	32160 MW	37220 TQ	USBLS	5/07
Metals and Plastics	Iowa	Y	32570 FQ	36310 MW	41190 TQ	USBLS	5/07
Metals and Plastics	Kansas	Y	27250 FQ	31790 MW	37270 TQ	USBLS	5/07
Metals and Plastics	Wichita MSA, KS	Y	27520 FQ	35110 MW	45970 TQ	USBLS	5/07
Metals and Plastics	Kentucky	Y	27686 FQ	36789 MW	45025 TQ	KYBLS	2008
Metals and Plastics	Louisville-Jefferson County MSA, KY-IN	Y	26990 FQ	33480 MW	39280 TQ	USBLS	5/07
Metals and Plastics	Owensboro MSA, KY	Y	39100 FQ	43210 MW	46870 TQ	USBLS	5/07
Metals and Plastics	Louisiana	H	11.80 FQ	14.25 MW	17.81 TQ	LABLS	1/08-3/08
Metals and Plastics	New Orleans-Metairie-Kenner MSA, LA	Y	28190 FQ	33280 MW	40900 TQ	USBLS	5/07
Metals and Plastics	Maryland	Y		42300 MW		MDBLS	3/08
Metals and Plastics	Massachusetts	Y	25110 FQ	29640 MW	36840 TQ	USBLS	5/07
Metals and Plastics	Boston-Cambridge-Quincy NECTA, MA	Y	25980 FQ	32370 MW	39580 TQ	USBLS	5/07
Metals and Plastics	Michigan	Y	27560 FQ	35950 MW	44320 TQ	USBLS	5/07
Metals and Plastics	Detroit-Warren-Livonia MSA, MI	Y	29870 FQ	39190 MW	46440 TQ	USBLS	5/07
Metals and Plastics	Grand Rapids-Wyoming MSA, MI	Y	32140 FQ	36490 MW	42520 TQ	USBLS	5/07
Metals and Plastics	Warren-Troy-Farmington Hills PMSA, MI	Y	26790 FQ	34630 MW	42040 TQ	USBLS	5/07
Metals and Plastics	Minnesota	Y	23605 FQ	32365 MW	45116 TQ	MNBLS	10/08-12/08
Metals and Plastics	Minneapolis-Saint Paul MSA, MN-WI	Y	25274 FQ	33702 MW	46453 TQ	MNBLS	10/08-12/08
Metals and Plastics	Mississippi	Y	25650 FQ	28680 MW	32840 TQ	USBLS	5/07
Metals and Plastics	Missouri	Y	24020 FQ	29850 MW	35070 TQ	USBLS	5/07
Metals and Plastics	St. Louis MSA, MO-IL	Y	26340 FQ	33070 MW	38620 TQ	USBLS	5/07
Metals and Plastics	Nebraska	Y	25240 FQ	29390 MW	69280 TQ	USBLS	5/07
Metals and Plastics	Omaha-Council Bluffs MSA, NE-IA	Y	23220 FQ	26430 MW	29270 TQ	USBLS	5/07
Metals and Plastics	Nevada	H	12.75 FQ	14.10 MW	15.35 TQ	NVBLS	5/08
Metals and Plastics	Las Vegas-Paradise MSA, NV	H	13.00 FQ	13.89 MW	14.77 TQ	NVBLS	5/08
Metals and Plastics	New Hampshire	H	10.37 AE	13.05 MW	15.83 AEX	NHBLS	6/08
Metals and Plastics	New Jersey	Y	21310 FQ	26150 MW	36850 TQ	USBLS	5/07
Metals and Plastics	Camden PMSA, NJ	Y	21350 FQ	24440 MW	33550 TQ	USBLS	5/07
Metals and Plastics	Edison PMSA, NJ	Y	22410 FQ	29800 MW	48390 TQ	USBLS	5/07
Metals and Plastics	Newark-Union PMSA, NJ-PA	Y	20520 FQ	23210 MW	27310 TQ	USBLS	5/07
Metals and Plastics	New York	Y	22270 FQ	30390 MW	38100 TQ	USBLS	5/07

AE	Average entry wage	AW	Average wage paid	FQ	First quartile wage	LO	Lowest wage paid	MTC	Median total compensation	TCC	Total cash compensation
AER	Average entry range	AWR	Average wage range	H	Hourly	LR	Low end range	MW	Median wage paid	TQ	Third quartile wage
AEX	Average experienced wage	AXR	Average experienced range	HI	Highest wage paid	M	Monthly	MWR	Median wage range	W	Weekly
ATC	Average total compensation	D	Daily	HR	High end range	MCC	Median cash compensation	S	See annotated source	Y	Yearly

Occupation/Type/Industry	Location	Per	Low	Mid	High	Source	Date
Rolling Machine Setter, Operator, and Tender							
Metals and Plastics	Buffalo-Niagara Falls MSA, NY	Y	27260 FQ	37100 MW	62500 TQ	USBLS	5/07
Metals and Plastics	Nassau-Suffolk PMSA, NY	Y	17300 FQ	21710 MW	28180 TQ	USBLS	5/07
Metals and Plastics	New York-Northern New Jersey-Long Island MSA, NY-NJ-PA	Y	20520 FQ	25880 MW	35100 TQ	USBLS	5/07
Metals and Plastics	Utica-Rome MSA, NY	Y	21520 FQ	24880 MW	34630 TQ	USBLS	5/07
Metals and Plastics	North Carolina	Y	23630 FQ	28100 MW	33780 TQ	USBLS	5/07
Metals and Plastics	Charlotte-Gastonia-Concord MSA, NC-SC	Y	28660 FQ	32520 MW	36620 TQ	USBLS	5/07
Metals and Plastics	Ohio	Y	26620 FQ	31280 MW	37510 TQ	USBLS	5/07
Metals and Plastics	Canton-Massillon MSA, OH	Y	26660 FQ	31640 MW	36670 TQ	USBLS	5/07
Metals and Plastics	Cincinnati-Middletown MSA, OH-KY-IN	Y	25600 FQ	29290 MW	34200 TQ	USBLS	5/07
Metals and Plastics	Cleveland-Elyria-Mentor MSA, OH	Y	27820 FQ	34460 MW	42160 TQ	USBLS	5/07
Metals and Plastics	Columbus MSA, OH	Y	24590 FQ	33210 MW	37010 TQ	USBLS	5/07
Metals and Plastics	Dayton MSA, OH	Y	25040 FQ	27900 MW	42820 TQ	USBLS	5/07
Metals and Plastics	Oklahoma	Y	22060 FQ	24750 MW	30400 TQ	USBLS	5/07
Metals and Plastics	Oklahoma City MSA, OK	Y	22040 FQ	23940 MW	26340 TQ	USBLS	5/07
Metals and Plastics	Tulsa MSA, OK	Y	22690 FQ	25770 MW	31430 TQ	USBLS	5/07
Metals and Plastics	Oregon	H	12.74 FQ	15.98 MW	20.30 TQ	ORBLS	5/08
Metals and Plastics	Portland-Vancouver-Beaverton MSA, OR-WA	Y	26700 FQ	32720 MW	39700 TQ	USBLS	5/07
Metals and Plastics	Pennsylvania	Y	26360 FQ	32290 MW	38540 TQ	USBLS	5/07
Metals and Plastics	Allentown-Bethlehem-Easton MSA, PA-NJ	Y	23840 FQ	28020 MW	33300 TQ	USBLS	5/07
Metals and Plastics	Philadelphia-Camden-Wilmington MSA, PA-NJ-DE-MD	Y	23270 FQ	29480 MW	36300 TQ	USBLS	5/07
Metals and Plastics	Pittsburgh MSA, PA	Y	28040 FQ	34990 MW	40280 TQ	USBLS	5/07
Metals and Plastics	Rhode Island	Y	32520 FQ	36360 MW	41050 TQ	USBLS	5/07
Metals and Plastics	Providence-Fall River-Warwick MSA, RI-MA	Y	28570 FQ	35280 MW	42370 TQ	USBLS	5/07
Metals and Plastics	South Carolina	Y	33720 FQ	40350 MW	45720 TQ	USBLS	5/07
Metals and Plastics	Columbia MSA, SC	Y	30280 FQ	34540 MW	38100 TQ	USBLS	5/07
Metals and Plastics	South Dakota	Y	22505 FQ	24660 MW	28142 TQ	SDBLS	7/08-9/08
Metals and Plastics	Tennessee	Y	22500 FQ	27310 MW	32130 TQ	USBLS	5/07
Metals and Plastics	Nashville-Davidson-Murfreesboro MSA, TN	Y	28110 FQ	30460 MW	32330 TQ	USBLS	5/07
Metals and Plastics	Texas	Y	20500 FQ	26550 MW	32690 TQ	USBLS	5/07
Metals and Plastics	Austin-Round Rock MSA, TX	Y	21460 FQ	26530 MW	31610 TQ	USBLS	5/07
Metals and Plastics	Dallas-Fort Worth-Arlington MSA, TX	Y	20610 FQ	26520 MW	32240 TQ	USBLS	5/07
Metals and Plastics	Houston-Sugar Land-Baytown MSA, TX	Y	17060 FQ	22170 MW	29970 TQ	USBLS	5/07
Metals and Plastics	San Antonio MSA, TX	Y	20590 FQ	26230 MW	33540 TQ	USBLS	5/07
Metals and Plastics	Virginia	Y	22860 FQ	29900 MW	36880 TQ	USBLS	5/07
Metals and Plastics	Richmond MSA, VA	Y	27580 FQ	33120 MW	39310 TQ	USBLS	5/07
Metals and Plastics	Virginia Beach-Norfolk-Newport News MSA, VA-NC	Y	20010 FQ	21920 MW	25130 TQ	USBLS	5/07
Metals and Plastics	Washington	H	16.28 FQ	18.75 MW	22.20 TQ	WABLS	3/08
Metals and Plastics	Seattle-Tacoma-Bellevue MSA, WA	Y	30570 FQ	41700 MW	61970 TQ	USBLS	5/07
Metals and Plastics	West Virginia	Y	27751 FQ	33362 MW	42758 TQ	WVBLS	7/08-9/08
Metals and Plastics	Wisconsin	Y	26980 FQ	31840 MW	36550 TQ	USBLS	5/07
Metals and Plastics	Milwaukee-Waukesha-West Allis MSA, WI	Y	26700 FQ	31920 MW	42950 TQ	USBLS	5/07
Roman Catholic Priest							
Congregation of the Great Spirit	Milwaukee, WI	S			65948 HI	LEDGE	2008
Diocese of San Diego	San Diego, CA	M			1535 HI	MSN03	2009
Roof Bolter							
Mining	Alabama	Y	40940 FQ	43490 MW	46050 TQ	USBLS	5/07
Mining	Colorado	Y	47270 FQ	51050 MW	55550 TQ	USBLS	5/07
Mining	Illinois	Y	39290 FQ	43400 MW	47500 TQ	USBLS	5/07
Mining	Indiana	Y	36750 FQ	40340 MW	44820 TQ	USBLS	5/07
Mining	Kentucky	Y	37511 FQ	41429 MW	47591 TQ	KYBLS	2008
Mining	Ohio	Y	43150 FQ	46040 MW	49070 TQ	USBLS	5/07

AE Average entry wage	**AW** Average wage paid	**FQ** First quartile wage	**LO** Lowest wage paid	**MTC** Median total compensation	**TCC** Total cash compensation
AER Average entry range	**AWR** Average wage range	**H** Hourly	**LR** Low end range	**MW** Median wage paid	**TQ** Third quartile wage
AEX Average experienced wage	**AXR** Average experienced range	**HI** Highest wage paid	**M** Monthly	**MWR** Median wage range	**W** Weekly
ATC Average total compensation	**D** Daily	**HR** High end range	**MCC** Median cash compensation	**S** See annotated source	**Y** Yearly

Occupation/Type/Industry	Location	Per	Low	Mid	High	Source	Date
Roof Bolter							
Mining	Pennsylvania	Y	40360 FQ	44200 MW	47840 TQ	USBLS	5/07
Mining	Utah	Y	39550 FQ	44480 MW	51100 TQ	USBLS	5/07
Mining	Virginia	Y	38630 FQ	42220 MW	46620 TQ	USBLS	5/07
Mining	Wyoming	Y	44474 FQ	53610 MW	71577 TQ	WYBLS	9/08
Roofer	Alabama	Y	21400 FQ	26240 MW	31490 TQ	USBLS	5/07
	Birmingham-Hoover MSA, AL	Y	23330 FQ	27200 MW	33230 TQ	USBLS	5/07
	Tuscaloosa MSA, AL	Y	23480 FQ	27120 MW	30690 TQ	USBLS	5/07
	Arizona	Y	22320 FQ	28770 MW	36350 TQ	USBLS	5/07
	Phoenix-Mesa-Scottsdale MSA, AZ	Y	21830 FQ	28250 MW	36290 TQ	USBLS	5/07
	Prescott MSA, AZ	Y	15390 FQ	33230 MW	38280 TQ	USBLS	5/07
	Tucson MSA, AZ	Y	23630 FQ	28980 MW	35200 TQ	USBLS	5/07
	Arkansas	Y	24450 FQ	29570 MW	36560 TQ	USBLS	5/07
	Fayetteville-Springdale-Rogers MSA, AR-MO	Y	25500 FQ	30440 MW	35920 TQ	USBLS	5/07
	Fort Smith MSA, AR-OK	Y	22130 FQ	25790 MW	32700 TQ	USBLS	5/07
	Little Rock-North Little Rock MSA, AR	Y	28850 FQ	34470 MW	41600 TQ	USBLS	5/07
	California	H	16.18 FQ	21.76 MW	25.47 TQ	CABLS	1/08-3/08
	Los Angeles-Long Beach-Glendale PMSA, CA	H	19.42 FQ	23.37 MW	27.54 TQ	CABLS	1/08-3/08
	Oakland-Fremont-Hayward MSA, CA	H	17.78 FQ	22.52 MW	26.27 TQ	CABLS	1/08-3/08
	Riverside-San Bernardino-Ontario MSA, CA	H	14.63 FQ	20.22 MW	22.95 TQ	CABLS	1/08-3/08
	Sacramento-Arden Arcade-Roseville MSA, CA	H	19.90 FQ	22.79 MW	26.03 TQ	CABLS	1/08-3/08
	San Diego-Carlsbad-San Marcos MSA, CA	H	14.60 FQ	18.90 MW	22.69 TQ	CABLS	1/08-3/08
	San Francisco-San Mateo-Redwood PMSA, CA	H	17.98 FQ	26.32 MW	31.97 TQ	CABLS	1/08-3/08
	San Jose-Sunnyvale-Santa Clara MSA, CA	H	21.43 FQ	24.97 MW	30.94 TQ	CABLS	1/08-3/08
	Santa Ana-Anaheim-Irvine PMSA, CA	Y	28070 FQ	35790 MW	46330 TQ	USBLS	5/07
	Colorado	Y	23490 FQ	29460 MW	36990 TQ	USBLS	5/07
	Denver-Aurora MSA, CO	Y	23870 FQ	29340 MW	35690 TQ	USBLS	5/07
	Connecticut	H	9.68 AE	16.92 MW		CTBLS	1/08-3/08
	Bridgeport-Stamford-Norwalk MSA, CT	Y	31570 FQ	34480 MW	37480 TQ	USBLS	5/07
	Hartford-West Hartford-East Hartford MSA, CT	Y	24010 FQ	36170 MW	49840 TQ	USBLS	5/07
	Delaware	Y	27930 FQ	34490 MW	41590 TQ	USBLS	5/07
	Wilmington PMSA, DE-MD-NJ	Y	29620 FQ	37840 MW	46110 TQ	USBLS	5/07
	Washington-Arlington-Alexandria MSA, DC-VA-MD-WV	Y	29760 FQ	36460 MW	46700 TQ	USBLS	5/07
	Florida	Y	25370 FQ	30430 MW	36780 TQ	USBLS	5/07
	Fort Lauderdale-Pompano Beach-Deerfield Beach PMSA, FL	Y	27540 FQ	33210 MW	39440 TQ	USBLS	5/07
	Jacksonville MSA, FL	Y	27000 FQ	31380 MW	35880 TQ	USBLS	5/07
	Miami-Fort Lauderdale-Miami Beach MSA, FL	Y	26170 FQ	31420 MW	37480 TQ	USBLS	5/07
	Orlando-Kissimmee MSA, FL	Y	24990 FQ	29550 MW	36110 TQ	USBLS	5/07
	Tampa-St. Petersburg-Clearwater MSA, FL	Y	25050 FQ	30290 MW	37580 TQ	USBLS	5/07
	West Palm Beach-Boca Raton-Boynton Beach PMSA, FL	Y	23910 FQ	28900 MW	34930 TQ	USBLS	5/07
	Georgia	Y	23700 FQ	28800 MW	35610 TQ	USBLS	5/07
	Athens-Clarke County MSA, GA	Y	26220 FQ	29070 MW	32000 TQ	USBLS	5/07
	Atlanta-Sandy Springs-Marietta MSA, GA	Y	24630 FQ	30000 MW	38470 TQ	USBLS	5/07
	Savannah MSA, GA	Y	26180 FQ	29280 MW	32550 TQ	USBLS	5/07
	Hawaii	Y	26990 FQ	37350 MW	59440 TQ	USBLS	5/07
	Honolulu MSA, HI	Y	28070 FQ	37000 MW	60550 TQ	USBLS	5/07
	Idaho	Y	27260 FQ	34770 MW	41510 TQ	USBLS	5/07
	Boise City-Nampa MSA, ID	Y	27040 FQ	33790 MW	41940 TQ	USBLS	5/07

AE	Average entry wage	AW	Average wage paid	FQ	First quartile wage	LO	Lowest wage paid	MTC	Median total compensation	TCC	Total cash compensation
AER	Average entry range	AWR	Average wage range	H	Hourly	LR	Low end range	MW	Median wage paid	TQ	Third quartile wage
AEX	Average experienced wage	AXR	Average experienced range	HI	Highest wage paid	M	Monthly	MWR	Median wage range	W	Weekly
ATC	Average total compensation	D	Daily	HR	High end range	MCC	Median cash compensation	S	See annotated source	Y	Yearly

Occupation/Type/Industry	Location	Per	Low	Mid	High	Source	Date
Roofer	Illinois	Y	30280 FQ	40350 MW	57320 TQ	USBLS	5/07
	Chicago-Naperville-Joliet MSA, IL-IN-WI	Y	30970 FQ	42110 MW	59770 TQ	USBLS	5/07
	Indiana	Y	26810 FQ	34140 MW	45100 TQ	USBLS	5/07
	Gary PMSA, IN	Y	31670 FQ	56250 MW	67070 TQ	USBLS	5/07
	Indianapolis-Carmel MSA, IN	Y	29740 FQ	35990 MW	44720 TQ	USBLS	5/07
	Iowa	Y	25360 FQ	30650 MW	37570 TQ	USBLS	5/07
	Des Moines-West Des Moines MSA, IA	Y	29090 FQ	35920 MW	43660 TQ	USBLS	5/07
	Dubuque MSA, IA	Y	27530 FQ	30990 MW	38420 TQ	USBLS	5/07
	Kansas	Y	23460 FQ	29270 MW	46370 TQ	USBLS	5/07
	Wichita MSA, KS	Y	21820 FQ	26390 MW	31330 TQ	USBLS	5/07
	Kentucky	Y	24443 FQ	30845 MW	37536 TQ	KYBLS	2008
	Louisville-Jefferson County MSA, KY-IN	Y	26010 FQ	31530 MW	36820 TQ	USBLS	5/07
	Louisiana	H	12.32 FQ	14.56 MW	17.12 TQ	LABLS	1/08-3/08
	Baton Rouge MSA, LA	Y	26970 FQ	30960 MW	35840 TQ	USBLS	5/07
	New Orleans-Metairie-Kenner MSA, LA	Y	26080 FQ	30210 MW	35370 TQ	USBLS	5/07
	Maine	Y	27030 FQ	30510 MW	36370 TQ	USBLS	5/07
	Portland-South Portland-Biddeford MSA, ME	Y	29960 FQ	34530 MW	39190 TQ	USBLS	5/07
	Maryland	Y		39875 MW		MDBLS	3/08
	Baltimore-Towson MSA, MD	Y	31180 FQ	38510 MW	47770 TQ	USBLS	5/07
	Bethesda-Gaithersburg-Frederick PMSA, MD	Y	29090 FQ	35830 MW	54640 TQ	USBLS	5/07
	Massachusetts	Y	33490 FQ	45190 MW	63890 TQ	USBLS	5/07
	Boston-Cambridge-Quincy NECTA, MA	Y	35760 FQ	51530 MW	87600 TQ	USBLS	5/07
	Worcester MSA, MA-CT	Y	36210 FQ	63350 MW	72710 TQ	USBLS	5/07
	Michigan	Y	28380 FQ	35940 MW	47460 TQ	USBLS	5/07
	Detroit-Warren-Livonia MSA, MI	Y	29520 FQ	40310 MW	53890 TQ	USBLS	5/07
	Grand Rapids-Wyoming MSA, MI	Y	22990 FQ	29930 MW	37410 TQ	USBLS	5/07
	Warren-Troy-Farmington Hills PMSA, MI	Y	29290 FQ	41910 MW	56520 TQ	USBLS	5/07
	Minnesota	Y	36169 FQ	52746 MW	63285 TQ	MNBLS	10/08-12/08
	Duluth-Superior MSA, MN-WI	Y	31626 FQ	57394 MW	65719 TQ	MNBLS	10/08-12/08
	Minneapolis-Saint Paul MSA, MN-WI	Y	45432 FQ	57689 MW	65561 TQ	MNBLS	10/08-12/08
	Rochester MSA, MN	Y	28605 FQ	31992 MW	37260 TQ	MNBLS	10/08-12/08
	Mississippi	Y	21200 FQ	25510 MW	31390 TQ	USBLS	5/07
	Jackson MSA, MS	Y	22480 FQ	24910 MW	30240 TQ	USBLS	5/07
	Missouri	Y	27560 FQ	41130 MW	55980 TQ	USBLS	5/07
	Jefferson City MSA, MO	Y	26080 FQ	33040 MW	54980 TQ	USBLS	5/07
	Kansas City MSA, MO-KS	Y	32870 FQ	48730 MW	59150 TQ	USBLS	5/07
	St. Louis MSA, MO-IL	Y	34400 FQ	50360 MW	58600 TQ	USBLS	5/07
	Montana	Y	23500 FQ	28950 MW	35700 TQ	USBLS	5/07
	Billings MSA, MT	Y	24400 FQ	29380 MW	34300 TQ	USBLS	5/07
	Nebraska	Y	23650 FQ	29220 MW	36860 TQ	USBLS	5/07
	Omaha-Council Bluffs MSA, NE-IA	Y	26240 FQ	31960 MW	37670 TQ	USBLS	5/07
	Nevada	H	15.17 FQ	17.94 MW	21.86 TQ	NVBLS	5/08
	Las Vegas-Paradise MSA, NV	H	15.07 FQ	18.50 MW	22.86 TQ	NVBLS	5/08
	New Hampshire	H	12.26 AE	14.87 MW	18.48 AEX	NHBLS	6/08
	Manchester MSA, NH	Y	25540 FQ	29280 MW	34380 TQ	USBLS	5/07
	New Jersey	Y	29050 FQ	37610 MW	49980 TQ	USBLS	5/07
	Camden PMSA, NJ	Y	33170 FQ	38800 MW	46720 TQ	USBLS	5/07
	Edison PMSA, NJ	Y	37310 FQ	43460 MW	49410 TQ	USBLS	5/07
	Newark-Union PMSA, NJ-PA	Y	26280 FQ	35480 MW	46720 TQ	USBLS	5/07
	New Mexico	Y	20430 FQ	23710 MW	29320 TQ	USBLS	5/07
	Albuquerque MSA, NM	Y	20410 FQ	23460 MW	28930 TQ	USBLS	5/07
	New York	Y	29290 FQ	36500 MW	49530 TQ	USBLS	5/07
	Albany-Schenectady-Troy MSA, NY	Y	28970 FQ	35500 MW	43410 TQ	USBLS	5/07
	Buffalo-Niagara Falls MSA, NY	Y	27550 FQ	32860 MW	39240 TQ	USBLS	5/07
	Nassau-Suffolk PMSA, NY	Y	31200 FQ	42400 MW	62990 TQ	USBLS	5/07
	New York-Northern New Jersey-Long Island MSA, NY-NJ-PA	Y	29590 FQ	37710 MW	59470 TQ	USBLS	5/07

AE	Average entry wage	AW	Average wage paid	FQ	First quartile wage	LO	Lowest wage paid	MTC	Median total compensation	TCC	Total cash compensation
AER	Average entry range	AWR	Average wage range	H	Hourly	LR	Low end range	MW	Median wage paid	TQ	Third quartile wage
AEX	Average experienced wage	AXR	Average experienced range	HI	Highest wage paid	M	Monthly	MWR	Median wage range	W	Weekly
ATC	Average total compensation	D	Daily	HR	High end range	MCC	Median cash compensation	S	See annotated source	Y	Yearly

Occupation/Type/Industry	Location	Per	Low	Mid	High	Source	Date
Roofer	North Carolina	Y	22650 FQ	27350 MW	31810 TQ	USBLS	5/07
	Charlotte-Gastonia-Concord MSA, NC-SC	Y	21780 FQ	26120 MW	31010 TQ	USBLS	5/07
	Durham MSA, NC	Y	26670 FQ	30930 MW	36540 TQ	USBLS	5/07
	Greensboro-High Point MSA, NC	Y	20530 FQ	24670 MW	29320 TQ	USBLS	5/07
	Raleigh-Cary MSA, NC	Y	24600 FQ	30190 MW	35610 TQ	USBLS	5/07
	North Dakota	Y	25510 FQ	29910 MW	36690 TQ	USBLS	5/07
	Fargo MSA, ND-MN	Y	25300 FQ	29660 MW	36760 TQ	USBLS	5/07
	Ohio	Y	26990 FQ	33920 MW	45150 TQ	USBLS	5/07
	Cincinnati-Middletown MSA, OH-KY-IN	Y	27060 FQ	34020 MW	45620 TQ	USBLS	5/07
	Cleveland-Elyria-Mentor MSA, OH	Y	28430 FQ	36460 MW	52440 TQ	USBLS	5/07
	Columbus MSA, OH	Y	23270 FQ	32370 MW	41970 TQ	USBLS	5/07
	Dayton MSA, OH	Y	26750 FQ	33460 MW	43700 TQ	USBLS	5/07
	Oklahoma	Y	21370 FQ	27010 MW	31470 TQ	USBLS	5/07
	Oklahoma City MSA, OK	Y	25090 FQ	28930 MW	35440 TQ	USBLS	5/07
	Tulsa MSA, OK	Y	20270 FQ	23550 MW	28320 TQ	USBLS	5/07
	Oregon	H	11.71 FQ	15.00 MW	18.42 TQ	ORBLS	5/08
	Portland-Vancouver-Beaverton MSA, OR-WA	Y	26830 FQ	33920 MW	42510 TQ	USBLS	5/07
	Pennsylvania	Y	29510 FQ	38120 MW	47550 TQ	USBLS	5/07
	Allentown-Bethlehem-Easton MSA, PA-NJ	Y	29510 FQ	39340 MW	51010 TQ	USBLS	5/07
	Philadelphia-Camden-Wilmington MSA, PA-NJ-DE-MD	Y	33870 FQ	41320 MW	50080 TQ	USBLS	5/07
	Pittsburgh MSA, PA	Y	27160 FQ	35070 MW	46050 TQ	USBLS	5/07
	Rhode Island	Y	26720 FQ	34680 MW	39900 TQ	USBLS	5/07
	Providence-Fall River-Warwick MSA, RI-MA	Y	27190 FQ	35220 MW	41880 TQ	USBLS	5/07
	South Carolina	Y	22160 FQ	25120 MW	29610 TQ	USBLS	5/07
	Charleston-North Charleston MSA, SC	Y	24580 FQ	28790 MW	32060 TQ	USBLS	5/07
	Columbia MSA, SC	Y	22240 FQ	26630 MW	30760 TQ	USBLS	5/07
	South Dakota	Y	22941 FQ	25211 MW	31308 TQ	SDBLS	7/08-9/08
	Sioux Falls MSA, SD	Y	24689 FQ	27475 MW	35155 TQ	SDBLS	7/08-9/08
	Tennessee	Y	24170 FQ	29320 MW	34880 TQ	USBLS	5/07
	Kingsport-Bristol-Bristol MSA, TN-VA	Y	22760 FQ	27680 MW	32660 TQ	USBLS	5/07
	Memphis MSA, TN-MS-AR	Y	26440 FQ	29770 MW	34960 TQ	USBLS	5/07
	Nashville-Davidson-Murfreesboro MSA, TN	Y	25050 FQ	30940 MW	36930 TQ	USBLS	5/07
	Texas	Y	20950 FQ	24930 MW	30230 TQ	USBLS	5/07
	Austin-Round Rock MSA, TX	Y	19910 FQ	24090 MW	30140 TQ	USBLS	5/07
	Dallas-Fort Worth-Arlington MSA, TX	Y	22120 FQ	26370 MW	30330 TQ	USBLS	5/07
	El Paso MSA, TX	Y	19260 FQ	20940 MW	22940 TQ	USBLS	5/07
	Houston-Sugar Land-Baytown MSA, TX	Y	22920 FQ	28800 MW	35150 TQ	USBLS	5/07
	San Antonio MSA, TX	Y	21060 FQ	24200 MW	29940 TQ	USBLS	5/07
	Utah	Y	28620 FQ	34530 MW	38990 TQ	USBLS	5/07
	Salt Lake City MSA, UT	Y	31190 FQ	35400 MW	39230 TQ	USBLS	5/07
	Vermont	Y	26020 FQ	29210 MW	33460 TQ	USBLS	5/07
	Burlington-South Burlington MSA, VT	Y	27130 FQ	30620 MW	34200 TQ	USBLS	5/07
	Virginia	Y	25960 FQ	31390 MW	38650 TQ	USBLS	5/07
	Richmond MSA, VA	Y	27970 FQ	31830 MW	38400 TQ	USBLS	5/07
	Virginia Beach-Norfolk-Newport News MSA, VA-NC	Y	25190 FQ	31960 MW	40830 TQ	USBLS	5/07
	Washington	H	16.50 FQ	21.86 MW	28.25 TQ	WABLS	3/08
	Seattle-Tacoma-Bellevue MSA, WA	Y	35990 FQ	51220 MW	61840 TQ	USBLS	5/07
	West Virginia	Y	20563 FQ	24706 MW	32022 TQ	WVBLS	7/08-9/08
	Charleston MSA, WV	Y	20030 FQ	23770 MW	29830 TQ	USBLS	5/07
	Wisconsin	Y	30450 FQ	38610 MW	46660 TQ	USBLS	5/07
	Milwaukee-Waukesha-West Allis MSA, WI	Y	33950 FQ	40990 MW	53600 TQ	USBLS	5/07
	Wyoming	Y	26988 FQ	31767 MW	39692 TQ	WYBLS	9/08
	Casper MSA, WY	Y	29686 FQ	32632 MW	39639 TQ	WYBLS	9/08
	Cheyenne MSA, WY	Y	27524 FQ	31439 MW	36138 TQ	WYBLS	9/08

AE Average entry wage	**AW** Average wage paid	**FQ** First quartile wage	**LO** Lowest wage paid	**MTC** Median total compensation	**TCC** Total cash compensation
AER Average entry range	**AWR** Average wage range	**H** Hourly	**LR** Low end range	**MW** Median wage paid	**TQ** Third quartile wage
AEX Average experienced wage	**AXR** Average experienced range	**HI** Highest wage paid	**M** Monthly	**MWR** Median wage range	**W** Weekly
ATC Average total compensation	**D** Daily	**HR** High end range	**MCC** Median cash compensation	**S** See annotated source	**Y** Yearly

Occupation/Type/Industry	Location	Per	Low	Mid	High	Source	Date
Roofer	Puerto Rico	Y	13230 FQ	15330 MW	19650 TQ	USBLS	5/07
	San Juan-Caguas-Guaynabo						
	MSA, PR	Y	13280 FQ	15480 MW	19330 TQ	USBLS	5/07
	Virgin Islands	Y	21770 FQ	32740 MW	37410 TQ	USBLS	5/07
Public Schools	North Carolina	M	2201 LO		3672 HI	NCSS	2008-2009
Rotary Drill Operator							
Oil and Gas	Alabama	Y	40490 FQ	51400 MW	67940 TQ	USBLS	5/07
Oil and Gas	Alaska	Y	40170 FQ	67670 MW	80680 TQ	USBLS	5/07
Oil and Gas	Arkansas	Y	32570 FQ	41340 MW	58280 TQ	USBLS	5/07
Oil and Gas	California	H	22.34 FQ	25.39 MW	28.59 TQ	CABLS	1/08-3/08
Oil and Gas	Colorado	Y	38400 FQ	44420 MW	50680 TQ	USBLS	5/07
Oil and Gas	Florida	Y	23180 FQ	27170 MW	31890 TQ	USBLS	5/07
Oil and Gas	Illinois	Y	28730 FQ	32140 MW	44600 TQ	USBLS	5/07
Oil and Gas	Kansas	Y	28400 FQ	34760 MW	41160 TQ	USBLS	5/07
Oil and Gas	Kentucky	Y	22102 FQ	25881 MW	47003 TQ	KYBLS	2008
Oil and Gas	Louisiana	H	15.97 FQ	20.66 MW	28.52 TQ	LABLS	1/08-3/08
Oil and Gas	Maryland	Y		23550 MW		MDBLS	3/08
Oil and Gas	Massachusetts	Y	53570 FQ	57040 MW	60510 TQ	USBLS	5/07
Oil and Gas	Michigan	Y	33500 FQ	40310 MW	49140 TQ	USBLS	5/07
Oil and Gas	Mississippi	Y	32980 FQ	36800 MW	41410 TQ	USBLS	5/07
Oil and Gas	Montana	Y	37880 FQ	48680 MW	67840 TQ	USBLS	5/07
Oil and Gas	New Mexico	Y	38300 FQ	48620 MW	61280 TQ	USBLS	5/07
Oil and Gas	North Dakota	Y	34890 FQ	46250 MW	56680 TQ	USBLS	5/07
Oil and Gas	Ohio	Y	26150 FQ	30340 MW	34290 TQ	USBLS	5/07
Oil and Gas	Oklahoma	Y	38920 FQ	48580 MW	58710 TQ	USBLS	5/07
Oil and Gas	Pennsylvania	Y	31100 FQ	38510 MW	56960 TQ	USBLS	5/07
Oil and Gas	Texas	Y	32020 FQ	42410 MW	56120 TQ	USBLS	5/07
Oil and Gas	Utah	Y	36080 FQ	41020 MW	52960 TQ	USBLS	5/07
Oil and Gas	Virginia	Y	22530 FQ	24980 MW	28650 TQ	USBLS	5/07
Oil and Gas	Washington	H	17.10 FQ	18.68 MW	23.83 TQ	WABLS	3/08
Oil and Gas	Wyoming	Y	44899 FQ	60473 MW	72506 TQ	WYBLS	9/08
Roustabout							
Oil and Gas	Alabama	Y	26970 FQ	31330 MW	63090 TQ	USBLS	5/07
Oil and Gas	Arkansas	Y	24910 FQ	28500 MW	33050 TQ	USBLS	5/07
Oil and Gas	California	H	14.83 FQ	20.00 MW	23.23 TQ	CABLS	1/08-3/08
Oil and Gas	Colorado	Y	25220 FQ	29100 MW	32880 TQ	USBLS	5/07
Oil and Gas	Illinois	Y	24150 FQ	27760 MW	31060 TQ	USBLS	5/07
Oil and Gas	Indiana	Y	20550 FQ	23930 MW	32270 TQ	USBLS	5/07
Oil and Gas	Kansas	Y	25120 FQ	31050 MW	36710 TQ	USBLS	5/07
Oil and Gas	Kentucky	Y	22032 FQ	29518 MW	35263 TQ	KYBLS	2008
Oil and Gas	Louisiana	H	11.06 FQ	13.43 MW	18.01 TQ	LABLS	1/08-3/08
Oil and Gas	Michigan	Y	25160 FQ	29070 MW	34630 TQ	USBLS	5/07
Oil and Gas	Mississippi	Y	23400 FQ	27590 MW	32530 TQ	USBLS	5/07
Oil and Gas	Montana	Y	28850 FQ	36260 MW	44690 TQ	USBLS	5/07
Oil and Gas	Nebraska	Y	26070 FQ	30680 MW	36190 TQ	USBLS	5/07
Oil and Gas	New Mexico	Y	21610 FQ	27940 MW	34410 TQ	USBLS	5/07
Oil and Gas	New York	Y	23440 FQ	28130 MW	32370 TQ	USBLS	5/07
Oil and Gas	North Dakota	Y	35180 FQ	41250 MW	50210 TQ	USBLS	5/07
Oil and Gas	Ohio	Y	21660 FQ	24300 MW	27450 TQ	USBLS	5/07
Oil and Gas	Oklahoma	Y	23420 FQ	29470 MW	38450 TQ	USBLS	5/07
Oil and Gas	Pennsylvania	Y	22680 FQ	25690 MW	29680 TQ	USBLS	5/07
Oil and Gas	Texas	Y	20850 FQ	25800 MW	33000 TQ	USBLS	5/07
Oil and Gas	Utah	Y	28050 FQ	35200 MW	46000 TQ	USBLS	5/07
Oil and Gas	Virginia	Y	17840 FQ	19730 MW	24280 TQ	USBLS	5/07
Oil and Gas	Wyoming	Y	28645 FQ	34283 MW	39952 TQ	WYBLS	9/08
Routemaker							
State Government	Ohio	H	14.85 LO		19.88 HI	ODAS	2008
Safety Director							
Municipal Government	Cincinnati, OH	Y	98374 LO		132805 HI	COHSS	10/08
Safety Officer							
Cruise Ship	United States	M	2400 LO		3100 HI	CRU02	2008
Safety Responsibility Evaluator							
State Government	Ohio	H	17.22 LO		21.77 HI	ODAS	2008
Sailor and Marine Oiler	Alabama	Y	18690 FQ	26720 MW	30080 TQ	USBLS	5/07
	Alaska	Y	32750 FQ	42250 MW	47610 TQ	USBLS	5/07
	Arkansas	Y	24250 FQ	30490 MW	35790 TQ	USBLS	5/07

AE	Average entry wage	AW	Average wage paid	FQ	First quartile wage	LO	Lowest wage paid	MTC	Median total compensation	TCC	Total cash compensation
AER	Average entry range	AWR	Average wage range	H	Hourly	LR	Low end range	MW	Median wage paid	TQ	Third quartile wage
AEX	Average experienced wage	AXR	Average experienced range	HI	Highest wage paid	M	Monthly	MWR	Median wage range	W	Weekly
ATC	Average total compensation	D	Daily	HR	High end range	MCC	Median cash compensation	S	See annotated source	Y	Yearly

1418

Occupation/Type/Industry	Location	Per	Low	Mid	High	Source	Date
Sailor and Marine Oiler	California	H	10.82 FQ	16.14 MW	22.44 TQ	CABLS	1/08-3/08
	Los Angeles-Long Beach-Glendale PMSA, CA	H	11.25 FQ	20.41 MW	24.83 TQ	CABLS	1/08-3/08
	Oakland-Fremont-Hayward MSA, CA	H	15.17 FQ	19.07 MW	23.59 TQ	CABLS	1/08-3/08
	San Diego-Carlsbad-San Marcos MSA, CA	H	11.25 FQ	14.13 MW	16.30 TQ	CABLS	1/08-3/08
	San Francisco-San Mateo-Redwood PMSA, CA	H	16.23 FQ	18.14 MW	21.36 TQ	CABLS	1/08-3/08
	Santa Ana-Anaheim-Irvine PMSA, CA	Y	15810 FQ	17900 MW	21190 TQ	USBLS	5/07
	Washington-Arlington-Alexandria MSA, DC-VA-MD-WV	Y	26530 FQ	31570 MW	38280 TQ	USBLS	5/07
	Florida	Y	27930 FQ	34800 MW	45830 TQ	USBLS	5/07
	Fort Lauderdale-Pompano Beach-Deerfield Beach PMSA, FL	Y	32570 FQ	42210 MW	48760 TQ	USBLS	5/07
	Jacksonville MSA, FL	Y	18330 FQ	39570 MW	64500 TQ	USBLS	5/07
	Miami-Fort Lauderdale-Miami Beach MSA, FL	Y	28840 FQ	34570 MW	44210 TQ	USBLS	5/07
	Tampa-St. Petersburg-Clearwater MSA, FL	Y	28220 FQ	42610 MW	50920 TQ	USBLS	5/07
	West Palm Beach-Boca Raton-Boynton Beach PMSA, FL	Y	25040 FQ	32690 MW	45420 TQ	USBLS	5/07
	Georgia	Y	18430 FQ	24220 MW	27250 TQ	USBLS	5/07
	Hawaii	Y	25670 FQ	28110 MW	34460 TQ	USBLS	5/07
	Honolulu MSA, HI	Y	25650 FQ	28050 MW	34480 TQ	USBLS	5/07
	Illinois	Y	23430 FQ	29900 MW	37040 TQ	USBLS	5/07
	Chicago-Naperville-Joliet MSA, IL-IN-WI	Y	24900 FQ	31550 MW	37650 TQ	USBLS	5/07
	Indiana	Y	23150 FQ	29790 MW	39150 TQ	USBLS	5/07
	Gary PMSA, IN	Y	24650 FQ	33580 MW	39550 TQ	USBLS	5/07
	Iowa	Y	19800 FQ	23950 MW	28490 TQ	USBLS	5/07
	Kentucky	Y	23226 FQ	27941 MW	34332 TQ	KYBLS	2008
	Louisville-Jefferson County MSA, KY-IN	Y	24100 FQ	29950 MW	41290 TQ	USBLS	5/07
	Louisiana	H	12.05 FQ	15.62 MW	19.33 TQ	LABLS	1/08-3/08
	Baton Rouge MSA, LA	Y	25660 FQ	31370 MW	39950 TQ	USBLS	5/07
	New Orleans-Metairie-Kenner MSA, LA	Y	22690 FQ	31000 MW	40010 TQ	USBLS	5/07
	Maine	Y	22140 FQ	27900 MW	35020 TQ	USBLS	5/07
	Portland-South Portland-Biddeford MSA, ME	Y	19040 FQ	28910 MW	35350 TQ	USBLS	5/07
	Maryland	Y		32000 MW		MDBLS	3/08
	Baltimore-Towson MSA, MD	Y	26840 FQ	33180 MW	39950 TQ	USBLS	5/07
	Massachusetts	Y	29640 FQ	34700 MW	39190 TQ	USBLS	5/07
	Boston-Cambridge-Quincy NECTA, MA	Y	32660 FQ	36150 MW	39860 TQ	USBLS	5/07
	Michigan	Y	20740 FQ	31840 MW	45800 TQ	USBLS	5/07
	Detroit-Warren-Livonia MSA, MI	Y	14730 FQ	15370 MW	21840 TQ	USBLS	5/07
	Warren-Troy-Farmington Hills PMSA, MI	Y	14730 FQ	15400 MW	21670 TQ	USBLS	5/07
	Mississippi	Y	26840 FQ	32380 MW	36090 TQ	USBLS	5/07
	Missouri	Y	25630 FQ	28470 MW	31720 TQ	USBLS	5/07
	St. Louis MSA, MO-IL	Y	14790 FQ	28010 MW	41770 TQ	USBLS	5/07
	New Jersey	Y	22260 FQ	28940 MW	36550 TQ	USBLS	5/07
	Edison PMSA, NJ	Y	20620 FQ	23030 MW	34720 TQ	USBLS	5/07
	New York	Y	22240 FQ	33640 MW	41010 TQ	USBLS	5/07
	Nassau-Suffolk PMSA, NY	Y	16620 FQ	24100 MW	34580 TQ	USBLS	5/07
	New York-Northern New Jersey-Long Island MSA, NY-NJ-PA	Y	23530 FQ	34280 MW	41160 TQ	USBLS	5/07
	North Carolina	Y	31410 FQ	37110 MW	42870 TQ	USBLS	5/07
	Ohio	Y	21610 FQ	32550 MW	50330 TQ	USBLS	5/07
	Cincinnati-Middletown MSA, OH-KY-IN	Y	19990 FQ	23430 MW	27400 TQ	USBLS	5/07
	Cleveland-Elyria-Mentor MSA, OH	Y	17250 FQ	18780 MW	22050 TQ	USBLS	5/07
	Oregon	H	12.98 FQ	15.71 MW	21.32 TQ	ORBLS	5/08

AE	Average entry wage	AW	Average wage paid	FQ	First quartile wage	LO	Lowest wage paid	MTC	Median total compensation	TCC	Total cash compensation
AER	Average entry range	AWR	Average wage range	H	Hourly	LR	Low end range	MW	Median wage paid	TQ	Third quartile wage
AEX	Average experienced wage	AXR	Average experienced range	HI	Highest wage paid	M	Monthly	MWR	Median wage range	W	Weekly
ATC	Average total compensation	D	Daily	HR	High end range	MCC	Median cash compensation	S	See annotated source	Y	Yearly

Occupation/Type/Industry	Location	Per	Low	Mid	High	Source	Date
Sailor and Marine Oiler	Portland-Vancouver-Beaverton						
	MSA, OR-WA	Y	26230 FQ	30600 MW	39100 TQ	USBLS	5/07
	Pennsylvania	Y	21220 FQ	27730 MW	32830 TQ	USBLS	5/07
	Pittsburgh MSA, PA	Y	26510 FQ	33270 MW	39260 TQ	USBLS	5/07
	Rhode Island	Y	20190 FQ	22330 MW	41730 TQ	USBLS	5/07
	Providence-Fall River-						
	Warwick MSA, RI-MA	Y	20870 FQ	22780 MW	43190 TQ	USBLS	5/07
	South Carolina	Y	23250 FQ	28540 MW	34380 TQ	USBLS	5/07
	Charleston-North Charleston						
	MSA, SC	Y	25810 FQ	30230 MW	36700 TQ	USBLS	5/07
	Tennessee	Y	32670 FQ	36600 MW	41620 TQ	USBLS	5/07
	Memphis MSA, TN-MS-AR	Y	32730 FQ	36270 MW	39820 TQ	USBLS	5/07
	Texas	Y	22480 FQ	26030 MW	41890 TQ	USBLS	5/07
	Corpus Christi MSA, TX	Y	21120 FQ	24120 MW	28830 TQ	USBLS	5/07
	Houston-Sugar Land-Baytown						
	MSA, TX	Y	22320 FQ	25350 MW	37520 TQ	USBLS	5/07
	Virginia	Y	30850 FQ	36990 MW	44440 TQ	USBLS	5/07
	Virginia Beach-Norfolk-						
	Newport News MSA, VA-NC	Y	30850 FQ	36990 MW	44440 TQ	USBLS	5/07
	Washington	H	16.94 FQ	20.64 MW	23.72 TQ	WABLS	3/08
	Seattle-Tacoma-Bellevue						
	MSA, WA	Y	35530 FQ	42730 MW	48800 TQ	USBLS	5/07
	West Virginia	Y	32069 FQ	36811 MW	40673 TQ	WVBLS	7/08-9/08
	Wisconsin	Y	17040 FQ	26000 MW	46280 TQ	USBLS	5/07
	Puerto Rico	Y	19660 FQ	30130 MW	36130 TQ	USBLS	5/07
	San Juan-Caguas-Guaynabo						
	MSA, PR	Y	27120 FQ	33720 MW	37260 TQ	USBLS	5/07
	Virgin Islands	Y	17560 FQ	20360 MW	23530 TQ	USBLS	5/07
	Guam	Y	18640 FQ	23560 MW	27470 TQ	USBLS	5/07
Sales Assistant	United States	Y		35800 AW		BUS201	2005-2006
Sales Engineer	Alabama	Y	55590 FQ	70620 MW	80030 TQ	USBLS	5/07
	Birmingham-Hoover MSA, AL	Y	63410 FQ	70600 MW	77670 TQ	USBLS	5/07
	Alaska	Y	48650 FQ	68780 MW	92420 TQ	USBLS	5/07
	Arizona	Y	44430 FQ	61600 MW	79660 TQ	USBLS	5/07
	Phoenix-Mesa-Scottsdale						
	MSA, AZ	Y	44810 FQ	63310 MW	81250 TQ	USBLS	5/07
	Tucson MSA, AZ	Y	42100 FQ	47500 MW	52430 TQ	USBLS	5/07
	Arkansas	Y	49250 FQ	58150 MW	80520 TQ	USBLS	5/07
	Little Rock-North Little Rock						
	MSA, AR	Y	50460 FQ	56660 MW	64500 TQ	USBLS	5/07
	California	H	34.69 FQ	45.17 MW	58.11 TQ	CABLS	1/08-3/08
	Los Angeles-Long Beach-						
	Glendale PMSA, CA	H	31.28 FQ	39.83 MW	51.83 TQ	CABLS	1/08-3/08
	Oakland-Fremont-Hayward						
	MSA, CA	H	36.19 FQ	47.16 MW	61.07 TQ	CABLS	1/08-3/08
	Riverside-San Bernardino-						
	Ontario MSA, CA	H	31.14 FQ	39.17 MW	52.04 TQ	CABLS	1/08-3/08
	Sacramento-Arden Arcade-						
	Roseville MSA, CA	H	33.69 FQ	41.63 MW	51.18 TQ	CABLS	1/08-3/08
	San Diego-Carlsbad-San						
	Marcos MSA, CA	H	32.66 FQ	39.34 MW	53.53 TQ	CABLS	1/08-3/08
	San Francisco-San Mateo-						
	Redwood PMSA, CA	H	37.36 FQ	46.68 MW	58.34 TQ	CABLS	1/08-3/08
	San Jose-Sunnyvale-Santa						
	Clara MSA, CA	H	38.92 FQ	49.61 MW	62.41 TQ	CABLS	1/08-3/08
	Santa Ana-Anaheim-Irvine						
	PMSA, CA	Y	61510 FQ	81150 MW	113650 TQ	USBLS	5/07
	Colorado	Y	63830 FQ	75420 MW	97720 TQ	USBLS	5/07
	Denver-Aurora MSA, CO	Y	64130 FQ	74890 MW	97760 TQ	USBLS	5/07
	Connecticut	H	27.04 AE	37.77 MW		CTBLS	1/08-3/08
	Bridgeport-Stamford-Norwalk						
	MSA, CT	Y	66880 FQ	81660 MW	99010 TQ	USBLS	5/07
	Hartford-West Hartford-East						
	Hartford MSA, CT	Y	62530 FQ	78440 MW	93350 TQ	USBLS	5/07
	Norwich-New London MSA,						
	CT-RI	Y	73150 FQ	86660 MW	97470 TQ	USBLS	5/07
	Delaware	Y	55440 FQ	79650 MW	96560 TQ	USBLS	5/07
	Wilmington PMSA, DE-MD-						
	NJ	Y	56240 FQ	80660 MW	96890 TQ	USBLS	5/07
	District of Columbia	Y	64150 FQ	75960 MW	102500 TQ	USBLS	5/07

AE	Average entry wage	AW	Average wage paid	FQ	First quartile wage	LO	Lowest wage paid	MTC	Median total compensation	TCC	Total cash compensation
AER	Average entry range	AWR	Average wage range	H	Hourly	LR	Low end range	MW	Median wage paid	TQ	Third quartile wage
AEX	Average experienced wage	AXR	Average experienced range	HI	Highest wage paid	M	Monthly	MWR	Median wage range	W	Weekly
ATC	Average total compensation	D	Daily	HR	High end range	MCC	Median cash compensation	S	See annotated source	Y	Yearly

1420

Sales Engineer

Occupation/Type/Industry	Location	Per	Low	Mid	High	Source	Date
Sales Engineer	Washington-Arlington-Alexandria MSA, DC-VA-MD-WV	Y	63480 FQ	85080 MW	105570 TQ	USBLS	5/07
	Florida	Y	56890 FQ	71860 MW	91400 TQ	USBLS	5/07
	Fort Lauderdale-Pompano Beach-Deerfield Beach PMSA, FL	Y	69560 FQ	84290 MW	98970 TQ	USBLS	5/07
	Jacksonville MSA, FL	Y	67630 FQ	82860 MW	103690 TQ	USBLS	5/07
	Miami-Fort Lauderdale-Miami Beach MSA, FL	Y	62430 FQ	79680 MW	97390 TQ	USBLS	5/07
	Orlando-Kissimmee MSA, FL	Y	55580 FQ	67620 MW	79690 TQ	USBLS	5/07
	Tampa-St. Petersburg-Clearwater MSA, FL	Y	50840 FQ	60590 MW	79230 TQ	USBLS	5/07
	West Palm Beach-Boca Raton-Boynton Beach PMSA, FL	Y	63380 FQ	82980 MW	101610 TQ	USBLS	5/07
	Georgia	Y	55780 FQ	74110 MW	94670 TQ	USBLS	5/07
	Atlanta-Sandy Springs-Marietta MSA, GA	Y	56830 FQ	75670 MW	96070 TQ	USBLS	5/07
	Hawaii	Y	47700 FQ	63140 MW	77560 TQ	USBLS	5/07
	Honolulu MSA, HI	Y	47150 FQ	61310 MW	76760 TQ	USBLS	5/07
	Idaho	Y	55640 FQ	67580 MW	78460 TQ	USBLS	5/07
	Boise City-Nampa MSA, ID	Y	51720 FQ	56040 MW	60600 TQ	USBLS	5/07
	Illinois	Y	55550 FQ	69430 MW	85630 TQ	USBLS	5/07
	Chicago-Naperville-Joliet MSA, IL-IN-WI	Y	56830 FQ	69890 MW	86230 TQ	USBLS	5/07
	Rockford MSA, IL	Y	58010 FQ	70750 MW	86370 TQ	USBLS	5/07
	Indiana	Y	57180 FQ	69040 MW	81250 TQ	USBLS	5/07
	Gary PMSA, IN	Y	64580 FQ	71880 MW	82200 TQ	USBLS	5/07
	Indianapolis-Carmel MSA, IN	Y	56290 FQ	69480 MW	80050 TQ	USBLS	5/07
	Iowa	Y	49260 FQ	65530 MW	81710 TQ	USBLS	5/07
	Des Moines-West Des Moines MSA, IA	Y	45080 FQ	60860 MW	77630 TQ	USBLS	5/07
	Kansas	Y	52520 FQ	65690 MW	80510 TQ	USBLS	5/07
	Wichita MSA, KS	Y	50600 FQ	65840 MW	80040 TQ	USBLS	5/07
	Kentucky	Y	54398 FQ	72490 MW	86082 TQ	KYBLS	2008
	Louisville-Jefferson County MSA, KY-IN	Y	57130 FQ	72190 MW	85400 TQ	USBLS	5/07
	Louisiana	H	28.41 FQ	34.55 MW	41.61 TQ	LABLS	1/08-3/08
	Baton Rouge MSA, LA	Y	74270 FQ	85340 MW	97630 TQ	USBLS	5/07
	New Orleans-Metairie-Kenner MSA, LA	Y	56570 FQ	65900 MW	78750 TQ	USBLS	5/07
	Maine	Y	51290 FQ	64910 MW	80150 TQ	USBLS	5/07
	Portland-South Portland-Biddeford MSA, ME	Y	55240 FQ	66210 MW	83680 TQ	USBLS	5/07
	Maryland	Y		75575 MW		MDBLS	3/08
	Baltimore-Towson MSA, MD	Y	51040 FQ	79090 MW	107440 TQ	USBLS	5/07
	Bethesda-Gaithersburg-Frederick PMSA, MD	Y	52620 FQ	77120 MW	95860 TQ	USBLS	5/07
	Massachusetts	Y	67100 FQ	86200 MW	114600 TQ	USBLS	5/07
	Boston-Cambridge-Quincy NECTA, MA	Y	68720 FQ	88170 MW	113530 TQ	USBLS	5/07
	Worcester MSA, MA-CT	Y	70860 FQ	85320 MW	114310 TQ	USBLS	5/07
	Michigan	Y	60810 FQ	79720 MW	100670 TQ	USBLS	5/07
	Detroit-Warren-Livonia MSA, MI	Y	65560 FQ	85480 MW	106330 TQ	USBLS	5/07
	Grand Rapids-Wyoming MSA, MI	Y	54240 FQ	66980 MW	80780 TQ	USBLS	5/07
	Southeast, MI	Y		93636 AW		MIOAKL03	2007
	Warren-Troy-Farmington Hills PMSA, MI	Y	66920 FQ	87150 MW	109210 TQ	USBLS	5/07
	Minnesota	Y	61854 FQ	76063 MW	98260 TQ	MNBLS	10/08-12/08
	Duluth-Superior MSA, MN-WI	Y	66042 FQ	72587 MW	79803 TQ	MNBLS	10/08-12/08
	Minneapolis-Saint Paul MSA, MN-WI	Y	62342 FQ	78644 MW	101695 TQ	MNBLS	10/08-12/08
	Mississippi	Y	54930 FQ	61230 MW	70770 TQ	USBLS	5/07
	Jackson MSA, MS	Y	54570 FQ	70290 MW	78580 TQ	USBLS	5/07
	Missouri	Y	51500 FQ	67060 MW	86920 TQ	USBLS	5/07
	Kansas City MSA, MO-KS	Y	55940 FQ	69320 MW	87080 TQ	USBLS	5/07
	St. Louis MSA, MO-IL	Y	52420 FQ	69170 MW	86270 TQ	USBLS	5/07
	Montana	Y	48100 FQ	59670 MW	73960 TQ	USBLS	5/07
	Nebraska	Y	51080 FQ	62540 MW	87460 TQ	USBLS	5/07

AE	Average entry wage	**AW**	Average wage paid	**FQ**	First quartile wage
AER	Average entry range	**AWR**	Average wage range	**H**	Hourly
AEX	Average experienced wage	**AXR**	Average experienced range	**HI**	Highest wage paid
ATC	Average total compensation	**D**	Daily	**HR**	High end range

LO	Lowest wage paid	**MTC**	Median total compensation	**TCC**	Total cash compensation
LR	Low end range	**MW**	Median wage paid	**TQ**	Third quartile wage
M	Monthly	**MWR**	Median wage range	**W**	Weekly
MCC	Median cash compensation	**S**	See annotated source	**Y**	Yearly

Occupation/Type/Industry	Location	Per	Low	Mid	High	Source	Date
Sales Engineer	Omaha-Council Bluffs MSA, NE-IA	Y	59010 FQ	77270 MW	95660 TQ	USBLS	5/07
	Nevada	H	24.62 FQ	30.98 MW	44.40 TQ	NVBLS	5/08
	Las Vegas-Paradise MSA, NV	H	24.89 FQ	30.65 MW	43.70 TQ	NVBLS	5/08
	New Hampshire	H	30.10 AE	43.19 MW	49.16 AEX	NHBLS	6/08
	Manchester MSA, NH	Y	73300 FQ	81900 MW	90290 TQ	USBLS	5/07
	Nashua NECTA, NH-MA	Y	72260 FQ	90500 MW	104330 TQ	USBLS	5/07
	New Jersey	Y	70380 FQ	96600 MW	124710 TQ	USBLS	5/07
	Camden PMSA, NJ	Y	61220 FQ	84400 MW	101030 TQ	USBLS	5/07
	Newark-Union PMSA, NJ-PA	Y	64910 FQ	81930 MW	109470 TQ	USBLS	5/07
	Trenton-Ewing MSA, NJ	Y	70400 FQ	85290 MW	96330 TQ	USBLS	5/07
	New Mexico	Y	51830 FQ	62150 MW	77150 TQ	USBLS	5/07
	Albuquerque MSA, NM	Y	52160 FQ	62780 MW	77680 TQ	USBLS	5/07
	New York	Y	64260 FQ	83430 MW	105690 TQ	USBLS	5/07
	Albany-Schenectady-Troy MSA, NY	Y	58710 FQ	80250 MW	101770 TQ	USBLS	5/07
	Binghamton MSA, NY	Y	59490 FQ	70900 MW	80890 TQ	USBLS	5/07
	Buffalo-Niagara Falls MSA, NY	Y	54030 FQ	67910 MW	91950 TQ	USBLS	5/07
	Nassau-Suffolk PMSA, NY	Y	71460 FQ	88950 MW	112680 TQ	USBLS	5/07
	New York-Northern New Jersey-Long Island MSA, NY-NJ-PA	Y	71640 FQ	92670 MW	118880 TQ	USBLS	5/07
	North Carolina	Y	53220 FQ	73650 MW	91870 TQ	USBLS	5/07
	Charlotte-Gastonia-Concord MSA, NC-SC	Y	54540 FQ	74850 MW	93760 TQ	USBLS	5/07
	Durham MSA, NC	Y	51110 FQ	74270 MW	102520 TQ	USBLS	5/07
	Raleigh-Cary MSA, NC	Y	55690 FQ	75710 MW	94100 TQ	USBLS	5/07
	Ohio	Y	58240 FQ	72530 MW	88070 TQ	USBLS	5/07
	Cincinnati-Middletown MSA, OH-KY-IN	Y	62150 FQ	75930 MW	92090 TQ	USBLS	5/07
	Cleveland-Elyria-Mentor MSA, OH	Y	55540 FQ	67830 MW	80850 TQ	USBLS	5/07
	Columbus MSA, OH	Y	52930 FQ	69870 MW	83780 TQ	USBLS	5/07
	Dayton MSA, OH	Y	68280 FQ	79780 MW	92280 TQ	USBLS	5/07
	Oklahoma	Y	39560 FQ	59050 MW	77580 TQ	USBLS	5/07
	Oklahoma City MSA, OK	Y	53710 FQ	65190 MW	76230 TQ	USBLS	5/07
	Tulsa MSA, OK	Y	37970 FQ	57550 MW	86590 TQ	USBLS	5/07
	Oregon	H	30.57 FQ	39.61 MW	51.18 TQ	ORBLS	5/08
	Portland-Vancouver-Beaverton MSA, OR-WA	Y	64460 FQ	83680 MW	107570 TQ	USBLS	5/07
	Pennsylvania	Y	53900 FQ	70350 MW	94510 TQ	USBLS	5/07
	Allentown-Bethlehem-Easton MSA, PA-NJ	Y	56660 FQ	65460 MW	96960 TQ	USBLS	5/07
	Philadelphia-Camden-Wilmington MSA, PA-NJ-DE-MD	Y	54450 FQ	70610 MW	94820 TQ	USBLS	5/07
	Pittsburgh MSA, PA	Y	50130 FQ	68420 MW	89570 TQ	USBLS	5/07
	Reading MSA, PA	Y	52800 FQ	72380 MW	95600 TQ	USBLS	5/07
	Rhode Island	Y	60830 FQ	71630 MW	88530 TQ	USBLS	5/07
	Providence-Fall River-Warwick MSA, RI-MA	Y	62050 FQ	74610 MW	96270 TQ	USBLS	5/07
	South Carolina	Y	57170 FQ	71000 MW	92850 TQ	USBLS	5/07
	Charleston-North Charleston MSA, SC	Y	37650 FQ	48260 MW	66360 TQ	USBLS	5/07
	Columbia MSA, SC	Y	59330 FQ	72660 MW	84940 TQ	USBLS	5/07
	Spartanburg MSA, SC	Y	56070 FQ	66280 MW	75720 TQ	USBLS	5/07
	South Dakota	Y	60955 FQ	71666 MW	83029 TQ	SDBLS	7/08-9/08
	Sioux Falls MSA, SD	Y	59259 FQ	71234 MW	87207 TQ	SDBLS	7/08-9/08
	Tennessee	Y	34010 FQ	48750 MW	77140 TQ	USBLS	5/07
	Nashville-Davidson-Murfreesboro MSA, TN	Y	30920 FQ	39120 MW	65740 TQ	USBLS	5/07
	Texas	Y	63700 FQ	87570 MW	114020 TQ	USBLS	5/07
	Austin-Round Rock MSA, TX	Y	53240 FQ	75160 MW	102330 TQ	USBLS	5/07
	Dallas-Fort Worth-Arlington MSA, TX	Y	60540 FQ	86460 MW	117540 TQ	USBLS	5/07
	Houston-Sugar Land-Baytown MSA, TX	Y	76900 FQ	93240 MW	118360 TQ	USBLS	5/07
	San Antonio MSA, TX	Y	47420 FQ	67410 MW	83670 TQ	USBLS	5/07
	Utah	Y	63860 FQ	80050 MW	91990 TQ	USBLS	5/07
	Salt Lake City MSA, UT	Y	68060 FQ	81700 MW	90920 TQ	USBLS	5/07
	Vermont	Y	54470 FQ	69190 MW	80410 TQ	USBLS	5/07

AE Average entry wage	**AW** Average wage paid	**FQ** First quartile wage	**LO** Lowest wage paid	**MTC** Median total compensation	**TCC** Total cash compensation
AER Average entry range	**AWR** Average wage range	**H** Hourly	**LR** Low end range	**MW** Median wage paid	**TQ** Third quartile wage
AEX Average experienced wage	**AXR** Average experienced range	**HI** Highest wage paid	**M** Monthly	**MWR** Median wage range	**W** Weekly
ATC Average total compensation	**D** Daily	**HR** High end range	**MCC** Median cash compensation	**S** See annotated source	**Y** Yearly

Occupation/Type/Industry	Location	Per	Low	Mid	High	Source	Date
Sales Engineer	Burlington-South Burlington MSA, VT	Y	51090 FQ	61450 MW	74660 TQ	USBLS	5/07
	Virginia	Y	64910 FQ	78830 MW	100050 TQ	USBLS	5/07
	Richmond MSA, VA	Y	60910 FQ	72350 MW	80980 TQ	USBLS	5/07
	Virginia Beach-Norfolk-Newport News MSA, VA-NC	Y	59580 FQ	70490 MW	81490 TQ	USBLS	5/07
	Washington	H	31.58 FQ	39.53 MW	52.49 TQ	WABLS	3/08
	Seattle-Tacoma-Bellevue MSA, WA	Y	67730 FQ	82860 MW	107720 TQ	USBLS	5/07
	West Virginia	Y	50855 FQ	75136 MW	97013 TQ	WVBLS	7/08-9/08
	Charleston MSA, WV	Y	49970 FQ	88980 MW	98260 TQ	USBLS	5/07
	Wisconsin	Y	59910 FQ	78620 MW	92670 TQ	USBLS	5/07
	Milwaukee-Waukesha-West Allis MSA, WI	Y	63140 FQ	82090 MW	93730 TQ	USBLS	5/07
	Wyoming	Y	72388 FQ	84770 MW	94972 TQ	WYBLS	9/08
	Puerto Rico	Y	41770 FQ	56890 MW	77800 TQ	USBLS	5/07
	San Juan-Caguas-Guaynabo MSA, PR	Y	41170 FQ	56500 MW	77660 TQ	USBLS	5/07
Sales Executive	United States	Y		147824 ATC		SMM	2006
Sales Manager	Alabama	Y	58550 FQ	85980 MW	116410 TQ	USBLS	5/07
	Birmingham-Hoover MSA, AL	Y	61450 FQ	90910 MW	120340 TQ	USBLS	5/07
	Mobile MSA, AL	Y	56340 FQ	74860 MW	107580 TQ	USBLS	5/07
	Tuscaloosa MSA, AL	Y	56210 FQ	90450 MW	143210 TQ	USBLS	5/07
	Alaska	Y	37840 FQ	55340 MW	80180 TQ	USBLS	5/07
	Anchorage MSA, AK	Y	36770 FQ	57420 MW	83420 TQ	USBLS	5/07
	Arizona	Y	49920 FQ	73520 MW	109790 TQ	USBLS	5/07
	Phoenix-Mesa-Scottsdale MSA, AZ	Y	51960 FQ	77300 MW	115160 TQ	USBLS	5/07
	Tucson MSA, AZ	Y	44190 FQ	61750 MW	84770 TQ	USBLS	5/07
	Arkansas	Y	56620 FQ	79230 MW	116460 TQ	USBLS	5/07
	Little Rock-North Little Rock MSA, AR	Y	64730 FQ	85430 MW	110320 TQ	USBLS	5/07
	California	H	32.32 FQ	50.22 MW		CABLS	1/08-3/08
	Fresno MSA, CA	H	29.95 FQ	42.67 MW	64.40 TQ	CABLS	1/08-3/08
	Los Angeles-Long Beach-Glendale PMSA, CA	H	32.63 FQ	49.67 MW		CABLS	1/08-3/08
	Oakland-Fremont-Hayward MSA, CA	H	34.97 FQ	52.17 MW		CABLS	1/08-3/08
	Riverside-San Bernardino-Ontario MSA, CA	H	25.70 FQ	41.97 MW	66.53 TQ	CABLS	1/08-3/08
	Sacramento-Arden Arcade-Roseville MSA, CA	H	29.28 FQ	42.55 MW	63.15 TQ	CABLS	1/08-3/08
	San Diego-Carlsbad-San Marcos MSA, CA	H	33.04 FQ	49.97 MW		CABLS	1/08-3/08
	San Francisco-San Mateo-Redwood PMSA, CA	H	41.49 FQ	62.95 MW		CABLS	1/08-3/08
	San Jose-Sunnyvale-Santa Clara MSA, CA	H	44.24 FQ	67.76 MW		CABLS	1/08-3/08
	Santa Ana-Anaheim-Irvine PMSA, CA	Y	75480 FQ	109210 MW		USBLS	5/07
	Colorado	Y	60680 FQ	92540 MW	128830 TQ	USBLS	5/07
	Denver-Aurora MSA, CO	Y	63880 FQ	95760 MW	130310 TQ	USBLS	5/07
	Connecticut	H	29.63 AE	48.98 MW		CTBLS	1/08-3/08
	Bridgeport-Stamford-Norwalk MSA, CT	Y	79750 FQ	108340 MW		USBLS	5/07
	Hartford-West Hartford-East Hartford MSA, CT	Y	70400 FQ	97310 MW	133330 TQ	USBLS	5/07
	Delaware	Y	71560 FQ	104990 MW	143480 TQ	USBLS	5/07
	Dover MSA, DE	Y	61110 FQ	107150 MW	129050 TQ	USBLS	5/07
	Wilmington PMSA, DE-MD-NJ	Y	73810 FQ	103380 MW	140000 TQ	USBLS	5/07
	District of Columbia	Y	60630 FQ	85590 MW	124810 TQ	USBLS	5/07
	Washington-Arlington-Alexandria MSA, DC-VA-MD-WV	Y	70260 FQ	108570 MW		USBLS	5/07
	Florida	Y	75200 FQ	109520 MW		USBLS	5/07
	Fort Lauderdale-Pompano Beach-Deerfield Beach PMSA, FL	Y	73710 FQ	108500 MW		USBLS	5/07
	Jacksonville MSA, FL	Y	73260 FQ	109250 MW		USBLS	5/07

AE Average entry wage	**AW** Average wage paid	**FQ** First quartile wage	**LO** Lowest wage paid	**MTC** Median total compensation	**TCC** Total cash compensation
AER Average entry range	**AWR** Average wage range	**H** Hourly	**LR** Low end range	**MW** Median wage paid	**TQ** Third quartile wage
AEX Average experienced wage	**AXR** Average experienced range	**HI** Highest wage paid	**M** Monthly	**MWR** Median wage range	**W** Weekly
ATC Average total compensation	**D** Daily	**HR** High end range	**MCC** Median cash compensation	**S** See annotated source	**Y** Yearly

Occupation/Type/Industry	Location	Per	Low	Mid	High	Source	Date
Sales Manager	Miami-Fort Lauderdale-Miami Beach MSA, FL	Y	76500 FQ	111250 MW		USBLS	5/07
	Orlando-Kissimmee MSA, FL	Y	68810 FQ	103640 MW		USBLS	5/07
	Tampa-St. Petersburg-Clearwater MSA, FL	Y	81630 FQ	113720 MW		USBLS	5/07
	West Palm Beach-Boca Raton-Boynton Beach PMSA, FL	Y	71110 FQ	110320 MW		USBLS	5/07
	Georgia	Y	62860 FQ	90310 MW	127690 TQ	USBLS	5/07
	Atlanta-Sandy Springs-Marietta MSA, GA	Y	65900 FQ	95110 MW	133010 TQ	USBLS	5/07
	Hawaii	Y	46780 FQ	68650 MW	106730 TQ	USBLS	5/07
	Honolulu MSA, HI	Y	48640 FQ	70690 MW	108860 TQ	USBLS	5/07
	Idaho	Y	43550 FQ	59640 MW	83710 TQ	USBLS	5/07
	Boise City-Nampa MSA, ID	Y	45130 FQ	60920 MW	85120 TQ	USBLS	5/07
	Illinois	Y	61580 FQ	93570 MW	133740 TQ	USBLS	5/07
	Chicago-Naperville-Joliet MSA, IL-IN-WI	Y	64880 FQ	97110 MW	138770 TQ	USBLS	5/07
	Indiana	Y	60500 FQ	82590 MW	117560 TQ	USBLS	5/07
	Gary PMSA, IN	Y	63650 FQ	76520 MW	119720 TQ	USBLS	5/07
	Indianapolis-Carmel MSA, IN	Y	64700 FQ	90040 MW	127410 TQ	USBLS	5/07
	South Bend-Mishawaka MSA, IN-MI	Y	57330 FQ	77830 MW	118060 TQ	USBLS	5/07
	Iowa	Y	60900 FQ	88890 MW	140460 TQ	USBLS	5/07
	Sioux City MSA, IA-NE-SD	Y	74560 FQ	121690 MW		USBLS	5/07
	Kansas	Y	56740 FQ	82480 MW	122420 TQ	USBLS	5/07
	Wichita MSA, KS	Y	56290 FQ	73870 MW	104600 TQ	USBLS	5/07
	Kentucky	Y	62341 FQ	86262 MW	122347 TQ	KYBLS	2008
	Elizabethtown MSA, KY	Y	71790 FQ	89500 MW	112870 TQ	USBLS	5/07
	Louisville-Jefferson County MSA, KY-IN	Y	62800 FQ	85290 MW	115400 TQ	USBLS	5/07
	Louisiana	H	24.50 FQ	34.80 MW	49.87 TQ	LABLS	1/08-3/08
	Baton Rouge MSA, LA	Y	49210 FQ	70240 MW	108280 TQ	USBLS	5/07
	Lake Charles MSA, LA	Y	45090 FQ	68750 MW	103590 TQ	USBLS	5/07
	New Orleans-Metairie-Kenner MSA, LA	Y	53050 FQ	78010 MW	112380 TQ	USBLS	5/07
	Shreveport-Bossier City MSA, LA	Y	51360 FQ	76290 MW	102170 TQ	USBLS	5/07
	Maine	Y	57460 FQ	72720 MW	99690 TQ	USBLS	5/07
	Portland-South Portland-Biddeford MSA, ME	Y	60680 FQ	82770 MW	112650 TQ	USBLS	5/07
	Maryland	Y		105275 MW		MDBLS	3/08
	Baltimore-Towson MSA, MD	Y	70850 FQ	105020 MW		USBLS	5/07
	Bethesda-Gaithersburg-Frederick PMSA, MD	Y	76560 FQ	111830 MW		USBLS	5/07
	Hagerstown-Martinsburg MSA, MD-WV	Y	51100 FQ	67660 MW	107210 TQ	USBLS	5/07
	Massachusetts	Y	78030 FQ	112040 MW		USBLS	5/07
	Barnstable Town MSA, MA	Y	72000 FQ	96730 MW	118520 TQ	USBLS	5/07
	Boston-Cambridge-Quincy NECTA, MA	Y	82770 FQ	120100 MW		USBLS	5/07
	Worcester MSA, MA-CT	Y	70530 FQ	99930 MW	136570 TQ	USBLS	5/07
	Michigan	Y	61310 FQ	89300 MW	123140 TQ	USBLS	5/07
	Detroit-Warren-Livonia MSA, MI	Y	71720 FQ	103500 MW	134390 TQ	USBLS	5/07
	Grand Rapids-Wyoming MSA, MI	Y	66880 FQ	84830 MW	113030 TQ	USBLS	5/07
	Muskegon-Norton Shores MSA, MI	Y	47220 FQ	65160 MW	100060 TQ	USBLS	5/07
	Warren-Troy-Farmington Hills PMSA, MI	Y	69560 FQ	101350 MW	134260 TQ	USBLS	5/07
	Minnesota	Y	76134 FQ	108905 MW	148734 TQ	MNBLS	10/08-12/08
	Duluth-Superior MSA, MN-WI	Y	55062 FQ	73788 MW	100032 TQ	MNBLS	10/08-12/08
	Minneapolis-Saint Paul MSA, MN-WI	Y	83537 FQ	114556 MW		MNBLS	10/08-12/08
	Rochester MSA, MN	Y	75080 FQ	104865 MW	144085 TQ	MNBLS	10/08-12/08
	Mississippi	Y	51830 FQ	73520 MW	100040 TQ	USBLS	5/07
	Jackson MSA, MS	Y	63540 FQ	80820 MW	107960 TQ	USBLS	5/07
	Missouri	Y	66990 FQ	94550 MW	133570 TQ	USBLS	5/07
	Jefferson City MSA, MO	Y	64020 FQ	88680 MW	129060 TQ	USBLS	5/07
	Kansas City MSA, MO-KS	Y	63810 FQ	93560 MW	131300 TQ	USBLS	5/07
	St. Louis MSA, MO-IL	Y	71370 FQ	98850 MW	140320 TQ	USBLS	5/07
	Montana	Y	43200 FQ	57830 MW	75060 TQ	USBLS	5/07

Occupation/Type/Industry	Location	Per	Low	Mid	High	Source	Date
Sales Manager	Billings MSA, MT	Y	37820 FQ	57520 MW	79110 TQ	USBLS	5/07
	Nebraska	Y	63520 FQ	86720 MW	122890 TQ	USBLS	5/07
	Omaha-Council Bluffs MSA, NE-IA	Y	66570 FQ	91350 MW	130570 TQ	USBLS	5/07
	Nevada	H	25.29 FQ	34.49 MW	48.32 TQ	NVBLS	5/08
	Las Vegas-Paradise MSA, NV	H	25.24 FQ	34.60 MW	48.35 TQ	NVBLS	5/08
	New Hampshire	H	31.28 AE	52.04 MW	67.55 AEX	NHBLS	6/08
	Manchester MSA, NH	Y	76040 FQ	103950 MW	138760 TQ	USBLS	5/07
	Nashua NECTA, NH-MA	Y	90910 FQ	119740 MW		USBLS	5/07
	New Jersey	Y	69440 FQ	111320 MW		USBLS	5/07
	Atlantic City MSA, NJ	Y	63250 FQ	82820 MW	127270 TQ	USBLS	5/07
	Camden PMSA, NJ	Y	63260 FQ	94640 MW		USBLS	5/07
	Edison PMSA, NJ	Y	64660 FQ	108530 MW		USBLS	5/07
	Newark-Union PMSA, NJ-PA	Y	76910 FQ	117890 MW		USBLS	5/07
	New Mexico	Y	45150 FQ	63070 MW	94530 TQ	USBLS	5/07
	Albuquerque MSA, NM	Y	46900 FQ	63850 MW	98700 TQ	USBLS	5/07
	New York	Y	100280 FQ	140210 MW		USBLS	5/07
	Albany-Schenectady-Troy MSA, NY	Y	65450 FQ	106060 MW		USBLS	5/07
	Buffalo-Niagara Falls MSA, NY	Y	73080 FQ	100640 MW	138330 TQ	USBLS	5/07
	Nassau-Suffolk PMSA, NY	Y	96220 FQ	144040 MW		USBLS	5/07
	New York-Northern New Jersey-Long Island MSA, NY-NJ-PA	Y	92970 FQ	134570 MW		USBLS	5/07
	North Carolina	Y	56000 FQ	84660 MW	122670 TQ	USBLS	5/07
	Charlotte-Gastonia-Concord MSA, NC-SC	Y	60320 FQ	90820 MW	127100 TQ	USBLS	5/07
	Raleigh-Cary MSA, NC	Y	59440 FQ	88740 MW	124920 TQ	USBLS	5/07
	Winston-Salem MSA, NC	Y	61020 FQ	83850 MW	114370 TQ	USBLS	5/07
	North Dakota	Y	50130 FQ	68590 MW	94820 TQ	USBLS	5/07
	Bismarck MSA, ND	Y	51000 FQ	62340 MW	80540 TQ	USBLS	5/07
	Fargo MSA, ND-MN	Y	51640 FQ	75680 MW	106010 TQ	USBLS	5/07
	Ohio	Y	66970 FQ	94860 MW	131640 TQ	USBLS	5/07
	Cincinnati-Middletown MSA, OH-KY-IN	Y	75490 FQ	104240 MW	139320 TQ	USBLS	5/07
	Cleveland-Elyria-Mentor MSA, OH	Y	78610 FQ	104560 MW	139180 TQ	USBLS	5/07
	Columbus MSA, OH	Y	67880 FQ	101160 MW	138850 TQ	USBLS	5/07
	Dayton MSA, OH	Y	60350 FQ	91820 MW	128530 TQ	USBLS	5/07
	Oklahoma	Y	47220 FQ	69150 MW	103490 TQ	USBLS	5/07
	Oklahoma City MSA, OK	Y	44520 FQ	68060 MW	106670 TQ	USBLS	5/07
	Tulsa MSA, OK	Y	56910 FQ	76790 MW	110220 TQ	USBLS	5/07
	Oregon	H	32.35 FQ	45.65 MW	63.99 TQ	ORBLS	5/08
	Portland-Vancouver-Beaverton MSA, OR-WA	Y	70870 FQ	101490 MW	133750 TQ	USBLS	5/07
	Pennsylvania	Y	64400 FQ	92830 MW	130080 TQ	USBLS	5/07
	Allentown-Bethlehem-Easton MSA, PA-NJ	Y	54710 FQ	82820 MW	122750 TQ	USBLS	5/07
	Philadelphia-Camden-Wilmington MSA, PA-NJ-DE-MD	Y	72800 FQ	105370 MW		USBLS	5/07
	Pittsburgh MSA, PA	Y	60460 FQ	87250 MW	118170 TQ	USBLS	5/07
	York-Hanover MSA, PA	Y	59200 FQ	82490 MW	108390 TQ	USBLS	5/07
	Rhode Island	Y	78100 FQ	105390 MW	142130 TQ	USBLS	5/07
	Providence-Fall River-Warwick MSA, RI-MA	Y	75390 FQ	103580 MW	140330 TQ	USBLS	5/07
	South Carolina	Y	56930 FQ	81040 MW	110780 TQ	USBLS	5/07
	Charleston-North Charleston MSA, SC	Y	65670 FQ	86960 MW	105860 TQ	USBLS	5/07
	Columbia MSA, SC	Y	56580 FQ	79710 MW	120370 TQ	USBLS	5/07
	South Dakota	Y	74701 FQ	94239 MW	118889 TQ	SDBLS	7/08-9/08
	Sioux Falls MSA, SD	Y	74125 FQ	93043 MW	110178 TQ	SDBLS	7/08-9/08
	Tennessee	Y	49700 FQ	72250 MW	101490 TQ	USBLS	5/07
	Memphis MSA, TN-MS-AR	Y	54400 FQ	77130 MW	111590 TQ	USBLS	5/07
	Nashville-Davidson-Murfreesboro MSA, TN	Y	51150 FQ	73720 MW	105200 TQ	USBLS	5/07
	Texas	Y	67780 FQ	97830 MW	137890 TQ	USBLS	5/07
	Austin-Round Rock MSA, TX	Y	68760 FQ	108300 MW		USBLS	5/07
	Dallas-Fort Worth-Arlington MSA, TX	Y	73840 FQ	103300 MW	142840 TQ	USBLS	5/07
	El Paso MSA, TX	Y	53940 FQ	73850 MW	110800 TQ	USBLS	5/07

AE	Average entry wage	AW	Average wage paid	FQ	First quartile wage
AER	Average entry range	AWR	Average wage range	H	Hourly
AEX	Average experienced wage	AXR	Average experienced range	HI	Highest wage paid
ATC	Average total compensation	D	Daily	HR	High end range

LO	Lowest wage paid	MTC	Median total compensation
LR	Low end range	MW	Median wage paid
M	Monthly	MWR	Median wage range
MCC	Median cash compensation	S	See annotated source

TCC	Total cash compensation		
TQ	Third quartile wage		
W	Weekly		
Y	Yearly		

Occupation/Type/Industry	Location	Per	Low	Mid	High	Source	Date
Sales Manager	Houston-Sugar Land-Baytown						
	MSA, TX	Y	71920 FQ	102060 MW	142610 TQ	USBLS	5/07
	San Antonio MSA, TX	Y	56490 FQ	79500 MW	116200 TQ	USBLS	5/07
	Utah	Y	62310 FQ	86540 MW	125410 TQ	USBLS	5/07
	Salt Lake City MSA, UT	Y	69180 FQ	94710 MW	137290 TQ	USBLS	5/07
	Vermont	Y	52100 FQ	88780 MW	124990 TQ	USBLS	5/07
	Burlington-South Burlington						
	MSA, VT	Y	72990 FQ	113350 MW	131440 TQ	USBLS	5/07
	Virginia	Y	63330 FQ	104120 MW		USBLS	5/07
	Richmond MSA, VA	Y	61560 FQ	104860 MW	140830 TQ	USBLS	5/07
	Virginia Beach-Norfolk-						
	Newport News MSA, VA-NC	Y	56910 FQ	90040 MW	128240 TQ	USBLS	5/07
	Washington	H	40.38 FQ	57.61 MW		WABLS	3/08
	Seattle-Tacoma-Bellevue						
	MSA, WA	Y	88150 FQ	125920 MW		USBLS	5/07
	Spokane MSA, WA	Y	60200 FQ	81220 MW	105530 TQ	USBLS	5/07
	West Virginia	Y	46631 FQ	71190 MW	105084 TQ	WVBLS	7/08-9/08
	Charleston MSA, WV	Y	45310 FQ	63700 MW	89600 TQ	USBLS	5/07
	Wisconsin	Y	63930 FQ	89920 MW	122520 TQ	USBLS	5/07
	Green Bay MSA, WI	Y	69390 FQ	89070 MW	119990 TQ	USBLS	5/07
	Milwaukee-Waukesha-West						
	Allis MSA, WI	Y	67660 FQ	100160 MW	135130 TQ	USBLS	5/07
	Wyoming	Y	47375 FQ	60643 MW	77703 TQ	WYBLS	9/08
	Cheyenne MSA, WY	Y	47701 FQ	56457 MW	79168 TQ	WYBLS	9/08
	Puerto Rico	Y	40160 FQ	56360 MW	80300 TQ	USBLS	5/07
	San Juan-Caguas-Guaynabo						
	MSA, PR	Y	40420 FQ	57910 MW	81900 TQ	USBLS	5/07
	Virgin Islands	Y	41250 FQ	50100 MW	65260 TQ	USBLS	5/07
	Guam	Y	29870 FQ	39250 MW	52420 TQ	USBLS	5/07
Copier Industry	United States	Y		48676 AW		COPIER	2008
Home Textiles Industry	United States	Y		166500 AW		HTT	2008
Sales Representative							
Wholesale and Manufacturing	Alabama	Y	32440 FQ	44500 MW	62500 TQ	USBLS	5/07
Wholesale and Manufacturing	Birmingham-Hoover MSA, AL	Y	33410 FQ	45620 MW	64460 TQ	USBLS	5/07
Wholesale and Manufacturing	Huntsville MSA, AL	Y	32290 FQ	41930 MW	63000 TQ	USBLS	5/07
Wholesale and Manufacturing	Alaska	Y	37360 FQ	49170 MW	62090 TQ	USBLS	5/07
Wholesale and Manufacturing	Anchorage MSA, AK	Y	38410 FQ	50200 MW	63040 TQ	USBLS	5/07
Wholesale and Manufacturing	Arizona	Y	32240 FQ	45500 MW	64730 TQ	USBLS	5/07
Wholesale and Manufacturing	Flagstaff MSA, AZ	Y	24040 FQ	35460 MW	50260 TQ	USBLS	5/07
Wholesale and Manufacturing	Phoenix-Mesa-Scottsdale						
	MSA, AZ	Y	32020 FQ	45930 MW	64710 TQ	USBLS	5/07
Wholesale and Manufacturing	Tucson MSA, AZ	Y	34050 FQ	41440 MW	59440 TQ	USBLS	5/07
Wholesale and Manufacturing	Arkansas	Y	32690 FQ	44240 MW	62060 TQ	USBLS	5/07
Wholesale and Manufacturing	Little Rock-North Little Rock						
	MSA, AR	Y	34660 FQ	45740 MW	61360 TQ	USBLS	5/07
Wholesale and Manufacturing	Pine Bluff MSA, AR	Y	23400 FQ	36450 MW	51530 TQ	USBLS	5/07
Wholesale and Manufacturing	California	H	18.84 FQ	26.40 MW	37.76 TQ	CABLS	1/08-3/08
Wholesale and Manufacturing	Los Angeles-Long Beach-						
	Glendale PMSA, CA	H	17.62 FQ	24.64 MW	35.55 TQ	CABLS	1/08-3/08
Wholesale and Manufacturing	Modesto MSA, CA	H	20.89 FQ	27.74 MW	38.14 TQ	CABLS	1/08-3/08
Wholesale and Manufacturing	Oakland-Fremont-Hayward						
	MSA, CA	H	20.80 FQ	28.49 MW	41.90 TQ	CABLS	1/08-3/08
Wholesale and Manufacturing	Riverside-San Bernardino-						
	Ontario MSA, CA	H	19.48 FQ	27.14 MW	37.40 TQ	CABLS	1/08-3/08
Wholesale and Manufacturing	Sacramento-Arden Arcade-						
	Roseville MSA, CA	H	18.35 FQ	24.94 MW	34.24 TQ	CABLS	1/08-3/08
Wholesale and Manufacturing	San Diego-Carlsbad-San						
	Marcos MSA, CA	H	19.32 FQ	27.58 MW	38.88 TQ	CABLS	1/08-3/08
Wholesale and Manufacturing	San Francisco-San Mateo-						
	Redwood PMSA, CA	H	20.04 FQ	27.67 MW	38.90 TQ	CABLS	1/08-3/08
Wholesale and Manufacturing	San Jose-Sunnyvale-Santa						
	Clara MSA, CA	H	21.72 FQ	31.41 MW	42.42 TQ	CABLS	1/08-3/08
Wholesale and Manufacturing	Santa Ana-Anaheim-Irvine						
	PMSA, CA	Y	40350 FQ	57510 MW	84790 TQ	USBLS	5/07
Wholesale and Manufacturing	Colorado	Y	33850 FQ	50710 MW	72780 TQ	USBLS	5/07
Wholesale and Manufacturing	Colorado Springs MSA, CO	Y	31380 FQ	45750 MW	64800 TQ	USBLS	5/07
Wholesale and Manufacturing	Denver-Aurora MSA, CO	Y	36250 FQ	53010 MW	74910 TQ	USBLS	5/07
Wholesale and Manufacturing	Pueblo MSA, CO	Y	27990 FQ	45860 MW	72100 TQ	USBLS	5/07
Wholesale and Manufacturing	Connecticut	H	17.81 AE	28.85 MW		CTBLS	1/08-3/08
Wholesale and Manufacturing	Bridgeport-Stamford-Norwalk						
	MSA, CT	Y	44380 FQ	64100 MW	103600 TQ	USBLS	5/07

AE	Average entry wage	AW	Average wage paid	FQ	First quartile wage
AER	Average entry range	AWR	Average wage range	H	Hourly
AEX	Average experienced wage	AXR	Average experienced range	HI	Highest wage paid
ATC	Average total compensation	D	Daily	HR	High end range

LO Lowest wage paid MTC Median total compensation TCC Total cash compensation
LR Low end range MW Median wage paid TQ Third quartile wage
M Monthly MWR Median wage range W Weekly
MCC Median cash compensation S See annotated source Y Yearly

Sales Representative

Occupation/Type/Industry	Location	Per	Low	Mid	High	Source	Date
Wholesale and Manufacturing	Hartford-West Hartford-East Hartford MSA, CT	Y	41610 FQ	58480 MW	84860 TQ	USBLS	5/07
Wholesale and Manufacturing	Delaware	Y	38140 FQ	55130 MW	74600 TQ	USBLS	5/07
Wholesale and Manufacturing	Wilmington PMSA, DE-MD-NJ	Y	42260 FQ	58620 MW	77960 TQ	USBLS	5/07
Wholesale and Manufacturing	District of Columbia	Y	41070 FQ	58980 MW	80470 TQ	USBLS	5/07
Wholesale and Manufacturing	Washington-Arlington-Alexandria MSA, DC-VA-MD-WV	Y	40660 FQ	56680 MW	81570 TQ	USBLS	5/07
Wholesale and Manufacturing	Florida	Y	32260 FQ	46670 MW	68360 TQ	USBLS	5/07
Wholesale and Manufacturing	Cape Coral-Fort Myers MSA, FL	Y	33770 FQ	48690 MW	75680 TQ	USBLS	5/07
Wholesale and Manufacturing	Fort Lauderdale-Pompano Beach-Deerfield Beach PMSA, FL	Y	31960 FQ	46210 MW	70630 TQ	USBLS	5/07
Wholesale and Manufacturing	Jacksonville MSA, FL	Y	32930 FQ	45990 MW	64960 TQ	USBLS	5/07
Wholesale and Manufacturing	Miami-Fort Lauderdale-Miami Beach MSA, FL	Y	30650 FQ	45370 MW	69380 TQ	USBLS	5/07
Wholesale and Manufacturing	Orlando-Kissimmee MSA, FL	Y	35390 FQ	50520 MW	73040 TQ	USBLS	5/07
Wholesale and Manufacturing	Tampa-St. Petersburg-Clearwater MSA, FL	Y	34920 FQ	49510 MW	65640 TQ	USBLS	5/07
Wholesale and Manufacturing	West Palm Beach-Boca Raton-Boynton Beach PMSA, FL	Y	30020 FQ	46330 MW	67630 TQ	USBLS	5/07
Wholesale and Manufacturing	Georgia	Y	35230 FQ	48710 MW	69590 TQ	USBLS	5/07
Wholesale and Manufacturing	Atlanta-Sandy Springs-Marietta MSA, GA	Y	36750 FQ	51100 MW	72370 TQ	USBLS	5/07
Wholesale and Manufacturing	Hawaii	Y	26220 FQ	40790 MW	56430 TQ	USBLS	5/07
Wholesale and Manufacturing	Honolulu MSA, HI	Y	25410 FQ	40880 MW	56760 TQ	USBLS	5/07
Wholesale and Manufacturing	Idaho	Y	34000 FQ	43190 MW	57500 TQ	USBLS	5/07
Wholesale and Manufacturing	Boise City-Nampa MSA, ID	Y	34870 FQ	44800 MW	58400 TQ	USBLS	5/07
Wholesale and Manufacturing	Illinois	Y	39380 FQ	56820 MW	82360 TQ	USBLS	5/07
Wholesale and Manufacturing	Champaign-Urbana MSA, IL	Y	33990 FQ	45070 MW	60700 TQ	USBLS	5/07
Wholesale and Manufacturing	Chicago-Naperville-Joliet MSA, IL-IN-WI	Y	42370 FQ	60710 MW	87440 TQ	USBLS	5/07
Wholesale and Manufacturing	Indiana	Y	35540 FQ	49990 MW	70070 TQ	USBLS	5/07
Wholesale and Manufacturing	Elkhart-Goshen MSA, IN	Y	34880 FQ	47860 MW	70910 TQ	USBLS	5/07
Wholesale and Manufacturing	Gary PMSA, IN	Y	35710 FQ	50490 MW	76950 TQ	USBLS	5/07
Wholesale and Manufacturing	Indianapolis-Carmel MSA, IN	Y	38090 FQ	52690 MW	72530 TQ	USBLS	5/07
Wholesale and Manufacturing	Terre Haute MSA, IN	Y	30930 FQ	40790 MW	60540 TQ	USBLS	5/07
Wholesale and Manufacturing	Iowa	Y	32290 FQ	44720 MW	60610 TQ	USBLS	5/07
Wholesale and Manufacturing	Des Moines-West Des Moines MSA, IA	Y	35060 FQ	48520 MW	66190 TQ	USBLS	5/07
Wholesale and Manufacturing	Dubuque MSA, IA	Y	33030 FQ	42690 MW	66430 TQ	USBLS	5/07
Wholesale and Manufacturing	Kansas	Y	34900 FQ	50070 MW	77160 TQ	USBLS	5/07
Wholesale and Manufacturing	Wichita MSA, KS	Y	30250 FQ	42400 MW	58900 TQ	USBLS	5/07
Wholesale and Manufacturing	Kentucky	Y	34238 FQ	47724 MW	69684 TQ	KYBLS	2008
Wholesale and Manufacturing	Bowling Green MSA, KY	Y	33790 FQ	41940 MW	52620 TQ	USBLS	5/07
Wholesale and Manufacturing	Louisville-Jefferson County MSA, KY-IN	Y	36170 FQ	48780 MW	70300 TQ	USBLS	5/07
Wholesale and Manufacturing	Louisiana	H	16.79 FQ	22.25 MW	29.78 TQ	LABLS	1/08-3/08
Wholesale and Manufacturing	Baton Rouge MSA, LA	Y	36520 FQ	46220 MW	60120 TQ	USBLS	5/07
Wholesale and Manufacturing	New Orleans-Metairie-Kenner MSA, LA	Y	36090 FQ	49780 MW	64800 TQ	USBLS	5/07
Wholesale and Manufacturing	Maine	Y	33820 FQ	47030 MW	65220 TQ	USBLS	5/07
Wholesale and Manufacturing	Portland-South Portland-Biddeford MSA, ME	Y	36230 FQ	52600 MW	72690 TQ	USBLS	5/07
Wholesale and Manufacturing	Maryland	Y		57500 MW		MDBLS	3/08
Wholesale and Manufacturing	Baltimore-Towson MSA, MD	Y	42970 FQ	59080 MW	81680 TQ	USBLS	5/07
Wholesale and Manufacturing	Bethesda-Gaithersburg-Frederick PMSA, MD	Y	41260 FQ	56790 MW	88280 TQ	USBLS	5/07
Wholesale and Manufacturing	Massachusetts	Y	44090 FQ	59840 MW	83520 TQ	USBLS	5/07
Wholesale and Manufacturing	Boston-Cambridge-Quincy NECTA, MA	Y	45660 FQ	62680 MW	89740 TQ	USBLS	5/07
Wholesale and Manufacturing	Worcester MSA, MA-CT	Y	41910 FQ	54350 MW	69270 TQ	USBLS	5/07
Wholesale and Manufacturing	Michigan	Y	36290 FQ	51730 MW	74860 TQ	USBLS	5/07
Wholesale and Manufacturing	Detroit-Warren-Livonia MSA, MI	Y	40000 FQ	57200 MW	81730 TQ	USBLS	5/07
Wholesale and Manufacturing	Grand Rapids-Wyoming MSA, MI	Y	37880 FQ	52680 MW	72390 TQ	USBLS	5/07
Wholesale and Manufacturing	Warren-Troy-Farmington Hills PMSA, MI	Y	42830 FQ	60680 MW	86180 TQ	USBLS	5/07

AE	Average entry wage	AW	Average wage paid	FQ	First quartile wage	LO	Lowest wage paid	MTC	Median total compensation	TCC	Total cash compensation
AER	Average entry range	AWR	Average wage range	H	Hourly	LR	Low end range	MW	Median wage paid	TQ	Third quartile wage
AEX	Average experienced wage	AXR	Average experienced range	HI	Highest wage paid	M	Monthly	MWR	Median wage range	W	Weekly
ATC	Average total compensation	D	Daily	HR	High end range	MCC	Median cash compensation	S	See annotated source	Y	Yearly

Sales Representative

Occupation/Type/Industry	Location	Per	Low	Mid	High	Source	Date
Sales Representative							
Wholesale and Manufacturing	Minnesota	Y	38905 FQ	53205 MW	74203 TQ	MNBLS	10/08-12/08
Wholesale and Manufacturing	Duluth-Superior MSA, MN-WI	Y	35033 FQ	44078 MW	57982 TQ	MNBLS	10/08-12/08
Wholesale and Manufacturing	Minneapolis-Saint Paul MSA, MN-WI	Y	40714 FQ	56315 MW	77821 TQ	MNBLS	10/08-12/08
Wholesale and Manufacturing	Rochester MSA, MN	Y	36841 FQ	44761 MW	53102 TQ	MNBLS	10/08-12/08
Wholesale and Manufacturing	Mississippi	Y	33170 FQ	44800 MW	59240 TQ	USBLS	5/07
Wholesale and Manufacturing	Hattiesburg MSA, MS	Y	32870 FQ	41700 MW	50300 TQ	USBLS	5/07
Wholesale and Manufacturing	Jackson MSA, MS	Y	34710 FQ	44920 MW	57570 TQ	USBLS	5/07
Wholesale and Manufacturing	Missouri	Y	33360 FQ	48240 MW	70510 TQ	USBLS	5/07
Wholesale and Manufacturing	Kansas City MSA, MO-KS	Y	36660 FQ	53380 MW	77130 TQ	USBLS	5/07
Wholesale and Manufacturing	St. Louis MSA, MO-IL	Y	36220 FQ	53090 MW	77490 TQ	USBLS	5/07
Wholesale and Manufacturing	Montana	Y	27570 FQ	36970 MW	49280 TQ	USBLS	5/07
Wholesale and Manufacturing	Billings MSA, MT	Y	28900 FQ	38750 MW	47520 TQ	USBLS	5/07
Wholesale and Manufacturing	Nebraska	Y	35350 FQ	47480 MW	62920 TQ	USBLS	5/07
Wholesale and Manufacturing	Omaha-Council Bluffs MSA, NE-IA	Y	37920 FQ	50700 MW	66740 TQ	USBLS	5/07
Wholesale and Manufacturing	Nevada	H	16.85 FQ	24.04 MW	32.64 TQ	NVBLS	5/08
Wholesale and Manufacturing	Las Vegas-Paradise MSA, NV	H	16.97 FQ	25.30 MW	34.34 TQ	NVBLS	5/08
Wholesale and Manufacturing	New Hampshire	H	17.06 AE	25.66 MW	38.61 AEX	NHBLS	6/08
Wholesale and Manufacturing	Manchester MSA, NH	Y	36100 FQ	49230 MW	68130 TQ	USBLS	5/07
Wholesale and Manufacturing	Nashua NECTA, NH-MA	Y	47590 FQ	62480 MW	86890 TQ	USBLS	5/07
Wholesale and Manufacturing	New Jersey	Y	42700 FQ	61820 MW	87830 TQ	USBLS	5/07
Wholesale and Manufacturing	Camden PMSA, NJ	Y	40890 FQ	59380 MW	84340 TQ	USBLS	5/07
Wholesale and Manufacturing	Edison PMSA, NJ	Y	44570 FQ	65260 MW	89730 TQ	USBLS	5/07
Wholesale and Manufacturing	Newark-Union PMSA, NJ-PA	Y	42480 FQ	58170 MW	83880 TQ	USBLS	5/07
Wholesale and Manufacturing	New Mexico	Y	27850 FQ	40670 MW	59130 TQ	USBLS	5/07
Wholesale and Manufacturing	Albuquerque MSA, NM	Y	29250 FQ	42340 MW	63170 TQ	USBLS	5/07
Wholesale and Manufacturing	Santa Fe MSA, NM	Y	32920 FQ	42840 MW	53130 TQ	USBLS	5/07
Wholesale and Manufacturing	New York	Y	38370 FQ	55950 MW	82270 TQ	USBLS	5/07
Wholesale and Manufacturing	Albany-Schenectady-Troy MSA, NY	Y	36030 FQ	48270 MW	65370 TQ	USBLS	5/07
Wholesale and Manufacturing	Buffalo-Niagara Falls MSA, NY	Y	37760 FQ	52830 MW	73070 TQ	USBLS	5/07
Wholesale and Manufacturing	Nassau-Suffolk PMSA, NY	Y	41060 FQ	61970 MW	91400 TQ	USBLS	5/07
Wholesale and Manufacturing	New York-Northern New Jersey-Long Island MSA, NY-NJ-PA	Y	40880 FQ	60240 MW	88940 TQ	USBLS	5/07
Wholesale and Manufacturing	North Carolina	Y	32340 FQ	45330 MW	65010 TQ	USBLS	5/07
Wholesale and Manufacturing	Charlotte-Gastonia-Concord MSA, NC-SC	Y	36500 FQ	50910 MW	76600 TQ	USBLS	5/07
Wholesale and Manufacturing	Raleigh-Cary MSA, NC	Y	32320 FQ	45350 MW	68290 TQ	USBLS	5/07
Wholesale and Manufacturing	North Dakota	Y	32790 FQ	42440 MW	57680 TQ	USBLS	5/07
Wholesale and Manufacturing	Fargo MSA, ND-MN	Y	35450 FQ	44520 MW	61810 TQ	USBLS	5/07
Wholesale and Manufacturing	Ohio	Y	39160 FQ	54440 MW	76570 TQ	USBLS	5/07
Wholesale and Manufacturing	Cincinnati-Middletown MSA, OH-KY-IN	Y	43850 FQ	60540 MW	80620 TQ	USBLS	5/07
Wholesale and Manufacturing	Cleveland-Elyria-Mentor MSA, OH	Y	39710 FQ	55360 MW	77940 TQ	USBLS	5/07
Wholesale and Manufacturing	Columbus MSA, OH	Y	40710 FQ	54340 MW	78850 TQ	USBLS	5/07
Wholesale and Manufacturing	Dayton MSA, OH	Y	35130 FQ	52070 MW	73750 TQ	USBLS	5/07
Wholesale and Manufacturing	Oklahoma	Y	30520 FQ	42680 MW	60120 TQ	USBLS	5/07
Wholesale and Manufacturing	Oklahoma City MSA, OK	Y	31080 FQ	43150 MW	61290 TQ	USBLS	5/07
Wholesale and Manufacturing	Tulsa MSA, OK	Y	33720 FQ	46650 MW	64860 TQ	USBLS	5/07
Wholesale and Manufacturing	Oregon	H	17.40 FQ	24.33 MW	36.52 TQ	ORBLS	5/08
Wholesale and Manufacturing	Portland-Vancouver-Beaverton MSA, OR-WA	Y	39150 FQ	55910 MW	82640 TQ	USBLS	5/07
Wholesale and Manufacturing	Pennsylvania	Y	37610 FQ	52340 MW	75270 TQ	USBLS	5/07
Wholesale and Manufacturing	Allentown-Bethlehem-Easton MSA, PA-NJ	Y	37700 FQ	50650 MW	70370 TQ	USBLS	5/07
Wholesale and Manufacturing	Philadelphia-Camden-Wilmington MSA, PA-NJ-DE-MD	Y	41060 FQ	57000 MW	81560 TQ	USBLS	5/07
Wholesale and Manufacturing	Pittsburgh MSA, PA	Y	39570 FQ	54400 MW	79200 TQ	USBLS	5/07
Wholesale and Manufacturing	York-Hanover MSA, PA	Y	36800 FQ	48570 MW	67960 TQ	USBLS	5/07
Wholesale and Manufacturing	Rhode Island	Y	41740 FQ	55520 MW	72940 TQ	USBLS	5/07
Wholesale and Manufacturing	Providence-Fall River-Warwick MSA, RI-MA	Y	41520 FQ	56050 MW	72340 TQ	USBLS	5/07
Wholesale and Manufacturing	South Carolina	Y	32920 FQ	45340 MW	67860 TQ	USBLS	5/07
Wholesale and Manufacturing	Charleston-North Charleston MSA, SC	Y	34740 FQ	46970 MW	65840 TQ	USBLS	5/07
Wholesale and Manufacturing	Columbia MSA, SC	Y	35600 FQ	49100 MW	76340 TQ	USBLS	5/07

AE	Average entry wage	AW	Average wage paid	FQ	First quartile wage	LO	Lowest wage paid	MTC	Median total compensation	TCC	Total cash compensation
AER	Average entry range	AWR	Average wage range	H	Hourly	LR	Low end range	MW	Median wage paid	TQ	Third quartile wage
AEX	Average experienced wage	AXR	Average experienced range	HI	Highest wage paid	M	Monthly	MWR	Median wage range	W	Weekly
ATC	Average total compensation	D	Daily	HR	High end range	MCC	Median cash compensation	S	See annotated source	Y	Yearly

Occupation/Type/Industry	Location	Per	Low	Mid	High	Source	Date
Sales Representative							
Wholesale and Manufacturing	Myrtle Beach-Conway-North Myrtle Beach MSA, SC	Y	30800 FQ	39690 MW	51880 TQ	USBLS	5/07
Wholesale and Manufacturing	South Dakota	Y	35851 FQ	45689 MW	61072 TQ	SDBLS	7/08-9/08
Wholesale and Manufacturing	Sioux Falls MSA, SD	Y	40737 FQ	52830 MW	72911 TQ	SDBLS	7/08-9/08
Wholesale and Manufacturing	Tennessee	Y	35090 FQ	48410 MW	69820 TQ	USBLS	5/07
Wholesale and Manufacturing	Johnson City MSA, TN	Y	25960 FQ	32810 MW	47790 TQ	USBLS	5/07
Wholesale and Manufacturing	Memphis MSA, TN-MS-AR	Y	37590 FQ	49240 MW	68280 TQ	USBLS	5/07
Wholesale and Manufacturing	Nashville-Davidson-Murfreesboro MSA, TN	Y	37060 FQ	51900 MW	73990 TQ	USBLS	5/07
Wholesale and Manufacturing	Texas	Y	34380 FQ	48010 MW	68830 TQ	USBLS	5/07
Wholesale and Manufacturing	Austin-Round Rock MSA, TX	Y	33300 FQ	47750 MW	67300 TQ	USBLS	5/07
Wholesale and Manufacturing	Dallas-Fort Worth-Arlington MSA, TX	Y	37300 FQ	51250 MW	74390 TQ	USBLS	5/07
Wholesale and Manufacturing	El Paso MSA, TX	Y	27640 FQ	39070 MW	54520 TQ	USBLS	5/07
Wholesale and Manufacturing	Houston-Sugar Land-Baytown MSA, TX	Y	36240 FQ	52020 MW	74830 TQ	USBLS	5/07
Wholesale and Manufacturing	San Antonio MSA, TX	Y	32180 FQ	43960 MW	59590 TQ	USBLS	5/07
Wholesale and Manufacturing	Utah	Y	35760 FQ	48650 MW	67630 TQ	USBLS	5/07
Wholesale and Manufacturing	Salt Lake City MSA, UT	Y	38000 FQ	51760 MW	70780 TQ	USBLS	5/07
Wholesale and Manufacturing	Vermont	Y	34760 FQ	47360 MW	64030 TQ	USBLS	5/07
Wholesale and Manufacturing	Burlington-South Burlington MSA, VT	Y	32770 FQ	46070 MW	62610 TQ	USBLS	5/07
Wholesale and Manufacturing	Virginia	Y	36650 FQ	50880 MW	74410 TQ	USBLS	5/07
Wholesale and Manufacturing	Richmond MSA, VA	Y	39060 FQ	54370 MW	78420 TQ	USBLS	5/07
Wholesale and Manufacturing	Virginia Beach-Norfolk-Newport News MSA, VA-NC	Y	34850 FQ	46450 MW	68260 TQ	USBLS	5/07
Wholesale and Manufacturing	Washington	H	18.61 FQ	24.20 MW	35.07 TQ	WABLS	3/08
Wholesale and Manufacturing	Olympia MSA, WA	Y	36750 FQ	48240 MW	76380 TQ	USBLS	5/07
Wholesale and Manufacturing	Seattle-Tacoma-Bellevue MSA, WA	Y	39160 FQ	50440 MW	73200 TQ	USBLS	5/07
Wholesale and Manufacturing	Charleston MSA, WV	Y	28900 FQ	40220 MW	60810 TQ	USBLS	5/07
Wholesale and Manufacturing	Wisconsin	Y	38270 FQ	52000 MW	74130 TQ	USBLS	5/07
Wholesale and Manufacturing	Milwaukee-Waukesha-West Allis MSA, WI	Y	42340 FQ	56410 MW	77200 TQ	USBLS	5/07
Wholesale and Manufacturing	Wyoming	Y	27748 FQ	36882 MW	48214 TQ	WYBLS	9/08
Wholesale and Manufacturing	Cheyenne MSA, WY	Y	29292 FQ	39427 MW	50231 TQ	WYBLS	9/08
Wholesale and Manufacturing	Puerto Rico	Y	15940 FQ	22740 MW	35300 TQ	USBLS	5/07
Wholesale and Manufacturing	San Juan-Caguas-Guaynabo MSA, PR	Y	15910 FQ	22710 MW	35220 TQ	USBLS	5/07
Wholesale and Manufacturing	Virgin Islands	Y	26260 FQ	28990 MW	32920 TQ	USBLS	5/07
Wholesale and Manufacturing	Guam	Y	17330 FQ	24140 MW	29160 TQ	USBLS	5/07
Wholesale and Manufacturing, Technical and Scientific Products	Alabama	Y	49720 FQ	74310 MW	98820 TQ	USBLS	5/07
Wholesale and Manufacturing, Technical and Scientific Products	Birmingham-Hoover MSA, AL	Y	55930 FQ	75820 MW	114170 TQ	USBLS	5/07
Wholesale and Manufacturing, Technical and Scientific Products	Huntsville MSA, AL	Y	36300 FQ	56310 MW	79350 TQ	USBLS	5/07
Wholesale and Manufacturing, Technical and Scientific Products	Alaska	Y	53820 FQ	66700 MW	82200 TQ	USBLS	5/07
Wholesale and Manufacturing, Technical and Scientific Products	Anchorage MSA, AK	Y	56240 FQ	69800 MW	84750 TQ	USBLS	5/07
Wholesale and Manufacturing, Technical and Scientific Products	Arizona	Y	37430 FQ	51300 MW	79300 TQ	USBLS	5/07
Wholesale and Manufacturing, Technical and Scientific Products	Flagstaff MSA, AZ	Y	29350 FQ	35910 MW	48790 TQ	USBLS	5/07
Wholesale and Manufacturing, Technical and Scientific Products	Phoenix-Mesa-Scottsdale MSA, AZ	Y	38020 FQ	52240 MW	80630 TQ	USBLS	5/07
Wholesale and Manufacturing, Technical and Scientific Products	Tucson MSA, AZ	Y	32540 FQ	45380 MW	72010 TQ	USBLS	5/07
Wholesale and Manufacturing, Technical and Scientific Products	Arkansas	Y	48370 FQ	56670 MW	74310 TQ	USBLS	5/07
Wholesale and Manufacturing, Technical and Scientific Products	Fort Smith MSA, AR-OK	Y	42800 FQ	78270 MW	89110 TQ	USBLS	5/07
Wholesale and Manufacturing, Technical and Scientific Products	Little Rock-North Little Rock MSA, AR	Y	51700 FQ	61170 MW	76810 TQ	USBLS	5/07
Wholesale and Manufacturing, Technical and Scientific Products	California	H	26.47 FQ	36.38 MW	49.79 TQ	CABLS	1/08-3/08

AE	Average entry wage	AW	Average wage paid	FQ	First quartile wage	LO	Lowest wage paid	MTC	Median total compensation	TCC	Total cash compensation
AER	Average entry range	AWR	Average wage range	H	Hourly	LR	Low end range	MW	Median wage paid	TQ	Third quartile wage
AEX	Average experienced wage	AXR	Average experienced range	HI	Highest wage paid	M	Monthly	MWR	Median wage range	W	Weekly
ATC	Average total compensation	D	Daily	HR	High end range	MCC	Median cash compensation	S	See annotated source	Y	Yearly

Occupation/Type/Industry	Location	Per	Low	Mid	High	Source	Date
Sales Representative							
Wholesale and Manufacturing, Technical and Scientific Products	Bakersfield MSA, CA	H	30.84 FQ	39.30 MW	51.40 TQ	CABLS	1/08-3/08
Wholesale and Manufacturing, Technical and Scientific Products	Los Angeles-Long Beach-Glendale PMSA, CA	H	23.22 FQ	32.30 MW	43.98 TQ	CABLS	1/08-3/08
Wholesale and Manufacturing, Technical and Scientific Products	Oakland-Fremont-Hayward MSA, CA	H	25.54 FQ	34.10 MW	45.91 TQ	CABLS	1/08-3/08
Wholesale and Manufacturing, Technical and Scientific Products	Riverside-San Bernardino-Ontario MSA, CA	H	23.78 FQ	32.63 MW	43.41 TQ	CABLS	1/08-3/08
Wholesale and Manufacturing, Technical and Scientific Products	Sacramento-Arden Arcade-Roseville MSA, CA	H	31.51 FQ	44.84 MW	59.98 TQ	CABLS	1/08-3/08
Wholesale and Manufacturing, Technical and Scientific Products	San Diego-Carlsbad-San Marcos MSA, CA	H	24.09 FQ	32.62 MW	44.23 TQ	CABLS	1/08-3/08
Wholesale and Manufacturing, Technical and Scientific Products	San Francisco-San Mateo-Redwood PMSA, CA	H	27.22 FQ	38.72 MW	54.50 TQ	CABLS	1/08-3/08
Wholesale and Manufacturing, Technical and Scientific Products	San Jose-Sunnyvale-Santa Clara MSA, CA	H	31.35 FQ	45.31 MW	60.18 TQ	CABLS	1/08-3/08
Wholesale and Manufacturing, Technical and Scientific Products	Santa Ana-Anaheim-Irvine PMSA, CA	Y	54960 FQ	74330 MW	105720 TQ	USBLS	5/07
Wholesale and Manufacturing, Technical and Scientific Products	Colorado	Y	49320 FQ	76750 MW	98180 TQ	USBLS	5/07
Wholesale and Manufacturing, Technical and Scientific Products	Boulder MSA, CO	Y	49110 FQ	79410 MW	120930 TQ	USBLS	5/07
Wholesale and Manufacturing, Technical and Scientific Products	Denver-Aurora MSA, CO	Y	52750 FQ	79970 MW	97280 TQ	USBLS	5/07
Wholesale and Manufacturing, Technical and Scientific Products	Fort Collins-Loveland MSA, CO	Y	38730 FQ	67440 MW	97480 TQ	USBLS	5/07
Wholesale and Manufacturing, Technical and Scientific Products	Connecticut	H	21.47 AE	36.69 MW		CTBLS	1/08-3/08
Wholesale and Manufacturing, Technical and Scientific Products	Bridgeport-Stamford-Norwalk MSA, CT	Y	66000 FQ	88190 MW	127800 TQ	USBLS	5/07
Wholesale and Manufacturing, Technical and Scientific Products	Danbury MSA, CT	Y	49810 FQ	71460 MW	91600 TQ	USBLS	5/07
Wholesale and Manufacturing, Technical and Scientific Products	Hartford-West Hartford-East Hartford MSA, CT	Y	53960 FQ	74170 MW	97530 TQ	USBLS	5/07
Wholesale and Manufacturing, Technical and Scientific Products	New Haven MSA, CT	Y	41580 FQ	57810 MW	94390 TQ	USBLS	5/07
Wholesale and Manufacturing, Technical and Scientific Products	Delaware	Y	64410 FQ	92820 MW	117070 TQ	USBLS	5/07
Wholesale and Manufacturing, Technical and Scientific Products	Wilmington PMSA, DE-MD-NJ	Y	63190 FQ	91750 MW	117080 TQ	USBLS	5/07
Wholesale and Manufacturing, Technical and Scientific Products	District of Columbia	Y	57030 FQ	71970 MW	90990 TQ	USBLS	5/07
Wholesale and Manufacturing, Technical and Scientific Products	Washington-Arlington-Alexandria MSA, DC-VA-MD-WV	Y	59420 FQ	79660 MW	106580 TQ	USBLS	5/07
Wholesale and Manufacturing, Technical and Scientific Products	Florida	Y	41300 FQ	59410 MW	86030 TQ	USBLS	5/07
Wholesale and Manufacturing, Technical and Scientific Products	Fort Lauderdale-Pompano Beach-Deerfield Beach PMSA, FL	Y	36970 FQ	54630 MW	79430 TQ	USBLS	5/07
Wholesale and Manufacturing, Technical and Scientific Products	Jacksonville MSA, FL	Y	40010 FQ	55440 MW	84110 TQ	USBLS	5/07
Wholesale and Manufacturing, Technical and Scientific Products	Miami-Fort Lauderdale-Miami Beach MSA, FL	Y	39770 FQ	57630 MW	80880 TQ	USBLS	5/07

Sales Representative

Occupation/Type/Industry	Location	Per	Low	Mid	High	Source	Date
Wholesale and Manufacturing, Technical and Scientific Products	Orlando-Kissimmee MSA, FL	Y	40230 FQ	59560 MW	84850 TQ	USBLS	5/07
Wholesale and Manufacturing, Technical and Scientific Products	Tampa-St. Petersburg-Clearwater MSA, FL	Y	42790 FQ	60730 MW	97290 TQ	USBLS	5/07
Wholesale and Manufacturing, Technical and Scientific Products	West Palm Beach-Boca Raton-Boynton Beach PMSA, FL	Y	50900 FQ	66730 MW	91400 TQ	USBLS	5/07
Wholesale and Manufacturing, Technical and Scientific Products	Georgia	Y	45800 FQ	70610 MW	106460 TQ	USBLS	5/07
Wholesale and Manufacturing, Technical and Scientific Products	Athens-Clarke County MSA, GA	Y	36340 FQ	72390 MW	92810 TQ	USBLS	5/07
Wholesale and Manufacturing, Technical and Scientific Products	Atlanta-Sandy Springs-Marietta MSA, GA	Y	48610 FQ	75610 MW	109640 TQ	USBLS	5/07
Wholesale and Manufacturing, Technical and Scientific Products	Hawaii	Y	35550 FQ	54750 MW	66310 TQ	USBLS	5/07
Wholesale and Manufacturing, Technical and Scientific Products	Honolulu MSA, HI	Y	35050 FQ	54300 MW	66430 TQ	USBLS	5/07
Wholesale and Manufacturing, Technical and Scientific Products	Idaho	Y	37590 FQ	72550 MW	92190 TQ	USBLS	5/07
Wholesale and Manufacturing, Technical and Scientific Products	Boise City-Nampa MSA, ID	Y	39220 FQ	72980 MW	92830 TQ	USBLS	5/07
Wholesale and Manufacturing, Technical and Scientific Products	Illinois	Y	46620 FQ	66330 MW	91740 TQ	USBLS	5/07
Wholesale and Manufacturing, Technical and Scientific Products	Chicago-Naperville-Joliet MSA, IL-IN-WI	Y	48940 FQ	69110 MW	93520 TQ	USBLS	5/07
Wholesale and Manufacturing, Technical and Scientific Products	Rockford MSA, IL	Y	39920 FQ	46210 MW	64990 TQ	USBLS	5/07
Wholesale and Manufacturing, Technical and Scientific Products	Indiana	Y	44700 FQ	63270 MW	85560 TQ	USBLS	5/07
Wholesale and Manufacturing, Technical and Scientific Products	Gary PMSA, IN	Y	58720 FQ	75490 MW	91380 TQ	USBLS	5/07
Wholesale and Manufacturing, Technical and Scientific Products	Indianapolis-Carmel MSA, IN	Y	44830 FQ	63080 MW	86530 TQ	USBLS	5/07
Wholesale and Manufacturing, Technical and Scientific Products	Iowa	Y	43110 FQ	58720 MW	81750 TQ	USBLS	5/07
Wholesale and Manufacturing, Technical and Scientific Products	Des Moines-West Des Moines MSA, IA	Y	49090 FQ	68610 MW	97870 TQ	USBLS	5/07
Wholesale and Manufacturing, Technical and Scientific Products	Dubuque MSA, IA	Y	14880 FQ	37960 MW	68010 TQ	USBLS	5/07
Wholesale and Manufacturing, Technical and Scientific Products	Kansas	Y	47390 FQ	65000 MW	88320 TQ	USBLS	5/07
Wholesale and Manufacturing, Technical and Scientific Products	Wichita MSA, KS	Y	48850 FQ	62530 MW	80110 TQ	USBLS	5/07
Wholesale and Manufacturing, Technical and Scientific Products	Kentucky	Y	51422 FQ	72599 MW	96833 TQ	KYBLS	2008
Wholesale and Manufacturing, Technical and Scientific Products	Louisville-Jefferson County MSA, KY-IN	Y	52180 FQ	78260 MW	119260 TQ	USBLS	5/07
Wholesale and Manufacturing, Technical and Scientific Products	Louisiana	H	19.99 FQ	27.12 MW	36.58 TQ	LABLS	1/08-3/08
Wholesale and Manufacturing, Technical and Scientific Products	Baton Rouge MSA, LA	Y	44490 FQ	62590 MW	75980 TQ	USBLS	5/07
Wholesale and Manufacturing, Technical and Scientific Products	New Orleans-Metairie-Kenner MSA, LA	Y	43890 FQ	56410 MW	76900 TQ	USBLS	5/07
Wholesale and Manufacturing, Technical and Scientific Products	Maine	Y	43970 FQ	57210 MW	79080 TQ	USBLS	5/07
Wholesale and Manufacturing, Technical and Scientific Products	Portland-South Portland-Biddeford MSA, ME	Y	41930 FQ	55060 MW	76690 TQ	USBLS	5/07
Wholesale and Manufacturing, Technical and Scientific Products	Maryland	Y		77850 MW		MDBLS	3/08
Wholesale and Manufacturing, Technical and Scientific Products	Baltimore-Towson MSA, MD	Y	54010 FQ	70710 MW	101380 TQ	USBLS	5/07

AE	Average entry wage	AW	Average wage paid	FQ	First quartile wage
AER	Average entry range	AWR	Average wage range	H	Hourly
AEX	Average experienced wage	AXR	Average experienced range	HI	Highest wage paid
ATC	Average total compensation	D	Daily	HR	High end range

LO	Lowest wage paid	MTC	Median total compensation
LR	Low end range	MW	Median wage paid
M	Monthly	MWR	Median wage range
MCC	Median cash compensation	S	See annotated source

TCC	Total cash compensation
TQ	Third quartile wage
W	Weekly
Y	Yearly

Occupation/Type/Industry	Location	Per	Low	Mid	High	Source	Date
Sales Representative							
Wholesale and Manufacturing, Technical and Scientific Products	Bethesda-Gaithersburg-Frederick PMSA, MD	Y	58120 FQ	89870 MW	114980 TQ	USBLS	5/07
Wholesale and Manufacturing, Technical and Scientific Products	Hagerstown-Martinsburg MSA, MD-WV	Y	47620 FQ	59950 MW	94090 TQ	USBLS	5/07
Wholesale and Manufacturing, Technical and Scientific Products	Massachusetts	Y	57010 FQ	79800 MW	108560 TQ	USBLS	5/07
Wholesale and Manufacturing, Technical and Scientific Products	Barnstable Town MSA, MA	Y	63400 FQ	76790 MW	117070 TQ	USBLS	5/07
Wholesale and Manufacturing, Technical and Scientific Products	Boston-Cambridge-Quincy NECTA, MA	Y	57320 FQ	81980 MW	114760 TQ	USBLS	5/07
Wholesale and Manufacturing, Technical and Scientific Products	Springfield MSA, MA-CT	Y	48030 FQ	57180 MW	73800 TQ	USBLS	5/07
Wholesale and Manufacturing, Technical and Scientific Products	Worcester MSA, MA-CT	Y	56900 FQ	76720 MW	102690 TQ	USBLS	5/07
Wholesale and Manufacturing, Technical and Scientific Products	Michigan	Y	51430 FQ	72660 MW	97870 TQ	USBLS	5/07
Wholesale and Manufacturing, Technical and Scientific Products	Detroit-Warren-Livonia MSA, MI	Y	55160 FQ	76310 MW	100990 TQ	USBLS	5/07
Wholesale and Manufacturing, Technical and Scientific Products	Grand Rapids-Wyoming MSA, MI	Y	47070 FQ	64670 MW	85950 TQ	USBLS	5/07
Wholesale and Manufacturing, Technical and Scientific Products	Warren-Troy-Farmington Hills PMSA, MI	Y	60640 FQ	80190 MW	103290 TQ	USBLS	5/07
Wholesale and Manufacturing, Technical and Scientific Products	Minnesota	Y	59151 FQ	79081 MW	103474 TQ	MNBLS	10/08-12/08
Wholesale and Manufacturing, Technical and Scientific Products	Duluth-Superior MSA, MN-WI	Y	54079 FQ	60950 MW	68420 TQ	MNBLS	10/08-12/08
Wholesale and Manufacturing, Technical and Scientific Products	Minneapolis-Saint Paul MSA, MN-WI	Y	60411 FQ	80830 MW	105781 TQ	MNBLS	10/08-12/08
Wholesale and Manufacturing, Technical and Scientific Products	Rochester MSA, MN	Y	44669 FQ	60274 MW	83480 TQ	MNBLS	10/08-12/08
Wholesale and Manufacturing, Technical and Scientific Products	Mississippi	Y	51640 FQ	66280 MW	84240 TQ	USBLS	5/07
Wholesale and Manufacturing, Technical and Scientific Products	Jackson MSA, MS	Y	55170 FQ	70740 MW	94560 TQ	USBLS	5/07
Wholesale and Manufacturing, Technical and Scientific Products	Missouri	Y	46800 FQ	65050 MW	93200 TQ	USBLS	5/07
Wholesale and Manufacturing, Technical and Scientific Products	Kansas City MSA, MO-KS	Y	51090 FQ	71190 MW	94560 TQ	USBLS	5/07
Wholesale and Manufacturing, Technical and Scientific Products	St. Louis MSA, MO-IL	Y	49090 FQ	69320 MW	96640 TQ	USBLS	5/07
Wholesale and Manufacturing, Technical and Scientific Products	Montana	Y	31560 FQ	45160 MW	62550 TQ	USBLS	5/07
Wholesale and Manufacturing, Technical and Scientific Products	Billings MSA, MT	Y	37770 FQ	48970 MW	59570 TQ	USBLS	5/07
Wholesale and Manufacturing, Technical and Scientific Products	Nebraska	Y	48600 FQ	63060 MW	81090 TQ	USBLS	5/07
Wholesale and Manufacturing, Technical and Scientific Products	Omaha-Council Bluffs MSA, NE-IA	Y	53580 FQ	66670 MW	90820 TQ	USBLS	5/07
Wholesale and Manufacturing, Technical and Scientific Products	Nevada	H	20.78 FQ	26.80 MW	45.77 TQ	NVBLS	5/08
Wholesale and Manufacturing, Technical and Scientific Products	Carson City MSA, NV	H	22.22 FQ	29.29 MW	50.55 TQ	NVBLS	5/08
Wholesale and Manufacturing, Technical and Scientific Products	Las Vegas-Paradise MSA, NV	H	19.44 FQ	23.35 MW	31.71 TQ	NVBLS	5/08
Wholesale and Manufacturing, Technical and Scientific Products	New Hampshire	H	20.78 AE	32.66 MW	46.62 AEX	NHBLS	6/08
Wholesale and Manufacturing, Technical and Scientific Products	Manchester MSA, NH	Y	56870 FQ	72650 MW	94020 TQ	USBLS	5/07
Wholesale and Manufacturing, Technical and Scientific Products	Nashua NECTA, NH-MA	Y	42650 FQ	59940 MW	85310 TQ	USBLS	5/07
Wholesale and Manufacturing, Technical and Scientific Products	New Jersey	Y	50070 FQ	73950 MW	107110 TQ	USBLS	5/07

AE	Average entry wage	AW	Average wage paid	FQ	First quartile wage
AER	Average entry range	AWR	Average wage range	H	Hourly
AEX	Average experienced wage	AXR	Average experienced range	HI	Highest wage paid
ATC	Average total compensation	D	Daily	HR	High end range

LO Lowest wage paid · LR Low end range · M Monthly · MCC Median cash compensation · MTC Median total compensation · MW Median wage paid · MWR Median wage range · S See annotated source · TCC Total cash compensation · TQ Third quartile wage · W Weekly · Y Yearly

Sales Representative

Occupation/Type/Industry	Location	Per	Low	Mid	High	Source	Date
Wholesale and Manufacturing, Technical and Scientific Products	Atlantic City MSA, NJ	Y	47470 FQ	67670 MW	77090 TQ	USBLS	5/07
Wholesale and Manufacturing, Technical and Scientific Products	Camden PMSA, NJ	Y	46070 FQ	65730 MW	97960 TQ	USBLS	5/07
Wholesale and Manufacturing, Technical and Scientific Products	Edison PMSA, NJ	Y	53880 FQ	84910 MW	120490 TQ	USBLS	5/07
Wholesale and Manufacturing, Technical and Scientific Products	Newark-Union PMSA, NJ-PA	Y	45820 FQ	62730 MW	97610 TQ	USBLS	5/07
Wholesale and Manufacturing, Technical and Scientific Products	Vineland-Millville-Bridgeton MSA, NJ	Y	40530 FQ	56420 MW	66470 TQ	USBLS	5/07
Wholesale and Manufacturing, Technical and Scientific Products	New Mexico	Y	38680 FQ	53370 MW	70630 TQ	USBLS	5/07
Wholesale and Manufacturing, Technical and Scientific Products	Albuquerque MSA, NM	Y	40470 FQ	54990 MW	75430 TQ	USBLS	5/07
Wholesale and Manufacturing, Technical and Scientific Products	New York	Y	49900 FQ	73400 MW	101090 TQ	USBLS	5/07
Wholesale and Manufacturing, Technical and Scientific Products	Albany-Schenectady-Troy MSA, NY	Y	40480 FQ	53350 MW	73480 TQ	USBLS	5/07
Wholesale and Manufacturing, Technical and Scientific Products	Buffalo-Niagara Falls MSA, NY	Y	36090 FQ	48200 MW	64350 TQ	USBLS	5/07
Wholesale and Manufacturing, Technical and Scientific Products	Ithaca MSA, NY	Y	55380 FQ	65690 MW	120860 TQ	USBLS	5/07
Wholesale and Manufacturing, Technical and Scientific Products	Nassau-Suffolk PMSA, NY	Y	49450 FQ	70090 MW	98190 TQ	USBLS	5/07
Wholesale and Manufacturing, Technical and Scientific Products	New York-Northern New Jersey-Long Island MSA, NY-NJ-PA	Y	50610 FQ	75230 MW	106670 TQ	USBLS	5/07
Wholesale and Manufacturing, Technical and Scientific Products	North Carolina	Y	38190 FQ	54320 MW	78950 TQ	USBLS	5/07
Wholesale and Manufacturing, Technical and Scientific Products	Charlotte-Gastonia-Concord MSA, NC-SC	Y	40260 FQ	54910 MW	79310 TQ	USBLS	5/07
Wholesale and Manufacturing, Technical and Scientific Products	Raleigh-Cary MSA, NC	Y	42440 FQ	56250 MW	85190 TQ	USBLS	5/07
Wholesale and Manufacturing, Technical and Scientific Products	North Dakota	Y	44360 FQ	60710 MW	87660 TQ	USBLS	5/07
Wholesale and Manufacturing, Technical and Scientific Products	Fargo MSA, ND-MN	Y	41800 FQ	71110 MW	92630 TQ	USBLS	5/07
Wholesale and Manufacturing, Technical and Scientific Products	Ohio	Y	47950 FQ	69720 MW	97020 TQ	USBLS	5/07
Wholesale and Manufacturing, Technical and Scientific Products	Cincinnati-Middletown MSA, OH-KY-IN	Y	57250 FQ	78220 MW	103590 TQ	USBLS	5/07
Wholesale and Manufacturing, Technical and Scientific Products	Cleveland-Elyria-Mentor MSA, OH	Y	48200 FQ	68060 MW	98330 TQ	USBLS	5/07
Wholesale and Manufacturing, Technical and Scientific Products	Columbus MSA, OH	Y	41930 FQ	68610 MW	94250 TQ	USBLS	5/07
Wholesale and Manufacturing, Technical and Scientific Products	Dayton MSA, OH	Y	42670 FQ	60090 MW	92690 TQ	USBLS	5/07
Wholesale and Manufacturing, Technical and Scientific Products	Oklahoma	Y	36380 FQ	47930 MW	73330 TQ	USBLS	5/07
Wholesale and Manufacturing, Technical and Scientific Products	Oklahoma City MSA, OK	Y	37490 FQ	47450 MW	66700 TQ	USBLS	5/07
Wholesale and Manufacturing, Technical and Scientific Products	Tulsa MSA, OK	Y	34690 FQ	48380 MW	83290 TQ	USBLS	5/07
Wholesale and Manufacturing, Technical and Scientific Products	Oregon	H	25.63 FQ	35.73 MW	47.63 TQ	ORBLS	5/08
Wholesale and Manufacturing, Technical and Scientific Products	Eugene-Springfield MSA, OR	Y	57560 FQ	81920 MW	96510 TQ	USBLS	5/07
Wholesale and Manufacturing, Technical and Scientific Products	Portland-Vancouver-Beaverton MSA, OR-WA	Y	51400 FQ	72280 MW	101630 TQ	USBLS	5/07
Wholesale and Manufacturing, Technical and Scientific Products	Pennsylvania	Y	50330 FQ	69560 MW	97850 TQ	USBLS	5/07

AE	Average entry wage	AW	Average wage paid	FQ	First quartile wage
AER	Average entry range	AWR	Average wage range	H	Hourly
AEX	Average experienced wage	AXR	Average experienced range	HI	Highest wage paid
ATC	Average total compensation	D	Daily	HR	High end range

LO Lowest wage paid
LR Low end range
M Monthly
MCC Median cash compensation

MTC Median total compensation
MW Median wage paid
MWR Median wage range
S See annotated source

TCC Total cash compensation
TQ Third quartile wage
W Weekly
Y Yearly

Occupation/Type/Industry	Location	Per	Low	Mid	High	Source	Date
Sales Representative							
Wholesale and Manufacturing, Technical and Scientific Products	Allentown-Bethlehem-Easton MSA, PA-NJ	Y	51350 FQ	79020 MW	120500 TQ	USBLS	5/07
Wholesale and Manufacturing, Technical and Scientific Products	Erie MSA, PA	Y	39310 FQ	58190 MW	74120 TQ	USBLS	5/07
Wholesale and Manufacturing, Technical and Scientific Products	Philadelphia-Camden-Wilmington MSA, PA-NJ-DE-MD	Y	54280 FQ	74130 MW	107180 TQ	USBLS	5/07
Wholesale and Manufacturing, Technical and Scientific Products	Pittsburgh MSA, PA	Y	46420 FQ	68540 MW	92940 TQ	USBLS	5/07
Wholesale and Manufacturing, Technical and Scientific Products	York-Hanover MSA, PA	Y	38410 FQ	59350 MW	89180 TQ	USBLS	5/07
Wholesale and Manufacturing, Technical and Scientific Products	Rhode Island	Y	47020 FQ	68990 MW	84190 TQ	USBLS	5/07
Wholesale and Manufacturing, Technical and Scientific Products	Providence-Fall River-Warwick MSA, RI-MA	Y	49260 FQ	71410 MW	91520 TQ	USBLS	5/07
Wholesale and Manufacturing, Technical and Scientific Products	South Carolina	Y	42920 FQ	60000 MW	78730 TQ	USBLS	5/07
Wholesale and Manufacturing, Technical and Scientific Products	Charleston-North Charleston MSA, SC	Y	42020 FQ	59650 MW	77750 TQ	USBLS	5/07
Wholesale and Manufacturing, Technical and Scientific Products	Columbia MSA, SC	Y	45590 FQ	67500 MW	80410 TQ	USBLS	5/07
Wholesale and Manufacturing, Technical and Scientific Products	Myrtle Beach-Conway-North Myrtle Beach MSA, SC	Y	39480 FQ	48280 MW	63270 TQ	USBLS	5/07
Wholesale and Manufacturing, Technical and Scientific Products	South Dakota	Y	40918 FQ	53691 MW	79977 TQ	SDBLS	7/08-9/08
Wholesale and Manufacturing, Technical and Scientific Products	Rapid City MSA, SD	Y	37645 FQ	56825 MW	90453 TQ	SDBLS	7/08-9/08
Wholesale and Manufacturing, Technical and Scientific Products	Sioux Falls MSA, SD	Y	45998 FQ	70354 MW	93720 TQ	SDBLS	7/08-9/08
Wholesale and Manufacturing, Technical and Scientific Products	Tennessee	Y	44330 FQ	64280 MW	90230 TQ	USBLS	5/07
Wholesale and Manufacturing, Technical and Scientific Products	Memphis MSA, TN-MS-AR	Y	48230 FQ	65680 MW	82850 TQ	USBLS	5/07
Wholesale and Manufacturing, Technical and Scientific Products	Nashville-Davidson-Murfreesboro MSA, TN	Y	44220 FQ	65240 MW	101110 TQ	USBLS	5/07
Wholesale and Manufacturing, Technical and Scientific Products	Texas	Y	53090 FQ	71130 MW	95690 TQ	USBLS	5/07
Wholesale and Manufacturing, Technical and Scientific Products	Austin-Round Rock MSA, TX	Y	61360 FQ	84920 MW	110550 TQ	USBLS	5/07
Wholesale and Manufacturing, Technical and Scientific Products	Dallas-Fort Worth-Arlington MSA, TX	Y	52660 FQ	69340 MW	92260 TQ	USBLS	5/07
Wholesale and Manufacturing, Technical and Scientific Products	El Paso MSA, TX	Y	26930 FQ	30030 MW	52170 TQ	USBLS	5/07
Wholesale and Manufacturing, Technical and Scientific Products	Houston-Sugar Land-Baytown MSA, TX	Y	55770 FQ	76070 MW	100950 TQ	USBLS	5/07
Wholesale and Manufacturing, Technical and Scientific Products	San Antonio MSA, TX	Y	47880 FQ	63520 MW	96950 TQ	USBLS	5/07
Wholesale and Manufacturing, Technical and Scientific Products	Utah	Y	44120 FQ	62460 MW	97140 TQ	USBLS	5/07
Wholesale and Manufacturing, Technical and Scientific Products	Salt Lake City MSA, UT	Y	42460 FQ	61410 MW	95260 TQ	USBLS	5/07
Wholesale and Manufacturing, Technical and Scientific Products	Vermont	Y	38280 FQ	49520 MW	68540 TQ	USBLS	5/07
Wholesale and Manufacturing, Technical and Scientific Products	Burlington-South Burlington MSA, VT	Y	39520 FQ	47500 MW	63240 TQ	USBLS	5/07
Wholesale and Manufacturing, Technical and Scientific Products	Virginia	Y	51810 FQ	70070 MW	95710 TQ	USBLS	5/07
Wholesale and Manufacturing, Technical and Scientific Products	Richmond MSA, VA	Y	48680 FQ	63700 MW	82770 TQ	USBLS	5/07

AE	Average entry wage	**AW**	Average wage paid	**FQ**	First quartile wage	**LO**	Lowest wage paid	**MTC** Median total compensation	**TCC** Total cash compensation
AER	Average entry range	**AWR**	Average wage range	**H**	Hourly	**LR**	Low end range	**MW** Median wage paid	**TQ** Third quartile wage
AEX	Average experienced wage	**AXR**	Average experienced range	**HI**	Highest wage paid	**M**	Monthly	**MWR** Median wage range	**W** Weekly
ATC	Average total compensation	**D**	Daily	**HR**	High end range	**MCC**	Median cash compensation	**S** See annotated source	**Y** Yearly

Occupation/Type/Industry	Location	Per	Low	Mid	High	Source	Date
Sales Representative							
Wholesale and Manufacturing, Technical and Scientific Products	Virginia Beach-Norfolk-Newport News MSA, VA-NC	Y	40990 FQ	57700 MW	84950 TQ	USBLS	5/07
Wholesale and Manufacturing, Technical and Scientific Products	Washington	H	23.77 FQ	34.09 MW	48.61 TQ	WABLS	3/08
Wholesale and Manufacturing, Technical and Scientific Products	Seattle-Tacoma-Bellevue MSA, WA	Y	51360 FQ	72080 MW	100320 TQ	USBLS	5/07
Wholesale and Manufacturing, Technical and Scientific Products	West Virginia	Y	48947 FQ	64436 MW	83977 TQ	WVBLS	7/08-9/08
Wholesale and Manufacturing, Technical and Scientific Products	Charleston MSA, WV	Y	41270 FQ	61190 MW	87090 TQ	USBLS	5/07
Wholesale and Manufacturing, Technical and Scientific Products	Wisconsin	Y	55290 FQ	72410 MW	92620 TQ	USBLS	5/07
Wholesale and Manufacturing, Technical and Scientific Products	Appleton MSA, WI	Y	52610 FQ	76720 MW	112470 TQ	USBLS	5/07
Wholesale and Manufacturing, Technical and Scientific Products	Milwaukee-Waukesha-West Allis MSA, WI	Y	58420 FQ	76060 MW	94600 TQ	USBLS	5/07
Wholesale and Manufacturing, Technical and Scientific Products	Racine MSA, WI	Y	48840 FQ	57820 MW	76230 TQ	USBLS	5/07
Wholesale and Manufacturing, Technical and Scientific Products	Wyoming	Y	42225 FQ	57702 MW	76331 TQ	WYBLS	9/08
Wholesale and Manufacturing, Technical and Scientific Products	Cheyenne MSA, WY	Y	31949 FQ	38052 MW	67599 TQ	WYBLS	9/08
Wholesale and Manufacturing, Technical and Scientific Products	Puerto Rico	Y	26710 FQ	40100 MW	55610 TQ	USBLS	5/07
Wholesale and Manufacturing, Technical and Scientific Products	San Juan-Caguas-Guaynabo MSA, PR	Y	27060 FQ	40930 MW	56240 TQ	USBLS	5/07
Wholesale and Manufacturing, Technical and Scientific Products	Virgin Islands	Y	31720 FQ	41290 MW	46400 TQ	USBLS	5/07
Wholesale and Manufacturing, Technical and Scientific Products	Guam	Y	21060 FQ	24590 MW	33000 TQ	USBLS	5/07
Sales Tax Manager							
Municipal Government	Colorado Springs, CO	M	6194 LO			COSPRS	1/1/09
Salvage Machine Operator							
State Government	Ohio	H	14.36 LO		15.41 HI	ODAS	2008
Sanitarian-In-Training	Cincinnati, OH	Y			42568 HI	COHSS	10/08
Sanitary Engineer	Rhode Island	Y	45773 LO		49775 HI	AFT02	3/1/08
Sanitation District General Manager	Orange County, CA	Y			289364 HI	LAT01	2008
Sanitation Specialist	Cincinnati, OH	Y	39917 LO		43264 HI	COHSS	10/08
Sanitation Superintendent	Walton County, GA	Y	34746 LO		52119 HI	GACTY03	2008
Sanitation Truck Driver	Cincinnati, OH	Y	37025 LO		39917 HI	COHSS	10/08
Sawing Machine Setter, Operator, and Tender, Wood	Alabama	Y	17350 FQ	20570 MW	26380 TQ	USBLS	5/07
	Birmingham-Hoover MSA, AL	Y	17260 FQ	21740 MW	25990 TQ	USBLS	5/07
	Alaska	Y	29010 FQ	33350 MW	37140 TQ	USBLS	5/07
	Arizona	Y	18380 FQ	22780 MW	29050 TQ	USBLS	5/07
	Phoenix-Mesa-Scottsdale MSA, AZ	Y	19210 FQ	24460 MW	29660 TQ	USBLS	5/07
	Tucson MSA, AZ	Y	18570 FQ	22470 MW	28260 TQ	USBLS	5/07
	Arkansas	Y	19160 FQ	23030 MW	28140 TQ	USBLS	5/07
	Little Rock-North Little Rock MSA, AR	Y	19050 FQ	22830 MW	29960 TQ	USBLS	5/07
	California	H	10.75 FQ	13.92 MW	17.20 TQ	CABLS	1/08-3/08
	Los Angeles-Long Beach-Glendale PMSA, CA	H	9.34 FQ	11.69 MW	15.23 TQ	CABLS	1/08-3/08
	Oakland-Fremont-Hayward MSA, CA	H	11.43 FQ	14.51 MW	21.51 TQ	CABLS	1/08-3/08

Occupation/Type/Industry	Location	Per	Low	Mid	High	Source	Date
Sawing Machine Setter, Operator, and Tender, Wood							
	Riverside-San Bernardino-Ontario MSA, CA	H	10.26 FQ	13.58 MW	16.60 TQ	CABLS	1/08-3/08
	Sacramento-Arden Arcade-Roseville MSA, CA	H	10.89 FQ	13.39 MW	16.46 TQ	CABLS	1/08-3/08
	San Diego-Carlsbad-San Marcos MSA, CA	H	12.72 FQ	16.51 MW	20.24 TQ	CABLS	1/08-3/08
	San Jose-Sunnyvale-Santa Clara MSA, CA	H	10.25 FQ	12.88 MW	17.87 TQ	CABLS	1/08-3/08
	Santa Ana-Anaheim-Irvine PMSA, CA	Y	18960 FQ	24050 MW	32430 TQ	USBLS	5/07
	Colorado	Y	19600 FQ	24980 MW	30250 TQ	USBLS	5/07
	Denver-Aurora MSA, CO	Y	20330 FQ	26270 MW	31930 TQ	USBLS	5/07
	Connecticut	H	10.19 AE	11.96 MW		CTBLS	1/08-3/08
	New Haven MSA, CT	Y	18950 FQ	22130 MW	25050 TQ	USBLS	5/07
	Washington-Arlington-Alexandria MSA, DC-VA-MD-WV	Y	20570 FQ	27520 MW	34940 TQ	USBLS	5/07
	Florida	Y	20010 FQ	24050 MW	30780 TQ	USBLS	5/07
	Fort Lauderdale-Pompano Beach-Deerfield Beach PMSA, FL	Y	22890 FQ	27530 MW	31870 TQ	USBLS	5/07
	Jacksonville MSA, FL	Y	26080 FQ	28970 MW	31540 TQ	USBLS	5/07
	Miami-Fort Lauderdale-Miami Beach MSA, FL	Y	20290 FQ	24660 MW	30750 TQ	USBLS	5/07
	Orlando-Kissimmee MSA, FL	Y	18220 FQ	30010 MW	34830 TQ	USBLS	5/07
	Tampa-St. Petersburg-Clearwater MSA, FL	Y	22920 FQ	27350 MW	31830 TQ	USBLS	5/07
	West Palm Beach-Boca Raton-Boynton Beach PMSA, FL	Y	19450 FQ	22290 MW	27990 TQ	USBLS	5/07
	Georgia	Y	18820 FQ	23980 MW	30120 TQ	USBLS	5/07
	Atlanta-Sandy Springs-Marietta MSA, GA	Y	18460 FQ	22330 MW	29000 TQ	USBLS	5/07
	Hawaii	Y	15080 FQ	26340 MW	32410 TQ	USBLS	5/07
	Idaho	Y	26820 FQ	35910 MW	43270 TQ	USBLS	5/07
	Boise City-Nampa MSA, ID	Y	18170 FQ	21660 MW	28110 TQ	USBLS	5/07
	Illinois	Y	21570 FQ	29110 MW	36030 TQ	USBLS	5/07
	Chicago-Naperville-Joliet MSA, IL-IN-WI	Y	20880 FQ	26530 MW	33230 TQ	USBLS	5/07
	Indiana	Y	19800 FQ	23770 MW	29150 TQ	USBLS	5/07
	Gary PMSA, IN	Y	17640 FQ	21080 MW	25070 TQ	USBLS	5/07
	Indianapolis-Carmel MSA, IN	Y	21230 FQ	29020 MW	35850 TQ	USBLS	5/07
	Iowa	Y	20700 FQ	23680 MW	28420 TQ	USBLS	5/07
	Kansas	Y	18880 FQ	22090 MW	25490 TQ	USBLS	5/07
	Wichita MSA, KS	Y	18880 FQ	22910 MW	27460 TQ	USBLS	5/07
	Kentucky	Y	16794 FQ	21540 MW	26892 TQ	KYBLS	2008
	Louisville-Jefferson County MSA, KY-IN	Y	20710 FQ	24650 MW	28450 TQ	USBLS	5/07
	Louisiana	H	9.38 FQ	12.27 MW	14.42 TQ	LABLS	1/08-3/08
	Maine	Y	21300 FQ	24790 MW	29970 TQ	USBLS	5/07
	Portland-South Portland-Biddeford MSA, ME	Y	21690 FQ	26230 MW	33090 TQ	USBLS	5/07
	Maryland	Y		28100 MW		MDBLS	3/08
	Baltimore-Towson MSA, MD	Y	21540 FQ	27250 MW	38030 TQ	USBLS	5/07
	Bethesda-Gaithersburg-Frederick PMSA, MD	Y	24850 FQ	36700 MW	44320 TQ	USBLS	5/07
	Massachusetts	Y	25150 FQ	28480 MW	35510 TQ	USBLS	5/07
	Michigan	Y	22780 FQ	27320 MW	32790 TQ	USBLS	5/07
	Detroit-Warren-Livonia MSA, MI	Y	28270 FQ	33470 MW	39060 TQ	USBLS	5/07
	Grand Rapids-Wyoming MSA, MI	Y	23260 FQ	29840 MW	34390 TQ	USBLS	5/07
	Warren-Troy-Farmington Hills PMSA, MI	Y	28230 FQ	34090 MW	40370 TQ	USBLS	5/07
	Minnesota	Y	24569 FQ	29234 MW	36387 TQ	MNBLS	10/08-12/08
	Duluth-Superior MSA, MN-WI	Y	21842 FQ	24050 MW	34314 TQ	MNBLS	10/08-12/08
	Minneapolis-Saint Paul MSA, MN-WI	Y	26725 FQ	32914 MW	41664 TQ	MNBLS	10/08-12/08
	Mississippi	Y	19230 FQ	23630 MW	28180 TQ	USBLS	5/07
	Jackson MSA, MS	Y	20370 FQ	27180 MW	35050 TQ	USBLS	5/07
	Missouri	Y	17980 FQ	21000 MW	26220 TQ	USBLS	5/07
	Kansas City MSA, MO-KS	Y	19210 FQ	23950 MW	27330 TQ	USBLS	5/07

AE Average entry wage	**AW** Average wage paid	**FQ** First quartile wage	**LO** Lowest wage paid	**MTC** Median total compensation	**TCC** Total cash compensation
AER Average entry range	**AWR** Average wage range	**H** Hourly	**LR** Low end range	**MW** Median wage paid	**TQ** Third quartile wage
AEX Average experienced wage	**AXR** Average experienced range	**HI** Highest wage paid	**M** Monthly	**MWR** Median wage range	**W** Weekly
ATC Average total compensation	**D** Daily	**HR** High end range	**MCC** Median cash compensation	**S** See annotated source	**Y** Yearly

Occupation/Type/Industry	Location	Per	Low	Mid	High	Source	Date
Sawing Machine Setter, Operator, and Tender, Wood	St. Joseph MSA, MO-KS	Y	14880 FQ	19690 MW	22640 TQ	USBLS	5/07
	St. Louis MSA, MO-IL	Y	18420 FQ	21280 MW	26060 TQ	USBLS	5/07
	Montana	Y	22040 FQ	30460 MW	35210 TQ	USBLS	5/07
	Nebraska	Y	17850 FQ	20900 MW	26210 TQ	USBLS	5/07
	Omaha-Council Bluffs MSA, NE-IA	Y	19900 FQ	26210 MW	30240 TQ	USBLS	5/07
	Nevada	H	10.91 FQ	13.02 MW	14.44 TQ	NVBLS	5/08
	Las Vegas-Paradise MSA, NV	H	9.70 FQ	12.73 MW	15.06 TQ	NVBLS	5/08
	New Hampshire	H	9.91 AE	12.01 MW	14.37 AEX	NHBLS	6/08
	Nashua NECTA, NH-MA	Y	26220 FQ	28200 MW	30180 TQ	USBLS	5/07
	New Jersey	Y	22310 FQ	26010 MW	28720 TQ	USBLS	5/07
	New Mexico	Y	19670 FQ	22530 MW	25370 TQ	USBLS	5/07
	Albuquerque MSA, NM	Y	22010 FQ	25040 MW	30960 TQ	USBLS	5/07
	New York	Y	19510 FQ	24630 MW	30600 TQ	USBLS	5/07
	Albany-Schenectady-Troy MSA, NY	Y	20370 FQ	22780 MW	28100 TQ	USBLS	5/07
	Binghamton MSA, NY	Y	18930 FQ	20870 MW	23150 TQ	USBLS	5/07
	Buffalo-Niagara Falls MSA, NY	Y	18820 FQ	23230 MW	27320 TQ	USBLS	5/07
	Glens Falls MSA, NY	Y	24730 FQ	28320 MW	36330 TQ	USBLS	5/07
	Nassau-Suffolk PMSA, NY	Y	16940 FQ	20970 MW	24710 TQ	USBLS	5/07
	New York-Northern New Jersey-Long Island MSA, NY-NJ-PA	Y	18350 FQ	24640 MW	30470 TQ	USBLS	5/07
	North Carolina	Y	20990 FQ	24640 MW	29380 TQ	USBLS	5/07
	Charlotte-Gastonia-Concord MSA, NC-SC	Y	22040 FQ	25570 MW	29670 TQ	USBLS	5/07
	Durham MSA, NC	Y	22750 FQ	27040 MW	29900 TQ	USBLS	5/07
	Raleigh-Cary MSA, NC	Y	18730 FQ	22130 MW	25810 TQ	USBLS	5/07
	Winston-Salem MSA, NC	Y	17800 FQ	20790 MW	25750 TQ	USBLS	5/07
	Ohio	Y	22390 FQ	28170 MW	35050 TQ	USBLS	5/07
	Cincinnati-Middletown MSA, OH-KY-IN	Y	24260 FQ	30500 MW	33920 TQ	USBLS	5/07
	Cleveland-Elyria-Mentor MSA, OH	Y	25590 FQ	31860 MW	37930 TQ	USBLS	5/07
	Columbus MSA, OH	Y	24540 FQ	28780 MW	35300 TQ	USBLS	5/07
	Oklahoma	Y	18980 FQ	24480 MW	29650 TQ	USBLS	5/07
	Oklahoma City MSA, OK	Y	21690 FQ	26100 MW	35000 TQ	USBLS	5/07
	Tulsa MSA, OK	Y	17950 FQ	20990 MW	27230 TQ	USBLS	5/07
	Oregon	H	11.78 FQ	14.36 MW	16.77 TQ	ORBLS	5/08
	Portland-Vancouver-Beaverton MSA, OR-WA	Y	24360 FQ	29420 MW	34970 TQ	USBLS	5/07
	Pennsylvania	Y	19880 FQ	25410 MW	29800 TQ	USBLS	5/07
	Philadelphia-Camden-Wilmington MSA, PA-NJ-DE-MD	Y	15080 FQ	26240 MW	36110 TQ	USBLS	5/07
	Pittsburgh MSA, PA	Y	16300 FQ	21260 MW	26930 TQ	USBLS	5/07
	Reading MSA, PA	Y	24610 FQ	30410 MW	34260 TQ	USBLS	5/07
	York-Hanover MSA, PA	Y	22750 FQ	29060 MW	34420 TQ	USBLS	5/07
	Rhode Island	Y	19420 FQ	21570 MW	23760 TQ	USBLS	5/07
	Providence-Fall River-Warwick MSA, RI-MA	Y	19420 FQ	21570 MW	23760 TQ	USBLS	5/07
	South Carolina	Y	20130 FQ	25460 MW	33250 TQ	USBLS	5/07
	Charleston-North Charleston MSA, SC	Y	21090 FQ	23390 MW	34700 TQ	USBLS	5/07
	Columbia MSA, SC	Y	23790 FQ	29080 MW	34240 TQ	USBLS	5/07
	South Dakota	Y	21309 FQ	24258 MW	28148 TQ	SDBLS	7/08-9/08
	Sioux Falls MSA, SD	Y	22179 FQ	24662 MW	28451 TQ	SDBLS	7/08-9/08
	Tennessee	Y	19340 FQ	23190 MW	27180 TQ	USBLS	5/07
	Memphis MSA, TN-MS-AR	Y	17770 FQ	20700 MW	25470 TQ	USBLS	5/07
	Nashville-Davidson-Murfreesboro MSA, TN	Y	18090 FQ	21870 MW	24580 TQ	USBLS	5/07
	Texas	Y	16820 FQ	20820 MW	26130 TQ	USBLS	5/07
	Austin-Round Rock MSA, TX	Y	16270 FQ	19830 MW	22440 TQ	USBLS	5/07
	Dallas-Fort Worth-Arlington MSA, TX	Y	17700 FQ	22380 MW	27230 TQ	USBLS	5/07
	El Paso MSA, TX	Y	14110 FQ	16550 MW	18560 TQ	USBLS	5/07
	Houston-Sugar Land-Baytown MSA, TX	Y	16240 FQ	19040 MW	25680 TQ	USBLS	5/07
	San Antonio MSA, TX	Y	17030 FQ	19180 MW	23020 TQ	USBLS	5/07
	Utah	Y	20040 FQ	23230 MW	32400 TQ	USBLS	5/07

AE Average entry wage	**AW** Average wage paid	**FQ** First quartile wage	**LO** Lowest wage paid	**MTC** Median total compensation	**TCC** Total cash compensation
AER Average entry range	**AWR** Average wage range	**H** Hourly	**LR** Low end range	**MW** Median wage paid	**TQ** Third quartile wage
AEX Average experienced wage	**AXR** Average experienced range	**HI** Highest wage paid	**M** Monthly	**MWR** Median wage range	**W** Weekly
ATC Average total compensation	**D** Daily	**HR** High end range	**MCC** Median cash compensation	**S** See annotated source	**Y** Yearly

Occupation/Type/Industry	Location	Per	Low	Mid	High	Source	Date
Sawing Machine Setter, Operator, and Tender, Wood	Salt Lake City MSA, UT	Y	20660 FQ	28080 MW	39290 TQ	USBLS	5/07
	Vermont	Y	21950 FQ	25330 MW	29720 TQ	USBLS	5/07
	Virginia	Y	19750 FQ	25340 MW	33500 TQ	USBLS	5/07
	Richmond MSA, VA	Y	19970 FQ	23660 MW	31160 TQ	USBLS	5/07
	Virginia Beach-Norfolk-Newport News MSA, VA-NC	Y	22530 FQ	44120 MW	49720 TQ	USBLS	5/07
	Washington	H	13.04 FQ	16.12 MW	19.07 TQ	WABLS	3/08
	Seattle-Tacoma-Bellevue MSA, WA	Y	26820 FQ	32470 MW	38230 TQ	USBLS	5/07
	West Virginia	Y	18494 FQ	21439 MW	25432 TQ	WVBLS	7/08-9/08
	Charleston MSA, WV	Y	17310 FQ	18690 MW	19930 TQ	USBLS	5/07
	Wisconsin	Y	21480 FQ	25630 MW	31070 TQ	USBLS	5/07
	Milwaukee-Waukesha-West Allis MSA, WI	Y	15050 FQ	20470 MW	24260 TQ	USBLS	5/07
	Wyoming	Y	18362 FQ	22726 MW	27769 TQ	WYBLS	9/08
Scale House Attendant	Harris County, GA	Y	19760 LO		20380 HI	GACTY03	2008
	Houston County, GA	Y	22984 LO		36795 HI	GACTY03	2008
Scale Maintenance Technician							
State Highway Patrol	Missouri	S	1393 LO		1966 HI	MSHPSS	7/1/08
Scenic River Coordinator							
State Government	Ohio	H	18.36 LO		23.87 HI	ODAS	2008
Scent Seeker							
P&G	Cincinnati, OH	S		25.00 AW		WSJ10	2009
Scheduler							
For United States Senator	United States	Y			59698 HI	WPOST	2006
White House Staff	United States	Y		35500-37500 HR		WPOST02	2008
School Board Member	Hillsborough County, FL	Y			40887 HI	TTRIB	2009
	Berkley, MI	S			30.00 HI	FREEP05	2007
	South Lyon, MI	S			30.00 HI	FREEP05	2007
School Bus Monitor							
Public Schools	Chicago, IL	H			9.87 HI	CPSSS	7/1/06
School Library Media Specialist	United States	Y		44348 AW		LIBJ	2007
School Lunch Manager							
Public Schools, Region 9	New York	Y		77355 AW		SAANYS	9/11/08
School Psychologist							
With Doctorate	North Carolina	M	4145 LO		6511 HI	NCSS	2008-2009
Science Public Information Officer	United States	Y	40000 LO		100000 HI	CASW	2008
Science Writer	United States	Y		48640 AW		OOSE03	2006
Scientific Instrument Technician							
Department of Environmental Quality	Oregon	M	2696 LO		3904 HI	ODEQSS	11/1/08
Seaman							
U.S. Navy, Active Duty, Pay Grade E-2	United States	M		1569 AW		DOD1	2009
U.S. Navy, Active Duty, Pay Grade E-3	United States	M	1650 LO		1860 HI	DOD1	2009
Seamstress							
New Hampshire Hospital	New Hampshire	Y		23967 AW		NHUL03	2008
Secondary School Teacher							
Except Special and Vocational Education	Alabama	Y	37360 FQ	43590 MW	49480 TQ	USBLS	5/07
Except Special and Vocational Education	Birmingham-Hoover MSA, AL	Y	38870 FQ	45190 MW	51670 TQ	USBLS	5/07
Except Special and Vocational Education	Alaska	Y	47050 FQ	56060 MW	65100 TQ	USBLS	5/07
Except Special and Vocational Education	Arizona	Y	32740 FQ	38070 MW	46750 TQ	USBLS	5/07
Except Special and Vocational Education	Flagstaff MSA, AZ	Y	33250 FQ	37600 MW	45100 TQ	USBLS	5/07
Except Special and Vocational Education	Phoenix-Mesa-Scottsdale MSA, AZ	Y	33910 FQ	39350 MW	48030 TQ	USBLS	5/07
Except Special and Vocational Education	Tucson MSA, AZ	Y	28460 FQ	34780 MW	43390 TQ	USBLS	5/07

Secondary School Teacher

Occupation/Type/Industry	Location	Per	Low	Mid	High	Source	Date
Except Special and Vocational Education	Arkansas	Y	•36260 FQ	42850 MW	50440 TQ	USBLS	5/07
Except Special and Vocational Education	Little Rock-North Little Rock MSA, AR	Y	37420 FQ	45950 MW	55300 TQ	USBLS	5/07
Except Special and Vocational Education	California	Y		63548 AW		CABLS	1/08-3/08
Except Special and Vocational Education	Los Angeles-Long Beach-Glendale PMSA, CA	Y		62021 AW		CABLS	1/08-3/08
Except Special and Vocational Education	Oakland-Fremont-Hayward MSA, CA	Y		64133 AW		CABLS	1/08-3/08
Except Special and Vocational Education	Riverside-San Bernardino-Ontario MSA, CA	Y		62400 AW		CABLS	1/08-3/08
Except Special and Vocational Education	Sacramento-Arden Arcade-Roseville MSA, CA	Y		59939 MW		CABLS	1/08-3/08
Except Special and Vocational Education	San Diego-Carlsbad-San Marcos MSA, CA	Y		64625 AW		CABLS	1/08-3/08
Except Special and Vocational Education	San Francisco-San Mateo-Redwood PMSA, CA	Y		64666 AW		CABLS	1/08-3/08
Except Special and Vocational Education	San Jose-Sunnyvale-Santa Clara MSA, CA	Y		67763 AW		CABLS	1/08-3/08
Except Special and Vocational Education	Santa Ana-Anaheim-Irvine PMSA, CA	Y	55740 FQ	68070 MW	82450 TQ	USBLS	5/07
Except Special and Vocational Education	Colorado	Y	37020 FQ	45240 MW	56650 TQ	USBLS	5/07
Except Special and Vocational Education	Denver-Aurora MSA, CO	Y	39470 FQ	49390 MW	60980 TQ	USBLS	5/07
Except Special and Vocational Education	Bridgeport-Stamford-Norwalk MSA, CT	Y	54230 FQ	69880 MW	83380 TQ	USBLS	5/07
Except Special and Vocational Education	Hartford-West Hartford-East Hartford MSA, CT	Y	49130 FQ	66230 MW	77610 TQ	USBLS	5/07
Except Special and Vocational Education	Waterbury MSA, CT	Y	47450 FQ	60640 MW	77000 TQ	USBLS	5/07
Except Special and Vocational Education	Delaware	Y	41630 FQ	54030 MW	67420 TQ	USBLS	5/07
Except Special and Vocational Education	Wilmington PMSA, DE-MD-NJ	Y	43570 FQ	55020 MW	69550 TQ	USBLS	5/07
Except Special and Vocational Education	District of Columbia	Y	38060 FQ	47860 MW	59000 TQ	USBLS	5/07
Except Special and Vocational Education	Washington-Arlington-Alexandria MSA, DC-VA-MD-WV	Y	46320 FQ	59240 MW	76410 TQ	USBLS	5/07
Except Special and Vocational Education	Florida	Y	40380 FQ	49550 MW	62470 TQ	USBLS	5/07
Except Special and Vocational Education	Jacksonville MSA, FL	Y	36890 FQ	41740 MW	56520 TQ	USBLS	5/07
Except Special and Vocational Education	Miami-Fort Lauderdale-Miami Beach MSA, FL	Y	42850 FQ	53290 MW	68570 TQ	USBLS	5/07
Except Special and Vocational Education	Orlando-Kissimmee MSA, FL	Y	38250 FQ	45170 MW	54880 TQ	USBLS	5/07
Except Special and Vocational Education	Tampa-St. Petersburg-Clearwater MSA, FL	Y	44990 FQ	53120 MW	65070 TQ	USBLS	5/07
Except Special and Vocational Education	West Palm Beach-Boca Raton-Boynton Beach PMSA, FL	Y	37560 FQ	45040 MW	58060 TQ	USBLS	5/07
Except Special and Vocational Education	Georgia	Y	38200 FQ	48030 MW	59290 TQ	USBLS	5/07
Except Special and Vocational Education	Atlanta-Sandy Springs-Marietta MSA, GA	Y	40480 FQ	49170 MW	59990 TQ	USBLS	5/07
Except Special and Vocational Education	Hawaii	Y	41930 FQ	49800 MW	61930 TQ	USBLS	5/07
Except Special and Vocational Education	Honolulu MSA, HI	Y	39890 FQ	52530 MW	68780 TQ	USBLS	5/07
Except Special and Vocational Education	Idaho	Y	43160 FQ	47010 MW	51430 TQ	USBLS	5/07
Except Special and Vocational Education	Boise City-Nampa MSA, ID	Y	43000 FQ	46330 MW	49880 TQ	USBLS	5/07
Except Special and Vocational Education	Illinois	Y	43960 FQ	59160 MW	80250 TQ	USBLS	5/07
Except Special and Vocational Education	Chicago-Naperville-Joliet MSA, IL-IN-WI	Y	49090 FQ	63920 MW	86080 TQ	USBLS	5/07
Except Special and Vocational Education	Indiana	Y	35830 FQ	47170 MW	60610 TQ	USBLS	5/07
Except Special and Vocational Education	Gary PMSA, IN	Y	37840 FQ	49330 MW	58930 TQ	USBLS	5/07
Except Special and Vocational Education	Indianapolis-Carmel MSA, IN	Y	33690 FQ	46230 MW	65770 TQ	USBLS	5/07
Except Special and Vocational Education	Terre Haute MSA, IN	Y	37440 FQ	49190 MW	61100 TQ	USBLS	5/07
Except Special and Vocational Education	Iowa	Y	29310 FQ	37320 MW	46880 TQ	USBLS	5/07
Except Special and Vocational Education	Des Moines-West Des Moines MSA, IA	Y	31010 FQ	39130 MW	49900 TQ	USBLS	5/07
Except Special and Vocational Education	Sioux City MSA, IA-NE-SD	Y	31130 FQ	37020 MW	45650 TQ	USBLS	5/07
Except Special and Vocational Education	Kansas	Y	32020 FQ	38430 MW	46110 TQ	USBLS	5/07
Except Special and Vocational Education	Topeka MSA, KS	Y	30150 FQ	38610 MW	46750 TQ	USBLS	5/07
Except Special and Vocational Education	Wichita MSA, KS	Y	34600 FQ	41830 MW	48180 TQ	USBLS	5/07
Except Special and Vocational Education	Kentucky	Y	39500 FQ	47187 MW	55312 TQ	KYBLS	2008
Except Special and Vocational Education	Louisville-Jefferson County MSA, KY-IN	Y	39570 FQ	48890 MW	58880 TQ	USBLS	5/07
Except Special and Vocational Education	Owensboro MSA, KY	Y	38970 FQ	47100 MW	56320 TQ	USBLS	5/07
Except Special and Vocational Education	Louisiana	Y		41963 AW		LABLS	1/08-3/08
Except Special and Vocational Education	Baton Rouge MSA, LA	Y	36270 FQ	41560 MW	47910 TQ	USBLS	5/07

AE	Average entry wage	AW	Average wage paid	FQ	First quartile wage	LO	Lowest wage paid	MTC	Median total compensation	TCC	Total cash compensation
AER	Average entry range	AWR	Average wage range	H	Hourly	LR	Low end range	MW	Median wage paid	TQ	Third quartile wage
AEX	Average experienced wage	AXR	Average experienced range	HI	Highest wage paid	M	Monthly	MWR	Median wage range	W	Weekly
ATC	Average total compensation	D	Daily	HR	High end range	MCC	Median cash compensation	S	See annotated source	Y	Yearly

Occupation/Type/Industry	Location	Per	Low	Mid	High	Source	Date
Secondary School Teacher							
Except Special and Vocational Education	New Orleans-Metairie-Kenner MSA, LA	Y	36390 FQ	42690 MW	49110 TQ	USBLS	5/07
Except Special and Vocational Education	Maine	Y	34510 FQ	42850 MW	51700 TQ	USBLS	5/07
Except Special and Vocational Education	Portland-South Portland-Biddeford MSA, ME	Y	37470 FQ	46060 MW	55260 TQ	USBLS	5/07
Except Special and Vocational Education	Maryland	Y		57025 MW		MDBLS	3/08
Except Special and Vocational Education	Baltimore-Towson MSA, MD	Y	46260 FQ	57480 MW	69930 TQ	USBLS	5/07
Except Special and Vocational Education	Bethesda-Gaithersburg-Frederick PMSA, MD	Y	45360 FQ	56230 MW	71210 TQ	USBLS	5/07
Except Special and Vocational Education	Cumberland MSA, MD-WV	Y	52710 FQ	63030 MW	70010 TQ	USBLS	5/07
Except Special and Vocational Education	Salisbury MSA, MD	Y	41960 FQ	52890 MW	62960 TQ	USBLS	5/07
Except Special and Vocational Education	Massachusetts	Y	45470 FQ	56970 MW	68240 TQ	USBLS	5/07
Except Special and Vocational Education	Boston-Cambridge-Quincy NECTA, MA	Y	47110 FQ	59850 MW	72710 TQ	USBLS	5/07
Except Special and Vocational Education	Worcester MSA, MA-CT	Y	46620 FQ	56600 MW	65040 TQ	USBLS	5/07
Except Special and Vocational Education	Michigan	Y	40400 FQ	51870 MW	66290 TQ	USBLS	5/07
Except Special and Vocational Education	Detroit-Warren-Livonia MSA, MI	Y	42580 FQ	53550 MW	72020 TQ	USBLS	5/07
Except Special and Vocational Education	Grand Rapids-Wyoming MSA, MI	Y	36870 FQ	47310 MW	58680 TQ	USBLS	5/07
Except Special and Vocational Education	Warren-Troy-Farmington Hills PMSA, MI	Y	43310 FQ	58800 MW	73540 TQ	USBLS	5/07
Except Special and Vocational Education	Minnesota	Y	39463 FQ	48387 MW	61005 TQ	MNBLS	10/08-12/08
Except Special and Vocational Education	Duluth-Superior MSA, MN-WI	Y	39641 FQ	50804 MW	61047 TQ	MNBLS	10/08-12/08
Except Special and Vocational Education	Minneapolis-Saint Paul MSA, MN-WI	Y	40154 FQ	49737 MW	65012 TQ	MNBLS	10/08-12/08
Except Special and Vocational Education	Rochester MSA, MN	Y	38557 FQ	46010 MW	55180 TQ	MNBLS	10/08-12/08
Except Special and Vocational Education	Mississippi	Y	33690 FQ	40100 MW	48360 TQ	USBLS	5/07
Except Special and Vocational Education	Jackson MSA, MS	Y	34960 FQ	40410 MW	48900 TQ	USBLS	5/07
Except Special and Vocational Education	Missouri	Y	33970 FQ	40660 MW	51550 TQ	USBLS	5/07
Except Special and Vocational Education	Kansas City MSA, MO-KS	Y	34380 FQ	40890 MW	50340 TQ	USBLS	5/07
Except Special and Vocational Education	St. Louis MSA, MO-IL	Y	36530 FQ	45610 MW	58300 TQ	USBLS	5/07
Except Special and Vocational Education	Montana	Y	27570 FQ	36580 MW	47490 TQ	USBLS	5/07
Except Special and Vocational Education	Billings MSA, MT	Y	33350 FQ	43820 MW	55510 TQ	USBLS	5/07
Except Special and Vocational Education	Nebraska	Y	34180 FQ	41360 MW	49470 TQ	USBLS	5/07
Except Special and Vocational Education	Omaha-Council Bluffs MSA, NE-IA	Y	34500 FQ	40610 MW	48720 TQ	USBLS	5/07
Except Special and Vocational Education	Nevada	Y	37298 FQ	45664 MW	54882 TQ	NVBLS	5/08
Except Special and Vocational Education	New Hampshire	Y	36844 AE	48956 MW	57411 AEX	NHBLS	6/08
Except Special and Vocational Education	Nashua NECTA, NH-MA	Y	40180 FQ	49660 MW	60970 TQ	USBLS	5/07
Except Special and Vocational Education	New Jersey	Y	47130 FQ	57840 MW	76040 TQ	USBLS	5/07
Except Special and Vocational Education	Camden PMSA, NJ	Y	47580 FQ	58240 MW	72180 TQ	USBLS	5/07
Except Special and Vocational Education	Edison PMSA, NJ	Y	46690 FQ	56080 MW	74460 TQ	USBLS	5/07
Except Special and Vocational Education	Newark-Union PMSA, NJ-PA	Y	47800 FQ	58490 MW	77270 TQ	USBLS	5/07
Except Special and Vocational Education	New Mexico	Y	36880 FQ	45320 MW	56140 TQ	USBLS	5/07
Except Special and Vocational Education	Albuquerque MSA, NM	Y	37960 FQ	46190 MW	57590 TQ	USBLS	5/07
Except Special and Vocational Education	Las Cruces MSA, NM	Y	34570 FQ	41610 MW	60680 TQ	USBLS	5/07
Except Special and Vocational Education	New York	Y	47250 FQ	60390 MW	77530 TQ	USBLS	5/07
Except Special and Vocational Education	Albany-Schenectady-Troy MSA, NY	Y	43620 FQ	55110 MW	71200 TQ	USBLS	5/07
Except Special and Vocational Education	Buffalo-Niagara Falls MSA, NY	Y	42610 FQ	52060 MW	69430 TQ	USBLS	5/07
Except Special and Vocational Education	Nassau-Suffolk PMSA, NY	Y	57600 FQ	74960 MW	99240 TQ	USBLS	5/07
Except Special and Vocational Education	New York-Northern New Jersey-Long Island MSA, NY-NJ-PA	Y	49880 FQ	63570 MW	81910 TQ	USBLS	5/07
Except Special and Vocational Education	North Carolina	Y	33780 FQ	40730 MW	48610 TQ	USBLS	5/07
Except Special and Vocational Education	Charlotte-Gastonia-Concord MSA, NC-SC	Y	34990 FQ	42200 MW	49270 TQ	USBLS	5/07
Except Special and Vocational Education	Raleigh-Cary MSA, NC	Y	36390 FQ	44170 MW	54170 TQ	USBLS	5/07
Except Special and Vocational Education	North Dakota	Y	32850 FQ	39420 MW	47230 TQ	USBLS	5/07
Except Special and Vocational Education	Fargo MSA, ND-MN	Y	34820 FQ	41290 MW	50230 TQ	USBLS	5/07
Except Special and Vocational Education	Grand Forks MSA, ND-MN	Y	36440 FQ	44940 MW	54750 TQ	USBLS	5/07
Except Special and Vocational Education	Ohio	Y	42180 FQ	53140 MW	64380 TQ	USBLS	5/07
Except Special and Vocational Education	Canton-Massillon MSA, OH	Y	41670 FQ	53170 MW	61880 TQ	USBLS	5/07
Except Special and Vocational Education	Cincinnati-Middletown MSA, OH-KY-IN	Y	42380 FQ	54140 MW	67460 TQ	USBLS	5/07
Except Special and Vocational Education	Cleveland-Elyria-Mentor MSA, OH	Y	47640 FQ	60370 MW	72870 TQ	USBLS	5/07
Except Special and Vocational Education	Columbus MSA, OH	Y	42040 FQ	53760 MW	67480 TQ	USBLS	5/07
Except Special and Vocational Education	Dayton MSA, OH	Y	42740 FQ	54210 MW	63440 TQ	USBLS	5/07

AE Average entry wage	AW Average wage paid	FQ First quartile wage	LO Lowest wage paid	MTC Median total compensation	TCC Total cash compensation
AER Average entry range	AWR Average wage range	H Hourly	LR Low end range	MW Median wage paid	TQ Third quartile wage
AEX Average experienced wage	AXR Average experienced range	HI Highest wage paid	M Monthly	MWR Median wage range	W Weekly
ATC Average total compensation	D Daily	HR High end range	MCC Median cash compensation	S See annotated source	Y Yearly

Occupation/Type/Industry	Location	Per	Low	Mid	High	Source	Date
Secondary School Teacher							
Except Special and Vocational Education	Oklahoma	Y	32610 FQ	37380 MW	43490 TQ	USBLS	5/07
Except Special and Vocational Education	Oklahoma City MSA, OK	Y	32290 FQ	36710 MW	42010 TQ	USBLS	5/07
Except Special and Vocational Education	Tulsa MSA, OK	Y	32620 FQ	39100 MW	47920 TQ	USBLS	5/07
Except Special and Vocational Education	Oregon	Y	40346 FQ	49055 MW	60055 TQ	ORBLS	5/08
Except Special and Vocational Education	Medford MSA, OR	Y	39820 FQ	50170 MW	61870 TQ	USBLS	5/07
Except Special and Vocational Education	Portland-Vancouver-Beaverton MSA, OR-WA	Y	40610 FQ	49190 MW	61290 TQ	USBLS	5/07
Except Special and Vocational Education	Salem MSA, OR	Y	40700 FQ	47800 MW	56410 TQ	USBLS	5/07
Except Special and Vocational Education	Pennsylvania	Y	39600 FQ	49730 MW	63420 TQ	USBLS	5/07
Except Special and Vocational Education	Allentown-Bethlehem-Easton MSA, PA-NJ	Y	39180 FQ	48150 MW	62580 TQ	USBLS	5/07
Except Special and Vocational Education	Philadelphia-Camden-Wilmington MSA, PA-NJ-DE-MD	Y	43800 FQ	53880 MW	69670 TQ	USBLS	5/07
Except Special and Vocational Education	Pittsburgh MSA, PA	Y	42140 FQ	51270 MW	64520 TQ	USBLS	5/07
Except Special and Vocational Education	Rhode Island	Y	47590 FQ	61290 MW	72200 TQ	USBLS	5/07
Except Special and Vocational Education	Providence-Fall River-Warwick MSA, RI-MA	Y	47480 FQ	60650 MW	71830 TQ	USBLS	5/07
Except Special and Vocational Education	South Carolina	Y	35660 FQ	43860 MW	53330 TQ	USBLS	5/07
Except Special and Vocational Education	Charleston-North Charleston MSA, SC	Y	36010 FQ	44250 MW	54260 TQ	USBLS	5/07
Except Special and Vocational Education	Columbia MSA, SC	Y	36280 FQ	44750 MW	55090 TQ	USBLS	5/07
Except Special and Vocational Education	South Dakota	Y	30781 FQ	36284 MW	42889 TQ	SDBLS	7/08-9/08
Except Special and Vocational Education	Sioux Falls MSA, SD	Y	30166 FQ	35919 MW	44212 TQ	SDBLS	7/08-9/08
Except Special and Vocational Education	Tennessee	Y	36810 FQ	42950 MW	50480 TQ	USBLS	5/07
Except Special and Vocational Education	Memphis MSA, TN-MS-AR	Y	36400 FQ	41630 MW	48850 TQ	USBLS	5/07
Except Special and Vocational Education	Nashville-Davidson-Murfreesboro MSA, TN	Y	36890 FQ	44270 MW	53270 TQ	USBLS	5/07
Except Special and Vocational Education	Texas	Y	39460 FQ	45940 MW	52660 TQ	USBLS	5/07
Except Special and Vocational Education	Austin-Round Rock MSA, TX	Y	37860 FQ	43830 MW	51010 TQ	USBLS	5/07
Except Special and Vocational Education	Corpus Christi MSA, TX	Y	36610 FQ	42560 MW	50490 TQ	USBLS	5/07
Except Special and Vocational Education	Dallas-Fort Worth-Arlington MSA, TX	Y	41070 FQ	46900 MW	53190 TQ	USBLS	5/07
Except Special and Vocational Education	El Paso MSA, TX	Y	41160 FQ	46440 MW	53240 TQ	USBLS	5/07
Except Special and Vocational Education	Houston-Sugar Land-Baytown MSA, TX	Y	41790 FQ	47450 MW	54720 TQ	USBLS	5/07
Except Special and Vocational Education	San Antonio MSA, TX	Y	42380 FQ	48400 MW	56730 TQ	USBLS	5/07
Except Special and Vocational Education	Utah	Y	37480 FQ	46920 MW	58470 TQ	USBLS	5/07
Except Special and Vocational Education	St. George MSA, UT	Y	35270 FQ	41640 MW	47590 TQ	USBLS	5/07
Except Special and Vocational Education	Salt Lake City MSA, UT	Y	39420 FQ	49160 MW	63000 TQ	USBLS	5/07
Except Special and Vocational Education	Vermont	Y	37780 FQ	47260 MW	58750 TQ	USBLS	5/07
Except Special and Vocational Education	Burlington-South Burlington MSA, VT	Y	38520 FQ	48940 MW	60780 TQ	USBLS	5/07
Except Special and Vocational Education	Virginia	Y	41120 FQ	51850 MW	67970 TQ	USBLS	5/07
Except Special and Vocational Education	Richmond MSA, VA	Y	42720 FQ	52430 MW	61110 TQ	USBLS	5/07
Except Special and Vocational Education	Roanoke MSA, VA	Y	38570 FQ	46740 MW	55480 TQ	USBLS	5/07
Except Special and Vocational Education	Virginia Beach-Norfolk-Newport News MSA, VA-NC	Y	38550 FQ	47340 MW	59400 TQ	USBLS	5/07
Except Special and Vocational Education	Washington	Y		54869 AW		WABLS	3/08
Except Special and Vocational Education	Seattle-Tacoma-Bellevue MSA, WA	Y	45880 FQ	55310 MW	65840 TQ	USBLS	5/07
Except Special and Vocational Education	West Virginia	Y	35944 FQ	42671 MW	48682 TQ	WVBLS	7/08-9/08
Except Special and Vocational Education	Charleston MSA, WV	Y	33980 FQ	41730 MW	47430 TQ	USBLS	5/07
Except Special and Vocational Education	Wisconsin	Y	36370 FQ	46160 MW	57890 TQ	USBLS	5/07
Except Special and Vocational Education	Milwaukee-Waukesha-West Allis MSA, WI	Y	40990 FQ	55080 MW	70590 TQ	USBLS	5/07
Except Special and Vocational Education	Wyoming	Y	40479 FQ	49823 MW	59018 TQ	WYBLS	9/08
Except Special and Vocational Education	Virgin Islands	Y	34930 FQ	42320 MW	52690 TQ	USBLS	5/07
Secretary							
Church of Christ	United States	Y	22000-27000 LR	26500-27333 AWR	27000-40000 HR	ACU	2008
Except Legal, Medical, and Executive	Alabama	Y	21710 FQ	26440 MW	31890 TQ	USBLS	5/07
Except Legal, Medical, and Executive	Birmingham-Hoover MSA, AL	Y	23530 FQ	28480 MW	34440 TQ	USBLS	5/07
Except Legal, Medical, and Executive	Alaska	Y	28770 FQ	34580 MW	40170 TQ	USBLS	5/07
Except Legal, Medical, and Executive	Anchorage MSA, AK	Y	27590 FQ	33800 MW	39770 TQ	USBLS	5/07
Except Legal, Medical, and Executive	Fairbanks MSA, AK	Y	28760 FQ	34160 MW	41900 TQ	USBLS	5/07
Except Legal, Medical, and Executive	Arizona	Y	22070 FQ	27570 MW	34020 TQ	USBLS	5/07
Except Legal, Medical, and Executive	Phoenix-Mesa-Scottsdale MSA, AZ	Y	23160 FQ	28770 MW	34920 TQ	USBLS	5/07
Except Legal, Medical, and Executive	Tucson MSA, AZ	Y	21590 FQ	26110 MW	33420 TQ	USBLS	5/07

AE Average entry wage	**AW** Average wage paid	**FQ** First quartile wage	**LO** Lowest wage paid	**MTC** Median total compensation	**TCC** Total cash compensation
AER Average entry range	**AWR** Average wage range	**H** Hourly	**LR** Low end range	**MW** Median wage paid	**TQ** Third quartile wage
AEX Average experienced wage	**AXR** Average experienced range	**HI** Highest wage paid	**M** Monthly	**MWR** Median wage range	**W** Weekly
ATC Average total compensation	**D** Daily	**HR** High end range	**MCC** Median cash compensation	**S** See annotated source	**Y** Yearly

Secretary

Occupation/Type/Industry	Location	Per	Low	Mid	High	Source	Date
Except Legal, Medical, and Executive	Arkansas	Y	19040 FQ	22870 MW	27860 TQ	USBLS	5/07
Except Legal, Medical, and Executive	Little Rock-North Little Rock MSA, AR	Y	20490 FQ	24480 MW	30810 TQ	USBLS	5/07
Except Legal, Medical, and Executive	California	H	12.71 FQ	15.98 MW	20.10 TQ	CABLS	1/08-3/08
Except Legal, Medical, and Executive	Bakersfield MSA, CA	H	12.14 FQ	15.35 MW	19.01 TQ	CABLS	1/08-3/08
Except Legal, Medical, and Executive	Los Angeles-Long Beach-Glendale PMSA, CA	H	12.35 FQ	15.28 MW	19.76 TQ	CABLS	1/08-3/08
Except Legal, Medical, and Executive	Oakland-Fremont-Hayward MSA, CA	H	15.10 FQ	18.77 MW	23.45 TQ	CABLS	1/08-3/08
Except Legal, Medical, and Executive	Riverside-San Bernardino-Ontario MSA, CA	H	12.21 FQ	15.08 MW	18.44 TQ	CABLS	1/08-3/08
Except Legal, Medical, and Executive	Sacramento-Arden Arcade-Roseville MSA, CA	H	12.94 FQ	16.65 MW	19.97 TQ	CABLS	1/08-3/08
Except Legal, Medical, and Executive	San Diego-Carlsbad-San Marcos MSA, CA	H	12.33 FQ	15.68 MW	20.41 TQ	CABLS	1/08-3/08
Except Legal, Medical, and Executive	San Francisco-San Mateo-Redwood PMSA, CA	H	15.82 FQ	19.12 MW	22.85 TQ	CABLS	1/08-3/08
Except Legal, Medical, and Executive	San Jose-Sunnyvale-Santa Clara MSA, CA	H	14.80 FQ	18.02 MW	21.56 TQ	CABLS	1/08-3/08
Except Legal, Medical, and Executive	Santa Ana-Anaheim-Irvine PMSA, CA	Y	26710 FQ	34140 MW	41980 TQ	USBLS	5/07
Except Legal, Medical, and Executive	Colorado	Y	24050 FQ	29560 MW	36100 TQ	USBLS	5/07
Except Legal, Medical, and Executive	Denver-Aurora MSA, CO	Y	26610 FQ	31520 MW	38050 TQ	USBLS	5/07
Except Legal, Medical, and Executive	Connecticut	H	11.84 AE	16.56 MW		CTBLS	1/08-3/08
Except Legal, Medical, and Executive	Bridgeport-Stamford-Norwalk MSA, CT	Y	28950 FQ	35590 MW	43430 TQ	USBLS	5/07
Except Legal, Medical, and Executive	Hartford-West Hartford-East Hartford MSA, CT	Y	26940 FQ	34480 MW	43400 TQ	USBLS	5/07
Except Legal, Medical, and Executive	Delaware	Y	25700 FQ	31160 MW	37980 TQ	USBLS	5/07
Except Legal, Medical, and Executive	Wilmington PMSA, DE-MD-NJ	Y	25240 FQ	30880 MW	38380 TQ	USBLS	5/07
Except Legal, Medical, and Executive	District of Columbia	Y	34880 FQ	41680 MW	49290 TQ	USBLS	5/07
Except Legal, Medical, and Executive	Washington-Arlington-Alexandria MSA, DC-VA-MD-WV	Y	31950 FQ	39250 MW	47270 TQ	USBLS	5/07
Except Legal, Medical, and Executive	Florida	Y	21160 FQ	26110 MW	31840 TQ	USBLS	5/07
Except Legal, Medical, and Executive	Cape Coral-Fort Myers MSA, FL	Y	21570 FQ	27100 MW	33040 TQ	USBLS	5/07
Except Legal, Medical, and Executive	Fort Lauderdale-Pompano Beach-Deerfield Beach PMSA, FL	Y	21470 FQ	27020 MW	33420 TQ	USBLS	5/07
Except Legal, Medical, and Executive	Jacksonville MSA, FL	Y	21420 FQ	26250 MW	32330 TQ	USBLS	5/07
Except Legal, Medical, and Executive	Miami-Fort Lauderdale-Miami Beach MSA, FL	Y	21990 FQ	27490 MW	33370 TQ	USBLS	5/07
Except Legal, Medical, and Executive	Orlando-Kissimmee MSA, FL	Y	20520 FQ	25590 MW	31110 TQ	USBLS	5/07
Except Legal, Medical, and Executive	Tampa-St. Petersburg-Clearwater MSA, FL	Y	20750 FQ	25120 MW	31380 TQ	USBLS	5/07
Except Legal, Medical, and Executive	West Palm Beach-Boca Raton-Boynton Beach PMSA, FL	Y	22300 FQ	27840 MW	33680 TQ	USBLS	5/07
Except Legal, Medical, and Executive	Georgia	Y	20160 FQ	25020 MW	31380 TQ	USBLS	5/07
Except Legal, Medical, and Executive	Atlanta-Sandy Springs-Marietta MSA, GA	Y	21970 FQ	27760 MW	34520 TQ	USBLS	5/07
Except Legal, Medical, and Executive	Hawaii	Y	26800 FQ	33130 MW	39370 TQ	USBLS	5/07
Except Legal, Medical, and Executive	Honolulu MSA, HI	Y	26350 FQ	32630 MW	39530 TQ	USBLS	5/07
Except Legal, Medical, and Executive	Idaho	Y	20000 FQ	24950 MW	31760 TQ	USBLS	5/07
Except Legal, Medical, and Executive	Boise City-Nampa MSA, ID	Y	21150 FQ	26680 MW	32660 TQ	USBLS	5/07
Except Legal, Medical, and Executive	Illinois	Y	22680 FQ	28390 MW	35220 TQ	USBLS	5/07
Except Legal, Medical, and Executive	Chicago-Naperville-Joliet MSA, IL-IN-WI	Y	24480 FQ	29880 MW	36950 TQ	USBLS	5/07
Except Legal, Medical, and Executive	Peoria MSA, IL	Y	20920 FQ	25330 MW	29960 TQ	USBLS	5/07
Except Legal, Medical, and Executive	Rockford MSA, IL	Y	22430 FQ	27170 MW	31670 TQ	USBLS	5/07
Except Legal, Medical, and Executive	Indiana	Y	22090 FQ	26550 MW	31510 TQ	USBLS	5/07
Except Legal, Medical, and Executive	Elkhart-Goshen MSA, IN	Y	23010 FQ	27130 MW	31410 TQ	USBLS	5/07
Except Legal, Medical, and Executive	Gary PMSA, IN	Y	22710 FQ	27490 MW	32780 TQ	USBLS	5/07
Except Legal, Medical, and Executive	Indianapolis-Carmel MSA, IN	Y	23040 FQ	27690 MW	32990 TQ	USBLS	5/07
Except Legal, Medical, and Executive	South Bend-Mishawaka MSA, IN-MI	Y	21450 FQ	25550 MW	30170 TQ	USBLS	5/07
Except Legal, Medical, and Executive	Iowa	Y	21220 FQ	25630 MW	31240 TQ	USBLS	5/07
Except Legal, Medical, and Executive	Des Moines-West Des Moines MSA, IA	Y	24910 FQ	29170 MW	35340 TQ	USBLS	5/07
Except Legal, Medical, and Executive	Waterloo-Cedar Falls MSA, IA	Y	20260 FQ	24260 MW	30000 TQ	USBLS	5/07

AE	Average entry wage	AW	Average wage paid	FQ	First quartile wage
AER	Average entry range	AWR	Average wage range	H	Hourly
AEX	Average experienced wage	AXR	Average experienced range	HI	Highest wage paid
ATC	Average total compensation	D	Daily	HR	High end range

LO	Lowest wage paid	MTC	Median total compensation	TCC	Total cash compensation
LR	Low end range	MW	Median wage paid	TQ	Third quartile wage
M	Monthly	MWR	Median wage range	W	Weekly
MCC	Median cash compensation	S	See annotated source	Y	Yearly

Secretary

Occupation/Type/Industry	Location	Per	Low	Mid	High	Source	Date
Except Legal, Medical, and Executive	Kansas	Y	19820 FQ	23720 MW	28740 TQ	USBLS	5/07
Except Legal, Medical, and Executive	Topeka MSA, KS	Y	20030 FQ	23480 MW	28290 TQ	USBLS	5/07
Except Legal, Medical, and Executive	Wichita MSA, KS	Y	20300 FQ	24410 MW	29720 TQ	USBLS	5/07
Except Legal, Medical, and Executive	Kentucky	Y	19735 FQ	24313 MW	30068 TQ	KYBLS	2008
Except Legal, Medical, and Executive	Louisville-Jefferson County MSA, KY-IN	Y	21220 FQ	25380 MW	31530 TQ	USBLS	5/07
Except Legal, Medical, and Executive	Louisiana	H	9.43 FQ	11.28 MW	13.85 TQ	LABLS	1/08-3/08
Except Legal, Medical, and Executive	Baton Rouge MSA, LA	Y	20950 FQ	24170 MW	29540 TQ	USBLS	5/07
Except Legal, Medical, and Executive	Lake Charles MSA, LA	Y	17800 FQ	21620 MW	26500 TQ	USBLS	5/07
Except Legal, Medical, and Executive	New Orleans-Metairie-Kenner MSA, LA	Y	21500 FQ	25420 MW	31270 TQ	USBLS	5/07
Except Legal, Medical, and Executive	Maine	Y	23960 FQ	28260 MW	32700 TQ	USBLS	5/07
Except Legal, Medical, and Executive	Portland-South Portland-Biddeford MSA, ME	Y	26170 FQ	30130 MW	35090 TQ	USBLS	5/07
Except Legal, Medical, and Executive	Maryland	Y		33700 MW		MDBLS	3/08
Except Legal, Medical, and Executive	Baltimore-Towson MSA, MD	Y	27200 FQ	33170 MW	39740 TQ	USBLS	5/07
Except Legal, Medical, and Executive	Bethesda-Gaithersburg-Frederick PMSA, MD	Y	28040 FQ	36240 MW	44880 TQ	USBLS	5/07
Except Legal, Medical, and Executive	Cumberland MSA, MD-WV	Y	20300 FQ	25020 MW	30990 TQ	USBLS	5/07
Except Legal, Medical, and Executive	Massachusetts	Y	28570 FQ	35010 MW	42120 TQ	USBLS	5/07
Except Legal, Medical, and Executive	Boston-Cambridge-Quincy NECTA, MA	Y	30170 FQ	37020 MW	44660 TQ	USBLS	5/07
Except Legal, Medical, and Executive	Lynn-Peabody-Salem NECTA, MA	Y	29430 FQ	35360 MW	41510 TQ	USBLS	5/07
Except Legal, Medical, and Executive	Worcester MSA, MA-CT	Y	27240 FQ	32530 MW	38640 TQ	USBLS	5/07
Except Legal, Medical, and Executive	Michigan	Y	25170 FQ	30820 MW	37310 TQ	USBLS	5/07
Except Legal, Medical, and Executive	Detroit-Warren-Livonia MSA, MI	Y	28160 FQ	33790 MW	39730 TQ	USBLS	5/07
Except Legal, Medical, and Executive	Flint MSA, MI	Y	24180 FQ	29390 MW	35230 TQ	USBLS	5/07
Except Legal, Medical, and Executive	Grand Rapids-Wyoming MSA, MI	Y	23690 FQ	29040 MW	35450 TQ	USBLS	5/07
Except Legal, Medical, and Executive	Warren-Troy-Farmington Hills PMSA, MI	Y	27780 FQ	33220 MW	39670 TQ	USBLS	5/07
Except Legal, Medical, and Executive	Minnesota	Y	30287 FQ	36042 MW	41527 TQ	MNBLS	10/08-12/08
Except Legal, Medical, and Executive	Duluth-Superior MSA, MN-WI	Y	28340 FQ	33867 MW	41267 TQ	MNBLS	10/08-12/08
Except Legal, Medical, and Executive	Minneapolis-Saint Paul MSA, MN-WI	Y	30599 FQ	36698 MW	42568 TQ	MNBLS	10/08-12/08
Except Legal, Medical, and Executive	Rochester MSA, MN	Y	31160 FQ	37344 MW	42603 TQ	MNBLS	10/08-12/08
Except Legal, Medical, and Executive	Mississippi	Y	19990 FQ	23760 MW	28750 TQ	USBLS	5/07
Except Legal, Medical, and Executive	Jackson MSA, MS	Y	21190 FQ	25810 MW	30440 TQ	USBLS	5/07
Except Legal, Medical, and Executive	Missouri	Y	21720 FQ	27100 MW	33090 TQ	USBLS	5/07
Except Legal, Medical, and Executive	Kansas City MSA, MO-KS	Y	22350 FQ	27560 MW	33180 TQ	USBLS	5/07
Except Legal, Medical, and Executive	St. Louis MSA, MO-IL	Y	23870 FQ	29250 MW	35750 TQ	USBLS	5/07
Except Legal, Medical, and Executive	Montana	Y	18130 FQ	22650 MW	28020 TQ	USBLS	5/07
Except Legal, Medical, and Executive	Billings MSA, MT	Y	18530 FQ	22730 MW	28340 TQ	USBLS	5/07
Except Legal, Medical, and Executive	Nebraska	Y	21070 FQ	25220 MW	30900 TQ	USBLS	5/07
Except Legal, Medical, and Executive	Omaha-Council Bluffs MSA, NE-IA	Y	22810 FQ	28120 MW	34230 TQ	USBLS	5/07
Except Legal, Medical, and Executive	Nevada	H	13.26 FQ	16.04 MW	19.45 TQ	NVBLS	5/08
Except Legal, Medical, and Executive	Las Vegas-Paradise MSA, NV	H	13.29 FQ	15.95 MW	19.34 TQ	NVBLS	5/08
Except Legal, Medical, and Executive	New Hampshire	H	10.61 AE	13.95 MW	15.96 AEX	NHBLS	6/08
Except Legal, Medical, and Executive	Manchester MSA, NH	Y	24500 FQ	29190 MW	35960 TQ	USBLS	5/07
Except Legal, Medical, and Executive	Nashua NECTA, NH-MA	Y	25340 FQ	29650 MW	35000 TQ	USBLS	5/07
Except Legal, Medical, and Executive	Rochester-Dover MSA, NH-ME	Y	23780 FQ	29350 MW	34340 TQ	USBLS	5/07
Except Legal, Medical, and Executive	New Jersey	Y	27780 FQ	34180 MW	41500 TQ	USBLS	5/07
Except Legal, Medical, and Executive	Camden PMSA, NJ	Y	26710 FQ	32950 MW	40500 TQ	USBLS	5/07
Except Legal, Medical, and Executive	Edison PMSA, NJ	Y	27380 FQ	33490 MW	40500 TQ	USBLS	5/07
Except Legal, Medical, and Executive	Newark-Union PMSA, NJ-PA	Y	28480 FQ	35060 MW	41830 TQ	USBLS	5/07
Except Legal, Medical, and Executive	Vineland-Millville-Bridgeton MSA, NJ	Y	24570 FQ	30480 MW	39090 TQ	USBLS	5/07
Except Legal, Medical, and Executive	New Mexico	Y	20060 FQ	25370 MW	31090 TQ	USBLS	5/07
Except Legal, Medical, and Executive	Albuquerque MSA, NM	Y	21300 FQ	26940 MW	31840 TQ	USBLS	5/07
Except Legal, Medical, and Executive	New York	Y	24950 FQ	30480 MW	37460 TQ	USBLS	5/07
Except Legal, Medical, and Executive	Albany-Schenectady-Troy MSA, NY	Y	25850 FQ	31170 MW	38060 TQ	USBLS	5/07
Except Legal, Medical, and Executive	Buffalo-Niagara Falls MSA, NY	Y	23010 FQ	27490 MW	32220 TQ	USBLS	5/07
Except Legal, Medical, and Executive	Nassau-Suffolk PMSA, NY	Y	25460 FQ	31220 MW	38190 TQ	USBLS	5/07

AE	Average entry wage	AW	Average wage paid	FQ	First quartile wage	LO	Lowest wage paid	MTC Median total compensation	TCC Total cash compensation
AER	Average entry range	AWR	Average wage range	H	Hourly	LR	Low end range	MW Median wage paid	TQ Third quartile wage
AEX	Average experienced wage	AXR	Average experienced range	HI	Highest wage paid	M	Monthly	MWR Median wage range	W Weekly
ATC	Average total compensation	D	Daily	HR	High end range	MCC	Median cash compensation	S See annotated source	Y Yearly

Occupation/Type/Industry	Location	Per	Low	Mid	High	Source	Date
Secretary							
Except Legal, Medical, and Executive	New York-Northern New Jersey-Long Island MSA, NY-NJ-PA	Y	26910 FQ	32760 MW	40290 TQ	USBLS	5/07
Except Legal, Medical, and Executive	North Carolina	Y	22390 FQ	27050 MW	31970 TQ	USBLS	5/07
Except Legal, Medical, and Executive	Charlotte-Gastonia-Concord MSA, NC-SC	Y	23360 FQ	28330 MW	33930 TQ	USBLS	5/07
Except Legal, Medical, and Executive	Raleigh-Cary MSA, NC	Y	24860 FQ	29040 MW	34280 TQ	USBLS	5/07
Except Legal, Medical, and Executive	North Dakota	Y	23370 FQ	28070 MW	33470 TQ	USBLS	5/07
Except Legal, Medical, and Executive	Fargo MSA, ND-MN	Y	25490 FQ	29710 MW	35220 TQ	USBLS	5/07
Except Legal, Medical, and Executive	Grand Forks MSA, ND-MN	Y	24200 FQ	28310 MW	32090 TQ	USBLS	5/07
Except Legal, Medical, and Executive	Ohio	Y	24200 FQ	29370 MW	35500 TQ	USBLS	5/07
Except Legal, Medical, and Executive	Cincinnati-Middletown MSA, OH-KY-IN	Y	24740 FQ	30180 MW	36450 TQ	USBLS	5/07
Except Legal, Medical, and Executive	Cleveland-Elyria-Mentor MSA, OH	Y	25820 FQ	31140 MW	37330 TQ	USBLS	5/07
Except Legal, Medical, and Executive	Columbus MSA, OH	Y	26590 FQ	31710 MW	37660 TQ	USBLS	5/07
Except Legal, Medical, and Executive	Dayton MSA, OH	Y	24770 FQ	30190 MW	36800 TQ	USBLS	5/07
Except Legal, Medical, and Executive	Oklahoma	Y	18000 FQ	22510 MW	28180 TQ	USBLS	5/07
Except Legal, Medical, and Executive	Lawton MSA, OK	Y	19210 FQ	24850 MW	35640 TQ	USBLS	5/07
Except Legal, Medical, and Executive	Oklahoma City MSA, OK	Y	18850 FQ	23760 MW	29620 TQ	USBLS	5/07
Except Legal, Medical, and Executive	Tulsa MSA, OK	Y	19110 FQ	23110 MW	28450 TQ	USBLS	5/07
Except Legal, Medical, and Executive	Oregon	H	11.42 FQ	14.11 MW	17.02 TQ	ORBLS	5/08
Except Legal, Medical, and Executive	Portland-Vancouver-Beaverton MSA, OR-WA	Y	25780 FQ	30930 MW	36890 TQ	USBLS	5/07
Except Legal, Medical, and Executive	Pennsylvania	Y	22320 FQ	27630 MW	33650 TQ	USBLS	5/07
Except Legal, Medical, and Executive	Allentown-Bethlehem-Easton MSA, PA-NJ	Y	23660 FQ	29090 MW	35180 TQ	USBLS	5/07
Except Legal, Medical, and Executive	Philadelphia-Camden-Wilmington MSA, PA-NJ-DE-MD	Y	25470 FQ	31010 MW	38120 TQ	USBLS	5/07
Except Legal, Medical, and Executive	Pittsburgh MSA, PA	Y	22200 FQ	27170 MW	32360 TQ	USBLS	5/07
Except Legal, Medical, and Executive	Rhode Island	Y	28840 FQ	33400 MW	38130 TQ	USBLS	5/07
Except Legal, Medical, and Executive	Providence-Fall River-Warwick MSA, RI-MA	Y	28180 FQ	32980 MW	37970 TQ	USBLS	5/07
Except Legal, Medical, and Executive	South Carolina	Y	22460 FQ	27010 MW	31800 TQ	USBLS	5/07
Except Legal, Medical, and Executive	Charleston-North Charleston MSA, SC	Y	24260 FQ	28720 MW	33680 TQ	USBLS	5/07
Except Legal, Medical, and Executive	Columbia MSA, SC	Y	22190 FQ	27190 MW	31800 TQ	USBLS	5/07
Except Legal, Medical, and Executive	South Dakota	Y	20282 FQ	23217 MW	26240 TQ	SDBLS	7/08-9/08
Except Legal, Medical, and Executive	Rapid City MSA, SD	Y	19564 FQ	23661 MW	27830 TQ	SDBLS	7/08-9/08
Except Legal, Medical, and Executive	Sioux Falls MSA, SD	Y	21329 FQ	24244 MW	27989 TQ	SDBLS	7/08-9/08
Except Legal, Medical, and Executive	Tennessee	Y	20320 FQ	24630 MW	30330 TQ	USBLS	5/07
Except Legal, Medical, and Executive	Memphis MSA, TN-MS-AR	Y	21210 FQ	25760 MW	31780 TQ	USBLS	5/07
Except Legal, Medical, and Executive	Nashville-Davidson-Murfreesboro MSA, TN	Y	21760 FQ	26920 MW	32440 TQ	USBLS	5/07
Except Legal, Medical, and Executive	Texas	Y	19850 FQ	25030 MW	30970 TQ	USBLS	5/07
Except Legal, Medical, and Executive	Austin-Round Rock MSA, TX	Y	21800 FQ	26410 MW	31620 TQ	USBLS	5/07
Except Legal, Medical, and Executive	Corpus Christi MSA, TX	Y	18760 FQ	23060 MW	28430 TQ	USBLS	5/07
Except Legal, Medical, and Executive	Dallas-Fort Worth-Arlington MSA, TX	Y	21640 FQ	27150 MW	32930 TQ	USBLS	5/07
Except Legal, Medical, and Executive	El Paso MSA, TX	Y	18240 FQ	22840 MW	28150 TQ	USBLS	5/07
Except Legal, Medical, and Executive	Houston-Sugar Land-Baytown MSA, TX	Y	21280 FQ	27110 MW	32880 TQ	USBLS	5/07
Except Legal, Medical, and Executive	San Antonio MSA, TX	Y	19870 FQ	24940 MW	30930 TQ	USBLS	5/07
Except Legal, Medical, and Executive	Utah	Y	21600 FQ	26520 MW	31370 TQ	USBLS	5/07
Except Legal, Medical, and Executive	St. George MSA, UT	Y	18670 FQ	22980 MW	27930 TQ	USBLS	5/07
Except Legal, Medical, and Executive	Salt Lake City MSA, UT	Y	22790 FQ	27660 MW	31960 TQ	USBLS	5/07
Except Legal, Medical, and Executive	Vermont	Y	23250 FQ	27570 MW	31410 TQ	USBLS	5/07
Except Legal, Medical, and Executive	Burlington-South Burlington MSA, VT	Y	24830 FQ	28820 MW	33390 TQ	USBLS	5/07
Except Legal, Medical, and Executive	Virginia	Y	26230 FQ	32970 MW	40760 TQ	USBLS	5/07
Except Legal, Medical, and Executive	Richmond MSA, VA	Y	24410 FQ	29500 MW	36610 TQ	USBLS	5/07
Except Legal, Medical, and Executive	Virginia Beach-Norfolk-Newport News MSA, VA-NC	Y	24580 FQ	30990 MW	37950 TQ	USBLS	5/07
Except Legal, Medical, and Executive	Washington	H	13.91 FQ	16.51 MW	19.02 TQ	WABLS	3/08
Except Legal, Medical, and Executive	Seattle-Tacoma-Bellevue MSA, WA	Y	30070 FQ	35300 MW	40600 TQ	USBLS	5/07
Except Legal, Medical, and Executive	West Virginia	Y	17847 FQ	22751 MW	29153 TQ	WVBLS	7/08-9/08
Except Legal, Medical, and Executive	Charleston MSA, WV	Y	19540 FQ	24390 MW	30070 TQ	USBLS	5/07
Except Legal, Medical, and Executive	Wisconsin	Y	24400 FQ	28930 MW	34170 TQ	USBLS	5/07

AE Average entry wage	**AW** Average wage paid	**FQ** First quartile wage	**LO** Lowest wage paid	**MTC** Median total compensation	**TCC** Total cash compensation
AER Average entry range	**AWR** Average wage range	**H** Hourly	**LR** Low end range	**MW** Median wage paid	**TQ** Third quartile wage
AEX Average experienced wage	**AXR** Average experienced range	**HI** Highest wage paid	**M** Monthly	**MWR** Median wage range	**W** Weekly
ATC Average total compensation **D** Daily		**HR** High end range	**MCC** Median cash compensation	**S** See annotated source	**Y** Yearly

Occupation/Type/Industry	Location	Per	Low	Mid	High	Source	Date
Secretary							
Except Legal, Medical, and Executive	Milwaukee-Waukesha-West Allis MSA, WI	Y	25970 FQ	30510 MW	36220 TQ	USBLS	5/07
Except Legal, Medical, and Executive	Wyoming	Y	20488 FQ	25023 MW	30419 TQ	WYBLS	9/08
Except Legal, Medical, and Executive	Cheyenne MSA, WY	Y	21825 FQ	27220 MW	31514 TQ	WYBLS	9/08
Except Legal, Medical, and Executive	Puerto Rico	Y	13640 FQ	16430 MW	20600 TQ	USBLS	5/07
Except Legal, Medical, and Executive	San Juan-Caguas-Guaynabo MSA, PR	Y	14060 FQ	17250 MW	21530 TQ	USBLS	5/07
Except Legal, Medical, and Executive	Virgin Islands	Y	23450 FQ	27440 MW	31200 TQ	USBLS	5/07
Except Legal, Medical, and Executive	Guam	Y	19820 FQ	27530 MW	35630 TQ	USBLS	5/07
Municipal Government	Reno, NV	Y			52505 HI	RGJ	2008
Secretary-General of the United Nations	United States	Y			225000 HI	ILLOOP	2009
Secretary of State							
Federal Government	United States	Y			186600 HI	NYT07	2009
Secretary of the Senate							
United States Senate	United States	Y			163700 HI	CRS01	2007
Securities, Commodities, and Financial Services Sales Agent	Alabama	Y	36740 FQ	50920 MW	99040 TQ	USBLS	5/07
	Birmingham-Hoover MSA, AL	Y	39200 FQ	51160 MW	86880 TQ	USBLS	5/07
	Alaska	Y	37330 FQ	50420 MW	81670 TQ	USBLS	5/07
	Arizona	Y	32870 FQ	54440 MW	92880 TQ	USBLS	5/07
	Phoenix-Mesa-Scottsdale MSA, AZ	Y	33320 FQ	55620 MW	95300 TQ	USBLS	5/07
	Prescott MSA, AZ	Y	27020 FQ	30170 MW	34700 TQ	USBLS	5/07
	Tucson MSA, AZ	Y	33750 FQ	59950 MW	81370 TQ	USBLS	5/07
	Arkansas	Y	36360 FQ	49190 MW	82900 TQ	USBLS	5/07
	Little Rock-North Little Rock MSA, AR	Y	34060 FQ	47870 MW	85290 TQ	USBLS	5/07
	California	H	22.78 FQ	34.82 MW	59.74 TQ	CABLS	1/08-3/08
	Los Angeles-Long Beach-Glendale PMSA, CA	H	21.55 FQ	33.94 MW	54.95 TQ	CABLS	1/08-3/08
	Oakland-Fremont-Hayward MSA, CA	H	24.10 FQ	44.41 MW		CABLS	1/08-3/08
	Riverside-San Bernardino-Ontario MSA, CA	H	21.29 FQ	27.74 MW	32.92 TQ	CABLS	1/08-3/08
	Sacramento-Arden Arcade-Roseville MSA, CA	H	16.18 FQ	25.33 MW	38.06 TQ	CABLS	1/08-3/08
	San Diego-Carlsbad-San Marcos MSA, CA	H	23.66 FQ	30.05 MW	48.74 TQ	CABLS	1/08-3/08
	San Francisco-San Mateo-Redwood PMSA, CA	H	31.96 FQ	54.08 MW		CABLS	1/08-3/08
	San Jose-Sunnyvale-Santa Clara MSA, CA	H	25.04 FQ	41.22 MW	65.12 TQ	CABLS	1/08-3/08
	Santa Ana-Anaheim-Irvine PMSA, CA	Y	44830 FQ	64260 MW	109700 TQ	USBLS	5/07
	Colorado	Y	36210 FQ	55240 MW	110920 TQ	USBLS	5/07
	Denver-Aurora MSA, CO	Y	36480 FQ	54030 MW	111020 TQ	USBLS	5/07
	Connecticut	H	31.58 AE			CTBLS	1/08-3/08
	Bridgeport-Stamford-Norwalk MSA, CT	Y	94810 FQ			USBLS	5/07
	Hartford-West Hartford-East Hartford MSA, CT	Y	59140 FQ	105460 MW		USBLS	5/07
	Delaware	Y	40830 FQ	59160 MW	94450 TQ	USBLS	5/07
	Wilmington PMSA, DE-MD-NJ	Y	41220 FQ	59550 MW	94490 TQ	USBLS	5/07
	District of Columbia	Y	45070 FQ	85040 MW	127900 TQ	USBLS	5/07
	Washington-Arlington-Alexandria MSA, DC-VA-MD-WV	Y	40360 FQ	56140 MW	91900 TQ	USBLS	5/07
	Florida	Y	38490 FQ	59440 MW	101000 TQ	USBLS	5/07
	Cape Coral-Fort Myers MSA, FL	Y	48180 FQ	111490 MW		USBLS	5/07
	Fort Lauderdale-Pompano Beach-Deerfield Beach PMSA, FL	Y	37790 FQ	59080 MW	79880 TQ	USBLS	5/07
	Jacksonville MSA, FL	Y	53120 FQ	70580 MW	107670 TQ	USBLS	5/07

AE	Average entry wage	**AW**	Average wage paid	**FQ**	First quartile wage
AER	Average entry range	**AWR**	Average wage range	**H**	Hourly
AEX	Average experienced wage	**AXR**	Average experienced range	**HI**	Highest wage paid
ATC	Average total compensation	**D**	Daily	**HR**	High end range

LO	Lowest wage paid	**MTC**	Median total compensation
LR	Low end range	**MW**	Median wage paid
M	Monthly	**MWR**	Median wage range
MCC	Median cash compensation	**S**	See annotated source
TCC	Total cash compensation	**TQ**	Third quartile wage
		W	Weekly
		Y	Yearly

Occupation/Type/Industry	Location	Per	Low	Mid	High	Source	Date
Securities, Commodities, and Financial Services Sales Agent	Miami-Fort Lauderdale-Miami Beach MSA, FL	Y	40650 FQ	64290 MW	106890 TQ	USBLS	5/07
	Orlando-Kissimmee MSA, FL	Y	36210 FQ	45840 MW	78300 TQ	USBLS	5/07
	Tallahassee MSA, FL	Y	29730 FQ	41040 MW	115110 TQ	USBLS	5/07
	Tampa-St. Petersburg-Clearwater MSA, FL	Y	36090 FQ	52530 MW	93320 TQ	USBLS	5/07
	West Palm Beach-Boca Raton-Boynton Beach PMSA, FL	Y	44600 FQ	93090 MW		USBLS	5/07
	Georgia	Y	41740 FQ	56590 MW	91620 TQ	USBLS	5/07
	Atlanta-Sandy Springs-Marietta MSA, GA	Y	44280 FQ	57840 MW	91820 TQ	USBLS	5/07
	Hawaii	Y	33750 FQ	52950 MW	68470 TQ	USBLS	5/07
	Honolulu MSA, HI	Y	38110 FQ	56170 MW	72390 TQ	USBLS	5/07
	Idaho	Y	29800 FQ	44250 MW	77640 TQ	USBLS	5/07
	Idaho Falls MSA, ID	Y	68530 FQ	77690 MW	110880 TQ	USBLS	5/07
	Illinois	Y	43920 FQ	69790 MW	113750 TQ	USBLS	5/07
	Chicago-Naperville-Joliet MSA, IL-IN-WI	Y	44100 FQ	69720 MW	114480 TQ	USBLS	5/07
	Peoria MSA, IL	Y	46340 FQ	69250 MW	88930 TQ	USBLS	5/07
	Indiana	Y	39490 FQ	57370 MW	95790 TQ	USBLS	5/07
	Fort Wayne MSA, IN	Y	35070 FQ	47750 MW	100030 TQ	USBLS	5/07
	Gary PMSA, IN	Y	37230 FQ	46800 MW	72120 TQ	USBLS	5/07
	Indianapolis-Carmel MSA, IN	Y	42970 FQ	74760 MW	108870 TQ	USBLS	5/07
	Iowa	Y	33530 FQ	47580 MW	79020 TQ	USBLS	5/07
	Des Moines-West Des Moines MSA, IA	Y	31770 FQ	41890 MW	65460 TQ	USBLS	5/07
	Iowa City MSA, IA	Y	85330 FQ	101890 MW	120870 TQ	USBLS	5/07
	Sioux City MSA, IA-NE-SD	Y	25390 FQ	41200 MW	106610 TQ	USBLS	5/07
	Wichita MSA, KS	Y	47640 FQ	64990 MW	119600 TQ	USBLS	5/07
	Kentucky	Y	41050 FQ	72677 MW	133585 TQ	KYBLS	2008
	Louisville-Jefferson County MSA, KY-IN	Y	41240 FQ	60100 MW	120210 TQ	USBLS	5/07
	Louisiana	H	22.54 FQ	31.64 MW	46.08 TQ	LABLS	1/08-3/08
	Baton Rouge MSA, LA	Y	44070 FQ	67720 MW	139290 TQ	USBLS	5/07
	New Orleans-Metairie-Kenner MSA, LA	Y	44850 FQ	59170 MW	85630 TQ	USBLS	5/07
	Maine	Y	44990 FQ	65230 MW	103750 TQ	USBLS	5/07
	Portland-South Portland-Biddeford MSA, ME	Y	46950 FQ	70160 MW	108080 TQ	USBLS	5/07
	Maryland	Y		59175 MW		MDBLS	3/08
	Baltimore-Towson MSA, MD	Y	46780 FQ	65160 MW	109090 TQ	USBLS	5/07
	Bethesda-Gaithersburg-Frederick PMSA, MD	Y	35100 FQ	51220 MW	67390 TQ	USBLS	5/07
	Massachusetts	Y	55590 FQ	84030 MW		USBLS	5/07
	Boston-Cambridge-Quincy NECTA, MA	Y	57990 FQ	86220 MW		USBLS	5/07
	Springfield MSA, MA-CT	Y	66320 FQ	83970 MW		USBLS	5/07
	Worcester MSA, MA-CT	Y	39730 FQ	66430 MW	99900 TQ	USBLS	5/07
	Michigan	Y	36820 FQ	63550 MW	113220 TQ	USBLS	5/07
	Detroit-Warren-Livonia MSA, MI	Y	37320 FQ	66250 MW	119440 TQ	USBLS	5/07
	Grand Rapids-Wyoming MSA, MI	Y	37070 FQ	69970 MW	123180 TQ	USBLS	5/07
	Warren-Troy-Farmington Hills PMSA, MI	Y	37250 FQ	66520 MW	132740 TQ	USBLS	5/07
	Minnesota	Y	45125 FQ	75565 MW	147573 TQ	MNBLS	10/08-12/08
	Duluth-Superior MSA, MN-WI	Y	37533 FQ	67576 MW	139463 TQ	MNBLS	10/08-12/08
	Minneapolis-Saint Paul MSA, MN-WI	Y	45288 FQ	75443 MW	145855 TQ	MNBLS	10/08-12/08
	Rochester MSA, MN	Y	77896 FQ	141333 MW		MNBLS	10/08-12/08
	Mississippi	Y	37740 FQ	64230 MW	93470 TQ	USBLS	5/07
	Jackson MSA, MS	Y	40970 FQ	70940 MW	114630 TQ	USBLS	5/07
	Missouri	Y	40190 FQ	58650 MW	92460 TQ	USBLS	5/07
	Joplin MSA, MO	Y	18960 FQ	81640 MW	95230 TQ	USBLS	5/07
	Kansas City MSA, MO-KS	Y	48120 FQ	72160 MW	139220 TQ	USBLS	5/07
	St. Louis MSA, MO-IL	Y	37350 FQ	52590 MW	80540 TQ	USBLS	5/07
	Montana	Y	27540 FQ	37580 MW	104020 TQ	USBLS	5/07
	Billings MSA, MT	Y	24300 FQ	44870 MW	104040 TQ	USBLS	5/07
	Nebraska	Y	31660 FQ	39960 MW	66740 TQ	USBLS	5/07
	Omaha-Council Bluffs MSA, NE-IA	Y	32370 FQ	39690 MW	63420 TQ	USBLS	5/07

AE	Average entry wage	**AW**	Average wage paid	**FQ**	First quartile wage	**LO**	Lowest wage paid	**MTC**	Median total compensation	**TCC** Total cash compensation
AER	Average entry range	**AWR**	Average wage range	**H**	Hourly	**LR**	Low end range	**MW**	Median wage paid	**TQ** Third quartile wage
AEX	Average experienced wage	**AXR**	Average experienced range	**HI**	Highest wage paid	**M**	Monthly	**MWR**	Median wage range	**W** Weekly
ATC	Average total compensation	**D**	Daily	**HR**	High end range	**MCC**	Median cash compensation	**S**	See annotated source	**Y** Yearly

Occupation/Type/Industry	Location	Per	Low	Mid	High	Source	Date
Securities, Commodities, and Financial Services Sales Agent	Nevada	H	12.60 FQ	16.76 MW	32.75 TQ	NVBLS	5/08
	Las Vegas-Paradise MSA, NV	H	12.44 FQ	22.52 MW	36.21 TQ	NVBLS	5/08
	New Hampshire	H	18.52 AE	25.57 MW	40.96 AEX	NHBLS	6/08
	Manchester MSA, NH	Y	47440 FQ	58830 MW	85970 TQ	USBLS	5/07
	Nashua NECTA, NH-MA	Y	37940 FQ	44390 MW	53190 TQ	USBLS	5/07
	New Jersey	Y	47740 FQ	82970 MW		USBLS	5/07
	Camden PMSA, NJ	Y	43640 FQ	79830 MW		USBLS	5/07
	Edison PMSA, NJ	Y	46870 FQ	73300 MW	138380 TQ	USBLS	5/07
	Newark-Union PMSA, NJ-PA	Y	48570 FQ	85450 MW	140680 TQ	USBLS	5/07
	New Mexico	Y	40010 FQ	68260 MW	109610 TQ	USBLS	5/07
	Albuquerque MSA, NM	Y	35680 FQ	70290 MW	101520 TQ	USBLS	5/07
	New York	Y	57410 FQ	96140 MW		USBLS	5/07
	Albany-Schenectady-Troy MSA, NY	Y	43160 FQ	56540 MW	80550 TQ	USBLS	5/07
	Buffalo-Niagara Falls MSA, NY	Y	46670 FQ	73060 MW	114950 TQ	USBLS	5/07
	Nassau-Suffolk PMSA, NY	Y	43630 FQ	65530 MW	129840 TQ	USBLS	5/07
	New York-Northern New Jersey-Long Island MSA, NY-NJ-PA	Y	56570 FQ	96590 MW		USBLS	5/07
	North Carolina	Y	53540 FQ	74660 MW	106700 TQ	USBLS	5/07
	Charlotte-Gastonia-Concord MSA, NC-SC	Y	56870 FQ	81530 MW	121090 TQ	USBLS	5/07
	Raleigh-Cary MSA, NC	Y	54270 FQ	66930 MW	90040 TQ	USBLS	5/07
	North Dakota	Y	33740 FQ	43660 MW	71800 TQ	USBLS	5/07
	Fargo MSA, ND-MN	Y	35290 FQ	42870 MW	60890 TQ	USBLS	5/07
	Ohio	Y	36340 FQ	52100 MW	83020 TQ	USBLS	5/07
	Cincinnati-Middletown MSA, OH-KY-IN	Y	36520 FQ	53260 MW	86230 TQ	USBLS	5/07
	Cleveland-Elyria-Mentor MSA, OH	Y	40120 FQ	57250 MW	90620 TQ	USBLS	5/07
	Columbus MSA, OH	Y	38340 FQ	56070 MW	90070 TQ	USBLS	5/07
	Dayton MSA, OH	Y	24530 FQ	39860 MW	68910 TQ	USBLS	5/07
	Oklahoma	Y	32430 FQ	50800 MW	81340 TQ	USBLS	5/07
	Oklahoma City MSA, OK	Y	33610 FQ	47580 MW	64630 TQ	USBLS	5/07
	Tulsa MSA, OK	Y	33050 FQ	55570 MW	98460 TQ	USBLS	5/07
	Oregon	H	20.08 FQ	32.85 MW	54.51 TQ	ORBLS	5/08
	Portland-Vancouver-Beaverton MSA, OR-WA	Y	40840 FQ	67390 MW	112350 TQ	USBLS	5/07
	Pennsylvania	Y	38860 FQ	57020 MW	103430 TQ	USBLS	5/07
	Allentown-Bethlehem-Easton MSA, PA-NJ	Y	31920 FQ	60430 MW	142830 TQ	USBLS	5/07
	Philadelphia-Camden-Wilmington MSA, PA-NJ-DE-MD	Y	40660 FQ	60260 MW	111040 TQ	USBLS	5/07
	Pittsburgh MSA, PA	Y	40460 FQ	59300 MW	100500 TQ	USBLS	5/07
	Rhode Island	Y	41880 FQ	62990 MW	114000 TQ	USBLS	5/07
	Providence-Fall River-Warwick MSA, RI-MA	Y	42120 FQ	64920 MW	114580 TQ	USBLS	5/07
	South Carolina	Y	34980 FQ	50050 MW	91010 TQ	USBLS	5/07
	Charleston-North Charleston MSA, SC	Y	38880 FQ	64220 MW	119650 TQ	USBLS	5/07
	Columbia MSA, SC	Y	39830 FQ	56040 MW	105060 TQ	USBLS	5/07
	South Dakota	Y	91196 FQ	123903 MW		SDBLS	7/08-9/08
	Sioux Falls MSA, SD	Y	98537 FQ	139094 MW		SDBLS	7/08-9/08
	Tennessee	Y	41720 FQ	82000 MW		USBLS	5/07
	Memphis MSA, TN-MS-AR	Y	52820 FQ	90640 MW		USBLS	5/07
	Nashville-Davidson-Murfreesboro MSA, TN	Y	34180 FQ	51330 MW	117750 TQ	USBLS	5/07
	Texas	Y	36220 FQ	62900 MW	121300 TQ	USBLS	5/07
	Austin-Round Rock MSA, TX	Y	34980 FQ	52520 MW	108710 TQ	USBLS	5/07
	Dallas-Fort Worth-Arlington MSA, TX	Y	37250 FQ	62300 MW	102380 TQ	USBLS	5/07
	El Paso MSA, TX	Y	35380 FQ	59380 MW	79060 TQ	USBLS	5/07
	Houston-Sugar Land-Baytown MSA, TX	Y	37570 FQ	77400 MW		USBLS	5/07
	San Antonio MSA, TX	Y	29110 FQ	46310 MW	75360 TQ	USBLS	5/07
	Utah	Y	34710 FQ	46980 MW	113140 TQ	USBLS	5/07
	Logan MSA, UT-ID	Y	43470 FQ	48880 MW	64400 TQ	USBLS	5/07
	Salt Lake City MSA, UT	Y	35800 FQ	50380 MW	135380 TQ	USBLS	5/07
	Vermont	Y	36360 FQ	57640 MW	87790 TQ	USBLS	5/07

AE Average entry wage	**AW** Average wage paid	**FQ** First quartile wage	**LO** Lowest wage paid	**MTC** Median total compensation	**TCC** Total cash compensation
AER Average entry range	**AWR** Average wage range	**H** Hourly	**LR** Low end range	**MW** Median wage paid	**TQ** Third quartile wage
AEX Average experienced wage	**AXR** Average experienced range	**HI** Highest wage paid	**M** Monthly	**MWR** Median wage range	**W** Weekly
ATC Average total compensation	**D** Daily	**HR** High end range	**MCC** Median cash compensation	**S** See annotated source	**Y** Yearly

Occupation/Type/Industry	Location	Per	Low	Mid	High	Source	Date
Securities, Commodities, and Financial Services Sales Agent	Burlington-South Burlington MSA, VT	Y	35140 FQ	47430 MW	80600 TQ	USBLS	5/07
	Virginia	Y	39180 FQ	55080 MW	92600 TQ	USBLS	5/07
	Richmond MSA, VA	Y	41820 FQ	54460 MW	102370 TQ	USBLS	5/07
	Roanoke MSA, VA	Y	34120 FQ	44880 MW	99850 TQ	USBLS	5/07
	Virginia Beach-Norfolk-Newport News MSA, VA-NC	Y	39430 FQ	59500 MW	92630 TQ	USBLS	5/07
	Washington	H	19.45 FQ	31.08 MW	46.97 TQ	WABLS	3/08
	Seattle-Tacoma-Bellevue MSA, WA	Y	40280 FQ	66720 MW	101490 TQ	USBLS	5/07
	Parkersburg-Marietta-Vienna MSA, WV-OH	Y	41800 FQ	78540 MW	96310 TQ	USBLS	5/07
	Wheeling MSA, WV-OH	Y	25830 FQ	43470 MW	77680 TQ	USBLS	5/07
	Wisconsin	Y	34700 FQ	46650 MW	94440 TQ	USBLS	5/07
	Green Bay MSA, WI	Y	47130 FQ	52450 MW	67140 TQ	USBLS	5/07
	Milwaukee-Waukesha-West Allis MSA, WI	Y	33650 FQ	44930 MW	92760 TQ	USBLS	5/07
	Wyoming	Y	34206 FQ	42605 MW	82415 TQ	WYBLS	9/08
	Casper MSA, WY	Y	35725 FQ	56897 MW	110088 TQ	WYBLS	9/08
	Puerto Rico	Y	20940 FQ	26200 MW	49370 TQ	USBLS	5/07
	San Juan-Caguas-Guaynabo MSA, PR	Y	21290 FQ	27950 MW	56280 TQ	USBLS	5/07
Security and Fire Alarm Systems Installer	Alabama	Y	24630 FQ	32450 MW	41070 TQ	USBLS	5/07
	Birmingham-Hoover MSA, AL	Y	22230 FQ	34350 MW	42730 TQ	USBLS	5/07
	Mobile MSA, AL	Y	36250 FQ	43450 MW	49350 TQ	USBLS	5/07
	Montgomery MSA, AL	Y	26390 FQ	28590 MW	30740 TQ	USBLS	5/07
	Alaska	Y	37650 FQ	50880 MW	76460 TQ	USBLS	5/07
	Arizona	Y	29260 FQ	38600 MW	49360 TQ	USBLS	5/07
	Phoenix-Mesa-Scottsdale MSA, AZ	Y	29040 FQ	39390 MW	50060 TQ	USBLS	5/07
	Tucson MSA, AZ	Y	31350 FQ	35920 MW	42060 TQ	USBLS	5/07
	Arkansas	Y	21590 FQ	28340 MW	33930 TQ	USBLS	5/07
	Fort Smith MSA, AR-OK	Y	18010 FQ	28240 MW	31440 TQ	USBLS	5/07
	Little Rock-North Little Rock MSA, AR	Y	22840 FQ	30310 MW	36880 TQ	USBLS	5/07
	California	H	15.39 FQ	18.85 MW	24.65 TQ	CABLS	1/08-3/08
	Los Angeles-Long Beach-Glendale PMSA, CA	H	15.39 FQ	19.01 MW	24.19 TQ	CABLS	1/08-3/08
	Oakland-Fremont-Hayward MSA, CA	H	17.85 FQ	22.44 MW	29.14 TQ	CABLS	1/08-3/08
	Riverside-San Bernardino-Ontario MSA, CA	H	14.10 FQ	16.85 MW	19.46 TQ	CABLS	1/08-3/08
	Sacramento-Arden Arcade-Roseville MSA, CA	H	12.35 FQ	17.33 MW	23.32 TQ	CABLS	1/08-3/08
	San Diego-Carlsbad-San Marcos MSA, CA	H	14.12 FQ	19.29 MW	24.08 TQ	CABLS	1/08-3/08
	San Francisco-San Mateo-Redwood PMSA, CA	H	18.87 FQ	22.83 MW	30.37 TQ	CABLS	1/08-3/08
	San Jose-Sunnyvale-Santa Clara MSA, CA	H	14.54 FQ	17.75 MW	24.31 TQ	CABLS	1/08-3/08
	Santa Ana-Anaheim-Irvine PMSA, CA	Y	32550 FQ	40870 MW	55690 TQ	USBLS	5/07
	Colorado	Y	29840 FQ	38340 MW	48000 TQ	USBLS	5/07
	Denver-Aurora MSA, CO	Y	30730 FQ	39080 MW	49700 TQ	USBLS	5/07
	Connecticut	H	15.53 AE	22.45 MW		CTBLS	1/08-3/08
	Bridgeport-Stamford-Norwalk MSA, CT	Y	41670 FQ	45420 MW	49180 TQ	USBLS	5/07
	Hartford-West Hartford-East Hartford MSA, CT	Y	36720 FQ	45870 MW	53050 TQ	USBLS	5/07
	New Haven MSA, CT	Y	35180 FQ	44940 MW	58850 TQ	USBLS	5/07
	Delaware	Y	29410 FQ	37170 MW	46670 TQ	USBLS	5/07
	Wilmington PMSA, DE-MD-NJ	Y	31000 FQ	39270 MW	49090 TQ	USBLS	5/07
	Washington-Arlington-Alexandria MSA, DC-VA-MD-WV	Y	33330 FQ	39950 MW	49540 TQ	USBLS	5/07
	Florida	Y	25710 FQ	31350 MW	38510 TQ	USBLS	5/07

AE Average entry wage	**AW** Average wage paid	**FQ** First quartile wage	**LO** Lowest wage paid	**MTC** Median total compensation	**TCC** Total cash compensation
AER Average entry range	**AWR** Average wage range	**H** Hourly	**LR** Low end range	**MW** Median wage paid	**TQ** Third quartile wage
AEX Average experienced wage	**AXR** Average experienced range	**HI** Highest wage paid	**M** Monthly	**MWR** Median wage range	**W** Weekly
ATC Average total compensation	**D** Daily	**HR** High end range	**MCC** Median cash compensation	**S** See annotated source	**Y** Yearly

1448

Occupation/Type/Industry	Location	Per	Low	Mid	High	Source	Date
Security and Fire Alarm Systems Installer	Fort Lauderdale-Pompano Beach-Deerfield Beach PMSA, FL	Y	27170 FQ	34230 MW	40260 TQ	USBLS	5/07
	Jacksonville MSA, FL	Y	24390 FQ	28410 MW	33040 TQ	USBLS	5/07
	Miami-Fort Lauderdale-Miami Beach MSA, FL	Y	24970 FQ	29520 MW	37420 TQ	USBLS	5/07
	Orlando-Kissimmee MSA, FL	Y	28920 FQ	34620 MW	44050 TQ	USBLS	5/07
	Tampa-St. Petersburg-Clearwater MSA, FL	Y	26110 FQ	33480 MW	40160 TQ	USBLS	5/07
	West Palm Beach-Boca Raton-Boynton Beach PMSA, FL	Y	23490 FQ	29430 MW	38750 TQ	USBLS	5/07
	Georgia	Y	26800 FQ	30820 MW	38900 TQ	USBLS	5/07
	Atlanta-Sandy Springs-Marietta MSA, GA	Y	27130 FQ	31050 MW	39580 TQ	USBLS	5/07
	Hawaii	Y	32300 FQ	38270 MW	45550 TQ	USBLS	5/07
	Honolulu MSA, HI	Y	32300 FQ	38640 MW	45980 TQ	USBLS	5/07
	Idaho	Y	23190 FQ	28510 MW	33910 TQ	USBLS	5/07
	Illinois	Y	33410 FQ	42560 MW	65490 TQ	USBLS	5/07
	Chicago-Naperville-Joliet MSA, IL-IN-WI	Y	33340 FQ	45060 MW	66960 TQ	USBLS	5/07
	Indiana	Y	23520 FQ	30560 MW	42580 TQ	USBLS	5/07
	Gary PMSA, IN	Y	25540 FQ	33710 MW	47280 TQ	USBLS	5/07
	Indianapolis-Carmel MSA, IN	Y	23990 FQ	30950 MW	44240 TQ	USBLS	5/07
	Iowa	Y	29500 FQ	37940 MW	46760 TQ	USBLS	5/07
	Des Moines-West Des Moines MSA, IA	Y	30470 FQ	39700 MW	50800 TQ	USBLS	5/07
	Kansas	Y	23940 FQ	30040 MW	37630 TQ	USBLS	5/07
	Wichita MSA, KS	Y	26660 FQ	32410 MW	38590 TQ	USBLS	5/07
	Kentucky	Y	25360 FQ	31313 MW	39232 TQ	KYBLS	2008
	Louisville-Jefferson County MSA, KY-IN	Y	24100 FQ	29890 MW	39050 TQ	USBLS	5/07
	Louisiana	H	12.59 FQ	15.53 MW	18.44 TQ	LABLS	1/08-3/08
	Baton Rouge MSA, LA	Y	25530 FQ	33110 MW	36860 TQ	USBLS	5/07
	New Orleans-Metairie-Kenner MSA, LA	Y	28450 FQ	36310 MW	46660 TQ	USBLS	5/07
	Maine	Y	31940 FQ	39970 MW	47220 TQ	USBLS	5/07
	Portland-South Portland-Biddeford MSA, ME	Y	34590 FQ	42070 MW	47630 TQ	USBLS	5/07
	Maryland	Y		39175 MW		MDBLS	3/08
	Baltimore-Towson MSA, MD	Y	32370 FQ	38540 MW	45580 TQ	USBLS	5/07
	Bethesda-Gaithersburg-Frederick PMSA, MD	Y	31700 FQ	36100 MW	41110 TQ	USBLS	5/07
	Massachusetts	Y	34170 FQ	46360 MW	55770 TQ	USBLS	5/07
	Boston-Cambridge-Quincy NECTA, MA	Y	40940 FQ	49950 MW	59310 TQ	USBLS	5/07
	Worcester MSA, MA-CT	Y	27540 FQ	30120 MW	43830 TQ	USBLS	5/07
	Michigan	Y	28450 FQ	37840 MW	44490 TQ	USBLS	5/07
	Detroit-Warren-Livonia MSA, MI	Y	31980 FQ	39560 MW	46000 TQ	USBLS	5/07
	Grand Rapids-Wyoming MSA, MI	Y	27200 FQ	37640 MW	43260 TQ	USBLS	5/07
	Warren-Troy-Farmington Hills PMSA, MI	Y	35750 FQ	41090 MW	46770 TQ	USBLS	5/07
	Minnesota	Y	32873 FQ	42010 MW	51461 TQ	MNBLS	10/08-12/08
	Duluth-Superior MSA, MN-WI	Y	28311 FQ	37866 MW	47475 TQ	MNBLS	10/08-12/08
	Minneapolis-Saint Paul MSA, MN-WI	Y	35727 FQ	45733 MW	54366 TQ	MNBLS	10/08-12/08
	Mississippi	Y	26570 FQ	34300 MW	41540 TQ	USBLS	5/07
	Jackson MSA, MS	Y	23200 FQ	27880 MW	33570 TQ	USBLS	5/07
	Missouri	Y	25860 FQ	29880 MW	38080 TQ	USBLS	5/07
	Joplin MSA, MO	Y	20980 FQ	23330 MW	26900 TQ	USBLS	5/07
	Kansas City MSA, MO-KS	Y	24670 FQ	30040 MW	36410 TQ	USBLS	5/07
	St. Louis MSA, MO-IL	Y	28230 FQ	34340 MW	45230 TQ	USBLS	5/07
	Montana	Y	26930 FQ	31340 MW	42130 TQ	USBLS	5/07
	Billings MSA, MT	Y	18590 FQ	33520 MW	38740 TQ	USBLS	5/07
	Nebraska	Y	29780 FQ	39370 MW	48320 TQ	USBLS	5/07
	Omaha-Council Bluffs MSA, NE-IA	Y	35040 FQ	43030 MW	51600 TQ	USBLS	5/07
	Nevada	H	17.96 FQ	21.25 MW	26.44 TQ	NVBLS	5/08
	Las Vegas-Paradise MSA, NV	H	18.44 FQ	22.30 MW	27.44 TQ	NVBLS	5/08
	New Hampshire	H	12.73 AE	17.15 MW	20.33 AEX	NHBLS	6/08

AE Average entry wage	**AW** Average wage paid	**FQ** First quartile wage	**LO** Lowest wage paid	**MTC** Median total compensation	**TCC** Total cash compensation
AER Average entry range	**AWR** Average wage range	**H** Hourly	**LR** Low end range	**MW** Median wage paid	**TQ** Third quartile wage
AEX Average experienced wage	**AXR** Average experienced range	**HI** Highest wage paid	**M** Monthly	**MWR** Median wage range	**W** Weekly
ATC Average total compensation	**D** Daily	**HR** High end range	**MCC** Median cash compensation	**S** See annotated source	**Y** Yearly

Occupation/Type/Industry	Location	Per	Low	Mid	High	Source	Date
Security and Fire Alarm Systems Installer							
	Manchester MSA, NH	Y	30510 FQ	35670 MW	39990 TQ	USBLS	5/07
	Nashua NECTA, NH-MA	Y	26020 FQ	34570 MW	46010 TQ	USBLS	5/07
	New Jersey	Y	29800 FQ	38830 MW	50480 TQ	USBLS	5/07
	Camden PMSA, NJ	Y	28300 FQ	33030 MW	47980 TQ	USBLS	5/07
	Edison PMSA, NJ	Y	29260 FQ	36660 MW	44680 TQ	USBLS	5/07
	Newark-Union PMSA, NJ-PA	Y	36300 FQ	45740 MW	55030 TQ	USBLS	5/07
	New Mexico	Y	24980 FQ	32160 MW	41180 TQ	USBLS	5/07
	Albuquerque MSA, NM	Y	26600 FQ	33800 MW	42150 TQ	USBLS	5/07
	New York	Y	27320 FQ	36040 MW	47370 TQ	USBLS	5/07
	Albany-Schenectady-Troy MSA, NY	Y	35240 FQ	41240 MW	52890 TQ	USBLS	5/07
	Buffalo-Niagara Falls MSA, NY	Y	29960 FQ	36650 MW	42360 TQ	USBLS	5/07
	Nassau-Suffolk PMSA, NY	Y	26650 FQ	31750 MW	42560 TQ	USBLS	5/07
	New York-Northern New Jersey-Long Island MSA, NY-NJ-PA	Y	28250 FQ	37380 MW	49190 TQ	USBLS	5/07
	North Carolina	Y	29280 FQ	34910 MW	41390 TQ	USBLS	5/07
	Charlotte-Gastonia-Concord MSA, NC-SC	Y	32000 FQ	39600 MW	53610 TQ	USBLS	5/07
	Raleigh-Cary MSA, NC	Y	28130 FQ	32160 MW	39500 TQ	USBLS	5/07
	North Dakota	Y	30330 FQ	35100 MW	43110 TQ	USBLS	5/07
	Fargo MSA, ND-MN	Y	31330 FQ	35580 MW	43160 TQ	USBLS	5/07
	Ohio	Y	24590 FQ	30810 MW	40620 TQ	USBLS	5/07
	Cincinnati-Middletown MSA, OH-KY-IN	Y	27600 FQ	34490 MW	40470 TQ	USBLS	5/07
	Cleveland-Elyria-Mentor MSA, OH	Y	19560 FQ	24130 MW	37640 TQ	USBLS	5/07
	Columbus MSA, OH	Y	24910 FQ	28860 MW	35980 TQ	USBLS	5/07
	Dayton MSA, OH	Y	26930 FQ	31960 MW	39170 TQ	USBLS	5/07
	Oklahoma	Y	28700 FQ	34410 MW	42670 TQ	USBLS	5/07
	Oklahoma City MSA, OK	Y	28950 FQ	34480 MW	42210 TQ	USBLS	5/07
	Tulsa MSA, OK	Y	30160 FQ	36200 MW	44940 TQ	USBLS	5/07
	Oregon	H	14.79 FQ	21.68 MW	27.98 TQ	ORBLS	5/08
	Portland-Vancouver-Beaverton MSA, OR-WA	Y	36090 FQ	46830 MW	57230 TQ	USBLS	5/07
	Pennsylvania	Y	32380 FQ	39040 MW	48450 TQ	USBLS	5/07
	Allentown-Bethlehem-Easton MSA, PA-NJ	Y	30960 FQ	38450 MW	53850 TQ	USBLS	5/07
	Philadelphia-Camden-Wilmington MSA, PA-NJ-DE-MD	Y	32820 FQ	42160 MW	56660 TQ	USBLS	5/07
	Pittsburgh MSA, PA	Y	33820 FQ	39600 MW	46510 TQ	USBLS	5/07
	Rhode Island	Y	33270 FQ	40480 MW	50130 TQ	USBLS	5/07
	Providence-Fall River-Warwick MSA, RI-MA	Y	32060 FQ	39540 MW	49820 TQ	USBLS	5/07
	South Carolina	Y	28050 FQ	33150 MW	38980 TQ	USBLS	5/07
	Columbia MSA, SC	Y	29260 FQ	35240 MW	42040 TQ	USBLS	5/07
	South Dakota	Y	29803 FQ	34438 MW	38953 TQ	SDBLS	7/08-9/08
	Tennessee	Y	26290 FQ	30410 MW	35830 TQ	USBLS	5/07
	Knoxville MSA, TN	Y	24460 FQ	28370 MW	33010 TQ	USBLS	5/07
	Memphis MSA, TN-MS-AR	Y	27780 FQ	30770 MW	36090 TQ	USBLS	5/07
	Nashville-Davidson-Murfreesboro MSA, TN	Y	26400 FQ	31260 MW	36110 TQ	USBLS	5/07
	Texas	Y	25880 FQ	31760 MW	38860 TQ	USBLS	5/07
	Austin-Round Rock MSA, TX	Y	29860 FQ	35680 MW	42730 TQ	USBLS	5/07
	Dallas-Fort Worth-Arlington MSA, TX	Y	27480 FQ	33990 MW	41070 TQ	USBLS	5/07
	El Paso MSA, TX	Y	23260 FQ	31630 MW	36720 TQ	USBLS	5/07
	Houston-Sugar Land-Baytown MSA, TX	Y	26950 FQ	30720 MW	36570 TQ	USBLS	5/07
	San Antonio MSA, TX	Y	32670 FQ	37570 MW	42810 TQ	USBLS	5/07
	Utah	Y	26580 FQ	35150 MW	42940 TQ	USBLS	5/07
	Ogden-Clearfield MSA, UT	Y	27100 FQ	29880 MW	37920 TQ	USBLS	5/07
	Salt Lake City MSA, UT	Y	25330 FQ	38030 MW	44240 TQ	USBLS	5/07
	Vermont	Y	29340 FQ	35990 MW	46210 TQ	USBLS	5/07
	Burlington-South Burlington MSA, VT	Y	28210 FQ	33840 MW	40610 TQ	USBLS	5/07
	Virginia	Y	28780 FQ	35800 MW	45060 TQ	USBLS	5/07
	Richmond MSA, VA	Y	28470 FQ	34160 MW	39470 TQ	USBLS	5/07

AE	Average entry wage	AW	Average wage paid	FQ	First quartile wage	LO	Lowest wage paid	MTC Median total compensation	TCC Total cash compensation
AER	Average entry range	AWR	Average wage range	H	Hourly	LR	Low end range	MW Median wage paid	TQ Third quartile wage
AEX	Average experienced wage	AXR	Average experienced range	HI	Highest wage paid	M	Monthly	MWR Median wage range	W Weekly
ATC	Average total compensation	D	Daily	HR	High end range	MCC	Median cash compensation	S See annotated source	Y Yearly

Occupation/Type/Industry	Location	Per	Low	Mid	High	Source	Date
Security and Fire Alarm Systems Installer							
	Virginia Beach-Norfolk- Newport News MSA, VA-NC	Y	29520 FQ	34870 MW	40770 TQ	USBLS	5/07
	Washington	H	14.89 FQ	19.63 MW	23.25 TQ	WABLS	3/08
	Seattle-Tacoma-Bellevue MSA, WA	Y	30470 FQ	40440 MW	47100 TQ	USBLS	5/07
	West Virginia	Y	24861 FQ	28949 MW	33923 TQ	WVBLS	7/08-9/08
	Charleston MSA, WV	Y	23260 FQ	26920 MW	30860 TQ	USBLS	5/07
	Wisconsin	Y	30500 FQ	35940 MW	42950 TQ	USBLS	5/07
	Milwaukee-Waukesha-West Allis MSA, WI	Y	36240 FQ	47280 MW	58670 TQ	USBLS	5/07
	Racine MSA, WI	Y	33170 FQ	36020 MW	38870 TQ	USBLS	5/07
	Wyoming	Y	31694 FQ	54777 MW	62496 TQ	WYBLS	9/08
	Puerto Rico	Y	13280 FQ	15510 MW	25290 TQ	USBLS	5/07
	San Juan-Caguas-Guaynabo MSA, PR	Y	12900 FQ	14550 MW	18390 TQ	USBLS	5/07
Security Architect	United States	Y		93900 AW		NWRLD	2009
Security Guard	Alabama	Y	14470 FQ	17740 MW	23190 TQ	USBLS	5/07
	Birmingham-Hoover MSA, AL	Y	14950 FQ	18010 MW	22230 TQ	USBLS	5/07
	Alaska	Y	25020 FQ	29630 MW	38150 TQ	USBLS	5/07
	Anchorage MSA, AK	Y	23050 FQ	28780 MW	37450 TQ	USBLS	5/07
	Fairbanks MSA, AK	Y	25790 FQ	28930 MW	35500 TQ	USBLS	5/07
	Arizona	Y	18040 FQ	21900 MW	26290 TQ	USBLS	5/07
	Phoenix-Mesa-Scottsdale MSA, AZ	Y	18420 FQ	22160 MW	26620 TQ	USBLS	5/07
	Tucson MSA, AZ	Y	16120 FQ	19710 MW	23520 TQ	USBLS	5/07
	Arkansas	Y	15570 FQ	18940 MW	26090 TQ	USBLS	5/07
	Little Rock-North Little Rock MSA, AR	Y	16050 FQ	19410 MW	27690 TQ	USBLS	5/07
	California	H	9.59 FQ	11.24 MW	13.71 TQ	CABLS	1/08-3/08
	Los Angeles-Long Beach- Glendale PMSA, CA	H	9.36 FQ	10.89 MW	12.95 TQ	CABLS	1/08-3/08
	Oakland-Fremont-Hayward MSA, CA	H	10.61 FQ	11.82 MW	13.95 TQ	CABLS	1/08-3/08
	Oxnard-Thousand Oaks- Ventura MSA, CA	H	9.66 FQ	11.35 MW	13.85 TQ	CABLS	1/08-3/08
	Riverside-San Bernardino- Ontario MSA, CA	H	9.05 FQ	10.43 MW	12.22 TQ	CABLS	1/08-3/08
	Sacramento-Arden Arcade- Roseville MSA, CA	H	9.85 FQ	11.22 MW	12.61 TQ	CABLS	1/08-3/08
	San Diego-Carlsbad-San Marcos MSA, CA	H	9.28 FQ	10.83 MW	12.48 TQ	CABLS	1/08-3/08
	San Francisco-San Mateo- Redwood PMSA, CA	H	11.86 FQ	13.74 MW	16.27 TQ	CABLS	1/08-3/08
	San Jose-Sunnyvale-Santa Clara MSA, CA	H	11.30 FQ	13.36 MW	15.86 TQ	CABLS	1/08-3/08
	Santa Ana-Anaheim-Irvine PMSA, CA	Y	19270 FQ	22410 MW	26420 TQ	USBLS	5/07
	Colorado	Y	19090 FQ	24020 MW	29590 TQ	USBLS	5/07
	Denver-Aurora MSA, CO	Y	18750 FQ	23920 MW	29220 TQ	USBLS	5/07
	Connecticut	H	9.73 AE	12.06 MW		CTBLS	1/08-3/08
	Bridgeport-Stamford-Norwalk MSA, CT	Y	19900 FQ	22970 MW	28230 TQ	USBLS	5/07
	Hartford-West Hartford-East Hartford MSA, CT	Y	21370 FQ	25460 MW	32880 TQ	USBLS	5/07
	Delaware	Y	19520 FQ	22930 MW	27030 TQ	USBLS	5/07
	Wilmington PMSA, DE-MD- NJ	Y	19790 FQ	23220 MW	27360 TQ	USBLS	5/07
	District of Columbia	Y	22300 FQ	29860 MW	36460 TQ	USBLS	5/07
	Washington-Arlington- Alexandria MSA, DC-VA- MD-WV	Y	22160 FQ	28770 MW	36560 TQ	USBLS	5/07
	Florida	Y	17470 FQ	20640 MW	24410 TQ	USBLS	5/07
	Fort Lauderdale-Pompano Beach-Deerfield Beach PMSA, FL	Y	17480 FQ	20390 MW	23570 TQ	USBLS	5/07
	Jacksonville MSA, FL	Y	17770 FQ	20440 MW	24060 TQ	USBLS	5/07
	Lakeland MSA, FL	Y	17630 FQ	19900 MW	23140 TQ	USBLS	5/07
	Miami-Fort Lauderdale-Miami Beach MSA, FL	Y	17520 FQ	20780 MW	24240 TQ	USBLS	5/07

AE	Average entry wage	AW	Average wage paid	FQ	First quartile wage	LO	Lowest wage paid	MTC	Median total compensation	TCC	Total cash compensation
AER	Average entry range	AWR	Average wage range	H	Hourly	LR	Low end range	MW	Median wage paid	TQ	Third quartile wage
AEX	Average experienced wage	AXR	Average experienced range	HI	Highest wage paid	M	Monthly	MWR	Median wage range	W	Weekly
ATC	Average total compensation	D	Daily	HR	High end range	MCC	Median cash compensation	S	See annotated source	Y	Yearly

Occupation/Type/Industry	Location	Per	Low	Mid	High	Source	Date
Security Guard	Orlando-Kissimmee MSA, FL	Y	18290 FQ	21610 MW	25050 TQ	USBLS	5/07
	Tampa-St. Petersburg- Clearwater MSA, FL	Y	16860 FQ	19240 MW	22880 TQ	USBLS	5/07
	West Palm Beach-Boca Raton- Boynton Beach PMSA, FL	Y	19480 FQ	22490 MW	25950 TQ	USBLS	5/07
	Georgia	Y	17240 FQ	21190 MW	27240 TQ	USBLS	5/07
	Atlanta-Sandy Springs- Marietta MSA, GA	Y	17960 FQ	21410 MW	25820 TQ	USBLS	5/07
	Hawaii	Y	20330 FQ	23970 MW	30190 TQ	USBLS	5/07
	Honolulu MSA, HI	Y	19830 FQ	23390 MW	29460 TQ	USBLS	5/07
	Idaho	Y	18410 FQ	22200 MW	28240 TQ	USBLS	5/07
	Boise City-Nampa MSA, ID	Y	18520 FQ	21470 MW	26710 TQ	USBLS	5/07
	Lewiston MSA, ID-WA	Y	14010 FQ	20500 MW	23340 TQ	USBLS	5/07
	Illinois	Y	19750 FQ	23520 MW	29580 TQ	USBLS	5/07
	Chicago-Naperville-Joliet MSA, IL-IN-WI	Y	19910 FQ	23620 MW	29590 TQ	USBLS	5/07
	Indiana	Y	18170 FQ	22100 MW	28490 TQ	USBLS	5/07
	Gary PMSA, IN	Y	18190 FQ	21740 MW	29800 TQ	USBLS	5/07
	Indianapolis-Carmel MSA, IN	Y	19350 FQ	22400 MW	27730 TQ	USBLS	5/07
	Terre Haute MSA, IN	Y	14620 FQ	18050 MW	24250 TQ	USBLS	5/07
	Iowa	Y	17220 FQ	20880 MW	26370 TQ	USBLS	5/07
	Cedar Rapids MSA, IA	Y	17190 FQ	19170 MW	23280 TQ	USBLS	5/07
	Des Moines-West Des Moines MSA, IA	Y	17410 FQ	21130 MW	28360 TQ	USBLS	5/07
	Sioux City MSA, IA-NE-SD	Y	17110 FQ	19730 MW	25730 TQ	USBLS	5/07
	Waterloo-Cedar Falls MSA, IA	Y	21000 FQ	23850 MW	33070 TQ	USBLS	5/07
	Kansas	Y	18410 FQ	23160 MW	31720 TQ	USBLS	5/07
	Wichita MSA, KS	Y	17940 FQ	20120 MW	30090 TQ	USBLS	5/07
	Kentucky	Y	17575 FQ	20508 MW	26086 TQ	KYBLS	2008
	Lexington-Fayette MSA, KY	Y	16570 FQ	19100 MW	22930 TQ	USBLS	5/07
	Louisville-Jefferson County MSA, KY-IN	Y	17750 FQ	20720 MW	24900 TQ	USBLS	5/07
	Louisiana	H	7.86 FQ	9.67 MW	12.28 TQ	LABLS	1/08-3/08
	Baton Rouge MSA, LA	Y	17310 FQ	21610 MW	28480 TQ	USBLS	5/07
	New Orleans-Metairie-Kenner MSA, LA	Y	16970 FQ	21050 MW	26040 TQ	USBLS	5/07
	Maine	Y	18870 FQ	22340 MW	28010 TQ	USBLS	5/07
	Portland-South Portland- Biddeford MSA, ME	Y	19270 FQ	22660 MW	27990 TQ	USBLS	5/07
	Maryland	Y		26625 MW		MDBLS	3/08
	Baltimore-Towson MSA, MD	Y	20490 FQ	24120 MW	32680 TQ	USBLS	5/07
	Bethesda-Gaithersburg- Frederick PMSA, MD	Y	22270 FQ	30700 MW	39100 TQ	USBLS	5/07
	Salisbury MSA, MD	Y	17250 FQ	21540 MW	33500 TQ	USBLS	5/07
	Massachusetts	Y	21470 FQ	24800 MW	29840 TQ	USBLS	5/07
	Boston-Cambridge-Quincy NECTA, MA	Y	21780 FQ	25000 MW	29850 TQ	USBLS	5/07
	Worcester MSA, MA-CT	Y	21500 FQ	24610 MW	28850 TQ	USBLS	5/07
	Michigan	Y	19290 FQ	24090 MW	30670 TQ	USBLS	5/07
	Detroit-Warren-Livonia MSA, MI	Y	19950 FQ	25560 MW	32210 TQ	USBLS	5/07
	Grand Rapids-Wyoming MSA, MI	Y	18220 FQ	21320 MW	26040 TQ	USBLS	5/07
	Lansing-East Lansing MSA, MI	Y	17880 FQ	20140 MW	24780 TQ	USBLS	5/07
	Warren-Troy-Farmington Hills PMSA, MI	Y	19740 FQ	24150 MW	29260 TQ	USBLS	5/07
	Minnesota	Y	22720 FQ	27091 MW	32789 TQ	MNBLS	10/08-12/08
	Duluth-Superior MSA, MN-WI	Y	18695 FQ	21936 MW	28418 TQ	MNBLS	10/08-12/08
	Minneapolis-Saint Paul MSA, MN-WI	Y	23347 FQ	27509 MW	33113 TQ	MNBLS	10/08-12/08
	Rochester MSA, MN	Y	22705 FQ	28124 MW	33805 TQ	MNBLS	10/08-12/08
	Mississippi	Y	15410 FQ	18360 MW	22510 TQ	USBLS	5/07
	Gulfport-Biloxi MSA, MS	Y	17010 FQ	20150 MW	26860 TQ	USBLS	5/07
	Jackson MSA, MS	Y	15330 FQ	17900 MW	20460 TQ	USBLS	5/07
	Missouri	Y	19120 FQ	23060 MW	30500 TQ	USBLS	5/07
	Kansas City MSA, MO-KS	Y	21830 FQ	26580 MW	35550 TQ	USBLS	5/07
	St. Louis MSA, MO-IL	Y	18620 FQ	22300 MW	29690 TQ	USBLS	5/07
	Montana	Y	16600 FQ	20310 MW	24160 TQ	USBLS	5/07
	Billings MSA, MT	Y	15190 FQ	19190 MW	22680 TQ	USBLS	5/07
	Nebraska	Y	18220 FQ	22980 MW	29740 TQ	USBLS	5/07
	Omaha-Council Bluffs MSA, NE-IA	Y	20640 FQ	24950 MW	30840 TQ	USBLS	5/07

AE	Average entry wage	AW	Average wage paid	FQ	First quartile wage	LO	Lowest wage paid	MTC	Median total compensation	TCC	Total cash compensation
AER	Average entry range	AWR	Average wage range	H	Hourly	LR	Low end range	MW	Median wage paid	TQ	Third quartile wage
AEX	Average experienced wage	AXR	Average experienced range	HI	Highest wage paid	M	Monthly	MWR	Median wage range	W	Weekly
ATC	Average total compensation	D	Daily	HR	High end range	MCC	Median cash compensation	S	See annotated source	Y	Yearly

Occupation/Type/Industry	Location	Per	Low	Mid	High	Source	Date
Security Guard	Nevada	H	9.65 FQ	11.65 MW	14.85 TQ	NVBLS	5/08
	Carson City MSA, NV	H	9.85 FQ	13.26 MW	17.66 TQ	NVBLS	5/08
	Las Vegas-Paradise MSA, NV	H	9.65 FQ	11.69 MW	14.86 TQ	NVBLS	5/08
	New Hampshire	H	10.45 AE	12.91 MW	15.10 AEX	NHBLS	6/08
	Manchester MSA, NH	Y	24040 FQ	26950 MW	30890 TQ	USBLS	5/07
	Nashua NECTA, NH-MA	Y	23770 FQ	27630 MW	32290 TQ	USBLS	5/07
	New Jersey	Y	19390 FQ	23700 MW	31000 TQ	USBLS	5/07
	Camden PMSA, NJ	Y	18200 FQ	21980 MW	27650 TQ	USBLS	5/07
	Edison PMSA, NJ	Y	20390 FQ	23980 MW	30430 TQ	USBLS	5/07
	Newark-Union PMSA, NJ-PA	Y	20220 FQ	25520 MW	33640 TQ	USBLS	5/07
	New Mexico	Y	17770 FQ	21690 MW	28770 TQ	USBLS	5/07
	Albuquerque MSA, NM	Y	17650 FQ	20960 MW	25510 TQ	USBLS	5/07
	New York	Y	19500 FQ	24550 MW	33470 TQ	USBLS	5/07
	Albany-Schenectady-Troy MSA, NY	Y	19560 FQ	24620 MW	30990 TQ	USBLS	5/07
	Buffalo-Niagara Falls MSA, NY	Y	15730 FQ	19090 MW	24890 TQ	USBLS	5/07
	Glens Falls MSA, NY	Y	16840 FQ	19900 MW	26130 TQ	USBLS	5/07
	Ithaca MSA, NY	Y	22660 FQ	28110 MW	33890 TQ	USBLS	5/07
	Nassau-Suffolk PMSA, NY	Y	21450 FQ	27740 MW	36690 TQ	USBLS	5/07
	New York-Northern New Jersey-Long Island MSA, NY-NJ-PA	Y	19910 FQ	24770 MW	33400 TQ	USBLS	5/07
	North Carolina	Y	17350 FQ	21060 MW	26590 TQ	USBLS	5/07
	Charlotte-Gastonia-Concord MSA, NC-SC	Y	17120 FQ	20760 MW	25490 TQ	USBLS	5/07
	Raleigh-Cary MSA, NC	Y	18070 FQ	21800 MW	25810 TQ	USBLS	5/07
	North Dakota	Y	18550 FQ	23060 MW	29330 TQ	USBLS	5/07
	Fargo MSA, ND-MN	Y	15930 FQ	19580 MW	23750 TQ	USBLS	5/07
	Ohio	Y	17730 FQ	21360 MW	27260 TQ	USBLS	5/07
	Cincinnati-Middletown MSA, OH-KY-IN	Y	18250 FQ	21870 MW	27920 TQ	USBLS	5/07
	Cleveland-Elyria-Mentor MSA, OH	Y	18170 FQ	21310 MW	26910 TQ	USBLS	5/07
	Columbus MSA, OH	Y	19770 FQ	22830 MW	27640 TQ	USBLS	5/07
	Dayton MSA, OH	Y	16770 FQ	20010 MW	26230 TQ	USBLS	5/07
	Oklahoma	Y	18230 FQ	21580 MW	29170 TQ	USBLS	5/07
	Oklahoma City MSA, OK	Y	18500 FQ	23060 MW	35770 TQ	USBLS	5/07
	Tulsa MSA, OK	Y	18310 FQ	20560 MW	24530 TQ	USBLS	5/07
	Oregon	H	9.22 FQ	10.80 MW	13.12 TQ	ORBLS	5/08
	Portland-Vancouver-Beaverton MSA, OR-WA	Y	18900 FQ	22260 MW	27040 TQ	USBLS	5/07
	Pennsylvania	Y	18100 FQ	21560 MW	26400 TQ	USBLS	5/07
	Allentown-Bethlehem-Easton MSA, PA-NJ	Y	18690 FQ	22970 MW	29220 TQ	USBLS	5/07
	Lancaster MSA, PA	Y	20700 FQ	24070 MW	29060 TQ	USBLS	5/07
	Philadelphia-Camden-Wilmington MSA, PA-NJ-DE-MD	Y	18330 FQ	21490 MW	25910 TQ	USBLS	5/07
	Pittsburgh MSA, PA	Y	17900 FQ	21940 MW	26760 TQ	USBLS	5/07
	Rhode Island	Y	19990 FQ	24600 MW	30950 TQ	USBLS	5/07
	Providence-Fall River-Warwick MSA, RI-MA	Y	19510 FQ	24040 MW	30480 TQ	USBLS	5/07
	South Carolina	Y	16910 FQ	20800 MW	28690 TQ	USBLS	5/07
	Charleston-North Charleston MSA, SC	Y	15900 FQ	19210 MW	25670 TQ	USBLS	5/07
	Columbia MSA, SC	Y	16160 FQ	20390 MW	27450 TQ	USBLS	5/07
	South Dakota	Y	18513 FQ	21633 MW	25476 TQ	SDBLS	7/08-9/08
	Sioux Falls MSA, SD	Y	19716 FQ	23410 MW	28942 TQ	SDBLS	7/08-9/08
	Tennessee	Y	16890 FQ	19450 MW	24190 TQ	USBLS	5/07
	Memphis MSA, TN-MS-AR	Y	16850 FQ	18940 MW	22730 TQ	USBLS	5/07
	Nashville-Davidson-Murfreesboro MSA, TN	Y	17420 FQ	19680 MW	25320 TQ	USBLS	5/07
	Texas	Y	17260 FQ	21020 MW	27200 TQ	USBLS	5/07
	Austin-Round Rock MSA, TX	Y	18430 FQ	22860 MW	27740 TQ	USBLS	5/07
	Dallas-Fort Worth-Arlington MSA, TX	Y	19160 FQ	22980 MW	29310 TQ	USBLS	5/07
	El Paso MSA, TX	Y	13850 FQ	17190 MW	23430 TQ	USBLS	5/07
	Houston-Sugar Land-Baytown MSA, TX	Y	17320 FQ	20210 MW	25770 TQ	USBLS	5/07
	San Antonio MSA, TX	Y	16550 FQ	19300 MW	24960 TQ	USBLS	5/07
	Utah	Y	19560 FQ	23220 MW	30340 TQ	USBLS	5/07

AE Average entry wage	**AW** Average wage paid	**FQ** First quartile wage	**LO** Lowest wage paid	**MTC** Median total compensation	**TCC** Total cash compensation
AER Average entry range	**AWR** Average wage range	**H** Hourly	**LR** Low end range	**MW** Median wage paid	**TQ** Third quartile wage
AEX Average experienced wage	**AXR** Average experienced range	**HI** Highest wage paid	**M** Monthly	**MWR** Median wage range	**W** Weekly
ATC Average total compensation	**D** Daily	**HR** High end range	**MCC** Median cash compensation	**S** See annotated source	**Y** Yearly

Occupation/Type/Industry	Location	Per	Low	Mid	High	Source	Date
Security Guard	Salt Lake City MSA, UT	Y	19390 FQ	22840 MW	30260 TQ	USBLS	5/07
	Vermont	Y	22270 FQ	26430 MW	33070 TQ	USBLS	5/07
	Burlington-South Burlington MSA, VT	Y	22040 FQ	25660 MW	29580 TQ	USBLS	5/07
	Virginia	Y	19410 FQ	24190 MW	32180 TQ	USBLS	5/07
	Richmond MSA, VA	Y	19370 FQ	23520 MW	30770 TQ	USBLS	5/07
	Virginia Beach-Norfolk-Newport News MSA, VA-NC	Y	16310 FQ	20490 MW	28780 TQ	USBLS	5/07
	Washington	H	10.38 FQ	12.36 MW	16.46 TQ	WABLS	3/08
	Seattle-Tacoma-Bellevue MSA, WA	Y	21730 FQ	25600 MW	34260 TQ	USBLS	5/07
	Spokane MSA, WA	Y	18630 FQ	21600 MW	27070 TQ	USBLS	5/07
	West Virginia	Y	15285 FQ	18357 MW	24197 TQ	WVBLS	7/08-9/08
	Charleston MSA, WV	Y	14400 FQ	16910 MW	22980 TQ	USBLS	5/07
	Huntington-Ashland MSA, WV-KY-OH	Y	14500 FQ	17370 MW	20470 TQ	USBLS	5/07
	Wisconsin	Y	18930 FQ	22840 MW	28800 TQ	USBLS	5/07
	Milwaukee-Waukesha-West Allis MSA, WI	Y	19880 FQ	23520 MW	29700 TQ	USBLS	5/07
	Wyoming	Y	20059 FQ	24582 MW	31255 TQ	WYBLS	9/08
	Cheyenne MSA, WY	Y	19119 FQ	23605 MW	34609 TQ	WYBLS	9/08
	Puerto Rico	Y	12680 FQ	14270 MW	16300 TQ	USBLS	5/07
	San Juan-Caguas-Guaynabo MSA, PR	Y	12640 FQ	14190 MW	16040 TQ	USBLS	5/07
	Virgin Islands	Y	14800 FQ	18470 MW	23620 TQ	USBLS	5/07
	Guam	Y	12520 FQ	13950 MW	15430 TQ	USBLS	5/07
Security Supervisor Municipal Government	Cincinnati, OH	Y	33351 LO		45924 HI	COHSS	10/08
Seed Analyst State Government	Ohio	H	17.22 LO		21.77 HI	ODAS	2008
Segmental Paver	Arizona	Y	27410 FQ	29150 MW	30890 TQ	USBLS	5/07
	California	H	12.67 FQ	17.53 MW	19.76 TQ	CABLS	1/08-3/08
	South Carolina	Y	18080 FQ	20130 MW	28790 TQ	USBLS	5/07
	Texas	Y	17820 FQ	23090 MW	29220 TQ	USBLS	5/07
Self-Enrichment Education Teacher	Alabama	Y	23290 FQ	35600 MW	45930 TQ	USBLS	5/07
	Birmingham-Hoover MSA, AL	Y	26440 FQ	38790 MW	47240 TQ	USBLS	5/07
	Tuscaloosa MSA, AL	Y	31950 FQ	34320 MW	36680 TQ	USBLS	5/07
	Alaska	Y	32340 FQ	43580 MW	49900 TQ	USBLS	5/07
	Anchorage MSA, AK	Y	39040 FQ	43990 MW	48700 TQ	USBLS	5/07
	Arizona	Y	25700 FQ	32610 MW	44020 TQ	USBLS	5/07
	Phoenix-Mesa-Scottsdale MSA, AZ	Y	27070 FQ	33140 MW	44730 TQ	USBLS	5/07
	Tucson MSA, AZ	Y	20590 FQ	30050 MW	39160 TQ	USBLS	5/07
	Arkansas	Y	24340 FQ	36320 MW	51400 TQ	USBLS	5/07
	Little Rock-North Little Rock MSA, AR	Y	27070 FQ	47400 MW	84460 TQ	USBLS	5/07
	California	H	12.35 FQ	16.74 MW	26.07 TQ	CABLS	1/08-3/08
	Los Angeles-Long Beach-Glendale PMSA, CA	H	12.91 FQ	16.63 MW	27.44 TQ	CABLS	1/08-3/08
	Oakland-Fremont-Hayward MSA, CA	H	14.81 FQ	20.87 MW	27.62 TQ	CABLS	1/08-3/08
	Oxnard-Thousand Oaks-Ventura MSA, CA	H	15.25 FQ	17.25 MW	20.11 TQ	CABLS	1/08-3/08
	Riverside-San Bernardino-Ontario MSA, CA	H	11.23 FQ	17.68 MW	25.20 TQ	CABLS	1/08-3/08
	Sacramento-Arden Arcade-Roseville MSA, CA	H	11.26 FQ	13.83 MW	20.85 TQ	CABLS	1/08-3/08
	San Diego-Carlsbad-San Marcos MSA, CA	H	13.93 FQ	20.54 MW	29.28 TQ	CABLS	1/08-3/08
	San Francisco-San Mateo-Redwood PMSA, CA	H	12.64 FQ	16.13 MW	23.76 TQ	CABLS	1/08-3/08
	San Jose-Sunnyvale-Santa Clara MSA, CA	H	13.97 FQ	18.05 MW	25.08 TQ	CABLS	1/08-3/08
	Santa Ana-Anaheim-Irvine PMSA, CA	Y	19630 FQ	25840 MW	38510 TQ	USBLS	5/07
	Colorado	Y	22570 FQ	29770 MW	43430 TQ	USBLS	5/07
	Denver-Aurora MSA, CO	Y	24880 FQ	32840 MW	49080 TQ	USBLS	5/07

AE Average entry wage	**AW** Average wage paid	**FQ** First quartile wage	**LO** Lowest wage paid	**MTC** Median total compensation	**TCC** Total cash compensation
AER Average entry range	**AWR** Average wage range	**H** Hourly	**LR** Low end range	**MW** Median wage paid	**TQ** Third quartile wage
AEX Average experienced wage	**AXR** Average experienced range	**HI** Highest wage paid	**M** Monthly	**MWR** Median wage range	**W** Weekly
ATC Average total compensation	**D** Daily	**HR** High end range	**MCC** Median cash compensation	**S** See annotated source	**Y** Yearly

Occupation/Type/Industry	Location	Per	Low	Mid	High	Source	Date
Self-Enrichment Education Teacher	Connecticut	H	13.82 AE	23.96 MW		CTBLS	1/08-3/08
	Bridgeport-Stamford-Norwalk MSA, CT	Y	30400 FQ	48110 MW	75810 TQ	USBLS	5/07
	Hartford-West Hartford-East Hartford MSA, CT	Y	30990 FQ	45710 MW	68540 TQ	USBLS	5/07
	Delaware	Y	32080 FQ	37970 MW	60780 TQ	USBLS	5/07
	Wilmington PMSA, DE-MD-NJ	Y	31140 FQ	37070 MW	52650 TQ	USBLS	5/07
	District of Columbia	Y	32950 FQ	42890 MW	55780 TQ	USBLS	5/07
	Washington-Arlington-Alexandria MSA, DC-VA-MD-WV	Y	26670 FQ	36520 MW	53420 TQ	USBLS	5/07
	Florida	Y	24580 FQ	33290 MW	47910 TQ	USBLS	5/07
	Fort Lauderdale-Pompano Beach-Deerfield Beach PMSA, FL	Y	25710 FQ	30510 MW	40230 TQ	USBLS	5/07
	Jacksonville MSA, FL	Y	21380 FQ	27050 MW	36110 TQ	USBLS	5/07
	Miami-Fort Lauderdale-Miami Beach MSA, FL	Y	29180 FQ	37180 MW	52090 TQ	USBLS	5/07
	Orlando-Kissimmee MSA, FL	Y	26390 FQ	34220 MW	52390 TQ	USBLS	5/07
	Tampa-St. Petersburg-Clearwater MSA, FL	Y	25490 FQ	33150 MW	48070 TQ	USBLS	5/07
	West Palm Beach-Boca Raton-Boynton Beach PMSA, FL	Y	33260 FQ	38070 MW	51760 TQ	USBLS	5/07
	Georgia	Y	24080 FQ	34450 MW	45620 TQ	USBLS	5/07
	Athens-Clarke County MSA, GA	Y	28360 FQ	35150 MW	53950 TQ	USBLS	5/07
	Atlanta-Sandy Springs-Marietta MSA, GA	Y	26380 FQ	34840 MW	42590 TQ	USBLS	5/07
	Hawaii	Y	27590 FQ	35320 MW	47880 TQ	USBLS	5/07
	Honolulu MSA, HI	Y	26220 FQ	34470 MW	49910 TQ	USBLS	5/07
	Idaho	Y	20470 FQ	24400 MW	32620 TQ	USBLS	5/07
	Boise City-Nampa MSA, ID	Y	19400 FQ	22680 MW	26520 TQ	USBLS	5/07
	Illinois	Y	26410 FQ	38010 MW	66030 TQ	USBLS	5/07
	Chicago-Naperville-Joliet MSA, IL-IN-WI	Y	30120 FQ	43920 MW	68270 TQ	USBLS	5/07
	Indiana	Y	22870 FQ	32350 MW	44680 TQ	USBLS	5/07
	Evansville MSA, IN-KY	Y	30950 FQ	36940 MW	67170 TQ	USBLS	5/07
	Gary PMSA, IN	Y	35380 FQ	40490 MW	59440 TQ	USBLS	5/07
	Indianapolis-Carmel MSA, IN	Y	14270 FQ	32160 MW	46150 TQ	USBLS	5/07
	Iowa	Y	21650 FQ	30000 MW	45770 TQ	USBLS	5/07
	Kansas	Y	29060 FQ	33510 MW	37550 TQ	USBLS	5/07
	Wichita MSA, KS	Y	26630 FQ	30470 MW	39670 TQ	USBLS	5/07
	Kentucky	Y	14663 FQ	23354 MW	41129 TQ	KYBLS	2008
	Lexington-Fayette MSA, KY	Y	13650 FQ	18040 MW	40900 TQ	USBLS	5/07
	Louisville-Jefferson County MSA, KY-IN	Y	22220 FQ	26390 MW	36540 TQ	USBLS	5/07
	Louisiana	H	16.29 FQ	19.01 MW	22.26 TQ	LABLS	1/08-3/08
	Baton Rouge MSA, LA	Y	33860 FQ	38480 MW	43430 TQ	USBLS	5/07
	New Orleans-Metairie-Kenner MSA, LA	Y	33940 FQ	41370 MW	48630 TQ	USBLS	5/07
	Maine	Y	22630 FQ	30540 MW	42550 TQ	USBLS	5/07
	Portland-South Portland-Biddeford MSA, ME	Y	23250 FQ	28430 MW	49490 TQ	USBLS	5/07
	Maryland	Y		32775 MW		MDBLS	3/08
	Baltimore-Towson MSA, MD	Y	25820 FQ	30360 MW	47440 TQ	USBLS	5/07
	Bethesda-Gaithersburg-Frederick PMSA, MD	Y	27880 FQ	37570 MW	47490 TQ	USBLS	5/07
	Massachusetts	Y	24730 FQ	34690 MW	48270 TQ	USBLS	5/07
	Boston-Cambridge-Quincy NECTA, MA	Y	23930 FQ	33390 MW	44750 TQ	USBLS	5/07
	Worcester MSA, MA-CT	Y	22450 FQ	36470 MW	48450 TQ	USBLS	5/07
	Michigan	Y	28110 FQ	37660 MW	47470 TQ	USBLS	5/07
	Ann Arbor MSA, MI	Y	29680 FQ	35620 MW	40310 TQ	USBLS	5/07
	Detroit-Warren-Livonia MSA, MI	Y	32410 FQ	40530 MW	50130 TQ	USBLS	5/07
	Grand Rapids-Wyoming MSA, MI	Y	24400 FQ	37430 MW	48280 TQ	USBLS	5/07
	Warren-Troy-Farmington Hills PMSA, MI	Y	31820 FQ	40190 MW	48030 TQ	USBLS	5/07
	Minnesota	Y	26783 FQ	33625 MW	51986 TQ	MNBLS	10/08-12/08

AE Average entry wage	**AW** Average wage paid	**FQ** First quartile wage	**LO** Lowest wage paid	**MTC** Median total compensation	**TCC** Total cash compensation
AER Average entry range	**AWR** Average wage range	**H** Hourly	**LR** Low end range	**MW** Median wage paid	**TQ** Third quartile wage
AEX Average experienced wage	**AXR** Average experienced range	**HI** Highest wage paid	**M** Monthly	**MWR** Median wage range	**W** Weekly
ATC Average total compensation	**D** Daily	**HR** High end range	**MCC** Median cash compensation	**S** See annotated source	**Y** Yearly

Occupation/Type/Industry	Location	Per	Low	Mid	High	Source	Date
Self-Enrichment Education Teacher	Duluth-Superior MSA, MN-WI	Y	27243 FQ	33133 MW	55554 TQ	MNBLS	10/08-12/08
	Minneapolis-Saint Paul MSA, MN-WI	Y	27494 FQ	33353 MW	52007 TQ	MNBLS	10/08-12/08
	Rochester MSA, MN	Y	20106 FQ	28995 MW	44836 TQ	MNBLS	10/08-12/08
	Mississippi	Y	22700 FQ	30620 MW	45840 TQ	USBLS	5/07
	Jackson MSA, MS	Y	26370 FQ	33560 MW	47770 TQ	USBLS	5/07
	Missouri	Y	21850 FQ	35600 MW	54180 TQ	USBLS	5/07
	Kansas City MSA, MO-KS	Y	24570 FQ	33540 MW	38310 TQ	USBLS	5/07
	St. Joseph MSA, MO-KS	Y	17110 FQ	18740 MW	25210 TQ	USBLS	5/07
	St. Louis MSA, MO-IL	Y	24490 FQ	44280 MW	59780 TQ	USBLS	5/07
	Montana	Y	15660 FQ	22980 MW	29760 TQ	USBLS	5/07
	Billings MSA, MT	Y	24570 FQ	27720 MW	30140 TQ	USBLS	5/07
	Nebraska	Y	20330 FQ	26060 MW	45760 TQ	USBLS	5/07
	Omaha-Council Bluffs MSA, NE-IA	Y	19880 FQ	27640 MW	45730 TQ	USBLS	5/07
	Nevada	H	14.45 FQ	18.58 MW	22.01 TQ	NVBLS	5/08
	Las Vegas-Paradise MSA, NV	H	14.08 FQ	18.53 MW	21.43 TQ	NVBLS	5/08
	New Hampshire	H	16.54 AE	25.49 MW	30.55 AEX	NHBLS	6/08
	Manchester MSA, NH	Y	56830 FQ	67080 MW	75780 TQ	USBLS	5/07
	Nashua NECTA, NH-MA	Y	41310 FQ	51760 MW	61770 TQ	USBLS	5/07
	New Jersey	Y	30570 FQ	47900 MW	63990 TQ	USBLS	5/07
	Camden PMSA, NJ	Y	38940 FQ	51320 MW	66620 TQ	USBLS	5/07
	Edison PMSA, NJ	Y	27310 FQ	40390 MW	57690 TQ	USBLS	5/07
	Newark-Union PMSA, NJ-PA	Y	38450 FQ	55230 MW	64450 TQ	USBLS	5/07
	Trenton-Ewing MSA, NJ	Y	27980 FQ	39540 MW	59020 TQ	USBLS	5/07
	New Mexico	Y	22850 FQ	35530 MW	53820 TQ	USBLS	5/07
	Albuquerque MSA, NM	Y	17920 FQ	28430 MW	61970 TQ	USBLS	5/07
	New York	Y	23320 FQ	32790 MW	53250 TQ	USBLS	5/07
	Albany-Schenectady-Troy MSA, NY	Y	24350 FQ	30070 MW	44930 TQ	USBLS	5/07
	Buffalo-Niagara Falls MSA, NY	Y	22580 FQ	28730 MW	34660 TQ	USBLS	5/07
	Ithaca MSA, NY	Y	35330 FQ	43410 MW	65950 TQ	USBLS	5/07
	Nassau-Suffolk PMSA, NY	Y	21330 FQ	30240 MW	42380 TQ	USBLS	5/07
	New York-Northern New Jersey-Long Island MSA, NY-NJ-PA	Y	25620 FQ	38080 MW	60130 TQ	USBLS	5/07
	Syracuse MSA, NY	Y	20930 FQ	24610 MW	32690 TQ	USBLS	5/07
	North Carolina	Y	25690 FQ	33110 MW	45150 TQ	USBLS	5/07
	Charlotte-Gastonia-Concord MSA, NC-SC	Y	22130 FQ	28800 MW	36240 TQ	USBLS	5/07
	Raleigh-Cary MSA, NC	Y	30350 FQ	45480 MW	53030 TQ	USBLS	5/07
	Ohio	Y	20410 FQ	27760 MW	44600 TQ	USBLS	5/07
	Cincinnati-Middletown MSA, OH-KY-IN	Y	21320 FQ	27220 MW	41010 TQ	USBLS	5/07
	Cleveland-Elyria-Mentor MSA, OH	Y	24220 FQ	40450 MW	51970 TQ	USBLS	5/07
	Columbus MSA, OH	Y	33060 FQ	52050 MW	61550 TQ	USBLS	5/07
	Dayton MSA, OH	Y	19630 FQ	23550 MW	38540 TQ	USBLS	5/07
	Springfield MSA, OH	Y	14920 FQ	19920 MW	37860 TQ	USBLS	5/07
	Oklahoma	Y	26690 FQ	33820 MW	41840 TQ	USBLS	5/07
	Oklahoma City MSA, OK	Y	24470 FQ	26830 MW	29170 TQ	USBLS	5/07
	Tulsa MSA, OK	Y	34370 FQ	38590 MW	47850 TQ	USBLS	5/07
	Oregon	H	12.69 FQ	15.76 MW	23.29 TQ	ORBLS	5/08
	Eugene-Springfield MSA, OR	Y	27470 FQ	33190 MW	39950 TQ	USBLS	5/07
	Portland-Vancouver-Beaverton MSA, OR-WA	Y	26720 FQ	33700 MW	48320 TQ	USBLS	5/07
	Salem MSA, OR	Y	22530 FQ	27210 MW	31040 TQ	USBLS	5/07
	Pennsylvania	Y	26750 FQ	36670 MW	50880 TQ	USBLS	5/07
	Allentown-Bethlehem-Easton MSA, PA-NJ	Y	28670 FQ	43190 MW	60440 TQ	USBLS	5/07
	Erie MSA, PA	Y	17520 FQ	20750 MW	33770 TQ	USBLS	5/07
	Philadelphia-Camden-Wilmington MSA, PA-NJ-DE-MD	Y	33540 FQ	44620 MW	57140 TQ	USBLS	5/07
	Pittsburgh MSA, PA	Y	24630 FQ	31220 MW	37520 TQ	USBLS	5/07
	Rhode Island	Y	17080 FQ	29610 MW	42120 TQ	USBLS	5/07
	Providence-Fall River-Warwick MSA, RI-MA	Y	20100 FQ	28040 MW	39990 TQ	USBLS	5/07
	South Carolina	Y	27610 FQ	37980 MW	49930 TQ	USBLS	5/07

AE Average entry wage	**AW** Average wage paid	**FQ** First quartile wage	**LO** Lowest wage paid	**MTC** Median total compensation	**TCC** Total cash compensation
AER Average entry range	**AWR** Average wage range	**H** Hourly	**LR** Low end range	**MW** Median wage paid	**TQ** Third quartile wage
AEX Average experienced wage	**AXR** Average experienced range	**HI** Highest wage paid	**M** Monthly	**MWR** Median wage range	**W** Weekly
ATC Average total compensation	**D** Daily	**HR** High end range	**MCC** Median cash compensation	**S** See annotated source	**Y** Yearly

Occupation/Type/Industry	Location	Per	Low	Mid	High	Source	Date
Self-Enrichment Education Teacher	Charleston-North Charleston MSA, SC	Y	23950 FQ	33340 MW	38960 TQ	USBLS	5/07
	Columbia MSA, SC	Y	29290 FQ	43770 MW	56080 TQ	USBLS	5/07
	South Dakota	Y	23875 FQ	27456 MW	32890 TQ	SDBLS	7/08-9/08
	Sioux Falls MSA, SD	Y	25722 FQ	29186 MW	35124 TQ	SDBLS	7/08-9/08
	Tennessee	Y	21900 FQ	29810 MW	38610 TQ	USBLS	5/07
	Memphis MSA, TN-MS-AR	Y	23610 FQ	33000 MW	43650 TQ	USBLS	5/07
	Nashville-Davidson-Murfreesboro MSA, TN	Y	25770 FQ	30880 MW	41280 TQ	USBLS	5/07
	Texas	Y	25100 FQ	32350 MW	48710 TQ	USBLS	5/07
	Austin-Round Rock MSA, TX	Y	26330 FQ	29350 MW	32370 TQ	USBLS	5/07
	Beaumont-Port Arthur MSA, TX	Y	30900 FQ	36610 MW	45500 TQ	USBLS	5/07
	Dallas-Fort Worth-Arlington MSA, TX	Y	25770 FQ	37630 MW	48780 TQ	USBLS	5/07
	El Paso MSA, TX	Y	30610 FQ	45480 MW	51860 TQ	USBLS	5/07
	Houston-Sugar Land-Baytown MSA, TX	Y	29690 FQ	41800 MW	62400 TQ	USBLS	5/07
	Midland MSA, TX	Y	16160 FQ	27130 MW	44160 TQ	USBLS	5/07
	San Antonio MSA, TX	Y	24280 FQ	44940 MW	55620 TQ	USBLS	5/07
	Utah	Y	20020 FQ	27060 MW	46310 TQ	USBLS	5/07
	Logan MSA, UT-ID	Y	19680 FQ	23390 MW	38680 TQ	USBLS	5/07
	Salt Lake City MSA, UT	Y	18450 FQ	43560 MW	53250 TQ	USBLS	5/07
	Vermont	Y	30910 FQ	40670 MW	47680 TQ	USBLS	5/07
	Burlington-South Burlington MSA, VT	Y	37050 FQ	43630 MW	49530 TQ	USBLS	5/07
	Virginia	Y	26520 FQ	42090 MW	59380 TQ	USBLS	5/07
	Richmond MSA, VA	Y	31400 FQ	50630 MW	60060 TQ	USBLS	5/07
	Roanoke MSA, VA	Y	20170 FQ	22740 MW	29530 TQ	USBLS	5/07
	Virginia Beach-Norfolk-Newport News MSA, VA-NC	Y	43710 FQ	52070 MW	62820 TQ	USBLS	5/07
	Washington	H	13.93 FQ	17.75 MW	23.29 TQ	WABLS	3/08
	Seattle-Tacoma-Bellevue MSA, WA	Y	29280 FQ	37510 MW	49440 TQ	USBLS	5/07
	West Virginia	Y	22235 FQ	25943 MW	30276 TQ	WVBLS	7/08-9/08
	Wisconsin	Y	24110 FQ	34120 MW	47300 TQ	USBLS	5/07
	Appleton MSA, WI	Y	29860 FQ	45180 MW	62090 TQ	USBLS	5/07
	Milwaukee-Waukesha-West Allis MSA, WI	Y	23970 FQ	37300 MW	48780 TQ	USBLS	5/07
	Puerto Rico	Y	17330 FQ	28960 MW	35550 TQ	USBLS	5/07
	San Juan-Caguas-Guaynabo MSA, PR	Y	17200 FQ	28970 MW	35000 TQ	USBLS	5/07
	Guam	Y	20530 FQ	23930 MW	29780 TQ	USBLS	5/07
Self-Reliance Specialist State Government	Idaho	Y	30472 LO		50793 HI	AFT02	3/1/08
Semiconductor Engineer Avionics Company	United States	Y		109814 AW		EDES	2008
Semiconductor Fab Technician	United States	Y			90000 HI	COMMN	2009
Semiconductor Processor	Arizona	Y	26210 FQ	31880 MW	40380 TQ	USBLS	5/07
	Phoenix-Mesa-Scottsdale MSA, AZ	Y	26710 FQ	32150 MW	40710 TQ	USBLS	5/07
	California	H	13.50 FQ	17.26 MW	22.49 TQ	CABLS	1/08-3/08
	Los Angeles-Long Beach-Glendale PMSA, CA	H	14.06 FQ	19.44 MW	29.11 TQ	CABLS	1/08-3/08
	Oakland-Fremont-Hayward MSA, CA	H	12.32 FQ	14.49 MW	17.58 TQ	CABLS	1/08-3/08
	Sacramento-Arden Arcade-Roseville MSA, CA	H	12.13 FQ	15.96 MW	19.42 TQ	CABLS	1/08-3/08
	San Jose-Sunnyvale-Santa Clara MSA, CA	H	15.09 FQ	19.25 MW	23.88 TQ	CABLS	1/08-3/08
	Santa Ana-Anaheim-Irvine PMSA, CA	Y	27010 FQ	31520 MW	40740 TQ	USBLS	5/07
	Colorado	Y	26990 FQ	35320 MW	45260 TQ	USBLS	5/07
	Connecticut	H	10.77 AE	14.54 MW		CTBLS	1/08-3/08
	Idaho	Y	25710 FQ	28230 MW	30760 TQ	USBLS	5/07
	Boise City-Nampa MSA, ID	Y	25800 FQ	28260 MW	30710 TQ	USBLS	5/07
	Illinois	Y	21380 FQ	22770 MW	24170 TQ	USBLS	5/07

AE	Average entry wage	**AW**	Average wage paid	**FQ**	First quartile wage	**LO**	Lowest wage paid
AER	Average entry range	**AWR**	Average wage range	**H**	Hourly	**LR**	Low end range
AEX	Average experienced wage	**AXR**	Average experienced range	**HI**	Highest wage paid	**M**	Monthly
ATC	Average total compensation	**D**	Daily	**HR**	High end range	**MCC**	Median cash compensation

MTC	Median total compensation	**TCC**	Total cash compensation	
MW	Median wage paid	**TQ**	Third quartile wage	
MWR	Median wage range	**W**	Weekly	
S	See annotated source	**Y**	Yearly	

Occupation/Type/Industry	Location	Per	Low	Mid	High	Source	Date
Semiconductor Processor	Chicago-Naperville-Joliet						
	MSA, IL-IN-WI	Y	21380 FQ	22770 MW	24170 TQ	USBLS	5/07
	Massachusetts	Y	33370 FQ	38940 MW	51660 TQ	USBLS	5/07
	Boston-Cambridge-Quincy						
	NECTA, MA	Y	37450 FQ	47910 MW	57500 TQ	USBLS	5/07
	Minnesota	Y	26974 FQ	34241 MW	39290 TQ	MNBLS	10/08-12/08
	Minneapolis-Saint Paul MSA,						
	MN-WI	Y	26300 FQ	32220 MW	38802 TQ	MNBLS	10/08-12/08
	New Hampshire	H	8.09 AE	9.07 MW	15.06 AEX	NHBLS	6/08
	New Jersey	Y	26490 FQ	32190 MW	39460 TQ	USBLS	5/07
	New York	Y	26400 FQ	33260 MW	40170 TQ	USBLS	5/07
	New York-Northern New						
	Jersey-Long Island MSA, NY-						
	NJ-PA	Y	25760 FQ	31610 MW	38940 TQ	USBLS	5/07
	Ohio	Y	22520 FQ	28620 MW	38630 TQ	USBLS	5/07
	Oregon	H	12.49 FQ	14.26 MW	17.13 TQ	ORBLS	5/08
	Portland-Vancouver-Beaverton						
	MSA, OR-WA	Y	23420 FQ	29220 MW	36030 TQ	USBLS	5/07
	Pennsylvania	Y	26720 FQ	34240 MW	39890 TQ	USBLS	5/07
	Pittsburgh MSA, PA	Y	19770 FQ	22100 MW	35330 TQ	USBLS	5/07
	Rhode Island	Y	21900 FQ	25750 MW	31090 TQ	USBLS	5/07
	Providence-Fall River-						
	Warwick MSA, RI-MA	Y	22370 FQ	26550 MW	31750 TQ	USBLS	5/07
	Texas	Y	25930 FQ	31130 MW	37680 TQ	USBLS	5/07
	Austin-Round Rock MSA, TX	Y	28920 FQ	35170 MW	42620 TQ	USBLS	5/07
	Dallas-Fort Worth-Arlington						
	MSA, TX	Y	25380 FQ	30110 MW	36020 TQ	USBLS	5/07
	Utah	Y	23440 FQ	31680 MW	37930 TQ	USBLS	5/07
	Virginia	Y	26630 FQ	30780 MW	38820 TQ	USBLS	5/07
	Washington	H	11.07 FQ	13.89 MW	18.11 TQ	WABLS	3/08
	Seattle-Tacoma-Bellevue						
	MSA, WA	Y	24210 FQ	30100 MW	38060 TQ	USBLS	5/07
	Wisconsin	Y	19990 FQ	27510 MW	36220 TQ	USBLS	5/07
Senate Legal Counsel							
United States Senate	United States	Y			163700 HI	CRS01	2007
Senate Staffer							
State Government	California	Y		60720 MW		SBEE	2008
Senator							
United States Senate	United States	Y			174000 HI	USSGOV	2009
Senior Accountant	Middle Atlantic	Y	53000 LO		65000 HI	ACTT	2009
State Government	Delaware	Y	32652 LO		48978 HI	AFT02	3/1/08
Senior Advisor Economist							
District Government	District of Columbia	Y	108507 LO		140602 HI	AFT02	3/1/08
Senior Applications Analyst							
Municipal Government	Carlsbad, CA	S	3270 LO		3975 HI	CCSS01	8/5/08
Senior Chief Petty Officer							
U.S. Navy, Active Duty, Pay Grade E-8	United States	M	3619 LO		5161 HI	DOD1	2009
Senior Criminalist							
Department of Justice	California	W	5279 LO		6534 HI	CAC	2006-2007
Senior Database Administrator							
Municipal Government	Carlsbad, CA	S	3403 LO		4137 HI	CCSS01	8/5/08
Senior DNA Analyst							
State Government	Wisconsin	Y	43764 LO		92125 HI	AFT02	3/1/08
Senior Hydrogeologist							
State Government	Wisconsin	Y	43764 LO		92125 HI	AFT02	3/1/08
Senior Master Sergeant							
U.S. Air Force, Active Duty, Pay Grade E-8	United States	M	3619 LO		5161 HI	DOD1	2009
Senior Minister							
Anglican	United States	Y		81113 AW		ANGJ	2008

AE Average entry wage	**AW** Average wage paid	**FQ** First quartile wage	**LO** Lowest wage paid	**MTC** Median total compensation	**TCC** Total cash compensation
AER Average entry range	**AWR** Average wage range	**H** Hourly	**LR** Low end range	**MW** Median wage paid	**TQ** Third quartile wage
AEX Average experienced wage	**AXR** Average experienced range	**HI** Highest wage paid	**M** Monthly	**MWR** Median wage range	**W** Weekly
ATC Average total compensation	**D** Daily	**HR** High end range	**MCC** Median cash compensation	**S** See annotated source	**Y** Yearly

Occupation/Type/Industry	Location	Per	Low	Mid	High	Source	Date
Senior Programmer Judicial Branch, State Government	New Hampshire	Y		54661 AW		NHUL03	2008
Senior Real Estate Specialist Municipal Government	Cincinnati, OH	Y	56332 LO		77569 HI	COHSS	10/08
Senior Revenue Tax Specialist State Government	Minnesota	Y	44850 LO		66106 HI	AFT02	3/1/08
Senior Security Trainer	United States	Y		55951 AW		IOMA04	2008
Senior Storm Drain Maintenance **Worker**	Carlsbad, CA	S	1782 LO		2166 HI	CCSS01	8/5/08
Senior Web Producer	United States	Y	85000 LO		110000 HI	COMMN	2009
Separating, Filtering, Clarifying, **Precipitating, and Still Machine** **Setter, Operator, and Tender**	Alabama	Y	23920 FQ	33110 MW	39810 TQ	USBLS	5/07
	Birmingham-Hoover MSA, AL	Y	34340 FQ	37080 MW	39560 TQ	USBLS	5/07
	Mobile MSA, AL	Y	39360 FQ	43630 MW	48550 TQ	USBLS	5/07
	Alaska	Y	36300 FQ	44470 MW	50840 TQ	USBLS	5/07
	Arizona	Y	27100 FQ	35510 MW	41280 TQ	USBLS	5/07
	Phoenix-Mesa-Scottsdale MSA, AZ	Y	20100 FQ	29910 MW	38250 TQ	USBLS	5/07
	Arkansas	Y	25700 FQ	32410 MW	36770 TQ	USBLS	5/07
	California	H	17.36 FQ	21.54 MW	26.62 TQ	CABLS	1/08-3/08
	Los Angeles-Long Beach- Glendale PMSA, CA	H	19.89 FQ	23.99 MW	27.84 TQ	CABLS	1/08-3/08
	Oakland-Fremont-Hayward MSA, CA	H	21.93 FQ	25.91 MW	29.10 TQ	CABLS	1/08-3/08
	Riverside-San Bernardino- Ontario MSA, CA	H	14.67 FQ	19.40 MW	25.77 TQ	CABLS	1/08-3/08
	Sacramento-Arden Arcade- Roseville MSA, CA	H	18.87 FQ	20.70 MW	22.54 TQ	CABLS	1/08-3/08
	San Diego-Carlsbad-San Marcos MSA, CA	H	18.19 FQ	20.92 MW	23.69 TQ	CABLS	1/08-3/08
	San Francisco-San Mateo- Redwood PMSA, CA	H	11.74 FQ	13.66 MW	17.81 TQ	CABLS	1/08-3/08
	San Jose-Sunnyvale-Santa Clara MSA, CA	H	14.69 FQ	18.24 MW	25.23 TQ	CABLS	1/08-3/08
	Santa Ana-Anaheim-Irvine PMSA, CA	Y	29170 FQ	35130 MW	42350 TQ	USBLS	5/07
	Colorado	Y	27840 FQ	33630 MW	39570 TQ	USBLS	5/07
	Colorado Springs MSA, CO	Y	23610 FQ	31920 MW	39040 TQ	USBLS	5/07
	Denver-Aurora MSA, CO	Y	28790 FQ	33080 MW	36950 TQ	USBLS	5/07
	Connecticut	H	12.29 AE	16.93 MW		CTBLS	1/08-3/08
	Washington-Arlington- Alexandria MSA, DC-VA- MD-WV	Y	26950 FQ	30360 MW	42320 TQ	USBLS	5/07
	Florida	Y	23420 FQ	33930 MW	43010 TQ	USBLS	5/07
	Jacksonville MSA, FL	Y	34010 FQ	40420 MW	45750 TQ	USBLS	5/07
	Miami-Fort Lauderdale-Miami Beach MSA, FL	Y	21240 FQ	28700 MW	42950 TQ	USBLS	5/07
	Orlando-Kissimmee MSA, FL	Y	17800 FQ	19620 MW	23700 TQ	USBLS	5/07
	Tampa-St. Petersburg- Clearwater MSA, FL	Y	15950 FQ	25180 MW	36540 TQ	USBLS	5/07
	West Palm Beach-Boca Raton- Boynton Beach PMSA, FL	Y	19500 FQ	25230 MW	40730 TQ	USBLS	5/07
	Georgia	Y	23860 FQ	37420 MW	43510 TQ	USBLS	5/07
	Atlanta-Sandy Springs- Marietta MSA, GA	Y	21720 FQ	32780 MW	39030 TQ	USBLS	5/07
	Savannah MSA, GA	Y	43870 FQ	48700 MW	53570 TQ	USBLS	5/07
	Idaho	Y	28970 FQ	34070 MW	41200 TQ	USBLS	5/07
	Illinois	Y	29610 FQ	37220 MW	48190 TQ	USBLS	5/07
	Chicago-Naperville-Joliet MSA, IL-IN-WI	Y	28820 FQ	38840 MW	51030 TQ	USBLS	5/07
	Indiana	Y	26890 FQ	35760 MW	44340 TQ	USBLS	5/07
	Gary PMSA, IN	Y	48410 FQ	53020 MW	57630 TQ	USBLS	5/07
	Indianapolis-Carmel MSA, IN	Y	18180 FQ	27100 MW	35550 TQ	USBLS	5/07
	Iowa	Y	24490 FQ	29460 MW	38280 TQ	USBLS	5/07

AE	Average entry wage	AW	Average wage paid	FQ	First quartile wage	LO	Lowest wage paid	MTC	Median total compensation	TCC	Total cash compensation
AER	Average entry range	AWR	Average wage range	H	Hourly	LR	Low end range	MW	Median wage paid	TQ	Third quartile wage
AEX	Average experienced wage	AXR	Average experienced range	HI	Highest wage paid	M	Monthly	MWR	Median wage range	W	Weekly
ATC	Average total compensation	D	Daily	HR	High end range	MCC	Median cash compensation	S	See annotated source	Y	Yearly

1459

Occupation/Type/Industry	Location	Per	Low	Mid	High	Source	Date
Separating, Filtering, Clarifying, Precipitating, and Still Machine Setter, Operator, and Tender							
	Des Moines-West Des Moines MSA, IA	Y	23070 FQ	26770 MW	30900 TQ	USBLS	5/07
	Kansas	Y	32500 FQ	36540 MW	42400 TQ	USBLS	5/07
	Kentucky	Y	31912 FQ	36431 MW	42676 TQ	KYBLS	2008
	Louisville-Jefferson County MSA, KY-IN	Y	32470 FQ	35940 MW	42250 TQ	USBLS	5/07
	Louisiana	H	10.35 FQ	14.82 MW	18.42 TQ	LABLS	1/08-3/08
	New Orleans-Metairie-Kenner MSA, LA	Y	21390 FQ	28430 MW	33950 TQ	USBLS	5/07
	Maine	Y	30000 FQ	34400 MW	39510 TQ	USBLS	5/07
	Portland-South Portland-Biddeford MSA, ME	Y	27570 FQ	36090 MW	42080 TQ	USBLS	5/07
	Maryland	Y		35700 MW		MDBLS	3/08
	Baltimore-Towson MSA, MD	Y	35070 FQ	39890 MW	45320 TQ	USBLS	5/07
	Massachusetts	Y	34550 FQ	41110 MW	48540 TQ	USBLS	5/07
	Boston-Cambridge-Quincy NECTA, MA	Y	35410 FQ	44740 MW	59700 TQ	USBLS	5/07
	Michigan	Y	24210 FQ	31050 MW	37410 TQ	USBLS	5/07
	Detroit-Warren-Livonia MSA, MI	Y	21380 FQ	29140 MW	40610 TQ	USBLS	5/07
	Grand Rapids-Wyoming MSA, MI	Y	22040 FQ	27060 MW	30170 TQ	USBLS	5/07
	Warren-Troy-Farmington Hills PMSA, MI	Y	28130 FQ	32500 MW	41220 TQ	USBLS	5/07
	Minnesota	Y	28850 FQ	33464 MW	39891 TQ	MNBLS	10/08-12/08
	Duluth-Superior MSA, MN-WI	Y	31483 FQ	36739 MW	46412 TQ	MNBLS	10/08-12/08
	Minneapolis-Saint Paul MSA, MN-WI	Y	35081 FQ	42483 MW	47998 TQ	MNBLS	10/08-12/08
	Mississippi	Y	18490 FQ	28670 MW	43220 TQ	USBLS	5/07
	Jackson MSA, MS	Y	23900 FQ	32700 MW	38050 TQ	USBLS	5/07
	Missouri	Y	22590 FQ	29570 MW	35540 TQ	USBLS	5/07
	Kansas City MSA, MO-KS	Y	21680 FQ	25950 MW	37850 TQ	USBLS	5/07
	St. Louis MSA, MO-IL	Y	22420 FQ	34180 MW	38710 TQ	USBLS	5/07
	Montana	Y	32490 FQ	36310 MW	40080 TQ	USBLS	5/07
	Nebraska	Y	21740 FQ	27460 MW	34300 TQ	USBLS	5/07
	Omaha-Council Bluffs MSA, NE-IA	Y	30440 FQ	32960 MW	35620 TQ	USBLS	5/07
	Nevada	H	14.95 FQ	19.01 MW	23.15 TQ	NVBLS	5/08
	Las Vegas-Paradise MSA, NV	H	13.93 FQ	15.95 MW	19.65 TQ	NVBLS	5/08
	New Hampshire	H	14.11 AE	17.38 MW	19.77 AEX	NHBLS	6/08
	New Jersey	Y	29370 FQ	43250 MW	52570 TQ	USBLS	5/07
	Camden PMSA, NJ	Y	29980 FQ	42340 MW	53280 TQ	USBLS	5/07
	Edison PMSA, NJ	Y	25070 FQ	41770 MW	49800 TQ	USBLS	5/07
	Newark-Union PMSA, NJ-PA	Y	27740 FQ	39350 MW	52260 TQ	USBLS	5/07
	New Mexico	Y	15530 FQ	27380 MW	35590 TQ	USBLS	5/07
	New York	Y	26840 FQ	34120 MW	40500 TQ	USBLS	5/07
	Albany-Schenectady-Troy MSA, NY	Y	30110 FQ	33900 MW	37420 TQ	USBLS	5/07
	Buffalo-Niagara Falls MSA, NY	Y	27780 FQ	37130 MW	52190 TQ	USBLS	5/07
	Nassau-Suffolk PMSA, NY	Y	34670 FQ	41280 MW	51300 TQ	USBLS	5/07
	New York-Northern New Jersey-Long Island MSA, NY-NJ-PA	Y	28360 FQ	36630 MW	47950 TQ	USBLS	5/07
	Syracuse MSA, NY	Y	18700 FQ	23150 MW	34810 TQ	USBLS	5/07
	North Carolina	Y	35920 FQ	42530 MW	51680 TQ	USBLS	5/07
	Charlotte-Gastonia-Concord MSA, NC-SC	Y	26930 FQ	29280 MW	33630 TQ	USBLS	5/07
	Raleigh-Cary MSA, NC	Y	38020 FQ	42860 MW	49140 TQ	USBLS	5/07
	North Dakota	Y	27210 FQ	31360 MW	36800 TQ	USBLS	5/07
	Ohio	Y	28260 FQ	36720 MW	49360 TQ	USBLS	5/07
	Cincinnati-Middletown MSA, OH-KY-IN	Y	34330 FQ	49280 MW	58230 TQ	USBLS	5/07
	Cleveland-Elyria-Mentor MSA, OH	Y	28690 FQ	32730 MW	39100 TQ	USBLS	5/07
	Columbus MSA, OH	Y	24040 FQ	30850 MW	47030 TQ	USBLS	5/07
	Dayton MSA, OH	Y	37410 FQ	40570 MW	43940 TQ	USBLS	5/07
	Oklahoma	Y	17690 FQ	20120 MW	32610 TQ	USBLS	5/07
	Oklahoma City MSA, OK	Y	17620 FQ	21030 MW	32290 TQ	USBLS	5/07

AE	Average entry wage	AW	Average wage paid	FQ	First quartile wage	LO	Lowest wage paid	MTC	Median total compensation	TCC	Total cash compensation
AER	Average entry range	AWR	Average wage range	H	Hourly	LR	Low end range	MW	Median wage paid	TQ	Third quartile wage
AEX	Average experienced wage	AXR	Average experienced range	HI	Highest wage paid	M	Monthly	MWR	Median wage range	W	Weekly
ATC	Average total compensation	D	Daily	HR	High end range	MCC	Median cash compensation	S	See annotated source	Y	Yearly

Occupation/Type/Industry	Location	Per	Low	Mid	High	Source	Date
Separating, Filtering, Clarifying, Precipitating, and Still Machine Setter, Operator, and Tender	Oregon	H	12.99 FQ	16.11 MW	19.84 TQ	ORBLS	5/08
	Portland-Vancouver-Beaverton MSA, OR-WA	Y	29820 FQ	36420 MW	44110 TQ	USBLS	5/07
	Pennsylvania	Y	29820 FQ	38110 MW	45500 TQ	USBLS	5/07
	Allentown-Bethlehem-Easton MSA, PA-NJ	Y	38510 FQ	43600 MW	47890 TQ	USBLS	5/07
	Erie MSA, PA	Y	22870 FQ	25390 MW	32970 TQ	USBLS	5/07
	Philadelphia-Camden-Wilmington MSA, PA-NJ-DE-MD	Y	32500 FQ	42210 MW	51490 TQ	USBLS	5/07
	Pittsburgh MSA, PA	Y	29480 FQ	36430 MW	43610 TQ	USBLS	5/07
	Providence-Fall River-Warwick MSA, RI-MA	Y	24920 FQ	29480 MW	40800 TQ	USBLS	5/07
	South Carolina	Y	28660 FQ	35110 MW	43980 TQ	USBLS	5/07
	Charleston-North Charleston MSA, SC	Y	28130 FQ	32310 MW	44510 TQ	USBLS	5/07
	Florence MSA, SC	Y	31850 FQ	34970 MW	37770 TQ	USBLS	5/07
	Spartanburg MSA, SC	Y	23770 FQ	33000 MW	37570 TQ	USBLS	5/07
	South Dakota	Y	22374 FQ	25843 MW	30505 TQ	SDBLS	7/08-9/08
	Sioux Falls MSA, SD	Y	29064 FQ	32389 MW	36897 TQ	SDBLS	7/08-9/08
	Tennessee	Y	29060 FQ	36620 MW	43280 TQ	USBLS	5/07
	Memphis MSA, TN-MS-AR	Y	27990 FQ	35840 MW	40540 TQ	USBLS	5/07
	Nashville-Davidson-Murfreesboro MSA, TN	Y	27560 FQ	36330 MW	41120 TQ	USBLS	5/07
	Texas	Y	25830 FQ	31810 MW	45100 TQ	USBLS	5/07
	Austin-Round Rock MSA, TX	Y	22030 FQ	26330 MW	29480 TQ	USBLS	5/07
	Beaumont-Port Arthur MSA, TX	Y	30200 FQ	43780 MW	57500 TQ	USBLS	5/07
	Dallas-Fort Worth-Arlington MSA, TX	Y	28300 FQ	38030 MW	49540 TQ	USBLS	5/07
	El Paso MSA, TX	Y	31470 FQ	34500 MW	37530 TQ	USBLS	5/07
	Houston-Sugar Land-Baytown MSA, TX	Y	26470 FQ	31680 MW	47840 TQ	USBLS	5/07
	San Antonio MSA, TX	Y	21930 FQ	27320 MW	31330 TQ	USBLS	5/07
	Utah	Y	27080 FQ	33510 MW	39100 TQ	USBLS	5/07
	Salt Lake City MSA, UT	Y	24050 FQ	31060 MW	38770 TQ	USBLS	5/07
	Vermont	Y	26300 FQ	30960 MW	34960 TQ	USBLS	5/07
	Burlington-South Burlington MSA, VT	Y	26250 FQ	31030 MW	35160 TQ	USBLS	5/07
	Virginia	Y	30080 FQ	36610 MW	45820 TQ	USBLS	5/07
	Richmond MSA, VA	Y	31530 FQ	40550 MW	53440 TQ	USBLS	5/07
	Virginia Beach-Norfolk-Newport News MSA, VA-NC	Y	33930 FQ	36190 MW	38450 TQ	USBLS	5/07
	Washington	H	14.06 FQ	18.23 MW	22.87 TQ	WABLS	3/08
	Seattle-Tacoma-Bellevue MSA, WA	Y	35070 FQ	41300 MW	49930 TQ	USBLS	5/07
	Spokane MSA, WA	Y	33640 FQ	39360 MW	44620 TQ	USBLS	5/07
	Wisconsin	Y	30050 FQ	36690 MW	44630 TQ	USBLS	5/07
	Milwaukee-Waukesha-West Allis MSA, WI	Y	40360 FQ	44420 MW	48450 TQ	USBLS	5/07
	Wyoming	Y	42529 FQ	54295 MW	61645 TQ	WYBLS	9/08
	Puerto Rico	Y	19080 FQ	27310 MW	33220 TQ	USBLS	5/07
	San Juan-Caguas-Guaynabo MSA, PR	Y	19750 FQ	27690 MW	33380 TQ	USBLS	5/07
Septic Tank Servicer and Sewer Pipe Cleaner	Alabama	Y	22880 FQ	29210 MW	38150 TQ	USBLS	5/07
	Birmingham-Hoover MSA, AL	Y	20570 FQ	25410 MW	34520 TQ	USBLS	5/07
	Alaska	Y	38060 FQ	44370 MW	48450 TQ	USBLS	5/07
	Arizona	Y	21670 FQ	27730 MW	38990 TQ	USBLS	5/07
	Phoenix-Mesa-Scottsdale MSA, AZ	Y	20020 FQ	32690 MW	42230 TQ	USBLS	5/07
	Arkansas	Y	22780 FQ	27140 MW	31700 TQ	USBLS	5/07
	Little Rock-North Little Rock MSA, AR	Y	23130 FQ	26900 MW	29780 TQ	USBLS	5/07
	California	H	15.04 FQ	18.73 MW	23.72 TQ	CABLS	1/08-3/08
	Los Angeles-Long Beach-Glendale PMSA, CA	H	14.05 FQ	18.00 MW	24.41 TQ	CABLS	1/08-3/08

AE	Average entry wage	AW	Average wage paid	FQ	First quartile wage	LO	Lowest wage paid	MTC	Median total compensation	TCC Total cash compensation
AER	Average entry range	AWR	Average wage range	H	Hourly	LR	Low end range	MW	Median wage paid	TQ Third quartile wage
AEX	Average experienced wage	AXR	Average experienced range	HI	Highest wage paid	M	Monthly	MWR	Median wage range	W Weekly
ATC	Average total compensation	D	Daily	HR	High end range	MCC	Median cash compensation	S	See annotated source	Y Yearly

Occupation/Type/Industry	Location	Per	Low	Mid	High	Source	Date
Septic Tank Servicer and Sewer Pipe Cleaner	Oakland-Fremont-Hayward MSA, CA	H	15.84 FQ	19.90 MW	26.63 TQ	CABLS	1/08-3/08
	Riverside-San Bernardino-Ontario MSA, CA	H	18.17 FQ	19.84 MW	28.19 TQ	CABLS	1/08-3/08
	Sacramento-Arden Arcade-Roseville MSA, CA	H	13.18 FQ	14.33 MW	20.22 TQ	CABLS	1/08-3/08
	San Diego-Carlsbad-San Marcos MSA, CA	H	13.04 FQ	15.08 MW	19.96 TQ	CABLS	1/08-3/08
	San Francisco-San Mateo-Redwood PMSA, CA	H	19.57 FQ	22.76 MW	25.09 TQ	CABLS	1/08-3/08
	San Jose-Sunnyvale-Santa Clara MSA, CA	H	18.07 FQ	21.32 MW	24.13 TQ	CABLS	1/08-3/08
	Santa Ana-Anaheim-Irvine PMSA, CA	Y	45710 FQ	54280 MW	60660 TQ	USBLS	5/07
	Colorado	Y	30410 FQ	38160 MW	51750 TQ	USBLS	5/07
	Colorado Springs MSA, CO	Y	33990 FQ	37180 MW	40370 TQ	USBLS	5/07
	Denver-Aurora MSA, CO	Y	33650 FQ	42860 MW	56190 TQ	USBLS	5/07
	Connecticut	H	16.75 AE	21.06 MW		CTBLS	1/08-3/08
	Bridgeport-Stamford-Norwalk MSA, CT	Y	41070 FQ	44970 MW	48980 TQ	USBLS	5/07
	Delaware	Y	27800 FQ	30860 MW	36620 TQ	USBLS	5/07
	Wilmington PMSA, DE-MD-NJ	Y	27310 FQ	31300 MW	38940 TQ	USBLS	5/07
	Washington-Arlington-Alexandria MSA, DC-VA-MD-WV	Y	26690 FQ	31620 MW	38790 TQ	USBLS	5/07
	Florida	Y	21850 FQ	26940 MW	32550 TQ	USBLS	5/07
	Fort Lauderdale-Pompano Beach-Deerfield Beach PMSA, FL	Y	23610 FQ	28050 MW	33440 TQ	USBLS	5/07
	Jacksonville MSA, FL	Y	20180 FQ	21580 MW	22980 TQ	USBLS	5/07
	Miami-Fort Lauderdale-Miami Beach MSA, FL	Y	24230 FQ	29850 MW	36320 TQ	USBLS	5/07
	Orlando-Kissimmee MSA, FL	Y	25730 FQ	29230 MW	33280 TQ	USBLS	5/07
	Pensacola-Ferry Pass-Brent MSA, FL	Y	23610 FQ	28410 MW	33130 TQ	USBLS	5/07
	Tampa-St. Petersburg-Clearwater MSA, FL	Y	24080 FQ	28140 MW	32030 TQ	USBLS	5/07
	West Palm Beach-Boca Raton-Boynton Beach PMSA, FL	Y	29950 FQ	34120 MW	38750 TQ	USBLS	5/07
	Georgia	Y	22940 FQ	31270 MW	38490 TQ	USBLS	5/07
	Atlanta-Sandy Springs-Marietta MSA, GA	Y	32450 FQ	37010 MW	43140 TQ	USBLS	5/07
	Idaho	Y	21930 FQ	27930 MW	35120 TQ	USBLS	5/07
	Illinois	Y	27740 FQ	36510 MW	45740 TQ	USBLS	5/07
	Chicago-Naperville-Joliet MSA, IL-IN-WI	Y	29020 FQ	36870 MW	46930 TQ	USBLS	5/07
	Indiana	Y	25930 FQ	33400 MW	39220 TQ	USBLS	5/07
	Gary PMSA, IN	Y	29920 FQ	37320 MW	45040 TQ	USBLS	5/07
	Indianapolis-Carmel MSA, IN	Y	22940 FQ	26220 MW	37620 TQ	USBLS	5/07
	Iowa	Y	26700 FQ	31540 MW	39310 TQ	USBLS	5/07
	Kansas	Y	26740 FQ	32030 MW	58770 TQ	USBLS	5/07
	Kentucky	Y	13899 FQ	16469 MW	24232 TQ	KYBLS	2008
	Louisiana	H	11.02 FQ	13.43 MW	17.48 TQ	LABLS	1/08-3/08
	New Orleans-Metairie-Kenner MSA, LA	Y	24830 FQ	27400 MW	30080 TQ	USBLS	5/07
	Maine	Y	26540 FQ	30300 MW	35830 TQ	USBLS	5/07
	Maryland	Y		36175 MW		MDBLS	3/08
	Baltimore-Towson MSA, MD	Y	31630 FQ	44470 MW	52750 TQ	USBLS	5/07
	Massachusetts	Y	33120 FQ	37810 MW	45540 TQ	USBLS	5/07
	Boston-Cambridge-Quincy NECTA, MA	Y	31570 FQ	39270 MW	48500 TQ	USBLS	5/07
	Worcester MSA, MA-CT	Y	35340 FQ	38160 MW	40970 TQ	USBLS	5/07
	Michigan	Y	26140 FQ	32130 MW	37370 TQ	USBLS	5/07
	Detroit-Warren-Livonia MSA, MI	Y	32330 FQ	35490 MW	39210 TQ	USBLS	5/07
	Grand Rapids-Wyoming MSA, MI	Y	25890 FQ	33110 MW	37560 TQ	USBLS	5/07
	Warren-Troy-Farmington Hills PMSA, MI	Y	34850 FQ	40560 MW	46760 TQ	USBLS	5/07
	Minnesota	Y	31468 FQ	40468 MW	47392 TQ	MNBLS	10/08-12/08

AE	Average entry wage	AW	Average wage paid	FQ	First quartile wage	LO	Lowest wage paid	MTC	Median total compensation	TCC	Total cash compensation
AER	Average entry range	AWR	Average wage range	H	Hourly	LR	Low end range	MW	Median wage paid	TQ	Third quartile wage
AEX	Average experienced wage	AXR	Average experienced range	HI	Highest wage paid	M	Monthly	MWR	Median wage range	W	Weekly
ATC	Average total compensation	D	Daily	HR	High end range	MCC	Median cash compensation	S	See annotated source	Y	Yearly

Occupation/Type/Industry	Location	Per	Low	Mid	High	Source	Date
Septic Tank Servicer and Sewer Pipe Cleaner	Duluth-Superior MSA, MN-WI	Y	26325 FQ	38318 MW	45696 TQ	MNBLS	10/08-12/08
	Minneapolis-Saint Paul MSA, MN-WI	Y	35926 FQ	40890 MW	47160 TQ	MNBLS	10/08-12/08
	Rochester MSA, MN	Y	35715 FQ	41199 MW	46296 TQ	MNBLS	10/08-12/08
	Mississippi	Y	17410 FQ	20610 MW	26020 TQ	USBLS	5/07
	Missouri	Y	22710 FQ	30300 MW	39030 TQ	USBLS	5/07
	Kansas City MSA, MO-KS	Y	18870 FQ	30570 MW	60750 TQ	USBLS	5/07
	St. Louis MSA, MO-IL	Y	24470 FQ	35040 MW	41900 TQ	USBLS	5/07
	Montana	Y	23330 FQ	27350 MW	32150 TQ	USBLS	5/07
	Great Falls MSA, MT	Y	26850 FQ	29220 MW	31570 TQ	USBLS	5/07
	Nebraska	Y	23540 FQ	31360 MW	43700 TQ	USBLS	5/07
	Omaha-Council Bluffs MSA, NE-IA	Y	26690 FQ	36760 MW	46110 TQ	USBLS	5/07
	Nevada	H	13.66 FQ	16.31 MW	19.73 TQ	NVBLS	5/08
	New Hampshire	H	11.81 AE	17.42 MW	20.42 AEX	NHBLS	6/08
	New Jersey	Y	34610 FQ	42230 MW	54310 TQ	USBLS	5/07
	Camden PMSA, NJ	Y	34360 FQ	37880 MW	42160 TQ	USBLS	5/07
	Edison PMSA, NJ	Y	38790 FQ	47000 MW	61080 TQ	USBLS	5/07
	Newark-Union PMSA, NJ-PA	Y	36590 FQ	43570 MW	50200 TQ	USBLS	5/07
	New Mexico	Y	19540 FQ	23410 MW	27790 TQ	USBLS	5/07
	New York	Y	27000 FQ	36120 MW	46090 TQ	USBLS	5/07
	Albany-Schenectady-Troy MSA, NY	Y	34290 FQ	39040 MW	47340 TQ	USBLS	5/07
	Buffalo-Niagara Falls MSA, NY	Y	30560 FQ	36440 MW	41220 TQ	USBLS	5/07
	Nassau-Suffolk PMSA, NY	Y	28180 FQ	35670 MW	41400 TQ	USBLS	5/07
	New York-Northern New Jersey-Long Island MSA, NY-NJ-PA	Y	32810 FQ	40850 MW	52560 TQ	USBLS	5/07
	North Carolina	Y	23690 FQ	28760 MW	39850 TQ	USBLS	5/07
	Charlotte-Gastonia-Concord MSA, NC-SC	Y	31980 FQ	37640 MW	42330 TQ	USBLS	5/07
	Raleigh-Cary MSA, NC	Y	23640 FQ	26870 MW	30370 TQ	USBLS	5/07
	North Dakota	Y	21310 FQ	28370 MW	38470 TQ	USBLS	5/07
	Ohio	Y	27330 FQ	32040 MW	41120 TQ	USBLS	5/07
	Canton-Massillon MSA, OH	Y	27900 FQ	31090 MW	40140 TQ	USBLS	5/07
	Cleveland-Elyria-Mentor MSA, OH	Y	30010 FQ	37730 MW	45210 TQ	USBLS	5/07
	Columbus MSA, OH	Y	27940 FQ	30990 MW	44850 TQ	USBLS	5/07
	Oklahoma	Y	22130 FQ	27090 MW	32640 TQ	USBLS	5/07
	Oklahoma City MSA, OK	Y	24580 FQ	33940 MW	38180 TQ	USBLS	5/07
	Tulsa MSA, OK	Y	21170 FQ	23100 MW	25030 TQ	USBLS	5/07
	Oregon	H	15.39 FQ	19.44 MW	26.46 TQ	ORBLS	5/08
	Portland-Vancouver-Beaverton MSA, OR-WA	Y	34600 FQ	40670 MW	56360 TQ	USBLS	5/07
	Pennsylvania	Y	29530 FQ	35720 MW	40920 TQ	USBLS	5/07
	Philadelphia-Camden-Wilmington MSA, PA-NJ-DE-MD	Y	32920 FQ	36680 MW	40320 TQ	USBLS	5/07
	Pittsburgh MSA, PA	Y	30580 FQ	38090 MW	48460 TQ	USBLS	5/07
	Rhode Island	Y	34560 FQ	39620 MW	46370 TQ	USBLS	5/07
	Providence-Fall River-Warwick MSA, RI-MA	Y	33730 FQ	38190 MW	45740 TQ	USBLS	5/07
	South Carolina	Y	19030 FQ	23730 MW	31050 TQ	USBLS	5/07
	Charleston-North Charleston MSA, SC	Y	21070 FQ	29540 MW	43970 TQ	USBLS	5/07
	Columbia MSA, SC	Y	28860 FQ	33720 MW	37590 TQ	USBLS	5/07
	South Dakota	Y	19461 FQ	22176 MW	25838 TQ	SDBLS	7/08-9/08
	Tennessee	Y	21590 FQ	27000 MW	31600 TQ	USBLS	5/07
	Memphis MSA, TN-MS-AR	Y	16480 FQ	17760 MW	19440 TQ	USBLS	5/07
	Nashville-Davidson-Murfreesboro MSA, TN	Y	32930 FQ	36420 MW	39980 TQ	USBLS	5/07
	Texas	Y	22130 FQ	27220 MW	32910 TQ	USBLS	5/07
	Austin-Round Rock MSA, TX	Y	27010 FQ	30000 MW	37050 TQ	USBLS	5/07
	Dallas-Fort Worth-Arlington MSA, TX	Y	26890 FQ	32900 MW	36050 TQ	USBLS	5/07
	Houston-Sugar Land-Baytown MSA, TX	Y	30350 FQ	33220 MW	36060 TQ	USBLS	5/07
	San Antonio MSA, TX	Y	19190 FQ	23550 MW	28370 TQ	USBLS	5/07
	Utah	Y	29550 FQ	36840 MW	54420 TQ	USBLS	5/07
	Vermont	Y	32130 FQ	35570 MW	40950 TQ	USBLS	5/07

AE	Average entry wage	AW	Average wage paid	FQ	First quartile wage
AER	Average entry range	AWR	Average wage range	H	Hourly
AEX	Average experienced wage	AXR	Average experienced range	HI	Highest wage paid
ATC	Average total compensation	D	Daily	HR	High end range

LO	Lowest wage paid	MTC	Median total compensation
LR	Low end range	MW	Median wage paid
M	Monthly	MWR	Median wage range
MCC	Median cash compensation	S	See annotated source

TCC	Total cash compensation
TQ	Third quartile wage
W	Weekly
Y	Yearly

Occupation/Type/Industry	Location	Per	Low	Mid	High	Source	Date
Septic Tank Servicer and Sewer Pipe Cleaner	Virginia	Y	24100 FQ	29140 MW	34040 TQ	USBLS	5/07
	Richmond MSA, VA	Y	26040 FQ	30540 MW	36780 TQ	USBLS	5/07
	Virginia Beach-Norfolk-Newport News MSA, VA-NC	Y	27690 FQ	32350 MW	36530 TQ	USBLS	5/07
	Washington	H	16.25 FQ	19.40 MW	23.95 TQ	WABLS	3/08
	Seattle-Tacoma-Bellevue MSA, WA	Y	37690 FQ	45600 MW	52400 TQ	USBLS	5/07
	West Virginia	Y	27815 FQ	31351 MW	34856 TQ	WVBLS	7/08-9/08
	Wisconsin	Y	25140 FQ	31320 MW	38090 TQ	USBLS	5/07
	Milwaukee-Waukesha-West Allis MSA, WI	Y	27130 FQ	29300 MW	31470 TQ	USBLS	5/07
	Wyoming	Y	32398 FQ	39936 MW	47739 TQ	WYBLS	9/08
	Puerto Rico	Y	13010 FQ	14860 MW	20410 TQ	USBLS	5/07
	San Juan-Caguas-Guaynabo MSA, PR	Y	12980 FQ	14840 MW	19360 TQ	USBLS	5/07
Sergeant							
Department of Corrections	New Hampshire	Y		62122 AW		NHUL03	2008
Police Department	Bainbridge, GA	Y	37084 LO		70762 HI	GACTY01	2008
U.S. Marines, Active Duty, Pay Grade E-4	United States	M	1827 LO		2219 HI	DOD1	2009
U.S. Marines, Active Duty, Pay Grade E-5	United States	M	1994 LO		2828 HI	DOD1	2009
Sergeant, Specialist 4							
U.S. Army, Active Duty, Pay Grade E-4	United States	M	1827 LO		2219 HI	DOD1	2009
Sergeant, Specialist 5							
U.S. Army, Active Duty, Pay Grade E-5	United States	M	1994 LO		2828 HI	DOD1	2009
Sergeant 1st Class							
U.S. Army, Active Duty, Pay Grade E-7	United States	M	2516 LO		4521 HI	DOD1	2009
Sergeant at Arms							
United States House of Representatives	United States	Y			167800 HI	CRS01	1/08
Sergeant at Arms and Doorkeeper							
United States Senate	United States	Y			163700 HI	CRS01	2007
Sergeant Major							
U.S. Army, Active Duty, Pay Grade E-9	United States	M	4421 LO		6863 HI	DOD1	2009
U.S. Marines, Active Duty, Pay Grade E-9	United States	M	4421 LO		6863 HI	DOD1	2009
Service Area Coordinator							
Municipal Government	Cincinnati, OH	Y	44033 LO		60634 HI	COHSS	10/08
Service Desk Manager	United States	Y		77270 MW		DATAM	2009
Service Manager							
Copier Industry	United States	Y		67739 AW		COPIER2	2008
Service Station Attendant	Alabama	Y	13560 FQ	16600 MW	19910 TQ	USBLS	5/07
	Birmingham-Hoover MSA, AL	Y	13780 FQ	17070 MW	21130 TQ	USBLS	5/07
	Montgomery MSA, AL	Y	13740 FQ	16190 MW	19210 TQ	USBLS	5/07
	Tuscaloosa MSA, AL	Y	17220 FQ	18570 MW	19920 TQ	USBLS	5/07
	Alaska	Y	18830 FQ	22310 MW	27210 TQ	USBLS	5/07
	Anchorage MSA, AK	Y	18030 FQ	20460 MW	23710 TQ	USBLS	5/07
	Arizona	Y	16690 FQ	19130 MW	23140 TQ	USBLS	5/07
	Phoenix-Mesa-Scottsdale MSA, AZ	Y	16440 FQ	18800 MW	23550 TQ	USBLS	5/07
	Tucson MSA, AZ	Y	20660 FQ	26030 MW	29770 TQ	USBLS	5/07
	Arkansas	Y	16340 FQ	18270 MW	20430 TQ	USBLS	5/07
	Little Rock-North Little Rock MSA, AR	Y	16840 FQ	18690 MW	20970 TQ	USBLS	5/07
	California	H	8.70 FQ	10.01 MW	13.83 TQ	CABLS	1/08-3/08
	Bakersfield MSA, CA	H	13.88 FQ	17.84 MW	19.80 TQ	CABLS	1/08-3/08
	Los Angeles-Long Beach-Glendale PMSA, CA	H	9.06 FQ	13.63 MW	16.44 TQ	CABLS	1/08-3/08
	Oakland-Fremont-Hayward MSA, CA	H	8.86 FQ	9.76 MW	11.09 TQ	CABLS	1/08-3/08
	Riverside-San Bernardino-Ontario MSA, CA	H	9.23 FQ	10.48 MW	11.71 TQ	CABLS	1/08-3/08
	Sacramento-Arden Arcade-Roseville MSA, CA	H	8.47 FQ	9.19 MW	9.86 TQ	CABLS	1/08-3/08

AE	Average entry wage	AW	Average wage paid	FQ	First quartile wage
AER	Average entry range	AWR	Average wage range	H	Hourly
AEX	Average experienced wage	AXR	Average experienced range	HI	Highest wage paid
ATC	Average total compensation	D	Daily	HR	High end range

LO	Lowest wage paid	MTC	Median total compensation	TCC	Total cash compensation
LR	Low end range	MW	Median wage paid	TQ	Third quartile wage
M	Monthly	MWR	Median wage range	W	Weekly
MCC	Median cash compensation	S	See annotated source	Y	Yearly

Occupation/Type/Industry	Location	Per	Low	Mid	High	Source	Date
Service Station Attendant	San Diego-Carlsbad-San Marcos MSA, CA	H	8.53 FQ	9.41 MW	11.28 TQ	CABLS	1/08-3/08
	San Francisco-San Mateo-Redwood PMSA, CA	H	8.91 FQ	9.69 MW	10.85 TQ	CABLS	1/08-3/08
	San Jose-Sunnyvale-Santa Clara MSA, CA	H	8.84 FQ	10.04 MW	12.02 TQ	CABLS	1/08-3/08
	Santa Ana-Anaheim-Irvine PMSA, CA	Y	16840 FQ	18080 MW	22540 TQ	USBLS	5/07
	Colorado	Y	17380 FQ	20110 MW	23890 TQ	USBLS	5/07
	Denver-Aurora MSA, CO	Y	17220 FQ	19730 MW	23370 TQ	USBLS	5/07
	Connecticut	H	8.56 AE	9.40 MW		CTBLS	1/08-3/08
	Bridgeport-Stamford-Norwalk MSA, CT	Y	17490 FQ	19630 MW	24260 TQ	USBLS	5/07
	Hartford-West Hartford-East Hartford MSA, CT	Y	16900 FQ	18090 MW	20010 TQ	USBLS	5/07
	Delaware	Y	17220 FQ	18880 MW	20400 TQ	USBLS	5/07
	Wilmington PMSA, DE-MD-NJ	Y	15800 FQ	17620 MW	19600 TQ	USBLS	5/07
	Washington-Arlington-Alexandria MSA, DC-VA-MD-WV	Y	17640 FQ	20510 MW	24940 TQ	USBLS	5/07
	Florida	Y	16770 FQ	19530 MW	23760 TQ	USBLS	5/07
	Fort Lauderdale-Pompano Beach-Deerfield Beach PMSA, FL	Y	14950 FQ	16500 MW	19600 TQ	USBLS	5/07
	Jacksonville MSA, FL	Y	17900 FQ	21220 MW	26800 TQ	USBLS	5/07
	Miami-Fort Lauderdale-Miami Beach MSA, FL	Y	15530 FQ	17540 MW	20350 TQ	USBLS	5/07
	Orlando-Kissimmee MSA, FL	Y	21530 FQ	26430 MW	33080 TQ	USBLS	5/07
	Tampa-St. Petersburg-Clearwater MSA, FL	Y	15850 FQ	17730 MW	21760 TQ	USBLS	5/07
	West Palm Beach-Boca Raton-Boynton Beach PMSA, FL	Y	16750 FQ	18140 MW	19650 TQ	USBLS	5/07
	Georgia	Y	15290 FQ	17860 MW	22280 TQ	USBLS	5/07
	Atlanta-Sandy Springs-Marietta MSA, GA	Y	15940 FQ	18290 MW	23060 TQ	USBLS	5/07
	Hawaii	Y	15860 FQ	18640 MW	29740 TQ	USBLS	5/07
	Honolulu MSA, HI	Y	17150 FQ	19280 MW	34640 TQ	USBLS	5/07
	Idaho	Y	16090 FQ	18910 MW	22780 TQ	USBLS	5/07
	Boise City-Nampa MSA, ID	Y	17560 FQ	20170 MW	22920 TQ	USBLS	5/07
	Illinois	Y	15050 FQ	16750 MW	21040 TQ	USBLS	5/07
	Chicago-Naperville-Joliet MSA, IL-IN-WI	Y	14760 FQ	16070 MW	19370 TQ	USBLS	5/07
	Indiana	Y	13790 FQ	16260 MW	19370 TQ	USBLS	5/07
	Gary PMSA, IN	Y	12780 FQ	14790 MW	17130 TQ	USBLS	5/07
	Indianapolis-Carmel MSA, IN	Y	13820 FQ	16000 MW	18330 TQ	USBLS	5/07
	Iowa	Y	15030 FQ	17000 MW	19810 TQ	USBLS	5/07
	Des Moines-West Des Moines MSA, IA	Y	14140 FQ	15370 MW	17940 TQ	USBLS	5/07
	Kansas	Y	14890 FQ	18340 MW	22960 TQ	USBLS	5/07
	Wichita MSA, KS	Y	16590 FQ	19240 MW	26640 TQ	USBLS	5/07
	Kentucky	Y	15217 FQ	18626 MW	24465 TQ	KYBLS	2008
	Louisville-Jefferson County MSA, KY-IN	Y	16470 FQ	19660 MW	26570 TQ	USBLS	5/07
	Louisiana	H	7.18 FQ	8.40 MW	9.68 TQ	LABLS	1/08-3/08
	Baton Rouge MSA, LA	Y	14120 FQ	17540 MW	23640 TQ	USBLS	5/07
	New Orleans-Metairie-Kenner MSA, LA	Y	13250 FQ	15300 MW	18050 TQ	USBLS	5/07
	Maine	Y	15140 FQ	16570 MW	18890 TQ	USBLS	5/07
	Portland-South Portland-Biddeford MSA, ME	Y	15880 FQ	18360 MW	20940 TQ	USBLS	5/07
	Maryland	Y		20150 MW		MDBLS	3/08
	Baltimore-Towson MSA, MD	Y	15280 FQ	18400 MW	24270 TQ	USBLS	5/07
	Bethesda-Gaithersburg-Frederick PMSA, MD	Y	16250 FQ	18710 MW	21830 TQ	USBLS	5/07
	Massachusetts	Y	17030 FQ	19530 MW	23130 TQ	USBLS	5/07
	Boston-Cambridge-Quincy NECTA, MA	Y	17730 FQ	20260 MW	23110 TQ	USBLS	5/07
	New Bedford MSA, MA	Y	21480 FQ	29710 MW	36300 TQ	USBLS	5/07
	Worcester MSA, MA-CT	Y	16580 FQ	18260 MW	20500 TQ	USBLS	5/07
	Michigan	Y	16910 FQ	19920 MW	25740 TQ	USBLS	5/07

AE	Average entry wage	AW	Average wage paid	FQ	First quartile wage	LO	Lowest wage paid	MTC	Median total compensation	TCC	Total cash compensation
AER	Average entry range	AWR	Average wage range	H	Hourly	LR	Low end range	MW	Median wage paid	TQ	Third quartile wage
AEX	Average experienced wage	AXR	Average experienced range	HI	Highest wage paid	M	Monthly	MWR	Median wage range	W	Weekly
ATC	Average total compensation	D	Daily	HR	High end range	MCC	Median cash compensation	S	See annotated source	Y	Yearly

Occupation/Type/Industry	Location	Per	Low	Mid	High	Source	Date
Service Station Attendant	Detroit-Warren-Livonia MSA, MI	Y	17550 FQ	22050 MW	28120 TQ	USBLS	5/07
	Grand Rapids-Wyoming MSA, MI	Y	15040 FQ	18620 MW	21970 TQ	USBLS	5/07
	Warren-Troy-Farmington Hills PMSA, MI	Y	19790 FQ	23830 MW	29060 TQ	USBLS	5/07
	Minnesota	Y	18174 FQ	21545 MW	24708 TQ	MNBLS	10/08-12/08
	Duluth-Superior MSA, MN-WI	Y	14783 FQ	15813 MW	17779 TQ	MNBLS	10/08-12/08
	Minneapolis-Saint Paul MSA, MN-WI	Y	20193 FQ	22804 MW	25384 TQ	MNBLS	10/08-12/08
	Rochester MSA, MN	Y	21003 FQ	25801 MW	30596 TQ	MNBLS	10/08-12/08
	Mississippi	Y	14560 FQ	17640 MW	21380 TQ	USBLS	5/07
	Jackson MSA, MS	Y	12970 FQ	14800 MW	19030 TQ	USBLS	5/07
	Missouri	Y	15090 FQ	17690 MW	22180 TQ	USBLS	5/07
	Kansas City MSA, MO-KS	Y	17410 FQ	20030 MW	25620 TQ	USBLS	5/07
	St. Louis MSA, MO-IL	Y	15290 FQ	18630 MW	22330 TQ	USBLS	5/07
	Springfield MSA, MO	Y	16570 FQ	17730 MW	19090 TQ	USBLS	5/07
	Montana	Y	14900 FQ	17100 MW	22460 TQ	USBLS	5/07
	Billings MSA, MT	Y	15550 FQ	20970 MW	31070 TQ	USBLS	5/07
	Nebraska	Y	13270 FQ	15640 MW	18910 TQ	USBLS	5/07
	Omaha-Council Bluffs MSA, NE-IA	Y	15210 FQ	18170 MW	20820 TQ	USBLS	5/07
	Nevada	H	7.88 FQ	8.77 MW	10.11 TQ	NVBLS	5/08
	Las Vegas-Paradise MSA, NV	H	7.69 FQ	8.54 MW	9.58 TQ	NVBLS	5/08
	New Hampshire	H	7.72 AE	9.67 MW	10.79 AEX	NHBLS	6/08
	Manchester MSA, NH	Y	16330 FQ	19080 MW	22710 TQ	USBLS	5/07
	Nashua NECTA, NH-MA	Y	17210 FQ	19420 MW	21830 TQ	USBLS	5/07
	Portsmouth MSA, NH-ME	Y	14780 FQ	19860 MW	23690 TQ	USBLS	5/07
	New Jersey	Y	15860 FQ	17450 MW	19300 TQ	USBLS	5/07
	Camden PMSA, NJ	Y	16800 FQ	18320 MW	19940 TQ	USBLS	5/07
	Edison PMSA, NJ	Y	15750 FQ	17140 MW	18800 TQ	USBLS	5/07
	Newark-Union PMSA, NJ-PA	Y	15710 FQ	17160 MW	19240 TQ	USBLS	5/07
	New Mexico	Y	14940 FQ	18560 MW	24240 TQ	USBLS	5/07
	Albuquerque MSA, NM	Y	16140 FQ	20830 MW	27030 TQ	USBLS	5/07
	New York	Y	15260 FQ	16330 MW	20590 TQ	USBLS	5/07
	Albany-Schenectady-Troy MSA, NY	Y	22620 FQ	25020 MW	34480 TQ	USBLS	5/07
	Buffalo-Niagara Falls MSA, NY	Y	15350 FQ	15840 MW	17220 TQ	USBLS	5/07
	Nassau-Suffolk PMSA, NY	Y	15330 FQ	17210 MW	21210 TQ	USBLS	5/07
	New York-Northern New Jersey-Long Island MSA, NY-NJ-PA	Y	15710 FQ	17210 MW*	19220 TQ	USBLS	5/07
	North Carolina	Y	14790 FQ	17010 MW	20250 TQ	USBLS	5/07
	Charlotte-Gastonia-Concord MSA, NC-SC	Y	16520 FQ	19110 MW	23710 TQ	USBLS	5/07
	Raleigh-Cary MSA, NC	Y	14000 FQ	15210 MW	18750 TQ	USBLS	5/07
	North Dakota	Y	15730 FQ	19330 MW	23670 TQ	USBLS	5/07
	Fargo MSA, ND-MN	Y	15660 FQ	18030 MW	21630 TQ	USBLS	5/07
	Ohio	Y	15120 FQ	16890 MW	19550 TQ	USBLS	5/07
	Cincinnati-Middletown MSA, OH-KY-IN	Y	15970 FQ	17810 MW	20240 TQ	USBLS	5/07
	Cleveland-Elyria-Mentor MSA, OH	Y	15480 FQ	17050 MW	19310 TQ	USBLS	5/07
	Columbus MSA, OH	Y	15470 FQ	17200 MW	19760 TQ	USBLS	5/07
	Dayton MSA, OH	Y	14720 FQ	16550 MW	18800 TQ	USBLS	5/07
	Oklahoma	Y	15010 FQ	18490 MW	21840 TQ	USBLS	5/07
	Oklahoma City MSA, OK	Y	14240 FQ	17630 MW	20260 TQ	USBLS	5/07
	Tulsa MSA, OK	Y	15680 FQ	21450 MW	23880 TQ	USBLS	5/07
	Oregon	H	8.41 FQ	8.96 MW	9.69 TQ	ORBLS	5/08
	Portland-Vancouver-Beaverton MSA, OR-WA	Y	17220 FQ	18400 MW	20140 TQ	USBLS	5/07
	Pennsylvania	Y	15600 FQ	18090 MW	22330 TQ	USBLS	5/07
	Allentown-Bethlehem-Easton MSA, PA-NJ	Y	16510 FQ	17930 MW	19690 TQ	USBLS	5/07
	Philadelphia-Camden-Wilmington MSA, PA-NJ-DE-MD	Y	16760 FQ	18640 MW	22520 TQ	USBLS	5/07
	Pittsburgh MSA, PA	Y	16240 FQ	18220 MW	21130 TQ	USBLS	5/07
	Rhode Island	Y	18240 FQ	20950 MW	24120 TQ	USBLS	5/07
	Providence-Fall River-Warwick MSA, RI-MA	Y	18090 FQ	20850 MW	23800 TQ	USBLS	5/07

AE Average entry wage	**AW** Average wage paid	**FQ** First quartile wage	**LO** Lowest wage paid	**MTC** Median total compensation	**TCC** Total cash compensation
AER Average entry range	**AWR** Average wage range	**H** Hourly	**LR** Low end range	**MW** Median wage paid	**TQ** Third quartile wage
AEX Average experienced wage	**AXR** Average experienced range	**HI** Highest wage paid	**M** Monthly	**MWR** Median wage range	**W** Weekly
ATC Average total compensation	**D** Daily	**HR** High end range	**MCC** Median cash compensation	**S** See annotated source	**Y** Yearly

Occupation/Type/Industry	Location	Per	Low	Mid	High	Source	Date
Service Station Attendant	South Carolina	Y	14110 FQ	17360 MW	21520 TQ	USBLS	5/07
	Charleston-North Charleston MSA, SC	Y	14250 FQ	17050 MW	19590 TQ	USBLS	5/07
	South Dakota	Y	17240 FQ	18710 MW	20512 TQ	SDBLS	7/08-9/08
	Sioux Falls MSA, SD	Y	17041 FQ	18415 MW	20416 TQ	SDBLS	7/08-9/08
	Tennessee	Y	13750 FQ	16700 MW	19520 TQ	USBLS	5/07
	Knoxville MSA, TN	Y	13930 FQ	16210 MW	18280 TQ	USBLS	5/07
	Memphis MSA, TN-MS-AR	Y	13370 FQ	15890 MW	19580 TQ	USBLS	5/07
	Nashville-Davidson-Murfreesboro MSA, TN	Y	16740 FQ	18920 MW	21430 TQ	USBLS	5/07
	Texas	Y	15300 FQ	17910 MW	21050 TQ	USBLS	5/07
	Austin-Round Rock MSA, TX	Y	13750 FQ	17200 MW	19920 TQ	USBLS	5/07
	Corpus Christi MSA, TX	Y	14690 FQ	17200 MW	19650 TQ	USBLS	5/07
	Dallas-Fort Worth-Arlington MSA, TX	Y	16600 FQ	18630 MW	22050 TQ	USBLS	5/07
	El Paso MSA, TX	Y	13650 FQ	16460 MW	19400 TQ	USBLS	5/07
	Houston-Sugar Land-Baytown MSA, TX	Y	14890 FQ	17970 MW	21480 TQ	USBLS	5/07
	San Antonio MSA, TX	Y	15840 FQ	18120 MW	21930 TQ	USBLS	5/07
	Utah	Y	16470 FQ	19210 MW	22160 TQ	USBLS	5/07
	Salt Lake City MSA, UT	Y	19150 FQ	21140 MW	23370 TQ	USBLS	5/07
	Vermont	Y	16720 FQ	18010 MW	19790 TQ	USBLS	5/07
	Burlington-South Burlington MSA, VT	Y	16750 FQ	18180 MW	20190 TQ	USBLS	5/07
	Virginia	Y	16130 FQ	18990 MW	23370 TQ	USBLS	5/07
	Richmond MSA, VA	Y	15120 FQ	17860 MW	22500 TQ	USBLS	5/07
	Virginia Beach-Norfolk-Newport News MSA, VA-NC	Y	15790 FQ	18760 MW	22260 TQ	USBLS	5/07
	Washington	H	8.91 FQ	10.21 MW	12.15 TQ	WABLS	3/08
	Seattle-Tacoma-Bellevue MSA, WA	Y	18400 FQ	21350 MW	25290 TQ	USBLS	5/07
	West Virginia	Y	13911 FQ	15015 MW	17173 TQ	WVBLS	7/08-9/08
	Wisconsin	Y	15750 FQ	17870 MW	20200 TQ	USBLS	5/07
	Milwaukee-Waukesha-West Allis MSA, WI	Y	15250 FQ	17150 MW	18870 TQ	USBLS	5/07
	Wyoming	Y	15097 FQ	19297 MW	27161 TQ	WYBLS	9/08
	Cheyenne MSA, WY	Y	17275 FQ	27578 MW	36524 TQ	WYBLS	9/08
	Puerto Rico	Y	12530 FQ	13910 MW	15720 TQ	USBLS	5/07
	San Juan-Caguas-Guaynabo MSA, PR	Y	12680 FQ	14190 MW	16480 TQ	USBLS	5/07
	Virgin Islands	Y	13700 FQ	14610 MW	17630 TQ	USBLS	5/07
	Guam	Y	12170 FQ	13230 MW	14290 TQ	USBLS	5/07
Service Technician Copier Industry	United States	Y		39865 AW		COPIER1	2008
Service Unit Operator Oil, Gas, and Mining	Alabama	Y	27870 FQ	33430 MW	38560 TQ	USBLS	5/07
Oil, Gas, and Mining	Arkansas	Y	29820 FQ	32900 MW	37300 TQ	USBLS	5/07
Oil, Gas, and Mining	California	H	16.30 FQ	20.48 MW	25.38 TQ	CABLS	1/08-3/08
Oil, Gas, and Mining	Colorado	Y	29390 FQ	36730 MW	47410 TQ	USBLS	5/07
Oil, Gas, and Mining	Illinois	Y	23640 FQ	27650 MW	32840 TQ	USBLS	5/07
Oil, Gas, and Mining	Kansas	Y	30480 FQ	34860 MW	39980 TQ	USBLS	5/07
Oil, Gas, and Mining	Kentucky	Y	24134 FQ	33357 MW	39342 TQ	KYBLS	2008
Oil, Gas, and Mining	Louisiana	H	13.90 FQ	17.00 MW	21.48 TQ	LABLS	1/08-3/08
Oil, Gas, and Mining	Michigan	Y	26110 FQ	29890 MW	35500 TQ	USBLS	5/07
Oil, Gas, and Mining	Mississippi	Y	33510 FQ	36820 MW	40180 TQ	USBLS	5/07
Oil, Gas, and Mining	Montana	Y	35740 FQ	44420 MW	53120 TQ	USBLS	5/07
Oil, Gas, and Mining	New Mexico	Y	32790 FQ	44960 MW	60890 TQ	USBLS	5/07
Oil, Gas, and Mining	New York	Y	28260 FQ	38820 MW	52530 TQ	USBLS	5/07
Oil, Gas, and Mining	North Dakota	Y	35260 FQ	39840 MW	48050 TQ	USBLS	5/07
Oil, Gas, and Mining	Ohio	Y	22030 FQ	25330 MW	30880 TQ	USBLS	5/07
Oil, Gas, and Mining	Oklahoma	Y	25960 FQ	33640 MW	47630 TQ	USBLS	5/07
Oil, Gas, and Mining	Pennsylvania	Y	22530 FQ	26250 MW	32410 TQ	USBLS	5/07
Oil, Gas, and Mining	Tennessee	Y	42990 FQ	47250 MW	51970 TQ	USBLS	5/07
Oil, Gas, and Mining	Texas	Y	26910 FQ	33550 MW	43270 TQ	USBLS	5/07
Oil, Gas, and Mining	Utah	Y	35960 FQ	43270 MW	58280 TQ	USBLS	5/07
Oil, Gas, and Mining	Wyoming	Y	33415 FQ	46578 MW	56546 TQ	WYBLS	9/08
Set and Exhibit Designer	Arizona	Y	29180 FQ	34370 MW	43940 TQ	USBLS	5/07
	Phoenix-Mesa-Scottsdale MSA, AZ	Y	27450 FQ	33440 MW	45670 TQ	USBLS	5/07

AE	Average entry wage	**AW**	Average wage paid	**FQ**	First quartile wage
AER	Average entry range	**AWR**	Average wage range	**H**	Hourly
AEX	Average experienced wage	**AXR**	Average experienced range	**HI**	Highest wage paid
ATC	Average total compensation	**D**	Daily	**HR**	High end range

LO	Lowest wage paid	**MTC**	Median total compensation	**TCC**	Total cash compensation
LR	Low end range	**MW**	Median wage paid	**TQ**	Third quartile wage
M	Monthly	**MWR**	Median wage range	**W**	Weekly
MCC	Median cash compensation	**S**	See annotated source	**Y**	Yearly

Occupation/Type/Industry	Location	Per	Low	Mid	High	Source	Date
Set and Exhibit Designer	Tucson MSA, AZ	Y	30330 FQ	34190 MW	40080 TQ	USBLS	5/07
	California	H	19.27 FQ	28.47 MW	38.78 TQ	CABLS	1/08-3/08
	Los Angeles-Long Beach-Glendale PMSA, CA	H	20.23 FQ	31.86 MW	42.26 TQ	CABLS	1/08-3/08
	Oakland-Fremont-Hayward MSA, CA	H	26.64 FQ	29.45 MW	32.35 TQ	CABLS	1/08-3/08
	Riverside-San Bernardino-Ontario MSA, CA	H	13.21 FQ	17.17 MW	26.13 TQ	CABLS	1/08-3/08
	Sacramento-Arden Arcade-Roseville MSA, CA	H	22.38 FQ	27.11 MW	30.22 TQ	CABLS	1/08-3/08
	San Diego-Carlsbad-San Marcos MSA, CA	H	20.02 FQ	27.38 MW	39.77 TQ	CABLS	1/08-3/08
	San Francisco-San Mateo-Redwood PMSA, CA	H	21.55 FQ	24.80 MW	30.23 TQ	CABLS	1/08-3/08
	San Jose-Sunnyvale-Santa Clara MSA, CA	H	21.31 FQ	34.60 MW	44.07 TQ	CABLS	1/08-3/08
	Santa Ana-Anaheim-Irvine PMSA, CA	Y	34640 FQ	38440 MW	56440 TQ	USBLS	5/07
	Colorado	Y	24820 FQ	27010 MW	29200 TQ	USBLS	5/07
	Denver-Aurora MSA, CO	Y	24310 FQ	29540 MW	51650 TQ	USBLS	5/07
	Connecticut	H	15.48 AE	21.08 MW		CTBLS	1/08-3/08
	Delaware	Y	39480 FQ	43930 MW	48770 TQ	USBLS	5/07
	Wilmington PMSA, DE-MD-NJ	Y	39350 FQ	43900 MW	49530 TQ	USBLS	5/07
	District of Columbia	Y	55160 FQ	67560 MW	75700 TQ	USBLS	5/07
	Washington-Arlington-Alexandria MSA, DC-VA-MD-WV	Y	38140 FQ	53490 MW	69590 TQ	USBLS	5/07
	Florida	Y	27100 FQ	36910 MW	48180 TQ	USBLS	5/07
	Miami-Fort Lauderdale-Miami Beach MSA, FL	Y	32060 FQ	37700 MW	48600 TQ	USBLS	5/07
	Orlando-Kissimmee MSA, FL	Y	32350 FQ	43720 MW	54570 TQ	USBLS	5/07
	West Palm Beach-Boca Raton-Boynton Beach PMSA, FL	Y	32140 FQ	35760 MW	40350 TQ	USBLS	5/07
	Georgia	Y	19890 FQ	23750 MW	36040 TQ	USBLS	5/07
	Atlanta-Sandy Springs-Marietta MSA, GA	Y	19420 FQ	23170 MW	34640 TQ	USBLS	5/07
	Hawaii	Y	30260 FQ	46340 MW	56120 TQ	USBLS	5/07
	Illinois	Y	32770 FQ	41230 MW	66670 TQ	USBLS	5/07
	Chicago-Naperville-Joliet MSA, IL-IN-WI	Y	33470 FQ	41770 MW	67440 TQ	USBLS	5/07
	Indiana	Y	31530 FQ	42990 MW	51930 TQ	USBLS	5/07
	Indianapolis-Carmel MSA, IN	Y	40080 FQ	46830 MW	52730 TQ	USBLS	5/07
	Kansas	Y	14110 FQ	21690 MW	28790 TQ	USBLS	5/07
	Kentucky	Y	16947 FQ	28683 MW	36219 TQ	KYBLS	2008
	Maryland	Y		52375 MW		MDBLS	3/08
	Baltimore-Towson MSA, MD	Y	38370 FQ	61700 MW	71030 TQ	USBLS	5/07
	Bethesda-Gaithersburg-Frederick PMSA, MD	Y	42630 FQ	53650 MW	66850 TQ	USBLS	5/07
	Massachusetts	Y	37860 FQ	62160 MW	73450 TQ	USBLS	5/07
	Boston-Cambridge-Quincy NECTA, MA	Y	39800 FQ	64860 MW	74300 TQ	USBLS	5/07
	Michigan	Y	31500 FQ	44090 MW	51210 TQ	USBLS	5/07
	Detroit-Warren-Livonia MSA, MI	Y	37450 FQ	46610 MW	52770 TQ	USBLS	5/07
	Minnesota	Y	37350 FQ	46023 MW	55847 TQ	MNBLS	10/08-12/08
	Minneapolis-Saint Paul MSA, MN-WI	Y	37507 FQ	45908 MW	55544 TQ	MNBLS	10/08-12/08
	Missouri	Y	29940 FQ	37690 MW	47740 TQ	USBLS	5/07
	St. Louis MSA, MO-IL	Y	27550 FQ	35630 MW	45560 TQ	USBLS	5/07
	Nevada	H	13.03 FQ	15.77 MW	20.46 TQ	NVBLS	5/08
	Las Vegas-Paradise MSA, NV	H	13.03 FQ	15.77 MW	20.46 TQ	NVBLS	5/08
	New Jersey	Y	24520 FQ	29540 MW	37450 TQ	USBLS	5/07
	New Mexico	Y	43010 FQ	51520 MW	58810 TQ	USBLS	5/07
	New York	Y	37180 FQ	48590 MW	63050 TQ	USBLS	5/07
	Nassau-Suffolk PMSA, NY	Y	41800 FQ	50310 MW	72600 TQ	USBLS	5/07
	New York-Northern New Jersey-Long Island MSA, NY-NJ-PA	Y	37170 FQ	48680 MW	63810 TQ	USBLS	5/07
	North Carolina	Y	33120 FQ	48450 MW	71350 TQ	USBLS	5/07
	Raleigh-Cary MSA, NC	Y	34310 FQ	38240 MW	50880 TQ	USBLS	5/07
	Ohio	Y	33580 FQ	45410 MW	60640 TQ	USBLS	5/07

AE Average entry wage	**AW** Average wage paid	**FQ** First quartile wage	**LO** Lowest wage paid	**MTC** Median total compensation	**TCC** Total cash compensation
AER Average entry range	**AWR** Average wage range	**H** Hourly	**LR** Low end range	**MW** Median wage paid	**TQ** Third quartile wage
AEX Average experienced wage	**AXR** Average experienced range	**HI** Highest wage paid	**M** Monthly	**MWR** Median wage range	**W** Weekly
ATC Average total compensation	**D** Daily	**HR** High end range	**MCC** Median cash compensation	**S** See annotated source	**Y** Yearly

Occupation/Type/Industry	Location	Per	Low	Mid	High	Source	Date
Set and Exhibit Designer	Cincinnati-Middletown MSA, OH-KY-IN	Y	34190 FQ	42420 MW	58110 TQ	USBLS	5/07
	Dayton MSA, OH	Y	52620 FQ	59040 MW	67930 TQ	USBLS	5/07
	Oklahoma	Y	28440 FQ	40250 MW	49260 TQ	USBLS	5/07
	Oregon	H	16.80 FQ	24.03 MW	31.31 TQ	ORBLS	5/08
	Portland-Vancouver-Beaverton MSA, OR-WA	Y	33730 FQ	54090 MW	63820 TQ	USBLS	5/07
	Pennsylvania	Y	33220 FQ	43150 MW	62870 TQ	USBLS	5/07
	Lancaster MSA, PA	Y	32920 FQ	41130 MW	53940 TQ	USBLS	5/07
	Philadelphia-Camden-Wilmington MSA, PA-NJ-DE-MD	Y	33670 FQ	40830 MW	56200 TQ	USBLS	5/07
	Pittsburgh MSA, PA	Y	50840 FQ	63520 MW	75970 TQ	USBLS	5/07
	South Carolina	Y	13630 FQ	16110 MW	29010 TQ	USBLS	5/07
	Tennessee	Y	30930 FQ	43430 MW	55860 TQ	USBLS	5/07
	Texas	Y	29560 FQ	36970 MW	56520 TQ	USBLS	5/07
	Dallas-Fort Worth-Arlington MSA, TX	Y	29210 FQ	36750 MW	57580 TQ	USBLS	5/07
	Houston-Sugar Land-Baytown MSA, TX	Y	32230 FQ	42270 MW	61860 TQ	USBLS	5/07
	Utah	Y	34100 FQ	37920 MW	47780 TQ	USBLS	5/07
	Salt Lake City MSA, UT	Y	34240 FQ	38000 MW	48270 TQ	USBLS	5/07
	Virginia	Y	25860 FQ	38810 MW	50130 TQ	USBLS	5/07
	Richmond MSA, VA	Y	17400 FQ	21970 MW	29690 TQ	USBLS	5/07
	Virginia Beach-Norfolk-Newport News MSA, VA-NC	Y	30100 FQ	43600 MW	51890 TQ	USBLS	5/07
	Washington	H	20.29 FQ	23.13 MW	26.75 TQ	WABLS	3/08
	Seattle-Tacoma-Bellevue MSA, WA	Y	42900 FQ	48730 MW	57090 TQ	USBLS	5/07
	Wisconsin	Y	28320 FQ	31060 MW	36310 TQ	USBLS	5/07
	Milwaukee-Waukesha-West Allis MSA, WI	Y	27990 FQ	30440 MW	33440 TQ	USBLS	5/07
	Wyoming	Y	20099 FQ	35870 MW	41343 TQ	WYBLS	9/08
Sewage Treatment Plant Superintendent	Fulton County, GA	Y	56286 LO		79925 HI	GACTY03	2008
Sewer							
Hand	Alabama	Y	15570 FQ	20840 MW	23780 TQ	USBLS	5/07
Hand	Arkansas	Y	22130 FQ	25240 MW	28960 TQ	USBLS	5/07
Hand	California	H	8.56 FQ	9.70 MW	11.67 TQ	CABLS	1/08-3/08
Hand	Los Angeles-Long Beach-Glendale PMSA, CA	H	8.61 FQ	9.75 MW	11.11 TQ	CABLS	1/08-3/08
Hand	Oakland-Fremont-Hayward MSA, CA	H	8.38 FQ	9.11 MW	11.56 TQ	CABLS	1/08-3/08
Hand	Riverside-San Bernardino-Ontario MSA, CA	H	9.80 FQ	10.76 MW	11.86 TQ	CABLS	1/08-3/08
Hand	San Diego-Carlsbad-San Marcos MSA, CA	H	8.87 FQ	10.41 MW	12.55 TQ	CABLS	1/08-3/08
Hand	San Francisco-San Mateo-Redwood PMSA, CA	H	8.45 FQ	9.20 MW	13.26 TQ	CABLS	1/08-3/08
Hand	San Jose-Sunnyvale-Santa Clara MSA, CA	H	14.83 FQ	17.06 MW	18.56 TQ	CABLS	1/08-3/08
Hand	Santa Ana-Anaheim-Irvine PMSA, CA	Y	16440 FQ	17980 MW	19580 TQ	USBLS	5/07
Hand	Colorado	Y	15200 FQ	17260 MW	21880 TQ	USBLS	5/07
Hand	Connecticut	H	9.40 AE	11.07 MW		CTBLS	1/08-3/08
Hand	Bridgeport-Stamford-Norwalk MSA, CT	Y	20030 FQ	22590 MW	25350 TQ	USBLS	5/07
Hand	Florida	Y	18390 FQ	21240 MW	25160 TQ	USBLS	5/07
Hand	Miami-Fort Lauderdale-Miami Beach MSA, FL	Y	19510 FQ	22210 MW	25940 TQ	USBLS	5/07
Hand	Orlando-Kissimmee MSA, FL	Y	17790 FQ	19630 MW	24780 TQ	USBLS	5/07
Hand	Tampa-St. Petersburg-Clearwater MSA, FL	Y	18120 FQ	20590 MW	26500 TQ	USBLS	5/07
Hand	Georgia	Y	15810 FQ	19960 MW	26050 TQ	USBLS	5/07
Hand	Atlanta-Sandy Springs-Marietta MSA, GA	Y	20960 FQ	24800 MW	28010 TQ	USBLS	5/07
Hand	Illinois	Y	17800 FQ	21850 MW	24360 TQ	USBLS	5/07
Hand	Chicago-Naperville-Joliet MSA, IL-IN-WI	Y	18330 FQ	22210 MW	24420 TQ	USBLS	5/07
Hand	Indiana	Y	21150 FQ	24150 MW	27740 TQ	USBLS	5/07

AE	Average entry wage	AW	Average wage paid	FQ	First quartile wage	LO	Lowest wage paid
AER	Average entry range	AWR	Average wage range	H	Hourly	LR	Low end range
AEX	Average experienced wage	AXR	Average experienced range	HI	Highest wage paid	M	Monthly
ATC	Average total compensation	D	Daily	HR	High end range	MCC	Median cash compensation

MTC	Median total compensation	TCC	Total cash compensation
MW	Median wage paid	TQ	Third quartile wage
MWR	Median wage range	W	Weekly
S	See annotated source	Y	Yearly

Sewer

Occupation/Type/Industry	Location	Per	Low	Mid	High	Source	Date
Sewer							
Hand	Indianapolis-Carmel MSA, IN	Y	22890 FQ	25250 MW	28680 TQ	USBLS	5/07
Hand	Kansas	Y	18170 FQ	22060 MW	25490 TQ	USBLS	5/07
Hand	Kentucky	Y	13363 FQ	15036 MW	18851 TQ	KYBLS	2008
Hand	Louisiana	H	8.34 FQ	9.82 MW	11.25 TQ	LABLS	1/08-3/08
Hand	New Orleans-Metairie-Kenner MSA, LA	Y	20450 FQ	22380 MW	24440 TQ	USBLS	5/07
Hand	Maine	Y	20910 FQ	24040 MW	27720 TQ	USBLS	5/07
Hand	Maryland	Y		23300 MW		MDBLS	3/08
Hand	Massachusetts	Y	17610 FQ	19610 MW	25050 TQ	USBLS	5/07
Hand	Boston-Cambridge-Quincy NECTA, MA	Y	17770 FQ	20640 MW	28220 TQ	USBLS	5/07
Hand	Michigan	Y	17820 FQ	20530 MW	22650 TQ	USBLS	5/07
Hand	Detroit-Warren-Livonia MSA, MI	Y	20540 FQ	21980 MW	23410 TQ	USBLS	5/07
Hand	Warren-Troy-Farmington Hills PMSA, MI	Y	20030 FQ	21340 MW	22650 TQ	USBLS	5/07
Hand	Minnesota	Y	15187 FQ	18494 MW	24610 TQ	MNBLS	10/08-12/08
Hand	Mississippi	Y	15760 FQ	17430 MW	19350 TQ	USBLS	5/07
Hand	Missouri	Y	20890 FQ	22730 MW	25380 TQ	USBLS	5/07
Hand	Kansas City MSA, MO-KS	Y	18700 FQ	22490 MW	26320 TQ	USBLS	5/07
Hand	St. Louis MSA, MO-IL	Y	21390 FQ	23310 MW	26850 TQ	USBLS	5/07
Hand	Nevada	H	10.52 FQ	11.57 MW	13.06 TQ	NVBLS	5/08
Hand	Las Vegas-Paradise MSA, NV	H	11.12 FQ	12.50 MW	14.47 TQ	NVBLS	5/08
Hand	New Jersey	Y	16570 FQ	19870 MW	26520 TQ	USBLS	5/07
Hand	Camden PMSA, NJ	Y	18520 FQ	23130 MW	37080 TQ	USBLS	5/07
Hand	Newark-Union PMSA, NJ-PA	Y	15910 FQ	18490 MW	24070 TQ	USBLS	5/07
Hand	New York	Y	17780 FQ	22700 MW	30740 TQ	USBLS	5/07
Hand	Nassau-Suffolk PMSA, NY	Y	20030 FQ	23070 MW	27570 TQ	USBLS	5/07
Hand	New York-Northern New Jersey-Long Island MSA, NY-NJ-PA	Y	17090 FQ	21730 MW	29310 TQ	USBLS	5/07
Hand	North Carolina	Y	17000 FQ	20970 MW	24800 TQ	USBLS	5/07
Hand	Charlotte-Gastonia-Concord MSA, NC-SC	Y	18860 FQ	21780 MW	24320 TQ	USBLS	5/07
Hand	Ohio	Y	18950 FQ	22110 MW	26140 TQ	USBLS	5/07
Hand	Cincinnati-Middletown MSA, OH-KY-IN	Y	19960 FQ	22690 MW	25680 TQ	USBLS	5/07
Hand	Columbus MSA, OH	Y	17630 FQ	19430 MW	22290 TQ	USBLS	5/07
Hand	Oregon	H	8.67 FQ	9.36 MW	10.56 TQ	ORBLS	5/08
Hand	Portland-Vancouver-Beaverton MSA, OR-WA	Y	17360 FQ	18480 MW	19620 TQ	USBLS	5/07
Hand	Pennsylvania	Y	16810 FQ	20650 MW	26180 TQ	USBLS	5/07
Hand	Philadelphia-Camden-Wilmington MSA, PA-NJ-DE-MD	Y	17620 FQ	21850 MW	28160 TQ	USBLS	5/07
Hand	Pittsburgh MSA, PA	Y	15040 FQ	18520 MW	22540 TQ	USBLS	5/07
Hand	Rhode Island	Y	16830 FQ	18750 MW	25770 TQ	USBLS	5/07
Hand	Providence-Fall River-Warwick MSA, RI-MA	Y	17600 FQ	21050 MW	27940 TQ	USBLS	5/07
Hand	South Carolina	Y	16610 FQ	22310 MW	27720 TQ	USBLS	5/07
Hand	South Dakota	Y	13649 FQ	15699 MW	18265 TQ	SDBLS	7/08-9/08
Hand	Sioux Falls MSA, SD	Y	17360 FQ	19283 MW	25383 TQ	SDBLS	7/08-9/08
Hand	Tennessee	Y	18100 FQ	21010 MW	23190 TQ	USBLS	5/07
Hand	Texas	Y	15870 FQ	19230 MW	23040 TQ	USBLS	5/07
Hand	Dallas-Fort Worth-Arlington MSA, TX	Y	18910 FQ	21990 MW	25260 TQ	USBLS	5/07
Hand	Houston-Sugar Land-Baytown MSA, TX	Y	13230 FQ	15590 MW	19030 TQ	USBLS	5/07
Hand	Utah	Y	15140 FQ	18550 MW	23110 TQ	USBLS	5/07
Hand	Salt Lake City MSA, UT	Y	17430 FQ	20820 MW	24790 TQ	USBLS	5/07
Hand	Vermont	Y	20910 FQ	23740 MW	30050 TQ	USBLS	5/07
Hand	Virginia	Y	17390 FQ	19740 MW	23350 TQ	USBLS	5/07
Hand	Virginia Beach-Norfolk-Newport News MSA, VA-NC	Y	17270 FQ	20150 MW	25820 TQ	USBLS	5/07
Hand	Washington	H	10.87 FQ	13.48 MW	16.50 TQ	WABLS	3/08
Hand	Seattle-Tacoma-Bellevue MSA, WA	Y	21860 FQ	25240 MW	29840 TQ	USBLS	5/07
Hand	Wisconsin	Y	21100 FQ	22770 MW	24470 TQ	USBLS	5/07
Hand	Puerto Rico	Y	12270 FQ	13560 MW	14850 TQ	USBLS	5/07
Sewer Construction Inspector	Cincinnati, OH	Y	45777 LO		49087 HI	COHSS	10/08

AE	Average entry wage	AW	Average wage paid	FQ	First quartile wage
AER	Average entry range	AWR	Average wage range	H	Hourly
AEX	Average experienced wage	AXR	Average experienced range	HI	Highest wage paid
ATC	Average total compensation	D	Daily	HR	High end range

LO	Lowest wage paid	MTC	Median total compensation
LR	Low end range	MW	Median wage paid
M	Monthly	MWR	Median wage range
MCC	Median cash compensation	S	See annotated source

TCC	Total cash compensation
TQ	Third quartile wage
W	Weekly
Y	Yearly

Occupation/Type/Industry	Location	Per	Low	Mid	High	Source	Date
Sewer Inspector	United States	Y		34960 AW		BWEEK01	2006
Sewer Maintenance Crew Leader	Cincinnati, OH	Y	38076 LO		51171 HI	COHSS	10/08
Sewer System Supervisor	Columbia County, GA	Y	36691 LO		55037 HI	GACTY03	2008
	Upson County, GA	Y	26802 LO		40783 HI	GACTY03	2008
	Walton County, GA	Y	33407 LO		56137 HI	GACTY03	2008
Sewing Machine Operator	Alabama	Y	15440 FQ	17890 MW	20990 TQ	USBLS	5/07
	Birmingham-Hoover MSA, AL	Y	14070 FQ	16810 MW	19180 TQ	USBLS	5/07
	Alaska	Y	19800 FQ	24500 MW	33070 TQ	USBLS	5/07
	Anchorage MSA, AK	Y	20900 FQ	23660 MW	33610 TQ	USBLS	5/07
	Arizona	Y	18430 FQ	22110 MW	25360 TQ	USBLS	5/07
	Phoenix-Mesa-Scottsdale MSA, AZ	Y	18880 FQ	22290 MW	25380 TQ	USBLS	5/07
	Tucson MSA, AZ	Y	16060 FQ	19040 MW	24120 TQ	USBLS	5/07
	Yuma MSA, AZ	Y	19120 FQ	21130 MW	23750 TQ	USBLS	5/07
	Arkansas	Y	15010 FQ	17470 MW	20700 TQ	USBLS	5/07
	Little Rock-North Little Rock MSA, AR	Y	19000 FQ	22060 MW	24880 TQ	USBLS	5/07
	Pine Bluff MSA, AR	Y	14170 FQ	15150 MW	16790 TQ	USBLS	5/07
	California	H	8.05 FQ	8.88 MW	10.42 TQ	CABLS	1/08-3/08
	Fresno MSA, CA	H	9.17 FQ	11.07 MW	13.69 TQ	CABLS	1/08-3/08
	Los Angeles-Long Beach-Glendale PMSA, CA	H	8.00 FQ	8.75 MW	10.07 TQ	CABLS	1/08-3/08
	Oakland-Fremont-Hayward MSA, CA	H	8.23 FQ	8.98 MW	9.84 TQ	CABLS	1/08-3/08
	Riverside-San Bernardino-Ontario MSA, CA	H	8.65 FQ	9.81 MW	11.84 TQ	CABLS	1/08-3/08
	Sacramento-Arden Arcade-Roseville MSA, CA	H	8.92 FQ	10.05 MW	11.19 TQ	CABLS	1/08-3/08
	San Diego-Carlsbad-San Marcos MSA, CA	H	8.83 FQ	10.09 MW	11.81 TQ	CABLS	1/08-3/08
	San Francisco-San Mateo-Redwood PMSA, CA	H	8.56 FQ	9.39 MW	10.67 TQ	CABLS	1/08-3/08
	San Jose-Sunnyvale-Santa Clara MSA, CA	H	8.47 FQ	9.40 MW	12.27 TQ	CABLS	1/08-3/08
	Santa Ana-Anaheim-Irvine PMSA, CA	Y	16550 FQ	17930 MW	19570 TQ	USBLS	5/07
	Colorado	Y	20020 FQ	22500 MW	25090 TQ	USBLS	5/07
	Denver-Aurora MSA, CO	Y	20460 FQ	22630 MW	24880 TQ	USBLS	5/07
	Connecticut	H	8.74 AE	10.86 MW		CTBLS	1/08-3/08
	Bridgeport-Stamford-Norwalk MSA, CT	Y	18490 FQ	22440 MW	30140 TQ	USBLS	5/07
	Hartford-West Hartford-East Hartford MSA, CT	Y	20580 FQ	23300 MW	31330 TQ	USBLS	5/07
	Delaware	Y	17860 FQ	20480 MW	26420 TQ	USBLS	5/07
	Wilmington PMSA, DE-MD-NJ	Y	19160 FQ	22960 MW	28000 TQ	USBLS	5/07
	District of Columbia	Y	17250 FQ	18530 MW	19810 TQ	USBLS	5/07
	Washington-Arlington-Alexandria MSA, DC-VA-MD-WV	Y	18440 FQ	22330 MW	28050 TQ	USBLS	5/07
	Florida	Y	16860 FQ	20290 MW	25320 TQ	USBLS	5/07
	Fort Lauderdale-Pompano Beach-Deerfield Beach PMSA, FL	Y	18120 FQ	22380 MW	28910 TQ	USBLS	5/07
	Jacksonville MSA, FL	Y	18500 FQ	23430 MW	29860 TQ	USBLS	5/07
	Miami-Fort Lauderdale-Miami Beach MSA, FL	Y	15650 FQ	18710 MW	23290 TQ	USBLS	5/07
	Orlando-Kissimmee MSA, FL	Y	18440 FQ	22340 MW	26670 TQ	USBLS	5/07
	Tampa-St. Petersburg-Clearwater MSA, FL	Y	17730 FQ	21050 MW	27550 TQ	USBLS	5/07
	West Palm Beach-Boca Raton-Boynton Beach PMSA, FL	Y	15990 FQ	20070 MW	27200 TQ	USBLS	5/07
	Georgia	Y	16430 FQ	20000 MW	24400 TQ	USBLS	5/07
	Atlanta-Sandy Springs-Marietta MSA, GA	Y	17360 FQ	20900 MW	25020 TQ	USBLS	5/07
	Hawaii	Y	15080 FQ	15880 MW	18550 TQ	USBLS	5/07
	Honolulu MSA, HI	Y	15080 FQ	15780 MW	18250 TQ	USBLS	5/07
	Idaho	Y	17090 FQ	20720 MW	23950 TQ	USBLS	5/07
	Boise City-Nampa MSA, ID	Y	17430 FQ	21390 MW	24200 TQ	USBLS	5/07
	Illinois	Y	16200 FQ	18840 MW	23490 TQ	USBLS	5/07

AE Average entry wage	**AW** Average wage paid	**FQ** First quartile wage	**LO** Lowest wage paid	**MTC** Median total compensation	**TCC** Total cash compensation
AER Average entry range	**AWR** Average wage range	**H** Hourly	**LR** Low end range	**MW** Median wage paid	**TQ** Third quartile wage
AEX Average experienced wage	**AXR** Average experienced range	**HI** Highest wage paid	**M** Monthly	**MWR** Median wage range	**W** Weekly
ATC Average total compensation	**D** Daily	**HR** High end range	**MCC** Median cash compensation	**S** See annotated source	**Y** Yearly

Occupation/Type/Industry	Location	Per	Low	Mid	High	Source	Date
Sewing Machine Operator	Chicago-Naperville-Joliet MSA, IL-IN-WI	Y	16180 FQ	18740 MW	23330 TQ	USBLS	5/07
	Indiana	Y	17430 FQ	21490 MW	26250 TQ	USBLS	5/07
	Gary PMSA, IN	Y	19160 FQ	20980 MW	22710 TQ	USBLS	5/07
	Indianapolis-Carmel MSA, IN	Y	19630 FQ	22270 MW	24960 TQ	USBLS	5/07
	Iowa	Y	16870 FQ	20590 MW	24250 TQ	USBLS	5/07
	Des Moines-West Des Moines MSA, IA	Y	18850 FQ	25050 MW	28770 TQ	USBLS	5/07
	Kansas	Y	16360 FQ	19710 MW	24870 TQ	USBLS	5/07
	Wichita MSA, KS	Y	15510 FQ	17640 MW	23360 TQ	USBLS	5/07
	Kentucky	Y	14420 FQ	17885 MW	23414 TQ	KYBLS	2008
	Lexington-Fayette MSA, KY	Y	15660 FQ	19590 MW	22510 TQ	USBLS	5/07
	Louisville-Jefferson County MSA, KY-IN	Y	18250 FQ	21820 MW	27270 TQ	USBLS	5/07
	Louisiana	H	7.23 FQ	8.41 MW	9.78 TQ	LABLS	1/08-3/08
	Baton Rouge MSA, LA	Y	17150 FQ	19970 MW	21980 TQ	USBLS	5/07
	New Orleans-Metairie-Kenner MSA, LA	Y	14540 FQ	17960 MW	20860 TQ	USBLS	5/07
	Maine	Y	18140 FQ	22440 MW	27200 TQ	USBLS	5/07
	Portland-South Portland-Biddeford MSA, ME	Y	19730 FQ	25530 MW	33140 TQ	USBLS	5/07
	Maryland	Y		22400 MW		MDBLS	3/08
	Baltimore-Towson MSA, MD	Y	19030 FQ	21920 MW	26450 TQ	USBLS	5/07
	Bethesda-Gaithersburg-Frederick PMSA, MD	Y	20400 FQ	25500 MW	31060 TQ	USBLS	5/07
	Salisbury MSA, MD	Y	14430 FQ	15760 MW	17290 TQ	USBLS	5/07
	Massachusetts	Y	18440 FQ	22710 MW	28390 TQ	USBLS	5/07
	Boston-Cambridge-Quincy NECTA, MA	Y	18920 FQ	23830 MW	32460 TQ	USBLS	5/07
	Worcester MSA, MA-CT	Y	16250 FQ	18670 MW	22200 TQ	USBLS	5/07
	Michigan	Y	19300 FQ	22740 MW	27340 TQ	USBLS	5/07
	Detroit-Warren-Livonia MSA, MI	Y	20560 FQ	24250 MW	28930 TQ	USBLS	5/07
	Grand Rapids-Wyoming MSA, MI	Y	20090 FQ	25440 MW	28990 TQ	USBLS	5/07
	Warren-Troy-Farmington Hills PMSA, MI	Y	20700 FQ	25380 MW	29290 TQ	USBLS	5/07
	Minnesota	Y	19769 FQ	24040 MW	29234 TQ	MNBLS	10/08-12/08
	Duluth-Superior MSA, MN-WI	Y	17602 FQ	19261 MW	21251 TQ	MNBLS	10/08-12/08
	Minneapolis-Saint Paul MSA, MN-WI	Y	22630 FQ	27212 MW	31411 TQ	MNBLS	10/08-12/08
	Rochester MSA, MN	Y	23375 FQ	27504 MW	31233 TQ	MNBLS	10/08-12/08
	Mississippi	Y	17310 FQ	22590 MW	28310 TQ	USBLS	5/07
	Jackson MSA, MS	Y	14420 FQ	18190 MW	24850 TQ	USBLS	5/07
	Missouri	Y	17100 FQ	20210 MW	23130 TQ	USBLS	5/07
	Kansas City MSA, MO-KS	Y	17790 FQ	21050 MW	25620 TQ	USBLS	5/07
	St. Louis MSA, MO-IL	Y	17810 FQ	20770 MW	23210 TQ	USBLS	5/07
	Montana	Y	15760 FQ	18590 MW	21760 TQ	USBLS	5/07
	Billings MSA, MT	Y	17640 FQ	20090 MW	22140 TQ	USBLS	5/07
	Nebraska	Y	17300 FQ	19700 MW	22980 TQ	USBLS	5/07
	Omaha-Council Bluffs MSA, NE-IA	Y	18170 FQ	20120 MW	22990 TQ	USBLS	5/07
	Nevada	H	8.21 FQ	9.98 MW	12.85 TQ	NVBLS	5/08
	Las Vegas-Paradise MSA, NV	H	8.08 FQ	9.79 MW	12.77 TQ	NVBLS	5/08
	New Hampshire	H	9.46 AE	11.66 MW	13.28 AEX	NHBLS	6/08
	Manchester MSA, NH	Y	16840 FQ	19820 MW	25970 TQ	USBLS	5/07
	Nashua NECTA, NH-MA	Y	26320 FQ	29330 MW	33070 TQ	USBLS	5/07
	New Jersey	Y	16800 FQ	19290 MW	24440 TQ	USBLS	5/07
	Camden PMSA, NJ	Y	19490 FQ	22660 MW	26780 TQ	USBLS	5/07
	Edison PMSA, NJ	Y	17270 FQ	22800 MW	29380 TQ	USBLS	5/07
	Newark-Union PMSA, NJ-PA	Y	18140 FQ	22090 MW	28610 TQ	USBLS	5/07
	New Mexico	Y	16460 FQ	18210 MW	19920 TQ	USBLS	5/07
	Albuquerque MSA, NM	Y	16530 FQ	18090 MW	19640 TQ	USBLS	5/07
	New York	Y	15810 FQ	19880 MW	26160 TQ	USBLS	5/07
	Albany-Schenectady-Troy MSA, NY	Y	20550 FQ	25020 MW	31120 TQ	USBLS	5/07
	Buffalo-Niagara Falls MSA, NY	Y	19830 FQ	25630 MW	35110 TQ	USBLS	5/07
	Nassau-Suffolk PMSA, NY	Y	19990 FQ	23760 MW	29280 TQ	USBLS	5/07
	New York-Northern New Jersey-Long Island MSA, NY-NJ-PA	Y	15820 FQ	19240 MW	25200 TQ	USBLS	5/07

AE Average entry wage	**AW** Average wage paid	**FQ** First quartile wage	**LO** Lowest wage paid	**MTC** Median total compensation	**TCC** Total cash compensation
AER Average entry range	**AWR** Average wage range	**H** Hourly	**LR** Low end range	**MW** Median wage paid	**TQ** Third quartile wage
AEX Average experienced wage	**AXR** Average experienced range	**HI** Highest wage paid	**M** Monthly	**MWR** Median wage range	**W** Weekly
ATC Average total compensation	**D** Daily	**HR** High end range	**MCC** Median cash compensation	**S** See annotated source	**Y** Yearly

Sewing Machine Operator

Occupation/Type/Industry	Location	Per	Low	Mid	High	Source	Date
Sewing Machine Operator	Syracuse MSA, NY	Y	18300 FQ	22760 MW	30210 TQ	USBLS	5/07
	North Carolina	Y	17110 FQ	21500 MW	27440 TQ	USBLS	5/07
	Charlotte-Gastonia-Concord MSA, NC-SC	Y	15160 FQ	19340 MW	22580 TQ	USBLS	5/07
	Greensboro-High Point MSA, NC	Y	18640 FQ	22560 MW	27920 TQ	USBLS	5/07
	Raleigh-Cary MSA, NC	Y	16270 FQ	18400 MW	22190 TQ	USBLS	5/07
	North Dakota	Y	17700 FQ	20590 MW	23410 TQ	USBLS	5/07
	Fargo MSA, ND-MN	Y	17290 FQ	21050 MW	24190 TQ	USBLS	5/07
	Ohio	Y	17810 FQ	21850 MW	26880 TQ	USBLS	5/07
	Cincinnati-Middletown MSA, OH-KY-IN	Y	18790 FQ	22260 MW	27280 TQ	USBLS	5/07
	Cleveland-Elyria-Mentor MSA, OH	Y	19640 FQ	25860 MW	38090 TQ	USBLS	5/07
	Columbus MSA, OH	Y	18760 FQ	21800 MW	24550 TQ	USBLS	5/07
	Dayton MSA, OH	Y	20060 FQ	24940 MW	28040 TQ	USBLS	5/07
	Oklahoma	Y	16190 FQ	18320 MW	21100 TQ	USBLS	5/07
	Oklahoma City MSA, OK	Y	16240 FQ	18360 MW	21280 TQ	USBLS	5/07
	Tulsa MSA, OK	Y	16330 FQ	18600 MW	22090 TQ	USBLS	5/07
	Oregon	H	8.81 FQ	9.79 MW	12.16 TQ	ORBLS	5/08
	Portland-Vancouver-Beaverton MSA, OR-WA	Y	18330 FQ	20770 MW	27450 TQ	USBLS	5/07
	Pennsylvania	Y	16510 FQ	19950 MW	24780 TQ	USBLS	5/07
	Allentown-Bethlehem-Easton MSA, PA-NJ	Y	16080 FQ	19280 MW	25470 TQ	USBLS	5/07
	Philadelphia-Camden-Wilmington MSA, PA-NJ-DE-MD	Y	18140 FQ	21980 MW	27080 TQ	USBLS	5/07
	Pittsburgh MSA, PA	Y	16910 FQ	19220 MW	22150 TQ	USBLS	5/07
	Rhode Island	Y	19140 FQ	22150 MW	27360 TQ	USBLS	5/07
	Providence-Fall River-Warwick MSA, RI-MA	Y	18940 FQ	21960 MW	26470 TQ	USBLS	5/07
	South Carolina	Y	17290 FQ	21050 MW	26340 TQ	USBLS	5/07
	Charleston-North Charleston MSA, SC	Y	17970 FQ	22810 MW	29780 TQ	USBLS	5/07
	Columbia MSA, SC	Y	17720 FQ	20870 MW	26440 TQ	USBLS	5/07
	South Dakota	Y	19492 FQ	21564 MW	23838 TQ	SDBLS	7/08-9/08
	Sioux Falls MSA, SD	Y	20480 FQ	23259 MW	27837 TQ	SDBLS	7/08-9/08
	Tennessee	Y	16630 FQ	19370 MW	23420 TQ	USBLS	5/07
	Memphis MSA, TN-MS-AR	Y	17900 FQ	20820 MW	26880 TQ	USBLS	5/07
	Nashville-Davidson-Murfreesboro MSA, TN	Y	18290 FQ	21080 MW	24610 TQ	USBLS	5/07
	Texas	Y	15170 FQ	18190 MW	21780 TQ	USBLS	5/07
	Austin-Round Rock MSA, TX	Y	14250 FQ	17730 MW	21640 TQ	USBLS	5/07
	Dallas-Fort Worth-Arlington MSA, TX	Y	16140 FQ	18770 MW	22570 TQ	USBLS	5/07
	El Paso MSA, TX	Y	12680 FQ	14270 MW	16360 TQ	USBLS	5/07
	Houston-Sugar Land-Baytown MSA, TX	Y	16590 FQ	20330 MW	23900 TQ	USBLS	5/07
	San Antonio MSA, TX	Y	14560 FQ	17140 MW	19840 TQ	USBLS	5/07
	Utah	Y	15500 FQ	18910 MW	26440 TQ	USBLS	5/07
	Salt Lake City MSA, UT	Y	15580 FQ	19930 MW	27620 TQ	USBLS	5/07
	Vermont	Y	19280 FQ	22630 MW	27080 TQ	USBLS	5/07
	Burlington-South Burlington MSA, VT	Y	20770 FQ	23770 MW	28400 TQ	USBLS	5/07
	Virginia	Y	16570 FQ	19100 MW	23020 TQ	USBLS	5/07
	Richmond MSA, VA	Y	18280 FQ	21360 MW	24950 TQ	USBLS	5/07
	Virginia Beach-Norfolk-Newport News MSA, VA-NC	Y	17840 FQ	20430 MW	23870 TQ	USBLS	5/07
	Washington	H	9.11 FQ	10.81 MW	13.97 TQ	WABLS	3/08
	Seattle-Tacoma-Bellevue MSA, WA	Y	18590 FQ	21980 MW	29070 TQ	USBLS	5/07
	West Virginia	Y	14346 FQ	15995 MW	19239 TQ	WVBLS	7/08-9/08
	Wisconsin	Y	18600 FQ	22790 MW	27890 TQ	USBLS	5/07
	Appleton MSA, WI	Y	21900 FQ	28970 MW	35330 TQ	USBLS	5/07
	Milwaukee-Waukesha-West Allis MSA, WI	Y	19050 FQ	22630 MW	27790 TQ	USBLS	5/07
	Wyoming	Y	17968 FQ	20093 MW	25781 TQ	WYBLS	9/08
	Puerto Rico	Y	12180 FQ	13270 MW	14360 TQ	USBLS	5/07
	San Juan-Caguas-Guaynabo MSA, PR	Y	12160 FQ	13240 MW	14320 TQ	USBLS	5/07

AE Average entry wage	**AW** Average wage paid	**FQ** First quartile wage	**LO** Lowest wage paid	**MTC** Median total compensation	**TCC** Total cash compensation
AER Average entry range	**AWR** Average wage range	**H** Hourly	**LR** Low end range	**MW** Median wage paid	**TQ** Third quartile wage
AEX Average experienced wage	**AXR** Average experienced range	**HI** Highest wage paid	**M** Monthly	**MWR** Median wage range	**W** Weekly
ATC Average total compensation	**D** Daily	**HR** High end range	**MCC** Median cash compensation	**S** See annotated source	**Y** Yearly

Occupation/Type/Industry	Location	Per	Low	Mid	High	Source	Date
Sexton							
Municipal Government	Hamburg Township, MI	Y			9007 HI	LCPP	2009
Shampooer	Alabama	Y	12870 FQ	14820 MW	17770 TQ	USBLS	5/07
	Birmingham-Hoover MSA, AL	Y	12620 FQ	14330 MW	16680 TQ	USBLS	5/07
	Arizona	Y	14720 FQ	16330 MW	19130 TQ	USBLS	5/07
	Phoenix-Mesa-Scottsdale MSA, AZ	Y	14800 FQ	16890 MW	19430 TQ	USBLS	5/07
	California	H	8.00 FQ	8.00 MW	8.64 TQ	CABLS	1/08-3/08
	Los Angeles-Long Beach-Glendale PMSA, CA	H	8.00 FQ	8.55 MW	9.21 TQ	CABLS	1/08-3/08
	San Diego-Carlsbad-San Marcos MSA, CA	H	8.00 FQ	8.00 MW	8.00 TQ	CABLS	1/08-3/08
	Colorado	Y	14830 FQ	15400 MW	16820 TQ	USBLS	5/07
	Connecticut	H	8.29 AE	9.06 MW		CTBLS	1/08-3/08
	Bridgeport-Stamford-Norwalk MSA, CT	Y	16210 FQ	17810 MW	19600 TQ	USBLS	5/07
	Hartford-West Hartford-East Hartford MSA, CT	Y	17160 FQ	18130 MW	19530 TQ	USBLS	5/07
	Delaware	Y	14730 FQ	15880 MW	18050 TQ	USBLS	5/07
	Wilmington PMSA, DE-MD-NJ	Y	14530 FQ	15360 MW	17260 TQ	USBLS	5/07
	District of Columbia	Y	20970 FQ	22820 MW	24670 TQ	USBLS	5/07
	Washington-Arlington-Alexandria MSA, DC-VA-MD-WV	Y	14580 FQ	17370 MW	21050 TQ	USBLS	5/07
	Florida	Y	15190 FQ	17090 MW	19560 TQ	USBLS	5/07
	Fort Lauderdale-Pompano Beach-Deerfield Beach PMSA, FL	Y	17530 FQ	19790 MW	22250 TQ	USBLS	5/07
	Miami-Fort Lauderdale-Miami Beach MSA, FL	Y	15170 FQ	16860 MW	19770 TQ	USBLS	5/07
	Tampa-St. Petersburg-Clearwater MSA, FL	Y	15240 FQ	17590 MW	19960 TQ	USBLS	5/07
	West Palm Beach-Boca Raton-Boynton Beach PMSA, FL	Y	14670 FQ	15470 MW	18310 TQ	USBLS	5/07
	Georgia	Y	13640 FQ	17480 MW	21010 TQ	USBLS	5/07
	Atlanta-Sandy Springs-Marietta MSA, GA	Y	14440 FQ	18640 MW	21690 TQ	USBLS	5/07
	Hawaii	Y	15460 FQ	15980 MW	17770 TQ	USBLS	5/07
	Honolulu MSA, HI	Y	15460 FQ	15980 MW	17770 TQ	USBLS	5/07
	Illinois	Y	14820 FQ	16090 MW	20800 TQ	USBLS	5/07
	Chicago-Naperville-Joliet MSA, IL-IN-WI	Y	14820 FQ	16160 MW	20990 TQ	USBLS	5/07
	Indiana	Y	14860 FQ	17080 MW	18980 TQ	USBLS	5/07
	Kentucky	Y	13661 FQ	16023 MW	21181 TQ	KYBLS	2008
	Louisiana	H	6.39 FQ	7.60 MW	8.79 TQ	LABLS	1/08-3/08
	Baton Rouge MSA, LA	Y	15660 FQ	17620 MW	19190 TQ	USBLS	5/07
	New Orleans-Metairie-Kenner MSA, LA	Y	12580 FQ	13770 MW	15180 TQ	USBLS	5/07
	Maryland	Y		15625 MW		MDBLS	3/08
	Baltimore-Towson MSA, MD	Y	14080 FQ	14920 MW	17210 TQ	USBLS	5/07
	Bethesda-Gaithersburg-Frederick PMSA, MD	Y	14540 FQ	16260 MW	21480 TQ	USBLS	5/07
	Massachusetts	Y	17240 FQ	18950 MW	21520 TQ	USBLS	5/07
	Boston-Cambridge-Quincy NECTA, MA	Y	17580 FQ	19710 MW	22350 TQ	USBLS	5/07
	Springfield MSA, MA-CT	Y	16880 FQ	17880 MW	18920 TQ	USBLS	5/07
	Michigan	Y	15410 FQ	16230 MW	18320 TQ	USBLS	5/07
	Detroit-Warren-Livonia MSA, MI	Y	15430 FQ	16350 MW	18390 TQ	USBLS	5/07
	Warren-Troy-Farmington Hills PMSA, MI	Y	15880 FQ	17270 MW	18810 TQ	USBLS	5/07
	Mississippi	Y	12170 FQ	13480 MW	14800 TQ	USBLS	5/07
	Missouri	Y	17580 FQ	19210 MW	20810 TQ	USBLS	5/07
	St. Louis MSA, MO-IL	Y	17280 FQ	19000 MW	20810 TQ	USBLS	5/07
	Las Vegas-Paradise MSA, NV	H	10.14 FQ	10.87 MW	11.60 TQ	NVBLS	5/08
	New Jersey	Y	15880 FQ	17450 MW	20370 TQ	USBLS	5/07
	Camden PMSA, NJ	Y	15840 FQ	17070 MW	18870 TQ	USBLS	5/07
	Edison PMSA, NJ	Y	15920 FQ	17620 MW	20370 TQ	USBLS	5/07
	Newark-Union PMSA, NJ-PA	Y	16660 FQ	19180 MW	21800 TQ	USBLS	5/07
	New York	Y	15920 FQ	18040 MW	20840 TQ	USBLS	5/07

AE	Average entry wage	AW	Average wage paid	FQ	First quartile wage	LO	Lowest wage paid	MTC	Median total compensation	TCC	Total cash compensation
AER	Average entry range	AWR	Average wage range	H	Hourly	LR	Low end range	MW	Median wage paid	TQ	Third quartile wage
AEX	Average experienced wage	AXR	Average experienced range	HI	Highest wage paid	M	Monthly	MWR	Median wage range	W	Weekly
ATC	Average total compensation	D	Daily	HR	High end range	MCC	Median cash compensation	S	See annotated source	Y	Yearly

Occupation/Type/Industry	Location	Per	Low	Mid	High	Source	Date
Shampooer	Albany-Schenectady-Troy MSA, NY	Y	17420 FQ	18720 MW	20010 TQ	USBLS	5/07
	Buffalo-Niagara Falls MSA, NY	Y	15610 FQ	17490 MW	18860 TQ	USBLS	5/07
	Nassau-Suffolk PMSA, NY	Y	15760 FQ	17950 MW	22440 TQ	USBLS	5/07
	New York-Northern New Jersey-Long Island MSA, NY-NJ-PA	Y	15910 FQ	17890 MW	21120 TQ	USBLS	5/07
	North Carolina	Y	17010 FQ	20250 MW	22160 TQ	USBLS	5/07
	Ohio	Y	14810 FQ	15600 MW	17460 TQ	USBLS	5/07
	Cleveland-Elyria-Mentor MSA, OH	Y	14700 FQ	15330 MW	17180 TQ	USBLS	5/07
	Pennsylvania	Y	14240 FQ	14970 MW	17020 TQ	USBLS	5/07
	Philadelphia-Camden-Wilmington MSA, PA-NJ-DE-MD	Y	14700 FQ	15840 MW	18080 TQ	USBLS	5/07
	Pittsburgh MSA, PA	Y	14090 FQ	14660 MW	15440 TQ	USBLS	5/07
	Tennessee	Y	17140 FQ	19920 MW	22950 TQ	USBLS	5/07
	Memphis MSA, TN-MS-AR	Y	15890 FQ	18590 MW	21950 TQ	USBLS	5/07
	Nashville-Davidson-Murfreesboro MSA, TN	Y	19370 FQ	21000 MW	23280 TQ	USBLS	5/07
	Texas	Y	12520 FQ	14090 MW	15750 TQ	USBLS	5/07
	Austin-Round Rock MSA, TX	Y	12000 FQ	13250 MW	14510 TQ	USBLS	5/07
	Dallas-Fort Worth-Arlington MSA, TX	Y	15580 FQ	19240 MW	21510 TQ	USBLS	5/07
	Houston-Sugar Land-Baytown MSA, TX	Y	12920 FQ	14660 MW	16520 TQ	USBLS	5/07
	Virginia	Y	13610 FQ	16220 MW	19560 TQ	USBLS	5/07
	Richmond MSA, VA	Y	12590 FQ	14070 MW	15590 TQ	USBLS	5/07
	Virginia Beach-Norfolk-Newport News MSA, VA-NC	Y	12450 FQ	13820 MW	15220 TQ	USBLS	5/07
	Wisconsin	Y	14220 FQ	14610 MW	15250 TQ	USBLS	5/07
	Puerto Rico	Y	12370 FQ	13430 MW	14490 TQ	USBLS	5/07
	San Juan-Caguas-Guaynabo MSA, PR	Y	12370 FQ	13430 MW	14490 TQ	USBLS	5/07
Sheet Metal Worker	Alabama	Y	25080 FQ	31590 MW	40240 TQ	USBLS	5/07
	Birmingham-Hoover MSA, AL	Y	28900 FQ	36070 MW	43740 TQ	USBLS	5/07
	Alaska	Y	37060 FQ	51900 MW	69070 TQ	USBLS	5/07
	Anchorage MSA, AK	Y	37190 FQ	51530 MW	69660 TQ	USBLS	5/07
	Arizona	Y	24140 FQ	32120 MW	43490 TQ	USBLS	5/07
	Phoenix-Mesa-Scottsdale MSA, AZ	Y	25880 FQ	34350 MW	44930 TQ	USBLS	5/07
	Tucson MSA, AZ	Y	22010 FQ	31150 MW	42620 TQ	USBLS	5/07
	Arkansas	Y	23330 FQ	28030 MW	35210 TQ	USBLS	5/07
	Jonesboro MSA, AR	Y	24410 FQ	28660 MW	35780 TQ	USBLS	5/07
	Little Rock-North Little Rock MSA, AR	Y	25750 FQ	32740 MW	38800 TQ	USBLS	5/07
	California	H	16.81 FQ	22.77 MW	30.94 TQ	CABLS	1/08-3/08
	Los Angeles-Long Beach-Glendale PMSA, CA	H	15.75 FQ	21.89 MW	32.55 TQ	CABLS	1/08-3/08
	Oakland-Fremont-Hayward MSA, CA	H	20.06 FQ	30.18 MW	36.47 TQ	CABLS	1/08-3/08
	Riverside-San Bernardino-Ontario MSA, CA	H	16.81 FQ	20.70 MW	27.93 TQ	CABLS	1/08-3/08
	Sacramento-Arden Arcade-Roseville MSA, CA	H	17.65 FQ	23.84 MW	32.65 TQ	CABLS	1/08-3/08
	San Diego-Carlsbad-San Marcos MSA, CA	H	17.73 FQ	22.37 MW	28.11 TQ	CABLS	1/08-3/08
	San Francisco-San Mateo-Redwood PMSA, CA	H	24.24 FQ	31.18 MW	37.34 TQ	CABLS	1/08-3/08
	San Jose-Sunnyvale-Santa Clara MSA, CA	H	17.40 FQ	27.74 MW	37.56 TQ	CABLS	1/08-3/08
	Santa Ana-Anaheim-Irvine PMSA, CA	Y	33810 FQ	40150 MW	54660 TQ	USBLS	5/07
	Colorado	Y	28710 FQ	36970 MW	48450 TQ	USBLS	5/07
	Denver-Aurora MSA, CO	Y	27170 FQ	33830 MW	45680 TQ	USBLS	5/07
	Connecticut	H	14.49 AE	20.94 MW		CTBLS	1/08-3/08
	Bridgeport-Stamford-Norwalk MSA, CT	Y	29050 FQ	36760 MW	49160 TQ	USBLS	5/07
	Hartford-West Hartford-East Hartford MSA, CT	Y	34080 FQ	43370 MW	55510 TQ	USBLS	5/07

AE	Average entry wage	AW	Average wage paid	FQ	First quartile wage
AER	Average entry range	AWR	Average wage range	H	Hourly
AEX	Average experienced wage	AXR	Average experienced range	HI	Highest wage paid
ATC	Average total compensation	D	Daily	HR	High end range

LO	Lowest wage paid	MTC	Median total compensation
LR	Low end range	MW	Median wage paid
M	Monthly	MWR	Median wage range
MCC	Median cash compensation	S	See annotated source

TCC	Total cash compensation
TQ	Third quartile wage
W	Weekly
Y	Yearly

Occupation/Type/Industry	Location	Per	Low	Mid	High	Source	Date
Sheet Metal Worker	Delaware	Y	32950 FQ	41370 MW	53890 TQ	USBLS	5/07
	Dover MSA, DE	Y	35220 FQ	43830 MW	55580 TQ	USBLS	5/07
	Wilmington PMSA, DE-MD-NJ	Y	36950 FQ	45810 MW	58310 TQ	USBLS	5/07
	Washington-Arlington-Alexandria MSA, DC-VA-MD-WV	Y	32000 FQ	39240 MW	49560 TQ	USBLS	5/07
	Florida	Y	26530 FQ	33430 MW	41260 TQ	USBLS	5/07
	Fort Lauderdale-Pompano Beach-Deerfield Beach PMSA, FL	Y	29100 FQ	35270 MW	41360 TQ	USBLS	5/07
	Jacksonville MSA, FL	Y	30770 FQ	40900 MW	46410 TQ	USBLS	5/07
	Miami-Fort Lauderdale-Miami Beach MSA, FL	Y	29400 FQ	36800 MW	44730 TQ	USBLS	5/07
	Orlando-Kissimmee MSA, FL	Y	25080 FQ	30910 MW	38060 TQ	USBLS	5/07
	Tampa-St. Petersburg-Clearwater MSA, FL	Y	28430 FQ	33980 MW	38940 TQ	USBLS	5/07
	West Palm Beach-Boca Raton-Boynton Beach PMSA, FL	Y	26130 FQ	35100 MW	43830 TQ	USBLS	5/07
	Georgia	Y	24660 FQ	33320 MW	45110 TQ	USBLS	5/07
	Atlanta-Sandy Springs-Marietta MSA, GA	Y	21500 FQ	31570 MW	45290 TQ	USBLS	5/07
	Augusta-Richmond County MSA, GA-SC	Y	22330 FQ	25810 MW	34350 TQ	USBLS	5/07
	Macon MSA, GA	Y	20160 FQ	30700 MW	36650 TQ	USBLS	5/07
	Hawaii	Y	37760 FQ	56980 MW	67210 TQ	USBLS	5/07
	Honolulu MSA, HI	Y	37120 FQ	56500 MW	65970 TQ	USBLS	5/07
	Idaho	Y	30060 FQ	39080 MW	52050 TQ	USBLS	5/07
	Boise City-Nampa MSA, ID	Y	30900 FQ	39550 MW	51390 TQ	USBLS	5/07
	Illinois	Y	34040 FQ	56530 MW	72140 TQ	USBLS	5/07
	Chicago-Naperville-Joliet MSA, IL-IN-WI	Y	37510 FQ	62140 MW	74660 TQ	USBLS	5/07
	Indiana	Y	29730 FQ	40580 MW	54540 TQ	USBLS	5/07
	Elkhart-Goshen MSA, IN	Y	22010 FQ	28330 MW	44100 TQ	USBLS	5/07
	Gary PMSA, IN	Y	42600 FQ	67070 MW	74370 TQ	USBLS	5/07
	Indianapolis-Carmel MSA, IN	Y	31320 FQ	41570 MW	54360 TQ	USBLS	5/07
	South Bend-Mishawaka MSA, IN-MI	Y	34100 FQ	39600 MW	49480 TQ	USBLS	5/07
	Iowa	Y	30690 FQ	40100 MW	56320 TQ	USBLS	5/07
	Des Moines-West Des Moines MSA, IA	Y	34190 FQ	40550 MW	60750 TQ	USBLS	5/07
	Kansas	Y	36020 FQ	46760 MW	55110 TQ	USBLS	5/07
	Wichita MSA, KS	Y	37420 FQ	46440 MW	52470 TQ	USBLS	5/07
	Kentucky	Y	26900 FQ	33076 MW	44223 TQ	KYBLS	2008
	Louisville-Jefferson County MSA, KY-IN	Y	26000 FQ	34810 MW	47260 TQ	USBLS	5/07
	Louisiana	H	12.84 FQ	16.37 MW	20.08 TQ	LABLS	1/08-3/08
	Baton Rouge MSA, LA	Y	30960 FQ	37270 MW	49260 TQ	USBLS	5/07
	New Orleans-Metairie-Kenner MSA, LA	Y	26880 FQ	34300 MW	42220 TQ	USBLS	5/07
	Maine	Y	28330 FQ	35650 MW	40770 TQ	USBLS	5/07
	Portland-South Portland-Biddeford MSA, ME	Y	23870 FQ	34460 MW	42100 TQ	USBLS	5/07
	Maryland	Y		41925 MW		MDBLS	3/08
	Baltimore-Towson MSA, MD	Y	33100 FQ	43540 MW	57040 TQ	USBLS	5/07
	Bethesda-Gaithersburg-Frederick PMSA, MD	Y	32030 FQ	38150 MW	44600 TQ	USBLS	5/07
	Cumberland MSA, MD-WV	Y	34550 FQ	44180 MW	51930 TQ	USBLS	5/07
	Massachusetts	Y	39380 FQ	52190 MW	66040 TQ	USBLS	5/07
	Boston-Cambridge-Quincy NECTA, MA	Y	43620 FQ	55380 MW	68670 TQ	USBLS	5/07
	Springfield MSA, MA-CT	Y	31470 FQ	43470 MW	53650 TQ	USBLS	5/07
	Worcester MSA, MA-CT	Y	45370 FQ	64160 MW	71330 TQ	USBLS	5/07
	Michigan	Y	35690 FQ	51460 MW	67260 TQ	USBLS	5/07
	Detroit-Warren-Livonia MSA, MI	Y	37300 FQ	55450 MW	71490 TQ	USBLS	5/07
	Grand Rapids-Wyoming MSA, MI	Y	33830 FQ	43980 MW	58090 TQ	USBLS	5/07
	Muskegon-Norton Shores MSA, MI	Y	27330 FQ	52670 MW	59510 TQ	USBLS	5/07
	Warren-Troy-Farmington Hills PMSA, MI	Y	38290 FQ	60410 MW	72640 TQ	USBLS	5/07

AE Average entry wage; AER Average entry range; AEX Average experienced wage; ATC Average total compensation; AW Average wage paid; AWR Average wage range; AXR Average experienced range; D Daily; FQ First quartile wage; H Hourly; HI Highest wage paid; HR High end range; LO Lowest wage paid; LR Low end range; M Monthly; MCC Median cash compensation; MTC Median total compensation; MW Median wage paid; MWR Median wage range; S See annotated source; TCC Total cash compensation; TQ Third quartile wage; W Weekly; Y Yearly

1476

Sheet Metal Worker

Occupation/Type/Industry	Location	Per	Low	Mid	High	Source	Date
Sheet Metal Worker	Minnesota	Y	41881 FQ	56961 MW	75288 TQ	MNBLS	10/08-12/08
	Duluth-Superior MSA, MN-WI	Y	54980 FQ	63021 MW	73212 TQ	MNBLS	10/08-12/08
	Minneapolis-Saint Paul MSA, MN-WI	Y	45917 FQ	67627 MW	78598 TQ	MNBLS	10/08-12/08
	Rochester MSA, MN	Y	47764 FQ	59237 MW	69405 TQ	MNBLS	10/08-12/08
	Mississippi	Y	23020 FQ	27320 MW	32260 TQ	USBLS	5/07
	Jackson MSA, MS	Y	21800 FQ	26770 MW	35440 TQ	USBLS	5/07
	Missouri	Y	29780 FQ	42310 MW	67330 TQ	USBLS	5/07
	Kansas City MSA, MO-KS	Y	31770 FQ	49890 MW	74620 TQ	USBLS	5/07
	St. Joseph MSA, MO-KS	Y	41670 FQ	68940 MW	75870 TQ	USBLS	5/07
	St. Louis MSA, MO-IL	Y	36590 FQ	56450 MW	69850 TQ	USBLS	5/07
	Montana	Y	23640 FQ	34560 MW	49280 TQ	USBLS	5/07
	Billings MSA, MT	Y	24310 FQ	36960 MW	52730 TQ	USBLS	5/07
	Nebraska	Y	32760 FQ	46370 MW	57450 TQ	USBLS	5/07
	Omaha-Council Bluffs MSA, NE-IA	Y	32610 FQ	46020 MW	59460 TQ	USBLS	5/07
	Nevada	H	15.05 FQ	21.48 MW	34.60 TQ	NVBLS	5/08
	Las Vegas-Paradise MSA, NV	H	16.38 FQ	23.27 MW	35.62 TQ	NVBLS	5/08
	Manchester MSA, NH	Y	33770 FQ	41350 MW	47860 TQ	USBLS	5/07
	Nashua NECTA, NH-MA	Y	28450 FQ	35680 MW	43090 TQ	USBLS	5/07
	New Jersey	Y	32450 FQ	50010 MW	74320 TQ	USBLS	5/07
	Camden PMSA, NJ	Y	33200 FQ	45920 MW	73310 TQ	USBLS	5/07
	Edison PMSA, NJ	Y	33520 FQ	50660 MW	70400 TQ	USBLS	5/07
	Newark-Union PMSA, NJ-PA	Y	26920 FQ	40880 MW	74150 TQ	USBLS	5/07
	New Mexico	Y	27570 FQ	34740 MW	46350 TQ	USBLS	5/07
	Albuquerque MSA, NM	Y	26810 FQ	35310 MW	47740 TQ	USBLS	5/07
	New York	Y	35040 FQ	55310 MW	74890 TQ	USBLS	5/07
	Albany-Schenectady-Troy MSA, NY	Y	45920 FQ	53920 MW	62730 TQ	USBLS	5/07
	Binghamton MSA, NY	Y	23310 FQ	33550 MW	46040 TQ	USBLS	5/07
	Buffalo-Niagara Falls MSA, NY	Y	28980 FQ	42570 MW	59560 TQ	USBLS	5/07
	Nassau-Suffolk PMSA, NY	Y	42480 FQ	66290 MW	85740 TQ	USBLS	5/07
	New York-Northern New Jersey-Long Island MSA, NY-NJ-PA	Y	36100 FQ	61520 MW	80670 TQ	USBLS	5/07
	North Carolina	Y	25350 FQ	30610 MW	37350 TQ	USBLS	5/07
	Charlotte-Gastonia-Concord MSA, NC-SC	Y	27180 FQ	31720 MW	37890 TQ	USBLS	5/07
	Raleigh-Cary MSA, NC	Y	25130 FQ	32740 MW	40880 TQ	USBLS	5/07
	North Dakota	Y	30250 FQ	36550 MW	44570 TQ	USBLS	5/07
	Fargo MSA, ND-MN	Y	29390 FQ	35530 MW	43610 TQ	USBLS	5/07
	Ohio	Y	32200 FQ	45750 MW	60800 TQ	USBLS	5/07
	Cincinnati-Middletown MSA, OH-KY-IN	Y	29970 FQ	39590 MW	54410 TQ	USBLS	5/07
	Cleveland-Elyria-Mentor MSA, OH	Y	36270 FQ	57610 MW	67490 TQ	USBLS	5/07
	Columbus MSA, OH	Y	35040 FQ	43380 MW	55590 TQ	USBLS	5/07
	Dayton MSA, OH	Y	31080 FQ	42000 MW	54370 TQ	USBLS	5/07
	Oklahoma	Y	28640 FQ	41650 MW	47980 TQ	USBLS	5/07
	Oklahoma City MSA, OK	Y	41730 FQ	45760 MW	49680 TQ	USBLS	5/07
	Tulsa MSA, OK	Y	20460 FQ	27360 MW	37270 TQ	USBLS	5/07
	Oregon	H	15.25 FQ	20.46 MW	29.14 TQ	ORBLS	5/08
	Portland-Vancouver-Beaverton MSA, OR-WA	Y	29810 FQ	40480 MW	61630 TQ	USBLS	5/07
	Pennsylvania	Y	34120 FQ	44940 MW	57840 TQ	USBLS	5/07
	Allentown-Bethlehem-Easton MSA, PA-NJ	Y	34100 FQ	47730 MW	66700 TQ	USBLS	5/07
	Philadelphia-Camden-Wilmington MSA, PA-NJ-DE-MD	Y	35310 FQ	45930 MW	67640 TQ	USBLS	5/07
	Pittsburgh MSA, PA	Y	37270 FQ	51180 MW	59950 TQ	USBLS	5/07
	Reading MSA, PA	Y	42340 FQ	56820 MW	64140 TQ	USBLS	5/07
	Rhode Island	Y	34570 FQ	41710 MW	46420 TQ	USBLS	5/07
	Providence-Fall River-Warwick MSA, RI-MA	Y	34630 FQ	41900 MW	46980 TQ	USBLS	5/07
	South Carolina	Y	26840 FQ	30940 MW	36580 TQ	USBLS	5/07
	Charleston-North Charleston MSA, SC	Y	26250 FQ	31240 MW	39310 TQ	USBLS	5/07
	Columbia MSA, SC	Y	30220 FQ	34190 MW	37730 TQ	USBLS	5/07
	Florence MSA, SC	Y	20990 FQ	26820 MW	32700 TQ	USBLS	5/07
	South Dakota	Y	24169 FQ	28711 MW	33654 TQ	SDBLS	7/08-9/08

AE	Average entry wage	AW	Average wage paid	FQ	First quartile wage
AER	Average entry range	AWR	Average wage range	H	Hourly
AEX	Average experienced wage	AXR	Average experienced range	HI	Highest wage paid
ATC	Average total compensation	D	Daily	HR	High end range

LO	Lowest wage paid	MTC	Median total compensation	TCC	Total cash compensation
LR	Low end range	MW	Median wage paid	TQ	Third quartile wage
M	Monthly	MWR	Median wage range	W	Weekly
MCC	Median cash compensation	S	See annotated source	Y	Yearly

Occupation/Type/Industry	Location	Per	Low	Mid	High	Source	Date
Sheet Metal Worker	Sioux Falls MSA, SD	Y	27315 FQ	31325 MW	36522 TQ	SDBLS	7/08-9/08
	Tennessee	Y	25320 FQ	32220 MW	41270 TQ	USBLS	5/07
	Memphis MSA, TN-MS-AR	Y	23100 FQ	28940 MW	37660 TQ	USBLS	5/07
	Nashville-Davidson-Murfreesboro MSA, TN	Y	25570 FQ	33770 MW	43070 TQ	USBLS	5/07
	Texas	Y	25760 FQ	31190 MW	40280 TQ	USBLS	5/07
	Austin-Round Rock MSA, TX	Y	28740 FQ	35400 MW	45330 TQ	USBLS	5/07
	Dallas-Fort Worth-Arlington MSA, TX	Y	23390 FQ	30440 MW	40920 TQ	USBLS	5/07
	El Paso MSA, TX	Y	22520 FQ	29190 MW	35280 TQ	USBLS	5/07
	Houston-Sugar Land-Baytown MSA, TX	Y	27150 FQ	31260 MW	39310 TQ	USBLS	5/07
	San Antonio MSA, TX	Y	28440 FQ	35110 MW	43780 TQ	USBLS	5/07
	Utah	Y	29480 FQ	42430 MW	52940 TQ	USBLS	5/07
	Salt Lake City MSA, UT	Y	30410 FQ	47590 MW	57850 TQ	USBLS	5/07
	Vermont	Y	27900 FQ	34500 MW	42310 TQ	USBLS	5/07
	Burlington-South Burlington MSA, VT	Y	30620 FQ	36890 MW	44530 TQ	USBLS	5/07
	Virginia	Y	28160 FQ	36050 MW	44710 TQ	USBLS	5/07
	Richmond MSA, VA	Y	27770 FQ	33920 MW	39500 TQ	USBLS	5/07
	Virginia Beach-Norfolk-Newport News MSA, VA-NC	Y	29620 FQ	38810 MW	46200 TQ	USBLS	5/07
	Washington	H	19.26 FQ	27.53 MW	34.66 TQ	WABLS	3/08
	Seattle-Tacoma-Bellevue MSA, WA	Y	44510 FQ	61870 MW	73800 TQ	USBLS	5/07
	West Virginia	Y	27220 FQ	39493 MW	50644 TQ	WVBLS	7/08-9/08
	Charleston MSA, WV	Y	22130 FQ	25770 MW	41310 TQ	USBLS	5/07
	Parkersburg-Marietta-Vienna MSA, WV-OH	Y	26600 FQ	38400 MW	50850 TQ	USBLS	5/07
	Wisconsin	Y	34470 FQ	49580 MW	62660 TQ	USBLS	5/07
	Milwaukee-Waukesha-West Allis MSA, WI	Y	44390 FQ	57960 MW	69760 TQ	USBLS	5/07
	Wyoming	Y	29491 FQ	38834 MW	47487 TQ	WYBLS	9/08
	Puerto Rico	Y	14990 FQ	17690 MW	20240 TQ	USBLS	5/07
	San Juan-Caguas-Guaynabo MSA, PR	Y	14420 FQ	17550 MW	20440 TQ	USBLS	5/07
	Virgin Islands	Y	35850 FQ	42480 MW	46980 TQ	USBLS	5/07
	Guam	Y	27590 FQ	31640 MW	36320 TQ	USBLS	5/07
Sheet Timer	United States	W		2000 MW		TAG	1/08
Sheriff	Gwinnett County, GA	Y			137469 HI	GACTY02	2008
	Spalding County, GA	Y			88529 HI	GACTY02	2008
	Harford County, MD	Y			104042 HI	BMAG	2009
Sheriff's Deputy	Fayette County, GA	Y	35500 LO		53250 HI	AREGC	2007
Shift Leader							
Casual Dining Restaurant	United States	H		12.41 AW		CLEAD	2008
Quick Service Restaurant	United States	H		9.60 AW		CLEAD	2008
Ship Engineer	Alabama	Y	35310 FQ	39840 MW	59430 TQ	USBLS	5/07
	Alaska	Y	46330 FQ	55300 MW	66370 TQ	USBLS	5/07
	California	H	23.33 FQ	28.27 MW	32.25 TQ	CABLS	1/08-3/08
	Connecticut	H	17.06 AE	26.86 MW		CTBLS	1/08-3/08
	Florida	Y	41360 FQ	54850 MW	80150 TQ	USBLS	5/07
	Georgia	Y	42680 FQ	53330 MW	59370 TQ	USBLS	5/07
	Hawaii	Y	36690 FQ	41140 MW	45100 TQ	USBLS	5/07
	Illinois	Y	39080 FQ	64240 MW	92690 TQ	USBLS	5/07
	Indiana	Y	50440 FQ	58820 MW	70930 TQ	USBLS	5/07
	Kentucky	Y	41124 FQ	55016 MW	69345 TQ	KYBLS	2008
	Louisiana	H	20.07 FQ	27.07 MW	36.15 TQ	LABLS	1/08-3/08
	Maryland	Y		113650 MW		MDBLS	3/08
	Massachusetts	Y	39730 FQ	46390 MW	71400 TQ	USBLS	5/07
	Michigan	Y	42870 FQ	48770 MW	62590 TQ	USBLS	5/07
	Mississippi	Y	40790 FQ	45770 MW	64020 TQ	USBLS	5/07
	New Jersey	Y	43510 FQ	61350 MW	86470 TQ	USBLS	5/07
	New York	Y	49270 FQ	60500 MW	74270 TQ	USBLS	5/07
	North Carolina	Y	35510 FQ	40540 MW	49620 TQ	USBLS	5/07
	Ohio	Y	39540 FQ	91530 MW	114330 TQ	USBLS	5/07
	Oregon	H	22.93 FQ	27.47 MW	32.08 TQ	ORBLS	5/08
	Pennsylvania	Y	40810 FQ	53160 MW	62720 TQ	USBLS	5/07
	South Carolina	Y	40860 FQ	54240 MW	61300 TQ	USBLS	5/07

AE	Average entry wage	AW	Average wage paid	FQ	First quartile wage	LO Lowest wage paid
AER	Average entry range	AWR	Average wage range	H	Hourly	LR Low end range
AEX	Average experienced wage	AXR	Average experienced range	HI	Highest wage paid	M Monthly
ATC	Average total compensation	D	Daily	HR	High end range	MCC Median cash compensation

MTC Median total compensation TCC Total cash compensation
MW Median wage paid TQ Third quartile wage
MWR Median wage range W Weekly
S See annotated source Y Yearly

Occupation/Type/Industry	Location	Per	Low	Mid	High	Source	Date
Ship Engineer	Texas	Y	42600 FQ	53230 MW	70450 TQ	USBLS	5/07
	Virginia	Y	39050 FQ	53940 MW	86250 TQ	USBLS	5/07
	Washington	H	28.51 FQ	32.57 MW	37.18 TQ	WABLS	3/08
	Puerto Rico	Y	28510 FQ	41130 MW	49320 TQ	USBLS	5/07
Shipping, Receiving, and Traffic Clerk	Alabama	Y	20400 FQ	25570 MW	31870 TQ	USBLS	5/07
	Birmingham-Hoover MSA, AL	Y	21180 FQ	26150 MW	32530 TQ	USBLS	5/07
	Alaska	Y	27380 FQ	34380 MW	44090 TQ	USBLS	5/07
	Anchorage MSA, AK	Y	27180 FQ	34150 MW	44400 TQ	USBLS	5/07
	Arizona	Y	16500 FQ	18790 MW	25410 TQ	USBLS	5/07
	Phoenix-Mesa-Scottsdale MSA, AZ	Y	16480 FQ	18650 MW	24730 TQ	USBLS	5/07
	Prescott MSA, AZ	Y	17840 FQ	22210 MW	27940 TQ	USBLS	5/07
	Tucson MSA, AZ	Y	16750 FQ	19060 MW	25610 TQ	USBLS	5/07
	Arkansas	Y	20230 FQ	24370 MW	29600 TQ	USBLS	5/07
	Little Rock-North Little Rock MSA, AR	Y	20130 FQ	24860 MW	30650 TQ	USBLS	5/07
	California	H	10.75 FQ	13.67 MW	17.47 TQ	CABLS	1/08-3/08
	Los Angeles-Long Beach-Glendale PMSA, CA	H	10.28 FQ	12.93 MW	16.81 TQ	CABLS	1/08-3/08
	Oakland-Fremont-Hayward MSA, CA	H	12.43 FQ	15.36 MW	18.85 TQ	CABLS	1/08-3/08
	Riverside-San Bernardino-Ontario MSA, CA	H	10.46 FQ	13.08 MW	15.84 TQ	CABLS	1/08-3/08
	Sacramento-Arden Arcade-Roseville MSA, CA	H	11.25 FQ	14.08 MW	17.94 TQ	CABLS	1/08-3/08
	San Diego-Carlsbad-San Marcos MSA, CA	H	11.26 FQ	13.82 MW	16.90 TQ	CABLS	1/08-3/08
	San Francisco-San Mateo-Redwood PMSA, CA	H	11.72 FQ	15.43 MW	20.17 TQ	CABLS	1/08-3/08
	San Jose-Sunnyvale-Santa Clara MSA, CA	H	13.06 FQ	16.19 MW	20.75 TQ	CABLS	1/08-3/08
	Santa Ana-Anaheim-Irvine PMSA, CA	Y	22290 FQ	27780 MW	34700 TQ	USBLS	5/07
	Colorado	Y	22320 FQ	28200 MW	34910 TQ	USBLS	5/07
	Denver-Aurora MSA, CO	Y	23460 FQ	29080 MW	36470 TQ	USBLS	5/07
	Connecticut	H	10.65 AE	14.78 MW		CTBLS	1/08-3/08
	Bridgeport-Stamford-Norwalk MSA, CT	Y	24470 FQ	31100 MW	38180 TQ	USBLS	5/07
	Hartford-West Hartford-East Hartford MSA, CT	Y	24530 FQ	30370 MW	36180 TQ	USBLS	5/07
	Norwich-New London MSA, CT-RI	Y	23250 FQ	28000 MW	32570 TQ	USBLS	5/07
	Delaware	Y	20970 FQ	27310 MW	36400 TQ	USBLS	5/07
	Wilmington PMSA, DE-MD-NJ	Y	22200 FQ	29190 MW	38340 TQ	USBLS	5/07
	District of Columbia	Y	25920 FQ	35900 MW	45710 TQ	USBLS	5/07
	Washington-Arlington-Alexandria MSA, DC-VA-MD-WV	Y	21940 FQ	28160 MW	37520 TQ	USBLS	5/07
	Florida	Y	20050 FQ	24910 MW	31160 TQ	USBLS	5/07
	Fort Lauderdale-Pompano Beach-Deerfield Beach PMSA, FL	Y	21660 FQ	26180 MW	30980 TQ	USBLS	5/07
	Jacksonville MSA, FL	Y	22710 FQ	28400 MW	36330 TQ	USBLS	5/07
	Miami-Fort Lauderdale-Miami Beach MSA, FL	Y	19670 FQ	24710 MW	31050 TQ	USBLS	5/07
	Orlando-Kissimmee MSA, FL	Y	18790 FQ	23600 MW	29320 TQ	USBLS	5/07
	Tampa-St. Petersburg-Clearwater MSA, FL	Y	20880 FQ	25700 MW	31580 TQ	USBLS	5/07
	West Palm Beach-Boca Raton-Boynton Beach PMSA, FL	Y	21150 FQ	28280 MW	34820 TQ	USBLS	5/07
	Georgia	Y	21150 FQ	26000 MW	31560 TQ	USBLS	5/07
	Athens-Clarke County MSA, GA	Y	20680 FQ	24180 MW	32420 TQ	USBLS	5/07
	Atlanta-Sandy Springs-Marietta MSA, GA	Y	21380 FQ	26450 MW	32010 TQ	USBLS	5/07
	Macon MSA, GA	Y	18430 FQ	22810 MW	28000 TQ	USBLS	5/07
	Hawaii	Y	19540 FQ	25380 MW	34140 TQ	USBLS	5/07
	Honolulu MSA, HI	Y	18800 FQ	25000 MW	34230 TQ	USBLS	5/07
	Idaho	Y	20620 FQ	24190 MW	29900 TQ	USBLS	5/07

AE	Average entry wage	**AW**	Average wage paid	**FQ**	First quartile wage
AER	Average entry range	**AWR**	Average wage range	**H**	Hourly
AEX	Average experienced wage	**AXR**	Average experienced range	**HI**	Highest wage paid
ATC	Average total compensation	**D**	Daily	**HR**	High end range

LO	Lowest wage paid	**MTC**	Median total compensation	**TCC**	Total cash compensation
LR	Low end range	**MW**	Median wage paid	**TQ**	Third quartile wage
M	Monthly	**MWR**	Median wage range	**W**	Weekly
MCC	Median cash compensation	**S**	See annotated source	**Y**	Yearly

Occupation/Type/Industry	Location	Per	Low	Mid	High	Source	Date
Shipping, Receiving, and Traffic Clerk	Boise City-Nampa MSA, ID	Y	21020 FQ	24040 MW	29850 TQ	USBLS	5/07
	Illinois	Y	21810 FQ	27480 MW	35210 TQ	USBLS	5/07
	Champaign-Urbana MSA, IL	Y	21400 FQ	25410 MW	31470 TQ	USBLS	5/07
	Chicago-Naperville-Joliet MSA, IL-IN-WI	Y	22110 FQ	27860 MW	35690 TQ	USBLS	5/07
	Indiana	Y	21600 FQ	26930 MW	33280 TQ	USBLS	5/07
	Gary PMSA, IN	Y	21440 FQ	27150 MW	35190 TQ	USBLS	5/07
	Indianapolis-Carmel MSA, IN	Y	21840 FQ	26940 MW	33340 TQ	USBLS	5/07
	Iowa	Y	21580 FQ	26320 MW	31960 TQ	USBLS	5/07
	Des Moines-West Des Moines MSA, IA	Y	23010 FQ	28530 MW	36010 TQ	USBLS	5/07
	Iowa City MSA, IA	Y	24570 FQ	29860 MW	34990 TQ	USBLS	5/07
	Kansas	Y	21200 FQ	26510 MW	33390 TQ	USBLS	5/07
	Wichita MSA, KS	Y	21110 FQ	26530 MW	37240 TQ	USBLS	5/07
	Kentucky	Y	22792 FQ	28240 MW	35510 TQ	KYBLS	2008
	Louisville-Jefferson County MSA, KY-IN	Y	22970 FQ	27840 MW	35420 TQ	USBLS	5/07
	Owensboro MSA, KY	Y	23360 FQ	28840 MW	34900 TQ	USBLS	5/07
	Louisiana	H	9.57 FQ	12.10 MW	15.24 TQ	LABLS	1/08-3/08
	Baton Rouge MSA, LA	Y	20270 FQ	25360 MW	33120 TQ	USBLS	5/07
	New Orleans-Metairie-Kenner MSA, LA	Y	20140 FQ	25370 MW	30990 TQ	USBLS	5/07
	Maine	Y	21010 FQ	26320 MW	31310 TQ	USBLS	5/07
	Portland-South Portland-Biddeford MSA, ME	Y	23260 FQ	27720 MW	32120 TQ	USBLS	5/07
	Maryland	Y		28075 MW		MDBLS	3/08
	Baltimore-Towson MSA, MD	Y	22380 FQ	28240 MW	35450 TQ	USBLS	5/07
	Bethesda-Gaithersburg-Frederick PMSA, MD	Y	21200 FQ	25920 MW	31710 TQ	USBLS	5/07
	Cumberland MSA, MD-WV	Y	20330 FQ	27780 MW	45290 TQ	USBLS	5/07
	Massachusetts	Y	24440 FQ	30910 MW	37940 TQ	USBLS	5/07
	Boston-Cambridge-Quincy NECTA, MA	Y	25360 FQ	32220 MW	40190 TQ	USBLS	5/07
	Lynn-Peabody-Salem NECTA, MA	Y	26210 FQ	31530 MW	40560 TQ	USBLS	5/07
	Worcester MSA, MA-CT	Y	23000 FQ	29150 MW	35780 TQ	USBLS	5/07
	Michigan	Y	23860 FQ	29490 MW	36540 TQ	USBLS	5/07
	Detroit-Warren-Livonia MSA, MI	Y	24740 FQ	30340 MW	38270 TQ	USBLS	5/07
	Grand Rapids-Wyoming MSA, MI	Y	24670 FQ	30100 MW	36510 TQ	USBLS	5/07
	Muskegon-Norton Shores MSA, MI	Y	25030 FQ	30120 MW	35740 TQ	USBLS	5/07
	Warren-Troy-Farmington Hills PMSA, MI	Y	24700 FQ	30040 MW	37170 TQ	USBLS	5/07
	Minnesota	Y	26228 FQ	31546 MW	38155 TQ	MNBLS	10/08-12/08
	Duluth-Superior MSA, MN-WI	Y	21211 FQ	27060 MW	34949 TQ	MNBLS	10/08-12/08
	Minneapolis-Saint Paul MSA, MN-WI	Y	27320 FQ	32691 MW	39040 TQ	MNBLS	10/08-12/08
	Rochester MSA, MN	Y	22838 FQ	27284 MW	34718 TQ	MNBLS	10/08-12/08
	Mississippi	Y	20430 FQ	24370 MW	29840 TQ	USBLS	5/07
	Gulfport-Biloxi MSA, MS	Y	20510 FQ	24570 MW	30630 TQ	USBLS	5/07
	Jackson MSA, MS	Y	21460 FQ	26620 MW	34690 TQ	USBLS	5/07
	Missouri	Y	20730 FQ	26040 MW	32930 TQ	USBLS	5/07
	Kansas City MSA, MO-KS	Y	22190 FQ	27200 MW	33950 TQ	USBLS	5/07
	St. Louis MSA, MO-IL	Y	21310 FQ	26850 MW	34350 TQ	USBLS	5/07
	Montana	Y	20590 FQ	24280 MW	30990 TQ	USBLS	5/07
	Billings MSA, MT	Y	19410 FQ	23420 MW	28170 TQ	USBLS	5/07
	Missoula MSA, MT	Y	20220 FQ	23270 MW	33170 TQ	USBLS	5/07
	Nebraska	Y	21720 FQ	27320 MW	33980 TQ	USBLS	5/07
	Omaha-Council Bluffs MSA, NE-IA	Y	22240 FQ	27530 MW	35110 TQ	USBLS	5/07
	Nevada	H	11.58 FQ	14.18 MW	17.87 TQ	NVBLS	5/08
	Las Vegas-Paradise MSA, NV	H	11.57 FQ	15.18 MW	18.71 TQ	NVBLS	5/08
	New Hampshire	H	10.65 AE	14.25 MW	16.44 AEX	NHBLS	6/08
	Manchester MSA, NH	Y	25590 FQ	30380 MW	35810 TQ	USBLS	5/07
	Nashua NECTA, NH-MA	Y	27020 FQ	31680 MW	36450 TQ	USBLS	5/07
	New Jersey	Y	23240 FQ	29850 MW	37940 TQ	USBLS	5/07
	Atlantic City MSA, NJ	Y	22160 FQ	28350 MW	35390 TQ	USBLS	5/07
	Camden PMSA, NJ	Y	24630 FQ	32040 MW	41720 TQ	USBLS	5/07
	Edison PMSA, NJ	Y	22380 FQ	28710 MW	36870 TQ	USBLS	5/07

AE	Average entry wage	AW	Average wage paid	FQ	First quartile wage	LO	Lowest wage paid	MTC	Median total compensation	TCC	Total cash compensation
AER	Average entry range	AWR	Average wage range	H	Hourly	LR	Low end range	MW	Median wage paid	TQ	Third quartile wage
AEX	Average experienced wage	AXR	Average experienced range	HI	Highest wage paid	M	Monthly	MWR	Median wage range	W	Weekly
ATC	Average total compensation	D	Daily	HR	High end range	MCC	Median cash compensation	S	See annotated source	Y	Yearly

1480

Shipping, Receiving, and Traffic Clerk

Occupation/Type/Industry	Location	Per	Low	Mid	High	Source	Date
Shipping, Receiving, and Traffic Clerk							
	Newark-Union PMSA, NJ-PA	Y	25240 FQ	30630 MW	37960 TQ	USBLS	5/07
	New Mexico	Y	20060 FQ	24650 MW	30690 TQ	USBLS	5/07
	Albuquerque MSA, NM	Y	20730 FQ	24630 MW	29930 TQ	USBLS	5/07
	New York	Y	20600 FQ	26740 MW	34730 TQ	USBLS	5/07
	Albany-Schenectady-Troy MSA, NY	Y	20550 FQ	26360 MW	33180 TQ	USBLS	5/07
	Buffalo-Niagara Falls MSA, NY	Y	20360 FQ	24820 MW	30620 TQ	USBLS	5/07
	Nassau-Suffolk PMSA, NY	Y	21060 FQ	27200 MW	36720 TQ	USBLS	5/07
	New York-Northern New Jersey-Long Island MSA, NY-NJ-PA	Y	21450 FQ	28230 MW	36820 TQ	USBLS	5/07
	North Carolina	Y	21760 FQ	26610 MW	32110 TQ	USBLS	5/07
	Charlotte-Gastonia-Concord MSA, NC-SC	Y	22890 FQ	27750 MW	33470 TQ	USBLS	5/07
	Greensboro-High Point MSA, NC	Y	22420 FQ	27510 MW	33480 TQ	USBLS	5/07
	Raleigh-Cary MSA, NC	Y	21920 FQ	26800 MW	32330 TQ	USBLS	5/07
	North Dakota	Y	20440 FQ	26780 MW	32430 TQ	USBLS	5/07
	Fargo MSA, ND-MN	Y	18700 FQ	25890 MW	30810 TQ	USBLS	5/07
	Ohio	Y	22660 FQ	27920 MW	33880 TQ	USBLS	5/07
	Cincinnati-Middletown MSA, OH-KY-IN	Y	23190 FQ	28530 MW	34930 TQ	USBLS	5/07
	Cleveland-Elyria-Mentor MSA, OH	Y	23700 FQ	28940 MW	35460 TQ	USBLS	5/07
	Columbus MSA, OH	Y	23340 FQ	28150 MW	33100 TQ	USBLS	5/07
	Dayton MSA, OH	Y	21420 FQ	26780 MW	34690 TQ	USBLS	5/07
	Springfield MSA, OH	Y	25490 FQ	28430 MW	31680 TQ	USBLS	5/07
	Oklahoma	Y	20010 FQ	25220 MW	32110 TQ	USBLS	5/07
	Oklahoma City MSA, OK	Y	19120 FQ	25580 MW	33580 TQ	USBLS	5/07
	Tulsa MSA, OK	Y	21560 FQ	25820 MW	31850 TQ	USBLS	5/07
	Oregon	H	11.20 FQ	13.73 MW	17.03 TQ	ORBLS	5/08
	Portland-Vancouver-Beaverton MSA, OR-WA	Y	23590 FQ	29000 MW	36080 TQ	USBLS	5/07
	Pennsylvania	Y	22130 FQ	28160 MW	35290 TQ	USBLS	5/07
	Allentown-Bethlehem-Easton MSA, PA-NJ	Y	21520 FQ	28340 MW	35380 TQ	USBLS	5/07
	Philadelphia-Camden-Wilmington MSA, PA-NJ-DE-MD	Y	23720 FQ	30680 MW	39320 TQ	USBLS	5/07
	Pittsburgh MSA, PA	Y	21310 FQ	26560 MW	32450 TQ	USBLS	5/07
	Rhode Island	Y	23490 FQ	28680 MW	34490 TQ	USBLS	5/07
	Providence-Fall River-Warwick MSA, RI-MA	Y	23010 FQ	28260 MW	34090 TQ	USBLS	5/07
	South Carolina	Y	20500 FQ	25600 MW	31550 TQ	USBLS	5/07
	Charleston-North Charleston MSA, SC	Y	20820 FQ	28190 MW	36470 TQ	USBLS	5/07
	Columbia MSA, SC	Y	20560 FQ	24730 MW	30940 TQ	USBLS	5/07
	South Dakota	Y	22585 FQ	25957 MW	30696 TQ	SDBLS	7/08-9/08
	Rapid City MSA, SD	Y	20917 FQ	24027 MW	29325 TQ	SDBLS	7/08-9/08
	Sioux Falls MSA, SD	Y	23351 FQ	26676 MW	31717 TQ	SDBLS	7/08-9/08
	Tennessee	Y	20990 FQ	25850 MW	31000 TQ	USBLS	5/07
	Memphis MSA, TN-MS-AR	Y	22510 FQ	26840 MW	31390 TQ	USBLS	5/07
	Nashville-Davidson-Murfreesboro MSA, TN	Y	20350 FQ	25580 MW	31880 TQ	USBLS	5/07
	Texas	Y	19850 FQ	24660 MW	30890 TQ	USBLS	5/07
	Austin-Round Rock MSA, TX	Y	20990 FQ	25490 MW	31010 TQ	USBLS	5/07
	Dallas-Fort Worth-Arlington MSA, TX	Y	20560 FQ	25410 MW	31990 TQ	USBLS	5/07
	El Paso MSA, TX	Y	15590 FQ	19550 MW	24180 TQ	USBLS	5/07
	Houston-Sugar Land-Baytown MSA, TX	Y	21160 FQ	25730 MW	31330 TQ	USBLS	5/07
	San Antonio MSA, TX	Y	19940 FQ	25050 MW	31290 TQ	USBLS	5/07
	Utah	Y	20400 FQ	24280 MW	30750 TQ	USBLS	5/07
	St. George MSA, UT	Y	20500 FQ	24890 MW	29990 TQ	USBLS	5/07
	Salt Lake City MSA, UT	Y	20950 FQ	24930 MW	31910 TQ	USBLS	5/07
	Vermont	Y	23450 FQ	28310 MW	33740 TQ	USBLS	5/07
	Burlington-South Burlington MSA, VT	Y	24290 FQ	29200 MW	35630 TQ	USBLS	5/07
	Virginia	Y	21130 FQ	27040 MW	34880 TQ	USBLS	5/07
	Richmond MSA, VA	Y	23840 FQ	30780 MW	36080 TQ	USBLS	5/07

AE Average entry wage	**AW** Average wage paid	**FQ** First quartile wage	**LO** Lowest wage paid	**MTC** Median total compensation	**TCC** Total cash compensation
AER Average entry range	**AWR** Average wage range	**H** Hourly	**LR** Low end range	**MW** Median wage paid	**TQ** Third quartile wage
AEX Average experienced wage	**AXR** Average experienced range	**HI** Highest wage paid	**M** Monthly	**MWR** Median wage range	**W** Weekly
ATC Average total compensation	**D** Daily	**HR** High end range	**MCC** Median cash compensation	**S** See annotated source	**Y** Yearly

Occupation/Type/Industry	Location	Per	Low	Mid	High	Source	Date
Shipping, Receiving, and Traffic Clerk							
	Virginia Beach-Norfolk-Newport News MSA, VA-NC	Y	19910 FQ	26120 MW	33870 TQ	USBLS	5/07
	Washington	H	11.92 FQ	14.59 MW	18.46 TQ	WABLS	3/08
	Bremerton-Silverdale MSA, WA	Y	28390 FQ	37710 MW	45440 TQ	USBLS	5/07
	Seattle-Tacoma-Bellevue MSA, WA	Y	25860 FQ	31220 MW	39340 TQ	USBLS	5/07
	West Virginia	Y	19677 FQ	27557 MW	36928 TQ	WVBLS	7/08-9/08
	Charleston MSA, WV	Y	19940 FQ	26910 MW	33060 TQ	USBLS	5/07
	Wisconsin	Y	23760 FQ	28480 MW	33520 TQ	USBLS	5/07
	Green Bay MSA, WI	Y	22210 FQ	27150 MW	32290 TQ	USBLS	5/07
	Milwaukee-Waukesha-West Allis MSA, WI	Y	24670 FQ	28750 MW	33940 TQ	USBLS	5/07
	Wyoming	Y	23018 FQ	28161 MW	32786 TQ	WYBLS	9/08
	Casper MSA, WY	Y	25231 FQ	29063 MW	32313 TQ	WYBLS	9/08
	Cheyenne MSA, WY	Y	22403 FQ	25960 MW	31061 TQ	WYBLS	9/08
	Puerto Rico	Y	13770 FQ	17120 MW	23250 TQ	USBLS	5/07
	Guayama MSA, PR	Y	13170 FQ	15060 MW	19130 TQ	USBLS	5/07
	San Juan-Caguas-Guaynabo MSA, PR	Y	14000 FQ	17650 MW	23690 TQ	USBLS	5/07
	Virgin Islands	Y	16590 FQ	19450 MW	25400 TQ	USBLS	5/07
	Guam	Y	18060 FQ	27000 MW	33680 TQ	USBLS	5/07
Shipping Packer							
Small Organization	United States	Y	24566 FQ	26431 MW	28296 TQ	ALA07	2008
Shoe and Leather Worker and Repairer							
	Alabama	Y	13360 FQ	15860 MW	22000 TQ	USBLS	5/07
	Arizona	Y	14660 FQ	17170 MW	21260 TQ	USBLS	5/07
	Phoenix-Mesa-Scottsdale MSA, AZ	Y	14550 FQ	15790 MW	20260 TQ	USBLS	5/07
	Arkansas	Y	16580 FQ	17990 MW	19610 TQ	USBLS	5/07
	California	H	8.85 FQ	10.18 MW	11.58 TQ	CABLS	1/08-3/08
	Los Angeles-Long Beach-Glendale PMSA, CA	H	8.89 FQ	10.20 MW	11.41 TQ	CABLS	1/08-3/08
	Colorado	Y	17860 FQ	20630 MW	30550 TQ	USBLS	5/07
	Connecticut	H	8.75 AE	9.73 MW		CTBLS	1/08-3/08
	Washington-Arlington-Alexandria MSA, DC-VA-MD-WV	Y	20260 FQ	22110 MW	24670 TQ	USBLS	5/07
	Florida	Y	20160 FQ	24840 MW	29400 TQ	USBLS	5/07
	Miami-Fort Lauderdale-Miami Beach MSA, FL	Y	21490 FQ	23360 MW	25640 TQ	USBLS	5/07
	Georgia	Y	20310 FQ	22990 MW	27580 TQ	USBLS	5/07
	Idaho	Y	18820 FQ	32590 MW	36700 TQ	USBLS	5/07
	Boise City-Nampa MSA, ID	Y	19820 FQ	35270 MW	38130 TQ	USBLS	5/07
	Illinois	Y	21400 FQ	24620 MW	28460 TQ	USBLS	5/07
	Chicago-Naperville-Joliet MSA, IL-IN-WI	Y	21980 FQ	24940 MW	28690 TQ	USBLS	5/07
	Indiana	Y	15270 FQ	26510 MW	31630 TQ	USBLS	5/07
	Kentucky	Y	16783 FQ	18756 MW	26635 TQ	KYBLS	2008
	Maine	Y	21240 FQ	25030 MW	29300 TQ	USBLS	5/07
	Massachusetts	Y	18050 FQ	19720 MW	33700 TQ	USBLS	5/07
	Michigan	Y	19290 FQ	23760 MW	31260 TQ	USBLS	5/07
	Minnesota	Y	20256 FQ	25077 MW	32157 TQ	MNBLS	10/08-12/08
	Minneapolis-Saint Paul MSA, MN-WI	Y	22236 FQ	24258 MW	26279 TQ	MNBLS	10/08-12/08
	Missouri	Y	19560 FQ	21670 MW	23750 TQ	USBLS	5/07
	St. Louis MSA, MO-IL	Y	18960 FQ	22060 MW	24980 TQ	USBLS	5/07
	Nevada	H	11.84 FQ	13.80 MW	16.34 TQ	NVBLS	5/08
	New Hampshire	H	8.09 AE	10.35 MW	11.79 AEX	NHBLS	6/08
	New Jersey	Y	17100 FQ	22140 MW	28020 TQ	USBLS	5/07
	New York	Y	19540 FQ	22550 MW	27610 TQ	USBLS	5/07
	Nassau-Suffolk PMSA, NY	Y	14910 FQ	16510 MW	18930 TQ	USBLS	5/07
	New York-Northern New Jersey-Long Island MSA, NY-NJ-PA	Y	19840 FQ	22720 MW	27520 TQ	USBLS	5/07
	North Carolina	Y	16770 FQ	19260 MW	22430 TQ	USBLS	5/07
	Ohio	Y	17120 FQ	22800 MW	29180 TQ	USBLS	5/07
	Oklahoma	Y	15390 FQ	16650 MW	17870 TQ	USBLS	5/07
	Oregon	H	9.51 FQ	13.09 MW	17.02 TQ	ORBLS	5/08

AE	Average entry wage	AW	Average wage paid	FQ	First quartile wage	LO	Lowest wage paid	MTC	Median total compensation	TCC	Total cash compensation
AER	Average entry range	AWR	Average wage range	H	Hourly	LR	Low end range	MW	Median wage paid	TQ	Third quartile wage
AEX	Average experienced wage	AXR	Average experienced range	HI	Highest wage paid	M	Monthly	MWR	Median wage range	W	Weekly
ATC	Average total compensation	D	Daily	HR	High end range	MCC	Median cash compensation	S	See annotated source	Y	Yearly

Occupation/Type/Industry	Location	Per	Low	Mid	High	Source	Date
Shoe and Leather Worker and Repairer	Portland-Vancouver-Beaverton MSA, OR-WA	Y	18810 FQ	28870 MW	35300 TQ	USBLS	5/07
	Pennsylvania	Y	16980 FQ	21500 MW	25100 TQ	USBLS	5/07
	Philadelphia-Camden-Wilmington MSA, PA-NJ-DE-MD	Y	15470 FQ	16030 MW	19310 TQ	USBLS	5/07
	South Carolina	Y	17050 FQ	20070 MW	27650 TQ	USBLS	5/07
	South Dakota	Y	19498 FQ	22331 MW	25053 TQ	SDBLS	7/08-9/08
	Tennessee	Y	20170 FQ	21830 MW	23490 TQ	USBLS	5/07
	Texas	Y	17350 FQ	20230 MW	26910 TQ	USBLS	5/07
	Dallas-Fort Worth-Arlington MSA, TX	Y	17740 FQ	20820 MW	29040 TQ	USBLS	5/07
	El Paso MSA, TX	Y	16880 FQ	18660 MW	25360 TQ	USBLS	5/07
	Houston-Sugar Land-Baytown MSA, TX	Y	18440 FQ	22740 MW	31630 TQ	USBLS	5/07
	Virginia	Y	17200 FQ	20750 MW	24080 TQ	USBLS	5/07
	Richmond MSA, VA	Y	16580 FQ	18810 MW	22040 TQ	USBLS	5/07
	Washington	H	9.44 FQ	10.34 MW	11.27 TQ	WABLS	3/08
	West Virginia	Y	14565 FQ	20122 MW	22997 TQ	WVBLS	7/08-9/08
	Wisconsin	Y	20560 FQ	23710 MW	27420 TQ	USBLS	5/07
	Milwaukee-Waukesha-West Allis MSA, WI	Y	25050 FQ	27030 MW	29040 TQ	USBLS	5/07
	Wyoming	Y	23729 FQ	26054 MW	31286 TQ	WYBLS	9/08
Shoe Machine Operator and Tender	Arkansas	Y	15530 FQ	18640 MW	23900 TQ	USBLS	5/07
	California	H	8.75 FQ	10.41 MW	12.20 TQ	CABLS	1/08-3/08
	Florida	Y	17390 FQ	21070 MW	31630 TQ	USBLS	5/07
	Illinois	Y	18160 FQ	26920 MW	34060 TQ	USBLS	5/07
	Massachusetts	Y	26330 FQ	28510 MW	30690 TQ	USBLS	5/07
	Michigan	Y	18680 FQ	22160 MW	26660 TQ	USBLS	5/07
	Minnesota	Y	27078 FQ	30053 MW	33132 TQ	MNBLS	10/08-12/08
	Missouri	Y	18480 FQ	23260 MW	27860 TQ	USBLS	5/07
	Pennsylvania	Y	18470 FQ	22470 MW	26580 TQ	USBLS	5/07
	Texas	Y	17050 FQ	24410 MW	29730 TQ	USBLS	5/07
	Puerto Rico	Y	12040 FQ	13180 MW	14310 TQ	USBLS	5/07
Shop Foreman Highway Department	Montague, MA	H			23.76 HI	FRCOG	2009
Shuttle Car Operator	Alabama	Y	38880 FQ	41720 MW	44630 TQ	USBLS	5/07
	Illinois	Y	38110 FQ	41670 MW	45700 TQ	USBLS	5/07
	Kentucky	Y	36894 FQ	40205 MW	44179 TQ	KYBLS	2008
	Ohio	Y	39150 FQ	41910 MW	44980 TQ	USBLS	5/07
	Pennsylvania	Y	37200 FQ	42960 MW	47140 TQ	USBLS	5/07
	Utah	Y	38640 FQ	43630 MW	51220 TQ	USBLS	5/07
	Virginia	Y	31230 FQ	42520 MW	47380 TQ	USBLS	5/07
	West Virginia	Y	39160 FQ	43596 MW	48004 TQ	WVBLS	7/08-9/08
	Wyoming	Y	40499 FQ	48064 MW	66272 TQ	WYBLS	9/08
Sign Fabrication Technician State Government	Ohio	H	16.78 LO		19.88 HI	ODAS	2008
Sign Language Interpreter Public Schools	Chicago, IL	H			28.00 HI	CPSSS	7/1/06
Sign Painter Municipal Government	Seattle, WA	H			25.87 HI	CSSS	2007
Signal and Track Switch Repairer	Arizona	Y	37240 FQ	41090 MW	47640 TQ	USBLS	5/07
	California	H	23.13 FQ	25.86 MW	28.51 TQ	CABLS	1/08-3/08
	Colorado	Y	41490 FQ	46190 MW	50860 TQ	USBLS	5/07
	Florida	Y	43080 FQ	46640 MW	50310 TQ	USBLS	5/07
	Georgia	Y	43130 FQ	46580 MW	50040 TQ	USBLS	5/07
	Illinois	Y	49760 FQ	56930 MW	70090 TQ	USBLS	5/07
	Indiana	Y	47180 FQ	51080 MW	56070 TQ	USBLS	5/07
	Iowa	Y	43620 FQ	48610 MW	56230 TQ	USBLS	5/07
	Kansas	Y	34290 FQ	47010 MW	56040 TQ	USBLS	5/07
	Louisiana	H	21.21 FQ	24.11 MW	26.78 TQ	LABLS	1/08-3/08
	Maryland	Y		52600 MW		MDBLS	3/08
	Massachusetts	Y	43770 FQ	48570 MW	53250 TQ	USBLS	5/07

AE Average entry wage	**AW** Average wage paid	**FQ** First quartile wage	**LO** Lowest wage paid	**MTC** Median total compensation	**TCC** Total cash compensation
AER Average entry range	**AWR** Average wage range	**H** Hourly	**LR** Low end range	**MW** Median wage paid	**TQ** Third quartile wage
AEX Average experienced wage	**AXR** Average experienced range	**HI** Highest wage paid	**M** Monthly	**MWR** Median wage range	**W** Weekly
ATC Average total compensation	**D** Daily	**HR** High end range	**MCC** Median cash compensation	**S** See annotated source	**Y** Yearly

Occupation/Type/Industry	Location	Per	Low	Mid	High	Source	Date
Signal and Track Switch Repairer	Minnesota	Y	45723 FQ	51083 MW	56307 TQ	MNBLS	10/08-12/08
	Mississippi	Y	46090 FQ	50300 MW	55510 TQ	USBLS	5/07
	Ohio	Y	41680 FQ	46690 MW	51720 TQ	USBLS	5/07
	Oklahoma	Y	40070 FQ	45150 MW	50340 TQ	USBLS	5/07
	Oregon	H	23.02 FQ	26.11 MW	29.28 TQ	ORBLS	5/08
	Pennsylvania	Y	46460 FQ	52160 MW	57710 TQ	USBLS	5/07
	Tennessee	Y	42400 FQ	51610 MW	57910 TQ	USBLS	5/07
	Texas	Y	45130 FQ	52650 MW	58210 TQ	USBLS	5/07
	Washington	H	19.78 FQ	25.29 MW	29.41 TQ	WABLS	3/08
	Wisconsin	Y	48460 FQ	52750 MW	57280 TQ	USBLS	5/07
Ski School Director							
Department of Resources and Economic Development	New Hampshire	Y			28198 HI	NHUL03	2008
Skin Care Specialist	Alabama	Y	14360 FQ	19650 MW	41260 TQ	USBLS	5/07
	Birmingham-Hoover MSA, AL	Y	13450 FQ	15840 MW	32510 TQ	USBLS	5/07
	Tuscaloosa MSA, AL	Y	12400 FQ	13420 MW	14450 TQ	USBLS	5/07
	Alaska	Y	18100 FQ	21370 MW	44750 TQ	USBLS	5/07
	Anchorage MSA, AK	Y	17870 FQ	20090 MW	42990 TQ	USBLS	5/07
	Arizona	Y	17420 FQ	21910 MW	28600 TQ	USBLS	5/07
	Phoenix-Mesa-Scottsdale MSA, AZ	Y	18390 FQ	22010 MW	27260 TQ	USBLS	5/07
	Tucson MSA, AZ	Y	18080 FQ	25090 MW	31730 TQ	USBLS	5/07
	Arkansas	Y	22220 FQ	28530 MW	33580 TQ	USBLS	5/07
	California	H	10.37 FQ	17.92 MW	26.72 TQ	CABLS	1/08-3/08
	Modesto MSA, CA	H	16.95 FQ	19.69 MW	21.69 TQ	CABLS	1/08-3/08
	Oakland-Fremont-Hayward MSA, CA	H	13.02 FQ	18.60 MW	21.87 TQ	CABLS	1/08-3/08
	Riverside-San Bernardino-Ontario MSA, CA	H	9.60 FQ	11.63 MW	17.85 TQ	CABLS	1/08-3/08
	Sacramento-Arden Arcade-Roseville MSA, CA	H	9.59 FQ	18.53 MW	27.99 TQ	CABLS	1/08-3/08
	San Diego-Carlsbad-San Marcos MSA, CA	H	8.00 FQ	11.32 MW	20.14 TQ	CABLS	1/08-3/08
	San Francisco-San Mateo-Redwood PMSA, CA	H	21.10 FQ	27.29 MW	31.77 TQ	CABLS	1/08-3/08
	San Jose-Sunnyvale-Santa Clara MSA, CA	H	12.09 FQ	26.79 MW	30.26 TQ	CABLS	1/08-3/08
	Santa Ana-Anaheim-Irvine PMSA, CA	Y	25690 FQ	29880 MW	37230 TQ	USBLS	
	Santa Rosa-Petaluma MSA, CA	H	8.60 FQ	9.46 MW	13.69 TQ	CABLS	1/08-3/08
	Colorado	Y	24140 FQ	34750 MW	42320 TQ	USBLS	5/07
	Boulder MSA, CO	Y	20020 FQ	26810 MW	30180 TQ	USBLS	5/07
	Denver-Aurora MSA, CO	Y	26320 FQ	35450 MW	42170 TQ	USBLS	5/07
	Connecticut	H	10.41 AE	16.21 MW		CTBLS	1/08-3/08
	Bridgeport-Stamford-Norwalk MSA, CT	Y	20800 FQ	29130 MW	37360 TQ	USBLS	5/07
	Hartford-West Hartford-East Hartford MSA, CT	Y	24260 FQ	33820 MW	38220 TQ	USBLS	5/07
	Norwich-New London MSA, CT-RI	Y	20460 FQ	39650 MW	43480 TQ	USBLS	5/07
	Delaware	Y	19640 FQ	26340 MW	36080 TQ	USBLS	5/07
	Wilmington PMSA, DE-MD-NJ	Y	22090 FQ	28420 MW	37380 TQ	USBLS	5/07
	Washington-Arlington-Alexandria MSA, DC-VA-MD-WV	Y	15690 FQ	19610 MW	42190 TQ	USBLS	5/07
	Florida	Y	18490 FQ	27910 MW	37920 TQ	USBLS	5/07
	Fort Lauderdale-Pompano Beach-Deerfield Beach PMSA, FL	Y	20270 FQ	33260 MW	48350 TQ	USBLS	5/07
	Jacksonville MSA, FL	Y	21540 FQ	30450 MW	55210 TQ	USBLS	5/07
	Miami-Fort Lauderdale-Miami Beach MSA, FL	Y	17610 FQ	27060 MW	37200 TQ	USBLS	5/07
	Orlando-Kissimmee MSA, FL	Y	19610 FQ	26300 MW	44410 TQ	USBLS	5/07
	Tampa-St. Petersburg-Clearwater MSA, FL	Y	18710 FQ	23720 MW	32680 TQ	USBLS	5/07
	West Palm Beach-Boca Raton-Boynton Beach PMSA, FL	Y	16460 FQ	22900 MW	30520 TQ	USBLS	5/07
	Georgia	Y	20380 FQ	25900 MW	33180 TQ	USBLS	5/07

Occupation/Type/Industry	Location	Per	Low	Mid	High	Source	Date
Skin Care Specialist	Atlanta-Sandy Springs-Marietta MSA, GA	Y	21330 FQ	26210 MW	32740 TQ	USBLS	5/07
	Hawaii	Y	19360 FQ	29600 MW	42040 TQ	USBLS	5/07
	Honolulu MSA, HI	Y	19100 FQ	28400 MW	39640 TQ	USBLS	5/07
	Idaho	Y	14630 FQ	24560 MW	35150 TQ	USBLS	5/07
	Illinois	Y	23250 FQ	30840 MW	38580 TQ	USBLS	5/07
	Chicago-Naperville-Joliet MSA, IL-IN-WI	Y	23790 FQ	31790 MW	39800 TQ	USBLS	5/07
	Indiana	Y	21700 FQ	24790 MW	36580 TQ	USBLS	5/07
	Gary PMSA, IN	Y	31020 FQ	38460 MW	42930 TQ	USBLS	5/07
	Indianapolis-Carmel MSA, IN	Y	18400 FQ	20680 MW	23780 TQ	USBLS	5/07
	Iowa	Y	23090 FQ	26830 MW	29690 TQ	USBLS	5/07
	Kansas	Y	22880 FQ	31390 MW	54250 TQ	USBLS	5/07
	Wichita MSA, KS	Y	23430 FQ	31050 MW	59570 TQ	USBLS	5/07
	Kentucky	Y	20289 FQ	23066 MW	29307 TQ	KYBLS	2008
	Louisiana	H	6.55 FQ	9.81 MW	11.84 TQ	LABLS	1/08-3/08
	New Orleans-Metairie-Kenner MSA, LA	Y	14190 FQ	21260 MW	24600 TQ	USBLS	5/07
	Maine	Y	14900 FQ	22250 MW	31530 TQ	USBLS	5/07
	Maryland	Y		29775 MW		MDBLS	3/08
	Baltimore-Towson MSA, MD	Y	22130 FQ	31610 MW	44440 TQ	USBLS	5/07
	Bethesda-Gaithersburg-Frederick PMSA, MD	Y	18280 FQ	32030 MW	45570 TQ	USBLS	5/07
	Massachusetts	Y	25090 FQ	34580 MW	41100 TQ	USBLS	5/07
	Boston-Cambridge-Quincy NECTA, MA	Y	30880 FQ	36040 MW	43150 TQ	USBLS	5/07
	Michigan	Y	21440 FQ	27360 MW	38920 TQ	USBLS	5/07
	Detroit-Warren-Livonia MSA, MI	Y	22050 FQ	27660 MW	43860 TQ	USBLS	5/07
	Grand Rapids-Wyoming MSA, MI	Y	21020 FQ	23300 MW	34210 TQ	USBLS	5/07
	Warren-Troy-Farmington Hills PMSA, MI	Y	21640 FQ	28820 MW	45240 TQ	USBLS	5/07
	Minnesota	Y	25219 FQ	31388 MW	44332 TQ	MNBLS	10/08-12/08
	Minneapolis-Saint Paul MSA, MN-WI	Y	25188 FQ	32747 MW	46831 TQ	MNBLS	10/08-12/08
	Missouri	Y	23880 FQ	32890 MW	40020 TQ	USBLS	5/07
	Kansas City MSA, MO-KS	Y	20410 FQ	31350 MW	48300 TQ	USBLS	5/07
	St. Louis MSA, MO-IL	Y	28610 FQ	34990 MW	42190 TQ	USBLS	5/07
	Nebraska	Y	27760 FQ	41090 MW	49820 TQ	USBLS	5/07
	Omaha-Council Bluffs MSA, NE-IA	Y	31630 FQ	44310 MW	51770 TQ	USBLS	5/07
	Las Vegas-Paradise MSA, NV	H	6.39 FQ	7.25 MW	9.49 TQ	NVBLS	5/08
	New Hampshire	H	8.76 AE	12.69 MW	15.22 AEX	NHBLS	6/08
	Manchester MSA, NH	Y	22450 FQ	40790 MW	44390 TQ	USBLS	5/07
	Nashua NECTA, NH-MA	Y	19340 FQ	25270 MW	27920 TQ	USBLS	5/07
	New Jersey	Y	24870 FQ	32340 MW	38520 TQ	USBLS	5/07
	Camden PMSA, NJ	Y	21900 FQ	33820 MW	41020 TQ	USBLS	5/07
	Edison PMSA, NJ	Y	28630 FQ	33200 MW	41640 TQ	USBLS	5/07
	Newark-Union PMSA, NJ-PA	Y	30390 FQ	34580 MW	41610 TQ	USBLS	5/07
	Trenton-Ewing MSA, NJ	Y	23190 FQ	34170 MW	38530 TQ	USBLS	5/07
	New Mexico	Y	18670 FQ	23500 MW	28610 TQ	USBLS	5/07
	New York	Y	20180 FQ	27100 MW	34840 TQ	USBLS	5/07
	Albany-Schenectady-Troy MSA, NY	Y	16250 FQ	19400 MW	26620 TQ	USBLS	5/07
	Buffalo-Niagara Falls MSA, NY	Y	24190 FQ	26740 MW	29070 TQ	USBLS	5/07
	Nassau-Suffolk PMSA, NY	Y	23700 FQ	28230 MW	33790 TQ	USBLS	5/07
	New York-Northern New Jersey-Long Island MSA, NY-NJ-PA	Y	21750 FQ	29310 MW	36720 TQ	USBLS	5/07
	North Carolina	Y	19080 FQ	24630 MW	48170 TQ	USBLS	5/07
	Charlotte-Gastonia-Concord MSA, NC-SC	Y	18600 FQ	22790 MW	30940 TQ	USBLS	5/07
	Raleigh-Cary MSA, NC	Y	47110 FQ	51100 MW	56380 TQ	USBLS	5/07
	Ohio	Y	15710 FQ	22280 MW	34790 TQ	USBLS	5/07
	Cincinnati-Middletown MSA, OH-KY-IN	Y	22400 FQ	32250 MW	49580 TQ	USBLS	5/07
	Cleveland-Elyria-Mentor MSA, OH	Y	20020 FQ	23600 MW	42090 TQ	USBLS	5/07
	Columbus MSA, OH	Y	15390 FQ	23590 MW	37100 TQ	USBLS	5/07
	Dayton MSA, OH	Y	14670 FQ	16690 MW	24600 TQ	USBLS	5/07

AE	Average entry wage	AW	Average wage paid	FQ	First quartile wage	LO	Lowest wage paid	MTC	Median total compensation	TCC	Total cash compensation
AER	Average entry range	AWR	Average wage range	H	Hourly	LR	Low end range	MW	Median wage paid	TQ	Third quartile wage
AEX	Average experienced wage	AXR	Average experienced range	HI	Highest wage paid	M	Monthly	MWR	Median wage range	W	Weekly
ATC	Average total compensation	D	Daily	HR	High end range	MCC	Median cash compensation	S	See annotated source	Y	Yearly

Occupation/Type/Industry	Location	Per	Low	Mid	High	Source	Date
Skin Care Specialist	Oklahoma	Y	12640 FQ	13770 MW	14900 TQ	USBLS	5/07
	Tulsa MSA, OK	Y	18220 FQ	28280 MW	35780 TQ	USBLS	5/07
	Oregon	H	12.00 FQ	18.19 MW	22.43 TQ	ORBLS	5/08
	Portland-Vancouver-Beaverton MSA, OR-WA	Y	24920 FQ	37680 MW	45510 TQ	USBLS	5/07
	Pennsylvania	Y	16650 FQ	19770 MW	23780 TQ	USBLS	5/07
	Allentown-Bethlehem-Easton MSA, PA-NJ	Y	14750 FQ	15940 MW	27110 TQ	USBLS	5/07
	Philadelphia-Camden-Wilmington MSA, PA-NJ-DE-MD	Y	18040 FQ	21630 MW	26850 TQ	USBLS	5/07
	Pittsburgh MSA, PA	Y	17780 FQ	21090 MW	24710 TQ	USBLS	5/07
	Rhode Island	Y	23830 FQ	33940 MW	40360 TQ	USBLS	5/07
	Providence-Fall River-Warwick MSA, RI-MA	Y	24040 FQ	34210 MW	40610 TQ	USBLS	5/07
	South Carolina	Y	23590 FQ	30610 MW	38640 TQ	USBLS	5/07
	Charleston-North Charleston MSA, SC	Y	19420 FQ	27360 MW	31870 TQ	USBLS	5/07
	Tennessee	Y	22230 FQ	30710 MW	50080 TQ	USBLS	5/07
	Memphis MSA, TN-MS-AR	Y	18590 FQ	30740 MW	53820 TQ	USBLS	5/07
	Nashville-Davidson-Murfreesboro MSA, TN	Y	22520 FQ	30310 MW	52960 TQ	USBLS	5/07
	Texas	Y	15380 FQ	24130 MW	34630 TQ	USBLS	5/07
	Austin-Round Rock MSA, TX	Y	15650 FQ	19860 MW	24920 TQ	USBLS	5/07
	Dallas-Fort Worth-Arlington MSA, TX	Y	18570 FQ	29220 MW	39420 TQ	USBLS	5/07
	Houston-Sugar Land-Baytown MSA, TX	Y	14490 FQ	26210 MW	35970 TQ	USBLS	5/07
	San Antonio MSA, TX	Y	18370 FQ	21340 MW	27100 TQ	USBLS	5/07
	Utah	Y	19070 FQ	23120 MW	30590 TQ	USBLS	5/07
	Salt Lake City MSA, UT	Y	20860 FQ	25990 MW	32630 TQ	USBLS	5/07
	Vermont	Y	24440 FQ	30180 MW	45530 TQ	USBLS	5/07
	Virginia	Y	16900 FQ	21400 MW	40850 TQ	USBLS	5/07
	Richmond MSA, VA	Y	14850 FQ	19520 MW	29800 TQ	USBLS	5/07
	Virginia Beach-Norfolk-Newport News MSA, VA-NC	Y	14600 FQ	28600 MW	39940 TQ	USBLS	5/07
	Washington	H	14.74 FQ	18.28 MW	22.78 TQ	WABLS	3/08
	Seattle-Tacoma-Bellevue MSA, WA	Y	33860 FQ	43400 MW	49840 TQ	USBLS	5/07
	West Virginia	Y	20447 FQ	26114 MW	32826 TQ	WVBLS	7/08-9/08
	Wisconsin	Y	18370 FQ	25850 MW	36330 TQ	USBLS	5/07
	Milwaukee-Waukesha-West Allis MSA, WI	Y	16750 FQ	18090 MW	19670 TQ	USBLS	5/07
	Wyoming	Y	18970 FQ	24265 MW	27136 TQ	WYBLS	9/08
	Puerto Rico	Y	13080 FQ	15020 MW	19530 TQ	USBLS	5/07
	San Juan-Caguas-Guaynabo MSA, PR	Y	13300 FQ	15530 MW	21010 TQ	USBLS	5/07
Sky Cap	United States	H		15.43 AW		AVJOB01	2009
Slaughterer and Meat Packer	Alabama	Y	17680 FQ	20930 MW	23150 TQ	USBLS	5/07
	Birmingham-Hoover MSA, AL	Y	18070 FQ	20930 MW	25920 TQ	USBLS	5/07
	Arkansas	Y	17160 FQ	19140 MW	22630 TQ	USBLS	5/07
	California	H	9.47 FQ	10.67 MW	11.73 TQ	CABLS	1/08-3/08
	Los Angeles-Long Beach-Glendale PMSA, CA	H	8.76 FQ	11.27 MW	20.44 TQ	CABLS	1/08-3/08
	Oakland-Fremont-Hayward MSA, CA	H	9.03 FQ	9.86 MW	11.64 TQ	CABLS	1/08-3/08
	Riverside-San Bernardino-Ontario MSA, CA	H	8.29 FQ	8.90 MW	10.71 TQ	CABLS	1/08-3/08
	San Jose-Sunnyvale-Santa Clara MSA, CA	H	8.50 FQ	9.27 MW	10.76 TQ	CABLS	1/08-3/08
	Colorado	Y	21380 FQ	23250 MW	25230 TQ	USBLS	5/07
	Denver-Aurora MSA, CO	Y	20940 FQ	22660 MW	24380 TQ	USBLS	5/07
	Connecticut	H	8.77 AE	9.56 MW		CTBLS	1/08-3/08
	Washington-Arlington-Alexandria MSA, DC-VA-MD-WV	Y	21960 FQ	23890 MW	26850 TQ	USBLS	5/07
	Florida	Y	16280 FQ	20890 MW	27480 TQ	USBLS	5/07
	Miami-Fort Lauderdale-Miami Beach MSA, FL	Y	15030 FQ	19960 MW	28910 TQ	USBLS	5/07
	Georgia	Y	16040 FQ	17910 MW	20050 TQ	USBLS	5/07

Occupation/Type/Industry	Location	Per	Low	Mid	High	Source	Date
Slaughterer and Meat Packer	Atlanta-Sandy Springs-Marietta MSA, GA	Y	16740 FQ	18110 MW	19930 TQ	USBLS	5/07
	Hawaii	Y	18920 FQ	21800 MW	25660 TQ	USBLS	5/07
	Honolulu MSA, HI	Y	16640 FQ	18850 MW	22540 TQ	USBLS	5/07
	Idaho	Y	17770 FQ	21150 MW	26010 TQ	USBLS	5/07
	Illinois	Y	17190 FQ	19930 MW	23060 TQ	USBLS	5/07
	Chicago-Naperville-Joliet MSA, IL-IN-WI	Y	17990 FQ	21270 MW	24030 TQ	USBLS	5/07
	Indiana	Y	20860 FQ	22870 MW	24990 TQ	USBLS	5/07
	Iowa	Y	21980 FQ	24570 MW	27620 TQ	USBLS	5/07
	Des Moines-West Des Moines MSA, IA	Y	22440 FQ	26000 MW	29180 TQ	USBLS	5/07
	Kansas	Y	24510 FQ	26300 MW	28110 TQ	USBLS	5/07
	Kentucky	Y	19421 FQ	23251 MW	26986 TQ	KYBLS	2008
	Louisville-Jefferson County MSA, KY-IN	Y	20410 FQ	22090 MW	24160 TQ	USBLS	5/07
	Louisiana	H	6.95 FQ	8.80 MW	10.46 TQ	LABLS	1/08-3/08
	Maryland	Y		22150 MW		MDBLS	3/08
	Baltimore-Towson MSA, MD	Y	17130 FQ	19320 MW	22680 TQ	USBLS	5/07
	Massachusetts	Y	22970 FQ	31070 MW	39270 TQ	USBLS	5/07
	Boston-Cambridge-Quincy NECTA, MA	Y	21240 FQ	24550 MW	41520 TQ	USBLS	5/07
	Michigan	Y	17950 FQ	23580 MW	27160 TQ	USBLS	5/07
	Minnesota	Y	23366 FQ	26155 MW	29649 TQ	MNBLS	10/08-12/08
	Minneapolis-Saint Paul MSA, MN-WI	Y	23574 FQ	26684 MW	30395 TQ	MNBLS	10/08-12/08
	Mississippi	Y	18390 FQ	22620 MW	27770 TQ	USBLS	5/07
	Jackson MSA, MS	Y	19980 FQ	21970 MW	23860 TQ	USBLS	5/07
	Missouri	Y	19180 FQ	22140 MW	25170 TQ	USBLS	5/07
	Kansas City MSA, MO-KS	Y	16560 FQ	18920 MW	23800 TQ	USBLS	5/07
	St. Louis MSA, MO-IL	Y	19000 FQ	21610 MW	25860 TQ	USBLS	5/07
	Montana	Y	18360 FQ	20990 MW	25010 TQ	USBLS	5/07
	Nebraska	Y	24530 FQ	26710 MW	28810 TQ	USBLS	5/07
	New Jersey	Y	21070 FQ	25510 MW	31890 TQ	USBLS	5/07
	Camden PMSA, NJ	Y	22020 FQ	26040 MW	30430 TQ	USBLS	5/07
	Edison PMSA, NJ	Y	19060 FQ	22250 MW	37300 TQ	USBLS	5/07
	New Mexico	Y	17200 FQ	20790 MW	25730 TQ	USBLS	5/07
	New York	Y	15510 FQ	20160 MW	24870 TQ	USBLS	5/07
	Albany-Schenectady-Troy MSA, NY	Y	18990 FQ	21810 MW	23970 TQ	USBLS	5/07
	New York-Northern New Jersey-Long Island MSA, NY-NJ-PA	Y	16210 FQ	21790 MW	27060 TQ	USBLS	5/07
	North Carolina	Y	17290 FQ	19440 MW	22780 TQ	USBLS	5/07
	Charlotte-Gastonia-Concord MSA, NC-SC	Y	19690 FQ	21100 MW	22460 TQ	USBLS	5/07
	Raleigh-Cary MSA, NC	Y	30190 FQ	32650 MW	35110 TQ	USBLS	5/07
	Ohio	Y	18120 FQ	22470 MW	26540 TQ	USBLS	5/07
	Cincinnati-Middletown MSA, OH-KY-IN	Y	19200 FQ	24050 MW	26850 TQ	USBLS	5/07
	Cleveland-Elyria-Mentor MSA, OH	Y	17880 FQ	20960 MW	24160 TQ	USBLS	5/07
	Dayton MSA, OH	Y	21460 FQ	24350 MW	34310 TQ	USBLS	5/07
	Oklahoma	Y	19770 FQ	21620 MW	23570 TQ	USBLS	5/07
	Oklahoma City MSA, OK	Y	23080 FQ	26200 MW	29920 TQ	USBLS	5/07
	Oregon	H	9.81 FQ	11.10 MW	13.91 TQ	ORBLS	5/08
	Portland-Vancouver-Beaverton MSA, OR-WA	Y	21030 FQ	24400 MW	30260 TQ	USBLS	5/07
	Pennsylvania	Y	20940 FQ	24070 MW	28650 TQ	USBLS	5/07
	Philadelphia-Camden-Wilmington MSA, PA-NJ-DE-MD	Y	22540 FQ	26890 MW	30110 TQ	USBLS	5/07
	Providence-Fall River-Warwick MSA, RI-MA	Y	20430 FQ	23880 MW	29650 TQ	USBLS	5/07
	South Carolina	Y	15080 FQ	17580 MW	20030 TQ	USBLS	5/07
	South Dakota	Y	23090 FQ	26109 MW	28991 TQ	SDBLS	7/08-9/08
	Tennessee	Y	19700 FQ	21120 MW	22550 TQ	USBLS	5/07
	Texas	Y	17650 FQ	20810 MW	24010 TQ	USBLS	5/07
	Dallas-Fort Worth-Arlington MSA, TX	Y	17290 FQ	20240 MW	23880 TQ	USBLS	5/07
	Houston-Sugar Land-Baytown MSA, TX	Y	19220 FQ	21970 MW	24570 TQ	USBLS	5/07

AE	Average entry wage	AW	Average wage paid	FQ	First quartile wage	LO	Lowest wage paid	MTC	Median total compensation	TCC	Total cash compensation
AER	Average entry range	AWR	Average wage range	H	Hourly	LR	Low end range	MW	Median wage paid	TQ	Third quartile wage
AEX	Average experienced wage	AXR	Average experienced range	HI	Highest wage paid	M	Monthly	MWR	Median wage range	W	Weekly
ATC	Average total compensation	D	Daily	HR	High end range	MCC	Median cash compensation	S	See annotated source	Y	Yearly

Occupation/Type/Industry	Location	Per	Low	Mid	High	Source	Date
Slaughterer and Meat Packer	San Antonio MSA, TX	Y	19380 FQ	22710 MW	26570 TQ	USBLS	5/07
	Utah	Y	19500 FQ	22240 MW	27000 TQ	USBLS	5/07
	Provo-Orem MSA, UT	Y	18170 FQ	21090 MW	25580 TQ	USBLS	5/07
	Salt Lake City MSA, UT	Y	17930 FQ	20830 MW	26210 TQ	USBLS	5/07
	Virginia	Y	20650 FQ	23230 MW	25570 TQ	USBLS	5/07
	Virginia Beach-Norfolk-Newport News MSA, VA-NC	Y	21040 FQ	24200 MW	26880 TQ	USBLS	5/07
	Seattle-Tacoma-Bellevue MSA, WA	Y	19880 FQ	22560 MW	25530 TQ	USBLS	5/07
	West Virginia	Y	18426 FQ	22818 MW	27151 TQ	WVBLS	7/08-9/08
	Wisconsin	Y	20200 FQ	24080 MW	27010 TQ	USBLS	5/07
	Milwaukee-Waukesha-West Allis MSA, WI	Y	17820 FQ	19780 MW	23440 TQ	USBLS	5/07
	Puerto Rico	Y	12670 FQ	14360 MW	16690 TQ	USBLS	5/07
	San Juan-Caguas-Guaynabo MSA, PR	Y	12840 FQ	14790 MW	17240 TQ	USBLS	5/07
Sleep Physician	New England	Y		96750 AW		SLEEP	2008
	Pacific	Y		165733 AW		SLEEP	2008
Sleep Technician	New England	Y		50000 AW		SLEEP	2008
	Pacific	Y		51430 AW		SLEEP	2008
Slot Key Person	Arizona	Y	19950 FQ	25670 MW	29720 TQ	USBLS	5/07
	California	H	9.81 FQ	11.60 MW	14.79 TQ	CABLS	1/08-3/08
	Colorado	Y	24190 FQ	28480 MW	36510 TQ	USBLS	5/07
	Florida	Y	24220 FQ	28340 MW	33150 TQ	USBLS	5/07
	Illinois	Y	34240 FQ	39050 MW	48110 TQ	USBLS	5/07
	Indiana	Y	20460 FQ	22820 MW	27620 TQ	USBLS	5/07
	Iowa	Y	20010 FQ	24620 MW	31050 TQ	USBLS	5/07
	Louisiana	H	10.30 FQ	11.31 MW	12.83 TQ	LABLS	1/08-3/08
	Michigan	Y	19450 FQ	21580 MW	24420 TQ	USBLS	5/07
	Minnesota	Y	19541 FQ	22950 MW	28481	MNBLS	10/08-12/08
	Mississippi	Y	20870 FQ	24700 MW	29950 TQ	USBLS	5/07
	Missouri	Y	29180 FQ	36420 MW	43000 TQ	USBLS	5/07
	New Jersey	Y	20850 FQ	24850 MW	30500 TQ	USBLS	5/07
	New Mexico	Y	14980 FQ	18050 MW	22910 TQ	USBLS	5/07
	New York	Y	22450 FQ	27080 MW	30450 TQ	USBLS	5/07
	North Dakota	Y	26480 FQ	29030 MW	31580 TQ	USBLS	5/07
	Oklahoma	Y	17440 FQ	18890 MW	20520 TQ	USBLS	5/07
	Oregon	H	10.76 FQ	12.20 MW	15.74 TQ	ORBLS	5/08
	South Dakota	Y	29005 FQ	32963 MW	37611 TQ	SDBLS	7/08-9/08
	Washington	H	9.50 FQ	11.69 MW	16.89 TQ	WABLS	3/08
	Wisconsin	Y	19030 FQ	22440 MW	29060 TQ	USBLS	5/07
	Puerto Rico	Y	17390 FQ	21740 MW	29750 TQ	USBLS	5/07
Soccer Player Women's Professional Soccer	United States	Y	40000 LO			SVSJBJ	2009
Social and Community Service Manager	Alabama	Y	34410 FQ	43980 MW	60530 TQ	USBLS	5/07
	Birmingham-Hoover MSA, AL	Y	37170 FQ	45880 MW	61740 TQ	USBLS	5/07
	Alaska	Y	39440 FQ	53950 MW	72780 TQ	USBLS	5/07
	Anchorage MSA, AK	Y	45270 FQ	56780 MW	75080 TQ	USBLS	5/07
	Arizona	Y	35880 FQ	46430 MW	61230 TQ	USBLS	5/07
	Phoenix-Mesa-Scottsdale MSA, AZ	Y	38050 FQ	48240 MW	66340 TQ	USBLS	5/07
	Tucson MSA, AZ	Y	33020 FQ	41840 MW	54360 TQ	USBLS	5/07
	Arkansas	Y	30760 FQ	40640 MW	53370 TQ	USBLS	5/07
	Fayetteville-Springdale-Rogers MSA, AR-MO	Y	34490 FQ	45530 MW	56090 TQ	USBLS	5/07
	Fort Smith MSA, AR-OK	Y	19510 FQ	26760 MW	38490 TQ	USBLS	5/07
	Little Rock-North Little Rock MSA, AR	Y	35220 FQ	45360 MW	65050 TQ	USBLS	5/07
	California	H	22.53 FQ	29.69 MW	39.78 TQ	CABLS	1/08-3/08
	Los Angeles-Long Beach-Glendale PMSA, CA	H	23.81 FQ	32.40 MW	40.52 TQ	CABLS	1/08-3/08
	Oakland-Fremont-Hayward MSA, CA	H	23.81 FQ	30.10 MW	43.03 TQ	CABLS	1/08-3/08
	Riverside-San Bernardino-Ontario MSA, CA	H	24.81 FQ	35.59 MW	45.28 TQ	CABLS	1/08-3/08

AE	Average entry wage	AW	Average wage paid	FQ	First quartile wage	LO	Lowest wage paid	MTC	Median total compensation	TCC	Total cash compensation
AER	Average entry range	AWR	Average wage range	H	Hourly	LR	Low end range	MW	Median wage paid	TQ	Third quartile wage
AEX	Average experienced wage	AXR	Average experienced range	HI	Highest wage paid	M	Monthly	MWR	Median wage range	W	Weekly
ATC	Average total compensation	D	Daily	HR	High end range	MCC	Median cash compensation	S	See annotated source	Y	Yearly

Occupation/Type/Industry	Location	Per	Low	Mid	High	Source	Date
Social and Community Service Manager	Sacramento-Arden Arcade-Roseville MSA, CA	H	21.28 FQ	28.85 MW	38.19 TQ	CABLS	1/08-3/08
	San Diego-Carlsbad-San Marcos MSA, CA	H	22.85 FQ	28.95 MW	36.76 TQ	CABLS	1/08-3/08
	San Francisco-San Mateo-Redwood PMSA, CA	H	23.92 FQ	30.30 MW	40.99 TQ	CABLS	1/08-3/08
	San Jose-Sunnyvale-Santa Clara MSA, CA	H	25.80 FQ	35.54 MW	45.74 TQ	CABLS	1/08-3/08
	Santa Ana-Anaheim-Irvine PMSA, CA	Y	42750 FQ	57750 MW	74640 TQ	USBLS	5/07
	Colorado	Y	42080 FQ	55590 MW	75110 TQ	USBLS	5/07
	Denver-Aurora MSA, CO	Y	45220 FQ	58200 MW	78980 TQ	USBLS	5/07
	Fort Collins-Loveland MSA, CO	Y	43230 FQ	52690 MW	82390 TQ	USBLS	5/07
	Connecticut	H	19.55 AE	27.11 MW		CTBLS	1/08-3/08
	Bridgeport-Stamford-Norwalk MSA, CT	Y	51610 FQ	64480 MW	79050 TQ	USBLS	5/07
	Danbury MSA, CT	Y	45230 FQ	55170 MW	63100 TQ	USBLS	5/07
	Hartford-West Hartford-East Hartford MSA, CT	Y	44150 FQ	55710 MW	73950 TQ	USBLS	5/07
	Delaware	Y	50300 FQ	58950 MW	69000 TQ	USBLS	5/07
	Dover MSA, DE	Y	53150 FQ	60660 MW	71530 TQ	USBLS	5/07
	Wilmington PMSA, DE-MD-NJ	Y	51140 FQ	59620 MW	71390 TQ	USBLS	5/07
	District of Columbia	Y	52510 FQ	63990 MW	81560 TQ	USBLS	5/07
	Washington-Arlington-Alexandria MSA, DC-VA-MD-WV	Y	52940 FQ	67570 MW	91070 TQ	USBLS	5/07
	Florida	Y	53380 FQ	68450 MW	92360 TQ	USBLS	5/07
	Cape Coral-Fort Myers MSA, FL	Y	54410 FQ	60740 MW	77670 TQ	USBLS	5/07
	Fort Lauderdale-Pompano Beach-Deerfield Beach PMSA, FL	Y	55150 FQ	72160 MW	94210 TQ	USBLS	5/07
	Jacksonville MSA, FL	Y	53980 FQ	64690 MW	91160 TQ	USBLS	5/07
	Miami-Fort Lauderdale-Miami Beach MSA, FL	Y	50320 FQ	71230 MW	97970 TQ	USBLS	5/07
	Orlando-Kissimmee MSA, FL	Y	51620 FQ	71060 MW	94350 TQ	USBLS	5/07
	Sarasota-Bradenton-Venice MSA, FL	Y	53310 FQ	65840 MW	95190 TQ	USBLS	5/07
	Tampa-St. Petersburg-Clearwater MSA, FL	Y	54860 FQ	65370 MW	91720 TQ	USBLS	5/07
	Georgia	Y	38680 FQ	48970 MW	72660 TQ	USBLS	5/07
	Atlanta-Sandy Springs-Marietta MSA, GA	Y	42250 FQ	50280 MW	75160 TQ	USBLS	5/07
	Hawaii	Y	42470 FQ	52440 MW	65680 TQ	USBLS	5/07
	Honolulu MSA, HI	Y	43160 FQ	54980 MW	68380 TQ	USBLS	5/07
	Idaho	Y	28860 FQ	40440 MW	58610 TQ	USBLS	5/07
	Boise City-Nampa MSA, ID	Y	34300 FQ	43120 MW	61610 TQ	USBLS	5/07
	Illinois	Y	36290 FQ	49220 MW	69280 TQ	USBLS	5/07
	Chicago-Naperville-Joliet MSA, IL-IN-WI	Y	40080 FQ	53220 MW	76140 TQ	USBLS	5/07
	Indiana	Y	35530 FQ	44520 MW	58790 TQ	USBLS	5/07
	Gary PMSA, IN	Y	36240 FQ	42100 MW	55750 TQ	USBLS	5/07
	Indianapolis-Carmel MSA, IN	Y	41710 FQ	51360 MW	71750 TQ	USBLS	5/07
	Iowa	Y	34190 FQ	45100 MW	61370 TQ	USBLS	5/07
	Des Moines-West Des Moines MSA, IA	Y	37290 FQ	48850 MW	71040 TQ	USBLS	5/07
	Kansas	Y	34880 FQ	44830 MW	57500 TQ	USBLS	5/07
	Wichita MSA, KS	Y	36170 FQ	51830 MW	64790 TQ	USBLS	5/07
	Kentucky	Y	37578 FQ	50118 MW	64038 TQ	KYBLS	2008
	Elizabethtown MSA, KY	Y	30660 FQ	35220 MW	46570 TQ	USBLS	5/07
	Louisville-Jefferson County MSA, KY-IN	Y	39450 FQ	49750 MW	63550 TQ	USBLS	5/07
	Louisiana	H	17.11 FQ	22.90 MW	31.17 TQ	LABLS	1/08-3/08
	Baton Rouge MSA, LA	Y	42340 FQ	53050 MW	68150 TQ	USBLS	5/07
	New Orleans-Metairie-Kenner MSA, LA	Y	40580 FQ	58070 MW	77610 TQ	USBLS	5/07
	Maine	Y	38950 FQ	47760 MW	59210 TQ	USBLS	5/07
	Portland-South Portland-Biddeford MSA, ME	Y	36890 FQ	50260 MW	63300 TQ	USBLS	5/07

AE	Average entry wage	**AW**	Average wage paid	**FQ**	First quartile wage
AER	Average entry range	**AWR**	Average wage range	**H**	Hourly
AEX	Average experienced wage	**AXR**	Average experienced range	**HI**	Highest wage paid
ATC	Average total compensation	**D**	Daily	**HR**	High end range

LO	Lowest wage paid	**MTC**	Median total compensation	**TCC**	Total cash compensation
LR	Low end range	**MW**	Median wage paid	**TQ**	Third quartile wage
M	Monthly	**MWR**	Median wage range	**W**	Weekly
MCC	Median cash compensation	**S**	See annotated source	**Y**	Yearly

Occupation/Type/Industry	Location	Per	Low	Mid	High	Source	Date
Social and Community Service Manager							
	Maryland	Y		60100 MW		MDBLS	3/08
	Baltimore-Towson MSA, MD	Y	48190 FQ	58130 MW	70210 TQ	USBLS	5/07
	Bethesda-Gaithersburg-Frederick PMSA, MD	Y	56180 FQ	66670 MW	86200 TQ	USBLS	5/07
	Massachusetts	Y	43340 FQ	54120 MW	71210 TQ	USBLS	5/07
	Barnstable Town MSA, MA	Y	45920 FQ	56440 MW	64660 TQ	USBLS	5/07
	Boston-Cambridge-Quincy NECTA, MA	Y	46700 FQ	58620 MW	77760 TQ	USBLS	5/07
	Worcester MSA, MA-CT	Y	42000 FQ	50930 MW	61440 TQ	USBLS	5/07
	Michigan	Y	41140 FQ	54430 MW	71430 TQ	USBLS	5/07
	Detroit-Warren-Livonia MSA, MI	Y	42840 FQ	55530 MW	71400 TQ	USBLS	5/07
	Grand Rapids-Wyoming MSA, MI	Y	42740 FQ	57530 MW	84600 TQ	USBLS	5/07
	Warren-Troy-Farmington Hills PMSA, MI	Y	40700 FQ	53030 MW	65280 TQ	USBLS	5/07
	Minnesota	Y	50860 FQ	63195 MW	78876 TQ	MNBLS	10/08-12/08
	Duluth-Superior MSA, MN-WI	Y	49077 FQ	60254 MW	78251 TQ	MNBLS	10/08-12/08
	Minneapolis-Saint Paul MSA, MN-WI	Y	52883 FQ	64436 MW	80555 TQ	MNBLS	10/08-12/08
	Rochester MSA, MN	Y	58115 FQ	71927 MW	83218 TQ	MNBLS	10/08-12/08
	Mississippi	Y	29040 FQ	35410 MW	44810 TQ	USBLS	5/07
	Jackson MSA, MS	Y	31510 FQ	38930 MW	49360 TQ	USBLS	5/07
	Missouri	Y	34220 FQ	39480 MW	50210 TQ	USBLS	5/07
	Kansas City MSA, MO-KS	Y	34360 FQ	44160 MW	57770 TQ	USBLS	5/07
	St. Louis MSA, MO-IL	Y	34340 FQ	42060 MW	56140 TQ	USBLS	5/07
	Montana	Y	29420 FQ	35870 MW	50030 TQ	USBLS	5/07
	Billings MSA, MT	Y	30540 FQ	36200 MW	42110 TQ	USBLS	5/07
	Missoula MSA, MT	Y	33090 FQ	39760 MW	51400 TQ	USBLS	5/07
	Nebraska	Y	34500 FQ	46270 MW	59420 TQ	USBLS	5/07
	Omaha-Council Bluffs MSA, NE-IA	Y	31250 FQ	44090 MW	62750 TQ	USBLS	5/07
	Nevada	H	18.90 FQ	27.81 MW	37.16 TQ	NVBLS	5/08
	Las Vegas-Paradise MSA, NV	H	17.96 FQ	26.22 MW	38.73 TQ	NVBLS	5/08
	New Hampshire	H	17.84 AE	24.81 MW	29.79 AEX	NHBLS	6/08
	Manchester MSA, NH	Y	44300 FQ	53310 MW	63960 TQ	USBLS	5/07
	Portsmouth MSA, NH-ME	Y	40840 FQ	51600 MW	64830 TQ	USBLS	5/07
	Rochester-Dover MSA, NH-ME	Y	31120 FQ	39200 MW	51870 TQ	USBLS	5/07
	New Jersey	Y	52820 FQ	68550 MW	85370 TQ	USBLS	5/07
	Atlantic City MSA, NJ	Y	48210 FQ	63040 MW	77670 TQ	USBLS	5/07
	Camden PMSA, NJ	Y	53080 FQ	64630 MW	81500 TQ	USBLS	5/07
	Edison PMSA, NJ	Y	54510 FQ	70620 MW	89170 TQ	USBLS	5/07
	Newark-Union PMSA, NJ-PA	Y	50330 FQ	67450 MW	83950 TQ	USBLS	5/07
	New Mexico	Y	35280 FQ	44680 MW	56140 TQ	USBLS	5/07
	Albuquerque MSA, NM	Y	38780 FQ	46680 MW	56680 TQ	USBLS	5/07
	New York	Y	52930 FQ	67880 MW	87480 TQ	USBLS	5/07
	Albany-Schenectady-Troy MSA, NY	Y	51850 FQ	64620 MW	84190 TQ	USBLS	5/07
	Buffalo-Niagara Falls MSA, NY	Y	44190 FQ	56440 MW	73670 TQ	USBLS	5/07
	Glens Falls MSA, NY	Y	53560 FQ	67720 MW	81900 TQ	USBLS	5/07
	Kingston MSA, NY	Y	46930 FQ	60140 MW	72260 TQ	USBLS	5/07
	Nassau-Suffolk PMSA, NY	Y	58850 FQ	72590 MW	88160 TQ	USBLS	5/07
	New York-Northern New Jersey-Long Island MSA, NY-NJ-PA	Y	57210 FQ	73350 MW	92520 TQ	USBLS	5/07
	North Carolina	Y	38300 FQ	49690 MW	62930 TQ	USBLS	5/07
	Charlotte-Gastonia-Concord MSA, NC-SC	Y	48450 FQ	57350 MW	65970 TQ	USBLS	5/07
	Raleigh-Cary MSA, NC	Y	33380 FQ	40390 MW	55320 TQ	USBLS	5/07
	North Dakota	Y	37680 FQ	48660 MW	59480 TQ	USBLS	5/07
	Fargo MSA, ND-MN	Y	33970 FQ	44000 MW	60360 TQ	USBLS	5/07
	Grand Forks MSA, ND-MN	Y	43000 FQ	55590 MW	72580 TQ	USBLS	5/07
	Ohio	Y	43250 FQ	52930 MW	68910 TQ	USBLS	5/07
	Cincinnati-Middletown MSA, OH-KY-IN	Y	43340 FQ	53290 MW	66380 TQ	USBLS	5/07
	Cleveland-Elyria-Mentor MSA, OH	Y	46990 FQ	57920 MW	73280 TQ	USBLS	5/07
	Columbus MSA, OH	Y	45020 FQ	55000 MW	76710 TQ	USBLS	5/07
	Dayton MSA, OH	Y	39670 FQ	47920 MW	65930 TQ	USBLS	5/07

AE	Average entry wage	AW	Average wage paid	FQ	First quartile wage	LO	Lowest wage paid	MTC	Median total compensation	TCC	Total cash compensation
AER	Average entry range	AWR	Average wage range	H	Hourly	LR	Low end range	MW	Median wage paid	TQ	Third quartile wage
AEX	Average experienced wage	AXR	Average experienced range	HI	Highest wage paid	M	Monthly	MWR	Median wage range	W	Weekly
ATC	Average total compensation	D	Daily	HR	High end range	MCC	Median cash compensation	S	See annotated source	Y	Yearly

1490

Occupation/Type/Industry	Location	Per	Low	Mid	High	Source	Date
Social and Community Service Manager							
	Oklahoma	Y	24450 FQ	39780 MW	50220 TQ	USBLS	5/07
	Oklahoma City MSA, OK	Y	33960 FQ	43440 MW	56300 TQ	USBLS	5/07
	Tulsa MSA, OK	Y	16790 FQ	37760 MW	49140 TQ	USBLS	5/07
	Oregon	H	18.57 FQ	24.32 MW	30.79 TQ	ORBLS	5/08
	Portland-Vancouver-Beaverton MSA, OR-WA	Y	39860 FQ	50630 MW	64900 TQ	USBLS	5/07
	Pennsylvania	Y	48360 FQ	57680 MW	64140 TQ	USBLS	5/07
	Allentown-Bethlehem-Easton MSA, PA-NJ	Y	34920 FQ	48400 MW	63450 TQ	USBLS	5/07
	Philadelphia-Camden-Wilmington MSA, PA-NJ-DE-MD	Y	54580 FQ	59520 MW	64570 TQ	USBLS	5/07
	Pittsburgh MSA, PA	Y	39400 FQ	51270 MW	65710 TQ	USBLS	5/07
	York-Hanover MSA, PA	Y	38830 FQ	48260 MW	61300 TQ	USBLS	5/07
	Rhode Island	Y	49070 FQ	64250 MW	83430 TQ	USBLS	5/07
	Providence-Fall River-Warwick MSA, RI-MA	Y	44810 FQ	60270 MW	80060 TQ	USBLS	5/07
	South Carolina	Y	33900 FQ	42490 MW	55590 TQ	USBLS	5/07
	Charleston-North Charleston MSA, SC	Y	37720 FQ	62760 MW	86020 TQ	USBLS	5/07
	Columbia MSA, SC	Y	35580 FQ	42060 MW	49580 TQ	USBLS	5/07
	South Dakota	Y	47253 FQ	56274 MW	65392 TQ	SDBLS	7/08-9/08
	Sioux Falls MSA, SD	Y	50115 FQ	59301 MW	66736 TQ	SDBLS	7/08-9/08
	Tennessee	Y	33760 FQ	44470 MW	55180 TQ	USBLS	5/07
	Memphis MSA, TN-MS-AR	Y	40440 FQ	46700 MW	54630 TQ	USBLS	5/07
	Nashville-Davidson-Murfreesboro MSA, TN	Y	39870 FQ	49130 MW	60200 TQ	USBLS	5/07
	Texas	Y	35220 FQ	44700 MW	58880 TQ	USBLS	5/07
	Austin-Round Rock MSA, TX	Y	38150 FQ	45210 MW	58930 TQ	USBLS	5/07
	Beaumont-Port Arthur MSA, TX	Y	29760 FQ	35730 MW	39620 TQ	USBLS	5/07
	Dallas-Fort Worth-Arlington MSA, TX	Y	39870 FQ	49920 MW	63530 TQ	USBLS	5/07
	El Paso MSA, TX	Y	33500 FQ	40800 MW	47660 TQ	USBLS	5/07
	Houston-Sugar Land-Baytown MSA, TX	Y	34700 FQ	45140 MW	62910 TQ	USBLS	5/07
	Midland MSA, TX	Y	27010 FQ	35740 MW	46370 TQ	USBLS	5/07
	San Antonio MSA, TX	Y	37720 FQ	49020 MW	62020 TQ	USBLS	5/07
	Utah	Y	41200 FQ	52750 MW	65430 TQ	USBLS	5/07
	Salt Lake City MSA, UT	Y	45980 FQ	55920 MW	71040 TQ	USBLS	5/07
	Vermont	Y	37010 FQ	48530 MW	64960 TQ	USBLS	5/07
	Burlington-South Burlington MSA, VT	Y	43610 FQ	56840 MW	70870 TQ	USBLS	5/07
	Virginia	Y	50320 FQ	68750 MW	89060 TQ	USBLS	5/07
	Richmond MSA, VA	Y	52740 FQ	71100 MW	87030 TQ	USBLS	5/07
	Virginia Beach-Norfolk-Newport News MSA, VA-NC	Y	54850 FQ	65400 MW	80540 TQ	USBLS	5/07
	Washington	H	32.87 FQ	39.18 MW	47.31 TQ	WABLS	3/08
	Seattle-Tacoma-Bellevue MSA, WA	Y	68990 FQ	82850 MW	100700 TQ	USBLS	5/07
	West Virginia	Y	35287 FQ	43310 MW	52426 TQ	WVBLS	7/08-9/08
	Charleston MSA, WV	Y	36320 FQ	44810 MW	55770 TQ	USBLS	5/07
	Wheeling MSA, WV-OH	Y	39220 FQ	45110 MW	51890 TQ	USBLS	5/07
	Wisconsin	Y	39040 FQ	49430 MW	62980 TQ	USBLS	5/07
	Milwaukee-Waukesha-West Allis MSA, WI	Y	41060 FQ	48430 MW	60450 TQ	USBLS	5/07
	Wyoming	Y	35464 FQ	42929 MW	57009 TQ	WYBLS	9/08
	Cheyenne MSA, WY	Y	36858 FQ	50699 MW	71888 TQ	WYBLS	9/08
	Puerto Rico	Y	24590 FQ	31050 MW	40680 TQ	USBLS	5/07
	San Juan-Caguas-Guaynabo MSA, PR	Y	28190 FQ	34000 MW	44070 TQ	USBLS	5/07
Social and Human Service Assistant							
	Alabama	Y	19240 FQ	26950 MW	35210 TQ	USBLS	5/07
	Birmingham-Hoover MSA, AL	Y	21240 FQ	26430 MW	32130 TQ	USBLS	5/07
	Alaska	Y	29140 FQ	35130 MW	41370 TQ	USBLS	5/07
	Anchorage MSA, AK	Y	30790 FQ	35820 MW	40930 TQ	USBLS	5/07
	Arizona	Y	22170 FQ	28900 MW	38920 TQ	USBLS	5/07
	Phoenix-Mesa-Scottsdale MSA, AZ	Y	22790 FQ	30630 MW	41820 TQ	USBLS	5/07

AE Average entry wage	**AW** Average wage paid	**FQ** First quartile wage	**LO** Lowest wage paid	**MTC** Median total compensation	**TCC** Total cash compensation
AER Average entry range	**AWR** Average wage range	**H** Hourly	**LR** Low end range	**MW** Median wage paid	**TQ** Third quartile wage
AEX Average experienced wage	**AXR** Average experienced range	**HI** Highest wage paid	**M** Monthly	**MWR** Median wage range	**W** Weekly
ATC Average total compensation	**D** Daily	**HR** High end range	**MCC** Median cash compensation	**S** See annotated source	**Y** Yearly

Occupation/Type/Industry	Location	Per	Low	Mid	High	Source	Date
Social and Human Service Assistant	Tucson MSA, AZ	Y	21130 FQ	26810 MW	36170 TQ	USBLS	5/07
	Arkansas	Y	18240 FQ	22330 MW	27510 TQ	USBLS	5/07
	Fort Smith MSA, AR-OK	Y	18630 FQ	22180 MW	28450 TQ	USBLS	5/07
	Little Rock-North Little Rock MSA, AR	Y	18680 FQ	22170 MW	26670 TQ	USBLS	5/07
	California	H	11.73 FQ	14.90 MW	19.17 TQ	CABLS	1/08-3/08
	Los Angeles-Long Beach-Glendale PMSA, CA	H	12.14 FQ	15.42 MW	18.50 TQ	CABLS	1/08-3/08
	Oakland-Fremont-Hayward MSA, CA	H	15.22 FQ	20.16 MW	26.89 TQ	CABLS	1/08-3/08
	Riverside-San Bernardino-Ontario MSA, CA	H	10.91 FQ	13.54 MW	15.83 TQ	CABLS	1/08-3/08
	Sacramento-Arden Arcade-Roseville MSA, CA	H	11.79 FQ	15.43 MW	21.19 TQ	CABLS	1/08-3/08
	San Diego-Carlsbad-San Marcos MSA, CA	H	9.74 FQ	13.47 MW	17.58 TQ	CABLS	1/08-3/08
	San Francisco-San Mateo-Redwood PMSA, CA	H	12.50 FQ	14.93 MW	20.66 TQ	CABLS	1/08-3/08
	San Jose-Sunnyvale-Santa Clara MSA, CA	H	12.11 FQ	15.13 MW	19.10 TQ	CABLS	1/08-3/08
	Santa Ana-Anaheim-Irvine PMSA, CA	Y	23740 FQ	28740 MW	35240 TQ	USBLS	5/07
	Santa Rosa-Petaluma MSA, CA	H	11.95 FQ	14.10 MW	16.07 TQ	CABLS	1/08-3/08
	Colorado	Y	22460 FQ	28330 MW	35610 TQ	USBLS	5/07
	Denver-Aurora MSA, CO	Y	25510 FQ	32010 MW	39260 TQ	USBLS	5/07
	Connecticut	H	12.70 AE	19.74 MW		CTBLS	1/08-3/08
	Bridgeport-Stamford-Norwalk MSA, CT	Y	34810 FQ	42090 MW	47350 TQ	USBLS	5/07
	Hartford-West Hartford-East Hartford MSA, CT	Y	29860 FQ	41180 MW	49690 TQ	USBLS	5/07
	Waterbury MSA, CT	Y	28370 FQ	34840 MW	42410 TQ	USBLS	5/07
	Delaware	Y	23270 FQ	28500 MW	34730 TQ	USBLS	5/07
	Wilmington PMSA, DE-MD-NJ	Y	22690 FQ	28000 MW	35450 TQ	USBLS	5/07
	District of Columbia	Y	26060 FQ	31790 MW	42980 TQ	USBLS	5/07
	Washington-Arlington-Alexandria MSA, DC-VA-MD-WV	Y	25830 FQ	33220 MW	41690 TQ	USBLS	5/07
	Florida	Y	22240 FQ	27930 MW	32390 TQ	USBLS	5/07
	Fort Lauderdale-Pompano Beach-Deerfield Beach PMSA, FL	Y	27250 FQ	31060 MW	37000 TQ	USBLS	5/07
	Jacksonville MSA, FL	Y	23800 FQ	28340 MW	33180 TQ	USBLS	5/07
	Miami-Fort Lauderdale-Miami Beach MSA, FL	Y	26290 FQ	29910 MW	35640 TQ	USBLS	5/07
	Orlando-Kissimmee MSA, FL	Y	25590 FQ	28710 MW	32180 TQ	USBLS	5/07
	Sarasota-Bradenton-Venice MSA, FL	Y	22410 FQ	28610 MW	34660 TQ	USBLS	5/07
	Tampa-St. Petersburg-Clearwater MSA, FL	Y	20450 FQ	26750 MW	31470 TQ	USBLS	5/07
	West Palm Beach-Boca Raton-Boynton Beach PMSA, FL	Y	25550 FQ	29920 MW	37590 TQ	USBLS	5/07
	Georgia	Y	21030 FQ	25140 MW	31180 TQ	USBLS	5/07
	Atlanta-Sandy Springs-Marietta MSA, GA	Y	22050 FQ	26280 MW	32470 TQ	USBLS	5/07
	Savannah MSA, GA	Y	21280 FQ	25080 MW	31020 TQ	USBLS	5/07
	Hawaii	Y	25310 FQ	30180 MW	35450 TQ	USBLS	5/07
	Honolulu MSA, HI	Y	26260 FQ	32180 MW	36340 TQ	USBLS	5/07
	Idaho	Y	16180 FQ	18950 MW	28920 TQ	USBLS	5/07
	Boise City-Nampa MSA, ID	Y	15710 FQ	18390 MW	25820 TQ	USBLS	5/07
	Illinois	Y	20680 FQ	27450 MW	34360 TQ	USBLS	5/07
	Chicago-Naperville-Joliet MSA, IL-IN-WI	Y	23290 FQ	29010 MW	36240 TQ	USBLS	5/07
	Indiana	Y	20790 FQ	24820 MW	30960 TQ	USBLS	5/07
	Evansville MSA, IN-KY	Y	19790 FQ	26320 MW	31330 TQ	USBLS	5/07
	Gary PMSA, IN	Y	20250 FQ	24820 MW	30020 TQ	USBLS	5/07
	Indianapolis-Carmel MSA, IN	Y	22860 FQ	27610 MW	34330 TQ	USBLS	5/07
	Iowa	Y	17880 FQ	25560 MW	34350 TQ	USBLS	5/07
	Des Moines-West Des Moines MSA, IA	Y	15660 FQ	28960 MW	35830 TQ	USBLS	5/07
	Sioux City MSA, IA-NE-SD	Y	19650 FQ	21820 MW	24640 TQ	USBLS	5/07

AE	Average entry wage	AW	Average wage paid	FQ	First quartile wage
AER	Average entry range	AWR	Average wage range	H	Hourly
AEX	Average experienced wage	AXR	Average experienced range	HI	Highest wage paid
ATC	Average total compensation	D	Daily	HR	High end range

LO	Lowest wage paid	MTC	Median total compensation	TCC	Total cash compensation
LR	Low end range	MW	Median wage paid	TQ	Third quartile wage
M	Monthly	MWR	Median wage range	W	Weekly
MCC	Median cash compensation	S	See annotated source	Y	Yearly

Occupation/Type/Industry	Location	Per	Low	Mid	High	Source	Date
Social and Human Service Assistant	Kansas	Y	19960 FQ	24660 MW	29410 TQ	USBLS	5/07
	Wichita MSA, KS	Y	21820 FQ	25900 MW	30200 TQ	USBLS	5/07
	Kentucky	Y	18811 FQ	23973 MW	30465 TQ	KYBLS	2008
	Louisville-Jefferson County MSA, KY-IN	Y	19950 FQ	24590 MW	30650 TQ	USBLS	5/07
	Louisiana	H	9.53 FQ	13.69 MW	18.36 TQ	LABLS	1/08-3/08
	Baton Rouge MSA, LA	Y	21120 FQ	27750 MW	37220 TQ	USBLS	5/07
	New Orleans-Metairie-Kenner MSA, LA	Y	21290 FQ	28870 MW	38830 TQ	USBLS	5/07
	Maine	Y	20820 FQ	23660 MW	27870 TQ	USBLS	5/07
	Portland-South Portland-Biddeford MSA, ME	Y	20670 FQ	22720 MW	25140 TQ	USBLS	5/07
	Maryland	Y		32675 MW		MDBLS	3/08
	Baltimore-Towson MSA, MD	Y	26300 FQ	32760 MW	42210 TQ	USBLS	5/07
	Bethesda-Gaithersburg-Frederick PMSA, MD	Y	24570 FQ	32650 MW	42290 TQ	USBLS	5/07
	Massachusetts	Y	23130 FQ	28300 MW	35810 TQ	USBLS	5/07
	Boston-Cambridge-Quincy NECTA, MA	Y	24640 FQ	30070 MW	37710 TQ	USBLS	5/07
	Worcester MSA, MA-CT	Y	22450 FQ	26250 MW	31770 TQ	USBLS	5/07
	Michigan	Y	21710 FQ	27410 MW	34970 TQ	USBLS	5/07
	Detroit-Warren-Livonia MSA, MI	Y	21480 FQ	27390 MW	34990 TQ	USBLS	5/07
	Grand Rapids-Wyoming MSA, MI	Y	20860 FQ	24980 MW	34650 TQ	USBLS	5/07
	Muskegon-Norton Shores MSA, MI	Y	21560 FQ	24730 MW	33880 TQ	USBLS	5/07
	Warren-Troy-Farmington Hills PMSA, MI	Y	19960 FQ	24820 MW	31600 TQ	USBLS	5/07
	Minnesota	Y	23299 FQ	27400 MW	33604 TQ	MNBLS	10/08-12/08
	Duluth-Superior MSA, MN-WI	Y	22054 FQ	25004 MW	32579 TQ	MNBLS	10/08-12/08
	Minneapolis-Saint Paul MSA, MN-WI	Y	24753 FQ	28530 MW	33426 TQ	MNBLS	10/08-12/08
	Rochester MSA, MN	Y	22724 FQ	26726 MW	32565 TQ	MNBLS	10/08-12/08
	Mississippi	Y	18350 FQ	24100 MW	30470 TQ	USBLS	5/07
	Jackson MSA, MS	Y	14680 FQ	20100 MW	32440 TQ	USBLS	5/07
	Missouri	Y	19350 FQ	24460 MW	30890 TQ	USBLS	5/07
	Kansas City MSA, MO-KS	Y	22150 FQ	26080 MW	31000 TQ	USBLS	5/07
	St. Louis MSA, MO-IL	Y	18110 FQ	21720 MW	29910 TQ	USBLS	5/07
	Montana	Y	18560 FQ	23020 MW	28000 TQ	USBLS	5/07
	Billings MSA, MT	Y	20150 FQ	23640 MW	27270 TQ	USBLS	5/07
	Nebraska	Y	20270 FQ	24300 MW	30270 TQ	USBLS	5/07
	Omaha-Council Bluffs MSA, NE-IA	Y	22790 FQ	28220 MW	34560 TQ	USBLS	5/07
	Nevada	H	10.84 FQ	12.51 MW	15.29 TQ	NVBLS	5/08
	Carson City MSA, NV	H	13.12 FQ	16.13 MW	18.53 TQ	NVBLS	5/08
	Las Vegas-Paradise MSA, NV	H	10.82 FQ	12.25 MW	15.17 TQ	NVBLS	5/08
	New Hampshire	H	9.88 AE	12.06 MW	14.04 AEX	NHBLS	6/08
	Manchester MSA, NH	Y	25090 FQ	27640 MW	30360 TQ	USBLS	5/07
	Nashua NECTA, NH-MA	Y	22250 FQ	26710 MW	34390 TQ	USBLS	5/07
	New Jersey	Y	23700 FQ	30010 MW	38000 TQ	USBLS	5/07
	Camden PMSA, NJ	Y	24050 FQ	29410 MW	37700 TQ	USBLS	5/07
	Edison PMSA, NJ	Y	23530 FQ	29610 MW	37260 TQ	USBLS	5/07
	Newark-Union PMSA, NJ-PA	Y	23340 FQ	28980 MW	36310 TQ	USBLS	5/07
	New Mexico	Y	20540 FQ	26330 MW	33840 TQ	USBLS	5/07
	Albuquerque MSA, NM	Y	21220 FQ	26070 MW	33780 TQ	USBLS	5/07
	New York	Y	21640 FQ	27140 MW	34910 TQ	USBLS	5/07
	Albany-Schenectady-Troy MSA, NY	Y	20500 FQ	25580 MW	35230 TQ	USBLS	5/07
	Buffalo-Niagara Falls MSA, NY	Y	16760 FQ	22350 MW	31060 TQ	USBLS	5/07
	Ithaca MSA, NY	Y	20490 FQ	28580 MW	37240 TQ	USBLS	5/07
	Nassau-Suffolk PMSA, NY	Y	21770 FQ	25470 MW	32020 TQ	USBLS	5/07
	New York-Northern New Jersey-Long Island MSA, NY-NJ-PA	Y	22610 FQ	27760 MW	34400 TQ	USBLS	5/07
	North Carolina	Y	21490 FQ	25530 MW	30650 TQ	USBLS	5/07
	Charlotte-Gastonia-Concord MSA, NC-SC	Y	21520 FQ	25420 MW	30660 TQ	USBLS	5/07
	Raleigh-Cary MSA, NC	Y	20630 FQ	24270 MW	29110 TQ	USBLS	5/07
	North Dakota	Y	20110 FQ	24970 MW	30290 TQ	USBLS	5/07

Social and Human Service Assistant

Occupation/Type/Industry	Location	Per	Low	Mid	High	Source	Date
	Fargo MSA, ND-MN	Y	19010 FQ	23910 MW	29480 TQ	USBLS	5/07
	Ohio	Y	20030 FQ	25210 MW	31650 TQ	USBLS	5/07
	Cincinnati-Middletown MSA, OH-KY-IN	Y	21310 FQ	25690 MW	31680 TQ	USBLS	5/07
	Cleveland-Elyria-Mentor MSA, OH	Y	20740 FQ	25820 MW	31130 TQ	USBLS	5/07
	Columbus MSA, OH	Y	21710 FQ	26390 MW	34210 TQ	USBLS	5/07
	Dayton MSA, OH	Y	21580 FQ	26790 MW	30860 TQ	USBLS	5/07
	Oklahoma	Y	19560 FQ	27130 MW	37550 TQ	USBLS	5/07
	Oklahoma City MSA, OK	Y	21800 FQ	30840 MW	43080 TQ	USBLS	5/07
	Tulsa MSA, OK	Y	19590 FQ	27370 MW	34100 TQ	USBLS	5/07
	Oregon	H	10.85 FQ	13.31 MW	16.64 TQ	ORBLS	5/08
	Portland-Vancouver-Beaverton MSA, OR-WA	Y	21970 FQ	25500 MW	31270 TQ	USBLS	5/07
	Pennsylvania	Y	20250 FQ	24680 MW	31300 TQ	USBLS	5/07
	Allentown-Bethlehem-Easton MSA, PA-NJ	Y	18220 FQ	22230 MW	28280 TQ	USBLS	5/07
	Philadelphia-Camden-Wilmington MSA, PA-NJ-DE-MD	Y	21560 FQ	26430 MW	34170 TQ	USBLS	5/07
	Pittsburgh MSA, PA	Y	18850 FQ	23780 MW	29590 TQ	USBLS	5/07
	Rhode Island	Y	23390 FQ	26940 MW	31020 TQ	USBLS	5/07
	Providence-Fall River-Warwick MSA, RI-MA	Y	22880 FQ	26390 MW	30740 TQ	USBLS	5/07
	South Carolina	Y	18410 FQ	22070 MW	27700 TQ	USBLS	5/07
	Charleston-North Charleston MSA, SC	Y	17120 FQ	19660 MW	24280 TQ	USBLS	5/07
	Columbia MSA, SC	Y	19850 FQ	23170 MW	28380 TQ	USBLS	5/07
	South Dakota	Y	19671 FQ	22340 MW	25266 TQ	SDBLS	7/08-9/08
	Rapid City MSA, SD	Y	19702 FQ	23198 MW	27508 TQ	SDBLS	7/08-9/08
	Sioux Falls MSA, SD	Y	20164 FQ	22180 MW	24333 TQ	SDBLS	7/08-9/08
	Tennessee	Y	20080 FQ	25310 MW	30430 TQ	USBLS	5/07
	Memphis MSA, TN-MS-AR	Y	18950 FQ	24610 MW	29670 TQ	USBLS	5/07
	Nashville-Davidson-Murfreesboro MSA, TN	Y	20400 FQ	24850 MW	31530 TQ	USBLS	5/07
	Texas	Y	16850 FQ	22500 MW	29690 TQ	USBLS	5/07
	Austin-Round Rock MSA, TX	Y	20790 FQ	24390 MW	30150 TQ	USBLS	5/07
	Dallas-Fort Worth-Arlington MSA, TX	Y	16850 FQ	22970 MW	32080 TQ	USBLS	5/07
	El Paso MSA, TX	Y	19680 FQ	24930 MW	29430 TQ	USBLS	5/07
	Houston-Sugar Land-Baytown MSA, TX	Y	21320 FQ	27300 MW	34290 TQ	USBLS	5/07
	San Antonio MSA, TX	Y	16500 FQ	21450 MW	24810 TQ	USBLS	5/07
	Utah	Y	18550 FQ	21640 MW	25010 TQ	USBLS	5/07
	Salt Lake City MSA, UT	Y	19680 FQ	22600 MW	26170 TQ	USBLS	5/07
	Vermont	Y	24770 FQ	29120 MW	35650 TQ	USBLS	5/07
	Burlington-South Burlington MSA, VT	Y	25180 FQ	28840 MW	34600 TQ	USBLS	5/07
	Virginia	Y	21920 FQ	26020 MW	33380 TQ	USBLS	5/07
	Richmond MSA, VA	Y	21430 FQ	24470 MW	29950 TQ	USBLS	5/07
	Virginia Beach-Norfolk-Newport News MSA, VA-NC	Y	24600 FQ	28580 MW	32780 TQ	USBLS	5/07
	Washington	H	10.53 FQ	12.68 MW	15.70 TQ	WABLS	3/08
	Bremerton-Silverdale MSA, WA	Y	21460 FQ	24100 MW	29750 TQ	USBLS	5/07
	Seattle-Tacoma-Bellevue MSA, WA	Y	23780 FQ	28860 MW	35270 TQ	USBLS	5/07
	West Virginia	Y	15345 FQ	17563 MW	20217 TQ	WVBLS	7/08-9/08
	Charleston MSA, WV	Y	15710 FQ	17730 MW	20230 TQ	USBLS	5/07
	Wisconsin	Y	24120 FQ	29580 MW	36760 TQ	USBLS	5/07
	Milwaukee-Waukesha-West Allis MSA, WI	Y	24250 FQ	29190 MW	35610 TQ	USBLS	5/07
	Wyoming	Y	21077 FQ	23183 MW	25796 TQ	WYBLS	9/08
	Cheyenne MSA, WY	Y	21121 FQ	22662 MW	24182 TQ	WYBLS	9/08
	Puerto Rico	Y	17780 FQ	21170 MW	24050 TQ	USBLS	5/07
	San Juan-Caguas-Guaynabo MSA, PR	Y	18140 FQ	21390 MW	24170 TQ	USBLS	5/07
	Virgin Islands	Y	17780 FQ	20730 MW	26490 TQ	USBLS	5/07
	Guam	Y	18820 FQ	24820 MW	29260 TQ	USBLS	5/07

Social Science Research Assistant

	Alabama	Y	28990 FQ	33860 MW	40680 TQ	USBLS	5/07

AE Average entry wage | AW Average wage paid | FQ First quartile wage | LO Lowest wage paid | MTC Median total compensation | TCC Total cash compensation
AER Average entry range | AWR Average wage range | H Hourly | LR Low end range | MW Median wage paid | TQ Third quartile wage
AEX Average experienced wage | AXR Average experienced range | HI Highest wage paid | M Monthly | MWR Median wage range | W Weekly
ATC Average total compensation | D Daily | HR High end range | MCC Median cash compensation | S See annotated source | Y Yearly

1494

Occupation/Type/Industry	Location	Per	Low	Mid	High	Source	Date
Social Science Research Assistant	Arizona	Y	26380 FQ	32170 MW	41350 TQ	USBLS	5/07
	Phoenix-Mesa-Scottsdale MSA, AZ	Y	29200 FQ	36460 MW	45810 TQ	USBLS	5/07
	Arkansas	Y	30760 FQ	38620 MW	54720 TQ	USBLS	5/07
	California	H	14.22 FQ	17.81 MW	22.35 TQ	CABLS	1/08-3/08
	Los Angeles-Long Beach-Glendale PMSA, CA	H	15.08 FQ	18.43 MW	23.01 TQ	CABLS	1/08-3/08
	Oakland-Fremont-Hayward MSA, CA	H	13.10 FQ	17.98 MW	23.01 TQ	CABLS	1/08-3/08
	Riverside-San Bernardino-Ontario MSA, CA	H	21.82 FQ	23.43 MW	25.03 TQ	CABLS	1/08-3/08
	Sacramento-Arden Arcade-Roseville MSA, CA	H	14.35 FQ	16.38 MW	18.91 TQ	CABLS	1/08-3/08
	San Diego-Carlsbad-San Marcos MSA, CA	H	10.74 FQ	14.08 MW	18.39 TQ	CABLS	1/08-3/08
	San Francisco-San Mateo-Redwood PMSA, CA	H	16.01 FQ	19.18 MW	24.83 TQ	CABLS	1/08-3/08
	Santa Ana-Anaheim-Irvine PMSA, CA	Y	27430 FQ	33630 MW	40280 TQ	USBLS	5/07
	Colorado	Y	30580 FQ	41550 MW	51290 TQ	USBLS	5/07
	Denver-Aurora MSA, CO	Y	34170 FQ	44550 MW	51650 TQ	USBLS	5/07
	Connecticut	H	13.13 AE	17.29 MW		CTBLS	1/08-3/08
	Delaware	Y	27180 FQ	28940 MW	30690 TQ	USBLS	5/07
	District of Columbia	Y	33390 FQ	37940 MW	46750 TQ	USBLS	5/07
	Washington-Arlington-Alexandria MSA, DC-VA-MD-WV	Y	34050 FQ	39770 MW	48730 TQ	USBLS	5/07
	Florida	Y	30090 FQ	39720 MW	51080 TQ	USBLS	5/07
	Jacksonville MSA, FL	Y	41800 FQ	45780 MW	49770 TQ	USBLS	5/07
	Miami-Fort Lauderdale-Miami Beach MSA, FL	Y	26360 FQ	31480 MW	38060 TQ	USBLS	5/07
	Tampa-St. Petersburg-Clearwater MSA, FL	Y	26910 FQ	31740 MW	36780 TQ	USBLS	5/07
	Georgia	Y	34030 FQ	44030 MW	55680 TQ	USBLS	5/07
	Atlanta-Sandy Springs-Marietta MSA, GA	Y	40270 FQ	49370 MW	61230 TQ	USBLS	5/07
	Hawaii	Y	33550 FQ	41180 MW	47540 TQ	USBLS	5/07
	Honolulu MSA, HI	Y	33320 FQ	41370 MW	47680 TQ	USBLS	5/07
	Illinois	Y	14900 FQ	15290 MW	36650 TQ	USBLS	5/07
	Chicago-Naperville-Joliet MSA, IL-IN-WI	Y	35030 FQ	43430 MW	60550 TQ	USBLS	5/07
	Indiana	Y	29070 FQ	40020 MW	48570 TQ	USBLS	5/07
	Iowa	Y	30930 FQ	36960 MW	44780 TQ	USBLS	5/07
	Des Moines-West Des Moines MSA, IA	Y	31860 FQ	35880 MW	39900 TQ	USBLS	5/07
	Kentucky	Y	22477 FQ	24734 MW	28417 TQ	KYBLS	2008
	Louisville-Jefferson County MSA, KY-IN	Y	21650 FQ	23570 MW	25770 TQ	USBLS	5/07
	Maine	Y	28500 FQ	31910 MW	36880 TQ	USBLS	5/07
	Portland-South Portland-Biddeford MSA, ME	Y	29250 FQ	33590 MW	37550 TQ	USBLS	5/07
	Maryland	Y		43925 MW		MDBLS	3/08
	Baltimore-Towson MSA, MD	Y	41460 FQ	48790 MW	59440 TQ	USBLS	5/07
	Bethesda-Gaithersburg-Frederick PMSA, MD	Y	34400 FQ	40730 MW	48520 TQ	USBLS	5/07
	Massachusetts	Y	35930 FQ	45870 MW	63520 TQ	USBLS	5/07
	Boston-Cambridge-Quincy NECTA, MA	Y	36670 FQ	46910 MW	65490 TQ	USBLS	5/07
	Michigan	Y	29580 FQ	36350 MW	43180 TQ	USBLS	5/07
	Ann Arbor MSA, MI	Y	29750 FQ	36950 MW	44150 TQ	USBLS	5/07
	Missouri	Y	30060 FQ	36020 MW	43550 TQ	USBLS	5/07
	Kansas City MSA, MO-KS	Y	31090 FQ	36840 MW	44720 TQ	USBLS	5/07
	St. Louis MSA, MO-IL	Y	36140 FQ	41270 MW	53560 TQ	USBLS	5/07
	Montana	Y	28430 FQ	32700 MW	38500 TQ	USBLS	5/07
	Nebraska	Y	32290 FQ	42150 MW	49770 TQ	USBLS	5/07
	New Jersey	Y	28930 FQ	33300 MW	42470 TQ	USBLS	5/07
	New Mexico	Y	26600 FQ	30480 MW	42970 TQ	USBLS	5/07
	New York	Y	26310 FQ	34340 MW	42970 TQ	USBLS	5/07
	Albany-Schenectady-Troy MSA, NY	Y	33190 FQ	41140 MW	48330 TQ	USBLS	5/07
	Buffalo-Niagara Falls MSA, NY	Y	21490 FQ	24130 MW	31810 TQ	USBLS	5/07

AE	Average entry wage	AW	Average wage paid	FQ	First quartile wage
AER	Average entry range	AWR	Average wage range	H	Hourly
AEX	Average experienced wage	AXR	Average experienced range	HI	Highest wage paid
ATC	Average total compensation	D	Daily	HR	High end range

LO	Lowest wage paid	MTC	Median total compensation	TCC	Total cash compensation
LR	Low end range	MW	Median wage paid	TQ	Third quartile wage
M	Monthly	MWR	Median wage range	W	Weekly
MCC	Median cash compensation	S	See annotated source	Y	Yearly

Social Science Research Assistant

Occupation/Type/Industry	Location	Per	Low	Mid	High	Source	Date
Social Science Research Assistant	Nassau-Suffolk PMSA, NY	Y	22950 FQ	31190 MW	40850 TQ	USBLS	5/07
	New York-Northern New Jersey-Long Island MSA, NY-NJ-PA	Y	25570 FQ	33140 MW	43530 TQ	USBLS	5/07
	North Carolina	Y	23310 FQ	28490 MW	36750 TQ	USBLS	5/07
	Charlotte-Gastonia-Concord MSA, NC-SC	Y	27140 FQ	29820 MW	38020 TQ	USBLS	5/07
	Greensboro-High Point MSA, NC	Y	28160 FQ	34060 MW	40790 TQ	USBLS	5/07
	Raleigh-Cary MSA, NC	Y	24850 FQ	35200 MW	43980 TQ	USBLS	5/07
	Ohio	Y	25080 FQ	33910 MW	40690 TQ	USBLS	5/07
	Cleveland-Elyria-Mentor MSA, OH	Y	30220 FQ	34300 MW	38220 TQ	USBLS	5/07
	Columbus MSA, OH	Y	22300 FQ	31680 MW	42330 TQ	USBLS	5/07
	Dayton MSA, OH	Y	27240 FQ	39070 MW	52220 TQ	USBLS	5/07
	Oklahoma	Y	27310 FQ	34700 MW	43800 TQ	USBLS	5/07
	Oregon	H	14.81 FQ	17.47 MW	20.60 TQ	ORBLS	5/08
	Portland-Vancouver-Beaverton MSA, OR-WA	Y	30750 FQ	34670 MW	39760 TQ	USBLS	5/07
	Pennsylvania	Y	38560 FQ	51190 MW	60190 TQ	USBLS	5/07
	Pittsburgh MSA, PA	Y	40360 FQ	45240 MW	50070 TQ	USBLS	5/07
	South Carolina	Y	26300 FQ	28760 MW	36730 TQ	USBLS	5/07
	South Dakota	Y	24912 FQ	26890 MW	29659 TQ	SDBLS	7/08-9/08
	Tennessee	Y	22820 FQ	26730 MW	35100 TQ	USBLS	5/07
	Texas	Y	34410 FQ	40630 MW	50300 TQ	USBLS	5/07
	Austin-Round Rock MSA, TX	Y	35620 FQ	44980 MW	52340 TQ	USBLS	5/07
	Dallas-Fort Worth-Arlington MSA, TX	Y	35010 FQ	40370 MW	48630 TQ	USBLS	5/07
	Houston-Sugar Land-Baytown MSA, TX	Y	34440 FQ	43900 MW	52810 TQ	USBLS	5/07
	San Antonio MSA, TX	Y	34670 FQ	39470 MW	47170 TQ	USBLS	5/07
	Utah	Y	20180 FQ	27620 MW	33030 TQ	USBLS	5/07
	Salt Lake City MSA, UT	Y	20450 FQ	28390 MW	33060 TQ	USBLS	5/07
	Virginia	Y	30510 FQ	40630 MW	51470 TQ	USBLS	5/07
	Virginia Beach-Norfolk-Newport News MSA, VA-NC	Y	24860 FQ	29790 MW	38250 TQ	USBLS	5/07
	Washington	H	14.86 FQ	17.58 MW	21.15 TQ	WABLS	3/08
	Olympia MSA, WA	Y	37730 FQ	44940 MW	52060 TQ	USBLS	5/07
	Seattle-Tacoma-Bellevue MSA, WA	Y	29640 FQ	34940 MW	40450 TQ	USBLS	5/07
	West Virginia	Y	29704 FQ	36800 MW	43575 TQ	WVBLS	7/08-9/08
	Wisconsin	Y	32000 FQ	34400 MW	36790 TQ	USBLS	5/07
Social Sciences Research Analyst							
State Government	Ohio	H	21.77 LO		31.86 HI	ODAS	2008
Social Work Teacher							
Postsecondary	Alabama	Y	39210 FQ	51410 MW	60380 TQ	USBLS	5/07
Postsecondary	Arizona	Y	33920 FQ	40840 MW	50570 TQ	USBLS	5/07
Postsecondary	California	Y		120575 AW		CABLS	1/08-3/08
Postsecondary	Los Angeles-Long Beach-Glendale PMSA, CA	Y		125425 AW		CABLS	1/08-3/08
Postsecondary	Colorado	Y	41110 FQ	55380 MW	73900 TQ	USBLS	5/07
Postsecondary	District of Columbia	Y	64880 FQ	80840 MW	102190 TQ	USBLS	5/07
Postsecondary	Washington-Arlington-Alexandria MSA, DC-VA-MD-WV	Y	62590 FQ	79300 MW	100540 TQ	USBLS	5/07
Postsecondary	Florida	Y	49110 FQ	57970 MW	73150 TQ	USBLS	5/07
Postsecondary	Georgia	Y	44340 FQ	56550 MW	70300 TQ	USBLS	5/07
Postsecondary	Atlanta-Sandy Springs-Marietta MSA, GA	Y	50690 FQ	60580 MW	69730 TQ	USBLS	5/07
Postsecondary	Illinois	Y	30090 FQ	50080 MW	71230 TQ	USBLS	5/07
Postsecondary	Chicago-Naperville-Joliet MSA, IL-IN-WI	Y	38040 FQ	51170 MW	75860 TQ	USBLS	5/07
Postsecondary	Indiana	Y	41890 FQ	47760 MW	56710 TQ	USBLS	5/07
Postsecondary	Iowa	Y	46870 FQ	57880 MW	79500 TQ	USBLS	5/07
Postsecondary	Kansas	Y	43190 FQ	58480 MW	82920 TQ	USBLS	5/07
Postsecondary	Kentucky	Y	39049 FQ	52854 MW	63517 TQ	KYBLS	2008
Postsecondary	Louisiana	Y		54610 AW		LABLS	1/08-3/08
Postsecondary	Portland-South Portland-Biddeford MSA, ME	Y	51540 FQ	62880 MW	76050 TQ	USBLS	5/07
Postsecondary	Maryland	Y		66350 MW		MDBLS	3/08

AE Average entry wage	AW Average wage paid	FQ First quartile wage	LO Lowest wage paid	MTC Median total compensation TCC Total cash compensation
AER Average entry range	AWR Average wage range	H Hourly	LR Low end range	MW Median wage paid TQ Third quartile wage
AEX Average experienced wage AXR Average experienced range	HI Highest wage paid	M Monthly	MWR Median wage range W Weekly
ATC Average total compensation D Daily	HR High end range	MCC Median cash compensation S See annotated source	Y Yearly

Occupation/Type/Industry	Location	Per	Low	Mid	High	Source	Date
Social Work Teacher							
Postsecondary	Baltimore-Towson MSA, MD	Y	55130 FQ	65920 MW	77630 TQ	USBLS	5/07
Postsecondary	Massachusetts	Y	41660 FQ	61070 MW	82430 TQ	USBLS	5/07
Postsecondary	Boston-Cambridge-Quincy NECTA, MA	Y	29900 FQ	60190 MW	82810 TQ	USBLS	5/07
Postsecondary	Michigan	Y	49590 FQ	60640 MW	75550 TQ	USBLS	5/07
Postsecondary	Detroit-Warren-Livonia MSA, MI	Y	30860 FQ	56070 MW	70280 TQ	USBLS	5/07
Postsecondary	Minnesota	Y	43627 FQ	54811 MW	71227 TQ	MNBLS	10/08-12/08
Postsecondary	Minneapolis-Saint Paul MSA, MN-WI	Y	42686 FQ	51903 MW	66414 TQ	MNBLS	10/08-12/08
Postsecondary	Mississippi	Y	42630 FQ	49070 MW	59350 TQ	USBLS	5/07
Postsecondary	Missouri	Y	44790 FQ	55350 MW	72130 TQ	USBLS	5/07
Postsecondary	Kansas City MSA, MO-KS	Y	46770 FQ	59270 MW	77380 TQ	USBLS	5/07
Postsecondary	St. Louis MSA, MO-IL	Y	46630 FQ	56640 MW	74650 TQ	USBLS	5/07
Postsecondary	Nebraska	Y	43710 FQ	52020 MW	62310 TQ	USBLS	5/07
Postsecondary	New Hampshire	Y	52658 AE	68063 MW	81680 AEX	NHBLS	6/08
Postsecondary	New Jersey	Y	44120 FQ	56880 MW	72830 TQ	USBLS	5/07
Postsecondary	Edison PMSA, NJ	Y	45790 FQ	58650 MW	75730 TQ	USBLS	5/07
Postsecondary	Newark-Union PMSA, NJ-PA	Y	43350 FQ	56250 MW	71780 TQ	USBLS	5/07
Postsecondary	New York	Y	40950 FQ	46010 MW	51730 TQ	USBLS	5/07
Postsecondary	New York-Northern New Jersey-Long Island MSA, NY-NJ-PA	Y	43810 FQ	49310 MW	66560 TQ	USBLS	5/07
Postsecondary	North Carolina	Y	46080 FQ	55500 MW	66670 TQ	USBLS	5/07
Postsecondary	Charlotte-Gastonia-Concord MSA, NC-SC	Y	41650 FQ	50400 MW	59700 TQ	USBLS	5/07
Postsecondary	North Dakota	Y	40180 FQ	45620 MW	58650 TQ	USBLS	5/07
Postsecondary	Ohio	Y	45540 FQ	59420 MW	78530 TQ	USBLS	5/07
Postsecondary	Cincinnati-Middletown MSA, OH-KY-IN	Y	35910 FQ	51980 MW	70710 TQ	USBLS	5/07
Postsecondary	Cleveland-Elyria-Mentor MSA, OH	Y	41820 FQ	49100 MW	67060 TQ	USBLS	5/07
Postsecondary	Columbus MSA, OH	Y	62920 FQ	78370 MW	93960 TQ	USBLS	5/07
Postsecondary	Dayton MSA, OH	Y	43980 FQ	59510 MW	79940 TQ	USBLS	5/07
Postsecondary	Portland-Vancouver-Beaverton MSA, OR-WA	Y	47360 FQ	68350 MW	77350 TQ	USBLS	5/07
Postsecondary	Pennsylvania	Y	50590 FQ	62490 MW	77930 TQ	USBLS	5/07
Postsecondary	Philadelphia-Camden-Wilmington MSA, PA-NJ-DE-MD	Y	52060 FQ	63170 MW	79290 TQ	USBLS	5/07
Postsecondary	Rhode Island	Y	47110 FQ	58210 MW	78700 TQ	USBLS	5/07
Postsecondary	Providence-Fall River-Warwick MSA, RI-MA	Y	47110 FQ	58210 MW	78700 TQ	USBLS	5/07
Postsecondary	South Carolina	Y	44830 FQ	54270 MW	64620 TQ	USBLS	5/07
Postsecondary	South Dakota	Y	42012 FQ	61641 MW	77413 TQ	SDBLS	7/08-9/08
Postsecondary	Tennessee	Y	46670 FQ	57550 MW	70840 TQ	USBLS	5/07
Postsecondary	Texas	Y	36680 FQ	52060 MW	69250 TQ	USBLS	5/07
Postsecondary	Dallas-Fort Worth-Arlington MSA, TX	Y	41970 FQ	54370 MW	66750 TQ	USBLS	5/07
Postsecondary	El Paso MSA, TX	Y	25010 FQ	45160 MW	58040 TQ	USBLS	5/07
Postsecondary	Vermont	Y	44020 FQ	48210 MW	52270 TQ	USBLS	5/07
Postsecondary	Virginia	Y	41070 FQ	49350 MW	61920 TQ	USBLS	5/07
Postsecondary	West Virginia	Y	44509 FQ	55898 MW	66912 TQ	WVBLS	7/08-9/08
Postsecondary	Wisconsin	Y	41090 FQ	53500 MW	68430 TQ	USBLS	5/07
Postsecondary	Milwaukee-Waukesha-West Allis MSA, WI	Y	46670 FQ	58900 MW	73750 TQ	USBLS	5/07
Postsecondary	Puerto Rico	Y	43570 FQ	60340 MW	76170 TQ	USBLS	5/07
Social Worker							
District Government	District of Columbia	Y	48623 LO		79959 HI	AFT02	3/1/08
Public Schools, Region 9	New York	Y		48218 AW		SAANYS	9/11/08
State Government	Idaho	Y	32385 LO		53996 HI	AFT02	3/1/08
Sociologist	Arizona	Y	43200 FQ	63800 MW	78940 TQ	USBLS	5/07
	Phoenix-Mesa-Scottsdale MSA, AZ	Y	48110 FQ	70530 MW	80900 TQ	USBLS	5/07
	California	H	23.35 FQ	31.21 MW	38.53 TQ	CABLS	1/08-3/08
	Oakland-Fremont-Hayward MSA, CA	H	36.85 FQ	47.03 MW	61.71 TQ	CABLS	1/08-3/08
	Sacramento-Arden Arcade-Roseville MSA, CA	H	28.75 FQ	33.03 MW	37.78 TQ	CABLS	1/08-3/08

AE	Average entry wage	**AW**	Average wage paid	**FQ**	First quartile wage
AER	Average entry range	**AWR**	Average wage range	**H**	Hourly
AEX	Average experienced wage	**AXR**	Average experienced range	**HI**	Highest wage paid
ATC	Average total compensation	**D**	Daily	**HR**	High end range

LO	Lowest wage paid	**MTC**	Median total compensation	**TCC** Total cash compensation
LR	Low end range	**MW**	Median wage paid	**TQ** Third quartile wage
M	Monthly	**MWR**	Median wage range	**W** Weekly
MCC	Median cash compensation	**S**	See annotated source	**Y** Yearly

Occupation/Type/Industry	Location	Per	Low	Mid	High	Source	Date
Sociologist	San Francisco-San Mateo-Redwood PMSA, CA	H	28.29 FQ	34.03 MW	40.03 TQ	CABLS	1/08-3/08
	Colorado	Y	37050 FQ	41420 MW	50390 TQ	USBLS	5/07
	Denver-Aurora MSA, CO	Y	37320 FQ	41140 MW	50440 TQ	USBLS	5/07
	District of Columbia	Y	50810 FQ	71490 MW	99130 TQ	USBLS	5/07
	Washington-Arlington-Alexandria MSA, DC-VA-MD-WV	Y	51000 FQ	72880 MW	100530 TQ	USBLS	5/07
	Florida	Y	46890 FQ	59270 MW	85600 TQ	USBLS	5/07
	Miami-Fort Lauderdale-Miami Beach MSA, FL	Y	48070 FQ	62590 MW	88300 TQ	USBLS	5/07
	Idaho	Y	48630 FQ	55060 MW	62310 TQ	USBLS	5/07
	Illinois	Y	55450 FQ	74630 MW	95140 TQ	USBLS	5/07
	Chicago-Naperville-Joliet MSA, IL-IN-WI	Y	52970 FQ	70630 MW	91170 TQ	USBLS	5/07
	Massachusetts	Y	63110 FQ	77270 MW	95120 TQ	USBLS	5/07
	Boston-Cambridge-Quincy NECTA, MA	Y	70230 FQ	81610 MW	96660 TQ	USBLS	5/07
	Michigan	Y	45180 FQ	55130 MW	61790 TQ	USBLS	5/07
	Minneapolis-Saint Paul MSA, MN-WI	Y	55313 FQ	84493 MW	120033 TQ	MNBLS	10/08-12/08
	New York	Y	52310 FQ	71290 MW	96930 TQ	USBLS	5/07
	Albany-Schenectady-Troy MSA, NY	Y	57720 FQ	69760 MW	78660 TQ	USBLS	5/07
	New York-Northern New Jersey-Long Island MSA, NY-NJ-PA	Y	51850 FQ	75060 MW	110660 TQ	USBLS	5/07
	North Carolina	Y	36050 FQ	45070 MW	56340 TQ	USBLS	5/07
	Raleigh-Cary MSA, NC	Y	34240 FQ	44080 MW	53550 TQ	USBLS	5/07
	Ohio	Y	37960 FQ	47140 MW	64900 TQ	USBLS	5/07
	Oregon	H	22.28 FQ	24.23 MW	27.07 TQ	ORBLS	5/08
	Pennsylvania	Y	41080 FQ	55270 MW	94670 TQ	USBLS	5/07
	Philadelphia-Camden-Wilmington MSA, PA-NJ-DE-MD	Y	41840 FQ	62850 MW	105860 TQ	USBLS	5/07
	Texas	Y	33420 FQ	41150 MW	52930 TQ	USBLS	5/07
	Utah	Y	40140 FQ	54780 MW	73940 TQ	USBLS	5/07
	Virginia	Y	53310 FQ	77570 MW	111200 TQ	USBLS	5/07
	Washington	H	19.59 FQ	27.86 MW	35.67 TQ	WABLS	3/08
	Wisconsin	Y	39490 FQ	45520 MW	56770 TQ	USBLS	5/07
Sociology Teacher							
Postsecondary	Alabama	Y	42190 FQ	52580 MW	65030 TQ	USBLS	5/07
Postsecondary	Arizona	Y	43150 FQ	53520 MW	70470 TQ	USBLS	5/07
Postsecondary	Phoenix-Mesa-Scottsdale MSA, AZ	Y	31460 FQ	45920 MW	53450 TQ	USBLS	5/07
Postsecondary	Arkansas	Y	39090 FQ	48960 MW	59700 TQ	USBLS	5/07
Postsecondary	California	Y		102455 AW		CABLS	1/08-3/08
Postsecondary	Los Angeles-Long Beach-Glendale PMSA, CA	Y		87288 AW		CABLS	1/08-3/08
Postsecondary	Oakland-Fremont-Hayward MSA, CA	Y		98855 AW		CABLS	1/08-3/08
Postsecondary	Riverside-San Bernardino-Ontario MSA, CA	Y		94784 AW		CABLS	1/08-3/08
Postsecondary	Sacramento-Arden Arcade-Roseville MSA, CA	Y		124062 AW		CABLS	1/08-3/08
Postsecondary	San Diego-Carlsbad-San Marcos MSA, CA	Y		94292 AW		CABLS	1/08-3/08
Postsecondary	San Francisco-San Mateo-Redwood PMSA, CA	Y		143894 AW		CABLS	1/08-3/08
Postsecondary	Santa Ana-Anaheim-Irvine PMSA, CA	Y	51410 FQ	75690 MW	112120 TQ	USBLS	5/07
Postsecondary	Colorado	Y	36400 FQ	52740 MW	65990 TQ	USBLS	5/07
Postsecondary	Denver-Aurora MSA, CO	Y	40920 FQ	55290 MW	64770 TQ	USBLS	5/07
Postsecondary	Delaware	Y	48490 FQ	63430 MW	91180 TQ	USBLS	5/07
Postsecondary	Wilmington PMSA, DE-MD-NJ	Y	50530 FQ	70150 MW	99160 TQ	USBLS	5/07
Postsecondary	District of Columbia	Y	54880 FQ	65160 MW	80890 TQ	USBLS	5/07
Postsecondary	Washington-Arlington-Alexandria MSA, DC-VA-MD-WV	Y	55170 FQ	66050 MW	81980 TQ	USBLS	5/07
Postsecondary	Florida	Y	44740 FQ	57690 MW	74970 TQ	USBLS	5/07

AE	Average entry wage	AW	Average wage paid	FQ	First quartile wage	LO	Lowest wage paid	MTC	Median total compensation	TCC	Total cash compensation
AER	Average entry range	AWR	Average wage range	H	Hourly	LR	Low end range	MW	Median wage paid	TQ	Third quartile wage
AEX	Average experienced wage	AXR	Average experienced range	HI	Highest wage paid	M	Monthly	MWR	Median wage range	W	Weekly
ATC	Average total compensation	D	Daily	HR	High end range	MCC	Median cash compensation	S	See annotated source	Y	Yearly

Sociology Teacher

Occupation/Type/Industry	Location	Per	Low	Mid	High	Source	Date
Sociology Teacher							
Postsecondary	Orlando-Kissimmee MSA, FL	Y	37270 FQ	50150 MW	69850 TQ	USBLS	5/07
Postsecondary	Tampa-St. Petersburg-Clearwater MSA, FL	Y	50730 FQ	60020 MW	75430 TQ	USBLS	5/07
Postsecondary	West Palm Beach-Boca Raton-Boynton Beach PMSA, FL	Y	44620 FQ	56430 MW	70090 TQ	USBLS	5/07
Postsecondary	Georgia	Y	41860 FQ	54300 MW	69800 TQ	USBLS	5/07
Postsecondary	Atlanta-Sandy Springs-Marietta MSA, GA	Y	49290 FQ	62770 MW	81920 TQ	USBLS	5/07
Postsecondary	Hawaii	Y	55020 FQ	67300 MW	77160 TQ	USBLS	5/07
Postsecondary	Honolulu MSA, HI	Y	60650 FQ	69640 MW	78250 TQ	USBLS	5/07
Postsecondary	Illinois	Y	37250 FQ	54300 MW	71990 TQ	USBLS	5/07
Postsecondary	Chicago-Naperville-Joliet MSA, IL-IN-WI	Y	42150 FQ	55940 MW	74710 TQ	USBLS	5/07
Postsecondary	Indiana	Y	47950 FQ	59370 MW	80300 TQ	USBLS	5/07
Postsecondary	Gary PMSA, IN	Y	43750 FQ	51400 MW	63000 TQ	USBLS	5/07
Postsecondary	Iowa	Y	43330 FQ	60270 MW	85450 TQ	USBLS	5/07
Postsecondary	Des Moines-West Des Moines MSA, IA	Y	42980 FQ	69990 MW	90560 TQ	USBLS	5/07
Postsecondary	Kansas	Y	36540 FQ	49950 MW	63720 TQ	USBLS	5/07
Postsecondary	Kentucky	Y	39011 FQ	54164 MW	67210 TQ	KYBLS	2008
Postsecondary	Louisiana	Y		54236 AW		LABLS	1/08-3/08
Postsecondary	Baton Rouge MSA, LA	Y	46340 FQ	53040 MW	61810 TQ	USBLS	5/07
Postsecondary	Maine	Y	48130 FQ	65450 MW	91420 TQ	USBLS	5/07
Postsecondary	Maryland	Y		61675 MW		MDBLS	3/08
Postsecondary	Baltimore-Towson MSA, MD	Y	44770 FQ	55400 MW	74220 TQ	USBLS	5/07
Postsecondary	Bethesda-Gaithersburg-Frederick PMSA, MD	Y	64850 FQ	80340 MW	129890 TQ	USBLS	5/07
Postsecondary	Massachusetts	Y	47910 FQ	61910 MW	80920 TQ	USBLS	5/07
Postsecondary	Boston-Cambridge-Quincy NECTA, MA	Y	44680 FQ	58620 MW	76630 TQ	USBLS	5/07
Postsecondary	Worcester MSA, MA-CT	Y	49080 FQ	60160 MW	75740 TQ	USBLS	5/07
Postsecondary	Michigan	Y	31930 FQ	50560 MW	70240 TQ	USBLS	5/07
Postsecondary	Detroit-Warren-Livonia MSA, MI	Y	27790 FQ	31190 MW	42520 TQ	USBLS	5/07
Postsecondary	Warren-Troy-Farmington Hills PMSA, MI	Y	25570 FQ	39920 MW	61480 TQ	USBLS	5/07
Postsecondary	Minnesota	Y	46504 FQ	57165 MW	70609 TQ	MNBLS	10/08-12/08
Postsecondary	Duluth-Superior MSA, MN-WI	Y	43481 FQ	52886 MW	63349 TQ	MNBLS	10/08-12/08
Postsecondary	Minneapolis-Saint Paul MSA, MN-WI	Y	48231 FQ	59729 MW	75359 TQ	MNBLS	10/08-12/08
Postsecondary	Mississippi	Y	43410 FQ	56810 MW	71880 TQ	USBLS	5/07
Postsecondary	Jackson MSA, MS	Y	41350 FQ	58180 MW	72460 TQ	USBLS	5/07
Postsecondary	Missouri	Y	39250 FQ	55110 MW	79910 TQ	USBLS	5/07
Postsecondary	Kansas City MSA, MO-KS	Y	37900 FQ	48070 MW	61740 TQ	USBLS	5/07
Postsecondary	St. Louis MSA, MO-IL	Y	25960 FQ	50260 MW	78900 TQ	USBLS	5/07
Postsecondary	Montana	Y	31570 FQ	46640 MW	54970 TQ	USBLS	5/07
Postsecondary	Nebraska	Y	44460 FQ	55990 MW	65670 TQ	USBLS	5/07
Postsecondary	Omaha-Council Bluffs MSA, NE-IA	Y	45940 FQ	58490 MW	70600 TQ	USBLS	5/07
Postsecondary	New Hampshire	Y	37073 AE	57744 MW	78341 AEX	NHBLS	6/08
Postsecondary	New Jersey	Y	46180 FQ	64520 MW	87850 TQ	USBLS	5/07
Postsecondary	Camden PMSA, NJ	Y	59840 FQ	75040 MW	97630 TQ	USBLS	5/07
Postsecondary	Edison PMSA, NJ	Y	65390 FQ	82610 MW	104760 TQ	USBLS	5/07
Postsecondary	Newark-Union PMSA, NJ-PA	Y	42250 FQ	58950 MW	80860 TQ	USBLS	5/07
Postsecondary	New Mexico	Y	53610 FQ	62880 MW	73390 TQ	USBLS	5/07
Postsecondary	New York	Y	49080 FQ	63900 MW	94230 TQ	USBLS	5/07
Postsecondary	Nassau-Suffolk PMSA, NY	Y	48160 FQ	59620 MW	79930 TQ	USBLS	5/07
Postsecondary	New York-Northern New Jersey-Long Island MSA, NY-NJ-PA	Y	50000 FQ	66010 MW	97090 TQ	USBLS	5/07
Postsecondary	North Carolina	Y	42330 FQ	53950 MW	65860 TQ	USBLS	5/07
Postsecondary	Charlotte-Gastonia-Concord MSA, NC-SC	Y	43900 FQ	55470 MW	67040 TQ	USBLS	5/07
Postsecondary	Raleigh-Cary MSA, NC	Y	37970 FQ	56190 MW	72440 TQ	USBLS	5/07
Postsecondary	North Dakota	Y	39010 FQ	50920 MW	61720 TQ	USBLS	5/07
Postsecondary	Fargo MSA, ND-MN	Y	43370 FQ	53850 MW	69430 TQ	USBLS	5/07
Postsecondary	Ohio	Y	42830 FQ	58140 MW	81060 TQ	USBLS	5/07
Postsecondary	Cincinnati-Middletown MSA, OH-KY-IN	Y	37690 FQ	50700 MW	70290 TQ	USBLS	5/07
Postsecondary	Cleveland-Elyria-Mentor MSA, OH	Y	50040 FQ	63930 MW	81930 TQ	USBLS	5/07

AE	Average entry wage	AW	Average wage paid	FQ	First quartile wage
AER	Average entry range	AWR	Average wage range	H	Hourly
AEX	Average experienced wage	AXR	Average experienced range	HI	Highest wage paid
ATC	Average total compensation	D	Daily	HR	High end range

LO	Lowest wage paid	MTC	Median total compensation	TCC	Total cash compensation
LR	Low end range	MW	Median wage paid	TQ	Third quartile wage
M	Monthly	MWR	Median wage range	W	Weekly
MCC	Median cash compensation	S	See annotated source	Y	Yearly

Occupation/Type/Industry	Location	Per	Low	Mid	High	Source	Date
Sociology Teacher							
Postsecondary	Columbus MSA, OH	Y	59150 FQ	78070 MW	95520 TQ	USBLS	5/07
Postsecondary	Dayton MSA, OH	Y	31160 FQ	46560 MW	64270 TQ	USBLS	5/07
Postsecondary	Oklahoma	Y	32280 FQ	39550 MW	48210 TQ	USBLS	5/07
Postsecondary	Oklahoma City MSA, OK	Y	32420 FQ	44700 MW	64000 TQ	USBLS	5/07
Postsecondary	Tulsa MSA, OK	Y	32220 FQ	38030 MW	44880 TQ	USBLS	5/07
Postsecondary	Portland-Vancouver-Beaverton MSA, OR-WA	Y	52230 FQ	67530 MW	97570 TQ	USBLS	5/07
Postsecondary	Pennsylvania	Y	45800 FQ	61060 MW	80430 TQ	USBLS	5/07
Postsecondary	Allentown-Bethlehem-Easton MSA, PA-NJ	Y	54460 FQ	65600 MW	85290 TQ	USBLS	5/07
Postsecondary	Philadelphia-Camden-Wilmington MSA, PA-NJ-DE-MD	Y	46380 FQ	61300 MW	84390 TQ	USBLS	5/07
Postsecondary	Pittsburgh MSA, PA	Y	46690 FQ	61160 MW	75550 TQ	USBLS	5/07
Postsecondary	Rhode Island	Y	55090 FQ	73100 MW	93700 TQ	USBLS	5/07
Postsecondary	Providence-Fall River-Warwick MSA, RI-MA	Y	55110 FQ	72760 MW	93480 TQ	USBLS	5/07
Postsecondary	South Carolina	Y	50010 FQ	59670 MW	71040 TQ	USBLS	5/07
Postsecondary	South Dakota	Y	39188 FQ	48659 MW	62323 TQ	SDBLS	7/08-9/08
Postsecondary	Tennessee	Y	44970 FQ	60800 MW	95310 TQ	USBLS	5/07
Postsecondary	Nashville-Davidson-Murfreesboro MSA, TN	Y	47910 FQ	64560 MW	104520 TQ	USBLS	5/07
Postsecondary	Texas	Y	27770 FQ	46250 MW	69240 TQ	USBLS	5/07
Postsecondary	Austin-Round Rock MSA, TX	Y	30680 FQ	72640 MW	99550 TQ	USBLS	5/07
Postsecondary	Dallas-Fort Worth-Arlington MSA, TX	Y	27570 FQ	42290 MW	64850 TQ	USBLS	5/07
Postsecondary	El Paso MSA, TX	Y	50980 FQ	64490 MW	77630 TQ	USBLS	5/07
Postsecondary	Houston-Sugar Land-Baytown MSA, TX	Y	30530 FQ	50020 MW	71650 TQ	USBLS	5/07
Postsecondary	San Antonio MSA, TX	Y	36900 FQ	47800 MW	61070 TQ	USBLS	5/07
Postsecondary	Utah	Y	48370 FQ	58240 MW	75960 TQ	USBLS	5/07
Postsecondary	Vermont	Y	40610 FQ	48150 MW	60260 TQ	USBLS	5/07
Postsecondary	Virginia	Y	42520 FQ	54600 MW	66760 TQ	USBLS	5/07
Postsecondary	Richmond MSA, VA	Y	35740 FQ	50990 MW	63410 TQ	USBLS	5/07
Postsecondary	Virginia Beach-Norfolk-Newport News MSA, VA-NC	Y	43340 FQ	51880 MW	66290 TQ	USBLS	5/07
Postsecondary	Washington	Y		65186 AW		WABLS	3/08
Postsecondary	Seattle-Tacoma-Bellevue MSA, WA	Y	47430 FQ	57950 MW	80460 TQ	USBLS	5/07
Postsecondary	West Virginia	Y	42456 FQ	52011 MW	71080 TQ	WVBLS	7/08-9/08
Postsecondary	Wisconsin	Y	45250 FQ	59580 MW	81630 TQ	USBLS	5/07
Postsecondary	Milwaukee-Waukesha-West Allis MSA, WI	Y	47120 FQ	73480 MW	102970 TQ	USBLS	5/07
Postsecondary	Wyoming	Y	41409 FQ	58780 MW	71826 TQ	WYBLS	9/08
Postsecondary	Puerto Rico	Y	44800 FQ	62750 MW	77030 TQ	USBLS	5/07
Postsecondary	San Juan-Caguas-Guaynabo MSA, PR	Y	47370 FQ	68820 MW	77850 TQ	USBLS	5/07
Software Development Manager	San Francisco, CA	Y		136000 AW		BWEEK	2008
Software Engineer							
Google	United States	Y		96000 AW		GLDR01	10/08
Yahoo!	United States	Y		98459 AW		GLDR02	10/08
Software Test Engineer	United States	Y		91733 AW		TMW	2008
Software User Assistance Professional	United States	Y		76044 AW		WRUA	12/1/07-1/25/08
Soil and Plant Scientist	Alabama	Y	50200 FQ	61730 MW	72820 TQ	USBLS	5/07
	Alaska	Y	58340 FQ	71630 MW	86070 TQ	USBLS	5/07
	Arizona	Y	47210 FQ	59770 MW	75430 TQ	USBLS	5/07
	California	H	26.99 FQ	34.27 MW	43.65 TQ	CABLS	1/08-3/08
	Los Angeles-Long Beach-Glendale PMSA, CA	H	24.34 FQ	33.56 MW	45.63 TQ	CABLS	1/08-3/08
	Oakland-Fremont-Hayward MSA, CA	H	36.92 FQ	44.01 MW	55.17 TQ	CABLS	1/08-3/08
	Riverside-San Bernardino-Ontario MSA, CA	H	26.94 FQ	36.32 MW	52.07 TQ	CABLS	1/08-3/08
	Sacramento-Arden Arcade-Roseville MSA, CA	H	30.03 FQ	36.07 MW	43.48 TQ	CABLS	1/08-3/08

AE	Average entry wage	AW	Average wage paid	FQ	First quartile wage	LO	Lowest wage paid	MTC	Median total compensation	TCC	Total cash compensation
AER	Average entry range	AWR	Average wage range	H	Hourly	LR	Low end range	MW	Median wage paid	TQ	Third quartile wage
AEX	Average experienced wage	AXR	Average experienced range	HI	Highest wage paid	M	Monthly	MWR	Median wage range	W	Weekly
ATC	Average total compensation	D	Daily	HR	High end range	MCC	Median cash compensation	S	See annotated source	Y	Yearly

Occupation/Type/Industry	Location	Per	Low	Mid	High	Source	Date
Soil and Plant Scientist	San Diego-Carlsbad-San Marcos MSA, CA	H	29.90 FQ	34.17 MW	37.65 TQ	CABLS	1/08-3/08
	San Francisco-San Mateo-Redwood PMSA, CA	H	27.67 FQ	34.03 MW	43.44 TQ	CABLS	1/08-3/08
	San Jose-Sunnyvale-Santa Clara MSA, CA	H	26.78 FQ	31.61 MW	37.87 TQ	CABLS	1/08-3/08
	Santa Ana-Anaheim-Irvine PMSA, CA	Y	27800 FQ	29750 MW	31700 TQ	USBLS	5/07
	Colorado	Y	40870 FQ	60180 MW	76690 TQ	USBLS	5/07
	Denver-Aurora MSA, CO	Y	39440 FQ	56930 MW	77020 TQ	USBLS	5/07
	Fort Collins-Loveland MSA, CO	Y	57670 FQ	66010 MW	77570 TQ	USBLS	5/07
	Connecticut	H	23.91 AE	30.95 MW		CTBLS	1/08-3/08
	Delaware	Y	38700 FQ	52550 MW	64100 TQ	USBLS	5/07
	District of Columbia	Y	58150 FQ	76970 MW	113800 TQ	USBLS	5/07
	Washington-Arlington-Alexandria MSA, DC-VA-MD-WV	Y	59190 FQ	80090 MW	111650 TQ	USBLS	5/07
	Georgia	Y	39900 FQ	67580 MW	81630 TQ	USBLS	5/07
	Atlanta-Sandy Springs-Marietta MSA, GA	Y	50410 FQ	71630 MW	78900 TQ	USBLS	5/07
	Hawaii	Y	46960 FQ	63820 MW	85570 TQ	USBLS	5/07
	Honolulu MSA, HI	Y	46330 FQ	63190 MW	87030 TQ	USBLS	5/07
	Idaho	Y	31260 FQ	54540 MW	71660 TQ	USBLS	5/07
	Boise City-Nampa MSA, ID	Y	27600 FQ	30240 MW	46540 TQ	USBLS	5/07
	Illinois	Y	49950 FQ	57620 MW	66900 TQ	USBLS	5/07
	Champaign-Urbana MSA, IL	Y	37430 FQ	56060 MW	77110 TQ	USBLS	5/07
	Chicago-Naperville-Joliet MSA, IL-IN-WI	Y	35220 FQ	55950 MW	65130 TQ	USBLS	5/07
	Indiana	Y	28330 FQ	35830 MW	49160 TQ	USBLS	5/07
	Indianapolis-Carmel MSA, IN	Y	35800 FQ	39270 MW	73690 TQ	USBLS	5/07
	Iowa	Y	46320 FQ	58600 MW	71380 TQ	USBLS	5/07
	Kansas	Y	41910 FQ	51850 MW	66990 TQ	USBLS	5/07
	Kentucky	Y	37705 FQ	51499 MW	59628 TQ	KYBLS	2008
	Louisville-Jefferson County MSA, KY-IN	Y	34670 FQ	37960 MW	60470 TQ	USBLS	5/07
	Louisiana	H	21.56 FQ	29.26 MW	36.33 TQ	LABLS	1/08-3/08
	Maryland	Y		75500 MW		MDBLS	3/08
	Massachusetts	Y	45820 FQ	52360 MW	65320 TQ	USBLS	5/07
	Boston-Cambridge-Quincy NECTA, MA	Y	45800 FQ	50370 MW	60010 TQ	USBLS	5/07
	Michigan	Y	41180 FQ	57260 MW	72320 TQ	USBLS	5/07
	Grand Rapids-Wyoming MSA, MI	Y	31700 FQ	36270 MW	46230 TQ	USBLS	5/07
	Minnesota	Y	40101 FQ	47948 MW	61078 TQ	MNBLS	10/08-12/08
	Duluth-Superior MSA, MN-WI	Y	51150 FQ	58682 MW	64782 TQ	MNBLS	10/08-12/08
	Minneapolis-Saint Paul MSA, MN-WI	Y	38124 FQ	43700 MW	53190 TQ	MNBLS	10/08-12/08
	Mississippi	Y	38340 FQ	54510 MW	76470 TQ	USBLS	5/07
	Missouri	Y	37740 FQ	45930 MW	60160 TQ	USBLS	5/07
	St. Louis MSA, MO-IL	Y	31150 FQ	44160 MW	71790 TQ	USBLS	5/07
	Montana	Y	36570 FQ	46940 MW	60360 TQ	USBLS	5/07
	Nebraska	Y	39550 FQ	46240 MW	59870 TQ	USBLS	5/07
	Nevada	H	68.49 FQ	67.40 AW		NVBLS	5/08
	Las Vegas-Paradise MSA, NV	H	69.63 FQ	70.44 AW		NVBLS	5/08
	New Jersey	Y	52620 FQ	63300 MW	80340 TQ	USBLS	5/07
	Edison PMSA, NJ	Y	53380 FQ	61310 MW	76990 TQ	USBLS	5/07
	New Mexico	Y	51530 FQ	64580 MW	75830 TQ	USBLS	5/07
	New York	Y	34990 FQ	43810 MW	61850 TQ	USBLS	5/07
	New York-Northern New Jersey-Long Island MSA, NY-NJ-PA	Y	55520 FQ	65800 MW	80930 TQ	USBLS	5/07
	North Carolina	Y	43080 FQ	55890 MW	75410 TQ	USBLS	5/07
	Charlotte-Gastonia-Concord MSA, NC-SC	Y	44370 FQ	53610 MW	65670 TQ	USBLS	5/07
	North Dakota	Y	32270 FQ	44480 MW	61990 TQ	USBLS	5/07
	Ohio	Y	38920 FQ	54270 MW	66400 TQ	USBLS	5/07
	Columbus MSA, OH	Y	31940 FQ	39720 MW	51870 TQ	USBLS	5/07
	Oklahoma	Y	63080 FQ	73180 MW	88600 TQ	USBLS	5/07
	Oklahoma City MSA, OK	Y	64910 FQ	73940 MW	87930 TQ	USBLS	5/07
	Oregon	H	24.07 FQ	28.65 MW	36.31 TQ	ORBLS	5/08

Occupation/Type/Industry	Location	Per	Low	Mid	High	Source	Date
Soil and Plant Scientist	Portland-Vancouver-Beaverton MSA, OR-WA	Y	47610 FQ	56290 MW	73960 TQ	USBLS	5/07
	Pennsylvania	Y	49120 FQ	61970 MW	76970 TQ	USBLS	5/07
	Philadelphia-Camden-Wilmington MSA, PA-NJ-DE-MD	Y	39160 FQ	56820 MW	69690 TQ	USBLS	5/07
	Pittsburgh MSA, PA	Y	71040 FQ	75700 MW	80350 TQ	USBLS	5/07
	South Carolina	Y	56920 FQ	68240 MW	97360 TQ	USBLS	5/07
	South Dakota	Y	40052 FQ	49756 MW	62520 TQ	SDBLS	7/08-9/08
	Sioux Falls MSA, SD	Y	59599 FQ	69505 MW	77266 TQ	SDBLS	7/08-9/08
	Tennessee	Y	38860 FQ	54370 MW	67040 TQ	USBLS	5/07
	Texas	Y	45220 FQ	56790 MW	74080 TQ	USBLS	5/07
	Utah	Y	39100 FQ	52190 MW	65040 TQ	USBLS	5/07
	Vermont	Y	42990 FQ	57640 MW	70440 TQ	USBLS	5/07
	Virginia	Y	45030 FQ	57840 MW	67620 TQ	USBLS	5/07
	Washington	H	25.10 FQ	30.19 MW	37.92 TQ	WABLS	3/08
	Seattle-Tacoma-Bellevue MSA, WA	Y	61790 FQ	73760 MW	98920 TQ	USBLS	5/07
	West Virginia	Y	53865 FQ	62484 MW	77340 TQ	WVBLS	7/08-9/08
	Wisconsin	Y	40420 FQ	45390 MW	53440 TQ	USBLS	5/07
	Wyoming	Y	44533 FQ	52093 MW	64708 TQ	WYBLS	9/08
	Puerto Rico	Y	26190 FQ	29570 MW	34510 TQ	USBLS	5/07
	San Juan-Caguas-Guaynabo MSA, PR	Y	26020 FQ	29260 MW	33030 TQ	USBLS	5/07
Soils Engineer							
Small Organization	United States	Y	58006 FQ	65415 MW	72824 TQ	ALA08	2008
Soils Resource Specialist							
State Government	Ohio	H	19.88 LO		26.28 HI	ODAS	2008
Solar Energy System Installer	Tech Valley, NY	Y	25000 LO		55000 HI	TVC01	2008
Solicitor							
State Court	DeKalb County, GA	Y			140145 HI	GACTY02	2008
State Court	Toombs County, GA	Y			30000 HI	GACTY02	2008
Solid Waste Administrator	Leverett, MA	Y			8829 HI	FRCOG	2009
Solid Waste Manager	Forsyth County, GA	Y	36512 LO		54768 HI	GACTY03	2008
Sound Editor							
Independent Motion Picture	West Coast	W			1945 HI	MPEG02	8/3/08-7/31/09
Sound Engineering Technician	Alabama	Y	14090 FQ	19760 MW	36770 TQ	USBLS	5/07
	Birmingham-Hoover MSA, AL	Y	13580 FQ	16920 MW	20940 TQ	USBLS	5/07
	Arizona	Y	18880 FQ	22370 MW	37920 TQ	USBLS	5/07
	Phoenix-Mesa-Scottsdale MSA, AZ	Y	18530 FQ	20470 MW	33830 TQ	USBLS	5/07
	Arkansas	Y	25090 FQ	30200 MW	43140 TQ	USBLS	5/07
	California	H	20.32 FQ	32.63 MW	44.73 TQ	CABLS	1/08-3/08
	Los Angeles-Long Beach-Glendale PMSA, CA	H	21.77 FQ	33.97 MW	45.85 TQ	CABLS	1/08-3/08
	Oakland-Fremont-Hayward MSA, CA	H	15.72 FQ	19.63 MW	26.24 TQ	CABLS	1/08-3/08
	Riverside-San Bernardino-Ontario MSA, CA	H	14.65 FQ	21.53 MW	25.53 TQ	CABLS	1/08-3/08
	Sacramento-Arden Arcade-Roseville MSA, CA	H	14.92 FQ	17.65 MW	22.65 TQ	CABLS	1/08-3/08
	San Diego-Carlsbad-San Marcos MSA, CA	H	15.78 FQ	24.57 MW	36.49 TQ	CABLS	1/08-3/08
	San Francisco-San Mateo-Redwood PMSA, CA	H	18.43 FQ	33.60 MW	46.83 TQ	CABLS	1/08-3/08
	San Jose-Sunnyvale-Santa Clara MSA, CA	H	15.01 FQ	16.80 MW	18.53 TQ	CABLS	1/08-3/08
	Santa Ana-Anaheim-Irvine PMSA, CA	Y	46280 FQ	52780 MW	57710 TQ	USBLS	5/07
	Colorado	Y	25380 FQ	32480 MW	42440 TQ	USBLS	5/07
	Denver-Aurora MSA, CO	Y	19990 FQ	28510 MW	43450 TQ	USBLS	5/07
	Connecticut	H	12.70 AE	20.70 MW		CTBLS	1/08-3/08
	Bridgeport-Stamford-Norwalk MSA, CT	Y	32520 FQ	36680 MW	43650 TQ	USBLS	5/07

Occupation/Type/Industry	Location	Per	Low	Mid	High	Source	Date
Sound Engineering Technician	Hartford-West Hartford-East Hartford MSA, CT	Y	27870 FQ	41190 MW	86380 TQ	USBLS	5/07
	District of Columbia	Y	29460 FQ	46340 MW	71890 TQ	USBLS	5/07
	Washington-Arlington-Alexandria MSA, DC-VA-MD-WV	Y	28960 FQ	41330 MW	61790 TQ	USBLS	5/07
	Florida	Y	26860 FQ	33380 MW	42680 TQ	USBLS	5/07
	Fort Lauderdale-Pompano Beach-Deerfield Beach PMSA, FL	Y	21450 FQ	28880 MW	41230 TQ	USBLS	5/07
	Jacksonville MSA, FL	Y	25660 FQ	29190 MW	32510 TQ	USBLS	5/07
	Miami-Fort Lauderdale-Miami Beach MSA, FL	Y	27920 FQ	37480 MW	45560 TQ	USBLS	5/07
	Orlando-Kissimmee MSA, FL	Y	32970 FQ	39250 MW	53390 TQ	USBLS	5/07
	Tampa-St. Petersburg-Clearwater MSA, FL	Y	27140 FQ	32900 MW	39930 TQ	USBLS	5/07
	West Palm Beach-Boca Raton-Boynton Beach PMSA, FL	Y	29060 FQ	38400 MW	48380 TQ	USBLS	5/07
	Hawaii	Y	23100 FQ	33070 MW	46420 TQ	USBLS	5/07
	Illinois	Y	36220 FQ	47430 MW	71480 TQ	USBLS	5/07
	Chicago-Naperville-Joliet MSA, IL-IN-WI	Y	37450 FQ	48800 MW	73040 TQ	USBLS	5/07
	Indiana	Y	22550 FQ	30060 MW	35140 TQ	USBLS	5/07
	Kansas	Y	16220 FQ	23890 MW	37880 TQ	USBLS	5/07
	Kentucky	Y	32148 FQ	34916 MW	37352 TQ	KYBLS	2008
	Louisiana	H	12.60 FQ	15.25 MW	23.63 TQ	LABLS	1/08-3/08
	Maryland	Y		38875 MW		MDBLS	3/08
	Baltimore-Towson MSA, MD	Y	26550 FQ	35490 MW	48500 TQ	USBLS	5/07
	Massachusetts	Y	33330 FQ	42830 MW	72140 TQ	USBLS	5/07
	Boston-Cambridge-Quincy NECTA, MA	Y	33210 FQ	41630 MW	73410 TQ	USBLS	5/07
	Michigan	Y	22740 FQ	45190 MW	71370 TQ	USBLS	5/07
	Detroit-Warren-Livonia MSA, MI	Y	19990 FQ	48800 MW	74840 TQ	USBLS	5/07
	Warren-Troy-Farmington Hills PMSA, MI	Y	18600 FQ	51940 MW	76810 TQ	USBLS	5/07
	Minnesota	Y	35278 FQ	47111 MW	54905 TQ	MNBLS	10/08-12/08
	Minneapolis-Saint Paul MSA, MN-WI	Y	44140 FQ	49957 MW	66581 TQ	MNBLS	10/08-12/08
	Mississippi	Y	26400 FQ	34720 MW	40950 TQ	USBLS	5/07
	Missouri	Y	30990 FQ	35950 MW	43100 TQ	USBLS	5/07
	Kansas City MSA, MO-KS	Y	27390 FQ	35080 MW	38650 TQ	USBLS	5/07
	St. Louis MSA, MO-IL	Y	30230 FQ	34450 MW	46890 TQ	USBLS	5/07
	Nebraska	Y	29420 FQ	34430 MW	42480 TQ	USBLS	5/07
	Omaha-Council Bluffs MSA, NE-IA	Y	29060 FQ	33660 MW	42510 TQ	USBLS	5/07
	Nevada	H	15.97 FQ	26.35 MW	32.80 TQ	NVBLS	5/08
	Las Vegas-Paradise MSA, NV	H	17.40 FQ	28.91 MW	34.44 TQ	NVBLS	5/08
	New Jersey	Y	44650 FQ	59550 MW	73310 TQ	USBLS	5/07
	Camden PMSA, NJ	Y	35170 FQ	50260 MW	66250 TQ	USBLS	5/07
	Edison PMSA, NJ	Y	40460 FQ	56260 MW	84180 TQ	USBLS	5/07
	Newark-Union PMSA, NJ-PA	Y	44210 FQ	50100 MW	72380 TQ	USBLS	5/07
	New York	Y	35920 FQ	49000 MW	78360 TQ	USBLS	5/07
	Albany-Schenectady-Troy MSA, NY	Y	39690 FQ	49430 MW	67250 TQ	USBLS	5/07
	Buffalo-Niagara Falls MSA, NY	Y	30560 FQ	47970 MW	63610 TQ	USBLS	5/07
	Nassau-Suffolk PMSA, NY	Y	31500 FQ	53630 MW	67960 TQ	USBLS	5/07
	New York-Northern New Jersey-Long Island MSA, NY-NJ-PA	Y	36470 FQ	50470 MW	81610 TQ	USBLS	5/07
	North Carolina	Y	30410 FQ	35800 MW	47300 TQ	USBLS	5/07
	Charlotte-Gastonia-Concord MSA, NC-SC	Y	34050 FQ	41690 MW	57160 TQ	USBLS	5/07
	Raleigh-Cary MSA, NC	Y	28460 FQ	31290 MW	38350 TQ	USBLS	5/07
	Ohio	Y	25950 FQ	35460 MW	53080 TQ	USBLS	5/07
	Cincinnati-Middletown MSA, OH-KY-IN	Y	31010 FQ	34620 MW	38660 TQ	USBLS	5/07
	Cleveland-Elyria-Mentor MSA, OH	Y	33550 FQ	39120 MW	53110 TQ	USBLS	5/07
	Oklahoma	Y	21220 FQ	27150 MW	36080 TQ	USBLS	5/07
	Oregon	H	20.30 FQ	24.03 MW	41.52 TQ	ORBLS	5/08

AE	Average entry wage	**AW**	Average wage paid	**FQ**	First quartile wage	**LO** Lowest wage paid	**MTC** Median total compensation	**TCC** Total cash compensation
AER	Average entry range	**AWR**	Average wage range	**H**	Hourly	**LR** Low end range	**MW** Median wage paid	**TQ** Third quartile wage
AEX	Average experienced wage	**AXR**	Average experienced range	**HI**	Highest wage paid	**M** Monthly	**MWR** Median wage range	**W** Weekly
ATC	Average total compensation	**D**	Daily	**HR**	High end range	**MCC** Median cash compensation	**S** See annotated source	**Y** Yearly

Occupation/Type/Industry	Location	Per	Low	Mid	High	Source	Date
Sound Engineering Technician	Portland-Vancouver-Beaverton MSA, OR-WA	Y	39760 FQ	47720 MW	65580 TQ	USBLS	5/07
	Pennsylvania	Y	28860 FQ	33330 MW	42210 TQ	USBLS	5/07
	Philadelphia-Camden-Wilmington MSA, PA-NJ-DE-MD	Y	29320 FQ	34080 MW	46760 TQ	USBLS	5/07
	Rhode Island	Y	26090 FQ	31080 MW	34960 TQ	USBLS	5/07
	Providence-Fall River-Warwick MSA, RI-MA	Y	26260 FQ	31170 MW	34860 TQ	USBLS	5/07
	South Carolina	Y	18590 FQ	23370 MW	32790 TQ	USBLS	5/07
	South Dakota	Y	22120 FQ	24173 MW	26357 TQ	SDBLS	7/08-9/08
	Sioux Falls MSA, SD	Y	23030 FQ	25165 MW	28692 TQ	SDBLS	7/08-9/08
	Tennessee	Y	26620 FQ	34910 MW	48390 TQ	USBLS	5/07
	Nashville-Davidson-Murfreesboro MSA, TN	Y	27300 FQ	39240 MW	49750 TQ	USBLS	5/07
	Texas	Y	24780 FQ	37170 MW	48530 TQ	USBLS	5/07
	Austin-Round Rock MSA, TX	Y	40560 FQ	46370 MW	50600 TQ	USBLS	5/07
	Dallas-Fort Worth-Arlington MSA, TX	Y	29920 FQ	37590 MW	50440 TQ	USBLS	5/07
	Houston-Sugar Land-Baytown MSA, TX	Y	19860 FQ	28720 MW	46470 TQ	USBLS	5/07
	Utah	Y	26820 FQ	35360 MW	49640 TQ	USBLS	5/07
	Virginia	Y	29860 FQ	39880 MW	59820 TQ	USBLS	5/07
	Virginia Beach-Norfolk-Newport News MSA, VA-NC	Y	37420 FQ	50910 MW	75650 TQ	USBLS	5/07
	Washington	H	15.55 FQ	23.48 MW	33.48 TQ	WABLS	3/08
	Seattle-Tacoma-Bellevue MSA, WA	Y	31400 FQ	45720 MW	68120 TQ	USBLS	5/07
	West Virginia	Y	14972 FQ	27819 MW	36531 TQ	WVBLS	7/08-9/08
	Wisconsin	Y	24620 FQ	36800 MW	56980 TQ	USBLS	5/07
	Puerto Rico	Y	20790 FQ	23780 MW	36250 TQ	USBLS	5/07
	San Juan-Caguas-Guaynabo MSA, PR	Y	20830 FQ	23700 MW	35970 TQ	USBLS	5/07
Sound Reader							
Feature Animation	West Coast	W			1311 HI	MPEG03	8/3/08-7/31/09
Space Planner							
State Government	Ohio	H	16.35 LO		19.88 HI	ODAS	2008
Spay and Neuter Technician							
Municipal Government	Seattle, WA	H	19.27 LO		20.80 HI	CSSS	2007
Speaker of the Assembly							
State Government	California	Y		133639 AW		CWCA	2008
Speaker of the House of Representatives							
Federal Government	United States	Y			217400 HI	OPM01	1/1/08
State Government	Washington	Y			50106 HI	WCC	9/1/08
Speaker of the Senate							
State Government	California	Y		133639 AW		CWCA	2008
Special Agent							
Federal Bureau of Investigation	United States	Y	61100-69900 LO			FBI	2009
U.S. Drug Enforcement Agency	United States	Y	49746-55483 LR		92592 HI	DEA	2008
Special Assistant and Personal Aide to the First Lady							
White House Staff	United States	Y			62700 HI	WPOST02	2008
Special Education Teacher							
Middle School	Alabama	Y	38330 FQ	43500 MW	47860 TQ	USBLS	5/07
Middle School	Birmingham-Hoover MSA, AL	Y	38290 FQ	43730 MW	48040 TQ	USBLS	5/07
Middle School	Alaska	Y	49820 FQ	58460 MW	66650 TQ	USBLS	5/07
Middle School	Arizona	Y	32480 FQ	37890 MW	46210 TQ	USBLS	5/07
Middle School	Phoenix-Mesa-Scottsdale MSA, AZ	Y	34260 FQ	39780 MW	47650 TQ	USBLS	5/07
Middle School	Tucson MSA, AZ	Y	30640 FQ	36120 MW	45750 TQ	USBLS	5/07

Occupation/Type/Industry	Location	Per	Low	Mid	High	Source	Date
Special Education Teacher							
Middle School	Arkansas	Y	37100 FQ	43170 MW	49590 TQ	USBLS	5/07
Middle School	Fort Smith MSA, AR-OK	Y	35360 FQ	39080 MW	43730 TQ	USBLS	5/07
Middle School	Little Rock-North Little Rock MSA, AR	Y	40590 FQ	48470 MW	57730 TQ	USBLS	5/07
Middle School	California	Y		61672 AW		CABLS	1/08-3/08
Middle School	Los Angeles-Long Beach-Glendale PMSA, CA	Y		60041 AW		CABLS	1/08-3/08
Middle School	Oakland-Fremont-Hayward MSA, CA	Y		57837 AW		CABLS	1/08-3/08
Middle School	Riverside-San Bernardino-Ontario MSA, CA	Y		60841 AW		CABLS	1/08-3/08
Middle School	Sacramento-Arden Arcade-Roseville MSA, CA	Y		60851 MW		CABLS	1/08-3/08
Middle School	San Diego-Carlsbad-San Marcos MSA, CA	Y		67753 AW		CABLS	1/08-3/08
Middle School	San Francisco-San Mateo-Redwood PMSA, CA	Y		63559 AW		CABLS	1/08-3/08
Middle School	San Jose-Sunnyvale-Santa Clara MSA, CA	Y		54237 AW		CABLS	1/08-3/08
Middle School	Santa Ana-Anaheim-Irvine PMSA, CA	Y	53200 FQ	64370 MW	78180 TQ	USBLS	5/07
Middle School	Colorado	Y	38570 FQ	47050 MW	57980 TQ	USBLS	5/07
Middle School	Denver-Aurora MSA, CO	Y	40140 FQ	50760 MW	62090 TQ	USBLS	5/07
Middle School	Bridgeport-Stamford-Norwalk MSA, CT	Y	53980 FQ	68440 MW	83650 TQ	USBLS	5/07
Middle School	Hartford-West Hartford-East Hartford MSA, CT	Y	52890 FQ	67400 MW	77740 TQ	USBLS	5/07
Middle School	Delaware	Y	43210 FQ	51660 MW	65360 TQ	USBLS	5/07
Middle School	Wilmington PMSA, DE-MD-NJ	Y	45240 FQ	55700 MW	73380 TQ	USBLS	5/07
Middle School	District of Columbia	Y	45980 FQ	54480 MW	71460 TQ	USBLS	5/07
Middle School	Washington-Arlington-Alexandria MSA, DC-VA-MD-WV	Y	43150 FQ	55680 MW	76910 TQ	USBLS	5/07
Middle School	Florida	Y	39400 FQ	48520 MW	60180 TQ	USBLS	5/07
Middle School	Miami-Fort Lauderdale-Miami Beach MSA, FL	Y	42670 FQ	51660 MW	63600 TQ	USBLS	5/07
Middle School	Orlando-Kissimmee MSA, FL	Y	37840 FQ	44640 MW	54420 TQ	USBLS	5/07
Middle School	Tampa-St. Petersburg-Clearwater MSA, FL	Y	44120 FQ	51080 MW	61110 TQ	USBLS	5/07
Middle School	Georgia	Y	40790 FQ	49380 MW	58850 TQ	USBLS	5/07
Middle School	Atlanta-Sandy Springs-Marietta MSA, GA	Y	40670 FQ	49810 MW	59910 TQ	USBLS	5/07
Middle School	Hawaii	Y	38950 FQ	45960 MW	51250 TQ	USBLS	5/07
Middle School	Illinois	Y	40730 FQ	52490 MW	67480 TQ	USBLS	5/07
Middle School	Chicago-Naperville-Joliet MSA, IL-IN-WI	Y	46110 FQ	58790 MW	73420 TQ	USBLS	5/07
Middle School	Indiana	Y	38560 FQ	47840 MW	59240 TQ	USBLS	5/07
Middle School	Fort Wayne MSA, IN	Y	37620 FQ	44990 MW	56330 TQ	USBLS	5/07
Middle School	Gary PMSA, IN	Y	39920 FQ	49840 MW	59300 TQ	USBLS	5/07
Middle School	Indianapolis-Carmel MSA, IN	Y	39580 FQ	51970 MW	63860 TQ	USBLS	5/07
Middle School	Terre Haute MSA, IN	Y	37490 FQ	51600 MW	62600 TQ	USBLS	5/07
Middle School	Iowa	Y	33100 FQ	40650 MW	50300 TQ	USBLS	5/07
Middle School	Davenport-Moline-Rock Island MSA, IA-IL	Y	33510 FQ	44460 MW	54520 TQ	USBLS	5/07
Middle School	Des Moines-West Des Moines MSA, IA	Y	34630 FQ	40850 MW	52910 TQ	USBLS	5/07
Middle School	Sioux City MSA, IA-NE-SD	Y	33520 FQ	40640 MW	49680 TQ	USBLS	5/07
Middle School	Kansas	Y	32770 FQ	38010 MW	45180 TQ	USBLS	5/07
Middle School	Wichita MSA, KS	Y	34490 FQ	40770 MW	47600 TQ	USBLS	5/07
Middle School	Kentucky	Y	37065 FQ	44083 MW	52184 TQ	KYBLS	2008
Middle School	Louisville-Jefferson County MSA, KY-IN	Y	39380 FQ	46490 MW	55620 TQ	USBLS	5/07
Middle School	Louisiana	Y		42613 AW		LABLS	1/08-3/08
Middle School	Baton Rouge MSA, LA	Y	48450 FQ	59020 MW	68800 TQ	USBLS	5/07
Middle School	Maine	Y	33960 FQ	42120 MW	50770 TQ	USBLS	5/07
Middle School	Portland-South Portland-Biddeford MSA, ME	Y	35600 FQ	44790 MW	52650 TQ	USBLS	5/07
Middle School	Maryland	Y		57500 MW		MDBLS	3/08
Middle School	Baltimore-Towson MSA, MD	Y	43720 FQ	53360 MW	64640 TQ	USBLS	5/07

AE	Average entry wage	AW	Average wage paid	FQ	First quartile wage
AER	Average entry range	AWR	Average wage range	H	Hourly
AEX	Average experienced wage	AXR	Average experienced range	HI	Highest wage paid
ATC	Average total compensation	D	Daily	HR	High end range

LO	Lowest wage paid	MTC	Median total compensation	TCC	Total cash compensation
LR	Low end range	MW	Median wage paid	TQ	Third quartile wage
M	Monthly	MWR	Median wage range	W	Weekly
MCC	Median cash compensation	S	See annotated source	Y	Yearly

Occupation/Type/Industry	Location	Per	Low	Mid	High	Source	Date
Special Education Teacher							
Middle School	Bethesda-Gaithersburg-Frederick PMSA, MD	Y	66330 FQ	82770 MW	93520 TQ	USBLS	5/07
Middle School	Cumberland MSA, MD-WV	Y	31910 FQ	41470 MW	54380 TQ	USBLS	5/07
Middle School	Massachusetts	Y	44790 FQ	55220 MW	65240 TQ	USBLS	5/07
Middle School	Boston-Cambridge-Quincy NECTA, MA	Y	45710 FQ	57830 MW	70290 TQ	USBLS	5/07
Middle School	New Bedford MSA, MA	Y	45730 FQ	58290 MW	67830 TQ	USBLS	5/07
Middle School	Worcester MSA, MA-CT	Y	44850 FQ	53600 MW	62230 TQ	USBLS	5/07
Middle School	Michigan	Y	41020 FQ	51730 MW	64920 TQ	USBLS	5/07
Middle School	Detroit-Warren-Livonia MSA, MI	Y	42070 FQ	52600 MW	70400 TQ	USBLS	5/07
Middle School	Grand Rapids-Wyoming MSA, MI	Y	37130 FQ	46570 MW	63230 TQ	USBLS	5/07
Middle School	Warren-Troy-Farmington Hills PMSA, MI	Y	42330 FQ	57410 MW	71380 TQ	USBLS	5/07
Middle School	Minnesota	Y	41482 FQ	50658 MW	62114 TQ	MNBLS	10/08-12/08
Middle School	Duluth-Superior MSA, MN-WI	Y	43732 FQ	51683 MW	61005 TQ	MNBLS	10/08-12/08
Middle School	Minneapolis-Saint Paul MSA, MN-WI	Y	42895 FQ	53043 MW	65075 TQ	MNBLS	10/08-12/08
Middle School	Rochester MSA, MN	Y	41124 FQ	50867 MW	62744 TQ	MNBLS	10/08-12/08
Middle School	Mississippi	Y	36200 FQ	42190 MW	48950 TQ	USBLS	5/07
Middle School	Jackson MSA, MS	Y	35660 FQ	39700 MW	49100 TQ	USBLS	5/07
Middle School	Missouri	Y	33960 FQ	41330 MW	51290 TQ	USBLS	5/07
Middle School	Joplin MSA, MO	Y	30950 FQ	35130 MW	40170 TQ	USBLS	5/07
Middle School	Kansas City MSA, MO-KS	Y	37480 FQ	44560 MW	53670 TQ	USBLS	5/07
Middle School	St. Louis MSA, MO-IL	Y	34860 FQ	42620 MW	54730 TQ	USBLS	5/07
Middle School	Springfield MSA, MO	Y	29840 FQ	35670 MW	42680 TQ	USBLS	5/07
Middle School	Montana	Y	31350 FQ	39910 MW	49510 TQ	USBLS	5/07
Middle School	Billings MSA, MT	Y	31890 FQ	40500 MW	50730 TQ	USBLS	5/07
Middle School	Nebraska	Y	36440 FQ	42530 MW	50130 TQ	USBLS	5/07
Middle School	Omaha-Council Bluffs MSA, NE-IA	Y	35710 FQ	41610 MW	49150 TQ	USBLS	5/07
Middle School	Nevada	Y	36184 FQ	43961 MW	52206 TQ	NVBLS	5/08
Middle School	New Hampshire	Y	36779 AE	51082 MW	58145 AEX	NHBLS	6/08
Middle School	Manchester MSA, NH	Y	35650 FQ	43030 MW	54760 TQ	USBLS	5/07
Middle School	Nashua NECTA, NH-MA	Y	44650 FQ	52840 MW	60420 TQ	USBLS	5/07
Middle School	New Jersey	Y	45530 FQ	53610 MW	67940 TQ	USBLS	5/07
Middle School	Atlantic City MSA, NJ	Y	44290 FQ	50010 MW	63210 TQ	USBLS	5/07
Middle School	Camden PMSA, NJ	Y	45420 FQ	52450 MW	68470 TQ	USBLS	5/07
Middle School	Edison PMSA, NJ	Y	45330 FQ	53370 MW	67650 TQ	USBLS	5/07
Middle School	Newark-Union PMSA, NJ-PA	Y	45800 FQ	53730 MW	65940 TQ	USBLS	5/07
Middle School	New Mexico	Y	35190 FQ	42730 MW	51120 TQ	USBLS	5/07
Middle School	Albuquerque MSA, NM	Y	35350 FQ	40740 MW	46970 TQ	USBLS	5/07
Middle School	New York	Y	48430 FQ	59210 MW	74590 TQ	USBLS	5/07
Middle School	Albany-Schenectady-Troy MSA, NY	Y	45590 FQ	56580 MW	72600 TQ	USBLS	5/07
Middle School	Buffalo-Niagara Falls MSA, NY	Y	42810 FQ	53160 MW	71520 TQ	USBLS	5/07
Middle School	Nassau-Suffolk PMSA, NY	Y	59940 FQ	74580 MW	91730 TQ	USBLS	5/07
Middle School	New York-Northern New Jersey-Long Island MSA, NY-NJ-PA	Y	48590 FQ	58980 MW	74630 TQ	USBLS	5/07
Middle School	North Carolina	Y	31950 FQ	38880 MW	47810 TQ	USBLS	5/07
Middle School	Charlotte-Gastonia-Concord MSA, NC-SC	Y	29200 FQ	36390 MW	46520 TQ	USBLS	5/07
Middle School	Raleigh-Cary MSA, NC	Y	38240 FQ	49660 MW	59080 TQ	USBLS	5/07
Middle School	Ohio	Y	42460 FQ	52610 MW	63370 TQ	USBLS	5/07
Middle School	Cincinnati-Middletown MSA, OH-KY-IN	Y	40410 FQ	51320 MW	63460 TQ	USBLS	5/07
Middle School	Cleveland-Elyria-Mentor MSA, OH	Y	48840 FQ	61810 MW	74400 TQ	USBLS	5/07
Middle School	Columbus MSA, OH	Y	42310 FQ	52920 MW	63260 TQ	USBLS	5/07
Middle School	Dayton MSA, OH	Y	42460 FQ	52220 MW	59880 TQ	USBLS	5/07
Middle School	Mansfield MSA, OH	Y	35990 FQ	43320 MW	49030 TQ	USBLS	5/07
Middle School	Oklahoma	Y	34200 FQ	38200 MW	44000 TQ	USBLS	5/07
Middle School	Oklahoma City MSA, OK	Y	34200 FQ	38060 MW	42810 TQ	USBLS	5/07
Middle School	Tulsa MSA, OK	Y	35810 FQ	41380 MW	50160 TQ	USBLS	5/07
Middle School	Oregon	Y	42848 FQ	50705 MW	60325 TQ	ORBLS	5/08
Middle School	Eugene-Springfield MSA, OR	Y	38690 FQ	44990 MW	55790 TQ	USBLS	5/07
Middle School	Portland-Vancouver-Beaverton MSA, OR-WA	Y	44180 FQ	52270 MW	59980 TQ	USBLS	5/07

AE	Average entry wage	AW	Average wage paid	LO	Lowest wage paid	MTC	Median total compensation	TCC	Total cash compensation
AER	Average entry range	AWR	Average wage range	LR	Low end range	MW	Median wage paid	TQ	Third quartile wage
AEX	Average experienced wage	AXR	Average experienced range	HI	Highest wage paid	MWR	Median wage range	W	Weekly
ATC	Average total compensation	D	Daily	HR	High end range	MCC	Median cash compensation	S	See annotated source	Y	Yearly

Occupation/Type/Industry	Location	Per	Low	Mid	High	Source	Date
Special Education Teacher							
Middle School	Pennsylvania	Y	41810 FQ	50420 MW	64320 TQ	USBLS	5/07
Middle School	Allentown-Bethlehem-Easton MSA, PA-NJ	Y	44060 FQ	50910 MW	64740 TQ	USBLS	5/07
Middle School	Philadelphia-Camden-Wilmington MSA, PA-NJ-DE-MD	Y	43510 FQ	52070 MW	68770 TQ	USBLS	5/07
Middle School	Pittsburgh MSA, PA	Y	41670 FQ	48980 MW	63480 TQ	USBLS	5/07
Middle School	Rhode Island	Y	49460 FQ	61420 MW	72980 TQ	USBLS	5/07
Middle School	Providence-Fall River-Warwick MSA, RI-MA	Y	49230 FQ	60920 MW	72670 TQ	USBLS	5/07
Middle School	South Carolina	Y	36820 FQ	43920 MW	51830 TQ	USBLS	5/07
Middle School	Charleston-North Charleston MSA, SC	Y	36940 FQ	44100 MW	52990 TQ	USBLS	5/07
Middle School	Columbia MSA, SC	Y	36080 FQ	41880 MW	51330 TQ	USBLS	5/07
Middle School	South Dakota	Y	31087 FQ	36183 MW	42005 TQ	SDBLS	7/08-9/08
Middle School	Tennessee	Y	35300 FQ	40700 MW	46540 TQ	USBLS	5/07
Middle School	Kingsport-Bristol-Bristol MSA, TN-VA	Y	35810 FQ	39230 MW	43290 TQ	USBLS	5/07
Middle School	Knoxville MSA, TN	Y	36790 FQ	43120 MW	50900 TQ	USBLS	5/07
Middle School	Memphis MSA, TN-MS-AR	Y	34340 FQ	39580 MW	45030 TQ	USBLS	5/07
Middle School	Nashville-Davidson-Murfreesboro MSA, TN	Y	35520 FQ	40390 MW	46650 TQ	USBLS	5/07
Middle School	Texas	Y	38950 FQ	44600 MW	50140 TQ	USBLS	5/07
Middle School	Austin-Round Rock MSA, TX	Y	38230 FQ	43210 MW	49550 TQ	USBLS	5/07
Middle School	Dallas-Fort Worth-Arlington MSA, TX	Y	42510 FQ	46820 MW	51340 TQ	USBLS	5/07
Middle School	El Paso MSA, TX	Y	36400 FQ	41650 MW	47070 TQ	USBLS	5/07
Middle School	Houston-Sugar Land-Baytown MSA, TX	Y	40300 FQ	45280 MW	51000 TQ	USBLS	5/07
Middle School	San Antonio MSA, TX	Y	41250 FQ	46250 MW	51460 TQ	USBLS	5/07
Middle School	Utah	Y	31590 FQ	40970 MW	48890 TQ	USBLS	5/07
Middle School	Salt Lake City MSA, UT	Y	30050 FQ	46320 MW	59730 TQ	USBLS	5/07
Middle School	Vermont	Y	40710 FQ	48170 MW	58230 TQ	USBLS	5/07
Middle School	Burlington-South Burlington MSA, VT	Y	43510 FQ	50670 MW	59720 TQ	USBLS	5/07
Middle School	Virginia	Y	38710 FQ	47110 MW	59160 TQ	USBLS	5/07
Middle School	Lynchburg MSA, VA	Y	34500 FQ	38100 MW	44240 TQ	USBLS	5/07
Middle School	Richmond MSA, VA	Y	40740 FQ	49370 MW	57970 TQ	USBLS	5/07
Middle School	Virginia Beach-Norfolk-Newport News MSA, VA-NC	Y	37500 FQ	43830 MW	49760 TQ	USBLS	5/07
Middle School	Washington	Y		52133 AW		WABLS	3/08
Middle School	Olympia MSA, WA	Y	46480 FQ	54480 MW	60930 TQ	USBLS	5/07
Middle School	Seattle-Tacoma-Bellevue MSA, WA	Y	42150 FQ	50630 MW	61090 TQ	USBLS	5/07
Middle School	West Virginia	Y	32730 FQ	38244 MW	44633 TQ	WVBLS	7/08-9/08
Middle School	Charleston MSA, WV	Y	35370 FQ	41260 MW	46710 TQ	USBLS	5/07
Middle School	Wheeling MSA, WV-OH	Y	35670 FQ	42450 MW	48990 TQ	USBLS	5/07
Middle School	Wisconsin	Y	37260 FQ	45220 MW	54490 TQ	USBLS	5/07
Middle School	Appleton MSA, WI	Y	36060 FQ	43650 MW	53190 TQ	USBLS	5/07
Middle School	Milwaukee-Waukesha-West Allis MSA, WI	Y	40310 FQ	47850 MW	58540 TQ	USBLS	5/07
Middle School	Wyoming	Y	43042 FQ	50730 MW	59968 TQ	WYBLS	9/08
Preschool, Kindergarten, and Elementary	Alabama	Y	37530 FQ	42990 MW	47920 TQ	USBLS	5/07
Preschool, Kindergarten, and Elementary	Birmingham-Hoover MSA, AL	Y	37990 FQ	43090 MW	47660 TQ	USBLS	5/07
Preschool, Kindergarten, and Elementary	Alaska	Y	49210 FQ	59080 MW	70020 TQ	USBLS	5/07
Preschool, Kindergarten, and Elementary	Arizona	Y	31110 FQ	37490 MW	45490 TQ	USBLS	5/07
Preschool, Kindergarten, and Elementary	Flagstaff MSA, AZ*	Y	22630 FQ	26620 MW	33110 TQ	USBLS	5/07
Preschool, Kindergarten, and Elementary	Phoenix-Mesa-Scottsdale MSA, AZ	Y	33300 FQ	38870 MW	47260 TQ	USBLS	5/07
Preschool, Kindergarten, and Elementary	Tucson MSA, AZ	Y	31510 FQ	36610 MW	44910 TQ	USBLS	5/07
Preschool, Kindergarten, and Elementary	Arkansas	Y	34500 FQ	41060 MW	47780 TQ	USBLS	5/07
Preschool, Kindergarten, and Elementary	Little Rock-North Little Rock MSA, AR	Y	36530 FQ	43360 MW	52070 TQ	USBLS	5/07
Preschool, Kindergarten, and Elementary	California	Y		61210 AW		CABLS	1/08-3/08
Preschool, Kindergarten, and Elementary	Los Angeles-Long Beach-Glendale PMSA, CA	Y		59570 AW		CABLS	1/08-3/08
Preschool, Kindergarten, and Elementary	Oakland-Fremont-Hayward MSA, CA	Y		56985 AW		CABLS	1/08-3/08
Preschool, Kindergarten, and Elementary	Riverside-San Bernardino-Ontario MSA, CA	Y		64174 AW		CABLS	1/08-3/08

AE	Average entry wage	AW	Average wage paid	FQ	First quartile wage	LO	Lowest wage paid	MTC	Median total compensation	TCC	Total cash compensation
AER	Average entry range	AWR	Average wage range	H	Hourly	LR	Low end range	MW	Median wage paid	TQ	Third quartile wage
AEX	Average experienced wage	AXR	Average experienced range	HI	Highest wage paid	M	Monthly	MWR	Median wage range	W	Weekly
ATC	Average total compensation	D	Daily	HR	High end range	MCC	Median cash compensation	S	See annotated source	Y	Yearly

Special Education Teacher

Occupation/Type/Industry	Location	Per	Low	Mid	High	Source	Date
Preschool, Kindergarten, and Elementary	Sacramento-Arden Arcade-Roseville MSA, CA	Y		56083 MW		CABLS	1/08-3/08
Preschool, Kindergarten, and Elementary	San Diego-Carlsbad-San Marcos MSA, CA	Y		69476 AW		CABLS	1/08-3/08
Preschool, Kindergarten, and Elementary	San Francisco-San Mateo-Redwood PMSA, CA	Y		61231 AW		CABLS	1/08-3/08
Preschool, Kindergarten, and Elementary	San Jose-Sunnyvale-Santa Clara MSA, CA	Y		64830 AW		CABLS	1/08-3/08
Preschool, Kindergarten, and Elementary	Santa Ana-Anaheim-Irvine PMSA, CA	Y	50050 FQ	63010 MW	83250 TQ	USBLS	5/07
Preschool, Kindergarten, and Elementary	Santa Rosa-Petaluma MSA, CA	Y		54053 AW		CABLS	1/08-3/08
Preschool, Kindergarten, and Elementary	Colorado	Y	38400 FQ	47370 MW	59130 TQ	USBLS	5/07
Preschool, Kindergarten, and Elementary	Boulder MSA, CO	Y	39720 FQ	51890 MW	63340 TQ	USBLS	5/07
Preschool, Kindergarten, and Elementary	Denver-Aurora MSA, CO	Y	41560 FQ	52900 MW	64750 TQ	USBLS	5/07
Preschool, Kindergarten, and Elementary	Fort Collins-Loveland MSA, CO	Y	37540 FQ	45390 MW	52530 TQ	USBLS	5/07
Preschool, Kindergarten, and Elementary	Bridgeport-Stamford-Norwalk MSA, CT	Y	51040 FQ	60570 MW	73890 TQ	USBLS	5/07
Preschool, Kindergarten, and Elementary	Hartford-West Hartford-East Hartford MSA, CT	Y	46130 FQ	62600 MW	74060 TQ	USBLS	5/07
Preschool, Kindergarten, and Elementary	Delaware	Y	37870 FQ	47760 MW	63740 TQ	USBLS	5/07
Preschool, Kindergarten, and Elementary	District of Columbia	Y	42350 FQ	48200 MW	54930 TQ	USBLS	5/07
Preschool, Kindergarten, and Elementary	Washington-Arlington-Alexandria MSA, DC-VA-MD-WV	Y	45280 FQ	58250 MW	79110 TQ	USBLS	5/07
Preschool, Kindergarten, and Elementary	Florida	Y	40990 FQ	49670 MW	61620 TQ	USBLS	5/07
Preschool, Kindergarten, and Elementary	Miami-Fort Lauderdale-Miami Beach MSA, FL	Y	41640 FQ	49440 MW	63360 TQ	USBLS	5/07
Preschool, Kindergarten, and Elementary	Orlando-Kissimmee MSA, FL	Y	37950 FQ	44970 MW	54230 TQ	USBLS	5/07
Preschool, Kindergarten, and Elementary	Tampa-St. Petersburg-Clearwater MSA, FL	Y	45660 FQ	52920 MW	63660 TQ	USBLS	5/07
Preschool, Kindergarten, and Elementary	Georgia	Y	40970 FQ	48570 MW	58030 TQ	USBLS	5/07
Preschool, Kindergarten, and Elementary	Atlanta-Sandy Springs-Marietta MSA, GA	Y	41280 FQ	48990 MW	58500 TQ	USBLS	5/07
Preschool, Kindergarten, and Elementary	Hawaii	Y	35730 FQ	45050 MW	50640 TQ	USBLS	5/07
Preschool, Kindergarten, and Elementary	Idaho	Y	28610 FQ	34350 MW	41430 TQ	USBLS	5/07
Preschool, Kindergarten, and Elementary	Illinois	Y	38510 FQ	51330 MW	67700 TQ	USBLS	5/07
Preschool, Kindergarten, and Elementary	Chicago-Naperville-Joliet MSA, IL-IN-WI	Y	41410 FQ	55170 MW	71330 TQ	USBLS	5/07
Preschool, Kindergarten, and Elementary	Indiana	Y	36940 FQ	47160 MW	58470 TQ	USBLS	5/07
Preschool, Kindergarten, and Elementary	Gary PMSA, IN	Y	38290 FQ	49110 MW	59480 TQ	USBLS	5/07
Preschool, Kindergarten, and Elementary	Indianapolis-Carmel MSA, IN	Y	35640 FQ	45360 MW	59880 TQ	USBLS	5/07
Preschool, Kindergarten, and Elementary	South Bend-Mishawaka MSA, IN-MI	Y	36220 FQ	44730 MW	55850 TQ	USBLS	5/07
Preschool, Kindergarten, and Elementary	Iowa	Y	33110 FQ	42280 MW	53380 TQ	USBLS	5/07
Preschool, Kindergarten, and Elementary	Des Moines-West Des Moines MSA, IA	Y	34440 FQ	39430 MW	47670 TQ	USBLS	5/07
Preschool, Kindergarten, and Elementary	Iowa City MSA, IA	Y	22520 FQ	25280 MW	40570 TQ	USBLS	5/07
Preschool, Kindergarten, and Elementary	Kansas	Y	34550 FQ	40270 MW	47650 TQ	USBLS	5/07
Preschool, Kindergarten, and Elementary	Wichita MSA, KS	Y	37320 FQ	43740 MW	50960 TQ	USBLS	5/07
Preschool, Kindergarten, and Elementary	Kentucky	Y	37698 FQ	44911 MW	52238 TQ	KYBLS	2008
Preschool, Kindergarten, and Elementary	Louisville-Jefferson County MSA, KY-IN	Y	40310 FQ	47640 MW	57730 TQ	USBLS	5/07
Preschool, Kindergarten, and Elementary	Louisiana	Y		38550 AW		LABLS	1/08-3/08
Preschool, Kindergarten, and Elementary	Baton Rouge MSA, LA	Y	34280 FQ	39750 MW	48020 TQ	USBLS	5/07
Preschool, Kindergarten, and Elementary	Lafayette MSA, LA	Y	31790 FQ	36630 MW	42930 TQ	USBLS	5/07
Preschool, Kindergarten, and Elementary	New Orleans-Metairie-Kenner MSA, LA	Y	35650 FQ	40650 MW	45590 TQ	USBLS	5/07
Preschool, Kindergarten, and Elementary	Maine	Y	34670 FQ	43490 MW	51730 TQ	USBLS	5/07
Preschool, Kindergarten, and Elementary	Bangor MSA, ME	Y	33850 FQ	42790 MW	51140 TQ	USBLS	5/07
Preschool, Kindergarten, and Elementary	Portland-South Portland-Biddeford MSA, ME	Y	39500 FQ	47010 MW	53920 TQ	USBLS	5/07
Preschool, Kindergarten, and Elementary	Maryland	Y		56125 MW		MDBLS	3/08
Preschool, Kindergarten, and Elementary	Baltimore-Towson MSA, MD	Y	44680 FQ	54340 MW	64050 TQ	USBLS	5/07
Preschool, Kindergarten, and Elementary	Massachusetts	Y	42510 FQ	53560 MW	63930 TQ	USBLS	5/07
Preschool, Kindergarten, and Elementary	Boston-Cambridge-Quincy NECTA, MA	Y	42340 FQ	54720 MW	67450 TQ	USBLS	5/07
Preschool, Kindergarten, and Elementary	Worcester MSA, MA-CT	Y	41820 FQ	52440 MW	61310 TQ	USBLS	5/07
Preschool, Kindergarten, and Elementary	Michigan	Y	41430 FQ	51340 MW	66400 TQ	USBLS	5/07
Preschool, Kindergarten, and Elementary	Detroit-Warren-Livonia MSA, MI	Y	42320 FQ	50860 MW	72570 TQ	USBLS	5/07

AE	Average entry wage	AW	Average wage paid	FQ	First quartile wage	LO	Lowest wage paid	MTC	Median total compensation	TCC	Total cash compensation
AER	Average entry range	AWR	Average wage range	H	Hourly	LR	Low end range	MW	Median wage paid	TQ	Third quartile wage
AEX	Average experienced wage	AXR	Average experienced range	HI	Highest wage paid	M	Monthly	MWR	Median wage range	W	Weekly
ATC	Average total compensation	D	Daily	HR	High end range	MCC	Median cash compensation	S	See annotated source	Y	Yearly

Occupation/Type/Industry	Location	Per	Low	Mid	High	Source	Date
Special Education Teacher							
Preschool, Kindergarten, and Elementary	Grand Rapids-Wyoming MSA, MI	Y	39520 FQ	52090 MW	60860 TQ	USBLS	5/07
Preschool, Kindergarten, and Elementary	Warren-Troy-Farmington Hills PMSA, MI	Y	46490 FQ	60150 MW	77770 TQ	USBLS	5/07
Preschool, Kindergarten, and Elementary	Minnesota	Y	42236 FQ	52426 MW	63485 TQ	MNBLS	10/08-12/08
Preschool, Kindergarten, and Elementary	Duluth-Superior MSA, MN-WI	Y	39474 FQ	51537 MW	61716 TQ	MNBLS	10/08-12/08
Preschool, Kindergarten, and Elementary	Minneapolis-Saint Paul MSA, MN-WI	Y	42895 FQ	54403 MW	66383 TQ	MNBLS	10/08-12/08
Preschool, Kindergarten, and Elementary	Rochester MSA, MN	Y	43550 FQ	50262 MW	59112 TQ	MNBLS	10/08-12/08
Preschool, Kindergarten, and Elementary	Mississippi	Y	35880 FQ	41420 MW	48650 TQ	USBLS	5/07
Preschool, Kindergarten, and Elementary	Jackson MSA, MS	Y	36870 FQ	42930 MW	51890 TQ	USBLS	5/07
Preschool, Kindergarten, and Elementary	Missouri	Y	34220 FQ	40970 MW	51950 TQ	USBLS	5/07
Preschool, Kindergarten, and Elementary	Jefferson City MSA, MO	Y	30240 FQ	34580 MW	41130 TQ	USBLS	5/07
Preschool, Kindergarten, and Elementary	Kansas City MSA, MO-KS	Y	36680 FQ	44540 MW	54010 TQ	USBLS	5/07
Preschool, Kindergarten, and Elementary	St. Louis MSA, MO-IL	Y	39200 FQ	48540 MW	60010 TQ	USBLS	5/07
Preschool, Kindergarten, and Elementary	Montana	Y	28730 FQ	35400 MW	46440 TQ	USBLS	5/07
Preschool, Kindergarten, and Elementary	Billings MSA, MT	Y	31870 FQ	39710 MW	53110 TQ	USBLS	5/07
Preschool, Kindergarten, and Elementary	Missoula MSA, MT	Y	25510 FQ	27520 MW	29470 TQ	USBLS	5/07
Preschool, Kindergarten, and Elementary	Nebraska	Y	34760 FQ	40380 MW	48050 TQ	USBLS	5/07
Preschool, Kindergarten, and Elementary	Omaha-Council Bluffs MSA, NE-IA	Y	38380 FQ	50490 MW	58920 TQ	USBLS	5/07
Preschool, Kindergarten, and Elementary	Nevada	Y	38116 FQ	45969 MW	55294 TQ	NVBLS	5/08
Preschool, Kindergarten, and Elementary	Las Vegas-Paradise MSA, NV	Y	38549 FQ	46193 MW	55846 TQ	NVBLS	5/08
Preschool, Kindergarten, and Elementary	New Hampshire	Y	35063 AE	47804 MW	55101 AEX	NHBLS	6/08
Preschool, Kindergarten, and Elementary	Manchester MSA, NH	Y	36230 FQ	44000 MW	55410 TQ	USBLS	5/07
Preschool, Kindergarten, and Elementary	Nashua NECTA, NH-MA	Y	37200 FQ	46120 MW	54980 TQ	USBLS	5/07
Preschool, Kindergarten, and Elementary	New Jersey	Y	44860 FQ	52510 MW	68370 TQ	USBLS	5/07
Preschool, Kindergarten, and Elementary	Camden PMSA, NJ	Y	45420 FQ	53100 MW	67240 TQ	USBLS	5/07
Preschool, Kindergarten, and Elementary	Edison PMSA, NJ	Y	44560 FQ	51240 MW	66110 TQ	USBLS	5/07
Preschool, Kindergarten, and Elementary	Newark-Union PMSA, NJ-PA	Y	45690 FQ	54410 MW	71210 TQ	USBLS	5/07
Preschool, Kindergarten, and Elementary	Vineland-Millville-Bridgeton MSA, NJ	Y	43450 FQ	48690 MW	66280 TQ	USBLS	5/07
Preschool, Kindergarten, and Elementary	New Mexico	Y	33880 FQ	40860 MW	48930 TQ	USBLS	5/07
Preschool, Kindergarten, and Elementary	Albuquerque MSA, NM	Y	34810 FQ	40410 MW	46030 TQ	USBLS	5/07
Preschool, Kindergarten, and Elementary	New York	Y	45960 FQ	60720 MW	77910 TQ	USBLS	5/07
Preschool, Kindergarten, and Elementary	Albany-Schenectady-Troy MSA, NY	Y	36170 FQ	45700 MW	61170 TQ	USBLS	5/07
Preschool, Kindergarten, and Elementary	Buffalo-Niagara Falls MSA, NY	Y	41610 FQ	53680 MW	72530 TQ	USBLS	5/07
Preschool, Kindergarten, and Elementary	Nassau-Suffolk PMSA, NY	Y	58920 FQ	74710 MW	94260 TQ	USBLS	5/07
Preschool, Kindergarten, and Elementary	New York-Northern New Jersey-Long Island MSA, NY-NJ-PA	Y	47860 FQ	63260 MW	80850 TQ	USBLS	5/07
Preschool, Kindergarten, and Elementary	North Carolina	Y	33200 FQ	39980 MW	47770 TQ	USBLS	5/07
Preschool, Kindergarten, and Elementary	Charlotte-Gastonia-Concord MSA, NC-SC	Y	32700 FQ	40860 MW	49010 TQ	USBLS	5/07
Preschool, Kindergarten, and Elementary	Durham MSA, NC	Y	36120 FQ	42860 MW	50540 TQ	USBLS	5/07
Preschool, Kindergarten, and Elementary	Raleigh-Cary MSA, NC	Y	36500 FQ	42480 MW	50300 TQ	USBLS	5/07
Preschool, Kindergarten, and Elementary	North Dakota	Y	36800 FQ	44470 MW	54240 TQ	USBLS	5/07
Preschool, Kindergarten, and Elementary	Fargo MSA, ND-MN	Y	43810 FQ	53450 MW	61530 TQ	USBLS	5/07
Preschool, Kindergarten, and Elementary	Ohio	Y	39470 FQ	50260 MW	61740 TQ	USBLS	5/07
Preschool, Kindergarten, and Elementary	Cincinnati-Middletown MSA, OH-KY-IN	Y	39250 FQ	50100 MW	64000 TQ	USBLS	5/07
Preschool, Kindergarten, and Elementary	Cleveland-Elyria-Mentor MSA, OH	Y	47120 FQ	59860 MW	72080 TQ	USBLS	5/07
Preschool, Kindergarten, and Elementary	Columbus MSA, OH	Y	39630 FQ	50180 MW	63150 TQ	USBLS	5/07
Preschool, Kindergarten, and Elementary	Dayton MSA, OH	Y	42240 FQ	50730 MW	60060 TQ	USBLS	5/07
Preschool, Kindergarten, and Elementary	Oklahoma	Y	34210 FQ	38170 MW	43410 TQ	USBLS	5/07
Preschool, Kindergarten, and Elementary	Oklahoma City MSA, OK	Y	33840 FQ	37680 MW	42200 TQ	USBLS	5/07
Preschool, Kindergarten, and Elementary	Tulsa MSA, OK	Y	35000 FQ	39550 MW	46040 TQ	USBLS	5/07
Preschool, Kindergarten, and Elementary	Oregon	Y	43278 FQ	52217 MW	62596 TQ	ORBLS	5/08
Preschool, Kindergarten, and Elementary	Portland-Vancouver-Beaverton MSA, OR-WA	Y	42440 FQ	49900 MW	61390 TQ	USBLS	5/07
Preschool, Kindergarten, and Elementary	Salem MSA, OR	Y	44220 FQ	51720 MW	59850 TQ	USBLS	5/07
Preschool, Kindergarten, and Elementary	Pennsylvania	Y	42480 FQ	52680 MW	66480 TQ	USBLS	5/07
Preschool, Kindergarten, and Elementary	Allentown-Bethlehem-Easton MSA, PA-NJ	Y	41620 FQ	50450 MW	63570 TQ	USBLS	5/07
Preschool, Kindergarten, and Elementary	Pittsburgh MSA, PA	Y	43590 FQ	51990 MW	67430 TQ	USBLS	5/07
Preschool, Kindergarten, and Elementary	Reading MSA, PA	Y	44560 FQ	52440 MW	63460 TQ	USBLS	5/07
Preschool, Kindergarten, and Elementary	Rhode Island	Y	46830 FQ	60040 MW	72610 TQ	USBLS	5/07

AE	Average entry wage	AW	Average wage paid	FQ	First quartile wage
AER	Average entry range	AWR	Average wage range	H	Hourly
AEX	Average experienced wage	AXR	Average experienced range	HI	Highest wage paid
ATC	Average total salaries	D	Daily	HR	High end range

LO	Lowest wage paid
LR	Low end range
M	Monthly
MCC	Median cash compensation

MTC	Median total compensation
MW	Median wage paid
MWR	Median wage range
S	See annotated source

TCC	Total cash compensation
TQ	Third quartile wage
W	Weekly
Y	Yearly

Special Education Teacher

Occupation/Type/Industry	Location	Per	Low	Mid	High	Source	Date
Special Education Teacher							
Preschool, Kindergarten, and Elementary	Providence-Fall River-Warwick MSA, RI-MA	Y	46510 FQ	59070 MW	71510 TQ	USBLS	5/07
Preschool, Kindergarten, and Elementary	South Carolina	Y	34910 FQ	43380 MW	52990 TQ	USBLS	5/07
Preschool, Kindergarten, and Elementary	Charleston-North Charleston MSA, SC	Y	33650 FQ	43510 MW	54480 TQ	USBLS	5/07
Preschool, Kindergarten, and Elementary	Columbia MSA, SC	Y	36660 FQ	45260 MW	54190 TQ	USBLS	5/07
Preschool, Kindergarten, and Elementary	Florence MSA, SC	Y	34240 FQ	45690 MW	54670 TQ	USBLS	5/07
Preschool, Kindergarten, and Elementary	South Dakota	Y	31237 FQ	35644 MW	40564 TQ	SDBLS	7/08-9/08
Preschool, Kindergarten, and Elementary	Sioux Falls MSA, SD	Y	32786 FQ	36453 MW	40503 TQ	SDBLS	7/08-9/08
Preschool, Kindergarten, and Elementary	Tennessee	Y	32350 FQ	39160 MW	47010 TQ	USBLS	5/07
Preschool, Kindergarten, and Elementary	Memphis MSA, TN-MS-AR	Y	29630 FQ	36990 MW	44180 TQ	USBLS	5/07
Preschool, Kindergarten, and Elementary	Nashville-Davidson-Murfreesboro MSA, TN	Y	34500 FQ	39950 MW	48190 TQ	USBLS	5/07
Preschool, Kindergarten, and Elementary	Texas	Y	38790 FQ	44510 MW	50410 TQ	USBLS	5/07
Preschool, Kindergarten, and Elementary	Austin-Round Rock MSA, TX	Y	36880 FQ	40940 MW	48030 TQ	USBLS	5/07
Preschool, Kindergarten, and Elementary	Dallas-Fort Worth-Arlington MSA, TX	Y	42010 FQ	46480 MW	51240 TQ	USBLS	5/07
Preschool, Kindergarten, and Elementary	El Paso MSA, TX	Y	36820 FQ	42670 MW	48830 TQ	USBLS	5/07
Preschool, Kindergarten, and Elementary	Houston-Sugar Land-Baytown MSA, TX	Y	40290 FQ	45770 MW	52350 TQ	USBLS	5/07
Preschool, Kindergarten, and Elementary	San Antonio MSA, TX	Y	40910 FQ	46300 MW	52090 TQ	USBLS	5/07
Preschool, Kindergarten, and Elementary	Utah	Y	32230 FQ	40350 MW	48060 TQ	USBLS	5/07
Preschool, Kindergarten, and Elementary	Salt Lake City MSA, UT	Y	35120 FQ	42790 MW	51650 TQ	USBLS	5/07
Preschool, Kindergarten, and Elementary	Vermont	Y	38510 FQ	46230 MW	56950 TQ	USBLS	5/07
Preschool, Kindergarten, and Elementary	Burlington-South Burlington MSA, VT	Y	41690 FQ	51580 MW	61680 TQ	USBLS	5/07
Preschool, Kindergarten, and Elementary	Virginia	Y	41320 FQ	50680 MW	66620 TQ	USBLS	5/07
Preschool, Kindergarten, and Elementary	Richmond MSA, VA	Y	41950 FQ	50550 MW	58670 TQ	USBLS	5/07
Preschool, Kindergarten, and Elementary	Virginia Beach-Norfolk-Newport News MSA, VA-NC	Y	39220 FQ	44710 MW	50600 TQ	USBLS	5/07
Preschool, Kindergarten, and Elementary	Washington	Y		51641 AW		WABLS	3/08
Preschool, Kindergarten, and Elementary	Seattle-Tacoma-Bellevue MSA, WA	Y	43690 FQ	52040 MW	62180 TQ	USBLS	5/07
Preschool, Kindergarten, and Elementary	West Virginia	Y	34797 FQ	40274 MW	47441 TQ	WVBLS	7/08-9/08
Preschool, Kindergarten, and Elementary	Charleston MSA, WV	Y	35220 FQ	41440 MW	47350 TQ	USBLS	5/07
Preschool, Kindergarten, and Elementary	Huntington-Ashland MSA, WV-KY-OH	Y	34680 FQ	40560 MW	47580 TQ	USBLS	5/07
Preschool, Kindergarten, and Elementary	Wisconsin	Y	38180 FQ	47850 MW	58290 TQ	USBLS	5/07
Preschool, Kindergarten, and Elementary	Milwaukee-Waukesha-West Allis MSA, WI	Y	41430 FQ	53950 MW	67260 TQ	USBLS	5/07
Preschool, Kindergarten, and Elementary	Wyoming	Y	38364 FQ	47230 MW	56588 TQ	WYBLS	9/08
Secondary School	Alabama	Y	39040 FQ	43930 MW	48380 TQ	USBLS	5/07
Secondary School	Birmingham-Hoover MSA, AL	Y	39950 FQ	44840 MW	50240 TQ	USBLS	5/07
Secondary School	Alaska	Y	48210 FQ	57610 MW	67960 TQ	USBLS	5/07
Secondary School	Arizona	Y	33590 FQ	40540 MW	50170 TQ	USBLS	5/07
Secondary School	Phoenix-Mesa-Scottsdale MSA, AZ	Y	34230 FQ	41700 MW	49870 TQ	USBLS	5/07
Secondary School	Tucson MSA, AZ	Y	31980 FQ	37830 MW	49050 TQ	USBLS	5/07
Secondary School	Arkansas	Y	37540 FQ	43960 MW	50800 TQ	USBLS	5/07
Secondary School	Fort Smith MSA, AR-OK	Y	36540 FQ	42020 MW	47640 TQ	USBLS	5/07
Secondary School	Little Rock-North Little Rock MSA, AR	Y	39730 FQ	47330 MW	55990 TQ	USBLS	5/07
Secondary School	California	Y		62646 AW		CABLS	1/08-3/08
Secondary School	Los Angeles-Long Beach-Glendale PMSA, CA	Y		62318 AW		CABLS	1/08-3/08
Secondary School	Oakland-Fremont-Hayward MSA, CA	Y		62113 AW		CABLS	1/08-3/08
Secondary School	Riverside-San Bernardino-Ontario MSA, CA	Y		52258 AW		CABLS	1/08-3/08
Secondary School	Sacramento-Arden Arcade-Roseville MSA, CA	Y		60123 MW		CABLS	1/08-3/08
Secondary School	San Diego-Carlsbad-San Marcos MSA, CA	Y		70419 AW		CABLS	1/08-3/08
Secondary School	San Francisco-San Mateo-Redwood PMSA, CA	Y		64594 AW		CABLS	1/08-3/08
Secondary School	San Jose-Sunnyvale-Santa Clara MSA, CA	Y		64892 AW		CABLS	1/08-3/08
Secondary School	Santa Ana-Anaheim-Irvine PMSA, CA	Y	52100 FQ	67330 MW	81560 TQ	USBLS	5/07
Secondary School	Colorado	Y	38890 FQ	48010 MW	60280 TQ	USBLS	5/07
Secondary School	Denver-Aurora MSA, CO	Y	41320 FQ	52710 MW	63800 TQ	USBLS	5/07

AE	Average entry wage	AW	Average wage paid	FQ	First quartile wage	LO	Lowest wage paid	MTC	Median total compensation	TCC	Total cash compensation
AER	Average entry range	AWR	Average wage range	H	Hourly	LR	Low end range	MW	Median wage paid	TQ	Third quartile wage
AEX	Average experienced wage	AXR	Average experienced range	HI	Highest wage paid	M	Monthly	MWR	Median wage range	W	Weekly
ATC	Average total compensation	D	Daily	HR	High end range	MCC	Median cash compensation	S	See annotated source	Y	Yearly

Special Education Teacher

Occupation/Type/Industry	Location	Per	Low	Mid	High	Source	Date
Special Education Teacher							
Secondary School	Bridgeport-Stamford-Norwalk MSA, CT	Y	58640 FQ	71450 MW	84980 TQ	USBLS	5/07
Secondary School	Hartford-West Hartford-East Hartford MSA, CT	Y	51270 FQ	66550 MW	76780 TQ	USBLS	5/07
Secondary School	Delaware	Y	44450 FQ	53940 MW	68070 TQ	USBLS	5/07
Secondary School	Wilmington PMSA, DE-MD-NJ	Y	46760 FQ	57080 MW	70560 TQ	USBLS	5/07
Secondary School	District of Columbia	Y	46200 FQ	54860 MW	71510 TQ	USBLS	5/07
Secondary School	Washington-Arlington-Alexandria MSA, DC-VA-MD-WV	Y	51380 FQ	65670 MW	84650 TQ	USBLS	5/07
Secondary School	Florida	Y	39720 FQ	48830 MW	60110 TQ	USBLS	5/07
Secondary School	Jacksonville MSA, FL	Y	37920 FQ	45900 MW	59540 TQ	USBLS	5/07
Secondary School	Miami-Fort Lauderdale-Miami Beach MSA, FL	Y	44630 FQ	54100 MW	65750 TQ	USBLS	5/07
Secondary School	Orlando-Kissimmee MSA, FL	Y	36280 FQ	41460 MW	52420 TQ	USBLS	5/07
Secondary School	Tampa-St. Petersburg-Clearwater MSA, FL	Y	44530 FQ	51100 MW	60910 TQ	USBLS	5/07
Secondary School	Georgia	Y	41180 FQ	49370 MW	59200 TQ	USBLS	5/07
Secondary School	Atlanta-Sandy Springs-Marietta MSA, GA	Y	41300 FQ	49280 MW	59730 TQ	USBLS	5/07
Secondary School	Hawaii	Y	39810 FQ	45950 MW	51180 TQ	USBLS	5/07
Secondary School	Idaho	Y	32180 FQ	35240 MW	42560 TQ	USBLS	5/07
Secondary School	Illinois	Y	42720 FQ	56830 MW	75510 TQ	USBLS	5/07
Secondary School	Chicago-Naperville-Joliet MSA, IL-IN-WI	Y	49760 FQ	63570 MW	81550 TQ	USBLS	5/07
Secondary School	Indiana	Y	37670 FQ	47260 MW	58760 TQ	USBLS	5/07
Secondary School	Gary PMSA, IN	Y	38420 FQ	47910 MW	58040 TQ	USBLS	5/07
Secondary School	Indianapolis-Carmel MSA, IN	Y	37650 FQ	47890 MW	61220 TQ	USBLS	5/07
Secondary School	Iowa	Y	32380 FQ	39580 MW	48050 TQ	USBLS	5/07
Secondary School	Cedar Rapids MSA, IA	Y	31920 FQ	37860 MW	46720 TQ	USBLS	5/07
Secondary School	Des Moines-West Des Moines MSA, IA	Y	35570 FQ	40620 MW	49570 TQ	USBLS	5/07
Secondary School	Kansas	Y	34110 FQ	40440 MW	47580 TQ	USBLS	5/07
Secondary School	Lawrence MSA, KS	Y	35670 FQ	41310 MW	47540 TQ	USBLS	5/07
Secondary School	Wichita MSA, KS	Y	34140 FQ	40880 MW	47490 TQ	USBLS	5/07
Secondary School	Kentucky	Y	38842 FQ	46174 MW	53721 TQ	KYBLS	2008
Secondary School	Louisville-Jefferson County MSA, KY-IN	Y	39890 FQ	47580 MW	57420 TQ	USBLS	5/07
Secondary School	Louisiana	Y		42400 AW		LABLS	1/08-3/08
Secondary School	Baton Rouge MSA, LA	Y	37270 FQ	42960 MW	49720 TQ	USBLS	5/07
Secondary School	New Orleans-Metairie-Kenner MSA, LA	Y	38900 FQ	44620 MW	49780 TQ	USBLS	5/07
Secondary School	Maine	Y	34830 FQ	42270 MW	50530 TQ	USBLS	5/07
Secondary School	Portland-South Portland-Biddeford MSA, ME	Y	37550 FQ	45500 MW	53940 TQ	USBLS	5/07
Secondary School	Maryland	Y		58750 MW		MDBLS	3/08
Secondary School	Baltimore-Towson MSA, MD	Y	47690 FQ	58500 MW	69350 TQ	USBLS	5/07
Secondary School	Bethesda-Gaithersburg-Frederick PMSA, MD	Y	49250 FQ	60160 MW	75630 TQ	USBLS	5/07
Secondary School	Massachusetts	Y	44930 FQ	55900 MW	66650 TQ	USBLS	5/07
Secondary School	Barnstable Town MSA, MA	Y	39900 FQ	49350 MW	60160 TQ	USBLS	5/07
Secondary School	Boston-Cambridge-Quincy NECTA, MA	Y	45560 FQ	57840 MW	71710 TQ	USBLS	5/07
Secondary School	Worcester MSA, MA-CT	Y	45400 FQ	54630 MW	63770 TQ	USBLS	5/07
Secondary School	Michigan	Y	41190 FQ	50570 MW	65190 TQ	USBLS	5/07
Secondary School	Detroit-Warren-Livonia MSA, MI	Y	40820 FQ	49600 MW	71650 TQ	USBLS	5/07
Secondary School	Flint MSA, MI	Y	46440 FQ	60480 MW	70650 TQ	USBLS	5/07
Secondary School	Grand Rapids-Wyoming MSA, MI	Y	38340 FQ	53200 MW	63260 TQ	USBLS	5/07
Secondary School	Warren-Troy-Farmington Hills PMSA, MI	Y	47740 FQ	61720 MW	76870 TQ	USBLS	5/07
Secondary School	Minnesota	Y	44182 FQ	54131 MW	65190 TQ	MNBLS	10/08-12/08
Secondary School	Duluth-Superior MSA, MN-WI	Y	46630 FQ	55669 MW	63254 TQ	MNBLS	10/08-12/08
Secondary School	Minneapolis-Saint Paul MSA, MN-WI	Y	44820 FQ	55638 MW	68904 TQ	MNBLS	10/08-12/08
Secondary School	Rochester MSA, MN	Y	44208 FQ	52625 MW	61372 TQ	MNBLS	10/08-12/08
Secondary School	Mississippi	Y	36510 FQ	42790 MW	49170 TQ	USBLS	5/07
Secondary School	Jackson MSA, MS	Y	36240 FQ	41060 MW	47270 TQ	USBLS	5/07
Secondary School	Missouri	Y	33890 FQ	39970 MW	49500 TQ	USBLS	5/07

AE	Average entry wage	AW	Average wage paid	FQ	First quartile wage	LO	Lowest wage paid	MTC	Median total compensation	TCC	Total cash compensation
AER	Average entry range	AWR	Average wage range	H	Hourly	LR	Low end range	MW	Median wage paid	TQ	Third quartile wage
AEX	Average experienced wage	AXR	Average experienced range	HI	Highest wage paid	M	Monthly	MWR	Median wage range	W	Weekly
ATC	Average total compensation	D	Daily	HR	High end range	MCC	Median cash compensation	S	See annotated source	Y	Yearly

Occupation/Type/Industry	Location	Per	Low	Mid	High	Source	Date
Special Education Teacher							
Secondary School	Kansas City MSA, MO-KS	Y	36450 FQ	43790 MW	53320 TQ	USBLS	5/07
Secondary School	St. Louis MSA, MO-IL	Y	38050 FQ	46800 MW	59910 TQ	USBLS	5/07
Secondary School	Montana	Y	28420 FQ	36660 MW	46310 TQ	USBLS	5/07
Secondary School	Billings MSA, MT	Y	26570 FQ	39400 MW	51370 TQ	USBLS	5/07
Secondary School	Nebraska	Y	36700 FQ	43040 MW	49770 TQ	USBLS	5/07
Secondary School	Omaha-Council Bluffs MSA, NE-IA	Y	36790 FQ	43890 MW	50760 TQ	USBLS	5/07
Secondary School	Nevada	Y	39747 FQ	46967 MW	55857 TQ	NVBLS	5/08
Secondary School	Las Vegas-Paradise MSA, NV	Y	38872 FQ	46094 MW	55020 TQ	NVBLS	5/08
Secondary School	New Hampshire	Y	37916 AE	49021 MW	55990 AEX	NHBLS	6/08
Secondary School	Nashua NECTA, NH-MA	Y	39920 FQ	47090 MW	56320 TQ	USBLS	5/07
Secondary School	New Jersey	Y	46830 FQ	58990 MW	78440 TQ	USBLS	5/07
Secondary School	Camden PMSA, NJ	Y	46030 FQ	55730 MW	71390 TQ	USBLS	5/07
Secondary School	Edison PMSA, NJ	Y	45920 FQ	55450 MW	73690 TQ	USBLS	5/07
Secondary School	Newark-Union PMSA, NJ-PA	Y	49520 FQ	64080 MW	82320 TQ	USBLS	5/07
Secondary School	Ocean City MSA, NJ	Y	47540 FQ	60450 MW	71700 TQ	USBLS	5/07
Secondary School	New Mexico	Y	38030 FQ	45020 MW	54270 TQ	USBLS	5/07
Secondary School	Albuquerque MSA, NM	Y	36110 FQ	42130 MW	47570 TQ	USBLS	5/07
Secondary School	New York	Y	50150 FQ	63670 MW	81720 TQ	USBLS	5/07
Secondary School	Albany-Schenectady-Troy MSA, NY	Y	43000 FQ	54640 MW	73390 TQ	USBLS	5/07
Secondary School	Buffalo-Niagara Falls MSA, NY	Y	44770 FQ	54130 MW	73420 TQ	USBLS	5/07
Secondary School	Glens Falls MSA, NY	Y	43390 FQ	50400 MW	64300 TQ	USBLS	5/07
Secondary School	Kingston MSA, NY	Y	53320 FQ	63240 MW	82350 TQ	USBLS	5/07
Secondary School	Nassau-Suffolk PMSA, NY	Y	66200 FQ	83680 MW	101660 TQ	USBLS	5/07
Secondary School	New York-Northern New Jersey-Long Island MSA, NY-NJ-PA	Y	52740 FQ	68310 MW	87020 TQ	USBLS	5/07
Secondary School	North Carolina	Y	33610 FQ	40400 MW	48610 TQ	USBLS	5/07
Secondary School	Asheville MSA, NC	Y	35340 FQ	42200 MW	50980 TQ	USBLS	5/07
Secondary School	Charlotte-Gastonia-Concord MSA, NC-SC	Y	31400 FQ	38800 MW	48090 TQ	USBLS	5/07
Secondary School	Durham MSA, NC	Y	37150 FQ	44400 MW	50980 TQ	USBLS	5/07
Secondary School	North Dakota	Y	36030 FQ	43430 MW	51610 TQ	USBLS	5/07
Secondary School	Bismarck MSA, ND	Y	39790 FQ	45850 MW	53000 TQ	USBLS	5/07
Secondary School	Fargo MSA, ND-MN	Y	50800 FQ	55420 MW	59770 TQ	USBLS	5/07
Secondary School	Ohio	Y	41120 FQ	51420 MW	62620 TQ	USBLS	5/07
Secondary School	Canton-Massillon MSA, OH	Y	44970 FQ	54670 MW	63080 TQ	USBLS	5/07
Secondary School	Cincinnati-Middletown MSA, OH-KY-IN	Y	41940 FQ	52010 MW	63920 TQ	USBLS	5/07
Secondary School	Cleveland-Elyria-Mentor MSA, OH	Y	49160 FQ	61160 MW	71970 TQ	USBLS	5/07
Secondary School	Columbus MSA, OH	Y	42790 FQ	53550 MW	67320 TQ	USBLS	5/07
Secondary School	Dayton MSA, OH	Y	42110 FQ	52520 MW	60880 TQ	USBLS	5/07
Secondary School	Oklahoma	Y	34850 FQ	39190 MW	45500 TQ	USBLS	5/07
Secondary School	Oklahoma City MSA, OK	Y	34280 FQ	38490 MW	43760 TQ	USBLS	5/07
Secondary School	Tulsa MSA, OK	Y	35100 FQ	40610 MW	51930 TQ	USBLS	5/07
Secondary School	Oregon	Y	42234 FQ	51446 MW	61780 TQ	ORBLS	5/08
Secondary School	Portland-Vancouver-Beaverton MSA, OR-WA	Y	41050 FQ	49920 MW	61600 TQ	USBLS	5/07
Secondary School	Pennsylvania	Y	41300 FQ	51910 MW	65290 TQ	USBLS	5/07
Secondary School	Allentown-Bethlehem-Easton MSA, PA-NJ	Y	42820 FQ	50720 MW	63090 TQ	USBLS	5/07
Secondary School	Philadelphia-Camden-Wilmington MSA, PA-NJ-DE-MD	Y	44280 FQ	54680 MW	70220 TQ	USBLS	5/07
Secondary School	Pittsburgh MSA, PA	Y	43910 FQ	55770 MW	71000 TQ	USBLS	5/07
Secondary School	Rhode Island	Y	53170 FQ	65130 MW	75540 TQ	USBLS	5/07
Secondary School	Providence-Fall River-Warwick MSA, RI-MA	Y	51980 FQ	64010 MW	75070 TQ	USBLS	5/07
Secondary School	South Carolina	Y	36590 FQ	45110 MW	53890 TQ	USBLS	5/07
Secondary School	Charleston-North Charleston MSA, SC	Y	31200 FQ	39470 MW	48820 TQ	USBLS	5/07
Secondary School	Columbia MSA, SC	Y	36290 FQ	46070 MW	55420 TQ	USBLS	5/07
Secondary School	South Dakota	Y	32322 FQ	36812 MW	42479 TQ	SDBLS	7/08-9/08
Secondary School	Sioux Falls MSA, SD	Y	34175 FQ	39115 MW	47047 TQ	SDBLS	7/08-9/08
Secondary School	Tennessee	Y	36290 FQ	41520 MW	47360 TQ	USBLS	5/07
Secondary School	Johnson City MSA, TN	Y	37570 FQ	44880 MW	53510 TQ	USBLS	5/07
Secondary School	Memphis MSA, TN-MS-AR	Y	37740 FQ	42910 MW	48090 TQ	USBLS	5/07

Occupation/Type/Industry	Location	Per	Low	Mid	High	Source	Date
Special Education Teacher							
Secondary School	Nashville-Davidson-Murfreesboro MSA, TN	Y	33640 FQ	37990 MW	44850 TQ	USBLS	5/07
Secondary School	Texas	Y	39490 FQ	45160 MW	50880 TQ	USBLS	5/07
Secondary School	Austin-Round Rock MSA, TX	Y	38990 FQ	44810 MW	51380 TQ	USBLS	5/07
Secondary School	Dallas-Fort Worth-Arlington MSA, TX	Y	43070 FQ	47750 MW	53010 TQ	USBLS	5/07
Secondary School	El Paso MSA, TX	Y	38320 FQ	43940 MW	49720 TQ	USBLS	5/07
Secondary School	Houston-Sugar Land-Baytown MSA, TX	Y	40940 FQ	45790 MW	51370 TQ	USBLS	5/07
Secondary School	San Antonio MSA, TX	Y	40850 FQ	46190 MW	51740 TQ	USBLS	5/07
Secondary School	Utah	Y	29870 FQ	39730 MW	50380 TQ	USBLS	5/07
Secondary School	Salt Lake City MSA, UT	Y	38210 FQ	46740 MW	64180 TQ	USBLS	5/07
Secondary School	Vermont	Y	39660 FQ	49260 MW	60710 TQ	USBLS	5/07
Secondary School	Burlington-South Burlington MSA, VT	Y	37180 FQ	48270 MW	62010 TQ	USBLS	5/07
Secondary School	Virginia	Y	41940 FQ	54260 MW	74330 TQ	USBLS	5/07
Secondary School	Charlottesville MSA, VA	Y	39990 FQ	47970 MW	58650 TQ	USBLS	5/07
Secondary School	Richmond MSA, VA	Y	41170 FQ	50410 MW	58980 TQ	USBLS	5/07
Secondary School	Virginia Beach-Norfolk-Newport News MSA, VA-NC	Y	39730 FQ	46520 MW	53660 TQ	USBLS	5/07
Secondary School	Washington	Y		53065 AW		WABLS	3/08
Secondary School	Seattle-Tacoma-Bellevue MSA, WA	Y	43420 FQ	53020 MW	64810 TQ	USBLS	5/07
Secondary School	West Virginia	Y	34591 FQ	40717 MW	47074 TQ	WVBLS	7/08-9/08
Secondary School	Charleston MSA, WV	Y	31520 FQ	37380 MW	44060 TQ	USBLS	5/07
Secondary School	Huntington-Ashland MSA, WV-KY-OH	Y	35820 FQ	42350 MW	48980 TQ	USBLS	5/07
Secondary School	Wheeling MSA, WV-OH	Y	30750 FQ	40200 MW	50770 TQ	USBLS	5/07
Secondary School	Wisconsin	Y	40670 FQ	49540 MW	59790 TQ	USBLS	5/07
Secondary School	Milwaukee-Waukesha-West Allis MSA, WI	Y	46010 FQ	58720 MW	71030 TQ	USBLS	5/07
Secondary School	Wyoming	Y	42763 FQ	50449 MW	58312 TQ	WYBLS	9/08
Secondary School	Virgin Islands	Y	38730 FQ	45880 MW	54310 TQ	USBLS	5/07
Special Events Manager							
State Lottery	Tennessee	Y			50607 HI	THETN	2008
Specialist 6							
U.S. Army, Active Duty, Pay Grade E-6	United States	M	2176 LO		3370 HI	DOD1	2009
Spectroscopist							
Female	United States	Y		65381 AW		SPECT	1/9/08-1/23/08
Male	United States	Y		81481 AW		SPECT	1/9/08-1/23/08
Speech-Language Pathologist	Alabama	Y	41960 FQ	49320 MW	61090 TQ	USBLS	5/07
	Birmingham-Hoover MSA, AL	Y	44040 FQ	55000 MW	63480 TQ	USBLS	5/07
	Alaska	Y	60180 FQ	70150 MW	79230 TQ	USBLS	5/07
	Anchorage MSA, AK	Y	65810 FQ	73610 MW	81480 TQ	USBLS	5/07
	Arizona	Y	38140 FQ	49490 MW	63060 TQ	USBLS	5/07
	Phoenix-Mesa-Scottsdale MSA, AZ	Y	39540 FQ	49360 MW	62720 TQ	USBLS	5/07
	Tucson MSA, AZ	Y	31430 FQ	46220 MW	62070 TQ	USBLS	5/07
	Arkansas	Y	44640 FQ	52110 MW	68800 TQ	USBLS	5/07
	Little Rock-North Little Rock MSA, AR	Y	47320 FQ	57920 MW	80260 TQ	USBLS	5/07
	California	H	29.87 FQ	35.91 MW	43.42 TQ	CABLS	1/08-3/08
	Los Angeles-Long Beach-Glendale PMSA, CA	H	31.52 FQ	37.58 MW	48.07 TQ	CABLS	1/08-3/08
	Oakland-Fremont-Hayward MSA, CA	H	30.73 FQ	38.81 MW	45.22 TQ	CABLS	1/08-3/08
	Riverside-San Bernardino-Ontario MSA, CA	H	30.03 FQ	37.18 MW	42.71 TQ	CABLS	1/08-3/08
	Sacramento-Arden Arcade-Roseville MSA, CA	H	27.66 FQ	33.55 MW	40.20 TQ	CABLS	1/08-3/08
	San Diego-Carlsbad-San Marcos MSA, CA	H	32.40 FQ	38.46 MW	44.97 TQ	CABLS	1/08-3/08
	San Francisco-San Mateo-Redwood PMSA, CA	H	31.06 FQ	36.32 MW	45.11 TQ	CABLS	1/08-3/08
	San Jose-Sunnyvale-Santa Clara MSA, CA	H	31.41 FQ	38.20 MW	43.91 TQ	CABLS	1/08-3/08

AE Average entry wage	**AW** Average wage paid	**FQ** First quartile wage	**LO** Lowest wage paid	**MTC** Median total compensation　**TCC** Total cash compensation
AER Average entry range	**AWR** Average wage range	**H** Hourly	**LR** Low end range	**MW** Median wage paid　**TQ** Third quartile wage
AEX Average experienced wage	**AXR** Average experienced range	**HI** Highest wage paid	**M** Monthly	**MWR** Median wage range　**W** Weekly
ATC Average total compensation	**D** Daily	**HR** High end range	**MCC** Median cash compensation	**S** See annotated source　**Y** Yearly

Speech-Language Pathologist

Occupation/Type/Industry	Location	Per	Low	Mid	High	Source	Date
Speech-Language Pathologist	Santa Ana-Anaheim-Irvine PMSA, CA	Y	63120 FQ	70890 MW	78240 TQ	USBLS	5/07
	Colorado	Y	55370 FQ	66900 MW	84500 TQ	USBLS	5/07
	Colorado Springs MSA, CO	Y	61220 FQ	73190 MW	89740 TQ	USBLS	5/07
	Denver-Aurora MSA, CO	Y	56300 FQ	68400 MW	86900 TQ	USBLS	5/07
	Connecticut	H	25.53 AE	35.35 MW		CTBLS	1/08-3/08
	Bridgeport-Stamford-Norwalk MSA, CT	Y	57100 FQ	77690 MW	107620 TQ	USBLS	5/07
	Hartford-West Hartford-East Hartford MSA, CT	Y	60320 FQ	70240 MW	80960 TQ	USBLS	5/07
	Delaware	Y	61290 FQ	72610 MW	80750 TQ	USBLS	5/07
	Wilmington PMSA, DE-MD-NJ	Y	60390 FQ	73160 MW	81990 TQ	USBLS	5/07
	District of Columbia	Y	57790 FQ	71780 MW	81080 TQ	USBLS	5/07
	Washington-Arlington-Alexandria MSA, DC-VA-MD-WV	Y	57580 FQ	70810 MW	85700 TQ	USBLS	5/07
	Florida	Y	49920 FQ	62320 MW	76760 TQ	USBLS	5/07
	Fort Lauderdale-Pompano Beach-Deerfield Beach PMSA, FL	Y	63720 FQ	73830 MW	86290 TQ	USBLS	5/07
	Jacksonville MSA, FL	Y	43290 FQ	57970 MW	69850 TQ	USBLS	5/07
	Miami-Fort Lauderdale-Miami Beach MSA, FL	Y	55830 FQ	67640 MW	80290 TQ	USBLS	5/07
	Orlando-Kissimmee MSA, FL	Y	44350 FQ	55240 MW	67220 TQ	USBLS	5/07
	Pensacola-Ferry Pass-Brent MSA, FL	Y	46240 FQ	56400 MW	69610 TQ	USBLS	5/07
	Tallahassee MSA, FL	Y	44990 FQ	54410 MW	64120 TQ	USBLS	5/07
	Tampa-St. Petersburg-Clearwater MSA, FL	Y	53950 FQ	67540 MW	85250 TQ	USBLS	5/07
	West Palm Beach-Boca Raton-Boynton Beach PMSA, FL	Y	52330 FQ	60300 MW	72700 TQ	USBLS	5/07
	Georgia	Y	47800 FQ	59150 MW	77940 TQ	USBLS	5/07
	Athens-Clarke County MSA, GA	Y	56610 FQ	106180 MW	118830 TQ	USBLS	5/07
	Atlanta-Sandy Springs-Marietta MSA, GA	Y	51000 FQ	65070 MW	83210 TQ	USBLS	5/07
	Macon MSA, GA	Y	42000 FQ	49350 MW	61660 TQ	USBLS	5/07
	Savannah MSA, GA	Y	46270 FQ	56860 MW	68370 TQ	USBLS	5/07
	Hawaii	Y	50270 FQ	57370 MW	64570 TQ	USBLS	5/07
	Honolulu MSA, HI	Y	52620 FQ	60340 MW	71160 TQ	USBLS	5/07
	Idaho	Y	44640 FQ	58030 MW	67470 TQ	USBLS	5/07
	Boise City-Nampa MSA, ID	Y	55520 FQ	61710 MW	72400 TQ	USBLS	5/07
	Idaho Falls MSA, ID	Y	28250 FQ	31530 MW	45050 TQ	USBLS	5/07
	Illinois	Y	48770 FQ	63590 MW	80930 TQ	USBLS	5/07
	Chicago-Naperville-Joliet MSA, IL-IN-WI	Y	52900 FQ	67340 MW	84240 TQ	USBLS	5/07
	Indiana	Y	48480 FQ	59420 MW	71220 TQ	USBLS	5/07
	Gary PMSA, IN	Y	45060 FQ	56210 MW	65160 TQ	USBLS	5/07
	Indianapolis-Carmel MSA, IN	Y	52440 FQ	62270 MW	74760 TQ	USBLS	5/07
	Iowa	Y	44270 FQ	53150 MW	60350 TQ	USBLS	5/07
	Des Moines-West Des Moines MSA, IA	Y	44620 FQ	53820 MW	62890 TQ	USBLS	5/07
	Iowa City MSA, IA	Y	52310 FQ	61050 MW	82010 TQ	USBLS	5/07
	Kansas	Y	42490 FQ	50470 MW	63600 TQ	USBLS	5/07
	Lawrence MSA, KS	Y	41240 FQ	46120 MW	51480 TQ	USBLS	5/07
	Topeka MSA, KS	Y	47460 FQ	57190 MW	73510 TQ	USBLS	5/07
	Wichita MSA, KS	Y	45060 FQ	52420 MW	60410 TQ	USBLS	5/07
	Kentucky	Y	45994 FQ	54434 MW	68478 TQ	KYBLS	2008
	Bowling Green MSA, KY	Y	88180 FQ	94680 MW	101190 TQ	USBLS	5/07
	Louisville-Jefferson County MSA, KY-IN	Y	55350 FQ	66950 MW	76850 TQ	USBLS	5/07
	Owensboro MSA, KY	Y	39220 FQ	49840 MW	62480 TQ	USBLS	5/07
	Louisiana	H	24.11 FQ	29.01 MW	35.66 TQ	LABLS	1/08-3/08
	Baton Rouge MSA, LA	Y	45610 FQ	54730 MW	64810 TQ	USBLS	5/07
	New Orleans-Metairie-Kenner MSA, LA	Y	55290 FQ	65590 MW	78350 TQ	USBLS	5/07
	Maine	Y	40770 FQ	49830 MW	59270 TQ	USBLS	5/07
	Portland-South Portland-Biddeford MSA, ME	Y	42140 FQ	51210 MW	59710 TQ	USBLS	5/07
	Maryland	Y		69275 MW		MDBLS	3/08
	Baltimore-Towson MSA, MD	Y	55170 FQ	66680 MW	77460 TQ	USBLS	5/07

AE Average entry wage	**AW** Average wage paid	**FQ** First quartile wage	**LO** Lowest wage paid	**MTC** Median total compensation	**TCC** Total cash compensation
AER Average entry range	**AWR** Average wage range	**H** Hourly	**LR** Low end range	**MW** Median wage paid	**TQ** Third quartile wage
AEX Average experienced wage	**AXR** Average experienced range	**HI** Highest wage paid	**M** Monthly	**MWR** Median wage range	**W** Weekly
ATC Average total compensation **D** Daily		**HR** High end range	**MCC** Median cash compensation	**S** See annotated source	**Y** Yearly

Occupation/Type/Industry	Location	Per	Low	Mid	High	Source	Date
Speech-Language Pathologist	Bethesda-Gaithersburg-Frederick PMSA, MD	Y	56910 FQ	68490 MW	82130 TQ	USBLS	5/07
	Massachusetts	Y	53460 FQ	64500 MW	78310 TQ	USBLS	5/07
	Boston-Cambridge-Quincy NECTA, MA	Y	54110 FQ	66010 MW	79520 TQ	USBLS	5/07
	Worcester MSA, MA-CT	Y	54580 FQ	62740 MW	75770 TQ	USBLS	5/07
	Michigan	Y	52890 FQ	66460 MW	81480 TQ	USBLS	5/07
	Detroit-Warren-Livonia MSA, MI	Y	53070 FQ	68090 MW	80570 TQ	USBLS	5/07
	Grand Rapids-Wyoming MSA, MI	Y	54660 FQ	72290 MW	103530 TQ	USBLS	5/07
	Warren-Troy-Farmington Hills PMSA, MI	Y	54150 FQ	69620 MW	89820 TQ	USBLS	5/07
	Minnesota	Y	48680 FQ	58201 MW	67439 TQ	MNBLS	10/08-12/08
	Duluth-Superior MSA, MN-WI	Y	52363 FQ	58212 MW	63840 TQ	MNBLS	10/08-12/08
	Minneapolis-Saint Paul MSA, MN-WI	Y	49193 FQ	59519 MW	69563 TQ	MNBLS	10/08-12/08
	Rochester MSA, MN	Y	48078 FQ	57785 MW	65639 TQ	MNBLS	10/08-12/08
	Mississippi	Y	43750 FQ	52360 MW	65940 TQ	USBLS	5/07
	Jackson MSA, MS	Y	45930 FQ	59170 MW	73650 TQ	USBLS	5/07
	Missouri	Y	43050 FQ	54070 MW	65450 TQ	USBLS	5/07
	Joplin MSA, MO	Y	32960 FQ	36560 MW	46760 TQ	USBLS	5/07
	Kansas City MSA, MO-KS	Y	45520 FQ	55640 MW	65430 TQ	USBLS	5/07
	St. Louis MSA, MO-IL	Y	46590 FQ	56920 MW	68360 TQ	USBLS	5/07
	Montana	Y	46070 FQ	55720 MW	62220 TQ	USBLS	5/07
	Billings MSA, MT	Y	55130 FQ	60050 MW	65330 TQ	USBLS	5/07
	Nebraska	Y	41330 FQ	49720 MW	60260 TQ	USBLS	5/07
	Omaha-Council Bluffs MSA, NE-IA	Y	38260 FQ	46590 MW	56100 TQ	USBLS	5/07
	Nevada	H	33.44 FQ	40.20 MW	63.28 TQ	NVBLS	5/08
	Las Vegas-Paradise MSA, NV	H	38.21 FQ	48.68 MW		NVBLS	5/08
	New Hampshire	H	21.82 AE	28.66 MW	32.77 AEX	NHBLS	6/08
	Manchester MSA, NH	Y	46070 FQ	55250 MW	62670 TQ	USBLS	5/07
	Nashua NECTA, NH-MA	Y	51220 FQ	57070 MW	65120 TQ	USBLS	5/07
	New Jersey	Y	57990 FQ	72940 MW	91940 TQ	USBLS	5/07
	Camden PMSA, NJ	Y	53010 FQ	70960 MW	87030 TQ	USBLS	5/07
	Edison PMSA, NJ	Y	56890 FQ	69560 MW	85320 TQ	USBLS	5/07
	Newark-Union PMSA, NJ-PA	Y	58090 FQ	72250 MW	94680 TQ	USBLS	5/07
	New Mexico	Y	44200 FQ	54940 MW	66010 TQ	USBLS	5/07
	Albuquerque MSA, NM	Y	41760 FQ	52850 MW	62980 TQ	USBLS	5/07
	Las Cruces MSA, NM	Y	56120 FQ	65210 MW	84700 TQ	USBLS	5/07
	New York	Y	52530 FQ	62900 MW	78590 TQ	USBLS	5/07
	Albany-Schenectady-Troy MSA, NY	Y	44050 FQ	53780 MW	64130 TQ	USBLS	5/07
	Buffalo-Niagara Falls MSA, NY	Y	46740 FQ	56320 MW	66490 TQ	USBLS	5/07
	Ithaca MSA, NY	Y	45160 FQ	52780 MW	59630 TQ	USBLS	5/07
	Nassau-Suffolk PMSA, NY	Y	59100 FQ	72310 MW	90730 TQ	USBLS	5/07
	New York-Northern New Jersey-Long Island MSA, NY-NJ-PA	Y	57840 FQ	70060 MW	86640 TQ	USBLS	5/07
	Syracuse MSA, NY	Y	48910 FQ	55550 MW	61930 TQ	USBLS	5/07
	North Carolina	Y	47440 FQ	58320 MW	73530 TQ	USBLS	5/07
	Charlotte-Gastonia-Concord MSA, NC-SC	Y	47160 FQ	56960 MW	72080 TQ	USBLS	5/07
	Raleigh-Cary MSA, NC	Y	51220 FQ	58900 MW	66220 TQ	USBLS	5/07
	North Dakota	Y	41230 FQ	47730 MW	57440 TQ	USBLS	5/07
	Fargo MSA, ND-MN	Y	44960 FQ	54990 MW	65210 TQ	USBLS	5/07
	Ohio	Y	57820 FQ	71960 MW	89880 TQ	USBLS	5/07
	Cincinnati-Middletown MSA, OH-KY-IN	Y	58590 FQ	75630 MW	95030 TQ	USBLS	5/07
	Cleveland-Elyria-Mentor MSA, OH	Y	62940 FQ	73620 MW	88660 TQ	USBLS	5/07
	Columbus MSA, OH	Y	62280 FQ	76950 MW	96290 TQ	USBLS	5/07
	Dayton MSA, OH	Y	55690 FQ	66650 MW	86600 TQ	USBLS	5/07
	Oklahoma	Y	36540 FQ	43970 MW	56990 TQ	USBLS	5/07
	Oklahoma City MSA, OK	Y	36700 FQ	45090 MW	60560 TQ	USBLS	5/07
	Tulsa MSA, OK	Y	36020 FQ	41700 MW	53920 TQ	USBLS	5/07
	Oregon	H	25.69 FQ	29.87 MW	35.92 TQ	ORBLS	5/08
	Portland-Vancouver-Beaverton MSA, OR-WA	Y	51720 FQ	61570 MW	74160 TQ	USBLS	5/07
	Pennsylvania	Y	47240 FQ	58970 MW	72780 TQ	USBLS	5/07

AE	Average entry wage	AW	Average wage paid	FQ	First quartile wage	LO	Lowest wage paid	MTC	Median total compensation	TCC	Total cash compensation
AER	Average entry range	AWR	Average wage range	H	Hourly	LR	Low end range	MW	Median wage paid	TQ	Third quartile wage
AEX	Average experienced wage	AXR	Average experienced range	HI	Highest wage paid	M	Monthly	MWR	Median wage range	W	Weekly
ATC	Average total compensation	D	Daily	HR	High end range	MCC	Median cash compensation	S	See annotated source	Y	Yearly

Occupation/Type/Industry	Location	Per	Low	Mid	High	Source	Date
Speech-Language Pathologist	Allentown-Bethlehem-Easton MSA, PA-NJ	Y	55530 FQ	68350 MW	78540 TQ	USBLS	5/07
	Philadelphia-Camden-Wilmington MSA, PA-NJ-DE-MD	Y	53850 FQ	65540 MW	80820 TQ	USBLS	5/07
	Pittsburgh MSA, PA	Y	42160 FQ	50770 MW	62870 TQ	USBLS	5/07
	Rhode Island	Y	55170 FQ	66710 MW	78370 TQ	USBLS	5/07
	Providence-Fall River-Warwick MSA, RI-MA	Y	54660 FQ	66500 MW	79700 TQ	USBLS	5/07
	South Carolina	Y	42760 FQ	51360 MW	63300 TQ	USBLS	5/07
	Charleston-North Charleston MSA, SC	Y	43890 FQ	52630 MW	63790 TQ	USBLS	5/07
	Columbia MSA, SC	Y	43240 FQ	55190 MW	68850 TQ	USBLS	5/07
	South Dakota	Y	37515 FQ	45020 MW	53382 TQ	SDBLS	7/08-9/08
	Sioux Falls MSA, SD	Y	41468 FQ	47227 MW	55202 TQ	SDBLS	7/08-9/08
	Tennessee	Y	42670 FQ	52430 MW	67630 TQ	USBLS	5/07
	Memphis MSA, TN-MS-AR	Y	44510 FQ	55220 MW	67720 TQ	USBLS	5/07
	Nashville-Davidson-Murfreesboro MSA, TN	Y	38760 FQ	49590 MW	59760 TQ	USBLS	5/07
	Texas	Y	45700 FQ	54610 MW	66100 TQ	USBLS	5/07
	Austin-Round Rock MSA, TX	Y	43350 FQ	50180 MW	62570 TQ	USBLS	5/07
	Corpus Christi MSA, TX	Y	40130 FQ	51920 MW	67060 TQ	USBLS	5/07
	Dallas-Fort Worth-Arlington MSA, TX	Y	46740 FQ	55070 MW	67920 TQ	USBLS	5/07
	El Paso MSA, TX	Y	55730 FQ	63050 MW	76040 TQ	USBLS	5/07
	Houston-Sugar Land-Baytown MSA, TX	Y	47880 FQ	57720 MW	70150 TQ	USBLS	5/07
	San Antonio MSA, TX	Y	49200 FQ	57030 MW	65870 TQ	USBLS	5/07
	Utah	Y	45220 FQ	57360 MW	70950 TQ	USBLS	5/07
	Salt Lake City MSA, UT	Y	51920 FQ	61860 MW	72350 TQ	USBLS	5/07
	Vermont	Y	45050 FQ	55010 MW	66570 TQ	USBLS	5/07
	Burlington-South Burlington MSA, VT	Y	50890 FQ	59140 MW	67600 TQ	USBLS	5/07
	Virginia	Y	50840 FQ	64980 MW	81480 TQ	USBLS	5/07
	Richmond MSA, VA	Y	52950 FQ	68640 MW	78390 TQ	USBLS	5/07
	Virginia Beach-Norfolk-Newport News MSA, VA-NC	Y	49090 FQ	63470 MW	89980 TQ	USBLS	5/07
	Washington	H	24.79 FQ	29.23 MW	34.16 TQ	WABLS	3/08
	Bremerton-Silverdale MSA, WA	Y	52900 FQ	58970 MW	67040 TQ	USBLS	5/07
	Seattle-Tacoma-Bellevue MSA, WA	Y	52090 FQ	61330 MW	71240 TQ	USBLS	5/07
	West Virginia	Y	40394 FQ	46992 MW	55155 TQ	WVBLS	7/08-9/08
	Charleston MSA, WV	Y	37840 FQ	43460 MW	48720 TQ	USBLS	5/07
	Wisconsin	Y	48120 FQ	57590 MW	67820 TQ	USBLS	5/07
	Milwaukee-Waukesha-West Allis MSA, WI	Y	51790 FQ	61020 MW	71430 TQ	USBLS	5/07
	Wyoming	Y	48985 FQ	58131 MW	66506 TQ	WYBLS	9/08
	Cheyenne MSA, WY	Y	58439 FQ	63983 MW	70967 TQ	WYBLS	9/08
	Puerto Rico	Y	26490 FQ	30740 MW	48660 TQ	USBLS	5/07
	San Juan-Caguas-Guaynabo MSA, PR	Y	26400 FQ	29950 MW	36770 TQ	USBLS	5/07
	Virgin Islands	Y	46080 FQ	51570 MW	56440 TQ	USBLS	5/07
MA Degree	United States	Y		63421 AW		SLPADV	2008
SLPD Degree	United States	Y		47333 AW		SLPADV	2008
Speechwriter							
White House Staff	United States	Y			59600 HI	WPOST02	2008
Speechwriter for the First Lady							
White House Staff	United States	Y			63000 HI	WPOST02	2008
Sports Nutritionist	United States	Y		30500 AW		DIETCEN	2008
SQL Server Expert	United States	Y		81220 AW		REDMAG	2008
Staff Accountant	Middle Atlantic	Y	43000 LO		56000 HI	ACTT	2009
Staff Nurse							
City-Run Hospital	United States	Y		66628 MW		CNYB	5/08
Private Hospital	United States	Y		74325 MW		CNYB	5/08
Public Health Agency	Georgia	Y		36753 AW		TMC01	2006

AE	Average entry wage	AW	Average wage paid	FQ	First quartile wage	LO	Lowest wage paid	MTC	Median total compensation	TCC	Total cash compensation
AER	Average entry range	AWR	Average wage range	H	Hourly	LR	Low end range	MW	Median wage paid	TQ	Third quartile wage
AEX	Average experienced wage	AXR	Average experienced range	HI	Highest wage paid	M	Monthly	MWR	Median wage range	W	Weekly
ATC	Average total compensation	D	Daily	HR	High end range	MCC	Median cash compensation	S	See annotated source	Y	Yearly

Occupation/Type/Industry	Location	Per	Low	Mid	High	Source	Date
Staff Pharmacist							
Hospital	United States	Y		105200 AW		DSN01	2008
Retail	United States	Y		108700 AW		DSN01	2008
Staff Sergeant							
U.S. Air Force, Active Duty, Pay Grade E-4	United States	M	1827 LO		2219 HI	DOD1	2009
U.S. Air Force, Active Duty, Pay Grade E-5	United States	M	1994 LO		2828 HI	DOD1	2009
U.S. Army, Active Duty, Pay Grade E-6	United States	M	2176 LO		3370 HI	DOD1	2009
U.S. Marines, Active Duty, Pay Grade E-6	United States	M	2176 LO		3370 HI	DOD1	2009
State Archivist							
Secretary of State	New Hampshire	Y			75382 HI	NHUL03	2008
State Education Superintendent	Louisiana	Y			355611 HI	DADV	2009
State Forms Administrator	Ohio	H	33.83 LO		44.38 HI	ODAS	2008
State Librarian							
Department of Cultural Resources	New Hampshire	Y			85958 HI	NHUL03	2008
State Procurement Analyst	Ohio	Y	52811 LO		70387 HI	AFT02	3/1/08
State Representative	Michigan	Y			79650 HI	FREEP02	2008
State Senator	Rhode Island	Y		14089 AW		RIM01	2009
State Veterinarian	Ohio	H	37.28 LO		48.86 HI	ODAS	2008
Stationary Engineer and Boiler Operator	Alabama	Y	28530 FQ	38390 MW	48650 TQ	USBLS	5/07
	Birmingham-Hoover MSA, AL	Y	28380 FQ	31900 MW	39280 TQ	USBLS	5/07
	Alaska	Y	52630 FQ	58420 MW	64490 TQ	USBLS	5/07
	Arizona	Y	36580 FQ	45290 MW	55810 TQ	USBLS	5/07
	Phoenix-Mesa-Scottsdale MSA, AZ	Y	37990 FQ	44720 MW	51400 TQ	USBLS	5/07
	Arkansas	Y	28240 FQ	34040 MW	44660 TQ	USBLS	5/07
	Little Rock-North Little Rock MSA, AR	Y	28920 FQ	34930 MW	41390 TQ	USBLS	5/07
	California	H	24.49 FQ	28.17 MW	31.43 TQ	CABLS	1/08-3/08
	Los Angeles-Long Beach-Glendale PMSA, CA	H	19.21 FQ	26.81 MW	30.94 TQ	CABLS	1/08-3/08
	Oakland-Fremont-Hayward MSA, CA	H	30.91 FQ	34.97 MW	38.19 TQ	CABLS	1/08-3/08
	Riverside-San Bernardino-Ontario MSA, CA	H	24.23 FQ	27.57 MW	30.21 TQ	CABLS	1/08-3/08
	Sacramento-Arden Arcade-Roseville MSA, CA	H	20.51 FQ	26.97 MW	29.70 TQ	CABLS	1/08-3/08
	San Diego-Carlsbad-San Marcos MSA, CA	H	22.75 FQ	25.92 MW	28.71 TQ	CABLS	1/08-3/08
	San Jose-Sunnyvale-Santa Clara MSA, CA	H	28.12 FQ	32.55 MW	36.74 TQ	CABLS	1/08-3/08
	Santa Ana-Anaheim-Irvine PMSA, CA	Y	51230 FQ	56870 MW	62830 TQ	USBLS	5/07
	Colorado	Y	40730 FQ	50410 MW	59770 TQ	USBLS	5/07
	Denver-Aurora MSA, CO	Y	41740 FQ	51120 MW	60450 TQ	USBLS	5/07
	Connecticut	H	20.60 AE	24.56 MW		CTBLS	1/08-3/08
	Bridgeport-Stamford-Norwalk MSA, CT	Y	41720 FQ	46660 MW	53300 TQ	USBLS	5/07
	Hartford-West Hartford-East Hartford MSA, CT	Y	45600 FQ	53740 MW	65000 TQ	USBLS	5/07
	Delaware	Y	55690 FQ	62920 MW	69680 TQ	USBLS	5/07
	Wilmington PMSA, DE-MD-NJ	Y	42490 FQ	56300 MW	64300 TQ	USBLS	5/07
	District of Columbia	Y	51500 FQ	57820 MW	67430 TQ	USBLS	5/07
	Washington-Arlington-Alexandria MSA, DC-VA-MD-WV	Y	49160 FQ	56130 MW	64320 TQ	USBLS	5/07
	Florida	Y	34240 FQ	42730 MW	52600 TQ	USBLS	5/07
	Jacksonville MSA, FL	Y	32530 FQ	41630 MW	55180 TQ	USBLS	5/07
	Miami-Fort Lauderdale-Miami Beach MSA, FL	Y	32120 FQ	37400 MW	45130 TQ	USBLS	5/07
	Orlando-Kissimmee MSA, FL	Y	37540 FQ	53780 MW	63500 TQ	USBLS	5/07

AE	Average entry wage	AW	Average wage paid	FQ	First quartile wage	LO	Lowest wage paid	MTC	Median total compensation
AER	Average entry range	AWR	Average wage range	H	Hourly	LR	Low end range	MW	Median wage paid
AEX	Average experienced wage	AXR	Average experienced range	HI	Highest wage paid	M	Monthly	MWR	Median wage range
ATC	Average total compensation	D	Daily	HR	High end range	MCC	Median cash compensation	S	See annotated source

TCC Total cash compensation
TQ Third quartile wage
W Weekly
Y Yearly

Occupation/Type/Industry	Location	Per	Low	Mid	High	Source	Date
Stationary Engineer and Boiler Operator							
	Tampa-St. Petersburg-Clearwater MSA, FL	Y	35320 FQ	43290 MW	50970 TQ	USBLS	5/07
	Georgia	Y	27980 FQ	34950 MW	44470 TQ	USBLS	5/07
	Atlanta-Sandy Springs-Marietta MSA, GA	Y	33770 FQ	38990 MW	48750 TQ	USBLS	5/07
	Idaho	Y	31350 FQ	37860 MW	42220 TQ	USBLS	5/07
	Illinois	Y	56340 FQ	67880 MW	75550 TQ	USBLS	5/07
	Chicago-Naperville-Joliet MSA, IL-IN-WI	Y	52910 FQ	65840 MW	74730 TQ	USBLS	5/07
	Indiana	Y	31920 FQ	44960 MW	60740 TQ	USBLS	5/07
	Fort Wayne MSA, IN	Y	29730 FQ	43580 MW	68640 TQ	USBLS	5/07
	Gary PMSA, IN	Y	37220 FQ	45310 MW	51250 TQ	USBLS	5/07
	Indianapolis-Carmel MSA, IN	Y	30710 FQ	44890 MW	62080 TQ	USBLS	5/07
	Iowa	Y	34260 FQ	39310 MW	54150 TQ	USBLS	5/07
	Des Moines-West Des Moines MSA, IA	Y	34760 FQ	37990 MW	42860 TQ	USBLS	5/07
	Kansas	Y	37070 FQ	44200 MW	58520 TQ	USBLS	5/07
	Kentucky	Y	27744 FQ	33276 MW	50655 TQ	KYBLS	2008
	Louisville-Jefferson County MSA, KY-IN	Y	27460 FQ	36670 MW	52720 TQ	USBLS	5/07
	Louisiana	H	14.55 FQ	17.11 MW	21.41 TQ	LABLS	1/08-3/08
	Baton Rouge MSA, LA	Y	32160 FQ	40010 MW	49630 TQ	USBLS	5/07
	New Orleans-Metairie-Kenner MSA, LA	Y	31630 FQ	34750 MW	38910 TQ	USBLS	5/07
	Maine	Y	33210 FQ	38830 MW	50520 TQ	USBLS	5/07
	Portland-South Portland-Biddeford MSA, ME	Y	27460 FQ	34650 MW	43320 TQ	USBLS	5/07
	Maryland	Y		46475 MW		MDBLS	3/08
	Baltimore-Towson MSA, MD	Y	39150 FQ	43100 MW	47280 TQ	USBLS	5/07
	Bethesda-Gaithersburg-Frederick PMSA, MD	Y	45810 FQ	55500 MW	62320 TQ	USBLS	5/07
	Massachusetts	Y	41920 FQ	47820 MW	55070 TQ	USBLS	5/07
	Boston-Cambridge-Quincy NECTA, MA	Y	43430 FQ	49120 MW	56760 TQ	USBLS	5/07
	Worcester MSA, MA-CT	Y	47780 FQ	52450 MW	58400 TQ	USBLS	5/07
	Michigan	Y	41770 FQ	49720 MW	61730 TQ	USBLS	5/07
	Detroit-Warren-Livonia MSA, MI	Y	43970 FQ	54350 MW	68810 TQ	USBLS	5/07
	Grand Rapids-Wyoming MSA, MI	Y	44340 FQ	49340 MW	55440 TQ	USBLS	5/07
	Warren-Troy-Farmington Hills PMSA, MI	Y	42640 FQ	54810 MW	70440 TQ	USBLS	5/07
	Minnesota	Y	44380 FQ	51740 MW	60967 TQ	MNBLS	10/08-12/08
	Duluth-Superior MSA, MN-WI	Y	42877 FQ	47873 MW	53088 TQ	MNBLS	10/08-12/08
	Minneapolis-Saint Paul MSA, MN-WI	Y	47137 FQ	55120 MW	62667 TQ	MNBLS	10/08-12/08
	Rochester MSA, MN	Y	47428 FQ	60677 MW	70212 TQ	MNBLS	10/08-12/08
	Mississippi	Y	28270 FQ	34990 MW	45420 TQ	USBLS	5/07
	Missouri	Y	30490 FQ	38420 MW	48810 TQ	USBLS	5/07
	Kansas City MSA, MO-KS	Y	41500 FQ	52780 MW	68650 TQ	USBLS	5/07
	St. Louis MSA, MO-IL	Y	41800 FQ	50880 MW	62170 TQ	USBLS	5/07
	Montana	Y	37070 FQ	44530 MW	54960 TQ	USBLS	5/07
	Billings MSA, MT	Y	38010 FQ	43210 MW	48670 TQ	USBLS	5/07
	Nebraska	Y	31490 FQ	37190 MW	42560 TQ	USBLS	5/07
	Omaha-Council Bluffs MSA, NE-IA	Y	33750 FQ	38020 MW	43170 TQ	USBLS	5/07
	Nevada	H	21.53 FQ	24.71 MW	31.14 TQ	NVBLS	5/08
	New Hampshire	H	16.86 AE	20.45 MW	22.66 AEX	NHBLS	6/08
	New Jersey	Y	41500 FQ	47320 MW	54920 TQ	USBLS	5/07
	Camden PMSA, NJ	Y	41500 FQ	45820 MW	50200 TQ	USBLS	5/07
	Edison PMSA, NJ	Y	39300 FQ	47480 MW	55320 TQ	USBLS	5/07
	Newark-Union PMSA, NJ-PA	Y	43250 FQ	50180 MW	60180 TQ	USBLS	5/07
	Trenton-Ewing MSA, NJ	Y	39620 FQ	45390 MW	51930 TQ	USBLS	5/07
	New Mexico	Y	38130 FQ	56160 MW	69790 TQ	USBLS	5/07
	New York	Y	44240 FQ	55330 MW	71350 TQ	USBLS	5/07
	Albany-Schenectady-Troy MSA, NY	Y	41000 FQ	45710 MW	50780 TQ	USBLS	5/07
	Buffalo-Niagara Falls MSA, NY	Y	37750 FQ	43840 MW	48760 TQ	USBLS	5/07
	Nassau-Suffolk PMSA, NY	Y	46320 FQ	57560 MW	67950 TQ	USBLS	5/07

AE Average entry wage	**AW** Average wage paid	**FQ** First quartile wage	**LO** Lowest wage paid	**MTC** Median total compensation	**TCC** Total cash compensation
AER Average entry range	**AWR** Average wage range	**H** Hourly	**LR** Low end range	**MW** Median wage paid	**TQ** Third quartile wage
AEX Average experienced wage	**AXR** Average experienced range	**HI** Highest wage paid	**M** Monthly	**MWR** Median wage range	**W** Weekly
ATC Average total compensation	**D** Daily	**HR** High end range	**MCC** Median cash compensation	**S** See annotated source	**Y** Yearly

Stationary Engineer and Boiler Operator

Occupation/Type/Industry	Location	Per	Low	Mid	High	Source	Date
Stationary Engineer and Boiler Operator	New York-Northern New Jersey-Long Island MSA, NY-NJ-PA	Y	46770 FQ	60270 MW	72590 TQ	USBLS	5/07
	North Carolina	Y	27700 FQ	35120 MW	46910 TQ	USBLS	5/07
	Charlotte-Gastonia-Concord MSA, NC-SC	Y	26780 FQ	32980 MW	39360 TQ	USBLS	5/07
	North Dakota	Y	30280 FQ	36270 MW	49320 TQ	USBLS	5/07
	Fargo MSA, ND-MN	Y	32210 FQ	41340 MW	46830 TQ	USBLS	5/07
	Ohio	Y	39950 FQ	46160 MW	55650 TQ	USBLS	5/07
	Cincinnati-Middletown MSA, OH-KY-IN	Y	40960 FQ	47780 MW	55310 TQ	USBLS	5/07
	Cleveland-Elyria-Mentor MSA, OH	Y	45070 FQ	54240 MW	66380 TQ	USBLS	5/07
	Columbus MSA, OH	Y	40140 FQ	45100 MW	50620 TQ	USBLS	5/07
	Dayton MSA, OH	Y	41290 FQ	49290 MW	58360 TQ	USBLS	5/07
	Oklahoma	Y	27940 FQ	34680 MW	43860 TQ	USBLS	5/07
	Oklahoma City MSA, OK	Y	31430 FQ	35470 MW	42010 TQ	USBLS	5/07
	Tulsa MSA, OK	Y	22590 FQ	35960 MW	57090 TQ	USBLS	5/07
	Oregon	H	18.60 FQ	24.39 MW	28.16 TQ	ORBLS	5/08
	Portland-Vancouver-Beaverton MSA, OR-WA	Y	40740 FQ	51740 MW	58080 TQ	USBLS	5/07
	Pennsylvania	Y	38550 FQ	46220 MW	54830 TQ	USBLS	5/07
	Allentown-Bethlehem-Easton MSA, PA-NJ	Y	34240 FQ	40580 MW	46590 TQ	USBLS	5/07
	Philadelphia-Camden-Wilmington MSA, PA-NJ-DE-MD	Y	41480 FQ	47400 MW	54040 TQ	USBLS	5/07
	Pittsburgh MSA, PA	Y	42570 FQ	50400 MW	64180 TQ	USBLS	5/07
	York-Hanover MSA, PA	Y	35530 FQ	44240 MW	50590 TQ	USBLS	5/07
	Rhode Island	Y	43100 FQ	49000 MW	57140 TQ	USBLS	5/07
	Providence-Fall River-Warwick MSA, RI-MA	Y	42790 FQ	48840 MW	56870 TQ	USBLS	5/07
	South Carolina	Y	30940 FQ	39760 MW	47470 TQ	USBLS	5/07
	Columbia MSA, SC	Y	26390 FQ	32160 MW	45200 TQ	USBLS	5/07
	South Dakota	Y	26493 FQ	36244 MW	45350 TQ	SDBLS	7/08-9/08
	Sioux Falls MSA, SD	Y	34524 FQ	41008 MW	46780 TQ	SDBLS	7/08-9/08
	Tennessee	Y	28730 FQ	44380 MW	59420 TQ	USBLS	5/07
	Memphis MSA, TN-MS-AR	Y	40090 FQ	48040 MW	60240 TQ	USBLS	5/07
	Nashville-Davidson-Murfreesboro MSA, TN	Y	35800 FQ	49110 MW	61190 TQ	USBLS	5/07
	Texas	Y	30890 FQ	39850 MW	48380 TQ	USBLS	5/07
	Austin-Round Rock MSA, TX	Y	36060 FQ	44380 MW	51360 TQ	USBLS	5/07
	Dallas-Fort Worth-Arlington MSA, TX	Y	33640 FQ	41770 MW	49240 TQ	USBLS	5/07
	El Paso MSA, TX	Y	30670 FQ	35990 MW	43770 TQ	USBLS	5/07
	Houston-Sugar Land-Baytown MSA, TX	Y	32310 FQ	40630 MW	47430 TQ	USBLS	5/07
	San Antonio MSA, TX	Y	26670 FQ	30510 MW	37680 TQ	USBLS	5/07
	Utah	Y	43860 FQ	54080 MW	65910 TQ	USBLS	5/07
	Ogden-Clearfield MSA, UT	Y	43120 FQ	48420 MW	55390 TQ	USBLS	5/07
	Salt Lake City MSA, UT	Y	38380 FQ	52760 MW	71100 TQ	USBLS	5/07
	Vermont	Y	29160 FQ	36350 MW	44540 TQ	USBLS	5/07
	Burlington-South Burlington MSA, VT	Y	34940 FQ	41480 MW	48690 TQ	USBLS	5/07
	Virginia	Y	32110 FQ	39660 MW	48600 TQ	USBLS	5/07
	Richmond MSA, VA	Y	29960 FQ	35870 MW	44260 TQ	USBLS	5/07
	Virginia Beach-Norfolk-Newport News MSA, VA-NC	Y	33940 FQ	40600 MW	46730 TQ	USBLS	5/07
	Washington	H	20.94 FQ	24.23 MW	28.51 TQ	WABLS	3/08
	Seattle-Tacoma-Bellevue MSA, WA	Y	45670 FQ	53210 MW	59650 TQ	USBLS	5/07
	West Virginia	Y	27331 FQ	40377 MW	55328 TQ	WVBLS	7/08-9/08
	Wisconsin	Y	37410 FQ	43840 MW	49710 TQ	USBLS	5/07
	Milwaukee-Waukesha-West Allis MSA, WI	Y	37920 FQ	43460 MW	49010 TQ	USBLS	5/07
	Wyoming	Y	50270 FQ	59117 MW	67215 TQ	WYBLS	9/08
	Puerto Rico	Y	26920 FQ	32970 MW	38450 TQ	USBLS	5/07
	San Juan-Caguas-Guaynabo MSA, PR	Y	28530 FQ	33950 MW	38940 TQ	USBLS	5/07
	Virgin Islands	Y	27730 FQ	31610 MW	36200 TQ	USBLS	5/07

AE	Average entry wage	AW	Average wage paid	FQ	First quartile wage	LO	Lowest wage paid	MTC	Median total compensation	TCC	Total cash compensation
AER	Average entry range	AWR	Average wage range	H	Hourly	LR	Low end range	MW	Median wage paid	TQ	Third quartile wage
AEX	Average experienced wage	AXR	Average experienced range	HI	Highest wage paid	M	Monthly	MWR	Median wage range	W	Weekly
ATC	Average total compensation	D	Daily	HR	High end range	MCC	Median cash compensation	S	See annotated source	Y	Yearly

Occupation/Type/Industry	Location	Per	Low	Mid	High	Source	Date
Statistical Assistant	Alabama	Y	24730 FQ	33930 MW	41740 TQ	USBLS	5/07
	Arizona	Y	26000 FQ	30640 MW	35970 TQ	USBLS	5/07
	Phoenix-Mesa-Scottsdale MSA, AZ	Y	26150 FQ	30860 MW	36250 TQ	USBLS	5/07
	California	H	15.38 FQ	18.73 MW	22.91 TQ	CABLS	1/08-3/08
	Los Angeles-Long Beach-Glendale PMSA, CA	H	14.55 FQ	16.69 MW	20.27 TQ	CABLS	1/08-3/08
	Oakland-Fremont-Hayward MSA, CA	H	17.45 FQ	21.56 MW	27.80 TQ	CABLS	1/08-3/08
	Riverside-San Bernardino-Ontario MSA, CA	H	16.22 FQ	19.94 MW	23.21 TQ	CABLS	1/08-3/08
	Sacramento-Arden Arcade-Roseville MSA, CA	H	17.25 FQ	19.94 MW	23.81 TQ	CABLS	1/08-3/08
	San Diego-Carlsbad-San Marcos MSA, CA	H	14.30 FQ	16.17 MW	22.04 TQ	CABLS	1/08-3/08
	San Francisco-San Mateo-Redwood PMSA, CA	H	19.85 FQ	23.55 MW	27.11 TQ	CABLS	1/08-3/08
	San Jose-Sunnyvale-Santa Clara MSA, CA	H	20.18 FQ	23.17 MW	26.53 TQ	CABLS	1/08-3/08
	Santa Ana-Anaheim-Irvine PMSA, CA	Y	30050 FQ	36260 MW	40580 TQ	USBLS	5/07
	Colorado	Y	35070 FQ	42760 MW	48750 TQ	USBLS	5/07
	Denver-Aurora MSA, CO	Y	35840 FQ	43910 MW	49000 TQ	USBLS	5/07
	Connecticut	H	13.97 AE	18.15 MW		CTBLS	1/08-3/08
	Bridgeport-Stamford-Norwalk MSA, CT	Y	32450 FQ	35950 MW	42430 TQ	USBLS	5/07
	Hartford-West Hartford-East Hartford MSA, CT	Y	30950 FQ	40450 MW	51280 TQ	USBLS	5/07
	District of Columbia	Y	37980 FQ	43160 MW	49150 TQ	USBLS	5/07
	Washington-Arlington-Alexandria MSA, DC-VA-MD-WV	Y	38240 FQ	44150 MW	50120 TQ	USBLS	5/07
	Florida	Y	27230 FQ	31460 MW	38310 TQ	USBLS	5/07
	Fort Lauderdale-Pompano Beach-Deerfield Beach PMSA, FL	Y	27940 FQ	33000 MW	38050 TQ	USBLS	5/07
	Miami-Fort Lauderdale-Miami Beach MSA, FL	Y	26160 FQ	31680 MW	38820 TQ	USBLS	5/07
	Orlando-Kissimmee MSA, FL	Y	26810 FQ	29620 MW	32750 TQ	USBLS	5/07
	Tampa-St. Petersburg-Clearwater MSA, FL	Y	29640 FQ	33110 MW	42120 TQ	USBLS	5/07
	Georgia	Y	21830 FQ	24320 MW	29420 TQ	USBLS	5/07
	Atlanta-Sandy Springs-Marietta MSA, GA	Y	22360 FQ	25170 MW	31500 TQ	USBLS	5/07
	Hawaii	Y	27000 FQ	30400 MW	38230 TQ	USBLS	5/07
	Honolulu MSA, HI	Y	27270 FQ	30890 MW	40440 TQ	USBLS	5/07
	Illinois	Y	35660 FQ	41930 MW	50030 TQ	USBLS	5/07
	Chicago-Naperville-Joliet MSA, IL-IN-WI	Y	31210 FQ	37540 MW	46120 TQ	USBLS	5/07
	Indiana	Y	27580 FQ	30220 MW	34760 TQ	USBLS	5/07
	Gary PMSA, IN	Y	27740 FQ	30050 MW	32510 TQ	USBLS	5/07
	Indianapolis-Carmel MSA, IN	Y	28020 FQ	31650 MW	41700 TQ	USBLS	5/07
	Iowa	Y	31430 FQ	41520 MW	55320 TQ	USBLS	5/07
	Kentucky	Y	40640 FQ	44140 MW	47821 TQ	KYBLS	2008
	Louisville-Jefferson County MSA, KY-IN	Y	27540 FQ	30130 MW	34640 TQ	USBLS	5/07
	Louisiana	H	15.22 FQ	21.85 MW	25.02 TQ	LABLS	1/08-3/08
	Maine	Y	28060 FQ	32340 MW	36520 TQ	USBLS	5/07
	Portland-South Portland-Biddeford MSA, ME	Y	28040 FQ	32000 MW	36090 TQ	USBLS	5/07
	Maryland	Y		40450 MW		MDBLS	3/08
	Baltimore-Towson MSA, MD	Y	29850 FQ	35860 MW	41590 TQ	USBLS	5/07
	Bethesda-Gaithersburg-Frederick PMSA, MD	Y	28420 FQ	35750 MW	54490 TQ	USBLS	5/07
	Massachusetts	Y	34550 FQ	39560 MW	46330 TQ	USBLS	5/07
	Boston-Cambridge-Quincy NECTA, MA	Y	34890 FQ	39540 MW	46240 TQ	USBLS	5/07
	Worcester MSA, MA-CT	Y	38830 FQ	45190 MW	53900 TQ	USBLS	5/07
	Michigan	Y	23840 FQ	28890 MW	37470 TQ	USBLS	5/07
	Detroit-Warren-Livonia MSA, MI	Y	33850 FQ	42900 MW	49610 TQ	USBLS	5/07

AE	Average entry wage	**AW**	Average wage paid	**FQ**	First quartile wage	**LO** Lowest wage paid	**MTC** Median total compensation **TCC** Total cash compensation
AER	Average entry range	**AWR**	Average wage range	**H**	Hourly	**LR** Low end range	**MW** Median wage paid **TQ** Third quartile wage
AEX	Average experienced wage	**AXR**	Average experienced range	**HI**	Highest wage paid	**M** Monthly	**MWR** Median wage range **W** Weekly
ATC	Average total compensation	**D**	Daily	**HR**	High end range	**MCC** Median cash compensation	**S** See annotated source **Y** Yearly

Statistical Assistant

Occupation/Type/Industry	Location	Per	Low	Mid	High	Source	Date
Statistical Assistant	Grand Rapids-Wyoming MSA, MI	Y	23770 FQ	33500 MW	38350 TQ	USBLS	5/07
	Warren-Troy-Farmington Hills PMSA, MI	Y	38330 FQ	43760 MW	48770 TQ	USBLS	5/07
	Minnesota	Y	34158 FQ	38571 MW	44181 TQ	MNBLS	10/08-12/08
	Minneapolis-Saint Paul MSA, MN-WI	Y	35845 FQ	40018 MW	46128 TQ	MNBLS	10/08-12/08
	Mississippi	Y	26940 FQ	31050 MW	43140 TQ	USBLS	5/07
	Missouri	Y	38380 FQ	44890 MW	51950 TQ	USBLS	5/07
	St. Louis MSA, MO-IL	Y	35680 FQ	45370 MW	52590 TQ	USBLS	5/07
	Nebraska	Y	19250 FQ	24710 MW	35650 TQ	USBLS	5/07
	Omaha-Council Bluffs MSA, NE-IA	Y	18760 FQ	24010 MW	35090 TQ	USBLS	5/07
	New Hampshire	H	13.85 AE	17.28 MW	19.89 AEX	NHBLS	6/08
	New Jersey	Y	33000 FQ	38440 MW	45690 TQ	USBLS	5/07
	Edison PMSA, NJ	Y	30370 FQ	36850 MW	44120 TQ	USBLS	5/07
	Newark-Union PMSA, NJ-PA	Y	29970 FQ	36950 MW	44300 TQ	USBLS	5/07
	New Mexico	Y	21960 FQ	31740 MW	37450 TQ	USBLS	5/07
	New York	Y	31910 FQ	38790 MW	50450 TQ	USBLS	5/07
	Albany-Schenectady-Troy MSA, NY	Y	29890 FQ	34780 MW	44110 TQ	USBLS	5/07
	Buffalo-Niagara Falls MSA, NY	Y	27450 FQ	35560 MW	45560 TQ	USBLS	5/07
	Nassau-Suffolk PMSA, NY	Y	33180 FQ	37490 MW	44150 TQ	USBLS	5/07
	New York-Northern New Jersey-Long Island MSA, NY-NJ-PA	Y	34080 FQ	39250 MW	48490 TQ	USBLS	5/07
	North Carolina	Y	25570 FQ	29880 MW	36460 TQ	USBLS	5/07
	Raleigh-Cary MSA, NC	Y	27900 FQ	31540 MW	39340 TQ	USBLS	5/07
	Ohio	Y	28120 FQ	32750 MW	38650 TQ	USBLS	5/07
	Cincinnati-Middletown MSA, OH-KY-IN	Y	32020 FQ	35470 MW	38760 TQ	USBLS	5/07
	Cleveland-Elyria-Mentor MSA, OH	Y	18800 FQ	28000 MW	36250 TQ	USBLS	5/07
	Columbus MSA, OH	Y	31870 FQ	41770 MW	49020 TQ	USBLS	5/07
	Dayton MSA, OH	Y	26490 FQ	29790 MW	33450 TQ	USBLS	5/07
	Oregon	H	15.49 FQ	18.63 MW	22.07 TQ	ORBLS	5/08
	Portland-Vancouver-Beaverton MSA, OR-WA	Y	33270 FQ	38550 MW	45270 TQ	USBLS	5/07
	Pennsylvania	Y	15490 FQ	31330 MW	42290 TQ	USBLS	5/07
	Allentown-Bethlehem-Easton MSA, PA-NJ	Y	25070 FQ	34800 MW	49780 TQ	USBLS	5/07
	Philadelphia-Camden-Wilmington MSA, PA-NJ-DE-MD	Y	28990 FQ	37360 MW	49860 TQ	USBLS	5/07
	Pittsburgh MSA, PA	Y	15180 FQ	28010 MW	36490 TQ	USBLS	5/07
	South Carolina	Y	26540 FQ	31980 MW	38150 TQ	USBLS	5/07
	Charleston-North Charleston MSA, SC	Y	29080 FQ	34780 MW	40540 TQ	USBLS	5/07
	Columbia MSA, SC	Y	28030 FQ	33780 MW	39010 TQ	USBLS	5/07
	South Dakota	Y	24731 FQ	28882 MW	42912 TQ	SDBLS	7/08-9/08
	Tennessee	Y	27420 FQ	35880 MW	41050 TQ	USBLS	5/07
	Nashville-Davidson-Murfreesboro MSA, TN	Y	29950 FQ	36150 MW	40520 TQ	USBLS	5/07
	Texas	Y	26880 FQ	36070 MW	48700 TQ	USBLS	5/07
	Austin-Round Rock MSA, TX	Y	42830 FQ	49420 MW	64860 TQ	USBLS	5/07
	Dallas-Fort Worth-Arlington MSA, TX	Y	24110 FQ	28980 MW	36830 TQ	USBLS	5/07
	Houston-Sugar Land-Baytown MSA, TX	Y	35880 FQ	43960 MW	50250 TQ	USBLS	5/07
	San Antonio MSA, TX	Y	42520 FQ	48170 MW	55350 TQ	USBLS	5/07
	Utah	Y	25820 FQ	33290 MW	44400 TQ	USBLS	5/07
	Ogden-Clearfield MSA, UT	Y	22060 FQ	29390 MW	44940 TQ	USBLS	5/07
	Salt Lake City MSA, UT	Y	27620 FQ	34160 MW	44220 TQ	USBLS	5/07
	Virginia	Y	37470 FQ	43660 MW	48480 TQ	USBLS	5/07
	Washington	H	14.41 FQ	17.12 MW	19.51 TQ	WABLS	3/08
	Seattle-Tacoma-Bellevue MSA, WA	Y	29510 FQ	35720 MW	41750 TQ	USBLS	5/07
	West Virginia	Y	29356 FQ	32804 MW	43938 TQ	WVBLS	7/08-9/08
	Wisconsin	Y	34030 FQ	38600 MW	44620 TQ	USBLS	5/07
	Milwaukee-Waukesha-West Allis MSA, WI	Y	39990 FQ	44360 MW	47890 TQ	USBLS	5/07

AE	Average entry wage	AW	Average wage paid	FQ	First quartile wage	LO	Lowest wage paid	MTC	Median total compensation	TCC	Total cash compensation
AER	Average entry range	AWR	Average wage range	H	Hourly	LR	Low end range	MW	Median wage paid	TQ	Third quartile wage
AEX	Average experienced wage	AXR	Average experienced range	HI	Highest wage paid	M	Monthly	MWR	Median wage range	W	Weekly
ATC	Average total compensation	D	Daily	HR	High end range	MCC	Median cash compensation	S	See annotated source	Y	Yearly

Occupation/Type/Industry	Location	Per	Low	Mid	High	Source	Date
Statistical Assistant	Puerto Rico	Y	15010 FQ	19510 MW	24370 TQ	USBLS	5/07
	San Juan-Caguas-Guaynabo MSA, PR	Y	14910 FQ	19110 MW	24390 TQ	USBLS	5/07
Department of Education	New Hampshire	Y			35059 HI	NHUL03	2008
Statistician	Alabama	Y	42990 FQ	53930 MW	68420 TQ	USBLS	5/07
	Arizona	Y	38060 FQ	59250 MW	90100 TQ	USBLS	5/07
	Phoenix-Mesa-Scottsdale MSA, AZ	Y	39760 FQ	65170 MW	93460 TQ	USBLS	5/07
	Tucson MSA, AZ	Y	33790 FQ	44790 MW	54770 TQ	USBLS	5/07
	California	H	31.93 FQ	40.78 MW	51.87 TQ	CABLS	1/08-3/08
	Los Angeles-Long Beach-Glendale PMSA, CA	H	29.13 FQ	36.90 MW	45.68 TQ	CABLS	1/08-3/08
	Oakland-Fremont-Hayward MSA, CA	H	34.95 FQ	45.12 MW	55.89 TQ	CABLS	1/08-3/08
	Riverside-San Bernardino-Ontario MSA, CA	H	28.07 FQ	36.59 MW	48.02 TQ	CABLS	1/08-3/08
	Sacramento-Arden Arcade-Roseville MSA, CA	H	25.81 FQ	31.79 MW	40.75 TQ	CABLS	1/08-3/08
	San Diego-Carlsbad-San Marcos MSA, CA	H	32.04 FQ	38.69 MW	50.63 TQ	CABLS	1/08-3/08
	San Francisco-San Mateo-Redwood PMSA, CA	H	33.52 FQ	46.16 MW	59.01 TQ	CABLS	1/08-3/08
	San Jose-Sunnyvale-Santa Clara MSA, CA	H	32.70 FQ	43.69 MW	55.62 TQ	CABLS	1/08-3/08
	Santa Ana-Anaheim-Irvine PMSA, CA	Y	74560 FQ	85990 MW	100900 TQ	USBLS	5/07
	Colorado	Y	54020 FQ	66210 MW	87340 TQ	USBLS	5/07
	Denver-Aurora MSA, CO	Y	55430 FQ	66360 MW	81620 TQ	USBLS	5/07
	Connecticut	H	29.49 AE	45.13 MW		CTBLS	1/08-3/08
	Bridgeport-Stamford-Norwalk MSA, CT	Y	85190 FQ	105160 MW	119640 TQ	USBLS	5/07
	Hartford-West Hartford-East Hartford MSA, CT	Y	71320 FQ	81880 MW	100140 TQ	USBLS	5/07
	Delaware	Y	40800 FQ	54750 MW	76670 TQ	USBLS	5/07
	District of Columbia	Y	80240 FQ	93610 MW	109750 TQ	USBLS	5/07
	Washington-Arlington-Alexandria MSA, DC-VA-MD-WV	Y	72750 FQ	89270 MW	103190 TQ	USBLS	5/07
	Florida	Y	39640 FQ	56390 MW	75580 TQ	USBLS	5/07
	Miami-Fort Lauderdale-Miami Beach MSA, FL	Y	47770 FQ	66900 MW	87260 TQ	USBLS	5/07
	Orlando-Kissimmee MSA, FL	Y	39420 FQ	62390 MW	81700 TQ	USBLS	5/07
	Tampa-St. Petersburg-Clearwater MSA, FL	Y	35200 FQ	53670 MW	67530 TQ	USBLS	5/07
	Georgia	Y	47790 FQ	69380 MW	91530 TQ	USBLS	5/07
	Atlanta-Sandy Springs-Marietta MSA, GA	Y	51070 FQ	72260 MW	92850 TQ	USBLS	5/07
	Hawaii	Y	47130 FQ	58620 MW	71480 TQ	USBLS	5/07
	Honolulu MSA, HI	Y	48330 FQ	59980 MW	72860 TQ	USBLS	5/07
	Illinois	Y	60640 FQ	75650 MW	93180 TQ	USBLS	5/07
	Chicago-Naperville-Joliet MSA, IL-IN-WI	Y	63680 FQ	77640 MW	94880 TQ	USBLS	5/07
	Indiana	Y	40640 FQ	61380 MW	77350 TQ	USBLS	5/07
	Indianapolis-Carmel MSA, IN	Y	40870 FQ	64400 MW	78240 TQ	USBLS	5/07
	Iowa	Y	45920 FQ	55890 MW	70020 TQ	USBLS	5/07
	Des Moines-West Des Moines MSA, IA	Y	44730 FQ	54230 MW	62100 TQ	USBLS	5/07
	Kansas	Y	34990 FQ	41950 MW	67740 TQ	USBLS	5/07
	Kentucky	Y	38664 FQ	58674 MW	79046 TQ	KYBLS	2008
	Louisville-Jefferson County MSA, KY-IN	Y	39130 FQ	58600 MW	75050 TQ	USBLS	5/07
	Louisiana	H	22.84 FQ	28.11 MW	35.64 TQ	LABLS	1/08-3/08
	New Orleans-Metairie-Kenner MSA, LA	Y	57390 FQ	68140 MW	78220 TQ	USBLS	5/07
	Maine	Y	45850 FQ	56620 MW	65440 TQ	USBLS	5/07
	Maryland	Y		89175 MW		MDBLS	3/08
	Baltimore-Towson MSA, MD	Y	56240 FQ	72750 MW	98020 TQ	USBLS	5/07
	Bethesda-Gaithersburg-Frederick PMSA, MD	Y	86180 FQ	100190 MW	118130 TQ	USBLS	5/07
	Massachusetts	Y	55340 FQ	75950 MW	100370 TQ	USBLS	5/07

AE	Average entry wage	AW	Average wage paid	FQ	First quartile wage	LO	Lowest wage paid	MTC	Median total compensation	TCC	Total cash compensation
AER	Average entry range	AWR	Average wage range	H	Hourly	LR	Low end range	MW	Median wage paid	TQ	Third quartile wage
AEX	Average experienced wage	AXR	Average experienced range	HI	Highest wage paid	M	Monthly	MWR	Median wage range	W	Weekly
ATC	Average total compensation	D	Daily	HR	High end range	MCC	Median cash compensation	S	See annotated source	Y	Yearly

Occupation/Type/Industry	Location	Per	Low	Mid	High	Source	Date
Statistician	Boston-Cambridge-Quincy NECTA, MA	Y	54560 FQ	74860 MW	100140 TQ	USBLS	5/07
	Worcester MSA, MA-CT	Y	52280 FQ	63450 MW	94400 TQ	USBLS	5/07
	Michigan	Y	48730 FQ	63510 MW	78660 TQ	USBLS	5/07
	Detroit-Warren-Livonia MSA, MI	Y	59990 FQ	71450 MW	82550 TQ	USBLS	5/07
	Grand Rapids-Wyoming MSA, MI	Y	36420 FQ	42350 MW	49360 TQ	USBLS	5/07
	Warren-Troy-Farmington Hills PMSA, MI	Y	57860 FQ	69880 MW	79970 TQ	USBLS	5/07
	Minnesota	Y	60409 FQ	76175 MW	95332 TQ	MNBLS	10/08-12/08
	Minneapolis-Saint Paul MSA, MN-WI	Y	63547 FQ	80674 MW	98251 TQ	MNBLS	10/08-12/08
	Mississippi	Y	49600 FQ	70750 MW	83950 TQ	USBLS	5/07
	Missouri	Y	43340 FQ	59480 MW	82400 TQ	USBLS	5/07
	Jefferson City MSA, MO	Y	34330 FQ	39030 MW	46040 TQ	USBLS	5/07
	Kansas City MSA, MO-KS	Y	50980 FQ	68140 MW	85430 TQ	USBLS	5/07
	St. Louis MSA, MO-IL	Y	57160 FQ	76190 MW	100950 TQ	USBLS	5/07
	Montana	Y	43310 FQ	51320 MW	69530 TQ	USBLS	5/07
	Nebraska	Y	35420 FQ	49190 MW	73960 TQ	USBLS	5/07
	Lincoln MSA, NE	Y	30790 FQ	39030 MW	55710 TQ	USBLS	5/07
	Omaha-Council Bluffs MSA, NE-IA	Y	38490 FQ	59490 MW	80320 TQ	USBLS	5/07
	Nevada	H	21.40 FQ	24.85 MW	39.45 TQ	NVBLS	5/08
	New Hampshire	H	18.86 AE	25.77 MW	32.60 AEX	NHBLS	6/08
	New Jersey	Y	60000 FQ	80040 MW	99000 TQ	USBLS	5/07
	Edison PMSA, NJ	Y	63680 FQ	84920 MW	100140 TQ	USBLS	5/07
	Newark-Union PMSA, NJ-PA	Y	60470 FQ	78090 MW	101740 TQ	USBLS	5/07
	New Mexico	Y	46730 FQ	79620 MW	94810 TQ	USBLS	5/07
	New York	Y	50850 FQ	66430 MW	81010 TQ	USBLS	5/07
	Albany-Schenectady-Troy MSA, NY	Y	42090 FQ	53390 MW	80670 TQ	USBLS	5/07
	Buffalo-Niagara Falls MSA, NY	Y	46590 FQ	57180 MW	76420 TQ	USBLS	5/07
	Nassau-Suffolk PMSA, NY	Y	47770 FQ	57260 MW	72610 TQ	USBLS	5/07
	New York-Northern New Jersey-Long Island MSA, NY-NJ-PA	Y	57400 FQ	73340 MW	92320 TQ	USBLS	5/07
	North Carolina	Y	51270 FQ	65800 MW	86410 TQ	USBLS	5/07
	Charlotte-Gastonia-Concord MSA, NC-SC	Y	46890 FQ	66230 MW	82440 TQ	USBLS	5/07
	Raleigh-Cary MSA, NC	Y	49900 FQ	59980 MW	77060 TQ	USBLS	5/07
	North Dakota	Y	42520 FQ	48640 MW	62670 TQ	USBLS	5/07
	Ohio	Y	50960 FQ	62410 MW	78640 TQ	USBLS	5/07
	Cincinnati-Middletown MSA, OH-KY-IN	Y	50050 FQ	68970 MW	90410 TQ	USBLS	5/07
	Cleveland-Elyria-Mentor MSA, OH	Y	54290 FQ	63080 MW	74800 TQ	USBLS	5/07
	Columbus MSA, OH	Y	49920 FQ	60350 MW	72150 TQ	USBLS	5/07
	Dayton MSA, OH	Y	53600 FQ	61900 MW	71750 TQ	USBLS	5/07
	Oklahoma	Y	33400 FQ	39390 MW	50110 TQ	USBLS	5/07
	Oklahoma City MSA, OK	Y	33260 FQ	39480 MW	50040 TQ	USBLS	5/07
	Oregon	H	23.26 FQ	27.72 MW	33.42 TQ	ORBLS	5/08
	Portland-Vancouver-Beaverton MSA, OR-WA	Y	48640 FQ	58230 MW	73200 TQ	USBLS	5/07
	Pennsylvania	Y	46920 FQ	66140 MW	98230 TQ	USBLS	5/07
	Philadelphia-Camden-Wilmington MSA, PA-NJ-DE-MD	Y	53530 FQ	79240 MW	110440 TQ	USBLS	5/07
	Pittsburgh MSA, PA	Y	38700 FQ	50710 MW	76270 TQ	USBLS	5/07
	Rhode Island	Y	66670 FQ	73660 MW	81590 TQ	USBLS	5/07
	Providence-Fall River-Warwick MSA, RI-MA	Y	66230 FQ	73300 MW	81300 TQ	USBLS	5/07
	South Carolina	Y	32170 FQ	41310 MW	51160 TQ	USBLS	5/07
	Charleston-North Charleston MSA, SC	Y	38500 FQ	45010 MW	54050 TQ	USBLS	5/07
	Columbia MSA, SC	Y	37020 FQ	45970 MW	59310 TQ	USBLS	5/07
	South Dakota	Y	39164 FQ	47032 MW	63182 TQ	SDBLS	7/08-9/08
	Sioux Falls MSA, SD	Y	41132 FQ	50214 MW	69630 TQ	SDBLS	7/08-9/08
	Tennessee	Y	37030 FQ	49910 MW	63570 TQ	USBLS	5/07
	Knoxville MSA, TN	Y	58600 FQ	78170 MW	93730 TQ	USBLS	5/07
	Memphis MSA, TN-MS-AR	Y	33370 FQ	43210 MW	50780 TQ	USBLS	5/07

AE	Average entry wage	AW	Average wage paid	FQ	First quartile wage	LO	Lowest wage paid	MTC	Median total compensation	TCC	Total cash compensation
AER	Average entry range	AWR	Average wage range	H	Hourly	LR	Low end range	MW	Median wage paid	TQ	Third quartile wage
AEX	Average experienced wage	AXR	Average experienced range	HI	Highest wage paid	M	Monthly	MWR	Median wage range	W	Weekly
ATC	Average total compensation	D	Daily	HR	High end range	MCC	Median cash compensation	S	See annotated source	Y	Yearly

Occupation/Type/Industry	Location	Per	Low	Mid	High	Source	Date
Statistician	Nashville-Davidson- Murfreesboro MSA, TN	Y	34960 FQ	41610 MW	58410 TQ	USBLS	5/07
	Texas	Y	50810 FQ	68550 MW	85670 TQ	USBLS	5/07
	Austin-Round Rock MSA, TX	Y	49970 FQ	74870 MW	93470 TQ	USBLS	5/07
	Dallas-Fort Worth-Arlington MSA, TX	Y	48790 FQ	67490 MW	91230 TQ	USBLS	5/07
	Houston-Sugar Land-Baytown MSA, TX	Y	59880 FQ	71490 MW	82450 TQ	USBLS	5/07
	San Antonio MSA, TX	Y	49630 FQ	64480 MW	80450 TQ	USBLS	5/07
	Utah	Y	47790 FQ	61910 MW	74130 TQ	USBLS	5/07
	Salt Lake City MSA, UT	Y	45450 FQ	57860 MW	71930 TQ	USBLS	5/07
	Vermont	Y	41820 FQ	47830 MW	56680 TQ	USBLS	5/07
	Virginia	Y	62520 FQ	83050 MW	100440 TQ	USBLS	5/07
	Richmond MSA, VA	Y	43770 FQ	53800 MW	72610 TQ	USBLS	5/07
	Washington	H	26.78 FQ	33.20 MW	39.84 TQ	WABLS	3/08
	Seattle-Tacoma-Bellevue MSA, WA	Y	53530 FQ	67380 MW	81710 TQ	USBLS	5/07
	West Virginia	Y	68845 FQ	84400 MW	99877 TQ	WVBLS	7/08-9/08
	Wisconsin	Y	51390 FQ	67930 MW	80960 TQ	USBLS	5/07
	Milwaukee-Waukesha-West Allis MSA, WI	Y	62650 FQ	73490 MW	83870 TQ	USBLS	5/07
	Cheyenne MSA, WY	Y	39546 FQ	53360 MW	76786 TQ	WYBLS	9/08
	Puerto Rico	Y	23250 FQ	27320 MW	31540 TQ	USBLS	5/07
	San Juan-Caguas-Guaynabo MSA, PR	Y	23350 FQ	27270 MW	31390 TQ	USBLS	5/07
State Government	Alabama	Y	30422 LO		48425 HI	AFT02	3/1/08
Statue/Decorative Artwork Restorer							
State Government	Ohio	H	23.04 LO		30.13 HI	ODAS	2008
Steeplejack							
Department of Transportation	Michigan	H	16.09 LO		24.71 HI	MDOT	10/1/07
Stenocaptioner	United States	Y		36224 AW		CBUILD02	12/08
Stock Clerk and Order Filler	Alabama	Y	15600 FQ	19290 MW	24310 TQ	USBLS	5/07
	Birmingham-Hoover MSA, AL	Y	16170 FQ	19800 MW	24900 TQ	USBLS	5/07
	Mobile MSA, AL	Y	15410 FQ	18720 MW	23260 TQ	USBLS	5/07
	Alaska	Y	21790 FQ	27930 MW	38710 TQ	USBLS	5/07
	Anchorage MSA, AK	Y	22500 FQ	28540 MW	39170 TQ	USBLS	5/07
	Arizona	Y	16650 FQ	18950 MW	23690 TQ	USBLS	5/07
	Phoenix-Mesa-Scottsdale MSA, AZ	Y	16760 FQ	18960 MW	23480 TQ	USBLS	5/07
	Prescott MSA, AZ	Y	16950 FQ	19960 MW	26380 TQ	USBLS	5/07
	Tucson MSA, AZ	Y	16400 FQ	18680 MW	23760 TQ	USBLS	5/07
	Arkansas	Y	15010 FQ	18020 MW	23020 TQ	USBLS	5/07
	Little Rock-North Little Rock MSA, AR	Y	15350 FQ	19130 MW	24190 TQ	USBLS	5/07
	California	H	8.84 FQ	10.62 MW	13.79 TQ	CABLS	1/08-3/08
	Los Angeles-Long Beach- Glendale PMSA, CA	H	8.65 FQ	10.03 MW	12.93 TQ	CABLS	1/08-3/08
	Oakland-Fremont-Hayward MSA, CA	H	9.38 FQ	11.60 MW	15.63 TQ	CABLS	1/08-3/08
	Oxnard-Thousand Oaks- Ventura MSA, CA	H	9.05 FQ	10.96 MW	13.80 TQ	CABLS	1/08-3/08
	Riverside-San Bernardino- Ontario MSA, CA	H	8.74 FQ	10.45 MW	13.75 TQ	CABLS	1/08-3/08
	Sacramento-Arden Arcade- Roseville MSA, CA	H	9.12 FQ	11.23 MW	14.21 TQ	CABLS	1/08-3/08
	San Diego-Carlsbad-San Marcos MSA, CA	H	8.80 FQ	10.62 MW	13.68 TQ	CABLS	1/08-3/08
	San Francisco-San Mateo- Redwood PMSA, CA	H	9.66 FQ	11.85 MW	15.88 TQ	CABLS	1/08-3/08
	San Jose-Sunnyvale-Santa Clara MSA, CA	H	9.04 FQ	11.04 MW	15.03 TQ	CABLS	1/08-3/08
	Santa Ana-Anaheim-Irvine PMSA, CA	Y	18160 FQ	21800 MW	27120 TQ	USBLS	5/07
	Stockton MSA, CA	H	8.86 FQ	10.68 MW	14.18 TQ	CABLS	1/08-3/08
	Colorado	Y	18790 FQ	23550 MW	32160 TQ	USBLS	5/07
	Boulder MSA, CO	Y	19340 FQ	25240 MW	33260 TQ	USBLS	5/07
	Denver-Aurora MSA, CO	Y	19210 FQ	24100 MW	33740 TQ	USBLS	5/07

AE	Average entry wage	**AW**	Average wage paid	**FQ**	First quartile wage
AER	Average entry range	**AWR**	Average wage range	**H**	Hourly
AEX	Average experienced wage	**AXR**	Average experienced range	**HI**	Highest wage paid
ATC	Average total compensation	**D**	Daily	**HR**	High end range

LO	Lowest wage paid	**MTC**	Median total compensation	**TCC**	Total cash compensation
LR	Low end range	**MW**	Median wage paid	**TQ**	Third quartile wage
M	Monthly	**MWR**	Median wage range	**W**	Weekly
MCC	Median cash compensation	**S**	See annotated source	**Y**	Yearly

Occupation/Type/Industry	Location	Per	Low	Mid	High	Source	Date
Stock Clerk and Order Filler	Connecticut	H	8.89 AE	11.34 MW		CTBLS	1/08-3/08
	Bridgeport-Stamford-Norwalk MSA, CT	Y	18930 FQ	22730 MW	29430 TQ	USBLS	5/07
	Hartford-West Hartford-East Hartford MSA, CT	Y	19440 FQ	23800 MW	30490 TQ	USBLS	5/07
	Delaware	Y	17380 FQ	21210 MW	26720 TQ	USBLS	5/07
	Wilmington PMSA, DE-MD-NJ	Y	17200 FQ	21140 MW	27250 TQ	USBLS	5/07
	District of Columbia	Y	17920 FQ	22560 MW	29710 TQ	USBLS	5/07
	Washington-Arlington-Alexandria MSA, DC-VA-MD-WV	Y	18360 FQ	22670 MW	29800 TQ	USBLS	5/07
	Florida	Y	16670 FQ	19530 MW	24040 TQ	USBLS	5/07
	Fort Lauderdale-Pompano Beach-Deerfield Beach PMSA, FL	Y	16580 FQ	19360 MW	24190 TQ	USBLS	5/07
	Jacksonville MSA, FL	Y	16980 FQ	20370 MW	25450 TQ	USBLS	5/07
	Miami-Fort Lauderdale-Miami Beach MSA, FL	Y	16560 FQ	19340 MW	24020 TQ	USBLS	5/07
	Orlando-Kissimmee MSA, FL	Y	17250 FQ	20300 MW	24460 TQ	USBLS	5/07
	Sarasota-Bradenton-Venice MSA, FL	Y	17160 FQ	20160 MW	24160 TQ	USBLS	5/07
	Tallahassee MSA, FL	Y	16040 FQ	18440 MW	22240 TQ	USBLS	5/07
	Tampa-St. Petersburg-Clearwater MSA, FL	Y	16270 FQ	18990 MW	23550 TQ	USBLS	5/07
	West Palm Beach-Boca Raton-Boynton Beach PMSA, FL	Y	16770 FQ	19930 MW	24250 TQ	USBLS	5/07
	Georgia	Y	17120 FQ	20680 MW	25420 TQ	USBLS	5/07
	Athens-Clarke County MSA, GA	Y	16720 FQ	20000 MW	24240 TQ	USBLS	5/07
	Atlanta-Sandy Springs-Marietta MSA, GA	Y	17660 FQ	21200 MW	25810 TQ	USBLS	5/07
	Hawaii	Y	18200 FQ	22380 MW	28600 TQ	USBLS	5/07
	Honolulu MSA, HI	Y	17920 FQ	21900 MW	28310 TQ	USBLS	5/07
	Idaho	Y	17200 FQ	20940 MW	26000 TQ	USBLS	5/07
	Boise City-Nampa MSA, ID	Y	18560 FQ	22190 MW	26690 TQ	USBLS	5/07
	Pocatello MSA, ID	Y	16530 FQ	18960 MW	23490 TQ	USBLS	5/07
	Illinois	Y	16840 FQ	19880 MW	25290 TQ	USBLS	5/07
	Chicago-Naperville-Joliet MSA, IL-IN-WI	Y	16980 FQ	19970 MW	25310 TQ	USBLS	5/07
	Peoria MSA, IL	Y	16860 FQ	20470 MW	27160 TQ	USBLS	5/07
	Indiana	Y	16940 FQ	20740 MW	26440 TQ	USBLS	5/07
	Gary PMSA, IN	Y	16230 FQ	19280 MW	23860 TQ	USBLS	5/07
	Indianapolis-Carmel MSA, IN	Y	17820 FQ	21850 MW	27740 TQ	USBLS	5/07
	Iowa	Y	16050 FQ	19270 MW	24400 TQ	USBLS	5/07
	Cedar Rapids MSA, IA	Y	16370 FQ	20040 MW	25250 TQ	USBLS	5/07
	Des Moines-West Des Moines MSA, IA	Y	16990 FQ	19610 MW	23920 TQ	USBLS	5/07
	Waterloo-Cedar Falls MSA, IA	Y	15350 FQ	18450 MW	23150 TQ	USBLS	5/07
	Kansas	Y	16580 FQ	20600 MW	27000 TQ	USBLS	5/07
	Wichita MSA, KS	Y	16930 FQ	21060 MW	30730 TQ	USBLS	5/07
	Kentucky	Y	16772 FQ	22050 MW	29822 TQ	KYBLS	2008
	Lexington-Fayette MSA, KY	Y	18060 FQ	24090 MW	35000 TQ	USBLS	5/07
	Louisville-Jefferson County MSA, KY-IN	Y	16810 FQ	21360 MW	26840 TQ	USBLS	5/07
	Louisiana	H	7.22 FQ	8.91 MW	11.37 TQ	LABLS	1/08-3/08
	Baton Rouge MSA, LA	Y	15380 FQ	18800 MW	23160 TQ	USBLS	5/07
	New Orleans-Metairie-Kenner MSA, LA	Y	16290 FQ	19950 MW	24840 TQ	USBLS	5/07
	Maine	Y	16980 FQ	19860 MW	24350 TQ	USBLS	5/07
	Portland-South Portland-Biddeford MSA, ME	Y	17510 FQ	20490 MW	25250 TQ	USBLS	5/07
	Maryland	Y		21800 MW		MDBLS	3/08
	Baltimore-Towson MSA, MD	Y	17140 FQ	21460 MW	28190 TQ	USBLS	5/07
	Bethesda-Gaithersburg-Frederick PMSA, MD	Y	17770 FQ	21280 MW	28810 TQ	USBLS	5/07
	Hagerstown-Martinsburg MSA, MD-WV	Y	17290 FQ	21270 MW	27140 TQ	USBLS	5/07
	Massachusetts	Y	18590 FQ	22460 MW	28900 TQ	USBLS	5/07
	Boston-Cambridge-Quincy NECTA, MA	Y	18720 FQ	22890 MW	30080 TQ	USBLS	5/07

AE	Average entry wage	AW	Average wage paid	FQ	First quartile wage
AER	Average entry range	AWR	Average wage range	H	Hourly
AEX	Average experienced wage	AXR	Average experienced range	HI	Highest wage paid
ATC	Average total compensation	D	Daily	HR	High end range

LO	Lowest wage paid	MTC	Median total compensation	TCC	Total cash compensation
LR	Low end range	MW	Median wage paid	TQ	Third quartile wage
M	Monthly	MWR	Median wage range	W	Weekly
MCC	Median cash compensation	S	See annotated source	Y	Yearly

Stock Clerk and Order Filler

Occupation/Type/Industry	Location	Per	Low	Mid	High	Source	Date
Stock Clerk and Order Filler	Lynn-Peabody-Salem NECTA, MA	Y	19370 FQ	23240 MW	30550 TQ	USBLS	5/07
	Worcester MSA, MA-CT	Y	18250 FQ	21590 MW	26450 TQ	USBLS	5/07
	Michigan	Y	17290 FQ	21960 MW	29490 TQ	USBLS	5/07
	Detroit-Warren-Livonia MSA, MI	Y	17700 FQ	23020 MW	30830 TQ	USBLS	5/07
	Grand Rapids-Wyoming MSA, MI	Y	18120 FQ	22460 MW	28950 TQ	USBLS	5/07
	Warren-Troy-Farmington Hills PMSA, MI	Y	17710 FQ	23040 MW	30470 TQ	USBLS	5/07
	Minnesota	Y	18130 FQ	22252 MW	28954 TQ	MNBLS	10/08-12/08
	Duluth-Superior MSA, MN-WI	Y	16736 FQ	20534 MW	26415 TQ	MNBLS	10/08-12/08
	Minneapolis-Saint Paul MSA, MN-WI	Y	18952 FQ	23615 MW	30464 TQ	MNBLS	10/08-12/08
	Rochester MSA, MN	Y	17865 FQ	21023 MW	28074 TQ	MNBLS	10/08-12/08
	Mississippi	Y	15520 FQ	19120 MW	24020 TQ	USBLS	5/07
	Jackson MSA, MS	Y	16770 FQ	20970 MW	26270 TQ	USBLS	5/07
	Missouri	Y	16530 FQ	20180 MW	26150 TQ	USBLS	5/07
	Kansas City MSA, MO-KS	Y	17750 FQ	21400 MW	26520 TQ	USBLS	5/07
	St. Louis MSA, MO-IL	Y	17200 FQ	21220 MW	28000 TQ	USBLS	5/07
	Montana	Y	16630 FQ	19710 MW	24710 TQ	USBLS	5/07
	Billings MSA, MT	Y	17150 FQ	20360 MW	25270 TQ	USBLS	5/07
	Nebraska	Y	16710 FQ	20040 MW	25040 TQ	USBLS	5/07
	Omaha-Council Bluffs MSA, NE-IA	Y	17280 FQ	20510 MW	25240 TQ	USBLS	5/07
	Nevada	H	9.04 FQ	11.02 MW	14.26 TQ	NVBLS	5/08
	Las Vegas-Paradise MSA, NV	H	8.98 FQ	10.92 MW	14.14 TQ	NVBLS	5/08
	New Hampshire	H	8.46 AE	11.25 MW	13.63 AEX	NHBLS	6/08
	Manchester MSA, NH	Y	18660 FQ	23450 MW	29360 TQ	USBLS	5/07
	Nashua NECTA, NH-MA	Y	18420 FQ	22680 MW	30150 TQ	USBLS	5/07
	Portsmouth MSA, NH-ME	Y	20430 FQ	24100 MW	29610 TQ	USBLS	5/07
	Rochester-Dover MSA, NH-ME	Y	19270 FQ	22500 MW	27890 TQ	USBLS	5/07
	New Jersey	Y	17160 FQ	20870 MW	28430 TQ	USBLS	5/07
	Camden PMSA, NJ	Y	17340 FQ	21190 MW	28180 TQ	USBLS	5/07
	Edison PMSA, NJ	Y	17180 FQ	20520 MW	28090 TQ	USBLS	5/07
	Newark-Union PMSA, NJ-PA	Y	17320 FQ	21350 MW	29450 TQ	USBLS	5/07
	New Mexico	Y	16460 FQ	19500 MW	24710 TQ	USBLS	5/07
	Albuquerque MSA, NM	Y	17240 FQ	20210 MW	25430 TQ	USBLS	5/07
	New York	Y	16390 FQ	19350 MW	25000 TQ	USBLS	5/07
	Albany-Schenectady-Troy MSA, NY	Y	17460 FQ	20690 MW	26270 TQ	USBLS	5/07
	Buffalo-Niagara Falls MSA, NY	Y	15800 FQ	18910 MW	24940 TQ	USBLS	5/07
	Nassau-Suffolk PMSA, NY	Y	17300 FQ	20240 MW	26060 TQ	USBLS	5/07
	New York-Northern New Jersey-Long Island MSA, NY-NJ-PA	Y	16830 FQ	19940 MW	26590 TQ	USBLS	5/07
	North Carolina	Y	17030 FQ	20790 MW	26120 TQ	USBLS	5/07
	Charlotte-Gastonia-Concord MSA, NC-SC	Y	17990 FQ	21890 MW	27270 TQ	USBLS	5/07
	Raleigh-Cary MSA, NC	Y	17450 FQ	20770 MW	25420 TQ	USBLS	5/07
	North Dakota	Y	16680 FQ	19480 MW	23950 TQ	USBLS	5/07
	Fargo MSA, ND-MN	Y	17060 FQ	19940 MW	24100 TQ	USBLS	5/07
	Ohio	Y	16380 FQ	20260 MW	27010 TQ	USBLS	5/07
	Cincinnati-Middletown MSA, OH-KY-IN	Y	16910 FQ	21940 MW	28950 TQ	USBLS	5/07
	Cleveland-Elyria-Mentor MSA, OH	Y	16740 FQ	20560 MW	27040 TQ	USBLS	5/07
	Columbus MSA, OH	Y	17270 FQ	21170 MW	28110 TQ	USBLS	5/07
	Dayton MSA, OH	Y	16220 FQ	20150 MW	26430 TQ	USBLS	5/07
	Oklahoma	Y	15970 FQ	19240 MW	25060 TQ	USBLS	5/07
	Oklahoma City MSA, OK	Y	16780 FQ	19910 MW	24980 TQ	USBLS	5/07
	Tulsa MSA, OK	Y	16780 FQ	20200 MW	27600 TQ	USBLS	5/07
	Oregon	H	9.48 FQ	11.53 MW	15.14 TQ	ORBLS	5/08
	Portland-Vancouver-Beaverton MSA, OR-WA	Y	19480 FQ	23870 MW	32040 TQ	USBLS	5/07
	Pennsylvania	Y	16330 FQ	19860 MW	25490 TQ	USBLS	5/07
	Allentown-Bethlehem-Easton MSA, PA-NJ	Y	15500 FQ	18480 MW	24460 TQ	USBLS	5/07

AE	Average entry wage	AW	Average wage paid	FQ	First quartile wage
AER	Average entry range	AWR	Average wage range	H	Hourly
AEX	Average experienced wage	AXR	Average experienced range	HI	Highest wage paid
ATC	Average total compensation	D	Daily	HR	High end range

LO	Lowest wage paid	MTC	Median total compensation	TCC	Total cash compensation
LR	Low end range	MW	Median wage paid	TQ	Third quartile wage
M	Monthly	MWR	Median wage range	W	Weekly
MCC	Median cash compensation	S	See annotated source	Y	Yearly

Occupation/Type/Industry	Location	Per	Low	Mid	High	Source	Date
Stock Clerk and Order Filler	Philadelphia-Camden-Wilmington MSA, PA-NJ-DE-MD	Y	17030 FQ	20610 MW	27190 TQ	USBLS	5/07
	Pittsburgh MSA, PA	Y	15550 FQ	18630 MW	23470 TQ	USBLS	5/07
	Rhode Island	Y	17380 FQ	20580 MW	26770 TQ	USBLS	5/07
	Providence-Fall River-Warwick MSA, RI-MA	Y	17530 FQ	20760 MW	26750 TQ	USBLS	5/07
	South Carolina	Y	16770 FQ	20360 MW	25650 TQ	USBLS	5/07
	Charleston-North Charleston MSA, SC	Y	16570 FQ	19770 MW	24870 TQ	USBLS	5/07
	Columbia MSA, SC	Y	16580 FQ	20480 MW	25750 TQ	USBLS	5/07
	Myrtle Beach-Conway-North Myrtle Beach MSA, SC	Y	17370 FQ	20350 MW	24390 TQ	USBLS	5/07
	South Dakota	Y	15586 FQ	18932 MW	23281 TQ	SDBLS	7/08-9/08
	Sioux Falls MSA, SD	Y	16928 FQ	20012 MW	24322 TQ	SDBLS	7/08-9/08
	Tennessee	Y	16240 FQ	19860 MW	25270 TQ	USBLS	5/07
	Memphis MSA, TN-MS-AR	Y	17490 FQ	21460 MW	27380 TQ	USBLS	5/07
	Nashville-Davidson-Murfreesboro MSA, TN	Y	16390 FQ	19900 MW	25370 TQ	USBLS	5/07
	Texas	Y	16340 FQ	19960 MW	25280 TQ	USBLS	5/07
	Austin-Round Rock MSA, TX	Y	18060 FQ	21970 MW	26990 TQ	USBLS	5/07
	Beaumont-Port Arthur MSA, TX	Y	15980 FQ	18540 MW	22770 TQ	USBLS	5/07
	Dallas-Fort Worth-Arlington MSA, TX	Y	17080 FQ	21020 MW	26730 TQ	USBLS	5/07
	El Paso MSA, TX	Y	13870 FQ	16960 MW	21560 TQ	USBLS	5/07
	Houston-Sugar Land-Baytown MSA, TX	Y	16670 FQ	20420 MW	25720 TQ	USBLS	5/07
	San Antonio MSA, TX	Y	16470 FQ	19650 MW	24610 TQ	USBLS	5/07
	Utah	Y	18210 FQ	21830 MW	25940 TQ	USBLS	5/07
	Ogden-Clearfield MSA, UT	Y	17840 FQ	21690 MW	26750 TQ	USBLS	5/07
	Salt Lake City MSA, UT	Y	19300 FQ	22530 MW	26050 TQ	USBLS	5/07
	Vermont	Y	17980 FQ	21300 MW	26880 TQ	USBLS	5/07
	Burlington-South Burlington MSA, VT	Y	17840 FQ	20660 MW	26900 TQ	USBLS	5/07
	Virginia	Y	17350 FQ	21520 MW	27880 TQ	USBLS	5/07
	Richmond MSA, VA	Y	18020 FQ	22670 MW	30470 TQ	USBLS	5/07
	Virginia Beach-Norfolk-Newport News MSA, VA-NC	Y	16460 FQ	20220 MW	25880 TQ	USBLS	5/07
	Washington	H	9.39 FQ	11.62 MW	15.62 TQ	WABLS	3/08
	Seattle-Tacoma-Bellevue MSA, WA	Y	19690 FQ	24930 MW	34400 TQ	USBLS	5/07
	West Virginia	Y	15677 FQ	19346 MW	26530 TQ	WVBLS	7/08-9/08
	Wisconsin	Y	16620 FQ	20290 MW	26070 TQ	USBLS	5/07
	Milwaukee-Waukesha-West Allis MSA, WI	Y	16800 FQ	20400 MW	26270 TQ	USBLS	5/07
	Wyoming	Y	18292 FQ	21788 MW	27684 TQ	WYBLS	9/08
	Casper MSA, WY	Y	20640 FQ	24303 MW	29559 TQ	WYBLS	9/08
	Cheyenne MSA, WY	Y	17849 FQ	20218 MW	24016 TQ	WYBLS	9/08
	Puerto Rico	Y	12950 FQ	14680 MW	18440 TQ	USBLS	5/07
	San Juan-Caguas-Guaynabo MSA, PR	Y	13050 FQ	14880 MW	18900 TQ	USBLS	5/07
	Virgin Islands	Y	14870 FQ	17090 MW	20150 TQ	USBLS	5/07
	Guam	Y	13760 FQ	17250 MW	26480 TQ	USBLS	5/07
Stockhandler							
Municipal Government	Cincinnati, OH	Y	33961 LO		34972 HI	COHSS	10/08
Stonemason	Alabama	Y	25250 FQ	35510 MW	45590 TQ	USBLS	5/07
	Birmingham-Hoover MSA, AL	Y	32990 FQ	44950 MW	54820 TQ	USBLS	5/07
	Arizona	Y	25460 FQ	30680 MW	38880 TQ	USBLS	5/07
	Phoenix-Mesa-Scottsdale MSA, AZ	Y	26740 FQ	32080 MW	40360 TQ	USBLS	5/07
	Tucson MSA, AZ	Y	18770 FQ	31620 MW	38920 TQ	USBLS	5/07
	Arkansas	Y	23610 FQ	28580 MW	34890 TQ	USBLS	5/07
	California	H	14.31 FQ	19.93 MW	24.77 TQ	CABLS	1/08-3/08
	Los Angeles-Long Beach-Glendale PMSA, CA	H	11.43 FQ	15.17 MW	32.48 TQ	CABLS	1/08-3/08
	Oakland-Fremont-Hayward MSA, CA	H	15.81 FQ	21.34 MW	25.01 TQ	CABLS	1/08-3/08
	Riverside-San Bernardino-Ontario MSA, CA	H	16.69 FQ	20.23 MW	23.10 TQ	CABLS	1/08-3/08

AE	Average entry wage	AW	Average wage paid	FQ	First quartile wage
AER	Average entry range	AWR	Average wage range	H	Hourly
AEX	Average experienced wage	AXR	Average experienced range	HI	Highest wage paid
ATC	Average total compensation	D	Daily	HR	High end range

LO	Lowest wage paid	MTC	Median total compensation	TCC	Total cash compensation
LR	Low end range	MW	Median wage paid	TQ	Third quartile wage
M	Monthly	MWR	Median wage range	W	Weekly
MCC	Median cash compensation	S	See annotated source	Y	Yearly

1527

Occupation/Type/Industry	Location	Per	Low	Mid	High	Source	Date
Stonemason	Sacramento-Arden Arcade-Roseville MSA, CA	H	16.96 FQ	22.01 MW	25.81 TQ	CABLS	1/08-3/08
	San Diego-Carlsbad-San Marcos MSA, CA	H	19.94 FQ	22.52 MW	25.25 TQ	CABLS	1/08-3/08
	San Francisco-San Mateo-Redwood PMSA, CA	H	16.72 FQ	23.13 MW	29.52 TQ	CABLS	1/08-3/08
	San Jose-Sunnyvale-Santa Clara MSA, CA	H	15.54 FQ	20.79 MW	24.43 TQ	CABLS	1/08-3/08
	Santa Ana-Anaheim-Irvine PMSA, CA	Y	24550 FQ	29060 MW	38400 TQ	USBLS	5/07
	Colorado	Y	36120 FQ	42920 MW	49840 TQ	USBLS	5/07
	Denver-Aurora MSA, CO	Y	33080 FQ	37460 MW	42280 TQ	USBLS	5/07
	Connecticut	H	16.24 AE	24.26 MW		CTBLS	1/08-3/08
	Bridgeport-Stamford-Norwalk MSA, CT	Y	38400 FQ	47970 MW	57020 TQ	USBLS	5/07
	Hartford-West Hartford-East Hartford MSA, CT	Y	38770 FQ	51650 MW	65750 TQ	USBLS	5/07
	Delaware	Y	26710 FQ	31240 MW	43680 TQ	USBLS	5/07
	Wilmington PMSA, DE-MD-NJ	Y	26240 FQ	29720 MW	38950 TQ	USBLS	5/07
	Washington-Arlington-Alexandria MSA, DC-VA-MD-WV	Y	28310 FQ	41020 MW	51400 TQ	USBLS	5/07
	Florida	Y	24770 FQ	30940 MW	35100 TQ	USBLS	5/07
	Miami-Fort Lauderdale-Miami Beach MSA, FL	Y	29400 FQ	32760 MW	35760 TQ	USBLS	5/07
	Georgia	Y	23000 FQ	28700 MW	35970 TQ	USBLS	5/07
	Atlanta-Sandy Springs-Marietta MSA, GA	Y	27640 FQ	32620 MW	36250 TQ	USBLS	5/07
	Macon MSA, GA	Y	26140 FQ	28120 MW	30090 TQ	USBLS	5/07
	Hawaii	Y	44860 FQ	50540 MW	63540 TQ	USBLS	5/07
	Honolulu MSA, HI	Y	44430 FQ	49680 MW	59500 TQ	USBLS	5/07
	Idaho	Y	27040 FQ	31440 MW	39470 TQ	USBLS	5/07
	Boise City-Nampa MSA, ID	Y	26320 FQ	30140 MW	35170 TQ	USBLS	5/07
	Illinois	Y	50180 FQ	69170 MW	76140 TQ	USBLS	5/07
	Chicago-Naperville-Joliet MSA, IL-IN-WI	Y	40250 FQ	67490 MW	75390 TQ	USBLS	5/07
	Indiana	Y	26010 FQ	36160 MW	45810 TQ	USBLS	5/07
	Indianapolis-Carmel MSA, IN	Y	44360 FQ	47520 MW	50680 TQ	USBLS	5/07
	Iowa	Y	29880 FQ	41100 MW	45980 TQ	USBLS	5/07
	Kansas	Y	18760 FQ	30550 MW	45660 TQ	USBLS	5/07
	Kentucky	Y	22147 FQ	24553 MW	39780 TQ	KYBLS	2008
	Louisville-Jefferson County MSA, KY-IN	Y	31420 FQ	41910 MW	46660 TQ	USBLS	5/07
	Louisiana	H	13.97 FQ	19.18 MW	21.75 TQ	LABLS	1/08-3/08
	Maine	Y	22680 FQ	25370 MW	31060 TQ	USBLS	5/07
	Maryland	Y		31725 MW		MDBLS	3/08
	Baltimore-Towson MSA, MD	Y	28510 FQ	32760 MW	47240 TQ	USBLS	5/07
	Bethesda-Gaithersburg-Frederick PMSA, MD	Y	24500 FQ	30350 MW	45610 TQ	USBLS	5/07
	Massachusetts	Y	36940 FQ	51160 MW	63450 TQ	USBLS	5/07
	Boston-Cambridge-Quincy NECTA, MA	Y	34830 FQ	51420 MW	68320 TQ	USBLS	5/07
	Michigan	Y	30500 FQ	37280 MW	49720 TQ	USBLS	5/07
	Minnesota	Y	40774 FQ	45169 MW	49806 TQ	MNBLS	10/08-12/08
	Minneapolis-Saint Paul MSA, MN-WI	Y	40605 FQ	54042 MW	61124 TQ	MNBLS	10/08-12/08
	Mississippi	Y	23030 FQ	29690 MW	40530 TQ	USBLS	5/07
	Jackson MSA, MS	Y	24220 FQ	28470 MW	36750 TQ	USBLS	5/07
	Missouri	Y	30710 FQ	36750 MW	53300 TQ	USBLS	5/07
	Kansas City MSA, MO-KS	Y	36370 FQ	45690 MW	54480 TQ	USBLS	5/07
	St. Louis MSA, MO-IL	Y	33710 FQ	37650 MW	52530 TQ	USBLS	5/07
	Montana	Y	35340 FQ	42130 MW	50350 TQ	USBLS	5/07
	Nevada	H	14.48 FQ	19.27 MW	24.58 TQ	NVBLS	5/08
	Las Vegas-Paradise MSA, NV	H	16.57 FQ	19.67 MW	24.46 TQ	NVBLS	5/08
	Reno-Sparks MSA, NV	H	13.15 FQ	14.26 MW	19.51 TQ	NVBLS	5/08
	New Hampshire	H	16.75 AE	18.46 MW	22.08 AEX	NHBLS	6/08
	New Jersey	Y	28730 FQ	42340 MW	54250 TQ	USBLS	5/07
	Camden PMSA, NJ	Y	25700 FQ	27380 MW	29060 TQ	USBLS	5/07
	Edison PMSA, NJ	Y	32980 FQ	46940 MW	56460 TQ	USBLS	5/07
	Newark-Union PMSA, NJ-PA	Y	38120 FQ	52680 MW	73090 TQ	USBLS	5/07
	New Mexico	Y	25470 FQ	30540 MW	40140 TQ	USBLS	5/07

AE	Average entry wage	AW	Average wage paid	FQ	First quartile wage
AER	Average entry range	AWR	Average wage range	H	Hourly
AEX	Average experienced wage	AXR	Average experienced range	HI	Highest wage paid
ATC	Average total compensation	D	Daily	HR	High end range

LO	Lowest wage paid	MTC	Median total compensation	TCC	Total cash compensation
LR	Low end range	MW	Median wage paid	TQ	Third quartile wage
M	Monthly	MWR	Median wage range	W	Weekly
MCC	Median cash compensation	S	See annotated source	Y	Yearly

Occupation/Type/Industry	Location	Per	Low	Mid	High	Source	Date
Stonemason	Albuquerque MSA, NM	Y	23700 FQ	26300 MW	31920 TQ	USBLS	5/07
	New York	Y	31330 FQ	39280 MW	48300 TQ	USBLS	5/07
	Albany-Schenectady-Troy MSA, NY	Y	25140 FQ	32370 MW	35520 TQ	USBLS	5/07
	Buffalo-Niagara Falls MSA, NY	Y	38300 FQ	41480 MW	45000 TQ	USBLS	5/07
	Nassau-Suffolk PMSA, NY	Y	43910 FQ	47840 MW	52670 TQ	USBLS	5/07
	New York-Northern New Jersey-Long Island MSA, NY-NJ-PA	Y	30730 FQ	43180 MW	61510 TQ	USBLS	5/07
	North Carolina	Y	26420 FQ	30540 MW	36820 TQ	USBLS	5/07
	Raleigh-Cary MSA, NC	Y	25060 FQ	31370 MW	43660 TQ	USBLS	5/07
	Ohio	Y	26540 FQ	31330 MW	41830 TQ	USBLS	5/07
	Cleveland-Elyria-Mentor MSA, OH	Y	28090 FQ	34250 MW	44850 TQ	USBLS	5/07
	Columbus MSA, OH	Y	29190 FQ	32350 MW	45460 TQ	USBLS	5/07
	Oklahoma	Y	27840 FQ	30750 MW	35040 TQ	USBLS	5/07
	Tulsa MSA, OK	Y	27440 FQ	29280 MW	31110 TQ	USBLS	5/07
	Oregon	H	14.77 FQ	16.96 MW	21.47 TQ	ORBLS	5/08
	Portland-Vancouver-Beaverton MSA, OR-WA	Y	29100 FQ	31970 MW	39600 TQ	USBLS	5/07
	Pennsylvania	Y	37870 FQ	49110 MW	58870 TQ	USBLS	5/07
	Philadelphia-Camden-Wilmington MSA, PA-NJ-DE-MD	Y	29610 FQ	49520 MW	59000 TQ	USBLS	5/07
	Pittsburgh MSA, PA	Y	49280 FQ	55810 MW	61320 TQ	USBLS	5/07
	Rhode Island	Y	37560 FQ	45470 MW	61120 TQ	USBLS	5/07
	Providence-Fall River-Warwick MSA, RI-MA	Y	38930 FQ	49330 MW	61960 TQ	USBLS	5/07
	South Carolina	Y	35530 FQ	39550 MW	45950 TQ	USBLS	5/07
	Tennessee	Y	24940 FQ	29810 MW	36370 TQ	USBLS	5/07
	Memphis MSA, TN-MS-AR	Y	19950 FQ	28660 MW	32400 TQ	USBLS	5/07
	Texas	Y	26880 FQ	34650 MW	42150 TQ	USBLS	5/07
	Dallas-Fort Worth-Arlington MSA, TX	Y	29490 FQ	36690 MW	45260 TQ	USBLS	5/07
	Houston-Sugar Land-Baytown MSA, TX	Y	29600 FQ	35320 MW	41610 TQ	USBLS	5/07
	San Antonio MSA, TX	Y	22130 FQ	33830 MW	39740 TQ	USBLS	5/07
	Utah	Y	29370 FQ	35150 MW	41850 TQ	USBLS	5/07
	Salt Lake City MSA, UT	Y	24230 FQ	33030 MW	46220 TQ	USBLS	5/07
	Vermont	Y	36120 FQ	39720 MW	45770 TQ	USBLS	5/07
	Burlington-South Burlington MSA, VT	Y	39160 FQ	47240 MW	56680 TQ	USBLS	5/07
	Virginia	Y	31040 FQ	39160 MW	47450 TQ	USBLS	5/07
	Richmond MSA, VA	Y	26970 FQ	34470 MW	39470 TQ	USBLS	5/07
	Virginia Beach-Norfolk-Newport News MSA, VA-NC	Y	29930 FQ	33490 MW	44730 TQ	USBLS	5/07
	Washington	H	19.62 FQ	27.02 MW	34.29 TQ	WABLS	3/08
	West Virginia	Y	24923 FQ	29471 MW	35581 TQ	WVBLS	7/08-9/08
	Wisconsin	Y	31730 FQ	38430 MW	52230 TQ	USBLS	5/07
	Wyoming	Y	34079 FQ	37418 MW	41041 TQ	WYBLS	9/08
	Puerto Rico	Y	14060 FQ	18160 MW	32270 TQ	USBLS	5/07
	San Juan-Caguas-Guaynabo MSA, PR	Y	14020 FQ	19940 MW	36270 TQ	USBLS	5/07
Store Director Nugget Market	Woodland, CA	Y		116444 AW		CNNM01	2009
Storm Chaser	United States	Y		60968 AW		CBUILD03	2009
Storm Drain Maintenance Worker	Carlsbad, CA	S	1551 LO		1885 HI	CCSS01	8/5/08
Storm Sewer Maintenance Specialist	Cincinnati, OH	Y	45777 LO		49087 HI	COHSS	10/08
Stormwater Business Administrator	Colorado Springs, CO	M	5939 LO			COSPRS	1/1/09
Stormwater Enterprise Manager	Colorado Springs, CO	M	7388 LO			COSPRS	1/1/09
Strategic Alliance Manager	United States	Y	87041-135000 FQ		140000-156250 TQ	ASAP	2008

AE	Average entry wage	AW	Average wage paid	FQ	First quartile wage	LO	Lowest wage paid	MTC	Median total compensation	TCC	Total cash compensation
AER	Average entry range	AWR	Average wage range	H	Hourly	LR	Low end range	MW	Median wage paid	TQ	Third quartile wage
AEX	Average experienced wage	AXR	Average experienced range	HI	Highest wage paid	M	Monthly	MWR	Median wage range	W	Weekly
ATC	Average total compensation	D	Daily	HR	High end range	MCC	Median cash compensation	S	See annotated source	Y	Yearly

Street Operations Manager

Occupation/Type/Industry	Location	Per	Low	Mid	High	Source	Date
Street Operations Manager	Colorado Springs, CO	M	6194 LO			COSPRS	1/1/09
Street Superintendent	Biloxi, MS	Y			50080 HI	MML	2008
	West, MS	Y			3000 HI	MML	2008
Street Sweeper Operator	Seaside, CA	S	2033 LO		2403 HI	SSSS	8/08
	Walnut Creek, CA	Y	56170 LO		66520 HI	WCSWP	6/27/08
Streets Manager	Colorado Springs, CO	M	7937 LO			COSPRS	1/1/09
Structural Designer							
Food and Beverage Packaging	United States	Y		70054 AW		FBPACK	12/06-12/07
Structural Engineer							
Municipal Government	Gresham, OR	Y	64284 LO		83544 HI	GOSS01	7/1/08
Structural Iron and Steel Worker	Alabama	Y	28540 FQ	33900 MW	39900 TQ	USBLS	5/07
	Birmingham-Hoover MSA, AL	Y	31170 FQ	36600 MW	45010 TQ	USBLS	5/07
	Alaska	Y	55600 FQ	66590 MW	73130 TQ	USBLS	5/07
	Arizona	Y	26740 FQ	32730 MW	38280 TQ	USBLS	5/07
	Phoenix-Mesa-Scottsdale MSA, AZ	Y	26540 FQ	32440 MW	37770 TQ	USBLS	5/07
	Tucson MSA, AZ	Y	27340 FQ	32980 MW	38640 TQ	USBLS	5/07
	Arkansas	Y	23350 FQ	28600 MW	35380 TQ	USBLS	5/07
	Fayetteville-Springdale-Rogers MSA, AR-MO	Y	25000 FQ	28420 MW	31610 TQ	USBLS	5/07
	Little Rock-North Little Rock MSA, AR	Y	24280 FQ	30920 MW	38260 TQ	USBLS	5/07
	California	H	15.64 FQ	24.33 MW	33.12 TQ	CABLS	1/08-3/08
	Los Angeles-Long Beach-Glendale PMSA, CA	H	15.57 FQ	25.88 MW	34.88 TQ	CABLS	1/08-3/08
	Oakland-Fremont-Hayward MSA, CA	H	28.69 FQ	34.13 MW	37.46 TQ	CABLS	1/08-3/08
	Riverside-San Bernardino-Ontario MSA, CA	H	14.02 FQ	17.89 MW	29.10 TQ	CABLS	1/08-3/08
	Sacramento-Arden Arcade-Roseville MSA, CA	H	23.13 FQ	30.51 MW	45.51 TQ	CABLS	1/08-3/08
	San Diego-Carlsbad-San Marcos MSA, CA	H	13.85 FQ	20.66 MW	31.39 TQ	CABLS	1/08-3/08
	San Francisco-San Mateo-Redwood PMSA, CA	H	19.26 FQ	23.77 MW	28.58 TQ	CABLS	1/08-3/08
	San Jose-Sunnyvale-Santa Clara MSA, CA	H	23.64 FQ	33.45 MW	36.56 TQ	CABLS	1/08-3/08
	Santa Ana-Anaheim-Irvine PMSA, CA	Y	25350 FQ	47650 MW	63710 TQ	USBLS	5/07
	Colorado	Y	29470 FQ	36380 MW	44830 TQ	USBLS	5/07
	Denver-Aurora MSA, CO	Y	31480 FQ	37990 MW	55390 TQ	USBLS	5/07
	Connecticut	H	17.75 AE	28.06 MW		CTBLS	1/08-3/08
	Hartford-West Hartford-East Hartford MSA, CT	Y	47300 FQ	60340 MW	67820 TQ	USBLS	5/07
	Delaware	Y	33310 FQ	39840 MW	47230 TQ	USBLS	5/07
	Wilmington PMSA, DE-MD-NJ	Y	34850 FQ	41130 MW	47340 TQ	USBLS	5/07
	Washington-Arlington-Alexandria MSA, DC-VA-MD-WV	Y	31380 FQ	38250 MW	49530 TQ	USBLS	5/07
	Florida	Y	30920 FQ	39860 MW	46900 TQ	USBLS	5/07
	Fort Lauderdale-Pompano Beach-Deerfield Beach PMSA, FL	Y	35660 FQ	40330 MW	45020 TQ	USBLS	5/07
	Jacksonville MSA, FL	Y	28190 FQ	32880 MW	43630 TQ	USBLS	5/07
	Miami-Fort Lauderdale-Miami Beach MSA, FL	Y	34420 FQ	42460 MW	49560 TQ	USBLS	5/07
	Orlando-Kissimmee MSA, FL	Y	30260 FQ	38200 MW	46240 TQ	USBLS	5/07
	Tampa-St. Petersburg-Clearwater MSA, FL	Y	29640 FQ	36070 MW	42890 TQ	USBLS	5/07
	West Palm Beach-Boca Raton-Boynton Beach PMSA, FL	Y	34770 FQ	44000 MW	52430 TQ	USBLS	5/07
	Georgia	Y	23760 FQ	30740 MW	39440 TQ	USBLS	5/07
	Atlanta-Sandy Springs-Marietta MSA, GA	Y	23850 FQ	30360 MW	39330 TQ	USBLS	5/07
	Hawaii	Y	45390 FQ	56610 MW	63120 TQ	USBLS	5/07
	Honolulu MSA, HI	Y	45650 FQ	56710 MW	64390 TQ	USBLS	5/07

Occupation/Type/Industry	Location	Per	Low	Mid	High	Source	Date
Structural Iron and Steel Worker	Idaho	Y	26190 FQ	34730 MW	43720 TQ	USBLS	5/07
	Boise City-Nampa MSA, ID	Y	25060 FQ	36260 MW	45950 TQ	USBLS	5/07
	Illinois	Y	58030 FQ	73160 MW	81670 TQ	USBLS	5/07
	Chicago-Naperville-Joliet MSA, IL-IN-WI	Y	66220 FQ	74260 MW	81790 TQ	USBLS	5/07
	Indiana	Y	31040 FQ	48790 MW	59300 TQ	USBLS	5/07
	Evansville MSA, IN-KY	Y	25330 FQ	42470 MW	56470 TQ	USBLS	5/07
	Gary PMSA, IN	Y	46760 FQ	61680 MW	70900 TQ	USBLS	5/07
	Indianapolis-Carmel MSA, IN	Y	33210 FQ	51110 MW	57010 TQ	USBLS	5/07
	South Bend-Mishawaka MSA, IN-MI	Y	41680 FQ	45070 MW	48460 TQ	USBLS	5/07
	Iowa	Y	36840 FQ	43320 MW	48510 TQ	USBLS	5/07
	Des Moines-West Des Moines MSA, IA	Y	40900 FQ	46910 MW	55120 TQ	USBLS	5/07
	Kansas	Y	24320 FQ	30980 MW	40250 TQ	USBLS	5/07
	Kentucky	Y	33453 FQ	42265 MW	49416 TQ	KYBLS	2008
	Louisville-Jefferson County MSA, KY-IN	Y	36360 FQ	43860 MW	50250 TQ	USBLS	5/07
	Owensboro MSA, KY	Y	29880 FQ	38300 MW	44260 TQ	USBLS	5/07
	Louisiana	H	14.79 FQ	18.41 MW	21.82 TQ	LABLS	1/08-3/08
	Baton Rouge MSA, LA	Y	32820 FQ	40080 MW	46030 TQ	USBLS	5/07
	New Orleans-Metairie-Kenner MSA, LA	Y	33260 FQ	40890 MW	45460 TQ	USBLS	5/07
	Maine	Y	29010 FQ	36030 MW	42250 TQ	USBLS	5/07
	Portland-South Portland-Biddeford MSA, ME	Y	39570 FQ	43100 MW	46700 TQ	USBLS	5/07
	Maryland	Y		52750 MW		MDBLS	3/08
	Baltimore-Towson MSA, MD	Y	38150 FQ	54560 MW	60070 TQ	USBLS	5/07
	Massachusetts	Y	55020 FQ	67190 MW	75310 TQ	USBLS	5/07
	Boston-Cambridge-Quincy NECTA, MA	Y	61770 FQ	69070 MW	76010 TQ	USBLS	5/07
	Worcester MSA, MA-CT	Y	54010 FQ	60430 MW	70370 TQ	USBLS	5/07
	Michigan	Y	38220 FQ	53090 MW	60980 TQ	USBLS	5/07
	Detroit-Warren-Livonia MSA, MI	Y	44450 FQ	57060 MW	64870 TQ	USBLS	5/07
	Grand Rapids-Wyoming MSA, MI	Y	53140 FQ	58450 MW	63670 TQ	USBLS	5/07
	Lansing-East Lansing MSA, MI	Y	28330 FQ	55170 MW	61150 TQ	USBLS	5/07
	Warren-Troy-Farmington Hills PMSA, MI	Y	31140 FQ	52670 MW	66050 TQ	USBLS	5/07
	Minnesota	Y	45748 FQ	61019 MW	75425 TQ	MNBLS	10/08-12/08
	Duluth-Superior MSA, MN-WI	Y	44231 FQ	65582 MW	76964 TQ	MNBLS	10/08-12/08
	Minneapolis-Saint Paul MSA, MN-WI	Y	63970 FQ	73181 MW	79672 TQ	MNBLS	10/08-12/08
	Mississippi	Y	21390 FQ	27430 MW	32050 TQ	USBLS	5/07
	Jackson MSA, MS	Y	20180 FQ	28320 MW	35360 TQ	USBLS	5/07
	Missouri	Y	32330 FQ	50110 MW	59840 TQ	USBLS	5/07
	Kansas City MSA, MO-KS	Y	39050 FQ	53760 MW	60730 TQ	USBLS	5/07
	St. Louis MSA, MO-IL	Y	46560 FQ	56940 MW	63150 TQ	USBLS	5/07
	Montana	Y	31230 FQ	40930 MW	45550 TQ	USBLS	5/07
	Billings MSA, MT	Y	32580 FQ	41370 MW	47340 TQ	USBLS	5/07
	Nebraska	Y	25300 FQ	40270 MW	47130 TQ	USBLS	5/07
	Omaha-Council Bluffs MSA, NE-IA	Y	38940 FQ	44610 MW	49390 TQ	USBLS	5/07
	Nevada	H	19.47 FQ	28.43 MW	37.64 TQ	NVBLS	5/08
	Las Vegas-Paradise MSA, NV	H	19.44 FQ	28.89 MW	37.87 TQ	NVBLS	5/08
	New Hampshire	H	14.92 AE	20.99 MW	24.87 AEX	NHBLS	6/08
	New Jersey	Y	35800 FQ	56660 MW	75030 TQ	USBLS	5/07
	Edison PMSA, NJ	Y	27980 FQ	48680 MW	71890 TQ	USBLS	5/07
	Newark-Union PMSA, NJ-PA	Y	36530 FQ	54280 MW	72390 TQ	USBLS	5/07
	New Mexico	Y	32930 FQ	43880 MW	54640 TQ	USBLS	5/07
	Albuquerque MSA, NM	Y	33610 FQ	46110 MW	56290 TQ	USBLS	5/07
	New York	Y	49170 FQ	72360 MW	90610 TQ	USBLS	5/07
	Albany-Schenectady-Troy MSA, NY	Y	38170 FQ	53520 MW	64710 TQ	USBLS	5/07
	Buffalo-Niagara Falls MSA, NY	Y	46500 FQ	54880 MW	60050 TQ	USBLS	5/07
	Nassau-Suffolk PMSA, NY	Y	68780 FQ	77450 MW	86020 TQ	USBLS	5/07
	New York-Northern New Jersey-Long Island MSA, NY-NJ-PA	Y	48110 FQ	72500 MW	86890 TQ	USBLS	5/07
	North Carolina	Y	27190 FQ	32040 MW	38110 TQ	USBLS	5/07

AE Average entry wage	**AW** Average wage paid	**FQ** First quartile wage	**LO** Lowest wage paid	**MTC** Median total compensation	**TCC** Total cash compensation
AER Average entry range	**AWR** Average wage range	**H** Hourly	**LR** Low end range	**MW** Median wage paid	**TQ** Third quartile wage
AEX Average experienced wage	**AXR** Average experienced range	**HI** Highest wage paid	**M** Monthly	**MWR** Median wage range	**W** Weekly
ATC Average total compensation	**D** Daily	**HR** High end range	**MCC** Median cash compensation	**S** See annotated source	**Y** Yearly

Occupation/Type/Industry	Location	Per	Low	Mid	High	Source	Date
Structural Iron and Steel Worker	Charlotte-Gastonia-Concord MSA, NC-SC	Y	28970 FQ	32750 MW	37380 TQ	USBLS	5/07
	Raleigh-Cary MSA, NC	Y	28460 FQ	34250 MW	45710 TQ	USBLS	5/07
	North Dakota	Y	31130 FQ	38010 MW	42310 TQ	USBLS	5/07
	Fargo MSA, ND-MN	Y	33860 FQ	37090 MW	40320 TQ	USBLS	5/07
	Ohio	Y	45800 FQ	53700 MW	59600 TQ	USBLS	5/07
	Cincinnati-Middletown MSA, OH-KY-IN	Y	41200 FQ	49230 MW	56410 TQ	USBLS	5/07
	Cleveland-Elyria-Mentor MSA, OH	Y	52250 FQ	58140 MW	66570 TQ	USBLS	5/07
	Columbus MSA, OH	Y	37530 FQ	52850 MW	59110 TQ	USBLS	5/07
	Dayton MSA, OH	Y	46890 FQ	52560 MW	59290 TQ	USBLS	5/07
	Oklahoma	Y	24330 FQ	33830 MW	44730 TQ	USBLS	5/07
	Oklahoma City MSA, OK	Y	22040 FQ	24860 MW	31330 TQ	USBLS	5/07
	Tulsa MSA, OK	Y	31090 FQ	42150 MW	47640 TQ	USBLS	5/07
	Oregon	H	19.95 FQ	22.95 MW	30.59 TQ	ORBLS	5/08
	Portland-Vancouver-Beaverton MSA, OR-WA	Y	46530 FQ	58810 MW	67210 TQ	USBLS	5/07
	Pennsylvania	Y	35480 FQ	46750 MW	62690 TQ	USBLS	5/07
	Allentown-Bethlehem-Easton MSA, PA-NJ	Y	40390 FQ	53670 MW	60280 TQ	USBLS	5/07
	Erie MSA, PA	Y	32540 FQ	37620 MW	50420 TQ	USBLS	5/07
	Philadelphia-Camden-Wilmington MSA, PA-NJ-DE-MD	Y	37320 FQ	48330 MW	76340 TQ	USBLS	5/07
	Pittsburgh MSA, PA	Y	38290 FQ	55080 MW	66990 TQ	USBLS	5/07
	Rhode Island	Y	37970 FQ	55460 MW	62490 TQ	USBLS	5/07
	Providence-Fall River-Warwick MSA, RI-MA	Y	36930 FQ	54950 MW	62570 TQ	USBLS	5/07
	South Carolina	Y	30130 FQ	35960 MW	41240 TQ	USBLS	5/07
	Charleston-North Charleston MSA, SC	Y	36000 FQ	41130 MW	45040 TQ	USBLS	5/07
	Columbia MSA, SC	Y	26970 FQ	32580 MW	37160 TQ	USBLS	5/07
	South Dakota	Y	24078 FQ	28903 MW	37002 TQ	SDBLS	7/08-9/08
	Sioux Falls MSA, SD	Y	35661 FQ	40434 MW	53694 TQ	SDBLS	7/08-9/08
	Tennessee	Y	30390 FQ	38250 MW	44580 TQ	USBLS	5/07
	Memphis MSA, TN-MS-AR	Y	32390 FQ	37640 MW	42950 TQ	USBLS	5/07
	Nashville-Davidson-Murfreesboro MSA, TN	Y	26580 FQ	31740 MW	42760 TQ	USBLS	5/07
	Texas	Y	23840 FQ	29700 MW	37540 TQ	USBLS	5/07
	Austin-Round Rock MSA, TX	Y	21990 FQ	31690 MW	38720 TQ	USBLS	5/07
	Beaumont-Port Arthur MSA, TX	Y	27570 FQ	31890 MW	41070 TQ	USBLS	5/07
	Corpus Christi MSA, TX	Y	22710 FQ	26820 MW	32590 TQ	USBLS	5/07
	Dallas-Fort Worth-Arlington MSA, TX	Y	22820 FQ	28740 MW	36780 TQ	USBLS	5/07
	Houston-Sugar Land-Baytown MSA, TX	Y	28400 FQ	35790 MW	43340 TQ	USBLS	5/07
	San Antonio MSA, TX	Y	21660 FQ	26890 MW	32680 TQ	USBLS	5/07
	Utah	Y	32340 FQ	43240 MW	48920 TQ	USBLS	5/07
	Salt Lake City MSA, UT	Y	33690 FQ	42780 MW	48580 TQ	USBLS	5/07
	Vermont	Y	25800 FQ	35060 MW	43720 TQ	USBLS	5/07
	Burlington-South Burlington MSA, VT	Y	33490 FQ	39350 MW	44950 TQ	USBLS	5/07
	Virginia	Y	29930 FQ	36280 MW	43410 TQ	USBLS	5/07
	Richmond MSA, VA	Y	35110 FQ	40560 MW	45260 TQ	USBLS	5/07
	Virginia Beach-Norfolk-Newport News MSA, VA-NC	Y	29710 FQ	36920 MW	44340 TQ	USBLS	5/07
	Washington	H	17.48 FQ	24.10 MW	32.16 TQ	WABLS	3/08
	Seattle-Tacoma-Bellevue MSA, WA	Y	36520 FQ	49880 MW	65390 TQ	USBLS	5/07
	West Virginia	Y	27335 FQ	36383 MW	55405 TQ	WVBLS	7/08-9/08
	Charleston MSA, WV	Y	40360 FQ	52590 MW	58190 TQ	USBLS	5/07
	Wisconsin	Y	37090 FQ	56250 MW	69700 TQ	USBLS	5/07
	Milwaukee-Waukesha-West Allis MSA, WI	Y	54190 FQ	66640 MW	74720 TQ	USBLS	5/07
	Wyoming	Y	27366 FQ	33298 MW	50031 TQ	WYBLS	9/08
	Puerto Rico	Y	14540 FQ	16850 MW	18650 TQ	USBLS	5/07
	San Juan-Caguas-Guaynabo MSA, PR	Y	14870 FQ	17040 MW	18800 TQ	USBLS	5/07
	Guam	Y	22080 FQ	23870 MW	25640 TQ	USBLS	5/07

AE	Average entry wage	AW	Average wage paid	FQ	First quartile wage	LO	Lowest wage paid	MTC Median total compensation TCC Total cash compensation
AER	Average entry range	AWR	Average wage range	H	Hourly	LR	Low end range	MW Median wage paid TQ Third quartile wage
AEX	Average experienced wage	AXR	Average experienced range	HI	Highest wage paid	M	Monthly	MWR Median wage range W Weekly
ATC	Average total compensation	D	Daily	HR	High end range	MCC	Median cash compensation	S See annotated source Y Yearly

Structural Metal Fabricator and Fitter

Occupation/Type/Industry	Location	Per	Low	Mid	High	Source	Date
Structural Metal Fabricator and Fitter	Alabama	Y	25300 FQ	30430 MW	35970 TQ	USBLS	5/07
	Birmingham-Hoover MSA, AL	Y	24650 FQ	30270 MW	35580 TQ	USBLS	5/07
	Mobile MSA, AL	Y	27740 FQ	32190 MW	37160 TQ	USBLS	5/07
	Alaska	Y	29640 FQ	37340 MW	43900 TQ	USBLS	5/07
	Anchorage MSA, AK	Y	36740 FQ	42210 MW	46310 TQ	USBLS	5/07
	Arizona	Y	22490 FQ	27910 MW	33060 TQ	USBLS	5/07
	Phoenix-Mesa-Scottsdale MSA, AZ	Y	24090 FQ	28890 MW	33750 TQ	USBLS	5/07
	Tucson MSA, AZ	Y	18130 FQ	21460 MW	25990 TQ	USBLS	5/07
	Arkansas	Y	22820 FQ	26990 MW	31470 TQ	USBLS	5/07
	Fayetteville-Springdale-Rogers MSA, AR-MO	Y	24040 FQ	27700 MW	31350 TQ	USBLS	5/07
	Little Rock-North Little Rock MSA, AR	Y	24520 FQ	27690 MW	30740 TQ	USBLS	5/07
	California	H	12.16 FQ	16.65 MW	22.09 TQ	CABLS	1/08-3/08
	Los Angeles-Long Beach-Glendale PMSA, CA	H	11.22 FQ	15.44 MW	20.63 TQ	CABLS	1/08-3/08
	Oakland-Fremont-Hayward MSA, CA	H	13.25 FQ	17.86 MW	26.70 TQ	CABLS	1/08-3/08
	Riverside-San Bernardino-Ontario MSA, CA	H	10.49 FQ	14.15 MW	20.04 TQ	CABLS	1/08-3/08
	Sacramento-Arden Arcade-Roseville MSA, CA	H	13.61 FQ	18.45 MW	23.47 TQ	CABLS	1/08-3/08
	San Diego-Carlsbad-San Marcos MSA, CA	H	15.98 FQ	20.00 MW	23.44 TQ	CABLS	1/08-3/08
	San Francisco-San Mateo-Redwood PMSA, CA	H	11.44 FQ	15.75 MW	20.73 TQ	CABLS	1/08-3/08
	San Jose-Sunnyvale-Santa Clara MSA, CA	H	13.37 FQ	16.84 MW	20.74 TQ	CABLS	1/08-3/08
	Santa Ana-Anaheim-Irvine PMSA, CA	Y	26110 FQ	35570 MW	45870 TQ	USBLS	5/07
	Colorado	Y	26390 FQ	33180 MW	39570 TQ	USBLS	5/07
	Denver-Aurora MSA, CO	Y	26590 FQ	33380 MW	39190 TQ	USBLS	5/07
	Connecticut	H	10.77 AE	14.91 MW		CTBLS	1/08-3/08
	Bridgeport-Stamford-Norwalk MSA, CT	Y	25390 FQ	32940 MW	40590 TQ	USBLS	5/07
	Hartford-West Hartford-East Hartford MSA, CT	Y	34170 FQ	41040 MW	49320 TQ	USBLS	5/07
	Delaware	Y	25480 FQ	30000 MW	37520 TQ	USBLS	5/07
	Wilmington PMSA, DE-MD-NJ	Y	31480 FQ	37220 MW	44110 TQ	USBLS	5/07
	Washington-Arlington-Alexandria MSA, DC-VA-MD-WV	Y	25590 FQ	32150 MW	38690 TQ	USBLS	5/07
	Florida	Y	24070 FQ	29210 MW	35280 TQ	USBLS	5/07
	Fort Lauderdale-Pompano Beach-Deerfield Beach PMSA, FL	Y	26330 FQ	29580 MW	38390 TQ	USBLS	5/07
	Jacksonville MSA, FL	Y	19940 FQ	24840 MW	31420 TQ	USBLS	5/07
	Lakeland MSA, FL	Y	25860 FQ	30300 MW	35580 TQ	USBLS	5/07
	Miami-Fort Lauderdale-Miami Beach MSA, FL	Y	24920 FQ	29750 MW	38210 TQ	USBLS	5/07
	Orlando-Kissimmee MSA, FL	Y	23980 FQ	29190 MW	35690 TQ	USBLS	5/07
	Tampa-St. Petersburg-Clearwater MSA, FL	Y	26010 FQ	30100 MW	34750 TQ	USBLS	5/07
	West Palm Beach-Boca Raton-Boynton Beach PMSA, FL	Y	26950 FQ	33900 MW	41390 TQ	USBLS	5/07
	Georgia	Y	22440 FQ	27710 MW	32980 TQ	USBLS	5/07
	Atlanta-Sandy Springs-Marietta MSA, GA	Y	23810 FQ	28730 MW	33990 TQ	USBLS	5/07
	Savannah MSA, GA	Y	20090 FQ	34410 MW	43120 TQ	USBLS	5/07
	Hawaii	Y	21840 FQ	45030 MW	57380 TQ	USBLS	5/07
	Honolulu MSA, HI	Y	49060 FQ	55150 MW	62440 TQ	USBLS	5/07
	Idaho	Y	21450 FQ	28440 MW	34700 TQ	USBLS	5/07
	Boise City-Nampa MSA, ID	Y	22080 FQ	27800 MW	34820 TQ	USBLS	5/07
	Illinois	Y	28680 FQ	35520 MW	52330 TQ	USBLS	5/07
	Chicago-Naperville-Joliet MSA, IL-IN-WI	Y	30610 FQ	37470 MW	54770 TQ	USBLS	5/07
	Indiana	Y	26070 FQ	32230 MW	39850 TQ	USBLS	5/07
	Elkhart-Goshen MSA, IN	Y	26620 FQ	35400 MW	52900 TQ	USBLS	5/07
	Evansville MSA, IN-KY	Y	26950 FQ	30250 MW	35550 TQ	USBLS	5/07

AE	Average entry wage	AW	Average wage paid	FQ	First quartile wage	LO	Lowest wage paid	MTC	Median total compensation	TCC	Total cash compensation
AER	Average entry range	AWR	Average wage range	H	Hourly	LR	Low end range	MW	Median wage paid	TQ	Third quartile wage
AEX	Average experienced wage	AXR	Average experienced range	HI	Highest wage paid	M	Monthly	MWR	Median wage range	W	Weekly
ATC	Average total compensation	D	Daily	HR	High end range	MCC	Median cash compensation	S	See annotated source	Y	Yearly

1533

Structural Metal Fabricator and Fitter

Occupation/Type/Industry	Location	Per	Low	Mid	High	Source	Date
Structural Metal Fabricator and Fitter	Gary PMSA, IN	Y	33980 FQ	37430 MW	46520 TQ	USBLS	5/07
	Indianapolis-Carmel MSA, IN	Y	25850 FQ	34200 MW	42100 TQ	USBLS	5/07
	Iowa	Y	25260 FQ	32240 MW	36300 TQ	USBLS	5/07
	Des Moines-West Des Moines MSA, IA	Y	21620 FQ	27530 MW	32780 TQ	USBLS	5/07
	Kansas	Y	24040 FQ	29190 MW	34870 TQ	USBLS	5/07
	Wichita MSA, KS	Y	22830 FQ	26400 MW	32470 TQ	USBLS	5/07
	Kentucky	Y	25653 FQ	32362 MW	37814 TQ	KYBLS	2008
	Louisville-Jefferson County MSA, KY-IN	Y	25880 FQ	32240 MW	38300 TQ	USBLS	5/07
	Louisiana	H	13.52 FQ	16.53 MW	19.52 TQ	LABLS	1/08-3/08
	Baton Rouge MSA, LA	Y	25920 FQ	31590 MW	43480 TQ	USBLS	5/07
	New Orleans-Metairie-Kenner MSA, LA	Y	30350 FQ	35740 MW	42490 TQ	USBLS	5/07
	Maine	Y	33500 FQ	36030 MW	38610 TQ	USBLS	5/07
	Portland-South Portland-Biddeford MSA, ME	Y	28730 FQ	33640 MW	38330 TQ	USBLS	5/07
	Maryland	Y		35275 MW		MDBLS	3/08
	Baltimore-Towson MSA, MD	Y	30150 FQ	36310 MW	41990 TQ	USBLS	5/07
	Bethesda-Gaithersburg-Frederick PMSA, MD	Y	27000 FQ	32010 MW	42010 TQ	USBLS	5/07
	Massachusetts	Y	29020 FQ	36340 MW	45680 TQ	USBLS	5/07
	Boston-Cambridge-Quincy NECTA, MA	Y	29470 FQ	37080 MW	45800 TQ	USBLS	5/07
	Worcester MSA, MA-CT	Y	28250 FQ	31480 MW	40240 TQ	USBLS	5/07
	Michigan	Y	29210 FQ	36120 MW	43980 TQ	USBLS	5/07
	Detroit-Warren-Livonia MSA, MI	Y	30440 FQ	38540 MW	46110 TQ	USBLS	5/07
	Grand Rapids-Wyoming MSA, MI	Y	33910 FQ	38550 MW	43590 TQ	USBLS	5/07
	Warren-Troy-Farmington Hills PMSA, MI	Y	31330 FQ	39480 MW	46450 TQ	USBLS	5/07
	Minnesota	Y	31898 FQ	37755 MW	44442 TQ	MNBLS	10/08-12/08
	Duluth-Superior MSA, MN-WI	Y	25460 FQ	32458 MW	38118 TQ	MNBLS	10/08-12/08
	Minneapolis-Saint Paul MSA, MN-WI	Y	35081 FQ	40109 MW	46857 TQ	MNBLS	10/08-12/08
	Mississippi	Y	27350 FQ	31930 MW	38150 TQ	USBLS	5/07
	Jackson MSA, MS	Y	26780 FQ	31780 MW	39040 TQ	USBLS	5/07
	Missouri	Y	25530 FQ	30470 MW	38730 TQ	USBLS	5/07
	Kansas City MSA, MO-KS	Y	29280 FQ	33440 MW	37430 TQ	USBLS	5/07
	St. Louis MSA, MO-IL	Y	29570 FQ	38040 MW	52540 TQ	USBLS	5/07
	Montana	Y	24650 FQ	29560 MW	35030 TQ	USBLS	5/07
	Billings MSA, MT	Y	23660 FQ	28910 MW	34980 TQ	USBLS	5/07
	Nebraska	Y	23300 FQ	27280 MW	34030 TQ	USBLS	5/07
	Omaha-Council Bluffs MSA, NE-IA	Y	26600 FQ	30780 MW	35300 TQ	USBLS	5/07
	Nevada	H	12.32 FQ	15.48 MW	19.12 TQ	NVBLS	5/08
	Las Vegas-Paradise MSA, NV	H	11.32 FQ	14.92 MW	19.37 TQ	NVBLS	5/08
	New Hampshire	H	12.20 AE	15.40 MW	17.49 AEX	NHBLS	6/08
	Nashua NECTA, NH-MA	Y	22880 FQ	27630 MW	33300 TQ	USBLS	5/07
	New Jersey	Y	25920 FQ	32800 MW	42420 TQ	USBLS	5/07
	Camden PMSA, NJ	Y	25570 FQ	33190 MW	41680 TQ	USBLS	5/07
	Edison PMSA, NJ	Y	28080 FQ	35630 MW	44630 TQ	USBLS	5/07
	Newark-Union PMSA, NJ-PA	Y	22770 FQ	31220 MW	40530 TQ	USBLS	5/07
	New Mexico	Y	22890 FQ	27270 MW	33270 TQ	USBLS	5/07
	Albuquerque MSA, NM	Y	23120 FQ	28290 MW	34830 TQ	USBLS	5/07
	New York	Y	23090 FQ	32070 MW	45320 TQ	USBLS	5/07
	Albany-Schenectady-Troy MSA, NY	Y	25960 FQ	33060 MW	39200 TQ	USBLS	5/07
	Buffalo-Niagara Falls MSA, NY	Y	27010 FQ	35690 MW	45180 TQ	USBLS	5/07
	Nassau-Suffolk PMSA, NY	Y	21790 FQ	27200 MW	35060 TQ	USBLS	5/07
	New York-Northern New Jersey-Long Island MSA, NY-NJ-PA	Y	23400 FQ	32300 MW	46850 TQ	USBLS	5/07
	Utica-Rome MSA, NY	Y	24390 FQ	35020 MW	51860 TQ	USBLS	5/07
	North Carolina	Y	26080 FQ	31440 MW	37240 TQ	USBLS	5/07
	Asheville MSA, NC	Y	27870 FQ	33630 MW	37090 TQ	USBLS	5/07
	Charlotte-Gastonia-Concord MSA, NC-SC	Y	28220 FQ	34080 MW	39460 TQ	USBLS	5/07
	Raleigh-Cary MSA, NC	Y	32250 FQ	35740 MW	38820 TQ	USBLS	5/07

AE	Average entry wage	AW	Average wage paid	FQ	First quartile wage	LO	Lowest wage paid	MTC	Median total compensation	TCC	Total cash compensation
AER	Average entry range	AWR	Average wage range	H	Hourly	LR	Low end range	MW	Median wage paid	TQ	Third quartile wage
AEX	Average experienced wage	AXR	Average experienced range	HI	Highest wage paid	M	Monthly	MWR	Median wage range	W	Weekly
ATC	Average total compensation	D	Daily	HR	High end range	MCC	Median cash compensation	S	See annotated source	Y	Yearly

1534

Occupation/Type/Industry	Location	Per	Low	Mid	High	Source	Date
Structural Metal Fabricator and Fitter	North Dakota	Y	25550 FQ	30250 MW	37140 TQ	USBLS	5/07
	Fargo MSA, ND-MN	Y	29130 FQ	37230 MW	42490 TQ	USBLS	5/07
	Ohio	Y	27450 FQ	31360 MW	37120 TQ	USBLS	5/07
	Cincinnati-Middletown MSA, OH-KY-IN	Y	28780 FQ	33080 MW	37400 TQ	USBLS	5/07
	Cleveland-Elyria-Mentor MSA, OH	Y	28530 FQ	33960 MW	39000 TQ	USBLS	5/07
	Columbus MSA, OH	Y	26780 FQ	30110 MW	34540 TQ	USBLS	5/07
	Dayton MSA, OH	Y	28120 FQ	31090 MW	35720 TQ	USBLS	5/07
	Oklahoma	Y	24480 FQ	29180 MW	34100 TQ	USBLS	5/07
	Oklahoma City MSA, OK	Y	24150 FQ	27900 MW	32340 TQ	USBLS	5/07
	Tulsa MSA, OK	Y	24960 FQ	30100 MW	34480 TQ	USBLS	5/07
	Oregon	H	12.93 FQ	16.42 MW	20.70 TQ	ORBLS	5/08
	Eugene-Springfield MSA, OR	Y	27460 FQ	33090 MW	39250 TQ	USBLS	5/07
	Portland-Vancouver-Beaverton MSA, OR-WA	Y	28000 FQ	37130 MW	45640 TQ	USBLS	5/07
	Pennsylvania	Y	27160 FQ	32150 MW	38150 TQ	USBLS	5/07
	Allentown-Bethlehem-Easton MSA, PA-NJ	Y	29570 FQ	33520 MW	37710 TQ	USBLS	5/07
	Philadelphia-Camden-Wilmington MSA, PA-NJ-DE-MD	Y	31300 FQ	37270 MW	43590 TQ	USBLS	5/07
	Pittsburgh MSA, PA	Y	24530 FQ	30260 MW	41530 TQ	USBLS	5/07
	Rhode Island	Y	24370 FQ	29450 MW	37430 TQ	USBLS	5/07
	Providence-Fall River-Warwick MSA, RI-MA	Y	24780 FQ	30330 MW	38480 TQ	USBLS	5/07
	South Carolina	Y	25520 FQ	30880 MW	37180 TQ	USBLS	5/07
	Charleston-North Charleston MSA, SC	Y	23450 FQ	33980 MW	38600 TQ	USBLS	5/07
	Columbia MSA, SC	Y	23270 FQ	26820 MW	31700 TQ	USBLS	5/07
	South Dakota	Y	24203 FQ	28901 MW	36923 TQ	SDBLS	7/08-9/08
	Sioux Falls MSA, SD	Y	26169 FQ	31202 MW	39469 TQ	SDBLS	7/08-9/08
	Tennessee	Y	25070 FQ	31290 MW	39230 TQ	USBLS	5/07
	Kingsport-Bristol-Bristol MSA, TN-VA	Y	24460 FQ	28060 MW	33010 TQ	USBLS	5/07
	Memphis MSA, TN-MS-AR	Y	24420 FQ	29100 MW	35440 TQ	USBLS	5/07
	Nashville-Davidson-Murfreesboro MSA, TN	Y	19290 FQ	28850 MW	34790 TQ	USBLS	5/07
	Texas	Y	21640 FQ	27470 MW	33640 TQ	USBLS	5/07
	Austin-Round Rock MSA, TX	Y	25300 FQ	28770 MW	32310 TQ	USBLS	5/07
	Dallas-Fort Worth-Arlington MSA, TX	Y	21440 FQ	26270 MW	32360 TQ	USBLS	5/07
	El Paso MSA, TX	Y	20850 FQ	26800 MW	32590 TQ	USBLS	5/07
	Houston-Sugar Land-Baytown MSA, TX	Y	20210 FQ	27110 MW	33640 TQ	USBLS	5/07
	San Antonio MSA, TX	Y	24990 FQ	28490 MW	32060 TQ	USBLS	5/07
	Utah	Y	24000 FQ	30900 MW	41740 TQ	USBLS	5/07
	Ogden-Clearfield MSA, UT	Y	23050 FQ	29720 MW	39800 TQ	USBLS	5/07
	Salt Lake City MSA, UT	Y	26230 FQ	38130 MW	45230 TQ	USBLS	5/07
	Vermont	Y	23720 FQ	27600 MW	34760 TQ	USBLS	5/07
	Virginia	Y	23650 FQ	28990 MW	36430 TQ	USBLS	5/07
	Richmond MSA, VA	Y	26780 FQ	33960 MW	40080 TQ	USBLS	5/07
	Roanoke MSA, VA	Y	21660 FQ	24200 MW	30580 TQ	USBLS	5/07
	Virginia Beach-Norfolk-Newport News MSA, VA-NC	Y	24800 FQ	32740 MW	43220 TQ	USBLS	5/07
	Washington	H	13.35 FQ	16.82 MW	20.04 TQ	WABLS	3/08
	Seattle-Tacoma-Bellevue MSA, WA	Y	27630 FQ	35190 MW	42460 TQ	USBLS	5/07
	West Virginia	Y	25880 FQ	29805 MW	34414 TQ	WVBLS	7/08-9/08
	Charleston MSA, WV	Y	25080 FQ	28570 MW	32340 TQ	USBLS	5/07
	Huntington-Ashland MSA, WV-KY-OH	Y	24350 FQ	29450 MW	42010 TQ	USBLS	5/07
	Wisconsin	Y	30250 FQ	35110 MW	40070 TQ	USBLS	5/07
	Milwaukee-Waukesha-West Allis MSA, WI	Y	32360 FQ	36550 MW	41940 TQ	USBLS	5/07
	Wyoming	Y	27036 FQ	36922 MW	45886 TQ	WYBLS	9/08
	Cheyenne MSA, WY	Y	25508 FQ	29714 MW	34689 TQ	WYBLS	9/08
	Puerto Rico	Y	12520 FQ	13940 MW	15530 TQ	USBLS	5/07
	San Juan-Caguas-Guaynabo MSA, PR	Y	12590 FQ	14080 MW	15870 TQ	USBLS	5/07
	Guam	Y	22520 FQ	27110 MW	33370 TQ	USBLS	5/07

AE	Average entry wage	**AW**	Average wage paid	**FQ**	First quartile wage	**LO**	Lowest wage paid	**MTC**	Median total compensation
AER	Average entry range	**AWR**	Average wage range	**H**	Hourly	**LR**	Low end range	**MW**	Median wage paid
AEX	Average experienced wage	**AXR**	Average experienced range	**HI**	Highest wage paid	**M**	Monthly	**MWR**	Median wage range
ATC	Average total compensation	**D**	Daily	**HR**	High end range	**MCC**	Median cash compensation	**S**	See annotated source

(continued)

TCC Total cash compensation
TQ Third quartile wage
W Weekly
Y Yearly

Occupation/Type/Industry	Location	Per	Low	Mid	High	Source	Date
Student Assistant							
Before and After School Programs, Public Schools	Wake County, NC	H			8.00 HI	WCPS01	2007-2008
Student Loan Auditor							
State Government	Ohio	H	17.22 LO		21.77 HI	ODAS	2008
Student Nutrition Director							
Area Public Schools	Brighton, MI	Y			56317 HI	LCPP	2009
Studio Manager							
Apparel Industry	United States	Y		84770 MW		247FASH	2009
Stunt Performer							
Basic and Theatrical Agreement, Weekly Basis	United States	W	2828 LO			SAG01	7/1/07-6/30/08
Subdivision Engineering Review Manager							
Municipal Government	Colorado Springs, CO	M	6687 LO			COSPRS	1/1/09
Subject Specialist							
University Libraries	East North Central	Y		58540 AW		ARL	2007-2008
University Libraries	East South Central	Y		50206 AW		ARL	2007-2008
University Libraries	Mountain	Y		61063 AW		ARL	2007-2008
University Libraries	New England	Y		71719 AW		ARL	2007-2008
University Libraries	Pacific	Y		68028 AW		ARL	2007-2008
University Libraries	West North Central	Y		61995 AW		ARL	2007-2008
University Libraries	West South Central	Y		53489 AW		ARL	2007-2008
Substance Abuse and Behavioral Disorder Counselor	Alabama	Y	27420 FQ	31020 MW	41790 TQ	USBLS	5/07
	Birmingham-Hoover MSA, AL	Y	27310 FQ	29880 MW	36470 TQ	USBLS	5/07
	Mobile MSA, AL	Y	27800 FQ	38300 MW	45570 TQ	USBLS	5/07
	Alaska	Y	35410 FQ	42400 MW	49720 TQ	USBLS	5/07
	Anchorage MSA, AK	Y	34100 FQ	40070 MW	47680 TQ	USBLS	5/07
	Arizona	Y	31670 FQ	39000 MW	48760 TQ	USBLS	5/07
	Phoenix-Mesa-Scottsdale MSA, AZ	Y	36750 FQ	45240 MW	58720 TQ	USBLS	5/07
	Tucson MSA, AZ	Y	26740 FQ	31020 MW	37090 TQ	USBLS	5/07
	Arkansas	Y	23800 FQ	26300 MW	33870 TQ	USBLS	5/07
	Little Rock-North Little Rock MSA, AR	Y	21490 FQ	23770 MW	42140 TQ	USBLS	5/07
	Pine Bluff MSA, AR	Y	26150 FQ	28320 MW	32510 TQ	USBLS	5/07
	California	H	13.04 FQ	15.84 MW	20.30 TQ	CABLS	1/08-3/08
	Los Angeles-Long Beach-Glendale PMSA, CA	H	12.37 FQ	14.66 MW	18.66 TQ	CABLS	1/08-3/08
	Oakland-Fremont-Hayward MSA, CA	H	12.13 FQ	15.81 MW	18.93 TQ	CABLS	1/08-3/08
	Riverside-San Bernardino-Ontario MSA, CA	H	13.51 FQ	15.59 MW	21.48 TQ	CABLS	1/08-3/08
	Sacramento-Arden Arcade-Roseville MSA, CA	H	12.86 FQ	16.26 MW	20.27 TQ	CABLS	1/08-3/08
	San Diego-Carlsbad-San Marcos MSA, CA	H	14.42 FQ	17.60 MW	20.72 TQ	CABLS	1/08-3/08
	San Francisco-San Mateo-Redwood PMSA, CA	H	12.19 FQ	15.79 MW	21.68 TQ	CABLS	1/08-3/08
	San Jose-Sunnyvale-Santa Clara MSA, CA	H	13.24 FQ	17.19 MW	22.51 TQ	CABLS	1/08-3/08
	Santa Ana-Anaheim-Irvine PMSA, CA	Y	26110 FQ	31300 MW	38180 TQ	USBLS	5/07
	Colorado	Y	24560 FQ	30190 MW	38930 TQ	USBLS	5/07
	Denver-Aurora MSA, CO	Y	24910 FQ	29910 MW	37030 TQ	USBLS	5/07
	Connecticut	H	13.98 AE	18.89 MW		CTBLS	1/08-3/08
	Bridgeport-Stamford-Norwalk MSA, CT	Y	29700 FQ	34380 MW	44770 TQ	USBLS	5/07
	Hartford-West Hartford-East Hartford MSA, CT	Y	30130 FQ	41140 MW	52400 TQ	USBLS	5/07
	Delaware	Y	28410 FQ	34690 MW	41640 TQ	USBLS	5/07
	Wilmington PMSA, DE-MD-NJ	Y	29370 FQ	35100 MW	43020 TQ	USBLS	5/07
	District of Columbia	Y	29970 FQ	37270 MW	44530 TQ	USBLS	5/07

AE	Average entry wage	AW	Average wage paid	FQ	First quartile wage	LO	Lowest wage paid	MTC	Median total compensation	TCC	Total cash compensation
AER	Average entry range	AWR	Average wage range	H	Hourly	LR	Low end range	MW	Median wage paid	TQ	Third quartile wage
AEX	Average experienced wage	AXR	Average experienced range	HI	Highest wage paid	M	Monthly	MWR	Median wage range	W	Weekly
ATC	Average total compensation	D	Daily	HR	High end range	MCC	Median cash compensation	S	See annotated source	Y	Yearly

Occupation/Type/Industry	Location	Per	Low	Mid	High	Source	Date
Substance Abuse and Behavioral Disorder Counselor	Washington-Arlington-Alexandria MSA, DC-VA-MD-WV	Y	32320 FQ	41970 MW	52890 TQ	USBLS	5/07
	Florida	Y	28440 FQ	35530 MW	48020 TQ	USBLS	5/07
	Fort Lauderdale-Pompano Beach-Deerfield Beach PMSA, FL	Y	32680 FQ	42090 MW	60290 TQ	USBLS	5/07
	Jacksonville MSA, FL	Y	28930 FQ	34710 MW	41210 TQ	USBLS	5/07
	Miami-Fort Lauderdale-Miami Beach MSA, FL	Y	31630 FQ	42390 MW	56840 TQ	USBLS	5/07
	Orlando-Kissimmee MSA, FL	Y	22870 FQ	34760 MW	45220 TQ	USBLS	5/07
	Tampa-St. Petersburg-Clearwater MSA, FL	Y	27850 FQ	31380 MW	43260 TQ	USBLS	5/07
	West Palm Beach-Boca Raton-Boynton Beach PMSA, FL	Y	26910 FQ	33950 MW	45200 TQ	USBLS	5/07
	Georgia	Y	28370 FQ	33860 MW	41280 TQ	USBLS	5/07
	Atlanta-Sandy Springs-Marietta MSA, GA	Y	29030 FQ	35790 MW	44920 TQ	USBLS	5/07
	Macon MSA, GA	Y	29300 FQ	35270 MW	43600 TQ	USBLS	5/07
	Hawaii	Y	34430 FQ	39990 MW	47470 TQ	USBLS	5/07
	Honolulu MSA, HI	Y	36050 FQ	44570 MW	50270 TQ	USBLS	5/07
	Idaho	Y	28570 FQ	32210 MW	40080 TQ	USBLS	5/07
	Boise City-Nampa MSA, ID	Y	28520 FQ	31240 MW	36020 TQ	USBLS	5/07
	Coeur d'Alene MSA, ID	Y	30450 FQ	34920 MW	41340 TQ	USBLS	5/07
	Illinois	Y	26770 FQ	31400 MW	37480 TQ	USBLS	5/07
	Chicago-Naperville-Joliet MSA, IL-IN-WI	Y	27030 FQ	31500 MW	37310 TQ	USBLS	5/07
	Indiana	Y	29120 FQ	37400 MW	50900 TQ	USBLS	5/07
	Gary PMSA, IN	Y	32320 FQ	36090 MW	40360 TQ	USBLS	5/07
	Indianapolis-Carmel MSA, IN	Y	44070 FQ	58920 MW	108570 TQ	USBLS	5/07
	Iowa	Y	26820 FQ	32590 MW	42150 TQ	USBLS	5/07
	Des Moines-West Des Moines MSA, IA	Y	21780 FQ	29350 MW	40240 TQ	USBLS	5/07
	Sioux City MSA, IA-NE-SD	Y	27010 FQ	29880 MW	35030 TQ	USBLS	5/07
	Kansas	Y	27580 FQ	31340 MW	37610 TQ	USBLS	5/07
	Wichita MSA, KS	Y	26670 FQ	29210 MW	31830 TQ	USBLS	5/07
	Kentucky	Y	28399 FQ	34876 MW	44906 TQ	KYBLS	2008
	Louisville-Jefferson County MSA, KY-IN	Y	30580 FQ	36400 MW	45490 TQ	USBLS	5/07
	Louisiana	H	11.25 FQ	13.99 MW	19.61 TQ	LABLS	1/08-3/08
	Baton Rouge MSA, LA	Y	26690 FQ	31560 MW	42690 TQ	USBLS	5/07
	New Orleans-Metairie-Kenner MSA, LA	Y	23450 FQ	26950 MW	44470 TQ	USBLS	5/07
	Maine	Y	33830 FQ	39350 MW	46220 TQ	USBLS	5/07
	Portland-South Portland-Biddeford MSA, ME	Y	35600 FQ	41380 MW	47780 TQ	USBLS	5/07
	Maryland	Y		39175 MW		MDBLS	3/08
	Baltimore-Towson MSA, MD	Y	32580 FQ	37420 MW	44990 TQ	USBLS	5/07
	Bethesda-Gaithersburg-Frederick PMSA, MD	Y	33300 FQ	37380 MW	42760 TQ	USBLS	5/07
	Massachusetts	Y	30840 FQ	39080 MW	46880 TQ	USBLS	5/07
	Boston-Cambridge-Quincy NECTA, MA	Y	28970 FQ	37500 MW	45280 TQ	USBLS	5/07
	Springfield MSA, MA-CT	Y	35200 FQ	41010 MW	47200 TQ	USBLS	5/07
	Worcester MSA, MA-CT	Y	28220 FQ	36460 MW	44220 TQ	USBLS	5/07
	Michigan	Y	24240 FQ	35180 MW	45590 TQ	USBLS	5/07
	Detroit-Warren-Livonia MSA, MI	Y	24190 FQ	35040 MW	46450 TQ	USBLS	5/07
	Grand Rapids-Wyoming MSA, MI	Y	18010 FQ	20360 MW	30730 TQ	USBLS	5/07
	Warren-Troy-Farmington Hills PMSA, MI	Y	31630 FQ	42020 MW	48920 TQ	USBLS	5/07
	Minnesota	Y	35718 FQ	42257 MW	50940 TQ	MNBLS	10/08-12/08
	Duluth-Superior MSA, MN-WI	Y	36764 FQ	43387 MW	54121 TQ	MNBLS	10/08-12/08
	Minneapolis-Saint Paul MSA, MN-WI	Y	35979 FQ	43271 MW	51620 TQ	MNBLS	10/08-12/08
	Rochester MSA, MN	Y	40379 FQ	51253 MW	61297 TQ	MNBLS	10/08-12/08
	Mississippi	Y	22730 FQ	25250 MW	34510 TQ	USBLS	5/07
	Jackson MSA, MS	Y	24420 FQ	28240 MW	35660 TQ	USBLS	5/07
	Missouri	Y	26590 FQ	32270 MW	40100 TQ	USBLS	5/07
	Kansas City MSA, MO-KS	Y	32110 FQ	38050 MW	45900 TQ	USBLS	5/07

AE	Average entry wage	AW	Average wage paid	FQ	First quartile wage	LO	Lowest wage paid
AER	Average entry range	AWR	Average wage range	H	Hourly	LR	Low end range
AEX	Average experienced wage	AXR	Average experienced range	HI	Highest wage paid	M	Monthly
ATC	Average total compensation	D	Daily	HR	High end range	MCC	Median cash compensation

MTC Median total compensation   TCC Total cash compensation
MW Median wage paid   TQ Third quartile wage
MWR Median wage range   W Weekly
S See annotated source   Y Yearly

Occupation/Type/Industry	Location	Per	Low	Mid	High	Source	Date
Substance Abuse and Behavioral Disorder Counselor	St. Louis MSA, MO-IL	Y	25020 FQ	30500 MW	37430 TQ	USBLS	5/07
	Montana	Y	32640 FQ	36320 MW	41350 TQ	USBLS	5/07
	Billings MSA, MT	Y	33860 FQ	37860 MW	41990 TQ	USBLS	5/07
	Missoula MSA, MT	Y	32650 FQ	36940 MW	43920 TQ	USBLS	5/07
	Nebraska	Y	28930 FQ	35380 MW	43190 TQ	USBLS	5/07
	Lincoln MSA, NE	Y	28910 FQ	34100 MW	39470 TQ	USBLS	5/07
	Omaha-Council Bluffs MSA, NE-IA	Y	28820 FQ	37250 MW	46430 TQ	USBLS	5/07
	Nevada	H	17.15 FQ	19.42 MW	22.88 TQ	NVBLS	5/08
	Las Vegas-Paradise MSA, NV	H	17.30 FQ	19.36 MW	23.04 TQ	NVBLS	5/08
	New Hampshire	H	13.70 AE	16.73 MW	19.31 AEX	NHBLS	6/08
	Manchester MSA, NH	Y	28720 FQ	31450 MW	35960 TQ	USBLS	5/07
	New Jersey	Y	31490 FQ	38530 MW	47610 TQ	USBLS	5/07
	Camden PMSA, NJ	Y	28660 FQ	34820 MW	43360 TQ	USBLS	5/07
	Edison PMSA, NJ	Y	33070 FQ	41170 MW	51610 TQ	USBLS	5/07
	Newark-Union PMSA, NJ-PA	Y	34100 FQ	40360 MW	48350 TQ	USBLS	5/07
	New Mexico	Y	27180 FQ	33260 MW	43710 TQ	USBLS	5/07
	Albuquerque MSA, NM	Y	25130 FQ	29480 MW	36310 TQ	USBLS	5/07
	New York	Y	31520 FQ	40300 MW	49330 TQ	USBLS	5/07
	Albany-Schenectady-Troy MSA, NY	Y	23740 FQ	27980 MW	35730 TQ	USBLS	5/07
	Buffalo-Niagara Falls MSA, NY	Y	28630 FQ	33560 MW	39510 TQ	USBLS	5/07
	Nassau-Suffolk PMSA, NY	Y	35000 FQ	43330 MW	54730 TQ	USBLS	5/07
	New York-Northern New Jersey-Long Island MSA, NY-NJ-PA	Y	34040 FQ	42310 MW	50890 TQ	USBLS	5/07
	North Carolina	Y	28930 FQ	36290 MW	42950 TQ	USBLS	5/07
	Charlotte-Gastonia-Concord MSA, NC-SC	Y	22550 FQ	34030 MW	40350 TQ	USBLS	5/07
	Durham MSA, NC	Y	27950 FQ	34660 MW	45270 TQ	USBLS	5/07
	Greensboro-High Point MSA, NC	Y	34590 FQ	40250 MW	44750 TQ	USBLS	5/07
	North Dakota	Y	36700 FQ	42220 MW	47930 TQ	USBLS	5/07
	Bismarck MSA, ND	Y	36820 FQ	43180 MW	49100 TQ	USBLS	5/07
	Fargo MSA, ND-MN	Y	36000 FQ	39760 MW	45000 TQ	USBLS	5/07
	Ohio	Y	32110 FQ	37530 MW	44010 TQ	USBLS	5/07
	Cincinnati-Middletown MSA, OH-KY-IN	Y	33410 FQ	38750 MW	46750 TQ	USBLS	5/07
	Cleveland-Elyria-Mentor MSA, OH	Y	32420 FQ	38470 MW	44150 TQ	USBLS	5/07
	Columbus MSA, OH	Y	31780 FQ	37520 MW	43830 TQ	USBLS	5/07
	Dayton MSA, OH	Y	31460 FQ	38080 MW	44930 TQ	USBLS	5/07
	Oklahoma	Y	25420 FQ	30520 MW	37430 TQ	USBLS	5/07
	Oklahoma City MSA, OK	Y	27550 FQ	31680 MW	38360 TQ	USBLS	5/07
	Tulsa MSA, OK	Y	30400 FQ	35560 MW	41890 TQ	USBLS	5/07
	Oregon	H	13.73 FQ	16.26 MW	20.75 TQ	ORBLS	5/08
	Medford MSA, OR	Y	21440 FQ	25170 MW	30140 TQ	USBLS	5/07
	Portland-Vancouver-Beaverton MSA, OR-WA	Y	29810 FQ	36320 MW	45550 TQ	USBLS	5/07
	Pennsylvania	Y	28610 FQ	36110 MW	46220 TQ	USBLS	5/07
	Allentown-Bethlehem-Easton MSA, PA-NJ	Y	30220 FQ	34810 MW	44630 TQ	USBLS	5/07
	Philadelphia-Camden-Wilmington MSA, PA-NJ-DE-MD	Y	28620 FQ	36620 MW	46090 TQ	USBLS	5/07
	Pittsburgh MSA, PA	Y	27430 FQ	32630 MW	39450 TQ	USBLS	5/07
	Rhode Island	Y	31940 FQ	38880 MW	46770 TQ	USBLS	5/07
	Providence-Fall River-Warwick MSA, RI-MA	Y	31930 FQ	39330 MW	47110 TQ	USBLS	5/07
	South Carolina	Y	31680 FQ	37960 MW	45470 TQ	USBLS	5/07
	Charleston-North Charleston MSA, SC	Y	39500 FQ	43920 MW	48130 TQ	USBLS	5/07
	Columbia MSA, SC	Y	30470 FQ	37270 MW	46550 TQ	USBLS	5/07
	Myrtle Beach-Conway-North Myrtle Beach MSA, SC	Y	30770 FQ	34160 MW	37790 TQ	USBLS	5/07
	South Dakota	Y	26627 FQ	32340 MW	39592 TQ	SDBLS	7/08-9/08
	Rapid City MSA, SD	Y	28036 FQ	32713 MW	37896 TQ	SDBLS	7/08-9/08
	Sioux Falls MSA, SD	Y	30721 FQ	38642 MW	48950 TQ	SDBLS	7/08-9/08
	Tennessee	Y	28720 FQ	35730 MW	44960 TQ	USBLS	5/07
	Memphis MSA, TN-MS-AR	Y	32440 FQ	42720 MW	46790 TQ	USBLS	5/07

AE	Average entry wage	AW	Average wage paid	FQ	First quartile wage
AER	Average entry range	AWR	Average wage range	H	Hourly
AEX	Average experienced wage	AXR	Average experienced range	HI	Highest wage paid
ATC	Average total compensation	D	Daily	HR	High end range

LO	Lowest wage paid	MTC	Median total compensation	TCC	Total cash compensation
LR	Low end range	MW	Median wage paid	TQ	Third quartile wage
M	Monthly	MWR	Median wage range	W	Weekly
MCC	Median cash compensation	S	See annotated source	Y	Yearly

Occupation/Type/Industry	Location	Per	Low	Mid	High	Source	Date
Substance Abuse and Behavioral Disorder Counselor	Nashville-Davidson-Murfreesboro MSA, TN	Y	30450 FQ	36510 MW	47540 TQ	USBLS	5/07
	Texas	Y	26670 FQ	32060 MW	37560 TQ	USBLS	5/07
	Austin-Round Rock MSA, TX	Y	25480 FQ	29040 MW	33950 TQ	USBLS	5/07
	Dallas-Fort Worth-Arlington MSA, TX	Y	28520 FQ	33860 MW	38210 TQ	USBLS	5/07
	El Paso MSA, TX	Y	25150 FQ	29950 MW	35360 TQ	USBLS	5/07
	Houston-Sugar Land-Baytown MSA, TX	Y	28160 FQ	33640 MW	38710 TQ	USBLS	5/07
	San Antonio MSA, TX	Y	28900 FQ	35670 MW	43730 TQ	USBLS	5/07
	Utah	Y	33400 FQ	38640 MW	46800 TQ	USBLS	5/07
	Salt Lake City MSA, UT	Y	32130 FQ	39020 MW	50790 TQ	USBLS	5/07
	Vermont	Y	33360 FQ	40950 MW	53970 TQ	USBLS	5/07
	Burlington-South Burlington MSA, VT	Y	34560 FQ	49110 MW	61700 TQ	USBLS	5/07
	Virginia	Y	31320 FQ	40230 MW	52640 TQ	USBLS	5/07
	Richmond MSA, VA	Y	27970 FQ	31770 MW	44650 TQ	USBLS	5/07
	Virginia Beach-Norfolk-Newport News MSA, VA-NC	Y	34620 FQ	38160 MW	41780 TQ	USBLS	5/07
	Washington	H	12.84 FQ	16.29 MW	20.87 TQ	WABLS	3/08
	Seattle-Tacoma-Bellevue MSA, WA	Y	28790 FQ	35130 MW	42820 TQ	USBLS	5/07
	West Virginia	Y	29961 FQ	34734 MW	40655 TQ	WVBLS	7/08-9/08
	Wisconsin	Y	31270 FQ	37670 MW	47400 TQ	USBLS	5/07
	Milwaukee-Waukesha-West Allis MSA, WI	Y	31980 FQ	36950 MW	46710 TQ	USBLS	5/07
	Wyoming	Y	34986 FQ	39417 MW	46833 TQ	WYBLS	9/08
	Puerto Rico	Y	16780 FQ	19900 MW	27370 TQ	USBLS	5/07
	San Juan-Caguas-Guaynabo MSA, PR	Y	16540 FQ	18830 MW	26770 TQ	USBLS	5/07
Substance Abuse/HIV Counselor							
State Government	Connecticut	Y	44837 LO		59505 HI	AFT02	3/1/08
Substitute Teacher							
Overseas Elementary and Secondary School, U.S. Department of Defense	United States	D			97.00 HI	CPMS01	2007-2008
Subway and Streetcar Operator	California	H	22.73 FQ	26.82 MW	29.05 TQ	CABLS	1/08-3/08
	Ohio	Y	34850 FQ	44060 MW	49570 TQ	USBLS	5/07
	Texas	Y	33360 FQ	36630 MW	39870 TQ	USBLS	5/07
Summer Associate							
Major Law Firm	Virginia	W		2354 AW		VLW	2008
Superintendent							
Canyons School District	Utah	Y			175000 HI	AMW	2008
Detroit Public Schools	Detroit, MI	Y			280000 HI	COD01	2008
Newburgh City School District	New York	Y			180000 HI	THREC1	2007
Public Schools	East Coast	Y		156000 AW		DPOST01	2008
Public Schools	Rocky Mountain Region	Y		110000 AW		DPOST01	2008
Public Schools	Spartanburg, SC	Y			183743 HI	GOUPS	2008-2009
Public Schools	Texas	Y		113334 AW		TASBN	2008-2009
Public Schools	Harlington, TX	Y			200000 HI	VMS01	2009-2010
State Police	Massachusetts	Y			210000 HI	BGLOBE1	2008
Tuxedo School District	New York	Y			180933 HI	THREC1	2007
Waste Water Treatment Facility	Montague, MA	Y			70286 HI	FRCOG	2009
Superintendent of Public Instruction	Washington	Y			121618 HI	WCC	9/1/08
Supervising Dietitian							
Municipal Government	Cincinnati, OH	Y	53522 LO		71929 HI	COHSS	10/08
Supervising Groundskeeper							
Municipal Government	Cincinnati, OH	Y	37647 LO		40748 HI	COHSS	10/08
Supervising Sanitarian							
Municipal Government	Cincinnati, OH	Y	47454 LO		65344 HI	COHSS	10/08

AE Average entry wage	AW Average wage paid	FQ First quartile wage	LO Lowest wage paid	MTC Median total compensation TCC Total cash compensation
AER Average entry range	AWR Average wage range	H Hourly	LR Low end range	MW Median wage paid TQ Third quartile wage
AEX Average experienced wage	AXR Average experienced range	HI Highest wage paid	M Monthly	MWR Median wage range W Weekly
ATC Average total compensation	D Daily	HR High end range	MCC Median cash compensation	S See annotated source Y Yearly

Occupation/Type/Industry	Location	Per	Low	Mid	High	Source	Date
Supervisor of Customer Service							
Municipal Government	Cincinnati, OH	Y	50721 LO		68164 HI	COHSS	10/08
Supervisor of Golf							
Municipal Government	Cincinnati, OH	Y	62598 LO		84507 HI	COHSS	10/08
Supervisor of Industrial Waste Disposal							
Municipal Government	Cincinnati, OH	Y	50721 LO		68164 HI	COHSS	10/08
Supervisor of Urban Forestry							
Municipal Government	Cincinnati, OH	Y	57719 LO		77569 HI	COHSS	10/08
Supplemental Income Claims Processor							
State Government	Ohio	H	15.62 LO		18.36 HI	ODAS	2008
Support Services Specialist							
Municipal Government	Cincinnati, OH	Y	32697 LO		60634 HI	COHSS	10/08
Supreme Court Justice	Michigan	Y			164610 HI	LSJ01	6/07
	Mississippi	Y			112530 HI	HATAM	7/08
Surgeon	Arizona	Y	128250 FQ			USBLS	5/07
	Phoenix-Mesa-Scottsdale MSA, AZ	Y	108540 FQ			USBLS	5/07
	California	H	62.94 FQ			CABLS	1/08-3/08
	Los Angeles-Long Beach-Glendale PMSA, CA	H	58.07 FQ			CABLS	1/08-3/08
	Oakland-Fremont-Hayward MSA, CA	H	28.81 FQ			CABLS	1/08-3/08
	San Jose-Sunnyvale-Santa Clara MSA, CA	H	56.01 FQ			CABLS	1/08-3/08
	Santa Ana-Anaheim-Irvine PMSA, CA	Y	108630 FQ			USBLS	5/07
	Denver-Aurora MSA, CO	Y	128970 FQ			USBLS	5/07
	Connecticut	H	75.21 AE	95.74 AW		CTBLS	1/08-3/08
	Hartford-West Hartford-East Hartford MSA, CT	Y	137410 FQ			USBLS	5/07
	District of Columbia	Y	85350 FQ	106280 MW		USBLS	5/07
	Washington-Arlington-Alexandria MSA, DC-VA-MD-WV	Y	101950 FQ			USBLS	5/07
	Florida	Y	109220 FQ			USBLS	5/07
	Fort Lauderdale-Pompano Beach-Deerfield Beach PMSA, FL	Y	53450 FQ	60290 MW		USBLS	5/07
	Miami-Fort Lauderdale-Miami Beach MSA, FL	Y	55240 FQ	95040 MW		USBLS	5/07
	West Palm Beach-Boca Raton-Boynton Beach PMSA, FL	Y	103540 FQ			USBLS	5/07
	Hawaii	Y	49070 FQ			USBLS	5/07
	Honolulu MSA, HI	Y	48540 FQ			USBLS	5/07
	Illinois	Y	110420 FQ			USBLS	5/07
	Chicago-Naperville-Joliet MSA, IL-IN-WI	Y	94100 FQ			USBLS	5/07
	Baton Rouge MSA, LA	Y	119720 FQ			USBLS	5/07
	Grand Rapids-Wyoming MSA, MI	Y	118740 FQ			USBLS	5/07
	Nebraska	Y	78820 FQ			USBLS	5/07
	Omaha-Council Bluffs MSA, NE-IA	Y	63910 FQ			USBLS	5/07
	North Dakota	Y	115230 FQ			USBLS	5/07
	Fargo MSA, ND-MN	Y	100130 FQ	114300 MW		USBLS	5/07
	Pennsylvania	Y	141050 FQ			USBLS	5/07
	Pittsburgh MSA, PA	Y	107820 FQ			USBLS	5/07
	Memphis MSA, TN-MS-AR	Y	55030 FQ			USBLS	5/07
	Vermont	Y	110630 FQ			USBLS	5/07
	Richmond MSA, VA	Y	119400 FQ			USBLS	5/07
	West Virginia	Y		204339 AW		WVBLS	7/08-9/08
	Puerto Rico	Y	133550 FQ	143190 MW		USBLS	5/07

Occupation/Type/Industry	Location	Per	Low	Mid	High	Source	Date
Surgical Technologist	Alabama	Y	24920 FQ	29960 MW	36290 TQ	USBLS	5/07
	Birmingham-Hoover MSA, AL	Y	26190 FQ	30670 MW	35920 TQ	USBLS	5/07
	Alaska	Y	40330 FQ	47900 MW	62860 TQ	USBLS	5/07
	Anchorage MSA, AK	Y	41790 FQ	50300 MW	65530 TQ	USBLS	5/07
	Arizona	Y	32750 FQ	39320 MW	45600 TQ	USBLS	5/07
	Phoenix-Mesa-Scottsdale MSA, AZ	Y	33800 FQ	40020 MW	45820 TQ	USBLS	5/07
	Tucson MSA, AZ	Y	34160 FQ	41610 MW	48330 TQ	USBLS	5/07
	Arkansas	Y	26400 FQ	30620 MW	36560 TQ	USBLS	5/07
	Little Rock-North Little Rock MSA, AR	Y	27100 FQ	30970 MW	37430 TQ	USBLS	5/07
	California	H	17.63 FQ	21.64 MW	26.28 TQ	CABLS	1/08-3/08
	Los Angeles-Long Beach-Glendale PMSA, CA	H	17.06 FQ	21.28 MW	25.55 TQ	CABLS	1/08-3/08
	Oakland-Fremont-Hayward MSA, CA	H	20.45 FQ	25.40 MW	31.51 TQ	CABLS	1/08-3/08
	Riverside-San Bernardino-Ontario MSA, CA	H	16.51 FQ	19.16 MW	22.67 TQ	CABLS	1/08-3/08
	Sacramento-Arden Arcade-Roseville MSA, CA	H	18.22 FQ	21.87 MW	25.35 TQ	CABLS	1/08-3/08
	San Diego-Carlsbad-San Marcos MSA, CA	H	16.63 FQ	20.64 MW	24.55 TQ	CABLS	1/08-3/08
	San Francisco-San Mateo-Redwood PMSA, CA	H	18.74 FQ	24.97 MW	30.29 TQ	CABLS	1/08-3/08
	San Jose-Sunnyvale-Santa Clara MSA, CA	H	19.89 FQ	23.72 MW	29.28 TQ	CABLS	1/08-3/08
	Santa Ana-Anaheim-Irvine PMSA, CA	Y	37980 FQ	45640 MW	53600 TQ	USBLS	5/07
	Colorado	Y	34590 FQ	41010 MW	47030 TQ	USBLS	5/07
	Denver-Aurora MSA, CO	Y	35400 FQ	41770 MW	47100 TQ	USBLS	5/07
	Pueblo MSA, CO	Y	31560 FQ	40910 MW	46780 TQ	USBLS	5/07
	Connecticut	H	15.81 AE	21.62 MW		CTBLS	1/08-3/08
	Bridgeport-Stamford-Norwalk MSA, CT	Y	38790 FQ	46330 MW	55110 TQ	USBLS	5/07
	Hartford-West Hartford-East Hartford MSA, CT	Y	41360 FQ	47390 MW	53990 TQ	USBLS	5/07
	New Haven MSA, CT	Y	31360 FQ	38370 MW	49590 TQ	USBLS	5/07
	Delaware	Y	35700 FQ	41580 MW	47560 TQ	USBLS	5/07
	Wilmington PMSA, DE-MD-NJ	Y	34880 FQ	40400 MW	46400 TQ	USBLS	5/07
	District of Columbia	Y	32830 FQ	39470 MW	46650 TQ	USBLS	5/07
	Washington-Arlington-Alexandria MSA, DC-VA-MD-WV	Y	37060 FQ	44400 MW	54750 TQ	USBLS	5/07
	Florida	Y	30230 FQ	35350 MW	40710 TQ	USBLS	5/07
	Cape Coral-Fort Myers MSA, FL	Y	32130 FQ	37550 MW	43800 TQ	USBLS	5/07
	Fort Lauderdale-Pompano Beach-Deerfield Beach PMSA, FL	Y	32200 FQ	36670 MW	41360 TQ	USBLS	5/07
	Jacksonville MSA, FL	Y	30870 FQ	34970 MW	38990 TQ	USBLS	5/07
	Miami-Fort Lauderdale-Miami Beach MSA, FL	Y	31400 FQ	36780 MW	42540 TQ	USBLS	5/07
	Orlando-Kissimmee MSA, FL	Y	28030 FQ	31820 MW	36870 TQ	USBLS	5/07
	Tampa-St. Petersburg-Clearwater MSA, FL	Y	30870 FQ	36200 MW	42080 TQ	USBLS	5/07
	West Palm Beach-Boca Raton-Boynton Beach PMSA, FL	Y	31960 FQ	37830 MW	43880 TQ	USBLS	5/07
	Georgia	Y	28620 FQ	34110 MW	39350 TQ	USBLS	5/07
	Atlanta-Sandy Springs-Marietta MSA, GA	Y	32200 FQ	36870 MW	41900 TQ	USBLS	5/07
	Hawaii	Y	38000 FQ	42640 MW	47050 TQ	USBLS	5/07
	Honolulu MSA, HI	Y	38540 FQ	43070 MW	47360 TQ	USBLS	5/07
	Idaho	Y	30840 FQ	35830 MW	44110 TQ	USBLS	5/07
	Boise City-Nampa MSA, ID	Y	29630 FQ	33550 MW	41260 TQ	USBLS	5/07
	Illinois	Y	34970 FQ	42380 MW	50830 TQ	USBLS	5/07
	Chicago-Naperville-Joliet MSA, IL-IN-WI	Y	35260 FQ	42280 MW	49410 TQ	USBLS	5/07
	Indiana	Y	32250 FQ	37100 MW	42490 TQ	USBLS	5/07
	Gary PMSA, IN	Y	32360 FQ	37250 MW	42870 TQ	USBLS	5/07
	Indianapolis-Carmel MSA, IN	Y	34740 FQ	40500 MW	47050 TQ	USBLS	5/07
	Iowa	Y	29040 FQ	33580 MW	38520 TQ	USBLS	5/07

AE Average entry wage	**AW** Average wage paid	**FQ** First quartile wage	**LO** Lowest wage paid	**MTC** Median total compensation	**TCC** Total cash compensation
AER Average entry range	**AWR** Average wage range	**H** Hourly	**LR** Low end range	**MW** Median wage paid	**TQ** Third quartile wage
AEX Average experienced wage	**AXR** Average experienced range	**HI** Highest wage paid	**M** Monthly	**MWR** Median wage range	**W** Weekly
ATC Average total compensation	**D** Daily	**HR** High end range	**MCC** Median cash compensation	**S** See annotated source	**Y** Yearly

Occupation/Type/Industry	Location	Per	Low	Mid	High	Source	Date
Surgical Technologist	Des Moines-West Des Moines MSA, IA	Y	29620 FQ	35950 MW	41970 TQ	USBLS	5/07
	Kansas	Y	28090 FQ	32340 MW	39690 TQ	USBLS	5/07
	Wichita MSA, KS	Y	28600 FQ	31970 MW	38490 TQ	USBLS	5/07
	Kentucky	Y	30079 FQ	35577 MW	40922 TQ	KYBLS	2008
	Louisville-Jefferson County MSA, KY-IN	Y	32410 FQ	37320 MW	43530 TQ	USBLS	5/07
	Louisiana	H	13.24 FQ	15.97 MW	18.75 TQ	LABLS	1/08-3/08
	Baton Rouge MSA, LA	Y	28890 FQ	34750 MW	40450 TQ	USBLS	5/07
	Lafayette MSA, LA	Y	28190 FQ	32730 MW	37010 TQ	USBLS	5/07
	New Orleans-Metairie-Kenner MSA, LA	Y	29150 FQ	35360 MW	41280 TQ	USBLS	5/07
	Shreveport-Bossier City MSA, LA	Y	23320 FQ	27090 MW	31760 TQ	USBLS	5/07
	Maine	Y	30670 FQ	35130 MW	41330 TQ	USBLS	5/07
	Portland-South Portland-Biddeford MSA, ME	Y	32040 FQ	36600 MW	43510 TQ	USBLS	5/07
	Maryland	Y		45325 MW		MDBLS	3/08
	Baltimore-Towson MSA, MD	Y	36110 FQ	43920 MW	50980 TQ	USBLS	5/07
	Bethesda-Gaithersburg-Frederick PMSA, MD	Y	47650 FQ	56610 MW	61390 TQ	USBLS	5/07
	Salisbury MSA, MD	Y	29930 FQ	35420 MW	41420 TQ	USBLS	5/07
	Massachusetts	Y	33950 FQ	41730 MW	51230 TQ	USBLS	5/07
	Boston-Cambridge-Quincy NECTA, MA	Y	34360 FQ	42730 MW	53310 TQ	USBLS	5/07
	Springfield MSA, MA-CT	Y	29830 FQ	38420 MW	45990 TQ	USBLS	5/07
	Worcester MSA, MA-CT	Y	32880 FQ	40100 MW	49110 TQ	USBLS	5/07
	Michigan	Y	33540 FQ	38870 MW	44900 TQ	USBLS	5/07
	Detroit-Warren-Livonia MSA, MI	Y	35240 FQ	40400 MW	46110 TQ	USBLS	5/07
	Grand Rapids-Wyoming MSA, MI	Y	36290 FQ	41620 MW	47320 TQ	USBLS	5/07
	Warren-Troy-Farmington Hills PMSA, MI	Y	34490 FQ	39600 MW	45750 TQ	USBLS	5/07
	Minnesota	Y	39285 FQ	46117 MW	52949 TQ	MNBLS	10/08-12/08
	Duluth-Superior MSA, MN-WI	Y	34410 FQ	40457 MW	47749 TQ	MNBLS	10/08-12/08
	Minneapolis-Saint Paul MSA, MN-WI	Y	41995 FQ	47613 MW	53211 TQ	MNBLS	10/08-12/08
	Rochester MSA, MN	Y	44893 FQ	51981 MW	57919 TQ	MNBLS	10/08-12/08
	Mississippi	Y	24350 FQ	28760 MW	34790 TQ	USBLS	5/07
	Jackson MSA, MS	Y	26520 FQ	32330 MW	39510 TQ	USBLS	5/07
	Missouri	Y	28310 FQ	34980 MW	42190 TQ	USBLS	5/07
	Kansas City MSA, MO-KS	Y	33400 FQ	39990 MW	46190 TQ	USBLS	5/07
	St. Louis MSA, MO-IL	Y	31110 FQ	36480 MW	42340 TQ	USBLS	5/07
	Springfield MSA, MO	Y	27970 FQ	34950 MW	43410 TQ	USBLS	5/07
	Montana	Y	28800 FQ	34880 MW	40090 TQ	USBLS	5/07
	Nebraska	Y	30400 FQ	35650 MW	41710 TQ	USBLS	5/07
	Omaha-Council Bluffs MSA, NE-IA	Y	31620 FQ	36450 MW	42910 TQ	USBLS	5/07
	Nevada	H	18.36 FQ	21.41 MW	24.65 TQ	NVBLS	5/08
	Las Vegas-Paradise MSA, NV	H	18.16 FQ	21.28 MW	24.80 TQ	NVBLS	5/08
	New Hampshire	H	15.99 AE	19.73 MW	21.15 AEX	NHBLS	6/08
	Manchester MSA, NH	Y	35140 FQ	41570 MW	46150 TQ	USBLS	5/07
	Nashua NECTA, NH-MA	Y	36550 FQ	40650 MW	46210 TQ	USBLS	5/07
	New Jersey	Y	38200 FQ	43720 MW	49800 TQ	USBLS	5/07
	Atlantic City MSA, NJ	Y	39640 FQ	44380 MW	49080 TQ	USBLS	5/07
	Camden PMSA, NJ	Y	37080 FQ	41490 MW	46520 TQ	USBLS	5/07
	Edison PMSA, NJ	Y	37990 FQ	43770 MW	49740 TQ	USBLS	5/07
	Newark-Union PMSA, NJ-PA	Y	36650 FQ	41580 MW	47690 TQ	USBLS	5/07
	New Mexico	Y	28100 FQ	32470 MW	38260 TQ	USBLS	5/07
	Albuquerque MSA, NM	Y	28740 FQ	33190 MW	38920 TQ	USBLS	5/07
	New York	Y	32930 FQ	38730 MW	46970 TQ	USBLS	5/07
	Albany-Schenectady-Troy MSA, NY	Y	28250 FQ	32860 MW	37480 TQ	USBLS	5/07
	Buffalo-Niagara Falls MSA, NY	Y	34530 FQ	38300 MW	43860 TQ	USBLS	5/07
	Nassau-Suffolk PMSA, NY	Y	35730 FQ	41680 MW	49140 TQ	USBLS	5/07
	New York-Northern New Jersey-Long Island MSA, NY-NJ-PA	Y	35200 FQ	41980 MW	49540 TQ	USBLS	5/07
	Syracuse MSA, NY	Y	32580 FQ	38530 MW	45470 TQ	USBLS	5/07
	North Carolina	Y	30270 FQ	35310 MW	40620 TQ	USBLS	5/07

AE	Average entry wage	**AW**	Average wage paid	**FQ**	First quartile wage
AER	Average entry range	**AWR**	Average wage range	**H**	Hourly
AEX	Average experienced wage	**AXR**	Average experienced range	**HI**	Highest wage paid
ATC	Average total compensation	**D**	Daily	**HR**	High end range

LO	Lowest wage paid	**MTC**	Median total compensation	**TCC**	Total cash compensation
LR	Low end range	**MW**	Median wage paid	**TQ**	Third quartile wage
M	Monthly	**MWR**	Median wage range	**W**	Weekly
MCC	Median cash compensation	**S**	See annotated source	**Y**	Yearly

Occupation/Type/Industry	Location	Per	Low	Mid	High	Source	Date
Surgical Technologist	Charlotte-Gastonia-Concord MSA, NC-SC	Y	29760 FQ	34680 MW	39710 TQ	USBLS	5/07
	Greensboro-High Point MSA, NC	Y	28400 FQ	33290 MW	39950 TQ	USBLS	5/07
	Raleigh-Cary MSA, NC	Y	34570 FQ	39710 MW	45170 TQ	USBLS	5/07
	North Dakota	Y	29950 FQ	35390 MW	42540 TQ	USBLS	5/07
	Fargo MSA, ND-MN	Y	31600 FQ	35900 MW	41740 TQ	USBLS	5/07
	Ohio	Y	30710 FQ	36410 MW	41760 TQ	USBLS	5/07
	Cincinnati-Middletown MSA, OH-KY-IN	Y	31950 FQ	37190 MW	43050 TQ	USBLS	5/07
	Cleveland-Elyria-Mentor MSA, OH	Y	31790 FQ	38620 MW	44320 TQ	USBLS	5/07
	Columbus MSA, OH	Y	29330 FQ	35000 MW	40150 TQ	USBLS	5/07
	Dayton MSA, OH	Y	34360 FQ	38820 MW	44630 TQ	USBLS	5/07
	Mansfield MSA, OH	Y	26250 FQ	28250 MW	30450 TQ	USBLS	5/07
	Oklahoma	Y	26530 FQ	31140 MW	37520 TQ	USBLS	5/07
	Oklahoma City MSA, OK	Y	28430 FQ	33390 MW	38950 TQ	USBLS	5/07
	Tulsa MSA, OK	Y	25890 FQ	30400 MW	38940 TQ	USBLS	5/07
	Oregon	H	18.42 FQ	21.00 MW	23.41 TQ	ORBLS	5/08
	Eugene-Springfield MSA, OR	Y	36200 FQ	41030 MW	45200 TQ	USBLS	5/07
	Portland-Vancouver-Beaverton MSA, OR-WA	Y	39280 FQ	43940 MW	48470 TQ	USBLS	5/07
	Salem MSA, OR	Y	38200 FQ	44760 MW	51010 TQ	USBLS	5/07
	Pennsylvania	Y	30330 FQ	35900 MW	41220 TQ	USBLS	5/07
	Allentown-Bethlehem-Easton MSA, PA-NJ	Y	31330 FQ	36910 MW	44410 TQ	USBLS	5/07
	Philadelphia-Camden-Wilmington MSA, PA-NJ-DE-MD	Y	34780 FQ	39630 MW	45870 TQ	USBLS	5/07
	Pittsburgh MSA, PA	Y	27390 FQ	32620 MW	38540 TQ	USBLS	5/07
	Rhode Island	Y	36340 FQ	43020 MW	49390 TQ	USBLS	5/07
	Providence-Fall River-Warwick MSA, RI-MA	Y	36320 FQ	43360 MW	50350 TQ	USBLS	5/07
	South Carolina	Y	29180 FQ	33710 MW	38250 TQ	USBLS	5/07
	Charleston-North Charleston MSA, SC	Y	26060 FQ	29690 MW	35160 TQ	USBLS	5/07
	Columbia MSA, SC	Y	30450 FQ	35310 MW	40220 TQ	USBLS	5/07
	South Dakota	Y	30051 FQ	34847 MW	40624 TQ	SDBLS	7/08-9/08
	Sioux Falls MSA, SD	Y	31601 FQ	36925 MW	42675 TQ	SDBLS	7/08-9/08
	Tennessee	Y	29980 FQ	35080 MW	40290 TQ	USBLS	5/07
	Memphis MSA, TN-MS-AR	Y	30560 FQ	35210 MW	39570 TQ	USBLS	5/07
	Nashville-Davidson-Murfreesboro MSA, TN	Y	32650 FQ	38110 MW	48060 TQ	USBLS	5/07
	Texas	Y	30790 FQ	36820 MW	44150 TQ	USBLS	5/07
	Austin-Round Rock MSA, TX	Y	32080 FQ	37140 MW	45170 TQ	USBLS	5/07
	Dallas-Fort Worth-Arlington MSA, TX	Y	31180 FQ	38100 MW	46090 TQ	USBLS	5/07
	El Paso MSA, TX	Y	29600 FQ	35450 MW	42070 TQ	USBLS	5/07
	Houston-Sugar Land-Baytown MSA, TX	Y	32380 FQ	37820 MW	44850 TQ	USBLS	5/07
	San Antonio MSA, TX	Y	33320 FQ	38370 MW	44820 TQ	USBLS	5/07
	Utah	Y	27680 FQ	31360 MW	37580 TQ	USBLS	5/07
	Salt Lake City MSA, UT	Y	28740 FQ	33470 MW	39950 TQ	USBLS	5/07
	Vermont	Y	33250 FQ	37160 MW	41630 TQ	USBLS	5/07
	Burlington-South Burlington MSA, VT	Y	34370 FQ	37410 MW	40690 TQ	USBLS	5/07
	Virginia	Y	33010 FQ	37840 MW	44690 TQ	USBLS	5/07
	Richmond MSA, VA	Y	31780 FQ	37100 MW	44300 TQ	USBLS	5/07
	Virginia Beach-Norfolk-Newport News MSA, VA-NC	Y	32690 FQ	36900 MW	42970 TQ	USBLS	5/07
	Washington	H	18.13 FQ	20.95 MW	23.73 TQ	WABLS	3/08
	Seattle-Tacoma-Bellevue MSA, WA	Y	40430 FQ	45960 MW	51560 TQ	USBLS	5/07
	West Virginia	Y	26996 FQ	30712 MW	36559 TQ	WVBLS	7/08-9/08
	Charleston MSA, WV	Y	25560 FQ	29400 MW	34490 TQ	USBLS	5/07
	Wisconsin	Y	36430 FQ	41680 MW	48000 TQ	USBLS	5/07
	Appleton MSA, WI	Y	36000 FQ	41070 MW	46200 TQ	USBLS	5/07
	Milwaukee-Waukesha-West Allis MSA, WI	Y	39200 FQ	44370 MW	50920 TQ	USBLS	5/07
	Racine MSA, WI	Y	35330 FQ	40440 MW	47700 TQ	USBLS	5/07
	Wyoming	Y	28819 FQ	34212 MW	43056 TQ	WYBLS	9/08
	Puerto Rico	Y	13060 FQ	14930 MW	18420 TQ	USBLS	5/07

AE	Average entry wage	**AW**	Average wage paid	**FQ**	First quartile wage	**LO**	Lowest wage paid	**MTC** Median total compensation	**TCC** Total cash compensation
AER	Average entry range	**AWR**	Average wage range	**H**	Hourly	**LR**	Low end range	**MW** Median wage paid	**TQ** Third quartile wage
AEX	Average experienced wage	**AXR**	Average experienced range	**HI**	Highest wage paid	**M**	Monthly	**MWR** Median wage range	**W** Weekly
ATC	Average total compensation	**D**	Daily	**HR**	High end range	**MCC**	Median cash compensation	**S** See annotated source	**Y** Yearly

Occupation/Type/Industry	Location	Per	Low	Mid	High	Source	Date
Surgical Technologist	San Juan-Caguas-Guaynabo MSA, PR	Y	13110 FQ	15020 MW	18710 TQ	USBLS	5/07
Surveillance Equipment Coordinator							
State Government	Ohio	H	17.78 LO		21.65 HI	ODAS	2008
Survey Party Chief							
Municipal Government	Walnut Creek, CA	Y	80165 LO		96785 HI	WCSWP	6/27/08
Survey Researcher	Alabama	Y	15000 FQ	18740 MW	35860 TQ	USBLS	5/07
	Birmingham-Hoover MSA, AL	Y	33960 FQ	40900 MW	49920 TQ	USBLS	5/07
	Arizona	Y	23290 FQ	29510 MW	49700 TQ	USBLS	5/07
	Phoenix-Mesa-Scottsdale MSA, AZ	Y	26890 FQ	34490 MW	56780 TQ	USBLS	5/07
	Tucson MSA, AZ	Y	16450 FQ	17840 MW	21420 TQ	USBLS	5/07
	Arkansas	Y	26740 FQ	29600 MW	33110 TQ	USBLS	5/07
	California	H	18.03 FQ	22.46 MW	34.49 TQ	CABLS	1/08-3/08
	Los Angeles-Long Beach-Glendale PMSA, CA	H	17.57 FQ	19.68 MW	28.67 TQ	CABLS	1/08-3/08
	Oakland-Fremont-Hayward MSA, CA	H	18.02 FQ	20.47 MW	28.62 TQ	CABLS	1/08-3/08
	Sacramento-Arden Arcade-Roseville MSA, CA	H	18.23 FQ	22.54 MW	35.40 TQ	CABLS	1/08-3/08
	San Diego-Carlsbad-San Marcos MSA, CA	H	9.41 FQ	15.29 MW	35.86 TQ	CABLS	1/08-3/08
	San Francisco-San Mateo-Redwood PMSA, CA	H	30.98 FQ	35.79 MW	40.75 TQ	CABLS	1/08-3/08
	San Jose-Sunnyvale-Santa Clara MSA, CA	H	27.87 FQ	33.39 MW	37.20 TQ	CABLS	1/08-3/08
	Santa Ana-Anaheim-Irvine PMSA, CA	Y	41830 FQ	47910 MW	54790 TQ	USBLS	5/07
	Colorado	Y	15390 FQ	21890 MW	28550 TQ	USBLS	5/07
	Denver-Aurora MSA, CO	Y	15310 FQ	22460 MW	29070 TQ	USBLS	5/07
	Connecticut	H	14.53 AE	25.72 MW		CTBLS	1/08-3/08
	Bridgeport-Stamford-Norwalk MSA, CT	Y	22720 FQ	35830 MW	64520 TQ	USBLS	5/07
	Hartford-West Hartford-East Hartford MSA, CT	Y	46520 FQ	58130 MW	72160 TQ	USBLS	5/07
	District of Columbia	Y	36550 FQ	47240 MW	63840 TQ	USBLS	5/07
	Washington-Arlington-Alexandria MSA, DC-VA-MD-WV	Y	41830 FQ	53780 MW	68960 TQ	USBLS	5/07
	Florida	Y	19610 FQ	36170 MW	49930 TQ	USBLS	5/07
	Miami-Fort Lauderdale-Miami Beach MSA, FL	Y	19190 FQ	39040 MW	50340 TQ	USBLS	5/07
	Georgia	Y	18280 FQ	23320 MW	32690 TQ	USBLS	5/07
	Atlanta-Sandy Springs-Marietta MSA, GA	Y	17970 FQ	21850 MW	31590 TQ	USBLS	5/07
	Hawaii	Y	30030 FQ	35030 MW	42220 TQ	USBLS	5/07
	Honolulu MSA, HI	Y	30120 FQ	35170 MW	42280 TQ	USBLS	5/07
	Idaho	Y	17700 FQ	21600 MW	36350 TQ	USBLS	5/07
	Illinois	Y	21820 FQ	31020 MW	48830 TQ	USBLS	5/07
	Chicago-Naperville-Joliet MSA, IL-IN-WI	Y	22090 FQ	31620 MW	49360 TQ	USBLS	5/07
	Indiana	Y	25390 FQ	41300 MW	53300 TQ	USBLS	5/07
	Indianapolis-Carmel MSA, IN	Y	20570 FQ	47300 MW	58390 TQ	USBLS	5/07
	Iowa	Y	35370 FQ	65460 MW	74690 TQ	USBLS	5/07
	Kansas	Y	34050 FQ	43970 MW	63280 TQ	USBLS	5/07
	Wichita MSA, KS	Y	18250 FQ	28620 MW	34630 TQ	USBLS	5/07
	Kentucky	Y	35176 FQ	39907 MW	48637 TQ	KYBLS	2008
	Maine	Y	29180 FQ	34220 MW	54050 TQ	USBLS	5/07
	Portland-South Portland-Biddeford MSA, ME	Y	28820 FQ	32430 MW	53650 TQ	USBLS	5/07
	Maryland	Y		56900 MW		MDBLS	3/08
	Baltimore-Towson MSA, MD	Y	18060 FQ	28630 MW	50000 TQ	USBLS	5/07
	Bethesda-Gaithersburg-Frederick PMSA, MD	Y	50460 FQ	60030 MW	72660 TQ	USBLS	5/07
	Massachusetts	Y	31560 FQ	37560 MW	53750 TQ	USBLS	5/07
	Boston-Cambridge-Quincy NECTA, MA	Y	31620 FQ	40540 MW	58680 TQ	USBLS	5/07
	Michigan	Y	30880 FQ	56000 MW	83690 TQ	USBLS	5/07

Survey Researcher

Occupation/Type/Industry	Location	Per	Low	Mid	High	Source	Date
Survey Researcher	Detroit-Warren-Livonia MSA, MI	Y	48710 FQ	75680 MW	100040 TQ	USBLS	5/07
	Grand Rapids-Wyoming MSA, MI	Y	23270 FQ	34890 MW	65590 TQ	USBLS	5/07
	Warren-Troy-Farmington Hills PMSA, MI	Y	44510 FQ	68370 MW	89300 TQ	USBLS	5/07
	Minnesota	Y	39850 FQ	51034 MW	63213 TQ	MNBLS	10/08-12/08
	Minneapolis-Saint Paul MSA, MN-WI	Y	40049 FQ	51202 MW	63296 TQ	MNBLS	10/08-12/08
	Missouri	Y	16700 FQ	28570 MW	45380 TQ	USBLS	5/07
	Kansas City MSA, MO-KS	Y	25040 FQ	38500 MW	76900 TQ	USBLS	5/07
	St. Louis MSA, MO-IL	Y	27090 FQ	30510 MW	39660 TQ	USBLS	5/07
	Montana	Y	13790 FQ	14790 MW	15800 TQ	USBLS	5/07
	Nebraska	Y	35840 FQ	51300 MW	77860 TQ	USBLS	5/07
	New Hampshire	H	10.59 AE	11.23 MW	13.03 AEX	NHBLS	6/08
	New Jersey	Y	20980 FQ	36180 MW	60620 TQ	USBLS	5/07
	Edison PMSA, NJ	Y	29370 FQ	53800 MW	66290 TQ	USBLS	5/07
	Newark-Union PMSA, NJ-PA	Y	27050 FQ	45250 MW	65500 TQ	USBLS	5/07
	New York	Y	37130 FQ	53930 MW	71480 TQ	USBLS	5/07
	Albany-Schenectady-Troy MSA, NY	Y	44740 FQ	59640 MW	74160 TQ	USBLS	5/07
	Nassau-Suffolk PMSA, NY	Y	43020 FQ	61990 MW	83430 TQ	USBLS	5/07
	New York-Northern New Jersey-Long Island MSA, NY-NJ-PA	Y	33530 FQ	50920 MW	69110 TQ	USBLS	5/07
	North Carolina	Y	32060 FQ	39600 MW	50730 TQ	USBLS	5/07
	Charlotte-Gastonia-Concord MSA, NC-SC	Y	28500 FQ	37630 MW	49550 TQ	USBLS	5/07
	Ohio	Y	24460 FQ	33960 MW	51160 TQ	USBLS	5/07
	Cincinnati-Middletown MSA, OH-KY-IN	Y	28510 FQ	38010 MW	57030 TQ	USBLS	5/07
	Cleveland-Elyria-Mentor MSA, OH	Y	19280 FQ	23850 MW	29140 TQ	USBLS	5/07
	Columbus MSA, OH	Y	35680 FQ	45480 MW	57610 TQ	USBLS	5/07
	Oklahoma	Y	27460 FQ	31760 MW	44540 TQ	USBLS	5/07
	Tulsa MSA, OK	Y	27380 FQ	31260 MW	47150 TQ	USBLS	5/07
	Oregon	H	15.19 FQ	17.40 MW	21.69 TQ	ORBLS	5/08
	Portland-Vancouver-Beaverton MSA, OR-WA	Y	32830 FQ	36680 MW	46370 TQ	USBLS	5/07
	Pennsylvania	Y	18130 FQ	21430 MW	36220 TQ	USBLS	5/07
	Philadelphia-Camden-Wilmington MSA, PA-NJ-DE-MD	Y	18760 FQ	23130 MW	38930 TQ	USBLS	5/07
	Pittsburgh MSA, PA	Y	15030 FQ	16880 MW	18740 TQ	USBLS	5/07
	Rhode Island	Y	32580 FQ	44080 MW	58030 TQ	USBLS	5/07
	Providence-Fall River-Warwick MSA, RI-MA	Y	32580 FQ	44080 MW	58030 TQ	USBLS	5/07
	South Carolina	Y	21050 FQ	23260 MW	31690 TQ	USBLS	5/07
	Columbia MSA, SC	Y	20730 FQ	22490 MW	25270 TQ	USBLS	5/07
	Tennessee	Y	19440 FQ	22070 MW	27530 TQ	USBLS	5/07
	Texas	Y	21830 FQ	26180 MW	38600 TQ	USBLS	5/07
	Austin-Round Rock MSA, TX	Y	22610 FQ	25790 MW	29940 TQ	USBLS	5/07
	Dallas-Fort Worth-Arlington MSA, TX	Y	37980 FQ	54520 MW	73440 TQ	USBLS	5/07
	Houston-Sugar Land-Baytown MSA, TX	Y	20320 FQ	23580 MW	29220 TQ	USBLS	5/07
	San Antonio MSA, TX	Y	20650 FQ	28140 MW	36490 TQ	USBLS	5/07
	Utah	Y	14070 FQ	17050 MW	20030 TQ	USBLS	5/07
	Vermont	Y	35660 FQ	40960 MW	47080 TQ	USBLS	5/07
	Virginia	Y	42650 FQ	47240 MW	52130 TQ	USBLS	5/07
	Washington	H	15.26 FQ	23.43 MW	28.98 TQ	WABLS	3/08
	Seattle-Tacoma-Bellevue MSA, WA	Y	33760 FQ	48600 MW	59820 TQ	USBLS	5/07
	West Virginia	Y	14273 FQ	15628 MW	26071 TQ	WVBLS	7/08-9/08
	Wisconsin	Y	37220 FQ	59720 MW	102640 TQ	USBLS	5/07
	Milwaukee-Waukesha-West Allis MSA, WI	Y	19440 FQ	41380 MW	64750 TQ	USBLS	5/07
	Puerto Rico	Y	18690 FQ	23580 MW	51870 TQ	USBLS	5/07
	San Juan-Caguas-Guaynabo MSA, PR	Y	18690 FQ	23580 MW	51870 TQ	USBLS	5/07

AE	Average entry wage	AW	Average wage paid	FQ	First quartile wage
AER	Average entry range	AWR	Average wage range	LR	Low end range
AEX	Average experienced wage	AXR	Average experienced range	HI	Hourly
ATC	Average total compensation D	Daily	HR	High end range

LO	Lowest wage paid	MTC	Median total compensation	TCC	Total cash compensation
LR	Low end range	MW	Median wage paid	TQ	Third quartile wage
M	Monthly	MWR	Median wage range	W	Weekly
MCC	Median cash compensation	S	See annotated source	Y	Yearly

Occupation/Type/Industry	Location	Per	Low	Mid	High	Source	Date
Surveying and Mapping Technician							
	Alabama	Y	21330 FQ	27510 MW	36540 TQ	USBLS	5/07
	Birmingham-Hoover MSA, AL	Y	23720 FQ	29450 MW	38000 TQ	USBLS	5/07
	Alaska	Y	38570 FQ	45770 MW	52350 TQ	USBLS	5/07
	Anchorage MSA, AK	Y	41660 FQ	47200 MW	53150 TQ	USBLS	5/07
	Arizona	Y	35060 FQ	43060 MW	51900 TQ	USBLS	5/07
	Phoenix-Mesa-Scottsdale MSA, AZ	Y	36130 FQ	44080 MW	53330 TQ	USBLS	5/07
	Tucson MSA, AZ	Y	33120 FQ	40380 MW	48280 TQ	USBLS	5/07
	Arkansas	Y	20980 FQ	26600 MW	34720 TQ	USBLS	5/07
	Little Rock-North Little Rock MSA, AR	Y	19550 FQ	27240 MW	34470 TQ	USBLS	5/07
	California	H	19.75 FQ	26.34 MW	32.40 TQ	CABLS	1/08-3/08
	Los Angeles-Long Beach-Glendale PMSA, CA	H	25.29 FQ	28.73 MW	31.91 TQ	CABLS	1/08-3/08
	Oakland-Fremont-Hayward MSA, CA	H	21.35 FQ	26.07 MW	33.67 TQ	CABLS	1/08-3/08
	Riverside-San Bernardino-Ontario MSA, CA	H	21.65 FQ	29.38 MW	35.69 TQ	CABLS	1/08-3/08
	Sacramento-Arden Arcade-Roseville MSA, CA	H	21.53 FQ	26.62 MW	33.61 TQ	CABLS	1/08-3/08
	San Diego-Carlsbad-San Marcos MSA, CA	H	20.96 FQ	25.44 MW	32.53 TQ	CABLS	1/08-3/08
	San Francisco-San Mateo-Redwood PMSA, CA	H	19.17 FQ	28.03 MW	34.67 TQ	CABLS	1/08-3/08
	San Jose-Sunnyvale-Santa Clara MSA, CA	H	19.36 FQ	31.18 MW	36.27 TQ	CABLS	1/08-3/08
	Santa Ana-Anaheim-Irvine PMSA, CA	Y	37930 FQ	45760 MW	61870 TQ	USBLS	5/07
	Colorado	Y	28490 FQ	37440 MW	48130 TQ	USBLS	5/07
	Colorado Springs MSA, CO	Y	28500 FQ	37030 MW	48650 TQ	USBLS	5/07
	Denver-Aurora MSA, CO	Y	29820 FQ	39400 MW	50220 TQ	USBLS	5/07
	Connecticut	H	14.15 AE	19.34 MW		CTBLS	1/08-3/08
	Bridgeport-Stamford-Norwalk MSA, CT	Y	42390 FQ	48360 MW	66370 TQ	USBLS	5/07
	Hartford-West Hartford-East Hartford MSA, CT	Y	33280 FQ	37620 MW	47300 TQ	USBLS	5/07
	Delaware	Y	27960 FQ	33060 MW	41180 TQ	USBLS	5/07
	Wilmington PMSA, DE-MD-NJ	Y	27990 FQ	35760 MW	46270 TQ	USBLS	5/07
	Washington-Arlington-Alexandria MSA, DC-VA-MD-WV	Y	31020 FQ	42190 MW	53640 TQ	USBLS	5/07
	Florida	Y	24620 FQ	30840 MW	39340 TQ	USBLS	5/07
	Cape Coral-Fort Myers MSA, FL	Y	24160 FQ	30800 MW	39470 TQ	USBLS	5/07
	Fort Lauderdale-Pompano Beach-Deerfield Beach PMSA, FL	Y	27520 FQ	35750 MW	46770 TQ	USBLS	5/07
	Jacksonville MSA, FL	Y	22850 FQ	28960 MW	36070 TQ	USBLS	5/07
	Miami-Fort Lauderdale-Miami Beach MSA, FL	Y	25620 FQ	32150 MW	40750 TQ	USBLS	5/07
	Orlando-Kissimmee MSA, FL	Y	26400 FQ	32690 MW	42310 TQ	USBLS	5/07
	Tampa-St. Petersburg-Clearwater MSA, FL	Y	23350 FQ	29560 MW	37780 TQ	USBLS	5/07
	West Palm Beach-Boca Raton-Boynton Beach PMSA, FL	Y	25490 FQ	31430 MW	38520 TQ	USBLS	5/07
	Georgia	Y	23070 FQ	29250 MW	35950 TQ	USBLS	5/07
	Atlanta-Sandy Springs-Marietta MSA, GA	Y	24800 FQ	31200 MW	37140 TQ	USBLS	5/07
	Augusta-Richmond County MSA, GA-SC	Y	21490 FQ	28840 MW	39860 TQ	USBLS	5/07
	Macon MSA, GA	Y	22160 FQ	28890 MW	36260 TQ	USBLS	5/07
	Hawaii	Y	25630 FQ	33600 MW	40950 TQ	USBLS	5/07
	Honolulu MSA, HI	Y	24270 FQ	32610 MW	41240 TQ	USBLS	5/07
	Idaho	Y	28220 FQ	35350 MW	44410 TQ	USBLS	5/07
	Boise City-Nampa MSA, ID	Y	30160 FQ	40140 MW	48430 TQ	USBLS	5/07
	Illinois	Y	32520 FQ	40230 MW	50600 TQ	USBLS	5/07
	Champaign-Urbana MSA, IL	Y	29230 FQ	34160 MW	39750 TQ	USBLS	5/07
	Chicago-Naperville-Joliet MSA, IL-IN-WI	Y	33930 FQ	40910 MW	48670 TQ	USBLS	5/07
	Indiana	Y	28360 FQ	33330 MW	39490 TQ	USBLS	5/07

AE	Average entry wage	AW	Average wage paid	FQ	First quartile wage	LO	Lowest wage paid	MTC Median total compensation TCC Total cash compensation
AER	Average entry range	AWR	Average wage range	H	Hourly	LR	Low end range	MW Median wage paid TQ Third quartile wage
AEX	Average experienced wage	AXR	Average experienced range	HI	Highest wage paid	M	Monthly	MWR Median wage range W Weekly
ATC	Average total compensation	D	Daily	HR	High end range	MCC	Median cash compensation	S See annotated source Y Yearly

Occupation/Type/Industry	Location	Per	Low	Mid	High	Source	Date
Surveying and Mapping Technician	Gary PMSA, IN	Y	26440 FQ	33480 MW	40950 TQ	USBLS	5/07
	Indianapolis-Carmel MSA, IN	Y	30560 FQ	36040 MW	43250 TQ	USBLS	5/07
	Iowa	Y	27820 FQ	33870 MW	39890 TQ	USBLS	5/07
	Des Moines-West Des Moines MSA, IA	Y	29230 FQ	35590 MW	43400 TQ	USBLS	5/07
	Kansas	Y	23010 FQ	31120 MW	41840 TQ	USBLS	5/07
	Wichita MSA, KS	Y	23140 FQ	27480 MW	32240 TQ	USBLS	5/07
	Kentucky	Y	23696 FQ	30721 MW	39024 TQ	KYBLS	2008
	Lexington-Fayette MSA, KY	Y	25590 FQ	30570 MW	37060 TQ	USBLS	5/07
	Louisville-Jefferson County MSA, KY-IN	Y	27210 FQ	32450 MW	38070 TQ	USBLS	5/07
	Louisiana	H	11.42 FQ	14.37 MW	19.43 TQ	LABLS	1/08-3/08
	Baton Rouge MSA, LA	Y	25870 FQ	30580 MW	38560 TQ	USBLS	5/07
	New Orleans-Metairie-Kenner MSA, LA	Y	28230 FQ	43640 MW	53170 TQ	USBLS	5/07
	Shreveport-Bossier City MSA, LA	Y	22300 FQ	27840 MW	33260 TQ	USBLS	5/07
	Maine	Y	28590 FQ	33210 MW	39510 TQ	USBLS	5/07
	Portland-South Portland-Biddeford MSA, ME	Y	30140 FQ	34150 MW	38460 TQ	USBLS	5/07
	Maryland	Y		35300 MW		MDBLS	3/08
	Baltimore-Towson MSA, MD	Y	26880 FQ	32860 MW	40430 TQ	USBLS	5/07
	Bethesda-Gaithersburg-Frederick PMSA, MD	Y	32150 FQ	44040 MW	54260 TQ	USBLS	5/07
	Massachusetts	Y	32320 FQ	41050 MW	51650 TQ	USBLS	5/07
	Boston-Cambridge-Quincy NECTA, MA	Y	35810 FQ	45540 MW	54610 TQ	USBLS	5/07
	Worcester MSA, MA-CT	Y	36390 FQ	39690 MW	47470 TQ	USBLS	5/07
	Michigan	Y	28270 FQ	37260 MW	45210 TQ	USBLS	5/07
	Detroit-Warren-Livonia MSA, MI	Y	28570 FQ	39240 MW	45700 TQ	USBLS	5/07
	Grand Rapids-Wyoming MSA, MI	Y	33220 FQ	40830 MW	47740 TQ	USBLS	5/07
	Warren-Troy-Farmington Hills PMSA, MI	Y	27240 FQ	36310 MW	45540 TQ	USBLS	5/07
	Minnesota	Y	39484 FQ	48147 MW	56339 TQ	MNBLS	10/08-12/08
	Duluth-Superior MSA, MN-WI	Y	36262 FQ	42978 MW	49768 TQ	MNBLS	10/08-12/08
	Minneapolis-Saint Paul MSA, MN-WI	Y	42717 FQ	49758 MW	57626 TQ	MNBLS	10/08-12/08
	Mississippi	Y	22390 FQ	29210 MW	41580 TQ	USBLS	5/07
	Jackson MSA, MS	Y	26000 FQ	30550 MW	41970 TQ	USBLS	5/07
	Missouri	Y	27040 FQ	34600 MW	45440 TQ	USBLS	5/07
	Kansas City MSA, MO-KS	Y	27080 FQ	36140 MW	46420 TQ	USBLS	5/07
	St. Louis MSA, MO-IL	Y	29690 FQ	36790 MW	46950 TQ	USBLS	5/07
	Montana	Y	23260 FQ	31000 MW	40510 TQ	USBLS	5/07
	Billings MSA, MT	Y	21640 FQ	30740 MW	40370 TQ	USBLS	5/07
	Nebraska	Y	26280 FQ	30940 MW	38760 TQ	USBLS	5/07
	Lincoln MSA, NE	Y	28450 FQ	32230 MW	39120 TQ	USBLS	5/07
	Omaha-Council Bluffs MSA, NE-IA	Y	31640 FQ	36470 MW	42430 TQ	USBLS	5/07
	Nevada	H	18.47 FQ	24.26 MW	30.28 TQ	NVBLS	5/08
	Las Vegas-Paradise MSA, NV	H	19.42 FQ	25.58 MW	31.43 TQ	NVBLS	5/08
	New Hampshire	H	11.80 AE	15.04 MW	18.18 AEX	NHBLS	6/08
	Nashua NECTA, NH-MA	Y	23860 FQ	29560 MW	47560 TQ	USBLS	5/07
	New Jersey	Y	29450 FQ	36520 MW	45770 TQ	USBLS	5/07
	Camden PMSA, NJ	Y	25970 FQ	32890 MW	42750 TQ	USBLS	5/07
	Edison PMSA, NJ	Y	30180 FQ	35770 MW	43960 TQ	USBLS	5/07
	Newark-Union PMSA, NJ-PA	Y	26670 FQ	32560 MW	43950 TQ	USBLS	5/07
	New Mexico	Y	26490 FQ	32060 MW	40080 TQ	USBLS	5/07
	Albuquerque MSA, NM	Y	26640 FQ	31490 MW	39450 TQ	USBLS	5/07
	Santa Fe MSA, NM	Y	26330 FQ	31270 MW	44510 TQ	USBLS	5/07
	New York	Y	28850 FQ	35920 MW	48190 TQ	USBLS	5/07
	Albany-Schenectady-Troy MSA, NY	Y	36060 FQ	44640 MW	53970 TQ	USBLS	5/07
	Buffalo-Niagara Falls MSA, NY	Y	26400 FQ	31220 MW	40180 TQ	USBLS	5/07
	Nassau-Suffolk PMSA, NY	Y	27860 FQ	39920 MW	63050 TQ	USBLS	5/07
	New York-Northern New Jersey-Long Island MSA, NY-NJ-PA	Y	30280 FQ	38990 MW	52330 TQ	USBLS	5/07
	Utica-Rome MSA, NY	Y	27240 FQ	29870 MW	32520 TQ	USBLS	5/07

AE Average entry wage	**AW** Average wage paid	**FQ** First quartile wage	**LO** Lowest wage paid	**MTC** Median total compensation	**TCC** Total cash compensation
AER Average entry range	**AWR** Average wage range	**H** Hourly	**LR** Low end range	**MW** Median wage paid	**TQ** Third quartile wage
AEX Average experienced wage	**AXR** Average experienced range	**HI** Highest wage paid	**M** Monthly	**MWR** Median wage range	**W** Weekly
ATC Average total compensation	**D** Daily	**HR** High end range	**MCC** Median cash compensation	**S** See annotated source	**Y** Yearly

Occupation/Type/Industry	Location	Per	Low	Mid	High	Source	Date
Surveying and Mapping Technician	North Carolina	Y	25470 FQ	31490 MW	38430 TQ	USBLS	5/07
	Charlotte-Gastonia-Concord MSA, NC-SC	Y	28720 FQ	33920 MW	40070 TQ	USBLS	5/07
	Raleigh-Cary MSA, NC	Y	29950 FQ	35710 MW	43010 TQ	USBLS	5/07
	North Dakota	Y	25270 FQ	30470 MW	39620 TQ	USBLS	5/07
	Fargo MSA, ND-MN	Y	29140 FQ	37380 MW	45980 TQ	USBLS	5/07
	Ohio	Y	28330 FQ	34820 MW	41820 TQ	USBLS	5/07
	Cincinnati-Middletown MSA, OH-KY-IN	Y	28320 FQ	33720 MW	39850 TQ	USBLS	5/07
	Cleveland-Elyria-Mentor MSA, OH	Y	28690 FQ	35970 MW	41780 TQ	USBLS	5/07
	Columbus MSA, OH	Y	31280 FQ	37890 MW	46930 TQ	USBLS	5/07
	Dayton MSA, OH	Y	34230 FQ	38340 MW	44660 TQ	USBLS	5/07
	Oklahoma	Y	26160 FQ	34310 MW	45710 TQ	USBLS	5/07
	Oklahoma City MSA, OK	Y	30220 FQ	42440 MW	50690 TQ	USBLS	5/07
	Tulsa MSA, OK	Y	31850 FQ	39440 MW	54350 TQ	USBLS	5/07
	Oregon	H	15.35 FQ	18.79 MW	23.12 TQ	ORBLS	5/08
	Portland-Vancouver-Beaverton MSA, OR-WA	Y	32360 FQ	38910 MW	47760 TQ	USBLS	5/07
	Pennsylvania	Y	25850 FQ	31540 MW	38720 TQ	USBLS	5/07
	Allentown-Bethlehem-Easton MSA, PA-NJ	Y	22240 FQ	24880 MW	33550 TQ	USBLS	5/07
	Philadelphia-Camden-Wilmington MSA, PA-NJ-DE-MD	Y	27640 FQ	34570 MW	44800 TQ	USBLS	5/07
	Pittsburgh MSA, PA	Y	25270 FQ	31650 MW	37540 TQ	USBLS	5/07
	Rhode Island	Y	34190 FQ	39590 MW	47250 TQ	USBLS	5/07
	Providence-Fall River-Warwick MSA, RI-MA	Y	34140 FQ	39150 MW	47310 TQ	USBLS	5/07
	South Carolina	Y	22510 FQ	30850 MW	39030 TQ	USBLS	5/07
	Charleston-North Charleston MSA, SC	Y	23910 FQ	30710 MW	39130 TQ	USBLS	5/07
	Columbia MSA, SC	Y	27080 FQ	34420 MW	38590 TQ	USBLS	5/07
	Spartanburg MSA, SC	Y	29690 FQ	35890 MW	40080 TQ	USBLS	5/07
	South Dakota	Y	24019 FQ	29611 MW	33730 TQ	SDBLS	7/08-9/08
	Tennessee	Y	25380 FQ	31310 MW	39260 TQ	USBLS	5/07
	Memphis MSA, TN-MS-AR	Y	27190 FQ	33160 MW	47410 TQ	USBLS	5/07
	Nashville-Davidson-Murfreesboro MSA, TN	Y	26410 FQ	33090 MW	40040 TQ	USBLS	5/07
	Texas	Y	21500 FQ	29160 MW	38200 TQ	USBLS	5/07
	Austin-Round Rock MSA, TX	Y	25390 FQ	30990 MW	37610 TQ	USBLS	5/07
	Brownsville-Harlingen MSA, TX	Y	20090 FQ	28040 MW	40410 TQ	USBLS	5/07
	Dallas-Fort Worth-Arlington MSA, TX	Y	24160 FQ	30610 MW	40280 TQ	USBLS	5/07
	El Paso MSA, TX	Y	21330 FQ	26580 MW	34280 TQ	USBLS	5/07
	Houston-Sugar Land-Baytown MSA, TX	Y	19570 FQ	31100 MW	42360 TQ	USBLS	5/07
	Midland MSA, TX	Y	12990 FQ	14820 MW	19080 TQ	USBLS	5/07
	San Antonio MSA, TX	Y	25040 FQ	29160 MW	34980 TQ	USBLS	5/07
	Utah	Y	21500 FQ	26140 MW	36170 TQ	USBLS	5/07
	Salt Lake City MSA, UT	Y	19220 FQ	23750 MW	29010 TQ	USBLS	5/07
	Vermont	Y	29850 FQ	35050 MW	39840 TQ	USBLS	5/07
	Virginia	Y	26400 FQ	33720 MW	45400 TQ	USBLS	5/07
	Richmond MSA, VA	Y	26540 FQ	31090 MW	38890 TQ	USBLS	5/07
	Virginia Beach-Norfolk-Newport News MSA, VA-NC	Y	23560 FQ	30390 MW	36970 TQ	USBLS	5/07
	Washington	H	16.26 FQ	20.23 MW	24.17 TQ	WABLS	3/08
	Bremerton-Silverdale MSA, WA	Y	24540 FQ	26540 MW	30380 TQ	USBLS	5/07
	Seattle-Tacoma-Bellevue MSA, WA	Y	35830 FQ	42820 MW	51060 TQ	USBLS	5/07
	Spokane MSA, WA	Y	24350 FQ	34510 MW	44300 TQ	USBLS	5/07
	West Virginia	Y	23048 FQ	30963 MW	42650 TQ	WVBLS	7/08-9/08
	Charleston MSA, WV	Y	25340 FQ	30280 MW	38290 TQ	USBLS	5/07
	Wisconsin	Y	29940 FQ	36270 MW	43330 TQ	USBLS	5/07
	Milwaukee-Waukesha-West Allis MSA, WI	Y	30230 FQ	38490 MW	49810 TQ	USBLS	5/07
	Wyoming	Y	23989 FQ	34856 MW	40872 TQ	WYBLS	9/08
	Puerto Rico	Y	15290 FQ	19760 MW	24170 TQ	USBLS	5/07

Occupation/Type/Industry	Location	Per	Low	Mid	High	Source	Date
Surveying and Mapping Technician	San Juan-Caguas-Guaynabo MSA, PR	Y	14960 FQ	20400 MW	24690 TQ	USBLS	5/07
Surveyor	Alabama	Y	30310 FQ	40130 MW	53930 TQ	USBLS	5/07
	Birmingham-Hoover MSA, AL	Y	30150 FQ	42630 MW	61730 TQ	USBLS	5/07
	Mobile MSA, AL	Y	29160 FQ	43580 MW	56360 TQ	USBLS	5/07
	Tuscaloosa MSA, AL	Y	32440 FQ	39830 MW	52540 TQ	USBLS	5/07
	Arizona	Y	35450 FQ	45800 MW	57410 TQ	USBLS	5/07
	Phoenix-Mesa-Scottsdale MSA, AZ	Y	35520 FQ	45940 MW	58330 TQ	USBLS	5/07
	Prescott MSA, AZ	Y	39770 FQ	47030 MW	58900 TQ	USBLS	5/07
	Tucson MSA, AZ	Y	34120 FQ	44630 MW	53880 TQ	USBLS	5/07
	Arkansas	Y	28150 FQ	38220 MW	48880 TQ	USBLS	5/07
	Little Rock-North Little Rock MSA, AR	Y	38790 FQ	48310 MW	58030 TQ	USBLS	5/07
	California	H	29.04 FQ	35.49 MW	40.55 TQ	CABLS	1/08-3/08
	Fresno MSA, CA	H	24.39 FQ	31.26 MW	37.86 TQ	CABLS	1/08-3/08
	Los Angeles-Long Beach-Glendale PMSA, CA	H	33.00 FQ	37.10 MW	41.86 TQ	CABLS	1/08-3/08
	Oakland-Fremont-Hayward MSA, CA	H	31.51 FQ	36.50 MW	41.03 TQ	CABLS	1/08-3/08
	Oxnard-Thousand Oaks-Ventura MSA, CA	H	28.31 FQ	34.31 MW	39.23 TQ	CABLS	1/08-3/08
	Riverside-San Bernardino-Ontario MSA, CA	H	30.01 FQ	36.04 MW	41.77 TQ	CABLS	1/08-3/08
	Sacramento-Arden Arcade-Roseville MSA, CA	H	29.61 FQ	36.75 MW	42.56 TQ	CABLS	1/08-3/08
	San Diego-Carlsbad-San Marcos MSA, CA	H	26.88 FQ	34.35 MW	38.77 TQ	CABLS	1/08-3/08
	San Francisco-San Mateo-Redwood PMSA, CA	H	26.01 FQ	33.70 MW	40.20 TQ	CABLS	1/08-3/08
	San Jose-Sunnyvale-Santa Clara MSA, CA	H	31.91 FQ	38.39 MW	45.26 TQ	CABLS	1/08-3/08
	Santa Ana-Anaheim-Irvine PMSA, CA	Y	65950 FQ	74160 MW	82380 TQ	USBLS	5/07
	Colorado	Y	42410 FQ	52370 MW	63730 TQ	USBLS	5/07
	Denver-Aurora MSA, CO	Y	43400 FQ	52570 MW	62300 TQ	USBLS	5/07
	Fort Collins-Loveland MSA, CO	Y	48690 FQ	58210 MW	70010 TQ	USBLS	5/07
	Connecticut	H	18.60 AE	27.21 MW		CTBLS	1/08-3/08
	Bridgeport-Stamford-Norwalk MSA, CT	Y	49810 FQ	57230 MW	64430 TQ	USBLS	5/07
	Hartford-West Hartford-East Hartford MSA, CT	Y	42100 FQ	53110 MW	65330 TQ	USBLS	5/07
	New Haven MSA, CT	Y	41820 FQ	64030 MW	76480 TQ	USBLS	5/07
	Delaware	Y	38970 FQ	47350 MW	57420 TQ	USBLS	5/07
	Wilmington PMSA, DE-MD-NJ	Y	43530 FQ	50680 MW	62160 TQ	USBLS	5/07
	District of Columbia	Y	46110 FQ	51610 MW	65990 TQ	USBLS	5/07
	Washington-Arlington-Alexandria MSA, DC-VA-MD-WV	Y	41550 FQ	52420 MW	71920 TQ	USBLS	5/07
	Florida	Y	36940 FQ	50690 MW	66310 TQ	USBLS	5/07
	Fort Lauderdale-Pompano Beach-Deerfield Beach PMSA, FL	Y	51680 FQ	57970 MW	73690 TQ	USBLS	5/07
	Jacksonville MSA, FL	Y	42090 FQ	56100 MW	63520 TQ	USBLS	5/07
	Miami-Fort Lauderdale-Miami Beach MSA, FL	Y	43070 FQ	54570 MW	68970 TQ	USBLS	5/07
	Orlando-Kissimmee MSA, FL	Y	31100 FQ	51970 MW	72410 TQ	USBLS	5/07
	Tampa-St. Petersburg-Clearwater MSA, FL	Y	38280 FQ	46970 MW	65830 TQ	USBLS	5/07
	West Palm Beach-Boca Raton-Boynton Beach PMSA, FL	Y	33870 FQ	48420 MW	62970 TQ	USBLS	5/07
	Georgia	Y	32060 FQ	38320 MW	47420 TQ	USBLS	5/07
	Atlanta-Sandy Springs-Marietta MSA, GA	Y	31850 FQ	37840 MW	46680 TQ	USBLS	5/07
	Athens-Clarke County, GA	Y			42074 HI	GACTY02	2008
	Brooks County, GA	Y			1800 HI	GACTY02	2008
	Hawaii	Y	42230 FQ	48910 MW	63750 TQ	USBLS	5/07
	Honolulu MSA, HI	Y	43290 FQ	51090 MW	65870 TQ	USBLS	5/07

AE Average entry wage	AW Average wage paid	FQ First quartile wage	LO Lowest wage paid	MTC Median total compensation	TCC Total cash compensation
AER Average entry range	AWR Average wage range	H Hourly	LR Low end range	MW Median wage paid	TQ Third quartile wage
AEX Average experienced wage	AXR Average experienced range	HI Highest wage paid	M Monthly	MWR Median wage range	W Weekly
ATC Average total compensation	D Daily	HR High end range	MCC Median cash compensation	S See annotated source	Y Yearly

Occupation/Type/Industry	Location	Per	Low	Mid	High	Source	Date
Surveyor	Idaho	Y	35590 FQ	47910 MW	66460 TQ	USBLS	5/07
	Boise City-Nampa MSA, ID	Y	39690 FQ	59380 MW	75020 TQ	USBLS	5/07
	Illinois	Y	42370 FQ	58180 MW	71340 TQ	USBLS	5/07
	Chicago-Naperville-Joliet MSA, IL-IN-WI	Y	47630 FQ	60810 MW	73430 TQ	USBLS	5/07
	Indiana	Y	33770 FQ	44000 MW	56520 TQ	USBLS	5/07
	Fort Wayne MSA, IN	Y	40420 FQ	46250 MW	56360 TQ	USBLS	5/07
	Gary PMSA, IN	Y	52040 FQ	66360 MW	74600 TQ	USBLS	5/07
	Indianapolis-Carmel MSA, IN	Y	41100 FQ	49340 MW	62250 TQ	USBLS	5/07
	Iowa	Y	35840 FQ	42530 MW	53220 TQ	USBLS	5/07
	Des Moines-West Des Moines MSA, IA	Y	35750 FQ	40560 MW	51900 TQ	USBLS	5/07
	Kansas	Y	32660 FQ	40700 MW	51170 TQ	USBLS	5/07
	Wichita MSA, KS	Y	29320 FQ	36670 MW	42060 TQ	USBLS	5/07
	Kentucky	Y	33872 FQ	42949 MW	55699 TQ	KYBLS	2008
	Louisville-Jefferson County MSA, KY-IN	Y	36470 FQ	45970 MW	58330 TQ	USBLS	5/07
	Owensboro MSA, KY	Y	33680 FQ	39260 MW	48310 TQ	USBLS	5/07
	Louisiana	H	13.31 FQ	19.95 MW	27.87 TQ	LABLS	1/08-3/08
	Baton Rouge MSA, LA	Y	36400 FQ	48810 MW	59460 TQ	USBLS	5/07
	Lake Charles MSA, LA	Y	19040 FQ	32370 MW	41610 TQ	USBLS	5/07
	New Orleans-Metairie-Kenner MSA, LA	Y	28270 FQ	41050 MW	63790 TQ	USBLS	5/07
	Maine	Y	35610 FQ	42210 MW	52980 TQ	USBLS	5/07
	Portland-South Portland-Biddeford MSA, ME	Y	36590 FQ	40350 MW	51170 TQ	USBLS	5/07
	Maryland	Y		56375 MW		MDBLS	3/08
	Baltimore-Towson MSA, MD	Y	41960 FQ	54710 MW	75670 TQ	USBLS	5/07
	Bethesda-Gaithersburg-Frederick PMSA, MD	Y	50110 FQ	68430 MW	79370 TQ	USBLS	5/07
	Massachusetts	Y	38810 FQ	49670 MW	64750 TQ	USBLS	5/07
	Boston-Cambridge-Quincy NECTA, MA	Y	38770 FQ	50910 MW	64470 TQ	USBLS	5/07
	Springfield MSA, MA-CT	Y	34060 FQ	37740 MW	56100 TQ	USBLS	5/07
	Worcester MSA, MA-CT	Y	41130 FQ	51390 MW	72640 TQ	USBLS	5/07
	Michigan	Y	40170 FQ	52550 MW	69110 TQ	USBLS	5/07
	Detroit-Warren-Livonia MSA, MI	Y	46930 FQ	58440 MW	74260 TQ	USBLS	5/07
	Grand Rapids-Wyoming MSA, MI	Y	40370 FQ	52970 MW	65850 TQ	USBLS	5/07
	Warren-Troy-Farmington Hills PMSA, MI	Y	45210 FQ	59230 MW	77200 TQ	USBLS	5/07
	Minnesota	Y	53388 FQ	64782 MW	78644 TQ	MNBLS	10/08-12/08
	Duluth-Superior MSA, MN-WI	Y	53838 FQ	69186 MW	84346 TQ	MNBLS	10/08-12/08
	Minneapolis-Saint Paul MSA, MN-WI	Y	56360 FQ	66257 MW	79680 TQ	MNBLS	10/08-12/08
	Mississippi	Y	25660 FQ	33350 MW	46780 TQ	USBLS	5/07
	Jackson MSA, MS	Y	32900 FQ	41480 MW	54810 TQ	USBLS	5/07
	Missouri	Y	34570 FQ	44170 MW	59170 TQ	USBLS	5/07
	Kansas City MSA, MO-KS	Y	34130 FQ	42330 MW	52040 TQ	USBLS	5/07
	St. Louis MSA, MO-IL	Y	41430 FQ	54550 MW	72930 TQ	USBLS	5/07
	Springfield MSA, MO	Y	27240 FQ	36200 MW	56990 TQ	USBLS	5/07
	Montana	Y	27950 FQ	40180 MW	57090 TQ	USBLS	5/07
	Billings MSA, MT	Y	45520 FQ	58680 MW	71800 TQ	USBLS	5/07
	Great Falls MSA, MT	Y	21480 FQ	28070 MW	35950 TQ	USBLS	5/07
	Nebraska	Y	33820 FQ	42750 MW	55220 TQ	USBLS	5/07
	Omaha-Council Bluffs MSA, NE-IA	Y	34070 FQ	42920 MW	55810 TQ	USBLS	5/07
	Nevada	H	20.01 FQ	29.21 MW	37.05 TQ	NVBLS	5/08
	Las Vegas-Paradise MSA, NV	H	18.31 FQ	28.57 MW	36.73 TQ	NVBLS	5/08
	New Hampshire	H	19.57 AE	24.29 MW	29.19 AEX	NHBLS	6/08
	Manchester MSA, NH	Y	47660 FQ	56550 MW	68190 TQ	USBLS	5/07
	Nashua NECTA, NH-MA	Y	45040 FQ	53250 MW	59560 TQ	USBLS	5/07
	New Jersey	Y	52270 FQ	65040 MW	77040 TQ	USBLS	5/07
	Camden PMSA, NJ	Y	44730 FQ	58520 MW	70570 TQ	USBLS	5/07
	Edison PMSA, NJ	Y	48970 FQ	58480 MW	71720 TQ	USBLS	5/07
	Newark-Union PMSA, NJ-PA	Y	50260 FQ	65360 MW	74720 TQ	USBLS	5/07
	New Mexico	Y	40310 FQ	51500 MW	63310 TQ	USBLS	5/07
	Albuquerque MSA, NM	Y	40910 FQ	52670 MW	66190 TQ	USBLS	5/07
	New York	Y	44660 FQ	58340 MW	75230 TQ	USBLS	5/07
	Albany-Schenectady-Troy MSA, NY	Y	57100 FQ	64110 MW	74660 TQ	USBLS	5/07

AE	Average entry wage	AW	Average wage paid	FQ	First quartile wage	LO Lowest wage paid	MTC Median total compensation	TCC Total cash compensation
AER	Average entry range	AWR	Average wage range	H	Hourly	LR Low end range	MW Median wage paid	TQ Third quartile wage
AEX	Average experienced wage	AXR	Average experienced range	HI	Highest wage paid	M Monthly	MWR Median wage range	W Weekly
ATC	Average total compensation	D	Daily	HR	High end range	MCC Median cash compensation	S See annotated source	Y Yearly

Surveyor

Occupation/Type/Industry	Location	Per	Low	Mid	High	Source	Date
Surveyor	Buffalo-Niagara Falls MSA, NY	Y	42840 FQ	55160 MW	63010 TQ	USBLS	5/07
	Nassau-Suffolk PMSA, NY	Y	55680 FQ	74690 MW	86370 TQ	USBLS	5/07
	New York-Northern New Jersey-Long Island MSA, NY-NJ-PA	Y	52930 FQ	67190 MW	79220 TQ	USBLS	5/07
	North Carolina	Y	42700 FQ	54770 MW	65550 TQ	USBLS	5/07
	Charlotte-Gastonia-Concord MSA, NC-SC	Y	35250 FQ	51980 MW	65170 TQ	USBLS	5/07
	Durham MSA, NC	Y	38080 FQ	46510 MW	59850 TQ	USBLS	5/07
	Raleigh-Cary MSA, NC	Y	46540 FQ	57840 MW	65520 TQ	USBLS	5/07
	North Dakota	Y	36280 FQ	45540 MW	60290 TQ	USBLS	5/07
	Ohio	Y	42670 FQ	55350 MW	67410 TQ	USBLS	5/07
	Cincinnati-Middletown MSA, OH-KY-IN	Y	43070 FQ	53530 MW	65670 TQ	USBLS	5/07
	Cleveland-Elyria-Mentor MSA, OH	Y	49500 FQ	59400 MW	68880 TQ	USBLS	5/07
	Columbus MSA, OH	Y	41720 FQ	51210 MW	64570 TQ	USBLS	5/07
	Dayton MSA, OH	Y	45730 FQ	55910 MW	72580 TQ	USBLS	5/07
	Oklahoma	Y	27220 FQ	35810 MW	49790 TQ	USBLS	5/07
	Oklahoma City MSA, OK	Y	26740 FQ	32750 MW	48790 TQ	USBLS	5/07
	Tulsa MSA, OK	Y	28130 FQ	39200 MW	50090 TQ	USBLS	5/07
	Oregon	H	24.13 FQ	30.42 MW	37.78 TQ	ORBLS	5/08
	Portland-Vancouver-Beaverton MSA, OR-WA	Y	57570 FQ	73060 MW	86120 TQ	USBLS	5/07
	Pennsylvania	Y	39240 FQ	48180 MW	57840 TQ	USBLS	5/07
	Allentown-Bethlehem-Easton MSA, PA-NJ	Y	46180 FQ	51860 MW	59980 TQ	USBLS	5/07
	Philadelphia-Camden-Wilmington MSA, PA-NJ-DE-MD	Y	43460 FQ	52060 MW	63470 TQ	USBLS	5/07
	Pittsburgh MSA, PA	Y	35770 FQ	41360 MW	52730 TQ	USBLS	5/07
	Rhode Island	Y	47010 FQ	53600 MW	63790 TQ	USBLS	5/07
	Providence-Fall River-Warwick MSA, RI-MA	Y	45860 FQ	53100 MW	64340 TQ	USBLS	5/07
	South Carolina	Y	30440 FQ	40310 MW	58070 TQ	USBLS	5/07
	Charleston-North Charleston MSA, SC	Y	39910 FQ	51580 MW	65120 TQ	USBLS	5/07
	Columbia MSA, SC	Y	29620 FQ	42480 MW	56420 TQ	USBLS	5/07
	South Dakota	Y	40104 FQ	51592 MW	62526 TQ	SDBLS	7/08-9/08
	Sioux Falls MSA, SD	Y	45221 FQ	60038 MW	65612 TQ	SDBLS	7/08-9/08
	Tennessee	Y	29400 FQ	40380 MW	60060 TQ	USBLS	5/07
	Johnson City MSA, TN	Y	29180 FQ	34220 MW	37520 TQ	USBLS	5/07
	Memphis MSA, TN-MS-AR	Y	32230 FQ	43040 MW	59250 TQ	USBLS	5/07
	Nashville-Davidson-Murfreesboro MSA, TN	Y	31590 FQ	52750 MW	76950 TQ	USBLS	5/07
	Texas	Y	38110 FQ	53850 MW	73410 TQ	USBLS	5/07
	Austin-Round Rock MSA, TX	Y	46800 FQ	59770 MW	83970 TQ	USBLS	5/07
	Corpus Christi MSA, TX	Y	38740 FQ	55150 MW	85790 TQ	USBLS	5/07
	Dallas-Fort Worth-Arlington MSA, TX	Y	39650 FQ	54620 MW	74540 TQ	USBLS	5/07
	El Paso MSA, TX	Y	46020 FQ	78010 MW	130630 TQ	USBLS	5/07
	Houston-Sugar Land-Baytown MSA, TX	Y	34640 FQ	57130 MW	74400 TQ	USBLS	5/07
	Midland MSA, TX	Y	30660 FQ	67010 MW	113110 TQ	USBLS	5/07
	San Antonio MSA, TX	Y	30830 FQ	49740 MW	77180 TQ	USBLS	5/07
	Utah	Y	35190 FQ	44610 MW	57820 TQ	USBLS	5/07
	Salt Lake City MSA, UT	Y	33060 FQ	43360 MW	57710 TQ	USBLS	5/07
	Vermont	Y	36940 FQ	44330 MW	54140 TQ	USBLS	5/07
	Burlington-South Burlington MSA, VT	Y	36250 FQ	41170 MW	46220 TQ	USBLS	5/07
	Virginia	Y	34250 FQ	45160 MW	59830 TQ	USBLS	5/07
	Charlottesville MSA, VA	Y	33440 FQ	39460 MW	47720 TQ	USBLS	5/07
	Richmond MSA, VA	Y	33770 FQ	45910 MW	66630 TQ	USBLS	5/07
	Virginia Beach-Norfolk-Newport News MSA, VA-NC	Y	44420 FQ	54300 MW	64180 TQ	USBLS	5/07
	Washington	H	26.72 FQ	32.02 MW	37.47 TQ	WABLS	3/08
	Seattle-Tacoma-Bellevue MSA, WA	Y	57220 FQ	68250 MW	78830 TQ	USBLS	5/07
	West Virginia	Y	25057 FQ	36671 MW	48105 TQ	WVBLS	7/08-9/08
	Charleston MSA, WV	Y	20370 FQ	35080 MW	46910 TQ	USBLS	5/07

AE	Average entry wage	**AW**	Average wage paid	**FQ**	First quartile wage	**LO** Lowest wage paid	**MTC** Median total compensation	**TCC** Total cash compensation
AER	Average entry range	**AWR**	Average wage range	**H**	Hourly	**LR** Low end range	**MW** Median wage paid	**TQ** Third quartile wage
AEX	Average experienced wage	**AXR**	Average experienced range	**HI**	Highest wage paid	**M** Monthly	**MWR** Median wage range	**W** Weekly
ATC	Average total compensation	**D**	Daily	**HR**	High end range	**MCC** Median cash compensation	**S** See annotated source	**Y** Yearly

Occupation/Type/Industry	Location	Per	Low	Mid	High	Source	Date
Surveyor	Huntington-Ashland MSA, WV-KY-OH	Y	37070 FQ	44920 MW	53170 TQ	USBLS	5/07
	Wisconsin	Y	38120 FQ	48090 MW	60270 TQ	USBLS	5/07
	Milwaukee-Waukesha-West Allis MSA, WI	Y	40550 FQ	48900 MW	60870 TQ	USBLS	5/07
	Wyoming	Y	34348 FQ	55046 MW	65778 TQ	WYBLS	9/08
	Cheyenne MSA, WY	Y	38198 FQ	64994 MW	75390 TQ	WYBLS	9/08
	Puerto Rico	Y	25870 FQ	31200 MW	39620 TQ	USBLS	5/07
	San Juan-Caguas-Guaynabo MSA, PR	Y	26810 FQ	31820 MW	40170 TQ	USBLS	5/07
Swim Team Coach	Montague, MA	H			10.50-11.50 HR	FRCOG	2009
Swine Herdsperson	United States	Y	25000 LO	31684 AW	40000 HI	AGRI	2008
Switchboard Operator	United States	Y	22000-28000 AER			IAAPHQ	2008
Including Answering Service	Alabama	Y	17300 FQ	20380 MW	24200 TQ	USBLS	5/07
Including Answering Service	Birmingham-Hoover MSA, AL	Y	17880 FQ	22000 MW	27160 TQ	USBLS	5/07
Including Answering Service	Huntsville MSA, AL	Y	17090 FQ	20010 MW	24000 TQ	USBLS	5/07
Including Answering Service	Alaska	Y	24390 FQ	28540 MW	32740 TQ	USBLS	5/07
Including Answering Service	Anchorage MSA, AK	Y	24050 FQ	27960 MW	31910 TQ	USBLS	5/07
Including Answering Service	Arizona	Y	20350 FQ	23100 MW	27020 TQ	USBLS	5/07
Including Answering Service	Phoenix-Mesa-Scottsdale MSA, AZ	Y	20810 FQ	23420 MW	27400 TQ	USBLS	5/07
Including Answering Service	Tucson MSA, AZ	Y	19000 FQ	22270 MW	26580 TQ	USBLS	5/07
Including Answering Service	Arkansas	Y	17570 FQ	20700 MW	25250 TQ	USBLS	5/07
Including Answering Service	Fort Smith MSA, AR-OK	Y	16620 FQ	18830 MW	22210 TQ	USBLS	5/07
Including Answering Service	Little Rock-North Little Rock MSA, AR	Y	19010 FQ	22800 MW	27770 TQ	USBLS	5/07
Including Answering Service	California	H	10.56 FQ	12.57 MW	15.16 TQ	CABLS	1/08-3/08
Including Answering Service	Fresno MSA, CA	H	9.59 FQ	11.49 MW	13.69 TQ	CABLS	1/08-3/08
Including Answering Service	Los Angeles-Long Beach-Glendale PMSA, CA	H	10.81 FQ	12.76 MW	15.02 TQ	CABLS	1/08-3/08
Including Answering Service	Oakland-Fremont-Hayward MSA, CA	H	13.21 FQ	16.17 MW	20.54 TQ	CABLS	1/08-3/08
Including Answering Service	Riverside-San Bernardino-Ontario MSA, CA	H	9.79 FQ	11.27 MW	13.18 TQ	CABLS	1/08-3/08
Including Answering Service	Sacramento-Arden Arcade-Roseville MSA, CA	H	10.11 FQ	12.27 MW	14.69 TQ	CABLS	1/08-3/08
Including Answering Service	San Diego-Carlsbad-San Marcos MSA, CA	H	10.12 FQ	11.73 MW	14.01 TQ	CABLS	1/08-3/08
Including Answering Service	San Francisco-San Mateo-Redwood PMSA, CA	H	13.88 FQ	16.52 MW	19.29 TQ	CABLS	1/08-3/08
Including Answering Service	San Jose-Sunnyvale-Santa Clara MSA, CA	H	10.34 FQ	13.48 MW	17.40 TQ	CABLS	1/08-3/08
Including Answering Service	Santa Ana-Anaheim-Irvine PMSA, CA	Y	22020 FQ	25380 MW	29760 TQ	USBLS	5/07
Including Answering Service	Colorado	Y	20810 FQ	23750 MW	27870 TQ	USBLS	5/07
Including Answering Service	Denver-Aurora MSA, CO	Y	21340 FQ	24440 MW	28810 TQ	USBLS	5/07
Including Answering Service	Connecticut	H	10.04 AE	13.39 MW		CTBLS	1/08-3/08
Including Answering Service	Bridgeport-Stamford-Norwalk MSA, CT	Y	21710 FQ	27290 MW	31450 TQ	USBLS	5/07
Including Answering Service	Hartford-West Hartford-East Hartford MSA, CT	Y	24380 FQ	29060 MW	33570 TQ	USBLS	5/07
Including Answering Service	Delaware	Y	20290 FQ	23930 MW	29250 TQ	USBLS	5/07
Including Answering Service	Wilmington PMSA, DE-MD-NJ	Y	21520 FQ	26400 MW	31190 TQ	USBLS	5/07
Including Answering Service	District of Columbia	Y	26240 FQ	30580 MW	36270 TQ	USBLS	5/07
Including Answering Service	Washington-Arlington-Alexandria MSA, DC-VA-MD-WV	Y	21800 FQ	26980 MW	32830 TQ	USBLS	5/07
Including Answering Service	Florida	Y	18020 FQ	21330 MW	24770 TQ	USBLS	5/07
Including Answering Service	Fort Lauderdale-Pompano Beach-Deerfield Beach PMSA, FL	Y	17930 FQ	21110 MW	24700 TQ	USBLS	5/07
Including Answering Service	Jacksonville MSA, FL	Y	19130 FQ	21480 MW	24260 TQ	USBLS	5/07
Including Answering Service	Lakeland MSA, FL	Y	18370 FQ	21630 MW	25300 TQ	USBLS	5/07
Including Answering Service	Miami-Fort Lauderdale-Miami Beach MSA, FL	Y	17630 FQ	21020 MW	24600 TQ	USBLS	5/07
Including Answering Service	Orlando-Kissimmee MSA, FL	Y	17840 FQ	20690 MW	25430 TQ	USBLS	5/07

AE	Average entry wage	AW	Average wage paid	FQ	First quartile wage	LO	Lowest wage paid	MTC	Median total compensation	TCC	Total cash compensation
AER	Average entry range	AWR	Average wage range	H	Hourly	LR	Low end range	MW	Median wage paid	TQ	Third quartile wage
AEX	Average experienced wage	AXR	Average experienced range	HI	Highest wage paid	M	Monthly	MWR	Median wage range	W	Weekly
ATC	Average total compensation	D	Daily	HR	High end range	MCC	Median cash compensation	S	See annotated source	Y	Yearly

1552

Switchboard Operator

Occupation/Type/Industry	Location	Per	Low	Mid	High	Source	Date
Switchboard Operator							
Including Answering Service	Tampa-St. Petersburg-Clearwater MSA, FL	Y	18920 FQ	22240 MW	25380 TQ	USBLS	5/07
Including Answering Service	West Palm Beach-Boca Raton-Boynton Beach PMSA, FL	Y	18870 FQ	22190 MW	26880 TQ	USBLS	5/07
Including Answering Service	Georgia	Y	18890 FQ	22820 MW	27730 TQ	USBLS	5/07
Including Answering Service	Atlanta-Sandy Springs-Marietta MSA, GA	Y	20730 FQ	24580 MW	29600 TQ	USBLS	5/07
Including Answering Service	Savannah MSA, GA	Y	17050 FQ	19340 MW	23350 TQ	USBLS	5/07
Including Answering Service	Hawaii	Y	24390 FQ	30210 MW	35640 TQ	USBLS	5/07
Including Answering Service	Honolulu MSA, HI	Y	21330 FQ	28460 MW	35600 TQ	USBLS	5/07
Including Answering Service	Idaho	Y	18230 FQ	22430 MW	27700 TQ	USBLS	5/07
Including Answering Service	Boise City-Nampa MSA, ID	Y	19380 FQ	23490 MW	29950 TQ	USBLS	5/07
Including Answering Service	Illinois	Y	20120 FQ	23730 MW	28870 TQ	USBLS	5/07
Including Answering Service	Chicago-Naperville-Joliet MSA, IL-IN-WI	Y	20820 FQ	24310 MW	29530 TQ	USBLS	5/07
Including Answering Service	Indiana	Y	19710 FQ	23030 MW	27380 TQ	USBLS	5/07
Including Answering Service	Evansville MSA, IN-KY	Y	17870 FQ	21000 MW	23660 TQ	USBLS	5/07
Including Answering Service	Gary PMSA, IN	Y	18730 FQ	21280 MW	23970 TQ	USBLS	5/07
Including Answering Service	Indianapolis-Carmel MSA, IN	Y	21570 FQ	25430 MW	29830 TQ	USBLS	5/07
Including Answering Service	Iowa	Y	19440 FQ	23110 MW	27010 TQ	USBLS	5/07
Including Answering Service	Davenport-Moline-Rock Island MSA, IA-IL	Y	18050 FQ	21450 MW	24520 TQ	USBLS	5/07
Including Answering Service	Des Moines-West Des Moines MSA, IA	Y	23300 FQ	27150 MW	30410 TQ	USBLS	5/07
Including Answering Service	Kansas	Y	19070 FQ	22380 MW	26950 TQ	USBLS	5/07
Including Answering Service	Wichita MSA, KS	Y	19920 FQ	23220 MW	27480 TQ	USBLS	5/07
Including Answering Service	Kentucky	Y	18682 FQ	21890 MW	26029 TQ	KYBLS	2008
Including Answering Service	Louisville-Jefferson County MSA, KY-IN	Y	20320 FQ	23600 MW	27670 TQ	USBLS	5/07
Including Answering Service	Louisiana	H	7.97 FQ	9.32 MW	11.14 TQ	LABLS	1/08-3/08
Including Answering Service	Baton Rouge MSA, LA	Y	18590 FQ	21850 MW	25260 TQ	USBLS	5/07
Including Answering Service	Houma-Bayou Cane-Thibodaux MSA, LA	Y	16240 FQ	18660 MW	22310 TQ	USBLS	5/07
Including Answering Service	New Orleans-Metairie-Kenner MSA, LA	Y	17540 FQ	20850 MW	24380 TQ	USBLS	5/07
Including Answering Service	Maine	Y	20270 FQ	22920 MW	26520 TQ	USBLS	5/07
Including Answering Service	Bangor MSA, ME	Y	18120 FQ	20710 MW	24210 TQ	USBLS	5/07
Including Answering Service	Portland-South Portland-Biddeford MSA, ME	Y	21080 FQ	23980 MW	27980 TQ	USBLS	5/07
Including Answering Service	Maryland	Y		24775 MW		MDBLS	3/08
Including Answering Service	Baltimore-Towson MSA, MD	Y	20290 FQ	23970 MW	28940 TQ	USBLS	5/07
Including Answering Service	Bethesda-Gaithersburg-Frederick PMSA, MD	Y	21510 FQ	26570 MW	31690 TQ	USBLS	5/07
Including Answering Service	Massachusetts	Y	22230 FQ	26150 MW	31030 TQ	USBLS	5/07
Including Answering Service	Boston-Cambridge-Quincy NECTA, MA	Y	23180 FQ	27300 MW	32160 TQ	USBLS	5/07
Including Answering Service	Worcester MSA, MA-CT	Y	20120 FQ	23370 MW	28740 TQ	USBLS	5/07
Including Answering Service	Michigan	Y	21020 FQ	25160 MW	29770 TQ	USBLS	5/07
Including Answering Service	Detroit-Warren-Livonia MSA, MI	Y	21720 FQ	26270 MW	30770 TQ	USBLS	5/07
Including Answering Service	Flint MSA, MI	Y	20460 FQ	23400 MW	28480 TQ	USBLS	5/07
Including Answering Service	Grand Rapids-Wyoming MSA, MI	Y	20260 FQ	24750 MW	28540 TQ	USBLS	5/07
Including Answering Service	Warren-Troy-Farmington Hills PMSA, MI	Y	22080 FQ	26470 MW	31230 TQ	USBLS	5/07
Including Answering Service	Minnesota	Y	23001 FQ	26352 MW	31421 TQ	MNBLS	10/08-12/08
Including Answering Service	Duluth-Superior MSA, MN-WI	Y	23511 FQ	27258 MW	30713 TQ	MNBLS	10/08-12/08
Including Answering Service	Minneapolis-Saint Paul MSA, MN-WI	Y	23376 FQ	26862 MW	32576 TQ	MNBLS	10/08-12/08
Including Answering Service	Rochester MSA, MN	Y	26955 FQ	30881 MW	34799 TQ	MNBLS	10/08-12/08
Including Answering Service	Mississippi	Y	17000 FQ	19880 MW	23390 TQ	USBLS	5/07
Including Answering Service	Jackson MSA, MS	Y	17500 FQ	20730 MW	23810 TQ	USBLS	5/07
Including Answering Service	Missouri	Y	19380 FQ	22450 MW	26430 TQ	USBLS	5/07
Including Answering Service	Kansas City MSA, MO-KS	Y	20130 FQ	23660 MW	28220 TQ	USBLS	5/07
Including Answering Service	St. Louis MSA, MO-IL	Y	20210 FQ	23120 MW	27290 TQ	USBLS	5/07
Including Answering Service	Montana	Y	18510 FQ	22020 MW	26270 TQ	USBLS	5/07
Including Answering Service	Billings MSA, MT	Y	19080 FQ	22700 MW	26200 TQ	USBLS	5/07
Including Answering Service	Nebraska	Y	19310 FQ	22670 MW	26500 TQ	USBLS	5/07
Including Answering Service	Lincoln MSA, NE	Y	20750 FQ	22850 MW	25060 TQ	USBLS	5/07
Including Answering Service	Omaha-Council Bluffs MSA, NE-IA	Y	19880 FQ	23660 MW	29380 TQ	USBLS	5/07

AE	Average entry wage	AW	Average wage paid	FQ	First quartile wage
AER	Average entry range	AWR	Average wage range	H	Hourly
AEX	Average experienced wage	AXR	Average experienced range	HI	Highest wage paid
ATC	Average total compensation	D	Daily	HR	High end range

LO	Lowest wage paid	MTC	Median total compensation	TCC	Total cash compensation
LR	Low end range	MW	Median wage paid	TQ	Third quartile wage
M	Monthly	MWR	Median wage range	W	Weekly
MCC	Median cash compensation	S	See annotated source	Y	Yearly

Switchboard Operator

Occupation/Type/Industry	Location	Per	Low	Mid	High	Source	Date
Including Answering Service	Nevada	H	10.85 FQ	13.36 MW	15.20 TQ	NVBLS	5/08
Including Answering Service	Las Vegas-Paradise MSA, NV	H	11.57 FQ	13.70 MW	15.42 TQ	NVBLS	5/08
Including Answering Service	New Hampshire	H	10.13 AE	12.66 MW	13.94 AEX	NHBLS	6/08
Including Answering Service	Manchester MSA, NH	Y	24400 FQ	27690 MW	31300 TQ	USBLS	5/07
Including Answering Service	Nashua NECTA, NH-MA	Y	24710 FQ	27030 MW	29310 TQ	USBLS	5/07
Including Answering Service	New Jersey	Y	21290 FQ	25260 MW	30110 TQ	USBLS	5/07
Including Answering Service	Camden PMSA, NJ	Y	18600 FQ	23120 MW	28650 TQ	USBLS	5/07
Including Answering Service	Edison PMSA, NJ	Y	20640 FQ	24450 MW	29010 TQ	USBLS	5/07
Including Answering Service	Newark-Union PMSA, NJ-PA	Y	22220 FQ	25450 MW	31460 TQ	USBLS	5/07
Including Answering Service	New Mexico	Y	17140 FQ	20630 MW	26810 TQ	USBLS	5/07
Including Answering Service	Albuquerque MSA, NM	Y	17320 FQ	21770 MW	28620 TQ	USBLS	5/07
Including Answering Service	New York	Y	20710 FQ	26490 MW	33890 TQ	USBLS	5/07
Including Answering Service	Albany-Schenectady-Troy MSA, NY	Y	21340 FQ	23980 MW	28410 TQ	USBLS	5/07
Including Answering Service	Binghamton MSA, NY	Y	24160 FQ	27470 MW	31270 TQ	USBLS	5/07
Including Answering Service	Buffalo-Niagara Falls MSA, NY	Y	16120 FQ	18820 MW	24580 TQ	USBLS	5/07
Including Answering Service	Glens Falls MSA, NY	Y	20200 FQ	23000 MW	27960 TQ	USBLS	5/07
Including Answering Service	Kingston MSA, NY	Y	19520 FQ	22840 MW	26680 TQ	USBLS	5/07
Including Answering Service	Nassau-Suffolk PMSA, NY	Y	22760 FQ	28020 MW	34200 TQ	USBLS	5/07
Including Answering Service	New York-Northern New Jersey-Long Island MSA, NY-NJ-PA	Y	23010 FQ	28580 MW	35810 TQ	USBLS	5/07
Including Answering Service	North Carolina	Y	19320 FQ	22570 MW	26500 TQ	USBLS	5/07
Including Answering Service	Charlotte-Gastonia-Concord MSA, NC-SC	Y	19380 FQ	22950 MW	27780 TQ	USBLS	5/07
Including Answering Service	Greensboro-High Point MSA, NC	Y	19450 FQ	22730 MW	26960 TQ	USBLS	5/07
Including Answering Service	Raleigh-Cary MSA, NC	Y	21690 FQ	24340 MW	28480 TQ	USBLS	5/07
Including Answering Service	North Dakota	Y	19660 FQ	22740 MW	26280 TQ	USBLS	5/07
Including Answering Service	Fargo MSA, ND-MN	Y	20720 FQ	23270 MW	26520 TQ	USBLS	5/07
Including Answering Service	Ohio	Y	19170 FQ	22920 MW	27730 TQ	USBLS	5/07
Including Answering Service	Canton-Massillon MSA, OH	Y	19160 FQ	22450 MW	26170 TQ	USBLS	5/07
Including Answering Service	Cincinnati-Middletown MSA, OH-KY-IN	Y	20320 FQ	24400 MW	30510 TQ	USBLS	5/07
Including Answering Service	Cleveland-Elyria-Mentor MSA, OH	Y	19540 FQ	24040 MW	28320 TQ	USBLS	5/07
Including Answering Service	Columbus MSA, OH	Y	20540 FQ	23590 MW	28610 TQ	USBLS	5/07
Including Answering Service	Dayton MSA, OH	Y	19710 FQ	22170 MW	26000 TQ	USBLS	5/07
Including Answering Service	Oklahoma	Y	17050 FQ	19880 MW	23310 TQ	USBLS	5/07
Including Answering Service	Oklahoma City MSA, OK	Y	18470 FQ	21470 MW	24310 TQ	USBLS	5/07
Including Answering Service	Tulsa MSA, OK	Y	18040 FQ	20600 MW	23560 TQ	USBLS	5/07
Including Answering Service	Oregon	H	10.35 FQ	12.38 MW	14.79 TQ	ORBLS	5/08
Including Answering Service	Medford MSA, OR	Y	20570 FQ	24520 MW	28560 TQ	USBLS	5/07
Including Answering Service	Portland-Vancouver-Beaverton MSA, OR-WA	Y	21770 FQ	25300 MW	29600 TQ	USBLS	5/07
Including Answering Service	Salem MSA, OR	Y	23280 FQ	27020 MW	31300 TQ	USBLS	5/07
Including Answering Service	Pennsylvania	Y	19820 FQ	23840 MW	28870 TQ	USBLS	5/07
Including Answering Service	Allentown-Bethlehem-Easton MSA, PA-NJ	Y	20780 FQ	25660 MW	29400 TQ	USBLS	5/07
Including Answering Service	Philadelphia-Camden-Wilmington MSA, PA-NJ-DE-MD	Y	21130 FQ	25460 MW	30770 TQ	USBLS	5/07
Including Answering Service	Pittsburgh MSA, PA	Y	19660 FQ	23700 MW	28740 TQ	USBLS	5/07
Including Answering Service	Rhode Island	Y	21660 FQ	25070 MW	29490 TQ	USBLS	5/07
Including Answering Service	Providence-Fall River-Warwick MSA, RI-MA	Y	21150 FQ	24540 MW	28870 TQ	USBLS	5/07
Including Answering Service	South Carolina	Y	19060 FQ	22420 MW	26260 TQ	USBLS	5/07
Including Answering Service	Charleston-North Charleston MSA, SC	Y	19330 FQ	21860 MW	24550 TQ	USBLS	5/07
Including Answering Service	Columbia MSA, SC	Y	18860 FQ	22540 MW	25770 TQ	USBLS	5/07
Including Answering Service	South Dakota	Y	22313 FQ	26336 MW	30653 TQ	SDBLS	7/08-9/08
Including Answering Service	Tennessee	Y	17960 FQ	21530 MW	25360 TQ	USBLS	5/07
Including Answering Service	Memphis MSA, TN-MS-AR	Y	20080 FQ	23790 MW	28590 TQ	USBLS	5/07
Including Answering Service	Nashville-Davidson-Murfreesboro MSA, TN	Y	17560 FQ	21780 MW	26160 TQ	USBLS	5/07
Including Answering Service	Texas	Y	17010 FQ	21460 MW	26110 TQ	USBLS	5/07
Including Answering Service	Austin-Round Rock MSA, TX	Y	20940 FQ	23800 MW	27430 TQ	USBLS	5/07
Including Answering Service	Brownsville-Harlingen MSA, TX	Y	14540 FQ	16850 MW	19350 TQ	USBLS	5/07

AE	Average entry wage	AW	Average wage paid	FQ	First quartile wage
AER	Average entry range	AWR	Average wage range	H	Hourly
AEX	Average experienced wage	AXR	Average experienced range	HI	Highest wage paid
ATC	Average total compensation	D	Daily	HR	High end range

LO	Lowest wage paid	MTC	Median total compensation	TCC	Total cash compensation
LR	Low end range	MW	Median wage paid	TQ	Third quartile wage
HI		M	Monthly	W	Weekly
MCC	Median cash compensation	S	See annotated source	Y	Yearly

Occupation/Type/Industry	Location	Per	Low	Mid	High	Source	Date
Switchboard Operator							
Including Answering Service	Dallas-Fort Worth-Arlington MSA, TX	Y	18790 FQ	23530 MW	28730 TQ	USBLS	5/07
Including Answering Service	El Paso MSA, TX	Y	13880 FQ	16450 MW	19280 TQ	USBLS	5/07
Including Answering Service	Houston-Sugar Land-Baytown MSA, TX	Y	20190 FQ	23660 MW	29230 TQ	USBLS	5/07
Including Answering Service	San Antonio MSA, TX	Y	18280 FQ	21320 MW	24580 TQ	USBLS	5/07
Including Answering Service	Utah	Y	18810 FQ	22560 MW	27300 TQ	USBLS	5/07
Including Answering Service	Salt Lake City MSA, UT	Y	20460 FQ	23900 MW	28260 TQ	USBLS	5/07
Including Answering Service	Vermont	Y	19590 FQ	22880 MW	26620 TQ	USBLS	5/07
Including Answering Service	Burlington-South Burlington MSA, VT	Y	21850 FQ	24440 MW	27900 TQ	USBLS	5/07
Including Answering Service	Virginia	Y	19610 FQ	22550 MW	26900 TQ	USBLS	5/07
Including Answering Service	Charlottesville MSA, VA	Y	18070 FQ	20330 MW	25340 TQ	USBLS	5/07
Including Answering Service	Richmond MSA, VA	Y	20240 FQ	23410 MW	28520 TQ	USBLS	5/07
Including Answering Service	Roanoke MSA, VA	Y	20310 FQ	22940 MW	26710 TQ	USBLS	5/07
Including Answering Service	Virginia Beach-Norfolk-Newport News MSA, VA-NC	Y	19330 FQ	21770 MW	24190 TQ	USBLS	5/07
Including Answering Service	Washington	H	11.18 FQ	13.11 MW	14.93 TQ	WABLS	3/08
Including Answering Service	Seattle-Tacoma-Bellevue MSA, WA	Y	24000 FQ	27790 MW	31670 TQ	USBLS	5/07
Including Answering Service	West Virginia	Y	16593 FQ	19359 MW	23719 TQ	WVBLS	7/08-9/08
Including Answering Service	Charleston MSA, WV	Y	15290 FQ	18040 MW	21830 TQ	USBLS	5/07
Including Answering Service	Wisconsin	Y	21280 FQ	24610 MW	28960 TQ	USBLS	5/07
Including Answering Service	Milwaukee-Waukesha-West Allis MSA, WI	Y	21940 FQ	26060 MW	30400 TQ	USBLS	5/07
Including Answering Service	Wyoming	Y	20156 FQ	23038 MW	25638 TQ	WYBLS	9/08
Including Answering Service	Cheyenne MSA, WY	Y	20196 FQ	23145 MW	25435 TQ	WYBLS	9/08
Including Answering Service	Puerto Rico	Y	13430 FQ	15800 MW	19590 TQ	USBLS	5/07
Including Answering Service	San Juan-Caguas-Guaynabo MSA, PR	Y	13580 FQ	16140 MW	19890 TQ	USBLS	5/07
Including Answering Service	Virgin Islands	Y	17370 FQ	19000 MW	23030 TQ	USBLS	5/07
Including Answering Service	Guam	Y	13830 FQ	16590 MW	22580 TQ	USBLS	5/07
System Developer	United States	Y		87211 AW		WSJO01	2008
Systems Administrator							
Municipal Government	Gresham, OR	Y	64512 LO		82368 HI	GOSS	1/1/09
Systems Analyst							
State Government	Rhode Island	Y	39838 LO		44440 HI	AFT02	3/1/08
Tailor, Dressmaker, and Custom Sewer	Alabama	Y	17110 FQ	20110 MW	26450 TQ	USBLS	5/07
	Birmingham-Hoover MSA, AL	Y	17930 FQ	20570 MW	23150 TQ	USBLS	5/07
	Arizona	Y	22290 FQ	26310 MW	35580 TQ	USBLS	5/07
	Phoenix-Mesa-Scottsdale MSA, AZ	Y	22650 FQ	29410 MW	36160 TQ	USBLS	5/07
	Tucson MSA, AZ	Y	20980 FQ	23560 MW	32470 TQ	USBLS	5/07
	Arkansas	Y	16760 FQ	19950 MW	23700 TQ	USBLS	5/07
	California	H	9.50 FQ	12.10 MW	16.11 TQ	CABLS	1/08-3/08
	Los Angeles-Long Beach-Glendale PMSA, CA	H	9.41 FQ	12.26 MW	15.66 TQ	CABLS	1/08-3/08
	Oakland-Fremont-Hayward MSA, CA	H	10.65 FQ	12.17 MW	14.66 TQ	CABLS	1/08-3/08
	Riverside-San Bernardino-Ontario MSA, CA	H	9.74 FQ	11.14 MW	12.60 TQ	CABLS	1/08-3/08
	Sacramento-Arden Arcade-Roseville MSA, CA	H	11.02 FQ	13.58 MW	17.09 TQ	CABLS	1/08-3/08
	San Diego-Carlsbad-San Marcos MSA, CA	H	8.60 FQ	9.33 MW	10.73 TQ	CABLS	1/08-3/08
	San Francisco-San Mateo-Redwood PMSA, CA	H	14.58 FQ	17.02 MW	20.70 TQ	CABLS	1/08-3/08
	San Jose-Sunnyvale-Santa Clara MSA, CA	H	10.21 FQ	14.45 MW	18.06 TQ	CABLS	1/08-3/08
	Santa Ana-Anaheim-Irvine PMSA, CA	Y	19230 FQ	23060 MW	33620 TQ	USBLS	5/07
	Colorado	Y	20910 FQ	25200 MW	31560 TQ	USBLS	5/07
	Colorado Springs MSA, CO	Y	22790 FQ	26540 MW	30080 TQ	USBLS	5/07
	Denver-Aurora MSA, CO	Y	20480 FQ	23310 MW	33540 TQ	USBLS	5/07
	Connecticut	H	10.36 AE	13.05 MW		CTBLS	1/08-3/08

AE	Average entry wage	AW	Average wage paid	FQ	First quartile wage	LO	Lowest wage paid	MTC	Median total compensation	TCC	Total cash compensation
AER	Average entry range	AWR	Average wage range	H	Hourly	LR	Low end range	MW	Median wage paid	TQ	Third quartile wage
AEX	Average experienced wage	AXR	Average experienced range	HI	Highest wage paid	M	Monthly	MWR	Median wage range	W	Weekly
ATC	Average total compensation	D	Daily	HR	High end range	MCC	Median cash compensation	S	See annotated source	Y	Yearly

Occupation/Type/Industry	Location	Per	Low	Mid	High	Source	Date
Tailor, Dressmaker, and Custom Sewer	Bridgeport-Stamford-Norwalk MSA, CT	Y	25310 FQ	27680 MW	30560 TQ	USBLS	5/07
	Hartford-West Hartford-East Hartford MSA, CT	Y	22730 FQ	25050 MW	28770 TQ	USBLS	5/07
	Delaware	Y	27170 FQ	29340 MW	31550 TQ	USBLS	5/07
	Wilmington PMSA, DE-MD-NJ	Y	26700 FQ	28810 MW	30910 TQ	USBLS	5/07
	District of Columbia	Y	37580 FQ	41450 MW	45450 TQ	USBLS	5/07
	Washington-Arlington-Alexandria MSA, DC-VA-MD-WV	Y	21570 FQ	28980 MW	36160 TQ	USBLS	5/07
	Florida	Y	16660 FQ	22410 MW	29450 TQ	USBLS	5/07
	Fort Lauderdale-Pompano Beach-Deerfield Beach PMSA, FL	Y	18550 FQ	22530 MW	25740 TQ	USBLS	5/07
	Jacksonville MSA, FL	Y	27840 FQ	37560 MW	45920 TQ	USBLS	5/07
	Miami-Fort Lauderdale-Miami Beach MSA, FL	Y	15270 FQ	19880 MW	25250 TQ	USBLS	5/07
	Orlando-Kissimmee MSA, FL	Y	19590 FQ	24840 MW	31290 TQ	USBLS	5/07
	Tampa-St. Petersburg-Clearwater MSA, FL	Y	18280 FQ	23040 MW	32100 TQ	USBLS	5/07
	West Palm Beach-Boca Raton-Boynton Beach PMSA, FL	Y	14800 FQ	15870 MW	26770 TQ	USBLS	5/07
	Georgia	Y	16400 FQ	19970 MW	23190 TQ	USBLS	5/07
	Atlanta-Sandy Springs-Marietta MSA, GA	Y	20150 FQ	22400 MW	27880 TQ	USBLS	5/07
	Hawaii	Y	18800 FQ	23920 MW	33290 TQ	USBLS	5/07
	Honolulu MSA, HI	Y	17440 FQ	21210 MW	25360 TQ	USBLS	5/07
	Idaho	Y	15100 FQ	17120 MW	20210 TQ	USBLS	5/07
	Boise City-Nampa MSA, ID	Y	15730 FQ	17180 MW	18690 TQ	USBLS	5/07
	Illinois	Y	20930 FQ	24740 MW	31320 TQ	USBLS	5/07
	Chicago-Naperville-Joliet MSA, IL-IN-WI	Y	23370 FQ	28170 MW	34170 TQ	USBLS	5/07
	Indiana	Y	17630 FQ	22620 MW	30250 TQ	USBLS	5/07
	Indianapolis-Carmel MSA, IN	Y	22270 FQ	28860 MW	41580 TQ	USBLS	5/07
	Terre Haute MSA, IN	Y	12720 FQ	14330 MW	15910 TQ	USBLS	5/07
	Iowa	Y	18100 FQ	21770 MW	25070 TQ	USBLS	5/07
	Des Moines-West Des Moines MSA, IA	Y	17880 FQ	21870 MW	25970 TQ	USBLS	5/07
	Kansas	Y	15920 FQ	18690 MW	22930 TQ	USBLS	5/07
	Wichita MSA, KS	Y	13760 FQ	16490 MW	21640 TQ	USBLS	5/07
	Kentucky	Y	22079 FQ	27907 MW	34372 TQ	KYBLS	2008
	Louisville-Jefferson County MSA, KY-IN	Y	18280 FQ	22770 MW	29050 TQ	USBLS	5/07
	Louisiana	H	8.20 FQ	9.86 MW	12.02 TQ	LABLS	1/08-3/08
	Baton Rouge MSA, LA	Y	13790 FQ	16540 MW	19150 TQ	USBLS	5/07
	New Orleans-Metairie-Kenner MSA, LA	Y	20550 FQ	22730 MW	29490 TQ	USBLS	5/07
	Maine	Y	19630 FQ	23490 MW	29760 TQ	USBLS	5/07
	Portland-South Portland-Biddeford MSA, ME	Y	21890 FQ	26110 MW	30630 TQ	USBLS	5/07
	Maryland	Y		25000 MW		MDBLS	3/08
	Baltimore-Towson MSA, MD	Y	21730 FQ	25920 MW	30540 TQ	USBLS	5/07
	Bethesda-Gaithersburg-Frederick PMSA, MD	Y	16620 FQ	18450 MW	30230 TQ	USBLS	5/07
	Massachusetts	Y	18920 FQ	23010 MW	28810 TQ	USBLS	5/07
	Boston-Cambridge-Quincy NECTA, MA	Y	18390 FQ	20850 MW	28220 TQ	USBLS	5/07
	Worcester MSA, MA-CT	Y	20500 FQ	25580 MW	31350 TQ	USBLS	5/07
	Michigan	Y	21440 FQ	26020 MW	30350 TQ	USBLS	5/07
	Ann Arbor MSA, MI	Y	23560 FQ	25920 MW	29040 TQ	USBLS	5/07
	Detroit-Warren-Livonia MSA, MI	Y	22710 FQ	26700 MW	30080 TQ	USBLS	5/07
	Grand Rapids-Wyoming MSA, MI	Y	22170 FQ	24810 MW	28750 TQ	USBLS	5/07
	Muskegon-Norton Shores MSA, MI	Y	36390 FQ	40350 MW	74360 TQ	USBLS	5/07
	Warren-Troy-Farmington Hills PMSA, MI	Y	24700 FQ	27680 MW	31070 TQ	USBLS	5/07
	Minnesota	Y	21542 FQ	31815 MW	40565 TQ	MNBLS	10/08-12/08

AE   Average entry wage   AW   Average wage paid   FQ   First quartile wage   LO   Lowest wage paid   MTC   Median total compensation   TCC   Total cash compensation
AER   Average entry range   AWR   Average wage range   H   Hourly   LR   Low end range   MW   Median wage paid   TQ   Third quartile wage
AEX   Average experienced wage   AXR   Average experienced range   HI   Highest wage paid   M   Monthly   MWR   Median wage range   W   Weekly
ATC   Average total compensation   D   Daily   HR   High end range   MCC   Median cash compensation   S   See annotated source   Y   Yearly

1556

Occupation/Type/Industry	Location	Per	Low	Mid	High	Source	Date
Tailor, Dressmaker, and Custom Sewer							
	Minneapolis-Saint Paul MSA, MN-WI	Y	29006 FQ	36864 MW	42078 TQ	MNBLS	10/08-12/08
	Rochester MSA, MN	Y	16642 FQ	18021 MW	23265 TQ	MNBLS	10/08-12/08
	Mississippi	Y	17460 FQ	20570 MW	23940 TQ	USBLS	5/07
	Jackson MSA, MS	Y	21150 FQ	23620 MW	26400 TQ	USBLS	5/07
	Missouri	Y	18290 FQ	22030 MW	27020 TQ	USBLS	5/07
	Kansas City MSA, MO-KS	Y	18670 FQ	23020 MW	32230 TQ	USBLS	5/07
	St. Louis MSA, MO-IL	Y	20450 FQ	22760 MW	26080 TQ	USBLS	5/07
	Montana	Y	19480 FQ	21790 MW	24350 TQ	USBLS	5/07
	Nebraska	Y	15830 FQ	19730 MW	24680 TQ	USBLS	5/07
	Omaha-Council Bluffs MSA, NE-IA	Y	18770 FQ	22210 MW	25780 TQ	USBLS	5/07
	Nevada	H	10.08 FQ	11.77 MW	14.28 TQ	NVBLS	5/08
	Las Vegas-Paradise MSA, NV	H	10.05 FQ	11.84 MW	14.75 TQ	NVBLS	5/08
	New Hampshire	H	10.88 AE	12.28 MW	13.28 AEX	NHBLS	6/08
	Manchester MSA, NH	Y	23280 FQ	26530 MW	29680 TQ	USBLS	5/07
	New Jersey	Y	17290 FQ	20650 MW	28880 TQ	USBLS	5/07
	Camden PMSA, NJ	Y	15880 FQ	19720 MW	25780 TQ	USBLS	5/07
	Edison PMSA, NJ	Y	18820 FQ	23330 MW	30400 TQ	USBLS	5/07
	Newark-Union PMSA, NJ-PA	Y	19470 FQ	27140 MW	34070 TQ	USBLS	5/07
	New Mexico	Y	16730 FQ	19330 MW	22790 TQ	USBLS	5/07
	New York	Y	23540 FQ	31480 MW	41960 TQ	USBLS	5/07
	Albany-Schenectady-Troy MSA, NY	Y	20960 FQ	22580 MW	24220 TQ	USBLS	5/07
	Nassau-Suffolk PMSA, NY	Y	23020 FQ	33830 MW	38930 TQ	USBLS	5/07
	New York-Northern New Jersey-Long Island MSA, NY-NJ-PA	Y	19870 FQ	28390 MW	37630 TQ	USBLS	5/07
	Syracuse MSA, NY	Y	17540 FQ	21660 MW	26760 TQ	USBLS	5/07
	North Carolina	Y	18100 FQ	22020 MW	26890 TQ	USBLS	5/07
	Charlotte-Gastonia-Concord MSA, NC-SC	Y	22300 FQ	25530 MW	28470 TQ	USBLS	5/07
	Greensboro-High Point MSA, NC	Y	17530 FQ	19540 MW	24160 TQ	USBLS	5/07
	Raleigh-Cary MSA, NC	Y	19990 FQ	23080 MW	27420 TQ	USBLS	5/07
	North Dakota	Y	17850 FQ	20620 MW	23740 TQ	USBLS	5/07
	Ohio	Y	20580 FQ	23300 MW	28660 TQ	USBLS	5/07
	Canton-Massillon MSA, OH	Y	18610 FQ	23810 MW	32170 TQ	USBLS	5/07
	Cincinnati-Middletown MSA, OH-KY-IN	Y	21620 FQ	23990 MW	28230 TQ	USBLS	5/07
	Cleveland-Elyria-Mentor MSA, OH	Y	20510 FQ	23360 MW	30410 TQ	USBLS	5/07
	Columbus MSA, OH	Y	20650 FQ	23400 MW	32770 TQ	USBLS	5/07
	Dayton MSA, OH	Y	21770 FQ	23630 MW	25770 TQ	USBLS	5/07
	Oklahoma	Y	17770 FQ	23900 MW	28700 TQ	USBLS	5/07
	Oklahoma City MSA, OK	Y	17170 FQ	23010 MW	26510 TQ	USBLS	5/07
	Tulsa MSA, OK	Y	22820 FQ	30790 MW	36740 TQ	USBLS	5/07
	Oregon	H	11.67 FQ	13.18 MW	14.62 TQ	ORBLS	5/08
	Portland-Vancouver-Beaverton MSA, OR-WA	Y	24540 FQ	27470 MW	30750 TQ	USBLS	5/07
	Pennsylvania	Y	21930 FQ	29120 MW	38940 TQ	USBLS	5/07
	Allentown-Bethlehem-Easton MSA, PA-NJ	Y	24610 FQ	29810 MW	43550 TQ	USBLS	5/07
	Philadelphia-Camden-Wilmington MSA, PA-NJ-DE-MD	Y	25440 FQ	31340 MW	39270 TQ	USBLS	5/07
	Pittsburgh MSA, PA	Y	19430 FQ	25580 MW	38560 TQ	USBLS	5/07
	Rhode Island	Y	23450 FQ	28180 MW	32460 TQ	USBLS	5/07
	Providence-Fall River-Warwick MSA, RI-MA	Y	23210 FQ	28000 MW	32360 TQ	USBLS	5/07
	South Carolina	Y	16620 FQ	21440 MW	28270 TQ	USBLS	5/07
	Charleston-North Charleston MSA, SC	Y	22910 FQ	27430 MW	29790 TQ	USBLS	5/07
	Columbia MSA, SC	Y	15900 FQ	22310 MW	29890 TQ	USBLS	5/07
	South Dakota	Y	18261 FQ	19997 MW	24043 TQ	SDBLS	7/08-9/08
	Tennessee	Y	16900 FQ	20700 MW	24100 TQ	USBLS	5/07
	Memphis MSA, TN-MS-AR	Y	17000 FQ	20310 MW	24240 TQ	USBLS	5/07
	Texas	Y	18800 FQ	23190 MW	28950 TQ	USBLS	5/07
	Austin-Round Rock MSA, TX	Y	14350 FQ	17390 MW	20150 TQ	USBLS	5/07
	Dallas-Fort Worth-Arlington MSA, TX	Y	20010 FQ	23780 MW	30970 TQ	USBLS	5/07

AE	Average entry wage	**AW**	Average wage paid	
AER	Average entry range	**AWR**	Average wage range	
AEX	Average experienced wage	**AXR**	Average experienced range	
ATC	Average total compensation	**D**	Daily	
FQ	First quartile wage	**LO**	Lowest wage paid	**MTC** Median total compensation **TCC** Total cash compensation
H	Hourly	**LR**	Low end range	**MW** Median wage paid **TQ** Third quartile wage
HI	Highest wage paid	**M**	Monthly	**MWR** Median wage range **W** Weekly
HR	High end range	**MCC**	Median cash compensation	**S** See annotated source **Y** Yearly

Occupation/Type/Industry	Location	Per	Low	Mid	High	Source	Date
Tailor, Dressmaker, and Custom Sewer	El Paso MSA, TX	Y	16560 FQ	18160 MW	20670 TQ	USBLS	5/07
	Houston-Sugar Land-Baytown MSA, TX	Y	20330 FQ	25120 MW	30150 TQ	USBLS	5/07
	San Antonio MSA, TX	Y	20260 FQ	22830 MW	26490 TQ	USBLS	5/07
	Utah	Y	17270 FQ	19180 MW	22790 TQ	USBLS	5/07
	Salt Lake City MSA, UT	Y	17470 FQ	19430 MW	23440 TQ	USBLS	5/07
	Virginia	Y	20410 FQ	25320 MW	30800 TQ	USBLS	5/07
	Richmond MSA, VA	Y	13970 FQ	18240 MW	26200 TQ	USBLS	5/07
	Virginia Beach-Norfolk-Newport News MSA, VA-NC	Y	21810 FQ	26090 MW	29030 TQ	USBLS	5/07
	Washington	H	12.28 FQ	14.59 MW	17.02 TQ	WABLS	3/08
	Seattle-Tacoma-Bellevue MSA, WA	Y	26150 FQ	31180 MW	36440 TQ	USBLS	5/07
	West Virginia	Y	17236 FQ	21033 MW	25888 TQ	WVBLS	7/08-9/08
	Huntington-Ashland MSA, WV-KY-OH	Y	20310 FQ	30790 MW	37720 TQ	USBLS	5/07
	Wisconsin	Y	21170 FQ	25910 MW	29380 TQ	USBLS	5/07
	Milwaukee-Waukesha-West Allis MSA, WI	Y	18240 FQ	25930 MW	30080 TQ	USBLS	5/07
	Wyoming	Y	21114 FQ	23847 MW	28299 TQ	WYBLS	9/08
	Puerto Rico	Y	13090 FQ	15180 MW	24080 TQ	USBLS	5/07
	San Juan-Caguas-Guaynabo MSA, PR	Y	14420 FQ	18070 MW	27160 TQ	USBLS	5/07
Talent Agent	United States	Y		39823 AW		NDAY01	2009
Tank Car, Truck, and Ship Loader	Alabama	Y	17300 FQ	23930 MW	34360 TQ	USBLS	5/07
	Arizona	Y	25210 FQ	33500 MW	44560 TQ	USBLS	5/07
	Phoenix-Mesa-Scottsdale MSA, AZ	Y	34170 FQ	43010 MW	47520 TQ	USBLS	5/07
	Arkansas	Y	20430 FQ	24930 MW	31650 TQ	USBLS	5/07
	California	H	13.74 FQ	17.60 MW	23.53 TQ	CABLS	1/08-3/08
	Los Angeles-Long Beach-Glendale PMSA, CA	H	14.23 FQ	20.41 MW	31.90 TQ	CABLS	1/08-3/08
	Oakland-Fremont-Hayward MSA, CA	H	15.67 FQ	17.73 MW	22.01 TQ	CABLS	1/08-3/08
	Riverside-San Bernardino-Ontario MSA, CA	H	13.50 FQ	16.65 MW	21.79 TQ	CABLS	1/08-3/08
	Sacramento-Arden Arcade-Roseville MSA, CA	H	12.99 FQ	14.99 MW	18.76 TQ	CABLS	1/08-3/08
	San Diego-Carlsbad-San Marcos MSA, CA	H	14.05 FQ	19.07 MW	31.15 TQ	CABLS	1/08-3/08
	Colorado	Y	23260 FQ	27470 MW	34610 TQ	USBLS	5/07
	Denver-Aurora MSA, CO	Y	23720 FQ	27970 MW	35050 TQ	USBLS	5/07
	Florida	Y	25550 FQ	31580 MW	38140 TQ	USBLS	5/07
	Jacksonville MSA, FL	Y	25390 FQ	28340 MW	31570 TQ	USBLS	5/07
	Orlando-Kissimmee MSA, FL	Y	20740 FQ	22500 MW	24250 TQ	USBLS	5/07
	Tampa-St. Petersburg-Clearwater MSA, FL	Y	28350 FQ	31540 MW	37340 TQ	USBLS	5/07
	Georgia	Y	18390 FQ	21260 MW	25040 TQ	USBLS	5/07
	Illinois	Y	28990 FQ	34050 MW	41750 TQ	USBLS	5/07
	Chicago-Naperville-Joliet MSA, IL-IN-WI	Y	28950 FQ	34070 MW	42010 TQ	USBLS	5/07
	Indiana	Y	30110 FQ	36520 MW	45480 TQ	USBLS	5/07
	Gary PMSA, IN	Y	31240 FQ	41700 MW	50520 TQ	USBLS	5/07
	Indianapolis-Carmel MSA, IN	Y	26300 FQ	30390 MW	34780 TQ	USBLS	5/07
	Iowa	Y	24710 FQ	27760 MW	32110 TQ	USBLS	5/07
	Kentucky	Y	24858 FQ	33714 MW	40415 TQ	KYBLS	2008
	Louisiana	H	8.41 FQ	12.59 MW	16.38 TQ	LABLS	1/08-3/08
	Baton Rouge MSA, LA	Y	16080 FQ	17280 MW	18480 TQ	USBLS	5/07
	New Orleans-Metairie-Kenner MSA, LA	Y	30890 FQ	34810 MW	39190 TQ	USBLS	5/07
	Maryland	Y		44650 MW		MDBLS	3/08
	Massachusetts	Y	27460 FQ	29730 MW	31920 TQ	USBLS	5/07
	Michigan	Y	20450 FQ	23810 MW	29840 TQ	USBLS	5/07
	Minnesota	Y	34716 FQ	39803 MW	47606 TQ	MNBLS	10/08-12/08
	Duluth-Superior MSA, MN-WI	Y	33301 FQ	35673 MW	38035 TQ	MNBLS	10/08-12/08
	Minneapolis-Saint Paul MSA, MN-WI	Y	38263 FQ	47262 MW	54743 TQ	MNBLS	10/08-12/08
	Mississippi	Y	24150 FQ	38330 MW	50380 TQ	USBLS	5/07

Occupation/Type/Industry	Location	Per	Low	Mid	High	Source	Date
Tank Car, Truck, and Ship Loader	Missouri	Y	19210 FQ	26030 MW	33090 TQ	USBLS	5/07
	St. Louis MSA, MO-IL	Y	27250 FQ	36380 MW	54800 TQ	USBLS	5/07
	Montana	Y	22640 FQ	25480 MW	27980 TQ	USBLS	5/07
	Nebraska	Y	16840 FQ	18840 MW	29100 TQ	USBLS	5/07
	Nevada	H	11.12 FQ	15.94 MW	20.38 TQ	NVBLS	5/08
	New Hampshire	H	21.11 AE	24.60 MW	26.32 AEX	NHBLS	6/08
	New Jersey	Y	41240 FQ	45200 MW	49290 TQ	USBLS	5/07
	Newark-Union PMSA, NJ-PA	Y	37690 FQ	41880 MW	46080 TQ	USBLS	5/07
	New Mexico	Y	23570 FQ	26260 MW	30380 TQ	USBLS	5/07
	New York	Y	37350 FQ	68680 MW	84310 TQ	USBLS	5/07
	New York-Northern New Jersey-Long Island MSA, NY-NJ-PA	Y	39520 FQ	47990 MW	68000 TQ	USBLS	5/07
	North Carolina	Y	29900 FQ	34150 MW	37660 TQ	USBLS	5/07
	Ohio	Y	27510 FQ	31610 MW	37520 TQ	USBLS	5/07
	Cincinnati-Middletown MSA, OH-KY-IN	Y	28510 FQ	32460 MW	36380 TQ	USBLS	5/07
	Cleveland-Elyria-Mentor MSA, OH	Y	26380 FQ	31480 MW	40500 TQ	USBLS	5/07
	Oklahoma	Y	25060 FQ	27210 MW	29280 TQ	USBLS	5/07
	Tulsa MSA, OK	Y	25390 FQ	27600 MW	29750 TQ	USBLS	5/07
	Portland-Vancouver-Beaverton MSA, OR-WA	Y	33650 FQ	48780 MW	65500 TQ	USBLS	5/07
	Pennsylvania	Y	29010 FQ	34840 MW	44370 TQ	USBLS	5/07
	Philadelphia-Camden-Wilmington MSA, PA-NJ-DE-MD	Y	40890 FQ	44370 MW	47890 TQ	USBLS	5/07
	Pittsburgh MSA, PA	Y	23970 FQ	41870 MW	53180 TQ	USBLS	5/07
	South Carolina	Y	25680 FQ	33840 MW	40010 TQ	USBLS	5/07
	Tennessee	Y	28180 FQ	33210 MW	36920 TQ	USBLS	5/07
	Memphis MSA, TN-MS-AR	Y	33960 FQ	36490 MW	38910 TQ	USBLS	5/07
	Nashville-Davidson-Murfreesboro MSA, TN	Y	24850 FQ	28210 MW	31060 TQ	USBLS	5/07
	Texas	Y	23530 FQ	32870 MW	48350 TQ	USBLS	5/07
	Dallas-Fort Worth-Arlington MSA, TX	Y	23820 FQ	29910 MW	35040 TQ	USBLS	5/07
	Houston-Sugar Land-Baytown MSA, TX	Y	26280 FQ	35150 MW	48860 TQ	USBLS	5/07
	Utah	Y	26440 FQ	32320 MW	40190 TQ	USBLS	5/07
	Virginia	Y	30000 FQ	36340 MW	44950 TQ	USBLS	5/07
	Virginia Beach-Norfolk-Newport News MSA, VA-NC	Y	31020 FQ	44160 MW	48590 TQ	USBLS	5/07
	Washington	H	19.64 FQ	30.28 MW	33.94 TQ	WABLS	3/08
	Seattle-Tacoma-Bellevue MSA, WA	Y	37990 FQ	60870 MW	69520 TQ	USBLS	5/07
	Charleston MSA, WV	Y	31540 FQ	35170 MW	42860 TQ	USBLS	5/07
	Huntington-Ashland MSA, WV-KY-OH	Y	18220 FQ	27670 MW	35620 TQ	USBLS	5/07
	Wisconsin	Y	29270 FQ	32620 MW	35940 TQ	USBLS	5/07
Taper	Alabama	Y	27420 FQ	30300 MW	34100 TQ	USBLS	5/07
	Birmingham-Hoover MSA, AL	Y	29990 FQ	32560 MW	35610 TQ	USBLS	5/07
	Arizona	Y	26090 FQ	30520 MW	36690 TQ	USBLS	5/07
	Phoenix-Mesa-Scottsdale MSA, AZ	Y	26030 FQ	30300 MW	36440 TQ	USBLS	5/07
	Tucson MSA, AZ	Y	25910 FQ	30070 MW	35990 TQ	USBLS	5/07
	Arkansas	Y	22200 FQ	24530 MW	28430 TQ	USBLS	5/07
	California	H	19.73 FQ	23.97 MW	28.83 TQ	CABLS	1/08-3/08
	Los Angeles-Long Beach-Glendale PMSA, CA	H	19.09 FQ	23.17 MW	28.60 TQ	CABLS	1/08-3/08
	Oakland-Fremont-Hayward MSA, CA	H	24.33 FQ	34.69 MW	40.21 TQ	CABLS	1/08-3/08
	Riverside-San Bernardino-Ontario MSA, CA	H	21.21 FQ	25.41 MW	28.41 TQ	CABLS	1/08-3/08
	Sacramento-Arden Arcade-Roseville MSA, CA	H	20.57 FQ	22.80 MW	25.17 TQ	CABLS	1/08-3/08
	San Diego-Carlsbad-San Marcos MSA, CA	H	19.55 FQ	22.47 MW	26.52 TQ	CABLS	1/08-3/08
	San Francisco-San Mateo-Redwood PMSA, CA	H	22.11 FQ	25.97 MW	34.56 TQ	CABLS	1/08-3/08

AE	Average entry wage	AW	Average wage paid	FQ	First quartile wage
AER	Average entry range	AWR	Average wage range	H	Hourly
AEX	Average experienced wage	AXR	Average experienced range	HI	Highest wage paid
ATC	Average total compensation	D	Daily	HR	High end range

LO	Lowest wage paid	MTC	Median total compensation
LR	Low end range	MW	Median wage paid
M	Monthly	MWR	Median wage range
MCC	Median cash compensation	S	See annotated source

TCC	Total cash compensation
TQ	Third quartile wage
W	Weekly
Y	Yearly

Occupation/Type/Industry	Location	Per	Low	Mid	High	Source	Date
Taper	San Jose-Sunnyvale-Santa Clara MSA, CA	H	23.46 FQ	28.26 MW	33.40 TQ	CABLS	1/08-3/08
	Santa Ana-Anaheim-Irvine PMSA, CA	Y	37990 FQ	45760 MW	54460 TQ	USBLS	5/07
	Colorado	Y	28220 FQ	34450 MW	41650 TQ	USBLS	5/07
	Denver-Aurora MSA, CO	Y	27500 FQ	33550 MW	41920 TQ	USBLS	5/07
	Connecticut	H	18.40 AE	26.58 MW		CTBLS	1/08-3/08
	Bridgeport-Stamford-Norwalk MSA, CT	Y	49310 FQ	55720 MW	61740 TQ	USBLS	5/07
	Hartford-West Hartford-East Hartford MSA, CT	Y	47090 FQ	54740 MW	61190 TQ	USBLS	5/07
	Washington-Arlington-Alexandria MSA, DC-VA-MD-WV	Y	33870 FQ	39040 MW	47950 TQ	USBLS	5/07
	Florida	Y	27440 FQ	34480 MW	42560 TQ	USBLS	5/07
	Jacksonville MSA, FL	Y	31610 FQ	33840 MW	36070 TQ	USBLS	5/07
	Miami-Fort Lauderdale-Miami Beach MSA, FL	Y	26840 FQ	29770 MW	42630 TQ	USBLS	5/07
	Orlando-Kissimmee MSA, FL	Y	33450 FQ	38140 MW	43360 TQ	USBLS	5/07
	Tampa-St. Petersburg-Clearwater MSA, FL	Y	30440 FQ	35560 MW	39880 TQ	USBLS	5/07
	Georgia	Y	30370 FQ	37510 MW	45490 TQ	USBLS	5/07
	Hawaii	Y	38780 FQ	55370 MW	72930 TQ	USBLS	5/07
	Honolulu MSA, HI	Y	40000 FQ	58360 MW	74580 TQ	USBLS	5/07
	Idaho	Y	30690 FQ	38580 MW	49440 TQ	USBLS	5/07
	Boise City-Nampa MSA, ID	Y	30560 FQ	38700 MW	50440 TQ	USBLS	5/07
	Illinois	Y	39050 FQ	62560 MW	71920 TQ	USBLS	5/07
	Chicago-Naperville-Joliet MSA, IL-IN-WI	Y	41230 FQ	64510 MW	72600 TQ	USBLS	5/07
	Indiana	Y	25590 FQ	40820 MW	52730 TQ	USBLS	5/07
	Gary PMSA, IN	Y	48910 FQ	53010 MW	57090 TQ	USBLS	5/07
	Indianapolis-Carmel MSA, IN	Y	23780 FQ	41550 MW	52030 TQ	USBLS	5/07
	Iowa	Y	33280 FQ	43880 MW	50970 TQ	USBLS	5/07
	Des Moines-West Des Moines MSA, IA	Y	41300 FQ	47860 MW	53710 TQ	USBLS	5/07
	Kansas	Y	33110 FQ	44310 MW	54890 TQ	USBLS	5/07
	Wichita MSA, KS	Y	33320 FQ	41520 MW	46300 TQ	USBLS	5/07
	Kentucky	Y	31326 FQ	38458 MW	48850 TQ	KYBLS	2008
	Louisville-Jefferson County MSA, KY-IN	Y	27940 FQ	33290 MW	45070 TQ	USBLS	5/07
	Louisiana	H	13.42 FQ	15.76 MW	20.15 TQ	LABLS	1/08-3/08
	Maine	Y	34230 FQ	39910 MW	47590 TQ	USBLS	5/07
	Maryland	Y		42025 MW		MDBLS	3/08
	Baltimore-Towson MSA, MD	Y	32100 FQ	38040 MW	44500 TQ	USBLS	5/07
	Bethesda-Gaithersburg-Frederick PMSA, MD	Y	36630 FQ	42640 MW	52320 TQ	USBLS	5/07
	Massachusetts	Y	55260 FQ	67570 MW	75260 TQ	USBLS	5/07
	Boston-Cambridge-Quincy NECTA, MA	Y	62880 FQ	72240 MW	78450 TQ	USBLS	5/07
	Michigan	Y	40790 FQ	51820 MW	58350 TQ	USBLS	5/07
	Detroit-Warren-Livonia MSA, MI	Y	51810 FQ	56460 MW	60820 TQ	USBLS	5/07
	Grand Rapids-Wyoming MSA, MI	Y	33840 FQ	41530 MW	48570 TQ	USBLS	5/07
	Warren-Troy-Farmington Hills PMSA, MI	Y	52580 FQ	56930 MW	61140 TQ	USBLS	5/07
	Minnesota	Y	49184 FQ	59280 MW	67426 TQ	MNBLS	10/08-12/08
	Duluth-Superior MSA, MN-WI	Y	36885 FQ	49026 MW	56519 TQ	MNBLS	10/08-12/08
	Minneapolis-Saint Paul MSA, MN-WI	Y	50143 FQ	59817 MW	67869 TQ	MNBLS	10/08-12/08
	Mississippi	Y	27210 FQ	32910 MW	41870 TQ	USBLS	5/07
	Jackson MSA, MS	Y	27760 FQ	33710 MW	44120 TQ	USBLS	5/07
	Missouri	Y	42800 FQ	52540 MW	59300 TQ	USBLS	5/07
	Kansas City MSA, MO-KS	Y	44550 FQ	54800 MW	60390 TQ	USBLS	5/07
	St. Louis MSA, MO-IL	Y	46260 FQ	54180 MW	60380 TQ	USBLS	5/07
	Montana	Y	27470 FQ	34730 MW	44080 TQ	USBLS	5/07
	Nebraska	Y	30480 FQ	37330 MW	43900 TQ	USBLS	5/07
	Omaha-Council Bluffs MSA, NE-IA	Y	29070 FQ	35080 MW	40440 TQ	USBLS	5/07
	Nevada	H	16.13 FQ	19.37 MW	24.63 TQ	NVBLS	5/08
	Las Vegas-Paradise MSA, NV	H	16.13 FQ	19.19 MW	24.79 TQ	NVBLS	5/08
	New Hampshire	H	14.25 AE	23.52 MW	30.06 AEX	NHBLS	6/08

AE	Average entry wage	AW	Average wage paid	FQ	First quartile wage	LO	Lowest wage paid	MTC	Median total compensation	TCC	Total cash compensation
AER	Average entry range	AWR	Average wage range	H	Hourly	LR	Low end range	MW	Median wage paid	TQ	Third quartile wage
AEX	Average experienced wage	AXR	Average experienced range	HI	Highest wage paid	M	Monthly	MWR	Median wage range	W	Weekly
ATC	Average total compensation	D	Daily	HR	High end range	MCC	Median cash compensation	S	See annotated source	Y	Yearly

Occupation/Type/Industry	Location	Per	Low	Mid	High	Source	Date
Taper	New Jersey	Y	60340 FQ	71330 MW	77430 TQ	USBLS	5/07
	Edison PMSA, NJ	Y	68700 FQ	73570 MW	78430 TQ	USBLS	5/07
	Newark-Union PMSA, NJ-PA	Y	42270 FQ	68960 MW	76290 TQ	USBLS	5/07
	New Mexico	Y	25660 FQ	30870 MW	43290 TQ	USBLS	5/07
	Albuquerque MSA, NM	Y	25660 FQ	30630 MW	42480 TQ	USBLS	5/07
	New York	Y	45260 FQ	56490 MW	68250 TQ	USBLS	5/07
	Albany-Schenectady-Troy MSA, NY	Y	38040 FQ	43900 MW	48410 TQ	USBLS	5/07
	Buffalo-Niagara Falls MSA, NY	Y	34240 FQ	41540 MW	46420 TQ	USBLS	5/07
	Nassau-Suffolk PMSA, NY	Y	55620 FQ	62420 MW	73190 TQ	USBLS	5/07
	New York-Northern New Jersey-Long Island MSA, NY-NJ-PA	Y	55180 FQ	67600 MW	75500 TQ	USBLS	5/07
	North Carolina	Y	27160 FQ	30920 MW	35410 TQ	USBLS	5/07
	Raleigh-Cary MSA, NC	Y	27880 FQ	31360 MW	35820 TQ	USBLS	5/07
	North Dakota	Y	25550 FQ	29010 MW	33010 TQ	USBLS	5/07
	Ohio	Y	29340 FQ	36880 MW	47740 TQ	USBLS	5/07
	Cincinnati-Middletown MSA, OH-KY-IN	Y	29290 FQ	36570 MW	47630 TQ	USBLS	5/07
	Cleveland-Elyria-Mentor MSA, OH	Y	29780 FQ	39090 MW	55570 TQ	USBLS	5/07
	Columbus MSA, OH	Y	30870 FQ	38940 MW	44470 TQ	USBLS	5/07
	Dayton MSA, OH	Y	28220 FQ	34210 MW	43880 TQ	USBLS	5/07
	Oklahoma	Y	32400 FQ	40860 MW	50080 TQ	USBLS	5/07
	Tulsa MSA, OK	Y	32880 FQ	38910 MW	48490 TQ	USBLS	5/07
	Oregon	H	15.39 FQ	22.29 MW	27.11 TQ	ORBLS	5/08
	Portland-Vancouver-Beaverton MSA, OR-WA	Y	35470 FQ	46250 MW	56600 TQ	USBLS	5/07
	Pennsylvania	Y	37590 FQ	45020 MW	55080 TQ	USBLS	5/07
	Philadelphia-Camden-Wilmington MSA, PA-NJ-DE-MD	Y	35640 FQ	54420 MW	66520 TQ	USBLS	5/07
	Pittsburgh MSA, PA	Y	39150 FQ	45200 MW	52000 TQ	USBLS	5/07
	Rhode Island	Y	30790 FQ	39570 MW	52620 TQ	USBLS	5/07
	Providence-Fall River-Warwick MSA, RI-MA	Y	30790 FQ	39570 MW	52620 TQ	USBLS	5/07
	South Carolina	Y	28450 FQ	31390 MW	36780 TQ	USBLS	5/07
	South Dakota	Y	22572 FQ	26760 MW	32753 TQ	SDBLS	7/08-9/08
	Tennessee	Y	29940 FQ	34650 MW	38840 TQ	USBLS	5/07
	Nashville-Davidson-Murfreesboro MSA, TN	Y	31300 FQ	35560 MW	39730 TQ	USBLS	5/07
	Texas	Y	22240 FQ	26850 MW	31060 TQ	USBLS	5/07
	Dallas-Fort Worth-Arlington MSA, TX	Y	23560 FQ	28330 MW	34600 TQ	USBLS	5/07
	El Paso MSA, TX	Y	19470 FQ	21790 MW	24100 TQ	USBLS	5/07
	Houston-Sugar Land-Baytown MSA, TX	Y	26560 FQ	28860 MW	31150 TQ	USBLS	5/07
	San Antonio MSA, TX	Y	25950 FQ	28610 MW	34600 TQ	USBLS	5/07
	Utah	Y	35200 FQ	40660 MW	45100 TQ	USBLS	5/07
	Salt Lake City MSA, UT	Y	36720 FQ	39860 MW	44620 TQ	USBLS	5/07
	Vermont	Y	29080 FQ	36590 MW	46680 TQ	USBLS	5/07
	Virginia	Y	25830 FQ	33580 MW	38560 TQ	USBLS	5/07
	Richmond MSA, VA	Y	19840 FQ	24370 MW	32430 TQ	USBLS	5/07
	Washington	H	14.95 FQ	21.59 MW	28.23 TQ	WABLS	3/08
	Seattle-Tacoma-Bellevue MSA, WA	Y	31680 FQ	47880 MW	61360 TQ	USBLS	5/07
	West Virginia	Y	25167 FQ	45008 MW	51505 TQ	WVBLS	7/08-9/08
	Wisconsin	Y	39120 FQ	46460 MW	52850 TQ	USBLS	5/07
	Milwaukee-Waukesha-West Allis MSA, WI	Y	41320 FQ	48750 MW	54960 TQ	USBLS	5/07
Tasting Room Manager	United States	Y		49519 AW		WINEB	2007
Tax Auditor Municipal Government	Seattle, WA	H	26.10 LO		30.39 HI	CSSS	2007
State Government	Arkansas	Y	35823 LO		48000 HI	AFT02	3/1/08
Tax Commissioner	Catoosa County, GA	Y			84505 HI	GACTY02	2008
Tax Examiner, Collector, and Revenue Agent	Alabama	Y	32200 FQ	45030 MW	65480 TQ	USBLS	5/07

AE Average entry wage; AER Average entry range; AEX Average experienced wage; ATC Average total compensation; AW Average wage paid; AWR Average wage range; AXR Average experienced range; D Daily; FQ First quartile wage; H Hourly; HI Highest wage paid; HR High end range; LO Lowest wage paid; LR Low end range; M Monthly; MCC Median cash compensation; MTC Median total compensation; MW Median wage paid; MWR Median wage range; S See annotated source; TCC Total cash compensation; TQ Third quartile wage; W Weekly; Y Yearly

Tax Examiner, Collector, and Revenue Agent

Occupation/Type/Industry	Location	Per	Low	Mid	High	Source	Date
Tax Examiner, Collector, and Revenue Agent	Birmingham-Hoover MSA, AL	Y	42780 FQ	57880 MW	77030 TQ	USBLS	5/07
	Alaska	Y	52310 FQ	76860 MW	92310 TQ	USBLS	5/07
	Arizona	Y	34800 FQ	46820 MW	63510 TQ	USBLS	5/07
	Phoenix-Mesa-Scottsdale MSA, AZ	Y	35790 FQ	47800 MW	64460 TQ	USBLS	5/07
	Arkansas	Y	23550 FQ	32100 MW	47440 TQ	USBLS	5/07
	Little Rock-North Little Rock MSA, AR	Y	24810 FQ	32730 MW	46520 TQ	USBLS	5/07
	California	H	21.11 FQ	27.94 MW	37.51 TQ	CABLS	1/08-3/08
	Fresno MSA, CA	H	18.81 FQ	21.67 MW	24.28 TQ	CABLS	1/08-3/08
	Oakland-Fremont-Hayward MSA, CA	H	24.75 FQ	32.30 MW	40.38 TQ	CABLS	1/08-3/08
	Oxnard-Thousand Oaks-Ventura MSA, CA	H	26.36 FQ	32.30 MW	41.98 TQ	CABLS	1/08-3/08
	Riverside-San Bernardino-Ontario MSA, CA	H	22.73 FQ	29.77 MW	39.12 TQ	CABLS	1/08-3/08
	Sacramento-Arden Arcade-Roseville MSA, CA	H	19.00 FQ	25.51 MW	32.06 TQ	CABLS	1/08-3/08
	San Diego-Carlsbad-San Marcos MSA, CA	H	25.51 FQ	33.22 MW	40.66 TQ	CABLS	1/08-3/08
	Colorado	Y	44380 FQ	56750 MW	77480 TQ	USBLS	5/07
	Denver-Aurora MSA, CO	Y	44320 FQ	56600 MW	79590 TQ	USBLS	5/07
	Connecticut	H	22.14 AE	35.46 MW		CTBLS	1/08-3/08
	Bridgeport-Stamford-Norwalk MSA, CT	Y	55650 FQ	79540 MW	94580 TQ	USBLS	5/07
	Hartford-West Hartford-East Hartford MSA, CT	Y	55750 FQ	71090 MW	84830 TQ	USBLS	5/07
	Delaware	Y	39260 FQ	47880 MW	59410 TQ	USBLS	5/07
	Wilmington PMSA, DE-MD-NJ	Y	43410 FQ	52850 MW	64980 TQ	USBLS	5/07
	Washington-Arlington-Alexandria MSA, DC-VA-MD-WV	Y	48140 FQ	60950 MW	81850 TQ	USBLS	5/07
	Florida	Y	29490 FQ	36350 MW	53970 TQ	USBLS	5/07
	Fort Lauderdale-Pompano Beach-Deerfield Beach PMSA, FL	Y	32450 FQ	53680 MW	82990 TQ	USBLS	5/07
	Miami-Fort Lauderdale-Miami Beach MSA, FL	Y	33440 FQ	52040 MW	78400 TQ	USBLS	5/07
	Orlando-Kissimmee MSA, FL	Y	29290 FQ	35900 MW	55830 TQ	USBLS	5/07
	Tampa-St. Petersburg-Clearwater MSA, FL	Y	31050 FQ	39920 MW	61490 TQ	USBLS	5/07
	Georgia	Y	29720 FQ	39990 MW	50550 TQ	USBLS	5/07
	Atlanta-Sandy Springs-Marietta MSA, GA	Y	32870 FQ	42180 MW	51220 TQ	USBLS	5/07
	Hawaii	Y	48320 FQ	66590 MW	86760 TQ	USBLS	5/07
	Idaho	Y	42120 FQ	51400 MW	63190 TQ	USBLS	5/07
	Boise City-Nampa MSA, ID	Y	43260 FQ	52780 MW	63860 TQ	USBLS	5/07
	Illinois	Y	45980 FQ	59400 MW	83510 TQ	USBLS	5/07
	Chicago-Naperville-Joliet MSA, IL-IN-WI	Y	51730 FQ	71840 MW	91840 TQ	USBLS	5/07
	Indiana	Y	27010 FQ	35240 MW	65730 TQ	USBLS	5/07
	Indianapolis-Carmel MSA, IN	Y	27420 FQ	33250 MW	56590 TQ	USBLS	5/07
	Iowa	Y	41640 FQ	54090 MW	67130 TQ	USBLS	5/07
	Kansas	Y	32050 FQ	41980 MW	51720 TQ	USBLS	5/07
	Wichita MSA, KS	Y	44130 FQ	66550 MW	85360 TQ	USBLS	5/07
	Lexington-Fayette MSA, KY	Y	37770 FQ	57450 MW	74400 TQ	USBLS	5/07
	Louisville-Jefferson County MSA, KY-IN	Y	34830 FQ	52020 MW	73910 TQ	USBLS	5/07
	Louisiana	H	14.96 FQ	20.58 MW	29.18 TQ	LABLS	1/08-3/08
	Baton Rouge MSA, LA	Y	29450 FQ	40090 MW	53440 TQ	USBLS	5/07
	New Orleans-Metairie-Kenner MSA, LA	Y	45080 FQ	63240 MW	82280 TQ	USBLS	5/07
	Shreveport-Bossier City MSA, LA	Y	27090 FQ	35700 MW	52580 TQ	USBLS	5/07
	Maine	Y	29890 FQ	36790 MW	46810 TQ	USBLS	5/07
	Portland-South Portland-Biddeford MSA, ME	Y	35690 FQ	45430 MW	59490 TQ	USBLS	5/07
	Maryland	Y		51750 MW		MDBLS	3/08
	Baltimore-Towson MSA, MD	Y	42780 FQ	49000 MW	63980 TQ	USBLS	5/07
	Massachusetts	Y	43670 FQ	58600 MW	78250 TQ	USBLS	5/07

Occupation/Type/Industry	Location	Per	Low	Mid	High	Source	Date
Tax Examiner, Collector, and Revenue Agent	Boston-Cambridge-Quincy NECTA, MA	Y	47240 FQ	65880 MW	81500 TQ	USBLS	5/07
	Worcester MSA, MA-CT	Y	44620 FQ	69640 MW	81510 TQ	USBLS	5/07
	Michigan	Y	43420 FQ	62200 MW	85540 TQ	USBLS	5/07
	Detroit-Warren-Livonia MSA, MI	Y	44310 FQ	63450 MW	87890 TQ	USBLS	5/07
	Warren-Troy-Farmington Hills PMSA, MI	Y	54780 FQ	73800 MW	90300 TQ	USBLS	5/07
	Minnesota	Y	42269 FQ	56219 MW	68512 TQ	MNBLS	10/08-12/08
	Duluth-Superior MSA, MN-WI	Y	40872 FQ	56000 MW	63591 TQ	MNBLS	10/08-12/08
	Minneapolis-Saint Paul MSA, MN-WI	Y	42602 FQ	56459 MW	72328 TQ	MNBLS	10/08-12/08
	Mississippi	Y	23070 FQ	29410 MW	47480 TQ	USBLS	5/07
	Jackson MSA, MS	Y	23130 FQ	29090 MW	47780 TQ	USBLS	5/07
	Missouri	Y	32410 FQ	41330 MW	52470 TQ	USBLS	5/07
	Kansas City MSA, MO-KS	Y	36060 FQ	43070 MW	49980 TQ	USBLS	5/07
	St. Louis MSA, MO-IL	Y	44320 FQ	61210 MW	82240 TQ	USBLS	5/07
	Montana	Y	35090 FQ	41620 MW	70150 TQ	USBLS	5/07
	Omaha-Council Bluffs MSA, NE-IA	Y	34090 FQ	53710 MW	82690 TQ	USBLS	5/07
	Nevada	H	22.42 FQ	27.94 MW	36.26 TQ	NVBLS	5/08
	Las Vegas-Paradise MSA, NV	H	24.38 FQ	30.42 MW	38.18 TQ	NVBLS	5/08
	New Hampshire	H	13.05 AE	19.38 MW	26.75 AEX	NHBLS	6/08
	Manchester MSA, NH	Y	41890 FQ	56320 MW	83930 TQ	USBLS	5/07
	Nashua NECTA, NH-MA	Y	34500 FQ	49830 MW	70850 TQ	USBLS	5/07
	New Jersey	Y	50960 FQ	67440 MW	86480 TQ	USBLS	5/07
	Camden PMSA, NJ	Y	46880 FQ	65060 MW	78620 TQ	USBLS	5/07
	Edison PMSA, NJ	Y	48140 FQ	65580 MW	87860 TQ	USBLS	5/07
	Newark-Union PMSA, NJ-PA	Y	57680 FQ	76970 MW	92240 TQ	USBLS	5/07
	New Mexico	Y	31350 FQ	50830 MW	74990 TQ	USBLS	5/07
	Albuquerque MSA, NM	Y	41330 FQ	61150 MW	77960 TQ	USBLS	5/07
	New York	Y	43300 FQ	53180 MW	70450 TQ	USBLS	5/07
	Albany-Schenectady-Troy MSA, NY	Y	38470 FQ	47540 MW	59600 TQ	USBLS	5/07
	Buffalo-Niagara Falls MSA, NY	Y	45810 FQ	56330 MW	69530 TQ	USBLS	5/07
	Nassau-Suffolk PMSA, NY	Y	43220 FQ	49140 MW	60880 TQ	USBLS	5/07
	New York-Northern New Jersey-Long Island MSA, NY-NJ-PA	Y	47690 FQ	61360 MW	85610 TQ	USBLS	5/07
	North Carolina	Y	32720 FQ	40800 MW	52010 TQ	USBLS	5/07
	Asheville MSA, NC	Y	33120 FQ	42470 MW	57340 TQ	USBLS	5/07
	Charlotte-Gastonia-Concord MSA, NC-SC	Y	34160 FQ	43610 MW	64870 TQ	USBLS	5/07
	Raleigh-Cary MSA, NC	Y	36990 FQ	43800 MW	51350 TQ	USBLS	5/07
	North Dakota	Y	37380 FQ	58090 MW	74710 TQ	USBLS	5/07
	Ohio	Y	39590 FQ	52190 MW	73990 TQ	USBLS	5/07
	Canton-Massillon MSA, OH	Y	34870 FQ	39610 MW	51130 TQ	USBLS	5/07
	Cincinnati-Middletown MSA, OH-KY-IN	Y	37830 FQ	44540 MW	51450 TQ	USBLS	5/07
	Cleveland-Elyria-Mentor MSA, OH	Y	45030 FQ	65690 MW	84310 TQ	USBLS	5/07
	Dayton MSA, OH	Y	39680 FQ	52330 MW	70730 TQ	USBLS	5/07
	Oklahoma	Y	26550 FQ	33640 MW	61760 TQ	USBLS	5/07
	Oklahoma City MSA, OK	Y	28550 FQ	39670 MW	69860 TQ	USBLS	5/07
	Tulsa MSA, OK	Y	31520 FQ	54040 MW	78200 TQ	USBLS	5/07
	Oregon	H	16.32 FQ	20.99 MW	28.78 TQ	ORBLS	5/08
	Portland-Vancouver-Beaverton MSA, OR-WA	Y	43550 FQ	53940 MW	72640 TQ	USBLS	5/07
	Pennsylvania	Y	26030 FQ	42030 MW	52120 TQ	USBLS	5/07
	Allentown-Bethlehem-Easton MSA, PA-NJ	Y	23010 FQ	42620 MW	56730 TQ	USBLS	5/07
	Lancaster MSA, PA	Y	15770 FQ	40470 MW	65850 TQ	USBLS	5/07
	Philadelphia-Camden-Wilmington MSA, PA-NJ-DE-MD	Y	40790 FQ	46880 MW	57750 TQ	USBLS	5/07
	Pittsburgh MSA, PA	Y	21440 FQ	42990 MW	61790 TQ	USBLS	5/07
	Rhode Island	Y	56330 FQ	77260 MW	91910 TQ	USBLS	5/07
	Providence-Fall River-Warwick MSA, RI-MA	Y	57320 FQ	74640 MW	88490 TQ	USBLS	5/07
	South Carolina	Y	29230 FQ	40170 MW	63800 TQ	USBLS	5/07

Occupation/Type/Industry	Location	Per	Low	Mid	High	Source	Date
Tax Examiner, Collector, and Revenue Agent	Columbia MSA, SC	Y	33300 FQ	54280 MW	72900 TQ	USBLS	5/07
	South Dakota	Y	33842 FQ	41379 TQ	50339 TQ	SDBLS	7/08-9/08
	Tennessee	Y	35840 FQ	43360 MW	53360 TQ	USBLS	5/07
	Memphis MSA, TN-MS-AR	Y	36600 FQ	42560 MW	48790 TQ	USBLS	5/07
	Nashville-Davidson-Murfreesboro MSA, TN	Y	39250 FQ	55390 MW	76550 TQ	USBLS	5/07
	Texas	Y	31570 FQ	42960 MW	64150 TQ	USBLS	5/07
	Austin-Round Rock MSA, TX	Y	32010 FQ	39340 MW	47480 TQ	USBLS	5/07
	Dallas-Fort Worth-Arlington MSA, TX	Y	40230 FQ	60680 MW	82310 TQ	USBLS	5/07
	El Paso MSA, TX	Y	28060 FQ	50020 MW	67520 TQ	USBLS	5/07
	Houston-Sugar Land-Baytown MSA, TX	Y	41480 FQ	67560 MW	91560 TQ	USBLS	5/07
	San Antonio MSA, TX	Y	35670 FQ	52140 MW	80280 TQ	USBLS	5/07
	Utah	Y	34330 FQ	40170 MW	47380 TQ	USBLS	5/07
	Vermont	Y	39630 FQ	46990 MW	59490 TQ	USBLS	5/07
	Virginia	Y	33890 FQ	45150 MW	62960 TQ	USBLS	5/07
	Richmond MSA, VA	Y	37220 FQ	47070 MW	64450 TQ	USBLS	5/07
	Virginia Beach-Norfolk-Newport News MSA, VA-NC	Y	31890 FQ	41560 MW	58310 TQ	USBLS	5/07
	Washington	H	20.95 FQ	24.19 MW	30.33 TQ	WABLS	3/08
	Seattle-Tacoma-Bellevue MSA, WA	Y	44010 FQ	51700 MW	70050 TQ	USBLS	5/07
	West Virginia	Y	21755 FQ	27313 MW	40216 TQ	WVBLS	7/08-9/08
	Charleston MSA, WV	Y	22980 FQ	29020 MW	44490 TQ	USBLS	5/07
	Wisconsin	Y	46260 FQ	58970 MW	79020 TQ	USBLS	5/07
	Milwaukee-Waukesha-West Allis MSA, WI	Y	56750 FQ	74370 MW	88620 TQ	USBLS	5/07
	Wyoming	Y	30946 FQ	39163 MW	72260 TQ	WYBLS	9/08
	Puerto Rico	Y	23900 FQ	30550 MW	38390 TQ	USBLS	5/07
	San Juan-Caguas-Guaynabo MSA, PR	Y	24200 FQ	29760 MW	35730 TQ	USBLS	5/07
Tax Preparer	Alabama	Y	16640 FQ	22360 MW	29910 TQ	USBLS	5/07
	Birmingham-Hoover MSA, AL	Y	13440 FQ	16090 MW	28100 TQ	USBLS	5/07
	Arizona	Y	25320 FQ	28910 MW	35050 TQ	USBLS	5/07
	Phoenix-Mesa-Scottsdale MSA, AZ	Y	25460 FQ	29450 MW	36350 TQ	USBLS	5/07
	Tucson MSA, AZ	Y	23810 FQ	27120 MW	29710 TQ	USBLS	5/07
	Arkansas	Y	19990 FQ	22710 MW	28200 TQ	USBLS	5/07
	Little Rock-North Little Rock MSA, AR	Y	18920 FQ	20670 MW	24080 TQ	USBLS	5/07
	California	H	15.23 FQ	23.96 MW	33.79 TQ	CABLS	1/08-3/08
	Los Angeles-Long Beach-Glendale PMSA, CA	H	18.27 FQ	26.75 MW	35.90 TQ	CABLS	1/08-3/08
	Oakland-Fremont-Hayward MSA, CA	H	10.94 FQ	23.89 MW	28.56 TQ	CABLS	1/08-3/08
	Riverside-San Bernardino-Ontario MSA, CA	H	14.64 FQ	18.29 MW	24.59 TQ	CABLS	1/08-3/08
	Sacramento-Arden Arcade-Roseville MSA, CA	H	15.62 FQ	20.32 MW	27.95 TQ	CABLS	1/08-3/08
	San Diego-Carlsbad-San Marcos MSA, CA	H	15.01 FQ	27.00 MW	37.57 TQ	CABLS	1/08-3/08
	San Francisco-San Mateo-Redwood PMSA, CA	H	21.46 FQ	29.15 MW	40.11 TQ	CABLS	1/08-3/08
	San Jose-Sunnyvale-Santa Clara MSA, CA	H	16.36 FQ	23.32 MW	43.86 TQ	CABLS	1/08-3/08
	Santa Ana-Anaheim-Irvine PMSA, CA	Y	31240 FQ	36660 MW	55070 TQ	USBLS	5/07
	Colorado	Y	15780 FQ	25120 MW	37580 TQ	USBLS	5/07
	Denver-Aurora MSA, CO	Y	14910 FQ	15540 MW	23070 TQ	USBLS	5/07
	Connecticut	H	10.16 AE	20.49 MW		CTBLS	1/08-3/08
	Bridgeport-Stamford-Norwalk MSA, CT	Y	21710 FQ	42910 MW	49970 TQ	USBLS	5/07
	Delaware	Y	23210 FQ	32770 MW	60060 TQ	USBLS	5/07
	Wilmington PMSA, DE-MD-NJ	Y	22550 FQ	35460 MW	60410 TQ	USBLS	5/07
	District of Columbia	Y	23450 FQ	40000 MW	46940 TQ	USBLS	5/07
	Washington-Arlington-Alexandria MSA, DC-VA-MD-WV	Y	23980 FQ	33490 MW	44010 TQ	USBLS	5/07

Tax Preparer

Occupation/Type/Industry	Location	Per	Low	Mid	High	Source	Date
Tax Preparer	Florida	Y	16860 FQ	22710 MW	30810 TQ	USBLS	5/07
	Fort Lauderdale-Pompano Beach-Deerfield Beach PMSA, FL	Y	15370 FQ	16820 MW	21300 TQ	USBLS	5/07
	Lakeland MSA, FL	Y	19010 FQ	26080 MW	30250 TQ	USBLS	5/07
	Miami-Fort Lauderdale-Miami Beach MSA, FL	Y	16900 FQ	23030 MW	34780 TQ	USBLS	5/07
	Orlando-Kissimmee MSA, FL	Y	16230 FQ	24310 MW	29880 TQ	USBLS	5/07
	Tampa-St. Petersburg-Clearwater MSA, FL	Y	21750 FQ	26300 MW	31590 TQ	USBLS	5/07
	West Palm Beach-Boca Raton-Boynton Beach PMSA, FL	Y	17050 FQ	19580 MW	25720 TQ	USBLS	5/07
	Georgia	Y	22050 FQ	30840 MW	43000 TQ	USBLS	5/07
	Atlanta-Sandy Springs-Marietta MSA, GA	Y	26350 FQ	33940 MW	46130 TQ	USBLS	5/07
	Hawaii	Y	33840 FQ	44230 MW	52530 TQ	USBLS	5/07
	Honolulu MSA, HI	Y	31600 FQ	44460 MW	53410 TQ	USBLS	5/07
	Idaho	Y	26310 FQ	30210 MW	35810 TQ	USBLS	5/07
	Illinois	Y	18330 FQ	27560 MW	38200 TQ	USBLS	5/07
	Chicago-Naperville-Joliet MSA, IL-IN-WI	Y	20210 FQ	30450 MW	40310 TQ	USBLS	5/07
	Indiana	Y	21210 FQ	27550 MW	35980 TQ	USBLS	5/07
	Gary PMSA, IN	Y	17740 FQ	22110 MW	29110 TQ	USBLS	5/07
	Indianapolis-Carmel MSA, IN	Y	18520 FQ	27280 MW	37670 TQ	USBLS	5/07
	South Bend-Mishawaka MSA, IN-MI	Y	27740 FQ	32580 MW	38750 TQ	USBLS	5/07
	Iowa	Y	18010 FQ	23310 MW	29840 TQ	USBLS	5/07
	Des Moines-West Des Moines MSA, IA	Y	25780 FQ	28640 MW	31510 TQ	USBLS	5/07
	Kansas	Y	19160 FQ	28150 MW	37630 TQ	USBLS	5/07
	Wichita MSA, KS	Y	18310 FQ	22000 MW	28530 TQ	USBLS	5/07
	Kentucky	Y	21641 FQ	29504 MW	34716 TQ	KYBLS	2008
	Bowling Green MSA, KY	Y	17570 FQ	20090 MW	43510 TQ	USBLS	5/07
	Louisville-Jefferson County MSA, KY-IN	Y	24030 FQ	29130 MW	48460 TQ	USBLS	5/07
	Louisiana	H	9.18 FQ	10.72 MW	13.72 TQ	LABLS	1/08-3/08
	Baton Rouge MSA, LA	Y	17050 FQ	22470 MW	28180 TQ	USBLS	5/07
	New Orleans-Metairie-Kenner MSA, LA	Y	20230 FQ	21900 MW	23550 TQ	USBLS	5/07
	Maine	Y	19730 FQ	23860 MW	42880 TQ	USBLS	5/07
	Maryland	Y		33275 MW		MDBLS	3/08
	Baltimore-Towson MSA, MD	Y	25030 FQ	40890 MW	53510 TQ	USBLS	5/07
	Bethesda-Gaithersburg-Frederick PMSA, MD	Y	25440 FQ	31460 MW	42860 TQ	USBLS	5/07
	Hagerstown-Martinsburg MSA, MD-WV	Y	23500 FQ	27660 MW	40030 TQ	USBLS	5/07
	Massachusetts	Y	42360 FQ	61980 MW	75170 TQ	USBLS	5/07
	Boston-Cambridge-Quincy NECTA, MA	Y	53690 FQ	68940 MW	77320 TQ	USBLS	5/07
	Springfield MSA, MA-CT	Y	34650 FQ	42590 MW	51400 TQ	USBLS	5/07
	Michigan	Y	19190 FQ	28620 MW	48960 TQ	USBLS	5/07
	Ann Arbor MSA, MI	Y	18040 FQ	25490 MW	42260 TQ	USBLS	5/07
	Detroit-Warren-Livonia MSA, MI	Y	17660 FQ	20640 MW	34890 TQ	USBLS	5/07
	Warren-Troy-Farmington Hills PMSA, MI	Y	22700 FQ	28340 MW	37600 TQ	USBLS	5/07
	Minnesota	Y	23835 FQ	28620 MW	40475 TQ	MNBLS	10/08-12/08
	Duluth-Superior MSA, MN-WI	Y	27442 FQ	31748 MW	38661 TQ	MNBLS	10/08-12/08
	Minneapolis-Saint Paul MSA, MN-WI	Y	23449 FQ	27161 MW	44698 TQ	MNBLS	10/08-12/08
	Mississippi	Y	16890 FQ	19470 MW	24920 TQ	USBLS	5/07
	Jackson MSA, MS	Y	18010 FQ	20140 MW	23870 TQ	USBLS	5/07
	Missouri	Y	22740 FQ	28980 MW	40410 TQ	USBLS	5/07
	Kansas City MSA, MO-KS	Y	22760 FQ	27000 MW	30310 TQ	USBLS	5/07
	St. Louis MSA, MO-IL	Y	21680 FQ	28440 MW	40080 TQ	USBLS	5/07
	Montana	Y	16990 FQ	24930 MW	35130 TQ	USBLS	5/07
	Nebraska	Y	19480 FQ	24450 MW	30410 TQ	USBLS	5/07
	Omaha-Council Bluffs MSA, NE-IA	Y	19400 FQ	23140 MW	29540 TQ	USBLS	5/07
	Nevada	H	13.43 FQ	33.77 MW	38.05 TQ	NVBLS	5/08
	Las Vegas-Paradise MSA, NV	H	26.98 FQ	35.40 MW	38.88 TQ	NVBLS	5/08
	New Hampshire	H	13.17 AE	20.49 MW	22.29 AEX	NHBLS	6/08

AE	Average entry wage	AW	Average wage paid	FQ	First quartile wage	LO	Lowest wage paid	MTC	Median total compensation	TCC	Total cash compensation
AER	Average entry range	AWR	Average wage range	H	Hourly	LR	Low end range	MW	Median wage paid	TQ	Third quartile wage
AEX	Average experienced wage	AXR	Average experienced range	HI	Highest wage paid	M	Monthly	MWR	Median wage range	W	Weekly
ATC	Average total compensation	D	Daily	HR	High end range	MCC	Median cash compensation	S	See annotated source	Y	Yearly

Occupation/Type/Industry	Location	Per	Low	Mid	High	Source	Date
Tax Preparer	Nashua NECTA, NH-MA	Y	42400 FQ	46100 MW	49790 TQ	USBLS	5/07
	New Jersey	Y	29200 FQ	37680 MW	45870 TQ	USBLS	5/07
	Camden PMSA, NJ	Y	26760 FQ	29970 MW	40700 TQ	USBLS	5/07
	Edison PMSA, NJ	Y	29720 FQ	36600 MW	45710 TQ	USBLS	5/07
	Newark-Union PMSA, NJ-PA	Y	41240 FQ	44680 MW	48340 TQ	USBLS	5/07
	New Mexico	Y	22680 FQ	29180 MW	36620 TQ	USBLS	5/07
	Albuquerque MSA, NM	Y	26300 FQ	29000 MW	31690 TQ	USBLS	5/07
	New York	Y	22610 FQ	26580 MW	36860 TQ	USBLS	5/07
	Albany-Schenectady-Troy MSA, NY	Y	22250 FQ	28490 MW	32730 TQ	USBLS	5/07
	Buffalo-Niagara Falls MSA, NY	Y	21490 FQ	23440 MW	33080 TQ	USBLS	5/07
	Nassau-Suffolk PMSA, NY	Y	23850 FQ	30920 MW	39930 TQ	USBLS	5/07
	New York-Northern New Jersey-Long Island MSA, NY-NJ-PA	Y	24820 FQ	29940 MW	43400 TQ	USBLS	5/07
	North Carolina	Y	17880 FQ	24330 MW	37970 TQ	USBLS	5/07
	Charlotte-Gastonia-Concord MSA, NC-SC	Y	22440 FQ	28870 MW	37850 TQ	USBLS	5/07
	Durham MSA, NC	Y	23910 FQ	37540 MW	45830 TQ	USBLS	5/07
	Raleigh-Cary MSA, NC	Y	35130 FQ	37420 MW	39710 TQ	USBLS	5/07
	Ohio	Y	18650 FQ	23420 MW	32210 TQ	USBLS	5/07
	Cincinnati-Middletown MSA, OH-KY-IN	Y	23180 FQ	26900 MW	30840 TQ	USBLS	5/07
	Cleveland-Elyria-Mentor MSA, OH	Y	19730 FQ	31730 MW	42840 TQ	USBLS	5/07
	Columbus MSA, OH	Y	17880 FQ	21310 MW	26370 TQ	USBLS	5/07
	Dayton MSA, OH	Y	22880 FQ	27520 MW	34630 TQ	USBLS	5/07
	Oklahoma	Y	17430 FQ	23180 MW	29610 TQ	USBLS	5/07
	Oklahoma City MSA, OK	Y	16450 FQ	21080 MW	38120 TQ	USBLS	5/07
	Tulsa MSA, OK	Y	15730 FQ	19370 MW	23040 TQ	USBLS	5/07
	Oregon	H	11.52 FQ	16.95 MW	21.68 TQ	ORBLS	5/08
	Portland-Vancouver-Beaverton MSA, OR-WA	Y	26770 FQ	38650 MW	46790 TQ	USBLS	5/07
	Pennsylvania	Y	19980 FQ	26180 MW	36480 TQ	USBLS	5/07
	Allentown-Bethlehem-Easton MSA, PA-NJ	Y	21940 FQ	26970 MW	30800 TQ	USBLS	5/07
	Philadelphia-Camden-Wilmington MSA, PA-NJ-DE-MD	Y	22280 FQ	29700 MW	46890 TQ	USBLS	5/07
	Pittsburgh MSA, PA	Y	19880 FQ	29440 MW	44420 TQ	USBLS	5/07
	Rhode Island	Y	18130 FQ	25780 MW	42270 TQ	USBLS	5/07
	Providence-Fall River-Warwick MSA, RI-MA	Y	18160 FQ	26160 MW	41360 TQ	USBLS	5/07
	South Carolina	Y	19080 FQ	23990 MW	29560 TQ	USBLS	5/07
	Charleston-North Charleston MSA, SC	Y	19390 FQ	22320 MW	25670 TQ	USBLS	5/07
	Columbia MSA, SC	Y	23500 FQ	29960 MW	38960 TQ	USBLS	5/07
	South Dakota	Y	24480 FQ	28618 MW	32255 TQ	SDBLS	7/08-9/08
	Tennessee	Y	18840 FQ	25650 MW	38420 TQ	USBLS	5/07
	Memphis MSA, TN-MS-AR	Y	20380 FQ	30370 MW	51040 TQ	USBLS	5/07
	Nashville-Davidson-Murfreesboro MSA, TN	Y	18920 FQ	26770 MW	47760 TQ	USBLS	5/07
	Texas	Y	20190 FQ	25530 MW	34000 TQ	USBLS	5/07
	Austin-Round Rock MSA, TX	Y	22510 FQ	28530 MW	36720 TQ	USBLS	5/07
	Corpus Christi MSA, TX	Y	20230 FQ	22200 MW	24690 TQ	USBLS	5/07
	Dallas-Fort Worth-Arlington MSA, TX	Y	18820 FQ	26160 MW	39370 TQ	USBLS	5/07
	El Paso MSA, TX	Y	18000 FQ	26000 MW	29810 TQ	USBLS	5/07
	Houston-Sugar Land-Baytown MSA, TX	Y	21620 FQ	25860 MW	30910 TQ	USBLS	5/07
	San Antonio MSA, TX	Y	24530 FQ	27890 MW	35460 TQ	USBLS	5/07
	Utah	Y	23770 FQ	31640 MW	37720 TQ	USBLS	5/07
	Salt Lake City MSA, UT	Y	25840 FQ	29900 MW	35060 TQ	USBLS	5/07
	Vermont	Y	26600 FQ	36080 MW	53160 TQ	USBLS	5/07
	Burlington-South Burlington MSA, VT	Y	25550 FQ	43100 MW	56770 TQ	USBLS	5/07
	Virginia	Y	19720 FQ	25690 MW	36430 TQ	USBLS	5/07
	Richmond MSA, VA	Y	22900 FQ	27950 MW	42810 TQ	USBLS	5/07
	Virginia Beach-Norfolk-Newport News MSA, VA-NC	Y	18010 FQ	20740 MW	30660 TQ	USBLS	5/07
	Washington	H	11.34 FQ	13.83 MW	18.42 TQ	WABLS	3/08

AE	Average entry wage	AW	Average wage paid	FQ	First quartile wage
AER	Average entry range	AWR	Average wage range	H	Hourly
AEX	Average experienced wage	AXR	Average experienced range	HI	Highest wage paid
ATC	Average total compensation	D	Daily	HR	High end range

LO Lowest wage paid　MTC Median total compensation　TCC Total cash compensation
LR Low end range　MW Median wage paid　TQ Third quartile wage
M Monthly　MWR Median wage range　W Weekly
MCC Median cash compensation　S See annotated source　Y Yearly

Occupation/Type/Industry	Location	Per	Low	Mid	High	Source	Date
Tax Preparer	Seattle-Tacoma-Bellevue MSA, WA	Y	24080 FQ	29530 MW	38960 TQ	USBLS	5/07
	West Virginia	Y	19829 FQ	23895 MW	29701 TQ	WVBLS	7/08-9/08
	Wisconsin	Y	27390 FQ	34400 MW	40760 TQ	USBLS	5/07
	Milwaukee-Waukesha-West Allis MSA, WI	Y	30870 FQ	36260 MW	49590 TQ	USBLS	5/07
	Wyoming	Y	18068 FQ	20692 MW	25476 TQ	WYBLS	9/08
Taxi Driver and Chauffeur	Alabama	Y	13380 FQ	15760 MW	19660 TQ	USBLS	5/07
	Birmingham-Hoover MSA, AL	Y	14240 FQ	17390 MW	23220 TQ	USBLS	5/07
	Huntsville MSA, AL	Y	13040 FQ	14970 MW	20080 TQ	USBLS	5/07
	Mobile MSA, AL	Y	12830 FQ	14540 MW	18130 TQ	USBLS	5/07
	Alaska	Y	20130 FQ	23080 MW	27120 TQ	USBLS	5/07
	Anchorage MSA, AK	Y	19220 FQ	22760 MW	27020 TQ	USBLS	5/07
	Arizona	Y	16210 FQ	19350 MW	24220 TQ	USBLS	5/07
	Phoenix-Mesa-Scottsdale MSA, AZ	Y	15860 FQ	19680 MW	24770 TQ	USBLS	5/07
	Prescott MSA, AZ	Y	16310 FQ	17570 MW	19210 TQ	USBLS	5/07
	Tucson MSA, AZ	Y	17290 FQ	19500 MW	24080 TQ	USBLS	5/07
	Arkansas	Y	15580 FQ	18180 MW	21090 TQ	USBLS	5/07
	Little Rock-North Little Rock MSA, AR	Y	16970 FQ	19220 MW	22080 TQ	USBLS	5/07
	California	H	9.23 FQ	11.22 MW	14.23 TQ	CABLS	1/08-3/08
	Los Angeles-Long Beach-Glendale PMSA, CA	H	9.26 FQ	11.36 MW	14.77 TQ	CABLS	1/08-3/08
	Oakland-Fremont-Hayward MSA, CA	H	9.74 FQ	12.17 MW	15.99 TQ	CABLS	1/08-3/08
	Riverside-San Bernardino-Ontario MSA, CA	H	8.99 FQ	11.20 MW	13.92 TQ	CABLS	1/08-3/08
	Sacramento-Arden Arcade-Roseville MSA, CA	H	8.63 FQ	10.69 MW	12.66 TQ	CABLS	1/08-3/08
	San Diego-Carlsbad-San Marcos MSA, CA	H	9.17 FQ	10.71 MW	13.07 TQ	CABLS	1/08-3/08
	San Francisco-San Mateo-Redwood PMSA, CA	H	10.66 FQ	13.15 MW	16.97 TQ	CABLS	1/08-3/08
	San Jose-Sunnyvale-Santa Clara MSA, CA	H	9.09 FQ	11.37 MW	14.81 TQ	CABLS	1/08-3/08
	Santa Ana-Anaheim-Irvine PMSA, CA	Y	18460 FQ	21560 MW	25440 TQ	USBLS	5/07
	Colorado	Y	18600 FQ	22290 MW	26230 TQ	USBLS	5/07
	Denver-Aurora MSA, CO	Y	19470 FQ	22830 MW	26810 TQ	USBLS	5/07
	Connecticut	H	9.58 AE	12.85 MW		CTBLS	1/08-3/08
	Bridgeport-Stamford-Norwalk MSA, CT	Y	24010 FQ	31640 MW	40030 TQ	USBLS	5/07
	Danbury MSA, CT	Y	24190 FQ	27220 MW	29830 TQ	USBLS	5/07
	Hartford-West Hartford-East Hartford MSA, CT	Y	19980 FQ	23560 MW	28670 TQ	USBLS	5/07
	Delaware	Y	17330 FQ	20700 MW	24620 TQ	USBLS	5/07
	Dover MSA, DE	Y	17830 FQ	20810 MW	24630 TQ	USBLS	5/07
	Wilmington PMSA, DE-MD-NJ	Y	17310 FQ	20520 MW	24570 TQ	USBLS	5/07
	District of Columbia	Y	25680 FQ	29910 MW	35470 TQ	USBLS	5/07
	Washington-Arlington-Alexandria MSA, DC-VA-MD-WV	Y	20160 FQ	24820 MW	31000 TQ	USBLS	5/07
	Florida	Y	16440 FQ	19040 MW	23200 TQ	USBLS	5/07
	Fort Lauderdale-Pompano Beach-Deerfield Beach PMSA, FL	Y	18290 FQ	21430 MW	25230 TQ	USBLS	5/07
	Jacksonville MSA, FL	Y	17510 FQ	19410 MW	22000 TQ	USBLS	5/07
	Miami-Fort Lauderdale-Miami Beach MSA, FL	Y	16800 FQ	18840 MW	22950 TQ	USBLS	5/07
	Orlando-Kissimmee MSA, FL	Y	14670 FQ	18060 MW	25460 TQ	USBLS	5/07
	Tampa-St. Petersburg-Clearwater MSA, FL	Y	17310 FQ	20870 MW	23870 TQ	USBLS	5/07
	West Palm Beach-Boca Raton-Boynton Beach PMSA, FL	Y	17950 FQ	20730 MW	25760 TQ	USBLS	5/07
	Georgia	Y	14550 FQ	17290 MW	19900 TQ	USBLS	5/07
	Atlanta-Sandy Springs-Marietta MSA, GA	Y	14790 FQ	17580 MW	19910 TQ	USBLS	5/07
	Hawaii	Y	17930 FQ	23320 MW	29940 TQ	USBLS	5/07
	Honolulu MSA, HI	Y	16750 FQ	20930 MW	26360 TQ	USBLS	5/07

AE Average entry wage	**AW** Average wage paid	**FQ** First quartile wage	**LO** Lowest wage paid	**MTC** Median total compensation	**TCC** Total cash compensation
AER Average entry range	**AWR** Average wage range	**H** Hourly	**LR** Low end range	**MW** Median wage paid	**TQ** Third quartile wage
AEX Average experienced wage	**AXR** Average experienced range	**HI** Highest wage paid	**M** Monthly	**MWR** Median wage range	**W** Weekly
ATC Average total compensation	**D** Daily	**HR** High end range	**MCC** Median cash compensation	**S** See annotated source	**Y** Yearly

Occupation/Type/Industry	Location	Per	Low	Mid	High	Source	Date
Taxi Driver and Chauffeur	Idaho	Y	16260 FQ	18640 MW	22730 TQ	USBLS	5/07
	Boise City-Nampa MSA, ID	Y	17820 FQ	21010 MW	25600 TQ	USBLS	5/07
	Illinois	Y	17520 FQ	20810 MW	25250 TQ	USBLS	5/07
	Chicago-Naperville-Joliet MSA, IL-IN-WI	Y	18030 FQ	21560 MW	26700 TQ	USBLS	5/07
	Indiana	Y	15660 FQ	17970 MW	21750 TQ	USBLS	5/07
	Gary PMSA, IN	Y	14370 FQ	19860 MW	27710 TQ	USBLS	5/07
	Indianapolis-Carmel MSA, IN	Y	17010 FQ	19210 MW	23350 TQ	USBLS	5/07
	Iowa	Y	16430 FQ	18520 MW	21880 TQ	USBLS	5/07
	Des Moines-West Des Moines MSA, IA	Y	17430 FQ	19300 MW	22290 TQ	USBLS	5/07
	Waterloo-Cedar Falls MSA, IA	Y	15650 FQ	17460 MW	19930 TQ	USBLS	5/07
	Kansas	Y	16450 FQ	19250 MW	22770 TQ	USBLS	5/07
	Wichita MSA, KS	Y	16780 FQ	18300 MW	19970 TQ	USBLS	5/07
	Kentucky	Y	15979 FQ	19156 MW	23327 TQ	KYBLS	2008
	Lexington-Fayette MSA, KY	Y	14380 FQ	18280 MW	21680 TQ	USBLS	5/07
	Louisville-Jefferson County MSA, KY-IN	Y	16150 FQ	18510 MW	23410 TQ	USBLS	5/07
	Louisiana	H	7.07 FQ	8.55 MW	11.71 TQ	LABLS	1/08-3/08
	Baton Rouge MSA, LA	Y	13030 FQ	14740 MW	21900 TQ	USBLS	5/07
	Houma-Bayou Cane-Thibodaux MSA, LA	Y	17290 FQ	20430 MW	24780 TQ	USBLS	5/07
	New Orleans-Metairie-Kenner MSA, LA	Y	16620 FQ	18790 MW	25870 TQ	USBLS	5/07
	Maine	Y	17360 FQ	20400 MW	24530 TQ	USBLS	5/07
	Portland-South Portland-Biddeford MSA, ME	Y	19060 FQ	21780 MW	25590 TQ	USBLS	5/07
	Maryland	Y		22875 MW		MDBLS	3/08
	Baltimore-Towson MSA, MD	Y	18240 FQ	22030 MW	25790 TQ	USBLS	5/07
	Bethesda-Gaithersburg-Frederick PMSA, MD	Y	21040 FQ	25700 MW	30820 TQ	USBLS	5/07
	Salisbury MSA, MD	Y	19960 FQ	21810 MW	23690 TQ	USBLS	5/07
	Massachusetts	Y	19590 FQ	23190 MW	28830 TQ	USBLS	5/07
	Boston-Cambridge-Quincy NECTA, MA	Y	20300 FQ	24270 MW	30320 TQ	USBLS	5/07
	Worcester MSA, MA-CT	Y	16700 FQ	18730 MW	23360 TQ	USBLS	5/07
	Michigan	Y	17390 FQ	20010 MW	23590 TQ	USBLS	5/07
	Detroit-Warren-Livonia MSA, MI	Y	17830 FQ	20470 MW	23780 TQ	USBLS	5/07
	Grand Rapids-Wyoming MSA, MI	Y	17880 FQ	20040 MW	24150 TQ	USBLS	5/07
	Warren-Troy-Farmington Hills PMSA, MI	Y	17890 FQ	20740 MW	23630 TQ	USBLS	5/07
	Minnesota	Y	19839 FQ	23605 MW	27746 TQ	MNBLS	10/08-12/08
	Duluth-Superior MSA, MN-WI	Y	18237 FQ	22689 MW	27902 TQ	MNBLS	10/08-12/08
	Minneapolis-Saint Paul MSA, MN-WI	Y	20817 FQ	24739 MW	28952 TQ	MNBLS	10/08-12/08
	Rochester MSA, MN	Y	19734 FQ	22664 MW	25465 TQ	MNBLS	10/08-12/08
	Mississippi	Y	16110 FQ	18960 MW	22820 TQ	USBLS	5/07
	Jackson MSA, MS	Y	14340 FQ	18190 MW	24400 TQ	USBLS	5/07
	Missouri	Y	16960 FQ	20340 MW	25650 TQ	USBLS	5/07
	Kansas City MSA, MO-KS	Y	19480 FQ	22810 MW	26720 TQ	USBLS	5/07
	St. Louis MSA, MO-IL	Y	17380 FQ	21650 MW	27710 TQ	USBLS	5/07
	Montana	Y	14460 FQ	17690 MW	23700 TQ	USBLS	5/07
	Billings MSA, MT	Y	14510 FQ	19640 MW	23960 TQ	USBLS	5/07
	Nebraska	Y	16120 FQ	19490 MW	22970 TQ	USBLS	5/07
	Omaha-Council Bluffs MSA, NE-IA	Y	16370 FQ	19750 MW	23490 TQ	USBLS	5/07
	Nevada	H	10.45 FQ	12.15 MW	15.62 TQ	NVBLS	5/08
	Las Vegas-Paradise MSA, NV	H	10.54 FQ	12.27 MW	15.73 TQ	NVBLS	5/08
	New Hampshire	H	7.75 AE	11.04 MW	12.62 AEX	NHBLS	6/08
	Manchester MSA, NH	Y	19590 FQ	23620 MW	30650 TQ	USBLS	5/07
	Nashua NECTA, NH-MA	Y	14370 FQ	21170 MW	27800 TQ	USBLS	5/07
	New Jersey	Y	19240 FQ	22970 MW	29340 TQ	USBLS	5/07
	Camden PMSA, NJ	Y	19910 FQ	23800 MW	29890 TQ	USBLS	5/07
	Edison PMSA, NJ	Y	20090 FQ	22950 MW	28830 TQ	USBLS	5/07
	Newark-Union PMSA, NJ-PA	Y	18630 FQ	22040 MW	28800 TQ	USBLS	5/07
	New Mexico	Y	15650 FQ	17600 MW	21160 TQ	USBLS	5/07
	Albuquerque MSA, NM	Y	15070 FQ	17440 MW	20170 TQ	USBLS	5/07
	New York	Y	19080 FQ	23210 MW	31340 TQ	USBLS	5/07
	Albany-Schenectady-Troy MSA, NY	Y	17010 FQ	20670 MW	24990 TQ	USBLS	5/07

AE	Average entry wage	AW	Average wage paid	FQ	First quartile wage	LO	Lowest wage paid	MTC	Median total compensation	TCC	Total cash compensation
AER	Average entry range	AWR	Average wage range	H	Hourly	LR	Low end range	MW	Median wage paid	TQ	Third quartile wage
AEX	Average experienced wage	AXR	Average experienced range	HI	Highest wage paid	M	Monthly	MWR	Median wage range	W	Weekly
ATC	Average total compensation	D	Daily	HR	High end range	MCC	Median cash compensation	S	See annotated source	Y	Yearly

Occupation/Type/Industry	Location	Per	Low	Mid	High	Source	Date
Taxi Driver and Chauffeur	Buffalo-Niagara Falls MSA, NY	Y	16210 FQ	19700 MW	24450 TQ	USBLS	5/07
	Nassau-Suffolk PMSA, NY	Y	21910 FQ	27090 MW	36670 TQ	USBLS	5/07
	New York-Northern New Jersey-Long Island MSA, NY-NJ-PA	Y	20140 FQ	24240 MW	31960 TQ	USBLS	5/07
	North Carolina	Y	16830 FQ	19500 MW	23110 TQ	USBLS	5/07
	Charlotte-Gastonia-Concord MSA, NC-SC	Y	17850 FQ	20570 MW	24580 TQ	USBLS	5/07
	Durham MSA, NC	Y	16840 FQ	18900 MW	23190 TQ	USBLS	5/07
	Raleigh-Cary MSA, NC	Y	17680 FQ	19860 MW	22470 TQ	USBLS	5/07
	North Dakota	Y	13340 FQ	16250 MW	20500 TQ	USBLS	5/07
	Bismarck MSA, ND	Y	16510 FQ	18480 MW	22000 TQ	USBLS	5/07
	Fargo MSA, ND-MN	Y	13010 FQ	15140 MW	22600 TQ	USBLS	5/07
	Ohio	Y	16100 FQ	19480 MW	23180 TQ	USBLS	5/07
	Cincinnati-Middletown MSA, OH-KY-IN	Y	17810 FQ	20760 MW	23930 TQ	USBLS	5/07
	Cleveland-Elyria-Mentor MSA, OH	Y	16760 FQ	20660 MW	25450 TQ	USBLS	5/07
	Columbus MSA, OH	Y	17460 FQ	20260 MW	22720 TQ	USBLS	5/07
	Dayton MSA, OH	Y	15970 FQ	17630 MW	19940 TQ	USBLS	5/07
	Mansfield MSA, OH	Y	14980 FQ	15940 MW	19720 TQ	USBLS	5/07
	Oklahoma	Y	15860 FQ	17800 MW	20480 TQ	USBLS	5/07
	Oklahoma City MSA, OK	Y	15760 FQ	17990 MW	22190 TQ	USBLS	5/07
	Tulsa MSA, OK	Y	15330 FQ	17190 MW	19660 TQ	USBLS	5/07
	Oregon	H	8.70 FQ	9.42 MW	10.79 TQ	ORBLS	5/08
	Medford MSA, OR	Y	17630 FQ	19500 MW	22290 TQ	USBLS	5/07
	Portland-Vancouver-Beaverton MSA, OR-WA	Y	18200 FQ	20090 MW	23500 TQ	USBLS	5/07
	Pennsylvania	Y	15310 FQ	18850 MW	23400 TQ	USBLS	5/07
	Allentown-Bethlehem-Easton MSA, PA-NJ	Y	15300 FQ	19870 MW	23390 TQ	USBLS	5/07
	Erie MSA, PA	Y	17890 FQ	21520 MW	24090 TQ	USBLS	5/07
	Philadelphia-Camden-Wilmington MSA, PA-NJ-DE-MD	Y	16230 FQ	20580 MW	25850 TQ	USBLS	5/07
	Pittsburgh MSA, PA	Y	14700 FQ	17640 MW	22140 TQ	USBLS	5/07
	Reading MSA, PA	Y	17100 FQ	20970 MW	24460 TQ	USBLS	5/07
	Rhode Island	Y	20110 FQ	23490 MW	27290 TQ	USBLS	5/07
	Providence-Fall River-Warwick MSA, RI-MA	Y	20080 FQ	23460 MW	27220 TQ	USBLS	5/07
	South Carolina	Y	14780 FQ	17860 MW	21560 TQ	USBLS	5/07
	Charleston-North Charleston MSA, SC	Y	16540 FQ	19460 MW	22730 TQ	USBLS	5/07
	Columbia MSA, SC	Y	16520 FQ	18790 MW	20970 TQ	USBLS	5/07
	South Dakota	Y	18237 FQ	20573 MW	23462 TQ	SDBLS	7/08-9/08
	Sioux Falls MSA, SD	Y	18609 FQ	21413 MW	23657 TQ	SDBLS	7/08-9/08
	Tennessee	Y	14480 FQ	18610 MW	21900 TQ	USBLS	5/07
	Memphis MSA, TN-MS-AR	Y	17700 FQ	20400 MW	23050 TQ	USBLS	5/07
	Nashville-Davidson-Murfreesboro MSA, TN	Y	13730 FQ	17060 MW	19500 TQ	USBLS	5/07
	Texas	Y	14900 FQ	18110 MW	22090 TQ	USBLS	5/07
	Austin-Round Rock MSA, TX	Y	15780 FQ	23030 MW	32910 TQ	USBLS	5/07
	Dallas-Fort Worth-Arlington MSA, TX	Y	16140 FQ	18280 MW	20830 TQ	USBLS	5/07
	El Paso MSA, TX	Y	12540 FQ	14280 MW	16490 TQ	USBLS	5/07
	Houston-Sugar Land-Baytown MSA, TX	Y	17770 FQ	21090 MW	27490 TQ	USBLS	5/07
	San Antonio MSA, TX	Y	14540 FQ	17540 MW	21680 TQ	USBLS	5/07
	Utah	Y	17600 FQ	20050 MW	23530 TQ	USBLS	5/07
	St. George MSA, UT	Y	16930 FQ	18560 MW	27120 TQ	USBLS	5/07
	Salt Lake City MSA, UT	Y	18100 FQ	19900 MW	22730 TQ	USBLS	5/07
	Vermont	Y	17550 FQ	20440 MW	24050 TQ	USBLS	5/07
	Burlington-South Burlington MSA, VT	Y	17070 FQ	20400 MW	28130 TQ	USBLS	5/07
	Virginia	Y	16720 FQ	19910 MW	24340 TQ	USBLS	5/07
	Richmond MSA, VA	Y	16390 FQ	20300 MW	23510 TQ	USBLS	5/07
	Virginia Beach-Norfolk-Newport News MSA, VA-NC	Y	15610 FQ	18570 MW	22890 TQ	USBLS	5/07
	Washington	H	9.11 FQ	11.18 MW	14.10 TQ	WABLS	3/08
	Seattle-Tacoma-Bellevue MSA, WA	Y	18680 FQ	24100 MW	30210 TQ	USBLS	5/07

AE	Average entry wage	AW	Average wage paid	FQ	First quartile wage
AER	Average entry range	AWR	Average wage range	H	Hourly
AEX	Average experienced wage	AXR	Average experienced range	HI	Highest wage paid
ATC	Average total compensation	D	Daily	HR	High end range

LO　Lowest wage paid　　　MTC　Median total compensation　TCC　Total cash compensation
LR　Low end range　　　　MW　Median wage paid　　　　TQ　Third quartile wage
M　Monthly　　　　　　MWR　Median wage range　　　W　Weekly
MCC　Median cash compensation　S　See annotated source　　Y　Yearly

Occupation/Type/Industry	Location	Per	Low	Mid	High	Source	Date
Taxi Driver and Chauffeur	Spokane MSA, WA	Y	17730 FQ	19030 MW	21790 TQ	USBLS	5/07
	West Virginia	Y	14307 FQ	16098 MW	19749 TQ	WVBLS	7/08-9/08
	Charleston MSA, WV	Y	14310 FQ	17340 MW	25600 TQ	USBLS	5/07
	Parkersburg-Marietta-Vienna MSA, WV-OH	Y	13860 FQ	15260 MW	17400 TQ	USBLS	5/07
	Wisconsin	Y	16370 FQ	19150 MW	22910 TQ	USBLS	5/07
	Milwaukee-Waukesha-West Allis MSA, WI	Y	17550 FQ	21230 MW	25550 TQ	USBLS	5/07
	Wyoming	Y	17333 FQ	20684 MW	25171 TQ	WYBLS	9/08
	Cheyenne MSA, WY	Y	16569 FQ	17948 MW	19279 TQ	WYBLS	9/08
	Puerto Rico	Y	12970 FQ	14860 MW	19030 TQ	USBLS	5/07
	San Juan-Caguas-Guaynabo MSA, PR	Y	13140 FQ	15350 MW	19770 TQ	USBLS	5/07
	Virgin Islands	Y	15410 FQ	18600 MW	23120 TQ	USBLS	5/07
	Guam	Y	13240 FQ	15270 MW	17610 TQ	USBLS	5/07
Teacher							
Alief Independent School District	Houston, TX	Y	43000 LO			TEACHH	2008
Area Public Schools	Brighton, MI	Y		67024 AW		LCPP	2009
Catholic High School	Rhode Island	Y		29500 AW		RIM01	2009
Community Schools	Fowlerville, MI	Y		56734 AW		LCPP	2009
Dayton Independent School District	Houston, TX	Y	38200 LO			TEACHH	2008
Deer Park Independent School District	Houston, TX	Y	44716 LO			TEACHH	2008
District 87	Bloomington, IL	Y	34565 LO		87270 HI	PGRAPH	10/08
Public Schools	Highlands County, FL	Y	34000 LO		54000 HI	HTOD	2007-2008
Public Schools	Louisiana	Y		48500 AW		KATC	2008-2009
Public Schools	New York, NY	Y	44500 LO		100000 HI	NYT05	2009
Public Schools	Sullivan County, NY	Y		61108 AW		THREC4	2008
Public Schools	Texas	Y		47545 AW		NEAT	2008
Public Schools	Utah	Y		41000 AW		AMW	2008
State Hospital	California	Y	57828 LO		73764 HI	AFT02	3/1/08
Teacher Assistant	Alabama	Y	14360 FQ	16590 MW	18550 TQ	USBLS	5/07
	Birmingham-Hoover MSA, AL	Y	16300 FQ	17560 MW	18810 TQ	USBLS	5/07
	Mobile MSA, AL	Y	14150 FQ	16580 MW	19140 TQ	USBLS	5/07
	Alaska	Y	27500 FQ	31560 MW	38290 TQ	USBLS	5/07
	Arizona	Y	16850 FQ	20450 MW	23930 TQ	USBLS	5/07
	Phoenix-Mesa-Scottsdale MSA, AZ	Y	16860 FQ	20500 MW	23940 TQ	USBLS	5/07
	Prescott MSA, AZ	Y	16630 FQ	19950 MW	23480 TQ	USBLS	5/07
	Tucson MSA, AZ	Y	17960 FQ	21400 MW	25290 TQ	USBLS	5/07
	Arkansas	Y	14390 FQ	15740 MW	18910 TQ	USBLS	5/07
	Little Rock-North Little Rock MSA, AR	Y	15710 FQ	17890 MW	20220 TQ	USBLS	5/07
	California	Y		28806 AW		CABLS	1/08-3/08
	Los Angeles-Long Beach-Glendale PMSA, CA	Y		29595 AW		CABLS	1/08-3/08
	Oakland-Fremont-Hayward MSA, CA	Y		30815 AW		CABLS	1/08-3/08
	Riverside-San Bernardino-Ontario MSA, CA	Y		27729 AW		CABLS	1/08-3/08
	Sacramento-Arden Arcade-Roseville MSA, CA	Y		26139 MW		CABLS	1/08-3/08
	San Diego-Carlsbad-San Marcos MSA, CA	Y		28693 AW		CABLS	1/08-3/08
	San Francisco-San Mateo-Redwood PMSA, CA	Y		31205 AW		CABLS	1/08-3/08
	San Jose-Sunnyvale-Santa Clara MSA, CA	Y		30539 AW		CABLS	1/08-3/08
	Santa Ana-Anaheim-Irvine PMSA, CA	Y	25570 FQ	31530 MW	36470 TQ	USBLS	5/07
	Colorado	Y	20010 FQ	23600 MW	27610 TQ	USBLS	5/07
	Denver-Aurora MSA, CO	Y	21700 FQ	25120 MW	29120 TQ	USBLS	5/07
	Bridgeport-Stamford-Norwalk MSA, CT	Y	20300 FQ	23930 MW	31590 TQ	USBLS	5/07
	Hartford-West Hartford-East Hartford MSA, CT	Y	21500 FQ	24960 MW	30900 TQ	USBLS	5/07
	Delaware	Y	20080 FQ	27380 MW	35650 TQ	USBLS	5/07
	Wilmington PMSA, DE-MD-NJ	Y	17950 FQ	23960 MW	31790 TQ	USBLS	5/07
	District of Columbia	Y	18580 FQ	21170 MW	25220 TQ	USBLS	5/07

AE	Average entry wage	AW	Average wage paid	FQ	First quartile wage	LO	Lowest wage paid	MTC	Median total compensation	TCC	Total cash compensation
AER	Average entry range	AWR	Average wage range	H	Hourly	LR	Low end range	MW	Median wage paid	TQ	Third quartile wage
AEX	Average experienced wage	AXR	Average experienced range	HI	Highest wage paid	M	Monthly	MWR	Median wage range	W	Weekly
ATC	Average total compensation	D	Daily	HR	High end range	MCC	Median cash compensation	S	See annotated source	Y	Yearly

Occupation/Type/Industry	Location	Per	Low	Mid	High	Source	Date
Teacher Assistant	Washington-Arlington-Alexandria MSA, DC-VA-MD-WV	Y	19590 FQ	25830 MW	31870 TQ	USBLS	5/07
	Florida	Y	17820 FQ	21420 MW	25560 TQ	USBLS	5/07
	Fort Lauderdale-Pompano Beach-Deerfield Beach PMSA, FL	Y	17610 FQ	20030 MW	24010 TQ	USBLS	5/07
	Jacksonville MSA, FL	Y	17410 FQ	19920 MW	26300 TQ	USBLS	5/07
	Miami-Fort Lauderdale-Miami Beach MSA, FL	Y	17040 FQ	20060 MW	24650 TQ	USBLS	5/07
	Orlando-Kissimmee MSA, FL	Y	18830 FQ	21760 MW	24700 TQ	USBLS	5/07
	Tampa-St. Petersburg-Clearwater MSA, FL	Y	18920 FQ	22220 MW	25850 TQ	USBLS	5/07
	West Palm Beach-Boca Raton-Boynton Beach PMSA, FL	Y	14890 FQ	16870 MW	22000 TQ	USBLS	5/07
	Georgia	Y	13690 FQ	16420 MW	20490 TQ	USBLS	5/07
	Atlanta-Sandy Springs-Marietta MSA, GA	Y	14180 FQ	18030 MW	22580 TQ	USBLS	5/07
	Hawaii	Y	18130 FQ	21470 MW	24850 TQ	USBLS	5/07
	Honolulu MSA, HI	Y	17050 FQ	19280 MW	22640 TQ	USBLS	5/07
	Idaho	Y	16960 FQ	21460 MW	24400 TQ	USBLS	5/07
	Boise City-Nampa MSA, ID	Y	13840 FQ	19000 MW	23120 TQ	USBLS	5/07
	Illinois	Y	16360 FQ	20360 MW	24850 TQ	USBLS	5/07
	Chicago-Naperville-Joliet MSA, IL-IN-WI	Y	17220 FQ	20920 MW	25490 TQ	USBLS	5/07
	Indiana	Y	17620 FQ	20820 MW	24050 TQ	USBLS	5/07
	Gary PMSA, IN	Y	16960 FQ	19190 MW	21600 TQ	USBLS	5/07
	Indianapolis-Carmel MSA, IN	Y	19750 FQ	23080 MW	26930 TQ	USBLS	5/07
	Iowa	Y	15990 FQ	19180 MW	22870 TQ	USBLS	5/07
	Des Moines-West Des Moines MSA, IA	Y	15900 FQ	19170 MW	22970 TQ	USBLS	5/07
	Kansas	Y	16160 FQ	18890 MW	22720 TQ	USBLS	5/07
	Wichita MSA, KS	Y	16840 FQ	21110 MW	25340 TQ	USBLS	5/07
	Kentucky	Y	18878 FQ	22626 MW	27050 TQ	KYBLS	2008
	Louisville-Jefferson County MSA, KY-IN	Y	20220 FQ	24970 MW	30790 TQ	USBLS	5/07
	Louisiana	Y		15918 AW		LABLS	1/08-3/08
	Baton Rouge MSA, LA	Y	13430 FQ	15730 MW	18570 TQ	USBLS	5/07
	New Orleans-Metairie-Kenner MSA, LA	Y	13740 FQ	16140 MW	19620 TQ	USBLS	5/07
	Maine	Y	22080 FQ	26020 MW	30320 TQ	USBLS	5/07
	Portland-South Portland-Biddeford MSA, ME	Y	24030 FQ	27800 MW	31590 TQ	USBLS	5/07
	Maryland	Y		24600 MW		MDBLS	3/08
	Baltimore-Towson MSA, MD	Y	18720 FQ	23070 MW	28030 TQ	USBLS	5/07
	Bethesda-Gaithersburg-Frederick PMSA, MD	Y	18370 FQ	24940 MW	30680 TQ	USBLS	5/07
	Massachusetts	Y	18900 FQ	23280 MW	28840 TQ	USBLS	5/07
	Boston-Cambridge-Quincy NECTA, MA	Y	19460 FQ	23590 MW	29180 TQ	USBLS	5/07
	New Bedford MSA, MA	Y	18330 FQ	22880 MW	27920 TQ	USBLS	5/07
	Worcester MSA, MA-CT	Y	18620 FQ	23460 MW	28980 TQ	USBLS	5/07
	Michigan	Y	18450 FQ	23280 MW	28350 TQ	USBLS	5/07
	Detroit-Warren-Livonia MSA, MI	Y	18690 FQ	24220 MW	28890 TQ	USBLS	5/07
	Grand Rapids-Wyoming MSA, MI	Y	19550 FQ	24970 MW	29800 TQ	USBLS	5/07
	Warren-Troy-Farmington Hills PMSA, MI	Y	20550 FQ	24760 MW	29390 TQ	USBLS	5/07
	Minnesota	Y	20955 FQ	25862 MW	31093 TQ	MNBLS	10/08-12/08
	Duluth-Superior MSA, MN-WI	Y	22891 FQ	27944 MW	32997 TQ	MNBLS	10/08-12/08
	Minneapolis-Saint Paul MSA, MN-WI	Y	20945 FQ	26500 MW	31533 TQ	MNBLS	10/08-12/08
	Rochester MSA, MN	Y	20465 FQ	24342 MW	29435 TQ	MNBLS	10/08-12/08
	Mississippi	Y	12890 FQ	14570 MW	16800 TQ	USBLS	5/07
	Jackson MSA, MS	Y	12930 FQ	14720 MW	17530 TQ	USBLS	5/07
	Missouri	Y	15290 FQ	18600 MW	23830 TQ	USBLS	5/07
	Kansas City MSA, MO-KS	Y	16030 FQ	19270 MW	23400 TQ	USBLS	5/07
	St. Louis MSA, MO-IL	Y	16000 FQ	20690 MW	26080 TQ	USBLS	5/07
	Montana	Y	15750 FQ	18180 MW	21190 TQ	USBLS	5/07
	Billings MSA, MT	Y	16740 FQ	18690 MW	20560 TQ	USBLS	5/07
	Missoula MSA, MT	Y	16160 FQ	18140 MW	20500 TQ	USBLS	5/07

AE	Average entry wage	AW	Average wage paid	FQ	First quartile wage
AER	Average entry range	AWR	Average wage range	H	Hourly
AEX	Average experienced wage	AXR	Average experienced range	HI	Highest wage paid
ATC	Average total compensation	D	Daily	HR	High end range

LO	Lowest wage paid	MTC	Median total compensation	TCC	Total cash compensation
LR	Low end range	MW	Median wage paid	TQ	Third quartile wage
M	Monthly	MWR	Median wage range	W	Weekly
MCC	Median cash compensation	S	See annotated source	Y	Yearly

Occupation/Type/Industry	Location	Per	Low	Mid	High	Source	Date
Teacher Assistant	Nebraska	Y	17130 FQ	19390 MW	22590 TQ	USBLS	5/07
	Omaha-Council Bluffs MSA, NE-IA	Y	17340 FQ	19340 MW	22380 TQ	USBLS	5/07
	Nevada	Y	23327 FQ	27148 MW	30348 TQ	NVBLS	5/08
	Las Vegas-Paradise MSA, NV	Y	23264 FQ	26653 MW	29567 TQ	NVBLS	5/08
	Reno-Sparks MSA, NV	Y	24372 FQ	28525 MW	31754 TQ	NVBLS	5/08
	New Hampshire	Y	18634 AE	25050 MW	28036 AEX	NHBLS	6/08
	Manchester MSA, NH	Y	19710 FQ	24070 MW	27980 TQ	USBLS	5/07
	Nashua NECTA, NH-MA	Y	20290 FQ	24850 MW	28680 TQ	USBLS	5/07
	Portsmouth MSA, NH-ME	Y	21080 FQ	25870 MW	29530 TQ	USBLS	5/07
	Rochester-Dover MSA, NH-ME	Y	18610 FQ	22720 MW	26590 TQ	USBLS	5/07
	New Jersey	Y	18800 FQ	23120 MW	28820 TQ	USBLS	5/07
	Camden PMSA, NJ	Y	17710 FQ	21740 MW	25660 TQ	USBLS	5/07
	Edison PMSA, NJ	Y	19500 FQ	24180 MW	31330 TQ	USBLS	5/07
	Newark-Union PMSA, NJ-PA	Y	18190 FQ	22710 MW	27720 TQ	USBLS	5/07
	Ocean City MSA, NJ	Y	18840 FQ	22590 MW	27000 TQ	USBLS	5/07
	New Mexico	Y	13610 FQ	16450 MW	21980 TQ	USBLS	5/07
	Albuquerque MSA, NM	Y	14210 FQ	17930 MW	22810 TQ	USBLS	5/07
	New York	Y	18260 FQ	23220 MW	29390 TQ	USBLS	5/07
	Albany-Schenectady-Troy MSA, NY	Y	17360 FQ	21970 MW	30040 TQ	USBLS	5/07
	Buffalo-Niagara Falls MSA, NY	Y	17390 FQ	21640 MW	27570 TQ	USBLS	5/07
	Nassau-Suffolk PMSA, NY	Y	18770 FQ	24280 MW	30140 TQ	USBLS	5/07
	New York-Northern New Jersey-Long Island MSA, NY-NJ-PA	Y	19780 FQ	24590 MW	30430 TQ	USBLS	5/07
	North Carolina	Y	16870 FQ	18850 MW	21680 TQ	USBLS	5/07
	Charlotte-Gastonia-Concord MSA, NC-SC	Y	17200 FQ	19720 MW	23100 TQ	USBLS	5/07
	Durham MSA, NC	Y	18400 FQ	21470 MW	24000 TQ	USBLS	5/07
	Raleigh-Cary MSA, NC	Y	16540 FQ	18410 MW	20510 TQ	USBLS	5/07
	North Dakota	Y	20980 FQ	24780 MW	29650 TQ	USBLS	5/07
	Fargo MSA, ND-MN	Y	21000 FQ	25560 MW	29640 TQ	USBLS	5/07
	Ohio	Y	20340 FQ	25670 MW	30580 TQ	USBLS	5/07
	Cincinnati-Middletown MSA, OH-KY-IN	Y	20410 FQ	25280 MW	30230 TQ	USBLS	5/07
	Cleveland-Elyria-Mentor MSA, OH	Y	22990 FQ	28630 MW	34230 TQ	USBLS	5/07
	Columbus MSA, OH	Y	22080 FQ	27240 MW	32340 TQ	USBLS	5/07
	Dayton MSA, OH	Y	19240 FQ	24770 MW	29930 TQ	USBLS	5/07
	Oklahoma	Y	13180 FQ	15070 MW	18820 TQ	USBLS	5/07
	Oklahoma City MSA, OK	Y	13010 FQ	14720 MW	17950 TQ	USBLS	5/07
	Tulsa MSA, OK	Y	13990 FQ	17390 MW	22420 TQ	USBLS	5/07
	Oregon	Y	21707 FQ	26218 MW	30901 TQ	ORBLS	5/08
	Portland-Vancouver-Beaverton MSA, OR-WA	Y	22290 FQ	27180 MW	31350 TQ	USBLS	5/07
	Pennsylvania	Y	15570 FQ	19010 MW	23590 TQ	USBLS	5/07
	Allentown-Bethlehem-Easton MSA, PA-NJ	Y	15730 FQ	19090 MW	23800 TQ	USBLS	5/07
	Philadelphia-Camden-Wilmington MSA, PA-NJ-DE-MD	Y	16580 FQ	20460 MW	25510 TQ	USBLS	5/07
	Pittsburgh MSA, PA	Y	14930 FQ	18030 MW	22920 TQ	USBLS	5/07
	Rhode Island	Y	20750 FQ	25580 MW	30560 TQ	USBLS	5/07
	Providence-Fall River-Warwick MSA, RI-MA	Y	19930 FQ	25060 MW	30190 TQ	USBLS	5/07
	South Carolina	Y	14000 FQ	16720 MW	19720 TQ	USBLS	5/07
	Charleston-North Charleston MSA, SC	Y	16000 FQ	18720 MW	22820 TQ	USBLS	5/07
	Columbia MSA, SC	Y	14540 FQ	17240 MW	19990 TQ	USBLS	5/07
	South Dakota	Y	18737 FQ	22025 MW	25732 TQ	SDBLS	7/08-9/08
	Sioux Falls MSA, SD	Y	18937 FQ	22538 MW	26823 TQ	SDBLS	7/08-9/08
	Tennessee	Y	14300 FQ	18040 MW	22120 TQ	USBLS	5/07
	Memphis MSA, TN-MS-AR	Y	14760 FQ	19510 MW	23580 TQ	USBLS	5/07
	Nashville-Davidson-Murfreesboro MSA, TN	Y	16350 FQ	20500 MW	23180 TQ	USBLS	5/07
	Texas	Y	14120 FQ	17120 MW	20550 TQ	USBLS	5/07
	Austin-Round Rock MSA, TX	Y	18050 FQ	21340 MW	24640 TQ	USBLS	5/07
	Corpus Christi MSA, TX	Y	14620 FQ	17580 MW	20110 TQ	USBLS	5/07

AE	Average entry wage	AW	Average wage paid	FQ	First quartile wage
AER	Average entry range	AWR	Average wage range	H	Hourly
AEX	Average experienced wage	AXR	Average experienced range	HI	Highest wage paid
ATC	Average total compensation	D	Daily	HR	High end range

LO	Lowest wage paid	MTC	Median total compensation	TCC	Total cash compensation
LR	Low end range	MW	Median wage paid	TQ	Third quartile wage
M	Monthly	MWR	Median wage range	W	Weekly
MCC	Median cash compensation	S	See annotated source	Y	Yearly

Occupation/Type/Industry	Location	Per	Low	Mid	High	Source	Date
Teacher Assistant	Dallas-Fort Worth-Arlington						
	MSA, TX	Y	14850 FQ	18010 MW	21990 TQ	USBLS	5/07
	El Paso MSA, TX	Y	17390 FQ	20880 MW	24450 TQ	USBLS	5/07
	Houston-Sugar Land-Baytown						
	MSA, TX	Y	14620 FQ	17330 MW	19870 TQ	USBLS	5/07
	San Antonio MSA, TX	Y	14720 FQ	17720 MW	20270 TQ	USBLS	5/07
	Utah	Y	17440 FQ	20840 MW	24550 TQ	USBLS	5/07
	Ogden-Clearfield MSA, UT	Y	20520 FQ	22900 MW	25400 TQ	USBLS	5/07
	Salt Lake City MSA, UT	Y	16980 FQ	20320 MW	24250 TQ	USBLS	5/07
	Vermont	Y	19950 FQ	23130 MW	26790 TQ	USBLS	5/07
	Burlington-South Burlington						
	MSA, VT	Y	19840 FQ	22860 MW	26140 TQ	USBLS	5/07
	Virginia	Y	16380 FQ	21250 MW	27660 TQ	USBLS	5/07
	Lynchburg MSA, VA	Y	12980 FQ	14730 MW	19980 TQ	USBLS	5/07
	Richmond MSA, VA	Y	16060 FQ	21040 MW	25370 TQ	USBLS	5/07
	Virginia Beach-Norfolk-						
	Newport News MSA, VA-NC	Y	16570 FQ	21860 MW	25930 TQ	USBLS	5/07
	Washington	Y		27717 AW		WABLS	3/08
	Seattle-Tacoma-Bellevue						
	MSA, WA	Y	25030 FQ	28520 MW	32130 TQ	USBLS	5/07
	West Virginia	Y	18185 FQ	22006 MW	25399 TQ	WVBLS	7/08-9/08
	Charleston MSA, WV	Y	16890 FQ	22030 MW	24990 TQ	USBLS	5/07
	Wisconsin	Y	20730 FQ	24240 MW	29350 TQ	USBLS	5/07
	Milwaukee-Waukesha-West						
	Allis MSA, WI	Y	22420 FQ	27100 MW	32780 TQ	USBLS	5/07
	Racine MSA, WI	Y	17930 FQ	21310 MW	25190 TQ	USBLS	5/07
	Wyoming	Y	18041 FQ	22534 MW	25963 TQ	WYBLS	9/08
	Cheyenne MSA, WY	Y	21704 FQ	23805 MW	25905 TQ	WYBLS	9/08
	Puerto Rico	Y	12790 FQ	14520 MW	16830 TQ	USBLS	5/07
	San Juan-Caguas-Guaynabo						
	MSA, PR	Y	12840 FQ	14630 MW	17080 TQ	USBLS	5/07
	Virgin Islands	Y	19450 FQ	26800 MW	32670 TQ	USBLS	5/07
	Guam	Y	15390 FQ	17450 MW	19130 TQ	USBLS	5/07
Teacher's Aide	Lake County, FL	Y			9000 HI	OSENT	2008
Team Assembler	Alabama	Y	19580 FQ	25330 MW	35830 TQ	USBLS	5/07
	Birmingham-Hoover MSA, AL	Y	15890 FQ	19430 MW	26160 TQ	USBLS	5/07
	Alaska	Y	24090 FQ	31570 MW	38350 TQ	USBLS	5/07
	Anchorage MSA, AK	Y	24040 FQ	29650 MW	37990 TQ	USBLS	5/07
	Arizona	Y	18110 FQ	22150 MW	28120 TQ	USBLS	5/07
	Phoenix-Mesa-Scottsdale						
	MSA, AZ	Y	17930 FQ	21920 MW	28330 TQ	USBLS	5/07
	Tucson MSA, AZ	Y	19080 FQ	22670 MW	26690 TQ	USBLS	5/07
	Arkansas	Y	19790 FQ	23670 MW	29780 TQ	USBLS	5/07
	Little Rock-North Little Rock						
	MSA, AR	Y	22570 FQ	29360 MW	35540 TQ	USBLS	5/07
	California	H	9.15 FQ	11.31 MW	14.33 TQ	CABLS	1/08-3/08
	Los Angeles-Long Beach-						
	Glendale PMSA, CA	H	8.59 FQ	10.09 MW	13.29 TQ	CABLS	1/08-3/08
	Oakland-Fremont-Hayward						
	MSA, CA	H	10.24 FQ	13.13 MW	17.27 TQ	CABLS	1/08-3/08
	Riverside-San Bernardino-						
	Ontario MSA, CA	H	9.03 FQ	10.97 MW	13.30 TQ	CABLS	1/08-3/08
	Sacramento-Arden Arcade-						
	Roseville MSA, CA	H	9.99 FQ	12.05 MW	14.88 TQ	CABLS	1/08-3/08
	San Diego-Carlsbad-San						
	Marcos MSA, CA	H	9.35 FQ	11.23 MW	13.83 TQ	CABLS	1/08-3/08
	San Francisco-San Mateo-						
	Redwood PMSA, CA	H	12.24 FQ	15.97 MW	19.00 TQ	CABLS	1/08-3/08
	San Jose-Sunnyvale-Santa						
	Clara MSA, CA	H	11.08 FQ	13.61 MW	16.46 TQ	CABLS	1/08-3/08
	Santa Ana-Anaheim-Irvine						
	PMSA, CA	Y	18730 FQ	22800 MW	28550 TQ	USBLS	5/07
	Colorado	Y	19780 FQ	24700 MW	29440 TQ	USBLS	5/07
	Denver-Aurora MSA, CO	Y	20290 FQ	25040 MW	29480 TQ	USBLS	5/07
	Connecticut	H	9.83 AE	13.84 MW		CTBLS	1/08-3/08
	Bridgeport-Stamford-Norwalk						
	MSA, CT	Y	19950 FQ	24700 MW	32660 TQ	USBLS	5/07
	Hartford-West Hartford-East						
	Hartford MSA, CT	Y	24480 FQ	31440 MW	37620 TQ	USBLS	5/07

AE	Average entry wage	AW	Average wage paid	FQ	First quartile wage
AER	Average entry range	AWR	Average wage range	H	Hourly
AEX	Average experienced wage	AXR	Average experienced range	HI	Highest wage paid
ATC	Average total compensation	D	Daily	HR	High end range

LO	Lowest wage paid	MTC	Median total compensation	TCC	Total cash compensation
LR	Low end range	MW	Median wage paid	TQ	Third quartile wage
M	Monthly	MWR	Median wage range	W	Weekly
MCC	Median cash compensation	S	See annotated source	Y	Yearly

Occupation/Type/Industry	Location	Per	Low	Mid	High	Source	Date
Team Assembler	Norwich-New London MSA, CT-RI	Y	21440 FQ	25890 MW	30590 TQ	USBLS	5/07
	Delaware	Y	26160 FQ	32190 MW	35870 TQ	USBLS	5/07
	Wilmington PMSA, DE-MD-NJ	Y	26940 FQ	32520 MW	36100 TQ	USBLS	5/07
	Washington-Arlington-Alexandria MSA, DC-VA-MD-WV	Y	20960 FQ	25100 MW	32220 TQ	USBLS	5/07
	Florida	Y	18190 FQ	22230 MW	27950 TQ	USBLS	5/07
	Fort Lauderdale-Pompano Beach-Deerfield Beach PMSA, FL	Y	18260 FQ	22200 MW	28200 TQ	USBLS	5/07
	Jacksonville MSA, FL	Y	19800 FQ	24220 MW	29980 TQ	USBLS	5/07
	Lakeland MSA, FL	Y	16150 FQ	20280 MW	24820 TQ	USBLS	5/07
	Miami-Fort Lauderdale-Miami Beach MSA, FL	Y	17030 FQ	20820 MW	26530 TQ	USBLS	5/07
	Orlando-Kissimmee MSA, FL	Y	17500 FQ	22350 MW	28940 TQ	USBLS	5/07
	Tampa-St. Petersburg-Clearwater MSA, FL	Y	18990 FQ	23000 MW	29510 TQ	USBLS	5/07
	West Palm Beach-Boca Raton-Boynton Beach PMSA, FL	Y	19230 FQ	23670 MW	32500 TQ	USBLS	5/07
	Georgia	Y	18880 FQ	23610 MW	29700 TQ	USBLS	5/07
	Atlanta-Sandy Springs-Marietta MSA, GA	Y	18180 FQ	22280 MW	28310 TQ	USBLS	5/07
	Macon MSA, GA	Y	24140 FQ	30150 MW	36840 TQ	USBLS	5/07
	Hawaii	Y	22260 FQ	29440 MW	38500 TQ	USBLS	5/07
	Honolulu MSA, HI	Y	21120 FQ	26660 MW	38760 TQ	USBLS	5/07
	Idaho	Y	20050 FQ	25310 MW	30680 TQ	USBLS	5/07
	Boise City-Nampa MSA, ID	Y	20650 FQ	25180 MW	30020 TQ	USBLS	5/07
	Illinois	Y	17210 FQ	22590 MW	29650 TQ	USBLS	5/07
	Chicago-Naperville-Joliet MSA, IL-IN-WI	Y	16050 FQ	20670 MW	27740 TQ	USBLS	5/07
	Indiana	Y	22010 FQ	27920 MW	34980 TQ	USBLS	5/07
	Gary PMSA, IN	Y	18750 FQ	28820 MW	35950 TQ	USBLS	5/07
	Indianapolis-Carmel MSA, IN	Y	21290 FQ	25720 MW	31060 TQ	USBLS	5/07
	Iowa	Y	21210 FQ	26860 MW	35190 TQ	USBLS	5/07
	Des Moines-West Des Moines MSA, IA	Y	21440 FQ	28630 MW	36760 TQ	USBLS	5/07
	Kansas	Y	19850 FQ	25390 MW	32480 TQ	USBLS	5/07
	Wichita MSA, KS	Y	18430 FQ	26690 MW	36660 TQ	USBLS	5/07
	Kentucky	Y	21542 FQ	27390 MW	33562 TQ	KYBLS	2008
	Louisville-Jefferson County MSA, KY-IN	Y	23130 FQ	29460 MW	36590 TQ	USBLS	5/07
	Owensboro MSA, KY	Y	24360 FQ	33990 MW	45110 TQ	USBLS	5/07
	Louisiana	H	9.21 FQ	11.69 MW	15.84 TQ	LABLS	1/08-3/08
	Baton Rouge MSA, LA	Y	21790 FQ	28930 MW	37770 TQ	USBLS	5/07
	Lafayette MSA, LA	Y	19610 FQ	23130 MW	29750 TQ	USBLS	5/07
	New Orleans-Metairie-Kenner MSA, LA	Y	19810 FQ	24560 MW	31150 TQ	USBLS	5/07
	Maine	Y	20830 FQ	23730 MW	28380 TQ	USBLS	5/07
	Portland-South Portland-Biddeford MSA, ME	Y	21770 FQ	24190 MW	28130 TQ	USBLS	5/07
	Maryland	Y		26325 MW		MDBLS	3/08
	Baltimore-Towson MSA, MD	Y	20060 FQ	25180 MW	35110 TQ	USBLS	5/07
	Bethesda-Gaithersburg-Frederick PMSA, MD	Y	20370 FQ	23710 MW	30780 TQ	USBLS	5/07
	Hagerstown-Martinsburg MSA, MD-WV	Y	25990 FQ	29920 MW	34110 TQ	USBLS	5/07
	Massachusetts	Y	21490 FQ	26580 MW	32760 TQ	USBLS	5/07
	Boston-Cambridge-Quincy NECTA, MA	Y	22450 FQ	27400 MW	33580 TQ	USBLS	5/07
	Worcester MSA, MA-CT	Y	22280 FQ	26280 MW	32120 TQ	USBLS	5/07
	Michigan	Y	20440 FQ	25900 MW	31710 TQ	USBLS	5/07
	Detroit-Warren-Livonia MSA, MI	Y	20780 FQ	25840 MW	33020 TQ	USBLS	5/07
	Grand Rapids-Wyoming MSA, MI	Y	22230 FQ	28480 MW	33830 TQ	USBLS	5/07
	Muskegon-Norton Shores MSA, MI	Y	18300 FQ	22140 MW	29990 TQ	USBLS	5/07
	Warren-Troy-Farmington Hills PMSA, MI	Y	21160 FQ	25850 MW	32220 TQ	USBLS	5/07
	Minnesota	Y	22734 FQ	26932 MW	33557 TQ	MNBLS	10/08-12/08

AE   Average entry wage   AW   Average wage paid   FQ   First quartile wage   LO   Lowest wage paid   MTC   Median total compensation   TCC   Total cash compensation
AER   Average entry range   AWR   Average wage range   H   Hourly   LR   Low end range   MW   Median wage paid   TQ   Third quartile wage
AEX   Average experienced wage   AXR   Average experienced range HI   Highest wage paid   M   Monthly   MWR   Median wage range   W   Weekly
ATC   Average total compensation D Daily   HR   High end range   MCC   Median cash compensation S   See annotated source   Y   Yearly

1574

Occupation/Type/Industry	Location	Per	Low	Mid	High	Source	Date
Team Assembler	Duluth-Superior MSA, MN-WI	Y	17167 FQ	19728 MW	22962 TQ	MNBLS	10/08-12/08
	Minneapolis-Saint Paul MSA, MN-WI	Y	22931 FQ	27243 MW	35350 TQ	MNBLS	10/08-12/08
	Rochester MSA, MN	Y	21293 FQ	24932 MW	33062 TQ	MNBLS	10/08-12/08
	Mississippi	Y	18250 FQ	22090 MW	26630 TQ	USBLS	5/07
	Jackson MSA, MS	Y	16560 FQ	20680 MW	25200 TQ	USBLS	5/07
	Missouri	Y	19230 FQ	23970 MW	30930 TQ	USBLS	5/07
	Kansas City MSA, MO-KS	Y	20580 FQ	26490 MW	35680 TQ	USBLS	5/07
	St. Louis MSA, MO-IL	Y	20690 FQ	25720 MW	32150 TQ	USBLS	5/07
	Montana	Y	20290 FQ	23340 MW	28830 TQ	USBLS	5/07
	Billings MSA, MT	Y	19430 FQ	22840 MW	27360 TQ	USBLS	5/07
	Nebraska	Y	23000 FQ	28030 MW	33940 TQ	USBLS	5/07
	Omaha-Council Bluffs MSA, NE-IA	Y	21830 FQ	30750 MW	38140 TQ	USBLS	5/07
	Nevada	H	10.07 FQ	11.96 MW	14.39 TQ	NVBLS	5/08
	Las Vegas-Paradise MSA, NV	H	9.90 FQ	12.04 MW	14.42 TQ	NVBLS	5/08
	New Hampshire	H	10.15 AE	13.28 MW	16.01 AEX	NHBLS	6/08
	Manchester MSA, NH	Y	23570 FQ	29660 MW	43020 TQ	USBLS	5/07
	Nashua NECTA, NH-MA	Y	22050 FQ	27640 MW	33490 TQ	USBLS	5/07
	New Jersey	Y	18660 FQ	24830 MW	30820 TQ	USBLS	5/07
	Camden PMSA, NJ	Y	17900 FQ	23450 MW	29270 TQ	USBLS	5/07
	Edison PMSA, NJ	Y	20530 FQ	26720 MW	32150 TQ	USBLS	5/07
	Newark-Union PMSA, NJ-PA	Y	16670 FQ	23630 MW	30510 TQ	USBLS	5/07
	New Mexico	Y	16780 FQ	19520 MW	24340 TQ	USBLS	5/07
	Albuquerque MSA, NM	Y	17280 FQ	20890 MW	27360 TQ	USBLS	5/07
	New York	Y	17310 FQ	22220 MW	29420 TQ	USBLS	5/07
	Albany-Schenectady-Troy MSA, NY	Y	20260 FQ	22940 MW	28520 TQ	USBLS	5/07
	Buffalo-Niagara Falls MSA, NY	Y	20680 FQ	25770 MW	31540 TQ	USBLS	5/07
	Nassau-Suffolk PMSA, NY	Y	15810 FQ	19560 MW	28220 TQ	USBLS	5/07
	New York-Northern New Jersey-Long Island MSA, NY-NJ-PA	Y	16850 FQ	22380 MW	30000 TQ	USBLS	5/07
	Utica-Rome MSA, NY	Y	16560 FQ	22820 MW	27780 TQ	USBLS	5/07
	North Carolina	Y	19550 FQ	24200 MW	30890 TQ	USBLS	5/07
	Charlotte-Gastonia-Concord MSA, NC-SC	Y	20820 FQ	25650 MW	32540 TQ	USBLS	5/07
	Raleigh-Cary MSA, NC	Y	18590 FQ	23520 MW	31410 TQ	USBLS	5/07
	North Dakota	Y	21350 FQ	25110 MW	31110 TQ	USBLS	5/07
	Fargo MSA, ND-MN	Y	21340 FQ	24520 MW	30700 TQ	USBLS	5/07
	Ohio	Y	20910 FQ	26190 MW	33000 TQ	USBLS	5/07
	Canton-Massillon MSA, OH	Y	17250 FQ	24360 MW	32540 TQ	USBLS	5/07
	Cincinnati-Middletown MSA, OH-KY-IN	Y	21200 FQ	26270 MW	33810 TQ	USBLS	5/07
	Cleveland-Elyria-Mentor MSA, OH	Y	20790 FQ	26090 MW	33820 TQ	USBLS	5/07
	Columbus MSA, OH	Y	19050 FQ	24180 MW	33270 TQ	USBLS	5/07
	Dayton MSA, OH	Y	20430 FQ	23520 MW	28120 TQ	USBLS	5/07
	Oklahoma	Y	18620 FQ	22950 MW	29030 TQ	USBLS	5/07
	Oklahoma City MSA, OK	Y	19130 FQ	23060 MW	28500 TQ	USBLS	5/07
	Tulsa MSA, OK	Y	19060 FQ	23600 MW	30290 TQ	USBLS	5/07
	Oregon	H	10.80 FQ	13.14 MW	15.34 TQ	ORBLS	5/08
	Portland-Vancouver-Beaverton MSA, OR-WA	Y	21430 FQ	26240 MW	32870 TQ	USBLS	5/07
	Pennsylvania	Y	21150 FQ	26840 MW	34430 TQ	USBLS	5/07
	Allentown-Bethlehem-Easton MSA, PA-NJ	Y	25310 FQ	34920 MW	43740 TQ	USBLS	5/07
	Philadelphia-Camden-Wilmington MSA, PA-NJ-DE-MD	Y	21860 FQ	28460 MW	36080 TQ	USBLS	5/07
	Pittsburgh MSA, PA	Y	19350 FQ	23910 MW	29990 TQ	USBLS	5/07
	Reading MSA, PA	Y	23170 FQ	28170 MW	32310 TQ	USBLS	5/07
	Rhode Island	Y	17290 FQ	21720 MW	28410 TQ	USBLS	5/07
	Providence-Fall River-Warwick MSA, RI-MA	Y	17230 FQ	21700 MW	28360 TQ	USBLS	5/07
	South Carolina	Y	20390 FQ	26260 MW	33160 TQ	USBLS	5/07
	Charleston-North Charleston MSA, SC	Y	19770 FQ	27830 MW	33570 TQ	USBLS	5/07
	Columbia MSA, SC	Y	19870 FQ	26420 MW	32000 TQ	USBLS	5/07
	South Dakota	Y	19993 FQ	23157 MW	26288 TQ	SDBLS	7/08-9/08
	Sioux Falls MSA, SD	Y	21420 FQ	24642 MW	28084 TQ	SDBLS	7/08-9/08

AE	Average entry wage	AW	Average wage paid	FQ	First quartile wage
AER	Average entry range	AWR	Average wage range	H	Hourly
AEX	Average experienced wage	AXR	Average experienced range	HI	Highest wage paid
ATC	Average total compensation	D	Daily	HR	High end range

LO	Lowest wage paid	MTC	Median total compensation
LR	Low end range	MW	Median wage paid
M	Monthly	MWR	Median wage range
MCC	Median cash compensation	S	See annotated source

TCC	Total cash compensation
TQ	Third quartile wage
W	Weekly
Y	Yearly

Occupation/Type/Industry	Location	Per	Low	Mid	High	Source	Date
Team Assembler	Tennessee	Y	20830 FQ	26610 MW	32820 TQ	USBLS	5/07
	Memphis MSA, TN-MS-AR	Y	19490 FQ	24510 MW	31790 TQ	USBLS	5/07
	Nashville-Davidson- Murfreesboro MSA, TN	Y	22620 FQ	32080 MW	54180 TQ	USBLS	5/07
	Texas	Y	16820 FQ	20550 MW	25880 TQ	USBLS	5/07
	Austin-Round Rock MSA, TX	Y	18800 FQ	22950 MW	28110 TQ	USBLS	5/07
	Dallas-Fort Worth-Arlington MSA, TX	Y	16840 FQ	20650 MW	25700 TQ	USBLS	5/07
	El Paso MSA, TX	Y	12770 FQ	14490 MW	17560 TQ	USBLS	5/07
	Houston-Sugar Land-Baytown MSA, TX	Y	17170 FQ	20520 MW	24970 TQ	USBLS	5/07
	San Antonio MSA, TX	Y	16060 FQ	20940 MW	33040 TQ	USBLS	5/07
	Utah	Y	19860 FQ	23780 MW	29190 TQ	USBLS	5/07
	Provo-Orem MSA, UT	Y	19520 FQ	22250 MW	24910 TQ	USBLS	5/07
	Salt Lake City MSA, UT	Y	19300 FQ	23920 MW	29700 TQ	USBLS	5/07
	Vermont	Y	22390 FQ	27030 MW	32510 TQ	USBLS	5/07
	Burlington-South Burlington MSA, VT	Y	26120 FQ	32510 MW	39210 TQ	USBLS	5/07
	Virginia	Y	20070 FQ	24770 MW	30700 TQ	USBLS	5/07
	Richmond MSA, VA	Y	18180 FQ	22620 MW	28390 TQ	USBLS	5/07
	Virginia Beach-Norfolk- Newport News MSA, VA-NC	Y	17810 FQ	21690 MW	28160 TQ	USBLS	5/07
	Washington	H	9.89 FQ	12.46 MW	15.83 TQ	WABLS	3/08
	Seattle-Tacoma-Bellevue MSA, WA	Y	20020 FQ	26840 MW	34320 TQ	USBLS	5/07
	West Virginia	Y	19052 FQ	25481 MW	38824 TQ	WVBLS	7/08-9/08
	Charleston MSA, WV	Y	38930 FQ	45230 MW	49820 TQ	USBLS	5/07
	Wisconsin	Y	21340 FQ	26310 MW	33380 TQ	USBLS	5/07
	Milwaukee-Waukesha-West Allis MSA, WI	Y	23040 FQ	28100 MW	34770 TQ	USBLS	5/07
	Wyoming	Y	18479 FQ	27213 MW	31091 TQ	WYBLS	9/08
	Cheyenne MSA, WY	Y	26126 FQ	28421 MW	30745 TQ	WYBLS	9/08
	Puerto Rico	Y	14270 FQ	16870 MW	18840 TQ	USBLS	5/07
	San Juan-Caguas-Guaynabo MSA, PR	Y	14390 FQ	17180 MW	19210 TQ	USBLS	5/07
Technical Sergeant U.S. Air Force, Active Duty, Pay Grade E-6	United States	M	2176 LO		3370 HI	DOD1	2009
Technical Systems Analyst Municipal Government	Cincinnati, OH	Y	60699 LO		81574 HI	COHSS	10/08
Technical Trainer	United States	Y		65452 AW		COWRLD	5/20/08-7/25/08
Technical Writer	Alabama	Y	41000 FQ	51000 MW	60450 TQ	USBLS	5/07
	Birmingham-Hoover MSA, AL	Y	32570 FQ	44290 MW	55120 TQ	USBLS	5/07
	Montgomery MSA, AL	Y	44510 FQ	51010 MW	60000 TQ	USBLS	5/07
	Alaska	Y	48200 FQ	57010 MW	64690 TQ	USBLS	5/07
	Anchorage MSA, AK	Y	52230 FQ	59320 MW	65750 TQ	USBLS	5/07
	Arizona	Y	47850 FQ	58910 MW	68010 TQ	USBLS	5/07
	Phoenix-Mesa-Scottsdale MSA, AZ	Y	48510 FQ	59560 MW	68340 TQ	USBLS	5/07
	Tucson MSA, AZ	Y	45170 FQ	56050 MW	66410 TQ	USBLS	5/07
	Arkansas	Y	27240 FQ	42950 MW	52420 TQ	USBLS	5/07
	Little Rock-North Little Rock MSA, AR	Y	42500 FQ	48580 MW	59230 TQ	USBLS	5/07
	California	H	28.11 FQ	36.23 MW	45.78 TQ	CABLS	1/08-3/08
	Los Angeles-Long Beach- Glendale PMSA, CA	H	26.97 FQ	33.69 MW	45.30 TQ	CABLS	1/08-3/08
	Oakland-Fremont-Hayward MSA, CA	H	30.09 FQ	37.86 MW	46.12 TQ	CABLS	1/08-3/08
	Riverside-San Bernardino- Ontario MSA, CA	H	23.27 FQ	32.02 MW	38.91 TQ	CABLS	1/08-3/08
	Sacramento-Arden Arcade- Roseville MSA, CA	H	24.85 FQ	29.27 MW	35.19 TQ	CABLS	1/08-3/08
	San Diego-Carlsbad-San Marcos MSA, CA	H	28.42 FQ	34.78 MW	40.80 TQ	CABLS	1/08-3/08
	San Francisco-San Mateo- Redwood PMSA, CA	H	30.35 FQ	39.81 MW	48.53 TQ	CABLS	1/08-3/08
	San Jose-Sunnyvale-Santa Clara MSA, CA	H	36.25 FQ	44.21 MW	52.61 TQ	CABLS	1/08-3/08

AE Average entry wage	**AW** Average wage paid	**FQ** First quartile wage	**LO** Lowest wage paid	**MTC** Median total compensation	**TCC** Total cash compensation
AER Average entry range	**AWR** Average wage range	**H** Hourly	**LR** Low end range	**MW** Median wage paid	**TQ** Third quartile wage
AEX Average experienced wage	**AXR** Average experienced range	**HI** Highest wage paid	**M** Monthly	**MWR** Median wage range	**W** Weekly
ATC Average total compensation	**D** Daily	**HR** High end range	**MCC** Median cash compensation	**S** See annotated source	**Y** Yearly

Occupation/Type/Industry	Location	Per	Low	Mid	High	Source	Date
Technical Writer	Santa Ana-Anaheim-Irvine PMSA, CA	Y	47820 FQ	63610 MW	78410 TQ	USBLS	5/07
	Colorado	Y	47980 FQ	61290 MW	76210 TQ	USBLS	5/07
	Denver-Aurora MSA, CO	Y	52110 FQ	64060 MW	77510 TQ	USBLS	5/07
	Connecticut	H	21.16 AE	28.82 MW		CTBLS	1/08-3/08
	Bridgeport-Stamford-Norwalk MSA, CT	Y	52060 FQ	64440 MW	76140 TQ	USBLS	5/07
	Hartford-West Hartford-East Hartford MSA, CT	Y	47060 FQ	54890 MW	67670 TQ	USBLS	5/07
	Delaware	Y	44710 FQ	59380 MW	69240 TQ	USBLS	5/07
	Wilmington PMSA, DE-MD-NJ	Y	46790 FQ	60080 MW	69330 TQ	USBLS	5/07
	District of Columbia	Y	49610 FQ	63720 MW	79580 TQ	USBLS	5/07
	Washington-Arlington-Alexandria MSA, DC-VA-MD-WV	Y	53950 FQ	66150 MW	80200 TQ	USBLS	5/07
	Florida	Y	45610 FQ	58570 MW	72650 TQ	USBLS	5/07
	Fort Lauderdale-Pompano Beach-Deerfield Beach PMSA, FL	Y	50390 FQ	62860 MW	74350 TQ	USBLS	5/07
	Jacksonville MSA, FL	Y	43290 FQ	54090 MW	61640 TQ	USBLS	5/07
	Miami-Fort Lauderdale-Miami Beach MSA, FL	Y	46110 FQ	58860 MW	70550 TQ	USBLS	5/07
	Orlando-Kissimmee MSA, FL	Y	46770 FQ	56670 MW	64010 TQ	USBLS	5/07
	Tampa-St. Petersburg-Clearwater MSA, FL	Y	57340 FQ	74180 MW	82780 TQ	USBLS	5/07
	West Palm Beach-Boca Raton-Boynton Beach PMSA, FL	Y	52430 FQ	59420 MW	67160 TQ	USBLS	5/07
	Georgia	Y	49350 FQ	64200 MW	79550 TQ	USBLS	5/07
	Atlanta-Sandy Springs-Marietta MSA, GA	Y	48890 FQ	59490 MW	74550 TQ	USBLS	5/07
	Idaho	Y	40900 FQ	50060 MW	61750 TQ	USBLS	5/07
	Boise City-Nampa MSA, ID	Y	42120 FQ	51390 MW	65900 TQ	USBLS	5/07
	Illinois	Y	53380 FQ	65840 MW	77820 TQ	USBLS	5/07
	Chicago-Naperville-Joliet MSA, IL-IN-WI	Y	55350 FQ	67950 MW	79640 TQ	USBLS	5/07
	Indiana	Y	44160 FQ	53900 MW	66380 TQ	USBLS	5/07
	Indianapolis-Carmel MSA, IN	Y	47790 FQ	56710 MW	70320 TQ	USBLS	5/07
	Iowa	Y	38910 FQ	47400 MW	57680 TQ	USBLS	5/07
	Des Moines-West Des Moines MSA, IA	Y	38570 FQ	44390 MW	50460 TQ	USBLS	5/07
	Kansas	Y	42140 FQ	49800 MW	59100 TQ	USBLS	5/07
	Wichita MSA, KS	Y	44390 FQ	50800 MW	58580 TQ	USBLS	5/07
	Kentucky	Y	39736 FQ	52786 MW	64200 TQ	KYBLS	2008
	Lexington-Fayette MSA, KY	Y	33960 FQ	48160 MW	60830 TQ	USBLS	5/07
	Louisville-Jefferson County MSA, KY-IN	Y	37430 FQ	51280 MW	61700 TQ	USBLS	5/07
	Louisiana	H	16.80 FQ	21.48 MW	26.92 TQ	LABLS	1/08-3/08
	New Orleans-Metairie-Kenner MSA, LA	Y	40790 FQ	52980 MW	66020 TQ	USBLS	5/07
	Maine	Y	36210 FQ	46060 MW	58180 TQ	USBLS	5/07
	Maryland	Y		65725 MW		MDBLS	3/08
	Baltimore-Towson MSA, MD	Y	52240 FQ	62050 MW	75290 TQ	USBLS	5/07
	Bethesda-Gaithersburg-Frederick PMSA, MD	Y	56610 FQ	67610 MW	81940 TQ	USBLS	5/07
	Massachusetts	Y	57030 FQ	72460 MW	90070 TQ	USBLS	5/07
	Boston-Cambridge-Quincy NECTA, MA	Y	56870 FQ	71540 MW	89540 TQ	USBLS	5/07
	Springfield MSA, MA-CT	Y	38860 FQ	54770 MW	65260 TQ	USBLS	5/07
	Worcester MSA, MA-CT	Y	56900 FQ	68690 MW	78220 TQ	USBLS	5/07
	Michigan	Y	46180 FQ	58090 MW	74710 TQ	USBLS	5/07
	Detroit-Warren-Livonia MSA, MI	Y	49220 FQ	61160 MW	76970 TQ	USBLS	5/07
	Grand Rapids-Wyoming MSA, MI	Y	48410 FQ	58440 MW	70750 TQ	USBLS	5/07
	Warren-Troy-Farmington Hills PMSA, MI	Y	49420 FQ	61730 MW	77170 TQ	USBLS	5/07
	Minnesota	Y	51484 FQ	62114 MW	75495 TQ	MNBLS	10/08-12/08
	Duluth-Superior MSA, MN-WI	Y	55910 FQ	62522 MW	73905 TQ	MNBLS	10/08-12/08
	Minneapolis-Saint Paul MSA, MN-WI	Y	53378 FQ	63621 MW	77117 TQ	MNBLS	10/08-12/08
	Rochester MSA, MN	Y	50083 FQ	57822 MW	66252 TQ	MNBLS	10/08-12/08

AE	Average entry wage	AW	Average wage paid	FQ	First quartile wage	LO	Lowest wage paid	MTC	Median total compensation	TCC	Total cash compensation
AER	Average entry range	AWR	Average wage range	H	Hourly	LR	Low end range	MW	Median wage paid	TQ	Third quartile wage
AEX	Average experienced wage	AXR	Average experienced range	HI	Highest wage paid	M	Monthly	MWR	Median wage range	W	Weekly
ATC	Average total compensation	D	Daily	HR	High end range	MCC	Median cash compensation	S	See annotated source	Y	Yearly

Occupation/Type/Industry	Location	Per	Low	Mid	High	Source	Date
Technical Writer	Mississippi	Y	42640 FQ	50670 MW	60040 TQ	USBLS	5/07
	Missouri	Y	43920 FQ	55330 MW	67410 TQ	USBLS	5/07
	Kansas City MSA, MO-KS	Y	42180 FQ	51460 MW	66030 TQ	USBLS	5/07
	St. Louis MSA, MO-IL	Y	48720 FQ	57830 MW	68630 TQ	USBLS	5/07
	Montana	Y	28410 FQ	45850 MW	59010 TQ	USBLS	5/07
	Nebraska	Y	36090 FQ	45540 MW	58520 TQ	USBLS	5/07
	Omaha-Council Bluffs MSA, NE-IA	Y	40160 FQ	51740 MW	61720 TQ	USBLS	5/07
	Nevada	H	23.04 FQ	29.03 MW	46.85 TQ	NVBLS	5/08
	Las Vegas-Paradise MSA, NV	H	23.32 FQ	29.09 MW	39.34 TQ	NVBLS	5/08
	New Hampshire	H	24.36 AE	33.11 MW	39.73 AEX	NHBLS	6/08
	Nashua NECTA, NH-MA	Y	66790 FQ	82950 MW	97320 TQ	USBLS	5/07
	New Jersey	Y	46520 FQ	61840 MW	78450 TQ	USBLS	5/07
	Camden PMSA, NJ	Y	46320 FQ	58090 MW	65470 TQ	USBLS	5/07
	Edison PMSA, NJ	Y	37890 FQ	60270 MW	77470 TQ	USBLS	5/07
	Newark-Union PMSA, NJ-PA	Y	54120 FQ	63800 MW	80090 TQ	USBLS	5/07
	Trenton-Ewing MSA, NJ	Y	53970 FQ	64710 MW	78580 TQ	USBLS	5/07
	New Mexico	Y	42460 FQ	59720 MW	77300 TQ	USBLS	5/07
	Albuquerque MSA, NM	Y	42400 FQ	60900 MW	82190 TQ	USBLS	5/07
	New York	Y	44560 FQ	59830 MW	77200 TQ	USBLS	5/07
	Albany-Schenectady-Troy MSA, NY	Y	45620 FQ	53370 MW	74280 TQ	USBLS	5/07
	Binghamton MSA, NY	Y	33280 FQ	42640 MW	51590 TQ	USBLS	5/07
	Buffalo-Niagara Falls MSA, NY	Y	40810 FQ	58450 MW	76870 TQ	USBLS	5/07
	Nassau-Suffolk PMSA, NY	Y	49020 FQ	61300 MW	73310 TQ	USBLS	5/07
	New York-Northern New Jersey-Long Island MSA, NY-NJ-PA	Y	47620 FQ	64430 MW	82000 TQ	USBLS	5/07
	Syracuse MSA, NY	Y	40840 FQ	54290 MW	66900 TQ	USBLS	5/07
	North Carolina	Y	44580 FQ	58460 MW	73560 TQ	USBLS	5/07
	Charlotte-Gastonia-Concord MSA, NC-SC	Y	45270 FQ	60780 MW	80480 TQ	USBLS	5/07
	Raleigh-Cary MSA, NC	Y	50450 FQ	64110 MW	77280 TQ	USBLS	5/07
	North Dakota	Y	41360 FQ	46760 MW	56250 TQ	USBLS	5/07
	Ohio	Y	43040 FQ	54370 MW	64860 TQ	USBLS	5/07
	Cincinnati-Middletown MSA, OH-KY-IN	Y	45760 FQ	55410 MW	63940 TQ	USBLS	5/07
	Cleveland-Elyria-Mentor MSA, OH	Y	36660 FQ	49140 MW	60900 TQ	USBLS	5/07
	Columbus MSA, OH	Y	53480 FQ	62010 MW	77310 TQ	USBLS	5/07
	Dayton MSA, OH	Y	41520 FQ	49520 MW	57250 TQ	USBLS	5/07
	Oklahoma	Y	34350 FQ	48250 MW	63780 TQ	USBLS	5/07
	Oklahoma City MSA, OK	Y	31090 FQ	47570 MW	62480 TQ	USBLS	5/07
	Tulsa MSA, OK	Y	40900 FQ	49120 MW	65140 TQ	USBLS	5/07
	Oregon	H	23.18 FQ	30.14 MW	37.47 TQ	ORBLS	5/08
	Eugene-Springfield MSA, OR	Y	34770 FQ	38150 MW	45180 TQ	USBLS	5/07
	Portland-Vancouver-Beaverton MSA, OR-WA	Y	52360 FQ	67440 MW	79220 TQ	USBLS	5/07
	Pennsylvania	Y	41730 FQ	57170 MW	70510 TQ	USBLS	5/07
	Allentown-Bethlehem-Easton MSA, PA-NJ	Y	55360 FQ	76970 MW	96710 TQ	USBLS	5/07
	Philadelphia-Camden-Wilmington MSA, PA-NJ-DE-MD	Y	48380 FQ	60790 MW	73950 TQ	USBLS	5/07
	Pittsburgh MSA, PA	Y	40300 FQ	51590 MW	63680 TQ	USBLS	5/07
	Rhode Island	Y	31850 FQ	40070 MW	60420 TQ	USBLS	5/07
	Providence-Fall River-Warwick MSA, RI-MA	Y	32680 FQ	47460 MW	60950 TQ	USBLS	5/07
	South Carolina	Y	42380 FQ	51330 MW	63680 TQ	USBLS	5/07
	Charleston-North Charleston MSA, SC	Y	44600 FQ	54790 MW	63940 TQ	USBLS	5/07
	Columbia MSA, SC	Y	43090 FQ	48770 MW	57850 TQ	USBLS	5/07
	South Dakota	Y	38086 FQ	45106 MW	52460 TQ	SDBLS	7/08-9/08
	Sioux Falls MSA, SD	Y	37913 FQ	43767 MW	51208 TQ	SDBLS	7/08-9/08
	Tennessee	Y	42630 FQ	52770 MW	64500 TQ	USBLS	5/07
	Memphis MSA, TN-MS-AR	Y	44290 FQ	54910 MW	65820 TQ	USBLS	5/07
	Nashville-Davidson-Murfreesboro MSA, TN	Y	35650 FQ	45440 MW	53270 TQ	USBLS	5/07
	Texas	Y	41510 FQ	53260 MW	66860 TQ	USBLS	5/07
	Austin-Round Rock MSA, TX	Y	41600 FQ	53360 MW	69190 TQ	USBLS	5/07

AE	Average entry wage	AW	Average wage paid	FQ	First quartile wage	LO	Lowest wage paid	MTC	Median total compensation	TCC	Total cash compensation
AER	Average entry range	AWR	Average wage range	H	Hourly	LR	Low end range	MW	Median wage paid	TQ	Third quartile wage
AEX	Average experienced wage	AXR	Average experienced range	HI	Highest wage paid	M	Monthly	MWR	Median wage range	W	Weekly
ATC	Average total compensation	D	Daily	HR	High end range	MCC	Median cash compensation	S	See annotated source	Y	Yearly

Occupation/Type/Industry	Location	Per	Low	Mid	High	Source	Date
Technical Writer	Dallas-Fort Worth-Arlington MSA, TX	Y	43370 FQ	56720 MW	72720 TQ	USBLS	5/07
	El Paso MSA, TX	Y	28100 FQ	44690 MW	70870 TQ	USBLS	5/07
	Houston-Sugar Land-Baytown MSA, TX	Y	42960 FQ	51800 MW	63920 TQ	USBLS	5/07
	San Antonio MSA, TX	Y	33980 FQ	48180 MW	59290 TQ	USBLS	5/07
	Utah	Y	41380 FQ	51070 MW	63740 TQ	USBLS	5/07
	Salt Lake City MSA, UT	Y	43280 FQ	56670 MW	68570 TQ	USBLS	5/07
	Vermont	Y	35200 FQ	47340 MW	61530 TQ	USBLS	5/07
	Burlington-South Burlington MSA, VT	Y	39770 FQ	47650 MW	59630 TQ	USBLS	5/07
	Virginia	Y	49660 FQ	63320 MW	78240 TQ	USBLS	5/07
	Richmond MSA, VA	Y	46830 FQ	61700 MW	78990 TQ	USBLS	5/07
	Virginia Beach-Norfolk-Newport News MSA, VA-NC	Y	44120 FQ	53350 MW	69760 TQ	USBLS	5/07
	Washington	H	27.96 FQ	35.81 MW	43.75 TQ	WABLS	3/08
	Bremerton-Silverdale MSA, WA	Y	41880 FQ	60660 MW	78000 TQ	USBLS	5/07
	Seattle-Tacoma-Bellevue MSA, WA	Y	61340 FQ	75880 MW	91380 TQ	USBLS	5/07
	West Virginia	Y	36405 FQ	42081 MW	55426 TQ	WVBLS	7/08-9/08
	Wisconsin	Y	44200 FQ	52660 MW	61300 TQ	USBLS	5/07
	Milwaukee-Waukesha-West Allis MSA, WI	Y	45510 FQ	53070 MW	60180 TQ	USBLS	5/07
	Puerto Rico	Y	30600 FQ	38200 MW	50120 TQ	USBLS	5/07
	San Juan-Caguas-Guaynabo MSA, PR	Y	31430 FQ	40640 MW	63950 TQ	USBLS	5/07
Technician/Lab Support Coatings Industry	United States	Y		46000 ATC		CWRLD01	2008
Telecommunication Linewire Worker Municipal Government	Cincinnati, OH	Y	41597 LO		44936 HI	COHSS	10/08
Telecommunications Equipment Installer and Repairer							
Except Line Installer	Alabama	Y	35360 FQ	48840 MW	57870 TQ	USBLS	5/07
Except Line Installer	Birmingham-Hoover MSA, AL	Y	47150 FQ	56020 MW	60880 TQ	USBLS	5/07
Except Line Installer	Mobile MSA, AL	Y	42970 FQ	47390 MW	52430 TQ	USBLS	5/07
Except Line Installer	Tuscaloosa MSA, AL	Y	34920 FQ	44560 MW	55920 TQ	USBLS	5/07
Except Line Installer	Alaska	Y	42590 FQ	58570 MW	71730 TQ	USBLS	5/07
Except Line Installer	Anchorage MSA, AK	Y	38700 FQ	59590 MW	72660 TQ	USBLS	5/07
Except Line Installer	Arizona	Y	41880 FQ	51990 MW	58140 TQ	USBLS	5/07
Except Line Installer	Phoenix-Mesa-Scottsdale MSA, AZ	Y	37010 FQ	49750 MW	57310 TQ	USBLS	5/07
Except Line Installer	Tucson MSA, AZ	Y	52080 FQ	56050 MW	60160 TQ	USBLS	5/07
Except Line Installer	Arkansas	Y	30560 FQ	44050 MW	56360 TQ	USBLS	5/07
Except Line Installer	Little Rock-North Little Rock MSA, AR	Y	30290 FQ	42620 MW	56170 TQ	USBLS	5/07
Except Line Installer	California	H	24.84 FQ	28.21 MW	31.05 TQ	CABLS	1/08-3/08
Except Line Installer	Los Angeles-Long Beach-Glendale PMSA, CA	H	25.20 FQ	28.57 MW	31.43 TQ	CABLS	1/08-3/08
Except Line Installer	Oakland-Fremont-Hayward MSA, CA	H	24.50 FQ	27.93 MW	30.68 TQ	CABLS	1/08-3/08
Except Line Installer	Oxnard-Thousand Oaks-Ventura MSA, CA	H	20.07 FQ	25.58 MW	29.16 TQ	CABLS	1/08-3/08
Except Line Installer	Riverside-San Bernardino-Ontario MSA, CA	H	18.81 FQ	26.15 MW	28.83 TQ	CABLS	1/08-3/08
Except Line Installer	Sacramento-Arden Arcade-Roseville MSA, CA	H	26.64 FQ	28.60 MW	30.65 TQ	CABLS	1/08-3/08
Except Line Installer	San Diego-Carlsbad-San Marcos MSA, CA	H	25.79 FQ	28.56 MW	31.15 TQ	CABLS	1/08-3/08
Except Line Installer	San Francisco-San Mateo-Redwood PMSA, CA	H	27.12 FQ	30.25 MW	32.95 TQ	CABLS	1/08-3/08
Except Line Installer	San Jose-Sunnyvale-Santa Clara MSA, CA	H	18.30 FQ	27.33 MW	30.85 TQ	CABLS	1/08-3/08
Except Line Installer	Santa Ana-Anaheim-Irvine PMSA, CA	Y	48230 FQ	57560 MW	63790 TQ	USBLS	5/07
Except Line Installer	Colorado	Y	48810 FQ	55520 MW	60900 TQ	USBLS	5/07
Except Line Installer	Denver-Aurora MSA, CO	Y	50040 FQ	56320 MW	61820 TQ	USBLS	5/07
Except Line Installer	Connecticut	H	17.02 FQ	24.19 MW		CTBLS	1/08-3/08

AE Average entry wage	**AW** Average wage paid	**FQ** First quartile wage	**LO** Lowest wage paid	**MTC** Median total compensation	**TCC** Total cash compensation
AER Average entry range	**AWR** Average wage range	**H** Hourly	**LR** Low end range	**MW** Median wage paid	**TQ** Third quartile wage
AEX Average experienced wage	**AXR** Average experienced range	**HI** Highest wage paid	**M** Monthly	**MWR** Median wage range	**W** Weekly
ATC Average total compensation	**D** Daily	**HR** High end range	**MCC** Median cash compensation	**S** See annotated source	**Y** Yearly

Occupation/Type/Industry	Location	Per	Low	Mid	High	Source	Date
Telecommunications Equipment Installer and Repairer							
Except Line Installer	Bridgeport-Stamford-Norwalk MSA, CT	Y	41970 FQ	49890 MW	60420 TQ	USBLS	5/07
Except Line Installer	Hartford-West Hartford-East Hartford MSA, CT	Y	42470 FQ	54890 MW	64770 TQ	USBLS	5/07
Except Line Installer	Delaware	Y	19580 FQ	36790 MW	50300 TQ	USBLS	5/07
Except Line Installer	Wilmington PMSA, DE-MD-NJ	Y	18650 FQ	45550 MW	57750 TQ	USBLS	5/07
Except Line Installer	District of Columbia	Y	54640 FQ	63300 MW	69900 TQ	USBLS	5/07
Except Line Installer	Florida	Y	34850 FQ	49200 MW	57650 TQ	USBLS	5/07
Except Line Installer	Fort Lauderdale-Pompano Beach-Deerfield Beach PMSA, FL	Y	45720 FQ	53090 MW	58150 TQ	USBLS	5/07
Except Line Installer	Jacksonville MSA, FL	Y	46530 FQ	53560 MW	58520 TQ	USBLS	5/07
Except Line Installer	Miami-Fort Lauderdale-Miami Beach MSA, FL	Y	36360 FQ	52110 MW	58960 TQ	USBLS	5/07
Except Line Installer	Orlando-Kissimmee MSA, FL	Y	29990 FQ	41870 MW	54010 TQ	USBLS	5/07
Except Line Installer	Tampa-St. Petersburg-Clearwater MSA, FL	Y	27090 FQ	44360 MW	54600 TQ	USBLS	5/07
Except Line Installer	West Palm Beach-Boca Raton-Boynton Beach PMSA, FL	Y	29510 FQ	38380 MW	51730 TQ	USBLS	5/07
Except Line Installer	Georgia	Y	42170 FQ	52110 MW	59570 TQ	USBLS	5/07
Except Line Installer	Atlanta-Sandy Springs-Marietta MSA, GA	Y	42680 FQ	52790 MW	60030 TQ	USBLS	5/07
Except Line Installer	Augusta-Richmond County MSA, GA-SC	Y	44280 FQ	53240 MW	59280 TQ	USBLS	5/07
Except Line Installer	Hawaii	Y	41860 FQ	53040 MW	60860 TQ	USBLS	5/07
Except Line Installer	Honolulu MSA, HI	Y	43600 FQ	53960 MW	61820 TQ	USBLS	5/07
Except Line Installer	Idaho	Y	47810 FQ	54820 MW	59770 TQ	USBLS	5/07
Except Line Installer	Boise City-Nampa MSA, ID	Y	31720 FQ	51520 MW	58200 TQ	USBLS	5/07
Except Line Installer	Illinois	Y	50590 FQ	59680 MW	66950 TQ	USBLS	5/07
Except Line Installer	Chicago-Naperville-Joliet MSA, IL-IN-WI	Y	51930 FQ	60000 MW	66810 TQ	USBLS	5/07
Except Line Installer	Peoria MSA, IL	Y	27470 FQ	38400 MW	69710 TQ	USBLS	5/07
Except Line Installer	Indiana	Y	43610 FQ	51330 MW	58800 TQ	USBLS	5/07
Except Line Installer	Gary PMSA, IN	Y	55770 FQ	60420 MW	64300 TQ	USBLS	5/07
Except Line Installer	Indianapolis-Carmel MSA, IN	Y	45050 FQ	50990 MW	57550 TQ	USBLS	5/07
Except Line Installer	South Bend-Mishawaka MSA, IN-MI	Y	44640 FQ	50880 MW	64580 TQ	USBLS	5/07
Except Line Installer	Iowa	Y	37990 FQ	49050 MW	55540 TQ	USBLS	5/07
Except Line Installer	Des Moines-West Des Moines MSA, IA	Y	45610 FQ	50680 MW	55860 TQ	USBLS	5/07
Except Line Installer	Kansas	Y	40730 FQ	48130 MW	54890 TQ	USBLS	5/07
Except Line Installer	Wichita MSA, KS	Y	43760 FQ	48210 MW	53500 TQ	USBLS	5/07
Except Line Installer	Kentucky	Y	38854 FQ	54895 MW	61278 TQ	KYBLS	2008
Except Line Installer	Louisville-Jefferson County MSA, KY-IN	Y	32290 FQ	53550 MW	59510 TQ	USBLS	5/07
Except Line Installer	Louisiana	H	15.14 FQ	22.46 MW	26.87 TQ	LABLS	1/08-3/08
Except Line Installer	Baton Rouge MSA, LA	Y	39910 FQ	48560 MW	56770 TQ	USBLS	5/07
Except Line Installer	Lafayette MSA, LA	Y	44170 FQ	51570 MW	56100 TQ	USBLS	5/07
Except Line Installer	New Orleans-Metairie-Kenner MSA, LA	Y	28430 FQ	42850 MW	52550 TQ	USBLS	5/07
Except Line Installer	Maine	Y	30160 FQ	41650 MW	55770 TQ	USBLS	5/07
Except Line Installer	Portland-South Portland-Biddeford MSA, ME	Y	27620 FQ	38720 MW	51210 TQ	USBLS	5/07
Except Line Installer	Maryland	Y		53075 MW		MDBLS	3/08
Except Line Installer	Baltimore-Towson MSA, MD	Y	39110 FQ	44570 MW	55200 TQ	USBLS	5/07
Except Line Installer	Massachusetts	Y	49090 FQ	62100 MW	71020 TQ	USBLS	5/07
Except Line Installer	Boston-Cambridge-Quincy NECTA, MA	Y	50050 FQ	61960 MW	71260 TQ	USBLS	5/07
Except Line Installer	Worcester MSA, MA-CT	Y	45790 FQ	57140 MW	67980 TQ	USBLS	5/07
Except Line Installer	Michigan	Y	48360 FQ	55870 MW	62430 TQ	USBLS	5/07
Except Line Installer	Detroit-Warren-Livonia MSA, MI	Y	49870 FQ	56960 MW	63980 TQ	USBLS	5/07
Except Line Installer	Grand Rapids-Wyoming MSA, MI	Y	38140 FQ	50650 MW	57250 TQ	USBLS	5/07
Except Line Installer	Lansing-East Lansing MSA, MI	Y	48320 FQ	54060 MW	60220 TQ	USBLS	5/07
Except Line Installer	Warren-Troy-Farmington Hills PMSA, MI	Y	45140 FQ	53190 MW	59060 TQ	USBLS	5/07
Except Line Installer	Minnesota	Y	48597 FQ	56642 MW	62569 TQ	MNBLS	10/08-12/08
Except Line Installer	Duluth-Superior MSA, MN-WI	Y	49845 FQ	57765 MW	63576 TQ	MNBLS	10/08-12/08

AE	Average entry wage	AW	Average wage paid	FQ	First quartile wage	LO	Lowest wage paid	MTC Median total compensation TCC Total cash compensation
AER	Average entry range	AWR	Average wage range	H	Hourly	LR	Low end range	MW Median wage paid TQ Third quartile wage
AEX	Average experienced wage	AXR	Average experienced range	HI	Highest wage paid	M	Monthly	MWR Median wage range W Weekly
ATC	Average total compensation	D	Daily	HR	High end range	MCC	Median cash compensation	S See annotated source Y Yearly

Occupation/Type/Industry	Location	Per	Low	Mid	High	Source	Date
Telecommunications Equipment Installer and Repairer							
Except Line Installer	Minneapolis-Saint Paul MSA, MN-WI	Y	49247 FQ	57251 MW	63429 TQ	MNBLS	10/08-12/08
Except Line Installer	Rochester MSA, MN	Y	35829 FQ	54139 MW	59446 TQ	MNBLS	10/08-12/08
Except Line Installer	Mississippi	Y	42210 FQ	53930 MW	60570 TQ	USBLS	5/07
Except Line Installer	Jackson MSA, MS	Y	41040 FQ	46570 MW	57280 TQ	USBLS	5/07
Except Line Installer	Missouri	Y	42850 FQ	51560 MW	58930 TQ	USBLS	5/07
Except Line Installer	Kansas City MSA, MO-KS	Y	39920 FQ	49980 MW	57230 TQ	USBLS	5/07
Except Line Installer	St. Louis MSA, MO-IL	Y	44250 FQ	51480 MW	59840 TQ	USBLS	5/07
Except Line Installer	Montana	Y	41430 FQ	53440 MW	58520 TQ	USBLS	5/07
Except Line Installer	Billings MSA, MT	Y	54530 FQ	58440 MW	62440 TQ	USBLS	5/07
Except Line Installer	Nebraska	Y	38460 FQ	50140 MW	56920 TQ	USBLS	5/07
Except Line Installer	Lincoln MSA, NE	Y	34570 FQ	39810 MW	45320 TQ	USBLS	5/07
Except Line Installer	Omaha-Council Bluffs MSA, NE-IA	Y	38690 FQ	51620 MW	57830 TQ	USBLS	5/07
Except Line Installer	Nevada	H	14.10 FQ	18.49 MW	25.08 TQ	NVBLS	5/08
Except Line Installer	Las Vegas-Paradise MSA, NV	H	14.26 FQ	18.10 MW	23.71 TQ	NVBLS	5/08
Except Line Installer	Reno-Sparks MSA, NV	H	7.06 FQ	21.52 MW	26.68 TQ	NVBLS	5/08
Except Line Installer	New Hampshire	H	16.43 AE	22.85 MW	28.62 AEX	NHBLS	6/08
Except Line Installer	Manchester MSA, NH	Y	61230 FQ	66570 MW	71800 TQ	USBLS	5/07
Except Line Installer	Nashua NECTA, NH-MA	Y	34630 FQ	38830 MW	54770 TQ	USBLS	5/07
Except Line Installer	New Jersey	Y	50280 FQ	58500 MW	65770 TQ	USBLS	5/07
Except Line Installer	Camden PMSA, NJ	Y	46690 FQ	58470 MW	66540 TQ	USBLS	5/07
Except Line Installer	Edison PMSA, NJ	Y	49060 FQ	58250 MW	65530 TQ	USBLS	5/07
Except Line Installer	Newark-Union PMSA, NJ-PA	Y	52130 FQ	59470 MW	65990 TQ	USBLS	5/07
Except Line Installer	New Mexico	Y	48920 FQ	55020 MW	59690 TQ	USBLS	5/07
Except Line Installer	Albuquerque MSA, NM	Y	50740 FQ	55270 MW	59610 TQ	USBLS	5/07
Except Line Installer	New York	Y	46830 FQ	64560 MW	73250 TQ	USBLS	5/07
Except Line Installer	Albany-Schenectady-Troy MSA, NY	Y	55740 FQ	70220 MW	76530 TQ	USBLS	5/07
Except Line Installer	Buffalo-Niagara Falls MSA, NY	Y	40570 FQ	46220 MW	57970 TQ	USBLS	5/07
Except Line Installer	Nassau-Suffolk PMSA, NY	Y	36680 FQ	66640 MW	74310 TQ	USBLS	5/07
Except Line Installer	New York-Northern New Jersey-Long Island MSA, NY-NJ-PA	Y	51760 FQ	63150 MW	72310 TQ	USBLS	5/07
Except Line Installer	North Carolina	Y	47180 FQ	54290 MW	59320 TQ	USBLS	5/07
Except Line Installer	Charlotte-Gastonia-Concord MSA, NC-SC	Y	40910 FQ	53980 MW	59820 TQ	USBLS	5/07
Except Line Installer	Raleigh-Cary MSA, NC	Y	43540 FQ	52580 MW	59300 TQ	USBLS	5/07
Except Line Installer	North Dakota	Y	47910 FQ	54830 MW	59720 TQ	USBLS	5/07
Except Line Installer	Fargo MSA, ND-MN	Y	49900 FQ	55210 MW	59680 TQ	USBLS	5/07
Except Line Installer	Ohio	Y	45120 FQ	53700 MW	60250 TQ	USBLS	5/07
Except Line Installer	Cincinnati-Middletown MSA, OH-KY-IN	Y	43560 FQ	52830 MW	59150 TQ	USBLS	5/07
Except Line Installer	Cleveland-Elyria-Mentor MSA, OH	Y	49160 FQ	55400 MW	60640 TQ	USBLS	5/07
Except Line Installer	Columbus MSA, OH	Y	44600 FQ	51110 MW	58890 TQ	USBLS	5/07
Except Line Installer	Dayton MSA, OH	Y	28870 FQ	51780 MW	59880 TQ	USBLS	5/07
Except Line Installer	Oklahoma	Y	36770 FQ	49300 MW	57930 TQ	USBLS	5/07
Except Line Installer	Oklahoma City MSA, OK	Y	32550 FQ	45730 MW	57320 TQ	USBLS	5/07
Except Line Installer	Tulsa MSA, OK	Y	43930 FQ	52190 MW	59650 TQ	USBLS	5/07
Except Line Installer	Oregon	H	23.70 FQ	26.67 MW	29.02 TQ	ORBLS	5/08
Except Line Installer	Eugene-Springfield MSA, OR	Y	52600 FQ	56310 MW	60270 TQ	USBLS	5/07
Except Line Installer	Medford MSA, OR	Y	42980 FQ	46300 MW	49620 TQ	USBLS	5/07
Except Line Installer	Portland-Vancouver-Beaverton MSA, OR-WA	Y	50890 FQ	55370 MW	59500 TQ	USBLS	5/07
Except Line Installer	Pennsylvania	Y	40180 FQ	52200 MW	61950 TQ	USBLS	5/07
Except Line Installer	Allentown-Bethlehem-Easton MSA, PA-NJ	Y	44540 FQ	52780 MW	60990 TQ	USBLS	5/07
Except Line Installer	Philadelphia-Camden-Wilmington MSA, PA-NJ-DE-MD	Y	42280 FQ	53770 MW	63070 TQ	USBLS	5/07
Except Line Installer	Pittsburgh MSA, PA	Y	41850 FQ	55000 MW	64690 TQ	USBLS	5/07
Except Line Installer	Rhode Island	Y	40760 FQ	55930 MW	62890 TQ	USBLS	5/07
Except Line Installer	Providence-Fall River-Warwick MSA, RI-MA	Y	40790 FQ	55730 MW	62950 TQ	USBLS	5/07
Except Line Installer	South Carolina	Y	41290 FQ	52440 MW	58930 TQ	USBLS	5/07
Except Line Installer	Charleston-North Charleston MSA, SC	Y	30130 FQ	48620 MW	59780 TQ	USBLS	5/07
Except Line Installer	Columbia MSA, SC	Y	50710 FQ	57640 MW	64070 TQ	USBLS	5/07

AE	Average entry wage	AW	Average wage paid	FQ	First quartile wage	LO	Lowest wage paid	MTC	Median total compensation	TCC	Total cash compensation
AER	Average entry range	AWR	Average wage range	H	Hourly	LR	Low end range	MW	Median wage paid	TQ	Third quartile wage
AEX	Average experienced wage	AXR	Average experienced range	HI	Highest wage paid	M	Monthly	MWR	Median wage range	W	Weekly
ATC	Average total compensation	D	Daily	HR	High end range	MCC	Median cash compensation	S	See annotated source	Y	Yearly

Occupation/Type/Industry	Location	Per	Low	Mid	High	Source	Date
Telecommunications Equipment Installer and Repairer							
Except Line Installer	South Dakota	Y	45728 FQ	55850 MW	63078 TQ	SDBLS	7/08-9/08
Except Line Installer	Sioux Falls MSA, SD	Y	45772 FQ	52615 MW	58821 TQ	SDBLS	7/08-9/08
Except Line Installer	Tennessee	Y	37760 FQ	52210 MW	58840 TQ	USBLS	5/07
Except Line Installer	Memphis MSA, TN-MS-AR	Y	35670 FQ	48900 MW	56620 TQ	USBLS	5/07
Except Line Installer	Nashville-Davidson-Murfreesboro MSA, TN	Y	45010 FQ	55660 MW	60980 TQ	USBLS	5/07
Except Line Installer	Texas	Y	38670 FQ	49910 MW	56700 TQ	USBLS	5/07
Except Line Installer	Austin-Round Rock MSA, TX	Y	40060 FQ	51370 MW	57280 TQ	USBLS	5/07
Except Line Installer	Dallas-Fort Worth-Arlington MSA, TX	Y	39170 FQ	49220 MW	56050 TQ	USBLS	5/07
Except Line Installer	El Paso MSA, TX	Y	36790 FQ	48730 MW	54380 TQ	USBLS	5/07
Except Line Installer	Houston-Sugar Land-Baytown MSA, TX	Y	40790 FQ	51950 MW	58640 TQ	USBLS	5/07
Except Line Installer	San Antonio MSA, TX	Y	38650 FQ	49600 MW	56590 TQ	USBLS	5/07
Except Line Installer	Utah	Y	39930 FQ	52630 MW	59820 TQ	USBLS	5/07
Except Line Installer	Salt Lake City MSA, UT	Y	42620 FQ	54090 MW	60930 TQ	USBLS	5/07
Except Line Installer	Vermont	Y	38380 FQ	52910 MW	61590 TQ	USBLS	5/07
Except Line Installer	Burlington-South Burlington MSA, VT	Y	42000 FQ	57040 MW	68910 TQ	USBLS	5/07
Except Line Installer	Virginia	Y	44330 FQ	54670 MW	63360 TQ	USBLS	5/07
Except Line Installer	Richmond MSA, VA	Y	43220 FQ	56390 MW	65940 TQ	USBLS	5/07
Except Line Installer	Virginia Beach-Norfolk-Newport News MSA, VA-NC	Y	41570 FQ	46780 MW	54030 TQ	USBLS	5/07
Except Line Installer	Washington	H	25.07 FQ	27.29 MW	29.48 TQ	WABLS	3/08
Except Line Installer	Seattle-Tacoma-Bellevue MSA, WA	Y	50340 FQ	55460 MW	60130 TQ	USBLS	5/07
Except Line Installer	West Virginia	Y	36329 FQ	47985 MW	63699 TQ	WVBLS	7/08-9/08
Except Line Installer	Charleston MSA, WV	Y	31610 FQ	45080 MW	60450 TQ	USBLS	5/07
Except Line Installer	Wisconsin	Y	41730 FQ	50460 MW	57200 TQ	USBLS	5/07
Except Line Installer	Milwaukee-Waukesha-West Allis MSA, WI	Y	46610 FQ	51550 MW	57870 TQ	USBLS	5/07
Except Line Installer	Wyoming	Y	50244 FQ	57664 MW	65222 TQ	WYBLS	9/08
Except Line Installer	Cheyenne MSA, WY	Y	47241 FQ	56035 MW	68205 TQ	WYBLS	9/08
Except Line Installer	Puerto Rico	Y	17100 FQ	21520 MW	33070 TQ	USBLS	5/07
Except Line Installer	San Juan-Caguas-Guaynabo MSA, PR	Y	17220 FQ	21170 MW	35020 TQ	USBLS	5/07
Telecommunications Line Installer and Repairer							
	Alabama	Y	30700 FQ	39890 MW	50910 TQ	USBLS	5/07
	Birmingham-Hoover MSA, AL	Y	26760 FQ	40420 MW	56080 TQ	USBLS	5/07
	Alaska	Y	44510 FQ	64380 MW	79110 TQ	USBLS	5/07
	Anchorage MSA, AK	Y	39280 FQ	60620 MW	74190 TQ	USBLS	5/07
	Arizona	Y	21020 FQ	28030 MW	40880 TQ	USBLS	5/07
	Phoenix-Mesa-Scottsdale MSA, AZ	Y	20660 FQ	27850 MW	40770 TQ	USBLS	5/07
	Tucson MSA, AZ	Y	25210 FQ	30670 MW	46450 TQ	USBLS	5/07
	Arkansas	Y	29660 FQ	41630 MW	54190 TQ	USBLS	5/07
	Little Rock-North Little Rock MSA, AR	Y	30680 FQ	48380 MW	56120 TQ	USBLS	5/07
	California	H	17.50 FQ	24.27 MW	30.27 TQ	CABLS	1/08-3/08
	Los Angeles-Long Beach-Glendale PMSA, CA	H	18.48 FQ	23.52 MW	30.32 TQ	CABLS	1/08-3/08
	Oakland-Fremont-Hayward MSA, CA	H	19.01 FQ	21.86 MW	30.10 TQ	CABLS	1/08-3/08
	Riverside-San Bernardino-Ontario MSA, CA	H	11.44 FQ	23.11 MW	29.71 TQ	CABLS	1/08-3/08
	Sacramento-Arden Arcade-Roseville MSA, CA	H	18.48 FQ	25.18 MW	29.43 TQ	CABLS	1/08-3/08
	San Diego-Carlsbad-San Marcos MSA, CA	H	21.95 FQ	28.23 MW	31.91 TQ	CABLS	1/08-3/08
	San Francisco-San Mateo-Redwood PMSA, CA	H	19.97 FQ	26.69 MW	31.86 TQ	CABLS	1/08-3/08
	San Jose-Sunnyvale-Santa Clara MSA, CA	H	20.37 FQ	27.38 MW	31.05 TQ	CABLS	1/08-3/08
	Santa Ana-Anaheim-Irvine PMSA, CA	Y	41740 FQ	53130 MW	61550 TQ	USBLS	5/07
	Colorado	Y	30240 FQ	37150 MW	49010 TQ	USBLS	5/07
	Denver-Aurora MSA, CO	Y	32600 FQ	40150 MW	50880 TQ	USBLS	5/07
	Connecticut	H	13.51 AE	19.07 MW		CTBLS	1/08-3/08

AE	Average entry wage	AW	Average wage paid	FQ	First quartile wage	LO	Lowest wage paid	MTC	Median total compensation	TCC	Total cash compensation
AER	Average entry range	AWR	Average wage range	H	Hourly	LR	Low end range	MW	Median wage paid	TQ	Third quartile wage
AEX	Average experienced wage	AXR	Average experienced range	HI	Highest wage paid	M	Monthly	MWR	Median wage range	W	Weekly
ATC	Average total compensation	D	Daily	HR	High end range	MCC	Median cash compensation	S	See annotated source	Y	Yearly

1582

Occupation/Type/Industry	Location	Per	Low	Mid	High	Source	Date
Telecommunications Line Installer and Repairer							
	Bridgeport-Stamford-Norwalk MSA, CT	Y	28650 FQ	35650 MW	42770 TQ	USBLS	5/07
	Hartford-West Hartford-East Hartford MSA, CT	Y	33710 FQ	41160 MW	54600 TQ	USBLS	5/07
	New Haven MSA, CT	Y	29370 FQ	38610 MW	55140 TQ	USBLS	5/07
	Delaware	Y	53420 FQ	58190 MW	62930 TQ	USBLS	5/07
	District of Columbia	Y	48670 FQ	55250 MW	60080 TQ	USBLS	5/07
	Washington-Arlington-Alexandria MSA, DC-VA-MD-WV	Y	36940 FQ	53690 MW	61320 TQ	USBLS	5/07
	Florida	Y	29010 FQ	42210 MW	53570 TQ	USBLS	5/07
	Fort Lauderdale-Pompano Beach-Deerfield Beach PMSA, FL	Y	28110 FQ	37380 MW	48240 TQ	USBLS	5/07
	Jacksonville MSA, FL	Y	25650 FQ	35240 MW	54600 TQ	USBLS	5/07
	Miami-Fort Lauderdale-Miami Beach MSA, FL	Y	30050 FQ	40960 MW	56240 TQ	USBLS	5/07
	Orlando-Kissimmee MSA, FL	Y	27430 FQ	36610 MW	46910 TQ	USBLS	5/07
	Tampa-St. Petersburg-Clearwater MSA, FL	Y	41220 FQ	48930 MW	55660 TQ	USBLS	5/07
	West Palm Beach-Boca Raton-Boynton Beach PMSA, FL	Y	26020 FQ	32740 MW	40150 TQ	USBLS	5/07
	Georgia	Y	29490 FQ	36690 MW	49600 TQ	USBLS	5/07
	Atlanta-Sandy Springs-Marietta MSA, GA	Y	32780 FQ	39020 MW	52170 TQ	USBLS	5/07
	Hawaii	Y	36530 FQ	42810 MW	50930 TQ	USBLS	5/07
	Honolulu MSA, HI	Y	37960 FQ	42650 MW	47540 TQ	USBLS	5/07
	Idaho	Y	26100 FQ	35730 MW	43010 TQ	USBLS	5/07
	Boise City-Nampa MSA, ID	Y	30580 FQ	35230 MW	38860 TQ	USBLS	5/07
	Illinois	Y	47190 FQ	56020 MW	63430 TQ	USBLS	5/07
	Chicago-Naperville-Joliet MSA, IL-IN-WI	Y	50210 FQ	59160 MW	65720 TQ	USBLS	5/07
	Indiana	Y	30190 FQ	37710 MW	49090 TQ	USBLS	5/07
	Evansville MSA, IN-KY	Y	26950 FQ	33060 MW	42280 TQ	USBLS	5/07
	Gary PMSA, IN	Y	48260 FQ	65500 MW	71140 TQ	USBLS	5/07
	Indianapolis-Carmel MSA, IN	Y	27860 FQ	33140 MW	40300 TQ	USBLS	5/07
	South Bend-Mishawaka MSA, IN-MI	Y	43850 FQ	50420 MW	57040 TQ	USBLS	5/07
	Iowa	Y	31740 FQ	40860 MW	49360 TQ	USBLS	5/07
	Des Moines-West Des Moines MSA, IA	Y	26720 FQ	35030 MW	44160 TQ	USBLS	5/07
	Kansas	Y	35130 FQ	45920 MW	56480 TQ	USBLS	5/07
	Wichita MSA, KS	Y	43590 FQ	51620 MW	57010 TQ	USBLS	5/07
	Kentucky	Y	26998 FQ	37539 MW	52534 TQ	KYBLS	2008
	Louisville-Jefferson County MSA, KY-IN	Y	26410 FQ	34470 MW	50280 TQ	USBLS	5/07
	Louisiana	H	12.52 FQ	15.98 MW	21.58 TQ	LABLS	1/08-3/08
	Baton Rouge MSA, LA	Y	24420 FQ	30420 MW	44090 TQ	USBLS	5/07
	New Orleans-Metairie-Kenner MSA, LA	Y	29430 FQ	39580 MW	50030 TQ	USBLS	5/07
	Maine	Y	38480 FQ	56120 MW	67030 TQ	USBLS	5/07
	Portland-South Portland-Biddeford MSA, ME	Y	35200 FQ	44790 MW	66610 TQ	USBLS	5/07
	Maryland	Y		57675 MW		MDBLS	3/08
	Baltimore-Towson MSA, MD	Y	40600 FQ	54500 MW	61020 TQ	USBLS	5/07
	Bethesda-Gaithersburg-Frederick PMSA, MD	Y	55370 FQ	61790 MW	67080 TQ	USBLS	5/07
	Massachusetts	Y	50850 FQ	62810 MW	70050 TQ	USBLS	5/07
	Boston-Cambridge-Quincy NECTA, MA	Y	48220 FQ	62190 MW	70040 TQ	USBLS	5/07
	Worcester MSA, MA-CT	Y	37080 FQ	50190 MW	61680 TQ	USBLS	5/07
	Michigan	Y	33060 FQ	45490 MW	53570 TQ	USBLS	5/07
	Detroit-Warren-Livonia MSA, MI	Y	26950 FQ	40050 MW	48750 TQ	USBLS	5/07
	Grand Rapids-Wyoming MSA, MI	Y	42220 FQ	45480 MW	48710 TQ	USBLS	5/07
	Warren-Troy-Farmington Hills PMSA, MI	Y	26600 FQ	38360 MW	48160 TQ	USBLS	5/07
	Minnesota	Y	33419 FQ	40038 MW	50601 TQ	MNBLS	10/08-12/08
	Minneapolis-Saint Paul MSA, MN-WI	Y	33293 FQ	38905 MW	47496 TQ	MNBLS	10/08-12/08

AE Average entry wage	**AW** Average wage paid	**FQ** First quartile wage	**LO** Lowest wage paid	**MTC** Median total compensation	**TCC** Total cash compensation
AER Average entry range	**AWR** Average wage range	**H** Hourly	**LR** Low end range	**MW** Median wage paid	**TQ** Third quartile wage
AEX Average experienced wage	**AXR** Average experienced range	**HI** Highest wage paid	**M** Monthly	**MWR** Median wage range	**W** Weekly
ATC Average total compensation	**D** Daily	**HR** High end range	**MCC** Median cash compensation	**S** See annotated source	**Y** Yearly

Occupation/Type/Industry	Location	Per	Low	Mid	High	Source	Date
Telecommunications Line Installer and Repairer							
	Mississippi	Y	25920 FQ	31760 MW	46670 TQ	USBLS	5/07
	Jackson MSA, MS	Y	24930 FQ	32310 MW	40760 TQ	USBLS	5/07
	Missouri	Y	33710 FQ	48900 MW	58030 TQ	USBLS	5/07
	Kansas City MSA, MO-KS	Y	39150 FQ	51950 MW	59390 TQ	USBLS	5/07
	St. Louis MSA, MO-IL	Y	36320 FQ	51550 MW	58420 TQ	USBLS	5/07
	Springfield MSA, MO	Y	20870 FQ	42450 MW	58850 TQ	USBLS	5/07
	Montana	Y	36570 FQ	47640 MW	56910 TQ	USBLS	5/07
	Nebraska	Y	26900 FQ	33560 MW	43690 TQ	USBLS	5/07
	Omaha-Council Bluffs MSA, NE-IA	Y	29390 FQ	36260 MW	43520 TQ	USBLS	5/07
	Nevada	H	16.07 FQ	20.79 MW	27.25 TQ	NVBLS	5/08
	Las Vegas-Paradise MSA, NV	H	15.13 FQ	20.16 MW	26.41 TQ	NVBLS	5/08
	New Hampshire	H	15.55 AE	24.36 MW	30.01 AEX	NHBLS	6/08
	Manchester MSA, NH	Y	41020 FQ	50240 MW	66220 TQ	USBLS	5/07
	New Jersey	Y	44330 FQ	60240 MW	66120 TQ	USBLS	5/07
	Camden PMSA, NJ	Y	52710 FQ	59670 MW	66520 TQ	USBLS	5/07
	Edison PMSA, NJ	Y	51910 FQ	60890 MW	66080 TQ	USBLS	5/07
	Newark-Union PMSA, NJ-PA	Y	39170 FQ	58110 MW	65510 TQ	USBLS	5/07
	New Mexico	Y	25450 FQ	31160 MW	41300 TQ	USBLS	5/07
	Albuquerque MSA, NM	Y	25660 FQ	29900 MW	35480 TQ	USBLS	5/07
	New York	Y	51340 FQ	66910 MW	73750 TQ	USBLS	5/07
	Albany-Schenectady-Troy MSA, NY	Y	50700 FQ	65620 MW	72280 TQ	USBLS	5/07
	Buffalo-Niagara Falls MSA, NY	Y	38620 FQ	63340 MW	71380 TQ	USBLS	5/07
	Nassau-Suffolk PMSA, NY	Y	54220 FQ	66780 MW	73800 TQ	USBLS	5/07
	New York-Northern New Jersey-Long Island MSA, NY-NJ-PA	Y	52010 FQ	65220 MW	72830 TQ	USBLS	5/07
	North Carolina	Y	30170 FQ	37390 MW	51160 TQ	USBLS	5/07
	Charlotte-Gastonia-Concord MSA, NC-SC	Y	30250 FQ	36370 MW	51210 TQ	USBLS	5/07
	Raleigh-Cary MSA, NC	Y	30770 FQ	34960 MW	42200 TQ	USBLS	5/07
	North Dakota	Y	29090 FQ	34300 MW	42460 TQ	USBLS	5/07
	Fargo MSA, ND-MN	Y	27790 FQ	32470 MW	36380 TQ	USBLS	5/07
	Ohio	Y	31440 FQ	40900 MW	51340 TQ	USBLS	5/07
	Cincinnati-Middletown MSA, OH-KY-IN	Y	34640 FQ	43540 MW	58480 TQ	USBLS	5/07
	Cleveland-Elyria-Mentor MSA, OH	Y	27080 FQ	38040 MW	49660 TQ	USBLS	5/07
	Columbus MSA, OH	Y	31470 FQ	43450 MW	50950 TQ	USBLS	5/07
	Dayton MSA, OH	Y	25960 FQ	30800 MW	39160 TQ	USBLS	5/07
	Mansfield MSA, OH	Y	27000 FQ	29080 MW	31060 TQ	USBLS	5/07
	Oklahoma	Y	33000 FQ	50700 MW	58460 TQ	USBLS	5/07
	Oklahoma City MSA, OK	Y	34570 FQ	49310 MW	57500 TQ	USBLS	5/07
	Tulsa MSA, OK	Y	40000 FQ	55400 MW	63900 TQ	USBLS	5/07
	Oregon	H	15.27 FQ	22.06 MW	27.61 TQ	ORBLS	5/08
	Portland-Vancouver-Beaverton MSA, OR-WA	Y	31990 FQ	44030 MW	55260 TQ	USBLS	5/07
	Pennsylvania	Y	37980 FQ	53350 MW	62250 TQ	USBLS	5/07
	Allentown-Bethlehem-Easton MSA, PA-NJ	Y	50360 FQ	57800 MW	62860 TQ	USBLS	5/07
	Philadelphia-Camden-Wilmington MSA, PA-NJ-DE-MD	Y	48850 FQ	59110 MW	65210 TQ	USBLS	5/07
	Pittsburgh MSA, PA	Y	33060 FQ	47820 MW	61310 TQ	USBLS	5/07
	Rhode Island	Y	61240 FQ	66210 MW	71750 TQ	USBLS	5/07
	Providence-Fall River-Warwick MSA, RI-MA	Y	61160 FQ	66170 MW	71710 TQ	USBLS	5/07
	South Carolina	Y	27020 FQ	34590 MW	47570 TQ	USBLS	5/07
	Charleston-North Charleston MSA, SC	Y	29080 FQ	36560 MW	45990 TQ	USBLS	5/07
	Columbia MSA, SC	Y	25750 FQ	33730 MW	52100 TQ	USBLS	5/07
	South Dakota	Y	28198 FQ	35144 MW	48044 TQ	SDBLS	7/08-9/08
	Sioux Falls MSA, SD	Y	27504 FQ	31637 MW	40087 TQ	SDBLS	7/08-9/08
	Tennessee	Y	32580 FQ	41930 MW	53240 TQ	USBLS	5/07
	Memphis MSA, TN-MS-AR	Y	33430 FQ	41330 MW	48170 TQ	USBLS	5/07
	Nashville-Davidson-Murfreesboro MSA, TN	Y	35170 FQ	48550 MW	55200 TQ	USBLS	5/07
	Texas	Y	29940 FQ	44320 MW	55870 TQ	USBLS	5/07
	Austin-Round Rock MSA, TX	Y	37300 FQ	51810 MW	58830 TQ	USBLS	5/07

AE Average entry wage	**AW** Average wage paid	**FQ** First quartile wage	**LO** Lowest wage paid	**MTC** Median total compensation	**TCC** Total cash compensation
AER Average entry range	**AWR** Average wage range	**H** Hourly	**LR** Low end range	**MW** Median wage paid	**TQ** Third quartile wage
AEX Average experienced wage	**AXR** Average experienced range	**HI** Highest wage paid	**M** Monthly	**MWR** Median wage range	**W** Weekly
ATC Average total compensation	**D** Daily	**HR** High end range	**MCC** Median cash compensation	**S** See annotated source	**Y** Yearly

Occupation/Type/Industry	Location	Per	Low	Mid	High	Source	Date
Telecommunications Line Installer and Repairer	Dallas-Fort Worth-Arlington MSA, TX	Y	31520 FQ	46530 MW	56000 TQ	USBLS	5/07
	El Paso MSA, TX	Y	26960 FQ	34060 MW	54130 TQ	USBLS	5/07
	Houston-Sugar Land-Baytown MSA, TX	Y	26250 FQ	34960 MW	53050 TQ	USBLS	5/07
	San Antonio MSA, TX	Y	29650 FQ	48090 MW	55690 TQ	USBLS	5/07
	Utah	Y	32150 FQ	40180 MW	47740 TQ	USBLS	5/07
	Salt Lake City MSA, UT	Y	32880 FQ	42350 MW	48420 TQ	USBLS	5/07
	Vermont	Y	51630 FQ	64520 MW	70960 TQ	USBLS	5/07
	Burlington-South Burlington MSA, VT	Y	50680 FQ	65330 MW	71170 TQ	USBLS	5/07
	Virginia	Y	34040 FQ	51980 MW	60550 TQ	USBLS	5/07
	Richmond MSA, VA	Y	40880 FQ	54660 MW	60120 TQ	USBLS	5/07
	Virginia Beach-Norfolk-Newport News MSA, VA-NC	Y	32100 FQ	53200 MW	60620 TQ	USBLS	5/07
	Washington	H	17.04 FQ	21.79 MW	26.56 TQ	WABLS	3/08
	Seattle-Tacoma-Bellevue MSA, WA	Y	37220 FQ	45790 MW	54900 TQ	USBLS	5/07
	West Virginia	Y	38377 FQ	52363 MW	61354 TQ	WVBLS	7/08-9/08
	Charleston MSA, WV	Y	34660 FQ	42950 MW	54770 TQ	USBLS	5/07
	Wisconsin	Y	34840 FQ	44450 MW	50490 TQ	USBLS	5/07
	Appleton MSA, WI	Y	35490 FQ	44360 MW	49910 TQ	USBLS	5/07
	Milwaukee-Waukesha-West Allis MSA, WI	Y	38840 FQ	45280 MW	50180 TQ	USBLS	5/07
	Wyoming	Y	27313 FQ	33150 MW	47160 TQ	WYBLS	9/08
	Cheyenne MSA, WY	Y	25768 FQ	29272 MW	33955 TQ	WYBLS	9/08
	Puerto Rico	Y	24070 FQ	31860 MW	38840 TQ	USBLS	5/07
	San Juan-Caguas-Guaynabo MSA, PR	Y	24160 FQ	31960 MW	39100 TQ	USBLS	5/07
	Guam	Y	21610 FQ	25640 MW	31330 TQ	USBLS	5/07
Telecommunications Specialist	United States	Y		49250-72500 AWR		CERT02	2008
Telecommunicator State Highway Patrol	Missouri	S	1192 LO		1676 HI	MSHPSS	7/1/08
Telemarketer	Alabama	Y	18570 FQ	20840 MW	23050 TQ	USBLS	5/07
	Birmingham-Hoover MSA, AL	Y	18100 FQ	21080 MW	23480 TQ	USBLS	5/07
	Mobile MSA, AL	Y	17910 FQ	20620 MW	23550 TQ	USBLS	5/07
	Arizona	Y	16820 FQ	20640 MW	24420 TQ	USBLS	5/07
	Phoenix-Mesa-Scottsdale MSA, AZ	Y	17950 FQ	21770 MW	25880 TQ	USBLS	5/07
	Tucson MSA, AZ	Y	15920 FQ	18650 MW	21810 TQ	USBLS	5/07
	Arkansas	Y	15720 FQ	20240 MW	23940 TQ	USBLS	5/07
	Little Rock-North Little Rock MSA, AR	Y	15360 FQ	20670 MW	23600 TQ	USBLS	5/07
	California	H	9.40 FQ	11.95 MW	15.25 TQ	CABLS	1/08-3/08
	Los Angeles-Long Beach-Glendale PMSA, CA	H	9.04 FQ	11.25 MW	14.27 TQ	CABLS	1/08-3/08
	Oakland-Fremont-Hayward MSA, CA	H	11.59 FQ	13.94 MW	17.32 TQ	CABLS	1/08-3/08
	Oxnard-Thousand Oaks-Ventura MSA, CA	H	8.96 FQ	13.03 MW	16.06 TQ	CABLS	1/08-3/08
	Riverside-San Bernardino-Ontario MSA, CA	H	8.85 FQ	10.95 MW	14.61 TQ	CABLS	1/08-3/08
	Sacramento-Arden Arcade-Roseville MSA, CA	H	10.13 FQ	11.80 MW	14.09 TQ	CABLS	1/08-3/08
	San Diego-Carlsbad-San Marcos MSA, CA	H	8.97 FQ	12.25 MW	15.94 TQ	CABLS	1/08-3/08
	San Francisco-San Mateo-Redwood PMSA, CA	H	10.54 FQ	12.27 MW	18.66 TQ	CABLS	1/08-3/08
	San Jose-Sunnyvale-Santa Clara MSA, CA	H	12.60 FQ	14.82 MW	17.44 TQ	CABLS	1/08-3/08
	Santa Ana-Anaheim-Irvine PMSA, CA	Y	20270 FQ	27070 MW	34450 TQ	USBLS	5/07
	Colorado	Y	18520 FQ	23010 MW	30960 TQ	USBLS	5/07
	Denver-Aurora MSA, CO	Y	19580 FQ	24800 MW	33940 TQ	USBLS	5/07
	Connecticut	H	9.18 AE	12.29 MW		CTBLS	1/08-3/08
	Bridgeport-Stamford-Norwalk MSA, CT	Y	21560 FQ	25750 MW	30130 TQ	USBLS	5/07

AE	Average entry wage	**AW**	Average wage paid	**FQ**	First quartile wage
AER	Average entry range	**AWR**	Average wage range	**H**	Hourly
AEX	Average experienced wage	**AXR**	Average experienced range	**HI**	Highest wage paid
ATC	Average total compensation	**D**	Daily	**HR**	High end range

LO	Lowest wage paid	**MTC**	Median total compensation	**TCC**	Total cash compensation
LR	Low end range	**MW**	Median wage paid	**TQ**	Third quartile wage
M	Monthly	**MWR**	Median wage range	**W**	Weekly
MCC	Median cash compensation	**S**	See annotated source	**Y**	Yearly

Occupation/Type/Industry	Location	Per	Low	Mid	High	Source	Date
Telemarketer	Hartford-West Hartford-East Hartford MSA, CT	Y	16510 FQ	24170 MW	32780 TQ	USBLS	5/07
	Delaware	Y	24720 FQ	29880 MW	37980 TQ	USBLS	5/07
	Wilmington PMSA, DE-MD-NJ	Y	23860 FQ	29670 MW	37680 TQ	USBLS	5/07
	District of Columbia	Y	15130 FQ	20560 MW	42390 TQ	USBLS	5/07
	Washington-Arlington-Alexandria MSA, DC-VA-MD-WV	Y	17550 FQ	22330 MW	36850 TQ	USBLS	5/07
	Florida	Y	17680 FQ	21280 MW	26580 TQ	USBLS	5/07
	Fort Lauderdale-Pompano Beach-Deerfield Beach PMSA, FL	Y	20560 FQ	24620 MW	30410 TQ	USBLS	5/07
	Jacksonville MSA, FL	Y	19930 FQ	23320 MW	28330 TQ	USBLS	5/07
	Miami-Fort Lauderdale-Miami Beach MSA, FL	Y	19580 FQ	23770 MW	29830 TQ	USBLS	5/07
	Orlando-Kissimmee MSA, FL	Y	18150 FQ	21090 MW	25940 TQ	USBLS	5/07
	Tampa-St. Petersburg-Clearwater MSA, FL	Y	16790 FQ	21000 MW	28420 TQ	USBLS	5/07
	West Palm Beach-Boca Raton-Boynton Beach PMSA, FL	Y	20190 FQ	23840 MW	31860 TQ	USBLS	5/07
	Georgia	Y	17710 FQ	20650 MW	27380 TQ	USBLS	5/07
	Athens-Clarke County MSA, GA	Y	17000 FQ	18390 MW	20020 TQ	USBLS	5/07
	Atlanta-Sandy Springs-Marietta MSA, GA	Y	17970 FQ	21320 MW	28400 TQ	USBLS	5/07
	Macon MSA, GA	Y	20220 FQ	22300 MW	24280 TQ	USBLS	5/07
	Hawaii	Y	18770 FQ	21990 MW	25230 TQ	USBLS	5/07
	Honolulu MSA, HI	Y	18450 FQ	21610 MW	24610 TQ	USBLS	5/07
	Idaho	Y	16870 FQ	21030 MW	24840 TQ	USBLS	5/07
	Boise City-Nampa MSA, ID	Y	16590 FQ	19010 MW	24830 TQ	USBLS	5/07
	Illinois	Y	17450 FQ	21420 MW	30710 TQ	USBLS	5/07
	Chicago-Naperville-Joliet MSA, IL-IN-WI	Y	17460 FQ	21260 MW	31770 TQ	USBLS	5/07
	Indiana	Y	17080 FQ	20470 MW	28680 TQ	USBLS	5/07
	Gary PMSA, IN	Y	13890 FQ	19280 MW	21940 TQ	USBLS	5/07
	Indianapolis-Carmel MSA, IN	Y	18370 FQ	21950 MW	31630 TQ	USBLS	5/07
	Iowa	Y	15840 FQ	19300 MW	24630 TQ	USBLS	5/07
	Des Moines-West Des Moines MSA, IA	Y	21190 FQ	26250 MW	29520 TQ	USBLS	5/07
	Kansas	Y	17450 FQ	19870 MW	27000 TQ	USBLS	5/07
	Wichita MSA, KS	Y	18160 FQ	21360 MW	24930 TQ	USBLS	5/07
	Kentucky	Y	16203 FQ	18431 MW	24728 TQ	KYBLS	2008
	Louisville-Jefferson County MSA, KY-IN	Y	16180 FQ	21020 MW	26430 TQ	USBLS	5/07
	Louisiana	H	7.30 FQ	10.45 MW	13.36 TQ	LABLS	1/08-3/08
	Baton Rouge MSA, LA	Y	15340 FQ	20440 MW	27210 TQ	USBLS	5/07
	New Orleans-Metairie-Kenner MSA, LA	Y	15350 FQ	24430 MW	34000 TQ	USBLS	5/07
	Maine	Y	17300 FQ	23680 MW	34320 TQ	USBLS	5/07
	Portland-South Portland-Biddeford MSA, ME	Y	18830 FQ	27810 MW	33770 TQ	USBLS	5/07
	Maryland	Y		23600 MW		MDBLS	3/08
	Baltimore-Towson MSA, MD	Y	18030 FQ	24050 MW	34860 TQ	USBLS	5/07
	Bethesda-Gaithersburg-Frederick PMSA, MD	Y	22140 FQ	26440 MW	36900 TQ	USBLS	5/07
	Massachusetts	Y	25800 FQ	32680 MW	43120 TQ	USBLS	5/07
	Boston-Cambridge-Quincy NECTA, MA	Y	27120 FQ	34780 MW	45830 TQ	USBLS	5/07
	Worcester MSA, MA-CT	Y	28310 FQ	35890 MW	44540 TQ	USBLS	5/07
	Michigan	Y	17310 FQ	21390 MW	25280 TQ	USBLS	5/07
	Detroit-Warren-Livonia MSA, MI	Y	17660 FQ	21450 MW	25700 TQ	USBLS	5/07
	Grand Rapids-Wyoming MSA, MI	Y	16880 FQ	20090 MW	23260 TQ	USBLS	5/07
	Lansing-East Lansing MSA, MI	Y	20340 FQ	22150 MW	23940 TQ	USBLS	5/07
	Warren-Troy-Farmington Hills PMSA, MI	Y	17270 FQ	21040 MW	25880 TQ	USBLS	5/07
	Minnesota	Y	18406 FQ	21739 MW	27299 TQ	MNBLS	10/08-12/08
	Duluth-Superior MSA, MN-WI	Y	17399 FQ	18782 MW	20164 TQ	MNBLS	10/08-12/08
	Minneapolis-Saint Paul MSA, MN-WI	Y	19818 FQ	24280 MW	29301 TQ	MNBLS	10/08-12/08

AE	Average entry wage	AW	Average wage paid	FQ	First quartile wage	LO	Lowest wage paid	MTC Median total compensation TCC Total cash compensation
AER	Average entry range	AWR	Average wage range	H	Hourly	LR	Low end range	MW Median wage paid TQ Third quartile wage
AEX	Average experienced wage	AXR	Average experienced range	HI	Highest wage paid	M	Monthly	MWR Median wage range W Weekly
ATC	Average total compensation	D	Daily	HR	High end range	MCC	Median cash compensation	S See annotated source Y Yearly

Telemarketer

Occupation/Type/Industry	Location	Per	Low	Mid	High	Source	Date
Telemarketer	Rochester MSA, MN	Y	17639 FQ	19122 MW	20980 TQ	MNBLS	10/08-12/08
	Mississippi	Y	14340 FQ	18080 MW	24170 TQ	USBLS	5/07
	Jackson MSA, MS	Y	21200 FQ	25480 MW	50580 TQ	USBLS	5/07
	Missouri	Y	16820 FQ	19070 MW	25870 TQ	USBLS	5/07
	Kansas City MSA, MO-KS	Y	18910 FQ	24340 MW	29390 TQ	USBLS	5/07
	St. Louis MSA, MO-IL	Y	17060 FQ	20170 MW	28060 TQ	USBLS	5/07
	Montana	Y	14310 FQ	15790 MW	22580 TQ	USBLS	5/07
	Billings MSA, MT	Y	14020 FQ	15240 MW	18800 TQ	USBLS	5/07
	Nebraska	Y	16210 FQ	18940 MW	24150 TQ	USBLS	5/07
	Omaha-Council Bluffs MSA, NE-IA	Y	15840 FQ	20180 MW	26140 TQ	USBLS	5/07
	Nevada	H	8.98 FQ	10.90 MW	13.46 TQ	NVBLS	5/08
	Las Vegas-Paradise MSA, NV	H	8.52 FQ	10.06 MW	12.46 TQ	NVBLS	5/08
	New Hampshire	H	9.71 AE	13.93 MW	16.34 AEX	NHBLS	6/08
	Manchester MSA, NH	Y	30080 FQ	32440 MW	35270 TQ	USBLS	5/07
	Nashua NECTA, NH-MA	Y	26410 FQ	28860 MW	31100 TQ	USBLS	5/07
	New Jersey	Y	22400 FQ	28140 MW	45850 TQ	USBLS	5/07
	Camden PMSA, NJ	Y	20970 FQ	23260 MW	26350 TQ	USBLS	5/07
	Edison PMSA, NJ	Y	22740 FQ	28030 MW	41490 TQ	USBLS	5/07
	Newark-Union PMSA, NJ-PA	Y	22740 FQ	27070 MW	36400 TQ	USBLS	5/07
	New Mexico	Y	14280 FQ	17770 MW	23180 TQ	USBLS	5/07
	Albuquerque MSA, NM	Y	15500 FQ	20810 MW	27170 TQ	USBLS	5/07
	New York	Y	18510 FQ	23810 MW	33670 TQ	USBLS	5/07
	Albany-Schenectady-Troy MSA, NY	Y	18420 FQ	22830 MW	28230 TQ	USBLS	5/07
	Buffalo-Niagara Falls MSA, NY	Y	17780 FQ	23010 MW	30000 TQ	USBLS	5/07
	Nassau-Suffolk PMSA, NY	Y	17950 FQ	22180 MW	26830 TQ	USBLS	5/07
	New York-Northern New Jersey-Long Island MSA, NY-NJ-PA	Y	20730 FQ	26650 MW	38470 TQ	USBLS	5/07
	North Carolina	Y	17950 FQ	20470 MW	24620 TQ	USBLS	5/07
	Charlotte-Gastonia-Concord MSA, NC-SC	Y	20880 FQ	27380 MW	36890 TQ	USBLS	5/07
	Raleigh-Cary MSA, NC	Y	19500 FQ	21680 MW	25340 TQ	USBLS	5/07
	Winston-Salem MSA, NC	Y	16600 FQ	18120 MW	19620 TQ	USBLS	5/07
	North Dakota	Y	16190 FQ	18560 MW	22180 TQ	USBLS	5/07
	Fargo MSA, ND-MN	Y	14380 FQ	17760 MW	21210 TQ	USBLS	5/07
	Ohio	Y	16840 FQ	19750 MW	24340 TQ	USBLS	5/07
	Cincinnati-Middletown MSA, OH-KY-IN	Y	21210 FQ	24510 MW	32100 TQ	USBLS	5/07
	Cleveland-Elyria-Mentor MSA, OH	Y	16690 FQ	19380 MW	24660 TQ	USBLS	5/07
	Columbus MSA, OH	Y	16500 FQ	20400 MW	23730 TQ	USBLS	5/07
	Dayton MSA, OH	Y	17600 FQ	19210 MW	22300 TQ	USBLS	5/07
	Oklahoma	Y	16160 FQ	18500 MW	22070 TQ	USBLS	5/07
	Oklahoma City MSA, OK	Y	14840 FQ	17640 MW	21750 TQ	USBLS	5/07
	Tulsa MSA, OK	Y	17730 FQ	20020 MW	23020 TQ	USBLS	5/07
	Oregon	H	8.87 FQ	10.26 MW	13.39 TQ	ORBLS	5/08
	Portland-Vancouver-Beaverton MSA, OR-WA	Y	18040 FQ	20320 MW	27630 TQ	USBLS	5/07
	Pennsylvania	Y	17060 FQ	21340 MW	30420 TQ	USBLS	5/07
	Allentown-Bethlehem-Easton MSA, PA-NJ	Y	20530 FQ	22940 MW	29340 TQ	USBLS	5/07
	Philadelphia-Camden-Wilmington MSA, PA-NJ-DE-MD	Y	19920 FQ	25440 MW	36350 TQ	USBLS	5/07
	Pittsburgh MSA, PA	Y	18540 FQ	22480 MW	29640 TQ	USBLS	5/07
	Rhode Island	Y	18030 FQ	21850 MW	27170 TQ	USBLS	5/07
	Providence-Fall River-Warwick MSA, RI-MA	Y	18210 FQ	22240 MW	27660 TQ	USBLS	5/07
	South Carolina	Y	17550 FQ	20850 MW	24520 TQ	USBLS	5/07
	Charleston-North Charleston MSA, SC	Y	16570 FQ	21330 MW	28620 TQ	USBLS	5/07
	Columbia MSA, SC	Y	18270 FQ	22600 MW	29580 TQ	USBLS	5/07
	South Dakota	Y	17877 FQ	20665 MW	25185 TQ	SDBLS	7/08-9/08
	Sioux Falls MSA, SD	Y	18831 FQ	22989 MW	28769 TQ	SDBLS	7/08-9/08
	Tennessee	Y	17380 FQ	22450 MW	30500 TQ	USBLS	5/07
	Memphis MSA, TN-MS-AR	Y	17190 FQ	22780 MW	32750 TQ	USBLS	5/07
	Nashville-Davidson-Murfreesboro MSA, TN	Y	19900 FQ	24740 MW	31850 TQ	USBLS	5/07
	Texas	Y	15760 FQ	18650 MW	24920 TQ	USBLS	5/07

AE	Average entry wage	AW	Average wage paid	FQ	First quartile wage	LO	Lowest wage paid	MTC	Median total compensation	TCC	Total cash compensation
AER	Average entry range	AWR	Average wage range	H	Hourly	LR	Low end range	MW	Median wage paid	TQ	Third quartile wage
AEX	Average experienced wage	AXR	Average experienced range	HI	Highest wage paid	M	Monthly	MWR	Median wage range	W	Weekly
ATC	Average total compensation	D	Daily	HR	High end range	MCC	Median cash compensation	S	See annotated source	Y	Yearly

Occupation/Type/Industry	Location	Per	Low	Mid	High	Source	Date
Telemarketer	Austin-Round Rock MSA, TX	Y	16510 FQ	19900 MW	26100 TQ	USBLS	5/07
	Beaumont-Port Arthur MSA, TX	Y	15710 FQ	19810 MW	24050 TQ	USBLS	5/07
	Dallas-Fort Worth-Arlington MSA, TX	Y	17600 FQ	23040 MW	30890 TQ	USBLS	5/07
	El Paso MSA, TX	Y	15040 FQ	16680 MW	18340 TQ	USBLS	5/07
	Houston-Sugar Land-Baytown MSA, TX	Y	17210 FQ	19460 MW	24750 TQ	USBLS	5/07
	San Antonio MSA, TX	Y	14810 FQ	16930 MW	19870 TQ	USBLS	5/07
	Utah	Y	18080 FQ	21170 MW	24900 TQ	USBLS	5/07
	Salt Lake City MSA, UT	Y	18910 FQ	21670 MW	25110 TQ	USBLS	5/07
	Vermont	Y	21620 FQ	25310 MW	38430 TQ	USBLS	5/07
	Burlington-South Burlington MSA, VT	Y	21530 FQ	23860 MW	29200 TQ	USBLS	5/07
	Virginia	Y	17760 FQ	22560 MW	28540 TQ	USBLS	5/07
	Richmond MSA, VA	Y	24140 FQ	29320 MW	38270 TQ	USBLS	5/07
	Virginia Beach-Norfolk-Newport News MSA, VA-NC	Y	14930 FQ	21430 MW	28490 TQ	USBLS	5/07
	Washington	H	9.09 FQ	10.79 MW	13.35 TQ	WABLS	3/08
	Seattle-Tacoma-Bellevue MSA, WA	Y	19850 FQ	24500 MW	30840 TQ	USBLS	5/07
	West Virginia	Y	17749 FQ	21250 MW	44780 TQ	WVBLS	7/08-9/08
	Charleston MSA, WV	Y	18430 FQ	40140 MW	45940 TQ	USBLS	5/07
	Wisconsin	Y	15570 FQ	19480 MW	25580 TQ	USBLS	5/07
	Milwaukee-Waukesha-West Allis MSA, WI	Y	14930 FQ	17960 MW	28410 TQ	USBLS	5/07
	Wyoming	Y	16972 FQ	18978 MW	30271 TQ	WYBLS	9/08
	Cheyenne MSA, WY	Y	19319 FQ	25835 MW	39313 TQ	WYBLS	9/08
	Puerto Rico	Y	12720 FQ	14150 MW	16030 TQ	USBLS	5/07
	San Juan-Caguas-Guaynabo MSA, PR	Y	12730 FQ	14170 MW	16110 TQ	USBLS	5/07
	Guam	Y	15800 FQ	21100 MW	31200 TQ	USBLS	5/07
Telephone Operator	Alabama	Y	17610 FQ	27440 MW	42500 TQ	USBLS	5/07
	Birmingham-Hoover MSA, AL	Y	39280 FQ	42190 MW	45010 TQ	USBLS	5/07
	Alaska	Y	23050 FQ	28930 MW	39070 TQ	USBLS	5/07
	Arizona	Y	24480 FQ	30540 MW	37560 TQ	USBLS	5/07
	Phoenix-Mesa-Scottsdale MSA, AZ	Y	23950 FQ	29150 MW	36210 TQ	USBLS	5/07
	California	H	11.78 FQ	19.05 MW	22.29 TQ	CABLS	1/08-3/08
	Sacramento-Arden Arcade-Roseville MSA, CA	H	13.30 FQ	18.37 MW	22.36 TQ	CABLS	1/08-3/08
	San Diego-Carlsbad-San Marcos MSA, CA	H	20.83 FQ	22.40 MW	23.97 TQ	CABLS	1/08-3/08
	San Francisco-San Mateo-Redwood PMSA, CA	H	10.58 FQ	13.31 MW	17.81 TQ	CABLS	1/08-3/08
	Santa Ana-Anaheim-Irvine PMSA, CA	Y	38640 FQ	41860 MW	45070 TQ	USBLS	5/07
	Denver-Aurora MSA, CO	Y	19000 FQ	22220 MW	27420 TQ	USBLS	5/07
	Connecticut	H	12.16 AE	14.44 MW		CTBLS	1/08-3/08
	Hartford-West Hartford-East Hartford MSA, CT	Y	24340 FQ	26690 MW	29740 TQ	USBLS	5/07
	Washington-Arlington-Alexandria MSA, DC-VA-MD-WV	Y	28000 FQ	38960 MW	44960 TQ	USBLS	5/07
	Florida	Y	18340 FQ	22290 MW	30140 TQ	USBLS	5/07
	Fort Lauderdale-Pompano Beach-Deerfield Beach PMSA, FL	Y	23420 FQ	26180 MW	28640 TQ	USBLS	5/07
	Miami-Fort Lauderdale-Miami Beach MSA, FL	Y	23350 FQ	28100 MW	43580 TQ	USBLS	5/07
	Orlando-Kissimmee MSA, FL	Y	21190 FQ	23590 MW	45390 TQ	USBLS	5/07
	Georgia	Y	17660 FQ	22290 MW	30020 TQ	USBLS	5/07
	Illinois	Y	23660 FQ	37400 MW	44360 TQ	USBLS	5/07
	Chicago-Naperville-Joliet MSA, IL-IN-WI	Y	31940 FQ	40350 MW	45960 TQ	USBLS	5/07
	Indiana	Y	25230 FQ	43520 MW	56320 TQ	USBLS	5/07
	Kansas	Y	35000 FQ	38010 MW	41540 TQ	USBLS	5/07
	Louisiana	H	9.99 FQ	15.14 MW	21.31 TQ	LABLS	1/08-3/08
	Maryland	Y		32500 MW		MDBLS	3/08
	Baltimore-Towson MSA, MD	Y	25310 FQ	32070 MW	39760 TQ	USBLS	5/07
	Massachusetts	Y	28080 FQ	41390 MW	45500 TQ	USBLS	5/07

AE Average entry wage	**AW** Average wage paid	**FQ** First quartile wage	**LO** Lowest wage paid	**MTC** Median total compensation	**TCC** Total cash compensation		
AER Average entry range	**AWR** Average wage range	**H** Hourly	**LR** Low end range	**MW** Median wage paid	**TQ** Third quartile wage		
AEX Average experienced wage	**AXR** Average experienced range	**HI** Highest wage paid	**M** Monthly	**MWR** Median wage range	**W** Weekly		
ATC Average total compensation	**D** Daily	**HR** High end range	**MCC** Median cash compensation	**S** See annotated source	**Y** Yearly		

Occupation/Type/Industry	Location	Per	Low	Mid	High	Source	Date
Telephone Operator	Boston-Cambridge-Quincy NECTA, MA	Y	17560 FQ	21850 MW	30510 TQ	USBLS	5/07
	Michigan	Y	38490 FQ	42840 MW	46300 TQ	USBLS	5/07
	Detroit-Warren-Livonia MSA, MI	Y	41150 FQ	44160 MW	46910 TQ	USBLS	5/07
	Warren-Troy-Farmington Hills PMSA, MI	Y	40280 FQ	42990 MW	45680 TQ	USBLS	5/07
	Minnesota	Y	17485 FQ	29319 MW	46180 TQ	MNBLS	10/08-12/08
	Minneapolis-Saint Paul MSA, MN-WI	Y	17391 FQ	29308 MW	46273 TQ	MNBLS	10/08-12/08
	Mississippi	Y	16290 FQ	21350 MW	35530 TQ	USBLS	5/07
	Missouri	Y	27190 FQ	37510 MW	46770 TQ	USBLS	5/07
	Kansas City MSA, MO-KS	Y	38170 FQ	44110 MW	48550 TQ	USBLS	5/07
	St. Louis MSA, MO-IL	Y	25310 FQ	28510 MW	33570 TQ	USBLS	5/07
	Nebraska	Y	23310 FQ	27460 MW	32240 TQ	USBLS	5/07
	Nevada	H	12.06 FQ	13.49 MW	14.81 TQ	NVBLS	5/08
	Las Vegas-Paradise MSA, NV	H	12.01 FQ	13.44 MW	14.73 TQ	NVBLS	5/08
	New Jersey	Y	30050 FQ	40750 MW	45000 TQ	USBLS	5/07
	Edison PMSA, NJ	Y	36540 FQ	41850 MW	45650 TQ	USBLS	5/07
	New York	Y	36300 FQ	42690 MW	47880 TQ	USBLS	5/07
	Albany-Schenectady-Troy MSA, NY	Y	21800 FQ	26550 MW	31560 TQ	USBLS	5/07
	Nassau-Suffolk PMSA, NY	Y	37800 FQ	43540 MW	47740 TQ	USBLS	5/07
	North Carolina	Y	18680 FQ	26340 MW	37900 TQ	USBLS	5/07
	North Dakota	Y	26100 FQ	27800 MW	29500 TQ	USBLS	5/07
	Fargo MSA, ND-MN	Y	26100 FQ	27800 MW	29500 TQ	USBLS	5/07
	Ohio	Y	19390 FQ	30060 MW	46410 TQ	USBLS	5/07
	Cincinnati-Middletown MSA, OH-KY-IN	Y	26260 FQ	42280 MW	48000 TQ	USBLS	5/07
	Pennsylvania	Y	22460 FQ	30110 MW	46040 TQ	USBLS	5/07
	Allentown-Bethlehem-Easton MSA, PA-NJ	Y	24270 FQ	42690 MW	48120 TQ	USBLS	5/07
	Philadelphia-Camden-Wilmington MSA, PA-NJ-DE-MD	Y	28500 FQ	35990 MW	43470 TQ	USBLS	5/07
	Pittsburgh MSA, PA	Y	21720 FQ	45330 MW	53850 TQ	USBLS	5/07
	Rhode Island	Y	35360 FQ	41070 MW	45350 TQ	USBLS	5/07
	Providence-Fall River-Warwick MSA, RI-MA	Y	36140 FQ	41470 MW	45130 TQ	USBLS	5/07
	South Carolina	Y	20230 FQ	22520 MW	25000 TQ	USBLS	5/07
	Columbia MSA, SC	Y	21710 FQ	23590 MW	25440 TQ	USBLS	5/07
	Tennessee	Y	17150 FQ	18760 MW	22570 TQ	USBLS	5/07
	Texas	Y	15040 FQ	24060 MW	44160 TQ	USBLS	5/07
	Austin-Round Rock MSA, TX	Y	42050 FQ	45660 MW	49300 TQ	USBLS	5/07
	Houston-Sugar Land-Baytown MSA, TX	Y	16810 FQ	21490 MW	42550 TQ	USBLS	5/07
	Utah	Y	25820 FQ	29520 MW	39740 TQ	USBLS	5/07
	Salt Lake City MSA, UT	Y	26510 FQ	30070 MW	40270 TQ	USBLS	5/07
	West Virginia	Y	40162 FQ	44262 MW	47754 TQ	WVBLS	7/08-9/08
	Wyoming	Y	25370 FQ	36219 MW	41765 TQ	WYBLS	9/08
	Puerto Rico	Y	21450 FQ	26000 MW	30260 TQ	USBLS	5/07
Municipal Government	Cincinnati, OH	Y	33961 LO		35480 HI	COHSS	10/08
Telephone Service Quality Coordinator							
State Government	Ohio	H	23.87 LO		35.02 HI	ODAS	2008
Television and Radio Project Manager							
State Government	Ohio	H	23.04 LO		30.13 HI	ODAS	2008
Television Photographer	Anchorage, AK	Y	28000 LO		35000 HI	BROLL	2009
	Detroit, MI	Y	65000 LO		110000 HI	BROLL	2009
	Billings, MT	Y	14000 LO		31000 HI	BROLL	2009
	New York, NY	Y	68000 LO		125000 HI	BROLL	2009
	Eugene, OR	Y	16000 LO		24000 HI	BROLL	2009
	Nashville, TN	Y	19000 LO		45000 HI	BROLL	2009
Television Producer	United States	H		31.65 MW		YAHHJ	2007
Teller	United States	Y	19000 AE			CCRUN02	2008
	Alabama	Y	18030 FQ	20590 MW	23380 TQ	USBLS	5/07

AE	Average entry wage	AW	Average wage paid	FQ First quartile wage
AER	Average entry range	AWR	Average wage range	H Hourly
AEX	Average experienced wage	AXR	Average experienced range	HI Highest wage paid
ATC	Average total compensation	D	Daily	HR High end range

LO	Lowest wage paid	MTC	Median total compensation	TCC	Total cash compensation
LR	Low end range	MW	Median wage paid	TQ	Third quartile wage
M	Monthly	MWR	Median wage range	W	Weekly
MCC	Median cash compensation	S	See annotated source	Y	Yearly

Occupation/Type/Industry	Location	Per	Low	Mid	High	Source	Date
Teller	Birmingham-Hoover MSA, AL	Y	18620 FQ	21360 MW	23890 TQ	USBLS	5/07
	Alaska	Y	23380 FQ	26890 MW	29840 TQ	USBLS	5/07
	Anchorage MSA, AK	Y	22590 FQ	26500 MW	29570 TQ	USBLS	5/07
	Arizona	Y	21090 FQ	23620 MW	28090 TQ	USBLS	5/07
	Phoenix-Mesa-Scottsdale MSA, AZ	Y	21220 FQ	23950 MW	28920 TQ	USBLS	5/07
	Tucson MSA, AZ	Y	20860 FQ	22980 MW	25550 TQ	USBLS	5/07
	Arkansas	Y	17540 FQ	19990 MW	23340 TQ	USBLS	5/07
	Fort Smith MSA, AR-OK	Y	17890 FQ	20670 MW	24060 TQ	USBLS	5/07
	Jonesboro MSA, AR	Y	17170 FQ	19540 MW	22870 TQ	USBLS	5/07
	Little Rock-North Little Rock MSA, AR	Y	18650 FQ	21460 MW	24370 TQ	USBLS	5/07
	California	H	10.76 FQ	12.38 MW	14.77 TQ	CABLS	1/08-3/08
	Los Angeles-Long Beach-Glendale PMSA, CA	H	10.78 FQ	12.43 MW	14.68 TQ	CABLS	1/08-3/08
	Oakland-Fremont-Hayward MSA, CA	H	11.50 FQ	13.39 MW	15.79 TQ	CABLS	1/08-3/08
	Riverside-San Bernardino-Ontario MSA, CA	H	10.76 FQ	12.29 MW	14.81 TQ	CABLS	1/08-3/08
	Sacramento-Arden Arcade-Roseville MSA, CA	H	10.73 FQ	12.19 MW	14.51 TQ	CABLS	1/08-3/08
	San Diego-Carlsbad-San Marcos MSA, CA	H	10.80 FQ	12.34 MW	14.45 TQ	CABLS	1/08-3/08
	San Francisco-San Mateo-Redwood PMSA, CA	H	12.25 FQ	14.11 MW	16.50 TQ	CABLS	1/08-3/08
	San Jose-Sunnyvale-Santa Clara MSA, CA	H	11.16 FQ	12.98 MW	16.41 TQ	CABLS	1/08-3/08
	Santa Ana-Anaheim-Irvine PMSA, CA	Y	22360 FQ	25360 MW	30280 TQ	USBLS	
	Colorado	Y	21590 FQ	24250 MW	28290 TQ	USBLS	5/07
	Denver-Aurora MSA, CO	Y	22450 FQ	25010 MW	29010 TQ	USBLS	5/07
	Connecticut	H	10.65 AE	12.91 MW		CTBLS	1/08-3/08
	Bridgeport-Stamford-Norwalk MSA, CT	Y	23600 FQ	27370 MW	31740 TQ	USBLS	5/07
	Hartford-West Hartford-East Hartford MSA, CT	Y	22710 FQ	25930 MW	29830 TQ	USBLS	5/07
	Delaware	Y	21350 FQ	23940 MW	27650 TQ	USBLS	5/07
	Wilmington PMSA, DE-MD-NJ	Y	21500 FQ	23980 MW	28070 TQ	USBLS	5/07
	District of Columbia	Y	21490 FQ	24700 MW	28610 TQ	USBLS	5/07
	Washington-Arlington-Alexandria MSA, DC-VA-MD-WV	Y	22480 FQ	25440 MW	28940 TQ	USBLS	5/07
	Florida	Y	20910 FQ	23510 MW	27490 TQ	USBLS	5/07
	Fort Lauderdale-Pompano Beach-Deerfield Beach PMSA, FL	Y	21310 FQ	23720 MW	27490 TQ	USBLS	5/07
	Jacksonville MSA, FL	Y	21800 FQ	24300 MW	27840 TQ	USBLS	5/07
	Miami-Fort Lauderdale-Miami Beach MSA, FL	Y	21380 FQ	24120 MW	28340 TQ	USBLS	5/07
	Orlando-Kissimmee MSA, FL	Y	20760 FQ	22960 MW	25870 TQ	USBLS	5/07
	Tampa-St. Petersburg-Clearwater MSA, FL	Y	20820 FQ	23900 MW	29220 TQ	USBLS	5/07
	West Palm Beach-Boca Raton-Boynton Beach PMSA, FL	Y	21610 FQ	24500 MW	28340 TQ	USBLS	5/07
	Georgia	Y	20570 FQ	23510 MW	27410 TQ	USBLS	5/07
	Athens-Clarke County MSA, GA	Y	20620 FQ	23310 MW	26210 TQ	USBLS	5/07
	Atlanta-Sandy Springs-Marietta MSA, GA	Y	22010 FQ	25270 MW	29070 TQ	USBLS	5/07
	Hawaii	Y	20320 FQ	23460 MW	27550 TQ	USBLS	5/07
	Honolulu MSA, HI	Y	19660 FQ	22710 MW	26350 TQ	USBLS	5/07
	Idaho	Y	18490 FQ	21210 MW	23880 TQ	USBLS	5/07
	Boise City-Nampa MSA, ID	Y	18490 FQ	21540 MW	24210 TQ	USBLS	5/07
	Illinois	Y	19260 FQ	22530 MW	26910 TQ	USBLS	5/07
	Chicago-Naperville-Joliet MSA, IL-IN-WI	Y	20110 FQ	23290 MW	28070 TQ	USBLS	5/07
	Rockford MSA, IL	Y	19080 FQ	21630 MW	24530 TQ	USBLS	5/07
	Indiana	Y	19320 FQ	21880 MW	24660 TQ	USBLS	5/07
	Gary PMSA, IN	Y	19130 FQ	21300 MW	23560 TQ	USBLS	5/07
	Indianapolis-Carmel MSA, IN	Y	20440 FQ	22620 MW	25210 TQ	USBLS	5/07
	Iowa	Y	20100 FQ	22970 MW	26350 TQ	USBLS	5/07

AE	Average entry wage	AW	Average wage paid	FQ	First quartile wage	LO	Lowest wage paid	MTC	Median total compensation	TCC	Total cash compensation
AER	Average entry range	AWR	Average wage range	H	Hourly	LR	Low end range	MW	Median wage paid	TQ	Third quartile wage
AEX	Average experienced wage	AXR	Average experienced range	HI	Highest wage paid	M	Monthly	MWR	Median wage range	W	Weekly
ATC	Average total compensation	D	Daily	HR	High end range	MCC	Median cash compensation	S	See annotated source	Y	Yearly

Occupation/Type/Industry	Location	Per	Low	Mid	High	Source	Date
Teller	Des Moines-West Des Moines MSA, IA	Y	22320 FQ	25290 MW	29440 TQ	USBLS	5/07
	Kansas	Y	18000 FQ	20720 MW	23810 TQ	USBLS	5/07
	Lawrence MSA, KS	Y	17640 FQ	19720 MW	22200 TQ	USBLS	5/07
	Wichita MSA, KS	Y	18090 FQ	20610 MW	23510 TQ	USBLS	5/07
	Kentucky	Y	18255 FQ	21234 MW	24356 TQ	KYBLS	2008
	Louisville-Jefferson County MSA, KY-IN	Y	20250 FQ	22510 MW	25270 TQ	USBLS	5/07
	Louisiana	H	8.57 FQ	9.85 MW	11.27 TQ	LABLS	1/08-3/08
	Baton Rouge MSA, LA	Y	17650 FQ	20050 MW	23070 TQ	USBLS	5/07
	New Orleans-Metairie-Kenner MSA, LA	Y	19420 FQ	21910 MW	24540 TQ	USBLS	5/07
	Shreveport-Bossier City MSA, LA	Y	17810 FQ	20260 MW	23120 TQ	USBLS	5/07
	Maine	Y	19300 FQ	21770 MW	24490 TQ	USBLS	5/07
	Bangor MSA, ME	Y	19300 FQ	21250 MW	23560 TQ	USBLS	5/07
	Portland-South Portland-Biddeford MSA, ME	Y	20650 FQ	23000 MW	25780 TQ	USBLS	5/07
	Maryland	Y		26275 MW		MDBLS	3/08
	Baltimore-Towson MSA, MD	Y	22220 FQ	25180 MW	29150 TQ	USBLS	5/07
	Bethesda-Gaithersburg-Frederick PMSA, MD	Y	23930 FQ	26560 MW	29410 TQ	USBLS	5/07
	Massachusetts	Y	22920 FQ	26270 MW	30380 TQ	USBLS	5/07
	Boston-Cambridge-Quincy NECTA, MA	Y	23060 FQ	26840 MW	31430 TQ	USBLS	5/07
	Lynn-Peabody-Salem NECTA, MA	Y	22610 FQ	25680 MW	30090 TQ	USBLS	5/07
	Worcester MSA, MA-CT	Y	22110 FQ	24680 MW	28570 TQ	USBLS	5/07
	Michigan	Y	19860 FQ	22850 MW	26520 TQ	USBLS	5/07
	Detroit-Warren-Livonia MSA, MI	Y	20600 FQ	23290 MW	27270 TQ	USBLS	5/07
	Grand Rapids-Wyoming MSA, MI	Y	18170 FQ	20570 MW	23900 TQ	USBLS	5/07
	Warren-Troy-Farmington Hills PMSA, MI	Y	20160 FQ	22600 MW	25550 TQ	USBLS	5/07
	Minnesota	Y	21377 FQ	23927 MW	27081 TQ	MNBLS	10/08-12/08
	Duluth-Superior MSA, MN-WI	Y	20420 FQ	22897 MW	25614 TQ	MNBLS	10/08-12/08
	Minneapolis-Saint Paul MSA, MN-WI	Y	22314 FQ	24843 MW	28757 TQ	MNBLS	10/08-12/08
	Rochester MSA, MN	Y	21830 FQ	23838 MW	26286 TQ	MNBLS	10/08-12/08
	Mississippi	Y	18790 FQ	21580 MW	24280 TQ	USBLS	5/07
	Jackson MSA, MS	Y	20180 FQ	22200 MW	24250 TQ	USBLS	5/07
	Missouri	Y	18060 FQ	21020 MW	24300 TQ	USBLS	5/07
	Kansas City MSA, MO-KS	Y	19720 FQ	22380 MW	25400 TQ	USBLS	5/07
	St. Louis MSA, MO-IL	Y	19520 FQ	22430 MW	25660 TQ	USBLS	5/07
	Montana	Y	19690 FQ	22490 MW	25700 TQ	USBLS	5/07
	Billings MSA, MT	Y	20600 FQ	25050 MW	29770 TQ	USBLS	5/07
	Missoula MSA, MT	Y	18780 FQ	21130 MW	23390 TQ	USBLS	5/07
	Nebraska	Y	18400 FQ	21140 MW	24350 TQ	USBLS	5/07
	Lincoln MSA, NE	Y	19340 FQ	22060 MW	26240 TQ	USBLS	5/07
	Omaha-Council Bluffs MSA, NE-IA	Y	19500 FQ	21930 MW	24440 TQ	USBLS	5/07
	Nevada	H	10.61 FQ	11.85 MW	13.84 TQ	NVBLS	5/08
	Las Vegas-Paradise MSA, NV	H	10.57 FQ	11.84 MW	13.72 TQ	NVBLS	5/08
	New Hampshire	H	10.12 AE	11.75 MW	13.08 AEX	NHBLS	6/08
	Manchester MSA, NH	Y	20920 FQ	23680 MW	27420 TQ	USBLS	5/07
	Nashua NECTA, NH-MA	Y	21810 FQ	24890 MW	28880 TQ	USBLS	5/07
	Portsmouth MSA, NH-ME	Y	20830 FQ	23010 MW	26260 TQ	USBLS	5/07
	New Jersey	Y	20860 FQ	23660 MW	28040 TQ	USBLS	5/07
	Camden PMSA, NJ	Y	18830 FQ	22570 MW	26680 TQ	USBLS	5/07
	Edison PMSA, NJ	Y	21390 FQ	23980 MW	28720 TQ	USBLS	5/07
	Newark-Union PMSA, NJ-PA	Y	21430 FQ	24160 MW	28010 TQ	USBLS	5/07
	New Mexico	Y	18160 FQ	21160 MW	24180 TQ	USBLS	5/07
	Albuquerque MSA, NM	Y	19210 FQ	21720 MW	24250 TQ	USBLS	5/07
	Las Cruces MSA, NM	Y	17330 FQ	20750 MW	25620 TQ	USBLS	5/07
	New York	Y	20630 FQ	23360 MW	27570 TQ	USBLS	5/07
	Albany-Schenectady-Troy MSA, NY	Y	20220 FQ	22630 MW	25370 TQ	USBLS	5/07
	Buffalo-Niagara Falls MSA, NY	Y	19980 FQ	23880 MW	28980 TQ	USBLS	5/07
	Nassau-Suffolk PMSA, NY	Y	21240 FQ	23840 MW	28260 TQ	USBLS	5/07

AE	Average entry wage	AW	Average wage paid	FQ	First quartile wage
AER	Average entry range	AWR	Average wage range	H	Hourly
AEX	Average experienced wage	AXR	Average experienced range	HI	Highest wage paid
ATC	Average total compensation	D	Daily	HR	High end range

LO	Lowest wage paid	MTC	Median total compensation	TCC	Total cash compensation
LR	Low end range	MW	Median wage paid	TQ	Third quartile wage
M	Monthly	MWR	Median wage range	W	Weekly
MCC	Median cash compensation	S	See annotated source	Y	Yearly

Occupation/Type/Industry	Location	Per	Low	Mid	High	Source	Date
Teller	New York-Northern New Jersey-Long Island MSA, NY-NJ-PA	Y	21120 FQ	23870 MW	28380 TQ	USBLS	5/07
	North Carolina	Y	21000 FQ	23200 MW	25990 TQ	USBLS	5/07
	Charlotte-Gastonia-Concord MSA, NC-SC	Y	21750 FQ	24010 MW	27670 TQ	USBLS	5/07
	Raleigh-Cary MSA, NC	Y	21220 FQ	23550 MW	27080 TQ	USBLS	5/07
	Winston-Salem MSA, NC	Y	21230 FQ	23300 MW	25820 TQ	USBLS	5/07
	North Dakota	Y	19100 FQ	22090 MW	25720 TQ	USBLS	5/07
	Fargo MSA, ND-MN	Y	20630 FQ	24660 MW	29850 TQ	USBLS	5/07
	Ohio	Y	18980 FQ	22050 MW	25340 TQ	USBLS	5/07
	Canton-Massillon MSA, OH	Y	17750 FQ	21300 MW	24740 TQ	USBLS	5/07
	Cincinnati-Middletown MSA, OH-KY-IN	Y	19440 FQ	22210 MW	25050 TQ	USBLS	5/07
	Cleveland-Elyria-Mentor MSA, OH	Y	20700 FQ	24160 MW	27640 TQ	USBLS	5/07
	Columbus MSA, OH	Y	20760 FQ	23080 MW	25930 TQ	USBLS	5/07
	Dayton MSA, OH	Y	20060 FQ	23170 MW	26740 TQ	USBLS	5/07
	Oklahoma	Y	17450 FQ	19960 MW	23250 TQ	USBLS	5/07
	Oklahoma City MSA, OK	Y	18280 FQ	20730 MW	23790 TQ	USBLS	5/07
	Tulsa MSA, OK	Y	18940 FQ	21670 MW	24110 TQ	USBLS	5/07
	Oregon	H	10.09 FQ	11.32 MW	13.09 TQ	ORBLS	5/08
	Medford MSA, OR	Y	21340 FQ	23440 MW	26310 TQ	USBLS	5/07
	Portland-Vancouver-Beaverton MSA, OR-WA	Y	21150 FQ	23750 MW	28010 TQ	USBLS	5/07
	Pennsylvania	Y	18680 FQ	21670 MW	24770 TQ	USBLS	5/07
	Allentown-Bethlehem-Easton MSA, PA-NJ	Y	19130 FQ	22190 MW	25580 TQ	USBLS	5/07
	Philadelphia-Camden-Wilmington MSA, PA-NJ-DE-MD	Y	19490 FQ	22410 MW	25480 TQ	USBLS	5/07
	Pittsburgh MSA, PA	Y	18430 FQ	21570 MW	25190 TQ	USBLS	5/07
	York-Hanover MSA, PA	Y	18700 FQ	21310 MW	24120 TQ	USBLS	5/07
	Rhode Island	Y	22210 FQ	25190 MW	29270 TQ	USBLS	5/07
	Providence-Fall River-Warwick MSA, RI-MA	Y	22250 FQ	25290 MW	29360 TQ	USBLS	5/07
	South Carolina	Y	20460 FQ	22810 MW	25470 TQ	USBLS	5/07
	Charleston-North Charleston MSA, SC	Y	20260 FQ	22780 MW	25800 TQ	USBLS	5/07
	Columbia MSA, SC	Y	20480 FQ	22630 MW	24910 TQ	USBLS	5/07
	South Dakota	Y	19307 FQ	22340 MW	25037 TQ	SDBLS	7/08-9/08
	Sioux Falls MSA, SD	Y	19160 FQ	22414 MW	25469 TQ	SDBLS	7/08-9/08
	Tennessee	Y	19200 FQ	22050 MW	24960 TQ	USBLS	5/07
	Memphis MSA, TN-MS-AR	Y	19850 FQ	22670 MW	25730 TQ	USBLS	5/07
	Nashville-Davidson-Murfreesboro MSA, TN	Y	20710 FQ	23230 MW	26650 TQ	USBLS	5/07
	Texas	Y	19290 FQ	22430 MW	26270 TQ	USBLS	5/07
	Austin-Round Rock MSA, TX	Y	20620 FQ	22970 MW	26070 TQ	USBLS	5/07
	Dallas-Fort Worth-Arlington MSA, TX	Y	21230 FQ	23660 MW	27740 TQ	USBLS	5/07
	El Paso MSA, TX	Y	17790 FQ	19880 MW	22760 TQ	USBLS	5/07
	Houston-Sugar Land-Baytown MSA, TX	Y	21020 FQ	24370 MW	28660 TQ	USBLS	5/07
	San Antonio MSA, TX	Y	20520 FQ	23660 MW	28700 TQ	USBLS	5/07
	Utah	Y	18680 FQ	21130 MW	24350 TQ	USBLS	5/07
	Salt Lake City MSA, UT	Y	18890 FQ	21170 MW	24270 TQ	USBLS	5/07
	Vermont	Y	21850 FQ	24480 MW	28550 TQ	USBLS	5/07
	Burlington-South Burlington MSA, VT	Y	22570 FQ	25630 MW	29220 TQ	USBLS	5/07
	Virginia	Y	20350 FQ	23020 MW	26380 TQ	USBLS	5/07
	Richmond MSA, VA	Y	21050 FQ	23430 MW	27190 TQ	USBLS	5/07
	Virginia Beach-Norfolk-Newport News MSA, VA-NC	Y	19440 FQ	22080 MW	24760 TQ	USBLS	5/07
	Washington	H	10.44 FQ	11.70 MW	13.72 TQ	WABLS	3/08
	Seattle-Tacoma-Bellevue MSA, WA	Y	21890 FQ	24560 MW	28650 TQ	USBLS	5/07
	Spokane MSA, WA	Y	21040 FQ	23560 MW	27130 TQ	USBLS	5/07
	West Virginia	Y	16543 FQ	19063 MW	22209 TQ	WVBLS	7/08-9/08
	Charleston MSA, WV	Y	16990 FQ	19220 MW	22330 TQ	USBLS	5/07
	Parkersburg-Marietta-Vienna MSA, WV-OH	Y	16450 FQ	18880 MW	22030 TQ	USBLS	5/07
	Wisconsin	Y	19730 FQ	22380 MW	25180 TQ	USBLS	5/07

AE	Average entry wage	AW	Average wage paid	FQ	First quartile wage
AER	Average entry range	AWR	Average wage range	H	Hourly
AEX	Average experienced wage	AXR	Average experienced range	HI	Highest wage paid
ATC	Average total compensation	D	Daily	HR	High end range

LO	Lowest wage paid	MTC	Median total compensation	TCC	Total cash compensation
LR	Low end range	MW	Median wage paid	TQ	Third quartile wage
M	Monthly	MWR	Median wage range	W	Weekly
MCC	Median cash compensation	S	See annotated source	Y	Yearly

Occupation/Type/Industry	Location	Per	Low	Mid	High	Source	Date
Teller	Milwaukee-Waukesha-West Allis MSA, WI	Y	19840 FQ	22420 MW	25100 TQ	USBLS	5/07
	Wyoming	Y	18561 FQ	21568 MW	25170 TQ	WYBLS	9/08
	Cheyenne MSA, WY	Y	18644 FQ	21357 MW	24158 TQ	WYBLS	9/08
	Puerto Rico	Y	12890 FQ	14630 MW	17140 TQ	USBLS	5/07
	San Juan-Caguas-Guaynabo MSA, PR	Y	12930 FQ	14690 MW	17160 TQ	USBLS	5/07
	Virgin Islands	Y	16660 FQ	18340 MW	20440 TQ	USBLS	5/07
	Guam	Y	19120 FQ	21760 MW	24110 TQ	USBLS	5/07
Tennis Instructor							
Municipal Government	Seattle, WA	H	17.56 LO		20.36 HI	CSSS	2008
Terrazzo Worker and Finisher	Alabama	Y	21200 FQ	24090 MW	43130 TQ	USBLS	5/07
	Arizona	Y	23100 FQ	29330 MW	35070 TQ	USBLS	5/07
	California	H	16.11 FQ	19.00 MW	23.94 TQ	CABLS	1/08-3/08
	Connecticut	H	15.92 AE	19.53 MW		CTBLS	1/08-3/08
	Florida	Y	22400 FQ	29470 MW	35830 TQ	USBLS	5/07
	Georgia	Y	22930 FQ	28790 MW	33820 TQ	USBLS	5/07
	Illinois	Y	32600 FQ	57700 MW	64990 TQ	USBLS	5/07
	Indiana	Y	33640 FQ	39960 MW	53880 TQ	USBLS	5/07
	Massachusetts	Y	38450 FQ	69990 MW	76640 TQ	USBLS	5/07
	Michigan	Y	29800 FQ	35980 MW	42670 TQ	USBLS	5/07
	Minnesota	Y	33471 FQ	39794 MW	54464 TQ	MNBLS	10/08-12/08
	Mississippi	Y	22500 FQ	27860 MW	31240 TQ	USBLS	5/07
	Missouri	Y	31860 FQ	39610 MW	60060 TQ	USBLS	5/07
	Nevada	H	14.39 FQ	21.69 MW	25.27 TQ	NVBLS	5/08
	New Hampshire	H	16.94 AE	20.35 MW	21.86 AEX	NHBLS	6/08
	New Jersey	Y	25900 FQ	27530 MW	29170 TQ	USBLS	5/07
	New York	Y	41260 FQ	61840 MW	76230 TQ	USBLS	5/07
	North Carolina	Y	27170 FQ	30030 MW	33220 TQ	USBLS	5/07
	Ohio	Y	27140 FQ	31750 MW	43850 TQ	USBLS	5/07
	Pennsylvania	Y	30200 FQ	52400 MW	60110 TQ	USBLS	5/07
	South Carolina	Y	23700 FQ	29270 MW	36890 TQ	USBLS	5/07
	Tennessee	Y	22980 FQ	27590 MW	33380 TQ	USBLS	5/07
	Texas	Y	25680 FQ	33550 MW	50730 TQ	USBLS	5/07
	Virginia	Y	37800 FQ	43620 MW	47590 TQ	USBLS	5/07
	Wisconsin	Y	27990 FQ	33470 MW	44010 TQ	USBLS	5/07
	Puerto Rico	Y	22170 FQ	28490 MW	35620 TQ	USBLS	5/07
Test Monitor							
State Government	Ohio	H	15.09 LO		17.03 HI	ODAS	2008
Textbook Specialist							
Public Schools	Baldwin County, AL	Y	33941 LO		41087 HI	BCPSSS	2008-2009
Textile Bleaching and Dyeing Machine Operator and Tender	Alabama	Y	19210 FQ	22040 MW	25160 TQ	USBLS	5/07
	California	H	8.60 FQ	9.61 MW	11.74 TQ	CABLS	1/08-3/08
	Connecticut	H	9.90 AE	12.61 MW		CTBLS	1/08-3/08
	Florida	Y	16240 FQ	19310 MW	30610 TQ	USBLS	5/07
	Georgia	Y	22840 FQ	26590 MW	29810 TQ	USBLS	5/07
	Maine	Y	21970 FQ	26480 MW	30290 TQ	USBLS	5/07
	Massachusetts	Y	21250 FQ	27010 MW	31700 TQ	USBLS	5/07
	Michigan	Y	20020 FQ	25230 MW	47780 TQ	USBLS	5/07
	Minnesota	Y	19499 FQ	23003 MW	29846 TQ	MNBLS	10/08-12/08
	Mississippi	Y	20170 FQ	26480 MW	29100 TQ	USBLS	5/07
	New Hampshire	H	9.62 AE	12.19 MW	14.14 AEX	NHBLS	6/08
	New Jersey	Y	19370 FQ	24280 MW	29160 TQ	USBLS	5/07
	New York	Y	24620 FQ	33240 MW	38270 TQ	USBLS	5/07
	North Carolina	Y	20160 FQ	24070 MW	27830 TQ	USBLS	5/07
	Ohio	Y	17610 FQ	20200 MW	23390 TQ	USBLS	5/07
	Pennsylvania	Y	22920 FQ	25760 MW	29120 TQ	USBLS	5/07
	Rhode Island	Y	25800 FQ	28970 MW	31830 TQ	USBLS	5/07
	South Carolina	Y	20820 FQ	23370 MW	27310 TQ	USBLS	5/07
	Tennessee	Y	21750 FQ	24570 MW	27320 TQ	USBLS	5/07
	Texas	Y	20890 FQ	25520 MW	28970 TQ	USBLS	5/07
	Virginia	Y	21380 FQ	23760 MW	26240 TQ	USBLS	5/07
	Wisconsin	Y	25470 FQ	28870 MW	32480 TQ	USBLS	5/07
Textile Cutting Machine Setter, Operator, and Tender	Alabama	Y	18540 FQ	21380 MW	23570 TQ	USBLS	5/07

AE	Average entry wage	AW	Average wage paid	LO	Lowest wage paid	MTC	Median total compensation	TCC	Total cash compensation
AER	Average entry range	AWR	Average wage range	LR	Low end range	MW	Median wage paid	TQ	Third quartile wage
AEX	Average experienced wage	AXR	Average experienced range	HI	Highest wage paid	MWR	Median wage range	W	Weekly
ATC	Average total compensation	D	Daily	HR	High end range	MCC	Median cash compensation	S	See annotated source	Y	Yearly
		FQ	First quartile wage				
		H	Hourly				
		M	Monthly				

Occupation/Type/Industry	Location	Per	Low	Mid	High	Source	Date
Textile Cutting Machine Setter, Operator, and Tender	Arkansas	Y	18070 FQ	22030 MW	34240 TQ	USBLS	5/07
	Little Rock-North Little Rock MSA, AR	Y	22240 FQ	34440 MW	37250 TQ	USBLS	5/07
	California	H	8.32 FQ	9.25 MW	11.67 TQ	CABLS	1/08-3/08
	Los Angeles-Long Beach-Glendale PMSA, CA	H	8.21 FQ	9.02 MW	10.76 TQ	CABLS	1/08-3/08
	Oakland-Fremont-Hayward MSA, CA	H	8.74 FQ	9.92 MW	13.17 TQ	CABLS	1/08-3/08
	Riverside-San Bernardino-Ontario MSA, CA	H	10.23 FQ	13.29 MW	15.96 TQ	CABLS	1/08-3/08
	San Diego-Carlsbad-San Marcos MSA, CA	H	8.57 FQ	9.49 MW	12.36 TQ	CABLS	1/08-3/08
	San Francisco-San Mateo-Redwood PMSA, CA	H	11.01 FQ	13.54 MW	17.51 TQ	CABLS	1/08-3/08
	Santa Ana-Anaheim-Irvine PMSA, CA	Y	20030 FQ	24190 MW	30500 TQ	USBLS	5/07
	Connecticut	H	9.88 AE	11.00 MW		CTBLS	1/08-3/08
	Washington-Arlington-Alexandria MSA, DC-VA-MD-WV	Y	19880 FQ	23520 MW	37260 TQ	USBLS	5/07
	Florida	Y	17630 FQ	21660 MW	26140 TQ	USBLS	5/07
	Fort Lauderdale-Pompano Beach-Deerfield Beach PMSA, FL	Y	17020 FQ	20670 MW	26650 TQ	USBLS	5/07
	Jacksonville MSA, FL	Y	21720 FQ	24230 MW	33430 TQ	USBLS	5/07
	Miami-Fort Lauderdale-Miami Beach MSA, FL	Y	17030 FQ	21260 MW	25760 TQ	USBLS	5/07
	Tampa-St. Petersburg-Clearwater MSA, FL	Y	17010 FQ	21640 MW	25580 TQ	USBLS	5/07
	West Palm Beach-Boca Raton-Boynton Beach PMSA, FL	Y	14750 FQ	16100 MW	17600 TQ	USBLS	5/07
	Georgia	Y	20390 FQ	25610 MW	29210 TQ	USBLS	5/07
	Atlanta-Sandy Springs-Marietta MSA, GA	Y	16280 FQ	19280 MW	25990 TQ	USBLS	5/07
	Illinois	Y	16970 FQ	21760 MW	28850 TQ	USBLS	5/07
	Chicago-Naperville-Joliet MSA, IL-IN-WI	Y	16870 FQ	22810 MW	29140 TQ	USBLS	5/07
	Indiana	Y	18640 FQ	21780 MW	25480 TQ	USBLS	5/07
	Indianapolis-Carmel MSA, IN	Y	18710 FQ	21000 MW	23250 TQ	USBLS	5/07
	Iowa	Y	17460 FQ	21180 MW	26700 TQ	USBLS	5/07
	Kansas	Y	15480 FQ	19270 MW	26970 TQ	USBLS	5/07
	Kentucky	Y	21564 FQ	24438 MW	28458 TQ	KYBLS	2008
	Louisiana	H	6.76 FQ	9.73 MW	10.81 TQ	LABLS	1/08-3/08
	Maine	Y	18320 FQ	24860 MW	29340 TQ	USBLS	5/07
	Maryland	Y		19175 MW		MDBLS	3/08
	Baltimore-Towson MSA, MD	Y	16060 FQ	17790 MW	19500 TQ	USBLS	5/07
	Massachusetts	Y	20610 FQ	25780 MW	31290 TQ	USBLS	5/07
	Boston-Cambridge-Quincy NECTA, MA	Y	17480 FQ	24250 MW	31030 TQ	USBLS	5/07
	Michigan	Y	21300 FQ	27400 MW	36980 TQ	USBLS	5/07
	Detroit-Warren-Livonia MSA, MI	Y	20740 FQ	24030 MW	37350 TQ	USBLS	5/07
	Grand Rapids-Wyoming MSA, MI	Y	19630 FQ	29930 MW	41080 TQ	USBLS	5/07
	Warren-Troy-Farmington Hills PMSA, MI	Y	20720 FQ	24100 MW	52660 TQ	USBLS	5/07
	Minnesota	Y	21614 FQ	27948 MW	35941 TQ	MNBLS	10/08-12/08
	Minneapolis-Saint Paul MSA, MN-WI	Y	20318 FQ	28923 MW	34448 TQ	MNBLS	10/08-12/08
	Mississippi	Y	20060 FQ	23030 MW	27630 TQ	USBLS	5/07
	Missouri	Y	19880 FQ	23940 MW	27030 TQ	USBLS	5/07
	Kansas City MSA, MO-KS	Y	17180 FQ	19340 MW	24390 TQ	USBLS	5/07
	St. Louis MSA, MO-IL	Y	20490 FQ	22520 MW	24560 TQ	USBLS	5/07
	Nebraska	Y	16360 FQ	21090 MW	24720 TQ	USBLS	5/07
	New Jersey	Y	19170 FQ	22740 MW	28340 TQ	USBLS	5/07
	Camden PMSA, NJ	Y	19640 FQ	23590 MW	31860 TQ	USBLS	5/07
	Edison PMSA, NJ	Y	18430 FQ	23640 MW	28540 TQ	USBLS	5/07
	Newark-Union PMSA, NJ-PA	Y	19210 FQ	22930 MW	28330 TQ	USBLS	5/07
	New York	Y	15710 FQ	19970 MW	29180 TQ	USBLS	5/07
	Buffalo-Niagara Falls MSA, NY	Y	19590 FQ	21750 MW	23740 TQ	USBLS	5/07

AE	Average entry wage	AW	Average wage paid	FQ	First quartile wage	LO	Lowest wage paid	MTC	Median total compensation	TCC	Total cash compensation
AER	Average entry range	AWR	Average wage range	H	Hourly	LR	Low end range	MW	Median wage paid	TQ	Third quartile wage
AEX	Average experienced wage	AXR	Average experienced range	HI	Highest wage paid	M	Monthly	MWR	Median wage range	W	Weekly
ATC	Average total compensation	D	Daily	HR	High end range	MCC	Median cash compensation	S	See annotated source	Y	Yearly

Occupation/Type/Industry	Location	Per	Low	Mid	High	Source	Date
Textile Cutting Machine Setter, Operator, and Tender	Nassau-Suffolk PMSA, NY	Y	20200 FQ	27910 MW	36190 TQ	USBLS	5/07
	New York-Northern New Jersey-Long Island MSA, NY-NJ-PA	Y	15780 FQ	20960 MW	29960 TQ	USBLS	5/07
	North Carolina	Y	20420 FQ	25210 MW	29590 TQ	USBLS	5/07
	Charlotte-Gastonia-Concord MSA, NC-SC	Y	20020 FQ	21830 MW	23670 TQ	USBLS	5/07
	Ohio	Y	20190 FQ	25400 MW	33620 TQ	USBLS	5/07
	Cincinnati-Middletown MSA, OH-KY-IN	Y	24840 FQ	30990 MW	36400 TQ	USBLS	5/07
	Cleveland-Elyria-Mentor MSA, OH	Y	16330 FQ	18310 MW	23160 TQ	USBLS	5/07
	Columbus MSA, OH	Y	20410 FQ	24580 MW	42000 TQ	USBLS	5/07
	Oklahoma	Y	15970 FQ	18080 MW	22170 TQ	USBLS	5/07
	Oregon	H	10.08 FQ	11.59 MW	13.31 TQ	ORBLS	5/08
	Portland-Vancouver-Beaverton MSA, OR-WA	Y	20150 FQ	23330 MW	26520 TQ	USBLS	5/07
	Pennsylvania	Y	19670 FQ	24070 MW	32820 TQ	USBLS	5/07
	Allentown-Bethlehem-Easton MSA, PA-NJ	Y	21920 FQ	26880 MW	32250 TQ	USBLS	5/07
	Philadelphia-Camden-Wilmington MSA, PA-NJ-DE-MD	Y	22290 FQ	29350 MW	35830 TQ	USBLS	5/07
	Pittsburgh MSA, PA	Y	17830 FQ	19650 MW	21570 TQ	USBLS	5/07
	Rhode Island	Y	18830 FQ	22170 MW	26730 TQ	USBLS	5/07
	Providence-Fall River-Warwick MSA, RI-MA	Y	19000 FQ	22230 MW	26750 TQ	USBLS	5/07
	South Carolina	Y	18360 FQ	20780 MW	25210 TQ	USBLS	5/07
	Tennessee	Y	19270 FQ	24020 MW	29130 TQ	USBLS	5/07
	Nashville-Davidson-Murfreesboro MSA, TN	Y	23670 FQ	27700 MW	38400 TQ	USBLS	5/07
	Texas	Y	17860 FQ	22260 MW	26960 TQ	USBLS	5/07
	Dallas-Fort Worth-Arlington MSA, TX	Y	20160 FQ	24540 MW	28000 TQ	USBLS	5/07
	Houston-Sugar Land-Baytown MSA, TX	Y	17660 FQ	25460 MW	29180 TQ	USBLS	5/07
	San Antonio MSA, TX	Y	13710 FQ	16140 MW	18430 TQ	USBLS	5/07
	Utah	Y	19080 FQ	23250 MW	27430 TQ	USBLS	5/07
	Salt Lake City MSA, UT	Y	19320 FQ	23630 MW	27700 TQ	USBLS	5/07
	Virginia	Y	17600 FQ	21180 MW	24010 TQ	USBLS	5/07
	Washington	H	9.84 FQ	11.73 MW	14.37 TQ	WABLS	3/08
	Seattle-Tacoma-Bellevue MSA, WA	Y	21850 FQ	25760 MW	30330 TQ	USBLS	5/07
	Wisconsin	Y	22120 FQ	25490 MW	28990 TQ	USBLS	5/07
	Milwaukee-Waukesha-West Allis MSA, WI	Y	19640 FQ	25560 MW	32940 TQ	USBLS	5/07
	Puerto Rico	Y	12520 FQ	13840 MW	15450 TQ	USBLS	5/07
	San Juan-Caguas-Guaynabo MSA, PR	Y	12520 FQ	13830 MW	15390 TQ	USBLS	5/07
Textile Designer	United States	Y		57000 MW		247FASH	2009
Textile Knitting and Weaving Machine Setter, Operator, and Tender	Alabama	Y	19400 FQ	22150 MW	25050 TQ	USBLS	5/07
	Arizona	Y	22290 FQ	25710 MW	28630 TQ	USBLS	5/07
	California	H	8.43 FQ	9.30 MW	11.27 TQ	CABLS	1/08-3/08
	Florida	Y	15370 FQ	17550 MW	27080 TQ	USBLS	5/07
	Georgia	Y	23240 FQ	26940 MW	30560 TQ	USBLS	5/07
	Illinois	Y	24640 FQ	27990 MW	32270 TQ	USBLS	5/07
	Iowa	Y	19300 FQ	25220 MW	34680 TQ	USBLS	5/07
	Kansas	Y	21970 FQ	23890 MW	25730 TQ	USBLS	5/07
	Kentucky	Y	19901 FQ	24251 MW	29072 TQ	KYBLS	2008
	Louisiana	H	6.40 FQ	7.48 MW	9.87 TQ	LABLS	1/08-3/08
	Maine	Y	21420 FQ	23830 MW	25710 TQ	USBLS	5/07
	Maryland	Y		25650 MW		MDBLS	3/08
	Massachusetts	Y	22950 FQ	26460 MW	29250 TQ	USBLS	5/07
	Michigan	Y	26380 FQ	28330 MW	30310 TQ	USBLS	5/07
	Minnesota	Y	24351 FQ	27834 MW	31369 TQ	MNBLS	10/08-12/08
	Mississippi	Y	19010 FQ	25240 MW	28580 TQ	USBLS	5/07

Occupation/Type/Industry	Location	Per	Low	Mid	High	Source	Date
Textile Knitting and Weaving Machine Setter, Operator, and Tender							
	Missouri	Y	14550 FQ	17800 MW	23250 TQ	USBLS	5/07
	New Hampshire	H	11.36 AE	14.54 MW	16.25 AEX	NHBLS	6/08
	New Jersey	Y	17740 FQ	23450 MW	30480 TQ	USBLS	5/07
	New Mexico	Y	14750 FQ	18920 MW	25140 TQ	USBLS	5/07
	New York	Y	20720 FQ	24260 MW	30110 TQ	USBLS	5/07
	North Carolina	Y	20430 FQ	24290 MW	28880 TQ	USBLS	5/07
	Ohio	Y	22070 FQ	27820 MW	32250 TQ	USBLS	5/07
	Pennsylvania	Y	20630 FQ	24240 MW	30060 TQ	USBLS	5/07
	Rhode Island	Y	19460 FQ	22110 MW	26330 TQ	USBLS	5/07
	South Carolina	Y	22060 FQ	25640 MW	28840 TQ	USBLS	5/07
	Tennessee	Y	19970 FQ	23390 MW	28190 TQ	USBLS	5/07
	Texas	Y	20120 FQ	23890 MW	28420 TQ	USBLS	5/07
	Utah	Y	19750 FQ	25320 MW	32870 TQ	USBLS	5/07
	Virginia	Y	19190 FQ	24290 MW	27900 TQ	USBLS	5/07
Textile Winding, Twisting, and Drawing Out Machine Setter, Operator, and Tender							
	Alabama	Y	21200 FQ	23090 MW	24920 TQ	USBLS	5/07
	Arkansas	Y	24020 FQ	32720 MW	36380 TQ	USBLS	5/07
	California	H	8.33 FQ	9.02 MW	10.21 TQ	CABLS	1/08-3/08
	Connecticut	H	10.78 AE	13.66 MW		CTBLS	1/08-3/08
	Florida	Y	19910 FQ	29450 MW	38010 TQ	USBLS	5/07
	Georgia	Y	22060 FQ	24750 MW	28140 TQ	USBLS	5/07
	Kansas	Y	17550 FQ	21210 MW	25840 TQ	USBLS	5/07
	Kentucky	Y	18413 FQ	21324 MW	25239 TQ	KYBLS	2008
	Louisiana	H	9.93 FQ	11.17 MW	13.09 TQ	LABLS	1/08-3/08
	Maine	Y	21010 FQ	25840 MW	29370 TQ	USBLS	5/07
	Massachusetts	Y	21110 FQ	25250 MW	27840 TQ	USBLS	5/07
	Michigan	Y	26590 FQ	29560 MW	41700 TQ	USBLS	5/07
	Minnesota	Y	27658 FQ	39227 MW	54622 TQ	MNBLS	10/08-12/08
	Mississippi	Y	17340 FQ	19530 MW	22100 TQ	USBLS	5/07
	Missouri	Y	22670 FQ	25010 MW	31530 TQ	USBLS	5/07
	New Hampshire	H	9.33 AE	11.48 MW	13.03 AEX	NHBLS	6/08
	New Jersey	Y	20960 FQ	25120 MW	29340 TQ	USBLS	5/07
	New Mexico	Y	20470 FQ	23430 MW	29820 TQ	USBLS	5/07
	New York	Y	20420 FQ	24240 MW	27570 TQ	USBLS	5/07
	North Carolina	Y	19480 FQ	22150 MW	25070 TQ	USBLS	5/07
	Pennsylvania	Y	19270 FQ	22680 MW	28560 TQ	USBLS	5/07
	Rhode Island	Y	17910 FQ	20340 MW	22880 TQ	USBLS	5/07
	South Carolina	Y	20290 FQ	22590 MW	25860 TQ	USBLS	5/07
	Tennessee	Y	21830 FQ	24530 MW	27580 TQ	USBLS	5/07
	Texas	Y	19030 FQ	22020 MW	29710 TQ	USBLS	5/07
	Utah	Y	23590 FQ	25570 MW	27910 TQ	USBLS	5/07
	Vermont	Y	20420 FQ	22210 MW	25060 TQ	USBLS	5/07
	Virginia	Y	20110 FQ	22940 MW	26580 TQ	USBLS	5/07
	Washington	H	9.43 FQ	10.80 MW	12.43 TQ	WABLS	3/08
	Wisconsin	Y	20280 FQ	24040 MW	35650 TQ	USBLS	5/07
Texture Painter	United States	W		1891 MW		TAG	1/08
Therapeutic Recreation Specialist							
Public Schools	North Carolina	M	2719 LO		4641 HI	NCSS	2008-2009
Therapeutic Recreational Program Coordinator							
Municipal Government	Cincinnati, OH	Y	37720 LO		50920 HI	COHSS	10/08
Therapy Aide							
State Government	Ohio	H	15.09 LO		17.03 HI	ODAS	2008
Ticket Office Clerk							
Municipal Government	Walnut Creek, CA	Y	43621 LO		52332 HI	WCSWP	6/27/08
Tile and Marble Setter							
	Alabama	Y	20060 FQ	28080 MW	35550 TQ	USBLS	5/07
	Birmingham-Hoover MSA, AL	Y	25930 FQ	30630 MW	39000 TQ	USBLS	5/07
	Arizona	Y	21610 FQ	27140 MW	39260 TQ	USBLS	5/07
	Phoenix-Mesa-Scottsdale MSA, AZ	Y	21510 FQ	25320 MW	36780 TQ	USBLS	5/07
	Tucson MSA, AZ	Y	20040 FQ	25760 MW	40050 TQ	USBLS	5/07

AE Average entry wage	**AW** Average wage paid	**FQ** First quartile wage	**LO** Lowest wage paid	**MTC** Median total compensation **TCC** Total cash compensation
AER Average entry range	**AWR** Average wage range	**H** Hourly	**LR** Low end range	**MW** Median wage paid **TQ** Third quartile wage
AEX Average experienced wage	**AXR** Average experienced range	**HI** Highest wage paid	**M** Monthly	**MWR** Median wage range **W** Weekly
ATC Average total compensation **D** Daily		**HR** High end range	**MCC** Median cash compensation	**S** See annotated source **Y** Yearly

Occupation/Type/Industry	Location	Per	Low	Mid	High	Source	Date
Tile and Marble Setter	Arkansas	Y	23570 FQ	33960 MW	45840 TQ	USBLS	5/07
	Little Rock-North Little Rock MSA, AR	Y	25850 FQ	44260 MW	48050 TQ	USBLS	5/07
	California	H	17.75 FQ	22.33 MW	26.72 TQ	CABLS	1/08-3/08
	Los Angeles-Long Beach-Glendale PMSA, CA	H	17.12 FQ	20.80 MW	24.88 TQ	CABLS	1/08-3/08
	Oakland-Fremont-Hayward MSA, CA	H	17.28 FQ	23.20 MW	31.38 TQ	CABLS	1/08-3/08
	Riverside-San Bernardino-Ontario MSA, CA	H	17.00 FQ	22.56 MW	26.81 TQ	CABLS	1/08-3/08
	Sacramento-Arden Arcade-Roseville MSA, CA	H	18.93 FQ	23.32 MW	27.47 TQ	CABLS	1/08-3/08
	San Diego-Carlsbad-San Marcos MSA, CA	H	20.29 FQ	22.69 MW	25.17 TQ	CABLS	1/08-3/08
	San Francisco-San Mateo-Redwood PMSA, CA	H	19.71 FQ	23.95 MW	32.05 TQ	CABLS	1/08-3/08
	San Jose-Sunnyvale-Santa Clara MSA, CA	H	19.67 FQ	26.58 MW	34.22 TQ	CABLS	1/08-3/08
	Santa Ana-Anaheim-Irvine PMSA, CA	Y	38380 FQ	47420 MW	56470 TQ	USBLS	5/07
	Colorado	Y	30880 FQ	38160 MW	50140 TQ	USBLS	5/07
	Denver-Aurora MSA, CO	Y	36130 FQ	42890 MW	57260 TQ	USBLS	5/07
	Connecticut	H	17.96 AE	27.20 MW		CTBLS	1/08-3/08
	Bridgeport-Stamford-Norwalk MSA, CT	Y	55930 FQ	60560 MW	78310 TQ	USBLS	5/07
	Hartford-West Hartford-East Hartford MSA, CT	Y	37200 FQ	56180 MW	61560 TQ	USBLS	5/07
	Washington-Arlington-Alexandria MSA, DC-VA-MD-WV	Y	36580 FQ	44200 MW	53590 TQ	USBLS	5/07
	Florida	Y	22920 FQ	32570 MW	40630 TQ	USBLS	5/07
	Fort Lauderdale-Pompano Beach-Deerfield Beach PMSA, FL	Y	22130 FQ	24010 MW	28270 TQ	USBLS	5/07
	Jacksonville MSA, FL	Y	22220 FQ	27860 MW	36610 TQ	USBLS	5/07
	Miami-Fort Lauderdale-Miami Beach MSA, FL	Y	21420 FQ	24790 MW	36840 TQ	USBLS	5/07
	Orlando-Kissimmee MSA, FL	Y	28200 FQ	35780 MW	39550 TQ	USBLS	5/07
	Tampa-St. Petersburg-Clearwater MSA, FL	Y	30530 FQ	35150 MW	40830 TQ	USBLS	5/07
	West Palm Beach-Boca Raton-Boynton Beach PMSA, FL	Y	35130 FQ	39320 MW	45370 TQ	USBLS	5/07
	Georgia	Y	20960 FQ	25340 MW	37470 TQ	USBLS	5/07
	Atlanta-Sandy Springs-Marietta MSA, GA	Y	23210 FQ	25760 MW	40550 TQ	USBLS	5/07
	Hawaii	Y	41120 FQ	57700 MW	65400 TQ	USBLS	5/07
	Honolulu MSA, HI	Y	45310 FQ	58900 MW	66070 TQ	USBLS	5/07
	Idaho	Y	24510 FQ	28340 MW	38310 TQ	USBLS	5/07
	Illinois	Y	42100 FQ	55960 MW	69620 TQ	USBLS	5/07
	Chicago-Naperville-Joliet MSA, IL-IN-WI	Y	43690 FQ	57230 MW	70380 TQ	USBLS	5/07
	Indiana	Y	25790 FQ	29100 MW	42620 TQ	USBLS	5/07
	Indianapolis-Carmel MSA, IN	Y	25770 FQ	28610 MW	43850 TQ	USBLS	5/07
	Iowa	Y	26750 FQ	36260 MW	52660 TQ	USBLS	5/07
	Kansas	Y	35620 FQ	44500 MW	51350 TQ	USBLS	5/07
	Kentucky	Y	24601 FQ	31000 MW	39190 TQ	KYBLS	2008
	Louisville-Jefferson County MSA, KY-IN	Y	25650 FQ	29220 MW	34820 TQ	USBLS	5/07
	Louisiana	H	11.66 FQ	15.42 MW	19.25 TQ	LABLS	1/08-3/08
	Baton Rouge MSA, LA	Y	25440 FQ	34230 MW	40390 TQ	USBLS	5/07
	New Orleans-Metairie-Kenner MSA, LA	Y	23140 FQ	31160 MW	39320 TQ	USBLS	5/07
	Maine	Y	27030 FQ	32570 MW	40990 TQ	USBLS	5/07
	Maryland	Y		45675 MW		MDBLS	3/08
	Baltimore-Towson MSA, MD	Y	35910 FQ	44030 MW	51530 TQ	USBLS	5/07
	Bethesda-Gaithersburg-Frederick PMSA, MD	Y	34280 FQ	45430 MW	51480 TQ	USBLS	5/07
	Massachusetts	Y	33960 FQ	44970 MW	61700 TQ	USBLS	5/07
	Boston-Cambridge-Quincy NECTA, MA	Y	36650 FQ	49590 MW	69010 TQ	USBLS	5/07
	Michigan	Y	34130 FQ	44200 MW	54880 TQ	USBLS	5/07

AE	Average entry wage	AW	Average wage paid	FQ	First quartile wage	LO	Lowest wage paid	MTC	Median total compensation	TCC	Total cash compensation
AER	Average entry range	AWR	Average wage range	H	Hourly	LR	Low end range	MW	Median wage paid	TQ	Third quartile wage
AEX	Average experienced wage	AXR	Average experienced range	HI	Highest wage paid	M	Monthly	MWR	Median wage range	W	Weekly
ATC	Average total compensation	D	Daily	HR	High end range	MCC	Median cash compensation	S	See annotated source	Y	Yearly

Occupation/Type/Industry	Location	Per	Low	Mid	High	Source	Date
Tile and Marble Setter	Detroit-Warren-Livonia MSA, MI	Y	35320 FQ	45660 MW	58750 TQ	USBLS	5/07
	Grand Rapids-Wyoming MSA, MI	Y	33920 FQ	42630 MW	47260 TQ	USBLS	5/07
	Warren-Troy-Farmington Hills PMSA, MI	Y	35340 FQ	45550 MW	58000 TQ	USBLS	5/07
	Minnesota	Y	36095 FQ	43008 MW	53262 TQ	MNBLS	10/08-12/08
	Minneapolis-Saint Paul MSA, MN-WI	Y	36885 FQ	43556 MW	53189 TQ	MNBLS	10/08-12/08
	Mississippi	Y	22160 FQ	27610 MW	34390 TQ	USBLS	5/07
	Missouri	Y	29840 FQ	39120 MW	56230 TQ	USBLS	5/07
	Kansas City MSA, MO-KS	Y	33350 FQ	41380 MW	50480 TQ	USBLS	5/07
	St. Louis MSA, MO-IL	Y	34430 FQ	53620 MW	59690 TQ	USBLS	5/07
	Springfield MSA, MO	Y	22550 FQ	32450 MW	47420 TQ	USBLS	5/07
	Montana	Y	22610 FQ	26360 MW	35430 TQ	USBLS	5/07
	Nebraska	Y	26810 FQ	35190 MW	45600 TQ	USBLS	5/07
	Omaha-Council Bluffs MSA, NE-IA	Y	25080 FQ	33580 MW	44850 TQ	USBLS	5/07
	Nevada	H	18.98 FQ	22.79 MW	26.08 TQ	NVBLS	5/08
	Las Vegas-Paradise MSA, NV	H	18.84 FQ	22.74 MW	25.99 TQ	NVBLS	5/08
	New Hampshire	H	13.21 AE	18.10 MW	20.24 AEX	NHBLS	6/08
	New Jersey	Y	35770 FQ	61250 MW	75890 TQ	USBLS	5/07
	Camden PMSA, NJ	Y	31060 FQ	34790 MW	38430 TQ	USBLS	5/07
	Edison PMSA, NJ	Y	36390 FQ	57870 MW	73690 TQ	USBLS	5/07
	Newark-Union PMSA, NJ-PA	Y	30710 FQ	60760 MW	82080 TQ	USBLS	5/07
	New Mexico	Y	22710 FQ	28070 MW	32040 TQ	USBLS	5/07
	Albuquerque MSA, NM	Y	22520 FQ	28600 MW	32640 TQ	USBLS	5/07
	Las Cruces MSA, NM	Y	18930 FQ	26920 MW	29570 TQ	USBLS	5/07
	New York	Y	36410 FQ	53190 MW	68380 TQ	USBLS	5/07
	Albany-Schenectady-Troy MSA, NY	Y	47500 FQ	52850 MW	64320 TQ	USBLS	5/07
	Buffalo-Niagara Falls MSA, NY	Y	23970 FQ	58070 MW	64700 TQ	USBLS	5/07
	Nassau-Suffolk PMSA, NY	Y	40870 FQ	74690 MW	89550 TQ	USBLS	5/07
	New York-Northern New Jersey-Long Island MSA, NY-NJ-PA	Y	38670 FQ	55880 MW	75740 TQ	USBLS	5/07
	North Carolina	Y	23510 FQ	28320 MW	35040 TQ	USBLS	5/07
	Charlotte-Gastonia-Concord MSA, NC-SC	Y	23950 FQ	28640 MW	35730 TQ	USBLS	5/07
	Raleigh-Cary MSA, NC	Y	26470 FQ	31170 MW	40340 TQ	USBLS	5/07
	North Dakota	Y	19690 FQ	36180 MW	44410 TQ	USBLS	5/07
	Ohio	Y	29090 FQ	41360 MW	50780 TQ	USBLS	5/07
	Cincinnati-Middletown MSA, OH-KY-IN	Y	29070 FQ	39790 MW	47640 TQ	USBLS	5/07
	Cleveland-Elyria-Mentor MSA, OH	Y	48370 FQ	51940 MW	56310 TQ	USBLS	5/07
	Columbus MSA, OH	Y	32660 FQ	40390 MW	46850 TQ	USBLS	5/07
	Dayton MSA, OH	Y	29820 FQ	33060 MW	42730 TQ	USBLS	5/07
	Oklahoma	Y	15340 FQ	27560 MW	34340 TQ	USBLS	5/07
	Tulsa MSA, OK	Y	16150 FQ	28120 MW	35100 TQ	USBLS	5/07
	Oregon	H	13.62 FQ	16.58 MW	20.67 TQ	ORBLS	5/08
	Portland-Vancouver-Beaverton MSA, OR-WA	Y	27890 FQ	33980 MW	43390 TQ	USBLS	5/07
	Pennsylvania	Y	33690 FQ	41620 MW	50420 TQ	USBLS	5/07
	Allentown-Bethlehem-Easton MSA, PA-NJ	Y	30150 FQ	35590 MW	41410 TQ	USBLS	5/07
	Lancaster MSA, PA	Y	33780 FQ	38210 MW	45540 TQ	USBLS	5/07
	Philadelphia-Camden-Wilmington MSA, PA-NJ-DE-MD	Y	34870 FQ	41750 MW	53440 TQ	USBLS	5/07
	Pittsburgh MSA, PA	Y	32860 FQ	43640 MW	51760 TQ	USBLS	5/07
	Rhode Island	Y	38910 FQ	45470 MW	51000 TQ	USBLS	5/07
	Providence-Fall River-Warwick MSA, RI-MA	Y	41530 FQ	45560 MW	49510 TQ	USBLS	5/07
	South Carolina	Y	21130 FQ	28170 MW	31940 TQ	USBLS	5/07
	Charleston-North Charleston MSA, SC	Y	29290 FQ	33750 MW	38110 TQ	USBLS	5/07
	Columbia MSA, SC	Y	26500 FQ	29390 MW	33040 TQ	USBLS	5/07
	Myrtle Beach-Conway-North Myrtle Beach MSA, SC	Y	17800 FQ	19420 MW	22550 TQ	USBLS	5/07
	South Dakota	Y	26275 FQ	29809 MW	33970 TQ	SDBLS	7/08-9/08

AE	Average entry wage	AW	Average wage paid	FQ	First quartile wage	LO	Lowest wage paid	MTC	Median total compensation	TCC	Total cash compensation
AER	Average entry range	AWR	Average wage range	H	Hourly	LR	Low end range	MW	Median wage paid	TQ	Third quartile wage
AEX	Average experienced wage	AXR	Average experienced range	HI	Highest wage paid	M	Monthly	MWR	Median wage range	W	Weekly
ATC	Average total compensation	D	Daily	HR	High end range	MCC	Median cash compensation	S	See annotated source	Y	Yearly

Occupation/Type/Industry	Location	Per	Low	Mid	High	Source	Date
Tile and Marble Setter	Tennessee	Y	23880 FQ	29690 MW	35120 TQ	USBLS	5/07
	Memphis MSA, TN-MS-AR	Y	23530 FQ	29500 MW	34970 TQ	USBLS	5/07
	Nashville-Davidson-Murfreesboro MSA, TN	Y	22870 FQ	27530 MW	31020 TQ	USBLS	5/07
	Texas	Y	20730 FQ	25880 MW	33370 TQ	USBLS	5/07
	Austin-Round Rock MSA, TX	Y	28660 FQ	32400 MW	37050 TQ	USBLS	5/07
	Dallas-Fort Worth-Arlington MSA, TX	Y	19250 FQ	24900 MW	33680 TQ	USBLS	5/07
	Houston-Sugar Land-Baytown MSA, TX	Y	21610 FQ	28180 MW	34510 TQ	USBLS	5/07
	San Antonio MSA, TX	Y	19720 FQ	23150 MW	28400 TQ	USBLS	5/07
	Utah	Y	29780 FQ	36290 MW	44870 TQ	USBLS	5/07
	Ogden-Clearfield MSA, UT	Y	30820 FQ	34300 MW	37610 TQ	USBLS	5/07
	Provo-Orem MSA, UT	Y	26030 FQ	29750 MW	33500 TQ	USBLS	5/07
	St. George MSA, UT	Y	28620 FQ	33350 MW	46860 TQ	USBLS	5/07
	Salt Lake City MSA, UT	Y	35120 FQ	43050 MW	53490 TQ	USBLS	5/07
	Virginia	Y	24860 FQ	36240 MW	48410 TQ	USBLS	5/07
	Richmond MSA, VA	Y	25560 FQ	35390 MW	41910 TQ	USBLS	5/07
	Virginia Beach-Norfolk-Newport News MSA, VA-NC	Y	30110 FQ	35470 MW	39850 TQ	USBLS	5/07
	Washington	H	19.08 FQ	26.77 MW	34.04 TQ	WABLS	3/08
	Seattle-Tacoma-Bellevue MSA, WA	Y	38100 FQ	55240 MW	70140 TQ	USBLS	5/07
	West Virginia	Y	28577 FQ	47141 MW	52357 TQ	WVBLS	7/08-9/08
	Wisconsin	Y	34590 FQ	48780 MW	58720 TQ	USBLS	5/07
	Appleton MSA, WI	Y	26440 FQ	40520 MW	56530 TQ	USBLS	5/07
	Milwaukee-Waukesha-West Allis MSA, WI	Y	33590 FQ	42630 MW	57120 TQ	USBLS	5/07
	Wyoming	Y	34983 FQ	45314 MW	52252 TQ	WYBLS	9/08
	Puerto Rico	Y	15240 FQ	17570 MW	19340 TQ	USBLS	5/07
	San Juan-Caguas-Guaynabo MSA, PR	Y	15130 FQ	17500 MW	19210 TQ	USBLS	5/07
Timing Device Assembler, Adjuster, and Calibrator	Arkansas	Y	27800 FQ	32500 MW	35860 TQ	USBLS	5/07
	California	H	12.16 FQ	15.37 MW	22.75 TQ	CABLS	1/08-3/08
	Connecticut	H	11.96 AE	14.16 MW		CTBLS	1/08-3/08
	Illinois	Y	22720 FQ	26000 MW	29020 TQ	USBLS	5/07
	Massachusetts	Y	25030 FQ	33270 MW	39240 TQ	USBLS	5/07
	Michigan	Y	27090 FQ	35150 MW	43820 TQ	USBLS	5/07
	Minnesota	Y	25968 FQ	30312 MW	35298 TQ	MNBLS	10/08-12/08
	New York	Y	24490 FQ	30840 MW	34590 TQ	USBLS	5/07
	Pennsylvania	Y	24930 FQ	30320 MW	36610 TQ	USBLS	5/07
	Tennessee	Y	22870 FQ	29510 MW	33520 TQ	USBLS	5/07
	Texas	Y	25850 FQ	35970 MW	49920 TQ	USBLS	5/07
	Utah	Y	22470 FQ	25240 MW	28770 TQ	USBLS	5/07
Tinsmith Municipal Government	Cincinnati, OH	Y			55978 HI	COHSS	10/08
Tire Builder	California	H	9.48 FQ	11.80 MW	14.22 TQ	CABLS	1/08-3/08
	Florida	Y	17690 FQ	22130 MW	28630 TQ	USBLS	5/07
	Georgia	Y	25000 FQ	32780 MW	38010 TQ	USBLS	5/07
	Illinois	Y	29600 FQ	42900 MW	48750 TQ	USBLS	5/07
	Kansas	Y	41520 FQ	47290 MW	54020 TQ	USBLS	5/07
	Kentucky	Y	23633 FQ	31848 MW	35767 TQ	KYBLS	2008
	Michigan	Y	17850 FQ	20500 MW	26690 TQ	USBLS	5/07
	Missouri	Y	25550 FQ	29060 MW	35490 TQ	USBLS	5/07
	Nebraska	Y	20490 FQ	24750 MW	28980 TQ	USBLS	5/07
	New Jersey	Y	17680 FQ	20300 MW	23140 TQ	USBLS	5/07
	New York	Y	41300 FQ	44280 MW	47240 TQ	USBLS	5/07
	Ohio	Y	31630 FQ	42800 MW	48580 TQ	USBLS	5/07
	Oklahoma	Y	43110 FQ	48290 MW	53490 TQ	USBLS	5/07
	Oregon	H	9.16 FQ	11.07 MW	13.69 TQ	ORBLS	5/08
	Pennsylvania	Y	26260 FQ	31730 MW	37650 TQ	USBLS	5/07
	South Carolina	Y	23660 FQ	39470 MW	44860 TQ	USBLS	5/07
	Texas	Y	18220 FQ	22050 MW	30540 TQ	USBLS	5/07
	Virginia	Y	29750 FQ	39640 MW	46000 TQ	USBLS	5/07
	Washington	H	10.52 FQ	12.52 MW	14.06 TQ	WABLS	3/08
	Wisconsin	Y	30450 FQ	43860 MW	47940 TQ	USBLS	5/07
Tire Repairer and Changer	Alabama	Y	16050 FQ	19330 MW	23970 TQ	USBLS	5/07

AE	Average entry wage	**AW**	Average wage paid	**FQ**	First quartile wage	**LO** Lowest wage paid	**MTC** Median total compensation	**TCC** Total cash compensation
AER	Average entry range	**AWR**	Average wage range	**H**	Hourly	**LR** Low end range	**MW** Median wage paid	**TQ** Third quartile wage
AEX	Average experienced wage	**AXR**	Average experienced range	**HI**	Highest wage paid	**M** Monthly	**MWR** Median wage range	**W** Weekly
ATC	Average total compensation	**D**	Daily	**HR**	High end range	**MCC** Median cash compensation	**S** See annotated source	**Y** Yearly

Occupation/Type/Industry	Location	Per	Low	Mid	High	Source	Date
Tire Repairer and Changer	Birmingham-Hoover MSA, AL	Y	13730 FQ	16500 MW	22660 TQ	USBLS	5/07
	Alaska	Y	19840 FQ	23180 MW	29350 TQ	USBLS	5/07
	Anchorage MSA, AK	Y	20290 FQ	23520 MW	31330 TQ	USBLS	5/07
	Arizona	Y	17800 FQ	21190 MW	29110 TQ	USBLS	5/07
	Phoenix-Mesa-Scottsdale MSA, AZ	Y	18830 FQ	23660 MW	33560 TQ	USBLS	5/07
	Tucson MSA, AZ	Y	16920 FQ	18330 MW	20770 TQ	USBLS	5/07
	Arkansas	Y	16560 FQ	19360 MW	23190 TQ	USBLS	5/07
	Little Rock-North Little Rock MSA, AR	Y	18560 FQ	22290 MW	26180 TQ	USBLS	5/07
	Pine Bluff MSA, AR	Y	14040 FQ	14930 MW	15820 TQ	USBLS	5/07
	California	H	9.39 FQ	11.37 MW	14.81 TQ	CABLS	1/08-3/08
	Los Angeles-Long Beach-Glendale PMSA, CA	H	9.57 FQ	11.34 MW	14.42 TQ	CABLS	1/08-3/08
	Oakland-Fremont-Hayward MSA, CA	H	10.58 FQ	12.82 MW	15.82 TQ	CABLS	1/08-3/08
	Riverside-San Bernardino-Ontario MSA, CA	H	8.95 FQ	10.88 MW	14.16 TQ	CABLS	1/08-3/08
	Sacramento-Arden Arcade-Roseville MSA, CA	H	8.96 FQ	10.58 MW	12.97 TQ	CABLS	1/08-3/08
	San Diego-Carlsbad-San Marcos MSA, CA	H	10.00 FQ	11.73 MW	14.59 TQ	CABLS	1/08-3/08
	San Francisco-San Mateo-Redwood PMSA, CA	H	12.26 FQ	14.80 MW	21.19 TQ	CABLS	1/08-3/08
	San Jose-Sunnyvale-Santa Clara MSA, CA	H	10.73 FQ	16.52 MW	18.81 TQ	CABLS	1/08-3/08
	Santa Ana-Anaheim-Irvine PMSA, CA	Y	18240 FQ	21640 MW	27010 TQ	USBLS	5/07
	Colorado	Y	19390 FQ	22690 MW	27300 TQ	USBLS	5/07
	Denver-Aurora MSA, CO	Y	20060 FQ	23250 MW	27500 TQ	USBLS	5/07
	Connecticut	H	8.84 AE	10.91 MW		CTBLS	1/08-3/08
	Bridgeport-Stamford-Norwalk MSA, CT	Y	20010 FQ	23510 MW	28470 TQ	USBLS	5/07
	Hartford-West Hartford-East Hartford MSA, CT	Y	18090 FQ	21190 MW	26880 TQ	USBLS	5/07
	Delaware	Y	16870 FQ	20760 MW	28110 TQ	USBLS	5/07
	Wilmington PMSA, DE-MD-NJ	Y	19270 FQ	21940 MW	26060 TQ	USBLS	5/07
	District of Columbia	Y	19680 FQ	22210 MW	24400 TQ	USBLS	5/07
	Washington-Arlington-Alexandria MSA, DC-VA-MD-WV	Y	19990 FQ	23250 MW	28020 TQ	USBLS	5/07
	Florida	Y	18320 FQ	21880 MW	26180 TQ	USBLS	5/07
	Fort Lauderdale-Pompano Beach-Deerfield Beach PMSA, FL	Y	17410 FQ	21030 MW	28180 TQ	USBLS	5/07
	Jacksonville MSA, FL	Y	19310 FQ	22640 MW	27220 TQ	USBLS	5/07
	Miami-Fort Lauderdale-Miami Beach MSA, FL	Y	17310 FQ	21420 MW	26870 TQ	USBLS	5/07
	Orlando-Kissimmee MSA, FL	Y	18160 FQ	21270 MW	24630 TQ	USBLS	5/07
	Tampa-St. Petersburg-Clearwater MSA, FL	Y	18590 FQ	22120 MW	25700 TQ	USBLS	5/07
	West Palm Beach-Boca Raton-Boynton Beach PMSA, FL	Y	17280 FQ	22420 MW	28560 TQ	USBLS	5/07
	Georgia	Y	17720 FQ	22480 MW	27510 TQ	USBLS	5/07
	Atlanta-Sandy Springs-Marietta MSA, GA	Y	21260 FQ	25620 MW	30410 TQ	USBLS	5/07
	Macon MSA, GA	Y	16800 FQ	18110 MW	19570 TQ	USBLS	5/07
	Savannah MSA, GA	Y	18300 FQ	21350 MW	32550 TQ	USBLS	5/07
	Hawaii	Y	19960 FQ	25620 MW	35380 TQ	USBLS	5/07
	Honolulu MSA, HI	Y	17070 FQ	22540 MW	29740 TQ	USBLS	5/07
	Idaho	Y	18670 FQ	23680 MW	28900 TQ	USBLS	5/07
	Boise City-Nampa MSA, ID	Y	21120 FQ	26320 MW	31140 TQ	USBLS	5/07
	Illinois	Y	17830 FQ	21620 MW	25160 TQ	USBLS	5/07
	Chicago-Naperville-Joliet MSA, IL-IN-WI	Y	17720 FQ	21450 MW	26880 TQ	USBLS	5/07
	Peoria MSA, IL	Y	20170 FQ	22220 MW	24280 TQ	USBLS	5/07
	Rockford MSA, IL	Y	17520 FQ	18990 MW	20230 TQ	USBLS	5/07
	Indiana	Y	17770 FQ	20870 MW	26040 TQ	USBLS	5/07
	Gary PMSA, IN	Y	17620 FQ	19770 MW	24740 TQ	USBLS	5/07
	Indianapolis-Carmel MSA, IN	Y	18370 FQ	21310 MW	27160 TQ	USBLS	5/07

AE	Average entry wage	AW	Average wage paid	FQ	First quartile wage	LO	Lowest wage paid	MTC	Median total compensation	TCC	Total cash compensation
AER	Average entry range	AWR	Average wage range	H	Hourly	LR	Low end range	MW	Median wage paid	TQ	Third quartile wage
AEX	Average experienced wage	AXR	Average experienced range	HI	Highest wage paid	M	Monthly	MWR	Median wage range	W	Weekly
ATC	Average total compensation	D	Daily	HR	High end range	MCC	Median cash compensation	S	See annotated source	Y	Yearly

1600

Occupation/Type/Industry	Location	Per	Low	Mid	High	Source	Date
Tire Repairer and Changer	South Bend-Mishawaka MSA, IN-MI	Y	16150 FQ	18680 MW	22400 TQ	USBLS	5/07
	Iowa	Y	18780 FQ	22190 MW	25710 TQ	USBLS	5/07
	Des Moines-West Des Moines MSA, IA	Y	19300 FQ	21680 MW	24070 TQ	USBLS	5/07
	Sioux City MSA, IA-NE-SD	Y	20120 FQ	23320 MW	28340 TQ	USBLS	5/07
	Kansas	Y	18040 FQ	21280 MW	25140 TQ	USBLS	5/07
	Wichita MSA, KS	Y	21690 FQ	23830 MW	25920 TQ	USBLS	5/07
	Kentucky	Y	17519 FQ	22237 MW	28431 TQ	KYBLS	2008
	Louisville-Jefferson County MSA, KY-IN	Y	18140 FQ	22410 MW	26200 TQ	USBLS	5/07
	Louisiana	H	7.88 FQ	9.15 MW	11.07 TQ	LABLS	1/08-3/08
	Baton Rouge MSA, LA	Y	17890 FQ	21120 MW	24510 TQ	USBLS	5/07
	New Orleans-Metairie-Kenner MSA, LA	Y	16730 FQ	18570 MW	21950 TQ	USBLS	5/07
	Maine	Y	17700 FQ	19920 MW	25510 TQ	USBLS	5/07
	Portland-South Portland-Biddeford MSA, ME	Y	18580 FQ	23700 MW	28270 TQ	USBLS	5/07
	Maryland	Y		22875 MW		MDBLS	3/08
	Baltimore-Towson MSA, MD	Y	20940 FQ	23200 MW	25310 TQ	USBLS	5/07
	Bethesda-Gaithersburg-Frederick PMSA, MD	Y	19410 FQ	21920 MW	24430 TQ	USBLS	5/07
	Massachusetts	Y	18060 FQ	20650 MW	26320 TQ	USBLS	5/07
	Boston-Cambridge-Quincy NECTA, MA	Y	18480 FQ	20500 MW	23260 TQ	USBLS	5/07
	Springfield MSA, MA-CT	Y	17220 FQ	18730 MW	25730 TQ	USBLS	5/07
	Worcester MSA, MA-CT	Y	19510 FQ	21360 MW	23210 TQ	USBLS	5/07
	Michigan	Y	18570 FQ	22010 MW	27450 TQ	USBLS	5/07
	Detroit-Warren-Livonia MSA, MI	Y	17880 FQ	20820 MW	24840 TQ	USBLS	5/07
	Grand Rapids-Wyoming MSA, MI	Y	21480 FQ	25060 MW	34970 TQ	USBLS	5/07
	Warren-Troy-Farmington Hills PMSA, MI	Y	18380 FQ	21660 MW	25560 TQ	USBLS	5/07
	Minnesota	Y	20643 FQ	24157 MW	29894 TQ	MNBLS	10/08-12/08
	Duluth-Superior MSA, MN-WI	Y	18020 FQ	21524 MW	25615 TQ	MNBLS	10/08-12/08
	Minneapolis-Saint Paul MSA, MN-WI	Y	21367 FQ	24555 MW	31027 TQ	MNBLS	10/08-12/08
	Rochester MSA, MN	Y	22314 FQ	25027 MW	29975 TQ	MNBLS	10/08-12/08
	Mississippi	Y	18330 FQ	22100 MW	25380 TQ	USBLS	5/07
	Jackson MSA, MS	Y	18350 FQ	22340 MW	25220 TQ	USBLS	5/07
	Missouri	Y	18010 FQ	22310 MW	27930 TQ	USBLS	5/07
	Kansas City MSA, MO-KS	Y	18740 FQ	21660 MW	25010 TQ	USBLS	5/07
	St. Louis MSA, MO-IL	Y	19190 FQ	24780 MW	31090 TQ	USBLS	5/07
	Montana	Y	18190 FQ	21420 MW	25200 TQ	USBLS	5/07
	Billings MSA, MT	Y	18050 FQ	19990 MW	25860 TQ	USBLS	5/07
	Great Falls MSA, MT	Y	16620 FQ	18010 MW	19960 TQ	USBLS	5/07
	Nebraska	Y	19310 FQ	22020 MW	24600 TQ	USBLS	5/07
	Omaha-Council Bluffs MSA, NE-IA	Y	21030 FQ	22770 MW	24620 TQ	USBLS	5/07
	Nevada	H	10.73 FQ	12.81 MW	16.94 TQ	NVBLS	5/08
	Las Vegas-Paradise MSA, NV	H	10.25 FQ	12.41 MW	16.37 TQ	NVBLS	5/08
	New Hampshire	H	9.35 AE	11.42 MW	12.87 AEX	NHBLS	6/08
	Manchester MSA, NH	Y	19660 FQ	22430 MW	26610 TQ	USBLS	5/07
	Nashua NECTA, NH-MA	Y	20260 FQ	22360 MW	24720 TQ	USBLS	5/07
	Portsmouth MSA, NH-ME	Y	24450 FQ	26860 MW	29100 TQ	USBLS	5/07
	New Jersey	Y	17480 FQ	22640 MW	28160 TQ	USBLS	5/07
	Camden PMSA, NJ	Y	20250 FQ	23720 MW	28440 TQ	USBLS	5/07
	Edison PMSA, NJ	Y	19850 FQ	23870 MW	28950 TQ	USBLS	5/07
	Newark-Union PMSA, NJ-PA	Y	15720 FQ	20490 MW	27620 TQ	USBLS	5/07
	New Mexico	Y	18440 FQ	21820 MW	25940 TQ	USBLS	5/07
	Albuquerque MSA, NM	Y	19590 FQ	22340 MW	25440 TQ	USBLS	5/07
	New York	Y	17810 FQ	21280 MW	27280 TQ	USBLS	5/07
	Albany-Schenectady-Troy MSA, NY	Y	17990 FQ	20870 MW	24880 TQ	USBLS	5/07
	Buffalo-Niagara Falls MSA, NY	Y	15830 FQ	17920 MW	22530 TQ	USBLS	5/07
	Nassau-Suffolk PMSA, NY	Y	24080 FQ	27990 MW	33870 TQ	USBLS	5/07
	New York-Northern New Jersey-Long Island MSA, NY-NJ-PA	Y	17770 FQ	22500 MW	28520 TQ	USBLS	5/07
	North Carolina	Y	18230 FQ	21370 MW	24940 TQ	USBLS	5/07

AE	Average entry wage	AW	Average wage paid	FQ	First quartile wage	LO	Lowest wage paid	MTC	Median total compensation
AER	Average entry range	AWR	Average wage range	H	Hourly	LR	Low end range	MW	Median wage paid
AEX	Average experienced wage	AXR	Average experienced range	HI	Highest wage paid	M	Monthly	MWR	Median wage range
ATC	Average total compensation	D	Daily	HR	High end range	MCC	Median cash compensation	S	See annotated source

TCC	Total cash compensation
TQ	Third quartile wage
W	Weekly
Y	Yearly

Occupation/Type/Industry	Location	Per	Low	Mid	High	Source	Date
Tire Repairer and Changer	Charlotte-Gastonia-Concord MSA, NC-SC	Y	18920 FQ	21830 MW	24920 TQ	USBLS	5/07
	Durham MSA, NC	Y	18430 FQ	21040 MW	24270 TQ	USBLS	5/07
	Raleigh-Cary MSA, NC	Y	19450 FQ	22410 MW	26110 TQ	USBLS	5/07
	Winston-Salem MSA, NC	Y	21370 FQ	29540 MW	55810 TQ	USBLS	5/07
	North Dakota	Y	17690 FQ	20170 MW	27030 TQ	USBLS	5/07
	Fargo MSA, ND-MN	Y	17350 FQ	19480 MW	23810 TQ	USBLS	5/07
	Ohio	Y	18380 FQ	22300 MW	27420 TQ	USBLS	5/07
	Cincinnati-Middletown MSA, OH-KY-IN	Y	18460 FQ	21660 MW	25350 TQ	USBLS	5/07
	Cleveland-Elyria-Mentor MSA, OH	Y	19760 FQ	27060 MW	34610 TQ	USBLS	5/07
	Columbus MSA, OH	Y	18870 FQ	23710 MW	26860 TQ	USBLS	5/07
	Dayton MSA, OH	Y	19990 FQ	23500 MW	28130 TQ	USBLS	5/07
	Oklahoma	Y	16740 FQ	19220 MW	23220 TQ	USBLS	5/07
	Oklahoma City MSA, OK	Y	18040 FQ	20670 MW	23510 TQ	USBLS	5/07
	Tulsa MSA, OK	Y	16420 FQ	18930 MW	26490 TQ	USBLS	5/07
	Oregon	H	9.76 FQ	12.27 MW	15.05 TQ	ORBLS	5/08
	Eugene-Springfield MSA, OR	Y	19910 FQ	23660 MW	30770 TQ	USBLS	5/07
	Portland-Vancouver-Beaverton MSA, OR-WA	Y	20830 FQ	24710 MW	29610 TQ	USBLS	5/07
	Pennsylvania	Y	18800 FQ	22700 MW	27570 TQ	USBLS	5/07
	Allentown-Bethlehem-Easton MSA, PA-NJ	Y	20600 FQ	24590 MW	27980 TQ	USBLS	5/07
	Philadelphia-Camden-Wilmington MSA, PA-NJ-DE-MD	Y	19200 FQ	23220 MW	30180 TQ	USBLS	5/07
	Pittsburgh MSA, PA	Y	18520 FQ	22260 MW	27280 TQ	USBLS	5/07
	York-Hanover MSA, PA	Y	19890 FQ	23000 MW	28330 TQ	USBLS	5/07
	Rhode Island	Y	22530 FQ	27800 MW	31970 TQ	USBLS	5/07
	Providence-Fall River-Warwick MSA, RI-MA	Y	20200 FQ	25900 MW	31150 TQ	USBLS	5/07
	South Carolina	Y	17760 FQ	21760 MW	26230 TQ	USBLS	5/07
	Charleston-North Charleston MSA, SC	Y	17700 FQ	22490 MW	33670 TQ	USBLS	5/07
	Columbia MSA, SC	Y	18450 FQ	21820 MW	25160 TQ	USBLS	5/07
	South Dakota	Y	19769 FQ	22485 MW	24830 TQ	SDBLS	7/08-9/08
	Sioux Falls MSA, SD	Y	19337 FQ	22225 MW	25256 TQ	SDBLS	7/08-9/08
	Tennessee	Y	18250 FQ	21350 MW	24820 TQ	USBLS	5/07
	Memphis MSA, TN-MS-AR	Y	19790 FQ	22550 MW	25780 TQ	USBLS	5/07
	Nashville-Davidson-Murfreesboro MSA, TN	Y	17950 FQ	20000 MW	23810 TQ	USBLS	5/07
	Texas	Y	16990 FQ	20260 MW	23710 TQ	USBLS	5/07
	Austin-Round Rock MSA, TX	Y	19910 FQ	22420 MW	24950 TQ	USBLS	5/07
	Dallas-Fort Worth-Arlington MSA, TX	Y	19320 FQ	22180 MW	25020 TQ	USBLS	5/07
	El Paso MSA, TX	Y	13940 FQ	16830 MW	19440 TQ	USBLS	5/07
	Houston-Sugar Land-Baytown MSA, TX	Y	16290 FQ	19500 MW	23390 TQ	USBLS	5/07
	San Antonio MSA, TX	Y	18180 FQ	20890 MW	23350 TQ	USBLS	5/07
	Utah	Y	16940 FQ	20030 MW	24040 TQ	USBLS	5/07
	Salt Lake City MSA, UT	Y	19790 FQ	22870 MW	26920 TQ	USBLS	5/07
	Vermont	Y	18850 FQ	22130 MW	43400 TQ	USBLS	5/07
	Burlington-South Burlington MSA, VT	Y	17810 FQ	19690 MW	23650 TQ	USBLS	5/07
	Virginia	Y	19900 FQ	23400 MW	28300 TQ	USBLS	5/07
	Richmond MSA, VA	Y	19220 FQ	22550 MW	27710 TQ	USBLS	5/07
	Virginia Beach-Norfolk-Newport News MSA, VA-NC	Y	18550 FQ	21480 MW	24060 TQ	USBLS	5/07
	Washington	H	9.99 FQ	11.96 MW	15.34 TQ	WABLS	3/08
	Seattle-Tacoma-Bellevue MSA, WA	Y	19920 FQ	23610 MW	30740 TQ	USBLS	5/07
	West Virginia	Y	16416 FQ	19740 MW	26693 TQ	WVBLS	7/08-9/08
	Charleston MSA, WV	Y	15260 FQ	17850 MW	25510 TQ	USBLS	5/07
	Wisconsin	Y	19630 FQ	23000 MW	27330 TQ	USBLS	5/07
	Milwaukee-Waukesha-West Allis MSA, WI	Y	19390 FQ	22310 MW	26180 TQ	USBLS	5/07
	Wyoming	Y	18135 FQ	20423 MW	23647 TQ	WYBLS	9/08
	Cheyenne MSA, WY	Y	17708 FQ	18872 MW	20035 TQ	WYBLS	9/08
	Puerto Rico	Y	12860 FQ	14590 MW	17330 TQ	USBLS	5/07
	Aguadilla-Isabela-San Sebastian MSA, PR	Y	12460 FQ	13770 MW	15090 TQ	USBLS	5/07

AE Average entry wage	**AW** Average wage paid	**FQ** First quartile wage	**LO** Lowest wage paid	**MTC** Median total compensation	**TCC** Total cash compensation
AER Average entry range	**AWR** Average wage range	**H** Hourly	**LR** Low end range	**MW** Median wage paid	**TQ** Third quartile wage
AEX Average experienced wage	**AXR** Average experienced range	**HI** Highest wage paid	**M** Monthly	**MWR** Median wage range	**W** Weekly
ATC Average total compensation	**D** Daily	**HR** High end range	**MCC** Median cash compensation	**S** See annotated source	**Y** Yearly

Occupation/Type/Industry	Location	Per	Low	Mid	High	Source	Date
Tire Repairer and Changer	Guayama MSA, PR	Y	12290 FQ	13650 MW	15010 TQ	USBLS	5/07
	San Juan-Caguas-Guaynabo MSA, PR	Y	13420 FQ	15890 MW	18700 TQ	USBLS	5/07
	Virgin Islands	Y	17420 FQ	19550 MW	23350 TQ	USBLS	5/07
	Guam	Y	13270 FQ	15170 MW	17770 TQ	USBLS	5/07
Title Agent							
State Government	Ohio	H	15.62 LO		18.36 HI	ODAS	2008
Title Examiner							
Municipal Government	Seattle, WA	H	20.80 LO		22.43 HI	CSSS	2007
Title Examiner, Abstractor, and Searcher							
	Alabama	Y	27520 FQ	35190 MW	40610 TQ	USBLS	5/07
	Birmingham-Hoover MSA, AL	Y	28780 FQ	36140 MW	41080 TQ	USBLS	5/07
	Alaska	Y	47720 FQ	59210 MW	69970 TQ	USBLS	5/07
	Arizona	Y	32120 FQ	38400 MW	47860 TQ	USBLS	5/07
	Phoenix-Mesa-Scottsdale MSA, AZ	Y	33440 FQ	39810 MW	50190 TQ	USBLS	5/07
	Tucson MSA, AZ	Y	30310 FQ	34390 MW	40340 TQ	USBLS	5/07
	Arkansas	Y	25530 FQ	29890 MW	36070 TQ	USBLS	5/07
	Fayetteville-Springdale-Rogers MSA, AR-MO	Y	27440 FQ	34140 MW	41580 TQ	USBLS	5/07
	Little Rock-North Little Rock MSA, AR	Y	27000 FQ	31060 MW	37490 TQ	USBLS	5/07
	California	H	18.82 FQ	25.10 MW	35.21 TQ	CABLS	1/08-3/08
	Los Angeles-Long Beach-Glendale PMSA, CA	H	18.33 FQ	23.77 MW	35.31 TQ	CABLS	1/08-3/08
	Oakland-Fremont-Hayward MSA, CA	H	20.60 FQ	25.36 MW	41.31 TQ	CABLS	1/08-3/08
	Riverside-San Bernardino-Ontario MSA, CA	H	20.29 FQ	24.13 MW	30.54 TQ	CABLS	1/08-3/08
	Sacramento-Arden Arcade-Roseville MSA, CA	H	18.82 FQ	24.23 MW	34.41 TQ	CABLS	1/08-3/08
	San Diego-Carlsbad-San Marcos MSA, CA	H	9.80 FQ	25.02 MW	38.55 TQ	CABLS	1/08-3/08
	San Francisco-San Mateo-Redwood PMSA, CA	H	16.19 FQ	25.54 MW	35.82 TQ	CABLS	1/08-3/08
	San Jose-Sunnyvale-Santa Clara MSA, CA	H	24.95 FQ	37.17 MW	44.47 TQ	CABLS	1/08-3/08
	Santa Ana-Anaheim-Irvine PMSA, CA	Y	40330 FQ	54410 MW	70890 TQ	USBLS	5/07
	Colorado	Y	34500 FQ	46250 MW	59750 TQ	USBLS	5/07
	Denver-Aurora MSA, CO	Y	38760 FQ	49470 MW	64330 TQ	USBLS	5/07
	Fort Collins-Loveland MSA, CO	Y	42400 FQ	49670 MW	58860 TQ	USBLS	5/07
	Connecticut	H	11.19 AE	21.77 MW		CTBLS	1/08-3/08
	Hartford-West Hartford-East Hartford MSA, CT	Y	38950 FQ	53110 MW	60580 TQ	USBLS	5/07
	Delaware	Y	26060 FQ	35300 MW	41400 TQ	USBLS	5/07
	Wilmington PMSA, DE-MD-NJ	Y	31690 FQ	37280 MW	43870 TQ	USBLS	5/07
	District of Columbia	Y	34840 FQ	42850 MW	69940 TQ	USBLS	5/07
	Washington-Arlington-Alexandria MSA, DC-VA-MD-WV	Y	31800 FQ	37390 MW	46420 TQ	USBLS	5/07
	Florida	Y	28930 FQ	37580 MW	48180 TQ	USBLS	5/07
	Fort Lauderdale-Pompano Beach-Deerfield Beach PMSA, FL	Y	31540 FQ	37960 MW	48180 TQ	USBLS	5/07
	Jacksonville MSA, FL	Y	32480 FQ	37240 MW	46660 TQ	USBLS	5/07
	Miami-Fort Lauderdale-Miami Beach MSA, FL	Y	28150 FQ	37230 MW	50350 TQ	USBLS	5/07
	Orlando-Kissimmee MSA, FL	Y	33000 FQ	40990 MW	52860 TQ	USBLS	5/07
	Sarasota-Bradenton-Venice MSA, FL	Y	34400 FQ	41430 MW	47930 TQ	USBLS	5/07
	Tampa-St. Petersburg-Clearwater MSA, FL	Y	29240 FQ	39710 MW	49100 TQ	USBLS	5/07
	West Palm Beach-Boca Raton-Boynton Beach PMSA, FL	Y	30520 FQ	38520 MW	45380 TQ	USBLS	5/07
	Georgia	Y	24000 FQ	31120 MW	43760 TQ	USBLS	5/07

AE	Average entry wage	AW	Average wage paid	FQ	First quartile wage
AER	Average entry range	AWR	Average wage range	H	Hourly
AEX	Average experienced wage	AXR	Average experienced range	HI	Highest wage paid
ATC	Average total compensation	D	Daily	HR	High end range

LO	Lowest wage paid	MTC	Median total compensation
LR	Low end range	MW	Median wage paid
M	Monthly	MWR	Median wage range
MCC	Median cash compensation	S	See annotated source

TCC	Total cash compensation
TQ	Third quartile wage
W	Weekly
Y	Yearly

Title Examiner, Abstractor, and Searcher

Occupation/Type/Industry	Location	Per	Low	Mid	High	Source	Date
Title Examiner, Abstractor, and Searcher	Atlanta-Sandy Springs-Marietta MSA, GA	Y	23390 FQ	30830 MW	44530 TQ	USBLS	5/07
	Hawaii	Y	31720 FQ	40300 MW	50020 TQ	USBLS	5/07
	Honolulu MSA, HI	Y	30100 FQ	38860 MW	48350 TQ	USBLS	5/07
	Idaho	Y	30790 FQ	36570 MW	43670 TQ	USBLS	5/07
	Boise City-Nampa MSA, ID	Y	34000 FQ	41440 MW	52580 TQ	USBLS	5/07
	Illinois	Y	22800 FQ	29830 MW	40280 TQ	USBLS	5/07
	Champaign-Urbana MSA, IL	Y	23780 FQ	29790 MW	39940 TQ	USBLS	5/07
	Chicago-Naperville-Joliet MSA, IL-IN-WI	Y	22220 FQ	28390 MW	41030 TQ	USBLS	5/07
	Indiana	Y	24990 FQ	32030 MW	40350 TQ	USBLS	5/07
	Gary PMSA, IN	Y	25140 FQ	30400 MW	35510 TQ	USBLS	5/07
	Indianapolis-Carmel MSA, IN	Y	26650 FQ	34300 MW	41060 TQ	USBLS	5/07
	Iowa	Y	22460 FQ	28950 MW	37740 TQ	USBLS	5/07
	Des Moines-West Des Moines MSA, IA	Y	23210 FQ	28870 MW	37550 TQ	USBLS	5/07
	Kansas	Y	19880 FQ	26910 MW	35090 TQ	USBLS	5/07
	Wichita MSA, KS	Y	23440 FQ	27850 MW	33210 TQ	USBLS	5/07
	Kentucky	Y	27193 FQ	35018 MW	39413 TQ	KYBLS	2008
	Louisville-Jefferson County MSA, KY-IN	Y	25580 FQ	33340 MW	39050 TQ	USBLS	5/07
	Louisiana	H	11.03 FQ	14.51 MW	18.54 TQ	LABLS	1/08-3/08
	Baton Rouge MSA, LA	Y	33720 FQ	37240 MW	41100 TQ	USBLS	5/07
	New Orleans-Metairie-Kenner MSA, LA	Y	23790 FQ	35780 MW	45240 TQ	USBLS	5/07
	Maine	Y	31070 FQ	34490 MW	38550 TQ	USBLS	5/07
	Portland-South Portland-Biddeford MSA, ME	Y	30200 FQ	33910 MW	40310 TQ	USBLS	5/07
	Maryland	Y		38100 MW		MDBLS	3/08
	Baltimore-Towson MSA, MD	Y	33910 FQ	37690 MW	45750 TQ	USBLS	5/07
	Bethesda-Gaithersburg-Frederick PMSA, MD	Y	33480 FQ	36920 MW	46590 TQ	USBLS	5/07
	Massachusetts	Y	37410 FQ	51200 MW	59590 TQ	USBLS	5/07
	Boston-Cambridge-Quincy NECTA, MA	Y	43340 FQ	51580 MW	68090 TQ	USBLS	5/07
	Worcester MSA, MA-CT	Y	50550 FQ	55290 MW	59840 TQ	USBLS	5/07
	Michigan	Y	29590 FQ	35780 MW	45420 TQ	USBLS	5/07
	Detroit-Warren-Livonia MSA, MI	Y	29560 FQ	35220 MW	43910 TQ	USBLS	5/07
	Grand Rapids-Wyoming MSA, MI	Y	29060 FQ	35010 MW	45790 TQ	USBLS	5/07
	Warren-Troy-Farmington Hills PMSA, MI	Y	28990 FQ	33320 MW	44010 TQ	USBLS	5/07
	Minnesota	Y	34002 FQ	40980 MW	51076 TQ	MNBLS	10/08-12/08
	Minneapolis-Saint Paul MSA, MN-WI	Y	37706 FQ	45709 MW	56736 TQ	MNBLS	10/08-12/08
	Rochester MSA, MN	Y	37233 FQ	45580 MW	61315 TQ	MNBLS	10/08-12/08
	Mississippi	Y	51480 FQ	56330 MW	61180 TQ	USBLS	5/07
	Jackson MSA, MS	Y	53410 FQ	57670 MW	61920 TQ	USBLS	5/07
	Missouri	Y	22530 FQ	28120 MW	35140 TQ	USBLS	5/07
	Kansas City MSA, MO-KS	Y	29330 FQ	34690 MW	40510 TQ	USBLS	5/07
	St. Louis MSA, MO-IL	Y	23100 FQ	28260 MW	36520 TQ	USBLS	5/07
	Montana	Y	31190 FQ	39860 MW	53950 TQ	USBLS	5/07
	Billings MSA, MT	Y	32020 FQ	42600 MW	56240 TQ	USBLS	5/07
	Nebraska	Y	25000 FQ	29830 MW	37510 TQ	USBLS	5/07
	Omaha-Council Bluffs MSA, NE-IA	Y	24670 FQ	29390 MW	36250 TQ	USBLS	5/07
	Nevada	H	20.53 FQ	24.32 MW	28.94 TQ	NVBLS	5/08
	Las Vegas-Paradise MSA, NV	H	20.86 FQ	24.42 MW	29.17 TQ	NVBLS	5/08
	New Hampshire	H	13.57 AE	18.23 MW	20.89 AEX	NHBLS	6/08
	New Jersey	Y	34430 FQ	40430 MW	46480 TQ	USBLS	5/07
	Camden PMSA, NJ	Y	33350 FQ	39480 MW	45090 TQ	USBLS	5/07
	Edison PMSA, NJ	Y	36080 FQ	41000 MW	45690 TQ	USBLS	5/07
	Newark-Union PMSA, NJ-PA	Y	32350 FQ	38740 MW	52200 TQ	USBLS	5/07
	Trenton-Ewing MSA, NJ	Y	31800 FQ	37660 MW	47430 TQ	USBLS	5/07
	New Mexico	Y	23170 FQ	30580 MW	47120 TQ	USBLS	5/07
	Albuquerque MSA, NM	Y	26360 FQ	36400 MW	62280 TQ	USBLS	5/07
	New York	Y	32740 FQ	38680 MW	47990 TQ	USBLS	5/07
	Albany-Schenectady-Troy MSA, NY	Y	39400 FQ	44120 MW	59280 TQ	USBLS	5/07

Occupation/Type/Industry	Location	Per	Low	Mid	High	Source	Date
Title Examiner, Abstractor, and Searcher							
	Buffalo-Niagara Falls MSA, NY	Y	33080 FQ	40570 MW	50650 TQ	USBLS	5/07
	Kingston MSA, NY	Y	37960 FQ	44390 MW	51340 TQ	USBLS	5/07
	Nassau-Suffolk PMSA, NY	Y	33350 FQ	38620 MW	47730 TQ	USBLS	5/07
	New York-Northern New Jersey-Long Island MSA, NY-NJ-PA	Y	33880 FQ	39540 MW	46990 TQ	USBLS	5/07
	North Carolina	Y	34730 FQ	44760 MW	49730 TQ	USBLS	5/07
	Charlotte-Gastonia-Concord MSA, NC-SC	Y	43940 FQ	47360 MW	50780 TQ	USBLS	5/07
	Raleigh-Cary MSA, NC	Y	33270 FQ	38600 MW	68860 TQ	USBLS	5/07
	Winston-Salem MSA, NC	Y	29350 FQ	33270 MW	37310 TQ	USBLS	5/07
	North Dakota	Y	19360 FQ	23820 MW	31630 TQ	USBLS	5/07
	Ohio	Y	29700 FQ	35450 MW	41400 TQ	USBLS	5/07
	Cincinnati-Middletown MSA, OH-KY-IN	Y	32860 FQ	36840 MW	43710 TQ	USBLS	5/07
	Cleveland-Elyria-Mentor MSA, OH	Y	30550 FQ	35420 MW	39460 TQ	USBLS	5/07
	Columbus MSA, OH	Y	30000 FQ	36810 MW	43410 TQ	USBLS	5/07
	Dayton MSA, OH	Y	23730 FQ	29770 MW	36010 TQ	USBLS	5/07
	Oklahoma	Y	23610 FQ	31390 MW	38050 TQ	USBLS	5/07
	Oklahoma City MSA, OK	Y	23880 FQ	32110 MW	37670 TQ	USBLS	5/07
	Tulsa MSA, OK	Y	29560 FQ	35620 MW	45870 TQ	USBLS	5/07
	Oregon	H	16.49 FQ	20.98 MW	28.83 TQ	ORBLS	5/08
	Portland-Vancouver-Beaverton MSA, OR-WA	Y	31570 FQ	42330 MW	57100 TQ	USBLS	5/07
	Pennsylvania	Y	26730 FQ	35880 MW	48560 TQ	USBLS	5/07
	Allentown-Bethlehem-Easton MSA, PA-NJ	Y	30300 FQ	38320 MW	45130 TQ	USBLS	5/07
	Philadelphia-Camden-Wilmington MSA, PA-NJ-DE-MD	Y	35160 FQ	42980 MW	55380 TQ	USBLS	5/07
	Pittsburgh MSA, PA	Y	25220 FQ	32120 MW	40400 TQ	USBLS	5/07
	Rhode Island	Y	34230 FQ	38640 MW	45980 TQ	USBLS	5/07
	Providence-Fall River-Warwick MSA, RI-MA	Y	34230 FQ	38640 MW	45980 TQ	USBLS	5/07
	South Carolina	Y	25450 FQ	30830 MW	36770 TQ	USBLS	5/07
	Charleston-North Charleston MSA, SC	Y	31820 FQ	36240 MW	40540 TQ	USBLS	5/07
	Columbia MSA, SC	Y	25800 FQ	30250 MW	35970 TQ	USBLS	5/07
	South Dakota	Y	27714 FQ	32521 MW	39301 TQ	SDBLS	7/08-9/08
	Sioux Falls MSA, SD	Y	29644 FQ	36866 MW	43932 TQ	SDBLS	7/08-9/08
	Tennessee	Y	24630 FQ	33830 MW	52110 TQ	USBLS	5/07
	Memphis MSA, TN-MS-AR	Y	27410 FQ	31370 MW	39840 TQ	USBLS	5/07
	Nashville-Davidson-Murfreesboro MSA, TN	Y	24920 FQ	36400 MW	56970 TQ	USBLS	5/07
	Texas	Y	28560 FQ	36210 MW	45780 TQ	USBLS	5/07
	Austin-Round Rock MSA, TX	Y	24010 FQ	30410 MW	39740 TQ	USBLS	5/07
	Dallas-Fort Worth-Arlington MSA, TX	Y	31770 FQ	38450 MW	47700 TQ	USBLS	5/07
	El Paso MSA, TX	Y	35620 FQ	40040 MW	52710 TQ	USBLS	5/07
	Houston-Sugar Land-Baytown MSA, TX	Y	30860 FQ	37890 MW	47980 TQ	USBLS	5/07
	San Antonio MSA, TX	Y	30760 FQ	36740 MW	45180 TQ	USBLS	5/07
	Utah	Y	31330 FQ	39250 MW	54930 TQ	USBLS	5/07
	Salt Lake City MSA, UT	Y	28620 FQ	38630 MW	52540 TQ	USBLS	5/07
	Virginia	Y	27250 FQ	34850 MW	44500 TQ	USBLS	5/07
	Richmond MSA, VA	Y	24230 FQ	30230 MW	42980 TQ	USBLS	5/07
	Virginia Beach-Norfolk-Newport News MSA, VA-NC	Y	23310 FQ	33280 MW	39500 TQ	USBLS	5/07
	Washington	H	16.31 FQ	19.60 MW	24.03 TQ	WABLS	3/08
	Seattle-Tacoma-Bellevue MSA, WA	Y	34120 FQ	41480 MW	49980 TQ	USBLS	5/07
	West Virginia	Y	26747 FQ	32191 MW	38631 TQ	WVBLS	7/08-9/08
	Wisconsin	Y	28810 FQ	34450 MW	39340 TQ	USBLS	5/07
	Milwaukee-Waukesha-West Allis MSA, WI	Y	29460 FQ	35150 MW	39760 TQ	USBLS	5/07
	Wyoming	Y	24949 FQ	41445 MW	69000 TQ	WYBLS	9/08
	Casper MSA, WY	Y	37685 FQ	44710 MW	59297 TQ	WYBLS	9/08
	Cheyenne MSA, WY	Y	27522 FQ	50013 MW	62166 TQ	WYBLS	9/08
	Puerto Rico	Y	21460 FQ	25300 MW	41830 TQ	USBLS	5/07

AE	Average entry wage	AW	Average wage paid	FQ	First quartile wage	LO	Lowest wage paid	MTC	Median total compensation	TCC	Total cash compensation
AER	Average entry range	AWR	Average wage range	H	Hourly	LR	Low end range	MW	Median wage paid	TQ	Third quartile wage
AEX	Average experienced wage	AXR	Average experienced range	HI	Highest wage paid	M	Monthly	MWR	Median wage range	W	Weekly
ATC	Average total compensation	D	Daily	HR	High end range	MCC	Median cash compensation	S	See annotated source	Y	Yearly

Occupation/Type/Industry	Location	Per	Low	Mid	High	Source	Date
Title Examiner, Abstractor, and Searcher	San Juan-Caguas-Guaynabo MSA, PR	Y	21460 FQ	25300 MW	41830 TQ	USBLS	5/07
Titles, Liens, and Collections Specialist							
Municipal Government	Gresham, OR	Y	42828 LO		54720 HI	GOSS	1/1/09
Toll Supervisor							
Department of Transportation	New Hampshire	Y		36893 AW		NHUL03	2008
Tomato Picker	Immokalee, FL	S			0.45 HI	NYT03	2007
Tool and Die Maker	Alabama	Y	33890 FQ	41520 MW	50980 TQ	USBLS	5/07
	Birmingham-Hoover MSA, AL	Y	37290 FQ	43800 MW	49510 TQ	USBLS	5/07
	Arizona	Y	35730 FQ	43080 MW	49710 TQ	USBLS	5/07
	Phoenix-Mesa-Scottsdale MSA, AZ	Y	35440 FQ	42840 MW	49980 TQ	USBLS	5/07
	Tucson MSA, AZ	Y	37230 FQ	44200 MW	49010 TQ	USBLS	5/07
	Arkansas	Y	29410 FQ	36550 MW	42540 TQ	USBLS	5/07
	Fayetteville-Springdale-Rogers MSA, AR-MO	Y	33490 FQ	37800 MW	42920 TQ	USBLS	5/07
	Little Rock-North Little Rock MSA, AR	Y	35200 FQ	42070 MW	48370 TQ	USBLS	5/07
	California	H	17.42 FQ	22.56 MW	27.44 TQ	CABLS	1/08-3/08
	Los Angeles-Long Beach-Glendale PMSA, CA	H	17.18 FQ	22.56 MW	27.29 TQ	CABLS	1/08-3/08
	Oakland-Fremont-Hayward MSA, CA	H	22.46 FQ	30.00 MW	34.20 TQ	CABLS	1/08-3/08
	Riverside-San Bernardino-Ontario MSA, CA	H	15.66 FQ	19.53 MW	24.03 TQ	CABLS	1/08-3/08
	Sacramento-Arden Arcade-Roseville MSA, CA	H	16.66 FQ	21.92 MW	27.01 TQ	CABLS	1/08-3/08
	San Diego-Carlsbad-San Marcos MSA, CA	H	15.46 FQ	21.87 MW	24.76 TQ	CABLS	1/08-3/08
	San Francisco-San Mateo-Redwood PMSA, CA	H	14.34 FQ	25.43 MW	29.49 TQ	CABLS	1/08-3/08
	San Jose-Sunnyvale-Santa Clara MSA, CA	H	19.29 FQ	22.62 MW	26.99 TQ	CABLS	1/08-3/08
	Santa Ana-Anaheim-Irvine PMSA, CA	Y	36600 FQ	46320 MW	55020 TQ	USBLS	5/07
	Colorado	Y	35190 FQ	45120 MW	55700 TQ	USBLS	5/07
	Denver-Aurora MSA, CO	Y	32960 FQ	41930 MW	53390 TQ	USBLS	5/07
	Fort Collins-Loveland MSA, CO	Y	43010 FQ	50810 MW	57030 TQ	USBLS	5/07
	Connecticut	H	20.23 AE	24.96 MW		CTBLS	1/08-3/08
	Bridgeport-Stamford-Norwalk MSA, CT	Y	43540 FQ	52190 MW	59530 TQ	USBLS	5/07
	Hartford-West Hartford-East Hartford MSA, CT	Y	44020 FQ	50050 MW	57880 TQ	USBLS	5/07
	Delaware	Y	45430 FQ	55500 MW	64530 TQ	USBLS	5/07
	Wilmington PMSA, DE-MD-NJ	Y	49060 FQ	60690 MW	66650 TQ	USBLS	5/07
	Washington-Arlington-Alexandria MSA, DC-VA-MD-WV	Y	39690 FQ	44750 MW	55860 TQ	USBLS	5/07
	Florida	Y	29090 FQ	38260 MW	46060 TQ	USBLS	5/07
	Fort Lauderdale-Pompano Beach-Deerfield Beach PMSA, FL	Y	33550 FQ	40910 MW	47830 TQ	USBLS	5/07
	Jacksonville MSA, FL	Y	35660 FQ	42850 MW	49200 TQ	USBLS	5/07
	Miami-Fort Lauderdale-Miami Beach MSA, FL	Y	29010 FQ	37350 MW	47400 TQ	USBLS	5/07
	Orlando-Kissimmee MSA, FL	Y	32420 FQ	40230 MW	45520 TQ	USBLS	5/07
	Tampa-St. Petersburg-Clearwater MSA, FL	Y	24620 FQ	34180 MW	43430 TQ	USBLS	5/07
	West Palm Beach-Boca Raton-Boynton Beach PMSA, FL	Y	21660 FQ	28010 MW	33120 TQ	USBLS	5/07
	Georgia	Y	33460 FQ	39880 MW	47340 TQ	USBLS	5/07
	Atlanta-Sandy Springs-Marietta MSA, GA	Y	34800 FQ	41350 MW	47640 TQ	USBLS	5/07
	Idaho	Y	32730 FQ	37230 MW	43630 TQ	USBLS	5/07

AE	Average entry wage	AW	Average wage paid	FQ	First quartile wage
AER	Average entry range	AWR	Average wage range	H	Hourly
AEX	Average experienced wage	AXR	Average experienced range	HI	Highest wage paid
ATC	Average total compensation	D	Daily	HR	High end range

LO	Lowest wage paid	MTC	Median total compensation	TCC	Total cash compensation
LR	Low end range	MW	Median wage paid	TQ	Third quartile wage
M	Monthly	MWR	Median wage range	W	Weekly
MCC	Median cash compensation	S	See annotated source	Y	Yearly

Occupation/Type/Industry	Location	Per	Low	Mid	High	Source	Date
Tool and Die Maker	Illinois	Y	36620 FQ	46330 MW	56660 TQ	USBLS	5/07
	Chicago-Naperville-Joliet MSA, IL-IN-WI	Y	36470 FQ	47660 MW	57770 TQ	USBLS	5/07
	Indiana	Y	37710 FQ	47300 MW	62990 TQ	USBLS	5/07
	Gary PMSA, IN	Y	37050 FQ	47820 MW	59730 TQ	USBLS	5/07
	Indianapolis-Carmel MSA, IN	Y	40890 FQ	62250 MW	72270 TQ	USBLS	5/07
	Terre Haute MSA, IN	Y	27830 FQ	33500 MW	37750 TQ	USBLS	5/07
	Iowa	Y	31300 FQ	40770 MW	47380 TQ	USBLS	5/07
	Des Moines-West Des Moines MSA, IA	Y	40510 FQ	44320 MW	48090 TQ	USBLS	5/07
	Kansas	Y	39170 FQ	51580 MW	58880 TQ	USBLS	5/07
	Wichita MSA, KS	Y	48460 FQ	53900 MW	58430 TQ	USBLS	5/07
	Kentucky	Y	36996 FQ	43915 MW	50924 TQ	KYBLS	2008
	Louisville-Jefferson County MSA, KY-IN	Y	34820 FQ	44090 MW	54530 TQ	USBLS	5/07
	Louisiana	H	18,89 FQ	23.62 MW	30.30 TQ	LABLS	1/08-3/08
	Maine	Y	42200 FQ	51670 MW	59710 TQ	USBLS	5/07
	Portland-South Portland-Biddeford MSA, ME	Y	36300 FQ	42640 MW	53020 TQ	USBLS	5/07
	Maryland	Y		46275 MW		MDBLS	3/08
	Baltimore-Towson MSA, MD	Y	40480 FQ	47140 MW	52820 TQ	USBLS	5/07
	Hagerstown-Martinsburg MSA, MD-WV	Y	39470 FQ	42180 MW	44900 TQ	USBLS	5/07
	Massachusetts	Y	38180 FQ	45000 MW	52620 TQ	USBLS	5/07
	Boston-Cambridge-Quincy NECTA, MA	Y	38120 FQ	44400 MW	52150 TQ	USBLS	5/07
	Worcester MSA, MA-CT	Y	38180 FQ	43940 MW	49430 TQ	USBLS	5/07
	Michigan	Y	42060 FQ	52980 MW	67710 TQ	USBLS	5/07
	Grand Rapids-Wyoming MSA, MI	Y	43380 FQ	51640 MW	69160 TQ	USBLS	5/07
	Warren-Troy-Farmington Hills PMSA, MI	Y	41400 FQ	53010 MW	65770 TQ	USBLS	5/07
	Minnesota	Y	41643 FQ	48526 MW	57286 TQ	MNBLS	10/08-12/08
	Minneapolis-Saint Paul MSA, MN-WI	Y	43664 FQ	50030 MW	57991 TQ	MNBLS	10/08-12/08
	Rochester MSA, MN	Y	36928 FQ	40789 MW	48871 TQ	MNBLS	10/08-12/08
	Mississippi	Y	32110 FQ	38150 MW	57060 TQ	USBLS	5/07
	Jackson MSA, MS	Y	39160 FQ	68720 MW	75740 TQ	USBLS	5/07
	Missouri	Y	37430 FQ	47790 MW	59600 TQ	USBLS	5/07
	Kansas City MSA, MO-KS	Y	43330 FQ	56610 MW	66390 TQ	USBLS	5/07
	St. Louis MSA, MO-IL	Y	44370 FQ	54080 MW	63270 TQ	USBLS	5/07
	Montana	Y	36370 FQ	43270 MW	50850 TQ	USBLS	5/07
	Nebraska	Y	34270 FQ	41420 MW	47850 TQ	USBLS	5/07
	Omaha-Council Bluffs MSA, NE-IA	Y	32220 FQ	37880 MW	44800 TQ	USBLS	5/07
	Nevada	H	16.86 FQ	22.51 MW	27.32 TQ	NVBLS	5/08
	Las Vegas-Paradise MSA, NV	H	16.43 FQ	23.57 MW	28.79 TQ	NVBLS	5/08
	New Hampshire	H	15.43 AE	20.63 MW	23.62 AEX	NHBLS	6/08
	Manchester MSA, NH	Y	42910 FQ	51420 MW	64660 TQ	USBLS	5/07
	Nashua NECTA, NH-MA	Y	38360 FQ	45480 MW	54660 TQ	USBLS	5/07
	New Jersey	Y	37980 FQ	47440 MW	57450 TQ	USBLS	5/07
	Camden PMSA, NJ	Y	30910 FQ	44510 MW	50840 TQ	USBLS	5/07
	Edison PMSA, NJ	Y	42830 FQ	52110 MW	58770 TQ	USBLS	5/07
	Newark-Union PMSA, NJ-PA	Y	35120 FQ	44460 MW	57900 TQ	USBLS	5/07
	New Mexico	Y	28550 FQ	43790 MW	65000 TQ	USBLS	5/07
	Albuquerque MSA, NM	Y	30910 FQ	44970 MW	65410 TQ	USBLS	5/07
	New York	Y	33020 FQ	43370 MW	55390 TQ	USBLS	5/07
	Albany-Schenectady-Troy MSA, NY	Y	27800 FQ	46400 MW	58780 TQ	USBLS	5/07
	Buffalo-Niagara Falls MSA, NY	Y	44710 FQ	56720 MW	72430 TQ	USBLS	5/07
	Nassau-Suffolk PMSA, NY	Y	39850 FQ	49200 MW	59480 TQ	USBLS	5/07
	New York-Northern New Jersey-Long Island MSA, NY-NJ-PA	Y	37790 FQ	47470 MW	57840 TQ	USBLS	5/07
	North Carolina	Y	32520 FQ	39850 MW	47330 TQ	USBLS	5/07
	Charlotte-Gastonia-Concord MSA, NC-SC	Y	32460 FQ	37770 MW	44500 TQ	USBLS	5/07
	Raleigh-Cary MSA, NC	Y	35070 FQ	41110 MW	48570 TQ	USBLS	5/07
	North Dakota	Y	31670 FQ	36460 MW	41970 TQ	USBLS	5/07
	Ohio	Y	35750 FQ	43590 MW	57920 TQ	USBLS	5/07
	Canton-Massillon MSA, OH	Y	34630 FQ	40300 MW	45930 TQ	USBLS	5/07

AE Average entry wage	**AW** Average wage paid	**FQ** First quartile wage	**LO** Lowest wage paid	**MTC** Median total compensation	**TCC** Total cash compensation
AER Average entry range	**AWR** Average wage range	**H** Hourly	**LR** Low end range	**MW** Median wage paid	**TQ** Third quartile wage
AEX Average experienced wage	**AXR** Average experienced range	**HI** Highest wage paid	**M** Monthly	**MWR** Median wage range	**W** Weekly
ATC Average total compensation	**D** Daily	**HR** High end range	**MCC** Median cash compensation	**S** See annotated source	**Y** Yearly

Occupation/Type/Industry	Location	Per	Low	Mid	High	Source	Date
Tool and Die Maker	Cincinnati-Middletown MSA, OH-KY-IN	Y	36190 FQ	43930 MW	58330 TQ	USBLS	5/07
	Cleveland-Elyria-Mentor MSA, OH	Y	36110 FQ	43660 MW	56430 TQ	USBLS	5/07
	Columbus MSA, OH	Y	35540 FQ	40630 MW	46400 TQ	USBLS	5/07
	Dayton MSA, OH	Y	31740 FQ	41170 MW	49720 TQ	USBLS	5/07
	Oklahoma	Y	32610 FQ	41000 MW	50720 TQ	USBLS	5/07
	Oklahoma City MSA, OK	Y	36460 FQ	45000 MW	54590 TQ	USBLS	5/07
	Tulsa MSA, OK	Y	29870 FQ	37000 MW	44030 TQ	USBLS	5/07
	Oregon	H	19.10 FQ	23.25 MW	28.47 TQ	ORBLS	5/08
	Portland-Vancouver-Beaverton MSA, OR-WA	Y	41930 FQ	51420 MW	60350 TQ	USBLS	5/07
	Pennsylvania	Y	34190 FQ	40320 MW	48500 TQ	USBLS	5/07
	Allentown-Bethlehem-Easton MSA, PA-NJ	Y	34030 FQ	38370 MW	46700 TQ	USBLS	5/07
	Philadelphia-Camden-Wilmington MSA, PA-NJ-DE-MD	Y	34940 FQ	43920 MW	54410 TQ	USBLS	5/07
	Pittsburgh MSA, PA	Y	33300 FQ	39260 MW	47000 TQ	USBLS	5/07
	Reading MSA, PA	Y	37160 FQ	46780 MW	57630 TQ	USBLS	5/07
	Rhode Island	Y	36160 FQ	43500 MW	51330 TQ	USBLS	5/07
	Providence-Fall River-Warwick MSA, RI-MA	Y	36130 FQ	43670 MW	51300 TQ	USBLS	5/07
	South Carolina	Y	34330 FQ	42370 MW	48420 TQ	USBLS	5/07
	Charleston-North Charleston MSA, SC	Y	24120 FQ	32630 MW	50570 TQ	USBLS	5/07
	Columbia MSA, SC	Y	34770 FQ	42880 MW	49350 TQ	USBLS	5/07
	South Dakota	Y	33976 FQ	38609 MW	45731 TQ	SDBLS	7/08-9/08
	Sioux Falls MSA, SD	Y	37662 FQ	45583 MW	52989 TQ	SDBLS	7/08-9/08
	Tennessee	Y	35030 FQ	41600 MW	48280 TQ	USBLS	5/07
	Memphis MSA, TN-MS-AR	Y	34860 FQ	39880 MW	46740 TQ	USBLS	5/07
	Nashville-Davidson-Murfreesboro MSA, TN	Y	36620 FQ	44010 MW	50260 TQ	USBLS	5/07
	Texas	Y	29840 FQ	40010 MW	48550 TQ	USBLS	5/07
	Austin-Round Rock MSA, TX	Y	28480 FQ	38640 MW	46060 TQ	USBLS	5/07
	Dallas-Fort Worth-Arlington MSA, TX	Y	31270 FQ	42440 MW	51320 TQ	USBLS	5/07
	El Paso MSA, TX	Y	23710 FQ	37730 MW	52820 TQ	USBLS	5/07
	Houston-Sugar Land-Baytown MSA, TX	Y	30360 FQ	38860 MW	46470 TQ	USBLS	5/07
	San Antonio MSA, TX	Y	27890 FQ	38180 MW	45580 TQ	USBLS	5/07
	Utah	Y	33700 FQ	44410 MW	53270 TQ	USBLS	5/07
	Salt Lake City MSA, UT	Y	36840 FQ	47210 MW	54380 TQ	USBLS	5/07
	Vermont	Y	37140 FQ	44860 MW	54160 TQ	USBLS	5/07
	Burlington-South Burlington MSA, VT	Y	32740 FQ	36260 MW	39950 TQ	USBLS	5/07
	Virginia	Y	35640 FQ	42180 MW	50440 TQ	USBLS	5/07
	Richmond MSA, VA	Y	33420 FQ	39400 MW	46990 TQ	USBLS	5/07
	Virginia Beach-Norfolk-Newport News MSA, VA-NC	Y	39640 FQ	48260 MW	58800 TQ	USBLS	5/07
	Washington	H	19.88 FQ	28.53 MW	32.76 TQ	WABLS	3/08
	Seattle-Tacoma-Bellevue MSA, WA	Y	51740 FQ	62690 MW	69810 TQ	USBLS	5/07
	West Virginia	Y	34198 FQ	42728 MW	48633 TQ	WVBLS	7/08-9/08
	Wisconsin	Y	38550 FQ	45550 MW	53460 TQ	USBLS	5/07
	Milwaukee-Waukesha-West Allis MSA, WI	Y	39640 FQ	46940 MW	55880 TQ	USBLS	5/07
	Puerto Rico	Y	20380 FQ	26930 MW	32830 TQ	USBLS	5/07
	San Juan-Caguas-Guaynabo MSA, PR	Y	20150 FQ	26230 MW	32150 TQ	USBLS	5/07
Tool Crib Attendant	Southeast, MI	H		16.46 AW		MIOAKL02	2007
Tool Grinder, Filer, and Sharpener	Alabama	Y	19420 FQ	24710 MW	31490 TQ	USBLS	5/07
	Birmingham-Hoover MSA, AL	Y	27650 FQ	32080 MW	36430 TQ	USBLS	5/07
	Arizona	Y	26900 FQ	29630 MW	32630 TQ	USBLS	5/07
	Phoenix-Mesa-Scottsdale MSA, AZ	Y	26980 FQ	29560 MW	32230 TQ	USBLS	5/07
	Arkansas	Y	24420 FQ	30760 MW	36160 TQ	USBLS	5/07
	Little Rock-North Little Rock MSA, AR	Y	30600 FQ	33700 MW	36550 TQ	USBLS	5/07

AE	Average entry wage	AW	Average wage paid	FQ	First quartile wage	LO	Lowest wage paid	MTC	Median total compensation	TCC	Total cash compensation
AER	Average entry range	AWR	Average wage range	H	Hourly	LR	Low end range	MW	Median wage paid	TQ	Third quartile wage
AEX	Average experienced wage	AXR	Average experienced range	HI	Highest wage paid	M	Monthly	MWR	Median wage range	W	Weekly
ATC	Average total compensation	D	Daily	HR	High end range	MCC	Median cash compensation	S	See annotated source	Y	Yearly

Occupation/Type/Industry	Location	Per	Low	Mid	High	Source	Date
Tool Grinder, Filer, and Sharpener	California	H	10.91 FQ	13.58 MW	17.44 TQ	CABLS	1/08-3/08
	Los Angeles-Long Beach-Glendale PMSA, CA	H	10.42 FQ	13.95 MW	17.81 TQ	CABLS	1/08-3/08
	Oakland-Fremont-Hayward MSA, CA	H	12.43 FQ	15.16 MW	17.58 TQ	CABLS	1/08-3/08
	Riverside-San Bernardino-Ontario MSA, CA	H	10.36 FQ	11.79 MW	14.79 TQ	CABLS	1/08-3/08
	Sacramento-Arden Arcade-Roseville MSA, CA	H	13.28 FQ	16.19 MW	19.06 TQ	CABLS	1/08-3/08
	San Diego-Carlsbad-San Marcos MSA, CA	H	10.71 FQ	13.87 MW	17.43 TQ	CABLS	1/08-3/08
	Santa Ana-Anaheim-Irvine PMSA, CA	Y	21950 FQ	25740 MW	36220 TQ	USBLS	5/07
	Colorado	Y	26360 FQ	31540 MW	36670 TQ	USBLS	5/07
	Denver-Aurora MSA, CO	Y	28710 FQ	33210 MW	37180 TQ	USBLS	5/07
	Connecticut	H	11.50 AE	17.81 MW		CTBLS	1/08-3/08
	Hartford-West Hartford-East Hartford MSA, CT	Y	27310 FQ	30680 MW	41780 TQ	USBLS	5/07
	Florida	Y	21420 FQ	24980 MW	31190 TQ	USBLS	5/07
	Orlando-Kissimmee MSA, FL	Y	21460 FQ	24840 MW	30450 TQ	USBLS	5/07
	Tampa-St. Petersburg-Clearwater MSA, FL	Y	20610 FQ	22790 MW	26870 TQ	USBLS	5/07
	Georgia	Y	25320 FQ	29320 MW	32450 TQ	USBLS	5/07
	Atlanta-Sandy Springs-Marietta MSA, GA	Y	28340 FQ	31030 MW	36670 TQ	USBLS	5/07
	Idaho	Y	25940 FQ	31780 MW	37240 TQ	USBLS	5/07
	Boise City-Nampa MSA, ID	Y	24620 FQ	29690 MW	34850 TQ	USBLS	5/07
	Illinois	Y	25670 FQ	32120 MW	41540 TQ	USBLS	5/07
	Indiana	Y	25500 FQ	29470 MW	35610 TQ	USBLS	5/07
	Indianapolis-Carmel MSA, IN	Y	25070 FQ	28900 MW	34330 TQ	USBLS	5/07
	Iowa	Y	24320 FQ	29990 MW	37650 TQ	USBLS	5/07
	Kansas	Y	25360 FQ	34210 MW	44010 TQ	USBLS	5/07
	Wichita MSA, KS	Y	34810 FQ	44030 MW	49190 TQ	USBLS	5/07
	Kentucky	Y	20927 FQ	27483 MW	39426 TQ	KYBLS	2008
	Louisville-Jefferson County MSA, KY-IN	Y	19940 FQ	25680 MW	31070 TQ	USBLS	5/07
	Louisiana	H	9.59 FQ	12.44 MW	16.07 TQ	LABLS	1/08-3/08
	Maine	Y	25610 FQ	29460 MW	34410 TQ	USBLS	5/07
	Maryland	Y		32525 MW		MDBLS	3/08
	Baltimore-Towson MSA, MD	Y	28760 FQ	32510 MW	39080 TQ	USBLS	5/07
	Massachusetts	Y	25840 FQ	29170 MW	35300 TQ	USBLS	5/07
	Boston-Cambridge-Quincy NECTA, MA	Y	24760 FQ	28800 MW	38940 TQ	USBLS	5/07
	Michigan	Y	28120 FQ	36460 MW	45830 TQ	USBLS	5/07
	Detroit-Warren-Livonia MSA, MI	Y	27430 FQ	36090 MW	47840 TQ	USBLS	5/07
	Grand Rapids-Wyoming MSA, MI	Y	37860 FQ	42700 MW	47500 TQ	USBLS	5/07
	Warren-Troy-Farmington Hills PMSA, MI	Y	25390 FQ	32520 MW	40590 TQ	USBLS	5/07
	Minnesota	Y	27679 FQ	32645 MW	44121 TQ	MNBLS	10/08-12/08
	Minneapolis-Saint Paul MSA, MN-WI	Y	27399 FQ	33992 MW	46795 TQ	MNBLS	10/08-12/08
	Mississippi	Y	20630 FQ	27310 MW	32240 TQ	USBLS	5/07
	Missouri	Y	24040 FQ	29650 MW	38460 TQ	USBLS	5/07
	Kansas City MSA, MO-KS	Y	24210 FQ	28860 MW	32770 TQ	USBLS	5/07
	St. Louis MSA, MO-IL	Y	27240 FQ	36940 MW	46300 TQ	USBLS	5/07
	Montana	Y	28070 FQ	36360 MW	42910 TQ	USBLS	5/07
	Nevada	H	10.39 FQ	13.10 MW	15.96 TQ	NVBLS	5/08
	New Hampshire	H	10.57 AE	14.18 MW	16.99 AEX	NHBLS	6/08
	New Jersey	Y	25740 FQ	30830 MW	40320 TQ	USBLS	5/07
	New Mexico	Y	24500 FQ	29370 MW	39300 TQ	USBLS	5/07
	Albuquerque MSA, NM	Y	27480 FQ	35590 MW	52560 TQ	USBLS	5/07
	New York	Y	25410 FQ	37110 MW	50090 TQ	USBLS	5/07
	Buffalo-Niagara Falls MSA, NY	Y	32290 FQ	45700 MW	57910 TQ	USBLS	5/07
	Nassau-Suffolk PMSA, NY	Y	31180 FQ	45170 MW	60280 TQ	USBLS	5/07
	New York-Northern New Jersey-Long Island MSA, NY-NJ-PA	Y	22980 FQ	30360 MW	42970 TQ	USBLS	5/07
	North Carolina	Y	23040 FQ	29410 MW	35290 TQ	USBLS	5/07

AE	Average entry wage	AW	Average wage paid	FQ	First quartile wage
AER	Average entry range	AWR	Average wage range	H	Hourly
AEX	Average experienced wage	AXR	Average experienced range	HI	Highest wage paid
ATC	Average total compensation	D	Daily	HR	High end range

LO	Lowest wage paid	MTC	Median total compensation	TCC	Total cash compensation
LR	Low end range	MW	Median wage paid	TQ	Third quartile wage
M	Monthly	MWR	Median wage range	W	Weekly
MCC	Median cash compensation	S	See annotated source	Y	Yearly

Occupation/Type/Industry	Location	Per	Low	Mid	High	Source	Date
Tool Grinder, Filer, and Sharpener	Charlotte-Gastonia-Concord MSA, NC-SC	Y	28910 FQ	32400 MW	37230 TQ	USBLS	5/07
	North Dakota	Y	21970 FQ	27830 MW	33220 TQ	USBLS	5/07
	Ohio	Y	25900 FQ	31950 MW	38280 TQ	USBLS	5/07
	Canton-Massillon MSA, OH	Y	18240 FQ	23740 MW	28010 TQ	USBLS	5/07
	Cincinnati-Middletown MSA, OH-KY-IN	Y	29300 FQ	33600 MW	38100 TQ	USBLS	5/07
	Cleveland-Elyria-Mentor MSA, OH	Y	29160 FQ	34540 MW	42250 TQ	USBLS	5/07
	Columbus MSA, OH	Y	28910 FQ	35560 MW	43480 TQ	USBLS	5/07
	Dayton MSA, OH	Y	33150 FQ	35530 MW	38180 TQ	USBLS	5/07
	Oklahoma	Y	22890 FQ	27410 MW	32590 TQ	USBLS	5/07
	Oklahoma City MSA, OK	Y	26460 FQ	28480 MW	30510 TQ	USBLS	5/07
	Tulsa MSA, OK	Y	22100 FQ	25440 MW	37380 TQ	USBLS	5/07
	Oregon	H	15.51 FQ	18.84 MW	22.21 TQ	ORBLS	5/08
	Portland-Vancouver-Beaverton MSA, OR-WA	Y	31520 FQ	41190 MW	48700 TQ	USBLS	5/07
	Pennsylvania	Y	26290 FQ	31120 MW	38890 TQ	USBLS	5/07
	Philadelphia-Camden-Wilmington MSA, PA-NJ-DE-MD	Y	27940 FQ	37840 MW	44910 TQ	USBLS	5/07
	Pittsburgh MSA, PA	Y	26950 FQ	34060 MW	39510 TQ	USBLS	5/07
	Rhode Island	Y	19860 FQ	25540 MW	31430 TQ	USBLS	5/07
	Providence-Fall River-Warwick MSA, RI-MA	Y	23150 FQ	27760 MW	31320 TQ	USBLS	5/07
	South Carolina	Y	21800 FQ	30360 MW	36980 TQ	USBLS	5/07
	South Dakota	Y	22487 FQ	25270 MW	31304 TQ	SDBLS	7/08-9/08
	Sioux Falls MSA, SD	Y	22670 FQ	24809 MW	30383 TQ	SDBLS	7/08-9/08
	Tennessee	Y	22550 FQ	28670 MW	41340 TQ	USBLS	5/07
	Nashville-Davidson-Murfreesboro MSA, TN	Y	25110 FQ	31900 MW	41590 TQ	USBLS	5/07
	Texas	Y	22050 FQ	29100 MW	37540 TQ	USBLS	5/07
	Dallas-Fort Worth-Arlington MSA, TX	Y	21470 FQ	26040 MW	31270 TQ	USBLS	5/07
	Houston-Sugar Land-Baytown MSA, TX	Y	22730 FQ	31220 MW	38470 TQ	USBLS	5/07
	Utah	Y	21270 FQ	23760 MW	29480 TQ	USBLS	5/07
	Provo-Orem MSA, UT	Y	22320 FQ	24880 MW	29870 TQ	USBLS	5/07
	Salt Lake City MSA, UT	Y	20710 FQ	22910 MW	36960 TQ	USBLS	5/07
	Vermont	Y	29850 FQ	33640 MW	37580 TQ	USBLS	5/07
	Virginia	Y	19350 FQ	23650 MW	31060 TQ	USBLS	5/07
	Washington	H	16.18 FQ	20.44 MW	24.87 TQ	WABLS	3/08
	Seattle-Tacoma-Bellevue MSA, WA	Y	32780 FQ	44520 MW	63930 TQ	USBLS	5/07
	West Virginia	Y	22189 FQ	28836 MW	34794 TQ	WVBLS	7/08-9/08
	Wisconsin	Y	30440 FQ	36310 MW	40850 TQ	USBLS	5/07
	Milwaukee-Waukesha-West Allis MSA, WI	Y	30430 FQ	35890 MW	40050 TQ	USBLS	5/07
	Wyoming	Y	23261 FQ	26727 MW	31685 TQ	WYBLS	9/08
Toolpusher							
Chesapeake Energy	Oklahoma City, OK	Y		178108 AW		CNNM01	2009
Toolroom Manager	United States	Y	56250 LO	83750 AW	117500 HI	SOPE	4/08-5/08
Top Aide to the Governor	New York	Y			178500 HI	RCITY	2009
Tour Coordinator							
State Government	Ohio	H	15.09 LO		17.03 HI	ODAS	2008
Tour Guide							
Metropolitan Area	Minnesota	H		13.78 AW		MMTHLY	2008
Municipal Government	Seattle, WA	H	14.83 LO		15.38 HI	CSSS	2008
Outstate Area	Minnesota	H		11.85 AW		MMTHLY	2008
State Capitol Building Tour	Ingham County, MI	Y			30622-41819 HR	LSJ01	6/07
Tour Guide and Escort	Birmingham-Hoover MSA, AL	Y	42490 FQ	45710 MW	48930 TQ	USBLS	5/07
	Alaska	Y	20070 FQ	26280 MW	33350 TQ	USBLS	5/07
	Arizona	Y	18260 FQ	25140 MW	30250 TQ	USBLS	5/07
	Flagstaff MSA, AZ	Y	23090 FQ	28020 MW	31300 TQ	USBLS	5/07

AE	Average entry wage	**AW**	Average wage paid	**FQ**	First quartile wage	**LO**	Lowest wage paid	**MTC** Median total compensation **TCC** Total cash compensation
AER	Average entry range	**AWR**	Average wage range	**H**	Hourly	**LR**	Low end range	**MW** Median wage paid **TQ** Third quartile wage
AEX	Average experienced wage	**AXR**	Average experienced range	**HI**	Highest wage paid	**M**	Monthly	**MWR** Median wage range **W** Weekly
ATC	Average total compensation	**D**	Daily	**HR**	High end range	**MCC**	Median cash compensation	**S** See annotated source **Y** Yearly

Occupation/Type/Industry	Location	Per	Low	Mid	High	Source	Date
Tour Guide and Escort	Phoenix-Mesa-Scottsdale MSA, AZ	Y	17160 FQ	21940 MW	25120 TQ	USBLS	5/07
	Tucson MSA, AZ	Y	14670 FQ	20110 MW	23190 TQ	USBLS	5/07
	Arkansas	Y	18520 FQ	26610 MW	30550 TQ	USBLS	5/07
	California	H	10.12 FQ	11.89 MW	15.65 TQ	CABLS	1/08-3/08
	Los Angeles-Long Beach-Glendale PMSA, CA	H	10.21 FQ	11.30 MW	13.37 TQ	CABLS	1/08-3/08
	Oakland-Fremont-Hayward MSA, CA	H	8.35 FQ	9.03 MW	12.31 TQ	CABLS	1/08-3/08
	Riverside-San Bernardino-Ontario MSA, CA	H	10.62 FQ	11.93 MW	13.79 TQ	CABLS	1/08-3/08
	Sacramento-Arden Arcade-Roseville MSA, CA	H	12.19 FQ	14.18 MW	17.09 TQ	CABLS	1/08-3/08
	San Diego-Carlsbad-San Marcos MSA, CA	H	10.47 FQ	11.81 MW	16.05 TQ	CABLS	1/08-3/08
	San Francisco-San Mateo-Redwood PMSA, CA	H	9.56 FQ	14.65 MW	20.00 TQ	CABLS	1/08-3/08
	San Jose-Sunnyvale-Santa Clara MSA, CA	H	9.16 FQ	10.12 MW	11.78 TQ	CABLS	1/08-3/08
	Santa Ana-Anaheim-Irvine PMSA, CA	Y	20660 FQ	25880 MW	34940 TQ	USBLS	5/07
	Santa Rosa-Petaluma MSA, CA	H	10.93 FQ	20.18 MW	22.45 TQ	CABLS	1/08-3/08
	Colorado	Y	20680 FQ	25230 MW	32730 TQ	USBLS	5/07
	Connecticut	H	8.49 AE	9.88 MW		CTBLS	1/08-3/08
	Hartford-West Hartford-East Hartford MSA, CT	Y	16960 FQ	18530 MW	22150 TQ	USBLS	5/07
	Delaware	Y	19050 FQ	26890 MW	31680 TQ	USBLS	5/07
	Wilmington PMSA, DE-MD-NJ	Y	18510 FQ	26240 MW	30950 TQ	USBLS	5/07
	District of Columbia	Y	21820 FQ	26990 MW	30110 TQ	USBLS	5/07
	Washington-Arlington-Alexandria MSA, DC-VA-MD-WV	Y	18930 FQ	23990 MW	30090 TQ	USBLS	5/07
	Florida	Y	15670 FQ	21870 MW	32050 TQ	USBLS	5/07
	Cape Coral-Fort Myers MSA, FL	Y	15040 FQ	23150 MW	28500 TQ	USBLS	5/07
	Jacksonville MSA, FL	Y	15490 FQ	17640 MW	37770 TQ	USBLS	5/07
	Orlando-Kissimmee MSA, FL	Y	14840 FQ	15820 MW	24410 TQ	USBLS	5/07
	Tampa-St. Petersburg-Clearwater MSA, FL	Y	15420 FQ	21650 MW	24440 TQ	USBLS	5/07
	West Palm Beach-Boca Raton-Boynton Beach PMSA, FL	Y	14800 FQ	15720 MW	21220 TQ	USBLS	5/07
	Georgia	Y	17250 FQ	21900 MW	25720 TQ	USBLS	5/07
	Atlanta-Sandy Springs-Marietta MSA, GA	Y	21730 FQ	27160 MW	34600 TQ	USBLS	5/07
	Hawaii	Y	19020 FQ	23300 MW	27990 TQ	USBLS	5/07
	Honolulu MSA, HI	Y	17490 FQ	22260 MW	26810 TQ	USBLS	5/07
	Idaho	Y	25000 FQ	28230 MW	32810 TQ	USBLS	5/07
	Illinois	Y	16880 FQ	19920 MW	25830 TQ	USBLS	5/07
	Chicago-Naperville-Joliet MSA, IL-IN-WI	Y	17260 FQ	20200 MW	25650 TQ	USBLS	5/07
	Indiana	Y	13460 FQ	15750 MW	21600 TQ	USBLS	5/07
	Gary PMSA, IN	Y	17490 FQ	19870 MW	22870 TQ	USBLS	5/07
	Indianapolis-Carmel MSA, IN	Y	23590 FQ	28410 MW	31640 TQ	USBLS	5/07
	Iowa	Y	16550 FQ	21800 MW	26220 TQ	USBLS	5/07
	Des Moines-West Des Moines MSA, IA	Y	20880 FQ	24180 MW	27810 TQ	USBLS	5/07
	Kansas	Y	13500 FQ	16710 MW	26710 TQ	USBLS	5/07
	Kentucky	Y	17385 FQ	21414 MW	27490 TQ	KYBLS	2008
	Louisville-Jefferson County MSA, KY-IN	Y	17890 FQ	20610 MW	24200 TQ	USBLS	5/07
	Louisiana	H	7.33 FQ	10.21 MW	13.00 TQ	LABLS	1/08-3/08
	New Orleans-Metairie-Kenner MSA, LA	Y	21710 FQ	24390 MW	29550 TQ	USBLS	5/07
	Maine	Y	17440 FQ	21960 MW	27990 TQ	USBLS	5/07
	Maryland	Y		17275 MW		MDBLS	3/08
	Baltimore-Towson MSA, MD	Y	14580 FQ	15810 MW	21690 TQ	USBLS	5/07
	Bethesda-Gaithersburg-Frederick PMSA, MD	Y	16650 FQ	17820 MW	18980 TQ	USBLS	5/07
	Massachusetts	Y	19800 FQ	25310 MW	30320 TQ	USBLS	5/07
	Boston-Cambridge-Quincy NECTA, MA	Y	23720 FQ	27890 MW	31740 TQ	USBLS	5/07

AE Average entry wage	**AW** Average wage paid	**FQ** First quartile wage	**LO** Lowest wage paid	**MTC** Median total compensation	**TCC** Total cash compensation
AER Average entry range	**AWR** Average wage range	**H** Hourly	**LR** Low end range	**MW** Median wage paid	**TQ** Third quartile wage
AEX Average experienced wage	**AXR** Average experienced range	**HI** Highest wage paid	**M** Monthly	**MWR** Median wage range	**W** Weekly
ATC Average total compensation	**D** Daily	**HR** High end range	**MCC** Median cash compensation	**S** See annotated source	**Y** Yearly

Occupation/Type/Industry	Location	Per	Low	Mid	High	Source	Date
Tour Guide and Escort	Worcester MSA, MA-CT	Y	19090 FQ	20350 MW	22300 TQ	USBLS	5/07
	Michigan	Y	16690 FQ	21360 MW	37720 TQ	USBLS	5/07
	Detroit-Warren-Livonia MSA, MI	Y	17330 FQ	25730 MW	33790 TQ	USBLS	5/07
	Warren-Troy-Farmington Hills PMSA, MI	Y	27210 FQ	33490 MW	43040 TQ	USBLS	5/07
	Minnesota	Y	21518 FQ	25794 MW	32914 TQ	MNBLS	10/08-12/08
	Duluth-Superior MSA, MN-WI	Y	17325 FQ	19761 MW	22866 TQ	MNBLS	10/08-12/08
	Minneapolis-Saint Paul MSA, MN-WI	Y	23557 FQ	28732 MW	35278 TQ	MNBLS	10/08-12/08
	Mississippi	Y	14340 FQ	26430 MW	30350 TQ	USBLS	5/07
	Missouri	Y	15440 FQ	18250 MW	22980 TQ	USBLS	5/07
	Kansas City MSA, MO-KS	Y	17920 FQ	19750 MW	25030 TQ	USBLS	5/07
	St. Louis MSA, MO-IL	Y	16350 FQ	19290 MW	25140 TQ	USBLS	5/07
	Montana	Y	14680 FQ	16240 MW	24140 TQ	USBLS	5/07
	Nebraska	Y	12590 FQ	14230 MW	15870 TQ	USBLS	5/07
	Las Vegas-Paradise MSA, NV	H	9.04 FQ	14.12 MW	17.03 TQ	NVBLS	5/08
	New Hampshire	H	8.37 AE	9.41 MW	10.74 AEX	NHBLS	6/08
	New Jersey	Y	16210 FQ	18830 MW	24130 TQ	USBLS	5/07
	Edison PMSA, NJ	Y	15220 FQ	17340 MW	23230 TQ	USBLS	5/07
	Newark-Union PMSA, NJ-PA	Y	18210 FQ	21080 MW	29250 TQ	USBLS	5/07
	New Mexico	Y	19680 FQ	21850 MW	24670 TQ	USBLS	5/07
	Albuquerque MSA, NM	Y	20320 FQ	22170 MW	24110 TQ	USBLS	5/07
	New York	Y	15730 FQ	22570 MW	31060 TQ	USBLS	5/07
	Albany-Schenectady-Troy MSA, NY	Y	18790 FQ	27170 MW	30290 TQ	USBLS	5/07
	Buffalo-Niagara Falls MSA, NY	Y	15820 FQ	17730 MW	19790 TQ	USBLS	5/07
	Nassau-Suffolk PMSA, NY	Y	23950 FQ	29020 MW	36340 TQ	USBLS	5/07
	New York-Northern New Jersey-Long Island MSA, NY-NJ-PA	Y	16070 FQ	22930 MW	31410 TQ	USBLS	5/07
	North Carolina	Y	16320 FQ	18660 MW	22820 TQ	USBLS	5/07
	North Dakota	Y	14520 FQ	18580 MW	22150 TQ	USBLS	5/07
	Ohio	Y	15650 FQ	18800 MW	26900 TQ	USBLS	5/07
	Cincinnati-Middletown MSA, OH-KY-IN	Y	14530 FQ	16470 MW	19570 TQ	USBLS	5/07
	Cleveland-Elyria-Mentor MSA, OH	Y	14960 FQ	22890 MW	28140 TQ	USBLS	5/07
	Oklahoma	Y	17910 FQ	19690 MW	30000 TQ	USBLS	5/07
	Oregon	H	9.71 FQ	11.56 MW	13.66 TQ	ORBLS	5/08
	Eugene-Springfield MSA, OR	Y	18590 FQ	20900 MW	23570 TQ	USBLS	5/07
	Portland-Vancouver-Beaverton MSA, OR-WA	Y	18860 FQ	21740 MW	26210 TQ	USBLS	5/07
	Pennsylvania	Y	19070 FQ	24040 MW	31680 TQ	USBLS	5/07
	Allentown-Bethlehem-Easton MSA, PA-NJ	Y	17010 FQ	22500 MW	31250 TQ	USBLS	5/07
	Lancaster MSA, PA	Y	17000 FQ	19180 MW	22820 TQ	USBLS	5/07
	Philadelphia-Camden-Wilmington MSA, PA-NJ-DE-MD	Y	22790 FQ	29200 MW	34920 TQ	USBLS	5/07
	Pittsburgh MSA, PA	Y	15950 FQ	18010 MW	20200 TQ	USBLS	5/07
	Rhode Island	Y	18080 FQ	20550 MW	23800 TQ	USBLS	5/07
	Providence-Fall River-Warwick MSA, RI-MA	Y	18070 FQ	20530 MW	23770 TQ	USBLS	5/07
	South Carolina	Y	13640 FQ	16290 MW	23500 TQ	USBLS	5/07
	Charleston-North Charleston MSA, SC	Y	13440 FQ	15780 MW	23750 TQ	USBLS	5/07
	South Dakota	Y	15145 FQ	18771 MW	23116 TQ	SDBLS	7/08-9/08
	Sioux Falls MSA, SD	Y	18366 FQ	19872 MW	21227 TQ	SDBLS	7/08-9/08
	Tennessee	Y	14210 FQ	17140 MW	26120 TQ	USBLS	5/07
	Memphis MSA, TN-MS-AR	Y	17550 FQ	20440 MW	23810 TQ	USBLS	5/07
	Texas	Y	15740 FQ	18840 MW	24850 TQ	USBLS	5/07
	Austin-Round Rock MSA, TX	Y	17210 FQ	18920 MW	21120 TQ	USBLS	5/07
	Dallas-Fort Worth-Arlington MSA, TX	Y	17240 FQ	23790 MW	37270 TQ	USBLS	5/07
	Houston-Sugar Land-Baytown MSA, TX	Y	16610 FQ	19140 MW	28210 TQ	USBLS	5/07
	San Antonio MSA, TX	Y	13460 FQ	15840 MW	21390 TQ	USBLS	5/07
	Utah	Y	18470 FQ	22790 MW	27050 TQ	USBLS	5/07
	Salt Lake City MSA, UT	Y	26660 FQ	29830 MW	32800 TQ	USBLS	5/07
	Vermont	Y	22140 FQ	24520 MW	28180 TQ	USBLS	5/07

AE	Average entry wage	AW	Average wage paid	FQ	First quartile wage	LO	Lowest wage paid	MTC	Median total compensation	TCC	Total cash compensation
AER	Average entry range	AWR	Average wage range	H	Hourly	LR	Low end range	MW	Median wage paid	TQ	Third quartile wage
AEX	Average experienced wage	AXR	Average experienced range	HI	Highest wage paid	M	Monthly	MWR	Median wage range	W	Weekly
ATC	Average total compensation	D	Daily	HR	High end range	MCC	Median cash compensation	S	See annotated source	Y	Yearly

Occupation/Type/Industry	Location	Per	Low	Mid	High	Source	Date
Tour Guide and Escort	Virginia	Y	15740 FQ	20380 MW	26940 TQ	USBLS	5/07
	Charlottesville MSA, VA	Y	16260 FQ	23060 MW	31290 TQ	USBLS	5/07
	Richmond MSA, VA	Y	14460 FQ	19430 MW	22190 TQ	USBLS	5/07
	Virginia Beach-Norfolk-Newport News MSA, VA-NC	Y	19400 FQ	23300 MW	30800 TQ	USBLS	5/07
	Washington	H	11.87 FQ	13.97 MW	15.85 TQ	WABLS	3/08
	Seattle-Tacoma-Bellevue MSA, WA	Y	27080 FQ	29600 MW	32550 TQ	USBLS	5/07
	West Virginia	Y	16241 FQ	24794 MW	43149 TQ	WVBLS	7/08-9/08
	Wisconsin	Y	14890 FQ	17930 MW	23880 TQ	USBLS	5/07
	Green Bay MSA, WI	Y	18880 FQ	21780 MW	24140 TQ	USBLS	5/07
	Milwaukee-Waukesha-West Allis MSA, WI	Y	15660 FQ	17680 MW	19930 TQ	USBLS	5/07
	Wyoming	Y	17154 FQ	28304 MW	45046 TQ	WYBLS	9/08
	Puerto Rico	Y	13860 FQ	16370 MW	22080 TQ	USBLS	5/07
	San Juan-Caguas-Guaynabo MSA, PR	Y	14920 FQ	20580 MW	24140 TQ	USBLS	5/07
	Virgin Islands	Y	19620 FQ	22000 MW	24040 TQ	USBLS	5/07
	Guam	Y	14330 FQ	17840 MW	24180 TQ	USBLS	5/07
Town Administrator	Ashfield, MA	Y			27351 HI	FRCOG	2009
Town Board Member	Tonawanda, NY	Y			19467 HI	BUFN	2009
Town Nurse	Charlemont, MA	H			18.00 HI	FRCOG	2009
	Rowe, MA	H			30.69 HI	FRCOG	2009
Town Secretary	Northfield, MA	H			15.78 HI	FRCOG	2009
Town Supervisor	New Windsor, NY	Y			91707 HI	THREC2	2007
	Wallkill, NY	Y			63466 HI	THREC2	2007
Township Clerk	Plainfield Township, MI	Y			65000 HI	TGRP	2008
Township Manager	Genoa Township, MI	Y			97000 HI	LCPP	2009
Township Supervisor	Macomb Township, MI	Y			80000 HI	FREEP03	2008
	Millcreek Township, PA	Y			66362 HI	ETNEWS	2009
Toy Designer	United States	Y	35000-45000 AER		135000 AEX	WSJ06	2007
Trade Show Manager		Y		58395 AW		TRADEW	2007
Association/Society/Institute	United States	Y		111833 AW		TRADEW1	11/08
Medical Industry	United States	Y		35000 AW		TRADEW1	11/08
Service Industry	United States						
Traffic Control Devices Technician							
State Government	Ohio	H	17.72 LO		21.77 HI	ODAS	2008
Traffic Engineer							
Municipal Government	Walnut Creek, CA	Y	101344 LO		123190 HI	WCSWP	7/11/08
Traffic Engineering Field Specialist							
Municipal Government	Colorado Springs, CO	M	3777 LO			COSPRS	1/1/09
Traffic Operations Technician							
Department of Transportation	New Hampshire	Y		50079 AW		NHUL03	2008
Traffic Signal Supervisor							
Municipal Government	Colorado Springs, CO	M	4442 LO			COSPRS	1/1/09
Traffic Technician	Alabama	Y	27460 FQ	35580 MW	45450 TQ	USBLS	5/07
	Arizona	Y	40830 FQ	60050 MW	74040 TQ	USBLS	5/07
	Phoenix-Mesa-Scottsdale MSA, AZ	Y	52240 FQ	66560 MW	75890 TQ	USBLS	5/07
	Arkansas	Y	31500 FQ	38070 MW	48570 TQ	USBLS	5/07
	California	H	21.06 FQ	23.54 MW	26.28 TQ	CABLS	1/08-3/08
	Oakland-Fremont-Hayward MSA, CA	H	27.44 FQ	31.63 MW	36.97 TQ	CABLS	1/08-3/08

Occupation/Type/Industry	Location	Per	Low	Mid	High	Source	Date
Traffic Technician	Riverside-San Bernardino-Ontario MSA, CA	H	11.30 FQ	12.49 MW	27.58 TQ	CABLS	1/08-3/08
	Sacramento-Arden Arcade-Roseville MSA, CA	H	13.68 FQ	14.73 MW	15.79 TQ	CABLS	1/08-3/08
	San Francisco-San Mateo-Redwood PMSA, CA	H	23.32 FQ	26.48 MW	31.43 TQ	CABLS	1/08-3/08
	Colorado	Y	38430 FQ	45470 MW	54580 TQ	USBLS	5/07
	Connecticut	H	11.78 AE	20.24 MW		CTBLS	1/08-3/08
	Washington-Arlington-Alexandria MSA, DC-VA-MD-WV	Y	40110 FQ	48820 MW	58850 TQ	USBLS	5/07
	Florida	Y	28010 FQ	33420 MW	39400 TQ	USBLS	5/07
	Miami-Fort Lauderdale-Miami Beach MSA, FL	Y	29890 FQ	38600 MW	50280 TQ	USBLS	5/07
	Orlando-Kissimmee MSA, FL	Y	22960 FQ	30470 MW	38290 TQ	USBLS	5/07
	Tampa-St. Petersburg-Clearwater MSA, FL	Y	27920 FQ	31790 MW	36220 TQ	USBLS	5/07
	Georgia	Y	26060 FQ	31520 MW	38400 TQ	USBLS	5/07
	Atlanta-Sandy Springs-Marietta MSA, GA	Y	27590 FQ	32330 MW	40010 TQ	USBLS	5/07
	Idaho	Y	27380 FQ	32070 MW	36960 TQ	USBLS	5/07
	Boise City-Nampa MSA, ID	Y	27750 FQ	33110 MW	38420 TQ	USBLS	5/07
	Illinois	Y	43730 FQ	49740 MW	64530 TQ	USBLS	5/07
	Indiana	Y	26930 FQ	33170 MW	41790 TQ	USBLS	5/07
	Kansas	Y	32720 FQ	37930 MW	45390 TQ	USBLS	5/07
	Louisiana	H	10.82 FQ	13.07 MW	15.73 TQ	LABLS	1/08-3/08
	Maryland	Y		44075 MW		MDBLS	3/08
	Baltimore-Towson MSA, MD	Y	25600 FQ	39000 MW	46480 TQ	USBLS	5/07
	Massachusetts	Y	38880 FQ	45350 MW	50510 TQ	USBLS	5/07
	Boston-Cambridge-Quincy NECTA, MA	Y	38570 FQ	45120 MW	50220 TQ	USBLS	5/07
	Michigan	Y	29770 FQ	37840 MW	48900 TQ	USBLS	5/07
	Minneapolis-Saint Paul MSA, MN-WI	Y	24437 FQ	30242 MW	41728 TQ	MNBLS	10/08-12/08
	Mississippi	Y	22420 FQ	26310 MW	33570 TQ	USBLS	5/07
	Missouri	Y	30640 FQ	35710 MW	40360 TQ	USBLS	5/07
	Kansas City MSA, MO-KS	Y	35250 FQ	39480 MW	46560 TQ	USBLS	5/07
	Nevada	H	27.01 FQ	33.83 MW	38.95 TQ	NVBLS	5/08
	Las Vegas-Paradise MSA, NV	H	27.01 FQ	33.83 MW	38.95 TQ	NVBLS	5/08
	New Jersey	Y	29490 FQ	42440 MW	58450 TQ	USBLS	5/07
	New Mexico	Y	24730 FQ	30740 MW	38210 TQ	USBLS	5/07
	Albuquerque MSA, NM	Y	32980 FQ	36650 MW	40320 TQ	USBLS	5/07
	New York	Y	28830 FQ	48400 MW	54730 TQ	USBLS	5/07
	Nassau-Suffolk PMSA, NY	Y	30070 FQ	36920 MW	47240 TQ	USBLS	5/07
	New York-Northern New Jersey-Long Island MSA, NY-NJ-PA	Y	28400 FQ	48420 MW	54650 TQ	USBLS	5/07
	North Carolina	Y	25420 FQ	30770 MW	39270 TQ	USBLS	5/07
	Ohio	Y	35400 FQ	43880 MW	50000 TQ	USBLS	5/07
	Columbus MSA, OH	Y	39220 FQ	44930 MW	49740 TQ	USBLS	5/07
	Oklahoma	Y	27160 FQ	30950 MW	40740 TQ	USBLS	5/07
	Tulsa MSA, OK	Y	27850 FQ	32170 MW	44200 TQ	USBLS	5/07
	Pennsylvania	Y	31260 FQ	43670 MW	50850 TQ	USBLS	5/07
	South Carolina	Y	33120 FQ	35720 MW	38320 TQ	USBLS	5/07
	Tennessee	Y	24830 FQ	31060 MW	37590 TQ	USBLS	5/07
	Johnson City MSA, TN	Y	24820 FQ	31350 MW	36640 TQ	USBLS	5/07
	Memphis MSA, TN-MS-AR	Y	26030 FQ	30060 MW	35060 TQ	USBLS	5/07
	Nashville-Davidson-Murfreesboro MSA, TN	Y	26120 FQ	35720 MW	45520 TQ	USBLS	5/07
	Texas	Y	27680 FQ	34100 MW	43890 TQ	USBLS	5/07
	Austin-Round Rock MSA, TX	Y	31550 FQ	38040 MW	46190 TQ	USBLS	5/07
	Dallas-Fort Worth-Arlington MSA, TX	Y	31140 FQ	39040 MW	47500 TQ	USBLS	5/07
	Houston-Sugar Land-Baytown MSA, TX	Y	28840 FQ	36350 MW	46500 TQ	USBLS	5/07
	San Antonio MSA, TX	Y	24670 FQ	29630 MW	37770 TQ	USBLS	5/07
	Utah	Y	27650 FQ	31740 MW	46700 TQ	USBLS	5/07
	Salt Lake City MSA, UT	Y	27100 FQ	30350 MW	37840 TQ	USBLS	5/07
	Virginia	Y	35120 FQ	40790 MW	49800 TQ	USBLS	5/07
	Virginia Beach-Norfolk-Newport News MSA, VA-NC	Y	32160 FQ	38320 MW	49380 TQ	USBLS	5/07
	Washington	H	20.34 FQ	22.55 MW	24.74 TQ	WABLS	3/08

Occupation/Type/Industry	Location	Per	Low	Mid	High	Source	Date
Traffic Technician	Wyoming	Y	36680 FQ	45644 MW	51077 TQ	WYBLS	9/08
Trailer Editor							
Major Motion Picture	West Coast	W			1790 HI	MPEG01	8/3/08-7/31/09
Training and Development Manager							
	Alabama	Y	52520 FQ	66220 MW	83660 TQ	USBLS	5/07
	Birmingham-Hoover MSA, AL	Y	51900 FQ	74070 MW	90130 TQ	USBLS	5/07
	Alaska	Y	58170 FQ	71090 MW	85600 TQ	USBLS	5/07
	Anchorage MSA, AK	Y	59100 FQ	77710 MW	94190 TQ	USBLS	5/07
	Arizona	Y	50160 FQ	70830 MW	94020 TQ	USBLS	5/07
	Phoenix-Mesa-Scottsdale MSA, AZ	Y	52880 FQ	73420 MW	96170 TQ	USBLS	5/07
	Tucson MSA, AZ	Y	38140 FQ	68330 MW	87780 TQ	USBLS	5/07
	Arkansas	Y	53690 FQ	68330 MW	87410 TQ	USBLS	5/07
	Little Rock-North Little Rock MSA, AR	Y	55320 FQ	65880 MW	84320 TQ	USBLS	5/07
	California	H	36.80 FQ	46.09 MW	58.72 TQ	CABLS	1/08-3/08
	Los Angeles-Long Beach-Glendale PMSA, CA	H	37.61 FQ	46.09 MW	55.56 TQ	CABLS	1/08-3/08
	Oakland-Fremont-Hayward MSA, CA	H	33.96 FQ	49.61 MW	62.55 TQ	CABLS	1/08-3/08
	Riverside-San Bernardino-Ontario MSA, CA	H	31.37 FQ	41.21 MW	53.20 TQ	CABLS	1/08-3/08
	Sacramento-Arden Arcade-Roseville MSA, CA	H	24.52 FQ	40.70 MW	50.19 TQ	CABLS	1/08-3/08
	San Diego-Carlsbad-San Marcos MSA, CA	H	39.37 FQ	44.94 MW	54.31 TQ	CABLS	1/08-3/08
	San Francisco-San Mateo-Redwood PMSA, CA	H	46.54 FQ	58.48 MW		CABLS	1/08-3/08
	San Jose-Sunnyvale-Santa Clara MSA, CA	H	41.38 FQ	50.82 MW	64.03 TQ	CABLS	1/08-3/08
	Santa Ana-Anaheim-Irvine PMSA, CA	Y	75260 FQ	94640 MW	126820 TQ	USBLS	5/07
	Santa Rosa-Petaluma MSA, CA	H	28.00 FQ	32.95 MW	44.29 TQ	CABLS	1/08-3/08
	Colorado	Y	67030 FQ	87670 MW	110430 TQ	USBLS	5/07
	Denver-Aurora MSA, CO	Y	69570 FQ	88130 MW	109050 TQ	USBLS	5/07
	Connecticut	H	25.66 AE	39.91 MW		CTBLS	1/08-3/08
	Bridgeport-Stamford-Norwalk MSA, CT	Y	59260 FQ	80080 MW	116820 TQ	USBLS	5/07
	Hartford-West Hartford-East Hartford MSA, CT	Y	62620 FQ	91140 MW	116040 TQ	USBLS	5/07
	Delaware	Y	61850 FQ	80420 MW	115350 TQ	USBLS	5/07
	Wilmington PMSA, DE-MD-NJ	Y	64050 FQ	90660 MW	121670 TQ	USBLS	5/07
	District of Columbia	Y	64590 FQ	84300 MW	131020 TQ	USBLS	5/07
	Washington-Arlington-Alexandria MSA, DC-VA-MD-WV	Y	70260 FQ	95490 MW	129690 TQ	USBLS	5/07
	Florida	Y	68610 FQ	88630 MW	112050 TQ	USBLS	5/07
	Fort Lauderdale-Pompano Beach-Deerfield Beach PMSA, FL	Y	69160 FQ	92830 MW	116100 TQ	USBLS	5/07
	Jacksonville MSA, FL	Y	66460 FQ	86840 MW	108890 TQ	USBLS	5/07
	Miami-Fort Lauderdale-Miami Beach MSA, FL	Y	70530 FQ	93230 MW	115570 TQ	USBLS	5/07
	Orlando-Kissimmee MSA, FL	Y	52030 FQ	81970 MW	109280 TQ	USBLS	5/07
	Tampa-St. Petersburg-Clearwater MSA, FL	Y	73740 FQ	90520 MW	116290 TQ	USBLS	5/07
	West Palm Beach-Boca Raton-Boynton Beach PMSA, FL	Y	76380 FQ	93260 MW	111810 TQ	USBLS	5/07
	Georgia	Y	61550 FQ	81550 MW	103260 TQ	USBLS	5/07
	Atlanta-Sandy Springs-Marietta MSA, GA	Y	66330 FQ	85230 MW	105080 TQ	USBLS	5/07
	Savannah MSA, GA	Y	57680 FQ	67160 MW	82300 TQ	USBLS	5/07
	Hawaii	Y	55690 FQ	67440 MW	82740 TQ	USBLS	5/07
	Honolulu MSA, HI	Y	56040 FQ	68070 MW	83800 TQ	USBLS	5/07
	Idaho	Y	29670 FQ	53660 MW	70590 TQ	USBLS	5/07
	Boise City-Nampa MSA, ID	Y	50880 FQ	66690 MW	77150 TQ	USBLS	5/07
	Illinois	Y	53570 FQ	76790 MW	101850 TQ	USBLS	5/07
	Chicago-Naperville-Joliet MSA, IL-IN-WI	Y	57110 FQ	79250 MW	104300 TQ	USBLS	5/07

AE	Average entry wage	**AW**	Average wage paid	**FQ**	First quartile wage
AER	Average entry range	**AWR**	Average wage range	**H**	Hourly
AEX	Average experienced wage	**AXR**	Average experienced range	**HI**	Highest wage paid
ATC	Average total compensation **D**	Daily		**HR**	High end range

LO	Lowest wage paid	**MTC**	Median total compensation	**TCC**	Total cash compensation
LR	Low end range	**MW**	Median wage paid	**TQ**	Third quartile wage
M	Monthly	**MWR**	Median wage range	**W**	Weekly
MCC	Median cash compensation	**S**	See annotated source	**Y**	Yearly

Occupation/Type/Industry	Location	Per	Low	Mid	High	Source	Date
Training and Development Manager							
	Peoria MSA, IL	Y	41390 FQ	55010 MW	79840 TQ	USBLS	5/07
	Indiana	Y	48610 FQ	65280 MW	86300 TQ	USBLS	5/07
	Gary PMSA, IN	Y	55940 FQ	70770 MW	88760 TQ	USBLS	5/07
	Indianapolis-Carmel MSA, IN	Y	46630 FQ	66230 MW	93370 TQ	USBLS	5/07
	Iowa	Y	57350 FQ	71220 MW	85980 TQ	USBLS	5/07
	Des Moines-West Des Moines MSA, IA	Y	61740 FQ	74440 MW	86770 TQ	USBLS	5/07
	Kansas	Y	58820 FQ	73700 MW	95850 TQ	USBLS	5/07
	Wichita MSA, KS	Y	48390 FQ	76470 MW	91770 TQ	USBLS	5/07
	Kentucky	Y	52066 FQ	65047 MW	82963 TQ	KYBLS	2008
	Louisville-Jefferson County MSA, KY-IN	Y	54600 FQ	68410 MW	82560 TQ	USBLS	5/07
	Louisiana	H	17.80 FQ	23.23 MW	32.37 TQ	LABLS	1/08-3/08
	Baton Rouge MSA, LA	Y	40750 FQ	54850 MW	64720 TQ	USBLS	5/07
	New Orleans-Metairie-Kenner MSA, LA	Y	38910 FQ	53670 MW	76070 TQ	USBLS	5/07
	Maine	Y	53140 FQ	66670 MW	97640 TQ	USBLS	5/07
	Portland-South Portland-Biddeford MSA, ME	Y	71140 FQ	87760 MW	107050 TQ	USBLS	5/07
	Maryland	Y		83325 MW		MDBLS	3/08
	Baltimore-Towson MSA, MD	Y	70030 FQ	81370 MW	102910 TQ	USBLS	5/07
	Bethesda-Gaithersburg-Frederick PMSA, MD	Y	71340 FQ	96480 MW	125570 TQ	USBLS	5/07
	Massachusetts	Y	85210 FQ	104260 MW	131030 TQ	USBLS	5/07
	Boston-Cambridge-Quincy NECTA, MA	Y	87940 FQ	108300 MW	135900 TQ	USBLS	5/07
	Worcester MSA, MA-CT	Y	71300 FQ	97000 MW	121220 TQ	USBLS	5/07
	Michigan	Y	60850 FQ	77740 MW	97370 TQ	USBLS	5/07
	Detroit-Warren-Livonia MSA, MI	Y	67880 FQ	81550 MW	102900 TQ	USBLS	5/07
	Grand Rapids-Wyoming MSA, MI	Y	59910 FQ	84710 MW	103380 TQ	USBLS	5/07
	Warren-Troy-Farmington Hills PMSA, MI	Y	68380 FQ	80910 MW	100470 TQ	USBLS	5/07
	Minnesota	Y	88208 FQ	109572 MW	132563 TQ	MNBLS	10/08-12/08
	Duluth-Superior MSA, MN-WI	Y	51454 FQ	61923 MW	109697 TQ	MNBLS	10/08-12/08
	Minneapolis-Saint Paul MSA, MN-WI	Y	89605 FQ	110917 MW	134366 TQ	MNBLS	10/08-12/08
	Mississippi	Y	53670 FQ	62000 MW	77260 TQ	USBLS	5/07
	Jackson MSA, MS	Y	51080 FQ	68730 MW	80160 TQ	USBLS	5/07
	Missouri	Y	53970 FQ	75050 MW	100740 TQ	USBLS	5/07
	Kansas City MSA, MO-KS	Y	59110 FQ	74880 MW	103950 TQ	USBLS	5/07
	St. Louis MSA, MO-IL	Y	63580 FQ	80480 MW	107750 TQ	USBLS	5/07
	Springfield MSA, MO	Y	33760 FQ	44960 MW	69770 TQ	USBLS	5/07
	Montana	Y	41230 FQ	58290 MW	73140 TQ	USBLS	5/07
	Nebraska	Y	57930 FQ	75750 MW	94910 TQ	USBLS	5/07
	Omaha-Council Bluffs MSA, NE-IA	Y	56020 FQ	76840 MW	95950 TQ	USBLS	5/07
	Nevada	H	27.92 FQ	33.62 MW	41.80 TQ	NVBLS	5/08
	Las Vegas-Paradise MSA, NV	H	28.28 FQ	34.70 MW	42.66 TQ	NVBLS	5/08
	New Hampshire	H	30.22 AE	40.10 MW	51.52 AEX	NHBLS	6/08
	Nashua NECTA, NH-MA	Y	72140 FQ	84840 MW	132540 TQ	USBLS	5/07
	New Jersey	Y	88430 FQ	106740 MW	137830 TQ	USBLS	5/07
	Camden PMSA, NJ	Y	83190 FQ	97880 MW	118130 TQ	USBLS	5/07
	Edison PMSA, NJ	Y	88570 FQ	107610 MW	144400 TQ	USBLS	5/07
	Newark-Union PMSA, NJ-PA	Y	89380 FQ	112420 MW		USBLS	5/07
	New Mexico	Y	41890 FQ	52410 MW	68970 TQ	USBLS	5/07
	Albuquerque MSA, NM	Y	38830 FQ	51090 MW	72300 TQ	USBLS	5/07
	New York	Y	83620 FQ	107410 MW	137440 TQ	USBLS	5/07
	Albany-Schenectady-Troy MSA, NY	Y	67480 FQ	84880 MW	112120 TQ	USBLS	5/07
	Buffalo-Niagara Falls MSA, NY	Y	69440 FQ	83910 MW	108650 TQ	USBLS	5/07
	Nassau-Suffolk PMSA, NY	Y	82300 FQ	101140 MW		USBLS	5/07
	New York-Northern New Jersey-Long Island MSA, NY-NJ-PA	Y	91700 FQ	113520 MW	144600 TQ	USBLS	5/07
	North Carolina	Y	71120 FQ	91460 MW	114930 TQ	USBLS	5/07
	Charlotte-Gastonia-Concord MSA, NC-SC	Y	69580 FQ	86500 MW	111710 TQ	USBLS	5/07
	Raleigh-Cary MSA, NC	Y	71630 FQ	90620 MW	111480 TQ	USBLS	5/07

AE Average entry wage	AW Average wage paid	FQ First quartile wage	LO Lowest wage paid	MTC Median total compensation	TCC Total cash compensation
AER Average entry range	AWR Average wage range	H Hourly	LR Low end range	MW Median wage paid	TQ Third quartile wage
AEX Average experienced wage	AXR Average experienced range	HI Highest wage paid	M Monthly	MWR Median wage range	W Weekly
ATC Average total compensation	D Daily	HR High end range	MCC Median cash compensation	S See annotated source	Y Yearly

Occupation/Type/Industry	Location	Per	Low	Mid	High	Source	Date
Training and Development Manager							
	North Dakota	Y	54000 FQ	66340 MW	78250 TQ	USBLS	5/07
	Ohio	Y	70240 FQ	85870 MW	106170 TQ	USBLS	5/07
	Cincinnati-Middletown MSA, OH-KY-IN	Y	66040 FQ	82430 MW	102950 TQ	USBLS	5/07
	Cleveland-Elyria-Mentor MSA, OH	Y	70290 FQ	86550 MW	105820 TQ	USBLS	5/07
	Columbus MSA, OH	Y	75220 FQ	91840 MW	124770 TQ	USBLS	5/07
	Dayton MSA, OH	Y	70990 FQ	81050 MW	96880 TQ	USBLS	5/07
	Oklahoma	Y	38540 FQ	56720 MW	77540 TQ	USBLS	5/07
	Oklahoma City MSA, OK	Y	37590 FQ	54140 MW	77240 TQ	USBLS	5/07
	Tulsa MSA, OK	Y	40680 FQ	61390 MW	79270 TQ	USBLS	5/07
	Oregon	H	29.90 FQ	38.92 MW	46.92 TQ	ORBLS	5/08
	Portland-Vancouver-Beaverton MSA, OR-WA	Y	59450 FQ	81360 MW	97330 TQ	USBLS	5/07
	Pennsylvania	Y	60340 FQ	80100 MW	101110 TQ	USBLS	5/07
	Allentown-Bethlehem-Easton MSA, PA-NJ	Y	61230 FQ	79260 MW	99780 TQ	USBLS	5/07
	Philadelphia-Camden-Wilmington MSA, PA-NJ-DE-MD	Y	66130 FQ	89710 MW	114640 TQ	USBLS	5/07
	Pittsburgh MSA, PA	Y	56410 FQ	70170 MW	89400 TQ	USBLS	5/07
	Rhode Island	Y	65980 FQ	85100 MW	105320 TQ	USBLS	5/07
	Providence-Fall River-Warwick MSA, RI-MA	Y	66080 FQ	85690 MW	108050 TQ	USBLS	5/07
	South Carolina	Y	51070 FQ	67650 MW	88050 TQ	USBLS	5/07
	Charleston-North Charleston MSA, SC	Y	59540 FQ	75040 MW	100680 TQ	USBLS	5/07
	Columbia MSA, SC	Y	56760 FQ	66110 MW	79540 TQ	USBLS	5/07
	South Dakota	Y	61885 FQ	72506 MW	85767 TQ	SDBLS	7/08-9/08
	Tennessee	Y	44970 FQ	63790 MW	84890 TQ	USBLS	5/07
	Memphis MSA, TN-MS-AR	Y	52950 FQ	63440 MW	86740 TQ	USBLS	5/07
	Nashville-Davidson-Murfreesboro MSA, TN	Y	50490 FQ	72130 MW	94010 TQ	USBLS	5/07
	Texas	Y	67340 FQ	87740 MW	112570 TQ	USBLS	5/07
	Austin-Round Rock MSA, TX	Y	61590 FQ	99180 MW	127420 TQ	USBLS	5/07
	Dallas-Fort Worth-Arlington MSA, TX	Y	73680 FQ	92360 MW	115870 TQ	USBLS	5/07
	Houston-Sugar Land-Baytown MSA, TX	Y	71840 FQ	87100 MW	110660 TQ	USBLS	5/07
	San Antonio MSA, TX	Y	63030 FQ	83010 MW	104030 TQ	USBLS	5/07
	Utah	Y	60400 FQ	79090 MW	97230 TQ	USBLS	5/07
	Salt Lake City MSA, UT	Y	60080 FQ	81490 MW	99980 TQ	USBLS	5/07
	Virginia	Y	68320 FQ	91920 MW	121160 TQ	USBLS	5/07
	Richmond MSA, VA	Y	68880 FQ	88650 MW	115850 TQ	USBLS	5/07
	Virginia Beach-Norfolk-Newport News MSA, VA-NC	Y	60110 FQ	75950 MW	92370 TQ	USBLS	5/07
	Washington	H	36.59 FQ	45.13 MW	54.46 TQ	WABLS	3/08
	Seattle-Tacoma-Bellevue MSA, WA	Y	78690 FQ	96210 MW	115660 TQ	USBLS	5/07
	West Virginia	Y	48187 FQ	60522 MW	75438 TQ	WVBLS	7/08-9/08
	Wisconsin	Y	57790 FQ	73610 MW	95940 TQ	USBLS	5/07
	Milwaukee-Waukesha-West Allis MSA, WI	Y	58760 FQ	71530 MW	97610 TQ	USBLS	5/07
	Wyoming	Y	38479 FQ	54494 MW	67821 TQ	WYBLS	9/08
	Puerto Rico	Y	44160 FQ	56420 MW	79270 TQ	USBLS	5/07
	San Juan-Caguas-Guaynabo MSA, PR	Y	43330 FQ	55050 MW	77380 TQ	USBLS	5/07
Training and Development Specialist							
	Alabama	Y	32640 FQ	42270 MW	56540 TQ	USBLS	5/07
	Birmingham-Hoover MSA, AL	Y	39200 FQ	50200 MW	65920 TQ	USBLS	5/07
	Alaska	Y	43720 FQ	52490 MW	63810 TQ	USBLS	5/07
	Anchorage MSA, AK	Y	42590 FQ	52010 MW	64170 TQ	USBLS	5/07
	Arizona	Y	34120 FQ	44420 MW	58250 TQ	USBLS	5/07
	Phoenix-Mesa-Scottsdale MSA, AZ	Y	36180 FQ	45720 MW	59430 TQ	USBLS	5/07
	Tucson MSA, AZ	Y	26420 FQ	35750 MW	47100 TQ	USBLS	5/07
	Arkansas	Y	29420 FQ	38690 MW	48510 TQ	USBLS	5/07
	Jonesboro MSA, AR	Y	29750 FQ	35000 MW	40080 TQ	USBLS	5/07

Occupation/Type/Industry	Location	Per	Low	Mid	High	Source	Date
Training and Development Specialist	Little Rock-North Little Rock MSA, AR	Y	31040 FQ	41140 MW	49860 TQ	USBLS	5/07
	California	H	21.74 FQ	29.17 MW	37.84 TQ	CABLS	1/08-3/08
	Los Angeles-Long Beach-Glendale PMSA, CA	H	20.68 FQ	27.52 MW	35.48 TQ	CABLS	1/08-3/08
	Oakland-Fremont-Hayward MSA, CA	H	25.52 FQ	33.79 MW	41.38 TQ	CABLS	1/08-3/08
	Riverside-San Bernardino-Ontario MSA, CA	H	19.23 FQ	23.85 MW	30.98 TQ	CABLS	1/08-3/08
	Sacramento-Arden Arcade-Roseville MSA, CA	H	19.52 FQ	26.35 MW	33.22 TQ	CABLS	1/08-3/08
	San Diego-Carlsbad-San Marcos MSA, CA	H	24.71 FQ	32.65 MW	43.71 TQ	CABLS	1/08-3/08
	San Francisco-San Mateo-Redwood PMSA, CA	H	27.56 FQ	35.17 MW	41.66 TQ	CABLS	1/08-3/08
	San Jose-Sunnyvale-Santa Clara MSA, CA	H	24.35 FQ	33.69 MW	45.74 TQ	CABLS	1/08-3/08
	Santa Ana-Anaheim-Irvine PMSA, CA	Y	50910 FQ	65240 MW	77990 TQ	USBLS	5/07
	Colorado	Y	39040 FQ	50620 MW	63650 TQ	USBLS	5/07
	Denver-Aurora MSA, CO	Y	40290 FQ	51860 MW	65200 TQ	USBLS	5/07
	Connecticut	H	17.79 AE	27.60 MW		CTBLS	1/08-3/08
	Bridgeport-Stamford-Norwalk MSA, CT	Y	49610 FQ	64010 MW	76570 TQ	USBLS	5/07
	Hartford-West Hartford-East Hartford MSA, CT	Y	42910 FQ	57120 MW	71750 TQ	USBLS	5/07
	New Haven MSA, CT	Y	36100 FQ	49560 MW	66260 TQ	USBLS	5/07
	Delaware	Y	42570 FQ	51800 MW	67680 TQ	USBLS	5/07
	Wilmington PMSA, DE-MD-NJ	Y	44780 FQ	58460 MW	73400 TQ	USBLS	5/07
	District of Columbia	Y	50640 FQ	69830 MW	89300 TQ	USBLS	5/07
	Washington-Arlington-Alexandria MSA, DC-VA-MD-WV	Y	43770 FQ	60300 MW	84010 TQ	USBLS	5/07
	Florida	Y	36570 FQ	46880 MW	60860 TQ	USBLS	5/07
	Fort Lauderdale-Pompano Beach-Deerfield Beach PMSA, FL	Y	36350 FQ	50280 MW	66130 TQ	USBLS	5/07
	Jacksonville MSA, FL	Y	39520 FQ	47150 MW	58120 TQ	USBLS	5/07
	Miami-Fort Lauderdale-Miami Beach MSA, FL	Y	38850 FQ	50460 MW	66410 TQ	USBLS	5/07
	Orlando-Kissimmee MSA, FL	Y	34040 FQ	45260 MW	59410 TQ	USBLS	5/07
	Tampa-St. Petersburg-Clearwater MSA, FL	Y	38290 FQ	46620 MW	57370 TQ	USBLS	5/07
	West Palm Beach-Boca Raton-Boynton Beach PMSA, FL	Y	42980 FQ	53280 MW	68400 TQ	USBLS	5/07
	Georgia	Y	41070 FQ	52380 MW	64850 TQ	USBLS	5/07
	Atlanta-Sandy Springs-Marietta MSA, GA	Y	45370 FQ	57010 MW	71480 TQ	USBLS	5/07
	Hawaii	Y	34410 FQ	43880 MW	58940 TQ	USBLS	5/07
	Honolulu MSA, HI	Y	34600 FQ	44420 MW	59850 TQ	USBLS	5/07
	Idaho	Y	30120 FQ	39310 MW	49190 TQ	USBLS	5/07
	Boise City-Nampa MSA, ID	Y	35110 FQ	41090 MW	53090 TQ	USBLS	5/07
	Illinois	Y	34130 FQ	49200 MW	63560 TQ	USBLS	5/07
	Chicago-Naperville-Joliet MSA, IL-IN-WI	Y	35560 FQ	50150 MW	64340 TQ	USBLS	5/07
	Indiana	Y	33170 FQ	45990 MW	60770 TQ	USBLS	5/07
	Gary PMSA, IN	Y	34550 FQ	45930 MW	56790 TQ	USBLS	5/07
	Indianapolis-Carmel MSA, IN	Y	36300 FQ	50260 MW	64650 TQ	USBLS	5/07
	Iowa	Y	33000 FQ	42600 MW	55220 TQ	USBLS	5/07
	Cedar Rapids MSA, IA	Y	34970 FQ	45670 MW	57550 TQ	USBLS	5/07
	Des Moines-West Des Moines MSA, IA	Y	40390 FQ	50230 MW	60020 TQ	USBLS	5/07
	Kansas	Y	34430 FQ	48440 MW	62690 TQ	USBLS	5/07
	Topeka MSA, KS	Y	41600 FQ	49110 MW	62140 TQ	USBLS	5/07
	Wichita MSA, KS	Y	28140 FQ	39830 MW	53180 TQ	USBLS	5/07
	Kentucky	Y	34266 FQ	44019 MW	57843 TQ	KYBLS	2008
	Louisville-Jefferson County MSA, KY-IN	Y	35130 FQ	43650 MW	56550 TQ	USBLS	5/07
	Louisiana	H	14.99 FQ	20.30 MW	26.45 TQ	LABLS	1/08-3/08
	Baton Rouge MSA, LA	Y	30560 FQ	40640 MW	55320 TQ	USBLS	5/07

AE Average entry wage	AW Average wage paid	FQ First quartile wage	LO Lowest wage paid	MTC Median total compensation	TCC Total cash compensation
AER Average entry range	AWR Average wage range	H Hourly	LR Low end range	MW Median wage paid	TQ Third quartile wage
AEX Average experienced wage	AXR Average experienced range	HI Highest wage paid	M Monthly	MWR Median wage range	W Weekly
ATC Average total compensation	D Daily	HR High end range	MCC Median cash compensation	S See annotated source	Y Yearly

Training and Development Specialist

Occupation/Type/Industry	Location	Per	Low	Mid	High	Source	Date
Training and Development Specialist	Lafayette MSA, LA	Y	34940 FQ	47630 MW	64520 TQ	USBLS	5/07
	Lake Charles MSA, LA	Y	27370 FQ	38620 MW	59720 TQ	USBLS	5/07
	New Orleans-Metairie-Kenner MSA, LA	Y	35430 FQ	45690 MW	56060 TQ	USBLS	5/07
	Maine	Y	33140 FQ	41220 MW	54390 TQ	USBLS	5/07
	Lewiston-Auburn MSA, ME	Y	35900 FQ	46410 MW	68770 TQ	USBLS	5/07
	Portland-South Portland-Biddeford MSA, ME	Y	34310 FQ	44070 MW	57650 TQ	USBLS	5/07
	Maryland	Y		48250 MW		MDBLS	3/08
	Baltimore-Towson MSA, MD	Y	38530 FQ	48630 MW	67730 TQ	USBLS	5/07
	Bethesda-Gaithersburg-Frederick PMSA, MD	Y	39870 FQ	46300 MW	74740 TQ	USBLS	5/07
	Massachusetts	Y	44520 FQ	58680 MW	76130 TQ	USBLS	5/07
	Boston-Cambridge-Quincy NECTA, MA	Y	45370 FQ	60410 MW	78920 TQ	USBLS	5/07
	Worcester MSA, MA-CT	Y	44010 FQ	54980 MW	70610 TQ	USBLS	5/07
	Michigan	Y	38010 FQ	51410 MW	68260 TQ	USBLS	5/07
	Detroit-Warren-Livonia MSA, MI	Y	38720 FQ	51750 MW	68760 TQ	USBLS	5/07
	Grand Rapids-Wyoming MSA, MI	Y	38030 FQ	46530 MW	61720 TQ	USBLS	5/07
	Warren-Troy-Farmington Hills PMSA, MI	Y	41400 FQ	53850 MW	68810 TQ	USBLS	5/07
	Minnesota	Y	44917 FQ	57742 MW	72600 TQ	MNBLS	10/08-12/08
	Duluth-Superior MSA, MN-WI	Y	40799 FQ	47524 MW	57846 TQ	MNBLS	10/08-12/08
	Minneapolis-Saint Paul MSA, MN-WI	Y	47419 FQ	60505 MW	74956 TQ	MNBLS	10/08-12/08
	Rochester MSA, MN	Y	44794 FQ	53536 MW	67253 TQ	MNBLS	10/08-12/08
	Mississippi	Y	30130 FQ	37420 MW	46970 TQ	USBLS	5/07
	Jackson MSA, MS	Y	32830 FQ	38140 MW	46500 TQ	USBLS	5/07
	Missouri	Y	34790 FQ	45250 MW	58710 TQ	USBLS	5/07
	Kansas City MSA, MO-KS	Y	38430 FQ	51220 MW	64580 TQ	USBLS	5/07
	St. Louis MSA, MO-IL	Y	36750 FQ	48100 MW	61430 TQ	USBLS	5/07
	Montana	Y	31870 FQ	38950 MW	49140 TQ	USBLS	5/07
	Billings MSA, MT	Y	33130 FQ	38240 MW	47690 TQ	USBLS	5/07
	Nebraska	Y	35100 FQ	42480 MW	54610 TQ	USBLS	5/07
	Omaha-Council Bluffs MSA, NE-IA	Y	35730 FQ	43160 MW	56010 TQ	USBLS	5/07
	Nevada	H	14.50 FQ	20.35 MW	28.45 TQ	NVBLS	5/08
	Las Vegas-Paradise MSA, NV	H	18.06 FQ	23.31 MW	31.25 TQ	NVBLS	5/08
	New Hampshire	H	15.37 AE	24.95 MW	30.83 AEX	NHBLS	6/08
	Manchester MSA, NH	Y	29480 FQ	48010 MW	57490 TQ	USBLS	5/07
	Nashua NECTA, NH-MA	Y	47470 FQ	66920 MW	84450 TQ	USBLS	5/07
	New Jersey	Y	47710 FQ	63560 MW	79090 TQ	USBLS	5/07
	Camden PMSA, NJ	Y	37970 FQ	49520 MW	66130 TQ	USBLS	5/07
	Edison PMSA, NJ	Y	52110 FQ	67370 MW	78760 TQ	USBLS	5/07
	Newark-Union PMSA, NJ-PA	Y	49770 FQ	64160 MW	80220 TQ	USBLS	5/07
	New Mexico	Y	31410 FQ	45820 MW	59560 TQ	USBLS	5/07
	Albuquerque MSA, NM	Y	30750 FQ	46690 MW	60230 TQ	USBLS	5/07
	New York	Y	42160 FQ	54420 MW	72730 TQ	USBLS	5/07
	Albany-Schenectady-Troy MSA, NY	Y	40350 FQ	51120 MW	64400 TQ	USBLS	5/07
	Buffalo-Niagara Falls MSA, NY	Y	40120 FQ	50070 MW	61320 TQ	USBLS	5/07
	Nassau-Suffolk PMSA, NY	Y	43320 FQ	52490 MW	65930 TQ	USBLS	5/07
	New York-Northern New Jersey-Long Island MSA, NY-NJ-PA	Y	45910 FQ	60530 MW	77990 TQ	USBLS	5/07
	North Carolina	Y	37410 FQ	47680 MW	61110 TQ	USBLS	5/07
	Charlotte-Gastonia-Concord MSA, NC-SC	Y	40040 FQ	50220 MW	66340 TQ	USBLS	5/07
	Durham MSA, NC	Y	42280 FQ	56540 MW	77840 TQ	USBLS	5/07
	Raleigh-Cary MSA, NC	Y	41880 FQ	52340 MW	62370 TQ	USBLS	5/07
	North Dakota	Y	30860 FQ	38000 MW	48130 TQ	USBLS	5/07
	Fargo MSA, ND-MN	Y	32370 FQ	37960 MW	45730 TQ	USBLS	5/07
	Ohio	Y	36990 FQ	48930 MW	61300 TQ	USBLS	5/07
	Canton-Massillon MSA, OH	Y	35340 FQ	52320 MW	63170 TQ	USBLS	5/07
	Cincinnati-Middletown MSA, OH-KY-IN	Y	39210 FQ	50440 MW	63410 TQ	USBLS	5/07
	Cleveland-Elyria-Mentor MSA, OH	Y	38960 FQ	48820 MW	61470 TQ	USBLS	5/07

AE	Average entry wage	AW	Average wage paid	FQ	First quartile wage	LO	Lowest wage paid	MTC	Median total compensation	TCC	Total cash compensation
AER	Average entry range	AWR	Average wage range	H	Hourly	LR	Low range	MW	Median wage paid	TQ	Third quartile wage
AEX	Average experienced wage	AXR	Average experienced range	HI	Highest wage paid	M	Monthly	MWR	Median wage range	W	Weekly
ATC	Average total compensation	D	Daily	HR	High end range	MCC	Median cash compensation	S	See annotated source	Y	Yearly

Occupation/Type/Industry	Location	Per	Low	Mid	High	Source	Date
Training and Development Specialist	Columbus MSA, OH	Y	37870 FQ	50550 MW	62110 TQ	USBLS	5/07
	Dayton MSA, OH	Y	39050 FQ	52010 MW	65920 TQ	USBLS	5/07
	Oklahoma	Y	26950 FQ	36420 MW	52490 TQ	USBLS	5/07
	Oklahoma City MSA, OK	Y	30370 FQ	39640 MW	60230 TQ	USBLS	5/07
	Tulsa MSA, OK	Y	27140 FQ	35130 MW	47660 TQ	USBLS	5/07
	Oregon	H	17.58 FQ	23.52 MW	30.43 TQ	ORBLS	5/08
	Portland-Vancouver-Beaverton MSA, OR-WA	Y	39940 FQ	52580 MW	68240 TQ	USBLS	5/07
	Pennsylvania	Y	34430 FQ	46490 MW	61170 TQ	USBLS	5/07
	Allentown-Bethlehem-Easton MSA, PA-NJ	Y	34200 FQ	46840 MW	60250 TQ	USBLS	5/07
	Philadelphia-Camden-Wilmington MSA, PA-NJ-DE-MD	Y	38380 FQ	50890 MW	67330 TQ	USBLS	5/07
	Pittsburgh MSA, PA	Y	33390 FQ	45950 MW	60130 TQ	USBLS	5/07
	Rhode Island	Y	43060 FQ	51640 MW	62860 TQ	USBLS	5/07
	Providence-Fall River-Warwick MSA, RI-MA	Y	42420 FQ	51560 MW	63060 TQ	USBLS	5/07
	South Carolina	Y	35220 FQ	46710 MW	60940 TQ	USBLS	5/07
	Charleston-North Charleston MSA, SC	Y	35960 FQ	49320 MW	58900 TQ	USBLS	5/07
	Columbia MSA, SC	Y	35190 FQ	45540 MW	56380 TQ	USBLS	5/07
	Florence MSA, SC	Y	34170 FQ	43690 MW	74180 TQ	USBLS	5/07
	South Dakota	Y	31521 FQ	37003 MW	43328 TQ	SDBLS	7/08-9/08
	Sioux Falls MSA, SD	Y	32941 FQ	37925 MW	45459 TQ	SDBLS	7/08-9/08
	Tennessee	Y	32590 FQ	44570 MW	60150 TQ	USBLS	5/07
	Knoxville MSA, TN	Y	32150 FQ	43590 MW	58380 TQ	USBLS	5/07
	Memphis MSA, TN-MS-AR	Y	38790 FQ	53640 MW	66800 TQ	USBLS	5/07
	Nashville-Davidson-Murfreesboro MSA, TN	Y	30070 FQ	43990 MW	59960 TQ	USBLS	5/07
	Texas	Y	37870 FQ	49230 MW	64530 TQ	USBLS	5/07
	Austin-Round Rock MSA, TX	Y	38480 FQ	51940 MW	69980 TQ	USBLS	5/07
	Dallas-Fort Worth-Arlington MSA, TX	Y	39330 FQ	49960 MW	65060 TQ	USBLS	5/07
	El Paso MSA, TX	Y	34140 FQ	45570 MW	56680 TQ	USBLS	5/07
	Houston-Sugar Land-Baytown MSA, TX	Y	42160 FQ	54740 MW	70310 TQ	USBLS	5/07
	San Antonio MSA, TX	Y	36620 FQ	45690 MW	56180 TQ	USBLS	5/07
	Utah	Y	32590 FQ	42030 MW	56090 TQ	USBLS	5/07
	Logan MSA, UT-ID	Y	37350 FQ	43880 MW	49630 TQ	USBLS	5/07
	Ogden-Clearfield MSA, UT	Y	28860 FQ	35910 MW	50120 TQ	USBLS	5/07
	Salt Lake City MSA, UT	Y	34300 FQ	43970 MW	61330 TQ	USBLS	5/07
	Vermont	Y	33860 FQ	41410 MW	56580 TQ	USBLS	5/07
	Burlington-South Burlington MSA, VT	Y	36160 FQ	45840 MW	61830 TQ	USBLS	5/07
	Virginia	Y	41650 FQ	54970 MW	73760 TQ	USBLS	5/07
	Richmond MSA, VA	Y	42180 FQ	55070 MW	67170 TQ	USBLS	5/07
	Virginia Beach-Norfolk-Newport News MSA, VA-NC	Y	37530 FQ	48510 MW	63160 TQ	USBLS	5/07
	Washington	H	21.39 FQ	27.65 MW	35.48 TQ	WABLS	3/08
	Seattle-Tacoma-Bellevue MSA, WA	Y	47650 FQ	60470 MW	76590 TQ	USBLS	5/07
	Spokane MSA, WA	Y	39130 FQ	46220 MW	54350 TQ	USBLS	5/07
	West Virginia	Y	28507 FQ	38540 MW	51643 TQ	WVBLS	7/08-9/08
	Charleston MSA, WV	Y	34090 FQ	40450 MW	55340 TQ	USBLS	5/07
	Wisconsin	Y	36490 FQ	45750 MW	57350 TQ	USBLS	5/07
	Milwaukee-Waukesha-West Allis MSA, WI	Y	38670 FQ	47890 MW	60240 TQ	USBLS	5/07
	Wyoming	Y	34517 FQ	40025 MW	50342 TQ	WYBLS	9/08
	Cheyenne MSA, WY	Y	33966 FQ	40688 MW	49104 TQ	WYBLS	9/08
	Puerto Rico	Y	22280 FQ	29820 MW	40980 TQ	USBLS	5/07
	San Juan-Caguas-Guaynabo MSA, PR	Y	22990 FQ	30470 MW	41480 TQ	USBLS	5/07
Training Officer Fire Department	Orange, MA	Y			2000 HI	FRCOG	2009
Transit and Railroad Police	Arizona	Y	15170 FQ	19370 MW	72840 TQ	USBLS	5/07
	Arkansas	Y	24570 FQ	44150 MW	54730 TQ	USBLS	5/07
	California	H	18.27 FQ	21.21 MW	24.97 TQ	CABLS	1/08-3/08
	Florida	Y	41930 FQ	46400 MW	50940 TQ	USBLS	5/07

AE	Average entry wage	AW	Average wage paid	FQ	First quartile wage	LO	Lowest wage paid	MTC	Median total compensation	TCC	Total cash compensation
AER	Average entry range	AWR	Average wage range	H	Hourly	LR	Low end range	MW	Median wage paid	TQ	Third quartile wage
AEX	Average experienced wage	AXR	Average experienced range	HI	Highest wage paid	M	Monthly	MWR	Median wage range	W	Weekly
ATC	Average total compensation	D	Daily	HR	High end range	MCC	Median cash compensation	S	See annotated source	Y	Yearly

Occupation/Type/Industry	Location	Per	Low	Mid	High	Source	Date
Transit and Railroad Police	Georgia	Y	43130 FQ	48250 MW	57640 TQ	USBLS	5/07
	Illinois	Y	35070 FQ	42590 MW	54430 TQ	USBLS	5/07
	Louisiana	H	18.34 FQ	22.71 MW	30.46 TQ	LABLS	1/08-3/08
	Maryland	Y		45700 MW		MDBLS	3/08
	Massachusetts	Y	44670 FQ	48320 MW	52020 TQ	USBLS	5/07
	Minnesota	Y	58573 FQ	62546 MW	66980 TQ	MNBLS	10/08-12/08
	New Jersey	Y	36220 FQ	46340 MW	77600 TQ	USBLS	5/07
	New York	Y	35310 FQ	43310 MW	51360 TQ	USBLS	5/07
	Ohio	Y	41450 FQ	46070 MW	50150 TQ	USBLS	5/07
	Pennsylvania	Y	35800 FQ	43650 MW	49300 TQ	USBLS	5/07
	Texas	Y	43770 FQ	52570 MW	66290 TQ	USBLS	5/07
	Utah	Y	23980 FQ	34270 MW	38240 TQ	USBLS	5/07
	West Virginia	Y	29229 FQ	36710 MW	58658 TQ	WVBLS	7/08-9/08
Transit Systems Manager Municipal Government	Colorado Springs, CO	M	7937 LO			COSPRS	1/1/09
Transplant Surgeon Kidney	United States	Y		386750 AW		CEJ01	2008
Transportation, Storage, and Distribution Manager	Alabama	Y	52170 FQ	70640 MW	91300 TQ	USBLS	5/07
	Birmingham-Hoover MSA, AL	Y	54980 FQ	77970 MW	96570 TQ	USBLS	5/07
	Alaska	Y	50100 FQ	67120 MW	86130 TQ	USBLS	5/07
	Anchorage MSA, AK	Y	47050 FQ	63960 MW	86250 TQ	USBLS	5/07
	Fairbanks MSA, AK	Y	61020 FQ	75650 MW	94770 TQ	USBLS	5/07
	Arizona	Y	46730 FQ	61280 MW	83990 TQ	USBLS	5/07
	Phoenix-Mesa-Scottsdale MSA, AZ	Y	47830 FQ	60520 MW	82350 TQ	USBLS	5/07
	Tucson MSA, AZ	Y	47170 FQ	63970 MW	87490 TQ	USBLS	5/07
	Arkansas	Y	49530 FQ	69140 MW	90390 TQ	USBLS	5/07
	Little Rock-North Little Rock MSA, AR	Y	47810 FQ	68400 MW	90120 TQ	USBLS	5/07
	California	H	30.72 FQ	38.41 MW	47.91 TQ	CABLS	1/08-3/08
	Los Angeles-Long Beach-Glendale PMSA, CA	H	29.84 FQ	37.25 MW	45.60 TQ	CABLS	1/08-3/08
	Oakland-Fremont-Hayward MSA, CA	H	30.56 FQ	42.21 MW	52.64 TQ	CABLS	1/08-3/08
	Oxnard-Thousand Oaks-Ventura MSA, CA	H	33.14 FQ	42.45 MW	53.33 TQ	CABLS	1/08-3/08
	Riverside-San Bernardino-Ontario MSA, CA	H	29.19 FQ	36.20 MW	44.62 TQ	CABLS	1/08-3/08
	Sacramento-Arden Arcade-Roseville MSA, CA	H	30.98 FQ	39.04 MW	46.98 TQ	CABLS	1/08-3/08
	San Diego-Carlsbad-San Marcos MSA, CA	H	31.21 FQ	39.09 MW	49.22 TQ	CABLS	1/08-3/08
	San Francisco-San Mateo-Redwood PMSA, CA	H	34.65 FQ	43.38 MW	51.89 TQ	CABLS	1/08-3/08
	San Jose-Sunnyvale-Santa Clara MSA, CA	H	35.19 FQ	44.50 MW	59.99 TQ	CABLS	1/08-3/08
	Santa Ana-Anaheim-Irvine PMSA, CA	Y	64660 FQ	78820 MW	100620 TQ	USBLS	5/07
	Santa Rosa-Petaluma MSA, CA	H	31.05 FQ	38.38 MW	47.29 TQ	CABLS	1/08-3/08
	Colorado	Y	61690 FQ	78900 MW	99900 TQ	USBLS	5/07
	Denver-Aurora MSA, CO	Y	61990 FQ	79460 MW	102230 TQ	USBLS	5/07
	Connecticut	H	25.74 AE	36.61 MW		CTBLS	1/08-3/08
	Bridgeport-Stamford-Norwalk MSA, CT	Y	63670 FQ	83150 MW	112280 TQ	USBLS	5/07
	Hartford-West Hartford-East Hartford MSA, CT	Y	57410 FQ	78400 MW	98170 TQ	USBLS	5/07
	Delaware	Y	64230 FQ	83680 MW	117300 TQ	USBLS	5/07
	Wilmington PMSA, DE-MD-NJ	Y	71660 FQ	91540 MW	128890 TQ	USBLS	5/07
	District of Columbia	Y	87110 FQ	107200 MW	130220 TQ	USBLS	5/07
	Washington-Arlington-Alexandria MSA, DC-VA-MD-WV	Y	71220 FQ	91380 MW	114420 TQ	USBLS	5/07
	Florida	Y	71420 FQ	89930 MW	114900 TQ	USBLS	5/07
	Fort Lauderdale-Pompano Beach-Deerfield Beach PMSA, FL	Y	58440 FQ	83250 MW	105380 TQ	USBLS	5/07
	Jacksonville MSA, FL	Y	69840 FQ	86810 MW	108130 TQ	USBLS	5/07

AE	Average entry wage	**AW**	Average wage paid	**FQ**	First quartile wage	**LO**	Lowest wage paid	**MTC** Median total compensation **TCC** Total cash compensation
AER	Average entry range	**AWR**	Average wage range	**H**	Hourly	**LR**	Low end range	**MW** Median wage paid **TQ** Third quartile wage
AEX	Average experienced wage	**AXR**	Average experienced range	**HI**	Highest wage paid	**M**	Monthly	**MWR** Median wage range **W** Weekly
ATC	Average total compensation	**D**	Daily	**HR**	High end range	**MCC**	Median cash compensation	**S** See annotated source **Y** Yearly

Occupation/Type/Industry	Location	Per	Low	Mid	High	Source	Date
Transportation, Storage, and Distribution Manager	Miami-Fort Lauderdale-Miami Beach MSA, FL	Y	70170 FQ	91400 MW	123630 TQ	USBLS	5/07
	Orlando-Kissimmee MSA, FL	Y	75960 FQ	93100 MW	115850 TQ	USBLS	5/07
	Tampa-St. Petersburg-Clearwater MSA, FL	Y	72510 FQ	88760 MW	105760 TQ	USBLS	5/07
	West Palm Beach-Boca Raton-Boynton Beach PMSA, FL	Y	79780 FQ	103350 MW		USBLS	5/07
	Georgia	Y	56770 FQ	73940 MW	94070 TQ	USBLS	5/07
	Atlanta-Sandy Springs-Marietta MSA, GA	Y	59490 FQ	76980 MW	97550 TQ	USBLS	5/07
	Hawaii	Y	54360 FQ	72310 MW	90190 TQ	USBLS	5/07
	Honolulu MSA, HI	Y	54470 FQ	73040 MW	91000 TQ	USBLS	5/07
	Idaho	Y	38700 FQ	49920 MW	79040 TQ	USBLS	5/07
	Boise City-Nampa MSA, ID	Y	40500 FQ	57860 MW	83950 TQ	USBLS	5/07
	Illinois	Y	61300 FQ	78830 MW	96970 TQ	USBLS	5/07
	Chicago-Naperville-Joliet MSA, IL-IN-WI	Y	64210 FQ	80860 MW	98840 TQ	USBLS	5/07
	Indiana	Y	55990 FQ	70780 MW	90810 TQ	USBLS	5/07
	Gary PMSA, IN	Y	57920 FQ	75850 MW	97740 TQ	USBLS	5/07
	Indianapolis-Carmel MSA, IN	Y	58690 FQ	72960 MW	91600 TQ	USBLS	5/07
	Iowa	Y	57190 FQ	69620 MW	81460 TQ	USBLS	5/07
	Des Moines-West Des Moines MSA, IA	Y	63350 FQ	70240 MW	77670 TQ	USBLS	5/07
	Sioux City MSA, IA-NE-SD	Y	38410 FQ	59650 MW	78980 TQ	USBLS	5/07
	Kansas	Y	58800 FQ	76240 MW	94660 TQ	USBLS	5/07
	Wichita MSA, KS	Y	56710 FQ	67650 MW	87150 TQ	USBLS	5/07
	Kentucky	Y	57543 FQ	75808 MW	94189 TQ	KYBLS	2008
	Bowling Green MSA, KY	Y	52380 FQ	59100 MW	83490 TQ	USBLS	5/07
	Louisville-Jefferson County MSA, KY-IN	Y	61170 FQ	79470 MW	96360 TQ	USBLS	5/07
	Louisiana	H	21.68 FQ	27.60 MW	36.49 TQ	LABLS	1/08-3/08
	Baton Rouge MSA, LA	Y	44790 FQ	56680 MW	70810 TQ	USBLS	5/07
	Houma-Bayou Cane-Thibodaux MSA, LA	Y	40590 FQ	57730 MW	79720 TQ	USBLS	5/07
	New Orleans-Metairie-Kenner MSA, LA	Y	46520 FQ	60010 MW	81400 TQ	USBLS	5/07
	Maine	Y	47490 FQ	62270 MW	82310 TQ	USBLS	5/07
	Bangor MSA, ME	Y	46240 FQ	53530 MW	76660 TQ	USBLS	5/07
	Portland-South Portland-Biddeford MSA, ME	Y	51130 FQ	72230 MW	87420 TQ	USBLS	5/07
	Maryland	Y		79725 MW		MDBLS	3/08
	Baltimore-Towson MSA, MD	Y	62800 FQ	76770 MW	94260 TQ	USBLS	5/07
	Bethesda-Gaithersburg-Frederick PMSA, MD	Y	61250 FQ	80010 MW	96370 TQ	USBLS	5/07
	Hagerstown-Martinsburg MSA, MD-WV	Y	55360 FQ	70010 MW	85880 TQ	USBLS	5/07
	Massachusetts	Y	59330 FQ	74990 MW	94540 TQ	USBLS	5/07
	Boston-Cambridge-Quincy NECTA, MA	Y	58350 FQ	73320 MW	92860 TQ	USBLS	5/07
	Worcester MSA, MA-CT	Y	66020 FQ	78320 MW	97470 TQ	USBLS	5/07
	Michigan	Y	60480 FQ	78850 MW	98700 TQ	USBLS	5/07
	Detroit-Warren-Livonia MSA, MI	Y	66350 FQ	82680 MW	105820 TQ	USBLS	5/07
	Grand Rapids-Wyoming MSA, MI	Y	60210 FQ	73020 MW	88760 TQ	USBLS	5/07
	Warren-Troy-Farmington Hills PMSA, MI	Y	62190 FQ	81860 MW	103390 TQ	USBLS	5/07
	Minnesota	Y	64905 FQ	83318 MW	105568 TQ	MNBLS	10/08-12/08
	Duluth-Superior MSA, MN-WI	Y	59493 FQ	80628 MW	94787 TQ	MNBLS	10/08-12/08
	Minneapolis-Saint Paul MSA, MN-WI	Y	66250 FQ	85330 MW	108310 TQ	MNBLS	10/08-12/08
	Rochester MSA, MN	Y	57506 FQ	67192 MW	86834 TQ	MNBLS	10/08-12/08
	Mississippi	Y	41730 FQ	57300 MW	74940 TQ	USBLS	5/07
	Jackson MSA, MS	Y	37900 FQ	54710 MW	75250 TQ	USBLS	5/07
	Missouri	Y	55160 FQ	72800 MW	93610 TQ	USBLS	5/07
	Joplin MSA, MO	Y	45680 FQ	51820 MW	76240 TQ	USBLS	5/07
	Kansas City MSA, MO-KS	Y	63690 FQ	80850 MW	97310 TQ	USBLS	5/07
	St. Louis MSA, MO-IL	Y	56310 FQ	73860 MW	95430 TQ	USBLS	5/07
	Montana	Y	51090 FQ	59710 MW	82810 TQ	USBLS	5/07
	Billings MSA, MT	Y	52660 FQ	58510 MW	68370 TQ	USBLS	5/07
	Nebraska	Y	61690 FQ	79200 MW	99410 TQ	USBLS	5/07

AE	Average entry wage	AW	Average wage paid	FQ	First quartile wage	LO	Lowest wage paid	MTC	Median total compensation	TCC Total cash compensation
AER	Average entry range	AWR	Average wage range	H	Hourly	LR	Low end range	MW	Median wage paid	TQ Third quartile wage
AEX	Average experienced wage	AXR	Average experienced range	HI	Highest wage paid	M	Monthly	MWR	Median wage range	W Weekly
ATC	Average total compensation D	Daily	HR	High end range	MCC	Median cash compensation	S	See annotated source	Y Yearly

1622

Occupation/Type/Industry	Location	Per	Low	Mid	High	Source	Date
Transportation, Storage, and Distribution Manager	Omaha-Council Bluffs MSA, NE-IA	Y	59900 FQ	73790 MW	94820 TQ	USBLS	5/07
	Nevada	H	25.71 FQ	32.88 MW	42.30 TQ	NVBLS	5/08
	Las Vegas-Paradise MSA, NV	H	24.73 FQ	31.32 MW	42.73 TQ	NVBLS	5/08
	New Hampshire	H	28.89 AE	40.85 MW	49.82 AEX	NHBLS	6/08
	Manchester MSA, NH	Y	63070 FQ	77180 MW	90240 TQ	USBLS	5/07
	Nashua NECTA, NH-MA	Y	68850 FQ	86770 MW	103620 TQ	USBLS	5/07
	New Jersey	Y	74690 FQ	92330 MW	119100 TQ	USBLS	5/07
	Camden PMSA, NJ	Y	72540 FQ	87050 MW	105470 TQ	USBLS	5/07
	Edison PMSA, NJ	Y	74540 FQ	91500 MW	114960 TQ	USBLS	5/07
	Newark-Union PMSA, NJ-PA	Y	74320 FQ	92890 MW	122820 TQ	USBLS	5/07
	New Mexico	Y	49470 FQ	71060 MW	92950 TQ	USBLS	5/07
	Albuquerque MSA, NM	Y	60160 FQ	82080 MW	98140 TQ	USBLS	5/07
	New York	Y	70300 FQ	89160 MW	113390 TQ	USBLS	5/07
	Albany-Schenectady-Troy MSA, NY	Y	65040 FQ	83640 MW	103710 TQ	USBLS	5/07
	Buffalo-Niagara Falls MSA, NY	Y	66540 FQ	79060 MW	94240 TQ	USBLS	5/07
	Nassau-Suffolk PMSA, NY	Y	70390 FQ	89290 MW	108360 TQ	USBLS	5/07
	New York-Northern New Jersey-Long Island MSA, NY-NJ-PA	Y	75650 FQ	93580 MW	121050 TQ	USBLS	5/07
	North Carolina	Y	53790 FQ	69940 MW	90980 TQ	USBLS	5/07
	Charlotte-Gastonia-Concord MSA, NC-SC	Y	53030 FQ	68180 MW	88790 TQ	USBLS	5/07
	Raleigh-Cary MSA, NC	Y	57940 FQ	71040 MW	89140 TQ	USBLS	5/07
	North Dakota	Y	50270 FQ	60610 MW	85550 TQ	USBLS	5/07
	Fargo MSA, ND-MN	Y	47230 FQ	55190 MW	66390 TQ	USBLS	5/07
	Ohio	Y	61020 FQ	76830 MW	97780 TQ	USBLS	5/07
	Cincinnati-Middletown MSA, OH-KY-IN	Y	62440 FQ	76860 MW	94990 TQ	USBLS	5/07
	Cleveland-Elyria-Mentor MSA, OH	Y	64500 FQ	84580 MW	105440 TQ	USBLS	5/07
	Columbus MSA, OH	Y	65210 FQ	80610 MW	102550 TQ	USBLS	5/07
	Dayton MSA, OH	Y	62440 FQ	82330 MW	99290 TQ	USBLS	5/07
	Oklahoma	Y	36930 FQ	51140 MW	74400 TQ	USBLS	5/07
	Oklahoma City MSA, OK	Y	36420 FQ	49340 MW	74110 TQ	USBLS	5/07
	Tulsa MSA, OK	Y	43400 FQ	65460 MW	87960 TQ	USBLS	5/07
	Oregon	H	28.67 FQ	35.68 MW	45.44 TQ	ORBLS	5/08
	Medford MSA, OR	Y	53770 FQ	73720 MW	97770 TQ	USBLS	5/07
	Portland-Vancouver-Beaverton MSA, OR-WA	Y	61940 FQ	76130 MW	96110 TQ	USBLS	5/07
	Pennsylvania	Y	62000 FQ	81100 MW	105100 TQ	USBLS	5/07
	Allentown-Bethlehem-Easton MSA, PA-NJ	Y	62900 FQ	88210 MW	111480 TQ	USBLS	5/07
	Erie MSA, PA	Y	59400 FQ	79610 MW	96390 TQ	USBLS	5/07
	Lancaster MSA, PA	Y	59260 FQ	81690 MW	104520 TQ	USBLS	5/07
	Philadelphia-Camden-Wilmington MSA, PA-NJ-DE-MD	Y	68570 FQ	86670 MW	112460 TQ	USBLS	5/07
	Pittsburgh MSA, PA	Y	63720 FQ	82990 MW	117490 TQ	USBLS	5/07
	York-Hanover MSA, PA	Y	63160 FQ	82890 MW	101500 TQ	USBLS	5/07
	Rhode Island	Y	56920 FQ	73100 MW	96220 TQ	USBLS	5/07
	Providence-Fall River-Warwick MSA, RI-MA	Y	56660 FQ	72570 MW	95350 TQ	USBLS	5/07
	South Carolina	Y	48440 FQ	63160 MW	82690 TQ	USBLS	5/07
	Charleston-North Charleston MSA, SC	Y	53910 FQ	66330 MW	81220 TQ	USBLS	5/07
	Columbia MSA, SC	Y	49060 FQ	66900 MW	90560 TQ	USBLS	5/07
	South Dakota	Y	62966 FQ	75324 MW	91932 TQ	SDBLS	7/08-9/08
	Sioux Falls MSA, SD	Y	65929 FQ	77078 MW	88925 TQ	SDBLS	7/08-9/08
	Tennessee	Y	47900 FQ	66310 MW	88470 TQ	USBLS	5/07
	Kingsport-Bristol-Bristol MSA, TN-VA	Y	63960 FQ	81160 MW	94240 TQ	USBLS	5/07
	Memphis MSA, TN-MS-AR	Y	57490 FQ	75110 MW	105210 TQ	USBLS	5/07
	Nashville-Davidson-Murfreesboro MSA, TN	Y	46710 FQ	66840 MW	87800 TQ	USBLS	5/07
	Texas	Y	55170 FQ	71840 MW	98140 TQ	USBLS	5/07
	Austin-Round Rock MSA, TX	Y	60160 FQ	77940 MW	103240 TQ	USBLS	5/07
	Dallas-Fort Worth-Arlington MSA, TX	Y	54650 FQ	70490 MW	93400 TQ	USBLS	5/07

AE	Average entry wage	AW	Average wage paid	FQ	First quartile wage
AER	Average entry range	AWR	Average wage range	H	Hourly
AEX	Average experienced wage	AXR	Average experienced range	HI	Highest wage paid
ATC	Average total compensation	D	Daily	HR	High end range

LO	Lowest wage paid	MTC	Median total compensation	TCC	Total cash compensation
LR	Low end range	MW	Median wage paid	TQ	Third quartile wage
M	Monthly	MWR	Median wage range	W	Weekly
MCC	Median cash compensation	S	See annotated source	Y	Yearly

Occupation/Type/Industry	Location	Per	Low	Mid	High	Source	Date
Transportation, Storage, and Distribution Manager	El Paso MSA, TX	Y	47220 FQ	66450 MW	90000 TQ	USBLS	5/07
	Houston-Sugar Land-Baytown MSA, TX	Y	59150 FQ	77950 MW	108250 TQ	USBLS	5/07
	San Antonio MSA, TX	Y	54670 FQ	75250 MW	98310 TQ	USBLS	5/07
	Utah	Y	56090 FQ	68530 MW	87990 TQ	USBLS	5/07
	Logan MSA, UT-ID	Y	48020 FQ	58410 MW	70840 TQ	USBLS	5/07
	Salt Lake City MSA, UT	Y	57330 FQ	71030 MW	92380 TQ	USBLS	5/07
	Vermont	Y	58740 FQ	72230 MW	90690 TQ	USBLS	5/07
	Burlington-South Burlington MSA, VT	Y	61050 FQ	76490 MW	93790 TQ	USBLS	5/07
	Virginia	Y	63390 FQ	82070 MW	99830 TQ	USBLS	5/07
	Richmond MSA, VA	Y	61940 FQ	81580 MW	97910 TQ	USBLS	5/07
	Virginia Beach-Norfolk-Newport News MSA, VA-NC	Y	68430 FQ	82220 MW	96580 TQ	USBLS	5/07
	Washington	H	32.91 FQ	42.55 MW	55.02 TQ	WABLS	3/08
	Seattle-Tacoma-Bellevue MSA, WA	Y	70110 FQ	91080 MW	117290 TQ	USBLS	5/07
	West Virginia	Y	44276 FQ	69040 MW	93663 TQ	WVBLS	7/08-9/08
	Charleston MSA, WV	Y	44950 FQ	63350 MW	84140 TQ	USBLS	5/07
	Wisconsin	Y	53770 FQ	70160 MW	91620 TQ	USBLS	5/07
	Milwaukee-Waukesha-West Allis MSA, WI	Y	59370 FQ	77520 MW	99070 TQ	USBLS	5/07
	Wyoming	Y	60763 FQ	84413 MW	101854 TQ	WYBLS	9/08
	Casper MSA, WY	Y	65231 FQ	87991 MW	98671 TQ	WYBLS	9/08
	Cheyenne MSA, WY	Y	48461 FQ	61018 MW	81041 TQ	WYBLS	9/08
	Puerto Rico	Y	36410 FQ	50770 MW	77100 TQ	USBLS	5/07
	San Juan-Caguas-Guaynabo MSA, PR	Y	36280 FQ	49550 MW	75560 TQ	USBLS	5/07
	Virgin Islands	Y	49870 FQ	62860 MW	74600 TQ	USBLS	5/07
	Guam	Y	39740 FQ	53610 MW	82310 TQ	USBLS	5/07
Transportation Attendant							
Except Flight Attendant and Baggage	Alaska	Y	28050 FQ	36010 MW	42060 TQ	USBLS	5/07
Except Flight Attendant and Baggage	Arizona	Y	15610 FQ	17520 MW	20990 TQ	USBLS	5/07
Except Flight Attendant and Baggage	Phoenix-Mesa-Scottsdale MSA, AZ	Y	15500 FQ	17350 MW	21620 TQ	USBLS	5/07
Except Flight Attendant and Baggage	Arkansas	Y	14720 FQ	20360 MW	23200 TQ	USBLS	5/07
Except Flight Attendant and Baggage	California	H	9.21 FQ	11.22 MW	16.46 TQ	CABLS	1/08-3/08
Except Flight Attendant and Baggage	Los Angeles-Long Beach-Glendale PMSA, CA	H	10.13 FQ	11.64 MW	17.14 TQ	CABLS	1/08-3/08
Except Flight Attendant and Baggage	Oakland-Fremont-Hayward MSA, CA	H	8.61 FQ	10.18 MW	16.08 TQ	CABLS	1/08-3/08
Except Flight Attendant and Baggage	San Diego-Carlsbad-San Marcos MSA, CA	H	8.34 FQ	8.94 MW	14.01 TQ	CABLS	1/08-3/08
Except Flight Attendant and Baggage	San Francisco-San Mateo-Redwood PMSA, CA	H	8.94 FQ	11.50 MW	16.01 TQ	CABLS	1/08-3/08
Except Flight Attendant and Baggage	Santa Ana-Anaheim-Irvine PMSA, CA	Y	16130 FQ	24930 MW	30990 TQ	USBLS	5/07
Except Flight Attendant and Baggage	Colorado	Y	17090 FQ	19520 MW	26370 TQ	USBLS	5/07
Except Flight Attendant and Baggage	Denver-Aurora MSA, CO	Y	17260 FQ	19760 MW	26670 TQ	USBLS	5/07
Except Flight Attendant and Baggage	Connecticut	H	10.11 AE	11.28 MW		CTBLS	1/08-3/08
Except Flight Attendant and Baggage	Delaware	Y	17530 FQ	23020 MW	28060 TQ	USBLS	5/07
Except Flight Attendant and Baggage	Wilmington PMSA, DE-MD-NJ	Y	17440 FQ	19150 MW	26020 TQ	USBLS	5/07
Except Flight Attendant and Baggage	Washington-Arlington-Alexandria MSA, DC-VA-MD-WV	Y	22540 FQ	26110 MW	29600 TQ	USBLS	5/07
Except Flight Attendant and Baggage	Florida	Y	17620 FQ	20840 MW	24640 TQ	USBLS	5/07
Except Flight Attendant and Baggage	Jacksonville MSA, FL	Y	14730 FQ	16900 MW	21230 TQ	USBLS	5/07
Except Flight Attendant and Baggage	Miami-Fort Lauderdale-Miami Beach MSA, FL	Y	17960 FQ	21150 MW	23640 TQ	USBLS	5/07
Except Flight Attendant and Baggage	Orlando-Kissimmee MSA, FL	Y	17220 FQ	19370 MW	24680 TQ	USBLS	5/07
Except Flight Attendant and Baggage	Tampa-St. Petersburg-Clearwater MSA, FL	Y	16960 FQ	19070 MW	23620 TQ	USBLS	5/07
Except Flight Attendant and Baggage	Georgia	Y	15140 FQ	21460 MW	33430 TQ	USBLS	5/07
Except Flight Attendant and Baggage	Atlanta-Sandy Springs-Marietta MSA, GA	Y	14640 FQ	22420 MW	34530 TQ	USBLS	5/07
Except Flight Attendant and Baggage	Hawaii	Y	21070 FQ	23660 MW	27490 TQ	USBLS	5/07
Except Flight Attendant and Baggage	Honolulu MSA, HI	Y	20810 FQ	25950 MW	30260 TQ	USBLS	5/07
Except Flight Attendant and Baggage	Illinois	Y	17030 FQ	18610 MW	20340 TQ	USBLS	5/07

Occupation/Type/Industry	Location	Per	Low	Mid	High	Source	Date
Transportation Attendant							
Except Flight Attendant and Baggage	Chicago-Naperville-Joliet MSA, IL-IN-WI	Y	17010 FQ	18500 MW	20050 TQ	USBLS	5/07
Except Flight Attendant and Baggage	Indiana	Y	22350 FQ	24470 MW	27880 TQ	USBLS	5/07
Except Flight Attendant and Baggage	Iowa	Y	14380 FQ	16200 MW	21260 TQ	USBLS	5/07
Except Flight Attendant and Baggage	Louisiana	H	6.37 FQ	7.48 MW	11.37 TQ	LABLS	1/08-3/08
Except Flight Attendant and Baggage	Maryland	Y		18925 MW		MDBLS	3/08
Except Flight Attendant and Baggage	Baltimore-Towson MSA, MD	Y	15800 FQ	18550 MW	23580 TQ	USBLS	5/07
Except Flight Attendant and Baggage	Massachusetts	Y	16500 FQ	18170 MW	20380 TQ	USBLS	5/07
Except Flight Attendant and Baggage	Boston-Cambridge-Quincy NECTA, MA	Y	16210 FQ	17700 MW	19190 TQ	USBLS	5/07
Except Flight Attendant and Baggage	Michigan	Y	15180 FQ	18080 MW	22290 TQ	USBLS	5/07
Except Flight Attendant and Baggage	Detroit-Warren-Livonia MSA, MI	Y	16190 FQ	21200 MW	24680 TQ	USBLS	5/07
Except Flight Attendant and Baggage	Warren-Troy-Farmington Hills PMSA, MI	Y	15400 FQ	20260 MW	24020 TQ	USBLS	5/07
Except Flight Attendant and Baggage	Minnesota	Y	20723 FQ	22772 MW	24769 TQ	MNBLS	10/08-12/08
Except Flight Attendant and Baggage	Minneapolis-Saint Paul MSA, MN-WI	Y	20566 FQ	22542 MW	24466 TQ	MNBLS	10/08-12/08
Except Flight Attendant and Baggage	Mississippi	Y	13770 FQ	18650 MW	27040 TQ	USBLS	5/07
Except Flight Attendant and Baggage	Missouri	Y	16560 FQ	20890 MW	23570 TQ	USBLS	5/07
Except Flight Attendant and Baggage	Kansas City MSA, MO-KS	Y	21300 FQ	22830 MW	24380 TQ	USBLS	5/07
Except Flight Attendant and Baggage	St. Louis MSA, MO-IL	Y	19180 FQ	21250 MW	23640 TQ	USBLS	5/07
Except Flight Attendant and Baggage	Montana	Y	18110 FQ	20260 MW	23900 TQ	USBLS	5/07
Except Flight Attendant and Baggage	Las Vegas-Paradise MSA, NV	H	7.61 FQ	9.54 MW	10.98 TQ	NVBLS	5/08
Except Flight Attendant and Baggage	New Jersey	Y	15950 FQ	18370 MW	22100 TQ	USBLS	5/07
Except Flight Attendant and Baggage	Camden PMSA, NJ	Y	15960 FQ	17300 MW	18640 TQ	USBLS	5/07
Except Flight Attendant and Baggage	Edison PMSA, NJ	Y	16220 FQ	17870 MW	19430 TQ	USBLS	5/07
Except Flight Attendant and Baggage	Newark-Union PMSA, NJ-PA	Y	15220 FQ	17620 MW	22130 TQ	USBLS	5/07
Except Flight Attendant and Baggage	New Mexico	Y	16500 FQ	19650 MW	25140 TQ	USBLS	5/07
Except Flight Attendant and Baggage	New York	Y	16270 FQ	18720 MW	24330 TQ	USBLS	5/07
Except Flight Attendant and Baggage	Buffalo-Niagara Falls MSA, NY	Y	17950 FQ	21180 MW	25160 TQ	USBLS	5/07
Except Flight Attendant and Baggage	New York-Northern New Jersey-Long Island MSA, NY-NJ-PA	Y	15530 FQ	18120 MW	22300 TQ	USBLS	5/07
Except Flight Attendant and Baggage	North Carolina	Y	20100 FQ	24410 MW	31410 TQ	USBLS	5/07
Except Flight Attendant and Baggage	Ohio	Y	15160 FQ	17350 MW	23400 TQ	USBLS	5/07
Except Flight Attendant and Baggage	Cleveland-Elyria-Mentor MSA, OH	Y	14870 FQ	15470 MW	23220 TQ	USBLS	5/07
Except Flight Attendant and Baggage	Columbus MSA, OH	Y	15750 FQ	19750 MW	23190 TQ	USBLS	5/07
Except Flight Attendant and Baggage	Oklahoma	Y	13590 FQ	16090 MW	21110 TQ	USBLS	5/07
Except Flight Attendant and Baggage	Pennsylvania	Y	16970 FQ	20380 MW	30940 TQ	USBLS	5/07
Except Flight Attendant and Baggage	Tennessee	Y	13080 FQ	15280 MW	27720 TQ	USBLS	5/07
Except Flight Attendant and Baggage	Nashville-Davidson-Murfreesboro MSA, TN	Y	12030 FQ	13340 MW	14650 TQ	USBLS	5/07
Except Flight Attendant and Baggage	Texas	Y	17640 FQ	21620 MW	25120 TQ	USBLS	5/07
Except Flight Attendant and Baggage	Dallas-Fort Worth-Arlington MSA, TX	Y	15210 FQ	20930 MW	25360 TQ	USBLS	5/07
Except Flight Attendant and Baggage	Houston-Sugar Land-Baytown MSA, TX	Y	19560 FQ	22600 MW	25540 TQ	USBLS	5/07
Except Flight Attendant and Baggage	Utah	Y	19890 FQ	24580 MW	29400 TQ	USBLS	5/07
Except Flight Attendant and Baggage	Salt Lake City MSA, UT	Y	22000 FQ	25670 MW	30590 TQ	USBLS	5/07
Except Flight Attendant and Baggage	Vermont	Y	19840 FQ	22700 MW	25260 TQ	USBLS	5/07
Except Flight Attendant and Baggage	Virginia	Y	19150 FQ	22420 MW	25540 TQ	USBLS	5/07
Except Flight Attendant and Baggage	Washington	H	9.72 FQ	11.13 MW	12.52 TQ	WABLS	3/08
Except Flight Attendant and Baggage	Seattle-Tacoma-Bellevue MSA, WA	Y	19290 FQ	22220 MW	24950 TQ	USBLS	5/07
Except Flight Attendant and Baggage	Wisconsin	Y	14830 FQ	16700 MW	18700 TQ	USBLS	5/07
Except Flight Attendant and Baggage	Milwaukee-Waukesha-West Allis MSA, WI	Y	14430 FQ	15020 MW	18700 TQ	USBLS	5/07
Except Flight Attendant and Baggage	Wyoming	Y	18576 FQ	23092 MW	27955 TQ	WYBLS	9/08
Except Flight Attendant and Baggage	Puerto Rico	Y	13700 FQ	16570 MW	23630 TQ	USBLS	5/07
Except Flight Attendant and Baggage	San Juan-Caguas-Guaynabo MSA, PR	Y	13420 FQ	15780 MW	23720 TQ	USBLS	5/07
Transportation Engineer							
Department of Transportation	Michigan	H	18.23 LO		32.47 HI	MDOT	10/1/07
State Government	South Dakota	Y	34818 LO		52228 HI	AFT02	3/1/08
Transportation Inspector	Alabama	Y	36280 FQ	42360 MW	51110 TQ	USBLS	5/07
	Birmingham-Hoover MSA, AL	Y	37900 FQ	62600 MW	88650 TQ	USBLS	5/07

AE	Average entry wage	AW	Average wage paid	FQ	First quartile wage	LO	Lowest wage paid	MTC	Median total compensation	TCC	Total cash compensation
AER	Average entry range	AWR	Average wage range	H	Hourly	LR	Low end range	MW	Median wage paid	TQ	Third quartile wage
AEX	Average experienced wage	AXR	Average experienced range	HI	Highest wage paid	M	Monthly	MWR	Median wage range	W	Weekly
ATC	Average total compensation	D	Daily	HR	High end range	MCC	Median cash compensation	S	See annotated source	Y	Yearly

Occupation/Type/Industry	Location	Per	Low	Mid	High	Source	Date
Transportation Inspector	Alaska	Y	63690 FQ	76920 MW	89750 TQ	USBLS	5/07
	Arizona	Y	47040 FQ	60350 MW	90180 TQ	USBLS	5/07
	Phoenix-Mesa-Scottsdale MSA, AZ	Y	53010 FQ	70870 MW	96100 TQ	USBLS	5/07
	Arkansas	Y	37960 FQ	42840 MW	55450 TQ	USBLS	5/07
	Little Rock-North Little Rock MSA, AR	Y	32660 FQ	46550 MW	78410 TQ	USBLS	5/07
	California	H	21.94 FQ	28.33 MW	39.71 TQ	CABLS	1/08-3/08
	Fresno MSA, CA	H	22.02 FQ	24.78 MW	40.63 TQ	CABLS	1/08-3/08
	Los Angeles-Long Beach-Glendale PMSA, CA	H	22.14 FQ	28.68 MW	45.19 TQ	CABLS	1/08-3/08
	Oakland-Fremont-Hayward MSA, CA	H	29.34 FQ	39.18 MW	52.74 TQ	CABLS	1/08-3/08
	Riverside-San Bernardino-Ontario MSA, CA	H	19.16 FQ	23.05 MW	35.61 TQ	CABLS	1/08-3/08
	Sacramento-Arden Arcade-Roseville MSA, CA	H	24.97 FQ	33.00 MW	45.40 TQ	CABLS	1/08-3/08
	San Diego-Carlsbad-San Marcos MSA, CA	H	22.45 FQ	26.03 MW	46.16 TQ	CABLS	1/08-3/08
	San Jose-Sunnyvale-Santa Clara MSA, CA	H	45.83 FQ	52.78 MW	58.57 TQ	CABLS	1/08-3/08
	Santa Ana-Anaheim-Irvine PMSA, CA	Y	33760 FQ	50480 MW	88560 TQ	USBLS	5/07
	Colorado	Y	46340 FQ	60820 MW	94650 TQ	USBLS	5/07
	Denver-Aurora MSA, CO	Y	55360 FQ	82740 MW	104730 TQ	USBLS	5/07
	Connecticut	H	19.78 AE	28.64 MW		CTBLS	1/08-3/08
	Hartford-West Hartford-East Hartford MSA, CT	Y	42130 FQ	53830 MW	60580 TQ	USBLS	5/07
	Wilmington PMSA, DE-MD-NJ	Y	28830 FQ	33150 MW	38070 TQ	USBLS	5/07
	Washington-Arlington-Alexandria MSA, DC-VA-MD-WV	Y	52920 FQ	86920 MW	111420 TQ	USBLS	5/07
	Florida	Y	30620 FQ	66020 MW	92120 TQ	USBLS	5/07
	Fort Lauderdale-Pompano Beach-Deerfield Beach PMSA, FL	Y	65750 FQ	82910 MW	104480 TQ	USBLS	5/07
	Jacksonville MSA, FL	Y	28290 FQ	41760 MW	49240 TQ	USBLS	5/07
	Miami-Fort Lauderdale-Miami Beach MSA, FL	Y	65160 FQ	83910 MW	101960 TQ	USBLS	5/07
	Orlando-Kissimmee MSA, FL	Y	63190 FQ	83890 MW	97390 TQ	USBLS	5/07
	Tampa-St. Petersburg-Clearwater MSA, FL	Y	19860 FQ	26360 MW	44970 TQ	USBLS	5/07
	Georgia	Y	38070 FQ	49320 MW	72960 TQ	USBLS	5/07
	Atlanta-Sandy Springs-Marietta MSA, GA	Y	34610 FQ	49020 MW	78560 TQ	USBLS	5/07
	Hawaii	Y	42170 FQ	51370 MW	73780 TQ	USBLS	5/07
	Honolulu MSA, HI	Y	42680 FQ	52970 MW	74970 TQ	USBLS	5/07
	Idaho	Y	39700 FQ	45680 MW	51480 TQ	USBLS	5/07
	Boise City-Nampa MSA, ID	Y	20280 FQ	53880 MW	85770 TQ	USBLS	5/07
	Illinois	Y	38490 FQ	48800 MW	78450 TQ	USBLS	5/07
	Chicago-Naperville-Joliet MSA, IL-IN-WI	Y	33040 FQ	56370 MW	82770 TQ	USBLS	5/07
	Indiana	Y	30680 FQ	39310 MW	72220 TQ	USBLS	5/07
	Indianapolis-Carmel MSA, IN	Y	37390 FQ	61150 MW	87910 TQ	USBLS	5/07
	Iowa	Y	38370 FQ	47750 MW	64320 TQ	USBLS	5/07
	Kansas	Y	38960 FQ	52060 MW	67180 TQ	USBLS	5/07
	Wichita MSA, KS	Y	50410 FQ	57580 MW	73610 TQ	USBLS	5/07
	Kentucky	Y	43763 FQ	50915 MW	79245 TQ	KYBLS	2008
	Louisville-Jefferson County MSA, KY-IN	Y	50030 FQ	73880 MW	93900 TQ	USBLS	5/07
	Louisiana	H	18.24 FQ	25.96 MW	37.87 TQ	LABLS	1/08-3/08
	Baton Rouge MSA, LA	Y	46280 FQ	72620 MW	93180 TQ	USBLS	5/07
	New Orleans-Metairie-Kenner MSA, LA	Y	27660 FQ	42400 MW	59650 TQ	USBLS	5/07
	Maine	Y	35520 FQ	42890 MW	92010 TQ	USBLS	5/07
	Maryland	Y		47225 MW		MDBLS	3/08
	Baltimore-Towson MSA, MD	Y	35270 FQ	42340 MW	53460 TQ	USBLS	5/07
	Massachusetts	Y	29220 FQ	41170 MW	76740 TQ	USBLS	5/07
	Boston-Cambridge-Quincy NECTA, MA	Y	78410 FQ	95000 MW	111210 TQ	USBLS	5/07
	Michigan	Y	41910 FQ	58530 MW	84950 TQ	USBLS	5/07

AE	Average entry wage	AW	Average wage paid	FQ	First quartile wage	LO	Lowest wage paid	MTC	Median total compensation	TCC	Total cash compensation
AER	Average entry range	AWR	Average wage range	H	Hourly	LR	Low end range	MW	Median wage paid	TQ	Third quartile wage
AEX	Average experienced wage	AXR	Average experienced range	HI	Highest wage paid	M	Monthly	MWR	Median wage range	W	Weekly
ATC	Average total compensation	D	Daily	HR	High end range	MCC	Median cash compensation	S	See annotated source	Y	Yearly

Transportation Inspector

Occupation/Type/Industry	Location	Per	Low	Mid	High	Source	Date
Transportation Inspector	Detroit-Warren-Livonia MSA, MI	Y	40960 FQ	59950 MW	87310 TQ	USBLS	5/07
	Grand Rapids-Wyoming MSA, MI	Y	58260 FQ	81070 MW	98010 TQ	USBLS	5/07
	Warren-Troy-Farmington Hills PMSA, MI	Y	32120 FQ	45530 MW	58410 TQ	USBLS	5/07
	Minnesota	Y	50113 FQ	72335 MW	99051 TQ	MNBLS	10/08-12/08
	Minneapolis-Saint Paul MSA, MN-WI	Y	62056 FQ	89542 MW	106916 TQ	MNBLS	10/08-12/08
	Mississippi	Y	36800 FQ	47450 MW	59450 TQ	USBLS	5/07
	Jackson MSA, MS	Y	47090 FQ	73180 MW	89630 TQ	USBLS	5/07
	Missouri	Y	29550 FQ	45680 MW	73310 TQ	USBLS	5/07
	Kansas City MSA, MO-KS	Y	24230 FQ	33370 MW	86820 TQ	USBLS	5/07
	St. Louis MSA, MO-IL	Y	34670 FQ	43970 MW	81310 TQ	USBLS	5/07
	Montana	Y	35310 FQ	41660 MW	71970 TQ	USBLS	5/07
	Billings MSA, MT	Y	34840 FQ	39400 MW	73120 TQ	USBLS	5/07
	Nebraska	Y	41400 FQ	52930 MW	70240 TQ	USBLS	5/07
	Nevada	H	18.07 FQ	27.00 MW	42.19 TQ	NVBLS	5/08
	Las Vegas-Paradise MSA, NV	H	16.98 FQ	24.87 MW	42.44 TQ	NVBLS	5/08
	New Jersey	Y	44720 FQ	64870 MW	81110 TQ	USBLS	5/07
	Edison PMSA, NJ	Y	34150 FQ	60420 MW	70000 TQ	USBLS	5/07
	Newark-Union PMSA, NJ-PA	Y	41990 FQ	56060 MW	88880 TQ	USBLS	5/07
	New Mexico	Y	29210 FQ	49780 MW	71510 TQ	USBLS	5/07
	Albany-Schenectady-Troy MSA, NY	Y	37080 FQ	48490 MW	75400 TQ	USBLS	5/07
	Buffalo-Niagara Falls MSA, NY	Y	41170 FQ	45720 MW	50340 TQ	USBLS	5/07
	Nassau-Suffolk PMSA, NY	Y	47010 FQ	78650 MW	100770 TQ	USBLS	5/07
	New York-Northern New Jersey-Long Island MSA, NY-NJ-PA	Y	48590 FQ	53100 MW	58010 TQ	USBLS	5/07
	North Carolina	Y	40840 FQ	50420 MW	59650 TQ	USBLS	5/07
	Charlotte-Gastonia-Concord MSA, NC-SC	Y	41090 FQ	44690 MW	65520 TQ	USBLS	5/07
	North Dakota	Y	46800 FQ	58670 MW	72740 TQ	USBLS	5/07
	Ohio	Y	31690 FQ	45850 MW	69380 TQ	USBLS	5/07
	Cincinnati-Middletown MSA, OH-KY-IN	Y	48860 FQ	74480 MW	92490 TQ	USBLS	5/07
	Cleveland-Elyria-Mentor MSA, OH	Y	22050 FQ	39480 MW	57680 TQ	USBLS	5/07
	Columbus MSA, OH	Y	43720 FQ	73020 MW	92120 TQ	USBLS	5/07
	Dayton MSA, OH	Y	43810 FQ	50190 MW	73790 TQ	USBLS	5/07
	Oklahoma	Y	38500 FQ	44580 MW	86940 TQ	USBLS	5/07
	Oklahoma City MSA, OK	Y	83580 FQ	96670 MW	112630 TQ	USBLS	5/07
	Tulsa MSA, OK	Y	35900 FQ	40050 MW	43650 TQ	USBLS	5/07
	Oregon	H	18.67 FQ	22.03 MW	28.14 TQ	ORBLS	5/08
	Portland-Vancouver-Beaverton MSA, OR-WA	Y	38550 FQ	56780 MW	81790 TQ	USBLS	5/07
	Pennsylvania	Y	36060 FQ	54440 MW	85800 TQ	USBLS	5/07
	Philadelphia-Camden-Wilmington MSA, PA-NJ-DE-MD	Y	27650 FQ	41450 MW	79130 TQ	USBLS	5/07
	Pittsburgh MSA, PA	Y	39340 FQ	56900 MW	93320 TQ	USBLS	5/07
	South Carolina	Y	41820 FQ	60540 MW	88340 TQ	USBLS	5/07
	Tennessee	Y	30180 FQ	49190 MW	75720 TQ	USBLS	5/07
	Memphis MSA, TN-MS-AR	Y	41880 FQ	61760 MW	80040 TQ	USBLS	5/07
	Texas	Y	29640 FQ	45560 MW	75280 TQ	USBLS	5/07
	Dallas-Fort Worth-Arlington MSA, TX	Y	22270 FQ	47450 MW	86360 TQ	USBLS	5/07
	El Paso MSA, TX	Y	24110 FQ	40730 MW	47370 TQ	USBLS	5/07
	Houston-Sugar Land-Baytown MSA, TX	Y	35090 FQ	56650 MW	82310 TQ	USBLS	5/07
	Utah	Y	36190 FQ	45600 MW	54950 TQ	USBLS	5/07
	Salt Lake City MSA, UT	Y	37520 FQ	49280 MW	70140 TQ	USBLS	5/07
	Vermont	Y	38580 FQ	44590 MW	50180 TQ	USBLS	5/07
	Virginia	Y	24990 FQ	39850 MW	83180 TQ	USBLS	5/07
	Virginia Beach-Norfolk-Newport News MSA, VA-NC	Y	17730 FQ	24530 MW	34980 TQ	USBLS	5/07
	Washington	H	22.18 FQ	29.63 MW	35.50 TQ	WABLS	3/08
	Seattle-Tacoma-Bellevue MSA, WA	Y	49980 FQ	64150 MW	74510 TQ	USBLS	5/07
	West Virginia	Y	68101 FQ	81849 MW	94142 TQ	WVBLS	7/08-9/08

Occupation/Type/Industry	Location	Per	Low	Mid	High	Source	Date
Transportation Inspector	Wisconsin	Y	41570 FQ	65510 MW	91710 TQ	USBLS	5/07
	Milwaukee-Waukesha-West Allis MSA, WI	Y	71610 FQ	86560 MW	99720 TQ	USBLS	5/07
	Wyoming	Y	35003 FQ	44877 MW	54506 TQ	WYBLS	9/08
	Puerto Rico	Y	21760 FQ	51370 MW	83970 TQ	USBLS	5/07
Transportation Mechanic							
Public Schools	North Carolina	M	2055-2719 LR		3403-4641 HR	NCSS	2008-2009
Transportation Planner							
Department of Transportation	Michigan	H	16.87 LO		31.85 HI	MDOT	10/1/07
Transportation Specialist							
Municipal Government	Walnut Creek, CA	Y	89412 LO		108677 HI	WCSWP	7/11/08
Travel Agent	Alabama	Y	23690 FQ	29810 MW	36860 TQ	USBLS	5/07
	Birmingham-Hoover MSA, AL	Y	25890 FQ	29990 MW	36770 TQ	USBLS	5/07
	Alaska	Y	24700 FQ	30050 MW	36580 TQ	USBLS	5/07
	Anchorage MSA, AK	Y	23530 FQ	29630 MW	36260 TQ	USBLS	5/07
	Arizona	Y	22620 FQ	28730 MW	36810 TQ	USBLS	5/07
	Phoenix-Mesa-Scottsdale MSA, AZ	Y	23410 FQ	30390 MW	38650 TQ	USBLS	5/07
	Prescott MSA, AZ	Y	16160 FQ	17890 MW	20770 TQ	USBLS	5/07
	Tucson MSA, AZ	Y	24520 FQ	27030 MW	29360 TQ	USBLS	5/07
	Arkansas	Y	22440 FQ	26710 MW	32390 TQ	USBLS	5/07
	Little Rock-North Little Rock MSA, AR	Y	23390 FQ	26910 MW	33370 TQ	USBLS	5/07
	California	H	12.08 FQ	15.21 MW	18.38 TQ	CABLS	1/08-3/08
	Los Angeles-Long Beach-Glendale PMSA, CA	H	11.87 FQ	14.51 MW	17.92 TQ	CABLS	1/08-3/08
	Oakland-Fremont-Hayward MSA, CA	H	15.28 FQ	17.24 MW	19.91 TQ	CABLS	1/08-3/08
	Riverside-San Bernardino-Ontario MSA, CA	H	14.35 FQ	16.48 MW	18.20 TQ	CABLS	1/08-3/08
	Sacramento-Arden Arcade-Roseville MSA, CA	H	10.80 FQ	14.30 MW	18.02 TQ	CABLS	1/08-3/08
	San Diego-Carlsbad-San Marcos MSA, CA	H	12.18 FQ	13.57 MW	15.02 TQ	CABLS	1/08-3/08
	San Francisco-San Mateo-Redwood PMSA, CA	H	11.13 FQ	13.73 MW	18.12 TQ	CABLS	1/08-3/08
	San Jose-Sunnyvale-Santa Clara MSA, CA	H	12.25 FQ	18.73 MW	23.13 TQ	CABLS	1/08-3/08
	Santa Ana-Anaheim-Irvine PMSA, CA	Y	30720 FQ	35120 MW	38980 TQ	USBLS	5/07
	Colorado	Y	25590 FQ	30190 MW	36890 TQ	USBLS	5/07
	Boulder MSA, CO	Y	25230 FQ	30370 MW	38330 TQ	USBLS	5/07
	Denver-Aurora MSA, CO	Y	27820 FQ	31420 MW	38580 TQ	USBLS	5/07
	Connecticut	H	9.89 AE	14.08 MW		CTBLS	1/08-3/08
	Bridgeport-Stamford-Norwalk MSA, CT	Y	20840 FQ	23970 MW	34700 TQ	USBLS	5/07
	Hartford-West Hartford-East Hartford MSA, CT	Y	21800 FQ	29630 MW	35450 TQ	USBLS	5/07
	Delaware	Y	25180 FQ	32750 MW	39630 TQ	USBLS	5/07
	Wilmington PMSA, DE-MD-NJ	Y	23120 FQ	32260 MW	40520 TQ	USBLS	5/07
	District of Columbia	Y	28690 FQ	36340 MW	43870 TQ	USBLS	5/07
	Washington-Arlington-Alexandria MSA, DC-VA-MD-WV	Y	23880 FQ'	34010 MW	43500 TQ	USBLS	5/07
	Florida	Y	21480 FQ	27180 MW	32470 TQ	USBLS	5/07
	Fort Lauderdale-Pompano Beach-Deerfield Beach PMSA, FL	Y	24760 FQ	28280 MW	31970 TQ	USBLS	5/07
	Jacksonville MSA, FL	Y	26690 FQ	31280 MW	36420 TQ	USBLS	5/07
	Miami-Fort Lauderdale-Miami Beach MSA, FL	Y	24630 FQ	28520 MW	33420 TQ	USBLS	5/07
	Orlando-Kissimmee MSA, FL	Y	18880 FQ	26550 MW	33430 TQ	USBLS	5/07
	Tampa-St. Petersburg-Clearwater MSA, FL	Y	20630 FQ	23520 MW	28440 TQ	USBLS	5/07
	West Palm Beach-Boca Raton-Boynton Beach PMSA, FL	Y	26410 FQ	29800 MW	34760 TQ	USBLS	5/07

AE	Average entry wage	AW	Average wage paid	FQ	First quartile wage
AER	Average entry range	AWR	Average wage range	H	Hourly
AEX	Average experienced wage	AXR	Average experienced range	HI	Highest wage paid
ATC	Average total compensation	D	Daily	HR	High end range

LO	Lowest wage paid	MTC	Median total compensation	TCC	Total cash compensation
LR	Low end range	MW	Median wage paid	TQ	Third quartile wage
M	Monthly	MWR	Median wage range	W	Weekly
MCC	Median cash compensation	S	See annotated source	Y	Yearly

Travel Agent

Occupation/Type/Industry	Location	Per	Low	Mid	High	Source	Date
Travel Agent	Georgia	Y	28260 FQ	33690 MW	38040 TQ	USBLS	5/07
	Atlanta-Sandy Springs- Marietta MSA, GA	Y	29220 FQ	34220 MW	38440 TQ	USBLS	5/07
	Hawaii	Y	19080 FQ	29230 MW	35190 TQ	USBLS	5/07
	Honolulu MSA, HI	Y	18500 FQ	27640 MW	36630 TQ	USBLS	5/07
	Idaho	Y	23040 FQ	29130 MW	35610 TQ	USBLS	5/07
	Boise City-Nampa MSA, ID	Y	25460 FQ	31730 MW	36790 TQ	USBLS	5/07
	Illinois	Y	23330 FQ	30690 MW	38600 TQ	USBLS	5/07
	Chicago-Naperville-Joliet MSA, IL-IN-WI	Y	24060 FQ	31140 MW	38960 TQ	USBLS	5/07
	Indiana	Y	20620 FQ	27030 MW	36900 TQ	USBLS	5/07
	Gary PMSA, IN	Y	14140 FQ	18630 MW	22480 TQ	USBLS	5/07
	Indianapolis-Carmel MSA, IN	Y	26290 FQ	32410 MW	38810 TQ	USBLS	5/07
	Iowa	Y	20750 FQ	28120 MW	37380 TQ	USBLS	5/07
	Des Moines-West Des Moines MSA, IA	Y	26320 FQ	32710 MW	41080 TQ	USBLS	5/07
	Kansas	Y	26070 FQ	30840 MW	36520 TQ	USBLS	5/07
	Wichita MSA, KS	Y	27720 FQ	31060 MW	36220 TQ	USBLS	5/07
	Kentucky	Y	28256 FQ	34491 MW	41655 TQ	KYBLS	2008
	Louisville-Jefferson County MSA, KY-IN	Y	28590 FQ	36580 MW	44920 TQ	USBLS	5/07
	Louisiana	H	8.62 FQ	11.68 MW	14.20 TQ	LABLS	1/08-3/08
	Baton Rouge MSA, LA	Y	17060 FQ	23070 MW	28010 TQ	USBLS	5/07
	New Orleans-Metairie-Kenner MSA, LA	Y	16320 FQ	26000 MW	30350 TQ	USBLS	5/07
	Maine	Y	17230 FQ	26680 MW	35570 TQ	USBLS	5/07
	Portland-South Portland- Biddeford MSA, ME	Y	14940 FQ	24840 MW	37510 TQ	USBLS	5/07
	Maryland	Y		32450 MW		MDBLS	3/08
	Baltimore-Towson MSA, MD	Y	26890 FQ	35910 MW	43810 TQ	USBLS	5/07
	Bethesda-Gaithersburg- Frederick PMSA, MD	Y	27330 FQ	34210 MW	43870 TQ	USBLS	5/07
	Massachusetts	Y	24730 FQ	31430 MW	39200 TQ	USBLS	5/07
	Boston-Cambridge-Quincy NECTA, MA	Y	24510 FQ	31110 MW	40450 TQ	USBLS	5/07
	Springfield MSA, MA-CT	Y	26060 FQ	30300 MW	35070 TQ	USBLS	5/07
	Worcester MSA, MA-CT	Y	26130 FQ	32610 MW	37790 TQ	USBLS	5/07
	Michigan	Y	22580 FQ	30370 MW	38580 TQ	USBLS	5/07
	Detroit-Warren-Livonia MSA, MI	Y	27770 FQ	35440 MW	44650 TQ	USBLS	5/07
	Grand Rapids-Wyoming MSA, MI	Y	25960 FQ	28900 MW	31910 TQ	USBLS	5/07
	Warren-Troy-Farmington Hills PMSA, MI	Y	29100 FQ	36310 MW	44700 TQ	USBLS	5/07
	Minnesota	Y	26902 FQ	31679 MW	39525 TQ	MNBLS	10/08-12/08
	Duluth-Superior MSA, MN-WI	Y	28650 FQ	31770 MW	34769 TQ	MNBLS	10/08-12/08
	Minneapolis-Saint Paul MSA, MN-WI	Y	27929 FQ	33143 MW	40348 TQ	MNBLS	10/08-12/08
	Rochester MSA, MN	Y	20822 FQ	27968 MW	32022 TQ	MNBLS	10/08-12/08
	Mississippi	Y	21660 FQ	25560 MW	31200 TQ	USBLS	5/07
	Jackson MSA, MS	Y	22200 FQ	26680 MW	30690 TQ	USBLS	5/07
	Missouri	Y	24920 FQ	31550 MW	38970 TQ	USBLS	5/07
	Kansas City MSA, MO-KS	Y	25860 FQ	32570 MW	38720 TQ	USBLS	5/07
	St. Louis MSA, MO-IL	Y	26150 FQ	32180 MW	38180 TQ	USBLS	5/07
	Montana	Y	21120 FQ	24840 MW	32780 TQ	USBLS	5/07
	Billings MSA, MT	Y	15370 FQ	21380 MW	27670 TQ	USBLS	5/07
	Nebraska	Y	22280 FQ	29750 MW	39720 TQ	USBLS	5/07
	Omaha-Council Bluffs MSA, NE-IA	Y	22320 FQ	30430 MW	40710 TQ	USBLS	5/07
	Nevada	H	11.19 FQ	13.54 MW	15.83 TQ	NVBLS	5/08
	Las Vegas-Paradise MSA, NV	H	11.28 FQ	13.64 MW	15.84 TQ	NVBLS	5/08
	New Hampshire	H	11.40 AE	17.96 MW	21.25 AEX	NHBLS	6/08
	Manchester MSA, NH	Y	34940 FQ	37960 MW	40410 TQ	USBLS	5/07
	Nashua NECTA, NH-MA	Y	22390 FQ	39280 MW	46370 TQ	USBLS	5/07
	New Jersey	Y	23150 FQ	29910 MW	38380 TQ	USBLS	5/07
	Camden PMSA, NJ	Y	17100 FQ	26010 MW	34990 TQ	USBLS	5/07
	Edison PMSA, NJ	Y	25740 FQ	32400 MW	42870 TQ	USBLS	5/07
	Newark-Union PMSA, NJ-PA	Y	18960 FQ	26260 MW	31400 TQ	USBLS	5/07
	New Mexico	Y	22680 FQ	25990 MW	29680 TQ	USBLS	5/07
	Albuquerque MSA, NM	Y	22490 FQ	25400 MW	29560 TQ	USBLS	5/07
	New York	Y	26980 FQ	34870 MW	45090 TQ	USBLS	5/07

AE	Average entry wage	AW	Average wage paid	FQ	First quartile wage
AER	Average entry range	AWR	Average wage range	H	Hourly
AEX	Average experienced wage	AXR	Average experienced range	HI	Highest wage paid
ATC	Average total compensation	D	Daily	HR	High end range

LO	Lowest wage paid	MTC	Median total compensation	TCC	Total cash compensation
LR	Low end range	MW	Median wage paid	TQ	Third quartile wage
M	Monthly	MWR	Median wage range	W	Weekly
MCC	Median cash compensation	S	See annotated source	Y	Yearly

Occupation/Type/Industry	Location	Per	Low	Mid	High	Source	Date
Travel Agent	Albany-Schenectady-Troy MSA, NY	Y	23390 FQ	27320 MW	31670 TQ	USBLS	5/07
	Buffalo-Niagara Falls MSA, NY	Y	25600 FQ	30590 MW	38550 TQ	USBLS	5/07
	Nassau-Suffolk PMSA, NY	Y	30240 FQ	36470 MW	46980 TQ	USBLS	5/07
	New York-Northern New Jersey-Long Island MSA, NY-NJ-PA	Y	26260 FQ	34340 MW	44500 TQ	USBLS	5/07
	North Carolina	Y	26550 FQ	32690 MW	39140 TQ	USBLS	5/07
	Charlotte-Gastonia-Concord MSA, NC-SC	Y	27090 FQ	37280 MW	45020 TQ	USBLS	5/07
	Raleigh-Cary MSA, NC	Y	28260 FQ	32840 MW	36160 TQ	USBLS	5/07
	Winston-Salem MSA, NC	Y	33200 FQ	35860 MW	38550 TQ	USBLS	5/07
	North Dakota	Y	18720 FQ	22490 MW	27140 TQ	USBLS	5/07
	Ohio	Y	21190 FQ	26060 MW	33450 TQ	USBLS	5/07
	Cincinnati-Middletown MSA, OH-KY-IN	Y	19500 FQ	29190 MW	37630 TQ	USBLS	5/07
	Cleveland-Elyria-Mentor MSA, OH	Y	22910 FQ	27620 MW	34860 TQ	USBLS	5/07
	Columbus MSA, OH	Y	21720 FQ	30750 MW	38410 TQ	USBLS	5/07
	Dayton MSA, OH	Y	20450 FQ	22700 MW	25150 TQ	USBLS	5/07
	Oklahoma	Y	24400 FQ	30470 MW	36840 TQ	USBLS	5/07
	Oklahoma City MSA, OK	Y	25550 FQ	30110 MW	36790 TQ	USBLS	5/07
	Tulsa MSA, OK	Y	29790 FQ	35070 MW	38290 TQ	USBLS	5/07
	Oregon	H	10.51 FQ	12.45 MW	15.28 TQ	ORBLS	5/08
	Eugene-Springfield MSA, OR	Y	21080 FQ	23470 MW	30090 TQ	USBLS	5/07
	Portland-Vancouver-Beaverton MSA, OR-WA	Y	22020 FQ	26130 MW	31860 TQ	USBLS	5/07
	Pennsylvania	Y	22530 FQ	30150 MW	38060 TQ	USBLS	5/07
	Allentown-Bethlehem-Easton MSA, PA-NJ	Y	22780 FQ	28130 MW	31920 TQ	USBLS	5/07
	Philadelphia-Camden-Wilmington MSA, PA-NJ-DE-MD	Y	22600 FQ	31080 MW	39090 TQ	USBLS	5/07
	Pittsburgh MSA, PA	Y	18990 FQ	27070 MW	33120 TQ	USBLS	5/07
	Rhode Island	Y	27610 FQ	31390 MW	36120 TQ	USBLS	5/07
	Providence-Fall River-Warwick MSA, RI-MA	Y	27010 FQ	30960 MW	35910 TQ	USBLS	5/07
	South Carolina	Y	19360 FQ	25820 MW	34110 TQ	USBLS	5/07
	Charleston-North Charleston MSA, SC	Y	18610 FQ	22920 MW	27810 TQ	USBLS	5/07
	Columbia MSA, SC	Y	23490 FQ	33430 MW	40440 TQ	USBLS	5/07
	South Dakota	Y	22195 FQ	25709 MW	30451 TQ	SDBLS	7/08-9/08
	Rapid City MSA, SD	Y	23915 FQ	28146 MW	31975 TQ	SDBLS	7/08-9/08
	Sioux Falls MSA, SD	Y	24818 FQ	28578 MW	31949 TQ	SDBLS	7/08-9/08
	Tennessee	Y	26230 FQ	32660 MW	39020 TQ	USBLS	5/07
	Memphis MSA, TN-MS-AR	Y	27830 FQ	34630 MW	39690 TQ	USBLS	5/07
	Nashville-Davidson-Murfreesboro MSA, TN	Y	28840 FQ	34920 MW	41620 TQ	USBLS	5/07
	Texas	Y	22810 FQ	30000 MW	37340 TQ	USBLS	5/07
	Austin-Round Rock MSA, TX	Y	27360 FQ	34520 MW	38450 TQ	USBLS	5/07
	Dallas-Fort Worth-Arlington MSA, TX	Y	21910 FQ	29390 MW	35310 TQ	USBLS	5/07
	El Paso MSA, TX	Y	21430 FQ	24070 MW	28570 TQ	USBLS	5/07
	Houston-Sugar Land-Baytown MSA, TX	Y	25750 FQ	34960 MW	45670 TQ	USBLS	5/07
	San Antonio MSA, TX	Y	22640 FQ	27630 MW	32020 TQ	USBLS	5/07
	Utah	Y	21890 FQ	25930 MW	32360 TQ	USBLS	5/07
	Salt Lake City MSA, UT	Y	21790 FQ	24320 MW	29860 TQ	USBLS	5/07
	Vermont	Y	25880 FQ	29770 MW	33990 TQ	USBLS	5/07
	Burlington-South Burlington MSA, VT	Y	29270 FQ	32960 MW	37090 TQ	USBLS	5/07
	Virginia	Y	20150 FQ	32680 MW	44010 TQ	USBLS	5/07
	Richmond MSA, VA	Y	19870 FQ	31820 MW	54310 TQ	USBLS	5/07
	Virginia Beach-Norfolk-Newport News MSA, VA-NC	Y	25580 FQ	33540 MW	42830 TQ	USBLS	5/07
	Washington	H	13.11 FQ	16.69 MW	22.50 TQ	WABLS	3/08
	Seattle-Tacoma-Bellevue MSA, WA	Y	29250 FQ	37290 MW	49010 TQ	USBLS	5/07
	Spokane MSA, WA	Y	20050 FQ	22980 MW	27980 TQ	USBLS	5/07
	West Virginia	Y	21672 FQ	27409 MW	33395 TQ	WVBLS	7/08-9/08
	Wisconsin	Y	22840 FQ	27910 MW	34100 TQ	USBLS	5/07

AE	Average entry wage	AW	Average wage paid	FQ	First quartile wage	LO	Lowest wage paid	MTC Median total compensation　TCC Total cash compensation
AER	Average entry range	AWR	Average wage range	H	Hourly	LR	Low end range	MW Median wage paid　TQ Third quartile wage
AEX	Average experienced wage	AXR	Average experienced range	HI	Highest wage paid	M	Monthly	MWR Median wage range　W Weekly
ATC	Average total compensation	D	Daily	HR	High end range	MCC	Median cash compensation	S See annotated source　Y Yearly

Occupation/Type/Industry	Location	Per	Low	Mid	High	Source	Date
Travel Agent	Appleton MSA, WI	Y	23260 FQ	27320 MW	34730 TQ	USBLS	5/07
	Milwaukee-Waukesha-West Allis MSA, WI	Y	21010 FQ	26180 MW	34370 TQ	USBLS	5/07
	Wyoming	Y	21543 FQ	26219 MW	32009 TQ	WYBLS	9/08
	Cheyenne MSA, WY	Y	17580 FQ	24944 MW	36215 TQ	WYBLS	9/08
	Puerto Rico	Y	14790 FQ	18000 MW	22820 TQ	USBLS	5/07
	San Juan-Caguas-Guaynabo MSA, PR	Y	15050 FQ	18350 MW	23150 TQ	USBLS	5/07
	Guam	Y	18400 FQ	22730 MW	28610 TQ	USBLS	5/07
Travel Guide	Alaska	Y	24700 FQ	29460 MW	43900 TQ	USBLS	5/07
	Arizona	Y	21580 FQ	35550 MW	39990 TQ	USBLS	5/07
	Phoenix-Mesa-Scottsdale MSA, AZ	Y	34190 FQ	38170 MW	42450 TQ	USBLS	5/07
	California	H	12.97 FQ	14.69 MW	17.28 TQ	CABLS	1/08-3/08
	Los Angeles-Long Beach-Glendale PMSA, CA	H	14.04 FQ	16.06 MW	21.63 TQ	CABLS	1/08-3/08
	San Francisco-San Mateo-Redwood PMSA, CA	H	11.87 FQ	13.26 MW	14.74 TQ	CABLS	1/08-3/08
	Colorado	Y	20880 FQ	22870 MW	24910 TQ	USBLS	5/07
	Florida	Y	36610 FQ	44570 MW	50390 TQ	USBLS	5/07
	Georgia	Y	14500 FQ	28020 MW	33140 TQ	USBLS	5/07
	Hawaii	Y	26660 FQ	29270 MW	33540 TQ	USBLS	5/07
	Illinois	Y	27110 FQ	30280 MW	37130 TQ	USBLS	5/07
	Chicago-Naperville-Joliet MSA, IL-IN-WI	Y	27730 FQ	30730 MW	38060 TQ	USBLS	5/07
	Kentucky	Y	16906 FQ	19220 MW	22600 TQ	KYBLS	2008
	Louisiana	H	27.65 FQ	31.83 MW	34.47 TQ	LABLS	1/08-3/08
	Maryland	Y		44875 MW		MDBLS	3/08
	Baltimore-Towson MSA, MD	Y	31070 FQ	43790 MW	47970 TQ	USBLS	5/07
	Massachusetts	Y	23330 FQ	28350 MW	33760 TQ	USBLS	5/07
	Michigan	Y	24050 FQ	27700 MW	31820 TQ	USBLS	5/07
	Minnesota	Y	19395 FQ	21999 MW	25721 TQ	MNBLS	10/08-12/08
	Mississippi	Y	17340 FQ	18720 MW	20100 TQ	USBLS	5/07
	New York	Y	30920 FQ	34550 MW	38270 TQ	USBLS	5/07
	New York-Northern New Jersey-Long Island MSA, NY-NJ-PA	Y	30920 FQ	34550 MW	38270 TQ	USBLS	5/07
	North Carolina	Y	27510 FQ	36250 MW	71820 TQ	USBLS	5/07
	Ohio	Y	20490 FQ	23580 MW	28540 TQ	USBLS	5/07
	Pennsylvania	Y	18180 FQ	28200 MW	37060 TQ	USBLS	5/07
	Allentown-Bethlehem-Easton MSA, PA-NJ	Y	16410 FQ	17880 MW	23930 TQ	USBLS	5/07
	Tennessee	Y	33590 FQ	36420 MW	39360 TQ	USBLS	5/07
	Nashville-Davidson-Murfreesboro MSA, TN	Y	33870 FQ	36680 MW	39630 TQ	USBLS	5/07
	Texas	Y	27470 FQ	38430 MW	56240 TQ	USBLS	5/07
	Dallas-Fort Worth-Arlington MSA, TX	Y	32910 FQ	49180 MW	56420 TQ	USBLS	5/07
	Utah	Y	21150 FQ	24850 MW	33390 TQ	USBLS	5/07
	Virginia	Y	20210 FQ	23910 MW	31300 TQ	USBLS	5/07
	Virginia Beach-Norfolk-Newport News MSA, VA-NC	Y	20120 FQ	22330 MW	24560 TQ	USBLS	5/07
	Washington	H	15.57 FQ	17.45 MW	20.17 TQ	WABLS	3/08
	Seattle-Tacoma-Bellevue MSA, WA	Y	32250 FQ	35690 MW	40260 TQ	USBLS	5/07
	Wisconsin	Y	25860 FQ	30350 MW	36940 TQ	USBLS	5/07
Travel Manager	United States	Y		100402 AW		BTN01	2008
Traveling Nurse	United States	Y		53735 AW		NDAY01	2009
Treasurer	United States	Y		98000 AW		BUSFIN	2008
Fire Department	Montague, MA	Y			1400 HI	FRCOG	2009
Municipal Government	Charlemont, MA	Y			14765 HI	FRCOG	2009
Municipal Government	Shutesbury, MA	Y			20495 HI	FRCOG	2009
Municipal Government	Taylor, MI	Y			68003 HI	NHERLD4	2009
Treasury Analyst	United States	Y		58000 AW		BUSFIN	2008
Treatment Plant Aide							
State Government	Ohio	H	15.41 LO		17.03 HI	ODAS	2008

AE Average entry wage	**AW** Average wage paid	**FQ** First quartile wage	**LO** Lowest wage paid	**MTC** Median total compensation	**TCC** Total cash compensation
AER Average entry range	**AWR** Average wage range	**H** Hourly	**LR** Low end range	**MW** Median wage paid	**TQ** Third quartile wage
AEX Average experienced wage	**AXR** Average experienced range	**HI** Highest wage paid	**M** Monthly	**MWR** Median wage range	**W** Weekly
ATC Average total compensation	**D** Daily	**HR** High end range	**MCC** Median cash compensation	**S** See annotated source	**Y** Yearly

Occupation/Type/Industry	Location	Per	Low	Mid	High	Source	Date
Treatment Plant Operator	Bismarck, ND	M	1082-1316 LO			NDLC01	2008
	Carrington, ND	M			3087 HI	NDLC01	2008
	Christine, ND	M			700 HI	NDLC02	2008
	Mayville, ND	M			3312 HI	NDLC01	2008
Treatment Superintendent							
Municipal Government	Cincinnati, OH	Y	75782 LO		102305 HI	COHSS	10/08
Tree Maintenance Worker							
Municipal Government	Cincinnati, OH	Y	37025 LO		39113 HI	COHSS	10/08
Tree Trimmer and Pruner	Alabama	Y	19990 FQ	25600 MW	30750 TQ	USBLS	5/07
	Arizona	Y	21200 FQ	26100 MW	31460 TQ	USBLS	5/07
	Phoenix-Mesa-Scottsdale MSA, AZ	Y	18840 FQ	23860 MW	31920 TQ	USBLS	5/07
	Arkansas	Y	22760 FQ	27020 MW	30280 TQ	USBLS	5/07
	Little Rock-North Little Rock MSA, AR	Y	23790 FQ	26880 MW	29580 TQ	USBLS	5/07
	California	H	12.91 FQ	17.40 MW	20.91 TQ	CABLS	1/08-3/08
	Los Angeles-Long Beach-Glendale PMSA, CA	H	13.78 FQ	15.73 MW	21.29 TQ	CABLS	1/08-3/08
	Oakland-Fremont-Hayward MSA, CA	H	11.53 FQ	13.77 MW	18.73 TQ	CABLS	1/08-3/08
	Riverside-San Bernardino-Ontario MSA, CA	H	18.04 FQ	22.07 MW	29.15 TQ	CABLS	1/08-3/08
	Sacramento-Arden Arcade-Roseville MSA, CA	H	17.79 FQ	20.01 MW	23.50 TQ	CABLS	1/08-3/08
	San Diego-Carlsbad-San Marcos MSA, CA	H	8.00 FQ	17.17 MW	20.80 TQ	CABLS	1/08-3/08
	San Francisco-San Mateo-Redwood PMSA, CA	H	16.95 FQ	18.74 MW	22.16 TQ	CABLS	1/08-3/08
	San Jose-Sunnyvale-Santa Clara MSA, CA	H	8.98 FQ	9.87 MW	11.71 TQ	CABLS	1/08-3/08
	Santa Ana-Anaheim-Irvine PMSA, CA	Y	18280 FQ	20120 MW	31200 TQ	USBLS	5/07
	Colorado	Y	25990 FQ	31810 MW	42770 TQ	USBLS	5/07
	Denver-Aurora MSA, CO	Y	29770 FQ	35640 MW	44870 TQ	USBLS	5/07
	Connecticut	H	16.62 AE	20.91 MW		CTBLS	1/08-3/08
	Bridgeport-Stamford-Norwalk MSA, CT	Y	35660 FQ	43210 MW	48300 TQ	USBLS	5/07
	Hartford-West Hartford-East Hartford MSA, CT	Y	35560 FQ	40060 MW	46240 TQ	USBLS	5/07
	Wilmington PMSA, DE-MD-NJ	Y	32960 FQ	37730 MW	41710 TQ	USBLS	5/07
	Washington-Arlington-Alexandria MSA, DC-VA-MD-WV	Y	29850 FQ	37010 MW	44130 TQ	USBLS	5/07
	Florida	Y	23870 FQ	29620 MW	39570 TQ	USBLS	5/07
	Jacksonville MSA, FL	Y	25120 FQ	26770 MW	28440 TQ	USBLS	5/07
	Miami-Fort Lauderdale-Miami Beach MSA, FL	Y	24550 FQ	32290 MW	42840 TQ	USBLS	5/07
	Orlando-Kissimmee MSA, FL	Y	15370 FQ	26960 MW	32840 TQ	USBLS	5/07
	Tampa-St. Petersburg-Clearwater MSA, FL	Y	27080 FQ	32720 MW	39910 TQ	USBLS	5/07
	West Palm Beach-Boca Raton-Boynton Beach PMSA, FL	Y	34260 FQ	41230 MW	46060 TQ	USBLS	5/07
	Georgia	Y	23960 FQ	28530 MW	35160 TQ	USBLS	5/07
	Atlanta-Sandy Springs-Marietta MSA, GA	Y	33450 FQ	37000 MW	40580 TQ	USBLS	5/07
	Hawaii	Y	29820 FQ	34820 MW	48940 TQ	USBLS	5/07
	Honolulu MSA, HI	Y	27560 FQ	30680 MW	34780 TQ	USBLS	5/07
	Idaho	Y	28880 FQ	34930 MW	38070 TQ	USBLS	5/07
	Illinois	Y	22120 FQ	28580 MW	36930 TQ	USBLS	5/07
	Chicago-Naperville-Joliet MSA, IL-IN-WI	Y	18270 FQ	23750 MW	35080 TQ	USBLS	5/07
	Indiana	Y	24830 FQ	29640 MW	35380 TQ	USBLS	5/07
	Gary PMSA, IN	Y	25390 FQ	29520 MW	33380 TQ	USBLS	5/07
	Indianapolis-Carmel MSA, IN	Y	35410 FQ	38220 MW	40490 TQ	USBLS	5/07
	Iowa	Y	22750 FQ	26710 MW	31910 TQ	USBLS	5/07
	Kansas	Y	24310 FQ	28660 MW	39130 TQ	USBLS	5/07
	Wichita MSA, KS	Y	25540 FQ	28960 MW	41840 TQ	USBLS	5/07

AE Average entry wage	**AW** Average wage paid	**FQ** First quartile wage	**LO** Lowest wage paid	**MTC** Median total compensation	**TCC** Total cash compensation
AER Average entry range	**AWR** Average wage range	**H** Hourly	**LR** Low end range	**MW** Median wage paid	**TQ** Third quartile wage
AEX Average experienced wage	**AXR** Average experienced range	**HI** Highest wage paid	**M** Monthly	**MWR** Median wage range	**W** Weekly
ATC Average total compensation	**D** Daily	**HR** High end range	**MCC** Median cash compensation	**S** See annotated source	**Y** Yearly

Occupation/Type/Industry	Location	Per	Low	Mid	High	Source	Date
Tree Trimmer and Pruner	Kentucky	Y	21825 FQ	25807 MW	29527 TQ	KYBLS	2008
	Louisiana	H	11.55 FQ	13.44 MW	14.83 TQ	LABLS	1/08-3/08
	Maine	Y	24720 FQ	38080 MW	42200 TQ	USBLS	5/07
	Maryland	Y		35275 MW		MDBLS	3/08
	Baltimore-Towson MSA, MD	Y	30100 FQ	34390 MW	39380 TQ	USBLS	5/07
	Bethesda-Gaithersburg-Frederick PMSA, MD	Y	30320 FQ	40240 MW	46140 TQ	USBLS	5/07
	Massachusetts	Y	28250 FQ	33040 MW	47940 TQ	USBLS	5/07
	Barnstable Town MSA, MA	Y	29240 FQ	32040 MW	36900 TQ	USBLS	5/07
	Boston-Cambridge-Quincy NECTA, MA	Y	22130 FQ	29730 MW	45320 TQ	USBLS	5/07
	Worcester MSA, MA-CT	Y	48320 FQ	52310 MW	56300 TQ	USBLS	5/07
	Michigan	Y	26820 FQ	32060 MW	41830 TQ	USBLS	5/07
	Detroit-Warren-Livonia MSA, MI	Y	32750 FQ	41360 MW	46250 TQ	USBLS	5/07
	Minnesota	Y	31388 FQ	37170 MW	42607 TQ	MNBLS	10/08-12/08
	Minneapolis-Saint Paul MSA, MN-WI	Y	31994 FQ	37379 MW	43527 TQ	MNBLS	10/08-12/08
	Rochester MSA, MN	Y	19137 FQ	21318 MW	38722 TQ	MNBLS	10/08-12/08
	Mississippi	Y	17550 FQ	19340 MW	23190 TQ	USBLS	5/07
	Missouri	Y	24450 FQ	31610 MW	35810 TQ	USBLS	5/07
	Kansas City MSA, MO-KS	Y	26410 FQ	31590 MW	40200 TQ	USBLS	5/07
	St. Louis MSA, MO-IL	Y	29130 FQ	32520 MW	36040 TQ	USBLS	5/07
	Montana	Y	32490 FQ	36150 MW	46210 TQ	USBLS	5/07
	Nevada	H	14.21 FQ	16.53 MW	19.09 TQ	NVBLS	5/08
	Las Vegas-Paradise MSA, NV	H	14.01 FQ	15.86 MW	18.82 TQ	NVBLS	5/08
	New Hampshire	H	15.86 AE	18.63 MW	20.19 AEX	NHBLS	6/08
	New Jersey	Y	15240 FQ	15600 MW	41050 TQ	USBLS	5/07
	Edison PMSA, NJ	Y	28820 FQ	33850 MW	40040 TQ	USBLS	5/07
	Newark-Union PMSA, NJ-PA	Y	15100 FQ	15330 MW	15560 TQ	USBLS	5/07
	New Mexico	Y	23800 FQ	27640 MW	32090 TQ	USBLS	5/07
	New York	Y	32310 FQ	38500 MW	46340 TQ	USBLS	5/07
	Buffalo-Niagara Falls MSA, NY	Y	39490 FQ	43920 MW	48210 TQ	USBLS	5/07
	Nassau-Suffolk PMSA, NY	Y	33710 FQ	38380 MW	44720 TQ	USBLS	5/07
	New York-Northern New Jersey-Long Island MSA, NY-NJ-PA	Y	24110 FQ	36880 MW	45490 TQ	USBLS	5/07
	North Carolina	Y	23890 FQ	27840 MW	31600 TQ	USBLS	5/07
	Raleigh-Cary MSA, NC	Y	24040 FQ	27370 MW	30680 TQ	USBLS	5/07
	North Dakota	Y	16230 FQ	23810 MW	31070 TQ	USBLS	5/07
	Ohio	Y	23990 FQ	29190 MW	35400 TQ	USBLS	5/07
	Cincinnati-Middletown MSA, OH-KY-IN	Y	27760 FQ	34590 MW	41800 TQ	USBLS	5/07
	Cleveland-Elyria-Mentor MSA, OH	Y	20210 FQ	23770 MW	34990 TQ	USBLS	5/07
	Columbus MSA, OH	Y	24740 FQ	28220 MW	31650 TQ	USBLS	5/07
	Oklahoma	Y	17350 FQ	23200 MW	31690 TQ	USBLS	5/07
	Oklahoma City MSA, OK	Y	16070 FQ	20210 MW	28840 TQ	USBLS	5/07
	Tulsa MSA, OK	Y	23050 FQ	29140 MW	35220 TQ	USBLS	5/07
	Oregon	H	12.04 FQ	14.91 MW	18.24 TQ	ORBLS	5/08
	Portland-Vancouver-Beaverton MSA, OR-WA	Y	29490 FQ	32560 MW	41680 TQ	USBLS	5/07
	Pennsylvania	Y	25280 FQ	31280 MW	38950 TQ	USBLS	5/07
	Philadelphia-Camden-Wilmington MSA, PA-NJ-DE-MD	Y	27900 FQ	36040 MW	43400 TQ	USBLS	5/07
	Pittsburgh MSA, PA	Y	28520 FQ	31260 MW	34360 TQ	USBLS	5/07
	Rhode Island	Y	28640 FQ	35520 MW	41020 TQ	USBLS	5/07
	Providence-Fall River-Warwick MSA, RI-MA	Y	28640 FQ	35520 MW	41020 TQ	USBLS	5/07
	South Carolina	Y	22440 FQ	26190 MW	30160 TQ	USBLS	5/07
	South Dakota	Y	23372 FQ	25926 MW	31876 TQ	SDBLS	7/08-9/08
	Sioux Falls MSA, SD	Y	24086 FQ	26617 MW	35044 TQ	SDBLS	7/08-9/08
	Tennessee	Y	23280 FQ	27040 MW	31270 TQ	USBLS	5/07
	Memphis MSA, TN-MS-AR	Y	25570 FQ	28730 MW	32770 TQ	USBLS	5/07
	Texas	Y	20210 FQ	23950 MW	28140 TQ	USBLS	5/07
	Austin-Round Rock MSA, TX	Y	23060 FQ	26470 MW	30390 TQ	USBLS	5/07
	Dallas-Fort Worth-Arlington MSA, TX	Y	19970 FQ	23810 MW	28170 TQ	USBLS	5/07
	Houston-Sugar Land-Baytown MSA, TX	Y	19990 FQ	22710 MW	25390 TQ	USBLS	5/07

AE Average entry wage	**AW** Average wage paid	**FQ** First quartile wage	**LO** Lowest wage paid	**MTC** Median total compensation	**TCC** Total cash compensation
AER Average entry range	**AWR** Average wage range	**H** Hourly	**LR** Low end range	**MW** Median wage paid	**TQ** Third quartile wage
AEX Average experienced wage	**AXR** Average experienced range	**HI** Highest wage paid	**M** Monthly	**MWR** Median wage range	**W** Weekly
ATC Average total compensation	**D** Daily	**HR** High end range	**MCC** Median cash compensation	**S** See annotated source	**Y** Yearly

Occupation/Type/Industry	Location	Per	Low	Mid	High	Source	Date
Tree Trimmer and Pruner	San Antonio MSA, TX	Y	23140 FQ	26540 MW	30440 TQ	USBLS	5/07
	Utah	Y	25430 FQ	27940 MW	33100 TQ	USBLS	5/07
	Ogden-Clearfield MSA, UT	Y	26630 FQ	31640 MW	37800 TQ	USBLS	5/07
	Salt Lake City MSA, UT	Y	25080 FQ	26820 MW	28540 TQ	USBLS	5/07
	Virginia	Y	29950 FQ	35350 MW	40340 TQ	USBLS	5/07
	Charlottesville MSA, VA	Y	34110 FQ	36650 MW	39180 TQ	USBLS	5/07
	Virginia Beach-Norfolk-Newport News MSA, VA-NC	Y	31250 FQ	37270 MW	44780 TQ	USBLS	5/07
	Washington	H	13.47 FQ	16.21 MW	19.36 TQ	WABLS	3/08
	Seattle-Tacoma-Bellevue MSA, WA	Y	36080 FQ	39660 MW	50120 TQ	USBLS	5/07
	Wisconsin	Y	28420 FQ	36340 MW	44730 TQ	USBLS	5/07
	Milwaukee-Waukesha-West Allis MSA, WI	Y	38580 FQ	44450 MW	48420 TQ	USBLS	5/07
	Wyoming	Y	26492 FQ	38372 MW	45301 TQ	WYBLS	9/08
	Puerto Rico	Y	26380 FQ	28470 MW	30560 TQ	USBLS	5/07
	San Juan-Caguas-Guaynabo MSA, PR	Y	27060 FQ	28920 MW	30780 TQ	USBLS	5/07
Tree Warden							
Highway Department	Bernardston, MA	Y			3000 HI	FRCOG	2009
Trial Court Judge	Massachusetts	Y			129694 HI	MLW	2008
Trial Court Services Director							
State Supreme Court	Michigan	Y			117137 HI	LSJ02	7/11/07
Trombone Player							
Department of Parks and Recreation	Kailua-Kona, HI	H			13.86 HI	CHDHR01	1/09
Trooper							
Highway Patrol	Florida	Y			34000 HI	CATHO	2008
Highway Patrol	Ohio	H	21.52 LO		27.37 HI	ODAS	2008
State Police	Michigan	Y	49318 LO		62535 HI	LCPP	2009
Truck Driver							
Heavy and Tractor-Trailer	Alabama	Y	26380 FQ	33680 MW	44000 TQ	USBLS	5/07
Heavy and Tractor-Trailer	Birmingham-Hoover MSA, AL	Y	29440 FQ	37590 MW	46940 TQ	USBLS	5/07
Heavy and Tractor-Trailer	Alaska	Y	35950 FQ	43110 MW	53440 TQ	USBLS	5/07
Heavy and Tractor-Trailer	Anchorage MSA, AK	Y	35030 FQ	42070 MW	51130 TQ	USBLS	5/07
Heavy and Tractor-Trailer	Arizona	Y	29630 FQ	36180 MW	44160 TQ	USBLS	5/07
Heavy and Tractor-Trailer	Phoenix-Mesa-Scottsdale MSA, AZ	Y	31660 FQ	37370 MW	45020 TQ	USBLS	5/07
Heavy and Tractor-Trailer	Tucson MSA, AZ	Y	28840 FQ	36250 MW	46170 TQ	USBLS	5/07
Heavy and Tractor-Trailer	Arkansas	Y	27430 FQ	36640 MW	46360 TQ	USBLS	5/07
Heavy and Tractor-Trailer	Little Rock-North Little Rock MSA, AR	Y	27170 FQ	33340 MW	41050 TQ	USBLS	5/07
Heavy and Tractor-Trailer	California	H	15.98 FQ	19.33 MW	22.94 TQ	CABLS	1/08-3/08
Heavy and Tractor-Trailer	Los Angeles-Long Beach-Glendale PMSA, CA	H	15.99 FQ	19.01 MW	22.47 TQ	CABLS	1/08-3/08
Heavy and Tractor-Trailer	Oakland-Fremont-Hayward MSA, CA	H	16.76 FQ	20.58 MW	24.20 TQ	CABLS	1/08-3/08
Heavy and Tractor-Trailer	Riverside-San Bernardino-Ontario MSA, CA	H	16.77 FQ	20.24 MW	24.48 TQ	CABLS	1/08-3/08
Heavy and Tractor-Trailer	Sacramento-Arden Arcade-Roseville MSA, CA	H	15.96 FQ	19.39 MW	22.59 TQ	CABLS	1/08-3/08
Heavy and Tractor-Trailer	San Diego-Carlsbad-San Marcos MSA, CA	H	16.88 FQ	20.48 MW	23.57 TQ	CABLS	1/08-3/08
Heavy and Tractor-Trailer	San Francisco-San Mateo-Redwood PMSA, CA	H	17.43 FQ	21.50 MW	25.73 TQ	CABLS	1/08-3/08
Heavy and Tractor-Trailer	San Jose-Sunnyvale-Santa Clara MSA, CA	H	15.50 FQ	19.45 MW	22.99 TQ	CABLS	1/08-3/08
Heavy and Tractor-Trailer	Santa Ana-Anaheim-Irvine PMSA, CA	Y	34040 FQ	40520 MW	46560 TQ	USBLS	5/07
Heavy and Tractor-Trailer	Colorado	Y	31070 FQ	36880 MW	45580 TQ	USBLS	5/07
Heavy and Tractor-Trailer	Boulder MSA, CO	Y	27890 FQ	33980 MW	40710 TQ	USBLS	5/07
Heavy and Tractor-Trailer	Denver-Aurora MSA, CO	Y	33140 FQ	39080 MW	47770 TQ	USBLS	5/07
Heavy and Tractor-Trailer	Fort Collins-Loveland MSA, CO	Y	31530 FQ	36270 MW	46390 TQ	USBLS	5/07
Heavy and Tractor-Trailer	Connecticut	H	15.12 AE	19.70 MW		CTBLS	1/08-3/08
Heavy and Tractor-Trailer	Bridgeport-Stamford-Norwalk MSA, CT	Y	33970 FQ	41380 MW	49510 TQ	USBLS	5/07

AE	Average entry wage	AW	Average wage paid	FQ	First quartile wage	LO	Lowest wage paid	MTC	Median total compensation	TCC	Total cash compensation
AER	Average entry range	AWR	Average wage range	H	Hourly	LR	Low end range	MW	Median wage paid	TQ	Third quartile wage
AEX	Average experienced wage	AXR	Average experienced range	HI	Highest wage paid	M	Monthly	MWR	Median wage range	W	Weekly
ATC	Average total compensation	D	Daily	HR	High end range	MCC	Median cash compensation	S	See annotated source	Y	Yearly

Occupation/Type/Industry	Location	Per	Low	Mid	High	Source	Date
Truck Driver							
Heavy and Tractor-Trailer	Hartford-West Hartford-East Hartford MSA, CT	Y	35850 FQ	42500 MW	50940 TQ	USBLS	5/07
Heavy and Tractor-Trailer	Delaware	Y	28830 FQ	35720 MW	43080 TQ	USBLS	5/07
Heavy and Tractor-Trailer	Wilmington PMSA, DE-MD-NJ	Y	32900 FQ	38830 MW	46980 TQ	USBLS	5/07
Heavy and Tractor-Trailer	District of Columbia	Y	34380 FQ	39700 MW	46120 TQ	USBLS	5/07
Heavy and Tractor-Trailer	Washington-Arlington-Alexandria MSA, DC-VA-MD-WV	Y	31320 FQ	37290 MW	45050 TQ	USBLS	5/07
Heavy and Tractor-Trailer	Florida	Y	26120 FQ	31670 MW	40570 TQ	USBLS	5/07
Heavy and Tractor-Trailer	Fort Lauderdale-Pompano Beach-Deerfield Beach PMSA, FL	Y	26440 FQ	31100 MW	39370 TQ	USBLS	5/07
Heavy and Tractor-Trailer	Jacksonville MSA, FL	Y	25290 FQ	34470 MW	45110 TQ	USBLS	5/07
Heavy and Tractor-Trailer	Miami-Fort Lauderdale-Miami Beach MSA, FL	Y	26630 FQ	32180 MW	40010 TQ	USBLS	5/07
Heavy and Tractor-Trailer	Orlando-Kissimmee MSA, FL	Y	26690 FQ	32330 MW	41270 TQ	USBLS	5/07
Heavy and Tractor-Trailer	Tampa-St. Petersburg-Clearwater MSA, FL	Y	26720 FQ	32940 MW	42430 TQ	USBLS	5/07
Heavy and Tractor-Trailer	West Palm Beach-Boca Raton-Boynton Beach PMSA, FL	Y	26620 FQ	31340 MW	39960 TQ	USBLS	5/07
Heavy and Tractor-Trailer	Georgia	Y	28280 FQ	35990 MW	45320 TQ	USBLS	5/07
Heavy and Tractor-Trailer	Atlanta-Sandy Springs-Marietta MSA, GA	Y	30740 FQ	38540 MW	47420 TQ	USBLS	5/07
Heavy and Tractor-Trailer	Macon MSA, GA	Y	26570 FQ	31910 MW	41440 TQ	USBLS	5/07
Heavy and Tractor-Trailer	Hawaii	Y	32040 FQ	37900 MW	47480 TQ	USBLS	5/07
Heavy and Tractor-Trailer	Honolulu MSA, HI	Y	29610 FQ	36520 MW	46420 TQ	USBLS	5/07
Heavy and Tractor-Trailer	Idaho	Y	26130 FQ	31120 MW	39160 TQ	USBLS	5/07
Heavy and Tractor-Trailer	Boise City-Nampa MSA, ID	Y	26500 FQ	29740 MW	36090 TQ	USBLS	5/07
Heavy and Tractor-Trailer	Lewiston MSA, ID-WA	Y	30320 FQ	36430 MW	44270 TQ	USBLS	5/07
Heavy and Tractor-Trailer	Illinois	Y	32400 FQ	39480 MW	49500 TQ	USBLS	5/07
Heavy and Tractor-Trailer	Chicago-Naperville-Joliet MSA, IL-IN-WI	Y	34910 FQ	42580 MW	52330 TQ	USBLS	5/07
Heavy and Tractor-Trailer	Indiana	Y	28300 FQ	36370 MW	46370 TQ	USBLS	5/07
Heavy and Tractor-Trailer	Gary PMSA, IN	Y	31570 FQ	41210 MW	52340 TQ	USBLS	5/07
Heavy and Tractor-Trailer	Indianapolis-Carmel MSA, IN	Y	27460 FQ	36420 MW	45800 TQ	USBLS	5/07
Heavy and Tractor-Trailer	Terre Haute MSA, IN	Y	29050 FQ	34040 MW	41080 TQ	USBLS	5/07
Heavy and Tractor-Trailer	Iowa	Y	27060 FQ	34440 MW	43390 TQ	USBLS	5/07
Heavy and Tractor-Trailer	Des Moines-West Des Moines MSA, IA	Y	30200 FQ	39290 MW	48010 TQ	USBLS	5/07
Heavy and Tractor-Trailer	Kansas	Y	27880 FQ	34320 MW	43570 TQ	USBLS	5/07
Heavy and Tractor-Trailer	Wichita MSA, KS	Y	26650 FQ	33890 MW	44990 TQ	USBLS	5/07
Heavy and Tractor-Trailer	Kentucky	Y	27569 FQ	33390 MW	42322 TQ	KYBLS	2008
Heavy and Tractor-Trailer	Elizabethtown MSA, KY	Y	28960 FQ	35190 MW	40420 TQ	USBLS	5/07
Heavy and Tractor-Trailer	Louisville-Jefferson County MSA, KY-IN	Y	28670 FQ	35230 MW	44620 TQ	USBLS	5/07
Heavy and Tractor-Trailer	Louisiana	H	11.93 FQ	14.56 MW	18.78 TQ	LABLS	1/08-3/08
Heavy and Tractor-Trailer	Baton Rouge MSA, LA	Y	26560 FQ	31440 MW	39020 TQ	USBLS	5/07
Heavy and Tractor-Trailer	New Orleans-Metairie-Kenner MSA, LA	Y	25590 FQ	31030 MW	42550 TQ	USBLS	5/07
Heavy and Tractor-Trailer	Maine	Y	25990 FQ	31140 MW	39070 TQ	USBLS	5/07
Heavy and Tractor-Trailer	Portland-South Portland-Biddeford MSA, ME	Y	28020 FQ	34400 MW	42090 TQ	USBLS	5/07
Heavy and Tractor-Trailer	Maryland	Y		38650 MW		MDBLS	3/08
Heavy and Tractor-Trailer	Baltimore-Towson MSA, MD	Y	31500 FQ	39050 MW	46660 TQ	USBLS	5/07
Heavy and Tractor-Trailer	Bethesda-Gaithersburg-Frederick PMSA, MD	Y	32030 FQ	36720 MW	43250 TQ	USBLS	5/07
Heavy and Tractor-Trailer	Hagerstown-Martinsburg MSA, MD-WV	Y	31450 FQ	36600 MW	45610 TQ	USBLS	5/07
Heavy and Tractor-Trailer	Massachusetts	Y	34150 FQ	40550 MW	48800 TQ	USBLS	5/07
Heavy and Tractor-Trailer	Boston-Cambridge-Quincy NECTA, MA	Y	35880 FQ	43180 MW	50310 TQ	USBLS	5/07
Heavy and Tractor-Trailer	Worcester MSA, MA-CT	Y	34730 FQ	40990 MW	51710 TQ	USBLS	5/07
Heavy and Tractor-Trailer	Michigan	Y	30410 FQ	37150 MW	45500 TQ	USBLS	5/07
Heavy and Tractor-Trailer	Detroit-Warren-Livonia MSA, MI	Y	33340 FQ	40060 MW	48060 TQ	USBLS	5/07
Heavy and Tractor-Trailer	Grand Rapids-Wyoming MSA, MI	Y	31770 FQ	37390 MW	47000 TQ	USBLS	5/07
Heavy and Tractor-Trailer	Warren-Troy-Farmington Hills PMSA, MI	Y	33330 FQ	39380 MW	48100 TQ	USBLS	5/07
Heavy and Tractor-Trailer	Minnesota	Y	31813 FQ	39397 MW	47491 TQ	MNBLS	10/08-12/08

AE	Average entry wage	AW	Average wage paid	FQ	First quartile wage
AER	Average entry range	AWR	Average wage range	H	Hourly
AEX	Average experienced wage	AXR	Average experienced range	HI	Highest wage paid
ATC	Average total compensation	D	Daily	HR	High end range

LO	Lowest wage paid	MTC	Median total compensation
LR	Low end range	MW	Median wage paid
M	Monthly	MWR	Median wage range
MCC	Median cash compensation	S	See annotated source

TCC	Total cash compensation
TQ	Third quartile wage
W	Weekly
Y	Yearly

Truck Driver

Occupation/Type/Industry	Location	Per	Low	Mid	High	Source	Date
Truck Driver							
Heavy and Tractor-Trailer	Duluth-Superior MSA, MN-WI	Y	33322 FQ	40084 MW	48043 TQ	MNBLS	10/08-12/08
Heavy and Tractor-Trailer	Minneapolis-Saint Paul MSA, MN-WI	Y	35746 FQ	42591 MW	49697 TQ	MNBLS	10/08-12/08
Heavy and Tractor-Trailer	Rochester MSA, MN	Y	33365 FQ	37983 MW	44080 TQ	MNBLS	10/08-12/08
Heavy and Tractor-Trailer	Mississippi	Y	26150 FQ	33380 MW	44650 TQ	USBLS	5/07
Heavy and Tractor-Trailer	Jackson MSA, MS	Y	27870 FQ	35040 MW	46650 TQ	USBLS	5/07
Heavy and Tractor-Trailer	Missouri	Y	27910 FQ	35370 MW	45410 TQ	USBLS	5/07
Heavy and Tractor-Trailer	Kansas City MSA, MO-KS	Y	31230 FQ	37070 MW	47060 TQ	USBLS	5/07
Heavy and Tractor-Trailer	St. Joseph MSA, MO-KS	Y	25160 FQ	31350 MW	41860 TQ	USBLS	5/07
Heavy and Tractor-Trailer	St. Louis MSA, MO-IL	Y	31670 FQ	38420 MW	47260 TQ	USBLS	5/07
Heavy and Tractor-Trailer	Montana	Y	26060 FQ	32780 MW	40150 TQ	USBLS	5/07
Heavy and Tractor-Trailer	Billings MSA, MT	Y	27300 FQ	33960 MW	41840 TQ	USBLS	5/07
Heavy and Tractor-Trailer	Nebraska	Y	29420 FQ	39120 MW	48590 TQ	USBLS	5/07
Heavy and Tractor-Trailer	Omaha-Council Bluffs MSA, NE-IA	Y	30910 FQ	38360 MW	47900 TQ	USBLS	5/07
Heavy and Tractor-Trailer	Nevada	H	16.97 FQ	19.76 MW	23.25 TQ	NVBLS	5/08
Heavy and Tractor-Trailer	Las Vegas-Paradise MSA, NV	H	16.71 FQ	19.49 MW	23.06 TQ	NVBLS	5/08
Heavy and Tractor-Trailer	New Hampshire	H	15.03 AE	18.20 MW	21.52 AEX	NHBLS	6/08
Heavy and Tractor-Trailer	Manchester MSA, NH	Y	32540 FQ	37480 MW	44620 TQ	USBLS	5/07
Heavy and Tractor-Trailer	Nashua NECTA, NH-MA	Y	34140 FQ	39420 MW	48890 TQ	USBLS	5/07
Heavy and Tractor-Trailer	New Jersey	Y	34000 FQ	40470 MW	47710 TQ	USBLS	5/07
Heavy and Tractor-Trailer	Camden PMSA, NJ	Y	35570 FQ	41670 MW	49860 TQ	USBLS	5/07
Heavy and Tractor-Trailer	Edison PMSA, NJ	Y	33500 FQ	39490 MW	46870 TQ	USBLS	5/07
Heavy and Tractor-Trailer	Newark-Union PMSA, NJ-PA	Y	33660 FQ	40100 MW	46850 TQ	USBLS	5/07
Heavy and Tractor-Trailer	New Mexico	Y	26570 FQ	33080 MW	42330 TQ	USBLS	5/07
Heavy and Tractor-Trailer	Albuquerque MSA, NM	Y	29610 FQ	36790 MW	47350 TQ	USBLS	5/07
Heavy and Tractor-Trailer	New York	Y	30620 FQ	38860 MW	49670 TQ	USBLS	5/07
Heavy and Tractor-Trailer	Albany-Schenectady-Troy MSA, NY	Y	34620 FQ	41590 MW	53320 TQ	USBLS	5/07
Heavy and Tractor-Trailer	Buffalo-Niagara Falls MSA, NY	Y	28720 FQ	34710 MW	40240 TQ	USBLS	5/07
Heavy and Tractor-Trailer	Nassau-Suffolk PMSA, NY	Y	35980 FQ	45600 MW	57510 TQ	USBLS	5/07
Heavy and Tractor-Trailer	New York-Northern New Jersey-Long Island MSA, NY-NJ-PA	Y	34160 FQ	41980 MW	50550 TQ	USBLS	5/07
Heavy and Tractor-Trailer	North Carolina	Y	28370 FQ	35810 MW	45640 TQ	USBLS	5/07
Heavy and Tractor-Trailer	Charlotte-Gastonia-Concord MSA, NC-SC	Y	29940 FQ	39100 MW	49810 TQ	USBLS	5/07
Heavy and Tractor-Trailer	Greensboro-High Point MSA, NC	Y	29350 FQ	35870 MW	44520 TQ	USBLS	5/07
Heavy and Tractor-Trailer	Raleigh-Cary MSA, NC	Y	28270 FQ	33780 MW	43220 TQ	USBLS	5/07
Heavy and Tractor-Trailer	North Dakota	Y	27080 FQ	33440 MW	41790 TQ	USBLS	5/07
Heavy and Tractor-Trailer	Fargo MSA, ND-MN	Y	28550 FQ	34280 MW	42940 TQ	USBLS	5/07
Heavy and Tractor-Trailer	Grand Forks MSA, ND-MN	Y	25740 FQ	31710 MW	39510 TQ	USBLS	5/07
Heavy and Tractor-Trailer	Ohio	Y	29550 FQ	36370 MW	45530 TQ	USBLS	5/07
Heavy and Tractor-Trailer	Cincinnati-Middletown MSA, OH-KY-IN	Y	29860 FQ	36140 MW	44400 TQ	USBLS	5/07
Heavy and Tractor-Trailer	Cleveland-Elyria-Mentor MSA, OH	Y	30730 FQ	37800 MW	46690 TQ	USBLS	5/07
Heavy and Tractor-Trailer	Columbus MSA, OH	Y	29680 FQ	36070 MW	45990 TQ	USBLS	5/07
Heavy and Tractor-Trailer	Dayton MSA, OH	Y	30190 FQ	37510 MW	46650 TQ	USBLS	5/07
Heavy and Tractor-Trailer	Oklahoma	Y	25870 FQ	31730 MW	41000 TQ	USBLS	5/07
Heavy and Tractor-Trailer	Oklahoma City MSA, OK	Y	27040 FQ	35830 MW	44370 TQ	USBLS	5/07
Heavy and Tractor-Trailer	Tulsa MSA, OK	Y	27510 FQ	33720 MW	42390 TQ	USBLS	5/07
Heavy and Tractor-Trailer	Oregon	H	14.47 FQ	17.35 MW	21.00 TQ	ORBLS	5/08
Heavy and Tractor-Trailer	Eugene-Springfield MSA, OR	Y	26540 FQ	31270 MW	38260 TQ	USBLS	5/07
Heavy and Tractor-Trailer	Portland-Vancouver-Beaverton MSA, OR-WA	Y	31170 FQ	37620 MW	44660 TQ	USBLS	5/07
Heavy and Tractor-Trailer	Pennsylvania	Y	29530 FQ	37280 MW	46810 TQ	USBLS	5/07
Heavy and Tractor-Trailer	Allentown-Bethlehem-Easton MSA, PA-NJ	Y	32170 FQ	38080 MW	45770 TQ	USBLS	5/07
Heavy and Tractor-Trailer	Philadelphia-Camden-Wilmington MSA, PA-NJ-DE-MD	Y	34030 FQ	40540 MW	48090 TQ	USBLS	5/07
Heavy and Tractor-Trailer	Pittsburgh MSA, PA	Y	28180 FQ	36150 MW	46180 TQ	USBLS	5/07
Heavy and Tractor-Trailer	Rhode Island	Y	33130 FQ	38560 MW	44980 TQ	USBLS	5/07
Heavy and Tractor-Trailer	Providence-Fall River-Warwick MSA, RI-MA	Y	32950 FQ	38440 MW	45140 TQ	USBLS	5/07
Heavy and Tractor-Trailer	South Carolina	Y	27080 FQ	33460 MW	43660 TQ	USBLS	5/07
Heavy and Tractor-Trailer	Charleston-North Charleston MSA, SC	Y	27360 FQ	33420 MW	40250 TQ	USBLS	5/07

AE	Average entry wage	AW	Average wage paid	FQ	First quartile wage	LO	Lowest wage paid	MTC	Median total compensation	TCC	Total cash compensation
AER	Average entry range	AWR	Average wage range	H	Hourly	LR	Low end range	MW	Median wage paid	TQ	Third quartile wage
AEX	Average experienced wage	AXR	Average experienced range	HI	Highest wage paid	M	Monthly	MWR	Median wage range	W	Weekly
ATC	Average total compensation	D	Daily	HR	High end range	MCC	Median cash compensation	S	See annotated source	Y	Yearly

Occupation/Type/Industry	Location	Per	Low	Mid	High	Source	Date
Truck Driver							
Heavy and Tractor-Trailer	Columbia MSA, SC	Y	28050 FQ	34950 MW	44440 TQ	USBLS	5/07
Heavy and Tractor-Trailer	Myrtle Beach-Conway-North Myrtle Beach MSA, SC	Y	23610 FQ	27250 MW	31580 TQ	USBLS	5/07
Heavy and Tractor-Trailer	Spartanburg MSA, SC	Y	25840 FQ	32770 MW	44570 TQ	USBLS	5/07
Heavy and Tractor-Trailer	South Dakota	Y	26757 FQ	31950 MW	39438 TQ	SDBLS	7/08-9/08
Heavy and Tractor-Trailer	Rapid City MSA, SD	Y	27206 FQ	31370 MW	40197 TQ	SDBLS	7/08-9/08
Heavy and Tractor-Trailer	Sioux Falls MSA, SD	Y	26846 FQ	32788 MW	41562 TQ	SDBLS	7/08-9/08
Heavy and Tractor-Trailer	Tennessee	Y	27330 FQ	36800 MW	46440 TQ	USBLS	5/07
Heavy and Tractor-Trailer	Memphis MSA, TN-MS-AR	Y	31540 FQ	41050 MW	50570 TQ	USBLS	5/07
Heavy and Tractor-Trailer	Nashville-Davidson-Murfreesboro MSA, TN	Y	29670 FQ	39000 MW	47990 TQ	USBLS	5/07
Heavy and Tractor-Trailer	Texas	Y	25810 FQ	32650 MW	42920 TQ	USBLS	5/07
Heavy and Tractor-Trailer	Austin-Round Rock MSA, TX	Y	26000 FQ	30100 MW	36830 TQ	USBLS	5/07
Heavy and Tractor-Trailer	Dallas-Fort Worth-Arlington MSA, TX	Y	29090 FQ	37170 MW	47410 TQ	USBLS	5/07
Heavy and Tractor-Trailer	El Paso MSA, TX	Y	29150 FQ	38720 MW	46160 TQ	USBLS	5/07
Heavy and Tractor-Trailer	Houston-Sugar Land-Baytown MSA, TX	Y	26130 FQ	32620 MW	41890 TQ	USBLS	5/07
Heavy and Tractor-Trailer	San Antonio MSA, TX	Y	23850 FQ	29780 MW	37300 TQ	USBLS	5/07
Heavy and Tractor-Trailer	Utah	Y	30710 FQ	36060 MW	43200 TQ	USBLS	5/07
Heavy and Tractor-Trailer	Salt Lake City MSA, UT	Y	31100 FQ	36360 MW	43360 TQ	USBLS	5/07
Heavy and Tractor-Trailer	Vermont	Y	28280 FQ	33590 MW	40790 TQ	USBLS	5/07
Heavy and Tractor-Trailer	Burlington-South Burlington MSA, VT	Y	28950 FQ	35430 MW	42910 TQ	USBLS	5/07
Heavy and Tractor-Trailer	Virginia	Y	27070 FQ	33940 MW	42710 TQ	USBLS	5/07
Heavy and Tractor-Trailer	Lynchburg MSA, VA	Y	22730 FQ	29860 MW	37470 TQ	USBLS	5/07
Heavy and Tractor-Trailer	Richmond MSA, VA	Y	28830 FQ	36950 MW	45910 TQ	USBLS	5/07
Heavy and Tractor-Trailer	Virginia Beach-Norfolk-Newport News MSA, VA-NC	Y	26710 FQ	31790 MW	40140 TQ	USBLS	5/07
Heavy and Tractor-Trailer	Washington	H	15.68 FQ	18.76 MW	22.41 TQ	WABLS	3/08
Heavy and Tractor-Trailer	Seattle-Tacoma-Bellevue MSA, WA	Y	34210 FQ	40210 MW	46830 TQ	USBLS	5/07
Heavy and Tractor-Trailer	West Virginia	Y	22755 FQ	29027 MW	39343 TQ	WVBLS	7/08-9/08
Heavy and Tractor-Trailer	Charleston MSA, WV	Y	22440 FQ	27350 MW	39120 TQ	USBLS	5/07
Heavy and Tractor-Trailer	Huntington-Ashland MSA, WV-KY-OH	Y	23620 FQ	30390 MW	40900 TQ	USBLS	5/07
Heavy and Tractor-Trailer	Wisconsin	Y	30260 FQ	36410 MW	45360 TQ	USBLS	5/07
Heavy and Tractor-Trailer	Appleton MSA, WI	Y	27480 FQ	35120 MW	44410 TQ	USBLS	5/07
Heavy and Tractor-Trailer	Milwaukee-Waukesha-West Allis MSA, WI	Y	31390 FQ	37290 MW	44980 TQ	USBLS	5/07
Heavy and Tractor-Trailer	Racine MSA, WI	Y	33920 FQ	39820 MW	48880 TQ	USBLS	5/07
Heavy and Tractor-Trailer	Wyoming	Y	30983 FQ	36328 MW	42604 TQ	WYBLS	9/08
Heavy and Tractor-Trailer	Cheyenne MSA, WY	Y	28111 FQ	31107 MW	37373 TQ	WYBLS	9/08
Heavy and Tractor-Trailer	Puerto Rico	Y	13010 FQ	14990 MW	18190 TQ	USBLS	5/07
Heavy and Tractor-Trailer	San German-Cabo Rojo MSA, PR	Y	12450 FQ	13940 MW	15560 TQ	USBLS	5/07
Heavy and Tractor-Trailer	San Juan-Caguas-Guaynabo MSA, PR	Y	13150 FQ	15340 MW	18630 TQ	USBLS	5/07
Heavy and Tractor-Trailer	Virgin Islands	Y	23270 FQ	27540 MW	34290 TQ	USBLS	5/07
Heavy and Tractor-Trailer	Guam	Y	20290 FQ	24630 MW	29320 TQ	USBLS	5/07
Light or Delivery Services	Alabama	Y	17830 FQ	23150 MW	31080 TQ	USBLS	5/07
Light or Delivery Services	Birmingham-Hoover MSA, AL	Y	19450 FQ	25090 MW	30790 TQ	USBLS	5/07
Light or Delivery Services	Alaska	Y	23360 FQ	29490 MW	39400 TQ	USBLS	5/07
Light or Delivery Services	Anchorage MSA, AK	Y	22980 FQ	28620 MW	37630 TQ	USBLS	5/07
Light or Delivery Services	Arizona	Y	21380 FQ	27010 MW	35170 TQ	USBLS	5/07
Light or Delivery Services	Phoenix-Mesa-Scottsdale MSA, AZ	Y	21700 FQ	27240 MW	35430 TQ	USBLS	5/07
Light or Delivery Services	Tucson MSA, AZ	Y	20080 FQ	25690 MW	32100 TQ	USBLS	5/07
Light or Delivery Services	Yuma MSA, AZ	Y	18430 FQ	26900 MW	38140 TQ	USBLS	5/07
Light or Delivery Services	Arkansas	Y	17410 FQ	21930 MW	28100 TQ	USBLS	5/07
Light or Delivery Services	Fayetteville-Springdale-Rogers MSA, AR-MO	Y	18140 FQ	22630 MW	28940 TQ	USBLS	5/07
Light or Delivery Services	Little Rock-North Little Rock MSA, AR	Y	19730 FQ	23830 MW	29390 TQ	USBLS	5/07
Light or Delivery Services	California	H	10.44 FQ	13.50 MW	17.46 TQ	CABLS	1/08-3/08
Light or Delivery Services	Los Angeles-Long Beach-Glendale PMSA, CA	H	10.37 FQ	13.49 MW	17.71 TQ	CABLS	1/08-3/08
Light or Delivery Services	Oakland-Fremont-Hayward MSA, CA	H	12.12 FQ	14.86 MW	18.85 TQ	CABLS	1/08-3/08
Light or Delivery Services	Riverside-San Bernardino-Ontario MSA, CA	H	10.13 FQ	13.88 MW	18.02 TQ	CABLS	1/08-3/08

AE	Average entry wage	AW	Average wage paid	FQ	First quartile wage
AER	Average entry range	AWR	Average wage range	H	Hourly
AEX	Average experienced wage	AXR	Average experienced range	HI	Highest wage paid
ATC	Average total compensation	D	Daily	HR	High end range

LO	Lowest wage paid	MTC	Median total compensation	TCC	Total cash compensation
LR	Low end range	MW	Median wage paid	TQ	Third quartile wage
M	Monthly	MWR	Median wage range	W	Weekly
MCC	Median cash compensation	S	See annotated source	Y	Yearly

Occupation/Type/Industry	Location	Per	Low	Mid	High	Source	Date
Truck Driver							
Light or Delivery Services	Sacramento-Arden Arcade-Roseville MSA, CA	H	10.23 FQ	13.75 MW	18.07 TQ	CABLS	1/08-3/08
Light or Delivery Services	San Diego-Carlsbad-San Marcos MSA, CA	H	9.67 FQ	12.28 MW	15.84 TQ	CABLS	1/08-3/08
Light or Delivery Services	San Francisco-San Mateo-Redwood PMSA, CA	H	13.06 FQ	15.99 MW	21.37 TQ	CABLS	1/08-3/08
Light or Delivery Services	San Jose-Sunnyvale-Santa Clara MSA, CA	H	11.81 FQ	14.33 MW	18.16 TQ	CABLS	1/08-3/08
Light or Delivery Services	Santa Ana-Anaheim-Irvine PMSA, CA	Y	20120 FQ	25720 MW	32410 TQ	USBLS	5/07
Light or Delivery Services	Stockton MSA, CA	H	11.60 FQ	13.61 MW	15.74 TQ	CABLS	1/08-3/08
Light or Delivery Services	Colorado	Y	23000 FQ	29120 MW	38060 TQ	USBLS	5/07
Light or Delivery Services	Colorado Springs MSA, CO	Y	21600 FQ	27150 MW	32470 TQ	USBLS	5/07
Light or Delivery Services	Denver-Aurora MSA, CO	Y	23790 FQ	29380 MW	38480 TQ	USBLS	5/07
Light or Delivery Services	Fort Collins-Loveland MSA, CO	Y	20750 FQ	26150 MW	34790 TQ	USBLS	5/07
Light or Delivery Services	Connecticut	H	9.73 AE	14.43 MW		CTBLS	1/08-3/08
Light or Delivery Services	Bridgeport-Stamford-Norwalk MSA, CT	Y	20260 FQ	28110 MW	38840 TQ	USBLS	5/07
Light or Delivery Services	Hartford-West Hartford-East Hartford MSA, CT	Y	22260 FQ	29120 MW	36680 TQ	USBLS	5/07
Light or Delivery Services	Delaware	Y	21230 FQ	28040 MW	37520 TQ	USBLS	5/07
Light or Delivery Services	Wilmington PMSA, DE-MD-NJ	Y	21970 FQ	28850 MW	37970 TQ	USBLS	5/07
Light or Delivery Services	District of Columbia	Y	25020 FQ	33030 MW	39960 TQ	USBLS	5/07
Light or Delivery Services	Washington-Arlington-Alexandria MSA, DC-VA-MD-WV	Y	20880 FQ	28130 MW	36910 TQ	USBLS	5/07
Light or Delivery Services	Florida	Y	20330 FQ	25660 MW	31800 TQ	USBLS	5/07
Light or Delivery Services	Fort Lauderdale-Pompano Beach-Deerfield Beach PMSA, FL	Y	23420 FQ	29120 MW	35190 TQ	USBLS	5/07
Light or Delivery Services	Jacksonville MSA, FL	Y	20910 FQ	25480 MW	31180 TQ	USBLS	5/07
Light or Delivery Services	Miami-Fort Lauderdale-Miami Beach MSA, FL	Y	21540 FQ	27160 MW	32900 TQ	USBLS	5/07
Light or Delivery Services	Orlando-Kissimmee MSA, FL	Y	20600 FQ	26630 MW	36690 TQ	USBLS	5/07
Light or Delivery Services	Tampa-St. Petersburg-Clearwater MSA, FL	Y	19600 FQ	24310 MW	29290 TQ	USBLS	5/07
Light or Delivery Services	West Palm Beach-Boca Raton-Boynton Beach PMSA, FL	Y	22390 FQ	28150 MW	34290 TQ	USBLS	5/07
Light or Delivery Services	Georgia	Y	19320 FQ	25470 MW	33830 TQ	USBLS	5/07
Light or Delivery Services	Atlanta-Sandy Springs-Marietta MSA, GA	Y	21530 FQ	27850 MW	36210 TQ	USBLS	5/07
Light or Delivery Services	Hawaii	Y	20280 FQ	25610 MW	33560 TQ	USBLS	5/07
Light or Delivery Services	Honolulu MSA, HI	Y	19600 FQ	24520 MW	32330 TQ	USBLS	5/07
Light or Delivery Services	Idaho	Y	18360 FQ	24050 MW	31880 TQ	USBLS	5/07
Light or Delivery Services	Boise City-Nampa MSA, ID	Y	20260 FQ	24280 MW	30290 TQ	USBLS	5/07
Light or Delivery Services	Illinois	Y	20290 FQ	28010 MW	37980 TQ	USBLS	5/07
Light or Delivery Services	Chicago-Naperville-Joliet MSA, IL-IN-WI	Y	21200 FQ	28780 MW	38840 TQ	USBLS	5/07
Light or Delivery Services	Indiana	Y	19450 FQ	25750 MW	34250 TQ	USBLS	5/07
Light or Delivery Services	Gary PMSA, IN	Y	17970 FQ	24480 MW	30410 TQ	USBLS	5/07
Light or Delivery Services	Indianapolis-Carmel MSA, IN	Y	19820 FQ	26770 MW	35610 TQ	USBLS	5/07
Light or Delivery Services	Iowa	Y	18480 FQ	23420 MW	32760 TQ	USBLS	5/07
Light or Delivery Services	Des Moines-West Des Moines MSA, IA	Y	21050 FQ	27220 MW	38660 TQ	USBLS	5/07
Light or Delivery Services	Kansas	Y	18020 FQ	22970 MW	30380 TQ	USBLS	5/07
Light or Delivery Services	Wichita MSA, KS	Y	17780 FQ	22040 MW	27880 TQ	USBLS	5/07
Light or Delivery Services	Kentucky	Y	19492 FQ	25138 MW	32881 TQ	KYBLS	2008
Light or Delivery Services	Louisville-Jefferson County MSA, KY-IN	Y	20520 FQ	25710 MW	32770 TQ	USBLS	5/07
Light or Delivery Services	Louisiana	H	8.09 FQ	10.86 MW	14.11 TQ	LABLS	1/08-3/08
Light or Delivery Services	Baton Rouge MSA, LA	Y	17870 FQ	24500 MW	30350 TQ	USBLS	5/07
Light or Delivery Services	New Orleans-Metairie-Kenner MSA, LA	Y	18980 FQ	24740 MW	31300 TQ	USBLS	5/07
Light or Delivery Services	Maine	Y	20350 FQ	25210 MW	35180 TQ	USBLS	5/07
Light or Delivery Services	Portland-South Portland-Biddeford MSA, ME	Y	19860 FQ	25200 MW	34490 TQ	USBLS	5/07
Light or Delivery Services	Maryland	Y		29325 MW		MDBLS	3/08
Light or Delivery Services	Baltimore-Towson MSA, MD	Y	22810 FQ	29520 MW	37370 TQ	USBLS	5/07

AE	Average entry wage	AW	Average wage paid	FQ	First quartile wage	LO	Lowest wage paid
AER	Average entry range	AWR	Average wage range	H	Hourly	LR	Low end range
AEX	Average experienced wage	AXR	Average experienced range	HI	Highest wage paid	M	Monthly
ATC	Average total compensation	D	Daily	HR	High end range	MCC	Median cash compensation

MTC Median total compensation TCC Total cash compensation
MW Median wage paid TQ Third quartile wage
MWR Median wage range W Weekly
S See annotated source Y Yearly

Occupation/Type/Industry	Location	Per	Low	Mid	High	Source	Date
Truck Driver							
Light or Delivery Services	Bethesda-Gaithersburg-Frederick PMSA, MD	Y	20390 FQ	27240 MW	35050 TQ	USBLS	5/07
Light or Delivery Services	Massachusetts	Y	23710 FQ	31100 MW	40450 TQ	USBLS	5/07
Light or Delivery Services	Boston-Cambridge-Quincy NECTA, MA	Y	23630 FQ	31700 MW	40860 TQ	USBLS	5/07
Light or Delivery Services	Worcester MSA, MA-CT	Y	26820 FQ	34000 MW	44820 TQ	USBLS	5/07
Light or Delivery Services	Michigan	Y	21620 FQ	29100 MW	38850 TQ	USBLS	5/07
Light or Delivery Services	Detroit-Warren-Livonia MSA, MI	Y	23070 FQ	30700 MW	40650 TQ	USBLS	5/07
Light or Delivery Services	Grand Rapids-Wyoming MSA, MI	Y	21970 FQ	28920 MW	39660 TQ	USBLS	5/07
Light or Delivery Services	Warren-Troy-Farmington Hills PMSA, MI	Y	22540 FQ	30000 MW	40120 TQ	USBLS	5/07
Light or Delivery Services	Minnesota	Y	23022 FQ	28723 MW	35995 TQ	MNBLS	10/08-12/08
Light or Delivery Services	Duluth-Superior MSA, MN-WI	Y	19267 FQ	25186 MW	32094 TQ	MNBLS	10/08-12/08
Light or Delivery Services	Minneapolis-Saint Paul MSA, MN-WI	Y	24229 FQ	30502 MW	37743 TQ	MNBLS	10/08-12/08
Light or Delivery Services	Rochester MSA, MN	Y	22885 FQ	27033 MW	30595 TQ	MNBLS	10/08-12/08
Light or Delivery Services	Mississippi	Y	19190 FQ	24170 MW	31800 TQ	USBLS	5/07
Light or Delivery Services	Gulfport-Biloxi MSA, MS	Y	18620 FQ	23510 MW	30970 TQ	USBLS	5/07
Light or Delivery Services	Hattiesburg MSA, MS	Y	22270 FQ	32330 MW	43620 TQ	USBLS	5/07
Light or Delivery Services	Jackson MSA, MS	Y	20330 FQ	24350 MW	30880 TQ	USBLS	5/07
Light or Delivery Services	Pascagoula MSA, MS	Y	19310 FQ	22520 MW	30810 TQ	USBLS	5/07
Light or Delivery Services	Missouri	Y	19820 FQ	25670 MW	34280 TQ	USBLS	5/07
Light or Delivery Services	Kansas City MSA, MO-KS	Y	19830 FQ	24900 MW	32000 TQ	USBLS	5/07
Light or Delivery Services	St. Louis MSA, MO-IL	Y	22140 FQ	28780 MW	37180 TQ	USBLS	5/07
Light or Delivery Services	Montana	Y	15320 FQ	21460 MW	29170 TQ	USBLS	5/07
Light or Delivery Services	Billings MSA, MT	Y	15510 FQ	21360 MW	28650 TQ	USBLS	5/07
Light or Delivery Services	Nebraska	Y	20080 FQ	26530 MW	35400 TQ	USBLS	5/07
Light or Delivery Services	Omaha-Council Bluffs MSA, NE-IA	Y	21440 FQ	27640 MW	34550 TQ	USBLS	5/07
Light or Delivery Services	Nevada	H	10.47 FQ	13.94 MW	18.69 TQ	NVBLS	5/08
Light or Delivery Services	Las Vegas-Paradise MSA, NV	H	10.54 FQ	13.89 MW	18.51 TQ	NVBLS	5/08
Light or Delivery Services	New Hampshire	H	9.74 AE	13.65 MW	17.65 AEX	NHBLS	6/08
Light or Delivery Services	Manchester MSA, NH	Y	24280 FQ	29180 MW	36790 TQ	USBLS	5/07
Light or Delivery Services	Nashua NECTA, NH-MA	Y	21070 FQ	28120 MW	36170 TQ	USBLS	5/07
Light or Delivery Services	Portsmouth MSA, NH-ME	Y	23090 FQ	28890 MW	39530 TQ	USBLS	5/07
Light or Delivery Services	New Jersey	Y	22670 FQ	30310 MW	39530 TQ	USBLS	5/07
Light or Delivery Services	Camden PMSA, NJ	Y	19370 FQ	27140 MW	34280 TQ	USBLS	5/07
Light or Delivery Services	Edison PMSA, NJ	Y	24050 FQ	32260 MW	41770 TQ	USBLS	5/07
Light or Delivery Services	Newark-Union PMSA, NJ-PA	Y	23700 FQ	30550 MW	38720 TQ	USBLS	5/07
Light or Delivery Services	Trenton-Ewing MSA, NJ	Y	21430 FQ	28720 MW	35610 TQ	USBLS	5/07
Light or Delivery Services	New Mexico	Y	18100 FQ	23880 MW	30780 TQ	USBLS	5/07
Light or Delivery Services	Albuquerque MSA, NM	Y	18270 FQ	23730 MW	30260 TQ	USBLS	5/07
Light or Delivery Services	Santa Fe MSA, NM	Y	21290 FQ	24180 MW	28130 TQ	USBLS	5/07
Light or Delivery Services	New York	Y	20950 FQ	29430 MW	41680 TQ	USBLS	5/07
Light or Delivery Services	Albany-Schenectady-Troy MSA, NY	Y	23040 FQ	28300 MW	36730 TQ	USBLS	5/07
Light or Delivery Services	Binghamton MSA, NY	Y	18240 FQ	23340 MW	32110 TQ	USBLS	5/07
Light or Delivery Services	Buffalo-Niagara Falls MSA, NY	Y	18790 FQ	25620 MW	33590 TQ	USBLS	5/07
Light or Delivery Services	Glens Falls MSA, NY	Y	18880 FQ	26500 MW	33750 TQ	USBLS	5/07
Light or Delivery Services	Nassau-Suffolk PMSA, NY	Y	24690 FQ	33820 MW	46100 TQ	USBLS	5/07
Light or Delivery Services	New York-Northern New Jersey-Long Island MSA, NY-NJ-PA	Y	23400 FQ	32440 MW	44000 TQ	USBLS	5/07
Light or Delivery Services	Utica-Rome MSA, NY	Y	16550 FQ	19000 MW	23370 TQ	USBLS	5/07
Light or Delivery Services	North Carolina	Y	21300 FQ	26530 MW	33000 TQ	USBLS	5/07
Light or Delivery Services	Charlotte-Gastonia-Concord MSA, NC-SC	Y	23010 FQ	28890 MW	36220 TQ	USBLS	5/07
Light or Delivery Services	Durham MSA, NC	Y	21120 FQ	25190 MW	32980 TQ	USBLS	5/07
Light or Delivery Services	Raleigh-Cary MSA, NC	Y	22300 FQ	27230 MW	32860 TQ	USBLS	5/07
Light or Delivery Services	North Dakota	Y	19180 FQ	24580 MW	33270 TQ	USBLS	5/07
Light or Delivery Services	Fargo MSA, ND-MN	Y	21350 FQ	26710 MW	41240 TQ	USBLS	5/07
Light or Delivery Services	Ohio	Y	19410 FQ	26090 MW	35350 TQ	USBLS	5/07
Light or Delivery Services	Cincinnati-Middletown MSA, OH-KY-IN	Y	21080 FQ	27370 MW	35580 TQ	USBLS	5/07
Light or Delivery Services	Cleveland-Elyria-Mentor MSA, OH	Y	19760 FQ	26620 MW	36140 TQ	USBLS	5/07
Light or Delivery Services	Columbus MSA, OH	Y	21440 FQ	28840 MW	38000 TQ	USBLS	5/07
Light or Delivery Services	Dayton MSA, OH	Y	18350 FQ	25360 MW	38400 TQ	USBLS	5/07

AE Average entry wage	**AW** Average wage paid	**FQ** First quartile wage	**LO** Lowest wage paid	**MTC** Median total compensation	**TCC** Total cash compensation
AER Average entry range	**AWR** Average wage range	**H** Hourly	**LR** Low end range	**MW** Median wage paid	**TQ** Third quartile wage
AEX Average experienced wage	**AXR** Average experienced range	**HI** Highest wage paid	**M** Monthly	**MWR** Median wage range	**W** Weekly
ATC Average total compensation	**D** Daily	**HR** High end range	**MCC** Median cash compensation	**S** See annotated source	**Y** Yearly

Truck Driver

Occupation/Type/Industry	Location	Per	Low	Mid	High	Source	Date
Light or Delivery Services	Oklahoma	Y	17710 FQ	22260 MW	29360 TQ	USBLS	5/07
Light or Delivery Services	Oklahoma City MSA, OK	Y	18240 FQ	22760 MW	31450 TQ	USBLS	5/07
Light or Delivery Services	Tulsa MSA, OK	Y	18020 FQ	22740 MW	28690 TQ	USBLS	5/07
Light or Delivery Services	Oregon	H	10.77 FQ	13.12 MW	16.19 TQ	ORBLS	5/08
Light or Delivery Services	Portland-Vancouver-Beaverton MSA, OR-WA	Y	22920 FQ	27980 MW	35470 TQ	USBLS	5/07
Light or Delivery Services	Pennsylvania	Y	19210 FQ	25850 MW	35280 TQ	USBLS	5/07
Light or Delivery Services	Allentown-Bethlehem-Easton MSA, PA-NJ	Y	21700 FQ	29480 MW	40330 TQ	USBLS	5/07
Light or Delivery Services	Philadelphia-Camden-Wilmington MSA, PA-NJ-DE-MD	Y	20810 FQ	28340 MW	38340 TQ	USBLS	5/07
Light or Delivery Services	Pittsburgh MSA, PA	Y	18550 FQ	25820 MW	36020 TQ	USBLS	5/07
Light or Delivery Services	Rhode Island	Y	22760 FQ	28740 MW	37870 TQ	USBLS	5/07
Light or Delivery Services	Providence-Fall River-Warwick MSA, RI-MA	Y	22560 FQ	28550 MW	36960 TQ	USBLS	5/07
Light or Delivery Services	South Carolina	Y	18280 FQ	23970 MW	31230 TQ	USBLS	5/07
Light or Delivery Services	Charleston-North Charleston MSA, SC	Y	17510 FQ	23360 MW	30120 TQ	USBLS	5/07
Light or Delivery Services	Columbia MSA, SC	Y	20600 FQ	25450 MW	31060 TQ	USBLS	5/07
Light or Delivery Services	Florence MSA, SC	Y	18280 FQ	23600 MW	37620 TQ	USBLS	5/07
Light or Delivery Services	South Dakota	Y	20941 FQ	25402 MW	33312 TQ	SDBLS	7/08-9/08
Light or Delivery Services	Rapid City MSA, SD	Y	22233 FQ	25488 MW	29130 TQ	SDBLS	7/08-9/08
Light or Delivery Services	Sioux Falls MSA, SD	Y	20867 FQ	26255 MW	35592 TQ	SDBLS	7/08-9/08
Light or Delivery Services	Tennessee	Y	19560 FQ	25210 MW	33320 TQ	USBLS	5/07
Light or Delivery Services	Kingsport-Bristol-Bristol MSA, TN-VA	Y	18780 FQ	23250 MW	29470 TQ	USBLS	5/07
Light or Delivery Services	Memphis MSA, TN-MS-AR	Y	21410 FQ	27200 MW	34400 TQ	USBLS	5/07
Light or Delivery Services	Nashville-Davidson-Murfreesboro MSA, TN	Y	21800 FQ	28130 MW	37460 TQ	USBLS	5/07
Light or Delivery Services	Texas	Y	19240 FQ	24660 MW	31610 TQ	USBLS	5/07
Light or Delivery Services	Austin-Round Rock MSA, TX	Y	21540 FQ	26490 MW	32360 TQ	USBLS	5/07
Light or Delivery Services	Dallas-Fort Worth-Arlington MSA, TX	Y	22000 FQ	27610 MW	34440 TQ	USBLS	5/07
Light or Delivery Services	El Paso MSA, TX	Y	15250 FQ	20490 MW	26620 TQ	USBLS	5/07
Light or Delivery Services	Houston-Sugar Land-Baytown MSA, TX	Y	20860 FQ	25370 MW	31550 TQ	USBLS	5/07
Light or Delivery Services	San Antonio MSA, TX	Y	18170 FQ	22370 MW	29330 TQ	USBLS	5/07
Light or Delivery Services	Utah	Y	17630 FQ	22890 MW	29210 TQ	USBLS	5/07
Light or Delivery Services	Provo-Orem MSA, UT	Y	14210 FQ	19330 MW	26800 TQ	USBLS	5/07
Light or Delivery Services	Salt Lake City MSA, UT	Y	19010 FQ	23180 MW	28820 TQ	USBLS	5/07
Light or Delivery Services	Vermont	Y	21670 FQ	28270 MW	39270 TQ	USBLS	5/07
Light or Delivery Services	Burlington-South Burlington MSA, VT	Y	23640 FQ	29750 MW	42020 TQ	USBLS	5/07
Light or Delivery Services	Virginia	Y	17980 FQ	24070 MW	31850 TQ	USBLS	5/07
Light or Delivery Services	Richmond MSA, VA	Y	18040 FQ	25050 MW	33560 TQ	USBLS	5/07
Light or Delivery Services	Virginia Beach-Norfolk-Newport News MSA, VA-NC	Y	17580 FQ	22260 MW	29830 TQ	USBLS	5/07
Light or Delivery Services	Washington	H	10.96 FQ	13.68 MW	17.12 TQ	WABLS	3/08
Light or Delivery Services	Seattle-Tacoma-Bellevue MSA, WA	Y	23850 FQ	29160 MW	35690 TQ	USBLS	5/07
Light or Delivery Services	Spokane MSA, WA	Y	19740 FQ	23990 MW	31280 TQ	USBLS	5/07
Light or Delivery Services	West Virginia	Y	15790 FQ	20702 MW	28765 TQ	WVBLS	7/08-9/08
Light or Delivery Services	Charleston MSA, WV	Y	17420 FQ	22940 MW	29270 TQ	USBLS	5/07
Light or Delivery Services	Wisconsin	Y	19620 FQ	25260 MW	32810 TQ	USBLS	5/07
Light or Delivery Services	Milwaukee-Waukesha-West Allis MSA, WI	Y	20240 FQ	27350 MW	36150 TQ	USBLS	5/07
Light or Delivery Services	Wyoming	Y	22937 FQ	30031 MW	34697 TQ	WYBLS	9/08
Light or Delivery Services	Cheyenne MSA, WY	Y	21547 FQ	31186 MW	35327 TQ	WYBLS	9/08
Light or Delivery Services	Puerto Rico	Y	12780 FQ	14450 MW	17010 TQ	USBLS	5/07
Light or Delivery Services	San Juan-Caguas-Guaynabo MSA, PR	Y	12930 FQ	14740 MW	17660 TQ	USBLS	5/07
Light or Delivery Services	Virgin Islands	Y	19570 FQ	22830 MW	28150 TQ	USBLS	5/07
Light or Delivery Services	Guam	Y	13240 FQ	15480 MW	20050 TQ	USBLS	5/07
Public Works	Camden County, GA	Y	23358 LO		36013 HI	GACTY03	2008
Public Works	Coweta County, GA	Y	29267 LO		43902 HI	GACTY03	2008

Trustee

Municipal Government	Cohoctah Township, MI	Y			1560 HI	LCPP	2009
Municipal Government	Green Oak Township, MI	Y			5000 HI	LCPP	2009
Municipal Government	Hartland Township, MI	Y			4000 HI	LCPP	2009

AE	Average entry wage	AW	Average wage paid	FQ	First quartile wage	LO Lowest wage paid	MTC Median total compensation	TCC Total cash compensation
AER	Average entry range	AWR	Average wage range	H	Hourly	LR Low end range	MW Median wage paid	TQ Third quartile wage
AEX	Average experienced wage	AXR	Average experienced range	HI	Highest wage paid	M Monthly	MWR Median wage range	W Weekly
ATC	Average total compensation	D	Daily	HR	High end range	MCC Median cash compensation	S See annotated source	Y Yearly

Occupation/Type/Industry	Location	Per	Low	Mid	High	Source	Date
Turbine Aircraft Mechanic	United States	H		24.00 AW		AVJOB07	2009
Turf Manager Municipal Government	Cincinnati, OH	Y	42428 LO		48214 HI	COHSS	10/08
Tutor Department of Regional Community Technical Colleges	New Hampshire	Y		8360 AW		NHUL03	2008
Typesetter and Pasteup Artist Municipal Government	Cincinnati, OH	Y	40748 LO		42428 HI	COHSS	10/08
Typesetting Machine Operator	Virginia	Y	20082-23999 LR		41214-49255 HR	VACG06	11/25/07
Typesetting Technician State Government	Ohio	H	16.78 LO		19.88 HI	ODAS	2008
Ultrasound Technologist	United States	Y			110000 HI	WXYZ01	2009
Umpire, Referee, and Other Sports Official	Arizona	Y	19780 FQ	27440 MW	34030 TQ	USBLS	5/07
	Phoenix-Mesa-Scottsdale MSA, AZ	Y	20100 FQ	27470 MW	33780 TQ	USBLS	5/07
	California	Y		32702 AW		CABLS	1/08-3/08
	Los Angeles-Long Beach-Glendale PMSA, CA	Y		35348 AW		CABLS	1/08-3/08
	Oakland-Fremont-Hayward MSA, CA	Y		28826 AW		CABLS	1/08-3/08
	Sacramento-Arden Arcade-Roseville MSA, CA	Y		35502 MW		CABLS	1/08-3/08
	San Diego-Carlsbad-San Marcos MSA, CA	Y		30682 AW		CABLS	1/08-3/08
	San Jose-Sunnyvale-Santa Clara MSA, CA	Y		36763 AW		CABLS	1/08-3/08
	Santa Ana-Anaheim-Irvine PMSA, CA	Y	19740 FQ	29070 MW	45200 TQ	USBLS	5/07
	Colorado	Y	15470 FQ	20380 MW	25440 TQ	USBLS	5/07
	Denver-Aurora MSA, CO	Y	19440 FQ	22140 MW	25740 TQ	USBLS	5/07
	Delaware	Y	14970 FQ	18810 MW	24170 TQ	USBLS	5/07
	Washington-Arlington-Alexandria MSA, DC-VA-MD-WV	Y	25090 FQ	33160 MW	37700 TQ	USBLS	5/07
	Florida	Y	21390 FQ	30450 MW	38930 TQ	USBLS	5/07
	Fort Lauderdale-Pompano Beach-Deerfield Beach PMSA, FL	Y	26270 FQ	29960 MW	48130 TQ	USBLS	5/07
	Miami-Fort Lauderdale-Miami Beach MSA, FL	Y	19630 FQ	28700 MW	40410 TQ	USBLS	5/07
	Georgia	Y	30870 FQ	34450 MW	38180 TQ	USBLS	5/07
	Idaho	Y	12780 FQ	14080 MW	20920 TQ	USBLS	5/07
	Illinois	Y	15000 FQ	16730 MW	25670 TQ	USBLS	5/07
	Chicago-Naperville-Joliet MSA, IL-IN-WI	Y	16160 FQ	19970 MW	27760 TQ	USBLS	5/07
	Indiana	Y	18550 FQ	22800 MW	29920 TQ	USBLS	5/07
	Indianapolis-Carmel MSA, IN	Y	20430 FQ	26360 MW	37080 TQ	USBLS	5/07
	Iowa	Y	15580 FQ	20310 MW	24450 TQ	USBLS	5/07
	Kansas	Y	15540 FQ	23380 MW	40400 TQ	USBLS	5/07
	Wichita MSA, KS	Y	21130 FQ	37810 MW	43160 TQ	USBLS	5/07
	Kentucky	Y	16417 FQ	18679 MW	26084 TQ	KYBLS	2008
	Louisville-Jefferson County MSA, KY-IN	Y	15760 FQ	18840 MW	27130 TQ	USBLS	5/07
	Louisiana	Y		24787 AW		LABLS	1/08-3/08
	Baton Rouge MSA, LA	Y	17520 FQ	18830 MW	20170 TQ	USBLS	5/07
	Maryland	Y		19950 MW		MDBLS	3/08
	Baltimore-Towson MSA, MD	Y	16860 FQ	18390 MW	20690 TQ	USBLS	5/07
	Massachusetts	Y	15820 FQ	18870 MW	33010 TQ	USBLS	5/07
	Boston-Cambridge-Quincy NECTA, MA	Y	15760 FQ	16490 MW	23000 TQ	USBLS	5/07
	Michigan	Y	15140 FQ	26740 MW	50850 TQ	USBLS	5/07
	Detroit-Warren-Livonia MSA, MI	Y	18720 FQ	40840 MW	48670 TQ	USBLS	5/07

Occupation/Type/Industry	Location	Per	Low	Mid	High	Source	Date
Umpire, Referee, and Other Sports Official							
	Warren-Troy-Farmington Hills PMSA, MI	Y	18720 FQ	40840 MW	48670 TQ	USBLS	5/07
	Minnesota	Y	19051 FQ	26448 MW	42110 TQ	MNBLS	10/08-12/08
	Minneapolis-Saint Paul MSA, MN-WI	Y	19491 FQ	33343 MW	46201 TQ	MNBLS	10/08-12/08
	Mississippi	Y	24120 FQ	27810 MW	31000 TQ	USBLS	5/07
	Missouri	Y	19920 FQ	26670 MW	31420 TQ	USBLS	5/07
	Kansas City MSA, MO-KS	Y	22990 FQ	33000 MW	43010 TQ	USBLS	5/07
	St. Louis MSA, MO-IL	Y	18970 FQ	28700 MW	32690 TQ	USBLS	5/07
	Nebraska	Y	13260 FQ	15550 MW	27070 TQ	USBLS	5/07
	New Hampshire	Y	14177 AE	23085 MW	38915 AEX	NHBLS	6/08
	New Jersey	Y	18470 FQ	23150 MW	32660 TQ	USBLS	5/07
	Edison PMSA, NJ	Y	17660 FQ	19420 MW	22750 TQ	USBLS	5/07
	New York	Y	19410 FQ	28930 MW	71670 TQ	USBLS	5/07
	Nassau-Suffolk PMSA, NY	Y	15510 FQ	18110 MW	24870 TQ	USBLS	5/07
	New York-Northern New Jersey-Long Island MSA, NY-NJ-PA	Y	17590 FQ	24790 MW	68820 TQ	USBLS	5/07
	Ohio	Y	17270 FQ	28040 MW	35220 TQ	USBLS	5/07
	Cincinnati-Middletown MSA, OH-KY-IN	Y	16370 FQ	20420 MW	28530 TQ	USBLS	5/07
	Cleveland-Elyria-Mentor MSA, OH	Y	18120 FQ	28460 MW	34560 TQ	USBLS	5/07
	Oklahoma	Y	20570 FQ	26960 MW	31370 TQ	USBLS	5/07
	Oklahoma City MSA, OK	Y	21350 FQ	26880 MW	31820 TQ	USBLS	5/07
	Tulsa MSA, OK	Y	18380 FQ	28460 MW	46130 TQ	USBLS	5/07
	Oregon	Y	18974 FQ	22728 MW	28666 TQ	ORBLS	5/08
	Portland-Vancouver-Beaverton MSA, OR-WA	Y	18500 FQ	23000 MW	28270 TQ	USBLS	5/07
	Philadelphia-Camden-Wilmington MSA, PA-NJ-DE-MD	Y	18870 FQ	22720 MW	32860 TQ	USBLS	5/07
	Pittsburgh MSA, PA	Y	26830 FQ	30570 MW	52540 TQ	USBLS	5/07
	Providence-Fall River-Warwick MSA, RI-MA	Y	15830 FQ	24780 MW	28460 TQ	USBLS	5/07
	South Carolina	Y	26060 FQ	40720 MW	51020 TQ	USBLS	5/07
	Tennessee	Y	17710 FQ	37400 MW	63130 TQ	USBLS	5/07
	Texas	Y	18990 FQ	28000 MW	33850 TQ	USBLS	5/07
	Dallas-Fort Worth-Arlington MSA, TX	Y	22180 FQ	29310 MW	34440 TQ	USBLS	5/07
	Houston-Sugar Land-Baytown MSA, TX	Y	17130 FQ	26440 MW	32130 TQ	USBLS	5/07
	Utah	Y	13600 FQ	16060 MW	20140 TQ	USBLS	5/07
	Richmond MSA, VA	Y	27320 FQ	29630 MW	31890 TQ	USBLS	5/07
	Washington	Y		48369 AW		WABLS	3/08
	Seattle-Tacoma-Bellevue MSA, WA	Y	35860 FQ	42670 MW	62190 TQ	USBLS	5/07
	Wisconsin	Y	20220 FQ	23790 MW	30660 TQ	USBLS	5/07
	Milwaukee-Waukesha-West Allis MSA, WI	Y	20410 FQ	23640 MW	31470 TQ	USBLS	5/07
Undersheriff	Livingston County, MI	Y			85181 HI	LCPP	2009
Upholsterer	Alabama	Y	18210 FQ	21540 MW	25730 TQ	USBLS	5/07
	Birmingham-Hoover MSA, AL	Y	25720 FQ	28510 MW	40980 TQ	USBLS	5/07
	Arizona	Y	20070 FQ	23250 MW	32050 TQ	USBLS	5/07
	Phoenix-Mesa-Scottsdale MSA, AZ	Y	18210 FQ	23210 MW	33170 TQ	USBLS	5/07
	Tucson MSA, AZ	Y	21110 FQ	23000 MW	24910 TQ	USBLS	5/07
	Arkansas	Y	21040 FQ	25950 MW	32870 TQ	USBLS	5/07
	Fayetteville-Springdale-Rogers MSA, AR-MO	Y	25740 FQ	27720 MW	29690 TQ	USBLS	5/07
	Little Rock-North Little Rock MSA, AR	Y	22540 FQ	31160 MW	37610 TQ	USBLS	5/07
	California	H	10.43 FQ	12.96 MW	16.54 TQ	CABLS	1/08-3/08
	Los Angeles-Long Beach-Glendale PMSA, CA	H	9.51 FQ	11.76 MW	14.84 TQ	CABLS	1/08-3/08
	Oakland-Fremont-Hayward MSA, CA	H	12.44 FQ	14.31 MW	17.54 TQ	CABLS	1/08-3/08
	Oxnard-Thousand Oaks-Ventura MSA, CA	H	12.19 FQ	14.81 MW	22.21 TQ	CABLS	1/08-3/08

AE Average entry wage	**AW** Average wage paid	**FQ** First quartile wage	**LO** Lowest wage paid	**MTC** Median total compensation **TCC** Total cash compensation
AER Average entry range	**AWR** Average wage range	**H** Hourly	**LR** Low end range	**MW** Median wage paid **TQ** Third quartile wage
AEX Average experienced wage	**AXR** Average experienced range	**HI** Highest wage paid	**M** Monthly	**MWR** Median wage range **W** Weekly
ATC Average total compensation	**D** Daily	**HR** High end range	**MCC** Median cash compensation	**S** See annotated source **Y** Yearly

Occupation/Type/Industry	Location	Per	Low	Mid	High	Source	Date
Upholsterer	Riverside-San Bernardino-Ontario MSA, CA	H	10.94 FQ	12.57 MW	14.92 TQ	CABLS	1/08-3/08
	Sacramento-Arden Arcade-Roseville MSA, CA	H	11.90 FQ	16.91 MW	18.51 TQ	CABLS	1/08-3/08
	San Diego-Carlsbad-San Marcos MSA, CA	H	12.77 FQ	16.43 MW	19.78 TQ	CABLS	1/08-3/08
	San Francisco-San Mateo-Redwood PMSA, CA	H	15.19 FQ	17.99 MW	21.03 TQ	CABLS	1/08-3/08
	San Jose-Sunnyvale-Santa Clara MSA, CA	H	11.06 FQ	13.59 MW	16.68 TQ	CABLS	1/08-3/08
	Santa Ana-Anaheim-Irvine PMSA, CA	Y	19080 FQ	24100 MW	29130 TQ	USBLS	5/07
	Colorado	Y	22260 FQ	26170 MW	30740 TQ	USBLS	5/07
	Denver-Aurora MSA, CO	Y	23880 FQ	27310 MW	31090 TQ	USBLS	5/07
	Connecticut	H	11.02 AE	14.96 MW		CTBLS	1/08-3/08
	Bridgeport-Stamford-Norwalk MSA, CT	Y	27540 FQ	31340 MW	40770 TQ	USBLS	5/07
	Delaware	Y	24670 FQ	40830 MW	55190 TQ	USBLS	5/07
	Wilmington PMSA, DE-MD-NJ	Y	34280 FQ	47100 MW	57820 TQ	USBLS	5/07
	Washington-Arlington-Alexandria MSA, DC-VA-MD-WV	Y	21110 FQ	25280 MW	33890 TQ	USBLS	5/07
	Florida	Y	20530 FQ	26310 MW	31660 TQ	USBLS	5/07
	Fort Lauderdale-Pompano Beach-Deerfield Beach PMSA, FL	Y	22770 FQ	25930 MW	34860 TQ	USBLS	5/07
	Jacksonville MSA, FL	Y	21980 FQ	26150 MW	32100 TQ	USBLS	5/07
	Miami-Fort Lauderdale-Miami Beach MSA, FL	Y	20850 FQ	25570 MW	32920 TQ	USBLS	5/07
	Orlando-Kissimmee MSA, FL	Y	24310 FQ	27670 MW	32860 TQ	USBLS	5/07
	Tampa-St. Petersburg-Clearwater MSA, FL	Y	18470 FQ	25750 MW	30150 TQ	USBLS	5/07
	West Palm Beach-Boca Raton-Boynton Beach PMSA, FL	Y	18220 FQ	24400 MW	30850 TQ	USBLS	5/07
	Georgia	Y	18330 FQ	24570 MW	35640 TQ	USBLS	5/07
	Atlanta-Sandy Springs-Marietta MSA, GA	Y	18910 FQ	26310 MW	35200 TQ	USBLS	5/07
	Hawaii	Y	21810 FQ	26590 MW	34810 TQ	USBLS	5/07
	Honolulu MSA, HI	Y	21310 FQ	25060 MW	31870 TQ	USBLS	5/07
	Idaho	Y	21410 FQ	25580 MW	30320 TQ	USBLS	5/07
	Boise City-Nampa MSA, ID	Y	24440 FQ	26880 MW	29500 TQ	USBLS	5/07
	Illinois	Y	26100 FQ	33390 MW	49360 TQ	USBLS	5/07
	Chicago-Naperville-Joliet MSA, IL-IN-WI	Y	27060 FQ	31950 MW	39090 TQ	USBLS	5/07
	Indiana	Y	19680 FQ	26180 MW	31430 TQ	USBLS	5/07
	Indianapolis-Carmel MSA, IN	Y	21870 FQ	27340 MW	35070 TQ	USBLS	5/07
	Iowa	Y	21940 FQ	27290 MW	32690 TQ	USBLS	5/07
	Kansas	Y	22600 FQ	28820 MW	40940 TQ	USBLS	5/07
	Topeka MSA, KS	Y	18070 FQ	27260 MW	36090 TQ	USBLS	5/07
	Wichita MSA, KS	Y	29320 FQ	42030 MW	48190 TQ	USBLS	5/07
	Kentucky	Y	27147 FQ	30227 MW	33550 TQ	KYBLS	2008
	Louisville-Jefferson County MSA, KY-IN	Y	25710 FQ	27960 MW	30300 TQ	USBLS	5/07
	Louisiana	H	8.63 FQ	10.96 MW	14.48 TQ	LABLS	1/08-3/08
	Baton Rouge MSA, LA	Y	17250 FQ	22060 MW	31490 TQ	USBLS	5/07
	Maine	Y	23650 FQ	27230 MW	33780 TQ	USBLS	5/07
	Maryland	Y		32150 MW		MDBLS	3/08
	Baltimore-Towson MSA, MD	Y	28370 FQ	32750 MW	38900 TQ	USBLS	5/07
	Bethesda-Gaithersburg-Frederick PMSA, MD	Y	14660 FQ	34180 MW	41750 TQ	USBLS	5/07
	Massachusetts	Y	26540 FQ	33460 MW	40640 TQ	USBLS	5/07
	Boston-Cambridge-Quincy NECTA, MA	Y	27850 FQ	34320 MW	41460 TQ	USBLS	5/07
	Michigan	Y	19640 FQ	25030 MW	31640 TQ	USBLS	5/07
	Detroit-Warren-Livonia MSA, MI	Y	25070 FQ	31170 MW	39040 TQ	USBLS	5/07
	Grand Rapids-Wyoming MSA, MI	Y	21200 FQ	25110 MW	31330 TQ	USBLS	5/07
	Warren-Troy-Farmington Hills PMSA, MI	Y	26690 FQ	32780 MW	40600 TQ	USBLS	5/07
	Minnesota	Y	25906 FQ	29991 MW	35412 TQ	MNBLS	10/08-12/08

AE Average entry wage	**AW** Average wage paid	**FQ** First quartile wage	**LO** Lowest wage paid	**MTC** Median total compensation	**TCC** Total cash compensation
AER Average entry range	**AWR** Average wage range	**H** Hourly	**LR** Low end range	**MW** Median wage paid	**TQ** Third quartile wage
AEX Average experienced wage	**AXR** Average experienced range	**HI** Highest wage paid	**M** Monthly	**MWR** Median wage range	**W** Weekly
ATC Average total compensation	**D** Daily	**HR** High end range	**MCC** Median cash compensation	**S** See annotated source	**Y** Yearly

Occupation/Type/Industry	Location	Per	Low	Mid	High	Source	Date
Upholsterer	Minneapolis-Saint Paul MSA, MN-WI	Y	27150 FQ	30737 MW	35703 TQ	MNBLS	10/08-12/08
	Mississippi	Y	21830 FQ	28060 MW	33890 TQ	USBLS	5/07
	Missouri	Y	21410 FQ	26920 MW	30900 TQ	USBLS	5/07
	Kansas City MSA, MO-KS	Y	24630 FQ	27440 MW	30530 TQ	USBLS	5/07
	St. Louis MSA, MO-IL	Y	25860 FQ	52210 MW	58720 TQ	USBLS	5/07
	Montana	Y	21560 FQ	28250 MW	38630 TQ	USBLS	5/07
	Nebraska	Y	14940 FQ	18440 MW	22900 TQ	USBLS	5/07
	Nevada	H	11.01 FQ	14.66 MW	22.66 TQ	NVBLS	5/08
	Las Vegas-Paradise MSA, NV	H	13.79 FQ	21.03 MW	24.32 TQ	NVBLS	5/08
	New Jersey	Y	24600 FQ	32030 MW	43510 TQ	USBLS	5/07
	Camden PMSA, NJ	Y	18460 FQ	21080 MW	30780 TQ	USBLS	5/07
	Edison PMSA, NJ	Y	21690 FQ	31100 MW	39240 TQ	USBLS	5/07
	Newark-Union PMSA, NJ-PA	Y	25050 FQ	30490 MW	37020 TQ	USBLS	5/07
	New Mexico	Y	17890 FQ	21790 MW	25190 TQ	USBLS	5/07
	Albuquerque MSA, NM	Y	20990 FQ	23590 MW	25300 TQ	USBLS	5/07
	New York	Y	26100 FQ	32530 MW	44770 TQ	USBLS	5/07
	Nassau-Suffolk PMSA, NY	Y	25370 FQ	28180 MW	30920 TQ	USBLS	5/07
	New York-Northern New Jersey-Long Island MSA, NY-NJ-PA	Y	26930 FQ	34780 MW	46980 TQ	USBLS	5/07
	North Carolina	Y	25980 FQ	33330 MW	40580 TQ	USBLS	5/07
	Charlotte-Gastonia-Concord MSA, NC-SC	Y	21580 FQ	26570 MW	35610 TQ	USBLS	5/07
	Raleigh-Cary MSA, NC	Y	22410 FQ	24330 MW	26990 TQ	USBLS	5/07
	North Dakota	Y	15790 FQ	20070 MW	24400 TQ	USBLS	5/07
	Ohio	Y	20180 FQ	27160 MW	34670 TQ	USBLS	5/07
	Cincinnati-Middletown MSA, OH-KY-IN	Y	25950 FQ	28430 MW	30920 TQ	USBLS	5/07
	Columbus MSA, OH	Y	26780 FQ	33520 MW	37170 TQ	USBLS	5/07
	Dayton MSA, OH	Y	26160 FQ	28570 MW	50860 TQ	USBLS	5/07
	Oklahoma	Y	20200 FQ	22980 MW	27620 TQ	USBLS	5/07
	Oklahoma City MSA, OK	Y	20470 FQ	23280 MW	27270 TQ	USBLS	5/07
	Tulsa MSA, OK	Y	20320 FQ	22770 MW	32880 TQ	USBLS	5/07
	Oregon	H	12.48 FQ	16.28 MW	18.08 TQ	ORBLS	5/08
	Portland-Vancouver-Beaverton MSA, OR-WA	Y	26630 FQ	33910 MW	37130 TQ	USBLS	5/07
	Pennsylvania	Y	21600 FQ	26790 MW	38710 TQ	USBLS	5/07
	Allentown-Bethlehem-Easton MSA, PA-NJ	Y	21860 FQ	24530 MW	31590 TQ	USBLS	5/07
	Philadelphia-Camden-Wilmington MSA, PA-NJ-DE-MD	Y	20700 FQ	27140 MW	40230 TQ	USBLS	5/07
	Pittsburgh MSA, PA	Y	21370 FQ	23190 MW	25100 TQ	USBLS	5/07
	Rhode Island	Y	26280 FQ	30650 MW	37940 TQ	USBLS	5/07
	South Carolina	Y	23640 FQ	30970 MW	48380 TQ	USBLS	5/07
	South Dakota	Y	23912 FQ	27052 MW	30075 TQ	SDBLS	7/08-9/08
	Tennessee	Y	23690 FQ	26640 MW	29350 TQ	USBLS	5/07
	Memphis MSA, TN-MS-AR	Y	21900 FQ	24780 MW	29260 TQ	USBLS	5/07
	Texas	Y	20760 FQ	26520 MW	30650 TQ	USBLS	5/07
	Austin-Round Rock MSA, TX	Y	26950 FQ	28940 MW	30810 TQ	USBLS	5/07
	Dallas-Fort Worth-Arlington MSA, TX	Y	21390 FQ	27070 MW	31510 TQ	USBLS	5/07
	Houston-Sugar Land-Baytown MSA, TX	Y	25780 FQ	28210 MW	30610 TQ	USBLS	5/07
	San Antonio MSA, TX	Y	21090 FQ	23080 MW	26030 TQ	USBLS	5/07
	Utah	Y	18650 FQ	25250 MW	29050 TQ	USBLS	5/07
	Salt Lake City MSA, UT	Y	20960 FQ	22940 MW	26710 TQ	USBLS	5/07
	Virginia	Y	19090 FQ	24740 MW	36660 TQ	USBLS	5/07
	Roanoke MSA, VA	Y	13520 FQ	23070 MW	28770 TQ	USBLS	5/07
	Washington	H	12.52 FQ	15.59 MW	18.92 TQ	WABLS	3/08
	Seattle-Tacoma-Bellevue MSA, WA	Y	26640 FQ	33340 MW	39960 TQ	USBLS	5/07
	West Virginia	Y	16712 FQ	22597 MW	35506 TQ	WVBLS	7/08-9/08
	Wisconsin	Y	25730 FQ	29100 MW	32960 TQ	USBLS	5/07
	Milwaukee-Waukesha-West Allis MSA, WI	Y	27270 FQ	29420 MW	31580 TQ	USBLS	5/07
	Puerto Rico	Y	12990 FQ	14940 MW	16980 TQ	USBLS	5/07
	San Juan-Caguas-Guaynabo MSA, PR	Y	13590 FQ	15630 MW	17660 TQ	USBLS	5/07
Urban and Regional Planner	Alabama	Y	40630 FQ	53980 MW	66680 TQ	USBLS	5/07

AE	Average entry wage	**AW**	Average wage paid	**FQ**	First quartile wage	**LO** Lowest wage paid	**MTC** Median total compensation	**TCC** Total cash compensation
AER	Average entry range	**AWR**	Average wage range	**H**	Hourly	**LR** Low end range	**MW** Median wage paid	**TQ** Third quartile wage
AEX	Average experienced wage	**AXR**	Average experienced range	**HI**	Highest wage paid	**M** Monthly	**MWR** Median wage range	**W** Weekly
ATC	Average total compensation	**D**	Daily	**HR**	High end range	**MCC** Median cash compensation	**S** See annotated source	**Y** Yearly

Occupation/Type/Industry	Location	Per	Low	Mid	High	Source	Date
Urban and Regional Planner	Birmingham-Hoover MSA, AL	Y	44260 FQ	53410 MW	63790 TQ	USBLS	5/07
	Alaska	Y	51420 FQ	60470 MW	72240 TQ	USBLS	5/07
	Anchorage MSA, AK	Y	53160 FQ	61880 MW	73140 TQ	USBLS	5/07
	Arizona	Y	43670 FQ	56060 MW	69380 TQ	USBLS	5/07
	Phoenix-Mesa-Scottsdale MSA, AZ	Y	45960 FQ	58570 MW	72320 TQ	USBLS	5/07
	Tucson MSA, AZ	Y	39800 FQ	50360 MW	61860 TQ	USBLS	5/07
	Arkansas	Y	38850 FQ	45390 MW	51950 TQ	USBLS	5/07
	California	H	26.53 FQ	32.78 MW	40.72 TQ	CABLS	1/08-3/08
	Los Angeles-Long Beach-Glendale PMSA, CA	H	25.70 FQ	31.25 MW	40.28 TQ	CABLS	1/08-3/08
	Oakland-Fremont-Hayward MSA, CA	H	31.37 FQ	37.04 MW	43.29 TQ	CABLS	1/08-3/08
	Riverside-San Bernardino-Ontario MSA, CA	H	25.01 FQ	31.65 MW	38.88 TQ	CABLS	1/08-3/08
	Sacramento-Arden Arcade-Roseville MSA, CA	H	27.20 FQ	32.82 MW	38.98 TQ	CABLS	1/08-3/08
	San Diego-Carlsbad-San Marcos MSA, CA	H	26.28 FQ	32.78 MW	39.59 TQ	CABLS	1/08-3/08
	San Francisco-San Mateo-Redwood PMSA, CA	H	36.10 FQ	43.13 MW	50.86 TQ	CABLS	1/08-3/08
	San Jose-Sunnyvale-Santa Clara MSA, CA	H	35.94 FQ	41.33 MW	49.13 TQ	CABLS	1/08-3/08
	Santa Ana-Anaheim-Irvine PMSA, CA	Y	46440 FQ	59980 MW	80860 TQ	USBLS	5/07
	Colorado	Y	51280 FQ	62880 MW	74980 TQ	USBLS	5/07
	Denver-Aurora MSA, CO	Y	54360 FQ	65660 MW	77300 TQ	USBLS	5/07
	Connecticut	H	23.38 AE	33.76 MW		CTBLS	1/08-3/08
	Bridgeport-Stamford-Norwalk MSA, CT	Y	56910 FQ	66080 MW	79920 TQ	USBLS	5/07
	Hartford-West Hartford-East Hartford MSA, CT	Y	57750 FQ	75070 MW	91580 TQ	USBLS	5/07
	Delaware	Y	48480 FQ	57790 MW	65590 TQ	USBLS	5/07
	Wilmington PMSA, DE-MD-NJ	Y	50850 FQ	57410 MW	63560 TQ	USBLS	5/07
	District of Columbia	Y	65820 FQ	83270 MW	101750 TQ	USBLS	5/07
	Washington-Arlington-Alexandria MSA, DC-VA-MD-WV	Y	53410 FQ	68000 MW	83020 TQ	USBLS	5/07
	Florida	Y	46110 FQ	56940 MW	71790 TQ	USBLS	5/07
	Fort Lauderdale-Pompano Beach-Deerfield Beach PMSA, FL	Y	52470 FQ	62230 MW	76230 TQ	USBLS	5/07
	Jacksonville MSA, FL	Y	44110 FQ	54270 MW	68020 TQ	USBLS	5/07
	Miami-Fort Lauderdale-Miami Beach MSA, FL	Y	52540 FQ	63370 MW	78400 TQ	USBLS	5/07
	Orlando-Kissimmee MSA, FL	Y	44510 FQ	52930 MW	66160 TQ	USBLS	5/07
	Sarasota-Bradenton-Venice MSA, FL	Y	43440 FQ	52960 MW	66980 TQ	USBLS	5/07
	Tampa-St. Petersburg-Clearwater MSA, FL	Y	48340 FQ	60610 MW	75540 TQ	USBLS	5/07
	West Palm Beach-Boca Raton-Boynton Beach PMSA, FL	Y	50590 FQ	61020 MW	75100 TQ	USBLS	5/07
	Georgia	Y	42680 FQ	52270 MW	63480 TQ	USBLS	5/07
	Atlanta-Sandy Springs-Marietta MSA, GA	Y	45510 FQ	54720 MW	65860 TQ	USBLS	5/07
	Hawaii	Y	50070 FQ	61410 MW	77100 TQ	USBLS	5/07
	Honolulu MSA, HI	Y	51330 FQ	62480 MW	79520 TQ	USBLS	5/07
	Idaho	Y	42120 FQ	52710 MW	62510 TQ	USBLS	5/07
	Boise City-Nampa MSA, ID	Y	46610 FQ	57150 MW	65880 TQ	USBLS	5/07
	Illinois	Y	48020 FQ	61260 MW	82350 TQ	USBLS	5/07
	Chicago-Naperville-Joliet MSA, IL-IN-WI	Y	48480 FQ	61680 MW	85480 TQ	USBLS	5/07
	Indiana	Y	36650 FQ	45060 MW	56460 TQ	USBLS	5/07
	Gary PMSA, IN	Y	37130 FQ	44200 MW	51910 TQ	USBLS	5/07
	Indianapolis-Carmel MSA, IN	Y	36290 FQ	44400 MW	53920 TQ	USBLS	5/07
	Iowa	Y	37070 FQ	51590 MW	62570 TQ	USBLS	5/07
	Des Moines-West Des Moines MSA, IA	Y	53040 FQ	59250 MW	70560 TQ	USBLS	5/07
	Kansas	Y	43700 FQ	51950 MW	65310 TQ	USBLS	5/07
	Kentucky	Y	35163 FQ	45276 MW	52379 TQ	KYBLS	2008

AE	Average entry wage	AW	Average wage paid	FQ	First quartile wage	LO	Lowest wage paid	MTC	Median total compensation	TCC	Total cash compensation
AER	Average entry range	AWR	Average wage range	H	Hourly	LR	Low end range	MW	Median wage paid	TQ	Third quartile wage
AEX	Average experienced wage	AXR	Average experienced range	HI	Highest wage paid	M	Monthly	MWR	Median wage range	W	Weekly
ATC	Average total compensation	D	Daily	HR	High end range	MCC	Median cash compensation	S	See annotated source	Y	Yearly

Occupation/Type/Industry	Location	Per	Low	Mid	High	Source	Date
Urban and Regional Planner	Louisville-Jefferson County MSA, KY-IN	Y	32610 FQ	43470 MW	52820 TQ	USBLS	5/07
	Louisiana	H	17.28 FQ	20.73 MW	26.90 TQ	LABLS	1/08-3/08
	New Orleans-Metairie-Kenner MSA, LA	Y	37230 FQ	44800 MW	58460 TQ	USBLS	5/07
	Maine	Y	44150 FQ	53830 MW	63590 TQ	USBLS	5/07
	Portland-South Portland-Biddeford MSA, ME	Y	48250 FQ	57820 MW	67020 TQ	USBLS	5/07
	Maryland	Y		60075 MW		MDBLS	3/08
	Baltimore-Towson MSA, MD	Y	48870 FQ	57700 MW	67040 TQ	USBLS	5/07
	Bethesda-Gaithersburg-Frederick PMSA, MD	Y	50410 FQ	66050 MW	76250 TQ	USBLS	5/07
	Massachusetts	Y	53550 FQ	67120 MW	79520 TQ	USBLS	5/07
	Boston-Cambridge-Quincy NECTA, MA	Y	55890 FQ	69920 MW	81710 TQ	USBLS	5/07
	Worcester MSA, MA-CT	Y	49100 FQ	59120 MW	72810 TQ	USBLS	5/07
	Michigan	Y	49800 FQ	58650 MW	70030 TQ	USBLS	5/07
	Detroit-Warren-Livonia MSA, MI	Y	50190 FQ	57840 MW	68220 TQ	USBLS	5/07
	Grand Rapids-Wyoming MSA, MI	Y	43870 FQ	58540 MW	78280 TQ	USBLS	5/07
	Warren-Troy-Farmington Hills PMSA, MI	Y	49420 FQ	58220 MW	67260 TQ	USBLS	5/07
	Minnesota	Y	52384 FQ	61863 MW	73371 TQ	MNBLS	10/08-12/08
	Duluth-Superior MSA, MN-WI	Y	49507 FQ	57333 MW	63401 TQ	MNBLS	10/08-12/08
	Minneapolis-Saint Paul MSA, MN-WI	Y	54843 FQ	64123 MW	77441 TQ	MNBLS	10/08-12/08
	Rochester MSA, MN	Y	51824 FQ	61277 MW	68670 TQ	MNBLS	10/08-12/08
	Mississippi	Y	32480 FQ	44270 MW	62670 TQ	USBLS	5/07
	Missouri	Y	43800 FQ	51890 MW	65600 TQ	USBLS	5/07
	Kansas City MSA, MO-KS	Y	44680 FQ	53470 MW	68160 TQ	USBLS	5/07
	St. Louis MSA, MO-IL	Y	44700 FQ	52240 MW	70900 TQ	USBLS	5/07
	Montana	Y	39150 FQ	45650 MW	51800 TQ	USBLS	5/07
	Nebraska	Y	45190 FQ	56580 MW	65670 TQ	USBLS	5/07
	Omaha-Council Bluffs MSA, NE-IA	Y	50730 FQ	59030 MW	65800 TQ	USBLS	5/07
	Nevada	H	27.54 FQ	34.79 MW	42.11 TQ	NVBLS	5/08
	Las Vegas-Paradise MSA, NV	H	29.42 FQ	36.01 MW	41.59 TQ	NVBLS	5/08
	Reno-Sparks MSA, NV	H	24.93 FQ	33.42 MW	46.67 TQ	NVBLS	5/08
	New Hampshire	H	19.21 AE	24.33 MW	28.08 AEX	NHBLS	6/08
	Manchester MSA, NH	Y	46090 FQ	55010 MW	63900 TQ	USBLS	5/07
	Nashua NECTA, NH-MA	Y	34850 FQ	40740 MW	52700 TQ	USBLS	5/07
	New Jersey	Y	53430 FQ	67070 MW	86070 TQ	USBLS	5/07
	Camden PMSA, NJ	Y	57290 FQ	74690 MW	95720 TQ	USBLS	5/07
	Edison PMSA, NJ	Y	51380 FQ	70030 MW	93150 TQ	USBLS	5/07
	Newark-Union PMSA, NJ-PA	Y	49320 FQ	57900 MW	75200 TQ	USBLS	5/07
	New Mexico	Y	41540 FQ	48500 MW	58820 TQ	USBLS	5/07
	Albuquerque MSA, NM	Y	43060 FQ	49430 MW	62800 TQ	USBLS	5/07
	New York	Y	48310 FQ	60750 MW	77930 TQ	USBLS	5/07
	Albany-Schenectady-Troy MSA, NY	Y	36030 FQ	45160 MW	59620 TQ	USBLS	5/07
	Buffalo-Niagara Falls MSA, NY	Y	45980 FQ	53630 MW	65710 TQ	USBLS	5/07
	Nassau-Suffolk PMSA, NY	Y	61420 FQ	72570 MW	87370 TQ	USBLS	5/07
	New York-Northern New Jersey-Long Island MSA, NY-NJ-PA	Y	53870 FQ	66450 MW	83970 TQ	USBLS	5/07
	North Carolina	Y	41840 FQ	49860 MW	62370 TQ	USBLS	5/07
	Asheville MSA, NC	Y	38860 FQ	46810 MW	55900 TQ	USBLS	5/07
	Charlotte-Gastonia-Concord MSA, NC-SC	Y	44530 FQ	55240 MW	69520 TQ	USBLS	5/07
	Raleigh-Cary MSA, NC	Y	41230 FQ	48740 MW	61310 TQ	USBLS	5/07
	North Dakota	Y	48330 FQ	53820 MW	59880 TQ	USBLS	5/07
	Fargo MSA, ND-MN	Y	49780 FQ	53920 MW	58320 TQ	USBLS	5/07
	Ohio	Y	44710 FQ	53640 MW	69370 TQ	USBLS	5/07
	Cincinnati-Middletown MSA, OH-KY-IN	Y	42770 FQ	62050 MW	73720 TQ	USBLS	5/07
	Cleveland-Elyria-Mentor MSA, OH	Y	45510 FQ	52580 MW	64870 TQ	USBLS	5/07
	Columbus MSA, OH	Y	44250 FQ	50780 MW	70970 TQ	USBLS	5/07
	Dayton MSA, OH	Y	41230 FQ	60680 MW	75700 TQ	USBLS	5/07
	Oklahoma	Y	46460 FQ	60940 MW	80390 TQ	USBLS	5/07

AE	Average entry wage	AW	Average wage paid	FQ	First quartile wage	LO	Lowest wage paid	MTC	Median total compensation	TCC	Total cash compensation
AER	Average entry range	AWR	Average wage range	H	Hourly	LR	Low end range	MW	Median wage paid	TQ	Third quartile wage
AEX	Average experienced wage	AXR	Average experienced range	HI	Highest wage paid	M	Monthly	MWR	Median wage range	W	Weekly
ATC	Average total compensation	D	Daily	HR	High end range	MCC	Median cash compensation	S	See annotated source	Y	Yearly

Occupation/Type/Industry	Location	Per	Low	Mid	High	Source	Date
Urban and Regional Planner	Oklahoma City MSA, OK	Y	56630 FQ	65270 MW	77570 TQ	USBLS	5/07
	Tulsa MSA, OK	Y	35350 FQ	41810 MW	52180 TQ	USBLS	5/07
	Oregon	H	23.98 FQ	29.55 MW	35.74 TQ	ORBLS	5/08
	Portland-Vancouver-Beaverton MSA, OR-WA	Y	51830 FQ	62910 MW	75400 TQ	USBLS	5/07
	Pennsylvania	Y	32870 FQ	44880 MW	56530 TQ	USBLS	5/07
	Allentown-Bethlehem-Easton MSA, PA-NJ	Y	35060 FQ	45090 MW	55900 TQ	USBLS	5/07
	Erie MSA, PA	Y	29940 FQ	39240 MW	44220 TQ	USBLS	5/07
	Philadelphia-Camden-Wilmington MSA, PA-NJ-DE-MD	Y	48570 FQ	59780 MW	74060 TQ	USBLS	5/07
	Pittsburgh MSA, PA	Y	42750 FQ	48120 MW	58200 TQ	USBLS	5/07
	Rhode Island	Y	56590 FQ	66350 MW	77590 TQ	USBLS	5/07
	Providence-Fall River-Warwick MSA, RI-MA	Y	55960 FQ	64780 MW	76570 TQ	USBLS	5/07
	South Carolina	Y	37540 FQ	45210 MW	54840 TQ	USBLS	5/07
	Charleston-North Charleston MSA, SC	Y	37970 FQ	45340 MW	55300 TQ	USBLS	5/07
	South Dakota	Y	30161 FQ	42573 MW	49056 TQ	SDBLS	7/08-9/08
	Tennessee	Y	38610 FQ	48940 MW	61250 TQ	USBLS	5/07
	Memphis MSA, TN-MS-AR	Y	47720 FQ	56910 MW	66900 TQ	USBLS	5/07
	Nashville-Davidson-Murfreesboro MSA, TN	Y	40670 FQ	49300 MW	60410 TQ	USBLS	5/07
	Texas	Y	41860 FQ	50790 MW	64690 TQ	USBLS	5/07
	Austin-Round Rock MSA, TX	Y	43690 FQ	50470 MW	64020 TQ	USBLS	5/07
	Dallas-Fort Worth-Arlington MSA, TX	Y	43040 FQ	54150 MW	69310 TQ	USBLS	5/07
	Houston-Sugar Land-Baytown MSA, TX	Y	46140 FQ	55020 MW	68370 TQ	USBLS	5/07
	San Antonio MSA, TX	Y	37600 FQ	45910 MW	56630 TQ	USBLS	5/07
	Utah	Y	44400 FQ	53900 MW	64830 TQ	USBLS	5/07
	Salt Lake City MSA, UT	Y	45860 FQ	54810 MW	64200 TQ	USBLS	5/07
	Vermont	Y	43430 FQ	50880 MW	63200 TQ	USBLS	5/07
	Burlington-South Burlington MSA, VT	Y	41320 FQ	52270 MW	58570 TQ	USBLS	5/07
	Virginia	Y	44050 FQ	56370 MW	71840 TQ	USBLS	5/07
	Richmond MSA, VA	Y	41840 FQ	53520 MW	64530 TQ	USBLS	5/07
	Virginia Beach-Norfolk-Newport News MSA, VA-NC	Y	41730 FQ	51310 MW	65780 TQ	USBLS	5/07
	Washington	H	26.47 FQ	31.24 MW	36.72 TQ	WABLS	3/08
	Seattle-Tacoma-Bellevue MSA, WA	Y	56550 FQ	67050 MW	77510 TQ	USBLS	5/07
	West Virginia	Y	39024 FQ	49447 MW	62849 TQ	WVBLS	7/08-9/08
	Wisconsin	Y	35390 FQ	49120 MW	66490 TQ	USBLS	5/07
	Milwaukee-Waukesha-West Allis MSA, WI	Y	45480 FQ	59070 MW	72820 TQ	USBLS	5/07
	Wyoming	Y	44486 FQ	52384 MW	64156 TQ	WYBLS	9/08
	Puerto Rico	Y	22980 FQ	30310 MW	46390 TQ	USBLS	5/07
	San Juan-Caguas-Guaynabo MSA, PR	Y	24060 FQ	32150 MW	50740 TQ	USBLS	5/07
Urban Conservator Municipal Government	Cincinnati, OH	Y	62598 LO		84507 HI	COHSS	10/08
Urban Design Planner Municipal Government	Seattle, WA	H	29.56 LO		34.48 HI	CSSS	2007
Urban Forester District Government	District of Columbia	Y	50510 LO		72199 HI	AFT02	3/1/08
Urban Forestry Specialist Municipal Government	Cincinnati, OH	Y	38076 LO		51171 HI	COHSS	10/08
Urban Planner	United States	Y		49880 AW		SUSA02	2008
Urologist	United States	Y	225000-275000 AE			UTIMES	2008
	Pennsylvania	Y		250000-300000 AW		UTIMES	2008
Usability Professional	United States	Y		94341 AW		UPA	2007

AE	Average entry wage	AW	Average wage paid	FQ	First quartile wage	LO	Lowest wage paid	MTC Median total compensation TCC Total cash compensation
AER	Average entry range	AWR	Average wage range	H	Hourly	LR	Low end range	MW Median wage paid TQ Third quartile wage
AEX	Average experienced wage	AXR	Average experienced range	HI	Highest wage paid	M	Monthly	MWR Median wage range W Weekly
ATC	Average total compensation	D	Daily	HR	High end range	MCC	Median cash compensation	S See annotated source Y Yearly

Occupation/Type/Industry	Location	Per	Low	Mid	High	Source	Date
Usability/User Experience Specialist	United States	Y		98800 MW		USNEWS02	2008
Usher, Lobby Attendant, and Ticket Taker							
	Alabama	Y	12310 FQ	13500 MW	14700 TQ	USBLS	5/07
	Birmingham-Hoover MSA, AL	Y	12430 FQ	13740 MW	15050 TQ	USBLS	5/07
	Alaska	Y	15770 FQ	16800 MW	20260 TQ	USBLS	5/07
	Anchorage MSA, AK	Y	15630 FQ	16930 MW	23140 TQ	USBLS	5/07
	Arizona	Y	14640 FQ	15370 MW	17860 TQ	USBLS	5/07
	Phoenix-Mesa-Scottsdale MSA, AZ	Y	14640 FQ	15370 MW	17930 TQ	USBLS	5/07
	Tucson MSA, AZ	Y	14570 FQ	15270 MW	16580 TQ	USBLS	5/07
	Arkansas	Y	14370 FQ	15600 MW	18350 TQ	USBLS	5/07
	Little Rock-North Little Rock MSA, AR	Y	15100 FQ	16850 MW	18560 TQ	USBLS	5/07
	California	H	8.08 FQ	8.96 MW	10.30 TQ	CABLS	1/08-3/08
	Los Angeles-Long Beach-Glendale PMSA, CA	H	8.10 FQ	8.91 MW	9.86 TQ	CABLS	1/08-3/08
	Oakland-Fremont-Hayward MSA, CA	H	8.22 FQ	10.05 MW	12.75 TQ	CABLS	1/08-3/08
	Riverside-San Bernardino-Ontario MSA, CA	H	8.00 FQ	8.54 MW	9.24 TQ	CABLS	1/08-3/08
	Sacramento-Arden Arcade-Roseville MSA, CA	H	8.02 FQ	8.73 MW	9.50 TQ	CABLS	1/08-3/08
	San Diego-Carlsbad-San Marcos MSA, CA	H	8.26 FQ	9.07 MW	10.30 TQ	CABLS	1/08-3/08
	San Francisco-San Mateo-Redwood PMSA, CA	H	8.82 FQ	10.36 MW	12.28 TQ	CABLS	1/08-3/08
	San Jose-Sunnyvale-Santa Clara MSA, CA	H	8.00 FQ	8.81 MW	9.80 TQ	CABLS	1/08-3/08
	Santa Ana-Anaheim-Irvine PMSA, CA	Y	16110 FQ	17540 MW	20130 TQ	USBLS	5/07
	Colorado	Y	14710 FQ	15270 MW	16120 TQ	USBLS	5/07
	Denver-Aurora MSA, CO	Y	14710 FQ	15270 MW	16110 TQ	USBLS	5/07
	Connecticut	H	7.92 AE	8.26 MW		CTBLS	1/08-3/08
	Bridgeport-Stamford-Norwalk MSA, CT	Y	16040 FQ	16470 MW	18780 TQ	USBLS	5/07
	Hartford-West Hartford-East Hartford MSA, CT	Y	16210 FQ	17080 MW	18630 TQ	USBLS	5/07
	Norwich-New London MSA, CT-RI	Y	15940 FQ	16570 MW	18170 TQ	USBLS	5/07
	Delaware	Y	15420 FQ	17180 MW	19230 TQ	USBLS	5/07
	Wilmington PMSA, DE-MD-NJ	Y	15740 FQ	17150 MW	18590 TQ	USBLS	5/07
	District of Columbia	Y	21620 FQ	23430 MW	25230 TQ	USBLS	5/07
	Washington-Arlington-Alexandria MSA, DC-VA-MD-WV	Y	14430 FQ	17090 MW	19870 TQ	USBLS	5/07
	Florida	Y	14690 FQ	15800 MW	18360 TQ	USBLS	5/07
	Fort Lauderdale-Pompano Beach-Deerfield Beach PMSA, FL	Y	14810 FQ	16920 MW	20160 TQ	USBLS	5/07
	Jacksonville MSA, FL	Y	14470 FQ	15360 MW	18080 TQ	USBLS	5/07
	Miami-Fort Lauderdale-Miami Beach MSA, FL	Y	14690 FQ	15770 MW	18010 TQ	USBLS	5/07
	Orlando-Kissimmee MSA, FL	Y	15330 FQ	17500 MW	20210 TQ	USBLS	5/07
	Tampa-St. Petersburg-Clearwater MSA, FL	Y	14610 FQ	15420 MW	17380 TQ	USBLS	5/07
	West Palm Beach-Boca Raton-Boynton Beach PMSA, FL	Y	14680 FQ	15520 MW	17920 TQ	USBLS	5/07
	Georgia	Y	13090 FQ	15050 MW	20000 TQ	USBLS	5/07
	Atlanta-Sandy Springs-Marietta MSA, GA	Y	13440 FQ	15850 MW	21330 TQ	USBLS	5/07
	Macon MSA, GA	Y	12260 FQ	13540 MW	14820 TQ	USBLS	5/07
	Hawaii	Y	15370 FQ	16010 MW	18370 TQ	USBLS	5/07
	Honolulu MSA, HI	Y	15330 FQ	15910 MW	17780 TQ	USBLS	5/07
	Idaho	Y	12940 FQ	14950 MW	17030 TQ	USBLS	5/07
	Boise City-Nampa MSA, ID	Y	13690 FQ	15700 MW	17470 TQ	USBLS	5/07
	Illinois	Y	14840 FQ	16120 MW	18540 TQ	USBLS	5/07
	Chicago-Naperville-Joliet MSA, IL-IN-WI	Y	14980 FQ	16600 MW	18980 TQ	USBLS	5/07

AE	Average entry wage	AW	Average wage paid	FQ	First quartile wage	LO	Lowest wage paid	MTC	Median total compensation	TCC	Total cash compensation
AER	Average entry range	AWR	Average wage range	H	Hourly	LR	Low end range	MW	Median wage paid	TQ	Third quartile wage
AEX	Average experienced wage	AXR	Average experienced range	HI	Highest wage paid	M	Monthly	MWR	Median wage range	W	Weekly
ATC	Average total compensation	D	Daily	HR	High end range	MCC	Median cash compensation	S	See annotated source	Y	Yearly

1648

Occupation/Type/Industry	Location	Per	Low	Mid	High	Source	Date
Usher, Lobby Attendant, and Ticket Taker	Peoria MSA, IL	Y	14510 FQ	14980 MW	15670 TQ	USBLS	5/07
	Indiana	Y	13330 FQ	15450 MW	17790 TQ	USBLS	5/07
	Gary PMSA, IN	Y	14450 FQ	18250 MW	21760 TQ	USBLS	5/07
	Indianapolis-Carmel MSA, IN	Y	13790 FQ	16040 MW	18080 TQ	USBLS	5/07
	South Bend-Mishawaka MSA, IN-MI	Y	12910 FQ	14670 MW	17080 TQ	USBLS	5/07
	Iowa	Y	13930 FQ	14970 MW	17940 TQ	USBLS	5/07
	Des Moines-West Des Moines MSA, IA	Y	14160 FQ	16340 MW	18400 TQ	USBLS	5/07
	Dubuque MSA, IA	Y	13670 FQ	14440 MW	15210 TQ	USBLS	5/07
	Kansas	Y	13210 FQ	15220 MW	17270 TQ	USBLS	5/07
	Wichita MSA, KS	Y	12930 FQ	14560 MW	16320 TQ	USBLS	5/07
	Kentucky	Y	13787 FQ	16039 MW	18835 TQ	KYBLS	2008
	Lexington-Fayette MSA, KY	Y	15430 FQ	17740 MW	19850 TQ	USBLS	5/07
	Louisville-Jefferson County MSA, KY-IN	Y	13220 FQ	15160 MW	17190 TQ	USBLS	5/07
	Louisiana	H	6.16 FQ	6.86 MW	7.96 TQ	LABLS	1/08-3/08
	Baton Rouge MSA, LA	Y	12800 FQ	14310 MW	16370 TQ	USBLS	5/07
	New Orleans-Metairie-Kenner MSA, LA	Y	13430 FQ	15780 MW	18390 TQ	USBLS	5/07
	Maine	Y	15400 FQ	16870 MW	18880 TQ	USBLS	5/07
	Portland-South Portland-Biddeford MSA, ME	Y	14720 FQ	15290 MW	16420 TQ	USBLS	5/07
	Maryland	Y		16875 MW		MDBLS	3/08
	Baltimore-Towson MSA, MD	Y	14180 FQ	15240 MW	18080 TQ	USBLS	5/07
	Bethesda-Gaithersburg-Frederick PMSA, MD	Y	14580 FQ	16570 MW	19520 TQ	USBLS	5/07
	Massachusetts	Y	16340 FQ	17950 MW	19610 TQ	USBLS	5/07
	Boston-Cambridge-Quincy NECTA, MA	Y	16400 FQ	17850 MW	19300 TQ	USBLS	5/07
	Worcester MSA, MA-CT	Y	16140 FQ	17720 MW	19570 TQ	USBLS	5/07
	Michigan	Y	15080 FQ	16370 MW	18580 TQ	USBLS	5/07
	Ann Arbor MSA, MI	Y	15940 FQ	17400 MW	18760 TQ	USBLS	5/07
	Detroit-Warren-Livonia MSA, MI	Y	15580 FQ	17150 MW	19020 TQ	USBLS	5/07
	Grand Rapids-Wyoming MSA, MI	Y	14870 FQ	15230 MW	18190 TQ	USBLS	5/07
	Warren-Troy-Farmington Hills PMSA, MI	Y	15460 FQ	16760 MW	18590 TQ	USBLS	5/07
	Minnesota	Y	14910 FQ	16300 MW	19636 TQ	MNBLS	10/08-12/08
	Minneapolis-Saint Paul MSA, MN-WI	Y	14962 FQ	16593 MW	19813 TQ	MNBLS	10/08-12/08
	Rochester MSA, MN	Y	14486 FQ	15194 MW	15998 TQ	MNBLS	10/08-12/08
	Mississippi	Y	13240 FQ	15360 MW	18620 TQ	USBLS	5/07
	Jackson MSA, MS	Y	12620 FQ	13950 MW	15430 TQ	USBLS	5/07
	Missouri	Y	15200 FQ	17740 MW	19990 TQ	USBLS	5/07
	Kansas City MSA, MO-KS	Y	14460 FQ	16320 MW	18490 TQ	USBLS	5/07
	St. Louis MSA, MO-IL	Y	15590 FQ	18230 MW	20240 TQ	USBLS	5/07
	Montana	Y	13680 FQ	14560 MW	15520 TQ	USBLS	5/07
	Billings MSA, MT	Y	13700 FQ	14600 MW	15510 TQ	USBLS	5/07
	Nebraska	Y	13730 FQ	16770 MW	20220 TQ	USBLS	5/07
	Las Vegas-Paradise MSA, NV	H	7.03 FQ	9.28 MW	12.67 TQ	NVBLS	5/08
	New Hampshire	H	6.57 AE	8.10 MW	10.01 AEX	NHBLS	6/08
	New Jersey	Y	15240 FQ	16060 MW	18710 TQ	USBLS	5/07
	Atlantic City MSA, NJ	Y	15220 FQ	15700 MW	19340 TQ	USBLS	5/07
	Camden PMSA, NJ	Y	15250 FQ	15710 MW	16260 TQ	USBLS	5/07
	Edison PMSA, NJ	Y	15440 FQ	16230 MW	18940 TQ	USBLS	5/07
	Newark-Union PMSA, NJ-PA	Y	15350 FQ	16360 MW	20790 TQ	USBLS	5/07
	New Mexico	Y	14720 FQ	16190 MW	17710 TQ	USBLS	5/07
	Albuquerque MSA, NM	Y	15160 FQ	16350 MW	17590 TQ	USBLS	5/07
	New York	Y	16780 FQ	20650 MW	27920 TQ	USBLS	5/07
	Albany-Schenectady-Troy MSA, NY	Y	15150 FQ	15600 MW	19500 TQ	USBLS	5/07
	Buffalo-Niagara Falls MSA, NY	Y	16020 FQ	19420 MW	24940 TQ	USBLS	5/07
	Nassau-Suffolk PMSA, NY	Y	16100 FQ	20710 MW	26150 TQ	USBLS	5/07
	New York-Northern New Jersey-Long Island MSA, NY-NJ-PA	Y	16910 FQ	21000 MW	29170 TQ	USBLS	5/07
	North Carolina	Y	13630 FQ	14470 MW	15470 TQ	USBLS	5/07

AE Average entry wage	**AW** Average wage paid	**FQ** First quartile wage	**LO** Lowest wage paid	**MTC** Median total compensation	**TCC** Total cash compensation
AER Average entry range	**AWR** Average wage range	**H** Hourly	**LR** Low end range	**MW** Median wage paid	**TQ** Third quartile wage
AEX Average experienced wage	**AXR** Average experienced range	**HI** Highest wage paid	**M** Monthly	**MWR** Median wage range	**W** Weekly
ATC Average total compensation	**D** Daily	**HR** High end range	**MCC** Median cash compensation	**S** See annotated source	**Y** Yearly

Occupation/Type/Industry	Location	Per	Low	Mid	High	Source	Date
Usher, Lobby Attendant, and Ticket Taker	Charlotte-Gastonia-Concord MSA, NC-SC	Y	13640 FQ	14500 MW	15580 TQ	USBLS	5/07
	North Dakota	Y	12990 FQ	14620 MW	17700 TQ	USBLS	5/07
	Fargo MSA, ND-MN	Y	13200 FQ	15030 MW	18290 TQ	USBLS	5/07
	Ohio	Y	14730 FQ	15510 MW	17930 TQ	USBLS	5/07
	Cincinnati-Middletown MSA, OH-KY-IN	Y	14650 FQ	15420 MW	16820 TQ	USBLS	5/07
	Cleveland-Elyria-Mentor MSA, OH	Y	14860 FQ	16240 MW	19510 TQ	USBLS	5/07
	Columbus MSA, OH	Y	14890 FQ	15720 MW	18250 TQ	USBLS	5/07
	Dayton MSA, OH	Y	14790 FQ	15580 MW	18220 TQ	USBLS	5/07
	Oklahoma	Y	12690 FQ	14280 MW	16230 TQ	USBLS	5/07
	Oklahoma City MSA, OK	Y	12570 FQ	14010 MW	15590 TQ	USBLS	5/07
	Tulsa MSA, OK	Y	12870 FQ	14840 MW	17310 TQ	USBLS	5/07
	Oregon	H	8.55 FQ	9.18 MW	10.27 TQ	ORBLS	5/08
	Portland-Vancouver-Beaverton MSA, OR-WA	Y	17450 FQ	18820 MW	21320 TQ	USBLS	5/07
	Pennsylvania	Y	14340 FQ	15220 MW	18710 TQ	USBLS	5/07
	Allentown-Bethlehem-Easton MSA, PA-NJ	Y	14280 FQ	15040 MW	15800 TQ	USBLS	5/07
	Philadelphia-Camden-Wilmington MSA, PA-NJ-DE-MD	Y	14470 FQ	15430 MW	19010 TQ	USBLS	5/07
	Pittsburgh MSA, PA	Y	14400 FQ	15700 MW	19120 TQ	USBLS	5/07
	Rhode Island	Y	15730 FQ	17180 MW	23370 TQ	USBLS	5/07
	Providence-Fall River-Warwick MSA, RI-MA	Y	15810 FQ	17370 MW	22200 TQ	USBLS	5/07
	South Carolina	Y	12660 FQ	14120 MW	15770 TQ	USBLS	5/07
	Charleston-North Charleston MSA, SC	Y	12820 FQ	14340 MW	16310 TQ	USBLS	5/07
	Columbia MSA, SC	Y	12510 FQ	13790 MW	15130 TQ	USBLS	5/07
	Myrtle Beach-Conway-North Myrtle Beach MSA, SC	Y	12880 FQ	14760 MW	16530 TQ	USBLS	5/07
	South Dakota	Y	14018 FQ	16550 MW	19008 TQ	SDBLS	7/08-9/08
	Sioux Falls MSA, SD	Y	14730 FQ	17512 MW	19485 TQ	SDBLS	7/08-9/08
	Tennessee	Y	12470 FQ	13820 MW	15200 TQ	USBLS	5/07
	Memphis MSA, TN-MS-AR	Y	13170 FQ	14540 MW	15920 TQ	USBLS	5/07
	Nashville-Davidson-Murfreesboro MSA, TN	Y	12750 FQ	14210 MW	15740 TQ	USBLS	5/07
	Texas	Y	12800 FQ	14360 MW	16690 TQ	USBLS	5/07
	Austin-Round Rock MSA, TX	Y	12650 FQ	14120 MW	15780 TQ	USBLS	5/07
	Corpus Christi MSA, TX	Y	12660 FQ	13910 MW	15220 TQ	USBLS	5/07
	Dallas-Fort Worth-Arlington MSA, TX	Y	13110 FQ	14960 MW	17960 TQ	USBLS	5/07
	Houston-Sugar Land-Baytown MSA, TX	Y	12590 FQ	13930 MW	15560 TQ	USBLS	5/07
	San Antonio MSA, TX	Y	13110 FQ	15200 MW	17390 TQ	USBLS	5/07
	Utah	Y	13560 FQ	16050 MW	18630 TQ	USBLS	5/07
	Salt Lake City MSA, UT	Y	13890 FQ	16630 MW	19020 TQ	USBLS	5/07
	Vermont	Y	16410 FQ	18390 MW	20570 TQ	USBLS	5/07
	Burlington-South Burlington MSA, VT	Y	16370 FQ	18170 MW	20130 TQ	USBLS	5/07
	Virginia	Y	12770 FQ	14330 MW	16270 TQ	USBLS	5/07
	Richmond MSA, VA	Y	12940 FQ	14750 MW	17390 TQ	USBLS	5/07
	Virginia Beach-Norfolk-Newport News MSA, VA-NC	Y	12600 FQ	13970 MW	15360 TQ	USBLS	5/07
	Washington	H	8.78 FQ	9.91 MW	11.40 TQ	WABLS	3/08
	Seattle-Tacoma-Bellevue MSA, WA	Y	18180 FQ	20850 MW	23600 TQ	USBLS	5/07
	Spokane MSA, WA	Y	18090 FQ	19700 MW	22830 TQ	USBLS	5/07
	West Virginia	Y	13864 FQ	14885 MW	15941 TQ	WVBLS	7/08-9/08
	Charleston MSA, WV	Y	13100 FQ	13870 MW	14640 TQ	USBLS	5/07
	Wisconsin	Y	14540 FQ	15410 MW	17800 TQ	USBLS	5/07
	Milwaukee-Waukesha-West Allis MSA, WI	Y	14810 FQ	16950 MW	20840 TQ	USBLS	5/07
	Wyoming	Y	12967 FQ	14069 MW	15173 TQ	WYBLS	9/08
	Puerto Rico	Y	12350 FQ	13540 MW	14740 TQ	USBLS	5/07
	San Juan-Caguas-Guaynabo MSA, PR	Y	12340 FQ	13540 MW	14740 TQ	USBLS	5/07

AE Average entry wage	**AW** Average wage paid	**FQ** First quartile wage	**LO** Lowest wage paid	**MTC** Median total compensation	**TCC** Total cash compensation
AER Average entry range	**AWR** Average wage range	**H** Hourly	**LR** Low end range	**MW** Median wage paid	**TQ** Third quartile wage
AEX Average experienced wage	**AXR** Average experienced range	**HI** Highest wage paid	**M** Monthly	**MWR** Median wage range	**W** Weekly
ATC Average total compensation	**D** Daily	**HR** High end range	**MCC** Median cash compensation	**S** See annotated source	**Y** Yearly

Occupation/Type/Industry	Location	Per	Low	Mid	High	Source	Date
Utility Attorney State Government	Ohio	H	26.28 LO		38.57 HI	ODAS	2008
Utility Director	Genoa Township, MI	Y			78500 HI	LCPP	2009
Utility Engineer Municipal Government Public Utilities Commission	Seaside, CA New Hampshire	S Y	2947 LO	63237 AW	3520 HI	SSSS NHUL03	8/08 2008
Valve Maintenance Worker Municipal Government	Carlsbad, CA	S	1730 LO		2103 HI	CCSS01	8/5/08
Varsity Basketball Coach Public High School	Baldwin County, AL	S	3371 LO		4494 HI	BCPSSS	2008-2009
Vascular Surgeon	Minnesota	Y		400000 AW		MMTHLY	2008
Vehicle Abatement Officer Municipal Government	Seaside, CA	S	1556 LO		1891 HI	SSSS	8/08
Vehicle Emission Technician Department of Environmental Quality	Oregon	M	2216 LO		3386 HI	ODEQSS	11/1/08
Venereal Disease Investigator Municipal Government	Cincinnati, OH	Y	34972 LO		36517 HI	COHSS	10/08
Veterans Affairs Director	Livingston County, MI	Y			60482 HI	LCPP	2009
Veterinarian	Alabama	Y	55510 FQ	68350 MW	89460 TQ	USBLS	5/07
	Birmingham-Hoover MSA, AL	Y	45300 FQ	63290 MW	78350 TQ	USBLS	5/07
	Mobile MSA, AL	Y	58410 FQ	66490 MW	89520 TQ	USBLS	5/07
	Montgomery MSA, AL	Y	71370 FQ	78440 MW	95820 TQ	USBLS	5/07
	Alaska	Y	68370 FQ	83550 MW	119360 TQ	USBLS	5/07
	Anchorage MSA, AK	Y	75700 FQ	100080 MW	131740 TQ	USBLS	5/07
	Arizona	Y	58460 FQ	75350 MW	92500 TQ	USBLS	5/07
	Phoenix-Mesa-Scottsdale MSA, AZ	Y	61290 FQ	74910 MW	91390 TQ	USBLS	5/07
	Prescott MSA, AZ	Y	28050 FQ	31150 MW	91890 TQ	USBLS	5/07
	Tucson MSA, AZ	Y	65130 FQ	84590 MW	97150 TQ	USBLS	5/07
	Arkansas	Y	51360 FQ	64510 MW	87250 TQ	USBLS	5/07
	Little Rock-North Little Rock MSA, AR	Y	46730 FQ	51770 MW	59380 TQ	USBLS	5/07
	California	H	34.81 FQ	45.05 MW	59.10 TQ	CABLS	1/08-3/08
	Los Angeles-Long Beach-Glendale PMSA, CA	H	37.18 FQ	49.67 MW	60.95 TQ	CABLS	1/08-3/08
	Oakland-Fremont-Hayward MSA, CA	H	40.18 FQ	48.75 MW		CABLS	1/08-3/08
	Riverside-San Bernardino-Ontario MSA, CA	H	32.07 FQ	39.72 MW	55.40 TQ	CABLS	1/08-3/08
	Sacramento-Arden Arcade-Roseville MSA, CA	H	33.01 FQ	44.96 MW	55.97 TQ	CABLS	1/08-3/08
	San Diego-Carlsbad-San Marcos MSA, CA	H	39.15 FQ	50.80 MW	63.31 TQ	CABLS	1/08-3/08
	San Francisco-San Mateo-Redwood PMSA, CA	H	38.09 FQ	45.47 MW	53.81 TQ	CABLS	1/08-3/08
	San Jose-Sunnyvale-Santa Clara MSA, CA	H	32.58 FQ	58.23 MW		CABLS	1/08-3/08
	Santa Ana-Anaheim-Irvine PMSA, CA	Y	82920 FQ	94590 MW	115330 TQ	USBLS	5/07
	Colorado	Y	49690 FQ	66730 MW	84940 TQ	USBLS	5/07
	Colorado Springs MSA, CO	Y	46840 FQ	65510 MW	78370 TQ	USBLS	5/07
	Denver-Aurora MSA, CO	Y	53810 FQ	68030 MW	85730 TQ	USBLS	5/07
	Connecticut	H	38.09 AE	47.06 MW		CTBLS	1/08-3/08
	Bridgeport-Stamford-Norwalk MSA, CT	Y	89210 FQ	106100 MW		USBLS	5/07
	Hartford-West Hartford-East Hartford MSA, CT	Y	83190 FQ	91390 MW	100850 TQ	USBLS	5/07
	Delaware	Y	73180 FQ	90520 MW	117530 TQ	USBLS	5/07
	Wilmington PMSA, DE-MD-NJ	Y	72700 FQ	89890 MW	105150 TQ	USBLS	5/07
	District of Columbia	Y	110930 FQ	127080 MW		USBLS	5/07

AE Average entry wage	**AW** Average wage paid	**FQ** First quartile wage	**LO** Lowest wage paid	**MTC** Median total compensation	**TCC** Total cash compensation
AER Average entry range	**AWR** Average wage range	**H** Hourly	**LR** Low end range	**MW** Median wage paid	**TQ** Third quartile wage
AEX Average experienced wage	**AXR** Average experienced range	**HI** Highest wage paid	**M** Monthly	**MWR** Median wage range	**W** Weekly
ATC Average total compensation	**D** Daily	**HR** High end range	**MCC** Median cash compensation	**S** See annotated source	**Y** Yearly

Veterinarian

Occupation/Type/Industry	Location	Per	Low	Mid	High	Source	Date
Veterinarian	Washington-Arlington-Alexandria MSA, DC-VA-MD-WV	Y	75660 FQ	96200 MW	126440 TQ	USBLS	5/07
	Florida	Y	57170 FQ	74560 MW	99520 TQ	USBLS	5/07
	Fort Lauderdale-Pompano Beach-Deerfield Beach PMSA, FL	Y	61010 FQ	72630 MW	90100 TQ	USBLS	5/07
	Jacksonville MSA, FL	Y	63770 FQ	78200 MW	126240 TQ	USBLS	5/07
	Miami-Fort Lauderdale-Miami Beach MSA, FL	Y	61380 FQ	80500 MW	109340 TQ	USBLS	5/07
	Orlando-Kissimmee MSA, FL	Y	37370 FQ	56570 MW	68620 TQ	USBLS	5/07
	Sarasota-Bradenton-Venice MSA, FL	Y	65410 FQ	98500 MW		USBLS	5/07
	Tampa-St. Petersburg-Clearwater MSA, FL	Y	63380 FQ	75060 MW	97320 TQ	USBLS	5/07
	West Palm Beach-Boca Raton-Boynton Beach PMSA, FL	Y	60140 FQ	81650 MW	99940 TQ	USBLS	5/07
	Georgia	Y	56210 FQ	72120 MW	86010 TQ	USBLS	5/07
	Atlanta-Sandy Springs-Marietta MSA, GA	Y	64110 FQ	74310 MW	86950 TQ	USBLS	5/07
	Hawaii	Y	69960 FQ	78200 MW	90160 TQ	USBLS	5/07
	Honolulu MSA, HI	Y	68740 FQ	75720 MW	84720 TQ	USBLS	5/07
	Idaho	Y	50250 FQ	64490 MW	82160 TQ	USBLS	5/07
	Boise City-Nampa MSA, ID	Y	63210 FQ	75580 MW	96080 TQ	USBLS	5/07
	Illinois	Y	55640 FQ	69290 MW	90520 TQ	USBLS	5/07
	Chicago-Naperville-Joliet MSA, IL-IN-WI	Y	57520 FQ	71310 MW	97710 TQ	USBLS	5/07
	Indiana	Y	56030 FQ	69870 MW	97890 TQ	USBLS	5/07
	Indianapolis-Carmel MSA, IN	Y	60470 FQ	80870 MW	114850 TQ	USBLS	5/07
	Iowa	Y	50210 FQ	60160 MW	74010 TQ	USBLS	5/07
	Des Moines-West Des Moines MSA, IA	Y	41810 FQ	54380 MW	61310 TQ	USBLS	5/07
	Sioux City MSA, IA-NE-SD	Y	58720 FQ	68560 MW	103110 TQ	USBLS	5/07
	Kansas	Y	52200 FQ	66150 MW	91220 TQ	USBLS	5/07
	Wichita MSA, KS	Y	58800 FQ	69280 MW	82170 TQ	USBLS	5/07
	Kentucky	Y	54100 FQ	74202 MW	99996 TQ	KYBLS	2008
	Louisville-Jefferson County MSA, KY-IN	Y	42120 FQ	66000 MW	90690 TQ	USBLS	5/07
	Louisiana	H	25.33 FQ	31.02 MW	38.53 TQ	LABLS	1/08-3/08
	Baton Rouge MSA, LA	Y	37930 FQ	50370 MW	73920 TQ	USBLS	5/07
	New Orleans-Metairie-Kenner MSA, LA	Y	56740 FQ	65580 MW	81300 TQ	USBLS	5/07
	Maine	Y	63350 FQ	74410 MW	92540 TQ	USBLS	5/07
	Portland-South Portland-Biddeford MSA, ME	Y	63190 FQ	75230 MW	97150 TQ	USBLS	5/07
	Maryland	Y		89550 MW		MDBLS	3/08
	Baltimore-Towson MSA, MD	Y	61070 FQ	84980 MW	115060 TQ	USBLS	5/07
	Bethesda-Gaithersburg-Frederick PMSA, MD	Y	74230 FQ	94360 MW	132600 TQ	USBLS	5/07
	Massachusetts	Y	52820 FQ	76500 MW	101540 TQ	USBLS	5/07
	Boston-Cambridge-Quincy NECTA, MA	Y	39340 FQ	74260 MW	101510 TQ	USBLS	5/07
	Lynn-Peabody-Salem NECTA, MA	Y	77640 FQ	106400 MW	127490 TQ	USBLS	5/07
	New Bedford MSA, MA	Y	63240 FQ	69750 MW	76260 TQ	USBLS	5/07
	Worcester MSA, MA-CT	Y	35810 FQ	61140 MW	90200 TQ	USBLS	5/07
	Michigan	Y	61860 FQ	73260 MW	91710 TQ	USBLS	5/07
	Ann Arbor MSA, MI	Y	66210 FQ	74080 MW	95990 TQ	USBLS	5/07
	Detroit-Warren-Livonia MSA, MI	Y	67990 FQ	79330 MW	104860 TQ	USBLS	5/07
	Grand Rapids-Wyoming MSA, MI	Y	55240 FQ	63440 MW	74740 TQ	USBLS	5/07
	Warren-Troy-Farmington Hills PMSA, MI	Y	67500 FQ	81390 MW	112100 TQ	USBLS	5/07
	Minnesota	Y	66916 FQ	77640 MW	93710 TQ	MNBLS	10/08-12/08
	Duluth-Superior MSA, MN-WI	Y	70107 FQ	79868 MW	108933 TQ	MNBLS	10/08-12/08
	Minneapolis-Saint Paul MSA, MN-WI	Y	67471 FQ	80046 MW	102781 TQ	MNBLS	10/08-12/08
	Rochester MSA, MN	Y	63669 FQ	73734 MW	85934 TQ	MNBLS	10/08-12/08
	Mississippi	Y	49000 FQ	64110 MW	90830 TQ	USBLS	5/07
	Jackson MSA, MS	Y	37280 FQ	45520 MW	62710 TQ	USBLS	5/07
	Missouri	Y	51060 FQ	66280 MW	84220 TQ	USBLS	5/07

AE   Average entry wage
AER   Average entry range
AEX   Average experienced wage
ATC   Average total compensation

AW   Average wage paid
AWR   Average wage range
AXR   Average experienced range
D   Daily

FQ   First quartile wage
H   Hourly
HI   Highest wage paid
HR   High end range

LO   Lowest wage paid
LR   Low end range
M   Monthly
MCC   Median cash compensation

MTC   Median total compensation
MW   Median wage paid
MWR   Median wage range
S   See annotated source

TCC   Total cash compensation
TQ   Third quartile wage
W   Weekly
Y   Yearly

1652

Occupation/Type/Industry	Location	Per	Low	Mid	High	Source	Date
Veterinarian	Jefferson City MSA, MO	Y	61210 FQ	75630 MW	88150 TQ	USBLS	5/07
	Kansas City MSA, MO-KS	Y	61760 FQ	85210 MW	107790 TQ	USBLS	5/07
	St. Louis MSA, MO-IL	Y	58960 FQ	70510 MW	81600 TQ	USBLS	5/07
	Montana	Y	39430 FQ	55080 MW	72140 TQ	USBLS	5/07
	Nebraska	Y	52140 FQ	61250 MW	73910 TQ	USBLS	5/07
	Omaha-Council Bluffs MSA, NE-IA	Y	31740 FQ	56550 MW	87390 TQ	USBLS	5/07
	Nevada	H	35.09 FQ	43.27 MW	58.56 TQ	NVBLS	5/08
	Las Vegas-Paradise MSA, NV	H	36.38 FQ	42.99 MW	50.05 TQ	NVBLS	5/08
	New Hampshire	H	26.56 AE	38.12 MW	46.44 AEX	NHBLS	6/08
	Nashua NECTA, NH-MA	Y	77350 FQ	101150 MW	119930 TQ	USBLS	5/07
	New Jersey	Y	74790 FQ	95580 MW	133710 TQ	USBLS	5/07
	Camden PMSA, NJ	Y	65980 FQ	76650 MW	91870 TQ	USBLS	5/07
	Edison PMSA, NJ	Y	76590 FQ	97560 MW	136380 TQ	USBLS	5/07
	Newark-Union PMSA, NJ-PA	Y	90960 FQ	116720 MW		USBLS	5/07
	New Mexico	Y	36390 FQ	52210 MW	74820 TQ	USBLS	5/07
	Albuquerque MSA, NM	Y	34710 FQ	37790 MW	61430 TQ	USBLS	5/07
	New York	Y	68320 FQ	88490 MW	123010 TQ	USBLS	5/07
	Buffalo-Niagara Falls MSA, NY	Y	62710 FQ	83050 MW	95270 TQ	USBLS	5/07
	Nassau-Suffolk PMSA, NY	Y	68080 FQ	85320 MW	127560 TQ	USBLS	5/07
	New York-Northern New Jersey-Long Island MSA, NY-NJ-PA	Y	77860 FQ	102120 MW	133900 TQ	USBLS	5/07
	North Carolina	Y	58610 FQ	77390 MW	96960 TQ	USBLS	5/07
	Charlotte-Gastonia-Concord MSA, NC-SC	Y	72190 FQ	85020 MW	102990 TQ	USBLS	5/07
	Raleigh-Cary MSA, NC	Y	62080 FQ	82250 MW	95800 TQ	USBLS	5/07
	North Dakota	Y	52540 FQ	60610 MW	70760 TQ	USBLS	5/07
	Fargo MSA, ND-MN	Y	57260 FQ	62240 MW	67860 TQ	USBLS	5/07
	Ohio	Y	60940 FQ	75870 MW	99670 TQ	USBLS	5/07
	Cincinnati-Middletown MSA, OH-KY-IN	Y	55370 FQ	72550 MW	96160 TQ	USBLS	5/07
	Cleveland-Elyria-Mentor MSA, OH	Y	68260 FQ	86800 MW	105190 TQ	USBLS	5/07
	Columbus MSA, OH	Y	66170 FQ	84840 MW		USBLS	5/07
	Dayton MSA, OH	Y	56030 FQ	62460 MW	72280 TQ	USBLS	5/07
	Oklahoma	Y	49680 FQ	64560 MW	76350 TQ	USBLS	5/07
	Oklahoma City MSA, OK	Y	50230 FQ	63330 MW	75100 TQ	USBLS	5/07
	Tulsa MSA, OK	Y	55240 FQ	67400 MW	85780 TQ	USBLS	5/07
	Oregon	H	29.13 FQ	36.20 MW	50.43 TQ	ORBLS	5/08
	Portland-Vancouver-Beaverton MSA, OR-WA	Y	65550 FQ	86460 MW	123110 TQ	USBLS	5/07
	Pennsylvania	Y	66280 FQ	86400 MW	115770 TQ	USBLS	5/07
	Allentown-Bethlehem-Easton MSA, PA-NJ	Y	56100 FQ	66970 MW	107980 TQ	USBLS	5/07
	Philadelphia-Camden-Wilmington MSA, PA-NJ-DE-MD	Y	68960 FQ	88590 MW	114170 TQ	USBLS	5/07
	Pittsburgh MSA, PA	Y	81490 FQ	101910 MW	124030 TQ	USBLS	5/07
	Rhode Island	Y	59850 FQ	77640 MW	96500 TQ	USBLS	5/07
	Providence-Fall River-Warwick MSA, RI-MA	Y	63660 FQ	78120 MW	97090 TQ	USBLS	5/07
	South Carolina	Y	51090 FQ	64480 MW	91630 TQ	USBLS	5/07
	Charleston-North Charleston MSA, SC	Y	47200 FQ	69750 MW	93760 TQ	USBLS	5/07
	Columbia MSA, SC	Y	38230 FQ	61460 MW	89990 TQ	USBLS	5/07
	South Dakota	Y	55259 FQ	63175 MW	76350 TQ	SDBLS	7/08-9/08
	Sioux Falls MSA, SD	Y	54406 FQ	59306 MW	65266 TQ	SDBLS	7/08-9/08
	Tennessee	Y	55050 FQ	69640 MW	85000 TQ	USBLS	5/07
	Memphis MSA, TN-MS-AR	Y	70780 FQ	89120 MW	108340 TQ	USBLS	5/07
	Nashville-Davidson-Murfreesboro MSA, TN	Y	30730 FQ	67940 MW	82760 TQ	USBLS	5/07
	Texas	Y	60740 FQ	74120 MW	94230 TQ	USBLS	5/07
	Austin-Round Rock MSA, TX	Y	63340 FQ	77260 MW	102960 TQ	USBLS	5/07
	Corpus Christi MSA, TX	Y	57070 FQ	73370 MW	84590 TQ	USBLS	5/07
	Dallas-Fort Worth-Arlington MSA, TX	Y	62180 FQ	77390 MW	95790 TQ	USBLS	5/07
	Houston-Sugar Land-Baytown MSA, TX	Y	61050 FQ	74640 MW	98540 TQ	USBLS	5/07
	San Antonio MSA, TX	Y	67870 FQ	77910 MW	95990 TQ	USBLS	5/07
	Utah	Y	52940 FQ	72410 MW	90740 TQ	USBLS	5/07

AE	Average entry wage	AW	Average wage paid	FQ	First quartile wage	LO	Lowest wage paid	MTC	Median total compensation	TCC	Total cash compensation
AER	Average entry range	AWR	Average wage range	H	Hourly	LR	Low end range	MW	Median wage paid	TQ	Third quartile wage
AEX	Average experienced wage	AXR	Average experienced range	HI	Highest wage paid	M	Monthly	MWR	Median wage range	W	Weekly
ATC	Average total compensation	D	Daily	HR	High end range	MCC	Median cash compensation	S	See annotated source	Y	Yearly

1653

Occupation/Type/Industry	Location	Per	Low	Mid	High	Source	Date
Veterinarian	Salt Lake City MSA, UT	Y	48230 FQ	71260 MW	91890 TQ	USBLS	5/07
	Vermont	Y	55690 FQ	72290 MW	88640 TQ	USBLS	5/07
	Burlington-South Burlington MSA, VT	Y	59830 FQ	77180 MW	88720 TQ	USBLS	5/07
	Virginia	Y	66500 FQ	81470 MW	101330 TQ	USBLS	5/07
	Lynchburg MSA, VA	Y	49590 FQ	58410 MW	67960 TQ	USBLS	5/07
	Richmond MSA, VA	Y	73020 FQ	86170 MW	100470 TQ	USBLS	5/07
	Roanoke MSA, VA	Y	61680 FQ	74460 MW	94420 TQ	USBLS	5/07
	Virginia Beach-Norfolk-Newport News MSA, VA-NC	Y	60280 FQ	72880 MW	88690 TQ	USBLS	5/07
	Washington	H	30.41 FQ	37.44 MW	45.46 MW	WABLS	3/08
	Seattle-Tacoma-Bellevue MSA, WA	Y	71510 FQ	85370 MW	99780 TQ	USBLS	5/07
	West Virginia	Y	57292 FQ	68089 MW	100101 TQ	WVBLS	7/08-9/08
	Charleston MSA, WV	Y	44720 FQ	57190 MW	64650 TQ	USBLS	5/07
	Wisconsin	Y	53320 FQ	67040 MW	81850 TQ	USBLS	5/07
	Appleton MSA, WI	Y	59370 FQ	76230 MW	103920 TQ	USBLS	5/07
	Green Bay MSA, WI	Y	42570 FQ	60810 MW	76520 TQ	USBLS	5/07
	Milwaukee-Waukesha-West Allis MSA, WI	Y	61960 FQ	77510 MW	97860 TQ	USBLS	5/07
	Wyoming	Y	37873 FQ	54139 MW	75494 TQ	WYBLS	9/08
	Puerto Rico	Y	40310 FQ	60210 MW	71000 TQ	USBLS	5/07
	San Juan-Caguas-Guaynabo MSA, PR	Y	38720 FQ	49420 MW	67120 TQ	USBLS	5/07
Employed in Spectator Sports	United States	Y		127090 AW		DVM	2008
Public Health	Ohio	H	24.90 LO		34.83 HI	ODAS	2008
Racing Commission	Ohio	H	19.70 LO		45.31 HI	ODAS	2008
Veterinary Assistant and Laboratory Animal Caretaker	Alabama	Y	14350 FQ	17270 MW	20420 TQ	USBLS	5/07
	Birmingham-Hoover MSA, AL	Y	17290 FQ	20030 MW	23120 TQ	USBLS	5/07
	Alaska	Y	21250 FQ	24610 MW	28660 TQ	USBLS	5/07
	Arizona	Y	16710 FQ	19470 MW	23790 TQ	USBLS	5/07
	Phoenix-Mesa-Scottsdale MSA, AZ	Y	17330 FQ	20580 MW	25510 TQ	USBLS	5/07
	Tucson MSA, AZ	Y	16260 FQ	19200 MW	22460 TQ	USBLS	5/07
	Arkansas	Y	15990 FQ	18700 MW	22080 TQ	USBLS	5/07
	Little Rock-North Little Rock MSA, AR	Y	17030 FQ	20110 MW	23040 TQ	USBLS	5/07
	California	H	9.37 FQ	11.29 MW	14.17 TQ	CABLS	1/08-3/08
	Los Angeles-Long Beach-Glendale PMSA, CA	H	9.01 FQ	10.69 MW	12.90 TQ	CABLS	1/08-3/08
	Oakland-Fremont-Hayward MSA, CA	H	8.48 FQ	11.31 MW	14.01 TQ	CABLS	1/08-3/08
	Riverside-San Bernardino-Ontario MSA, CA	H	10.73 FQ	13.09 MW	14.66 TQ	CABLS	1/08-3/08
	Sacramento-Arden Arcade-Roseville MSA, CA	H	9.39 FQ	11.19 MW	13.86 TQ	CABLS	1/08-3/08
	San Diego-Carlsbad-San Marcos MSA, CA	H	10.37 FQ	12.82 MW	17.73 TQ	CABLS	1/08-3/08
	San Francisco-San Mateo-Redwood PMSA, CA	H	10.61 FQ	12.52 MW	19.31 TQ	CABLS	1/08-3/08
	San Jose-Sunnyvale-Santa Clara MSA, CA	H	10.65 FQ	11.93 MW	15.60 TQ	CABLS	1/08-3/08
	Santa Ana-Anaheim-Irvine PMSA, CA	Y	17520 FQ	19270 MW	22610 TQ	USBLS	5/07
	Stockton MSA, CA	H	11.04 FQ	11.98 MW	13.06 TQ	CABLS	1/08-3/08
	Colorado	Y	17450 FQ	20660 MW	26140 TQ	USBLS	5/07
	Denver-Aurora MSA, CO	Y	18310 FQ	22080 MW	25920 TQ	USBLS	5/07
	Connecticut	H	9.15 AE	11.38 MW		CTBLS	1/08-3/08
	Bridgeport-Stamford-Norwalk MSA, CT	Y	21090 FQ	25720 MW	33280 TQ	USBLS	5/07
	Hartford-West Hartford-East Hartford MSA, CT	Y	18680 FQ	20950 MW	23730 TQ	USBLS	5/07
	Delaware	Y	20010 FQ	23740 MW	28070 TQ	USBLS	5/07
	Wilmington PMSA, DE-MD-NJ	Y	19830 FQ	24020 MW	27970 TQ	USBLS	5/07
	District of Columbia	Y	23080 FQ	27410 MW	33100 TQ	USBLS	5/07
	Washington-Arlington-Alexandria MSA, DC-VA-MD-WV	Y	20190 FQ	24070 MW	29470 TQ	USBLS	5/07
	Florida	Y	17070 FQ	19540 MW	23120 TQ	USBLS	5/07

AE	Average entry wage	AW	Average wage paid	FQ	First quartile wage	LO	Lowest wage paid	MTC	Median total compensation	TCC	Total cash compensation
AER	Average entry range	AWR	Average wage range	H	Hourly	LR	Low end range	MW	Median wage paid	TQ	Third quartile wage
AEX	Average experienced wage	AXR	Average experienced range	HI	Highest wage paid	M	Monthly	MWR	Median wage range	W	Weekly
ATC	Average total compensation	D	Daily	HR	High end range	MCC	Median cash compensation	S	See annotated source	Y	Yearly

1654

Occupation/Type/Industry	Location	Per	Low	Mid	High	Source	Date
Veterinary Assistant and Laboratory Animal Caretaker	Cape Coral-Fort Myers MSA, FL	Y	18220 FQ	22520 MW	27070 TQ	USBLS	5/07
	Fort Lauderdale-Pompano Beach-Deerfield Beach PMSA, FL	Y	17060 FQ	18450 MW	19940 TQ	USBLS	5/07
	Jacksonville MSA, FL	Y	18850 FQ	21200 MW	23710 TQ	USBLS	5/07
	Miami-Fort Lauderdale-Miami Beach MSA, FL	Y	17460 FQ	19170 MW	23740 TQ	USBLS	5/07
	Orlando-Kissimmee MSA, FL	Y	15540 FQ	18060 MW	21380 TQ	USBLS	5/07
	Tampa-St. Petersburg-Clearwater MSA, FL	Y	17690 FQ	20920 MW	23450 TQ	USBLS	5/07
	West Palm Beach-Boca Raton-Boynton Beach PMSA, FL	Y	18150 FQ	20570 MW	23530 TQ	USBLS	5/07
	Georgia	Y	15090 FQ	17560 MW	20610 TQ	USBLS	5/07
	Athens-Clarke County MSA, GA	Y	15070 FQ	17730 MW	20850 TQ	USBLS	5/07
	Atlanta-Sandy Springs-Marietta MSA, GA	Y	14880 FQ	17280 MW	19750 TQ	USBLS	5/07
	Hawaii	Y	17810 FQ	20460 MW	24220 TQ	USBLS	5/07
	Honolulu MSA, HI	Y	18350 FQ	20960 MW	24220 TQ	USBLS	5/07
	Idaho	Y	16880 FQ	19680 MW	22500 TQ	USBLS	5/07
	Boise City-Nampa MSA, ID	Y	18160 FQ	20500 MW	22850 TQ	USBLS	5/07
	Idaho Falls MSA, ID	Y	18200 FQ	21850 MW	23860 TQ	USBLS	5/07
	Illinois	Y	17490 FQ	20620 MW	25010 TQ	USBLS	5/07
	Chicago-Naperville-Joliet MSA, IL-IN-WI	Y	18390 FQ	22170 MW	26190 TQ	USBLS	5/07
	Indiana	Y	16620 FQ	20000 MW	23670 TQ	USBLS	5/07
	Gary PMSA, IN	Y	15220 FQ	17290 MW	20470 TQ	USBLS	5/07
	Indianapolis-Carmel MSA, IN	Y	18580 FQ	22270 MW	25610 TQ	USBLS	5/07
	Iowa	Y	15670 FQ	18200 MW	22360 TQ	USBLS	5/07
	Des Moines-West Des Moines MSA, IA	Y	16720 FQ	18300 MW	20180 TQ	USBLS	5/07
	Kansas	Y	14330 FQ	17490 MW	21310 TQ	USBLS	5/07
	Wichita MSA, KS	Y	13780 FQ	16820 MW	21420 TQ	USBLS	5/07
	Kentucky	Y	18494 FQ	21358 MW	24300 TQ	KYBLS	2008
	Lexington-Fayette MSA, KY	Y	18040 FQ	21010 MW	23850 TQ	USBLS	5/07
	Louisville-Jefferson County MSA, KY-IN	Y	18390 FQ	20800 MW	23460 TQ	USBLS	5/07
	Louisiana	H	7.60 FQ	9.74 MW	12.10 TQ	LABLS	1/08-3/08
	Baton Rouge MSA, LA	Y	16820 FQ	21310 MW	23960 TQ	USBLS	5/07
	New Orleans-Metairie-Kenner MSA, LA	Y	16680 FQ	20260 MW	27960 TQ	USBLS	5/07
	Maine	Y	20220 FQ	23720 MW	28830 TQ	USBLS	5/07
	Portland-South Portland-Biddeford MSA, ME	Y	21040 FQ	25780 MW	29410 TQ	USBLS	5/07
	Maryland	Y		23375 MW		MDBLS	3/08
	Baltimore-Towson MSA, MD	Y	17420 FQ	21530 MW	28180 TQ	USBLS	5/07
	Bethesda-Gaithersburg-Frederick PMSA, MD	Y	23650 FQ	29990 MW	43080 TQ	USBLS	5/07
	Massachusetts	Y	22160 FQ	27750 MW	35080 TQ	USBLS	5/07
	Boston-Cambridge-Quincy NECTA, MA	Y	25270 FQ	30550 MW	38790 TQ	USBLS	5/07
	Springfield MSA, MA-CT	Y	19700 FQ	23320 MW	27940 TQ	USBLS	5/07
	Worcester MSA, MA-CT	Y	22320 FQ	26950 MW	32980 TQ	USBLS	5/07
	Michigan	Y	18640 FQ	22120 MW	26970 TQ	USBLS	5/07
	Ann Arbor MSA, MI	Y	21810 FQ	30060 MW	34380 TQ	USBLS	5/07
	Detroit-Warren-Livonia MSA, MI	Y	18100 FQ	21550 MW	26460 TQ	USBLS	5/07
	Flint MSA, MI	Y	21080 FQ	22860 MW	24770 TQ	USBLS	5/07
	Grand Rapids-Wyoming MSA, MI	Y	18840 FQ	22010 MW	27410 TQ	USBLS	5/07
	Lansing-East Lansing MSA, MI	Y	18730 FQ	22230 MW	31560 TQ	USBLS	5/07
	Warren-Troy-Farmington Hills PMSA, MI	Y	18320 FQ	21610 MW	26010 TQ	USBLS	5/07
	Minnesota	Y	20117 FQ	24163 MW	29004 TQ	MNBLS	10/08-12/08
	Duluth-Superior MSA, MN-WI	Y	20869 FQ	25292 MW	30959 TQ	MNBLS	10/08-12/08
	Minneapolis-Saint Paul MSA, MN-WI	Y	20033 FQ	24142 MW	29171 TQ	MNBLS	10/08-12/08
	Rochester MSA, MN	Y	20344 FQ	23649 MW	27284 TQ	MNBLS	10/08-12/08
	Mississippi	Y	15760 FQ	18600 MW	22260 TQ	USBLS	5/07
	Jackson MSA, MS	Y	17520 FQ	19370 MW	22540 TQ	USBLS	5/07

AE	Average entry wage	AW	Average wage paid	FQ	First quartile wage	LO	Lowest wage paid	MTC	Median total compensation	TCC	Total cash compensation
AER	Average entry range	AWR	Average wage range	H	Hourly	LR	Low end range	MW	Median wage paid	TQ	Third quartile wage
AEX	Average experienced wage	AXR	Average experienced range	HI	Highest wage paid	M	Monthly	MWR	Median wage range	W	Weekly
ATC	Average total compensation	D	Daily	HR	High end range	MCC	Median cash compensation	S	See annotated source	Y	Yearly

Occupation/Type/Industry	Location	Per	Low	Mid	High	Source	Date
Veterinary Assistant and Laboratory Animal Caretaker	Missouri	Y	15900 FQ	18750 MW	22600 TQ	USBLS	5/07
	Kansas City MSA, MO-KS	Y	14880 FQ	18780 MW	23320 TQ	USBLS	5/07
	St. Louis MSA, MO-IL	Y	16000 FQ	18560 MW	22810 TQ	USBLS	5/07
	Montana	Y	16710 FQ	18240 MW	20150 TQ	USBLS	5/07
	Billings MSA, MT	Y	16860 FQ	18290 MW	19840 TQ	USBLS	5/07
	Missoula MSA, MT	Y	17210 FQ	18960 MW	23130 TQ	USBLS	5/07
	Nebraska	Y	14790 FQ	17400 MW	21780 TQ	USBLS	5/07
	Omaha-Council Bluffs MSA, NE-IA	Y	13470 FQ	15480 MW	21030 TQ	USBLS	5/07
	Nevada	H	8.19 FQ	9.86 MW	12.73 TQ	NVBLS	5/08
	Las Vegas-Paradise MSA, NV	H	8.86 FQ	11.14 MW	13.67 TQ	NVBLS	5/08
	New Hampshire	H	7.14 AE	9.97 MW	11.71 AEX	NHBLS	6/08
	Nashua NECTA, NH-MA	Y	15590 FQ	17220 MW	18780 TQ	USBLS	5/07
	Rochester-Dover MSA, NH-ME	Y	17280 FQ	20800 MW	25820 TQ	USBLS	5/07
	New Jersey	Y	17410 FQ	20240 MW	23380 TQ	USBLS	5/07
	Camden PMSA, NJ	Y	17960 FQ	20680 MW	22980 TQ	USBLS	5/07
	Edison PMSA, NJ	Y	18570 FQ	21250 MW	24980 TQ	USBLS	5/07
	Newark-Union PMSA, NJ-PA	Y	16290 FQ	19470 MW	22680 TQ	USBLS	5/07
	Trenton-Ewing MSA, NJ	Y	16810 FQ	18200 MW	19570 TQ	USBLS	5/07
	New Mexico	Y	16960 FQ	20380 MW	23830 TQ	USBLS	5/07
	Albuquerque MSA, NM	Y	19290 FQ	22000 MW	24710 TQ	USBLS	5/07
	Las Cruces MSA, NM	Y	12950 FQ	15020 MW	17150 TQ	USBLS	5/07
	Santa Fe MSA, NM	Y	21120 FQ	25330 MW	33590 TQ	USBLS	5/07
	New York	Y	18810 FQ	23390 MW	29950 TQ	USBLS	5/07
	Albany-Schenectady-Troy MSA, NY	Y	19290 FQ	26050 MW	29650 TQ	USBLS	5/07
	Buffalo-Niagara Falls MSA, NY	Y	17860 FQ	19560 MW	25490 TQ	USBLS	5/07
	Glens Falls MSA, NY	Y	19180 FQ	21540 MW	23900 TQ	USBLS	5/07
	Nassau-Suffolk PMSA, NY	Y	20060 FQ	24480 MW	29140 TQ	USBLS	5/07
	New York-Northern New Jersey-Long Island MSA, NY-NJ-PA	Y	18930 FQ	23320 MW	30640 TQ	USBLS	5/07
	North Carolina	Y	16460 FQ	19040 MW	23410 TQ	USBLS	5/07
	Charlotte-Gastonia-Concord MSA, NC-SC	Y	17660 FQ	20020 MW	24160 TQ	USBLS	5/07
	Greensboro-High Point MSA, NC	Y	16930 FQ	19540 MW	27490 TQ	USBLS	5/07
	Raleigh-Cary MSA, NC	Y	15820 FQ	18220 MW	21470 TQ	USBLS	5/07
	North Dakota	Y	16180 FQ	19020 MW	26250 TQ	USBLS	5/07
	Fargo MSA, ND-MN	Y	17710 FQ	22690 MW	33930 TQ	USBLS	5/07
	Ohio	Y	17910 FQ	21960 MW	25780 TQ	USBLS	5/07
	Cincinnati-Middletown MSA, OH-KY-IN	Y	18820 FQ	22620 MW	25690 TQ	USBLS	5/07
	Cleveland-Elyria-Mentor MSA, OH	Y	19770 FQ	23280 MW	27050 TQ	USBLS	5/07
	Columbus MSA, OH	Y	18060 FQ	22280 MW	26700 TQ	USBLS	5/07
	Dayton MSA, OH	Y	16400 FQ	21720 MW	28710 TQ	USBLS	5/07
	Oklahoma	Y	14460 FQ	18080 MW	22860 TQ	USBLS	5/07
	Oklahoma City MSA, OK	Y	16650 FQ	18720 MW	25170 TQ	USBLS	5/07
	Tulsa MSA, OK	Y	13360 FQ	16860 MW	22050 TQ	USBLS	5/07
	Oregon	H	9.63 FQ	11.10 MW	12.77 TQ	ORBLS	5/08
	Portland-Vancouver-Beaverton MSA, OR-WA	Y	20270 FQ	22820 MW	26410 TQ	USBLS	5/07
	Salem MSA, OR	Y	18590 FQ	21690 MW	25000 TQ	USBLS	5/07
	Pennsylvania	Y	18750 FQ	22900 MW	28880 TQ	USBLS	5/07
	Allentown-Bethlehem-Easton MSA, PA-NJ	Y	19280 FQ	21210 MW	23480 TQ	USBLS	5/07
	Philadelphia-Camden-Wilmington MSA, PA-NJ-DE-MD	Y	18370 FQ	22230 MW	27960 TQ	USBLS	5/07
	Pittsburgh MSA, PA	Y	20240 FQ	24490 MW	29610 TQ	USBLS	5/07
	Reading MSA, PA	Y	21940 FQ	23860 MW	25870 TQ	USBLS	5/07
	Rhode Island	Y	19530 FQ	23310 MW	27860 TQ	USBLS	5/07
	Providence-Fall River-Warwick MSA, RI-MA	Y	18770 FQ	22290 MW	25900 TQ	USBLS	5/07
	South Carolina	Y	17640 FQ	20940 MW	25890 TQ	USBLS	5/07
	Charleston-North Charleston MSA, SC	Y	16270 FQ	19510 MW	22930 TQ	USBLS	5/07
	Columbia MSA, SC	Y	13310 FQ	15770 MW	22680 TQ	USBLS	5/07

AE	Average entry wage	AW	Average wage paid	FQ	First quartile wage
AER	Average entry range	AWR	Average wage range	H	Hourly
AEX	Average experienced wage	AXR	Average experienced range	HI	Highest wage paid
ATC	Average total compensation	D	Daily	HR	High end range

LO	Lowest wage paid	MTC	Median total compensation	TCC	Total cash compensation
LR	Low end range	MW	Median wage paid	TQ	Third quartile wage
M	Monthly	MWR	Median wage range	W	Weekly
MCC	Median cash compensation	S	See annotated source	Y	Yearly

Occupation/Type/Industry	Location	Per	Low	Mid	High	Source	Date
Veterinary Assistant and Laboratory Animal Caretaker	South Dakota	Y	17208 FQ	19091 MW	21688 TQ	SDBLS	7/08-9/08
	Sioux Falls MSA, SD	Y	17630 FQ	19347 MW	21369 TQ	SDBLS	7/08-9/08
	Tennessee	Y	17030 FQ	19810 MW	23580 TQ	USBLS	5/07
	Memphis MSA, TN-MS-AR	Y	17890 FQ	19860 MW	24160 TQ	USBLS	5/07
	Nashville-Davidson-Murfreesboro MSA, TN	Y	16750 FQ	20130 MW	23100 TQ	USBLS	5/07
	Texas	Y	15810 FQ	19260 MW	23440 TQ	USBLS	5/07
	Austin-Round Rock MSA, TX	Y	17050 FQ	19270 MW	21590 TQ	USBLS	5/07
	Dallas-Fort Worth-Arlington MSA, TX	Y	16220 FQ	20640 MW	24580 TQ	USBLS	5/07
	Houston-Sugar Land-Baytown MSA, TX	Y	14740 FQ	20400 MW	24430 TQ	USBLS	5/07
	San Antonio MSA, TX	Y	16410 FQ	18590 MW	22130 TQ	USBLS	5/07
	Utah	Y	16820 FQ	19950 MW	24780 TQ	USBLS	5/07
	Salt Lake City MSA, UT	Y	16790 FQ	20470 MW	25470 TQ	USBLS	5/07
	Vermont	Y	17200 FQ	20240 MW	26240 TQ	USBLS	5/07
	Burlington-South Burlington MSA, VT	Y	17680 FQ	19720 MW	24020 TQ	USBLS	5/07
	Virginia	Y	17880 FQ	21120 MW	25030 TQ	USBLS	5/07
	Charlottesville MSA, VA	Y	17970 FQ	20830 MW	23130 TQ	USBLS	5/07
	Richmond MSA, VA	Y	16880 FQ	19270 MW	22440 TQ	USBLS	5/07
	Virginia Beach-Norfolk-Newport News MSA, VA-NC	Y	18140 FQ	21080 MW	25140 TQ	USBLS	5/07
	Washington	H	9.90 FQ	11.20 MW	12.80 TQ	WABLS	3/08
	Seattle-Tacoma-Bellevue MSA, WA	Y	21420 FQ	24280 MW	28270 TQ	USBLS	5/07
	West Virginia	Y	16409 FQ	19129 MW	22132 TQ	WVBLS	7/08-9/08
	Charleston MSA, WV	Y	15880 FQ	17630 MW	19280 TQ	USBLS	5/07
	Wisconsin	Y	18430 FQ	21210 MW	24060 TQ	USBLS	5/07
	Milwaukee-Waukesha-West Allis MSA, WI	Y	18880 FQ	20850 MW	23070 TQ	USBLS	5/07
	Wyoming	Y	15361 FQ	18603 MW	21575 TQ	WYBLS	9/08
	Puerto Rico	Y	12770 FQ	14490 MW	16080 TQ	USBLS	5/07
	San Juan-Caguas-Guaynabo MSA, PR	Y	12640 FQ	14230 MW	15680 TQ	USBLS	5/07
Veterinary Bacteriologist State Government	Ohio	H	37.28 LO		48.86 HI	ODAS	2008
Veterinary Pathologist Academia	Middle Atlantic	Y		80000-149999 MWR		ACVPSS	2006
Academia	North Central	Y		60000-129999 MWR		ACVPSS	2006
Academia	Northeast	Y		70000-169999 MWR		ACVPSS	2006
Academia	South	Y		90000-149999 MWR		ACVPSS	2006
Academia	West	Y		80000-159999 MWR		ACVPSS	2006
Industry	Middle Atlantic	Y		130000-179000 MWR		ACVPSS	2006
Industry	North Central	Y		120000-179000 MWR		ACVPSS	2006
Industry	Northeast	Y		130000-189000 MWR		ACVPSS	2006
Industry	South	Y		170000-179999 MWR		ACVPSS	2006
Industry	West	Y		120000-219999 MWR		ACVPSS	2006
Veterinary Technologist and Technician	Alabama	Y	19680 FQ	23790 MW	29430 TQ	USBLS	5/07
	Birmingham-Hoover MSA, AL	Y	19880 FQ	23120 MW	26040 TQ	USBLS	5/07
	Mobile MSA, AL	Y	17200 FQ	22980 MW	27600 TQ	USBLS	5/07
	Alaska	Y	27620 FQ	33980 MW	38300 TQ	USBLS	5/07
	Anchorage MSA, AK	Y	31150 FQ	35690 MW	39490 TQ	USBLS	5/07
	Arizona	Y	22620 FQ	26380 MW	30760 TQ	USBLS	5/07
	Phoenix-Mesa-Scottsdale MSA, AZ	Y	23140 FQ	27130 MW	31370 TQ	USBLS	5/07
	Tucson MSA, AZ	Y	22210 FQ	24950 MW	29720 TQ	USBLS	5/07

AE	Average entry wage	AW	Average wage paid	FQ	First quartile wage	LO	Lowest wage paid	MTC	Median total compensation	TCC	Total cash compensation
AER	Average entry range	AWR	Average wage range	H	Hourly	LR	Low end range	MW	Median wage paid	TQ	Third quartile wage
AEX	Average experienced wage	AXR	Average experienced range	HI	Highest wage paid	M	Monthly	MWR	Median wage range	W	Weekly
ATC	Average total compensation	D	Daily	HR	High end range	MCC	Median cash compensation	S	See annotated source	Y	Yearly

Occupation/Type/Industry	Location	Per	Low	Mid	High	Source	Date
Veterinary Technologist and Technician							
	Arkansas	Y	18950 FQ	22680 MW	26530 TQ	USBLS	5/07
	California	H	12.65 FQ	15.80 MW	19.34 TQ	CABLS	1/08-3/08
	Los Angeles-Long Beach-Glendale PMSA, CA	H	11.27 FQ	14.74 MW	18.71 TQ	CABLS	1/08-3/08
	Oakland-Fremont-Hayward MSA, CA	H	16.18 FQ	19.56 MW	23.07 TQ	CABLS	1/08-3/08
	Riverside-San Bernardino-Ontario MSA, CA	H	11.45 FQ	14.12 MW	16.88 TQ	CABLS	1/08-3/08
	Sacramento-Arden Arcade-Roseville MSA, CA	H	14.37 FQ	17.29 MW	20.68 TQ	CABLS	1/08-3/08
	San Diego-Carlsbad-San Marcos MSA, CA	H	13.78 FQ	17.82 MW	24.33 TQ	CABLS	1/08-3/08
	San Francisco-San Mateo-Redwood PMSA, CA	H	14.52 FQ	17.35 MW	20.08 TQ	CABLS	1/08-3/08
	San Jose-Sunnyvale-Santa Clara MSA, CA	H	15.59 FQ	18.52 MW	21.53 TQ	CABLS	1/08-3/08
	Santa Ana-Anaheim-Irvine PMSA, CA	Y	24530 FQ	30040 MW	36740 TQ	USBLS	5/07
	Stockton MSA, CA	H	13.78 FQ	14.70 MW	15.60 TQ	CABLS	1/08-3/08
	Colorado	Y	24410 FQ	28790 MW	33090 TQ	USBLS	5/07
	Boulder MSA, CO	Y	27430 FQ	32080 MW	36860 TQ	USBLS	5/07
	Denver-Aurora MSA, CO	Y	24370 FQ	28660 MW	32610 TQ	USBLS	5/07
	Connecticut	H	12.32 AE	16.99 MW		CTBLS	1/08-3/08
	Bridgeport-Stamford-Norwalk MSA, CT	Y	27520 FQ	36050 MW	44180 TQ	USBLS	5/07
	Hartford-West Hartford-East Hartford MSA, CT	Y	30650 FQ	37690 MW	43010 TQ	USBLS	5/07
	Delaware	Y	24520 FQ	31660 MW	37730 TQ	USBLS	5/07
	Wilmington PMSA, DE-MD-NJ	Y	25810 FQ	33080 MW	38050 TQ	USBLS	5/07
	District of Columbia	Y	24710 FQ	32260 MW	42960 TQ	USBLS	5/07
	Washington-Arlington-Alexandria MSA, DC-VA-MD-WV	Y	26270 FQ	33560 MW	39910 TQ	USBLS	5/07
	Florida	Y	20300 FQ	24100 MW	29410 TQ	USBLS	5/07
	Fort Lauderdale-Pompano Beach-Deerfield Beach PMSA, FL	Y	22210 FQ	25740 MW	29540 TQ	USBLS	5/07
	Jacksonville MSA, FL	Y	20300 FQ	22740 MW	26050 TQ	USBLS	5/07
	Miami-Fort Lauderdale-Miami Beach MSA, FL	Y	21190 FQ	25740 MW	30600 TQ	USBLS	5/07
	Orlando-Kissimmee MSA, FL	Y	20390 FQ	23670 MW	30150 TQ	USBLS	5/07
	Tampa-St. Petersburg-Clearwater MSA, FL	Y	19760 FQ	24030 MW	30060 TQ	USBLS	5/07
	West Palm Beach-Boca Raton-Boynton Beach PMSA, FL	Y	20930 FQ	25270 MW	30650 TQ	USBLS	5/07
	Georgia	Y	20120 FQ	25260 MW	30380 TQ	USBLS	5/07
	Atlanta-Sandy Springs-Marietta MSA, GA	Y	22490 FQ	27150 MW	31370 TQ	USBLS	5/07
	Hawaii	Y	22350 FQ	26960 MW	31150 TQ	USBLS	5/07
	Honolulu MSA, HI	Y	23230 FQ	27460 MW	31390 TQ	USBLS	5/07
	Idaho	Y	23220 FQ	26760 MW	30930 TQ	USBLS	5/07
	Boise City-Nampa MSA, ID	Y	24270 FQ	27460 MW	31010 TQ	USBLS	5/07
	Illinois	Y	26020 FQ	33170 MW	38400 TQ	USBLS	5/07
	Chicago-Naperville-Joliet MSA, IL-IN-WI	Y	28100 FQ	34980 MW	39340 TQ	USBLS	5/07
	Indiana	Y	22850 FQ	27680 MW	32600 TQ	USBLS	5/07
	Gary PMSA, IN	Y	20280 FQ	22860 MW	25370 TQ	USBLS	5/07
	Indianapolis-Carmel MSA, IN	Y	23740 FQ	28760 MW	33980 TQ	USBLS	5/07
	Iowa	Y	22760 FQ	27140 MW	33380 TQ	USBLS	5/07
	Davenport-Moline-Rock Island MSA, IA-IL	Y	22820 FQ	25590 MW	29400 TQ	USBLS	5/07
	Des Moines-West Des Moines MSA, IA	Y	22600 FQ	25450 MW	29240 TQ	USBLS	5/07
	Kansas	Y	22570 FQ	26670 MW	30870 TQ	USBLS	5/07
	Wichita MSA, KS	Y	20400 FQ	22860 MW	28400 TQ	USBLS	5/07
	Kentucky	Y	18494 FQ	22737 MW	26722 TQ	KYBLS	2008
	Louisville-Jefferson County MSA, KY-IN	Y	17200 FQ	22490 MW	27120 TQ	USBLS	5/07
	Louisiana	H	8.78 FQ	10.32 MW	12.40 TQ	LABLS	1/08-3/08
	Baton Rouge MSA, LA	Y	18830 FQ	22080 MW	26620 TQ	USBLS	5/07

AE Average entry wage	**AW** Average wage paid	**FQ** First quartile wage	**LO** Lowest wage paid	**MTC** Median total compensation	**TCC** Total cash compensation
AER Average entry range	**AWR** Average wage range	**H** Hourly	**LR** Low end range	**MW** Median wage paid	**TQ** Third quartile wage
AEX Average experienced wage	**AXR** Average experienced range	**HI** Highest wage paid	**M** Monthly	**MWR** Median wage range	**W** Weekly
ATC Average total compensation	**D** Daily	**HR** High end range	**MCC** Median cash compensation	**S** See annotated source	**Y** Yearly

Occupation/Type/Industry	Location	Per	Low	Mid	High	Source	Date
Veterinary Technologist and Technician	New Orleans-Metairie-Kenner MSA, LA	Y	17950 FQ	21580 MW	26640 TQ	USBLS	5/07
	Maine	Y	24330 FQ	28730 MW	33900 TQ	USBLS	5/07
	Portland-South Portland-Biddeford MSA, ME	Y	25630 FQ	30880 MW	36500 TQ	USBLS	5/07
	Maryland	Y		28350 MW		MDBLS	3/08
	Baltimore-Towson MSA, MD	Y	21920 FQ	27540 MW	32610 TQ	USBLS	5/07
	Bethesda-Gaithersburg-Frederick PMSA, MD	Y	25120 FQ	31860 MW	38790 TQ	USBLS	5/07
	Massachusetts	Y	27240 FQ	32110 MW	38110 TQ	USBLS	5/07
	Boston-Cambridge-Quincy NECTA, MA	Y	27880 FQ	33150 MW	39530 TQ	USBLS	5/07
	Worcester MSA, MA-CT	Y	29970 FQ	34410 MW	38680 TQ	USBLS	5/07
	Michigan	Y	27190 FQ	32910 MW	38870 TQ	USBLS	5/07
	Detroit-Warren-Livonia MSA, MI	Y	25630 FQ	32820 MW	38040 TQ	USBLS	5/07
	Grand Rapids-Wyoming MSA, MI	Y	24620 FQ	28890 MW	32610 TQ	USBLS	5/07
	Warren-Troy-Farmington Hills PMSA, MI	Y	23670 FQ	31960 MW	38270 TQ	USBLS	5/07
	Minnesota	Y	25716 FQ	30215 MW	35801 TQ	MNBLS	10/08-12/08
	Duluth-Superior MSA, MN-WI	Y	21102 FQ	24952 MW	30277 TQ	MNBLS	10/08-12/08
	Minneapolis-Saint Paul MSA, MN-WI	Y	26699 FQ	31250 MW	37318 TQ	MNBLS	10/08-12/08
	Rochester MSA, MN	Y	30426 FQ	35491 MW	41849 TQ	MNBLS	10/08-12/08
	Mississippi	Y	20790 FQ	25800 MW	32110 TQ	USBLS	5/07
	Gulfport-Biloxi MSA, MS	Y	20970 FQ	23020 MW	25260 TQ	USBLS	5/07
	Jackson MSA, MS	Y	24090 FQ	31220 MW	36880 TQ	USBLS	5/07
	Missouri	Y	18630 FQ	24610 MW	31290 TQ	USBLS	5/07
	Kansas City MSA, MO-KS	Y	22710 FQ	28090 MW	32250 TQ	USBLS	5/07
	St. Louis MSA, MO-IL	Y	22490 FQ	26940 MW	30890 TQ	USBLS	5/07
	Montana	Y	19210 FQ	23520 MW	27850 TQ	USBLS	5/07
	Billings MSA, MT	Y	17890 FQ	22730 MW	26550 TQ	USBLS	5/07
	Nebraska	Y	21190 FQ	24020 MW	29850 TQ	USBLS	5/07
	Omaha-Council Bluffs MSA, NE-IA	Y	23160 FQ	27810 MW	31440 TQ	USBLS	5/07
	Nevada	H	13.68 FQ	15.57 MW	18.89 TQ	NVBLS	5/08
	Las Vegas-Paradise MSA, NV	H	13.82 FQ	15.79 MW	19.50 TQ	NVBLS	5/08
	Reno-Sparks MSA, NV	H	13.30 FQ	14.70 MW	16.19 TQ	NVBLS	5/08
	New Hampshire	H	11.70 AE	14.87 MW	16.24 AEX	NHBLS	6/08
	Manchester MSA, NH	Y	27050 FQ	31160 MW	34570 TQ	USBLS	5/07
	Nashua NECTA, NH-MA	Y	26670 FQ	30490 MW	35140 TQ	USBLS	5/07
	New Jersey	Y	24940 FQ	29210 MW	35530 TQ	USBLS	5/07
	Camden PMSA, NJ	Y	25330 FQ	28630 MW	32170 TQ	USBLS	5/07
	Edison PMSA, NJ	Y	23390 FQ	30120 MW	38170 TQ	USBLS	5/07
	Newark-Union PMSA, NJ-PA	Y	26740 FQ	30290 MW	37410 TQ	USBLS	5/07
	New Mexico	Y	24830 FQ	30630 MW	36110 TQ	USBLS	5/07
	Albuquerque MSA, NM	Y	25800 FQ	31980 MW	36740 TQ	USBLS	5/07
	New York	Y	27040 FQ	31870 MW	37890 TQ	USBLS	5/07
	Albany-Schenectady-Troy MSA, NY	Y	24300 FQ	28810 MW	35050 TQ	USBLS	5/07
	Buffalo-Niagara Falls MSA, NY	Y	26410 FQ	29400 MW	33330 TQ	USBLS	5/07
	Ithaca MSA, NY	Y	26690 FQ	33230 MW	38040 TQ	USBLS	5/07
	Nassau-Suffolk PMSA, NY	Y	30960 FQ	35140 MW	39050 TQ	USBLS	5/07
	New York-Northern New Jersey-Long Island MSA, NY-NJ-PA	Y	26560 FQ	32200 MW	38560 TQ	USBLS	5/07
	North Carolina	Y	21670 FQ	25860 MW	30600 TQ	USBLS	5/07
	Charlotte-Gastonia-Concord MSA, NC-SC	Y	25510 FQ	29130 MW	33810 TQ	USBLS	5/07
	Raleigh-Cary MSA, NC	Y	19280 FQ	23880 MW	31140 TQ	USBLS	5/07
	North Dakota	Y	24050 FQ	27240 MW	30430 TQ	USBLS	5/07
	Fargo MSA, ND-MN	Y	25970 FQ	28200 MW	30430 TQ	USBLS	5/07
	Ohio	Y	24350 FQ	28420 MW	32240 TQ	USBLS	5/07
	Cincinnati-Middletown MSA, OH-KY-IN	Y	22970 FQ	27560 MW	31070 TQ	USBLS	5/07
	Cleveland-Elyria-Mentor MSA, OH	Y	26610 FQ	29680 MW	32950 TQ	USBLS	5/07
	Columbus MSA, OH	Y	26050 FQ	29110 MW	32330 TQ	USBLS	5/07
	Dayton MSA, OH	Y	22330 FQ	26580 MW	32090 TQ	USBLS	5/07

AE	Average entry wage	AW	Average wage paid	FQ	First quartile wage	LO	Lowest wage paid	MTC	Median total compensation	TCC	Total cash compensation
AER	Average entry range	AWR	Average wage range	H	Hourly	LR	Low end range	MW	Median wage paid	TQ	Third quartile wage
AEX	Average experienced wage	AXR	Average experienced range	HI	Highest wage paid	M	Monthly	MWR	Median wage range	W	Weekly
ATC	Average total compensation	D	Daily	HR	High end range	MCC	Median cash compensation	S	See annotated source	Y	Yearly

Occupation/Type/Industry	Location	Per	Low	Mid	High	Source	Date
Veterinary Technologist and Technician							
	Oklahoma	Y	18420 FQ	24040 MW	29670 TQ	USBLS	5/07
	Oklahoma City MSA, OK	Y	19860 FQ	25470 MW	29390 TQ	USBLS	5/07
	Tulsa MSA, OK	Y	15320 FQ	18780 MW	22550 TQ	USBLS	5/07
	Oregon	H	12.47 FQ	15.26 MW	17.83 TQ	ORBLS	5/08
	Portland-Vancouver-Beaverton MSA, OR-WA	Y	26430 FQ	32110 MW	37100 TQ	USBLS	5/07
	Pennsylvania	Y	23580 FQ	28390 MW	34460 TQ	USBLS	5/07
	Allentown-Bethlehem-Easton MSA, PA-NJ	Y	24740 FQ	28880 MW	33560 TQ	USBLS	5/07
	Philadelphia-Camden-Wilmington MSA, PA-NJ-DE-MD	Y	25720 FQ	30710 MW	36360 TQ	USBLS	5/07
	Pittsburgh MSA, PA	Y	24060 FQ	28750 MW	34090 TQ	USBLS	5/07
	Rhode Island	Y	26930 FQ	30720 MW	35460 TQ	USBLS	5/07
	Providence-Fall River-Warwick MSA, RI-MA	Y	26960 FQ	30480 MW	35180 TQ	USBLS	5/07
	South Carolina	Y	21160 FQ	27250 MW	32360 TQ	USBLS	5/07
	Charleston-North Charleston MSA, SC	Y	25010 FQ	28860 MW	33260 TQ	USBLS	5/07
	Columbia MSA, SC	Y	18760 FQ	22800 MW	27780 TQ	USBLS	5/07
	Spartanburg MSA, SC	Y	17400 FQ	19540 MW	23760 TQ	USBLS	5/07
	South Dakota	Y	22409 FQ	24423 MW	26980 TQ	SDBLS	7/08-9/08
	Sioux Falls MSA, SD	Y	22939 FQ	25907 MW	30339 TQ	SDBLS	7/08-9/08
	Tennessee	Y	19610 FQ	23240 MW	27350 TQ	USBLS	5/07
	Memphis MSA, TN-MS-AR	Y	19310 FQ	22300 MW	25430 TQ	USBLS	5/07
	Nashville-Davidson-Murfreesboro MSA, TN	Y	20990 FQ	24170 MW	28650 TQ	USBLS	5/07
	Texas	Y	19210 FQ	24150 MW	30130 TQ	USBLS	5/07
	Austin-Round Rock MSA, TX	Y	21760 FQ	26180 MW	30250 TQ	USBLS	5/07
	Brownsville-Harlingen MSA, TX	Y	13860 FQ	32380 MW	39970 TQ	USBLS	5/07
	Dallas-Fort Worth-Arlington MSA, TX	Y	21120 FQ	25930 MW	30910 TQ	USBLS	5/07
	El Paso MSA, TX	Y	19010 FQ	22720 MW	29440 TQ	USBLS	5/07
	Houston-Sugar Land-Baytown MSA, TX	Y	16950 FQ	22560 MW	31350 TQ	USBLS	5/07
	San Antonio MSA, TX	Y	19160 FQ	25350 MW	29440 TQ	USBLS	5/07
	Utah	Y	22150 FQ	26140 MW	29440 TQ	USBLS	5/07
	Salt Lake City MSA, UT	Y	24180 FQ	27140 MW	29720 TQ	USBLS	5/07
	Vermont	Y	24240 FQ	28170 MW	32140 TQ	USBLS	5/07
	Burlington-South Burlington MSA, VT	Y	24130 FQ	28540 MW	32780 TQ	USBLS	5/07
	Virginia	Y	24520 FQ	30280 MW	37530 TQ	USBLS	5/07
	Richmond MSA, VA	Y	23960 FQ	28580 MW	33810 TQ	USBLS	5/07
	Virginia Beach-Norfolk-Newport News MSA, VA-NC	Y	24680 FQ	29230 MW	36070 TQ	USBLS	5/07
	Washington	H	12.81 FQ	14.77 MW	17.13 TQ	WABLS	3/08
	Seattle-Tacoma-Bellevue MSA, WA	Y	28010 FQ	31900 MW	37020 TQ	USBLS	5/07
	West Virginia	Y	16048 FQ	19325 MW	23133 TQ	WVBLS	7/08-9/08
	Charleston MSA, WV	Y	15190 FQ	19960 MW	22440 TQ	USBLS	5/07
	Wisconsin	Y	24980 FQ	29580 MW	36510 TQ	USBLS	5/07
	Milwaukee-Waukesha-West Allis MSA, WI	Y	22890 FQ	26290 MW	29780 TQ	USBLS	5/07
	Wyoming	Y	26081 FQ	31146 MW	37600 TQ	WYBLS	9/08
	Puerto Rico	Y	17850 FQ	23660 MW	40560 TQ	USBLS	5/07
	San Juan-Caguas-Guaynabo MSA, PR	Y	17750 FQ	22590 MW	31100 TQ	USBLS	5/07
Veterinary Toxicologist Department of Agriculture	Ohio	Y	66144 LO		97406 HI	OHCS	5/08
Veterinary Virologist State Government	Ohio	H	37.28 LO		48.86 HI	ODAS	2008
Vice President of Legal Services for Corporate Compliance State Lottery	Tennessee	Y			102336 HI	THETN	2008

AE	Average entry wage	**AW**	Average wage paid	**FQ**	First quartile wage	**LO**	Lowest wage paid	**MTC**	Median total compensation	**TCC**	Total cash compensation
AER	Average entry range	**AWR**	Average wage range	**H**	Hourly	**LR**	Low end range	**MW**	Median wage paid	**TQ**	Third quartile wage
AEX	Average experienced wage	**AXR**	Average experienced range	**HI**	Highest wage paid	**M**	Monthly	**MWR**	Median wage range	**W**	Weekly
ATC	Average total compensation	**D**	Daily	**HR**	High end range	**MCC**	Median cash compensation	**S**	See annotated source	**Y**	Yearly

Occupation/Type/Industry	Location	Per	Low	Mid	High	Source	Date
Vice President of Loss Prevention Food Retailing	United States	Y		125000- 210000 AWR		SMNEWS	2008
Vice President of Public Safety Wayne County Airport Authority	Wayne County, MI	Y			150094 HI	FREEP06	2006
Vice President of Risk Management Food Retailing	United States	Y		125000- 195000 AWR		SMNEWS	2008
Vice President of Sales and Marketing Printing Industry	United States	Y		87550 AW		GRAM	2006
Vice President of the United States	United States	Y			227300 HI	NYT08	2009
Victim Advocate Municipal Government	Seattle, WA	H	23.28 LO		27.09 HI	CSSS	2008
Victim/Witness Specialist Department of Justice	New Hampshire	Y		64573 AW		NHUL03	2008
Video Game Developer	United States Maryland	Y Y		73000 MW 75000 AW		MSN02 WTGMD	2009 2009
Video Game Player Professional	United States	Y			90000 HI	CSM02	2008
Video Game Programmer	United States	Y		83383 AW		GAMS	2007
Video Game Tester	United States	Y		39063 AW		GAMS	2007
Video Production Specialist Municipal Government	Cincinnati, OH	Y	36485 LO		49033 HI	COHSS	10/08
Video Specialist Municipal Government	Colorado Springs, CO	M	2935 LO			COSPRS	1/1/09
Videographer State Government	Ohio	H	21.77 LO		31.86 HI	ODAS	2008
Village Clerk	Milford Village, MI	Y	43000 LO		48000 HI	SPO02	2009
Village Manager	Fowlerville, MI	Y			72450 HI	LCPP	2009
Village President	Fowlerville, MI Pinckney, MI	Y Y			6277 HI 20000 HI	LCPP LCPP	2009 2009
Virtual Assistant	United States	H	30.00 LO			YVR01	2009
Visitor Assistance Coordinator Municipal Government	Seattle, WA	H	21.18 LO		24.63 HI	CSSS	2008
Visual Display Designer Apparel Industry	United States	Y		38000 MW		247FASH	2009
Visual Merchandiser Apparel Industry	United States	Y		58100 MW		247FASH	2009
Vital Statistics Coordinator Municipal Government	Cincinnati, OH	Y	52236 LO		71929 HI	COHSS	10/08
Vocational Education Teacher Middle School Middle School Middle School Middle School Middle School Middle School	Alabama Alaska Arizona Phoenix-Mesa-Scottsdale MSA, AZ Tucson MSA, AZ Arkansas	Y Y Y Y Y Y	37580 FQ 44780 FQ 30550 FQ 30970 FQ 31840 FQ 37950 FQ	42790 MW 51680 MW 34730 MW 36620 MW 34790 MW 43770 MW	48390 TQ 61050 TQ 40030 TQ 41570 TQ 38490 TQ 50510 TQ	USBLS USBLS USBLS USBLS USBLS USBLS	5/07 5/07 5/07 5/07 5/07 5/07

AE Average entry wage	**AW** Average wage paid	**FQ** First quartile wage	**LO** Lowest wage paid	**MTC** Median total compensation	**TCC** Total cash compensation
AER Average entry range	**AWR** Average wage range	**H** Hourly	**LR** Low end range	**MW** Median wage paid	**TQ** Third quartile wage
AEX Average experienced wage	**AXR** Average experienced range	**HI** Highest wage paid	**M** Monthly	**MWR** Median wage range	**W** Weekly
ATC Average total compensation	**D** Daily	**HR** High end range	**MCC** Median cash compensation	**S** See annotated source	**Y** Yearly

Vocational Education Teacher

Occupation/Type/Industry	Location	Per	Low	Mid	High	Source	Date
Middle School	Little Rock-North Little Rock MSA, AR	Y	40140 FQ	52110 MW	58780 TQ	USBLS	5/07
Middle School	California	Y		56401 AW		CABLS	1/08-3/08
Middle School	Los Angeles-Long Beach-Glendale PMSA, CA	Y*		58278 AW		CABLS	1/08-3/08
Middle School	Oakland-Fremont-Hayward MSA, CA	Y		48648 AW		CABLS	1/08-3/08
Middle School	Riverside-San Bernardino-Ontario MSA, CA	Y		48125 AW		CABLS	1/08-3/08
Middle School	Sacramento-Arden Arcade-Roseville MSA, CA	Y		52279 MW		CABLS	1/08-3/08
Middle School	Santa Ana-Anaheim-Irvine PMSA, CA	Y	56220 FQ	66420 MW	82260 TQ	USBLS	5/07
Middle School	Colorado	Y	33300 FQ	41680 MW	58270 TQ	USBLS	5/07
Middle School	Bridgeport-Stamford-Norwalk MSA, CT	Y	50350 FQ	66990 MW	76770 TQ	USBLS	5/07
Middle School	Hartford-West Hartford-East Hartford MSA, CT	Y	52260 FQ	71100 MW	80070 TQ	USBLS	5/07
Middle School	New Haven MSA, CT	Y	43500 FQ	56190 MW	68260 TQ	USBLS	5/07
Middle School	Washington-Arlington-Alexandria MSA, DC-VA-MD-WV	Y	44400 FQ	58030 MW	82270 TQ	USBLS	5/07
Middle School	Florida	Y	44180 FQ	54350 MW	69230 TQ	USBLS	5/07
Middle School	Miami-Fort Lauderdale-Miami Beach MSA, FL	Y	48380 FQ	61780 MW	77060 TQ	USBLS	5/07
Middle School	Orlando-Kissimmee MSA, FL	Y	43110 FQ	53460 MW	60540 TQ	USBLS	5/07
Middle School	Tampa-St. Petersburg-Clearwater MSA, FL	Y	45520 FQ	51910 MW	66590 TQ	USBLS	5/07
Middle School	Georgia	Y	43530 FQ	53600 MW	61210 TQ	USBLS	5/07
Middle School	Atlanta-Sandy Springs-Marietta MSA, GA	Y	43030 FQ	56090 MW	64720 TQ	USBLS	5/07
Middle School	Hawaii	Y	33980 FQ	40040 MW	48540 TQ	USBLS	5/07
Middle School	Honolulu MSA, HI	Y	33600 FQ	39290 MW	48400 TQ	USBLS	5/07
Middle School	Illinois	Y	34300 FQ	44430 MW	58830 TQ	USBLS	5/07
Middle School	Chicago-Naperville-Joliet MSA, IL-IN-WI	Y	36700 FQ	49370 MW	60570 TQ	USBLS	5/07
Middle School	Indiana	Y	44160 FQ	53880 MW	61060 TQ	USBLS	5/07
Middle School	Gary PMSA, IN	Y	38700 FQ	48200 MW	58430 TQ	USBLS	5/07
Middle School	Iowa	Y	31090 FQ	39710 MW	49530 TQ	USBLS	5/07
Middle School	Kansas	Y	36250 FQ	41410 MW	46490 TQ	USBLS	5/07
Middle School	Wichita MSA, KS	Y	33870 FQ	38120 MW	44990 TQ	USBLS	5/07
Middle School	Kentucky	Y	37504 FQ	46384 MW	60662 TQ	KYBLS	2008
Middle School	Louisiana	Y		41800 AW		LABLS	1/08-3/08
Middle School	Baton Rouge MSA, LA	Y	38100 FQ	42750 MW	48010 TQ	USBLS	5/07
Middle School	New Orleans-Metairie-Kenner MSA, LA	Y	40700 FQ	45750 MW	50400 TQ	USBLS	5/07
Middle School	Maine	Y	43250 FQ	49510 MW	57330 TQ	USBLS	5/07
Middle School	Maryland	Y		54825 MW		MDBLS	3/08
Middle School	Baltimore-Towson MSA, MD	Y	44440 FQ	60020 MW	77740 TQ	USBLS	5/07
Middle School	Bethesda-Gaithersburg-Frederick PMSA, MD	Y	18710 FQ	54690 MW	75110 TQ	USBLS	5/07
Middle School	Massachusetts	Y	52460 FQ	60750 MW	67780 TQ	USBLS	5/07
Middle School	Boston-Cambridge-Quincy NECTA, MA	Y	43620 FQ	55130 MW	69680 TQ	USBLS	5/07
Middle School	Michigan	Y	36180 FQ	39620 MW	48170 TQ	USBLS	5/07
Middle School	Detroit-Warren-Livonia MSA, MI	Y	43130 FQ	50020 MW	69230 TQ	USBLS	5/07
Middle School	Warren-Troy-Farmington Hills PMSA, MI	Y	43780 FQ	55540 MW	71670 TQ	USBLS	5/07
Middle School	Minnesota	Y	42131 FQ	53221 MW	60660 TQ	MNBLS	10/08-12/08
Middle School	Minneapolis-Saint Paul MSA, MN-WI	Y	40666 FQ	49057 MW	60210 TQ	MNBLS	10/08-12/08
Middle School	Mississippi	Y	35320 FQ	41210 MW	50260 TQ	USBLS	5/07
Middle School	Missouri	Y	36480 FQ	44130 MW	54180 TQ	USBLS	5/07
Middle School	Kansas City MSA, MO-KS	Y	39040 FQ	48860 MW	59280 TQ	USBLS	5/07
Middle School	St. Louis MSA, MO-IL	Y	40100 FQ	51890 MW	58990 TQ	USBLS	5/07
Middle School	Montana	Y	23060 FQ	30610 MW	39380 TQ	USBLS	5/07
Middle School	Nebraska	Y	39790 FQ	47390 MW	56990 TQ	USBLS	5/07
Middle School	Nevada	Y	44196 FQ	54108 MW	59736 TQ	NVBLS	5/08
Middle School	New Hampshire	Y	35815 AE	49502 MW	55711 AEX	NHBLS	6/08
Middle School	New Jersey	Y	48040 FQ	60780 MW	72690 TQ	USBLS	5/07

AE	Average entry wage	AW	Average wage paid	FQ	First quartile wage	LO	Lowest wage paid	MTC	Median total compensation	TCC	Total cash compensation
AER	Average entry range	AWR	Average wage range	H	Hourly	LR	Low end range	MW	Median wage paid	TQ	Third quartile wage
AEX	Average experienced wage	AXR	Average experienced range	HI	Highest wage paid	M	Monthly	MWR	Median wage range	W	Weekly
ATC	Average total compensation	D	Daily	HR	High end range	MCC	Median cash compensation	S	See annotated source	Y	Yearly

Occupation/Type/Industry	Location	Per	Low	Mid	High	Source	Date
Vocational Education Teacher							
Middle School	New Mexico	Y	34910 FQ	45160 MW	61020 TQ	USBLS	5/07
Middle School	New York	Y	41900 FQ	51460 MW	66250 TQ	USBLS	5/07
Middle School	Albany-Schenectady-Troy MSA, NY	Y	39720 FQ	45920 MW	56370 TQ	USBLS	5/07
Middle School	Buffalo-Niagara Falls MSA, NY	Y	40660 FQ	50270 MW	63690 TQ	USBLS	5/07
Middle School	Nassau-Suffolk PMSA, NY	Y	50360 FQ	61580 MW	81890 TQ	USBLS	5/07
Middle School	New York-Northern New Jersey-Long Island MSA, NY-NJ-PA	Y	48560 FQ	62860 MW	80400 TQ	USBLS	5/07
Middle School	North Carolina	Y	33670 FQ	42360 MW	50610 TQ	USBLS	5/07
Middle School	Charlotte-Gastonia-Concord MSA, NC-SC	Y	38960 FQ	48030 MW	57710 TQ	USBLS	5/07
Middle School	Greensboro-High Point MSA, NC	Y	29760 FQ	36820 MW	46600 TQ	USBLS	5/07
Middle School	Raleigh-Cary MSA, NC	Y	43320 FQ	52530 MW	61580 TQ	USBLS	5/07
Middle School	Ohio	Y	46940 FQ	57660 MW	68070 TQ	USBLS	5/07
Middle School	Cleveland-Elyria-Mentor MSA, OH	Y	55780 FQ	61790 MW	73220 TQ	USBLS	5/07
Middle School	Columbus MSA, OH	Y	46330 FQ	61840 MW	72740 TQ	USBLS	5/07
Middle School	Dayton MSA, OH	Y	30820 FQ	37450 MW	47500 TQ	USBLS	5/07
Middle School	Oklahoma	Y	35840 FQ	41700 MW	47440 TQ	USBLS	5/07
Middle School	Oklahoma City MSA, OK	Y	31850 FQ	35640 MW	40140 TQ	USBLS	5/07
Middle School	Oregon	Y	42729 FQ	48964 MW	57807 TQ	ORBLS	5/08
Middle School	Portland-Vancouver-Beaverton MSA, OR-WA	Y	39650 FQ	46990 MW	58830 TQ	USBLS	5/07
Middle School	Pennsylvania	Y	42940 FQ	53870 MW	65650 TQ	USBLS	5/07
Middle School	Allentown-Bethlehem-Easton MSA, PA-NJ	Y	40690 FQ	52940 MW	63370 TQ	USBLS	5/07
Middle School	Philadelphia-Camden-Wilmington MSA, PA-NJ-DE-MD	Y	46040 FQ	55580 MW	66940 TQ	USBLS	5/07
Middle School	Pittsburgh MSA, PA	Y	44350 FQ	55860 MW	69860 TQ	USBLS	5/07
Middle School	South Carolina	Y	40130 FQ	48460 MW	57720 TQ	USBLS	5/07
Middle School	South Dakota	Y	33820 FQ	36809 MW	39809 TQ	SDBLS	7/08-9/08
Middle School	Tennessee	Y	35970 FQ	43640 MW	52460 TQ	USBLS	5/07
Middle School	Memphis MSA, TN-MS-AR	Y	36140 FQ	43040 MW	51680 TQ	USBLS	5/07
Middle School	Nashville-Davidson-Murfreesboro MSA, TN	Y	36020 FQ	44030 MW	51140 TQ	USBLS	5/07
Middle School	Texas	Y	40270 FQ	46560 MW	53860 TQ	USBLS	5/07
Middle School	Austin-Round Rock MSA, TX	Y	38920 FQ	44540 MW	51160 TQ	USBLS	5/07
Middle School	Beaumont-Port Arthur MSA, TX	Y	36950 FQ	44390 MW	51630 TQ	USBLS	5/07
Middle School	Dallas-Fort Worth-Arlington MSA, TX	Y	41430 FQ	47300 MW	54440 TQ	USBLS	5/07
Middle School	Houston-Sugar Land-Baytown MSA, TX	Y	42440 FQ	48930 MW	57780 TQ	USBLS	5/07
Middle School	San Antonio MSA, TX	Y	43270 FQ	48480 MW	55560 TQ	USBLS	5/07
Middle School	Utah	Y	31230 FQ	39060 MW	51320 TQ	USBLS	5/07
Middle School	Salt Lake City MSA, UT	Y	28120 FQ	31430 MW	43270 TQ	USBLS	5/07
Middle School	Vermont	Y	41460 FQ	47040 MW	54400 TQ	USBLS	5/07
Middle School	Virginia	Y	37440 FQ	47570 MW	61830 TQ	USBLS	5/07
Middle School	Lynchburg MSA, VA	Y	38940 FQ	44260 MW	51340 TQ	USBLS	5/07
Middle School	Richmond MSA, VA	Y	38520 FQ	47310 MW	56930 TQ	USBLS	5/07
Middle School	Virginia Beach-Norfolk-Newport News MSA, VA-NC	Y	23260 FQ	25570 MW	43910 TQ	USBLS	5/07
Middle School	Washington	Y		55210 AW		WABLS	3/08
Middle School	Seattle-Tacoma-Bellevue MSA, WA	Y	45930 FQ	57760 MW	67130 TQ	USBLS	5/07
Middle School	Wisconsin	Y	38250 FQ	49020 MW	59560 TQ	USBLS	5/07
Middle School	Milwaukee-Waukesha-West Allis MSA, WI	Y	37030 FQ	47850 MW	60190 TQ	USBLS	5/07
Middle School	Wyoming	Y	44071 FQ	52831 MW	60677 TQ	WYBLS	9/08
Middle School	Virgin Islands	Y	43300 FQ	60500 MW	73280 TQ	USBLS	5/07
Middle School	Alabama	Y	31670 FQ	44470 MW	55630 TQ	USBLS	5/07
Postsecondary	Birmingham-Hoover MSA, AL	Y	29460 FQ	36980 MW	50660 TQ	USBLS	5/07
Postsecondary	Alaska	Y	54450 FQ	64020 MW	78770 TQ	USBLS	5/07
Postsecondary	Anchorage MSA, AK	Y	58730 FQ	70000 MW	80960 TQ	USBLS	5/07
Postsecondary	Arizona	Y	32660 FQ	45470 MW	65230 TQ	USBLS	5/07
Postsecondary	Phoenix-Mesa-Scottsdale MSA, AZ	Y	32760 FQ	46350 MW	69710 TQ	USBLS	5/07

Occupation/Type/Industry	Location	Per	Low	Mid	High	Source	Date
Vocational Education Teacher							
Postsecondary	Tucson MSA, AZ	Y	34900 FQ	45000 MW	57260 TQ	USBLS	5/07
Postsecondary	Arkansas	Y	26550 FQ	36590 MW	47220 TQ	USBLS	5/07
Postsecondary	Little Rock-North Little Rock MSA, AR	Y	36260 FQ	56220 MW	61890 TQ	USBLS	5/07
Postsecondary	California	Y		64133 AW		CABLS	1/08-3/08
Postsecondary	Los Angeles-Long Beach-Glendale PMSA, CA	H	19.26 FQ	27.53 MW	40.27 TQ	CABLS	1/08-3/08
Postsecondary	Modesto MSA, CA	H	14.05 FQ	16.50 MW	21.18 TQ	CABLS	1/08-3/08
Postsecondary	Oakland-Fremont-Hayward MSA, CA	H	25.99 FQ	31.35 MW	37.95 TQ	CABLS	1/08-3/08
Postsecondary	Riverside-San Bernardino-Ontario MSA, CA	H	20.96 FQ	24.84 MW	36.24 TQ	CABLS	1/08-3/08
Postsecondary	Sacramento-Arden Arcade-Roseville MSA, CA	H	19.65 FQ	24.33 MW	43.24 TQ	CABLS	1/08-3/08
Postsecondary	San Diego-Carlsbad-San Marcos MSA, CA	H	21.84 FQ	33.05 MW	52.65 TQ	CABLS	1/08-3/08
Postsecondary	San Francisco-San Mateo-Redwood PMSA, CA	H	22.37 FQ	32.16 MW	52.25 TQ	CABLS	1/08-3/08
Postsecondary	San Jose-Sunnyvale-Santa Clara MSA, CA	H	19.84 FQ	23.17 MW	51.27 TQ	CABLS	1/08-3/08
Postsecondary	Santa Ana-Anaheim-Irvine PMSA, CA	Y	35510 FQ	48300 MW	60450 TQ	USBLS	5/07
Postsecondary	Colorado	Y	29050 FQ	36100 MW	46990 TQ	USBLS	5/07
Postsecondary	Denver-Aurora MSA, CO	Y	30140 FQ	36550 MW	46360 TQ	USBLS	5/07
Postsecondary	Connecticut	H	16.26 AE	22.32 MW		CTBLS	1/08-3/08
Postsecondary	Bridgeport-Stamford-Norwalk MSA, CT	Y	37390 FQ	45380 MW	56780 TQ	USBLS	5/07
Postsecondary	Hartford-West Hartford-East Hartford MSA, CT	Y	31200 FQ	42160 MW	48810 TQ	USBLS	5/07
Postsecondary	New Haven MSA, CT	Y	44480 FQ	56390 MW	69560 TQ	USBLS	5/07
Postsecondary	Delaware	Y	33980 FQ	38930 MW	46810 TQ	USBLS	5/07
Postsecondary	Wilmington PMSA, DE-MD-NJ	Y	32120 FQ	35850 MW	39450 TQ	USBLS	5/07
Postsecondary	District of Columbia	Y	46700 FQ	53330 MW	61040 TQ	USBLS	5/07
Postsecondary	Washington-Arlington-Alexandria MSA, DC-VA-MD-WV	Y	33150 FQ	40940 MW	53890 TQ	USBLS	5/07
Postsecondary	Florida	Y	35590 FQ	49050 MW	66050 TQ	USBLS	5/07
Postsecondary	Fort Lauderdale-Pompano Beach-Deerfield Beach PMSA, FL	Y	42880 FQ	60290 MW	72950 TQ	USBLS	5/07
Postsecondary	Jacksonville MSA, FL	Y	34930 FQ	43450 MW	66360 TQ	USBLS	5/07
Postsecondary	Orlando-Kissimmee MSA, FL	Y	33940 FQ	44420 MW	60500 TQ	USBLS	5/07
Postsecondary	Tampa-St. Petersburg-Clearwater MSA, FL	Y	30690 FQ	38610 MW	46580 TQ	USBLS	5/07
Postsecondary	West Palm Beach-Boca Raton-Boynton Beach PMSA, FL	Y	35720 FQ	42970 MW	49610 TQ	USBLS	5/07
Postsecondary	Georgia	Y	39050 FQ	46090 MW	54760 TQ	USBLS	5/07
Postsecondary	Atlanta-Sandy Springs-Marietta MSA, GA	Y	39960 FQ	46820 MW	54900 TQ	USBLS	5/07
Postsecondary	Hawaii	Y	40870 FQ	54210 MW	66480 TQ	USBLS	5/07
Postsecondary	Honolulu MSA, HI	Y	42290 FQ	54030 MW	67090 TQ	USBLS	5/07
Postsecondary	Boise City-Nampa MSA, ID	Y	25920 FQ	33270 MW	51910 TQ	USBLS	5/07
Postsecondary	Illinois	Y	35260 FQ	47450 MW	59840 TQ	USBLS	5/07
Postsecondary	Chicago-Naperville-Joliet MSA, IL-IN-WI	Y	41450 FQ	51450 MW	66300 TQ	USBLS	5/07
Postsecondary	Indiana	Y	31140 FQ	45760 MW	66620 TQ	USBLS	5/07
Postsecondary	Gary PMSA, IN	Y	32910 FQ	66510 MW	75190 TQ	USBLS	5/07
Postsecondary	Indianapolis-Carmel MSA, IN	Y	28510 FQ	34420 MW	45510 TQ	USBLS	5/07
Postsecondary	Iowa	Y	32510 FQ	43810 MW	54070 TQ	USBLS	5/07
Postsecondary	Des Moines-West Des Moines MSA, IA	Y	43830 FQ	49710 MW	60140 TQ	USBLS	5/07
Postsecondary	Kansas	Y	30970 FQ	50880 MW	63790 TQ	USBLS	5/07
Postsecondary	Wichita MSA, KS	Y	53960 FQ	60480 MW	66990 TQ	USBLS	5/07
Postsecondary	Kentucky	Y	34175 FQ	40961 MW	50621 TQ	KYBLS	2008
Postsecondary	Lexington-Fayette MSA, KY	Y	33390 FQ	36260 MW	39130 TQ	USBLS	5/07
Postsecondary	Louisville-Jefferson County MSA, KY-IN	Y	34840 FQ	42650 MW	51240 TQ	USBLS	5/07
Postsecondary	Louisiana	Y		33980 AW		LABLS	1/08-3/08
Postsecondary	New Orleans-Metairie-Kenner MSA, LA	Y	27150 FQ	32220 MW	40950 TQ	USBLS	5/07

AE Average entry wage	**AW** Average wage paid	**FQ** First quartile wage	**LO** Lowest wage paid	**MTC** Median total compensation	**TCC** Total cash compensation
AER Average entry range	**AWR** Average wage range	**H** Hourly	**LR** Low end range	**MW** Median wage paid	**TQ** Third quartile wage
AEX Average experienced wage	**AXR** Average experienced range	**HI** Highest wage paid	**M** Monthly	**MWR** Median wage range	**W** Weekly
ATC Average total compensation	**D** Daily	**HR** High end range	**MCC** Median cash compensation	**S** See annotated source	**Y** Yearly

Occupation/Type/Industry	Location	Per	Low	Mid	High	Source	Date
Vocational Education Teacher							
Postsecondary	Maine	Y	36100 FQ	47550 MW	57260 TQ	USBLS	5/07
Postsecondary	Portland-South Portland-Biddeford MSA, ME	Y	42970 FQ	49730 MW	57660 TQ	USBLS	5/07
	Maryland	Y		46675 MW		MDBLS	3/08
Postsecondary	Baltimore-Towson MSA, MD	Y	26030 FQ	43680 MW	59620 TQ	USBLS	5/07
Postsecondary	Massachusetts	Y	32290 FQ	45760 MW	65660 TQ	USBLS	5/07
Postsecondary	Boston-Cambridge-Quincy NECTA, MA	Y	31920 FQ	52760 MW	80140 TQ	USBLS	5/07
Postsecondary	Springfield MSA, MA-CT	Y	32150 FQ	39000 MW	48660 TQ	USBLS	5/07
Postsecondary	Worcester MSA, MA-CT	Y	37760 FQ	44900 MW	57180 TQ	USBLS	5/07
Postsecondary	Michigan	Y	31990 FQ	50220 MW	69400 TQ	USBLS	5/07
Postsecondary	Detroit-Warren-Livonia MSA, MI	Y	31670 FQ	44720 MW	64230 TQ	USBLS	5/07
Postsecondary	Warren-Troy-Farmington Hills PMSA, MI	Y	38470 FQ	50910 MW	69260 TQ	USBLS	5/07
Postsecondary	Minnesota	Y	44360 FQ	60022 MW	71268 TQ	MNBLS	10/08-12/08
Postsecondary	Duluth-Superior MSA, MN-WI	Y	55041 FQ	66111 MW	74010 TQ	MNBLS	10/08-12/08
Postsecondary	Minneapolis-Saint Paul MSA, MN-WI	Y	42884 FQ	59655 MW	74083 TQ	MNBLS	10/08-12/08
Postsecondary	Rochester MSA, MN	Y	36419 FQ	48988 MW	77447 TQ	MNBLS	10/08-12/08
Postsecondary	Mississippi	Y	37270 FQ	50650 MW	60790 TQ	USBLS	5/07
Postsecondary	Jackson MSA, MS	Y	32660 FQ	36560 MW	52090 TQ	USBLS	5/07
Postsecondary	Missouri	Y	29730 FQ	40730 MW	60330 TQ	USBLS	5/07
Postsecondary	Kansas City MSA, MO-KS	Y	32250 FQ	41950 MW	55260 TQ	USBLS	5/07
Postsecondary	St. Louis MSA, MO-IL	Y	30660 FQ	41160 MW	61040 TQ	USBLS	5/07
Postsecondary	Montana	Y	22090 FQ	37180 MW	48640 TQ	USBLS	5/07
Postsecondary	Nebraska	Y	40250 FQ	53780 MW	68140 TQ	USBLS	5/07
Postsecondary	Omaha-Council Bluffs MSA, NE-IA	Y	43420 FQ	55270 MW	72050 TQ	USBLS	5/07
Postsecondary	Nevada	H	14.85 FQ	17.63 MW	28.46 TQ	NVBLS	5/08
Postsecondary	Las Vegas-Paradise MSA, NV	H	14.51 FQ	16.90 MW	28.31 TQ	NVBLS	5/08
Postsecondary	New Hampshire	H	14.38 AE	20.42 MW	24.63 AEX	NHBLS	6/08
Postsecondary	New Jersey	Y	38120 FQ	46700 MW	58870 TQ	USBLS	5/07
Postsecondary	Camden PMSA, NJ	Y	39970 FQ	47280 MW	60830 TQ	USBLS	5/07
Postsecondary	Edison PMSA, NJ	Y	38220 FQ	50930 MW	59190 TQ	USBLS	5/07
Postsecondary	Newark-Union PMSA, NJ-PA	Y	29140 FQ	44730 MW	64130 TQ	USBLS	5/07
Postsecondary	New Mexico	Y	32700 FQ	40230 MW	50500 TQ	USBLS	5/07
Postsecondary	Albuquerque MSA, NM	Y	31430 FQ	36210 MW	43050 TQ	USBLS	5/07
Postsecondary	Santa Fe MSA, NM	Y	29550 FQ	35320 MW	63440 TQ	USBLS	5/07
Postsecondary	New York	Y	35190 FQ	48820 MW	60900 TQ	USBLS	5/07
Postsecondary	Albany-Schenectady-Troy MSA, NY	Y	27250 FQ	36420 MW	50140 TQ	USBLS	5/07
Postsecondary	Buffalo-Niagara Falls MSA, NY	Y	30800 FQ	42860 MW	54670 TQ	USBLS	5/07
Postsecondary	Nassau-Suffolk PMSA, NY	Y	27790 FQ	33300 MW	64540 TQ	USBLS	5/07
Postsecondary	New York-Northern New Jersey-Long Island MSA, NY-NJ-PA	Y	35770 FQ	48700 MW	62140 TQ	USBLS	5/07
Postsecondary	North Carolina	Y	36690 FQ	44050 MW	52130 TQ	USBLS	5/07
Postsecondary	Charlotte-Gastonia-Concord MSA, NC-SC	Y	34260 FQ	42180 MW	53550 TQ	USBLS	5/07
Postsecondary	Raleigh-Cary MSA, NC	Y	37220 FQ	44160 MW	54640 TQ	USBLS	5/07
Postsecondary	North Dakota	Y	33430 FQ	43030 MW	51120 TQ	USBLS	5/07
Postsecondary	Fargo MSA, ND-MN	Y	39790 FQ	48100 MW	64350 TQ	USBLS	5/07
Postsecondary	Ohio	Y	30800 FQ	43220 MW	59590 TQ	USBLS	5/07
Postsecondary	Cincinnati-Middletown MSA, OH-KY-IN	Y	30760 FQ	39850 MW	55640 TQ	USBLS	5/07
Postsecondary	Cleveland-Elyria-Mentor MSA, OH	Y	29810 FQ	37370 MW	63930 TQ	USBLS	5/07
Postsecondary	Columbus MSA, OH	Y	26720 FQ	40610 MW	56190 TQ	USBLS	5/07
Postsecondary	Dayton MSA, OH	Y	27500 FQ	43870 MW	58160 TQ	USBLS	5/07
Postsecondary	Oklahoma	Y	33190 FQ	44340 MW	53150 TQ	USBLS	5/07
Postsecondary	Oklahoma City MSA, OK	Y	38480 FQ	46730 MW	57240 TQ	USBLS	5/07
Postsecondary	Tulsa MSA, OK	Y	31100 FQ	43330 MW	52440 TQ	USBLS	5/07
Postsecondary	Portland-Vancouver-Beaverton MSA, OR-WA	Y	34540 FQ	46050 MW	68840 TQ	USBLS	5/07
Postsecondary	Pennsylvania	Y	36460 FQ	45350 MW	57210 TQ	USBLS	5/07
Postsecondary	Allentown-Bethlehem-Easton MSA, PA-NJ	Y	32950 FQ	41440 MW	51030 TQ	USBLS	5/07

AE Average entry wage	**AW** Average wage paid	**FQ** First quartile wage	**LO** Lowest wage paid	**MTC** Median total compensation	**TCC** Total cash compensation
AER Average entry range	**AWR** Average wage range	**H** Hourly	**LR** Low end range	**MW** Median wage paid	**TQ** Third quartile wage
AEX Average experienced wage	**AXR** Average experienced range	**HI** Highest wage paid	**M** Monthly	**MWR** Median wage range	**W** Weekly
ATC Average total compensation	**D** Daily	**HR** High end range	**MCC** Median cash compensation	**S** See annotated source	**Y** Yearly

Vocational Education Teacher

Occupation/Type/Industry	Location	Per	Low	Mid	High	Source	Date
Postsecondary	Philadelphia-Camden-Wilmington MSA, PA-NJ-DE-MD	Y	37700 FQ	47060 MW	62200 TQ	USBLS	5/07
Postsecondary	Pittsburgh MSA, PA	Y	36480 FQ	43720 MW	52640 TQ	USBLS	5/07
Postsecondary	Rhode Island	Y	33200 FQ	50900 MW	80540 TQ	USBLS	5/07
Postsecondary	Providence-Fall River-Warwick MSA, RI-MA	Y	33300 FQ	49780 MW	80240 TQ	USBLS	5/07
Postsecondary	South Carolina	Y	27280 FQ	36210 MW	51840 TQ	USBLS	5/07
Postsecondary	Charleston-North Charleston MSA, SC	Y	40760 FQ	50570 MW	59300 TQ	USBLS	5/07
Postsecondary	Columbia MSA, SC	Y	25670 FQ	28050 MW	30450 TQ	USBLS	5/07
Postsecondary	South Dakota	Y	36742 FQ	46221	56788 TQ	SDBLS	7/08-9/08
Postsecondary	Rapid City MSA, SD	Y	33012 FQ	46572 MW	58899 TQ	SDBLS	7/08-9/08
Postsecondary	Sioux Falls MSA, SD	Y	37096 FQ	41643 MW	50961 TQ	SDBLS	7/08-9/08
Postsecondary	Tennessee	Y	32260 FQ	43230 MW	52120 TQ	USBLS	5/07
Postsecondary	Kingsport-Bristol-Bristol MSA, TN-VA	Y	28430 FQ	40920 MW	53080 TQ	USBLS	5/07
Postsecondary	Memphis MSA, TN-MS-AR	Y	46540 FQ	55030 MW	63180 TQ	USBLS	5/07
Postsecondary	Nashville-Davidson-Murfreesboro MSA, TN	Y	31510 FQ	39890 MW	47550 TQ	USBLS	5/07
Postsecondary	Texas	Y	28220 FQ	40740 MW	55030 TQ	USBLS	5/07
Postsecondary	Austin-Round Rock MSA, TX	Y	21760 FQ	31950 MW	42850 TQ	USBLS	5/07
Postsecondary	Beaumont-Port Arthur MSA, TX	Y	29100 FQ	33290 MW	39710 TQ	USBLS	5/07
Postsecondary	Dallas-Fort Worth-Arlington MSA, TX	Y	24650 FQ	33790 MW	46240 TQ	USBLS	5/07
Postsecondary	El Paso MSA, TX	Y	27420 FQ	41490 MW	51620 TQ	USBLS	5/07
Postsecondary	Houston-Sugar Land-Baytown MSA, TX	Y	39180 FQ	52660 MW	64390 TQ	USBLS	5/07
Postsecondary	San Antonio MSA, TX	Y	26870 FQ	37200 MW	49900 TQ	USBLS	5/07
Postsecondary	Utah	Y	28660 FQ	40280 MW	52810 TQ	USBLS	5/07
Postsecondary	Provo-Orem MSA, UT	Y	37440 FQ	45520 MW	52380 TQ	USBLS	5/07
Postsecondary	Salt Lake City MSA, UT	Y	23430 FQ	33390 MW	52850 TQ	USBLS	5/07
Postsecondary	Vermont	Y	34440 FQ	41960 MW	49950 TQ	USBLS	5/07
Postsecondary	Burlington-South Burlington MSA, VT	Y	31480 FQ	42070 MW	48030 TQ	USBLS	5/07
Postsecondary	Virginia	Y	30950 FQ	40660 MW	53200 TQ	USBLS	5/07
Postsecondary	Richmond MSA, VA	Y	41720 FQ	52240 MW	59520 TQ	USBLS	5/07
Postsecondary	Virginia Beach-Norfolk-Newport News MSA, VA-NC	Y	28390 FQ	38520 MW	50970 TQ	USBLS	5/07
Postsecondary	Washington	H	17.34 FQ	22.13 MW	28.28 TQ	WABLS	3/08
Postsecondary	Bremerton-Silverdale MSA, WA	Y	29250 FQ	39880 MW	59060 TQ	USBLS	5/07
Postsecondary	Seattle-Tacoma-Bellevue MSA, WA	Y	38940 FQ	47620 MW	61100 TQ	USBLS	5/07
Postsecondary	West Virginia	Y	17353 FQ	33911 MW	46076 TQ	WVBLS	7/08-9/08
Postsecondary	Charleston MSA, WV	Y	18890 FQ	29640 MW	42980 TQ	USBLS	5/07
Postsecondary	Parkersburg-Marietta-Vienna MSA, WV-OH	Y	33250 FQ	46550 MW	56170 TQ	USBLS	5/07
Postsecondary	Wisconsin	Y	49460 FQ	63960 MW	75550 TQ	USBLS	5/07
Postsecondary	Green Bay MSA, WI	Y	37840 FQ	50080 MW	70750 TQ	USBLS	5/07
Postsecondary	Milwaukee-Waukesha-West Allis MSA, WI	Y	55250 FQ	62870 MW	74170 TQ	USBLS	5/07
Postsecondary	Wyoming	Y	33836 FQ	43297 MW	51708 TQ	WYBLS	9/08
Postsecondary	Puerto Rico	Y	19480 FQ	25450 MW	32810 TQ	USBLS	5/07
Postsecondary	San Juan-Caguas-Guaynabo MSA, PR	Y	21640 FQ	27360 MW	36130 TQ	USBLS	5/07
Secondary School	Alabama	Y	42070 FQ	47810 MW	55380 TQ	USBLS	5/07
Secondary School	Birmingham-Hoover MSA, AL	Y	42670 FQ	50140 MW	58420 TQ	USBLS	5/07
Secondary School	Alaska	Y	50370 FQ	60400 MW	69560 TQ	USBLS	5/07
Secondary School	Arizona	Y	35260 FQ	41970 MW	49030 TQ	USBLS	5/07
Secondary School	Phoenix-Mesa-Scottsdale MSA, AZ	Y	40250 FQ	46000 MW	51900 TQ	USBLS	5/07
Secondary School	Tucson MSA, AZ	Y	33460 FQ	37500 MW	44980 TQ	USBLS	5/07
Secondary School	Arkansas	Y	38930 FQ	44460 MW	50610 TQ	USBLS	5/07
Secondary School	Fayetteville-Springdale-Rogers MSA, AR-MO	Y	41110 FQ	45850 MW	51070 TQ	USBLS	5/07
Secondary School	Fort Smith MSA, AR-OK	Y	39860 FQ	44170 MW	48620 TQ	USBLS	5/07
Secondary School	Little Rock-North Little Rock MSA, AR	Y	40910 FQ	47510 MW	57740 TQ	USBLS	5/07
Secondary School	California	Y		59682 AW		CABLS	1/08-3/08

AE Average entry wage	AW Average wage paid	FQ First quartile wage	LO Lowest wage paid	MTC Median total compensation	TCC Total cash compensation
AER Average entry range	AWR Average wage range	H Hourly	LR Low end range	MW Median wage paid	TQ Third quartile wage
AEX Average experienced wage	AXR Average experienced range	HI Highest wage paid	M Monthly	MWR Median wage range	W Weekly
ATC Average total compensation	D Daily	HR High end range	MCC Median cash compensation	S See annotated source	Y Yearly

Occupation/Type/Industry	Location	Per	Low	Mid	High	Source	Date
Vocational Education Teacher							
Secondary School	Fresno MSA, CA	Y		71763 AW		CABLS	1/08-3/08
Secondary School	Los Angeles-Long Beach-Glendale PMSA, CA	Y		62123 AW		CABLS	1/08-3/08
Secondary School	Oakland-Fremont-Hayward MSA, CA	Y		63169 AW		CABLS	1/08-3/08
Secondary School	Riverside-San Bernardino-Ontario MSA, CA	Y		63354 AW		CABLS	1/08-3/08
Secondary School	Sacramento-Arden Arcade-Roseville MSA, CA	Y		55160 MW		CABLS	1/08-3/08
Secondary School	San Diego-Carlsbad-San Marcos MSA, CA	Y		60585 AW		CABLS	1/08-3/08
Secondary School	San Francisco-San Mateo-Redwood PMSA, CA	Y		46618 AW		CABLS	1/08-3/08
Secondary School	San Jose-Sunnyvale-Santa Clara MSA, CA	Y		57703 AW		CABLS	1/08-3/08
Secondary School	Santa Ana-Anaheim-Irvine PMSA, CA	Y	51480 FQ	66710 MW	77810 TQ	USBLS	5/07
Secondary School	Stockton MSA, CA	Y		68727 AW		CABLS	1/08-3/08
Secondary School	Colorado	Y	40290 FQ	49340 MW	59850 TQ	USBLS	5/07
Secondary School	Colorado Springs MSA, CO	Y	38340 FQ	44630 MW	52600 TQ	USBLS	5/07
Secondary School	Denver-Aurora MSA, CO	Y	46160 FQ	56040 MW	66510 TQ	USBLS	5/07
Secondary School	Bridgeport-Stamford-Norwalk MSA, CT	Y	44780 FQ	60720 MW	75080 TQ	USBLS	5/07
Secondary School	Hartford-West Hartford-East Hartford MSA, CT	Y	44530 FQ	66070 MW	76440 TQ	USBLS	5/07
Secondary School	Delaware	Y	54810 FQ	64870 MW	75210 TQ	USBLS	5/07
Secondary School	Wilmington PMSA, DE-MD-NJ	Y	47280 FQ	58710 MW	70550 TQ	USBLS	5/07
Secondary School	Washington-Arlington-Alexandria MSA, DC-VA-MD-WV	Y	47700 FQ	61070 MW	78470 TQ	USBLS	5/07
Secondary School	Florida	Y	44330 FQ	54480 MW	66530 TQ	USBLS	5/07
Secondary School	Jacksonville MSA, FL	Y	40800 FQ	51770 MW	60680 TQ	USBLS	5/07
Secondary School	Orlando-Kissimmee MSA, FL	Y	42170 FQ	48770 MW	61750 TQ	USBLS	5/07
Secondary School	Tallahassee MSA, FL	Y	27480 FQ	31960 MW	42510 TQ	USBLS	5/07
Secondary School	Tampa-St. Petersburg-Clearwater MSA, FL	Y	45780 FQ	52930 MW	68050 TQ	USBLS	5/07
Secondary School	Georgia	Y	42430 FQ	50290 MW	61610 TQ	USBLS	5/07
Secondary School	Atlanta-Sandy Springs-Marietta MSA, GA	Y	42250 FQ	50080 MW	62280 TQ	USBLS	5/07
Secondary School	Hawaii	Y	40480 FQ	45250 MW	49410 TQ	USBLS	5/07
Secondary School	Illinois	Y	38620 FQ	48970 MW	63810 TQ	USBLS	5/07
Secondary School	Champaign-Urbana MSA, IL	Y	32630 FQ	37800 MW	46580 TQ	USBLS	5/07
Secondary School	Chicago-Naperville-Joliet MSA, IL-IN-WI	Y	45750 FQ	59870 MW	89760 TQ	USBLS	5/07
Secondary School	Indiana	Y	41940 FQ	52510 MW	61660 TQ	USBLS	5/07
Secondary School	Gary PMSA, IN	Y	42300 FQ	57260 MW	67330 TQ	USBLS	5/07
Secondary School	Indianapolis-Carmel MSA, IN	Y	43330 FQ	53390 MW	64010 TQ	USBLS	5/07
Secondary School	Iowa	Y	33010 FQ	39760 MW	48080 TQ	USBLS	5/07
Secondary School	Cedar Rapids MSA, IA	Y	34240 FQ	40440 MW	48250 TQ	USBLS	5/07
Secondary School	Davenport-Moline-Rock Island MSA, IA-IL	Y	34140 FQ	41790 MW	54770 TQ	USBLS	5/07
Secondary School	Des Moines-West Des Moines MSA, IA	Y	34070 FQ	38120 MW	45260 TQ	USBLS	5/07
Secondary School	Waterloo-Cedar Falls MSA, IA	Y	27280 FQ	39370 MW	45660 TQ	USBLS	5/07
Secondary School	Kansas	Y	35600 FQ	42250 MW	48860 TQ	USBLS	5/07
Secondary School	Wichita MSA, KS	Y	39500 FQ	46740 MW	53530 TQ	USBLS	5/07
Secondary School	Kentucky	Y	43705 FQ	52343 MW	62425 TQ	KYBLS	2008
Secondary School	Louisville-Jefferson County MSA, KY-IN	Y	46740 FQ	56090 MW	64850 TQ	USBLS	5/07
Secondary School	Louisiana	Y		43962 AW		LABLS	1/08-3/08
Secondary School	Baton Rouge MSA, LA	Y	39860 FQ	45620 MW	51530 TQ	USBLS	5/07
Secondary School	New Orleans-Metairie-Kenner MSA, LA	Y	41530 FQ	46550 MW	51590 TQ	USBLS	5/07
Secondary School	Maine	Y	37420 FQ	46260 MW	53830 TQ	USBLS	5/07
Secondary School	Portland-South Portland-Biddeford MSA, ME	Y	37440 FQ	48430 MW	55560 TQ	USBLS	5/07
Secondary School	Maryland	Y		57175 MW		MDBLS	3/08
Secondary School	Baltimore-Towson MSA, MD	Y	46300 FQ	55710 MW	66100 TQ	USBLS	5/07
Secondary School	Bethesda-Gaithersburg-Frederick PMSA, MD	Y	41460 FQ	52470 MW	69440 TQ	USBLS	5/07

AE Average entry wage	**AW** Average wage paid	**FQ** First quartile wage	**LO** Lowest wage paid	**MTC** Median total compensation	**TCC** Total cash compensation
AER Average entry range	**AWR** Average wage range	**H** Hourly	**LR** Low end range	**MW** Median wage paid	**TQ** Third quartile wage
AEX Average experienced wage	**AXR** Average experienced range	**HI** Highest wage paid	**M** Monthly	**MWR** Median wage range	**W** Weekly
ATC Average total compensation	**D** Daily	**HR** High end range	**MCC** Median cash compensation	**S** See annotated source	**Y** Yearly

Vocational Education Teacher

Occupation/Type/Industry	Location	Per	Low	Mid	High	Source	Date
Vocational Education Teacher							
Secondary School	Massachusetts	Y	52160 FQ	61090 MW	71710 TQ	USBLS	5/07
Secondary School	Boston-Cambridge-Quincy NECTA, MA	Y	54950 FQ	65490 MW	75430 TQ	USBLS	5/07
Secondary School	Worcester MSA, MA-CT	Y	50910 FQ	58010 MW	65020 TQ	USBLS	5/07
Secondary School	Michigan	Y	41930 FQ	52140 MW	64260 TQ	USBLS	5/07
Secondary School	Detroit-Warren-Livonia MSA, MI	Y	42430 FQ	49460 MW	62940 TQ	USBLS	5/07
Secondary School	Grand Rapids-Wyoming MSA, MI	Y	45210 FQ	54900 MW	64830 TQ	USBLS	5/07
Secondary School	Warren-Troy-Farmington Hills PMSA, MI	Y	42650 FQ	53440 MW	72650 TQ	USBLS	5/07
Secondary School	Minnesota	Y	42958 FQ	52269 MW	63349 TQ	MNBLS	10/08-12/08
Secondary School	Duluth-Superior MSA, MN-WI	Y	38197 FQ	47948 MW	60545 TQ	MNBLS	10/08-12/08
Secondary School	Minneapolis-Saint Paul MSA, MN-WI	Y	44119 FQ	54905 MW	67104 TQ	MNBLS	10/08-12/08
Secondary School	Rochester MSA, MN	Y	43353 FQ	50105 MW	56707 TQ	MNBLS	10/08-12/08
Secondary School	Mississippi	Y	38550 FQ	44750 MW	51400 TQ	USBLS	5/07
Secondary School	Jackson MSA, MS	Y	35730 FQ	41260 MW	48150 TQ	USBLS	5/07
Secondary School	Pascagoula MSA, MS	Y	40840 FQ	45800 MW	50690 TQ	USBLS	5/07
Secondary School	Missouri	Y	35180 FQ	41810 MW	52330 TQ	USBLS	5/07
Secondary School	Kansas City MSA, MO-KS	Y	38140 FQ	46300 MW	55240 TQ	USBLS	5/07
Secondary School	St. Louis MSA, MO-IL	Y	39200 FQ	49230 MW	62230 TQ	USBLS	5/07
Secondary School	Springfield MSA, MO	Y	34450 FQ	46020 MW	64910 TQ	USBLS	5/07
Secondary School	Montana	Y	31300 FQ	40960 MW	49860 TQ	USBLS	5/07
Secondary School	Billings MSA, MT	Y	32280 FQ	41040 MW	51550 TQ	USBLS	5/07
Secondary School	Nebraska	Y	36200 FQ	44910 MW	53240 TQ	USBLS	5/07
Secondary School	Omaha-Council Bluffs MSA, NE-IA	Y	36490 FQ	43430 MW	51130 TQ	USBLS	5/07
Secondary School	Nevada	Y	44006 FQ	51015 MW	58431 TQ	NVBLS	5/08
Secondary School	New Hampshire	Y	42116 AE	53261 MW	59645 AEX	NHBLS	6/08
Secondary School	Rochester-Dover MSA, NH-ME	Y	43770 FQ	50150 MW	58850 TQ	USBLS	5/07
Secondary School	New Jersey	Y	48030 FQ	60830 MW	73530 TQ	USBLS	5/07
Secondary School	Camden PMSA, NJ	Y	45590 FQ	55950 MW	71320 TQ	USBLS	5/07
Secondary School	Edison PMSA, NJ	Y	46160 FQ	52870 MW	63870 TQ	USBLS	5/07
Secondary School	Newark-Union PMSA, NJ-PA	Y	65620 FQ	71210 MW	76810 TQ	USBLS	5/07
Secondary School	New Mexico	Y	39990 FQ	46900 MW	57000 TQ	USBLS	5/07
Secondary School	New York	Y	48350 FQ	62310 MW	80150 TQ	USBLS	5/07
Secondary School	Albany-Schenectady-Troy MSA, NY	Y	45840 FQ	56770 MW	73800 TQ	USBLS	5/07
Secondary School	Buffalo-Niagara Falls MSA, NY	Y	39900 FQ	49910 MW	68340 TQ	USBLS	5/07
Secondary School	Nassau-Suffolk PMSA, NY	Y	59670 FQ	78750 MW	96540 TQ	USBLS	5/07
Secondary School	New York-Northern New Jersey-Long Island MSA, NY-NJ-PA	Y	53730 FQ	69660 MW	83540 TQ	USBLS	5/07
Secondary School	North Carolina	Y	36550 FQ	44180 MW	51420 TQ	USBLS	5/07
Secondary School	Asheville MSA, NC	Y	40880 FQ	47850 MW	56990 TQ	USBLS	5/07
Secondary School	Charlotte-Gastonia-Concord MSA, NC-SC	Y	37510 FQ	46110 MW	54730 TQ	USBLS	5/07
Secondary School	North Dakota	Y	36760 FQ	44460 MW	51720 TQ	USBLS	5/07
Secondary School	Bismarck MSA, ND	Y	36240 FQ	46560 MW	56470 TQ	USBLS	5/07
Secondary School	Fargo MSA, ND-MN	Y	42700 FQ	55410 MW	64540 TQ	USBLS	5/07
Secondary School	Ohio	Y	47200 FQ	57540 MW	67930 TQ	USBLS	5/07
Secondary School	Cincinnati-Middletown MSA, OH-KY-IN	Y	50910 FQ	59460 MW	70550 TQ	USBLS	5/07
Secondary School	Cleveland-Elyria-Mentor MSA, OH	Y	54060 FQ	64740 MW	75860 TQ	USBLS	5/07
Secondary School	Columbus MSA, OH	Y	49230 FQ	59000 MW	69950 TQ	USBLS	5/07
Secondary School	Dayton MSA, OH	Y	51210 FQ	61950 MW	74610 TQ	USBLS	5/07
Secondary School	Oklahoma	Y	36680 FQ	43470 MW	50860 TQ	USBLS	5/07
Secondary School	Oklahoma City MSA, OK	Y	39350 FQ	46580 MW	53730 TQ	USBLS	5/07
Secondary School	Tulsa MSA, OK	Y	37280 FQ	43790 MW	52750 TQ	USBLS	5/07
Secondary School	Oregon	Y	44258 FQ	54047 MW	62403 TQ	ORBLS	5/08
Secondary School	Portland-Vancouver-Beaverton MSA, OR-WA	Y	47060 FQ	55850 MW	64320 TQ	USBLS	5/07
Secondary School	Pennsylvania	Y	41350 FQ	51830 MW	63410 TQ	USBLS	5/07
Secondary School	Allentown-Bethlehem-Easton MSA, PA-NJ	Y	43230 FQ	54330 MW	65110 TQ	USBLS	5/07
Secondary School	Erie MSA, PA	Y	41540 FQ	47970 MW	56000 TQ	USBLS	5/07

AE	Average entry wage	AW	Average wage paid	FQ	First quartile wage	LO	Lowest wage paid	MTC	Median total compensation	TCC	Total cash compensation
AER	Average entry range	AWR	Average wage range	H	Hourly	LR	Low end range	MW	Median wage paid	TQ	Third quartile wage
AEX	Average experienced wage	AXR	Average experienced range	HI	Highest wage paid	M	Monthly	MWR	Median wage range	W	Weekly
ATC	Average total compensation	D	Daily	HR	High end range	MCC	Median cash compensation	S	See annotated source	Y	Yearly

Occupation/Type/Industry	Location	Per	Low	Mid	High	Source	Date
Vocational Education Teacher							
Secondary School	Philadelphia-Camden-Wilmington MSA, PA-NJ-DE-MD	Y	43010 FQ	54750 MW	68000 TQ	USBLS	5/07
Secondary School	Pittsburgh MSA, PA	Y	42520 FQ	50330 MW	59040 TQ	USBLS	5/07
Secondary School	Rhode Island	Y	52870 FQ	64650 MW	73810 TQ	USBLS	5/07
Secondary School	Providence-Fall River-Warwick MSA, RI-MA	Y	52210 FQ	60730 MW	70240 TQ	USBLS	5/07
Secondary School	South Carolina	Y	38300 FQ	46130 MW	55200 TQ	USBLS	5/07
Secondary School	Columbia MSA, SC	Y	40730 FQ	46120 MW	55100 TQ	USBLS	5/07
Secondary School	South Dakota	Y	33482 FQ	37894 MW	42551 TQ	SDBLS	7/08-9/08
Secondary School	Sioux Falls MSA, SD	Y	32272 FQ	36956 MW	41655 TQ	SDBLS	7/08-9/08
Secondary School	Tennessee	Y	35810 FQ	41500 MW	48630 TQ	USBLS	5/07
Secondary School	Memphis MSA, TN-MS-AR	Y	37680 FQ	43910 MW	50160 TQ	USBLS	5/07
Secondary School	Nashville-Davidson-Murfreesboro MSA, TN	Y	35800 FQ	41520 MW	50470 TQ	USBLS	5/07
Secondary School	Texas	Y	41010 FQ	47310 MW	54930 TQ	USBLS	5/07
Secondary School	Austin-Round Rock MSA, TX	Y	38560 FQ	44920 MW	52040 TQ	USBLS	5/07
Secondary School	Brownsville-Harlingen MSA, TX	Y	42090 FQ	49030 MW	57200 TQ	USBLS	5/07
Secondary School	Dallas-Fort Worth-Arlington MSA, TX	Y	44320 FQ	49570 MW	57560 TQ	USBLS	5/07
Secondary School	El Paso MSA, TX	Y	41620 FQ	47700 MW	55550 TQ	USBLS	5/07
Secondary School	Houston-Sugar Land-Baytown MSA, TX	Y	43750 FQ	49990 MW	59040 TQ	USBLS	5/07
Secondary School	San Antonio MSA, TX	Y	41810 FQ	48110 MW	56230 TQ	USBLS	5/07
Secondary School	Utah	Y	36920 FQ	45260 MW	53970 TQ	USBLS	5/07
Secondary School	Salt Lake City MSA, UT	Y	36720 FQ	45280 MW	54670 TQ	USBLS	5/07
Secondary School	Vermont	Y	41920 FQ	50150 MW	60410 TQ	USBLS	5/07
Secondary School	Virginia	Y	41470 FQ	51860 MW	67340 TQ	USBLS	5/07
Secondary School	Lynchburg MSA, VA	Y	38520 FQ	44600 MW	51510 TQ	USBLS	5/07
Secondary School	Richmond MSA, VA	Y	47070 FQ	56200 MW	67390 TQ	USBLS	5/07
Secondary School	Virginia Beach-Norfolk-Newport News MSA, VA-NC	Y	36550 FQ	43930 MW	52780 TQ	USBLS	5/07
Secondary School	Washington	Y		56672 AW		WABLS	3/08
Secondary School	Seattle-Tacoma-Bellevue MSA, WA	Y	46060 FQ	56420 MW	65920 TQ	USBLS	5/07
Secondary School	West Virginia	Y	36987 FQ	44593 MW	50314 TQ	WVBLS	7/08-9/08
Secondary School	Charleston MSA, WV	Y	38790 FQ	44480 MW	49490 TQ	USBLS	5/07
Secondary School	Wisconsin	Y	37740 FQ	46410 MW	56200 TQ	USBLS	5/07
Secondary School	Appleton MSA, WI	Y	37110 FQ	47350 MW	58090 TQ	USBLS	5/07
Secondary School	Milwaukee-Waukesha-West Allis MSA, WI	Y	42090 FQ	52210 MW	62680 TQ	USBLS	5/07
Secondary School	Wyoming	Y	44698 FQ	51596 MW	59579 TQ	WYBLS	9/08
Secondary School	Virgin Islands	Y	44640 FQ	51090 MW	60700 TQ	USBLS	5/07
Vocational Rehabilitation Specialist							
Department of Education	New Hampshire	Y			58750 HI	NHUL03	2008
State Government	Iowa	Y	37024 LO		55931 HI	AFT02	3/1/08
Voice Actor							
"The Simpsons" Television Show	Los Angeles, CA	S			400000 HI	UPI01	2008
Volcanologist	United States	Y		30000-90000 AW		OSTATE	2008
Volleyball Referee							
Parks and Recreation Department	Minneapolis, MN	Y			2400 HI	MMTHLY	2008
Volunteer Coordinator							
Municipal Government	Seaside, CA	S	1148 LO		1395 HI	SSSS	8/08
Volunteer Program Manager							
State Government	Ohio	H	20.89 LO		26.11 HI	ODAS	2008
Waiter and Waitress	Alabama	Y	12490 FQ	13810 MW	15180 TQ	USBLS	5/07
	Birmingham-Hoover MSA, AL	Y	12490 FQ	13810 MW	15200 TQ	USBLS	5/07
	Mobile MSA, AL	Y	12290 FQ	13520 MW	14740 TQ	USBLS	5/07
	Alaska	Y	15970 FQ	17350 MW	19560 TQ	USBLS	5/07
	Anchorage MSA, AK	Y	15880 FQ	17080 MW	19060 TQ	USBLS	5/07
	Arizona	Y	14550 FQ	15090 MW	16410 TQ	USBLS	5/07

AE	Average entry wage	AW	Average wage paid	FQ	First quartile wage
AER	Average entry range	AWR	Average wage range	H	Hourly
AEX	Average experienced wage	AXR	Average experienced range	HI	Highest wage paid
ATC	Average total compensation	D	Daily	HR	High end range

LO	Lowest wage paid	MTC	Median total compensation	TCC	Total cash compensation
LR	Low end range	MW	Median wage paid	TQ	Third quartile wage
M	Monthly	MWR	Median wage range	W	Weekly
MCC	Median cash compensation	S	See annotated source	Y	Yearly

Occupation/Type/Industry	Location	Per	Low	Mid	High	Source	Date
Waiter and Waitress	Phoenix-Mesa-Scottsdale MSA, AZ	Y	14570 FQ	15180 MW	17910 TQ	USBLS	5/07
	Tucson MSA, AZ	Y	14480 FQ	14910 MW	15720 TQ	USBLS	5/07
	Yuma MSA, AZ	Y	14510 FQ	14990 MW	15770 TQ	USBLS	5/07
	Arkansas	Y	14060 FQ	14880 MW	16190 TQ	USBLS	5/07
	Little Rock-North Little Rock MSA, AR	Y	14130 FQ	15080 MW	16970 TQ	USBLS	5/07
	California	H	8.00 FQ	8.52 MW	9.32 TQ	CABLS	1/08-3/08
	Los Angeles-Long Beach-Glendale PMSA, CA	H	8.00 FQ	8.49 MW	9.25 TQ	CABLS	1/08-3/08
	Oakland-Fremont-Hayward MSA, CA	H	8.00 FQ	8.68 MW	9.46 TQ	CABLS	1/08-3/08
	Riverside-San Bernardino-Ontario MSA, CA	H	8.00 FQ	8.43 MW	9.21 TQ	CABLS	1/08-3/08
	Sacramento-Arden Arcade-Roseville MSA, CA	H	8.00 FQ	8.40 MW	9.19 TQ	CABLS	1/08-3/08
	San Diego-Carlsbad-San Marcos MSA, CA	H	8.00 FQ	8.43 MW	9.20 TQ	CABLS	1/08-3/08
	San Francisco-San Mateo-Redwood PMSA, CA	H	8.41 FQ	9.31 MW	10.83 TQ	CABLS	1/08-3/08
	San Jose-Sunnyvale-Santa Clara MSA, CA	H	8.00 FQ	8.55 MW	9.26 TQ	CABLS	1/08-3/08
	Santa Ana-Anaheim-Irvine PMSA, CA	Y	16040 FQ	17120 MW	18910 TQ	USBLS	5/07
	Colorado	Y	14720 FQ	15470 MW	21630 TQ	USBLS	5/07
	Colorado Springs MSA, CO	Y	14710 FQ	15360 MW	19470 TQ	USBLS	5/07
	Denver-Aurora MSA, CO	Y	14750 FQ	15620 MW	22340 TQ	USBLS	5/07
	Pueblo MSA, CO	Y	14650 FQ	15060 MW	15730 TQ	USBLS	5/07
	Connecticut	H	7.97 AE	8.80 MW		CTBLS	1/08-3/08
	Bridgeport-Stamford-Norwalk MSA, CT	Y	16180 FQ	17650 MW	21680 TQ	USBLS	5/07
	Hartford-West Hartford-East Hartford MSA, CT	Y	16130 FQ	18580 MW	25100 TQ	USBLS	5/07
	Delaware	Y	14830 FQ	16820 MW	22510 TQ	USBLS	5/07
	Wilmington PMSA, DE-MD-NJ	Y	15060 FQ	17600 MW	23690 TQ	USBLS	5/07
	District of Columbia	Y	15690 FQ	18720 MW	24240 TQ	USBLS	5/07
	Washington-Arlington-Alexandria MSA, DC-VA-MD-WV	Y	14430 FQ	16270 MW	22580 TQ	USBLS	5/07
	Florida	Y	14880 FQ	18100 MW	23180 TQ	USBLS	5/07
	Cape Coral-Fort Myers MSA, FL	Y	14760 FQ	17160 MW	22190 TQ	USBLS	5/07
	Fort Lauderdale-Pompano Beach-Deerfield Beach PMSA, FL	Y	14820 FQ	18270 MW	23320 TQ	USBLS	5/07
	Jacksonville MSA, FL	Y	15230 FQ	19080 MW	23050 TQ	USBLS	5/07
	Miami-Fort Lauderdale-Miami Beach MSA, FL	Y	14970 FQ	18790 MW	23690 TQ	USBLS	5/07
	Orlando-Kissimmee MSA, FL	Y	14790 FQ	16610 MW	22990 TQ	USBLS	5/07
	Tampa-St. Petersburg-Clearwater MSA, FL	Y	14780 FQ	17840 MW	22920 TQ	USBLS	5/07
	West Palm Beach-Boca Raton-Boynton Beach PMSA, FL	Y	14910 FQ	19780 MW	25290 TQ	USBLS	5/07
	Georgia	Y	12740 FQ	14270 MW	17360 TQ	USBLS	5/07
	Athens-Clarke County MSA, GA	Y	12450 FQ	13850 MW	15330 TQ	USBLS	5/07
	Atlanta-Sandy Springs-Marietta MSA, GA	Y	12810 FQ	14390 MW	18700 TQ	USBLS	5/07
	Savannah MSA, GA	Y	12990 FQ	14710 MW	22190 TQ	USBLS	5/07
	Hawaii	Y	15640 FQ	20930 MW	31040 TQ	USBLS	5/07
	Honolulu MSA, HI	Y	15490 FQ	19360 MW	29420 TQ	USBLS	5/07
	Idaho	Y	12680 FQ	14220 MW	16850 TQ	USBLS	5/07
	Boise City-Nampa MSA, ID	Y	12610 FQ	14110 MW	16000 TQ	USBLS	5/07
	Coeur d'Alene MSA, ID	Y	12470 FQ	13790 MW	15240 TQ	USBLS	5/07
	Illinois	Y	14680 FQ	15390 MW	19440 TQ	USBLS	5/07
	Chicago-Naperville-Joliet MSA, IL-IN-WI	Y	14650 FQ	15450 MW	20560 TQ	USBLS	5/07
	Indiana	Y	12890 FQ	14600 MW	18050 TQ	USBLS	5/07
	Gary PMSA, IN	Y	12860 FQ	14570 MW	17670 TQ	USBLS	5/07
	Indianapolis-Carmel MSA, IN	Y	13180 FQ	15280 MW	20360 TQ	USBLS	5/07
	Iowa	Y	13800 FQ	14710 MW	15990 TQ	USBLS	5/07

AE	Average entry wage	**AW**	Average wage paid	**FQ**	First quartile wage	**LO**	Lowest wage paid
AER	Average entry range	**AWR**	Average wage range	**H**	Hourly	**LR**	Low end range
AEX	Average experienced wage	**AXR**	Average experienced range	**HI**	Highest wage paid	**M**	Monthly
ATC	Average total compensation **D**	Daily		**HR**	High end range	**MCC**	Median cash compensation

MTC	Median total compensation	**TCC**	Total cash compensation
MW	Median wage paid	**TQ**	Third quartile wage
MWR	Median wage range	**W**	Weekly
S	See annotated source	**Y**	Yearly

Occupation/Type/Industry	Location	Per	Low	Mid	High	Source	Date
Waiter and Waitress	Des Moines-West Des Moines MSA, IA	Y	13890 FQ	14890 MW	18090 TQ	USBLS	5/07
	Dubuque MSA, IA	Y	13840 FQ	14770 MW	16010 TQ	USBLS	5/07
	Kansas	Y	12730 FQ	14280 MW	16860 TQ	USBLS	5/07
	Topeka MSA, KS	Y	12580 FQ	14030 MW	15630 TQ	USBLS	5/07
	Wichita MSA, KS	Y	12460 FQ	13770 MW	15120 TQ	USBLS	5/07
	Kentucky	Y	13053 FQ	14586 MW	16450 TQ	KYBLS	2008
	Lexington-Fayette MSA, KY	Y	12810 FQ	14500 MW	17450 TQ	USBLS	5/07
	Louisville-Jefferson County MSA, KY-IN	Y	12710 FQ	14270 MW	16740 TQ	USBLS	5/07
	Louisiana	H	6.07 FQ	6.79 MW	7.64 TQ	LABLS	1/08-3/08
	Baton Rouge MSA, LA	Y	12680 FQ	14240 MW	16160 TQ	USBLS	5/07
	New Orleans-Metairie-Kenner MSA, LA	Y	12790 FQ	14480 MW	17520 TQ	USBLS	5/07
	Maine	Y	14810 FQ	15700 MW	25410 TQ	USBLS	5/07
	Portland-South Portland-Biddeford MSA, ME	Y	14880 FQ	15880 MW	25010 TQ	USBLS	5/07
	Maryland	Y		15325 MW		MDBLS	3/08
	Baltimore-Towson MSA, MD	Y	14020 FQ	14860 MW	17420 TQ	USBLS	5/07
	Bethesda-Gaithersburg-Frederick PMSA, MD	Y	14330 FQ	15760 MW	21920 TQ	USBLS	5/07
	Salisbury MSA, MD	Y	14020 FQ	14840 MW	16430 TQ	USBLS	5/07
	Massachusetts	Y	16730 FQ	23350 MW	28650 TQ	USBLS	5/07
	Boston-Cambridge-Quincy NECTA, MA	Y	17280 FQ	25140 MW	29400 TQ	USBLS	5/07
	New Bedford MSA, MA	Y	15950 FQ	18260 MW	23110 TQ	USBLS	5/07
	Worcester MSA, MA-CT	Y	16240 FQ	19640 MW	27830 TQ	USBLS	5/07
	Michigan	Y	14950 FQ	15550 MW	17880 TQ	USBLS	5/07
	Detroit-Warren-Livonia MSA, MI	Y	15020 FQ	15680 MW	18730 TQ	USBLS	5/07
	Flint MSA, MI	Y	14930 FQ	15480 MW	17980 TQ	USBLS	5/07
	Grand Rapids-Wyoming MSA, MI	Y	15050 FQ	15680 MW	18660 TQ	USBLS	5/07
	Warren-Troy-Farmington Hills PMSA, MI	Y	14980 FQ	15690 MW	19900 TQ	USBLS	5/07
	Minnesota	Y	15108 FQ	17001 MW	27300 TQ	MNBLS	10/08-12/08
	Duluth-Superior MSA, MN-WI	Y	14962 FQ	16039 MW	22626 TQ	MNBLS	10/08-12/08
	Minneapolis-Saint Paul MSA, MN-WI	Y	15223 FQ	19217 MW	29014 TQ	MNBLS	10/08-12/08
	Rochester MSA, MN	Y	15297 FQ	18818 MW	28231 TQ	MNBLS	10/08-12/08
	Mississippi	Y	12530 FQ	13860 MW	15250 TQ	USBLS	5/07
	Jackson MSA, MS	Y	12460 FQ	13720 MW	14980 TQ	USBLS	5/07
	Missouri	Y	14230 FQ	14950 MW	16660 TQ	USBLS	5/07
	Kansas City MSA, MO-KS	Y	13870 FQ	14720 MW	16200 TQ	USBLS	5/07
	St. Louis MSA, MO-IL	Y	14430 FQ	15270 MW	19190 TQ	USBLS	5/07
	Montana	Y	13780 FQ	14760 MW	16220 TQ	USBLS	5/07
	Billings MSA, MT	Y	13810 FQ	14820 MW	16310 TQ	USBLS	5/07
	Missoula MSA, MT	Y	13720 FQ	14650 MW	15880 TQ	USBLS	5/07
	Nebraska	Y	12610 FQ	14080 MW	15760 TQ	USBLS	5/07
	Omaha-Council Bluffs MSA, NE-IA	Y	12920 FQ	14280 MW	15880 TQ	USBLS	5/07
	Nevada	H	6.68 FQ	8.12 MW	10.96 TQ	NVBLS	5/08
	Las Vegas-Paradise MSA, NV	H	6.91 FQ	9.10 MW	11.30 TQ	NVBLS	5/08
	New Hampshire	H	6.50 AE	7.67 MW	10.89 AEX	NHBLS	6/08
	Manchester MSA, NH	Y	13520 FQ	16250 MW	24460 TQ	USBLS	5/07
	Nashua NECTA, NH-MA	Y	13430 FQ	16970 MW	26040 TQ	USBLS	5/07
	New Jersey	Y	16040 FQ	21430 MW	27130 TQ	USBLS	5/07
	Camden PMSA, NJ	Y	15840 FQ	20380 MW	25460 TQ	USBLS	5/07
	Edison PMSA, NJ	Y	17860 FQ	22590 MW	27670 TQ	USBLS	5/07
	Newark-Union PMSA, NJ-PA	Y	15820 FQ	21470 MW	27540 TQ	USBLS	5/07
	New Mexico	Y	12620 FQ	14050 MW	15720 TQ	USBLS	5/07
	Albuquerque MSA, NM	Y	12570 FQ	13930 MW	15450 TQ	USBLS	5/07
	New York	Y	16100 FQ	21400 MW	28670 TQ	USBLS	5/07
	Albany-Schenectady-Troy MSA, NY	Y	15660 FQ	19520 MW	25880 TQ	USBLS	5/07
	Buffalo-Niagara Falls MSA, NY	Y	15060 FQ	16640 MW	23130 TQ	USBLS	5/07
	Nassau-Suffolk PMSA, NY	Y	16390 FQ	21270 MW	26800 TQ	USBLS	5/07
	New York-Northern New Jersey-Long Island MSA, NY-NJ-PA	Y	17510 FQ	22900 MW	30500 TQ	USBLS	5/07
	Syracuse MSA, NY	Y	15660 FQ	18810 MW	24760 TQ	USBLS	5/07

AE	Average entry wage	AW	Average wage paid	FQ	First quartile wage	LO	Lowest wage paid	MTC	Median total compensation	TCC	Total cash compensation
AER	Average entry range	AWR	Average wage range	H	Hourly	LR	Low end range	MW	Median wage paid	TQ	Third quartile wage
AEX	Average experienced wage	AXR	Average experienced range	HI	Highest wage paid	M	Monthly	MWR	Median wage range	W	Weekly
ATC	Average total compensation	D	Daily	HR	High end range	MCC	Median cash compensation	S	See annotated source	Y	Yearly

1671

Occupation/Type/Industry	Location	Per	Low	Mid	High	Source	Date
Waiter and Waitress	North Carolina	Y	13800 FQ	14800 MW	16690 TQ	USBLS	5/07
	Charlotte-Gastonia-Concord MSA, NC-SC	Y	13780 FQ	14880 MW	17900 TQ	USBLS	5/07
	Greensboro-High Point MSA, NC	Y	13750 FQ	14710 MW	16090 TQ	USBLS	5/07
	Raleigh-Cary MSA, NC	Y	13840 FQ	14890 MW	18460 TQ	USBLS	5/07
	North Dakota	Y	12660 FQ	14130 MW	15970 TQ	USBLS	5/07
	Bismarck MSA, ND	Y	12600 FQ	13970 MW	15640 TQ	USBLS	5/07
	Fargo MSA, ND-MN	Y	13070 FQ	14560 MW	18400 TQ	USBLS	5/07
	Ohio	Y	14670 FQ	15170 MW	16140 TQ	USBLS	5/07
	Cincinnati-Middletown MSA, OH-KY-IN	Y	14540 FQ	15180 MW	17460 TQ	USBLS	5/07
	Cleveland-Elyria-Mentor MSA, OH	Y	14700 FQ	15260 MW	16240 TQ	USBLS	5/07
	Columbus MSA, OH	Y	14700 FQ	15240 MW	16230 TQ	USBLS	5/07
	Dayton MSA, OH	Y	14650 FQ	15110 MW	15870 TQ	USBLS	5/07
	Oklahoma	Y	12770 FQ	14320 MW	16650 TQ	USBLS	5/07
	Oklahoma City MSA, OK	Y	12800 FQ	14370 MW	17000 TQ	USBLS	5/07
	Tulsa MSA, OK	Y	13100 FQ	14980 MW	18350 TQ	USBLS	5/07
	Oregon	H	8.62 FQ	9.28 MW	10.57 TQ	ORBLS	5/08
	Portland-Vancouver-Beaverton MSA, OR-WA	Y	17600 FQ	19210 MW	23650 TQ	USBLS	5/07
	Pennsylvania	Y	14300 FQ	15120 MW	17580 TQ	USBLS	5/07
	Allentown-Bethlehem-Easton MSA, PA-NJ	Y	14260 FQ	15000 MW	16240 TQ	USBLS	5/07
	Erie MSA, PA	Y	14200 FQ	14870 MW	16410 TQ	USBLS	5/07
	Philadelphia-Camden-Wilmington MSA, PA-NJ-DE-MD	Y	14750 FQ	16100 MW	21460 TQ	USBLS	5/07
	Pittsburgh MSA, PA	Y	14220 FQ	14930 MW	16120 TQ	USBLS	5/07
	Rhode Island	Y	15670 FQ	16430 MW	19920 TQ	USBLS	5/07
	Providence-Fall River-Warwick MSA, RI-MA	Y	15750 FQ	17130 MW	22600 TQ	USBLS	5/07
	South Carolina	Y	12690 FQ	14170 MW	16100 TQ	USBLS	5/07
	Charleston-North Charleston MSA, SC	Y	12950 FQ	14740 MW	17320 TQ	USBLS	5/07
	Columbia MSA, SC	Y	12570 FQ	13850 MW	15220 TQ	USBLS	5/07
	South Dakota	Y		14580 MW	16255 TQ	SDBLS	7/08-9/08
	Sioux Falls MSA, SD	Y		14644 MW	16413 TQ	SDBLS	7/08-9/08
	Tennessee	Y	12680 FQ	14220 MW	16480 TQ	USBLS	5/07
	Memphis MSA, TN-MS-AR	Y	12930 FQ	14600 MW	18230 TQ	USBLS	5/07
	Nashville-Davidson-Murfreesboro MSA, TN	Y	12750 FQ	14350 MW	17920 TQ	USBLS	5/07
	Texas	Y	12690 FQ	14200 MW	16130 TQ	USBLS	5/07
	Austin-Round Rock MSA, TX	Y	12650 FQ	14120 MW	15950 TQ	USBLS	5/07
	Corpus Christi MSA, TX	Y	12520 FQ	13820 MW	15160 TQ	USBLS	5/07
	Dallas-Fort Worth-Arlington MSA, TX	Y	12790 FQ	14400 MW	17720 TQ	USBLS	5/07
	El Paso MSA, TX	Y	12520 FQ	13920 MW	15410 TQ	USBLS	5/07
	Houston-Sugar Land-Baytown MSA, TX	Y	12790 FQ	14420 MW	16910 TQ	USBLS	5/07
	San Antonio MSA, TX	Y	12790 FQ	14370 MW	17120 TQ	USBLS	5/07
	Utah	Y	13630 FQ	16490 MW	22500 TQ	USBLS	5/07
	Salt Lake City MSA, UT	Y	13750 FQ	17090 MW	24440 TQ	USBLS	5/07
	Vermont	Y	16280 FQ	18470 MW	25320 TQ	USBLS	5/07
	Burlington-South Burlington MSA, VT	Y	16770 FQ	20060 MW	31000 TQ	USBLS	5/07
	Virginia	Y	13150 FQ	15180 MW	19610 TQ	USBLS	5/07
	Richmond MSA, VA	Y	13090 FQ	14960 MW	19360 TQ	USBLS	5/07
	Virginia Beach-Norfolk-Newport News MSA, VA-NC	Y	13040 FQ	14870 MW	18650 TQ	USBLS	5/07
	Washington	H	11.67 FQ	13.55 MW	15.18 TQ	WABLS	3/08
	Seattle-Tacoma-Bellevue MSA, WA	Y	23430 FQ	27910 MW	31530 TQ	USBLS	5/07
	West Virginia	Y	14044 FQ	15168 MW	16694 TQ	WVBLS	7/08-9/08
	Charleston MSA, WV	Y	13610 FQ	14810 MW	16970 TQ	USBLS	5/07
	Wheeling MSA, WV-OH	Y	14030 FQ	14700 MW	15430 TQ	USBLS	5/07
	Wisconsin	Y	14490 FQ	15320 MW	18380 TQ	USBLS	5/07
	Green Bay MSA, WI	Y	14480 FQ	15260 MW	18610 TQ	USBLS	5/07
	Milwaukee-Waukesha-West Allis MSA, WI	Y	14530 FQ	15390 MW	18190 TQ	USBLS	5/07
	Wyoming	Y	13145 FQ	14632 MW	16441 TQ	WYBLS	9/08

AE	Average entry wage	AW	Average wage paid	FQ	First quartile wage
AER	Average entry range	AWR	Average wage range	H	Hourly
AEX	Average experienced wage	AXR	Average experienced range	HI	Highest wage paid
ATC	Average total compensation	D	Daily	HR	High end range

LO	Lowest wage paid	MTC	Median total compensation
LR	Low end range	MW	Median wage paid
M	Monthly	MWR	Median wage range
MCC	Median cash compensation	S	See annotated source

TCC	Total cash compensation
TQ	Third quartile wage
W	Weekly
Y	Yearly

Occupation/Type/Industry	Location	Per	Low	Mid	High	Source	Date
Waiter and Waitress	Cheyenne MSA, WY	Y	12851 FQ	14191 MW	15531 TQ	WYBLS	9/08
	Puerto Rico	Y	12430 FQ	13650 MW	14870 TQ	USBLS	5/07
	San Juan-Caguas-Guaynabo MSA, PR	Y	12470 FQ	13720 MW	14980 TQ	USBLS	5/07
	Virgin Islands	Y	13710 FQ	14630 MW	16120 TQ	USBLS	5/07
	Guam	Y	12500 FQ	13830 MW	15210 TQ	USBLS	5/07
Wall Street Trader	New York, NY	S	80000 LO		600000 HI	BBERG	2008
Ward Clerk							
Glencliff Home for the Elderly	New Hampshire	Y			30519 HI	NHUL03	2008
New Hampshire Hospital	New Hampshire	Y		28723 AW		NHUL03	2008
Warden							
State Prison - Men	New Hampshire	Y			97444 HI	NHUL03	2008
State Prison - Women	New Hampshire	Y			107488 HI	NHUL03	2008
Warehouse Superintendent							
Liquor Commission	New Hampshire	Y			58376 HI	NHUL03	2008
Warrant Officer							
Military, Active Duty, Pay Grade W-1	United States	M	2593 LO		4484 HI	DOD1	2009
Military, Active Duty, Pay Grade W-2	United States	M	2938 LO		4935 HI	DOD1	2009
Military, Active Duty, Pay Grade W-3	United States	M	3340 LO		5861 HI	DOD1	2009
Military, Active Duty, Pay Grade W-4	United States	M	3658 LO		6815 HI	DOD1	2009
Military, Active Duty, Pay Grade W-5	United States	M	6506 LO		8513 HI	DOD1	2009
Military, Reserve, Pay Grade W-1	United States	S	5364 LO		9268 HI	DOD2	2009
Military, Reserve, Pay Grade W-2	United States	S	6110 LO		10199 HI	DOD2	2009
Military, Reserve, Pay Grade W-3	United States	S	6904 LO		12112 HI	DOD2	2009
Military, Reserve, Pay Grade W-4	United States	S	7561 LO		13809 HI	DOD2	2009
Military, Reserve, Pay Grade W-5	United States	S	13445 LO		15197 HI	DOD2	2009
Municipal Government	Seattle, WA	H	18.98 LO		22.04 HI	CSSS	2007
Watch Repairer	Arizona	Y	17100 FQ	19610 MW	27750 TQ	USBLS	5/07
	Phoenix-Mesa-Scottsdale MSA, AZ	Y	16690 FQ	18460 MW	23800 TQ	USBLS	5/07
	California	H	11.44 FQ	13.95 MW	16.51 TQ	CABLS	1/08-3/08
	Connecticut	H	16.94 AE	17.92 MW		CTBLS	1/08-3/08
	Florida	Y	21960 FQ	28260 MW	42230 TQ	USBLS	5/07
	Orlando-Kissimmee MSA, FL	Y	21650 FQ	33380 MW	43170 TQ	USBLS	5/07
	Tampa-St. Petersburg-Clearwater MSA, FL	Y	21790 FQ	23300 MW	24810 TQ	USBLS	5/07
	Georgia	Y	16230 FQ	41940 MW	46450 TQ	USBLS	5/07
	Illinois	Y	32540 FQ	37590 MW	45250 TQ	USBLS	5/07
	Chicago-Naperville-Joliet MSA, IL-IN-WI	Y	32930 FQ	38050 MW	45650 TQ	USBLS	5/07
	Indiana	Y	33760 FQ	37820 MW	41440 TQ	USBLS	5/07
	Michigan	Y	17730 FQ	25960 MW	42080 TQ	USBLS	5/07
	Minnesota	Y	35412 FQ	40331 MW	45933 TQ	MNBLS	10/08-12/08
	Minneapolis-Saint Paul MSA, MN-WI	Y	35412 FQ	40331 MW	45933 TQ	MNBLS	10/08-12/08
	Nebraska	Y	31550 FQ	33630 MW	35730 TQ	USBLS	5/07
	New Hampshire	H	9.21 AE	11.00 MW	16.03 AEX	NHBLS	6/08
	New Jersey	Y	35760 FQ	46360 MW	56680 TQ	USBLS	5/07
	New York	Y	30760 FQ	56140 MW	81220 TQ	USBLS	5/07
	New York-Northern New Jersey-Long Island MSA, NY-NJ-PA	Y	39460 FQ	55420 MW	75540 TQ	USBLS	5/07
	Ohio	Y	33240 FQ	49400 MW	54850 TQ	USBLS	5/07
	Pennsylvania	Y	31410 FQ	39830 MW	53150 TQ	USBLS	5/07
	Philadelphia-Camden-Wilmington MSA, PA-NJ-DE-MD	Y	45360 FQ	51620 MW	57740 TQ	USBLS	5/07
	Texas	Y	18430 FQ	25370 MW	29720 TQ	USBLS	5/07
	Austin-Round Rock MSA, TX	Y	18130 FQ	20260 MW	29070 TQ	USBLS	5/07
	Washington	H	20.97 FQ	22.59 MW	24.21 TQ	WABLS	3/08
	Puerto Rico	Y	13410 FQ	16070 MW	19930 TQ	USBLS	5/07
Water and Liquid Waste Treatment Plant and System Operator	Alabama	Y	27350 FQ	33990 MW	41940 TQ	USBLS	5/07
	Birmingham-Hoover MSA, AL	Y	30760 FQ	36700 MW	45610 TQ	USBLS	5/07

AE	Average entry wage	**AW**	Average wage paid	**FQ**	First quartile wage	**LO** Lowest wage paid	**MTC** Median total compensation	**TCC** Total cash compensation
AER	Average entry range	**AWR**	Average wage range	**H**	Hourly	**LR** Low end range	**MW** Median wage paid	**TQ** Third quartile wage
AEX	Average experienced wage	**AXR**	Average experienced range	**HI**	Highest wage paid	**M** Monthly	**MWR** Median wage range	**W** Weekly
ATC	Average total compensation	**D**	Daily	**HR**	High end range	**MCC** Median cash compensation	**S** See annotated source	**Y** Yearly

Occupation/Type/Industry	Location	Per	Low	Mid	High	Source	Date
Water and Liquid Waste Treatment Plant and System Operator							
	Alaska	Y	30340 FQ	48230 MW	63780 TQ	USBLS	5/07
	Anchorage MSA, AK	Y	51190 FQ	59850 MW	69560 TQ	USBLS	5/07
	Arizona	Y	33970 FQ	41410 MW	50850 TQ	USBLS	5/07
	Phoenix-Mesa-Scottsdale MSA, AZ	Y	37690 FQ	45450 MW	55380 TQ	USBLS	5/07
	Tucson MSA, AZ	Y	31110 FQ	36700 MW	45980 TQ	USBLS	5/07
	Arkansas	Y	23740 FQ	29110 MW	36580 TQ	USBLS	5/07
	Fayetteville-Springdale-Rogers MSA, AR-MO	Y	26580 FQ	32110 MW	38470 TQ	USBLS	5/07
	Little Rock-North Little Rock MSA, AR	Y	23320 FQ	27830 MW	35150 TQ	USBLS	5/07
	California	H	20.70 FQ	25.66 MW	31.04 TQ	CABLS	1/08-3/08
	Los Angeles-Long Beach-Glendale PMSA, CA	H	22.35 FQ	26.62 MW	31.80 TQ	CABLS	1/08-3/08
	Oakland-Fremont-Hayward MSA, CA	H	28.55 FQ	33.74 MW	37.80 TQ	CABLS	1/08-3/08
	Riverside-San Bernardino-Ontario MSA, CA	H	18.86 FQ	23.69 MW	28.31 TQ	CABLS	1/08-3/08
	Sacramento-Arden Arcade-Roseville MSA, CA	H	20.14 FQ	25.63 MW	30.75 TQ	CABLS	1/08-3/08
	San Diego-Carlsbad-San Marcos MSA, CA	H	22.29 FQ	26.73 MW	30.93 TQ	CABLS	1/08-3/08
	San Francisco-San Mateo-Redwood PMSA, CA	H	23.88 FQ	27.78 MW	32.05 TQ	CABLS	1/08-3/08
	San Jose-Sunnyvale-Santa Clara MSA, CA	H	27.13 FQ	31.52 MW	35.13 TQ	CABLS	1/08-3/08
	Santa Ana-Anaheim-Irvine PMSA, CA	Y	39170 FQ	49800 MW	61350 TQ	USBLS	5/07
	Colorado	Y	32900 FQ	41140 MW	51240 TQ	USBLS	5/07
	Boulder MSA, CO	Y	33160 FQ	38760 MW	47640 TQ	USBLS	5/07
	Denver-Aurora MSA, CO	Y	35930 FQ	45700 MW	55860 TQ	USBLS	5/07
	Connecticut	H	17.19 AE	23.15 MW		CTBLS	1/08-3/08
	Bridgeport-Stamford-Norwalk MSA, CT	Y	36180 FQ	43370 MW	53610 TQ	USBLS	5/07
	Hartford-West Hartford-East Hartford MSA, CT	Y	41960 FQ	48860 MW	56920 TQ	USBLS	5/07
	Delaware	Y	29970 FQ	38310 MW	47430 TQ	USBLS	5/07
	Wilmington PMSA, DE-MD-NJ	Y	37740 FQ	46180 MW	53670 TQ	USBLS	5/07
	District of Columbia	Y	37470 FQ	43270 MW	51220 TQ	USBLS	5/07
	Washington-Arlington-Alexandria MSA, DC-VA-MD-WV	Y	34790 FQ	42320 MW	50160 TQ	USBLS	5/07
	Florida	Y	32950 FQ	40020 MW	48740 TQ	USBLS	5/07
	Fort Lauderdale-Pompano Beach-Deerfield Beach PMSA, FL	Y	38220 FQ	45730 MW	53130 TQ	USBLS	5/07
	Jacksonville MSA, FL	Y	35480 FQ	46830 MW	58590 TQ	USBLS	5/07
	Miami-Fort Lauderdale-Miami Beach MSA, FL	Y	37950 FQ	45720 MW	54570 TQ	USBLS	5/07
	Orlando-Kissimmee MSA, FL	Y	32890 FQ	39740 MW	49140 TQ	USBLS	5/07
	Tallahassee MSA, FL	Y	33450 FQ	39510 MW	46130 TQ	USBLS	5/07
	Tampa-St. Petersburg-Clearwater MSA, FL	Y	30610 FQ	37570 MW	45970 TQ	USBLS	5/07
	West Palm Beach-Boca Raton-Boynton Beach PMSA, FL	Y	37120 FQ	44450 MW	52980 TQ	USBLS	5/07
	Georgia	Y	25890 FQ	30590 MW	37630 TQ	USBLS	5/07
	Atlanta-Sandy Springs-Marietta MSA, GA	Y	28720 FQ	33860 MW	40460 TQ	USBLS	5/07
	Hawaii	Y	35660 FQ	42970 MW	48390 TQ	USBLS	5/07
	Honolulu MSA, HI	Y	41970 FQ	45820 MW	49680 TQ	USBLS	5/07
	Idaho	Y	25390 FQ	30850 MW	36600 TQ	USBLS	5/07
	Boise City-Nampa MSA, ID	Y	31910 FQ	35660 MW	39400 TQ	USBLS	5/07
	Coeur d'Alene MSA, ID	Y	24370 FQ	31610 MW	41340 TQ	USBLS	5/07
	Illinois	Y	36600 FQ	47200 MW	61900 TQ	USBLS	5/07
	Chicago-Naperville-Joliet MSA, IL-IN-WI	Y	37450 FQ	52130 MW	65360 TQ	USBLS	5/07
	Indiana	Y	29600 FQ	34590 MW	40000 TQ	USBLS	5/07
	Fort Wayne MSA, IN	Y	27640 FQ	34920 MW	43200 TQ	USBLS	5/07

AE Average entry wage	**AW** Average wage paid	**FQ** First quartile wage	**LO** Lowest wage paid	**MTC** Median total compensation	**TCC** Total cash compensation
AER Average entry range	**AWR** Average wage range	**H** Hourly	**LR** Low end range	**MW** Median wage paid	**TQ** Third quartile wage
AEX Average experienced wage	**AXR** Average experienced range	**HI** Highest wage paid	**M** Monthly	**MWR** Median wage range	**W** Weekly
ATC Average total compensation	**D** Daily	**HR** High end range	**MCC** Median cash compensation	**S** See annotated source	**Y** Yearly

Occupation/Type/Industry	Location	Per	Low	Mid	High	Source	Date
Water and Liquid Waste Treatment Plant and System Operator							
	Gary PMSA, IN	Y	30950 FQ	34050 MW	37260 TQ	USBLS	5/07
	Indianapolis-Carmel MSA, IN	Y	32560 FQ	39370 MW	46920 TQ	USBLS	5/07
	Iowa	Y	28030 FQ	34550 MW	40580 TQ	USBLS	5/07
	Des Moines-West Des Moines MSA, IA	Y	35030 FQ	41250 MW	48260 TQ	USBLS	5/07
	Dubuque MSA, IA	Y	39190 FQ	43910 MW	48140 TQ	USBLS	5/07
	Kansas	Y	26520 FQ	31560 MW	37440 TQ	USBLS	5/07
	Wichita MSA, KS	Y	27720 FQ	32220 MW	37330 TQ	USBLS	5/07
	Kentucky	Y	23949 FQ	30069 MW	37071 TQ	KYBLS	2008
	Louisville-Jefferson County MSA, KY-IN	Y	27850 FQ	32890 MW	39020 TQ	USBLS	5/07
	Louisiana	H	10.57 FQ	13.08 MW	16.13 TQ	LABLS	1/08-3/08
	Baton Rouge MSA, LA	Y	24890 FQ	30120 MW	36360 TQ	USBLS	5/07
	Houma-Bayou Cane-Thibodaux MSA, LA	Y	20940 FQ	27770 MW	34930 TQ	USBLS	5/07
	New Orleans-Metairie-Kenner MSA, LA	Y	26120 FQ	31190 MW	38670 TQ	USBLS	5/07
	Maine	Y	31810 FQ	35690 MW	39780 TQ	USBLS	5/07
	Portland-South Portland-Biddeford MSA, ME	Y	35150 FQ	39940 MW	46090 TQ	USBLS	5/07
	Maryland	Y		41525 MW		MDBLS	3/08
	Baltimore-Towson MSA, MD	Y	33480 FQ	40740 MW	49310 TQ	USBLS	5/07
	Bethesda-Gaithersburg-Frederick PMSA, MD	Y	37460 FQ	47720 MW	57010 TQ	USBLS	5/07
	Cumberland MSA, MD-WV	Y	22800 FQ	29280 MW	38690 TQ	USBLS	5/07
	Massachusetts	Y	36320 FQ	42510 MW	49500 TQ	USBLS	5/07
	Boston-Cambridge-Quincy NECTA, MA	Y	38480 FQ	44710 MW	50710 TQ	USBLS	5/07
	Worcester MSA, MA-CT	Y	33420 FQ	40380 MW	47660 TQ	USBLS	5/07
	Michigan	Y	33360 FQ	39260 MW	46050 TQ	USBLS	5/07
	Detroit-Warren-Livonia MSA, MI	Y	36320 FQ	43430 MW	49390 TQ	USBLS	5/07
	Grand Rapids-Wyoming MSA, MI	Y	35660 FQ	41290 MW	47560 TQ	USBLS	5/07
	Warren-Troy-Farmington Hills PMSA, MI	Y	41530 FQ	45850 MW	50440 TQ	USBLS	5/07
	Minnesota	Y	38875 FQ	45168 MW	51294 TQ	MNBLS	10/08-12/08
	Duluth-Superior MSA, MN-WI	Y	43042 FQ	47687 MW	53233 TQ	MNBLS	10/08-12/08
	Minneapolis-Saint Paul MSA, MN-WI	Y	43146 FQ	48599 MW	53295 TQ	MNBLS	10/08-12/08
	Rochester MSA, MN	Y	37555 FQ	43654 MW	55069 TQ	MNBLS	10/08-12/08
	Mississippi	Y	22280 FQ	28650 MW	35250 TQ	USBLS	5/07
	Jackson MSA, MS	Y	21650 FQ	29430 MW	42370 TQ	USBLS	5/07
	Missouri	Y	25870 FQ	31850 MW	38600 TQ	USBLS	5/07
	Kansas City MSA, MO-KS	Y	26240 FQ	33720 MW	42120 TQ	USBLS	5/07
	St. Louis MSA, MO-IL	Y	34910 FQ	44250 MW	64070 TQ	USBLS	5/07
	Montana	Y	27430 FQ	34610 MW	40350 TQ	USBLS	5/07
	Billings MSA, MT	Y	34890 FQ	39700 MW	43940 TQ	USBLS	5/07
	Nebraska	Y	28180 FQ	34700 MW	43470 TQ	USBLS	5/07
	Omaha-Council Bluffs MSA, NE-IA	Y	34720 FQ	44350 MW	52430 TQ	USBLS	5/07
	Nevada	H	21.76 FQ	27.37 MW	31.36 TQ	NVBLS	5/08
	Las Vegas-Paradise MSA, NV	H	25.58 FQ	29.10 MW	33.03 TQ	NVBLS	5/08
	New Hampshire	H	15.46 AE	19.45 MW	22.71 AEX	NHBLS	6/08
	Manchester MSA, NH	Y	35680 FQ	41490 MW	50940 TQ	USBLS	5/07
	Nashua NECTA, NH-MA	Y	37110 FQ	42640 MW	47700 TQ	USBLS	5/07
	New Jersey	Y	42600 FQ	50240 MW	58950 TQ	USBLS	5/07
	Camden PMSA, NJ	Y	41360 FQ	46260 MW	51880 TQ	USBLS	5/07
	Edison PMSA, NJ	Y	42470 FQ	51740 MW	59620 TQ	USBLS	5/07
	Newark-Union PMSA, NJ-PA	Y	43220 FQ	50920 MW	61130 TQ	USBLS	5/07
	New Mexico	Y	22120 FQ	27920 MW	35400 TQ	USBLS	5/07
	Albuquerque MSA, NM	Y	25710 FQ	30910 MW	36350 TQ	USBLS	5/07
	New York	Y	35880 FQ	43510 MW	50230 TQ	USBLS	5/07
	Albany-Schenectady-Troy MSA, NY	Y	33100 FQ	39350 MW	46370 TQ	USBLS	5/07
	Buffalo-Niagara Falls MSA, NY	Y	37630 FQ	44550 MW	50530 TQ	USBLS	5/07
	Ithaca MSA, NY	Y	32710 FQ	35750 MW	38900 TQ	USBLS	5/07
	Nassau-Suffolk PMSA, NY	Y	41070 FQ	50980 MW	59450 TQ	USBLS	5/07

AE	Average entry wage	AW	Average wage paid	FQ	First quartile wage	LO	Lowest wage paid	MTC Median total compensation	TCC Total cash compensation
AER	Average entry range	AWR	Average wage range	H	Hourly	LR	Low end range	MW Median wage paid	TQ Third quartile wage
AEX	Average experienced wage	AXR	Average experienced range	HI	Highest wage paid	M	Monthly	MWR Median wage range	W Weekly
ATC	Average total compensation	D	Daily	HR	High end range	MCC Median cash compensation	S See annotated source	Y Yearly

Occupation/Type/Industry	Location	Per	Low	Mid	High	Source	Date
Water and Liquid Waste Treatment Plant and System Operator							
	New York-Northern New Jersey-Long Island MSA, NY-NJ-PA	Y	43450 FQ	49840 MW	58250 TQ	USBLS	5/07
	North Carolina	Y	27290 FQ	32590 MW	38650 TQ	USBLS	5/07
	Asheville MSA, NC	Y	27120 FQ	32090 MW	36250 TQ	USBLS	5/07
	Charlotte-Gastonia-Concord MSA, NC-SC	Y	28110 FQ	33440 MW	39550 TQ	USBLS	5/07
	Raleigh-Cary MSA, NC	Y	30220 FQ	35770 MW	41510 TQ	USBLS	5/07
	North Dakota	Y	29920 FQ	35920 MW	44040 TQ	USBLS	5/07
	Fargo MSA, ND-MN	Y	36830 FQ	41780 MW	47210 TQ	USBLS	5/07
	Ohio	Y	33270 FQ	39390 MW	45860 TQ	USBLS	5/07
	Cincinnati-Middletown MSA, OH-KY-IN	Y	33250 FQ	40650 MW	47300 TQ	USBLS	5/07
	Cleveland-Elyria-Mentor MSA, OH	Y	36710 FQ	42770 MW	47770 TQ	USBLS	5/07
	Columbus MSA, OH	Y	32970 FQ	38260 MW	45190 TQ	USBLS	5/07
	Dayton MSA, OH	Y	35740 FQ	42320 MW	49020 TQ	USBLS	5/07
	Oklahoma	Y	21690 FQ	26050 MW	32000 TQ	USBLS	5/07
	Oklahoma City MSA, OK	Y	22550 FQ	27490 MW	36370 TQ	USBLS	5/07
	Tulsa MSA, OK	Y	23920 FQ	28920 MW	35010 TQ	USBLS	5/07
	Oregon	H	17.10 FQ	20.65 MW	24.46 TQ	ORBLS	5/08
	Medford MSA, OR	Y	39220 FQ	43580 MW	47930 TQ	USBLS	5/07
	Portland-Vancouver-Beaverton MSA, OR-WA	Y	34840 FQ	43190 MW	51300 TQ	USBLS	5/07
	Pennsylvania	Y	29890 FQ	38270 MW	46460 TQ	USBLS	5/07
	Allentown-Bethlehem-Easton MSA, PA-NJ	Y	34040 FQ	41080 MW	47500 TQ	USBLS	5/07
	Philadelphia-Camden-Wilmington MSA, PA-NJ-DE-MD	Y	34990 FQ	42900 MW	49440 TQ	USBLS	5/07
	Pittsburgh MSA, PA	Y	14430 FQ	34870 MW	47620 TQ	USBLS	5/07
	Rhode Island	Y	35420 FQ	40240 MW	49320 TQ	USBLS	5/07
	Providence-Fall River-Warwick MSA, RI-MA	Y	34790 FQ	39760 MW	48340 TQ	USBLS	5/07
	South Carolina	Y	25310 FQ	32430 MW	40680 TQ	USBLS	5/07
	Charleston-North Charleston MSA, SC	Y	25370 FQ	32290 MW	41420 TQ	USBLS	5/07
	Columbia MSA, SC	Y	18260 FQ	26480 MW	37040 TQ	USBLS	5/07
	Spartanburg MSA, SC	Y	31390 FQ	37810 MW	42000 TQ	USBLS	5/07
	South Dakota	Y	28443 FQ	33361 MW	39481 TQ	SDBLS	7/08-9/08
	Sioux Falls MSA, SD	Y	32367 FQ	37536 MW	48122 TQ	SDBLS	7/08-9/08
	Tennessee	Y	24900 FQ	31720 MW	39310 TQ	USBLS	5/07
	Memphis MSA, TN-MS-AR	Y	27900 FQ	37150 MW	51010 TQ	USBLS	5/07
	Nashville-Davidson-Murfreesboro MSA, TN	Y	26590 FQ	33330 MW	42160 TQ	USBLS	5/07
	Texas	Y	24210 FQ	30120 MW	37050 TQ	USBLS	5/07
	Austin-Round Rock MSA, TX	Y	26020 FQ	31130 MW	37060 TQ	USBLS	5/07
	Beaumont-Port Arthur MSA, TX	Y	32890 FQ	38870 MW	46300 TQ	USBLS	5/07
	Dallas-Fort Worth-Arlington MSA, TX	Y	28700 FQ	34670 MW	40940 TQ	USBLS	5/07
	El Paso MSA, TX	Y	25820 FQ	29570 MW	34520 TQ	USBLS	5/07
	Houston-Sugar Land-Baytown MSA, TX	Y	27140 FQ	32190 MW	38990 TQ	USBLS	5/07
	San Antonio MSA, TX	Y	26100 FQ	30670 MW	35950 TQ	USBLS	5/07
	Utah	Y	32290 FQ	37390 MW	43630 TQ	USBLS	5/07
	St. George MSA, UT	Y	30540 FQ	35720 MW	40370 TQ	USBLS	5/07
	Salt Lake City MSA, UT	Y	34900 FQ	39870 MW	46610 TQ	USBLS	5/07
	Vermont	Y	25640 FQ	34360 MW	40340 TQ	USBLS	5/07
	Burlington-South Burlington MSA, VT	Y	27380 FQ	35990 MW	42710 TQ	USBLS	5/07
	Virginia	Y	29210 FQ	36050 MW	44680 TQ	USBLS	5/07
	Richmond MSA, VA	Y	29770 FQ	38190 MW	46780 TQ	USBLS	5/07
	Virginia Beach-Norfolk-Newport News MSA, VA-NC	Y	31740 FQ	37930 MW	46960 TQ	USBLS	5/07
	Washington	H	20.78 FQ	24.44 MW	28.38 TQ	WABLS	3/08
	Seattle-Tacoma-Bellevue MSA, WA	Y	49320 FQ	56400 MW	63090 TQ	USBLS	5/07
	West Virginia	Y	22496 FQ	28785 MW	36984 TQ	WVBLS	7/08-9/08

Occupation/Type/Industry	Location	Per	Low	Mid	High	Source	Date
Water and Liquid Waste Treatment Plant and System Operator	Charleston MSA, WV	Y	22850 FQ	27130 MW	34720 TQ	USBLS	5/07
	Wisconsin	Y	32190 FQ	38740 MW	45640 TQ	USBLS	5/07
	Milwaukee-Waukesha-West Allis MSA, WI	Y	42210 FQ	47030 MW	54260 TQ	USBLS	5/07
	Wyoming	Y	36108 FQ	43131 MW	50813 TQ	WYBLS	9/08
	Puerto Rico	Y	16980 FQ	22330 MW	29080 TQ	USBLS	5/07
	San Juan-Caguas-Guaynabo MSA, PR	Y	17000 FQ	22270 MW	29020 TQ	USBLS	5/07
	Virgin Islands	Y	21080 FQ	30220 MW	36470 TQ	USBLS	5/07
Water Conservation Specialist Municipal Government	Carlsbad, CA	Y	1646 LO		2001 HI	CCSS01	8/5/08
Water Meter Repairer Municipal Government	Cincinnati, OH	Y	37025 LO		38340 HI	COHSS	10/08
Water Plant Aide State Government	Ohio	H	15.41 LO		17.03 HI	ODAS	2008
Water Quality Analyst Municipal Government	Seattle, WA	H	24.65 LO		28.79 HI	CSSS	2007
Water Quality Chemist Municipal Government	Seattle, WA	H	27.63 LO		32.19 HI	CSSS	2008
Water Quality Engineer State Government	Ohio	H	27.93 LO		36.59 HI	ODAS	2008
Water Quality Specialist Municipal Government	Gresham, OR	Y	45096 LO		57576 HI	GOSS	1/1/09
Water Safety Instructor Municipal Government	Seaside, CA	S	856 LO		1206 HI	SSSS	8/08
Water Superintendent Municipal Government	Gresham, OR	Y	57996 LO		75420 HI	GOSS01	7/1/08
Water/Wastewater Lab Technician	Columbia County, GA	Y	24835 LO		37253 HI	GACTY03	2008
	Walton County, GA	Y	33407 LO		58146 HI	GACTY03	2008
Water/Wastewater Superintendent	Gwinnett County, GA	Y	52272 LO		86248 HI	GACTY03	2008
	Newton County, GA	Y	32094 LO		48173 HI	GACTY03	2008
Water/Wastewater Treatment Plant Manager	Fayette County, GA	Y	55090 LO		83826 HI	GACTY03	2008
	Pickens County, GA	Y	27833 LO		42351 HI	GACTY03	2008
Water/Wastewater Treatment Plant Operator	Fayette County, GA	Y	37110 LO		56468 HI	GACTY03	2008
	Newton County, GA	Y	23962 LO		35942 HI	GACTY03	2008
Water Works Dispatcher Municipal Government	Cincinnati, OH	Y	41597 LO		44100 HI	COHSS	10/08
Watershed Inspector Municipal Government	Seattle, WA	H	20.57 LO		23.94 HI	CSSS	2007
Web Application Development Strategist	United States	Y		105200 AW		NWRLD	2009
Web Contact Administrator	Southeast, MI	Y		57187 AW		MIOAKL01	2008
Web Designer Flash	United States	Y		42786 AW		IOMA05	2008
Hospital	United States	Y		52500 AW		IOMA05	2008
HTML	United States	Y		41260 AW		IOMA05	2008
Microsoft Office	United States	Y		39734 AW		IOMA05	2008

AE Average entry wage	**AW** Average wage paid	**FQ** First quartile wage	**LO** Lowest wage paid	**MTC** Median total compensation	**TCC** Total cash compensation
AER Average entry range	**AWR** Average wage range	**H** Hourly	**LR** Low end range	**MW** Median wage paid	**TQ** Third quartile wage
AEX Average experienced wage	**AXR** Average experienced range	**HI** Highest wage paid	**M** Monthly	**MWR** Median wage range	**W** Weekly
ATC Average total compensation	**D** Daily	**HR** High end range	**MCC** Median cash compensation	**S** See annotated source	**Y** Yearly

Occupation/Type/Industry	Location	Per	Low	Mid	High	Source	Date
Web Designer							
Self-Employed	United States	Y		24104 AW		IOMA05	2008
Web Developer	United States	Y	60000-89750 LR			PRN01	2009
Web Master							
Printing Industry	United States	Y		41714 AW		GRAM	2006
Website Assistant							
White House Staff	United States	Y			34300 HI	WPOST02	2008
Website Coordinator							
Judicial Branch, State Government	New Hampshire	Y			26728 HI	NHUL03	2008
Wedding Photographer	Rhode Island	Y		70000-100000 AWR		RIM01	2009
Weigher, Measurer, Checker, and Sampler, Recordkeeping	Alabama	Y	20870 FQ	24030 MW	30560 TQ	USBLS	5/07
	Birmingham-Hoover MSA, AL	Y	20640 FQ	23610 MW	29310 TQ	USBLS	5/07
	Alaska	Y	22860 FQ	30030 MW	36010 TQ	USBLS	5/07
	Anchorage MSA, AK	Y	30570 FQ	34230 MW	39170 TQ	USBLS	5/07
	Arizona	Y	23320 FQ	31950 MW	37860 TQ	USBLS	5/07
	Phoenix-Mesa-Scottsdale MSA, AZ	Y	23240 FQ	31400 MW	37430 TQ	USBLS	5/07
	Tucson MSA, AZ	Y	31380 FQ	37150 MW	43560 TQ	USBLS	5/07
	Arkansas	Y	20640 FQ	23290 MW	28530 TQ	USBLS	5/07
	Little Rock-North Little Rock MSA, AR	Y	21450 FQ	24250 MW	31680 TQ	USBLS	5/07
	California	H	9.26 FQ	11.71 MW	15.58 TQ	CABLS	1/08-3/08
	Fresno MSA, CA	H	9.19 FQ	10.80 MW	13.15 TQ	CABLS	1/08-3/08
	Los Angeles-Long Beach-Glendale PMSA, CA	H	8.97 FQ	11.11 MW	14.99 TQ	CABLS	1/08-3/08
	Oakland-Fremont-Hayward MSA, CA	H	10.92 FQ	12.60 MW	17.57 TQ	CABLS	1/08-3/08
	Riverside-San Bernardino-Ontario MSA, CA	H	9.38 FQ	12.35 MW	16.72 TQ	CABLS	1/08-3/08
	Sacramento-Arden Arcade-Roseville MSA, CA	H	9.31 FQ	12.54 MW	16.01 TQ	CABLS	1/08-3/08
	San Diego-Carlsbad-San Marcos MSA, CA	H	9.28 FQ	11.27 MW	15.33 TQ	CABLS	1/08-3/08
	San Francisco-San Mateo-Redwood PMSA, CA	H	9.53 FQ	12.25 MW	19.46 TQ	CABLS	1/08-3/08
	San Jose-Sunnyvale-Santa Clara MSA, CA	H	8.79 FQ	9.71 MW	12.14 TQ	CABLS	1/08-3/08
	Santa Ana-Anaheim-Irvine PMSA, CA	Y	19150 FQ	26180 MW	35100 TQ	USBLS	5/07
	Colorado	Y	19090 FQ	24100 MW	33030 TQ	USBLS	5/07
	Colorado Springs MSA, CO	Y	26440 FQ	32270 MW	38020 TQ	USBLS	5/07
	Denver-Aurora MSA, CO	Y	17490 FQ	21110 MW	29070 TQ	USBLS	5/07
	Connecticut	H	10.60 AE	14.16 MW		CTBLS	1/08-3/08
	Bridgeport-Stamford-Norwalk MSA, CT	Y	18160 FQ	23940 MW	31470 TQ	USBLS	5/07
	Hartford-West Hartford-East Hartford MSA, CT	Y	25760 FQ	31370 MW	40960 TQ	USBLS	5/07
	New Haven MSA, CT	Y	21970 FQ	25050 MW	33760 TQ	USBLS	5/07
	Delaware	Y	21800 FQ	27170 MW	34940 TQ	USBLS	5/07
	Wilmington PMSA, DE-MD-NJ	Y	23020 FQ	30760 MW	40330 TQ	USBLS	5/07
	Washington-Arlington-Alexandria MSA, DC-VA-MD-WV	Y	25620 FQ	31330 MW	39830 TQ	USBLS	5/07
	Florida	Y	21130 FQ	26060 MW	30830 TQ	USBLS	5/07
	Fort Lauderdale-Pompano Beach-Deerfield Beach PMSA, FL	Y	24830 FQ	28790 MW	32470 TQ	USBLS	5/07
	Jacksonville MSA, FL	Y	21240 FQ	26410 MW	32310 TQ	USBLS	5/07
	Miami-Fort Lauderdale-Miami Beach MSA, FL	Y	22270 FQ	27760 MW	31950 TQ	USBLS	5/07
	Orlando-Kissimmee MSA, FL	Y	21850 FQ	25200 MW	29620 TQ	USBLS	5/07

AE   Average entry wage   AW   Average wage paid   FQ   First quartile wage   LO   Lowest wage paid   MTC Median total compensation   TCC Total cash compensation
AER Average entry range   AWR Average wage range   H   Hourly   LR   Low end range   MW   Median wage paid   TQ   Third quartile wage
AEX Average experienced wage   AXR Average experienced range HI Highest wage paid   M   Monthly   MWR Median wage range   W   Weekly
ATC Average total compensation D   Daily   HR   High end range   MCC Median cash compensation S   See annotated source   Y   Yearly

1678

Occupation/Type/Industry	Location	Per	Low	Mid	High	Source	Date
Weigher, Measurer, Checker, and Sampler, Recordkeeping	Tampa-St. Petersburg-Clearwater MSA, FL	Y	22730 FQ	28150 MW	33060 TQ	USBLS	5/07
	West Palm Beach-Boca Raton-Boynton Beach PMSA, FL	Y	18170 FQ	26700 MW	30580 TQ	USBLS	5/07
	Georgia	Y	21480 FQ	26530 MW	33490 TQ	USBLS	5/07
	Atlanta-Sandy Springs-Marietta MSA, GA	Y	22930 FQ	28620 MW	35880 TQ	USBLS	5/07
	Hawaii	Y	23830 FQ	28700 MW	35510 TQ	USBLS	5/07
	Honolulu MSA, HI	Y	23460 FQ	28450 MW	34970 TQ	USBLS	5/07
	Idaho	Y	21240 FQ	27060 MW	30970 TQ	USBLS	5/07
	Boise City-Nampa MSA, ID	Y	25980 FQ	28910 MW	36090 TQ	USBLS	5/07
	Illinois	Y	24700 FQ	29190 MW	36120 TQ	USBLS	5/07
	Chicago-Naperville-Joliet MSA, IL-IN-WI	Y	23990 FQ	28560 MW	35120 TQ	USBLS	5/07
	Indiana	Y	19320 FQ	24490 MW	31090 TQ	USBLS	5/07
	Gary PMSA, IN	Y	19290 FQ	23320 MW	35200 TQ	USBLS	5/07
	Indianapolis-Carmel MSA, IN	Y	17930 FQ	22190 MW	28400 TQ	USBLS	5/07
	Iowa	Y	23600 FQ	27750 MW	32530 TQ	USBLS	5/07
	Cedar Rapids MSA, IA	Y	21380 FQ	24920 MW	34280 TQ	USBLS	5/07
	Des Moines-West Des Moines MSA, IA	Y	27660 FQ	34030 MW	41220 TQ	USBLS	5/07
	Kansas	Y	19430 FQ	25600 MW	30420 TQ	USBLS	5/07
	Wichita MSA, KS	Y	28410 FQ	35600 MW	47170 TQ	USBLS	5/07
	Kentucky	Y	21859 FQ	25701 MW	34021 TQ	KYBLS	2008
	Louisville-Jefferson County MSA, KY-IN	Y	20950 FQ	23350 MW	27890 TQ	USBLS	5/07
	Louisiana	H	9.14 FQ	12.92 MW	15.69 TQ	LABLS	1/08-3/08
	Baton Rouge MSA, LA	Y	18020 FQ	25330 MW	32430 TQ	USBLS	5/07
	Houma-Bayou Cane-Thibodaux MSA, LA	Y	13550 FQ	16860 MW	26640 TQ	USBLS	5/07
	New Orleans-Metairie-Kenner MSA, LA	Y	24260 FQ	27010 MW	30000 TQ	USBLS	5/07
	Maine	Y	22250 FQ	28060 MW	33770 TQ	USBLS	5/07
	Portland-South Portland-Biddeford MSA, ME	Y	20460 FQ	22180 MW	24030 TQ	USBLS	5/07
	Baltimore-Towson MSA, MD	Y	25310 FQ	34750 MW	50630 TQ	USBLS	5/07
	Bethesda-Gaithersburg-Frederick PMSA, MD	Y	31200 FQ	41390 MW	52180 TQ	USBLS	5/07
	Massachusetts	Y	27830 FQ	35130 MW	43000 TQ	USBLS	5/07
	Boston-Cambridge-Quincy NECTA, MA	Y	28520 FQ	37360 MW	45300 TQ	USBLS	5/07
	Worcester MSA, MA-CT	Y	24820 FQ	29720 MW	38490 TQ	USBLS	5/07
	Michigan	Y	22690 FQ	31270 MW	38740 TQ	USBLS	5/07
	Detroit-Warren-Livonia MSA, MI	Y	28220 FQ	34400 MW	41650 TQ	USBLS	5/07
	Grand Rapids-Wyoming MSA, MI	Y	22260 FQ	27550 MW	35550 TQ	USBLS	5/07
	Muskegon-Norton Shores MSA, MI	Y	15440 FQ	16110 MW	30770 TQ	USBLS	5/07
	Warren-Troy-Farmington Hills PMSA, MI	Y	26550 FQ	32440 MW	39670 TQ	USBLS	5/07
	Minnesota	Y	25884 FQ	31546 MW	39196 TQ	MNBLS	10/08-12/08
	Duluth-Superior MSA, MN-WI	Y	30068 FQ	34460 MW	38842 TQ	MNBLS	10/08-12/08
	Minneapolis-Saint Paul MSA, MN-WI	Y	26852 FQ	32223 MW	41194 TQ	MNBLS	10/08-12/08
	Rochester MSA, MN	Y	27972 FQ	31081 MW	35808 TQ	MNBLS	10/08-12/08
	Mississippi	Y	18180 FQ	22270 MW	27880 TQ	USBLS	5/07
	Jackson MSA, MS	Y	20180 FQ	23990 MW	28440 TQ	USBLS	5/07
	Missouri	Y	25080 FQ	28960 MW	34410 TQ	USBLS	5/07
	Kansas City MSA, MO-KS	Y	25970 FQ	29710 MW	35440 TQ	USBLS	5/07
	St. Louis MSA, MO-IL	Y	25800 FQ	28630 MW	33670 TQ	USBLS	5/07
	Montana	Y	21940 FQ	29040 MW	33600 TQ	USBLS	5/07
	Nebraska	Y	21310 FQ	26130 MW	32270 TQ	USBLS	5/07
	Omaha-Council Bluffs MSA, NE-IA	Y	22590 FQ	26520 MW	32180 TQ	USBLS	5/07
	Nevada	H	11.23 FQ	13.42 MW	16.10 TQ	NVBLS	5/08
	Las Vegas-Paradise MSA, NV	H	10.94 FQ	12.68 MW	15.72 TQ	NVBLS	5/08
	New Hampshire	H	10.46 AE	12.45 MW	14.81 AEX	NHBLS	6/08
	Nashua NECTA, NH-MA	Y	20040 FQ	28730 MW	34230 TQ	USBLS	5/07
	New Jersey	Y	23900 FQ	30990 MW	39020 TQ	USBLS	5/07
	Camden PMSA, NJ	Y	23040 FQ	30770 MW	38390 TQ	USBLS	5/07

AE Average entry wage	**AW** Average wage paid	**FQ** First quartile wage	**LO** Lowest wage paid	**MTC** Median total compensation	**TCC** Total cash compensation
AER Average entry range	**AWR** Average wage range	**H** Hourly	**LR** Low end range	**MW** Median wage paid	**TQ** Third quartile wage
AEX Average experienced wage	**AXR** Average experienced range	**HI** Highest wage paid	**M** Monthly	**MWR** Median wage range	**W** Weekly
ATC Average total compensation	**D** Daily	**HR** High end range	**MCC** Median cash compensation	**S** See annotated source	**Y** Yearly

Occupation/Type/Industry	Location	Per	Low	Mid	High	Source	Date
Weigher, Measurer, Checker, and Sampler, Recordkeeping	Edison PMSA, NJ	Y	26150 FQ	32120 MW	38700 TQ	USBLS	5/07
	Newark-Union PMSA, NJ-PA	Y	22820 FQ	33100 MW	43120 TQ	USBLS	5/07
	New Mexico	Y	23300 FQ	27450 MW	31480 TQ	USBLS	5/07
	Albuquerque MSA, NM	Y	24440 FQ	27540 MW	30580 TQ	USBLS	5/07
	New York	Y	19140 FQ	24610 MW	33960 TQ	USBLS	5/07
	Albany-Schenectady-Troy MSA, NY	Y	23010 FQ	30120 MW	36100 TQ	USBLS	5/07
	Buffalo-Niagara Falls MSA, NY	Y	22540 FQ	27560 MW	37590 TQ	USBLS	5/07
	Nassau-Suffolk PMSA, NY	Y	19960 FQ	30590 MW	40740 TQ	USBLS	5/07
	New York-Northern New Jersey-Long Island MSA, NY-NJ-PA	Y	20800 FQ	28340 MW	37630 TQ	USBLS	5/07
	North Carolina	Y	19210 FQ	23120 MW	29230 TQ	USBLS	5/07
	Charlotte-Gastonia-Concord MSA, NC-SC	Y	18510 FQ	22290 MW	27670 TQ	USBLS	5/07
	Raleigh-Cary MSA, NC	Y	22460 FQ	28440 MW	34550 TQ	USBLS	5/07
	North Dakota	Y	22340 FQ	25680 MW	34690 TQ	USBLS	5/07
	Fargo MSA, ND-MN	Y	25200 FQ	31520 MW	39910 TQ	USBLS	5/07
	Ohio	Y	23370 FQ	28040 MW	33490 TQ	USBLS	5/07
	Cincinnati-Middletown MSA, OH-KY-IN	Y	23390 FQ	27350 MW	31610 TQ	USBLS	5/07
	Cleveland-Elyria-Mentor MSA, OH	Y	22280 FQ	26280 MW	31860 TQ	USBLS	5/07
	Columbus MSA, OH	Y	25960 FQ	29800 MW	35810 TQ	USBLS	5/07
	Dayton MSA, OH	Y	22440 FQ	26760 MW	30600 TQ	USBLS	5/07
	Oklahoma	Y	16970 FQ	22150 MW	27890 TQ	USBLS	5/07
	Oklahoma City MSA, OK	Y	15000 FQ	21810 MW	29180 TQ	USBLS	5/07
	Tulsa MSA, OK	Y	15430 FQ	22920 MW	28650 TQ	USBLS	5/07
	Oregon	H	9.89 FQ	12.76 MW	16.73 TQ	ORBLS	5/08
	Portland-Vancouver-Beaverton MSA, OR-WA	Y	21630 FQ	27900 MW	35670 TQ	USBLS	5/07
	Pennsylvania	Y	21940 FQ	24950 MW	31670 TQ	USBLS	5/07
	Allentown-Bethlehem-Easton MSA, PA-NJ	Y	21030 FQ	23420 MW	26050 TQ	USBLS	5/07
	Philadelphia-Camden-Wilmington MSA, PA-NJ-DE-MD	Y	23020 FQ	28460 MW	36490 TQ	USBLS	5/07
	Pittsburgh MSA, PA	Y	23080 FQ	28600 MW	38810 TQ	USBLS	5/07
	Rhode Island	Y	19860 FQ	25750 MW	31960 TQ	USBLS	5/07
	Providence-Fall River-Warwick MSA, RI-MA	Y	30240 FQ	34090 MW	38410 TQ	USBLS	5/07
	South Carolina	Y	19320 FQ	25070 MW	33790 TQ	USBLS	5/07
	Charleston-North Charleston MSA, SC	Y	20870 FQ	31120 MW	49160 TQ	USBLS	5/07
	Columbia MSA, SC	Y	18620 FQ	22490 MW	28100 TQ	USBLS	5/07
	South Dakota	Y	24165 FQ	27242 MW	29925 TQ	SDBLS	7/08-9/08
	Tennessee	Y	22240 FQ	28020 MW	33190 TQ	USBLS	5/07
	Memphis MSA, TN-MS-AR	Y	19580 FQ	26470 MW	32940 TQ	USBLS	5/07
	Nashville-Davidson-Murfreesboro MSA, TN	Y	23500 FQ	28780 MW	34960 TQ	USBLS	5/07
	Texas	Y	18290 FQ	23380 MW	30010 TQ	USBLS	5/07
	Austin-Round Rock MSA, TX	Y	22330 FQ	25860 MW	30620 TQ	USBLS	5/07
	Corpus Christi MSA, TX	Y	16910 FQ	18250 MW	20040 TQ	USBLS	5/07
	Dallas-Fort Worth-Arlington MSA, TX	Y	20570 FQ	27130 MW	33590 TQ	USBLS	5/07
	El Paso MSA, TX	Y	20400 FQ	24530 MW	30750 TQ	USBLS	5/07
	Houston-Sugar Land-Baytown MSA, TX	Y	19670 FQ	23730 MW	29560 TQ	USBLS	5/07
	San Antonio MSA, TX	Y	19200 FQ	24610 MW	31210 TQ	USBLS	5/07
	Utah	Y	25070 FQ	27850 MW	32350 TQ	USBLS	5/07
	Salt Lake City MSA, UT	Y	24420 FQ	30140 MW	38150 TQ	USBLS	5/07
	Vermont	Y	21490 FQ	27280 MW	31780 TQ	USBLS	5/07
	Virginia	Y	21640 FQ	26470 MW	32450 TQ	USBLS	5/07
	Richmond MSA, VA	Y	20450 FQ	24590 MW	32270 TQ	USBLS	5/07
	Virginia Beach-Norfolk-Newport News MSA, VA-NC	Y	22750 FQ	29240 MW	35270 TQ	USBLS	5/07
	Washington	H	12.36 FQ	15.61 MW	18.76 TQ	WABLS	3/08
	Seattle-Tacoma-Bellevue MSA, WA	Y	28730 FQ	35320 MW	40100 TQ	USBLS	5/07
	West Virginia	Y	19087 FQ	25902 MW	35183 TQ	WVBLS	7/08-9/08

AE	Average entry wage	AW	Average wage paid	FQ	First quartile wage
AER	Average entry range	AWR	Average wage range	H	Hourly
AEX	Average experienced wage	AXR	Average experienced range	HI	Highest wage paid
ATC	Average total compensation	D	Daily	HR	High end range

LO	Lowest wage paid	MTC	Median total compensation
LR	Low end range	MW	Median wage paid
M	Monthly	MWR	Median wage range
MCC	Median cash compensation	S	See annotated source

TCC	Total cash compensation
TQ	Third quartile wage
W	Weekly
Y	Yearly

Occupation/Type/Industry	Location	Per	Low	Mid	High	Source	Date
Weigher, Measurer, Checker, and Sampler, Recordkeeping	Charleston MSA, WV	Y	21650 FQ	31970 MW	41890 TQ	USBLS	5/07
	Wisconsin	Y	22280 FQ	27790 MW	34480 TQ	USBLS	5/07
	Milwaukee-Waukesha-West Allis MSA, WI	Y	20580 FQ	23560 MW	31270 TQ	USBLS	5/07
	Wyoming	Y	21600 FQ	24172 MW	28918 TQ	WYBLS	9/08
	Cheyenne MSA, WY	Y	22861 FQ	26093 MW	29467 TQ	WYBLS	9/08
	Puerto Rico	Y	14000 FQ	17700 MW	24400 TQ	USBLS	5/07
	San Juan-Caguas-Guaynabo MSA, PR	Y	13910 FQ	17800 MW	25230 TQ	USBLS	5/07
Weights and Measures Inspector Municipal Government	Cincinnati, OH	Y	40748 LO		45777 HI	COHSS	10/08
Weights and Measures Metrologist Department of Agriculture	New Hampshire	Y			32888 HI	NHUL03	2008
Weights and Measures Technologist State Government	Ohio	H	18.36 LO		23.87 HI	ODAS	2008
Welder Municipal Government	Cincinnati, OH	Y	44100 LO		47537 HI	COHSS	10/08
Solar Power Manufacturing	New York	H		16.00 AW		GCJR	2008
Welder, Cutter, Solderer, and Brazer	Alabama	Y	24780 FQ	29720 MW	36510 TQ	USBLS	5/07
	Birmingham-Hoover MSA, AL	Y	26210 FQ	31150 MW	37270 TQ	USBLS	5/07
	Alaska	Y	40440 FQ	48990 MW	62910 TQ	USBLS	5/07
	Anchorage MSA, AK	Y	39640 FQ	46810 MW	59190 TQ	USBLS	5/07
	Arizona	Y	24150 FQ	30440 MW	38550 TQ	USBLS	5/07
	Phoenix-Mesa-Scottsdale MSA, AZ	Y	23710 FQ	29570 MW	37200 TQ	USBLS	5/07
	Tucson MSA, AZ	Y	23440 FQ	29560 MW	36300 TQ	USBLS	5/07
	Arkansas	Y	23290 FQ	28040 MW	34520 TQ	USBLS	5/07
	Little Rock-North Little Rock MSA, AR	Y	24000 FQ	28390 MW	37370 TQ	USBLS	5/07
	Pine Bluff MSA, AR	Y	30370 FQ	33190 MW	35920 TQ	USBLS	5/07
	California	H	12.55 FQ	15.89 MW	20.65 TQ	CABLS	1/08-3/08
	Fresno MSA, CA	H	12.12 FQ	14.78 MW	17.28 TQ	CABLS	1/08-3/08
	Los Angeles-Long Beach-Glendale PMSA, CA	H	10.68 FQ	13.71 MW	18.11 TQ	CABLS	1/08-3/08
	Oakland-Fremont-Hayward MSA, CA	H	16.71 FQ	20.65 MW	24.47 TQ	CABLS	1/08-3/08
	Riverside-San Bernardino-Ontario MSA, CA	H	12.69 FQ	15.31 MW	18.88 TQ	CABLS	1/08-3/08
	Sacramento-Arden Arcade-Roseville MSA, CA	H	13.56 FQ	15.96 MW	18.78 TQ	CABLS	1/08-3/08
	San Diego-Carlsbad-San Marcos MSA, CA	H	13.29 FQ	17.03 MW	22.38 TQ	CABLS	1/08-3/08
	San Francisco-San Mateo-Redwood PMSA, CA	H	13.93 FQ	20.78 MW	27.98 TQ	CABLS	1/08-3/08
	San Jose-Sunnyvale-Santa Clara MSA, CA	H	16.90 FQ	20.31 MW	24.21 TQ	CABLS	1/08-3/08
	Santa Ana-Anaheim-Irvine PMSA, CA	Y	26060 FQ	31810 MW	40970 TQ	USBLS	5/07
	Stockton MSA, CA	H	11.39 FQ	15.81 MW	19.12 TQ	CABLS	1/08-3/08
	Colorado	Y	27060 FQ	33840 MW	42730 TQ	USBLS	5/07
	Boulder MSA, CO	Y	35950 FQ	41650 MW	48340 TQ	USBLS	5/07
	Denver-Aurora MSA, CO	Y	26260 FQ	32960 MW	39780 TQ	USBLS	5/07
	Connecticut	H	13.42 AE	17.96 MW		CTBLS	1/08-3/08
	Bridgeport-Stamford-Norwalk MSA, CT	Y	30920 FQ	40280 MW	46680 TQ	USBLS	5/07
	Hartford-West Hartford-East Hartford MSA, CT	Y	31060 FQ	37370 MW	45340 TQ	USBLS	5/07
	New Haven MSA, CT	Y	29210 FQ	36650 MW	49210 TQ	USBLS	5/07
	Delaware	Y	26490 FQ	35940 MW	47920 TQ	USBLS	5/07
	Wilmington PMSA, DE-MD-NJ	Y	32520 FQ	39800 MW	50020 TQ	USBLS	5/07
	District of Columbia	Y	48180 FQ	55390 MW	60830 TQ	USBLS	5/07

AE	Average entry wage	AW	Average wage paid	FQ	First quartile wage	LO	Lowest wage paid	MTC	Median total compensation	TCC	Total cash compensation
AER	Average entry range	AWR	Average wage range	H	Hourly	LR	Low end range	MW	Median wage paid	TQ	Third quartile wage
AEX	Average experienced wage	AXR	Average experienced range	HI	Highest wage paid	M	Monthly	MWR	Median wage range	W	Weekly
ATC	Average total compensation	D	Daily	HR	High end range	MCC	Median cash compensation	S	See annotated source	Y	Yearly

Occupation/Type/Industry	Location	Per	Low	Mid	High	Source	Date
Welder, Cutter, Solderer, and Brazer							
	Washington-Arlington-Alexandria MSA, DC-VA-MD-WV	Y	33030 FQ	39080 MW	48290 TQ	USBLS	5/07
	Florida	Y	25880 FQ	32200 MW	38610 TQ	USBLS	5/07
	Fort Lauderdale-Pompano Beach-Deerfield Beach PMSA, FL	Y	27440 FQ	34420 MW	40320 TQ	USBLS	5/07
	Jacksonville MSA, FL	Y	28010 FQ	32890 MW	38440 TQ	USBLS	5/07
	Miami-Fort Lauderdale-Miami Beach MSA, FL	Y	25730 FQ	32780 MW	39340 TQ	USBLS	5/07
	Orlando-Kissimmee MSA, FL	Y	27310 FQ	34200 MW	43380 TQ	USBLS	5/07
	Tampa-St. Petersburg-Clearwater MSA, FL	Y	27470 FQ	32790 MW	37370 TQ	USBLS	5/07
	West Palm Beach-Boca Raton-Boynton Beach PMSA, FL	Y	29780 FQ	36030 MW	43580 TQ	USBLS	5/07
	Georgia	Y	25590 FQ	29090 MW	34250 TQ	USBLS	5/07
	Atlanta-Sandy Springs-Marietta MSA, GA	Y	25530 FQ	28870 MW	34510 TQ	USBLS	5/07
	Augusta-Richmond County MSA, GA-SC	Y	26370 FQ	31380 MW	39780 TQ	USBLS	5/07
	Hawaii	Y	41160 FQ	51290 MW	61350 TQ	USBLS	5/07
	Honolulu MSA, HI	Y	42470 FQ	52600 MW	62000 TQ	USBLS	5/07
	Idaho	Y	20210 FQ	26860 MW	33380 TQ	USBLS	5/07
	Boise City-Nampa MSA, ID	Y	18730 FQ	25710 MW	32540 TQ	USBLS	5/07
	Illinois	Y	26730 FQ	32460 MW	39050 TQ	USBLS	5/07
	Chicago-Naperville-Joliet MSA, IL-IN-WI	Y	27170 FQ	34510 MW	42750 TQ	USBLS	5/07
	Indiana	Y	26200 FQ	31330 MW	37680 TQ	USBLS	5/07
	Gary PMSA, IN	Y	27780 FQ	35500 MW	46180 TQ	USBLS	5/07
	Indianapolis-Carmel MSA, IN	Y	28200 FQ	34710 MW	41830 TQ	USBLS	5/07
	Iowa	Y	26230 FQ	30890 MW	36450 TQ	USBLS	5/07
	Davenport-Moline-Rock Island MSA, IA-IL	Y	25750 FQ	33540 MW	41890 TQ	USBLS	5/07
	Des Moines-West Des Moines MSA, IA	Y	29170 FQ	34200 MW	39610 TQ	USBLS	5/07
	Iowa City MSA, IA	Y	27680 FQ	30590 MW	35630 TQ	USBLS	5/07
	Waterloo-Cedar Falls MSA, IA	Y	28250 FQ	32240 MW	35550 TQ	USBLS	5/07
	Kansas	Y	23390 FQ	27970 MW	33930 TQ	USBLS	5/07
	Wichita MSA, KS	Y	22670 FQ	28130 MW	36130 TQ	USBLS	5/07
	Kentucky	Y	25518 FQ	31183 MW	37171 TQ	KYBLS	2008
	Louisville-Jefferson County MSA, KY-IN	Y	25210 FQ	29420 MW	36350 TQ	USBLS	5/07
	Louisiana	H	14.84 FQ	17.83 MW	21.33 TQ	LABLS	1/08-3/08
	Baton Rouge MSA, LA	Y	33430 FQ	41870 MW	47550 TQ	USBLS	5/07
	New Orleans-Metairie-Kenner MSA, LA	Y	30720 FQ	36020 MW	41790 TQ	USBLS	5/07
	Maine	Y	29880 FQ	38030 MW	46190 TQ	USBLS	5/07
	Portland-South Portland-Biddeford MSA, ME	Y	33500 FQ	38800 MW	50100 TQ	USBLS	5/07
	Maryland	Y		35650 MW		MDBLS	3/08
	Baltimore-Towson MSA, MD	Y	28050 FQ	33710 MW	40830 TQ	USBLS	5/07
	Bethesda-Gaithersburg-Frederick PMSA, MD	Y	29910 FQ	38290 MW	46750 TQ	USBLS	5/07
	Massachusetts	Y	33100 FQ	39410 MW	47380 TQ	USBLS	5/07
	Boston-Cambridge-Quincy NECTA, MA	Y	33970 FQ	40540 MW	50810 TQ	USBLS	5/07
	Worcester MSA, MA-CT	Y	33090 FQ	40530 MW	47930 TQ	USBLS	5/07
	Michigan	Y	28000 FQ	36120 MW	50160 TQ	USBLS	5/07
	Detroit-Warren-Livonia MSA, MI	Y	30310 FQ	44510 MW	58200 TQ	USBLS	5/07
	Grand Rapids-Wyoming MSA, MI	Y	30840 FQ	38600 MW	45380 TQ	USBLS	5/07
	Warren-Troy-Farmington Hills PMSA, MI	Y	31120 FQ	47730 MW	57260 TQ	USBLS	5/07
	Minnesota	Y	30861 FQ	36698 MW	44276 TQ	MNBLS	10/08-12/08
	Duluth-Superior MSA, MN-WI	Y	29649 FQ	37859 MW	46899 TQ	MNBLS	10/08-12/08
	Minneapolis-Saint Paul MSA, MN-WI	Y	33806 FQ	40969 MW	47728 TQ	MNBLS	10/08-12/08
	Rochester MSA, MN	Y	32918 FQ	37847 MW	45112 TQ	MNBLS	10/08-12/08
	Mississippi	Y	26530 FQ	31620 MW	36390 TQ	USBLS	5/07
	Hattiesburg MSA, MS	Y	27360 FQ	30310 MW	33550 TQ	USBLS	5/07

AE	Average entry wage	AW	Average wage paid	FQ	First quartile wage
AER	Average entry range	AWR	Average wage range	H	Hourly
AEX	Average experienced wage	AXR	Average experienced range	HI	Highest wage paid
ATC	Average total compensation	D	Daily	HR	High end range

LO	Lowest wage paid	MTC	Median total compensation	TCC	Total cash compensation
LR	Low end range	MW	Median wage paid	TQ	Third quartile wage
M	Monthly	MWR	Median wage range	W	Weekly
MCC	Median cash compensation	S	See annotated source	Y	Yearly

Occupation/Type/Industry	Location	Per	Low	Mid	High	Source	Date
Welder, Cutter, Solderer, and Brazer	Jackson MSA, MS	Y	27370 FQ	32530 MW	36930 TQ	USBLS	5/07
	Missouri	Y	24860 FQ	30540 MW	37990 TQ	USBLS	5/07
	Jefferson City MSA, MO	Y	29260 FQ	33260 MW	36480 TQ	USBLS	5/07
	Kansas City MSA, MO-KS	Y	27270 FQ	33430 MW	43480 TQ	USBLS	5/07
	St. Louis MSA, MO-IL	Y	25700 FQ	31910 MW	39460 TQ	USBLS	5/07
	Montana	Y	26450 FQ	32980 MW	45370 TQ	USBLS	5/07
	Billings MSA, MT	Y	27700 FQ	32220 MW	38830 TQ	USBLS	5/07
	Missoula MSA, MT	Y	24110 FQ	28440 MW	39880 TQ	USBLS	5/07
	Nebraska	Y	24730 FQ	29010 MW	35100 TQ	USBLS	5/07
	Omaha-Council Bluffs MSA, NE-IA	Y	24940 FQ	29380 MW	35890 TQ	USBLS	5/07
	Nevada	H	14.33 FQ	17.86 MW	23.13 TQ	NVBLS	5/08
	Las Vegas-Paradise MSA, NV	H	15.32 FQ	17.82 MW	20.58 TQ	NVBLS	5/08
	New Hampshire	H	13.32 AE	17.16 MW	20.84 AEX	NHBLS	6/08
	Manchester MSA, NH	Y	32580 FQ	46180 MW	53940 TQ	USBLS	5/07
	Nashua NECTA, NH-MA	Y	30570 FQ	35250 MW	41170 TQ	USBLS	5/07
	New Jersey	Y	29260 FQ	36660 MW	45350 TQ	USBLS	5/07
	Camden PMSA, NJ	Y	34370 FQ	40560 MW	47470 TQ	USBLS	5/07
	Edison PMSA, NJ	Y	26560 FQ	35330 MW	45300 TQ	USBLS	5/07
	Newark-Union PMSA, NJ-PA	Y	28680 FQ	36040 MW	45970 TQ	USBLS	5/07
	New Mexico	Y	26030 FQ	32330 MW	43000 TQ	USBLS	5/07
	Albuquerque MSA, NM	Y	25730 FQ	28760 MW	35580 TQ	USBLS	5/07
	New York	Y	27400 FQ	33760 MW	42500 TQ	USBLS	5/07
	Albany-Schenectady-Troy MSA, NY	Y	32520 FQ	37570 MW	54550 TQ	USBLS	5/07
	Buffalo-Niagara Falls MSA, NY	Y	29040 FQ	35850 MW	46080 TQ	USBLS	5/07
	Kingston MSA, NY	Y	26240 FQ	30820 MW	36420 TQ	USBLS	5/07
	Nassau-Suffolk PMSA, NY	Y	27110 FQ	30970 MW	37280 TQ	USBLS	5/07
	New York-Northern New Jersey-Long Island MSA, NY-NJ-PA	Y	27410 FQ	34330 MW	44360 TQ	USBLS	5/07
	North Carolina	Y	26910 FQ	32400 MW	38510 TQ	USBLS	5/07
	Charlotte-Gastonia-Concord MSA, NC-SC	Y	27910 FQ	33740 MW	39860 TQ	USBLS	5/07
	Raleigh-Cary MSA, NC	Y	29340 FQ	34650 MW	39140 TQ	USBLS	5/07
	North Dakota	Y	26760 FQ	31170 MW	36960 TQ	USBLS	5/07
	Fargo MSA, ND-MN	Y	28420 FQ	33120 MW	36910 TQ	USBLS	5/07
	Grand Forks MSA, ND-MN	Y	25680 FQ	28810 MW	34310 TQ	USBLS	5/07
	Ohio	Y	26250 FQ	31740 MW	38340 TQ	USBLS	5/07
	Cincinnati-Middletown MSA, OH-KY-IN	Y	29620 FQ	34760 MW	40810 TQ	USBLS	5/07
	Cleveland-Elyria-Mentor MSA, OH	Y	26400 FQ	32310 MW	40130 TQ	USBLS	5/07
	Columbus MSA, OH	Y	26010 FQ	30480 MW	36500 TQ	USBLS	5/07
	Dayton MSA, OH	Y	28150 FQ	34080 MW	43250 TQ	USBLS	5/07
	Oklahoma	Y	24350 FQ	29810 MW	35540 TQ	USBLS	5/07
	Lawton MSA, OK	Y	24760 FQ	28490 MW	31640 TQ	USBLS	5/07
	Oklahoma City MSA, OK	Y	23450 FQ	28010 MW	32760 TQ	USBLS	5/07
	Tulsa MSA, OK	Y	28200 FQ	33070 MW	37440 TQ	USBLS	5/07
	Oregon	H	13.29 FQ	16.09 MW	19.73 TQ	ORBLS	5/08
	Portland-Vancouver-Beaverton MSA, OR-WA	Y	28850 FQ	35750 MW	42800 TQ	USBLS	5/07
	Pennsylvania	Y	27700 FQ	33580 MW	39750 TQ	USBLS	5/07
	Allentown-Bethlehem-Easton MSA, PA-NJ	Y	30440 FQ	35670 MW	41080 TQ	USBLS	5/07
	Philadelphia-Camden-Wilmington MSA, PA-NJ-DE-MD	Y	32740 FQ	38360 MW	45960 TQ	USBLS	5/07
	Pittsburgh MSA, PA	Y	26640 FQ	31140 MW	37260 TQ	USBLS	5/07
	Rhode Island	Y	31810 FQ	37360 MW	41980 TQ	USBLS	5/07
	Providence-Fall River-Warwick MSA, RI-MA	Y	31400 FQ	36990 MW	41810 TQ	USBLS	5/07
	South Carolina	Y	26910 FQ	31480 MW	38070 TQ	USBLS	5/07
	Charleston-North Charleston MSA, SC	Y	28220 FQ	33240 MW	38150 TQ	USBLS	5/07
	Columbia MSA, SC	Y	27800 FQ	31450 MW	37170 TQ	USBLS	5/07
	South Dakota	Y	25044 FQ	28500 MW	31929 TQ	SDBLS	7/08-9/08
	Sioux Falls MSA, SD	Y	26801 FQ	29850 MW	33490 TQ	SDBLS	7/08-9/08
	Tennessee	Y	25950 FQ	30690 MW	36140 TQ	USBLS	5/07
	Memphis MSA, TN-MS-AR	Y	26930 FQ	31310 MW	36490 TQ	USBLS	5/07

AE	Average entry wage	AW	Average wage paid	FQ First quartile wage
AER	Average entry range	AWR	Average wage range	H Hourly
AEX	Average experienced wage	AXR	Average experienced range	HI Highest wage paid
ATC	Average total compensation	D	Daily	HR High end range

LO	Lowest wage paid	MTC	Median total compensation	TCC	Total cash compensation
LR	Low end range	MW	Median wage paid	TQ	Third quartile wage
M	Monthly	MWR	Median wage range	W	Weekly
MCC	Median cash compensation	S	See annotated source	Y	Yearly

Occupation/Type/Industry	Location	Per	Low	Mid	High	Source	Date
Welder, Cutter, Solderer, and Brazer	Nashville-Davidson-Murfreesboro MSA, TN	Y	25820 FQ	29550 MW	34740 TQ	USBLS	5/07
	Texas	Y	24720 FQ	30600 MW	38420 TQ	USBLS	5/07
	Austin-Round Rock MSA, TX	Y	22230 FQ	28660 MW	36260 TQ	USBLS	5/07
	Beaumont-Port Arthur MSA, TX	Y	31260 FQ	38030 MW	45360 TQ	USBLS	5/07
	Dallas-Fort Worth-Arlington MSA, TX	Y	24050 FQ	29380 MW	36470 TQ	USBLS	5/07
	El Paso MSA, TX	Y	19360 FQ	22060 MW	27600 TQ	USBLS	5/07
	Houston-Sugar Land-Baytown MSA, TX	Y	27630 FQ	34060 MW	42250 TQ	USBLS	5/07
	Midland MSA, TX	Y	23800 FQ	28710 MW	36080 TQ	USBLS	5/07
	San Antonio MSA, TX	Y	22240 FQ	26030 MW	31010 TQ	USBLS	5/07
	Utah	Y	27180 FQ	32070 MW	39630 TQ	USBLS	5/07
	Salt Lake City MSA, UT	Y	27440 FQ	32700 MW	40100 TQ	USBLS	5/07
	Vermont	Y	27320 FQ	31400 MW	37920 TQ	USBLS	5/07
	Burlington-South Burlington MSA, VT	Y	29950 FQ	35500 MW	45320 TQ	USBLS	5/07
	Virginia	Y	28980 FQ	35280 MW	42950 TQ	USBLS	5/07
	Richmond MSA, VA	Y	28110 FQ	35010 MW	41670 TQ	USBLS	5/07
	Virginia Beach-Norfolk-Newport News MSA, VA-NC	Y	32850 FQ	40020 MW	46780 TQ	USBLS	5/07
	Washington	H	15.90 FQ	19.33 MW	23.56 TQ	WABLS	3/08
	Seattle-Tacoma-Bellevue MSA, WA	Y	35680 FQ	42610 MW	49720 TQ	USBLS	5/07
	West Virginia	Y	27108 FQ	31945 MW	38772 TQ	WVBLS	7/08-9/08
	Charleston MSA, WV	Y	27160 FQ	31920 MW	46100 TQ	USBLS	5/07
	Huntington-Ashland MSA, WV-KY-OH	Y	29060 FQ	34570 MW	38420 TQ	USBLS	5/07
	Wisconsin	Y	28870 FQ	33810 MW	38890 TQ	USBLS	5/07
	Milwaukee-Waukesha-West Allis MSA, WI	Y	28850 FQ	33550 MW	38960 TQ	USBLS	5/07
	Wyoming	Y	32937 FQ	40520 MW	48887 TQ	WYBLS	9/08
	Cheyenne MSA, WY	Y	28361 FQ	33536 MW	42297 TQ	WYBLS	9/08
	Puerto Rico	Y	15940 FQ	18510 MW	22840 TQ	USBLS	5/07
	San Juan-Caguas-Guaynabo MSA, PR	Y	15970 FQ	18460 MW	22590 TQ	USBLS	5/07
	Virgin Islands	Y	41340 FQ	44800 MW	48270 TQ	USBLS	5/07
	Guam	Y	24990 FQ	29700 MW	35280 TQ	USBLS	5/07
Welder-Diver	United States	Y	15000 LO		100000 HI	AWS	2008
Welding, Soldering, and Brazing Machine Setter, Operator, and Tender	Alabama	Y	27240 FQ	52880 MW	59840 TQ	USBLS	5/07
	Birmingham-Hoover MSA, AL	Y	21830 FQ	26390 MW	32240 TQ	USBLS	5/07
	Arizona	Y	25630 FQ	31450 MW	41240 TQ	USBLS	5/07
	Phoenix-Mesa-Scottsdale MSA, AZ	Y	25300 FQ	30890 MW	43150 TQ	USBLS	5/07
	Tucson MSA, AZ	Y	25650 FQ	31330 MW	36330 TQ	USBLS	5/07
	Arkansas	Y	23610 FQ	27710 MW	32770 TQ	USBLS	5/07
	Little Rock-North Little Rock MSA, AR	Y	30740 FQ	35180 MW	38470 TQ	USBLS	5/07
	California	H	10.98 FQ	13.69 MW	17.59 TQ	CABLS	1/08-3/08
	Los Angeles-Long Beach-Glendale PMSA, CA	H	11.09 FQ	13.79 MW	17.80 TQ	CABLS	1/08-3/08
	Modesto MSA, CA	H	11.94 FQ	13.84 MW	17.46 TQ	CABLS	1/08-3/08
	Oakland-Fremont-Hayward MSA, CA	H	10.24 FQ	12.15 MW	17.64 TQ	CABLS	1/08-3/08
	Riverside-San Bernardino-Ontario MSA, CA	H	10.17 FQ	12.75 MW	15.81 TQ	CABLS	1/08-3/08
	Sacramento-Arden Arcade-Roseville MSA, CA	H	11.25 FQ	14.36 MW	20.38 TQ	CABLS	1/08-3/08
	San Diego-Carlsbad-San Marcos MSA, CA	H	10.90 FQ	15.00 MW	18.48 TQ	CABLS	1/08-3/08
	San Jose-Sunnyvale-Santa Clara MSA, CA	H	10.47 FQ	11.59 MW	15.84 TQ	CABLS	1/08-3/08
	Santa Ana-Anaheim-Irvine PMSA, CA	Y	24350 FQ	29060 MW	35040 TQ	USBLS	5/07
	Colorado	Y	29170 FQ	36610 MW	48780 TQ	USBLS	5/07

AE Average entry wage	**AW** Average wage paid	**FQ** First quartile wage	**LO** Lowest wage paid	**MTC** Median total compensation	**TCC** Total cash compensation
AER Average entry range	**AWR** Average wage range	**H** Hourly	**LR** Low end range	**MW** Median wage paid	**TQ** Third quartile wage
AEX Average experienced wage	**AXR** Average experienced range	**HI** Highest wage paid	**M** Monthly	**MWR** Median wage range	**W** Weekly
ATC Average total compensation	**D** Daily	**HR** High end range	**MCC** Median cash compensation	**S** See annotated source	**Y** Yearly

Occupation/Type/Industry	Location	Per	Low	Mid	High	Source	Date
Welding, Soldering, and Brazing Machine Setter, Operator, and Tender	Denver-Aurora MSA, CO	Y	28300 FQ	37570 MW	50610 TQ	USBLS	5/07
	Connecticut	H	12.43 AE	17.93 MW		CTBLS	1/08-3/08
	Hartford-West Hartford-East Hartford MSA, CT	Y	27390 FQ	36520 MW	45360 TQ	USBLS	5/07
	Delaware	Y	33130 FQ	39660 MW	51870 TQ	USBLS	5/07
	Wilmington PMSA, DE-MD-NJ	Y	35000 FQ	41250 MW	52220 TQ	USBLS	5/07
	Washington-Arlington-Alexandria MSA, DC-VA-MD-WV	Y	26520 FQ	30800 MW	40720 TQ	USBLS	5/07
	Florida	Y	22320 FQ	26650 MW	33970 TQ	USBLS	5/07
	Fort Lauderdale-Pompano Beach-Deerfield Beach PMSA, FL	Y	23980 FQ	28770 MW	33430 TQ	USBLS	5/07
	Jacksonville MSA, FL	Y	21760 FQ	23420 MW	25070 TQ	USBLS	5/07
	Miami-Fort Lauderdale-Miami Beach MSA, FL	Y	26980 FQ	32670 MW	37470 TQ	USBLS	5/07
	Orlando-Kissimmee MSA, FL	Y	23360 FQ	28170 MW	35950 TQ	USBLS	5/07
	Tampa-St. Petersburg-Clearwater MSA, FL	Y	23080 FQ	26860 MW	30930 TQ	USBLS	5/07
	Georgia	Y	23940 FQ	28480 MW	33790 TQ	USBLS	5/07
	Atlanta-Sandy Springs-Marietta MSA, GA	Y	23640 FQ	27950 MW	32200 TQ	USBLS	5/07
	Idaho	Y	28500 FQ	32510 MW	36350 TQ	USBLS	5/07
	Boise City-Nampa MSA, ID	Y	29530 FQ	32580 MW	35620 TQ	USBLS	5/07
	Illinois	Y	25680 FQ	31750 MW	39530 TQ	USBLS	5/07
	Chicago-Naperville-Joliet MSA, IL-IN-WI	Y	21850 FQ	28300 MW	37860 TQ	USBLS	5/07
	Rockford MSA, IL	Y	33010 FQ	63100 MW	74030 TQ	USBLS	5/07
	Indiana	Y	25730 FQ	29130 MW	34030 TQ	USBLS	5/07
	Elkhart-Goshen MSA, IN	Y	26850 FQ	29510 MW	32020 TQ	USBLS	5/07
	Gary PMSA, IN	Y	22080 FQ	25750 MW	34400 TQ	USBLS	5/07
	Indianapolis-Carmel MSA, IN	Y	28610 FQ	34160 MW	38070 TQ	USBLS	5/07
	Iowa	Y	28010 FQ	32910 MW	37210 TQ	USBLS	5/07
	Kansas	Y	24120 FQ	30340 MW	41980 TQ	USBLS	5/07
	Wichita MSA, KS	Y	29460 FQ	42140 MW	47320 TQ	USBLS	5/07
	Kentucky	Y	24575 FQ	29454 MW	33660 TQ	KYBLS	2008
	Lexington-Fayette MSA, KY	Y	36220 FQ	39860 MW	44330 TQ	USBLS	5/07
	Louisville-Jefferson County MSA, KY-IN	Y	27860 FQ	31280 MW	34590 TQ	USBLS	5/07
	Louisiana	H	13.87 FQ	16.76 MW	18.92 TQ	LABLS	1/08-3/08
	Baton Rouge MSA, LA	Y	31070 FQ	34870 MW	38700 TQ	USBLS	5/07
	New Orleans-Metairie-Kenner MSA, LA	Y	29800 FQ	34540 MW	38640 TQ	USBLS	5/07
	Maine	Y	29610 FQ	36960 MW	44750 TQ	USBLS	5/07
	Maryland	Y		34800 MW		MDBLS	3/08
	Baltimore-Towson MSA, MD	Y	30870 FQ	34270 MW	37210 TQ	USBLS	5/07
	Massachusetts	Y	29050 FQ	35430 MW	48110 TQ	USBLS	5/07
	Boston-Cambridge-Quincy NECTA, MA	Y	30620 FQ	38170 MW	51910 TQ	USBLS	5/07
	Worcester MSA, MA-CT	Y	21810 FQ	23570 MW	25540 TQ	USBLS	5/07
	Michigan	Y	26960 FQ	35070 MW	52190 TQ	USBLS	5/07
	Detroit-Warren-Livonia MSA, MI	Y	31160 FQ	40200 MW	57340 TQ	USBLS	5/07
	Grand Rapids-Wyoming MSA, MI	Y	27870 FQ	33500 MW	42360 TQ	USBLS	5/07
	Warren-Troy-Farmington Hills PMSA, MI	Y	28080 FQ	33610 MW	45570 TQ	USBLS	5/07
	Minnesota	Y	28456 FQ	34718 MW	41456 TQ	MNBLS	10/08-12/08
	Minneapolis-Saint Paul MSA, MN-WI	Y	36045 FQ	41601 MW	46733 TQ	MNBLS	10/08-12/08
	Mississippi	Y	24310 FQ	27700 MW	30620 TQ	USBLS	5/07
	Missouri	Y	22750 FQ	27710 MW	33770 TQ	USBLS	5/07
	Kansas City MSA, MO-KS	Y	23440 FQ	28030 MW	33700 TQ	USBLS	5/07
	St. Louis MSA, MO-IL	Y	25300 FQ	30630 MW	35470 TQ	USBLS	5/07
	Montana	Y	25930 FQ	29430 MW	33070 TQ	USBLS	5/07
	Nebraska	Y	25790 FQ	29060 MW	33820 TQ	USBLS	5/07
	Omaha-Council Bluffs MSA, NE-IA	Y	22990 FQ	28480 MW	33710 TQ	USBLS	5/07

AE	Average entry wage	AW	Average wage paid	FQ	First quartile wage
AER	Average entry range	AWR	Average wage range	H	Hourly
AEX	Average experienced wage	AXR	Average experienced range	HI	Highest wage paid
ATC	Average total compensation	D	Daily	HR	High end range

LO	Lowest wage paid	MTC	Median total compensation	TCC	Total cash compensation
LR	Low end range	MW	Median wage paid	TQ	Third quartile wage
M	Monthly	MWR	Median wage range	W	Weekly
MCC	Median cash compensation	S	See annotated source	Y	Yearly

Occupation/Type/Industry	Location	Per	Low	Mid	High	Source	Date
Welding, Soldering, and Brazing Machine Setter, Operator, and Tender							
	Nevada	H	10.74 FQ	15.27 MW	17.84 TQ	NVBLS	5/08
	Las Vegas-Paradise MSA, NV	H	8.87 FQ	12.08 MW	17.19 TQ	NVBLS	5/08
	Reno-Sparks MSA, NV	H	13.94 FQ	16.27 MW	18.53 TQ	NVBLS	5/08
	New Hampshire	H	12.63 AE	15.87 MW	17.26 AEX	NHBLS	6/08
	Manchester MSA, NH	Y	27400 FQ	30320 MW	33730 TQ	USBLS	5/07
	Nashua NECTA, NH-MA	Y	29730 FQ	32500 MW	35480 TQ	USBLS	5/07
	New Jersey	Y	27110 FQ	33550 MW	38260 TQ	USBLS	5/07
	Camden PMSA, NJ	Y	33850 FQ	36580 MW	39550 TQ	USBLS	5/07
	Edison PMSA, NJ	Y	29470 FQ	34760 MW	38830 TQ	USBLS	5/07
	Newark-Union PMSA, NJ-PA	Y	22160 FQ	29050 MW	37400 TQ	USBLS	5/07
	New Mexico	Y	18310 FQ	21440 MW	32570 TQ	USBLS	5/07
	New York	Y	27960 FQ	35880 MW	54520 TQ	USBLS	5/07
	Albany-Schenectady-Troy MSA, NY	Y	38160 FQ	53210 MW	59910 TQ	USBLS	5/07
	Nassau-Suffolk PMSA, NY	Y	23550 FQ	29690 MW	36490 TQ	USBLS	5/07
	New York-Northern New Jersey-Long Island MSA, NY-NJ-PA	Y	26030 FQ	31850 MW	38970 TQ	USBLS	5/07
	North Carolina	Y	26510 FQ	30650 MW	35470 TQ	USBLS	5/07
	Charlotte-Gastonia-Concord MSA, NC-SC	Y	27430 FQ	31570 MW	35380 TQ	USBLS	5/07
	Fargo MSA, ND-MN	Y	28410 FQ	34270 MW	44750 TQ	USBLS	5/07
	Ohio	Y	26520 FQ	30940 MW	37740 TQ	USBLS	5/07
	Cincinnati-Middletown MSA, OH-KY-IN	Y	24950 FQ	32470 MW	37890 TQ	USBLS	5/07
	Cleveland-Elyria-Mentor MSA, OH	Y	27100 FQ	30600 MW	36830 TQ	USBLS	5/07
	Columbus MSA, OH	Y	25690 FQ	29800 MW	36960 TQ	USBLS	5/07
	Dayton MSA, OH	Y	28550 FQ	32310 MW	36440 TQ	USBLS	5/07
	Oklahoma	Y	25710 FQ	29920 MW	35710 TQ	USBLS	5/07
	Oklahoma City MSA, OK	Y	25990 FQ	28720 MW	31390 TQ	USBLS	5/07
	Tulsa MSA, OK	Y	25460 FQ	30880 MW	36730 TQ	USBLS	5/07
	Oregon	H	11.38 FQ	15.65 MW	19.60 TQ	ORBLS	5/08
	Eugene-Springfield MSA, OR	Y	23450 FQ	30310 MW	35030 TQ	USBLS	5/07
	Portland-Vancouver-Beaverton MSA, OR-WA	Y	22630 FQ	29990 MW	38480 TQ	USBLS	5/07
	Pennsylvania	Y	25930 FQ	31190 MW	38510 TQ	USBLS	5/07
	Philadelphia-Camden-Wilmington MSA, PA-NJ-DE-MD	Y	25680 FQ	33610 MW	41100 TQ	USBLS	5/07
	Pittsburgh MSA, PA	Y	27630 FQ	32380 MW	38250 TQ	USBLS	5/07
	Rhode Island	Y	18450 FQ	24870 MW	30750 TQ	USBLS	5/07
	Providence-Fall River-Warwick MSA, RI-MA	Y	20470 FQ	26200 MW	33670 TQ	USBLS	5/07
	South Carolina	Y	24920 FQ	29390 MW	36990 TQ	USBLS	5/07
	Charleston-North Charleston MSA, SC	Y	22420 FQ	27100 MW	34500 TQ	USBLS	5/07
	Columbia MSA, SC	Y	28020 FQ	31860 MW	37440 TQ	USBLS	5/07
	South Dakota	Y	27727 FQ	32298 MW	36799 TQ	SDBLS	7/08-9/08
	Sioux Falls MSA, SD	Y	25861 FQ	29885 MW	34127 TQ	SDBLS	7/08-9/08
	Tennessee	Y	22280 FQ	26550 MW	32120 TQ	USBLS	5/07
	Memphis MSA, TN-MS-AR	Y	21330 FQ	23350 MW	26550 TQ	USBLS	5/07
	Nashville-Davidson-Murfreesboro MSA, TN	Y	24410 FQ	28020 MW	31360 TQ	USBLS	5/07
	Texas	Y	22020 FQ	26220 MW	32970 TQ	USBLS	5/07
	Austin-Round Rock MSA, TX	Y	20680 FQ	25790 MW	37990 TQ	USBLS	5/07
	Dallas-Fort Worth-Arlington MSA, TX	Y	20560 FQ	24370 MW	32380 TQ	USBLS	5/07
	Houston-Sugar Land-Baytown MSA, TX	Y	22330 FQ	26720 MW	34190 TQ	USBLS	5/07
	San Antonio MSA, TX	Y	22840 FQ	25710 MW	28600 TQ	USBLS	5/07
	Utah	Y	22340 FQ	24860 MW	33630 TQ	USBLS	5/07
	Provo-Orem MSA, UT	Y	23890 FQ	28940 MW	41910 TQ	USBLS	5/07
	Salt Lake City MSA, UT	Y	24380 FQ	28240 MW	35880 TQ	USBLS	5/07
	Vermont	Y	24910 FQ	32640 MW	37580 TQ	USBLS	5/07
	Virginia	Y	28110 FQ	32660 MW	42830 TQ	USBLS	5/07
	Richmond MSA, VA	Y	30480 FQ	33420 MW	36070 TQ	USBLS	5/07
	Virginia Beach-Norfolk-Newport News MSA, VA-NC	Y	35250 FQ	43660 MW	47950 TQ	USBLS	5/07

Occupation/Type/Industry	Location	Per	Low	Mid	High	Source	Date
Welding, Soldering, and Brazing Machine Setter, Operator, and Tender	Washington	H	15.82 FQ	18.02 MW	29.38 TQ	WABLS	3/08
	Seattle-Tacoma-Bellevue MSA, WA	Y	33170 FQ	49880 MW	67860 TQ	USBLS	5/07
	West Virginia	Y	22054 FQ	31141 MW	36209 TQ	WVBLS	7/08-9/08
	Wisconsin	Y	28430 FQ	33910 MW	38970 TQ	USBLS	5/07
	Milwaukee-Waukesha-West Allis MSA, WI	Y	26110 FQ	32130 MW	37350 TQ	USBLS	5/07
	Wyoming	Y	21884 FQ	24563 MW	37410 TQ	WYBLS	9/08
	Puerto Rico	Y	14790 FQ	17280 MW	19650 TQ	USBLS	5/07
	San Juan-Caguas-Guaynabo MSA, PR	Y	13960 FQ	16770 MW	19960 TQ	USBLS	5/07
Wellhead Pumper	Alabama	Y	41310 FQ	50950 MW	62150 TQ	USBLS	5/07
	Arkansas	Y	24090 FQ	30850 MW	39390 TQ	USBLS	5/07
	California	H	14.26 FQ	18.77 MW	22.49 TQ	CABLS	1/08-3/08
	Colorado	Y	33520 FQ	39510 MW	50010 TQ	USBLS	5/07
	Illinois	Y	16410 FQ	26260 MW	29880 TQ	USBLS	5/07
	Indiana	Y	14590 FQ	18160 MW	27360 TQ	USBLS	5/07
	Kansas	Y	26490 FQ	30450 MW	41670 TQ	USBLS	5/07
	Kentucky	Y	20393 FQ	27676 MW	37471 TQ	KYBLS	2008
	Louisiana	H	14.67 FQ	17.45 MW	19.57 TQ	LABLS	1/08-3/08
	Michigan	Y	25480 FQ	30080 MW	35570 TQ	USBLS	5/07
	Mississippi	Y	33110 FQ	55040 MW	61080 TQ	USBLS	5/07
	Montana	Y	34390 FQ	40570 MW	55060 TQ	USBLS	5/07
	New Mexico	Y	29760 FQ	40020 MW	49970 TQ	USBLS	5/07
	New York	Y	25140 FQ	26750 MW	28360 TQ	USBLS	5/07
	North Dakota	Y	44780 FQ	52200 MW	57730 TQ	USBLS	5/07
	Ohio	Y	23070 FQ	28800 MW	39210 TQ	USBLS	5/07
	Oklahoma	Y	32640 FQ	41870 MW	50430 TQ	USBLS	5/07
	Pennsylvania	Y	28290 FQ	33400 MW	38600 TQ	USBLS	5/07
	Texas	Y	30100 FQ	37700 MW	46790 TQ	USBLS	5/07
	Utah	Y	25130 FQ	28170 MW	31400 TQ	USBLS	5/07
	Virginia	Y	27930 FQ	30430 MW	34180 TQ	USBLS	5/07
	West Virginia	Y	20204 FQ	30258 MW	49564 TQ	WVBLS	7/08-9/08
	Wyoming	Y	30797 FQ	42380 MW	51453 TQ	WYBLS	9/08
Wellness Coach	United States	H			150.00 HI	EZART1	2007
West Wing Receptionist White House Staff	United States	Y			47000 HI	WPOST02	2008
Wholesale and Retail Buyer							
Except Farm Products	Alabama	Y	31290 FQ	39290 MW	51720 TQ	USBLS	5/07
Except Farm Products	Birmingham-Hoover MSA, AL	Y	36180 FQ	46840 MW	57370 TQ	USBLS	5/07
Except Farm Products	Alaska	Y	34420 FQ	46280 MW	69740 TQ	USBLS	5/07
Except Farm Products	Anchorage MSA, AK	Y	34060 FQ	48760 MW	71410 TQ	USBLS	5/07
Except Farm Products	Arizona	Y	31860 FQ	42360 MW	61570 TQ	USBLS	5/07
Except Farm Products	Phoenix-Mesa-Scottsdale MSA, AZ	Y	32550 FQ	45500 MW	63560 TQ	USBLS	5/07
Except Farm Products	Tucson MSA, AZ	Y	29670 FQ	36720 MW	51500 TQ	USBLS	5/07
Except Farm Products	Arkansas	Y	32590 FQ	48210 MW	77420 TQ	USBLS	5/07
Except Farm Products	Fort Smith MSA, AR-OK	Y	27890 FQ	34370 MW	50370 TQ	USBLS	5/07
Except Farm Products	Little Rock-North Little Rock MSA, AR	Y	36450 FQ	47490 MW	87750 TQ	USBLS	5/07
Except Farm Products	California	H	18.28 FQ	23.98 MW	31.98 TQ	CABLS	1/08-3/08
Except Farm Products	Bakersfield MSA, CA	H	14.08 FQ	18.39 MW	27.25 TQ	CABLS	1/08-3/08
Except Farm Products	Los Angeles-Long Beach-Glendale PMSA, CA	H	17.68 FQ	23.50 MW	32.48 TQ	CABLS	1/08-3/08
Except Farm Products	Oakland-Fremont-Hayward MSA, CA	H	19.29 FQ	24.52 MW	33.31 TQ	CABLS	1/08-3/08
Except Farm Products	Riverside-San Bernardino-Ontario MSA, CA	H	16.74 FQ	20.87 MW	27.69 TQ	CABLS	1/08-3/08
Except Farm Products	Sacramento-Arden Arcade-Roseville MSA, CA	H	20.04 FQ	27.53 MW	36.03 TQ	CABLS	1/08-3/08
Except Farm Products	San Diego-Carlsbad-San Marcos MSA, CA	H	19.71 FQ	25.93 MW	32.87 TQ	CABLS	1/08-3/08
Except Farm Products	San Francisco-San Mateo-Redwood PMSA, CA	H	18.61 FQ	24.46 MW	30.97 TQ	CABLS	1/08-3/08
Except Farm Products	San Jose-Sunnyvale-Santa Clara MSA, CA	H	20.20 FQ	28.34 MW	39.33 TQ	CABLS	1/08-3/08

AE Average entry wage	AW Average wage paid	FQ First quartile wage	LO Lowest wage paid	MTC Median total compensation	TCC Total cash compensation
AER Average entry range	AWR Average wage range	H Hourly	LR Low end range	MW Median wage paid	TQ Third quartile wage
AEX Average experienced wage	AXR Average experienced range	HI Highest wage paid	M Monthly	MWR Median wage range	W Weekly
ATC Average total compensation	D Daily	HR High end range	MCC Median cash compensation	S See annotated source	Y Yearly

Occupation/Type/Industry	Location	Per	Low	Mid	High	Source	Date
Wholesale and Retail Buyer							
Except Farm Products	Santa Ana-Anaheim-Irvine PMSA, CA	Y	42150 FQ	52650 MW	64810 TQ	USBLS	5/07
Except Farm Products	Colorado	Y	34360 FQ	45610 MW	63850 TQ	USBLS	5/07
Except Farm Products	Denver-Aurora MSA, CO	Y	37180 FQ	47990 MW	66730 TQ	USBLS	5/07
Except Farm Products	Connecticut	H	17.87 AE	25.71 MW		CTBLS	1/08-3/08
Except Farm Products	Bridgeport-Stamford-Norwalk MSA, CT	Y	47960 FQ	60050 MW	110000 TQ	USBLS	5/07
Except Farm Products	Hartford-West Hartford-East Hartford MSA, CT	Y	39110 FQ	48300 MW	60340 TQ	USBLS	5/07
Except Farm Products	New Haven MSA, CT	Y	36310 FQ	49480 MW	62790 TQ	USBLS	5/07
Except Farm Products	Delaware	Y	34470 FQ	46480 MW	58920 TQ	USBLS	5/07
Except Farm Products	Dover MSA, DE	Y	33000 FQ	55790 MW	83120 TQ	USBLS	5/07
Except Farm Products	Wilmington PMSA, DE-MD-NJ	Y	34330 FQ	44900 MW	57970 TQ	USBLS	5/07
Except Farm Products	District of Columbia	Y	35210 FQ	50010 MW	63810 TQ	USBLS	5/07
Except Farm Products	Washington-Arlington-Alexandria MSA, DC-VA-MD-WV	Y	35790 FQ	49970 MW	66510 TQ	USBLS	5/07
Except Farm Products	Florida	Y	36220 FQ	46660 MW	61340 TQ	USBLS	5/07
Except Farm Products	Fort Lauderdale-Pompano Beach-Deerfield Beach PMSA, FL	Y	39720 FQ	48710 MW	61600 TQ	USBLS	5/07
Except Farm Products	Jacksonville MSA, FL	Y	40590 FQ	50130 MW	62580 TQ	USBLS	5/07
Except Farm Products	Miami-Fort Lauderdale-Miami Beach MSA, FL	Y	35460 FQ	46340 MW	59670 TQ	USBLS	5/07
Except Farm Products	Orlando-Kissimmee MSA, FL	Y	38340 FQ	47140 MW	64270 TQ	USBLS	5/07
Except Farm Products	Tampa-St. Petersburg-Clearwater MSA, FL	Y	37850 FQ	49380 MW	67480 TQ	USBLS	5/07
Except Farm Products	West Palm Beach-Boca Raton-Boynton Beach PMSA, FL	Y	39540 FQ	49750 MW	63920 TQ	USBLS	5/07
Except Farm Products	Georgia	Y	35760 FQ	45220 MW	60670 TQ	USBLS	5/07
Except Farm Products	Atlanta-Sandy Springs-Marietta MSA, GA	Y	36100 FQ	45910 MW	61750 TQ	USBLS	5/07
Except Farm Products	Hawaii	Y	31970 FQ	39600 MW	51550 TQ	USBLS	5/07
Except Farm Products	Honolulu MSA, HI	Y	33120 FQ	41320 MW	53800 TQ	USBLS	5/07
Except Farm Products	Idaho	Y	22750 FQ	31830 MW	49800 TQ	USBLS	5/07
Except Farm Products	Boise City-Nampa MSA, ID	Y	25620 FQ	35610 MW	52550 TQ	USBLS	5/07
Except Farm Products	Illinois	Y	34500 FQ	44640 MW	62480 TQ	USBLS	5/07
Except Farm Products	Chicago-Naperville-Joliet MSA, IL-IN-WI	Y	35140 FQ	46360 MW	65710 TQ	USBLS	5/07
Except Farm Products	Peoria MSA, IL	Y	33280 FQ	47560 MW	60950 TQ	USBLS	5/07
Except Farm Products	Indiana	Y	33600 FQ	45320 MW	58280 TQ	USBLS	5/07
Except Farm Products	Evansville MSA, IN-KY	Y	32680 FQ	45570 MW	55390 TQ	USBLS	5/07
Except Farm Products	Fort Wayne MSA, IN	Y	33370 FQ	40540 MW	53870 TQ	USBLS	5/07
Except Farm Products	Gary PMSA, IN	Y	32730 FQ	49140 MW	58860 TQ	USBLS	5/07
Except Farm Products	Indianapolis-Carmel MSA, IN	Y	35420 FQ	48270 MW	59100 TQ	USBLS	5/07
Except Farm Products	Iowa	Y	30040 FQ	42480 MW	56300 TQ	USBLS	5/07
Except Farm Products	Des Moines-West Des Moines MSA, IA	Y	38090 FQ	47990 MW	57290 TQ	USBLS	5/07
Except Farm Products	Dubuque MSA, IA	Y	37210 FQ	50890 MW	65890 TQ	USBLS	5/07
Except Farm Products	Kansas	Y	31000 FQ	39790 MW	51290 TQ	USBLS	5/07
Except Farm Products	Wichita MSA, KS	Y	32650 FQ	40760 MW	51530 TQ	USBLS	5/07
Except Farm Products	Kentucky	Y	31984 FQ	41978 MW	55406 TQ	KYBLS	2008
Except Farm Products	Louisville-Jefferson County MSA, KY-IN	Y	35530 FQ	46090 MW	55610 TQ	USBLS	5/07
Except Farm Products	Louisiana	H	12.35 FQ	17.57 MW	27.92 TQ	LABLS	1/08-3/08
Except Farm Products	Baton Rouge MSA, LA	Y	33190 FQ	53700 MW	82850 TQ	USBLS	5/07
Except Farm Products	New Orleans-Metairie-Kenner MSA, LA	Y	25550 FQ	35660 MW	48510 TQ	USBLS	5/07
Except Farm Products	Maine	Y	31250 FQ	38660 MW	48760 TQ	USBLS	5/07
Except Farm Products	Bangor MSA, ME	Y	34990 FQ	40020 MW	58660 TQ	USBLS	5/07
Except Farm Products	Portland-South Portland-Biddeford MSA, ME	Y	34330 FQ	41730 MW	51870 TQ	USBLS	5/07
Except Farm Products	Maryland	Y		49325 MW		MDBLS	3/08
Except Farm Products	Baltimore-Towson MSA, MD	Y	35630 FQ	45770 MW	62260 TQ	USBLS	5/07
Except Farm Products	Bethesda-Gaithersburg-Frederick PMSA, MD	Y	36000 FQ	55380 MW	66520 TQ	USBLS	5/07
Except Farm Products	Massachusetts	Y	40780 FQ	52060 MW	68550 TQ	USBLS	5/07
Except Farm Products	Boston-Cambridge-Quincy NECTA, MA	Y	42890 FQ	52310 MW	67370 TQ	USBLS	5/07
Except Farm Products	Worcester MSA, MA-CT	Y	40920 FQ	54960 MW	72820 TQ	USBLS	5/07

AE	Average entry wage	AW	Average wage paid	FQ	First quartile wage
AER	Average entry range	AWR	Average wage range	H	Hourly
AEX	Average experienced wage	AXR	Average experienced range	HI	Highest wage paid
ATC	Average total compensation	D	Daily	HR	High end range

LO	Lowest wage paid	MTC	Median total compensation	TCC	Total cash compensation
LR	Low end range	MW	Median wage paid	TQ	Third quartile wage
M	Monthly	MWR	Median wage range	W	Weekly
MCC	Median cash compensation	S	See annotated source	Y	Yearly

Occupation/Type/Industry	Location	Per	Low	Mid	High	Source	Date
Wholesale and Retail Buyer							
Except Farm Products	Michigan	Y	35130 FQ	47470 MW	66280 TQ	USBLS	5/07
Except Farm Products	Detroit-Warren-Livonia MSA, MI	Y	38680 FQ	51630 MW	72980 TQ	USBLS	5/07
Except Farm Products	Grand Rapids-Wyoming MSA, MI	Y	40440 FQ	55940 MW	76940 TQ	USBLS	5/07
Except Farm Products	Warren-Troy-Farmington Hills PMSA, MI	Y	37100 FQ	50170 MW	69680 TQ	USBLS	5/07
Except Farm Products	Minnesota	Y	43478 FQ	53498 MW	68523 TQ	MNBLS	10/08-12/08
Except Farm Products	Duluth-Superior MSA, MN-WI	Y	35001 FQ	40757 MW	54395 TQ	MNBLS	10/08-12/08
Except Farm Products	Minneapolis-Saint Paul MSA, MN-WI	Y	45647 FQ	55427 MW	71140 TQ	MNBLS	10/08-12/08
Except Farm Products	Rochester MSA, MN	Y	42438 FQ	48876 MW	60711 TQ	MNBLS	10/08-12/08
Except Farm Products	Mississippi	Y	30310 FQ	39670 MW	49580 TQ	USBLS	5/07
Except Farm Products	Jackson MSA, MS	Y	38270 FQ	44760 MW	50570 TQ	USBLS	5/07
Except Farm Products	Missouri	Y	31610 FQ	40810 MW	53530 TQ	USBLS	5/07
Except Farm Products	Kansas City MSA, MO-KS	Y	35630 FQ	44540 MW	54800 TQ	USBLS	5/07
Except Farm Products	St. Louis MSA, MO-IL	Y	33980 FQ	43160 MW	55260 TQ	USBLS	5/07
Except Farm Products	Montana	Y	29670 FQ	39760 MW	54070 TQ	USBLS	5/07
Except Farm Products	Billings MSA, MT	Y	33160 FQ	41950 MW	59430 TQ	USBLS	5/07
Except Farm Products	Nebraska	Y	33770 FQ	42450 MW	57280 TQ	USBLS	5/07
Except Farm Products	Omaha-Council Bluffs MSA, NE-IA	Y	34850 FQ	44640 MW	63780 TQ	USBLS	5/07
Except Farm Products	Nevada	H	17.48 FQ	24.20 MW	44.13 TQ	NVBLS	5/08
Except Farm Products	Las Vegas-Paradise MSA, NV	H	17.22 FQ	24.33 MW	45.14 TQ	NVBLS	5/08
Except Farm Products	New Hampshire	H	17.07 AE	25.18 MW	36.10 AEX	NHBLS	6/08
Except Farm Products	Manchester MSA, NH	Y	43170 FQ	53130 MW	66730 TQ	USBLS	5/07
Except Farm Products	Nashua NECTA, NH-MA	Y	49190 FQ	56080 MW	83140 TQ	USBLS	5/07
Except Farm Products	New Jersey	Y	44060 FQ	59270 MW	76800 TQ	USBLS	5/07
Except Farm Products	Camden PMSA, NJ	Y	40250 FQ	49940 MW	67690 TQ	USBLS	5/07
Except Farm Products	Edison PMSA, NJ	Y	41350 FQ	59490 MW	77250 TQ	USBLS	5/07
Except Farm Products	Newark-Union PMSA, NJ-PA	Y	44250 FQ	60570 MW	75130 TQ	USBLS	5/07
Except Farm Products	Ocean City MSA, NJ	Y	27230 FQ	31430 MW	51340 TQ	USBLS	5/07
Except Farm Products	Trenton-Ewing MSA, NJ	Y	39240 FQ	49750 MW	69840 TQ	USBLS	5/07
Except Farm Products	New Mexico	Y	31730 FQ	40740 MW	50960 TQ	USBLS	5/07
Except Farm Products	Albuquerque MSA, NM	Y	35310 FQ	43970 MW	54540 TQ	USBLS	5/07
Except Farm Products	New York	Y	40700 FQ	54410 MW	73320 TQ	USBLS	5/07
Except Farm Products	Albany-Schenectady-Troy MSA, NY	Y	35360 FQ	46340 MW	59530 TQ	USBLS	5/07
Except Farm Products	Binghamton MSA, NY	Y	33940 FQ	40880 MW	56750 TQ	USBLS	5/07
Except Farm Products	Buffalo-Niagara Falls MSA, NY	Y	32270 FQ	47360 MW	58980 TQ	USBLS	5/07
Except Farm Products	Nassau-Suffolk PMSA, NY	Y	45270 FQ	60540 MW	76190 TQ	USBLS	5/07
Except Farm Products	New York-Northern New Jersey-Long Island MSA, NY-NJ-PA	Y	45690 FQ	59860 MW	78850 TQ	USBLS	5/07
Except Farm Products	North Carolina	Y	33750 FQ	44740 MW	60700 TQ	USBLS	5/07
Except Farm Products	Charlotte-Gastonia-Concord MSA, NC-SC	Y	35430 FQ	48090 MW	62880 TQ	USBLS	5/07
Except Farm Products	Raleigh-Cary MSA, NC	Y	39540 FQ	50410 MW	64290 TQ	USBLS	5/07
Except Farm Products	North Dakota	Y	37500 FQ	46530 MW	72490 TQ	USBLS	5/07
Except Farm Products	Fargo MSA, ND-MN	Y	36890 FQ	45220 MW	57010 TQ	USBLS	5/07
Except Farm Products	Ohio	Y	32120 FQ	42580 MW	57760 TQ	USBLS	5/07
Except Farm Products	Cincinnati-Middletown MSA, OH-KY-IN	Y	36800 FQ	50990 MW	71750 TQ	USBLS	5/07
Except Farm Products	Cleveland-Elyria-Mentor MSA, OH	Y	35440 FQ	45780 MW	58080 TQ	USBLS	5/07
Except Farm Products	Columbus MSA, OH	Y	33550 FQ	45280 MW	58980 TQ	USBLS	5/07
Except Farm Products	Dayton MSA, OH	Y	30920 FQ	35980 MW	46200 TQ	USBLS	5/07
Except Farm Products	Mansfield MSA, OH	Y	26220 FQ	29480 MW	74430 TQ	USBLS	5/07
Except Farm Products	Oklahoma	Y	28240 FQ	40380 MW	55310 TQ	USBLS	5/07
Except Farm Products	Oklahoma City MSA, OK	Y	29550 FQ	42920 MW	55620 TQ	USBLS	5/07
Except Farm Products	Tulsa MSA, OK	Y	25430 FQ	38620 MW	57730 TQ	USBLS	5/07
Except Farm Products	Oregon	H	16.77 FQ	20.31 MW	26.86 TQ	ORBLS	5/08
Except Farm Products	Portland-Vancouver-Beaverton MSA, OR-WA	Y	35440 FQ	43490 MW	56720 TQ	USBLS	5/07
Except Farm Products	Pennsylvania	Y	35960 FQ	47680 MW	63670 TQ	USBLS	5/07
Except Farm Products	Allentown-Bethlehem-Easton MSA, PA-NJ	Y	40310 FQ	47010 MW	57760 TQ	USBLS	5/07
Except Farm Products	Philadelphia-Camden-Wilmington MSA, PA-NJ-DE-MD	Y	38690 FQ	50670 MW	68830 TQ	USBLS	5/07

AE	Average entry wage	AW	Average wage paid	FQ	First quartile wage
AER	Average entry range	AWR	Average wage range	H	Hourly
AEX	Average experienced wage	AXR	Average experienced range	HI	Highest wage paid
ATC	Average total compensation	D	Daily	HR	High end range

LO	Lowest wage paid	MTC	Median total compensation
LR	Low end range	MW	Median wage paid
M	Monthly	MWR	Median wage range
MCC	Median cash compensation	S	See annotated source

TCC	Total cash compensation
TQ	Third quartile wage
W	Weekly
Y	Yearly

Occupation/Type/Industry	Location	Per	Low	Mid	High	Source	Date
Wholesale and Retail Buyer							
Except Farm Products	Pittsburgh MSA, PA	Y	34950 FQ	46290 MW	57640 TQ	USBLS	5/07
Except Farm Products	Rhode Island	Y	36390 FQ	55210 MW	64060 TQ	USBLS	5/07
Except Farm Products	Providence-Fall River-Warwick MSA, RI-MA	Y	35520 FQ	50130 MW	62000 TQ	USBLS	5/07
Except Farm Products	South Carolina	Y	35250 FQ	47330 MW	62200 TQ	USBLS	5/07
Except Farm Products	Charleston-North Charleston MSA, SC	Y	30650 FQ	41800 MW	55820 TQ	USBLS	5/07
Except Farm Products	Columbia MSA, SC	Y	37480 FQ	51210 MW	60460 TQ	USBLS	5/07
Except Farm Products	South Dakota	Y	37682 FQ	45200 MW	53939 TQ	SDBLS	7/08-9/08
Except Farm Products	Sioux Falls MSA, SD	Y	38484 FQ	46391 MW	54113 TQ	SDBLS	7/08-9/08
Except Farm Products	Tennessee	Y	32120 FQ	41270 MW	61650 TQ	USBLS	5/07
Except Farm Products	Memphis MSA, TN-MS-AR	Y	35840 FQ	48420 MW	71140 TQ	USBLS	5/07
Except Farm Products	Nashville-Davidson-Murfreesboro MSA, TN	Y	33980 FQ	44440 MW	60420 TQ	USBLS	5/07
Except Farm Products	Texas	Y	37330 FQ	49100 MW	69980 TQ	USBLS	5/07
Except Farm Products	Austin-Round Rock MSA, TX	Y	37410 FQ	72500 MW	108300 TQ	USBLS	5/07
Except Farm Products	Corpus Christi MSA, TX	Y	38930 FQ	47120 MW	62120 TQ	USBLS	5/07
Except Farm Products	Dallas-Fort Worth-Arlington MSA, TX	Y	40240 FQ	52090 MW	72090 TQ	USBLS	5/07
Except Farm Products	El Paso MSA, TX	Y	28010 FQ	39860 MW	62640 TQ	USBLS	5/07
Except Farm Products	Houston-Sugar Land-Baytown MSA, TX	Y	37770 FQ	48670 MW	65640 TQ	USBLS	5/07
Except Farm Products	San Antonio MSA, TX	Y	35260 FQ	43630 MW	57490 TQ	USBLS	5/07
Except Farm Products	Utah	Y	33470 FQ	42360 MW	55190 TQ	USBLS	5/07
Except Farm Products	Salt Lake City MSA, UT	Y	36050 FQ	43330 MW	52510 TQ	USBLS	5/07
Except Farm Products	Vermont	Y	30230 FQ	40680 MW	51030 TQ	USBLS	5/07
Except Farm Products	Burlington-South Burlington MSA, VT	Y	30510 FQ	41780 MW	49060 TQ	USBLS	5/07
Except Farm Products	Virginia	Y	32890 FQ	43940 MW	63780 TQ	USBLS	5/07
Except Farm Products	Charlottesville MSA, VA	Y	24910 FQ	36300 MW	52740 TQ	USBLS	5/07
Except Farm Products	Richmond MSA, VA	Y	36830 FQ	54070 MW	76990 TQ	USBLS	5/07
Except Farm Products	Virginia Beach-Norfolk-Newport News MSA, VA-NC	Y	30660 FQ	38340 MW	49960 TQ	USBLS	5/07
Except Farm Products	Washington	H	16.45 FQ	20.77 MW	28.18 TQ	WABLS	3/08
Except Farm Products	Seattle-Tacoma-Bellevue MSA, WA	Y	34850 FQ	44170 MW	58510 TQ	USBLS	5/07
Except Farm Products	West Virginia	Y	27766 FQ	36876 MW	48634 TQ	WVBLS	7/08-9/08
Except Farm Products	Charleston MSA, WV	Y	22260 FQ	30890 MW	38770 TQ	USBLS	5/07
Except Farm Products	Wisconsin	Y	33120 FQ	42250 MW	57130 TQ	USBLS	5/07
Except Farm Products	Milwaukee-Waukesha-West Allis MSA, WI	Y	34750 FQ	43590 MW	57310 TQ	USBLS	5/07
Except Farm Products	Racine MSA, WI	Y	32540 FQ	39260 MW	75620 TQ	USBLS	5/07
Except Farm Products	Wyoming	Y	23745 FQ	34124 MW	46530 TQ	WYBLS	9/08
Except Farm Products	Cheyenne MSA, WY	Y	24334 FQ	33805 MW	37256 TQ	WYBLS	9/08
Except Farm Products	Puerto Rico	Y	21620 FQ	27900 MW	38260 TQ	USBLS	5/07
Except Farm Products	San Juan-Caguas-Guaynabo MSA, PR	Y	21940 FQ	28350 MW	39470 TQ	USBLS	5/07
Except Farm Products	Virgin Islands	Y	31500 FQ	34930 MW	39570 TQ	USBLS	5/07
Except Farm Products	Guam	Y	20270 FQ	27780 MW	39640 TQ	USBLS	5/07
WIC Program Coordinator							
Municipal Government	Cincinnati, OH	Y	44033 LO		60634 HI	COHSS	10/08
Wide Area Network Engineer							
Public Schools	North Carolina	M	3870 LO		6949 HI	NCSS	2008-2009
Wildlife Area Coordinator							
State Government	Ohio	H	16.35 LO		19.88 HI	ODAS	2008
Wildlife Biology Program Administrator							
State Government	Ohio	H	25.40 LO		33.16 HI	ODAS	2008
Wildlife Communications Specialist							
State Government	Ohio	H	18.36 LO		23.87 HI	ODAS	2008
Wildlife Investigator							
State Government	Ohio	H	20.41 LO		25.73 HI	ODAS	2008

Occupation/Type/Industry	Location	Per	Low	Mid	High	Source	Date
Wildlife Research Technician							
State Government	Ohio	Y	34611 LO		39957 HI	AFT02	3/1/08
Wind Energy Research Specialist	Albany, NY	Y		100000 AW		TVC06	2008
Windows Home Server Expert	United States	Y		69935 AW		REDMAG	2008
Windows Vista Expert	United States	Y		75818 AW		REDMAG	2008
Wine-Spirits Marketing Specialist							
Liquor Commission	New Hampshire	Y		59368 AW		NHUL03	2008
Winemaker	United States	Y		94447 AW		WINEB	2007
Wire Harness Manufacturing Worker	United States	H		27.75 AW		AVJOB06	2009
Wooden Boat Carpenter	Rhode Island	H		28.00 AW		RIM01	2009
Woodworking Machine Setter, Operator, and Tender							
Except Sawing	Alabama	Y	17200 FQ	19980 MW	24790 TQ	USBLS	5/07
Except Sawing	Birmingham-Hoover MSA, AL	Y	17550 FQ	23620 MW	29170 TQ	USBLS	5/07
Except Sawing	Huntsville MSA, AL	Y	16710 FQ	18930 MW	24540 TQ	USBLS	5/07
Except Sawing	Arizona	Y	18230 FQ	22140 MW	25730 TQ	USBLS	5/07
Except Sawing	Phoenix-Mesa-Scottsdale MSA, AZ	Y	18460 FQ	22350 MW	26440 TQ	USBLS	5/07
Except Sawing	Tucson MSA, AZ	Y	16580 FQ	19820 MW	23910 TQ	USBLS	5/07
Except Sawing	Arkansas	Y	18290 FQ	22560 MW	27700 TQ	USBLS	5/07
Except Sawing	Little Rock-North Little Rock MSA, AR	Y	27020 FQ	33640 MW	37090 TQ	USBLS	5/07
Except Sawing	California	H	9.63 FQ	11.80 MW	14.70 TQ	CABLS	1/08-3/08
Except Sawing	Los Angeles-Long Beach-Glendale PMSA, CA	H	8.80 FQ	10.27 MW	12.14 TQ	CABLS	1/08-3/08
Except Sawing	Modesto MSA, CA	H	8.97 FQ	10.95 MW	13.36 TQ	CABLS	1/08-3/08
Except Sawing	Oakland-Fremont-Hayward MSA, CA	H	10.55 FQ	13.03 MW	15.39 TQ	CABLS	1/08-3/08
Except Sawing	Riverside-San Bernardino-Ontario MSA, CA	H	10.47 FQ	12.81 MW	15.18 TQ	CABLS	1/08-3/08
Except Sawing	Sacramento-Arden Arcade-Roseville MSA, CA	H	10.24 FQ	12.06 MW	14.99 TQ	CABLS	1/08-3/08
Except Sawing	San Diego-Carlsbad-San Marcos MSA, CA	H	11.95 FQ	14.05 MW	16.70 TQ	CABLS	1/08-3/08
Except Sawing	San Francisco-San Mateo-Redwood PMSA, CA	H	11.50 FQ	14.49 MW	20.39 TQ	CABLS	1/08-3/08
Except Sawing	San Jose-Sunnyvale-Santa Clara MSA, CA	H	13.47 FQ	14.82 MW	17.44 TQ	CABLS	1/08-3/08
Except Sawing	Santa Ana-Anaheim-Irvine PMSA, CA	Y	20820 FQ	24010 MW	28220 TQ	USBLS	5/07
Except Sawing	Stockton MSA, CA	H	8.78 FQ	10.58 MW	13.44 TQ	CABLS	1/08-3/08
Except Sawing	Colorado	Y	21820 FQ	26330 MW	31050 TQ	USBLS	5/07
Except Sawing	Boulder MSA, CO	Y	21750 FQ	25590 MW	29120 TQ	USBLS	5/07
Except Sawing	Denver-Aurora MSA, CO	Y	21710 FQ	26020 MW	30230 TQ	USBLS	5/07
Except Sawing	Connecticut	H	11.18 AE	14.46 MW		CTBLS	1/08-3/08
Except Sawing	Bridgeport-Stamford-Norwalk MSA, CT	Y	24450 FQ	27720 MW	31610 TQ	USBLS	5/07
Except Sawing	Hartford-West Hartford-East Hartford MSA, CT	Y	26080 FQ	33520 MW	39490 TQ	USBLS	5/07
Except Sawing	Delaware	Y*	25820 FQ	28390 MW	31320 TQ	USBLS	5/07
Except Sawing	Wilmington PMSA, DE-MD-NJ	Y	21570 FQ	24200 MW	28280 TQ	USBLS	5/07
Except Sawing	Washington-Arlington-Alexandria MSA, DC-VA-MD-WV	Y	19460 FQ	23220 MW	28860 TQ	USBLS	5/07
Except Sawing	Florida	Y	19000 FQ	22670 MW	27980 TQ	USBLS	5/07
Except Sawing	Cape Coral-Fort Myers MSA, FL	Y	23210 FQ	27820 MW	30970 TQ	USBLS	5/07
Except Sawing	Fort Lauderdale-Pompano Beach-Deerfield Beach PMSA, FL	Y	14830 FQ	19380 MW	22460 TQ	USBLS	5/07
Except Sawing	Jacksonville MSA, FL	Y	20080 FQ	23270 MW	29080 TQ	USBLS	5/07

Occupation/Type/Industry	Location	Per	Low	Mid	High	Source	Date
Woodworking Machine Setter, Operator, and Tender							
Except Sawing	Miami-Fort Lauderdale-Miami Beach MSA, FL	Y	17200 FQ	21030 MW	25330 TQ	USBLS	5/07
Except Sawing	Orlando-Kissimmee MSA, FL	Y	21550 FQ	26050 MW	31060 TQ	USBLS	5/07
Except Sawing	Tampa-St. Petersburg-Clearwater MSA, FL	Y	18230 FQ	21020 MW	25680 TQ	USBLS	5/07
Except Sawing	West Palm Beach-Boca Raton-Boynton Beach PMSA, FL	Y	21610 FQ	24370 MW	29270 TQ	USBLS	5/07
Except Sawing	Georgia	Y	18080 FQ	21680 MW	25990 TQ	USBLS	5/07
Except Sawing	Atlanta-Sandy Springs-Marietta MSA, GA	Y	18510 FQ	22380 MW	27170 TQ	USBLS	5/07
Except Sawing	Hawaii	Y	20430 FQ	27090 MW	34170 TQ	USBLS	5/07
Except Sawing	Honolulu MSA, HI	Y	16150 FQ	21040 MW	28130 TQ	USBLS	5/07
Except Sawing	Idaho	Y	20440 FQ	26080 MW	33650 TQ	USBLS	5/07
Except Sawing	Boise City-Nampa MSA, ID	Y	18260 FQ	23160 MW	30810 TQ	USBLS	5/07
Except Sawing	Illinois	Y	19810 FQ	26330 MW	34790 TQ	USBLS	5/07
Except Sawing	Chicago-Naperville-Joliet MSA, IL-IN-WI	Y	23410 FQ	29030 MW	36560 TQ	USBLS	5/07
Except Sawing	Indiana	Y	20430 FQ	24160 MW	28930 TQ	USBLS	5/07
Except Sawing	Gary PMSA, IN	Y	20880 FQ	27270 MW	30840 TQ	USBLS	5/07
Except Sawing	Indianapolis-Carmel MSA, IN	Y	20020 FQ	22150 MW	25590 TQ	USBLS	5/07
Except Sawing	Iowa	Y	18800 FQ	23380 MW	29610 TQ	USBLS	5/07
Except Sawing	Des Moines-West Des Moines MSA, IA	Y	19780 FQ	27040 MW	31740 TQ	USBLS	5/07
Except Sawing	Waterloo-Cedar Falls MSA, IA	Y	20730 FQ	23240 MW	28710 TQ	USBLS	5/07
Except Sawing	Kansas	Y	20580 FQ	24460 MW	28380 TQ	USBLS	5/07
Except Sawing	Wichita MSA, KS	Y	21270 FQ	25000 MW	28450 TQ	USBLS	5/07
Except Sawing	Kentucky	Y	18468 FQ	23247 MW	29199 TQ	KYBLS	2008
Except Sawing	Louisville-Jefferson County MSA, KY-IN	Y	19840 FQ	25300 MW	31960 TQ	USBLS	5/07
Except Sawing	Louisiana	H	9.94 FQ	12.32 MW	15.89 TQ	LABLS	1/08-3/08
Except Sawing	Maine	Y	19410 FQ	23040 MW	28300 TQ	USBLS	5/07
Except Sawing	Bangor MSA, ME	Y	16420 FQ	17780 MW	20350 TQ	USBLS	5/07
Except Sawing	Portland-South Portland-Biddeford MSA, ME	Y	18360 FQ	22790 MW	31130 TQ	USBLS	5/07
Except Sawing	Maryland	Y		25475 MW		MDBLS	3/08
Except Sawing	Baltimore-Towson MSA, MD	Y	21030 FQ	25190 MW	29650 TQ	USBLS	5/07
Except Sawing	Bethesda-Gaithersburg-Frederick PMSA, MD	Y	17280 FQ	21340 MW	28400 TQ	USBLS	5/07
Except Sawing	Massachusetts	Y	23770 FQ	31120 MW	36510 TQ	USBLS	5/07
Except Sawing	Boston-Cambridge-Quincy NECTA, MA	Y	22490 FQ	29330 MW	37890 TQ	USBLS	5/07
Except Sawing	Worcester MSA, MA-CT	Y	23490 FQ	34200 MW	38530 TQ	USBLS	5/07
Except Sawing	Michigan	Y	22520 FQ	27860 MW	34390 TQ	USBLS	5/07
Except Sawing	Detroit-Warren-Livonia MSA, MI	Y	26270 FQ	50660 MW	55440 TQ	USBLS	5/07
Except Sawing	Warren-Troy-Farmington Hills PMSA, MI	Y	38000 FQ	51570 MW	55900 TQ	USBLS	5/07
Except Sawing	Minnesota	Y	25149 FQ	31131 MW	40969 TQ	MNBLS	10/08-12/08
Except Sawing	Duluth-Superior MSA, MN-WI	Y	19551 FQ	21687 MW	24154 TQ	MNBLS	10/08-12/08
Except Sawing	Minneapolis-Saint Paul MSA, MN-WI	Y	25916 FQ	32935 MW	42472 TQ	MNBLS	10/08-12/08
Except Sawing	Rochester MSA, MN	Y	24982 FQ	27985 MW	30698 TQ	MNBLS	10/08-12/08
Except Sawing	Mississippi	Y	19190 FQ	22830 MW	27760 TQ	USBLS	5/07
Except Sawing	Jackson MSA, MS	Y	17210 FQ	21010 MW	24880 TQ	USBLS	5/07
Except Sawing	Missouri	Y	18230 FQ	21820 MW	27130 TQ	USBLS	5/07
Except Sawing	Kansas City MSA, MO-KS	Y	22640 FQ	26180 MW	28970 TQ	USBLS	5/07
Except Sawing	St. Louis MSA, MO-IL	Y	16760 FQ	20420 MW	27210 TQ	USBLS	5/07
Except Sawing	Montana	Y	20760 FQ	25410 MW	33170 TQ	USBLS	5/07
Except Sawing	Nebraska	Y	20940 FQ	24450 MW	30800 TQ	USBLS	5/07
Except Sawing	Omaha-Council Bluffs MSA, NE-IA	Y	22640 FQ	25380 MW	30920 TQ	USBLS	5/07
Except Sawing	Nevada	H	8.84 FQ	10.52 MW	13.52 TQ	NVBLS	5/08
Except Sawing	Las Vegas-Paradise MSA, NV	H	8.80 FQ	10.14 MW	13.28 TQ	NVBLS	5/08
Except Sawing	New Hampshire	H	9.79 AE	13.06 MW	15.14 AEX	NHBLS	6/08
Except Sawing	Nashua NECTA, NH-MA	Y	20780 FQ	22990 MW	25790 TQ	USBLS	5/07
Except Sawing	New Jersey	Y	22100 FQ	27650 MW	43850 TQ	USBLS	5/07
Except Sawing	Camden PMSA, NJ	Y	18670 FQ	29870 MW	36030 TQ	USBLS	5/07
Except Sawing	Edison PMSA, NJ	Y	22970 FQ	40380 MW	52960 TQ	USBLS	5/07
Except Sawing	Newark-Union PMSA, NJ-PA	Y	18090 FQ	24060 MW	29330 TQ	USBLS	5/07
Except Sawing	New Mexico	Y	16280 FQ	20660 MW	29410 TQ	USBLS	5/07

AE	Average entry wage	AW	Average wage paid	FQ	First quartile wage	LO	Lowest wage paid	MTC	Median total compensation	TCC	Total cash compensation
AER	Average entry range	AWR	Average wage range	H	Hourly	LR	Low end range	MW	Median wage paid	TQ	Third quartile wage
AEX	Average experienced wage	AXR	Average experienced range	HI	Highest wage paid	M	Monthly	MWR	Median wage range	W	Weekly
ATC	Average total compensation	D	Daily	HR	High end range	MCC	Median cash compensation	S	See annotated source	Y	Yearly

1692

Occupation/Type/Industry	Location	Per	Low	Mid	High	Source	Date
Woodworking Machine Setter, Operator, and Tender							
Except Sawing	Albuquerque MSA, NM	Y	14170 FQ	18040 MW	29650 TQ	USBLS	5/07
Except Sawing	New York	Y	19590 FQ	25530 MW	30000 TQ	USBLS	5/07
Except Sawing	Albany-Schenectady-Troy MSA, NY	Y	23830 FQ	30250 MW	35290 TQ	USBLS	5/07
Except Sawing	Buffalo-Niagara Falls MSA, NY	Y	27220 FQ	29270 MW	31300 TQ	USBLS	5/07
Except Sawing	Nassau-Suffolk PMSA, NY	Y	17050 FQ	20100 MW	27990 TQ	USBLS	5/07
Except Sawing	New York-Northern New Jersey-Long Island MSA, NY-NJ-PA	Y	19690 FQ	26260 MW	36340 TQ	USBLS	5/07
Except Sawing	Syracuse MSA, NY	Y	17510 FQ	19640 MW	24920 TQ	USBLS	5/07
Except Sawing	North Carolina	Y	20510 FQ	24630 MW	29450 TQ	USBLS	5/07
Except Sawing	Charlotte-Gastonia-Concord MSA, NC-SC	Y	18670 FQ	22250 MW	27720 TQ	USBLS	5/07
Except Sawing	North Dakota	Y	21060 FQ	24310 MW	28940 TQ	USBLS	5/07
Except Sawing	Ohio	Y	21200 FQ	25220 MW	30710 TQ	USBLS	5/07
Except Sawing	Cincinnati-Middletown MSA, OH-KY-IN	Y	21470 FQ	26370 MW	31670 TQ	USBLS	5/07
Except Sawing	Cleveland-Elyria-Mentor MSA, OH	Y	22990 FQ	27530 MW	34120 TQ	USBLS	5/07
Except Sawing	Columbus MSA, OH	Y	22410 FQ	24720 MW	29990 TQ	USBLS	5/07
Except Sawing	Dayton MSA, OH	Y	22570 FQ	25220 MW	35200 TQ	USBLS	5/07
Except Sawing	Oklahoma	Y	18480 FQ	23210 MW	26940 TQ	USBLS	5/07
Except Sawing	Oklahoma City MSA, OK	Y	18850 FQ	21160 MW	23400 TQ	USBLS	5/07
Except Sawing	Tulsa MSA, OK	Y	16010 FQ	18700 MW	26230 TQ	USBLS	5/07
Except Sawing	Oregon	H	11.79 FQ	14.58 MW	17.27 TQ	ORBLS	5/08
Except Sawing	Portland-Vancouver-Beaverton MSA, OR-WA	Y	21990 FQ	27760 MW	34710 TQ	USBLS	5/07
Except Sawing	Pennsylvania	Y	21680 FQ	26480 MW	31550 TQ	USBLS	5/07
Except Sawing	Allentown-Bethlehem-Easton MSA, PA-NJ	Y	20030 FQ	23410 MW	27950 TQ	USBLS	5/07
Except Sawing	Erie MSA, PA	Y	18900 FQ	22190 MW	27340 TQ	USBLS	5/07
Except Sawing	Philadelphia-Camden-Wilmington MSA, PA-NJ-DE-MD	Y	24220 FQ	32860 MW	44140 TQ	USBLS	5/07
Except Sawing	Pittsburgh MSA, PA	Y	19360 FQ	22170 MW	24890 TQ	USBLS	5/07
Except Sawing	Rhode Island	Y	20310 FQ	28010 MW	36820 TQ	USBLS	5/07
Except Sawing	Providence-Fall River-Warwick MSA, RI-MA	Y	21050 FQ	28760 MW	36600 TQ	USBLS	5/07
Except Sawing	South Carolina	Y	20000 FQ	23720 MW	30580 TQ	USBLS	5/07
Except Sawing	Charleston-North Charleston MSA, SC	Y	19940 FQ	22200 MW	25300 TQ	USBLS	5/07
Except Sawing	South Dakota	Y	21408 FQ	24532 MW	28935 TQ	SDBLS	7/08-9/08
Except Sawing	Sioux Falls MSA, SD	Y	22134 FQ	24442 MW	28727 TQ	SDBLS	7/08-9/08
Except Sawing	Tennessee	Y	18590 FQ	22110 MW	27100 TQ	USBLS	5/07
Except Sawing	Memphis MSA, TN-MS-AR	Y	18350 FQ	23690 MW	30490 TQ	USBLS	5/07
Except Sawing	Nashville-Davidson-Murfreesboro MSA, TN	Y	20170 FQ	23750 MW	27430 TQ	USBLS	5/07
Except Sawing	Texas	Y	16840 FQ	20000 MW	24810 TQ	USBLS	5/07
Except Sawing	Austin-Round Rock MSA, TX	Y	17280 FQ	19520 MW	23170 TQ	USBLS	5/07
Except Sawing	Dallas-Fort Worth-Arlington MSA, TX	Y	16750 FQ	19890 MW	24570 TQ	USBLS	5/07
Except Sawing	El Paso MSA, TX	Y	16180 FQ	19210 MW	22950 TQ	USBLS	5/07
Except Sawing	Houston-Sugar Land-Baytown MSA, TX	Y	16270 FQ	20370 MW	25330 TQ	USBLS	5/07
Except Sawing	San Antonio MSA, TX	Y	18150 FQ	21250 MW	25250 TQ	USBLS	5/07
Except Sawing	Utah	Y	19890 FQ	24090 MW	29050 TQ	USBLS	5/07
Except Sawing	Ogden-Clearfield MSA, UT	Y	20370 FQ	22440 MW	24800 TQ	USBLS	5/07
Except Sawing	Salt Lake City MSA, UT	Y	22440 FQ	26190 MW	30300 TQ	USBLS	5/07
Except Sawing	Vermont	Y	22290 FQ	26630 MW	29780 TQ	USBLS	5/07
Except Sawing	Virginia	Y	19690 FQ	23590 MW	28770 TQ	USBLS	5/07
Except Sawing	Richmond MSA, VA	Y	20710 FQ	24620 MW	28620 TQ	USBLS	5/07
Except Sawing	Roanoke MSA, VA	Y	20850 FQ	23490 MW	26910 TQ	USBLS	5/07
Except Sawing	Virginia Beach-Norfolk-Newport News MSA, VA-NC	Y	20240 FQ	25300 MW	34580 TQ	USBLS	5/07
Except Sawing	Washington	H	12.95 FQ	15.71 MW	18.51 TQ	WABLS	3/08
Except Sawing	Seattle-Tacoma-Bellevue MSA, WA	Y	24720 FQ	28830 MW	35020 TQ	USBLS	5/07
Except Sawing	West Virginia	Y	17272 FQ	19402 MW	25355 TQ	WVBLS	7/08-9/08
Except Sawing	Wisconsin	Y	20830 FQ	25050 MW	30910 TQ	USBLS	5/07

AE	Average entry wage	AW	Average wage paid	FQ	First quartile wage	LO	Lowest wage paid	MTC	Median total compensation	TCC	Total cash compensation
AER	Average entry range	AWR	Average wage range	H	Hourly	LR	Low end range	MW	Median wage paid	TQ	Third quartile wage
AEX	Average experienced wage	AXR	Average experienced range	HI	Highest wage paid	M	Monthly	MWR	Median wage range	W	Weekly
ATC	Average total compensation	D	Daily	HR	High end range	MCC	Median cash compensation	S	See annotated source	Y	Yearly

Occupation/Type/Industry	Location	Per	Low	Mid	High	Source	Date
Woodworking Machine Setter, Operator, and Tender							
Except Sawing	Green Bay MSA, WI	Y	24300 FQ	30350 MW	34210 TQ	USBLS	5/07
Except Sawing	Milwaukee-Waukesha-West Allis MSA, WI	Y	18470 FQ	21460 MW	25590 TQ	USBLS	5/07
Except Sawing	Wyoming	Y	20923 FQ	23040 MW	26556 TQ	WYBLS	9/08
Except Sawing	Puerto Rico	Y	12460 FQ	13860 MW	15500 TQ	USBLS	5/07
Except Sawing	San Juan-Caguas-Guaynabo MSA, PR	Y	12530 FQ	14040 MW	15760 TQ	USBLS	5/07
Word Processor and Typist	Alabama	Y	21260 FQ	26470 MW	33230 TQ	USBLS	5/07
	Birmingham-Hoover MSA, AL	Y	23670 FQ	28070 MW	33670 TQ	USBLS	5/07
	Alaska	Y	27690 FQ	33980 MW	38800 TQ	USBLS	5/07
	Anchorage MSA, AK	Y	26960 FQ	34000 MW	38440 TQ	USBLS	5/07
	Arizona	Y	23620 FQ	28540 MW	34950 TQ	USBLS	5/07
	Phoenix-Mesa-Scottsdale MSA, AZ	Y	23890 FQ	28990 MW	35540 TQ	USBLS	5/07
	Tucson MSA, AZ	Y	22420 FQ	25670 MW	31890 TQ	USBLS	5/07
	Arkansas	Y	20630 FQ	23170 MW	29200 TQ	USBLS	5/07
	Little Rock-North Little Rock MSA, AR	Y	21700 FQ	25220 MW	31530 TQ	USBLS	5/07
	California	H	14.25 FQ	16.83 MW	19.54 TQ	CABLS	1/08-3/08
	Los Angeles-Long Beach-Glendale PMSA, CA	H	15.35 FQ	17.61 MW	19.52 TQ	CABLS	1/08-3/08
	Modesto MSA, CA	H	13.48 FQ	15.33 MW	17.55 TQ	CABLS	1/08-3/08
	Oakland-Fremont-Hayward MSA, CA	H	14.40 FQ	16.96 MW	22.58 TQ	CABLS	1/08-3/08
	Riverside-San Bernardino-Ontario MSA, CA	H	13.85 FQ	15.54 MW	17.75 TQ	CABLS	1/08-3/08
	Sacramento-Arden Arcade-Roseville MSA, CA	H	13.25 FQ	15.02 MW	17.50 TQ	CABLS	1/08-3/08
	San Diego-Carlsbad-San Marcos MSA, CA	H	14.07 FQ	17.57 MW	21.10 TQ	CABLS	1/08-3/08
	San Francisco-San Mateo-Redwood PMSA, CA	H	15.13 FQ	18.75 MW	24.25 TQ	CABLS	1/08-3/08
	San Jose-Sunnyvale-Santa Clara MSA, CA	H	16.21 FQ	20.26 MW	28.85 TQ	CABLS	1/08-3/08
	Santa Ana-Anaheim-Irvine PMSA, CA	Y	29370 FQ	36020 MW	42880 TQ	USBLS	5/07
	Colorado	Y	28680 FQ	35190 MW	42110 TQ	USBLS	5/07
	Colorado Springs MSA, CO	Y	30340 FQ	35380 MW	40590 TQ	USBLS	5/07
	Denver-Aurora MSA, CO	Y	29910 FQ	37520 MW	43580 TQ	USBLS	5/07
	Fort Collins-Loveland MSA, CO	Y	25910 FQ	28780 MW	31510 TQ	USBLS	5/07
	Connecticut	H	13.21 AE	16.01 MW		CTBLS	1/08-3/08
	Bridgeport-Stamford-Norwalk MSA, CT	Y	31700 FQ	38170 MW	45560 TQ	USBLS	5/07
	Hartford-West Hartford-East Hartford MSA, CT	Y	27830 FQ	31490 MW	36790 TQ	USBLS	5/07
	Delaware	Y	27870 FQ	33010 MW	39060 TQ	USBLS	5/07
	Dover MSA, DE	Y	25050 FQ	31440 MW	36030 TQ	USBLS	5/07
	Wilmington PMSA, DE-MD-NJ	Y	28150 FQ	33310 MW	39810 TQ	USBLS	5/07
	District of Columbia	Y	27030 FQ	30830 MW	37620 TQ	USBLS	5/07
	Washington-Arlington-Alexandria MSA, DC-VA-MD-WV	Y	26070 FQ	30150 MW	37010 TQ	USBLS	5/07
	Florida	Y	22130 FQ	25570 MW	31630 TQ	USBLS	5/07
	Fort Lauderdale-Pompano Beach-Deerfield Beach PMSA, FL	Y	23930 FQ	28610 MW	32190 TQ	USBLS	5/07
	Jacksonville MSA, FL	Y	22930 FQ	26830 MW	32790 TQ	USBLS	5/07
	Miami-Fort Lauderdale-Miami Beach MSA, FL	Y	23230 FQ	28940 MW	37030 TQ	USBLS	5/07
	Orlando-Kissimmee MSA, FL	Y	22540 FQ	27580 MW	33030 TQ	USBLS	5/07
	Sarasota-Bradenton-Venice MSA, FL	Y	23310 FQ	27000 MW	31160 TQ	USBLS	5/07
	Tampa-St. Petersburg-Clearwater MSA, FL	Y	22300 FQ	25430 MW	31680 TQ	USBLS	5/07
	West Palm Beach-Boca Raton-Boynton Beach PMSA, FL	Y	23160 FQ	28010 MW	36630 TQ	USBLS	5/07
	Georgia	Y	15570 FQ	18800 MW	31530 TQ	USBLS	5/07

AE	Average entry wage	AW	Average wage paid	FQ	First quartile wage	LO
AER	Average entry range	AWR	Average wage range	H	Hourly	LR
AEX	Average experienced wage	AXR	Average experienced range	HI	Highest wage paid	M
ATC	Average total compensation	D	Daily	HR	High end range	MCC

AE Average entry wage   AW Average wage paid   FQ First quartile wage   LO Lowest wage paid   MTC Median total compensation   TCC Total cash compensation
AER Average entry range   AWR Average wage range   H Hourly   LR Low end range   MW Median wage paid   TQ Third quartile wage
AEX Average experienced wage   AXR Average experienced range   HI Highest wage paid   M Monthly   MWR Median wage range   W Weekly
ATC Average total compensation   D Daily   HR High end range   MCC Median cash compensation   S See annotated source   Y Yearly

Occupation/Type/Industry	Location	Per	Low	Mid	High	Source	Date
Word Processor and Typist	Atlanta-Sandy Springs-Marietta MSA, GA	Y	16770 FQ	18660 MW	29720 TQ	USBLS	5/07
	Augusta-Richmond County MSA, GA-SC	Y	20690 FQ	25270 MW	29670 TQ	USBLS	5/07
	Hawaii	Y	25230 FQ	28430 MW	31690 TQ	USBLS	5/07
	Honolulu MSA, HI	Y	25160 FQ	28500 MW	32030 TQ	USBLS	5/07
	Idaho	Y	22060 FQ	27760 MW	35070 TQ	USBLS	5/07
	Boise City-Nampa MSA, ID	Y	26260 FQ	33660 MW	43070 TQ	USBLS	5/07
	Illinois	Y	27030 FQ	34180 MW	46250 TQ	USBLS	5/07
	Chicago-Naperville-Joliet MSA, IL-IN-WI	Y	28560 FQ	37460 MW	48920 TQ	USBLS	5/07
	Indiana	Y	21980 FQ	26910 MW	33240 TQ	USBLS	5/07
	Gary PMSA, IN	Y	20760 FQ	23850 MW	28720 TQ	USBLS	5/07
	Indianapolis-Carmel MSA, IN	Y	23390 FQ	28030 MW	33090 TQ	USBLS	5/07
	Iowa	Y	21970 FQ	29020 MW	35400 TQ	USBLS	5/07
	Des Moines-West Des Moines MSA, IA	Y	25450 FQ	31520 MW	36620 TQ	USBLS	5/07
	Kansas	Y	21030 FQ	26330 MW	33780 TQ	USBLS	5/07
	Wichita MSA, KS	Y	17520 FQ	19740 MW	33650 TQ	USBLS	5/07
	Kentucky	Y	23127 FQ	27274 MW	32573 TQ	KYBLS	2008
	Louisville-Jefferson County MSA, KY-IN	Y	24350 FQ	27690 MW	31880 TQ	USBLS	5/07
	Louisiana	H	9.86 FQ	11.26 MW	15.50 TQ	LABLS	1/08-3/08
	Baton Rouge MSA, LA	Y	20880 FQ	24750 MW	30790 TQ	USBLS	5/07
	New Orleans-Metairie-Kenner MSA, LA	Y	25090 FQ	34910 MW	44570 TQ	USBLS	5/07
	Maine	Y	22670 FQ	25320 MW	29070 TQ	USBLS	5/07
	Portland-South Portland-Biddeford MSA, ME	Y	21860 FQ	24300 MW	28050 TQ	USBLS	5/07
	Maryland	Y		31800 MW		MDBLS	3/08
	Baltimore-Towson MSA, MD	Y	27330 FQ	33320 MW	37810 TQ	USBLS	5/07
	Bethesda-Gaithersburg-Frederick PMSA, MD	Y	24520 FQ	29700 MW	39020 TQ	USBLS	5/07
	Massachusetts	Y	28280 FQ	33500 MW	40010 TQ	USBLS	5/07
	Boston-Cambridge-Quincy NECTA, MA	Y	28450 FQ	33440 MW	39980 TQ	USBLS	5/07
	Worcester MSA, MA-CT	Y	25850 FQ	30820 MW	36330 TQ	USBLS	5/07
	Michigan	Y	28340 FQ	34660 MW	38910 TQ	USBLS	5/07
	Ann Arbor MSA, MI	Y	27860 FQ	34380 MW	40370 TQ	USBLS	5/07
	Detroit-Warren-Livonia MSA, MI	Y	28040 FQ	34820 MW	39680 TQ	USBLS	5/07
	Grand Rapids-Wyoming MSA, MI	Y	29740 FQ	35210 MW	38560 TQ	USBLS	5/07
	Lansing-East Lansing MSA, MI	Y	33290 FQ	36520 MW	39870 TQ	USBLS	5/07
	Warren-Troy-Farmington Hills PMSA, MI	Y	28950 FQ	35640 MW	40790 TQ	USBLS	5/07
	Minnesota	Y	24875 FQ	32889 MW	41715 TQ	MNBLS	10/08-12/08
	Duluth-Superior MSA, MN-WI	Y	27716 FQ	34710 MW	39133 TQ	MNBLS	10/08-12/08
	Minneapolis-Saint Paul MSA, MN-WI	Y	29121 FQ	37239 MW	44879 TQ	MNBLS	10/08-12/08
	Rochester MSA, MN	Y	28915 FQ	35977 MW	44680 TQ	MNBLS	10/08-12/08
	Mississippi	Y	19330 FQ	22830 MW	28660 TQ	USBLS	5/07
	Gulfport-Biloxi MSA, MS	Y	22160 FQ	25020 MW	30940 TQ	USBLS	5/07
	Jackson MSA, MS	Y	19310 FQ	22200 MW	26870 TQ	USBLS	5/07
	Missouri	Y	21950 FQ	23940 MW	27380 TQ	USBLS	5/07
	Kansas City MSA, MO-KS	Y	22890 FQ	26270 MW	34010 TQ	USBLS	5/07
	St. Louis MSA, MO-IL	Y	22600 FQ	25270 MW	30810 TQ	USBLS	5/07
	Montana	Y	22840 FQ	26980 MW	31030 TQ	USBLS	5/07
	Billings MSA, MT	Y	23830 FQ	28100 MW	31460 TQ	USBLS	5/07
	Nebraska	Y	23170 FQ	27520 MW	31570 TQ	USBLS	5/07
	Lincoln MSA, NE	Y	22070 FQ	26900 MW	31690 TQ	USBLS	5/07
	Omaha-Council Bluffs MSA, NE-IA	Y	24950 FQ	28830 MW	32470 TQ	USBLS	5/07
	Nevada	H	12.12 MW	13.65 MW	15.23 TQ	NVBLS	5/08
	Las Vegas-Paradise MSA, NV	H	11.96 FQ	13.53 MW	14.96 TQ	NVBLS	5/08
	New Hampshire	H	10.27 AE	13.27 MW	14.62 AEX	NHBLS	6/08
	New Jersey	Y	27220 FQ	32410 MW	39280 TQ	USBLS	5/07
	Camden PMSA, NJ	Y	26690 FQ	31810 MW	37510 TQ	USBLS	5/07
	Edison PMSA, NJ	Y	26560 FQ	31470 MW	38760 TQ	USBLS	5/07
	Newark-Union PMSA, NJ-PA	Y	28350 FQ	34490 MW	41370 TQ	USBLS	5/07
	New Mexico	Y	22400 FQ	27830 MW	33360 TQ	USBLS	5/07
	Albuquerque MSA, NM	Y	22440 FQ	27580 MW	32060 TQ	USBLS	5/07

AE Average entry wage	**AW** Average wage paid	**FQ** First quartile wage	**LO** Lowest wage paid	**MTC** Median total compensation **TCC** Total cash compensation
AER Average entry range	**AWR** Average wage range	**H** Hourly	**LR** Low end range	**MW** Median wage paid **TQ** Third quartile wage
AEX Average experienced wage	**AXR** Average experienced range	**HI** Highest wage paid	**M** Monthly	**MWR** Median wage range **W** Weekly
ATC Average total compensation	**D** Daily	**HR** High end range	**MCC** Median cash compensation	**S** See annotated source **Y** Yearly

Word Processor and Typist

Occupation/Type/Industry	Location	Per	Low	Mid	High	Source	Date
Word Processor and Typist	New York	Y	25450 FQ	30450 MW	37190 TQ	USBLS	5/07
	Albany-Schenectady-Troy MSA, NY	Y	26120 FQ	29960 MW	34920 TQ	USBLS	5/07
	Buffalo-Niagara Falls MSA, NY	Y	25780 FQ	29500 MW	34110 TQ	USBLS	5/07
	Glens Falls MSA, NY	Y	23350 FQ	27160 MW	30380 TQ	USBLS	5/07
	Nassau-Suffolk PMSA, NY	Y	27020 FQ	32010 MW	39000 TQ	USBLS	5/07
	New York-Northern New Jersey-Long Island MSA, NY-NJ-PA	Y	26460 FQ	32540 MW	40630 TQ	USBLS	5/07
	North Carolina	Y	23290 FQ	27760 MW	33870 TQ	USBLS	5/07
	Charlotte-Gastonia-Concord MSA, NC-SC	Y	28120 FQ	36340 MW	44360 TQ	USBLS	5/07
	Raleigh-Cary MSA, NC	Y	24570 FQ	27970 MW	32550 TQ	USBLS	5/07
	North Dakota	Y	21450 FQ	24850 MW	30490 TQ	USBLS	5/07
	Fargo MSA, ND-MN	Y	19220 FQ	21250 MW	23270 TQ	USBLS	5/07
	Ohio	Y	25290 FQ	31920 MW	36930 TQ	USBLS	5/07
	Cincinnati-Middletown MSA, OH-KY-IN	Y	26800 FQ	32740 MW	36710 TQ	USBLS	5/07
	Cleveland-Elyria-Mentor MSA, OH	Y	25340 FQ	33130 MW	37630 TQ	USBLS	5/07
	Columbus MSA, OH	Y	27700 FQ	34510 MW	39150 TQ	USBLS	5/07
	Dayton MSA, OH	Y	27100 FQ	31850 MW	37140 TQ	USBLS	5/07
	Oklahoma	Y	22690 FQ	27670 MW	33370 TQ	USBLS	5/07
	Lawton MSA, OK	Y	19790 FQ	28530 MW	34390 TQ	USBLS	5/07
	Oklahoma City MSA, OK	Y	24960 FQ	29340 MW	36280 TQ	USBLS	5/07
	Tulsa MSA, OK	Y	22510 FQ	27040 MW	31890 TQ	USBLS	5/07
	Oregon	H	12.16 FQ	15.57 MW	19.00 TQ	ORBLS	5/08
	Portland-Vancouver-Beaverton MSA, OR-WA	Y	26230 FQ	33030 MW	39440 TQ	USBLS	5/07
	Pennsylvania	Y	25270 FQ	29120 MW	34030 TQ	USBLS	5/07
	Allentown-Bethlehem-Easton MSA, PA-NJ	Y	26050 FQ	29470 MW	34570 TQ	USBLS	5/07
	Philadelphia-Camden-Wilmington MSA, PA-NJ-DE-MD	Y	27230 FQ	31220 MW	37800 TQ	USBLS	5/07
	Pittsburgh MSA, PA	Y	20830 FQ	25970 MW	31510 TQ	USBLS	5/07
	Rhode Island	Y	31370 FQ	35950 MW	40490 TQ	USBLS	5/07
	Providence-Fall River-Warwick MSA, RI-MA	Y	31280 FQ	35890 MW	40450 TQ	USBLS	5/07
	South Carolina	Y	21710 FQ	26120 MW	32710 TQ	USBLS	5/07
	Charleston-North Charleston MSA, SC	Y	26730 FQ	33180 MW	37790 TQ	USBLS	5/07
	Columbia MSA, SC	Y	23400 FQ	28150 MW	33030 TQ	USBLS	5/07
	South Dakota	Y	18319 FQ	19922 MW	22748 TQ	SDBLS	7/08-9/08
	Tennessee	Y	21460 FQ	26010 MW	33830 TQ	USBLS	5/07
	Memphis MSA, TN-MS-AR	Y	24520 FQ	29940 MW	36390 TQ	USBLS	5/07
	Texas	Y	25530 FQ	30760 MW	37980 TQ	USBLS	5/07
	Austin-Round Rock MSA, TX	Y	24960 FQ	31460 MW	40180 TQ	USBLS	5/07
	Dallas-Fort Worth-Arlington MSA, TX	Y	28190 FQ	33500 MW	42450 TQ	USBLS	5/07
	El Paso MSA, TX	Y	19680 FQ	25660 MW	32310 TQ	USBLS	5/07
	Houston-Sugar Land-Baytown MSA, TX	Y	26720 FQ	34530 MW	43430 TQ	USBLS	5/07
	San Antonio MSA, TX	Y	27680 FQ	30770 MW	34380 TQ	USBLS	5/07
	Salt Lake City MSA, UT	Y	27950 FQ	34750 MW	44550 TQ	USBLS	5/07
	Vermont	Y	23220 FQ	28200 MW	35190 TQ	USBLS	5/07
	Virginia	Y	25340 FQ	30010 MW	36770 TQ	USBLS	5/07
	Lynchburg MSA, VA	Y	21280 FQ	24470 MW	28430 TQ	USBLS	5/07
	Richmond MSA, VA	Y	27600 FQ	33550 MW	40300 TQ	USBLS	5/07
	Virginia Beach-Norfolk-Newport News MSA, VA-NC	Y	23640 FQ	30310 MW	35910 TQ	USBLS	5/07
	Washington	H	13.14 FQ	15.54 MW	19.35 TQ	WABLS	3/08
	Seattle-Tacoma-Bellevue MSA, WA	Y	28000 FQ	33880 MW	43980 TQ	USBLS	5/07
	West Virginia	Y	25494 FQ	31475 MW	37227 TQ	WVBLS	7/08-9/08
	Parkersburg-Marietta-Vienna MSA, WV-OH	Y	29700 FQ	33770 MW	37070 TQ	USBLS	5/07
	Wisconsin	Y	26600 FQ	30420 MW	35030 TQ	USBLS	5/07
	Milwaukee-Waukesha-West Allis MSA, WI	Y	26620 FQ	30460 MW	35260 TQ	USBLS	5/07
	Wyoming	Y	24258 FQ	29178 MW	34340 TQ	WYBLS	9/08

AE Average entry wage	**AW** Average wage paid	**FQ** First quartile wage	**LO** Lowest wage paid	**MTC** Median total compensation	**TCC** Total cash compensation
AER Average entry range	**AWR** Average wage range	**H** Hourly	**LR** Low end range	**MW** Median wage paid	**TQ** Third quartile wage
AEX Average experienced wage	**AXR** Average experienced range	**HI** Highest wage paid	**M** Monthly	**MWR** Median wage range	**W** Weekly
ATC Average total compensation	**D** Daily	**HR** High end range	**MCC** Median cash compensation	**S** See annotated source	**Y** Yearly

Occupation/Type/Industry	Location	Per	Low	Mid	High	Source	Date
Word Processor and Typist	Cheyenne MSA, WY	Y	27389 FQ	33251 MW	37450 TQ	WYBLS	9/08
	Puerto Rico	Y	16980 FQ	19150 MW	22510 TQ	USBLS	5/07
	San Juan-Caguas-Guaynabo MSA, PR	Y	17190 FQ	19300 MW	22600 TQ	USBLS	5/07
	Virgin Islands	Y	17110 FQ	20940 MW	24780 TQ	USBLS	5/07
Work Adjustment Specialist							
State Government	Ohio	H	16.51 LO		19.78 HI	ODAS	2008
Workforce Coordinator							
State Government	Nebraska	Y	31179 LO		44054 HI	AFT02	3/1/08
Working Foreman							
Highway Department	Montague, MA	H			22.71 HI	FRCOG	2009
Writer and Author	Alabama	Y	27600 FQ	37200 MW	58950 TQ	USBLS	5/07
	Birmingham-Hoover MSA, AL	Y	30850 FQ	36830 MW	50730 TQ	USBLS	5/07
	Mobile MSA, AL	Y	29890 FQ	35980 MW	47450 TQ	USBLS	5/07
	Arizona	Y	26470 FQ	35020 MW	47020 TQ	USBLS	5/07
	Phoenix-Mesa-Scottsdale MSA, AZ	Y	27320 FQ	34930 MW	45960 TQ	USBLS	5/07
	Tucson MSA, AZ	Y	15030 FQ	29820 MW	55000 TQ	USBLS	5/07
	Arkansas	Y	27420 FQ	40550 MW	48970 TQ	USBLS	5/07
	Little Rock-North Little Rock MSA, AR	Y	24290 FQ	36380 MW	48410 TQ	USBLS	5/07
	California	H	22.94 FQ	32.99 MW	57.07 TQ	CABLS	1/08-3/08
	Los Angeles-Long Beach-Glendale PMSA, CA	H	25.21 FQ	37.47 MW		CABLS	1/08-3/08
	Oakland-Fremont-Hayward MSA, CA	H	22.71 FQ	31.58 MW	51.91 TQ	CABLS	1/08-3/08
	Riverside-San Bernardino-Ontario MSA, CA	H	15.71 FQ	21.65 MW	31.80 TQ	CABLS	1/08-3/08
	Sacramento-Arden Arcade-Roseville MSA, CA	H	18.64 FQ	25.99 MW	31.24 TQ	CABLS	1/08-3/08
	San Diego-Carlsbad-San Marcos MSA, CA	H	17.40 FQ	27.92 MW	59.04 TQ	CABLS	1/08-3/08
	San Francisco-San Mateo-Redwood PMSA, CA	H	23.99 FQ	31.07 MW	44.28 TQ	CABLS	1/08-3/08
	San Jose-Sunnyvale-Santa Clara MSA, CA	H	28.11 FQ	38.02 MW	46.73 TQ	CABLS	1/08-3/08
	Santa Ana-Anaheim-Irvine PMSA, CA	Y	44550 FQ	60050 MW	90130 TQ	USBLS	5/07
	Santa Rosa-Petaluma MSA, CA	H	13.32 FQ	14.65 MW	15.94 TQ	CABLS	1/08-3/08
	Colorado	Y	37350 FQ	54310 MW	69520 TQ	USBLS	5/07
	Denver-Aurora MSA, CO	Y	38440 FQ	55460 MW	71970 TQ	USBLS	5/07
	Connecticut	H	16.86 AE	27.00 MW		CTBLS	1/08-3/08
	Bridgeport-Stamford-Norwalk MSA, CT	Y	36120 FQ	53600 MW	64070 TQ	USBLS	5/07
	Hartford-West Hartford-East Hartford MSA, CT	Y	35700 FQ	56310 MW	75980 TQ	USBLS	5/07
	New Haven MSA, CT	Y	42590 FQ	47650 MW	68690 TQ	USBLS	5/07
	Delaware	Y	40410 FQ	54460 MW	62630 TQ	USBLS	5/07
	Wilmington PMSA, DE-MD-NJ	Y	38780 FQ	47960 MW	60400 TQ	USBLS	5/07
	District of Columbia	Y	48770 FQ	59840 MW	77730 TQ	USBLS	5/07
	Washington-Arlington-Alexandria MSA, DC-VA-MD-WV	Y	48420 FQ	60920 MW	79100 TQ	USBLS	5/07
	Florida	Y	32140 FQ	45810 MW	59170 TQ	USBLS	5/07
	Fort Lauderdale-Pompano Beach-Deerfield Beach PMSA, FL	Y	33800 FQ	43900 MW	50960 TQ	USBLS	5/07
	Jacksonville MSA, FL	Y	34840 FQ	42610 MW	52370 TQ	USBLS	5/07
	Miami-Fort Lauderdale-Miami Beach MSA, FL	Y	34630 FQ	46980 MW	70310 TQ	USBLS	5/07
	Orlando-Kissimmee MSA, FL	Y	26490 FQ	37550 MW	59290 TQ	USBLS	5/07
	Sarasota-Bradenton-Venice MSA, FL	Y	32020 FQ	45510 MW	54180 TQ	USBLS	5/07
	Tampa-St. Petersburg-Clearwater MSA, FL	Y	40340 FQ	46110 MW	55490 TQ	USBLS	5/07
	West Palm Beach-Boca Raton-Boynton Beach PMSA, FL	Y	41230 FQ	48190 MW	67870 TQ	USBLS	5/07

AE	Average entry wage	**AW**	Average wage paid	**FQ**	First quartile wage	**LO**	Lowest wage paid	**MTC**	Median total compensation	**TCC**	Total cash compensation
AER	Average entry range	**AWR**	Average wage range	**H**	Hourly	**LR**	Low end range	**MW**	Median wage paid	**TQ**	Third quartile wage
AEX	Average experienced wage	**AXR**	Average experienced range	**HI**	Highest wage paid	**M**	Monthly	**MWR**	Median wage range	**W**	Weekly
ATC	Average total compensation	**D**	Daily	**HR**	High end range	**MCC**	Median cash compensation	**S**	See annotated source	**Y**	Yearly

Occupation/Type/Industry	Location	Per	Low	Mid	High	Source	Date
Writer and Author	Georgia	Y	34480 FQ	47040 MW	60150 TQ	USBLS	5/07
	Atlanta-Sandy Springs-Marietta MSA, GA	Y	40300 FQ	50720 MW	62120 TQ	USBLS	5/07
	Hawaii	Y	29490 FQ	41820 MW	55970 TQ	USBLS	5/07
	Honolulu MSA, HI	Y	37060 FQ	49340 MW	65860 TQ	USBLS	5/07
	Idaho	Y	41880 FQ	51290 MW	58130 TQ	USBLS	5/07
	Boise City-Nampa MSA, ID	Y	45000 FQ	51820 MW	59230 TQ	USBLS	5/07
	Illinois	Y	34430 FQ	49960 MW	73280 TQ	USBLS	5/07
	Chicago-Naperville-Joliet MSA, IL-IN-WI	Y	37550 FQ	51230 MW	76150 TQ	USBLS	5/07
	Peoria MSA, IL	Y	37300 FQ	46590 MW	58480 TQ	USBLS	5/07
	Indiana	Y	25620 FQ	36060 MW	47150 TQ	USBLS	5/07
	Gary PMSA, IN	Y	35040 FQ	40230 MW	48830 TQ	USBLS	5/07
	Indianapolis-Carmel MSA, IN	Y	36420 FQ	42720 MW	67260 TQ	USBLS	5/07
	Iowa	Y	24700 FQ	38840 MW	52280 TQ	USBLS	5/07
	Cedar Rapids MSA, IA	Y	30980 FQ	38860 MW	49050 TQ	USBLS	5/07
	Des Moines-West Des Moines MSA, IA	Y	36740 FQ	45430 MW	60600 TQ	USBLS	5/07
	Kansas	Y	30690 FQ	41260 MW	53010 TQ	USBLS	5/07
	Wichita MSA, KS	Y	17490 FQ	20320 MW	36880 TQ	USBLS	5/07
	Kentucky	Y	29936 FQ	41207 MW	57059 TQ	KYBLS	2008
	Lexington-Fayette MSA, KY	Y	34110 FQ	41080 MW	56140 TQ	USBLS	5/07
	Louisville-Jefferson County MSA, KY-IN	Y	29520 FQ	38270 MW	55350 TQ	USBLS	5/07
	Louisiana	H	13.71 FQ	18.47 MW	25.92 TQ	LABLS	1/08-3/08
	Baton Rouge MSA, LA	Y	24900 FQ	36980 MW	47910 TQ	USBLS	5/07
	New Orleans-Metairie-Kenner MSA, LA	Y	39890 FQ	48720 MW	67110 TQ	USBLS	5/07
	Maine	Y	43680 FQ	50960 MW	60090 TQ	USBLS	5/07
	Portland-South Portland-Biddeford MSA, ME	Y	44450 FQ	50950 MW	59560 TQ	USBLS	5/07
	Maryland	Y		52900 MW		MDBLS	3/08
	Baltimore-Towson MSA, MD	Y	36900 FQ	45860 MW	61320 TQ	USBLS	5/07
	Bethesda-Gaithersburg-Frederick PMSA, MD	Y	48100 FQ	68600 MW	83820 TQ	USBLS	5/07
	Massachusetts	Y	39240 FQ	53100 MW	70990 TQ	USBLS	5/07
	Boston-Cambridge-Quincy NECTA, MA	Y	39550 FQ	54440 MW	72810 TQ	USBLS	5/07
	Worcester MSA, MA-CT	Y	43740 FQ	57700 MW	91970 TQ	USBLS	5/07
	Michigan	Y	30820 FQ	45430 MW	65400 TQ	USBLS	5/07
	Detroit-Warren-Livonia MSA, MI	Y	45020 FQ	63180 MW	82320 TQ	USBLS	5/07
	Grand Rapids-Wyoming MSA, MI	Y	29530 FQ	37480 MW	46730 TQ	USBLS	5/07
	Warren-Troy-Farmington Hills PMSA, MI	Y	43260 FQ	61860 MW	84230 TQ	USBLS	5/07
	Minnesota	Y	38427 FQ	50177 MW	67575 TQ	MNBLS	10/08-12/08
	Duluth-Superior MSA, MN-WI	Y	36366 FQ	48220 MW	57280 TQ	MNBLS	10/08-12/08
	Minneapolis-Saint Paul MSA, MN-WI	Y	42131 FQ	53263 MW	71091 TQ	MNBLS	10/08-12/08
	Rochester MSA, MN	Y	30262 FQ	56927 MW	69028 TQ	MNBLS	10/08-12/08
	Mississippi	Y	31470 FQ	40970 MW	58200 TQ	USBLS	5/07
	Jackson MSA, MS	Y	34170 FQ	40450 MW	50390 TQ	USBLS	5/07
	Missouri	Y	34760 FQ	45510 MW	57940 TQ	USBLS	5/07
	Kansas City MSA, MO-KS	Y	39790 FQ	48610 MW	60030 TQ	USBLS	5/07
	St. Joseph MSA, MO-KS	Y	39030 FQ	55450 MW	65100 TQ	USBLS	5/07
	St. Louis MSA, MO-IL	Y	35060 FQ	45190 MW	57430 TQ	USBLS	5/07
	Springfield MSA, MO	Y	33980 FQ	40230 MW	59310 TQ	USBLS	5/07
	Montana	Y	24950 FQ	38690 MW	50160 TQ	USBLS	5/07
	Nebraska	Y	23390 FQ	39960 MW	58580 TQ	USBLS	5/07
	Omaha-Council Bluffs MSA, NE-IA	Y	33110 FQ	46190 MW	63000 TQ	USBLS	5/07
	Nevada	H	19.17 FQ	23.96 MW	29.14 TQ	NVBLS	5/08
	Las Vegas-Paradise MSA, NV	H	19.72 FQ	25.86 MW	30.04 TQ	NVBLS	5/08
	Reno-Sparks MSA, NV	H	19.23 FQ	22.19 MW	26.19 TQ	NVBLS	5/08
	New Hampshire	H	14.37 AE	22.73 MW	31.89 AEX	NHBLS	6/08
	New Jersey	Y	33710 FQ	48690 MW	70590 TQ	USBLS	5/07
	Camden PMSA, NJ	Y	46720 FQ	53190 MW	59900 TQ	USBLS	5/07
	Newark-Union PMSA, NJ-PA	Y	27490 FQ	32470 MW	51090 TQ	USBLS	5/07
	Trenton-Ewing MSA, NJ	Y	43520 FQ	49760 MW	59800 TQ	USBLS	5/07
	New Mexico	Y	35010 FQ	42850 MW	58440 TQ	USBLS	5/07
	Albuquerque MSA, NM	Y	34310 FQ	40180 MW	51450 TQ	USBLS	5/07

AE	Average entry wage	AW	Average wage paid	FQ	First quartile wage	LO	Lowest wage paid	MTC	Median total compensation	TCC	Total cash compensation
AER	Average entry range	AWR	Average wage range	H	Hourly	LR	Low end range	MW	Median wage paid	TQ	Third quartile wage
AEX	Average experienced wage	AXR	Average experienced range	HI	Highest wage paid	M	Monthly	MWR	Median wage range	W	Weekly
ATC	Average total compensation	D	Daily	HR	High end range	MCC	Median cash compensation	S	See annotated source	Y	Yearly

Occupation/Type/Industry	Location	Per	Low	Mid	High	Source	Date
Writer and Author	New York	Y	41970 FQ	57810 MW	81360 TQ	USBLS	5/07
	Albany-Schenectady-Troy MSA, NY	Y	39990 FQ	52520 MW	61460 TQ	USBLS	5/07
	Nassau-Suffolk PMSA, NY	Y	30860 FQ	44730 MW	63220 TQ	USBLS	5/07
	New York-Northern New Jersey-Long Island MSA, NY-NJ-PA	Y	42090 FQ	58060 MW	81170 TQ	USBLS	5/07
	North Carolina	Y	36000 FQ	46860 MW	57530 TQ	USBLS	5/07
	Charlotte-Gastonia-Concord MSA, NC-SC	Y	29270 FQ	45720 MW	59360 TQ	USBLS	5/07
	Raleigh-Cary MSA, NC	Y	37130 FQ	46380 MW	57130 TQ	USBLS	5/07
	North Dakota	Y	26920 FQ	31890 MW	36520 TQ	USBLS	5/07
	Ohio	Y	33390 FQ	44540 MW	59590 TQ	USBLS	5/07
	Cincinnati-Middletown MSA, OH-KY-IN	Y	18740 FQ	40720 MW	59380 TQ	USBLS	5/07
	Cleveland-Elyria-Mentor MSA, OH	Y	44060 FQ	55950 MW	63750 TQ	USBLS	5/07
	Columbus MSA, OH	Y	33440 FQ	46340 MW	61360 TQ	USBLS	5/07
	Dayton MSA, OH	Y	40170 FQ	43720 MW	47320 TQ	USBLS	5/07
	Oklahoma	Y	30260 FQ	47180 MW	112310 TQ	USBLS	5/07
	Oklahoma City MSA, OK	Y	27710 FQ	35230 MW	47360 TQ	USBLS	5/07
	Tulsa MSA, OK	Y	46550 FQ	110700 MW	131270 TQ	USBLS	5/07
	Oregon	H	18.68 FQ	23.78 MW	28.93 TQ	ORBLS	5/08
	Portland-Vancouver-Beaverton MSA, OR-WA	Y	40790 FQ	50270 MW	60320 TQ	USBLS	5/07
	Pennsylvania	Y	35170 FQ	47290 MW	67450 TQ	USBLS	5/07
	Allentown-Bethlehem-Easton MSA, PA-NJ	Y	42230 FQ	64420 MW	71180 TQ	USBLS	5/07
	Philadelphia-Camden-Wilmington MSA, PA-NJ-DE-MD	Y	36920 FQ	48310 MW	65910 TQ	USBLS	5/07
	Pittsburgh MSA, PA	Y	37180 FQ	54230 MW	71120 TQ	USBLS	5/07
	Rhode Island	Y	35560 FQ	58450 MW	72000 TQ	USBLS	5/07
	Providence-Fall River-Warwick MSA, RI-MA	Y	37480 FQ	60380 MW	72460 TQ	USBLS	5/07
	South Carolina	Y	30270 FQ	39490 MW	52070 TQ	USBLS	5/07
	Columbia MSA, SC	Y	22290 FQ	25070 MW	39110 TQ	USBLS	5/07
	South Dakota	Y	34236 FQ	37184 MW	40147 TQ	SDBLS	7/08-9/08
	Sioux Falls MSA, SD	Y	33237 FQ	37391 MW	41579 TQ	SDBLS	7/08-9/08
	Tennessee	Y	29120 FQ	39100 MW	53650 TQ	USBLS	5/07
	Memphis MSA, TN-MS-AR	Y	38510 FQ	57450 MW	76490 TQ	USBLS	5/07
	Nashville-Davidson-Murfreesboro MSA, TN	Y	27780 FQ	36780 MW	46520 TQ	USBLS	5/07
	Texas	Y	36270 FQ	49640 MW	68990 TQ	USBLS	5/07
	Austin-Round Rock MSA, TX	Y	37550 FQ	56860 MW	84150 TQ	USBLS	5/07
	Dallas-Fort Worth-Arlington MSA, TX	Y	39390 FQ	56980 MW	75630 TQ	USBLS	5/07
	El Paso MSA, TX	Y	30330 FQ	48040 MW	66880 TQ	USBLS	5/07
	Houston-Sugar Land-Baytown MSA, TX	Y	36610 FQ	48170 MW	57940 TQ	USBLS	5/07
	San Antonio MSA, TX	Y	15660 FQ	49730 MW	63640 TQ	USBLS	5/07
	Utah	Y	37170 FQ	50320 MW	69680 TQ	USBLS	5/07
	Provo-Orem MSA, UT	Y	34800 FQ	49580 MW	62420 TQ	USBLS	5/07
	Salt Lake City MSA, UT	Y	44370 FQ	60810 MW	95990 TQ	USBLS	5/07
	Vermont	Y	29380 FQ	43170 MW	71090 TQ	USBLS	5/07
	Burlington-South Burlington MSA, VT	Y	34240 FQ	46090 MW	60670 TQ	USBLS	5/07
	Virginia	Y	40360 FQ	53310 MW	69720 TQ	USBLS	5/07
	Richmond MSA, VA	Y	43430 FQ	51640 MW	68230 TQ	USBLS	5/07
	Virginia Beach-Norfolk-Newport News MSA, VA-NC	Y	36550 FQ	47530 MW	58350 TQ	USBLS	5/07
	Washington	H	21.43 FQ	28.59 MW	36.97 TQ	WABLS	3/08
	Seattle-Tacoma-Bellevue MSA, WA	Y	44740 FQ	60320 MW	76510 TQ	USBLS	5/07
	West Virginia	Y	19711 FQ	30890 MW	42326 TQ	WVBLS	7/08-9/08
	Wisconsin	Y	27060 FQ	40090 MW	56210 TQ	USBLS	5/07
	Milwaukee-Waukesha-West Allis MSA, WI	Y	27560 FQ	35880 MW	52530 TQ	USBLS	5/07
	Wyoming	Y	35885 FQ	51879 MW	58918 TQ	WYBLS	9/08
	Puerto Rico	Y	26550 FQ	29630 MW	38910 TQ	USBLS	5/07
	San Juan-Caguas-Guaynabo MSA, PR	Y	26620 FQ	29660 MW	38800 TQ	USBLS	5/07

AE	Average entry wage	AW	Average wage paid	FQ	First quartile wage
AER	Average entry range	AWR	Average wage range	H	Hourly
AEX	Average experienced wage	AXR	Average experienced range	HI	Highest wage paid
ATC	Average total compensation	D	Daily	HR	High end range

LO	Lowest wage paid	MTC	Median total compensation	TCC	Total cash compensation
LR	Low end range	MW	Median wage paid	TQ	Third quartile wage
M	Monthly	MWR	Median wage range	W	Weekly
MCC	Median cash compensation	S	See annotated source	Y	Yearly

Occupation/Type/Industry	Location	Per	Low	Mid	High	Source	Date
X-Ray and EKG Technician							
New Hampshire Hospital	New Hampshire	Y			53729 HI	NHUL03	2008
Yoga Instructor	United States	Y		30000-40000 AWR		DJS	2008
Zoning Hearing Examiner	Cincinnati, OH	Y	77518 LO		104649 HI	COHSS	10/08
Zoning Supervisor	Cincinnati, OH	Y	49502 LO		68164 HI	COHSS	10/08
Zoologist and Wildlife Biologist	Alaska	Y	44960 FQ	56230 MW	68000 TQ	USBLS	5/07
	Arizona	Y	41900 FQ	55160 MW	64300 TQ	USBLS	5/07
	Phoenix-Mesa-Scottsdale MSA, AZ	Y	40560 FQ	55330 MW	68480 TQ	USBLS	5/07
	Arkansas	Y	43700 FQ	53230 MW	62790 TQ	USBLS	5/07
	California	H	25.01 FQ	34.21 MW	44.29 TQ	CABLS	1/08-3/08
	Los Angeles-Long Beach-Glendale PMSA, CA	H	22.82 FQ	30.02 MW	38.49 TQ	CABLS	1/08-3/08
	Oakland-Fremont-Hayward MSA, CA	H	33.56 FQ	43.30 MW	50.55 TQ	CABLS	1/08-3/08
	Riverside-San Bernardino-Ontario MSA, CA	H	23.58 FQ	30.73 MW	38.46 TQ	CABLS	1/08-3/08
	Sacramento-Arden Arcade-Roseville MSA, CA	H	22.48 FQ	29.81 MW	37.68 TQ	CABLS	1/08-3/08
	San Diego-Carlsbad-San Marcos MSA, CA	H	19.26 FQ	25.66 MW	37.70 TQ	CABLS	1/08-3/08
	San Francisco-San Mateo-Redwood PMSA, CA	H	29.73 FQ	34.43 MW	40.76 TQ	CABLS	1/08-3/08
	Santa Ana-Anaheim-Irvine PMSA, CA	Y	41520 FQ	55660 MW	73420 TQ	USBLS	5/07
	Colorado	Y	38870 FQ	52980 MW	68540 TQ	USBLS	5/07
	Denver-Aurora MSA, CO	Y	36230 FQ	53670 MW	73420 TQ	USBLS	5/07
	Connecticut	H	30.02 AE	34.96 MW		CTBLS	1/08-3/08
	Hartford-West Hartford-East Hartford MSA, CT	Y	63930 FQ	69170 MW	74310 TQ	USBLS	5/07
	District of Columbia	Y	77180 FQ	106900 MW	124950 TQ	USBLS	5/07
	Washington-Arlington-Alexandria MSA, DC-VA-MD-WV	Y	55770 FQ	87470 MW	110970 TQ	USBLS	5/07
	Florida	Y	37580 FQ	48160 MW	61080 TQ	USBLS	5/07
	Miami-Fort Lauderdale-Miami Beach MSA, FL	Y	43720 FQ	55350 MW	75240 TQ	USBLS	5/07
	Orlando-Kissimmee MSA, FL	Y	43230 FQ	54620 MW	64470 TQ	USBLS	5/07
	Tampa-St. Petersburg-Clearwater MSA, FL	Y	37010 FQ	47650 MW	59630 TQ	USBLS	5/07
	West Palm Beach-Boca Raton-Boynton Beach PMSA, FL	Y	38690 FQ	47420 MW	57520 TQ	USBLS	5/07
	Georgia	Y	32580 FQ	42060 MW	50640 TQ	USBLS	5/07
	Atlanta-Sandy Springs-Marietta MSA, GA	Y	29500 FQ	38600 MW	47700 TQ	USBLS	5/07
	Hawaii	Y	45610 FQ	58050 MW	71090 TQ	USBLS	5/07
	Idaho	Y	38710 FQ	51290 MW	63080 TQ	USBLS	5/07
	Boise City-Nampa MSA, ID	Y	40620 FQ	51140 MW	64070 TQ	USBLS	5/07
	Illinois	Y	46010 FQ	56800 MW	68290 TQ	USBLS	5/07
	Indiana	Y	46260 FQ	63980 MW	79920 TQ	USBLS	5/07
	Indianapolis-Carmel MSA, IN	Y	49250 FQ	66450 MW	82030 TQ	USBLS	5/07
	Iowa	Y	42180 FQ	53670 MW	60910 TQ	USBLS	5/07
	Louisiana	H	20.92 FQ	28.23 MW	36.16 TQ	LABLS	1/08-3/08
	Maine	Y	42470 FQ	49910 MW	58730 TQ	USBLS	5/07
	Maryland	Y		87300 MW		MDBLS	3/08
	Baltimore-Towson MSA, MD	Y	52140 FQ	76220 MW	95450 TQ	USBLS	5/07
	Bethesda-Gaithersburg-Frederick PMSA, MD	Y	65420 FQ	90190 MW	106330 TQ	USBLS	5/07
	Massachusetts	Y	58870 FQ	77390 MW	88520 TQ	USBLS	5/07
	Boston-Cambridge-Quincy NECTA, MA	Y	65330 FQ	80530 MW	89380 TQ	USBLS	5/07
	Michigan	Y	51470 FQ	58900 MW	67540 TQ	USBLS	5/07
	Minnesota	Y	44192 FQ	54477 MW	65451 TQ	MNBLS	10/08-12/08
	Minneapolis-Saint Paul MSA, MN-WI	Y	41148 FQ	48503 MW	57898 TQ	MNBLS	10/08-12/08
	Mississippi	Y	38920 FQ	52910 MW	77360 TQ	USBLS	5/07
	Jackson MSA, MS	Y	34600 FQ	40460 MW	47550 TQ	USBLS	5/07
	Missouri	Y	35860 FQ	44150 MW	54860 TQ	USBLS	5/07

AE	Average entry wage	AW	Average wage paid	FQ	First quartile wage	LO	Lowest wage paid	MTC	Median total compensation	TCC	Total cash compensation
AER	Average entry range	AWR	Average wage range	H	Hourly	LR	Low end range	MW	Median wage paid	TQ	Third quartile wage
AEX	Average experienced wage	AXR	Average experienced range	HI	Highest wage paid	M	Monthly	MWR	Median wage range	W	Weekly
ATC	Average total compensation	D	Daily	HR	High end range	MCC	Median cash compensation	S	See annotated source	Y	Yearly

1700

Occupation/Type/Industry	Location	Per	Low	Mid	High	Source	Date
Zoologist and Wildlife Biologist	Kansas City MSA, MO-KS	Y	37530 FQ	48270 MW	59410 TQ	USBLS	5/07
	St. Louis MSA, MO-IL	Y	34920 FQ	41900 MW	52410 TQ	USBLS	5/07
	Montana	Y	39360 FQ	48440 MW	60200 TQ	USBLS	5/07
	Nevada	H	22.15 FQ	27.15 MW	31.15 TQ	NVBLS	5/08
	Las Vegas-Paradise MSA, NV	H	22.97 FQ	27.60 MW	32.43 TQ	NVBLS	5/08
	New Jersey	Y	53610 FQ	69050 MW	80230 TQ	USBLS	5/07
	Edison PMSA, NJ	Y	67200 FQ	77570 MW	88940 TQ	USBLS	5/07
	New Mexico	Y	52530 FQ	60600 MW	72780 TQ	USBLS	5/07
	New York	Y	46290 FQ	56870 MW	66130 TQ	USBLS	5/07
	Albany-Schenectady-Troy MSA, NY	Y	53190 FQ	61060 MW	71050 TQ	USBLS	5/07
	Nassau-Suffolk PMSA, NY	Y	48680 FQ	59180 MW	72350 TQ	USBLS	5/07
	New York-Northern New Jersey-Long Island MSA, NY-NJ-PA	Y	41440 FQ	61770 MW	78270 TQ	USBLS	5/07
	North Carolina	Y	42920 FQ	50310 MW	64480 TQ	USBLS	5/07
	Charlotte-Gastonia-Concord MSA, NC-SC	Y	55800 FQ	63700 MW	73180 TQ	USBLS	5/07
	Ohio	Y	34240 FQ	43740 MW	54240 TQ	USBLS	5/07
	Columbus MSA, OH	Y	32690 FQ	42330 MW	52930 TQ	USBLS	5/07
	Oklahoma	Y	41920 FQ	47630 MW	53910 TQ	USBLS	5/07
	Oregon	H	22.23 FQ	27.37 MW	32.48 TQ	ORBLS	5/08
	Portland-Vancouver-Beaverton MSA, OR-WA	Y	50470 FQ	58990 MW	68930 TQ	USBLS	5/07
	Philadelphia-Camden-Wilmington MSA, PA-NJ-DE-MD	Y	29340 FQ	41660 MW	74320 TQ	USBLS	5/07
	South Carolina	Y	40220 FQ	47990 MW	58100 TQ	USBLS	5/07
	South Dakota	Y	38861 FQ	47196 MW	57856 TQ	SDBLS	7/08-9/08
	Tennessee	Y	35420 FQ	48720 MW	71910 TQ	USBLS	5/07
	Texas	Y	44410 FQ	56780 MW	77920 TQ	USBLS	5/07
	Austin-Round Rock MSA, TX	Y	40620 FQ	50610 MW	72140 TQ	USBLS	5/07
	Dallas-Fort Worth-Arlington MSA, TX	Y	44080 FQ	52470 MW	64050 TQ	USBLS	5/07
	Houston-Sugar Land-Baytown MSA, TX	Y	59430 FQ	76830 MW	135280 TQ	USBLS	5/07
	Utah	Y	37390 FQ	45340 MW	58200 TQ	USBLS	5/07
	Vermont	Y	45530 FQ	55670 MW	61690 TQ	USBLS	5/07
	Virginia	Y	38460 FQ	50070 MW	64580 TQ	USBLS	5/07
	Richmond MSA, VA	Y	41180 FQ	49630 MW	60510 TQ	USBLS	5/07
	Virginia Beach-Norfolk-Newport News MSA, VA-NC	Y	42490 FQ	49480 MW	62210 TQ	USBLS	5/07
	Washington	H	23.89 FQ	28.63 MW	34.36 TQ	WABLS	3/08
	Seattle-Tacoma-Bellevue MSA, WA	Y	46410 FQ	59130 MW	78080 TQ	USBLS	5/07
	West Virginia	Y	36815 FQ	46318 MW	59565 TQ	WVBLS	7/08-9/08
	Wisconsin	Y	42720 FQ	48420 MW	59000 TQ	USBLS	5/07
	Wyoming	Y	40624 FQ	49151 MW	59160 TQ	WYBLS	9/08
	Cheyenne MSA, WY	Y	44391 FQ	54369 MW	64701 TQ	WYBLS	9/08

AE	Average entry wage	AW	Average wage paid	FQ	First quartile wage	LO	Lowest wage paid	MTC	Median total compensation	TCC	Total cash compensation
AER	Average entry range	AWR	Average wage range	H	Hourly	LR	Low end range	MW	Median wage paid	TQ	Third quartile wage
AEX	Average experienced wage	AXR	Average experienced range	HI	Highest wage paid	M	Monthly	MWR	Median wage range	W	Weekly
ATC	Average total compensation	D	Daily	HR	High end range	MCC	Median cash compensation	S	See annotated source	Y	Yearly

1701

247FASH

WWD Apparel & Retail Industry Salary and Job Satisfaction Survey 2009, January 12, 2009, pp. 36-61.

Online: http://www.24seveninc.com/2009salarysurvey/
Survey Period: 2009

Note: Data were downloaded on January 12, 2009.

4NTAX

"New York City Area Nanny Salary Survey Results Sept 2007-Feb 2008," February 23, 2009.

Online: http://www.4nannytaxes.com
Survey Period: September 2007-February 2008

Note: Data were downloaded on February 23, 2009.

4NTAX01

"Washington DC Area Salary Survey Results Sept 2007-Feb 2008," February 23, 2009.

Online: http://www.4nannytaxes.com
Survey Period: September 2007-February 2008

Note: Data were downloaded on February 23, 2009.

AACSB

2007-2008 US Salary Survey Report, January 2008.

The Association to Advance Collegiate Schools of Business
777 South Harbour Island Boulevard
Suite 750
Tampa, FL 33602-5730
Online: http://www.aacsb.edu
Survey Period: 2007-2008

AAHS

"Compare Top Health Care Jobs," *AllAlliedHealthSchools*, January 22, 2009.

Online: http://www.allalliedhealthschools.com
Survey Period: 2009

Note: Data were downloaded on January 22, 2009 and were considered current by the source.

AAPC

Brad Ericson, "2008 Salary Survey: Sunlight on Coders' Compensation," *AAPC Coding Edge*, October 2008, pp. 18-22.

American Academy of Professional Coders
2480 South 3850 West, Suite B
Salt Lake City, UT 84120
Telephone: (800) 626-CODE
Fax: (801) 236-2258
Survey Period: 2008

AAPG

"Geologist Pay Reflects Demand," *AAPG Explorer*, April 2008.

American Association of Petroleum Geologists
1444 South Boulder Avenue
Tulsa, OK 74119
Telephone: (800) 364-2274
Fax: (918) 560-2665
Online: http://www.aapg.org
Survey Period: 2008

AASH

Higher Education Sustainability Officer Position and Salary Survey, January 2008.

Association for the Advancement of Sustainability in
Higher Education
213 1/2 North Limestone
Lexington, KY 40507
Telephone: (859) 402-9272
Online: http://www.aashe.org
Survey Period: 2007

AASTATE

Kirk Bohls, "He May be Horns' 'Other' Coordinator, But Davis is Working Magic," *Austin American-Statesman*, October 10, 2008.

Online: http://www.statesman.com
Survey Period: 2008

AAUP

"Table B: Average Salary for Division I-A Football Head Coaches and Full Professors, by Conference, 2006-07 and 2007-08," January 6, 2009.

American Association of University Professors
1133 Nineteenth Street, NW, Suite 200
Washington, DC 20036
Telephone: (202) 737-5900
Fax: (202) 737-5526
Online: http://www.aaup.org
Email: aaup@aaup.org
Survey Period: 2007-2008

ABAJ

"A Flush Start," *ABA Journal*, January 2008, p. 13.

Survey Period: 2008

ABCN

John Berman, "Even Santa's Job Isn't Safe," *ABC News*, December 9, 2008.

Online: http://abcnews.go.com
Survey Period: December 2008

ABCN01

Sharon Alfonso, "Behind the Scenes at Westminster," *World News*, February 10, 2009.

Online: http://abcnews.go.com
Survey Period: 2009

Note: According to the source, top dog handlers can earn more than $100,000 per year.

ABCN02

Tory Johnson, "Unemployment Rescue: Five Part-Time Jobs You Can Get Now," *ABC News*, February 10, 2009.

Online: http://abcnews.go.com
Survey Period: 2009

ABJ

"ADM Chooses Interim Director," *Akron Beacon Journal*, October 7, 2008.

Online: http://www.ohio.com
Survey Period: 2008

ACONT

Kelli Michael, "Odd Jobs: Crime-Scene Cleaner," *Associated Content*, January 30, 2009.

Online: http://www.associatedcontent.com
Survey Period: 2009

Note: Data were downloaded on January 30, 2009 and were considered current by the source.

ACTECH

"Tough Times Ahead?" *Accounting Technology 2009 The Year Ahead*, December 2008, pp. 4-6.

Survey Period: 2009

ACTT

Daniel Hood, "Acc'ts May Escape Salary Woes in 2009," *Accounting Today*, November 17, 2008-December 14, 2008, p. 8.

Survey Period: 2009

ACU

"2008 Salary Survey Results," October 13, 2008.

Abilene Christian University
Abilene, TX 79699
Telephone: (325) 674-2000
Online: http://www.acu.edu
Survey Period: 2008

Note: Data were downloaded on October 13, 2008.

ACVPSS

American College of Veterinary Pathologists 2006 Salary Survey, January 26, 2009.

American College of Veterinary Pathologists
2810 Crossroads Drive, Suite 3800
Madison, WI 53718
Telephone: (608) 443-2466
Fax: (608) 443-2474
Online: http://www.avcp.org
Survey Period: 2006

ADA

"Night Nanny," October 13, 2008.

American Domestic Agency Inc.
3519 Silverside Road
Suite 101-D Ridgely Building
Wilmington, DE 19810
Telephone: (302) 478-6340
Fax: (302) 478-6350
Online: http://www.americandomestic.com
Email: Melissa@AmericanDomestic.com
Survey Period: 2008

Note: Data were downloaded on October 13, 2008 and were considered current by the source.

ADA01

"Registered Dietitian Information Sheet," October 24, 2008.

> American Dietetic Association
> 120 South Riverside Plaza, Suite 200
> Chicago, IL 60606-6995
> **Telephone:** (800) 877-1600
> **Online:** http://www.eatright.org
> **Survey Period:** 2007

Note: Data were downloaded on October 24, 2008.

ADAGE01

Bradley Johnson, "CMOs Snag an Average of $1.5 Million a Year," *Advertising Age*, July 28, 2008, p. 1.

> **Survey Period:** 2007

ADGAZ

Charlie Frago, "Justices: Low Pay Threatens Judiciary," *Arkansas Democrat Gazette*, September 25, 2008.

> **Online:** http://www.nwanews.com
> **Survey Period:** 2008

ADT01

Keith Ward, "Salary Survey: IT Workers Continue to Flourish," *Application Development Trends*, September 6, 2007.

> **Online:** http://adtmag.com
> **Survey Period:** 2007

ADVN

Adrianne O'Brien, "ADVANCE Salary Survey 2008: Nursing Shortage Begins to Level Out," *ADVANCE for Nurses*, October 2008.

> **Online:** http://nursing.advanceweb.com
> **Survey Period:** 2008

AEA

"Become an Electrologist," October 28, 2008.

> American Electrology Association
> **Online:** http://www.electrology.com
> **Email:** infoaea@electrology.com
> **Survey Period:** 2008

Note: Data were downloaded on October 28, 2008 and were considered current by the source.

AFNP

Jill Rollet and Sarah Lebo, "A Decade of Growth: Salaries Increase as Profession Matures," *ADVANCE for Nurse Practitioners*, January 2008, pp. 29-35.

> **Online:** http://www.advancefornp.com
> **Survey Period:** 2007

AFP

Billy Treger, "Despite Slowing Economy, Compensation Growth for Financial Professionals Surpassed that of National Average in 2007," July 17, 2008.

> Association for Financial Professionals
> 4520 East West Highway, Suite 750
> Bethesda, MD 20814
> **Telephone:** (301) 907-2862
> **Fax:** (301) 907-2864
> **Online:** http://www.afponline.org
> **Survey Period:** 2008

Note: Press release.

AFT01

"2008 AFT Public Employees Compensation Survey: Private Sector vs. State Employee Average Salary Comparisons, 2008," September 25, 2008.

> American Federation of Teachers
> 555 New Jersey Avenue NW
> Washington, DC 20001
> **Online:** http://www.aft.org
> **Survey Period:** 2008

AFT02

AFT Public Employees Compensation Survey 2008, September 2008.

> American Federation of Teachers
> 555 New Jersey Avenue NW
> Washington, DC 20001
> **Online:** http://www.aft.org
> **Survey Period:** March 1, 2008

AFTRA1

"2006-2008 Extension to the AFTRA Radio Recorded Commercials Contract Schedule of Minimum Fees," February 12, 2009.

> American Federation of Television & Radio Artists
> 5757 Wilshire Boulevard, 9th Floor
> Los Angeles, CA 90036-3689
> **Telephone:** (323) 634-8193
> **Fax:** (323) 634-8194
> **Online:** http://www.aftra.org
> **Survey Period:** October 30, 2006-October 29, 2008

Note: According to the source, an actor working on a network program commercial gets paid differently depending on how many weeks the commercial is used. If the commercial is used for one week, then the actor is paid a minimum of $422. If the commercial is used for thirteen weeks then the actor is paid a minimum of $1,354. Salary data are rounded to the nearest dollar.

AFTRA2

"Infomercial Rates," February 12, 2009.

> American Federation of Television & Radio Artists
> 5757 Wilshire Boulevard, 9th Floor
> Los Angeles, CA 90036-3689
> **Telephone:** (323) 634-8193
> **Fax:** (323) 634-8194
> **Online:** http://www.aftra.org
> **Survey Period:** October 30, 2006-October 29, 2008

Note: According to the source, on-camera infomercial hosts receive a minimum of $1,134 for the first day of work and a minimum of $567 for each additional day after that. Salary data are rounded to the nearest dollar.

AGO

"2009 Salary Guide for Musicians Employed by Religious Institutions," November 20, 2008.

> American Guild of Organists
> 475 Riverside Drive, Suite 1260
> New York, NY 10115
> **Telephone:** (212) 870-2310
> **Fax:** (212) 870-2163
> **Online:** http://www.agohq.org
> **Survey Period:** 2009

Note: Salary data are for the 2009 contract year.

AGPRO

Colleen Scherer, "Salary Survey 2007," *Ag Professional*, May 2007.

> **Online:** http://www.agprofessional.com
> **Survey Period:** 2007

AGRI

"2008 Salary Schedule," *Farm Production Salary Survey*, October 2008.

> AGRIcareers, Inc.
> Highway 92 West
> Massena, IA 50853
> **Telephone:** (800) 633-8387
> **Fax:** (712) 779-3366
> **Online:** http://www.agricareersinc.com
> **Survey Period:** 2008

AHIP

Lynn Jusinski, "2008 Salary Survey Results," *ADVANCE for Health Information Professionals*, December 15, 2008.

> **Online:** http://health-information.advanceweb.com
> **Survey Period:** 2008

Note: Salary data combine both full- and part-time registrar salaries.

AIFS

"Au Pair in America Program Fees," October 9, 2008.

American Institute for Foreign Study
Au Pair in America
River Plaza, 9 West Broad Street
Stamford, CT 06902
Telephone: (800) 928-7247
Fax: (203) 399-5592
Online: http://www.aupairinamerica.com
Survey Period: July 24, 2008-July 23, 2009

Note: The minimum weekly stipend for au pairs is established by the United States government based on the 2007 minimum wage law less an allowance for room and board. The 2007 minimum wage law provides for a 3-year phased increase. On July 24, 2009, the weekly stipend for au pairs will increase to $195.75. The weekly stipend for au pairs extraordinaire is set by Au Pair in America.

AIGA01

AIGA/AQUENT Survey of Design Salaries 2008, October 2008.

AIGA
164 Fifth Avenue
New York, NY 10010
Telephone: (212) 807-1990
Online: http://www.designsalaries.org
Survey Period: 2008

ALA01

Jenifer Grady, "Librarian Salary Survey Reports Mean Librarian Salary Up 2 Percent to $58,960 in 2008," August 8, 2008.

ALA-APA
50 East Huron
Chicago, IL 60611
Telephone: (312) 280-2424
Online: http://ala-apa.org
Email: jgrady@ala.org
Survey Period: 2008

Note: Press release.

ALA02

Food & Beverage Processing, 2008.

Abbott, Langer Association Surveys
1725 I Street NW, Suite 300
Washington, DC 20006
Telephone: (877) 210-6563
Fax: (877) 239-2457
Online: http://www.abbott-langer.com
Survey Period: 2008

ALA03

Biotechnology, 2008.

Abbott, Langer Association Surveys
1725 I Street NW, Suite 300
Washington, DC 20006
Telephone: (877) 210-6563
Fax: (877) 239-2457
Online: http://www.abbott-langer.com
Survey Period: 2008

ALA04

Publishing, 2008.

Abbott, Langer Association Surveys
1725 I Street NW, Suite 300
Washington, DC 20006
Telephone: (877) 210-6563
Fax: (877) 239-2457
Online: http://www.abbott-langer.com
Survey Period: 2008

ALA05

Manufacturing, 2008.

Abbott, Langer Association Surveys
1725 I Street NW, Suite 300
Washington, DC 20006
Telephone: (877) 210-6563
Fax: (877) 239-2457
Online: http://www.abbott-langer.com
Survey Period: 2008

ALA06

Consulting Engineering and Land Surveying, 2008.

    Abbott, Langer Association Surveys
1725 I Street NW, Suite 300
Washington, DC 20006
Telephone: (877) 210-6563
Fax: (877) 239-2457
Online: http://www.abbott-langer.com
Survey Period: 2008

ALA07

Wholesaling and Manufacturer's Representatives, 2008.

    Abbott, Langer Association Surveys
1725 I Street NW, Suite 300
Washington, DC 20006
Telephone: (877) 210-6563
Fax: (877) 239-2457
Online: http://www.abbott-langer.com
Survey Period: 2008

ALA08

Petroleum Products, 2008.

    Abbott, Langer Association Surveys
1725 I Street NW, Suite 300
Washington, DC 20006
Telephone: (877) 210-6563
Fax: (877) 239-2457
Online: http://www.abbott-langer.com
Survey Period: 2008

ALTC

Liz Rosto, "2007 Long-Term Care Salary Survey," *ADVANCE for Long-Term Care Management*, October 13, 2008, pp. 27-28.

    Online: http://www.advanceforltc.com
Survey Period: July 2007-August 2007

Note: Data were downloaded on October 13, 2008.

AMIW01

Natalie Wade, "Auburn U: $60K Salary Increase for Auburn U. Lobbyist Raises Criticism," *The America's Intelligence Wire*, September 20, 2008.

    Survey Period: 2008

AMLIB

"APA Report Shows Librarian Salary Rise," *American Libraries*, March 12, 2008.

    Survey Period: 2007

AMNUR

"2007 Wage & Benefits Survey," *American Nurseryman*, April 15, 2008, pp. 38-43.

    Survey Period: 2007

AMT

Barb Zyehlke, "Salary Snapshot," *Aircraft Maintenance Technology*, August 14, 2008.

    Online: http://www.amtonline.com
Survey Period: 2008

AMW

Kirsten Stewart, "Canyons School District Pays Well for Top Talent: Priorities? Some Board Members Say Salaries Too High," *The America's Intelligence Wire*, December 19, 2008.

    Survey Period: 2008

ANCDN

"Editorial: Pay Raise in Juneau? Give Legislators Flat Pay Rates, Even Though It Means Raises," *Anchorage Daily News*, February 21, 2009.

Survey Period: 2008

Note: Salary data include basic pay only.

ANGJ

"Ministers' Salaries," *Anglican Journal*, October 1, 2008.

Online: http://www.anglicanjournal.com
Survey Period: 2008

ANISR

Sarah Jane Udall, "Digital Video Editing," *Animation School Review*, January 30, 2006.

Online: http://www.animationschoolreview.com
Survey Period: 2006

AORN01

Donald Bacon, "Results of the 2007 AORN Salary Survey," *AORN Journal*, December 2007, pp. 944-957.

Survey Period: 2007

APA01

"Salary Survey Summary," February 2, 2009.

American Planning Association
122 South Michigan Avenue, Suite 1600
Chicago, IL 60603
Telephone: (312) 431-9100
Fax: (312) 431-9985
Online: http://www.planning.org
Survey Period: 2008

Note: Data were downloaded on February 2, 2009.

APACWS

Xiaofan Li, Marlene Wicherski, and Jessica L. Kohout, *Salaries in Psychology 2007: Report of the 2007 APA Salary Survey*, October 2008.

American Psychological Association
Center for Workforce Studies
750 First Street, NE
Washington, DC 20002-4242
Telephone: (202) 336-5980
Fax: (202) 336-6148
Online: http://research.apa.org/salaries07.html
Email: cws@apa.org
Survey Period: 2007

APC

Airline Pilot Pay Snapshot, July 30, 2008.

Online: http://airlinepilotcentral.com
Survey Period: July 2008

APDEM

Howard Yune, "Sutter Supervisors Will Pay Themselves More: Hike Salaries in 3 Other Departments," *Appeal-Democrat*, December 31, 2008.

Survey Period: March 14, 2009

Note: Salary for County Supervisor took effect on March 14, 2009.

APHYS

"Physician Salaries and Salary Surveys," June 2006.

Allied Physicians, Inc.
4590 Highway 1 #131
Rehoboth Beach, DE 19971
Online: http://www.allied-physicians.com
Survey Period: June 2003-June 2006

APP

Todd B. Bates and Paul D'Ambrosio, "State Workers at $100G on Rise," *Asbury Park Press*, October 22, 2008.

Online: http://www.app.com
Survey Period: 2008

AREGC

2007 Regional Salary Survey, February 24, 2009.

Atlanta Regional Commission
40 Courtland Street, NE
Atlanta, GA 30303
Telephone: (404) 463-3100
Fax: (404) 463-3205
Online: http://www.atlantaregional.com
Survey Period: 2007

Note: Salary data are rounded to the nearest dollar.

ARL

Martha Kyrillidou, et. al., *ARL Annual Salary Survey 2007-2008*, 2008.

Association of Research Libraries
21 Dupont Circle, NW, Suite 800
Washington, DC 20036
Telephone: (202) 296-2296
Fax: (202) 872-0884
Online: http://www.arl.org
Survey Period: 2007-2008

ASAP

Jay Ennesser, et. al., *Alliance Management Compensation — A Groundbreaking Report*, May 12, 2008.

Association of Strategic Alliance Professionals
Silicon Valley/NorCal Chapter
250 First Avenue, Suite 300
Needham, MA 02494
Fax: (781) 972-5425
Online: http://www.strategic-alliances.org
Email: info@strategic-alliances.org
Survey Period: 2008

Note: Webinar on April 29, 2008. Published on May 12, 2008. Average first and third quartile salaries for Alliance Manager I are $87,041 and $140,000, respectively. Average first and third quartile salaries for Alliance Manager III are $135,000 and $156,250, respectively, according to the source.

ASKM

Austin Silver, "What's a Male Model's Salary?" *AskMen.com*, November 7, 2008.

Online: http://www.askmen.com
Survey Period: 2008

Note: Data were downloaded on November 7, 2008 and were considered current by the source.

ASP01

2008 Technical Support Salary Survey, 2008.

The Association of Support Professionals
122 Barnard Avenue
Watertown, MA 02472
Telephone: (617) 924-3944
Fax: (617) 924-7288
Online: http://www.asponline.com
Survey Period: 2008

ASPORT

"Professional Skateboarders," January 9, 2009.

Online: http://www.adventurousport.com
Survey Period: 2009

Note: Data were downloaded on January 9, 2009 and were considered current by the source.

AUDDEV

"2008 Circulation Salary Survey," *Audience Development*, December 3, 2008.

Online: http://www.audiencedevelopment.com
Survey Period: 2008

AUTOM

"Automation.com 2008 Salary Survey Results," February 17, 2009.

Online: http://www.automation.com
Survey Period: 2008

Note: Data were downloaded on February 17, 2009.

AVJOB01

"Airport Salaries, Wages and Pay," February 17, 2009.

Online: http://www.aviationsalary.com
Survey Period: 2009

AVJOB02

"Dispatch Salaries, Wages and Pay," February 17, 2009.

Online: http://www.aviationsalary.com
Survey Period: 2009

Note: Salary data are rounded to the nearest dollar.

AVJOB03

"Ground & Ramp Salaries, Wages and Pay," February 17, 2009.

Online: http://www.aviationsalary.com
Survey Period: 2009

AVJOB04

"Airline & Aerospace Executive Salaries, Wages and Pay," February 17, 2009.

Online: http://www.aviationsalary.com
Survey Period: 2009

Note: Salary data are rounded to the nearest dollar.

AVJOB05

"Reservations & Travel Agent Salaries, Wages and Pay," February 17, 2009.

Online: http://www.aviationsalary.com
Survey Period: 2009

AVJOB06

"Avionics Salaries, Wages and Pay," February 17, 2009.

Online: http://www.aviationsalary.com
Survey Period: 2009

AVJOB07

"A&P Mechanic Salaries, Wages and Pay," February 17, 2009.

Online: http://www.aviationsalary.com
Survey Period: 2009

AVWK

Carole R. Hedden, "A&D Workforce in Depth," *Aviation Week & Space Technology*, August 18, 2008, pp. 72-75.

Survey Period: 2007

Note: The Average Entry Wage (AE) is for engineers with 0 to 5 years experience. The Average Experienced Wage (AEX) is for engineers with 26 to 30 years experience.

AWS

"Taking the Plunge: A Guide to Starting an Underwater Welding Career," November 13, 2008.

American Welding Society
550 LeJeune Road
Miami, FL 33126
Telephone: (305) 443-9353
Fax: (305) 443-7559
Online: http://www.aws.org
Email: info@aws.org
Survey Period: 2008

Note: Data were downloaded on November 13, 2008 and were considered current by the source. Most welder-divers are paid on a project-by-project basis. In some cases welder-divers can earn more than $100,000 per year.

AZREP

Russ Wiles, "IRS Hiring in Phoenix," *The Arizona Republic*, February 2, 2009.

Online: http://www.azcentral.com
Survey Period: 2009

BALRA

Eva Wisnik, *Bay Area Legal Recruitment Association Salary Survey 2007*, 2007.

Survey Period: October 2007

BBERG

Christine Harper and Serena Saitto, "Broken Securities Industry Still Has $20 Billion to Pay Bonuses," *Bloomberg.com*, October 27, 2008.

Online: http://www.bloomberg.com
Survey Period: 2008

Note: Salary range includes the salaries for Wall Street bankers.

BBF

G. Scott Thomas, "Select Buffalo Salaries Among Nation's Best," *Buffalo Business First*, January 23, 2009.

Online: http://buffalo.bizjournals.com
Survey Period: 2009

BCPSSS

Dr. Faron Hollinger and Lester Smith, *Baldwin County Public Schools 2008-2009 Salary Schedule*, 2008.

Baldwin County Public Schools
Baldwin County Board of Education
2600 North Hand Avenue
Bay Minette, AL 36507
Telephone: (251) 937-0306
Online: http://www.bcbe.org
Survey Period: 2008-2009

Note: Salary data for Athletic Director, coaches and Band Director are supplemental pay amounts.

BDPLAN

Zelda Bronstein, "The Public Eye: Mayor Bates: Raise City Manager Salary to $232,020 (and Counting)," *The Berkeley Daily Planet*, January 21, 2009.

Online: http://www.berkeleydailyplanet.com
Survey Period: 2009

BEA

Peter B. Orlik, "2007-2008 National Salary Survey Results Broadcast Education Association," October 30, 2008.

Broadcast Education Association
1771 N Street, NW
Washington, DC 20036-2891
Telephone: (202) 429-3935
Online: http://www.beaweb.org
Email: BEAMemberServices@nab.org
Survey Period: September 2007-December 2007

BGLOBE

Alison Lobron, "Reawakening the Two-Party System in Mass.," *The Boston Globe*, February 4, 2009, p. A15.

Survey Period: 2009

BGLOBE1

Andrea Estes, "Umass Employees Top List of Highest-Paid State Workers," *The Boston Globe*, February 11, 2009.

Online: http://www.boston.com
Survey Period: 2008

BGLOBE2

Rachana Rathi, "Newton's Payroll Defies '08 Trend," *The Boston Globe*, February 4, 2009, p. B3.

Survey Period: 2008

BGLOBE3

Peter Schworm, "Umass Has Most of State's Top-Paid Workers," *The Boston Globe*, February 17, 2009.

Online: http://www.boston.com
Survey Period: 2009

Note: Salary data are rounded to the nearest dollar.

BGLOBE4

Brian R. Ballou, "Top Salaries at MSPCA Questioned," *The Boston Globe*, February 20, 2009.

Online: http://www.boston.com
Survey Period: 2009

Note: Data includes salary and benefits.

BHM

"Public Health Informatics Specialist," October 8, 2006.

Online: http://www.biohealthmatics.com
Survey Period: 2006

BIZJ01

Jane Meyer Brahm, "Companies Balk at High Starting Salaries for Associates," *Puget Sound Business Journal*, August 22, 2008.

Online: http://www.bizjournals.com
Survey Period: 2008

BMAG

Christina Breda Antoniades, "2009 Salary Survey," *Baltimore Magazine*, January 12, 2009.

Online: http://www.baltimoremagazine.net
Survey Period: 2009

Note: Data were downloaded on January 12, 2009.

BOM

Brandon Lorenz, "New Survey Reports on Industry Job Satisfaction, Job Security and FM Pay," *Building Operating Management*, October 28, 2008.

Online: http://www.facilitiesnet.com
Survey Period: May 2008-July 2008

Note: Data were downloaded on October 28, 2008.

BOPP01

"Salaries in the Parish Ministry: 2008 Salary Study," October 24, 2008.

Online: http://web.pensions.org
Survey Period: May 1, 2008

Note: Data were downloaded on October 23, 2008.

BPHARM

Laura Bush, "Satisfied, Well Paid, and Secure," *Biopharm International*, January 2008, pp. 38-41.

Survey Period: September 2007-December 2007

Note: Salary survey was conducted in the Fall of 2007.

BRADEH

Grace Gagliano, "Census to Hire 400-500 Workers Locally: Manatee, Sarasota Have Part-Time, Full-Time Postions," *Bradenton Herald*, January 6, 2009.

Survey Period: 2009

BROLL

Kevin Johnson, "b-roll.net Market Salary Survey," January 20, 2009.

Online: http://www.b-roll.net/info/salary/
Survey Period: 2009

Note: Data were downloaded on January 20, 2009 and were considered current by the source.

BSB

"Personnel Profile," *Body Shop Business*, May 2007, p. 58.

Survey Period: 2007

BSO

"New Contract, New Leadership, Bright Future," October 27, 2008.

Online: http://www.bsomusicians.org
Email: pc@bsomusicians.org
Survey Period: 2007-2008

Note: Data were downloaded on October 27, 2008.

BTN01

"BTN's 2008 Travel Manager Salary & Attitude Survey," *Business Travel News*, July 21, 2008.

Survey Period: 2008

BTRIB

Crystal R. Reid, "Bismarck-Mandan Fourth in Average Wages in North Dakota," *Bismarck Tribune*, January 14, 2009.

Survey Period: 2007

BUFN

Janice L. Habuda, "Most Officials Get Pay Raises, But Not Board," *Buffalo News*, January 6, 2009.

Survey Period: 2009

BUS201

"The Hottest Salaries," *Business 2.0*, April 7, 2007.

Online: http://money.cnn.com
Survey Period: 2005-2006

BUS202

Michael Copeland and Kevin Kelleher, "The New New Careers," *Business 2.0*, April 7, 2007.

Online: http://money.cnn.com
Survey Period: 2007

BUSFIN

Karen Kroll, "Second Life: Wall Street is Dead, and a New Breed of Treasurer is Being Born," *Business Finance*, October 2008, pp. 24-28.

Survey Period: 2008

BWEEK

Douglas MacMillan, "Highest IT Salaries: San Francisco, London," *BusinessWeek*, January 21, 2009.

Online: http://www.businessweek.com
Survey Period: 2008

BWEEK01

Kerry Miller, "Worst Jobs With The Best Pay," *BusinessWeek*, September 14, 2006.

Online: http://www.businessweek.com
Survey Period: 2006

BWEEK02

Judy Warner, "Directors' Pay: The Median is the Message," *BusinessWeek*, February 3, 2009.

Online: http://www.businessweek.com
Survey Period: 2008

BWEEK03

Ellen Gibson, "College Campuses Debate Administrators' Lofty Pay," *BusinessWeek*, February 16, 2009.

Online: http://www.businessweek.com
Survey Period: 2007-2008

CABLS

California Occupational Employment Statistics (OES) Survey Results, July 2008.

Employment Development Department
Labor Market Information Division
P.O. Box 826880, MIC 57
Sacramento, CA 94280-0001
Telephone: (916) 262-2162
Fax: (916) 262-2352
Online: http://www.calmis.ca.gov
Survey Period: January 2008-March 2008

Note: All data are provided by the State Employment Security Administration to the Occupational Employment Statistics (OES) survey conducted by the U.S. Department of Labor, Bureau of Labor Statistics. May 2007 Occupational Employment and Wage Estimates have been adjusted to the first quarter of 2008 using the Employment Cost Index.

CAC

California Association of Criminalists 2006-2007 Salary Survey, October 9, 2008.

California Association of Criminalists
California Department of Justice — Riverside
1500 Castellano Road
Riverside, CA 92509
Telephone: (909) 782-4170
Fax: (909) 782-4128
Online: http://www.cacnews.org
Survey Period: 2006-2007

Note: Data were downloaded on October 9, 2008.

CASW

"A Guide to Careers in Science Writing," *Council for the Advancement of Science Writing*, February 3, 2009.

Council for the Advancement of Science Writing
P.O. Box 910
Hedgesville, WV 25427
Telephone: (304) 754-5077
Online: http://casw.org/booklet.htm
Survey Period: 2008

Note: Data were downloaded on February 3, 2009.

CATHO

Ina Paiva Cordle, "Need a Good Job? Become a Police Officer," *Catholic Online*, December 30, 2008.

Online: http://www.catholic.org
Survey Period: 2008

CBSTV

Bennett Cunningham, "Big Spending, Big Salaries at DFW Airport," *CBS11TV.com*, September 24, 2008.

Online: http://cbs11tv.com
Survey Period: 2008

CBUILD

Mary Lorenz, "Five Jobs for Daredevils," *AOL Find a Job*, October 6, 2008.

Online: http://jobs.aol.com
Survey Period: 2008

CBUILD01

Selena Dehne, "Top 10 Low-Stress Jobs for Baby Boomers," *CareerBuilder*, September 10, 2008.

Online: http://www.careerbuilder.com
Survey Period: 2008

CBUILD02

Rachel Zupek, "15 'Normal' Jobs You Can't Pronounce," *CareerBuilder*, December 22, 2008.

Online: http://www.careerbuilder.com
Survey Period: December 2008

CBUILD03

Rachel Zupek, "10 Jobs Cooler Than Yours," *CareerBuilder*, March 12, 2009.

Online: http://www.careerbuilder.com
Survey Period: 2009

CCRUN01

"Nursing Salaries List," *College Crunch*, December 18, 2008.

Online: http://www.collegecrunch.org
Survey Period: 2008

CCRUN02

"52 Career Starting Salaries," *College Crunch*, November 2, 2008.

Online: http://www.collegecrunch.org
Survey Period: 2008

CCSS

Hourly Salary Schedule, February 20, 2009.

City of Carlsbad
1200 Carlsbad Village Drive
Carlsbad, CA 92008-1949
Telephone: (760) 434-2820
Online: http://www.carlsbadca.gov
Survey Period: January 1, 2008

Note: Data were downloaded on February 20, 2009. Salaries went into effect on January 1, 2008.

CCSS01

Salary Schedule — General Employees, August 21, 2008.

City of Carlsbad
1200 Carlsbad Village Drive
Carlsbad, CA 92008-1949
Telephone: (760) 434-2820
Online: http://www.carlsbadca.gov
Survey Period: August 5, 2008

Note: Salary data are biweekly and are rounded to the nearest dollar.

CEJ01

"2008 Physician Compensation Survey, by the American Medical Group Association (AMGA)," January 30, 2009.

Online: http://www.cejkasearch.com
Survey Period: 2008

Note: Data were downloaded on January 30, 2009.

CERT01

Daniel Margolis, et. al., "CertMag's 2007 Salary Survey," *Certification Magazine*, December 2007, pp. 18-31.

Survey Period: August 1, 2007-September 5, 2007

CERT02

Katherine Spencer Lee, "Hottest Jobs Involve Wireless and Mobile Technology," *Certification Magazine*, June 2008.

Online: http://www.certmag.com
Survey Period: 2008

CERT03

Agatha Gilmore, et. al., "Salary Survey 2008," *Certification Magazine*, December 2008, pp. 22-47.

Survey Period: 2008

CFR

"Computer Forensic Salaries by State," February 3, 2009.

Online: http://www.computer-forensics-recruiter.com
Survey Period: 2009

Note: Data were downloaded on February 3, 2009 and were considered current by the source.

CHAROB

Karen Sullivan, "CPCC's Pastry Program Sweet as Cherry Pie, or Torte, or …," *Charlotte Observer*, February 8, 2009.

Online: http://www.charlotteobserver.com
Survey Period: 2009

CHDHR01

"Musician I," January 15, 2009.

> Department of Human Resources, County of Hawai'i
> Aupuni Center
> 101 Pauahi Street, Suite 2
> Hilo, HI 96720
> **Telephone:** (808) 961-8361
> **Online:** http://co.hawaii.hi.us
> **Survey Period:** January 2009

CHDHR02

"School Crossing Guard," January 15, 2009.

> Department of Human Resources, County of Hawai'i
> Aupuni Center
> 101 Pauahi Street, Suite 2
> Hilo, HI 96720
> **Telephone:** (808) 961-8361
> **Online:** http://co.hawaii.hi.us
> **Survey Period:** January 2009

CHE

Audrey Williams June, "Law, Business, and Engineering Professors are Found to be Highest Paid," *Chronicle of Higher Education*, March 14, 2008, p. A10.

> **Survey Period:** 2007-2008

CHEMPR

Ken Schnepf, "How Much Do Chemical Engineers Make? Chemical Processing Reveals All in 2008 Salary Survey," *Chemical Processing*, October 28, 2008.

> **Online:** http://www.chemicalprocessing.com
> **Survey Period:** 2008

Note: Data were downloaded on October 28, 2008.

CHIRO

"11th Annual Salary & Expense Survey: Is This Year's Picture in Focus?" *Chiropractic Economics*, May 2008.

> **Online:** http://www.chiroeco.com
> **Survey Period:** 2008

CHITRI

"Comparison of Automakers' Wages, Labor Costs," *Chicago Tribune*, December 12, 2008.

> **Online:** http://archives.chicagotribune.com/
> **Survey Period:** 2008

Note: Salary data for Autoworkers do not include benefits. Toyota's wages do not include profit sharing. Honda's wages do include profit sharing.

CHNAV

"2008 CEO Compensation Study," *Charity Navigator*, August 1, 2008.

> Charity Navigator
> 1200 MacArthur Boulevard, Second Floor
> Mahwah, NJ 07430
> **Telephone:** (201) 818-1288
> **Fax:** (201) 818-4694
> **Online:** http://www.charitynavigator.org
> **Survey Period:** 2008

CHTW

Philip Mattera, *High Road or Low Road? Job Quality in the New Green Economy*, February 3, 2009.

> Good Jobs First
> 1616 P Street NW, Suite 210
> Washington, DC 20036
> **Telephone:** (202) 232-1616
> **Online:** http://www.changetowin.org
> **Survey Period:** 2008

CIA01

"Paramilitary Operations Officer/Specialized Skills Officer," *Careers at CIA*, November 13, 2008.

> Central Intelligence Agency
> Office of Public Affairs
> Washington, DC 20505
> **Telephone:** (703) 482-0623
> **Fax:** (703) 482-1739
> **Online:** http://www.cia.gov
> **Survey Period:** 2008

Note: Data were downloaded on November 13, 2008 and were considered current by the source.

CIA02

"Military Analyst," *Careers at CIA*, November 13, 2008.

> Central Intelligence Agency
> Office of Public Affairs
> Washington, DC 20505
> **Telephone:** (703) 482-0623
> **Fax:** (703) 482-1739
> **Online:** http://www.cia.gov
> **Survey Period:** 2008

Note: Data were downloaded on November 13, 2008 and were considered current by the source. Military analysts with the most experience can earn salaries greater than $90,698.

CIA03

"Polygraph Examiner," *Careers at CIA*, November 13, 2008.

> Central Intelligence Agency
> Office of Public Affairs
> Washington, DC 20505
> **Telephone:** (703) 482-0623
> **Fax:** (703) 482-1739
> **Online:** http://www.cia.gov
> **Survey Period:** 2008

Note: Data were downloaded on November 13, 2008 and were considered current by the source. Polygraph examiners with the most experience can earn salaries greater than $107,854.

CIRMGT

"The 2007 Circulation Salary Survey," *Circulation Management*, December 2007, pp. 34-37.

> **Survey Period:** 2007

CLEAD

David Farkas, "New Parameters for Payday," *Chain Leader*, September 1, 2008.

> **Online:** http://www.chainleader.com
> **Survey Period:** 2008

CLJOBS

Security Clearance Jobs Salary Survey Results, October 2008.

> **Online:** http://www.clearancejobs.com
> **Survey Period:** March 20, 2007-February 20, 2008

CNASTP

Albert Kim, "Comic Genius," *Condé Nast Portfolio.com*, April 28, 2008.

> **Online:** http://www.portfolio.com
> **Survey Period:** 2008

Note: According to the source, an elite comic book illustrator can earn $1,000 per page.

CNN01

Amy Sabha, "Postal Service Hits Back at Criticism of Postmaster's Pay," *CNN.com*, February 17, 2009.

> **Online:** http://www.cnn.com
> **Survey Period:** 2008

Note: Total compensation for the Postmaster General was nearly $800,000 in 2008.

CNNM

Chris Isidore, "GM Offers Buyouts to 74,000," *CNNMoney.com*, February 12, 2008.

> **Online:** http://money.cnn.com
> **Survey Period:** 2008

CNNM01

"25 Top Paying Companies," *CNNMoney.com*, January 23, 2009.

> **Online:** http://money.cnn.com
> **Survey Period:** 2009

Note: Data were last updated on January 23, 2009.

CNNM02

Jennifer Merritt, et. al., "Best Jobs in America: Young and Restless — Top 20 Jobs," *CNNMoney.com*, July 3, 2007.

> **Online:** http://money.cnn.com
> **Survey Period:** 2007

CNNM03

Jennifer Merritt, et. al., "Best Jobs in America: Retired from the Military — Top 20 Jobs," *CNNMoney.com*, July 3, 2007.

> **Online:** http://money.cnn.com
> **Survey Period:** 2007

CNNM04

Jennifer Merritt, et. al., "Best Jobs in America: If You're Over 50 — Top 20 Jobs for a Change," *CNNMoney.com*, July 3, 2007.

> **Online:** http://money.cnn.com
> **Survey Period:** 2007

CNYB

Gale Scott, "Black Nurses Earn Less Than Whites," *Crain's New York Business*, July 7, 2008-July 13, 2008, pp. 1, 6.

> **Survey Period:** May 2008

COD01

"DPS Superintendent Reprimanded by School Board," *ClickOnDetroit.com*, September 12, 2008.

> **Online:** http://www.clickondetroit.com
> **Survey Period:** 2008

COHSS

City of Cincinnati Salary Grade/Step Schedule, October 29, 2008.

> City of Cincinnati
> Human Resources Department
> 805 Central Avenue, Cent. II, Suite 200
> Cincinnati, OH 45202
> **Telephone:** (513) 352-2400
> **Fax:** (513) 352-5223
> **Online:** http://www.cincinnati-oh.gov
> **Survey Period:** October 2008

Note: Salary data are rounded to the nearest dollar.

COMMN

John Rossheim, "Nontraditional Jobs That Pay $100K," *comcast.net Jobs*, January 13, 2009.

> **Online:** http://content.comcast.monster.com/salary-trends/
> **Survey Period:** 2009

Note: Data were downloaded on January 13, 2009 and were considered current by the source. Salary for Semiconductor Fab Technician includes overtime.

COPIER

Scott Cullen, "2008 Sales Management Salary Survey," *Copier Careers*, May 2008.

>   **Online:** http://www.copiercareers.com
>   **Survey Period:** 2008

COPIER1

Scott Cullen, "2008 Service Technician Salary Survey," *Copier Careers*, May 2008.

>   **Online:** http://www.copiercareers.com
>   **Survey Period:** 2008

COPIER2

Scott Cullen, "2008 Service Manager Salary Survey," *Copier Careers*, June 2008.

>   **Online:** http://www.copiercareers.com
>   **Survey Period:** 2008

COSOC

"Oceanographers," January 26, 2009.

>   **Online:** http://www.oceancareers.com
>   **Survey Period:** November 2006

Note: Data were downloaded on January 26, 2009.

COSPRS

City of Colorado Springs — 2009 Salary Schedule, December 12, 2008.

>   City of Colorado Springs
>   107 North Nevada Avenue
>   Colorado Springs, CO 80901-1575
>   **Telephone:** (719) 385-CITY
>   **Online:** http://www.springsgov.com
>   **Email:** AskCity@SpringsGov.com
>   **Survey Period:** January 1, 2009

Note: Salary data became effective on January 1, 2009.

COWRLD

"Salary Survey 2008: Staff and Entry-Level Positions," *ComputerWorld*, November 10, 2008.

>   **Online:** http://www.computerworld.com
>   **Survey Period:** May 20, 2008-July 25, 2008

COWRLD1

"Salary Survey 2008: Middle Management," *ComputerWorld*, November 10, 2008.

>   **Online:** http://www.computerworld.com
>   **Survey Period:** May 20, 2008-July 25, 2008

COWRLD2

"Salary Survey 2008: Senior Management," *ComputerWorld*, November 10, 2008.

>   **Online:** http://www.computerworld.com
>   **Survey Period:** May 20, 2008-July 25, 2008

CPHIL

Holly Hall, "Salaries of Fund Raisers Rose by 5% Last Year, a New Study Finds," *The Chronicle of Philanthropy*, May 29, 2008, p. 1.

>   **Survey Period:** 2007

CPMS01

R. Craig Jerabek, "Schedule A: Elementary and Secondary Substitute Teacher Schedule," *Overseas Educators School Year 2007-2008 Salary Schedule*, August 1, 2007.

United States Department of Defense
Civilian Personnel Management Service
1400 Key Boulevard, Suite B200
Arlington, VA 22209-5144
Online: http://www.cpms.osd.mil
Survey Period: 2007-2008

CPSSS

"Miscellaneous Positions: Paytable 60," February 20, 2009.

Chicago Public Schools
Department of Human Resources
125 South Clark Street, 2nd Floor
Chicago, IL 60603
Telephone: (773) 553-1000
Online: http://www.cps-humanresources.org
Survey Period: July 1, 2006

Note: Salary data were downloaded on February 20, 2009. Salaries went into effect on July 1, 2006.

CRDB01

Julie Yolles, "Detroit Musicians Tune in Cash with Touring Productions," *Crain's Detroit Business*, February 8, 2009.

Online: http://www.crainsdetroit.com
Survey Period: 2009

Note: The union rate for Local 5 musicians is $151 per show. The wage is based on an eight-show performance week. Salary data are rounded to the nearest dollar.

CRDB02

"Border Patrol is Hiring," *Crain's Detroit Business*, February 8, 2009.

Online: http://www.crainsdetroit.com
Survey Period: 2009

CRDB03

Elizabeth Gardner, "Practice Managers' Dilemma: Cut Costs, Not Quality," *Crain's Detroit Business*, January 18, 2009.

Online: http://www.crainsdetroit.com
Survey Period: 2009

Note: Salary data include total compensation.

CRS01

Ida A. Brudnick, "Congressional Salaries and Allowances," *CRS Report for Congress RL30064*, October 1, 2008.

Congressional Research Service
Library of Congress
101 Independence Avenue, SE
Washington, DC 20540-7500
Online: http://www.thecapitol.net
Survey Period: 2007-2008

CRS02

Barbara L. Schwemle, "Legislative, Executive, and Judicial Officials: Process for Adjusting Pay and Current Salaries," *CRS Report for Congress RL33245*, July 28, 2008.

Congressional Research Service
Library of Congress
101 Independence Avenue, SE
Washington, DC 20540-7500
Online: http://senate.gov
Survey Period: January 2008

CRU01

"Cruise Ship Jobs — Casino, Croupier and Cashier," October 24, 2008.

Online: http://www.cruiseshipjob.com
Survey Period: 2008

Note: Data were downloaded on October 24, 2008 and were considered current by the source.

CRU02

"Cruise Ship Jobs — Deck Department," October 24, 2008.

Online: http://www.cruiseshipjob.com
Survey Period: 2008

Note: Data were downloaded on October 24, 2008 and were considered current by the source.

CRU03

"Cruise Ship Jobs — Photography Jobs," October 24, 2008.

Online: http://www.cruiseshipjob.com
Survey Period: 2008

Note: Data were downloaded on October 24, 2008 and were considered current by the source.

CRU04

"Cruise Ship Jobs — Spa and Beauty Salon Jobs," October 24, 2008.

Online: http://www.cruiseshipjob.com
Survey Period: 2008

Note: Data were downloaded on October 24, 2008 and were considered current by the source.

CSENET

"The Facts About Esthetician Careers," January 16, 2008.

Online: http://www.collegesearchengine.net
Survey Period: 2008

CSM01

"College Football Coaches Receive CEO-like Salaries," *The Christian Science Monitor*, September 22, 2008.

Online: http://www.csmonitor.com
Survey Period: 2008

CSM02

Gloria Goodale, "Video-gaming Strives for Respect. Is It a Sport?" *The Christian Science Monitor*, August 4, 2008.

Online: http://www.csmonitor.com
Survey Periód: 2006-2008

CSM03

Mark Trumbull, "Understaffed Fed Raises Worries," *The Christian Science Monitor*, June 17, 2008.

Online: http://www.csmonitor.com
Survey Period: 2008

CSSS

2008 Salary Schedule and Compensation Plan, February 14, 2008.

City of Seattle Personnel Department
Seattle Municipal Tower
700 5th Avenue, Suite 5500
Seattle, WA 98124-4028
Telephone: (206) 684-7999
Fax: (206) 684-4157
Online: http://www.seattle.gov
Survey Period: 2006-2008

CTBLS

Connecticut Occupational Employment & Wages: Statewide 2008, October 23, 2008.

Connecticut Department of Labor
Office of Research/OES Unit
200 Folly Brook Boulevard
Wethersfield, CT 06109
Telephone: (860) 263-6285
Fax: (860) 263-6263
Online: http://www.ctdol.state.ct.us
Email: dol.lmi@ct.gov
Survey Period: January 2008-March 2008

Note: All data are provided by the State Employment Security Administration to the Occupational Employment Statistics (OES) survey conducted by the U.S. Department of Labor, Bureau of Labor Statistics. May 2007 Occupational Employment and Wage Estimates have been adjusted to the first quarter of 2008 using the Employment Cost Index. The Average Entry Wage (AE) is the mean wage of the lowest third of the population, according to the source.

CTRLR01

"Staying Current: Controller Salaries at $114K at Cos. with 500 FTEs," *The Controller's Report*, November 2008, pp. 1-2.

Survey Period: February 2008

CTRLRPT

"Controller Salaries," *The Controller's Report*, March 2007, pp. 5-6.

Survey Period: March 2007

CUMGT

Karen Bankston, "Feeling the Squeeze?" *Credit Union Management*, July 2008, pp. 14-18.

Survey Period: 2008

CUMGT1

Karen Bankston, "Rough Road to Retirement?" *Credit Union Management*, December 2008, pp. 26-29.

Survey Period: 2008

Note: Salary data are for median base salary plus bonus.

CVERT

Mark Spaulding, "2008 Salary & Career Survey: Overworked...but Not Necessarily Underpaid," *Converting Magazine*, July 1, 2008.

Online: http://www.convertingmagazine.com
Survey Period: 2007

CVOICE

"County Clerk of Courts Asks for Pay Increase," *CitizensVoice.com*, October 14, 2008.

Online: http://www.citizensvoice.com
Survey Period: 2008

CWCA

"Average Capitol Pay Level at $61,000 a Year," *Capitol Weekly*, November 13, 2008.

Online: http://www.capitolweekly.net
Survey Period: 2008

CWRLD01

"7th Annual Salary Survey," *Coatings World*, November 2008, pp. 31-36.

Survey Period: 2008

DADM

Alan Dessoff, "8th Annual Salary Survey: A Guide to the Going Rate for Education Leaders Nationwide," *District Administration*, August 2008, pp. 22-30.

Survey Period: 2007-2008

DADV

Melinda Deslatte, "Commentary: Budget Plans Don't Include CEO's Salaries," *The Daily Advertiser*, January 19, 2009.

Online: http://www.theadvertiser.com
Survey Period: 2009

DATAM

James Maguire, "Inside the 'IT Salaries are Rising' Report," *Datamation*, February 17, 2009.

Online: http://itmanagement.earthweb.com
Survey Period: 2009

DEA

"Questions and Answers," November 13, 2008.

U.S. Drug Enforcement Agency
Office of Personnel
8701 Morrissette Drive
Springfield, VA 22152
Telephone: (800) DEA-4288
Online: http://www.usdoj.com
Survey Period: 2008

Note: Data were downloaded on November 13, 2008 and were considered current by the source.

DIETCEN

"2008 Salary Survey Results," October 28, 2008.

Online: http://www.dietitiancentral.com
Survey Period: 2008

Note: Data were downloaded on October 28, 2008.

DJS

Brian Braiker, "Dream Job: Yoga Instructor," *Salary.com*, October 21, 2008.

Online: http://www.salary.com/careers/
Survey Period: 2008

Note: Data were downloaded October 21, 2008 and were considered current by the source.

DMA01

Laura E. Vasilion, "DMA's 2008 Salary Survey: A Year of Promise," November 2008-December 2008.

Dietary Managers Association
406 Surrey Woods Drive
St. Charles, IL 60174
Telephone: (800) 323-1908
Fax: (630) 587-6308
Online: http://www.dmaonline.org
Survey Period: July 2008-August 2008

DNEWS01

"Southfield's Cost Cuts Would Favor Students," *The Detroit News*, April 6, 2008, p. 5C.

Survey Period: 2008

DNEWS02

Mike Wilkerson, "Metro Job Seekers Swamp Census Bureau System," *The Detroit News*, November 20, 2008.

Online: http://www.detnews.com
Survey Period: 2008-2009

DOD1

"Monthly Basic Pay Table," *Military Compensation*, January 7, 2009.

U.S. Department of Defense, Office of the Under Secretary of Defense for Personnel and Readiness
4000 Defense Pentagon
Washington, DC 20301-4000
Online: http://www.defenselink.mil
Survey Period: 2009

DOD2

"Reserve Pay for Four Drills," *Military Compensation*, January 7, 2009.

U.S. Department of Defense, Office of the Under Secretary of Defense for Personnel and Readiness
4000 Defense Pentagon
Washington, DC 20301-4000
Online: http://www.defenselink.mil
Survey Period: 2009

DOKL

Bryan Dean, "Staffing and Salary Top Oklahoma County Jail Woes: Fundsreport Cites Salary as Big Reason for Turnover," *Daily Oklahoman*, January 18, 2009.

Survey Period: 2009

DPOST

"Editorial: A 43 Percent Raise? In a Recession, It's Excessive. District Attorney Mitch Morrissey May Deserve Such a Big Pay Increase, but with People Losing Their Jobs, the Timing is Wrong," *The Denver Post*, January 7, 2009, p. B-14.

Survey Period: 2009

DPOST01

Jeremy P. Meyer, "DPS Chief a Bargain for District," *The Denver Post*, February 2, 2009.

Online: http://www.denverpost.com
Survey Period: 2008

DREG

Jason Clayworth, "4 Coaches in Top 6 for State Employee Salaries," *Des Moines Register*, November 2, 2008.

Online: http://www.desmoinesregister.com
Survey Period: 2008

DRJ01

"2007 Compensation Report," *Disaster Recovery Journal*, January 12, 2009.

Online: http://www.drj.com
Survey Period: 2006-2007

Note: Data were downloaded on January 12, 2009.

DSN01

Jim Frederick, "Pharmacy Pay Renews Surge," *Drug Store News*, September 8, 2008, p. 27.

Survey Period: 2008

DVM

James M. Lewis, "Veterinary Salaries Remain Modest — But Job Security's Great," *DVM Newsmagazine*, August 1, 2008.

Survey Period: 2008

EDES

Jay McSherry, "What's in Your Paycheck?" *Electronic Design*, October 23, 2008, pp. 26-31.

Survey Period: 2008

EDPUB

"AP and Guild Reach Tentative Agreement — 2% Raise Coming," *Editor & Publisher*, February 7, 2009.

Online: http://editorandpublisher.com
Survey Period: March 2009

Note: The salary for experienced newsperson went into effect on March 2, 2009.

EE01

Judy Bokorney, "Communicating with Your Boss is Important," *EE-Evaluation Engineering*, April 1, 2008.

Survey Period: 2008

ELCA

"Missionary Sponsorship," November 6, 2008.

Evangelical Lutheran Church in America
8765 West Higgins Road
Chicago, IL 60631
Telephone: (800) 638-3522
Fax: (773) 380-1465
Online: http://archive.elca.org
Email: info@elca.org
Survey Period: 2008

Note: Data were downloaded on November 6, 2008 and were considered current by the source. Salary data include housing, baggage shipment, pension, social security contributions, local transportation, and international travel. Missionary families' salary averages $79,000 per year.

ENR01

Bruce Buckley, "Market Shifts are Still Driving Up Costs as Candidates Hedge New Job Offers," *ENR: Engineering News-Record*, June 16, 2008, p. 65.

Survey Period: 2007

ENR02

Bruce Buckley, "Tight Labor Markets Push Wages Up," *ENR: Engineering News-Record*, September 29, 2008, pp. 39-42.

Survey Period: September 2008

Note: Salaries are a 20-city average.

EPROT

L.K. Williams, "2008 Salary Survey: Basic Training and Then Some," *Environmental Protection*, September 29, 2008.

Online: http://www.eponline.com
Survey Period: 2008

ESECP

James Maguire, "2009 Salaries for IT Security Professionals," *eSecurity Planet*, November 18, 2008.

Online: http://www.esecurityplanet.com
Survey Period: 2009

ETNEWS

John Guerriero, "Millcreek Township, Pa., Supervisors Get 3.75 Percent Pay Hike," *Erie Times-News*, January 7, 2009.

Survey Period: 2009

EWHOL

"Salary Survey Includes Electrical Workers," *Electrical Wholesaling*, September 1, 2008.

Survey Period: 2008

EXHC

"Medical Librarian," May 14, 2008.

American Dental Education Association
1400 K Street, NW, Suite 1100
Washington, DC 20005
Telephone: (202) 289-7201
Online: http://www.explorehealthcareers.org
Survey Period: May 2008

EZART

Sally Weaver, "Nurse Manager Salaries," *Ezine @rticles*, January 5, 2009.

Online: http://ezinearticles.com
Survey Period: 2009

EZART1

Roslyn J. Randle, "Wellness Coaching — The New Hourly Pay Boom for Wellness Coaches," *Ezine @rticles*, October 18, 2007.

Online: http://ezinearticles.com
Survey Period: 2007

FBI

"Special Agent Frequently Asked Questions," January 6, 2009.

Online: http://www.fbijobs.gov
Survey Period: 2009

Note: Data were downloaded on January 6, 2009 and were considered current by the source.

FBPACK

Pan Demetrakakes, "Packaging Salaries Outstrip Inflation," *Food & Beverage Packaging*, October 28, 2008.

Online: http://www.foodandbeveragepackaging.com
Survey Period: December 2006-December 2007

Note: Data were downloaded on October 28, 2008.

FCHF

"Fire Protection Engineers Among Highest Paid," *Fire Chief*, May 26, 2006.

Survey Period: 2006

FELS

"FELS Wage & Benefit Surveys," October 28, 2008.

    Farm Employers Labor Service
2300 River Plaza Drive
Sacramento, CA 95833
Telephone: (800) 753-9073
Fax: (916) 561-5696
Online: http://www.fels.org
Survey Period: 2008

Note: Data were downloaded on October 28, 2008.

FHA

"Facts About Florida's Health Care System — Updated Oct. 2008," October 2008.

    Florida Hospital Association
307 Park Lake Circle
Orlando, FL 32803
Telephone: (407) 841-6230
Survey Period: 2007

FIREH

Elizabeth Neroulas and Kevin Roche, "2005 National Run Survey, Part 4," *Firehouse Magazine*, September 2006, pp. 64-73.

    Survey Period: 2006

FLKK

Ryan McCarthy, "Marathon City Manager Burnett Up for Job Review: City Manager Could See Salary Bump," *Florida Keys Keynoter*, February 21, 2009.

    Survey Period: 2008

FLOOP

"Average Salary for a Music Producer," January 6, 2009.

    Online: http://free-loops.com
Survey Period: 2007

Note: Data were downloaded on January 6, 2009.

FOLIO

Joanna Pettas, "Salary by Category: Editorial Director," *Folio: The Magazine for Magazine Management*, July 29, 2008.

    Online: http://www.foliomag.com
Survey Period: 2008

FOLIO01

Joanna Pettas, "Advertising Sales Salary Survey," *Folio: The Magazine for Magazine Management*, June 2008, pp. 44-46, 48.

    Survey Period: February 25, 2008-April 9, 2008

FOLIO02

Vanessa Voltolina, "Circulation Manager," *Folio: The Magazine for Magazine Management*, December 4, 2008.

    Online: http://www.foliomag.com
Survey Period: August 12, 2008-September 24, 2008

FORB01

Steve McGookin, "Surprising Six-Figure Jobs: Near the Head of the Salary Class," *Forbes*, June 19, 2007.

    Online: http://www.forbes.com
Survey Period: 2007

FORB02

Klaus Kneale, "Six-Figure Jobs You Don't Need a College Degree For," *Forbes*, January 12, 2009.

Online: http://www.forbes.com
Survey Period: 2009

FRCOG

2009 Franklin County Wage and Salary Survey, December 29, 2008.

Franklin Regional Council of Governments
425 Main Street, Suite 20
Greenfield, MA 01301-3313
Telephone: (413) 774-3167
Online: http://www.frcog.org
Email: info@frcog.org
Survey Period: 2009

FREEP01

"Judicial Workers' Salaries Available to Web Users," *Detroit Free Press*, July 15, 2007, p. 4B.

Survey Period: 2007

FREEP02

"The Best Choices for Oakland County State House Seats," *Detroit Free Press*, October 15, 2008.

Online: http://www.freep.com
Survey Period: 2008

FREEP03

Steve Neavling, "Misuse of Macomb Township Supervisor's Office Probed," *Detroit Free Press*, October 15, 2008.

Online: http://www.freep.com/
Survey Period: 2008

FREEP04

"The Best Choices for Metro Area Judicial Seats," *Detroit Free Press*, October 23, 2008.

Online: http://www.freep.com/
Survey Period: 2008

FREEP05

"Tabulated Oakland County Results," *Detroit Free Press*, November 6, 2007.

Online: http://www.freep.com
Survey Period: 2007

Note: Berkley school board members receive $30.00 per meeting. Birmingham city commissioners receive $5.00 per meeting. Royal Oak city commissioners receive $20.00 per meeting. South Lyon school board members receive $30.00 per meeting.

FREEP06

Jennifer Dixon, "1st Class Perks for Airport Execs," *Detroit Free Press*, June 15, 2008, pp. 1A, 14A.

Survey Period: 2008

FREEP07

Chastity Pratt Dawsey, "Schools' Money Manager Praised," *Detroit Free Press*, February 1, 2009, p. B1.

Survey Period: 2009

FREEP08

"Tag! It's Not a Bad Time to be IT," *Detroit Free Press*, February 8, 2009, p. K1.

Survey Period: 2009

FREEP09

Kathleen Gray, "I Don't Want a Free Ride," *Detroit Free Press*, February 19, 2009, p. A11.

Survey Period: 2009

FREEP10

Kathleen Gray, "Census to Hire 4,000 Workers," *Detroit Free Press*, February 19, 2009, p. D1.

Survey Period: 2009

FREEP11

John Gallagher, "Despite Pain, Openings Remain," *Detroit Free Press,* April 5, 2009, pp. B1, B3.

Survey Period: 2009

FURNT

"Employees & Payroll, 2007," *Furniture Today*, September 8, 2008, pp. 24-25.

Survey Period: 2007

GACTY01

2008 Municipal Wage and Salary Survey: Public Safety, September 2008.

Georgia Department of Community Affairs
Office of Research
60 Executive Park South
Atlanta, GA 30329-2231
Telephone: (404) 679-4940
Online: http://www.dca.state.ga.us
Survey Period: 2008

GACTY02

2008 Wage and Salary Survey: Compensation of Elected County Officials, September 2008.

Georgia Department of Community Affairs
Office of Research
60 Executive Park South
Atlanta, GA 30329-2231
Telephone: (404) 679-4940
Online: http://www.dca.state.ga.us
Survey Period: 2008

GACTY03

2008 County Wage and Salary Survey: Public Works/Solid Waste Positions, September 2008.

Georgia Department of Community Affairs
Office of Research
60 Executive Park South
Atlanta, GA 30329-2231
Telephone: (404) 679-4940
Online: http://www.dca.state.ga.us
Survey Period: 2008

GACTY04

2008 Wage and Salary Survey: Compensation of Municipal Elected Officials, September 2008.

Georgia Department of Community Affairs
Office of Research
60 Executive Park South
Atlanta, GA 30329-2231
Telephone: (404) 679-4940
Online: http://www.dca.state.ga.us
Survey Period: 2008

GAMS

"Game Developer Debuts 2007 Salary Survey," *Gamasutra*, April 15, 2008.

Online: http://www.gamasutra.com
Survey Period: 2007

GCJR

Green Collar Jobs Roundtable Briefing Packet, May 24, 2008.

Urban Agenda
275 7th Avenue, 18th Floor
New York, NY 10001
Telephone: (212) 206-8747
Online: http://www.urbanagenda.org
Email: info@urbanagenda.org
Survey Period: 2008

GCM

"What Income Can You Expect?" *Greeting Card Markets*, October 28, 2008.

Online: http://www.greetingcardmarkets.com
Survey Period: 2008

Note: Data were downloaded on October 28, 2008 and were considered current by the source. Salary data are on a per card written basis.

GLDR01

"Salaries," October 8, 2008.

Online: http://www.glassdoor.com
Survey Period: October 2008

GLDR02

"Yahoo! Salaries," October 8, 2008.

Online: http://www.glassdoor.com
Survey Period: October 2008

GLKNO

2008 IT Skills and Salary Report: A Joint Study by Global Knowledge and TechRepublic, 2008.

Online: http://images.globalknowledge.com
Survey Period: October 11, 2007-October 26, 2007

GLKNO1

2009 IT Skills and Salary Report: A Comprehensive Survey from Global Knowledge and TechRepublic, 2009.

Online: http://downloads.techrepublic.com.com
Survey Period: October 20, 2008-November 11, 2008

GOSS

Teamsters Local 223, General Unit Employees Salary Schedule, February 20, 2009.

City of Gresham
1333 NW Eastman Parkway
Gresham, OR 97030
Telephone: (503) 661-3000
Online: http://www.greshamoregon.gov
Survey Period: January 1, 2009

Note: Data were downloaded on February 20, 2009. Salaries went into effect on January 1, 2009

GOSS01

Management, Supervisory, Confidential Salary Schedule, February 20, 2009.

City of Gresham
1333 NW Eastman Parkway
Gresham, OR 97030
Telephone: (503) 661-3000
Online: http://www.greshamoregon.gov
Survey Period: July 1, 2008

Note: Data were downloaded on February 20, 2009. Salaries went into effect on July 1, 2008.

GOUPS

Lynne P. Shackleford, "School Superintendents are Among Top Earners in Area," *GoUpstate.com*, February 15, 2009.

Online: http://www.goupstate.com
Survey Period: 2008-2009

GOVAUD

Jeff Litchfield, "Association of Local Government Auditors 2008 Salary Survey," May 30, 2008.

Association of Local Government Auditors
449 Lewis Hargett Circle, Suite 290
Lexington, KY 40503-3590
Telephone: (859) 276-0686
Online: http://www.governmentauditors.org
Survey Period: 2008

GRAM

"Salary Survey," *Graphic Arts Online*, April 8, 2008.

Online: http://www.graphicartsonline.com
Survey Period: 2006

HATAM

Earlesha Butler, "Judges Face Unfilled Promises," *Hattiesburg American*, February 2, 2009.

Online: http://www.hattiesburgamerican.com
Survey Period: July 2008

HBJ

"Survey: Houston Salaries to Rise for Some Job Seekers," *Houston Business Journal*, March 27, 2008.

Online: http://houston.bizjournals.com
Survey Period: 2008

HCC01

"Perfusionist," January 20, 2009.

Health Careers Center
Mississippi Hospital Association
116 Woodgreen Crossing
Madison, MS 39130-1909
Telephone: (601) 982-3251
Fax: (601) 368-3200
Online: http://www.mshealthcareers.com
Survey Period: 2009

Note: Data were downloaded on January 20, 2009 and were considered current by the source.

HCC02

"Admitting and Discharging Clerk," January 21, 2009.

Health Careers Center
Mississippi Hospital Association
116 Woodgreen Crossing
Madison, MS 39130-1909
Telephone: (601) 982-3251
Fax: (601) 368-3200
Online: http://www.mshealthcareers.com
Survey Period: 2009

Note: Data were downloaded on January 21, 2009 and were considered current by the source.

HCC03

"Cytogenetic Technologist," January 21, 2009.

Health Careers Center
Mississippi Hospital Association
116 Woodgreen Crossing
Madison, MS 39130-1909
Telephone: (601) 982-3251
Fax: (601) 368-3200
Online: http://www.mshealthcareers.com
Survey Period: 2009

Note: Data were downloaded on January 21, 2009 and were considered current by the source.

HCC04

"Pastoral Counselor," January 21, 2009.

> Health Careers Center
> Mississippi Hospital Association
> 116 Woodgreen Crossing
> Madison, MS 39130-1909
> **Telephone:** (601) 982-3251
> **Fax:** (601) 368-3200
> **Online:** http://www.mshealthcareers.com
> **Survey Period:** 2009

Note: Data were downloaded on January 21, 2009 and were considered current by the source.

HCC05

"Creative Arts Therapist," January 21, 2009.

> Health Careers Center
> Mississippi Hospital Association
> 116 Woodgreen Crossing
> Madison, MS 39130-1909
> **Telephone:** (601) 982-3251
> **Fax:** (601) 368-3200
> **Online:** http://www.mshealthcareers.com
> **Survey Period:** 2009

Note: Data were downloaded on January 21, 2009 and were considered current by the source.

HCCD01

"Blood Bank Technology-Specialist," *Health Care Careers Directory 2008-2009*, October 13, 2008.

> American Medical Association
> 515 North State Street
> Chicago, IL 60611
> **Telephone:** (800) 621-8335
> **Online:** http://www.ama-assn.org
> **Survey Period:** 2008

Note: Data were downloaded on October 13, 2008 and were considered current by the source.

HCHRON

Zen T. C. Zheng, "Emergency Management Office Positions Reclassified; County Raises Salaries, Changes Job Descriptions," *The Houston Chronicle*, January 15, 2009.

> **Survey Period:** 2009

HCOUR

Jeffrey B. Cohen, "Hartford Residents Approve City Council Salary Increases," *The Hartford Courant*, November 5, 2008.

> **Online:** http://www.courant.com
> **Survey Period:** 2008

HED01

"Faculty Median Salaries by Discipline and Rank (2007-08)," *HigherEdJobs.com*, October 2008.

> **Online:** http://www.higheredjobs.com
> **Survey Period:** 2007-2008

HERLD

Matt Garfield, "City Manager Gets Pay Raise, Rebuke from Councilman," *The Herald*, February 11, 2009.

> **Survey Period:** 2009

HERT

Nicole Brooks, "Ivy Tech in Bloomington, Ind., Seeks Salary Freeze for 2009," *Herald-Times*, January 2, 2009.

> **Survey Period:** 2008-2009

HISTORY

Robert B. Townsend, "Barely Keeping Up?" *Perspectives on History*, May 2008.

American Historical Association
400 A Street, SE
Washington, DC 20003-3889
Telephone: (202) 544-2422
Fax: (202) 544-8307
Online: http://www.historians.org
Survey Period: 2007-2008

HLIFE

Pat Murphy, "New Administrator's Job: Help Southfield Neighborhoods," *HOMETOWNlife.com*, October 9, 2008.

Online: http://www.hometownlife.com
Survey Period: 2008

HLIFE01

Karen Smith, "Berkley Officers Receive 2-Percent Raises," *HOMETOWNlife.com*, October 7, 2008.

Online: http://www.hometownlife.com
Survey Period: 2008

HOMECARE

"Salaries Under Siege," *HomeCare*, October 29, 2008.

Online: http://www.homecaremag.com
Survey Period: August 25, 2008-September 24, 2008

HOOPS

"2007-08 NBA Salaries," *Hoopsworld.com*, September 16, 2008.

Online: http://www.hoopsworld.com
Survey Period: 2007-2008

Note: Data were extrapolated using the full salary listing for the 2007-2008 season.

HPS

Chris Graham and Andy King, "The 2007 HPS Salary Survey," *Health Physics News*, March 2008, pp. 10-13.

Online: http://hps.org
Survey Period: 2007

HPURCH01

Rick Dana Barlow, "Glimmer of Hope Amid the Gloom: Salaries Continue Sliding, but Pay Hikes Rebounding," *Healthcare Purchasing News*, July 2008, pp. 20-21.

Survey Period: 2008

HRFOC

"HR Recruiters Lead in Salaries & Rewards," *HR Focus*, June 2008, pp. 5-6.

Survey Period: 2008

HTOD

Marc Valero, "Teacher Salaries Continue to Lag National Average," *Highlands Today*, January 3, 2009.

Survey Period: 2007-2008

HTT

James Mammarella, "Gains Seen in Salary Survey," *Home Textiles Today*, June 9, 2008.

Online: http://www.hometextilestoday.com
Survey Period: 2008

IAAPHQ

"Average Starting Salaries for Administrative Support Staff — 2008," January 30, 2009.

International Association of Administrative Professionals
105 NW Ambassador Drive
Kansas City, MO 64153
Telephone: (816) 891-6600
Fax: (816) 891-9118
Online: http://www.iaap-hq.org
Survey Period: 2008

Note: Data were downloaded on January 30, 2009.

IAI

"Salary Survey, 2007," October 29, 2008.

The Information Architecture Institute
Online: http://www.iainstitute.org
Survey Period: June 2007-October 2007

Note: Salaries were downloaded from the Excel file on October 29, 2008.

IHOOPS

"WNBA Basketball," *InsideHoops.com*, October 17, 2008.

Online: http://www.insidehoops.com/wnba/
Survey Period: 2008

Note: Data were downloaded October 20, 2008.

ILLOOP

"Salaries and Pensions," February 17, 2009.

Online: http://www.illinoisloop.org
Survey Period: 2009

Note: Data were downloaded on February 17, 2009 and were considered current by the source.

IMM

Woodruff Imberman, "Injection Molding Industry Salary Survey," *Injection Molding*, April 1, 2008.

Online: http://imm.plasticstoday.com
Survey Period: January 14, 2008-February 20, 2008

INPRIS

"Average Salary of a Crime Scene Investigator," October 27, 2008.

Online: http://www.insideprison.com
Survey Period: 2006

Note: Data were downloaded on October 27, 2008.

INSJ01

Andrea Ortega-Wells, "Insurance Journal's Exclusive Agency Salary Survey," *Insurance Journal*, March 12, 2007.

Online: http://www.insurancejournal.com
Survey Period: 2006

Note: Average salary range based on premium volume. The higher the premium volume, the higher the average salary of the line managers.

IOMA01

"Hospital Nurse Aides Earn More Than Nurse Aides in Other Fields," *Report on Salary Surveys*, February 2007, p. 8.

Survey Period: 2007

IOMA02

"4 Surveys Find Increased Competition & Pay for Engineering Professionals," *Report on Salary Surveys*, March 2007, pp. 1, 6-11.

Survey Period: 2007

IOMA03

"Study Covers Comp in Manufacturing Industry," *Report on Salary Surveys*, October 2008, p. 3.

Survey Period: 2008

IOMA04

"Study Shows Staff Positions Experiencing Greatest Salary Growth," *Security Director's Report*, November 2008, p. 8.

Survey Period: 2008

IOMA05

"Web Designer Salaries Vary Slightly by Skill," *Report on Salary Surveys*, November 2008, pp. 3-4.

Survey Period: 2008

IOMA06

"3 Surveys Examine Pay for Call Center Reps & Managers," *Report on Salary Surveys*, December 2008, pp. 1, 7, 10.

Survey Period: 2008

IOMA07

"Finance Pros See Mixed Pay Trends — But Companies Still Hiring," *Report on Salary Surveys*, December 2008, pp. 2-5.

Survey Period: 2009

IPL

"Salaries and Retirement Benefits of U.S. Presidents and Other Federal Government Employees," October 27, 2008.

The Internet Public Library, Drexel University
College of Information Science and Technology
3141 Chestnut Street
Philadelphia, PA 19104-2875
Online: http://www.ipl.org
Survey Period: 2008

Note: Data were downloaded on October 27, 2008 and were considered current by the source.

IREM01

"New Study Shows Rising Compensation Levels of the Accredited Residential Manager®," November 6, 2007.

Institute of Real Estate Management
430 North Michigan Avenue
Chicago, IL 60611
Telephone: (800) 837-0706
Fax: (800) 338-4736
Online: http://www.irem.org
Email: custserv@irem.org
Survey Period: 2006

Note: Press release.

ISHN01

Karen Jenkins, "State of the EHS Nation: Exclusive Results from ISHN's 23rd Annual White Paper," *Industrial Safety & Hygiene News*, January 2007, p. 24.

Survey Period: 2007

IWEEK

David Blanchard, "IndustryWeek's 2008 Salary Survey: Are You Worth What They're Paying You?" *IndustryWeek*, March 1, 2008.

Online: http://www.industryweek.com
Survey Period: 2008

IWEEK01

David Blanchard, "IndustryWeek's 2009 Salary Survey: Rebuilding Manufacturing from Scratch," *IndustryWeek*, March 1, 2009.

Online: http://www.industryweek.com
Survey Period: 2009

JEMS

David M. Williams, "JEMS 2008 Salary & Workplace Survey: So, Remind Me Again Why EMS is a Good Job?" *JEMS*, October 2008, pp. 49-64.

Survey Period: 2008

JEWEL

"JCK's Annual Salary Survey," *JCKonline.com*, November 2008.

Online: http://www.jckonline.com
Survey Period: 2008

JWRLD

Mike Belt, "Wage Survey Gives Salary Details: State's 10 Highest Paying Occupations Found in Health Care," *Journal-World*, September 25, 2008.

Survey Period: April 2007-June 2007

JYI

Aleksandra Dabkowska, "Interdisciplinary Science: Astrobiology," *The Journal of Young Investigators*, October 30, 2008.

Online: http://www.jyi.com
Survey Period: 2008

Note: Data were downloaded on October 30, 2008 and were considered current by the source.

KATC

"La. Teachers Need Raise to Keep Southern Average," *KATC.com*, January 22, 2009.

Online: http://www.katc.com
Survey Period: 2008-2009

Note: Data were downloaded on January 22, 2009.

KLIB

Holly Smith, "Administrators, Not Teachers, Reap Rewards of Increased School Spending," *Kansas Liberty*, January 5, 2009.

Online: http://www.kansasliberty.com
Survey Period: 2007-2008

Note: The original article was published on January 5, 2009. Data were updated on January 11, 2009.

KNOXN

Michael Collins, "TVA Salary Raise Blasted: Lawmakers Say Increasing CEO's Pay Now is Bad Timing," *Knoxville News Sentinel*, November 1, 2008.

Online: http://www.knoxnews.com
Survey Period: 2008-2009

KPSC

"Electrophysiology," February 9, 2009.

Online: http://residency.kp.org
Survey Period: 2008-2009

KYBLS

Kentucky Occupational Wages (OES), October 15, 2008.

> Office of Employment and Training
> Research and Statistics Branch
> 275 East Main Street
> Frankfort, KY 40621
> **Telephone:** (502) 564-7976
> **Fax:** (502) 564-2937
> **Online:** http://www.workforcekentucky.ky.gov
> **Survey Period:** 2008

Note: All data are provided by the State Employment Security Administration to the Occupational Employment Statistics (OES) survey conducted by the U.S. Department of Labor, Bureau of Labor Statistics. May 2007 Occupational Employment and Wage Estimates have been adjusted to 2008 using the Employment Cost Index. Data were downloaded on October 15, 2008.

LABLS

Louisiana Occupational Employment Wage Survey — 2008, September 30, 2008.

> Louisiana Workforce Commission
> 1001 North 23rd Street
> Baton Rouge, LA 70804-9094
> **Telephone:** (888) 302-7662
> **Online:** http://www.laworks.net
> **Survey Period:** January 2008-March 2008

Note: All data are provided by the State Employment Security Administration to the Occupational Employment Statistics (OES) survey conducted by the U.S. Department of Labor, Bureau of Labor Statistics. May 2007 Occupational Employment and Wage Estimates have been adjusted to the first quarter of 2008 using the Employment Cost Index.

LANDL

Marisa Palmieri, "Labor in Limbo," *Lawn and Landscape Magazine*, October 2007, pp. S14-S17.

> **Survey Period:** 2007

LAT01

Christian Berthelsen, "Orange County Sanitation District Manager's Salary Hike Raises a Bit of a Stink," *Los Angeles Times*, August 29, 2008.

> **Online:** http://www.latimes.com
> **Survey Period:** 2008

Note: Salary data include benefits.

LAT02

Swati Pandey, "Cash In, Mr. Chips," *Los Angeles Times*, March 9, 2008.

> **Online:** http://www.latimes.com
> **Survey Period:** 2005-2007

Note: Salary data include benefits.

LAT03

Jeremy Scahill, "Bush's Rent-an-Army," *Los Angeles Times*, January 25, 2007, p. A-23.

> **Online:** http://www.latimes.com
> **Survey Period:** 2007

LCPP

"Livingston County Public Payroll 2009," *Daily Press & Argus*, February 22, 2009.

> **Online:** http://www.livingstondaily.com
> **Survey Period:** 2009

LCT01

Martin Romjue, "Operators, Revenues Rise," *LCT Fact Book 2008-2009*, June 2008, pp. 26, 35-36.

> **Survey Period:** 2008

LEDGE

Georgia Pabst, "A Home for the Great Spirit: American Indian Parish Fights Closure," *Ledger-Enquirer.com*, October 27, 2008.

Online: http://www.ledger-enquirer.com
Survey Period: 2008

Note: Salary data include benefits.

LIBJ

Stephanie Maatta, "Placements & Salary Survey 2008: Jobs and Pay Both Up," *Library Journal*, October 15, 2008.

Online: http://www.libraryjournal.com
Survey Period: 2007

LLIFE

"Decline in Primary Care Physicians Correspondents to Lower Salaries," *Locum Life*, October 2008, p. 5.

Survey Period: 2008

LSJ01

"State of Michigan Salary Search," *Lansing State Journal*, October 20, 2008.

Online: http://db.lsj.com
Survey Period: June 2007

Note: Data were downloaded on October 20, 2008. Salary ranges are rounded to the nearest dollar.

LSJ02

"Michigan Supreme Court and Michigan Court of Appeals Salaries as of July 11, 2007 Presented on an Annualized Basis," *Lansing State Journal*, October 20, 2008.

Online: http://www.lansingstatejournal.com
Survey Period: July 11, 2007

Note: Data were downloaded on October 20, 2008. Average salaries were extrapolated.

LTEL

Liam Marlaire, "State Lawmakers Split on Salary Increase," *The Leader-Telegram*, January 4, 2009.

Survey Period: 2009

LVSUN

Cy Ryan, "Governor: Salary Cuts Possible, Any Tax Hike Must be Temporary," *Las Vegas Sun*, November 10, 2008.

Online: http://www.lasvegassun.com
Survey Period: 2008

MAG

Kevin Benson, "Harvest Season Weekly Report," October 2, 2008.

Online: http://www.michaglabor.org
Survey Period: October 2008

Note: The wage for a chestnut harvester was 50 cents per pound in October 2008.

MANDP

Joel Crews and Marjorie Troxel Hellmer, "Cold Cash," *Meat & Poultry*, July 2008, pp. 26-42.

Survey Period: 2008

MASS

"Average Salary by Job Title — FY 2008," January 6, 2009.

Online: http://www.mass.gov
Survey Period: 2008

Note: Salary data are for fiscal year 2008.

MCP

"The 13th Annual Salary Survey: IT Salaries on the Rise," *Microsoft Certified Professional Magazine Online*, September 2008.

Online: http://mcpmag.com
Survey Period: 2008

MDBLS

Maryland Occupational Wage Estimates, October 15, 2008.

Maryland Department of Labor, Licensing & Regulation
Office of Workforce Information and Performance
1100 North Eutaw Street, Room 316
Baltimore, MD 21201
Telephone: (410) 767-2250
Fax: (410) 767-2219
Online: http://www.dllr.state.md.us/lmi/wages/
Survey Period: March 2008

Note: All data are provided by the State Employment Security Administration to the Occupational Employment Statistics (OES) survey conducted by the U.S. Department of Labor, Bureau of Labor Statistics. May 2007 Occupational Employment and Wage Estimates have been adjusted to March 2008 using the Employment Cost Index. Data were downloaded on October 15, 2008.

MDES

"What's Hot, What's Not," *Machine Design*, April 21, 2008.

Online: http://machinedesign.com
Survey Period: 2008

MDOT

"MDOT Careers & Salary," October 20, 2008.

Online: http://www.michigan.gov
Survey Period: October 1, 2007

Note: Data were downloaded on October 20, 2008.

MEDEC01

Ken Terry, "2008 Exclusive Survey — Earnings: Good News for Primary Care Income," *Medical Economics*, August 1, 2008.

Online: http://medicaleconomics.modernmedicine.com/
Survey Period: 2007

MEP01

2008 Salary Survey Report, July 2008.

MEP Jobs
6200 Aurora Avenue, Suite 405E
Urbandale, IA 50322
Telephone: (888) 482-6025
Online: http://www.mepjobs.com
Survey Period: 2008

MGREEN

George! "Motown Voters Nix Mayor Pay Raise; Mayor Vows to Keep Trying," *Morristown Green*, November 4, 2008.

Online: http://www.nj.com
Survey Period: 2008

MHLTH01

Melanie Evans, "'We Just Don't Get a Slowdown': Not-For-Profit Execs Still See Wage Gains as Tax-Reporting Changes Loom," *Modern Healthcare*, July 28, 2008, p. S1.

Survey Period: 2008

MIOAKL01

2008 Salary Survey, Southeast Michigan Region, October 29, 2008.

Online: http://www.oakgov.com
Survey Period: 2008

Note: Data were downloaded on October 29, 2008.

MIOAKL02

2007 Production, Service, and Trade Wage and Salary Survey, Southeast Michigan Region, October 29, 2008.

Online: http://www.oakgov.com
Survey Period: 2007

Note: Data were downloaded on October 29, 2008.

MIOAKL03

2007 Engineering Survey, Southeast Michigan Region, October 29, 2008.

Online: http://www.oakgov.com
Survey Period: 2007

Note: Data were downloaded on October 29, 2008.

MJSENT

Patrick Marley, "State Fired, Then Rehired Tech Expert at Six-Figure Salary," *Milwaukee Journal Sentinel*, January 12, 2009.

Survey Period: 2009

MLBPA

Average Salaries in Major League Baseball 1967-2009, January 30, 2009.

Major League Baseball Players Association
12 East 49th Street
New York, NY 10017
Telephone: (212) 826-0808
Fax: (212) 752-3649
Online: http://hosted.ap.org
Survey Period: 2008

Note: Data were downloaded on January 30, 2009.

MLTCN01

Brett Bakshis, "Top Salaries Rise Further," *McKnight's Long-Term Care News*, August 2008, p. 1.

Survey Period: 2008

MLTCN02

"Salary Snapshot: Activity Director," *McKnight's Long-Term Care News*, September 2008, p. 74.

Survey Period: 2008

MLTCN03

"Salary Snapshot: Director of Dining/Food Services," *McKnight's Long-Term Care News*, October 2008, p. 72.

Survey Period: 2008-2009

MLTCN04

"Salary Snapshot: Admissions Coordinator," *McKnight's Long-Term Care News*, February 2009, p. 32.

Survey Period: 2008-2009

MLW

"Taken Under Advisement: Mass. Judges Making a Case for Another Salary Boost," *Massachusetts Lawyers Weekly*, February 11, 2008.

Survey Period: 2008

MMH

Corinne Kator, "Modern's First Salary Survey," *Modern Materials Handling*, June 2008, pp. 27-31.

Survey Period: 2008

MMH01

Allison Manning, "Workforce: Lower Turnover, Higher Wages for Warehouse Workers," *Modern Materials Handling*, September 29, 2008.

Online: http://www.mmh.com
Survey Period: 2008

MML

Jeff Markham, et. al., *2008 Municipal Salary and Benefits Survey*, June 2008.

Online: http://www.msgovt.org
Survey Period: 2008

MMM

Ben Comer, "Career & Salary Survey: Down in the Count," *Medical Marketing & Media*, September 2008, pp. 40-53.

Survey Period: 2008

MMTHLY

David Brauer, et. al., "Who Makes What?" *Minnesota Monthly*, January 2008.

Online: http://www.minnesotamonthly.com
Survey Period: 2008

MNBLS

Minnesota Occupation Employment Statistics, March 2009.

Minnesota Department of Employment and Economic Development
1st National Bank Building
332 Minnesota Street, Suite E200
Saint Paul, MN 55101-1351
Telephone: (651) 259-7114
Online: http://www.deed.state.mn.us/lmi/wages.htm
Email: deed.customerservice@state.mn.us
Survey Period: October 2008-December 2008

Note: All data are provided by the State Employment Security Administration to the Occupational Employment Statistics (OES) survey conducted by the U.S. Department of Labor, Bureau of Labor Statistics. May 2007 Occupational Employment and Wage Estimates have been adjusted to the fourth quarter of 2008 using the Employment Cost Index. Data were downloaded in March 2009.

MODPHY

"By the Numbers," *Modern Physician Online*, October 30, 2008.

Online: http://modernphysician.com
Survey Period: 2007-2008

MORNC

Nicole Radzievich, "Bethlehem City Council Grants Raise for Mayor: 3% Annual Pay Hike for Net 4 Years OK'd for Top Executive," *The Morning Call*, February 18, 2009.

Survey Period: 2009

MPEG01

"Majors Post Production Agreement," October 30, 2008.

Motion Picture Editor's Guild
7715 Sunset Boulevard, Suite 200
Hollywood, CA 90046
Telephone: (800) 705-8700
Fax: (323) 876-0861
Online: http://www.editorsguild.com
Survey Period: August 3, 2008-July 31, 2009

MPEG02

"Independent Post Production Agreement," October 30, 2008.

Motion Picture Editor's Guild
7715 Sunset Boulevard, Suite 200
Hollywood, CA 90046
Telephone: (800) 705-8700
Fax: (323) 876-0861
Online: http://www.editorsguild.com
Survey Period: August 3, 2008-July 31, 2009

MPEG03

"Feature Animation Agreement," October 30, 2008.

Motion Picture Editor's Guild
7715 Sunset Boulevard, Suite 200
Hollywood, CA 90046
Telephone: (800) 705-8700
Fax: (323) 876-0861
Online: http://www.editorsguild.com
Survey Period: August 3, 2008-July 31, 2009

MPEG04

"East Coast Majors Feature Agreement," October 30, 2008.

Motion Picture Editor's Guild
7715 Sunset Boulevard, Suite 200
Hollywood, CA 90046
Telephone: (800) 705-8700
Fax: (323) 876-0861
Online: http://www.editorsguild.com
Survey Period: August 3, 2008-July 31, 2009

MPEG05

"East Coast Independent Feature Agreement," October 30, 2008.

Motion Picture Editor's Guild
7715 Sunset Boulevard, Suite 200
Hollywood, CA 90046
Telephone: (800) 705-8700
Fax: (323) 876-0861
Online: http://www.editorsguild.com
Survey Period: August 3, 2008-July 31, 2009

MSHPSS

"Civilian Employee Salary Schedule," February 24, 2009.

Missouri State Highway Patrol
1510 East Elm Street
Jefferson City, MO 65102
Telephone: (573) 751-3313
Online: http://www.mshp.dps.missouri.gov
Survey Period: July 1, 2008

Note: Data were downloaded on February 24, 2009. Salaries became effective on July 1, 2008. Salary data are bimonthly and are rounded to the nearest dollar.

MSN01

Matthew Kirdahy, "Jobs That Earn a Surprising Six-Figures," *MSNBC.com*, February 1, 2009.

Online: http://www.msnbc.msn.com
Survey Period: 2009

Note: Article was updated February 1, 2009.

MSN02

Kristin Kalning, "Sure, It's a Cool Job. But Do Games Pay?" *MSNBC.com*, February 1, 2009.

Online: http://www.msnbc.msn.com
Survey Period: 2009

Note: Article was updated February 1, 2009.

MSN03

"Priests Asked to Help Pay Abuse Settlement," *MSNBC.com*, January 30, 2009.

   Online: http://www.msnbc.msn.com
   Survey Period: 2009

Note: Article was updated January 30, 2009.

MSN04

Chris Dannen, "What are the Best Jobs of 2008?" *MSNBC.com*, January 30, 2009.

   Online: http://www.msnbc.msn.com
   Survey Period: 2008

Note: Article was updated January 30, 2009.

MTSDB

Collective Bargaining Agreement Between The State of Montana, Board of Public Education; Montana State School for the Deaf and Blind; and Montana School for the Deaf and Blind Federation of Teachers Local #4027, MEA-MFT, AFT, AFL-CIO, December 5, 2007.

   Montana Department of Labor and Industry
   Employment Relations Division
   1805 Prospect
   Helena, MT 59601
   Telephone: (406) 444-2718
   Fax: (406) 444-4140
   Online: http://laborrelations.mt.gov/
   Survey Period: October 2008-June 2009

Note: Salary data for Goal Ball Coach are supplementary pay amounts.

NALC

"City Carrier Wage Schedule: Effective August 30, 2008," *Postal Record*, August 2008-September 2008, p. 112.

   National Association of Letter Carriers AFL-CIO
   100 Indiana Avenue, NW
   Washington, DC 20001-2144
   Telephone: (202) 393-4695
   Online: http://www.nalc.org
   Survey Period: August 30, 2008

Note: Salary data do not include overtime.

NAOT

"Orthotech Pay Increases by 3% in 2008," July 3, 2008.

   National Association of Orthopaedic Technologists
   8365 Keystone Crossing, Suite 107
   Indianapolis, IN 46240
   Telephone: (317) 205-9484
   Fax: (317) 205-9481
   Online: http://www.naot.org
   Email: naot@hp-assoc.com
   Survey Period: 2008

NASA

"Frequently Asked Questions," October 14, 2008.

   Online: http://www.nasa.gov
   Survey Period: 2008

Note: Data were downloaded on October 14, 2008 and were considered current by the source.

NAYGN

2007 Recruitment & Retention Benchmarking Survey Report, February 2008.

   North American Young Generation in Nuclear
   P.O. Box 10014
   La Grange, IL 60525
   Telephone: (877) 526-2946
   Online: http://www.na-ygn.org
   Survey Period: 2007

NBJ

Todd Stringer, "Education in Law, Sciences Pays Off for Patent Attorneys," *Nashville Business Journal*, December 19, 2008.

Online: http://nashville.bizjournals.com
Survey Period: 2008

NBREW

"Brewpubs Operational Survey," *The New Brewer*, September 2008-October 2008, pp. 55-61.

Survey Period: 2008

NBREW1

Pete Johnson, "The Results are in: BA's Packaging Brewers Survey," *The New Brewer*, January 2009-February 2009, pp. 55-64.

Survey Period: August 2008-September 2008

Note: Salary data is based on brewery size in barrels produced. Brewery managers working in breweries that produce 0-5,000 barrels receive an average salary of $42,700. The salary increases as the size of the brewery increases.

NCBSC

"Animal Behaviorist," January 26, 2009.

North Carolina Association for Biomedical Research
P.O. Box 19469
Raleigh, NC 27619-9469
Telephone: (919) 785-1304
Fax: (919) 785-1306
Online: http://www.aboutbioscience.org
Email: dhowles@ncabr.org
Survey Period: 2006

Note: Most animal behaviorists earn from $35,000 to $90,000, according to the source.

NCLW

Diana Smith, "N.C. Bar Assn. Targets Injustice of Low Judicial Salaries," *North Carolina Lawyers Weekly*, July 21, 2008.

Survey Period: 2008

NCSS

Fiscal Year 2008-2009 North Carolina Public School Salary Schedules, July 1, 2008.

North Carolina Department of Public Instruction
Financial & Business Services
301 North Wilmington Street
Raleigh, NC 27601
Telephone: (919) 807-3300
Online: http://www.ncpublicschools.org
Email: information@dpi.state.nc.us
Survey Period: 2008-2009

Note: Curriculum support and maintenance personnel salaries are rounded to the nearest dollar.

NDAY01

"10 Jobs with Great Employee Rewards," *Newsday.com*, February 1, 2009.

Online: http://www.newsday.com
Survey Period: 2009

NDLC01

"North Dakota League of Cities 2008 Salary Survey: Cities 1,000 and Over," October 20, 2008.

North Dakota League of Cities
410 East Front Avenue
Bismarck, ND 58504
Telephone: (701) 223-3518
Fax: (701) 223-5174
Online: http://www.ndlc.org
Survey Period: 2008

NDLC02

"North Dakota League of Cities 2008 Salary Survey: Cities Under 1,000," October 20, 2008.

North Dakota League of Cities
410 East Front Avenue
Bismarck, ND 58504
Telephone: (701) 223-3518
Fax: (701) 223-5174
Online: http://www.ndlc.org
Survey Period: 2008

NEAT

"The Leverage of a Wage Campaign," *NEA Today*, November 1, 2008.

Survey Period: 2008

NEST

State of Nebraska Personnel Almanac, Twenty Fourth Edition, July 2008.

State Personnel Division
Department of Administrative Services
P.O. Box 94905
Lincoln, NE 68509-4905
Fax: (402) 471-8392
Online: http://www.nlc.state.ne.us
Survey Period: 2008

NEWG

"2008 Reporter Top Salaries," January 20, 2009.

The Newspaper Guild
501 3rd Street NW
Washington, DC 20001-2797
Telephone: (202) 434-7177
Fax: (202) 434-1472
Online: http://newsguild.org/scales/index.php?ID=4937
Email: guild@cwa-union.org
Survey Period: 2008

Note: Data were downloaded on January 20, 2009. Salary data are rounded to the nearest dollar. Salaries represent minimum levels of pay according to the individual Newspaper Guild collective bargaining agreements with the magazines and newspapers.

NFDA

Celine Clark and Jessica Koth, "NFDA Releases Results of Member Compensation Survey," April 15, 2008.

National Funeral Directors Association
13625 Bishop's Drive
Brookfield, WI 53005-6607
Telephone: (800) 228-6332
Fax: (262) 789-6977
Online: http://www.nfda.org
Email: nfda@nfda.org
Survey Period: 2006

Note: Press release.

NHBLS

New Hampshire Occupational Employment & Wages — 2008, September 25, 2008.

> Economic and Labor Market Information Bureau
> New Hampshire Employment Security
> 32 South Main Street
> Concord, NH 03301
> **Telephone:** (603) 228-4124
> **Fax:** (603) 228-4172
> **Online:** http://www.nh.gov
> **Email:** elmi@nhes.nh.gov
> **Survey Period:** June 2008

Note: All data are provided by the State Employment Security Administration to the Occupational Employment Statistics (OES) survey conducted by the U.S. Department of Labor, Bureau of Labor Statistics. May 2007 Occupational Employment and Wage Estimates have been adjusted to June 2008 using the Employment Cost Index. The Average Entry Wage (AE) is the mean wage of the lowest third of the population and the Average Experienced Wage (AEX) is the mean wage of the top two-thirds of the population, according to the source.

NHERLD1

Rene Cizio, "Allen Park: City Prepares for Development," *The News Herald*, January 2, 2009.

> **Online:** http://www.thenewsherald.com
> **Survey Period:** 2009

NHERLD2

Jason Alley, "Lincoln Park: Department Heads Reappointed," *The News Herald*, January 2, 2009.

> **Online:** http://www.thenewsherald.com
> **Survey Period:** 2009

NHERLD3

Dave Gorgon, "Taylor: Election Worker is an Iron Woman," *The News Herald*, November 4, 2008.

> **Online:** http://www.thenewsherald.com
> **Survey Period:** 2008

NHERLD4

Anne Sullivan, "Taylor: Info Packets Available for Those Eyeing Public Office," *The News Herald*, February 6, 2009.

> **Online:** http://www.thenewsherald.com
> **Survey Period:** 2009

NHERLD5

Jason Alley, "Lincoln Park: Mayor's Holiday Cards Questioned," *The News Herald*, January 17, 2009.

> **Online:** http://www.thenewsherald.com
> **Survey Period:** 2009

NHUL01

Michael Cousineau, "UNH Coach Umile Tops Pay List," *New Hampshire Union Leader*, January 25, 2009.

> **Online:** http://www.unionleader.com
> **Survey Period:** 2008

Note: Salary data are base salaries and do not include deferred compensation.

NHUL02

Michael Cousineau, "Hefty Paycheck on the Way Out the Door for Budget Assistant," *New Hampshire Union Leader*, January 25, 2009.

> **Online:** http://www.unionleader.com
> **Survey Period:** 2008

NHUL03

"State of New Hampshire 2008 Annual Salaries," January 26, 2009.

Online: http://www.unionleader.com
Survey Period: 2008

Note: Data were downloaded on January 26, 2009. Average wage data were extrapolated by the editor. High wages are actual wages of employees in state government.

NOAO

"Frequently Asked Questions About…Being an Astronomer," November 6, 2008.

National Optical Astronomy Observatory
950 North Cherry Avenue
Tucson AZ 85719
Telephone: (520) 318-8000
Online: http://www.noao.edu
Survey Period: 2008

Note: Data were downloaded on November 6, 2008 and were considered current by the source.

NTOP

Nathan Key, "Rolling Back Salaries: The Real Effect," *News-Topic*, February 15, 2009.

Survey Period: November 2008

Note: Salary data are rounded to the nearest dollar.

NVBLS

Nevada 2008 Occupational Employment and Wages, January 2009.

Nevada Department of Employment, Training & Rehabilitation
Information Development & Processing Division, Research and Analysis Bureau
500 East Third Street
Carson City, NV 89713
Telephone: (775) 684-0450
Online: http://detr.state.nv.us/lmi/
Survey Period: May 2008

Note: All data are provided by the State Employment Security Administration to the Occupational Employment Statistics (OES) survey conducted by the U.S. Department of Labor, Bureau of Labor Statistics. May 2007 Occupational Employment and Wage Estimates have been adjusted to May 2008 using the Employment Cost Index. Data were downloaded in January 2009.

NWRLD

Beth Schultz, "Annual Raises Fall Short, Leaving IT Pros to Grin and Bear," *NetworkWorld*, January 5, 2009.

Online: http://www.networkworld.com
Survey Period: 2009

NYDN

Alison Gendar, "Bigger NYPD Salaries Lead to a Surge in New Police Recruits," *New York Daily News*, October 12, 2008.

Online: http://www.nydailynews.com
Survey Period: 2008

Note: Starting salary in the police academy is $41,975. After six months, the salary increases to $43,644.

NYDN01

Andy Martino, "Arena Football League Players Cry Foul at Owners, Try to Survive Shutdown," *New York Daily News*, January 21, 2009.

Online: http://www.nydailynews.com
Survey Period: 2008

Note: Most Arena Football League players earned between $40,000 and $50,000 per season.

NYPH

Susan Evans, Ph. D., *Training Programs in Clinical Psychology: 2008-2009*, February 16, 2009.

Online: http://nypsychiatry.com
Survey Period: 2007-2008

Note: Data were downloaded on February 16, 2009.

NYT01

David Koeppel, "To Land a High-Paying Job, Some Try an Executive Coach," *The New York Times*, May 13, 2007, p. 5.

Survey Period: 2007

NYT02

Harry Hurt III, "Executive Pursuits: Paper Balanchine," *The New York Times*, March 10, 2007, p. B5.

Survey Period: 2007

NYT03

Steven Greenhouse, "Tomato Pickers' Wages Fight Faces Obstacles," *The New York Times*, December 24, 2007.

Online: http://www.nytimes.com
Survey Period: 2007

Note: Wages for tomato pickers in 2007 were 45 cents per 32-pound bucket of tomatoes. In 1980, wages were 40 cents per 32-pound bucket.

NYT04

Harry Hurt III, "Executive Pursuits: Drag, Water, Repeat: Caring for Major League Dirt," *The New York Times*, June 28, 2008, p. B5.

Survey Period: 2008

NYT05

Michael Winerip, "Generation B: Still Doing the Math, but for $100K a Year," *The New York Times*, February 1, 2009.

Online: http://www.nytimes.com
Survey Period: 2009

Note: The salary for a teacher with 30 years experience in New York City is $100,000.

NYT06

Adam Liptak, "On the Subject of Judicial Salaries, a Sharp Difference of Opinion," *The New York Times*, January 20, 2009, p. A14.

Survey Period: 2006

NYT07

Sarah Wheaton, "Congress Cuts a Salary; Helping Hillary Clinton," *The New York Times*, December 11, 2008.

Online: http://www.nytimes.com
Survey Period: 2009

NYT08

Ben Geman and Katherine Ling, "Senate Energy Policy Mark-up Begins, but Heavy Lifting is Weeks Away," *The New York Times*, March 30, 2009.

Online: http://www.nytimes.com
Survey Period: 2009

OCREG

Tony Saavedra, "Boy Scouts Cut $600,000 and 11 Positions," *The Orange County Register*, June 5, 2008.

Online: http://www.ocregister.com
Survey Period: 2008

ODAS

Pay Range Classification Booklet, July 1, 2008.

Online: http://das.ohio.gov
Survey Period: 2008

ODEQSS

"Salary Schedule," November 20, 2008.

Oregon Department of Environmental Quality
811 SW 6th Avenue
Portland, OR 97204-1390
Telephone: (800) 452-4011
Fax: (503) 229-6124
Online: http://www.deq.state.or.us
Email: deq.info@deq.state.or.us
Survey Period: November 1, 2008

Note: Salaries became effective on November 1, 2008.

OHCS

"Veterinary Toxicologist," May 8, 2008.

Ohio Hiring Management System
Telephone: (800) 409-1205
Online: http://agency.governmentjobs.com
Email: careers@ohio.gov
Survey Period: May 2008

Note: Salary data are rounded to the nearest dollar.

OMAG

Sari Harrar, "Medical Bills: Let Someone Else Fight Your Battles," *O, The Oprah Magazine*, January 2008, pp. 119-120.

Survey Period: 2008

OOH01

"Science Technicians," *Occupational Outlook Handbook 2008-09 Edition*, 2008.

U.S. Bureau of Labor Statistics
Office of Occupational Statistics and Employment Projections
2 Massachusetts Avenue, NE, Suite 2135
Washington, DC 20212-0001
Telephone: (202) 691-5700
Fax: (202) 691-5745
Online: http://www.bls.gov
Survey Period: 2007

OOH02

"Interpreters and Translators," *Occupational Outlook Handbook 2008-09 Edition*, 2008.

U.S. Bureau of Labor Statistics
Office of Occupational Statistics and Employment Projections
2 Massachusetts Avenue, NE, Suite 2135
Washington, DC 20212-0001
Telephone: (202) 691-5700
Fax: (202) 691-5745
Online: http://www.bls.gov
Survey Period: 2007

OOH03

"Biological Scientists," *Occupational Outlook Handbook 2008-09 Edition*, 2008.

    U.S. Bureau of Labor Statistics
Office of Occupational Statistics and Employment Projections
2 Massachusetts Avenue, NE, Suite 2135
Washington, DC 20212-0001
Telephone: (202) 691-5700
Fax: (202) 691-5745
Online: http://www.bls.gov/oco/pdf/ocos047.pdf
Survey Period: 2007

OOSE01

"Athletic Trainer," *LifeWorks*, October 30, 2008.

    National Institutes of Health
Office of Science Education
Bethesda, MD 20892
Online: http://science.education.nih.gov
Survey Period: May 2006

Note: Data were downloaded on October 30, 2008.

OOSE02

"Electroneurodiagnostic Technologist," *LifeWorks*, October 30, 2008.

    National Institutes of Health
Office of Science Education
Bethesda, MD 20892
Online: http://science.education.nih.gov
Survey Period: 2006

Note: Data were downloaded on October 30, 2008.

OOSE03

"Science Writer," *LifeWorks*, October 30, 2008.

    National Institutes of Health
Office of Science Education
Bethesda, MD 20892
Online: http://science.education.nih.gov
Survey Period: 2006

Note: Data were downloaded on October 30, 2008.

OPM01

"Executive Order 13454 Adjustments of Certain Rates of Pay," October 27, 2008.

    U.S. Office of Personnel Management
1900 E Street NW
Washington, DC 20415
Telephone: (202) 606-1800
Online: http://www.opm.gov
Email: General@opm.gov
Survey Period: January 1, 2008

Note: Data were downloaded on October 27, 2008.

OPOL

John A. Challenger, "Looking for a Job? Go Green Collar," *Office-Politics*, August 10, 2008.

    Online: http://www.officepolitics.com
Survey Period: 2008

ORBLS

2008 Oregon Wage Information: Statewide & Regional, June 2008.

> Oregon Employment Department
> Workforce and Economic Research
> 875 Union Street NE
> Salem, OR 97311
> **Telephone:** (503) 947-1261
> **Online:** http://www.qualityinfo.org
> **Email:** lmipubs.emp@state.or.us
> **Survey Period:** May 2008

Note: All data are provided by the State Employment Security Administration to the Occupational Employment Statistics (OES) survey conducted by the U.S. Department of Labor, Bureau of Labor Statistics. May 2007 Occupational Employment and Wage Estimates have been adjusted to May 2008 using the Employment Cost Index. Data were downloaded on October 15, 2008.

OSENT

Lauren Ritchie, "Tiny Groveland's Big Council Salaries are Poor Use of Taxpayer Cash," *Orlando Sentinel*, November 5, 2008.

> **Online:** http://www.orlandosentinel.com/
> **Survey Period:** 2008

OSTATE

"How Much Do Volcanologists Make?" October 27, 2008.

> **Online:** http://volcano.oregonstate.edu
> **Survey Period:** 2008

Note: Data were downloaded on October 27, 2008 and were considered current by the source.

PARD01

Meg Massey, "How Much Do the VP Candidates Earn?" *PARADE*, October 7, 2008.

> **Online:** http://www.parade.com
> **Survey Period:** 2008

PARD02

Lynn Brenner, "How Does Your Salary Stack Up?" *PARADE*, April 13, 2008.

> **Online:** http://www.parade.com
> **Survey Period:** 2008

PCHIEF

Jeff Tucker, "Realignment Could Save Pueblo Almost $325,000; City Council President Details Savings Through a Combination of Moves That Eliminates Salaries for Four Positions in 2009," *Pueblo Chieftain*, February 18, 2009.

> **Survey Period:** 2009

PCMAN

"Independent Pharmacists' Average Salary: $109,618," November 3, 2008.

> Pharmaceutical Care Management Association
> 601 Pennsylvania Avenue, NW, Suite 740
> Washington, DC 20004
> **Telephone:** (202) 207-3610
> **Fax:** (202) 207-3623
> **Online:** http://www.pcmanet.org
> **Email:** info@pcmanet.org
> **Survey Period:** 2008

PCMEM

Monique A. Moyer, "Memorandum," September 4, 2008.

> **Online:** http://www.sfgov.org
> **Survey Period:** 2008

Note: Memorandum was prepared by Lavena Holmes-Williams.

PGRAPH

Phyllis Coulter, "B-N Teacher Salaries Stack Up Well, Though Economy Complicates Talks," *Pantagraph*, February 14, 2009.

Survey Period: October 2008

Note: Some teachers in the district earn more than $90,000 per year.

PHBJ

Mike Sunnucks, "Corporate Board Pay Increases Despite Economy," *Phoenix Business Journal*, December 9, 2008.

Online: http://phoenix.bizjournals.com
Survey Period: 2008

PLANTE

Bob Vavra, "Productivity, Salary Gains Support Manufacturing Growth," *Plant Engineering*, January 15, 2008.

Online: http://www.plantengineering.com
Survey Period: 2007

PLIVE

Al Winn, "Council Moves to Raise Lebanon Mayor's Salary," *The Patriot-News*, May 22, 2008.

Online: http://www.pennlive.com
Survey Period: 2008

PMGT

"2007 Manager Salaries," *Public Management*, April 2008, p. 41.

Survey Period: 2007

PPGAZ

Ron Cook, "Successful Coaches Deserve High-End Salaries," *Pittsburgh Post-Gazette*, February 24, 2009.

Online: http://www.post-gazette.com
Survey Period: 2009

PRINC

Willa D. Cooke and Chris Licciardi, "Principals' Salaries, 2007-2008," *Principal*, May 2008-June 2008, pp. 46-51.

Survey Period: 2007-2008

PRN01

"2009 Robert Half Salary Guides Identify Job Market Bright Spots: Research Reveals In-Demand Accounting, Technology and Office-Support Positions," *PRNewswire*, October 23, 2008.

Online: http://www.prnewswire.com
Survey Period: 2009

PRN02

"The Rich Get Richer: PARADE's 25th Annual 'What People Earn' Salary Survey Finds Celebs, CEOs, Athletes and… a Dog…are Raking in the Dough," *PRNewswire*, April 10, 2008.

Survey Period: 2008

PROMO

Larry Jaffee, "24/7: Promo Marketers' Salary Survey," *PROMO*, July 1, 2007.

Online: http://www.promomagazine.com
Survey Period: May 9, 2007-May 23, 2007

PSEARCH

"Physician Compensation Survey — In Practice Three Plus Years," October 1, 2008.

Physician Search
5581 East Stetson Court
Anaheim, CA 92807-4650
Telephone: (800) 748-6320
Online: http://www.physicianssearch.com
Survey Period: 2008

Note: Data were downloaded on October 1, 2008 and were considered current by the source.

PSTAN

Meghan Rubado, "A Week After Getting Pay Increase, Syracuse Garage Workers See Their Hours Cut," *The Post Standard*, December 22, 2008.

Online: http://blog.syracuse.com
Survey Period: 2008

QDIG

Mike Richmond, "2008 Salary Survey," *Quality Digest*, August 2008, pp. 36-39.

Survey Period: 2008

QUAL

Gillian Campbell, "Quality Professionals Still Satisfied: Notwithstanding the Challenges, Quality Professionals are Still Satisfied with Their Jobs, According to Annual Survey," *Quality*, July 2008, pp. 54-58.

Survey Period: 2008

RADM

Erin Shipps, "Salary Survey," *Radio Magazine*, October 1, 2008.

Online: http://www.radiomagazine.com
Survey Period: 2008

RCITY

Mary Anna Towler, "Politics: Governor Hands Out Goodies While State Suffers," *Rochester City Newspaper*, February 17, 2009.

Online: http://rochestercitynewspaper.com
Survey Period: 2009

RD01

Cathie Gandel, et. al., "9 Recession-Proof Careers," *Reader's Digest*, March 2009.

Online: http://www.rd.com
Survey Period: 2009

REDMAG

Michael Domingo, "Cover Story: IT Salaries on the Rise," *Redmondmag.com*, September 2008.

Online: http://redmondmag.com
Survey Period: 2008

RFIDU

"'RFID Strategist' Named as a Top In-Demand Executive Job," *RFID Update*, February 10, 2005.

Online: http://www.rfidupdate.com
Survey Period: 2005

RGJ

Susan Voyles, "Reno Struggles to Pay Competitive Wages in Poor Economy," *Reno Gazette-Journal*, October 27, 2008.

Online: http://www.rgj.com
Survey Period: 2008

RIM01

Chris Museler, "Salary Survey 2009," *Rhode Island Monthly*, February 2009.

Online: http://www.rimonthly.com
Survey Period: 2009

RIMAG

Derek Gale, "Mean Salaries: Is Foodservice's Low Pay Balanced by Growth Opportunity?" *Restaurants & Institutions*, June 19, 2007.

Online: http://www.rimag.com
Survey Period: 2007

RIMS

"2008 Risk Management Compensation Survey Executive Summary," October 24, 2008.

Risk and Insurance Management Society, Inc.
1065 Avenue of the Americas, 13th Floor
New York, NY 10018
Telephone: (212) 286-9292
Online: http://www.rims.org
Survey Period: May 5, 2008-June 30, 2008

Note: Press release.

RORB

"Public, Private Sectors Seek Digital Asset Manager," *RedOrbit*, February 8, 2009.

Online: http://www.redorbit.com
Survey Period: 2009

RTODAY

"2007 Technologist Salary Survey," *Radiology Today*, May 7, 2007, p. 24.

Online: http://www.radiologytoday.net
Survey Period: 2007

SAANYS

"Average Administrative Salary by Title," January 30, 2009.

School Administrators Association of New York State
8 Airport Park Boulevard
Albany Airport Park
Latham, NY 12110
Telephone: (518) 782-0600
Fax: (518) 782-9552
Online: http://www.saanys.org
Survey Period: September 11, 2008

Note: Data were downloaded on January 30, 2009. Salaries are rounded to the nearest dollar.

SABJ

Catherine Dominguez, "IT Starting Salaries Here Lag National Average, but BRAC Offers Hope," *San Antonio Business Journal*, February 22, 2008.

Online: http://sanantonio.bizjournals.com
Survey Period: 2008

SAEN

Melissa Ludwig, "Paying the Price for a Hot Career," *San Antonio Express-News*, January 21, 2009.

Online: http://www.mysanantonio.com
Survey Period: 2009

Note: Salary data are for a nursing professor with a master's degree.

SAG01

"2005-2008 TV-Theatrical Rates," July 2005.

Screen Actors Guild
5757 Wilshire Boulevard, 7th Floor
Los Angeles, CA 90036-3600
Telephone: (323) 954-1600
Online: http://www.sag.org
Survey Period: July 1, 2007-June 30, 2008

SALEX

"Salary Survey Summary Data for Astronomer," *Salary Expert*, July 11, 2008.

SalaryExpert.com
9817 NE 54th Street, Suite 101
Vancouver, WA 98662
Telephone: (877) 799-3427
Fax: (360) 733-5550
Online: http://www.salaryexpert.com
Survey Period: July 2008

SBEE

"Top Legislative Staff High on Salary List," *The Sacramento Bee*, March 15, 2008.

Online: http://www.sacbee.com
Survey Period: 2008

SBEE01

"State Salaries Results," *The Sacramento Bee*, October 20, 2008.

Online: http://www.sacbee.com
Survey Period: 2008

Note: Data were downloaded October 20, 2008.

SBJ

Robert Celaschi, "Salaries Hold Steady," *Sacramento Business Journal*, February 13, 2009.

Online: http://sacramento.bizjournals.com
Survey Period: 2008

SCI01

Edyta Zielinska, "The Scientist 2008 Life Science Salary Survey," *The Scientist*, September 2008, p. 45.

Online: http://www.the-scientist.com
Survey Period: 2008

SCMAG

Illena Armstrong, "More Than Money: Information Security Pros Neither Face Wage Bonus Nor Badlands This Year," *SC Magazine*, July 2008, pp. 26-31.

Survey Period: 2008

SCOMP

Roger L. Brauer, "Career Success: Lessons Learned from a New CSP Salary and Demographic Survey," *Safety Compliance Letter*, September 1, 2008, pp. 7, 10-11, 16.

Survey Period: January 2008

SDBJ01

Emily Knight, "Highest Paid Elected Officials: Ranked by Salary for the 2007 Fiscal Year," *San Diego Business Journal*, December 31, 2007.

Survey Period: 2007

SDBJ02

Emily Knight and Andrew Schweizer, "Highest Paid Public Employees: Ranked by Salary for 2007-2008 Fiscal Year," *San Diego Business Journal*, December 31, 2007.

Survey Period: 2007-2008

SDBLS

South Dakota Occupational Wage Estimates, January 2009.

Labor Market Information Center
South Dakota Department of Labor
P.O. Box 4730
Aberdeen, SD 57402-4730
Telephone: (605) 626-2314
Fax: (605) 626-2322
Online: http://dol.sd.gov/lmic/
Survey Period: July 2008-September 2008

Note: All data are provided by the State Employment Security Administration to the Occupational Employment Statistics (OES) survey conducted by the U.S. Department of Labor, Bureau of Labor Statistics. May 2007 Occupational Employment and Wage Estimates have been adjusted to the third quarter of 2008 using the Employment Cost Index. Data were downloaded in January 2009.

SFCHN

"Autoworker Wage and Benefit Differences," *San Francisco Chronicle*, December 11, 2008.

Online: http://sfgate.com
Survey Period: 2008

SFMS

"Mayor's Salary & Benefits," October 2008.

Online: http://www.siouxfalls.org
Survey Period: 2008

SFSUNS

Megan O'Matz and Josh Hafenbrack, "Fla. Lieutenant Governor's $127,399 Position Comes with a Light Workload," *South Florida Sun-Sentinel*, February 14, 2009.

Online: http://www.sun-sentinel.com
Survey Period: 2009

SLEEP

"Salary Survey," *Sleep Review*, September 2008, p. 25.

Survey Period: 2008

SLPADV

Jason Mosheim, "2008 Salary Survey," *ADVANCE for Speech-Language Pathologists and Audiologists*, December 2, 2008.

Online: http://speech-language-pathology-audiology.advanceweb.com
Survey Period: 2008

SMM

Joseph Kornik, "What's it All Worth?" *Sales & Marketing Management*, May 2007, pp. 27-35.

Survey Period: 2006

SMNEWS

"Food Retailing Salaries 2008," *Supermarket News*, September 29, 2008.

Online: http://subscribers.supermarketnews.com
Survey Period: 2008

SOPE

"2008 Salary Calculator," *PlasticsJOBS.com*, October 13, 2008.

    Gros Executive Recruiters, Inc.
1616 Westgate Circle
Brentwood, TN 37027
Telephone: (800) 283-5643
Fax: (615) 661-4568
Online: http://www.plasticsjobs.com
Survey Period: April 2008-May 2008

Note: Data were downloaded on October 13, 2008.

SPDR

"Average Salary for Peds Derms Exceeds $200K in 2008," *SPDreview*, July 2008, pp. 1-4.

    Society for Pediatric Dermatology
8365 Keystone Crossing, Suite 107
Indianapolis, IN 46240
Telephone: (317) 202-0224
Fax: (317) 205-9841
Online: http://www.pedsderm.net
Email: spd@hp-assoc.com
Survey Period: 2008

SPE

Annual Membership Salary Survey: Highlight Report, September 2008.

    The Society of Petroleum Engineers
P.O. Box 833836
Richardson, TX 75083-3836
Telephone: (800) 456-6863
Fax: (972) 852-9435
Online: http://www.spe.org
Email: service@spe.org
Survey Period: June 2008-July 2008

SPECT

Brian Johnson, "2008 Salary Survey: Salaries and Stress Shrink," *Spectroscopy*, March 1, 2008.

    Survey Period: January 9, 2008-January 23, 2008

SPO01

Andrew Sawmiller, "Jamian Appointed to County Road Board," *Spinal Column Online*, February 11, 2009.

    Online: http://www.spinalcolumnonline.com
Survey Period: 2009

SPO02

Michael Shelton, "Village Council Votes to Rehire Frazer as Clerk," *Spinal Column Online*, January 28, 2009.

    Online: http://www.spinalcolumnonline.com
Survey Period: 2009

SPO03

Andrew Sawmiller, "Commissioners' Pay Frozen for 2009 Fiscal Year," *Spinal Column Online*, September 24, 2008.

    Online: http://www.spinalcolumnonline.com
Survey Period: 2008

SSSS

"Job Class Code Listing," August 21, 2008.

    City of Seaside
Personnel Office
440 Harcourt Avenue
Seaside, CA 93955
Telephone: (831) 899-6711
Online: http://www.ci.seaside.ca.us
Survey Period: August 2008

Note: Salary data are biweekly and are rounded to the nearest dollar.

STARB

"Legislators Should Refuse Enormous Salary Increases," *Star Bulletin*, October 14, 2008.

> **Online:** http://www.starbulletin.com
> **Survey Period:** 2008

STARC

Heather Sperling and JJ Proville, "2007 StarChefs.com Salary Survey," *StarChefs.com*, May 2008.

> **Online:** http://www.starchefs.com
> **Survey Period:** 2007

STFIN

Karl E. Reichardt and David L. Schroeder, "IMA 2007 Salary Survey," *Strategic Finance*, June 2008, pp. 26-43.

> **Survey Period:** 2007

STLEG1

"Louisiana Lawmakers, Who Have Not Seen a Pay Increase Since 1980, Voted to Raise Their Salaries by July 1 from $16,800 to $50,700, Only to See the Measure Vetoed by Governor Bobby Jindal," *State Legislatures*, July 2008-August 2008, p. 15.

> **Survey Period:** 2008

STLEG2

"Former House Appropriations Committee Chair Brett Feese is Drawing the Highest Salary in Pennsylvania State Government, and it is Raising the Ire of Governor Ed Rendell," *State Legislatures*, February 2008, p. 7.

> **Survey Period:** 2008.

SUSA01

"Pet Groomer," October 28, 2008.

> **Online:** http://www.schoolsintheusa.com
> **Survey Period:** 2008

Note: Data were downloaded on October 28, 2008 and were considered current by the source.

SUSA02

"Career Search Results: Social Science and Religion," October 28, 2008.

> **Online:** http://www.schoolsintheusa.com
> **Survey Period:** 2008

Note: Data were downloaded on October 28, 2008 and were considered current by the source.

SUSA03

"Career Search Results: Occupations in Resource-Based In- dustries," October 28, 2008.

> **Online:** http://www.schoolsintheusa.com
> **Survey Period:** 2008

Note: Data were downloaded on October 28, 2008 and were considered current by the source.

SUSA04

"Astrophysicist," January 22, 2009.

> **Online:** http://www.schoolsintheusa.com
> **Survey Period:** 2009

Note: Data were downloaded on January 22, 2009 and were considered current by the source.

SUSA05

"Geochemical Technician," January 22, 2009.

  Online: http://www.schoolsintheusa.com
  Survey Period: 2009

Note: Data were downloaded on January 22, 2009 and were considered current by the source.

SUSA06

"Job Analyst," January 22, 2009.

  Online: http://www.schoolsintheusa.com
  Survey Period: 2009

Note: Data were downloaded on January 22, 2009 and were considered current by the source.

SVSJBJ

Eric Young, "Women's Soccer League Guarantees Salaries of National Team Players," *Silicon Valley/San Jose Business Journal*, February 16, 2009.

  Online: http://sanjose.bizjournals.com
  Survey Period: 2009

TAG

"Member Wage Survey, January 2008," October 22, 2008.

  The Animation Guild and Affiliated Optical Electronic and Graphic Arts
  Local 839 IATSE
  4729 Lankershim Boulevard
  North Hollywood, CA 91602-1864
  Telephone: (818) 766-7151
  Fax: (818) 506-4805
  Online: http://www.animationguild.org
  Email: info@animationguild.org
  Survey Period: January 2008

TASBN

Mary Elizabeth Barrett, "Statewide Superintendent Salary Survey Released," *TASB News*, December 2008.

  Texas Association of School Boards
  P.O. Box 400
  Austin, TX 78767-0400
  Telephone: (512) 467-0222
  Online: http://www.tasb.org
  Survey Period: 2008-2009

Note: Press release.

TBLADE

"Panel Promises No Increase in Pay for Toledo Mayor, Councilmen," *Toledo Blade*, February 24, 2009.

  Online: http://www.toledoblade.com
  Survey Period: 2009

TCN

Jerry J. Sweet, et. al., "The TCN/AACN 2005 'Salary Survey': Professional Practices, Beliefs, and Incomes of U.S. Neuropsychologists," *The Clinical Neuropsychologist*, September 1, 2006.

  Online: http://napnet.org
  Survey Period: February 2005-May 31, 2005

TCRE

"Panel Delays Vote on Lawmaker Pay Cut," *Traverse City Record-Eagle*, February 13, 2009.

  Online: http://www.record-eagle.com
  Survey Period: 2009

TDI

Rick Dandes, "Ohio Man Hired as City Manager," *The Daily Item*, February 24, 2009.

Online: http://www.dailyitem.com
Survey Period: 2009

TEACHH

"School District Salaries," February 17, 2009.

The University of Houston, teachHouston
304 D Farish Hall
Houston, TX 77204-5027
Telephone: (713) 743-4969
Online: http://teachhouston.uh.edu
Survey Period: 2008

Note: Data were downloaded on February 17, 2009.

TEL01

Linda N. Weller, "Officials' Salaries Won't Change," *The Telegraph*, September 24, 2008.

Online: http://www.thetelegraph.com
Survey Period: 2008

TGRP

Paul Kopenkoskey, "'I Am Overqualified,' for Clerk's Pay; Plainfield Primary Victor Defends His Credentials as Board Considers Cutting Job's Salary," *The Grand Rapids Press*, October 21, 2008, p. B3.

Survey Period: 2008

THETN

"Tennessee Lottery Employee Salaries," *The Tennessean*, December 11, 2008.

Online: http://data.tennessean.com
Survey Period: 2008

THREC1

Matt King, "Salary, School District Size Disconnected When it Comes to Superintendents' Pay: Job Duties Secondary for School Execs," *Times Herald-Record*, October 6, 2008.

Online: http://www.recordonline.com
Survey Period: 2007

THREC2

Matt King, "No Logic to Town Supervisors' Salaries: What Towns Offer in Pay Doesn't Jibe with Duties," *Times Herald-Record*, October 6, 2008.

Online: http://www.recordonline.com
Survey Period: 2007

THREC3

Chris McKenna, "High Salaries in KJ School District: School Clerk Draws $137,000 Salary," *Times Herald-Record*, October 20, 2008.

Online: http://www.recordonline.com
Survey Period: 2008

THREC4

"K-12 Teacher Pay by County," *Times Herald-Record*, October 6, 2008.

Online: http://www.recordonline.com
Survey Period: 2008

TLEAD

Terrie Morgan-Besecker, "Court Officer's Paid Leave of Absence 4 Months Long: Administrator Sharkey Has Been Collecting Full $97,000 Salary While on Medical Leave," *Times Leader*, January 8, 2009.

Survey Period: 2009

TLEAD01

Jennifer Learn-Andes, "Judges Cut $2.8M from Luzerne County Payroll: Unprecedented Reductions Made Through Layoffs, Eliminating Vacant Posts, Salary Reductions," *Times Leader*, February 14, 2009.

Survey Period: 2009

TMC

"WVU Raises: Merit & the Market: Figures Can Range from $8K to $550K," *TMCnews*, December 29, 2008.

Online: http://www.tmcnet.com
Survey Period: 2008

TMC01

"2008 Salary Survey Results: Family Planning Providers Record Little Uptick in 2008 Paychecks," *TMCnews*, January 24, 2009.

Online: http://www.tmcnet.com
Survey Period: 2006

TME01

Frances Romero, "How Much Do Plumbers Really Make?" *Time*, October 17, 2008.

Online: http://www.time.com
Survey Period: 2008

TMW

"Salary Survey 2008," *Test & Measurement World*, October 1, 2008.

Online: http://www.tmworld.com
Survey Period: 2008

Note: Data were downloaded on October 1, 2008 and were considered current by the source.

TRADEW

"Salary Gap Getting Wider," *Tradeshow Week*, January 7, 2008.

Survey Period: 2007

TRADEW1

Kerry Zerlin, "Salaries are Movin' on Up," *Tradeshow Week*, January 5, 2009, pp. 5-6.

Survey Period: November 2008

TRAIN

"The Bucks Stop Here," *Training*, October 2008, pp. 22-28.

Survey Period: 2008

TSEAT

Rob Hotakainen, "Congress Urged to Rescind Pay Raise Amid Recession," *The Seattle Times*, December 31, 2008, p. A4.

Survey Period: 2009

TTRIB

Adam Emerson, "School Board Pay Cuts Pressed," *The Tampa Tribune*, January 15, 2009, p. 4.

Survey Period: 2009

TVC01

"PV (Solar Energy System) Installer," October 23, 2008.

Online: http://www.techvalleycareers.org
Email: contact@techvalleycareers.org
Survey Period: 2008

Note: Data were downloaded on October 23, 2008 and were considered current by the source.

TVC02

"Fuel Cell Engineer," October 23, 2008.

> **Online:** http://www.techvalleycareers.org
> **Email:** contact@techvalleycareers.org
> **Survey Period:** 2008

Note: Data were downloaded on October 23, 2008 and were considered current by the source.

TVC03

"Geothermal Senior Reservoir Engineer," October 23, 2008.

> **Online:** http://www.techvalleycareers.org
> **Email:** contact@techvalleycareers.org
> **Survey Period:** 2008

Note: Data were downloaded on October 23, 2008 and were considered current by the source.

TVC04

"Geophysicist," October 23, 2008.

> **Online:** http://www.techvalleycareers.org
> **Email:** contact@techvalleycareers.org
> **Survey Period:** 2008

Note: Data were downloaded on October 23, 2008 and were considered current by the source.

TVC05

"Bioenergy Process Engineer," October 23, 2008.

> **Online:** http://www.techvalleycareers.org
> **Email:** contact@techvalleycareers.org
> **Survey Period:** 2008

Note: Data were downloaded on October 23, 2008 and were considered current by the source.

TVC06

"Wind Energy Research Specialist," October 23, 2008.

> **Online:** http://www.techvalleycareers.org
> **Email:** contact@techvalleycareers.org
> **Survey Period:** 2008

Note: Data were downloaded on October 23, 2008 and were considered current by the source.

TVC07

"Computer Forensic Technician," October 23, 2008.

> **Online:** http://www.techvalleycareers.org
> **Email:** contact@techvalleycareers.org
> **Survey Period:** 2008

Note: Data were downloaded on October 23, 2008 and were considered current by the source.

TWST

Kristin Bull, "Doling Out Comfort," *Twist*, July 27, 2008-August 2, 2008, pp. 8-9.

> **Survey Period:** 2008

Note: Salary data are fees per client.

UCSC1

"Joint Senate — Administration Task Force on Faculty Salaries Report," September 10, 2008, pp. 2-3.

> UC Santa Cruz Academic Senate
> 125 Kerr Hall, 1156 High Street
> Santa Cruz, CA 95064-1077
> **Telephone:** (831) 459-2089
> **Online:** http://senate.ucsc.edu
> **Survey Period:** 2008

UNCHC

"Benefits for Residents: Salaries," *Graduate Medical Education*, January 23, 2009.

Online: http://gme.unchealthcare.org/benefits/salaries
Survey Period: July 1, 2008

Note: Data were downloaded on January 23, 2009.

UPA

UPA 2007 Salary Survey: Free Version, February 15, 2008.

Usability Professionals' Association
140 North Bloomingdale Road
Bloomingdale, IL 60108-1017
Telephone: (630) 980-4997
Fax: (630) 351-8490
Online: http://www.usabilityprofessionals.org
Email: office@usabilityprofessionals.org
Survey Period: 2007

UPI01

"'Simpsons' Voice Actors Make Deal with Fox," *UPI.com*, June 2, 2008.

Online: http://www.upi.com
Survey Period: 2008

Note: The actors' salaries are $400,000 per episode.

UPI02

"Ohio State Gives Tressel Rich New Contract," *UPI.com*, August 29, 2008.

Online: http://www.upi.com
Survey Period: 2008

USATOD01

Erik Brady, "Pay Gap Could Mean Schools are in Violation," *USA TODAY*, May 23, 2008, p. 10C.

Survey Period: 2006

USATOD02

Rita Rubin, "Boomers May See Doctor Shortage," *USA TODAY*, September 10, 2008, p. 1A.

Survey Period: 2007

USATOD03

Jay Yang and Karl Gelles, "Compensation for Executives," *USA TODAY*, September 10, 2008, p. 1B.

Survey Period: 2008

USATOD04

Thomas Frank, "TSA Struggles to Reduce Persistent Turnover," *USA TODAY*, February 25, 2008, p. 4A.

Survey Period: 2008

USATOD05

"Football," *USA TODAY Salaries Databases*, October 17, 2008.

Online: http://content.usatoday.com
Survey Period: 2007

Note: Median salaries range from the Green Bay Packers' $440,520 to the Pittsburgh Steelers' $1,102,880.

USATOD06

"Hockey," *USA TODAY Salaries Databases*, October 17, 2008.

Online: http://content.usatoday.com
Survey Period: 2007-2008

Note: Median salaries range from the San Jose Sharks' $800,000 to the Carolina Hurricanes' $2,200,000.

USATOD07

"Baseball," *USA TODAY Salaries Databases*, October 17, 2008.

Online: http://content.usatoday.com
Survey Period: 2008

Note: Median salaries range from the Florida Marlins' $395,000 to the Chicago Cubs' $3,175,000.

USATOD08

Michael McCarthy, "Goodell Cuts, Freezes Salary," *USA TODAY*, February 13, 2009, p. 7C.

Survey Period: 2006-2009

USBLS

May 2007 National Occupational Employment and Wage Estimates, May 2008.

U.S. Bureau of Labor Statistics
Division of Occupational Employment Statistics
2 Massachusetts Avenue, NE, Suite 2135
Washington, DC 20212-0001
Telephone: (202) 691-6569
Fax: (202) 691-6444
Online: http://www.bls.gov
Survey Period: May 2007

USNEWS01

Sarah Baldauf, "Seeing the Big Picture," *U.S. News & World Report*, April 9, 2007.

Survey Period: 2007

USNEWS02

Liz Wolgemuth, et. al., "Career Guide 2008," *U.S. News & World Report*, March 24, 2008, pp. 45-61.

Survey Period: 2008

USNEWS03

Lucia Graves, "An Education Evolution," *U.S. News & World Report*, October 27, 2008, pp. 62-66.

Survey Period: 2008

USNEWS04

Paul Raeburn, "Doing Battle with Your Plan," *U.S. News & World Report*, November 17, 2008-November 24, 2008, pp. 68-70.

Survey Period: 2008

USNEWS05

Kim Clark, "How Much Do College Presidents Earn?" *U.S. News & World Report*, November 17, 2008.

Survey Period: 2006-2007

Note: The latest year for which private university salaries were available was 2006.

USNEWS06

Marty Nemko, "Best Careers 2009: Genetic Counselor," *U.S. News & World Report*, December 11, 2008.

Online: http://www.usnews.com
Survey Period: 2008

Note: Salary data are for genetic counselors with eight years experience.

USNEWS07

Marty Nemko, "Best Careers 2009: Locksmith/Security System Technician," *U.S. News & World Report*, December 11, 2008.

Online: http://www.usnews.com
Survey Period: 2008

Note: Salary data are for locksmiths/security system technicians with eight years experience.

USSGOV

"Senate Salaries Since 1789," March 30, 2009.

United States Senate
Washington, DC 20510
Online: http://www.senate.gov
Survey Period: 2009

Note: Data were downloaded on March 30, 2009.

UTIMES

"Low Salaries Causing Urologist Shortage in PA," *Urology Times*, March 1, 2008.

Survey Period: 2008

VACG01

"Career Guide for Environmental Compliance Inspector," January 21, 2009.

Online: http://jobs.virginia.gov/careerguides/
Survey Period: November 25, 2007

Note: Data were downloaded on January 21, 2009. Salaries became effective on November 25, 2007.

VACG02

"Career Guide for Exhibit Designer," January 21, 2009.

Online: http://jobs.virginia.gov/careerguides/
Survey Period: November 25, 2007

Note: Data were downloaded on January 21, 2009. Salaries became effective on November 25, 2007.

VACG03

"Career Guide for Horseracing Steward," January 21, 2009.

Online: http://jobs.virginia.gov/careerguides/
Survey Period: November 25, 2007

Note: Data were downloaded on January 21, 2009. Salaries became effective on November 25, 2007.

VACG04

"Career Guide for Hospital Quality Assurance Coordinator," January 21, 2009.

Online: http://jobs.virginia.gov/careerguides/
Survey Period: November 25, 2007

Note: Data were downloaded on January 21, 2009. Salaries became effective on November 25, 2007.

VACG05

"Career Guide Reimbursement Analyst," January 21, 2009.

Online: http://jobs.virginia.gov/careerguides/
Survey Period: November 25, 2007

Note: Data were downloaded on January 21, 2009. Salaries became effective on November 25, 2007.

VACG06

"Career Guide for Typesetting Machine Operator," January 21, 2009.

Online: http://jobs.virginia.gov/careerguides/
Survey Period: November 25, 2007

Note: Data were downloaded on January 21, 2009. Salaries became effective on November 25, 2007.

VAPLT

Deirdre Fernandes, "Beach City Council Pay Cuts Proposed as Symbolic Gesture," *Virginian-Pilot*, February 14, 2009.

Survey Period: 2009

VLW

"Summer Associates Salary Survey 2008," *Virginia Lawyers Weekly*, October 2008.

Online: http://www.valawyersweekly.com
Survey Period: 2008

VMS01

Allen Essex, "Brief: Flores' Salary Raised to $200,000," *Valley Morning Star*, February 12, 2009.

Survey Period: 2009-2010

WABLS

Washington Occupational Employment and Wage Estimates, October 15, 2008.

Employment Security Department
Labor Market and Economic Analysis Branch
P.O. Box 9046
Olympia, WA 98507-9046
Telephone: (800) 215-1617
Fax: (360) 438-4109
Online: http://www.workforceexplorer.com
Email: Jwines@esd.wa.gov
Survey Period: March 2008

Note: All data are provided by the State Employment Security Administration to the Occupational Employment Statistics (OES) survey conducted by the U.S. Department of Labor, Bureau of Labor Statistics. May 2007 Occupational Employment and Wage Estimates have been adjusted to March 2008 using the Employment Cost Index. Data were downloaded on October 15, 2008.

WATIME

Jim McElhatton, "In Hard Times, Postmaster Earned $800,000 in Pay, Perks; Raise Came Amid Calls for Cuts in Delivery," *The Washington Times*, February 17, 2009, p. A1.

Survey Period: 2008

Note: Salary data include total compensation for 2008.

WCC

"Washington Citizens' Commission on Salaries for Elected Officials 2007-08 Salary Schedule," May 15, 2007.

Washington Citizens' Commission on Salaries for Elected Officials
General Administration Building, Room 301A
210 11th Avenue SW
Olympia, WA 98504
Telephone: (866) 809-8116
Fax: (360) 586-7544
Online: http://www.salaries.wa.gov/
Survey Period: September 1, 2008

Note: Salary data became effective on September 1, 2008.

WCPS

"2008-09 Salaries: Speech Language Pathologists and Audiologists (Master's Degree)," 2008.

   Wake County Public School System
   3600 Wake Forest Road
   Raleigh, NC 27609
   Telephone: (919) 850-1600
   Online: http://www.wcpss.net
   Survey Period: 2008-2009

Note: Salary data are rounded to the nearest dollar.

WCPS01

"Salaries 2007-08: Special Hourly Assignments," 2008.

   Wake County Public School System
   3600 Wake Forest Road
   Raleigh, NC 27609
   Telephone: (919) 850-1600
   Online: http://www.wcpss.net
   Survey Period: 2007-2008

WCPS02

"Technology Salary Schedules: 2008-09," 2008.

   Wake County Public School System
   3600 Wake Forest Road
   Raleigh, NC 27609
   Telephone: (919) 850-1600
   Online: http://www.wcpss.net
   Survey Period: 2008-2009

WCSWP

"City of Walnut Creek Salary and Wage Plan," September 5, 2008.

   City of Walnut Creek
   1666 North Main Street
   Walnut Creek, CA 94596
   Telephone: (925) 943-5899
   Fax: (925) 943-5897
   Online: http://www.walnutcreek.org
   Survey Period: 2007-2008

WFMGMT

Fay Hansen, "Balancing the Global Workforce," *Workforce Management*, December 11, 2006, pp. 44-67.

   Survey Period: September 1, 2006

WIHC

"Orthoptist," February 9, 2009.

   Online: http://www.wihealthcareers.org
   Survey Period: 2007

Note: Data were downloaded on February 9, 2009.

WINEB

Mary-Colleen Tinney, "2007 Salary Survey Report: Salaries Up 3.8 Percent," *Wine Business.com*, October 15, 2007.

   Online: http://www.winebusiness.com
   Survey Period: 2007

WPOST

"A Closer Look at Congressional Staff Salaries," *Washington Post*, January 1, 2007.

   Online: http://www.washingtonpost.com
   Survey Period: 2006

WPOST01

Nancy Trejos, "More Than a Day Job," *Washington Post*, January 4, 2009.

   Online: http://www.washingtonpost.com
   Survey Period: 2009

Note: The salary for Pedicab Driver was based on an actual wage earned by one driver.

WPOST02

Dan Froomkin, "2008 White House Office Staff List - Title," *Washington Post*, July 24, 2008.

Online: http://www.washingtonpost.com
Survey Period: 2008

Note: On January 21, 2009, President Barack Obama signed an executive order freezing salaries for senior White House staff that make more than $100,000.

WPOST03

Raymond McCaffrey, "Salaries, Strong Recruitment Ease Area Paramedic Shortage," *Washington Post*, April 4, 2008, p. A01.

Online: http://www.washingtonpost.com
Survey Period: 2008

WRUA

"The 2008 WritersUA Salary Survey," January 29, 2008.

Online: http://www.writersua.com
Email: info@writersua.com
Survey Period: December 1, 2007-January 25, 2008

WSJ01

Sarah E. Needleman, "Pay Grade: Rocket Scientist," *The Wall Street Journal*, January 22, 2008, p. B4.

Survey Period: 2008

WSJ02

Simona Covel, "Three Approaches to Reining in Customer Debt," *The Wall Street Journal*, September 24, 2007, p. B4.

Survey Period: 2007

WSJ03

Sarah E. Needleman, "Pay Grade: Public Places, Personal Touches," *The Wall Street Journal*, September 25, 2007, p. B6.

Survey Period: 2007

WSJ04

Sarah E. Needleman, "If You Want to Stand Out, Join the Crowd," *The Wall Street Journal*, August 14, 2007, p. B6.

Survey Period: 2007

WSJ05

Sarah E. Needleman, "Pay Grade: Turning a Seasonal Hem," *The Wall Street Journal*, August 7, 2007, p. B6.

Survey Period: 2007

WSJ06

Sarah E. Needleman, "Pay Grade: Work and Play," *The Wall Street Journal*, December 18, 2007, p. B6.

Survey Period: 2007

WSJ07

Sarah E. Needleman, "Pay Grade," *The Wall Street Journal*, May 27, 2008, p. D4.

Survey Period: 2008

WSJ08

Sarah E. Needleman, "Pay Grade," *The Wall Street Journal*, August 26, 2008, p. D5.

Survey Period: 2008

WSJ09

Sarah E. Needleman, "Doing the Math to Find the Good Jobs," *The Wall Street Journal*, January 6, 2009.

Online: http://www.wsj.com
Survey Period: 2009

WSJ10

Ellen Byron, "Is the Smell of Moroccan Bazaar Too Edgy for American Homes?" *The Wall Street Journal*, February 3, 2009.

Online: http://www.wsj.com
Survey Period: 2009

Note: Scent Seekers are paid test participants. Each Scent Seeker is paid on average $25.00 to test fragrances in cleaning products in P&G's research facility near Cincinnati, Ohio.

WSJ11

Richard Gibson, "Sizing Up Salaries Inside Franchisers," *The Wall Street Journal*, December 30, 2008, p. B2.

Survey Period: August 2007-July 2008

Note: Salary data are for the 12 months ended July 1, 2008.

WSJ12

Sarah E. Needleman, "Pay Grade," *The Wall Street Journal*, December 30, 2008, p. D5.

Survey Period: 2008

WSJO01

Ben Worthen, "Tech Workers Get a Raise," *The Wall Street Journal Online*, January 21, 2009.

Online: http://blogs.wsj.com/digits/
Survey Period: 2008

WTGMD

"How Much Can I Make?" *Way 2 Go Maryland*, January 19, 2009.

University System of Maryland
3300 Metzerott Road
Adelphi, MD 20783-1690
Telephone: (301) 445-2740
Online: http://www.way2gomaryland.org/howmuch/
Survey Period: 2009

Note: Data were downloaded on January 19, 2009 and were considered current by the source.

WVBLS

Comparative Occupational Wages 2008, January 9, 2009.

WORKFORCE West Virginia
Research Information and Analysis
112 California Avenue
Charleston, WV 25305-0112
Telephone: (304) 558-2660
Fax: (304) 558-1343
Online: http://www.wvbep.org/bep/lmi/
Survey Period: July 2008-September 2008

Note: All data are provided by the State Employment Security Administration to the Occupational Employment Statistics (OES) survey conducted by the U.S. Department of Labor, Bureau of Labor Statistics. May 2007 Occupational Employment and Wage Estimates have been adjusted to the third quarter of 2008 using the Employment Cost Index. Data were downloaded on January 9, 2009.

WXYZ

"Anthony Adam's Salary Secret," July 23, 2008.

Online: http://www.wxyz.com
Survey Period: 2008

WXYZ01

"Landing a 6-Figure Job Without a Degree," January 26, 2009.

Online: http://www.wxyz.com
Survey Period: 2009

WYBLS

Wyoming Occupational Employment and Wages September 2008, January 2009.

Wyoming Department of Employment
Research & Planning
246 South Cedar Street
Casper, WY 82602
Telephone: (307) 473-3807
Online: http://doe.state.wy.us/lmi/oes.htm
Survey Period: September 2008

Note: All data are provided by the State Employment Security Administration to the Occupational Employment Statistics (OES) survey conducted by the U.S. Department of Labor, Bureau of Labor Statistics. May 2007 Occupational Employment and Wage Estimates have been adjusted to September 2008 using the Employment Cost Index. Data were downloaded in January 2009.

YAHHJ

Clare Kaufman, "10 Careers That Top $30 Per Hour," *Yahoo! hotjobs*, January 23, 2009.

Online: http://hotjobs.yahoo.com
Survey Period: 2007

Note: Data were downloaded on January 23, 2009.

YVR01

"What is the Cost or Salary of Hiring an Office Assistant vs the Average Salary or Cost of Partnering with a VA?" January 26, 2009.

Online: http://www.yourvirtualresource.com
Survey Period: 2009

Note: Data were downloaded on January 26, 2009 and were considered current by the source.

ZBB

"Illinois Technology Association Releases Results from Third Annual Salary Survey," January 14, 2009.

Online: http://www.zibb.com
Survey Period: 2008

Note: Salary data do not include non-cash compensation.

Appendix II

SALARY CONVERSION TABLE

Hour	Week	Month	Year	Hour	Week	Month	Year	Hour	Week	Month	Year	Hour	Week	Month	Year
2.00	80	346	4,157	4.10	164	710	8,521	6.20	248	1,074	12,886	8.30	332	1,438	17,251
2.05	82	355	4,261	4.15	166	719	8,625	6.25	250	1,083	12,990	8.35	334	1,446	17,355
2.10	84	364	4,365	4.20	168	727	8,729	6.30	252	1,091	13,094	8.40	336	1,455	17,459
2.15	86	372	4,469	4.25	170	736	8,833	6.35	254	1,100	13,198	8.45	338	1,464	17,562
2.20	88	381	4,572	4.30	172	745	8,937	6.40	256	1,108	13,302	8.50	340	1,472	17,666
2.25	90	390	4,676	4.35	174	753	9,041	6.45	258	1,117	13,406	8.55	342	1,481	17,770
2.30	92	398	4,780	4.40	176	762	9,145	6.50	260	1,126	13,510	8.60	344	1,490	17,874
2.35	94	407	4,884	4.45	178	771	9,249	6.55	262	1,134	13,614	8.65	346	1,498	17,978
2.40	96	416	4,988	4.50	180	779	9,353	6.60	264	1,143	13,717	8.70	348	1,507	18,082
2.45	98	424	5,092	4.55	182	788	9,457	6.65	266	1,152	13,821	8.75	350	1,516	18,186
2.50	100	433	5,196	4.60	184	797	9,561	6.70	268	1,160	13,925	8.80	352	1,524	18,290
2.55	102	442	5,300	4.65	186	805	9,665	6.75	270	1,169	14,029	8.85	354	1,533	18,394
2.60	104	450	5,404	4.70	188	814	9,768	6.80	272	1,178	14,133	8.90	356	1,541	18,498
2.65	106	459	5,508	4.75	190	823	9,872	6.85	274	1,186	14,237	8.95	358	1,550	18,602
2.70	108	468	5,612	4.80	192	831	9,976	6.90	276	1,195	14,341	9.00	360	1,559	18,706
2.75	110	476	5,716	4.85	194	840	10,080	6.95	278	1,204	14,445	9.05	362	1,567	18,810
2.80	112	485	5,820	4.90	196	849	10,184	7.00	280	1,212	14,549	9.10	364	1,576	18,913
2.85	114	494	5,923	4.95	198	857	10,288	7.05	282	1,221	14,653	9.15	366	1,585	19,017
2.90	116	502	6,027	5.00	200	866	10,392	7.10	284	1,230	14,757	9.20	368	1,593	19,121
2.95	118	511	6,131	5.05	202	875	10,496	7.15	286	1,238	14,861	9.25	370	1,602	19,225
3.00	120	520	6,235	5.10	204	883	10,600	7.20	288	1,247	14,964	9.30	372	1,611	19,329
3.05	122	528	6,339	5.15	206	892	10,704	7.25	290	1,256	15,068	9.35	374	1,619	19,433
3.10	124	537	6,443	5.20	208	901	10,808	7.30	292	1,264	15,172	9.40	376	1,628	19,537
3.15	126	546	6,547	5.25	210	909	10,912	7.35	294	1,273	15,276	9.45	378	1,637	19,641
3.20	128	554	6,651	5.30	212	918	11,016	7.40	296	1,282	15,380	9.50	380	1,645	19,745
3.25	130	563	6,755	5.35	214	927	11,119	7.45	298	1,290	15,484	9.55	382	1,654	19,849
3.30	132	572	6,859	5.40	216	935	11,223	7.50	300	1,299	15,588	9.60	384	1,663	19,953
3.35	134	580	6,963	5.45	218	944	11,327	7.55	302	1,308	15,692	9.65	386	1,671	20,057
3.40	136	589	7,067	5.50	220	953	11,431	7.60	304	1,316	15,796	9.70	388	1,680	20,160
3.45	138	598	7,170	5.55	222	961	11,535	7.65	306	1,325	15,900	9.75	390	1,689	20,264
3.50	140	606	7,274	5.60	224	970	11,639	7.70	308	1,334	16,004	9.80	392	1,697	20,368
3.55	142	615	7,378	5.65	226	979	11,743	7.75	310	1,342	16,108	9.85	394	1,706	20,472
3.60	144	624	7,482	5.70	228	987	11,847	7.80	312	1,351	16,212	9.90	396	1,715	20,576
3.65	146	632	7,586	5.75	230	996	11,951	7.85	314	1,360	16,315	9.95	398	1,723	20,680
3.70	148	641	7,690	5.80	232	1,005	12,055	7.90	316	1,368	16,419	10.00	400	1,732	20,784
3.75	150	649	7,794	5.85	234	1,013	12,159	7.95	318	1,377	16,523	10.05	402	1,741	20,888
3.80	152	658	7,898	5.90	236	1,022	12,263	8.00	320	1,386	16,627	10.10	404	1,749	20,992
3.85	154	667	8,002	5.95	238	1,031	12,366	8.05	322	1,394	16,731	10.15	406	1,758	21,096
3.90	156	675	8,106	6.00	240	1,039	12,470	8.10	324	1,403	16,835	10.20	408	1,767	21,200
3.95	158	684	8,210	6.05	242	1,048	12,574	8.15	326	1,412	16,939	10.25	410	1,775	21,304
4.00	160	693	8,314	6.10	244	1,057	12,678	8.20	328	1,420	17,043	10.30	412	1,784	21,408
4.05	162	701	8,418	6.15	246	1,065	12,782	8.25	330	1,429	17,147	10.35	414	1,793	21,511

Hour	Week	Month	Year	Hour	Week	Month	Year	Hour	Week	Month	Year	Hour	Week	Month	Year
10.40	416	1,801	21,615	13.20	528	2,286	27,435	16.00	640	2,771	33,254	18.80	752	3,256	39,074
10.45	418	1,810	21,719	13.25	530	2,295	27,539	16.05	642	2,780	33,358	18.85	754	3,265	39,178
10.50	420	1,819	21,823	13.30	532	2,304	27,643	16.10	644	2,789	33,462	18.90	756	3,273	39,282
10.55	422	1,827	21,927	13.35	534	2,312	27,747	16.15	646	2,797	33,566	18.95	758	3,282	39,386
10.60	424	1,836	22,031	13.40	536	2,321	27,851	16.20	648	2,806	33,670	19.00	760	3,291	39,490
10.65	426	1,845	22,135	13.45	538	2,330	27,954	16.25	650	2,815	33,774	19.05	762	3,299	39,594
10.70	428	1,853	22,239	13.50	540	2,338	28,058	16.30	652	2,823	33,878	19.10	764	3,308	39,697
10.75	430	1,862	22,343	13.55	542	2,347	28,162	16.35	654	2,832	33,982	19.15	766	3,317	39,801
10.80	432	1,871	22,447	13.60	544	2,356	28,266	16.40	656	2,840	34,086	19.20	768	3,325	39,905
10.85	434	1,879	22,551	13.65	546	2,364	28,370	16.45	658	2,849	34,190	19.25	770	3,334	40,009
10.90	436	1,888	22,655	13.70	548	2,373	28,474	16.50	660	2,858	34,294	19.30	772	3,343	40,113
10.95	438	1,897	22,758	13.75	550	2,382	28,578	16.55	662	2,866	34,398	19.35	774	3,351	40,217
11.00	440	1,905	22,862	13.80	552	2,390	28,682	16.60	664	2,875	34,501	19.40	776	3,360	40,321
11.05	442	1,914	22,966	13.85	554	2,399	28,786	16.65	666	2,884	34,605	19.45	778	3,369	40,425
11.10	444	1,923	23,070	13.90	556	2,407	28,890	16.70	668	2,892	34,709	19.50	780	3,377	40,529
11.15	446	1,931	23,174	13.95	558	2,416	28,994	16.75	670	2,901	34,813	19.55	782	3,386	40,633
11.20	448	1,940	23,278	14.00	560	2,425	29,098	16.80	672	2,910	34,917	19.60	784	3,395	40,737
11.25	450	1,949	23,382	14.05	562	2,433	29,202	16.85	674	2,918	35,021	19.65	786	3,403	40,841
11.30	452	1,957	23,486	14.10	564	2,442	29,305	16.90	676	2,927	35,125	19.70	788	3,412	40,944
11.35	454	1,966	23,590	14.15	566	2,451	29,409	16.95	678	2,936	35,229	19.75	790	3,421	41,048
11.40	456	1,974	23,694	14.20	568	2,459	29,513	17.00	680	2,944	35,333	19.80	792	3,429	41,152
11.45	458	1,983	23,798	14.25	570	2,468	29,617	17.05	682	2,953	35,437	19.85	794	3,438	41,256
11.50	460	1,992	23,902	14.30	572	2,477	29,721	17.10	684	2,962	35,541	19.90	796	3,447	41,360
11.55	462	2,000	24,006	14.35	574	2,485	29,825	17.15	686	2,970	35,645	19.95	798	3,455	41,464
11.60	464	2,009	24,109	14.40	576	2,494	29,929	17.20	688	2,979	35,748	20.00	800	3,464	41,568
11.65	466	2,018	24,213	14.45	578	2,503	30,033	17.25	690	2,988	35,852	20.05	802	3,473	41,672
11.70	468	2,026	24,317	14.50	580	2,511	30,137	17.30	692	2,996	35,956	20.10	804	3,481	41,776
11.75	470	2,035	24,421	14.55	582	2,520	30,241	17.35	694	3,005	36,060	20.15	806	3,490	41,880
11.80	472	2,044	24,525	14.60	584	2,529	30,345	17.40	696	3,014	36,164	20.20	808	3,499	41,984
11.85	474	2,052	24,629	14.65	586	2,537	30,449	17.45	698	3,022	36,268	20.25	810	3,507	42,088
11.90	476	2,061	24,733	14.70	588	2,546	30,552	17.50	700	3,031	36,372	20.30	812	3,516	42,192
11.95	478	2,070	24,837	14.75	590	2,555	30,656	17.55	702	3,040	36,476	20.35	814	3,525	42,295
12.00	480	2,078	24,941	14.80	592	2,563	30,760	17.60	704	3,048	36,580	20.40	816	3,533	42,399
12.05	482	2,087	25,045	14.85	594	2,572	30,864	17.65	706	3,057	36,684	20.45	818	3,542	42,503
12.10	484	2,096	25,149	14.90	596	2,581	30,968	17.70	708	3,066	36,788	20.50	820	3,551	42,607
12.15	486	2,104	25,253	14.95	598	2,589	31,072	17.75	710	3,074	36,892	20.55	822	3,559	42,711
12.20	488	2,113	25,356	15.00	600	2,598	31,176	17.80	712	3,083	36,996	20.60	824	3,568	42,815
12.25	490	2,122	25,460	15.05	602	2,607	31,280	17.85	714	3,092	37,099	20.65	826	3,577	42,919
12.30	492	2,130	25,564	15.10	604	2,615	31,384	17.90	716	3,100	37,203	20.70	828	3,585	43,023
12.35	494	2,139	25,668	15.15	606	2,624	31,488	17.95	718	3,109	37,307	20.75	830	3,594	43,127
12.40	496	2,148	25,772	15.20	608	2,633	31,592	18.00	720	3,118	37,411	20.80	832	3,603	43,231
12.45	498	2,156	25,876	15.25	610	2,641	31,696	18.05	722	3,126	37,515	20.85	834	3,611	43,335
12.50	500	2,165	25,980	15.30	612	2,650	31,800	18.10	724	3,135	37,619	20.90	836	3,620	43,439
12.55	502	2,174	26,084	15.35	614	2,659	31,903	18.15	726	3,144	37,723	20.95	838	3,629	43,542
12.60	504	2,182	26,188	15.40	616	2,667	32,007	18.20	728	3,152	37,827	21.00	840	3,637	43,646
12.65	506	2,191	26,292	15.45	618	2,676	32,111	18.25	730	3,161	37,931	21.05	842	3,646	43,750
12.70	508	2,200	26,396	15.50	620	2,685	32,215	18.30	732	3,170	38,035	21.10	844	3,655	43,854
12.75	510	2,208	26,500	15.55	622	2,693	32,319	18.35	734	3,178	38,139	21.15	846	3,663	43,958
12.80	512	2,217	26,604	15.60	624	2,702	32,423	18.40	736	3,187	38,243	21.20	848	3,672	44,062
12.85	514	2,226	26,707	15.65	626	2,711	32,527	18.45	738	3,196	38,346	21.25	850	3,680	44,166
12.90	516	2,234	26,811	15.70	628	2,719	32,631	18.50	740	3,204	38,450	21.30	852	3,689	44,270
12.95	518	2,243	26,915	15.75	630	2,728	32,735	18.55	742	3,213	38,554	21.35	854	3,698	44,374
13.00	520	2,252	27,019	15.80	632	2,737	32,839	18.60	744	3,222	38,658	21.40	856	3,706	44,478
13.05	522	2,260	27,123	15.85	634	2,745	32,943	18.65	746	3,230	38,762	21.45	858	3,715	44,582
13.10	524	2,269	27,227	15.90	636	2,754	33,047	18.70	748	3,239	38,866	21.50	860	3,724	44,686
13.15	526	2,278	27,331	15.95	638	2,763	33,150	18.75	750	3,248	38,970	21.55	862	3,732	44,790

Hour	Week	Month	Year	Hour	Week	Month	Year	Hour	Week	Month	Year	Hour	Week	Month	Year
21.60	864	3,741	44,893	24.40	976	4,226	50,713	27.20	1,088	4,711	56,532	30.00	1,200	5,196	62,352
21.65	866	3,750	44,997	24.45	978	4,235	50,817	27.25	1,090	4,720	56,636	30.05	1,202	5,205	62,456
21.70	868	3,758	45,101	24.50	980	4,243	50,921	27.30	1,092	4,728	56,740	30.10	1,204	5,213	62,560
21.75	870	3,767	45,205	24.55	982	4,252	51,025	27.35	1,094	4,737	56,844	30.15	1,206	5,222	62,664
21.80	872	3,776	45,309	24.60	984	4,261	51,129	27.40	1,096	4,746	56,948	30.20	1,208	5,231	62,768
21.85	874	3,784	45,413	24.65	986	4,269	51,233	27.45	1,098	4,754	57,052	30.25	1,210	5,239	62,872
21.90	876	3,793	45,517	24.70	988	4,278	51,336	27.50	1,100	4,763	57,156	30.30	1,212	5,248	62,976
21.95	878	3,802	45,621	24.75	990	4,287	51,440	27.55	1,102	4,772	57,260	30.35	1,214	5,257	63,079
22.00	880	3,810	45,725	24.80	992	4,295	51,544	27.60	1,104	4,780	57,364	30.40	1,216	5,265	63,183
22.05	882	3,819	45,829	24.85	994	4,304	51,648	27.65	1,106	4,789	57,468	30.45	1,218	5,274	63,287
22.10	884	3,828	45,933	24.90	996	4,313	51,752	27.70	1,108	4,798	57,572	30.50	1,220	5,283	63,391
22.15	886	3,836	46,037	24.95	998	4,321	51,856	27.75	1,110	4,806	57,676	30.55	1,222	5,291	63,495
22.20	888	3,845	46,140	25.00	1,000	4,330	51,960	27.80	1,112	4,815	57,780	30.60	1,224	5,300	63,599
22.25	890	3,854	46,244	25.05	1,002	4,339	52,064	27.85	1,114	4,824	57,883	30.65	1,226	5,309	63,703
22.30	892	3,862	46,348	25.10	1,004	4,347	52,168	27.90	1,116	4,832	57,987	30.70	1,228	5,317	63,807
22.35	894	3,871	46,452	25.15	1,006	4,356	52,272	27.95	1,118	4,841	58,091	30.75	1,230	5,326	63,911
22.40	896	3,880	46,556	25.20	1,008	4,365	52,376	28.00	1,120	4,850	58,195	30.80	1,232	5,335	64,015
22.45	898	3,888	46,660	25.25	1,010	4,373	52,480	28.05	1,122	4,858	58,299	30.85	1,234	5,343	64,119
22.50	900	3,897	46,764	25.30	1,012	4,382	52,584	28.10	1,124	4,867	58,403	30.90	1,236	5,352	64,223
22.55	902	3,906	46,868	25.35	1,014	4,391	52,687	28.15	1,126	4,876	58,507	30.95	1,238	5,361	64,326
22.60	904	3,914	46,972	25.40	1,016	4,399	52,791	28.20	1,128	4,884	58,611	31.00	1,240	5,369	64,430
22.65	906	3,923	47,076	25.45	1,018	4,408	52,895	28.25	1,130	4,893	58,715	31.05	1,242	5,378	64,534
22.70	908	3,932	47,180	25.50	1,020	4,417	52,999	28.30	1,132	4,902	58,819	31.10	1,244	5,387	64,638
22.75	910	3,940	47,284	25.55	1,022	4,425	53,103	28.35	1,134	4,910	58,923	31.15	1,246	5,395	64,742
22.80	912	3,949	47,388	25.60	1,024	4,434	53,207	28.40	1,136	4,919	59,027	31.20	1,248	5,404	64,846
22.85	914	3,958	47,491	25.65	1,026	4,443	53,311	28.45	1,138	4,928	59,130	31.25	1,250	5,412	64,950
22.90	916	3,966	47,595	25.70	1,028	4,451	53,415	28.50	1,140	4,936	59,234	31.30	1,252	5,421	65,054
22.95	918	3,975	47,699	25.75	1,030	4,460	53,519	28.55	1,142	4,945	59,338	31.35	1,254	5,430	65,158
23.00	920	3,984	47,803	25.80	1,032	4,469	53,623	28.60	1,144	4,954	59,442	31.40	1,256	5,438	65,262
23.05	922	3,992	47,907	25.85	1,034	4,477	53,727	28.65	1,146	4,962	59,546	31.45	1,258	5,447	65,366
23.10	924	4,001	48,011	25.90	1,036	4,486	53,831	28.70	1,148	4,971	59,650	31.50	1,260	5,456	65,470
23.15	926	4,010	48,115	25.95	1,038	4,495	53,934	28.75	1,150	4,979	59,754	31.55	1,262	5,464	65,574
23.20	928	4,018	48,219	26.00	1,040	4,503	54,038	28.80	1,152	4,988	59,858	31.60	1,264	5,473	65,677
23.25	930	4,027	48,323	26.05	1,042	4,512	54,142	28.85	1,154	4,997	59,962	31.65	1,266	5,482	65,781
23.30	932	4,036	48,427	26.10	1,044	4,521	54,246	28.90	1,156	5,005	60,066	31.70	1,268	5,490	65,885
23.35	934	4,044	48,531	26.15	1,046	4,529	54,350	28.95	1,158	5,014	60,170	31.75	1,270	5,499	65,989
23.40	936	4,053	48,635	26.20	1,048	4,538	54,454	29.00	1,160	5,023	60,274	31.80	1,272	5,508	66,093
23.45	938	4,062	48,738	26.25	1,050	4,546	54,558	29.05	1,162	5,031	60,378	31.85	1,274	5,516	66,197
23.50	940	4,070	48,842	26.30	1,052	4,555	54,662	29.10	1,164	5,040	60,481	31.90	1,276	5,525	66,301
23.55	942	4,079	48,946	26.35	1,054	4,564	54,766	29.15	1,166	5,049	60,585	31.95	1,278	5,534	66,405
23.60	944	4,088	49,050	26.40	1,056	4,572	54,870	29.20	1,168	5,057	60,689	32.00	1,280	5,542	66,509
23.65	946	4,096	49,154	26.45	1,058	4,581	54,974	29.25	1,170	5,066	60,793	32.05	1,282	5,551	66,613
23.70	948	4,105	49,258	26.50	1,060	4,590	55,078	29.30	1,172	5,075	60,897	32.10	1,284	5,560	66,717
23.75	950	4,113	49,362	26.55	1,062	4,598	55,182	29.35	1,174	5,083	61,001	32.15	1,286	5,568	66,821
23.80	952	4,122	49,466	26.60	1,064	4,607	55,285	29.40	1,176	5,092	61,105	32.20	1,288	5,577	66,924
23.85	954	4,131	49,570	26.65	1,066	4,616	55,389	29.45	1,178	5,101	61,209	32.25	1,290	5,586	67,028
23.90	956	4,139	49,674	26.70	1,068	4,624	55,493	29.50	1,180	5,109	61,313	32.30	1,292	5,594	67,132
23.95	958	4,148	49,778	26.75	1,070	4,633	55,597	29.55	1,182	5,118	61,417	32.35	1,294	5,603	67,236
24.00	960	4,157	49,882	26.80	1,072	4,642	55,701	29.60	1,184	5,127	61,521	32.40	1,296	5,612	67,340
24.05	962	4,165	49,986	26.85	1,074	4,650	55,805	29.65	1,186	5,135	61,625	32.45	1,298	5,620	67,444
24.10	964	4,174	50,089	26.90	1,076	4,659	55,909	29.70	1,188	5,144	61,728	32.50	1,300	5,629	67,548
24.15	966	4,183	50,193	26.95	1,078	4,668	56,013	29.75	1,190	5,153	61,832	32.55	1,302	5,638	67,652
24.20	968	4,191	50,297	27.00	1,080	4,676	56,117	29.80	1,192	5,161	61,936	32.60	1,304	5,646	67,756
24.25	970	4,200	50,401	27.05	1,082	4,685	56,221	29.85	1,194	5,170	62,040	32.65	1,306	5,655	67,860
24.30	972	4,209	50,505	27.10	1,084	4,694	56,325	29.90	1,196	5,179	62,144	32.70	1,308	5,664	67,964
24.35	974	4,217	50,609	27.15	1,086	4,702	56,429	29.95	1,198	5,187	62,248	32.75	1,310	5,672	68,068

Hour	Week	Month	Year	Hour	Week	Month	Year	Hour	Week	Month	Year	Hour	Week	Month	Year
32.80	1,312	5,681	68,172	35.60	1,424	6,166	73,991	38.40	1,536	6,651	79,811	41.20	1,648	7,136	85,630
32.85	1,314	5,690	68,275	35.65	1,426	6,175	74,095	38.45	1,538	6,660	79,914	41.25	1,650	7,144	85,734
32.90	1,316	5,698	68,379	35.70	1,428	6,183	74,199	38.50	1,540	6,668	80,018	41.30	1,652	7,153	85,838
32.95	1,318	5,707	68,483	35.75	1,430	6,192	74,303	38.55	1,542	6,677	80,122	41.35	1,654	7,162	85,942
33.00	1,320	5,716	68,587	35.80	1,432	6,201	74,407	38.60	1,544	6,686	80,226	41.40	1,656	7,170	86,046
33.05	1,322	5,724	68,691	35.85	1,434	6,209	74,511	38.65	1,546	6,694	80,330	41.45	1,658	7,179	86,150
33.10	1,324	5,733	68,795	35.90	1,436	6,218	74,615	38.70	1,548	6,703	80,434	41.50	1,660	7,188	86,254
33.15	1,326	5,742	68,899	35.95	1,438	6,227	74,718	38.75	1,550	6,711	80,538	41.55	1,662	7,196	86,358
33.20	1,328	5,750	69,003	36.00	1,440	6,235	74,822	38.80	1,552	6,720	80,642	41.60	1,664	7,205	86,461
33.25	1,330	5,759	69,107	36.05	1,442	6,244	74,926	38.85	1,554	6,729	80,746	41.65	1,666	7,214	86,565
33.30	1,332	5,768	69,211	36.10	1,444	6,253	75,030	38.90	1,556	6,737	80,850	41.70	1,668	7,222	86,669
33.35	1,334	5,776	69,315	36.15	1,446	6,261	75,134	38.95	1,558	6,746	80,954	41.75	1,670	7,231	86,773
33.40	1,336	5,785	69,419	36.20	1,448	6,270	75,238	39.00	1,560	6,755	81,058	41.80	1,672	7,240	86,877
33.45	1,338	5,794	69,522	36.25	1,450	6,278	75,342	39.05	1,562	6,763	81,162	41.85	1,674	7,248	86,981
33.50	1,340	5,802	69,626	36.30	1,452	6,287	75,446	39.10	1,564	6,772	81,265	41.90	1,676	7,257	87,085
33.55	1,342	5,811	69,730	36.35	1,454	6,296	75,550	39.15	1,566	6,781	81,369	41.95	1,678	7,266	87,189
33.60	1,344	5,820	69,834	36.40	1,456	6,304	75,654	39.20	1,568	6,789	81,473	42.00	1,680	7,274	87,293
33.65	1,346	5,828	69,938	36.45	1,458	6,313	75,758	39.25	1,570	6,798	81,577	42.05	1,682	7,283	87,397
33.70	1,348	5,837	70,042	36.50	1,460	6,322	75,862	39.30	1,572	6,807	81,681	42.10	1,684	7,292	87,501
33.75	1,350	5,845	70,146	36.55	1,462	6,330	75,966	39.35	1,574	6,815	81,785	42.15	1,686	7,300	87,605
33.80	1,352	5,854	70,250	36.60	1,464	6,339	76,069	39.40	1,576	6,824	81,889	42.20	1,688	7,309	87,708
33.85	1,354	5,863	70,354	36.65	1,466	6,348	76,173	39.45	1,578	6,833	81,993	42.25	1,690	7,318	87,812
33.90	1,356	5,871	70,458	36.70	1,468	6,356	76,277	39.50	1,580	6,841	82,097	42.30	1,692	7,326	87,916
33.95	1,358	5,880	70,562	36.75	1,470	6,365	76,381	39.55	1,582	6,850	82,201	42.35	1,694	7,335	88,020
34.00	1,360	5,889	70,666	36.80	1,472	6,374	76,485	39.60	1,584	6,859	82,305	42.40	1,696	7,344	88,124
34.05	1,362	5,897	70,770	36.85	1,474	6,382	76,589	39.65	1,586	6,867	82,409	42.45	1,698	7,352	88,228
34.10	1,364	5,906	70,873	36.90	1,476	6,391	76,693	39.70	1,588	6,876	82,512	42.50	1,700	7,361	88,332
34.15	1,366	5,915	70,977	36.95	1,478	6,400	76,797	39.75	1,590	6,885	82,616	42.55	1,702	7,370	88,436
34.20	1,368	5,923	71,081	37.00	1,480	6,408	76,901	39.80	1,592	6,893	82,720	42.60	1,704	7,378	88,540
34.25	1,370	5,932	71,185	37.05	1,482	6,417	77,005	39.85	1,594	6,902	82,824	42.65	1,706	7,387	88,644
34.30	1,372	5,941	71,289	37.10	1,484	6,426	77,109	39.90	1,596	6,911	82,928	42.70	1,708	7,396	88,748
34.35	1,374	5,949	71,393	37.15	1,486	6,434	77,213	39.95	1,598	6,919	83,032	42.75	1,710	7,404	88,852
34.40	1,376	5,958	71,497	37.20	1,488	6,443	77,316	40.00	1,600	6,928	83,136	42.80	1,712	7,413	88,956
34.45	1,378	5,967	71,601	37.25	1,490	6,452	77,420	40.05	1,602	6,937	83,240	42.85	1,714	7,422	89,059
34.50	1,380	5,975	71,705	37.30	1,492	6,460	77,524	40.10	1,604	6,945	83,344	42.90	1,716	7,430	89,163
34.55	1,382	5,984	71,809	37.35	1,494	6,469	77,628	40.15	1,606	6,954	83,448	42.95	1,718	7,439	89,267
34.60	1,384	5,993	71,913	37.40	1,496	6,478	77,732	40.20	1,608	6,963	83,552	43.00	1,720	7,448	89,371
34.65	1,386	6,001	72,017	37.45	1,498	6,486	77,836	40.25	1,610	6,971	83,656	43.05	1,722	7,456	89,475
34.70	1,388	6,010	72,120	37.50	1,500	6,495	77,940	40.30	1,612	6,980	83,760	43.10	1,724	7,465	89,579
34.75	1,390	6,019	72,224	37.55	1,502	6,504	78,044	40.35	1,614	6,989	83,863	43.15	1,726	7,474	89,683
34.80	1,392	6,027	72,328	37.60	1,504	6,512	78,148	40.40	1,616	6,997	83,967	43.20	1,728	7,482	89,787
34.85	1,394	6,036	72,432	37.65	1,506	6,521	78,252	40.45	1,618	7,006	84,071	43.25	1,730	7,491	89,891
34.90	1,396	6,045	72,536	37.70	1,508	6,530	78,356	40.50	1,620	7,015	84,175	43.30	1,732	7,500	89,995
34.95	1,398	6,053	72,640	37.75	1,510	6,538	78,460	40.55	1,622	7,023	84,279	43.35	1,734	7,508	90,099
35.00	1,400	6,062	72,744	37.80	1,512	6,547	78,564	40.60	1,624	7,032	84,383	43.40	1,736	7,517	90,203
35.05	1,402	6,071	72,848	37.85	1,514	6,556	78,667	40.65	1,626	7,041	84,487	43.45	1,738	7,526	90,306
35.10	1,404	6,079	72,952	37.90	1,516	6,564	78,771	40.70	1,628	7,049	84,591	43.50	1,740	7,534	90,410
35.15	1,406	6,088	73,056	37.95	1,518	6,573	78,875	40.75	1,630	7,058	84,695	43.55	1,742	7,543	90,514
35.20	1,408	6,097	73,160	38.00	1,520	6,582	78,979	40.80	1,632	7,067	84,799	43.60	1,744	7,552	90,618
35.25	1,410	6,105	73,264	38.05	1,522	6,590	79,083	40.85	1,634	7,075	84,903	43.65	1,746	7,560	90,722
35.30	1,412	6,114	73,368	38.10	1,524	6,599	79,187	40.90	1,636	7,084	85,007	43.70	1,748	7,569	90,826
35.35	1,414	6,123	73,471	38.15	1,526	6,608	79,291	40.95	1,638	7,093	85,110	43.75	1,750	7,577	90,930
35.40	1,416	6,131	73,575	38.20	1,528	6,616	79,395	41.00	1,640	7,101	85,214	43.80	1,752	7,586	91,034
35.45	1,418	6,140	73,679	38.25	1,530	6,625	79,499	41.05	1,642	7,110	85,318	43.85	1,754	7,595	91,138
35.50	1,420	6,149	73,783	38.30	1,532	6,634	79,603	41.10	1,644	7,119	85,422	43.90	1,756	7,603	91,242
35.55	1,422	6,157	73,887	38.35	1,534	6,642	79,707	41.15	1,646	7,127	85,526	43.95	1,758	7,612	91,346

Hour	Week	Month	Year	Hour	Week	Month	Year	Hour	Week	Month	Year	Hour	Week	Month	Year
44.00	1,760	7,621	91,450	46.80	1,872	8,106	97,269	49.60	1,984	8,591	103,089	52.40	2,096	9,076	108,908
44.05	1,762	7,629	91,554	46.85	1,874	8,114	97,373	49.65	1,986	8,599	103,193	52.45	2,098	9,084	109,012
44.10	1,764	7,638	91,657	46.90	1,876	8,123	97,477	49.70	1,988	8,608	103,296	52.50	2,100	9,093	109,116
44.15	1,766	7,647	91,761	46.95	1,878	8,132	97,581	49.75	1,990	8,617	103,400	52.55	2,102	9,102	109,220
44.20	1,768	7,655	91,865	47.00	1,880	8,140	97,685	49.80	1,992	8,625	103,504	52.60	2,104	9,110	109,324
44.25	1,770	7,664	91,969	47.05	1,882	8,149	97,789	49.85	1,994	8,634	103,608	52.65	2,106	9,119	109,428
44.30	1,772	7,673	92,073	47.10	1,884	8,158	97,893	49.90	1,996	8,643	103,712	52.70	2,108	9,128	109,532
44.35	1,774	7,681	92,177	47.15	1,886	8,166	97,997	49.95	1,998	8,651	103,816	52.75	2,110	9,136	109,636
44.40	1,776	7,690	92,281	47.20	1,888	8,175	98,100	50.00	2,000	8,660	103,920	52.80	2,112	9,145	109,740
44.45	1,778	7,699	92,385	47.25	1,890	8,184	98,204	50.05	2,002	8,669	104,024	52.85	2,114	9,154	109,843
44.50	1,780	7,707	92,489	47.30	1,892	8,192	98,308	50.10	2,004	8,677	104,128	52.90	2,116	9,162	109,947
44.55	1,782	7,716	92,593	47.35	1,894	8,201	98,412	50.15	2,006	8,686	104,232	52.95	2,118	9,171	110,051
44.60	1,784	7,725	92,697	47.40	1,896	8,210	98,516	50.20	2,008	8,695	104,336	53.00	2,120	9,180	110,155
44.65	1,786	7,733	92,801	47.45	1,898	8,218	98,620	50.25	2,010	8,703	104,440	53.05	2,122	9,188	110,259
44.70	1,788	7,742	92,904	47.50	1,900	8,227	98,724	50.30	2,012	8,712	104,544	53.10	2,124	9,197	110,363
44.75	1,790	7,751	93,008	47.55	1,902	8,236	98,828	50.35	2,014	8,721	104,647	53.15	2,126	9,206	110,467
44.80	1,792	7,759	93,112	47.60	1,904	8,244	98,932	50.40	2,016	8,729	104,751	53.20	2,128	9,214	110,571
44.85	1,794	7,768	93,216	47.65	1,906	8,253	99,036	50.45	2,018	8,738	104,855	53.25	2,130	9,223	110,675
44.90	1,796	7,777	93,320	47.70	1,908	8,262	99,140	50.50	2,020	8,747	104,959	53.30	2,132	9,232	110,779
44.95	1,798	7,785	93,424	47.75	1,910	8,270	99,244	50.55	2,022	8,755	105,063	53.35	2,134	9,240	110,883
45.00	1,800	7,794	93,528	47.80	1,912	8,279	99,348	50.60	2,024	8,764	105,167	53.40	2,136	9,249	110,987
45.05	1,802	7,803	93,632	47.85	1,914	8,288	99,451	50.65	2,026	8,773	105,271	53.45	2,138	9,258	111,090
45.10	1,804	7,811	93,736	47.90	1,916	8,296	99,555	50.70	2,028	8,781	105,375	53.50	2,140	9,266	111,194
45.15	1,806	7,820	93,840	47.95	1,918	8,305	99,659	50.75	2,030	8,790	105,479	53.55	2,142	9,275	111,298
45.20	1,808	7,829	93,944	48.00	1,920	8,314	99,763	50.80	2,032	8,799	105,583	53.60	2,144	9,284	111,402
45.25	1,810	7,837	94,048	48.05	1,922	8,322	99,867	50.85	2,034	8,807	105,687	53.65	2,146	9,292	111,506
45.30	1,812	7,846	94,152	48.10	1,924	8,331	99,971	50.90	2,036	8,816	105,791	53.70	2,148	9,301	111,610
45.35	1,814	7,855	94,255	48.15	1,926	8,340	100,075	50.95	2,038	8,825	105,894	53.75	2,150	9,309	111,714
45.40	1,816	7,863	94,359	48.20	1,928	8,348	100,179	51.00	2,040	8,833	105,998	53.80	2,152	9,318	111,818
45.45	1,818	7,872	94,463	48.25	1,930	8,357	100,283	51.05	2,042	8,842	106,102	53.85	2,154	9,327	111,922
45.50	1,820	7,881	94,567	48.30	1,932	8,366	100,387	51.10	2,044	8,851	106,206	53.90	2,156	9,335	112,026
45.55	1,822	7,889	94,671	48.35	1,934	8,374	100,491	51.15	2,046	8,859	106,310	53.95	2,158	9,344	112,130
45.60	1,824	7,898	94,775	48.40	1,936	8,383	100,595	51.20	2,048	8,868	106,414	54.00	2,160	9,353	112,234
45.65	1,826	7,907	94,879	48.45	1,938	8,392	100,698	51.25	2,050	8,876	106,518	54.05	2,162	9,361	112,338
45.70	1,828	7,915	94,983	48.50	1,940	8,400	100,802	51.30	2,052	8,885	106,622	54.10	2,164	9,370	112,441
45.75	1,830	7,924	95,087	48.55	1,942	8,409	100,906	51.35	2,054	8,894	106,726	54.15	2,166	9,379	112,545
45.80	1,832	7,933	95,191	48.60	1,944	8,418	101,010	51.40	2,056	8,902	106,830	54.20	2,168	9,387	112,649
45.85	1,834	7,941	95,295	48.65	1,946	8,426	101,114	51.45	2,058	8,911	106,934	54.25	2,170	9,396	112,753
45.90	1,836	7,950	95,399	48.70	1,948	8,435	101,218	51.50	2,060	8,920	107,038	54.30	2,172	9,405	112,857
45.95	1,838	7,959	95,502	48.75	1,950	8,443	101,322	51.55	2,062	8,928	107,142	54.35	2,174	9,413	112,961
46.00	1,840	7,967	95,606	48.80	1,952	8,452	101,426	51.60	2,064	8,937	107,245	54.40	2,176	9,411	113,070
46.05	1,842	7,976	95,710	48.85	1,954	8,461	101,530	51.65	2,066	8,946	107,349	54.45	2,178	9,420	113,174
46.10	1,844	7,985	95,814	48.90	1,956	8,469	101,634	51.70	2,068	8,954	107,453	54.50	2,180	9,429	113,278
46.15	1,846	7,993	95,918	48.95	1,958	8,478	101,738	51.75	2,070	8,963	107,557	54.55	2,182	9,437	113,382
46.20	1,848	8,002	96,022	49.00	1,960	8,487	101,842	51.80	2,072	8,972	107,661	54.60	2,184	9,446	113,486
46.25	1,850	8,010	96,126	49.05	1,962	8,495	101,946	51.85	2,074	8,980	107,765	54.65	2,186	9,454	113,590
46.30	1,852	8,019	96,230	49.10	1,964	8,504	102,049	51.90	2,076	8,989	107,869	54.70	2,188	9,463	113,694
46.35	1,854	8,028	96,334	49.15	1,966	8,513	102,153	51.95	2,078	8,998	107,973	54.75	2,190	9,472	113,798
46.40	1,856	8,036	96,438	49.20	1,968	8,521	102,257	52.00	2,080	9,006	108,077	54.80	2,192	9,480	113,902
46.45	1,858	8,045	96,542	49.25	1,970	8,530	102,361	52.05	2,082	9,015	108,181	54.85	2,194	9,489	114,006
46.50	1,860	8,054	96,646	49.30	1,972	8,539	102,465	52.10	2,084	9,024	108,285	54.90	2,196	9,498	114,110
46.55	1,862	8,062	96,750	49.35	1,974	8,547	102,569	52.15	2,086	9,032	108,389	54.95	2,198	9,506	114,214
46.60	1,864	8,071	96,853	49.40	1,976	8,556	102,673	52.20	2,088	9,041	108,492	55.00	2,200	9,515	114,318
46.65	1,866	8,080	96,957	49.45	1,978	8,565	102,777	52.25	2,090	9,050	108,596	55.05	2,202	9,524	114,421
46.70	1,868	8,088	97,061	49.50	1,980	8,573	102,881	52.30	2,092	9,058	108,700	55.10	2,204	9,532	114,525
46.75	1,870	8,097	97,165	49.55	1,982	8,582	102,985	52.35	2,094	9,067	108,804	55.15	2,206	9,541	114,629

Hour	Week	Month	Year	Hour	Week	Month	Year	Hour	Week	Month	Year	Hour	Week	Month	Year
55.20	2,208	9,550	114,733	58.00	2,320	10,034	120,553	60.80	2,432	10,518	126,373	63.60	2,544	11,003	132,193
55.25	2,210	9,558	114,837	58.05	2,322	10,043	120,657	60.85	2,434	10,527	126,477	63.65	2,546	11,011	132,297
55.30	2,212	9,567	114,941	58.10	2,324	10,051	120,761	60.90	2,436	10,536	126,581	63.70	2,548	11,020	132,400
55.35	2,214	9,576	115,045	58.15	2,326	10,060	120,865	60.95	2,438	10,544	126,685	63.75	2,550	11,029	132,504
55.40	2,216	9,584	115,149	58.20	2,328	10,069	120,969	61.00	2,440	10,553	126,788	63.80	2,552	11,037	132,608
55.45	2,218	9,593	115,253	58.25	2,330	10,077	121,073	61.05	2,442	10,562	126,892	63.85	2,554	11,046	132,712
55.50	2,220	9,602	115,357	58.30	2,332	10,086	121,177	61.10	2,444	10,570	126,996	63.90	2,556	11,055	132,816
55.55	2,222	9,610	115,461	58.35	2,334	10,095	121,280	61.15	2,446	10,579	127,100	63.95	2,558	11,063	132,920
55.60	2,224	9,619	115,565	58.40	2,336	10,103	121,384	61.20	2,448	10,588	127,204	64.00	2,560	11,072	133,024
55.65	2,226	9,627	115,669	58.45	2,338	10,112	121,488	61.25	2,450	10,596	127,308	64.05	2,562	11,081	133,128
55.70	2,228	9,636	115,772	58.50	2,340	10,121	121,592	61.30	2,452	10,605	127,412	64.10	2,564	11,089	133,232
55.75	2,230	9,645	115,876	58.55	2,342	10,129	121,696	61.35	2,454	10,614	127,516	64.15	2,566	11,098	133,336
55.80	2,232	9,653	115,980	58.60	2,344	10,138	121,800	61.40	2,456	10,622	127,620	64.20	2,568	11,107	133,440
55.85	2,234	9,662	116,084	58.65	2,346	10,146	121,904	61.45	2,458	10,631	127,724	64.25	2,570	11,115	133,544
55.90	2,236	9,671	116,188	58.70	2,348	10,155	122,008	61.50	2,460	10,640	127,828	64.30	2,572	11,124	133,648
55.95	2,238	9,679	116,292	58.75	2,350	10,164	122,112	61.55	2,462	10,648	127,932	64.35	2,574	11,133	133,751
56.00	2,240	9,688	116,396	58.80	2,352	10,172	122,216	61.60	2,464	10,657	128,036	64.40	2,576	11,141	133,855
56.05	2,242	9,697	116,500	58.85	2,354	10,181	122,320	61.65	2,466	10,665	128,140	64.45	2,578	11,150	133,959
56.10	2,244	9,705	116,604	58.90	2,356	10,190	122,424	61.70	2,468	10,674	128,243	64.50	2,580	11,158	134,063
56.15	2,246	9,714	116,708	58.95	2,358	10,198	122,528	61.75	2,470	10,683	128,347	64.55	2,582	11,167	134,167
56.20	2,248	9,723	116,812	59.00	2,360	10,207	122,632	61.80	2,472	10,691	128,451	64.60	2,584	11,176	134,271
56.25	2,250	9,731	116,916	59.05	2,362	10,216	122,735	61.85	2,474	10,700	128,555	64.65	2,586	11,184	134,375
56.30	2,252	9,740	117,020	59.10	2,364	10,224	122,839	61.90	2,476	10,709	128,659	64.70	2,588	11,193	134,479
56.35	2,254	9,749	117,123	59.15	2,366	10,233	122,943	61.95	2,478	10,717	128,763	64.75	2,590	11,202	134,583
56.40	2,256	9,757	117,227	59.20	2,368	10,242	123,047	62.00	2,480	10,726	128,867	64.80	2,592	11,210	134,687
56.45	2,258	9,766	117,331	59.25	2,370	10,250	123,151	62.05	2,482	10,735	128,971	64.85	2,594	11,219	134,791
56.50	2,260	9,775	117,435	59.30	2,372	10,259	123,255	62.10	2,484	10,743	129,075	64.90	2,596	11,228	134,895
56.55	2,262	9,783	117,539	59.35	2,374	10,268	123,359	62.15	2,486	10,752	129,179	64.95	2,598	11,236	134,999
56.60	2,264	9,792	117,643	59.40	2,376	10,276	123,463	62.20	2,488	10,761	129,283	65.00	2,600	11,245	135,102
56.65	2,266	9,800	117,747	59.45	2,378	10,285	123,567	62.25	2,490	10,769	129,387	65.05	2,602	11,254	135,206
56.70	2,268	9,809	117,851	59.50	2,380	10,294	123,671	62.30	2,492	10,778	129,491	65.10	2,604	11,262	135,310
56.75	2,270	9,818	117,955	59.55	2,382	10,302	123,775	62.35	2,494	10,787	129,594	65.15	2,606	11,271	135,414
56.80	2,272	9,826	118,059	59.60	2,384	10,311	123,879	62.40	2,496	10,795	129,698	65.20	2,608	11,280	135,518
56.85	2,274	9,835	118,163	59.65	2,386	10,319	123,983	62.45	2,498	10,804	129,802	65.25	2,610	11,288	135,622
56.90	2,276	9,844	118,267	59.70	2,388	10,328	124,086	62.50	2,500	10,812	129,906	65.30	2,612	11,297	135,726
56.95	2,278	9,852	118,371	59.75	2,390	10,337	124,190	62.55	2,502	10,821	130,010	65.35	2,614	11,306	135,830
57.00	2,280	9,861	118,475	59.80	2,392	10,345	124,294	62.60	2,504	10,830	130,114	65.40	2,616	11,314	135,934
57.05	2,282	9,870	118,578	59.85	2,394	10,354	124,398	62.65	2,506	10,838	130,218	65.45	2,618	11,323	136,038
57.10	2,284	9,878	118,682	59.90	2,396	10,363	124,502	62.70	2,508	10,847	130,322	65.50	2,620	11,331	136,142
57.15	2,286	9,887	118,786	59.95	2,398	10,371	124,606	62.75	2,510	10,856	130,426	65.55	2,622	11,340	136,246
57.20	2,288	9,896	118,890	60.00	2,400	10,380	124,710	62.80	2,512	10,864	130,530	65.60	2,624	11,349	136,350
57.25	2,290	9,904	118,994	60.05	2,402	10,389	124,814	62.85	2,514	10,873	130,634	65.65	2,626	11,357	136,454
57.30	2,292	9,913	119,098	60.10	2,404	10,397	124,918	62.90	2,516	10,882	130,738	65.70	2,628	11,366	136,557
57.35	2,294	9,922	119,202	60.15	2,406	10,406	125,022	62.95	2,518	10,890	130,842	65.75	2,630	11,375	136,661
57.40	2,296	9,930	119,306	60.20	2,408	10,415	125,126	63.00	2,520	10,899	130,945	65.80	2,632	11,383	136,765
57.45	2,298	9,939	119,410	60.25	2,410	10,423	125,230	63.05	2,522	10,908	131,049	65.85	2,634	11,392	136,869
57.50	2,300	9,947	119,514	60.30	2,412	10,432	125,334	63.10	2,524	10,916	131,153	65.90	2,636	11,401	136,973
57.55	2,302	9,956	119,618	60.35	2,414	10,441	125,437	63.15	2,526	10,925	131,257	65.95	2,638	11,409	137,077
57.60	2,304	9,965	119,722	60.40	2,416	10,449	125,541	63.20	2,528	10,934	131,361	66.00	2,640	11,418	137,181
57.65	2,306	9,973	119,826	60.45	2,418	10,458	125,645	63.25	2,530	10,942	131,465	66.05	2,642	11,427	137,285
57.70	2,308	9,982	119,929	60.50	2,420	10,467	125,749	63.30	2,532	10,951	131,569	66.10	2,644	11,435	137,389
57.75	2,310	9,991	120,033	60.55	2,422	10,475	125,853	63.35	2,534	10,960	131,673	66.15	2,646	11,444	137,493
57.80	2,312	9,999	120,137	60.60	2,424	10,484	125,957	63.40	2,536	10,968	131,777	66.20	2,648	11,453	137,597
57.85	2,314	10,008	120,241	60.65	2,426	10,492	126,061	63.45	2,538	10,977	131,881	66.25	2,650	11,461	137,701
57.90	2,316	10,017	120,345	60.70	2,428	10,501	126,165	63.50	2,540	10,985	131,985	66.30	2,652	11,470	137,805
57.95	2,318	10,025	120,449	60.75	2,430	10,510	126,269	63.55	2,542	10,994	132,089	66.35	2,654	11,479	137,908

Hour	Week	Month	Year	Hour	Week	Month	Year	Hour	Week	Month	Year	Hour	Week	Month	Year
66.40	2,656	11,487	138,012	69.20	2,768	11,972	143,832	72.00	2,880	12,456	149,652	74.80	2,992	12,940	155,472
66.45	2,658	11,496	138,116	69.25	2,770	11,980	143,936	72.05	2,882	12,465	149,756	74.85	2,994	12,949	155,576
66.50	2,660	11,504	138,220	69.30	2,772	11,989	144,040	72.10	2,884	12,473	149,860	74.90	2,996	12,958	155,680
66.55	2,662	11,513	138,324	69.35	2,774	11,998	144,144	72.15	2,886	12,482	149,964	74.95	2,998	12,966	155,784
66.60	2,664	11,522	138,428	69.40	2,776	12,006	144,248	72.20	2,888	12,491	150,068	75.00	3,000	12,975	155,887
66.65	2,666	11,530	138,532	69.45	2,778	12,015	144,352	72.25	2,890	12,499	150,172	75.05	3,002	12,984	155,991
66.70	2,668	11,539	138,636	69.50	2,780	12,023	144,456	72.30	2,892	12,508	150,276	75.10	3,004	12,992	156,095
66.75	2,670	11,548	138,740	69.55	2,782	12,032	144,560	72.35	2,894	12,517	150,379	75.15	3,006	13,001	156,199
66.80	2,672	11,556	138,844	69.60	2,784	12,041	144,664	72.40	2,896	12,525	150,483	75.20	3,008	13,010	156,303
66.85	2,674	11,565	138,948	69.65	2,786	12,049	144,768	72.45	2,898	12,534	150,587	75.25	3,010	13,018	156,407
66.90	2,676	11,574	139,052	69.70	2,788	12,058	144,871	72.50	2,900	12,542	150,691	75.30	3,012	13,027	156,511
66.95	2,678	11,582	139,156	69.75	2,790	12,067	144,975	72.55	2,902	12,551	150,795	75.35	3,014	13,036	156,615
67.00	2,680	11,591	139,259	69.80	2,792	12,075	145,079	72.60	2,904	12,560	150,899	75.40	3,016	13,044	156,719
67.05	2,682	11,600	139,363	69.85	2,794	12,084	145,183	72.65	2,906	12,568	151,003	75.45	3,018	13,053	156,823
67.10	2,684	11,608	139,467	69.90	2,796	12,093	145,287	72.70	2,908	12,577	151,107	75.50	3,020	13,061	156,927
67.15	2,686	11,617	139,571	69.95	2,798	12,101	145,391	72.75	2,910	12,586	151,211	75.55	3,022	13,070	157,031
67.20	2,688	11,626	139,675	70.00	2,800	12,110	145,495	72.80	2,912	12,594	151,315	75.60	3,024	13,079	157,135
67.25	2,690	11,634	139,779	70.05	2,802	12,119	145,599	72.85	2,914	12,603	151,419	75.65	3,026	13,087	157,239
67.30	2,692	11,643	139,883	70.10	2,804	12,127	145,703	72.90	2,916	12,612	151,523	75.70	3,028	13,096	157,342
67.35	2,694	11,652	139,987	70.15	2,806	12,136	145,807	72.95	2,918	12,620	151,627	75.75	3,030	13,105	157,446
67.40	2,696	11,660	140,091	70.20	2,808	12,145	145,911	73.00	2,920	12,629	151,730	75.80	3,032	13,113	157,550
67.45	2,698	11,669	140,195	70.25	2,810	12,153	146,015	73.05	2,922	12,638	151,834	75.85	3,034	13,122	157,654
67.50	2,700	11,677	140,299	70.30	2,812	12,162	146,119	73.10	2,924	12,646	151,938	75.90	3,036	13,131	157,758
67.55	2,702	11,686	140,403	70.35	2,814	12,171	146,222	73.15	2,926	12,655	152,042	75.95	3,038	13,139	157,862
67.60	2,704	11,695	140,507	70.40	2,816	12,179	146,326	73.20	2,928	12,664	152,146	76.00	3,040	13,148	157,966
67.65	2,706	11,703	140,611	70.45	2,818	12,188	146,430	73.25	2,930	12,672	152,250	76.05	3,042	13,157	158,070
67.70	2,708	11,712	140,714	70.50	2,820	12,196	146,534	73.30	2,932	12,681	152,354	76.10	3,044	13,165	158,174
67.75	2,710	11,721	140,818	70.55	2,822	12,205	146,638	73.35	2,934	12,690	152,458	76.15	3,046	13,174	158,278
67.80	2,712	11,729	140,922	70.60	2,824	12,214	146,742	73.40	2,936	12,698	152,562	76.20	3,048	13,183	158,382
67.85	2,714	11,738	141,026	70.65	2,826	12,222	146,846	73.45	2,938	12,707	152,666	76.25	3,050	13,191	158,486
67.90	2,716	11,747	141,130	70.70	2,828	12,231	146,950	73.50	2,940	12,715	152,770	76.30	3,052	13,200	158,590
67.95	2,718	11,755	141,234	70.75	2,830	12,240	147,054	73.55	2,942	12,724	152,874	76.35	3,054	13,209	158,693
68.00	2,720	11,764	141,338	70.80	2,832	12,248	147,158	73.60	2,944	12,733	152,978	76.40	3,056	13,217	158,797
68.05	2,722	11,773	141,442	70.85	2,834	12,257	147,262	73.65	2,946	12,741	153,082	76.45	3,058	13,226	158,901
68.10	2,724	11,781	141,546	70.90	2,836	12,266	147,366	73.70	2,948	12,750	153,185	76.50	3,060	13,234	159,005
68.15	2,726	11,790	141,650	70.95	2,838	12,274	147,470	73.75	2,950	12,759	153,289	76.55	3,062	13,243	159,109
68.20	2,728	11,799	141,754	71.00	2,840	12,283	147,573	73.80	2,952	12,767	153,393	76.60	3,064	13,252	159,213
68.25	2,730	11,807	141,858	71.05	2,842	12,292	147,677	73.85	2,954	12,776	153,497	76.65	3,066	13,260	159,317
68.30	2,732	11,816	141,962	71.10	2,844	12,300	147,781	73.90	2,956	12,785	153,601	76.70	3,068	13,269	159,421
68.35	2,734	11,825	142,065	71.15	2,846	12,309	147,885	73.95	2,958	12,793	153,705	76.75	3,070	13,278	159,525
68.40	2,736	11,833	142,169	71.20	2,848	12,318	147,989	74.00	2,960	12,802	153,809	76.80	3,072	13,286	159,629
68.45	2,738	11,842	142,273	71.25	2,850	12,326	148,093	74.05	2,962	12,811	153,913	76.85	3,074	13,295	159,733
68.50	2,740	11,850	142,377	71.30	2,852	12,335	148,197	74.10	2,964	12,819	154,017	76.90	3,076	13,304	159,837
68.55	2,742	11,859	142,481	71.35	2,854	12,344	148,301	74.15	2,966	12,828	154,121	76.95	3,078	13,312	159,941
68.60	2,744	11,868	142,585	71.40	2,856	12,352	148,405	74.20	2,968	12,837	154,225	77.00	3,080	13,321	160,044
68.65	2,746	11,876	142,689	71.45	2,858	12,361	148,509	74.25	2,970	12,845	154,329	77.05	3,082	13,330	160,148
68.70	2,748	11,885	142,793	71.50	2,860	12,369	148,613	74.30	2,972	12,854	154,433	77.10	3,084	13,338	160,252
68.75	2,750	11,894	142,897	71.55	2,862	12,378	148,717	74.35	2,974	12,863	154,536	77.15	3,086	13,347	160,356
68.80	2,752	11,902	143,001	71.60	2,864	12,387	148,821	74.40	2,976	12,871	154,640	77.20	3,088	13,356	160,460
68.85	2,754	11,911	143,105	71.65	2,866	12,395	148,925	74.45	2,978	12,880	154,744	77.25	3,090	13,364	160,564
68.90	2,756	11,920	143,209	71.70	2,868	12,404	149,028	74.50	2,980	12,888	154,848	77.30	3,092	13,373	160,668
68.95	2,758	11,928	143,313	71.75	2,870	12,413	149,132	74.55	2,982	12,897	154,952	77.35	3,094	13,382	160,772
69.00	2,760	11,937	143,416	71.80	2,872	12,421	149,236	74.60	2,984	12,906	155,056	77.40	3,096	13,390	160,876
69.05	2,762	11,946	143,520	71.85	2,874	12,430	149,340	74.65	2,986	12,914	155,160	77.45	3,098	13,399	160,980
69.10	2,764	11,954	143,624	71.90	2,876	12,439	149,444	74.70	2,988	12,923	155,264	77.50	3,100	13,407	161,084
69.15	2,766	11,963	143,728	71.95	2,878	12,447	149,548	74.75	2,990	12,932	155,368	77.55	3,102	13,416	161,188

Hour	Week	Month	Year	Hour	Week	Month	Year	Hour	Week	Month	Year	Hour	Week	Month	Year
77.60	3,104	13,425	161,292	80.40	3,216	13,909	167,111	83.20	3,328	14,394	172,931	86.00	3,440	14,878	178,751
77.65	3,106	13,433	161,396	80.45	3,218	13,918	167,215	83.25	3,330	14,402	173,035	86.05	3,442	14,887	178,855
77.70	3,108	13,442	161,499	80.50	3,220	13,926	167,319	83.30	3,332	14,411	173,139	86.10	3,444	14,895	178,959
77.75	3,110	13,451	161,603	80.55	3,222	13,935	167,423	83.35	3,334	14,420	173,243	86.15	3,446	14,904	179,063
77.80	3,112	13,459	161,707	80.60	3,224	13,944	167,527	83.40	3,336	14,428	173,347	86.20	3,448	14,913	179,167
77.85	3,114	13,468	161,811	80.65	3,226	13,952	167,631	83.45	3,338	14,437	173,451	86.25	3,450	14,921	179,271
77.90	3,116	13,477	161,915	80.70	3,228	13,961	167,735	83.50	3,340	14,445	173,555	86.30	3,452	14,930	179,375
77.95	3,118	13,485	162,019	80.75	3,230	13,970	167,839	83.55	3,342	14,454	173,659	86.35	3,454	14,939	179,478
78.00	3,120	13,494	162,123	80.80	3,232	13,978	167,943	83.60	3,344	14,463	173,763	86.40	3,456	14,947	179,582
78.05	3,122	13,503	162,227	80.85	3,234	13,987	168,047	83.65	3,346	14,471	173,867	86.45	3,458	14,956	179,686
78.10	3,124	13,511	162,331	80.90	3,236	13,996	168,151	83.70	3,348	14,480	173,970	86.50	3,460	14,964	179,790
78.15	3,126	13,520	162,435	80.95	3,238	14,004	168,255	83.75	3,350	14,489	174,074	86.55	3,462	14,973	179,894
78.20	3,128	13,529	162,539	81.00	3,240	14,013	168,358	83.80	3,352	14,497	174,178	86.60	3,464	14,982	179,998
78.25	3,130	13,537	162,643	81.05	3,242	14,022	168,462	83.85	3,354	14,506	174,282	86.65	3,466	14,990	180,102
78.30	3,132	13,546	162,747	81.10	3,244	14,030	168,566	83.90	3,356	14,515	174,386	86.70	3,468	14,999	180,206
78.35	3,134	13,555	162,850	81.15	3,246	14,039	168,670	83.95	3,358	14,523	174,490	86.75	3,470	15,008	180,310
78.40	3,136	13,563	162,954	81.20	3,248	14,048	168,774	84.00	3,360	14,532	174,594	86.80	3,472	15,016	180,414
78.45	3,138	13,572	163,058	81.25	3,250	14,056	168,878	84.05	3,362	14,541	174,698	86.85	3,474	15,025	180,518
78.50	3,140	13,580	163,162	81.30	3,252	14,065	168,982	84.10	3,364	14,549	174,802	86.90	3,476	15,034	180,622
78.55	3,142	13,589	163,266	81.35	3,254	14,074	169,086	84.15	3,366	14,558	174,906	86.95	3,478	15,042	180,726
78.60	3,144	13,598	163,370	81.40	3,256	14,082	169,190	84.20	3,368	14,567	175,010	87.00	3,480	15,051	180,829
78.65	3,146	13,606	163,474	81.45	3,258	14,091	169,294	84.25	3,370	14,575	175,114	87.05	3,482	15,060	180,933
78.70	3,148	13,615	163,578	81.50	3,260	14,099	169,398	84.30	3,372	14,584	175,218	87.10	3,484	15,068	181,037
78.75	3,150	13,624	163,682	81.55	3,262	14,108	169,502	84.35	3,374	14,593	175,321	87.15	3,486	15,077	181,141
78.80	3,152	13,632	163,786	81.60	3,264	14,117	169,606	84.40	3,376	14,601	175,425	87.20	3,488	15,086	181,245
78.85	3,154	13,641	163,890	81.65	3,266	14,125	169,710	84.45	3,378	14,610	175,529	87.25	3,490	15,094	181,349
78.90	3,156	13,650	163,994	81.70	3,268	14,134	169,813	84.50	3,380	14,618	175,633	87.30	3,492	15,103	181,453
78.95	3,158	13,658	164,098	81.75	3,270	14,143	169,917	84.55	3,382	14,627	175,737	87.35	3,494	15,112	181,557
79.00	3,160	13,667	164,201	81.80	3,272	14,151	170,021	84.60	3,384	14,636	175,841	87.40	3,496	15,120	181,661
79.05	3,162	13,676	164,305	81.85	3,274	14,160	170,125	84.65	3,386	14,644	175,945	87.45	3,498	15,129	181,765
79.10	3,164	13,684	164,409	81.90	3,276	14,169	170,229	84.70	3,388	14,653	176,049	87.50	3,500	15,137	181,869
79.15	3,166	13,693	164,513	81.95	3,278	14,177	170,333	84.75	3,390	14,662	176,153	87.55	3,502	15,146	181,973
79.20	3,168	13,702	164,617	82.00	3,280	14,186	170,437	84.80	3,392	14,670	176,257	87.60	3,504	15,155	182,077
79.25	3,170	13,710	164,721	82.05	3,282	14,195	170,541	84.85	3,394	14,679	176,361	87.65	3,506	15,163	182,181
79.30	3,172	13,719	164,825	82.10	3,284	14,203	170,645	84.90	3,396	14,688	176,465	87.70	3,508	15,172	182,284
79.35	3,174	13,728	164,929	82.15	3,286	14,212	170,749	84.95	3,398	14,696	176,569	87.75	3,510	15,181	182,388
79.40	3,176	13,736	165,033	82.20	3,288	14,221	170,853	85.00	3,400	14,705	176,672	87.80	3,512	15,189	182,492
79.45	3,178	13,745	165,137	82.25	3,290	14,229	170,957	85.05	3,402	14,714	176,776	87.85	3,514	15,198	182,596
79.50	3,180	13,753	165,241	82.30	3,292	14,238	171,061	85.10	3,404	14,722	176,880	87.90	3,516	15,207	182,700
79.55	3,182	13,762	165,345	82.35	3,294	14,247	171,164	85.15	3,406	14,731	176,984	87.95	3,518	15,215	182,804
79.60	3,184	13,771	165,449	82.40	3,296	14,255	171,268	85.20	3,408	14,740	177,088	88.00	3,520	15,224	182,908
79.65	3,186	13,779	165,553	82.45	3,298	14,264	171,372	85.25	3,410	14,748	177,192	88.05	3,522	15,233	183,012
79.70	3,188	13,788	165,656	82.50	3,300	14,272	171,476	85.30	3,412	14,757	177,296	88.10	3,524	15,241	183,116
79.75	3,190	13,797	165,760	82.55	3,302	14,281	171,580	85.35	3,414	14,766	177,400	88.15	3,526	15,250	183,220
79.80	3,192	13,805	165,864	82.60	3,304	14,290	171,684	85.40	3,416	14,774	177,504	88.20	3,528	15,259	183,324
79.85	3,194	13,814	165,968	82.65	3,306	14,298	171,788	85.45	3,418	14,783	177,608	88.25	3,530	15,267	183,428
79.90	3,196	13,823	166,072	82.70	3,308	14,307	171,892	85.50	3,420	14,791	177,712	88.30	3,532	15,276	183,532
79.95	3,198	13,831	166,176	82.75	3,310	14,316	171,996	85.55	3,422	14,800	177,816	88.35	3,534	15,285	183,635
80.00	3,200	13,840	166,280	82.80	3,312	14,324	172,100	85.60	3,424	14,809	177,920	88.40	3,536	15,293	183,739
80.05	3,202	13,849	166,384	82.85	3,314	14,333	172,204	85.65	3,426	14,817	178,024	88.45	3,538	15,302	183,843
80.10	3,204	13,857	166,488	82.90	3,316	14,342	172,308	85.70	3,428	14,826	178,127	88.50	3,540	15,310	183,947
80.15	3,206	13,866	166,592	82.95	3,318	14,350	172,412	85.75	3,430	14,835	178,231	88.55	3,542	15,319	184,051
80.20	3,208	13,875	166,696	83.00	3,320	14,359	172,515	85.80	3,432	14,843	178,335	88.60	3,544	15,328	184,155
80.25	3,210	13,883	166,800	83.05	3,322	14,368	172,619	85.85	3,434	14,852	178,439	88.65	3,546	15,336	184,259
80.30	3,212	13,892	166,904	83.10	3,324	14,376	172,723	85.90	3,436	14,861	178,543	88.70	3,548	15,345	184,363
80.35	3,214	13,901	167,007	83.15	3,326	14,385	172,827	85.95	3,438	14,869	178,647	88.75	3,550	15,354	184,467

Hour	Week	Month	Year	Hour	Week	Month	Year	Hour	Week	Month	Year	Hour	Week	Month	Year
88.80	3,552	15,362	184,571	91.60	3,664	15,847	190,391	94.40	3,776	16,331	196,210	97.20	3,888	16,816	202,030
88.85	3,554	15,371	184,675	91.65	3,666	15,855	190,495	94.45	3,778	16,340	196,314	97.25	3,890	16,824	202,134
88.90	3,556	15,380	184,779	91.70	3,668	15,864	190,598	94.50	3,780	16,348	196,418	97.30	3,892	16,833	202,238
88.95	3,558	15,388	184,883	91.75	3,670	15,873	190,702	94.55	3,782	16,357	196,522	97.35	3,894	16,842	202,342
89.00	3,560	15,397	184,986	91.80	3,672	15,881	190,806	94.60	3,784	16,366	196,626	97.40	3,896	16,850	202,446
89.05	3,562	15,406	185,090	91.85	3,674	15,890	190,910	94.65	3,786	16,374	196,730	97.45	3,898	16,859	202,550
89.10	3,564	15,414	185,194	91.90	3,676	15,899	191,014	94.70	3,788	16,383	196,834	97.50	3,900	16,867	202,654
89.15	3,566	15,423	185,298	91.95	3,678	15,907	191,118	94.75	3,790	16,392	196,938	97.55	3,902	16,876	202,758
89.20	3,568	15,432	185,402	92.00	3,680	15,916	191,222	94.80	3,792	16,400	197,042	97.60	3,904	16,885	202,862
89.25	3,570	15,440	185,506	92.05	3,682	15,925	191,326	94.85	3,794	16,409	197,146	97.65	3,906	16,893	202,966
89.30	3,572	15,449	185,610	92.10	3,684	15,933	191,430	94.90	3,796	16,418	197,250	97.70	3,908	16,902	203,069
89.35	3,574	15,458	185,714	92.15	3,686	15,942	191,534	94.95	3,798	16,426	197,354	97.75	3,910	16,911	203,173
89.40	3,576	15,466	185,818	92.20	3,688	15,951	191,638	95.00	3,800	16,435	197,457	97.80	3,912	16,919	203,277
89.45	3,578	15,475	185,922	92.25	3,690	15,959	191,742	95.05	3,802	16,444	197,561	97.85	3,914	16,928	203,381
89.50	3,580	15,483	186,026	92.30	3,692	15,968	191,846	95.10	3,804	16,452	197,665	97.90	3,916	16,937	203,485
89.55	3,582	15,492	186,130	92.35	3,694	15,977	191,949	95.15	3,806	16,461	197,769	97.95	3,918	16,945	203,589
89.60	3,584	15,501	186,234	92.40	3,696	15,985	192,053	95.20	3,808	16,470	197,873	98.00	3,920	16,954	203,693
89.65	3,586	15,509	186,338	92.45	3,698	15,994	192,157	95.25	3,810	16,478	197,977	98.05	3,922	16,963	203,797
89.70	3,588	15,518	186,441	92.50	3,700	16,002	192,261	95.30	3,812	16,487	198,081	98.10	3,924	16,971	203,901
89.75	3,590	15,527	186,545	92.55	3,702	16,011	192,365	95.35	3,814	16,496	198,185	98.15	3,926	16,980	204,005
89.80	3,592	15,535	186,649	92.60	3,704	16,020	192,469	95.40	3,816	16,504	198,289	98.20	3,928	16,989	204,109
89.85	3,594	15,544	186,753	92.65	3,706	16,028	192,573	95.45	3,818	16,513	198,393	98.25	3,930	16,997	204,213
89.90	3,596	15,553	186,857	92.70	3,708	16,037	192,677	95.50	3,820	16,521	198,497	98.30	3,932	17,006	204,317
89.95	3,598	15,561	186,961	92.75	3,710	16,046	192,781	95.55	3,822	16,530	198,601	98.35	3,934	17,015	204,420
90.00	3,600	15,570	187,065	92.80	3,712	16,054	192,885	95.60	3,824	16,539	198,705	98.40	3,936	17,023	204,524
90.05	3,602	15,579	187,169	92.85	3,714	16,063	192,989	95.65	3,826	16,547	198,809	98.45	3,938	17,032	204,628
90.10	3,604	15,587	187,273	92.90	3,716	16,072	193,093	95.70	3,828	16,556	198,912	98.50	3,940	17,040	204,732
90.15	3,606	15,596	187,377	92.95	3,718	16,080	193,197	95.75	3,830	16,565	199,016	98.55	3,942	17,049	204,836
90.20	3,608	15,605	187,481	93.00	3,720	16,089	193,300	95.80	3,832	16,573	199,120	98.60	3,944	17,058	204,940
90.25	3,610	15,613	187,585	93.05	3,722	16,098	193,404	95.85	3,834	16,582	199,224	98.65	3,946	17,066	205,044
90.30	3,612	15,622	187,689	93.10	3,724	16,106	193,508	95.90	3,836	16,591	199,328	98.70	3,948	17,075	205,148
90.35	3,614	15,631	187,792	93.15	3,726	16,115	193,612	95.95	3,838	16,599	199,432	98.75	3,950	17,084	205,252
90.40	3,616	15,639	187,896	93.20	3,728	16,124	193,716	96.00	3,840	16,608	199,536	98.80	3,952	17,092	205,356
90.45	3,618	15,648	188,000	93.25	3,730	16,132	193,820	96.05	3,842	16,617	199,640	98.85	3,954	17,101	205,460
90.50	3,620	15,656	188,104	93.30	3,732	16,141	193,924	96.10	3,844	16,625	199,744	98.90	3,956	17,110	205,564
90.55	3,622	15,665	188,208	93.35	3,734	16,150	194,028	96.15	3,846	16,634	199,848	98.95	3,958	17,118	205,668
90.60	3,624	15,674	188,312	93.40	3,736	16,158	194,132	96.20	3,848	16,643	199,952	99.00	3,960	17,127	205,771
90.65	3,626	15,682	188,416	93.45	3,738	16,167	194,236	96.25	3,850	16,651	200,056	99.05	3,962	17,136	205,875
90.70	3,628	15,691	188,520	93.50	3,740	16,175	194,340	96.30	3,852	16,660	200,160	99.10	3,964	17,144	205,979
90.75	3,630	15,700	188,624	93.55	3,742	16,184	194,444	96.35	3,854	16,669	200,263	99.15	3,966	17,153	206,083
90.80	3,632	15,708	188,728	93.60	3,744	16,193	194,548	96.40	3,856	16,677	200,367	99.20	3,968	17,162	206,187
90.85	3,634	15,717	188,832	93.65	3,746	16,201	194,652	96.45	3,858	16,686	200,471	99.25	3,970	17,170	206,291
90.90	3,636	15,726	188,936	93.70	3,748	16,210	194,755	96.50	3,860	16,694	200,575	99.30	3,972	17,179	206,395
90.95	3,638	15,734	189,040	93.75	3,750	16,219	194,859	96.55	3,862	16,703	200,679	99.35	3,974	17,188	206,499
91.00	3,640	15,743	189,143	93.80	3,752	16,227	194,963	96.60	3,864	16,712	200,783	99.40	3,976	17,196	206,603
91.05	3,642	15,752	189,247	93.85	3,754	16,236	195,067	96.65	3,866	16,720	200,887	99.45	3,978	17,205	206,707
91.10	3,644	15,760	189,351	93.90	3,756	16,245	195,171	96.70	3,868	16,729	200,991	99.50	3,980	17,213	206,811
91.15	3,646	15,769	189,455	93.95	3,758	16,253	195,275	96.75	3,870	16,738	201,095	99.55	3,982	17,222	206,915
91.20	3,648	15,778	189,559	94.00	3,760	16,262	195,379	96.80	3,872	16,746	201,199	99.60	3,984	17,231	207,019
91.25	3,650	15,786	189,663	94.05	3,762	16,271	195,483	96.85	3,874	16,755	201,303	99.65	3,986	17,239	207,123
91.30	3,652	15,795	189,767	94.10	3,764	16,279	195,587	96.90	3,876	16,764	201,407	99.70	3,988	17,248	207,226
91.35	3,654	15,804	189,871	94.15	3,766	16,288	195,691	96.95	3,878	16,772	201,511	99.75	3,990	17,257	207,330
91.40	3,656	15,812	189,975	94.20	3,768	16,297	195,795	97.00	3,880	16,781	201,614	99.80	3,992	17,265	207,434
91.45	3,658	15,821	190,079	94.25	3,770	16,305	195,899	97.05	3,882	16,790	201,718	99.85	3,994	17,274	207,538
91.50	3,660	15,829	190,183	94.30	3,772	16,314	196,003	97.10	3,884	16,798	201,822	99.90	3,996	17,283	207,642
91.55	3,662	15,838	190,287	94.35	3,774	16,323	196,106	97.15	3,886	16,807	201,926	99.95	3,998	17,291	207,746

Hour	Week	Month	Year	Hour	Week	Month	Year	Hour	Week	Month	Year	Hour	Week	Month	Year
100.00	4,000	17,300	207,850	102.80	4,112	17,784	213,670	105.60	4,224	18,269	219,490	108.40	4,336	18,753	225,309
100.05	4,002	17,309	207,954	102.85	4,114	17,793	213,774	105.65	4,226	18,277	219,594	108.45	4,338	18,762	225,413
100.10	4,004	17,317	208,058	102.90	4,116	17,802	213,878	105.70	4,228	18,286	219,697	108.50	4,340	18,770	225,517
100.15	4,006	17,326	208,162	102.95	4,118	17,810	213,982	105.75	4,230	18,295	219,801	108.55	4,342	18,779	225,621
100.20	4,008	17,335	208,266	103.00	4,120	17,819	214,085	105.80	4,232	18,303	219,905	108.60	4,344	18,788	225,725
100.25	4,010	17,343	208,370	103.05	4,122	17,828	214,189	105.85	4,234	18,312	220,009	108.65	4,346	18,796	225,829
100.30	4,012	17,352	208,474	103.10	4,124	17,836	214,293	105.90	4,236	18,321	220,113	108.70	4,348	18,805	225,933
100.35	4,014	17,361	208,577	103.15	4,126	17,845	214,397	105.95	4,238	18,329	220,217	108.75	4,350	18,814	226,037
100.40	4,016	17,369	208,681	103.20	4,128	17,854	214,501	106.00	4,240	18,338	220,321	108.80	4,352	18,822	226,141
100.45	4,018	17,378	208,785	103.25	4,130	17,862	214,605	106.05	4,242	18,347	220,425	108.85	4,354	18,831	226,245
100.50	4,020	17,386	208,889	103.30	4,132	17,871	214,709	106.10	4,244	18,355	220,529	108.90	4,356	18,840	226,349
100.55	4,022	17,395	208,993	103.35	4,134	17,880	214,813	106.15	4,246	18,364	220,633	108.95	4,358	18,848	226,453
100.60	4,024	17,404	209,097	103.40	4,136	17,888	214,917	106.20	4,248	18,373	220,737	109.00	4,360	18,857	226,556
100.65	4,026	17,412	209,201	103.45	4,138	17,897	215,021	106.25	4,250	18,381	220,841	109.05	4,362	18,866	226,660
100.70	4,028	17,421	209,305	103.50	4,140	17,905	215,125	106.30	4,252	18,390	220,945	109.10	4,364	18,874	226,764
100.75	4,030	17,430	209,409	103.55	4,142	17,914	215,229	106.35	4,254	18,399	221,048	109.15	4,366	18,883	226,868
100.80	4,032	17,438	209,513	103.60	4,144	17,923	215,333	106.40	4,256	18,407	221,152	109.20	4,368	18,892	226,972
100.85	4,034	17,447	209,617	103.65	4,146	17,931	215,437	106.45	4,258	18,416	221,256	109.25	4,370	18,900	227,076
100.90	4,036	17,456	209,721	103.70	4,148	17,940	215,540	106.50	4,260	18,424	221,360	109.30	4,372	18,909	227,180
100.95	4,038	17,464	209,825	103.75	4,150	17,949	215,644	106.55	4,262	18,433	221,464	109.35	4,374	18,918	227,284
101.00	4,040	17,473	209,928	103.80	4,152	17,957	215,748	106.60	4,264	18,442	221,568	109.40	4,376	18,926	227,388
101.05	4,042	17,482	210,032	103.85	4,154	17,966	215,852	106.65	4,266	18,450	221,672	109.45	4,378	18,935	227,492
101.10	4,044	17,490	210,136	103.90	4,156	17,975	215,956	106.70	4,268	18,459	221,776	109.50	4,380	18,943	227,596
101.15	4,046	17,499	210,240	103.95	4,158	17,983	216,060	106.75	4,270	18,468	221,880	109.55	4,382	18,952	227,700
101.20	4,048	17,508	210,344	104.00	4,160	17,992	216,164	106.80	4,272	18,476	221,984	109.60	4,384	18,961	227,804
101.25	4,050	17,516	210,448	104.05	4,162	18,001	216,268	106.85	4,274	18,485	222,088	109.65	4,386	18,969	227,908
101.30	4,052	17,525	210,552	104.10	4,164	18,009	216,372	106.90	4,276	18,494	222,192	109.70	4,388	18,978	228,011
101.35	4,054	17,534	210,656	104.15	4,166	18,018	216,476	106.95	4,278	18,502	222,296	109.75	4,390	18,987	228,115
101.40	4,056	17,542	210,760	104.20	4,168	18,027	216,580	107.00	4,280	18,511	222,399	109.80	4,392	18,995	228,219
101.45	4,058	17,551	210,864	104.25	4,170	18,035	216,684	107.05	4,282	18,520	222,503	109.85	4,394	19,004	228,323
101.50	4,060	17,559	210,968	104.30	4,172	18,044	216,788	107.10	4,284	18,528	222,607	109.90	4,396	19,013	228,427
101.55	4,062	17,568	211,072	104.35	4,174	18,053	216,891	107.15	4,286	18,537	222,711	109.95	4,398	19,021	228,531
101.60	4,064	17,577	211,176	104.40	4,176	18,061	216,995	107.20	4,288	18,546	222,815	110.00	4,400	19,030	228,635
101.65	4,066	17,585	211,280	104.45	4,178	18,070	217,099	107.25	4,290	18,554	222,919	110.05	4,402	19,039	228,739
101.70	4,068	17,594	211,383	104.50	4,180	18,078	217,203	107.30	4,292	18,563	223,023	110.10	4,404	19,047	228,843
101.75	4,070	17,603	211,487	104.55	4,182	18,087	217,307	107.35	4,294	18,572	223,127	110.15	4,406	19,056	228,947
101.80	4,072	17,611	211,591	104.60	4,184	18,096	217,411	107.40	4,296	18,580	223,231	110.20	4,408	19,065	229,051
101.85	4,074	17,620	211,695	104.65	4,186	18,104	217,515	107.45	4,298	18,589	223,335	110.25	4,410	19,073	229,155
101.90	4,076	17,629	211,799	104.70	4,188	18,113	217,619	107.50	4,300	18,597	223,439	110.30	4,412	19,082	229,259
101.95	4,078	17,637	211,903	104.75	4,190	18,122	217,723	107.55	4,302	18,606	223,543	110.35	4,414	19,091	229,362
102.00	4,080	17,646	212,007	104.80	4,192	18,130	217,827	107.60	4,304	18,615	223,647	110.40	4,416	19,099	229,466
102.05	4,082	17,655	212,111	104.85	4,194	18,139	217,931	107.65	4,306	18,623	223,751	110.45	4,418	19,108	229,570
102.10	4,084	17,663	212,215	104.90	4,196	18,148	218,035	107.70	4,308	18,632	223,854	110.50	4,420	19,116	229,674
102.15	4,086	17,672	212,319	104.95	4,198	18,156	218,139	107.75	4,310	18,641	223,958	110.55	4,422	19,125	229,778
102.20	4,088	17,681	212,423	105.00	4,200	18,165	218,242	107.80	4,312	18,649	224,062	110.60	4,424	19,134	229,882
102.25	4,090	17,689	212,527	105.05	4,202	18,174	218,346	107.85	4,314	18,658	224,166	110.65	4,426	19,142	229,986
102.30	4,092	17,698	212,631	105.10	4,204	18,182	218,450	107.90	4,316	18,667	224,270	110.70	4,428	19,151	230,090
102.35	4,094	17,707	212,734	105.15	4,206	18,191	218,554	107.95	4,318	18,675	224,374	110.75	4,430	19,160	230,194
102.40	4,096	17,715	212,838	105.20	4,208	18,200	218,658	108.00	4,320	18,684	224,478	110.80	4,432	19,168	230,298
102.45	4,098	17,724	212,942	105.25	4,210	18,208	218,762	108.05	4,322	18,693	224,582	110.85	4,434	19,177	230,402
102.50	4,100	17,732	213,046	105.30	4,212	18,217	218,866	108.10	4,324	18,701	224,686	110.90	4,436	19,186	230,506
102.55	4,102	17,741	213,150	105.35	4,214	18,226	218,970	108.15	4,326	18,710	224,790	110.95	4,438	19,194	230,610
102.60	4,104	17,750	213,254	105.40	4,216	18,234	219,074	108.20	4,328	18,719	224,894	111.00	4,440	19,203	230,713
102.65	4,106	17,758	213,358	105.45	4,218	18,243	219,178	108.25	4,330	18,727	224,998	111.05	4,442	19,212	230,817
102.70	4,108	17,767	213,462	105.50	4,220	18,251	219,282	108.30	4,332	18,736	225,102	111.10	4,444	19,220	230,921
102.75	4,110	17,776	213,566	105.55	4,222	18,260	219,386	108.35	4,334	18,745	225,205	111.15	4,446	19,229	231,025

Appendix III

ABBREVIATIONS

Acronyms used to abbreviate data sources may be found in Appendix I.

2D	Two Dimensional	**HVAC**	Heating, Ventilation, and Air Conditioning
3D	Three Dimensional	**IRA**	Individual Retirement Account
A&M	Agricultural and Mechanical	**K-12**	Kindergarten through Twelfth Grade
A&P	Airframe and Powerplant	**LLC**	Limited Liability Company
ADA	Americans with Disabilities Act	**LO**	Lowest wage paid
AE	Average entry wage	**LR**	Low end rage
AER	Average entry range	**M**	Monthly
AEX	Average experienced wage	**MA**	Master of Arts
ATC	Average total compensation	**MCC**	Median cash compensation
AW	Average wage	**MCDST**	Microsoft Certified Desktop Support Technician
AWR	Average wage range	**MCSE**	Microsoft Certified Systems Engineer
AXR	Average experienced range	**MSA**	Metropolitan Statistical Area
CAGO	Collegue, American Guild of Organists	**MTC**	Median total compensation
CDL	Commercial Driver's License	**MW**	Median wage
CEO	Chief Executive Officer	**MWR**	Median wage range
D	Daily	**NECTA**	New England City and Town Area
DNA	Deoxyribonucleic Acid	**P&G**	Procter and Gamble
EKG	Electrocardiogram	**PMSA**	Primary Metropolitan Statistical Area
EMS	Emergency Medical Service	**R&D**	Research and Development
FAGO	Fellowship, American Guild of Organists	**RFID**	Radio Frequency Identification
FQ	First quartile wage	**ROTC**	Reserve Officer's Training Corps
GED	General Educational Development	**S**	See annotated source
GIS	Geographic Information System	**SLPD**	Doctor of Speech-Language Pathology
H	Hourly	**SQL**	Structured Query Language
HACCP	Hazard Analysis and Critical Control Point	**TCC**	Total cash compensation
HI	Highest wage paid	**TQ**	Third quartile wage
HIV	Human Immunodeficiency Virus	**UNC**	University of North Carolina
HR	High end range	**W**	Weekly
HTML	Hypertext Markup Language		

Appendix IV

EMPLOYMENT BY OCCUPATION - 2006 AND 2016

This appendix displays data from the *National Industry-Occupational Matrix* prepared by the Department of Labor (DOL) from time to time. The data show employment by occupation for 2006 with DOL projections to 2016. The appendix is divided into three parts. The first part shows the occupations in alphabetical order using occupation titles as defined by DOL. The only exceptions are cases where the DOL refers to ''All Other'' followed by an occupation. These have been rendered by the name of the occupation, followed by the abbreviation 'nsk' to indicate 'not specified by kind.' The second arrangement shows occupations by 2006 employment, largest category first. The third sort is by rate of growth, 2006 to 2016, the fastest growing occupation shown first. Data were released in October 2007 and are referred to as *National OES Matrices*.

Alphabetical Order

Total Employment 2006	2016	% Change	Occupation
1,274,357	1,499,932	17.7	Accountants and auditors
70,030	78,141	11.6	Actors
18,137	22,438	23.7	Actuaries
15,479	15,487	0.1	Administrative law judges, adjudicators, and hearing officers
247,103	276,048	11.7	Administrative services managers
75,847	86,628	14.2	Adult literacy, remedial education, and GED teachers and instructors
47,296	50,247	6.2	Advertising and promotions managers
170,479	205,119	20.3	Advertising sales agents
8,512	9,400	10.4	Aerospace engineering and operations technicians
89,831	98,993	10.2	Aerospace engineers
24,870	27,259	9.6	Agents and business managers of artists, performers, and athletes
25,804	27,516	6.6	Agricultural and food science technicians
3,133	3,401	8.6	Agricultural engineers
59,451	56,482	-5.0	Agricultural equipment operators
16,176	15,998	-1.1	Agricultural inspectors
20,350	20,360	0.0	Agricultural workers, nsk
25,223	27,795	10.2	Air traffic controllers
5,792	7,140	23.3	Aircraft cargo handling supervisors
122,472	135,495	10.6	Aircraft mechanics and service technicians
28,083	31,681	12.8	Aircraft structure, surfaces, rigging, and systems assemblers
4,891	5,469	11.8	Airfield operations specialists
79,444	89,678	12.9	Airline pilots, copilots, and flight engineers
21,538	26,209	21.7	Ambulance drivers and attendants, except emergency medical technicians
247,497	307,572	24.3	Amusement and recreation attendants
10,505	10,967	4.4	Animal breeders
15,202	17,097	12.5	Animal control workers
5,371	5,900	9.8	Animal scientists
42,924	52,682	22.7	Animal trainers
5,545	6,377	15.0	Anthropologists and archeologists
101,125	118,197	16.9	Appraisers and assessors of real estate
8,469	9,363	10.6	Arbitrators, mediators, and conciliators
131,873	155,258	17.7	Architects, except landscape and naval
115,522	122,541	6.1	Architectural and civil drafters
6,449	7,379	14.4	Archivists
77,898	84,870	8.9	Art directors
13,799	14,955	8.4	Artists and related workers, nsk
291,591	266,264	-8.7	Assemblers and fabricators, nsk
1,656	1,748	5.5	Astronomers
17,524	20,891	19.2	Athletes and sports competitors

Total Employment 2006	2016	% Change	Occupation
17,117	21,271	24.3	Athletic trainers
8,759	9,684	10.6	Atmospheric and space scientists
49,881	61,971	24.2	Audio and video equipment technicians
12,253	13,454	9.8	Audiologists
7,305	6,298	-13.8	Audio-visual collections specialists
182,676	203,800	11.6	Automotive body and related repairers
23,610	28,033	18.7	Automotive glass installers and repairers
772,675	883,131	14.3	Automotive service technicians and mechanics
15,709	16,987	8.1	Avionics technicians
49,319	53,739	9.0	Baggage porters and bellhops
18,608	20,688	11.2	Bailiffs
149,266	164,263	10.0	Bakers
60,034	60,678	1.1	Barbers
495,307	550,952	11.2	Bartenders
8,644	9,267	7.2	Bicycle repairers
434,200	533,636	22.9	Bill and account collectors
541,869	565,622	4.4	Billing and posting clerks and machine operators
64,859	50,697	-21.8	Bindery workers
20,131	23,326	15.9	Biochemists and biophysicists
29,067	30,138	3.7	Biological scientists, nsk
78,690	91,288	16.0	Biological technicians
14,379	17,415	21.1	Biomedical engineers
17,571	20,034	14.0	Boilermakers
7,211	5,995	-16.9	Bookbinders
2,113,780	2,377,315	12.5	Bookkeeping, accounting, and auditing clerks
158,316	173,596	9.7	Brickmasons and blockmasons
3,926	3,799	-3.2	Bridge and lock tenders
7,724	8,184	6.0	Broadcast news analysts
37,881	42,479	12.1	Broadcast technicians
73,309	87,999	20.0	Brokerage clerks
61,858	66,260	7.1	Budget analysts
15,649	18,011	15.1	Building cleaning workers, nsk
274,876	306,383	11.5	Bus and truck mechanics and diesel engine specialists
454,800	497,252	9.3	Bus drivers, school
198,488	223,311	12.5	Bus drivers, transit and intercity
1,043,120	1,261,364	20.9	Business operation specialists, nsk
131,352	133,852	1.9	Butchers and meat cutters
149,047	153,146	2.8	Cabinetmakers and bench carpenters
4,403	4,309	-2.1	Camera and photographic equipment repairers
26,897	30,001	11.5	Camera operators, television, video, and motion picture
33,617	39,628	17.9	Captains, mates, and pilots of water vessels
45,378	56,956	25.5	Cardiovascular technologists and technicians

Total Employment		%		Total Employment		%	
2006	2016	Change	Occupation	2006	2016	Change	Occupation
85,985	100,154	16.5	Cargo and freight agents	42,991	43,132	0.3	Control and valve installers and repairers, except mechanical door
1,462,071	1,612,072	10.3	Carpenters				
73,205	72,324	-1.2	Carpet installers	49,677	46,026	-7.3	Conveyor operators and tenders
12,184	14,656	20.3	Cartographers and photogrammetrists	629,405	681,455	8.3	Cooks, fast food
3,500,169	3,381,931	-3.4	Cashiers, except gaming	401,027	444,521	10.8	Cooks, institution and cafeteria
221,539	246,791	11.4	Cement masons and concrete finishers	15,588	16,122	3.4	Cooks, nsk
23,362	21,209	-9.2	Cementing and gluing machine operators and tenders	4,927	5,360	8.8	Cooks, private household
				850,343	948,167	11.5	Cooks, restaurant
114,784	123,521	7.6	Chefs and head cooks	195,495	204,959	4.8	Cooks, short order
30,444	32,842	7.9	Chemical engineers	10,677	9,956	-6.8	Cooling and freezing equipment operators and tenders
52,737	50,688	-3.9	Chemical equipment operators and tenders				
53,243	45,094	-15.3	Chemical plant and system operators	441,761	516,309	16.9	Correctional officers and jailers
61,228	64,793	5.8	Chemical technicians	17,445	19,531	12.0	Correspondence clerks
83,697	91,340	9.1	Chemists	221,100	262,007	18.5	Cost estimators
402,246	410,478	2.0	Chief executives	4,328	4,940	14.1	Costume attendants
1,388,168	1,635,947	17.8	Child care workers	27,306	31,835	16.6	Counselors, nsk
282,424	336,376	19.1	Child, family, and school social workers	476,623	585,824	22.9	Counter and rental clerks
52,725	60,339	14.4	Chiropractors	532,840	586,935	10.2	Counter attendants, cafeteria, food concession, and coffee shop
20,429	20,927	2.4	Choreographers				
90,650	99,888	10.2	Civil engineering technicians	133,770	133,551	-0.2	Couriers and messengers
256,330	302,409	18.0	Civil engineers	19,101	23,790	24.5	Court reporters
305,169	332,419	8.9	Claims adjusters, examiners, and investigators	114,584	124,628	8.8	Court, municipal, and license clerks
368,216	419,928	14.0	Cleaners of vehicles and equipment	8,816	9,522	8.0	Craft artists
15,914	14,348	-9.8	Cleaning, washing, and metal pickling equipment operators and tenders	46,393	47,691	2.8	Crane and tower operators
				67,132	68,398	1.9	Credit analysts
404,396	480,687	18.9	Clergy	68,975	63,204	-8.4	Credit authorizers, checkers, and clerks
152,381	176,462	15.8	Clinical, counseling, and school psychologists	69,320	70,619	1.9	Crossing guards
216,780	248,530	14.6	Coaches and scouts	42,485	37,440	-11.9	Crushing, grinding, and polishing machine setters, operators, and tenders
106,426	92,743	-12.9	Coating, painting, and spraying machine setters, operators, and tenders				
				10,362	12,772	23.3	Curators
22,835	15,879	-30.5	Coil winders, tapers, and finishers	2,202,271	2,747,432	24.8	Customer service representatives
47,928	46,498	-3.0	Coin, vending, and amusement machine servicers and repairers	28,633	26,901	-6.0	Cutters and trimmers, hand
				78,794	71,486	-9.3	Cutting and slicing machine setters, operators, and tenders
2,502,891	2,954,811	18.1	Combined food preparation and serving workers, including fast food	271,745	231,384	-14.9	Cutting, punching, and press machine setters, operators, and tenders, metal and plastic
47,978	51,412	7.2	Commercial and industrial designers				
3,133	3,688	17.7	Commercial divers	19,767	21,643	9.5	Dancers
27,596	31,236	13.2	Commercial pilots	313,355	298,680	-4.7	Data entry keyers
4,346	4,667	7.4	Communications equipment operators, nsk	119,415	153,523	28.6	Database administrators
118,012	147,644	25.1	Community and social service specialists, nsk	104,769	123,670	18.0	Demonstrators and product promoters
49,087	54,996	12.0	Compensation and benefits managers	279,828	361,549	29.2	Dental assistants
109,916	130,153	18.4	Compensation, benefits, and job analysis specialists	167,017	217,220	30.1	Dental hygienists
				53,439	55,393	3.7	Dental laboratory technicians
237,035	248,709	4.9	Compliance officers, except agriculture, construction, health and safety, and transportation	136,323	148,893	9.2	Dentists, general
				6,928	7,398	6.8	Dentists, nsk
				18,784	17,694	-5.8	Derrick operators, oil and gas
25,261	30,701	21.5	Computer and information scientists, research	16,041	17,931	11.8	Designers, nsk
263,695	306,829	16.4	Computer and information systems managers	31,833	32,137	1.0	Desktop publishers
78,525	82,137	4.6	Computer hardware engineers	106,336	124,776	17.3	Detectives and criminal investigators
129,997	97,943	-24.7	Computer operators	45,668	54,384	19.1	Diagnostic medical sonographers
435,076	417,065	-4.1	Computer programmers	25,083	28,789	14.8	Dietetic technicians
506,751	732,510	44.6	Computer software engineers, applications	57,126	62,038	8.6	Dietitians and nutritionists
350,048	448,679	28.2	Computer software engineers, systems software	416,276	465,502	11.8	Dining room and cafeteria attendants and bartender helpers
135,949	156,509	15.1	Computer specialists, nsk	99,230	118,730	19.7	Directors, religious activities and education
552,458	623,634	12.9	Computer support specialists	517,358	571,223	10.4	Dishwashers
503,631	649,571	29.0	Computer systems analysts	190,231	193,125	1.5	Dispatchers, except police, fire, and ambulance
174,961	180,211	3.0	Computer, automated teller, and office machine repairers				
				199,552	206,890	3.7	Door-to-door sales workers, news and street vendors, and related workers
140,510	136,339	-3.0	Computer-controlled machine tool operators, metal and plastic				
				24,521	27,215	11.0	Drafters, nsk
19,753	22,547	14.1	Concierges	2,142	2,285	6.7	Dredge operators
19,777	20,830	5.3	Conservation scientists	42,686	33,215	-22.2	Drilling and boring machine tool setters, operators, and tenders, metal and plastic
109,730	129,739	18.2	Construction and building inspectors				
62,455	67,974	8.8	Construction and related workers, nsk	445,092	421,337	-5.3	Driver/sales workers
1,232,002	1,366,496	10.9	Construction laborers	185,864	199,393	7.3	Drywall and ceiling tile installers
487,077	563,584	15.7	Construction managers	21,681	23,099	6.5	Earth drillers, except oil and gas
10,043	10,504	4.6	Continuous mining machine operators	14,792	15,900	7.5	Economists

Total Employment 2006	2016	% Change	Occupation
121,511	124,275	2.3	Editors
225,905	243,048	7.6	Education administrators, elementary and secondary school
29,714	33,462	12.6	Education administrators, nsk
131,293	149,980	14.2	Education administrators, postsecondary
56,064	69,246	23.5	Education administrators, preschool and child care center/program
99,216	109,591	10.5	Education, training, and library workers, nsk
259,543	292,352	12.6	Educational, vocational, and school counselors
25,474	24,398	-4.2	Electric motor, power tool, and related repairers
170,433	176,530	3.6	Electrical and electronic engineering technicians
213,381	156,167	-26.8	Electrical and electronic equipment assemblers
34,848	36,286	4.1	Electrical and electronics drafters
21,079	21,978	4.3	Electrical and electronics installers and repairers, transportation equipment
80,226	85,688	6.8	Electrical and electronics repairers, commercial and industrial equipment
22,300	21,261	-4.7	Electrical and electronics repairers, powerhouse, substation, and relay
153,375	162,965	6.3	Electrical engineers
112,183	120,294	7.2	Electrical power-line installers and repairers
705,015	757,438	7.4	Electricians
60,298	54,800	-9.1	Electromechanical equipment assemblers
15,739	16,155	2.6	Electro-mechanical technicians
20,017	20,936	4.6	Electronic equipment installers and repairers, motor vehicles
39,700	40,908	3.0	Electronic home entertainment equipment installers and repairers
137,868	142,954	3.7	Electronics engineers, except computer
1,540,159	1,749,333	13.6	Elementary school teachers, except special education
21,830	23,753	8.8	Elevator installers and repairers
112,418	115,907	3.1	Eligibility interviewers, government programs
9,028	10,316	14.3	Embalmers
11,725	13,172	12.3	Emergency management specialists
201,099	239,762	19.2	Emergency medical technicians and paramedics
196,892	233,035	18.4	Employment, recruitment, and placement specialists
45,265	41,368	-8.6	Engine and other machine assemblers
187,089	200,669	7.3	Engineering managers
81,824	83,443	2.0	Engineering technicians, except drafters, nsk
170,305	179,675	5.5	Engineers, nsk
77,075	89,272	15.8	Entertainers and performers, sports and related workers, nsk
21,126	26,362	24.8	Environmental engineering technicians
54,341	68,161	25.4	Environmental engineers
36,500	46,701	28.0	Environmental science and protection technicians, including health
83,267	104,142	25.1	Environmental scientists and specialists, including health
4,507	5,119	13.6	Epidemiologists
13,625	12,969	-4.8	Etchers and engravers
80,157	86,818	8.3	Excavating and loading machine and dragline operators
1,618,018	1,857,071	14.8	Executive secretaries and administrative assistants
5,334	5,407	1.4	Explosives workers, ordnance handling experts, and blasters
9,750	9,784	0.4	Extraction workers, nsk
93,869	87,146	-7.2	Extruding and drawing machine setters, operators, and tenders, metal and plastic
17,682	14,573	-17.6	Extruding and forming machine setters, operators, and tenders, synthetic and glass fibers
81,193	74,657	-8.1	Extruding, forming, pressing, and compacting machine setters, operators, and tenders
9,209	6,578	-28.6	Fabric and apparel patternmakers
1,809	1,781	-1.5	Fabric menders, except garment
13,085	12,112	-7.4	Fallers
14,969	15,735	5.1	Farm and home management advisors
30,672	31,087	1.4	Farm equipment mechanics
258,156	261,032	1.1	Farm, ranch, and other agricultural managers
1,058,444	968,838	-8.5	Farmers and ranchers
603,083	582,746	-3.4	Farmworkers and laborers, crop, nursery, and greenhouse
106,843	109,772	2.7	Farmworkers, farm and ranch animals
20,411	21,428	5.0	Fashion designers
32,470	35,908	10.6	Fence erectors
33,294	35,346	6.2	Fiberglass laminators and fabricators
233,808	137,245	-41.3	File clerks
20,544	23,150	12.7	Film and video editors
220,568	295,157	33.8	Financial analysts
25,588	28,326	10.7	Financial examiners
506,347	570,362	12.6	Financial managers
129,135	144,378	11.8	Financial specialists, nsk
30,323	33,337	9.9	Fine artists, including painters, sculptors, and illustrators
292,876	328,189	12.1	Fire fighters
13,805	15,327	11.0	Fire inspectors and investigators
771,796	841,777	9.1	First-line supervisors/managers of construction trades and extraction workers
39,584	44,538	12.5	First-line supervisors/managers of correctional officers
52,468	58,483	11.5	First-line supervisors/managers of fire fighting and prevention workers
817,108	909,458	11.3	First-line supervisors/managers of food preparation and serving workers
181,954	204,647	12.5	First-line supervisors/managers of helpers, laborers, and material movers, hand
282,237	318,009	12.7	First-line supervisors/managers of housekeeping and janitorial workers
201,840	237,416	17.6	First-line supervisors/managers of landscaping, lawn service, and groundskeeping workers
464,881	498,976	7.3	First-line supervisors/managers of mechanics, installers, and repairers
529,958	549,430	3.7	First-line supervisors/managers of non-retail sales workers
1,418,494	1,500,083	5.8	First-line supervisors/managers of office and administrative support workers
214,810	248,153	15.5	First-line supervisors/managers of personal service workers
93,018	101,529	9.2	First-line supervisors/managers of police and detectives
699,259	665,489	-4.8	First-line supervisors/managers of production and operating workers
1,675,937	1,747,019	4.2	First-line supervisors/managers of retail sales workers
226,065	249,171	10.2	First-line supervisors/managers of transportation and material-moving machine and vehicle operators
48,019	54,989	14.5	First-line supervisors/managers, protective service workers, nsk
8,030	8,017	-0.2	Fish and game wardens
38,372	32,179	-16.1	Fishers and related fishing workers
234,841	297,845	26.8	Fitness trainers and aerobics instructors
96,730	106,949	10.6	Flight attendants
28,991	25,450	-12.2	Floor layers, except carpet, wood, and hard tiles
14,319	14,064	-1.8	Floor sanders and finishers
86,909	79,184	-8.9	Floral designers
18,876	20,921	10.8	Food and tobacco roasting, baking, and drying machine operators and tenders
94,921	105,275	10.9	Food batchmakers

Total Employment 2006	2016	% Change	Occupation
44,393	42,310	-4.7	Food cooking machine operators and tenders
56,326	63,628	13.0	Food preparation and serving related workers, nsk
901,660	1,039,744	15.3	Food preparation workers
11,782	13,002	10.3	Food scientists and technologists
189,234	219,155	15.8	Food servers, nonrestaurant
350,259	367,782	5.0	Food service managers
13,051	17,063	30.7	Forensic science technicians
33,829	33,166	-2.0	Forest and conservation technicians
19,844	20,939	5.5	Forest and conservation workers
1,815	1,853	2.1	Forest fire inspectors and prevention specialists
13,188	13,868	5.2	Foresters
31,068	21,640	-30.3	Forging machine setters, operators, and tenders, metal and plastic
14,523	11,229	-22.7	Foundry mold and coremakers
32,807	37,486	14.3	Funeral attendants
28,770	32,358	12.5	Funeral directors
31,596	28,834	-8.7	Furnace, kiln, oven, drier, and kettle operators and tenders
31,326	30,348	-3.1	Furniture finishers
18,463	23,637	28.0	Gaming and sports book writers and runners
18,033	20,077	11.3	Gaming cage workers
27,109	28,924	6.7	Gaming change persons and booth cashiers
83,523	103,670	24.1	Gaming dealers
3,997	4,974	24.4	Gaming managers
14,644	18,475	26.2	Gaming service workers, nsk
33,887	41,831	23.4	Gaming supervisors
8,658	11,565	33.6	Gaming surveillance officers and gaming investigators
4,154	3,427	-17.5	Gas compressor and gas pumping station operators
12,261	11,044	-9.9	Gas plant operators
1,720,460	1,746,324	1.5	General and operations managers
1,096	1,162	6.1	Geographers
11,818	12,838	8.6	Geological and petroleum technicians
31,061	37,850	21.9	Geoscientists, except hydrologists and geographers
54,992	61,552	11.9	Glaziers
42,091	41,332	-1.8	Graders and sorters, agricultural products
260,831	286,424	9.8	Graphic designers
44,776	41,586	-7.1	Grinding and polishing workers, hand
101,441	85,499	-15.7	Grinding, lapping, polishing, and buffing machine tool setters, operators, and tenders, metal and plastic
27,873	32,513	16.6	Grounds maintenance workers, nsk
617,452	694,225	12.4	Hairdressers, hairstylists, and cosmetologists
39,497	43,929	11.2	Hazardous materials removal workers
25,380	27,823	9.6	Health and safety engineers, except mining safety engineers and inspectors
64,876	72,513	11.8	Health diagnosing and treating practitioners, nsk
61,546	77,664	26.2	Health educators
52,768	60,579	14.8	Healthcare practitioners and technical workers, nsk
204,428	236,300	15.6	Healthcare support workers, nsk
79,344	91,208	15.0	Healthcare technologists and technicians, nsk
27,122	23,107	-14.8	Heat treating equipment setters, operators, and tenders, metal and plastic
291,861	317,359	8.7	Heating, air conditioning, and refrigeration mechanics and installers
37,564	42,282	12.6	Helpers, construction trades, nsk
65,364	72,568	11.0	Helpers—Brickmasons, blockmasons, stonemasons, and tile and marble setters
109,060	121,817	11.7	Helpers—Carpenters
105,340	112,487	6.8	Helpers—Electricians
25,016	24,964	-0.2	Helpers—Extraction workers
163,379	182,599	11.8	Helpers—Installation, maintenance, and repair

Total Employment 2006	2016	% Change	Occupation
			workers
24,455	24,286	-0.7	Helpers—Painters, paperhangers, plasterers, and stucco masons
84,643	94,731	11.9	Helpers—Pipelayers, plumbers, pipefitters, and steamfitters
541,605	538,831	-0.5	Helpers—Production workers
21,769	23,228	6.7	Helpers—Roofers
145,216	158,140	8.9	Highway maintenance workers
3,446	3,716	7.8	Historians
3,017	2,980	-1.2	Hoist and winch operators
57,364	58,239	1.5	Home appliance repairers
787,315	1,170,935	48.7	Home health aides
351,188	387,759	10.4	Hosts and hostesses, restaurant, lounge, and coffee shop
218,776	256,806	17.4	Hotel, motel, and resort desk clerks
168,201	187,125	11.3	Human resources assistants, except payroll and timekeeping
58,233	64,849	11.4	Human resources managers, nsk
214,383	249,735	16.5	Human resources, training, and labor relations specialists, nsk
474	384	-19.0	Hunters and trappers
8,315	10,337	24.3	Hydrologists
74,915	82,364	9.9	Industrial engineering technicians
201,311	242,263	20.3	Industrial engineers
260,727	284,283	9.0	Industrial machinery mechanics
157,341	148,094	-5.9	Industrial production managers
637,034	624,181	-2.0	Industrial truck and tractor operators
1,943	2,356	21.3	Industrial-organizational psychologists
244,584	212,988	-12.9	Information and record clerks, nsk
491,417	456,817	-7.0	Inspectors, testers, sorters, samplers, and weighers
168,431	181,134	7.5	Installation, maintenance, and repair workers, nsk
129,430	158,530	22.5	Instructional coordinators
32,414	35,130	8.4	Insulation workers, floor, ceiling, and wall
28,446	30,898	8.6	Insulation workers, mechanical
13,399	15,078	12.5	Insurance appraisers, auto damage
253,949	250,613	-1.3	Insurance claims and policy processing clerks
436,100	492,434	12.9	Insurance sales agents
104,477	111,063	6.3	Insurance underwriters
71,856	85,853	19.5	Interior designers
41,193	50,916	23.6	Interpreters and translators
220,911	241,968	9.5	Interviewers, except eligibility and loan
2,386,570	2,731,507	14.5	Janitors and cleaners, except maids and housekeeping cleaners
52,219	51,047	-2.2	Jewelers and precious stone and metal workers
48,240	43,749	-9.3	Job printers
27,192	28,580	5.1	Judges, magistrate judges, and magistrates
170,234	198,000	16.3	Kindergarten teachers, except special education
2,416,034	2,465,805	2.1	Laborers and freight, stock, and material movers, hand
27,839	32,402	16.4	Landscape architects
1,220,054	1,441,326	18.1	Landscaping and groundskeeping workers
67,760	51,976	-23.3	Lathe and turning machine tool setters, operators, and tenders, metal and plastic
238,681	261,781	9.7	Laundry and dry-cleaning workers
36,689	36,235	-1.2	Law clerks
760,672	844,195	11.0	Lawyers
10,153	8,144	-19.8	Lay-out workers, metal and plastic
275,269	307,533	11.7	Legal secretaries
47,878	50,311	5.1	Legal support workers, nsk
64,507	65,171	1.0	Legislators
158,373	164,127	3.6	Librarians
116,009	125,127	7.9	Library assistants, clerical
121,256	131,534	8.5	Library technicians
748,605	853,703	14.0	Licensed practical and licensed vocational nurses

Total Employment 2006	2016	% Change	Occupation
14,027	16,179	15.3	Life scientists, nsk
66,177	72,695	9.8	Life, physical, and social science technicians, nsk
114,189	135,539	18.7	Lifeguards, ski patrol, and other recreational protective service workers
3,085	3,224	4.5	Loading machine operators, underground mining
33,396	34,730	4.0	Loan counselors
256,023	253,765	-0.9	Loan interviewers and clerks
372,544	415,225	11.5	Loan officers
19,383	23,567	21.6	Locker room, coatroom, and dressing room attendants
26,018	31,768	22.1	Locksmiths and safe repairers
70,988	79,651	12.2	Lodging managers
7,115	6,741	-5.3	Log graders and scalers
40,496	39,980	-1.3	Logging equipment operators
7,935	7,470	-5.9	Logging workers, nsk
83,443	97,856	17.3	Logisticians
147,763	125,360	-15.2	Machine feeders and offbearers
396,539	384,120	-3.1	Machinists
1,469,519	1,655,518	12.7	Maids and housekeeping cleaners
152,064	134,414	-11.6	Mail clerks and mail machine operators, except postal service
1,390,952	1,530,861	10.1	Maintenance and repair workers, general
84,291	83,348	-1.1	Maintenance workers, machinery
2,146	3,000	39.8	Makeup artists, theatrical and performance
678,188	826,839	21.9	Management analysts
869,558	929,743	6.9	Managers, nsk
78,121	99,680	27.6	Manicurists and pedicurists
11,803	11,462	-2.9	Manufactured building and mobile home installers
9,196	10,199	10.9	Marine engineers and naval architects
234,354	281,397	20.1	Market research analysts
167,464	191,549	14.4	Marketing managers
24,701	32,051	29.8	Marriage and family therapists
117,696	141,547	20.3	Massage therapists
53,588	53,964	0.7	Material moving workers, nsk
21,616	22,482	4.0	Materials engineers
9,695	10,536	8.7	Materials scientists
10,390	12,607	21.3	Mathematical scientists, nsk
1,302	1,405	7.9	Mathematical technicians
3,033	3,342	10.2	Mathematicians
144,228	159,947	10.9	Meat, poultry, and fish cutters and trimmers
15,399	17,698	14.9	Mechanical door repairers
78,340	82,437	5.2	Mechanical drafters
47,792	50,848	6.4	Mechanical engineering technicians
225,797	235,169	4.2	Mechanical engineers
18,779	20,701	10.2	Media and communication equipment workers, nsk
35,660	39,848	11.7	Media and communication workers, nsk
151,366	174,060	15.0	Medical and clinical laboratory technicians
167,207	187,960	12.4	Medical and clinical laboratory technologists
261,925	304,910	16.4	Medical and health services managers
123,643	153,526	24.2	Medical and public health social workers
12,323	13,488	9.4	Medical appliance technicians
416,882	564,558	35.4	Medical assistants
45,247	51,655	14.2	Medical equipment preparers
37,645	45,799	21.7	Medical equipment repairers
169,742	199,966	17.8	Medical records and health information technicians
87,402	105,039	20.2	Medical scientists, except epidemiologists
408,369	476,591	16.7	Medical secretaries
98,454	111,747	13.5	Medical transcriptionists
50,962	61,095	19.9	Meeting and convention planners
122,272	158,844	29.9	Mental health and substance abuse social workers
99,794	129,759	30.0	Mental health counselors
87,001	96,285	10.7	Merchandise displayers and window trimmers

Total Employment 2006	2016	% Change	Occupation
48,661	36,431	-25.1	Metal workers and plastic workers, nsk
18,386	14,896	-19.0	Metal-refining furnace operators and tenders
46,574	41,800	-10.3	Meter readers, utilities
17,357	19,306	11.2	Microbiologists
658,060	731,803	11.2	Middle school teachers, except special and vocational education
29,211	23,071	-21.0	Milling and planing machine setters, operators, and tenders, metal and plastic
54,884	58,062	5.8	Millwrights
7,918	8,218	3.8	Mine cutting and channeling machine operators
7,070	7,774	10.0	Mining and geological engineers, including mining safety engineers
2,989	3,134	4.9	Mining machine operators, nsk
142,842	135,544	-5.1	Mixing and blending machine setters, operators, and tenders
130,570	146,656	12.3	Mobile heavy equipment mechanics, except engines
8,791	8,240	-6.3	Model makers, metal and plastic
1,888	1,118	-40.8	Model makers, wood
2,003	2,200	9.8	Models
55,928	56,646	1.3	Molders, shapers, and casters, except metal and plastic
156,842	136,758	-12.8	Molding, coremaking, and casting machine setters, operators, and tenders, metal and plastic
11,493	10,532	-8.4	Motion picture projectionists
75,942	84,575	11.4	Motor vehicle operators, nsk
24,114	28,704	19.0	Motorboat mechanics
2,978	3,302	10.9	Motorboat operators
21,211	23,858	12.5	Motorcycle mechanics
87,296	109,845	25.8	Multi-media artists and animators
96,553	96,846	0.3	Multiple machine tool setters, operators, and tenders, metal and plastic
10,676	12,376	15.9	Museum technicians and conservators
68,005	76,763	12.9	Music directors and composers
5,998	6,167	2.8	Musical instrument repairers and tuners
196,330	216,172	10.1	Musicians and singers
40,743	45,381	11.4	Natural sciences managers
309,201	392,536	27.0	Network and computer systems administrators
261,793	401,626	53.4	Network systems and data communications analysts
81,422	68,135	-16.3	New accounts clerks
156,624	185,414	18.4	Nonfarm animal caretakers
15,273	16,377	7.2	Nuclear engineers
19,850	22,783	14.8	Nuclear medicine technologists
3,794	4,195	10.6	Nuclear power reactor operators
6,502	6,939	6.7	Nuclear technicians
17,980	16,474	-8.4	Numerical tool and process control programmers
1,447,233	1,710,876	18.2	Nursing aides, orderlies, and attendants
45,206	48,882	8.1	Occupational health and safety specialists
10,468	11,992	14.6	Occupational health and safety technicians
8,235	10,035	21.9	Occupational therapist aides
24,981	31,332	25.4	Occupational therapist assistants
98,858	121,709	23.1	Occupational therapists
319,970	290,221	-9.3	Office and administrative support workers, nsk
3,200,245	3,603,802	12.6	Office clerks, general
93,926	91,393	-2.7	Office machine operators, except computer
424,152	459,649	8.4	Operating engineers and other construction equipment operators
58,353	64,552	10.6	Operations research analysts
29,064	30,970	6.6	Ophthalmic laboratory technicians
65,904	71,631	8.7	Opticians, dispensing
32,740	36,445	11.3	Optometrists
7,698	8,396	9.1	Oral and maxillofacial surgeons
270,869	204,918	-24.3	Order clerks
9,179	10,026	9.2	Orthodontists

Total Employment		%		Total Employment		%	
2006	2016	Change	Occupation	2006	2016	Change	Occupation
5,706	6,379	11.8	Orthotists and prosthetists	94,445	104,742	10.9	Probation officers and correctional treatment specialists
32,892	34,706	5.5	Outdoor power equipment and other small engine mechanics	77,798	76,196	-2.1	Procurement clerks
385,988	365,058	-5.4	Packaging and filling machine operators and tenders	93,074	103,360	11.1	Producers and directors
				304,906	311,981	2.3	Production workers, nsk
833,812	730,180	-12.4	Packers and packagers, hand	292,794	305,123	4.2	Production, planning, and expediting clerks
462,833	517,319	11.8	Painters, construction and maintenance	17,856	18,995	6.4	Proofreaders and copy markers
54,322	58,883	8.4	Painters, transportation equipment	328,928	378,593	15.1	Property, real estate, and community association managers
30,885	31,988	3.6	Painting, coating, and decorating workers				
113,107	92,563	-18.2	Paper goods machine setters, operators, and tenders	999	1,106	10.7	Prosthodontists
				82,703	93,157	12.6	Protective service workers, nsk
9,899	8,691	-12.2	Paperhangers	61,735	61,694	-0.1	Psychiatric aides
237,703	290,570	22.2	Paralegals and legal assistants	62,098	60,073	-3.3	Psychiatric technicians
10,520	11,814	12.3	Parking enforcement workers	11,591	12,503	7.9	Psychologists, nsk
135,204	151,574	12.1	Parking lot attendants	11,960	11,934	-0.2	Public address system and other announcers
238,015	232,849	-2.2	Parts salespersons	49,575	57,966	16.9	Public relations managers
7,429	7,025	-5.4	Patternmakers, metal and plastic	243,275	286,145	17.6	Public relations specialists
2,279	1,369	-39.9	Patternmakers, wood	10,544	9,225	-12.5	Pump operators, except wellhead pumpers
64,255	70,056	9.0	Paving, surfacing, and tamping equipment operators	15,904	14,536	-8.6	Purchasing agents and buyers, farm products
				287,429	287,810	0.1	Purchasing agents, except wholesale, retail, and farm products
213,612	220,246	3.1	Payroll and timekeeping clerks				
767,257	1,155,795	50.6	Personal and home care aides	69,526	71,910	3.4	Purchasing managers
86,431	75,299	-12.9	Personal care and service workers, nsk	14,627	18,248	24.8	Radiation therapists
176,220	248,405	41.0	Personal financial advisors	58,905	54,020	-8.3	Radio and television announcers
69,722	80,500	15.5	Pest control workers	6,533	6,268	-4.1	Radio mechanics
30,605	34,893	14.0	Pesticide handlers, sprayers, and applicators, vegetation	1,548	1,296	-16.3	Radio operators
				196,200	225,877	15.1	Radiologic technologists and technicians
17,355	18,251	5.2	Petroleum engineers	26,578	27,926	5.1	Rail car repairers
41,970	36,367	-13.4	Petroleum pump system operators, refinery operators, and gaugers	6,772	5,506	-18.7	Rail transportation workers, nsk
				24,609	21,799	-11.4	Railroad brake, signal, and switch operators
243,482	296,364	21.7	Pharmacists	40,152	43,795	9.1	Railroad conductors and yardmasters
50,394	44,807	-11.1	Pharmacy aides	14,635	15,334	4.8	Rail-track laying and maintenance equipment operators
285,035	376,364	32.0	Pharmacy technicians				
122,480	135,138	10.3	Photographers	131,239	145,770	11.1	Real estate brokers
23,684	15,090	-36.3	Photographic process workers	432,291	478,135	10.6	Real estate sales agents
49,304	24,742	-49.8	Photographic processing machine operators	1,172,666	1,374,666	17.2	Receptionists and information clerks
23,881	25,350	6.2	Physical scientists, nsk	319,818	360,485	12.7	Recreation workers
46,242	57,512	24.4	Physical therapist aides	25,115	26,046	3.7	Recreational therapists
60,296	79,821	32.4	Physical therapist assistants	13,998	16,542	18.2	Recreational vehicle service technicians
172,948	219,752	27.1	Physical therapists	3,478	3,079	-11.5	Refractory materials repairers, except brickmasons
65,628	83,353	27.0	Physician assistants				
16,516	17,641	6.8	Physicists	135,970	146,047	7.4	Refuse and recyclable material collectors
5,584	6,050	8.3	Pile-driver operators	2,504,664	3,092,013	23.5	Registered nurses
66,590	72,401	8.7	Pipelayers	140,732	173,042	23.0	Rehabilitation counselors
14,132	13,772	-2.6	Plant and system operators, nsk	30,162	33,633	11.5	Reinforcing iron and rebar workers
61,148	66,106	8.1	Plasterers and stucco masons	39,194	46,922	19.7	Religious workers, nsk
41,898	36,788	-12.2	Plating and coating machine setters, operators, and tenders, metal and plastic	59,212	59,921	1.2	Reporters and correspondents
				165,345	167,127	1.1	Reservation and transportation ticket agents and travel clerks
502,201	555,431	10.6	Plumbers, pipefitters, and steamfitters				
11,944	13,076	9.5	Podiatrists	56,845	67,347	18.5	Residential advisors
648,418	718,516	10.8	Police and sheriff's patrol officers	102,406	125,563	22.6	Respiratory therapists
99,053	112,512	13.6	Police, fire, and ambulance dispatchers	19,167	19,334	0.9	Respiratory therapy technicians
4,694	4,945	5.3	Political scientists	4,476,942	5,033,766	12.4	Retail salespersons
79,505	80,435	1.2	Postal service clerks	12,315	12,284	-0.3	Riggers
337,768	341,299	1.0	Postal service mail carriers	3,883	4,858	25.1	Rock splitters, quarry
197,714	181,173	-8.4	Postal service mail sorters, processors, and processing machine operators	35,853	31,611	-11.8	Rolling machine setters, operators, and tenders, metal and plastic
25,870	25,653	-0.8	Postmasters and mail superintendents	4,291	4,345	1.2	Roof bolters, mining
14,791	12,212	-17.4	Pourers and casters, metal	156,284	178,697	14.3	Roofers
8,571	8,153	-4.9	Power distributors and dispatchers	19,923	18,853	-5.4	Rotary drill operators, oil and gas
34,759	35,701	2.7	Power plant operators	44,085	42,663	-3.2	Roustabouts, oil and gas
16,327	17,036	4.3	Precision instrument and equipment repairers, nsk	32,981	38,167	15.7	Sailors and marine oilers
				179,564	204,740	14.0	Sales and related workers, nsk
70,899	55,959	-21.1	Prepress technicians and workers	75,795	82,255	8.5	Sales engineers
437,088	551,985	26.3	Preschool teachers, except special education	318,329	350,838	10.2	Sales managers
77,182	73,762	-4.4	Pressers, textile, garment, and related materials	539,732	690,262	27.9	Sales representatives, services, nsk
197,594	186,337	-5.7	Printing machine operators	1,562,254	1,693,014	8.4	Sales representatives, wholesale and manufacturing, except technical and
51,693	61,124	18.2	Private detectives and investigators				

Total Employment 2006	2016	% Change	Occupation	Total Employment 2006	2016	% Change	Occupation
			scientific products	54,312	58,169	7.1	Tapers
410,948	461,852	12.4	Sales representatives, wholesale and manufacturing, technical and scientific products	80,726	82,455	2.1	Tax examiners, collectors, and revenue agents
				100,415	91,946	-8.4	Tax preparers
65,032	67,501	3.8	Sawing machine setters, operators, and tenders, wood	228,531	258,200	13.0	Taxi drivers and chauffeurs
				1,312,222	1,448,763	10.4	Teacher assistants
1,037,547	1,096,096	5.6	Secondary school teachers, except special and vocational education	740,916	805,252	8.7	Teachers and instructors, nsk
				1,274,303	1,275,052	0.1	Team assemblers
1,939,837	1,962,267	1.2	Secretaries, except legal, medical, and executive	49,151	58,741	19.5	Technical writers
				197,993	203,035	2.5	Telecommunications equipment installers and repairers, except line installers
319,943	399,430	24.8	Securities, commodities, and financial services sales agents	162,317	169,802	4.6	Telecommunications line installers and repairers
56,959	68,438	20.2	Security and fire alarm systems installers	394,783	355,732	-9.9	Telemarketers
1,040,287	1,215,755	16.9	Security guards	26,681	16,137	-39.5	Telephone operators
957	1,055	10.3	Segmental pavers	607,609	689,400	13.5	Tellers
261,496	321,980	23.1	Self-enrichment education teachers	6,769	7,508	10.9	Terrazzo workers and finishers
42,397	36,930	-12.9	Semiconductor processors	19,420	13,551	-30.2	Textile bleaching and dyeing machine operators and tenders
44,289	42,873	-3.2	Separating, filtering, clarifying, precipitating, and still machine setters, operators, and tenders	18,687	13,565	-27.4	Textile cutting machine setters, operators, and tenders
23,774	26,199	10.2	Septic tank servicers and sewer pipe cleaners	40,145	27,739	-30.9	Textile knitting and weaving machine setters, operators, and tenders
96,199	108,325	12.6	Service station attendants				
27,905	26,400	-5.4	Service unit operators, oil, gas, and mining	43,340	32,801	-24.3	Textile winding, twisting, and drawing out machine setters, operators, and tenders
12,205	14,373	17.8	Set and exhibit designers	24,379	20,765	-14.8	Textile, apparel, and furnishings workers, nsk
23,440	20,580	-12.2	Sewers, hand	34,562	38,005	10.0	Therapists, nsk
232,810	169,526	-27.2	Sewing machine operators	79,183	91,398	15.4	Tile and marble setters
29,428	33,328	13.3	Shampooers	2,527	2,336	-7.6	Timing device assemblers, adjusters, and calibrators
188,655	201,382	6.7	Sheet metal workers				
14,797	16,888	14.1	Ship engineers	22,664	19,939	-12.0	Tire builders
768,974	797,286	3.7	Shipping, receiving, and traffic clerks	105,842	127,182	20.2	Tire repairers and changers
15,575	13,977	-10.3	Shoe and leather workers and repairers	69,009	68,167	-1.2	Title examiners, abstractors, and searchers
4,089	2,627	-35.7	Shoe machine operators and tenders	100,788	91,101	-9.6	Tool and die makers
2,886	2,647	-8.3	Shuttle car operators	21,930	17,681	-19.4	Tool grinders, filers, and sharpeners
7,165	6,799	-5.1	Signal and track switch repairers	40,381	48,929	21.2	Tour guides and escorts
38,209	51,308	34.3	Skin care specialists	6,916	7,602	9.9	Traffic technicians
122,074	137,614	12.7	Slaughterers and meat packers	28,878	33,388	15.6	Training and development managers
19,658	21,841	11.1	Slot key persons	210,342	248,832	18.3	Training and development specialists
130,018	162,139	24.7	Social and community service managers	5,551	5,906	6.4	Transit and railroad police
338,743	452,618	33.6	Social and human service assistants	20,830	23,746	14.0	Transportation attendants, except flight attendants and baggage porters
17,777	19,977	12.4	Social science research assistants				
35,994	37,684	4.7	Social scientists and related workers, nsk	26,400	30,742	16.4	Transportation inspectors
66,220	78,001	17.8	Social workers, nsk	43,608	49,400	13.3	Transportation workers, nsk
3,702	4,072	10.0	Sociologists	94,012	101,858	8.3	Transportation, storage, and distribution managers
15,790	17,110	8.4	Soil and plant scientists				
16,124	17,598	9.1	Sound engineering technicians	101,167	102,215	1.0	Travel agents
102,165	118,352	15.8	Special education teachers, middle school	4,672	5,162	10.5	Travel guides
218,850	261,799	19.6	Special education teachers, preschool, kindergarten, and elementary school	40,560	45,071	11.1	Tree trimmers and pruners
				1,859,848	2,052,860	10.4	Truck drivers, heavy and tractor-trailer
137,901	149,657	8.5	Special education teachers, secondary school	1,051,159	1,139,965	8.4	Truck drivers, light or delivery services
109,677	121,288	10.6	Speech-language pathologists	18,699	21,698	16.0	Umpires, referees, and other sports officials
45,389	46,951	3.4	Stationary engineers and boiler operators	54,809	49,890	-9.0	Upholsterers
22,507	24,208	7.6	Statistical assistants	33,809	38,716	14.5	Urban and regional planners
22,416	24,324	8.5	Statisticians	103,166	120,602	16.9	Ushers, lobby attendants, and ticket takers
1,704,921	1,574,199	-7.7	Stock clerks and order fillers	62,196	83,956	35.0	Veterinarians
23,844	26,218	10.0	Stonemasons	74,534	86,228	15.7	Veterinary assistants and laboratory animal caretakers
71,736	76,052	6.0	Structural iron and steel workers				
103,008	102,790	-0.2	Structural metal fabricators and fitters	71,178	100,373	41.0	Veterinary technologists and technicians
83,343	111,971	34.3	Substance abuse and behavioral disorder counselors	15,805	15,003	-5.1	Vocational education teachers, middle school
6,937	7,773	12.1	Subway and streetcar operators	95,534	91,133	-4.6	Vocational education teachers, secondary school
86,197	107,274	24.5	Surgical technologists				
26,853	31,128	15.9	Survey researchers	2,360,630	2,615,309	10.8	Waiters and waitresses
75,555	90,189	19.4	Surveying and mapping technicians	3,814	3,619	-5.1	Watch repairers
60,032	74,243	23.7	Surveyors	110,840	126,111	13.8	Water and liquid waste treatment plant and system operators
177,485	162,575	-8.4	Switchboard operators, including answering service	79,021	70,058	-11.3	Weighers, measurers, checkers, and samplers, recordkeeping
53,910	54,931	1.9	Tailors, dressmakers, and custom sewers				
16,295	17,799	9.2	Tank car, truck, and ship loaders	409,024	429,732	5.1	Welders, cutters, solderers, and brazers

Total Employment 2006	2016	% Change	Occupation
52,803	54,397	3.0	Welding, soldering, and brazing machine setters, operators, and tenders
14,411	12,698	-11.9	Wellhead pumpers
156,568	156,379	-0.1	Wholesale and retail buyers, except farm products
20,486	20,819	1.6	Woodworkers, nsk
99,518	105,870	6.4	Woodworking machine setters, operators, and tenders, except sawing
178,998	158,198	-11.6	Word processors and typists
135,246	152,552	12.8	Writers and authors
20,091	21,830	8.7	Zoologists and wildlife biologists

Employment Order - 2006

4,476,942	5,033,766	12.4	Retail salespersons
3,500,169	3,381,931	-3.4	Cashiers, except gaming
3,200,245	3,603,802	12.6	Office clerks, general
2,504,664	3,092,013	23.5	Registered nurses
2,502,891	2,954,811	18.1	Combined food preparation and serving workers, including fast food
2,416,034	2,465,805	2.1	Laborers and freight, stock, and material movers, hand
2,386,570	2,731,507	14.5	Janitors and cleaners, except maids and housekeeping cleaners
2,360,630	2,615,309	10.8	Waiters and waitresses
2,202,271	2,747,432	24.8	Customer service representatives
2,113,780	2,377,315	12.5	Bookkeeping, accounting, and auditing clerks
1,939,837	1,962,267	1.2	Secretaries, except legal, medical, and executive
1,859,848	2,052,860	10.4	Truck drivers, heavy and tractor-trailer
1,720,460	1,746,324	1.5	General and operations managers
1,704,921	1,574,199	-7.7	Stock clerks and order fillers
1,675,937	1,747,019	4.2	First-line supervisors/managers of retail sales workers
1,618,018	1,857,071	14.8	Executive secretaries and administrative assistants
1,562,254	1,693,014	8.4	Sales representatives, wholesale and manufacturing, except technical and scientific products
1,540,159	1,749,333	13.6	Elementary school teachers, except special education
1,469,519	1,655,518	12.7	Maids and housekeeping cleaners
1,462,071	1,612,072	10.3	Carpenters
1,447,233	1,710,876	18.2	Nursing aides, orderlies, and attendants
1,418,494	1,500,083	5.8	First-line supervisors/managers of office and administrative support workers
1,390,952	1,530,861	10.1	Maintenance and repair workers, general
1,388,168	1,635,947	17.8	Child care workers
1,312,222	1,448,763	10.4	Teacher assistants
1,274,357	1,499,932	17.7	Accountants and auditors
1,274,303	1,275,052	0.1	Team assemblers
1,232,002	1,366,496	10.9	Construction laborers
1,220,054	1,441,326	18.1	Landscaping and groundskeeping workers
1,172,666	1,374,666	17.2	Receptionists and information clerks
1,058,444	968,838	-8.5	Farmers and ranchers
1,051,159	1,139,965	8.4	Truck drivers, light or delivery services
1,043,120	1,261,364	20.9	Business operation specialists, nsk
1,040,287	1,215,755	16.9	Security guards
1,037,547	1,096,096	5.6	Secondary school teachers, except special and vocational education
901,660	1,039,744	15.3	Food preparation workers
869,558	929,743	6.9	Managers, nsk
850,343	948,167	11.5	Cooks, restaurant
833,812	730,180	-12.4	Packers and packagers, hand
817,108	909,458	11.3	First-line supervisors/managers of food preparation and serving workers

Total Employment 2006	2016	% Change	Occupation
787,315	1,170,935	48.7	Home health aides
772,675	883,131	14.3	Automotive service technicians and mechanics
771,796	841,777	9.1	First-line supervisors/managers of construction trades and extraction workers
768,974	797,286	3.7	Shipping, receiving, and traffic clerks
767,257	1,155,795	50.6	Personal and home care aides
760,672	844,195	11.0	Lawyers
748,605	853,703	14.0	Licensed practical and licensed vocational nurses
740,916	805,252	8.7	Teachers and instructors, nsk
705,015	757,438	7.4	Electricians
699,259	665,489	-4.8	First-line supervisors/managers of production and operating workers
678,188	826,839	21.9	Management analysts
658,060	731,803	11.2	Middle school teachers, except special and vocational education
648,418	718,516	10.8	Police and sheriff's patrol officers
637,034	624,181	-2.0	Industrial truck and tractor operators
629,405	681,455	8.3	Cooks, fast food
617,452	694,225	12.4	Hairdressers, hairstylists, and cosmetologists
607,609	689,400	13.5	Tellers
603,083	582,746	-3.4	Farmworkers and laborers, crop, nursery, and greenhouse
552,458	623,634	12.9	Computer support specialists
541,869	565,622	4.4	Billing and posting clerks and machine operators
541,605	538,831	-0.5	Helpers—Production workers
539,732	690,262	27.9	Sales representatives, services, nsk
532,840	586,935	10.2	Counter attendants, cafeteria, food concession, and coffee shop
529,958	549,430	3.7	First-line supervisors/managers of non-retail sales workers
517,358	571,223	10.4	Dishwashers
506,751	732,510	44.6	Computer software engineers, applications
506,347	570,362	12.6	Financial managers
503,631	649,571	29.0	Computer systems analysts
502,201	555,431	10.6	Plumbers, pipefitters, and steamfitters
495,307	550,952	11.2	Bartenders
491,417	456,817	-7.0	Inspectors, testers, sorters, samplers, and weighers
487,077	563,584	15.7	Construction managers
476,623	585,824	22.9	Counter and rental clerks
464,881	498,976	7.3	First-line supervisors/managers of mechanics, installers, and repairers
462,833	517,319	11.8	Painters, construction and maintenance
454,800	497,252	9.3	Bus drivers, school
445,092	421,337	-5.3	Driver/sales workers
441,761	516,309	16.9	Correctional officers and jailers
437,088	551,985	26.3	Preschool teachers, except special education
436,100	492,434	12.9	Insurance sales agents
435,076	417,065	-4.1	Computer programmers
434,200	533,636	22.9	Bill and account collectors
432,291	478,135	10.6	Real estate sales agents
424,152	459,649	8.4	Operating engineers and other construction equipment operators
416,882	564,558	35.4	Medical assistants
416,276	465,502	11.8	Dining room and cafeteria attendants and bartender helpers
410,948	461,852	12.4	Sales representatives, wholesale and manufacturing, technical and scientific products
409,024	429,732	5.1	Welders, cutters, solderers, and brazers
408,369	476,591	16.7	Medical secretaries
404,396	480,687	18.9	Clergy
402,246	410,478	2.0	Chief executives
401,027	444,521	10.8	Cooks, institution and cafeteria
396,539	384,120	-3.1	Machinists
394,783	355,732	-9.9	Telemarketers

Total Employment 2006	2016	% Change	Occupation
385,988	365,058	-5.4	Packaging and filling machine operators and tenders
372,544	415,225	11.5	Loan officers
368,216	419,928	14.0	Cleaners of vehicles and equipment
351,188	387,759	10.4	Hosts and hostesses, restaurant, lounge, and coffee shop
350,259	367,782	5.0	Food service managers
350,048	448,679	28.2	Computer software engineers, systems software
338,743	452,618	33.6	Social and human service assistants
337,768	341,299	1.0	Postal service mail carriers
328,928	378,593	15.1	Property, real estate, and community association managers
319,970	290,221	-9.3	Office and administrative support workers, nsk
319,943	399,430	24.8	Securities, commodities, and financial services sales agents
319,818	360,485	12.7	Recreation workers
318,329	350,838	10.2	Sales managers
313,355	298,680	-4.7	Data entry keyers
309,201	392,536	27.0	Network and computer systems administrators
305,169	332,419	8.9	Claims adjusters, examiners, and investigators
304,906	311,981	2.3	Production workers, nsk
292,876	328,189	12.1	Fire fighters
292,794	305,123	4.2	Production, planning, and expediting clerks
291,861	317,359	8.7	Heating, air conditioning, and refrigeration mechanics and installers
291,591	266,264	-8.7	Assemblers and fabricators, nsk
287,429	287,810	0.1	Purchasing agents, except wholesale, retail, and farm products
285,035	376,364	32.0	Pharmacy technicians
282,424	336,376	19.1	Child, family, and school social workers
282,237	318,009	12.7	First-line supervisors/managers of housekeeping and janitorial workers
279,828	361,549	29.2	Dental assistants
275,269	307,533	11.7	Legal secretaries
274,876	306,383	11.5	Bus and truck mechanics and diesel engine specialists
271,745	231,384	-14.9	Cutting, punching, and press machine setters, operators, and tenders, metal and plastic
270,869	204,918	-24.3	Order clerks
263,695	306,829	16.4	Computer and information systems managers
261,925	304,910	16.4	Medical and health services managers
261,793	401,626	53.4	Network systems and data communications analysts
261,496	321,980	23.1	Self-enrichment education teachers
260,831	286,424	9.8	Graphic designers
260,727	284,283	9.0	Industrial machinery mechanics
259,543	292,352	12.6	Educational, vocational, and school counselors
258,156	261,032	1.1	Farm, ranch, and other agricultural managers
256,330	302,409	18.0	Civil engineers
256,023	253,765	-0.9	Loan interviewers and clerks
253,949	250,613	-1.3	Insurance claims and policy processing clerks
247,497	307,572	24.3	Amusement and recreation attendants
247,103	276,048	11.7	Administrative services managers
244,584	212,988	-12.9	Information and record clerks, nsk
243,482	296,364	21.7	Pharmacists
243,275	286,145	17.6	Public relations specialists
238,681	261,781	9.7	Laundry and dry-cleaning workers
238,015	232,849	-2.2	Parts salespersons
237,703	290,570	22.2	Paralegals and legal assistants
237,035	248,709	4.9	Compliance officers, except agriculture, construction, health and safety, and transportation
234,841	297,845	26.8	Fitness trainers and aerobics instructors
234,354	281,397	20.1	Market research analysts
233,808	137,245	-41.3	File clerks
232,810	169,526	-27.2	Sewing machine operators
228,531	258,200	13.0	Taxi drivers and chauffeurs

Total Employment 2006	2016	% Change	Occupation
226,065	249,171	10.2	First-line supervisors/managers of transportation and material-moving machine and vehicle operators
225,905	243,048	7.6	Education administrators, elementary and secondary school
225,797	235,169	4.2	Mechanical engineers
221,539	246,791	11.4	Cement masons and concrete finishers
221,100	262,007	18.5	Cost estimators
220,911	241,968	9.5	Interviewers, except eligibility and loan
220,568	295,157	33.8	Financial analysts
218,850	261,799	19.6	Special education teachers, preschool, kindergarten, and elementary school
218,776	256,806	17.4	Hotel, motel, and resort desk clerks
216,780	248,530	14.6	Coaches and scouts
214,810	248,153	15.5	First-line supervisors/managers of personal service workers
214,383	249,735	16.5	Human resources, training, and labor relations specialists, nsk
213,612	220,246	3.1	Payroll and timekeeping clerks
213,381	156,167	-26.8	Electrical and electronic equipment assemblers
210,342	248,832	18.3	Training and development specialists
204,428	236,300	15.6	Healthcare support workers, nsk
201,840	237,416	17.6	First-line supervisors/managers of landscaping, lawn service, and groundskeeping workers
201,311	242,263	20.3	Industrial engineers
201,099	239,762	19.2	Emergency medical technicians and paramedics
199,552	206,890	3.7	Door-to-door sales workers, news and street vendors, and related workers
198,488	223,311	12.5	Bus drivers, transit and intercity
197,993	203,035	2.5	Telecommunications equipment installers and repairers, except line installers
197,714	181,173	-8.4	Postal service mail sorters, processors, and processing machine operators
197,594	186,337	-5.7	Printing machine operators
196,892	233,035	18.4	Employment, recruitment, and placement specialists
196,330	216,172	10.1	Musicians and singers
196,200	225,877	15.1	Radiologic technologists and technicians
195,495	204,959	4.8	Cooks, short order
190,231	193,125	1.5	Dispatchers, except police, fire, and ambulance
189,234	219,155	15.8	Food servers, nonrestaurant
188,655	201,382	6.7	Sheet metal workers
187,089	200,669	7.3	Engineering managers
185,864	199,393	7.3	Drywall and ceiling tile installers
182,676	203,800	11.6	Automotive body and related repairers
181,954	204,647	12.5	First-line supervisors/managers of helpers, laborers, and material movers, hand
179,564	204,740	14.0	Sales and related workers, nsk
178,998	158,198	-11.6	Word processors and typists
177,485	162,575	-8.4	Switchboard operators, including answering service
176,220	248,405	41.0	Personal financial advisors
174,961	180,211	3.0	Computer, automated teller, and office machine repairers
172,948	219,752	27.1	Physical therapists
170,479	205,119	20.3	Advertising sales agents
170,433	176,530	3.6	Electrical and electronic engineering technicians
170,305	179,675	5.5	Engineers, nsk
170,234	198,000	16.3	Kindergarten teachers, except special education
169,742	199,966	17.8	Medical records and health information technicians
168,431	181,134	7.5	Installation, maintenance, and repair workers, nsk
168,201	187,125	11.3	Human resources assistants, except payroll and

Total Employment 2006	2016	% Change	Occupation	Total Employment 2006	2016	% Change	Occupation
			timekeeping	114,189	135,539	18.7	Lifeguards, ski patrol, and other recreational protective service workers
167,464	191,549	14.4	Marketing managers				
167,207	187,960	12.4	Medical and clinical laboratory technologists	113,107	92,563	-18.2	Paper goods machine setters, operators, and tenders
167,017	217,220	30.1	Dental hygienists				
165,345	167,127	1.1	Reservation and transportation ticket agents and travel clerks	112,418	115,907	3.1	Eligibility interviewers, government programs
				112,183	120,294	7.2	Electrical power-line installers and repairers
163,379	182,599	11.8	Helpers—Installation, maintenance, and repair workers	110,840	126,111	13.8	Water and liquid waste treatment plant and system operators
162,317	169,802	4.6	Telecommunications line installers and repairers	109,916	130,153	18.4	Compensation, benefits, and job analysis specialists
158,373	164,127	3.6	Librarians	109,730	129,739	18.2	Construction and building inspectors
158,316	173,596	9.7	Brickmasons and blockmasons	109,677	121,288	10.6	Speech-language pathologists
157,341	148,094	-5.9	Industrial production managers	109,060	121,817	11.7	Helpers—Carpenters
156,842	136,758	-12.8	Molding, coremaking, and casting machine setters, operators, and tenders, metal and plastic	106,843	109,772	2.7	Farmworkers, farm and ranch animals
				106,426	92,743	-12.9	Coating, painting, and spraying machine setters, operators, and tenders
156,624	185,414	18.4	Nonfarm animal caretakers	106,336	124,776	17.3	Detectives and criminal investigators
156,568	156,379	-0.1	Wholesale and retail buyers, except farm products	105,842	127,182	20.2	Tire repairers and changers
				105,340	112,487	6.8	Helpers—Electricians
156,284	178,697	14.3	Roofers	104,769	123,670	18.0	Demonstrators and product promoters
153,375	162,965	6.3	Electrical engineers	104,477	111,063	6.3	Insurance underwriters
152,381	176,462	15.8	Clinical, counseling, and school psychologists	103,166	120,602	16.9	Ushers, lobby attendants, and ticket takers
152,064	134,414	-11.6	Mail clerks and mail machine operators, except postal service	103,008	102,790	-0.2	Structural metal fabricators and fitters
				102,406	125,563	22.6	Respiratory therapists
151,366	174,060	15.0	Medical and clinical laboratory technicians	102,165	118,352	15.8	Special education teachers, middle school
149,266	164,263	10.0	Bakers	101,441	85,499	-15.7	Grinding, lapping, polishing, and buffing machine tool setters, operators, and tenders, metal and plastic
149,041	153,146	2.8	Cabinetmakers and bench carpenters				
147,763	125,360	-15.2	Machine feeders and offbearers				
145,216	158,140	8.9	Highway maintenance workers	101,167	102,215	1.0	Travel agents
144,228	159,947	10.9	Meat, poultry, and fish cutters and trimmers	101,125	118,197	16.9	Appraisers and assessors of real estate
142,842	135,544	-5.1	Mixing and blending machine setters, operators, and tenders	100,788	91,101	-9.6	Tool and die makers
				100,415	91,946	-8.4	Tax preparers
140,732	173,042	23.0	Rehabilitation counselors	99,794	129,759	30.0	Mental health counselors
140,510	136,339	-3.0	Computer-controlled machine tool operators, metal and plastic	99,518	105,870	6.4	Woodworking machine setters, operators, and tenders, except sawing
137,901	149,657	8.5	Special education teachers, secondary school	99,230	118,730	19.7	Directors, religious activities and education
137,868	142,954	3.7	Electronics engineers, except computer	99,216	109,591	10.5	Education, training, and library workers, nsk
136,323	148,893	9.2	Dentists, general	99,053	112,512	13.6	Police, fire, and ambulance dispatchers
135,970	146,047	7.4	Refuse and recyclable material collectors	98,858	121,709	23.1	Occupational therapists
135,949	156,509	15.1	Computer specialists, nsk	98,454	111,747	13.5	Medical transcriptionists
135,246	152,552	12.8	Writers and authors	96,730	106,949	10.6	Flight attendants
135,204	151,574	12.1	Parking lot attendants	96,553	96,846	0.3	Multiple machine tool setters, operators, and tenders, metal and plastic
133,770	133,551	-0.2	Couriers and messengers				
131,873	155,258	17.7	Architects, except landscape and naval	96,199	108,325	12.6	Service station attendants
131,352	133,852	1.9	Butchers and meat cutters	95,534	91,133	-4.6	Vocational education teachers, secondary school
131,293	149,980	14.2	Education administrators, postsecondary				
131,239	145,770	11.1	Real estate brokers	94,921	105,275	10.9	Food batchmakers
130,570	146,656	12.3	Mobile heavy equipment mechanics, except engines	94,445	104,742	10.9	Probation officers and correctional treatment specialists
130,018	162,139	24.7	Social and community service managers	94,012	101,858	8.3	Transportation, storage, and distribution managers
129,997	97,943	-24.7	Computer operators				
129,430	158,530	22.5	Instructional coordinators	93,926	91,393	-2.7	Office machine operators, except computer
129,135	144,378	11.8	Financial specialists, nsk	93,869	87,146	-7.2	Extruding and drawing machine setters, operators, and tenders, metal and plastic
123,643	153,526	24.2	Medical and public health social workers				
122,480	135,138	10.3	Photographers	93,074	103,360	11.1	Producers and directors
122,472	135,495	10.6	Aircraft mechanics and service technicians	93,018	101,529	9.2	First-line supervisors/managers of police and detectives
122,272	158,844	29.9	Mental health and substance abuse social workers	90,650	99,888	10.2	Civil engineering technicians
122,074	137,614	12.7	Slaughterers and meat packers	89,831	98,993	10.2	Aerospace engineers
121,511	124,275	2.3	Editors	87,402	105,039	20.2	Medical scientists, except epidemiologists
121,256	131,534	8.5	Library technicians	87,296	109,845	25.8	Multi-media artists and animators
119,415	153,523	28.6	Database administrators	87,001	96,285	10.7	Merchandise displayers and window trimmers
118,012	147,644	25.1	Community and social service specialists, nsk	86,909	79,184	-8.9	Floral designers
117,696	141,547	20.3	Massage therapists	86,431	75,299	-12.9	Personal care and service workers, nsk
116,009	125,127	7.9	Library assistants, clerical	86,197	107,274	24.5	Surgical technologists
115,522	122,541	6.1	Architectural and civil drafters	85,985	100,154	16.5	Cargo and freight agents
114,784	123,521	7.6	Chefs and head cooks	84,643	94,731	11.9	Helpers—Pipelayers, plumbers, pipefitters, and steamfitters
114,584	124,628	8.8	Court, municipal, and license clerks				

Total Employment		%	
2006	2016	Change	Occupation
84,291	83,348	-1.1	Maintenance workers, machinery
83,697	91,340	9.1	Chemists
83,523	103,670	24.1	Gaming dealers
83,443	97,856	17.3	Logisticians
83,343	111,971	34.3	Substance abuse and behavioral disorder counselors
83,267	104,142	25.1	Environmental scientists and specialists, including health
82,703	93,157	12.6	Protective service workers, nsk
81,824	83,443	2.0	Engineering technicians, except drafters, nsk
81,422	68,135	-16.3	New accounts clerks
81,193	74,657	-8.1	Extruding, forming, pressing, and compacting machine setters, operators, and tenders
80,726	82,455	2.1	Tax examiners, collectors, and revenue agents
80,226	85,688	6.8	Electrical and electronics repairers, commercial and industrial equipment
80,157	86,818	8.3	Excavating and loading machine and dragline operators
79,505	80,435	1.2	Postal service clerks
79,444	89,678	12.9	Airline pilots, copilots, and flight engineers
79,344	91,208	15.0	Healthcare technologists and technicians, nsk
79,183	91,398	15.4	Tile and marble setters
79,021	70,058	-11.3	Weighers, measurers, checkers, and samplers, recordkeeping
78,794	71,486	-9.3	Cutting and slicing machine setters, operators, and tenders
78,690	91,288	16.0	Biological technicians
78,525	82,137	4.6	Computer hardware engineers
78,340	82,437	5.2	Mechanical drafters
78,121	99,680	27.6	Manicurists and pedicurists
77,898	84,870	8.9	Art directors
77,798	76,196	-2.1	Procurement clerks
77,182	73,762	-4.4	Pressers, textile, garment, and related materials
77,075	89,272	15.8	Entertainers and performers, sports and related workers, nsk
75,942	84,575	11.4	Motor vehicle operators, nsk
75,847	86,628	14.2	Adult literacy, remedial education, and GED teachers and instructors
75,795	82,255	8.5	Sales engineers
75,555	90,189	19.4	Surveying and mapping technicians
74,915	82,364	9.9	Industrial engineering technicians
74,534	86,228	15.7	Veterinary assistants and laboratory animal caretakers
73,309	87,999	20.0	Brokerage clerks
73,205	72,324	-1.2	Carpet installers
71,856	85,853	19.5	Interior designers
71,736	76,052	6.0	Structural iron and steel workers
71,178	100,373	41.0	Veterinary technologists and technicians
70,988	79,651	12.2	Lodging managers
70,899	55,959	-21.1	Prepress technicians and workers
70,030	78,141	11.6	Actors
69,722	80,500	15.5	Pest control workers
69,526	71,910	3.4	Purchasing managers
69,320	70,619	1.9	Crossing guards
69,009	68,167	-1.2	Title examiners, abstractors, and searchers
68,975	63,204	-8.4	Credit authorizers, checkers, and clerks
68,005	76,763	12.9	Music directors and composers
67,760	51,976	-23.3	Lathe and turning machine tool setters, operators, and tenders, metal and plastic
67,132	68,398	1.9	Credit analysts
66,590	72,401	8.7	Pipelayers
66,220	78,001	17.8	Social workers, nsk
66,177	72,695	9.8	Life, physical, and social science technicians, nsk
65,904	71,631	8.7	Opticians, dispensing
65,628	83,353	27.0	Physician assistants
65,364	72,568	11.0	Helpers—Brickmasons, blockmasons, stonemasons, and tile and marble setters

Total Employment		%	
2006	2016	Change	Occupation
65,032	67,501	3.8	Sawing machine setters, operators, and tenders, wood
64,876	72,513	11.8	Health diagnosing and treating practitioners, nsk
64,859	50,697	-21.8	Bindery workers
64,507	65,171	1.0	Legislators
64,255	70,056	9.0	Paving, surfacing, and tamping equipment operators
62,455	67,974	8.8	Construction and related workers, nsk
62,196	83,956	35.0	Veterinarians
62,098	60,073	-3.3	Psychiatric technicians
61,858	66,260	7.1	Budget analysts
61,735	61,694	-0.1	Psychiatric aides
61,546	77,664	26.2	Health educators
61,228	64,793	5.8	Chemical technicians
61,148	66,106	8.1	Plasterers and stucco masons
60,298	54,800	-9.1	Electromechanical equipment assemblers
60,296	79,821	32.4	Physical therapist assistants
60,034	60,678	1.1	Barbers
60,032	74,243	23.7	Surveyors
59,451	56,482	-5.0	Agricultural equipment operators
59,212	59,921	1.2	Reporters and correspondents
58,905	54,020	-8.3	Radio and television announcers
58,353	64,552	10.6	Operations research analysts
58,233	64,849	11.4	Human resources managers, nsk
57,364	58,239	1.5	Home appliance repairers
57,126	62,038	8.6	Dietitians and nutritionists
56,959	68,438	20.2	Security and fire alarm systems installers
56,845	67,347	18.5	Residential advisors
56,326	63,628	13.0	Food preparation and serving related workers, nsk
56,064	69,246	23.5	Education administrators, preschool and child care center/program
55,928	56,646	1.3	Molders, shapers, and casters, except metal and plastic
54,992	61,552	11.9	Glaziers
54,884	58,062	5.8	Millwrights
54,809	49,890	-9.0	Upholsterers
54,341	68,161	25.4	Environmental engineers
54,322	58,883	8.4	Painters, transportation equipment
54,312	58,169	7.1	Tapers
53,910	54,931	1.9	Tailors, dressmakers, and custom sewers
53,588	53,964	0.7	Material moving workers, nsk
53,439	55,393	3.7	Dental laboratory technicians
53,243	45,094	-15.3	Chemical plant and system operators
52,803	54,397	3.0	Welding, soldering, and brazing machine setters, operators, and tenders
52,768	60,579	14.8	Healthcare practitioners and technical workers, nsk
52,737	50,688	-3.9	Chemical equipment operators and tenders
52,725	60,339	14.4	Chiropractors
52,468	58,483	11.5	First-line supervisors/managers of fire fighting and prevention workers
52,219	51,047	-2.2	Jewelers and precious stone and metal workers
51,693	61,124	18.2	Private detectives and investigators
50,962	61,095	19.9	Meeting and convention planners
50,394	44,807	-11.1	Pharmacy aides
49,881	61,971	24.2	Audio and video equipment technicians
49,677	46,026	-7.3	Conveyor operators and tenders
49,575	57,966	16.9	Public relations managers
49,319	53,739	9.0	Baggage porters and bellhops
49,304	24,742	-49.8	Photographic processing machine operators
49,151	58,741	19.5	Technical writers
49,087	54,996	12.0	Compensation and benefits managers
48,661	36,431	-25.1	Metal workers and plastic workers, nsk
48,240	43,749	-9.3	Job printers
48,019	54,989	14.5	First-line supervisors/managers, protective service workers, nsk

Total Employment 2006	2016	% Change	Occupation
47,978	51,412	7.2	Commercial and industrial designers
47,928	46,498	-3.0	Coin, vending, and amusement machine servicers and repairers
47,878	50,311	5.1	Legal support workers, nsk
47,792	50,848	6.4	Mechanical engineering technicians
47,296	50,247	6.2	Advertising and promotions managers
46,574	41,800	-10.3	Meter readers, utilities
46,393	47,691	2.8	Crane and tower operators
46,242	57,512	24.4	Physical therapist aides
45,668	54,384	19.1	Diagnostic medical sonographers
45,389	46,951	3.4	Stationary engineers and boiler operators
45,378	56,956	25.5	Cardiovascular technologists and technicians
45,265	41,368	-8.6	Engine and other machine assemblers
45,247	51,655	14.2	Medical equipment preparers
45,206	48,882	8.1	Occupational health and safety specialists
44,776	41,586	-7.1	Grinding and polishing workers, hand
44,393	42,310	-4.7	Food cooking machine operators and tenders
44,289	42,873	-3.2	Separating, filtering, clarifying, precipitating, and still machine setters, operators, and tenders
44,085	42,663	-3.2	Roustabouts, oil and gas
43,608	49,400	13.3	Transportation workers, nsk
43,340	32,801	-24.3	Textile winding, twisting, and drawing out machine setters, operators, and tenders
42,991	43,132	0.3	Control and valve installers and repairers, except mechanical door
42,924	52,682	22.7	Animal trainers
42,686	33,215	-22.2	Drilling and boring machine tool setters, operators, and tenders, metal and plastic
42,485	37,440	-11.9	Crushing, grinding, and polishing machine setters, operators, and tenders
42,397	36,930	-12.9	Semiconductor processors
42,091	41,332	-1.8	Graders and sorters, agricultural products
41,970	36,367	-13.4	Petroleum pump system operators, refinery operators, and gaugers
41,898	36,788	-12.2	Plating and coating machine setters, operators, and tenders, metal and plastic
41,193	50,916	23.6	Interpreters and translators
40,743	45,381	11.4	Natural sciences managers
40,560	45,071	11.1	Tree trimmers and pruners
40,496	39,980	-1.3	Logging equipment operators
40,381	48,929	21.2	Tour guides and escorts
40,152	43,795	9.1	Railroad conductors and yardmasters
40,145	27,739	-30.9	Textile knitting and weaving machine setters, operators, and tenders
39,700	40,908	3.0	Electronic home entertainment equipment installers and repairers
39,584	44,538	12.5	First-line supervisors/managers of correctional officers
39,497	43,929	11.2	Hazardous materials removal workers
39,194	46,922	19.7	Religious workers, nsk
38,372	32,179	-16.1	Fishers and related fishing workers
38,209	51,308	34.3	Skin care specialists
37,881	42,479	12.1	Broadcast technicians
37,645	45,799	21.7	Medical equipment repairers
37,564	42,282	12.6	Helpers, construction trades, nsk
36,689	36,235	-1.2	Law clerks
36,500	46,701	28.0	Environmental science and protection technicians, including health
35,994	37,684	4.7	Social scientists and related workers, nsk
35,853	31,611	-11.8	Rolling machine setters, operators, and tenders, metal and plastic
35,660	39,848	11.7	Media and communication workers, nsk
34,848	36,286	4.1	Electrical and electronics drafters
34,759	35,701	2.7	Power plant operators
34,562	38,005	10.0	Therapists, nsk
33,887	41,831	23.4	Gaming supervisors
33,829	33,166	-2.0	Forest and conservation technicians

Total Employment 2006	2016	% Change	Occupation
33,809	38,716	14.5	Urban and regional planners
33,617	39,628	17.9	Captains, mates, and pilots of water vessels
33,396	34,730	4.0	Loan counselors
33,294	35,346	6.2	Fiberglass laminators and fabricators
32,981	38,167	15.7	Sailors and marine oilers
32,892	34,706	5.5	Outdoor power equipment and other small engine mechanics
32,807	37,486	14.3	Funeral attendants
32,740	36,445	11.3	Optometrists
32,470	35,908	10.6	Fence erectors
32,414	35,130	8.4	Insulation workers, floor, ceiling, and wall
31,833	32,137	1.0	Desktop publishers
31,596	28,834	-8.7	Furnace, kiln, oven, drier, and kettle operators and tenders
31,326	30,348	-3.1	Furniture finishers
31,068	21,640	-30.3	Forging machine setters, operators, and tenders, metal and plastic
31,061	37,850	21.9	Geoscientists, except hydrologists and geographers
30,885	31,988	3.6	Painting, coating, and decorating workers
30,672	31,087	1.4	Farm equipment mechanics
30,605	34,893	14.0	Pesticide handlers, sprayers, and applicators, vegetation
30,444	32,842	7.9	Chemical engineers
30,323	33,337	9.9	Fine artists, including painters, sculptors, and illustrators
30,162	33,633	11.5	Reinforcing iron and rebar workers
29,714	33,462	12.6	Education administrators, nsk
29,428	33,328	13.3	Shampooers
29,211	23,071	-21.0	Milling and planing machine setters, operators, and tenders, metal and plastic
29,067	30,138	3.7	Biological scientists, nsk
29,064	30,970	6.6	Ophthalmic laboratory technicians
28,991	25,450	-12.2	Floor layers, except carpet, wood, and hard tiles
28,878	33,388	15.6	Training and development managers
28,770	32,358	12.5	Funeral directors
28,633	26,901	-6.0	Cutters and trimmers, hand
28,446	30,898	8.6	Insulation workers, mechanical
28,083	31,681	12.8	Aircraft structure, surfaces, rigging, and systems assemblers
27,905	26,400	-5.4	Service unit operators, oil, gas, and mining
27,873	32,513	16.6	Grounds maintenance workers, nsk
27,839	32,402	16.4	Landscape architects
27,596	31,236	13.2	Commercial pilots
27,306	31,835	16.6	Counselors, nsk
27,192	28,580	5.1	Judges, magistrate judges, and magistrates
27,122	23,107	-14.8	Heat treating equipment setters, operators, and tenders, metal and plastic
27,109	28,924	6.7	Gaming change persons and booth cashiers
26,897	30,001	11.5	Camera operators, television, video, and motion picture
26,853	31,128	15.9	Survey researchers
26,681	16,137	-39.5	Telephone operators
26,578	27,926	5.1	Rail car repairers
26,400	30,742	16.4	Transportation inspectors
26,018	31,768	22.1	Locksmiths and safe repairers
25,870	25,653	-0.8	Postmasters and mail superintendents
25,804	27,516	6.6	Agricultural and food science technicians
25,588	28,326	10.7	Financial examiners
25,474	24,398	-4.2	Electric motor, power tool, and related repairers
25,380	27,823	9.6	Health and safety engineers, except mining safety engineers and inspectors
25,261	30,701	21.5	Computer and information scientists, research
25,223	27,795	10.2	Air traffic controllers
25,115	26,046	3.7	Recreational therapists
25,083	28,789	14.8	Dietetic technicians

Total Employment 2006	2016	% Change	Occupation
25,016	24,964	-0.2	Helpers—Extraction workers
24,981	31,332	25.4	Occupational therapist assistants
24,870	27,259	9.6	Agents and business managers of artists, performers, and athletes
24,701	32,051	29.8	Marriage and family therapists
24,609	21,799	-11.4	Railroad brake, signal, and switch operators
24,521	27,215	11.0	Drafters, nsk
24,455	24,286	-0.7	Helpers—Painters, paperhangers, plasterers, and stucco masons
24,379	20,765	-14.8	Textile, apparel, and furnishings workers, nsk
24,114	28,704	19.0	Motorboat mechanics
23,881	25,350	6.2	Physical scientists, nsk
23,844	26,218	10.0	Stonemasons
23,774	26,199	10.2	Septic tank servicers and sewer pipe cleaners
23,684	15,090	-36.3	Photographic process workers
23,610	28,033	18.7	Automotive glass installers and repairers
23,440	20,580	-12.2	Sewers, hand
23,362	21,209	-9.2	Cementing and gluing machine operators and tenders
22,835	15,879	-30.5	Coil winders, tapers, and finishers
22,664	19,939	-12.0	Tire builders
22,507	24,208	7.6	Statistical assistants
22,416	24,324	8.5	Statisticians
22,300	21,261	-4.7	Electrical and electronics repairers, powerhouse, substation, and relay
21,930	17,681	-19.4	Tool grinders, filers, and sharpeners
21,830	23,753	8.8	Elevator installers and repairers
21,769	23,228	6.7	Helpers—Roofers
21,681	23,099	6.5	Earth drillers, except oil and gas
21,616	22,482	4.0	Materials engineers
21,538	26,209	21.7	Ambulance drivers and attendants, except emergency medical technicians
21,211	23,858	12.5	Motorcycle mechanics
21,126	26,362	24.8	Environmental engineering technicians
21,079	21,978	4.3	Electrical and electronics installers and repairers, transportation equipment
20,830	23,746	14.0	Transportation attendants, except flight attendants and baggage porters
20,544	23,150	12.7	Film and video editors
20,486	20,819	1.6	Woodworkers, nsk
20,429	20,927	2.4	Choreographers
20,411	21,428	5.0	Fashion designers
20,350	20,360	0.0	Agricultural workers, nsk
20,131	23,326	15.9	Biochemists and biophysicists
20,091	21,830	8.7	Zoologists and wildlife biologists
20,017	20,936	4.6	Electronic equipment installers and repairers, motor vehicles
19,923	18,853	-5.4	Rotary drill operators, oil and gas
19,850	22,783	14.8	Nuclear medicine technologists
19,844	20,939	5.5	Forest and conservation workers
19,777	20,830	5.3	Conservation scientists
19,767	21,643	9.5	Dancers
19,753	22,547	14.1	Concierges
19,658	21,841	11.1	Slot key persons
19,420	13,551	-30.2	Textile bleaching and dyeing machine operators and tenders
19,383	23,567	21.6	Locker room, coatroom, and dressing room attendants
19,167	19,334	0.9	Respiratory therapy technicians
19,101	23,790	24.5	Court reporters
18,876	20,921	10.8	Food and tobacco roasting, baking, and drying machine operators and tenders
18,784	17,694	-5.8	Derrick operators, oil and gas
18,779	20,701	10.2	Media and communication equipment workers, nsk
18,699	21,698	16.0	Umpires, referees, and other sports officials
18,687	13,565	-27.4	Textile cutting machine setters, operators, and tenders

Total Employment 2006	2016	% Change	Occupation
18,608	20,688	11.2	Bailiffs
18,463	23,637	28.0	Gaming and sports book writers and runners
18,386	14,896	-19.0	Metal-refining furnace operators and tenders
18,137	22,438	23.7	Actuaries
18,033	20,077	11.3	Gaming cage workers
17,980	16,474	-8.4	Numerical tool and process control programmers
17,856	18,995	6.4	Proofreaders and copy markers
17,777	19,977	12.4	Social science research assistants
17,682	14,573	-17.6	Extruding and forming machine setters, operators, and tenders, synthetic and glass fibers
17,571	20,034	14.0	Boilermakers
17,524	20,891	19.2	Athletes and sports competitors
17,445	19,531	12.0	Correspondence clerks
17,357	19,306	11.2	Microbiologists
17,355	18,251	5.2	Petroleum engineers
17,117	21,271	24.3	Athletic trainers
16,516	17,641	6.8	Physicists
16,327	17,036	4.3	Precision instrument and equipment repairers, nsk
16,295	17,799	9.2	Tank car, truck, and ship loaders
16,176	15,998	-1.1	Agricultural inspectors
16,124	17,598	9.1	Sound engineering technicians
16,041	17,931	11.8	Designers, nsk
15,914	14,348	-9.8	Cleaning, washing, and metal pickling equipment operators and tenders
15,904	14,536	-8.6	Purchasing agents and buyers, farm products
15,805	15,003	-5.1	Vocational education teachers, middle school
15,790	17,110	8.4	Soil and plant scientists
15,739	16,155	2.6	Electro-mechanical technicians
15,709	16,987	8.1	Avionics technicians
15,649	18,011	15.1	Building cleaning workers, nsk
15,588	16,122	3.4	Cooks, nsk
15,575	13,977	-10.3	Shoe and leather workers and repairers
15,479	15,487	0.1	Administrative law judges, adjudicators, and hearing officers
15,399	17,698	14.9	Mechanical door repairers
15,273	16,377	7.2	Nuclear engineers
15,202	17,097	12.5	Animal control workers
14,969	15,735	5.1	Farm and home management advisors
14,797	16,888	14.1	Ship engineers
14,792	15,900	7.5	Economists
14,791	12,212	-17.4	Pourers and casters, metal
14,644	18,475	26.2	Gaming service workers, nsk
14,635	15,334	4.8	Rail-track laying and maintenance equipment operators
14,627	18,248	24.8	Radiation therapists
14,523	11,229	-22.7	Foundry mold and coremakers
14,411	12,698	-11.9	Wellhead pumpers
14,379	17,415	21.1	Biomedical engineers
14,319	14,064	-1.8	Floor sanders and finishers
14,132	13,772	-2.6	Plant and system operators, nsk
14,027	16,179	15.3	Life scientists, nsk
13,998	16,542	18.2	Recreational vehicle service technicians
13,805	15,327	11.0	Fire inspectors and investigators
13,799	14,955	8.4	Artists and related workers, nsk
13,625	12,969	-4.8	Etchers and engravers
13,399	15,078	12.5	Insurance appraisers, auto damage
13,188	13,868	5.2	Foresters
13,085	12,112	-7.4	Fallers
13,051	17,063	30.7	Forensic science technicians
12,323	13,488	9.4	Medical appliance technicians
12,315	12,284	-0.3	Riggers
12,261	11,044	-9.9	Gas plant operators
12,253	13,454	9.8	Audiologists
12,205	14,373	17.8	Set and exhibit designers
12,184	14,656	20.3	Cartographers and photogrammetrists

Total Employment 2006	2016	% Change	Occupation
11,960	11,934	-0.2	Public address system and other announcers
11,944	13,076	9.5	Podiatrists
11,818	12,838	8.6	Geological and petroleum technicians
11,803	11,462	-2.9	Manufactured building and mobile home installers
11,782	13,002	10.3	Food scientists and technologists
11,725	13,172	12.3	Emergency management specialists
11,591	12,503	7.9	Psychologists, nsk
11,493	10,532	-8.4	Motion picture projectionists
10,677	9,956	-6.8	Cooling and freezing equipment operators and tenders
10,676	12,376	15.9	Museum technicians and conservators
10,544	9,225	-12.5	Pump operators, except wellhead pumpers
10,520	11,814	12.3	Parking enforcement workers
10,505	10,967	4.4	Animal breeders
10,468	11,992	14.6	Occupational health and safety technicians
10,390	12,607	21.3	Mathematical scientists, nsk
10,362	12,772	23.3	Curators
10,153	8,144	-19.8	Lay-out workers, metal and plastic
10,043	10,504	4.6	Continuous mining machine operators
9,899	8,691	-12.2	Paperhangers
9,750	9,784	0.4	Extraction workers, nsk
9,695	10,536	8.7	Materials scientists
9,209	6,578	-28.6	Fabric and apparel patternmakers
9,196	10,199	10.9	Marine engineers and naval architects
9,179	10,026	9.2	Orthodontists
9,028	10,316	14.3	Embalmers
8,816	9,522	8.0	Craft artists
8,791	8,240	-6.3	Model makers, metal and plastic
8,759	9,684	10.6	Atmospheric and space scientists
8,658	11,565	33.6	Gaming surveillance officers and gaming investigators
8,644	9,267	7.2	Bicycle repairers
8,571	8,153	-4.9	Power distributors and dispatchers
8,512	9,400	10.4	Aerospace engineering and operations technicians
8,469	9,363	10.6	Arbitrators, mediators, and conciliators
8,315	10,337	24.3	Hydrologists
8,235	10,035	21.9	Occupational therapist aides
8,030	8,017	-0.2	Fish and game wardens
7,935	7,470	-5.9	Logging workers, nsk
7,918	8,218	3.8	Mine cutting and channeling machine operators
7,724	8,184	6.0	Broadcast news analysts
7,698	8,396	9.1	Oral and maxillofacial surgeons
7,429	7,025	-5.4	Patternmakers, metal and plastic
7,305	6,298	-13.8	Audio-visual collections specialists
7,211	5,995	-16.9	Bookbinders
7,165	6,799	-5.1	Signal and track switch repairers
7,115	6,741	-5.3	Log graders and scalers
7,070	7,774	10.0	Mining and geological engineers, including mining safety engineers
6,937	7,773	12.1	Subway and streetcar operators
6,928	7,398	6.8	Dentists, nsk
6,916	7,602	9.9	Traffic technicians
6,772	5,506	-18.7	Rail transportation workers, nsk
6,769	7,508	10.9	Terrazzo workers and finishers
6,533	6,268	-4.1	Radio mechanics
6,502	6,939	6.7	Nuclear technicians
6,449	7,379	14.4	Archivists
5,998	6,167	2.8	Musical instrument repairers and tuners
5,792	7,140	23.3	Aircraft cargo handling supervisors
5,706	6,379	11.8	Orthotists and prosthetists
5,584	6,050	8.3	Pile-driver operators
5,551	5,906	6.4	Transit and railroad police
5,545	6,377	15.0	Anthropologists and archeologists
5,371	5,900	9.8	Animal scientists
5,334	5,407	1.4	Explosives workers, ordnance handling

Total Employment 2006	2016	% Change	Occupation
			experts, and blasters
4,927	5,360	8.8	Cooks, private household
4,891	5,469	11.8	Airfield operations specialists
4,694	4,945	5.3	Political scientists
4,672	5,162	10.5	Travel guides
4,507	5,119	13.6	Epidemiologists
4,403	4,309	-2.1	Camera and photographic equipment repairers
4,346	4,667	7.4	Communications equipment operators, nsk
4,328	4,940	14.1	Costume attendants
4,291	4,345	1.2	Roof bolters, mining
4,154	3,427	-17.5	Gas compressor and gas pumping station operators
4,089	2,627	-35.7	Shoe machine operators and tenders
3,997	4,974	24.4	Gaming managers
3,926	3,799	-3.2	Bridge and lock tenders
3,883	4,858	25.1	Rock splitters, quarry
3,814	3,619	-5.1	Watch repairers
3,794	4,195	10.6	Nuclear power reactor operators
3,702	4,072	10.0	Sociologists
3,478	3,079	-11.5	Refractory materials repairers, except brickmasons
3,446	3,716	7.8	Historians
3,133	3,401	8.6	Agricultural engineers
3,133	3,688	17.7	Commercial divers
3,085	3,224	4.5	Loading machine operators, underground mining
3,033	3,342	10.2	Mathematicians
3,017	2,980	-1.2	Hoist and winch operators
2,989	3,134	4.9	Mining machine operators, nsk
2,978	3,302	10.9	Motorboat operators
2,886	2,647	-8.3	Shuttle car operators
2,527	2,336	-7.6	Timing device assemblers, adjusters, and calibrators
2,279	1,369	-39.9	Patternmakers, wood
2,146	3,000	39.8	Makeup artists, theatrical and performance
2,142	2,285	6.7	Dredge operators
2,003	2,200	9.8	Models
1,943	2,356	21.3	Industrial-organizational psychologists
1,888	1,118	-40.8	Model makers, wood
1,815	1,853	2.1	Forest fire inspectors and prevention specialists
1,809	1,781	-1.5	Fabric menders, except garment
1,656	1,748	5.5	Astronomers
1,548	1,296	-16.3	Radio operators
1,302	1,405	7.9	Mathematical technicians
1,096	1,162	6.1	Geographers
999	1,106	10.7	Prosthodontists
957	1,055	10.3	Segmental pavers
474	384	-19.0	Hunters and trappers

Growth/Decline Order - 2006 to 2016

2006	2016	% Change	Occupation
261,793	401,626	53.4	Network systems and data communications analysts
767,257	1,155,795	50.6	Personal and home care aides
787,315	1,170,935	48.7	Home health aides
506,751	732,510	44.6	Computer software engineers, applications
176,220	248,405	41.0	Personal financial advisors
71,178	100,373	41.0	Veterinary technologists and technicians
2,146	3,000	39.8	Makeup artists, theatrical and performance
416,882	564,558	35.4	Medical assistants
62,196	83,956	35.0	Veterinarians
38,209	51,308	34.3	Skin care specialists
83,343	111,971	34.3	Substance abuse and behavioral disorder counselors
220,568	295,157	33.8	Financial analysts

Total Employment 2006	2016	% Change	Occupation
8,658	11,565	33.6	Gaming surveillance officers and gaming investigators
338,743	452,618	33.6	Social and human service assistants
60,296	79,821	32.4	Physical therapist assistants
285,035	376,364	32.0	Pharmacy technicians
13,051	17,063	30.7	Forensic science technicians
167,017	217,220	30.1	Dental hygienists
99,794	129,759	30.0	Mental health counselors
122,272	158,844	29.9	Mental health and substance abuse social workers
24,701	32,051	29.8	Marriage and family therapists
279,828	361,549	29.2	Dental assistants
503,631	649,571	29.0	Computer systems analysts
119,415	153,523	28.6	Database administrators
350,048	448,679	28.2	Computer software engineers, systems software
36,500	46,701	28.0	Environmental science and protection technicians, including health
18,463	23,637	28.0	Gaming and sports book writers and runners
539,732	690,262	27.9	Sales representatives, services, nsk
78,121	99,680	27.6	Manicurists and pedicurists
172,948	219,752	27.1	Physical therapists
309,201	392,536	27.0	Network and computer systems administrators
65,628	83,353	27.0	Physician assistants
234,841	297,845	26.8	Fitness trainers and aerobics instructors
437,088	551,985	26.3	Preschool teachers, except special education
14,644	18,475	26.2	Gaming service workers, nsk
61,546	77,664	26.2	Health educators
87,296	109,845	25.8	Multi-media artists and animators
45,378	56,956	25.5	Cardiovascular technologists and technicians
54,341	68,161	25.4	Environmental engineers
24,981	31,332	25.4	Occupational therapist assistants
118,012	147,644	25.1	Community and social service specialists, nsk
83,267	104,142	25.1	Environmental scientists and specialists, including health
3,883	4,858	25.1	Rock splitters, quarry
2,202,271	2,747,432	24.8	Customer service representatives
21,126	26,362	24.8	Environmental engineering technicians
14,627	18,248	24.8	Radiation therapists
319,943	399,430	24.8	Securities, commodities, and financial services sales agents
130,018	162,139	24.7	Social and community service managers
19,101	23,790	24.5	Court reporters
86,197	107,274	24.5	Surgical technologists
3,997	4,974	24.4	Gaming managers
46,242	57,512	24.4	Physical therapist aides
247,497	307,572	24.3	Amusement and recreation attendants
17,117	21,271	24.3	Athletic trainers
8,315	10,337	24.3	Hydrologists
49,881	61,971	24.2	Audio and video equipment technicians
123,643	153,526	24.2	Medical and public health social workers
83,523	103,670	24.1	Gaming dealers
18,137	22,438	23.7	Actuaries
60,032	74,243	23.7	Surveyors
41,193	50,916	23.6	Interpreters and translators
56,064	69,246	23.5	Education administrators, preschool and child care center/program
2,504,664	3,092,013	23.5	Registered nurses
33,887	41,831	23.4	Gaming supervisors
5,792	7,140	23.3	Aircraft cargo handling supervisors
10,362	12,772	23.3	Curators
98,858	121,709	23.1	Occupational therapists
261,496	321,980	23.1	Self-enrichment education teachers
140,732	173,042	23.0	Rehabilitation counselors
434,200	533,636	22.9	Bill and account collectors
476,623	585,824	22.9	Counter and rental clerks
42,924	52,682	22.7	Animal trainers
102,406	125,563	22.6	Respiratory therapists
129,430	158,530	22.5	Instructional coordinators
237,703	290,570	22.2	Paralegals and legal assistants
26,018	31,768	22.1	Locksmiths and safe repairers
31,061	37,850	21.9	Geoscientists, except hydrologists and geographers
678,188	826,839	21.9	Management analysts
8,235	10,035	21.9	Occupational therapist aides
21,538	26,209	21.7	Ambulance drivers and attendants, except emergency medical technicians
37,645	45,799	21.7	Medical equipment repairers
243,482	296,364	21.7	Pharmacists
19,383	23,567	21.6	Locker room, coatroom, and dressing room attendants
25,261	30,701	21.5	Computer and information scientists, research
1,943	2,356	21.3	Industrial-organizational psychologists
10,390	12,607	21.3	Mathematical scientists, nsk
40,381	48,929	21.2	Tour guides and escorts
14,379	17,415	21.1	Biomedical engineers
1,043,120	1,261,364	20.9	Business operation specialists, nsk
170,479	205,119	20.3	Advertising sales agents
12,184	14,656	20.3	Cartographers and photogrammetrists
201,311	242,263	20.3	Industrial engineers
117,696	141,547	20.3	Massage therapists
87,402	105,039	20.2	Medical scientists, except epidemiologists
56,959	68,438	20.2	Security and fire alarm systems installers
105,842	127,182	20.2	Tire repairers and changers
234,354	281,397	20.1	Market research analysts
73,309	87,999	20.0	Brokerage clerks
50,962	61,095	19.9	Meeting and convention planners
99,230	118,730	19.7	Directors, religious activities and education
39,194	46,922	19.7	Religious workers, nsk
218,850	261,799	19.6	Special education teachers, preschool, kindergarten, and elementary school
71,856	85,853	19.5	Interior designers
49,151	58,741	19.5	Technical writers
75,555	90,189	19.4	Surveying and mapping technicians
17,524	20,891	19.2	Athletes and sports competitors
201,099	239,762	19.2	Emergency medical technicians and paramedics
282,424	336,376	19.1	Child, family, and school social workers
45,668	54,384	19.1	Diagnostic medical sonographers
24,114	28,704	19.0	Motorboat mechanics
404,396	480,687	18.9	Clergy
23,610	28,033	18.7	Automotive glass installers and repairers
114,189	135,539	18.7	Lifeguards, ski patrol, and other recreational protective service workers
221,100	262,007	18.5	Cost estimators
56,845	67,347	18.5	Residential advisors
109,916	130,153	18.4	Compensation, benefits, and job analysis specialists
196,892	233,035	18.4	Employment, recruitment, and placement specialists
156,624	185,414	18.4	Nonfarm animal caretakers
210,342	248,832	18.3	Training and development specialists
109,730	129,739	18.2	Construction and building inspectors
1,447,233	1,710,876	18.2	Nursing aides, orderlies, and attendants
51,693	61,124	18.2	Private detectives and investigators
13,998	16,542	18.2	Recreational vehicle service technicians
2,502,891	2,954,811	18.1	Combined food preparation and serving workers, including fast food
1,220,054	1,441,326	18.1	Landscaping and groundskeeping workers
256,330	302,409	18.0	Civil engineers
104,769	123,670	18.0	Demonstrators and product promoters
33,617	39,628	17.9	Captains, mates, and pilots of water vessels
1,388,168	1,635,947	17.8	Child care workers
169,742	199,966	17.8	Medical records and health information technicians
12,205	14,373	17.8	Set and exhibit designers

Total Employment 2006	2016	% Change	Occupation
66,220	78,001	17.8	Social workers, nsk
1,274,357	1,499,932	17.7	Accountants and auditors
131,873	155,258	17.7	Architects, except landscape and naval
3,133	3,688	17.7	Commercial divers
201,840	237,416	17.6	First-line supervisors/managers of landscaping, lawn service, and groundskeeping workers
243,275	286,145	17.6	Public relations specialists
218,776	256,806	17.4	Hotel, motel, and resort desk clerks
106,336	124,776	17.3	Detectives and criminal investigators
83,443	97,856	17.3	Logisticians
1,172,666	1,374,666	17.2	Receptionists and information clerks
101,125	118,197	16.9	Appraisers and assessors of real estate
441,761	516,309	16.9	Correctional officers and jailers
49,575	57,966	16.9	Public relations managers
1,040,287	1,215,755	16.9	Security guards
103,166	120,602	16.9	Ushers, lobby attendants, and ticket takers
408,369	476,591	16.7	Medical secretaries
27,306	31,835	16.6	Counselors, nsk
27,873	32,513	16.6	Grounds maintenance workers, nsk
85,985	100,154	16.5	Cargo and freight agents
214,383	249,735	16.5	Human resources, training, and labor relations specialists, nsk
263,695	306,829	16.4	Computer and information systems managers
27,839	32,402	16.4	Landscape architects
261,925	304,910	16.4	Medical and health services managers
26,400	30,742	16.4	Transportation inspectors
170,234	198,000	16.3	Kindergarten teachers, except special education
78,690	91,288	16.0	Biological technicians
18,699	21,698	16.0	Umpires, referees, and other sports officials
20,131	23,326	15.9	Biochemists and biophysicists
10,676	12,376	15.9	Museum technicians and conservators
26,853	31,128	15.9	Survey researchers
152,381	176,462	15.8	Clinical, counseling, and school psychologists
77,075	89,272	15.8	Entertainers and performers, sports and related workers, nsk
189,234	219,155	15.8	Food servers, nonrestaurant
102,165	118,352	15.8	Special education teachers, middle school
487,077	563,584	15.7	Construction managers
32,981	38,167	15.7	Sailors and marine oilers
74,534	86,228	15.7	Veterinary assistants and laboratory animal caretakers
204,428	236,300	15.6	Healthcare support workers, nsk
28,878	33,388	15.6	Training and development managers
214,810	248,153	15.5	First-line supervisors/managers of personal service workers
69,722	80,500	15.5	Pest control workers
79,183	91,398	15.4	Tile and marble setters
901,660	1,039,744	15.3	Food preparation workers
14,027	16,179	15.3	Life scientists, nsk
15,649	18,011	15.1	Building cleaning workers, nsk
135,949	156,509	15.1	Computer specialists, nsk
328,928	378,593	15.1	Property, real estate, and community association managers
196,200	225,877	15.1	Radiologic technologists and technicians
5,545	6,377	15.0	Anthropologists and archeologists
79,344	91,208	15.0	Healthcare technologists and technicians, nsk
151,366	174,060	15.0	Medical and clinical laboratory technicians
15,399	17,698	14.9	Mechanical door repairers
25,083	28,789	14.8	Dietetic technicians
1,618,018	1,857,071	14.8	Executive secretaries and administrative assistants
52,768	60,579	14.8	Healthcare practitioners and technical workers, nsk
19,850	22,783	14.8	Nuclear medicine technologists
216,780	248,530	14.6	Coaches and scouts
10,468	11,992	14.6	Occupational health and safety technicians
48,019	54,989	14.5	First-line supervisors/managers, protective

Total Employment 2006	2016	% Change	Occupation
			service workers, nsk
2,386,570	2,731,507	14.5	Janitors and cleaners, except maids and housekeeping cleaners
33,809	38,716	14.5	Urban and regional planners
6,449	7,379	14.4	Archivists
52,725	60,339	14.4	Chiropractors
167,464	191,549	14.4	Marketing managers
772,675	883,131	14.3	Automotive service technicians and mechanics
9,028	10,316	14.3	Embalmers
32,807	37,486	14.3	Funeral attendants
156,284	178,697	14.3	Roofers
75,847	86,628	14.2	Adult literacy, remedial education, and GED teachers and instructors
131,293	149,980	14.2	Education administrators, postsecondary
45,247	51,655	14.2	Medical equipment preparers
19,753	22,547	14.1	Concierges
4,328	4,940	14.1	Costume attendants
14,797	16,888	14.1	Ship engineers
17,571	20,034	14.0	Boilermakers
368,216	419,928	14.0	Cleaners of vehicles and equipment
748,605	853,703	14.0	Licensed practical and licensed vocational nurses
30,605	34,893	14.0	Pesticide handlers, sprayers, and applicators, vegetation
179,564	204,740	14.0	Sales and related workers, nsk
20,830	23,746	14.0	Transportation attendants, except flight attendants and baggage porters
110,840	126,111	13.8	Water and liquid waste treatment plant and system operators
1,540,159	1,749,333	13.6	Elementary school teachers, except special education
4,507	5,119	13.6	Epidemiologists
99,053	112,512	13.6	Police, fire, and ambulance dispatchers
98,454	111,747	13.5	Medical transcriptionists
607,609	689,400	13.5	Tellers
29,428	33,328	13.3	Shampooers
43,608	49,400	13.3	Transportation workers, nsk
27,596	31,236	13.2	Commercial pilots
56,326	63,628	13.0	Food preparation and serving related workers, nsk
228,531	258,200	13.0	Taxi drivers and chauffeurs
79,444	89,678	12.9	Airline pilots, copilots, and flight engineers
552,458	623,634	12.9	Computer support specialists
436,100	492,434	12.9	Insurance sales agents
68,005	76,763	12.9	Music directors and composers
28,083	31,681	12.8	Aircraft structure, surfaces, rigging, and systems assemblers
135,246	152,552	12.8	Writers and authors
20,544	23,150	12.7	Film and video editors
282,237	318,009	12.7	First-line supervisors/managers of housekeeping and janitorial workers
1,469,519	1,655,518	12.7	Maids and housekeeping cleaners
319,818	360,485	12.7	Recreation workers
122,074	137,614	12.7	Slaughterers and meat packers
29,714	33,462	12.6	Education administrators, nsk
259,543	292,352	12.6	Educational, vocational, and school counselors
506,347	570,362	12.6	Financial managers
37,564	42,282	12.6	Helpers, construction trades, nsk
3,200,245	3,603,802	12.6	Office clerks, general
82,703	93,157	12.6	Protective service workers, nsk
96,199	108,325	12.6	Service station attendants
15,202	17,097	12.5	Animal control workers
2,113,780	2,377,315	12.5	Bookkeeping, accounting, and auditing clerks
198,488	223,311	12.5	Bus drivers, transit and intercity
39,584	44,538	12.5	First-line supervisors/managers of correctional officers
181,954	204,647	12.5	First-line supervisors/managers of helpers, laborers, and material movers, hand

Total Employment 2006	2016	% Change	Occupation
28,770	32,358	12.5	Funeral directors
13,399	15,078	12.5	Insurance appraisers, auto damage
21,211	23,858	12.5	Motorcycle mechanics
617,452	694,225	12.4	Hairdressers, hairstylists, and cosmetologists
167,207	187,960	12.4	Medical and clinical laboratory technologists
4,476,942	5,033,766	12.4	Retail salespersons
410,948	461,852	12.4	Sales representatives, wholesale and manufacturing, technical and scientific products
17,777	19,977	12.4	Social science research assistants
11,725	13,172	12.3	Emergency management specialists
130,570	146,656	12.3	Mobile heavy equipment mechanics, except engines
10,520	11,814	12.3	Parking enforcement workers
70,988	79,651	12.2	Lodging managers
37,881	42,479	12.1	Broadcast technicians
292,876	328,189	12.1	Fire fighters
135,204	151,574	12.1	Parking lot attendants
6,937	7,773	12.1	Subway and streetcar operators
49,087	54,996	12.0	Compensation and benefits managers
17,445	19,531	12.0	Correspondence clerks
54,992	61,552	11.9	Glaziers
84,643	94,731	11.9	Helpers—Pipelayers, plumbers, pipefitters, and steamfitters
4,891	5,469	11.8	Airfield operations specialists
16,041	17,931	11.8	Designers, nsk
416,276	465,502	11.8	Dining room and cafeteria attendants and bartender helpers
129,135	144,378	11.8	Financial specialists, nsk
64,876	72,513	11.8	Health diagnosing and treating practitioners, nsk
163,379	182,599	11.8	Helpers—Installation, maintenance, and repair workers
5,706	6,379	11.8	Orthotists and prosthetists
462,833	517,319	11.8	Painters, construction and maintenance
247,103	276,048	11.7	Administrative services managers
109,060	121,817	11.7	Helpers—Carpenters
275,269	307,533	11.7	Legal secretaries
35,660	39,848	11.7	Media and communication workers, nsk
70,030	78,141	11.6	Actors
182,676	203,800	11.6	Automotive body and related repairers
274,876	306,383	11.5	Bus and truck mechanics and diesel engine specialists
26,897	30,001	11.5	Camera operators, television, video, and motion picture
850,343	948,167	11.5	Cooks, restaurant
52,468	58,483	11.5	First-line supervisors/managers of fire fighting and prevention workers
372,544	415,225	11.5	Loan officers
30,162	33,633	11.5	Reinforcing iron and rebar workers
221,539	246,791	11.4	Cement masons and concrete finishers
58,233	64,849	11.4	Human resources managers, nsk
75,942	84,575	11.4	Motor vehicle operators, nsk
40,743	45,381	11.4	Natural sciences managers
817,108	909,458	11.3	First-line supervisors/managers of food preparation and serving workers
18,033	20,077	11.3	Gaming cage workers
168,201	187,125	11.3	Human resources assistants, except payroll and timekeeping
32,740	36,445	11.3	Optometrists
18,608	20,688	11.2	Bailiffs
495,307	550,952	11.2	Bartenders
39,497	43,929	11.2	Hazardous materials removal workers
17,357	19,306	11.2	Microbiologists
658,060	731,803	11.2	Middle school teachers, except special and vocational education
93,074	103,360	11.1	Producers and directors
131,239	145,770	11.1	Real estate brokers
19,658	21,841	11.1	Slot key persons
40,560	45,071	11.1	Tree trimmers and pruners
24,521	27,215	11.0	Drafters, nsk
13,805	15,327	11.0	Fire inspectors and investigators
65,364	72,568	11.0	Helpers—Brickmasons, blockmasons, stonemasons, and tile and marble setters
760,672	844,195	11.0	Lawyers
1,232,002	1,366,496	10.9	Construction laborers
94,921	105,275	10.9	Food batchmakers
9,196	10,199	10.9	Marine engineers and naval architects
144,228	159,947	10.9	Meat, poultry, and fish cutters and trimmers
2,978	3,302	10.9	Motorboat operators
94,445	104,742	10.9	Probation officers and correctional treatment specialists
6,769	7,508	10.9	Terrazzo workers and finishers
401,027	444,521	10.8	Cooks, institution and cafeteria
18,876	20,921	10.8	Food and tobacco roasting, baking, and drying machine operators and tenders
648,418	718,516	10.8	Police and sheriff's patrol officers
2,360,630	2,615,309	10.8	Waiters and waitresses
25,588	28,326	10.7	Financial examiners
87,001	96,285	10.7	Merchandise displayers and window trimmers
999	1,106	10.7	Prosthodontists
122,472	135,495	10.6	Aircraft mechanics and service technicians
8,469	9,363	10.6	Arbitrators, mediators, and conciliators
8,759	9,684	10.6	Atmospheric and space scientists
32,470	35,908	10.6	Fence erectors
96,730	106,949	10.6	Flight attendants
3,794	4,195	10.6	Nuclear power reactor operators
58,353	64,552	10.6	Operations research analysts
502,201	555,431	10.6	Plumbers, pipefitters, and steamfitters
432,291	478,135	10.6	Real estate sales agents
109,677	121,288	10.6	Speech-language pathologists
99,216	109,591	10.5	Education, training, and library workers, nsk
4,672	5,162	10.5	Travel guides
8,512	9,400	10.4	Aerospace engineering and operations technicians
517,358	571,223	10.4	Dishwashers
351,188	387,759	10.4	Hosts and hostesses, restaurant, lounge, and coffee shop
1,312,222	1,448,763	10.4	Teacher assistants
1,859,848	2,052,860	10.4	Truck drivers, heavy and tractor-trailer
1,462,071	1,612,072	10.3	Carpenters
11,782	13,002	10.3	Food scientists and technologists
122,480	135,138	10.3	Photographers
957	1,055	10.3	Segmental pavers
89,831	98,993	10.2	Aerospace engineers
25,223	27,795	10.2	Air traffic controllers
90,650	99,888	10.2	Civil engineering technicians
532,840	586,935	10.2	Counter attendants, cafeteria, food concession, and coffee shop
226,065	249,171	10.2	First-line supervisors/managers of transportation and material-moving machine and vehicle operators
3,033	3,342	10.2	Mathematicians
18,779	20,701	10.2	Media and communication equipment workers, nsk
318,329	350,838	10.2	Sales managers
23,774	26,199	10.2	Septic tank servicers and sewer pipe cleaners
1,390,952	1,530,861	10.1	Maintenance and repair workers, general
196,330	216,172	10.1	Musicians and singers
149,266	164,263	10.0	Bakers
7,070	7,774	10.0	Mining and geological engineers, including mining safety engineers
3,702	4,072	10.0	Sociologists
23,844	26,218	10.0	Stonemasons
34,562	38,005	10.0	Therapists, nsk
30,323	33,337	9.9	Fine artists, including painters, sculptors, and

Total Employment 2006	2016	% Change	Occupation
			illustrators
74,915	82,364	9.9	Industrial engineering technicians
6,916	7,602	9.9	Traffic technicians
5,371	5,900	9.8	Animal scientists
12,253	13,454	9.8	Audiologists
260,831	286,424	9.8	Graphic designers
66,177	72,695	9.8	Life, physical, and social science technicians, nsk
2,003	2,200	9.8	Models
158,316	173,596	9.7	Brickmasons and blockmasons
238,681	261,781	9.7	Laundry and dry-cleaning workers
24,870	27,259	9.6	Agents and business managers of artists, performers, and athletes
25,380	27,823	9.6	Health and safety engineers, except mining safety engineers and inspectors
19,767	21,643	9.5	Dancers
220,911	241,968	9.5	Interviewers, except eligibility and loan
11,944	13,076	9.5	Podiatrists
12,323	13,488	9.4	Medical appliance technicians
454,800	497,252	9.3	Bus drivers, school
136,323	148,893	9.2	Dentists, general
93,018	101,529	9.2	First-line supervisors/managers of police and detectives
9,179	10,026	9.2	Orthodontists
16,295	17,799	9.2	Tank car, truck, and ship loaders
83,697	91,340	9.1	Chemists
771,796	841,777	9.1	First-line supervisors/managers of construction trades and extraction workers
7,698	8,396	9.1	Oral and maxillofacial surgeons
40,152	43,795	9.1	Railroad conductors and yardmasters
16,124	17,598	9.1	Sound engineering technicians
49,319	53,739	9.0	Baggage porters and bellhops
260,727	284,283	9.0	Industrial machinery mechanics
64,255	70,056	9.0	Paving, surfacing, and tamping equipment operators
77,898	84,870	8.9	Art directors
305,169	332,419	8.9	Claims adjusters, examiners, and investigators
145,216	158,140	8.9	Highway maintenance workers
62,455	67,974	8.8	Construction and related workers, nsk
4,927	5,360	8.8	Cooks, private household
114,584	124,628	8.8	Court, municipal, and license clerks
21,830	23,753	8.8	Elevator installers and repairers
291,861	317,359	8.7	Heating, air conditioning, and refrigeration mechanics and installers
9,695	10,536	8.7	Materials scientists
65,904	71,631	8.7	Opticians, dispensing
66,590	72,401	8.7	Pipelayers
740,916	805,252	8.7	Teachers and instructors, nsk
20,091	21,830	8.7	Zoologists and wildlife biologists
3,133	3,401	8.6	Agricultural engineers
57,126	62,038	8.6	Dietitians and nutritionists
11,818	12,838	8.6	Geological and petroleum technicians
28,446	30,898	8.6	Insulation workers, mechanical
121,256	131,534	8.5	Library technicians
75,795	82,255	8.5	Sales engineers
137,901	149,657	8.5	Special education teachers, secondary school
22,416	24,324	8.5	Statisticians
13,799	14,955	8.4	Artists and related workers, nsk
32,414	35,130	8.4	Insulation workers, floor, ceiling, and wall
424,152	459,649	8.4	Operating engineers and other construction equipment operators
54,322	58,883	8.4	Painters, transportation equipment
1,562,254	1,693,014	8.4	Sales representatives, wholesale and manufacturing, except technical and scientific products
15,790	17,110	8.4	Soil and plant scientists
1,051,159	1,139,965	8.4	Truck drivers, light or delivery services
629,405	681,455	8.3	Cooks, fast food

Total Employment 2006	2016	% Change	Occupation
80,157	86,818	8.3	Excavating and loading machine and dragline operators
5,584	6,050	8.3	Pile-driver operators
94,012	101,858	8.3	Transportation, storage, and distribution managers
15,709	16,987	8.1	Avionics technicians
45,206	48,882	8.1	Occupational health and safety specialists
61,148	66,106	8.1	Plasterers and stucco masons
8,816	9,522	8.0	Craft artists
30,444	32,842	7.9	Chemical engineers
116,009	125,127	7.9	Library assistants, clerical
1,302	1,405	7.9	Mathematical technicians
11,591	12,503	7.9	Psychologists, nsk
3,446	3,716	7.8	Historians
114,784	123,521	7.6	Chefs and head cooks
225,905	243,048	7.6	Education administrators, elementary and secondary school
22,507	24,208	7.6	Statistical assistants
14,792	15,900	7.5	Economists
168,431	181,134	7.5	Installation, maintenance, and repair workers, nsk
4,346	4,667	7.4	Communications equipment operators, nsk
705,015	757,438	7.4	Electricians
135,970	146,047	7.4	Refuse and recyclable material collectors
185,864	199,393	7.3	Drywall and ceiling tile installers
187,089	200,669	7.3	Engineering managers
464,881	498,976	7.3	First-line supervisors/managers of mechanics, installers, and repairers
8,644	9,267	7.2	Bicycle repairers
47,978	51,412	7.2	Commercial and industrial designers
112,183	120,294	7.2	Electrical power-line installers and repairers
15,273	16,377	7.2	Nuclear engineers
61,858	66,260	7.1	Budget analysts
54,312	58,169	7.1	Tapers
869,558	929,743	6.9	Managers, nsk
6,928	7,398	6.8	Dentists, nsk
80,226	85,688	6.8	Electrical and electronics repairers, commercial and industrial equipment
105,340	112,487	6.8	Helpers—Electricians
16,516	17,641	6.8	Physicists
2,142	2,285	6.7	Dredge operators
27,109	28,924	6.7	Gaming change persons and booth cashiers
21,769	23,228	6.7	Helpers—Roofers
6,502	6,939	6.7	Nuclear technicians
188,655	201,382	6.7	Sheet metal workers
25,804	27,516	6.6	Agricultural and food science technicians
29,064	30,970	6.6	Ophthalmic laboratory technicians
21,681	23,099	6.5	Earth drillers, except oil and gas
47,792	50,848	6.4	Mechanical engineering technicians
17,856	18,995	6.4	Proofreaders and copy markers
5,551	5,906	6.4	Transit and railroad police
99,518	105,870	6.4	Woodworking machine setters, operators, and tenders, except sawing
153,375	162,965	6.3	Electrical engineers
104,477	111,063	6.3	Insurance underwriters
47,296	50,247	6.2	Advertising and promotions managers
33,294	35,346	6.2	Fiberglass laminators and fabricators
23,881	25,350	6.2	Physical scientists, nsk
115,522	122,541	6.1	Architectural and civil drafters
1,096	1,162	6.1	Geographers
7,724	8,184	6.0	Broadcast news analysts
71,736	76,052	6.0	Structural iron and steel workers
61,228	64,793	5.8	Chemical technicians
1,418,494	1,500,083	5.8	First-line supervisors/managers of office and administrative support workers
54,884	58,062	5.8	Millwrights
1,037,547	1,096,096	5.6	Secondary school teachers, except special and vocational education

Total Employment 2006	2016	% Change	Occupation
1,656	1,748	5.5	Astronomers
170,305	179,675	5.5	Engineers, nsk
19,844	20,939	5.5	Forest and conservation workers
32,892	34,706	5.5	Outdoor power equipment and other small engine mechanics
19,777	20,830	5.3	Conservation scientists
4,694	4,945	5.3	Political scientists
13,188	13,868	5.2	Foresters
78,340	82,437	5.2	Mechanical drafters
17,355	18,251	5.2	Petroleum engineers
14,969	15,735	5.1	Farm and home management advisors
27,192	28,580	5.1	Judges, magistrate judges, and magistrates
47,878	50,311	5.1	Legal support workers, nsk
26,578	27,926	5.1	Rail car repairers
409,024	429,732	5.1	Welders, cutters, solderers, and brazers
20,411	21,428	5.0	Fashion designers
350,259	367,782	5.0	Food service managers
237,035	248,709	4.9	Compliance officers, except agriculture, construction, health and safety, and transportation
2,989	3,134	4.9	Mining machine operators, nsk
195,495	204,959	4.8	Cooks, short order
14,635	15,334	4.8	Rail-track laying and maintenance equipment operators
35,994	37,684	4.7	Social scientists and related workers, nsk
78,525	82,137	4.6	Computer hardware engineers
10,043	10,504	4.6	Continuous mining machine operators
20,017	20,936	4.6	Electronic equipment installers and repairers, motor vehicles
162,317	169,802	4.6	Telecommunications line installers and repairers
3,085	3,224	4.5	Loading machine operators, underground mining
10,505	10,967	4.4	Animal breeders
541,869	565,622	4.4	Billing and posting clerks and machine operators
21,079	21,978	4.3	Electrical and electronics installers and repairers, transportation equipment
16,327	17,036	4.3	Precision instrument and equipment repairers, nsk
1,675,937	1,747,019	4.2	First-line supervisors/managers of retail sales workers
225,797	235,169	4.2	Mechanical engineers
292,794	305,123	4.2	Production, planning, and expediting clerks
34,848	36,286	4.1	Electrical and electronics drafters
33,396	34,730	4.0	Loan counselors
21,616	22,482	4.0	Materials engineers
7,918	8,218	3.8	Mine cutting and channeling machine operators
65,032	67,501	3.8	Sawing machine setters, operators, and tenders, wood
29,067	30,138	3.7	Biological scientists, nsk
53,439	55,393	3.7	Dental laboratory technicians
199,552	206,890	3.7	Door-to-door sales workers, news and street vendors, and related workers
137,868	142,954	3.7	Electronics engineers, except computer
529,958	549,430	3.7	First-line supervisors/managers of non-retail sales workers
25,115	26,046	3.7	Recreational therapists
768,974	797,286	3.7	Shipping, receiving, and traffic clerks
170,433	176,530	3.6	Electrical and electronic engineering technicians
158,373	164,127	3.6	Librarians
30,885	31,988	3.6	Painting, coating, and decorating workers
15,588	16,122	3.4	Cooks, nsk
69,526	71,910	3.4	Purchasing managers
45,389	46,951	3.4	Stationary engineers and boiler operators
112,418	115,907	3.1	Eligibility interviewers, government programs
213,612	220,246	3.1	Payroll and timekeeping clerks
174,961	180,211	3.0	Computer, automated teller, and office machine repairers
39,700	40,908	3.0	Electronic home entertainment equipment installers and repairers
52,803	54,397	3.0	Welding, soldering, and brazing machine setters, operators, and tenders
149,047	153,146	2.8	Cabinetmakers and bench carpenters
46,393	47,691	2.8	Crane and tower operators
5,998	6,167	2.8	Musical instrument repairers and tuners
106,843	109,772	2.7	Farmworkers, farm and ranch animals
34,759	35,701	2.7	Power plant operators
15,739	16,155	2.6	Electro-mechanical technicians
197,993	203,035	2.5	Telecommunications equipment installers and repairers, except line installers
20,429	20,927	2.4	Choreographers
121,511	124,275	2.3	Editors
304,906	311,981	2.3	Production workers, nsk
1,815	1,853	2.1	Forest fire inspectors and prevention specialists
2,416,034	2,465,805	2.1	Laborers and freight, stock, and material movers, hand
80,726	82,455	2.1	Tax examiners, collectors, and revenue agents
402,246	410,478	2.0	Chief executives
81,824	83,443	2.0	Engineering technicians, except drafters, nsk
131,352	133,852	1.9	Butchers and meat cutters
67,132	68,398	1.9	Credit analysts
69,320	70,619	1.9	Crossing guards
53,910	54,931	1.9	Tailors, dressmakers, and custom sewers
20,486	20,819	1.6	Woodworkers, nsk
190,231	193,125	1.5	Dispatchers, except police, fire, and ambulance
1,720,460	1,746,324	1.5	General and operations managers
57,364	58,239	1.5	Home appliance repairers
5,334	5,407	1.4	Explosives workers, ordnance handling experts, and blasters
30,672	31,087	1.4	Farm equipment mechanics
55,928	56,646	1.3	Molders, shapers, and casters, except metal and plastic
79,505	80,435	1.2	Postal service clerks
59,212	59,921	1.2	Reporters and correspondents
4,291	4,345	1.2	Roof bolters, mining
1,939,837	1,962,267	1.2	Secretaries, except legal, medical, and executive
60,034	60,678	1.1	Barbers
258,156	261,032	1.1	Farm, ranch, and other agricultural managers
165,345	167,127	1.1	Reservation and transportation ticket agents and travel clerks
31,833	32,137	1.0	Desktop publishers
64,507	65,171	1.0	Legislators
337,768	341,299	1.0	Postal service mail carriers
101,167	102,215	1.0	Travel agents
19,167	19,334	0.9	Respiratory therapy technicians
53,588	53,964	0.7	Material moving workers, nsk
9,750	9,784	0.4	Extraction workers, nsk
42,991	43,132	0.3	Control and valve installers and repairers, except mechanical door
96,553	96,846	0.3	Multiple machine tool setters, operators, and tenders, metal and plastic
15,479	15,487	0.1	Administrative law judges, adjudicators, and hearing officers
287,429	287,810	0.1	Purchasing agents, except wholesale, retail, and farm products
1,274,303	1,275,052	0.1	Team assemblers
20,350	20,360	0.0	Agricultural workers, nsk
61,735	61,694	-0.1	Psychiatric aides
156,568	156,379	-0.1	Wholesale and retail buyers, except farm products

Total Employment 2006	2016	% Change	Occupation
133,770	133,551	-0.2	Couriers and messengers
8,030	8,017	-0.2	Fish and game wardens
25,016	24,964	-0.2	Helpers—Extraction workers
11,960	11,934	-0.2	Public address system and other announcers
103,008	102,790	-0.2	Structural metal fabricators and fitters
12,315	12,284	-0.3	Riggers
541,605	538,831	-0.5	Helpers—Production workers
24,455	24,286	-0.7	Helpers—Painters, paperhangers, plasterers, and stucco masons
25,870	25,653	-0.8	Postmasters and mail superintendents
256,023	253,765	-0.9	Loan interviewers and clerks
16,176	15,998	-1.1	Agricultural inspectors
84,291	83,348	-1.1	Maintenance workers, machinery
73,205	72,324	-1.2	Carpet installers
3,017	2,980	-1.2	Hoist and winch operators
36,689	36,235	-1.2	Law clerks
69,009	68,167	-1.2	Title examiners, abstractors, and searchers
253,949	250,613	-1.3	Insurance claims and policy processing clerks
40,496	39,980	-1.3	Logging equipment operators
1,809	1,781	-1.5	Fabric menders, except garment
14,319	14,064	-1.8	Floor sanders and finishers
42,091	41,332	-1.8	Graders and sorters, agricultural products
33,829	33,166	-2.0	Forest and conservation technicians
637,034	624,181	-2.0	Industrial truck and tractor operators
4,403	4,309	-2.1	Camera and photographic equipment repairers
77,798	76,196	-2.1	Procurement clerks
52,219	51,047	-2.2	Jewelers and precious stone and metal workers
238,015	232,849	-2.2	Parts salespersons
14,132	13,772	-2.6	Plant and system operators, nsk
93,926	91,393	-2.7	Office machine operators, except computer
11,803	11,462	-2.9	Manufactured building and mobile home installers
47,928	46,498	-3.0	Coin, vending, and amusement machine servicers and repairers
140,510	136,339	-3.0	Computer-controlled machine tool operators, metal and plastic
31,326	30,348	-3.1	Furniture finishers
396,539	384,120	-3.1	Machinists
3,926	3,799	-3.2	Bridge and lock tenders
44,085	42,663	-3.2	Roustabouts, oil and gas
44,289	42,873	-3.2	Separating, filtering, clarifying, precipitating, and still machine setters, operators, and tenders
62,098	60,073	-3.3	Psychiatric technicians
3,500,169	3,381,931	-3.4	Cashiers, except gaming
603,083	582,746	-3.4	Farmworkers and laborers, crop, nursery, and greenhouse
52,737	50,688	-3.9	Chemical equipment operators and tenders
435,076	417,065	-4.1	Computer programmers
6,533	6,268	-4.1	Radio mechanics
25,474	24,398	-4.2	Electric motor, power tool, and related repairers
77,182	73,762	-4.4	Pressers, textile, garment, and related materials
95,534	91,133	-4.6	Vocational education teachers, secondary school
313,355	298,680	-4.7	Data entry keyers
22,300	21,261	-4.7	Electrical and electronics repairers, powerhouse, substation, and relay
44,393	42,310	-4.7	Food cooking machine operators and tenders
13,625	12,969	-4.8	Etchers and engravers
699,259	665,489	-4.8	First-line supervisors/managers of production and operating workers
8,571	8,153	-4.9	Power distributors and dispatchers
59,451	56,482	-5.0	Agricultural equipment operators
142,842	135,544	-5.1	Mixing and blending machine setters, operators, and tenders
7,165	6,799	-5.1	Signal and track switch repairers
15,805	15,003	-5.1	Vocational education teachers, middle school

Total Employment 2006	2016	% Change	Occupation
3,814	3,619	-5.1	Watch repairers
445,092	421,337	-5.3	Driver/sales workers
7,115	6,741	-5.3	Log graders and scalers
385,988	365,058	-5.4	Packaging and filling machine operators and tenders
7,429	7,025	-5.4	Patternmakers, metal and plastic
19,923	18,853	-5.4	Rotary drill operators, oil and gas
27,905	26,400	-5.4	Service unit operators, oil, gas, and mining
197,594	186,337	-5.7	Printing machine operators
18,784	17,694	-5.8	Derrick operators, oil and gas
157,341	148,094	-5.9	Industrial production managers
7,935	7,470	-5.9	Logging workers, nsk
28,633	26,901	-6.0	Cutters and trimmers, hand
8,791	8,240	-6.3	Model makers, metal and plastic
10,677	9,956	-6.8	Cooling and freezing equipment operators and tenders
491,417	456,817	-7.0	Inspectors, testers, sorters, samplers, and weighers
44,776	41,586	-7.1	Grinding and polishing workers, hand
93,869	87,146	-7.2	Extruding and drawing machine setters, operators, and tenders, metal and plastic
49,677	46,026	-7.3	Conveyor operators and tenders
13,085	12,112	-7.4	Fallers
2,527	2,336	-7.6	Timing device assemblers, adjusters, and calibrators
1,704,921	1,574,199	-7.7	Stock clerks and order fillers
81,193	74,657	-8.1	Extruding, forming, pressing, and compacting machine setters, operators, and tenders
58,905	54,020	-8.3	Radio and television announcers
2,886	2,647	-8.3	Shuttle car operators
68,975	63,204	-8.4	Credit authorizers, checkers, and clerks
11,493	10,532	-8.4	Motion picture projectionists
17,980	16,474	-8.4	Numerical tool and process control programmers
197,714	181,173	-8.4	Postal service mail sorters, processors, and processing machine operators
177,485	162,575	-8.4	Switchboard operators, including answering service
100,415	91,946	-8.4	Tax preparers
1,058,444	968,838	-8.5	Farmers and ranchers
45,265	41,368	-8.6	Engine and other machine assemblers
15,904	14,536	-8.6	Purchasing agents and buyers, farm products
291,591	266,264	-8.7	Assemblers and fabricators, nsk
31,596	28,834	-8.7	Furnace, kiln, oven, drier, and kettle operators and tenders
86,909	79,184	-8.9	Floral designers
54,809	49,890	-9.0	Upholsterers
60,298	54,800	-9.1	Electromechanical equipment assemblers
23,362	21,209	-9.2	Cementing and gluing machine operators and tenders
78,794	71,486	-9.3	Cutting and slicing machine setters, operators, and tenders
48,240	43,749	-9.3	Job printers
319,970	290,221	-9.3	Office and administrative support workers, nsk
100,788	91,101	-9.6	Tool and die makers
15,914	14,348	-9.8	Cleaning, washing, and metal pickling equipment operators and tenders
12,261	11,044	-9.9	Gas plant operators
394,783	355,732	-9.9	Telemarketers
46,574	41,800	-10.3	Meter readers, utilities
15,575	13,977	-10.3	Shoe and leather workers and repairers
50,394	44,807	-11.1	Pharmacy aides
79,021	70,058	-11.3	Weighers, measurers, checkers, and samplers, recordkeeping
24,609	21,799	-11.4	Railroad brake, signal, and switch operators
3,478	3,079	-11.5	Refractory materials repairers, except brickmasons
152,064	134,414	-11.6	Mail clerks and mail machine operators,

Total Employment 2006	2016	% Change	Occupation
			except postal service
178,998	158,198	-11.6	Word processors and typists
35,853	31,611	-11.8	Rolling machine setters, operators, and tenders, metal and plastic
42,485	37,440	-11.9	Crushing, grinding, and polishing machine setters, operators, and tenders
14,411	12,698	-11.9	Wellhead pumpers
22,664	19,939	-12.0	Tire builders
28,991	25,450	-12.2	Floor layers, except carpet, wood, and hard tiles
9,899	8,691	-12.2	Paperhangers
41,898	36,788	-12.2	Plating and coating machine setters, operators, and tenders, metal and plastic
23,440	20,580	-12.2	Sewers, hand
833,812	730,180	-12.4	Packers and packagers, hand
10,544	9,225	-12.5	Pump operators, except wellhead pumpers
156,842	136,758	-12.8	Molding, coremaking, and casting machine setters, operators, and tenders, metal and plastic
106,426	92,743	-12.9	Coating, painting, and spraying machine setters, operators, and tenders
244,584	212,988	-12.9	Information and record clerks, nsk
86,431	75,299	-12.9	Personal care and service workers, nsk
42,397	36,930	-12.9	Semiconductor processors
41,970	36,367	-13.4	Petroleum pump system operators, refinery operators, and gaugers
7,305	6,298	-13.8	Audio-visual collections specialists
27,122	23,107	-14.8	Heat treating equipment setters, operators, and tenders, metal and plastic
24,379	20,765	-14.8	Textile, apparel, and furnishings workers, nsk
271,745	231,384	-14.9	Cutting, punching, and press machine setters, operators, and tenders, metal and plastic
147,763	125,360	-15.2	Machine feeders and offbearers
53,243	45,094	-15.3	Chemical plant and system operators
101,441	85,499	-15.7	Grinding, lapping, polishing, and buffing machine tool setters, operators, and tenders, metal and plastic
38,372	32,179	-16.1	Fishers and related fishing workers
81,422	68,135	-16.3	New accounts clerks
1,548	1,296	-16.3	Radio operators
7,211	5,995	-16.9	Bookbinders
14,791	12,212	-17.4	Pourers and casters, metal
4,154	3,427	-17.5	Gas compressor and gas pumping station operators
17,682	14,573	-17.6	Extruding and forming machine setters, operators, and tenders, synthetic and glass fibers
113,107	92,563	-18.2	Paper goods machine setters, operators, and tenders
6,772	5,506	-18.7	Rail transportation workers, nsk
474	384	-19.0	Hunters and trappers
18,386	14,896	-19.0	Metal-refining furnace operators and tenders
21,930	17,681	-19.4	Tool grinders, filers, and sharpeners
10,153	8,144	-19.8	Lay-out workers, metal and plastic
29,211	23,071	-21.0	Milling and planing machine setters, operators, and tenders, metal and plastic
70,899	55,959	-21.1	Prepress technicians and workers
64,859	50,697	-21.8	Bindery workers
42,686	33,215	-22.2	Drilling and boring machine tool setters, operators, and tenders, metal and plastic
14,523	11,229	-22.7	Foundry mold and coremakers
67,760	51,976	-23.3	Lathe and turning machine tool setters, operators, and tenders, metal and plastic
270,869	204,918	-24.3	Order clerks
43,340	32,801	-24.3	Textile winding, twisting, and drawing out machine setters, operators, and tenders
129,997	97,943	-24.7	Computer operators
48,661	36,431	-25.1	Metal workers and plastic workers, nsk
213,381	156,167	-26.8	Electrical and electronic equipment assemblers
232,810	169,526	-27.2	Sewing machine operators
18,687	13,565	-27.4	Textile cutting machine setters, operators, and tenders
9,209	6,578	-28.6	Fabric and apparel patternmakers
19,420	13,551	-30.2	Textile bleaching and dyeing machine operators and tenders
31,068	21,640	-30.3	Forging machine setters, operators, and tenders, metal and plastic
22,835	15,879	-30.5	Coil winders, tapers, and finishers
40,145	27,739	-30.9	Textile knitting and weaving machine setters, operators, and tenders
4,089	2,627	-35.7	Shoe machine operators and tenders
23,684	15,090	-36.3	Photographic process workers
26,681	16,137	-39.5	Telephone operators
2,279	1,369	-39.9	Patternmakers, wood
1,888	1,118	-40.8	Model makers, wood
233,808	137,245	-41.3	File clerks
49,304	24,742	-49.8	Photographic processing machine operators